THE COMMON LAW LIBRARY

THE LAW OF CONTRACTS

VOLUME I

GENERAL PRINCIPLES

OTHER VOLUMES IN THE COMMON LAW LIBRARY

Clerk & Lindsell on Torts

Chitty & Jacob's Queen's Bench Forms

Bullen & Leake & Jacob's Precedents of Pleadings

Charlesworth and Percy on Negligence

Bowstead and Reynolds on Agency

Gatley on Libel and Slander

McGregor on Damages

Phipson on Evidence

Benjamin's Sale of Goods

Jackson & Powell on Professional Negligence

Goff & Jones, The Law of Restitution

Arlidge, Eady & Smith on Contempt

THE COMMON LAW LIBRARY

CHITTY ON CONTRACTS

THIRTIETH EDITION

VOLUME I

GENERAL PRINCIPLES

SWEET & MAXWELL
THOMSON REUTERS

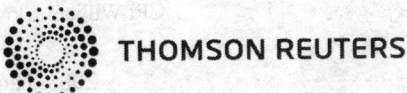

First Edition	(1826)	By Joseph Chitty, Junior
Second Edition	(1834)	" " "
Third Edition	(1841)	By Thompson Chitty
Fourth Edition	(1850)	By His Hon. Judge J. A. Russell, Q.C.
Fifth Edition	(1853)	" " "
Sixth Edition	(1857)	" " "
Seventh Edition	(1863)	" " "
Eighth Edition	(1868)	" " "
Ninth Edition	(1871)	" " "
Tenth Edition	(1876)	" " "
Eleventh Edition	(1881)	" " "
Twelfth Edition	(1890)	By J. M. Lely and Sir William Geary
Thirteenth Edition	(1896)	By J. M. Lely
Fourteenth Edition	(1904)	" "
Fifteenth Edition	(1909)	By W. Wyatt Paine
Sixteenth Edition	(1912)	" "
Seventeenth Edition	(1921)	" "
Eighteenth Edition	(1930)	By W. A. MacFarlane and G. W. Wrangham
Nineteenth Edition	(1937)	General Editor: Harold Potter
Twentieth Edition	(1947)	" " "
Twenty-first Edition	(1955)	Under the General Editorship of John Burke and Peter Allsop
Twenty-second Edition	(1961)	General Editor: John Morris
Twenty-third Edition	(1968)	General Editor: A. G. Guest
Second Impression	(1972)	" " "
Twenty-fourth Edition	(1977)	" " "
Second Impression	(1979)	" " "
Third Impression	(1980)	" " "
Twenty-fifth Edition	(1983)	" " "
Twenty-sixth Edition	(1989)	" " "
Second Impression	(1990)	" " "
Third Impression	(1991)	" " "
Twenty-seventh Edition	(1994)	" " "
Second Impression	(1995)	" " "
Third Impression	(1997)	" " "
Fourth Impression	(1998)	" " "
Twenty-eighth Edition	(1999)	General Editor: H. G. Beale
Second Impression	(2001)	" " "
Twenty-ninth Edition	(2004)	" " "
Thirtieth Edition	(2008)	" " "

Published in 2008 by
Thomson Reuters (Legal) Limited
(Registered in England & Wales, Company No 1679046.
Registered Office and address for service: 100 Avenue Road, London, NW3 3PF)
trading as Sweet & Maxwell
For further information on our products and services,
visit *www.sweetandmaxwell.co.uk*
Computerset by
Interactive Sciences, Gloucester
Printed in the UK by
CPI William Clowes Beccles NR34 7TL

GENERAL EDITOR

H. G. BEALE, Q.C. (Hon.), B.A., F.B.A.
Honorary Bencher of Lincoln's Inn; Professor of Law in the University of Warwick

EDITORS

A. S. BURROWS, Q.C. (Hon.), B.C.L., LL.M., M.A., F.B.A.
of the Middle Temple, Honorary Bencher; Fellow of St Hugh's College and Norton Rose Professor of Commercial Law in the University of Oxford

M. R. FREEDLAND, LL.B., M.A., D.Phil., F.B.A.
Bencher of Gray's Inn; Professor of Employment Law in the University of Oxford and Fellow of St John's College, Oxford

A. G. GUEST, C.B.E., Q.C., M.A., F.B.A.
Bencher of Gray's Inn; formerly Professor of English Law in the University of London; Fellow of the Chartered Institute of Arbitrators

R. J. A. HOOLEY, M.A.
of the Middle Temple, Barrister; Professor of Law, King's College London; Fellow of Fitzwilliam College, Cambridge

EVA LOMNICKA, M.A.
of the Middle Temple, Barrister; Professor of Law, King's College London

DAVID McCLEAN, C.B.E., Q.C. (Hon.), D.C.L., F.B.A.
Bencher of Gray's Inn; Emeritus Professor of Law, University of Sheffield; Chancellor of the Dioceses of Newcastle and Sheffield

P. J. S. MACDONALD EGGERS, LL.B. (Syd.), LL.M. (Cantab.)
of the Middle Temple, Barrister; Solicitor of the Supreme Court of New South Wales; Visiting Lecturer, University College London

E. G. McKENDRICK, LL.B., B.C.L., M.A.
of Gray's Inn, Barrister; Pro-Vice-Chancellor and Herbert Smith Professor of English Private Law in the University of Oxford and Fellow of Lady Margaret Hall

PAUL MITCHELL, B.A., D.Phil. (Oxon)
Reader in Law, King's College London

VINCENT MORAN, M.A. (Cantab.)
of Gray's Inn, Barrister

C. G. J. MORSE, B.C.L., M.A.
of the Middle Temple, Barrister; Professor of Law, King's College London

D. D. PRENTICE, LL.B., J.D., M.A.
of Lincoln's Inn, Barrister; Emeritus Fellow of Pembroke College and formerly Allen & Overy Professor of Corporate Law in the University of Oxford

F. M. B. REYNOLDS, Q.C. (Hon.), D.C.L., F.B.A.
Honorary Bencher of the Inner Temple; Emeritus Fellow of Worcester College and Professor of Law Emeritus in the University of Oxford

SIR GUENTER TREITEL, Q.C., D.C.L., F.B.A.
Honorary Bencher of Gray's Inn; Formerly Vinerian Professor of English Law in the University of Oxford

JOHN UFF, C.B.E., Q.C., Ph.D., B.Sc., F.I.C.E., F.C.I.Arb., F.R.Eng.
Bencher of Gray's Inn; Emeritus Professor of Engineering Law, King's College London

G. J. VIRGO, M.A. (Cantab.), B.C.L. (Oxon)
of Lincoln's Inn, Barrister; Professor of English Private Law in the University of Cambridge and Fellow of Downing College Cambridge

R. P. WHISH, B.A., B.C.L. (Oxon)
Solicitor of the Supreme Court of Judicature; Professor of Law, King's College London

S. J. WHITTAKER, B.C.L., M.A., D.Phil.
of Lincoln's Inn, Barrister; Fellow of St John's College and Professor of European Comparative Law in the University of Oxford

NOTE TO READERS

Chitty on Contracts, 30th edition, consists of two volumes. Volume I sets out the *General Principles* and Volume II deals with *Specific Contracts*. Customers may choose to purchase either Volume I alone or both Volumes together.

Please note that Volume I contains Chapters 1 to 30 and an Index which relates to Volume I only.

Volume II contains Chapters 31 to 44 and an Index which relates to both Volumes I and II.

No natural forests were destroyed to make this product;
only farmed timber was used and replanted

A CIP catalogue record for
this book is available
from the British Library

ISBN Volume I 9781847035479

PREFACE

For the 30th edition of *Chitty on Contracts* there have been a number of changes to the editorial team. Professor Sue Arrowsmith, who contributed valuably to the chapter on the Crown, Public Authorities and the European Community, has resigned from the editorship because of the pressure of other work. Mr Donald Harris has retired from editing the chapter on damage in Volume I and the section on remedies in the chapter on sale of goods in Volume II. His contribution to the development of those chapters and to the book as a whole over many editions were enormous and will be missed very much. Mr Simon Hughes has found the pressures of practice too great to continue as co-editor of the chapter on construction contracts, which he had done a great deal to develop. We are very grateful to them all.

We are delighted that Dr Paul Mitchell of King's College London has agreed to take the place of Professor Arrowsmith and that Mr Hughes' place has been taken by Mr Vince Moran of the same Chambers. Lastly, Professor Eva Lomnicka, also of King's College London, has joined the team, taking over the chapter on credit and security from Professor Tony Guest. We welcome them all as great additions to the team. I have taken over those parts of the work previously edited by Donald Harris.

The four years since the 29th edition have seen a large number of developments. Some of the more important changes are as follows:

Volume I

Chapter 1, Introduction: the Regulatory Reform (Execution of Deeds and Documents) Order 2005 makes significant changes to the formal requirements for deeds.

Chapter 2, The Agreement: the effect of a change in a company's capacity on an offer by or to the company has been rewritten in the light of Companies Act 2006. Cases include *Datec Electronic Holdings Ltd v United Parcels Ltd* on when communications in the course of negotiations amount to offer or acceptance and *L.J. Korbetis Ltd v Transgrain Shipping BV* on the effect of a misdirected fax.

Chapter 3, Consideration: the decision of the House of Lords in *Cobbe v Yeomans Row Management Ltd* became available while the new edition was in proof and have led to important changes in the account of promissory estoppel. *Collier v P & M.J. Wright (Holdings) Ltd* discusses, not uncontroversially, when a creditor may resile from a promise to accept part payment of a debt in full satisfaction.

Chapter 4, Form: *Kinane v Mackie-Conteh* considers the application of proprietary estoppel to cases within Law of Property (Miscellaneous Provisions) Act 1989, s.2.

Chapter 5, Mistake: the section on common mistake has been rewritten to bring greater clarity and to deal with mistakes of law in the light of *Brennan v Bolt Burdon*. Other sections seek to explain apparent inconsistencies in the treatment of mistakes over the terms of the contract at common law and in the equitable rectification cases.

Chapter 6, Misrepresentation: there are a number of cases on what amounts to a misrepresentation and on the effects of no-reliance clauses, including *IFE Fund SA v Goldman Sachs International*.

Chapter 7, Duress and Undue Influence: *Turkey v Awadh* is important on the meaning of "a transaction that calls for explanation", and *Yorkshire Bank Plc v Tinsley* deals with the effect of undue influence on replacement mortgages.

Chapter 8, Personal Incapacity: the impact of the Mental Capacity Act 2005 on contractual capacity is explained.

Chapter 9, Corporations and Unincorporated Associations: the changes made by Companies Act 2006 are set out.

Chapter 10, The Crown, Public Authorities and the European Community: this has been re-written. Controversy over specific remedies against Crown servants, raised in *Davidson v Scottish Ministers*, has been left unresolved by *Beggs v Scottish Ministers*. The new Directive on procurement contracts is noted, particularly its potential to make contracts unenforceable.

Chapter 12, Express Terms: what were previously called "rules" of construction are now re-named "principles", in the light of recent cases; their strength is undoubtedly in decline in the face of Lord Hoffmann's general test, laid down in the *Investors Compensation Scheme* case, that words are to be taken to bear the meaning they would convey to a reasonable person against the relevant background of the transaction.

Chapter 14, Exemption Clauses: the role of the Unfair Contract Terms Act 1977 in consumer contracts has been largely superseded by the Unfair Terms in Consumer Contracts Regulations 1999 and, so far as business to business contracts are concerned, the trickle of decided cases suggest that where a contract is concluded between experienced businessmen representing companies of equal bargaining power, they are the best judges of what is a fair and reasonable term to be included in the contract.

Chapter 15, Unfair Terms: here the most important development is *OFT v Abbey National Plc*, the "bank charges" case.

Chapter 18, Third Parties: a number of cases, in particular *Offer-Hoare v Larkstore Ltd* and *Smithkline Beecham Plc v Apotex Europe Ltd* discuss the extent to which a promise can recover damages in respect of loss suffered by a third person. There are cases interpreting the Contracts (Rights of Third Parties) Act 1999 and an explanation of the repercussions on contracts involving third parties of the decision of the House of Lords in *OBG Ltd v Allen* on the torts of inducing breach of contract and intimidation.

Chapter 19, Assignment: the effect of prohibitions on assignment is discussed in the light of *Barbados Trust Company Ltd v Bank of Zambia*.

Chapter 22, Discharge by Agreement: *State Securities Plc v Initial Industry Ltd* on waiver is considered.

Chapter 23, Discharge by Frustration: the decision in *Edwinton Commercial Corp v Tsavliris Russ (Worldwide Salvage & Towage) Ltd (The Sea Angel)* is examined.

Chapter 26, Damages: the important and controversial decision of the House of Lords in

Transfield Shipping Inc v Mercator Shipping Inc (The Achilleas), that a party who is in breach may not be liable even for usual types of loss if in the circumstances it was not reasonable to think that he was accepting responsibility for the loss, appeared while the 30th edition was in proof. A new section dealing with the case has been inserted.

Chapter 27, Third Parties: this considers *Thames Valley Power Ltd v Total Gas & Power Ltd* on specific relief in a contract for the sale of unascertained goods, and *Lauritzencool AB v Lady Navigation Inc* of the availability of specific relief in respect of an obligation to render services that are not of a personal nature.

Chapter 29, Restitution: the major developments here are *Deutsche Morgan Grenfell Group Plc v IRC* on recovery of mistaken tax payments; *Sempra Metals Ltd v IRC* on the use of interest to identify an enrichment and the award of interest generally for restitutionary claims; *Niru Battery Manufacturing Co v Milestone Trading Ltd (No.2)* on recoupment, subrogation and contribution; *WWF—World Wide Fund for Nature v World Wrestling Federation Entertainment Inc* on the characterisation of remedies for breach of contract; and *Commerzbank AG v Gareth Price-Jones* on change of position.

Chapter 30, Conflict of Laws: this contains a full discussion of Regulation (EC) 593/2008 of the European Parliament and of The Council of June 17, 2008 on the law applicable to contractual obligations (Rome I).

Volume II

Chapter 31, Agency: the chapter has been quite extensively revised, and new material on the Commercial Agents Regulations incorporated, particularly the House of Lords decision on the calculation of compensation on termination of agency in *Lonsdale v Howard & Hallam Ltd*.

Chapter 32, Arbitration: reference to over fifty cases have been incorporated, including *Premium Nafta Products Ltd v Fili Shipping Co Ltd* (construction of arbitration clauses and separability); *West Tankers Inc v RAS Riunione Adriatica de Sicurta SA* (anti-suit injunctions); and *Lesotho Highlands Development Authority v Impreglio SpA* (relationship between errors of law and serious irregularity.) It is now clear that s.68 of the Arbitration Act 1996 is the most favoured ground for attempting to challenge an award. *Stretford v Football Association Ltd* and *Sumukan Ltd v Commonwealth Secretariat* further emphasise that deployment of the Human Rights Act 1998 to attack the arbitral process is, fortunately, unlikely to be successful.

Chapter 34, Bills of Exchange and Banking: the section on commercial credits has been re-written in the light of UCP 600. Significant cases include *Architects of Wine Ltd v Barclays Bank Plc* (on Cheques Act 1957, s.4) and *Office of Fair Trading v Abbey National Plc* (on overdraft charges).

Chapter 36, Carriage by Land: here there have been a number of cases: *T Comedy (UK) Ltd v Easy Managed Transport Ltd* (incorporation of RHA Conditions, consistency with the CMR Convention, liens); *Datec Electronic Holdings Ltd v United Parcels Service Ltd* (CMR, limitation of liability, wilful misconduct); *Royal & Sun Alliance Insurance Plc v MK Digital Fze (Cyprus) Ltd* (application of CMR, jurisdiction); and *Rosewood Trucking Limited v Balaam* (claim by one carrier against another under CMR). The Railways (Convention on International Carriage by Rail) Regulations 2005 have enacted the Vilnius Protocol to COTIF.

Chapter 37, Construction Contracts: cases include *Reinwood Ltd v L Brown & Sons Ltd* (liquidated damages) and *Melville Dundas Ltd v George Wimpey UK Ltd* (determination).

Chapter 38, Credit and Security has been largely rewritten to take account of Consumer Credit Act 2006.

Chapter 39, Employment, deals with Employment Equality (Age) Regulations 2006. (It should be noted that if and when the Employment Bill 2007–8 is passed, provisions of the Employment Act 2002 concerning dispute resolution, and the Regulations of 2004 fleshing out those provisions, may be downgraded or repealed.)

Chapter 40, Gaming and Wagering, takes account of the fundamental changes brought about by the Gambling Act 2005, which from September 1, 2007 rendered gambling contracts legally enforceable (as a general rule).

Chapter 41, Insurance, also considers the impact of the Gambling Act 2005, and of possible reforms canvassed by the Law Commissions' Consultation Paper on misrepresentation, non-disclosure and breach of warranty by the insured. Cases include *HLB Kidsons v Lloyd's Underwriters* (notification under liability policies—the Court of Appeal's decision is pending); *Limit No.2 Limited v AXA Versicherung AG* (misrepresentation—appeal also pending); *Kosmar Villa Holidays Plc v Trustees of Syndicate 1243* (waiver of condition precedents); *Tesco Stores Ltd v Constable* (scope of liability cover); *WASA International Insurance Co Ltd v Lexington Insurance Co* (relationship between reinsurance and original insurance—appeal pending); and *Byrne v Motor Insurers Bureau* (claims against MIB).

Chapter 43, Sale of Goods: the chapter takes account of some of the many points raised in *Balmoral Group Ltd v Borealis (UK) Ltd* and of the problems arising from re-tender of repaired goods considered in *J.H. Ritchie Ltd v Lloyd Ltd.*

As usual, the publishers have taken responsibility for the tables and the index. I would like to put on record how grateful we are for this and for all their hard work on this new 30th edition of *Chitty on Contracts*.

Lastly, it cannot go unremarked that during the lifetime of the 29th edition, *Chitty on Contracts* was made available in a digital edition to subscribers of the relevant services from Westlaw. The 30th edition will also be available. To your Editors the digital format appears to work very well. We are very grateful to the staff at Sweet & Maxwell who developed the format and put the book "on-line".

It has been our aim to deal with developments that occurred and cases that appeared by May 1, 2008. It has been possible to incorporate some subsequent developments at the proof stage. It is our aim to produce the first Annual Supplement in 2009.

Hugh Beale

Warwick, October 14, 2008

TABLE OF CONTENTS

VOLUME I

	Page
Preface	ix
Table of Statutes	xxi
Table of Statutory Instruments	xlix
Table of European Community Legislation	lvii
Table of International Statutory Material	lxvii
Table of Cases	lxix
Table of European Community Cases	cdliii

PART ONE

INTRODUCTION

		Para.
1. Introductory	*S. J. Whittaker*	1–001
1. Definitions of Contract		1–001
2. Fundamental Principles of Contract Law		1–010
3. The Human Rights Act 1998 and Contracts		1–035
4. Classification of Contracts		1–067
5. Contracts Contained in Deeds		1–085
6. The Relationship between Contract and Tort		1–117
7. Contract and other Legal Categories		1–188

PART TWO

FORMATION OF CONTRACT

2. The Agreement	*G. H. Treitel*	2–001
1. Preliminary		2–001
2. The Offer		2–003
3. The Acceptance		2–027
4. Termination of the Offer		2–087
5. Special Cases		2–110
6. Incomplete Agreement		2–112
7. Certainty of Terms		2–139
8. Conditional Agreements		2–147

9. Contractual Intention 2–158

3. CONSIDERATION *G. H. Treitel* 3–001
1. Introduction 3–001
2. Definitions 3–004
3. Adequacy of Consideration 3–014
4. The Concept of "Valuable" Consideration 3–022
5. Past Consideration 3–026
6. Consideration must Move from the Promisee 3–036
7. Compromise and Forbearance to Sue 3–046
8. Existing Duties as Consideration 3–061
9. Discharge and Variation of Existing Contractual Duties 3–076
10. Part Payment of a Debt 3–115
11. Proprietary Estoppel 3–137
12. Special Cases 3–165

4. FORM *S. J. Whittaker* 4–001
1. In General 4–001
2. Contracts for the Sale or other Disposition of an Interest in Land 4–009

5. MISTAKE *H. G. Beale* 5–001
1. Introduction 5–001
2. Common Mistake 5–017
3. Mistakes in "Communication" 5–066
4. *Non est Factum* 5–101
5. Rectification of Written Agreements 5–107

6. MISREPRESENTATION *H. G. Beale* 6–001
1. In General 6–001
2. What Constitutes Effective Misrepresentation 6–006
3. Damages for Misrepresentation 6–041
4. Rescission for Misrepresentation 6–103
5. Exclusion of Liability for Misrepresentation 6–134
6. Contracts *Uberrimae Fidei* 6–142

7. DURESS AND UNDUE INFLUENCE *H. G. Beale* 7–001
1. Introduction 7–001
2. Duress 7–003
3. Undue Influence 7–056
4. Unconscionable Bargains and Inequality of Bargaining Power 7–126

PART THREE

CAPACITY OF PARTIES

8. PERSONAL INCAPACITY *S. J. Whittaker* 8–001
1. In General 8–001
2. Minors 8–002

3. Persons Lacking Mental Capacity 8–068
4. Drunken Persons 8–080

9. CORPORATIONS AND UNINCORPORATED ASSOCIATIONS *D. D. Prentice* 9–001
1. Corporations 9–001
2. Unincorporated Associations 9–064

10. THE CROWN, PUBLIC AUTHORITIES AND THE EUROPEAN COMMUNITY *P. Mitchell* 10–001
1. Introduction 10–001
2. Crown Contracts 10–004
3. Public Authorities 10–020
4. Tender Process Contracts 10–035
5. Estoppel 10–039
6. Public Procurement 10–044

11. POLITICAL IMMUNITY AND INCAPACITY *C. G. J. Morse* 11–001
1. Foreign States, Sovereigns, Ambassadors and International Organisations 11–001
2. Alien Enemies 11–024

PART FOUR

THE TERMS OF THE CONTRACT

12. EXPRESS TERMS *A. G. Guest* 12–001
1. Proof of Terms 12–002
2. Classification of Terms 12–019
3. Construction of Terms 12–041
4. Admissibility of Extrinsic Evidence 12–095

13. IMPLIED TERMS *A. G. Guest* 13–001

14. EXEMPTION CLAUSES *A. G. Guest* 14–001
1. In General 14–001
2. Principles of Construction 14–005
3. Fundamental Breach 14–020
4. Application of Principles of Construction to Particular Contracts 14–025
5. Exemption Clauses and Third Parties 14–039
6. Statutory Control of Exemption Clauses 14–059
7. Common Law Qualifications 14–132
8. *Force Majeure* Clauses 14–137

15. UNFAIR TERMS IN CONSUMER CONTRACTS — *S. J. Whittaker* 15–001
1. Introduction 15–001
2. The EC Directive on Unfair Terms in Consumer Contracts and the UK Regulations 15–004
3. The Temporal Application of the Regulations 15–011
4. The Types of Contracts Governed by the Regulations 15–016
5. Contract Terms Excluded from the Regulations 15–038
6. The Requirement of Fairness 15–044
7. The Requirement of Plain and Intelligible Language 15–128
8. Choice of Law Clauses 15–131
9. The Prevention of Unfair Terms 15–132

PART FIVE

ILLEGALITY AND PUBLIC POLICY

16. ILLEGALITY AND PUBLIC POLICY — *D. D. Prentice* 16–001
1. Introduction 16–001
2. The Position at Common Law 16–003
3. Contracts Unenforceable by Statute 16–142
4. Enforcement of Collateral and Proprietary Rights 16–164
5. Severance 16–194
6. Pleading and Practice 16–204

PART SIX

JOINT OBLIGATIONS, THIRD PARTIES AND ASSIGNMENT

17. JOINT OBLIGATIONS — *A. S. Burrows* 17–001

18. THIRD PARTIES — *G. H. Treitel* 18–001
1. Introduction 18–001
2. The Common Law Doctrine 18–003
3. Scope 18–021
4. Contracts for the Benefit of Third Parties 18–043
5. Enforcement Against Third Parties 18–133

19. ASSIGNMENT — *A. S. Burrows* 19–001
1. Assignment 19–001
2. Vicarious Performance 19–081
3. Assignment and Negotiability 19–085
4. Assignment, Novation and Acknowledgment 19–086

20. DEATH AND BANKRUPTCY — *D. D. Prentice* 20–001
1. Death 20–001
2. Bankruptcy 20–015

PART SEVEN

PERFORMANCE AND DISCHARGE

21. PERFORMANCE *E. G. McKendrick* 21–001
1. In General 21–001
2. Time of Performance 21–011
3. Partial Performance of an Entire Obligation 21–027
4. Payment 21–039
5. Tender 21–083

22. DISCHARGE BY AGREEMENT *E. G. McKendrick* 22–001
1. In General 22–001
2. Release 22–003
3. Accord and Satisfaction 22–012
4. Rescission 22–025
5. Variation 22–032
6. Waiver 22–040
7. Provision for Discharge in the Contract Itself 22–048

23. DISCHARGE BY FRUSTRATION *E. G. McKendrick* 23–001
1. Introduction 23–001
2. The Test for Frustration 23–007
3. Illustrations of the Doctrine 23–020
4. The Limits of Frustration 23–058
5. The Legal Consequences of Frustration 23–070

24. DISCHARGE BY BREACH *E. G. McKendrick* 24–001
1. In General 24–001
2. Renunciation 24–018
3. Impossibility Created by One Party 24–028
4. Failure of Performance 24–034
5. Consequences of Discharge 24–047

25. OTHER MODES OF DISCHARGE *E. G. McKendrick* 25–001
1. Merger 25–001
2. Alteration or Cancellation of a Written Instrument 25–020
3. Miscellaneous Modes of Discharge 25–028

PART EIGHT

REMEDIES FOR BREACH OF CONTRACT

26. DAMAGES *H. G. Beale* 26–001
1. Nature and Kinds of Damages 26–001
2. Causation and Contributory Negligence 26–032
3. Remoteness of Damage 26–051
4. Illustrations of the Remoteness of Damage and the Assessment of Damages 26–088

5. Assumption of Responsibility 26–100A
6. Mitigation of Damage 26–101
7. Penalty or Liquidated Damages 26–125
8. The Tax Element in Damages 26–157
9. Interest and Rate of Exchange 26–167

27. SPECIFIC PERFORMANCE AND INJUNCTION *G. H. Treitel* 27–001
1. Introduction 27–001
2. The "Adequacy" of Damages 27–005
3. Contracts Not Specifically Enforceable 27–020
4. Other Grounds for Refusing Specific Performance 27–030
5. Mutuality of Remedy 27–046
6. Specific Performance and Third Parties 27–049
7. Specific Performance with Compensation 27–054
8. Injunction 27–060
9. Damages and Specific Performance or Injunction 27–077

28. LIMITATION OF ACTIONS *A. S. Burrows* 28–001
1. Periods of Limitation 28–001
2. Accrual of the Cause of Action 28–031
3. Computation of the Period 28–062
4. The Running of Time 28–064
5. Extension of the Period 28–071
6. Abridgement of the Period 28–112
7. Commencement of Proceedings 28–116
8. The Statute Bars the Remedy, Not the Right 28–126
9. Limitation in Equity 28–134

PART NINE

RESTITUTION

29. RESTITUTION *G. Virgo* 29–001
1. Introduction 29–001
2. Unjust Enrichment 29–018
3. Restitution for Wrongs 29–139
4. Proprietary Restitutionary Claims 29–158
5. Defences 29–176
6. Miscellaneous Restitutionary Claims 29–191

PART TEN

CONFLICT OF LAWS

30. CONFLICT OF LAWS *C. G. J. Morse* 30–001
1. Preliminary Considerations 30–001
2. Common Law: The Doctrine of the Proper Law of a Contract 30–005

3. The Rome Convention 30–017
4. The Rome I Regulation 30–130
5. Scope of the Applicable Law 30–303

Page
Index 2151

VOLUME II

31. Agency

32. Arbitration

33. Bailment

34. Bills of Exchange and Banking

35. Carriage by Air

36. Carriage by Land

37. Construction Contracts

38. Credit and Security

39. Employment

40. Gaming and Wagering

41. Insurance

42. Restrictive Agreements and Competition

43. Sale of Goods

44. Suretyship

Please note that Volume I is available for sale separately from Volume II, so you will only have access to the above contents of Volume II if you have purchased both Volumes.

TABLE OF STATUTES

[Where a reference indicates significant discussion of the statute in the text, it is in **bold**. Where a reference is to a footnote, it is *italic*.]

1551 Sale of Offices Act (5 & 6 Edw.6 c.16) *16–022*
1562 5 Eliz. c.4 .... *8–023*
1623 Limitation Act (21 Jac.1 c.16) 28–077, 28–092
1677 Statute of Frauds (29 Car.2 c.3) *3–143*, 4–009, 4–066, 4–073, *4–075*, 20–014, 22–001, 22–030
s.4 ...*1–084*, 1–104, 3–168, *4–004*, 4–006, 4–009, 4–010, 4–011, 4–014, 4–059, *4–075*, 4–081, 5–112, *9–015*, *12–102*, *22–030*, *22–033*, *30–311*
s.17 ....4–009, *22–030*, *22–043*
1688 Bill of Rights (1 Will. & Mar. Sess.2 c.2)
art.4 .... *10–006*, 29–083
1774 Life Assurance Act (14 Geo.3 c.48)
s.1 .... *16–186*
Fires Prevention (Metropolis) Act (14 Geo.3 c.78)
s.83 .... *18–129*
1814 Apprentices Act (54 Geo.3 c.96)
s.2 .... *8–023*
1828 Statute of Frauds Amendment Act (Lord Tenterden's Act) (9 Geo.4 c.14) *6–015*, *6–070*
s.1 .... *28–092*
s.5 .... *8–042*
s.6 .... *6–041*
1830 Carriers Act (11 Geo.4 & 1 Will.4 c.68)
s.4 12–018
s.5 .... *17–010*
1833 Real Property Limitation Act (3 & 4 Will.4 c.27)
s.16 .... *28–076*
Civil Procedure Act (3 & 4 Will.4 c.42) ...28–092, *28–101*
s.8 .... *17–010*
1837 Wills Act (7 Will.4 & 1 Vict. c.26)
s.18 .... *16–073*
s.20 .... *16–073*
1838 Judgments Act (1 & 2 Vict c.110) 26–179
s.17 ....*26–179*, *26–184*, *30–378*
1842 Ecclesiastical Leasing Act (5 & 6 Vict. c.108) *9–006*
1845 Companies Clauses Consolidation Act (8 & 9 Vict. c.16) 8–037
s.79 .... *8–037*
Gaming Act (8 & 9 Vict. c.109) 16–144, 29–039, 29–075
s.18 3–169
Real Property Act (8 & 9 Vict.)
s.5 ....1–109, 18–123, 18–124, *18–125*
1852 Common Law Procedure Act (6 & 7 Vict. c.76) 29–007
s.34 .... *1–118*
s.35 .... *1–118*
s.41 .... *1–118*
s.74 .... *1–118*
1855 Bills of Lading Act (9 & 10 Vict. c.111) *14–055*
s.1 .... *18–034*, *18–052*
1856 Mercantile Law Amendment Act (19 & 20 Vict. c.97) *12–102*
s.2 .... *27–014*
s.5 .... *29–110*
s.13 .... *28–092*
1858 Chancery Amendment Act (Lord Cairns' Act) (21 & 22 Vict. c.27) *6–100*
s.2 27–077
Ecclesiastical Leasing Act (21 & 22 Vict. c.57) *9–006*
1860 Petitions of Right Act (23 & 24 Vict. c.34) 10–015

1861 Ecclesiastical Leases Act (24 & 25 Vict. c.105) *9–006*
1862 Ecclesiastical Leases Act (25 & 26 Vict. c.52) *9–006*
Companies Act (25 & 26 Vict. c.89)
s.53 .... *9–040*
1865 Ecclesiastical Leases Act (28 & 29 Vict.) *9–006*
1867 Sale of Land by Auction Act (30 & 31 Vict. c.48)
ss.4–7 .... *29–148*
s.5 .... *2–012*
Policies of Assurance Act (30 & 31 Vict. c.144)
s.1 .... *19–003*
1870 Apportionment Act (33 & 34 Vict. c.35) *29–070*
s.2 21–030
1871 ..... Trade Union Act (34 & 35 Vict. c.31) .. *16–127*, 29–192
s.3 .... *9–084*, *16–133*
s.4 .... *16–133*
1873 Supreme Court of Judicature Act (36 & 37 Vict. c.66) ...5–124, 7–010, 16–062, *17–027*, 18–086, 19–038, 19–040, 22–030
s.24 .... *28–123*
s.25 19–004
(7) *21–012*
(11) *18–086*
1874 Infants' Relief Act (37 & 38 Vict. c.62) 8–005, *8–066*, *29–081*
s.1 ....*8–005*, *8–020*, 8–045, *8–065*
s.2 8–044
1875 Public Health Act (38 & 39 Vict. c.55)
s.174 5–113
1876 Treasury Solicitor Act (39 & 40 Vict. c.18)
s.1 .... *8–002*
Trade Union Act Amendment Act (39 & 40 Vict. c.22) *16–127*, *16–133*
s.9 .... *8–060*
1881 Conveyancing Act (44 & 45 Vict. c.41)
s.58 .... *1–109*
s.60 .... *3–044*
1882 Bills of Sale Act (1878) Amendment Act (45 & 46 Vict. c.43)
s.9 .... *4–003*, *21–058*
Municipal Corporations Act (45 & 46 Vict. c.50) 16–019
Bills of Exchange Act (45 & 46 Vict. c.61) *19–003*, 21–080
s.10(1)(a) *28–042*
s.11(1) *28–041*
s.12 .... *12–110*
s.13(1) *12–110*
s.14(2) *28–041*
(3) *28–041*
(4) 21–026
s.19(2)(c) *28–041*, *28–042*
s.20 .... *12–110*
s.22(2) *8–020*
s.26(1) *20–011*
s.27(1)(b) 3–034
s.29 .... *19–085*
s.30 .... *19–085*
(2) *7–052*
s.31(5) *20–011*
s.36(2) *19–085*
s.38 .... *19–085*
(2) *19–072*
s.39(1) *28–041*
s.43 .... *28–043*
s.45 .... *21–010*
s.47 .... *28–043*
s.48 .... *21–009*, *28–043*
s.49 .... *21–009*
s.50(2) *28–043*
s.52 .... *28–041*
(1) 21–010
(2) *28–042*
s.53(1) *19–015*
(2) *19–015*
s.55 .... *28–043*
(1) *28–044*
(2) *28–044*
s.57 .... *26–010*, *26–098*, *26–174*, *28–044*, *29–108*
s.59 .... *28–044*
(2) *29–108*
s.61 25–004
s.62 .... *3–078*, *3–126*, 22–009, *22–020*
(2) *22–009*
s.63 .... *25–026*
s.64 .... *21–081*
(1) 25–024
(2) *25–024*
s.65(1) *29–133*
s.66(1) *29–133*
s.68(3) *29–109*
(4) *29–109*
(5) *29–133*
s.69 .... *21–056*, *21–080*, 25–027
s.70 .... *25–027*
s.85(1) *17–005*
(2) *17–005*
s.87 .... *21–010*, *28–041*
(1) *28–042*

(2) *28–043*
(3) *28–043*
s.89 .... *22–020*
s.90 .... *9–033*
Married Women's Property Act (45 & 46 Vict. c.75)
s.11 .... *18–084*, 18–126
1883 Trial of Lunatics Act (46 & 47 Vict. c.38)
s.2 .... *16–169*
1890 Lunacy Act (53 & 54 Vict. c.5) 8–077
Inland Revenue Regulation Act (53 & 54 Vict. c.21)
s.1(2) *10–021*
Partnership Act (53 & 54 Vict. c.39) 24–049
ss.1–3 .... *3–175*
s.6(3) *3–175*
s.7(3) *22–031*
s.9 .... *17–005*, *17–012*
ss.9–12 .... *29–127*
s.12 .... *17–005*
s.17(3) *3–175*
s.24(1) *29–127*
(2) *29–127*
s.26(1) *15–100*
s.28 6–162
s.29 6–162
s.30 6–162
s.40 .... *29–060*
s.44 .... *29–127*
Directors' Liability Act (53 & 54 Vict.) *6–090*, *6–153*
1891 Stamp Act (54 & 55 Vict. c.39)
s.14 .... *21–058*
(4) *29–192*
s.103 .... *21–093*
1892 Gaming Act (55 & 56 Vict. c.9) 16–144
1893 Sale of Goods Act (56 & 57 Vict. c.71) *1–070*, 8–007, 24–038, 26–088
s.2 .... *8–007*, 8–010, 8–074
s.4 .... 22–030, *22–043*
s.6 5–023
s.7 .... *23–005*
s.11(1) 12–036
(c) *12–023*
ss.12–15 .... *24–038*
s.14 .... *1–017*
s.22 .... *2–117*
s.23 .... *2–117*
s.24 .... *2–117*
s.50 26–088
s.51 26–088
s.53 26–088
s.54 26–088
s.55 .... 14–090, *14–091*, *14–101*
(3) *14–081*
(4) *14–081*
(5) *14–085*
1897 Police (Property) Act (60 & 61 Vict. c.30) *29–139*
1906 Marine Insurance Act (6 Edw.7 c.41) 6–144
s.1 .... *1–069*
s.4 3–169
s.14(2) *18–128*
s.18(1) *6–148*
(2) 6–145
s.20(2) *6–037*
(4) 6–020
(5) 6–009
s.31(2) *2–129*
ss.33–41 .... *12–026*, *12–031*
s.34(3) *6–149*
s.50 .... *19–072*
(2) *19–003*, *19–072*
s.66(1) *29–129*
s.80 .... *29–128*
Sch.I r.12 .... *12–087*
Trade Disputes Act (6 Edw.7 c.47)
s.4 .... *29–143*
Public Trustee Act (6 Edw.7 c.55)
s.1 .... *9–002*
1914 Aliens Restriction Act (4 & 5 Geo.5 c.12) 11–027
Deeds of Arrangement Act (4 & 5 Geo.5 c.47) *3–125*, *18–122*, *20–051*
s.1 .... *20–051*
s.2 20–051
Bankruptcy Act (4 & 5 Geo.5 c.59) *20–020*
s.30(1) *1–125*
s.34 .... *20–032*
s.37 .... *20–019*
s.42 .... *18–079*
s.46 .... *20–019*
1915 Legal Proceedings against Alien Enemies Act (9 & 10 Geo.5) *11–030*
1920 Administration of Justice Act (10 & 11 Geo.5 c.81) *11–004*, *11–005*, *25–017*, *28–016*
s.9(2)(a) *25–017*
(b) *25–017*
(c) *25–017*
(d) *25–017*
(f) *25–017*

1924 Carriage of Goods by Sea Act (14 & 15 Geo.5 c.22)
Sch. *18–034*
1925 Settled Land Act (15 & 16 Geo.5 c.18)
s.1 .... *3–157*
s.19 .... *8–034*
s.20 .... *8–034*
s.26 .... *8–034*
s.27 .... *8–034*
(1) 8–034
Trustee Act (15 & 16 Geo.5 c.19)
s.13 .... *3–019*
s.15 20–014
s.23(3)(a) *21–043*
s.27 20–013
(2) *20–013*
Law of Property Act (15 & 16 Geo.5 c.20) 1–098, 4–010, 4–054, 13–031
s.1(6) *8–034*
s.19 .... *8–034*
s.22(1) 8–079
(2) 8–079
s.34 .... *29–118*
s.40 .. *3–143*, *4–002*, *4–003*, 4–009, **4–010**, 4–011, *4–013*, 4–014, 4–015, 4–019, 4–022, 4–029, 4–031, *4–036*, 4–041, 4–044, 4–052, *4–056*, 4–059, 4–060, *4–072*, 4–073, 4–075, 4–084, 4–087, 4–088, *12–102*, *19–006*, *27–037*
(1) 4–010, 4–043, *22–033*
(2) *4–010*, 4–042
s.41 .... *12–037*, **21–012**, 21–018
s.46 .... *2–049*
s.47 .... *18–128*
s.49(2) *4–041*, *4–084*, *24–053*, 26–146, **26–152**, *29–064*
ss.51—55 4–055
s.52 .... *4–002*, *4–003*
s.53 .... *19–006*
(1)(a) *4–059*
(b) *18–079*, *19–025*
(c) 4–013, *4–028*, *4–055*, 19–025, 19–026
(2) *4–013*, *19–025*
s.54 .... *4–002*, *4–003*
(2) *4–068*
s.55(d) 4–042
s.56 18–124
(1) 1–109, 18–020, **18–122**, 18–124, 18–125
(2) *18–122*
s.58 12–068
s.61 .... 12–061, 12–026
s.67 .... *12–108*
s.68 .... *12–108*
s.69 .... *21–043*
s.73 .... *1–086*, 4–040
s.74 1–095
(1) 1–091, 1–094, *1–100*
(1A) *1–098*
s.74A(1) *1–100*
(2) *1–100*
s.77 .... *29–106*
s.78 .... *1–109*
s.81 3–044
s.82 .... *9–071*, 17–007
s.84(7) *3–020*
s.108 .... *18–128*
s.136 ..... 16–061, 16–062, 19–004, **19–006**, *19–017*, 19–041, 19–042, *19–059*, 19–066, 19–070
(1) *18–100*
s.137(3) 19–069
s.139 1–047
s.141 1–047
s.146 .... *22–048*, *26–147*
s.172 .... *1–108*, *3–019*
s.173 .... *1–108*, *3–019*
(1) *29–147*
s.180(1) *9–002*
(3) *9–002*
s.185 .... *25–004*
s.191 .... *27–026*
s.196(3) *2–060*
s.205(1)(ii) *4–011*
(xx) ... 1–109, *9–002*, *18–124*, *18–128*
(xxi) *3–019*
Land Registration Act (15 & 16 Geo.5 c.21) *4–013*
s.70(1) *4–013*
Land Charges Act (15 & 16 Geo.5 c.22) *4–013*
s.10 .... *4–013*
(1) 4–057
s.13(2) 3–020
Administration of Estates Act (15 & 16 Geo.5 c.23)
s.21 .... *20–004*
s.21A *17–023*, 28–065
(1) *28–065*
(b) *17–023*
(2) *28–065*
(3) *28–065*
s.27(2) 21–049
s.28 .... *20–012*
s.33(1) *20–010*
s.34(2) *25–006*
s.38 .... *20–013*
s.55(1)(xi) *21–049*
(xx) *21–049*

Supreme Court of Judicature (Consolidation) Act (15 & 16 Geo.5 c.49)
s.38 ... *28–123*
s.41 ... *28–123*
s.43 ... 5–124
Honours (Prevention of Abuses) Act (15 & 16 Geo.5) ... *16–021*
1926 Fertilisers and Feeding Stuffs Act (16 & 17 Geo.5 c.45)
s.1(2) ... *16–153*
1927 Auctions (Bidding Agreements) Act (17 & 18 Geo.5 c.12) ... *27–015*
s.1 ... *16–135*
Moneylenders Act (17 & 18 Geo.5 c.21)
s.6 ... *29–173*
1930 Mental Treatment Act (20 & 21 Geo.5 c.23) ... 8–077, 28–006
Third Parties (Rights against Insurers) Act (20 & 21 Geo.5 c.35) ... *18–131*
1932 Solicitors Act (22 & 23 Geo.5 c.37)
s.47(3) ... *16–019*
1933 Children and Young Persons Act (23 & 24 Geo.5 c.12)
s.18(1) ... *8–025*
Foreign Judgments (Reciprocal Enforcement) Act (23 & 24 Geo.5 c.13) ... *25–017*, *28–016*
s.2(a) ... *25–017*
s.4(1)(a) ... *25–017*
s.8(1) ... *25–017*
(2) ... *25–017*
1934 Law Reform (Miscellaneous Provisions) Act (24 & 25 Geo.5 c.41) ... 20–006, *29–141*
s.1 ... *1–118*, 28–064, 28–072
(1) ... 20–001
(3) ... *1–118*, *29–143*
s.3 ... *26–174*
(1) ... *26–174*
(c) ... *26–174*
Road Traffic Act (24 & 25 Geo.5 c.50)
s.8 ... *16–147*
Betting and Lotteries Act (24 & 25 Geo.5 c.58)
s.13 ... *29–150*
1935 Law Reform (Married Women and Tortfeasors) Act (25 & 26 Geo.5 c.30) ... *8–001*
s.1(c) ... *8–001*
s.6 ... 17–033, 17–034
(2) ... *29–121*
1938 Inheritance (Family Provision) Act (1 & 2 Geo.6 c.45) ... *18–047*
1939 Limitation Act (2 & 3 Geo.6 c.21) ... 28–086, 28–123
s.26(b) ... 28–086, *28–087*
(c) ... *28–088*
Trading with the Enemy Act (2 & 3 Geo.6 c.89) ... *11–025*, 11–026, 11–028, **16–162**
s.1 ... 16–162
(2) ... 16–162
s.2 ... *11–026*, *23–030*
(1) ... 16–163
(2) ... *16–163*
s.15(1) ... 16–163
(1A) ... *16–163*
1943 Law Reform (Frustrated Contracts) Act (6 & 7 Geo.6 c.40) ... *2–099*, 18–117, *21–026*, *21–031*, *23–024*, 23–056, 23–070, **23–074**, *23–082*, 23–087, 23–098, *29–056*, 29–060, *30–373*
s.1 ... *23–071*
(1) ... 23–074
(2) ... *1–034*, **23–076**, 23–077, 23–078, 23–079, 23–080, *23–082*, *29–059*
(3) ... *1–034*, *1–059*, *15–116*, *23–073*, *23–078*, 23–079, **23–084**, *23–085*, 23–086, 23–088, 23–090, 23–095, *29–014*, 29–060
(a) ... 23–089
(b) ... 23–086
(4) ... *23–083*
(5) ... *23–093*
(6) ... 23–095
s.2(2) ... 23–095
(3) ... **23–092**, *29–058*
(4) ... **23–091**
(5) ... 23–096
(c) ... *23–096*
s.6(3) ... *29–059*
1945 Limitation (Enemies and War Prisoners) Act (8 & 9 Geo.6 c.16) ... 11–031, 28–069

Law Reform (Contributory Negligence) Act (8 & 9 Geo.6 c.28) ...*1–122*, 6–040, 6–064, 6–074, 17–034, 26–049
s.1 .... 1–166, 6–074
(1) 6–064, *26–049*
s.4 6–064
Bretton Woods Agreements Act (9 & 10 Geo.6 c.19) *16–011*, *16–159*
1946 National Health Service Act (9 & 10 Geo.6 c.81)
s.13 10–010
1947 Crown Proceedings Act (10 & 11 Geo.6 c.44) **10–015**, 10–045, *29–141*
s.1 10–015
s.2(1) 10–016
s.17 10–010
(2) *10–010*
(3) *10–010*
s.21 10–019
(1) **10–016**, 10–017, 10–018
(2) **10–018**, 10–019
s.25(4) *10–010*
s.38(2) *10–018*
s.40(1) *10–015*
(2)(b) *10–015*
(3) *10–015*
1948 National Assistance Act (11 & 12 Geo.6 c.29)
s.21 .... *1–053*, 1–054
Companies Act (11 & 12 Geo.6 c.38) 28–004
s.20(1) *28–004*
s.54 ....*9–038*, *16–165*, 16–193, *16–201*
(2) *16–193*
s.242(2)(a) *16–063*
Law Reform (Personal Injuries) Act (11 & 12 Geo.6 c.41)
s.1(3) 14–121
Agricultural Holdings Act (11 & 12 Geo.6 c.63)
s.24 16–016
1950 Statute Law Revision Act 1950 (13 & 14 Geo.6 c.6)
s.1 ....*10–015*
Arbitration Act (13 &14 Geo.6 c.27) 11–019
s.13A *2–006*
s.19 ....*29–094*
s.20 ....*26–184*
s.27 28–115
1952 Income Tax Act (15 & 16 Geo.6 & 1 Eliz.2 c.10)
s.173 ....*29–107*
Diplomatic Immunities (Commonwealth Countries and Republic of Ireland) Act (15 & 16 Geo.6 & 1 Eliz.2 c.18) 11–017
s.1(1) 11–009
(2) *11–017*
Defamation Act (15 & 16 Geo.6 & 1 Eliz.2 c.66)
s.11 16–175
1954 Currency and Bank Notes Act (2 & 3 Eliz.2 c.12)
s.1(2) 21–086
(6) 21–086
Agriculture (Miscellaneous Provisions) Act (2 & 3 Eliz.2 c.39)
s.12(1) *16–153*
Landlord and Tenant Act (2 & 3 Eliz.2 c.56)
Pt II 1–047
s.29(3) *21–026*
1955 Army Act (3 & 4 Eliz.2 c.18)
s.203 ....*16–022*
Air Force Act (3 & 4 Eliz.2 c.19)
s.203 ....*16–022*
1957 Occupiers' Liability Act (5 & 6 Eliz.2 c.31) 14–053, 14–060, 18–132
s.1(2) *1–119*
s.2(1) *13–014*
(2) *13–014*, *29–013*
s.3(1) *14–053*, *18–132*
(1)–(4) *13–014*
(4) *13–017*
s.5(1) *13–014*
(2) *13–014*
(3) *13–014*
Maintenance Agreements Act (5 & 6 Eliz.2 c.35)
s.1 .... *3–055*
Cheques Act (5 & 6 Eliz.2 c.36)
s.3 ....*21–058*
s.4(3) *29–036*
1959 Mental Health Act (7 & 8 Eliz.2 c.72)
Sch.8 .... *8–077*

1960 Road Traffic Act (8 & 9 Eliz.2 c.16)
s.151 .... *3–181*
Carriage by Air Act (8 & 9 Eliz.2 c.27) 14–118
Corporate Bodies' Contracts Act (8 & 9 Eliz.2 c.46) *3–167*, *4–001*
Betting and Gaming Act (8 & 9 Eliz.2 c.60) 16–143
1961 Diplomatic Immunities (Conference with Commonwealth Countries and Republic of Ireland) Act (9 & 10 Eliz.2 c.11) 11–019
Restriction of Offensive Weapons Act (9 & 10 Eliz.2 c.22)
s.1 .... *2–014*
Carriage by Air Act (c.27) 28–024, 28–126
s.5 .... *28–024*
(3) *28–024*
Sch.1 art.22(5) *30–377*
art.26 .... *28–024*
art.29 .... *28–024*, *28–126*
Suicide Act (c.60)
s.1 16–171
Housing Act (c.65)
s.32 .... *21–009*
1962 Carriage by Air (Supplementary Provisions) Act (10 & 11 Eliz.2 c.43)
s.3(2) *28–024*
Landlord and Tenant Act (10 & 11 Eliz.2 c.50)
s.1 .... *4–003*
1963 Stock Transfer Act (c.18) ... *19–003*
Limitation Act (c.47)
s.4(4) *28–024*
1964 Plant Varieties and Seeds Act (c.14) 14–124
s.16 .... *14–124*
s.17 .... *14–124*
Hire Purchase Act (c.53)
s.27 5–095
Diplomatic Privileges Act (c.81) 11–008, 11–009, 11–022
s.2(3) *11–022*
s.4 .... *11–015*
s.8(4) *11–009*
Sch.1 11–008
art.1 .... *11–010*
art.32 .... *11–022*
Sch.2 .... *11–009*
1965 Industrial and Provident Societies Act (c.12) 9–063
s.20 .... *8–060*
Carriage of Goods by Road Act (c.37) 14–116, 28–026
Sch. *28–026*, *28–068*, *28–124*
Redundancy Payments Act (c.62) *9–047*
Hire Purchase Act (c.66) ... *4–002*
1966 Commonwealth Secretariat Act (c.10) 11–023
s.1(2) *11–019*, *11–023*
Sch. *11–019*
para.8 .... *11–023*
Arbitration (International Investment Disputes) Act (c.41) 11–023
s.4 .... *11–019*
Sch. *11–019*
art.20 .... *11–023*
art.21 .... *11–023*
1967 Misrepresentation Act (c.7) 1–131, 1–132, 1–136, 6–001, 6–004, 6–017, 6–041, 6–042, 6–088, 6–103, 6–104, 6–123, 6–133, 6–139, 6–152, 12–005, **14–114**, 18–117
s.1 .... *23–056*
(a) *1–131*, **6–105**, 6–106, 6–108, *6–125*, *6–140*, *14–114*, *27–058*
(b) *6–114*, 6–133, *27–155*
s.2 .... 1–122, *6–068*
(1) *1–131*, *1–133*, 1–165, *5–047*, 6–001, 6–019, 6–040, 6–041, 6–042, *6–054*, **6–068**, 6–069, 6–070, 6–072, 6–073, 6–074, 6–076, 6–077, 6–078, 6–097, 6–099, *6–100*, *6–101*, *6–134*, 6–142, 6–143, *12–005*, *26–049*, *28–010*, 28–034, 28–083
(2) 1–034, 1–059, *1–131*, *6–025*, 6–072, 6–094, **6–096**, 6–097, 6–098, 6–099, 6–100, 6–101, 6–102, 6–107, 6–108, 6–109, *6–111*, 6–133, 6–152, *14–114*, *23–056*, 27–055, 27–058
(3) *6–096*, 6–099
s.3 ...*1–132*, *6–134*, *6–135*, **6–136**, 6–137, 6–138, *6–139*, 6–141, *12–104*, 14–085, 14–090, *14–092*, 14–114, 27–058, 28–113
s.84 .... *6–111*
Sch.2 ground 5 .... *6–111*

Uniform Laws on International Sales Act (c.45) 28–027, *30–002*, *30–015*, *30–027*
Sch.1 ...... *28–027*, *28–114*, *30–015*
Criminal Law Act (c.58) ... 16–048
s.1 .... *3–062*
(1) *16–037*
(2) *16–037*
s.5 .... 16–036, 16–037, 16–038
(1) *3–062, 7–049*, *16–036*
(3) *16–036*
(5) *7–049*
s.13(1)(a) *16–048*
(b) *16–048*
s.14 .... *30–366*
(1) *16–048*
(2) 16–048, 16–049, *16–057*, 19–053
Sch.4 .... *16–048*
1968 Consular Relations Act (c.18) 11–017, 11–022
s.1(5) *11–022*
s.12 .... *11–017*
Sch.I art.1 .... *11–017*
art.45 .... *11–022*
Trade Descriptions Act (c.29) *6–012*, *6–016*
s.14(1)(b) *2–020*
s.35 .... *16–144*
International Organisations Act (c.48) ... 11–018, 11–019, 11–023
s.12(5) *11–019*
Hovercraft Act (c.59)
s.1 .... *14–106*
Theft Act (c.60)
s.3(1) *2–015*
1969 Family Law Reform Act (c.46)
s.1 8–002
s.9 8–002
s.11 .... *8–023*
s.19(1) *18–126*
Auctions (Bidding Agreements) Act (c.56)
s.3(1) *1–082*, *16–135*
Employers' Liability (Compulsory Insurance) Act (c.57) *13–010*, *16–173*
1970 Taxes Management Act (c.9)
s.33 29–085
Proceedings against Estates Act (c.17)
s.2 .... *28–031*
Administration of Justice Act (c.31)
s.40 .... *21–010*
s.44A *30–378*
Law Reform (Miscellaneous Provisions) Act (c.33)
s.1 .... *3–073*, 16–070, *23–037*, *26–019*, *28–086*
s.2 16–070
s.6 .... *28–086*
s.7(2) *28–086*
Agriculture Act (c.40) 14–124
s.68(6) *14–124*
s.72(3) *14–124*
Equal Pay Act (c.41) 28–030, 30–115
s.1(1) *1–017*, *30–114*, *30–115*
s.2(5) *28–030*
Matrimonial Proceedings and Property Act (c.45)
s.41 .... *8–019*
1971 Carriage of Goods by Sea Act (c.19) *14–106*, *14–111*, 14–117, *18–034*, 28–022, 28–115, 28–126, *30–008*, *30–026*
s.1 .... *1–069*, 28–022
(2) *18–032*
s.2 .... *28–022*
s.3 .... *14–032*
s.4 .... *28–022*
s.5 .... *28–022*
Sch. *14*–042, 18–*032*, *28–022*, *28–126*
art.I(b) *1–069*
art.III(1) *14–032*
Coinage Act (c.24)
s.2 21–086
(1) *21–086*
(1B) *21–086*
s.3(e) *21–086*
(EE) *21–086*
Unsolicited Goods and Services Act (c.30) *29–133*
s.3A *4–002*
Industrial Relations Act (c.72) 9–083
1972 Summer Time Act (c.6)
s.3(1) *21–023*
Superannuation Act (c.11)
s.5(1) *19–047*
Defective Premises Act (c.35) 13–015, 18–132, *28–010*
s.1 .... *1–173*, *13–015*, *18–132*, 28–056
(5) *28–056*
s.2 .... *13–015*
s.3 .... *13–015*
s.4 .... *1–173*, *18–132*
(2) *21–009*

(4) ... *13–016*
s.6 ... *13–015*
(3) ... 14–120
European Communities Act (c.68)
s.2 ... *16–005*
s.3 ... *16–005*
s.9(1) ... 9–027
(2) ... 9–012
Local Government Act (c.70)
s.94 ... *16–020*
s.111 ... 10–022
(1) ... 10–023
s.123 ... *3–019*
(2) ... *3–019*, *3–022*
s.117 ... *16–020*
Sch.13 Pt 1 ... *10–022*, 10–024
1973 Supply of Goods (Implied Terms) Act (c.13) ... 12–036
s.8(3) ... *12–031*
ss.8–11 ... *1–017*, 13–029, 14–028, 14–078
s.10(2D) ... *2–020*, *2–165*
Matrimonial Causes Act (c.18)
s.1(2)(d) ... 16–043
s.12 ... *7–010*
s.25 ... *6–155*
s.34 ... *3–055*, *3–166*, 3–168, *16–044*, *16–201*
s.35 ... *16–044*, *23–040*
Fair Trading Act (c.41) ... 14–131, *16–139*
Pt XI ... *16–017*
s.26 ... *16–144*
ss.34–43 ... *14–131*
Domicile and Matrimonial Proceedings Act (c.45)
s.5(2) ... *30–079*
1974 Consumer Credit Act (c.39) .. 1–021, 1–037, 1–044, 1–045, 1–048, *1–073*, *2–159*, 7–138, 14–126, 14–128, *15–003*, *15–079*, 18–006, 26–001, 26–146, **26–155**, *30–008*, *30–102*, *30–341*
Pt III ... *16–147*
s.8 ... *1–069*
s.16(6C) ... *26–155*
s.21 ... *16–147*
s.40(1) ... *16–147*, 16–155
s.45 ... *2–020*
s.46 ... *2–020*
s.56(2) ... *18–006*, *30–084*
s.59 ... *2–135*
s.60 ... *1–084*, *4–001*, 4–002
ss.60–65 ... *30–311*
s.61 ... *1–084*, *4–001*
s.65 ... *1–084*, *4–003*
(1) ... 1–037
s.67 ... *14–128*
ss.67–73 ... *1–082*
s.69(1)(ii) ... *2–089*
(7) ... *2–089*
s.73(1) ... *14–126*
s.75 ... *18–006*, *30–084*, *30–102*
(1) ... *30–065*
s.76 ... *22–048*
s.81 ... *21–059*
s.82 ... *22–033*
s.86 ... *22–048*
s.87 ... *22–048*
s.98 ... *22–048*
s.100(1) ... 26–155
(3) ... 26–155
s.105 ... *4–001*
s.106 ... *1–044*
s.113 ... *1–044*
(7) ... *8–045*
s.125 ... *19–085*
s.127 ... *4–003*
(3) ... 1–037, 1–044
s.129 ... *15–082*
s.132 ... *26–155*
s.136 ... *15–082*
ss.137–139 ... 20–030
ss.137–140 ... *7–126*, *7–138*, *26–167*, *26–182*
s.139(1)(a) ... *20–030*
s.140A(1) ... *1–021*, *26–155*
ss.140A–140D ... *1–021*, *7–126*, *7–138*, 26–155, 26–167
s.140B(1) ... *1–021*, *26–155*
s.140C(4) ... *26–155*
s.171(4)(b) ... *30–352*
s.172 ... *29–176*
(3) ... *29–176*
s.173(1) ... *14–128*
s.189(1) ... *26–155*
Friendly Societies Act (c.46)
s.7(2)(d) ... *9–072*
Solicitors Act (c.47) ... 14–122
s.22 ... *16–019*
s.33 ... *29–198*
s.37 ... 18–130
s.56(6) ... *16–064*
s.57 ... *16–056*
(5) ... *14–122*
s.59 ... *16–055*, *16–056*
(1) ... *16–056*
ss.59–63 ... *16–056*
ss.59–66 ... *14–122*
s.60 ... *16–056*
(5) ... *14–122*
(6) ... *14–122*
s.61 ... *16–056*

(2) *14–122*
s.65(1) *16–064*
s.69 .... *28–053*
s.140 .... *14–122*
Trade Union and Labour Relations Act (c.52) 7–017, 9–082
s.2 .... *9–081*
s.13(1) *29–143*
Rehabilitation of Offenders Act (c.53)
s.4(2) *6–147*
(3) *6–147*
1975 Social Security Act (c.14)
s.24(1) *16–169*
Inheritance (Provision for Family and Dependants) Act (c.63) *3–015*, *16–170*, *18–047*
s.1(3) *3–020*
s.10(2)(b) *3–019*
(5)(b) *3–019*
s.11(2)(c) *3–019*
Sex Discrimination Act (c.65) *16–167*, 28–030, *30–114*
Pt II *27–074*
Pt III *27–074*
s.6(1)(c) *1–016*
s.8 .... *1–119*
s.13 .... *27–075*
s.65 .... *27–074*, *27–078*
(1)(c) *27–022*
(3)(a) *27–022*
s.66 .... *27–074*
s.71(1) *27–022*
s.76 .... *28–030*
s.77 .... *14–121*
s.82(1) *2–181*
Policyholders Protection Act (c.75)
s.7 .... *18–131*
1976 Fatal Accidents Act (c.30) 28–007, 28–009, *28–024*, 28–072, 28–078, 28–091, 28–104
s.12 .... *28–007*, *28–009*
s.13 .... *28–007*, *28–009*
s.14 .... *28–007*, *28–009*
s.33 .... *28–008*
Race Relations Act (c.74) *11–018*, 28–030, *30–114*
Pt II *27–074*
Pt III *27–074*
s.4 .... *30–115*
(1)(c) *1–016*
s.8(1) *30–115*
(1A) *30–115*
s.17 .... *1–016*
s.20 .... *1–016*
s.21 .... *1–016*
s.25 9–076
s.56 .... *27–074*
(1)(c) *27–022*
(4) *27–022*
s.57 .... *27–074*, *27–078*
s.68 .... *28–030*
s.72 .... *14–121*, *27–074*
(1) 1–084
(2) *1–084*
1977 Torts (Interference with Goods) Act (c.32) *29–023*, 29–052, *29–076*
s.2 .... *1–003*
(1) *8–047*
(2) *29–142*
s.3 .... *29–158*, *29–171*
(2) 29–052
s.6 29–052
(1) 29–052
(2) 29–052
(3) 29–052
s.7(4) 29–014, 29–100
s.12 .... *29–052*
(5)(a) *29–052*
Patents Act (c.37)
s.30 .... *19–003*
s.32 .... *19–003*
ss.39–43 .... *30–114*
s.44 .... 16–131, *30–008*, *30–114*
ss.61–62 .... *29–142*
Estate Agents Act (c.38)
s.18 .... *4–002*
Rent Act (c.42) 1–049, 16–185
s.57 .... *29–042*
ss.119–125 .... *16–185*
Sch.I para.2 .... *1–049*
para.3 .... *1–049*
Unfair Contract Terms Act (c.50) ..1–021, 1–178, 6–029, 6–083, *7–126*, 14–003, *14–023*, 14–029, 14–034, **14–059**, 14–064, 14–065, 14–066, 14–092, 14–100, 14–101, 14–102, 14–104, 14–115, 14–125, 14–131, 14–135, 14–137, 14–152, 15–003, 15–010, 15–023, 15–027, 15–028, 15–029, *15–032*, **15–037**, 15–038, 15–067, 15–080, 15–090, 15–092, 15–093, 15–099, 15–116, 15–120, 15–132, 18–110, 18–117, 22–048, 26–001, 26–012, *26–125*, 26–142, 26–144, *26–173*, 28–113, 30–008, *30–102*, 30–103

Pt I *14–059*, 14–062
Pt II *14–059*
Pt III *14–059*
s.1 .... *13–014*
(1) *1–151*, *14–060*
(a) *18–118*
(2) *14–105*, *15–037*
(3) *14–065*, *14–075*, *15–023*
(4) 1–146, *14–041*
s.2 .... 1–151, *1–157*, *13–014*, *14–015*, *14–029*, *14–034*, *14–051*, *14–060*, *14–063*, 14–071, 14–076, 14–105, 14–106, *15–037*, **18–118**
(1) 1–021, 6–030, *8–009*, *8–025*, *14–041*, *14–061*, *14–071*, 14–106, 14–108, 14–109, 18–118
(2) *1–021*, *1–132*, *1–186*, *6–029*, *6–031*, 6–083, 6–141, *14–041*, *14–071*, 14–107, 14–108, 18–118
(3) *14–071*, 14–083
ss.2–4 .... *15–037*, 27–057
ss.2–7 14–113
s.3 .... *1–021*, *13–014*, *14–029*, *14–034*, 14–041, 14–043, **14–072**, 14–073, 14–105, 14–106, 14–107, 14–110, 14–152, *15–026*, *15–036*, *15–037*, 15–046, 18–118, *21–008*, 27–057
(1) *14–060*
(2) 15–093
(a) *14–060*, *14–073*
(b) *2–176*, *14–059*, *14–060*, *14–062*, *14–073*, *14–081*, *14–152*, *15–099*, *21–001*, *22–048*
(3) *14–014*
s.4 .... *14–015*, *14–059*, *14–060*, *14–062*, 14–075, 14–076, 14–105, 14–106, 14–107, 14–110, *15*–003
(1) *14–075*
(2) *14–075*
s.5 .... *14–060*, *14–061*, 14–077
(2) *14–077*
(a) *14–077*
(b) *14–077*
ss.5–7 .... *14–063*
s.6 .... *1–119*, 14–028, *14–060*, *14–065*, 14–078, 14–085, *15–037*
(1) 14–026, *14–061*
(2) 1–002, 1–021, 14–027, *14–061*
(3) *1–021*
(4) *14–078*
s.7 .... *14–060*, *14–067*, **14–079**, 14–085, 14–106
(2) *14–041*, *14–061*, *14–079*
(3) *14–079*
(3A) *14–061*, *14–079*
(4) *14–041*, *14–079*
(5) *14–079*
s.9(1) *14–022*, *14–080*
(2) *14–080*
s.10 .... *14–051*, *14–060*, *14–062*, *14–064*, *14–073*, **14–081**
s.11 .... *1–021*, 6–141, *14–091*, 14–092, *15–072*, *21–001*
(1) *1–064*, 6–136, 6–139, *14–084*, *14–087*, 14–114, *15–067*
(2) *14–059*, 14–085
(3) *14–084*
(4) 14–087
(5) *6–083*, *14–088*, 15–118, *15–120*, *30–352*
s.12 .... *1–073*, *14–027*, *15–026*, *15–028*, *15–029*, *15–037*, *21–001*, *30–008*
(1) *30–093*
(a) *14–066*
(b) *14–066*
(c) *14–067*
(1A) *14–067*
(2) *14–068*, *15–028*, *30–353*
(3) *14–070*, *30–352*
s.13 .... *6–083*, *6–137*, *14–081*, *15–093*
(1) 1–147, 14–062, *14–063*
(2) *14–004*, *14–062*
s.14 .... *14–065*, *14–071*, *14–077*, *15–023*, *15–037*
s.17 .... *14–072*
s.26 .... *14–026*, *14–027*, 14–110, *30–008*, *30–068*, 30–103
(3) 14–110
(4) 14–110
s.27 .... *15–132*, *30–008*, *30–341*
(1) 14–113, *30–008*, *30–068*, *30–341*
(2) 14–082, *30–065*, *30–068*, *30–103*, *30–342*
(a) *30–008*
(b) *30–008*, *30–094*
s.28 .... *14–111*
s.29(1) 14–111
(2) 14–112
(3) *14–111*, *14–112*
Sch.1 .... **14–105**
para.1 14–105
(a) *15–037*
(b) *15–037*
(c) *15–037*, *27–057*
para.2 .... *14–029*, 14–106
para.3 .... *14–029*, 14–107

para.4 14–108
para.5 .... *14–081*
Sch.2 ..... 14–085, 14–086, 14–109, *15–067*, *15–080*
1978 Interpretation Act (c.30) 21–023
s.5 .... 4–006, *12–061*, *14–113*
s.9 .... *21–023*
s.23(3) *21–023*
Sch.1 ...... *12–061*, *14–113*, *21–026*
State Immunity Act (c.33) **11–002**, **11–004**, 11–006, 11–008, 11–021
s.1 .... *11–004*
s.2 .... *11–005*, *11–021*
(2) *11–014*, *11–016*, *11–021*
(3) *11–021*
(a) *11–021*
(b) *11–021*
(4) *11–021*
(5) *11–021*
(6) *11–016*, *11–021*
(7) *11–021*
s.3(1)(a) *11–004*, *11–005*
(3) *11–005*
s.4 .... *11–005*
s.5 .... *11–005*
s.6 .... *11–005*
(3) *11–005*
s.7 .... *11–005*
s.8 .... *11–005*
s.10 .... *11–005*
s.9 .... *11–005*, *11–021*
s.11 .... *11–005*
ss.12–14 .... *11–006*
s.13(2) *11–021*
(b) *11–021*
(3) *11–021*
s.14 .... *11–004*, *11–008*
(4) 11–003
s.15 .... *11–006*
s.16(1) *11–014*
ss.18–19 .... *11–006*
s.20 .... *11–008*
(1) *11–008*
s.21(a) *11–006*
s.22(3) *11–002*
Employment Protection (Consolidation) Act (c.44)
Sch.13 para.17 .... *9–047*
Civil Liability (Contribution) Act (c.47) *16–164*, *16–173*, 17–004, 17–009, 17–015, 17–034, 17–035, *28–015*, 29–014, 29–121
s.1 .... **17–029**, 28–015, 28–051, 28–078, 28–104, 28–124
(1) 17–029, 17–030, *29–099*
(2) 17–029
(3) 17–029, 17–033
(4) *17–032*
(5) *17–032*
(6) *17–032*
s.2(1) 17–031, *29–121*, *29–123*, 29–125
s.3 .... *17–015*, 17–016
s.4 .... *17–009*, *17–016*
s.6(1) 29–121
s.7(3)(b) *29–121*
1979 International Monetary Fund Act (c.29)
s.5(1) *11–019*
Estate Agents Act (c.38)
s.13 .... *29–198*
s.14 .... *29–198*
Merchant Shipping Act (c.39)
s.17 .... *18–032*
Sch.4 .... *18–032*
Sale of Goods Act (c.54) *1–017*, 2–126, 2–131, 12–036, 14–006, 14–093, 14–094, 28–052
Pt 5A *26–003*
s.2(1) 1–069
s.3 ... *8–007*, 8–010, 8–011, 8–012, 8–074, 8–075, 8–081, *29–135*
(2) *8–011*, *8–074*
(3) 8–010
s.6 ... *5–023*, *5–040*, 5–045, 5–046, 5–047
(3) *14–027*
s.7 .... *5–047*, 23–047
s.8(2) *2–031*, 2–113, *29–071*
s.9(1) *2–131*
s.10 21–013
(1) 21–053
(3) *12–061*, *21–026*
s.11(2) ... *12–031*, *22–046*, *22–047*, *24–007*, *24–009*
(3) *12–026*, *12–031*, *12–034*, *24–037*
(4) *12–023*, *12–031*, 24–005
s.12 14–026
(1) *28–052*
(2)(b) *28–052*
(5A) *12–026*, *12–034*
ss.12–15 ... *1–017*, 13–029, 14–078
s.13(1A) *12–026*, *12–034*
ss.13–15 14–027
s.14 .. *1–002*, 1–021, *1–119*, *1–147*, *1–149*, *5–008*, 14–063
(1) *15–026*
(2D) *2–020*, *2–165*
(5) *14–069*
(6) *12–026*, *12–034*
s.15(3) *12–026*, *12–034*

s.15A *1–034*, *12–034*
s.16 .... *27–015*
s.18 .... 1–190, *2–154*
s.20A *27–015*
(1) *27–016*
(2) *27–016*
s.28 ....*12–029*, *21–027*, *28–052*
s.29(1) *21–005*
(2) *21–005*
(3) *21–020*
(5) *28–062*
s.30 .... *21–001*
(1) *21–035*, *23–068*, *29–070*
(2A) *23–068*
s.31 .... *21–027*
(2) *24–044*
s.35 .... 6–125, 12–023
s.41(1)(c) *20–033*
ss.44–46 .... *20–033*
s.48(3) *21–013*, *21–014*
s.48A(2)(a) *27–019*
s.48B *27–019*
(3)(a) *27–019*
(b) *27–019*
s.48C *27–019*
s.48E(2) *27–019*
(3) *27–019*
(4) *27–019*
s.49 .... *27–013*
(1) *28–052*
(2) *28–052*
s.50(3) *26–110*, *26–111*, *26–117*, *28–052*
s.51(2) 26–100E, *30–337*
(3) *26–110*, *28–052*, *30–337*
s.52 ....**27–013**, 27–014, 27–015, 27–016, 27–017, 27–018, 27–019, *27–052*
s.53(1) 28–123
(3) *1–122*
s.55 .... *5–047*, *14–023*
s.57(2) 2–011
s.61 4–019
(1) *12–026*, *12–031*, *24–037*, *27–016*
(5A) *27–019*
Sch.1 para.11 .... *14–023*

1980 Protection of Trading Interests Act (c.11) *16–033*
Limitation Amendment Act (c.24) *28–093*
Transport Act (c.34)
s.61 .... *18–127*
Housing Act (c.51)
s.79 .... *16–185*

Limitation Act (c.58) 1–084, 1–124, 17–010, 17–026, 20–014, 21–063, **28–001**, 28–070, 28–071, 28–114, 28–127, 28–134, *29–085*
s.2 ....*1–124*, *28–010*, 28–014
s.3(2) *28–107*, *28–126*
s.5 ....*1–124*, 28–002, *28–010*, *28–014*, 28–018, 28–031, 28–134, *28–135*
s.6 .... *28–014*, 28–036
(1) *28–014*
s.7 ....*28–017*, *28–018*, *28–134*
s.8 ....28–003, 28–018, 28–134
(1) *1–116*, *28–003*
(2) *1–116*, *28–003*, *28–006*, *28–014*
s.9 ....*28–003*, *28–004*, *28–018*, *28–134*
s.10 ....*17–029*, *28–015*, *28–022*, *28–078*
(1) *28–051*
(2) *28–051*
(3) *28–051*
(4) *28–051*
(5) *28–104*
s.11 ....*1–124*, 28–006, *28–010*, *28–024*, *28–078*, 28–120
(2) *28–006*
(5) *28–031*, *28–064*, *28–072*
s.11A *28–078*
(3) *28–064*, *28–072*, *28–080*, *28–091*, *28–126*
s.12 28–120
(1) *28–024*, *28–080*
(2) *28–031*, *28–078*
(3) *28–091*, *28–104*
s.13(1)(a) *28–113*
(b) *28–113*
(4) *28–115*
s.14 ....*28–006*, *28–064*, *28–072*
(1) *28–004*, *28–125*
(2) *28–004*
s.14A *1–124*, *6–068*, **28–010**, 28–011, 28–012, 28–013, *28–056*, 28–072, *28–091*
(1) *28–010*
(2) *28–010*
(4)(a) *28–011*
(b) *28–011*, 28–079
(5) *28–011*
(6) *28–011*
(7) *28–011*
(8) *28–011*, 28–012
(a) 28–012
(9) *28–011*, 28–012
(10) 28–011
s.14B *28–010*, *28–080*, *28–091*

(1) *28–013*
(2)(a) *28–013*
(b) *28–013*
s.16 .... *28–134*
s.17 .... *28–107*, *28–126*
s.19 .... *28–003*
s.20 .... *28–004*, *28–134*
(1) *28–004*
(5) *28–004*, *28–035*
(6) *28–035*
(7) *28–035*
s.21 .... 28–019, *28–134*
(1) *28–019*, 28–139
(3) 28–019
s.22 .... *28–134*
s.23 .... *28–002*
s.24 .... *28–016*, *28–018*, *28–134*
(1) 28–016
(2) 28–016
s.26 .... *20–004*, *28–031*
s.28 .... **28–075**, 28–076, 28–078, 28–079, 28–080, *28–123*
(1) *28–075*
(2) *28–075*, *28–080*
(3) *28–076*
(4) *28–080*
(5) *28–078*
(6) *28–078*
(7)(a) *28–080*
(b) *28–078*
s.28A **28–079**, 28–080
(1) *28–079*
s.29 .... *1–084*, **28–093**
(5) 3–035, *28–093*, 28–097
(6) *28–093*
(7) *3–033*, *3–035*, *28–093*
s.30(1) *3–035*, *28–094*
(2) *17–026*, *28–100*
s.31(6) *17–010*, *17–026*, *28–103*
(7) *17–026*, *28–103*
(9) *28–103*
s.32 .... *28–052*, **28–081**, 28–082, 28–085, 28–090, **28–091**
(1) 28–082, *28–087*, 28–089, *28–091*, 29–045
(a) *28–082*, 28–083, *28–088*, 28–091
(b) 28–010, *28–082*, 28–084, 28–086
(c) *28–082*, 28–088, 29–084
(2) *28–084*
(3) 28–090
(4A) *28–091*
(5) *28–010*, *28–013*, *28–091*
s.33 .... *28–023*, *28–120*
(2) *28–024*
s.35 .... *28–118*, *28–119*, 28–122
(1) 28–124
(a) *28–124*
(b) *28–022*
(2) *28–122*, *28–124*
(a) *28–118*
(b) *28–119*
(3) *28–122*
(5)(a) *28–118*
(b) *28–118*
(6) *28–119*
(7) *28–118*
(8) *28–118*, *28–119*
s.36 .... *28–135*
(1) *28–018*, 28–019, *28–134*, *28–135*
(2) *28–018*, *28–123*, *28–134*, *28–136*, *28–139*
s.37(1) *28–001*
s.38(1) *28–002*, *28–006*, *28–070*, *28–116*
(2) *28–074*
(3) *28–074*
(4) *28–074*
(5) *28–087*, *28–090*
(9) *28–084*
s.39 .... *28–001*, *28–020*, *28–024*, *28–075*, *28–091*, *28–104*, *28–118*, *28–122*, *28–124*
s.40(1) *28–093*, *28–122*
(2) *28–125*
Sch.2 para.5 .... *28–093*
para.6 .... *28–022*
para.8(2) *28–022*
Sch.3 para.5 .... *28–125*
para.6 .... *28–125*
Overseas Development and Co-operation Act (c.63)
s.9 .... *11–019*
1981 International Organisations Act (c.9) 11–018, 11–019
s.1 .... *11–018*, *11–019*
(1) *11–018*
(2)(b) *11–018*
(c) *11–018*
(d) *11–018*
(3) *11–018*
(4) *11–018*
(6)(b) *11–018*
s.2(1) *11–019*
s.4 .... *11–018*, *11–019*
s.4A *11–019*
s.5 .... *11–019*
s.5A *11–018*, *11–019*
s.6 .... *11–019*
Sch.1 Pt I para.1 .... *11–018*
Pt II para.9 .... *11–018*
Pt III para.14 .... *11–018*
Pt IV para.20 .... *11–018*
para.21 .... *11–018*
para.23 .... *11–018*
Merchant Shipping Act (c.10) *14–106*, *14–111*

ss.2–5 ..... *14–117*
Public Passenger Vehicles Act (c.14) 14–116
s.29 ..... *3–181*, *14–116*
Supreme Court Act (c.54)
s.15(1) 2–113
s.19 ..... *22–013*
s.30 ..... *1–197*
s.35A *1–124*, *26–174*, 26–179, *29–085*
(1) *26–174*
(2) *26–174*
(3) *26–174*
(4) *26–177*, *26–182*
(5) *26–179*
(6) *26–178*
(7) *26–174*
(8) *26–174*
s.49 ..... *1–115*, *22–006*, 27–077, *28–123*
(1) *18–086*
(2) *18–070*
(3) *18–070*
s.50 ..... *26–023*, 27–077, *27–079*
s.51 ..... *16–053*
s.61 5–131
Sch.1 5–131
British Nationality Act (c.61)
s.51(3) *11–016*
1982 Civil Jurisdiction and Judgments Act (c.27) *19–079*, 30–080
Pt I *28–016*
Pt II *28–016*
s.2(1) *25–017*
(2) *25–017*
s.3(1) *25–017*
(3) *30–019*
s.3A *25–017*
s.18 ..... *25–017*
s.19 ..... *25–017*
(1) *25–017*
(2) *25–017*
(3) *25–017*
s.31 ..... *11–004*
s.32 ..... *25–017*
s.33 ..... *25–017*
s.34 25–016
s.42 ..... *30–080*
s.50 ..... *25–016*, *25–017*
Sch.1 ..... *25–017*
para.26 ..... *25–017*
para.29 ..... *25–017*
para.30 ..... *25–017*
Sch.2 ..... *25–017*
Sch.3 ..... *25–017*
Sch.3A *30–031*
Sch.3C *25–017*
para.26 ..... *25–017*
para.29 ..... *25–017*
para.30 ..... *25–017*
Sch.4 ..... *30–033*
Sch.6 ..... *25–017*
Sch.7 ..... *25–017*
Supply of Goods and Services Act (c.29)
s.2 14–079
ss.2–5 ..... 13–030, 14–079
s.4 ..... *1–149*
(2B) *2–165*
ss.7–10 ..... 13–029, 14–079
s.11D(3A) *2–020*
s.12(2), (4) *13–032*
s.13 13–032
s.14 13–033
s.15 13–033
(1) *2–031*, *2–126*
s.16 ..... *13–032*
s.18(1) *13–032*
Forfeiture Act (c.34) **16–170**
s.1(1) 16–170
s.2(2) 16–170
s.5 ..... *16–170*
Insurance Companies Act (c.50) *30–008*
1984 Occupiers' Liability Act (c.3)
s.1(1) *1–119*
Foreign Limitation Periods Act (c.16) ... 28–115, *28–118*, 30–347
s.1(1) *30–347*
(3) *30–347*
(5) *30–347*
s.2(1) *30–347*
(2) 30–347
(3) *30–347*
(4) *30–347*
s.4 ..... *30–347*
(2) *30–347*
(3) *30–348*
Public Health (Control of Disease) Act (c.22)
ss.46–48 ..... *29–132*
County Courts Act (c.28)
s.1(2) *25–010*
s.21 ..... *5–132*
s.23 5–132
s.35 ..... *25–007*, *25–008*, *26–011*
s.38 ..... *5–132*
s.48(1) *17–009*
(2) *17–027*
s.69 ..... *26–174*, 26–179
(1) *26–174*
(2) *26–174*
(3) *26–174*
(4) *26–177*, *26–182*
(5) *26–178*
(6) *26–174*

(7) ... *26–174*
s.74 ... *26–184*
(5A) ... *30–378*
ss.112–117 ... *20–050*
s.147(1) ... 5–132
Inheritance Tax Act (c.51)
s.241 ... *29–085*
Police and Criminal Evidence Act (c.60)
s.24 ... *3–062*
(1) ... *16–036*
1985 Companies Act (c.6) ... 1–087, 1–096, 8–037, 9–003, 16–156, 28–004
Pt XII ... *9–046*
s.2(1)(c) ... *9–021*
(5)(a) ... *30–376*
s.14 ... *9–061*, *18–010*, 18–113
s.22 ... *9–060*
s.34 ... *9–017*
s.35 ... 9–027
ss.35–35C ... 9–020
ss.35–36C ... *9–020*
s.35A ... *9–027*, 9–032
(1) ... 9–032
s.35B ... 9–032
s.36(4) ... 9–012
s.36A ... *1–095*, *4–040*
(2) ... 1–086
(3) ... *1–091*
(4) ... *1–086*, *1–091*
(5) ... *1–086*, *1–091*, *1–094*
(6) ... *1–091*
(7) ... *1–098*
s.36AA(1) ... *1–100*
(2) ... *1–100*
s.36C ... *1–091*, 9–012, 9–013, *18–094*
(1) ... *4–074*
ss.82–86 ... *9–060*
s.103 ... *3–019*
s.111A ... *9–060*
s.182(1) ... *19–003*
s.317 ... *9–055*
s.320 ... *3–019*
s.395(1) ... *16–156*
ss.395–398 ... *19–003*, *19–065*, 19–066
s.409 ... 19–066
s.425 ... *30–376*
s.427 ... *9–047*
s.651 ... 28–070
s.716 ... *9–064*
Business Names Act (c.7) ... 9–008
s.4 ... *1–125*
s.5 ... *1–125*
Company Securities (Insider Dealing) Act (c.8)
s.8(3) ... *16–145*
Reserve Forces (Safeguard of Employment) Act (c.17)
s.10 ... *27–022*
s.17 ... *27–022*
s.18 ... *27–022*
Enduring Powers of Attorney Act (c.29) ... 8–078
Child Abduction and Custody Act (c.60) ... *11–011*
Pt I ... *30–079*
Insolvency Act (c.65)
s.163 ... *1–125*
s.211(1) ... *1–125*
(2) ... *1–125*
(3) ... *1–125*
s.339 ... *3–168*
Housing Act (c.68) ... 8–035
Pt V ... *1–015*
s.62 ... *8–003*
s.89 ... *8–035*
s.90 ... *8–035*
s.125(4A) ... *6–014*
Landlord and Tenant Act (c.70)
s.4 ... *4–001*, *4–002*
s.8 ... *13–016*
s.9 ... *13–016*
s.10 ... *13–016*
s.11 ... *21–009*
(1)(a) ... 1–049
ss.11–17 ... *13–016*
s.17 ... *27–028*
1986 Agricultural Holdings Act (c.5)
s.24 ... *26–127*
Drug Trafficking Offences Act (c.32)
s.1 ... *20–046*
Latent Damage Act (c.37) ... 1–124, 1–167
s.1 ... *28–010*
s.2(2) ... *28–010*
s.3 ... *18–034*, *28–075*
(3) ... *28–075*
Gas Act (c.44)
s.10 ... *1–015*
Insolvency Act (c.45) ... 17–025, *20–015*, 20–038, 29–104, *30–376*
Pt I ... *3–125*
Pt II ... 9–053
Pt VIII ... *3–125*, 20–050
s.5(2) ... *3–125*
s.19 ... *9–050*
s.29 ... *9–050*
(2) ... *9–050*
s.44 ... *27–026*
(1)(a) ... 9–050
(b) ... *9–050*, *9–051*

(2) *9–050*
ss.72C–72H *9–050*
s.91(2) *9–047*
s.103 .... *9–047*
s.127 .... *9–049, 20–019*
s.166 .... *16–063*
s.167 .... *16–063*, *19–049*
s.178 .... *9–048*
s.214 .... *16–063*
s.233 .... *20–056*
s.238 .... *3–008*, *3–019*
(5) *9–021*
ss.238–246 .... *19–065*
s.239 .... *3–019*
s.244 .... *26–167*, *26–182*
s.251 .... *9–050*
s.252 .... *20–050*
s.253 .... *20–050*
(1) *20–050*
s.255 .... *20–050*
s.258(4) *20–050*
s.260 .... *20–050*
(2) *3–125*
(3) *20–051*
s.262 .... *20–050*
s.263 .... *20–050*
s.267 .... *20–018*
(2) *20–018*
s.268(1) *20–018*
(2) *20–018*
s.269 .... *20–018*
s.272 .... *20–018*
s.278 .... *20–030*
(a) *20–015, 20–019*
(b) *20–019*
s.279 20–045
(1) *20–045*
(2) *20–045*
(3)–(5) *20–045*
s.281(3) *20–046*
(4) *20–046*
(5)(a) *20–046*
(b) *20–046*, *20–049*
(6) *20–046*
(7) *17–024*, *20–047*
s.281A *20–045*
s.283 .... 20–019, *20–026*
(2) *20–019*
s.283A *20–026*
s.284(1) *19–064*, *20–019*
(2) *20–019*
(4) *19–064, 20–019*, 20–021
(5) *20–019*, *20–048*
s.285 .... *20–019*
(3) *20–048*
s.286 .... *20–024*
s.287 .... *20–024*
s.292(2) *20–024*
ss.292–294 .... *20–024*
s.303 .... *20–019*
s.305 .... *20–017*
s.306 ...... *20–019*, *20–024*, *21–050*
s.307 ...... *20–024*, *20–035*, *20–054*
(2) *20–054*
(3) *20–054*
(4) *20–054*
s.308 .... *20–019*, *20–035*
s.309 20–054
(1) *20–054*
s.310 .... *20–054*, 20–057
(2) *20–054*
s.313 .... *20–036*
s.313A *20–036*
s.314 ..... *19–049*, *20–026*, *20–032*, 20–056, *21–050*
(1) *16–063*
s.315 20–035
(2) *20–035*
(3) *20–035*
(a) *20–035*
(4) *20–035*
(5) *20–035*
s.316 .... *20–035*
s.317 .... *20–035*
s.318 .... *20–035*
s.322 .... *20–037*
(2) *20–049*
s.323 ...... 19–009, 20–040, 20–041
(1) 20–040
(2) 20–040
(3) 20–040
s.328 .... *20–038*
(3) *20–037*
(4) *20–049*
(5) *20–049*
s.334 20–057
(2) *20–057*
(3) *20–057*
s.335 20–057
(1) *20–057*
(3) *20–057*
(5) *20–057*
(6) *20–057*
s.336(2) *20–036*
(4)(a) *20–036*
(c) *20–036*
(d) *20–036*
s.337 .... *20–036*
(2)(a) *20–036*
(5) *20–036*
(6) *20–036*
s.339 .... *3–008*, *18–079*, 20–028
(2) *20–028*
(3) *20–028*
ss.339–349 .... *19–063*
s.340(3) *20–029*
(5) *20–029*
(6) *20–029*
s.341(1) *20–028*
(b) *20–029*

(c) *20–029*
(2) *20–028*
(3) *20–028*, *20–029*
s.342 .... *20–028*, *20–029*
(2)(b) *20–028*
(4) *20–028*
s.343 .... *20–030*, *26–167*, *26–182*
(2) *20–030*
(3) *20–030*
(4) *20–030*
(6) *20–030*
s.344 .... *19–003*, 19–062, 19–065, *20–026*
(2) *20–026*
(3)(b) *19–062*, *20–026*
s.345 .... *20–033*
(4) *17–010*
s.348 .... *20–032*
s.370 .... *20–024*
s.372 20–056
(1) *20–056*
(2)(a) *20–056*
(b) *20–056*
(5) *20–056*
s.382 .... 8–052, *20–046*, 20–049, *29–141*
(1)(a) *20–049*
(b) *20–049*
(3) *20–049*, *29–104*
(4) *8–052*, *20–037*, *20–049*, 29–014, *29–104*
s.384(1) *20–046*
s.386 .... *20–038*
s.388 .... *20–024*
(2)(b) *20–051*
s.390 .... *20–024*
s.421 .... *20–005*
s.423 .... *3–019*, 20–031, *28–003*, *28–084*
(1) *20–031*
(3) *20–031*
ss.423–425 .... *19–063*, *19–065*
s.424 .... *20–031*
s.435 .... *20–028*, *20–029*
s.436 .... *1–191*, *16–063*, *19–049*, *20–019*
(4) *20–026*
Sch.B1 paras 42–45 .... *9–053*
Sch.4 .... *16–063*, *19–049*, *20–045*
Sch.5 .... *19–049*, *20–026*
Pt I *20–032*, 20–056
Pt II para.10 .... *20–032*, *21–050*
Sch.6 .... *20–038*
Company Directors Disqualification Act (c.46)
s.11 16–005
Building Societies Act (c.53)
Sch.2 para.5(3) *8–060*
1987 Minors' Contracts Act (c.13) *8–001*, 8–005, 8–055, *29–081*
s.1 .... *3–033*, *8–044*
s.2 .... 8–045, *17–008*
(1) *8–063*
s.3 .... 8–047, **8–054**, 8–057
(1) 8–047, 29–081
(2) *29–081*
s.4 .... *3–033*, *17–008*
Banking Act (c.22)
s.58 .... *19–020*
Landlord and Tenant Act (c.31)
Pt IV *13–017*
Consumer Protection Act (c.43) *16–147*
Pt I *1–124*, 14–126, *18–026*, 28–009, 28–072, 28–078, 28–080, 28–091, 28–126
s.2(2) *28–009*
s.4 .... *28–009*
(2)(b) *28–009*
s.5(5) *1–124*
s.7 .... *14–126*
s.11A *28–009*
(3) *28–009*
s.14 .... *28–009*
s.20 .... *2–020*
(1) 2–015
s.33 .... *28–009*
(1A) *28–009*
Diplomatic and Consular Premises Act (c.46) 11–012
1988 Multilateral Investment Guarantee Agency Act (c.8)
s.3 .... *11–019*
Local Government Act (c.9) 10–048
s.17 .... *10–048*
ss.17—23 1–201
Criminal Justice Act (c.33)
s.14A(1) *2–014*
Legal Aid Act (c.34)
s.2(11) *16–063*
Education Reform Act (c.40) *15–024*
Copyright, Designs and Patents Act (c.48)
s.90 .... *19–003*, *19–055*
(3) *19–025*
s.94 .... *19–003*
s.96 .... *29–142*
s.97 .... *29–142*
s.229 .... *29–142*
Housing Act (c.50)
ss.27–28 .... *29–142*
Road Traffic Act (c.52)
s.18(4) *16–147*

s.75(7) *16–147*
s.145 .... *2–168*
s.148 14–119
(7) *18–127*
s.149 .... *2–168*, *14–116*
(3) *14–014*
s.150 .... *2–168*
ss.151–153 .... *18–131*
ss.157–159 .... *29–132*
Sch.1 .... *16–147*

1989 Electricity Act (c.29)
s.16 .... *1–015*, *15–035*
s.22 .... *15–035*
Sch.3 para.3 .... *1–015*

Law of Property (Miscellaneous Provisions) Act (c.34) .. 1–093, 1–099, 1–100, 1–104, *4–044*, 4–074, 4–077, 4–080, 4–086, 12–101, *28–003*
s.1 ... 1–086, 1–090, *1–095*, *1–109*, *4–040*, 4–055, *4–060*, *22–003*
(1) 1–003
(2) 1–096, 9–010
(a) 1–087, 1–090, 1–096
(b) 1–096, *1–098*, *1–100*
(2A) *1–097*
(3) *1–090*, *1–104*
(b) *1–090*, *1–093*, *1–099*
(4) *1–090*
(b) *1–099*
(4A) *1–098*
(5) *1–093*
(7) *3–044*
(9) *1–092*
(10) *1–092*
(11) *1–090*
s.2 ... 1–081, *2–120*, *2–171*, 3–140, *4–003*, 4–006, *4–010*, *4–011*, *4–013*, **4–052**, 4–053, 4–054, 4–055, 4–056, 4–057, 4–058, 4–059, 4–060, 4–061, 4–062, 4–063, 4–064, 4–065, 4–066, 4–067, *4–068*, 4–069, 4–070, 4–071, 4–073, *4–074*, 4–075, 4–076, 4–077, 4–078, 4–079, 4–080, 4–081, 4–082, 4–083, 4–085, 4–086, 4–087, 4–088
(1) *2–119*, *2–171*, *3–113*, **4–052**, *4–054*, 4–058, 4–063, *4–069*, *4–070*, *4–071*, 4–074, 4–076, 4–077, 4–081, 5–112, *12–101*, *22–014*, *22–030*, *27–037*, *27–047*, *30–314*
(1)–(3) *3–143*
(2) *12–101*
(3) *2–119*, 4–063, 4–072, 4–074
(4) *4–070*, *12–101*
(5) *2–171*, *3–113*, *4–063*, 4–068, 4–075, 4–077, 4–081
(6) *3–143*, 4–054, 4–064, *4–068*
(8) *4–052*
s.3 .... *6–052*, *26–091*
s.5(3) *4–052*
(4) *4–052*

Companies Act (c.40) *1–089*
Pt IV *9–046*
ss.108–109 .... *9–020*

Children Act (c.41) 16–074
s.2(1) *16–074*
(2) *16–074*
(9) *16–074*
s.4(1)(b) *16–074*
s.15(1) *8–061*
s.20(8) *16–074*
s.22 .... *8–023*
s.23(9) *8–023*
s.24(2) *8–023*
Sch.1 para.1 .... *8–061*
Sch.2 para.18(1) *8–023*

1990 Town and Country Planning Act (c.8)
s.106 4–061

Contracts (Applicable Law) Act (c.36) *1–125*, *1–169*, *16–027*, 30–002, 30–017, 30–026, 30–046
s.2(1) *30–017*, *30–026*
(a) *30–046*
(2) 23–029, *30–017*, *30–026*, *30–033*, *30–063*, *30–102*, *30–112*, *30–327*, *30–359*
(3) *30–025*, *30–026*
s.3 30–019
(2) *30–019*
(3)(a) 30–026
s.5 .... *30–026*
Sch.1 .... *21–069*, *23–027*, *30–359*
Sch.2 .... *30–017*
Sch.3 .... 30–017, *30–026*
Sch.3A *30–017*
Sch.3B *30–017*
Sch.4 .... *30–026*

Human Fertilisation and Embryology Act (c.37)
s.36 .... *16–074*
Sch.3 para.4(1) *3–087*

Courts and Legal Services Act (c.41)
s.58 16–056
(1) *15–063*, *16–056*
(2)(a) *15–063*, *16–056*
(b) *16–056*
(3) *15–063*, *16–056*
(c) *15–063*

(4) *15–063*
(b) *16–056*
(c) *16–056*
s.58A *16–049*, 16–056
(4) *16–049*
(6) *15–127*
s.61 .... *3–029*
s.62 .... *1–154*
1991 Property Misdescriptions Act (c.29)
s.1 .... *6–010*, 6–091
(4) *6–091*
s.2 .... *6–091*
Child Support Act (c.48) ... 16–074
Water Industry Act (c.56)
ss.53–56 .... *15–035*
1992 Social Security Administration Act (c.5)
ss.105–108 .... *8–061*
s.187 .... *19–047*
Taxation of Chargeable Gains Act (c.12)
s.1(1) *26–166*
s.23 .... *26–166*
s.37 .... *26–166*
s.51(2) *26–166*
ss.152–154 .... *26–166*
Timeshare Act (c.35) 4–002, 14–129, *30–084*
s.1A *6–014*
(1) 4–002
s.5(2) *4–003*
s.5A *4–003*
Sch.1 .... *4–002*
Friendly Societies Act (c.40) *9–072*
s.7(2)(b) *9–072*
s.10 .... *9–072*
s.119A(1)(a) *8–060*
Sch.2 Pt D *9–072*
Carriage of Goods by Sea Act (c.50) ... *14–055*, *18–052*, 18–112, *19–003*, *30–066*
s.1(5) *18–112*
s.2 .... *2–160*, *18–034*
(4) *18–034*
s.3 .... *2–160*, *18–134*
Trade Union and Labour Relations (Consolidation) Act (c.52) 2–177, *7–045*
Ch.V *9–085*
s.1 16–136
s.4(2) *9–082*
s.10 .... *9–064*, 9–081
(1) *9–081*
(a) *9–081*
(b) *9–081*
(2) *9–081*
s.11 .... *9–081*, *9–084*, 16–136
s.12(1) *9–081*
(2) *9–081*
s.46 9–082
(1)(b) *9–082*
ss.47–52 .... *9–082*
s.62(7) *2–182*
s.122 16–133
s.128 16–133
ss.152–167 .... *27–022*
s.178(1) *2–177*
(2) *2–177*
s.179(1) *2–177*
(2) *2–177*
s.174 .... *8–060*
s.188 .... *30–116*
s.219 .... *18–040*
s.226 .... *27–022*
s.235A *18–040*, *27–022*
s.236 27–022
s.245 .... *2–182*
s.285(2) *30–114*
s.287 .... *30–114*
s.288 .... *14–121*
s.289 .... *30–114*
1993 Charities Act (c.10) 1–086, 1–092, 9–006
s.50 .... *1–086*, *1–092*
s.60 .... *1–086*, *1–092*
s.61(1)(a) *3–020*
s.64 .... *2–104*
s.65(1)(a) *3–019*
Leasehold Reform, Housing and Urban Development Act (c.28) *21–016*
Criminal Justice Act (c.36)
s.52 .... *6–014*
s.63(2) *6–014*, *16–145*
Railways Act (c.43)
s.123 .... *2–021*
1994 Value Added Tax Act (c.23)
s.80 .... *29–085*
(3) *29–014*, 29–086
Law of Property (Miscellaneous Provisions) Act (c.36) 13–031
s.1(4) *13–031*
1995 Merchant Shipping Act (c.21)
s.25 .... *3–070*
s.34(1)(c) *19–055*
s.38 .... *21–030*
s.40 .... *29–130*
s.73(2) *29–131*
s.183 .... *14–117*
s.185 .... *18–032*
ss.187–189 .... *29–121*
s.190 .... *28–118*
s.224 .... *7–047*

s.210 .... *14–131*
(7) *14–131*
ss.210–236 .... *14–131*
s.211 .... *14–131*
(1)(c) *15–139*
(2)(g) *14–131*
s.212 .... *14–131*, *15–139*
(1) *15–139*
s.213(1) *14–131*
(1)–(13) *14–131*
(5A) *14–131*, *15–139*
s.214 .... *15–139*
s.217 .... *14–131*, *15–139*
s.250 9–050
Sch.13 .... *14–131*
Sch.16 .... *9–053*
2003 Income Tax (Earnings and Pensions) Act (c.1)
s.309 .... *26–158*
s.401(1) 26–158
ss.401–403 .... *26–158*
ss.401–406 .... *26–158*
s.403(1) 26–158
2004 Civil Partnership Act (c.33) 2–170, *30–154*
s.1 .... *2–170*
(1) *2–171*
s.70 .... *2–170*, 18–126
s.73 .... *2–170*, *3–073*
Housing Act (c.34)
Pt 5 .... *6–093*, *6–156*
2005 Income Tax (Trading and Other Income) Act (c.5)
s.751(1) *26–157*
Mental Capacity Act (c.9) ...8–003, **8–073**, 8–075, 8–077, 8–078, 8–079
s.1 .... *8–073*, *8–075*
s.2 .... *2–102*, *8–003*
(1) *8–073*
s.3(1) *8–073*
s.4 .... *8–073*
s.7 ....*8–003*, *8–007*, *8–013*, 8–075
(1), (2) *8–075*
s.9(1) *8–078*
(2)(c) *8–078*
ss.9–14 .... *8–078*
s.13(2) *8–078*
s.15 .... *8–073*, *8–077*
ss.15–19 .... *8–073*
s.16 .... *8–077*
(1) 8–073
(2)(a) *8–073*
(b) *8–073*
(3) *8–073*
ss.16–21 .... *8–073*
s.17 .... *8–073*
s.18 .... *8–073*, *8–077*
s.20(6) *8–073*
s.42 .... *8–075*
Sch.6 para.4(2)(c) *8–079*
Sch.7 para.1 .... *8–077*
Disability Discrimination Act (c.13) *1–016*
Gambling Act (c.19) *29–197*
s.2 .... *3–169*
s.33(2) *3–169*
s.42 .... *3–169*
s.334(1) *3–169*
s.335(1) *3–009*, *3–016*, *3–017*, *3–050*, 3–169
s.356(1) *3–169*
(2) *3–169*
(3) *3–169*
Sch.16 .... *3–169*
International Organisations Act (c.20) *11–019*
2006 Equality Act (c.3) *30–114*
Pt 2 .... *27–074*
Pt 3 .... *27–074*
s.1 .... *27–074*
s.23(1)(a) *27–074*
(3)(a) *27–074*
s.24 .... *27–074*
s.33 .... *27–074*
(1)(g) *27–074*
(h) *27–074*
s.34 .... *27–074*
s.46 .... *27–074*
s.47 .... *27–074*
s.65 .... *27–078*
s.66 .... *27–074*, *27–078*
s.81(1) *27–074*
Consumer Credit Act (c.14) 1–021
s.2 2–159
Fraud Act (c.35) 6–003, *6–047*
s.2 .... *3–136*, *6–047*
Companies Act (c.46) *1–090*, 2–103, **2–104**, 2–105, **9–003**, 9–005, *9–064*
Pt 1 Ch.1 .... *9–004*
Ch.2 .... *9–004*
Pt 10 .... *9–028*, *9–055*
Pt 18 Ch.1 .... *9–038*
Ch.2 .... *9–038*, *16–193*
Pt 25 9–046
Pt 33 .... *9–016*
Pt 41 9–008
Ch.1 9–008
s.1 .... *2–104*, *9–016*
s.2 .... *9–008*
s.7 .... *9–028*
s.8 .... *9–019*, 9–028
(1) *9–028*
s.17 .... *2–105*, *9–028*
(a) 2–104
(b) *2–104*
s.21 .... *2–104*

s.28 .... *9–028*, *9–061*
s.29 .... *2–104*, *2–105*
s.31 .... *2–104*, 2–105, *9–019*
(1) 9–028
(2) *2–104*
(c) *9–028*
(3) 2–104, 2–105, 2–106, 2–107
(4) *2–104*, *2–105*, *9–028*
s.33 .... *9–020*, *9–028*, 9–061, 18–113
(1) 9–028, 18–010, 18–113, *28–004*
s.39 .. 9–005, 9–029, 9–037, *9–039*, *9–056*
(1) 2–104, 2–105, 2–106, 2–107
(2) *2–104*
ss.39–40 .... *9–019*, 9–042, 9–043
ss.39–42 .... **9–027**
s.40 .. 2–104, 2–105, 2–106, 9–032, 9–034, 9–036, 9–037, 9–040, 9–042, *9–056*
(1) 2–104, 2–105, 2–106, 2–107, 9–032, 9–035
(2) 9–032, 9–040
(a) 9–032
(b) 9–033
(3) *9–032*
(a) 2–105
(4) 2–104, 2–105, *2–106*, 9–034
(6) *2–105*
(a) 2–104
(b) *2–104*
s.41 .. *2–104*, *2–105*, *9–037*, 9–041, *9–056*
(1) *9–036*
(2) *9–036*
(3) *9–036*
(4) *9–036*
(6) *9–036*
s.42 .... *2–104*, *2–105*, *9–037*
(2) *9–037*
(3) *9–037*
(4) *9–037*
s.43 .... *9–009*, *30–325*
ss.43–47 .... *28–003*
s.44 .... *30–325*
(2) *1–100*
(6) *1–100*
ss.44–47 9–010
s.45(1) *30–325*
s.46 9–010
s.47 .... *9–010*
s.51 .... 9–012, *9–016*, *18–094*, *30–325*
s.82 .... *9–008*
s.83 9–008
s.112 9–060
s.157 .... *9–044*
s.159 .... *9–044*
s.160 .... *9–044*
s.161 .... **9–044**
(1)(b) *9–044*
(c) *9–044*
s.168 9–058
s.171 .... 9–028, *9–034*
(a) 9–030
s.177 .... *9–055*, 9–056
s.182 .... *9–055*
ss.182–186 .... *9–056*
s.187 .... *9–056*
s.190 9–055
s.195 .... *9–055*
s.197 .... *9–056*
s.214 .... *9–056*
ss.215–219 .... *9–056*
s.227 .... *9–058*
ss.228–229 .... *9–058*
s.230 .... *9–058*
s.239 .... *9–055*
s.252 .... *9–055*
s.318 .... *9–056*
s.489(1) *9–062*
(3) *9–062*
(4) *9–062*
s.492 .... *9–062*
s.495 .... *9–062*
s.510 .... *9–062*
ss.510–513 .... *9–062*
ss.516–518 .... *9–062*
s.542(3) *30–376*
s.544 .... *19–003*
s.551(17) *2–024*
s.578 .... *2–024*
s.655 .... *6–042*, 9–060
s.756 .... *2–024*
s.761 .... *9–019*
(2) *9–019*
s.765 .... *30–376*
s.767 .... *9–019*
s.860 9–046
ss.860–861 .... *19–003*, *19–065*, *19–066*
ss.860–894 .... *29–158*, *29–168*
s.861(7) *9–046*
s.863 ...... *19–003*, *19–065*, *19–066*
ss.866–867 .... *19–003*, *19–065*, *19–066*
s.870 .... *9–046*
s.873 9–046
s.874 .... *9–046*, *19–003*, *19–065*, *19–066*
s.894 .... *9–046*
s.895 .... *30–376*
s.896(6)(b) *9–046*
s.900 9–047
s.1043 .... *9–004*
s.1052 .... *19–066*

s.1085 .... *9–021*
s.1192(1) *9–008*
s.1200 .... *9–008*
s.1202 .... *9–008*
s.1205 .... *9–008*
s.1206 .... *9–008*
s.1297 9–003
(5) 18–113
Sch.16 .... *9–037*
2007 Appropriation Act (c.1) *10–006*

TABLE OF STATUTORY INSTRUMENTS

[Where a reference indicates significant discussion of the statutory instrument in the text, it is in **bold**. Where a reference is to a footnote, it is *italic*.]

1939 Control of Timber (No.4) Order 23–025

1965 Rules of the Supreme Court (SI 1965/1776) 8–062

Ord.6 r.8(1) *21–024*

Ord.9 r.14(b) *11–030*

Ord.15 r.6(6) *28–119*

r.7 .... *28–119*

r.12 .... 9–065, *9–068*

Ord.16 r.9 .... *9–068*

Ord.20 r.5 ....*20–004*

Ord.37 r.6 ....*26–015*

Ord.53 ....1–193, 1–194, **1–195**, 1–197

Ord.80 r.1 .... *8–062*

r.2 .... *8–062*

r.10 .... *8–062*

r.11 .... *8–062*

1971 Hovercraft (Civil Liability) Order (SI 1971/720) ...*14–106*

1976 Consumer Transactions (Restrictions on Statements) Order (SI 1976/1813) *14–131*

1977 Business Advertisements (Disclosure) Order (SI 1977/1918) *14–131*

1981 County Courts Jurisdiction Order (SI 1981/1123) *5–132*

County Court Rules (SI 1981/1687) 8–062

Ord.10 r.1 .... *8–062*

r.10 .... *8–062*

Transfer of Undertakings (Protection of Employment) Regulations (SI 1981/1794) *9–047*, *9–050*

1982 Supply of Services (Exclusion of Implied Terms) Order (SI 1982/1771) *13–032*

1983 Supply of Services (Exclusion of Implied Terms) Order (SI 1983/902) ...*13–032*

Consumer Credit (Agreements) Regulations (SI 1983/1553) *2–159*, *4–002*

Sch.5 .... *4–001*

1985 Supply of Services (Exclusion of Implied Terms) Order (SI 1985/1) *13–032*

Companies (Tables A to F) Regulations (SI 1995/805)

art.70 .... *9–007*

1986 Insolvency Rules (SI 1986/1925)

r.4.90 ....*30–350*

r.4.91 ....*30–377*

r.6.111 ....*30–377*

r.6.223 ....*20–046*

r.12.3 ....*20–049*

(2) *20–049*

r.13.1 ....*29–141*

r.13.12 ....*29–141*

Administration of Insolvent Estates of Deceased Persons Order (SI 1986/1999) *20–005*

Insurance Companies (Winding-up) (Amendment) Rules (SI 1986/2002)

r.6.178(4) *20–035*

1987 Carriage of Passengers and their Luggage by Sea (Domestic Carriage) Order (SI 1987/670) ... 14–116

Consumer Protection (Cancellation of Contracts Concluded away from Business Premises) Regulations (SI 1987/2117) 14–129

1989 European Economic Interest Grouping Regulations (SI 1989/638) *9–001*

Supply of Beer (Tied Estate) Order (SI 1989/2390) *16–125*

Supply of Beer (Loan Ties, Licensed Premises and Wholesale Prices) Order (SI 1989/2258) *16–125*

1991 Arrangements for Placement of Children (General) Regulations (SI 1991/890) *16–074*

County Courts (Interest on Judgment Debts) Order (SI 1991/1184) *26–184*

Parental Responsibility Agreement Regulations (SI 1991/1478) ... *16–074*

Public Works Contracts Regulations (SI 1991/2680) *1–201*

1992 Council Tax (Administration and Enforcement) Regulations (SI 1992/613) *29–085*

Property Misdescriptions (Specified Matters) Order (SI 1992/2834) *6–091*

Utilities Supply and Works Contracts Regulations (SI 1992/3279) *1–201*

Package Travel, Package Holidays and Package Tours Regulations (SI 1992/3288) ... 6–092, 13–034, 14–127, *30–235*

reg.9 .... *4–001*, *13–034*

reg.10 .... *13–034*

reg.12 .... *13–034*

reg.13 .... *13–034*

(3)(b) *14–149*

reg.14 .... *13–034*

reg.15 .... *13–034*, 14–127

(2)(c) *14–149*

(5) *14–127*

1993 Judgment Debts (Rate of Interest) Order (SI 1993/564) *26–184*

Commercial Agents (Council Directive) Regulations (SI 1993/3053) ...1–027, *30–042*, *30–065*

reg.1(2) *30–042*

(3)(a) *30–042*

(b) *30–042*

reg.3(1) *1–027*

regs 3–22 .... *30–042*

reg.17 .... *30–065*

reg.18 .... *30–065*

1994 Contracts (Applicable Law) Act 1990 (Amendment) Order (SI 1994/1900) *30–017*

Solicitors (Non-Contentious Business) Remuneration Order (SI 1994/2616) *16–064*

Unfair Terms in Consumer Contracts Regulations (SI 1994/3159) **15–003**, 15–004, 15–006, 15–007, 15–011, 15–012, 15–013, 15–014, 15–015, 15–016, **15–017**, 15–021, 15–022, 15–024, 15–026, 15–032, 15–033, 15–034, 15–035, **15–036**, 15–037, **15–038**, 15–039, 15–043, 15–044, 15–045, 15–046, 15–047, *15–055*, 15–070, 15–071, 15–072, 15–074, 15–076, 15–077, 15–078, **15–080**, 15–081, 15–087, 15–089, 15–090, 15–091, 15–093, 15–098, 15–102, 15–108, 15–114, 15–116, 15–118, 15–122, 15–126, 15–127, 15–129, 15–130, 15–133, 15–136, 15–138

reg.1 .... *15–011*, *15–014*

reg.2 .... *15–019*, *15–023*, *15–028*

(1) *15–017*

reg.3 .... *15–038*, *15–046*

(1) *15–036*, *15–039*, *15–042*

(2) *15–049*, *15–062*

(b) 15–051, *15–056*

(3) *15–047*, *15–080*

(4) *15–047*

(5) *15–047*

reg.4(1) *15–064*, *15–074*

(2) *15–054*, *15–064*, *15–080*

(4) *15–054*, *15–091*

reg.5(1) *15–012*, *15–077*

reg.6 .... *15–012*, *15–038*, *15–129*

reg.7 .... *15–132*, *30–068*

reg.8 .... *15–003*, *15–009*, *15–133*

reg.12 .... *15–120*

Sch.1 paras (a)–(d) *15–036*

para.(e)(i) *15–039*

(ii) *15–042*

Sch.2 .... *15–067*, **15–080**

Sch.3 .... *15–054*, *15–064*

para.1 .... *15–091*

(i) 15–076

(l) *15–054*

para.2 .... *15–100*, *15–103*

(b) *15–103*

1995 Public Supply Contracts Regulations (SI 1995/201) *1–201*
1996 Utilities Contracts Regulations (SI 1996/2911) ... *1–201*
1997 Timeshare Regulations (SI 1997/1081) *30–236*
reg.6 .... *4–001*
1998 Air Carrier Liability Order (SI 1998/1751) *14–118*
Working Time Regulations (SI 1998/1833) *30–116*
County Courts (Interest on Judgment Debts) (Amendment) Order (SI 1998/2400) *26–184*
Carriage of Passengers and their Luggage by Sea (United Kingdom Carriers) Order (SI 1998/2917) ... *14–111*, *14–117*
Civil Procedure Rules (SI 1998/3132) 8–062, 8–064, 19–039, 26–179, **28–118**, 28–119
Pt 1 .... *1–194*
r.2.2 17–009
r.2.8(5) *28–063*
r.3.1(2)(f) *28–111*
(g) *25–007*
r.3.4 .... *28–107*
(2)(a) *25–007*
r.6.5 .... *22–011*, *22–023*
r.6.20 .... *17–010*
(5)(a) *30–023*
r.6.21(2A) *30–023*
r.7.5 .... *28–116*
(3) *28–116*
r.7.6(1) *28–116*
(2) *28–116*
(3) *28–116*
Pt 7 PD *28–116*
Pt 11 28–116
r.12.6 .... *26–179*
(2) *26–179*
r.12.7 .... *26–179*
r.15.4 .... *28–116*
r.16.4(2) *26–174*
r.16.5 ....*8–064*, *25–013*, *28–107*
r.16.6 .... *20–031*, *28–123*
Pt 16 PD *28–107*
r.17.4 .... *20–004*, *28–117*
(2) *28–118*
(4) *28–118*
r.19.2(2)(a) *18–089*
rr.19.2–3 .... *19–039*
r.19.5 .... *28–119*
r.19.8 .... *28–031*, *28–064*
Pt 20 28–124
r.20.2 .... *25–031*
r.20.9(1) *28–122*
Pt 21 .... *8–062*
r.21.1(2) *8–062*
r.21.10(2) *8–043*
Pt 24 .... *1–197*, *26–009*
Pt 25 PD *16–092*
r.25.1 .... *10–017*
r.26.4 .... *28–111*
Pt 36 ....3–046, **4–065**, *21–089*, 26–179
r.36.22 .... *26–179*
(2) *26–179*
r.40.2(3) *30–377*
r.40.8 .... *26–184*
Pts 43–47 PD on Costs para.9.1 .... *15–127*
Pt 44.3A *15–127*
r.48.5 .... *8–062*
r.52.10 .... *26–030*
r.52.11 .... *26–030*
Pt 54 .... 1–194, **1–197**
r.54.1(2) *1–197*
r.54.2 .... *1–197*
r.54.3 .... *1–197*
(2) *29–085*
r.54.4 .... *1–197*
r.54.5 .... *1–197*
r.54.20 .... *1–197*
Pt 72 .... *21–051*
Sch.1 Ord.15 r.6A para.3 .... *20–005*
Ord.45 r.9 .... *27–050*
1999 Carriage by Air Acts (Implementation of Protocol No.4 of Montreal, 1975) Order (SI 1999/1312) *14–118*
Unfair Terms in Consumer Contracts Regulations (SI 1999/2083) *1–017*, 1–021, 1–064, *1–073*, *1–151*, 6–141, *6–149*, *7–126*, *7–137*, 8–001, *8–009*, *13–009*, *14–004*, *14–015*, *14–074*, *14–105*, 14–125, 14–131, 14–135, **14–153**, **15–001**, 15–004, 15–006, 15–007, **15–009**, 15–010, 15–011, **15–012**, 15–013, 15–015, 15–016, **15–017**, 15–019, 15–021, 15–022, 15–024, 15–026, 15–030, 15–032, 15–033, 15–034, 15–035, 15–036, 15–037, **15–038**, 15–039, 15–043, 15–044, 15–045, 15–046, 15–047, 15–048, 15–049, *15–055*, 15–063, *15–067*, 15–070, 15–071, 15–072, 15–074, 15–076, 15–077, 15–078, 15–080,

15–086, 15–087, 15–089, 15–090, 15–091, 15–093, *15–095*, 15–098, 15–102, 15–108, 15–109, 15–114, 15–116, 15–118, 15–122, 15–126, 15–127, 15–130, 15–133, 15–134, 15–135, 15–136, 15–138, *21–001*, 22–039, 22–048, *26–001*, 26–012, *26–125*, *26–127*, 26–142, *26–151*, 26–156, *26–182*, *27–057*, *28–113*, *30–008*, *30–065*, 30–103

reg.1 .... *15–011*, *15–138*

reg.2 .... *15–011*

reg.3(1) ... *1–025*, *15–017*, 15–023, 15–028

reg.4 .... *15–043*

(1) *15–038*

(2)(a) *15–039*, *15–063*

(b) *15–042*

reg.5 .... *14–153*, *15–043*

(1) *1–021*, *1–025*, *1–064*, *6–141*, *15–038*, *15–046*, 15–051, 15–064, *15–077*, 15–086

(1)–(4) *15–048*

(2) *15–047*

(3) *15–047*

(4) *15–047*, *15–120*, *30*–352, *30–353*

(5) *2–131*, *15–054*, *15–091*

reg.6(1) 15–064, *15–074*, *15–080*, *15–090*, 15–111

(2) *1–021*, *7–137*, 15–031, *15–038*, *15–043*, 15–049, **15–051**, 15–053, 15–054, 15–056, **15–057**, 15–058, 15–059, 15–060, *15–061*, *15–062*, *15–098*, *15–131*

(b) ... *3–014*, **15–052**, 15–053, 15–059

reg.7 ...... *12–084*, *14–153*, *15–012*, *15–038*, **15–129**, 15–130, 15–131

reg.8 .... *1–084*, *14–125*, 15–123, 15–125

(1) *15–012*

reg.9 .... **15–132**, *30–065*, *30–103*

reg.10(1) *15–135*

(2) *15–135*, *15–138*

(3) *15–135*, *15–138*

regs 10–13 .... *15–113*

regs 10–14 .... *14–125*

reg.11(1) *15–138*

(2) *15–138*

reg.12 ..... *15–009*, 15–113, *15–136*

(1) *15–012*, *15–135*

(2) *15–138*

(3) *15–135*, *15–138*

(4) *15–135*

regs 12–14 .... *15–134*

reg.13 .... *15–135*

(5) *15–138*

reg.15 .... *14–125*

(3) *15–135*

Sch.1 Pt 1 .... *14–125*

Sch.2 ...... *2–176*, 15–021, 15–054, 15–064

para.1 .... *15–091*, 15–092

(b) *15–109*

(c) *3–025*

(f) *3–025*, *14–153*, *22–048*

(g) *14–153*

(h) *14–153*

(j) *14–153*, *22–039*

(k) *14–153*, *22–039*

(i) *15–076*

(l) ... *15–054*, *15–072*, *22–039*

(p) *19–047*

para.2 .... *15–103*

(a) *15–100*

(b) ... *2–131*, *15–098*, *15–100*, *22–039*

(c) *15–021*, *22–039*

(d) *22–039*

(e) 15–098

(g) 15–100

(j) 15–103

(l) 15–103

Unfair Arbitration Agreements (Specified Amount) Order (SI 1999/2167) .. *15–089*, *15–094*

Maternity and Parental Leave etc Regulations (SI 1999/3312)

reg.18 .... *27–022*

2000 Competition Act 1998 (Land and Vertical Agreements Exclusion) Order (SI 2000/310) *16–121*

Conditional Fee Agreements Regulations (SI 2000/692) *15–063*

Contracts (Applicable Law) Act 1990 (Amendment) Order (SI 2000/1825) *30–017*

Consumer Protection (Distance Selling) Regulations (SI 2000/2334) ...1–077, 2–062, 2–064, *4–002*, 14–129, **14–154**, 30–103

reg.3 .... *1–077*, *2–064*

(1) *1–077*

reg.5 .... *1–077*

reg.6 .... *1–077*, *2–064*

(1) *30–084*

reg.7 14–154

(1)(b) *14–154*

(c) *14–154*

(2) *14–154*
regs 7–8 .... *1–077*
regs 7–20 .... *30–084*
regs 10–18 .... *1–077*
reg.13(1)(b) *2–062*
reg.19 .... *1–077*
(1) *14–154*
(2) *14–154*
(7) 14–154
reg.21(1) *30–352*
(2) *30–352*
(3) *30–352*
reg.22 .... *2–005*
reg.24 .... *2–005*
reg.25(5) *30–008*, *30–065*, *30–068*, *30–103*
Sch.1 .... *2–064*
Sch.2 .... *1–077*

2001 Stop Now Orders (EC Directive) Regulations (SI 2001/1422) 14–131
Financial Services and Markets Act 2000 (Law Applicable to Contracts of Insurance) Regulations (SI 2001/2635) .. *30–045*, **30–046**, 30–252, *30–258*, 30–274
reg.2(1) *30–046*
(2)(a) *30–046*
(b) *30–046*
(c) *30–046*
(d) *30–046*
(3)(a) *30–046*
reg.4(5) *30–272*
reg.7(3) *30–272*
Civil Jurisdiction and Judgments Order (SI 2001/3929) *30–018*
art.3 .... *25–017*
art.67 .... *25–017*
art.68 .... *25–017*
Sch.1 .... *25–017*
para.33 .... *25–017*
para.36 .... *25–017*
para.37 .... *25–017*
Sch.2 .... *25–017*

2002 Carriage by Air Acts (Implementation of the Montreal Convention 1999) Order (SI 2002/263) *14–118*
Electronic Signatures Regulations (SI 2002/318) 4–006, *4–007*
Late Payment of Commercial Debts (Interest) Act 1998 (Commencement No.5) Order (SI 2002/1673) *26–172*
Late Payment of Commercial Debts Regulations (SI 2002/1674) *14–130*
Late Payment of Commercial Debts (Rate of Interest) (No.3) Order (SI 2002/1675) *26–172*
International Maritime Organisation (Immunities and Privileges) Order (SI 2002/1826) *11–019*
Electronic Commerce (EC Directive) Regulations (SI 2002/2013) *2–064*, *30–062*
reg.4(4) *30–097*
reg.9 .... *2–051*
(4) *2–051*
reg.10 .... *2–064*
(2) *2–064*
reg.11 .... *2–027*, *2–051*
(2)(a) *2–051*, *2–064*, *30–096*, *30–101*
(3) *2–051*, *2–064*
(12) *2–064*
reg.13 .... *2–064*
reg.17 .... *2–064*
Sch. *30–097*
Fixed-term Employees (Prevention of Less Favourable Treatment) Regulations (SI 2002/2034) *30–115*
Sale and Supply of Goods to Consumers Regulations (SI 2002/3045) ... 2–020, 2–167, 3–027, 6–086, *14–077*, *27–019*, *30–008*, *30–065*, *30–068*, 30–103
reg.2 .... *2–020*, *2–167*, *3–027*, *14–134*, *18–005*
reg.15 .... *2–020*, *2–167*, *3–027*, *14–134*
(1) *3–027*, *6–086*

2003 Enterprise Act 2002 (Part 8 Community Infringements Specified UK Laws) Order (SI 2003/1374) .. *14–131*, *30–103*
art.3 .... *15–139*
Enterprise Act 2002 (Part 8 Notice to OFT of Intended Prosecution Specified Enactments, Revocation and Transitional Provision) Order (SI 2003/1376) 14–131

Enterprise Act 2002 (Part 8 Designated Enforcers Criteria for Designation, Designation of Public Bodies as Designated Enforcers and Transitional Provisions) Order (SI 2003/1399)
art.5 .... *15–139*
Sch.1 .... *15–139*
Enterprise Act 2002 (Part 8 Domestic Infringements) Order (SI 2003/1593) *30–103*
Employment Equality (Religion or Belief) Regulations (SI 2003/1660) *1–016*, *30–114*
Employment Equality (Sexual Orientation) Regulations (SI 2003/1661) *1–016*, *30–114*
Disability Discrimination Act (Amendment) Regulations (SI 2003/1673) *1–016*
Enterprise Act 2002 (Commencement No.4 and Transitional Provisions and Savings) Order (SI 2003/2093) *9–050*
2004 Enterprise Act 2002 (Part 8) (Designation of the Financial Services Authority as a Designated Enforcer) Order 2004 (SI 2004/935) *14–131*
Air Carrier Liability Regulations (SI 2004/1418) *14–118*
Carriage by Air Acts (Application of Provisions) Order (SI 2004/1899) .. 14–118, 28–024
Financial Services (Distance Marketing) Regulations (SI 2004/2095) ... *1–025*, *1–077*, *30–103*
reg.16(3) *30–065*
reg.24 .... *15–089*
Life Assurance Consolidation Directive (Consequential Amendments) Regulations 2004 (SI 2004/3379) *30–045*
2005 Enterprise Act 2002 (Part 8) (Designation of the Consumers' Association) Order 2005 (SI 2005/917) *14–131*
Regulatory Reform (Execution of Deeds and Documents) Order (SI 2005/1906) 1–087, 1–089, **1–095**, 1–096, 1–098, 1–099, 1–100
art.1(1) *1–087*
(2) *1–087*
art.4 .... *1–095*
art.6 .... *1–095*
art.7(3) *1–096*, *1–097*
Railways (Convention on International Carriage by Rail) Regulations (SI 2005/2092) *14–116*, 28–025
Medicines (Marketing Authorisations Etc.) Amendment Regulations (SI 2005/2759) ... 14–131
2006 Public Contracts Regulations (SI 2006/5) *10–003*, *10–044*
reg.8 .... *10–044*
reg.12 .... *10–044*
reg.15(2) *10–044*
reg.30 .... *10–044*
reg.32 .... *10–044*
reg.47 .... *10–045*
(9) *10–045*
(10) *10–045*
Utilities Contracts Regulations (SI 2006/6) *10–003*, *10–044*
reg.11 .... *10–044*
reg.14 .... *10–044*
reg.16 .... *10–044*
reg.30 .... *10–044*
reg.33 .... *10–044*
reg.45 .... *10–045*
(9) *10–045*
(10) *10–045*
Transfer of Undertakings (Protection of Employment) Regulations (SI 2006/246) *19–055*, *30–116*
Employment Equality (Age) Regulations (SI 2006/1031) .. *27–074*, *30–114*
Home Information Pack Regulations (SI 2006/1503)
reg.8 .... *6–093*, *6–156*

Enterprise Act 2002 (Amendment) Regulations (SI 2006/3363) ... 14–131
Enterprise Act 2002 (Part 8 Community Infringements Specified UK Laws) Order (SI 2006/3372) *14–131*
2007 Government of Wales Act 2006 (Local Government (Contracts) Act 1997) (Modifications) Order (SI 2007/1182 .... *10–034*
Equality Act (Sexual Orientation) Regulations (SI 2007/1263)
reg.34 .... *30–115*
Home Information Pack (No.2) Regulations (SI 2007/1667)
reg.9 .... *6–093*, *6–156*
Sch.9 art.2 .... *6–093*
art.3 .... *6–093*
Public Contracts and Utilities Contracts (Amendment) Regulations (SI 2007/3542) ... 10–044
2008 Business Protection from Misleading Marketing Regulations (SI 2008/1276) *2–020*, *14–129*
reg.29 .... *6–002*, *7–002*
Consumer Protection from Unfair Trading Regulations (SI 2008/1277) *1–018*, *2–020*, *14–077*, *14–128*, *14–129*, 14–131, *15–114*, *30–013*, 30–103
reg.2(1) *1–025*
reg.2 .... *2–015*
reg.3(3) *1–018*, *1–025*
(4)(d) *1–018*, *2–005*, *2–020*
reg.5 .... *1–018*
reg.6 .... *1–018*
reg.7 .... *1–018*
reg.29 .... *1–018*, *6–002*, *7–002*
reg.30(1) *2–005*, *2–020*, *2–064*, *3–027*
Sch.1 .... *1–018*
para.6 .... *2–015*, *2–020*
para.29 .... *2–005*
Sch.2, para.96 .... *2–005*
para.97 .... *14–143*
para.110 .... *20–020*, *2–064*
Cancellation of Contracts made in a Consumer's Home or Place of Work etc. Regulations (SI 2008/1816) *30–103*

TABLE OF EUROPEAN COMMUNITY LEGISLATION

[Where a reference indicates significant discussion of the legislation in the text, it is in **bold**. Where a reference is to a footnote, it is *italic*.]

Treaties and Conventions

1957 Treaty establishing the European Community (post Treaty of Amsterdam) (as consolidated and further amended) *16–133*, 30–130
art.12 ..... *30–103*
art.28 ..... *30–103*
art.29 ..... *30–103*
art.30 15–040
art.39 1–007
art.49 ..... *30–103*
art.61(c) 30–132
art.65 ..... *30–130*, 30–132
art.65B *30–130*
art.81 ..... *1–018*, *16–091*, *16–095*, *16–096*, *16–116*, *16–119*, *16–121*, *16–122*, *16–128*, *16–130*, 16–138, *16–158*, *16–205*
(1) 16–076, *16–121*, *16–122*, 16–124, 16–131, *19–043*
(3) *16–121*
art.82 ..... *1–018*, *16–095*, *16–096*, *16–121*, *16–130*, 16–134, *27–011*
art.95 15–005
(3) *15–005*
art.234 ..... *30–019*, 20–134
art.249 ..... *15–006*
art.282 ..... *10–002*
art.288 ..... *15–015*
(1) 10–002
art.299 30–136
1968 Brussels Convention on Jurisdiction and Enforcement of Judgments in Civil and Commercial Matters 1–007, *11–003*, 25–017, 30–018, *30–019*, 30–070, *30–084*, *30–093*
art.5(1) 1–007, 1–168, *30–031*, *30–032*, 30–033, *30–110*
(3) 1–168
art.13 ..... 15–029, 15–030, 15–095
art.16(1) *30–084*
art.17 ..... *19–079*, 30–040
art.27 ..... *25–017*
(1) *30–070*
art.28 ..... *25–017*
1971 Protocol to the 1968 Brussels Convention on Jurisdiction and Enforcement of Judgments in Civil and Commercial Matters *25–017*
art.2(2) *30–019*
1972 European Convention on State Immunity *11–004*
1980 Convention on the Law applicable to Contractual Obligations (Rome Convention) *1–125*, 1–169, *15–132*, 16–027, 16–031, *16–032*, 30–002, 30–003, 30–004, *30–005*, *30–009*, *30–010*, *30–012*, *30–013*, *30–015*, **30–017**, 30–018, 30–019, 30–020, 30–021, 30–026, 30–029, 30–031, 30–032, 30–038, 30–039, 30–040, 30–041, 30–042, 30–060, 30–087, 30–121, 30–130, 30–133, 30–136, 30–141, 30–143, 30–144, *30–145*, 30–147, 30–151, 30–152, 30–162, 30–163, 30–165, 30–167, *30–168*, 30–172, 30–173, 30–174, 30–175, 30–186, *30–217*, *30–272*, 30–322, *30–377*
Preamble *30–019*
art.1 ..... *30–082*, *30–123*
(1) 30–022, 30–023, 30–024, 30–030, 30–048
(2) 30–030, 30–035

(a) ..*30–036*, 30–153, *30–323*
(b) ..30–037, 30–154, 30–155
(c) *30–039*, 30–156
(d) *30–040*, 30–157
(e) ..*30–041*, 30–042, 30–158, *30–323*, 30–325, *30–345*
(f) ...*30–041*, 30–042, 30–159, *30–323*, 30–325
(g) ..30–043, 30–160, 30–325
(h) 30–044, 30–049, 30–161, *30–339*
(3) 30–045, 30–046, *30–093*, 30–252
(4) *30–045*, *30–252*
art.2 30–023
art.3 ....*30–051*, 30–093, 30–094, 30–108, 30–109, 30–111, 30–170, 30–209, 30–221, 30–252
(1) 30–047, **30–049**, 30–050, 30–051, 30–052, 30–056, 30–058, 30–071, *30–112*, *30–305*, 30–317, *30–331*, 30–341, 30–342, 30–371
(2) 30–058, 30–176, 30–316
(3) **30–061**, 30–062, 30–063, 30–064, 30–065, 30–066, 30–067, 30–068, 30–102, 30–112, 30–177, 30–178, 30–280, 30–303
(4) *30–006*, 30–059, 30–184, *30–304*, *30–308*
art.4 ......30–054, 30–055, 30–057, 30–058, 30–059, *30–068*, **30–071**, 30–072, 30–090, 30–093, 30–107, 30–109, 30–111, 30–231, 30–252, 30–305, 30–341, 30–342, 30–343
(1) 30–071, 30–188, 30–317
(2) 30–073, 30–074, 30–076, 30–078, 30–079, 30–082, 30–083, 30–085, *30–086*, 30–088, 30–090, 30–091, *30–109*, *30–189*, 30–190, 30–191, 30–193, 30–198, 30–209, 30–210, 30–221, *30–256*, 30–341
(2)–(4) 30–072, 30–090, *30–125*, 30–203
(3) *30–072*, 30–076, 30–082, 30–083, 30–084, 30–192, *30–314*
(4) *30–072*, 30–076, 30–085, 30–086, 30–209, 30–213, *30–216*
(5) *30–072*, 30–076, *30–077*, 30–083, 30–088, 30–090, 30–091, 30–207, 30–209, 30–221
art.5 ....*30–047*, *30–061*, 30–063, **30–092**, 30–093, 30–094, 30–095, 30–097, 30–102, 30–104, 30–107, 30–209, 30–231, 30–234, 30–243, 30–245, 30–249, 30–252, 30–303, *30–305*, 30–313
(1) *15–032*, *30–093*, *30–240*
(2) *15–132*, *30–094*, 30–095, **30–096**, 30–097, 30–098, 30–099, 30–100, 30–101, 30–102, 30–104, *30–242*, *30–244*
(3) *30–031*, 30–107, 30–313
(4)(a) *30–093*, *30–221*
(b) ..*30–093*, *30–234*, *30–235*
(5) *30–093*, *30–235*
art.6 ....*30–047*, *30–061*, 30–063, 30–092, **30–108**, 30–109, 30–110, 30–111, 30–113, 30–114, 30–120, 30–276, 30–277, 30–278, 30–303, *30–305*
(1) *30–108*, **30–112**, 30–117, 30–118, 30–276, *30–277*, 30–280
(2) *30–108*, **30–119**, *30–120*, 30–285
(a) ..*30–108*, 30–119, 30–120, 30–276, 30–282
(b) *30–108*, 30–119, 30–120, *30–276*
art.7(1) ...*15–026*, *16–033*, *23–029*, *30–017*, *30–061*, 30–063, *30–068*, *30–102*, *30–112*, 30–182, 30–359, 30–360, 30–365
(2) 16–030, *16–033*, *23–029*, *30–061*, 30–063, 30–068, 30–104, *30–112*, 30–118, *30–120*, 30–181, 30–303, 30–311, 30–357, 30–359
art.8 ....*16–027*, *23–027*, *30–006*, 30–303
(1) *21–069*, *30–059*, **30–304**, 30–305, 30–306, 30–307, 30–308, 30–309, *30–356*
(2) 30–306, 30–307, 30–308
art.9 .... 30–303, 30–310, *30–311*, 30–319, 30–354
(1) *30–312*, 30–318
(1)–(3) *30–310*, *30–315*
(1)–(4) *30–314*
(2).....................*30–312*, 30–318
(3) *30–312*, 30–318
(4).......*30–310*, *30–315*, 30–319
(5) *30–310*, *30–313*
(6) *30–061*, *30–063*, *30–310*, 30–314, 30–321
art.10 ......*16–027*, 30–303, **30–326**

(1) **30–326**, 30–329, 30–330, 30–350
(a) ..*21–069*, *30–326*, *30–331*, *30–372*
(b) *21–069*, *30–326*, 30–332, 30–339, 30–345, *30–370*, *30–374*
(c) ..*30–326*, **30–336**, 30–337, 30–338, 30–339, 30–340, 30–348, *30–373*
(d) 30–299, *30–326*, 30–345, 30–347, 30–348
(e) ..*30–017*, 30–033, 30–034, *30–326*, 30–327, *30–329*, 10–349
(2) *23–029*, *30–326*, 30–332, 30–333, 30–335, 30–359, 30–374
art.11 .....30–036, 30–303, 30–324, *30–325*
art.12 .....**30–123**, 30–124, *30–125*, 30–126, 30–288, 30–289
(1) *30–125*, 30–288, 30–290
(2) **30–125**, 30–126, 30–288, 30–291, 30–292
art.13 .... 30–127, 30–293
(1) 30–127, 30–128, 30–293, 30–294
(2) *30–129*, 30–293, 30–296, *30–297*, 30–298
art.14 .... 30–303, **30–351**
(1) *30–351*, 30–352, 30–353
(2) *30–311*, *30–351*, 30–354
art.15 30–028
art.16 ..... 16–029, 16–030, *23–029*, 30–069, 30–070, 30–113, 30–183, 30–303, *30–309*, 30–347, 30–359, **30–366**, 30–368
art.17 .....*30–002*, *30–017*, *30–026*, *30–123*
art.18 .... 30–020, *30–044*
art.19(1) 30–024
(2) 30–025
art.20 .... 30–027, *30–108*
art.21 .... 30–027, *30–087*
art.22 ......*30–017*, *30–063*, *30–359*
(1) *30–033*
(b) *30–327*
Brussels Protocol on implementing the Convention on the Law applicable to Contractual Obligations (Rome Convention) *30–017*, 30–019, 30–020, *30–025*
art.1 ....*30–019*
art.2 ....*30–019*
(a) *30–019*
(b) 30–019
art.3 ....*30–020*
1988 Lugano Convention on Jurisdiction and Enforcement of Judgments in Civil and Commercial Matters 25–017, *30–084*
art.5(1) *30–031*
art.16(1) *30–084*
art.27 ....*25–017*
art.28 ....*25–017*
art.54B *25–017*
1992 Agreement on the European Economic Area *30–045*
1996 Convention providing for the Accession to the Convention on the Law applicable to Contractual Obligations (Rome Convention) of Austria, Finland and Sweden *30–017*
2005 Convention providing for the Accession to the Convention on the Law applicable to Contractual Obligations (Rome Convention) of the Czech Republic, Estonia, Cyprus, Latvia, Lithuania, Hungary, Malta, Poland, Slovenia and the Slovak Republic ... *30–017*
2007 Charter of Fundamental Rights of the European Union
art.16 1–013

Regulations

1971 Reg.1408/71 on social security schemes [1971] OJ L149/366 ....*30–078*
1983 Reg.1984/83 on exclusive purchase agreements [1983] OJ L173/5 ......*16–122*, 16–124
1996 Reg.240/96 on technology transfer agreements [1996] OJ L31/2 16–131
1999 Reg.2790/1999 on categories of vertical agreements [1999] OJ L336/21 .... *16–121*, *16–124*
art.5(a) *16–122*
2000 Reg.1346/2000 on insolvency proceedings [2000] OJ L160/1 30–301

art.3 .... *30–301*
art.4(1) *30–301*
(2)(d) *30–301*
art.6(1) 30–301
2001 Reg.44/2001 on jurisdiction and the recognition and enforcement of judgments in civil and commercial matters [2001] OJ L12/1 ....*1–007*, *1–125*, 1–168, 1–169, *15–029*, *15–095*, 25–017, *30–018*, *30–019*, 30–134, 30–139, 30–141, 30–142
art.1(1) *30–142*
art.5 .... *30–190*, *30–191*
(1) *1–125*, *1–168*, *18–117*
(3) *1–125*, *1–168*
(5) 30–166
art.15(1) 30–240
(c) ..30–242, 30–243, 30–247
(3) *30–097*
art.18 .... *30–278*
art.22(1) 30–192
art.23 12–011
art.34 .... *25–017*
(1) *30–070*
art.35 .... *25–017*
art.60(1)(b) *30–080*
(c) *30–164*
art.65 .... *30–019*
art.68 .... *30–019*
2004 Reg.2006/2004 on consumer protection co-operation [2004] OJ L346/1 .... 15–139, *30–103*
art.4(6) *15–139*
art.13(4) *15–139*
2007 Reg.864/2007 on the law applicable to non-contractual obligations (Rome II) [2007] OJ L199/40 .... *1–125*, 1–169, 30–031, 30–032, **30–034**, 30–122, 30–134, 30–139, 30–141, 30–142, 30–148, 30–287, 30–327, 30–328
Recital 11 .... *1–169*, *30–031*, *30–032*, *30–122*
Recital 30 .... *30–149*
art.1(1) *30–141*, *30–142*
art.4(1) *1–169*
(3) *1–169*
art.5 .... *1–169*
art.10 .... 30–034, 30–150
(1) *30–034*, 30–150
(2) *30–034*
(2)–(4) *30–150*
(3) *30–034*
(4) *30–034*
art.12 .... *1–169*, *30–031*, 30–149, 30–162
(1) 30–149
art.14 .... *1–169*, 30–178
(2) 30–178
art.23 .... *30–164*
(1) *30–166*
2008 Reg.593/2008 on the law applicable to non-contractual obligations (Rome I) [2008] OJ L177/6 .... *1–125*, *1–169*, *15–132*, 30–002, 30–003, 30–004, *30–005*, *30–012*, *30–013*, *30–015*, 30–130, 30–131, 30–132, 30–133, 30–134, 30–139, 30–141, 30–148, 30–287, 30–311, 30–318, 30–323, 30–328, 30–377
Ch.I 30–133
Ch.II 30–133
Ch.III 30–133
Ch.IV 30–133
Preamble *30–132*
Recital 1 .... *30–132*
Recital 2 .... *30–132*
Recital 3 .... *30–132*, *30–237*
Recital 4 .... *30–132*
Recital 5 .... *30–130*
Recital 6 30–132
Recital 7 .... *30–134*, 30–139, *30–166*, *30–192*, *30–240*, *30–242*, *30–243*, *30–278*
Recitals 7–10 .... *30–134*
Recital 8 .... *30–134*, 30–154, 30–155
Recital 9 30–156
Recital 10 .... *30–031*, *30–149*, *30–162*
Recital 11 30–170
Recital 12 .... 30–174, *30–178*, *30–214*
Recital 13 .... *30–144*, *30–171*
Recital 14 .... *30–144*, *30–171*
Recital 15 .... *30–134*, 30–178
Recital 16 .... 30–188, *30–203*, *30–220*
Recital 17 .... *30–189*, *30–190*, *30–191*
Recital 19 .... *30–197*, *30–200*, 30–201
Recital 20 .... 30–203, 30–204

Recital 21 .... 30–206, 30–207
Recital 22 .... 30–213, 30–217, 30–218
Recital 23 .... *30–231*, *30–240*, *30–256*
Recital 24 .... *30–231*, *30–232*, *30–240*, *30–242*, *30–243*, *30–245*, 30–247, *30–248*
Recital 25 .... *30–249*
Recital 26 .... *30–237*
Recital 27 .... *30–236*
Recital 28 .... 30–237, *30–238*
Recital 29 30–237
Recital 31 .... *30–238*
Recital 32 .... *30–210*, *30–222*, *30–239*, *30–256*
Recital 33 .... *30–274*
Recital 34 .... *30–280*
Recital 36 30–283
Recital 37 .... *30–180*, *30–249*, *30–361*, *30–364*, *30–366*, *30–368*
Recital 38 30–290
Recital 39 30–164
Recital 40 .... 30–135, *30–280*
Recital 41 .... *30–137*, 30–211
Recital 42 .... *30–137*
Recital 44 .... *30–132*
Recital 45 .... *30–130*
Recital 46 .... *30–132*
art.1(1) 30–139, 30–144
(2) **30–152**
(b) *30–134*, 30–154
(c) *30–134*, 30–155
(d) 30–156
(e) 30–157
(f) ... 30–158, *30–323*, 30–325, *30–345*
(g) 30–159, *30–323*, 30–325, *30–350*
(h) 30–160
(i) *30–149*, 30–162
(j) ... 30–162, 30–163, **30–255**
(k) *30–045*
(3) *30–143*, 30–152, 30–161, *30–171*, *30–179*, *30–300*
(4) 30–258
art.2 .... 30–143, 30–144
art.3 .... 30–133, *30–157*, **30–170**, 30–177, 30–189, 30–210, 30–215, 30–226, 30–234, 30–236, 30–249, 30–250, 30–256, 30–261, 30–263, 30–264, 30–266, 30–272, 30–274, 30–279
(1) **30–171**, 30–172, 30–173, 30–175, 30–214, *30–305*, 30–322, *30–331*, 30–341, 30–342, 30–371
(2) **30–176**, 30–322
(3) *30–134*, *30–177*, **30–178**, 30–180, 30–303, 30–361
(4) *30–144*, *30–177*, **30–179**, 30–180, 30–303
(5) *30–006*, 30–184, *30–304*, *30–308*
arts 3–8 .... *30–144*
art.4 .... 30–133, *30–164*, 30–186, **30–187**, 30–188, *30–190*, 30–234, 30–236, 30–250, 30–256, 30–274, 30–305, 30–322, 30–341, 30–342, 30–343
(1) 30–187, 30–189, **30–197**, 30–198, 30–199, 30–200, 30–203, 30–204, 30–205, 30–206, 30–256, 30–264
(a) .. 30–190, 30–194, 30–200, 30–341
(b) .. 30–191, 30–198, 30–200
(c) .. *30–084*, 30–192, 30–236
(d) .. *30–084*, 30–192, 30–236
(f) 30–194
(g) 30–195
(h) 30–195, 30–238
(2) 30–187, 30–194, 30–197, 30–199, 30–200, 30–203, 30–204, 30–205, 30–206
(e) 30–193
(3) 30–187, 30–203, 30–205, 30–220, 30–256, 30–264, *30–285*
(4) 30–187, 30–201, 30–206, 30–207, 30–208, *30–285*
(5) 30–203
art.5 .... *30–085*, 30–133, *30–164*, 30–209, **30–210**, *30–216*, *30–221*, 30–235, 30–305
(1) 30–210, 30–212, 30–215, 30–219, 30–220, *30–225*, 30–230
(2) 30–210, 30–221, **30–222**, 30–223, 30–225, 30–226, 30–227, 30–228, 30–229, 30–230
(3) 30–210, 30–212, 30–219, 30–220, 30–221, 30–222, 30–230
arts 5–8 .... 30–187, *30–189*
art.6 .... 30–095, *30–097*, 30–133, 30–138, *30–164*, *30–195*, *30–222*, 30–231, **30–232**, 30–233, 30–234, 30–235, 30–236, 30–237, 30–238, **30–239**, 30–240, 30–245, 30–246, 30–251, *30–256*, 30–303, 30–305, 30–320, *30–321*

(1) 30–232, 30–239, 30–240, 30–243, 30–245, 30–248, 30–249, *30–256*
(a) .. 30–232, 30–241, 30–242, 30–244, 30–248, 30–250
(b) 30–232, 30–241, 30–243, 30–245, 30–247, 30–248, 30–250
(2) 30–232, *30–241*, 30–249, *30–277*
(3) 30–232, 30–250
(4) 30–232, 30–233, 30–259
(a) *30–233*
(b) *30–210*, *30–222*
(c) .. *30–084*, 30–236, *30–321*
(d) 30–237
(e) *30–238*
art.7 .... *30–045*, 30–133, *30–135*, *30–144*, 30–163, *30–164*, *30–198*, 30–239, 30–252, **30–253**, 30–254, 30–256, 30–257, 30–258
(1) *30–045*, 30–253, 30–254, 30–257, 30–265, 30–305
(2) 30–253, 30–254, 30–260, 30–261, 30–263, 30–264, **30–265**, *30–273*, 30–275
(3) 30–146, 30–253, 30–260, 30–265, **30–266**, 30–271, 30–272, 30–273, 30–274, 30–275
(a) 30–267, 30–272
(b) 30–268, 30–272
(c) 30–269
(d) 30–270
(e) .. *30–270*, 30–271, 30–272
(4) 30–253, 30–275
(a) 30–275
(b) 30–275
(5) 30–253, 30–273, 30–274, 30–275
(6) 30–253, 30–259
art.8 .... *30–108*, 30–133, 30–276, **30–277**, 30–278, *30–286*, 30–303, 30–305
(1) 30–277, 30–279, 30–280
(2) 30–277, 30–281, **30–282**, 30–283, 30–284, 30–285
(3) 30–277, 30–281, 30–284, 30–285
(4) 30–277, 30–281, 30–282, 30–285
art.9 .... *30–063*, 30–133, *30–177*, 30–180, *30–249*, 30–303
(1) *30–063*, 30–180, *30–357*, 30–361
(2) 30–181, 30–211, 30–311, 30–357
(3) 30–182, **30–360**, 30–362, 30–364, 30–365
art.10 ..... *30–006*, 30–133, *30–164*, 30–184, 30–237, 30–303
(1) *30–169*, **30–304**, 30–306, 30–308, 30–309, 30–328, *30–356*
(2) 30–306, 30–307, 30–308
arts 10–13 30–133
art.11 ..... 30–133, *30–164*, 30–176, 30–184, 30–237, 30–303, 30–310, 30–354
(1) **30–318**
(1)–(3) 30–320
(2) **30–318**
(3) **30–319**
(4) *30–241*, **30–320**
(5) **30–321**
art.12 ..... 30–133, 30–237, 30–303, 30–326
(1) *30–150*, 30–329, 30–330, 30–348, 30–350
(a) .. *30–326*, *30–331*, *30–372*
(b) *30–326*, 30–332, 30–339, 30–345, *30–370*, *30–374*
(c) .. *30–326*, **30–336**, 30–337, 30–338, 30–339, 30–340, 30–348, *30–373*
(d) *30–326*, 30–345, 30–347, 30–348
(e) .. 30–034, 30–150, *30–326*, 30–328, *30–329*, 30–349
(2) *30–150*, *30–326*, 30–332, 30–333, 30–335, 30–374
(i) *30–339*
art.13 ..... 30–133, 30–153, 30–184, 30–237, 30–303, 30–324, *30–325*
art.14 ..... 30–123, 30–133, 30–288, 30–289, 30–295
(1) 30–288, 30–290
(2) 30–291, 30–292
(3) 30–288, 30–289, *30–292*
arts 14–17 30–133
art.15 ..... 30–133, *30–290*, 30–293, **30–294**, 30–295
art.16 ..... 30–133, 30–293, **30–296**, 30–297, 30–298
art.17 ..... 30–133, **30–299**, 30–300, 30–301, 30–302, 30–346, *30–350*
art.18 ..... 30–133, 30–161, 30–303, **30–351**
(1) 30–351, 30–352, 30–353
(2) *30–351*, 30–354
art.19 ..... *30–079*, 30–133, **30–164**, 30–229, *30–256*
(1) *30–080*, 30–165, *30–167*, 30–224, 30–225, 30–241
(2) 30–166, 30–225, 30–229
(3) 30–169, *30–224*, *30–242*

art.20 .... 30–133, 30–146
art.21 .....30–133, *30–177*, 30–183, 30–303, *30–309*, 30–347, 30–366, 30–369
art.22 30–133
(1) *30–145*
(2) *30–130*
art.23 .... 30–133, *30–135*
art.24 .... 30–133, 30–136
(1) *30–136*
(2) *30–136*
art.25 30–133
(1) 30–137, 30–211
(2) *30–137*, 30–211
art.26 .... 30–133, *30–137*
(1) 30–137
(2) *30–137*
art.27 .... 30–133, 30–138
(1) *30–138*, 30–251
(i) *30–138*
(ii) *30–138*
(2) *30–138*, *30–288*, *30–292*
art.28 .....*30–002*, *30–017*, *30–130*, 30–133
art.29 .....*30–002*, *30–017*, *30–130*, 30–133

Directives

1968 Dir.68/151 First Directive on company law [1968] OJ L65/8
art.7 9–012
art.9 9–027
(1) 9–029
(2) 9–033
1973 Dir.73/239 First non-life insurance Directive [1973] OJ L228/3 30–265
art.5(d) 30–261, 30–262
(i) *30–262*
(ii) *30–262*
(iii) *30–262*, *30–265*
1979 Dir.79/7 on equal treatment of men and women in social security [1979] OJ 6/24 .... *15–014*
1984 Dir.84/5 on motor insurance [1984] OJ L8/17 .... *28–078*
1985 Dir.85/374 on liability for defective products [1985] OJ L210/29 ....*15–024*, 28–009
art.9 .... *15–126*
Dir.85/577 on contracts negotiated away from business premises [1985] OJ L372/31
art.2 .... *15–029*
art.7(c) 15–024
Dir.85/611 on collective investment in transferable securities (UCITS) [1985] OJ L375/3 30–237
1986 Dir.86/653 on self-employed commercial agents [1986] OJ L L382/17 .... *1–025*, *30–042*, *30–065*
art.3(1) *1–025*, *1–027*
art.17 .... *30–065*
art.18 .... *30–065*
1988 Dir.88/357 Second non-life insurance Directive [1988] OJ L127/1 ...... *30–045*
art.2(d) 30–259
art.7 .... *30–045*
1989 Dir.89/665 on review procedures for the award of public supply and public works contracts [1989] OJ L395/33 .... *10–044*
art.2 .... *10–045*
art.2a *10–046*
art.2d *10–046*
(2) *10–046*
(3) *10–046*
art.2e(2) *10–046*
1990 Dir.90/314 on package travel, package holidays and package tours [1990] OJ L158/59 ......*6–092*, *13–034*, 30–235
art.4(6) *14–149*
art.6(4) *30–235*
Dir.90/619 Second life insurance Directive [1990] OJ L330/50 .... *30–045*
art.4 .... *30–045*
1991 Dir.91/533 on employer's obligation to inform employees of conditions applicable to contract or employment relationship [1991] OJ L288/32 ......1–007, 1–008
1992 Dir.92/13 on procurement procedures of entities operating in the water, energy, transport and telecommunications sectors [1992] OJ L76/14 .... *10–044*
art.2 .... *10–045*
Dir.92/49 Third non-life insurance Directive [1992] OJ L228/1 ...... *30–045*

Dir.92/96 Third life insurance Directive [1992] OJ L360/1 .... *30–045*

1993 Dir.93/13 on unfair terms in consumer contracts [1993] OJ L95/29 ....1–009, *1–021*, 7–137, 14–125, 14–131, **15–004**, 15–010, **15–014**, 15–015, 15–016, 15–019, 15–021, 15–023, 15–025, 15–026, 15–029, 15–030, 15–031, 15–034, 15–035, 15–036, 15–046, 15–048, 15–065, 15–069, 15–070, 15–077, *15–091*, *15–094*, 15–111, 15–112, 15–113, 15–115, 15–117, 15–118, 15–139, 30–103

Preamble 1–064, 15–005, 15–039, *15–067*, 15–080

Recital 1 .... *15–019*, *15–050*

Recitals 1–2 .... *15–025*

Recital 2 .... *15–005*, *15–019*, *15–050*

Recital 5 .... *15–005*, *15–019*, *15–026*

Recital 6 .... *15–026*, *15–050*

Recital 7 .... *15–005*, *15–019*, *15–050*

Recital 9 .... *15–005*

Recital 10 .... *3–014*, 15–018, *15–019*, *15–026*, 15–036

Recital 11 .... *15–038*

Recital 13 .... 15–039, 15–041

Recital 14 15–039

Recital 16 .... *1–064*, *15–050*, 15–066, *15–067*, *15–069*, 15–080, 15–081, 15–084

Recital 19 .... *3–014*, *15–018*, *15–019*, 15–050, 15–051, 15–053, 15–054, 15–055, 15–078, *15–080*, 15–084

art.1 .... 15–032, 15–036

(1) 15–043

(2) *15–004*, 15–039, 15–040, 15–041, 15–042

art.2 ....*15–018*, 15–032, 15–035

(a) *15–038*

(b) *15–008*

(c) *15–017*, 15–024

art.3 .... 7–137, 15–095

(1) *1–025*, *15–038*, *15–048*, 15–053, 15–080, 15–115

(2) *15–048*, *15–118*, *15–120*, *15–121*

art.4(1) ...*15–018*, *15–019*, *15–050*, 15–053, 15–067, *15–111*

(2) *3–014*, *7–137*, *15–007*, 15–049, **15–050**, 15–051, 15–053, *15–054*, 15–055, 15–056, *15–058*

art.5 15–134

(1) *15–034*

(2) 15–134

art.6 15–119

(1) 15–123, 15–126

(2) 15–132, *30–008*

art.7 ....*15–006*, *15–014*, 15–114, *15–123*, 15–133, 15–134

(1) *15–113*

(2) *15–113*, 15–134

art.8 .... *15–004*, *15–005*

art.10 15–014

(1) *15–014*, *15–015*

Annex 15–021, *15–091*

para.1(q) 15–095

para.2 .... *15–018*

1994 Dir.94/47 on contracts on using immovable properties on a timeshare basis [1994] OJ L280/83 ....*30–084*, 30–236

1996 Dir.96/71 on the posting of workers [1997] OJ L18/1 .... *30–108*, *30–115*, *30–276*

Preamble para.(18) *30–117*

art.2(2) *30–110*

art.3(7) *30–117*

1997 Dir.97/7 on protection of consumers in respect of distance contracts [1997] OJ L144/19 ......*2–005*, *30–065*, *30–103*

art.2(1) *1–077*

art.10(2) *30–008*

1998 Dir.98/26 on payment and securities settlement systems [1998] OJ L166/45

art.2(a) *30–238*

Dir.98/27 on injunctions for protection of consumers' interests [1998] OJ L166/51 ....*14–131*, *15–134*, *15–139*, *30–103*

art.1(2) *15–134*

art.4 .... *15–139*

Annex No.9 .... *15–134*

1999 Dir.1999/44 on sale of consumer goods and guarantees [1999] OJ L171/7 ....*2–165*, *15–028*, *27–019*, *30–065*, *30–103*

art.2(e) *18–005*

art.6 .... *18–005*

art.7 .... *3–027*
(2) *30–008*, *30–065*, *30–103*
Dir.1999/93 on a Community framework for electronic signatures [2000] OJ L13/12 4–007
2000 Dir.2000/31 on electronic commerce [2000] OJ L178/1 ....*2–027*, *2–064*, *12–048*, *30–062*, *30–096*, *30–135*
Recital 19 ....*30–101*
Recital 23 ....*30–097*
Recital 34 .... *9–005*
Recital 55 ....*30–097*
art.1(4) *30–097*
art.3(3) *30–097*
art.9 .... 4–005, **4–006**
(1) 4–005
(2)(a) *4–005*, *4–006*
(d) *4–005*, *4–006*
art.11(1) ...*2–051*, *30–097*, *30–101*
(3) *30–097*
Annex *30–097*
Dir.2000/78 on equal treatment in employment and occupation [2000] OJ L303/16 ....*27–074*
2002 Dir.2002/65 on distance marketing of consumer financial services [2002] OJ L271/16 ....15–089, *30–103*
art.3(2) *1–025*
art.12(2) *30–065*
Dir.2002/83 on life insurance [2002] OJ L345/1
art.1(1)(c) *30–259*
(g) 30–259
art.2 30–163
art.3(3) *30–163*
art.32 ....*30–045*
2004 Dir.2004/17 on procurement procedures of entities operating in water, energy, transport and postal services sectors [2004] OJ L134/1 ....*10–044*
Preamble para.(14) *10–047*
art.10 ....*10–044*
arts 16–27 ....*10–044*
art.40 ....*10–044*
arts 41–44 ....*10–044*
art.49 ....*10–044*
art.55(1) *10–044*
Dir.2004/18 on procedures for the award of public works contracts, public supply contracts and public service contracts [2004] OJ L134/114 ....*10–044*
Preamble para.(7) *10–047*
art.2 ....*10–044*
arts 7–9 ....*10–044*
art.28 ....*10–044*
arts 29–30 ....*10–044*
arts 35–37 ....*10–044*
art.41 ....*10–044*
art.53 ....*10–044*
Dir.2004/39 on markets in financial instruments [2004] OJ L145/1
Recital 18 ....*30–196*
Recital 30 ....*30–196*
art.4 ....*30–237*
(1)(15) *30–196*
(17) 30–196, *30–237*
(18) *30–237*
Annex I section A 30–237
section B 30–237
section C *30–196*
2005 Dir.2005/29 on unfair commercial practices [2005] OJ L149/22 ......1–018, 6–002, 7–002, 14–129, 15–031, 15–114, *30–103*
Recital 18 ....*15–031*
art.3(1) *6–002*, *15–114*
(2) 1–018, *15–031*
art.5 .... *1–018*, *1–025*
(3) *15–031*, *15–087*
(5) *1–018*
arts 5–9 ....*15–114*
art.6 .... *1–018*, *6–002*
art.7 .... *1–018*, *6–002*
art.8 .... *7–002*
art.9 .... *7–002*
Annex I *1–018*

TABLE OF INTERNATIONAL STATUTORY MATERIAL

[Where a reference indicates significant discussion of the legislation in the text, it is in **bold**. Where a reference is to a footnote, it is *italic*.]

Statutes

Civil Code (France) 1–019, 15–065
art.1101 .... *1–068*
art.1134 .... *15–065*
art.1134.1 .... *1–019*
art.1147 30–352
art.1152 .... *1–019*
art.1152.1 .... *1–019*
art.1174 .... *15–096*
art.1226 .... *1–019*
art.1249 .... *30–289*, *30–295*
art.1250 .... *30–289*
art.1251 .... *30–295*
arts 1382—1383 .... *1–136*
Civil Code (Germany) 15–065
para.242 .... *15–065*
para.307(1) *15–065*
para.308(3) *15–096*
Consumer Code (Law No.95–96) (France)
art.L.132–1 .... *16–055*, *15–065*, *15–118*
Sherman Act (US) *16–033*
Uniform Commercial Code (US)
s.1–203 .... *1–024*
s.2–202 .... *12–104*
s.2–302 7–136
s.2–328(3) *2–012*
s.2–613 .... *5–048*
s.2–615(b) *14–151*
(c) *14–151*
1908 Limitation Act (India)
s.19 .... *28–101*
1937 Gold Clauses Act (Canada) *21–069*
1956 Frustrated Contracts Act (Newfoundland) *23–086*
1958 Judicature Amendment Act (New Zealand)
s.94A *29–045*
s.94B *29–179*
1959 Frustrated Contracts Act (Victoria) 23–082
1962 Property, Perpetuities and Succession Act (Western Australia)
s.23 .... *29–045*
s.24 .... *29–045*
1974 Frustrated Contracts Act (British Columbia)
s.5(3) *23–081*
1976 Standard Contracts Act (Germany) ... *15–036*, *15–065*
paras 9–11 .... *15–065*
para.10.3 .... *15–096*
1978 Law No.78–23
arts 35–38 .... *15–068*
1984 Insurance Contracts Act (Australia)
s.8 .... *30–008*
1987 Private International Law Act (Switzerland)
art.117(3)(d) *30–077*

International Conventions

1924 International Convention on Bills of Lading (Hague Rules) 14–117, *18–034*, *28–123*, *28–126*
art.III r.6 28–115
r.8 .... *18–110*
1929 Warsaw Convention on International Carriage by Air ... *14–095*, 14–118, 15–042
1950 European Convention on Human Rights 1–013, 1–035, 12–049, 30–070
art.6 .... *1–040*, 1–044, 1–049, 1–051, 11–003, *11–018*, *25–013*
(1) 1–037, 1–044, 1–061
art.8 .... 1–049, 1–055, 1–065
art.10 1–065
art.14 1–049

Protocol 1 art.1 ...... 1–037, 1–038, *1–040*, 1–044, **1–045**, 1–046, 1–047, 1–048, 1–051, 1–191, 10–033
1955 Convention on the Law applicable to International Sales of Goods (Hague III) *30–027*
1956 Convention on the Contract for the International Carriage of Goods by Road (CMR) *14–095*, 28–026, 28–068
art.32(2) *28–068*
(4) *28–123*
1958 Convention on the Recognition and Enforcement of Foreign Arbitral Awards (United Nations) *30–040*
1961 Vienna Convention on Diplomatic Relations 11–008, 11–009
art.22 .... *11–012*
art.30 .... *11–012*
art.31 .... *11–011*
art.37 .... *11–016*
(1) *11–011*
(2) *11–013*
(3) *11–013*
art.38(1) *11–016*
(2) *11–016*
art.39(1) *11–014*
(2) *11–014*
(3) *11–014*
1963 Vienna Convention on Consular Relations 11–017
art.43 .... *11–017*
art.57 .... *11–017*
1964 Convention relating to a Uniform Law on the International Sale of Goods 28–027, *30–027*
art.39 28–027
(1) *28–027*
art.49(1) *28–027*
(2) *28–027*
1968 Protocol to the Hague Rules (Hague-Visby Rules) *14–008*, *14–016*, *14–032*, *14–095*, 14–117, 28–022, *30–026*
art.III r.6 .... *28–022*, 28–115
r.6*bis* *28–022*
r.8 .... *14–117*
art.IV*bis*(2) *14–042*
1974 Athens Convention relating to the Carriage of Passengers and their Luggage by their Sea *13–034*, 14–111, 14–117, 28–023
art.16 .... *28–023*
art.18 .... *14–117*
1976 Protocol to the Athens Convention relating to the Carriage of Passengers and their Luggage by Sea 14–117
1980 Convention on the Civil Aspects of International Child Abduction (Hague XXVIII) *30–079*
Convention on Contracts for the International Sale of Goods (United Nations) 2–063, 3–173, *30–027*, *30–028*
art.10(a) *30–079*
art.15(1) *2–063*
art.16(1) *2–063*, *2–089*
(2) *2–088*, *3–173*
art.18(2) *2–063*, *2–089*
art.19(2) *2–032*, *2–092*
art.21(1) *2–096*
(2) *2–032*
art.22 .... *2–032*
art.24 .... *2–032*, *2–089*
Convention concerning International Carriage by Rail (COTIF) 14–116, 28–025, 28–068
Appendix A (CIV) *14–116*
art.47 .... *28–025*
art.58 .... *28–025*
art.60(1) *28–025*
(2) *28–025*
(3) *28–025*
(4) *28–068*
Appendix B (CIM)
art.48(2) *28–025*
(3) *28–068*
art.59 .... *28–025*
1989 International Convention on Salvage *7–047*
art.7 .... *7–047*
art.13 .... *7–047*
art.23 28–021
2001 UNCITRAL Convention on the Assignment of Receivables in International Trade
art.2 .... *30–289*
2004 Convention on Jurisdictional Immunities of States and their Property (United Nations) *11–003*

TABLE OF CASES

Where a reference indicates significant discussion of the case in the text, it is in **bold**. Where a reference is to a footnote, it is *italic*.

1 Pump Court Chambers v Horton; sub nom. Higham v Horton; Horton v 1 Pump Court Chambers; Horton v Higham [2004] EWCA Civ 941; [2004] 3 All E.R. 852; [2005] I.C.R. 292; (2004) 101(33) L.S.G. 34; (2004) 148 S.J.L.B. 911, CA (Civ Div) *3–038*

21st Century Logistic Solutions Ltd (In Liquidation) v Madysen Ltd [2004] EWHC 231 (QB); [2004] 2 Lloyd's Rep. 92; [2004] S.T.C. 1535; [2004] B.T.C. 5720; [2004] B.V.C. 779; [2004] S.T.I. 497; (2004) 101(12) L.S.G. 35, QBD *16–017*

24 Seven Utility Services Ltd v Rosekey Ltd (t/a Atwasl Builders) [2003] EWHC 3415; [2004] All E.R. (D) 288 (Feb), QBD *16–057*, *19–050*

56 Denton Road, Twickenham, Re; sub nom. War Damage Act 1943, Re [1953] Ch. 51; [1952] 2 All E.R. 799; [1952] 2 T.L.R. 676; [1952] W.N. 472, Ch D *10–041*

A v A (Child Abduction) (Habitual Residence) [1993] 2 F.L.R. 225; [1993] 1 F.C.R. 829 .... *30–079*

A v B Plc; sub nom. B and C v A; A v B (A Firm) [2002] EWCA Civ 337; [2003] Q.B. 195; [2002] 3 W.L.R. 542; [2002] 2 All E.R. 545; [2002] E.M.L.R. 21; [2002] 1 F.L.R. 1021; [2002] 2 F.C.R. 158; [2002] H.R.L.R. 25; [2002] U.K.H.R.R. 457; 12 B.H.R.C. 466; [2002] Fam. Law 415; (2002) 99(17) L.S.G. 36; (2002) 152 N.L.J. 434; (2002) 146 S.J.L.B. 77, CA (Civ Div) *1–060*, *1–066*

A v C. [1985] F.L.R. 4451 .... *16–074*

A v Hayden (No.2) (1985) 59 A.L.J.R. 6 .... *10–008*, *16–035*

A v Lord Grey's School. *See* Ali v Lord Grey School Governors

A&J Fabrications (Batley) Ltd v Grant Thornton (A Firm) (No.1) [1999] B.C.C. 807; [1998] 2 B.C.L.C. 227; [2000] Lloyd's Rep. P.N. 565, Ch D *1–184*

A&J Inglis v John Buttery & Co (1877–78) L.R. 3 App. Cas. 552; (1878) 5 R. (H.L.) 87, HL *12–069*, *12–096*, *12–118*, *12–119*

A&TG Ridgway, Re (1891) 8 Morr. 289 .... *20–032*

A Company Ltd v Republic of X [1990] 2 Lloyd's Rep. 520, QBD (Comm) *11–004*, *11–005*, *11–021*, *11–022*

A Davies & Co (Shopfitters) v Old (William), 67 L.G.R. 395; (1969) 113 S.J. 262 .... *2–036*

A Debtor, Re [1908] 1 K.B. 344 .... *21–074*

A Debtor, Re [1937] Ch. 156 .... *29–113*

A Hamson & Son (London) Ltd v S Martin Johnson & Co Ltd [1953] 1 Lloyd's Rep. 553, QBD *13–012*

A Roberts & Co v Leicestershire CC [1961] Ch. 555; [1961] 2 W.L.R. 1000; [1961] 2 All E.R. 545; 59 L.G.R. 349; (1961) 105 S.J. 425, Ch D *5–076*, 5–115

A Schroeder Music Publishing Co Ltd v Macaulay (formerly Instone); sub nom. Macaulay (formerly Instone) v A Schroeder Music Publishing Co Ltd [1974] 1 W.L.R. 1308; [1974] 3 All E.R. 616; (1974) 118 S.J. 734, HL; affirming [1974] 1 All E.R. 171, CA (Civ Div) *7–126*, *7–139*, *16–006*, 16–084, *16–086*, *16–088*, *16–090*, *16–094*, *16–096*, *16–115*, *16–121*, *27–068*

A Smith & Son (Bognor Regis) v Walker [1952] 2 Q.B. 319; [1952] 1 All E.R. 1008; [1952] 1 T.L.R. 1089; (1952) 96 S.J. 260, CA *12–081*, *16–154*, *21–062*

A Solicitor, Re (1913) 29 T.L.R. 354 .... *16–055*

A to Z Bazaars (Pty) v Minister of Agriculture (1974) (4) S.A. 392 (c) *2–060*
AB v South West Water Services Ltd; Gibbons v South West Water Services Ltd [1993] Q.B. 507; [1993] 2 W.L.R. 507; [1993] 1 All E.R. 609; [1993] Env. L.R. 266; [1993] P.I.Q.R. P167; (1993) 143 N.L.J. 235; [1992] N.P.C. 146, CA (Civ Div) 6–063
AB Bofors-UVA CAV Ltd v AB Skandia Transport; sub nom. AB Bofors-Ura v Skandia AB Transport [1982] 1 Lloyd's Rep. 410; [1982] Com. L.R. 63, QBD (Comm) *30–331*
AB Corp v CD Co; The Sine Nomine [2002] 1 Lloyd's Rep. 805, Arbitration *26–025*, *29–154*
AB Kemp Ltd v Tolland (t/a James Tolland & Co) [1956] 2 Lloyd's Rep. 681, QBD *26–175*
AB Marintrans v Comet Shipping Co Ltd; The Shinjitsu Maru No.5 [1985] 1 W.L.R. 1270; [1985] 3 All E.R. 442; [1985] 1 Lloyd's Rep. 568; (1986) 83 L.S.G. 43, QBD (Comm) *26–049*
ABC Coupler and Engineering Co (No.3), Re [1970] 1 W.L.R. 702; [1970] 1 All E.R. 650; (1970) 114 S.J. 242, Ch D *9–048*
ABCI (formerly Arab Business Consortium International Finance & Investment Co) v Banque Franco-Tunisienne (Costs); sub nom. ABCI v BFT (Costs) [2003] EWCA Civ 205; [2003] 2 Lloyd's Rep. 146, CA (Civ Div) *11–006*
ABD (Metals and Waste) Ltd v Anglo Chemical & Ore Co Ltd [1955] 2 Lloyd's Rep. 456, QBD *26–113*
AC Yule & Son Ltd v Speedwell Roofing & Cladding Ltd [2007] EWHC 1360 (TCC); [2007] B.L.R. 499; [2007] C.I.L.L. 2489, QBD (TCC) *2–073*, *2–077*
ACE Insurance SA-NV (formerly Cigna Insurance Co of Europe SA NV) v Zurich Insurance Co [2001] EWCA Civ 173; [2001] 1 All E.R. (Comm) 802; [2001] 1 Lloyd's Rep. 618; [2001] C.L.C. 526; [2001] I.L.Pr. 41; [2001] Lloyd's Rep. I.R. 504; (2001) 98(8) L.S.G. 46, CA (Civ Div) *30–011*, *30–051*
AE Realisations (1985) Ltd, Re [1988] 1 W.L.R. 200; [1987] 3 All E.R. 83; (1987) 3 B.C.C. 136; [1987] B.C.L.C. 486; [1988] P.C.C. 48; (1988) 85(2) L.S.G. 35; (1988) 132 S.J. 51, Ch D (Companies Ct) *9–048*, *20–035*
AEG (UK) Ltd v Logic Resource Ltd [1996] C.L.C. 265, CA (Civ Div) ..*12–015*, *14–085*, *14–088*, 14–093
AEM (Avon) Ltd v Bristol City Council [1999] B.L.G.R. 93; [1998] R.A. 89; [1998] E.G. 31 (C.S.), QBD *29–084*
AF Colverd & Co Ltd v Anglo Overseas Transport Co Ltd [1961] 2 Lloyd's Rep. 352; (1961) 105 S.J. 1010, QBD *14–016*, *14–030*
AG Securities v Vaughan; Antoniades v Villiers [1990] 1 A.C. 417; [1988] 3 W.L.R. 1205; [1988] 3 All E.R. 1058; (1989) 21 H.L.R. 79; (1989) 57 P. & C.R. 17; [1988] 47 E.G. 193; [1988] E.G. 153 (C.S.); (1989) 86(1) L.S.G. 39; (1988) 138 N.L.J. Rep. 325; (1988) 132 S.J. 1638, HL; reversing [1988] 2 W.L.R. 689; [1988] 2 All E.R. 173; (1988) 20 H.L.R. 212; (1988) 56 P. & C.R. 168; [1988] 06 E.G. 112; (1988) 85(7) L.S.G. 38; (1988) 138 N.L.J. Rep. 23; (1988) 132 S.J. 301, CA (Civ Div) *1–069*, *2–161*, *12–126*
AIB Finance Ltd v Alsop; sub nom. AIB Finance Ltd v Debtors [1998] 2 All E.R. 929; [1998] Lloyd's Rep. Bank. 102; [1998] B.C.C. 780; [1998] 1 B.C.L.C. 665; [1998] B.P.I.R. 533; (1998) 95(14) L.S.G. 22; (1998) 142 S.J.L.B. 108, CA (Civ Div) *1–148*
AIB Group (UK) Plc (formerly Allied Irish Banks Plc and AIB Finance Ltd) v Martin; sub nom. AIB Group (UK) Ltd v Martin; AIB Group (UK) Plc (formerly Allied Irish Bank Plc and AIB Finance Ltd) v Martin; AIB Group (UK) Plc (formerly Allied Irish Bank Plc and AIB Finance Ltd) v Gold [2001] UKHL 63; [2002] 1 W.L.R. 94; [2002] 1 All E.R. 353; [2002] 1 All E.R. (Comm) 209; [2002] 1 E.G. 75 (C.S.); (2002) 99(7) L.S.G. 34; (2002) 146 S.J.L.B. 13; [2001] N.P.C. 183, HL *12–100*, *17–005*
AIC Ltd v ITS Testing Services (UK) Ltd; The Kriti Palm [2006] EWCA Civ 1601; [2007] 1 All E.R. (Comm) 667; [2007] 1 Lloyd's Rep. 555; [2007] 2 C.L.C. 223, CA (Civ Div) *28–086*
AIC Ltd v Nigeria [2003] EWHC 1357, QBD *11–004*, *11–005*

AIG Capital Partners Inc v Kazakhstan [2005] EWHC 2239 (Comm); [2006] 1 W.L.R. 1420; [2006] 1 All E.R. 284; [2006] 1 All E.R. (Comm) 1; [2006] 1 Lloyd's Rep. 45, QBD (Comm) *11–003*, *11–004*
AKAS Jamal v Moolla Dawood Sons & Co [1916] 1 A.C. 175, PC (Burma) *26–100*, *26–117*
AL Barnes Ltd v Time Talk (UK) Ltd [2003] EWCA Civ 402; [2003] B.L.R. 331; (2003) 147 S.J.L.B. 385, CA (Civ Div) *16–176*
AL Gullison & Sons v Corey (1980) 29 N.B.R. (2d.) 86 .... *6–085*
AL Underwood Ltd v Bank of Liverpool and Martins; AL Underwood Ltd v Barclays Bank [1924] 1 K.B. 775, CA *9–041*
AMEC Properties v Planning Research & Systems [1992] B.C.L.C. 1149; [1992] 1 E.G.L.R. 70; [1992] 13 E.G. 109, CA (Civ Div) *27–007*, *27–015*
AMEV-UDC Finance v Austin (1987) 68 A.L.R. 185, HC (Aus) *26–126*, *26–140*
AMF International v Magnet Bowling [1968] 1 W.L.R. 1028; [1968] 2 All E.R. 789; 66 L.G.R. 706; (1968) 112 S.J. 522, QBD *14–013*, *14–015*
AMP (UK) Plc v Barker [2001] O.P.L.R. 197; [2001] Pens. L.R. 77; [2001] W.T.L.R. 1237; (2000–01) 3 I.T.E.L.R. 414, Ch D *5–114*
AR Dennis & Co Ltd v Campbell [1978] Q.B. 365; [1978] 2 W.L.R. 429; [1978] 1 All E.R. 1215; [1978] I.C.R. 862; (1977) 121 S.J. 790, CA (Civ Div) [1977] Q.B. 158; [1976] 3 W.L.R. 501; [1977] 1 All E.R. 138; [1976] I.C.R. 465; (1976) 120 S.J. 690, QBD *16–013*
AR Wright & Son v Romford BC [1957] 1 Q.B. 431; [1956] 3 W.L.R. 896; [1956] 3 All E.R. 785; (1957) 121 J.P. 44; 54 L.G.R. 647; (1956) 100 S.J. 859, QBD *9–009*
A/S Awilco of Oslo v Fulvia SpA di Navigazione of Cagliari; The Chikuma. *See* Awilco of Oslo A/S v Fulvia SpA di Navigazione of Cagliari
AS James Pty v SB Duncan [1970] V.R. 705 .... *26–049*
A/S Tankexpress v Compagnie Financiere Belge des Petroles SA [1949] A.C. 76; [1948] 2 All E.R. 939; (1948–49) 82 Ll. L. Rep. 43; [1949] L.J.R. 170; (1949) 93 S.J. 26, HL *3–091*, *12–118*, *21–056*, *22–042*
AT Poeton (Gloucester Plating) Ltd v Horton; sub nom. Poeton Industries Ltd v Horton [2000] I.C.R. 1208; [2001] F.S.R. 14; (2000) 23(8) I.P.D. 23060, CA (Civ Div) *16–108*
AV Pound & Co v MW Hardy & Co Inc [1956] A.C. 588; [1956] 2 W.L.R. 683; [1956] 1 All E.R. 639; [1956] 1 Lloyd's Rep. 255; (1956) 100 S.J. 208, HL; affirming [1955] 1 Q.B. 499; [1955] 2 W.L.R. 589; [1955] 1 All E.R. 666; [1955] 1 Lloyd's Rep. 155; (1955) 99 S.J. 204, CA; reversing [1954] 2 Lloyd's Rep. 428, QBD *2–155*, *13–011*, *13–013*, *23–027*, *23–047*, *30–334*
AW Gamage Ltd v Charlesworth; sub nom. AW Gamage Ltd v Charlesworth's Trustee, 1910 S.C. 257; 1910 1 S.L.T. 11, IH (1 Div) *20–039*
AXA Reinsurance (UK) Ltd v Field [1996] 1 W.L.R. 1026; [1996] 3 All E.R. 517; [1996] 2 Lloyd's Rep. 233; [1996] C.L.C. 1169; [1996] 5 Re. L.R. 184; (1996) 93(33) L.S.G. 24; (1996) 146 N.L.J. 1093; (1996) 140 S.J.L.B. 155, HL; reversing [1996] 1 Lloyd's Rep. 26; [1995] C.L.C. 1504; [1995] 4 Re. L.R. 384, CA (Civ Div) *12–057*
AY Bank Ltd (In Liquidation), Re; sub nom. AY Bank Ltd (In Liquidation) v Bosnia and Herzegovina [2006] EWHC 830; [2006] 2 All E.R. (Comm) 463, Ch D (Companies Ct) *11–007*
Aaron's Reefs v Twiss [1896] A.C. 273; 65 L.J.P.C. 54; 74 L.T. 794, HL (UK-Irl) *6–127*, *9–060*, *28–144*
Admiralty Commissioners v Owners of the SS Amerika [1917] A.C. 38; 86 L.J.P. 58; 116 L.T. 34, HL *18–047*
Abbey National Bank Plc v Matthews & Son; sub nom. Abbey National Bank Plc v David Gouldman & Co [2003] EWHC 925 (Ch); [2003] 1 W.L.R. 2042; [2003] P.N.L.R. 21; (2003) 100(14) L.S.G. 28, Ch D *17–034*
Abbey National Business Equipment Leasing Ltd v Dora Ife (t/a Hair Expressions) [2003] C.L.Y. 723, CC (Shoreditch) *14–095*
Abbott v Hendrix (1840) 1 M. & G. 791; Drinkwater 31; 2 Scott N.R. 183; 133 E.R. 551 .... *12–108*
Abbott v Middleton (1858) 7 H.L.C. 68; 28 L.J.Ch. 110; 115 R.R. 38 .... *12–055*

Abbott v Parfitt (1871) L.R. 6 Q.B. 346; 40 L.J.Q.B. 115; 24 L.T. 469 .... *20–002*
Abbott v Sullivan; Abbott v Isett Cornporters Committee Members [1952] 1 K.B. 189; [1952] 1 All E.R. 226; [1951] 2 Lloyd's Rep. 573; [1952] 1 T.L.R. 133; (1952) 96 S.J. 119, CA *9–071*, 9–074
Abbotts v Barry (1820) 2 Brod. B. 369 .... *29–148*
Aberdeen Varieties Ltd v James F Donald (Aberdeen Cinemas) Ltd, 1940 S.C. (H.L.) 52; 1940 S.L.T. 374, HL; reversing, 1939 S.C. 788; 1940 S.L.T. 58, IH (2 Div) *16–085*
Aberfoyle Plantations Ltd v Cheng [1960] A.C. 115; [1959] 3 W.L.R. 1011; [1959] 3 All E.R. 910; (1959) 103 S.J. 1045, PC (FMS) *12–027*, *12–028*
Abnett v British Airways Plc; Sidhu v British Airways Plc [1997] A.C. 430; [1997] 2 W.L.R. 26; [1997] 1 All E.R. 193; [1997] 2 Lloyd's Rep. 76; 1997 S.C. (H.L.) 26; 1997 S.L.T. 492; 1997 S.C.L.R. 114; (1997) 94(2) L.S.G. 26; (1996) 146 N.L.J. 1851; (1997) 141 S.J.L.B. 26, HL; affirming [1995] P.I.Q.R. P427, CA (Civ Div) *18–034*
Abouloff v Oppenheimer & Co (1882–83) L.R. 10 Q.B.D. 295, CA *25–015*
Abou-Rahmah v Abacha [2006] EWCA Civ 1492; [2007] Bus. L.R. 220; [2007] 1 All E.R. (Comm) 827; [2007] 1 Lloyd's Rep. 115; [2007] W.T.L.R. 1; (2006–07) 9 I.T.E.L.R. 401, CA (Civ Div); affirming [2005] EWHC 2662 (QB); [2006] 1 All E.R. (Comm) 247; [2006] 1 Lloyd's Rep. 484; [2006] W.T.L.R. 377, QBD *18–031*, *29–174*, *29–183*
Abraham v Thompson [1997] 4 All E.R. 362; [1997] C.L.C. 1,377; (1997) 94(37) L.S.G. 41; (1997) 141 S.J.L.B. 217, CA; reversing [1997] C.L.C. 1,370; (1997) 141 S.J.L.B. 114; (1997) 94(23) L.S.G. 27, Ch D *16–053*, 16–054
Abrahams v Herbert Reiach Ltd [1922] 1 K.B. 477, CA *26–048*
Abram SS Co v Westville Shipping Co [1923] A.C. 773; 93 L.J.P.C. 39 .... *6–111*, *6–132*
Abrey v Crux (1869) L.R. 6 C.P. 37; 39 L.J.P.C. 9; 18 W.R. 63 .... *12–101*, *12–108*
Absalom v TCRU Ltd (formerly Monument Insurance Brokers Ltd) [2005] EWCA Civ 1586; [2006] 1 All E.R. (Comm) 375; [2006] 2 Lloyd's Rep. 129; [2006] 1 C.L.C. 648, CA (Civ Div); affirming [2005] EWHC 1090; [2005] 2 Lloyd's Rep. 735, QBD (Comm) *12–050*, *12–057*, *12–119*
Abu Dhabi National Tanker Co v Product Star Shipping; The Product Star (No.2) [1993] 1 Lloyd's Rep. 397, CA (Civ Div); reversing [1991] 2 Lloyd's Rep. 468, QBD (Comm) *2–154*, *12–063*, *13–026*
Academy of Health and Fitness Pty v Power [1973] V.R. 254 .... *6–104*, *6–109*
Ace London Services Ltd v Charman, unreported, October 1, 2001, QBD *16–102*
Achille Lauro Fu Gioacchino & C v Total Societa Italiana Per Azioni [1969] 2 Lloyd's Rep. 65, CA (Civ Div) *23–044*
Ackbar v CF Green & Co Ltd [1975] Q.B. 582; [1975] 2 W.L.R. 773; [1975] 2 All E.R. 65; [1975] 1 Lloyd's Rep. 673; (1975) 119 S.J. 219, QBD *12–082*, *28–006*
Ackland v Lutley, 112 E.R. 1446; (1839) 9 Ad. & El. 879; (1839) 8 L.J. Q.B. 164, QB *12–093*
A'Court v Cross (1825) 3 Bing. 329 .... *28–001*
Acrow (Automation) Ltd v Rex Chainbelt Inc [1971] 1 W.L.R. 1676; [1971] 3 All E.R. 1175; (1971) 115 S.J. 642, CA (Civ Div) *27–076*
Actionstrength Ltd (t/a Vital Resources) v International Glass Engineering IN.GL.EN SpA [2003] UKHL 17; [2003] 2 A.C. 541; [2003] 2 W.L.R. 1060; [2003] 2 All E.R. 615; [2003] 2 All E.R. (Comm) 331; [2005] 1 B.C.L.C. 606; [2003] 1 C.L.C. 1003; [2003] B.L.R. 207; 88 Con. L.R. 208; (2003) 153 N.L.J. 563; (2003) 147 S.J.L.B. 418, HL *1–023*, 1–104, 4–004, 4–075, *4–078*, 4–081
Actis Co v Sanko Steamship Co; The Aquacharm [1982] 1 W.L.R. 119; [1982] 1 All E.R. 390; [1982] 1 Lloyd's Rep. 7; [1981] Com. L.R. 274; (1981) 125 S.J. 790, CA (Civ Div); affirming [1980] 2 Lloyd's Rep. 237, QBD (Comm) *14–015*
Active Estates Ltd v Parness [2002] EWHC 893 (Ch); [2002] B.P.I.R. 865; [2003] L. & T.R. 21; [2002] 3 E.G.L.R. 13; [2002] 36 E.G. 147; [2002] N.P.C. 122, Ch D *4–058*
Acton v Symon (1635) Cro. Car. 414 .... *25–001*

Adam v Newbigging; sub nom. Newbigging v Adam (1888) L.R. 13 App. Cas. 308, HL; affirming (1887) L.R. 34 Ch. D. 582, CA *6–097*, *6–103*, 6–115, 6–117, *6–121*
Adam Opel GmbH v Mitras Automotive (UK) Ltd [2007] EWHC 3252 (QB), [2007] All ER (D) 272 .... *7–031*, *7–041*
Adamastos Shipping Co Ltd v Anglo Saxon Petroleum Co Ltd; sub nom. Anglo Saxon Petroleum Co Ltd v Adamastos Shipping Co Ltd [1959] A.C. 133; [1958] 2 W.L.R. 688; [1958] 1 All E.R. 725; [1958] 1 Lloyd's Rep. 73; (1958) 102 S.J. 290, HL *12–075*, *12–078*, *12–079*
Adami v Lincoln Grange Management Ltd (1998) 30 H.L.R. 982; [1998] 1 E.G.L.R. 58; [1998] 17 E.G. 148; [1997] E.G. 182 (C.S.); (1998) 95(3) L.S.G. 25; (1998) 142 S.J.L.B. 37; [1997] N.P.C. 180 , CA (Civ Div) *13–016*
Adams v Adams (Separation Agreement) [1941] 1 K.B. 536, CA *23–040*
Adams v British Airways Plc [1996] I.R.L.R. 574, CA (Civ Div); reversing [1995] I.R.L.R. 577, QBD *12–118*
Adams v Cape Industries Plc [1990] Ch. 433; [1990] 2 W.L.R. 657; [1991] 1 All E.R. 929; [1990] B.C.C. 786; [1990] B.C.L.C. 479, CA (Civ Div) .. *9–002*, *30–081*
Adams v Hall (1877) 37 L.T. 70 .... *12–115*
Adams v Lindsell (1818) 1 B. & Ald. 681; 19 R.R. 515; 106 E.R. 250, KB 2–026, *2–048*, *2–089*
Adams v National Bank of Greece and Athens SA; Darling v National Bank of Greece SA; sub nom. Prudential Assurance Co Ltd v National Bank of Greece and Athens SA [1961] A.C. 255; [1960] 3 W.L.R. 8; [1960] 2 All E.R. 421; (1960) 104 S.J. 489, HL *30–345*
Adams v Richardson & Starling [1969] 1 W.L.R. 1645; [1969] 2 All E.R. 1221; (1969) 113 S.J. 832, CA (Civ Div) *12–085*, *14–009*
Adams v Wordley (1836) 1 M. & W. 374; 2 Gaale 29; 150 E.R. 479 .... *12–101*
Adams (Durham) v Trust Houses [1960] 1 Lloyd's Rep. 380 .... *12–017*
Adamson v Jarvis (1827) 4 Bing. 66; 12 Moore C.P. 241 .... *16–175*
Adderley v Dixon (1824) 1 S. & S. 607 .... *27–005*, *27–007*, *27–008*, *27–017*
Addey and Stanhope School Governing Body v Vakante [2003] I.C.R. 290, EAT *16–166*
Addis v Burrows [1948] 1 K.B. 444; [1948] 1 All E.R. 177; 64 T.L.R. 169; [1948] L.J.R. 1033; (1948) 92 S.J. 124, CA *22–051*
Addis v Gramophone Co [1909] A.C. 488; 78 L.J.K.B. 1122; 101 L.T. 466, HL *1–123*, 26–019, *26–032*, *26–083*
Addison v Brown [1954] 1 W.L.R. 779; [1954] 2 All E.R. 213; (1954) 98 S.J. 338, QBD *13–006*, *13–026*, *16–029*, *16–044*, *21–068*, *30–367*, *30–368*
Addlestone Linoleum Co, Re (1888) L.R. 37 Ch. D. 191; 57 L.J.Ch. 249; 36 W.R. 227, CA *9–060*
Adelaide Electric Supply Co Ltd v Prudential Assurance Co Ltd [1934] A.C. 122, HL *30–012*, *30–372*, *30–374*
Adelfamar SA v Silos e Mangimi Martini SpA; The Adelfa [1988] 2 Lloyd's Rep. 466, QBD (Comm) *23–035*, *23–040*, *23–059*
Adelson v Associated Newspapers Ltd [2007] EWCA Civ 701; [2008] 1 W.L.R. 585; [2007] 4 All E.R. 330; [2007] C.P. Rep. 40; [2008] E.M.L.R. 9, CA (Civ Div) *28–119*
Adlard v Booth (1835) 7 C.P. 108 .... *21–030*
Adler v Dickson (No.1) [1955] 1 Q.B. 158; [1954] 3 W.L.R. 696; [1954] 3 All E.R. 397; [1954] 2 Lloyd's Rep. 267; (1954) 98 S.J. 787, CA *14–042*, *14–047*, *18–094*
Admiralty Commissioners v Owners of the SS Susquehanna [1926] A.C. 655; (1926) 25 Ll. L. Rep. 205; 42 T.L.R. 639; [1926] W.N. 200; 95 L.J. P. 128; 135 L.T. 456, HL *26–006*
Adriatic, The [1931] P. 241, PDAD *30–011*
Adsett v Hives (1863) 33 Beav. 52; 9 Jur. 1065; 140 R.R. 14 .... *4–034*
Advanced Technology Structures Ltd v Cray Valley Products Ltd [1993] B.C.L.C. 723, CA (Civ Div) *16–059*
Advantage Business Systems Ltd v Hopley [2007] EWHC (QB) 1783, [2007] All E.R. (D) 339(Jul), QBD *16–097*

Aectra Refining & Marketing Inc v Exmar NV; The New Vanguard and The Pacifica [1994] 1 W.L.R. 1634; [1995] 1 All E.R. 641; [1995] 1 Lloyd's Rep. 191, CA (Civ Div) *3–119*
Aegnoussiotis Shipping Corp of Monrovia v Kristian Jebsens Rederi of Bergen AS; The Aegnoussiotis [1977] 1 Lloyd's Rep. 268, QBD (Comm) *22–051*, *24–013*
Aeolian Shipping SA v ISS Machinery Services Ltd; The Aeolian; sub nom. ISS Machinery Services Ltd v Aeolian Shipping SA; The Aeolian [2001] EWCA Civ 1162; [2001] 2 Lloyd's Rep. 641; [2001] C.L.C. 1708, CA (Civ Div) *30–020*, *30–023*, *30–051*, *30–058*, *30–077*, *30–090*
Aer Lingus Plc v Gildacroft Ltd [2006] EWCA Civ 4; [2006] 1 W.L.R. 1173; [2006] 2 All E.R. 290; [2006] C.P. Rep. 21; [2006] P.I.Q.R. P16; (2006) 103(6) L.S.G. 32; (2006) 156 N.L.J. 147; (2006) 150 S.J.L.B. 129; [2006] N.P.C. 4, CA (Civ Div) *28–051*
Aerial Advertising v Batchelors Peas Ltd (Manchester) [1938] 2 All E.R. 788; 82 S.J. 567, KBD *1–123*, *26–006*
Affleck v Hammond [1912] 3 K.B. 162; 81 L.J.K.B. 565; 106 L.T. 8, CA *20–055*
Afovos Shipping Co SA v R Pagnan & Fratelli; The Afovos [1983] 1 W.L.R. 195; [1983] 1 All E.R. 449; [1983] 1 Lloyd's Rep. 335; [1983] Com. L.R. 83; (1983) 127 S.J. 98, HL; affirming [1982] 1 W.L.R. 848; [1982] 3 All E.R. 18; [1982] 1 Lloyd's Rep. 562; [1982] Com. L.R. 128; (1982) 126 S.J. 242, CA (Civ Div); reversing [1980] 2 Lloyd's Rep. 469, QBD (Comm) *21–013*, *21–022*, *21–046*, *22–048*, *22–049*, *22–051*, *24–018*, *24–028*, *24–031*, *28–062*
Agbeyegbe v Ikomi [1953] 1 W.L.R. 263; (1953) 97 S.J. 78, PC (West Africa) *28–138*
Agbor v Commissioner of Police of the Metropolis [1969] 1 W.L.R. 703; [1969] 2 All E.R. 707; (1969) 113 S.J. 227, CA (Civ Div) *11–012*
Agip (Africa) Ltd v Jackson [1991] Ch. 547; [1991] 3 W.L.R. 116; [1992] 4 All E.R. 451; (1991) 135 S.J. 117, CA (Civ Div); affirming [1990] Ch. 265; [1989] 3 W.L.R. 1367; [1992] 4 All E.R. 385; (1989) 86(3) L.S.G. 34; (1990) 134 S.J. 198, Ch D 5–116, *29–049*, *29–163*, *29–165*, *29–166*, *29–172*, *29–182*
Agip SpA v Navigazione Alta Italia SpA; The Nai Genova and The Nai Superba [1984] 1 Lloyd's Rep. 353, CA (Civ Div); affirming [1983] 2 Lloyd's Rep. 333; [1983] Com. L.R. 170; (1983) 133 N.L.J. 621, QBD (Comm) *3–092*, *5–107*, *5–116*, *5–118*
Agnew v Lansforsakringsbolagens AB [2001] 1 A.C. 223; [2000] 2 W.L.R. 497; [2000] 1 All E.R. 737; [2000] 1 All E.R. (Comm) 321; [2000] C.L.C. 848; [2001] I.L.Pr. 25; [2000] Lloyd's Rep. I.R. 317; (2000) 97(9) L.S.G. 39; (2000) 144 S.J.L.B. 109, HL *30–031*
Agra & Masterman's Bank Ex p. Asiatic Banking Corp, Re (1866–67) L.R. 2 Ch. App. 391, CA in Chancery *19–072*
Agra Bank Ex p. Tondeur, Re (1867–68) L.R. 5 Eq. 160, Ct of Chancery *24–028*
Agricultural Mortgage Corp Plc v Woodward [1994] B.C.C. 688; [1995] 1 B.C.L.C. 1; [1996] 1 F.L.R. 226; [1996] 2 F.C.R. 796; (1995) 70 P. & C.R. 53; [1995] 1 E.G.L.R. 1; [1995] 04 E.G. 143; [1996] Fam. Law 149; [1994] E.G. 98 (C.S.), CA (Civ Div) *3–019*, *20–031*
Agriculturists Cattle Insurance Co, Re; sub nom. Smallcombe's Case; Evans v Smallcombe (1868) L.R. 3 H.L. 249, HL; affirming (1866–67) L.R. 3 Eq. 769, Ct of Chancery *9–039*
Agroexport State Enterprise for Foreign Trade v Compagnie Europeene de Cereales [1974] 1 Lloyd's Rep. 499, QBD (Comm) *2–155*
Agrokor AG v Tradigrain SA [2000] 1 Lloyd's Rep. 497, QBD (Comm) *14–140*
Agromet Motoimport Ltd v Maulden Engineering Co (Beds) Ltd [1985] 1 W.L.R. 762; [1985] 2 All E.R. 436, QBD *28–060*
Ahmed v Saudi Arabia [1996] 2 All E.R. 248; [1996] I.C.R. 25, CA (Civ Div) *11–005*, *11–014*, *11–021*
Aiken v Short, 156 E.R. 1180; (1856) 1 Hurl. & N. 210, QB 29–030, 29–032, 29–038
Aiken v Stewart Wrightson Members Agency Ltd [1996] 2 Lloyd's Rep. 577; [1997] 6 Re. L.R. 79, CA (Civ Div); affirming [1995] 1 W.L.R. 1281; [1995] 3 All E.R. 449; [1995] 2 Lloyd's Rep. 618; [1995] C.L.C. 318, QBD (Comm) *1–116*, 1–150, *18–022*, *28–003*

Ailion v Spiekermann [1976] Ch. 158; [1976] 2 W.L.R. 556; [1976] 1 All E.R. 497; (1976) 31 P. & C.R. 369; (1975) 238 E.G. 48; (1975) 120 S.J. 9, Ch D *16–146, 16–158*, *16–185*, *16–201*
Ailsa Craig Fishing Co Ltd v Malvern Fishing Co Ltd; The Strathallan; Malvern Fishing Co Ltd v Ailsa Craig Fishing Co Ltd; The Strathallan [1983] 1 W.L.R. 964; [1983] 1 All E.R. 101; [1983] 1 Lloyd's Rep. 183 (Note); 1982 S.C. (H.L.) 14; 1982 S.L.T. 377; (1983) 80 L.S.G. 2516; (1983) 127 S.J. 508, HL; affirming, 1981 S.L.T. 130, IH (1 Div) *12–022*, *14–005*, *14–007*, *14–009*, *14–010*, *14–022*
Ainsworth, Re; Millington v Ainsworth [1922] 1 Ch. 22; 91 L.J.Ch. 51; 66 S.J. 107, Ch D *20–048*
Aiolos, The. *See* Central Insurance Co v Seacalf Shipping Corp.
Air Canada v British Columbia (1989) 59 D.L.R. (4th) 161; [1989] 1 S.C.R. 1161; [1989] 4 W.W.R. 97, Sup Ct (Can) *29–034*, *29–045*, *29–086*
Air Great Lakes v KS Easter (Holdings) Pty (1985) 2 N.S.W.L.R. 309 .... *12–098*
Air Jamaica Ltd v Charlton; Air Jamaica Ltd v Clarke; Air Jamaica Ltd v Goodall; Air Jamaica Ltd v Philpotts [1999] 1 W.L.R. 1399; [1999] O.P.L.R. 11; [1999] Pens. L.R. 247; (1999–2000) 2 I.T.E.L.R. 244, PC (Jam) *29–159*
Air New Zealand v Nippon Credit Bank [1997] 1 N.Z.L.R. 218 .... *12–094*
Airedale Cooperative Worsted Manufacturing Society Ltd, Re [1933] Ch. 639; 102 L.J.Ch. 229; B. & C.R. 114; 77 S.J. 267, Ch D *9–025*
Airline Engineering v Itercon Cattle Meat, unreported, January 24, 1983, CA *14–011*
Airlines Airspares v Handley Page [1970] Ch. 193; [1970] 2 W.L.R. 163; [1970] 1 All E.R. 29, Ch D *9–051*
AirNew Zealand Ltd v Nippon Credit Bank Ltd [1997] N.Z.L.R. 218 .... *12–104*
Aitken Lilburn & Co v Ernsthausen & Co [1894] 1 Q.B. 773, CA *26–090*
Ajayi (t/a Colony Carrier Co) v RT Briscoe (Nigeria) Ltd [1964] 1 W.L.R. 1326; [1964] 3 All E.R. 556; (1964) 108 S.J. 857, PC (Nig) *3–096*, *3–129*, *3–130*, *3–132*, *3–135*
Ajit (Chintaminie) v Sammy (Joseph Mootoo) [1967] 1 A.C. 255; [1966] 3 W.L.R. 983; (1966) 110 S.J. 790, PC (BG) *21–014*
Akai Pty Ltd v People's Insurance Co Ltd [1998] 1 Lloyd's Rep. 90; [1997] C.L.C. 1508; [1999] I.L.Pr. 24, QBD (Comm) *30–007*, *30–008*, *30–046*, *30–065*, *30–068*
Aker Oil & Gas Technology UK Plc v Sovereign Corporate Ltd [2002] C.L.C. 557, QBD (TCC) *3–094*
Akerblom v Price Potter Walker & Co (1880–81) L.R. 7 Q.B.D. 129; 50 L.J.Q.B. 629; 44 L.T. 837; 29 W.R. 797, CA *7–047*
Akerhielm v De Mare; sub nom. Baron Uno Carl Samuel Akerhielm v Rolf de Mare [1959] A.C. 789; [1959] 3 W.L.R. 108; [1959] 3 All E.R. 485; (1959) 103 S.J. 527, PC (EA) *6–047*
Akerib v Booth & Others Ltd [1961] 1 W.L.R. 367; [1961] 1 All E.R. 380; (1961) 105 S.J. 231, CA; reversing [1960] 1 W.L.R. 454; [1960] 1 All E.R. 481; (1960) 104 S.J. 350, Assizes (Manchester) *14–011*
Akerman, Re; sub nom. Akerman v Akerman [1891] 3 Ch. 212, Ch D *28–130*
Akiens v Salomon (1993) 65 P. & C.R. 364; [1993] 14 E.G. 97; [1992] E.G. 131 (C.S.), CA (Civ Div) *3–144*
Akt Dampskibbs Steinstad v William Pearson Co (1927) 137 L.T. 533 .... *29–188*
Akties Nord-Osterso Rederiet v EA Casper Edgar & Co Ltd (1923) 14 Ll. L. Rep. 203, HL *23–030*
Aktieselkab Helios v Ekman & Co [1897] 2 Q.B. 83; 66 L.J.Q.B. 538; 76 L.T. 537; 2 Com. Cas. 263, CA *12–058*, *12–130*
Aktieselskabet Dampskibs Steinstad v W Pearson & Co (1927) 28 Ll. L. Rep. 69, KBD *29–109*
Aktieselskabet Dampskibsselskabet Primula A/S v Horsley & Co (1923–24) 17 Ll. L. Rep. 30; (1923) 40 T.L.R. 11; 68 S.J. 253, KBD *12–059*
Aktieselskabet Dampskibsselskabet Svendborg v Mobil North Sea Ltd; sub nom. Aktielselkabet Dampskibsselskabel Svendborg v Mobil North Sea Ltd; Aktieselskabet Dampskibsselskabet Svendorg v Mobil North Sea Ltd [2001] 2 All E.R. (Comm) 553; [2001] 2 Lloyd's Rep. 127, QBD (Comm) *22–048*

Aktieselskabet Frank v Namaqua Copper Co Ltd (1920) 90 L.J.K.B. 36; 123 L.T. 523; (1920) 25 Com. Cas. 212 .... *12–087*
Aktieselskabet Olivebank v Danck Svovlsyre Fabrik. *See* Olivebank A/S v Dansk Svovlsyre Fabrik.
Aktieselskabet Reidar v Arcos Ltd; sub nom. Reidar A/S v Acros Ltd [1927] 1 K.B. 352; (1926) 25 Ll. L. Rep. 513, CA *26–011*, *26–125*
Aktion Maritime Corp of Liberia v S Kasmas & Brothers; The Aktion [1987] 1 Lloyd's Rep. 283, QBD (Comm) *12–034*, *12–036*, *19–086*, *22–031*, *24–018*
Akumah v Hackney LBC [2005] UKHL 17; [2005] 1 W.L.R. 985; [2005] 2 All E.R. 148; [2005] H.L.R. 26; [2005] B.L.G.R. 399; [2005] 10 E.G. 155 (C.S.); (2005) 102(17) L.S.G. 31; (2005) 149 S.J.L.B. 299; [2005] N.P.C. 31, HL; affirming [2002] EWCA Civ 582; [2003] H.L.R. 5, CA (Civ Div) *10–023*, *10–025*
Al Nakib Investments (Jersey) Ltd v Longcroft [1990] 1 W.L.R. 1390; [1990] 3 All E.R. 321; [1990] B.C.C. 517; [1991] B.C.L.C. 7; (1990) 87(42) L.S.G. 37; (1990) 140 N.L.J. 741, Ch D *6–028*
Al-Adsani v Kuwait (1996) 107 I.L.R. 536, CA (Civ Div) *11–003*
Alan Estates Ltd v WG Stores Ltd [1982] Ch. 511; [1981] 3 W.L.R. 892; [1981] 3 All E.R. 481; (1982) 43 P. & C.R. 192; (1981) 260 E.G. 173; (1981) 125 S.J. 567, CA (Civ Div) *1–107*, *2–152*
Albany Home Loans Ltd v Massey; sub nom. Massey v Albany Life Assurance Co Ltd [1997] 2 All E.R. 609; [1997] 2 F.L.R. 305; [1997] 2 F.C.R. 145; (1997) 29 H.L.R. 902; (1997) 73 P. & C.R. 509; [1997] Fam. Law 404; (1997) 94(8) L.S.G. 27; (1997) 141 S.J.L.B. 44; [1997] N.P.C. 17A, CA (Civ Div) *1–027*
Albazero, The. *See* Owners of Cargo Laden on Board the Albacruz v Owners of the Albazero
Albeko Schuhmaschinen AG v Kamborian Shoe Machine Co (1961) 111 L.J. 519 .... *30–306*
Alberg v Chandler (1948) 64 T.L.R. 394 .... *29–192*
Albermarle Supply Co Ltd v Hind Co [1928] 1 K.B. 307 .... *21–061*
Albert (Men's Wear) v Prevezer (1949) 154 E.G. 424 .... *4–028*
Albion Sugar Co v William Tankers [1977] 2 Lloyd's Rep. 457, QBD (Comm) ... *2–154*
Albon (t/a NA Carriage Co) v Naza Motor Trading Sdn Bhd [2007] EWHC 9 (Ch); [2007] 1 W.L.R. 2489; [2007] 2 All E.R. 719; [2007] 1 All E.R. (Comm) 795; [2007] 1 Lloyd's Rep. 297; [2007] Bus. L.R. D87, Ch D *30–077*
Albright & Wilson UK Ltd v Biachem Ltd [2002] UKHL 37; [2002] 2 All E.R. (Comm) 753; [2003] 1 C.L.C. 637; (2002) 146 S.J.L.B. 241, HL *21–001*
Alcenius v Nigren (1854) 1 E. & B. 217; 24 L.J.Q.B. 19; 3 W.R. 25 .... *11–027*
Alcoa Minerals of Jamaica Inc v Broderick [2002] 1 A.C. 371; [2000] 3 W.L.R. 23; [2000] B.L.R. 279; (2000) 2 T.C.L.R. 850; [2000] Env. L.R. 734; (2000) 144 S.J.L.B. 182, PC (Jam) *26–018*, *26–064*, *26–109*, *26–110*
Alcock v Chief Constable of South Yorkshire; sub nom. Jones v Wright; Penk v Wright; Jones v Chief Constable of South Yorkshire; Copoc v Chief Constable of South Yorkshire [1992] 1 A.C. 310; [1991] 3 W.L.R. 1057; [1991] 4 All E.R. 907; [1992] P.I.Q.R. P1; (1992) 89(3) L.S.G. 34; (1991) 141 N.L.J. 166; (1992) 136 S.J.L.B. 9, HL; affirming [1991] 3 All E.R. 88, CA (Civ Div); affirming [1991] 2 W.L.R. 814; [1991] 1 All E.R. 353; (1990) 140 N.L.J. 1717, QBD *1–123*
Alcom v Columbia [1984] A.C. 580; [1984] 2 W.L.R. 750; [1984] 2 All E.R. 6; [1984] 2 Lloyd's Rep. 24; (1984) 81 L.S.G. 1837, HL; reversing [1983] 3 W.L.R. 906; [1984] 1 All E.R. 1; [1984] 1 Lloyd's Rep. 368; (1984) 128 S.J. 315, CA (Civ Div); reversing [1984] 2 Lloyd's Rep. 31 (Note), QBD *11–001*, *11–005*, *11–006*, *11–011*, *11–021*
Alder v Moore [1961] 2 Q.B. 57; [1961] 2 W.L.R. 426; [1961] 1 All E.R. 1; [1960] 2 Lloyd's Rep. 325; (1961) 105 S.J. 280, CA *26–009*, *26–127*, *26–145*
Alderslade v Hendon Laundry Ltd [1945] K.B. 189; [1945] 1 All E.R. 244; 114 L.J.K.B. 114; 172 L.T. 153; 89 S.J. 164, CA *12–021*, *14–008*, *14–012*, 14–013, *14–035*

Alderson v Beetham Organisation Ltd [2003] EWCA Civ 408; [2003] 1 W.L.R. 1686; [2003] B.L.R. 217; [2003] H.L.R. 60; (2003) 100(23) L.S.G. 39; (2003) 147 S.J.L.B. 418; [2003] N.P.C. 47, CA (Civ Div) *28–056*
Alderson v Langdale (1832) 3 B. Ad. 660 .... *21–081*
Aldhous, Re; sub nom. Noble v Treasury Solicitor [1955] 1 W.L.R. 459; [1955] 2 All E.R. 80; (1955) 99 S.J. 276, Ch D *20–013*
Aldora, The. *See* Tyne Tugs v Owners of the MV Aldora; The MV Aldora
Aldou's Case (1868) L.R. 3 Q.B. 753 .... *1–114*
Aldous v Cornwell (1867–68) L.R. 3 Q.B. 573, QB *25–023*
Alec Lobb Garages Ltd v Total Oil Great Britain Ltd [1985] 1 W.L.R. 173; [1985] 1 All E.R. 303; [1985] 1 E.G.L.R. 33; (1985) 273 E.G. 659; (1985) 82 L.S.G. 45; (1985) 129 S.J. 83, CA (Civ Div); affirming [1983] 1 W.L.R. 87; [1983] 1 All E.R. 944; (1983) 133 N.L.J. 401; (1982) 126 S.J. 768, Ch D *5–013*, *7–018*, *7–045*, *7–126*, *7–128*, *7–130*, *7–131*, *7–132*, *7–133*, 16–085, *16–085*, *16–090*, *16–095*, 16–123
Alev, The. *See* Vantage Navigation Corp v Suhail and Saud Bahwan Materials; Aalev, The.
Alexander v Brown (1824) 1 C.P. 288 .... *21–088*
Alexander v Mercouris [1979] 1 W.L.R. 1270; [1979] 3 All E.R. 305; (1979) 252 E.G. 911; (1979) 123 S.J. 604, CA (Civ Div) *13–015*
Alexander v Railway Executive [1951] 2 K.B. 882; [1951] 2 All E.R. 442; [1951] 2 T.L.R. 69; (1951) 95 S.J. 369, KBD ... *12–009*, *14–016*, *14–033*, *14–034*, *14–036*
Alexander v Rayson [1936] 1 K.B. 169; 114 A.L.R. 357, CA *16–010*, *16–017*, *16–167*, *16–176*, *16–179*, *16–205*
Alexander v Standard Telephone and Cables ltd [1990] I.C.R. 291 .... *27–064*
Alexander v Steinhardt Walker & Co [1903] 2 K.B. 208, KBD (Comm Ct) *19–023*
Alexander Hamilton Institute v Jones (1924) 234 Ill App. 444 .... *2–072*
Alexander Philp & Co v Knoblauch, 1907 S.C. 994; (1907) 15 S.L.T. 61, IH (2 Div) *2–007*
Alexander's Timber Co, Re (1901) 70 L.J.Ch. 767; 8 Manson 372 .... *9–058*
Alexandra Palace Co (No.2), Re (1882) L.R. 21 Ch. D. 149, Ch D *29–126*
Alexandra Park Co, Re (1868) L.R. 6 Eq. 512 .... *8–037*
Alexandria Cotton & Trading Co (Sudan) Ltd v Cotton Co of Ethiopia Ltd [1965] 2 Lloyd's Rep. 447, CA *26–144*
Alexiadi v Robinson (1861) 2 F.F. 679 .... *21–021*
Alf Vaughan & Co Ltd (In Receivership) v Royscot Trust Plc [1999] 1 All E.R. (Comm.) 856, Ch D *7–046*
Al-Fayed v Advocate General for Scotland; sub nom. Al-Fayed v Inland Revenue Commissioners; Ali Fayed v Advocate General for Scotland; Fayed v Inland Revenue Commissioners [2004] S.T.C. 1703; 2004 S.C. 745; 2004 S.L.T. 798; 77 T.C. 273; [2006] B.T.C. 70; [2004] S.T.I. 1723; 2004 G.W.D. *22–491*, IH (1 Div); affirming [2002] S.T.C. 910; 2003 S.C. 1; 2003 S.L.T. 747; [2002] B.T.C. 428; 4 I.T.L. Rep. 831; [2002] S.T.I. 880; 2002 G.W.D. *19–633*, OH *10–021*, *10–030*, *10–033*
Al-Fayed v Al-Tajir [1988] Q.B. 712; [1987] 3 W.L.R. 102; [1987] 2 All E.R. 396; [1987] 1 F.T.L.R. 441; (1987) 84 L.S.G. 1055; (1987) 131 S.J. 744, CA (Civ Div) *11–021*
Alfred C Toepfer International GmbH v Itex Itagrani Export SA [1993] 1 Lloyd's Rep. 360, QBD (Comm) *24–019*, *24–028*, *24–030*
Alfred C Toepfer v Peter Cremer GmbH & Co; sub nom. Toepfer v Cremer [1975] 2 Lloyd's Rep. 118; (1975) 119 S.J. 506, CA (Civ Div); affirming [1975] 1 Lloyd's Rep. 406, QBD (Comm) *12–082*, *14–144*, *14–148*, *22–052*, *24–006*, *24–008*, *24–019*
Alfred McAlpine Capital Projects Ltd v Tilebox Ltd [2005] EWHC 281 (TCC); [2005] B.L.R. 271; 104 Con. L.R. 39; (2005) 21 Const. L.J. 539, QBD (TCC) *26–126*, *26–135*

Alfred McAlpine Construction Ltd v Panatown Ltd (No.1); sub nom. Panatown Ltd v Alfred McAlpine Construction Ltd [2001] 1 A.C. 518; [2000] 3 W.L.R. 946; [2000] 4 All E.R. 97; [2000] C.L.C. 1604; [2000] B.L.R. 331; (2000) 2 T.C.L.R. 547; 71 Con. L.R. 1; [2000] E.G. 102 (C.S.); (2000) 97(38) L.S.G. 43; (2000) 150 N.L.J. 1299; (2000) 144 S.J.L.B. 240; [2000] N.P.C. 89, HL; reversing [1998] C.L.C. 636; 88 B.L.R. 67; 58 Con. L.R. 46; (1998) 14 Const. L.J. 267; [1998] E.G. 19 (C.S.); [1998] N.P.C. 17, CA (Civ Div) *18–002*, *18–047*, *18–051*, *18–052*, *18–054*, *18–055*, *18–056*, 18–058, 18–059, 18–060, *18–061*, 18–062, 18–065, *18–066*, *18–068*, 18–093, *19–076*, *26–003*, *26–128*

Alfred McAlpine Construction Ltd v Panatown Ltd (No.2) [2001] EWCA Civ 485; 76 Con. L.R. 224, CA (Civ Div) *2–129*

Alfred McAlpine Plc v BAI (Run-Off) Ltd [2000] 1 All E.R. (Comm) 545; [2000] 1 Lloyd's Rep. 437; [2000] C.L.C. 812; (2001) 3 T.C.L.R. 5; 69 Con. L.R. 87; [2000] Lloyd's Rep. I.R. 352, CA (Civ Div) *24–040*

Alghussein Establishment v Eton College [1988] 1 W.L.R. 587; [1991] 1 All E.R. 267; [1988] E.G. 69 (C.S.); (1988) 132 S.J. 750, HL; affirming, *The Times*, February 16, 1987, CA (Civ Div) *1–031*, *12–082*, *22–055*

Alhambra, The (1881) L.R. 6 P.D. 68, CA; reversing (1879–80) L.R. 5 P.D. 256, PDAD *12–057*

Ali v Ahmed (1996) 71 P. & C.R. D39, CA (Civ Div) *2–162*

Ali v Christian Salvesen Food Services Ltd; sub nom. Christian Salvesen Food Services Ltd v Ali [1997] 1 All E.R. 721; [1997] I.C.R. 25; [1997] I.R.L.R. 17; (1996) 93(41) L.S.G. 29; (1996) 140 S.J.L.B. 231, CA (Civ Div); reversing [1996] I.C.R. 1; [1995] I.R.L.R. 624, EAT *1–156*, *13–010*

Ali v Lane [2006] EWCA Civ 1532; [2007] 1 P. & C.R. 26; [2007] 2 E.G. 126; [2006] 48 E.G. 231 (C.S.); [2006] N.P.C. 124, CA (Civ Div) *12–126*

Ali v Lord Grey School Governors; sub nom. A v Headteacher and Governors of Lord Grey School [2006] UKHL 14; [2006] 2 A.C. 363; [2006] 2 W.L.R. 690; [2006] 2 All E.R. 457; [2006] H.R.L.R. 20; [2006] U.K.H.R.R. 591; 20 B.H.R.C. 295; [2006] E.L.R. 223, HL *27–024*

Ali Shipping Corp v Shipyard Trogir [1999] 1 W.L.R. 314; [1998] 2 All E.R. 136; [1998] 1 Lloyd's Rep. 643; [1998] C.L.C. 566, CA (Civ Div) *13–003*

Aliakmon, The. *See* Leigh and Sillivan Ltd v Aliakmon Shipping Co Ltd.

Alicia Hosiery v Brown Shipley & Co [1970] 1 Q.B. 195; [1969] 2 W.L.R. 1268; [1969] 2 All E.R. 504; [1969] 2 Lloyd's Rep. 179; (1969) 113 S.J. 466, QBD 18–009

Al-Kadhimi v Government of Saudi Arabia [2003] EWCA Civ 1689 ..... *11–005*

Al-Kandari v JR Brown & Co [1988] Q.B. 665; [1988] 2 W.L.R. 671; [1988] 1 All E.R. 833; [1988] Fam. Law 382; (1988) 85(14) L.S.G. 50; (1988) 138 N.L.J. Rep. 62; (1988) 132 S.J. 462, CA (Civ Div); reversing [1987] Q.B. 514; [1987] 2 W.L.R. 469; [1987] 2 All E.R. 302; (1987) 84 L.S.G. 825; (1987) 137 N.L.J. 36; (1987) 131 S.J. 225, QBD *1–134*, *18–022*

Al-Kishtaini v Shanshal; sub nom. Shanshal v Al-Kishtaini [2001] EWCA Civ 264; [2001] 2 All E.R. (Comm) 601; [2001] Lloyd's Rep. Bank. 174; (2001) 98(17) L.S.G. 38, CA (Civ Div) *30–357*

Allam & Co v Europa Poster Services [1968] 1 W.L.R. 638; [1968] 1 All E.R. 826; (1968) 112 S.J. 86, Ch D *22–051*

Allan Bros and Co v James Bros & Co (1897) 3 Com. Cas. 10 ..... *14–011*

Allan J Panozza & Co Pty Ltd v Allied Interstate (Queensland) Pty Ltd [1976] 2 N.S.W.L.R. 192 ..... *30–337*, *30–347*

Allan Janes LLP v Johal [2006] EWHC 286 (Ch); [2006] I.C.R. 742; [2006] I.R.L.R. 599; (2006) 156 N.L.J. 373, Ch D *16–104*

Allard v Bourne (1863) 15 C.B. (N.S.) 468 ..... *9–039*

Allardyce v Roebuck; sub nom. Gray (Deceased), Re [2004] EWHC 1538 (Ch); [2005] 1 W.L.R. 815; [2004] 3 All E.R. 754; [2004] W.T.L.R. 779; (2004–05) 7 I.T.E.L.R. 232; [2004] N.P.C. 109, Ch D *2–127*, *3–172*

Allcard v Skinner (1887) L.R. 36 Ch. D. 145, CA 7–057, *7–058*, 7–059, 7–063, *7–064*, *7–069*, 7–071, *7–077*, 7–086, 7–094, *7–097*, 7–103, *28–140*, 28–145, *29–137*

Allcard v Walker [1896] 2 Ch. 369, Ch D 5–054, 5–062, 29–043
Allen v Cameron (1833) 1 C. & M. 832 12–064
Allen v Dundas (1789) 3 T.R. 125 21–049
Allen v Flood; sub nom. Flood v Jackson [1898] A.C. 1, HL; reversing [1895] 2 Q.B. 21, CA 7–045
Allen v Pink (1838) 4 M. & W. 140 12–107
Allen v Rescous (1676) 2 Lev. 179 16–018
Allen v Richardson (1879–80) L.R. 13 Ch. D. 524, Ch D 29–057
Allen v Robles [1969] 1 W.L.R. 1193; [1969] 3 All E.R. 154; [1969] 2 Lloyd's Rep. 61; (1969) 113 S.J. 484, CA (Civ Div) 24–003
Allen v Royal Bank of Canada (1925) 41 T.L.R. 625; [1925] CarswellFor 3; [1925] 3 W.W.R. 67; (1925) 95 L.J. P.C. 17, PC (Wind) 21–073, 21–074
Allen v Taylor (1871) 39 L.J.Ch. 627 16–114
Allen v Waters & Co [1935] 1 K.B. 200, CA 18–076
Allen v Wingrove (1901) 17 T.L.R. 261 29–117
Allhusen v Borrie (1867) 15 W.R. 739 27–038
Alliance & Leicester Building Society v Edgestop Ltd (Application for Leave); Alliance & Leicester Building Society v Dhanoa; Alliance & Leicester Building Society v Samra; Mercantile Credit Co Ltd v Lancaster; Alliance & Leicester Building Society v Hamptons, LTA 94/5856/B, CA (Civ Div); affirming [1993] 1 W.L.R. 1462; [1994] 2 All E.R. 38; [1994] 2 E.G.L.R. 229; [1993] E.G. 93 (C.S.); [1993] N.P.C. 79, Ch D 6–040, 6–064, 6–074
Alliance Bank Ltd v Broom, 62 E.R. 631; (1864) 2 Drew. & Sm. 289, QB ...3–057, 3–058, 3–060
Alliance Paper Group Plc v Prestwich (No.1) [1996] I.R.L.R. 25, Ch D 16–120
Allied Air Conditioning v British Columbia (1992) 76 B.C.L.R. 2d 218 29–086
Allied Carpets Group Plc v Macfarlane (t/a Whicheloe Macfarlane Partnership) [2002] EWHC 1155; [2002] B.L.R. 433; [2002] P.N.L.R. 38, QBD (TCC) 19–021, 19–025
Allied Dunbar (Frank Weisinger) Ltd v Frank Weisinger [1988] I.R.L.R. 60 .....16–092, 16–104, 16–116
Allied Irish Bank Plc v Byrne [1995] 2 F.L.R. 325; [1995] 1 F.C.R. 430; [1995] Fam. Law 609, Ch D 7–113
Allied Maples Group Ltd v Simmons & Simmons [1995] 1 W.L.R. 1602; [1995] 4 All E.R. 907; [1996] C.L.C. 153; 46 Con. L.R. 134; [1955–95] P.N.L.R. 701; (1995) 145 N.L.J. 1646; [1995] N.P.C. 83; (1995) 70 P. & C.R. D14, CA (Civ Div) 26–043, 26–044, 26–045
Allied Marine Transport v Vale do Rio Doce Navegacao SA; The Leonidas D; Vale do Rio Doce Navegacao SA v Ocean Freighters Corp [1985] 1 W.L.R. 925; [1985] 2 All E.R. 796; [1985] 2 Lloyd's Rep. 18; (1985) 82 L.S.G. 2160; (1985) 129 S.J. 431, CA (Civ Div); reversing [1984] 1 W.L.R. 1; [1983] 3 All E.R. 737; [1983] 2 Lloyd's Rep. 411; (1983) 127 S.J. 729, QBD (Comm) 1–004, 2–004, 2–006, 2–045, 2–071, 2–076, 3–047, 3–092, 5–067, 22–027, 22–044
Allis Chalmers Co v Maryland Fidelity and Deposit Co (1916) 114 L.T. 433 6–151
Allseas International Management v Panroy Bulk Transport SA; The Star Gazer and The Star Delta [1985] 1 Lloyd's Rep. 370, QBD (Comm) 27–014
Allsopp v Orchard [1923] 1 Ch. 323, Ch D 22–046
Alma Shipping Corp v Union of India; The Astraea [1971] 2 Lloyd's Rep. 494, QBD (Comm) 24–006, 28–022, 28–109
Alma Shipping Corp of Monrovia v Mantovani; The Dione [1975] 1 Lloyd's Rep. 115; (1974) 119 S.J. 164, CA (Civ Div); reversing [1974] 1 Lloyd's Rep. 86, QBD (Comm) 12–093
Alman and Benson v Associated Newspapers Group, unreported, June 20, 1980 12–104
Almatrans SA v Steamship Mutual Underwriting Association (Bermuda) Ltd; The Tutova [2006] EWHC 2223 (Comm); [2007] 1 Lloyd's Rep. 104, QBD (Comm) 12–075, 12–122, 12–124

Alpenstow Ltd v Regalian Properties Plc [1985] 1 W.L.R. 721; [1985] 2 All E.R. 545; [1985] 1 E.G.L.R. 164; (1984) 274 E.G. 1141; (1985) 82 L.S.G. 2241; (1985) 135 N.L.J. 205; (1985) 129 S.J. 400, Ch D *2–120*, *27–042*
Alpha Trading Ltd v Dunnshaw-Patten Ltd [1981] Q.B. 290; [1981] 2 W.L.R. 169; [1981] 1 All E.R. 482; [1981] 1 Lloyd's Rep. 122; (1980) 124 S.J. 827, CA (Civ Div); affirming [1980] 2 Lloyd's Rep. 284, QBD (Comm) *2–156*, *13–004*, *13–006*, *13–007*
Alstom Signalling Ltd (t/a Alstom Transport Information Solutions) v Jarvis Facilities Ltd [2004] EWHC 1232 (TCC); 95 Con. L.R. 55, QBD (TCC) *2–131*, *2–140*
Aluminium Industrie Vaassen BV v Romalpa Aluminium [1976] 1 W.L.R. 676; [1976] 2 All E.R. 552; [1976] 1 Lloyd's Rep. 443; (1976) 120 S.J. 95, CA (Civ Div) *29–164*, *29–168*
Amalgamated Building Contractors v Waltham Holy Cross Urban DC [1952] 2 All E.R. 452; [1952] 2 T.L.R. 269; 50 L.G.R. 667; [1952] W.N. 400; (1952) 96 S.J. 530, CA; affirming [1952] 1 T.L.R. 1165; 50 L.G.R. 429 .. *12–082*, *13–012*
Amalgamated General Finance Co Ltd v CE Golding & Co Ltd [1964] 2 Lloyd's Rep. 163, QBD (Comm) *19–016*
Amalgamated Investment & Property Co Ltd (In Liquidation) v Texas Commerce International Bank Ltd [1982] Q.B. 84; [1981] 3 W.L.R. 565; [1981] 3 All E.R. 577; [1982] 1 Lloyd's Rep. 27; [1981] Com. L.R. 236; (1981) 125 S.J. 623, CA (Civ Div); affirming [1981] 2 W.L.R. 554; [1981] 1 All E.R. 923; [1981] Com. L.R. 37; (1981) 125 S.J. 133, QBD (Comm) *1–112*, *3–103*, 3–108, *3–110*, 3–111, 3–113, *3–138*, *3–141*, *3–163*, 9–014, *12–126*, *28–136*
Amalgamated Investment & Property Co v John Walker & Sons [1977] 1 W.L.R. 164; [1976] 3 All E.R. 509; (1976) 32 P. & C.R. 278; (1976) 239 E.G. 277; (1976) 120 S.J. 252, CA (Civ Div) *5–016*, *23–002*, *23–034*, *23–057*
Amalgamated Metal Trading Ltd v Department of Trade and Industry, *The Times*, March 21, 1989*; Financial Times*, February 28, 1989, QBD *11–005*
Amalgamated Society of Carpenters Cabinet Makers & Joiners v Braithwaite; sub nom. Braithwaite v Amalgamated Society of Carpenters Cabinet Makers & Joiners; General Union of Operative Carpenters & Joiners v Ashley [1922] 2 A.C. 440, HL; affirming [1921] 2 Ch. 399, CA 9–074
Amalgamated Society of Railway Servants v Osborne (No.2); sub nom. Osborne v Amalgamated Society of Railway Servants (No.2) [1911] 1 Ch. 540, CA 9–074, *16–200*
Amalgamated Society of Railway Servants v Osborne. *See* Osborne v Amalgamated Society of Railway Servants (No.1).
Aman v Southern Railway Co [1926] 1 K.B. 59, CA *25–007*
Amantilla v Telefusion (1987) 9 Con. L.R. 139 .... *3–120*
Amar Singh v Kulubya [1964] A.C. 142; [1963] 3 W.L.R. 513; [1963] 3 All E.R. 499; (1963) 107 S.J. 616, PC (EA) *16–178*
Amatrudi v Watson (1952) 88 A. 2d 7 .... *29–144*
Ambatielos v Anton Jurgens Margarine Works [1923] A.C. 175; (1922) 13 Ll. L. Rep. 357, HL; affirming [1922] 2 K.B. 185; (1922) 10 Ll. L. Rep. 781, CA; reversing (1922) 10 Ll. L. Rep. 125, KBD *12–069*, *12–090*
Ambrose v Kerrison (1851) 10 C.B. 776 .... *29–132*, *29–134*
Amec Developments Ltd v Jury's Hotel Management (UK) Ltd [2002] T.C.L.R. 13; (2001) 82 P. & C.R. 22; [2001] 1 E.G.L.R. 81; [2001] 07 E.G. 163; [2000] E.G. 138 (C.S.); [2000] N.P.C. 125, Ch D *29–151*
American Airlines Inc v Hope; sub nom. Banque Sabbag SAL v Hope [1974] 2 Lloyd's Rep. 301, HL; affirming [1973] 1 Lloyd's Rep. 233, CA (Civ Div); affirming [1972] 1 Lloyd's Rep. 253, QBD (Comm) *2–129*
American Cyanamid Co (No.1) v Ethicon Ltd [1975] A.C. 396; [1975] 2 W.L.R. 316; [1975] 1 All E.R. 504; [1975] F.S.R. 101; [1975] R.P.C. 513; (1975) 119 S.J. 136, HL *27–061*
American Home Assurance Co v Tjmond Properties [1986] B.C.L.C. 181, CA (NZ) *9–023*

American Motorists Insurance Co (AMICO) v Cellstar Corp [2003] EWCA Civ 206; [2003] 2 C.L.C. 599; [2003] I.L.Pr. 22; [2003] Lloyd's Rep. I.R. 295; (2003) 100(18) L.S.G. 35, CA (Civ Div) ..*30–045*, *30–051*, *30–053*, *30–055*, *30–056*, *30–071*, *30–077*, *30–273*
Amherst v James Walker Goldsmith & Silversmith Ltd [1983] Ch. 305; [1983] 3 W.L.R. 334; [1983] 2 All E.R. 1067; (1984) 47 P. & C.R. 85; (1982) 267 E.G. 163; (1983) 127 S.J. 391, CA (Civ Div) *2–004*, *2–006*, *3–092*, *3–103*, *21–018*
Amicable Society v Bolland (1830) 2 Dow. & Cl. 1 16–172
Amin v Brown [2005] EWHC 1670; [2006] I.L.Pr. 5; [2005] A.C.D. 95; (2005) 155 N.L.J. 1278; [2005] N.P.C. 104, Ch D *11–024*, *11–028*
Amin Rasheed Shipping Corp v Kuwait Insurance Co; The Al Wahab [1984] A.C. 50; [1983] 3 W.L.R. 241; [1983] 2 All E.R. 884; [1983] 2 Lloyd's Rep. 365; (1983) 127 S.J. 492, HL *30–005*, *30–009*, *30–010*, *30–011*, *30–012*, *30–013*, *30–016*, *30–051*, *30–055*
Amiri Flight Authority v BAE Systems Plc [2003] EWCA Civ 1447; [2004] 1 All E.R. (Comm) 385; [2003] 2 Lloyd's Rep. 767; [2003] 2 C.L.C. 662, CA (Civ Div); reversing [2002] EWHC 2481 (Comm); [2003] 1 All E.R. (Comm) 1; [2003] 1 Lloyd's Rep. 50, QBD (Comm) *12–015*, *14–005*, *18–031*, *30–008*, *30–068*, *30–309*
Amoco Australian Pty Ltd v Rocca Bros Motor Engineering Co Pty Ltd; sub nom. Amoco Australia Pty v Rocco Bros Motor Engineering Co Pty [1975] A.C. 561; [1975] 2 W.L.R. 779; [1975] 1 All E.R. 968; (1975) 119 S.J. 301, PC (Aus) 16–085, *16–122*, *16–129*
Amoco (UK) Exploration Co v British American Offshore Ltd, unreported, November 16, 2001, QBD (Comm) *24–017*, *24–018*
Amontilla Ltd v Telefusion Plc (1987) 9 Con. L.R. 139 .... *28–093*
Amory v Brodrick (1822) 5 B.A. 712 .... *24–028*
Amos and Wood v Kaprow, 64 T.L.R. 110; [1948] W.N. 71; (1948) 92 S.J. 153, CA *24–044*
Amsprop Trading Ltd v Harris Distribution Ltd [1997] 1 W.L.R. 1025; [1997] 2 All E.R. 990; [1997] 2 E.G.L.R. 78; [1997] 47 E.G. 127; [1996] N.P.C. 154, Ch D *18–019*, *18–125*
Amstrad Plc v Seagate Technology Inc, 86 B.L.R. 34; [1998] Masons C.L.R. Rep. 1, QBD *26–165*
Anangel Atlas Compania Naviera SA v Ishikawajima-Harima Heavy Industries Co (No.2) [1990] 2 Lloyd's Rep. 526, QBD (Comm) *2–140*, *3–068*, *3–118*, 3–123, *12–118*, *22–035*
Anchor Brewhouse Developments Ltd v Berkeley House (Docklands) Developments Ltd (1987) 284 E.G. 626 .... *29–144*
Anchor Line v Keith Rowell; The Hazelmoor [1980] 2 Lloyd's Rep. 351, CA (Civ Div) *24–018*, *24–019*
And So To Bed Ltd v Dixon [2001] F.S.R. 47, Ch D *18–049*
Anders Utkilens Rederi A/S v O/Y Lovisa Stevedoring Co A/B and Keller Bryant Transport Co; The Golfstraum [1985] 2 All E.R. 669; [1985] S.T.C. 301, Ch D *22–024*
Anderson v Anderson [1895] 1 Q.B. 749, CA *12–089*, *14–138*
Anderson v Commercial Union Assurance Co (1885) 55 L.J.Q.B. 146 21–007
Anderson v Equitable Life Assurance Society of the United States (1929) 45 T.L.R. 468 .... *30–370*
Anderson v Fitzgerald (1853) 4 H.L.C. 484 .... *6–149*
Anderson v Hillies (1852) 12 C.B. 499 .... *21–075*
Anderson v Martindale (1801) 1 East. 497 ....*3–042*, *3–044*
Anderson v Pacific Fire & Marine Insurance Co (1871–72) L.R. 7 C.P. 65, CCP *6–009*
Anderson v Radcliffe (1858) E.B. & E. 806 ....*16–054*, *16–064*
Anderson v Sutherland (1897) 2 Com. Cas. 65 .... *21–044*
Anderson v Thornton (1835) 8 Ex. 425 .... *29–082*
Anderton & Rowland v Rowland, *The Times*, November 5, 1999, QBD (Merc) *2–110*, *18–010*
Anderson (A Bankrupt), Re [1911] 1 K.B. 896, KBD *19–068*

Anderson Ltd v Daniel [1924] 1 K.B. 138, CA *16–150*, *16–153*, *16–158*
Andrabell, Re [1984] 3 All E.R. 407, Ch D *29–169*
André et Cie SA v Cook Industries Inc [1987] 2 Lloyd's Rep. 463, CA (Civ Div); reversing [1986] 2 Lloyd's Rep. 200, QBD *2–003*, *14–150*, *24–014*
Andre et Cie SA v Etablissements Michel Blanc et Fils [1979] 2 Lloyd's Rep. 427, CA (Civ Div); affirming [1977] 2 Lloyd's Rep. 166, QBD (Comm) *1–122*, *1–131*, *6–013*, *6–069*, *6–088*, *14–140*, *14–141*
Andre et Cie SA v JH Vantol Ltd [1952] 2 Lloyd's Rep. 282, QBD *26–070*
Andre et Cie SA v Marine Transocean Ltd; The Splendid Sun [1981] Q.B. 694; [1981] 3 W.L.R. 43; [1981] 2 All E.R. 993; [1981] 2 Lloyd's Rep. 29; [1981] Com. L.R. 95; (1981) 125 S.J. 395, CA (Civ Div); affirming [1980] 1 Lloyd's Rep. 333, QBD (Comm) *2–004*, *2–006*, *2–071*, *2–076*, *22–027*
Andre et Cie SA v Tradax Export SA [1983] 1 Lloyd's Rep. 254; [1983] Com. L.R. 2, CA (Civ Div); reversing [1981] 2 Lloyd's Rep. 352, QBD (Comm) ... *14–141*
Andre (Trevor) v Bashford [1965] C.L.Y. 1984, CC *16–102*
Andrew v St Olave's Board of Works [1898] 1 Q.B. 775, QBD *29–096*
Andrew Millar & Co Ltd v Taylor & Co Ltd [1916] 1 K.B. 402, CA *23–035*
Andrew Weir & Co v Dobell & Co [1916] 1 K.B. 722, KBD *26–104*
Andrews v Hopkinson [1957] 1 Q.B. 229; [1956] 3 W.L.R. 732; [1956] 3 All E.R. 422; (1956) 100 S.J. 768, Assizes (Leeds) *12–007*, *18–006*
Andrews v Schooling [1991] 1 W.L.R. 783; [1991] 3 All E.R. 723; 53 B.L.R. 68; 26 Con. L.R. 33; (1991) 23 H.L.R. 316; (1991) 135 S.J. 446, CA (Civ Div) *1–173*, *13–015*
Andrews Bros (Bournemouth) Ltd v Singer & Co Ltd [1934] 1 K.B. 17, CA ... *14–006*, *14–027*
Aneco Reinsurance Underwriting Ltd (In Liquidation) v Johnson & Higgins Ltd; sub nom. Aneco Reinsurance Underwriting Ltd v Johnson & Higgs Ltd [2001] UKHL 51; [2001] 2 All E.R. (Comm) 929; [2002] 1 Lloyd's Rep. 157; [2002] C.L.C. 181; [2002] Lloyd's Rep. I.R. 91; [2002] P.N.L.R. 8, HL *26–079*
Angel v Jay [1911] 1 K.B. 666, KBD *5–132*
Angelic Star, The. *See* Oresundsvarvet AB v Lemos; The Angelic Star
Angell v Duke (1874–75) L.R. 10 Q.B. 174, QBD *4–016*, *12–103*
Angell v Duke (1875) 32 L.T. 320 .... *12–100*, *12–103*
Anglesey, Re. *See* Marquis of Anglesey, Re
Anglesey (Marquis of), Re; sub nom. Willmot v Gardner [1901] 2 Ch. 548, CA *13–022*, *26–167*
Anglia Commercial Properties v North East Essex Building Co (1983) 266 E.G. 1096 .... *12–031*
Anglia Television Ltd v Reed [1972] 1 Q.B. 60; [1971] 3 W.L.R. 528; [1971] 3 All E.R. 690; (1971) 115 S.J. 723, CA (Civ Div) *26–073*, 26–076, *26–077*
Anglo African Shipping Co of New York Inc v J Mortner Ltd [1962] 1 Lloyd's Rep. 610, CA *24–010*, *26–104*, *26–122*
Anglo-American Asphalt Co Ltd v Crowley, Russell Co Ltd (1945) 173 L.T. 228 .... *29–191*
Anglo-Australian Life Assurance Co v British Provident Life and Fire Society (1862) 3 Giff. 521 .... *27–008*
Anglo-Austrian Bank (Vogel's Application), Re; Dresdner Bank (Ellert's Application), Re; Direction Der Disconto Gesellschaft (Gutschow's Application), Re [1920] 1 Ch. 69, Ch D *30–012*, *30–345*
Anglo Auto Finance Co v James [1963] 1 W.L.R. 1042; [1963] 3 All E.R. 566; (1963) 107 S.J. 534, CA *22–049*, *26–131*, *26–155*
Anglo Cyprian Trade Agencies v Paphos Wine Industries [1951] 1 All E.R. 873; [1951] W.N. 205; (1951) 95 S.J. 336, KBD *26–006*, *26–008*
Anglo Group Plc v Winther Browne & Co Ltdl; sub nom. Winther Brown & Co Ltd v Anglo Group Plc 72 Con. L.R. 118; [1999–2000] Info. T.L.R. 61; [2000] I.T.C.L.R. 559; [2000] Masons C.L.R. 13; (2000) 144 S.J.L.B. 197, QBD (TCC) *24–040*
Anglo-Moravian Hungarian Junction Railway Co Ex p. Watkin, Re (1875–76) L.R. 1 Ch. D. 130, CA *9–048*

Anglo-Overseas Agencies v Green [1961] 1 Q.B. 1; [1960] 3 W.L.R. 561; 104 S.J. 756; [1960] 3 All E.R. 244 .... *9–022*
Anglo Petroleum Ltd v TFB (Mortgages) Ltd; TFB (Mortgages) Ltd v Sutton; TFB (Mortgages) Ltd v Anglo Petroleum Ltd [2007] EWCA Civ 456; [2007] All E.R. (D) 243; [2007] B.C.C. 407; [2008] 1 B.C.L.C. 185, CA (Civ Div); affirming [2006] EWHC 258 (Ch), Ch D *16–011*
Anglo-Russian Merchant Traders and John Batt & Co (London), Re [1917] 2 K.B. 679 .... *2–155*, *13–013*, *14–141*
Anglo Scottish Beet Sugar Corp Ltd v Spalding Urban DC [1937] 2 K.B. 607, KBD *28–058*, *29–031*, *29–040*, *29–043*
Angus v Clifford [1891] 2 Ch. 449, CA *6–010*
Annamunthodo v Oilfields Workers Trade Union [1961] A.C. 945; [1961] 3 W.L.R. 650; [1961] 3 All E.R. 621; (1961) 105 S.J. 706, PC (WI) *9–083*
Annandale, Marchioness of (1728) 1 Bro.P.C. 250; 2 P.Wms. 432 .... *16–067*
Annangel Glory Compania Naviera SA v M Golodetz Ltd; The Annangel Glory [1988] 1 Lloyd's Rep. 45; [1988] P.C.C. 37, QBD (Comm) *19–032*, *19–066*
Anning v Anning (1907) 4 C.L.R. 1049 .... *19–036*
Anns v Merton LBC; sub nom. Anns v Walcroft Property Co Ltd [1978] A.C. 728; [1977] 2 W.L.R. 1024; [1977] 2 All E.R. 492; 75 L.G.R. 555; (1977) 243 E.G. 523; (1988) 4 Const. L.J. 100; [1977] J.P.L. 514; (1987) 84 L.S.G. 319; (1987) 137 N.L.J. 794; (1977) 121 S.J. 377, HL; affirming [1976] Q.B. 882; [1976] 2 W.L.R. 512; 74 L.G.R. 374; (1976) 241 E.G. 311; (1976) 120 S.J. 216, CA (Civ Div); reversing unreported, October 24, 1975, HC *1–124*, *1–177*, *18–027*
Anon (1700) 12 Mod. 415 .... *29–140*
Anon. v White (1709) 3 Swan. 108 .... *27–040*
Anonima Petroli Italiana SpA and Neste Oy v Marlucidez Armadora SA; The Filiatra Legacy [1991] 2 Lloyd's Rep. 337, CA (Civ Div); reversing [1990] 1 Lloyd's Rep. 354, QBD (Comm) *18–034*
Ansell v Baker (1850) 15 Q.B. 20 .... *25–001*
Ansell v Waterhouse (1817) 6 M. & S. 385 .... *1–128*
Anstey v British National Premium Life Association (1908) 99 L.T. 765 .... *6–149*
Antaios Compania Naviera SA v Salen Rederierna AB; The Antaios [1985] A.C. 191; [1984] 3 W.L.R. 592; [1984] 3 All E.R. 229; [1984] 2 Lloyd's Rep. 235; (1984) 81 L.S.G. 2776; (1984) 128 S.J. 564, HL; affirming [1983] 1 W.L.R. 1362; [1983] 3 All E.R. 777; [1983] 2 Lloyd's Rep. 473; [1983] Com. L.R. 262; (1983) 127 S.J. 730, CA (Civ Div) *12–040*, *12–055*, 12–057
Antclizo Shipping Corp v Food Corp of India; The Antclizo [1992] 1 Lloyd's Rep. 558, CA (Civ Div); affirming [1991] 2 Lloyd's Rep. 485, QBD (Comm) *12–082*
Anton Durbeck GmbH v Den Norske Bank ASA [2005] EWHC 2497 (Comm); [2006] 1 Lloyd's Rep. 93; [2005] 2 C.L.C. 783, QBD (Comm) *18–143*, *18–145*
Antoniades v Villiers. *See* AG Securities v Vaughan; Antoniades v Villiers
Anziani, Re; sub nom. Herbert v Christopherson [1930] 1 Ch. 407, Ch D *30–123*
Apex Supply Co, Re [1942] Ch. 108, Ch D *26–145*
Apley Estates Co Ltd v De Bernales [1947] Ch. 217; [1947] 1 All E.R. 213; 63 T.L.R. 71; [1947] L.J.R. 705; 176 L.T. 182; (1947) 91 S.J. 12, CA; affirming [1946] 2 All E.R. 338, Ch D *17–018*
Apple Corps Ltd v Apple Computer Inc [2004] EWHC 768; [2004] 2 C.L.C. 720; [2004] I.L.Pr. 34, Ch D *30–020*, *30–076*, *30–089*
Applebee, Re; sub nom. Leveson v Beales [1891] 3 Ch. 422, Ch D *17–023*, *25–005*
Appleby v Dods (1807) 8 East 300 .... *21–030*
Appleby v Myers; sub nom. Appleby v Meyers (1866–67) L.R. 2 C.P. 651, Ex Chamber *21–029*, *21–030*, *21–031*, *21–033*, *21–037*, *23–005*, *23–021*, 23–049, *23–073*, *23–086*
Applegate v Moss; sub nom. Archer v Moss [1971] 1 Q.B. 406; [1971] 2 W.L.R. 541; [1971] 1 All E.R. 747; 3 B.L.R. 1; (1970) 114 S.J. 971, CA (Civ Div) *28–086*, *28–087*
Appleson v Littlewood [1939] 1 All E.R. 464 .... *2–162*
Appleton v Cambell (1862) 2 C. & P. 347 .... *16–069*

Apthorp v Neville (1907) 23 T.L.R. 575 .... *16–010*, *16–018*
Apthorpe v Apthorpe (1887) L.R. 12 P.D. 192, CA *16–022*
Aqua Design & Play International Ltd (t/a Aqua Design) (In Liquidation) v Kier Regional Ltd (t/a French Kier Anglia); Fenlock Hansen Ltd (t/a Fendor Hansen) v Kier Regional Ltd (t/a French Kier Anglia) [2002] EWCA Civ 797; [2003] B.L.R. 111; 82 Con. L.R. 107, CA (Civ Div); reversing HT–01–160, HT–01–232, QBD (TCC) *12–083*, *12–119*
Aquaflite v Jaymar International Freight Consultants [1980] 1 Lloyd's Rep. 36, CA (Civ Div) *3–098*
Arab Bank v Ross [1952] 2 Q.B. 216; [1952] 1 All E.R. 709; [1952] 1 T.L.R. 811; (1952) 96 S.J. 229, CA *25–025*
Arab Bank Ltd v Barclays Bank (Dominion, Colonial and Overseas) [1954] A.C. 495; [1954] 2 W.L.R. 1022; [1954] 2 All E.R. 226; (1954) 98 S.J. 350, HL *21–010*, *23–031*, *28–039*
Arab Bank Plc v John D Wood (Commercial) Ltd; Arab Bank Plc v Browne [2000] 1 W.L.R. 857; [2000] Lloyd's Rep. I.R. 471; [2000] Lloyd's Rep. P.N. 173; [1999] E.G. 133 (C.S.); (1999) 96(47) L.S.G. 30; (2000) 144 S.J.L.B. 6; [1999] N.P.C. 134, CA (Civ Div) *26–094*, *26–117*
Arab Monetary Fund v Hashim (No.3) [1991] 2 A.C. 114; [1991] 2 W.L.R. 729; [1991] 1 All E.R. 871; [1991] B.C.C. 180; (1991) 135 S.J.L.B. 311, HL; reversing [1990] 3 W.L.R. 139; [1990] 2 All E.R. 769; [1990] B.C.C. 499, CA (Civ Div); reversing [1990] 1 All E.R. 685; [1990] B.C.C. 52; (1990) 87(14) L.S.G. 42, Ch D *11–007*, *11–019*
Arab Monetary Fund v Hashim (No.9) [1996] 1 Lloyd's Rep. 589, CA (Civ Div) [1993] 1 Lloyd's Rep. 543, QBD (Comm) *11–007*, *11–019*, *11–023*, *28–061*, *28–118*, *29–156*, *30–347*
Arab Republic of Egypt v Gamal-Eldin. *See* Egypt v Gamal-Eldin
Aramark Plc v Sommerville, 1995 S.L.T. 749, OH *16–111*
Aramis, The [1989] 1 Lloyd's Rep. 213, CA (Civ Div); reversing [1987] 2 Lloyd's Rep. 58, QBD (Admlty) *2–003*, *2–111*, *2–160*, *3–008*, *3–073*, *18–005*
Aratra Potato Co Ltd v Taylor Joynson Garrett [1995] 4 All E.R. 695; (1995) 145 N.L.J. 1402, QBD *16–066*, *29–079*
Arbitration between Comptoir Commercial Anversois and Power Son & Co, Re [1920] 1 K.B. 868; (1919) 1 Ll. L. Rep. 266, CA *12–026*, *13–003*, *13–009*, *14–141*, *23–047*
Arbitration between L Sutro & Co and Heilbut Symons & Co, Re [1917] 2 K.B. 348, CA *12–057*, *12–070*, *12–128*, *13–023*, *21–002*, *21–004*
Arbuthnot Leasing International Ltd v Havelet Leasing Ltd (No.2) [1990] B.C.C. 636, Ch D *20–031*
Arbuthnott v Fagan; Deeny v Gooda Walker Ltd (Agency Agreement: Construction) [1996] L.R.L.R. 135; [1995] C.L.C. 1396, CA (Civ Div) *12–050*
Archbishop of Canterbury's Case (1596) 2 Co. Rep. 46a *12–089*
Archbold v Scully (1861) 9 H.L.C. 360 .... *28–035*, *28–136*, *28–139*
Archbolds (Freightage) Ltd v S Spanglett Ltd [1961] 1 Q.B. 374; [1961] 2 W.L.R. 170; [1961] 1 All E.R. 417; (1961) 105 S.J. 149, CA 16–011, *16–142*, *16–144*, *16–146*, *16–159*, *16–176*, *16–180*, *16–204*
Archer v Brown [1985] Q.B. 401; [1984] 3 W.L.R. 350; [1984] 2 All E.R. 267; (1984) 81 L.S.G. 2770; (1984) 134 N.L.J. 235; (1984) 128 S.J. 532, QBD ...*1–131*, *1–133*, *6–042*, *6–061*, *6–063*, *16–148*, *26–083*
Archer v Cutler [1980] 1 N.Z.L.R. 386 .... *7–132*, *8–068*
Archer v Hudson (1844) 7 Beav. 551 .... *7–074*, *7–075*
Archer (Lady) v Williams [2003] EWHC 1670 (QB); [2003] E.M.L.R. 38, QBD *1–060*, *1–066*
Architype Projects Ltd v Dewhurst Macfarlane & Partners [2003] EWHC 3341; 96 Con. L.R. 35; [2004] P.N.L.R. 38, QBD (TCC) *18–032*
Arcos Ltd v EA Ronaasen & Son; sub nom. Ronaasen & Son v Arcos Ltd [1933] A.C. 470; (1933) 45 Ll. L. Rep. 33, HL *21–002*, *21–004*
Arcos v Aronson (1930) 36 Ll. L. Rep. 108 .... *2–131*
Ardennes, The. *See* Owners of Cargo Lately Laden on Board the Ardennes v Owners of the Ardennes.

Arenson v Arenson. *See* Arenson v Casson, Beckman, Rutley & Co.
Argentum Reductions (UK) Ltd, Re [1975] 1 W.L.R. 186; [1975] 1 All E.R. 608; (1974) 119 S.J. 97, Ch D *9–049*
Argo Fund Ltd v Essar Steel Ltd; sub nom. Essar Steel Ltd v Argo Fund Ltd [2006] EWCA Civ 241; [2006] 2 All E.R. (Comm) 104; [2006] 2 Lloyd's Rep. 134; [2006] 1 C.L.C. 546, CA (Civ Div); affirming [2005] EWHC 600 (Comm); [2006] 1 All E.R. (Comm) 56; [2005] 2 Lloyd's Rep. 203; [2005] 2 C.L.C. 209, QBD (Comm) 2–047, *3–077*
Argo Hellas, The. *See* Adler (Richard) v Soutos (Hellas) Maritime Corp.
Argy Trading Development Co v Lapid Developments [1977] 1 W.L.R. 444; [1977] 3 All E.R. 785; [1977] 1 Lloyd's Rep. 67, QBD *1–134*, *3–004*, *3–098*, *3–103*, *3–178*, *6–085*
Aribisala v St James Homes (Grosvenor Dock) Ltd [2008] EWHC 456 (Ch); [2008] 12 E.G. 96 (C.S.); (2008) 105(14) L.S.G. 29; [2008] N.P.C. 32, Ch D *26–152*
Aries Tanker Corp v Total Transport Ltd; The Aries [1977] 1 W.L.R. 185; [1977] 1 All E.R. 398; [1977] 1 Lloyd's Rep. 334; (1977) 121 S.J. 117, HL *28–022*, *28–123*, *28–126*
Ark Therapeutics Plc v True North Capital Ltd [2005] EWHC 1585; [2006] 1 All E.R. (Comm) 138, QBD (Comm) *30–075*, *30–077*, *30–308*, *30–309*
Arkwright v Newbold (1881) L.R. 17 Ch. D. 301, CA *6–017*
Armadora Occidental SA v Horace Mann Insurance Co [1977] 1 W.L.R. 1098; [1978] 1 All E.R. 407; [1977] 2 Lloyd's Rep. 406; (1977) 121 S.J. 406, CA (Civ Div) *30–005*, *30–011*
Armagas Ltd v Mundogas SA; The Ocean Frost [1986] A.C. 717; [1986] 2 W.L.R. 1063; [1986] 2 All E.R. 385; [1986] 2 Lloyd's Rep. 109; (1986) 2 B.C.C. 99197; (1986) 83 L.S.G. 2002; (1986) 130 S.J. 430, HL; affirming [1985] 3 W.L.R. 640; [1985] 3 All E.R. 795; [1985] 1 Lloyd's Rep. 1; (1984) 81 L.S.G. 2169; (1984) 129 S.J. 362, CA (Civ Div) *9–043*
Armar Shipping Co v Caisse Algerienne d'Assurance et de Reassurance; The Armar [1981] 1 W.L.R. 207; [1981] 1 All E.R. 498; [1980] 2 Lloyd's Rep. 450, CA (Civ Div) *30–005*, *30–015*
Armfield v Allport (1857) 27 L.J.Ex. 42 ..... *12–110*
Armitage Ex p. Good, Re (1877) L.R. 5 Ch. D. 46, CA *17–017*, *17–018*
Armitage v Nurse [1998] Ch. 241; [1997] 3 W.L.R. 1046; [1997] 2 All E.R. 705; (1997) 74 P. & C.R. D13, CA (Civ Div); affirming [1995] N.P.C. 110, Ch D ... *14–136*, *28–019*
Armitage v Staveley Industries Plc [2005] EWCA Civ 792; [2005] O.P.L.R. 177; [2006] Pens. L.R. 191, CA (Civ Div); reversing [2004] EWHC 2320; [2005] O.P.L.R. 165; [2004] Pens. L.R. 385, Ch D *12–055*, *12–080*, *13–009*
Armour Hick Northern Ltd v Whitehouse; sub nom. Armour Hick Northern Ltd v Armour Trust [1980] 1 W.L.R. 1520; [1980] 3 All E.R. 833; (1980) 124 S.J. 864, Ch D *9–038*, *16–193*
Armstrong v Jackson [1917] 2 K.B. 822, KBD *6–117*, *6–127*, *6–133*, *28–135*, *28–140*
Armstrong v Sheppard & Short [1959] 2 Q.B. 384; [1959] 3 W.L.R. 84; [1959] 2 All E.R. 651; (1959) 123 J.P. 401; (1959) 103 S.J. 508, CA *3–139*, *3–151*
Armstrong v Strain [1952] 1 K.B. 232; [1952] 1 All E.R. 139; [1952] 1 T.L.R. 82, CA *6–048*, *6–071*
Armstrong & Holmes Ltd v Holmes; Armstrong & Holmes Ltd v Dodds [1993] 1 W.L.R. 1482; [1994] 1 All E.R. 826, Ch D *3–172*
Arnison v Smith (1889) L.R. 41 Ch. D. 348, CA *6–035*
Arnold v National Westminster Bank Plc (No.1) [1991] 2 A.C. 93; [1991] 2 W.L.R. 1177; [1991] 3 All E.R. 41; (1991) 62 P. & C.R. 490; [1991] 2 E.G.L.R. 109; [1991] 30 E.G. 57; [1991] E.G. 49 (C.S.); (1991) 135 S.J. 574, HL *25–011*, *25–013*, *25–014*
Arnold v Poole Corp (1842) 4 M.G. 860 ..... *21–063*
Arnott v Holden (1852) 18 Q.B. 593 ..... *28–035*
Aroso v Coutts & Co [2002] 1 All E.R. (Comm) 241; [2001] W.T.L.R. 797, Ch D *3–044*
Arpad, The (No.2) [1934] P. 189; (1934) 49 Ll. L. Rep. 313, CA *26–089*

Arrale v Costain Civil Engineer [1976] 1 Lloyd's Rep. 98; (1975) 119 S.J. 527, CA (Civ Div) *3–024*, 3–121, *3–129*, *3–136*, *7–045*, *7–139*, *12–119*, *12–126*
Art Reproduction Co Ltd, Re [1952] Ch. 89; [1951] 2 All E.R. 984; [1951] 2 T.L.R. 979; (1951) 95 S.J. 745, Ch D *28–070*
Arthur, Re; sub nom. Arthur v Wayne (1880) L.R. 14 Ch. D. 603, Ch D *23–004*
Arthur JS Hall & Co v Simons; sub nom. Harris v Scholfield Roberts & Hall; Barratt v Ansell (t/a Woolf Seddon); Barratt v Woolf Seddon; Cockbone v Atkinson Dacre & Slack; Harris v Scholfield Roberts & Hill [2002] 1 A.C. 615; [2000] 3 W.L.R. 543; [2000] 3 All E.R. 673; [2000] B.L.R. 407; [2000] E.C.C. 487; [2000] 2 F.L.R. 545; [2000] 2 F.C.R. 673; [2001] P.N.L.R. 6; [2000] Fam. Law 806; [2000] E.G. 99 (C.S.); (2000) 97(32) L.S.G. 38; (2000) 150 N.L.J. 1147; (2000) 144 S.J.L.B. 238; [2000] N.P.C. 87, HL; affirming [1999] 3 W.L.R. 873; [1999] 1 F.L.R. 536; [1999] 2 F.C.R. 193; [1999] Lloyd's Rep. P.N. 47; [1999] P.N.L.R. 374; [1999] Fam. Law 215; [1998] N.P.C. 162, CA (Civ Div); affirming [1998] 2 F.L.R. 679; [1999] P.N.L.R. 208; [1998] Fam. Law 524, QBD 1–142, *1–154*, *3–029*
Arthur White (Contractors) Ltd v Tarmac Civil Engineering Ltd; sub nom. Spalding v Tarmac Civil Engineering Ltd [1967] 1 W.L.R. 1508; [1967] 3 All E.R. 586; (1967) 111 S.J. 831, HL; reversing [1966] 1 W.L.R. 156; [1966] 1 All E.R. 209; 64 L.G.R. 111; (1965) 109 S.J. 995, CA *14–015*
Artisans' Land and Mortgage Corp, Re [1904] 1 Ch. 796, Ch D 28–004, *28–045*
Artistic Upholstery Ltd v Art Forma (Furniture) Ltd [1999] 4 All E.R. 277; [2000] F.S.R. 311; (1999) 22(12) I.P.D. 22118, Ch D *2–110*
Aruna Mills Ltd v Dhanrajmal Gobindram [1968] 1 Q.B. 655; [1968] 2 W.L.R. 101; [1968] 1 All E.R. 113; [1968] 1 Lloyd's Rep. 304; (1967) 111 S.J. 924, QBD (Comm) *26–081*
Asamera Oil Corp v Sea Oil & General Corp (1978) 89 D.L.R. (3d) 1, Sup Ct (Can) *24–010*, *26–109*
Ascherson v Tredegar Dry Dock & Wharf Co Ltd [1909] 2 Ch. 401, Ch D *27–008*
Ash & Newman v Creative Devices Research [1991] B.C.L.C. 403 .... *9–051*
Ashbourne v Department of Education and Skills; Collins v Department of Education & Skills (2007) UKEAT/0207/09, EAT *30–115*, *30–116*
Ashburn Anstalt v WJ Arnold & Co [1989] Ch. 1; [1988] 2 W.L.R. 706; [1988] 2 All E.R. 147; (1988) 55 P. & C.R. 137; (1987) 284 E.G. 1375; (1988) 132 S.J. 416, CA (Civ Div); affirming (1988) 55 P. & C.R. 13, Ch D *2–080*, *2–141*, *18–135*, *27–007*
Ashbury Railway Carriage & Iron Co Ltd v Riche; sub nom. Riche v Ashbury Railway Carriage & Iron Co Ltd (1874–75) L.R. 7 H.L. 653, HL; reversing (1873–74) L.R. 9 Ex. 224, Ex Chamber *9–005*, 9–020, *9–024*, 10–027
Ashbury v Watson (1885) L.R. 30 Ch. D. 376, CA; affirming (1885) L.R. 28 Ch. D. 56, Ch D *9–061*
Ashby v Ashby (1827) 7 B. & C. 444 .... *17–027*
Ashby v Costin (1888) L.R. 21 Q.B.D. 401, QBD *18–073*
Ashby v James (1843) 11 M. & W. 542 ....*28–129*, *29–191*
Ashby v Tolhurst [1937] 2 K.B. 242; [1937] 2 All E.R. 837, CA *14–011*, *14–036*
Ashby v White, 92 E.R. 126; (1703) 2 Ld. Raym. 938; (1703) 1 Smith L.C. 253, KB *26–008*
Ashdown v Samuel Williams & Sons Ltd [1957] 1 Q.B. 409; [1956] 3 W.L.R. 1104; [1957] 1 All E.R. 35; (1956) 100 S.J. 945, CA; reversing in part [1956] 2 Q.B. 580; [1956] 3 W.L.R. 128; [1956] 2 All E.R. 384; (1956) 100 S.J. 420, QBD *12–017*, *13–014*
Ashenden v London Brighton & South Coast Railway Co (1879–80) L.R. 5 Ex. D. 190, Exchequer Div *14–011*
Asher v Wallis (1707) 11 Mod. 146 ....*29–140*, *29–142*
Ashhurst v Mason; Ashhurst v Fowler (1875) L.R. 20 Eq. 225, Ct of Chancery *29–126*
Ashington Piggeries Ltd v Christopher Hill Ltd; Christopher Hill Ltd v Fur Farm Supplies Ltd, Norsildmel (Third Parties); sub nom. Christopher Hill Ltd v Ashington Piggeries Ltd [1972] A.C. 441; [1971] 2 W.L.R. 1051; [1971] 1 All E.R. 847; [1971] 1 Lloyd's Rep. 245; (1971) 115 S.J. 223, HL *26–058*, *26–059*
Ashmole v Wainwright (1842) 2 Q.B. 837 ....*29–088*, *29–092*

Ashmore v Corp of Lloyd's (No.2) [1992] 2 Lloyd's Rep. 620, QBD (Comm) ...*1–070*, *1–134*, *13–003*, *13–004*, *13–009*
Ashmore v Corp of Lloyd's [1992] 1 W.L.R. 446; [1992] 2 All E.R. 486; [1992] 2 Lloyd's Rep. 1; (1992) 136 S.J.L.B. 113, HL *1–134*
Ashmore & Son v CS Cox & Co [1899] 1 Q.B. 436, QBD (Comm) *14–142*
Ashmore Benson Pease & Co Ltd v AV Dawson Ltd [1973] 1 W.L.R. 828; [1973] 2 All E.R. 856; [1973] 2 Lloyd's Rep. 21; [1973] R.T.R. 473; (1973) 117 S.J. 203, CA (Civ Div) 16–010, *16–011*, *16–142*, *16–153*
Ashton v Corrigan (1871–72) L.R. 13 Eq. 76, Ct of Chancery *27–008*
Ashurst v Pollard; sub nom. Pollard v Ashurst [2001] Ch. 595; [2001] 2 W.L.R. 722; [2001] 2 All E.R. 75; [2001] B.P.I.R. 131; (2001) 98(3) L.S.G. 42; (2000) 150 N.L.J. 1787, CA (Civ Div) *30–082*
Ashwell. *See* R. v Ashwell
Askey v Golden Wine Co Ltd [1948] 2 All E.R. 35; 64 T.L.R. 379; (1948) 92 S.J. 411, KBD *16–014*, 16–173
Aspden v Seddon; Preston v Seddon (1875–76) L.R. 1 Ex. D. 496, CA *19–079*
Aspdin v Austin, 114 E.R. 1402; (1844) 5 Q.B. 671, QB *12–092*, *13–012*, *13–024*
Aspinall v Wake (1833) 10 Bing. 51 .... *20–002*
Aspinall's Club Ltd v Al-Zayat [2007] EWCA Civ 1001; [2008] Bus. L.R. D13, CA (Civ Div); reversing [2007] EWHC 362 (Comm); [2007] Bus. L.R. D92, QBD (Comm) *2–076*, *3–015*
Asset Recovery Agency v Singh [2005] EWCA Civ 580 .... *29–138*
Associated Distributors Ltd v Hall [1938] 2 K.B. 83, CA *26–136*
Associated Japanese Bank (International) Ltd v Crédit du Nord SA [1989] 1 W.L.R. 255; [1988] 3 All E.R. 902; [1989] Fin. L.R. 117; (1989) 86(8) L.S.G. 43; (1988) 138 N.L.J. Rep. 109; (1989) 133 S.J. 81, QBD *5–012*, *5–016*, *5–024*, **5–035**, *5–038*, 5–039, *5–040*, *5–053*, *5–055*, 5–058, 5–059, *5–064*, 5–065, *13–004*, *23–002*
Associated Newspapers Group Ltd v Wade [1979] 1 W.L.R. 697; [1979] I.C.R. 664; [1979] I.R.L.R. 201; (1979) 123 S.J. 250, CA (Civ Div) *16–136*
Associated Newspapers Ltd v Dingle; sub nom. Dingle v Associated Newspapers Ltd [1964] A.C. 371; [1962] 3 W.L.R. 229; [1962] 2 All E.R. 737; (1962) 106 S.J. 488, HL *26–030*
Associated Oil Carriers Ltd v Union Insurance Society of Canton Ltd [1917] 2 K.B. 184, KBD *6–147*
Associated Portland Cement Manufacturers (1900) Ltd v Houlder Bros Co Ltd (1917) 86 L.J.K.B. 1495 .... *26–040*
Associated Portland Cement Manufacturers Ltd v Teigland Shipping A/S; The Oakworth [1975] 1 Lloyd's Rep. 581; (1974) 119 S.J. 97, CA (Civ Div) ...*27–008*, *27–070*
Association of British Travel Agents Ltd v British Airways Plc [2000] 2 All E.R. (Comm) 204; [2000] 2 Lloyd's Rep. 209, CA (Civ Div); affirming [2000] 1 Lloyd's Rep. 169, QBD (Comm) *12–050*, *12–118*, *13–004*
Assunzione, The (No.1) [1954] P. 150; [1954] 2 W.L.R. 234; [1954] 1 All E.R. 278; [1953] 2 Lloyd's Rep. 716; (1954) 98 S.J. 107, CA *30–005*, *30–011*, *30–012*
Astbury v Astbury [1898] 2 Ch. 111, Ch D *28–131*
Astea (UK) Ltd v Time Group Ltd [2003] EWHC 725, QBD (TCC) .. *21–017*, *21–020*, *24–002*, *24–017*, *24–040*
Astilleros Canarios SA v Cape Hatteras Shipping Co Inc; The Cape Hatteras [1982] 1 Lloyd's Rep. 518, QBD (Comm) *3–108*, *3–109*, *22–038*
Astley v Austrust Ltd [1999] Lloyd's Rep. P.N. 758, HC (Bar) *26–049*
Astley v Gurney (1868–69) L.R. 4 C.P. 714, Ex Chamber *20–041*
Astley v Reynolds (1731) 2 Str. 915 ...*7–012*, *7–026*, *29–006*, *29–088*, 29–092, *29–150*
Astley v Weldon (1801) 2 B.P. 346 .... *26–127*
Astley Industrial Trust v Grimley [1963] 1 W.L.R. 584; [1963] 2 All E.R. 33; (1963) 107 S.J. 474, CA *12–026*, *14–020*, *14–028*, *18–006*, *24–040*

Aston Cantlow and Wilmcote with Billesley Parochial Church Council v Wallbank; sub nom. Wallbank v Aston Cantlow and Wilmcote with Billesley Parochial Church Council [2003] UKHL 37; [2004] 1 A.C. 546; [2003] 3 W.L.R. 283; [2003] 3 All E.R. 1213; [2003] H.R.L.R. 28; [2003] U.K.H.R.R. 919; [2003] 27 E.G. 137 (C.S.); (2003) 100(33) L.S.G. 28; (2003) 153 N.L.J. 1030; (2003) 147 S.J.L.B. 812; [2003] N.P.C. 80, HL; reversing [2001] EWCA Civ 713; [2002] Ch. 51; [2001] 3 W.L.R. 1323; [2001] 3 All E.R. 393; [2002] 1 P. & C.R. 5; 4 I.T.L. Rep. 353; [2002] S.T.I. 168; [2001] 21 E.G. 167 (C.S.); (2001) 98(22) L.S.G. 37; (2001) 98(25) L.S.G. 46; (2001) 145 S.J.L.B. 140, CA (Civ Div); reversing (2001) 81 P. & C.R. 14; [2000] 2 E.G.L.R. 149; (2000) 97(17) L.S.G. 32; (2000) 144 S.J.L.B. 181; [2000] N.P.C. 33, Ch D *1–050*, 1–051
Astor Chemical Ltd v Synthetic Technology Ltd [1990] B.C.C. 97; [1990] B.C.L.C. 1, Ch D *9–051*
Astor Properties Ltd v Tunbridge Wells Equitable Friendly Society [1936] 1 All E.R. 531 .... *26–099*
Astra SA Insurance and Reinsurance Co v Sphere Drake Insurance Ltd (formerly Sphere Drake Insurance Plc, Sphere Insurance Plc and Odyssey Re (London) Ltd) [2000] 2 Lloyd's Rep. 550, QBD (Comm) *30–345*
Astra Trust v Adams and Williams [1969] 1 Lloyd's Rep. 81, QBD (Comm) *2–154*
Astro Exito Navegacion SA v Southland Enterprise Co; The Messiniaki Tolmi (No.2) [1983] 2 A.C. 787; [1983] 3 W.L.R. 130; [1983] 2 All E.R. 725; [1983] Com. L.R. 217; (1983) 80 L.S.G. 3083; (1983) 127 S.J. 461, HL *27–002*, *27–013*
Astro Venturoso Compania Naviera v Hellenic Shipyards SA; The Mariannina [1983] 1 Lloyd's Rep. 12, CA (Civ Div) *30–005*, *30–010*, *30–305*
Asty Maritime Co Ltd v Rocco Guiseppe & Figli SNC; The Astyanax [1985] 2 Lloyd's Rep. 109, CA (Civ Div); reversing [1984] 2 Lloyd's Rep. 459, QBD (Comm) *2–029*
Aswan Engineering Establishment Co v Lupdine Ltd. *See* M/S Aswan Engineering Establishment Co v Lupdine Ltd
Ateni Maritime Corp v Great Marine Ltd; The Great Marine (No.2) [1991] 1 Lloyd's Rep. 421, CA (Civ Div); reversing [1990] 2 Lloyd's Rep. 250, QBD (Comm) *2–116*
Athlumney Ex p. Wilson, Re [1898] 2 Q.B. 547, QBD *16–161*
Atkin v Acton (1830) 4 C.P. 208 .... *21–085*
Atkins v Hill (1775) 1 Cowp. 284 .... *3–032*
Atkinson v Denby (1862) 7 H. & N. 934 .... *7–049*, 16–186
Atkinson v Hawdon (1835) 2 A.E. 628 .... *21–081*
Atkinson v Ritchie (1809) 10 East 530 .... *23–004*, *23–005*
Atkyns v Kinnier (1850) 4 Exch. 776 .... *16–113*
Atlantic and Pacific Fibre Importing and Manufacturing Co Ltd, Re; sub nom. Viscount Burnham v Atlantic and Pacific Fibre Importing and Manufacturing Co Ltd [1928] Ch. 836, Ch D *28–101*
Atlantic Computer Systems Plc, Re [1992] Ch. 505; [1992] 2 W.L.R. 367; [1992] 1 All E.R. 476; [1990] B.C.C. 859; [1991] B.C.L.C. 606, CA (Civ Div); reversing [1990] B.C.C. 439; [1990] B.C.L.C. 729, Ch D (Companies Ct) *9–050*
Atlantic Lines & Navigation Co Inc v Hallam Ltd; The Lucy [1983] 1 Lloyd's Rep. 188, QBD (Comm) 6–098, *6–102*, *6–111*, *6–116*, *6–119*, *12–103*
Atlantic Marine Transport Corp v Coscol Petroleum Corp; The Pina [1992] 2 Lloyd's Rep. 103, CA (Civ Div); affirming [1991] 1 Lloyd's Rep. 246, QBD (Comm) *2–116*, *5–122*, *12–030*
Atlantic Maritime Co Inc v Gibbon [1954] 1 Q.B. 88; [1953] 3 W.L.R. 714; [1953] 2 All E.R. 1086; [1953] 2 Lloyd's Rep. 294; (1953) 97 S.J. 760, CA *23–040*
Atlantic Paper Stock Ltd v St Anne Nackawic Pulp and Paper Co Ltd (1975) 56 D.L.R. (3d) 409 .... *14–148*
Atlantic Scout, The. *See* Société Dunkerquoise de Remorquage et de Sauvetage v Owners of Atlantic Scout.

Atlantic Shipping & Trading Co Ltd v Louis Dreyfus & Co; The Quantock; sub nom. Louis Dreyfus & Co v Atlantic Shipping & Trading Co Ltd [1922] 2 A.C. 250; (1922) 10 Ll. L. Rep. 707, HL; affirming (1921) 6 Ll. L. Rep. 194, CA; reversing (1920) 4 Ll. L. Rep. 424, KBD *3–078*, *14–004*, *14–032*, *16–045*, *28–112*
Atlantic Telecom GmbH, Noter, 2004 S.L.T. 1031; 2004 G.W.D. 30–623, OH *30–020*, *30–031*, *30–041*, *30–077*
Atlas Express Ltd v Kafco (Importers and Distributors) Ltd [1989] Q.B. 833; [1989] 3 W.L.R. 389; [1989] 1 All E.R. 641; (1990) 9 Tr. L.R. 56; (1989) 139 N.L.J. 111; (1989) 133 S.J. 977, QBD (Comm) *3–066*, *3–067*, *7–018*, 7–042, *29–088*
Atlas Shipping Agency (UK) Ltd v Suisse Atlantique Societe d'Armement Maritime SA; The Gulf Grain and The El Amaan [1995] 2 Lloyd's Rep. 188; [1995] C.L.C. 633; [1995] I.L.Pr. 600, QBD (Comm) *18–078*, *18–083*, *30–031*, *30–350*
Atlee v Backhouse, 150 E.R. 1298; (1838) 3 M. & W. 633, Ex Ct *7–012*, *29–088*, *29–092*, *29–094*, *29–189*
Attfield v DJ Plant Hire & General Contractors Co Ltd [1987] Ch. 141; [1986] 3 W.L.R. 432; [1986] 3 All E.R. 273; (1986) 83 L.S.G. 2922; (1986) 130 S.J. 633, Ch D *27–007*
Attica Sea Carriers Corp v Ferrostaal Poseidon Bulk Reederei GmbH, The Puerto Buitrago [1976] 1 Lloyd's Rep. 250, CA (Civ Div) *13–007*, *24–010*, *26–122*, *26–123*, *26–124*
Attika Hope, The. *See* G&N Angelakis Shipping Co SA v Compagnie National Algerienne de Navigation.
Attock Cement Co Ltd v Romanian Bank for Foreign Trade [1989] 1 W.L.R. 1147; [1989] 1 All E.R. 1189; [1989] 1 Lloyd's Rep. 572; (1989) 86(39) L.S.G. 36; (1989) 133 S.J. 1298, CA (Civ Div) *30–011*, *30–012*
Attorney General v Barker (Worldwide Injunction) [1990] 3 All E.R. 257, CA (Civ Div) *1–066*, *27–060*, *27–061*
Attorney General v Blake [2001] 1 A.C. 268; [2000] 3 W.L.R. 625; [2000] 4 All E.R. 385; [2000] 2 All E.R. (Comm) 487; [2001] I.R.L.R. 36; [2001] Emp. L.R. 329; [2000] E.M.L.R. 949; (2000) 23(12) I.P.D. 23098; (2000) 97(32) L.S.G. 37; (2000) 150 N.L.J. 1230; (2000) 144 S.J.L.B. 242, HL; affirming [1998] Ch. 439; [1998] 2 W.L.R. 805; [1998] 1 All E.R. 833; [1998] E.M.L.R. 309; (1998) 95(4) L.S.G. 33; (1998) 148 N.L.J. 15; (1998) 142 S.J.L.B. 35, CA (Civ Div); reversing [1997] Ch. 84; [1996] 3 W.L.R. 741; [1996] 3 All E.R. 903; [1996] E.M.L.R. 382; [1996] F.S.R. 727; (1996) 19(7) I.P.D. 19066, Ch D .. *1–019*, *1–123*, *2–136*, 6–062, 26–001, 26–003, 26–020, 26–021, 26–023, **26–024**, 26–025, 26–026, *26–027*, 26–028, *26–029*, *26–084*, *27–079*, *27–080*, *29–152*, **29–153**
Attorney General v Brown [1921] 3 K.B. 29; (1921) 7 Ll. L. Rep. 210, CA; reversing [1920] 1 K.B. 773; (1919–20) 1 Ll. L. Rep. 641, KBD *12–087*
Attorney General v Canter [1939] 1 K.B. 318, CA; affirming in part [1938] 2 K.B. 826, KBD *1–118*
Attorney General v Cocke [1988] Ch. 414; [1988] 2 W.L.R. 542; [1988] 2 All E.R. 391; (1988) 85(14) L.S.G. 46; (1988) 132 S.J. 418, Ch D *28–002*
Attorney General v Crayford Urban DC [1962] Ch. 575; [1962] 2 W.L.R. 998; [1962] 2 All E.R. 147; [1962] 1 Lloyd's Rep. 163; (1962) 126 J.P. 308; 60 L.G.R. 261; (1962) 106 S.J. 175, CA; affirming [1962] Ch. 246; [1961] 3 W.L.R. 1198; [1961] 3 All E.R. 1002; [1961] 2 Lloyd's Rep. 267; (1962) 126 J.P. 24; 59 L.G.R. 576; (1961) 105 S.J. 968, Ch D *9–020*
Attorney General v Ewelme Hospital (1853) 17 Beav. 366 .... *12–086*
Attorney General v Fulham Corp [1921] 1 Ch. 440, Ch D *10–025*
Attorney General v Goddard (1929) 45 T.L.R. 609 .... *29–156*
Attorney General v Great Eastern Railway Co (1879–80) L.R. 5 App. Cas. 473, HL; affirming (1879) L.R. 11 Ch. D. 449, CA *9–020*, *9–022*, 10–023, 10–027
Attorney General v Great Southern & Western Railway Co; sub nom. Great Southern & Western Railway Co of Ireland [1924] 2 K.B. 450, CA; reversing [1924] 1 K.B. 154, KBD 10–006

Attorney General v London CC. *See* London CC v Attorney General
Attorney General v Manchester Corp [1906] 1 Ch. 643, Ch D *9–004*, *10–021*, 10–025, *10–026*
Attorney General v Mersey Railway Co [1907] A.C. 415, HL; reversing [1907] 1 Ch. 81, CA; reversing [1906] 1 Ch. 811, Ch D *9–020*, *9–021*, *10–025*
Attorney General v Nissan; sub nom. Nissan v Attorney General [1970] A.C. 179; [1969] 2 W.L.R. 926; [1969] 1 All E.R. 629; (1969) 113 S.J. 207, HL; affirming [1968] 1 Q.B. 286; [1967] 3 W.L.R. 1044; [1967] 2 All E.R. 1238; (1967) 111 S.J. 544, CA (Civ Div); reversing in part [1967] 3 W.L.R. 109; [1967] 2 All E.R. 200; (1967) 111 S.J. 195, QBD *11–007*, *29–008*, *29–011*, *29–144*
Attorney General v Observer Ltd; Attorney General v Times Newspapers Ltd (No.2); Attorney General v Guardian Newspapers Ltd (No.2) [1990] 1 A.C. 109; [1988] 3 W.L.R. 776; [1988] 3 All E.R. 545; [1989] 2 F.S.R. 181; (1988) 85(42) L.S.G. 45; (1988) 138 N.L.J. Rep. 296; (1988) 132 S.J. 1496, HL; affirming [1988] 2 W.L.R. 805; (1988) 138 N.L.J. Rep. 47; (1988) 132 S.J. 566, CA (Civ Div); affirming, *The Times*, December 22, 1987, Ch D *1–066*, *16–035*, *29–145*, *29–155*, *29–160*
Attorney General v Odell [1906] 2 Ch. 47, CA *29–120*
Attorney General v Parker (1747) 3 Atk. 576 .... *12–126*
Attorney General v Plymouth Corp (1845) 9 Beav. 67 .... *10–030*
Attorney General v Smethwick Corp [1932] 1 Ch. 562, CA *10–025*
Attorney General v Tomline (No.2) (1877–78) L.R. 7 Ch. D. 388, Ch D *5–062*
Attorney General v Wilts United Dairies Ltd (1922) 38 T.L.R. 781, HL; affirming (1921) 37 T.L.R. 884, CA *10–023*, *29–083*, *29–084*
Attorney General for England and Wales v R. *See* R v Attorney General of England and Wales.
Attorney General of Australia v Adelaide Steamship [1913] A.C. 781, PC (Aus) ...*16–093*, *16–095*, *16–134*
Attorney General of Canada v Standard Trust Co of New York [1911] A.C. 498, PC (Can) *9–054*
Attorney General of Ceylon v Silva (AD) [1953] A.C. 461; [1953] 2 W.L.R. 1185; [1953] 1 Lloyd's Rep. 563; (1953) 97 S.J. 384, PC (Cey) ...*10–009*, 10–012
Attorney General of Ghana v Texaco Overseas Tankships Ltd; The Texaco Melbourne [1994] 1 Lloyd's Rep. 473; [1994] C.L.C. 155, HL *30–373*
Attorney General of Hong Kong v Humphreys Estate (Queen's Gardens) Ltd [1987] A.C. 114; [1987] 2 W.L.R. 343; [1987] 2 All E.R. 387; (1987) 54 P. & C.R. 96; (1987) 84 L.S.G. 574; (1987) 131 S.J. 194, PC (HK) *2–120*, *3–106*, *3–138*, *3–144*, *3–145*, *3–147*, *28–136*
Attorney General of Hong Kong v Reid [1994] 1 A.C. 324; [1993] 3 W.L.R. 1143; [1994] 1 All E.R. 1; (1993) 143 N.L.J. 1569; (1993) 137 S.J.L.B. 251; [1993] N.P.C. 144, PC (NZ) *29–156*, *29–160*
Attorney General of New Brunswick v St John [1948] 3 D.L.R. 693, Sup Ct (NB) *9–004*
Attorney General of New South Wales v Perpetual Trustee Co [1955] A.C. 457; [1955] 2 W.L.R. 707; [1955] 1 All E.R. 846; (1955) 99 S.J. 233, PC (Aus) *29–101*
Attorney General of New Zealand v Ortiz [1984] A.C. 1; [1983] 2 W.L.R. 809; [1983] 2 All E.R. 93; [1983] 2 Lloyd's Rep. 265; (1983) 133 N.L.J. 537; (1983) 127 S.J. 307, HL; affirming [1982] 3 W.L.R. 570; [1982] 3 All E.R. 432; [1982] 2 Lloyd's Rep. 224; [1982] Com. L.R. 156; (1982) 79 L.S.G. 919; (1982) 126 S.J. 429, CA (Civ Div); reversing [1982] Q.B. 349; [1982] 2 W.L.R. 10; [1982] 1 Lloyd's Rep. 173; (1981) 125 S.J. 530, QBD (Comm) *16–029*, *16–031*, *16–031*
Attorney General's Reference No.1 of 1987 (1987) 47 S.A.S.R. 152 .... *30–068*
Attwood v Emery (1856) 1 C.B.(N.S.) 11 .... *21–021*
Attwood v Lamont [1920] 3 K.B. 571, CA; reversing [1920] 2 K.B. 146, KBD *16–095*, *16–104*, *16–105*, *16–106*, *16–110*, *16–116*, *16–198*, *16–203*
Attwood v Small (1838) 6 Cl. & F. 232 ....*6–032*, *6–033*, *6–097*
Auckland Corp v Alliance Assurance Co Ltd. *See* Mayor of Auckland v Alliance Assurance Co Ltd

Auckland Harbour Board v King, The [1924] A.C. 318, PC (NZ); affirming [1919] N.Z.L.R. 419, Sup Ct (NZ) *10–006*, *29–043*, *29–083*
Auerbach v Nelson [1919] 2 Ch. 383, Ch D *4–010*, *4–029*, *12–123*
August Leonhard, The. *See* K Lokumal & Sons (London) Ltd v Lotte Shipping Co Pte Ltd.
Auriena Ltd v Haigh and Ringrose Ltd (1988) Const. L.J. 200 .... *22–022*
Austin v Great Western Railway; sub nom. Austin v Great Western Railway Co (1866–67) L.R. 2 Q.B. 442, QB *18–022*
Austin v Manchester Sheffield & Lincolnshire Railway Co (1852) 10 C.B. 454 ... *14–011*
Austin v Mills (1853) 9 Exch. 288 .... *25–010*
Austin v Zurich General Accident & Liability Insurance Co Ltd [1945] K.B. 250; (1945) 78 Ll. L. Rep. 185, CA; affirming [1944] 2 All E.R. 243; (1944) 77 Ll. L. Rep. 409, KBD *18–127*
Austin Hall Building Ltd v Buckland Securities Ltd [2001] B.L.R. 272; (2001) 3 T.C.L.R. 18; 80 Con. L.R. 115; (2001) 17 Const. L.J. 325; [2001] 25 E.G. 155 (C.S.), QBD (TCC) *1–049*
Austin Knight (UK) Ltd v Hinds [1994] F.S.R. 52, Ch D *16–111*
Australia & New Zealand Banking Group v Westpac Banking Corp, 164 C.L.R. 662, HC (Aus) *29–032*, *29–033*, *29–182*
Australia and New Zealand Banking Group Ltd v Compagnie Noga d'Importation et d'Exportation SA [2007] EWHC 293 (Comm); [2007] 1 Lloyd's Rep. 487, QBD (Comm) *16–039*
Australian Blue Metal v Hughes [1963] A.C. 74; [1962] 3 W.L.R. 802; [1962] 3 All E.R. 335; (1962) 106 S.J. 628, PC (Aus) *13–027*, *13–028*
Australian Consolidated Press Ltd v Uren (Thomas) [1969] 1 A.C. 590; [1967] 3 W.L.R. 1338; [1967] 3 All E.R. 523; (1967) 111 S.J. 741, PC (Aus) *26–019*
Australian Joint Stock Bank Ltd v Bailey [1899] A.C. 396, PC (Aus) *12–066*
Australian Woollen Mills Pty v The Commonwealth (1954) 92 C.L.R. 424 ...... *3–060*
Australian Workers Union v Bowen (1948) 77 C.L.R. 601 .... *9–083*
Automatic Tube Co Pty Ltd v Adelaide Steamship (Operations) Ltd; The Beltana [1967] 1 Lloyd's Rep. 531; 117 N.L.J. 914, Sup Ct (WA) (Sgl judge) 28–022
Automobile Carriage Builders Ltd v Sayers (1909) 101 L.T. 419 .... *16–099*, *16–114*
Auty v Hutchinson (1848) 6 C.B. 266 .... *10–013*
Aveline v Whisson (1842) 4 Man. & G. 801 .... *4–040*
Avery v Bowden (1855) 5 E.B. 714 .... *24–001*, *24–011*, 24–024
Avimex SA v Dewulf & Cie [1979] 2 Lloyd's Rep. 57, QBD (Comm) ... *3–090*, *3–091*, *14–140*, *14–141*, *14–144*, *14–148*, *14–151*, *22–044*, *22–052*, *24–006*, *24–008*
Avintair v Avill, 1995 S.C.L.R. 1012, OH *2–112*
Avon CC v Howlett [1983] 1 W.L.R. 605; [1983] 1 All E.R. 1073; [1983] I.R.L.R. 171; 81 L.G.R. 555; (1983) 133 N.L.J. 377; (1983) 127 S.J. 173, CA (Civ Div) *6–015*, *29–036*, *29–176*, *29–177*, 29–178, *29–181*, *29–185*, *29–188*
Avon Finance Co v Bridger [1985] 2 All E.R. 281; (1979) 123 S.J. 705, CA (Civ Div) *7–074*, *7–112*
Avon Insurance Plc v Swire Fraser Ltd [2000] 1 All E.R. (Comm) 573; [2000] C.L.C. 665; [2000] Lloyd's Rep. I.R. 535, QBD (Comm) *6–001*, 6–020, *6–037*, *6–070*
Avraamides v Colwill [2006] EWCA Civ 1533; [2007] B.L.R. 76; (2006) 103(46) L.S.G. 31; [2006] N.P.C. 120, CA (Civ Div) *18–091*
Awilco of Oslo A/S v Fulvia SpA di Navigazione of Cagliari; The Chikuma [1981] 1 W.L.R. 314; [1981] 1 All E.R. 652; [1981] 1 Lloyd's Rep. 371; [1981] Com. L.R. 64; (1981) 125 S.J. 184, HL; reversing [1980] 2 Lloyd's Rep. 409, CA (Civ Div); reversing [1979] 1 Lloyd's Rep. 367, QBD (Comm) *7–126*, *12–034*, *12–037*, *21–045*
Awwad v Geraghty & Co; sub nom. Geraghty & Co v Awwad [2001] Q.B. 570; [2000] 3 W.L.R. 1041; [2000] 1 All E.R. 608; [2000] 1 Costs L.R. 105; [1999] N.P.C. 148, CA (Civ Div) *16–049*, *16–054*, 16–055
Axel Johnson Petroleum AB v MG Mineral Group [1992] 1 W.L.R. 270; [1992] 2 All E.R. 163; (1991) 135 S.J.L.B. 60, CA (Civ Div) *28–123*
Axiom Business Computers Ltd v Kenny, unreported, November 20, 2003, OH ... *16–106*

Ayala Holdings, Re [1993] B.C.L.C. 256, Ch D *20–031*
Ayerst v Jenkins (1873) L.R. 16 Eq. 275, Lord Chancellor *16–067*, *16–167*
Aylesbury Football Club (1997) Ltd v Watford Association Football Club Ltd, unreported, 2000, QBD *8–022*
Aylesford (Earl of) v Morris (1872–73) L.R. 8 Ch. App. 484, CA in Chancery ...*7–128*, *7–135*
Aylmer, Re; Ex p. Aylmer (1894) 70 L.T. 244[10] R. 473 .... *20–048*
Ayr Harbour Trustees v Oswald (1882–83) L.R. 8 App. Cas. 623, HL *10–028*, 10–029
Ayres v South Australian Banking Corp (1871) L.R. 3 P.C. 548 .... *9–026*
Azemar v Casella (1866–67) L.R. 2 C.P. 677, Ex Chamber; affirming (1866–67) L.R. 2 C.P. 431, CCP *14–027*
Aziz v Aziz [2007] EWCA Civ 712; [2008] 2 All E.R. 501; [2007] Fam. Law 1047, CA (Civ Div) *11–003*, *11–008*
Aziz v Yemen; sub nom. Yemen v Aziz [2005] EWCA Civ 745; [2005] I.C.R. 1391, CA (Civ Div) *11–004*, *11–005*, *11–021*
Azov Shipping Co v Baltic Shipping Co (No.3) [1999] 2 All E.R. (Comm) 453; [1999] 2 Lloyd's Rep. 159; [1999] C.L.C. 1425, QBD (Comm) *2–110*, *3–090*, *3–098*, *3–100*, *3–113*, *11–007*, *30–325*
B (A Child) (Care Proceedings: Diplomatic Immunity), Re [2002] EWHC 1751; [2003] Fam. 16; [2003] 2 W.L.R. 168; [2003] 1 F.L.R. 241; [2003] Fam. Law 8; (2002) 99(41) L.S.G. 27, Fam Div *11–005*, *11–013*
B (Minors) (Care Proceedings: Issue Estoppel), Re; sub nom. B (Minors) (Care Proceedings: Evidence), Re; B (Minors: Issue Estoppel), Re; B (Children Act Proceedings: Issue Estoppel), Re [1997] Fam. 117; [1997] 3 W.L.R. 1; [1997] 2 All E.R. 29; [1997] 1 F.L.R. 285; [1997] 1 F.C.R. 477; [1997] Fam. Law 235; (1997) 161 J.P.N. 358; (1996) 93(44) L.S.G. 30; (1996) 140 S.J.L.B. 252, Fam Div *25–011*
B&B Viennese Fashions v Losane [1952] 1 All E.R. 909; [1952] 1 T.L.R. 750, CA *16–153*
B&S Contracts and Design v Victor Green Publications [1984] I.C.R. 419; (1984) 81 L.S.G. 893; (1984) 128 S.J. 279, CA (Civ Div); affirming [1982] I.C.R. 654, QBD *3–067*, *3–074*, *7–005*, 7–018, *7–031*, *7–040*, *7–041*, *14–138*, *14–140*, *14–146*, *14–148*, *29–088*
BBC v Johns [1965] Ch. 32; [1964] 2 W.L.R. 1071; [1964] 1 All E.R. 923; [1964] R.V.R. 579; 10 R.R.C. 239; 41 T.C. 471; (1964) 43 A.T.C. 38; [1964] T.R. 45; (1964) 108 S.J. 217, CA; reversing [1963] R.A. 337; [1963] R.V.R. 695; 10 R.R.C. 164; (1963) 42 A.T.C. 341; [1963] T.R. 369, Ch D *10–010*, *10–018*
B Liggett (Liverpool) Ltd v Barclays Bank Ltd [1928] 1 K.B. 48, KBD *9–025*, *9–041*, *29–115*
B Sunley & Co Ltd v Cunard White Star Ltd; sub nom. Sunley & Co Ltd v Cunard White Star Line Ltd [1940] 1 K.B. 740; (1940) 66 Ll. L. Rep. 134, CA *26–006*, *26–070*
BC Checo International Ltd v British Colombia Hydro & Power Authority (1993) 99 D.L.R. (4th) 477 .... *1–126*
BC Sawmills v Nettleship (1868) L.R. 3 C.P. 499 .... *26–006*
BCCI SA, Re. *See* Malik v Bank of Credit and Commerce International SA (In Liquidation)
BCT Software Solutions Ltd v Arnold Laver & Co Ltd [2002] EWHC 1298; [2002] 2 All E.R. (Comm) 85; [2002] Masons C.L.R. 53, Ch D *12–079*
BDG Roof Bond Ltd (In Liquidation) v Douglas [2000] B.C.C. 770; [2000] 1 B.C.L.C. 401; [2000] Lloyd's Rep. P.N. 273; [2000] P.N.L.R. 397, Ch D *1–184*
BG Transport Services Ltd v Marston Motor Co Ltd [1970] 1 Lloyd's Rep. 371, QBD *14–036*
BHP Petroleum Ltd v British Steel Plc [2000] 2 All E.R. (Comm) 133; [2000] 2 Lloyd's Rep. 277; [2000] C.L.C. 1162; 74 Con. L.R. 63, CA (Civ Div); affirming [1999] 2 All E.R. (Comm) 544; [1999] 2 Lloyd's Rep. 583, QBD (Comm) *14–006*, *14–010*, *14–011*, *14–062*

BICC Plc v Burndy Corp [1985] Ch. 232; [1985] 2 W.L.R. 132; [1985] 1 All E.R. 417; [1985] R.P.C. 273; (1984) 81 L.S.G. 3011; (1984) 128 S.J. 750, CA (Civ Div) *3–104*, *21–038*, *22–047*, *26–148*
BP Exploration Co (Libya) Ltd v Hunt (No.2) [1983] 2 A.C. 352; [1982] 2 W.L.R. 253; [1982] 1 All E.R. 925, HL; affirming [1981] 1 W.L.R. 232; (1981) 125 S.J. 165, CA (Civ Div); affirming [1979] 1 W.L.R. 783; (1979) 123 S.J. 455, QBD *3–086*, *3–090*, *3–103*, *23–021*, *23–071*, *23–074*, *23–074*, 23–075, *23–077*, *23–078*, *23–079*, 23–081, 23–084, *23–085*, 23–086, *23–087*, 23–088, *23–089*, *23–090*, *23–092*, *24–004*, *24–006*, *24–014*, *24–046*, *26–174*, *26–176*, *29–011*, *29–014*, *29–021*, *29–053*, *29–059*, *29–060*, *29–069*, *29–182*, *30–373*, *30–376*
BP Exploration Operating Co Ltd v Chevron Shipping Co; sub nom. BP Exploration Operating Co Ltd v Chevron Transport (Scotland); BP Exploration Operating Co Ltd v Chevron Tankers (Bermuda) Ltd; BP Exploration Operating Co Ltd v Chevron Transport Corp [2001] UKHL 50; [2003] 1 A.C. 197; [2001] 3 W.L.R. 949; [2002] 1 All E.R. (Comm) 1; [2002] 1 Lloyd's Rep. 77; 2001 S.C. (H.L.) 19; 2001 S.L.T. 1394; 2001 S.C.L.R. 1029; (2001) 98(45) L.S.G. 26; (2001) 145 S.J.L.B. 244; 2001 G.W.D. 33–1316, HL; reversing, 2000 S.L.T. 1374; 2000 S.C.L.R. 580; 2000 G.W.D. 14–559, IH (1 Div); reversing in part, 2000 S.L.T. 201; 1999 S.C.L.R. 438; 1999 G.W.D. 7–355, OH *18–146*
BP Exploration Operating Co Ltd v Kvaerner Oilfield Products Ltd [2004] EWHC 999; [2004] 2 All E.R. (Comm) 266; [2005] 1 Lloyd's Rep. 307, QBD (Comm) *12–050*, *12–051*, *12–055*, *12–080*
BP Plc v AON Ltd (No.2) [2006] EWHC 424 (Comm); [2006] 1 All E.R. (Comm) 789; [2006] 1 C.L.C. 881; [2006] Lloyd's Rep. I.R. 577; (2006) 103(14) L.S.G. 31, QBD (Comm) *1–184*, *18–031*
BP Refinery (Westenport) Pty Ltd v Shire of Hastings, 80 C.L.R. 266; (1978) 52 A.L.J.R. 20 .... *13–004*, *13–009*
BRS v Arthur v Crutchley. *See* British Road Services Ltd v Arthur V Crutchley & Co Ltd (No.1)
BS&N Ltd (BVI) v Micado Shipping Ltd (Malta); The Seaflower (No.1) [2001] 1 All E.R. (Comm) 240; [2001] 1 Lloyd's Rep. 341; [2001] C.L.C. 421, CA (Civ Div); reversing [2000] C.L.C. 795, QBD (Comm) *12–037*, *12–040*, *21–013*
BS&N Ltd (BVI) v Micado Shipping Ltd (Malta); The Seaflower (No.2) [2000] 2 All E.R. (Comm) 169; [2000] 2 Lloyd's Rep. 37; [2000] C.L.C. 802, QBD (Comm) *2–155*
BSC v Cleveland Bridge. *See* British Steel Corp v Cleveland Bridge & Engineering Co.
BV Oliehandel Jongkind v Coastal International Ltd [1983] 2 Lloyd's Rep. 463, QBD (Comm) *2–154*, *24–012*, *24–018*
Babanaft International Co SA v Avanti Petroleum Inc; The Oltenia; sub nom. Babanaft International Co SA v Avant Petroleum Inc [1982] 1 W.L.R. 871; [1982] 3 All E.R. 244; [1982] 2 Lloyd's Rep. 99; [1982] Com. L.R. 104; [1983] E.C.C. 365; (1982) 79 L.S.G. 953; (1982) 126 S.J. 361, CA (Civ Div) *28–112*
Babcock v Lawson (1879–80) L.R. 5 Q.B.D. 284, CA; affirming (1878–79) L.R. 4 Q.B.D. 394, QBD *6–129*
Baber v Kenwood Manufacturing Co [1978] 1 Lloyd's Rep. 175; (1977) 121 S.J. 606, CA (Civ Div) *2–131*
Bacal Contracting Ltd v Modern Engineering (Bristol) Ltd [1980] 2 All E.R. 655, QBD *9–051*
Bacardi-Martini Beverages Ltd v Thomas Hardy Packaging Ltd; sub nom. Messer UK Ltd v Bacardi-Martini Beverages Ltd; Messer UK Ltd v Thomas Hardy Packaging Ltd [2002] EWCA Civ 549; [2002] 2 All E.R. (Comm) 335; [2002] 2 Lloyd's Rep. 379, CA (Civ Div); affirming [2002] 1 Lloyd's Rep. 62, QBD (Comm) *6–139*, 14–094, *14–096*, *14–100*, *14–103*
Baccus Srl v Servicio Nacional del Trigo [1957] 1 Q.B. 438; [1956] 3 W.L.R. 948; [1956] 3 All E.R. 715; [1956] 2 Lloyd's Rep. 448; (1956) 100 S.J. 872, CA *11–001*, *11–020*

Backhouse v Backhouse; sub nom. B v B [1978] 1 W.L.R. 243; [1978] 1 All E.R. 1158; (1977) 7 Fam. Law 212; (1977) 121 S.J. 710, Fam Div *7–085*, *7–128*, *7–130*
Bacon v Cooper (Metals) Ltd [1982] 1 All E.R. 397, QBD *26–078*, 26–107, *26–116*, *26–169*
Badeley v Consolidated Bank (1888) L.R. 38 Ch. D. 238, CA; affirming (1887) L.R. 34 Ch. D. 536, Ch D *17–015*
Baden v Société Générale pour Favoriser le Developpement du Commerce et de l'Industrie en France SA [1993] 1 W.L.R. 509; [1992] 4 All E.R. 161, Ch D 5–116
Badgerhill Properties Ltd v Cottrell [1991] B.C.C. 463; [1991] B.C.L.C. 805; 54 B.L.R. 23, CA (Civ Div) *9–012*
Badische Co Ltd, Re; Bayer Co Ltd, Re; Griesheim Elektron Ltd, Re; Kalle & Co Ltd, Re; Berlin Aniline Co Ltd, Re; Meister Lucius & Bruning Ltd, Re [1921] 2 Ch. 331; (1921) 9 Ll. L. Rep. 20, Ch D *23–030*, *23–047*
Bagge v Slade (1616) 3 Bulst. 162 .... *3–115*
Baglehole v Walter (1811) 3 Camp. 154 .... *6–016*
Bagley v Winsome and National Provincial Bank Ltd [1952] 2 Q.B. 236 .... *21–010*
Bagley and Shoesmith's Contract (1918) 87 L.J. Ch. 626 .... *21–014*
Bagot v Chapman [1907] 2 Ch. 222, Ch D *5–103*
Bagot v Stevens Scanlan & Co Ltd [1966] 1 Q.B. 197; [1964] 3 W.L.R. 1162; [1964] 3 All E.R. 577; [1964] 2 Lloyd's Rep. 353; 2 B.L.R. 67; (1964) 108 S.J. 604, QBD *1–124*, *28–033*, 28–053
Bagot Pneumatic Tyre Co v Clipper Pneumatic Tyre Co [1902] 1 Ch. 146, CA; affirming [1901] 1 Ch. 196, Ch D *9–014*
Bagueley v Hawley (1867) L.R. 2 C.P. 625 .... *14–026*
Bahamas Oil Refining Co v Kristiansands Tank Rederie; The Polyduke [1978] 1 Lloyd's Rep. 211, QBD (Comm) *2–159*, *12–002*
Bahamas Sisal Plantation v Griffin (1897) 14 T.L.R. 139 .... *26–099*
Bahia and San Francisco Railway Co Ltd, Re (1867–68) L.R. 3 Q.B. 584, QB *6–095*
Bahin v Hughes (1886) L.R. 31 Ch. D. 390, CA *29–125*
Bailey v Bowen (1867–68) L.R. 3 Q.B. 133, QB *22–006*
Bailey v Bullock [1950] 2 All E.R. 1167; 66 T.L.R. (Pt. 2) 791; [1950] W.N. 482; (1950) 94 S.J. 689, KBD *26–082*, *26–083*
Bailey v Finch (1871–72) L.R. 7 Q.B. 34; (1871) 41 L.J. Q.B. 83, QB *20–041*, *20–044*
Bailey v Haines (1849) 13 Q.B. 815 .... *29–116*
Bailey v HSS Alarms Ltd, *The Times*, June 20, 2000, CA (Civ Div) *18–022*
Bailey v Sweeting (1861) 9 C.B. (N.S.) 843 .... *4–027*
Bailey v Thurston & Co Ltd [1903] 1 K.B. 137, CA; affirming [1902] 2 K.B. 397, KBD *20–026*, *20–034*, *20–055*
Bailey Hay & Co, Re [1971] 1 W.L.R. 1357; [1971] 3 All E.R. 693; (1971) 115 S.J. 639, Ch D *9–039*
Bailey Sons & Co v Ross, Smythe & Co. *See* Ross T Smyth & Co Ltd v TD Bailey & Co.
Baillie v Kell (1838) 4 Bing N.C. 638 .... *24–014*
Baily v De Crespigny (1868–69) L.R. 4 Q.B. 180, QB 23–022
Bain v Field & Co Fruit Merchants Ltd (1920) 5 Ll. L. Rep. 16, CA *30–373*
Bain v Fothergill; Paterson v Hankey (1874–75) L.R. 7 H.L. 158, HL; affirming (1870–71) L.R. 6 Ex. 59, Ex Chamber *6–052*, *21–018*, 26–091
Bainbridge v Smith (1889) L.R. 41 Ch. D. 462, CA *27–021*
Bainbrigge v Browne (1880–81) L.R. 18 Ch. D. 188, Ch D *7–074*
Bainbrigge v Firmstone (1838) 8 A. & E.743 .... *3–004*, *3–016*, 3–177
Bainbrigge v Pickering (1780) 2 W.Bl. 1325 .... *8–008*
Baindail v Baindail [1946] P. 122, CA *30–324*
Baines & Ernst Ltd v Customs and Excise Commissioners; sub nom. Baines & Ernst Ltd v Revenue and Customs Commissioners [2006] EWCA Civ 1040; [2006] S.T.C. 1632; [2006] B.T.C. 5649; [2006] B.V.C. 719; [2006] S.T.I. 1987, CA (Civ Div) *29–086*
Baird v Wells (1890) L.R. 44 Ch. D. 661, Ch D 9–074, *9–080*, *16–108*, *16–198*

Baird Textile Holdings Ltd v Marks & Spencer Plc; sub nom. Baird Textiles Holdings Ltd v Marks & Spencer Plc [2001] EWCA Civ 274; [2002] 1 All E.R. (Comm) 737; [2001] C.L.C. 999, CA (Civ Div); affirming, 2000 Folio No. 22, QBD (Comm) *2–136*, *2–142*, *2–158*, *2–160*, *2–161*, 2–164, *2–183*, *3–088*, *3–090*, *3–098*, *3–099*, *3–100*, *3–101*, *3–103*, *3–107*, *3–113*, *3–129*, *3–146*, *28–136*
Bairstow Eves London Central Ltd v Smith [2004] EWHC 263 (QB); [2004] 2 E.G.L.R. 25; [2004] 29 E.G. 118, QBD 15–057
Bajwa v Furini [2004] EWCA Civ 412; [2004] 1 W.L.R. 1971, CA (Civ Div) *28–118*
Bake v French (No.1) [1907] 1 Ch. 428, Ch D *25–008*
Baker, Re (1881) 20 Ch. D. 230 ..... *28–139*
Baker v Baker [1993] 2 F.L.R. 247; (1993) 25 H.L.R. 408; [1993] E.G. 35 (C.S.); (1993) 137 S.J.L.B. 60; [1993] N.P.C. 32, CA (Civ Div) *3–157*, *3–158*
Baker v Black Sea & Baltic General Insurance Co Ltd; sub nom. Black Sea & Baltic General Insurance Co Ltd v Baker [1998] 1 W.L.R. 974; [1998] 2 All E.R. 833; [1998] C.L.C. 820; [1998] Lloyd's Rep. I.R. 327; (1998) 95(23) L.S.G. 26; (1998) 148 N.L.J. 782; (1998) 142 S.J.L.B. 171, HL; reversing in part [1996] L.R.L.R. 353; [1996] 5 Re. L.R. 202, CA (Civ Div); affirming [1995] L.R.L.R. 261, QBD (Comm) *13–010*, *13–018*
Baker v Bradley (1855) 7 De. G. M. & G. 597 ..... *7–074*
Baker v Courage & Co [1910] 1 K.B. 56, KBD *28–058*, *29–040*
Baker v Dening (1838) 8 A. & E. 94 ..... *4–034*
Baker v Dewey (1823) 1 B. & C. 704 ..... *1–112*
Baker v Greenhill (1842) 3 Q.B. 148 ..... *29–107*
Baker v Hedgecock (1888) L.R. 39 Ch. D. 520, Ch D *16–112*, *16–194*, *16–198*
Baker v Jones [1954] 1 W.L.R. 1005; [1954] 2 All E.R. 553; (1954) 98 S.J. 473, QBD *9–075*, *16–047*, *16–052*
Baker v Kaye [1997] I.R.L.R. 219; (1998) 39 B.M.L.R. 12, QBD *18–031*
Baker v Lipton Ltd (1899) 15 T.L.R. 435 ..... *21–056*
Baker v Lloyd's Bank Ltd [1920] 2 K.B. 322, KBD *20–041*
Baker v Monk (1864) 4 De. G.J. & S. 388 ..... *7–128*
Baker v St Quintin (1844) 12 M. & W. 441 ..... *22–003*
Baker v Walker (1845) 14 M. &W. 465 ..... *3–057*
Baker v Walker, 153 E.R. 558; (1845) 14 M. & W. 465, Ex Ct *21–076*
Baker v White (1690) 2 Vern. 215 ..... *16–072*
Baker & Davies Plc v Leslie Wilks Associates [2005] EWHC 1179 (TCC); [2005] 3 All E.R. 603; [2005] B.L.R. 425; 101 Con. L.R. 82; [2006] P.N.L.R. 3, QBD (TCC) *17–032*
Bal v Van Staden [1902] T.S. 128 ..... *2–047*
Balabel v Air India [1988] Ch. 317; [1988] 2 W.L.R. 1036; [1988] 2 All E.R. 246; [1988] E.G. 38 (C.S.); (1988) 138 N.L.J. Rep. 85; (1988) 132 S.J. 699, CA (Civ Div) *4–036*
Balder London, The. *See* Gatoil Anstalt v Omenial Ltd
Baldney v Richie (1816) 1 Stark. 338 ..... *17–010*
Baldry v Marshall [1925] 1 K.B. 260, CA *14–006*, *29–058*, *29–059*
Balfour v Balfour [1919] 2 K.B. 571, CA *2–168*, 2–169, *2–170*
Balfour v Sea Fire and Life Assurance Co (1857) 3 C.B. (N.S.) 300 ..... *5–076*
Balfour Beatty Construction (Scotland) Ltd v Scottish Power Plc, 1994 S.C. (H.L.) 20; 1994 S.L.T. 807; [1994] C.L.C. 321, HL *26–057*, *26–060*
Balkis Consolidated, Re (1888) 58 L.T. 300 ..... *1–092*
Balkis Consolidated Co Ltd v Tomkinson [1893] A.C. 396, HL; affirming [1891] 2 Q.B. 614, CA *6–095*
Ball (Inspector of Taxes) v National & Grindlay's Bank Ltd [1973] Ch. 127; [1972] 3 W.L.R. 17; [1971] 3 All E.R. 485; 47 T.C. 287; [1971] T.R. 203; (1972) 116 S.J. 508, CA (Civ Div); affirming [1971] 2 W.L.R. 1129, Ch D *3–014*
Ballachulish Slate Quarries Co Ltd v Grant (1903) 5 F. 1105; (1903) 11 S.L.T. 230; 1903 S.L.R. 791, IH (2 Div) *16–110*

Ballard (Kent) Ltd v Oliver Ashworth (Holdings) Ltd; sub nom. Oliver Ashworth (Holdings) Ltd v Ballard (Kent) Ltd [2000] Ch. 12; [1999] 3 W.L.R. 57; [1999] 2 All E.R. 791; [1999] L. & T.R. 400; [1999] 2 E.G.L.R. 23; [1999] 19 E.G. 161; (1999) 96(16) L.S.G. 36; (1999) 149 N.L.J. 521; [1999] N.P.C. 36, CA (Civ Div); reversing [1998] 3 E.G.L.R. 60; [1998] 46 E.G. 190, Ch D *3–081*, *3–104*
Ballett v Mingay [1943] K.B. 281, CA *1–162*, *8–047*
Balli Trading Ltd v Afalona Shipping Ltd; The Coral [1993] 1 Lloyd's Rep. 1; (1992) 89(34) L.S.G. 40; (1992) 136 S.J.L.B. 259, CA (Civ Div); reversing [1992] 2 Lloyd's Rep. 158, QBD (Admlty) *12–079*
Balmoral Group Ltd v Borealis (UK) Ltd [2006] EWHC 1900 (Comm); [2006] 2 Lloyd's Rep. 629; [2006] 2 C.L.C. 220, QBD (Comm) *12–011*, *12–012*, *14–084*, *14–085*, *14–086*, *14–087*, *14–094*, *14–099*, *14–113*, *30–008*, *30–068*
Balsamo v Medici [1984] 1 W.L.R. 951; [1984] 2 All E.R. 304; (1984) 81 L.S.G. 2700; (1984) 128 S.J. 500, Ch D 1–177, *18–019*, *18–022*, *18–031*, 18–032, *18–036*
Balston Ltd v Headline Filters Ltd (No.1) [1987] F.S.R. 330, Ch D *16–107*, *16–109*
Baltic SS Co v Dillon (1993) 67 AL.J.R. 228 .... *29–061*
Baly v Barrett, *The Times*, May 19, 1989; *Independent*, June 26, 1989; *Financial Times*, May 24, 1989, HL (NI) *28–116*
Bamberger v Commercial Credit Co (1855) 15 C.B. 676 .... *25–026*
Banbury v Bank of Montreal [1918] A.C. 626, HL; affirming [1917] 1 K.B. 409, CA *6–041*
Banco Central SA v Lingoss & Falce Ltd; The Raven [1980] 2 Lloyd's Rep. 266, QBD (Comm) *12–055*, *12–119*, *19–070*, *19–073*, *28–123*
Banco de Bilbao v Sancha; Banco de Bilbao v Rey [1938] 2 K.B. 176, CA *30–325*
Banco de Portugal v Waterlow & Sons Ltd; Waterlow & Sons Ltd v Banco de Portugal [1932] A.C. 452; [1932] All E.R. Rep. 181, HL *13–006*, *18–047*, *26–001*, *26–104*
Banco Exterior Internacional SA v Thomas [1997] 1 W.L.R. 221; [1997] 1 All E.R. 46; [1997] 1 F.L.R. 703; [1997] 2 F.C.R. 429; [1997] Fam. Law 326, CA (Civ Div) 6–026, *7–120*
Banco Santander SA v Bayfern Ltd; sub nom. Banco Santander SA v Banque Paribas [2000] 1 All E.R. (Comm) 776; [2000] Lloyd's Rep. Bank. 165; [2000] C.L.C. 906, CA (Civ Div); affirming [1999] 2 All E.R. (Comm) 18; [1999] Lloyd's Rep. Bank. 239; [1999] C.L.C. 1321; (1999) 96(26) L.S.G. 27, QBD (Comm) *17–014*, *19–070*
Bandar Property Holdings Ltd v JS Darwen (Successors) Ltd [1968] 2 All E.R. 305; (1968) 19 P. & C.R. 785, QBD *13–009*
Bangladesh Chemical Industries Corp v Henry Stephens Shipping Co and Tex-Bilan Shipping Co; The SLS Everest [1981] 2 Lloyd's Rep. 389; [1981] Com. L.R. 176, CA (Civ Div) *30–010*
Bangladesh Export Import Co Ltd v Sucden Kerry SA [1995] 2 Lloyd's Rep. 1, CA (Civ Div) *23–029*, *23–058*, *30–364*
Banham Marshalls Services Unlimited v Lincolnshire CC [2007] EWHC 402 (QB), QBD *24–013*
Banister, Re; sub nom. Broad v Munton (1879) L.R. 12 Ch. D. 131, CA *14–136*
Bank für Gemeinwirtschaft AG v City of London Garages Ltd [1971] 1 W.L.R. 149; [1971] 1 All E.R. 541; (1970) 114 S.J. 970, CA (Civ Div) 16–011
Bank Line Ltd v Arthur Capel & Co [1919] A.C. 435, HL *23–007*, *23–010*, *23–012*, 23–041, 23–042, 23–043, *23–058*, *23–059*, *23–061*
Bank Negara Indonesia v Philip Hoalim [1973] 2 M.L.J. 3 .... *12–103*
Bank of America National Trust and Savings Association v Chrismas; The Kyriaki [1994] 1 All E.R. 401; [1993] 1 Lloyd's Rep. 137, QBD (Comm) *28–050*, *28–119*
Bank of Australasia v Clan Line Steamers Ltd [1916] 1 K.B. 39, CA *14–032*
Bank of Australasia v Harding (1850) 9 C.B. 661 .... *25–016*
Bank of Australasia v Nias (1851) 16 Q.B. 717 .... *25–016*
Bank of Australasia v Palmer [1897] A.C. 540, PC (Aus) *12–096*

Bank of Baroda v Mahomed; sub nom. Mahomed v Bank of Baroda [1999] Lloyd's Rep. Bank. 14; [1999] C.L.C. 463; (1998) 95(47) L.S.G. 29, CA (Civ Div) *28–039*
Bank of Baroda v Patel [1996] 1 Lloyd's Rep. 391, QBD *28–046*
Bank of Baroda v Vysya Bank Ltd [1994] 2 Lloyd's Rep. 87; [1994] 3 Bank. L.R. 216; [1994] C.L.C. 41, QBD (Comm) .. *30–012*, *30–023*, *30–077*, *30–090*, *30–091*, *30–204*
Bank of Boston Connecticut (formerly Colonial Bank) v European Grain & Shipping Ltd; The Dominique; sub nom. Colonial Bank v European Grain & Shipping Ltd [1989] A.C. 1056; [1989] 2 W.L.R. 440; [1989] 1 All E.R. 545; [1989] 1 Lloyd's Rep. 431; (1989) 86(11) L.S.G. 43; (1989) 133 S.J. 219, HL; reversing [1988] 3 W.L.R. 60; [1988] 3 All E.R. 233; [1988] 1 Lloyd's Rep. 215; [1988] 1 F.T.L.R. 327; (1988) 132 S.J. 896, CA (Civ Div); reversing [1987] 1 Lloyd's Rep. 239, QBD (Comm) *19–070*, *19–071*, *24–001*, *24–047*, *24–048*
Bank of Credit & Commerce Hong Kong Ltd (In Liquidation) v Sonali Bank [1995] 1 Lloyd's Rep. 227; [1994] C.L.C. 1171, QBD (Comm) ... *30–012*, *30–051*, *30–077*, *30–091*
Bank of Credit and Commerce International (Overseas) Ltd (In Liquidation) v Price Waterhouse (No.1) [1997] 4 All E.R. 108, Ch D *11–004*, *11–008*
Bank of Credit and Commerce International (Overseas) Ltd (In Liquidation) v Price Waterhouse (No.2) [1998] Lloyd's Rep. Bank. 85; [1998] B.C.C. 617; [1998] E.C.C. 410; [1998] P.N.L.R. 564; (1998) 95(15) L.S.G. 32; (1998) 142 S.J.L.B. 86, CA (Civ Div); reversing [1997] B.C.C. 584, Ch D *1–179*, *1–184*
Bank of Credit and Commerce International (Overseas) Ltd v Akindele; sub nom. BCCI v Chief Labode Onadimaki Akindele [2001] Ch. 437; [2000] 3 W.L.R. 1423; [2000] 4 All E.R. 221; [2000] Lloyd's Rep. Bank. 292; [2000] B.C.C. 968; [2000] W.T.L.R. 1049; (1999–2000) 2 I.T.E.L.R. 788; (2000) 97(26) L.S.G. 36; (2000) 150 N.L.J. 950, CA (Civ Div) *29–174*
Bank of Credit and Commerce International SA (In Liquidation) (No.11), Re [1997] Ch. 213; [1997] 2 W.L.R. 172; [1996] 4 All E.R. 796; [1996] B.C.C. 980; [1997] 1 B.C.L.C. 80, Ch D *30–350*
Bank of Credit and Commerce International SA (In Liquidation) v Ali (No.1) [2001] UKHL 8; [2002] 1 A.C. 251; [2001] 2 W.L.R. 735; [2001] 1 All E.R. 961; [2001] I.C.R. 337; [2001] I.R.L.R. 292; [2001] Emp. L.R. 359; (2001) 98(15) L.S.G. 32; (2001) 151 N.L.J. 351; (2001) 145 S.J.L.B. 67; (2001) 145 S.J.L.B. 70, HL; affirming [2000] 3 All E.R. 51; [2000] I.C.R. 1410; [2000] I.R.L.R. 398, CA (Civ Div); reversing [1999] 2 All E.R. 1005; [1999] I.C.R. 1068; [1999] I.R.L.R. 226; (1999) 96(7) L.S.G. 35; (1999) 149 N.L.J. 53, Ch D 3–048, 3–049, 5–013, *5–055*, *5–076*, *6–124*, 6–164, *7–129*, *12–042*, *12–050*, *12–119*, *12–120*, *22–004*, *22–005*, 22–012
Bank of Credit and Commerce International SA (In Liquidation) v Ali (No.3); sub nom. BCCI SA v Ali; Husain v Bank of Credit and Commerce International SA [2002] EWCA Civ 82; [2002] 3 All E.R. 750; [2002] I.C.R. 1258; [2002] I.R.L.R. 460; [2002] Emp. L.R. 406, CA (Civ Div) *26–044*, *26–086*
Bank of Credit and Commerce International SA v Aboody [1990] 1 Q.B. 923; [1989] 2 W.L.R. 759; [1992] 4 All E.R. 955; [1990] 1 F.L.R. 354; [1989] C.C.L.R. 63; [1989] Fam. Law 435; (1988) 132 S.J. 1754, CA (Civ Div) ....*6–021*, *7–059*, *7–061*, *7–062*, 7–064, 7–065, 7–068, 7–091, 7–101 , *7–104*
Bank of England v Cutler [1908] 2 K.B. 208, CA *29–120*
Bank of England v Vagliano Bros; sub nom. Vagliano Bros v Bank of England [1891] A.C. 107, HL *29–191*
Bank of India v Morris. *See* Morris v Bank of India
Bank of India v Trans Continental Commodity Merchants Ltd; sub nom. Bank of India v Patel [1983] 2 Lloyd's Rep. 298, CA (Civ Div); affirming [1982] 1 Lloyd's Rep. 506, QBD (Comm) *16–205*
Bank of Ireland v M'Manamy [1916] 2 I.R. 161 .... *5–101*
Bank of Liverpool and Martins v Holland (1926) 43 T.L.R. 29 .... *19–012*

Bank of Montreal v Snoxell (1982) 143 D.L.R. (3d) 349 .... *30–007*, *30–311*
Bank of Montreal v Stuart [1911] A.C. 120, PC (Can) *7–064*, 7–065
Bank of New South Wales v Murphett [1983] V.R. 489, Sup Ct (Vic) *29–033*
Bank of New Zealand v Simpson [1900] A.C. 182, PC (NZ) *12–118*
Bank of Nova Scotia v Hellenic Mutual War Risk Association (Bermuda) Ltd; The Good Luck [1992] 1 A.C. 233; [1991] 2 W.L.R. 1279; [1991] 3 All E.R. 1; [1991] 2 Lloyd's Rep. 191; (1991) 141 N.L.J. 779, HL; reversing [1990] 1 Q.B. 818; [1990] 2 W.L.R. 547; [1989] 3 All E.R. 628; [1989] 2 Lloyd's Rep. 238; (1990) 87(10) L.S.G. 34, CA (Civ Div); reversing [1988] 1 Lloyd's Rep. 514, QBD (Comm) *1–146*, 1–154, 1–155, *1–158*, *6–149*, *12–026*, *12–031*, *13–010*, *26–034*, *26–049*, *26–050*, *26–059*, *26–060*
Bank of Scotland Plc v King [2007] EWHC 2747 (Ch); [2007] All E.R. (D) 376 (Nov); [2008] 13 E.G. 150, Ch D *1–106*, *1–107*
Bank of Scotland v Henry Butcher & Co [2003] EWCA Civ 67; [2003] 2 All E.R. (Comm) 557; [2003] 1 B.C.L.C. 575; (2003) 100(13) L.S.G. 29, CA (Civ Div) *25–020*
Bank of Scotland v Hill [2002] EWCA Civ 1081; [2002] 29 E.G. 152 (C.S.); [2003] 1 P. & C.R. DG7, CA (Civ Div) *7–115*
Bank of Scotland v Singh, unreported, June 17, 2005, QBD *15–032*
Bank Tejarat v Hong Kong and Shanghai Banking Corp (CI) Ltd [1995] 1 Lloyd's Rep. 239, QBD (Comm) *29–182*
Bank voor Handel en Scheepvaart NV v Slatford (No.2); sub nom. Bank voor Handel en Scheepvaart NV v Administrator of Hungarian Property [1954] A.C. 584; [1954] 2 W.L.R. 867; [1954] 1 All E.R. 969; 47 R. & I.T. 373; 35 T.C. 311; (1954) 33 A.T.C. 102; [1954] T.R. 115; (1954) 98 S.J. 301, HL; reversing [1953] 1 Q.B. 248; [1952] 2 All E.R. 956; [1952] 2 T.L.R. 861; 46 R. & I.T. 120; (1952) 31 A.T.C. 535; [1952] T.R. 493; (1952) 96 S.J. 784, CA; affirming [1952] 1 All E.R. 314; [1952] 1 T.L.R. 341; [1952] W.N. 75, KBD 10–010
Bankers Insurance Co Ltd v South [2003] EWHC 380 (QB); [2003] P.I.Q.R. P28 .... *15–055*, *15–062*
Bankers Trust Co v PT Jakarta International Hotels and Development [1999] 1 All E.R. (Comm) 785; [1999] 1 Lloyd's Rep. 910, QBD (Comm) *27–005*, *27–070*
Bankers Trust Co v State Bank of India [1991] 2 Lloyd's Rep. 443, CA (Civ Div); affirming [1991] 1 Lloyd's Rep. 587, QBD (Comm) *12–057*, *12–118*
Bankes, Re; sub nom. Reynolds v Ellis [1902] 2 Ch. 333, Ch D *30–310*
Bankruptcy Notice (No.62 of 1924), Re [1924] 2 Ch. 76, CA *1–112*
Bankway Properties Ltd v Penfold-Dunsford; sub nom. Bankway Properties Ltd v Dunsford; Dunsford v Bankway Properties Ltd [2001] EWCA Civ 528; [2001] 1 W.L.R. 1369; [2002] H.L.R. 42; [2001] L. & T.R. 27; [2001] 2 E.G.L.R. 36; [2001] 26 E.G. 164; [2001] 16 E.G. 145 (C.S.); [2001] N.P.C. 74, CA (Civ Div) *3–014*, *12–126*
Bannatyne v D&C MacIver [1906] 1 K.B. 103, CA *29–173*
Banner, Ex p. *See* Blythe Ex p. Banner, Re.
Banner Homes Group Plc v Luff Developments Ltd. *See* Banner Homes Holdings Ltd (formerly Banner Homes Group Plc) v Luff Developments Ltd
Banner Homes Holdings Ltd (formerly Banner Homes Group Plc) v Luff Developments Ltd (No.2) [2000] Ch. 372; [2000] 2 W.L.R. 772, CA (Civ Div) *2–116*, *3–140*, *4–077*, *29–160*
Banner Industrial & Commercial Properties v Clark Paterson [1990] 2 E.G.L.R. 139; [1990] 47 E.G. 64, Ch D *3–095*
Bannerman v White (1861) 10 C.B. (N.S.) 844 .... *12–003*
Banning v Wright [1972] 1 W.L.R. 972; [1972] 2 All E.R. 987; 48 T.C. 421; [1972] T.R. 105; (1972) 116 S.J. 509, HL; reversing (1970) 49 A.T.C. 330; [1970] T.R. 331, CA (Civ Div) *3–082*, *3–096*, *3–130*

Bannister v Bannister [1948] 2 All E.R. 133; [1948] W.N. 261; (1948) 92 S.J. 377, CA *13–028*, *29–160*
Banque Belge pour l'Etranger v Hambrouck [1921] 1 K.B. 321, CA *29–163*
Banque Bruxelles Lambert SA v Eagle Star Insurance Co Ltd; Mortgage Express Ltd v Bowerman & Partners (No.2); BNP Mortgages Ltd v Goadsby & Harding Ltd; BNP Mortgages Ltd v Key Surveyors Nationwide Ltd; Nykredit Mortgage Bank Plc v Edward Erdman Group Ltd; United Bank of Kuwait Plc v Prudential Property Services Ltd [1995] Q.B. 375; [1995] 2 W.L.R. 607; [1995] 2 All E.R. 769; [1995] L.R.L.R. 195; [1996] 5 Bank. L.R. 64; [1995] C.L.C. 410; 73 B.L.R. 47; [1995] E.C.C. 398; [1996] 5 Re. L.R. 23; [1995] 1 E.G.L.R. 129; [1995] 12 E.G. 144; [1995] E.G. 31 (C.S.); (1995) 92(12) L.S.G. 34; (1995) 145 N.L.J. 343; (1995) 139 S.J.L.B. 56; [1995] N.P.C. 32; (1995) 69 P. & C.R. D37, CA (Civ Div); reversing [1995] L.R.L.R. 17; 68 B.L.R. 39; [1994] 31 E.G. 68; [1994] 32 E.G. 89, QBD (Comm) *1–164*, *1–165*
Banque de l'Indochine et de Suez SA v JH Rayner (Mincing Lane) Ltd [1983] Q.B. 711; [1983] 2 W.L.R. 841; [1983] 1 All E.R. 1137; [1983] 1 Lloyd's Rep. 228; (1983) 127 S.J. 361, CA (Civ Div); affirmin [1983] 2 W.L.R. 841; [1983] 1 All E.R. 468; [1982] 2 Lloyd's Rep. 476; [1982] Com. L.R. 205, QBD (Comm) *3–047*
Banque Financiere de la Cite SA (formerly Banque Keyser Ullmann SA) v Westgate Insurance Co (formerly Hodge General & Mercantile Co Ltd); sub nom. Banque Keyser Ullmann SA v Skandia (UK) Insurance Co; Skandia (UK) Insurance Co v Chemical Bank; Skandia (UK) Insurance Co v Credit Lyonnais Bank Nederland NV [1991] 2 A.C. 249; [1990] 3 W.L.R. 364; [1990] 2 All E.R. 947; [1990] 2 Lloyd's Rep. 377; (1990) 87(35) L.S.G. 36; (1990) 140 N.L.J. 1074; (1990) 134 S.J. 1265, HL; affirming [1990] 1 Q.B. 665; [1989] 3 W.L.R. 25; [1989] 2 All E.R. 952; [1988] 2 Lloyd's Rep. 513; [1989] Fin. L.R. 1; (1989) 133 S.J. 817, CA (Civ Div); reversing [1987] 2 W.L.R. 1300; [1987] 2 All E.R. 923; [1987] 1 Lloyd's Rep. 69; [1987] Fin. L.R. 134; (1987) 84 L.S.G. 1965; (1987) 131 S.J. 775, QBD (Comm) ...*1–022*, *1–029*, *1–126*, *1–131*, *1–134*, *1–135*, *1–154*, *6–017*, *6–030*, *6–073*, *6–085*, *6–095*, *6–142*, *6–143*, *6–146*, *12–027*, *18–022*, *26–041*, *26–049*
Banque Financiere de la Cite SA v Parc (Battersea) Ltd [1999] 1 A.C. 221; [1998] 2 W.L.R. 475; [1998] 1 All E.R. 737; [1998] C.L.C. 520; [1998] E.G. 36 (C.S.); (1998) 95(15) L.S.G. 31; (1998) 148 N.L.J. 365; (1998) 142 S.J.L.B. 101, HL *18–021*, *29–001*, *29–018*, *29–034*, *29–049*, *29–109*, *29–173*
Banque Internationale de Commerce de Petrograd v Goukassow. *See* La Banque Internationale de Commerce de Petrograd v Goukassow
Banque Keyser Ullmann SA v Skandia (UK) Insurance Co. *See* Banque Financiere de la Cite SA (formerly Banque Keyser Ullmann SA) v Westgate Insurance Co (formerly Hodge General & Mercantile Co Ltd)
Banque Paribas v Cargill International SA [1992] 2 Lloyd's Rep. 19, CA (Civ Div); affirming [1992] 1 Lloyd's Rep. 96, QBD (Comm) *12–011*
Barbados Trust Co Ltd (formerly CI Trustees (Asia Pacific) Ltd) v Bank of Zambia [2007] EWCA Civ 148; [2007] 2 All E.R. (Comm) 445; [2007] 1 Lloyd's Rep. 495; [2007] 1 C.L.C. 434; (2006–07) 9 I.T.E.L.R. 689, CA (Civ Div); affirming [2006] EWHC 222 (Comm); [2006] 1 Lloyd's Rep. 723; [2006] 1 C.L.C. 311; (2005–06) 8 I.T.E.L.R. 739, QBD (Comm) *18–078*, *18–083*, *18–086*, 19–046
Barber v Brown (1856) 1 C.B.(N.S.) 121 .... *29–042*
Barber v Fox (1670) 2 Wms.Saund.134 .... *3–004*, *3–036*
Barber v Manchester Regional Hospital Board [1958] 1 W.L.R. 181; [1958] 1 All E.R. 322; (1958) 122 J.P. 124; (1958) 102 S.J. 140, QBD *1–017*, *27–023*
Barber v NWS Bank Plc [1996] 1 W.L.R. 641; [1996] 1 All E.R. 906; [1996] R.T.R. 388; [1996] C.C.L.R. 30; (1995) 145 N.L.J. 1814, CA (Civ Div) *12–040*, *29–057*, *29–180*
Barber v Rowe; sub nom. Barker v Rowe [1948] 2 All E.R. 1050; [1948] W.N. 423; (1948) 92 S.J. 718, CA *4–030*

Barber v Somerset CC; Baker Refractories Ltd v Bishop; Sutherland v Hatton; Sandwell MBC v Jones; sub nom. Jones v Sandwell MBC; Hatton v Sutherland; Bishop v Baker Refractories Ltd; Somerset CC v Barber [2004] UKHL 13; [2004] 1 W.L.R. 1089; [2004] 2 All E.R. 385; [2004] I.C.R. 457; [2004] I.R.L.R. 475; [2004] E.L.R. 199; [2004] P.I.Q.R. P31; (2004) 77 B.M.L.R. 219; (2004) 101(18) L.S.G. 34; (2004) 148 S.J.L.B. 419, HL *26–083*

Barclay v Messenger (1874) 43 L.J. Ch. 449 .... *21–019*

Barclay v Pearson [1893] 2 Ch. 154, Ch D *16–185*

Barclay v Prospect Mortgages, Ltd [1974] 1 W.L.R. 837; [1974] 2 All E.R. 672; (1974) 118 S.J. 441, Ch D *16–185*

Barclays Bank International Ltd v Levin Bros (Bradford) Ltd [1977] Q.B. 270; [1976] 3 W.L.R. 852; [1976] 3 All E.R. 900; [1977] 1 Lloyd's Rep. 51; (1976) 120 S.J. 801, QBD (Comm) *30–375*, *30–376*

Barclays Bank Ltd v Beck [1952] 2 Q.B. 47; [1952] 1 All E.R. 549; [1952] 1 T.L.R. 595; (1952) 96 S.J. 194, CA *25–001*, *25–002*, *25–003*

Barclays Bank Ltd v Okenhare [1966] 2 Lloyd's Rep. 87, QBD *5–092*

Barclays Bank Ltd v Quistclose Investments Ltd; sub nom. Quistclose Investments Ltd v Rolls Razor Ltd (In Voluntary Liquidation) [1970] A.C. 567; [1968] 3 W.L.R. 1097; [1968] 3 All E.R. 651; (1968) 112 S.J. 903, HL; affirming [1968] Ch. 540; [1968] 2 W.L.R. 478; [1968] 1 All E.R. 613; (1967) 118 N.L.J. 13; (1968) 112 S.J. 85, CA (Civ Div); reversing [1967] Ch. 910; [1967] 2 W.L.R. 1064; [1967] 1 All E.R. 864; (1967) 111 S.J. 190, Ch D 1–189

Barclays Bank Ltd v Roberts [1954] 1 W.L.R. 1212; [1954] 3 All E.R. 107; (1954) 98 S.J. 589, CA *20–020*

Barclays Bank Ltd v TOSG Trust Fund Ltd [1984] A.C. 626; [1984] 2 W.L.R. 650; [1984] 1 All E.R. 1060; (1984) 1 B.C.C. 99081; (1984) 81 L.S.G. 1360; (1984) 134 N.L.J. 656; (1984) 128 S.J. 261, HL; affirming [1984] 2 W.L.R. 49; [1984] 1 All E.R. 628; (1984) 1 B.C.C. 99017; (1983) 127 S.J. 730, CA (Civ Div) *9–033*

Barclays Bank Ltd v WJ Simms Son & Cooke (Southern) Ltd [1980] Q.B. 677; [1980] 2 W.L.R. 218; [1979] 3 All E.R. 522; [1980] 1 Lloyd's Rep. 225; (1979) 123 S.J. 785, QBD (Comm) *23–080*, *29–030*, *29–033*, 29–034, 29–037, *29–038*, *29–040*, *29–179*

Barclays Bank Plc v Boulter [1999] 1 W.L.R. 1919; [1999] 4 All E.R. 513; [2000] Lloyd's Rep. Bank. 29; [2000] C.P. Rep. 16; [1999] 2 F.L.R. 986; [1999] 3 F.C.R. 529; (2000) 32 H.L.R. 170; [1999] 3 E.G.L.R. 88; [1999] 49 E.G. 97; [2000] Fam. Law 25; [1999] E.G. 121 (C.S.); (1999) 96(42) L.S.G. 41; (1999) 96(42) L.S.G. 44; (1999) 149 N.L.J. 1645; (1999) 143 S.J.L.B. 250; [1999] N.P.C. 124; (2000) 79 P. & C.R. D1, HL; affirming [1998] 1 W.L.R. 1; [1997] 2 All E.R. 1002; [1997] 2 F.L.R. 157; [1997] 3 F.C.R. 252; (1998) 30 H.L.R. 134; [1997] Fam. Law 545; [1997] N.P.C. 63; (1997) 74 P. & C.R. D11, CA (Civ Div) *6–027*, *6–130*, *7–119*

Barclays Bank Plc v Caplan [1998] 1 F.L.R. 532; (1999) 78 P. & C.R. 153; [1998] Fam. Law 257; [1997] N.P.C. 164, Ch D *6–025*

Barclays Bank Plc v Coleman [2001] Q.B. 20; [2000] 3 W.L.R. 405; [2000] 1 All E.R. 385; [2000] Lloyd's Rep. Bank. 67; [2000] 1 F.L.R. 343; [2000] 1 F.C.R. 398; (2001) 33 H.L.R. 8; [2000] Fam. Law 245; [2000] E.G. 4 (C.S.); (2000) 97(3) L.S.G. 37; (2000) 144 S.J.L.B. 42; [2000] N.P.C. 2; (2000) 79 P. & C.R. D28, CA (Civ Div) *7–063*

Barclays Bank Plc v Eustice [1995] 1 W.L.R. 1238; [1995] 4 All E.R. 511; [1995] B.C.C. 978; [1995] 2 B.C.L.C. 630; (1995) 145 N.L.J. 1503; (1995) 70 P. & C.R. D29, CA (Civ Div) *3–019*, *20–031*

Barclays Bank Plc v Fairclough Building Ltd (No.1) [1995] Q.B. 214; [1994] 3 W.L.R. 1057; [1995] 1 All E.R. 289; [1994] C.L.C. 529; 68 B.L.R. 1; 38 Con. L.R. 86; (1995) 11 Const. L.J. 35; [1995] E.G. 10 (C.S.); (1994) 91(25) L.S.G. 30; (1994) 138 S.J.L.B. 118, CA (Civ Div); reversing (1994) 10 Const. L.J. 48, QBD *1–122*, *1–143*, *1–166*, *26–049*

Barclays Bank Plc v Fairclough Building Ltd (No.2); Carne (Structural Repair) Co Ltd v Trendleway Ltd, 76 B.L.R. 1; 44 Con. L.R. 35; [1995] I.R.L.R. 605; [1995] P.I.Q.R. P152, CA (Civ Div); reversing [1994] C.L.C. 756; 39 Con. L.R. 144; [1994] E.G. 141 (C.S.), QBD (OR) *1–122*, *1–141*, 1–143, *1–166*

Barclays Bank Plc v Khaira [1993] 1 F.L.R. 343; [1993] Fam. Law 124, CA (Civ Div); reversing [1992] 1 W.L.R. 623; [1996] 5 Bank. L.R. 196; (1992) 89(17) L.S.G. 50; [1991] N.P.C. 141, Ch D *1–134*

Barclays Bank Plc v Kingston [2006] EWHC 533; [2006] 1 All E.R. (Comm) 519; [2006] 2 Lloyd's Rep. 59; [2006] 12 E.G. 223 (C.S.), QBD *12–118*

Barclays Bank Plc v O'Brien [1994] 1 A.C. 180; [1993] 3 W.L.R. 786; [1993] 4 All E.R. 417; [1994] 1 F.L.R. 1; [1994] 1 F.C.R. 357; (1994) 26 H.L.R. 75; (1994) 13 Tr. L.R. 165; [1994] C.C.L.R. 94; [1994] Fam. Law 78; [1993] E.G. 169 (C.S.); (1993) 143 N.L.J. 1511; (1993) 137 S.J.L.B. 240; [1993] N.P.C. 135, HL; affirming [1993] Q.B. 109; [1992] 3 W.L.R. 593; [1992] 4 All E.R. 983; [1993] 1 F.L.R. 124; [1993] 1 F.C.R. 97; (1993) 25 H.L.R. 7; (1993) 66 P. & C.R. 135; (1992) 11 Tr. L.R. 153; [1992] C.C.L.R. 37; [1993] Fam. Law 62; (1992) 89(27) L.S.G. 34; (1992) 142 N.L.J. 1040; (1992) 136 S.J.L.B. 175; [1992] N.P.C. 74, CA (Civ Div) *6–021*, 6–023, 6–024, 6–025, 6–026, 7–059, 7–069, *7–070*, 7–080, 7–085, *7–089*, *7–104*, **7–106**, *7–107*, 7–108, 7–109, 7–110, *7–112*, 7–113, *7–114*, 7–115, *7–124*, *7–136*, *8–001*, *16–068*

Barclays Bank Plc v Rivett [1999] 1 F.L.R. 730; [1998] 3 F.C.R. 304; (1997) 29 H.L.R. 893; [1999] Fam. Law 308; [1997] N.P.C. 18, CA (Civ Div) *7–085*

Barclays Bank Plc v Savile Estates Ltd; sub nom. Barclays Bank Plc v Saville Estates Ltd [2002] EWCA Civ 589; [2003] 2 P. & C.R. 28; [2002] L. & T.R. 28; [2002] 2 E.G.L.R. 16; [2002] 24 E.G. 152; [2002] 18 E.G. 152 (C.S.), CA (Civ Div) *21–014*

Barclays Bank Plc v Schwartz, *The Times*, August 2, 1995, CA (Civ Div) *7–131*, 8–001, 8–080

Barclays Bank Plc v Taylor; Trustee Savings Bank of Wales and Border Counties v Taylor [1989] 1 W.L.R. 1066; [1989] 3 All E.R. 563; [1989] Fin. L.R. 304; (1990) 87(4) L.S.G. 66; (1989) 133 S.J. 1372, CA (Civ Div) *13–004*

Barclays Bank Plc v Thomson [1997] 4 All E.R. 816; [1996] 5 Bank. L.R. 402; [1997] 1 F.L.R. 156; [1997] 1 F.C.R. 541; (1998) 75 P. & C.R. 5; [1997] Fam. Law 245; (1996) 146 N.L.J. 1778; [1996] N.P.C. 155; (1997) 73 P. & C.R. D21, CA (Civ Div) *7–118*

Barclays Bank Plc v Weeks Legg & Dean; sub nom. Barclays Bank Plc v Dean; Barclays Bank Plc v Layton Lougher & Co; Mohamed v Fahiya; Barclays Bank Plc v NE Hopkin John & Co [1999] Q.B. 309; [1998] 3 W.L.R. 656; [1998] 3 All E.R. 213; [1998] P.N.L.R. 729; (1999) 77 P. & C.R. 320; [1998] 3 E.G.L.R. 103; [1998] 40 E.G. 182; (1998) 95(21) L.S.G. 38; (1998) 95(25) L.S.G. 33; (1998) 142 S.J.L.B. 180; [1998] N.P.C. 89; (1998) 76 P. & C.R. D27, CA (Civ Div); affirming [1996] 5 Bank. L.R. 162; [1996] E.C.C. 396; [1996] E.G. 29 (C.S.); [1996] N.P.C. 15, QBD *3–039*

Barder v Caluori; sub nom. Barder v Barder [1988] A.C. 20; [1987] 2 W.L.R. 1350; [1987] 2 All E.R. 440; [1987] 2 F.L.R. 480; [1988] Fam. Law 18; (1987) 84 L.S.G. 2046; (1987) 137 N.L.J. 497; (1987) 131 S.J. 776, HL *29–032*

Bardwell v Lydall (1831) 7 Bing. 489 .... *21–065*

Barex Brokers Ltd v Morris Dean & Co [1999] P.N.L.R. 344, CA (Civ Div) *1–184*, *18–029*

Baring Bros & Co Ltd v Cunninghame DC [1997] C.L.C. 108, OH *30–327*

Barings Plc (In Administration) v Coopers & Lybrand [1997] B.C.C. 498; [1997] 1 B.C.L.C. 427; [1997] E.C.C. 372; [1997] I.L.Pr. 576; [1997] P.N.L.R. 179, CA (Civ Div); affirming [1997] I.L.Pr. 12; (1996) 93(39) L.S.G. 27; (1996) 140 S.J.L.B. 210, Ch D *18–022*

Barings Plc (In Liquidation) v Coopers & Lybrand (No.5); Barings Futures (Singapore) Pte Ltd (In Liquidation) v Mattar (No.4) [2002] EWHC 461 (Ch); [2002] 2 B.C.L.C. 410; [2002] Lloyd's Rep. P.N. 395; [2002] P.N.L.R. 39, Ch D *6–009*, *6–035*

Barker v Allanson [1937] 1 K.B. 463, CA *9–065*, *9–067*

Barker v Birt (1842) 10 M.W. 61 .... *29–191*
Barker v Greenwood (1837) 2 Y.C. Ex. 414 .... *21–044*
Barker v Hodgson (1814) 3 M.S. 267 .... *23–004*
Barker v Stickney [1919] 1 K.B. 121, CA; affirming [1918] 2 K.B. 356, KBD *18–139*
Barker's Estate, Re (1875) 44 L.J. Ch. 487 3–031
Barking and Dagenham LBC v Stamford Asphalt Co Ltd [1997] C.L.C. 929; 82 B.L.R. 25; 54 Con. L.R. 1, CA (Civ Div) *12–087*
Barkworth v Young (1856) 26 L.J. Ch. 153 .... *21–007*
Barlow Clowes International Ltd (In Liquidation) v Vaughan; sub nom. Vaughan v Barlow Clowes International Ltd [1992] 4 All E.R. 22; [1992] B.C.L.C. 910, CA (Civ Div) *21–066*, *29–167*, *29–172*, *29–174*, *29–183*
Barnard, Re; sub nom. Edwards v Barnard (1886) L.R. 32 Ch. D. 447, CA *17–005*
Barnes v Richards (1902) 71 L.J.K.B. 341 .... *7–049*
Barnes v St Helens MBC; sub nom. St Helens MBC v Barnes [2006] EWCA Civ 1372; [2007] 1 W.L.R. 879; [2007] 3 All E.R. 525; [2007] C.P. Rep. 7; [2007] P.I.Q.R. P10, CA (Civ Div) *28–116*
Barnes & Co v Toye (1883–84) L.R. 13 Q.B.D. 410, QBD *8–008*
Barnett Ex p. *See* Deveze Ex p.
Barnett v Ira L&AC Berk Pty Ltd (1952) 52 S.R. (N.S.W.) 268 .... *14–138*
Barnett v Javeri & Co [1916] 2 K.B. 390, KBD *26–064*
Barnstaple Boat Co Ltd v Jones [2007] EWCA Civ 727; [2008] 1 All E.R. 1124; (2007) 151 S.J.L.B. 987, CA (Civ Div) *28–083*
Baroness Wenlock v River Dee Co (No.1) (1884–85) L.R. 10 App. Cas. 354, HL *10–024*, *10–027*
Baroness Wenlock v River Dee Co (No.2) (1887) L.R. 19 Q.B.D. 155, CA *29–173*
Barque Quilpue Ltd v Brown [1904] 2 K.B. 264, CA *13–012*, *21–020*
Barr v Craven (1904) 89 L.T. 574 .... *16–110*
Barr v Gibson (1838) 3 M. & W. 390; 150 E.R. 1196 .... 5–021, *5–022*
Barratt v Gough Thomas [1951] 2 All E.R. 48; [1951] 2 T.L.R. 106; [1951] W.N. 309; (1951) 95 S.J. 381, Ch D *21–084*
Barratt Southampton v Fairclough Building Ltd, 27 Con. L.R. 62, QBD (OR) *13–010*
Barrett v Deere (1828) Moo. M 200 .... *21–043*
Barrett v GN Railway (1904) 20 T.L.R. 175 .... *14–047*
Barrett v Lounava (1982) Ltd [1990] 1 Q.B. 348 .... *27–026*, *27–028*
Barrett v Universal-Island Records Ltd [2006] EWHC 1009 (Ch); [2006] E.M.L.R. 21, Ch D *21–049*
Barrett Bros (Taxis) Ltd v Davies; sub nom. Lickiss v Milestone Motor Policies at Lloyds [1966] 1 W.L.R. 1334; [1966] 2 All E.R. 972; [1966] 2 Lloyd's Rep. 1; (1966) 110 S.J. 600, CA 22–46
Barron v Willis. *See* Willis v Barron.
Barros Mattos Junior v MacDaniels Ltd; Barros Mattos Junior v General Securities & Finance Co Ltd; sub nom. Mattos Junior v MacDaniels Ltd [2004] EWHC 1188 (Ch); [2005] 1 W.L.R. 247; [2004] 3 All E.R. 299; [2004] 2 All E.R. (Comm) 501; [2004] 2 Lloyd's Rep. 475, Ch D *29–179*, *29–183*, *30–347*, *30–355*, *30–356*, *30–367*
Barrow v Arnaud (1846) 8 Q.B. 595 .... *26–088*
Barrow v Bankside Members Agency Ltd; sub nom. Barrow v Bankside Underwriting Management Ltd [1996] 1 W.L.R. 257; [1996] 1 All E.R. 981; [1996] 1 Lloyd's Rep. 278; [1996] C.L.C. 413; [1996] 5 Re. L.R. 1, CA (Civ Div) *25–013*
Barrow v Chappel & Co, unreported *27–025*
Barrow Lane & Ballard Ltd v Phillip Phillips & Co Ltd [1929] 1 K.B. 574; (1928) 32 Ll. L. Rep. 228, KBD *5–044*, *5–048*, *23–068*
Barr's Contract, Re; sub nom. Moorwell Buildings Ltd v Barr; Moorwell Holdings Ltd v Barr [1956] Ch. 551; [1956] 1 W.L.R. 918; [1956] 2 All E.R. 853; (1956) 100 S.J. 550, Ch D *21–014*
Barry v Davies (t/a Heathcote Ball & Co); sub nom. Barry v Heathcote Ball & Co (Commercial Auctions) Ltd; Heathcote Ball & Co (Commercial Auctions) Ltd v Barry [2000] 1 W.L.R. 1962; [2001] 1 All E.R. 944; [2000] 3 E.G.L.R. 7; [2000] 47 E.G. 178; (2000) 97(39) L.S.G. 41; (2000) 150 N.L.J. 1377; (2000) 144 S.J.L.B. 249, CA (Civ Div) *2–012*, *3–174*

Bart v British West Indian Airways [1967] 1 Lloyd's Rep. 239, CA (Guy) *14–054*, *18–022*
Bart v Purnell (1836) 4 A. & E. 792 .... *4–038*
Bart v Wells (1862) 1 B. & S. 836 .... *8–050*
Bartlett v Pentland (1830) 10 B.C. 760 .... *21–044*
Barton v County Natwest Ltd; sub nom. County Natwest Ltd v Barton [2002] 4 All E.R. 494 (Note); [1999] Lloyd's Rep. Bank. 408; [1999] E.G. 103 (C.S.); (1999) 96(33) L.S.G. 31, CA (Civ Div) *6–036*
Barton v Fincham [1921] 2 K.B. 291, CA *16–016*
Barton v Fitzgerald (1812) 15 East. 529 .... *12–063*, *12–078*
Barton v North Staffordshire Railway Co (1888) L.R. 38 Ch. D. 458, Ch D *28–057*
Barton (Alexander) v Armstrong (Alexander Ewan) [1976] A.C. 104; [1975] 2 W.L.R. 1050; [1975] 2 All E.R. 465; (1973) 119 S.J. 286, PC (Aus) *6–035*, *7–004*, 7–007, *7–008*, 7–025, *7–026*, *7–053*, *29–088*
Barton (Deceased), Re; sub nom. Tod v Barton [2002] EWHC 264 (Ch); [2002] W.T.L.R. 469; (2001–02) 4 I.T.E.L.R. 715, Ch D *30–037*, *30–043*
Barton Thompson & Co Ltd v Stapling Machines Co [1966] Ch. 499; [1966] 2 W.L.R. 1429; [1966] 2 All E.R. 222; (1966) 110 S.J. 313, Ch D *26–155*
Barwick v English Joint Stock Bank (1866–67) L.R. 2 Ex. 259; (1867) 36 L.J. Ex. 147, Ex Chamber *6–017*, *22–047*
Baschet v London Illustrated Standard Co [1900] 1 Ch. 73, Ch D *30–338*
Base Metal Trading Ltd v Shamurin [2004] EWCA Civ 1316; [2005] 1 W.L.R. 1157; [2005] 1 All E.R. (Comm) 17; [2005] B.C.C. 325; [2005] 2 B.C.L.C. 171; [2004] 2 C.L.C. 916; (2004) 148 S.J.L.B. 1281, CA (Civ Div) *30–020*, *30–031*, *30–032*, *30–041*, *30–110*, *30–012*, *30–120*, *30–121*, *30–147*
Basham (Deceased), Re [1986] 1 W.L.R. 1498; [1987] 1 All E.R. 405; [1987] 2 F.L.R. 264; [1987] Fam. Law 310; (1987) 84 L.S.G. 112; (1986) 130 S.J. 986, Ch D *3–146*, *3–147*, *3–148*
Bashir v Commissioner of Lands [1960] A.C. 44; [1959] 3 W.L.R. 996; [1960] 1 All E.R. 117; (1959) 103 S.J. 1045, PC (EA) *12–030*
Basildon DC v JE Lesser (Properties) Ltd [1985] Q.B. 839; [1984] 3 W.L.R. 812; [1985] 1 All E.R. 20; 8 Con. L.R. 89; (1984) 1 Const. L.J. 57; (1984) 81 L.S.G. 1437; (1984) 134 N.L.J. 330, QBD *26–049*
Baskomb v Beckwith (1869) L.R. 8 Eq. 100 .... *5–077*
Basma (Abdul Karim) v Weekes [1950] A.C. 441; [1950] 2 All E.R. 146; 66 T.L.R. (Pt. 1) 1047, PC (West Africa) *8–042*
Basnett v J&A Jackson Ltd [1976] I.C.R. 63; [1976] I.R.L.R. 154, HC *26–158*
Bastable Ex p. Trustee, Re [1901] 2 K.B. 518, CA *20–035*
Basten v Butter (1806) 7 East 479 .... *21–033*
Bastone & Firminger Ltd v Nasima Enterprises (Nigeria) Ltd [1996] C.L.C. 1902, QBD *30–012*, *30–051*, *30–077*, *30–091*
Batard v Hawes (1853) 2 E. & B. 287 .... *17–027*
Batchelor v Middleton (1848) 6 Hare 75 .... *28–100*
Bate, Ex p. (1838) 3 Deac. 358 .... *25–002*
Bateman v Ball (1887) 56 L.J.Q.B. 291 .... *9–048*
Bateman v Hunt [1904] 2 K.B. 530, CA *19–016*, *19–059*
Bateman v Phillips (1812) 15 East 272 .... *12–114*
Bateman v Service (1880–81) L.R. 6 App. Cas. 386, PC (Aus) *30–325*
Bates v Hudson (1825) 6 Dow. Ry. K.B. 3 .... *21–030*
Bates v Townley (1848) 2 Ex. 152 .... *29–109*, *29–191*
Bateson v Gosling (1871–72) L.R. 7 C.P. 9, CCP *17–018*
Bath's Case. *See* Norwich Provident Insurance Society, Re
Bathynay v Bouch (1881) 50 L.J.Q.B. 221 .... *27–014*
Batis Maritime Corp v Petroleos Mediterraneo SA; The Batis [1990] 1 Lloyd's Rep. 345, QBD (Comm) *29–073*
Battersby v Anglo American Oil Co Ltd [1945] K.B. 23, CA *28–116*
Battle's Feed Mills, Re (1975) 59 D.L.R. (3d) 488 .... *19–008*
Battley v Faulkner (1820) 3 B. & Ald. 288 .... *1–124*, *28–032*, *28–052*
Batts Combe Quarry Ltd v Ford [1943] Ch. 51; [1942] 2 All E.R. 639, CA *16–117*

Batty v Metropolitan Property Realisations Ltd [1978] Q.B. 554; [1978] 2 W.L.R. 500; [1978] 2 All E.R. 445; 7 B.L.R. 1; (1977) 245 E.G. 43; (1978) 122 S.J. 63, CA (Civ Div) *29–121*
Baumwoll v Gilchrest & Co. *See* Baumwoll Manufactur Von Carl Scheibler v Furness.
Baumwoll Manufactur Von Carl Scheibler v Furness; sub nom. Baumvoll Manufactur Von Scheibler v Gilchrest & Co; Baumvoll Manufactur Von Scheibler v Gilchrist & Co [1893] A.C. 8, HL; affirming [1892] 1 Q.B. 253, CA; reversing [1891] 2 Q.B. 310, QBD *12–055*, *12–069*, *12–073*, *18–146*
Bavins & Sims v London & South Western Bank Ltd [1900] 1 Q.B. 270, CA *29–141*
Bawden v London, Edinburgh and Glasgow Assurance Co [1892] 2 Q.B. 534, CA *6–149*
Baxter v Camden LBC (No.2) [2001] Q.B. 1; [1999] 2 W.L.R. 566; [1999] 1 All E.R. 237; [1999] Env. L.R. 561; (1999) 31 H.L.R. 356; [1999] B.L.G.R. 239; [1999] L. & T.R. 136; [1998] E.G. 157 (C.S.); (1998) 95(45) L.S.G. 41; (1999) 143 S.J.L.B. 11; [1998] N.P.C. 147; [1999] E.H.L.R. Dig. 205, CA (Civ Div) *1–154*
Baxter v Connolly (1820) 1 J. & W. 576 .... *27–043*
Bay Ridge, The. *See* Manatee Towing Co Ltd v Oceanbulk Maritime SA.
Baybut v Eccle Riggs Country Park Ltd, *The Times*, November 13, 2006, Ch D *13–009*, 15–043, *15–061*
Bayleaf v Butterworth (1847) 1 Exch. 425 .... *13–018*
Bayley v Homan (1837) 3 Bing.N.C. 915 .... *22–015*
Baylis v Bishop of London [1913] 1 Ch. 127, CA *29–012*, *29–179*, *29–182*, 29–190
Baylis v Lintott (1872–73) L.R. 8 C.P. 345, CCP *1–129*
Baynham v Philips Electronic (UK) Ltd [1995] O.P.L.R. 253, QBD *2–141*
Bayoil SA v Seawind Tankers Corp; The Leonidas [2001] 1 All E.R. (Comm) 392; [2001] 1 Lloyd's Rep. 533; [2001] C.L.C. 1800, QBD (Comm) *12–079*
Bayoumi v Women's Total Abstinence Educational Union Ltd; sub nom. Perkins v Women's Total Abstinence Educational Union Ltd [2003] EWCA Civ 1548; [2004] Ch. 46; [2004] 2 W.L.R. 181; [2004] 3 All E.R. 110; [2004] 2 P. & C.R. 11; [2004] W.T.L.R. 133; (2003) 100(47) L.S.G. 21; (2003) 147 S.J.L.B. 1307; [2003] N.P.C. 135; [2004] 1 P. & C.R. DG9, CA (Civ Div); reversing [2003] EWHC 212 (Ch); [2003] Ch. 283; [2003] 2 W.L.R. 1287; [2003] 1 All E.R. 864; [2003] W.T.L.R. 317; (2003) 100(10) L.S.G. 27; [2003] N.P.C. 4; [2003] 1 P. & C.R. DG21, Ch D *3–019*
Baytur SA v Finagro Holdings SA [1992] Q.B. 610; [1991] 3 W.L.R. 866; [1991] 4 All E.R. 129; [1992] 1 Lloyd's Rep. 134; (1991) 135 S.J.L.B. 52, CA (Civ Div) *19–055*
Bazeley v Forder (1867–68) L.R. 3 Q.B. 559, QB *8–061*
Beach v Reed Corrugated Cases [1956] 1 W.L.R. 807; [1956] 2 All E.R. 652; 49 R. & I.T. 757; (1956) 35 A.T.C. 126; [1956] T.R. 215; (1956) 100 S.J. 472, QBD *26–048*, *26–159*
Beadling v Goll (1922) 39 T.L.R. 128 .... *16–161*
Beale v Kyte [1907] 1 Ch. 564, Ch D *5–119*, *5–129*, *5–133*
Beale v Nind (1821) 4 B. & A. 566 .... *28–061*
Beale v Taylor [1967] 1 W.L.R. 1193; [1967] 3 All E.R. 253; (1967) 111 S.J. 668, CA (Civ Div) *12–003*
Beaman v ARTS [1949] 1 K.B. 550; [1949] 1 All E.R. 465; 65 T.L.R. 389; (1949) 93 S.J. 236, CA; reversing [1948] 2 All E.R. 89; 64 T.L.R. 285; [1948] W.N. 224, KBD *1–124*, *28–083*, *28–086*, *29–140*
Bean v Wade (1885) 2 T.L.R. 157 .... *28–033*
Beaney (Deceased), Re; sub nom. Beaney v Beaney [1978] 1 W.L.R. 770; [1978] 2 All E.R. 595; (1977) 121 S.J. 832, Ch D *8–069*, *8–070*, *8–071*
Bear Stearns Bank Plc v Forum Global Equity Ltd [2007] EWHC 1576 (Comm), QBD (Comm) *2–113*, *2–114*, *2–142*, *2–161*, *2–183*, *3–109*, *24–003*
Beard v Moira Colliery Co Ltd [1915] 1 Ch. 257, CA *12–051*
Beardmore v TD Burgess Co, 226 A. 2d 329 (1967) *6–052*
Beaton v McDivitt (1988) 13 N.S.W.L.R. 162 .... *2–080*, *3–002*, *3–024*

Beaton v Nationwide Anglia Building Society (formerly Nationwide Building Society) [1991] 2 E.G.L.R. 145; [1991] 38 E.G. 218, DC *14–092*
Beattie v E&F Beattie Ltd [1938] Ch. 708; [1938] 3 All E.R. 214, CA *9–061*, *18–113*
Beattie v Lord Ebury (1874–75) L.R. 7 H.L. 102, HL; affirming (1871–72) L.R. 7 Ch. App. 777, CA in Chancery *6–013*
Beatty v Beatty [1924] 1 K.B. 807, CA *25–017*
Beauchamp Ex p. Beauchamp, Re [1904] 1 K.B. 572, CA *20–049*
Beauchamp v Winn; sub nom. Earl Beauchamp v Winn (1873) L.R. 6 H.L. 223, HL; affirming (1868–69) L.R. 4 Ch. App. 562, CA in Chancery *5–027*, *5–128*, *28–141*
Beaufort (Duke of) v Swansea Corp (1849) 3 Exch. 413 .... *12–126*
Beaufort Developments (NI) Ltd v Gilbert-Ash (NI) Ltd [1999] 1 A.C. 266; [1998] 2 W.L.R. 860; [1998] 2 All E.R. 778; [1998] N.I. 144; [1998] C.L.C. 830; 88 B.L.R. 1; 59 Con. L.R. 66; (1998) 14 Const. L.J. 280; [1998] E.G. 85 (C.S.); (1998) 95(24) L.S.G. 33; (1998) 95(31) L.S.G. 34; (1998) 148 N.L.J. 869; (1998) 142 S.J.L.B. 172; [1998] N.P.C. 91; [1998] N.P.C. 93, HL (NI); reversing [1997] N.I. 142; 83 B.L.R. 1; (1997) 13 Const. L.J. 321, CA (NI) *12–091*
Beaumont v Greathead (1846) 2 C.B. 494 .... *26–008*
Beaumont v Humberts (A Firm) [1990] 49 E.G. 46; [1990] E.G. 97 (C.S.), CA (Civ Div); affirming [1988] 29 E.G. 104; [1988] E.G. 13 (C.S.), QBD *18–022*
Beaumont v Reeve (1846) 8 Q.B. 483 .... *16–067*
Beaumont (Deceased), Re; sub nom. Martin v Midland Bank Trust Co [1980] Ch. 444; [1979] 3 W.L.R. 818; [1980] 1 All E.R. 266; (1979) 123 S.J. 803, Ch D *2–158*, *2–169*
Beauvale Furnishings Ltd v Chapman [2000] All E.R. (D) 2038; [2001] Emp. L.R. 501, EAT *16–017*
Beavan v M'Donnell (1854) 9 Exch. 309 .... *8–068*
Beavan (No.1), Re; sub nom. Davies Banks & Co v Beavan (No.1) [1912] 1 Ch. 196, Ch D *28–100*
Beazer Homes Ltd v Stroude. *See* Stroude v Beazer Homes Ltd
Becher v Roplak Enterprises. *See* Kurt A Becher GmbH & Co KG v Roplak Enterprises SA; The World Navigator
Beck v Value Capital Ltd (No.2) [1976] 1 W.L.R. 572; [1976] 2 All E.R. 102; (1976) 120 S.J. 252, CA (Civ Div); affirming [1975] 1 W.L.R. 6; [1974] 3 All E.R. 442; (1974) 119 S.J. 32, Ch D *20–004*, *28–118*
Becker v Partridge [1966] 2 Q.B. 155; [1966] 2 W.L.R. 803; [1966] 2 All E.R. 266; (1966) 110 S.J. 187, CA *6–157*
Becket v Cohen; sub nom. Beckett v Cohen [1972] 1 W.L.R. 1593; [1973] 1 All E.R. 120; 71 L.G.R. 46; (1972) 116 S.J. 882, DC *6–012*
Beckett Financial Services v Atkinson, unreported, November 6, 2001, QBD *16–102*
Beckett Investment Management Group Ltd v Hall [2007] EWCA Civ 613; [2007] I.C.R. 1539; [2007] I.R.L.R. 793; (2007) 151 S.J.L.B. 891, CA (Civ Div); reversing [2007] EWHC 241 (QB), QBD *12–081*, *16–097*, *16–196*
Beckett v Nurse [1948] 1 K.B. 535; [1948] 1 All E.R. 81; 64 T.L.R. 95; [1948] L.J.R. 450; (1948) 92 S.J. 54, CA *4–026*, *12–102*, *12–107*
Beckford v Wade (1805) 17 Ves. 87 .... *28–134*
Beckham v Drake, 9 E.R. 1213; (1849) 2 H.L. Cas. 579; (1841) 9 M. & W. 79, HL *20–034*, *20–055*, *26–103*
Beckhuson & Gibbs v Hamblet [1901] 2 K.B. 73, CA *29–117*
Becton Dickinson UK v Zwebner [1989] Q.B. 208; [1988] 3 W.L.R. 1376; [1989] 13 E.G. 65; (1988) 132 S.J. 1638, QBD *29–106*
Bedford Insurance Co Ltd v Instituto de Resseguros do Brasil [1985] Q.B. 966; [1984] 3 W.L.R. 726; [1984] 3 All E.R. 766; [1984] 1 Lloyd's Rep. 210; [1985] Fin. L.R. 49; (1985) 82 L.S.G. 37; (1984) 134 N.L.J. 34; (1984) 128 S.J. 701, QBD (Comm) *16–147*
Bedfordshire CC v Fitzpatrick Contractors Ltd, 62 Con. L.R. 64, QBD (TCC) ...*1–032*, *13–007*, *13–009*, *13–010*, *21–014*
Beech v Ford (1848) 7 Hare 208 .... *22–006*

Beer v Bowden [1981] 1 W.L.R. 522; [1981] 1 All E.R. 1070; (1981) 41 P. & C.R. 317, CA (Civ Div) ... *2–128*, *2–132*
Beesly v Hallwood Estates Ltd [1961] Ch. 105; [1961] 2 W.L.R. 36; [1961] 1 All E.R. 90; (1961) 105 S.J. 61, CA; affirming [1960] 1 W.L.R. 549; [1960] 2 All E.R. 314; (1960) 104 S.J. 407, Ch D ... *1–093*, *1–105*, *1–106*, *2–180*, *3–098*, *3–172*, *5–054*, *6–013*
Beeston and Stapleford Urban DC v Smith [1949] 1 K.B. 656; [1949] 1 All E.R. 394; 65 T.L.R. 154; 47 L.G.R. 199; [1949] L.J.R. 984; (1949) 93 S.J. 73, DC ... *16–019*
Beevor v Marler (1898) 14 T.L.R. 289 ... *29–036*
Begbie v Phosphate Sewage Co Ltd (1875–76) L.R. 1 Q.B.D. 679, CA; affirming (1874–75) L.R. 10 Q.B. 491, QBD ... *16–017*
Beggs v Scottish Ministers [2007] UKHL 3; [2007] 1 W.L.R. 455; 2007 S.L.T. 235; 2007 S.C.L.R. 287; (2007) 151 S.J.L.B. 258; 2007 G.W.D. 5–72, HL ... *10–019*
Behn v Burness (1863) 3 B. & S. 751 ... *12–031*, *12–037*
Behnke v Bede Shipping Co Ltd [1927] 1 K.B. 649; (1927) 27 Ll. L. Rep. 24, KBD ... *4–032*, *4–034*, *27–014*
Behrend & Co Ltd v Produce Brokers Co Ltd [1920] 3 K.B. 530; (1920) 4 Ll. L. Rep. 228, KBD ... *29–062*
Behrend's Trust, Re; sub nom. Surman v Biddell [1911] 1 Ch. 687, Ch D ... *20–054*
Behzadi v Shaftesbury Hotels Ltd [1992] Ch. 1; [1991] 2 W.L.R. 1251; [1991] 2 All E.R. 477; (1991) 62 P. & C.R. 163; [1990] E.G. 111 (C.S.); (1990) 140 N.L.J. 1385, CA (Civ Div) ... *12–038*, *21–014*, *21–017*
Belcham and Gawley's Contract, Re [1930] 1 Ch. 56, Ch D ... *27–055*
Belcore Maritime Corp v Fratelli Moretti Cereali SpA; The Mastro Giorgis [1983] 2 Lloyd's Rep. 66, QBD (Comm) ... *12–089*
Belgravia Navigation Co SA v Cannor Shipping; The Troll Park [1988] 2 Lloyd's Rep. 423, CA (Civ Div); affirming [1988] 1 Lloyd's Rep. 55, QBD (Comm) ... *12–046*
Bell v Balls [1897] 1 Ch. 663, Ch D ... *4–038*
Bell v Banks (1841) 3 M.G. 258 ... *25–001*
Bell v Buckley (1856) 11 Exch. 631 ... *21–078*
Bell v Cundall (1750) Amb. 101 ... *5–130*
Bell v Gardiner (1842) 4 M.G. 11 ... *29–036*
Bell v Holmes [1956] 1 W.L.R. 1359; [1956] 3 All E.R. 449; (1956) 100 S.J. 801, Assizes (Leeds) ... *25–012*
Bell v Lever Brothers Ltd; sub nom. Lever Bros Ltd v Bell [1932] A.C. 161, HL; reversing [1931] 1 K.B. 557, CA ... *1–082*, *3–026*, *5–001*, *5–008*, *5–009*, *5–012*, 5–018, *5–021*, **5–028**, *5–029*, *5–030*, 5–032, *5–035*, *5–044*, *5–049*, *5–050*, 5–051, 5–053, 5–058, 5–061, *6–142*, *6–162*, *22–021*, *29–043*, *29–074*
Bell v London and North Western Railway (1852) 15 Beav. 548 ... *19–022*
Bell v Peter Browne & Co [1990] 2 Q.B. 495; [1990] 3 W.L.R. 510; [1990] 3 All E.R. 124; (1990) 140 N.L.J. 701, CA (Civ Div) ... *1–136*, *1–167*, *18–026*, *28–033*, *28–034*
Bell & Co v Antwerp, London & Brazil Line [1891] 1 Q.B. 103, CA ... *21–010*
Bell Bros Pty v Shire of Serpentine Jarrahdale (1969) 44 A.L.J.R. 26, HC (Aus) ... *29–094*
Bell Houses Ltd v City Wall Properties Ltd (No.1) [1966] 2 Q.B. 656; [1966] 2 W.L.R. 1323; [1966] 2 All E.R. 674; (1967) 205 E.G. 535; (1966) 110 S.J. 268, CA; reversing [1966] 1 Q.B. 207; [1965] 3 W.L.R. 1065; [1965] 3 All E.R. 427; (1965) 109 S.J. 898, QBD ... *9–023*
Bell River Community Arena Inc v Kaufmann Co (1978) 87 D.l.R. (3d) 761 ... *5–074*
Bellhouse v Mellor Proudman & Mellor (1859) 4 H. & N. 116 ... *12–093*
Bellingham v Dhillon [1973] Q.B. 304; [1972] 3 W.L.R. 730; [1973] 1 All E.R. 20; (1972) 116 S.J. 566, QBD ... *26–115*
Bellshill & Mossend Cooperative Society Ltd v Dalziel Cooperative Society Ltd [1960] A.C. 832; [1960] 2 W.L.R. 580; [1960] 1 All E.R. 673; 1960 S.C. (H.L.) 64; 1960 S.L.T. 165; (1960) 104 S.J. 248, HL; affirming, 1958 S.C. 400; 1959 S.L.T. 150, IH (1 Div) ... *16–045*, *16–117*

Belmont Finance Corp v Williams Furniture Ltd (No.2) [1980] 1 All E.R. 393, CA (Civ Div) *16–193*
Belshaw v Bush, 138 E.R. 444; (1851) 11 C.B. 191, CCP *21–041*, *21–073*, *21–074*, *21–076*
Beltana, The. *See* Automatic Tube Co Pty Ltd v Adelaide Steamship (Operations) Ltd; The Beltana
Belvoir Finance Co Ltd v Harold G Cole & Co Ltd [1969] 1 W.L.R. 1877; [1969] 2 All E.R. 904, QBD *16–180*
Belvoir Finance Co Ltd v Stapleton [1971] 1 Q.B. 210; [1970] 3 W.L.R. 530; [1970] 3 All E.R. 664; (1970) 114 S.J. 719, CA (Civ Div) *16–167*, *16–178*
Bem Dis A Turk Ticaret S/A TR v International Agri Trade Co Ltd; The Selda [1999] 1 All E.R. (Comm.) 619; [1999] 1 Lloyd's Rep. 729; [1999] C.L.C. 813, CA (Civ Div); affirming [1998] 1 Lloyd's Rep. 416, QBD (Comm) *14–005*
Ben Shipping Co (Pte) Ltd v An Bord Bainne; The C Joyce; sub nom. Benline Shipping v An Bord Bainne [1986] 2 All E.R. 177; [1986] 2 Lloyd's Rep. 285, QBD (Comm) *12–069*, *13–010*
Benabu & Co v Produce Brokers Co (1921) 37 T.L.R. 609, KBD *12–036*
Benaim & Co v Debono [1924] A.C. 514, PC (M) *30–012*
Bence v Shearman [1898] 2 Ch. 582, CA *19–017*, *19–085*
Bence Graphics International Ltd v Fasson UK Ltd [1998] Q.B. 87; [1997] 3 W.L.R. 205; [1997] 1 All E.R. 979; [1997] C.L.C. 373; (1996) 93(40) L.S.G. 24; (1996) 146 N.L.J. 1577; (1996) 140 S.J.L.B. 227, CA (Civ Div) *26–060*, *26–089*, *26–117*
Benham v Gambling [1941] A.C. 157, HL *26–030*
Beningfield v Baxter (1887) L.R. 12 App. Cas. 167, PC (Natal) *7–077*
Benjamin Developments Ltd v Robt. Jones (Pacific) Ltd [1994] 3 N.Z.L.R. 189 .... *12–055*
Benmax v Austin Motor Co Ltd [1955] A.C. 370; [1955] 2 W.L.R. 418; [1955] 1 All E.R. 326; (1955) 72 R.P.C. 39; (1955) 99 S.J. 129, HL; affirming (1953) 70 R.P.C. 284, CA; reversing (1953) 70 R.P.C. 143, Ch D *8–014*
Bennett Ex p. Official Receiver, Re [1907] 1 K.B. 149, KBD *20–054*
Bennett v Bennett [1952] 1 K.B. 249; [1952] 1 All E.R. 413; [1952] 1 T.L.R. 400, CA; affirming [1951] 2 K.B. 572; [1951] 1 All E.R. 1088; [1951] 1 T.L.R. 873; (1951) 115 J.P. 355; (1951) 95 S.J. 286, KBD *16–044*, *16–199*, *16–201*, *16–202*
Bennett v Bennett [1969] 1 W.L.R. 430; [1969] 1 All E.R. 539; (1969) 113 S.J. 284, PDAD *8–069*
Bennett v Clough (1818) 1 B. & Ald. 461 .... *16–204*
Bennett v Fowler (1840) 2 Beav. 302 .... *22–046*
Bennett v Greenland Houchen & Co [1998] P.N.L.R. 458, CA (Civ Div) *28–006*
Bennett v Griffin Finance (A Firm) [1967] 2 Q.B. 46; [1967] 2 W.L.R. 561; [1967] 1 All E.R. 515; (1967) 111 S.J. 150, CA *21–041*
Bennett v Parker (1867) Ir. 2 C.L. 89 .... *21–089*
Bennett v Tugwell [1971] 2 Q.B. 267; [1971] 2 W.L.R. 847; [1971] 2 All E.R. 248; [1971] 1 Lloyd's Rep. 333; [1971] R.T.R. 221; (1971) 115 S.J. 289, QBD *14–014*
Bennett Walden & Co v Wood [1950] 2 All E.R. 134; 66 T.L.R. (Pt. 2) 3; [1950] W.N. 329, CA *2–118*
Bensley v Burdon (1830) 8 L.J. (O.S.) Ch. 85 .... *1–112*
Bent v Wakefield and Barnsley Union Bank (1878–79) L.R. 4 C.P.D. 1, CPD *2–043*, *3–062*
Bentall Horsley & Baldry v Vicary [1931] 1 K.B. 253, KBD *2–084*
Bentinck v Fenn; sub nom. Cape Breton Co, Re (1887) L.R. 12 App. Cas. 652, HL; affirming (1885) L.R. 29 Ch. D. 795, CA; affirming (1884) L.R. 26 Ch. D. 221, Ch D *6–128*, *9–055*
Bentley v Craven (1853) 18 Beav. 75 .... *6–162*
Benton v Campbell Parker & Co Ltd [1925] 2 K.B. 410, KBD *21–048*
Bentsen v Taylor Sons & Co (No.2) [1893] 2 Q.B. 274, CA *12–026*, *24–001*, *24–002*, *24–003*, *24–004*, *24–010*, *24–038*
Bentworth Finance v Lubert [1968] 1 Q.B. 680 .... *2–150*

Benyon v Nettlefold (1850) 3 Mac. & G. 94 .... *16–067*
Benzon, Re; sub nom. Bower v Chetwynd [1914] 2 Ch. 68, CA *28–064*
Beoco Ltd v Alfa Laval Co Ltd [1995] Q.B. 137; [1994] 3 W.L.R. 1179; [1994] 4 All E.R. 464; [1994] C.L.C. 111; 66 B.L.R. 1; (1994) 144 N.L.J. 233, CA (Civ Div) *1–122*, *26–037*, *26–040*
Berdoe v Dawson (1865) 34 Beav. 603 .... *7–074*
Beresford v Royal Insurance Co Ltd [1938] A.C. 586, HL; affirming [1937] 2 K.B. 197, CA *16–168*, *16–170*, *16–171*, *16–172*
Berg v Sadler and Moore [1937] 2 K.B. 158, CA *6–109*, *16–017*
Berg & Son Ltd v Vanden Avenne-Izegem PVBA. *See* V Berg & Son v Vanden Avenne-Izegem PVBA
Berge Sisar, The. *See* Borealis AB (formerly Borealis Petrokemi AB and Statoil Petrokemi AB) v Stargas Ltd.
Berger and Light Diffusers Pty Ltd v Pollock [1973] 2 Lloyd's Rep. 442, QBD (Comm) *6–019*
Bergerco USA v Vegoil Ltd [1984] 1 Lloyd's Rep. 440, QBD (Comm) *12–036*
Bergmann v Kenburn Waste Management Ltd. *See* Kenburn Waste Management Ltd v Bergmann
Berkeley v Hardy (1826) 5 B. & C. 355 .... *1–109*, *18–122*
Berkeley Applegate (Investment Consultants) Ltd (No.1), Re; Harris v Conway [1989] Ch. 32; [1988] 3 W.L.R. 95; [1988] 3 All E.R. 71; (1988) 4 B.C.C. 274; [1989] B.C.L.C. 28; [1989] P.C.C. 261; (1988) 132 S.J. 896, Ch D (Companies Ct) *16–165*, *29–022*, *29–112*, *29–115*, *29–133*, *29–157*
Berkeley Community Villages Ltd v Pullen [2007] EWHC 1330 (Ch); [2007] 24 E.G. 169 (C.S.); [2007] 3 E.G.L.R. 101; [2007] N.P.C. 71, Ch D *1–030*, *24–021*
Berkshire, The [1974] 1 Lloyd's Rep. 185, QBD (Admlty) *14–038*
Berliner Industriebank AG v Jost [1971] 2 Q.B. 463; [1971] 3 W.L.R. 61; [1971] 2 All E.R. 1513; (1971) 115 S.J. 505, CA (Civ Div) *25–017*
Berlitz Schools of Languages Ltd v Duchene (1903) 6 F. 181; (1903) 11 S.L.T. 491, IH (1 Div) *16–099*
Bermingham v Sheridan, Waterloo Life Assurance Co (No.4) (1864) 33 Beav. 660 .... *27–011*
Bernard v Josephs [1982] Ch. 391; [1982] 2 W.L.R. 1052; [1982] 3 All E.R. 162; (1983) 4 F.L.R. 178; (1982) 126 S.J. 361, CA (Civ Div) *16–068*
Bernard & Shaw Ltd v Shaw [1951] 2 All E.R. 267; 44 R. & I.T. 397; (1951) 30 A.T.C. 187; [1951] T.R. 205; [1951] W.N. 340; (1951) 95 S.J. 530, KBD *29–107*
Bernhard Schulte GmbH & Co KG v Nile Holdings Ltd [2004] EWHC 977 (Comm); [2004] 2 Lloyd's Rep. 352, QBD (Comm) *1–022*, *1–032*
Bernstein v Pamson Motors (Golders Green) Ltd [1987] 2 All E.R. 220; [1987] R.T.R. 384, QBD *6–127*
Bernuth Lines Ltd v High Seas Shipping Ltd; The Eastern Navigator [2005] EWHC 3020; [2006] 1 All E.R. (Comm) 359; [2006] 1 Lloyd's Rep. 537; [2006] 1 C.L.C. 403; [2006] C.I.L.L. 2343; (2006) 156 N.L.J. 64, QBD (Comm) *2–051*, *2–091*
Berridge v Fitzgerald (1868–69) L.R. 4 Q.B. 639, QB *21–056*
Berry v Berry [1929] 2 K.B. 316, KBD *1–115*, *22–030*, 22–032, *22–033*
Berry Ltd v Brighton and Sussex Building Society [1939] 3 All E.R. 217, Ch D ... *2–118*
Bertel v Neveux (1878) 39 L.T. 257 .... *2–129*
Berwick v Horsfall (1858) 4 C.B. (N.S.) 450 .... *12–047*
Berwick v Lloyds TSB Bank Plc, unreported May 15, 2007, CC (Birmingham) ... *15–098*
Besant v Cross (1851) 10 C.B. 895 .... *12–101*
Besseler Waechter Glover & Co v South Derwent Coal Co Ltd [1938] 1 K.B. 408; (1937) 59 Ll. L. Rep. 104, KBD 22–041, *22–042*
Best v Glenville [1960] 1 W.L.R. 1198; [1960] 3 All E.R. 478; 58 L.G.R. 333; (1961) 12 P. & C.R. 48; (1960) 104 S.J. 934, CA *16–012*
Best v Hamand (1879) L.R. 12 Ch. D. 1, CA *26–152*
Best's Case (1865) 2 D.J. & S. 650 .... *2–045*

Beswick v Beswick [1968] A.C. 58; [1967] 3 W.L.R. 932; [1967] 2 All E.R. 1197; (1967) 111 S.J. 540, HL; affirming [1966] Ch. 538; [1966] 3 W.L.R. 396; [1966] 3 All E.R. 1; (1966) 110 S.J. 507, CA; reversing [1965] 3 All E.R. 858; (1965) 116 N.L.J. 245, Chancery Ct of Lancaster 1–109, *1–188*, **18–020**, 18–042, 18–044, *18–046*, 18–047, 18–049, 18–051, 18–054, 18–062, *18–063*, 18–071, 18–073, 18–075, *18–076*, *18–079*, *18–081*, 18–083, 18–093, *18–122*, 18–124, 18–125, *21–003*, *27–005*, *27–006*, *27–008*, 27–009, *27–034*, 27–043, 27–050, 27–051, *27–0–52*
Beta Computers (Europe) Ltd v Adobe Systems (Europe) Ltd, 1996 S.L.T. 604; [1996] C.L.C. 821; [1997–98] Info. T.L.R. 73; [1996] F.S.R. 367; [1998] Masons C.L.R. Rep. 104, OH *2–030*
Bethell, Re; sub nom. Bethell v Bethell (1887) L.R. 34 Ch. D. 561, Ch D *28–042*
Betjemann v Betjemann [1895] 2 Ch. 474, CA *28–057*, *28–089*
Betterbee v Davis (1811) 3 Camp. 70 ..... *21–085*
Bettini v Gye (1875–76) L.R. 1 Q.B.D. 183, QBD *12–040*, 24–038
Betts & Drew v Gibbins (1834) 2 A. & E. 57 ..... *16–175*
Bevan v Bevan (No.1) [1955] 2 Q.B. 227; [1955] 2 W.L.R. 948; [1955] 2 All E.R. 206; (1955) 99 S.J. 306, QBD *16–026*, *23–031*
Bevan v Waters (1828) 3 C.P. 520 ..... *29–103*
Bevan Ashford v Geoff Yeandle (Contractors) Ltd (In Liquidation) [1999] Ch. 239; [1998] 3 W.L.R. 172; [1998] 3 All E.R. 238; 59 Con. L.R. 1; [1998] 2 Costs L.R. 15; (1998) 95(16) L.S.G. 27; (1998) 148 N.L.J. 587; (1998) 142 S.J.L.B. 151; [1998] N.P.C. 69, Ch D *16–049*
Bevan Ashford v Malin [1995] I.C.R. 453; [1995] I.R.L.R. 360, EAT *12–093*
Bevan Investments Ltd v Blackhall & Struthers (No.2), 11 B.L.R. 78; [1978] 2 N.Z.L.R. 97, CA (NZ) *26–016*, *26–018*
Bevans v Rees (1839) 5 M.W. 306 ..... *21–085*, *21–090*
Beverley Corp v Richard Hodgson & Sons (1972) 225 E.G. 799 ..... *13–027*, *22–054*
Beves & Co Ltd v Farkas [1953] 1 Lloyd's Rep. 103, QBD *23–047*
Beyers v Green [1936] 1 All E.R. 613 ..... *28–086*
Beyfus v Lodge [1925] Ch. 350, Ch D *26–152*, *27–057*
Beyfus and Masters's Contract, Re (1888) L.R. 39 Ch. D. 110, CA *27–056*
Bhowampur Banking Corp Ltd v Sreemati Durgesh Nandini Dasi (1941) 68 L.R.I.A. 144 ..... *16–037*
Bidaisee v Sampath [1995] N.P.C. 59, PC (Trin) *21–014*, *21–016*
Bidder v Bridges (No.3) (1888) L.R. 37 Ch. D. 406, CA *3–129*
Biddulph and District Agricultural Society Ltd v Agricultural Wholesale Society Ltd; sub nom. Agricultural Wholesale Society Ltd v Biddulph and District Agricultural Society Ltd [1927] A.C. 76, HL; affirming [1925] Ch. 769, CA *9–063*
Bielecki v Suffolk Coastal CC [2004] EWHC 3142, QBD *10–024*
Biffin v Bignell (1862) 7 H. & N. 877 ..... *7–040*
Bigg v Boyd Gibbins [1971] 1 W.L.R. 913; [1971] 2 All E.R. 183; (1971) 115 S.J. 406, CA (Civ Div) *2–009*
Biggerstaff v Rowatt's Wharf Ltd; Howard v Rowatt's Wharf Ltd [1896] 2 Ch. 93, CA *9–042*, *19–070*, *29–054*, *29–059*, *29–062*
Biggin v Minton [1977] 1 W.L.R. 701; [1977] 2 All E.R. 647; (1977) 34 P. & C.R. 1; (1977) 121 S.J. 254, Ch D *27–079*, *27–082*
Biggin & Co Ltd v Permanite Ltd [1951] 2 K.B. 314; [1951] 2 All E.R. 191; [1951] 2 T.L.R. 159; (1951) 95 S.J. 414, CA *26–060*, *26–078*
Biggin Hill Airport Ltd v Bromley LBC [2001] EWCA Civ 1089; (2001) 98(33) L.S.G. 30, CA (Civ Div); reversing (2001) 98(3) L.S.G. 42; [2000] N.P.C. 130, Ch D 1–043, 1–057, *1–061*
Bigos v Bousted [1951] 1 All E.R. 92, KBD *16–010*, *16–014*, *16–165*, *16–177*, *16–180*, *16–186*, 16–190
Bilbie v Lumley (1802) 2 East. 469 ..... *5–054*, *29–041*, 29–044
Bilke v Havelock (1813) 3 Camp. 374 ..... *3–062*
Billing v Ries (1841) Car. M. 26 ..... *29–147*

Billyack v Leyland Construction Co [1968] 1 W.L.R. 471; [1968] 1 All E.R. 783; 66 L.G.R. 506; (1968) 112 S.J. 274, QBD *13–015*, *14–009*
Bilston Corp v Wolverhampton Corp [1942] Ch. 391, Ch D *16–025*
Bim Kemi AB v Blackburn Chemicals Ltd (Application to Strike Out); sub nom. Blackburn Chemicals Ltd v Bim Kemi AB (Application to Strike Out) [2004] EWCA Civ 1490; [2005] U.K.C.L.R. 1; [2005] Eu. L.R. 176; (2004) 101(46) L.S.G. 34, CA (Civ Div); affirming [2004] EWHC 166 (Comm); [2004] U.K.C.L.R. 364; [2004] Eu. L.R. 575, QBD (Comm) *16–205*
Binder v Alachouzos [1972] 2 Q.B. 151; [1972] 2 W.L.R. 947; [1972] 2 All E.R. 189; [1972] 1 Lloyd's Rep. 524; (1972) 116 S.J. 139, CA (Civ Div) ...16–013, *29–098*
Bingham v Allport (1833) 1 Nev. M. 398 .... *21–094*
Bingham v Bingham, 27 E.R. 934; (1748) 1 Ves. Sen. 126, Ct of Chancery *5–026*
Binions v Evans [1972] Ch. 359; [1972] 2 W.L.R. 729; [1972] 2 All E.R. 70; (1972) 23 P. & C.R. 192; (1972) 116 S.J. 122, CA (Civ Div) ...1–006, *1–188*, *13–028*, *18–135*
Binns v Nichols (1866) L.R. 2 Eq. 256, Ct of Chancery *28–031*
Birch v Birch [1902] P. 130, CA *25–015*
Birch v Paramount Estate (1956) 167 E.G. 396 .... *12–004*
Birch v Thomas [1972] 1 W.L.R. 294; [1972] 1 All E.R. 905; [1972] 1 Lloyd's Rep. 209; [1972] R.T.R. 130; (1971) 115 S.J. 968, CA (Civ Div) *12–017*, *14–014*
Birchall, Re; sub nom. Wilson v Birchall (1880–81) L.R. 16 Ch. D. 41, CA *8–062*
Bircham & Co Nominees (No.2) Ltd v Worrell Holdings Ltd [2001] EWCA Civ 775; (2001) 82 P. & C.R. 34; [2001] 3 E.G.L.R. 83; [2001] 47 E.G. 149; [2001] 22 E.G. 153 (C.S.); [2001] N.P.C. 94; (2001) 82 P. & C.R. DG18, CA (Civ Div) *2–032*, *2–088*, *2–127*, *3–172*, 4–058
Bird v Boulter (1833) 4 B. & Ad. 443 .... *4–038*
Bird v Gammon (1837) 3 Bing. N.C. 883 .... *28–094*
Bird v Hildage [1948] 1 K.B. 91; [1947] 2 All E.R. 7; 63 T.L.R. 405; [1948] L.J.R. 196; 177 L.T. 97; (1947) 91 S.J. 559, CA *21–019*
Bird & Co v Thomas Cook & Son [1937] 2 All E.R. 227 .... *12–122*
Birkbeck Permanent Benefit Building Society (No.2), Re [1915] 1 Ch. 91, Ch D *29–043*
Birkdale District Electric Supply Co Ltd v Southport Corp; sub nom. Southport Corp v Birkdale District Electric Supply Co Ltd [1926] A.C. 355, HL; affirming [1925] Ch. 794, CA; reversing [1925] Ch. 63, Ch D *10–027*, *10–028*, *10–029*, 10–030
Birkenhead, etc., Ry v Pilcher (1850) 5 Exch. 121 .... *8–037*
Birkett v Acorn Business Machines Ltd [1999] 2 All E.R. (Comm) 429; (1999) 96(31) L.S.G. 35 , CA (Civ Div) *16–205*
Birkin v Wing (1890) 63 L.T. 80 .... *8–070*
Birkley v Presgrave (1801) 1 East 220 .... *29–129*
Birks, Re; sub nom. Kenyon v Birks [1900] 1 Ch. 417, CA; reversing [1899] 1 Ch. 703, Ch D *12–055*
Birmingham & District Land Co v London & North Western Railway Co (No.2) (1889) L.R. 40 Ch. D. 268, CA; affirming (1887) L.R. 36 Ch. D. 650, Ch D ... 3–097
Birmingham City Council v C Bryant & Son and Bison Concrete, 9 Con. L.R. 128 ....*28–118*, *28–119*
Birmingham Midshires Building Society v Infields (A Firm), 66 Con. L.R. 20; [1999] Lloyd's Rep. P.N. 874; [1999] E.G. 77 (C.S.), QBD (TCC) *28–011*
Birmingham Mosque Trust v Alavi [1992] I.C.R. 435, EAT *2–181*
Birrell v Dryer; sub nom. Birell v Dryer (1883–84) L.R. 9 App. Cas. 345, HL *12–083*
Birtley & District Co-operative Society Ltd v Windy Nook and District Industrial Co-operative Soc. Ltd (No. 2) [1960] 2 Q.B. 1; [1959] 2 W.L.R. 415; 103 S.J. 240; [1959] 1 All E.R. 623 .... *16–045*
Bishop, Ex p. *See* Fox Walker & Co Ex p. Bishop, Re
Bishop v Bonham [1988] 1 W.L.R. 742; (1988) 4 B.C.C. 347; [1988] B.C.L.C. 656; [1988] F.L.R. 282; (1988) 132 S.J. 933, CA (Civ Div); reversing (1988) 4 B.C.C. 265, Ch D *14–011*
Bishop v Chambre (1827) Moo. M 116 ....*25–021*, 25–022
Bishop v Church (1748) 3 Atk. 691 .... *20–044*

Bishop v Consolidated London Properties Ltd [1933] All E.R. Rep. 963, KBD ... *21–009*
Bishop v Cunard White Star Ltd; The Queen Mary; Appleby v Cunard White Star Ltd [1950] P. 240; [1950] 2 All E.R. 22; (1949–50) 83 Ll. L. Rep. 415; 66 T.L.R. (Pt. 1) 828; (1950) 94 S.J. 305, PDAD ... *26–080*
Bishop v Smedley (1846) 2 C.B. 90 ... *21–088*
Bishop & Baxter v Anglo-Eastern Trading Co [1944] K.B. 12 ... *2–141*
Bishop of Crediton v Bishop of Exeter [1905] 2 Ch. 455, Ch D ... *25–023*
Bishopsgate Investment Management Ltd (In Liquidation) v Homan [1995] Ch. 211; [1994] 3 W.L.R. 1270; [1995] 1 All E.R. 347; [1994] B.C.C. 868; (1994) 91(36) L.S.G. 37; (1994) 138 S.J.L.B. 176, CA (Civ Div) ... *29–164*, *29–167*
Bishun Chand Firm v Seth Girdhari Lal (1934) 50 T.L.R. 465 ... *29–191*
Bisset v Wilkinson [1927] A.C. 177, PC (NZ) ... *6–009*, *6–012*
Bize v Dickason, 99 E.R. 1097; (1786) 1 Term Rep. 285, KB ... *28–127*
Blachford v Preston (1799) 8 T.R. 89 ... *16–019*
Black v Davies [2005] EWCA Civ 531; [2005] All E.R. (D) 78 (May), CA (Civ Div) ... 6–065
Black v Gompertz (1852) 7 Exch. 862 ... *4–034*
Black v Smallwood (1865–66) 117 C.L.R. 52 ... *9–012*
Black v Smith (1791) Peake 121 ... *21–085*
Black v Wilcox (1976) 30 D.L.R. (3d) 192 ... *7–136*
Black v Yates [1992] Q.B. 526; [1991] 3 W.L.R. 90; [1991] 4 All E.R. 722; [1991] 1 Lloyd's Rep. 181, QBD ... *25–016*, *25–018*
Black Clawson International Ltd v Papierwerke Waldhof-Aschaffenburg AG [1975] A.C. 591; [1975] 2 W.L.R. 513; [1975] 1 All E.R. 810; [1975] 2 Lloyd's Rep. 11; (1975) 119 S.J. 221, HL ... *25–017*
Black Clawson International Ltd v Papierwerke Waldhof-Aschaffenburg AG [1981] 2 Lloyd's Rep. 446; [1981] Com. L.R. 61, QBD (Comm) ... *30–005*
Blackburn v Flavelle (1880–81) L.R. 6 App. Cas. 628, PC (Aus) ... *12–091*
Blackburn and District Benefit Building Society v Cunliffe Brooks & Co. *See* Cunliffe Brooks & Co v Blackburn and District Benefit Building Society
Blackburn Bobbin Co Ltd v TW Allen & Sons Ltd [1918] 2 K.B. 467; 3 A.L.R. 11, CA ... *23–028*, *23–047*, *26–111*
Blackburn Low & Co v Vigors (1887) L.R. 12 App. Cas. 531, HL; reversing (1886) L.R. 17 Q.B.D. 553, CA ... *6–144*, *6–148*
Blackett v Bates (1865–66) L.R. 1 Ch. App. 117, Lord Chancellor ... *27–026*, *27–046*
Blackett v Royal Exchange Assurance Co (1832) 2 Cr. App. R. & J. 244 ... *12–085*, *12–118*
Blackler v New Zealand Rugby Football League (Incorporated) [1968] N.Z.L.R. 547 ... *16–091*
Blackley v National Mutual Life Association of Australasia [1972] N.Z.L.R. 1038 ... *6–151*
Blackpool and Fylde Aero Club v Blackpool BC [1990] 1 W.L.R. 1195; [1990] 3 All E.R. 25; 88 L.G.R. 864; (1991) 3 Admin. L.R. 322; (1991) 155 L.G. Rev. 246, CA (Civ Div) ... 1–136, *2–022*, *2–160*, *3–172*, 10–035, 10–037, 10–038
Blackwood v Robertson, 1984 S.L.T. (Sh. Ct.) 68, Sh Ct (Lothian) ... *1–147*
Blaenau Gwent BC v Robinson Jones Design Partnership Ltd, 53 Con. L.R. 31, QBD (OR) ... *28–109*
Blagden v Bradbear (1806) 12 Ves. 466 ... *4–025*
Blake, Re; sub nom. Minahan, Re [1932] 1 Ch. 54, Ch D ... *28–058*, *28–134*
Blake v Concannon (1870) 4 Ir.Rep.C.L. 323 ... *8–033*
Blake v Gale (1886) L.R. 32 Ch. D. 571, CA ... *28–141*
Blake v Richards & Wallington Industries and Fram Siegwart (1974) 16 K.I.R. 151 ... *14–015*
Blake & Co v Sohn [1969] 1 W.L.R. 1412; [1969] 3 All E.R. 123; (1969) 113 S.J. 690, QBD ... *2–153*
Blake (Valuation Officer) v Hendon Corp (No.1) [1962] 1 Q.B. 283; [1961] 3 W.L.R. 951; [1961] 3 All E.R. 601; (1961) 125 J.P. 620; 59 L.G.R. 515; [1961] R.V.R. 552; (1961) 105 S.J. 666, CA; reversing 175 E.G. 981; 7 R.R.C. 159; 53 R. & I.T. 409; [1960] J.P.L. 429, Lands Tr ... *10–029*
Blakeley v Muller [1903] 2 K.B. 760 ... *23–033*, *23–072*

Blakely Ordnance Co, Re; sub nom. Ex p. New Zealand Banking Corp (1867–68) L.R. 3 Ch. App. 154, CA in Chancery *19–072*
Blakely Ordnance Co, Re; sub nom. Lumsden's Case (1868–69) L.R. 4 Ch. App. 31, CA in Chancery *8–038*
Blane Steamships Ltd v Minister of Transport [1951] 2 K.B. 965; [1951] 2 Lloyd's Rep. 155; [1951] 2 T.L.R. 763; (1951) 95 S.J. 577, CA *23–040*
Blankenstein, The. *See* Damon Compania Naviera SA v Hapag-Lloyd International SA.
Bleakley v Smith (1840) 11 Sim. 150 .... *12–123*
Bleuse v MBT Transport Ltd [2008] I.R.L.R. 264, EAT *30–112*, *30–115*, *30–116*, *30–117*
Blewett, In the Goods of (1879–80) L.R. 5 P.D. 116, PDAD *4–034*
Bliss v South East Thames RHA [1987] I.C.R. 700; [1985] I.R.L.R. 308, CA (Civ Div); reversing (1984) 134 N.L.J. 121, QBD *1–123*, *26–019*, *26–083*
Blisset v Danie, E.R. 1022; (1853) 10 Hare 493, Ct of Chancery *1–027*
Blohn v Desser [1962] 2 Q.B. 116; [1961] 3 W.L.R. 719; [1961] 3 All E.R. 1; (1961) 105 S.J. 724, QBD *25–017*
Blomley v Ryan (1956) 99 C.L.R. 362 .... *7–130*, 7–131, *7–136*, *8–080*
Bloom v American Swiss Watch Co (1915) App.Div. 100 .... *2–041*
Bloomer v Bernstein (1873–74) L.R. 9 C.P. 588, CCP *24–018*, *24–044*
Bloomer v Spittle (1871–72) L.R. 13 Eq. 427, Ct of Chancery 5–119
Blow v Russell (1824) 1 C.P. 365 .... *21–085*
Bloxam v Metropolitan Railway Co (1867–68) L.R. 3 Ch. App. 337, Lord Chancellor *16–060*
Bloxham's Case (1864) 33 Beav. 529 .... *2–045*
Bluck v Gompertz (1852) 7 Exch. 362 .... *22–037*
Blue Haven Enterprises Ltd v Tully [2006] UKPC 17, PC (Jam) *3–138*, *29–003*
Blue Wave, The [1982] 1 Lloyd's Rep. 151; [1981] Com. L.R. 131, QBD (Admlty) *30–005*, *30–006*
Bluett v Stutchbury's (1908) 24 T.L.R. 469 .... *9–058*
Blumberg v Life Interests and Reversionary Securities Corp [1898] 1 Ch. 27, CA *21–044*, *21–087*
Blyth v Fladgate; Morgan v Blyth; Smith v Blyth [1891] 1 Ch. 337, Ch D *17–016*
Blythe Ex p. Banner, Re; sub nom. Blythe, Re v Ex p. Banner (1881) L.R. 17 Ch. D. 480, CA *3–051*, *20–049*
Blythe & Co v Richards Turpin & Co (1916) 114 L.T. 753 .... *14–141*
Boake Allen Ltd v Revenue and Customs Commissioners; sub nom. NEC Semi Conductors Ltd v Revenue and Customs Commissioners [2007] UKHL 25; [2007] 1 W.L.R. 1386; [2007] 3 All E.R. 605; [2007] S.T.C. 1265; [2007] 3 C.M.L.R. 6; [2007] Eu. L.R. 701; [2007] B.T.C. 414; 9 I.T.L. Rep. 995; [2007] S.T.I. 1585; (2007) 104(23) L.S.G. 30; (2007) 151 S.J.L.B. 707, HL ...*29–016*, *29–085*
Board v Hoey, 65 T.L.R. 43; [1948] W.N. 448; (1948) 92 S.J. 661 .... *3–047*
Board of Trade v Cayzer Irvine & Co Ltd; sub nom. Cayzer Irvine & Co Ltd v Board of Trade; Cayzer, Irvine & Co Ltd v Board of Trade [1927] A.C. 610; (1927) 28 Ll. L. Rep. 113, HL *28–031*, *28–059*, *28–125*
Board of Trade v Temperley Steam Shipping Co Ltd (1927) 27 Ll. L. Rep. 230, CA; affirming (1926) 26 Ll. L. Rep. 76, KBD *10–007*
Board of Works for the Greenwich District v Maudslay (1869–70) L.R. 5 Q.B. 397, QB *10–027*
Boardman v Phipps; sub nom. Phipps v Boardman [1967] 2 A.C. 46; [1966] 3 W.L.R. 1009; [1966] 3 All E.R. 721; (1966) 110 S.J. 853, HL *29–155*, *29–156*, *29–157*, *29–160*
Boast v Firth (1868–69) L.R. 4 C.P. 1, CCP *23–038*
Boats Park Ltd v Hutchinson [1999] 2 N.Z.L.R. 1129 .... *12–050*
Boatwright v Boatwright (1873–74) L.R. 17 Eq. 71, Ct of Chancery *28–064*
Bocking Garage v Mazurk, *The Times*, February 4, 1954, CA *21–043*
Bocock v Enfield Rolling Mills [1954] 1 W.L.R. 1303; [1954] 3 All E.R. 94; [1954] 2 Lloyd's Rep. 103; (1954) 98 S.J. 716, CA *26–030*
Boddington v Lawton [1994] I.C.R. 478, Ch D *1–081*, *16–075*, *16–140*

Bodega Co Ltd, Re [1904] 1 Ch. 276, Ch D *29–030*
Bodenham v Purchas (1818) 2 B. Ald 39 .... *21–039*, *21–066*
Bodger v Arch, 156 E.R. 472; (1854) 10 Ex. 333, Ex Ct *28–099*
Bodley Head Ltd v Alec Flegon (t/a Flegon Press) [1972] 1 W.L.R. 680; [1972] F.S.R. 21; [1972] R.P.C. 587; (1971) 115 S.J. 909, Ch D *30–324*
Bodwell v Parsons (1808) 10 East 359 .... *24–028*
Boissevain v Weil [1950] A.C. 327; [1950] 1 All E.R. 728; 66 T.L.R. (Pt. 1) 771; (1950) 94 S.J. 319, HL; affirming [1949] 1 K.B. 482; [1949] 1 All E.R. 146; 65 T.L.R. 197; (1949) 93 S.J. 133, CA; reversing [1948] 1 All E.R. 893, KBD *16–029*, *30–07*, *30–013*, *30–3570*
Bojczuk v Gregorcewicz [1961] S.A.S.R. 128 .... *8–028*
Bolam v Friern Hospital Management Committee [1957] 1 W.L.R. 582; [1957] 2 All E.R. 118; [1955–95] P.N.L.R. 7; (1957) 101 S.J. 357, QBD *13–032*
Bolands Ltd v London & Lancashire Fire Insurance Co Ltd; sub nom. London and Lancashire Fire Insurance Co Ltd v Bolands Ltd [1924] A.C. 836; (1924) 19 Ll. L. Rep. 1, HL (UK-Irl); reversing (1922) 13 Ll. L. Rep. 413, HC (Irl) *12–083*, *14–146*
Bold v Brough, Nicholson & Hall, Ltd [1964] 1 W.L.R. 201; [1963] 3 All E.R. 849; (1964) 43 A.T.C. 13; [1964] T.R. 17; (1964) 108 S.J. 177, QBD *26–158*
Bold v Rayner (1836) 1 M. & W. 343 .... *12–132*
Bolitho (Deceased) v City and Hackney HA [1998] A.C. 232; [1997] 3 W.L.R. 1151; [1997] 4 All E.R. 771; [1998] P.I.Q.R. P10; [1998] Lloyd's Rep. Med. 26; (1998) 39 B.M.L.R. 1; [1998] P.N.L.R. 1; (1997) 94(47) L.S.G. 30; (1997) 141 S.J.L.B. 238, HL; affirming [1993] P.I.Q.R. P334; [1993] 4 Med. L.R. 381, CA (Civ Div) *13–032*
Bolivia v Indemnity Mutual Marine Assurance Co Ltd [1909] 1 K.B. 785, CA *12–087*
Bolivia Exploration Syndicate Ltd, Re [1914] 1 Ch. 139; 83 L.J.Ch. 226; 109 L.T. 741; 110 L.T. 141; 58 S.J. 173; 30 T.L.R. 78, Ch D *9–055*, *11–020*
Bols Distilleries BV (t/a Bols Royal Distilleries) v Superior Yacht Services Ltd [2006] UKPC 45; [2007] 1 W.L.R. 12; [2007] 1 All E.R. (Comm) 461; [2007] 1 Lloyd's Rep. 683; [2007] 1 C.L.C. 308; [2007] I.L.Pr. 46, PC (Gib) *2–112*
Bolt & Nut Co (Tipton) Ltd v Rowlands Nicholls & Co Ltd [1964] 2 Q.B. 10; [1964] 2 W.L.R. 98; [1964] 1 All E.R. 137; (1963) 107 S.J. 909, CA *21–074*, *21–076*
Bolton v Madden (1873–74) L.R. 9 Q.B. 55, QB *3–004*, *3–006*, 3–040
Bolton v Mahadeva [1972] 1 W.L.R. 1009; [1972] 2 All E.R. 1322; (1972) 116 S.J. 564, CA (Civ Div) *21–030*, *21–031*, *21–032*, *21–033*, *24–043*
Bolton (Duke of) v Williams (1793) 2 Ves. 138 .... *12–067*
Bolton MBC v Torkington [2003] EWCA Civ 1634; [2004] Ch. 66; [2004] 2 W.L.R. 426; [2004] 4 All E.R. 238; [2004] 1 P. & C.R. 9; [2004] 1 E.G.L.R. 28; [2004] 07 E.G. 132; [2003] 46 E.G. 130 (C.S.); (2003) 100(43) L.S.G. 33; (2003) 147 S.J.L.B. 1304, CA (Civ Div) .. 1–094, *1–100*, *2–119*, *2–180*, *3–172*
Bolton Partners v Lambert (1889) L.R. 41 Ch. D. 295, CA *2–123*
Bonacina, Re; sub nom. Le Brasseur v Bonacina [1912] 2 Ch. 394, CA; reversing [1912] 2 Ch. 68, Ch D *3–033*, *20–048*, *30–031*, *30–066*, *30–306*, *30–315*, *30–366*
Bonanza Creek Gold Mining Co Ltd v King, The [1916] 1 A.C. 566, PC (Can) *9–004*
Bond v Barrow Haematite Steel Co; sub nom. Bond v Barrow H'matite Steel Co [1902] 1 Ch. 353, Ch D *28–045*
Bond Worth Ltd, Re [1980] Ch. 228; [1979] 3 W.L.R. 629; [1979] 3 All E.R. 919; (1979) 123 S.J. 216, Ch D *19–066*, *29–158*, *29–168*
Bondholders Securities Corp v Manville [1933] 4 D.L.R. 609 .... *30–324*
Bone v Eckles (1860) 5 H. & N. 925 .... *16–192*
Bone v Ekless (1860) 29 L.J. Ex. 438 .... *16–188*
Bone v Seale [1975] 1 W.L.R. 797; [1975] 1 All E.R. 787; (1974) 119 S.J. 137, CA (Civ Div) *26–030*
Bonelli's Telegraph Co, Re; sub nom. Collie's Claim (1871) L.R. 12 Eq. 246, Ct of Chancery *9–039*
Bonhote v Henderson [1895] 2 Ch. 202, CA; affirming [1895] 1 Ch. 742, Ch D *5–122*, *5–136*

Bonnard v Dott [1906] 1 Ch. 740, CA *16–185*
Bonner v Cox; sub nom. Bonner v Cox Dedicated Corporate Member Ltd [2005] EWCA Civ 1512; [2006] 1 All E.R. (Comm) 565; [2006] 2 Lloyd's Rep. 152; [2006] 1 C.L.C. 126; [2006] Lloyd's Rep. I.R. 385, CA (Civ Div); affirming [2004] EWHC 2963 (Comm); [2005] Lloyd's Rep. I.R. 569, QBD (Comm) *13–010*
Bonner v Tottenham and Edmonton Permanent Investment Building Society [1899] 1 Q.B. 161, CA *29–102*
Bonomi v Backhouse (1859) E.B. & E. 646 .... *1–124*
Bonsor v Musicians Union [1956] A.C. 104; [1955] 3 W.L.R. 788; [1955] 3 All E.R. 518; (1955) 99 S.J. 814, HL; reversing [1954] Ch. 479; [1954] 2 W.L.R. 687; [1954] 1 All E.R. 822; (1954) 98 S.J. 248, CA *9–071*, *9–082*, *9–083*
Bontex Knitting Works Ltd v St. John's Garage [1944] All E.R. 381n; 60 T.L.R. 253, CA; affirming [1943] 2 All E.R. 690, KBD *14–030*
Bonython v Australia [1951] A.C. 201; 66 T.L.R. (Pt. 2) 969; [1948] 2 D.L.R. 672; (1950) 94 S.J. 821, PC (Aus) *21–068*, *30–005*, *30–012*, *30–013*, *30–331*, *30–332*, *30–372*
Bonzi v Stewart (1842) 4 M.G. 295 .... *29–147*
Boodle Hatfield & Co v British Films [1986] P.C.C. 176; [1986] Fin. L.R. 134; (1986) 136 N.L.J. 117, Ch D *29–173*
Booker v Palmer [1942] 2 All E.R. 674, CA *2–183*
Bookmakers Afternoon Greyhound Services Ltd v Wilf Gilbert (Staffordshire) Ltd [1994] F.S.R. 723, Ch D *29–021*, *29–073*
Boomer v Muir (1933) 24 P. 2d 570 .... *29–068*
Boone v Eyre (1777) 1 H.Bl. 273 .... *12–026*, *21–033*, 24–037
Boorne v Wicker [1927] 1 Ch. 667, Ch D *16–119*
Boosey v Wood (1865) 3 H. & C. 484 .... *22–006*
Boot v Boot [1996] 2 F.C.R. 713; (1997) 73 P. & C.R. 137; [1996] C.C.L.R. 68; (1996) 72 P. & C.R. D30, CA (Civ Div) *28–036*
Booth v Alcock (1872–73) L.R. 8 Ch. App. 663, CA in Chancery *12–062*
Booth v Bowron (1892) 8 T.L.R. 641 .... *24–018*
Booth v Earl of Warrington (1714) 4 Bro. P.C. 163 .... *28–140*
Booth v Phillips [2004] EWHC 1437 (Comm); [2004] 1 W.L.R. 3292; [2004] 2 Lloyd's Rep. 457; (2004) 101(30) L.S.G. 29; (2004) 154 N.L.J. 1050, QBD (Comm) *30–032*, *30–119*, *30–120*, *30–121*
Boothbey v Snowden (1812) 3 Camp. 175 .... *3–125*
Borden (UK) Ltd v Scottish Timber Products Ltd [1981] Ch. 25; [1979] 3 W.L.R. 672; [1979] 3 All E.R. 961; [1980] 1 Lloyd's Rep. 160; (1979) 123 S.J. 688, CA (Civ Div); reversing [1979] 2 Lloyd's Rep. 168; (1978) 122 S.J. 825, Ch D *19–066*, *29–158*, *29–164*, *29–165*, *29–166*, *29–168*
Borders (UK) Ltd v Commissioner of Police of the Metropolis [2005] EWCA Civ 197; [2005] Po. L.R. 1; (2005) 149 S.J.L.B. 301, CA (Civ Div) *26–019*, *26–025*
Borealis AB (formerly Borealis Petrokemi AB and Statoil Petrokemi AB) v Stargas Ltd; The Berge Sisar [2001] UKHL 17; [2002] 2 A.C. 205; [2001] 2 W.L.R. 1118; [2001] 2 All E.R. 193; [2001] 1 All E.R. (Comm) 673; [2001] 1 Lloyd's Rep. 663; [2001] C.L.C. 1084; (2001) 98(20) L.S.G. 43; (2001) 145 S.J.L.B. 93, HL; affirming [1999] Q.B. 863; [1998] 3 W.L.R. 1353; [1998] 4 All E.R. 821; [1998] 2 Lloyd's Rep. 475; [1998] C.L.C. 1589, CA (Civ Div); reversing [1997] 1 Lloyd's Rep. 642 (Note), QBD (Comm) *14–055*
Borgivigilant, The. *See* Owners of the Borvigilant v Owners of the Romina G
Borradaile v Hunter (1843) 5 M. & G. 639 .... *12–083*
Borries v Hutchinson (1865) 19 C.B.(N.S.) 445 .... *26–078*
Borries v Imperial Ottoman Bank (1873–74) L.R. 9 C.P. 38, CCP *21–044*
Borrowman Phillips & Co v Free & Hollis (1878–79) L.R. 4 Q.B.D. 500, CA *21–090*
Borrows v Ellison (1870–71) L.R. 6 Ex. 128, Ex Ct *28–076*
Borys v Canadian Pacific Railway Co [1953] A.C. 217; [1953] 2 W.L.R. 224; [1953] 1 All E.R. 451; (1953) 97 S.J. 78, PC (Can); affirming [1952] 3 D.L.R. 218, CA (Alta) *12–052*
Bos v Helsham (1866–67) L.R. 2 Ex. 72, Ex Ct *27–058*

Boscawen v Bajwa; Abbey National Plc v Boscawen [1996] 1 W.L.R. 328; [1995] 4 All E.R. 769; (1995) 70 P. & C.R. 391; (1995) 92(21) L.S.G. 37; (1995) 139 S.J.L.B. 111, CA (Civ Div) *29–164*, *29–173*, *29–185*
Boshali v Allied Commercial Exporters (1961) 105 S.J. 987, PC *14–027*
Bosma v Larsen [1966] 1 Lloyd's Rep. 22, QBD (Comm) *28–049*
Bossevain v Weil [1950] A.C. 327 ....*29–008*, *29–011*, *29–019*, *30–068*
Bostel Bros v Hurlock [1949] 1 K.B. 74; [1948] 2 All E.R. 312; 64 T.L.R. 495; [1948] L.J.R. 1846; (1948) 92 S.J. 361, CA *16–154*
Bostock v Jardine (1865) 3 H.C. 700 .... *29–056*
Boston v Boston [1904] 1 K.B. 124, CA *4–016*
Boston Deep Sea Fishing & Ice Co v Ansell (1888) L.R. 39 Ch. D. 339, CA ...*21–030*, *24–014*, *29–156*
Bosun v Sandford (1691) 2 Salk 440 .... *1–118*
Boswell v Coaks (No.2) (1894) 6 R. 167; (1894) 86 L.T. 365, HL *25–015*
Bottiglieri di Navigazione SpA v Cosco Qingdao Ocean Shipping Co; The Bunga Saga Lima [2005] EWHC 244; [2005] 2 Lloyd's Rep. 1, QBD (Comm) *3–083*, *3–094*, *3–097*, *3–130*
Bottomley v Bannister [1932] 1 K.B. 458, CA *13–016*
Bottomley v Nuttall (1858) 5 C.B.(N.S.) 122 .... *21–074*
Boulter v Peplow (1850) 9 C.B. 493 .... *17–027*
Boulton v Jones (1857) 2 H. & N. 564; (1857) 6 W.R. 107 ....5–090, 5–098, *19–083*
Boulton v Jones (1857) 27 L.J. Ex. 117 ....*29–076*, 29–182
Boulton v Reynolds (1859) 29 L.J.Q.B. 11 .... *21–094*
Bourgeois v Wilson Holgate & Co Ltd (1920) 4 Ll. L. Rep. 1, CA *26–144*
Bourne v Colodense [1985] I.C.R. 291; [1985] I.R.L.R. 339; (1985) 82 L.S.G. 923; (1985) 129 S.J. 153, CA (Civ Div) *19–050*
Bourne v Mason (1668) 1 Ventris 6 .... *18–019*
Bourne v McDonald [1950] 2 K.B. 422; [1950] 2 All E.R. 183; 66 T.L.R. (Pt. 2) 226; (1951) 95 S.J. 435, CA *5–132*
Bourne v McEvoy Timber Preservation (1975) 237 E.G. 496 .... *18–022*
Bourne (Thomas), Re [1906] 1 Ch. 697, CA *17–023*, *25–005*
Bournemouth & Boscombe Athletic Football Club v Manchester United Football Club, *The Times*, May 22, 1980, CA (Civ Div) *2–153*, *2–156*
Boussmaker, Ex p. (1806) 13 Ves. 71 .... *11–030*
Boustany v Piggott (1995) 69 P. & C.R. 298; [1993] E.G. 85 (C.S.); [1993] N.P.C. 75, PC (Ant) *5–013*, *7–128*, 7–130, 7–132, 7–134
Bovis International Inc (formerly L/M International Construction Inc) v Circle Ltd Partnership, 49 Con. L.R. 12; [1995] N.P.C. 128, CA (Civ Div) *14–017*
Bovis Lend Lease Ltd (formerly Bovis Construction Ltd) v Saillard Fuller & Partners, 77 Con. L.R. 134, QBD (TCC) *17–030*, *17–032*
Bowen v Owen (1847) 11. Q.B. 130 .... *21–092*
Bower v Bantam Investments [1972] 1 W.L.R. 1120; [1972] 3 All E.R. 349; (1972) 116 S.J. 633, Ch D *27–071*
Bowerbank v Monteiro (1813) 4 Taunt. 844 .... *12–101*
Bowerman v Association of British Travel Agents Ltd [1996] C.L.C. 451; (1995) 145 N.L.J. 1815, CA (Civ Div); reversing (1995) 14 Tr. L.R. 246, QBD *2–003*, 2–018, *2–078*, *2–161*, *2–165*, *18–012*
Bowes v Chaleyer (1923) 32 C.L.R. 159 .... *24–011*
Bowes v Foster (1858) 2 H.N. 779 ....*12–106*, *21–058*
Bowes v Shand; sub nom. Shand v Bowes (1876–77) L.R. 2 App. Cas. 455, HL; reversing (1876–77) L.R. 2 Q.B.D. 112, CA; reversing (1875–76) L.R. 1 Q.B.D. 470, QBD *12–036*, *12–037*, *12–046*, *14–027*, *21–013*
Bowie v Southorns [2002] EWHC 1389; [2002] Lloyd's Rep. P.N. 564; [2003] P.N.L.R. 7; (2002) 152 N.L.J. 1240; [2002] N.P.C. 94, QBD *28–011*
Bowker v Burdekin, 152 E.R. 744; (1843) 11 M. & W. 128, Ex Ct *1–105*
Bowlby v Bell (1846) 3 C.B. 284 .... *29–117*
Bowler v Lovegrove [1921] 1 Ch. 642, Ch D *16–106*, *16–114*
Bowmakers Ltd v Barnet Instruments Ltd [1945] K.B. 65, CA *16–007*, *16–167*, *16–178*0, 16–180, 16–181, 16–184, *16–185*

Bowman v Secular Society Ltd; sub nom. Secular Society Ltd v Bowman; Bowman, Re [1917] A.C. 406, HL; affirming [1915] 2 Ch. 447, CA *16–014*
Bowman v Taylor (1834) 2 Ad. & El. 278 .... *1–112*
Bowring-Hanbury's Trustee v Bowring-Hanbury [1943] Ch. 104, CA *25–006*, *28–064*, *28–065*, *28–094*, *28–100*, *28–101*
Bowry v Bennet (1808) 1 Camp. 348 .... *16–069*
Bowskill v Dawson (No.1); National Provincial Bank v Dawson (No.1) [1954] 1 Q.B. 288; [1953] 3 W.L.R. 969; [1953] 2 All E.R. 1393; (1953) 97 S.J. 815, QBD *18–079*
Bowyer v Woodman Ex p. Clarke (1866–67) L.R. 3 Eq. 313, Ct of Chancery *28–035*
Box v Midland Bank Ltd [1981] 1 Lloyd's Rep. 434, CA (Civ Div); reversing [1979] 2 Lloyd's Rep. 391, QBD (Comm) *1–122*, 6–012, 6–087
Boyce v Edbrooke [1903] 1 Ch. 836, Ch D *17–007*
Boyd v Hind (1857) 1 H. & N. 938 .... *3–125*
Boyd and Forrest v Glasgow Railway. *See* Glasgow & South Western Railway Co v Boyd & Forrest (A Firm) (No.3)
Boydell v Drummond (1809) 11 East 142 .... *4–029*
Boyo v Lambeth LBC [1994] I.C.R. 727; [1995] I.R.L.R. 50, CA (Civ Div) *24–010*, *24–013*
Boys, Re. *See* Eedes v Boys
Boys v Chaplin; sub nom. Chaplin v Boys [1971] A.C. 356; [1969] 3 W.L.R. 322; [1969] 2 All E.R. 1085; [1969] 2 Lloyd's Rep. 487; (1969) 113 S.J. 608, HL *26–051*, *30–337*, *30–338*
Boys and Girls Welfare Society v McDonald [1997] I.C.R. 693; [1996] I.R.L.R. 129, EAT *15–121*
Bozon v Farlow (1816) 1 Mer. 459 .... *27–043*
Brabant, The [1967] 1 Q.B. 588; [1966] 2 W.L.R. 909; 110 S.J. 265; [1966] 1 All E.R. 961; [1965] 2 Lloyd's Rep. 546 .... *12–070*
Brace v Calder [1895] 2 Q.B. 253, CA *26–103*, *26–113*
Bracewell v Appleby [1975] Ch. 408; [1975] 2 W.L.R. 282; [1975] 1 All E.R. 993; (1975) 29 P. & C.R. 204; (1974) 119 S.J. 114, Ch D *26–023*, *29–142*
Bracken v Billinghurst [2003] EWHC 1333 (TCC); [2003] All E.R. (D) 488 (Jul); [2004] T.C.L.R. 4; [2003] C.I.L.L. 2039, QBD (TCC) *3–126*, *22–022*
Bradburn v Great Western Railway Co (1874–75) L.R. 10 Ex. 1, Ex Ct *26–117*
Bradburne v Batfield (1845) 14 M. & W. 559 .... *3–044*
Bradbury v Morgan (1862) 1 H. & C. 249 .... *2–100*
Braddon Towers Ltd v International Stores Ltd [1987] 1 E.G.L.R. 209 .... *27–026*
Bradford & Bingley Plc v Rashid [2006] UKHL 37; [2006] 1 W.L.R. 2066; [2006] 4 All E.R. 705; [2006] 2 All E.R. (Comm) 951; [2006] 29 E.G. 132 (C.S.); (2006) 103(30) L.S.G. 30; (2006) 156 N.L.J. 1172; (2006) 150 S.J.L.B. 983, HL; reversing [2005] EWCA Civ 1080, CA (Civ Div) ...*3–035*, *28–094*, *28–095*
Bradford (Earl of) v Earl of Romney (1862) 30 Beav. 431 .... *5–122*
Bradford Old Bank Ltd v Sutcliffe [1918] 2 K.B. 833, CA *21–066*, *28–036*, *28–046*
Bradford Sons v Price Bros (1923) 92 L.J.K.B. 871 .... *21–044*
Bradlaugh v Newdegate (1882–83) L.R. 11 Q.B.D. 1, QBD *16–051*, *16–053*
Bradley v Eagle Star Insurance Co Ltd [1989] A.C. 957; [1989] 2 W.L.R. 568; [1989] 1 All E.R. 961; [1989] 1 Lloyd's Rep. 465; [1989] B.C.L.C. 469; [1989] I.C.R. 301; [1989] Fin. L.R. 253; (1989) 86(17) L.S.G. 38; (1989) 86(3) L.S.G. 43; (1989) 139 N.L.J. 330; (1989) 133 S.J. 359, HL *18–131*, *28–049*
Bradley v Gregory (1810) 2 Camp. 383 .... *3–125*
Bradley v H Newsom Sons & Co; sub nom. H Newsum & Co Ltd v Bradley [1919] A.C. 16, HL *24–021*
Bradley Egg Farm v Clifford [1943] 2 All E.R. 378 .... *9–064*
Bradshaw v Beard (1862) 12 C.B.(N.S.) 344 .... *29–132*
Bradstock Trustee Services Ltd v Nabarro Nathanson [1995] 1 W.L.R. 1405; [1995] 4 All E.R. 888; [1995] C.L.C. 1495; [1996] O.P.L.R. 247, Ch D *18–083*, *28–011*, *28–119*
Bradstreets British Ltd v Mitchell; Bradstreets British Ltd v Carapanayoti & Co Ltd [1933] Ch. 190, Ch D *16–175*

Brady v Brady [1989] A.C. 755; [1988] 2 W.L.R. 1308; [1988] 2 All E.R. 617; (1988) 4 B.C.C. 390; [1988] B.C.L.C. 579; [1988] P.C.C. 316; [1988] 2 F.T.L.R. 181; (1988) 132 S.J. 820, HL; reversing (1987) 3 B.C.C. 535; [1988] B.C.L.C. 20; [1977] P.C.C. 434; [1987] 2 F.T.L.R. 414; (1987) 137 N.L.J. 898, CA (Civ Div) *3–014*, *3–023*
Brady v St Margaret's Trust [1963] 2 Q.B. 494; [1963] 2 W.L.R. 1162; [1963] 2 All E.R. 275, CA *22–049*, *26–141*
Bragg v Oceanus Mutual Underwriting Association (Bermuda) Ltd; Ulster Marine Insurance Co Ltd v Oceanus Mutual Underwriting Association (Bermuda) Ltd [1982] 2 Lloyd's Rep. 132; [1982] Com. L.R. 165, CA (Civ Div) *25–013*
Braithwaite v Foreign Hardwood Co [1905] 2 K.B. 543, CA 24–011, *24–023*, *24–024*
Brake Bros Ltd v Ungless [2004] EWHC 2799; [2004] All E.R. (D) 686, QBD *16–108*
Branca v Cobarro [1947] K.B. 854; [1947] 2 All E.R. 101; 63 T.L.R. 408; [1948] L.J.R. 43; 177 L.T. 332, CA *2–116*, 2–123
Branchett v Beaney [1992] 3 All E.R. 910; (1992) 24 H.L.R. 348; [1992] 28 E.G. 107; [1992] E.G. 15 (C.S.); [1992] N.P.C. 14, CA (Civ Div) *26–085*
Brandon v Newington (1842) 3 Q.B. 915 .... *21–095*
Brand's Estate, Re [1936] 3 All E.R. 374 .... *2–175*
Brandt v Liverpool Brazil & River Plate Steam Navigation Co Ltd; sub nom. Brandt & Co v River Plate Steam Navigation Co Ltd [1924] 1 K.B. 575; [1923] All E.R. Rep. 656; (1923–24) 17 Ll. L. Rep. 142, CA; affirming (1923) 15 Ll. L. Rep. 123, KBD *3–073*, *14–030*, *14–055*, *18–058*
Brandt's Sons & Co v Dunlop Rubber Co. *See* William Brandt's Sons & Co v Dunlop Rubber Co Ltd.
Braniff v Holland & Hannen and Cubitts (Southern) Ltd [1969] 1 W.L.R. 1533; [1969] 3 All E.R. 959; (1969) 113 S.J. 836, CA (Civ Div) *28–119*
Branwhite v Worcester Works Finance Ltd [1969] 1 A.C. 552; [1968] 3 W.L.R. 760; [1968] 3 All E.R. 104; (1968) 112 S.J. 758, HL *18–006*, *29–029*, *29–054*, *29–074*
Bratton Seymour Service Co Ltd v Oxborough [1992] B.C.C. 471; [1992] B.C.L.C. 693; [1992] E.G. 28 (C.S.), CA (Civ Div) *9–061*
Brauer & Co (Great Britain) Ltd v James Clark (Brush Materials) Ltd [1952] 2 All E.R. 497; [1952] 2 Lloyd's Rep. 147; [1952] 2 T.L.R. 349; [1952] W.N. 422; (1952) 96 S.J. 548, CA; reversing [1952] 1 All E.R. 981; [1952] 1 Lloyd's Rep. 385; [1952] 1 T.L.R. 953; [1952] W.N. 187; (1952) 96 S.J. 246, QBD *2–155*, *13–013*, *14–141*, *14–148*
Braymist Ltd v Wise Finance Co Ltd; sub nom. Wise Finance Ltd v Braymist Ltd [2002] EWCA Civ 127; [2002] Ch. 273; [2002] 3 W.L.R. 322; [2002] 2 All E.R. 333; [2002] B.C.C. 514; [2002] 1 B.C.L.C. 415; [2002] 9 E.G. 220 (C.S.); (2002) 99(13) L.S.G. 25; (2002) 146 S.J.L.B. 60; [2002] N.P.C. 25, CA (Civ Div); affirming [2001] 11 E.G. 174 (C.S.); [2001] N.P.C. 55, Ch D *4–074*, *9–012*
Brayshaw v Eaton (1839) 7 Scott 183 .... *8–008*
Brazier v Bramwell Scaffolding Ltd [2001] UKPC 59, PC (NZ) *16–102*
Breen v Amalgamated Engineering Union [1971] 2 Q.B. 175; [1971] 2 W.L.R. 742; [1971] 1 All E.R. 1148; 10 K.I.R. 120; (1971) 115 S.J. 203, CA (Civ Div) *9–083*
Brekkes Ltd v Cattel [1972] Ch. 105; [1971] 2 W.L.R. 647; [1971] 1 All E.R. 1031; (1971) 115 S.J. 10, Ch D *16–075*
Bremer Handels GmbH v C Mackprang Jr [1979] 1 Lloyd's Rep. 221, CA (Civ Div); reversing in part [1977] 2 Lloyd's Rep. 467, QBD (Comm) *3–089*, *3–091*, *3–104*, *14–141*, *14–144*, *14–150*, *14–151*, *22–044*, *22–052*, *23–064*, *24–008*
Bremer Handels GmbH v Continental Grain Corp [1983] 1 Lloyd's Rep. 269, CA (Civ Div); affirming [1982] Com. L.R. 145, QBD (Comm) ..*14–141*, *14–151*, *23–064*
Bremer Handels GmbH v Deutsche Conti-Handels GmbH (Non Delivery) [1983] 2 Lloyd's Rep. 45, CA (Civ Div); affirming [1981] 2 Lloyd's Rep. 112, QBD (Comm) *22–044*, *22–052*, *22–053*, *24–003*, *24–008*

Bremer Handels GmbH v Deutsche Conti-Handels GmbH (Shipment Period) [1983] 1 Lloyd's Rep. 689, QBD (Comm) *3–090*, *3–093*, *3–095*, *14–151*
Bremer Handels GmbH v Finagrain Compagnie Commerciale Agricole et Financière SA [1981] 2 Lloyd's Rep. 259, CA (Civ Div); reversing [1981] 1 Lloyd's Rep. 224, QBD (Comm) *3–090*, *3–104*, *14–137*, *14–151*, *22–044*, *22–052*, *22–055*
Bremer Handels GmbH v JH Rayner & Co [1979] 2 Lloyd's Rep. 216, CA (Civ Div); reversing [1978] 2 Lloyd's Rep. 73, QBD (Comm) *12–078*
Bremer Handels GmbH v Mackprang [1981] 1 Lloyd's Rep. 292, CA (Civ Div); affirming [1980] 1 Lloyd's Rep. 210, QBD (Comm) *14–141*, *14–150*, *14–151*, *22–052*
Bremer Handels GmbH v Raiffeisen Hauptgenossenschaft eG (No.1) [1982] 1 Lloyd's Rep. 599, CA (Civ Div); affirming [1982] 1 Lloyd's Rep. 210, QBD (Comm) *3–091*, *14–141*, *14–151*, *22–044*
Bremer Handels GmbH v Vanden-Avenne Izegem PVBA [1978] 2 Lloyd's Rep. 109, HL; reversing [1977] 2 Lloyd's Rep. 329, CA (Civ Div); reversing [1977] 1 Lloyd's Rep. 133, QBD (Comm) *3–089*, *3–090*, *3–091*, 10–039, *12–034*, *12–039*, *12–040*, *14–140*, *14–141*, *14–144*, *14–148*, *14–150*, *14–151*, *21–002*, *22–041*, *22–044*, *22–051*, *22–052*, *24–008*, *28–062*
Bremer Handels GmbH v Westzucker GmbH (No.1) [1981] 1 Lloyd's Rep. 207, QBD (Comm) *3–090*, *3–091*, *3–104*, *14–141*, *22–044*, *22–052*
Bremer Handels GmbH v Westzucker GmbH (No.3) [1989] 1 Lloyd's Rep. 582, CA (Civ Div); affirming [1989] 1 Lloyd's Rep. 198, QBD (Comm) ...*14–141*, *14–150*
Bremer Handelsgesellschaft mbH v Bunge Corp [1983] 1 Lloyd's Rep. 476; [1983] Com. L.R. 103, CA (Civ Div); affirming [1982] 1 Lloyd's Rep. 108, QBD (Comm) *3–091*, *3–093*, *3–095*, *3–104*, *14–141*, *14–150*, *14–151*, *22–052*
Bremer Handelsgesellschaft mbH v Westzucker GmbH (No.2); sub nom. Bunge GmbH v Westzucker GmbH [1981] 2 Lloyd's Rep. 130; [1981] Com. L.R. 179, CA (Civ Div); affirming [1981] 1 Lloyd's Rep. 214, QBD (Comm) ...*14–141*, *22–052*
Bremer Vulkan Schiffbau und Maschinenfabrik v South India Shipping Corp Ltd; sub nom. Bremer Vulcan Schiffbau und Maschinenfabrik v South India Shipping Corp; Gregg v Raytheon [1981] A.C. 909; [1981] 2 W.L.R. 141; [1981] 2 All E.R. 289; [1981] 1 Lloyd's Rep. 253; [1981] Com. L.R. 19; [1981] E.C.C. 151; (1981) 125 S.J. 114, HL; affirming [1980] 2 W.L.R. 905; [1980] 1 All E.R. 420; [1980] 1 Lloyd's Rep. 255; (1980) 124 S.J. 396, CA (Civ Div); affirming [1979] 3 W.L.R. 471; [1979] 3 All E.R. 194; (1979) 76 L.S.G. 834; (1979) 123 S.J. 504, QBD *13–010*, *23–040*, *24–016*, *24–032*
Brennan v Bolt Burdon; sub nom. Brennan v Bolt Burden; Brennan v Islington LBC [2004] EWCA Civ 1017; [2005] Q.B. 303; [2004] 3 W.L.R. 1321; [2004] C.P. Rep. 43; (2004) 101(34) L.S.G. 31; (2004) 148 S.J.L.B. 972; [2004] N.P.C. 133, CA (Civ Div); reversing [2003] EWHC 2493 (QB); [2004] 1 W.L.R. 1240, QBD *5–054*, 5–055, 5–056, *22–021*, *29–046*, *29–047*, *29–187*, *29–189*
Brennan v Bolton (1842) 2 Dr. & War. 349 .... *4–048*
Brennan v Brighton BC (No.2) [1997] E.G. 76 (C.S.), CA (Civ Div) *18–042*
Bret v JS (1600) Cr.Eliz.755 .... *3–022*
Brett v East India Shipping Co (1864) 2 H. & C. 404 .... *27–021*
Brett v Schneideman Bros Ltd [1923] N.Z.L.R. 938 .... *24–011*
Brewer Street Investments Ltd v Barclays Woollen Co Ltd [1954] 1 Q.B. 428; [1953] 3 W.L.R. 869; [1953] 2 All E.R. 1330; (1953) 97 S.J. 796, CA 4–088, *29–021*, *29–071*, *29–116*
Brewin v Briscoe (1859) 28 L.J.Q.B. 329 .... *20–020*
Brice v Bannister (1877–78) L.R. 3 Q.B.D. 569, CA *19–008*, *19–014*, *19–015*, *19–017*, *19–020*
Brickfield Properties v Newton; Rosebell Holdings v Newton [1971] 1 W.L.R. 862; [1971] 3 All E.R. 328; (1971) 115 S.J. 307, CA (Civ Div) *28–118*
Brickles v Snell [1916] 2 A.C. 599, PC (Can) *21–013*

Bridge Oil Ltd v Owners and/or Demise Charterers of the Ship Guiseppe di Vittorio (No.1); The Guiseppe di Vittorio [1998] 1 Lloyd's Rep. 136; [1998] C.L.C. 149; (1997) 94(44) L.S.G. 35; (1997) 141 S.J.L.B. 223, CA (Civ Div) *18–146*
Bridge v Campbell Discount Co Ltd; sub nom. Campbell Discount Co Ltd v Bridge [1962] A.C. 600; [1962] 2 W.L.R. 439; [1962] 1 All E.R. 385; (1962) 106 S.J. 94, HL; reversing [1961] 1 Q.B. 445; [1961] 2 W.L.R. 596; [1961] 2 All E.R. 97; (1961) 105 S.J. 232, CA *7–126*, *22–054*, *26–127*, *26–135*, 26–136, *26–137*, *26–155*
Bridge v Deacons [1984] A.C. 705; [1984] 2 W.L.R. 837; [1984] 2 All E.R. 19; (1984) 81 L.S.G. 1291; (1984) 134 N.L.J. 723; (1984)128 S.J. 263, PC (HK) *16–081*, *16–092*, 16–119
Bridgeman v Green; sub nom. Green v Bridgeman (1755) 2 Ves.Sen. 627; 97 E.R. 22; (1757) Wilm. 58, KB *7–064*, *7–125*
Bridger v Savage (1884–85) L.R. 15 Q.B.D. 363, CA *16–192*
Bridges v Berry (1810) 3 Taunt 130 .... *21–079*
Bridges v Garrett (1869–70) L.R. 5 C.P. 451, Ex Chamber *21–044*
Bridgewater v Griffiths [2000] 1 W.L.R. 524; [1999] 2 Costs L.R. 52, QBD *29–021*
Bridgewater v Leahy [1988] H.C.A. 66; 158 A.L.R. 66 .... *7–129*, *7–136*
Briess v Woolley; sub nom. Briess v Rosher [1954] A.C. 333; [1954] 2 W.L.R. 832; [1954] 1 All E.R. 909; (1954) 98 S.J. 286, HL; reversing [1953] 2 Q.B. 218; [1953] 2 W.L.R. 608; [1953] 1 All E.R. 717; (1953) 97 S.J. 209, CA *6–019*, *6–048*
Briggs v Calverly (1800) 8 T.R. 629 .... *21–089*
Briggs v Oates [1991] 1 All E.R. 407; [1990] I.C.R. 473; [1990] I.R.L.R. 472; (1990) 140 N.L.J. 208, Ch D *16–100*
Briggs v Rowan [1991] E.G. 6 (C.S.), Ch D *2–172*
Briggs v Wilson (1854) 5 De G.M. & G. 12 .... *28–131*
Brightlife Ltd, Re [1987] Ch. 200; [1987] 2 W.L.R. 197; [1986] 3 All E.R. 673; (1986) 2 B.C.C. 99359; [1986] P.C.C. 435; (1987) 84 L.S.G. 653; (1987) 131 S.J. 132, Ch D (Companies Ct) *20–026*
Brightman & Co v Bunge y Born Limitada Sociedad. *See* HA Brightman & Co v Bunge y Born Limitada Sociedad
Brighton, The. *See* Bugsier Reederei und Bergungs A/G v Owners of the SS Brighton
Brighty v Norton, 122 E.R. 116; (1862) 3 B. & S. 312, QB *21–053*
Brikom Investments Ltd v Carr; Brikom Investments Ltd v Roddy; Brikom Investments Ltd v Hickey [1979] Q.B. 467; [1979] 2 W.L.R. 737; [1979] 2 All E.R. 753; (1979) 38 P. & C.R. 326; (1979) 251 E.G. 359, CA (Civ Div) *3–024*, 3–080, *3–081*, *3–085*, *3–093*, *3–098*, *3–103*, *3–104*, *3–115*, *3–124*, *3–127*, 3–133, *12–004*, *12–103*, *12–103*, *18–007*, *22–036*
Brikom Investments Ltd v Seaford [1981] 1 W.L.R. 863; [1981] 2 All E.R. 783; (1981–82) 1 H.L.R. 21; (1981) 42 P. & C.R. 190; (1981) 258 E.G. 750; (1981) 125 S.J. 240, CA (Civ Div) *3–096*, *3–098*, *6–013*, *6–095*
Brilliant v Michaels [1945] 1 All E.R. 121, Ch D *2–118*
Brimnes, The. *See* Tenax Steamship Co v Owners of the Motor Vessel Brimnes
Brinkibon v Stahag Stahl und Stahlwarenhandels GmbH; sub nom. Brinkibon Ltd v Stahag Stahl und Stahlwarenhandelsgesellschaft mbH [1983] 2 A.C. 34; [1982] 2 W.L.R. 264; [1982] 1 All E.R. 293; [1982] 1 Lloyd's Rep. 217; [1982] Com. L.R. 72; [1982] E.C.C. 322; (1982) 126 S.J. 116, HL; affirming [1980] 2 Lloyd's Rep. 556, CA (Civ Div) *2–032*, *2–045*, *2–048*, *2–050*, *2–051*, *2–053*, *2–091*, *24–018*
Brinnand v Ewens (1987) 19 H.L.R. 415; (1987) 284 E.G. 1052, CA (Civ Div) *3–138*, *3–144*
Brisbane v Dacres (1813) 5 Taunt. 143 .... *29–041*
Brisbane City Council v Attorney General of Queensland; Myer Shopping Centres Pty Ltd v Attorney General of Queensland [1979] A.C. 411; [1978] 3 W.L.R. 299; [1978] 3 All E.R. 30; (1978) 122 S.J. 506, PC (Aus) *25–013*

Briscoe v Lubrizol Ltd (No.1) [2000] I.C.R. 694; [2000] P.I.Q.R. P39; (1999) 96(41) L.S.G. 36, CA (Civ Div) *1–179*, 1–184, *18–029*
Briscoe v Stephens, 130 E.R. 288; (1824) 2 Bing. 213, KB *25–010*
Bristol & West Building Society v Mothew (t/a Stapley & Co); sub nom. Mothew v Bristol & West Building Society [1998] Ch. 1; [1997] 2 W.L.R. 436; [1996] 4 All E.R. 698; [1997] P.N.L.R. 11; (1998) 75 P. & C.R. 241; [1996] E.G. 136 (C.S.); (1996) 146 N.L.J. 1273; (1996) 140 S.J.L.B. 206; [1996] N.P.C. 126, CA (Civ Div) *6–059*, *6–130*, *29–162*, *29–165*
Bristol & West Plc v Bartlett; Paragon Finance Plc v Banks; Halifax Plc v Grant [2002] EWCA Civ 1181; [2003] 1 W.L.R. 284; [2002] 4 All E.R. 544; [2002] 2 All E.R. (Comm) 1105; [2003] H.L.R. 22; [2003] 1 E.G.L.R. 85; [2003] 01 E.G. 69; [2002] 33 E.G. 97 (C.S.); (2002) 99(38) L.S.G. 34; [2002] N.P.C. 109, CA (Civ Div) *25–001*, *28–003*
Bristol and West Building Society v Fancy & Jackson [1997] 4 All E.R. 582; [1997] N.P.C. 109, Ch D *26–079*, *26–096*
Bristol Cardiff & Swansea Aerated Bread Co v Maggs (1890) L.R. 44 Ch. D. 616, Ch D *2–029*
Bristow v Eastman (1794) 1 Esp. 172 .... *1–118*, *8–046*, *8–047*, *8–049*
Bristowe v Fairclough (1840) 1 M.G. 143 .... *25–008*
Britain v Rossiter (1882–83) L.R. 11 Q.B.D. 123, CA *4–017*, *4–042*, *4–049*, *27–021*, *29–019*
Britain & Overseas Trading (Bristles) Ltd v Brooks Wharf & Bull Wharf Ltd [1967] 2 Lloyd's Rep. 51, QBD *19–079*
British & American Telegraph Co Ltd v Colson (1870–71) L.R. 6 Ex. 108, Ex Ct ...*1–004*, *1–011*, *2–056*
British & Beningtons Ltd v North West Cachar Tea Co Ltd; sub nom. Baintgoorie (Dooars) Tea Co Ltd v British & Beningtons Ltd; Mazdehee Tea Co Ltd v British & Beningtons Ltd; North-Western Cachar Tea Co Ltd v British & Beningtons Ltd; British & Beningtons Ltd v Baintgoorie (Dooars) Tea Co Ltd; British & Beningtons Ltd v Mazdahee Tea Co Ltd; North-Western Cachar Tea Co Ltd v Same [1923] A.C. 48; (1922) 13 Ll. L. Rep. 67, HL; affirming (1922) 10 Ll. L. Rep. 381, CA; reversing (1921) 8 Ll. L. Rep. 219, KBD *22–028*, *22–033*, *22–034*, *24–014*, *24–023*, *24–028*, *24–029*
British & Commonwealth Holdings Plc (No.3), Re [1992] 1 W.L.R. 672; [1992] B.C.C. 58; [1992] B.C.L.C. 322, Ch D *20–025*
British & Commonwealth Holdings Plc v Quadrex Holdings Inc (No.1) [1989] Q.B. 842; [1989] 3 W.L.R. 723; [1989] 3 All E.R. 492; (1989) 86(23) L.S.G. 42; (1989) 133 S.J. 694, CA (Civ Div) *21–012*, *21–013*
British & Commonwealth Holdings Plc v Quadrex Holdings Inc, unreported, April 10, 1985, CA *6–102*
British & Mexican Shipping Co v Lockett Bros & Co; sub nom. British & Mexican Shipping Co Ltd v Lockett Bros & Co Ltd [1911] 1 K.B. 264, CA *12–130*
British and French Trust Corp v New Brunswick Railway [1936] 1 All E.R. 13 .... *21–071*
British and Foreign Cork Co, Re; sub nom. British and Foreign Cork Co Re v Leifchild's Case; Leifchild's Case (1865–66) L.R. 1 Eq. 231, Ct of Chancery *9–022*, *12–106*
British and North European Bank Ltd v Zalzstein [1927] 2 K.B. 92, KBD *29–029*
British Airways Board v Taylor [1976] 1 W.L.R. 13; [1976] 1 All E.R. 65; [1976] 1 Lloyd's Rep. 167; (1976) 62 Cr. App. R. 174; [1977] Crim. L.R. 372; 18 Man. Law 146; (1975) 120 S.J. 7, HL; affirming [1975] 1 W.L.R. 1197; [1975] 3 All E.R. 307; [1975] 2 Lloyd's Rep. 434; [1975] Crim. L.R. 471; 18 Man. Law 46; (1975) 119 S.J. 559, DC *2–021*, *6–012*
British American Continental Bank v British Bank for Foreign Trade [1926] 1 K.B. 328, CA *29–031*, *29–038*
British Anzani (Felixstowe) Ltd v International Marine Management (UK) Ltd [1980] Q.B. 137; [1979] 3 W.L.R. 451; [1979] 2 All E.R. 1063; (1980) 39 P. & C.R. 189; (1978) 250 E.G. 1183; (1979) 123 S.J. 64, QBD *21–038*, *28–123*
British Association of Advisers and Lecturers in Physical Education v National Union of Teachers [1986] I.R.L.R. 497, CA (Civ Div) *9–064*

British Bank for Foreign Trade v Novinex [1949] 1 K.B. 623; [1949] 1 All E.R. 155; [1949] L.J.R. 658; (1949) 93 S.J. 146, CA *2–113*, *2–128*
British Bank for Foreign Trade v Russian Commercial & Industrial Bank (1921) 9 Ll. L. Rep. 155, Ch D *21–068*
British Bank of the Middle East v Sun Life Assurance Co of Canada (UK) [1983] 2 Lloyd's Rep. 9; [1983] Com. L.R. 187; (1983) 133 N.L.J. 575, HL *9–042*
British Berna Motor Lorries Ltd v Inter-Transport Co Ltd (1915) 31 T.L.R. 200 ... *23–052*
British Car Auctions v Wright [1972] 1 W.L.R. 1519; [1972] 3 All E.R. 462; [1972] R.T.R. 540; [1972] Crim. L.R. 562; (1972) 116 S.J. 583, QBD *2–011*
British Cash & Parcel Conveyors Ltd v Lamson Store Service Co Ltd [1908] 1 K.B. 1006, CA *16–049*, *16–050*, *16–057*
British Columbia Saw Mill Co Ltd v Nettleship (1867–68) L.R. 3 C.P. 499, CCP *26–062*, *26–070*, *26–175*
British Controlled Oilfields v Stagg [1921] W.N. 31 .... *30–007*
British Crane Hire Corp Ltd v Ipswich Plant Hire Ltd [1975] Q.B. 303; [1974] 2 W.L.R. 856; [1974] 1 All E.R. 1059; (1973) 118 S.J. 387, CA (Civ Div) *12–012*, *13–018*, *14–015*
British Eagle International Airlines Ltd v Compagnie Nationale Air France [1975] 1 W.L.R. 758; [1975] 2 All E.R. 390; [1975] 2 Lloyd's Rep. 43; (1975) 119 S.J. 368, HL; reversing in part [1974] 1 Lloyd's Rep. 429, CA (Civ Div); affirming [1973] 1 Lloyd's Rep. 414, Ch D *19–022*, *20–025*
British Electrical and Associated Industries (Cardiff) Ltd v Patley Pressings Ltd [1953] 1 W.L.R. 280; [1953] 1 All E.R. 94; (1953) 97 S.J. 96, QBD *2–141*, *12–077*, *14–137*
British Energy Power & Energy Trading Ltd v Credit Suisse [2008] EWCA Civ 53; [2008] 1 Lloyd's Rep. 413, CA (Civ Div); affirming [2007] EWHC 1428 (Comm); [2007] 2 Lloyd's Rep. 427, QBD (Comm) *19–043*
British Fermentation Products Ltd v Compair Reavell Ltd [1999] 2 All E.R. (Comm) 389; [1999] B.L.R. 352; (2000) 2 T.C.L.R. 704; 66 Con. L.R. 1, QBD (TCC) *14–072*, *14–085*, 14–097
British Gas Trading v Eastern Electricity Plc, unreported, December 18, 1996, CA (Civ Div) *19–044*
British Guiana Credit Corp v Da Silva [1965] 1 W.L.R. 248; (1965) 109 S.J. 30, PC (BG) *2–029*
British Homes Assurance Corp Ltd v Paterson [1902] 2 Ch. 404, Ch D *19–087*
British Homophone v Kunz (1935) 152 L.T. 589 .... *2–126*
British Industrial Plastics Ltd v Ferguson [1940] 1 All E.R. 479, HL ...*18–135*, *22–055*
British Medical Association v Greater Glasgow Health Board [1989] A.C. 1211; [1989] 2 W.L.R. 660; [1989] 1 All E.R. 984; 1989 S.C. (H.L.) 65; 1989 S.L.T. 493; (1989) 133 S.J. 456, HL; affirming, 1988 S.L.T. 538; 1988 S.C.L.R. 403, IH (2 Div); affirming 1988 S.L.T. 130, OH 10–018, *10–019*
British Motor Trade Association v Gilbert [1951] 2 All E.R. 641; [1951] 2 T.L.R. 514; [1951] W.N. 454; (1951) 95 S.J. 595, Ch D *16–121*
British Motor Trade Association v Gray, 1951 S.C. 586; 1951 S.L.T. 247, IH (1 Div); affirming, 1950 S.L.T. (Notes) 61, OH *16–077*
British Motor Trade Association v Salvadori [1949] Ch. 556; [1949] 1 All E.R. 208; 65 T.L.R. 44; [1949] L.J.R. 1304, Ch D 18–141
British Movietonews v London and District Cinemas [1952] A.C. 166; [1951] 2 All E.R. 617; [1951] 2 T.L.R. 571; (1951) 95 S.J. 499, HL; reversing [1951] 1 K.B. 190; [1950] 2 All E.R. 390; 66 T.L.R. (Pt. 2) 203; (1950) 94 S.J. 504, CA *1–020*, *12–043*, *13–009*, *23–008*, *23–010*, *23–012*, *23–059*
British Murac Syndicate Ltd v Alperton Rubber Co Ltd [1915] 2 Ch. 186, Ch D *27–021*
British Nylon Spinners v ICI [1953] Ch. 19; [1952] 2 All E.R. 780; [1952] 2 T.L.R. 669; (1952) 69 R.P.C. 288, CA *16–033*, *30–367*
British Oxygen Co Ltd v South of Scotland Electricity Board (No.2); sub nom. British Oxygen Gases Ltd v South of Scotland Electricity Board (No.2) [1959] 1 W.L.R. 587; [1959] 2 All E.R. 225; 1959 S.C. (H.L.) 17; 1959 S.L.T. 181; (1959) 103 S.J. 370, HL *29–084*, *29–094*, *29–095*, *29–097*

British Racing Drivers Club Ltd v Hextall Erskine & Co [1996] 3 All E.R. 667; [1996] B.C.C. 727; [1997] 1 B.C.L.C. 182; [1996] P.N.L.R. 523, Ch D *26–032*, *26–120*
British Red Cross Balkan Fund, Re; sub nom. British Red Cross Society v Johnson [1914] 2 Ch. 419; [1914–15] All E.R. Rep. 459, Ch D *21–066*
British Reinforced Concrete Engineering Co Ltd v Schelff [1921] 2 Ch. 563, Ch D *16–093*, *16–117*, *16–194*, *16–198*
British Road Services Ltd v Arthur V Crutchley & Co Ltd (No.1) [1968] 1 All E.R. 811; [1968] 1 Lloyd's Rep. 271, CA (Civ Div); reversing [1967] 2 All E.R. 785, Assizes (Liverpool) 2–036
British Russian Gazette & Trade Outlook Ltd v Associated Newspapers Ltd; Talbot v Associated Newspapers Ltd [1933] 2 K.B. 616, CA *22–012*, *22–013*, *22–015*
British Ry Traffic and Electric Co v Roper (1939) 162 L.T. 217 .... *5–105*
British School of Motoring Ltd v Simms [1971] 1 All E.R. 317; [1971] R.T.R. 190, Assizes (Winchester) *13–006*
British South Africa Co v De Beers Consolidated Mines Ltd. *See* De Beers Consolidated Mines Ltd v British South Africa Co
British Stamp and Ticket Automatic Delivery Co v Haynes [1921] 1 K.B. 377, KBD *26–103*
British Steel Corp v Cleveland Bridge & Engineering Co Ltd [1984] 1 All E.R. 504; [1982] Com. L.R. 54; 24 B.L.R. 94, QBD ...*2–042*, *2–085*, *2–113*, *2–116*, *2–183*, *29–011*, *29–021*, *29–071*, *29–080*
British Steel Plc v Customs and Excise Commissioners (No.1) [1997] 2 All E.R. 366, CA (Civ Div) *29–083*, *29–085*
British Sugar Plc v NEI Power Projects Ltd, 87 B.L.R. 42; [1997–98] Info. T.L.R. 353; [1998] I.T.C.L.R. 125; (1998) 14 Const. L.J. 365, CA (Civ Div); affirming [1997] C.L.C. 622, QBD *12–053*, *14–006*
British Telecommunications Plc v James Thomson & Sons (Engineers) Ltd [1999] 1 W.L.R. 9; [1999] 2 All E.R. 241; 1999 S.C. (H.L.) 9; 1999 S.L.T. 224; 1999 S.C.L.R. 126; [1999] B.L.R. 35; (1999) 1 T.C.L.R. 1; 61 Con. L.R. 1; [1999] Lloyd's Rep. I.R. 105; (1999) 96(4) L.S.G. 40; (1999) 143 S.J.L.B. 28; [1998] N.P.C. 161; 1999 G.W.D. 1–47, HL; reversing, 1997 S.C. 59; 1997 S.L.T. 767; 1997 S.C.L.R. 228; 82 B.L.R. 1; 54 Con. L.R. 108; [1997] 6 Re. L.R. 325; 1997 Rep. L.R. 23; (1997) 13 Const. L.J. 332; 1997 G.W.D. 3–77, IH (2 Div); affirming, 49 Con. L.R. 163, OH *1–187*, *18–022*
British Telecommunications Plc v Sun Life Assurance Society Plc [1996] Ch. 69; [1995] 3 W.L.R. 622; [1995] 4 All E.R. 44; (1997) 73 P. & C.R. 475; [1995] 2 E.G.L.R. 44; [1995] 45 E.G. 133; (1995) 145 N.L.J. 1366; (1995) 139 S.J.L.B. 203; [1995] N.P.C. 140, CA (Civ Div) *21–009*
British Thomson Houston Co Ltd v Federated European Bank Ltd [1932] 2 K.B. 176, CA *9–042*, *9–043*
British Trade Corp Ltd, Re [1932] 2 Ch. 1, CA *28–042*
British Transport Commission v Gourley [1956] A.C. 185; [1956] 2 W.L.R. 41; [1955] 3 All E.R. 796; [1955] 2 Lloyd's Rep. 475; 49 R. & I.T. 11; (1955) 34 A.T.C. 305; [1955] T.R. 303; (1956) 100 S.J. 12, HL 26–157, 26–158, 26–159, 26–160, 26–161, 26–162, 26–163, 26–164, 26–166
British Transport Commission v Westmorland CC; British Transport Commission v Worcestershire CC [1958] A.C. 126; [1957] 2 W.L.R. 1032; [1957] 2 All E.R. 353; (1957) 121 J.P. 394; (1957) 101 S.J. 445, HL; affirming [1956] 2 Q.B. 214; [1956] 2 W.L.R. 1022; [1956] 2 All E.R. 129; 54 L.G.R. 311; (1956) 100 S.J. 317, CA; affirming [1956] 2 W.L.R. 428; [1956] 1 All E.R. 321; 54 L.G.R. 130; (1956) 100 S.J. 112, DC *10–027*, *10–028*
British Union & National Insurance Co v Rawson [1916] 2 Ch. 476, CA; affirming [1916] 2 Ch. 152, Ch D *19–055*
British Waggon Co v Lea & Co; Parkgate Waggon Co v Lea & Co (1879–80) L.R. 5 Q.B.D. 149, QBD *9–048*, 19–083
British Westinghouse Electric & Manufacturing Co Ltd v Underground Electric Railways Co of London Ltd (No.2) [1912] A.C. 673, HL; reversing [1912] 3 K.B. 128, CA *1–164*, *26–001*, *26–074*, *26–103*, *26–104*, *26–115*, 26–116, *26–119*

Brittain v Lloyd, 153 E.R. 683; (1854) 14 M. & W. 762, Ex Ct *29–113*
Britvic Soft Drinks Ltd v Messer UK Ltd; sub nom. Messer UK Ltd v Britvic Soft Drinks Ltd [2002] EWCA Civ 548; [2002] 2 All E.R. (Comm) 321; [2002] 2 Lloyd's Rep. 368, CA (Civ Div); affirming [2002] 1 Lloyd's Rep. 20, QBD *2–116*, *14–007*, *14–085*, 14–094, 14–096, *14–103*
Broadwater Manor School v Davis [1999] C.L.Y. 1801, CC (Worthing) *15–099*
Broadwick Financial Services Ltd v Spencer [2002] EWCA Civ 35; [2002] 1 All E.R. (Comm) 446; (2002) 99(11) L.S.G. 36; (2002) 146 S.J.L.B. 53, CA (Civ Div) *2–162*
Brocklebank Ltd, Re [1925] 1 K.B. 52 .... *29–083*, *29–084*, *29–094*, *29–143*
Brocklehurst (Deceased) (Estate of), Re; sub nom. Hall v Roberts; Estate of Sir Philip Lee Brocklehurst (Deceased), Re [1978] Ch. 14; [1977] 3 W.L.R. 696; [1978] 1 All E.R. 767; (1977) 121 S.J. 633, CA (Civ Div) *7–064*, *7–093*
Brocklesby v Armitage & Guest [2002] 1 W.L.R. 598; [2001] 1 All E.R. 172; [1999] Lloyd's Rep. P.N. 888; [2000] P.N.L.R. 33; [2001] 1 E.G.L.R. 67; [2001] 14 E.G. 150, CA (Civ Div) 28–085
Brockman, Re [1909] 2 Ch. 170, CA *28–133*
Brocks v Phillips (1599) Cro.Eliz. 683 .... *11–029*
Broderick, Re [1986] N.I.J.B. 36 .... *3–115*
Brodie, Re; sub nom. Brodie v Brodie [1917] P. 271, PDAD *16–070*
Brodie v Cardiff Corp; sub nom. Arbitration Between Nott and the Cardiff Corp, Re [1919] A.C. 337, HL *29–101*
Brodin v A/R Seljan, 1973 S.C. 213; 1973 S.L.T. 198; 1973 S.L.T. (Notes) 59, OH *16–030*
Brogden v Metropolitan Railway Co (1876–77) L.R. 2 App. Cas. 666, HL *2–030*, 2–031, *2–045*
Broggi v Robins (1899) 15 T.L.R. 224 .... *21–009*
Brokaw v Seatrain UK Ltd; sub nom. United States v Brokaw [1971] 2 Q.B. 476; [1971] 2 W.L.R. 791; [1971] 2 All E.R. 98; [1971] 1 Lloyd's Rep. 337; [1971] T.R. 71; (1971) 115 S.J. 172, CA (Civ Div) *16–031*
Broken Hill Proprietary Co Pty Ltd v Xenakis [1982] 2 Lloyd's Rep. 304; [1982] Com. L.R. 152, QBD (Comm) *30–011*, *30–012*
Bromley LBC v A Ellis (Luff & Sons, Third Party) [1971] 1 Lloyd's Rep. 97; (1970) 114 S.J. 906, CA (Civ Div) *29–096*
Bromley v Smith [1909] 2 K.B. 235, KBD *8–026*, *16–102*, *16–112*, *16–198*
Bronester v Priddle [1961] 1 W.L.R. 1294; [1961] 3 All E.R. 471; (1961) 105 S.J. 683, CA *13–007*
Brook v Hook (1870–71) L.R. 6 Ex. 89, Ex Ct *12–047*, *16–037*
Brooke v Rounthwaite (1846) 5 Hare 298 .... *27–057*
Brooker v Scott (1843) 11 M. & W. 67 .... *8–008*
Brooker v Seddon (1858) 1 F. & F. 196 .... *12–108*
Brookman's Trust, Re (1869–70) L.R. 5 Ch. App. 182, CA in Chancery ... *16–073*, *21–006*
Brooks v Beirnstein [1909] 1 K.B. 98, KBD *24–051*, *25–008*
Brooks v Muckleston [1909] 2 Ch. 519, Ch D *28–142*
Brooks v Olyslager Oms (UK) Ltd [1998] I.R.L.R. 590, CA (Civ Div) *16–107*
Brooks Wharf and Bull Wharf Ltd v Goodman Bros [1937] 1 K.B. 534 ... *29–008*, *29–011*, *29–020*, *29–025*, *29–026*, *29–099*, 29–102
Brooksbank v Smith (1836) 2 Y. & C. Ex. 58 .... *28–140*
Broom v Batchelor (1856) 1 H. & N. 255 .... *12–081*
Broom v Davis (1794) 7 East 480 .... *21–033*
Broome v Cassell & Co Ltd (No.1) [1972] A.C. 1027; [1972] 2 W.L.R. 645; [1972] 1 All E.R. 801; (1972) 116 S.J. 199, HL; affirming [1971] 2 Q.B. 354; [1971] 2 W.L.R. 853; [1971] 2 All E.R. 187; (1971) 115 S.J. 289, CA (Civ Div); affirming [1971] 1 All E.R. 262, QBD *1–123*, *1–133*, 6–063, *26–019*, *29–145*
Broome v Pardess Co-operative Societyof Orange Growers Ltd [1940] 1 All E.R. 603, CA *12–092*
Brough v Nettleton [1921] 2 Ch. 25, Ch D *4–047*, *4–050*
Broughton v Snook [1938] Ch. 505, Ch D *4–045*, *4–046*, *4–049*
Brown v Boorman (1842) L.R. 3 Q.B. 511; (1844) 11 Cl. & Fin. 1, HL 1–129, 1–145
Brown v Brine (1875–76) L.R. 1 Ex. D. 5, Exchequer Div *3–062*, *16–005*

Brown v Byrne (1854) 3 E. & B. 703 .... *12–127*, *12–128*
Brown v Dean (1833) 5 B. Ad. 848 .... *21–010*
Brown v Dixon (1786) 1 T.R. 274 .... *1–128*
Brown v Gould [1972] Ch. 53; [1971] 3 W.L.R. 334; [1971] 2 All E.R. 1505; (1971) 22 P. & C.R. 871; (1971) 115 S.J. 406, Ch D *2–127*, *2–128*, *2–130*, *2–132*, *2–140*
Brown v Great Eastern Railway Co (1876–77) L.R. 2 Q.B.D. 406, QBD *21–010*
Brown v Harper (1893) 68 L.T. 488 .... *8–023*, *8–045*
Brown v Heathlands Mental Health NHS Trust [1996] 1 All E.R. 133; (1996) 31 B.M.L.R. 57, Ch D *27–062*
Brown v Howard (1820) 2 Brod. & B. 73 .... *28–033*
Brown v Inland Revenue Commissioners [1965] A.C. 244; [1964] 3 W.L.R. 511; [1964] 3 All E.R. 119; 1964 S.C. (H.L.) 180; 1964 S.L.T. 302; 42 T.C. 42; (1964) 43 A.T.C. 244; [1964] T.R. 269; (1964) 108 S.J. 636, HL *29–198*
Brown v Jodrell (1827) M. & M. 105 .... *8–068*
Brown v KMR Services Ltd (formerly HG Poland (Agencies) Ltd); Sword Daniels v Pitel [1995] 4 All E.R. 598; [1995] 2 Lloyd's Rep. 513; [1995] C.L.C. 1418; [1995] 4 Re. L.R. 241, CA (Civ Div) *26–043*, *26–054*, *26–059*, *26–066*, *26–117*
Brown v Knowsley BC [1986] I.R.L.R. 102, EAT *2–149*
Brown v Muller (1871–72) L.R. 7 Ex. 319, Ex Ct *24–011*, *26–112*
Brown v Overbury (1856) 11 Exch. 715 .... *16–047*
Brown v Raphael [1958] Ch. 636; [1958] 2 W.L.R. 647; [1958] 2 All E.R. 79; (1958) 102 S.J. 269, CA *6–007*, *6–009*, 6–009, *6–010*, 6–011
Brown v Royal Insurance Society (1859) 1 E.E. 853 .... *21–006*, *23–004*
Brown v Sheen and Richmond Car Sales Ltd [1950] 1 All E.R. 1102; [1950] W.N. 316, KBD *1–133*, *12–007*, *18–006*
Brown v Watts (1808) 1 Taunt. 353 .... *21–078*
Brown & Davis Ltd v Galbraith [1972] 1 W.L.R. 997; [1972] 3 All E.R. 31; [1972] 2 Lloyd's Rep. 1; [1972] R.T.R. 523; (1972) 116 S.J. 545, CA (Civ Div) *12–007*, *18–008*, *29–019*, *29–133*
Brown & Green v Hays (1920) 36 T.L.R. 330 .... *9–059*
Brown Boveri (Australia) Pty v Baltic Shipping Co; The Nadezhda Krupskaya [1989] 1 Lloyd's Rep. 518, CA (NSW) *21–070*
Brown Green Ltd v Hays (1920) 36 T.L.R. 330 .... *29–142*
Brown Jenkinson & Co Ltd v Percy Dalton (London) Ltd [1957] 2 Q.B. 621; [1957] 3 W.L.R. 403; [1957] 2 All E.R. 844; [1957] 2 Lloyd's Rep. 1; (1957) 101 S.J. 610, CA; reversing [1957] 1 Lloyd's Rep. 31, MCLC *6–028*, *6–046*, *16–017*, *16–018*, *16–175*
Brown Shipley & Co v Kough (1885) L.R. 29 Ch. D. 848, CA *19–024*
Browne v La Trinidad (1888) L.R. 37 Ch. D. 1, CA *9–061*
Browning v Baldwin (1879) 40 L.T. 248 .... *21–064*, *21–066*
Browning v Morris, 98 E.R. 1364; (1778) 2 Cowp. 790, KB 16–185
Browning v Wright, 126 E.R. 1128; (1799) 2 Bos. & P. 13, KB *12–063*
Brownlie v Campbell (1879–80) L.R. 5 App. Cas. 925, HL *29–036*
Brown's Estate, Re; sub nom. Brown v Brown [1893] 2 Ch. 300, Ch D *28–036*, *28–042*, *28–046*
Brownton Ltd v Edward Moore Inbucom Ltd [1985] 3 All E.R. 499; (1985) 82 L.S.G. 1165, CA (Civ Div) *16–052*, 16–059, 16–060, *19–050*
Bruce, Re; sub nom. Lawford v Bruce [1908] 2 Ch. 682, CA *28–130*
Bruce v Hunter (1813) 3 Camp. 467 .... *13–022*
Bruner v Moore [1904] 1 Ch. 305, Ch D *2–048*, *22–041*, *22–042*
Brunning Group v Bentley [1966] C.L.Y. 4489 .... *16–108*
Brunsden v Humphrey (1884–85) L.R. 14 Q.B.D. 141, CA *25–008*
Brunswick (Duke of) v King of Hanover, 49 E.R. 724; (1844) 6 Beav. 1, Ct of Chancery *11–001*, *11–007*, *11–020*

Bruton v London & Quadrant Housing Trust; sub nom. Bruton v Quadrant Housing Trust [2000] 1 A.C. 406; [1999] 3 W.L.R. 150; [1999] 3 All E.R. 481; (1999) 31 H.L.R. 902; [1999] L. & T.R. 469; [1999] 2 E.G.L.R. 59; [1999] 30 E.G. 91; [1999] E.G. 90 (C.S.); (1999) 96(28) L.S.G. 26; (1999) 149 N.L.J. 1001; (1999) 143 S.J.L.B. 195; [1999] N.P.C. 73; (1999) 78 P. & C.R. D21, HL; reversing [1998] Q.B. 834; [1998] 3 W.L.R. 438; [1997] 4 All E.R. 970; (1998) 30 H.L.R. 658; [1997] 2 E.G.L.R. 91; [1997] 50 E.G. 87; [1997] E.G. 125 (C.S.); (1997) 147 N.L.J. 1385; [1997] N.P.C. 124; (1998) 75 P. & C.R. D1, CA (Civ Div) *2–161*
Brutus v Cozens [1973] A.C. 854; [1972] 3 W.L.R. 521; [1972] 2 All E.R. 1297; (1972) 56 Cr. App. R. 799; [1973] Crim. L.R. 56; (1972) 116 S.J. 647, HL; reversing [1972] 1 W.L.R. 484; [1972] 2 All E.R. 1; (1972) 116 S.J. 217, QBD *12–046*
Bryan v Maloney, 74 B.L.R. 35; 51 Con. L.R. 29; 182 C.L.R. 609; (1995) 11 Const. L.J. 274, HC (Aus) *1–126*, *18–027*
Bryanston Finance Ltd v De Vries (No.1) [1975] Q.B. 703; [1975] 2 W.L.R. 718; [1975] 2 All E.R. 609; (1975) 119 S.J. 287, CA (Civ Div) *17–018*
Bryant v Herbert (1877–78) L.R. 3 C.P.D. 389, CA; reversing (1877–78) L.R. 3 C.P.D. 189, CPD *1–118*
Bryant v Richardson (1866) L.R. 3 Ex. 93 .... *8–016*
Bryen & Langley Ltd v Boston [2005] EWCA Civ 973; [2005] B.L.R. 508, CA (Civ Div); reversing [2004] EWHC 2450 (TCC); [2005] B.L.R. 28; 98 Con. L.R. 82; [2004] N.P.C. 165, QBD (TCC) *2–116*, 15–048, 15–075, *15–094*
Bua International Ltd v Hai Hing Shipping Co Ltd; The Hai Hing [2000] 1 Lloyd's Rep. 300; [2000] C.P. Rep. 68; [2000] C.L.C. 603, QBD (Comm) *28–116*, *28–126*
Buchanan v Alba Diagnostics Ltd [2004] UKHL 5; 2004 S.C. (H.L.) 9; 2004 S.L.T. 255; 2004 S.C.L.R. 273; [2004] R.P.C. 34; (2004) 27(4) I.P.D. 27034; (2004) 148 S.J.L.B. 183; 2004 G.W.D. 5–95, HL; affirming 2001 S.C.L.R. 307; [2001] R.P.C. 43; 2001 G.W.D. 6–234, IH (1 Div); affirming [2000] R.P.C. 367; 1999 G.W.D. 24–1170, OH 16–120, *16–121*
Buck v Robson (1870) L.R. 10 Eq. 629, Ct of Chancery *28–004*
Buck v Robson (1877–78) L.R. 3 Q.B.D. 686, QBD *19–008*
Buckland v Farmar & Moody [1979] 1 W.L.R. 221; [1978] 3 All E.R. 929; (1978) 36 P. & C.R. 330; (1978) 122 S.J. 211, CA (Civ Div) *21–014*, *22–042*
Buckland v Palmer [1984] 1 W.L.R. 1109; [1984] 3 All E.R. 554; [1985] R.T.R. 5; (1984) 81 L.S.G. 2300; (1984) 128 S.J. 565, CA (Civ Div) *25–007*
Buckley v Tuttey (1971) 125 C.L.R. 353 .... *16–137*
Buckmaster v Harrop (1807) 13 Ves. 456 .... *4–050*
Buckpitt v Oates [1968] 1 All E.R. 1145, Assizes (Devon) ..*2–168*, *8–009*, *8–025*, *14–014*
Budd v Peninsular and Oriental Steam Navigation Co [1969] 2 Lloyd's Rep. 262, QBD *12–014*
Budget Rent A Car International Inc v Mamos Slough (1977) 121 S.J. 374, CA (Civ Div) *16–138*
Budgett v Budgett [1895] 1 Ch. 202, Ch D *28–132*
Budgett v Stratford Co-operative and Industrail Society Ltd (1916) 32 T.L.R. 378, KBD *3–008*
Budgett & Co v Binnington & Co [1891] 1 Q.B. 35, CA 23–045
Buehler AG v Chronos Richardson Ltd [1998] 2 All E.R. 960; [1998] R.P.C. 609; (1998) 21(7) I.P.D. 21076; (1998) 95(16) L.S.G. 25; (1998) 142 S.J.L.B. 133, CA (Civ Div) *25–012*
Buenaventura v Ocean Trade Co [1984] E.C.C. 183, Hof (Den Haag) *30–336*
Bugsier Reederei und Bergungs A/G v Owners of the SS Brighton; The Brighton [1951] 2 Lloyd's Rep. 65; [1951] 2 T.L.R. 409; [1951] W.N. 370; (1951) 95 S.J. 547, PDAD *11–027*
Bulk Oil (Zug) v Sun International Ltd and Sun Oil Trading Co Ltd (No.2) [1984] 1 Lloyd's Rep. 531, QBD (Comm) *24–012*
Bulk Shipping AG v Ipco Trading SA; The Jasmine B; sub nom. Jasmine B, The [1992] 1 Lloyd's Rep. 39, QBD (Comm) *12–082*, *13–012*

Bulk Trading Corp Ltd v Zenziper Grains and Feed Stuffs; sub nom. Zenziper Grains and Feed Stuffs v Bulk Trading Corp Ltd [2001] 1 All E.R. (Comm) 385; [2001] 1 Lloyd's Rep. 357; [2001] C.L.C. 496, CA (Civ Div) *2–143*
Bulk Transport Group Shipping Co Ltd v Seacrystal Shipping Ltd; The Kyzikos; sub nom. Seacrystal Shipping Ltd v Bulk Transport Group Shipping Co Ltd; The Kyzikos [1989] A.C. 1264; [1988] 3 W.L.R. 858; [1988] 3 All E.R. 745; [1989] 1 Lloyd's Rep. 1; (1988) 85(41) L.S.G. 47; (1988) 132 S.J. 1526, HL; reversing [1987] 1 W.L.R. 1565; [1987] 3 All E.R. 222; [1987] 2 Lloyd's Rep. 122; [1987] F.T.L.R. 171; (1987) 131 S.J. 1550, CA (Civ Div); reversing [1987] 1 Lloyd's Rep. 48, QBD (Comm) *12–057*
Bull v Nottinghamshire and City of Nottingham Fire and Rescue Authority; Lincolnshire CC v Fire Brigades Union [2007] EWCA Civ 240; [2007] I.C.R. 1631; [2007] B.L.G.R. 439; (2007) 151 S.J.L.B. 333, CA (Civ Div); affirming [2006] EWHC 2749 (QB), QBD *12–118*, *13–008*
Bull v Pitney Bowes Ltd [1967] 1 W.L.R. 273; [1966] 3 All E.R. 384; 1 K.I.R. 342; (1967) 111 S.J. 32, QBD *16–091*, *16–095*, *16–104*, *16–105*
Buller v Harrison, 98 E.R. 1243; (1777) 2 Cowp. 565, KB *29–031*, *29–182*
Bulli Coal Mining Co v Osborne [1899] A.C. 351, PC (Aus) *28–086*
Bullock v Lloyds Bank Ltd [1955] Ch. 317; [1955] 2 W.L.R. 1; [1954] 3 All E.R. 726; (1955) 99 S.J. 28, Ch D *7–058*, *7–074*, *7–097*, *28–140*, 28–145
Bunbury v Lautro Ltd [1996] C.L.C. 1273, Ch D *9–076*
Bunbury Foods Proprietary v National Bank of Australasia, 153 C.L.R. 491; (1984) 51 A.L.R. 609, HC (Aus) *21–053*
Bunge AG v Giuseppe Rocco & Figli; The Istros II [1973] 2 Lloyd's Rep. 152, QBD (Comm) *29–115*
Bunge Corp v Tradax Export SA [1981] 1 W.L.R. 711; [1981] 2 All E.R. 540; [1981] 2 Lloyd's Rep. 1; (1981) 125 S.J. 373, HL; affirming [1981] 2 All E.R. 524; [1980] 1 Lloyd's Rep. 294, CA (Civ Div); reversing [1979] 2 Lloyd's Rep. 477, QBD (Comm) *12–026*, *12–034*, *12–037*, *12–040*, *21–013*, *26–048*
Bunge Corp v Vegetable Vitamin Foods (Pte) Ltd [1985] 1 Lloyd's Rep. 613; (1984) 134 N.L.J. 125, QBD (Comm) *24–011*
Bunge GmbH v Alfred C Toepfer [1979] 1 Lloyd's Rep. 554, CA (Civ Div); affirming [1978] 1 Lloyd's Rep. 506, QBD (Comm) *14–148*, *14–150*, *22–052*, *24–006*
Bunge GmbH v CCV Landbouwberlang GA [1980] 1 Lloyd's Rep. 458, CA (Civ Div); affirming [1978] 1 Lloyd's Rep. 217, QBD (Comm) ... *12–037*, *14–150*, *24–044*
Bunge SA v Compagnie Europeene de Cereales [1982] 1 Lloyd's Rep. 306, QBD (Comm) *3–091*, *14–151*, *22–052*
Bunge SA v Deutsche Conti-Handels GmbH (No.1) [1979] 2 Lloyd's Rep. 435, CA (Civ Div) *14–151*
Bunge SA v Deutsche Conti-Handelsgesellschaft GmbH (No.2) [1981] 1 Lloyd's Rep. 352 .... *28–113*
Bunge SA v Kruse (No.2) [1980] 2 Lloyd's Rep. 142, CA (Civ Div); affirming [1979] 1 Lloyd's Rep. 279, QBD (Comm) *12–118*, *14–141*, *14–150*, *14–151*, *22–022*, *22–051*
Bunge SA v Schleswig-Holsteinische Landwirtschaftliche Hauptgenossenschaft Eingetr GmbH [1978] 1 Lloyd's Rep. 480, QBD (Comm) *22–044*, *24–008*
Burchell v Clark (1876–77) L.R. 2 C.P.D. 88, CA; reversing (1875–76) L.R. 1 C.P.D. 602, CPD *12–067*
Burchell v Gowrie & Blockhouse Collieries Ltd [1910] A.C. 614, PC (Can) *29–068*, *29–069*
Burchell v Thompson [1920] 2 K.B. 80, CA *21–058*
Burchfield v Moore (1854) 23 L.J.Q.B. 261 .... *25–024*
Burdick v Garrick (1869–70) L.R. 5 Ch. App. 233, CA in Chancery *28–031*
Burge v Ashley & Smith Ltd [1900] 1 Q.B. 744, CA *16–192*
Burge v Ashley Ltd [1990] 1 Q.B. 744 .... *29–197*
Burges v Wickham (1863) 3 B. & S. 669 .... *12–062*, *12–118*, *12–123*
Burgess' Policy, Re (1915) 113 L.T. 443 .... *18–081*, *18–086*

Burgess v Cox [1951] Ch. 383; [1950] 2 All E.R. 1212; [1951] 1 T.L.R. 531, Ch D ... *4–024*, *4–026*, *4–027*, *4–028*, *22–046*
Burgess v Merrill (1812) 4 Taunt. 468 ... *8–063*, *17–008*, *17–010*
Burgh v Legge (1839) 5 M.W. 418 ... *29–191*
Burland v Earle [1902] A.C. 83, PC (Can) ... *9–054*, *9–055*
Burlinson v Hall (1883–84) L.R. 12 Q.B.D. 347, QBD ... *19–012*
Burmah Oil Co Ltd v Bank of England (1981) 125 S.J. 528, Ch D ... *7–126*
Burmah Steam Ship Co v Inland Revenue Commissioners, 1931 S.C. 156; 1931 S.L.T. 116, IH (1 Div) ... *26–163*
Burn v National Amalgamated Labourers Union of Great Britain and Ireland [1920] 2 Ch. 364, Ch D ... *9–083*
Burnaby v Equitable Reversionary Interest Society (1885) L.R. 28 Ch. D. 416, Ch D ... *8–036*
Burnard v Haggis, 143 E.R. 360; (1863) 14 C.B. N.S. 45, CCP ... *1–162*, *8–047*
Burnett v British Waterways Board [1973] 1 W.L.R. 700; [1973] 2 All E.R. 631; [1973] 2 Lloyd's Rep. 137; (1973) 117 S.J. 203, CA (Civ Div); affirming [1972] 1 W.L.R. 1329; [1972] 2 All E.R. 1353; [1972] 2 Lloyd's Rep. 222; (1972) 116 S.J. 783, QBD ... *12–017*, *14–014*
Burnett v Westminster Bank Ltd [1966] 1 Q.B. 742; [1965] 3 W.L.R. 863; [1965] 3 All E.R. 81; [1965] 2 Lloyd's Rep. 218; (1965) 109 S.J. 533, QBD (Comm) ... *12–009*, *12–013*
Burns v Burns [1984] Ch. 317; [1984] 2 W.L.R. 582; [1984] 1 All E.R. 244; [1984] Fam. Law 244; (1984) 81 L.S.G. 893; (1984) 128 S.J. 173, CA (Civ Div) ... *2–171*
Burns v Campbell [1952] 1 K.B. 15; [1951] 2 All E.R. 965; [1951] 2 T.L.R. 1007; (1951) 95 S.J. 743, CA ... *20–004*
Burns v Shuttlehurst Ltd; sub nom. Burns v General Accident Fire and Life Assurance Corp Plc [1999] 1 W.L.R. 1449; [1999] 2 All E.R. 27; [1999] P.I.Q.R. P229; (1999) 96(6) L.S.G. 35, CA (Civ Div) ... *28–006*
Buron v Denman, 154 E.R. 327; (1848) 2 Ex. 167, Ex Ct ... *11–007*
Burrell & Son v Leven (1926) 42 T.L.R. 407 ... *3–050*
Burrell & Sons v Hind Rolph & Co; sub nom. Burrell & Sons v F Green & Co [1915] 1 K.B. 391, CA; reversing in part [1914] 1 K.B. 293, KBD ... *12–077*
Burroughes v Abbott [1922] 1 Ch. 86, Ch D ... *5–108*, *5–109*, *28–146*
Burrow v Scammell (1881–82) L.R. 19 Ch. D. 175, Ch D ... 5–077, *27–054*
Burrowes v Lock (1805) Ves. 470 ... *3–101*, *3–113*, *6–095*
Burrows, Re (1856) 8 De. G. M. & G. 254 ... *8–040*, *8–065*
Burrows v Brent LBC [1996] 1 W.L.R. 1448; [1996] 4 All E.R. 577; [1997] 1 F.L.R. 178; [1997] 2 F.C.R. 43; (1997) 29 H.L.R. 167; [1997] 1 E.G.L.R. 32; [1997] 11 E.G. 150; [1997] Fam. Law 246; (1996) 93(43) L.S.G. 26; (1996) 146 N.L.J. 1616; (1996) 140 S.J.L.B. 239; [1996] N.P.C. 149, HL; reversing (1995) 27 H.L.R. 748; (1996) 72 P. & C.R. 261; [1995] E.G. 128 (C.S.); [1995] N.P.C. 124, CA (Civ Div) ... *2–185*, *3–087*, *3–136*
Burrows v Jamaica Private Power Co Ltd [2002] 1 All E.R. (Comm) 374; [2002] C.L.C. 255; [2002] Lloyd's Rep. I.R. 466, QBD (Comm) ... *30–023*, *30–051*
Burrows v Rhodes; sub nom. Burroughs v Rhodes [1899] 1 Q.B. 816, QBD ... *16–176*
Burrows v Sharp (1991) 23 H.L.R. 82; [1991] Fam. Law 67; [1989] E.G. 51 (C.S.), CA (Civ Div) ... *3–157*, *3–158*, *27–024*
Burstein v Times Newspapers Ltd. *See* Times Newspapers Ltd v Burstein (Costs: Champertous Retainer)
Burston Finance Ltd v Speirway Ltd [1974] 1 W.L.R. 1648; [1974] 3 All E.R. 735; (1975) 29 P. & C.R. 34; (1974) 118 S.J. 882, Ch D ... *29–173*
Burt Boulton & Hayward v Bull [1895] 1 Q.B. 276, CA ... *9–051*
Burton v Pinkerton (1866–67) L.R. 2 Ex. 340, Ex Ct ... *26–082*
Burton v Watkins (1851) 14 Beav. 425 ... *12–078*
Burton & Co v English & Co (1883–84) L.R. 12 Q.B.D. 218, CA; reversing (1882–83) L.R. 10 Q.B.D. 426, QBD ... *14–011*
Burton & Deakin Ltd, Re [1977] 1 W.L.R. 390; [1977] 1 All E.R. 631; (1977) 121 S.J. 169, Ch D ... *9–049*

Burton Marsden Douglas, Re. *See* Marsden v Guide Dogs for the Blind Association
Busby v Cooper; Busby v Abbey National Plc; Busby v Lumby [1996] C.L.C. 1425; 52 Con. L.R. 94; [1996] E.G. 64 (C.S.), CA (Civ Div) *28–011*
Busch v Stevens [1963] 1 Q.B. 1; [1962] 2 W.L.R. 511; [1962] 1 All E.R. 412; (1962) 106 S.J. 153, QBD *28–105*
Bush v Canfield (1818) 2 Conn. 485 .... *29–059*
Bushell v Faith [1970] A.C. 1099; [1970] 2 W.L.R. 272; [1970] 1 All E.R. 53; (1970) 114 S.J. 54, HL; affirming [1969] 2 Ch. 438; [1969] 2 W.L.R. 1067; [1969] 1 All E.R. 1002; (1969) 113 S.J. 262, CA (Civ Div) *9–058*
Bushwall Properties Ltd v Vortex Properties Ltd [1976] 1 W.L.R. 591; [1976] 2 All E.R. 283; (1976) 32 P. & C.R. 334; (1976) 120 S.J. 183, CA (Civ Div); reversing [1975] 1 W.L.R. 1649; [1975] 2 All E.R. 214; (1974) 119 S.J. 846, Ch D *2–112*, *2–143*, *12–126*, *26–174*, *26–175*
Business Computers International Ltd v Registrar of Companies [1988] Ch. 229; [1987] 3 W.L.R. 1134; [1987] 3 All E.R. 465; (1987) 3 B.C.C. 395; [1987] B.C.L.C. 621; [1988] P.C.C. 16; (1988) 85(4) L.S.G. 35; (1987) 137 N.L.J. 758; (1987) 131 S.J. 1628, Ch D *1–176*
Business Computers Ltd v Anglo-African Leasing Ltd [1977] 1 W.L.R. 578; [1977] 2 All E.R. 741; (1977) 121 S.J. 201, Ch D 19–070, *26–175*
Business Environment Bow Lane Ltd v Deanwater Estates Ltd [2007] EWCA Civ 622; [2007] L. & T.R. 26; [2007] 32 E.G. 90; [2007] 27 E.G. 303 (C.S.); [2007] N.P.C. 79, CA (Civ Div); reversing [2006] EWHC 3363 (Ch); [2007] L. & T.R. 12; [2007] 19 E.G. 166, Ch D *2–166*, *3–080*, *3–127*, 4–076, *12–004*
Business Seating (Renovations) Ltd v Broad [1989] I.C.R. 729, HC ... *16–097*, *16–103*, *16–104*, *16–111*, *16–112*, *16–197*
Bute (Marquis of) v Thompson (1844) 13 M.W. 487 .... *21–007*, *23–004*
Butler v Butler (1885–86) L.R. 16 Q.B.D. 374, CA; affirming (1884–85) L.R. 14 Q.B.D. 831, QBD *8–001*
Butler v Miller (1867) L.R. 1 Eq. 195 .... *3–021*
Butler v Mulvihill (1823) 1 Bligh 137 .... *8–080*
Butler Machine Tool Co v Ex-cell-o Corp (England) [1979] 1 W.L.R. 401; [1979] 1 All E.R. 965; (1977) 121 S.J. 406, CA (Civ Div) *2–032*, 2–037, *2–111*
Butlin's Settlement Trusts (Rectification), Re; sub nom. Butlin v Butlin (Rectification) [1976] Ch. 251; [1976] 2 W.L.R. 547; [1976] 2 All E.R. 483; (1975) 119 S.J. 794, Ch D *5–123*, *5–136*, *29–029*, *29–032*, *29–033*
Butterfield v Sibbitt [1950] 4 D.L.R. 302, HC (Ont) *8–025*
Butterworth v Kingsway Motors Ltd [1954] 1 W.L.R. 1286; [1954] 2 All E.R. 694; (1954) 98 S.J. 717, Assizes (Liverpool) *12–023*, *29–057*
Buttery v Pickard (1946) 62 T.L.R. 241 .... *3–128*
Buttes Gas & Oil Co v Hammer (No.3); Occidental Petroleum Corp v Buttes Gas & Oil Co (No.2) [1982] A.C. 888; [1981] 3 W.L.R. 787; [1981] 3 All E.R. 616; [1981] Com. L.R. 257; (1981) 125 S.J. 776 [1981] Q.B. 223; [1980] 3 W.L.R. 668; [1980] 3 All E.R. 475; (1980) 124 S.J. 630, CA (Civ Div) *11–007*
Button Ex p. Haviside, Re [1907] 2 K.B. 180, CA *29–104*
Button's Lease, Re; sub nom. Inman v Button [1964] Ch. 263; [1963] 3 W.L.R. 903; [1963] 3 All E.R. 708; (1963) 107 S.J. 830, Ch D *3–172*
Butwick v Grant [1924] 2 K.B. 483, KBD *21–043*
Buxton v Lister (1746) 3 At6k. 383 .... *27–002*, *27–011*, *27–017*
Buxton v Rust (1871–72) L.R. 7 Ex. 279, Ex Chamber; affirming (1871–72) L.R. 7 Ex. 1, Ex Ct *4–027*, *4–031*
Byfield (A Bankrupt), Re; sub nom. Hill Samuel & Co Ltd v Trustee of the Property of the Bankrupt [1982] Ch. 267; [1982] 2 W.L.R. 613; [1982] 1 All E.R. 249, Ch D *20–022*, *20–023*, *29–043*, *29–165*, *29–173*
Byford (Deceased), Re; sub nom. Byford v Butler [2003] EWHC 1267 (Ch); [2004] 1 F.L.R. 56; [2004] 2 F.C.R. 454; [2003] B.P.I.R. 1089; [2004] 1 P. & C.R. 12; [2004] Fam. Law 14; (2003) 100(24) L.S.G. 38; (2003) 100(31) L.S.G. 32; [2003] N.P.C. 77, Ch D *20–026*
Byrn v Godfrey (1798) 4 Ves. 6 .... *22–004*
Byrne v Australian Airlines Ltd (1995) 185 C.L.R. 410 .... *13–004*

Byrne v Hall Pain & Foster [1999] 1 W.L.R. 1849; [1999] 2 All E.R. 400; 68 Con. L.R. 110; [1999] Lloyd's Rep. P.N. 147; [1999] P.N.L.R. 565; [1999] 1 E.G.L.R. 73; [1999] 12 E.G. 165; (1999) 15 Const. L.J. 388; [1998] E.G. 182 (C.S.); (1999) 96(5) L.S.G. 37; (1999) 143 S.J.L.B. 36; [1998] N.P.C. 164, CA (Civ Div) *28–034*
Byrne v Motor Insurers Bureau [2008] EWCA Civ 574; [2008] 2 W.L.R. 234; [2007] 3 All E.R. 499; [2008] R.T.R. 1; [2007] 3 C.M.L.R. 15; [2007] Eu. L.R. 739; [2008] Lloyd's Rep. I.R. 61; [2007] P.I.Q.R. P25; (2007) 104(25) L.S.G. 38; (2007) 157 N.L.J. 858; (2007) 151 S.J.L.B. 811, QBD *28–078*
Byrne & Co v Leon Van Tien Hoven & Co (1879–80) L.R. 5 C.P.D. 344, CPD *1–004*, *2–054*, 2–089, 2–090, *2–099*
C (A Minor) v Hackney LBC [1996] 1 W.L.R. 789; [1996] 1 All E.R. 973; [1996] 1 F.L.R. 427; [1996] 1 F.C.R. 653; (1996) 28 H.L.R. 423; [1996] Fam. Law 278, CA (Civ Div) *25–012*
C Czarnikow Ltd v Centrala Handlu Zagranicznego Rolimpex (CHZ) [1979] A.C. 351; [1978] 3 W.L.R. 274; [1978] 2 All E.R. 1043; [1978] 2 Lloyd's Rep. 305; (1978) 122 S.J. 506, HL; affirming [1978] Q.B. 176; [1977] 3 W.L.R. 677; [1978] 1 All E.R. 81; [1977] 2 Lloyd's Rep. 201; (1977) 128 N.L.J. 578; (1977) 121 S.J. 527, CA (Civ Div) *2–155*, *14–141*, *23–047*
C Czarnikow Ltd v Koufos. *See* Koufos v C Czarnikow Ltd
C Davis Metal Producers Ltd v Gilyott & Scott Ltd. *See* Chas Davis (Metal Brokers) Ltd v Gilyott & Scott Ltd
C Itoh & Co Ltd v Companhia De Navegacao Lloyd Brasileiro; The Rio Assu (No.1) [1999] 1 Lloyd's Rep. 201, QBD (Comm) *30–345*
C Itoh & Co Ltd v Companhia De Navegacao Lloyd Brasileiro; The Rio Assu (No.2); C Itoh & Co Ltd v Republica Federativa Do Brasil; The Rio Assu (No.2) [1999] 1 Lloyd's Rep. 115, CA (Civ Div) *12–118*, *13–004*, *13–007*
C Sharpe & Co Ltd v Nosawa & Co [1917] 2 K.B. 814, KBD *26–109*
C v D [2007] EWCA Civ 1282; [2008] 1 Lloyd's Rep. 239; [2008] C.P. Rep. 11; [2007] 2 C.L.C. 930; 116 Con. L.R. 230, CA (Civ Div) *30–010*
C Wilh Svenssons Travarnaktiebolag v Cliffe Steamship Co; sub nom. Svenssons Travaruaktiebolag v Cliffe Steamship Co Ltd [1932] 1 K.B. 490; (1931) 41 Ll. L. Rep. 262, KBD *14–011*
C&P Haulage v Middleton [1983] 1 W.L.R. 1461; [1983] 3 All E.R. 94; (1983) 127 S.J. 730, CA (Civ Div) *26–073*, *26–075*
CA Venezolana de Navegacion v Bank Line; The Roachbank [1988] 2 Lloyd's Rep. 337, CA (Civ Div); affirming [1987] 2 Lloyd's Rep. 498, QBD (Comm) *12–089*
CA Webber (Transport) Ltd v Railtrack Plc; sub nom. CA Webber (Transport) Ltd v Network Rail Infrastructure Ltd (formerly Railtrack Plc) [2003] EWCA Civ 1167; [2004] 1 W.L.R. 320; [2004] 3 All E.R. 202; [2004] 1 P. & C.R. 20; [2004] L. & T.R. 2; [2004] 1 E.G.L.R. 49; [2004] 14 E.G. 142; (2003) 100(36) L.S.G. 40; (2003) 147 S.J.L.B. 902; [2003] 2 P. & C.R. DG21, CA (Civ Div) *1–047*
CBS/Sony Hong Kong Ltd v Television Broadcasts Ltd [1987] F.S.R. 262, HC (HK) *9–066*
CCC Films (London) v Impact Quadrant Films [1985] Q.B. 16; [1984] 3 W.L.R. 245; [1984] 3 All E.R. 298; (1984) 81 L.S.G. 1046; (1984) 134 N.L.J. 657; (1984) 128 S.J. 297, QBD ...*3–014*, *3–177*, *26–073*, *26–075*, 26-*076*, *26–077*, *29–059*
CEL Group Ltd v Nedlloyd Lines UK Ltd [2003] EWCA Civ 1716; [2004] 1 All E.R. (Comm) 689; [2004] 1 Lloyd's Rep. 381; (2003) 147 S.J.L.B. 1399, CA (Civ Div) *2–153*, *13–005*, *13–012*
CFW Architects v Cowlin Construction Ltd [2006] EWHC 6 (TCC); 105 Con. L.R. 116; [2006] C.I.L.L. 2335, QBD (TCC) *13–006*
CGU International Insurance Plc v AstraZeneca Insurance Co Ltd [2005] EWHC 2755; [2006] 1 C.L.C. 162; [2006] Lloyd's Rep. I.R. 409, QBD (Comm) *30–331*
CGU International Insurance Plc v Szabo [2002] 1 All E.R. (Comm) 83; [2002] C.L.C. 265; [2002] Lloyd's Rep. I.R. 196, QBD (Comm) *30–056*, *30–071*
CH Giles & Co Ltd v Morris [1972] 1 W.L.R. 307; [1972] 1 All E.R. 960; (1971) 116 S.J. 176, Ch D *27–023*, *27–024*

CIA Barca de Panama SA v George Wimpey & Co Ltd (No.1) [1980] 1 Lloyd's Rep. 598, CA (Civ Div) *2–153*, *26–178*
CIBC Mellon Trust Co v Stolzenberg (Costs) [2005] EWCA Civ 628; [2005] C.P. Rep. 45; [2005] 2 B.C.L.C. 618; [2005] 4 Costs L.R. 617, CA (Civ Div); reversing [2004] EWHC 413, Ch D *16–053*
CIBC Mortgages Plc v Pitt [1994] 1 A.C. 200; [1993] 3 W.L.R. 802; [1993] 4 All E.R. 433; [1994] 1 F.L.R. 17; [1994] 1 F.C.R. 374; (1994) 26 H.L.R. 90; (1994) 13 Tr. L.R. 180; [1994] C.C.L.R. 68; [1993] Fam. Law 79; [1993] E.G. 174 (C.S.); (1993) 143 N.L.J. 1514; (1993) 137 S.J.L.B. 240; [1993] N.P.C. 136, HL; affirming (1993) 25 H.L.R. 439; (1993) 66 P. & C.R. 179; [1993] E.G. 66 (C.S.); [1993] N.P.C. 61, CA (Civ Div) *6–023*, *7–058*, *7–061*, *7–062*, 7–063, *7–065*, 7–067, *7–068*, *7–105*, *7–107*, 7–113
CMS Dolphin Ltd v Simonet [2002] B.C.C. 600; [2001] 2 B.C.L.C. 704; [2001] Emp. L.R. 895, Ch D *16–107*
CN Marine Inc v Stena Line A/B; The Stena Nautica (No.2) [1982] 2 Lloyd's Rep. 336; [1982] Com. L.R. 203; (1982) 79 L.S.G. 922, CA (Civ Div) *18–138*, 18–147, *27–006*, *27–014*
COLT Telecom Group Plc. *See* Highberry Ltd v Colt Telecom Group Plc (No.2)
CPC Consolidated Pool Carriers GmbH v CTM CIA Transmediterreanea SA; The CPC Gallia [1994] 1 Lloyd's Rep. 68, QBD (Comm) *2–116*
CR Smith Glaziers (Dunfermline) Ltd v Customs and Excise Commissioners; sub nom. CR Smith Glaziers (Dunfermline) Ltd v Edinburgh VAT and Duties Tribunal [2003] UKHL 7; [2003] 1 W.L.R. 656; [2003] 1 All E.R. 801; [2003] S.T.C. 419; 2003 S.C. (H.L.) 21; 2003 S.L.T. 355; 2003 S.C.L.R. 222; [2003] 1 C.M.L.R. 37; [2003] B.T.C. 5193; [2003] B.V.C. 249; [2003] S.T.I. 267; (2003) 147 S.J.L.B. 232; 2003 G.W.D. 8–239, HL; reversing [2001] S.T.C. 770; 2001 S.C. 646; 2002 S.L.T. 81; [2001] S.T.I. 830; 2001 G.W.D. 7–290, IH (Ex Div); affirming [2000] B.V.C. 2146; [2000] S.T.I. 264, V&DTr *2–116*
CTI Group Inc v Transclear SA; The Mary Nour [2007] EWHC 2070 (Comm); [2008] 1 All E.R. (Comm) 192; [2008] 1 Lloyd's Rep. 179; [2007] 2 C.L.C. 518; (2007) 104(38) L.S.G. 35, QBD (Comm) *23–047*
CTN Cash and Carry Ltd v Gallaher Ltd [1994] 4 All E.R. 714, CA (Civ Div) *7–018*, *7–020*, 7–046, *29–028*, *29–088*
CVG Siderurgicia del Orinoco SA v London Steamship Owners Mutual Insurance Association Ltd; The Vainqueur Jose [1979] 1 Lloyd's Rep. 557, QBD (Comm) *26–138*
Cabell v Vaughan (1669) 1 Wms. Saund.290a *17–009*, *17–011*
Cable & Montanari Inc v American Export Imbrandtsen Lines Ltd [1968] 1 Lloyd's Rep. 260, affirmed, 386 F. 2d 839 (1967); cert. denied 309 U.S. 1013 (1968) *14–042*
Cable & Wireless Plc v IBM United Kingdom Ltd; sub nom. Cable & Wireless Plc v IBM UK Ltd [2002] EWHC 2059 (Comm); [2002] 2 All E.R. (Comm) 1041; [2002] C.L.C. 1319; [2003] B.L.R. 89; [2002] Masons C.L.R. 58; (2002) 152 N.L.J. 1652, QBD (Comm) *2–131*
Cable & Wireless Plc v Muscat; sub nom. Muscat v Cable & Wireless Plc [2006] EWCA Civ 220; [2006] I.C.R. 975; [2006] I.R.L.R. 354; (2006) 103(12) L.S.G. 30; (2006) 150 S.J.L.B. 362, CA (Civ Div) *18–005*
Cable (Lord) (Deceased) Will Trusts, Re (No.1); sub nom. Garratt v Waters; Lord Cable (Deceased), Re [1977] 1 W.L.R. 7; [1976] 3 All E.R. 417; (1976) 120 S.J. 317, Ch D *16–027*, *30–367*
Cabot Corp v Moore McCormack Lines Inc; The Mormacscan [1971] 2 Lloyd's Rep. 351, US Ct *14–042*
Cadaval (Duke) v Collins (1836) 4 A. & E. 858 .... *7–048*, *29–098*
Caddick v Skidmore (1857) 2 De. G. & J. 52 .... *4–012*, *4–026*, *12–123*
Cade & Sons Ltd v Daly & Co Ltd [1910] 1 I.R. 306 .... *16–134*
Cadle Co v Hearley [2002] 1 Lloyd's Rep. 143, QBD (Merc) *28–094*

Cadogan Estates Ltd v McMahon [2001] 1 A.C. 378; [2000] 3 W.L.R. 1555; [2000] 4 All E.R. 897; [2001] B.P.I.R. 17; (2001) 33 H.L.R. 42; [2001] L. & T.R. 2; [2001] 1 E.G.L.R. 47; [2001] 06 E.G. 164; [2000] E.G. 119 (C.S.); (2000) 97(43) L.S.G. 39; (2000) 97(44) L.S.G. 45; (2000) 150 N.L.J. 1625; (2000) 144 S.J.L.B. 281; [2000] N.P.C. 110; (2001) 81 P. & C.R. DG11, HL; affirming [1999] 1 W.L.R. 1689; [1999] B.P.I.R. 849; (2000) 32 H.L.R. 433; [1999] L. & T.R. 481; [1999] 2 E.G.L.R. 67; [1999] 31 E.G. 92; [1999] E.G. 80 (C.S.); (1999) 96(22) L.S.G. 35; (1999) 96(23) L.S.G. 36, CA (Civ Div) *20–033*
Cadre SA v Astra Asigurari [2005] EWHC 2504, QBD (Comm) *30–055*
Caffin v Aldridge [1895] 2 Q.B. 648 .... *12–069*
Caine v Coulton (1863) 1 H.C. 764 .... *21–077*, *21–094*
Caines v Smith (1846) 15 M.W. 189 .... *21–010*, *24–028*
Caird v Moss (1886) L.R. 33 Ch. D. 22, CA *5–129*, *29–098*
Cairns v Visteon UK Ltd [2007] I.C.R. 616; [2007] I.R.L.R. 175, EAT *2–160*, *18–005*
Calabar Properties Ltd v Stitcher [1984] 1 W.L.R. 287; [1983] 3 All E.R. 759; (1984) 11 H.L.R. 20; (1984) 47 P. & C.R. 285; (1983) 268 E.G. 697; (1983) 80 L.S.G. 3163; (1983) 127 S.J. 785, CA (Civ Div) *18–050*, *26–078*, *26–082*
Calaminus v Dowlais Iron Co Ltd (1878) 47 L.J.Q.B. 575 .... *21–006*
Calder v Rutherford (1882) 3 Brod. & Bing. 302 .... *17–012*
Caldwell v Parker (1869) 3 I.R. Eq. 519 .... *25–023*
Caledonia Ltd v Orbit Value Co Europe. *See* EE Caledonia Ltd (formerly Occidental Petroleum (Caledonia) Ltd) v Orbit Valve Co Europe Plc
Caledonia North Sea Ltd v London Bridge Engineering Ltd; sub nom. Caledonia North Sea Ltd v BT Plc; Caledonia North Sea Ltd v British Telecommunications Plc; Caledonia North Sea Ltd v Norton (No.2) Ltd (In Liquidation); EE Caledonia Ltd v London Bridge Engineering Ltd [2002] UKHL 4; [2002] 1 All E.R. (Comm) 321; [2002] 1 Lloyd's Rep. 553; 2002 S.C. (H.L.) 117; 2002 S.L.T. 278; 2002 S.C.L.R. 346; [2002] C.L.C. 741; [2002] B.L.R. 139; [2002] Lloyd's Rep. I.R. 261; 2002 G.W.D. 6–178, HL; affirming, 2000 S.L.T. 1123; [2000] Lloyd's Rep. I.R. 249; 2000 G.W.D. 3–84, IH (1 Div); reversing in part, 1997 G.W.D. 33–1658, OH *14–006*
Caledonia Subsea Ltd v Micoperi Srl; sub nom. Caledonia Subsea Ltd v Microperi Srl, 2003 S.C. 70; 2002 S.L.T. 1022; 2003 S.C.L.R. 20; 2002 G.W.D. 25–842, IH (1 Div) *30–020*, *30–077*, *30–090*, *30–188*
Caledonian Railway Co v North British Railway Co (1880–81) L.R. 6 App. Cas. 114, HL *12–053*
Calico Printers Association Ltd v Barclays Bank Ltd (1931) 36 Com. Cas. 197 .... *14–021*
Callaghan v Dominion Insurance Co Ltd [1997] 2 Lloyd's Rep. 541, QBD *28–050*
Callander v Howard (1850) 10 C.B. 290 .... *21–039*
Callisher v Bischoffsheim (1869–70) L.R. 5 Q.B. 449, QB *3–050*, *3–052*, *29–088*, *29–189*
Calton v Bragg (1812) 15 East 223 .... *13–022*
Calvert v Baker (1838) 4 M.W. 417 .... *29–191*
Cambridge v Callaghan. *See* Cambridge v Motor Insurers Bureau
Cambridge v Motor Insurers Bureau; sub nom. Cambridge v Callaghan [1998] R.T.R. 365 , CA (Civ Div) *18–123*
Cambridge Antibody Technology Ltd v Abbott Biotechnology Ltd [2004] EWHC 2974; [2005] F.S.R. 27, Ch D (Patents Ct) *5–114*
Cambridge Display Technology Ltd v EI Dupont de Nemours & Co [2005] EWCA Civ 224, CA (Civ Div); affirming [2004] EWHC 1415 (Ch); [2005] F.S.R. 14, Ch D *12–076*
Cambridge Nutrition Ltd v BBC [1990] 3 All E.R. 523, CA (Civ Div) *3–025*, *27–061*
Cambro Contractors v John Kennelly Sales, *The Times*, April 4, 1994, CA (Civ Div) *5–122*
Camden LBC v McBride (1999) 1 C.L. 284, CC (Clerkenwell) *15–020*
Camdex International Ltd v Bank of Zambia (No.1) [1998] Q.B. 22; [1996] 3 W.L.R. 759; [1996] 3 All E.R. 431; [1996] C.L.C. 1477, CA (Civ Div) *16–049*, 16–061, *19–049*, *30–367*
Cameron v Cameron (No.1), 1996 S.C. 17; 1996 S.L.T. 306, IH (2 Div) *30–079*

Cameron-Head v Cameron & Co, 1919 S.C. 627; 1919 2 S.L.T. 133, IH (1 Div) *26–127*
Camidge v Allenby (1827) 6 B.C. 373 .... *21–078*, *21–079*
Camillo Tank Steamship Co v Alexandria Engineering Works; sub nom. Alexandria Engineering Works Ltd v Camillo Tank Steamship Co Ltd (1921) 9 Ll. L. Rep. 307, HL *29–190*
Campanari v Woodburn (1854) 15 C.B. 400 .... *20–009*
Campbell, Ex p. Wolverhampton and Staffordshire Banking Co, Re (1884–85) L.R. 14 Q.B.D. 32, QBD *16–038*
Campbell v Edwards [1976] 1 W.L.R. 403; [1976] 1 All E.R. 785; [1976] 1 Lloyd's Rep. 522; (1975) 119 S.J. 845, CA (Civ Div) *2–131*
Campbell v Fleming (1834) 1 A.E. 40 .... *29–149*
Campbell v Frisbee [2002] EWCA Civ 1374; [2003] I.C.R. 141; [2003] E.M.L.R. 3; (2002) 146 S.J.L.B. 233, CA (Civ Div); reversing [2002] EWHC 328 (Ch); [2002] E.M.L.R. 31, Ch D *1–066*, *24–047*
Campbell v Griffin [2001] EWCA Civ 990; [2001] W.T.L.R. 981; [2001] N.P.C. 102; (2001) 82 P. & C.R. DG23, CA (Civ Div) *3–141*, *3–157*
Campbell v Hodgson (1819) Gow. 74 .... *12–101*
Campbell v Mirror Group Newspapers Ltd; sub nom. Campbell v MGN Ltd [2004] UKHL 22; [2004] 2 A.C. 457; [2004] 2 W.L.R. 1232; [2004] 2 All E.R. 995; [2004] E.M.L.R. 15; [2004] H.R.L.R. 24; [2004] U.K.H.R.R. 648; 16 B.H.R.C. 500; (2004) 101(21) L.S.G. 36; (2004) 154 N.L.J. 733; (2004) 148 S.J.L.B. 572, HL; reversing [2002] EWCA Civ 1373; [2003] Q.B. 633; [2003] 2 W.L.R. 80; [2003] 1 All E.R. 224; [2003] E.M.L.R. 2; [2003] H.R.L.R. 2; (2002) 99(42) L.S.G. 38; (2002) 146 S.J.L.B. 234, CA (Civ Div); reversing [2002] EWHC 499 (QB); [2002] E.M.L.R. 30; [2002] H.R.L.R. 28; (2002) 99(19) L.S.G. 28; (2002) 146 S.J.L.B. 107, QBD ...*1–060*, *1–066*
Campbell v Thompson [1953] 1 Q.B. 445; [1953] 2 W.L.R. 656; [1953] 1 All E.R. 831; (1953) 97 S.J. 229, QBD *9–067*
Campbell Connelly & Co v Noble [1963] 1 W.L.R. 252; [1963] 1 All E.R. 237; (1963) 107 S.J. 135, Ch D *19–032*, *30–123*, 30–125
Campbell Discount Co Ltd v Gall [1961] 1 Q.B. 431; [1961] 2 W.L.R. 514; [1961] 2 All E.R. 104; (1961) 105 S.J. 232, CA *5–105*, *5–106*, *12–106*, *18–006*
Campden Hill Ltd v Chakrani [2005] EWHC 911 (Ch); [2005] N.P.C. 65, Ch D *29–165*, *29–167*
Campos v Kentucky & Indiana Terminal Railroad Co [1962] 2 Lloyd's Rep. 459; (1962) 106 S.J. 469, QBD (Comm) *21–070*, *21–071*
Can v Read (1749) 3 Atk. 695 .... *21–049*
Canada Rice Mills Ltd v Union Marine & General Insurance Co Ltd [1941] A.C. 55; [1940] 4 All E.R. 169; (1940) 67 Ll. L. Rep. 549; 1940 A.M.C. 1673, PC (Can) *14–146*
Canada Steamship Lines Ltd v King, The [1952] A.C. 192; [1952] 1 All E.R. 305; [1952] 1 Lloyd's Rep. 1; [1952] 1 T.L.R. 261; (1952) 96 S.J. 72, PC (Can) 14–010, *14–013*, 14–015
Canadian General Electric Co v Lake Bosomtwe, The (No.1); Canadian General Electric Co v Pickford & Black Ltd [1970] 2 Lloyd's Rep. 81, Sup Ct (Can); affirming [1969] 1 Lloyd's Rep. 164, Ex Ct (Can) *14–042*
Canadian Pacific Hotels Ltd v Bank of Montreal (1988) 40 D.L.R. (4th) 385 ... *1–126*
Canadian Pacific Railway Co v King, The [1931] A.C. 414, PC (Can) ... *3–139*, *3–142*, *3–151*
Cancol Ltd, Re; sub nom. Cazaly Irving Holdings Ltd v Cancol Ltd [1996] 1 All E.R. 37; [1995] B.C.C. 1133; [1996] 1 B.C.L.C. 101; [1996] B.P.I.R. 252; [1995] E.G. 146 (C.S.); [1995] N.P.C. 156, Ch D (Companies Ct) *3–125*
Candler v Crane Christmas & Co [1951] 2 K.B. 164; [1951] 1 All E.R. 426; [1951] 1 T.L.R. 371; (1951) 95 S.J. 171, CA *6–081*, *18–022*
Candlewood Navigation Corp v Mitsui Osk Lines; The Mineral Transporter and The Ibaraki Maru [1986] A.C. 1; [1985] 3 W.L.R. 381; [1985] 2 All E.R. 935; [1985] 2 Lloyd's Rep. 303; (1985) 82 L.S.G. 2912; (1985) 135 N.L.J. 677; (1985) 129 S.J. 506, PC (Aus) *1–176*, *18–034*, *18–036*, *18–144*

Cane v Jones [1980] 1 W.L.R. 1451; [1981] 1 All E.R. 533; (1980) 124 S.J. 542, Ch D *9–032*, *9–055*
Canmer International Inc v UK Mutual Steamship Assurance Association (Bermuda) Ltd; The Rays [2005] EWHC 1694; [2005] 2 Lloyd's Rep. 479, QBD (Comm) *3–107*, *12–050*, *12–055*, *12–118*, *21–084*
Canning v Farquhar (1885–86) L.R. 16 Q.B.D. 727, CA *2–098*
Cannon v Hartley [1949] Ch. 213; [1949] 1 All E.R. 50; 65 T.L.R. 63; [1949] L.J.R. 370; (1948) 92 S.J. 719, Ch D *27–034*
Canterbury Golf International Ltd v Yoshimoto [2002] UKPC 40; [2001] N.Z.L.R. 523, PC (NZ) *12–119*
Cantieri Navali Riuniti SpA v Omne Justitia NV; The Stolt Marmaro [1985] 2 Lloyd's Rep. 428, CA (Civ Div) *30–005*, *30–012*
Cantor Fitzgerald International v Bird [2002] I.R.L.R. 867; [2002] Emp. L.R. 1171, QBD *24–003*
Cantor Index Ltd v Shortall [2002] All E.R. (D) (Nov) 161, QBD *7–018*
Cap Palos, The. *See* Owners of the Cap Palos v Alder
Caparo Industries Plc v Dickman [1990] 2 A.C. 605; [1990] 2 W.L.R. 358; [1990] 1 All E.R. 568; [1990] B.C.C. 164; [1990] B.C.L.C. 273; [1990] E.C.C. 313; [1955–95] P.N.L.R. 523; (1990) 87(12) L.S.G. 42; (1990) 140 N.L.J. 248; (1990) 134 S.J. 494, HL; affirming [1989] Q.B. 653; [1989] 2 W.L.R. 316; [1989] 1 All E.R. 798; (1989) 5 B.C.C. 105; [1989] B.C.L.C. 154; [1989] P.C.C. 125; (1988) 138 N.L.J. Rep. 289; (1989) 133 S.J. 221, CA (Civ Div); reversing in part (1988) 4 B.C.C. 144; [1988] B.C.L.C. 387, QBD *1–141*, 1–160, *1–177*, 1–184, 6–029, 6–082, 6–086, *18–022*, *18–032*
Cape Asbestos Co v Lloyds Bank [1921] W.N. 274 .... *3–091*
Cape Breton Co, Re. *See* Bentinck v Fenn
Capital & Counties Bank Ltd v Rhodes [1903] 1 Ch. 631, CA *25–004*
Capital & Suburban Properties Ltd v Swycher [1976] Ch. 319; [1976] 2 W.L.R. 822; [1976] 1 All E.R. 881; (1976) 32 P. & C.R. 101; [1976] J.P.L. 374; (1976) 120 S.J. 251, CA (Civ Div) *27–082*
Capital and Counties Plc v Hampshire CC; John Munroe (Acrylics) Ltd v London Fire and Civil Defence Authority; Church of Jesus Christ of Latter Day Saints (Great Britain) v West Yorkshire Fire and Civil Defence Authority; Digital Equipment Co Ltd v Hampshire CC [1997] Q.B. 1004; [1997] 3 W.L.R. 331; [1997] 2 All E.R. 865; [1997] 2 Lloyd's Rep. 161; (1997) 147 N.L.J. 599; (1997) 141 S.J.L.B. 92, CA (Civ Div); affirming [1996] 1 W.L.R. 1553; [1996] 4 All E.R. 336; (1996) 146 N.L.J. 1543, QBD (OR) *2–042*
Capital Finance Co Ltd v Bray [1964] 1 W.L.R. 323; [1964] 1 All E.R. 603; (1964) 108 S.J. 95, CA *2–030*, *2–031*
Capital Finance Co Ltd v Donati (1977) 121 S.J. 270, CA (Civ Div) *26–141*
Capital Finance Co Ltd v Stokes; sub nom. City Field Properties, Re [1969] 1 Ch. 261; [1968] 3 W.L.R. 899; [1968] 3 All E.R. 625; (1968) 19 P. & C.R. 791; (1968) 112 S.J. 746, CA (Civ Div) *29–173*
Capital Fire Insurance Association (Winding Up Petition), Re (1882) L.R. 21 Ch. D. 209, Ch D *12–067*
Capital Structures Plc v Time & Tide Construction Ltd [2006] EWHC 591 (TCC); [2006] B.L.R. 226; [2006] C.I.L.L. 2345, QBD (TCC) *7–053*
Capital Trust Investments Ltd v Radio Design TJ AB; sub nom. Capital Trusts Investments Ltd v Radio Design TJ AB [2002] EWCA Civ 135; [2002] 2 All E.R. 159; [2002] 1 All E.R. (Comm) 514; [2002] C.L.C. 787, CA (Civ Div); affirming [2001] 3 All E.R. 756; [2001] 1 All E.R. (Comm) 1079, Ch D *3–048*
Capper's Case. *See* China Steamship and Labuan Coal Co, Re
Car & Universal Finance Co Ltd v Caldwell [1965] 1 Q.B. 525; [1964] 2 W.L.R. 600; [1964] 1 All E.R. 290; (1964) 108 S.J. 15, CA; affirming [1963] 2 All E.R. 547; (1963) 107 S.J. 738, QBD 6–110, *6–114*
Caraman Rowley & May v Aperghis (1923–24) 17 Ll. L. Rep. 183; (1923) 40 T.L.R. 124, KBD *5–133*
Caramba-Coker v Military Affairs Office of the Kuwait Embassy; sub nom. Military Affairs Office of the Kuwait Embassy v Caramba-Coker, April 10, 2003, EAT *11–004*, *11–005*

Carapanayoti & Co v Comptoir Commercial & Cie SA [1972] 1 Lloyd's Rep. 139; (1972) 116 S.J. 96, CA (Civ Div); reversing [1971] 1 Lloyd's Rep. 327, QBD (Comm) *12–093*, *21–024*
Cardinal Financial Investment Corp v Central Bank of Yemen (No.1); sub nom. Central Bank of Yemen v Cardinal Financial Investments Corp [2001] Lloyd's Rep. Bank. 1, CA (Civ Div); affirming, 1999 Folio No.1195, QBD (Comm) *11–005*
Care Shipping Corp v Itex Itagrani Export SA. *See* Itex Itagrani Export SA v Care Shipping Corp
Care Shipping Corp v Latin American Shipping Corp; The Cebu [1983] Q.B. 1005; [1983] 2 W.L.R. 829; [1983] 1 All E.R. 1121; [1983] 1 Lloyd's Rep. 302; [1983] Com. L.R. 5; (1983) 127 S.J. 104, QBD (Comm) *19–012*
Carew v White (1829) 2 Moo. P 558 .... *25–026*
Carga Del Sur Campania Naviera SA v Ross T Smyth & Co Ltd; The Seafort [1962] 2 Lloyd's Rep. 147; (1962) 106 S.J. 651, QBD (Comm) *12–077*
Cargill International SA v Bangladesh Sugar & Food Industries Corp [1998] 1 W.L.R. 461; [1998] 2 All E.R. 406; [1998] C.L.C. 399; (1998) 95(3) L.S.G. 25; (1998) 142 S.J.L.B. 14, CA (Civ Div); affirming [1996] 4 All E.R. 563; [1996] 2 Lloyd's Rep. 524, QBD (Comm) *1–031*, *13–007*, *26–125*
Cargill SRL (Milan) (formerly Cargill SpA) v P Kadinopoulos SA [1992] 1 Lloyd's Rep. 1, HL; affirming [1991] 1 Lloyd's Rep. 364, CA (Civ Div); affirming [1990] 2 Lloyd's Rep. 32, QBD (Comm) *2–006*
Caribonum Co Ltd v Le Couch (1913) 109 L.T. 385 .... *16–092*, *16–108*, *16–198*
Carillion Construction Ltd v Felix (UK) Ltd [2001] B.L.R. 1; 74 Con. L.R. 144, QBD (TCC) *7–018*, *7–044*
Cariss v Tatterswell (1841) 2 M.G 890 .... *25–022*
Carl Zeiss Stiftung v Rayner & Keeler Ltd (Pleadings: Striking Out) [1970] Ch. 506; [1969] 3 W.L.R. 991; [1969] 3 All E.R. 897; [1969] R.P.C. 194; (1969) 113 S.J. 922, Ch D *25–011*, *25–012*, *25–013*
Carl Zeiss Stiftung v Rayner & Keeler Ltd; Rayner & Keeler Ltd v Courts & Co [1967] 1 A.C. 853; [1966] 3 W.L.R. 125; [1966] 2 All E.R. 536; [1967] R.P.C. 497; (1966) 110 S.J. 425, HL *25–011*, *25–012*, *25–014*, *25–016*, *25–017*, *25–018*, *30–325*
Carlill v Carbolic Smoke Ball Co [1893] 1 Q.B. 256, CA; affirming [1892] 2 Q.B. 484, QBD *1–003*, *1–079*, 2–018, 2–019, 2–043, 2–047, *2–078*, *2–161*, 2–165, *3–008*, 3–012
Carlish v Salt [1906] 1 Ch. 335, Ch D *6–156*
Carlisle & Cumberland Banking Co v Bragg [1911] 1 K.B. 489, CA *5–103*, 5–106
Carlton Contractors v Bexley Corp (1962) 106 S.J. 391; 60 L.G.R.331 .... *5–113*
Carlton Steamship Co Ltd v Castle Mail Packets Co Ltd [1898] A.C. 486, HL *21–020*
Carlyle Finance Ltd v Pallas Industrial Finance Ltd [1999] 1 All E.R. (Comm) 659; [1999] R.T.R. 281; [1999] C.C.L.R. 85, CA (Civ Div) *2–030*, *2–069*
Carmel Exporters & Importers Ltd v HE Daniels Ltd (No.2); sub nom. HE Daniels Ltd v Carmel Exporters & Importers Ltd [1953] 2 Q.B. 242; [1953] 3 W.L.R. 216; [1953] 3 All E.R. 401; [1953] 2 Lloyd's Rep. 103; (1953) 97 S.J. 473, QBD *26–013*, *26–014*
Carmichael v National Power Plc [1999] 1 W.L.R. 2042; [1999] 4 All E.R. 897; [1999] I.C.R. 1226; [2000] I.R.L.R. 43; (1999) 96(46) L.S.G. 38; (1999) 143 S.J.L.B. 281, HL; reversing [1998] I.C.R. 1167; [1998] I.R.L.R. 301; (1998) 95(19) L.S.G. 23; (1998) 142 S.J.L.B. 140, CA (Civ Div) *2–175*, *3–110*, *12–126*
Carnac Ex p. Simmonds, Re (1885–86) L.R. 16 Q.B.D. 308, CA *29–043*
Carnegie v Giessen [2005] EWCA Civ 191; [2005] 1 W.L.R. 2510; [2005] C.P. Rep. 24; [2005] 1 C.L.C. 259; (2005) 102(18) L.S.G. 23, CA (Civ Div) *30–376*
Carnell v Harrison [1916] 1 Ch. 328, CA *8–041*
Carnes v Nesbitt (1862) 7 H.N. 778 .... *26–011*
Carney v Herbert [1985] A.C. 301; [1984] 3 W.L.R. 1303; [1985] 1 All E.R. 438; (1984) 81 L.S.G. 3500, PC (Aus) *16–195*
Carpenter v Buller (1841) 8 M. & W. 209 .... *1–112*
Carpenters Estates Ltd v Davies [1940] Ch. 160, Ch D *27–028*
Carr v Fracis Times & Co [1902] A.C. 176, HL *11–007*, *25–019*

Carr v Jackson (1852) 7 Exch. 392 .... *12–115*
Carr v L&NW Ry (1875) L.R. 10 C.P. 310 .... *3–094*
Carr v Lynch [1900] 1 Ch. 613, Ch D *4–023*, *12–122*
Carr-Glynn v Frearsons [1999] Ch. 326; [1999] 2 W.L.R. 1046; [1998] 4 All E.R. 225; [1999] 1 F.L.R. 8; [1998] 3 F.C.R. 487; [1999] P.N.L.R. 13; [1998] Fam. Law 739; [1998] E.G. 128 (C.S.); (1998) 148 N.L.J. 1487; [1998] N.P.C. 136, CA (Civ Div); reversing [1997] 2 All E.R. 614; [1997] P.N.L.R. 343, Ch D 18–038
Carrier Australia v Hunt (1935) 61 C.L.R. 534 .... *9–058*
Carrington v Roots (1837) 2 M. & W. 248 .... *4–041*
Carr-Saunders v Dick McNeill Associates [1986] 1 W.L.R. 922 .... *29–142*, *29–144*
Carter v Boehm (1766) 3 Burr. 1905 .... *1–022*, *1–071*, *6–144*, *6–146*, *15–069*
Carter v Carter (1829) 5 Bing. 406 .... *29–105*
Carter v Silber. *See* Edwards v Carter
Cartledge v E Jopling & Sons Ltd [1963] A.C. 758; [1963] 2 W.L.R. 210; [1963] 1 All E.R. 341; [1963] 1 Lloyd's Rep. 1; (1963) 107 S.J. 73, HL; affirming [1962] 1 Q.B. 189; [1961] 3 W.L.R. 838; [1961] 3 All E.R. 482; [1961] 2 Lloyd's Rep. 61; (1961) 105 S.J. 884, CA *1–124*, 28–061
Cartwright v Cartwright (1853) 3 De. G.M. & G. 382 .... *16–072*
Cartwright v Cooke (1832) 3 B. & Ad. 701 .... *22–015*
Cartwright v Hoogstoel (1911) 195 L.T. 628 .... *2–090*
Cartwright v MacCormack [1963] 1 W.L.R. 18; [1963] 1 All E.R. 11; [1962] 2 Lloyd's Rep. 328; (1962) 106 S.J. 957, CA *12–093*, *21–022*, *21–024*, *21–026*
Cases of Taffs Well Ltd, Re [1992] Ch. 179; [1991] 3 W.L.R. 731; [1991] B.C.C. 582; [1992] B.C.L.C. 11, Ch D (Companies Ct) *28–070*
Casey's Patents, Re; sub nom. Stewart v Casey [1892] 1 Ch. 104, CA *3–029*
Casillo Grani v Napier Shipping Co; The World Ares [1984] 2 Lloyd's Rep. 481, QBD (Comm) *28–022*, *28–118*, *28–123*, *28–126*
Cassel v Inglis [1916] 2 Ch. 211, Ch D *9–077*
Cassell & Co v Broome. *See* Broome v Cassell & Co Ltd (No.1)
Cassidy (Peter) Seed Co Ltd v Osuustukkukauppa I.L. [1957] 1 W.L.R. 273; 101 S.J. 149; [1957] 1 All E.R. 484; [1957] 1 Lloyd's Rep. 25 .... *2–155*, *13–013*
Cassir, Moore & Co Ltd v Eastcheap Dried Fruit Co [1962] 1 Lloyd's Rep. 400, QBD *26–144*
Casson v Ostley PJ Ltd [2001] EWCA Civ 1013; [2003] B.L.R. 147; 85 Con. L.R. 18; (2002) 18 Const. L.J. 145; [2001] N.P.C. 105, CA (Civ Div); reversing [2001] B.L.R. 126, QBD *14–013*
Castle v Wilkinson (1869–70) L.R. 5 Ch. App. 534, CA in Chancery *27–041*, *27–055*
Castle Insurance Co v Hong Kong Islands Shipping Co; The Potoi Chau [1984] A.C. 226; [1983] 3 W.L.R. 524; [1983] 3 All E.R. 706; [1983] 2 Lloyd's Rep. 376; (1983) 127 S.J. 616, PC (HK) *28–050*
Castlegate Steamship Co Ltd v Dempsey [1892] 1 Q.B. 854, CA *21–020*
Castlereagh Motels v Davies-Roe (1966) 67 S.R. (N.S.W.) 279 .... *9–055*
Castrique v Imrie (1869–70) L.R. 4 H.L. 414, HL *25–019*
Caterpillar Financial Services Corp v SNC Passion [2004] EWHC 569; [2004] 2 Lloyd's Rep. 99, QBD (Comm) *30–033*, *30–061*, *30–062*, *30–328*
Catling v King (1877) L.R. 5 Ch. D. 660, CA *4–023*
Cato v Thompson (1881–82) L.R. 9 Q.B.D. 616, CA *27–055*
Caton v Caton; sub nom. Caton v Cassidy (1867) L.R. 2 H.L. 127; (1867) 16 W.R. 1; (1867) 36 L.J. Ch. 886, HL; affirming (1865–66) L.R. 1 Ch. App. 137, Lord Chancellor *4–032*, *4–042*, *4–044*, *4–045*, 4–073
Cator v Croydon Canal Co (1841) 4 Y. & C. Ex. 405 .... *19–040*
Catt v Tourle (1868–69) L.R. 4 Ch. App. 654, CA in Chancery *16–102*, *16–125*, *16–126*, *27–042*
Catterall v Hindle (1866–67) L.R. 2 C.P. 368, Ex Chamber *21–043*, *21–044*
Cattle v Stockton Waterworks Co (1874–75) L.R. 10 Q.B. 453; [1874–80] All E.R. Rep. 492, QBD *1–154*, *18–034*
Cattley v Pollard [2006] EWHC 3130 (Ch); [2007] Ch. 353; [2007] 3 W.L.R. 317; [2007] 2 All E.R. 1086; [2007] P.N.L.R. 19; [2007] W.T.L.R. 245; (2007–08) 10 I.T.E.L.R. 1, Ch D *28–019*

Cavalier Insurance Co Ltd, Re [1989] 2 Lloyd's Rep. 430, Ch D *29–082*
Cavalier v Pope; sub nom. Cavalier and Wife v Pope [1906] A.C. 428, HL; affirming [1905] 2 K.B. 757, CA 1–154
Cavanagh v Ulster Weaving Co Ltd [1960] A.C. 145; [1959] 3 W.L.R. 262; [1959] 2 All E.R. 745; [1959] 2 Lloyd's Rep. 165; (1959) 103 S.J. 581, HL (NI) *26–030*
Cave v Hastings (1880–81) L.R. 7 Q.B.D. 125, QBD *4–028*, *4–029*
Cave v Robinson Jarvis & Rolf; sub nom. Robinson Jarvis & Rolf v Cave; Cave v Robinson Jarvis & Rolfe [2002] UKHL 18; [2003] 1 A.C. 384; [2002] 2 W.L.R. 1107; [2002] 2 All E.R. 641; [2003] 1 C.L.C. 101; 81 Con. L.R. 25; [2002] P.N.L.R. 25; [2002] 19 E.G. 146 (C.S.); (2002) 99(20) L.S.G. 32; (2002) 152 N.L.J. 671; (2002) 146 S.J.L.B. 109, HL *28–084*, 28–085, *28–086*
Cavendish-Woodhouse Ltd v Manley (1984) 148 J.P. 299; 82 L.G.R. 376; [1984] Crim. L.R. 239, DC *14–006*
Cedar Trading Co Ltd v Transworld Oil Ltd; The Gudermes [1985] 2 Lloyd's Rep. 623, QBD (Comm) *2–126*
Cehave NV v Bremer Handels GmbH; The Hansa Nord; sub nom. Cehave NV v Bremer Handelgesellschaft mbH; The Hansa Nord [1976] Q.B. 44; [1975] 3 W.L.R. 447; [1975] 3 All E.R. 739; [1975] 2 Lloyd's Rep. 445; (1975) 119 S.J. 678, CA (Civ Div); reversing [1974] 2 Lloyd's Rep. 216, QBD (Comm) *12–026*, *12–034*, 12–036, *12–040*, *24–037*, *24–040*, *26–064*
Cellulose Acetate Silk Co Ltd v Widnes Foundry (1925) Ltd; sub nom. Widnes Foundry (1925) Ltd v Cellulose Acetate Silk Co Ltd [1933] A.C. 20, HL *26–135*, *26–142*, *26–143*
Cementation Piling and Foundations Ltd v Commercial Union Insurance Co Plc; Cementation Piling and Foundations Ltd v Aegon Insurance Ltd [1995] 1 Lloyd's Rep. 97; 74 B.L.R. 98; 47 Con. L.R. 14, CA (Civ Div); affirming [1993] 1 Lloyd's Rep. 526; (1994) 10 Const. L.J. 301, QBD *12–063*
Cemp Properties (UK) Ltd v Dentsply Research & Development Corp (No.1) [1989] 35 E.G. 99, Ch D *1–131*
Cemp Properties (UK) Ltd v Dentsply Research & Development Corp (No.2) [1991] 2 E.G.L.R. 197; [1991] 34 E.G. 62, CA (Civ Div); reversing [1989] 36 E.G. 90; [1989] 37 E.G. 126; [1989] E.G. 29 (C.S.), Ch D *6–100*
Central Electricity Generating Board v Halifax Corp [1963] A.C. 785; [1962] 3 W.L.R. 1313; [1962] 3 All E.R. 915; 61 L.G.R. 125; (1962) 106 S.J. 936, HL *28–031*
Central Insurance Co Ltd v Seacalf Shipping Corp; The Aiolos [1983] 2 Lloyd's Rep. 25, CA (Civ Div) *19–038*, *19–039*, *28–022*
Central London Property Trust v High Trees House Ltd [1947] K.B. 130; [1956] 1 All E.R. 256 (Note); 62 T.L.R. 557; [1947] L.J.R. 77; 175 L.T. 333, KBD *3–089*, *3–098*, *3–099*, *3–103*, *3–104*, *3–117*, 3–128, 3–129, *3–130*, 3–132, 3–133, 3–135, 3–136, 3–146, 3–172, *19–038*, *19–039*, 22–018
Central Trust & Safe Deposit Co v Snider [1916] 1 A.C. 266, PC (Can) *16–073*
Central Trust Co v Rafuse (1986) 31 D.L.R. (4th) 481, Sup Ct (Can) *1–126*, 1–150
Centrax Ltd v Citibank NA [1999] 1 All E.R. (Comm) 557, CA (Civ Div) *30–015*, *30–024*, *30–046*, *30–056*, *30–071*
Centre Reinsurance International Co v Curzon Insurance Ltd; Centre Reinsurance International Co v Freakley; Freakley v Centre Reinsurance International Co [2006] UKHL 45; [2007] Bus. L.R. 284; [2006] 1 W.L.R. 2863; [2006] 4 All E.R. 1153; [2006] 2 All E.R. (Comm) 943; [2006] B.C.C. 971; [2007] 1 B.C.L.C. 85; [2006] B.P.I.R. 1405; [2007] Lloyd's Rep. I.R. 32; (2006) 103(41) L.S.G. 35; (2006) 156 N.L.J. 1613; (2006) 150 S.J.L.B. 1395, HL; reversing [2005] EWCA Civ 115; [2005] 2 All E.R. (Comm) 65; [2006] 1 B.C.L.C. 225; [2005] 1 C.L.C. 78; [2006] B.P.I.R. 1122; [2005] Lloyd's Rep. I.R. 303, CA (Civ Div); affirming in part [2004] EWHC 200 (Ch); [2004] 2 All E.R. (Comm) 28; [2006] 1 B.C.L.C. 187; [2004] 2 C.L.C. 586; [2004] Lloyd's Rep. I.R. 622; (2004) 101(11) L.S.G. 34, Ch D *18–131*
Centrepoint Custodians Pty v Lidgerwood Investments Pty [1990] V.R. 411 .... *12–069*
Centrovincial Estates v Merchant Investors Assurance Co [1983] Com. L.R. 158, CA (Civ Div) *2–003*, *3–047*, 5–075

Cereal Investments Co (CIC) SA v ED&F Man Sugar Ltd [2007] EWHC 2843 (Comm); [2008] 1 Lloyd's Rep. 355; [2007] 2 C.L.C. 959, QBD (Comm) *12–080*
Cerealmangimi SpA v Alfred C Toepfer; The Eurometal [1981] 3 All E.R. 533; [1981] 1 Lloyd's Rep. 337; [1981] Com. L.R. 13, QBD (Comm) *12–037*, *22–044*, *24–011*
Cerium Investments v Evans (1991) 62 P. & C.R. 203; [1991] 20 E.G. 189; (1991) 135 S.J.L.B. 217, CA (Div) *12–082*
Cero Navigation Corp v Jean Lion & Cie; The Solon [2000] 1 All E.R. (Comm) 214; [2000] 1 Lloyd's Rep. 292; [2000] C.L.C. 593, QBD (Comm) *12–053*, *14–004*, *14–005*, *14–137*
Cesarini v Ronzani (1858) 1 F.F. 339 ..... *21–058*
Ceylon v Chandris [1965] 3 All E.R. 48; [1965] 2 Lloyd's Rep. 204, QBD (Comm) *26–008*, *26–037*
Chadwick v Manning [1896] A.C. 231, PC (Aus) *3–103*
Chafer v Lilley [1947] L.J.R. 231; 176 L.T. 22 ..... *16–105*
Chakki v United Yeast Co Ltd [1981] 2 All E.R. 446; [1982] I.C.R. 140, EAT *23–039*
Challoner v Bower (1984) 269 E.G. 725 ..... *2–004*
Chalmers, Ex p. *See* Edwards Ex p. Chalmers, Re
Chalmers v Pardoe [1963] 1 W.L.R. 677; [1963] 3 All E.R. 552; (1963) 107 S.J. 435, PC (Fiji) *29–161*
Chamber Colliery Co Ltd v Twyerould [1915] 1 Ch. 268 (Note), HL *12–063*
Chamberlain v Boodle & King [1982] 1 W.L.R. 1443; [1982] 3 All E.R. 188; (1981) 125 S.J. 257, CA (Civ Div); affirming (1980) 124 S.J. 186, QBD *2–113*
Chamberlain v Napier (1880) L.R. 15 Ch. D. 614, Ch D *30–011*, *30–015*
Chambers v Miller, 143 E.R. 50; (1862) 13 C.B. N.S. 125, CCP *29–030*
Champanhac & Co Ltd v Waller & Co Ltd [1948] 2 All E.R. 724, KBD *14–027*
Champion Investments Ltd v Ahmed [2004] EWHC 1956 (QB); [2004] All E.R. (D) 28 (Aug), QBD *22–021*
Chan Kit San v Ho Fung Hang [1902] A.C. 257, PC (HK) *28–031*
Chandler v Kerley [1978] 1 W.L.R. 693; [1978] 2 All E.R. 942; (1978) 8 Fam. Law 108; (1978) 122 S.J. 332, CA (Civ Div) *13–028*, *16–068*
Chandler v Webster [1904] 1 K.B. 493, CA 23–033, 23–072, 23–073, *23–074*
Chandler Bros Ltd v Boswell [1936] 3 All E.R. 179 ..... *23–059*
Chandris v Argo Insurance Co Ltd [1963] 2 Lloyd's Rep. 65; (1963) 107 S.J. 575, QBD (Comm) *28–050*, *28–061*
Chandris v Isbrandtsen Moller Co Inc [1951] 1 K.B. 240; [1950] 2 All E.R. 618; (1950) 84 Ll. L. Rep. 347; 66 T.L.R. (Pt. 2) 358; (1950) 94 S.J. 534, CA; reversing in part [1950] 1 All E.R. 768; (1949–50) 83 Ll. L. Rep. 385; 66 T.L.R. (Pt. 1) 971; (1950) 94 S.J. 303, KBD *12–065*, *12–077*, *12–088*, *12–089*, *14–138*, *22–050*, *24–001*, *24–003*, *24–010*, *29–073*
Chanel Ltd v FW Woolworth & Co Ltd [1981] 1 W.L.R. 485; [1981] 1 All E.R. 745; [1981] F.S.R. 196; (1981) 125 S.J. 202, CA (Div) *5–062*
Chaney v Maclow [1929] 1 Ch. 461, CA *4–038*
Channel Home Centers Division of Grace Retail Corp v Grossman (1986) 795 F. 2d 291 ..... *2–138*
Channel Island Ferries Ltd v Cenargo Navigation Ltd; The Rozel [1994] 2 Lloyd's Rep. 161; [1994] C.L.C. 168, QBD (Comm) *26–017*
Channel Island Ferries Ltd v Sealink UK Ltd [1988] 1 Lloyd's Rep. 323, CA (Civ Div); affirming [1987] 1 Lloyd's Rep. 559, QBD (Comm) *3–090*, *12–069*, 14–140, *14–141*, *14–142*, *14–146*
Channel Tunnel Group Ltd v Balfour Beatty Construction Ltd; France Manche SA v Balfour Beatty Construction Ltd [1993] A.C. 334; [1993] 2 W.L.R. 262; [1993] 1 All E.R. 664; [1993] 1 Lloyd's Rep. 291; 61 B.L.R. 1; 32 Con. L.R. 1; [1993] I.L.Pr. 607; (1993) 137 S.J.L.B. 36; [1993] N.P.C. 8, HL *27–028*, *27–061*
Chanter v Hopkins (1838) 4 M. & W. 399 ..... *12–021*
Chanter v Leese (1839) 5 M.W. 698 ..... *21–030*
Chapelton v Barry Urban DC [1940] 1 K.B. 532, CA *2–016*, *12–009*
Chaplin v Hicks [1911] 2 K.B. 786, CA *26–007*, 26–044

Chaplin v Leslie Frewin (Publishers) Ltd [1966] Ch. 71; [1966] 2 W.L.R. 40; [1965] 3 All E.R. 764; (1965) 109 S.J. 871, CA; reversing (1965) 109 S.J. 776, Ch D *8–022*, *8–028*, 8–066
Chapman v Bluck (1838) 4 Bing.N.C. 187 .... *12–126*
Chapman v Ellesmere; sub nom. Chapman v Lord Ellesmere [1932] 2 K.B. 431, CA 1–153
Chapman v Honig [1963] 2 Q.B. 502; [1963] 3 W.L.R. 19; [1963] 2 All E.R. 513; (1963) 107 S.J. 374, CA *7–045*
Chapman v Michaelson [1909] 1 Ch. 238, CA; affirming [1908] 2 Ch. 612, Ch D *16–185*
Chapman v Smith [1907] 2 Ch. 97, Ch D *12–122*
Chapman v Speller (1850) 14 Q.B. 621 .... *14–026*
Chappell v Cooper; sub nom. Player v Bruguiere [1980] 1 W.L.R. 958; [1980] 2 All E.R. 463; (1980) 124 S.J. 544, CA (Civ Div) *28–116*
Chappell v Somers & Blake [2003] EWHC 1644 (Ch); [2004] Ch. 19; [2003] 3 W.L.R. 1233; [2003] 3 All E.R. 1076; [2003] P.N.L.R. 37; [2003] W.T.L.R. 1085; (2003) 147 S.J.L.B. 1148; [2003] N.P.C. 87, Ch D *18–038*, *18–047*
Chappell v Times Newspapers Ltd [1975] 1 W.L.R. 482; [1975] 2 All E.R. 233; [1975] I.C.R. 145; [1975] I.R.L.R. 90; 18 Man. Law 5; (1975) 119 S.J. 82, CA (Civ Div) *27–021*, *27–035*, *27–064*
Chappell & Co Ltd v Nestlé Co Ltd [1960] A.C. 87; [1959] 3 W.L.R. 168; [1959] 2 All E.R. 701; (1959) 103 S.J. 561, HL; reversing [1958] Ch. 529; [1958] 2 W.L.R. 657; [1958] 2 All E.R. 155; (1958) 102 S.J. 270, CA 3–016
Chapple v Cooper (1844) 13 M. & W. 252 .... *8–013*, *8–019*
Chaproniere v Lambert [1917] 2 Ch. 356, CA *4–049*
Charfield v Paxton (1799) 2 East 471 .... *29–187*
Charge Card Services Ltd (No.2), Re [1989] Ch. 497; [1988] 3 W.L.R. 764; [1988] 3 All E.R. 702; (1988) 4 B.C.C. 524; [1988] B.C.L.C. 711; [1988] P.C.C. 390; [1988] Fin. L.R. 308; (1989) 8 Tr. L.R. 86; (1988) 85(42) L.S.G. 46; (1988) 138 N.L.J. Rep. 201; (1988) 132 S.J. 1458, CA (Civ Div); affirming [1987] Ch. 150; [1986] 3 W.L.R. 697; [1986] 3 All E.R. 289; (1986) 2 B.C.C. 99373; [1987] B.C.L.C. 17; [1987] P.C.C. 36; [1987] E.C.C. 91; [1987] Fin. L.R. 1; (1986) 83 L.S.G. 3424; (1986) 130 S.J. 801, Ch D (Companies Ct) *2–014*, *2–030*, *3–015*, *3–039*, *18–007*, *19–087*, *20–040*, *20–041*, *21–039*, *21–057*, *21–073*, *21–074*, *21–082*
Charles v Blackwell (1876–77) L.R. 2 C.P.D. 151, CA *21–044*
Charles Church Developments Ltd v Stent Foundations Ltd [2006] EWHC 3158 (TCC); [2007] 1 W.L.R. 1203; [2007] B.L.R. 81; [2007] T.C.L.R. 2; [2007] C.I.L.L. 2408, QBD (TCC) *28–118*
Charles Duval & Co v Gans [1904] 2 K.B. 685, CA *21–054*
Charles Rickards Ltd v Oppenheim; sub nom. Rickards (Charles) v Oppenhaim [1950] 1 K.B. 616; [1950] 1 All E.R. 420; 66 T.L.R. (Pt. 1) 435; (1950) 94 S.J. 161, CA 3–082, *3–085*, *21–014*, *22–042*
Charles Roberts & Co v British Railways Board [1965] 1 W.L.R. 396; [1964] 3 All E.R. 651; (1964) 108 S.J. 502, Ch D *9–020*
Charlesworth v Holt (1873–74) L.R. 9 Ex. 38, Ex Ct *23–040*
Charlotte Thirty and Bison v Croker, 24 Con. L.R. 46, QBD (OR) *12–002*, *13–030*, *14–073*, *14–079*, *14–085*, 14–092, *14–132*, *19–055*
Charlson v Warner [2000] C.L.Y. 4043, CC (West London) *13–034*, *14–149*
Charlton v Earl of Durham (1868–69) L.R. 4 Ch. App. 433, Lord Chancellor *21–049*
Charlton v Fisher; sub nom. Churchill Insurance v Charlton [2001] EWCA Civ 112; [2002] Q.B. 578; [2001] 3 W.L.R. 1435; [2001] 1 All E.R. (Comm) 769; [2001] R.T.R. 33; [2001] Lloyd's Rep. I.R. 387; [2001] P.I.Q.R. P23; (2001) 98(10) L.S.G. 45, CA (Div) *16–168*, *16–173*, *18–131*
Charm Maritime Inc v Kyriakou [1987] 1 Lloyd's Rep. 433; [1987] 1 F.T.L.R. 265, CA (Civ Div) *25–017*
Charnock v Liverpool Corp [1968] 1 W.L.R. 1498; [1968] 3 All E.R. 473; [1968] 2 Lloyd's Rep. 113; (1968) 112 S.J. 781, CA (Civ Div) *3–177*, 12–007, 18–008, *21–020*
Charrington & Co Ltd v Wooder [1914] A.C. 71, HL *12–118*

Charron v Montreal Trust Co (1958) 15 D.L.R. (2d) 240, CA (Ont) *30–324*
Chartbrook Ltd v Persimmon Homes Ltd [2008] EWCA Civ 183; [2008] 11 E.G. 92 (C.S.); [2008] N.P.C. 30, CA (Civ Div); affirming [2007] EWHC 409 (Ch); [2007] 1 All E.R. (Comm) 1083; [2007] 2 P. & C.R. 9; [2007] 11 E.G. 160 (C.S.), Ch D *5–084*, *12–119*
Charter Plc v City Index Ltd. *See* City Index Ltd v Gawler
Charter Reinsurance Co Ltd (In Liquidation) v Fagan [1997] A.C. 313; [1996] 2 W.L.R. 726; [1996] 3 All E.R. 46; [1996] 2 Lloyd's Rep. 113; [1996] C.L.C. 977; [1996] 5 Re. L.R. 411; (1996) 140 S.J.L.B. 148, HL; affirming [1996] 1 All E.R. 406; [1996] 1 Lloyd's Rep. 261; [1995] C.L.C. 1345; [1996] 5 Re. L.R. 7; (1995) 139 S.J.L.B. 246, CA (Civ Div) ... *1–031*, *12–051*, *12–055*, *12–057*
Charter v Sullivan [1957] 2 Q.B. 117; [1957] 2 W.L.R. 528; [1957] 1 All E.R. 809, CA *26–069*, *26–111*
Charterbridge Corp v Lloyds Bank Ltd [1970] Ch. 62; [1969] 3 W.L.R. 122; [1969] 2 All E.R. 1185; [1969] 2 Lloyd's Rep. 24; (1968) 113 S.J. 465, Ch D *9–038*
Chartered Bank of India Australia and China v British India Steam Navigation Co Ltd [1909] A.C. 369, PC (Straits Settlements) *14–016*, *14–032*, *14–033*
Chartered Mercantile Bank of India, London and China v Netherlands India Steam Navigation Co Ltd (1882–83) L.R. 10 Q.B.D. 521, CA *30–005*
Chartered Trust Plc v Davies (1998) 76 P. & C.R. 396; [1997] 2 E.G.L.R. 83; [1997] 49 E.G. 135; [1997] N.P.C. 125; (1998) 75 P. & C.R. D6, CA (Civ Div) *6–006*
Charterhouse Credit Co v Tolly [1963] 2 Q.B. 683; [1963] 2 W.L.R. 1168; [1963] 2 All E.R. 432; (1963) 107 S.J. 234, CA *14–020*, *14–028*, *26–141*
Chas Davis (Metal Brokers) Ltd v Gilyott & Scott Ltd [1975] 2 Lloyd's Rep. 422, QBD *14–015*, *14–054*
Chase v Ram Technical Services Ltd [2000] 2 Lloyd's Rep. 418, QBD (Comm) *30–011*
Chase Manhattan Bank NA v Israel-British Bank (London) Ltd [1981] Ch. 105; [1980] 2 W.L.R. 202; [1979] 3 All E.R. 1025; (1980) 124 S.J. 99, Ch D ...*29–036*, *29–049*, *29–164*, *29–165*, *29–172*
Chase Manhattan Equities Ltd v Goodman [1991] B.C.C. 308; [1991] B.C.L.C. 897, Ch D *16–085*, *16–145*
Chatenay v Brazilian Submarine Telegraph Co Ltd [1891] 1 Q.B. 79, CA *12–046*, *30–011*, *30–012*
Chater v Mortgage Agency Services Number Two Ltd; sub nom. Charter v Mortgage Agency Services; Mortgage Agency Services Number Two Ltd v Chater [2003] EWCA Civ 490; [2003] H.L.R. 61; [2004] 1 P. & C.R. 4; [2003] 15 E.G. 138 (C.S.); (2003) 147 S.J.L.B. 417; [2003] N.P.C. 48; [2003] 2 P. & C.R. DG9, CA (Civ Div) 7–088, *7–113*
Chatsworth Investments v Cussins (Contractors) [1969] 1 W.L.R. 1; [1969] 1 All E.R. 143; (1968) 112 S.J. 843, CA (Civ Div) *19–087*, *22–031*, *28–118*
Chatterton v Gerson [1981] Q.B. 432; [1980] 3 W.L.R. 1003; [1981] 1 All E.R. 257; (1980) 124 S.J. 885, QBD *1–153*
Chatterton v Maclean [1951] 1 All E.R. 761, KBD *24–051*
Chattey v Farndale Holdings Inc (1998) 75 P. & C.R. 298; [1997] 1 E.G.L.R. 153; [1997] 06 E.G. 152; [1996] N.P.C. 136, CA (Civ Div) *27–039*
Chaudhry v Prabhakar [1989] 1 W.L.R. 29; [1988] 3 All E.R. 718; (1988) 138 N.L.J. Rep. 172; (1989) 133 S.J. 82, CA (Civ Div) *3–179*
Cheale v Kenward (1858) 3 D. & J. 27 .... *3–008*, *3–021*, *3–179*, *27–011*
Cheall v Association of Professional, Executive, Clerical and Computer Staff (APEX) [1983] 2 A.C. 180; [1983] 2 W.L.R. 679; [1983] 1 All E.R. 1130; [1983] I.C.R. 398; [1983] I.R.L.R. 215; (1983) 133 N.L.J. 538, HL; reversing [1983] Q.B. 126; [1982] 3 W.L.R. 685; [1982] 3 All E.R. 855; [1982] I.C.R. 543; [1982] I.R.L.R. 362; (1982) 79 L.S.G. 921; (1982) 126 S.J. 623, CA (Civ Div); reversing [1982] I.C.R. 231, QBD *12–082*, *22–055*, *23–061*
Cheang Thye Phin v Lam Kin Sang [1929] A.C. 670, PC (Shanghai) *28–038*

Cheese v Thomas [1994] 1 W.L.R. 129; [1994] 1 All E.R. 35; [1994] 1 F.L.R. 118; [1995] 1 F.C.R. 162; (1994) 26 H.L.R. 426; (1995) 69 P. & C.R. 316; [1994] Fam. Law 80; [1993] E.G. 149 (C.S.); (1993) 143 N.L.J. 1368, CA (Civ Div) ... *3–157*, *7–058*, *7–092*, *7–102*
Cheetham v Ward (1797) 1 Bos. & P. 630 ... *25–005*
Chellaram v Chellaram (No.2) [2002] EWHC 632 (Ch); [2002] 3 All E.R. 17; [2002] W.T.L.R. 675; (2001–02) 4 I.T.E.L.R. 729; (2002) 152 N.L.J. 639, Ch D ... *30–043*
Chellaram & Sons (London) v Butlers Warehousing & Distribution. *See* K Chellaram & Sons (London) v Butlers Warehousing & Distribution
Chelmsford Auctions Ltd v Poole [1973] Q.B. 542; [1973] 2 W.L.R. 219; [1973] 1 All E.R. 810; (1972) 117 S.J. 219, CA (Civ Div) ... *18–005*
Chelsea & Waltham Green Building Society v Armstrong [1951] Ch. 853; [1951] 2 All E.R. 250; [1951] 2 T.L.R. 313, Ch D ... *18–122*
Cheltenham & Gloucester Building Society v Ebbage [1994] C.L.Y. 3292, CC (Portsmouth) ... *14–105*
Cheltenham & Gloucester Plc v Appleyard [2004] EWCA Civ 291; [2004] 13 E.G. 127 (C.S.); (2004) 101(13) L.S.G. 37; (2004) 101(14) L.S.G. 26; (2004) 148 S.J.L.B. 356; [2004] N.P.C. 42, CA (Civ Div) ... 29–173
Chemco Leasing SpA v Rediffusion [1987] 1 F.T.L.R. 201, CA (Civ Div) ... *2–125*
Chemidus Wavin Ltd v Societe pour la Transformation et l'Exploitation des Resines Industrielles SA [1978] 3 C.M.L.R. 514; [1977] F.S.R. 181, CA (Civ Div); affirming [1976] 2 C.M.L.R. 387; [1977] F.S.R. 19, Ch D ... *16–195*, *16–201*
Cheminant v Thornton (1825) 2 C.P. 50 ... *21–090*
Cherry v Boultbee (1839) 4 My. & Cr. 442 ... *20–044*
Cherry v Hemming (1849) 4 Exch. 631 ... *4–040*
Cheslyn v Dalby (1840) 4 Y. & C. Ex. 238 ... *28–094*
Chesnau v Interhomes (1983) 134 N.L.J. 341 ... *6–069*
Chester Grosvenor Hotel Co v Alfred McAlpine Management, 56 B.L.R. 115 ... *14–072*
Chesterfield (Earl of) v Janssen, 26 E.R. 191; (1750) 1 Atk. 301, Ct of Chancery ... *29–138*
Chesterman's Trusts, Re; Mott v Browning [1923] 2 Ch. 466, CA ... *21–068*, *30–009*, *30–370*
Chesworth v Farrar [1967] 1 Q.B. 407; [1966] 2 W.L.R. 1073; [1966] 2 All E.R. 107; (1966) 110 S.J. 307, QBD ... *1–124*, *29–140*, *29–142*, *29–143*
Chetham v Hoare (1869–70) L.R. 9 Eq. 571, Ct of Chancery ... *28–089*
Chettiar (ARPL Palaniappa) v Chettiar (PLAR Arunasalam); sub nom. Chettiar v Chettiar [1962] A.C. 294; [1962] 2 W.L.R. 548; [1962] 1 All E.R. 494; (1962) 106 S.J. 110, PC (FMS) ... *16–014*, *16–178*, *16–188*, *16–205*
Chetty v Chetty [1916] 1 A.C. 603, PC (Sing) ... *28–031*
Chetty (Deceased) v Vijayaraghavachariar [1922] 1 A.C. 488, PC (Ind) ... *28–057*
Chetwynd v Allen [1899] 1 Ch. 353, Ch D ... *25–001*
Chetwynd's Estate, Re; sub nom. Dunn's Trust Ltd v Brown [1938] Ch. 13, CA ... *29–109*
Cheverny Consulting Ltd v Whitehead Mann Ltd [2006] EWCA Civ 1303; [2007] 1 All E.R. (Comm) 124, CA (Civ Div); reversing [2005] EWHC 2431 (Ch), Ch D ... *2–116*
Chevron International Oil Co Ltd v A/S Sea Team; The TS Havprins [1983] 2 Lloyd's Rep. 356; [1983] Com. L.R. 172, QBD (Comm) ... *12–012*, *30–006*, *30–305*
Chichester v Cobb (1866) 14 L.T. 433 ... *3–073*, *4–034*
Chief Constable of Leicestershire v M [1989] 1 W.L.R. 20; [1988] 3 All E.R. 1015; (1988) 138 N.L.J. Rep. 295, Ch D ... *29–143*
Chief Constable of North Wales v Evans. *See* R. v Chief Constable of North Wales Ex p. Evans
Chiemgauer Membran und Zeltbau GmbH (formerly Koch Hightex GmbH) v New Millennium Experience Co Ltd (formerly Millennium Central Ltd) (No.2); sub nom. Chiemguaer Membran und Zeltbau GmbH (formerly Koch Hightex GmbH) v New Millennium Experience Co Ltd (formerly Millennium Central Ltd) [2002] B.P.I.R. 42; (2001) 98(5) L.S.G. 36, Ch D ... *24–022*, *24–023*

Chikuma, The. *See* Awilco of Oslo A/S v Fulvia SpA di Navigazione of Cagliari
Childs v Monins (1821) 2 B. & B. 460 .... *20–011*
Chilean Nitrate Sales Corp v Marine Transportation Co Ltd; The Hermosa; Marine Transportation Co Ltd v Pansuiza Compania de Navegacion SA; Nitrate Corp of Chile Ltd v Pansuiza Compania de Navegacion SA [1982] 1 Lloyd's Rep. 570, CA (Civ Div); affirming [1980] 1 Lloyd's Rep. 638, QBD (Comm) *12–035*, *24–018*, *24–040*, *24–046*
Chillingworth v Chambers [1896] 1 Ch. 685, CA *29–125*
Chillingworth v Esche; sub nom. Challingworth v Esche [1924] 1 Ch. 97; [1923] All E.R. Rep. 97, CA; reversing [1923] 1 Ch. 576, Ch D *2–118*, *2–119*, *2–136*, *29–054*, *29–064*
Chin Keow v Government of Malaysia [1967] 1 W.L.R. 813; (1967) 111 S.J. 333, PC (Mal) *13–032*
China and South Seas Bank Ltd v Tan [1990] 1 A.C. 536; [1990] 2 W.L.R. 56; [1989] 3 All E.R. 839; [1990] 1 Lloyd's Rep. 113; (1989) 86(46) L.S.G. 37; (1989) 139 N.L.J. 1669; (1990) 134 S.J. 165, PC (HK) *1–148*
China National Foreign Trade Transportation Corp v Evlogia Shipping Co SA of Panama; The Mihalios Xilas [1979] 1 W.L.R. 1018; [1979] 2 All E.R. 1044; [1979] 2 Lloyd's Rep. 303; (1979) 123 S.J. 521, HL; reversing [1978] 1 W.L.R. 1257; [1979] 1 All E.R. 657; [1978] 2 Lloyd's Rep. 397; (1978) 122 S.J. 591, CA (Civ Div); reversing [1976] 3 All E.R. 865; [1976] 2 Lloyd's Rep. 697, QBD (Comm) *3–090*, *3–091*, *22–048*, *22–053*
China National Foreign Trade Transportation Corp v Evlogia Shipping Co SA of Panama; The Mihalios Xilas [1979] 1 W.L.R. 1018; [1979] 2 All E.R. 1044; [1979] 2 Lloyd's Rep. 303; (1979) 123 S.J. 521, HL *24–003*, *24–007*, *24–051*
China Ocean Shipping Co; The Xingcheng v Andros; The Andros [1987] 1 W.L.R. 1213; [1987] 2 Lloyd's Rep. 210; (1987) 84 L.S.G. 2364; (1987) 131 S.J. 972, PC (HK) *28–022*
China Shipbuilding Corp v Nippon Yusen Kabukishi Kaisha; The Seta Maru, The Saikyo and The Suma [2000] 1 Lloyd's Rep. 367; [2000] C.L.C. 566, QBD (Comm) *14–024*, *14–133*
China Steamship and Labuan Coal Co, Re; sub nom. Capper's Case (1867–68) L.R. 3 Ch. App. 458, CA in Chancery *8–038*
China-Pacific SA v Food Corp of India; The Winson [1982] A.C. 939; [1981] 3 W.L.R. 860; [1981] 3 All E.R. 688; [1982] 1 Lloyd's Rep. 117; (1981) 125 S.J. 808, HL; reversing [1981] Q.B. 403; [1980] 3 W.L.R. 891; [1980] 3 All E.R. 556; [1980] 2 Lloyd's Rep. 213; (1980) 124 S.J. 614, CA (Civ Div); reversing [1979] 2 All E.R. 35; [1979] 1 Lloyd's Rep. 167, QBD (Comm) *3–090*, *3–091*, *3–103*, *6–013*, *6–095*, *14–054*, *29–131*, *29–136*
Chinery v Viall (1860) 5 H. & N. 28; 29 L.J. Ex. 1 .... *1–133*
Chinn v Hochstrasser (Inspector of Taxes); sub nom. Chinn v Collins (Inspector of Taxes) [1981] A.C. 533; [1981] 2 W.L.R. 14; [1981] 1 All E.R. 189; [1981] S.T.C. 1; 54 T.C. 311; [1980] T.R. 467; (1981) 125 S.J. 49, HL *27–011*
Chinnery v Evans (1864) 11 H.L.C. 115 .... *28–100*
Chinnock v Ely, Marchioness (1865) 4 De. G.J. & S. 638 .... *2–118*
Chinnock v Sainsbury (1861) 30 L.J. Ch. 409 .... *27–024*
Chippendale v Thurston (1829) 4 C.P. 98 .... *21–006*
Chippenham Golf Club v North Wilts RDC. *See* Farrage v North Wiltshire DC
Chiron Corp v Organon Teknika Ltd (No.2); sub nom. Chiron Corp v Murex Diagnostics Ltd (No.1) [1993] F.S.R. 567, CA (Civ Div) *30–008*, *30–068*, *30–114*
Chisman v Count (1841) 2 M.G. 307 .... *29–191*
Chiswell Shipping and Liberian Jaguar Transports Inc v National Iranian Tankers Co; The World Symphony and The World Renown [1992] 2 Lloyd's Rep. 115, CA (Civ Div); affirming [1991] 2 Lloyd's Rep. 251, QBD (Comm) *12–053*
Chitholie v Nash & Co (1973) 229 E.G. 786 .... *26–091*
Chohan v Saggar [1992] B.C.C. 750; [1993] B.C.L.C. 661, Ch D *20–031*
Chohan v Times Newspapers Ltd. *See* Times Newspapers Ltd v Chohan (Limitation Periods)

Choice Investments v Jeromnimon [1981] Q.B. 149; [1980] 2 W.L.R. 80; [1981] 1 All E.R. 225; (1980) 124 S.J. 883, CA (Civ Div) *30–376*
Cholmondeley v Clinton, 37 E.R. 527; (1820) 2 Jac. & W. 1, Ct of Chancery *12–042*, *28–001*, *28–134*
Chris Hart (Business Sales) Ltd v Niven, 1992 S.L.T. (Sh. Ct.) 53; 1992 S.C.L.R. 534, Sh Pr *30–093*
Christian v Queen, The; sub nom. R. v Christian (Stevens Raymond) [2006] UKPC 47; [2007] 2 A.C. 400; [2007] 2 W.L.R. 120; (2006) 150 S.J.L.B. 146, PC (PI) *11–007*
Christian Salvesen (Properties) Ltd v Central Electricity Generating Board (1984) 48 P. & C.R. 465; [1984] R.V.R. 185; [1984] J.P.L. 669, Lands Tr *28–125*
Christie v Taunton Delmard Lane & Co; Taunton Delmard Lane & Co, Re [1893] 2 Ch. 175, Ch D *19–070*
Christie v Wilson, 1915 S.C. 645; 1915 1 S.L.T. 265, IH (Ex Div) *21–006*
Christie Owen & Davies v Rapacioli [1974] Q.B. 781; [1974] 2 W.L.R. 723; [1974] 2 All E.R. 311; (1974) 118 S.J. 167, CA (Civ Div) *2–110*
Christie Owen & Davies v Stockton [1953] 1 W.L.R. 1353; [1953] 2 All E.R. 1149; (1953) 97 S.J. 781, QBD *2–118*
Christina, The. *See* Compania Naviera Vascongada v Cristina, The
Christopher & Co v Essig [1948] W.N. 461; (1948) 92 S.J. 675 .... *2–084*
Christopher Hill Ltd v Ashington Piggeries Ltd. *See* Ashington Piggeries Ltd v Christopher Hill Ltd
Christopher Moran Holdings Ltd v Bairstow. *See* Park Air Services Plc, Re
Christos v Secretary of State for the Environment, Transport and the Regions; sub nom. Secretary of State for Transport v Christos [2003] EWCA Civ 1073; [2004] 1 P. & C.R. 17; [2004] 1 E.G.L.R. 5; [2004] 10 E.G. 186; [2003] R.V.R. 307; [2003] 31 E.G. 68 (C.S.); [2003] N.P.C. 96, CA (Civ Div); reversing in part [2003] R.V.R. 191, Lands Tr *2–119*, *2–120*, *3–144*
Christy v Row, 127 E.R. 849; (1808) 1 Taunt. 300, CCP *21–035*
Chung Kwok Hotel Co v Field (No.1) [1960] 1 W.L.R. 1112; [1960] 3 All E.R. 143; (1960) 104 S.J. 847, CA *19–049*
Churchill & Co v Lonberg [1914] 3 All E.R. 137 .... *11–030*
Churchill (Lord) v Whetnall (1918) 87 L.J. Ch. 524 .... 9–068, *9–069*
Churchward v Queen, The (1865–66) L.R. 1 Q.B. 173, QB *2–039*, 10–006
Churton v Douglas, 70 E.R. 385; (1859) John. 174, QB *16–118*, *16–119*
Chwee Kin Keong v Digilandmall.com Pte Ltd [2005] S.G.C.A. 2; [2005] 1 S.L.R. 502 .... *5–057*, *5–074*, *5–075*
Cia de Seguros Imperio v Heath (REBX) Ltd (formerly CE Heath & Co (America) Ltd); sub nom. Companhia de Seguros Imperio v Heath (REBX) Ltd [2001] 1 W.L.R. 112; [2000] 2 All E.R. (Comm) 787; [2000] C.L.C. 1543; [2001] Lloyd's Rep. I.R. 109; [2000] Lloyd's Rep. P.N. 795; (2000–01) 3 I.T.E.L.R. 134, CA (Civ Div) *28–019*, *28–135*
Cia Portorafti Commerciale SA v Ultramar Panama Inc; The Captain Gregos (No.1) [1990] 3 All E.R. 967; [1990] 1 Lloyd's Rep. 310, CA (Civ Div); reversing [1989] 2 All E.R. 54; [1989] 2 Lloyd's Rep. 63, QBD (Comm) *14–008*, *14–016*, *14–136*, *18–019*
Cia Portorafti Commerciale SA v Ultramar Panama Inc; The Captain Gregos (No.2) [1990] 2 Lloyd's Rep. 395, CA (Civ Div) .... *2–180*, *3–109*, *14–054* , *14–055*
Ciampa v British Steam Navigation Co Ltd [1915] 2 K.B. 774, KBD *14–140*
Ciavarella v Balmer (1983) 153 C.L.R. 438 .... *26–148*
Cie Commerciale Sucres et Denrees v C Czarnikow Ltd; The Naxos [1990] 1 W.L.R. 1337; [1990] 3 All E.R. 641; [1991] 1 Lloyd's Rep. 29; (1990) 134 S.J. 1301, HL *12–026*, *12–034*, *12–037*
Cil v Owners of the Turiddu; The Turiddu; sub nom. Cil v First National Bank of Maryland; The Turiddu [1999] 2 All E.R. (Comm) 161; [1999] 2 Lloyd's Rep. 401; [1999] C.L.C. 1737; [2000] I.C.R. 354, CA (Civ Div); affirming [1998] 2 Lloyd's Rep. 278; [1998] C.L.C. 1043, QBD (Admlty) .. *16–047*, *18–046*, *18–074*
Circle Freight International Ltd v Medeast Gulf Exports Ltd [1988] 2 Lloyd's Rep. 427, CA (Civ Div) *12–011*, *12–014*, *14–017*

Circle Sales & Import Ltd v The Tarantel [1978] 1 F.C. 269 .... *14–042*, *14–048*
Circuit Systems Ltd (In Liquidation) v Zuken-Redac (UK) Ltd [1997] 1 W.L.R. 721; [1996] 3 All E.R. 748; [1996] 2 B.C.L.C. 349; 80 B.L.R. 25; (1996) 93(16) L.S.G. 30; (1996) 140 S.J.L.B. 99, CA (Civ Div); reversing, 72 B.L.R. 106; (1995) 11 Const. L.J. 201, QBD (OR) *16–052*, *19–043*
Citadel Insurance Co v Atlantic Union Insurance Co SA [1982] 2 Lloyd's Rep. 543; [1982] Com. L.R. 213; [1984] E.C.C. 191, CA (Civ Div) .. *2–039*, *2–117*, *3–025*, *3–173*
Citibank NA v Brown Shipley & Co Ltd; Midland Bank Plc v Brown Shipley & Co Ltd [1991] 2 All E.R. 690; [1991] 1 Lloyd's Rep. 576; (1990) 140 N.L.J. 1753, QBD (Comm) *5–097*, *29–159*
Citizen's Bank of Louisiana v First National Bank of New Orleans; New Orleans Canal and Banking Co v First National Bank of New Orleans (1873) L.R. 6 H.L. 352, HL *3–103*, *14–133*
City Alliance Ltd v Oxford Forecasting Services Ltd [2001] 1 All E.R. (Comm) 233, CA (Civ Div) *12–055*, *12–076*
City and Hackney HA v National Union of Public Employees; sub nom. City and Hackney HA v NUPE [1985] I.R.L.R. 252; (1985) 82 L.S.G. 118, CA (Civ Div) *27–064*
City and Westminster Properties (1934) Ltd v Mudd [1959] Ch. 129; [1958] 3 W.L.R. 312; [1958] 2 All E.R. 733; (1958) 102 S.J. 582, Ch D *12–004*, *12–069*, 12–103, *22–036*
City Bank of Sydney v McLaughlin (1909) 9 C.L.R. 615 .... *29–116*
City Discount Co Ltd v McLean (1873–74) L.R. 9 C.P. 692, Ex Chamber *21–066*
City Equitable Fire Insurance Co Ltd, Re [1925] Ch. 407; [1924] All E.R. Rep. 485, CA *14–017*
City Equitable Fire Insurance Co Ltd, Re; sub nom. City Equitable Fire Insurance Co Ltd v Liverpool and London Globe Insurance Co Ltd [1930] 2 Ch. 293, CA *20–041*
City Index Ltd v Gawler; sub nom. Charter Plc v City Index Ltd [2007] EWCA Civ 1382; [2008] 2 W.L.R. 950; [2007] 2 C.L.C. 968; [2008] P.N.L.R. 16; (2008) 105(2) L.S.G. 27, CA (Civ Div) *17–030*, *29–121*
City Life Assurance Co Ltd, Re; sub nom. Grandfield's Case, Re [1926] Ch. 191; [1925] All E.R. Rep. 453, CA *19–020*, *20–041*, 20–043
City of London v Goree (1677) 2 Levinz 174 .... *29–006*
City of London v Reeve & Co Ltd; G Lawrence Wholesale Meat Co Ltd v Citigen (London) Ltd [2000] C.P. Rep. 73; [2000] B.L.R. 211, QBD (TCC) ...*12–050*, *28–049*
City of York v Toun (1700) 5 Mod. 444 .... *29–006*
Civil Service & General Store, Re (1887) 57 L.J. Ch. 119 .... *9–049*
Civil Service Cooperative Society v General Steam Navigation Co [1903] 2 K.B. 756, CA *23–034*, *23–072*
Claim by Helbert Wagg & Co Ltd, Re; sub nom. Prudential Assurance Co Ltd, Re [1956] Ch. 323; [1956] 2 W.L.R. 183; [1956] 1 All E.R. 129; (1956) 100 S.J. 53, Ch D *23–031*, *30–005*, *30–007*, *30–009*, *30–011*, *30–015*, *30–345*, *30–356*, *30–367*
Clan Line Steamers Ltd v Liverpool and London War Risks Insurance Association Ltd [1943] K.B. 209; (1942) 73 Ll. L. Rep. 165, KBD *14–146*
Clare v Lamb (1874–75) L.R. 10 C.P. 334; (1875) 23 W.R. 389, CCP *29–057*
Clarion Ltd v National Provident Institution [2000] 1 W.L.R. 1888; [2000] 2 All E.R. 265, Ch D *5–058*, *5–078*, *13–007*
Clark v Chandler; sub nom. Chandler v Clark [2002] EWCA Civ 1249; [2003] 1 P. & C.R. 15; (2002) 99(28) L.S.G. 33, CA (Civ Div) *4–055*
Clark v Clark (Costs) [1906] P. 331, PDAD *19–047*
Clark v Clark [2006] EWHC 275; [2006] 1 F.C.R. 421; [2006] W.T.L.R. 823; [2006] 2 P. & C.R. DG10, Ch D *3–151*, *3–154*
Clark v Cutland [2003] EWCA Civ 810; [2004] 1 W.L.R. 783; [2003] 4 All E.R. 733; [2004] B.C.C. 27; [2003] 2 B.C.L.C. 393; [2003] O.P.L.R. 343; [2003] Pens. L.R. 179; [2003] W.T.L.R. 1413; [2004] W.T.L.R. 629; (2003) 147 S.J.L.B. 781, CA (Civ Div) *29–160*

Clark v Electronic Applications (Commercial) [1963] R.P.C. 234 .... *16–108*, *16–111*
Clark v Forbes Stuart (Thames Street) Ltd [1964] 1 W.L.R. 836; [1964] 2 All E.R. 282; (1964) 108 S.J. 422, CA *28–031*
Clark v Kirby Smith [1964] Ch. 506; [1964] 3 W.L.R. 239; [1964] 2 All E.R. 835; [1964] 2 Lloyd's Rep. 172; (1964) 108 S.J. 462, Ch D *28–033*
Clark v Lindsay (1903) 19 T.L.R. 202 .... *5–025*
Clark v Lindsay (1903) 88 L.T. 198 .... *23–033*
Clark v Malpas (1862) 4 De. G. F. & J. 401 .... *7–128*
Clark v Sir William Arrol & Co Ltd, 1974 S.C. 17; 1974 S.L.T. 90, OH *14–011*
Clark v University of Lincolnshire and Humberside [2000] 1 W.L.R. 1988; [2000] 3 All E.R. 752; [2000] Ed. C.R. 553; [2000] E.L.R. 345; [2000] C.O.D. 293; (2000) 150 N.L.J. 616; (2000) 144 S.J.L.B. 220, CA (Civ Div) *1–196*, *1–197*
Clark v Urquhart; Stracey v Urquhart; sub nom. Urquhart v Clark; Urquhart v Stracey [1930] A.C. 28; (1929) 34 Ll. L. Rep. 359, HL (NI) *25–008*
Clark v Woor [1965] 1 W.L.R. 650; [1965] 2 All E.R. 353; (1965) 109 S.J. 251, QBD *28–086*
Clark (A Bankrupt), Re; sub nom. Trustees Ex p. v Texaco [1975] 1 W.L.R. 559; [1975] 1 All E.R. 453; (1974) 118 S.J. 862, Ch D *20–022*, *20–023*, *29–043*
Clarke, Re; sub nom. Debtor Ex p. v S Aston & Son Ltd [1967] Ch. 1121; [1966] 3 W.L.R. 1101; [1966] 3 All E.R. 622; (1966) 110 S.J. 923, DC *6–129*
Clarke v Bruce Lance & Co [1988] 1 W.L.R. 881; [1988] 1 All E.R. 364; (1988) 85(2) L.S.G. 37; (1987) 137 N.L.J. 1064; (1987) 131 S.J. 1698; (1988) 7 Tr. L. 200, CA (Civ Div) *18–022*, *20–003*
Clarke v Burn (1866) 14 L.T. 439 .... *24–044*
Clarke v Cobley (1789) 2 Cox. 173 8–053
Clarke v Dickson (1858) E.B. & E. 148 ....6–115, 6–117
Clarke v Dickson, 120 E.R. 463; (1858) El. Bl. & El. 148, QB *29–149*
Clarke v Earl of Dunraven; The Satanita [1897] A.C. 59, HL; affirming [1895] P. 248, CA *2–110*, *18–011*
Clarke v Nationwide Anglia Building Society [1998] E.G. 47 (C.S.); (1998) 95(12) L.S.G. 29; [1998] N.P.C. 45; (1998) 76 P. & C.R. D5, CA (Civ Div) *2–185*
Clarke v Newland [1991] 1 All E.R. 397, CA (Civ Div) *16–097*
Clarke v Prus [1995] N.P.C. 41, Ch D *8–069*
Clarke v Ramuz [1891] 2 Q.B. 456, CA *25–003*
Clarke v Shee and Johnson, 98 E.R. 1041; (1774) 1 Cowp. 197, KB ..*29–150*, *29–166*, *29–170*
Clarke v Watson (1865) 18 C.B. (N.S.) 278 .... *12–028*
Clarke v West Ham Corp [1909] 2 K.B. 858, CA *1–015*
Clarke v Yorke (1882) 47 L.T. 381 .... *26–013*
Clarke & Sons (Coaches) v Axtell Yates Hallett, 30 Con. L.R. 123, QBD (OR) *28–118*
Clarkson v Davies [1923] A.C. 100, PC (Can) *9–055*
Clay v Ray (1864) 17 C.B.(N.S.) 188 .... *16–166*
Clay v Yates (1856) 1 H. & N. 73 .... *16–011*, *29–078*
Clay Hill Brick Tile Co Ltd v Rawlings [1938] 4 All E.R. 100 ....*9–043*, *21–044*
Clay's Policy of Assurance Re [1937] 2 All E.R. 548 .....*18–079*, *18–082*, *18–086*, *18–126*
Clayton & Jack Waller Ltd v Oliver. *See* Herbert Clayton & Jack Waller Ltd v Oliver
Clayton v Ashdown (1714) 9 Vin. Abr. 393 .... *27–047*
Clayton v Gregson (1836) 5 A. & E. 302 .... *12–058*
Clayton v Illingworth (1853) 10 Hare 451 .... *27–038*
Clayton v Jennings (1760) 2 W.Bl. 706 .... *3–168*
Clayton v Kynaston (1699) 12 Mod. R. 221 .... *22–006*
Clayton v Leech (1889) L.R. 41 Ch. D. 103, CA *27–055*, *29–057*
Clayton v Nugent, Lord (1844) 13 M. & W. 200 .... *12–125*
Clayton (Lucy) v Kynaston (1699) 12 Mod. 221 .... *17–017*
Clayton's Case; sub nom. Devaynes v Noble [1814–23] All E.R. Rep. 1; 35 E.R. 781; (1816) 1 Mer. 572 ....**21–066**, 28–098, 29–167

Clea Shipping Corp v Bulk Oil International; The Alaskan Trader (No.2) [1984] 1 All E.R. 129; [1983] 2 Lloyd's Rep. 645, QBD (Comm) ...*24–010*, *26–122*, *26–123*, *26–124*
Cleadon Trust Ltd, Re [1939] Ch. 286, CA *29–109*, 29–112, *29–115*, *29–116*, *29–133*, *29–173*
Cleadon Trust v Davies [1940] 1 Ch. 940 .... *27–047*
Cleaver v Mutual Reserve Fund Life Association [1892] 1 Q.B. 147, CA *16–169*, *18–046*, 18–084
Cleeves Western Valleys Anthracite Collieries Ltd v Owners of The Penelope [1928] P. 180; (1928) 31 Ll. L. Rep. 96, PDAD *23–035*, 23–045, *23–058*
Clef Aquitaine Sarl v Laporte Materials (Barrow) Ltd; sub nom. Clef Aquitaine Sarl v Sovereign Chemical Industries Ltd [2001] Q.B. 488; [2000] 3 W.L.R. 1760; [2000] 3 All E.R. 493, CA (Civ Div) *1–133*, *6–028*, *6–052*, *6–065*, *28–083*, *28–089*
Clegg v Andersson (t/a Nordic Marine) [2003] EWCA Civ 320; [2003] 1 All E.R. (Comm) 721; [2003] 2 Lloyd's Rep. 32; (2003) 100(20) L.S.G. 28, CA (Civ Div); reversing [2002] EWHC 943 (QB), QBD *6–127*
Clegg v Edmonson (1857) 8 De G.M. & G. 787 ....*28–142*, *28–143*
Clegg v Hands (1890) L.R. 44 Ch. D. 503, CA *16–125*
Clement v Gibb [1996] C.L.Y. 1209 .... *2–140*
Clements v London & North Western Railway Co [1894] 2 Q.B. 482, CA ...8–021, *8–025*, *8–029*
Clerk v Wright (1737) 1 Atk. 12 .... *4–048*
Cleveland Petroleum Co Ltd v Dartstone Ltd (No.1) [1969] 1 W.L.R. 116; [1969] 1 All E.R. 201; (1969) 20 P. & C.R. 235; (1968) 112 S.J. 962, CA (Civ Div) *16–085*, *16–122*, *16–129*
Cleveland Trust Plc, Re [1991] B.C.C. 33; [1991] B.C.L.C. 424, Ch D (Companies Ct) *5–035*
Clifford v Parker (1841) 2 M.G. 909 .... *25–022*
Clifford v Turrell, 62 E.R. 826; (1841) 1 Y. & C. Ch. 138, Ct of Chancery *12–108*, *27–007*
Clifford Davis Management Ltd v WEA Records Ltd [1975] 1 W.L.R. 61; [1975] 1 All E.R. 237; (1974) 118 S.J. 775, CA (Civ Div) *16–083*, *16–115*, *16–121*, *27–061*, *27–068*
Clifford Maersk, The [1982] 1 W.L.R. 1292; [1982] 3 All E.R. 905; [1982] 2 Lloyd's Rep. 251; (1982) 79 L.S.G. 988; (1982) 126 S.J. 446, QBD (Admlty) *28–022*, *28–063*
Clifton v Palumbo [1944] 2 All E.R. 497, CA *2–009*
Clifton Place Garage, Re [1970] Ch. 477; [1970] 2 W.L.R. 243; [1970] 1 All E.R. 353; (1969) 113 S.J. 895, CA (Civ Div); reversing [1969] 3 All E.R. 892; (1969) 113 S.J. 832, Ch D *9–049*
Clipper Maritime Ltd v Shirlstar Container Transport Ltd; The Anemone [1987] 1 Lloyd's Rep. 546, QBD (Comm) *2–116*, *3–106*, *4–027*
Clipsham v Vertue (1843) 5 Q.B. 565 .... *12–035*
Clive v Beaumont (1847) 1 De G. & Sm. 397 .... *2–032*
Cloncurry, Lord v Laffan [1924] 1 Ir.R. 78 .... *4–010*
Clore v Theatrical Properties Ltd; sub nom. Clore v Westby & Co Ltd [1936] 3 All E.R. 483, CA *18–139*
Close v Close (1853) 4 De G.M. & G. 176 .... *20–052*
Close Invoice Finance Ltd v Belmont Bleaching and Dyeing Co Ltd [2003] All E.R. (D) 304 .... *21–033*
Close v Phipps (1844) 7 M. & G. 586 ....*7–015*, *29–093*
Clough v Killey [1996] N.P.C. 38; (1996) 72 P. & C.R. D22, CA (Civ Div) *3–139*, *3–157*
Clough v London & North Western Railway Co (1871–72) L.R. 7 Ex. 26, Ex Chamber *6–109*, *6–124*, 6–127, *6–128*, *6–130*, *24–003*
Clough v Samuel; sub nom. Reis Ex p. Clough, Re [1905] A.C. 442, HL; affirming [1904] 2 K.B. 769, CA; reversing [1904] 1 K.B. 451, KBD *20–047*

Clough Mill Ltd v Martin [1985] 1 W.L.R. 111; [1984] 3 All E.R. 982; (1985) 82 L.S.G. 1075; (1985) 82 L.S.G. 116; (1984) 128 S.J. 850, CA (Civ Div); reversing [1984] 1 W.L.R. 1067; [1984] 1 All E.R. 721; (1984) 81 L.S.G. 2375; (1984) 128 S.J. 564, Ch D 1–189, 29–158, 29–165, 29–166, 29–168

Clowes v Brook (1739) 2 Str. 1101 8–016

Clugas v Penaluna (1791) 4 Term Rep. 466 .... 16–014, 30–357

Clyde Cycle Co v Hargreaves (1898) 78 L.T. 296 8–016

Clydebank Engineering & Shipbuilding Co Ltd v Don Jose Ramos Yzquierdo y Castaneda; sub nom. Castaneda v Clydebank Engineering & Shipbuilding Co Ltd [1905] A.C. 6; (1904) 7 F. (H.L.) 77; (1904) 12 S.L.T. 498, HL 26–125, 26–127, 26–135

Clydesdale Bank Ltd v Schroder & Co [1913] 2 K.B. 1, KBD 29–098

Coach v Goodman (1842) 2 Q.B. 580 4–040

Coal Cliff Collieries Pty Ltd v Sijehama Pty Ltd (1991) 24 N.S.W.L.R. 1 1–024

Coast Lines v Hudig & Veder Chartering NV [1972] 2 Q.B. 34; [1972] 2 W.L.R. 280; [1972] 1 All E.R. 451; [1972] 1 Lloyd's Rep. 53; (1971) 116 S.J. 119 [1971] 2 Lloyd's Rep. 390, QBD (Comm) 2–159, 14–148, 30–005, 30–011, 30–012, 30–013, 30–014, 30–072, 30–309

Coaten v PBS Corp [2006] EWHC 1781 (Ch); [2006] 3 E.G.L.R. 43; [2006] 44 E.G. 198; [2007] 1 P. & C.R. DG11, Ch D 2–127, 2–131, 3–172

Coates v Coates (1864) 33 Beav. 249 28–130

Coates v Wilson (1804) 5 Esp. 152 8–016

Cobb v Beake (1845) 6 Q.B. 930 29–026

Cobb v Great Western Railway Co [1894] A.C. 419, HL 26–035

Cobbe v Yeoman's Row Management Ltd; sub nom. Yeoman's Row Management Ltd v Cobbe [2008] UKHL 55; [2008] 1 W.L.R. 1752; [2006] EWCA Civ 1139; [2006] 1 W.L.R. 2964; [2007] 1 P. & C.R. 8; [2006] 3 E.G.L.R. 107; [2006] W.T.L.R. 1473; [2007] 1 P. & C.R. DG14, CA (Civ Div); affirming [2005] EWHC 266 (Ch); [2005] W.T.L.R. 625; [2005] N.P.C. 29; [2005] 2 P. & C.R. DG1, Ch D 2–112, 2–113, 2–120, 2–137, 2–164, 2–171, 3–090, 3–103, 3–106, 3–114, 3–137, 3–140, 3–141, 3–143, 3–144, 3–146, 3–147, 3–148, 3–151, 3–153, 3–154, 3–155, 3–157, 3–160, 3–162, 3–163, 4–082

Cobbett v Brock (1855) 20 Beav. 524 .... 7–077, 7–125

Cobbold v Bakewell Management Ltd [2003] EWHC 2289, Ch D 29–035, 29–160, 29–187

Cobec Brazilian Trading & Warehousing Corp v Toepfer [1983] 2 Lloyd's Rep. 386, CA (Civ Div) 24–003, 24–008

Cobelfret NV v Cyclades Shipping Co Ltd; The Linardos [1994] 1 Lloyd's Rep. 28, QBD (Comm) 1–031

Coburn v Colledge [1897] 1 Q.B. 702, CA 28–031, 28–053

Cochrane v Willis (1865–66) L.R. 1 Ch. App. 58, CA in Chancery 5–026

Cock v Richards (1805) 10 Ves. 429 16–072

Cockburn v Alexander (1848) 6 C.B. 791 12–128

Cockell v Taylor (1851) 15 Beav. 103 3–014

Cockerall v Aucompte (1857) 2 C.B. (N.S.) 440 9–073

Cockerton v Naviera Aznar, SA [1960] 2 Lloyd's Rep. 450, QBD 2–021, 12–009, 12–010, 12–011, 12–014, 13–022, 14–040, 14–132

Cocking v Pratt (1749) 1 Ves.Sen. 400 .... 5–026, 7–074

Cocking v Ward (1845) 1 C.B. 858 .... 4–011, 4–016, 29–192

Cocks v Masterman (1829) 9 B.C. 902 .... 29–040, 29–182

Cocks v Thanet DC [1983] 2 A.C. 286; [1982] 3 W.L.R. 1121; [1982] 3 All E.R. 1135; (1983) 6 H.L.R. 15; 81 L.G.R. 81; [1984] R.V.R. 31; (1982) 126 S.J. 820, HL 1–193, 1–194

Cockshott v Bennett, 100 E.R. 411; (1788) 2 Term Rep. 763, KB 16–017

Coddington v Paleologo (1866–67) L.R. 2 Ex. 193, Ex Ct 24–044

Codelfa Construction Property Ltd v State Rail Authority of New South Wales, 149 C.L.R. 337, HC (Aus) 12–118, 13–002, 13–004, 13–007, 23–098

Codrington v Codrington (1874–75) L.R. 7 H.L. 854, HL 8–036

Cogan v Duffield (1875–76) L.R. 2 Ch. D. 44, CA; affirming (1875) L.R. 20 Eq. 789, Ct of Chancery *5–134*
Coggs v Bernard (1703) 2 Ld. Raym. 909 .... *3–177*
Cohen Co v Ockerby Co Ltd (1917) 24 C.L.R. 288 .... *24–011*
Cohen v Hale (1877–78) L.R. 3 Q.B.D. 371, QBD *16–185*, *21–074*
Cohen v Kittell (1889) L.R. 22 Q.B.D. 680, QBD *16–192*
Cohen v Nessdale Ltd [1982] 2 All E.R. 97, CA (Civ Div); affirming [1981] 3 All E.R. 118; (1982) 263 E.G. 437, QBD *2–119*, *2–120*, *4–027*, *4–049*
Cohen v Roche [1927] 1 K.B. 169, KBD *4–032*, *4–034*, *4–038*, *16–135*, *21–087*, *27–005*, 27–015
Cointat v Myham & Son [1913] 2 K.B. 220, KBD; reversing (1914) 30 T.L.R. 282 .... *16–173*, *26–087*
Colbeam Palmer v Stock Affiliates Pty [1972] R.P.C. 303 .... *29–145*
Colburn v Patmore, 149 E.R. 999; (1834) 1 Cr. M & R. 72; (1834) 4 Tyr. 677, KB *16–173*
Colburn v Simms (1843) 2 Ha. 543 .... *29–142*
Colchester BC v Smith; Colchester BC v Tillson [1992] Ch. 421; [1992] 2 W.L.R. 728; [1992] 2 All E.R. 561, CA (Civ Div); affirming [1991] Ch. 448; [1991] 2 W.L.R. 540; [1991] 2 All E.R. 29; (1991) 62 P. & C.R. 242; [1990] E.G. 83 (C.S.), Ch D *3–024*, *3–051*, *3–053*, *3–107*, *6–135*, *14–133*
Coldunell v Gallon [1986] Q.B. 1184; [1986] 2 W.L.R. 466; [1986] 1 All E.R. 429; [1986] F.L.R. 183; (1986) 83 L.S.G. 520; (1986) 130 S.J. 88, CA (Civ Div) *6–023*, *7–064*, *7–105*
Cole, Re; sub nom. Trustee in Bankruptcy v Public Trustee [1931] 2 Ch. 174, Ch D *3–052*
Cole v Booker (1913) 29 T.L.R. 295 .... *16–052*, *16–053*
Cole v Gibson (1750) 1 Ves.Sen. 503 .... *16–191*, *22–005*
Cole v Kernot (1872) L.R. 7 Q.B. 534n *20–047*
Cole v Lynn [1942] 1 K.B. 142, CA *20–052*
Cole v Wellington Dairy Farmers' Co-op Association [1917] N.Z.U.L.R. 372 .... *19–055*
Colebrook's Conveyances, Re; sub nom. Taylor v Taylor [1972] 1 W.L.R. 1397; [1973] 1 All E.R. 132; (1972) 24 P. & C.R. 249; (1972) 116 S.J. 784, Ch D ... *5–111*
Coleman Engineering v North American Aviation (1967) 420 P2d 713 .... *29–021*
Coleman v Bucks and Oxon Union Bank [1897] 2 Ch. 243, Ch D *29–164*
Coleman v Myers [1977] 2 N.Z.L.R. 225 .... *6–014*
Cole-McIntyre-Norfleet Co v Holloway, 141 Tenn. 679; 214 S.W. 87 (1919) ... *2–072*
Colen v Cebrian (UK) Ltd [2003] EWCA Civ 1676; [2004] I.C.R. 568; [2004] I.R.L.R. 210; (2004) 101(2) L.S.G. 27, CA (Civ Div) *16–007*
Coles v Hulme (1828) 8 B. & C. 568 .... *12–063*, *12–064*, *12–076*
Coles v Pack (1869–70) L.R. 5 C.P. 65, CCP *3–047*
Coles v Trecothick (1804) 9 Ves. 234 .... *27–033*
Coliseum (Barrow) Ltd, Re [1930] 2 Ch. 44, Ch D *28–101*
Collard v South Eastern Railway (1861) 7 H.N. 79 .... *26–089*
Colley v Overseas Exporters (1919) Ltd [1921] 3 K.B. 302; (1921) 8 Ll. L. Rep. 127, KBD *2–153*, *13–011*, *24–032*
Collidge v Freeport Plc [2008] EWCA Civ 485, CA (Civ Div) *24–051*
Collier v Brown (1788) 1 Cox C.C. 428 .... *27–033*
Collier v Collier [2002] EWCA Civ 1095; [2002] B.P.I.R. 1057; [2003] W.T.L.R. 617; (2003–04) 6 I.T.E.L.R. 270; [2003] 1 P. & C.R. DG3, CA (Civ Div); reversing, HC 99 04609, Ch D *16–182*
Collier v Hollinshead (1984) 272 E.G. 941, Ch D *2–174*
Collier v P&MJ Wright (Holdings) Ltd [2007] EWCA Civ 1329; [2008] 1 W.L.R. 643; [2007] B.P.I.R. 1452; [2007] N.P.C. 136, CA (Civ Div) *3–010*, *3–117*, 3–132
Collier v Sunday Referee Publishing Co Ltd [1940] 2 K.B. 647, KBD *26–118*
Collin v Duke of Westminster [1985] Q.B. 581; [1985] 2 W.L.R. 553; [1985] 1 All E.R. 463; (1985) 17 H.L.R. 246; (1985) 50 P. & C.R. 380; [1985] 1 E.G.L.R. 109; (1985) 273 E.G. 881; [1985] R.V.R. 4; (1985) 82 L.S.G. 767; (1985) 129 S.J. 116, CA (Civ Div) ... *2–006*, *2–076*, *3–077*, *3–089*, *3–092*, *22–027*, *28–003*

Collins, Re [1925] Ch. 556, Ch D *19–061*, *20–026*, *20–034*
Collins v Associated Greyhound Racecourses Ltd [1930] 1 Ch. 1, CA .. *9–060*, *12–114*, *20–007*
Collins v Blantern (1767) 2 Wils. K.B. 341 .... *1–112*, *12–112*, *16–039*, *16–195*
Collins v Brebner [2000] Lloyd's Rep. P.N. 587, CA (Civ Div) *29–148*
Collins v Brook (1860) 5 H. & N. 700 .... *8–042*
Collins v Cory (1901) 17 T.L.R. 242 .... *8–061*
Collins v Godefroy (1831) 1 B. & Ad. 950 3–062
Collins v Hertfordshire CC [1947] K.B. 598; [1947] 1 All E.R. 633; 63 T.L.R. 317; (1947) 111 J.P. 272; [1947] L.J.R. 789; 176 L.T. 456, KBD *29–121*
Collins v Hopkins [1923] 2 K.B. 617; 34 A.L.R. 703, KBD *13–016*
Collins v Howard [1949] 2 All E.R. 324; (1949) 65 T.L.R. 598; (1949) 93 S.J. 482, CA *26–052*
Collins v Howell-Jones (1981) 259 E.G. 331 .... *14–063*
Collins v Jackson (1862) 31 Beav. 645 .... *16–022*
Collins v Locke (1878–79) L.R. 4 App. Cas. 674, PC (Aus) *16–138*, *16–200*
Collins v Plumb (1810) 16 Ves. 454 .... *27–042*
Collyer v Isaacs (1881–82) L.R. 19 Ch. D. 342, CA *20–047*
Colonia Versicherung AG v Amoco Oil Co; The Wind Star [1997] 1 Lloyd's Rep. 261; [1997] C.L.C. 454; [1997] 6 Re. L.R. 86, CA (Civ Div); affirming [1995] 1 Lloyd's Rep. 570; [1995] C.L.C. 51, QBD (Comm) *3–007*, *3–051*, *18–128*
Colonial Bank v Exchange Bank of Yarmouth, Nova Scotia (1886) L.R. 11 App. Cas. 84, PC (Can) *29–030*, *29–031*, *29–040*
Colonial Mutual General Insurance Co Ltd v ANZ Banking Group (New Zealand) Ltd [1995] 1 W.L.R. 1140; [1995] 3 All E.R. 987; [1995] 2 Lloyd's Rep. 433; [1995] C.L.C. 1047; [1995] 4 Re. L.R. 275; (1995) 92(28) L.S.G. 39; (1995) 139 S.J.L.B. 152; [1995] N.P.C. 111, PC (NZ) *19–025*
Coloniale Import-Export v Loumidis Sons [1978] 2 Lloyd's Rep. 560, QBD (Comm) *2–155*, *13–013*, *14–148*
Colpoys v Colpoys (1822) Jac. 451 .... *12–117*, *12–125*
Colquhoun v Brooks (1889) L.R. 14 App. Cas. 493; 2 T.C. 490, HL; affirming (1888) L.R. 21 Q.B.D. 52, CA; reversing (1887) L.R. 19 Q.B.D. 400, QBD *12–088*, *12–091*
Colt v Nettervill (1725) 2 P. Wms. 301 .... *27–002*
Colt Industries Inc v Sarlie (No.2) [1966] 1 W.L.R. 1287; [1966] 3 All E.R. 85; [1966] 2 Lloyd's Rep. 163; (1966) 110 S.J. 468, CA *25–017*
Columbus Co Ltd v Clowes [1903] 1 K.B. 244, KBD *26–008*
Colyear v Mulgrave (1836) 2 Keen 81 .... *18–086*
Combe v Combe; sub nom. Coombe v Coombe [1951] 2 K.B. 215; [1951] 1 All E.R. 767; [1951] 1 T.L.R. 811; (1951) 95 S.J. 317, CA; reversing [1950] 2 All E.R. 1115; 66 T.L.R. (Pt. 2) 983; [1950] W.N. 552; (1951) 95 S.J. 30, KBD 3–060, 3–098, 3–099, *3–100*, *3–113*, *3–128*, *3–135*
Comber v Leyland [1898] A.C. 524, HL *21–005*
Comdel Commodities Ltd v Siporex Trade SA [1997] 1 Lloyd's Rep. 424, CA (Civ Div) *26–125*
Comet Products (UK) Ltd v Hawkex Plastics Ltd [1971] 2 Q.B. 67; [1971] 2 W.L.R. 361; [1971] 1 All E.R. 1141; [1971] F.S.R. 7; [1972] R.P.C. 691; (1970) 114 S.J. 975, CA (Civ Div) *22–054*
Comfort v Betts [1891] 1 Q.B. 737, CA *19–012*, *19–049*
Commercial Air Hire Ltd v Wrightways Ltd [1938] 1 All E.R. 89, KBD *16–205*
Commercial Bank of Australia Ltd v Official Assignee of the Estate of EJohn Wilson & Co [1893] A.C. 181, PC (Aus) *21–042*
Commercial Bank of Australia v Amadio (1983) 151 C.L.R. 447 .....*5–013*, *7–058*, *7–130*, 7–131, *7–136*
Commercial Bank of Australia v Younis [1979] 1 N.S.W.L.R. 444 .... *29–030*
Commercial Banking Co of Sydney Ltd v Mann [1961] A.C. 1; [1960] 3 W.L.R. 726; [1960] 3 All E.R. 482; (1960) 104 S.J. 846, PC (Aus) *29–140*
Commercial Banking Co of Sydney v RH Brown & Co [1972] 2 Lloyd's Rep. 360; (1972) 126 C.L.R. 13, HC (Aus) *6–028*, *6–029*

Commercial Cable Co v Newfoundland [1916] 2 A.C. 610, PC (Can) *10–005*, *10–006*, *10–013*
Commercial Credit Services v Knowles [1978] 6 C.L. 64 .... *1–092*
Commercial Plastics Ltd v Vincent [1965] 1 Q.B. 623; [1964] 3 W.L.R. 820; 108 S.J. 599; [1964] 3 All E.R. 546 ... *16–088*, 16–091, *16–092*, *16–104*, *16–108*, *16–110*, *16–111*, *16–112*
Commercial Steamship Co v Boulton (1874–75) L.R. 10 Q.B. 346, QBD *21–022*
Commercial Union Assurance Co Plc v NRG Victory Reinsurance Ltd; Skandia International Insurance Corp v NRG Victory Reinsurance Ltd [1998] 2 All E.R. 434; [1998] 2 Lloyd's Rep. 600; [1998] C.L.C. 920; [1998] Lloyd's Rep. I.R. 439, CA (Civ Div) *30–011*
Commercial Union Assurance Co Plc v Sun Alliance Insurance Group Plc; Commercial Union Assurance Co Plc v Guardian Royal Exchange Plc [1992] 1 Lloyd's Rep. 475, QBD (Comm) *3–107*, *12–077*
Commercial Union Assurance Co v Hayden [1977] Q.B. 804; [1977] 2 W.L.R. 272; [1977] 1 All E.R. 441; [1977] 1 Lloyd's Rep. 1; (1976) 120 S.J. 855, CA (Civ Div) *29–128*
Commerzbank AG v Gareth Price-Jones. *See* Jones v Commerzbank AG
Commerzbank AG v IMB Morgan Plc [2004] EWHC 2771 (Ch); [2005] 2 All E.R. (Comm) 564; [2005] 1 Lloyd's Rep. 298; [2005] W.T.L.R. 1485; [2005] 1 P. & C.R. DG17, Ch D *21–066*, *29–160*, *29–167*
Commerzbank AG v Keen. *See* . See Keen v Commerzbank AG
Commission for the New Towns v Cooper (Great Britain) Ltd (formerly Coopind UK); sub nom. Milton Keynes Development Corp v Cooper (Great Britain) [1995] Ch. 259; [1995] 2 W.L.R. 677; [1995] 2 All E.R. 929; (1996) 72 P. & C.R. 270; [1995] 2 E.G.L.R. 113; [1995] E.G. 30 (C.S.); (1995) 139 S.J.L.B. 87; [1995] N.P.C. 34; (1995) 69 P. & C.R. D40, CA (Civ Div); affirming in part (1995) 69 P. & C.R. 221; [1993] E.G. 142 (C.S.); [1993] N.P.C. 115, Ch D ... *2–110*, *2–119*, *2–162*, 4–071, *5–074*, *5–078*, *5–116*, 5–117, 5–121
Commissioner of Police of the Metropolis v Charles (Derek Michael); sub nom. R. v Charles (Derek Michael) [1977] A.C. 177; [1976] 3 W.L.R. 431; [1976] 3 All E.R. 112; (1976) 63 Cr. App. R. 252; [1977] Crim. L.R. 615; (1976) 120 S.J. 588, HL; affirming [1976] 1 W.L.R. 248; [1976] 1 All E.R. 659; [1976] Crim. L.R. 196; (1975) 120 S.J. 147, CA (Crim Div) 6–015
Commissioner of Public Works v Hills; sub nom. Public Works Commissioners v Hills [1906] A.C. 368; (1906) 22 T.L.R. 589, PC (Cape) ...*26–127*, *26–130*, *26–135*, *26–146*, *26–150*, *29–064*
Commissioner of Stamp Duties v Bone [1977] A.C. 511; [1976] 2 W.L.R. 968; [1976] 2 All E.R. 354; [1976] S.T.C. 145; [1976] T.R. 117; (1976) 120 S.J. 421, PC (Aus) *3–115*
Commissioner of Stamps v Hope [1891] A.C. 476, PC (Aus) *25–002*
Commissioner of State Revenue (Vic) v Royal Insurance Australia Ltd (1994) 182 C.L.R. 51 ....*29–075*, *29–086*
Commissioners of Crown Lands v Page. *See* Crown Lands Commissioners v Page
Commissioners of Customs & Excise v TH Knitwear (Wholesale). *See* TH Knitwear (Wholesale) Ltd, Re
Commonwealth of Australia v McCormack (1982) 69 F.L.R. 9 ...*29–036*, *29–037*, *29–038*
Commonwealth of Australia v Verwayen (1990) 170 C.L.R. 394 ....*3–101*, *3–106*
Commonwealth v Verwayen (1990) 64 A.L.J.R. 540 .... *28–109*
Compagnie Algerienne de Meunerie v Katana Societa di Navigatione Marittima SpA; The Nizetti [1960] 2 Q.B. 115; [1960] 2 W.L.R. 719; [1960] 2 All E.R. 55; [1960] 1 Lloyd's Rep. 132; (1960) 104 S.J. 327, CA; affirming [1959] 1 Q.B. 527; [1959] 2 W.L.R. 366; [1959] 1 All E.R. 272; [1958] 2 Lloyd's Rep. 502; (1959) 103 S.J. 178, QBD *13–007*, *13–013*
Compagnie de Commerce et Commission, SARL v Parkinson Stove Co [1953] 2 Lloyd's Rep. 487, CA; reversing [1953] 1 Lloyd's Rep. 532, QBD *2–028*
Compagnie Europeene de Cereals SA v Tradax Export SA [1986] 2 Lloyd's Rep. 301, QBD (Comm) *28–125*

Compagnie Francaise des Chemins de Fer Paris-Orleans v Leeston Shipping Co Ltd (1919) 1 Ll. L. Rep. 235, KBD (Comm Ct) *6–104*, *6–117*

Compagnie Francaise d'Importation et de Distribution SA v Deutsche Conti-Handels GmbH [1985] 2 Lloyd's Rep. 592, QBD (Comm) ...*2–004*, *2–006*, *2–071*, *3–092*, *22–027*

Compagnie Generale Maritime v Diakan Spirit SA; The Ymnos (No.2) [1982] 2 Lloyd's Rep. 574; [1982] Com. L.R. 228, QBD (Comm) *12–035*

Compagnie Noga d'Importation et d'Exportation SA v Abacha (No.4) [2003] EWCA Civ 1100; [2003] 2 All E.R. (Comm) 915, CA (Civ Div) *2–112*, *3–069*, *3–071*, *3–079*, *12–123*, *22–028*

Compagnie Tunisienne de Navigation SA v Compagnie d'Armement Maritime SA; sub nom. Compagnie d'Armement Maritime SA v Compagnie Tunisienne de Navigation SA [1971] A.C. 572; [1970] 3 W.L.R. 389; [1970] 3 All E.R. 71; [1970] 2 Lloyd's Rep. 99; (1970) (1970) 114 S.J. 618, HL *30–005*, *30–006*, *30–010*, *30–011*, *30–012*, *30–013*, *30–052*, *30–060*

Compania Colombiana de Seguros v Pacific Steam Navigation Co; The Colombiana; Empressa de Telefona de Bogota v Pacific Steam Navigation Co; The Colombiana [1965] 1 Q.B. 101; [1964] 2 W.L.R. 484; [1964] 1 All E.R. 216; [1963] 2 Lloyd's Rep. 479; (1964) 108 S.J. 75, QBD (Comm) *16–060*, *16–062*, *19–008*, *19–016*, *19–039*, *19–049*, *28–022*, *28–117*

Compania Continental del Peru SA v Evelpis Shipping Corp; The Agia Skepi [1992] 2 Lloyd's Rep. 467, QBD (Comm) *3–177*

Compania de Electricidad de la Provincia de Buenos Aires Ltd, Re [1980] Ch. 146; [1979] 2 W.L.R. 316; [1978] 3 All E.R. 668; (1978) 122 S.J. 145, Ch D *28–003*, 28–004, *28–045*, *28–100*, *28–101*

Compania de Naveira Nedelka SA v Tradex Internacional SA; The Tres Flores [1974] Q.B. 264; [1973] 3 W.L.R. 545; [1973] 3 All E.R. 967; [1973] 2 Lloyd's Rep. 247; (1973) 117 S.J. 649, CA (Civ Div); affirming [1972] 2 Lloyd's Rep. 384, QBD (Comm) *12–037*

Compania Financiera Soleada SA v Hamoor Tanker Corp Inc; The Borag [1981] 1 W.L.R. 274; [1981] 1 All E.R. 856; [1981] 1 Lloyd's Rep. 483; [1981] Com. L.R. 29; (1981) 125 S.J. 185, CA (Civ Div) 26–108, *26–120*, *26–169*

Compania Naviera General SA v Kerametal; The Lorna I [1983] 1 Lloyd's Rep. 373; [1982] Com. L.R. 257; (1983) 80 L.S.G. 36, CA (Civ Div) *23–072*

Compania Naviera Maropan SA v Bowaters Lloyd Pulp & Paper Mills Ltd [1955] 2 Q.B. 68; [1955] 2 W.L.R. 998; [1955] 2 All E.R. 241; [1955] 1 Lloyd's Rep. 349; (1955) 99 S.J. 336, CA *26–038*

Compania Naviera Micro SA v Shipley International Inc; The Parouth [1982] 2 Lloyd's Rep. 351, CA (Civ Div) *30–006*, *30–010*, *30–305*, *30–306*

Compania Naviera Termar SA v Tradax Export SA [1966] 1 Lloyd's Rep. 566; 116 N.L.J. 809, HL; affirming [1965] 2 Lloyd's Rep. 79, CA; reversing [1965] 1 Lloyd's Rep. 198, QBD (Comm) *12–069*

Compania Naviera Vascongada v Cristina, The [1938] A.C. 485; [1938] 1 All E.R. 719; (1938) 60 Ll. L. Rep. 147, HL; affirming [1937] 4 All E.R. 313; (1937) 59 Ll. L. Rep. 47, CA; affirming (1937) 59 Ll. L. Rep. 1, PDAD *11–001*

Compania Portorafti Commerciale SA v Ultramar Panama Inc. *See* Cia Portorafti Commerciale SA v Ultramar Panama Inc

Compaq Computer Ltd v Abercorn Group Ltd (t/a Osiris) [1991] B.C.C. 484; [1993] B.C.L.C. 603, Ch D *19–068*

Comptoir Commercial Anversois and Power Son & Co, Re. *See* Arbitration between Comptoir Commercial Anversois and Power Son & Co, Re

Comptoir d'Achat et de Vente du Boerenbond Belge SA v Luis de Ridder Limitada; The Julia [1949] A.C. 293; [1949] 1 All E.R. 269; (1948–49) 82 Ll. L. Rep. 270; 65 T.L.R. 126; [1949] L.J.R. 513; (1949) 93 S.J. 101, HL *29–054*, *29–056*

Compton v Bagley [1892] 1 Ch. 313, Ch D *21–014*

Computastaff v Ingledew Brown Bennison & Garrett (1983) 133 N.L.J. 598; 268 E.G. 598, QBD *6–085*

Comyn Ching & Co (London) Ltd v Oriental Tube Co Ltd [1981] Com. L.R. 67; 17 B.L.R. 47, CA (Civ Div) *14–015*

Concadoro, The [1916] 2 A.C. 199, PC (Egy) *14–148*
Concord Trust v Law Debenture Trust Corp Plc [2005] UKHL 27; [2005] 1 W.L.R. 1591; [2005] 1 All E.R. (Comm) 699; [2005] 2 Lloyd's Rep. 221; [2006] 1 B.C.L.C. 616; [2005] 1 C.L.C. 631; (2005) 155 N.L.J. 692, HL; reversing [2004] EWCA Civ 1001; [2004] 2 All E.R. (Comm) 737; [2005] 1 Lloyd's Rep. 113; (2004) 148 S.J.L.B. 1062, CA (Civ Div); reversing in part [2004] EWHC 1216 (Ch), Ch D *13–005*
Condogianis v Guardian Assurance Co Ltd [1921] 2 A.C. 125; (1921) 7 Ll. L. Rep. 155, PC (Aus) *6–149*
Condon Ex p. James, Re (1873–74) L.R. 9 Ch. App. 609; [1874–80] All E.R. Rep. 388, CA in Chancery *20–017*, **20–022**, *20–023*, 29–043, *29–165*
Condon v Basi [1985] 1 W.L.R. 866; [1985] 2 All E.R. 453; (1985) 135 N.L.J. 485; (1985) 129 S.J. 382, CA (Civ Div) *1–119*
Condor v The Barron Knights Ltd [1966] 1 W.L.R. 87; (1966) 110 S.J. 71, Assizes (Bedford) *23–038*
Coney (A Bankrupt), Re [1998] B.P.I.R. 333, Ch D *20–018*
Coneys v Morris [1922] 1 Ir. R. 81 .... *28–047*, *28–128*
Confetti Records v Warner Music UK Ltd (t/a East West Records) [2003] EWHC 1274 (Ch); [2003] E.C.D.R. 31; [2003] E.M.L.R. 35, Ch D *2–005*, *2–030*, *2–162*
Congimex Companhia Geral de Comercia Importadora e Exportadora Sarl v Tradax Export SA [1983] 1 Lloyd's Rep. 250, CA (Civ Div); affirming [1981] 2 Lloyd's Rep. 687, QBD (Comm) *2–155*, *13–013*, *23–034*
Congreve v Home Office [1976] Q.B. 629; [1976] 2 W.L.R. 291; [1976] 1 All E.R. 697; (1975) 119 S.J. 847, CA (Civ Div) *29–083*
Conlan v Carlow County Council [1912] 2 I.R. 535 .... *19–014*
Conlon v Simms; sub nom. Simms v Conlon [2006] EWCA Civ 1749; [2008] 1 W.L.R. 484; [2007] 3 All E.R. 802, CA (Civ Div); reversing [2006] EWHC 401 (Ch); [2006] 2 All E.R. 1024; (2006) 103(13) L.S.G. 25, Ch D *1–027*, 6–143, *6–162*
Conner v Fitzgerald (1883) 11 L.R. Ir. 106 .... *4–048*
Connex South Eastern Ltd v MJ Building Services Group Plc [2005] EWCA Civ 193; [2005] 1 W.L.R. 3323; [2005] 2 All E.R. 871; [2005] B.L.R. 201; 100 Con. L.R. 16; (2005) 102(18) L.S.G. 23; (2005) 149 S.J.L.B. 296, CA (Civ Div) *24–048*
Connolly Ltd v Bellway Homes Ltd [2007] EWHC 895, [2007] All E.R. (D) 182, Ch D *6–007*
Connolly Shaw Ltd v A/S Det Nordenfjeldske D/S (1934) 49 Ll. L. Rep. 183, KBD *14–007*, *14–021*
Connolly-Martin v Davis; sub nom. Connolly-Martin v D [1999] Lloyd's Rep. P.N. 790; [1999] P.N.L.R. 826; (1999) 96(23) L.S.G. 35, CA (Civ Div); reversing [1999] P.N.L.R. 350, Ch D *1–184*, *18–029*
Connors Bros Ltd v Connors [1940] 4 All E.R. 179 .... *16–117*
Conquer v Boot [1928] 2 K.B. 336, KBD *25–008*, *26–013*
Conquest's Case. *See* European Assurance Society Arbitration Acts, Re
Conservative and Unionist Central Office v Burrell [1982] 1 W.L.R. 522; [1982] 2 All E.R. 1; [1982] S.T.C. 317; 55 T.C. 671; [1981] T.R. 543, CA (Civ Div); affirming [1980] 3 All E.R. 42; [1980] S.T.C. 400; [1980] T.R. 143, Ch D *18–076*
Consistent Group Ltd v Kalwak; sub nom. Consistent Group Ltd v Welsh Country Foods Ltd [2008] EWCA Civ 430; [2008] I.R.L.R. 505, CA (Civ Div); reversing [2007] I.R.L.R. 560, EAT *18–005*
Consolidated Agencies Ltd v Bertram Ltd [1965] A.C. 470; [1964] 3 W.L.R. 671; [1964] 3 All E.R. 282; (1964) 108 S.J. 578, PC (EA) *28–095*, *28–101*
Consolidated Exploration and Finance Co v Musgrave [1900] 1 Ch. 37, Ch D *16–039*
Consolidated Investment & Contracting v Saponaria Shipping Co; The Virgo [1978] 1 W.L.R. 986; [1978] 3 All E.R. 988; [1978] 2 Lloyd's Rep. 167; (1978) 122 S.J. 540, CA (Civ Div) *28–115*
Consort Deep Level Gold Mines Ltd Ex p. Stark, Re [1897] 1 Ch. 575, CA *2–045*
Constan Industries of Australia Pty Ltd v Norwich Winterthur Insurance (Aust) Ltd (1986) 160 C.L.R. 226 .... *13–018*
Constantine v Imperial Hotels Ltd [1944] K.B. 693, KBD *26–008*, *27–074*

Constantinidi v Ralli [1935] Ch. 427, Ch D *5–108*, *5–122*
Construction Industry Training Board v Labour Force Ltd [1970] 3 All E.R. 220; 9 K.I.R. 269; (1970) 4 I.T.R. 290; (1970) 114 S.J. 704, DC *18–009*
Container Transport International Inc v Oceanus Mutual Underwriting Association (Bermuda) Ltd (No.1) [1984] 1 Lloyd's Rep. 476, CA (Civ Div); reversing [1982] 2 Lloyd's Rep. 178; [1982] Com. L.R. 68, QBD (Comm) *2–029*, *6–126*
Contex Drouzhba v Wiseman [2007] EWCA Civ 1201; (2007) 157 N.L.J. 1695, CA (Civ Div); affirming [2006] EWHC 2708 (QB); [2007] All E.R. (D) 293; [2007] 1 B.C.L.C. 758, QBD *6–015*, *6–041*
Continental Caoutchoue v Kleinwort (1904) 90 L.T. 474 .... *29–182*
Continental Contractors Ltd v Medway Oil & Storage Co Ltd (1926) 25 Ll. L. Rep. 288, HL *24–023*
Continental Enterprises Ltd v Shandong Zhucheng Foreign Trade Group Co [2005] EWHC 92, QBD (Comm) *30–041*, *30–325*, *30–358*, *30–366*, *30–368*
Continental Grain Co v Bremer Handelsgesellschaft mbH (No.2) [1984] 1 Lloyd's Rep. 121 .... *26–184*
Continental Grain Export Corp v STM Grain Ltd (Charles E Ford Ltd) [1979] 2 Lloyd's Rep. 460, QBD (Comm) ...*3–079*, *14–137*, *14–140*, *14–141*, *22–055*, *23–064*
Continental Illinois National Bank & Trust Co of Chicago v Papanicolaou; The Fedora, The Tatiana and The Eretrea II [1986] 2 Lloyd's Rep. 441; [1986] Fin. L.R. 373; (1986) 83 L.S.G. 2569, CA (Civ Div) *14–010*
Continental Tyre Co v Heath (1913) 29 T.L.R. 308 .... *16–110*, *16–198*
Contract Corp, Re; sub nom. Gooch's Case (1872–73) L.R. 8 Ch. App. 266, CA in Chancery *8–038*
Convenience Co Ltd v Roberts [2001] F.S.R. 625 16–120
Cooden Engineering Co v Stanford [1953] 1 Q.B. 86; [1952] 2 All E.R. 915; [1952] 2 T.L.R. 822; (1952) 96 S.J. 802, CA *26–127*, *26–136*, *26–155*
Cook v Fearn (1878) 48 L.J. Ch. 63 .... *5–122*
Cook v Field (1850) 15 Q.B. 460 .... *16–006*
Cook v Lister, 143 E.R. 215; (1863) 13 C.B. N.S. 543, CCP *3–125*, *3–126*
Cook v S. *See* Cook v Swinfen
Cook v Swinfen; sub nom. Cook v S [1967] 1 W.L.R. 457; [1967] 1 All E.R. 299; (1966) 110 S.J. 964, CA; reversing in part [1966] 1 W.L.R. 635; [1966] 1 All E.R. 248; (1965) 109 S.J. 972, QBD *1–123*, *26–034*, *26–044*, *26–083*, *28–033*
Cook v Taylor [1942] Ch. 349, Ch D *23–057*, *27–007*
Cook v Whellock (1890) L.R. 24 Q.B.D. 658, CA *20–055*
Cook v Wright (1861) 1 B. & S. 559 ....*3–052*, *3–053*, *29–189*
Cook Industries Inc v Meunerie Liegeois SA [1981] 1 Lloyd's Rep. 359, QBD (Comm) *3–091*, *3–093*, *14–141*, *22–044*, *22–052*
Cook Industries Inc v Tradax Export SA [1985] 2 Lloyd's Rep. 454, CA (Civ Div); affirming [1983] 1 Lloyd's Rep. 327, QBD (Comm) *3–092*, *14–141*
Cooke v Clayworth (1811) 18 Ves. 12 .... *8–080*
Cooke v Football Association [1972] C.L.Y. 516 ....*16–075*, *16–091*, *16–137*
Cooke v Gill (1872–73) L.R. 8 C.P. 107, CCP *28–031*
Cooke v Head (No.1) [1972] 1 W.L.R. 518; [1972] 2 All E.R. 38; (1972) 116 S.J. 298, CA (Civ Div) *16–068*
Cooke v Oxley (1790) 3 T.R. 653 ....*2–088*, *3–004*, *3–172*
Cooke v Riddelien (1844) 1 C. & K. 561 .... *12–133*
Cooke v Routledge [1998] N.I. 174, CA (NI) 16–174
Cooke & Sons v Eshelby. *See* Isaac Cooke & Sons v Eshelby
Cooker v Child, 83 E.R. 456; (1673) 2 Lev. 74, KB *18–122*
Cooke's Trusts, Re, (1887) 3 T.L.R. 558 .... *30–324*
Cook's Mortgage (No.2), Re [1896] 1 Ch. 923, Ch D *29–118*
Cook's Settlement Trusts, Re; sub nom. Royal Exchange Assurance v Cook [1965] Ch. 902; [1965] 2 W.L.R. 179; [1964] 3 All E.R. 898; (1965) 109 S.J. 77, Ch D *18–082*, *18–087*
Cookson v Harewood [1932] 2 K.B. 478 (Note), CA *9–074*

Cookson & Clegg Ltd v Ministry of Defence [2005] EWCA Civ 811; [2006] Eu. L.R. 1092; (2005) 149 S.J.L.B. 771, CA (Civ Div); affirming [2005] EWHC 38 (Admin); [2005] Eu. L.R. 517; [2005] A.C.D. 48, QBD (Admin) *10–036*
Coole, Re; sub nom. Coole v Flight [1920] 2 Ch. 536, Ch D *28–084*
Coomber, Re; sub nom. Coomber v Coomber [1911] 1 Ch. 723, CA; affirming [1911] 1 Ch. 174, Ch D *7–093*, 7–095
Coombes v Quinney (1916) 142 L.T.J. 23 4
Coombes v Smith [1986] 1 W.L.R. 808; [1987] 1 F.L.R. 352; [1987] Fam. Law 123; (1986) 130 S.J. 482, Ch D *2–171*, *3–039*, *3–138*, *3–147*, *13–028*
Coombs v Wilkes [1891] 3 Ch. 77, Ch D *4–023*
Coope v Ridout [1921] 1 Ch. 291, CA; affirming [1920] 2 Ch. 411, Ch D *2–119*
Coope v Twynam (1823) Turn. & R. 426 .... *17–027*
Cooper Ex p. Hall, Re (1881–82) L.R. 19 Ch. D. 580; 51 L.J.Ch. 556; 46 L.T. 549, CA *7–050*
Cooper v Chitty (1756) 1 Burr. 20 .... *1–118*
Cooper v Cooper (1888) L.R. 13 App. Cas. 88, HL *8–036*, *30–324*
Cooper v Critchley [1955] Ch. 431; [1955] 2 W.L.R. 510; [1955] 1 All E.R. 520; (1955) 99 S.J. 148, CA *4–011*, *4–013*
Cooper v Firth Brown, Ltd [1963] 1 W.L.R. 418; [1963] 2 All E.R. 31; (1963) 107 S.J. 295, Assizes (Sheffield) *26–162*
Cooper v Micklefield Coal and Lime Co (1912) 107 L.T. 457 .... *19–055*
Cooper v National Provincial Bank Ltd [1946] K.B. 1, KBD *6–159*
Cooper v Parker (1855) 15 C.B. 822 .... *3–052*, *3–118*
Cooper v Phibbs (1867) L.R. 2 H.L. 149, HL (UK-Irl) 5–027, 5–049, *5–054*, 5–058, 5–061, 5–062, *5–075*, 6–013, 29–043, *29–044*
Cooper v Phillips (1831) 4 C. & P. 581 .... *8–061*
Cooper v Simmons (1862) 7 H. & N. 707 .... *8–022*
Cooper v Tamms [1988] 1 E.G.L.R. 257, DC *6–032*, *6–069*, *6–075*, *6–139*
Cooper v Turner (1819) 2 Stark. 497 .... *21–058*
Cooper Ewing & Co Ltd v Hamel & Horley Ltd (1922) 13 Ll. L. Rep. 590, KBD *24–023*
Cooperative Bank Plc v Tipper [1996] 4 All E.R. 366, Ch D *25–020*
Cooperative Insurance Society corp v Freeman Fox & Partners (1976) 241 E.G. 391 .... *16–114*
Cooperative Insurance Society Ltd v Argyll Stores (Holdings) Ltd [1998] A.C. 1; [1997] 2 W.L.R. 898; [1997] 3 All E.R. 297; [1997] C.L.C. 1114; [1997] 1 E.G.L.R. 52; [1997] 23 E.G. 141; [1997] E.G. 81 (C.S.); (1997) 94(26) L.S.G. 30; (1997) 147 N.L.J. 845; (1997) 141 S.J.L.B. 131; [1997] N.P.C. 79, HL *27–002*, *27–005*, *27–026*, 27–027, *27–030*, *27–071*
Cooperative Retail Services Ltd v Taylor Young Partnership Ltd; Cooperative Retail Services Ltd v Hoare Lea & Partners; Cooperative Retail Services Ltd v Carillion Construction Ltd (formerly Tarmac Construction (Contracts) Ltd); Cooperative Retail Services Ltd v East Midlands Electricity Electrical Installations Services Ltd (t/a Hall Electrical) (In Liquidation) [2002] UKHL 17; [2002] 1 W.L.R. 1419; [2002] 1 All E.R. (Comm) 918; [2003] 1 C.L.C. 75; [2002] B.L.R. 272; [2002] T.C.L.R. 9; 82 Con. L.R. 1; [2002] Lloyd's Rep. I.R. 555, HL; affirming [2000] 2 All E.R. 865; [2000] B.L.R. 461; (2001) 3 T.C.L.R. 4; 74 Con. L.R. 12; [2001] Lloyd's Rep. I.R. 122; (2000) 16 Const. L.J. 347, CA (Civ Div); affirming [2000] 1 All E.R. (Comm) 721; (2000) 16 Const. L.J. 204; [2000] E.G. 6 (C.S.), QBD (TCC) *17–029*
Cooperative Wholesale Society Ltd (t/a CWS Engineering Group) v Birse Construction Ltd (formerly Peter Birse Ltd); sub nom. Birse Construction Ltd (formerly Peter Birse Ltd) v Cooperative Wholesale Society Ltd (t/a CWS Engineering Group) [1997] C.L.C. 1290; 84 B.L.R. 58; 57 Con. L.R. 98; (1997) 94(29) L.S.G. 29, CA (Civ Div); affirming, 46 Con. L.R. 110, QBD *18–021*
Coore v Calloway (1794) 1 Esp. 115 .... *21–095*
Cooter & Green v Tyrrell [1962] 2 Lloyd's Rep. 377, CA *18–008*
Cooth v Jackson (1801) 6 Ves.12 .... *4–048*
Cope v Doherty (1858) 2 De G. & J. 614 .... *30–337*

Cope v Rowlands, 150 E.R. 707; (1836) 2 M. & W. 149, Ex Ct *16–147*
Coppock v Bower (1838) 4 M. & W. 361 .... *16–040*
Coral (UK) Ltd v Rechtman and Altro Mozart Food Handels GmbH [1996] 1 Lloyd's Rep. 235, QBD (Comm) *12–075*
Coral Leisure Group v Barnett [1981] I.C.R. 503; [1981] I.R.L.R. 204; (1981) 125 S.J. 374, EAT *16–007*, *16–010*, *16–067*, *16–069*, *16–157*,
Corbett v Bond Pearce (A Firm) [2001] EWCA Civ 531; [2001] 3 All E.R. 769; [2001] Lloyd's Rep. P.N. 501; [2001] P.N.L.R. 31; [2001] W.T.L.R. 419; (2001) 151 N.L.J. 609, CA (Civ Div); reversing [2000] Lloyd's Rep. P.N. 805; [2001] P.N.L.R. 24; [2000] W.T.L.R. 655, QBD *18–038*
Corbett v The Commissioners of Her Majesty's Works and Public Buildings (1868) 18 L.T. 548 .... *10–016*
Corby v Morrison (t/a the Card Shop) [1980] I.C.R. 564; [1980] I.R.L.R. 218, EAT *16–011*
Cordwell's Estate, Re; sub nom. White v Cordwell (1875) L.R. 20 Eq. 644, Ct of Chancery *28–130*
Corin v Patton (1990) 169 C.L.R. 540 HC (Aus) *19–036*
Cork and Bandon Railway v Goode (1853) 13 C.B. 826 .... *28–004*
Cork and Bandon Ry Co v Cazenove (1847) 10 Q.B. 935 ....*8–030*, *8–038*, *8–040*
Cork and Youghal Railway Co, Re (1868–69) L.R. 4 Ch. App. 748, CA in Chancery *9–025*, *29–173*
Cork v Rawlins; sub nom. Rawlins, Re [2001] EWCA Civ 202; [2001] Ch. 792; [2001] 3 W.L.R. 300; [2001] 4 All E.R. 50; [2001] B.P.I.R. 222; [2001] Lloyd's Rep. I.R. 587; (2001) 98(18) L.S.G. 44, CA (Civ Div); affirming [2000] B.P.I.R. 654; (2000) 97(27) L.S.G. 38, Ch D *20–034*
Corkling v Massey (1872–73) L.R. 8 C.P. 395, CCP *13–024*
Cormier Enterprises Ltd v Costello (1980) 108 D.L.R. (3d) 472 .... *26–018*
Corn v Matthews [1893] 1 Q.B. 310, CA *8–022*, *8–029*, *16–102*
Corner v Munday [1987] C.L.Y. 479 .... *6–019*
Cornfoot v Fowke, 151 E.R. 450; (1840) 6 M. & W. 358, Ex Ct *6–048*
Cornfoot v Royal Exchange Assurance Corp [1904] 1 K.B. 40, CA; affirming [1903] 2 K.B. 363, KBD *12–093*, *21–022*
Cornish v Abington (1859) 4 H. & N. 549 .... *5–067*
Cornish v Accident Insurance Co Ltd (1889) L.R. 23 Q.B.D. 453, CA *12–081*, *12–083*
Cornish v Midland Bank Plc; sub nom. Midland Bank Plc v Cornish [1985] 3 All E.R. 513; [1985] F.L.R. 298; (1985) 135 N.L.J. 869, CA (Civ Div) *1–134*, *6–085*, *7–082*
Cornwall v Hawkins (1872) 41 L.J. Ch. 435 .... *8–023*
Cornwall v Henson [1900] 2 Ch. 298, CA *24–018*, *24–044*
Cornwall CC v Prater; sub nom. Prater v Cornwall CC [2006] EWCA Civ 102; [2006] 2 All E.R. 1013; [2006] I.C.R. 731; [2006] I.R.L.R. 362; [2006] B.L.G.R. 479; (2006) 156 N.L.J. 372, CA (Civ Div) *2–175*
Corocraft Ltd v Pan American Airways Inc; sub nom. Corocraft v Pan American World Airways Inc; Corocraft and Vendome Jewels v Pan American Airways Inc [1969] 1 Q.B. 616; [1968] 3 W.L.R. 1273; [1969] 1 All E.R. 82; [1968] 2 Lloyd's Rep. 459; (1968) 112 S.J. 903, CA (Civ Div) *30–068*
Corpe v Overton (1833) 10 Bing. 252 .... *8–065*
Corporacion Nacional del Cobre de Chile v Sogemin Metals Ltd [1997] 1 W.L.R. 1396; [1997] 2 All E.R. 917; [1997] C.L.C. 435; (1996) 93(46) L.S.G. 29; (1997) 167 N.L.J. 161, Ch D *6–064*
Cort v Ambergate etc Railway Co (1851) 17 Q.B. 127 .... *24–027*
Cory, Re (1912) 29 T.L.R. 18 .... *3–002*
Cory v Cory (1747) 1 Ves.Sen. 19 .... *8–080*
Cory v Gertcken (1816) 2 Madd. 40 .... *8–053*
Cory v Patton (Demurrer and Joinder) (1871–72) L.R. 7 Q.B. 304, QB ... *2–117*, *6–019*
Cory v Thames Ironworks & Shipbuilding Co Ltd (1867–68) L.R. 3 Q.B. 181, QB *26–066*, *26–067*
Cory Bros & Co Ltd v Owners of the Turkish Steamship Mecca [1897] A.C. 286, HL *21–059*, *21–061*, *21–066*
Cosgrove v Horsefall (1945) 62 T.L.R. 140 ....*14–042*, *14–052*

Coslake v Till (1826) 1 Russ. 376 .... *27–043*
Cossill v Stangman [1963] N.S.W.R. 1695 .... *19–018*
Costa Rica Railway Co Ltd v Forwood [1901] 1 Ch. 746, CA; affirming [1900] 1 Ch. 756, Ch D *9–055*
Costello v Chief Constable of Derbyshire [2001] EWCA Civ 381; [2001] 1 W.L.R. 1437; [2001] 3 All E.R. 150; [2001] 2 Lloyd's Rep. 216; [2001] Po. L.R. 83, CA (Civ Div) *16–180*, *29–159*
Cotman v Brougham; sub nom. Anglo Cuban Oil Bitumen and Asphalt Co Ltd, Re [1918] A.C. 514, HL; affirming [1917] 1 Ch. 477, CA *9–021*, *9–022*
Cotronic (UK) Ltd v Dezonie (t/a Wendaland Builders Ltd) [1991] B.C.C. 200; [1991] B.C.L.C. 721, CA (Civ Div) *9–012*, *9–017*, *29–076*
Cotswold Developments Construction Ltd v Williams [2006] I.R.L.R. 181, EAT *3–025*
Cottage Club Estates Ltd v Woodside Estates Co (Amersham) Ltd [1928] 2 K.B. 463, KBD *19–055*
Cottee v Seaton (Douglas) (Used Cars) [1972] 1 W.L.R. 1408; [1972] 3 All E.R. 750; [1972] R.T.R. 509; [1972] Crim. L.R. 590; (1972) 116 S.J. 821, DC *6–016*
Cotterrell v Leeds Day; sub nom. Cotterell v Leeds Day [2001] W.T.L.R. 435, CA (Civ Div) *28–109*
Cotton v Godwin (1840) 7 M.W. 147 .... *21–085*, *21–095*
Cotton v Heyl [1930] 1 Ch. 510, Ch D *19–025*, *19–032*
Cottrell v King; sub nom. TA King (Services) Ltd, Re [2004] EWHC 397; [2004] B.C.C. 307; [2004] 2 B.C.L.C. 413; [2005] W.T.L.R. 63, Ch D *2–127*
Cottrill v Steyning and Littlehampton Building Society [1966] 1 W.L.R. 753; [1966] 2 All E.R. 295; 184 E.G. 253; (1962) 106 S.J. 736, QBD .. *26–068*, *26–091*
Couchman v Hill [1947] K.B. 554; [1947] 1 All E.R. 103; 63 T.L.R. 81; [1948] L.J.R. 295; 176 L.T. 278, CA *12–004*, *12–103*, *14–134*
Couldery v Bartrum (1881–82) L.R. 19 Ch. D. 394, CA *3–117*
Coull v Kolbuc (1969) 68 W.W.R. 76, DC (Alberta) *8–016*
Coulls v Bagot's Executor and Trustee Co (No.1) [1967] A.L.R. 385; 119 C.L.R. 460; (1967) 40 A.L.J.R. 471, HC (Aus) ... *3–042*, *3–044*, *18–046*, *18–049*, 18–074, *18–076*, *18–084*, *19–022*, *27–005*, *27–051*
Coulter v Chief Constable of Dorset [2004] EWCA Civ 1259; [2005] 1 W.L.R. 130; [2005] B.P.I.R. 62; (2004) 101(40) L.S.G. 28; (2004) 148 S.J.L.B. 1213, CA (Civ Div); affirming [2003] EWHC 3391 (Ch); [2004] 1 W.L.R. 1425; [2004] B.P.I.R. 462; [2004] Po. L.R. 56, Ch D *19–025*, *20–018*
Coulthard v Disco Mix Club Ltd [2000] 1 W.L.R. 707; [1999] 2 All E.R. 457; [1999] E.M.L.R. 434; [1999] F.S.R. 900, Ch D *28–019*, *28–135*
Coulthart v Clementson (1879–80) L.R. 5 Q.B.D. 42, QBD *2–100*
Council of Civil Service Unions v Minister for the Civil Service [1985] A.C. 374; [1984] 3 W.L.R. 1174; [1984] 3 All E.R. 935; [1985] I.C.R. 14; [1985] I.R.L.R. 28; (1985) 82 L.S.G. 437; (1984) 128 S.J. 837, HL; reversing [1984] I.R.L.R. 353, CA (Civ Div); reversing [1984] I.R.L.R. 309, DC *1–194*
Council of the City of Sydney v Goldspar Australia Pty Ltd [2006] F.C.A. 472 .... *12–126*
Country & Metropolitan Homes Surrey Ltd v Topclaim Ltd [1996] Ch. 307; [1996] 3 W.L.R. 525; [1997] 1 All E.R. 254, Ch D *21–014*, *26–152*
Countrywide Assured Financial Services Ltd v Smart [2004] EWHC 1214, Ch D *16–093*
Countrywide Communications Ltd v ICL Pathway Ltd [2000] C.L.C. 324, QBD *3–106*, *29–021*, *29–071*
County & District Properties Ltd v C Jenner & Son [1976] 2 Lloyd's Rep. 728; 3 B.L.R. 38; (1974) 230 E.G. 1589, QBD *28–049*
County Hotel & Wine Co Ltd v London & North Western Railway Co [1921] 1 A.C. 85, HL; affirming [1919] 2 K.B. 29, CA; affirming in part [1918] 2 K.B. 251, KBD *16–061*, *19–049*
County Ltd v Girozentrale Securities [1996] 3 All E.R. 834; [1996] 1 B.C.L.C. 653, CA (Civ Div) *2–162*, *2–185*, *3–173*, *26–032*, *26–041*
County Natwest Bank Ltd v Barton. *See* Barton v County Natwest Ltd
County of Gloucester Bank v Rudry Merthyr Steam & House Coal Colliery Co [1895] 1 Ch. 629, CA *9–040*

County Personnel (Employment Agency) Ltd v Alan R Pulver & Co [1987] 1 W.L.R. 916; [1987] 1 All E.R. 289; [1986] 2 E.G.L.R. 246; (1987) 84 L.S.G. 1409; (1986) 136 N.L.J. 1138; (1987) 131 S.J. 474, CA (Civ Div) *1–164*, *26–064*, 26–079, *26–120*

Coupland v Arabian Gulf Oil Co [1983] 1 W.L.R. 1136; [1983] 3 All E.R. 226; (1983) 133 N.L.J. 893; (1983) 127 S.J. 597, CA (Civ Div); affirming [1983] 1 W.L.R. 1136; [1983] 2 All E.R. 434; (1983) 127 S.J. 393, QBD ... *1–168*, *1–169*, *30–032*, *30–120*, *30–121*, *30–309*

Courage & Co Ltd v Carpenter [1910] 1 Ch. 262, Ch D *16–126*

Courage Ltd v Crehan (No.1); sub nom. Crehan v Courage Ltd; Byrne v Inntrepreneur Beer Supply Co Ltd; Inntrepreneur Beer Supply Co Ltd v Langton; Greenalls Management Ltd v Smith; Walker Cain Ltd v McCaughey [1999] U.K.C.L.R. 110; [1999] E.C.C. 455; [1999] Eu. L.R. 834; [1999] 2 E.G.L.R. 145; [1999] E.G. 85 (C.S.); [1999] E.G. 86 (C.S.); (1999) 96(25) L.S.G. 29; (1999) 143 S.J.L.B. 182, CA (Civ Div); affirming [1999] Eu. L.R. 409; [1998] E.G. 171 (C.S.), Ch D *16–123*

Courcier and Harrold's Contract, Re [1923] 1 Ch. 565, Ch D *27–056*, *27–057*, *27–058*

Court Line Ltd v Dant & Russell Inc (1939) 64 Ll. L. Rep. 212, KBD *23–040*, *23–043*

Court Line v Gotaverken AB; The Halcyon the Great [1984] 1 Lloyd's Rep. 283; (1984) 134 N.L.J. 203, QBD (Comm) *19–012*, *19–017*, *19–055*

Courtenay v Williams (1844) 3 Hare 539 .... *28–130*

Courtney v Taylor (1843) 6 M. & G. 851 .... *13–024*

Courtney & Fairbairn Ltd v Tolaini Brothers (Hotels) Ltd; sub nom. Courtney & Fairburn v Tolaini Bros (Hotels) [1975] 1 W.L.R. 297; [1975] 1 All E.R. 716; 2 B.L.R. 97; (1974) 119 S.J. 134, CA (Civ Div) *2–113*, *2–136*

Courts (Emergency Powers) Act 1939, Re; S Brown & Co (General Warehousemen) Ltd. Re [1940] Ch. 961, Ch D *9–051*

Coutts & Co v Browne Lecky [1947] K.B. 104; [1946] 2 All E.R. 207; 62 T.L.R. 421; 115 L.J. K.B. 508; (1946) 90 S.J. 489, KBD *8–045*, *8–063*, *17–008*

Coutts & Co v Stock [2000] 1 W.L.R. 906; [2000] 2 All E.R. 56; [2000] Lloyd's Rep. Bank. 14; [2000] B.C.C. 247; [2000] 1 B.C.L.C. 183; [2000] B.P.I.R. 400; (1999) 96(48) L.S.G. 39; (2000) 144 S.J.L.B. 24, Ch D *12–085*

Couturier v Hastie, 10 E.R. 1065; (1856) 5 H.L. Cas. 673, QB 5–020, 5–021, 5–023, 5–033, 5–048, *5–049*

Coventry City Council v J Hepworth & Sons (1983) 46 P. & C.R. 170; (1983) 265 E.G. 608, CA (Civ Div) *21–013*

Covington Marine Corp v Xiamen Shipbuilding Industry Co Ltd [2005] EWHC 2912; [2006] 1 Lloyd's Rep. 745; [2006] 1 C.L.C. 624, QBD (Comm) *2–003*, *2–004*, *2–136*, *2–139*, *2–149*, *2–153*

Cowan v Milbourn (1866–67) L.R. 2 Ex. 230, Ex Ct *16–014*

Cowan v O'Connor (1888) L.R. 20 Q.B.D. 640, QBD *2–048*

Cowan de Groot Properties v Eagle Trust [1992] 4 All E.R. 700; [1991] B.C.L.C. 1045, Ch D *29–164*

Coward v Motor Insurers Bureau [1963] 1 Q.B. 259; [1962] 2 W.L.R. 663; [1962] 1 All E.R. 531; [1962] 1 Lloyd's Rep. 1; (1962) 106 S.J. 34, CA; affirming [1961] 1 Lloyd's Rep. 583, QBD *2–168*

Cowell v Rosehill Racecourse Ltd (1936) 56 C.L.R. 605 .... *13–028*

Cowen v Truefitt Ltd [1899] 2 Ch. 309, CA; affirming [1898] 2 Ch. 551, Ch D *5–112*, *12–075*

Cowern v Nield [1912] 2 K.B. 419, KBD *8–004*, *8–017*, *8–018*, *8–028*, *8–047*, *8–049*, *29–081*

Cowey v Liberian Operations [1966] 2 Lloyd's Rep. 45, MCLC *22–032*

Cowley v Watts (1853) 17 Jur. 172 .... *12–123*

Cowling v Beacham (1823) 7 Moore 465 .... *29–197*

Cox v Bankside Members Agency Ltd [1995] 2 Lloyd's Rep. 437; [1995] C.L.C. 671, CA (Civ Div); affirming [1995] C.L.C. 180, QBD (Comm) *8–131*

Cozens v Brutus. *See* Brutus v Cozens

Crabb v Arun DC [1976] Ch. 179; [1975] 3 W.L.R. 847; [1975] 3 All E.R. 865; (1976) 32 P. & C.R. 70; (1975) 119 S.J. 711, CA (Civ Div) 1–006, 3–141, 3–143, *3–146*, 3–149, *3–150*, *3–153*, 3–156, *3–162*, 3–163, 3–164, *10–039*, *29–161*
Craddock Bros Ltd v Hunt [1923] 2 Ch. 136, CA; affirming [1922] 2 Ch. 809, Ch D *5–112*, *5–124*, *5–130*, *5–133*, *12–112*
Crage v Fry (1903) 67 J.P. 240 .... *16–173*
Craig (Deceased), Re; sub nom. Meneces v Middleton; Craig, Re [1971] Ch. 95; [1970] 2 W.L.R. 1219; [1970] 2 All E.R. 390; (1970) 114 S.J. 171, Ch D ...*7–064*, *7–082*
Crampton v Varna Railway Co (1871–72) L.R. 7 Ch. App. 562, Lord Chancellor *9–040*, *27–006*
Crane v Hegeman Harris Co Inc [1939] 4 All E.R. 68, CA; affirming [1971] 1 W.L.R. 1390; [1939] 1 All E.R. 662, Ch D *5–113*
Crane Co v Wittenborg A/S, unreported, December 21, 1999, CA (Civ Div) *19–057*, *22–048*
Cranleigh Precision Engineering Ltd v Bryant [1965] 1 W.L.R. 1293; [1964] 3 All E.R. 289; [1966] R.P.C. 81; (1965) 109 S.J. 830, QBD *2–029*, *2–123*, *24–001*, *24–003*, *24–013*, *27–070*
Cranley v Hillary (1813) 2 M.S. 120 .... *21–005*
Crantrave Ltd (In Liquidation) v Lloyds Bank Plc [2000] Q.B. 917; [2000] 3 W.L.R. 877; [2000] 4 All E.R. 473; [2000] 2 All E.R. (Comm) 89; [2000] Lloyd's Rep. Bank. 181; [2000] C.L.C. 1194; [2001] B.P.I.R. 57; (2000) 97(20) L.S.G. 42; (2000) 144 S.J.L.B. 219, CA (Civ Div) *18–021*
Craven Ellis v Canons Ltd [1936] 2 K.B. 403, CA *9–059*, *29–008*, *29–022*, 29–076, *29–142*
Crawford & Rowat v Wilson Sons & Co (1896) 12 T.L.R. 170 .... *14–143*
Craxford's (Ramsgate) Ltd v Williams & Steer Manufacturing Co Ltd [1954] 1 W.L.R. 1130; [1954] 3 All E.R. 17; (1954) 98 S.J. 576, QBD *16–161*
Crears v Hunter (1887) L.R. 19 Q.B.D. 341, CA *3–047*, *3–060*
Crédit Lyonnais v New Hampshire Insurance Co Ltd [1997] 2 Lloyd's Rep. 1; [1997] C.L.C. 909; [1997] 2 C.M.L.R. 610, CA (Civ Div) ...*30–020*, *30–045*, *30–077*, *30–090*, *30–347*
Crédit Lyonnais v PT Barnard & Associates Ltd [1976] 1 Lloyd's Rep. 557, QBD (Comm) *16–011*
Crédit Lyonnais Bank Nederland NV (now Generale Bank Nederland NV) v Export Credits Guarantee Department; sub nom. Generale Bank Nederland NV (formerly Credit Lyonnais Bank Nederland NV) v Export Credits Guarantee Department [2000] 1 A.C. 486; [1999] 2 W.L.R. 540; [1999] 1 All E.R. 929; [1999] 1 Lloyd's Rep. 563; [1999] C.L.C. 823; (1999) 96(10) L.S.G. 30; (1999) 143 S.J.L.B. 89, HL; affirming [1998] 1 Lloyd's Rep. 19; [1997] 6 Bank. L.R. 355; (1997) 94(34) L.S.G. 29; (1997) 141 S.J.L.B. 194, CA (Civ Div); affirming [1996] 1 Lloyd's Rep. 200; [1996] C.L.C. 11, QBD (Comm) *6–009*, *6–024*, *6–134*, 6–159
Crédit Lyonnais Bank Nederland NV v Burch [1997] 1 All E.R. 144; [1996] 5 Bank. L.R. 233; [1997] C.L.C. 95; [1997] 1 F.L.R. 11; [1997] 2 F.C.R. 1; (1997) 29 H.L.R. 513; (1997) 74 P. & C.R. 384; [1997] Fam. Law 168; (1996) 93(32) L.S.G. 33; (1996) 146 N.L.J. 1421; (1996) 140 S.J.L.B. 158; [1996] N.P.C. 99; (1996) 72 P. & C.R. D33, CA (Div) ...*7–083*, *7–091*, 7–128, *7–130*, *7–131*, 7–133, 7–134
Crédit Suisse v Allerdale BC [1997] Q.B. 306; [1996] 3 W.L.R. 894; [1996] 4 All E.R. 129; [1996] 2 Lloyd's Rep. 241; [1996] 5 Bank. L.R. 249; (1997) 161 J.P. Rep. 88, CA (Civ Div); affirming [1995] 1 Lloyd's Rep. 315; (1995) 159 L.G. Rev. 549, QBD (Comm) *3–107*, *3–108*, *10–027*, *10–032*
Crédit Suisse v Waltham Forest LBC [1997] Q.B. 362; [1996] 3 W.L.R. 943; [1996] 4 All E.R. 176; (1997) 29 H.L.R. 115; 94 L.G.R. 686; (1997) 9 Admin. L.R. 517, CA (Civ Div); reversing [1994] 3 Bank. L.R. 201; [1994] N.P.C. 137, QBD *3–107*, *3–108*, *10–024*
Crédit Suisse Financial Products v Societe Generale d'Enterprises [1996] 5 Bank. L.R. 220; [1997] C.L.C. 168; [1997] I.L.Pr. 165, CA (Civ Div) *12–014*

Crédit Suisse First Boston (Europe) Ltd v Seagate Trading Co Ltd [1999] 1 All E.R. (Comm.) 261; [1999] 1 Lloyd's Rep. 784; [1999] C.L.C. 600, QBD (Comm) *30–305*, *30–308*
Crediton Gas Co v Crediton Urban DC [1928] Ch. 447, CA; affirming [1928] Ch. 174, Ch D *13–027*, *22–054*
Crehan v Inntrepreneur Pub Co (CPC); sub nom. Inntrepreneur Pub Co (CPC) v Crehan [2006] UKHL 38; [2007] 1 A.C. 333; [2006] 3 W.L.R. 148; [2006] 4 All E.R. 465; [2006] U.K.C.L.R. 1232; [2007] E.C.C. 2; [2006] Eu. L.R. 1189; [2006] I.C.R. 1344; [2006] 30 E.G. 103 (C.S.); (2006) 150 S.J.L.B. 983; [2006] N.P.C. 85, HL; reversing [2004] EWCA Civ 637; [2004] 2 C.L.C. 803; [2004] U.K.C.L.R. 1500; [2004] E.C.C. 28; [2004] Eu. L.R. 693; [2004] 3 E.G.L.R. 128; [2004] 23 E.G. 120 (C.S.); (2004) 148 S.J.L.B. 662; [2004] N.P.C. 83, CA (Civ Div); reversing [2003] EWHC 1510 (Ch); [2003] U.K.C.L.R. 834; [2004] E.C.C. 8; [2003] Eu. L.R. 663; [2003] 27 E.G. 138 (C.S.); (2003) 100(27) L.S.G. 39; (2003) 100(33) L.S.G. 28, Ch D *16–158*
Cremdean Properties v Nash (1977) 244 E.G. 547, CA (Civ Div); affirming (1977) 241 E.G. 837 .... *6–138*, *14–062*, *14–063*, *27–058*
Cremer v General Carriers SA. *See* Peter Cremer GmbH v General Carriers SA; The Dona Mari
Crenver & Wheal Abraham United Mining Co Ex p. Wilson, Re (1872–73) L.R. 8 Ch. App. 45, CA in Chancery *8–038*
Crescendo Management Pty Ltd v Westpac Banking Corp (1988) 19 N.S.W.L.R. 40 .... *7–005*, *7–027*, *29–088*
Crescent Oil & Shipping Services Ltd v Importang UEE (No.1) [1998] 1 W.L.R. 919; [1997] 3 All E.R. 428; [1997] C.L.C. 1198, QBD (Comm) *11–006*, *12–114*
Cressman v Coys of Kensington (Sales) Ltd; sub nom. Coys of Kensington (Sales) Ltd v McDonald; McDonald v Coys of Kensington Holdings Ltd [2004] EWCA Civ 47; [2004] 1 W.L.R. 2775; (2004) 101(10) L.S.G. 29; (2004) 148 S.J.L.B. 182, CA (Civ Div) *29–018*, *29–021*, *29–022*, *29–183*
Cresspark Ltd v Wymering Mansions Ltd [1996] E.G. 63 (C.S.), Ch D *12–118*
Cresswell v Potter [1978] 1 W.L.R. 255, Ch D *7–085*, *7–128*, *7–130*
Cretanor Maritime Co Ltd v Irish Marine Management Ltd; The Cretan Harmony [1978] 1 W.L.R. 966; [1978] 3 All E.R. 164; [1978] 1 Lloyd's Rep. 425; (1978) 122 S.J. 298, CA (Civ Div) *29–158*
Creyke v Corp of the Level of Hatfield Chase (1896) 12 T.L.R. 383 .... *10–028*
Cricklewood Property & Investment Trust Ltd v Leighton's Investment Trust Ltd; sub nom. Leighton's Investment Trust Ltd v Cricklewood Property & Investment Trust Ltd [1945] A.C. 221; [1945] 1 All E.R. 252, HL *23–025*, 23–052, *23–053*, 23–055, *23–066*, *23–068*
Cripps v Reade (1796) 6 T.R. 606 .... *29–042*
Crisdee v Bolton (1827) 3 C.P. 240 .... *26–134*
Cristel v Cristel [1951] 2 K.B. 725; [1951] 2 All E.R. 574; (1951) 95 S.J. 561, CA *22–024*
Criterion Properties Plc v Stratford UK Properties LLC [2004] UKHL 28; [2004] 1 W.L.R. 1846; [2004] B.C.C. 570; [2006] 1 B.C.L.C. 729; (2004) 101(26) L.S.G. 27; (2004) 148 S.J.L.B. 760; [2004] N.P.C. 96, HL; affirming [2002] EWCA Civ 1883; [2003] 1 W.L.R. 2108; [2003] B.C.C. 50; [2003] 2 B.C.L.C. 129, CA (Civ Div); reversing [2002] EWHC 496 (Ch); [2002] 2 B.C.L.C. 151, Ch D 9–031, *9–038*, *29–174*
Crittall Windows v Stormseal (UPVC) Window Systems [1991] R.P.C. 265, Ch D *26–148*
Crocker v British Coal Corp (1996) 29 B.M.L.R. 159, QBD *28–061*
Crocker v Sundance Northwest Resorts (1988) 51 D.L.R. (4th) 321 .... *12–002*
Crockford v Winter (1807) 1 Camp. 124 .... *29–147*
Crofter Hand Woven Harris Tweed Co Ltd v Veitch [1942] A.C. 435; [1942] 1 All E.R. 147; 1942 S.C. (H.L.) 1; 1943 S.L.T. 2, HL *29–088*
Crofton v Ormsby (1806) 2 Sch. & L. 583 .... *28–143*
Croke v Hydro Aluminium Worcester Ltd [2007] I.C.R. 1303, EAT *18–005*
Crompton v Jarratt (1885) L.R. 30 Ch. D. 298, CA *12–089*

Croockewit v Fletcher (1857) 1 H.N. 893 ....*25–020*, *25–021*, *25–023*
Crooks & Co v Allan; sub nom. Crooks v Allan (1879–80) L.R. 5 Q.B.D. 38, QBD *12–107*
Cropp v Hambleton (1586) Cro. Eliz. 48 .... *21–095*
Crosby v Wadworth (1805) 6 East 602 .... *4–018*
Cross v Imperial Continental Gas Association [1923] 2 Ch. 553, Ch D *9–020*
Cross v Sprigg (1849) 6 Hare 552, reversed (1850) 2 Mac. & G. 113 .... *22–004*
Crossley v Faithful & Gould Holdings Ltd [2004] EWCA Civ 293; [2004] 4 All E.R. 447; [2004] I.C.R. 1615; [2004] I.R.L.R. 377; (2004) 101(14) L.S.G. 26; (2004) 154 N.L.J. 653; (2004) 148 S.J.L.B. 356, CA (Civ Div) ...*13–008*, *13–009*, *13–010*
Crossley v Magnac [1893] 1 Ch. 594 .... *21–044*
Crouch v Crouch [1912] 1 K.B. 378, KBD *12–066*
Crouch v London North Western Railway (1849) 2 C.K. 789 .... *26–089*
Crouch & Lees v Haridas; sub nom. Crouch & Lees (A Firm) v Haridas [1972] 1 Q.B. 158; [1971] 3 W.L.R. 532; [1971] 3 All E.R. 172; (1971) 115 S.J. 528, CA (Civ Div) *16–205*
Croudace Construction Ltd v Cawoods Concrete Products Ltd [1978] 2 Lloyd's Rep. 55; 8 B.L.R. 20, CA (Civ Div) *14–006*
Crow v Rogers (1726) 1 Stra. 592 .... *18–019*
Crowden v Aldridge [1993] 1 W.L.R. 433; [1993] 3 All E.R. 603; [1992] N.P.C. 152, Ch D *2–116*, *2–161*, *18–078*
Crowe v Clay (1854) 9 Exch. 604 .... *21–080*
Crowhurst Park, Re; Suis-Hilditch v Simmons [1974] 1 W.L.R. 583; (1973) 118 S.J. 331; [1974] 1 All E.R. 991 .... *20–004*
Crown Dilmun v Sutton [2004] EWHC 52 (Ch); [2004] 1 B.C.L.C. 468; [2004] W.T.L.R. 497; (2004) 101(7) L.S.G. 34, Ch D *29–155*, *29–174*
Crown Dilmun, Dilmun Investments Ltd v Nicholas Sutton, Fulham River. *See* Crown Dilmun v Sutton
Crown Estate Commissioners v John Mowlem & Co Ltd, 70 B.L.R. 1; 40 Con. L.R. 36; (1994) 10 Const. L.J. 311, CA (Civ Div) *28–112*
Crown Estates Commissioners v Dorset County Council [1990] Ch. 297 .... *25–012*
Crown Lands Commissioners v Page; sub nom. Commissioners of Crown Lands v Page [1960] 2 Q.B. 274; [1960] 3 W.L.R. 446; [1960] 2 All E.R. 726; (1960) 104 S.J. 642, CA 10–007, 10–008
Crowson Fabrics Ltd v Rider [2007] EWHC 2942 (Ch); [2008] I.R.L.R. 288; [2008] F.S.R. 17, Ch D *16–107*
Crowther v Farrer (1850) 15 Q.B. 677 ....*3–047*, *22–015*
Croxford v Universal Insurance Co Ltd; Norman v Gresham Fire and Accident Insurance Society Ltd [1936] 2 K.B. 253; (1936) 54 Ll. L. Rep. 171, CA; reversing [1935] 2 K.B. 409; (1935) 52 Ll. L. Rep. 258, KBD *16–161*
Crozer v Pilling (1825) 4 B.C. 26 .... *21–094*
Cruikshanks v Rose (1831) 1 Moo. Rob. 100 .... *21–063*
Crumpston v Haigh (1836) 2 Scott. 684 .... *12–085*
Crusader, The [1907] P. 196, CA; affirming [1907] P. 15, PDAD *7–047*
Cruttwell v Lye (1810) 17 Ves. 335 .... *16–118*
Cryne v Barclays Bank [1987] B.C.L.C. 548, CA (Civ Div) *13–010*
Crystal Palace FC (2000) Ltd v Dowie [2007] All E.R. (D) 135 .... *7–054*
Cubitt v Gamble (1919) 35 T.L.R. 223 .... *21–087*
Cuckmere Brick Co v Mutual Finance [1971] Ch. 949; [1971] 2 W.L.R. 1207; [1971] 2 All E.R. 633; (1971) 22 P. & C.R. 624; (1971) 115 S.J. 288, CA (Civ Div) *1–148*
Cud v Rutter (1719) 1 P. Wms. 570 .... *27–011*
Cudgen Rutile (No.2) Pty Ltd v Chalk; Queensland Titanium Mines Pty v Chalk; Cudgen Rutile (No.2) Pty Ltd v Queensland Titanium Mines Pty [1975] A.C. 520; [1975] 2 W.L.R. 1; (1974) 119 S.J. 31, PC (Aus) *10–005*
Cullard v Butler (1816) 5 M. & S. 461 .... *12–087*
Cullard v Elwin (1904) 90 L.T. 840 .... *16–140*

Cullard v Taylor (1887) 3 T.L.R. 698 .... *16–110*

Cullard v Thomson (1862) 6 L.T. 870 6–030

Cullen v Barclay (1881) 10 L.R. Ir. 224 .... *21–010*

Cullinane v British Rema Manufacturing Co Ltd [1954] 1 Q.B. 292; [1953] 3 W.L.R. 923; [1953] 2 All E.R. 1257; (1953) 97 S.J. 811, CA *26–002*, *26–074*, *26–075*, *26–077*

Cullwick, Re; sub nom. R. v Cullwick Ex p. London Senior Official Receiver [1918] 1 K.B. 646, KBD *28–070*

Cumber v Wane (1721) 1 Stra. 426 .... *3–115*, *22–016*

Cumbrian Newspapers Group Ltd v Cumberland & Westmorland Herald Newspaper & Printing Co Ltd [1987] Ch. 1; [1986] 3 W.L.R. 26; [1986] 2 All E.R. 816; (1986) 2 B.C.C. 99227; [1987] P.C.C. 12; (1986) 83 L.S.G. 1719; (1986) 130 S.J. 446, Ch D *9–058*, *9–061*

Cumming v Ince (1847) 11 Q.B. 112 .... *7–052*

Cumming v Roebuck (1816) Holt N.P.C. 172 .... *20–055*

Cunard Steamship Co Ltd v Buerger; sub nom. Buerger v Cunard Steamship Co Ltd [1927] A.C. 1; (1926) 25 Ll. L. Rep. 215, HL; affirming [1925] 2 K.B. 646; (1925) 22 Ll. L. Rep. 6, CA; reversing (1925) 21 Ll. L. Rep. 38, KBD *14–021*, *14–029*, *14–030*

Cundy v Lindsay; sub nom. Lindsay v Cundy (1877–78) L.R. 3 App. Cas. 459; [1874–80] All E.R. Rep. 1149; (1878) 42 J.P. 483; (1878) 14 Cox C.C. 93; (1878) 26 W.R. 406; (1878) 47 L.J. Q.B. 481; (1878) 38 L.T. 573; 15 Sask. R. 233, HL; affirming (1876–77) L.R. 2 Q.B.D. 96, CA; reversing (1875–76) L.R. 1 Q.B.D. 348, QBD *1–082*, *5–009*, 5–088, 5–094, 5–095, 5–096, *6–129*, *29–076*

Cundy v Marriott, 109 E.R. 945; (1831) 1 B. & Ad. 696, KB *21–078*

Cunigunda, In the Estate of; sub nom. Crippen, In the Estate of [1911] P. 108, PDAD *16–168*

Cunliffe Brooks & Co v Blackburn and District Benefit Building Society; sub nom. Blackburn and District Benefit Building Society v Cunliffe Brooks & Co (1883–84) L.R. 9 App. Cas. 857, HL; affirming (1883) L.R. 22 Ch. D. 61, CA *9–025*, *29–173*

Cunliffe-Owen v Teather & Greenwood; Cunliffe Owen v Schaverien Habermann, Simon & Co; Cunliffe Owen v LA Seligmann & Co [1967] 1 W.L.R. 1421; [1967] 3 All E.R. 561; (1967) 111 S.J. 866, Ch D *12–129*, *13–018*

Cunningham v Harrison [1973] Q.B. 942; [1973] 3 W.L.R. 97; [1973] 3 All E.R. 463; (1973) 117 S.J. 547, CA (Civ Div) *18–076*, *29–133*

Cunningham-Reid v Public Trustee [1944] K.B. 602, KBD *17–027*

Curfew, The [1891] P. 131, PDAD *12–118*

Curl Bros Ltd v Webster [1904] 1 Ch. 685, Ch D *16–119*

Curran v Newpark Cinemas [1951] 1 All E.R. 295, CA *19–015*, *19–018*, *19–022*, *19–023*

Currie v Misa. *See* Misa v Currie

Curtice v London City & Midland Bank Ltd [1908] 1 K.B. 293, CA *2–091*

Curtis v Chemical Cleaning & Dyeing Co [1951] 1 K.B. 805; [1951] 1 All E.R. 631; [1951] 1 T.L.R. 452; (1951) 95 S.J. 253, CA *6–013*, *6–017*, 14–132

Curtis v Curtis [1969] 1 W.L.R. 422; [1969] 2 All E.R. 207; (1969) 113 S.J. 242, CA (Civ Div) *20–046*

Curtis & Sons v Mathews [1919] 1 K.B. 425, CA; affirming [1918] 2 K.B. 825, KBD *14–146*

Curtis's Case. *See* Imperial Mercantile Credit Association, Re

Curwin v Milburn (1889) 42 Ch. D. 424 .... *28–133*

Cushen v City of Hamilton (1902) 4 Ont L.R. 265 .... *29–187*

Cushla, Re [1979] 3 All E.R. 415; [1979] S.T.C. 615, Ch D *20–023*, *20–041*, *20–043*

Customs and Excise Commissioners v Barclays Bank Plc [2006] UKHL 28; [2007] 1 A.C. 181; [2006] 3 W.L.R. 1; [2006] 4 All E.R. 256; [2006] 2 All E.R. (Comm) 831; [2006] 2 Lloyd's Rep. 327; [2006] 1 C.L.C. 1096; (2006) 103(27) L.S.G. 33; (2006) 156 N.L.J. 1060; (2006) 150 S.J.L.B. 859, HL; reversing [2004] EWCA Civ 1555; [2005] 1 W.L.R. 2082; [2005] 3 All E.R. 852; [2005] 1 Lloyd's Rep. 165; (2004) 154 N.L.J. 1831; (2004) 148 S.J.L.B. 1402; [2004] N.P.C. 175, CA (Civ Div); reversing [2004] EWHC 122 (Comm); [2004] 1 W.L.R. 2027; [2004] 2 All E.R. 789; [2004] 1 All E.R. (Comm) 960; [2004] 1 Lloyd's Rep. 572; [2004] 2 C.L.C. 1; (2004) 101(7) L.S.G. 35; (2004) 154 N.L.J. 224, QBD (Comm) 1–184, *18–031*
Customs and Excise Commissioners v Diners Club Ltd; Customs and Excise Commissioners v Cardholder Services [1989] 1 W.L.R. 1196; [1989] 2 All E.R. 385; [1989] S.T.C. 407; [1989] C.C.L.R. 107, CA (Civ Div); affirming [1988] 2 All E.R. 1016; [1988] S.T.C. 416; [1988] Fin. L.R. 218, QBD; reversing [1987] V.A.T.T.R. 10, VAT Tr *3–039*, *18–007*, *18–008*
Customs and Excise Commissioners v National Westminster Bank Plc (Authorisation: Mistake) [2002] EWHC 2204; [2003] 1 All E.R. (Comm) 327; (2002) 99(48) L.S.G. 27, Ch D *29–038*
Customs and Excise Commissioners v Telemed Ltd [1992] S.T.C. 89, QBD; affirming [1989] V.A.T.T.R. 238, VAT Tr *3–036*
Cuthbertson v Friends Provident Life Office [2006] CSOH 74; 2006 S.L.T. 567; 2006 S.C.L.R. 697, OH *6–037*
Cutler v Goodwin (1721) 11 Mod.R. 344 .... *22–005*
Cutler v McPhail [1962] 2 Q.B. 292; [1962] 2 W.L.R. 1135; [1962] 2 All E.R. 474; (1962) 106 S.J. 391, QBD *17–017*
Cutler v Southern (1668) 1 Wms. Saund. 116 .... *21–009*
Cutsforth v Mansfield Inns Ltd; sub nom. Cutsforth (t/a for Amusement Only) v Mansfield Inns Ltd [1986] 1 W.L.R. 558; [1986] 1 All E.R. 577; [1986] 1 C.M.L.R. 1; (1986) 83 L.S.G. 1232; (1986) 130 S.J. 314, QBD *16–076*, *16–125*
Cutter v Powell, 101 E.R. 573; (1795) 6 Term Rep. 320, KB *12–026*, *21–029*, 21–030, 21–032, *21–033*, 24–037
Cuxon v Chadley (1824) 3 B. & C. 591 .... *19–088*
Cyril Leonard & Co v Simo Securities Trust Ltd [1972] 1 W.L.R. 80; [1971] 3 All E.R. 1318; (1971) 115 S.J. 911, CA (Civ Div) *24–014*
Czarnikow Ltd v Roth Schmidt & Co [1922] 2 K.B. 478; (1922) 12 Ll. L. Rep. 195, CA; affirming (1922) 10 Ll. L. Rep. 687, KBD *14–136*, *16–202*
D v D (Custody: Jurisdiction) [1996] 1 F.L.R. 574; [1996] 3 F.C.R. 19; [1996] Fam. Law 272; (1996) 146 N.L.J. 917, Fam Div *30–079*
D v M [1996] I.R.L.R. 192, QBD *16–101*
D&C Builders Ltd v Rees [1966] 2 Q.B. 617; [1966] 2 W.L.R. 288; [1965] 3 All E.R. 837; (1965) 109 S.J. 971, CA *1–145*, *3–095*, 3–116, 3–120, *3–122*, *3–129*, 3–132, 3–136, *3–175*, *7–015*, 7–019, *21–077*, *22–016*, *22–021*
D&F Estates Ltd v Church Commissioners for England [1989] A.C. 177; [1988] 3 W.L.R. 368; [1988] 2 All E.R. 992; 41 B.L.R. 1; 15 Con. L.R. 35; [1988] 2 E.G.L.R. 213; (1988) 4 Const. L.J. 100; [1988] E.G. 113 (C.S.); (1988) 85(33) L.S.G. 46; (1988) 138 N.L.J. Rep. 210; (1988) 132 S.J. 1092, HL; affirming 36 B.L.R. 72; 11 Con. L.R. 12; [1987] 1 F.T.L.R. 405; (1987) 3 Const. L.J. 110, CA (Civ Div); affirming in part 7 Con. L.R. 40, OR ...*1–176*, *14–056*, *18–027*, *18–033*, *18–036*
D&J Nicol v Dundee Harbour Trustees; sub nom. Dundee Harbour Trustees v D&J Nicol [1915] A.C. 550; 1915 S.C. (H.L.) 7; (1914) 2 S.L.T.418, HL; affirming 1914 S.C. 374; (1914) 1 S.L.T.205, IH (2 Div); affirming (1913) 1 S.L.T.203, OH *9–022*, *10–027*
D&M Trailers (Halifax) Ltd v Stirling [1978] R.T.R. 468; (1978) 248 E.G. 597; (1978) 122 S.J. 625, CA (Civ Div) *2–031*, *13–028*
D Owen & Co v Cronk [1895] 1 Q.B. 265, CA *29–090*
DC Thomson & Co Ltd v Deakin [1952] Ch. 646; [1952] 2 All E.R. 361; [1952] 2 T.L.R. 105, CA; affirming [1952] 1 T.L.R. 1397, Ch D *18–135*
DE Bernardy v Harding (1853) 8 Exch. 822 .... *29–066*, *29–068*

DEG-Deutsche Investitions und Entwicklungsgesellschaft mbH v Koshy (Account of Profits: Limitations); sub nom. Gwembe Valley Development Co Ltd (In Receivership) v Koshy (Account of Profits: Limitations) [2003] EWCA Civ 1048; [2004] 1 B.C.L.C. 131; [2004] W.T.L.R. 97; (2003) 147 S.J.L.B. 1086, CA (Civ Div) *28–019*, *28–135*
DH Curtis (Builders) Ltd, Re [1978] Ch. 162; [1978] 2 W.L.R. 28; [1978] 2 All E.R. 183; (1977) 121 S.J. 707, Ch D *20–041*
DR Insurance Co v Central National Insurance Co of Omaha (In Rehabilitation) [1996] 1 Lloyd's Rep. 74; [1996] C.L.C. 64; [1996] 5 Re. L.R. 482, QBD (Comm) *16–144*, *16–164*, *30–008*, *30–009*, *30–011*, *30–012*, *30–051*, *30–068*
DRC Distribution Ltd v Ulva Ltd [2007] EWHC 1716 (QB), QBD *24–015*
DO Ferguson Associates v Sohl, 62 B.L.R. 95, CA (Civ Div) *29–063*
D/S A/S Gulnes v ICI Ltd (1937) 59 Ll. L. Rep. 144, KBD *23–059*
DSND Subsea Ltd (formerly DSND Oceantech Ltd) v Petroleum Geo Services ASA [2000] B.L.R. 530, QBD (TCC) *7–032*, *7–041*, *7–044*, *7–097*
DSV Silo und Verwaltungsgesellschaft mbH v Owners of the Sennar; The Sennar (No.2) [1985] 1 W.L.R. 490; [1985] 2 All E.R. 104; [1985] 1 Lloyd's Rep. 521; (1985) 82 L.S.G. 1863; (1985) 135 N.L.J. 316; (1985) 129 S.J. 248, HL *25–012*, *25–017*, *25–018*
DW Moore v Ferrier [1988] 1 W.L.R. 267; [1988] 1 All E.R. 400; (1988) 132 S.J. 227, CA (Civ Div) *1–124*, *1–167*, *28–033*, *28–034*
Da Costa v Davis (1798) 1 B.P. 242 .... *21–007*
Dacas v Brook Street Bureau (UK) Ltd; sub nom. Brook Street Bureau (UK) Ltd v Dacas [2004] EWCA Civ 217; [2004] I.C.R. 1437; [2004] I.R.L.R. 358, CA (Civ Div); reversing [2003] I.R.L.R. 190, EAT *18–005*
Dadourian Group International Inc v Simms (Damages) [2006] EWHC 2973, [2006] All E.R. (D) 351, Ch D *6–035*
Daewoo Heavy Industries Ltd v Klipriver Shipping Ltd; The Kapitan Petko Voivoda [2003] EWCA Civ 451; [2003] 1 All E.R. (Comm) 801; [2003] 2 Lloyd's Rep. 1; [2003] 1 C.L.C. 1092, CA (Civ Div); affirming [2002] EWHC 1306 (Comm); [2002] 2 All E.R. (Comm) 560, QBD (Comm) *2–188*, *14–008*, *14–029*, *14–031*, *18–052*
Dagenham (Thames) Dock Co Ex p. Hulse, Re (1872–73) L.R. 8 Ch. App. 1022, CA in Chancery *21–016*, *26–147*
Dahl (t/a Dahl & Co) v Nelson, Donkin & Co; sub nom. Nelson v Dahl (1880–81) L.R. 6 App. Cas. 38, HL; affirming (1879) L.R. 12 Ch. D. 568, CA *13–011*, *13–018*, 23–011, *23–040*
Daido Asia Japan Co Ltd v Rothen [2002] B.C.C. 589, Ch D *16–001*
Daily Mirror Newspapers Ltd v Exclusive News Agency (1937) 81 S.J. 924 ... *16–175*
Daily Telegraph Newspaper Co Ltd v McLaughain [1904] A.C. 776, PC (Aus) *8–071*
Daimler Co Ltd v Continental Tyre & Rubber Co (Great Britain) Ltd; sub nom. Continental Tyre & Rubber Co (Great Britain) Ltd v Daimler Co Ltd; Continental Tyre & Rubber Co (Great Britain) Ltd v Thomas Tilling Ltd [1916] 2 A.C. 307, HL; reversing [1915] 1 K.B. 893, CA *11–025*
Dairy Containers Ltd v Tasman Orient Line CV; The Tasman Discoverer [2004] UKPC 22; [2005] 1 W.L.R. 215; [2004] 2 All E.R. (Comm) 667; [2004] 2 Lloyd's Rep. 647; [2004] 2 C.L.C. 794, PC (NZ); affirming [2002] 2 Lloyd's Rep. 528; [2002] 3 N.Z.L.R. 353, CA (NZ); reversing [2001] 2 Lloyd's Rep. 665; [2002] 1 N.Z.L.R. 265, HC (NZ) ... *12–050*, *12–083*, *14–005*, *14–009*, *21–070*
Dairy Crest v Pigott [1989] I.C.R. 92, CA (Civ Div) *16–110*
Dakin v Oxley, 143 E.R. 938; (1864) 15 C.B. N.S. 646, CCP *21–032*, *21–034*
Dakins v Wagner (1835) 3 Dowl. 535 .... *12–093*
Dale v Hamilton (1846) 5 Hare 369 .... *4–012*, *4–066*
Dale v Humfrey (1858) E.B. & E. 1004 .... *12–133*, *13–018*
Dale (Deceased), Re; sub nom. Estate of Monica Dale (Deceased), Re; Proctor v Dale [1994] Ch. 31; [1993] 3 W.L.R. 652; [1993] 4 All E.R. 129; [1994] Fam. Law 77; (1993) 137 S.J.L.B. 83, Ch D .. *3–005*, *3–008*, *3–015*, *3–140*, *3–167*
Dale SS Co Ltd v Northern SS Co Ltd (1918) 34 T.L.R. 271 .... *23–047*

Dalkia Utilities Services Plc v Celtech International Ltd [2006] EWHC 63 (Comm); [2006] 1 Lloyd's Rep. 599; [2006] 2 P. & C.R. 9, QBD (Comm) *5–110*, *12–037*, *12–038*, *12–075*, *21–017*, *22–048*, *22–049*, *24–013*, *24–018*, *24–019*

Dallal v Bank Mellat [1986] Q.B. 441; [1986] 2 W.L.R. 745; [1986] 1 All E.R. 239; (1986) 83 L.S.G. 779; (1985) 130 S.J. 185, QBD (Comm) *25–012*, *25–013*

Dallas, Re [1904] 2 Ch. 385, CA *19–069*

D'Almeida Araujo v Becker. *See* J D'Almeida Araujo LDA v Sir Frederick Becker & Co Ltd

Dalmia Dairy Industries v National Bank of Pakistan [1978] 2 Lloyd's Rep. 223; (1977) 121 S.J. 442, CA (Civ Div) *23–047*

Dalrymple v Dalrymple (1811) 2 Hag. Con. 54 .... *2–165*

Dal-Sterling Group Plc v WSP South & West Ltd [2002] T.C.L.R. 20, QBD (TCC) *16–056*

Dalton (A Bankrupt), Re; sub nom. Herrington & Carmichael Ex p. v Trustee [1963] Ch. 336; [1962] 3 W.L.R. 140; [1962] 2 All E.R. 499; (1962) 106 S.J. 510, Ch D *20–019*, *20–020*, *20–021*

Dalton (Smith's Administratrix) v Inland Revenue Commissioners (1958) 37 A.T.C. 49; [1958] T.R. 45 .... *19–058*

Daly v General Steam Navigation Co; The Dragon [1981] 1 W.L.R. 120; [1980] 3 All E.R. 696; [1980] 2 Lloyd's Rep. 415; (1981) 125 S.J. 100, CA (Civ Div); affirming [1979] 1 Lloyd's Rep. 257, QBD (Admlty) ...*2–021*, *12–010*, *18–012*, *18–049*

Damon Compania Naviera SA v Hapag-Lloyd International SA; The Blankenstein [1985] 1 W.L.R. 435; [1985] 1 All E.R. 475; [1985] 1 Lloyd's Rep. 93; (1985) 82 L.S.G. 1644; (1985) 129 S.J. 218, CA (Civ Div); affirming [1983] 3 All E.R. 510; [1983] 2 Lloyd's Rep. 522; [1983] Com. L.R. 204, QBD (Comm) *2–116*, *2–156*, *12–027*, *19–086*, *22–031*, 24–051, *26–009*, *29–064*

D'Angibau, Re; sub nom. Andrews v Andrews (1880) L.R. 15 Ch. D. 228, CA *8–059*, *18–087*

Daniel v O'Leary (1976) 14 N.B.R. (2d) 564 .... *29–144*

Daniel, Re; sub nom. Daniel v Vassall [1917] 2 Ch. 405, Ch D *26–091*

Daniels v Trefusis [1914] 1 Ch. 788, Ch D *4–027*, *4–036*, *4–047*

Danish Bacon Co Ltd Staff Pension Fund Trusts, Re; sub nom. Christensen v Arnett [1971] 1 W.L.R. 248; [1971] 1 All E.R. 486, Ch D *4–028*, *19–022*, *19–026*

Danka Rentals Ltd v Xi Software Ltd (1998) 17 Tr. L.R. 74, QBD *14–079*

Dann v Curzon (1910) 104 L.T. 66 .... *16–039*

Danowski v Henry Moore Foundation [1996] E.C.C. 380; [1996] E.M.L.R. 364; (1996) 140 S.J.L.B. 101, CA (Civ Div) *12–128*, *13–018*

Danziger v Thompson [1944] K.B. 654, KBD *12–114*

Daraydan Holdings Ltd v Solland International Ltd [2004] EWHC 622 (Ch); [2005] Ch. 119; [2004] 3 W.L.R. 1106; [2005] 4 All E.R. 73; [2004] W.T.L.R. 815; [2004] N.P.C. 49, Ch D *29–156*, *29–160*

Darbey v Whitaker, 62 E.R. 52; (1857) 4 Drew. 134, QB *27–043*

Darbishire v Warran [1963] 1 W.L.R. 1067; [1963] 3 All E.R. 310; [1963] 2 Lloyd's Rep. 187; (1963) 107 S.J. 631, CA *26–103*

Darby v Boucher (1694) 1 Salk. 279 .... *8–020*

D'Arcy v Adamson (1913) 29 T.L.R. 367 .... *9–075*

Darley Main Colliery Co v Mitchell; sub nom. Mitchell v Darley Main Colliery Co (1886) L.R. 11 App. Cas. 127, HL *25–008*, *26–013*, *28–061*

Darlington BC v Wiltshier Northern Ltd [1995] 1 W.L.R. 68; [1995] 3 All E.R. 895; [1994] C.L.C. 691; 69 B.L.R. 1; (1995) 11 Const. L.J. 36; (1994) 91(37) L.S.G. 49; (1994) 138 S.J.L.B. 161, CA (Civ Div); reversing 37 Con. L.R. 29, QBD *18–051*, *19–076*, *18–020*, *18–054*, *18–055*, 18–056, *18–058*, 18–059, *18–062*, *18–065*, *18–068*, *18–093*

Darlington Futures Ltd v Delco Australia Pty Ltd (1987) A.L.R. 385 ....*14–005*, *14–007*, *14–008*

Dashwood v Magniac [1891] 3 Ch. 306, CA *12–131*

Dashwood (formerly Kaye) v Fleurets Ltd [2007] EWHC 1610 (QB); [2007] 34 E.G. 84; [2007] 28 E.G. 120 (C.S.), QBD *13–010*

Datec Electronic Holdings Ltd v United Parcels Service Ltd [2007] UKHL 23; [2007] Bus. L.R. 1291; [2007] 1 W.L.R. 1325; [2007] 4 All E.R. 765; [2007] 2 All E.R. (Comm) 1067; [2007] 2 Lloyd's Rep. 114; [2007] 1 C.L.C. 720; [2007] R.T.R. 40; (2007) 151 S.J.L.B. 670, HL; affirming [2005] EWCA Civ 1418; [2006] 2 All E.R. (Comm) 350; [2006] 1 Lloyd's Rep. 279; [2005] 2 C.L.C. 1025, CA (Civ Div); reversing [2005] EWHC 221 (Comm); [2005] 1 Lloyd's Rep. 470, QBD (Comm) 2–009, *2–030*
Daulia Ltd v Four Millbank Nominees Ltd [1978] Ch. 231; [1978] 2 W.L.R. 621; [1978] 2 All E.R. 557; (1978) 36 P. & C.R. 244; (1977) 121 S.J. 851, CA (Civ Div) *2–078*, *2–080*, *2–120*, *3–170*, *4–027*, *4–028*, *4–048*, *12–103*
Daun v City of London Brewery Co (1869) L.R. 8 Eq. 155, Ct of Chancery *12–129*, *13–018*
Daval Aciers D'Usinor et de Sacilor v Armare Srl; The Nerarno [1996] 1 Lloyd's Rep. 1, CA (Civ Div); affirming [1994] 2 Lloyd's Rep. 50, QBD (Admlty) *3–093*, *3–104*
Davenport, Re; sub nom. Bankrupt Ex p. v Eric Street Properties [1963] 1 W.L.R. 817; [1963] 2 All E.R. 850; (1963) 107 S.J. 457, CA *8–018*, *8–043*
David Securities Pty v Commonwealth Bank of Australia, 175 C.L.R. 353, HC (Aus) *29–030*, *29–033*, *29–034*, *29–036*, *29–045*, *29–046*, *29–063*, *29–086*, *29–179*, *29–181*, *29–186*, *29–187*, *29–188*
David T Boyd & Co v Louis Louca [1973] 1 Lloyd's Rep. 209, QBD (Comm) *2–143*
David Taylor & Son v Barnett Trading Co [1953] 1 W.L.R. 562; [1953] 1 All E.R. 843; [1953] 1 Lloyd's Rep. 181; (1953) 97 S.J. 226, CA *16–045*
Davidson v Cooper (1844) M. & W. 343 .... *4–035*, *25–021*, *25–023*
Davidson v Gwynne, 104 E.R. 149; (1810) 12 East 381, KB *24–040*
Davidson v Pillay [1979] I.R.L.R. 275, EAT *16–011*
Davidson v Scottish Ministers (Incidental Petition: Dismissal of Appeal); sub nom. Davidson, Petitioner (No.3) [2005] UKHL 74; 2005 1 S.C. (H.L.) 1, HL *10–015*, *10–018*, 10–019
Davidson v Tullock (1860) 3 Macq. 783 .... *1–122*
Davie v New Merton Board Mills Ltd [1959] A.C. 604; [1959] 2 W.L.R. 331; [1959] 1 All E.R. 346; [1959] 2 Lloyd's Rep. 587; (1959) 103 S.J. 177, HL; affirming [1958] 1 Q.B. 210; [1958] 2 W.L.R. 21; [1958] 1 All E.R. 67; (1958) 102 S.J. 14, CA; reversing [1957] 2 Q.B. 368; [1957] 2 W.L.R. 747; [1957] 2 All E.R. 38; (1957) 101 S.J. 321, QBD *1–147*, *1–152*
Davies Ex p. Cleland, Re (1866–67) L.R. 2 Ch. App. 808, CA in Chancery *20–041*
Davies, Re [1892] 3 Ch. 63 .... *18–073*
Davies, Re; sub nom. Davies v Davies [1892] 3 Ch. 63, Ch D *8–033*, *8–034*
Davies v Collins [1945] 1 All E.R. 247, CA *14–008*, *14–038*, *19–081*, 19–082, *21–004*
Davies v Davies (1887) L.R. 36 Ch. D. 359, CA *2–139*, *16–097*, *16–099*
Davies v Directloans Ltd; sub nom. Davies and Hedley-Cheney v Directloans Ltd [1986] 1 W.L.R. 823; [1986] 2 All E.R. 783; [1986] F.L.R. 382, Ch D *7–138*
Davies v Humphreys, 151 E.R. 361; (1840) 6 M. & W. 153, Ex Ct *17–028*, *28–048*
Davies v Idris Parry (1988) 20 E.G. 92 .... *14–092*
Davies v Leighton (1979) 68 Cr. App. R. 4; [1978] Crim. L.R. 575; (1978) 122 S.J. 641, DC *2–014*
Davies v London and Provincial Marine Insurance Co (1878) L.R. 8 Ch. D. 469; (1878) 26 W.R. 794, Ch D *6–019*, *7–049*, *16–186*
Davies v McLean (1873) 21 W.R. 264 .... *21–009*
Davies v Parry (1988) 20 H.L.R. 452; [1988] 20 E.G. 92; [1988] 21 E.G. 74, QBD *18–022*
Davies v Powell Duffryn Associated Collieries Ltd [1942] A.C. 601, HL *26–030*
Davies v Presbyterian Church of Wales [1986] 1 W.L.R. 323; [1986] 1 All E.R. 705; [1986] I.C.R. 280; [1986] I.R.L.R. 194; (1986) 83 L.S.G. 968; (1986) 130 S.J. 203, HL *2–181*
Davies v Rees (1886) L.R. 17 Q.B.D. 408, CA *29–076*
Davies v Rhondda UDC (1917) 87 L.J.K.B. 166 .... *2–047*

Davies v Sumner; sub nom. Sumner v Davies [1984] 1 W.L.R. 1301; [1984] 3 All E.R. 831; (1985) 149 J.P. 110; [1985] R.T.R. 95; 84 L.G.R. 123; (1985) 149 J.P.N. 11; (1985) 82 L.S.G. 45; (1984) 128 S.J. 814; (1985) 4 Tr. L. 1, HL; affirming [1984] 1 W.L.R. 405; (1984) 81 L.S.G. 360; (1984) 128 S.J. 18, QBD *14–065*
Davies v Swan Motor Co (Swansea) Ltd [1949] 2 K.B. 291; [1949] 1 All E.R. 620; 65 T.L.R. 278, CA *17–035*
Davies v Sweet [1962] 2 Q.B. 300; [1962] 2 W.L.R. 525; [1962] 1 All E.R. 92; (1961) 105 S.J. 1083, CA *2–029*, *4–036*, *4–037*
Davies v Taylor [1974] A.C. 207; [1972] 3 W.L.R. 801; [1972] 3 All E.R. 836; (1972) 116 S.J. 864, HL *26–042*, *26–045*
Davies v Thomas (Restraint of Trade) [1920] 2 Ch. 189, CA; affirming [1920] 1 Ch. 217, Ch D *16–137*
Davis v Churchward, unreported, May 6, 1993 .... *6–052*
Davis v Freethy (1890) L.R. 24 Q.B.D. 519, CA *16–064*
Davis v Garrett (1830) 6 Bing. 716 .... *14–029*
Davis v Gyde, 111 E.R. 240; (1835) 2 Ad. & El. 623, KB *21–076*
Davis v Jones (1856) 17 C.B. 625 .... *1–105*, *12–110*
Davis v Radcliffe [1990] 1 W.L.R. 821; [1990] 2 All E.R. 536; [1990] B.C.C. 472; [1990] B.C.L.C. 647; (1990) 87(19) L.S.G. 43; (1990) 134 S.J. 1078, PC (IoM) *18–036*
Davis v Reilly [1898] 1 Q.B. 1, QBD *21–074*
Davis v Street (1823) 1 C. & P. 18 .... *22–025*, *22–026*
Davis v Temco [1992] 11 C.L. 208, CC (City of London) *12–132*
Davis & Co (Wines) Ltd v Afa-Minerva (EMI) Ltd [1974] 2 Lloyd's Rep. 27; 9 B.L.R. 99, QBD *6–069*, *6–100*, *13–030*
Davis & Co Ex p. Rawlings, Re (1889) L.R. 22 Q.B.D. 193, CA *20–026*
Davis & Primrose Ltd v Clyde Shipbuilding & Engineering Co Ltd, 1917 1 S.L.T. 297, OH *23–082*
Davis Contractors v Fareham Urban DC [1956] A.C. 696; [1956] 3 W.L.R. 37; [1956] 2 All E.R. 145; 54 L.G.R. 289; (1956) 100 S.J. 378, HL; affirming [1955] 1 Q.B. 302; [1955] 2 W.L.R. 388; [1955] 1 All E.R. 275; (1955) 99 S.J. 109, CA .. 1–020, *12–119*, *23–007*, 23–011, 23–012, 23–014, 23–015, *23–016*, *23–021*, *23–035*, *23–047*, 23–050, *23–059*, *24–003*
Davstone Estates Ltd's Leases, Re; sub nom. Manprop Ltd v O'Dell [1969] 2 Ch. 378; [1969] 2 W.L.R. 1287; [1969] 2 All E.R. 849; (1969) 20 P. & C.R. 395; (1969) 113 S.J. 366, Ch D *16–048*
Davy Offshore Ltd v Emerald Field Contracting Ltd [1992] 2 Lloyd's Rep. 142, CA (Civ Div); affirming 55 B.L.R. 1; 27 Con. L.R. 138, QBD *12–073*, *13–011*, *13–012*
Dawes Ex p. *See* Husband Ex p. Dawes, Re
Dawes v Tredwell (1880–81) L.R. 18 Ch. D. 354, CA *12–066*, *13–025*
Dawkins v Antrobus (1881) L.R. 17 Ch. D. 615, Ch D *9–075*
Dawnay Day & Co Ltd v de Braconier d'Alphen [1998] I.C.R. 1068; [1997] I.R.L.R. 442; (1997) 94(26) L.S.G. 30; (1997) 141 S.J.L.B. 129, CA (Civ Div); affirming [1997] I.R.L.R. 285, Ch D *16–093*, *16–119*
Dawson v Great Northern & City Railway Co [1905] 1 K.B. 260, CA; reversing [1904] 1 K.B. 277, KBD *16–060*, *19–008*, *19–049*, 19–074
Dawson v Linton (1822) 5 B. Ald. 521 .... *29–103*, *29–107*
Dawson v Remnant (1806) 6 Esp. 24 .... *29–191*
Dawson v Wrench (1849) 3 Exch. 359 .... *21–009*
Dawson v Yeoward [1961] 1 Lloyd's Rep. 431, CA *12–003*
Dawson (Bradford) Ltd v Dove [1971] 1 Q.B. 330; [1971] 2 W.L.R. 1; [1971] 1 All E.R. 554; (1970) 114 S.J. 974, QBD *20–004*, *20–005*
Dawsons Ltd v Bonnin [1922] 2 A.C. 413; (1922) 12 Ll. L. Rep. 237; 1922 S.C. (H.L.) 156; 1922 S.L.T. 444, HL; affirming, 1921 S.C. 511; 1921 1 S.L.T. 324, IH (2 Div) *6–147*, *6–149*, *12–026*
Day v McLea (1889) L.R. 22 Q.B.D. 610, CA *22–022*

Day & Dent Constructions Pty (In Liquidation) v North Australian Properties Pty (Provisional Liquidator Appointed) (1982) 40 A.L.R. 399 .... *20–041*

Day v William Hill (Park Lane) Ltd [1949] 1 K.B. 632; [1949] 1 All E.R. 219; 65 T.L.R. 73; [1949] L.J.R. 689; (1949) 93 S.J. 163, CA *29–191*

Day's Will Trusts, Re; sub nom. Day's Will Trusts, Re, Lloyds Bank v Shafe [1962] 1 W.L.R. 1419; 106 S.J. 856; [1962] 3 All E.R. 699 .... *2–112*

Days Medical Aids Ltd v Pihsiang Machinery Manufacturing Co Ltd [2004] EWHC 44 (Comm); [2004] 1 All E.R. (Comm) 991; [2004] 2 C.L.C. 489; [2004] U.K.C.L.R. 384; [2004] E.C.C. 21; [2004] Eu. L.R. 477, QBD (Comm) *16–105*, *16–121*

De Beers Consolidated Mines Ltd v British South Africa Co; sub nom. British South Africa Co v De Beers Consolidated Mines Ltd [1912] A.C. 52, HL; reversing [1910] 2 Ch. 502, CA; affirming [1910] 1 Ch. 354, Ch D *9–004*, *30–011*, *30–012*, *30–015*, *30–082*

De Bueger v J Ballantyne & Co Ltd [1938] A.C. 452, PC (NZ) *30–370*

De Bussche v Alt (1878) L.R. 8 Ch. D. 286, CA *22–004*, *28–136*

De Cicco v Schweitzer (1917) 221 N.Y. 413; 117 N.E. 807 .... *3–073*

De Francesco v Barnum (1890) L.R. 45 Ch. D. 430, Ch D *8–023*, *8–029*, *8–045*

De Jongh Weill v Mean Fiddler Holdings [2005] All E.R. (D) 331 ...... 18–048, *27–040*

De la Bere v Pearson Ltd [1908] 1 K.B. 280, CA; affirming [1907] 1 K.B. 483, KBD *3–178*, *26–035*

de la Warr (Earl) v Miles (1881) L.R. 17 Ch. D. 535, CA *12–126*

De Lasala v De Lasala [1980] A.C. 546; [1979] 3 W.L.R. 390; [1979] 2 All E.R. 1146; [1980] F.S.R. 443; (1979) 123 S.J. 301, PC (HK) *5–062*

De Lassalle v Guildford [1901] 2 K.B. 215, CA *5–062*, *12–003*, 12–004, *12–006*, *12–103*, *22–036*

De Marney, Re; sub nom. Official Receiver, Ex p. v Salaman [1943] Ch. 126, Ch D *20–026*

De Mattos v Benjamin (1894) 63 L.J.Q.B. 248 .... *16–192*

De Mattos v Gibson, 45 E.R. 108; (1858) 4 De G. & J. 276, QB ... 1–188, 18–139, 18–140, *18–143*, *27–026*, *27–070*

De Mautort v Saunders (1830) 1 B. & Ad. 399 .... *17–010*

De Meza & Stuart v Apple van Straten Shena & Stone [1975] 1 Lloyd's Rep. 498, CA (Civ Div) *26–049*

De Molestina v Ponton [2002] 1 Lloyd's Rep. 271, QBD (Comm) 6–118

De Nicols v Curlier (No.2); sub nom. De Nicols, Re [1900] 2 Ch. 410, Ch D *4–012*

De Pina v MS Birka Beutler Schiffahrts KG; The Birka [1996] 1 Lloyd's Rep. 31, CA (Civ Div) *28–116*

De Roo v Foster (1862) 12 C.B. (N.S.) 272 .... *8–050*

De Rosaz, In the Goods of (1876–77) L.R. 2 P.D. 66, PDAD *12–125*

De Serville v Argee Ltd [2001] N.P.C. 82; (2001) 82 P. & C.R. DG12, Ch D *4–059*, *4–071*

De Stacpoole v De Stacpoole; sub nom. De Stacpoole v Seymour; De Stacpoole v Stapleton; De Stacpoole, Re (1888) L.R. 37 Ch. D. 139, Ch D *8–013*

De Tchihatchef v Salerni Coupling Ltd [1932] 1 Ch. 330, Ch D *6–013*

De Wütz v Hendricks (1824) 2 Bing. 314 .... 16–031, *30–367*

Dean v Ainley [1987] 1 W.L.R. 1729; [1987] 3 All E.R. 748; (1987) 284 E.G. 1244; (1987) 84 L.S.G. 2450; (1987) 131 S.J. 1589, CA (Civ Div) *26–008*

Dean v Allin & Watts [2001] EWCA Civ 758; [2001] 2 Lloyd's Rep. 249; [2001] Lloyd's Rep. P.N. 605; [2001] P.N.L.R. 39; (2001) 98(31) L.S.G. 36; (2001) 145 S.J.L.B. 157, CA (Civ Div); reversing [2000] Lloyd's Rep. P.N. 469; [2000] P.N.L.R. 690; [2000] E.G. 5 (C.S.), Ch D *1–184*, *4–059*, *18–029*, *18–038*

Dean v James (1833) 4 B. Ad. 546 .... *21–085*

Dean v Newhall (1799) 8 T.R. 168 .... *17–017*

Deanplan Ltd v Mahmoud [1993] Ch. 151; [1992] 3 W.L.R. 467; [1992] 3 All E.R. 945; (1992) 64 P. & C.R. 409; [1992] 1 E.G.L.R. 79; [1992] 16 E.G. 100; [1992] E.G. 30 (C.S.); [1992] N.P.C. 31, Ch D *17–001*, *17–017*, *17–020*

Dearle v Hall, 38 E.R. 475; (1828) 3 Russ. 1, Ch D 19–068, 19–085

Deaway Trading v Calverley [1973] 3 All E.R. 776; [1973] I.C.R. 546; [1973] I.T.R. 562, NIRC *9–050*

Debenham v Ox (1749) 1 Ves.Sen. 276 .... *16–006*

Debenham v Sawbridge [1901] 2 Ch. 98, Ch D *27–056*, *29–057*

Debtor (No.82 of 1926), Re [1927] 1 Ch. 410, Ch D *20–041*

Debtor (No.229 of 1927), Re [1927] 2 Ch. 367, CA *20–049*

Debtor (No.564 of 1949), Re; sub nom. Customs and Excise Commissioners, Ex p. v Debtor [1950] Ch. 282; [1950] 1 All E.R. 308; 66 T.L.R. (Pt. 1) 313; (1950) 94 S.J. 113, CA *8–018*

Debtor (No.66 of 1955), Re; sub nom. Debtor v Waite's Trustee; Debtor, Ex p. v Trustee of the Property of Waite (A Bankrupt) [1956] 1 W.L.R. 1226; [1956] 3 All E.R. 225; (1956) 100 S.J. 649, CA; affirming [1956] 1 W.L.R. 480; [1956] 2 All E.R. 94; (1956) 100 S.J. 320, Ch D *20–041*

Debtor (No.1 of 1987), Re [1989] 1 W.L.R. 271; [1989] 2 All E.R. 46; (1989) 86(16) L.S.G. 35; (1989) 133 S.J. 290, CA (Civ Div); affirmi [1988] 1 W.L.R. 419; [1988] 1 All E.R. 959; (1988) 132 S.J. 375, Ch D *20–018*

Debtor (No.2389 of 1989), Re A [1991] Fam. Law 326; [1991] 2 W.L.R. 578; [1990] 3 All E.R. 984 .... *20–050*

Debtor (No.259 of 1990), Re [1992] 1 W.L.R. 226; [1992] 1 All E.R. 641, Ch D *3–125*, *20–050*

Debtor (No.51/SD/1991), Re [1992] 1 W.L.R. 1294; [1993] 2 All E.R. 40, Ch D *20–018*, *30–376*

Debtor (No.50A-SD–1995), Re; sub nom. Jelly v All Type Roofing Co [1997] Ch. 310; [1997] 2 W.L.R. 57; [1997] 2 All E.R. 789; [1997] B.C.C. 465; [1997] 1 B.C.L.C. 280; [1996] B.P.I.R. 565, Ch D *28–070*

Debtors (Nos.4449 and 4450 of 1998), Re; sub nom. McAllister v Society of Lloyd's [1999] 1 All E.R. (Comm) 149; [1999] B.P.I.R. 548; [1999] Lloyd's Rep. I.R. 487, Ch D *2–136*, *2–138*

Decoma UK Ltd v Haden DrysysInternational Ltd [2005] EWHC 2948 (TCC), (2005) 103 Const. L.R. 1 .... *12–082*

Decouvreur v Jordan, *The Times*, May 25, 1987, CA (Civ Div) *4–034*

Decroix v Meyer. *See* H Meyer & Co Ltd v Jules Decroix Verley et Cie

Decro-Wall International SA v Practitioners in Marketing [1971] 1 W.L.R. 361; [1971] 2 All E.R. 216; (1970) 115 S.J. 171, CA (Civ Div) *21–013*, *24–001*, *24–010*, *24–040*, *27–008*, *27–070*

Deeley v Lloyds Bank Ltd [1912] A.C. 756, HL *21–061*, *21–066*

Deeny v Gooda Walker Ltd (No.2); Albert v Gooda Walker Ltd; Brownrigg v Gooda Walker Ltd [1996] 1 W.L.R. 426; [1996] 1 All E.R. 933; [1996] L.R.L.R. 109; [1996] S.T.C. 299; [1996] 5 Re. L.R. 43; (1996) 93(15) L.S.G. 32; (1996) 146 N.L.J. 369; (1996) 140 S.J.L.B. 92, HL *26–160*, *26–163*

Deeny v Gooda Walker Ltd (No.3) [1995] 1 W.L.R. 1206; [1995] 4 All E.R. 289; [1996] L.R.L.R. 176; [1995] C.L.C. 623; [1995] 4 Re. L.R. 117, QBD (Comm) *26–013*

Deep Vein Thrombosis and Air Travel Group Litigation, Re [2005] UKHL 72; [2006] 1 A.C. 495; [2005] 3 W.L.R. 1320; [2006] 1 All E.R. 786; [2006] 1 All E.R. (Comm) 313; [2006] 1 Lloyd's Rep. 231; [2005] 2 C.L.C. 1083; [2006] P.I.Q.R. P14; (2006) 87 B.M.L.R. 1; (2006) 103(3) L.S.G. 26; (2005) 155 N.L.J. 1925; (2006) 150 S.J.L.B. 29, HL; affirming [2003] EWCA Civ 1005; [2004] Q.B. 234; [2003] 3 W.L.R. 956; [2004] 1 All E.R. 445; [2004] 1 All E.R. (Comm) 459; [2004] 1 Lloyd's Rep. 316; [2003] 2 C.L.C. 884; [2003] P.I.Q.R. P35; (2004) 76 B.M.L.R. 38; (2003) 100(35) L.S.G. 34; (2003) 147 S.J.L.B. 869, CA (Civ Div); affirming [2002] EWHC 2825 (QB); [2003] 1 All E.R. 935; [2003] 1 All E.R. (Comm) 418; (2003) 71 B.M.L.R. 82, QBD *18–034*

Deepak Fertilisers & Petrochemicals Corp Ltd v Davy McKee (London) Ltd; sub nom. Deepak Fertilisers & Petrochemicals Corp Ltd v ICI Chemicals & Polymers Ltd; Deepak Fertilisers & Petrochemical Corp Ltd v Davy McKee (UK) London Ltd [1999] 1 All E.R. (Comm.) 69; [1999] 1 Lloyd's Rep. 387; [1999] B.L.R. 41; (1999) 1 T.C.L.R. 200; 62 Con. L.R. 86, CA (Civ Div); reversing in part [1998] 2 Lloyd's Rep. 139, QBD (Comm) *12–104*, *14–006*, *14–015*, *14–042*, *14–050*, *14–051*, *18–070*, *30–309*
Deering v Earl of Winchelsea (1787) 1 Cox 318; 2 Bos. & P. 270 .... *17–027*
Definitely Maybe (Touring) Ltd v Marek Lieberberg Konzertagentur GmbH (No.2); sub nom. Definitely Maybe (Touring) Ltd v Marck Lieberberg Konzertagentur GmbH (No.2) [2001] 1 W.L.R. 1745; [2001] 4 All E.R. 283; [2001] 2 All E.R. (Comm) 1; [2001] 2 Lloyd's Rep. 455; [2002] C.L.C. 360; [2002] I.L.Pr. 9, QBD (Comm) *30–020*, *30–077*, *30–090*
Defries v Davis (1835) 1 Scott. 594 .... *8–046*
Defries v Milne [1913] 1 Ch. 98, CA *16–060*, *19–049*
Deglman v Guaranty Trust Co of Canada and Constantineau [1954] 3 D.L.R. 78; [1954] S.C.R. 725 .... 4–087, *29–015*, 29–080
Deichland, The. *See* Owners of Cargo Lately Laden on Board the Deichland v Owners and/or Demise Charterers of the Deichland; The Deichland
Delaney v Staples (t/a De Montfort Recruitment) [1992] 1 A.C. 687; [1992] 2 W.L.R. 451; [1992] 1 All E.R. 944; [1992] I.C.R. 483; [1992] I.R.L.R. 191; (1992) 142 N.L.J. 384, HL *27–066*, *27–068*
Delaney v TP Smith Ltd [1946] K.B. 393, CA *4–041*
Delauney v Strickland (1818) 2 Stark. 416 .... *9–073*
Deloitte Haskins & Sells v National Mutual Life Nominees [1993] A.C. 774; [1993] 3 W.L.R. 347; [1993] 2 All E.R. 1015; [1993] B.C.L.C. 1174; (1993) 143 N.L.J. 883; (1993) 137 S.J.L.B. 152, PC (NZ) *18–036*
Delzenne (Francis) v Klee (1968) 112 S.J. 583 .... *16–197*
Demerara Bauxite Co Ltd v Hubbard [1923] A.C. 673, PC (WI) *7–062*, *7–076*
Den Norske Bank ASA v Acemex Management Co Ltd; The Tropical Reefer [2003] EWCA Civ 1559; [2004] 1 All E.R. (Comm) 904; [2004] 1 Lloyd's Rep. 1; [2005] 1 B.C.L.C. 274; [2003] 2 C.L.C. 910, CA (Civ Div); affirming [2003] EWHC 326; [2003] 2 All E.R. (Comm) 318, QBD (Comm) *18–143*
Denaby Main Colliery Co Ltd v Manchester Sheffield and Lincolnshire Railway Co; sub nom. Manchester, Sheffield and Lincolnshire Railway Co v Denaby Main Colliery Co (1886) L.R. 11 App. Cas. 97, HL *29–097*
Denby v Moore, 106 E.R. 46; (1817) 1 B. & Ald. 123, KB *29–111*
Dendy v Henderson (1855) 11 Ech. 194 .... *16–110*
Denfleet InternationalLtd v TNT Global SPA. *See* TNT Global SpA v Denfleet International Ltd
Denham v Midland Employers Mutual Assurance [1955] 2 Q.B. 437; [1955] 3 W.L.R. 84; [1955] 2 All E.R. 561; [1955] 1 Lloyd's Rep. 467; (1955) 99 S.J. 417, CA; affirming [1955] 1 Lloyd's Rep. 245, QBD *19–055*
Denholm Fishselling Ltd v Anderson, 1991 S.L.T. (Sh. Ct.) 24, Sh Pr *14–085*
Denison v Ralphson (1682) 1 Vent. 365 .... *1–118*
Denman v Brise [1949] 1 K.B. 22; [1948] 2 All E.R. 141; 64 T.L.R. 335; [1948] L.J.R. 1388; (1948) 92 S.J. 349, CA *23–055*
Denmark Productions v Boscobel Productions [1969] 1 Q.B. 699; [1968] 3 W.L.R. 841; [1968] 3 All E.R. 513; (1968) 112 S.J. 761, CA (Civ Div); affirming in part (1967) 111 S.J. 715 .... *8–028*, *8–058*, *13–006*, *23–061*, *24–003*, *24–010*, *24–013*, *24–014*, *24–035*
Dennant v Skinner and Collom [1948] 2 K.B. 164; [1948] 2 All E.R. 29; [1948] L.J.R. 1576, KBD *5–089*, *5–092*
Denne v Light, 44 E.R. 588; (1857) 8 De G.M. & G. 774, QB 27–031
Denney v John Hudson & Co *See* SA&D Wright Ltd, Re
Dennis v London Passenger Transport Board [1948] 1 All E.R. 779; 64 T.L.R. 269; (1948) 92 S.J. 350, KBD *18–076*
Dennis & Co v Munn [1949] 2 K.B. 327; [1949] 1 All E.R. 616; 65 T.L.R. 251; [1949] L.J.R. 857; (1949) 93 S.J. 181, CA *16–154*

Dennis (A Bankrupt), Re; sub nom. Dennis v Goodman [1996] Ch. 80; [1995] 3 W.L.R. 367; [1995] 3 All E.R. 171; [1995] 2 F.L.R. 387; [1995] 3 F.C.R. 760; [1995] Fam. Law 611; [1995] N.P.C. 61, CA (Civ Div); reversing [1993] Ch. 72; [1992] 3 W.L.R. 204; [1992] 3 All E.R. 436; [1993] 1 F.L.R. 313; [1993] 1 F.C.R. 941, Ch D *20–019*
Denny Mott & Dickson Ltd v James B Fraser & Co Ltd; sub nom. James B Fraser & Co Ltd v Denny Mott & Dickson Ltd [1944] A.C. 265; 1944 S.C. (H.L.) 35; 1945 S.L.T. 2, HL; affirming 1943 S.C. 293; 1944 S.L.T. 139, IH (2 Div) ...*1–020*, *23–007*, *23–011*, *23–016*, 23–025, *23–047*, *23–057*, *23–058*
Denny v Conklin [1913] 3 K.B. 177, KBD *19–016*
Denny v Hancock (No.1) (1870–71) L.R. 6 Ch. App. 1, CA in Chancery *5–077*
Dent v Bennett (1839) 4 My. & Cr. App. R. 269 .... *3–026*
Dent v Davis Blank Furniss [2001] Lloyd's Rep. P.N. 534, Ch D *26–093*
Denton v GN Ry (1856) 5 E. & B. 860 ....*2–021*, *3–015*, *6–046*
Denys v Shuckburgh (1840) 4 Y. & C. Ex. 42 .... *28–140*
Department of the Environment v Thomas Bates & Sons Ltd [1991] 1 A.C. 499; [1990] 3 W.L.R. 457; [1990] 2 All E.R. 943; 50 B.L.R. 61; 21 Con. L.R. 54; [1990] 46 E.G. 115; [1990] E.G. 104 (C.S.); (1990) 134 S.J. 1077, HL; affirming [1989] 1 All E.R. 1075; 44 B.L.R. 88; 13 Con. L.R. 1; [1989] 26 E.G. 121; [1988] E.G. 165 (C.S.); (1989) 139 N.L.J. 39, CA (Civ Div); affirming 36 B.L.R. 104; (1987) 3 Const. L.J. 130, QBD (OR) *1–176*, *14–056*, *18–027*, *18–036*, *28–055*
Deposit Protection Board v Barclays Bank Plc; sub nom. Deposit Protection Board v Dalia; Depositors Protection Fund v Barclays Bank Plc [1994] 2 A.C. 367; [1994] 2 W.L.R. 732; [1994] 2 All E.R. 577; [1994] 2 B.C.L.C. 227; (1994) 91(25) L.S.G. 30; (1994) 138 S.J.L.B. 123, HL; reversing [1994] 1 All E.R. 539; (1993) 143 N.L.J. 781; (1993) 137 S.J.L.B. 143, CA (Civ Div); affirming [1993] Ch. 243; [1992] 3 W.L.R. 945; [1993] 1 All E.R. 599; [1994] 1 B.C.L.C. 510; (1992) 89(42) L.S.G. 36; [1992] N.P.C. 90, Ch D *19–020*
Deputy Commissioner of Taxation (NSW) v Chamberlain (1990) 93 A.L.R. 729, Fed Ct (Aus) *5–074*, *5–078*
Derby & Co Ltd v Weldon (No.9), *The Times*, November 9, 1990, CA (Civ Div); affirming [1991] 1 W.L.R. 652; [1991] 2 All E.R. 901, Ch D *12–048*
Derby Resources AG v Blue Corinth Marine Co Ltd; The Athenian Harmony (No.2) [1998] 2 Lloyd's Rep. 425, QBD (Comm) *26–178*
Dermatine Co v Ashworth (1905) 21 T.L.R. 510 .... *12–122*
Derrick v Williams [1939] 2 All E.R. 559; (1939) 55 T.L.R. 676, CA *29–047*
Derry v Peek; sub nom. Peek v Derry (1889) L.R. 14 App. Cas. 337; (1889) 5 T.L.R. 625, HL; reversing (1888) L.R. 37 Ch. D. 541, CA *1–122*, *1–131*, 5–026, 6–043, 6–044, 6–067, 6–079, *6–090*, *6–153*
Desert Sun Loan Corp v Hill [1996] 2 All E.R. 847; [1996] 5 Bank. L.R. 98; [1996] C.L.C. 1132; [1996] I.L.Pr. 406; (1996) 140 S.J.L.B. 64, CA (Civ Div) *25–018*
Design Company, The v Elizabeth King, unreported, July 7, 1992, CA *24–019*
Despina R, The. *See* Owners of the Eleftherotria v Owners of the Despina R
Deuchar v Gas Light & Coke Co [1925] A.C. 691, HL; affirming [1924] 2 Ch. 426, CA; affirming [1924] 1 Ch. 422, Ch D *9–022*, *10–025*
Deutsche Bank (London Agency) v Beriro & Co (1895) 1 Com. Cas. 123 ....*29–030*, *29–176*, *29–178*
Deutsche Bank AG v Ibrahim, *Financial Times*, December 13, 1991; *Financial Times*, December 13, 1991 ....*4–014*, 4–059
Deutsche Conti-Handelsgesellschaft m.b.H. v Bremer Handelsgesellschaft mbH [1984] 1 Lloyd's Rep. 447 .... *14–141*
Deutsche Genossenschaftsbank v Burnhope [1995] 1 W.L.R. 1580; [1995] 4 All E.R. 717; [1996] 1 Lloyd's Rep. 113; [1996] 5 Bank. L.R. 109; [1996] B.C.C. 180; (1995) 145 N.L.J. 1719; (1996) 140 S.J.L.B. 21, HL; reversing [1995] B.C.C. 488, CA (Civ Div); reversing [1993] 2 Lloyd's Rep. 518, QBD (Comm) *12–043*, *12–061*

Deutsche Morgan Grenfell Group Plc v Inland Revenue Commissioners; sub nom. Inland Revenue Commissioners v Deutsche Morgan Grenfell Group Plc; Deutsche Morgan Grenfell Group Plc v Revenue and Customs Commissioners [2006] UKHL 49; [2007] 1 A.C. 558; [2006] 3 W.L.R. 781; [2007] 1 All E.R. 449; [2007] S.T.C. 1; [2007] 1 C.M.L.R. 14; [2007] Eu. L.R. 226; 78 T.C. 120; [2006] B.T.C. 781; 9 I.T.L. Rep. 201; [2006] S.T.I. 2386; (2006) 103(43) L.S.G. 29; (2006) 150 S.J.L.B. 1430, HL; reversing [2005] EWCA Civ 78; [2006] Ch. 243; [2006] 2 W.L.R. 103; [2005] 3 All E.R. 1025; [2005] S.T.C. 329; [2005] Eu. L.R. 553; [2005] B.T.C. 126; 7 I.T.L. Rep. 476; [2005] S.T.I. 194; (2005) 102(10) L.S.G. 30; [2005] N.P.C. 18, CA (Civ Div); reversing in part [2003] EWHC 1779 (Ch); [2003] 4 All E.R. 645; [2003] S.T.C. 1017; [2003] Eu. L.R. 838; [2003] B.T.C. 497; 5 I.T.L. Rep. 1067; [2003] S.T.I. 1269; (2003) 100(36) L.S.G. 41; (2003) 153 N.L.J. 1171, Ch D *4–086*, *28–088*, *29–001*, 29–016, *29–034*, 29–035, *29–043*, *29–045*, *29–047*, *29–048*, 29–084, *29–085*, *29–086*, *29–187*
Deutsche Schachtbau- und Tiefbohrgesellschaft mbH v Ras Al-Khaimah National Oil Co; sub nom. DST v Rakoil; Deutsche Schachtbau- und Tiefbohrgesellschaft mbH v Ras Al-Khaimah National Oil Co (Garnishee Proceedings); Deutsche Schachtbau- und Tiefbohrgesellschaft mbH v Shell International Petroleum Co Ltd (Nos.1 and 2) [1990] 1 A.C. 295; [1988] 3 W.L.R. 230; [1988] 2 All E.R. 833; [1988] 2 Lloyd's Rep. 293; (1988) 85(28) L.S.G. 45, HL; reversing [1987] 3 W.L.R. 1023; [1987] 2 All E.R. 769; [1987] 2 Lloyd's Rep. 246; [1987] 1 F.T.L.R. 17; (1987) 131 S.J. 1486, CA (Civ Div) *2–140*
Deux v Jefferies (1594) Cro.Eliz. 352 .... *22–006*
Deveaux v Conolly (1849) 8 C.B. 640 .... *29–062*
Dever re Suse and Sibeth, Ex p. *See* Suse & Sibeth Ex p. Dever, Re
Deveze Ex p. Barnett, Re (1873–74) L.R. 9 Ch. App. 293, CA in Chancery *20–041*
Devine v Jefferys (A Firm) [2001] Lloyd's Rep. P.N. 301; [2001] P.N.L.R. 16, QBD (Merc) *26–093*
Devonald v Rosser & Sons [1906] 2 K.B. 728, CA *12–091*, *12–129*
Dew v Parsons (1819) 2 B. Ald. 562 .... *29–094*
Dewar v Mintoft [1912] 2 K.B. 373, KBD *4–023*, *4–038*, *24–051*
Dews v National Coal Board [1988] A.C. 1; [1987] 3 W.L.R. 38; [1987] 2 All E.R. 545; [1987] I.C.R. 602; [1987] I.R.L.R. 330; [1987] 2 F.T.L.R. 284; (1987) 84 L.S.G. 2044; (1987) 137 N.L.J. 545, HL *26–162*
Dextra Bank & Trust Co Ltd v Bank of Jamaica [2002] 1 All E.R. (Comm) 193, PC (Jam) *29–033*, *29–034*, 29–036, *29–179*, *29–180*, *29–183*, 29–184
Dey v Pullinger Engineering Co [1921] 1 K.B. 77, KBD *9–042*
Deyong v Shenburn [1946] K.B. 227, CA *13–010*
Di Ferdinando v Simon Smits & Co Ltd [1920] 3 K.B. 409; (1920) 4 Ll. L. Rep. 264; 11 A.L.R. 358, CA *26–080*, *30–376*
Di Sora v Phillips (1863) 10 H.L.C. 624 .... *12–121*
Diamond, The [1906] P. 282, PDAD *14–146*
Diamond v Bank of London and Montreal [1979] Q.B. 333; [1979] 2 W.L.R. 228; [1979] 1 All E.R. 561; [1979] 1 Lloyd's Rep. 335; (1978) 122 S.J. 814, CA (Civ Div) *2–050*
Diamond v Campbell Jones [1961] Ch. 22; [1960] 2 W.L.R. 568; [1960] 1 All E.R. 583; 53 R. & I.T. 502; (1960) 39 A.T.C. 103; [1960] T.R. 131; (1960) 104 S.J. 249, Ch D *26–040*, *26–060*, *26–068*, *26–091*, *26–163*
Diamond Cutting Works Federation Ltd v Triefus & Co Ltd [1956] 1 Lloyd's Rep. 216, QBD *26–111*
Dibbins v Dibbins [1896] 2 Ch. 348, Ch D *21–013*
Dibbs v Goren (1849) 11 Beav. 439 .... *29–043*
Dick v US, 82 F.Supp. 326 (1949) *2–058*
Dick Bentley Productions Ltd v Harold Smith (Motors) Ltd [1965] 1 W.L.R. 623; [1965] 2 All E.R. 65; (1965) 109 S.J. 329, CA *6–094*, 12–003

Dicker v Scammell; sub nom. Scammell v Dicker [2005] EWCA Civ 405; [2005] 3 All E.R. 838; [2006] 1 P. & C.R. 4; [2005] 3 E.G.L.R. 61; [2005] 42 E.G. 236, CA (Civ Div); reversing [2003] EWHC 1601 (QB); [2003] N.P.C. 90, QBD *2–088*, *2–115*, *2–128*, *2–139*, *2–140*, *2–142*, 2–145
Dickinson v Abel [1969] 1 W.L.R. 295; [1969] 1 All E.R. 484; 45 T.C. 353; [1968] T.R. 419; (1968) 112 S.J. 967, Ch D *3–013*, *3–036*
Dickinson v Barrow [1904] 2 Ch. 339, Ch D *4–042*, *4–047*
Dickinson v Burrell; Stourton v Burrell; Dickinson (Ann) v Burrell (1865–66) L.R. 1 Eq. 337, Ct of Chancery *16–061*, *19–049*
Dickinson v Del Solar [1930] 1 K.B. 376; (1929) 34 Ll. L. Rep. 445, KBD *11–020*
Dickinson v Dodds (1875–76) L.R. 2 Ch. D. 463, CA 2–088, *2–089*, 2–090, *2–099*, *3–172*
Dickinson v Jones Alexander & Co [1993] 2 F.L.R. 521; [1990] Fam. Law 137; (1989) 139 N.L.J. 1525, QBD *26–044*, *26–165*
Dickinson v Shee (1801) 4 Esp. 67 .... *21–088*
Dickinson UK v Zwebner. *See* Becton Dickinson UK v Zwebner
Dickson v Pharmaceutical Society of Great Britain. *See* Pharmaceutical Society of Great Britain v Dickson
Didymi Corp v Atlantic Lines and Navigation Co Inc; The Didymi [1988] 2 Lloyd's Rep. 108, CA (Civ Div); affirming [1987] 2 Lloyd's Rep. 166, QBD (Comm) *2–130*, *2–131*, *2–140*
Dies v British & International Mining and Finance Corp Ltd [1939] 1 K.B. 724, KBD *24–051*, *26–150*, 26–154, *29–058*, *29–061*, *29–065*
Diesen v Samson, 1971 S.L.T. (Sh. Ct.) 49, Sh Ct (Glasgow) *26–083*
Diestal v Stevenson [1906] 2 K.B. 345, KBD *26–129*, *26–135*
Dietmann v Brent LBC; sub nom. Dietman v Brent LBC [1988] I.C.R. 842; [1988] I.R.L.R. 299, CA (Civ Div); affirming [1987] I.C.R. 737; [1987] I.R.L.R. 259, QBD *1–195*
Dietz v Lennig Chemicals Ltd [1969] 1 A.C. 170; [1967] 3 W.L.R. 165; [1967] 2 All E.R. 282; (1967) 111 S.J. 354, HL; affirming [1966] 1 W.L.R. 1349; [1966] 2 All E.R. 962; (1966) 110 S.J. 448, CA *5–062*, *6–114*, *22–021*
Digby v General Accident Fire and Life Assurance Corp Ltd [1943] A.C. 121; [1942] 2 All E.R. 319; (1942) 73 Ll. L. Rep. 175, HL; reversing [1940] 2 K.B. 226; [1940] 3 All E.R. 190; (1940) 67 Ll. L. Rep. 205, CA; reversing [1940] 1 K.B. 643; [1940] 1 All E.R. 514; (1940) 66 Ll. L. Rep. 89, KBD *12–057*
Diggle v Higgs (1876–77) L.R. 2 Ex. D. 422, CA *29–197*
Dillingham v Harrison [1917] W.N. 305 .... *8–022*
Dillon, Re; sub nom. Duffin v Duffin (1890) L.R. 44 Ch. D. 76, CA *28–039*
Dillon v Baltic Shipping Co; The Mikhail Lermontov [1991] 2 Lloyd's Rep. 155, CA (NSW); affirming [1990] 1 Lloyd's Rep. 579, Sup Ct (NSW) .. *2–021*, *12–010*, *12–015*
Dillwyn v Llewelyn, 45 E.R. 1285; (1862) 4 De G.F. & J. 517, QB *3–106*, 3–139, 3–141, 3–142, *3–143*, 3–149, 3–151, *3–162*, *3–163*, *29–161*
Dilmitis v Niland (1965) (3) S.A. 492 .... *29–144*
Dimmock v Hallett (1866–67) L.R. 2 Ch. App. 21; (1866) 12 Jur. N.S. 953; (1866) 15 W.R. 93, CA in Chancery *6–006*, *27–057*
Dimond v Lovell [2002] 1 A.C. 384; [2000] 2 W.L.R. 1121; [2000] 2 All E.R. 897; [2000] R.T.R. 243; [2000] C.C.L.R. 57; 2000 Rep. L.R. 62; (2000) 97(22) L.S.G. 47; (2000) 150 N.L.J. 740, HL *26–115*, *29–079*, *29–133*
Dimsdale Developments (South East) Ltd v De Haan (1984) 47 P. & C.R. 1, Ch D *21–014*
Dimskal Shipping Co SA v International Transport Workers Federation; The Evia Luck (No.2) [1992] 2 A.C. 152; [1991] 3 W.L.R. 875; [1991] 4 All E.R. 871; [1992] 1 Lloyd's Rep. 115; [1992] I.C.R. 37; [1992] I.R.L.R. 78, HL; affirming [1990] 1 Lloyd's Rep. 319; [1990] I.C.R. 694; [1990] I.R.L.R. 102, CA (Civ Div); reversing [1989] 1 Lloyd's Rep. 166, QBD (Comm) *7–005*, *7–013*, 7–018, *7–024*, *7–026*, 7–027, *7–037*, *7–055*, *29–088*, *29–143*, *29–150*, *30–109*, *30–305*, *30–308*, *30–367*
Dingle v Associated Newspapers Ltd. *See* Associated Newspapers Ltd v Dingle

Dinkha Latchin v General Mediterranean Holdings SA. *See* Latchin (t/a Dinkha Latchin Associates) v General Mediterranean Holdings SA
Diocese of Southwark v Coker; sub nom. Coker v Diocese of Southwark [1998] I.C.R. 140; (1997) 94(29) L.S.G. 29; (1997) 141 S.J.L.B. 169, CA (Civ Div); affirming [1996] I.C.R. 896, EAT; reversing [1995] I.C.R. 563, IT *2–181*
Diplock, Re. *See* Ministry of Health v Simpson
Diptford Parish Lands, Re; sub nom. Charitable Trusts Act 1853 to 1925, Re [1934] Ch. 151, Ch D *19–006*
Direct Travel Insurance v McGeown. *See* McGeown v Direct Travel Insurance
Director General of Fair Trading v First National Bank Plc [2001] UKHL 52; [2002] 1 A.C. 481; [2001] 3 W.L.R. 1297; [2002] 1 All E.R. 97; [2001] 2 All E.R. (Comm) 1000; [2002] 1 Lloyd's Rep. 489; [2002] E.C.C. 22; (2001) 151 N.L.J. 1610, HL; reversing [2000] Q.B. 672; [2000] 2 W.L.R. 1353; [2000] 2 All E.R. 759; [2000] 1 All E.R. (Comm) 371; [2000] Lloyd's Rep. Bank. 130; [2000] C.C.L.R. 31; (2000) 97(7) L.S.G. 39, CA (Civ Div); reversing [2000] 1 W.L.R. 98; [2000] 1 All E.R. 240; [1999] Lloyd's Rep. Bank. 427; [2000] E.C.C. 169; (1999) 18 Tr. L.R. 245, Ch D *1–022*, *1–025*, *3–014*, *15–007*, 15–009, 15–020, 15–051, *15–054*, **15–056**, 15–057, **15–069**, **15–082**, 15–094, 15–110, *15–115*, *15–116*, *15–122*, *15–137*, *26–182*
DPP for Northern Ireland v Lynch [1975] A.C. 653; [1975] 2 W.L.R. 641; [1975] 1 All E.R. 913; (1975) 61 Cr. App. R. 6; [1975] Crim. L.R. 707; (1975) 119 S.J. 233, HL 7–004, 7–005, 7–006, 7–007, *7–014*, *7–053*
DPP v Bhagwan. *See* R. v Bhagwan (Dharam Singh)
DPP v Hutchinson; sub nom. R. v Secretary of State for Defence Ex p. Parker; R. v Secretary of State for Defence Ex p. Hayman; DPP v Smith (Georgina) [1990] 2 A.C. 783; [1990] 3 W.L.R. 196; (1991) 155 J.P. 71; 89 L.G.R. 1; (1990) 2 Admin. L.R. 741; [1991] C.O.D. 4; (1990) 154 J.P.N. 674; (1990) 154 L.G. Rev. 872; (1990) 140 N.L.J. 1035; (1990) 134 S.J. 1041, HL; reversing [1989] Q.B. 583; [1989] 3 W.L.R. 281; [1989] 1 All E.R. 1060; (1989) 153 J.P. 453; 87 L.G.R. 347; [1989] Crim. L.R. 208; [1989] C.O.D. 251; (1989) 153 J.P.N. 631; (1989) 153 L.G. Rev. 609; (1989) 133 S.J. 946, QBD *4–061*
DPP v Ray; sub nom. Ray v Sempers [1974] A.C. 370; [1973] 3 W.L.R. 359; [1973] 3 All E.R. 131; (1974) 58 Cr. App. R. 130; [1974] Crim. L.R. 181; (1973) 117 S.J. 663, HL; reversing [1973] 1 W.L.R. 317; [1973] 1 All E.R. 860; (1973) 57 Cr. App. R. 324; [1973] Crim. L.R. 182, DC *6–010*, *6–015*, *6–018*, *6–019*
DPP v Turner; sub nom. R. v Turner (John Eric) [1974] A.C. 357; [1973] 3 W.L.R. 352; [1973] 3 All E.R. 124; (1973) 57 Cr. App. R. 932; [1974] Crim. L.R. 186; (1973) 117 S.J. 664, HL *21–074*
DPP v Withers (Ian Douglas); sub nom. R. v Withers (Ian Douglas); R. v Gearing (Helen); R. v Withers (Stuart Robert); R. v Withers (Helen); R. v Withers (Phyllis May) [1975] A.C. 842; [1974] 3 W.L.R. 751; [1974] 3 All E.R. 984; (1974) 60 Cr. App. R. 85; [1975] Crim. L.R. 95; (1974) 118 S.J. 862, HL; reversing [1974] Q.B. 414; [1974] 2 W.L.R. 26; (1974) 58 Cr. App. R. 187, CA (Crim Div) *16–015*
Distributors and Warehousing Ltd, Re (1985) 1 B.C.C. 99570; [1986] 1 E.G.L.R. 90; (1986) 278 E.G. 1363, Ch D *20–035*
Dixon, Ex p. (1876) 4 Ch. D. 133 .... *21–044*
Dixon v Broomfield (1814) 2 Chit. 205 .... *4–039*
Dixon v Clarke, 136 E.R. 919; (1848) 5 C.B. 365, QB ..*21–083*, *21–084*, *21–085*, *21–089*, *21–090*, *21–095*
Dixon v Evans; sub nom. Agriculturist Cattle Insurance Co, Re; Dixon's Case (1871–72) L.R. 5 H.L. 606, HL; reversing (1869–70) L.R. 5 Ch. App. 79, CA in Chancery *9–022*
Dixon v Holdroyd (1857) 7 E.B. 903 .... *21–001*
Dobell v Hutchinson (1835) 3 A. & E. 355 .... *4–027*
Dobell v Stevens (1825) 3 B. & C. 623 .... *6–039*, *12–112*
Dobell & Co v Steamship Rossmore Co Ltd [1895] 2 Q.B. 408, CA *30–009*

Dobie v Larkam (1855) 10 Exch. 776 ... *21–090*
Doble v Haymills (Contractors) Ltd (1988) 85(30) L.S.G. 38; (1988) 132 S.J. 1063, CA (Civ Div) ... *28–116*
Dobson v Keys (1610) Cro.Jac. 261 ... *12–076*
Dockpride Pty Ltd v Subiaco Redevelopment Authority [2005] WASC 211, Sup Ct (West Aus) ... *10–037*
Dodd v Churton [1897] 1 Q.B. 562, CA ... *12–055*, *13–012*, *22–032*, *22–038*
Dodd v Wilson [1946] 2 All E.R. 691, Assizes (Chester) ... *13–030*
Dodd Properties (Kent) Ltd v Canterbury City Council [1980] 1 W.L.R. 433; [1980] 1 All E.R. 928; 13 B.L.R. 45; (1979) 253 E.G. 1335; (1980) 124 S.J. 84, CA (Civ Div) ... *26–016*, *26–018*, *26–064*, *26–065*, *26–120*
Dodds v Walker [1981] 1 W.L.R. 1027; [1981] 2 All E.R. 609; (1981) 42 P. & C.R. 131; (1981) 125 S.J. 463, HL; affirming [1980] 1 W.L.R. 1061; [1980] 2 All E.R. 507; (1980) 40 P. & C.R. 487; (1980) 255 E.G. 53; (1980) 124 S.J. 575, CA (Civ Div) ... *12–061*, *12–093*, *21–024*, *21–026*
Dodson v Downey [1901] 2 Ch. 620, Ch D ... *27–024*
Dodsworth v Dodsworth [1973] E.G.D. 233; (1973) 228 E.G. 1115, CA (Civ Div) ... 3–157, 3–158, *29–161*
Doe d. Bryan v Bancks (1821) 4 B. & Ald. 401 ... *12–082*, *22–055*
Doe d. Chandler v Ford (1853) 3 A. & E. 649 ... *12–112*
Doe d. Garnons v Knight (1826) 5 B. & C. 671 ... *1–093*
Doe d. Leicester v Biggs (1809) 2 Taunt. 109 ... *12–078*
Doe d. Muston v Gladwin (1845) 6 Q.B. 953 ... *21–003*
Doe d. Norton v Webster (1840) 12 A. & E. 442 ... *12–123*
Doe d. Pearson v Ries (1832) 8 Bing. 178 ... *12–126*
Doe d. Preece v Howells (1831) 2 B. & Ad. 744 ... *1–112*
Doe d. Tatum v Catomore (1851) 16 Q.B. 745 ... *25–022*
Doe d. Thomas v Roberts (1847) 16 M. & W. 778 ... *8–058*
Doe d. Thompson v Pitcher (1815) 6 Taunt. 359 ... *16–195*
Doherty v Allman (1877–78) L.R. 3 App. Cas. 709, HL ... *27–060*
Doherty v Monroe Eckstein Brewing Co (1921) 191 N.Y.S. 59 ... *23–054*
Dollfus Mieg et Compagnie SA v Bank of England (No.1); sub nom. United States v Dollfus Mieg et Cie SA [1952] A.C. 582; [1952] 1 All E.R. 572; [1952] 1 T.L.R. 541; (1952) 96 S.J. 180, HL; reversing in part [1950] Ch. 333; [1950] 1 All E.R. 747; 66 T.L.R. (Pt. 1) 675; (1950) 94 S.J. 285, CA; reversing [1949] Ch. 369; [1949] 1 All E.R. 946; 66 T.L.R. (Pt. 2) 559; [1949] L.J.R. 1496; (1949) 93 S.J. 265, Ch D ... *11–004*
Dolphin Quays Developments Ltd v Mills [2006] EWHC 931 (Ch); [2007] 1 P. & C.R. 12, Ch D ... *4–067*, *4–069*
Domansa v Derin Shipping & Trading Co Inc; The Sletreal [2001] 1 Lloyd's Rep. 362; [2001] C.L.C. 211, QBD (Comm) ... *30–081*
Domb v Isoz [1980] Ch. 548; [1980] 2 W.L.R. 565; [1980] 1 All E.R. 942; (1980) 40 P. & C.R. 516; (1979) 123 S.J. 838, CA (Civ Div) ... *2–033*, *2–119*
Domicrest Ltd v Swiss Bank Corp [1999] Q.B. 548; [1999] 2 W.L.R. 364; [1998] 3 All E.R. 577; [1999] 1 Lloyd's Rep. 80; [1998] C.L.C. 1451; [1999] I.L.Pr. 146, QBD ... *1–168*
Dominion Coal Co Ltd v Dominion Iron & Steel Co Ltd [1909] A.C. 293, PC (Can) ... *3–025*, *24–018*, *24–022*, *24–044*, *27–017*, *27–026*, *27–084*
Dominique, The. *See* Bank of Boston Connecticut (formerly Colonial Bank) v European Grain & Shipping Ltd
Domsalla (t/a Domsalla Building Services) v Dyason [2007] EWHC 1174 (TCC); [2007] B.L.R. 348; [2007] T.C.L.R. 5; 112 Con. L.R. 95; [2007] C.I.L.L. 2501, QBD (TCC) ... *15–033*, *15–069*, *15–079*, *15–086*, *15–093*
Don King Productions Inc v Warren (No.1) [2000] Ch. 291; [1999] 3 W.L.R. 276; [1999] 2 All E.R. 218; [1999] 1 Lloyd's Rep. 588; [2000] 1 B.C.L.C. 607; [1999] E.M.L.R. 402, CA (Civ Div); affirming [1998] 2 All E.R. 608; [1998] 2 Lloyd's Rep. 176; [1998] 2 B.C.L.C. 132; [1998] R.P.C. 817; (1998) 95(21) L.S.G. 24; (1998) 142 S.J.L.B. 162, Ch D ... *12–045*, *12–118*, *19–046*, *19–055*
Donaldson v Donaldson (1854) Kay 711 ... *19–040*

Doncaster and Retford Cooperative Societies Agreement, Re [1960] 1 W.L.R. 1186; [1960] 3 All E.R. 541; (1960) 104 S.J. 913, Ch D (RPC) *16–117*
Donegal International Ltd v Zambia [2007] EWHC 197 (Comm); [2007] 1 Lloyd's Rep. 397, QBD (Comm) *3–103*, *5–076*, *6–014*, *6–125*, *6–135*, *11–004*, *11–005*, *11–021*, *30–355*, *30–367*
Donnell v Bennett (1883) L.R. 22 Ch. D. 835, Ch D *3–025*, *27–017*, *27–070*
Donnelly v Joyce [1974] Q.B. 454; [1973] 3 W.L.R. 514; [1973] 3 All E.R. 475; [1973] 2 Lloyd's Rep. 130; (1973) 117 S.J. 488, CA (Civ Div) *2–174*, *18–076*, *29–133*
Donoghue v Stevenson; sub nom. McAlister v Stevenson [1932] A.C. 562; 1932 S.C. (H.L.) 31; 1932 S.L.T. 317; [1932] W.N. 139, HL 1–174, *18–026*
Donovan v Northlea Farms [1976] 1 N.Z.L.R. 180 .... *12–103*
Donwin Productions v EMI Films, *The Times*, March 9, 1984 .... *2–138*
Dornoch Ltd v Mauritius Union Assurance Co Ltd [2006] EWCA Civ 389; [2006] 2 All E.R. (Comm) 385; [2006] 2 Lloyd's Rep. 475; [2006] 1 C.L.C. 714; [2006] Lloyd's Rep. I.R. 786, CA (Civ Div); affirming [2005] EWHC 1887 (Comm); [2006] Lloyd's Rep. I.R. 127; (2005) 102(35) L.S.G. 42, QBD (Comm) *12–119*, *30–051*, *30–055*, *30–077*, *30–305*
Dorset CC v Southern Felt Roofing Co, 48 B.L.R. 96; (1990) 10 Tr. L.R. 96; (1990) 6 Const. L.J. 37, CA (Civ Div); affirming 26 Con. L.R. 128, QBD 14–013, *14–015*
Dorset Yacht Co v Home Office. *See* Home Office v Dorset Yacht Co Ltd
Dott v Brickwell (1906) 23 T.L.R. 61 .... *16–176*
Doughboy Industries Inc., Matter of, 233 N.Y.S. 2d 488 (1962) *2–037*
Douglas Ex p. Snowball, Re (1871–72) L.R. 7 Ch. App. 534, CA in Chancery *20–020*
Douglas v Forrest (1828) 4 Bing. 686 .... *28–031*
Douglas v Hello! Ltd (No.1) [2001] Q.B. 967; [2001] 2 W.L.R. 992; [2001] 2 All E.R. 289; [2001] E.M.L.R. 9; [2001] 1 F.L.R. 982; [2002] 1 F.C.R. 289; [2001] H.R.L.R. 26; [2001] U.K.H.R.R. 223; 9 B.H.R.C. 543; [2001] F.S.R. 40, CA (Civ Div) *1–060*, *1–065*, *1–066*
Douglas v Hello! Ltd (No.3). *See* Douglas v Hello! Ltd (No.6)
Douglas v Hello! Ltd (No.6); sub nom. Douglas v Hello! Ltd; Trial Action: Breach of Confidence (No.3) [2005] EWCA Civ 595; [2006] Q.B. 125; [2005] 3 W.L.R. 881; [2005] 4 All E.R. 128; [2005] E.M.L.R. 28; [2005] 2 F.C.R. 487; [2005] H.R.L.R. 27; (2005) 28(8) I.P.D. 28057; (2005) 155 N.L.J. 828, CA (Civ Div); reversing in part [2003] EWHC 786 (Ch); [2003] 3 All E.R. 996; [2003] E.M.L.R. 31; (2003) 153 N.L.J. 595, Ch D ... *1–060*, *1–066*
Douglas v Lloyds Bank Ltd (1929) 34 Com. Cas. 263 .... *21–058*, *28–039*
Douglas v Patrick (1790) 3 T.R. 683 .... *21–085*, *21–088*, *21–094*
Dove v Banhams Patent Locks Ltd [1983] 1 W.L.R. 1436; [1983] 2 All E.R. 833; (1983) 133 N.L.J. 538; (1983) 127 S.J. 748, QBD *18–022*, *18–026*, *28–055*
Dow Jones v Gutnick. *See* Gutnick v Dow Jones
Dowden & Pook Ltd v Pook [1904] 1 K.B. 45, CA *16–091*, *16–097*
Down v Hatcher (1839) 10 A. & E. 121 .... *22–016*
Downing v Al Tameer Establishment [2002] EWCA Civ 721; [2002] 2 All E.R. (Comm) 545; [2002] C.L.C. 1291; [2002] B.L.R. 323, CA (Civ Div) *2–076*
Downs v Chappell; Downs v Stephenson Smart [1997] 1 W.L.R. 426; [1996] 3 All E.R. 344; [1996] C.L.C. 1492, CA (Civ Div) 6–057, 6–059, *6–060*, *6–101*, 17–037
Downsview Nominees Ltd v First City Corp Ltd; sub nom. First City Corp Ltd v Downsview Nominees Ltd [1993] A.C. 295; [1993] 2 W.L.R. 86; [1993] 3 All E.R. 626; [1993] B.C.C. 46; [1994] 2 B.C.L.C. 49; (1992) 89(45) L.S.G. 26; (1992) 136 S.J.L.B. 324, PC (NZ); reversing in part [1990] 3 N.Z.L.R. 265, CA (NZ) *1–027*, *1–148*
Dowse v Gorton; sub nom. Gorton, Re [1891] A.C. 190, HL; reversing in part (1889) L.R. 40 Ch. D. 536, CA *20–010*
Dowson & Mason v Potter [1986] 1 W.L.R. 1419; [1986] 2 All E.R. 418; (1986) 83 L.S.G. 3429; (1986) 130 S.J. 841, CA (Civ Div) *16–107*
Dowty Boulton Paul Ltd v Wolverhampton Corp (No.1) [1971] 1 W.L.R. 204; [1971] 2 All E.R. 277; 69 L.G.R. 192; (1970) 115 S.J. 76, Ch D .. *10–031*, *27–026*

Dowty Boulton Paul Ltd v Wolverhampton Corp (No.2) [1976] Ch. 13; [1973] 2 W.L.R. 68; 117 S.J. 304; 71 L.G.R. 323 .... *10–031*
Doyle v Olby (Ironmongers) Ltd [1969] 2 Q.B. 158; [1969] 2 W.L.R. 673; [1969] 2 All E.R. 119; (1969) 113 S.J. 128, CA (Civ Div) ...*1–122*, *1–131*, *1–132*, *1–165*, 6–049, 6–050, 6–051
Doyle v White City Stadium Ltd [1935] 1 K.B. 110, CA *8–011*, *8–017*, *8–028*, *8–029*
Drain v Harvey (1855) 17 C.B. 257 .... *12–101*
Drake v Mitchell (1803) 3 East 251 .... *17–015*, *21–076*, *25–001*
Drake Insurance Plc (In Provisional Liquidation) v Provident Insurance Plc [2003] EWCA Civ 1834; [2004] Q.B. 601; [2004] 2 W.L.R. 530; [2004] 2 All E.R. (Comm) 65; [2004] 1 Lloyd's Rep. 268; [2004] 1 C.L.C. 574; [2004] R.T.R. 19; [2004] Lloyd's Rep. I.R. 277, CA (Civ Div); reversing [2003] EWHC 109 (Comm); [2003] 1 All E.R. (Comm) 759; [2004] R.T.R. 11; [2003] Lloyd's Rep. I.R. 781, QBD (Comm) *2–029*
Drake v Whipp [1996] 1 F.L.R. 826; [1996] 2 F.C.R. 296; (1996) 28 H.L.R. 531; [1995] N.P.C. 188; (1996) 71 P. & C.R. D32, CA (Civ Div) *3–140*
Drakeford v Piercy (1866) 7 B.S. 515 .... *21–043*
Drane v Evangelou [1978] 1 W.L.R. 455; [1978] 2 All E.R. 437; (1978) 36 P. & C.R. 270; (1977) 246 E.G. 137; (1977) 121 S.J. 793, CA (Civ Div) *26–019*
Dranez Anstalt v Hayek [2002] EWCA Civ 1729; [2003] 1 B.C.L.C. 278; [2003] F.S.R. 32; (2002) 146 S.J.L.B. 273, CA (Civ Div); reversing [2002] 1 B.C.L.C. 693, Ch D *16–106*, *16–108*, *16–109*
Draper v Earl Manvers (1892) 9 T.L.R. 73 .... *9–073*
Drayton v Dale (1823) 2 B. & C. 293 .... *20–055*
Drennan v Star Paving Co, 51 Cal. 2d. 409; 333 P. 2d. 757 (1958) *3–173*
Dresser UK Ltd v Falcongate Freight Management Ltd; The Duke of Yare [1992] Q.B. 502; [1992] 2 W.L.R. 319; [1992] 2 All E.R. 450; [1991] 2 Lloyd's Rep. 557; [1992] I.L.Pr. 164; (1991) 135 S.J.L.B. 126, CA (Civ Div) *14–054*
Drew v Daniel; sub nom. Daniel v Drew [2005] EWCA Civ 507; [2005] 2 F.C.R. 365; [2005] W.T.L.R. 807; [2005] 2 P. & C.R. DG14, CA (Civ Div) *7–050*, *7–064*
Drew v Nunn (1878–79) L.R. 4 Q.B.D. 661, CA *8–076*
Drew & Co v Josolyne (1887) L.R. 18 Q.B.D. 590, CA *19–061*
Drew Brown Ltd v Owners of the Orient Trader; The Orient Trader [1973] 2 Lloyd's Rep. 174, Sup Ct (Can); affirming [1972] 1 Lloyd's Rep. 35, Ex Ct (Can) *14–029*
Drexel Burnham Lambert International BV v Nasr [1986] 1 Lloyd's Rep. 356, QBD (Comm) *3–089*, *3–090*, *3–098*
Drexel v Drexel [1916] 1 Ch. 251, Ch D *21–054*
Drimmie v Davies [1899] I.T.R. 176 .... *18–079*, *18–086*, *27–050*
Drive Yourself Hire Co (London) Ltd v Strutt [1954] 1 Q.B. 250; [1953] 3 W.L.R. 1111; [1953] 2 All E.R. 1475; (1953) 97 S.J. 874, CA; reversing [1953] 2 W.L.R. 953; [1953] 1 All E.R. 1036; (1953) 97 S.J. 317, QBD *18–019*, *18–124*
Driver v Broad [1893] 1 Q.B. 744, CA; affirming [1893] 1 Q.B. 539, QBD *4–012*
Driver v William Willett (Contractors), Ltd [1969] 1 All E.R. 665, Assizes (Sussex) *18–022*
Drogheda Steam Packet Co, Re [1903] 1 Ir. R. 512 .... *28–004*
Druiff v Lord Parker (1867–68) L.R. 5 Eq. 131, Ct of Chancery *5–133*, *12–112*
Drury v Victor Buckland Ltd [1941] 1 All E.R. 269, CA *12–007*
Dryden Construction Co Ltd v Hydro Electric Power Commission of Ontario (1957) 10 D.L.R. (2D) 124 .... *23–050*
D'Silva v Lister House Developments Ltd [1971] Ch. 17; [1970] 2 W.L.R. 563; [1970] 1 All E.R. 858; (1970) 21 P. & C.R. 230; (1969) 113 S.J. 921, Ch D ... *1–105*
Duarte v Black & Decker Corp [2007] EWHC 2720 (QB); [2008] 1 All E.R. (Comm) 401, QBD *30–068*, *30–069*, *30–110*, *30–111*, *30–112*, *30–113*, *30–118*, *30–278*, *30–309*, *30–367*

Dubai Aluminium Co Ltd v Salaam; Dubai Aluminium Co Ltd v Amhurst Brown Martin & Nicholson [2002] UKHL 48; [2003] 2 A.C. 366; [2002] 3 W.L.R. 1913; [2003] 1 All E.R. 97; [2003] 2 All E.R. (Comm) 451; [2003] 1 Lloyd's Rep. 65; [2003] 1 B.C.L.C. 32; [2003] 1 C.L.C. 1020; [2003] I.R.L.R. 608; [2003] W.T.L.R. 163; (2003) 100(7) L.S.G. 36; (2002) 146 S.J.L.B. 280, HL; reversing [2001] Q.B. 113; [2000] 3 W.L.R. 910; [2000] 2 Lloyd's Rep. 168; [2000] Lloyd's Rep. P.N. 497; [2000] P.N.L.R. 578, CA (Civ Div); reversing [1999] 1 Lloyd's Rep. 415; (1998) 148 N.L.J. 1301, QBD (Comm) *16–168*, *17–034*, *29–014*, *29–121*
Dubai Electricity Co v Islamic Republic of Iran Shipping Lines; The Iran Vojdan [1984] 2 Lloyd's Rep. 380, QBD (Comm) *8–037*, *8–038*, *30–305*
Dubey v Revenue and Customs Commissioners; sub nom. Dubey v Hall; Farepak Food and Gifts Ltd (In Administration), Re [2006] EWHC 3272 (Ch); [2008] B.C.C. 22; [2007] 2 B.C.L.C. 1; [2007] W.T.L.R. 1407, Ch D (Companies Ct) *29–059*, *29–160*
Dubowski & Sons v Goldstein [1896] 1 Q.B. 478, CA *16–113*, *16–198*
Duchess of Kingston's Case [1775–1802] All E.R. Rep. 623; (1776) 2 Smith L.C. 644 ....*25–011*, *25–015*
Duck v Mayeu [1892] 2 Q.B. 511, CA *17–018*
Duckwari Plc (No.2), Re; sub nom. Duckwari Plc v Offerventure Ltd (No.2) [1999] Ch. 253; [1998] 3 W.L.R. 913; [1999] B.C.C. 11; [1998] 2 B.C.L.C. 315; (1998) 95(20) L.S.G. 36; (1998) 95(22) L.S.G. 28; (1998) 142 S.J.L.B. 163, CA (Civ Div); reversing [1997] Ch. 201; [1997] 2 W.L.R. 48; [1997] B.C.C. 45; [1997] 2 B.C.L.C. 729, Ch D (Companies Ct) *9–055*
Dudgeon v Pembroke (1876–77) L.R. 2 App. Cas. 284, HL; reversing (1875–76) L.R. 1 Q.B.D. 96, Ex Chamber; reversing (1873–74) L.R. 9 Q.B. 581, QB *12–073*
Duff Development Co Ltd v Kelantan [1924] A.C. 797, HL *11–020*, *11–021*, *11–022*
Duff Development Co Ltd v Kelantan Government [1923] 1 Ch. 385, CA *11–020*, *11–021*, *11–022*
Duffen v FRA BO SpA (No.2); sub nom. Duffen v Frabo SpA (No.2) [2000] 1 Lloyd's Rep. 180; [2000] E.C.C. 61; [2000] Eu. L.R. 167; (1999) 18 Tr. L.R. 342, CC (Central London) *24–048*
Duffner v Bowyer (1924) 40 T.L.R. 700 .... *17–015*
Dufour v Pereira, 21 E.R. 332; (1769) Dick. 419, Ct of Chancery *16–073*
Dugdale v Lovering (1874–75) L.R. 10 C.P. 196, CCP *29–120*
Dumford Trading AG v OAO Atlantrybflot [2005] EWCA Civ 24; [2005] 1 Lloyd's Rep. 289, CA (Civ Div); reversing [2004] EWHC 1099 (Comm); [2004] 2 Lloyd's Rep. 157, QBD (Comm) *3–113*, *12–075*, *12–122*, 12–124
Dunbar Bank Plc v Nadeem [1998] 3 All E.R. 876; [1998] 2 F.L.R. 457; [1998] 3 F.C.R. 629; (1999) 31 H.L.R. 402; [1998] Fam. Law 595; (1999) 77 P. & C.R. D8, CA (Civ Div); affirming [1997] 2 All E.R. 253; [1997] 1 F.L.R. 318; [1997] 1 F.C.R. 197; [1997] Fam. Law 247; (1997) 147 N.L.J. 217; [1996] N.P.C. 156, Ch D *6–025*, *7–057*, *7–065*, *7–067*, *7–098*
Dunbar v Plant [1998] Ch. 412; [1997] 3 W.L.R. 1261; [1997] 4 All E.R. 289; [1998] 1 F.L.R. 157; [1997] 3 F.C.R. 669; [1998] Fam. Law 139; (1997) 94(36) L.S.G. 44; (1997) 141 S.J.L.B. 191, CA (Civ Div) *16–170*
Dunbeth, The [1897] P. 133, PDAD *14–029*
Duncan v Café (1837) 2 M.W. 244 .... *29–198*
Duncan v Dixon (1890) L.R. 44 Ch. D. 211, Ch D *8–036*
Duncan v Hill; Duncan v Beeson (1872–73) L.R. 8 Ex. 242, Ex Chamber *29–117*
Duncan v Motherwell Bridge & Engineering Co Ltd, 1952 S.C. 131; 1952 S.L.T. 433, IH (2 Div) *30–068*
Duncan v Topham (1849) 8 C.B. 225 .... *21–021*
Duncan Co, Re. *See* WW Duncan & Co, Re
Duncan Stevenson Macmillan v AW Knott Becker Scott. *See* Macmillan v AW Knott Becker Scott Ltd
Duncuft v Albrecht (1841) 12 Sim. 189 .... *27–011*
Dundee Harbour Trustees v Nicol. *See* D&J Nicol v Dundee Harbour Trustees
Dungate v Dungate [1965] 1 W.L.R. 1477; [1965] 3 All E.R. 818; (1965) 109 S.J. 715, CA *28–094*, *28–095*

Dungate v Lee [1969] 1 Ch. 545; [1967] 2 W.L.R. 670; [1967] 1 All E.R. 241; (1967) 111 S.J. 134, Ch D ... *16–008*, *16–143*, *16–157*
Dunk v George Waller & Son [1970] 2 Q.B. 163; [1970] 2 W.L.R. 1241; [1970] 2 All E.R. 630; (1970) 114 S.J. 356, CA (Civ Div) ... *26–019*
Dunkirk Colliery Co v Lever (1878) L.R. 9 Ch. D. 20, CA ... *26–104*, *26–110*
Dunlop v Higgins, 9 E.R. 805; (1848) 1 H.L. Cas. 381, QB ... *2–055*
Dunlop v Lambert (1839) 2 Cl. & F. 626 ... *18–052*, *19–076*
Dunlop Pneumatic Tyre Co Ltd v New Garage & Motor Co Ltd [1915] A.C. 79, HL ... *26–126*, 26–127, *26–129*, 26–132, 26–133, *26–134*
Dunlop Pneumatic Tyre Co Ltd v Selfridge & Co Ltd [1915] A.C. 847, HL; affirming [1914] W.N. 59, CA ... *1–188*, *3–007*, *18–019*, *18–086*, *18–124*
Dunmore v Alexander (1830) 9 Shaw 190 ... *2–060*
Dunn v Macdonald [1897] 1 Q.B. 555, CA; affirming [1897] 1 Q.B. 401, QBD ... 10–013, *10–014*
Dunnachie v Kingston upon Hull City Council; Williams v Southampton Institute; Dawson v Stonham Housing Association; sub nom. Kingston Upon Hull City Council v Dunnachie (No.1) [2004] UKHL 36; [2005] 1 A.C. 226; [2004] 3 W.L.R. 310; [2004] 3 All E.R. 1011; [2004] I.C.R. 1052; [2004] I.R.L.R. 727; (2004) 101(33) L.S.G. 34; (2004) 154 N.L.J. 1156; (2004) 148 S.J.L.B. 909, HL ... *26–086*
Dunne v English (1874) L.R. 18 Eq. 524, Ct of Chancery ... *6–162*
Duomatic Ltd, Re [1969] 2 Ch. 365; [1969] 2 W.L.R. 114; [1969] 1 All E.R. 161; (1968) 112 S.J. 922, Ch D ... *9–039*
Dupen v Keeling (1829) 4 C.P. 102 ... *29–148*
Durant v Heritage [1994] E.G. 134 (C.S.); [1994] N.P.C. 117 ... *3–139*, *3–151*
Durham v Legard (1865) 34 Beav. 611 ... *27–055*
Durham Bros v Robertson [1898] 1 Q.B. 765, CA ... *19–012*, *19–013*, *19–014*
Durham Fancy Goods Ltd v Michael Jackson (Fancy Goods) Ltd [1968] 2 Q.B. 839; [1968] 3 W.L.R. 225; [1968] 2 All E.R. 987; [1968] 2 Lloyd's Rep. 98; (1968) 112 S.J. 582, QBD (Comm) ... *3–086*
Durrant v Ecclesiastical Comm (1880) 6 Q.B.D. 234 ... *29–036*, *29–179*
Durrell v Evans (1862) 1 H. & C. 174 ... *4–032*, *4–034*, *4–038*
Duthie v Hilton (1868–69) L.R. 4 C.P. 138, CCP ... *12–029*
Dutton v Bognor Regis Urban DC [1972] 1 Q.B. 373; [1972] 2 W.L.R. 299; [1972] 1 All E.R. 462; [1972] 1 Lloyd's Rep. 227; 3 B.L.R. 11; 70 L.G.R. 57; (1971) 116 S.J. 16, CA (Civ Div); affirming [1971] 2 All E.R. 1003, QBD ... *18–027*
Dutton v Manchester Airport Plc. *See* Manchester Airport Plc v Dutton
Dutton v Poole, 83 E.R. 523; (1677) 2 Lev. 210; affirmed T.Raym. 302 ... *3–022*, *18–019*, *18–087*
Dyas v Stafford (1881) 7 L.R. Ir. 590 ... *4–034*
Dyer v Hargrave (1805) 10 Ves. 505 ... *6–033*, *6–039*
Dymocks Franchise Systems (NSW) Pty Ltd v Todd [2002] UKPC 50; [2002] 2 All E.R. (Comm) 849, PC (NZ) ... *1–024*, *1–032*, *24–032*
Dymond Plc v Reeve. *See* Dyno Rod Plc v Reeve
Dynamics Corp of America (In Liquidation) (No.2), Re [1976] 1 W.L.R. 757; [1976] 2 All E.R. 669; (1976) 120 S.J. 450, Ch D ... *30–376*, *30–377*
Dynamit A/G v Rio Tinto Co Ltd [1918] A.C. 260 ... *30–367*
Dyno Rod Plc v Reeve [1999] F.S.R. 148, Ch D ... 16–120
Dyson v Forster; sub nom. Forster v Elvet Colliery Co; Quin v Elvet Colliery Co; Seed v Elvet Colliery Co; Morgan v Elvet Colliery Co; Dyson v Seed [1909] A.C. 98, HL; affirming [1908] 1 K.B. 629, CA ... *1–109*, *18–123*
Dyster v Randall & Sons [1926] Ch. 932, Ch D ... *5–099*, *6–156*, *20–055*
E&L Berg Homes v Grey (1979) 253 E.G. 473, CA (Civ Div) ... *3–148*
E Dibbens & Sons (In Liquidation), Re [1990] B.C.L.C. 577, Ch D ... *1–189*
E Hulton & Co v Chadwick Taylor (1918) 34 T.L.R. 230 ... *3–071*
E Johnson & Co (Barbados) Ltd v NSR Ltd [1997] A.C. 400; [1996] 3 W.L.R. 583; [1996] E.G. 133 (C.S.); (1996) 140 S.J.L.B. 183; [1996] N.P.C. 114, PC (Bar) ... *23–057*, *27–007*, *27–048*

E Pfeiffer Weinkellerei-Weineinkauf GmbH & Co v Arbuthnot Factors Ltd [1988] 1 W.L.R. 150; (1987) 3 B.C.C. 608; [1987] B.C.L.C. 522, QBD *19–025*, *19–028*, *19–066*, 19–068, *29–168*
E Underwood & Son Ltd v Barker [1899] 1 Ch. 300, CA *16–110*, *16–198*
EA Grimstead & Son Ltd v McGarrigan [1998–99] Info. T.L.R. 384, CA (Civ Div) *6–135*, *6–139*, *14–063*, *14–133*
ED&F Man (Sugar) Ltd v Haryanto (No.1) [1986] 2 Lloyd's Rep. 44, CA (Civ Div) *2–159*, *12–097*, *12–099*
ED&F Man Ltd v Nigerian Sweets & Confectionery Co [1977] 2 Lloyd's Rep. 50, QBD (Comm) *21–074*
ED Sassoon & Co v Western Assurance Co [1912] A.C. 561, PC (Shanghai) *14–146*
EE & Brian Smith (1928) Ltd v Wheatsheaf Mills Ltd [1939] 2 K.B. 302; (1939) 63 Ll. L. Rep. 237, KBD *13–018*
EE Caledonia Ltd (formerly Occidental Petroleum (Caledonia) Ltd) v Orbit Valve Co Europe Plc; sub nom. Elf Enterprise Caledonia Ltd (formerly Occidental Petroleum (Caledonia)) v Orbit Valve Co Europe Plc [1994] 1 W.L.R. 1515; [1995] 1 All E.R. 174; [1994] 2 Lloyd's Rep. 239; [1994] C.L.C. 647, CA (Civ Div); affirming [1994] 1 W.L.R. 221; [1993] 4 All E.R. 165; [1993] 2 Lloyd's Rep. 418, QBD (Comm) *14–011*, *14–013*, *14–015*
EETPU v Times Newspapers. *See* Electrical, Electronic, Telecommunication and Plumbing Union v Times Newspapers
EI Du Pont de Nemours & Co v Agnew (No.1) [1987] 2 Lloyd's Rep. 585; [1987] F.L.R. 376; [1987] 2 F.T.L.R. 487, CA (Civ Div) *30–005*, *30–016*
EIC Services Ltd v Phipps [2004] EWCA Civ 1069; [2005] 1 W.L.R. 1377; [2005] 1 All E.R. 338; [2004] B.C.C. 814; [2004] 2 B.C.L.C. 589; (2004) 148 S.J.L.B. 1118, CA (Civ Div); reversing [2003] EWHC 1507 (Ch); [2003] 1 W.L.R. 2360; [2003] 3 All E.R. 804; [2003] B.C.C. 931, Ch D 9–032
EJ Riley Investments Ltd v Eurostile Holdings Ltd [1985] 1 W.L.R. 1139; [1985] 3 All E.R. 181; (1986) 51 P. & C.R. 36; [1985] 2 E.G.L.R. 124; (1985) 82 L.S.G. 2500; (1985) 135 N.L.J. 887; (1985) 129 S.J. 523, CA (Civ Div) *21–026*
EJR Lovelock v Exportles [1968] 1 Lloyd's Rep. 163, CA (Civ Div) *2–144*
EMI Records Ltd v Riley [1981] 1 W.L.R. 923; [1981] 2 All E.R. 838; [1981] F.S.R. 503; (1981) 125 S.J. 412, Ch D *9–067*
ER Ives Investment Ltd v High [1967] 2 Q.B. 379; [1967] 2 W.L.R. 789; [1967] 1 All E.R. 504; (1966) 110 S.J. 963, CA *2–116*, *2–123*, *3–141*, *3–142*, *3–153*, *13–028*, *29–161*
ERDC Group Ltd v Brunel University [2006] EWHC 687 (TCC); [2006] B.L.R. 255; 109 Con. L.R. 114; [2006] C.I.L.L. 2348, QBD (TCC) *29–069*
ERG Raffinerie Mediterranee SpA v Chevron USA Inc (t/a Chevron Texaco Global Trading) [2007] EWCA Civ 494; [2007] 2 All E.R. (Comm) 548; [2007] 2 Lloyd's Rep. 542; [2007] 1 C.L.C. 807, CA (Civ Div); affirming [2006] EWHC 1322 (Comm); [2006] 2 All E.R. (Comm) 913; [2006] 2 Lloyd's Rep. 543, QBD (Comm) *12–037*
EW Savory Ltd v World of Golf Ltd [1914] 2 Ch. 566, Ch D *12–123*
Eadie v Township of Brantford [1967] S.C.R. 573 .... *29–043*
Eads v Williams, 43 E.R. 671; (1854) 4 De G.M. & G. 674, QB *28–143*
Eagle Star Insurance v Karasiewicz. *See* Karasiewicz v Eagle Star Insurance Co Ltd
Eagle Star Insurance Co Ltd v Green [2001] EWCA Civ 1389, CA (Civ Div) 4–055
Eagle Star Insurance Co Ltd v Provincial Insurance [1994] 1 A.C. 130; [1993] 3 W.L.R. 257; [1993] 3 All E.R. 1; [1993] 2 Lloyd's Rep. 143; [1993] R.T.R. 328; (1993) 143 N.L.J. 920; (1993) 137 S.J.L.B. 143, PC (Bah) *18–131*, *29–128*
Eagle Star Life Assurance Co Ltd v Griggs [1998] 1 Lloyd's Rep. 256, CA (Civ Div) *13–032*
Eaglehill Ltd v J Needham Builders Ltd [1973] A.C. 992; [1972] 3 W.L.R. 789; [1972] 3 All E.R. 895; [1973] 1 Lloyd's Rep. 143; (1972) 116 S.J. 861, HL; reversing [1972] 2 Q.B. 8; [1972] 2 W.L.R. 136; [1972] 1 All E.R. 417; [1972] 1 Lloyd's Rep. 128; (1971) 116 S.J. 95, CA (Civ Div) *2–091*, *21–022*
Eaglesfield v Marquis of Londonderry (1876–77) L.R. 4 Ch. D. 693, CA *29–041*

Earl v Slater and Wheeler (Airlyne) Ltd [1973] 1 W.L.R. 51; [1973] All E.R. 145; [1972] I.C.R. 508; [1972] I.R.L.R. 115; 13 K.I.R. 319; [1973] I.T.R. 33; (1973) 117 S.J. 14, NIRC *24–014*
Earle v Hopwood(1861) 9 C.B. (N.S.) 566 .... *16–055*
Earle v Peale (1712) 10 Mod. 67 .... *8–020*
Ease Faith Ltd v Leonis Marine Management Ltd [2006] EWHC 232; [2006] 2 All E.R. (Comm) 422; [2006] 1 Lloyd's Rep. 673; [2006] 1 C.L.C. 345, QBD (Comm) *3–107*, *13–006*, *14–006*
East, Re (1914) 111 L.T. 101 .... *20–010*
East v Maurer [1991] 1 W.L.R. 461; [1991] 2 All E.R. 733, CA (Civ Div) ...*1–122*, *1–133*, 6–052
East v Pantiles (Plant Hire) [1982] 2 E.G.L.R. 111; (1982) 263 E.G. 61, CA (Civ Div) 5–110, *12–075*
East Essex Farmers Ltd v Holder [1926] W.N. 230 .... *16–198*
East Ham Corp v Bernard Sunley & Sons [1966] A.C. 406; [1965] 3 W.L.R. 1096; [1965] 3 All E.R. 619; [1965] 2 Lloyd's Rep. 425; 64 L.G.R. 43; (1965) 109 S.J. 874, HL *26–016*, *26–034*, *26–054*, *26–064*, *26–109*
East India Co v Paul (1850) 7 Moo. P.C. 85 .... *28–108*
East India Co v Tritton (1854) 3 B.C. 280 .... *29–041*
East West Corp v DKBS 1912; sub nom. East West Corp v Dampskibsselskabet AF 1912 A/S; P&O Nedlloyd BV v Utaniko Ltd; Dampskibsselskabet AF 1912 A/S v East West Corp; Utaniko Ltd v P&O Nedlloyd BV [2003] EWCA Civ 83; [2003] Q.B. 1509; [2003] 3 W.L.R. 916; [2003] 2 All E.R. 700; [2003] 1 All E.R. (Comm) 524; [2003] 1 Lloyd's Rep. 239; [2003] 1 C.L.C. 797; (2003) 100(12) L.S.G. 31, CA (Civ Div); affirming [2002] EWHC 83 (Comm); [2002] 1 All E.R. (Comm) 676; [2002] 2 Lloyd's Rep. 182, QBD (Comm) *14–007*, *14–033*, *14–054*, *18–034*, *18–133*, *30–332*, *30–334*
Eastbourne BC v Foster (No.1) [2001] EWCA Civ 1091; [2002] I.C.R. 234; [2001] Emp. L.R. 1079; (2001) 3 L.G.L.R. 53; [2001] B.L.G.R. 529; (2001) 98(33) L.S.G. 30, CA (Civ Div) *29–058*, *29–075*
Easterby v Sampson (1830) 6 Bing. 644 .... *13–024*
Eastern Distributors v Goldring [1957] 2 Q.B. 600; [1957] 3 W.L.R. 237; [1957] 2 All E.R. 525; (1957) 101 S.J. 553, CA *5–105*, *16–144*
Eastes v Russ [1914] 1 Ch. 468, CA *16–110*
Eastgate Ex p. Ward, Re [1905] 1 K.B. 465, KBD *20–033*, *20–039*
Eastgate Group Ltd v Lindsey Morden Group Inc [2001] EWCA Civ 1446; [2002] 1 W.L.R. 642; [2001] 2 All E.R. (Comm) 1050; [2002] C.P. Rep. 7; [2001] C.P.L.R. 525; [2002] C.L.C. 144; [2002] Lloyd's Rep. P.N. 11; [2002] P.N.L.R. 9; (2001) 98(43) L.S.G. 34; (2001) 145 S.J.L.B. 243, CA (Civ Div); reversing [2001] Lloyd's Rep. P.N. 511; [2001] P.N.L.R. 40; (2001) 151 N.L.J. 458, QBD (Comm) *17–029*, 17–030
Eastham v Newcastle United Football Club [1964] Ch. 413; [1963] 3 W.L.R. 574; [1963] 3 All E.R. 139; (1963) 107 S.J. 574, Ch D ...*16–075*, *16–105*, *16–137*, *27–068*, *27–078*
Eastham (Inspector of Taxes) v Leigh London and Provincial Properties Ltd [1971] Ch. 871; [1971] 2 W.L.R. 1149; [1971] 2 All E.R. 887; 46 T.C. 687; (1971) 50 A.T.C. 53; [1971] T.R. 33; (1971) 115 S.J. 266, CA (Civ Div); reversing [1970] 3 W.L.R. 848; [1971] 1 All E.R. 87; [1970] T.R. 203; (1970) 114 S.J. 809, Ch D *12–028*
Eastman Chemical International AG v NMT Trading and Eagle Transport [1972] 2 Lloyd's Rep. 25, QBD *12–011*, *13–032*, *14–022*
Easton v Brown [1981] 3 All E.R. 278, Ch D *27–031*
Easton v Hitchcock [1912] 1 K.B. 535, KBD *13–010*
Eastwood v Ashton [1915] A.C. 900, HL; reversing [1914] 1 Ch. 68, CA; reversing [1913] 2 Ch. 39, Ch D *12–075*
Eastwood v Kenyon (1840) 11 Ad. & E. 438 .... *3–002*, *3–026*, 3–032, 3–033

Eastwood v Magnox Electric Plc; McCabe v Cornwall CC [2004] UKHL 35; [2005] 1 A.C. 503; [2004] 3 W.L.R. 322; [2004] 3 All E.R. 991; [2004] I.C.R. 1064; [2004] I.R.L.R. 733; (2004) 101(32) L.S.G. 36; (2004) 154 N.L.J. 1155; (2004) 148 S.J.L.B. 909, HL; reversing [2002] EWCA Civ 463; [2003] I.C.R. 520; [2002] I.R.L.R. 447; [2002] Emp. L.R. 795, CA (Civ Div) *1–032*, *1–123*, *1–155*, *26–083*, *26–086*
Eastwood v McNab [1914] 2 K.B. 361, KBD *29–107*
Eaton v Lyon (1798) 3 Ves. 690 .... *12–042*
Ebbetts v Conquest (1900) 82 L.T. 560 .... *25–008*
Ebbw Vale Steel Co v Blaina Iron Co (1901) 6 Com. Cas. 33 .... *24–018*, *24–043*
Eberle's Hotels and Restaurant Co v Jonas; sub nom. Eberle's Hotels & Restaurant Co v E Jonas & Bros (1887) L.R. 18 Q.B.D. 459, CA *20–041*
Ebrahim Dawood Ltd v Heath (Est 1927) Ltd; Oosman v Heath (Est 1927) Ltd [1961] 2 Lloyd's Rep. 512, QBD (Comm) *29–054*, *29–062*
Eccles v Bryant [1948] Ch. 93; [1947] 2 All E.R. 865; [1948] L.J.R. 418; 177 L.T. 247, CA; reversing [1947] Ch. 661, Ch D *2–119*
Ecclesiastical Commissioners for England v North Eastern Railway Co (1876–77) L.R. 4 Ch. D. 845, Ch D *28–089*
Ecclesiastical Commissioners for England's Conveyance, Re; sub nom. Law of Property Act 1925, Re [1936] Ch. 430; (1957) 7 P. & C.R. 298, Ch D *18–125*
Economic Life Assurance Society v Usborne; sub nom. Usborne v Limerick Market Trustees [1902] A.C. 147, HL *25–007*, *25–009*, *26–182*
Economides v Commercial Union Assurance Co Plc [1998] Q.B. 587; [1997] 3 W.L.R. 1066; [1997] 3 All E.R. 636; [1997] C.L.C. 1169; [1998] Lloyd's Rep. I.R. 9, CA (Civ Div) *6–007*, 6–009, *6–148*
Ecuador v Occidental Exploration & Production Co; sub nom. Occidental Exploration & Production Co v Ecuador [2005] EWCA Civ 1116; [2006] Q.B. 432; [2006] 2 W.L.R. 70; [2006] 2 All E.R. 225; [2005] 2 All E.R. (Comm) 689; [2005] 2 Lloyd's Rep. 707; [2005] 2 C.L.C. 457; (2005) 102(37) L.S.G. 31, CA (Civ Div); affirming [2005] EWHC 774; [2005] 2 Lloyd's Rep. 240, QBD (Comm) *11–007*
Eddis v Chichester Constable [1969] 2 Ch. 345; [1969] 3 W.L.R. 48; [1969] 2 All E.R. 912; (1969) 113 S.J. 386, CA (Civ Div) *28–081*, *28–087*, *28–090*
Edge v Strafford (1831) 1 Cr. App. R. & J. 391 .... *4–011*
Edgell v Day (1865) L.R. 1 C.P. 80 .... *29–198*
Edger v Knapp (1843) 5 M.G. 753 .... *29–124*
Edgington v Fitzmaurice (1885) L.R. 29 Ch. D. 459, CA *6–010*, 6–034, *6–035*
Edis v Bury (1827) 6 B. & C. 433 .... *12–085*
Edler v Auerbach [1950] 1 K.B. 359; [1949] 2 All E.R. 692; 65 T.L.R. 645; (1949–51) 1 P. & C.R. 10; (1949) 93 S.J. 727, KBD *13–016*, *16–010*, *16–011*, *16–167*, *16–186*, *16–204*, *16–205*
Edm JM Mertens & Co PVBA v Veevoeder Import Export Vimex BV [1979] 2 Lloyd's Rep. 372, QBD (Comm) *3–091*, *24–004*
Edmonds v Lawson; sub nom. Edmunds v Lawson [2000] Q.B. 501; [2000] 2 W.L.R. 1091; [2000] I.C.R. 567; [2000] I.R.L.R. 391; (2000) 97(14) L.S.G. 42; (2000) 144 S.J.L.B. 151, CA (Civ Div); reversing [2000] I.R.L.R. 18; (1999) 96(39) L.S.G. 38; (1999) 143 S.J.L.B. 234, QBD 2–161, 3–038
Edmondson v Copland [1911] 2 Ch. 301, Ch D *21–084*
Edmonton Corp v WM Knowles & Son, 60 L.G.R. 124 .... *13–016*
Edmund Murray v BSP International Foundations, 33 Con. L.R. 1, CA (Civ Div) ... *2–067*, *14–085*, 14–093, *14–103*
Edmunds v Downes (1834) 1 Cr. & M. 459 .... *28–094*
Edmunds v Lloyds Italico & l'Ancora Compagnia di Assicurazioni & Riassicurazione SpA [1986] 1 W.L.R. 492; [1986] 2 All E.R. 249; [1986] 1 Lloyd's Rep. 326; (1986) 83 L.S.G. 876; (1986) 130 S.J. 242, CA (Civ Div) *21–040*, *26–174*, *26–183*
Edmunds v Simmonds [2001] 1 W.L.R. 1003; [2001] R.T.R. 24; [2001] P.I.Q.R. P21, QBD *30–337*
Edmunds v Wallingford (1884–85) L.R. 14 Q.B.D. 811, CA *29–103*
Edmunds v Waugh (1865–66) L.R. 1 Eq. 418, Ct of Chancery *28–003*

Edmundson v Longton Corp (1902) 19 T.L.R. 15 .... *21–001*, *21–057*
Edmundson v Render [1905] 2 Ch. 320, Ch D *16–114*
Edward Lloyd Ltd v Sturgeon Falls Pulp Co (1901) 85 L.T. 162 .... *12–118*
Edwards Ex p. Chalmers, Re (1872–73) L.R. 8 Ch. App. 289, CA in Chancery *20–032*, *20–033*
Edwards v Aberayron Mutual Ship Insurance Society Ltd (1875–76) L.R. 1 Q.B.D. 563, Ex Chamber *16–045*
Edwards v Bates, 135 E.R. 238; (1844) 7 Man. & G. 590, CCP *29–013*
Edwards v Baugh (1843) 11 M. & W. 641 .... *3–050*
Edwards v Carter; sub nom. Carter v Silber; Carter v Hasluck; Edwards v Earl of Lisburne [1893] A.C. 360, HL; affirming [1892] 2 Ch. 278, CA; reversing [1891] 3 Ch. 553, Ch D *8–036*, *8–041*
Edwards v Grace (1836) 2 M. & W. 190 .... *20–002*
Edwards v Grand Junction Ry Co (1836) My. & Cr. 650 .... *16–025*
Edwards v Hancher (1875–76) L.R. 1 C.P.D. 111, CPD *22–015*
Edwards v Jones (1921) 124 L.T. 740 .... *4–026*
Edwards v Lee's Administrators (1936) 265 Ky. 418 .... *29–144*
Edwards v Mallan [1908] 1 K.B. 1002, CA *1–118*
Edwards v Newland & Co (E Burchett, Third Party) [1950] 2 K.B. 534; [1950] 1 All E.R. 1072; 66 T.L.R. (Pt. 2) 321; (1950) 94 S.J. 351, CA *19–082*, *21–004*
Edwards v O'Connor [1991] 2 N.Z.L.R. 542, CA (NZ) *12–096*
Edwards v Skyways [1964] 1 W.L.R. 349; [1964] 1 All E.R. 494; (1964) 108 S.J. 279, QBD *2–159*, 2–163
Edwards v Society of Graphical and Allied Trades [1971] Ch. 354; [1970] 3 W.L.R. 713; [1970] 3 All E.R. 689; 8 K.I.R. 1; (1970) 114 S.J. 618, CA (Civ Div); reversing in part [1970] 1 W.L.R. 379; [1970] 1 All E.R. 905; 7 K.I.R. 499; (1970) 114 S.J. 107, Ch D 9–082, *16–136*, *26–019*, *26–030*, *26–103*, *26–113*
Edwards v West Herts Group Hospital Committee [1957] 1 W.L.R. 415; 121 J.P. 212; 101 S.J. 190; [1957] 1 All E.R. 541 .... *13–010*
Edwards v Worboys [1984] A.C. 724; [1984] 2 W.L.R. 850; [1983] Com. L.R. 151, CA (Civ Div) *16–104*, *16–119*
Edwards' Will Trusts, Re; sub nom. Brewer v Gething [1937] Ch. 553, Ch D *28–100*
Edwin Hill & Partners v First National Finance Corp [1989] 1 W.L.R. 225; [1988] 3 All E.R. 801; [1989] B.C.L.C. 89; [1988] 48 E.G. 83; [1988] E.G. 116 (C.S.); (1988) 85(32) L.S.G. 44; (1988) 138 N.L.J. Rep. 268; (1988) 122 S.J. 1389, CA (Civ Div) *9–051*, *18–145*
Edwin Shirley Productions Ltd v Workspace Management Ltd [2001] 2 E.G.L.R. 16; [2001] 23 E.G. 158, Ch D *3–144*
Edwinton Commercial Corp v Tsavliris Russ (Worldwide Salvage & Towage) Ltd; The Sea Angel [2007] EWCA Civ 547; [2007] 2 All E.R. (Comm) 634; [2007] 2 Lloyd's Rep. 517; [2007] 1 C.L.C. 876, CA (Civ Div) ... *23–003*, *23–007*, *23–008*, *23–019*, *23–035*, *23–044*, 23–046, *23–058*, *23–059*, *23–060*, *23–061*, *23–065*
Ee v Kakar (1980) 40 P. & C.R. 223; (1979) 255 E.G. 879; (1980) 124 S.J. 327, Ch D *2–154*, *3–172*
Eedes v Boys; sub nom. Boys Ex p. Hop Planters Co, Re (1870) L.R. 10 Eq. 467, Ct of Chancery *21–073*
Effort Shipping Co Ltd v Linden Management SA; The Giannis NK [1998] A.C. 605; [1998] 2 W.L.R. 206; [1998] 1 All E.R. 495; [1998] 1 Lloyd's Rep. 337; [1998] C.L.C. 374; 1998 A.M.C. 1050; (1998) 95(7) L.S.G. 32; (1998) 148 N.L.J. 121; (1998) 142 S.J.L.B. 54, HL; affirming [1996] 1 Lloyd's Rep. 577; [1996] C.L.C. 943, CA (Civ Div); affirming [1994] 2 Lloyd's Rep. 171; [1994] C.L.C. 386, QBD (Comm) *18–019*
Egan v Static Control Components (Europe) Ltd. *See* Static Control Components (Europe) Ltd v Egan
Egerton v Earl Brownlow (1853) 4 H.L.C. 1 .... *16–004*, *16–021*
Egg v Craig (1903) 89 L.T. 41 .... *21–066*
Egg Stores (Stamford Hill) v Leibovici [1977] I.C.R. 260; [1976] I.R.L.R. 376; (1976) 11 I.T.R. 289, EAT *23–038*
Egham Staines Electricity Co Ltd v Egham UDC [1944] 1 All E.R. 107 23–067

Egon Oldendorff v Libera Corp (No.1) [1995] 2 Lloyd's Rep. 64; [1996] C.L.C. 482, QBD (Comm) *30–052*, *30–059*, *30–305*, 30–306, *30–309*
Egon Oldendorff v Libera Corp (No.2) [1996] 1 Lloyd's Rep. 380; [1996] C.L.C. 482, QBD (Comm) *30–020*, *30–023*, *30–051*, *30–052*, *30–054*, *30–059*, *30–305*
Egypt v Gamal-Eldin [1996] 2 All E.R. 237; [1996] I.C.R. 13, EAT *11–005*, *11–021*
Egyptian International Foreign Trade Co v Soplex Wholesale Supplies Ltd; The Raffaella; sub nom. Soplex Wholesale Supplies Ltd v Egyptian International Foreign Trade Co [1985] 2 Lloyd's Rep. 36; [1985] Fin. L.R. 123, CA (Civ Div); affirming [1984] 1 Lloyd's Rep. 102, QBD (Comm) *9–043*
Ehrman v Bartholomew [1898] 1 Ch. 671, Ch D *16–102*, *16–112*, *27–065*
Ehrmann Brothers Ltd, Re; sub nom. Albert v Ehrmann Bros Ltd [1906] 2 Ch. 697, CA *19–065*
Eiccholz v Bannister (1864) 17 C.B. (N.S.) 708 .... *14–026*
Eichengruen v Mond [1940] Ch. 785, CA *11–027*
Eider, The [1893] P. 119, CA *21–054*
Eisen und Metall AG v Ceres Stevedoring Co and Canadian Overseas Shipping [1977] 1 Lloyd's Rep. 665, CA (Que) *14–042*
El Ajou v Dollar Land Holdings Plc (No.1) [1994] 2 All E.R. 685; [1994] B.C.C. 143; [1994] 1 B.C.L.C. 464; [1993] N.P.C. 165, CA (Civ Div) *29–160*, *29–165*
El Awadi v Bank of Credit and Commerce International SA Ltd; sub nom. Elawadi v Bank of Credit and Commerce International SA [1990] 1 Q.B. 606; [1989] 3 W.L.R. 220; [1989] 1 All E.R. 242; [1989] Fin. L.R. 192; (1988) 138 N.L.J. Rep. 298; (1989) 133 S.J. 784, QBD *2–154*
Elbe Maru, The. *See* Nippon Yusen Kaisha v International Import and Export Co
Elbinger AG fur Fabricatien von Eisenbahn Materiel v Armstrong (1873–74) L.R. 9 Q.B. 473, QB *26–062*
Elder v Northcott [1930] 2 Ch. 422, Ch D *28–038*
Elder Dempster & Co Ltd v Paterson Zochonis & Co Ltd. *See* Paterson Zochonis & Co Ltd v Elder Dempster & Co Ltd
Elder Dempster Lines v Zaki Ishag; The Lycaon [1983] 2 Lloyd's Rep. 548, QBD (Comm) *18–073*
Elderslie Steamship Co Ltd v Borthwick; sub nom. Borthwick v Elderslie Steamship Co Ltd (No.1) [1905] A.C. 93, HL; affirming [1904] 1 K.B. 319, CA *14–032*
Eldon (Lord) v Hedley Bros [1935] 2 K.B. 1, CA *13–018*
Electra Private Equity Partners v KPMG Peat Marwick [2000] B.C.C. 368; [2001] 1 B.C.L.C. 589; [1999] Lloyd's Rep. P.N. 670; [2000] P.N.L.R. 247, CA (Civ Div); reversing [1998] P.N.L.R. 135, Ch D *1–183*
Electric Transmission v Dannenberg (1949) 66 R.P.C. 183, CA *16–106*
Electrical Trades Union v Tarlo (No.2) [1964] Ch. 720; [1964] 2 W.L.R. 1041; [1964] 2 All E.R. 1; (1964) 108 S.J. 217, Ch D *16–056*, *16–195*
Electrical, Electronic, Telecommunication and Plumbing Union v Times Newspapers [1980] Q.B. 585; [1980] 3 W.L.R. 98; [1980] 1 All E.R. 1097; (1980) 124 S.J. 31, QBD *9–064*, *9–067*
Electricity Supply Nominees Ltd v IAF Group Ltd [1993] 1 W.L.R. 1059; [1993] 3 All E.R. 372; (1994) 67 P. & C.R. 28; [1993] 2 E.G.L.R. 95; [1993] 37 E.G. 155; [1992] E.G. 145 (C.S.), QBD *14–105*
Electrosteel Castings Ltd v Scan Trans Shipping & Chartering Sdn Bhd [2002] EWHC 1993; [2002] 2 All E.R. (Comm) 1064; [2003] 1 Lloyd's Rep. 190; 87 Con. L.R. 50, QBD (Comm) *2–112*, *12–115*, *12–119*
Elektronska Industrija Oour TVA v Transped Oour Kintinentalna Spedicna [1986] 1 Lloyd's Rep. 49, QBD (Comm) *18–013*
Eley v Positive Government Security Life Assurance Co Ltd (1875–76) L.R. 1 Ex. D. 88, CA; affirming (1875–76) L.R. 1 Ex. D. 20, Exchequer Div *9–061*
Elias v George Sahely & Co (Barbados) [1983] 1 A.C. 646; [1982] 3 W.L.R. 956; [1982] 3 All E.R. 801; (1982) 126 S.J. 708, PC (Bar) *2–114*, *2–116*, *2–118*, *2–123*, *4–028*, *4–041*, *12–102*
Eliason v Henshaw (1819) 4 Wheat. 225, US Ct *2–065*
Elizabeth Jones v Christos Emmanuel Cleanthi [2006] EWCA Civ 171 .... *23–055*

Elkington & Co v Amery [1936] 2 All E.R. 86 .... *8–011*, *8–016*
Elkington v Cooke-Hill (1914) 30 T.L.R. 670 .... *3–057*
Ellen v Great Northern Railway (1901) 17 T.L.R. 453 .... *21–058*
Ellen v Topp (1851) 6 Exch. 424 .... *24–036*
Ellenborough, Re; sub nom. Towry Law v Burne [1903] 1 Ch. 697, Ch D *19–028*
Ellerman Lines Ltd v Lancaster Maritime Co Ltd; The Lancaster [1980] 2 Lloyd's Rep. 497, QBD (Comm) *18–146*, *19–068*
Ellesmere (Earl of) v Wallace [1929] 2 Ch. 1, CA *18–011*
Elli 2, The. *See* Ilyssia Compania Naviera SA v Ahmed Abdul-Qawi Bamaodah; The Elli 2
Elliman Sons & Co v Carrington & Son Ltd [1901] 2 Ch. 275, Ch D *16–121*
Elliot, Ex p. (1838) 3 Deac. 343 .... *29–103*
Elliott v Ince (1857) 7 De. G.M. & G. 475 .... *8–070*
Elliott v Pierson [1948] Ch. 452; [1948] 1 All E.R. 939; [1948] L.J.R. 1452; (1948) 92 S.J. 271, Ch D *4–029*, *27–013*, *27–041*
Elliott v Richardson (1869–70) L.R. 5 C.P. 744, CCP *16–041*
Elliott Steam Tug Co Ltd v Shipping Controller [1922] 1 K.B. 127; (1921) 8 Ll. L. Rep. 462, CA *26–104*
Elliott's Case (1777) 2 East P.C. 951 .... *12–076*
Ellis v Barker (1871–72) L.R. 7 Ch. App. 104, CA in Chancery *7–058*, *7–077*
Ellis v Bromley RDC. *See* Bromley LBC v A Ellis (Luff & Sons, Third Party)
Ellis v Chief Adjudication Officer [1998] 1 F.L.R. 184; [1998] 2 F.C.R. 51; [1997] Fam. Law 794, CA (Civ Div) *2–174*, *3–012*
Ellis v Earl Grey (1833) 6 Sim 214 .... *10–019*
Ellis v Ellis (1689) Comb. 482 .... *8–020*
Ellis v Emmanuel (1876) 1 Ex. D. 157 .... *21–065*
Ellis v Hamlen (1810) 3 Taunt. 52 .... *29–021*
Ellis v Kerr [1910] 1 Ch. 529, Ch D *17–007*
Ellis v Torrington [1920] 1 K.B. 399, CA *16–051*, *16–060*, 16–061, *19–049*
Ellis & Co's Trustee v Dixon-Johnson [1925] A.C. 489, HL; affirming [1924] 2 Ch. 451, CA; affirming [1924] 1 Ch. 342, Ch D *20–041*
Ellis Tylin Ltd v Cooperative Retail Services Ltd [1999] B.L.R. 205; 68 Con. L.R. 137, QBD *22–049*, *22–051*
Ellwood, Re [1927] 1 Ch. 455 .... *12–088*
Elphick v Barnes (1879–80) L.R. 5 C.P.D. 321, CPD *23–047*
Elphinstone (Lord) v Monkland Iron & Coal Co Ltd; sub nom. Lord Elphinstone v Markland Iron & Coal Co Ltd (1886) L.R. 11 App. Cas. 332, HL ...*26–127*, *26–135*, *26–143*
Elsden v Pick [1980] 1 W.L.R. 898; 124 S.J. 312; [1980] 3 All E.R. 235; (1980) 254 E.G. 503 .... *4–045*, *4–048*
Elsey v JG Collins Insurance Agencies Ltd (1978) 83 D.L.R. (3.d) 1 .... *26–126*
Elsley v Collins Insurance Agencies (1978) 83 D.L.R. (3d) 1, Sup Ct (Can) *26–011*, *26–143*
Elson (Inspector of Taxes) v Prices Tailors Ltd [1963] 1 W.L.R. 287; [1963] 1 All E.R. 231; 40 T.C. 671; (1962) 41 A.T.C. 345; [1962] T.R. 359; (1963) 107 S.J. 195, Ch D *29–065*
Elton Cop Dyeing Co v Broadbent & Son (1920) 89 L.J. K.B. 186 .... *22–015*
Elves v Crofts (1850) 10 C.B. 241 .... *16–099*
Embiricos v Sydney Reid & Co [1914] 3 K.B. 45, KBD *23–035*, *24–030*
Emcor Drake & Scull Ltd v Sir Robert McAlpine Ltd [2004] EWCA Civ 1733; 98 Con. L.R. 1, CA (Civ Div); affirming [2004] EWHC 1017 (TCC), QBD (TCC) *2–116*
Emerald Construction Co v Lowthian [1966] 1 W.L.R. 691; [1966] 1 All E.R. 1013; 1 K.I.R. 200; (1966) 110 S.J. 226, CA 18–132
Emery v Day (1834) 1 Cr. M. & R. 245 .... *28–053*
Emery's Investment Trusts, Re; sub nom. Emery v Emery [1959] Ch. 410; [1959] 2 W.L.R. 461; [1959] 1 All E.R. 577; (1959) 103 S.J. 257, Ch D *16–031*, *30–367*
Emma Silver Mining Co Ltd v Lewis & Son (1878–79) L.R. 4 C.P.D. 396, CPD *9–054*
Emmerson v Heelis (1809) 2 Taunt. 38 .... *4–036*, *4–038*

Employers Liability Assurance Corp Ltd v Sedgwick Collins & Co Ltd; sub nom. Sedgwick Collins & Co Ltd v Rossia Insurance Co of Petrograd (Employers Liability Assurance Corp Ltd) [1927] A.C. 95; (1926) 25 Ll. L. Rep. 453 HL *21–051*
Empresa Cubana de Fletes v Lagonisi Shipping Co Ltd; The Georgios C [1971] 1 Q.B. 488; [1971] 2 W.L.R. 221; [1971] 1 All E.R. 193; [1971] 1 Lloyd's Rep. 7; (1970) 114 S.J. 862, CA (Civ Div) *21–088*
Empresa Cubana Importadora de Alimentos v Octavia Shipping Co SA; The Kefalonia Wind [1986] 1 Lloyd's Rep. 273, QBD (Comm) *28–118*
Empresa Exportadora De Azucar (CUBAZUCAR) v Industria Azucarera Nacional SA (IANSA); The Playa Larga and Marble Islands [1983] 2 Lloyd's Rep. 171; [1983] Com. L.R. 58, CA (Civ Div) ... *11–007*, *14–141*, *23–047*, *23–058*, *30–356*
Empresa Lineas Maritimas Argentinas v Oceanus Mutual Underwriting Association (Bermuda) Ltd [1984] 2 Lloyd's Rep. 517; (1984) 134 N.L.J. 724, QBD (Comm) *3–109*, *18–004*
Empress Engineering Co, Re (1880–81) L.R. 16 Ch. D. 125, CA *9–015*
Empson v Smith [1966] 1 Q.B. 426; [1965] 3 W.L.R. 380; [1965] 2 All E.R. 881; (1965) 109 S.J. 493, CA *11–009*
Enderby Town Football Club v Football Association [1971] Ch. 591; [1970] 3 W.L.R. 1021; [1971] 1 All E.R. 215; (1970) 114 S.J. 827, CA (Civ Div) *9–075*, *16–003*
Enfield LBC v Arajah [1995] E.G. 164 (C.S.), CA (Civ Div) *2–116*, 4–053, *4–070*
Enfield LBC v Castles Estate Agents Ltd (1996) 160 J.P. 618; [1996] P.N.L.R. 422; (1997) 73 P. & C.R. 343; [1996] 2 E.G.L.R. 21; [1996] 36 E.G. 145; (1996) 160 J.P.N. 760; [1996] E.G. 30 (C.S.); [1996] N.P.C. 24, QBD *6–091*
Enfield LBC v Mahoney [1983] 1 W.L.R. 749; [1983] 2 All E.R. 901; (1983) 127 S.J. 392, CA (Civ Div) *27–002*
Enfield LBC v Sivanandan. *See* Sivanandan v Enfield LBC
Enfield Technical Services Ltd v Payne; Grace v BF Components Ltd [2008] EWCA Civ 393; [2008] I.R.L.R. 500, CA (Civ Div); affirming [2008] I.C.R. 30; [2007] I.R.L.R. 840, EAT *16–012*
Engel v Fitch; sub nom. Engell v Fitch 1868–69) L.R. 4 Q.B. 659, Ex Chamber ... *26–091*
Engelbach's Estate, Re; sub nom. Tibbetts v Englebach [1924] 2 Ch. 348, Ch D ...*18–073*, *18–079*, *18–126*
Engelke v Musmann; sub nom. Musmann v Engelke [1928] A.C. 433, HL; reversing [1928] 1 K.B. 90, CA *11–015*
England v Curling (1844) 8 Beav. 129 .... *27–024*
England v Davidson (1840) 11 A. & E. 856 ....*2–043*, *3–062*
England v Downs (1840) 2 Beav. 522 .... *12–123*
England v Marsden (1865–66) L.R. 1 C.P. 529, CCP *29–103*
English v Cliff [1914] 2 Ch. 376, Ch D *12–093*, *21–024*
English v Dedham Vale Properties; sub nom. English v Denham Vale Properties [1978] 1 W.L.R. 93; [1978] 1 All E.R. 382; (1978) 35 P. & C.R. 148; 245 E.G. 747; [1978] J.P.L. 315; (1977) 121 S.J. 320, Ch D *6–157*, *7–094*, *29–140*, *29–145*, *29–160*, *29–165*
English v Donnelly, 1958 S.C. 494; 1959 S.L.T. 2, IH (1 Div) *16–030*, *30–007*, *30–008*, *30–068*, *30–311*
English & Colonial Produce Co Ltd, Re [1906] 2 Ch. 435, CA *9–015*, *9–016*
English and Scottish Marine Insurance Co Ex p. Maclure, Re (1869–70) L.R. 5 Ch. App. 737, CA in Chancery *9–047*
English Hop Growers v Dering; sub nom. English Hop Growers Ltd v Dering [1928] 2 K.B. 174, CA *16–095*, *16–127*, *26–127*, *26–129*, *26–134*
English Industrial Estates Corp v George Wimpey & Co Ltd [1973] 1 Lloyd's Rep. 118; 7 B.L.R. 122; 71 L.G.R. 127; (1972) 116 S.J. 945, CA (Civ Div) *12–070*, *12–126*
English Joint Stock Bank Ex p. Harding, Re; sub nom. English Joint Stock Bank Ltd Ex p. Harding, Re (1866–67) L.R. 3 Eq. 341, Ct of Chancery *9–047*

Ennstone Building Products Ltd v Stanger Ltd; sub nom. Ennstone Building Products Ltd (formerly Natural Stone Products Ltd) v Stanger Ltd (formerly TBV Stanger Ltd) (No.2) [2002] EWCA Civ 916; [2002] 1 W.L.R. 3059; [2002] 2 All E.R. (Comm) 479; [2003] 1 C.L.C. 265; [2002] B.L.R. 347; [2002] T.C.L.R. 23; [2002] P.N.L.R. 42; (2002) 99(35) L.S.G. 34; (2002) 146 S.J.L.B. 200, CA (Civ Div) .. *13–007*, *30–020*, *30–025*, *30–032*, *30–077*, *30–078*, *30–082*, *30–090*, *30–347*
Enrico Furst & Co v WE Fischer Ltd [1960] 2 Lloyd's Rep. 340, QBD (Comm) *22–042*
Entico Corp Ltd v United Nations Educational Scientific and Cultural Association [2008] EWHC 531 (Comm); [2008] 1 Lloyd's Rep. 673; (2008) 105(14) L.S.G. 30; (2008) 158 N.L.J. 447, QBD (Comm) *11–003*, *11–018*
Entores Ltd v Miles Far East Corp; sub nom. Newcomb v De Roos [1955] 2 Q.B. 327; [1955] 3 W.L.R. 48; [1955] 2 All E.R. 493; [1955] 1 Lloyd's Rep. 511; (1955) 99 S.J. 384, CA *2–046*, *2–047*, *2–050*, *2–051*
Epps v Rothnie [1945] K.B. 562, CA *12–114*
Epsilon Rosa, The. *See*. Welex AG v Rosa Maritime Ltd; The Epsilon Rosa (No.2)
Equitable Fire and Accident Office Ltd v Ching Wo Hong [1907] A.C. 96, PC (Sing) *12–108*
Equitable Life Assurance Society v Hyman [2002] 1 A.C. 408; [2000] 3 W.L.R. 529; [2000] 3 All E.R. 961; [2001] Lloyd's Rep. I.R. 99; [2000] O.P.L.R. 101; [2000] Pens. L.R. 249; (2000) 144 S.J.L.B. 239, HL; affirming [2000] 2 W.L.R. 798; [2000] 2 All E.R. 331; [2000] O.P.L.R. 71; [2000] Pens. L.R. 129; (2000) 97(5) L.S.G. 34; (2000) 144 S.J.L.B. 57, CA (Civ Div); reversing [1999] O.P.L.R. 213; [1999] Pens. L.R. 297, Ch D *2–175*, *13–002*, *13–003*, *13–007*
Eric Gnapp v Petroleum Board [1949] 1 All E.R. 980; [1949] W.N. 180; (1949) 93 S.J. 338, CA *7–045*
Eridania SpA (formerly Cereol Italia Srl) v Oetker; The Fjord Wind [2000] 2 All E.R. (Comm) 108; [2000] 2 Lloyd's Rep. 191; [2000] C.L.C. 1376, CA (Civ Div); affirming [1999] 1 Lloyd's Rep. 307; [1998] C.L.C. 1186, QBD (Comm) *12–050*, *12–118*, *23–035*
Erie County Natural Gas & Fuel Co Ltd v Carroll [1911] A.C. 105, PC (Can) *26–008*, *26–111*, *26–115*, *26–120*
Erlanger v New Sombrero Phosphate Co; sub nom. New Sombrero Phosphate Co v Erlanger (1877–78) L.R. 3 App. Cas. 1218, HL; affirming (1877) L.R. 5 Ch. D. 73, CA .. 6–116, *6–127*, *6–128*, *6–153*, *6–154*, *7–054*, *9–054*, *28–134*, 28–138, *28–144*
Ernest v Nicholls (1857) 6 H.L. Cas. 401 .... *9–021*
Ernest Beck & Co v K Szymanowski & Co; sub nom. Szymonowski & Co v Beck & Co [1924] A.C. 43; (1923–24) 17 Ll. L. Rep. 97, HL; affirming [1923] 1 K.B. 457; (1923) 14 Ll. L. Rep. 84, CA *14–006*, *14–027*
Ernest Scragg & Sons v Perseverance Banking and Trust Co [1973] 2 Lloyd's Rep. 101, CA (Civ Div) *5–122*, *29–146*
Ernst & Young v Butte Mining Plc (No.2); sub nom. Butte Mining Plc v Ernst & Young (No.2) [1997] 1 W.L.R. 1485; [1997] 2 All E.R. 471; [1997] 1 Lloyd's Rep. 313, Ch D *28–122*
Errington v Errington and Woods [1952] 1 K.B. 290; [1952] 1 All E.R. 149; [1952] 1 T.L.R. 231; (1952) 96 S.J. 119, CA 2–080, *3–142*, *13–028*, *18–135*, *19–059*
Erskine v Adeane (1872–73) L.R. 8 Ch. App. 756, CA in Chancery *4–016*, *12–004*, *12–103*, *22–036*
Erskine Macdonald Ltd v Eyles [1921] 1 Ch. 631, Ch D *18–138*
Ertel Bieber & Co v Rio Tinto Co Ltd; Dynamit AG (Vormals Alfred Nobel Co) v Rio Tinto Co Ltd; Vereingte Koenigs v Rio Tinto Co Ltd [1918] A.C. 260, HL *16–026*, *23–024*, *23–030*, *23–058*, *23–059*
Erven Warnink BV v J Townend & Sons (Hull) Ltd (No.2) [1982] 3 All E.R. 312; [1982] Com. L.R. 184; [1982] R.P.C. 511; (1982) 79 L.S.G. 987; (1982) 126 S.J. 465, CA (Civ Div) *26–184*

Erwin v Snelgrove [1927] 4 D.L.R. 1028 .... *16–186*

Esanda Finance Corp v Plessnig, 166 C.L.R. 131, HC (Aus) *26–140*, *26–125*

Escalera Silver Lead Mining Co (1908) 25 T.L.R. 87 .... *21–054*

Eshelby v Federated European Bank Ltd [1932] 1 K.B. 423, CA *21–030*, *21–031*, *24–043*

Eshun v Moorgate Mercantile Co [1971] 1 W.L.R. 722; [1971] 2 All E.R. 402; (1971) 115 S.J. 301, CA (Civ Div) *12–038*

Esmail v J Rosenthal Sons Ltd. *See* J Rosenthal & Sons v Esmail (t/a HMH Esmail & Sons)

Essex Strategic HA (formerly North Essex HA) v David-John; sub nom. North Essex HA v David-John [2004] I.C.R. 112; [2003] Lloyd's Rep. Med. 586, EAT *2–182A*

Esso Petroleum Co Ltd v Addison; sub nom. Addison v Esso Petroleum Co Ltd [2004] EWCA Civ 1470; (2004) 101(46) L.S.G. 33; (2004) 148 S.J.L.B. 1400, CA (Civ Div); affirming [2003] EWHC 1730, QBD (Comm) *22–039*

Esso Petroleum Co Ltd v Alstonbridge Properties Ltd [1975] 1 W.L.R. 1474; [1975] 3 All E.R. 358; (1975) 30 P. & C.R. 170; (1975) 237 E.G. 881; (1975) 119 S.J. 727, Ch D *28–046*

Esso Petroleum Co Ltd v Customs and Excise Commissioners [1976] 1 W.L.R. 1; [1976] 1 All E.R. 117; (1975) 120 S.J. 49, HL; affirming [1975] 1 W.L.R. 406; (1975) 119 S.J. 205, CA (Civ Div); reversing [1973] 1 W.L.R. 1240; (1973) 117 S.J. 680, DC *2–014*, 2–186

Esso Petroleum Co Ltd v Hall Russell & Co Ltd; The Esso Bernicia [1989] A.C. 643; [1988] 3 W.L.R. 730; [1989] 1 All E.R. 37; [1989] 1 Lloyd's Rep. 8; 1988 S.L.T. 874; (1988) 85(42) L.S.G. 48; (1988) 132 S.J. 1459, HL; affirming in part 1988 S.L.T. 33, IH (1 Div) *18–019*, *18–047*, *29–019*, *29–109*, *29–112*, *29–173*

Esso Petroleum Co Ltd v Harper's Garage (Stourport) Ltd [1968] A.C. 269; [1967] 2 W.L.R. 871; [1967] 1 All E.R. 699; (1967) 111 S.J. 174, HL; reversing in part [1966] 2 Q.B. 514; [1966] 2 W.L.R. 1043; [1966] 1 All E.R. 725; (1966) 110 S.J. 265, CA; reversing [1965] 3 W.L.R. 469; [1965] 2 All E.R. 933; (1965) 109 S.J. 511, QBD *16–004*, *16–075*, 16–077, *16–078*, *16–081*, *16–082*, *16–083*, *16–084*, 16–085, *16–086*, *16–092*, *16–093*, *16–095*, *16–098*, *16–114*, *16–115*, *16–121*, 16–122, *16–125*, *16–126*, *16–127*, *16–128*, *16–129*, *16–130*, *16–137*, *16–194*, *16–199*, *27–068*

Esso Petroleum Co Ltd v Kingswood Motors (Addlestone) Ltd [1974] Q.B. 142; [1973] 3 W.L.R. 780; [1973] 3 All E.R. 1057; [1973] C.M.L.R. 665; (1973) 117 S.J. 852, QBD *18–141*

Esso Petroleum Co Ltd v Mardon [1976] Q.B. 801; [1976] 2 W.L.R. 583; [1976] 2 All E.R. 5; [1976] 2 Lloyd's Rep. 305; 2 B.L.R. 82; (1976) 120 S.J. 131, CA (Civ Div); reversing in part [1975] Q.B. 819; [1975] 2 W.L.R. 147; [1975] 1 All E.R. 203; (1974) 119 S.J. 81, QBD *1–122*, *1–129*, *1–131*, 1–133, *1–136*, *1–177*, 6–012, *6–049*, *6–052*, *6–069*, *6–084*, 6–085, *12–003*, *12–004*, *12–004*, *12–005*, *12–033*

Esso Petroleum Co Ltd v Milton [1997] 1 W.L.R. 1060; [1997] 1 W.L.R. 938; [1997] 2 All E.R. 593; [1997] C.L.C. 634; (1997) 16 Tr. L.R. 250, CA (Civ Div) *14–062*, *14–092*

Esso Petroleum Co Ltd v Niad Ltd [2001] All E.R. (D) 324, Ch D *16–122*, *26–025*, *26–028*, *29–154*

Estate of Arnandh v Barnet Primary Health Care Trust [2004]EWCA Civ 5; [2004] All E.R. (D) 242, CA (Civ Div) *16–147*

Esterhuizen v Allied Dunbar Assurance Plc [1998] 2 F.L.R. 668; [1998] Fam. Law 527, QBD *18–037*

Etablissements Chainbaux SARL v Harbormaster Ltd [1955] 1 Lloyd's Rep. 303, QBD *24–014*

Etablissements Levy (Georges et Paul) v Adderley Navigation Co Panama SA; The Olympic Pride [1980] 2 Lloyd's Rep. 67, QBD (Comm) *5–111*

Etablissements Soules et Cie v International Trade Development Co [1980] 1 Lloyd's Rep. 129, CA (Civ Div); affirming [1979] 2 Lloyd's Rep. 122, QBD (Comm) *3–093*, *3–103*

Etzin v Reece [2003] 1 P. & C.R. DG9; [2002] All E.R. (D) 405 (July), Ch D *21–014*, *21–016*, *21–017*, *22–048*

Eugenia, The. *See* Ocean Tramp Tankers Corp v V/O Sovfracht; The Eugenia

Eurasian Dream. The. *See* Papera Traders Co Ltd v Hyundai Merchant Marine Co Ltd

Eurico SpA v Philipp Bros; The Epaphus [1987] 2 Lloyd's Rep. 215; [1987] 2 F.T.L.R. 213, CA (Civ Div); affirming [1986] 2 Lloyd's Rep. 387, QBD (Comm) *1–012*, *12–055*, *13–006*, *13–009*

Euro Cellular (Distribution) Plc v Danzas Ltd (t/a Danzas AEI Intercontinental) [2003] EWHC 3161; [2004] 1 Lloyd's Rep. 521, QBD (Comm) ...*14–018*, *14–019*

Euro London Appointments Ltd v Claessens International Ltd [2006] EWCA Civ 385; [2006] 2 Lloyd's Rep. 436, CA (Civ Div) *26–126*, *26–136*, *26–137*

Eurodata Systems Plc v Michael Gerson (Finance) Plc; sub nom. Eurodata Systems Plc v Michael Gershon (Finance) Plc, *The Times*, March 25, 2003, QBD *2–116*

Euro-Diam Ltd v Bathurst [1990] 1 Q.B. 1; [1988] 2 W.L.R. 517; [1988] 2 All E.R. 23; [1988] 1 Lloyd's Rep. 228; [1988] F.T.L.R. 242; [1988] Fin. L.R. 27; (1988) 85(9) L.S.G. 45; (1988) 132 S.J. 372, CA (Civ Div); affirming [1987] 2 W.L.R. 1368; [1987] 2 All E.R. 113; [1987] 1 Lloyd's Rep. 178; [1987] Fin. L.R. 247; (1987) 84 L.S.G. 1732; (1987) 131 S.J. 775, QBD (Comm) 16–007, *16–164*, *16–165*, 16–167, *16–181*, *30–367*

Europa, The [1908] P. 84, PDAD *14–032*

European Asian Bank AG v Punjab & Sind Bank [1982] 2 Lloyd's Rep. 356; [1982] Com. L.R. 76, CA (Civ Div); affirming [1981] 2 Lloyd's Rep. 651; [1981] Com. L.R. 246, QBD (Comm) *14–051*, *18–070*, *30–077*

European Assurance Society Arbitration Acts, Re; sub nom. Conquest's Case; Wellington Reversionary Annuity and Life Assurance Society, Re (1875–76) L.R. 1 Ch. D. 334, CA *19–087*, *22–031*

European Assurance Society, Re; sub nom. Miller's Case (1876) L.R. 3 Ch. D. 391, CA *19–087*, *22–031*

European Bank for Reconstruction & Development v Tekoglu [2004] EWHC 846, QBD (Comm) *30–020*, *30–051*

European Central Railway Co Ex p. Oriental Financial Corp, Re (1876–77) L.R. 4 Ch. D. 33; (1876) 25 W.R. 92; (1876) 46 L.J. Ch. 57; (1876) 35 L.T. 583, CA *25–007*

European etc Mail Co v Royal Mail Steam Packet Co (1861) 30 L.J.P.C. 247 .... *13–012*

European Gas Turbines Ltd (formerly Ruston Gas Turbines Ltd) v MSAS Cargo International Inc [2001] C.L.C. 880, QBD *1–184*, *18–031*

European Gateway, The. *See* Speedlink Vanguard, The and European Gateway, The

European Grain & Shipping Ltd v Peter Cremer GmbH & Co [1983] 1 Lloyd's Rep. 211, QBD (Comm) *24–009*

European International Reinsurance Co Ltd v Curzon Insurance Ltd [2003] EWCA Civ 1074; [2003] Lloyd's Rep. I.R. 793; (2003) 100(36) L.S.G. 43; (2003) 147 S.J.L.B. 906, CA (Civ Div); affirming [2003] EWHC 321 (Comm); [2003] Lloyd's Rep. I.R. 454, QBD (Comm) *1–184*

Eurosteel Ltd v Stinnes AG [2000] 1 All E.R. (Comm) 964; [2000] C.L.C. 470, QBD (Comm) *30–345*

Eustace, Re; sub nom. Lee v McMillan [1912] 1 Ch. 561, Ch D *28–142*

Evans, Re; sub nom. Evans v Evans (1887) L.R. 34 Ch. D. 597, CA *20–010*

Evans v Amicus Healthcare Ltd; Hadley v Midland Fertility Services Ltd [2004] EWCA Civ 727; [2005] Fam. 1; [2004] 3 W.L.R. 681; [2004] 3 All E.R. 1025; [2004] 2 F.L.R. 766; [2004] 2 F.C.R. 530; (2004) 78 B.M.L.R. 181; [2004] Fam. Law 647; (2004) 148 S.J.L.B. 823, CA (Civ Div); affirming [2003] EWHC 2161 (Fam); [2004] 2 W.L.R. 713; [2003] 4 All E.R. 903; [2004] 1 F.L.R. 67; [2003] 3 F.C.R. 577; (2004) 75 B.M.L.R. 115; [2003] Fam. Law 879; (2003) 100(39) L.S.G. 38; (2003) 153 N.L.J. 1519; (2003) 147 S.J.L.B. 1150, Fam Div *3–087*, *3–088*, *3–090*, *3–095*, *3–101*
Evans v Brunner Mond & Co Ltd [1921] 1 Ch. 359, Ch D *9–022*
Evans v Chapman (1902) 86 L.T. 381 .... *5–135*
Evans v Cherry Tree Finance Ltd, unreported April 13, 2007 Ch D (Leeds) *15–029*, *15–098*
Evans v Edmonds (1853) 13 C.B. 777 .... *6–045*
Evans v Hoare [1892] 1 Q.B. 593, QBD *4–032*, *4–034*, *4–073*
Evans v Hooper (1875–76) L.R. 1 Q.B.D. 45, CA *18–010*
Evans v HSBC Trust Co (UK) Ltd [2005] W.T.L.R. 1289, Ch D *3–141*, *3–148*, *3–155*, *3–157*, *3–160*
Evans v Judkins (1815) 4 Camp. 156 .... *21–090*
Evans v Kosmar Villa Holiday Plc; sub nom. Evans v Kosmar Villa Ltd [2007] EWCA Civ 1003; [2008] 1 W.L.R. 297; [2008] 1 All E.R. 530; [2008] 1 All E.R. (Comm) 721; [2008] P.I.Q.R. P7; (2007) 104(43) L.S.G. 31; (2007) 151 S.J.L.B. 1404; [2007] N.P.C. 109, CA (Civ Div); reversing [2006] EWHC 3417 (Comm), QBD (Comm) *13–034*
Evans v Llewellin, 29 E.R. 1191; (1787) 1 Cox Eq. Cas. 333, Ct of Chancery *27–032*
Evans v Motor Insurers Bureau. *See* White (Brian) v White
Evans v Richardson (1817) 3 Mer. 469 .... *16–205*
Evans v Roe (1871–72) L.R. 7 C.P. 138, CCP *12–096*
Evans v Secretary of State for the Environment, Transport and the Regions [2001] EWCA Civ 32; [2001] 2 C.M.L.R. 10; [2002] Lloyd's Rep. I.R. 1, CA (Civ Div); affirming [2001] P.I.Q.R. P3, QBD *18–131*
Evans v Smallcombe. *See* Agriculturists Cattle Insurance Co, Re
Evans v Ware [1892] 3 Ch. 502, Ch D *8–023*
Evans Construction Co Ltd v Charrington & Co Ltd; Evans Construction Co Ltd v Bass Holdings Ltd [1983] Q.B. 810; [1983] 2 W.L.R. 117; [1983] 1 All E.R. 310; (1982) 264 E.G. 347; (1982) 79 L.S.G. 1138, CA (Civ Div) *28–118*
Evans Marshall & Co v Bertola SA (No.1) [1973] 1 W.L.R. 349; [1973] 1 All E.R. 992; [1973] 1 Lloyd's Rep. 453; (1972) 117 S.J. 225, CA (Civ Div) *27–005*, *27–008*, *27–061*, *27–064*, *27–070*, *30–010*
Evanthia M, The. *See* Petroleo Brasileiro SA—Petrobras Franto National de Peroleiros—Fronape v Elounda Shipping Co
Evenden v Guildford City Association Football Club [1975] Q.B. 917; [1975] 3 W.L.R. 251; [1975] 3 All E.R. 269; [1975] I.C.R. 367; [1975] I.R.L.R. 213; [1975] I.T.R. 95; 18 Man. Law 92; (1975) 119 S.J. 460, CA (Civ Div); reversing [1974] I.C.R. 554; [1974] I.R.L.R. 285, NIRC *3–088*, *3–098*
Evening Standard Co Ltd v Henderson [1987] I.C.R. 588; [1987] I.R.L.R. 64; [1987] F.S.R. 165, CA (Civ Div) *16–102*, *27–061*, *27–066*
Everett v Collins (1810) 2 Camp. 515 .... *21–075*
Evergos Naftiki Eteria v Cargill Plc; The Voltaz [1997] 1 Lloyd's Rep. 35, CC (Central London) *12–070*
Eves v Eves [1975] 1 W.L.R. 1338; [1975] 3 All E.R. 768; (1975) 119 S.J. 394, CA (Civ Div) *2–171*, *3–139*, *3–142*, *3–158*, *3–162*, *16–068*
Evialis SA v SIAT [2003] EWHC 863; [2003] 2 Lloyd's Rep. 377; [2003] 2 C.L.C. 802; [2003] I.L.Pr. 43; [2004] Lloyd's Rep. I.R. 187, QBD (Comm) ...*30–051*, *30–273*
Ewin v Lancaster (1865) 6 B. & S. 571 .... *12–116*
Ewing v Osbaladiston (1836) 2 My. & Cr. 53 .... *16–008*
Ewing & Co v Ewing; sub nom. Orr Ewing & Co v Orr Ewing (1882–83) L.R. 8 App. Cas. 822, HL 12–080
Exall v Partridge, 101 E.R. 1405; (1799) 8 Term Rep. 308, KB *29–020*, *29–103*

Excomm v Guan Guan Shipping Pte Ltd; The Golden Bear [1987] 1 Lloyd's Rep. 330; [1987] 1 F.T.L.R. 61, QBD (Comm) *2–004*, *2–006*, *2–071*, *2–076*, *22–027*
Exercise Shipping Co Ltd v Bay Maritime Lines Ltd; The Fantasy [1992] 1 Lloyd's Rep. 235, CA (Civ Div); affirming [1991] 2 Lloyd's Rep. 391, QBD (Comm) *14–011*
Eximenco Handels AG v Partredereit Oro Chief and Levantes Maritime Corp; The Oro Chief [1983] 2 Lloyd's Rep. 509; (1983) 133 N.L.J. 642, QBD (Comm) *22–053*, *27–008*, *27–014*
Exmar NV v BP Shipping; The Gas Enterprise [1993] 2 Lloyd's Rep. 352, CA (Civ Div) *2–071*
Experience Hendrix LLC v PPX Enterprises Inc [2003] EWCA Civ 323; [2003] 1 All E.R. (Comm) 830; [2003] E.M.L.R. 25; [2003] F.S.R. 46; (2003) 26(7) I.P.D. 26046; (2003) 100(22) L.S.G. 29; (2003) 147 S.J.L.B. 509, CA (Civ Div); reversing [2002] EWHC 1353 (QB), QBD *16–100*, *16–122*, *26–022*, 26–025, 26–026, 26–027, 26–028, 26–029, *27–081*, 29–154
Expo Fabrics (UK) Ltd v Martin [2003] EWCA Civ 1165, CA (Civ Div) *14–092*
Expo Fabrics (UK) Ltd v Naughty Clothing. *See* Expo Fabrics (UK) Ltd v Martin
Export Credits Guarantee Department v Universal Oil Products Co [1983] 1 W.L.R. 399; [1983] 2 All E.R. 205; [1983] 2 Lloyd's Rep. 152; 23 B.L.R. 106; (1983) 133 N.L.J. 662; (1983) 127 S.J. 408, HL *26–136*, 26–137
Exportelisa SA v Rocco Giuseppe & Figli Soc Coll [1978] 1 Lloyd's Rep. 433, CA (Civ Div); affirming [1977] 2 Lloyd's Rep. 494, QBD (Comm) *14–141*
Exposito v Bowden (1857) 7 E.B. 763 .... *23–030*
Express Dairy Co v Jackson (1930) 99 L.J.K.B. 181 ..... *8–026*, *8–029*, *16–097*, *16–111*, *16–198*
Express Newspapers Plc v Silverstone Circuits, *The Times*, June 20, 1989; *Independent*, June 16, 1989, CA (Civ Div) *13–009*
Extec Screens & Crushers Ltd v Rice [2007] EWHC 1043 (QB), QBD *16–107*
Exxonmobil Sales & Supply Corp v Texaco Ltd [2003] EWHC 1964; [2004] 1 All E.R. (Comm) 435; [2003] 2 Lloyd's Rep. 686, QBD (Comm) *12–104*, *13–018*
Eyestorm Ltd v Hoptonacre Homes Ltd [2007] EWCA Civ 1366; [2007] All ER (D) 284, CA (Civ Div) *4–056*
Eyles v Ellis, 130 E.R. 710; (1827) 4 Bing. 112, KB *21–047*, *21–058*
Eyre v Johnson [1946] K.B. 481; [1946] 1 All E.R. 719; 62 T.L.R. 400; [1947] L.J.R. 433; 175 L.T. 132; (1946) 90 S.J. 516, KBD *23–025*, *23–055*, *23–066*
Eyre v Measday [1986] 1 All E.R. 488; (1986) 136 N.L.J. 91, CA (Civ Div) *2–002*
Ezekiel v Lehrer [2002] EWCA Civ 16; [2002] Lloyd's Rep. P.N. 260, CA (Civ Div) *28–089*
Ezekiel v Orakpo [1997] 1 W.L.R. 340; [1996] N.P.C. 108, CA (Civ Div) *28–003*
F, Re *See* F. v West Berkshire HA
F v West Berkshire HA; sub nom. F (Mental Patient: Sterilisation), Re [1990] 2 A.C. 1; [1989] 2 W.L.R. 1025; [1989] 2 All E.R. 545; [1989] 2 F.L.R. 376; (1989) 139 N.L.J. 789; (1989) 133 S.J. 785, HL; affirming (1989) 86(10) L.S.G. 42, CA (Civ Div) *8–068*, *29–133*
F (Mental Patient: Sterilisation), Re. *See* F v West Berkshire HA
F&G Sykes (Wessex) Ltd v Fine Fare Ltd [1967] 1 Lloyd's Rep. 53, CA; reversing in part [1966] 2 Lloyd's Rep. 205, QBD (Comm) *2–128*
F&H Entertainments v Leisure Enterprises; sub nom. F&B Entertainments v Leisure Enterprises (1976) 240 E.G. 455; (1976) 120 S.J. 331 ...*6–069*, *6–072*, *6–097*, *6–136*, *6–157*
F&K Jabbour v Custodian of Israeli Absentee Property [1954] 1 W.L.R. 139; [1954] 1 All E.R. 145; [1953] 2 Lloyd's Rep. 760; (1954) 98 S.J. 45, QBD ... *30–009*
F Gliksten & Son Ltd v State Assurance Co (1922) 10 Ll. L. Rep. 604, KBD *2–129*
F Goldsmith (Sicklesmere) Ltd v Baxter [1970] Ch. 85; [1969] 3 W.L.R. 522; [1969] 3 All E.R. 733; (1969) 20 P. & C.R. 787; (1969) 113 S.J. 705, Ch D *4–023*, *12–075*
FA Tamplin Steamship Co Ltd v Anglo Mexican Petroleum Products Co Ltd [1916] 2 A.C. 397, HL; affirming [1916] 1 K.B. 485, CA; affirming [1915] 3 K.B. 668, KBD *5–025*, 23–010, 23–017, 23–042, 23–043, *23–059*

FAI General Insurance Co Ltd v Ocean Marine Mutual Protection and Indemnity Association (No.2) [1998] Lloyd's Rep. I.R. 24, HC (Aus) *6–112*
FC Shepherd & Co v Jerrom [1987] Q.B. 301; [1986] 3 W.L.R. 801; [1986] 3 All E.R. 589; [1986] I.C.R. 802; [1986] I.R.L.R. 358; (1986) 130 S.J. 665, CA (Civ Div) *23–016*, *23–039*, *23–065*, *24–030*
FE Napier v Dexters Ltd (1926) 26 Ll.L.R. 62 .... *22–046*
FG Whitley & Sons v Bickerto, [1993] 07 E.G. 100; [1992] E.G. 25 (C.S.) *1–167*
FJ Bloemen Pty Ltd (formerly Canterbury Pipelines (Australia) Pty Ltd) v Council of the City of Gold Coast [1973] A.C. 115; [1972] 3 W.L.R. 43; [1972] 3 All E.R. 357; (1972) 116 S.J. 395, PC (Aus) *24–048*
FP&CH Matthews Ltd, Re [1982] Ch. 257; [1982] 2 W.L.R. 495; [1982] 1 All E.R. 338, CA (Civ Div) *20–029*
FSS Travel & Leisure Systems Ltd v Johnson [1998] I.R.L.R. 382; [1999] I.T.C.L.R. 218; [1999] F.S.R. 505, CA (Civ Div) *16–109*
FW Moore & Co Ltd v Landauer & Co; sub nom. Arbitration Between Moore & Co Ltd and Landauer & Co Re [1921] 2 K.B. 519; (1921) 6 Ll. L. Rep. 384, CA; affirming [1921] 1 K.B. 73; (1920) 5 Ll. L. Rep. 69, KBD (Comm Ct) ... *6–108*
Faccenda Chicken Ltd v Fowler; Fowler v Faccenda Chicken Ltd [1987] Ch. 117; [1986] 3 W.L.R. 288; [1986] 1 All E.R. 617; [1986] I.C.R. 297; [1986] I.R.L.R. 69; [1986] F.S.R. 291; (1986) 83 L.S.G. 288; (1986) 136 N.L.J. 71; (1986) 130 S.J. 573, CA (Civ Div); affirming [1985] 1 All E.R. 724; [1984] I.C.R. 589; [1984] I.R.L.R. 61; [1985] F.S.R. 105; (1984) 134 N.L.J. 255, Ch D *16–107*, 16–108, 16–109
Facer v Vehicle & General Insurance Co Ltd [1965] 1 Lloyd's Rep. 113, QBD *6–149*
Factortame Ltd v Secretary of State for the Environment, Transport and the Regions (Costs) (No.2); sub nom. R. (on the application of Factortame Ltd) v Secretary of State for Transport, Local Government and the Regions (Costs: Champertous Agreement) [2002] EWCA Civ 932; [2003] Q.B. 381; [2002] 3 W.L.R. 1104; [2002] 4 All E.R. 97; [2003] B.L.R. 1; [2002] 3 Costs L.R. 467; (2002) 99(35) L.S.G. 34; (2002) 152 N.L.J. 1313; (2002) 146 S.J.L.B. 178, CA (Civ Div) *16–056*
Fagan v Green & Edwards Ltd [1926] 1 K.B. 102, KBD *14–012*
Fahey v Frawley (1890) 26 L.R. Ir. 78 .... *29–113*
Fairclough Building Ltd v Port Talbot BC, 62 B.L.R. 82; 33 Con. L.R. 24, CA (Civ Div) *2–022*, 10–038
Fairclough Dodd & Jones v Vantol (JH) [1957] 1 W.L.R. 136; [1956] 3 All E.R. 921; [1956] 2 Lloyd's Rep. 437; (1957) 101 S.J. 86, HL; reversing [1955] 1 W.L.R. 1302; [1955] 3 All E.R. 750; [1955] 2 Lloyd's Rep. 489; (1955) 99 S.J. 888, CA; affirming [1955] 1 W.L.R. 642; [1955] 2 All E.R. 516; [1955] 1 Lloyd's Rep. 546; (1955) 99 S.J. 386, QBD *14–004*, *14–137*, *14–141*, *14–143*, *14–148*
Fairfax Gerrard Holdings Ltd v Capital Bank Plc [2007] EWCA Civ 1226; [2008] 1 All E.R. (Comm) 632; [2008] 1 Lloyd's Rep. 297; [2007] 2 C.L.C. 896; [2008] B.P.I.R. 332, CA (Civ Div); reversing [2006] EWHC 3439 (Comm); [2007] 1 Lloyd's Rep. 171; [2007] B.P.I.R. 330, QBD (Comm) *13–009*
Fairlie v Fenton (1869–70) L.R. 5 Ex. 169, Ex Ct *12–115*
Fairline Shipping Corp v Adamson [1975] Q.B. 180; [1974] 2 W.L.R. 824; [1974] 2 All E.R. 967; [1974] 1 Lloyd's Rep. 133; (1973) 118 S.J. 406, QBD *2–075*
Fairport, The (No.5) [1967] 2 Lloyd's Rep. 162, PDAD *8–020*
Fairtitle v Gilbert (1787) 2 T.R. 169 .... *10–040*
Faith v EIC (1821) 4 B. & Ald. 630 .... *18–135*
Falck v Williams [1900] A.C. 176, PC (Aus) *2–002*, *5–067*, *5–071*
Falcke v Gray (1859) 3 Drew. 651 ....*18–138*, *27–014*, *27–033*
Falcke v Scottish Imperial Insurance Co (1887) L.R. 34 Ch. D. 234, CA *29–019*, *29–053*, *29–073*, *29–109*, *29–115*, *29–131*, *29–133*, *29–136*
Falco Finance Ltd v Gough (1999) 17 Tr. L.R. 526; [1999] C.C.L.R. 16, CC (Macclesfield) *15–020*
Fallick v Barber (1813) 1 M. & S. 108 .... *2–043*

Falmouth Boat Construction Co Ltd v Howell. *See* Howell v Falmouth Boat Construction Co Ltd
Famosa Shipping Co Ltd v Armada Bulk Carriers Ltd; The Fanis [1994] 1 Lloyd's Rep. 633, QBD (Comm) *26–117*
Fane v Fane (1875) L.R. 20 Eq. 698, Ct of Chancery *6–155*
Fannon v Backhouse, *The Times*, August 22, 1987, CA (Civ Div) *28–118*
Fanti and the Padre Island (No.2), The. *See* Firma C-Trade SA v Newcastle Protection and Indemnity Association
Far Eastern Shipping Plc v Scales Trading Ltd; sub nom. Scales Trading Ltd v Far Eastern Shipping Plc [2001] 1 All E.R. (Comm) 319; [2001] Lloyd's Rep. Bank. 29; [2001] C.L.C. 412, PC (NZ) 6–118
Faraday v Tamworth Union (1916) 86 L.J.Ch. 436 , QBD *5–113*
Farah Constructions Pty Ltd v Say-Dee Pty Ltd [2007] HCA 22; (2007–08) 10 I.T.E.L.R. 136, HC (Aus) *29–015*, *29–174*
Faramus v Film Artistes Association [1964] A.C. 925; [1964] 2 W.L.R. 126; [1964] 1 All E.R. 25; (1964) 108 S.J. 13, HL; affirming [1963] 2 Q.B. 527; [1963] 2 W.L.R. 504; [1963] 1 All E.R. 636; (1963) 107 S.J. 93, CA *9–075*, *9–076*, *9–082*, *9–083*, 16–133
Farebrother v Simmons, 106 E.R. 1213; (1822) 5 B. & Ald. 333, KB *4–039*
Farepak Food and Gifts Ltd. *See* Dubey v Revenue and Customs Commissioners
Farey v Cooper [1927] 2 K.B. 384, CA *16–118*
Farjab v Smyth, unreported, August 28, 1998, CA *16–066*
Farley, Re (1852) 2 De G.M.G. 936 .... *21–088*
Farley v Housing & Commercial Developments Ltd (1984) 1 B.C.C. 99150; [1984] B.C.L.C. 442; 26 B.L.R. 66; (1984) 81 L.S.G. 2216, QBD *19–009*
Farley v Skinner (No.2); sub nom. Skinner v Farley [2001] UKHL 49; [2002] 2 A.C. 732; [2001] 3 W.L.R. 899; [2001] 4 All E.R. 801; [2002] B.L.R. 1; [2002] T.C.L.R. 6; 79 Con. L.R. 1; [2002] H.L.R. 5; [2002] P.N.L.R. 2; [2001] 3 E.G.L.R. 57; [2001] 48 E.G. 131; [2001] 49 E.G. 120; [2001] 42 E.G. 139 (C.S.); (2001) 98(40) L.S.G. 41; (2001) 145 S.J.L.B. 230; [2001] N.P.C. 146, HL *26–082*, *26–083*, *26–084*, 26–085, *26–093*, *26–104*
Farmer v Moseley (Holdings) Ltd (Security for Costs) [2001] 2 B.C.L.C. 572; [2002] B.P.I.R. 473, Ch D *16–063*
Farmer v Russell (1798) 1 B. & P. 296 .... *16–192*
Farmers Mart Ltd v Milne [1915] A.C. 106; 1914 S.C. (H.L.) 84; 1914 2 S.L.T. 153, HL; affirming, 1914 S.C. 129; 1913 2 S.L.T. 410, IH (2 Div); reversing, 1913 2 S.L.T. 305, OH *16–042*
Farmizer (Products) Ltd, Re; sub nom. Moore v Gadd [1997] B.C.C. 655; [1997] 1 B.C.L.C. 589; (1997) 94(8) L.S.G. 27; (1997) 141 S.J.L.B. 45, CA (Civ Div) *28–003*
Farnworth Finance Facilities Ltd v Attryde [1970] 1 W.L.R. 1053; [1970] 2 All E.R. 774; [1970] R.T.R. 352; (1970) 114 S.J. 354, CA (Civ Div) *12–021*, *14–022*, *14–028*
Farquharson v Pearl Assurance Co Ltd [1937] 3 All E.R. 124 ....*21–088*, *21–095*
Farr (AE) v Admiralty [1953] 1 W.L.R. 965; [1953] 2 All E.R. 512; [1953] 2 Lloyd's Rep. 173; (1953) 97 S.J. 491, QBD *13–012*, *14–011*, *14–015*
Farr Smith & Co Ltd v Messers Ltd [1928] 1 K.B. 397, KBD *4–027*, *4–036*
Farra v Hetherington (1931) 40 Ll. L. Rep. 132; (1931) 47 T.L.R. 465, KBD *6–147*
Farrage v North Wiltshire DC; sub nom. Trustees of Chippenham Golf Club v North Wiltshire DC (1992) 64 P. & C.R. 527; (1992) 156 L.G. Rev. 863; [1991] E.G. 135 (C.S.); [1991] N.P.C. 139, CA (Civ Div); reversing 89 L.G.R. 785; (1991) 62 P. & C.R. 643, Ch D *3–172*, *4–058*
Farrall v Hilditch (1859) 5 C.B.(N.S.) 840 .... *13–024*
Farrant v Woodroffe School [1998] I.C.R. 184; [1998] I.R.L.R. 176, EAT *24–019*
Farrar v Hutchinson (1839) 9 A.E. 641 .... *21–058*
Farrell v Alexander [1977] A.C. 59; [1976] 3 W.L.R. 145; [1976] 2 All E.R. 721; (1976) 32 P. & C.R. 292; (1976) 120 S.J. 451, HL; reversing [1976] Q.B. 345; [1975] 3 W.L.R. 642; [1976] 1 All E.R. 129; (1976) 31 P. & C.R. 1; (1975) 119 S.J. 543, CA (Civ Div) *16–185*

Farrell v Green (1974) 232 E.G. 587 .... *4–026*
Farrow v Mayes (1852) 18 Q.B. 516 .... *29–098*
Farrow v Wilson (1868–69) L.R. 4 C.P. 744, CCP *20–006*
Fast Ferries One SA v Ferries Australia Pty Ltd [2000] 1 Lloyd's Rep. 534, QBD (Comm) *13–009*
Fastframe Ltd v Lochinski, unreported, March 3, 1993, CA *14–062*, *14–092*
Faulkner v Llewellin (1862) 31 L.J.Ch 549 .... *4–048*
Faulkner v Lowe (1848) 2 Exch. 595 .... *17–007*
Faure Electric Accumulator Co, Re (1889) L.R. 40 Ch. D. 141, Ch D *9–030*
Fawcett v Saint Merat. *See* Fawcett v Star Car Sales
Fawcett v Smethurst (1914) 84 L.J.K.B. 473 .... *8–009*, *8–016*, *8–046*
Fawcett v Star Car Sales; sub nom. Fawcett v Saint Merat [1960] N.Z.L.R. 406, CA; affirming [1959] N.Z.L.R. 952 .... *5–092*, 5–098
Fawcett and Holmes Contract, Re (1889) L.R. 42 Ch. D. 150, CA *27–055*, *27–057*
Fay v Miller, Wilkins & Co [1941] Ch. 360, CA *4–023*, *4–028*
Fayed v Al-Tajir. *See* Al-Fayed v Al- Tajir
Fearon v Earl of Aylesford (1884–85) L.R. 14 Q.B.D. 792, CA 24–036
Feather v Queen, The, 122 E.R. 1191; (1865) 6 B. & S. 257, QB *12–086*
Federal Commerce & Navigation Co Ltd v Molena Alpha Inc; The Nanfri; Federal Commerce & Navigation Co Ltd v Molena Beta Inc; The Benfri; Federal Commerce & Navigation Co Ltd v Molena Gamma Inc; The Lorfri [1979] A.C. 757; [1978] 3 W.L.R. 991; [1979] 1 All E.R. 307; [1979] 1 Lloyd's Rep. 201; (1978) 122 S.J. 843, HL; affirming in part [1978] Q.B. 927; [1978] 3 W.L.R. 309; [1978] 3 All E.R. 1066; [1978] 2 Lloyd's Rep. 132; (1978) 122 S.J. 347, CA (Civ Div); reversing [1978] 1 Lloyd's Rep. 581, QBD (Comm) *12–035*, *24–018*, *24–019*, *24–040*, *28–123*
Federal Commerce & Navigation Co Ltd v Tradax Export SA; The Maratha Envoy [1978] A.C. 1; [1977] 3 W.L.R. 126; [1977] 2 All E.R. 849; [1977] 2 Lloyd's Rep. 301; (1977) 121 S.J. 459, HL; reversing [1977] Q.B. 324; [1977] 2 W.L.R. 122; [1977] 2 All E.R. 41; [1977] 1 Lloyd's Rep. 217; (1976) 120 S.J. 834, CA (Civ Div); reversing [1975] 1 W.L.R. 1372; [1976] 1 All E.R. 293; [1975] 2 Lloyd's Rep. 223; (1975) 119 S.J. 641, QBD (Comm) *13–007*, *30–376*
Federal Steam Navigation Co Ltd v Raylton Dixon & Co Ltd (1919) 1 Ll. L. Rep. 63, HL *23–049*
Federal Sugar Refining Co v United States Sugar Equalisation Board (1920) 268 F. 575 .... *29–145*
Fehmarn, The. *See* Owners of Cargo Lately on Board the Fehmarn v Owners of the Fehmarn; The Fehmarn
Feist v Societe Intercommunale Belge d'Electricite; sub nom. Societe Intercommunale Belge d'Electricite, Re [1934] A.C. 161; 88 A.L.R. 1524, HL *21–069*, 21–070, 21–071, *30–331*
Feldarol Foundry Plc v Hermes Leasing (London) Ltd; sub nom. Feldaroll Foundry Plc v Hermes Leasing (London) Ltd; Feldarol Foundry Plc v Amari Sant Agata Classics [2004] EWCA Civ 747; (2004) 101(24) L.S.G. 32; (2004) 148 S.J.L.B. 630, CA (Civ Div) *14–066*
Felix Hadley & Co v Hadley [1898] 2 Ch. 680; (1897) 77 L.T. 131, Ch D *21–074*
Felixstowe Dock & Railway Co v British Transport Docks Board; sub nom. European Ferries Ltd v British Transport Docks Board [1976] 2 Lloyd's Rep. 656; [1976] 2 C.M.L.R. 655, CA (Civ Div); affirming [1976] 2 C.M.L.R. 405, QBD *2–152*
Fell v Whittaker (1871–72) L.R. 7 Q.B. 120, QB *29–090*, *29–091*
Fellowes v Clyde Helicopters Ltd; sub nom. Herd v Clyde Helicopters Ltd [1997] A.C. 534; [1997] 2 W.L.R. 380; [1997] 1 All E.R. 775; 1997 S.C. (H.L.) 86; 1997 S.L.T. 672; 1997 S.C.L.R. 308; (1997) 94(12) L.S.G. 22; (1997) 141 S.J.L.B. 64; 1997 G.W.D. 9–360, HL; affirming 1996 S.L.T. 976, IH (2 Div) *18–133*
Fellowes & Son v Fisher [1976] Q.B. 122; [1975] 3 W.L.R. 184; [1975] 2 All E.R. 829; (1975) 119 S.J. 390, CA (Civ Div) *27–061*
Fellows v Wood (1888) 59 L.T. 513 .... *8–023*

Feltham v Terry (1772) Lofft. 207 .... *29–141*
Felthouse v Bindley, 142 E.R. 1037; (1862) 11 C.B. N.S. 869; (1862) 6 L.T. 157, CCP *1–004*, 2–070, 2–072, 2–075
Fender v St John Mildmay; sub nom. Fender v Mildmay [1938] A.C. 1, HL; reversing [1936] 1 K.B. 111, CA; affirming [1935] 2 K.B. 334, KBD *16–070*
Fenn v Bittleston (1851) 7 Exch. 152 .... *14–034*
Fenner v Blake [1900] 1 Q.B. 426, QBD *22–032*
Fennon v Anthony Hodari & Co [2001] Lloyd's Rep. P.N. 183, CA (Civ Div) *28–011*
Fenny v Brice (1865) 18 C.B.(N.S.) 393 .... *28–064*
Fentem (Deceased), Re; sub nom. Cockerton v Fentem [1950] 2 All E.R. 1073; [1950] W.N. 543; (1950) 94 S.J. 779, Ch D *16–072*
Fenton v Fenton (1837) 1 Dr. & W. 66 .... *12–074*
Fenton v Holloway (1815) 1 Stark. 126 .... *8–080*
Fenton Insurance Co v Gothaer Versicherungsbank VVaG [1991] 1 Lloyd's Rep. 172, QBD (Comm) *2–006*
Fenton Textile Association v Thomas (1929) 45 T.L.R. 264 .... *29–142*
Fenwick v Macdonald, Fraser & Co Ltd; sub nom. Fenwick v Macdonald, Fraser & Co (1904) 6 F. 850; (1904) 12 S.L.T. 227, IH (2 Div); affirming (1904) 11 S.L.T. 734, OH *2–012*
Fenwick v Schmalz (1868) L.R. 3 C.P. 313 .... *12–087*
Fercometal Sarl v MSC Mediterranean Shipping Co SA; The Simona [1989] A.C. 788; [1988] 3 W.L.R. 200; [1988] 2 All E.R. 742; [1988] 2 Lloyd's Rep. 199; (1988) 138 N.L.J. Rep. 178; (1988) 132 S.J. 966, HL .. *24–001*, *24–002*, *24–011*, *24–012*, *24–015*, 24–025, *26–121*
Feret v Hill (1854) 15 C.B. 207 .... *16–167*, *16–178*
Ferguson v Davies [1997] 1 All E.R. 315, CA (Civ Div) *3–118*, *22–016*, *22–022*
Ferguson v John Dawson & Partners (Contractors) Ltd [1976] 1 W.L.R. 1213; [1976] 3 All E.R. 817; [1976] 2 Lloyd's Rep. 669; 8 B.L.R. 38; [1976] I.R.L.R. 346; (1976) 120 S.J. 603, CA (Civ Div); affirming [1976] 1 Lloyd's Rep. 143, QBD *12–126*
Ferguson v Littlewoods Pools Ltd, 1997 S.L.T. 309, OH *2–162*
Ferguson v Wilson (1866–67) L.R. 2 Ch. App. 77, CA in Chancery *9–030*
Ferguson Shipbuilders Ltd v Voith Hydro GmbH & Co KG, 2000 S.L.T. 229; 1999 G.W.D. 31–1500, OH *30–059*, *30–077*, *30–090*
Fergusson v Fyffe (1841) 8 Cl. & Fin. 121 .... *28–064*
Fernley v Branson (1851) 20 L.J.Q.B. 178 .... *7–015*
Ferns v Carr (1885) L.R. 28 Ch. D. 409, Ch D 29–060
Ferryways NV v Associated British Ports [2008] EWHC Comm 225; [2008] 1 Lloyd's Rep. 638 .... *12–114*, *14–006*, *14–072*
Fesenmayer v Adcock (1847) 16 M.W. 449 .... *29–191*
Fessard v Mugnier (1865) 18 C.B.(N.S.) 286 .... *21–054*
Fewings, Ex p. *See* Sneyd Ex p. Fewings, Re
Fibrenetix Storage Ltd v Davis; Fibrenetix Storage Ltd v Lapis Solutions Ltd [2004] EWHC 1359; [2004] All E.R. (D) 99, QBD *16–108*
Fibrosa Spolka Akcyjna v Fairbairn Lawson Combe Barbour Ltd; sub nom. Fibrosa Societe Anonyme v Fairbairn Lawson Combe Barbour Ltd [1943] A.C. 32; [1942] 2 All E.R. 122; (1942) 73 Ll. L. Rep. 45; 144 A.L.R. 1298, HL; reversing [1942] 1 K.B. 12; (1941) 70 Ll. L. Rep. 30, CA; affirming (1941) 69 Ll. L. Rep. 97, KBD *11–027*, *23–030*, *23–047*, *23–058*, 23–072, 23–073, 23–077, 23–094, *24–050*, *26–154*, *29–001*, *29–007*, *29–011*, *29–054*, *29–055*, *29–056*, *29–058*, *29–060*, *29–062*, *29–065*
Ficom SA v Sociedad Cadex Ltda [1980] 2 Lloyd's Rep. 118, QBD (Comm) *3–079*, *3–082*, *22–042*
Fidelitas Shipping Co Ltd v V/O Exportchleb [1966] 1 Q.B. 630; [1965] 2 W.L.R. 1059; [1965] 2 All E.R. 4; [1965] 1 Lloyd's Rep. 223; (1965) 109 S.J. 191, CA *25–011*, *25–012*, *25–013*
Field v Carr (1828) 5 Bing. 13 .... *21–066*
Field v Moore (1854) 7 De. G.M. & G. 691 .... *8–043*
Field v Newport, etc. Railway (1858) 3 H.N. 409 .... *21–091*
Field Common Ltd v Elmbridge Borough Council [2008] EWHC 2079 .... *29–142*

Fielding & Platt Ltd v Selim Najjar [1969] 1 W.L.R. 357; [1969] 2 All E.R. 150; (1969) 113 S.J. 160, CA (Civ Div) *16–031*, 16–034
Figgis, Re; sub nom. Roberts v MacLaren [1969] 1 Ch. 123; [1968] 2 W.L.R. 1173; [1968] 1 All E.R. 999; (1968) 112 S.J. 156, Ch D *12–093*
Filby v Hounsell [1896] 2 Ch. 737, Ch D *2–116*, *2–123*, *4–029*, *4–036*
Filby v Mortgage Express (No.2) Ltd [2004] EWCA Civ 759; (2004) 101(29) L.S.G. 30; [2004] N.P.C. 98; [2004] 2 P. & C.R. DG16, CA (Civ Div) *29–173*
Filiatra Legacy, The. *See* Anonima Petroli Italiana SpA and Neste Oy v Marlucidez Armadora SA
Films Rover International Ltd v Cannon Film Sales Ltd [1987] 1 W.L.R. 670; [1986] 3 All E.R. 772, Ch D 9–014
Filross Securities Ltd v Midgeley (1999) 31 H.L.R. 465; [1998] 3 E.G.L.R. 43; [1998] 43 E.G. 134; [1998] E.G. 124 (C.S.); (1998) 95(30) L.S.G. 26, CA (Civ Div) *28–123*
Finagra (UK) Ltd v OT Africa Line Ltd [1998] 2 Lloyd's Rep. 622; [1998] C.L.C. 1419, QBD (Comm) *12–079*
Finagrain SA Geneva v P Kruse Hamburg [1976] 2 Lloyd's Rep. 508, CA (Civ Div) *3–090*, *3–091*, *3–104*, *14–150*, *22–044*, *24–008*
Finance for Mortgages Ltd v Farley & Co [1998] P.N.L.R. 145; [1996] E.G. 35 (C.S.); [1996] N.P.C. 19, QBD *28–011*
Finance Ltd v Bank of New Zealand (1993) 32 N.S.W.L.R. 50 .... *7–018*
Financial Collection Agencies (UK) v Batey (1973) 117 S.J. 416, CA (Civ Div) *16–113*
Financial Services Compensation Scheme Ltd v Larnell (Insurances) Ltd (In Liquidation); sub nom. Financial Services Compensation Scheme v Larnell Insurance [2005] EWCA Civ 1408; [2006] Q.B. 808; [2006] 2 W.L.R. 751; [2006] C.P. Rep. 14; [2006] B.C.C. 690; [2006] B.P.I.R. 1370; [2006] Lloyd's Rep. I.R. 448; [2006] P.N.L.R. 13, CA (Civ Div) *28–013*
Financial Techniques (Planning Services) v Hughes [1981] I.R.L.R. 32, CA (Civ Div) *2–070*, *2–159*
Financings v Stimson [1962] 1 W.L.R. 1184; [1962] 3 All E.R. 386, CA *2–008*, *2–065*, *2–069*, *2–098*, 5–065
Financings Ltd v Baldock [1963] 2 Q.B. 104; [1963] 2 W.L.R. 359; [1963] 1 All E.R. 443; (1963) 107 S.J. 15, CA *12–037*, *12–040*, *22–047*, *22–049*, *26–141*
Finch v Boning (1878–79) L.R. 4 C.P.D. 143, CPD *21–094*
Finch v Brook (1834) 1 Bing. N.C. 253 .... *21–088*, *21–095*
Finch v Miller (1848) 5 C.B. 428 .... *21–091*
Finch v Oake [1896] 1 Ch. 409, CA *16–200*
Finchbourne Ltd v Rodrigues [1976] 3 All E.R. 581, CA (Civ Div) *2–142*
Finck v Tranter [1905] 1 K.B. 427, KBD *29–042*
Finelli v Dee (1968) 67 D.L.R. (2d) 393, CA (Ont) *24–010*, *27–029*
Finelvet AG v Vinava Shipping Co Ltd; The Chrysalis [1983] 1 W.L.R. 1469; [1983] 2 All E.R. 658; [1983] 1 Lloyd's Rep. 503; [1983] Com. L.R. 126; (1983) 80 L.S.G. 2684; (1983) 127 S.J. 680, QBD *23–030*, *23–044*, *23–080*
Finkeilkraut v Monohan [1949] 2 All E.R. 235 .... *21–014*, *26–152*
Finlan v Eyton Morris Winfield (A Firm) [2007] EWHC 914 (Ch); [2007] 4 All E.R. 143, Ch D *19–025*, *28–118*
Finland Steamship Co Ltd v Felixstowe Dock & Railway Co [1980] 2 Lloyd's Rep. 287, QBD (Comm) *3–071*
Finlay & Co Ltd v NV Kwik Hoo Tung HM. *See* James Finlay & Co Ltd v NV Kwik Hoo Tung Handel Maatschappij
Finley v Connell Associates (Application to Strike Out) [1999] Lloyd's Rep. P.N. 895; (1999) 96(26) L.S.G. 27, QBD *17–020*
Finnegan v Allen [1943] K.B. 425; [1943] 1 All E.R. 493, CA *12–031*
Finnegan v Cementation Co Ltd [1953] 1 Q.B. 688; [1953] 2 W.L.R. 1015; [1953] 1 All E.R. 1130; (1953) 97 S.J. 332, CA *20–004*
Finzel, Berry & Co v Eastcheap Dried Fruit Co [1962] 2 Lloyd's Rep. 11, CA; affirming [1962] 1 Lloyd's Rep. 370, QBD (Comm) *12–069*, *12–114*

Fiona Trust & Holding Corp v Privalov; sub nom. Premium Nafta Products Ltd v Fili Shipping Co Ltd [2007] UKHL 40; [2007] Bus. L.R. 1719; [2007] 4 All E.R. 951; [2007] 2 All E.R. (Comm) 1053; [2008] 1 Lloyd's Rep. 254; [2007] 2 C.L.C. 553; 114 Con. L.R. 69; [2007] C.I.L.L. 2528; (2007) 104(42) L.S.G. 34; (2007) 151 S.J.L.B. 1364, HL *30–046*
Firchuk and Firchuk (t/a Atlas Textile Wholesale) v Waterfront Cartage, Division of Waterfront Investments and Cartage Ltd [1969] 2 Lloyd's Rep. 533; 1970 A.M.C. 80, CC (Ont) *12–016*
Firestone Tyre & Rubber Co Ltd v Vokins & Co Ltd [1951] 1 Lloyd's Rep. 32, KBD *3–025*, 14–018
Firma C-Trade SA v Newcastle Protection and Indemnity Association; The Fanti; Socony Mobil Oil Co Inc v West of England Shipowners Mutual Insurance Association (London) Ltd; The Padre Island (No.2) [1991] 2 A.C. 1; [1990] 3 W.L.R. 78; [1990] 2 All E.R. 705; [1990] 2 Lloyd's Rep. 191; [1990] B.C.L.C. 625; 1991 A.M.C. 607; (1990) 134 S.J. 833, HL; reversing [1989] 1 Lloyd's Rep. 239, CA (Civ Div); reversing in part [1987] 2 Lloyd's Rep. 299, QBD (Comm) *18–131*, *28–049*, *28–050*
First Energy (UK) Ltd v Hungarian International Bank Ltd [1993] 2 Lloyd's Rep. 194; [1993] B.C.C. 533; [1993] B.C.L.C. 1409; [1993] N.P.C. 34, CA (Civ Div) *2–003*, *2–113*, *6–021*, *9–043*
First Interstate Bank of California v Cohen Arnold & Co [1996] 5 Bank. L.R. 150; [1996] C.L.C. 174; [1996] P.N.L.R. 17; [1995] E.G. 188 (C.S.); (1996) 140 S.J.L.B. 12, CA (Civ Div) *26–045*
First National Bank Plc v Achampong [2003] EWCA Civ 487; [2004] 1 F.C.R. 18; (2003) 147 S.J.L.B. 419; [2003] N.P.C. 46; [2003] 2 P. & C.R. DG11, CA (Civ Div) *7–123*
First National Bank Plc v Thompson [1996] Ch. 231; [1996] 2 W.L.R. 293; [1996] 1 All E.R. 140; [1996] 5 Bank. L.R. 113; (1996) 72 P. & C.R. 118; (1995) 92(28) L.S.G. 30; (1995) 139 S.J.L.B. 189; [1995] N.P.C. 130; (1996) 71 P. & C.R. D14, CA (Civ Div) *3–103*
First National Bank Plc v Walker [2001] 1 F.L.R. 505; [2001] 1 F.C.R. 21; [2001] Fam. Law 182, CA (Civ Div) 7–122
First National City Bank of Chicago v West of England Shipowners Mutual Protection and Indemnity Association (Luxembourg); The Evelpidis Era [1981] 1 Lloyd's Rep. 54, QBD (Comm) *19–070*, *19–072*
First National Commercial Bank Plc v Loxleys [1997] P.N.L.R. 211; [1996] E.G. 174 (C.S.); (1996) 93(43) L.S.G. 26; (1997) 141 S.J.L.B. 6; [1996] N.P.C. 158, CA (Civ Div) *14–084*
First National Reinsurance Co Ltd v JH Greenfield [1921] 2 K.B. 260; (1920) 5 Ll. L. Rep. 402, KBD *6–127*, *9–060*, *28–144*
First National Securities Ltd v Jones [1978] Ch. 109; [1978] 2 W.L.R. 475; [1978] 2 All E.R. 221; (1977) 121 S.J. 760, CA (Civ Div) *1–092*, *1–097*
First Realty Plc v Norton Rose [1999] 2 B.C.L.C. 428; [1999] N.P.C. 53, CA (Civ Div) *12–050*
First Sport Ltd v Barclays Bank Plc [1993] 1 W.L.R. 1229; [1993] 3 All E.R. 789; (1993) 12 Tr. L.R. 69, CA (Civ Div) *2–047*, *18–007*
Firstpost Homes Ltd v Johnson [1995] 1 W.L.R. 1567; [1995] 4 All E.R. 355; [1996] 1 E.G.L.R. 175; [1996] 13 E.G. 125; (1995) 92(28) L.S.G. 30; (1995) 139 S.J.L.B. 187; [1995] N.P.C. 135, CA (Civ Div) ...*4–006*, 4–009, 4–070, 4–073, *4–086*
Firth v Midland Railway Co (1875) L.R. 20 Eq. 100, Ct of Chancery *22–029*
Fischer v Toumazos [1991] 2 E.G.L.R. 204; [1991] 48 E.G. 123, CA (Civ Div) ... *2–155*
Fischer (Great Britain) Ltd v Multi Construction Ltd. *See* George Fischer (Great Britain) Ltd v Multi Construction Ltd
Fisher v Bell [1961] 1 Q.B. 394; [1960] 3 W.L.R. 919; [1960] 3 All E.R. 731; (1961) 125 J.P. 101; (1960) 104 S.J. 981, DC *2–014*
Fisher v Bridges, 118 E.R. 1283; (1854) 3 El. & Bl. 642, QB *16–165*
Fisher & Co v Apollinaris Co (1874–75) L.R. 10 Ch. App. 297, CA in Chancery *7–049*
Fisher & Sons, Re [1912] 2 K.B. 491, KBD *20–010*

Fisher (Louis Walter) v Keane (1879) L.R. 11 Ch. D. 353, Ch D *9–075*
Fishmonger's Corp v Robertson (1843) 5 Man. & G. 131 .... *3–167*
Fitch v Dewes; sub nom. Dewes v Fitch [1921] 2 A.C. 158, HL; affirming [1920] 2 Ch. 159, CA *16–092*, *16–108*, *16–110*, *16–113*
Fitch v Sutton (1804) 5 East 23 *004*, *22–016*
Fitzgerald, Re; sub nom. Surman v Fitzgerald [1904] 1 Ch. 573, CA *30–012*
Fitzgerald v Leonard (1893) 32 L.R.Ir. 675 .... *16–173*
Fitzgerald v Masters (1956) 95 C.L.R. 420 .... *28–142*
Fitzpatrick v Sterling Housing Association Ltd [2001] 1 A.C. 27; [1999] 3 W.L.R. 1113; [1999] 4 All E.R. 705; [1999] 2 F.L.R. 1027; [2000] 1 F.L.R. 271; [2000] 1 F.C.R. 21; [2000] U.K.H.R.R. 25; 7 B.H.R.C. 200; (2000) 32 H.L.R. 178; [2000] L. & T.R. 44; [2000] Fam. Law 14; [1999] E.G. 125 (C.S.); (1999) 96(43) L.S.G. 3; [1999] N.P.C. 127; (2000) 79 P. & C.R. D4, HL; reversing [1998] Ch. 304; [1998] 2 W.L.R. 225; [1997] 4 All E.R. 991; [1998] 1 F.L.R. 6; [1998] 1 F.C.R. 417; (1998) 30 H.L.R. 576; [1997] Fam. Law 784; [1997] E.G. 122 (C.S.); (1997) 147 N.L.J. 1275; [1997] N.P.C. 118, CA (Civ Div) *16–068*
Fitzroy v Cave [1905] 2 K.B. 364, CA *16–060*, *19–012*, *19–049*, *19–054*
Five Steel Barges, Re (1890) L.R. 15 P.D. 142, PDAD 29–136
Fjord Wind. The. *See* Eridania SpA (formerly Cereol Italia Srl) v Oetker
Flamar Interocean v Denmac; The Flamar Pride and The Flamar Progress [1990] 1 Lloyd's Rep. 434, QBD (Comm) *13–007*, *14–071*, *14–072*, *14–084*, *14–085*, *14–087*
Flamar Pride, The. *See* Flamar Interocean Ltd v Denmac Ltd
Flanagan v Great Western Railway Co (1868–69) L.R. 7 Eq. 116, Ct of Chancery *9–055*
Flarty v Odlum (1790) 3 T.R. 681 .... *16–022*
Flavell, Re; sub nom. Murray v Flavell (1884) L.R. 25 Ch. D. 89, CA *18–079*, *18–080*, *18–083*
Flaviis v Pauley (t/a Banjax Bike Hire) [2002] All E.R. (D) 436 (Oct), QBD *16–166*
Fleet v Murton (1871–72) L.R. 7 Q.B. 126, QB *12–133*
Fleet v Perrins; sub nom. Fleet (Ross's Administratrix) v Perrins (1868–69) L.R. 4 Q.B. 500, Ex Ct *29–195*
Fleetwood's Policy, Re [1926] Ch. 48, Ch D *3–036*, *18–081*
Flemyng v Hector (1836) 2 M. & W. 172 .... *9–073*
Fletamentos Maritimos SA v Effjohn International BV [1995] 1 Lloyd's Rep. 311, QBD (Comm) *13–007*
Fletcher v Fletcher (1844) 4 Hare 67 .... *18–079*, *27–034*
Fletcher v Tayleur (1855) 17 C.B. 21 .... *26–066*, *26–175*
Flight v Bolland (1828) 4 Russ. 298 .... *8–042*, *27–046*, *27–048*
Flight v Booth, 131 E.R. 1160; (1834) 1 Bing. N.C. 370, CCP *27–055*, *27–057*
Flight v Leman (1843) 4 Q.B. 883 .... *16–050*
Flight v Reed (1863) 1 H. & C. 703 3–033
Flint v Barnard (1889) L.R. 22 Q.B.D. 90, CA *20–049*
Flint v Brandon (1803) 8 Ves. 159 .... *27–026*
Flint v Lovell [1935] 1 K.B. 354; 97 A.L.R. 815, CA *26–030*
Flintoff, Ex p. (1844) 3 M.D. De.G 726 .... *25–001*
Flittens v Allfrey (1874) L.R. 10 C.P. 29 .... *25–011*
Floating Dock Ltd v Hong Kong and Shanghai Banking Corp [1986] 1 Lloyd's Rep. 65, QBD (Comm) *2–004*
Flockton v Hall (1849) 14 Q.B. 380 .... *22–023*
Flood v Patterson, 54 E.R. 640; (1861) 29 Beav. 295, Ct of Chancery *28–031*
Flood v Shand Construction Ltd [1997] C.L.C. 588; 81 B.L.R. 31; 54 Con. L.R. 125; [1996] N.P.C. 185, CA (Civ Div) *19–043*
Floods of Queensferry Ltd v Shand Construction Ltd (No.3) [2000] B.L.R. 81, QBD (TCC) 6–098
Flower v London & North Western Railway Co [1894] 2 Q.B. 65, CA ... 8–009, *8–024*, *8–029*
Flower v Marten (1837) 2 My. & Cr. 459 .... *22–004*

Flower v Sadler (1882–83) L.R. 10 Q.B.D. 572, CA; affirming (1881–82) L.R. 9 Q.B.D. 83, QBD *7–048*, *7–049*, *16–036*
Floydd v Cheney; Cheney v Floydd [1970] Ch. 602; [1970] 2 W.L.R. 314; [1970] 1 All E.R. 446; (1970) 114 S.J. 70, Ch D *1–027*
Fluck v Tollemache (1823) 1 C. & P. 5 .... *8–061*
Flynn (Deceased), Re (No.2); sub nom. Flynn v Flynn (No.2) [1969] 2 Ch. 403; [1969] 2 W.L.R. 1148; [1969] 2 All E.R. 557; (1969) 113 S.J. 428, Ch D *25–016*, *28–016*, *28–094*, *28–095*
Flynn and Newman's Contract, Re [1948] I.R. 104 .... *6–157*
Foakes v Beer; sub nom. Beer v Foakes (1883–84) L.R. 9 App. Cas. 605, HL; affirming (1882–83) L.R. 11 Q.B.D. 221, CA *3–037*, 3–115, 3–116, 3–117, 3–118, 3–120, 3–123, 3–125, 3–128, 3–129, 3–132, *12–066*, *22–004*, *22–016*
Foamcrete (UK) Ltd v Thrust Engineering Ltd [2002] B.C.C. 221, CA (Civ Div) *19–043*
Foaminol Laboratories v British Arid Plastics [1941] 2 All E.R. 393, QBD *26–083*
Foley v Classique Coaches Ltd [1934] 2 K.B. 1, CA 2–128, *29–071*
Foley v Fletcher (1858) 3 H. & N. 769 .... *22–006*
Foley v Hill, 9 E.R. 1002; (1848) 2 H.L. Cas. 28, QB *28–039*
Fontana NV v Mautner (1979) 254 E.G. 199 .... *3–093*, *3–094*, *3–137*
Food Corp of India v Antclizo Shipping Corp; The Antclizo [1988] 1 W.L.R. 603; [1988] 2 All E.R. 513; [1988] 2 Lloyd's Rep. 93; [1988] 2 F.T.L.R. 124; [1988] E.G. 62 (C.S.); (1988) 138 N.L.J. Rep. 135; (1988) 132 S.J. 752, HL, affirming [1987] 2 Lloyd's Rep. 130; [1987] 2 F.T.L.R. 114, CA (Civ Div); affirming [1986] 1 Lloyd's Rep. 181, QBD (Comm) *2–003*, *2–004*, *2–006*, *2–071*, *3–090*, *3–092*, *22–027*
Food Corp of India v Marastro Cia Naviera SA; The Trade Fortitude (No.1); Food Corp of India v Marastro Cia Naviera SA; The Trade Fortitude (No.2) [1987] 1 W.L.R. 134; [1986] 2 All E.R. 500; [1986] 2 Lloyd's Rep. 209; (1986) 83 L.S.G. 2919; (1986) 136 N.L.J. 607; (1986) 130 S.J. 649, CA (Civ Div) *26–183*
Foord v Noll (1842) 2 Dowl.(N.S.) 617 .... *21–091*
Foote v Hayne (1824) 1 C. & P. 545 .... *6–021*
Footman Bower & Co Ltd, Re [1961] Ch. 443; [1961] 2 W.L.R. 667; [1961] 2 All E.R. 161; (1961) 105 S.J. 282, Ch D *21–060*, *21–066*, *28–096*, *28–097*, *28–098*
Foran v Wight (1989) 168 C.L.R. 385 .... *24–011*, *24–012*
Forbes Abbott & Lennard v Great Western Railway (1928) 138 L.T. 286 .... *14–011*, *14–012*
Forbes v Git [1922] 1 A.C. 256, PC (Can) *12–078*
Ford v Beech (1848) 11 Q.B. 852 .... *12–044*, *22–006*, *22–015*
Ford v Cotesworth (1869–70) L.R. 5 Q.B. 544, Ex Ct *21–020*
Ford v Stuart (1852) 15 Beav. 493 .... *12–067*
Ford v White & Co [1964] 1 W.L.R. 885; [1964] 2 All E.R. 755; (1964) 108 S.J. 542, Ch D 1–164
Ford & Co Ltd v Cie Furness. *See* H Ford & Co v Compagnie Furness
Ford Hunt v Singh (Raghbir) [1973] 1 W.L.R. 738; [1973] 2 All E.R. 700; (1973) 117 S.J. 341, Ch D *27–081*
Ford Motor Co v Armstrong (1915) 31 T.L.R. 267 .... *26–127*, 26–133
Ford Motor Co Ltd v Amalgamated Union of Engineering and Foundry Workers [1969] 2 Q.B. 303; [1969] 1 W.L.R. 339; [1969] 2 All E.R. 481; (1969) 6 K.I.R. 50; (1969) 113 S.J. 203, QBD 2–177
Forder v GW Ry [1905] 2 K.B. 532 .... *14–017*
Fores v Johnes (1802) 4 Esp. 97 .... *16–014*
Forestry Commission of New South Wales v Stefanetto, 133 C.L.R. 507, HC (Aus) *26–138*
Forman & Co Proprietary Ltd v Liddesdale, The [1900] A.C. 190, PC (Aus) .... *21–004* , *21–029*, *21–031*, *21–035*, *29–053*, *29–073*
Formby Bros v Formby (1910) 102 L.T. 116 .... *12–114*
Forrer v Nash, 55 E.R. 858; (1865) 35 Beav. 167, Ct of Chancery *27–041*

Forrest v Glasser [2006] EWCA Civ 1086; [2006] 2 Lloyd's Rep. 392; (2006) 150 S.J.L.B. 1052, CA (Civ Div) *12–050*, *12–051*, *12–055*
Forsikringsaktieselskapet Vesta v Butcher [1989] A.C. 852; [1989] 2 W.L.R. 290; [1989] 1 All E.R. 402; [1989] 1 Lloyd's Rep. 331; [1989] Fin. L.R. 223; (1989) 133 S.J. 184, HL; affirming [1988] 3 W.L.R. 565; [1988] 2 All E.R. 43; [1988] 1 Lloyd's Rep. 19; [1988] 1 F.T.L.R. 78; [1988] Fin. L.R. 67; (1988) 4 Const. L.J. 75; (1988) 85(31) L.S.G. 33; (1988) 132 S.J. 1181, CA (Civ Div); affirming [1986] 2 All E.R. 488; [1986] 2 Lloyd's Rep. 179, QBD (Comm) *1–122*, *1–143*, 1–166, *6–064*, *12–055*, *12–072*, *12–118*, *18–023*, 26–049, *30–011*, *30–012*, *30–015*
Forslind v Bechely-Crundall, 1922 S.C. (H.L.) 173; 1922 S.L.T. 496, HL *24–018*, *24–021*
Forster v Baker [1910] 2 K.B. 636, CA *19–014*
Forster v Elvet Colliery Co. *See* Dyson v Forster
Forster v Hale (1800) 5 Ves. 308 .... *4–012*, *4–066*
Forster v Outred & Co [1982] 1 W.L.R. 86; [1982] 2 All E.R. 753; (1981) 125 S.J. 309, CA (Civ Div) *1–124*, *1–167*, *28–033*, *28–034*
Forster v Silvermere Golf and Equestrian Centre (1981) 42 P. & C.R. 255; (1981) 125 S.J. 397, Ch D 18–051, *18–068*
Forsyth-Grant v Allen [2008] EWCA Civ 505; [2008] 15 E.G. 172 (C.S.), CA (Civ Div) *29–142*
Fortescue v Barnett (1834) 3 My. & K. 36 .... *19–033*
Fortisbank SA v Trenwick International Ltd [2005] EWHC 399; [2005] Lloyd's Rep. I.R. 464, QBD (Comm) *3–090*, *3–094*, *3–104*, *3–109*
Fortman Holdings Ltd v Modem Holdings Ltd [2001] EWCA Civ 1235, CA (Civ Div) *22–048*
Forum Craftsman, The [1985] 1 Lloyd's Rep. 291, CA (Civ Div); affirming [1984] 2 Lloyd's Rep. 102, QBD (Admlty) *18–019*
Fosbroke-Hobbes v Airwork Ltd [1937] 1 All E.R. 108 .... *14–040*
Foskett v McKeown [2001] 1 A.C. 102; [2000] 2 W.L.R. 1299; [2000] 3 All E.R. 97; [2000] Lloyd's Rep. I.R. 627; [2000] W.T.L.R. 667; (1999–2000) 2 I.T.E.L.R. 711; (2000) 97(23) L.S.G. 44, HL *29–001*, *29–010*, *29–017*, *29–158*, *29–159*, *29–162*, *29–165*, *29–166*, 29–172, *29–174*, *29–175*, *29–179*
Foster, Re; sub nom. Hudson v Foster [1938] 3 All E.R. 357, Ch D ... *18–079*, *18–082*, *18–125*
Foster v Bates (1843) 12 M. & W. 226 .... *20–004*, *20–009*
Foster v Dawber (1861) 6 Exch. 838 .... *3–015*, *3–077*, *22–003*, *22–004*, *22–025*
Foster v Driscoll; Lindsay v Attfield; Lindsay v Driscoll [1929] 1 K.B. 470, CA ...*16–031*, *30–363*, *30–367*
Foster v Foster [1916] 1 Ch. 532, Ch D *9–058*
Foster v Jolly (1835) 1 C.M. & R. 703 .... *12–101*
Foster v London Chatham & Dover Railway Co [1895] 1 Q.B. 711, CA *10–027*
Foster v Mackinnon (1868–69) L.R. 4 C.P. 704, CCP 5–101, *5–103*, *12–106*
Foster v Mentor Life Assurance Co (1854) 3 E. & B. 48 .... *4–032*
Foster v Redgrave (1867) L.R. 4 Ex. 35n *8–008*
Foster v Robinson [1951] 1 K.B. 149; [1950] 2 All E.R. 342; 66 T.L.R. (Pt. 2) 120; (1950) 94 S.J. 474, CA *13–028*
Foster v Stewart (1814) 3 M.S. 191 .... *29–142*
Foster Clark's Indenture Trust, Re; sub nom. Loveland v Horscroft [1966] 1 W.L.R. 125; [1966] 1 All E.R. 43; (1966) 110 S.J. 108, Ch D *9–050*
Foster's Policy, Re; sub nom. Menneer v Foster [1966] 1 W.L.R. 222; [1966] 1 All E.R. 432; (1966) 110 S.J. 151, Ch D *18–079*, *18–080*, *18–126*
Fothergill v Rowland (1873–74) L.R. 17 Eq. 132, Ct of Chancery *27–017*, *27–070*
Foundling Hospital (Governors and Guardians) v Crane; sub nom. Governors and Guardians of the Foundling Hospital v Crane [1911] 2 K.B. 367, CA *1–105*
Fountaine v Carmarthen Railway Co (1867–68) L.R. 5 Eq. 316, Ct of Chancery *9–040*
Four Point Garage v Carter, *The Times*, November 19, 1984, QBD *29–168*
Fowell v Forrest (1670) 2 Wms.Saund. 47 .... *22–006*

Fowkes v Manchester Assurance Association, 122 E.R. 343; (1863) 3 B. & S. 917; (1863) 32 L.J. Q.B. 153, KBD ... *5–067*
Fowler v Bratt [1950] 2 K.B. 96; [1950] 1 All E.R. 662; 66 T.L.R. (Pt. 1) 889; (1950) 94 S.J. 269, CA ... *4–028*
Fowler v Broad's Patent Night Light Co [1893] 1 Ch. 724, Ch D ... *9–047*
Fowler v Commercial Timber Co Ltd [1930] 2 K.B. 1, CA ... *9–047*
Fowler v Fowler (1859) 4 De. G. & J. 250 ... *5–122*
Fowler v Hunter (1829) 3 Y. & J. 506 ... *12–067*
Fowler v Midland Electric Corp for Power Distribution Ltd [1917] 1 Ch. 656, CA ... *21–054*
Fox v Henderson Investment Fund Ltd [1999] 2 Lloyd's Rep. 303, QBD (Comm) ... *23–028*, *30–364*, *30–365*, *30–367*
Fox Brothers (Clothes) Ltd v Bryant [1979] I.C.R. 64; [1978] I.R.L.R. 485; (1978) 13 I.T.R. 593; (1978) 122 S.J. 759, EAT ... *9–047*
Fox Walker & Co Ex p. Bishop, Re (1880) L.R. 15 Ch. D. 400, CA ... *29–108*
Fox-Bourne v Vernon & Co Ltd (1894) 10 T.L.R. 647 ... *13–018*
Fracis Times & Co v Carr. *See* Carr v Fracis Times & Co
Francis v Cockrell (1869–70) L.R. 5 Q.B. 501, Ex Chamber; affirming (1869–70) L.R. 5 Q.B. 184, QB ... *13–014*
Francis v Cowcliffe Ltd (1977) 33 P. & C.R. 368; 239 E.G. 977, Ch D ... *27–031*
Francis v Kuala Lumpur Councillors. *See* Francis v Municipal Councillors of Kuala Lumpur
Francis v Municipal Councillors of Kuala Lumpur [1962] 1 W.L.R. 1411; [1962] 3 All E.R. 633; (1962) 106 S.J. 833, PC (FMS) ... *27–022*
Francis Delzene v Klee (1968) S.J. 583 ... *16–203*
Franco-British Ship Store Co v Compagnie des Chargeurs Française (1926) 42 T.L.R. 735 ... *4–028*
Frank Pais, The [1986] 1 Lloyd's Rep. 529, QBD (Admlty) ... *30–005*
Frank v Knight (1937) O.P.D. 113 ... *2–065*
Frank W Clifford Ltd v Garth [1956] 1 W.L.R. 570; [1956] 2 All E.R. 323; (1956) 100 S.J. 379, CA ... *16–154*, *16–195*
Franklin v Attorney General [1974] Q.B. 185; [1973] 2 W.L.R. 225; [1973] 1 All E.R. 879; (1972) 117 S.J. 143, QBD ... *10–015*
Franklin v Miller (1836) 4 A.E. 499 ... *24–018*
Franks v Reuters Ltd [2003] EWCA Civ 417; [2003] I.C.R. 1166; [2003] I.R.L.R. 423; (2003) 100(25) L.S.G. 45; (2003) 147 S.J.L.B. 474, CA (Civ Div) ... *2–175*
Frans Maas (UK) Ltd v Samsung Electronics (UK) Ltd [2004] EWHC 1502; [2005] 2 All E.R. (Comm) 783; [2004] 2 Lloyd's Rep. 251; [2005] 1 C.L.C. 647, QBD (Comm) ... *14–010*, *14–011*, *14–016*, *14–085*, *14–087*, 14–096, *14–099*
Fraser v Buckle [1996] 1 I.R. 1 ... *30–367*
Fraser v Evans [1969] 1 Q.B. 349; [1968] 3 W.L.R. 1172; [1969] 1 All E.R. 8; (1968) 112 S.J. 805, CA (Civ Div) ... *1–066*
Fraser v Pendlebury (1861) 31 L.J.C.P. 1 ... *29–093*
Fraser v Thames Television Ltd [1984] Q.B. 44; [1983] 2 W.L.R. 917; [1983] 2 All E.R. 101; (1983) 133 N.L.J. 281; (1983) 127 S.J. 379, QBD ... *2–127*
Fraser River Pile & Dredge Ltd v Can-Dive Services Ltd [2000] 1 Lloyd's Rep. 199, Sup Ct (Can) ... *18–020*
Fratelli Moretti SpA v Nidera Handelscompagnie BV [1981] 2 Lloyd's Rep. 47, CA (Civ Div) ... *26–138*
Fratelli Sorrentino v Buerger [1915] 3 K.B. 367, CA; affirming [1915] 1 K.B. 307, KBD ... *19–082*, *19–083*
Frawley v Neill [2000] C.P. Rep. 20; (1999) 96(12) L.S.G. 33; (1999) 143 S.J.L.B. 98, CA (Civ Div) ... *28–138*
Freakley v Fox (1829) 9 B.C. 130 ... *25–005*
Fred Drughorn Ltd v Rederiaktiebolaget Transatlantic; sub nom. Rederi Aktienbolaget Transatlantic v Fred Drughorn Ltd [1919] A.C. 203, HL; affirming [1918] 1 K.B. 394, CA ... *12–114*

Frederick E Rose (London) Ltd v William H Pim Junior & Co Ltd [1953] 2 Q.B. 450; [1953] 3 W.L.R. 497; [1953] 2 All E.R. 739; [1953] 2 Lloyd's Rep. 238; (1953) 70 R.P.C. 238; (1953) 97 S.J. 556, CA; reversing [1953] 1 Lloyd's Rep. 84, QBD *5–113*, 5–123
Free v Hawkins (1817) 8 Taunt. 92 .... *12–101*
Freedman (t/a John Freedman & Co) v Union Group Plc [1997] E.G. 28 (C.S.), CA (Civ Div) *3–052*
Freedom General Shipping SA v Tokai Shipping Co; The Khian Zephyr [1982] 1 Lloyd's Rep. 73, QBD (Comm) *28–022*
Freedom Maritime Corp v International Bulk Carriers; The Khian Captain (No.2) [1986] 1 Lloyd's Rep. 429, QBD (Comm) *19–070*
Freeguard v Rogers (No.1) [1999] 1 W.L.R. 375; [1998] E.G. 145 (C.S.); (1998) 95(45) L.S.G. 40; (1999) 143 S.J.L.B. 12, CA (Civ Div) *12–123*
Freehold Land Investments Ltd v Queensland Estates Ltd (1970) 123 C.L.R. 418 .... *30–007*, *30–311*
Freeland, Re; sub nom. Jackson v Rodgers [1952] Ch. 110; [1952] 1 All E.R. 16; [1951] 2 T.L.R. 1076; (1951) 95 S.J. 802, CA *25–005*
Freeman v Cooke, 154 E.R. 652; (1848) 2 Ex. 654, Ex Ct *3–103*
Freeman v Fox. *See* Cooperative Insurance Society corp v Freeman Fox & Partners
Freeman v Home Office [1984] Q.B. 524; [1984] 2 W.L.R. 802; [1984] 1 All E.R. 1036; (1984) 81 L.S.G. 1045; (1984) 128 S.J. 298, CA (Civ Div); affirming [1984] 2 W.L.R. 130; [1983] 3 All E.R. 589; (1983) 133 N.L.J. 726; (1983) 127 S.J. 825, QBD *1–153*
Freeman v Jeffries (1868–69) L.R. 4 Ex. 189, Ex Ct *29–013*, *29–040*
Freeman v Read (1863) 4 B.S. 174 .... *21–026*
Freeman v Taylor (1831) 8 Bing. 124 .... *12–035*, *14–030*, *24–040*
Freeman & Lockyer v Buckhurst Park Properties (Mangal) Ltd [1964] 2 Q.B. 480; [1964] 2 W.L.R. 618; [1964] 1 All E.R. 630; (1964) 108 S.J. 96, CA *9–021*, *9–040*, *9–042*, 9–043
Freeth v Burr (1873–74) L.R. 9 C.P. 208, CCP *24–018*, *24–019*, *24–044*
Freightex Ltd v International Express Co Ltd, unreported, April 15, 1980, CA *16–063*, *19–049*
Freights Queen, The. *See* Mineracoas Brasilieras Reunidas v EF Marine SA; The Freights Queen
French Marine v Compagnie Napolitaine d'Eclairage et de Chauffage par le Gaz; Compagnie Napolitaine d'Eclairage et du Chauffage Par Gaz v French Marine; sub nom. Stella Shipping Co Ltd v RWJ Sutherland & Co [1921] 2 A.C. 494; (1921) 8 Ll. L. Rep. 345, HL *23–072*
French v Barclays Bank Plc [1998] I.R.L.R. 646, CA (Civ Div) *26–083*
French's (Wine Bar) Ltd, Re (1987) 3 B.C.C. 173; [1987] B.C.L.C. 499, Ch D (Companies Ct) *9–049*
Frenkel v MacAndrews & Co Ltd [1929] A.C. 545; (1929) 33 Ll. L. Rep. 191, HL; affirming (1928) 31 Ll. L. Rep. 92, CA; reversing (1928) 30 Ll. L. Rep. 173, KBD *14–021*
Frewen, Re (1889) 60 L.T. 953 .... *20–013*
Friedeberg Seeley v Klass (1957) 101 S.J. 275 .... *7–011*
Friend v Harrison (1827) 2 Car. & P. 584 .... *16–067*
Friend v Young [1897] 2 Ch. 421, Ch D *28–128*
Friends Provident Life Office v Hillier Parker May & Rowden [1997] Q.B. 85; [1996] 2 W.L.R. 123; [1995] 4 All E.R. 260; [1995] C.L.C. 592; (1996) 71 P. & C.R. 286; [1995] E.G. 64 (C.S.); [1995] N.P.C. 63, CA (Civ Div) *17–030*, *29–045*, *29–049*, *29–075*, *29–121*
Frisby v BBC [1967] Ch. 932; [1967] 2 W.L.R. 1204; [1967] 2 All E.R. 106; (1967) 111 S.J. 91, Ch D *12–004*, *12–103*
Frisia, The [1960] 1 Lloyd's Rep. 90, CA *26–164*
Frith v Frith [1906] A.C. 254, PC (TCI) *12–108*
Frobisher (Second Investments) Ltd v Kiloran Trust Co Ltd [1980] 1 W.L.R. 425; [1980] 1 All E.R. 488; (1980) 40 P. & C.R. 442, Ch D *13–007*

Front Carriers Ltd v Atlantic and Orient Shipping Corp (Double Happiness) [2007] EWHC 421 (Comm); [2007] 2 Lloyd's Rep. 131, QBD (Comm) *2–071*, *3–092*, *12–075*
Frontier International Shipping Corp v Swissmarine Corp Inc; The Cape Equinox [2005] EWHC 8; [2005] 1 All E.R. (Comm) 528; [2005] 1 Lloyd's Rep. 390; [2005] 1 C.L.C. 1, QBD (Comm) *14–138*
Frost v Aylesbury Dairy Co Ltd [1905] 1 K.B. 608, CA *18–026*
Frost v Knight (1871–72) L.R. 7 Ex. 111, Ex Chamber *24–001*, *24–011*, *24–022*
Frota Oceanica Brasiliera SA v Steamship Mutual Underwriting Association (Bermuda) Ltd; The Frotanorte [1996] 2 Lloyd's Rep. 461; [1997] C.L.C. 230, CA (Civ Div); affirming [1995] 2 Lloyd's Rep. 254; [1995] C.L.C. 999, QBD (Comm) *2–029*
Fry v Lane; sub nom. Whittet v Bush; Fry, Re (1889) L.R. 40 Ch. D. 312, Ch D 7–128, *7–131*
Fry (Deceased), Re; Chase National Executors and Trustees Corp v Fry [1946] Ch. 312, Ch D *1–108*, *19–034*
Fuji Seal Europe Ltd v Catalytic Combustion Corp [2005] EWHC 1659 (TCC); 102 Con. L.R. 47, QBD (TCC) *18–009*
Fulham Football Club Ltd v Cabra Estates Plc [1992] B.C.C. 863; [1994] 1 B.C.L.C. 363; (1993) 65 P. & C.R. 284; [1993] 1 P.L.R. 29; (1992) 136 S.J.L.B. 267, CA (Civ Div); reversing [1992] N.P.C. 115, Ch D *16–039*
Full Metal Jacket Ltd v Gowlain Building Group [2005] EWCA Civ 1809, CA (Civ Div) *12–126*
Fuller v Happy Shopper Markets Ltd [2001] 1 W.L.R. 1681; [2001] 2 Lloyd's Rep. 49; [2001] L. & T.R. 16; [2001] 2 E.G.L.R. 32; [2001] 25 E.G. 159; [2001] 9 E.G. 226 (C.S.); (2001) 98(11) L.S.G. 43; (2001) 145 S.J.L.B. 62; [2001] N.P.C. 35, Ch D *28–058*, *28–123*, *29–040*
Fuller v Redman (No.2) (1859) 26 Beav. 614 ....*28–131*, *28*
Fullerton v Provincial Bank of Ireland [1903] A.C. 309, HL (UK-Irl) *3–047*, *3–057*, *3–060*
Fullwood v Fullwood (1878) L.R. 9 Ch. D. 176, Ch D *28–135*, *28–139*
Furini v Bajwa. *See* Bajwa v Furini
Furlong v Burns & Co (1964) 43 D.L.R. (2d) 689, HC (Ont) *16–201*
Furness Withy (Australia) Ltd v Metal Distributors (UK) Ltd; The Amazonia [1990] 1 Lloyd's Rep. 236, CA (Civ Div); affirming [1989] 1 Lloyd's Rep. 403, QBD (Comm) *2–004*, *2–180*, *3–115*, *5–054*
Furness Withy Co v Hall (1909) 25 T.L.R. 233 ....*25–008*, *26–013*
Furnival v Bogle (1827) 4 Russ. 142 .... *5–062*
Furnivall v Coombes (1843) 5 M. & G. 736 .... *12–078*
Furtado v Rogers (1802) 3 Bos & Pul. 191 .... *16–026*
Fusion Interactive Communication Solutions Ltd v Venture Investment Placement Ltd (No.2) [2005] EWHC 736; [2006] B.C.C. 187; [2005] 2 B.C.L.C. 571, Ch D *21–074*
Fyffes Group Ltd v Templeman [2000] 2 Lloyd's Rep. 643; (2000) 97(25) L.S.G. 40, QBD (Comm) *29–156*
Fyson v Chambers (1842) 9 M. & W. 460 .... *20–055*
G (A) v G (T); sub nom. G v G [1970] 2 Q.B. 643; [1970] 3 W.L.R. 132; [1970] 3 All E.R. 546; (1970) 114 S.J. 493, CA (Civ Div) *8–058*, *8–065*
G&C Kreglinger v New Patagonia Meat & Cold Storage Co Ltd; sub nom. Kreglinger v New Patagonia Meat & Cold Storage Co Ltd [1914] A.C. 25, HL *21–016*
G&H Montage GmbH (formerly Grunzweig und Hartmann Montage GmbH) v Irvani [1990] 1 W.L.R. 667; [1990] 2 All E.R. 225; [1990] 1 Lloyd's Rep. 14; [1989] Fin. L.R. 390; (1990) 87(8) L.S.G. 44; (1990) 134 S.J. 425, CA (Civ Div) *30–311*
G&K Ladenbau (UK) Ltd v Crawley & de Reya [1978] 1 W.L.R. 266; [1978] 1 All E.R. 682, QBD *26–068*
G&N Angelakis Shipping Co SA v Compagnie National Algerienne de Navigation; The Attika Hope [1988] 1 Lloyd's Rep. 439, QBD (Comm) ... *3–047*, *19–068*
G&T Earle v Hemsworth RDC (1928) 44 T.L.R. 605 ....*19–008*, *19–014*

G Percy Trentham Ltd v Archital Luxfer Ltd [1993] 1 Lloyd's Rep. 25; 63 B.L.R. 44, CA (Civ Div) *2–003*, *2–028*, *2–032*, *2–111*
G Scammell and Nephew Ltd v HC&JG Ouston [1941] A.C. 251, HL *2–128*, 2–139
GE Commercial Finance Ltd v Gee [2005] EWHC 2056; [2006] 1 Lloyd's Rep. 337, QBD *6–048*
GE Crane Sales Pty v Commissioner of Taxation (1971) 126 C.L.R. 177 .... *19–021*, *19–049*
GF Sharp & Co Ltd v McMillan [1998] I.R.L.R. 632, EAT *2–180*, *23–007*, *23–038*
GFI Group Inc v Eaglestone [1994] I.R.L.R. 119; [1994] F.S.R. 535, QBD *27–061*
GH Myers & Co v Brent Cross Service Co [1934] 1 K.B. 46, KBD *13–030*
GH Renton & Co Ltd v Palmyra Trading Corp of Panama; The Caspiana [1957] A.C. 149; [1957] 2 W.L.R. 45; [1956] 3 All E.R. 957; [1956] 2 Lloyd's Rep. 379, HL; affirming [1956] 1 Q.B. 462; [1956] 2 W.L.R. 232; [1956] 1 All E.R. 209; [1955] 2 Lloyd's Rep. 722; (1957) 101 S.J. 43, CA; reversing [1955] 3 W.L.R. 535; [1955] 3 All E.R. 251; [1955] 2 Lloyd's Rep. 301; (1955) 99 S.J. 762, QBD *12–073*, *14–007*
GKN Centrax Gears Ltd v Matbro Ltd [1976] 2 Lloyd's Rep. 555; (1976) 120 S.J. 401, CA (Civ Div) *26–087*
GKN Distributors, Ltd v Tyne Tees Fabrication, Ltd (1985) 50 P. & C.R. 403; [1985] 2 E.G.L.R. 181; (1985) 275 E.G. 53, Ch D *27–083*
GL Baker Ltd v Medway Building and Supplies Ltd [1958] 1 W.L.R. 1216; [1958] 3 All E.R. 540; (1958) 102 S.J. 877, Gadderer v Dawes (1847) 10 L.T.(O.S.) 109 .... *21–058*
GLC v Connolly. *See* Greater London Council v Connolly
GS Fashions v B&Q Plc [1995] 1 W.L.R. 1088; [1995] 4 All E.R. 899; [1995] 1 E.G.L.R. 62; [1995] 09 E.G. 324; [1994] E.G. 161 (C.S.); [1994] N.P.C. 128; (1994) 68 P. & C.R. D24, Ch D *5–076*
GUS Property Management Ltd v Littlewoods Mail Order Stores Ltd; sub nom. J Dykes Ltd v Littlewoods Mail Order Stores Ltd, 1982 S.C. (H.L.) 157; 1982 S.L.T. 533, HL; reversing unreported, March 12, 1981, IH (1 Div); reversing 1982 S.L.T. 50, OH *19–049*, *19–075*
GW Atkins v Scott (1991) 7 Const. L.J. 215, CA (Civ Div) *26–016*
GW Plowman & Son Ltd v Ash; sub nom. Plowman (GW) & Son v Ash [1964] 1 W.L.R. 568; [1964] 2 All E.R. 10; (1964) 108 S.J. 216, CA *16–110*, *16–111*, *16–112*, *16–113*
Gabriel v Dresser (1855) 15 C.B. 622 .... *22–015*
Gadd v Thompson [1911] 1 K.B. 304, KBD *8–013*, *8–023*, *8–026*, *16–102*
Gafford v Graham (1999) 77 P. & C.R. 73; [1999] 3 E.G.L.R. 75; [1999] 41 E.G. 159; (1998) 95(21) L.S.G. 36; (1999) 96(40) L.S.G. 44; (1998) 142 S.J.L.B. 155; [1998] N.P.C. 66; (1998) 76 P. & C.R. D18, CA (Civ Div) *27–063*
Gage v King (Quantum) [1961] 1 Q.B. 188; [1960] 3 W.L.R. 460; [1960] 3 All E.R. 62; (1960) 104 S.J. 644, QBD *2–169*
Gaiman v National Association for Mental Health [1971] Ch. 317; [1970] 3 W.L.R. 42; [1970] 2 All E.R. 362; (1970) 114 S.J. 416, Ch D *9–075*
Gaisberg v Storr [1950] 1 K.B. 107; [1949] 2 All E.R. 411; 65 T.L.R. 485; [1949] W.N. 337; (1949) 93 S.J. 600, CA *12–126*
Galaxy Energy International Ltd v Assuranceforeningen Skuld (Ejensidie); The Oakwell [1999] 1 Lloyd's Rep. 249; [1999] C.L.C. 216, QBD (Comm) *12–118*
Galaxy Energy International Ltd v Novorossiysk Shipping Co; The Petr Schmidt [1998] 2 Lloyd's Rep. 1; [1998] C.L.C. 894, CA (Civ Div); affirming [1997] 1 Lloyd's Rep. 284; [1997] C.L.C. 402, QBD (Comm) *2–047*
Galbraith & Grant Ltd v Block [1922] 2 K.B. 155, KBD *21–043*
Galbraith v Mitchenall Estates [1965] 2 Q.B. 473; [1964] 3 W.L.R. 454; [1964] 2 All E.R. 653; (1964) 108 S.J. 749, QBD *22–048*, *24–051*, *26–150*, *26–155*, *29–061*
Gale v Williamson (1841) 8 M. & W. 405; 10 L.J.Ex. 446 .... *12–108*
Gallagher Switchboard Corp v Heckler Electric Co (1962) 229 N.Y.S. 2d. 623 ..... *7–031*
Gallaher Ltd v Gallaher Pensions Ltd [2005] EWHC 42 (Ch); [2005] All E.R. (D) 177; [2005] O.P.L.R. 57; [2005] Pens. L.R. 103, Ch D *5–114*

Galliard Homes Ltd v Jarvis Interiors Ltd. *See* Jarvis Interiors Ltd v Galliard Homes Ltd
Gallie v Lee. *See* Saunders (Executrix of the Estate of Rose Maud Gallie) v Anglia Building Society
Galloway v Galloway (1914) 30 T.L.R. 531 .... *5–024*
Galloway v Guardian Royal Exchange (UK) Ltd [1999] Lloyd's Rep. I.R. 209, CA (Civ Div) *16–060*
Galoo Ltd v Bright Grahame Murray [1994] 1 W.L.R. 1360; [1995] 1 All E.R. 16; [1994] B.C.C. 319, CA (Civ Div) *1–122*, *1–165*, *6–029*, *26–032*, *26–037*, *26–100B*
Galsworthy v Strutt (1848) 1 Ex. 659 .... *26–134*
Gamerco SA v ICM/Fair Warning (Agency) Ltd [1995] 1 W.L.R. 1226; [1995] C.L.C. 536; [1995] E.M.L.R. 263, QBD *2–155*, *23–002*, 23–081, 23–082
Gan Insurance Co Ltd v Tai Ping Insurance Co Ltd (No.1); Royal Reinsurance Co Ltd v Central Insurance Co Ltd [1999] 2 All E.R. (Comm) 54; [1999] C.L.C. 1270; [1999] I.L.Pr. 729; [1999] Lloyd's Rep. I.R. 472, CA (Civ Div) *30–011*, *30–012*, *30–015*, *30–023*, *30–051*
Gandy v Gandy (1885) L.R. 30 Ch. D. 57, CA 1*8–019*, *18–079*
Garcia v National Australian Bank Ltd [1998] 155 A.L.R. 614, HC (Aus) *7–107*, *7–136*
Garden Cottage Foods Ltd v Milk Marketing Board [1984] A.C. 130; [1983] 3 W.L.R. 143; [1983] 2 All E.R. 770; [1983] Com. L.R. 198; [1983] 3 C.M.L.R. 43; [1984] F.S.R. 23; (1983) 127 S.J. 460, HL *27–011*, *27–074*, *27–078*
Garden Neptune Shipping v Occidental Worldwide Investment Corp and Concord Petroleum Corp [1990] 1 Lloyd's Rep. 330, CA (Civ Div); reversing [1989] 1 Lloyd's Rep. 305, QBD *6–069*
Garden v Bruce (1867–68) L.R. 3 C.P. 300, CCP *28–036*
Gardiner v Moore (No.2) [1969] 1 Q.B. 55; [1966] 3 W.L.R. 786; [1966] 1 All E.R. 365; (1965) 110 S.J. 34, QBD *13–007*, *17–018*
Gardner v Brooke [1897] 2 Ir.R. 6 .... *17–027*
Gardner v Lachlan (1836) 8 Sim.123; Donnelly 119 .... *18–122*
Gardner v Marsh & Parsons [1997] 1 W.L.R. 489; [1997] 3 All E.R. 871; [1997] P.N.L.R. 362; (1998) 75 P. & C.R. 319; [1997] 1 E.G.L.R. 111; [1997] 15 E.G. 137; [1996] E.G. 186 (C.S.); (1996) 93(46) L.S.G. 28; (1996) 140 S.J.L.B. 262; [1996] N.P.C. 162, CA (Civ Div) *26–093*, *26–117*
Gardner v Moore [1984] A.C. 548; [1984] 2 W.L.R. 714; [1984] 1 All E.R. 1100; [1984] 2 Lloyd's Rep. 135; [1984] R.T.R. 209; (1984) 81 L.S.G. 1444; (1984) 128 S.J. 282, HL *16–173*, *18–131*
Gardner v Walsh (1855) 5 E. & B. 83; 24 L.J.Q.B. 285; 25 L.T. (O.S.) 155; 1 Jur. (N.S.) 428; 3 W.R. 460; 3 C.L.R. 1235 .... *17–022*
Garland v Consumer's Gas Distributors Inc [2004] 1 S.C.R. 629 .... *29–015*
Garnac Grain Co Inc v HMF Faure & Fairclough Ltd; sub nom. Bunge Corp v HMF Faure & Fairclough Ltd [1968] A.C. 1130; [1967] 3 W.L.R. 143; [1967] 2 All E.R. 353; [1967] 1 Lloyd's Rep. 495; (1967) 111 S.J. 434, HL; affirming [1966] 1 Q.B. 650; [1965] 3 W.L.R. 934; [1965] 3 All E.R. 273; [1965] 2 Lloyd's Rep. 229; (1965) 109 S.J. 571, CA; reversing [1965] 2 W.L.R. 696; [1965] 1 All E.R. 47; [1964] 2 Lloyd's Rep. 296; (1964) 108 S.J. 693, QBD (Comm) *6–021*, *6–076*, *24–003*, *24–022*
Garnett, Re; sub nom. Gandy v Macaulay (1886) L.R. 31 Ch. D. 1, CA *5–129*, *28–141*, *28–145*
Garnham, Harris & Elton v Ellis (Alfred W) (Transport) [1967] 1 W.L.R. 940; [1967] 2 All E.R. 940; [1967] 2 Lloyd's Rep. 22; (1967) 111 S.J. 558, QBD *14–008*, *14–034*, *14–038*
Garrard v Frankel (1862) 30 Beav. 445; 31 L.J. Ch. 604; 8 Jur. 985; 132 R.R. 352, Ct of Chancery 5–119, 5–120
Garrett v Noble (1834) 6 Sim. 504; 3 L.J. Ch. 159; 58 E.R. 683 .... *20–010*
Gartside v Outram (1857) 26 L.J. Ch. 113; 28 L.T. (O.S.) 120; 3 Jur. (N.S.) 5 W.R. 35 .... *16–035*
Gasbourne Pty Ltd [1984] V.R. 801 .... *29–099*, *29–109*
Gaskell v King (1809) 11 East 165; 10 R.R. 462 .... *16–195*

Gastronome (UK) Ltd v Anglo Dutch Meats (UK) Ltd [2006] EWCA Civ 1233; [2006] 2 Lloyd's Rep. 587, CA (Civ Div); affirming [2005] EWHC 3237 (QB), QBD *12–050*, *12–075*, *12–118*, *12–122*, *12–124*
Gates v City Mutual Life Assurance Society Ltd (1986) C.L.R. 1 .... *1–122*
Gath v Lees (1865) 3 H.C. 558 .... *21–006*
Gatoil Anstalt v Omenial Ltd; The Balder London (No.1) [1980] 2 Lloyd's Rep. 489, QBD (Comm) *19–012*, *19–013*, *19–016*
Gator Shipping Corp v Trans-Asiatic Oil SA; The Odenfeld [1978] 2 Lloyd's Rep. 357, QBD (Comm) *24–010*
Gaumont-British Pictures Corp v Alexander [1936] 2 All E.R. 1686; 80 S.J. 816 .... *3–014*
Gavaghan v Edwards [1961] 2 Q.B. 220; [1961] 2 W.L.R. 948; [1961] 2 All E.R. 477; (1961) 105 S.J. 405, CA *4–036*, *4–038*
Gawthrop v Boulton [1979] 1 W.L.R. 268; [1978] 3 All E.R. 615; (1978) 122 S.J. 297, Ch D *28–119*
Geary v Physic (1826) 5 B. & C. 234; 7 D. & R. 653; 4 L.J.K.B. 147; 29 R.R. 255 .... *4–034*
Gebhardt v Saunders [1892] 2 Q.B. 452, QBD *29–020*, *29–096*, *29–107*
Gebr Van Weelde Scheepvaart Kantoor BV v Compania Naviera Sea Orient SA; The Agrabele (No.2) [1987] 2 Lloyd's Rep. 223, CA (Civ Div); reversing [1985] 2 Lloyd's Rep. 496, QBD (Comm) *2–004*, *2–006*, *2–071*, *2–072*, *22–027*
Gebruder Metelmann GmbH v NBR (London) Ltd [1984] 1 Lloyd's Rep. 614 ..... *26–078*
Gedge v Royal Exchange Assurance Corp [1900] 2 Q.B. 214; 69 L.J.Q.B. 506; 82 L.T. 463; 16 T.L.R. 344; 9 Asp. M.C. 57; 5 Com. Cas. 229, QBD (Comm) *16–205*
Gee v Lancs Yorks Railway (1860) 6 H.N. 211 .... *26–070*
Gee v Liddell (1866) L.R. 2 Eq. 341, Ct of Chancery *28–130*
Gee & Co (Woolwich) Ltd, Re [1975] Ch. 52; [1974] 2 W.L.R. 515; [1974] 1 All E.R. 1149; (1973) 118 S.J. 65, Ch D *28–094*, *28–095*, *28–101*
Geere v Mare (1863) 2 H. & C. 339; 33 L.J. Ex. 50; 8 L.T. 463; 12 W.R. 17; 133 R.R. 707 .... *16–165*
Geest Plc v Fyffes Plc [1999] 1 All E.R. (Comm) 672, QBD (Comm Ct) *6–012*, *6–034*, *6–109*, *6–116*, *6–159*, *27–035*
Geier (otherwise Braun) v Kujawa, Weston and Warne Bros (Transport) [1970] 1 Lloyd's Rep. 364, QBD *2–002*, *12–016*
Geipel v Smith (1871–72) L.R. 7 Q.B. 404, QB *23–040*
Geiringer v Swiss Bank Corp [1940] 1 All E.R. 406; 84 S.J. 151 .... *11–027*
Geismar v Sun Alliance and London Insurance Ltd [1978] Q.B. 383; [1978] 2 W.L.R. 38; [1977] 3 All E.R. 570; [1977] 2 Lloyd's Rep. 62; [1977] Crim. L.R. 475; (1977) 121 S.J. 201, QBD *16–146*, *16–165*, *16–167*, *16–168*, *16–173*
Gelmini v Moriggia [1913] 2 K.B. 549, KBD *28–062*, *28–063*
General Accident Assurance Corp v Noel [1902] 1 K.B. 377; 71 L.J.K.B. 236; 86 L.T. 555; 18 T.L.R. 164; 50 W.R. 381, KBD *16–102*, *26–011*
General Accident Fire & Life Assurance Corp Ltd v Tanter; sub nom. The Zephyr [1985] 2 Lloyd's Rep. 529, CA (Civ Div); reversing in part [1984] 1 W.L.R. 100; [1984] 1 All E.R. 35; [1984] 1 Lloyd's Rep. 58; (1984) 134 N.L.J. 35; (1983) 127 S.J. 733, QBD (Comm) *2–117*, *2–159*, *3–180*, *18–024*
General Auction Estate & Monetary Co v Smith [1891] 3 Ch. 432; 60 L.J. Ch. 723; 65 L.T. 188; 40 W.R. 106 .... *9–022*
General Billposting Co Ltd v Atkinson [1909] A.C. 118; L.J. Ch. 77; 99 L.T. 943; 25 T.L.R. 178 .... *16–100*, 16–101, *24–003*, 24–036, *24–047*, *24–048*
General Finance, Mortgage and Discount Co v Liberator Permanent Benefit Building Society (1878–79) L.R. 10 Ch. D. 15, Ch D *1–112*
General Reinsurance Corp v Forsakringsaktiebolaget Fennia Patria [1983] Q.B. 856; [1983] 3 W.L.R. 318; [1983] 2 Lloyd's Rep. 287; (1983) 127 S.J. 389, CA (Civ Div); reversing [1982] Q.B. 1022; [1982] 2 W.L.R. 518; [1982] 1 Lloyd's Rep. 87; [1981] Com. L.R. 280; (1982) 126 S.J. 32, QBD (Comm) *2–117*, *3–173*, *13–018*

General Rolling Stock Co, Re; sub nom. General Rolling Stock Co Re v Chapman's Case; Chapman's Case (1865–66) L.R. 1 Eq. 346, Ct of Chancery 9–049
General Rolling Stock Co, Re; sub nom. Joint Stock Discount Co's Claim (1871–72) L.R. 7 Ch. App. 646, CA in Chancery *28–070*
General Steam Navigation Co v Guillou (1843) 11 M. & W. 877 .... *30–325*
General Tire & Rubber Co Ltd v Firestone Tyre & Rubber Co Ltd (No.2) [1975] 1 W.L.R. 819; [1975] 2 All E.R. 173; [1975] F.S.R. 273; [1976] R.P.C. 197; (1975) 119 S.J. 389, HL *26–176*
Genys v Matthews [1966] 1 W.L.R. 758; [1965] 3 All E.R. 24; [1965] 2 Lloyd's Rep. 449; (1966) 110 S.J. 332, Ct of Passage (Liverpool) *14–042*
George v Davies [1911] 2 K.B. 445; 80 L.J.K.B. 924; 104 L.T. 648; 27 T.L.R. 415, KBD *12–129*
George Veflings Rederi A/S v President of India; The Bellami; Monrovia Tramp Shipping Co v President of India; The Pearl Merchant; Marperfecta Compania Naviera SA v President of India; The Doric Chariot [1979] 1 W.L.R. 59; [1979] 1 All E.R. 380; [1979] 1 Lloyd's Rep. 123; (1978) 122 S.J. 843, CA (Civ Div) *30–375*, *30–376*
George Barker (Transport) Ltd v Eynon [1974] 1 W.L.R. 462; [1974] 1 All E.R. 900; [1974] 1 Lloyd's Rep. 65; (1973) 118 S.J. 240, CA (Civ Div); reversing [1973] 1 W.L.R. 1461; [1973] 3 All E.R. 374; (1973) 117 S.J. 631, QBD *9–051*, *19–070*
George Fischer (Great Britain) Ltd v Multi Construction Ltd [1995] B.C.C. 310; [1995] 1 B.C.L.C. 260, CA (Civ Div) *16–052*, *18–050*
George Mitchell (Chesterhall) Ltd v Finney Lock Seeds Ltd [1983] 2 A.C. 803; [1983] 3 W.L.R. 163; [1983] 2 All E.R. 737; [1983] 2 Lloyd's Rep. 272; [1983] Com. L.R. 209, HL; affirming [1983] Q.B. 284; [1982] 3 W.L.R. 1036; [1983] 1 All E.R. 108; [1983] 1 Lloyd's Rep. 168; (1982) 79 L.S.G. 1444; (1982) 126 S.J. 689, CA (Civ Div); affirming [1981] 1 Lloyd's Rep. 476, QBD (Comm) *12–011*, *12–022*, *14–005*, *14–006*, *14–008*, *14–009*, *14–010*, *14–011*, **14–023**, *14–027*, *14–085*, *14–087*, 14–091, *14–101*, *14–102*, *14–103*, *15–116*, *27–057*
George Trollope & Sons v Martyn Bros [1934] 2 K.B. 436, CA *13–009*, *13–012*
George Wills & Sons Ltd v RS Cunningham Son & Co Ltd [1924] 2 K.B. 220, KBD *14–142*
George Wimpey & Co Ltd v British Overseas Airways Corp (BOAC); Littlewood v British Overseas Airways Corp; Littlewood v George Wimpey & Co Ltd [1955] A.C. 169; [1954] 3 W.L.R. 932; [1954] 3 All E.R. 661; (1954) 98 S.J. 868, HL; affirming [1953] 2 Q.B. 501; [1953] 3 W.L.R. 553; [1953] 2 All E.R. 915; (1953) 117 J.P. 484; 51 L.G.R. 557; (1953) 97 S.J. 587, CA; affirming [1953] 1 W.L.R. 426; [1953] 1 All E.R. 583; (1953) 97 S.J. 152, QBD *17–033*
George Wimpey UK Ltd (formerly Wimpey Homes Holdings Ltd) v VI Construction Ltd (formerly VI Components Ltd); sub nom. George Wimpey UK Ltd (formerly Wimpey Homes Holdings Ltd) v VIC Construction Ltd (formerly Vic Components Ltd) [2005] EWCA Civ 77; [2005] B.L.R. 135; 103 Con. L.R. 67; (2005) 102(9) L.S.G. 28; (2005) 149 S.J.L.B. 182; [2005] 2 P. & C.R. DG5, CA (Civ Div); reversing [2004] EWHC 1374 (Ch), Ch D 5–116
Geraghty v Minter(1979–80) 142 C.L.R. 177 .... *16–119*
Gerald Cooper Chemicals Ltd, Re [1978] Ch. 262; [1978] 2 W.L.R. 866; [1978] 2 All E.R. 49; (1977) 121 S.J. 848, Ch D *6–010*, *6–015*
Gerald McDonald & Co v Nash & Co [1924] A.C. 625, HL; reversing (1922) 12 Ll. L. Rep. 464, CA *12–116*
German Date Coffee Co, Re (1881–82) L.R. 20 Ch. D. 169; 51 L.J. Ch. 564; 46 L.T. 327; 30 W.R. 717, CA *9–022*
German v Yates (1915) 32 T.L.R. 52 .... *19–033*, *19–036*, *19–059*
Gess, Re; Gess v Royal Exchange Assurance [1942] Ch. 37; 111 L.J. Ch. 117, Ch D *20–013*
Gething v Kilner [1972] 1 W.L.R. 337; [1972] 1 All E.R. 1166; (1971) 116 S.J. 74, Ch D *6–014*

Getreide Importgesellschaft mbH v Contimar SA Compania Industrial Commercial y Maritima SA [1953] 1 W.L.R. 793; [1953] 2 All E.R. 223; [1953] 1 Lloyd's Rep. 572; (1953) 97 S.J. 434, CA; affirming [1953] 1 W.L.R. 207; [1953] 1 All E.R. 257; [1952] 2 Lloyd's Rep. 551; (1953) 97 S.J. 66, QBD ... *2–058*
Ghaidan v Godin-Mendoza; sub nom. Mendoza v Ghaidan; Ghaidan v Mendoza; Godin-Mendoza v Ghaidan [2004] UKHL 30; [2004] 2 A.C. 557; [2004] 3 W.L.R. 113; [2004] 3 All E.R. 411; [2004] 2 F.L.R. 600; [2004] 2 F.C.R. 481; [2004] H.R.L.R. 31; [2004] U.K.H.R.R. 827; 16 B.H.R.C. 671; [2004] H.L.R. 46; [2005] 1 P. & C.R. 18; [2005] L. & T.R. 3; [2004] 2 E.G.L.R. 132; [2004] Fam. Law 641; [2004] 27 E.G. 128 (C.S.); (2004) 101(27) L.S.G. 30; (2004) 154 N.L.J. 1013; (2004) 148 S.J.L.B. 792; [2004] N.P.C. 100; [2004] 2 P. & C.R. DG17, HL; affirming [2002] EWCA Civ 1533; [2003] Ch. 380; [2003] 2 W.L.R. 478; [2002] 4 All E.R. 1162; [2002] 3 F.C.R. 591; [2003] U.K.H.R.R. 254; 13 B.H.R.C. 608; [2003] H.L.R. 35; [2003] L. & T.R. 14; [2003] A.C.D. 12; [2003] Fam. Law 87; [2002] 46 E.G. 197 (C.S.); (2003) 100(1) L.S.G. 24; (2002) 152 N.L.J. 1718; (2002) 146 S.J.L.B. 253; [2002] N.P.C. 138; [2003] 1 P. & C.R. DG14, CA (Civ Div) 1–049, *16–068*
Ghosh v D'Rozario [1963] 1 Q.B. 106; [1962] 3 W.L.R. 405; [1962] 2 All E.R. 640; (1962) 106 S.J. 352, CA *11–014*
Gibaud v Great Eastern Railway Co [1921] 2 K.B. 426, CA; affirming [1920] 3 K.B. 689, KBD *14–008*, *14–011*, *14–021*, *14–035*
Gibbon v Mitchell [1990] 1 W.L.R. 1304; [1990] 3 All E.R. 338, Ch D *29–029*, *29–043*
Gibbon v Young (1818) 8 Taunt. 254; 2 Moore 224; 19 R.R. 510 .... *12–057*
Gibbons v Hooper (1831) 2 B. & Ad. 734; 9 L.J.K.B. 69; 36 R.R. 726 .... *16–195*
Gibbons v Nelsons (A Firm) [2000] Lloyd's Rep. P.N. 603; [2000] P.N.L.R. 734; [2000] W.T.L.R. 453; (2000) 97(19) L.S.G. 44, Ch D *18–037*
Gibbons v Proctor (1891) 64 L.T. 594; 55 J.P. 616 .... *2–019*, 2–041
Gibbons v Wright (1954) 91 C.L.R. 423 .... *8–068*, *8–069*
Gibbs v Arnold Son & Hockley [1989] 45 E.G. 156, DC *14–063*
Gibbs v David (1875) L.R. 20 Eq. 373, Ct of Chancery *27–026*
Gibbs v Guild (1881–82) L.R. 9 Q.B.D. 59; 51 L.J.Q.B. 313; 46 L.T. 248; 30 W.R. 591, CA; affirming (1881–82) L.R. 8 Q.B.D. 296, QBD *1–124*, *28–032*, *28–134*, *28–140*
Gibbs v Merrill (1810) 3 Taunt. 307 .... *17–008*, *17–010*
Gibbs v Southam (1834) 5 B. Ad. 911 .... *21–010*
Giblin v Murdoch, 1979 S.L.T. (Sh. Ct.) 5, Sh Ct (Glasgow) *16–117*
Gibraltar v Kenney [1956] 2 Q.B. 410; [1956] 3 W.L.R. 466; [1956] 3 All E.R. 22; (1956) 100 S.J. 551, QBD *23–097*
Gibson v Carruthers (1841) 8 M. & W. 321; 11 L.J.Ex. 138; 58 R.R. 713 .... *20–034*
Gibson v Dickie (1815) 3 M. & S. 463; 16 R.R. 333 .... *16–067*
Gibson v Holland (1865) L.R. 1 C.P. 1; Har. & Ruth. 1; 35 L.J.C.P. 5; 13 L.T. 293; 11 Jur. (N.S.) 1022; 14 W.R. 86 .... *4–027*
Gibson v Manchester City Council [1979] 1 W.L.R. 294; [1979] 1 All E.R. 972; 77 L.G.R. 405; [1979] J.P.L. 532; (1979) 123 S.J. 201, HL; reversing [1978] 1 W.L.R. 520; [1978] 2 All E.R. 583; 76 L.G.R. 365; [1978] J.P.L. 246; (1978) 122 S.J. 80, CA (Civ Div) *2–007*, *2–093*, *2–111*
Gibson v Small (1853) 4 H.L.C. 353; 1 C.L.R. 363; 17 Jur. 1134; 66 R.R. 376 .... *12–057*, *13–018*
Gidley v Lord Palmerston (1822) 3 B. & B. 275 .... *10–013*
Gifford v Whittaker (1844) 6 Q.B. 249; 13 L.J.Q.B. 325; 8 Jur. 1134; 66 R.R. 376 .... *22–015*
Gifford v Willoughby's Mashonaland Expedition Co (1899) 16 T.L.R. 24 .... *9–054*
Gil v Baygreen Properties Ltd [2004] EWHC 1732; [2005] B.P.I.R. 95, Ch D *20–031*
Gilbert v Brett (le case de Mixt Moneys) (1604) Davis 18 .... *21–068*, *30–370*
Gilbert v Endean (1878) 9 Ch. D. 259; 39 L.T. 404; 27 W.R. 252 .... *22–021*
Gilbert v Ruddeard (1608) 3 Dy. 276b(n) *3–015*
Gilbert v Trinity House Corp (1886) L.R. 17 Q.B.D. 795, QBD 10–010
Gilbert & Partners v Knight; sub nom. Gilbert & Partners (A Firm) v Knight [1968] 2 All E.R. 248; (1968) 112 S.J. 155, CA (Civ Div) *29–019*, *29–072*

Gilbert Ash (Northern) Ltd v Modern Engineering (Bristol) Ltd; sub nom. Modern Engineering (Bristol) Ltd v Gilbert Ash (Northern) Ltd [1974] A.C. 689; [1973] 3 W.L.R. 421; [1973] 3 All E.R. 195; 1 B.L.R. 73; 72 L.G.R. 1; (1973) 117 S.J. 745, HL; reversing 71 L.G.R. 162, CA (Civ Div) *14–005*, *26–138*, *26–141*
Gilbert Rowe, The. *See* Rowan Companies Inc. v Lambert Eggink Offshore Transport Consultants vof
Gilbert Stokes and Kerr Pty v Dalgety & Co (1947–48) 81 Ll. L. Rep. 337, Sup Ct (NSW) *14–046*
Gilchester Properties Ltd v Gomm [1948] 1 All E.R. 493; 64 T.L.R. 235; [1948] W.N. 71; (1948) 92 S.J. 220, Ch D *6–094*, *12–003*, *27–055*
Gilchrist Watt & Sanderson Pty Ltd v York Products Pty Ltd. *See* York Products Pty v Gilchrist Watt & Sanderson Pty
Giles, Re; sub nom. Giles v Giles [1972] Ch. 544; [1971] 3 W.L.R. 640; [1971] 3 All E.R. 1141; (1971) 115 S.J. 428, Ch D *16–168*, *16–169*
Giles v Perkins (1807) East 12 ...... *29–171*
Giles v Rhind [2008] EWCA Civ 118, CA (Civ Div) *28–003*, *28–084*
Giles v Rhind, unreported, February 9, 2000 ...... *16–120*
Giles v Thompson; Devlin v Baslington; Sanders v Templar [1994] 1 A.C. 142; [1993] 2 W.L.R. 908; [1993] 3 All E.R. 321; [1993] R.T.R. 289; (1993) 143 N.L.J. 884; (1993) 137 S.J.L.B. 151, HL; affirming (1993) 143 N.L.J. 284, CA (Civ Div) *16–049*, *16–050*, *16–051*, *16–052*, 16–054, *16–058*, *16–064*, *19–049*
Gilford Motor Co Ltd v Horne [1933] Ch. 935, CA *16–111*, *16–114*, *16–198*
Gill v M'Dowell [1903] 2 Ir.Rep. 463; 36 I.L.T. 191 ...... *5–076*, *6–015*
Gill & Duffus Landauer Ltd v London Export Corp [1982] 2 Lloyd's Rep. 627, QBD (Comm) *2–050*, *2–053*, *30–012*
Gill & Duffus SA v Berger & Co Inc; sub nom. Berger & Co v Gill & Duffus SA [1984] A.C. 382; [1984] 2 W.L.R. 95; [1984] 1 All E.R. 438; [1984] 1 Lloyd's Rep. 227; (1984) 81 L.S.G. 429; (1984) 128 S.J. 47, HL .. *24–011*, *24–023*
Gill & Duffus SA v Rionda Futures Ltd [1994] 2 Lloyd's Rep. 67, QBD (Comm Ct) *3–005*
Gill & Duffus SA v Société pour l'Exportation des Sucres SA [1986] 1 Lloyd's Rep. 322, CA (Civ Div); affirming [1985] 1 Lloyd's Rep. 621, QBD (Comm) *12–037*, *12–118*, *21–013*
Gillatt v Sky Television Ltd (formerly Sky Television Plc) [2000] 1 All E.R. (Comm) 461; [2000] 2 B.C.L.C. 103, CA (Civ Div) *2–130*, *2–131*
Gillespie v Great Atlantic & Pacific Stores, 187 S.E. 3d 441 (1972) *2–015*
Gillespie Bros & Co v Chevey Eggar & Co [1896] 2 Q.B. 59; 65 L.J.Q.B. 552; 12 T.L.R. 274; 40 S.J. 354; 1 Com. Cas. 373, QBD 12–097, *12–100*
Gillespie Bros & Co Ltd v Roy Bowles Transport Ltd [1973] Q.B. 400; [1972] 3 W.L.R. 1003; [1973] 1 All E.R. 193; [1973] 1 Lloyd's Rep. 10; [1973] R.T.R. 95; (1972) 116 S.J. 861, CA (Civ Div); reversing [1971] 2 Lloyd's Rep. 521; [1972] R.T.R. 65, QBD *12–011*, *13–022*, *14–010*, *14–012*, *14–015*, *14–054*, *14–135*
Gillett v Holt [2001] Ch. 210; [2000] 3 W.L.R. 815; [2000] 2 All E.R. 289; [2000] 2 F.L.R. 266; [2000] 1 F.C.R. 705; [2000] W.T.L.R. 195; [2000] Fam. Law 714; (2000) 97(12) L.S.G. 40; (2000) 144 S.J.L.B. 141; [2000] N.P.C. 25; (2000) 80 P. & C.R. D3, CA (Civ Div); reversing [1998] 3 All E.R. 917; [1998] 2 F.L.R. 470; [1998] Fam. Law 596; (1998) 95(26) L.S.G. 31, Ch D *2–111*, *2–171*, *2–183*, *3–015*, 3–143, *3–144*, *3–147*, *3–148*, *3–154*, *3–156*, 3–158, *29–161*
Gillick v West Norfolk and Wisbech Area Health Authority and the D.H.S.S. [1986] A.C. 112; [1985] 3 W.L.R. 830; (1985) 129 S.J. 738; [1985] 3 All E.R. 402; [1986] Crim. L.R. 113; (1985) 135 New L.J. 1055; (1985) 82 L.S.Gaz. 3531, HL *8–011*
Gillin v Lloyds TSB Bank Plc, unreported June 26, 2007, CC (Coventry) *15–098*
Gillott's Settlement, Re; sub nom. Chattock v Reid [1934] Ch. 97, Ch D *19–032*
Gillow v Lillie (1835) 4 L.J.C.P. 2221 Scott. 597; 1 Bing N.C. 695; 1 Hodges 160 ...... *8–063*
Ginsberg v Parker. *See* Rex Stewart Jefferies Parker Ginsberg v Parker.

Girardy v Richardson (1793) 1 Esp. 13; 1 B. & P. 340 .... *16–069*
Girdlestone v Brighton Aquarium Co (1878–79) L.R. 4 Ex. D. 107, CA *25–015*
Gladwell v Steggall (1839) 5 Bing (N.C.) 733; 8 Scott 60; 9 L.J.P.C. 361; 3 Jur. 535; 132 E.R. 1283 .... *1–174*
Glaholm v Hays (1841) 2 M. & G. 257; 2 Scott W.R. 471; 10 L.J.C.P. 98; 58 R.R. 399 .... *12–026*
Glamorgan Coal Co v South Wales Miners Federation. *See* South Wales Miners Federation v Glamorgan Coal Co Ltd
Glasbrook Bros Ltd v Glamorgan CC; sub nom. Glamorgan CC v Glasbrook Bros Ltd [1925] A.C. 270, HL; affirming [1924] 1 K.B. 879, CA 3–063
Glasgow & South Western Railway Co v Boyd & Forrest (A Firm) (No.3); sub nom. Boyd & Forrest (A Firm) v Glasgow & South Western Railway Co (No.3) [1915] A.C. 526; 1915 S.C. (H.L.) 20; 1915 1 S.L.T. 114, HL; reversing, 1914 S.C. 472; 1914 1 S.L.T. 171, IH (2 Div) 6–119, 6–120, *6–134*
Glasgow Lord Provost and Magistrates v Farie; sub nom. Glasgow Corp v Farie; Lord Provost and Magistrates of Glasgow v Farie (1888) L.R. 13 App. Cas. 657, HL; reversing (1887) 14 R. 346, IH (1 Div) *12–052*
Glatzer v Bradston Ltd; The Ocean Enterprise [1997] 1 Lloyd's Rep. 449, QBD (Admlty) *2–185*
GlaxoSmithKline Ltd v Department of Health [2007] EWHC 1470 (Comm); [2007] 2 All E.R. (Comm) 1140, QBD (Comm) *2–163*
Glebe Island Terminals Pty v Continental Seagram Pty; The Antwerpen [1994] 1 Lloyd's Rep. 213, CA (NSW) *3–074*, *14–007*, *14–008*, *14–015*, *14–019*
Gledhow Autoparts v Delaney [1965] 1 W.L.R. 1366; [1965] 3 All E.R. 288; (1965) 109 S.J. 571, CA *16–088*, *16–111*, *27–069*
Gledstane v Hewitt (1831) 1 C. & J. 566; 1 Tyr. 445; 9 L.J.O.S. Ex. 145; 148 E.R. 1548 .... *1–118*
Gleeson v J Wippell & Co Ltd [1977] 1 W.L.R. 510; [1977] 3 All E.R. 54; [1977] F.S.R. 301; (1977) 121 S.J. 157, Ch D *25–012*
Glegg v Bromley [1912] 3 K.B. 474; 81 L.J.K.B. 1081; 106 L.T. 825, CA *16–060*, *16–061*, *16–063*, *19–027*, 19–030, *19–032*, *19–033*, *19–049*, *19–052*
Glen Courtney v Corp Ltd [2006] EWCA Civ 518 .... *4–056*, *4–069*
Glencore Grain Ltd v Flacker Shipping Ltd; The Happy Day; sub nom. Flacker Shipping Ltd v Glencore Grain Ltd; The Happy Day [2002] EWCA Civ 1068; [2002] 2 All E.R. (Comm) 896; [2002] 2 Lloyd's Rep. 487; [2003] 1 C.L.C. 537, CA (Civ Div); reversing [2001] 1 All E.R. (Comm) 659; [2001] 1 Lloyd's Rep. 754; [2001] C.L.C. 813, QBD (Comm) *2–180*, *3–081*, *3–104*
Glencore Grain Rotterdam BV v Lebanese Organisation for International Commerce; The Lorico [1997] 4 All E.R. 514; [1997] 2 Lloyd's Rep. 386; [1997] C.L.C. 1274, CA (Civ Div) *24–004*, *24–006*, *24–007*, *24–014*
Glencore International AG v Metro Trading International Inc (No.1); Metro Trading International Inc v Itochu Petroleum Co (S) PTE Ltd (No.1) [1999] 2 All E.R. (Comm) 899; [1999] 2 Lloyd's Rep. 632; [2000] C.P. Rep. 26; [2000] C.L.C. 83; [2000] I.L.Pr. 358, QBD (Comm) *19–079*
Glencore International AG v Metro Trading International Inc (No.2); sub nom. Glencore International AG v Metro Trading International Inc (formerly Metro Bunkering & Trading Co) (No.2) [2001] 1 All E.R. (Comm) 103; [2001] 1 Lloyd's Rep. 284; [2001] C.L.C. 1732, QBD (Comm) *30–016*, *30–031*
Glendarroch, The [1894] P. 226; [1891–94] All E.R. 484; 63 L.J.P. 89; 70 L.T. 344; 10 T.L.R. 269; 38 S.J. 362; 7 Asp. M.L.C. 420; 6 R. 686, CA *14–018*, *14–019*, *14–146*
Glengate-KG Properties Ltd v Norwich Union Fire Insurance Society Ltd [1996] 2 All E.R. 487; [1996] 1 Lloyd's Rep. 614; [1996] C.L.C. 676; 49 Con. L.R. 78; [1996] 5 Re. L.R. 50; (1996) 12 Const. L.J. 266, CA (Civ Div); affirming [1995] 1 Lloyd's Rep. 278; (1995) 11 Const. L.J. 233; [1994] N.P.C. 103, QBD (Comm) *18–128*
Glenroy, The [1943] P. 109; 113 L.J.P.4; 170 L.T. 273; 60 T.L.R. 8, PDAD *11–029*
Glessing v Green [1975] 1 W.L.R. 863; [1975] 2 All E.R. 696; (1975) 29 P. & C.R. 461; (1975) 119 S.J. 369, CA (Civ Div) *1–105*, *1–106*

Glicksman v Lancashire & General Assurance Co Ltd [1927] A.C. 139; (1926) 26 Ll. L. Rep. 69, HL; affirming [1925] 2 K.B. 593; (1925) 22 Ll. L. Rep. 179, CA; reversing (1925) 21 Ll. L. Rep. 352, KBD *6–147*, *6–150*

Glissen v Ogden (1731) 2 Atk. 258 .... *7–074*

Global Container Lines Ltd v State Black Sea Shipping Co [1999] 1 Lloyd's Rep. 127, CA (Civ Div) *2–128*

Global Tankers Inc v Amercoat Europe [1975] 1 Lloyd's Rep. 666, QBD *2–032*

Globe Master Management Ltd v Boulus-Gad Ltd [2002] EWCA Civ 313, CA (Civ Div) *23–012*

Glossop v Ashley [1922] 1 K.B. 1; 90 L.J.K.B. 1237; 125 L.T. 842; 85 J.P. 234; 37 T.L.R. 327; 66 S.J. 695; 19 L.G.R. 593, CA; affirming [1921] 2 K.B. 451, KBD *2–047*

Gloucestershire CC v Richardson (t/a WJ Richardson & Son) [1969] 1 A.C. 480; [1968] 3 W.L.R. 645; [1968] 2 All E.R. 1181; 67 L.G.R. 15; (1968) 112 S.J. 759, HL; affirming [1967] 3 All E.R. 458, CA (Civ Div) *5–016*, *13–030*

Glover v Glover [1951] 1 D.L.R. 657 .... *7–075*

Gloyne v Richardson [2001] EWCA Civ 716; [2001] 2 B.C.L.C. 669, CA (Civ Div) *3–054*, *3–109*

Gluckstein v Barnes; sub nom. Olympia Ltd, Re [1900] A.C. 240; 69 L.J.Ch. 385; 82 L.T. 393; 16 T.L.R. 321; 7 Manson 321; affirming [1898] 2 Ch. 153, CA *6–154*, *9–054*

Glynn v Keele University; sub nom. Glynn v University of Keele [1971] 1 W.L.R. 487; [1971] 2 All E.R. 89; (1970) 115 S.J. 173, Ch D *27–072*

Glynn v Margetson & Co; sub nom. Margetson v Glynn [1893] A.C. 351, HL; affirming [1892] 1 Q.B. 337, CA *12–057*, *12–063*, *12–069*, *12–070*, 12–073, *14–007*, *14–029*

Glynn v Thomas, 156 E.R. 1085; (1856) 11 Ex. 870, Ex Ct *29–091*

Godard v Gray (1870–71) L.R. 6 Q.B. 139, QB *30–066*

Goddard's Case (1584) 2 Co.Rep. 46 .... *1–100*

Godden v Merthyr Tydfil Housing Association (1997) 74 P. & C. R. D1; [1997] N.P.C. 1, CA *3–115*, *4–052*, 4–061, 4–067, 4–079, *4–080*, 4–086

Godfrey Davis Ltd v Culling [1962] 2 Lloyd's Rep. 349; (1962) 106 S.J. 918, CA *18–008*

Godfrey v Britannic Assurance Co Ltd [1963] 2 Lloyd's Rep. 515; (1963) 107 S.J. 536, QBD *6–147*

Godina v Patrick Operations Pty Ltd [1984] 1 Lloyd's Rep. 333, CA (NSW) *14–042*

Godley v Perry [1960] 1 W.L.R. 9; [1960] 1 All E.R. 36; (1960) 104 S.J. 16, QBD *26–082*

Godwin v Francis (1869–70) L.R. 5 C.P. 295; 39 L.J.C.P. 121; 33 L.T. 338, CCP *4–034*, *26–091*

Goebel v Linn (1882) 11 N.W. *7–041*

Goel v Pick; sub nom. Pick (Virdi's Trustee) v Goel [2006] EWHC 833 (Ch); [2007] 1 All E.R. 982; [2006] R.T.R. 28; [2006] B.P.I.R. 827, Ch D *19–010*

Goetz v Rogers; sub nom. Rogers v Von Goetz, unreported, July 29, 1998, CA (Civ Div) *28–037*

Goff v Gauthier (1991) 62 P. & C.R. 388, Ch D *6–010*, *6–038*, *6–139*

Gold v Patman & Fotheringham [1958] 1 W.L.R. 697; [1958] 2 All E.R. 497; [1958] 1 Lloyd's Rep. 587; (1958) 102 S.J. 470, CA; reversing [1957] 2 Lloyd's Rep. 319, QBD *12–070*

Goldcorp Exchange Ltd (In Receivership), Re; sub nom. Kensington v Liggett; Goldcorp Finance Ltd, Re [1995] 1 A.C. 74; [1994] 3 W.L.R. 199; [1994] 2 All E.R. 806; [1994] 2 B.C.L.C. 578; [1994] C.L.C. 591; (1994) 13 Tr. L.R. 434; (1994) 91(24) L.S.G. 46; (1994) 144 N.L.J. 792; (1994) 138 S.J.L.B. 127, PC (NZ) *27–015*, *29–049*, *29–165*, *29–167*

Golden Acres Ltd v Queensland Estates Ltd [1969] St. R. Od. 378 ...... *30–007*, *30–311*

Golden Strait Corp v Nippon Yusen Kubishika Kaisha; The Golden Victory [2007] UKHL 12; [2007] 2 A.C. 353; [2007] Bus. L.R. 997; [2007] 2 W.L.R. 691; [2007] 3 All E.R. 1; [2007] 2 All E.R. (Comm) 97; [2007] 2 Lloyd's Rep. 164; [2007] 1 C.L.C. 352; (2007) 157 N.L.J. 518; (2007) 151 S.J.L.B. 468, HL; affirming [2005] EWCA Civ 1190; [2006] 1 W.L.R. 533; [2006] 1 All E.R. (Comm) 235; [2005] 2 Lloyd's Rep. 747; [2005] 2 C.L.C. 576; (2005) 102(43) L.S.G. 31, CA (Civ Div); affirming [2005] EWHC 161 (Comm); [2005] 1 All E.R. (Comm) 467; [2005] 1 Lloyd's Rep. 443; [2005] 1 C.L.C. 138, QBD (Comm) *2–149*, *24–022*, *24–048*, *26–001*, *26–047*, *26–048*, *26–064*
Goldenglow Nut Food Co Ltd v Commodin (Produce) Ltd; Goldenglow Nut Food Co Ltd v Societe Generale de Surveillance SA; Goldenglow Nut Food Co Ltd v New Hampshire Insurance Co Ltd [1987] 2 Lloyd's Rep. 569, CA (Civ Div) *28–116*
Goldfoot v Welch [1914] 1 Ch. 213; 83 L.J. Ch. 360; 109 L.T. 820, Ch D *12–103*
Goldrei Foucard & Son v Sinclair [1918] 1 K.B. 180; 87 L.J.K.B. 261; 118 L.T. 147; 34 T.L.R. 74, CA *17–015*
Goldshede v Cottrell (1836) 2 M.W. 20 ..... *21–073*
Goldshede v Swan (1847) 1 Ex. 154; 16 L.J.Ex. 284; 9 L.T. (O.S.) 248; 154 E.R. 65 ..... *3–028*, *12–081*, *12–108*
Goldsmith v Rodger [1962] 2 Lloyd's Rep. 249, CA 6–017
Goldsmiths Co v West Metropolitan Railway Co [1904] 1 K.B. 1; 72 L.J.K.B. 931; 89 L.T. 428; 20 T.L.R. 7; 52 W.R. 21; 68 J.P. 41, CA *12–093*, *21–024*
Goldsoll v Goldman [1915] 1 Ch. 292; 84 L.J. Ch. 228; 112 L.T. 494, CA; affirming [1914] 2 Ch. 603, Ch D *16–075*, *16–091*, *16–117*, 16–197, 16–198, *16–203*
Goldsworthy v Brickell [1987] Ch. 378; [1987] 2 W.L.R. 133; [1987] 1 All E.R. 853; (1987) 84 L.S.G. 654; (1987) 131 S.J. 102, CA (Civ Div) *3–090*, *7–060*, *7–073*, *7–097*
Gompertz v Bartlett (1853) 2 E. & B. 849; 2 C.L.R. 395; 23 L.J.Q.B. 65; 18 Jur. 266; 2 W.R. 43; 22 L.T. 99; 95 R.R. 851, QB 5–019, 5–021
Gompertz v Denton (1832) 1 C. & M. 207; 1 Dowl. 623; 3 Tyr. 232; 2 L.J. Ex. 82; 149 E.R. 376 ..... *22–026*
Gonin (Deceased); sub nom. Gonin v Garmeson [1979] Ch. 16; [1977] 3 W.L.R. 379; [1977] 2 All E.R. 720; (1977) 121 S.J. 558, Ch D *4–045*, *4–046*, *4–049*
Gonty and Manchester Sheffield and Lincolnshire Railway Co's Arbitration, Re [1896] 2 Q.B. 439, CA *10–027*
Gooch's Case. *See* Contract Corp, Re
Good v Cheesman (1831) 2 B. & Ad. 328; 4 C. & P. 513; 9 L.J.K.B. 234; 36 R.R. 574 ..... *3–125*, *22–015*
Good v Parry [1963] 2 Q.B. 418; [1963] 2 W.L.R. 846; [1963] 2 All E.R. 59; (1963) 107 S.J. 194, CA *28–095*
Good Challenger Navegante SA v Metalexportimport SA [2003] EWCA Civ 1668; [2004] 1 Lloyd's Rep. 67; (2004) 101(2) L.S.G. 27, CA (Civ Div); affirming [2003] EWHC 10 (Comm); [2003] 1 Lloyd's Rep. 471, QBD (Comm) *3–035*, *28–094*
Goodchild, Re *See* Goodchild v Goodchild
Goodchild v Goodchild; sub nom. Goodchild (Deceased), Re [1997] 1 W.L.R. 1216; [1997] 3 All E.R. 63; [1997] 2 F.L.R. 644; [1997] 3 F.C.R. 601; [1997] Fam. Law 660; (1997) 147 N.L.J. 759, CA (Civ Div); affirming [1996] 1 W.L.R. 694; [1996] 1 All E.R. 670; [1996] 1 F.L.R. 591; [1997] 1 F.C.R. 45; [1996] Fam. Law 209, Ch D *2–183*, *3–015*, *4–063*
Goode v Harrison (1821) 5 B. & Ald. 147; 24 R.R. 307 ..... *8–039*
Goode v Job (1858) 1 E. & E. 6 ..... *28–094*
Goode v Martin [2001] EWCA Civ 1899; [2002] 1 W.L.R. 1828; [2002] 1 All E.R. 620; [2002] C.P. Rep. 16; [2002] C.P.L.R. 74; [2002] C.L.C. 420; [2002] P.I.Q.R. P24; (2002) 152 N.L.J. 109, CA (Civ Div) *28–118*
Goodfellow (Charles) Lumber Sales v Verreault Hovington & Verreault Navigation Inc [1971] 1 Lloyd's Rep. 185, Sup Ct (Can) *14–146*
Gooding v White (1913) 29 T.L.R. 312 ..... *6–146*

Goodinson v Goodinson [1954] 2 Q.B. 118; [1954] 2 W.L.R. 1121; [1954] 2 All E.R. 255; (1954) 98 S.J. 369, CA *3–166*, 16–201, *16–202*
Goodman v Pocock (1850) 15 Q.B. 576 .... *29–058*
Goodson v Baker (1908) 98 L.T. 41524 T.L.R. 338; 52 S.J. 302 .... *3–050*
Goodway v Zurich Insurance Co [2004] EWHC 137; 96 Con. L.R. 49, QBD (TCC) *13–011*
Goodwill v British Pregnancy Advisory Service [1996] 1 W.L.R. 1397; [1996] 2 All E.R. 161; [1996] 2 F.L.R. 55; [1996] 2 F.C.R. 680; [1996] P.I.Q.R. P197; [1996] 7 Med. L.R. 129; (1996) 31 B.M.L.R. 83; (1996) 93(5) L.S.G. 31; (1996) 146 N.L.J. 173; (1996) 140 S.J.L.B. 37, CA (Civ Div) 18–039
Goodwin v Coates (1832) 1 M. Rob. 221 .... *21–079*
Goodyear Tyre & Rubber Co (Great Britain) Ltd v Lancashire Batteries LtdL.R. 1 R.P. 22; [1958] 1 W.L.R. 857; [1958] 3 All E.R. 7; (1958) 102 S.J. 581, CA; reversing [1958] 1 W.L.R. 655; [1958] 2 All E.R. 324; (1958) 102 S.J. 453, Ch D *12–017*
Goose v Wilson Sandford & Co (No.2) [2000] All E.R. (D.) 324; [2001] Lloyd's Rep. P.N. 189, CA (Civ Div) *6–030*
Gopala Chetty v Vijayaraghavachariar. *See* Chetty (Deceased) v Vijayaraghavachariar
Gophir Diamond Co v Wood [1902] 1 Ch. 950; 71 L.J.Ch. 550; 861 L.T. 801; 18 T.L.R. 492; 50 W.R. 603, Ch D *16–114*
Gordian Knot Ltd v Towers, unreported, December 6, 2001, QBD *16–105*
Gordon, Re; Lloyds Bank and Parratt v Lloyd and Gordon [1940] Ch. 851, Ch D *18–079*, *18–083*
Gordon v Cox (1835) 7 C.P. 172 .... *21–090*
Gordon v Gordon (1816–19) 3 Swans 400; 19 R.R. 230 6–155
Gordon v Selico Ltd (1986) 18 H.L.R. 219; [1986] 1 E.G.L.R. 71; (1986) 278 E.G. 53, CA (Civ Div) *27–028*
Gordon v Strange (1847) 1 Exch. 477 .... *21–073*
Gordon v Street [1899] 2 Q.B. 641; 69 L.J.Q.B. 45; 81 L.T. 237; 48 W.R. 158, CA *5–099*
Gore v Gibson (1845) 13 M. & W. 623; 14 L.J.Ex. 151; 9 Jur. 140; 67 R.R. 762 .... *8–080*
Gore v Hawsey (1862) 3 F. & F. 509; 130 R.R. 888 .... *8–061*
Gore v Van der Lann; sub nom. Gore v Van der Lann Corp of Liverpool (Interveners) [1967] 2 Q.B. 31; [1967] 2 W.L.R. 358; [1967] 1 All E.R. 360; [1967] 1 Lloyd's Rep. 145; 65 L.G.R. 94; (1966) 110 S.J. 928, CA *2–021*, 2–178, *3–004*, *3–126*, 3–181, *14–042*, *14–051*, 18–070, 18–071
Gorham v British Telecommunications Plc [2000] 1 W.L.R. 2129; [2000] 4 All E.R. 867; [2001] Lloyd's Rep. I.R. 531; [2000] Lloyd's Rep. P.N. 897; [2001] P.N.L.R. 2; [2000] Pens. L.R. 293; (2000) 97(38) L.S.G. 44; (2000) 144 S.J.L.B. 251, CA (Civ Div) *1–184*, 18–038
Goring v British Actors Equity Association [1987] I.R.L.R. 122, Ch D *9–074*, *9–084*
Goring v Goring (1602) Yelv. 11 .... *22–015*
Goring, The [1988] A.C. 831; [1988] 2 W.L.R. 460; [1988] 1 All E.R. 641; [1988] 1 Lloyd's Rep. 397; [1988] F.T.L.R. 524; (1988) 85(14) L.S.G. 50; (1988) 138 N.L.J. Rep. 61; (1988) 132 S.J. 334, HL *29–131*, *29–136*
Gorringe v Irwell India Rubber and Gutta Percha Works (1887) L.R. 34 Ch. D. 128; 56 L.J.Ch. 85; 55 L.T. 572; 35 W.R. 86, CA *19–020*
Gorton v Macintosh [1883] W.N. 103 .... *14–027*
Gosbell v Archer (1835) 2 A. & E. 500; 4 N. & M. 485; 5 N. & M. 525; 1 H. & N. 559; 4 L.J.K.B. 78; 41 R.R. 475 .... *4–033*
Goshawk Dedicated Ltd v Tyser & Co Ltd [2006] EWCA Civ 54; [2006] 1 All E.R. (Comm) 501; [2006] 1 Lloyd's Rep. 566; [2006] 1 C.L.C. 198; [2007] Lloyd's Rep. I.R. 224, CA (Civ Div); reversing [2005] EWHC 461 (Comm); [2005] 2 All E.R. (Comm) 115; [2005] Lloyd's Rep. I.R. 379, QBD (Comm) *2–160*, *13–006*
Gosling v Anderson [1972] C.L.Y. 492, CA (Civ Div) *6–071*, *6–076*
Gosling v Burrard-Lucas [1999] 1 C.L. 197, CC (Tunbridge Wells) *15–098*
Gosling v Gaskell; sub nom. Gaskell v Gosling [1897] A.C. 575; 66 L.J.Q.B. 848; 77 L.T. 314, HL; reversing [1896] 1 Q.B. 669, CA *9–047*, *9–051*

Gosling v Gosling [1968] P. 1; [1967] 2 W.L.R. 1219; [1967] 2 All E.R. 510; (1967) 111 S.J. 192, CA (Civ Div) *16–043*
Goss v Chilcott [1996] A.C. 788; [1996] 3 W.L.R. 180; [1997] 2 All E.R. 110; (1996) 93(22) L.S.G. 26; (1996) 140 S.J.L.B. 176; [1996] N.P.C. 93, PC (NZ) *4–085*, *24–050*, *29–054*, 29–062, *29–063*
Goss v Lord Nugent (1833) 5 B. & Ad. 58; 2 N. & M. 28; 2 L.J.K.B. 127; 39 R.R. 392 .... *12–096*, *12–111*, *22–032*, 22–033
Gotham v Doode; sub nom. Doodes v Gotham [2006] EWCA Civ 1080; [2007] 1 W.L.R. 86; [2007] 1 All E.R. 527; [2007] 1 F.L.R. 373; [2007] 2 F.C.R. 712; [2006] B.P.I.R. 1178; [2007] Fam. Law 15; (2006) 156 N.L.J. 1325; [2006] N.P.C. 89, CA (Civ Div) *28–003*
Goulandris Bros Ltd v B Goldman & Sons Ltd [1958] 1 Q.B. 74; [1957] 3 W.L.R. 596; [1957] 3 All E.R. 100; [1957] 2 Lloyd's Rep. 207; (1957) 101 S.J. 762, QBD *28–126*
Gould v Gould [1970] 1 Q.B. 275; [1969] 3 W.L.R. 490; [1969] 3 All E.R. 728; (1969) 113 S.J. 508, CA (Civ Div) *2–169*, *2–183*
Gould v Johnson (1702) 2 Salk. 422 .... *28–032*
Gould v Skinner [1983] Qd. 377 .... *19–052*
Gould v Webb (1855) 4 E.B. 933 .... *21–051*
Goulden v Wilson Barca (A Firm); sub nom. Wilson Barca (A Firm) v Goulden [2000] 1 W.L.R. 167; (1999) 96(31) L.S.G. 35; (1999) 143 S.J.L.B. 212, CA (Civ Div) *3–062*
Government of Ceylon v Chandris. *See* Ceylon v Chandris
Government of India v Taylor. *See* India v Taylor
Government of Sierra Leone v Marmaro Shipping Co Ltd. *See* Sierra Leone v Marmaro Shipping Co; The Amazona and The Yayamaria
Governor & Company of Bank of Scotland of the Mound v Butcher, July 28, 1998, CA *30–070*, *30–076*
Governor and Co of the Bank of Scotland v Henry Butcher & Co. *See* Bank of Scotland v Henry Butcher & Co
Governors of the Peabody Donation Fund v Sir Lindsay Parkinson & Co Ltd [1985] A.C. 210; [1984] 3 W.L.R. 953; [1984] 3 All E.R. 529; 28 B.L.R. 1; 83 L.G.R. 1; [1984] C.I.L.L. 128; (1984) 81 L.S.G. 3179; (1984) 128 S.J. 753, HL; affirming [1983] 3 W.L.R. 754; [1983] 3 All E.R. 417; 25 B.L.R. 108; 82 L.G.R. 138; (1984) 47 P. & C.R. 402; (1983) 127 S.J. 749, CA (Civ Div) *1–176*, *1–177*, *1–187*
Govett v Radnidge Pulman & Gimblett (1802) 3 East 62; 102 E.R. 520 .... *1–128*
Gowers v Lloyds & National Provincial Foreign Bank Ltd [1938] 1 All E.R. 766, CA *29–182*
Gozney v Bristol Trade & Provident Society [1909] 1 K.B. 901, CA *16–140*
Gozzett, Re [1936] 1 All E.R. 79; 80 S.J. 146, CA *20–023*
Grace Shipping and Hai Nguan v CF Sharp (Malaya) Pte [1987] 1 Lloyd's Rep. 207, PC (Sing) *2–140*
Grady v Prison Service [2003] EWCA Civ 527; [2003] 3 All E.R. 745; [2003] I.C.R. 753; [2003] I.R.L.R. 474; [2003] B.P.I.R. 823; (2003) 100(25) L.S.G. 45; (2003) 147 S.J.L.B. 540, CA (Civ Div) 20–034, *27–022*, *27–023*
Graham v Belfast & Northern Counties Ry. Co [1901] 2 I.R. 13 .... *14–017*
Graham v Entec Europe Ltd (t/a Exploration Associates) [2003] EWCA Civ 1177; [2003] 4 All E.R. 1345; [2003] 2 All E.R. (Comm) 811; 92 Con. L.R. 35; [2004] Lloyd's Rep. I.R. 660, CA (Civ Div) *28–011*
Graham v Ewart (1856) 1 H. & N. 550; 26 L.J.Ex. 97; 3 Jur. 163; 108 R.R. 714 .... *12–052*
Graham v Musson (1839) 5 Bing. N.C. 603; 8 Sco. 769; 8 L.J.C.P. 324; 50 R.R. 807 .... *4–036*, *4–039*
Graham v Pitkin [1992] 1 W.L.R. 403; [1992] 2 All E.R. 235; (1992) 64 P. & C.R. 522; (1992) 136 S.J.L.B. 97; [1992] N.P.C. 37, PC (UK) *2–154*
Graham v Public Works Commissioners; sub nom. Graham v HM's Commissioners of Public Works and Buildings [1901] 2 K.B. 781; 70 L.J.K.B. 860; 85 L.T. 96; 50 W.R. 122, KBD 10–013, *10–016*
Graham v Seal (1918) 88 L.J. Ch. 31 .... *21–084*, *21–092*

Graham & Scott (Southgate) Ltd v Oxlade [1950] 2 K.B. 257; [1950] 1 All E.R. 856; 66 T.L.R. (Pt. 1) 808; (1950) 94 S.J. 209, CA; affirming [1950] 1 All E.R. 91, KBD *2–118*
Grainger & Son v Gough (Surveyor of Taxes) [1896] A.C. 325; 65 L.J.Q.B. 410; 74 L.T. 435; 44 W.R. 561; 60 J.P. 692, HL; reversing [1895] 1 Q.B. 71, CA *2–017*
Grains & Fourrages SA v Huyton [1997] 1 Lloyd's Rep. 628, QBD (Comm) *3–054*, *5–016*, *5–035*, *29–039*
Gran Gelato Ltd v Richcliff (Group) Ltd [1992] Ch. 560; [1992] 2 W.L.R. 867; [1992] 1 All E.R. 865; [1992] 1 E.G.L.R. 297; [1991] E.G. 136 (C.S.); (1992) 142 N.L.J. 51, Ch D *1–166*, *1–177*, *6–040*, 6–074, *6–085*, *18–022*, *26–049*
Granada Theatres Ltd v Freehold Investment (Leytonstone) Ltd [1959] Ch. 592; [1959] 1 W.L.R. 570; [1959] 2 All E.R. 176; (1959) 103 S.J. 392, CA *21–038*
Grand Junction Canal Co v Petty (1888) L.R. 21 Q.B.D. 273, CA *10–027*
Grand Metropolitan Plc v William Hill Group Ltd [1997] 1 B.C.L.C. 390, Ch D *5–114*
Grand Trunk Railway Co of Canada v Robinson [1915] A.C. 740; 84 L.J.C. 194; 113 L.T. 350; 31 T.L.R. 395, PC (Can) *14–135*
Granit SA v Benship International Inc [1994] 1 Lloyd's Rep. 526, QBD (Comm) *2–128*
Grant v Australian Knitting Mills Ltd; sub nom. Australian Knitting Mills v Grant Ltd [1936] A.C. 85; 105 L.J.P.C. 6; 154 L.T. 18; 52 T.L.R. 38; 79 S.J. 815, PC (Aus); reversing (1933) 50 C.L.R. 387, Sup Ct (SAus) *1–174*, *26–078*, *26–082*
Grant v Cigman; sub nom. Grant v Lapid Developments Ltd [1996] B.C.C. 410; [1996] 2 B.C.L.C. 24, Ch D *21–013*, *27–011*
Grant v Dawkins [1973] 1 W.L.R. 1406; [1973] 3 All E.R. 897; (1974) 27 P. & C.R. 158; (1973) 117 S.J. 665, Ch D *26–091*, *27–079*, *27–081*
Grant v Easton (1883–84) L.R. 13 Q.B.D. 302, CA *28–016*
Grant v Edmonson [1931] 1 Ch. 1; 100 L.J. Ch. 1; 143 L.T. 749, CA; affirming [1930] 2 Ch. 245, Ch D *18–123*
Grant v Edwards [1986] Ch. 638; [1986] 3 W.L.R. 114; [1986] 2 All E.R. 426; [1987] 1 F.L.R. 87; [1986] Fam. Law 300; (1986) 83 L.S.G. 1996; (1986) 136 N.L.J. 439; (1986) 130 S.J. 408, CA (Civ Div) *2–171*, *3–141*, *3–147*, *13–028*, *29–161*
Grant v Grant (1870) L.R. 5 C.P. 727; 39 L.J.P.C. 272; 22 L.T. 829; 18 W.R.951, Ex Chamber; affirming (1869–70) L.R. 5 C.P. 380, CCP *12–120*
Grant v John Grant & Sons Pty Ltd (1954) 91 C.L.R. 112, HC (Aus) *22–005*
Grant v Maddox (1846) 15 M. & W. 737; 16 L.J. Ex. 227; 71 R.R. 815 .... *12–132*
Grant v United Kingdom Switchback Railways Co (1889) L.R. 40 Ch. D. 135; 58 L.J.Ch. 211; 60 L.T. 525; 37 W.R. 312; 1 Meg. 117, CA *9–039*
Grant Smith & Co v Seattle Construction & Dry Dock Co; McDonnell Ltd v Seattle Construction & Dry Dock Co [1920] A.C. 162; [1918–19] All E.R. 378; 89 L.J.P.C. 17; 122 L.T. 203, PC (Can) *14–146*
Granville Oil & Chemicals Ltd v Davies Turner & Co Ltd; sub nom. Granville Oils & Chemicals Ltd v Davis Turner & Co Ltd [2003] EWCA Civ 570; [2003] 1 All E.R. (Comm) 819; [2003] 2 Lloyd's Rep. 356; [2003] 2 C.L.C. 418; (2003) 147 S.J.L.B. 505, CA (Civ Div) *14–062*, *14–085*, *14–095*, *14–099*, *14–103*
Graumann v Treitel [1940] 2 All E.R. 188 .... *30–375*
Gravely v Barnard (1874) L.R. 18 Eq. 518; 43 L.J. Ch. 659; 30 L.T. 863; 22 W.R. 891, Ct of Chancery *3–014*, *16–090*
Graves v Cohen (1829) 46 T.L.R. 121 ....*20–006*, 23–037
Graves v Graves [2007] EWCA Civ 660; [2007] All E.R. (D) 32; [2007] 3 F.C.R. 26; [2008] H.L.R. 10; [2008] L. & T.R. 15; (2007) 151 S.J.L.B. 926, CA (Civ Div) *5–016*, *5–039*, *5–064*, 5–065, 23–053
Graves v Key (1832) 3 B. & Ad. 313 ....*12–107*, *21–058*
Graves v Legg, 156 E.R. 304; (1854) 9 Ex. 709, Ex Ct *24–038*
Gravgaard v Aldridge & Brownlee (A Firm) [2004] EWCA Civ 1529; [2005] P.N.L.R. 19; (2005) 149 S.J.L.B. 27; [2004] N.P.C. 187, CA (Civ Div) *28–011*

Gray, Re. *See* Allardyce v Roebuck.
Gray v Allison (1909) 25 T.L.R. 531 .... *9–075*
Gray v Barr [1971] 2 Q.B. 554; [1971] 2 W.L.R. 1334; [1971] 2 All E.R. 949; [1971] 2 Lloyd's Rep. 1; (1971) 115 S.J. 364, CA (Civ Div); affirming [1970] 2 Q.B. 626; [1970] 3 W.L.R. 108; [1970] 2 All E.R. 702; [1970] 2 Lloyd's Rep. 69; (1970) 114 S.J. 413, QBD *16–168*, 16–173, 16–174
Gray v Carr (1870–71) L.R. 6 Q.B. 522, Ex Chamber *12–069*, *12–077*
Gray v Marlborough College [2006] EWCA Civ 1262; [2006] E.L.R. 516; (2006) 150 S.J.L.B. 1289, CA (Civ Div) 1–030
Gray v Mathias (1800) 5 Ves. 286; 5 R.R. 48 .... *16–067*
Gray v Pearson (1869–70) L.R. 5 C.P. 568; 23 L.T. 416, CCP *18–010*
Gray v Smith (1890) L.R. 43 Ch. D. 208; 59 L.J. Ch. 145; 61 L.T. 481; 62 L.T. 335; 38 W.R. 310, CA *2–123*, *4–012*
Gray v Southouse [1949] 2 All E.R. 1019, KBD *16–185*
Gray v Spyer [1922] 2 Ch. 22, CA *27–038*
Gray v Taylor [1998] 1 W.L.R. 1093; [1998] 4 All E.R. 17; (1999) 31 H.L.R. 262; [1998] L. & T.R. 50; [1998] E.G. 62 (C.S.); (1998) 95(20) L.S.G. 34; (1998) 142 S.J.L.B. 141; [1998] N.P.C. 60, CA (Civ Div) *15–035*
Gray v TP Bennett & Son, 43 B.L.R. 63 .... *28–086*
Gray v Trinity College, Dublin [1910] 1 Ir. R. 370 .... *9–004*
Gray's Inn Construction Co Ltd, Re [1980] 1 W.L.R. 711; [1980] 1 All E.R. 814; (1980) 124 S.J. 463, CA (Civ Div) *9–049*
Greasley v Cooke [1980] 1 W.L.R. 1306; [1980] 3 All E.R. 710; (1980) 124 S.J. 629, CA (Civ Div) *3–137*, *3–141*, *3–147*, *3–151*, *13–028*
Great China Metal Industries Co Ltd v Malaysian International Shipping Corp Bhd; The Bunga Seroja [1999] 1 Lloyd's Rep. 512; 1999 A.M.C. 427, HC (Aus); affirming [1994] 1 Lloyd's Rep. 455, Sup Ct (NSW) *14–146*
Great Future International Ltd v Sealand Housing Corp [2002] All E.R. (D) 28 .... *6–054*
Great North Eastern Railway Ltd v Avon Insurance Plc; sub nom. GNER v Avon Insurance Plc; Great Northern Eastern Railway Ltd v Avon Insurance Plc [2001] EWCA Civ 780; [2001] 2 All E.R. (Comm) 526; [2001] 2 Lloyd's Rep. 649; [2001] Lloyd's Rep. I.R. 793, CA (Civ Div) *12–126*
Great North West Central Railway Co v Charlebois [1899] A.C. 114; 68 L.J.P.C. 25; 79 L.T. 35, PC (Can) *9–024*
Great Northern Railway Co v Harrison (1852) 12 C.B.(N.S.) 576; 22 L.J.C.P. 49; 16 Jur. 565; 19 L.T. 259; 92 R.R. 786 .... *13–024*
Great Northern Railway Co v Swaffield (1873–74) L.R. 9 Ex. 132, Ex Ct *29–019*, *29–022*, *29–115*, *29–133*, *29–136*
Great Northern Railway Co v Witham (1873) L.R. 9 C.P. 16; 43 L.J.C.P. 1; 29 L.T. 471, CCP *2–039*, *2–078*
Great Peace Shipping Ltd v Tsavliris Salvage (International) Ltd [2002] EWCA Civ 1407; [2003] Q.B. 679; [2002] 3 W.L.R. 1617; [2002] 4 All E.R. 689; [2002] 2 All E.R. (Comm) 999; [2002] 2 Lloyd's Rep. 653; [2003] 2 C.L.C. 16; (2002) 99(43) L.S.G. 34; (2002) 152 N.L.J. 1616; [2002] N.P.C. 127, CA (Civ Div); affirming [2001] All E.R. (D) 152, QBD (Comm) *1–083*, *5–001*, *5–012*, *5–016*, *5–018*, *5–022*, *5–023*, *5–026*, **5–036**, *5–037*, 5–039, 5–043, 5–046, 5–052, 5–053, 5–057, *5–058*, 5–060, *5–061*, **5–062**, 5–063, *22–021*, *23–002*, *27–033*
Great Western and Metropolitan Dairies Ltd v Gibbs (1918) 34 T.L.R. 344 ..... *16–110*
Great Western Insurance Co v Cunliffe (1873–74) L.R. 9 Ch. App. 525, CA in Chancery *26–167*
Great Western Railway v Oxford (1853) 3 De G.M. & G. 341 .... *28–135*
Great Western Railway Co v Bristol Corp (1918) 87 L.J.Ch. 414 .... *12–118*, *12–124*
Great Western Railway Co v London & County Banking Co Ltd [1901] A.C. 414; 68 L.J.Q.B. 959; 81 L.T. 310, HL; reversing [1900] 2 Q.B. 464, CA; affirming [1899] 2 Q.B. 172, QBD (Comm) *4–036*
Great Western Railway Co v Solihull Rural DC (1902) 86 L.T. 852 .....*10–027*, *10–028*
Great Western Railway Co v Sutton (1869–70) L.R. 4 H.L. 226, HL *7–015*, *29–092*, *29–097*

Greater London Council v Connolly [1970] 2 Q.B. 100; [1970] 2 W.L.R. 658; [1970] 1 All E.R. 870; (1970) 114 S.J. 108, CA (Civ Div) *2–142*

Greater Nottingham Cooperative Society v Cementation Piling & Foundations Ltd [1989] Q.B. 71; [1988] 3 W.L.R. 396; [1988] 2 All E.R. 971; 41 B.L.R. 43; (1988) 4 Const. L.J. 216; (1988) 138 N.L.J. Rep. 112; (1988) 132 S.J. 754, CA (Civ Div) *1–158*, *1–176*, *1–177*, *14–056*, *18–005*, *18–023*, *18–031*, *18–036*, *18–059*

Greathead v Bromley (1798) 7 T.R. 455 .... *25–007*

Greaves & Co (Contractors) Ltd v Baynham Meikle & Partners [1975] 1 W.L.R. 1095; [1975] 3 All E.R. 99; [1975] 2 Lloyd's Rep. 325; 4 B.L.R. 56; (1975) 119 S.J. 372, CA (Civ Div); affirming [1974] 1 W.L.R. 1261; [1974] 3 All E.R. 666; [1975] 1 Lloyd's Rep. 31; (1974) 118 S.J. 595, QBD *13–003*, *13–032*

Grecoair Inc v Tilling [2004] EWHC 2851; [2005] Lloyd's Rep. I.R. 151, QBD (Comm) *18–004*

Green v Arcos Ltd (1931) 47 T.L.R. 336 .... *14–027*

Green v Baverstock (1863) 14 C.B.(N.S.) 204 .... *29–148*

Green v Duckett (1882–83) L.R. 11 Q.B.D. 275, QBD *29–091*, *29–092*

Green v Gaul; sub nom. Loftus (Deceased), Re [2006] EWCA Civ 1124; [2007] 1 W.L.R. 591; [2006] 4 All E.R. 1110; [2006] W.T.L.R. 1391; (2006–07) 9 I.T.E.L.R. 107; (2006) 156 N.L.J. 1365; [2007] 1 P. & C.R. DG12, CA (Civ Div) *28–019*, *28–134*, *28–139*

Green v Greenbank (1816) 2 Marsh 485; 17 R.R. 529 .... *8–043*

Green v Hampshire CC, unreported, July 14, 1980, CA (Civ Div) *25–012*, *25–013*

Green v Horn (1694) 1 Salk. 197 .... *18–122*

Green v Low (1856) 22 Beav. 625 .... *21–003*

Green v Patterson (1886) L.R. 32 Ch. D. 95; 56 L.J. Ch. 181; 54 L.T. 738; 34 W.R. 724, CA *18–087*

Green v Portsmouth Stadium [1953] 2 Q.B. 190; [1953] 2 W.L.R. 1206; [1953] 2 All E.R. 102; (1953) 97 S.J. 386, CA; reversing [1953] 1 W.L.R. 487; [1953] 1 All E.R. 642; (1953) 97 S.J. 172, QBD *16–185*, *29–084*, *29–150*

Green v Rozen [1955] 1 W.L.R. 741; [1955] 2 All E.R. 797; (1955) 99 S.J. 473, QBD *22–015*

Green v Russell, McCarthy (Third Party) [1959] 2 Q.B. 226; [1959] 3 W.L.R. 17; [1959] 2 All E.R. 525; (1959) 103 S.J. 489, CA; affirming [1959] 1 Q.B. 28; [1958] 3 W.L.R. 371; [1958] 3 All E.R. 44; (1958) 102 S.J. 620, QBD *18–019*, *18–079*, *18–082*, *18–086*

Green v Sevin (1879–80) L.R. 13 Ch. D. 589, Ch D *21–014*

Green v Thompson [1899] 2 Q.B. 1; 68 L.J.Q.B. 719; 80 L.T. 691; 48 W.R. 31, QBD *8–022*

Green & Sons (Northampton) Ltd v Morris [1914] 1 Ch. 562; 83 L.J.H. 559; 110 L.T. 508; 30 T.L.R. 301; 58 S.J. 398, Ch D *16–118*

Green (Deceased), Re; sub nom. Lindner v Green [1951] Ch. 148; [1950] 2 All E.R. 913; 66 T.L.R. (Pt. 2) 819; (1950) 94 S.J. 742, Ch D *29–160*

Greenaway Harrison Ltd v Wiles [1994] I.R.L.R. 380, EAT *24–021*

Greene, Re; sub nom. Greene v Greene [1949] Ch. 333; [1949] 1 All E.R. 167; (1949) 93 S.J. 27, Ch D *9–061*

Greene v Chelsea BC [1954] 2 Q.B. 127; [1954] 3 W.L.R. 12; [1954] 2 All E.R. 318; (1954) 118 J.P. 346; 52 L.G.R. 352; (1954) 98 S.J. 389, CA *1–174*

Greene v Church Commissioners for England [1974] Ch. 467; [1974] 3 W.L.R. 349; [1974] 3 All E.R. 609; (1975) 29 P. & C.R. 285; (1974) 118 S.J. 700, CA (Civ Div) *3–047*, *3–172*

Greenhalgh v Mallard [1943] 2 All E.R. 234, CA *18–139*, *25–013*

Greening Industries Ltd v Penny (1965) 53 D.L.R. (2d) 643 .... *16–117*

Greenman v, Yuba Power Products, 377 P.2d 897 (1963)..................................... *6–086*

Greenmast Shipping Co SA v Jean Lion et Cie; The Saronikos [1986] 2 Lloyd's Rep. 277, QBD (Comm) *2–005*, *2–030*

Greenock Corp v Caledonian Railway Co; sub nom. Caledonian Railway Co v Corp of Greenock; Greenock Corp v Glasgow & South Western Railway Co [1917] A.C. 556; 1917 S.C. (H.L.) 56; 1917 2 S.L.T. 67, HL *14–146*

Greenshields v Johnston (1981) 119 D.L.R. (3d) 714 .... *30–007*, *30–311*

Greenslade v Dare (1855) 20 Beav. 284; 24 L.J.Ch. 490; 1 Jur. 294; 3 W.R. 220; 109 R.R. 416 .... *8–070*

Greenspan v Slate (1953) 97 A. 2d. 390 .... *8–061*

Greenwich Marine Inc v Federal Commerce & Navigation Co Ltd; The Mavro Vetranic [1985] 1 Lloyd's Rep. 580, QBD (Comm) *12–037*, *12–040*

Greenwood v Bennett [1973] Q.B. 195; [1972] 3 W.L.R. 691; [1972] 3 All E.R. 586; [1972] R.T.R. 535; (1972) 116 S.J. 762, CA (Civ Div) *29–021*, *29–022*, *29–052*, 29–053, *29–133*

Greenwood v Bishop of London (1814) 5 Taunt. 727; 1 Marsh 292; 15 R.R. 627 ... *16–167*, *16–195*

Greenwood v Martins Bank Ltd [1933] A.C. 51; [1932] All E.R. Rep. 318; 101 L.J.K.B. 623; 147 L.T. 441; 48 T.L.R. 601; 76 S.J. 544; 38 Com. Cas. 54, HL *6–095*, *20–009*

Greenwood v Sutcliffe [1892] 1 Ch. 1, CA *21–084*, *21–092*

Greenwood v Turner [1891] 2 Ch. 144, Ch D *27–007*

Greer v Downs Supply Co [1927] 2 K.B. 28, CA *21–044*

Greer v Kettle [1938] A.C. 156; 107 L.J.Ch. 56; 158 L.T. 433; 54 T.L.R. 143; 82 S.J. 133; [1937] 4 All E.R. 397, CA *1–112*

Greg, Re; sub nom. Fordham v Greg [1921] 2 Ch. 243, Ch D *28–065*

Gregory v Ford [1951] 1 All E.R. 121, Assizes (Nottingham) *16–173*

Gregory v Wallace [1998] I.R.L.R. 387, CA (Civ Div) *22–046*

Gregory v Williams (1817) Mer. 582 .... *18–078*

Gregory v Wilson (1851) 9 Hare 683 .... *27–040*

Greig v Insole; World Series Cricket Pty v Insole [1978] 1 W.L.R. 302; [1978] 3 All E.R. 449; (1978) 122 S.J. 162, Ch D .. *9–084*, *16–075*, *16–105*, *16–115*, *16–133*, *16–136*, *16–137*

Greig v National Aamalgamated Union of Shop Assistants (1906) 22 T.L.R. 274 .... *16–050*

Grell v Levy (1864) 16 C.B.(N.S.) 73; 10 Jur. 210; 9 L.T. 721; 2 W.R. 378; 139 R.R. 414 .... *16–029*, *16–055*, *16–057*

Grell v Levy, 143 E.R. 1052; (1864) 16 C.B. N.S. 73, CCP *30–367*

Grenfell v The Dean and Canons of Windsor (1840) 2 Beav. 544 .... *16–022*

Gresley v Mousley (1859) 4 De G. & J. 78 .... *28–141*

Greville v Venables [2007] EWCA Civ 878; (2007) 104(37) L.S.G. 36, CA (Civ Div) *10–037*

Grey v Australian Motorists & General Insurance Co Pty. [1976] 1 N.S.W.L.R. 669 .... *19–013*, *19–015*, *19–016*

Grey v Inland Revenue Commissioners; sub nom. Grey and Randolph (Hunter's Nominees) v Inland Revenue Commissioners [1960] A.C. 1; [1959] 3 W.L.R. 759; [1959] 3 All E.R. 603; (1959) 38 A.T.C. 313; [1959] T.R. 311; (1959) 103 S.J. 896, HL; affirming [1958] Ch. 690; [1958] 3 W.L.R. 45; [1958] 2 All E.R. 428; (1958) 37 A.T.C. 136; [1958] T.R. 165; (1958) 102 S.J. 469, CA; reversing [1958] Ch. 375; [1958] 2 W.L.R. 168; [1958] 1 All E.R. 246; (1957) 36 A.T.C. 296; [1957] T.R. 293; (1958) 102 S.J. 84, Ch D *19–025*

Grey v Pearson (1857) 6 H.L.C. 61; 26 L.J. Ch. 473; 3 Jur. 823; 5 W.R. 454; 108 R.R. 19 .... *12–051*, *12–055*

Grice v Kenrick (1869–70) L.R. 5 Q.B. 340, QB *21–048*

Grieves v FT Everard & Sons Ltd; Quinn v George Clark & Nem Ltd; Mears v RG Carter Ltd; Jackson v Brock Plc; Rothwell v Chemical & Insulating Co Ltd; Downey v Charles Evans Shopfitters Ltd; Storey v Clellands Shipbuilders Ltd; Topping v Benchtown Ltd (formerly Jones Bros (Preston) Ltd); Johnston v NEI International Combustion Ltd; Hindson v Pipe House Wharf (Swansea) Ltd [2007] UKHL 39; [2008] 1 A.C. 281; [2007] 3 W.L.R. 876; [2007] 4 All E.R. 1047; [2007] I.C.R. 1745; [2008] P.I.Q.R. P6; [2008] LS Law Medical 1; (2008) 99 B.M.L.R. 139; (2007) 104(42) L.S.G. 34; (2007) 157 N.L.J. 1542; (2007) 151 S.J.L.B. 1366, HL; affirming [2006] EWCA Civ 27; [2006] 4 All E.R. 1161; [2006] I.C.R. 1458; (2006) 90 B.M.L.R. 88; (2006) 103(7) L.S.G. 25; (2006) 156 N.L.J. 185; (2006) 150 S.J.L.B. 164, CA (Civ Div); reversing [2005] EWHC 88 (QB); [2005] P.I.Q.R. P25, QBD *18–026*
Griffin, Re; sub nom. Griffin v. Griffin [1899] 1 Ch. 408; 68 L.J. Ch. 220; 79 L.T. 442; 15 T.L.R. 78, Ch D *19–022*, *19–046*
Griffin v Pillet [1926] 1 K.B. 17, KBD *21–009*
Griffin v Weatherby (1868) L.R. 3 Q.B. 753 29–194
Griffith v Brymer (1903) 19 T.L.R. 434 .... *5–005*, 5–025, 5–041, *5–053*, *23–033*
Griffith v Griffith [1944] I.R. 35 .... *7–010*
Griffith v Ystradyfodwg School Board (1890) L.R. 24 Q.B.D. 307, QBD *21–084*
Griffiths v Owen (1844) 13 M. & W. 58; 2 D. & L. 190; 13 L.J. Ex. 345; 67 R.R. 5101 .... *22–015*, *21–074*
Griffiths v Secretary of State for Social Services [1974] Q.B. 468; [1973] 3 W.L.R. 831; [1973] 3 All E.R. 1184; (1973) 117 S.J. 873, QBD *9–050*, *19–057*
Griffiths v Tower Publishing Co [1897] 1 Ch. 21; 66 L.J. Ch. 12; 15 L.T. 330; 45 W.R. 73, Ch D *19–055*, *19–057*
Griffiths v Williams [1978] E.G.D. 919; (1977) 248 E.G. 947, CA (Civ Div) *3–139*, *3–151*, *3–156*, *3–157*, *3–163*
Griffiths v Young [1970] Ch. 675; [1970] 3 W.L.R. 246; [1970] 3 All E.R. 601; (1970) 21 P. & C.R. 770; [1971] J.P.L. 117; (1970) 114 S.J. 571, CA (Civ Div) *4–027*, *4–028*
Grigby v Cox (1750) 1 Ves. Sen. 517 .... *7–085*
Grimston v Cunningham [1894] 1 Q.B. 125 .... *27–064*
Grindell v Bass [1920] 2 Ch. 487; 89 L.J. Ch. 591; 124 L.T. 211; 36 T.L.R. 867, Ch D *4–027*, *4–036*, *28–094*
Grist v Bailey [1967] Ch. 532; [1966] 3 W.L.R. 618; [1966] 2 All E.R. 875; (1966) 110 S.J. 791, Ch D *5–058*, 5–059
Grogan v Robin Meredith Plant Hire [1996] C.L.C. 1127; 53 Con. L.R. 87; (1996) 15 Tr. L.R. 371; (1996) 140 S.J.L.B. 57, CA (Civ Div) *12–008*, *12–009*, *12–012*
Groom v Crocker [1939] 1 K.B. 194; (1938) 60 Ll. L. Rep. 393, CA *26–083*, *28–033*
Gross v Lewis Hillman Ltd [1970] Ch. 445; [1969] 3 W.L.R. 787; [1969] 3 All E.R. 1476; (1969) 113 S.J. 737, CA (Civ Div) 6–028, *6–047*
Grossman v Hooper [2001] EWCA Civ 615; [2001] 3 F.C.R. 662; [2001] 2 E.G.L.R. 82; [2001] 27 E.G. 135, CA (Civ Div) 4–067
Grosvenor Casinos Ltd v National Bank of Abu Dhabi [2008] EWHC 511 (Comm); [2008] 1 C.L.C. 399, QBD (Comm) *18–004*, *18–013*
Grosvenor v Sherratt (1860) 28 Beav. 659; 3 L.T. 76; 6 Jur. (N.S.) 1288; 8 W.R. 682 .... *7–075*, *7–084*
Group Josi Re Co SA v Walbrook Insurance Co Ltd; Deutsche Ruckversicherung AG v Walbrook Insurance Co Ltd; sub nom. Group Josi Re (formerly Group Josi Reassurance SA) v Walbrook Insurance Co Ltd [1996] 1 W.L.R. 1152; [1996] 1 All E.R. 791; [1996] 1 Lloyd's Rep. 345; [1995] C.L.C. 1532; [1996] 5 Re. L.R. 91, CA (Civ Div) *27–061*
Groupama Navigation et Transports v Catatumbo CA Seguros [2000] 2 All E.R. (Comm) 193; [2000] 2 Lloyd's Rep. 350; [2000] C.L.C. 1534; [2001] Lloyd's Rep. I.R. 141, CA (Civ Div) *30–011*
Groves v Groves (1829) 3 Y. & J. 163; 32 R.R. 782 .... *1–108*

Grovewood Holdings Plc v James Capel & Co Ltd [1995] Ch. 80; [1995] 2 W.L.R. 70; [1994] 4 All E.R. 417; [1995] B.C.C. 760; [1994] 2 B.C.L.C. 782; [1994] E.G. 136 (C.S.); (1994) 144 N.L.J. 1405, Ch D *16–053*, *16–063*, *19–049*
Grovit v De Nederlandsche Bank; Thorncroft v De Nederlandsche Bank [2007] EWCA Civ 953; [2008] 1 W.L.R. 51; [2008] 1 All E.R. (Comm) 106; [2008] I.L.Pr. 19, CA (Civ Div); affirming [2005] EWHC 2944 (QB); [2006] 1 W.L.R. 3323; [2006] 1 All E.R. (Comm) 397; [2006] 1 Lloyd's Rep. 636; [2006] Eu. L.R. 731; [2006] I.L.Pr. 22, QBD *11–003*, *11–004*
Grupo Torras SA v Al-Sabah (No.5); Bonafonte v Grupo Torras SA; sub nom. Al-Sabah v Grupo Torras SA [2001] Lloyd's Rep. Bank. 36; [2001] C.L.C. 221; [2001] Lloyd's Rep. P.N. 117, CA (Civ Div) *30–325*
Gryf-Lowczowski v Hinchingbrooke Healthcare NHS Trust [2005] EWHC 2407; [2006] I.C.R. 425; [2006] I.R.L.R. 100; [2006] Lloyd's Rep. Med. 199; (2006) 87 B.M.L.R. 46, QBD *27–023*
Guarantee Trust of Jersey v Gardner (1973) 117 S.J. 564, CA (Civ Div) *14–028*
Guardian Ocean Cargoes Ltd v Banco do Brasil SA; The Golden Med (No.1) [1994] 2 Lloyd's Rep. 152; [1994] C.L.C. 243, CA (Civ Div); reversing in part [1991] 2 Lloyd's Rep. 68, QBD (Comm) *12–043*, *12–107*
Guardian Permanent Benefit Building Society, Re (1883) L.R. 23 Ch. D. 440, CA *9–025*
Guardian Trust and Executors Co of New Zealand Ltd v Public Trustee of New Zealand [1942] A.C. 115; 111 L.J.P.C. 119; 167 L.T. 162; 58 T.L.R. 132; [1942] 1 All E.R. 598, PC (NZ) *20–013*
Guardians of Pontypridd Union v Drew; sub nom. Pontypridd Union Guardians v Drew [1927] 1 K.B. 214; 95 L.J.K.B. 1030; 136 L.T. 83; 42 T.L.R. 677, CA; reversing [1926] 1 K.B. 567, KBD *8–011*
Gudermes, The. *See* Mitsui & Co Ltd v Novorossiysk Shipping Co
Gueprate v Young (1851) 4 De G. & Sm. 217 .... *30–310*
Guest v Empire Pools (No.2) (1964) 108 S.J. 98, Ch D *2–162*
Guildford v Lockyer [1975] Crim. L.R. 235; (1975) 119 S.J. 353, DC *2–016*
Guildford BC v Hein [2005] EWCA Civ 979; [2005] B.L.G.R. 797, CA (Civ Div) *29–130*
Guiness Mahon Co Ltd v Kensington Chelsea RLBC [1998] 2 All E.R. 272 .....*29–056*, *29–075*
Guinness Mahon & Co Ltd v Kensington and Chelsea RLBC [1999] Q.B. 215; [1998] 3 W.L.R. 829; [1998] 2 All E.R. 272; [1998] Lloyd's Rep. Bank. 109; [1998] C.L.C. 662; (1998) 95(13) L.S.G. 28; (1998) 148 N.L.J. 366; (1998) 142 S.J.L.B. 92, CA (Civ Div) *3–004*, *3–007*, *10–046*
Guinness Peat Aviation (Belgium) NV v Hispania Lineas Aereas SA [1992] 1 Lloyd's Rep. 190, QBD (Comm) *18–145*
Guinness Plc v Saunders; Guinness v Ward [1990] 2 A.C. 663; [1990] 2 W.L.R. 324; [1990] 1 All E.R. 652; [1990] B.C.C. 205; [1990] B.C.L.C. 402; (1990) 87(9) L.S.G. 42; (1990) 134 S.J. 457, HL; affirming [1988] 1 W.L.R. 863; [1988] 2 All E.R. 940; (1988) 4 B.C.C. 377; [1988] B.C.L.C. 607; [1988] P.C.C. 270; (1988) 138 N.L.J. Rep. 142; (1988) 132 S.J. 820, CA (Civ Div); affirming (1987) 3 B.C.C. 520; [1988] B.C.L.C. 43; 1987 P.C.C. 413, Ch D *9–055*, *29–002*, *29–008*, *29–011*, *29–076*, *29–156*, *29–157*, *29–160*
Guiseppe di Vittorio, The. *See* Bridge Oil Ltd v Owners and/or Demise Charterers of the Ship Guiseppe di Vittorio (No.1)
Gulf Azov Shipping Co Ltd v Chief Idisi (No.2); United Kingdom Mutual Steamship Assurance Association (Bermuda) Ltd v Lonestar Drilling Nigeria Ltd; Gulf Azov Shipping Co Ltd v Lonestar Drilling Nigeria Ltd; United Kingdom Mutual Steamship Assurance Association (Bermuda) Ltd v Lonestar Overseas Ltd [2001] EWCA Civ 505; [2001] 2 All E.R. (Comm) 673; [2001] 1 Lloyd's Rep. 727, CA (Civ Div) *7–011*, *7–051*
Gulf Steel Co Ltd v Al Khalifa Shipping Co Ltd; The Anwar Al Sabar [1980] 2 Lloyd's Rep. 261, QBD (Comm) *2–021*
Gulnes (D/S A/S/) v ICI Ltd. *See* D/S A/S Gulnes v ICI Ltd
Gunatunga v DeAlwis (1996) 72 P. & C.R. 161, CA (Civ Div) *24–040*, *25–003*

Gundry v Sainsbury [1910] 1 K.B. 645; [1997] Costs L.R. (Core Vol.) 1, CA; affirming [1910] 1 K.B. 99, KBD *16–056*
Gunn v Bolckow Vaughan & Co (1874–75) L.R. 10 Ch. App. 491, CA in Chancery *21–074*
Gunn's Case. *See* Universal Banking Corp, Re
Gunsbourg Re (1919) 88 L.J.K.B. 479; [1918–19] B. & C.R. 99 .... *19–022*
Gunton v Richmond upon Thames LBC [1981] Ch. 448; [1980] 3 W.L.R. 714; [1980] 3 All E.R. 577; [1980] I.C.R. 755; [1980] I.R.L.R. 321; 79 L.G.R. 241; (1980) 124 S.J. 792, CA (Civ Div) *24–013*, *27–022*
Gunyon v South Eastern and Chatham Railway Companies Managing Committee [1915] 2 K.B. 370; 84 L.J.K.B. 1212; 113 L.T. 282; 31 T.L.R. 334, KBD *14–029*
Gurney v Womersley (1854) 24 L.J.Q.B. 46; 4 E. & B. 133; C.L.R. 3; 1 Jur. 328; 99 R.R. 390, QB *5–021*
Gurney v Womersley, 119 E.R. 51; (1854) 4 El. & Bl. 133, QB *29–056*
Gurtner v Circuit [1968] 2 Q.B. 587; [1968] 2 W.L.R. 668; [1968] 1 All E.R. 328; [1968] 1 Lloyd's Rep. 171; (1968) 112 S.J. 63; (1968) 112 S.J. 73, CA (Civ Div) *18–075*, *18–131*, *27–034*, *27–052*
Gurwicz Ex p. Trustee, Re [1919] 1 K.B. 675, KBD *16–039*
Gustavson Drilling (1964) Ltd v Minister of National Revenue [1977] 1 S.C.R. 271 .... *1–040*
Gutnick v Dow Jones [2002] HCA 56, HC (Aus) *30–097*
Guy v Churchill (1889) L.R. 40 Ch. D. 481; 58 L.J. Ch. 545; 60 L.T. 473, Ch D *16–063*, *19–049*, *20–032*
Guy-Pell v Foster [1930] 2 Ch. 169, CA *24–030*, *24–035*, *24–040*
Gwembe Valley Development Co Ltd v Koshy. *See* DEG-Deutsche Investitions und Entwicklungsgesellschaft mbH v Koshy (Account of Profits: Limitations)
Gwyn v Neath Canal Navigation Co (1867–68) L.R. 3 Ex. 209; 37 L.J. Ex. 122; 18 L.T. 688; 16 W.R. 1209, Ex Ct *12–072*
Gyles v Hall, 24 E.R. 774; (1726) 2 P. Wms. 378, Ch D *21–054*
Gyllenhammar & Partners International Ltd v Sour Brodogradevna Industrija [1989] 2 Lloyd's Rep. 403, QBD (Comm) *2–149*, *2–155*, *12–082*, *13–009*, *14–138*, *27–014*

H v H [1954] P. 258; [1953] 3 W.L.R. 849; [1953] 2 All E.R. 1229; (1953) 97 S.J. 782, PDAD *7–010*
H v M (Property Occupied by Wife's Parents); sub nom. JH v AM [2004] EWHC 625 (Fam); [2004] 2 F.L.R. 16; [2004] Fam. Law 485, Fam Div *3–147*
H Cousins & Co v D&C Carriers [1971] 2 Q.B. 230; [1971] 2 W.L.R. 85; [1971] 1 All E.R. 55; [1970] 2 Lloyd's Rep. 397; (1970) 114 S.J. 882, CA (Civ Div) *26–176*
H Dakin & Co v Lee; sub nom. Dakin & Co v Lee [1916] 1 K.B. 566, CA *21–031*, *21–032*, *21–033*, *24–043*
H Ford & Co v Compagnie Furness [1922] 2 K.B. 797; (1922) 12 Ll. L. Rep. 281, KBD *14–004*
H Meyer & Co Ltd v Jules Decroix Verley et Cie; sub nom. Decroix Verley & Cie v Meyer & Co Ltd [1891] A.C. 520, HL *25–023*
H Parsons (Livestock) Ltd v Uttley Ingham & Co Ltd. *See* Parsons (Livestock) Ltd v Uttley Ingham & Co Ltd
HA Brightman & Co v Bunge y Born Limitada Sociedad; sub nom. Brightman & Co v Bunge y Born Limitada Sociedad; Bunge y Born Limitada Sociedad v HA Brightman & Co [1925] A.C. 799; (1925) 22 Ll. L. Rep. 395, HL *21–006*, *21–007*
HC Smith Ltd v Great Western Railway Co Ltd [1922] 1 A.C. 178, HL; affirming [1921] 2 K.B. 237, CA *14–018*
HE Daniels Ltd v Carmel Exporters & Importers Ltd. *See* Carmel Exporters & Importers Ltd v HE Daniels Ltd (No.2)
HE Thorne & Son Ltd, Re [1914] 2 Ch. 438, Ch D *20–041*
HF Pension Trustees Ltd v Ellison [1999] Lloyd's Rep. P.N. 489; [1999] P.N.L.R. 894; [1999] O.P.L.R. 67; (1999) 96(8) L.S.G. 30, Ch D *28–012*

HIB v Guardian Insurance Co Inc. *See* Hogg Insurance Brokers Ltd v Guardian Insurance Co Inc
HIH Casualty & General Insurance Ltd v Axa Corporate Solutions (formerly Axa Reassurance SA); HIH Casualty & General Insurance Ltd v New Hampshire Insurance Co [2002] EWCA Civ 1253; [2002] 2 All E.R. (Comm) 1053; [2003] Lloyd's Rep. I.R. 1, CA (Civ Div); affirming [2002] Lloyd's Rep. I.R. 325, QBD *3–092*, *3–109*
HIH Casualty & General Insurance Ltd v Chase Manhattan Bank; Chase Manhattan Bank v HIH Casualty & General Insurance Ltd [2003] UKHL 6; [2003] 1 All E.R. (Comm) 349; [2003] 2 Lloyd's Rep. 61; [2003] 1 C.L.C. 358; [2003] Lloyd's Rep. I.R. 230; (2003) 147 S.J.L.B. 264, HL; reversing in part [2001] EWCA Civ 1250; [2001] 2 Lloyd's Rep. 483; [2001] C.L.C. 1853; [2001] Lloyd's Rep. I.R. 703, CA (Civ Div); reversing in part [2001] 1 All E.R. (Comm) 719; [2001] 1 Lloyd's Rep. 30; [2001] C.L.C. 48; [2001] Lloyd's Rep. I.R. 191, QBD (Comm) *6–134*, *6–143*, *14–010*, *14–011*, *14–013*, *14–136*
HIH Casualty & General Insurance Ltd v New Hampshire Insurance Co [2001] EWCA Civ 735; [2001] 2 All E.R. (Comm) 39; [2001] 2 Lloyd's Rep. 161; [2001] C.L.C. 1480; [2001] Lloyd's Rep. I.R. 596, CA (Civ Div); affirming [2001] 1 Lloyd's Rep. 378; [2001] C.L.C. 481, QBD (Comm) *2–117*, *12–015*, *12–069*, *12–096*, *12–119*, *14–013*
HL Estates Ltd v Parker-Lake Homes Ltd; sub nom. HL Estates Ltd v Parker-Lane Homes Ltd [2003] EWHC 604; [2003] All E.R. (D) 245,, Ch D *4–056*
HO Brandt & Co v HN Morris & Co; sub nom. HO Brandt & Co v HN Morris & Co Ltd [1917] 2 K.B. 784, CA *2–155*, *13–013*
HOK Sport Ltd (formerly Lobb Partnership Ltd) v Aintree Racecourse Co Ltd [2002] EWHC 3094 (TCC); [2003] B.L.R. 155; 86 Con. L.R. 165; [2003] Lloyd's Rep. P.N. 148, QBD (TCC) *26–079*
HPC Productions Ltd, Re [1962] Ch. 466; [1962] 2 W.L.R. 51; [1962] 1 All E.R. 37; (1962) 106 S.J. 36, Ch D *16–145*, *29–113*
HR&S Sainsbury Ltd v Street [1972] 1 W.L.R. 834; [1972] 3 All E.R. 1127; (1972) 116 S.J. 483, Assizes (Bristol) *23–047*, 23–068, 23–069, *23–096*
HSBC Bank Plc v Liberty Mutual Insurance Co (UK) Ltd; Liberty Mutual Insurance Co (UK) Ltd v HSBC Bank Plc [2002] EWCA Civ 691, CA (Civ Div) *12–050*
HSBC Rail (UK) Ltd v Network Rail Infrastructure Ltd (formerly Railtrack Plc) [2005] EWCA Civ 1437; [2006] 1 W.L.R. 643; [2006] 1 All E.R. 343; [2006] 1 All E.R. (Comm) 345; [2006] 1 Lloyd's Rep. 358; [2006] 1 C.L.C. 991; (2006) 103(1) L.S.G. 17, CA (Civ Div); affirming [2005] EWHC 403 (Comm); [2005] 1 All E.R. (Comm) 689; [2005] 2 Lloyd's Rep. 343, QBD (Comm) *18–055*
HSBC Trust Co (UK) Ltd v Quinn [2007] EWHC 1543 (Ch); [2007] All E.R. (D) 125 (Jul), Ch D *1–090*
Habib Bank Ltd v Central Bank of Sudan [2006] EWHC 1767 (Comm); [2007] 1 W.L.R. 470; [2007] 1 All E.R. (Comm) 53; [2006] 2 Lloyd's Rep. 412; [2006] 2 C.L.C. 176, QBD (Comm) *28–095*, *30–012*, *30–077*
Habib Bank Ltd v Habib Bank AG [1981] 1 W.L.R. 1265; [1981] 2 All E.R. 650; [1982] R.P.C. 1; (1981) 125 S.J. 512, CA (Civ Div) *28–136*
Habib Bank Ltd v Tufail [2006] EWCA Civ 374; [2006] All E.R. (D) 92; [2006] 2 P. & C.R. DG14, CA (Civ Div) *6–126*, *7–097*
Hack v Hack (1976) 6 Fam. Law 177 .... *30–079*
Hackett v Smith [1917] 2 L.R. 508 .... *29–107*
Hackney LBC v Dore [1922] 1 K.B. 431; 91 L.J.K.B. 109; 126 L.T. 375; 86 J.P. 45; 38 T.L.R. 93; 20 L.G.R. 88, DC *14–147*, *14–148*
Hackney LBC v Thompson [2001] L. & T.R. 7, CA (Civ Div) *2–140*, *2–142*
Hadenfayre v British National Insurance Society; Trident General Insurance Co v Lombard Elizabethan Insurance Co [1984] 2 Lloyd's Rep. 393; (1984) 134 N.L.J. 1017, QBD (Comm) *2–117*
Hadjipateras v Weigall & Co (1918) 34 T.L.R. 360 .... *12–070*, *12–087*

Hadley v Baxendale (1854) 9 Exch. 341; 23 L.J. Ex. 179; 2 C.L.R. 517; 18 Jur.358; 2 W.R. 302; 2 Sm. L.C. (13th ed.) 529; 3 L.T. 69; R.R. 742 ....*1–164*, *26–006*, *26–051*, **26–052**, *26–053*, 26–054, *26–055*, 26–057, *26–059*, 26–061, *26–062*, 26–063, *26–066*, *26–070*, 26–098, 26–100C, *26–100D*, 26–105, 26–106, *26–107*, 26–169
Hadley v Green (1832) 2 Cr. J. 374 .... *25–007*
Hadley v Kemp [1999] E.M.L.R. 589, Ch D *2–112*, *2–168*, *3–011*, *3–066*
Hadley Design Associates Ltd v Westminster City Council [2003] EWHC 1617 (TCC); [2004] T.C.L.R. 1; [2004] Masons C.L.R. 3, QBD (TCC) *13–009*, *14–072*, *14–074*
Hadsley v Dayer-Smith [1914] A.C. 979; 83 L.J. Ch. 770; 111 L.T. 479; 30 T.L.R. 524, HL *16–114*
Hadwen v Mendisabal (1825) 10 Moore C.P. 477 .... *21–074*
Haggar v De Placido [1972] 1 W.L.R. 716; [1972] 2 All E.R. 1029; (1972) 116 S.J. 396, Crown Ct (Chester) *2–174*
Haigh v Brooks (1893) 9 L.J.Q.B. 99; (1839) 10 A. & E. 309; 2 P. & D. 477; 50 R.R. 399, QB *3–014*, *3–015*, 3–051, *12–081*, *29–189*
Haigh v Royal Mail Steam Packet Co (1883) 52 L.J.Q.B. 640; 49 L.T. 802; 48 J.P. 230; 5 Asp. M.L.C. 189 .... *14–011*
Hain Steamship Co v Tate & Lyle Ltd. *See* Tate & Lyle Ltd v Hain Steamship Co Ltd
Halcyon Skies, The. *See* Powell v Owners of the Proceeds of Sale of the Halcyon Skies (No.2)
Haldane v Johnson (1853) 8 Exch. 689 .... *21–054*, *21–094*
Hale v Ruthven (1869) 20 L.T. 404 .... *8–042*
Hales v Freeman (1819) 1 B.B. 391 .... *29–107*
Hales v London North Western Railway (1863) 4 B.S. 66 .... *26–089*
Halifax Building Society v Edell [1992] Ch. 436; [1992] 3 W.L.R. 136; [1992] 3 All E.R. 389; [1993] E.C.C. 462; [1992] 1 E.G.L.R. 195; [1992] 18 E.G. 151; (1993) 12 Tr. L.R. 117; [1992] E.G. 33 (C.S.); [1992] N.P.C. 38, Ch D *2–180*, *3–027*, *18–014*, *18–015*, *18–022*
Halifax Building Society v Thomas [1996] Ch. 217; [1996] 2 W.L.R. 63; [1995] 4 All E.R. 673; [1995] N.P.C. 112, CA (Civ Div) 6–062, *29–025*, *29–140*, *29–143*, *29–146*, *29–147*, *29–149*, *29–160*
Halifax Financial Services Ltd v Intuitive Systems Ltd [1999] 1 All E.R. (Comm) 303; (2000) 2 T.C.L.R. 35; [1999] C.I.L.L. 1467, QBD *2–136*
Halifax Mortgage Services Ltd (formerly BNP Mortgages Ltd) v Stepsky [1996] Ch. 207; [1996] 2 W.L.R. 230; [1996] 2 All E.R. 277; [1996] 1 F.L.R. 620; [1996] 2 F.C.R. 97; (1996) 28 H.L.R. 522; [1996] Fam. Law 279; (1996) 93(1) L.S.G. 21; (1996) 140 S.J.L.B. 9; [1995] N.P.C. 184, CA (Civ Div); affirming [1996] Ch. 1; [1995] 3 W.L.R. 701; [1995] 4 All E.R. 656; (1995) 92(27) L.S.G. 31, Ch D *7–117*
Halifax Plc v Omar [2002] EWCA Civ 121; [2002] 2 P. & C.R. 26; [2002] 16 E.G. 180 (C.S.), CA (Civ Div) *29–173*
Halkett v Earl of Dudley [1907] 1 Ch. 590, Ch D *27–047*
Hall Ex p. Re Whiting (1878–79) L.R. 10 Ch. D. 615; 48 L.J.Bk. 79; 40 L.T. 179; 39 L.T. 259; 27 W.R. 64, 385, CA *4–012*, *19–022*
Hall v Cazenove (1804) 4 East 477; 1 Smith 272; 7 R.R. 611 .... *12–110*
Hall v Hallett (1784) 1 Cox 134 .... *16–064*
Hall v Herbert [1993] 2 S.C.R. 159 .... *16–164*
Hall v Levy (1875) L.R. 10 C.P. 154; 44 L.J.C.P. 89; 31 L.T. 727; 23 W.R. 393, CCP *22–008*
Hall v Meyrick [1957] 2 Q.B. 455; [1957] 3 W.L.R. 273; [1957] 2 All E.R. 722; (1957) 101 S.J. 574, CA *26–044*
Hall v North Eastern Ry Co (1875) L.R. 10 Q.B. 437; 44 L.J.Q.B. 164; 33 L.T. 306; 39 J.P. 724; 23 W.R. 860 .... *14–047*
Hall v Palmer (1844) 3 Hare 532; 13 L.J. Ch. 353; 8 Jur. 459; 64 R.R. 399 .... *16–067*
Hall v Swansea Corp (1844) 5 Q.B. 526 .... *29–142*
Hall v Warren (1804) 9 Ves. Jun. 605; 7 R.R. 306 .... *8–070*, *8–070*
Hall v Wells [1962] Tas.S.R. 122 .... *8–047*

Hall v Woolston Hall Leisure Ltd [2001] 1 W.L.R. 225; [2000] 4 All E.R. 787; [2001] I.C.R. 99; [2000] I.R.L.R. 578; (2000) 97(24) L.S.G. 39; (2000) 150 N.L.J. 833, CA (Civ Div); reversing [1998] I.C.R. 651, EAT *16–010*, *16–011*, *16–012*, *16–165*, *16–167*
Hall v Wright (1858) E.B.E. 746 .... *23–005*, 23–037
Hall & Co v Pearlberg [1956] 1 W.L.R. 244; [1956] 1 All E.R. 297 (Note); (1956) 100 S.J. 187, QBD *26–157*
Hall (Deceased), Re; sub nom. Hall v Knight; Hall, In the Estate of [1914] P. 1, CA *16–169*
Hallam-Eames v Merrett Syndicates Ltd (No.1) [1995] C.L.C. 173; [1996] 5 Re. L.R. 110; [1996] 7 Med. L.R. 122; [2001] Lloyd's Rep. P.N. 178; [1955–95] P.N.L.R. 672, CA (Civ Div) *28–012*
Hallen v Runder (1834) 1 Cr. M. & R. 266; 3 Tyr. 959; 3 L.J. Ex. 260 .... *4–020*
Hallen v Spaeth [1923] A.C. 684; 92 L.J.P.C. 181; 129 L.T. 803, PC (Fiji) *16–045*
Hallett's Estate, Re; sub nom. Knatchbull v Hallett (1879–80) L.R. 13 Ch. D. 696; 48 L.J. Ch. 415; 42 L.T. 421; 28 W.R. 732, CA *9–025*, *29–166*, *29–167*, *29–172*
Halley v Law Society [2003] EWCA Civ 97; [2003] W.T.L.R. 845; (2003–04) 6 I.T.E.L.R. 40; (2003) 153 N.L.J. 262, CA (Civ Div); affirming [2002] EWHC 255 (Ch), Ch D *16–178*, *29–160*
Halpern v Halpern [2007] EWCA Civ 291; [2008] Q.B. 195; [2007] 3 W.L.R. 849; [2007] 3 All E.R. 478; [2007] 2 All E.R. (Comm) 330; [2007] 2 Lloyd's Rep. 56; [2007] 1 C.L.C. 527, CA (Civ Div); affirming [2006] EWHC 603 (Comm); [2006] 2 All E.R. (Comm) 251; [2006] 2 Lloyd's Rep. 83; [2006] 3 F.C.R. 76, QBD (Comm) *2–131*, *2–140*, *6–120*, *7–054*, *29–088*, *30–009*, *30–022*, *30–026*, *30–029*, *30–037*, *30–040*, *30–048*, *30–071*, *30–075*, *30–077*, *30–308*
Halsey v Lowenfeld [1916] 2 K.B. 707; 85 L.J.K.B. 1498; 115 L.T. 617; 32 T.L.R. 709, CA; affirming [1916] 1 K.B. 143, KBD *11–030*
Halycon, The. *See* Court Line Ltd v Aktieblaget Gotaverken
Hamble Fisheries Ltd v L Gardner & Sons Ltd; The Rebecca Elaine [1999] 2 Lloyd's Rep. 1; (1999) 15 Const. L.J. 152; (1999) 96(6) L.S.G. 34, CA (Civ Div) *1–184*, *3–180*, *18–031*
Hambly v Trott (1776) 1 Cowp. 371 .... *1–118*, *1–128*, *20–001*
Hambros Bank Ltd v British Historic Buildings Trust [1995] N.P.C. 179, CA (Civ Div) *5–104*, *5–106*, *8–001*
Hamburg Star, The [1994] 1 Lloyd's Rep. 399, QBD (Admlty) *18–034*
Hamed el Chiaty & Co (t/a Travco Nile Cruise Lines) v Thomas Cook Group Ltd; The Nile Rhapsody [1994] 1 Lloyd's Rep. 382; [1994] I.L.Pr. 367, CA (Civ Div); affirming [1992] 2 Lloyd's Rep. 399, QBD (Comm) *3–115*, *5–108*, *12–112*, *12–118*
Hamelin v Bruck (1846) 9 Q.B. 306 .... *25–020*
Hamer v Sidway, 124 N.Y. 538 (1881) *2–078*
Hamilton, Re Fitz George v Fitz George (1921) 124 L.T. 737 .... *19–023*
Hamilton v Bennett (1930) 94 J.P.N. 136; 74 S.J. 122 .... *8–011*, *8–016*, *8–027*
Hamilton v Hamilton [1892] 1 Ch. 396; 61 L.J. Ch. 220; 66 L.T. 112; 40 W.R. 312, Ch D *8–036*
Hamilton v Spottiswoode (1849) 4 Ex. 200 .... *29–194*
Hamilton v Vaughan-Sherrin Electrical Engineering Co [1894] 3 Ch. 589; 63 L.J. Ch. 795; 71 L.T. 325; 43 W.R. 126, Ch D *8–037*, *8–038*, *8–040*
Hamilton Fraser & Co v Pandorf & Co; sub nom. Pandorf & Co v Hamilton Fraser & Co (1887) L.R. 12 App. Cas. 518, HL; reversing (1886) L.R. 17 Q.B.D. 670, CA; reversing (1885–86) L.R. 16 Q.B.D. 629, QBD *14–146*
Hamilton Jones v David & Snape (A Firm) [2003] EWHC 3147; [2004] 1 W.L.R. 924; [2004] 1 All E.R. 657; [2004] 1 F.L.R. 774; [2004] 1 F.C.R. 243; [2004] P.N.L.R. 21; [2004] Fam. Law 246; (2004) 101(4) L.S.G. 31; (2004) 154 N.L.J. 55, Ch D *26–083*
Hamlet v Richardson (1833) 9 Bing. 644 .... *29–098*

Hamlin v Edwin Evans (A Firm), 80 B.L.R. 85; 52 Con. L.R. 106; (1997) 29 H.L.R. 414; [1996] P.N.L.R. 398; [1996] 2 E.G.L.R. 106; [1996] 47 E.G. 141; [1996] E.G. 120 (C.S.); (1996) 93(27) L.S.G. 29; (1996) 140 S.J.L.B. 167; [1996] N.P.C. 110, CA (Civ Div) *28–011*
Hamlin v Great Northern Railway Co, 156 E.R. 1261; (1856) 1 Hurl. & N. 408, QB *26–083*
Hamlyn v Wood [1891] 2 Q.B. 488; 60 L.J.Q.B. 734; 65 L.T. 286; 40 W.R. 24, CA *13–004*, *13–009*, *13–010*, *13–012*
Hamlyn & Co v Talisker Distillery; sub nom. Talisker Distillery v Hamlyn & Co [1894] A.C. 202; (1894) 21 R. (H.L.) 21; (1894) 2 S.L.T.12, HL *30–005*, *30–010*, *30–012*, *30–015*
Hammersley v Baron De Biel (1845) 12 Cl. & F. 45; 3 Beav. 469; 69 R.R. 18 .... *16–073*
Hammersmith and Fulham LBC v Top Shop Centres Ltd; Hammersmith and Fulham LBC v Glassgrove [1990] Ch. 237; [1989] 2 W.L.R. 643; [1989] 2 All E.R. 655; [1989] 41 E.G. 121; (1989) 133 S.J. 877, Ch D *3–141*, *3–147*
Hammersmith and Fulham LBC. *See* R. v Hammersmith and Fulham LBC Ex p. Beddowes
Hammond and Nevard, Re; sub nom. Hammond, Ex p. (1873) L.R. 16 Eq. 614; 42 L.J. Bk. 97; 29 L.T. 72, Ct of Chancery *20–047*
Hammond Ex p. *See* Hammond and Nevard, Re
Hammond v Allen [1994] 1 All E.R. 307; (1993) 65 P. & C.R. 18; [1993] 08 E.G. 122, QBD *21–012*
Hammond v Messenger (1838) 9 Sim.327; 7 L.J. Ch. 310; 2 Jur. 655 .... *19–002*
Hammond v Mitchell [1991] 1 W.L.R. 1127; [1992] 2 All E.R. 109, Fam Div ...*3–147*, *13–028*
Hammond v Osborn [2002] EWCA Civ 885; [2002] W.T.L.R. 1125; (2002) 99(34) L.S.G. 29; (2002) 146 S.J.L.B. 176; [2002] 2 P. & C.R. DG20, CA (Civ Div) *7–058*, *7–094*
Hammond v Schofield [1891] 1 Q.B. 453; 60 L.J.Q.B. 539, QBD *17–015*
Hampden v Walsh (1875–76) L.R. 1 Q.B.D. 189; 45 L.J.Q.B. 238; 33 L.T. 852; 24 W.R. 607, QBD *16–192*, *29–197*
Hampshire CC v Supportways Community Services Ltd. *See* R. (on the application of Supportways Community Services Ltd) v Hampshire CC
Hampstead & Suburban Properties Ltd v Diomedous (No.1) [1969] 1 Ch. 248; [1968] 3 W.L.R. 990; [1968] 3 All E.R. 545; (1968) 19 P. & C.R. 880; (1968) 112 S.J. 656, Ch D *27–061*
Hampton & Sons Ltd v George [1939] 3 All E.R. 627, KBD *2–084*
Hampton v Minns [2002] 1 W.L.R. 1; [2002] 1 All E.R. (Comm) 481; (2001) 98(20) L.S.G. 41, Ch D *17–029*, *28–015*
Hanak v Green [1958] 2 Q.B. 9; [1958] 2 W.L.R. 755; [1958] 2 All E.R. 141; 1 B.L.R. 1; (1958) 102 S.J. 329, CA *28–123*
Hancock v BW Brazier (Anerley) Ltd [1966] 1 W.L.R. 1317; [1966] 2 All E.R. 901, CA; affirming [1966] 2 All E.R. 1; (1966) 110 S.J. 368, QBD *13–015*, *25–003*
Hancock v Smith (1889) L.R. 41 Ch. D. 456, CA *29–167*
Hancock Shipping Co Ltd v Deacon & Trysail (Private) Ltd; The Casper Trader [1991] 2 Lloyd's Rep. 550, QBD (Comm) *14–015*, *14–071*, *14–076*
Hancock Shipping Co Ltd v Kawasaki Heavy Industries Ltd; The Casper Trader [1992] 1 W.L.R. 1025; [1992] 3 All E.R. 132; [1991] 2 Lloyd's Rep. 237; (1991) 135 S.J.L.B. 77, CA (Civ Div) *20–004*, *28–118*, *28–119*
Handel (NV) My J Smits Import-Export v English Exporters Ltd. *See* NV Handel My J Smits Import-Export v English Exporters (London) Ltd
Handley Page v Customs and Excise Commissioners; Rockwell Machine Tool Co v Customs and Excise Commissioners [1971] 2 Lloyd's Rep. 298, CA (Civ Div) *27–012*, *27–035*
Handley v Marston (1962) 106 S.J. 327, CA *14–028*
Hands v Burton (1808) 9 East 349 .... *21–039*
Hangkam Kwingtong Woo v Lin Lan Fong (Alias Liu Ah Lan) [1951] A.C. 707; [1951] 2 All E.R. 567; [1951] 2 T.L.R. 442; (1951) 95 S.J. 544, PC (HK) *23–021*, *23–039*
Hanif v Middleweeks (A Firm) [2000] Lloyd's Rep. P.N. 920, CA (Civ Div) *26–044*

Hanjin Shipping Co Ltd v Zenith Chartering Corp; The Mercedes Envoy [1995] 2 Lloyd's Rep. 559, QBD (Comm) *2–140*, 2–163
Hanley v Pearson (1879–80) L.R. 13 Ch. D. 545, Ch D *5–122*, *5–134*
Hannah Blumenthal, The *See* Paal Wilson & Co A/S v Partenreederei Hannah Blumenthal; Hannah Blumenthal, The.
Hannam v Bradford Corp; sub nom. Hannam v Bradford City Council [1970] 1 W.L.R. 937; [1970] 2 All E.R. 690; 68 L.G.R. 498; (1970) 114 S.J. 414, CA (Civ Div) *18–009*
Hanover Insurance Brokers Ltd v Schapiro [1994] I.R.L.R. 82, CA (Civ Div) *16–097*
Hans Place Ltd, Re [1992] B.C.C. 737; [1993] B.C.L.C. 768; [1992] 44 E.G. 143, Ch D (Companies Ct) *9–048*, *20–035*
Hanson v Royden (1867) L.R. 3 C.P. 47, CCP *3–070*
Happy Day, The. *See* Glencore Grain Ltd v Flacker Shipping Ltd
Happy Ranger, The. *See* Parsons Corp v CV Scheepvaartonderneming Happy Ranger
Haq v Singh [2001] EWCA Civ 957; [2001] 1 W.L.R. 1594; [2001] C.P. Rep. 95; [2001] B.P.I.R. 1002, CA (Civ Div) *28–118*
Harb v Aziz (No.1); sub nom. Harb v King Fahd Bin Abdul Aziz (No.1) [2005] EWCA Civ 632; [2005] 2 F.L.R. 1108; [2005] 2 F.C.R. 342; [2005] Fam. Law 778, CA (Civ Div) *11–004*
Harbinger UK Ltd v GE Information Services Ltd [2000] 1 All E.R. (Comm) 166; (2000) 2 T.C.L.R. 463; [2000] I.T.C.L.R. 501, CA (Civ Div); reversing [1999] Masons C.L.R. 335, QBD (TCC) *12–050*, *12–055*, *13–027*
Harbutt's Plasticine Ltd v Wayne Tank & Pump Co Ltd; sub nom. Harbutts Plasticine v Wayne Tank & Pump Co Ltd [1970] 1 Q.B. 447; [1970] 2 W.L.R. 198; [1970] 1 All E.R. 225; [1970] 1 Lloyd's Rep. 15; (1969) 119 N.L.J. 1164; (1970) 114 S.J. 29, CA (Civ Div) *14–022*, *24–001*, 24–047, *26–016*, *26–078*, *26–082*, *26–116*, *26–175*, *26–176*
Hardie & Lane Ltd v Chiltern (Tort) [1928] 1 K.B. 663, CA *29–143*
Hardie & Lane Ltd v Chilton (Fixed Price Agreement) [1928] 2 K.B. 306, CA *7–045*, *9–068*
Harding v Davis (1825) 2 C.P. 77 .... *21–088*
Harding v Harding (1886) L.R. 17 Q.B.D. 442, QBD *19–015*, *19–019*, *19–027*, *19–033*
Harding v Wealands [2006] UKHL 32; [2007] 2 A.C. 1; [2006] 3 W.L.R. 83; [2006] 4 All E.R. 1; [2006] 2 C.L.C. 193; [2006] R.T.R. 35; (2006) 156 N.L.J. 1136; (2006) 150 S.J.L.B. 917, HL; reversing [2004] EWCA Civ 1735; [2005] 1 W.L.R. 1539; [2005] 1 All E.R. 415; [2005] 2 C.L.C. 411; [2005] R.T.R. 20; (2005) 155 N.L.J. 59, CA (Civ Div); reversing [2004] EWHC 1957 (QB), QBD *30–337*, *30–338*, *30–347*
Hardingham v Allen (1848) 5 C.B. 793 .... *21–085*
Hardman v Booth, 158 E.R. 1107; (1863) 1 Hurl. & C. 803, QB *5–009*, *5–097*, *6–129*
Hardwick v Johnson [1978] 1 W.L.R. 683; [1978] 2 All E.R. 935; (1978) 122 S.J. 162, CA (Civ Div) *2–174*, *3–130*, *13–028*
Hardwick Game Farm v Suffolk Agricultural and Poultry Producers Association Ltd. *See* Henry Kendall & Sons v William Lillico & Sons Ltd
Hardy v Elphick [1974] Ch. 65; [1973] 2 W.L.R. 824; [1973] 2 All E.R. 914; (1973) 117 S.J. 373, CA (Civ Div) *4–027*
Hardy v Motor Insurers Bureau [1964] 2 Q.B. 745; [1964] 3 W.L.R. 433; [1964] 2 All E.R. 742; [1964] 1 Lloyd's Rep. 397; (1964) 108 S.J. 422, CA *16–173*, *16–173*, *16–175*, *18–131*
Hare v Gocher [1962] 2 Q.B. 641; [1962] 3 W.L.R. 339; [1962] 2 All E.R. 763; (1962) 126 J.P. 395; 60 L.G.R. 278; (1962) 13 P. & C.R. 298; (1962) 106 S.J. 531, DC *12–093*, *21–024*
Hare v Horton (1833) 5 B. & Ad. 715 .... *12–091*
Hare v Murphy Bros [1974] 3 All E.R. 940; [1974] I.C.R. 603; [1974] I.R.L.R. 342; 18 K.I.R. 31; (1975) 10 I.T.R. 1; (1974) 118 S.J. 596, CA (Civ Div) *23–039*, *23–065*
Hare v Nicoll; sub nom. Hare v Nichol [1966] 2 Q.B. 130; [1966] 2 W.L.R. 441; [1966] 1 All E.R. 285; (1966) 110 S.J. 11, CA *21–013*
Harewood v Retese [1990] 1 W.L.R. 333; (1990) 134 S.J. 166, PC (Trin) *12–123*

Hargreave v Smee (1829) 6 Bing. 244 .... *12–085*
Hargreaves Transport Ltd v Lynch [1969] 1 W.L.R. 215; [1969] 1 All E.R. 455; (1969) 20 P. & C.R. 143; (1968) 112 S.J. 54, CA (Civ Div) *2–155*, *13–011*
Hargrove, Re; sub nom. Hargrove v Pain [1915] 1 Ch. 398, Ch D *8–036*
Harington v Hoggart, 109 E.R. 902; (1830) 1 B. & Ad. 577, KB *29–198*
Harington v Sendall [1903] 1 Ch. 921, Ch D *9–074*
Harley v Greenwood (1821) 5 B. Ald. 95 .... *25–007*
Harling v Eddy [1951] 2 K.B. 739; [1951] 2 All E.R. 212; [1951] 2 T.L.R. 245; (1951) 95 S.J. 501, CA *12–004*, *12–017*, *12–103*, *14–134*, *29–059*
Harlingdon and Leinster Enterprises Ltd v Christopher Hull Fine Art Ltd [1991] 1 Q.B. 564; [1990] 3 W.L.R. 13; [1990] 1 All E.R. 737; (1991) 10 Tr. L.R. 65; [1989] E.G. 176 (C.S.); (1990) 140 N.L.J. 90, CA (Civ Div) *6–012*
Harlow & Jones Ltd v Panex (International) Ltd [1967] 2 Lloyd's Rep. 509; (1967) 118 N.L.J. 38, QBD (Comm) *26–078*
Harlow Development Corp v Kingsgate (Clothing Productions) (1973) 226 E.G. 1960 .... *5–108*
Harmer v Armstrong [1934] Ch. 65, CA *18–082*
Harmer v Steele (1849) 4 Exch. 1 .... *25–004*
Harmon CFEM Facades (UK) Ltd v Corporate Officer of the House of Commons, 67 Con. L.R. 1; (2000) 2 L.G.L.R. 372, QBD (TCC) *10–025*, 10–036, *10–037*, 10–038
Harmony & Montague Tin and Copper Mining Co, Re; sub nom. Spargo's Case (1872–73) L.R. 8 Ch. App. 407; [1861–73] All E.R. Rep. 261, CA in Chancery *21–039*
Harmony Shipping Co SA v Davis; Harmony Shipping Co SA v Saudi Europe Line Ltd; Harmony Shipping Co SA v Orri (t/a Saudi Europe Line Ltd) [1979] 1 W.L.R. 1380; [1979] 3 All E.R. 177; [1980] 1 Lloyd's Rep. 44, CA (Civ Div) *2–029*, *2–111*, *2–126*, *12–118*, *12–119*, *12–126*, *13–009*, *13–010*
Harmony Shipping Co SA v Saudi-Europe Line Ltd [1981] 1 Lloyd's Rep. 409 ... *12–126*
Harmony Shipping Co SA v Saudi Europe Line Ltd; The Good Helmsman [1981] 1 Lloyd's Rep. 377; (1979) 123 S.J. 691, CA (Civ Div) *12–118*, *12–119*
Harnett v Yielding (1805) 2 Sch. & Lef. 549 .... *27–005*
Harold Wood Brick Co Ltd v Ferris [1935] 2 K.B. 198, CA *21–013*
Harper v Gray & Walker [1985] 1 W.L.R. 1196; [1985] 2 All E.R. 507; (1983) 1 Const. L.J. 46; [1984] C.I.L.L. 106; (1985) 82 L.S.G. 3532; (1985) 129 S.J. 776, QBD *17–034*
Harper & Co v Vigers Bros [1909] 2 K.B. 549, KBD *12–115*
Harries v Edmunds (1845) 1 Car. Kir. 686 .... *26–103*
Harrington v Kloprogge (1785) 2 B. & B. 678 .... *12–081*
Harris v Brisco (1886) L.R. 17 Q.B.D. 504, CA *16–052*
Harris v Carter (1854) 3 E. & B. 559 .... *3–066*
Harris v Goodwyn (1841) 2 M. & G. 405 .... *22–004*
Harris v Great Western Railway Co (1875–76) L.R. 1 Q.B.D. 515, QBD *14–035*
Harris v Nickerson (1873) L.R. 8 Q.B. 286, QBD *2–012*, *3–174*
Harris v Pepperell (1867) L.R. 5 Eq. 1, Ct of Chancery 5–119, *5–122*
Harris v Quine; sub nom. Harris & Adams v Quine (1868–69) L.R. 4 Q.B. 653, QB *25–017*
Harris v Rickett (1859) 4 H. & N. 1 .... *12–097*, *12–098*
Harris v Sheffield United Football Club Ltd; sub nom. Sheffield United Football Club v South Yorkshire Police Authority [1988] Q.B. 77; [1987] 3 W.L.R. 305; [1987] 2 All E.R. 838; 85 L.G.R. 696; (1987) 151 L.G. Rev. 810; (1987) 84 L.S.G. 1327, CA (Civ Div); affirming, *The Times*, April 4, 1986, QBD *3–063*
Harris v United Kingdom etc Society (1899) 87 L.T.J. 272 .... *18–073*
Harris v Watson (1791) Peake 102 .... *3–066*
Harris v Wyre Forest DC. *See* Smith v Eric Bush
Harris Calculating Machine Co, Re; sub nom. Sumner v Harris Calculating Machine Co, Re [1914] 1 Ch. 920, Ch D *21–054*
Harrison v Battye [1975] 1 W.L.R. 58; [1974] 3 All E.R. 830; (1974) 119 S.J. 31, CA (Civ Div); affirming [1974] 2 All E.R. 1201, Ch D *2–032*, *2–120*
Harrison v Blackburn (1864) 17 C.B. (N.S.) 678 .... *12–087*

Harrison v Cage (1698) 12 Mod. 214 .... *3–008*
Harrison v Dodd (1914) 111 L.T. 47 .... *3–066*
Harrison v Fane (1840) 1 M. & G. 550 .... *8–008*, *8–016*
Harrison v Guest (1860) 8 H.L.C. 481 .... *7–128*
Harrison v Holland & Hannen & Cubitts Ltd [1922] 1 K.B. 211, CA *29–064*
Harrison v James (1862) 7 H.N. 804 .... *29–058*
Harrison v Mexican Railway Co (1874–75) L.R. 19 Eq. 358, Ct of Chancery *12–067*
Harrison v Norwest Holst Group Administration *See* Norwest Holst Group Administration v Harrison
Harrison v Walker [1919] 2 K.B. 453; 89 L.J.K.B. 105; 121 L.T. 251, KBD *13–011*
Harrison (Properties) Ltd v Harrison. *See* JJ Harrison (Properties) Ltd v Harrison
Harris's Case. *See* Imperial Land Co of Marseilles, Re [1961] 1 Lloyd's Rep. 251, QBD *14–011*, *14–015*, *14–054*
Harriss v Fawcett (1872–73) L.R. 8 Ch. App. 866, CA in Chancery; affirming (1872–73) L.R. 15 Eq. 311, Ct of Chancery *2–100*
Harrop (John) v Harrop (Mabel) [1920] 3 K.B. 386, KBD *25–017*
Harry Parker Ltd v Mason [1940] 2 K.B. 590, CA *16–014*, *16–189*, *16–192*, *29–043*
Harse v Pearl Life Assurance Co [1904] 1 K.B. 558, CA; reversing [1903] 2 K.B. 92, KBD *6–013*, *16–186*
Hart v Hall & Pickles; Geoffrey Reyner & Co (Third Party) [1969] 1 Q.B. 405; [1968] 3 W.L.R. 744; [1968] 3 All E.R. 291; (1968) 112 S.J. 786, CA (Civ Div) *17–033*
Hart v Hart (1880–81) L.R. 18 Ch. D. 670, Ch D *2–141*
Hart v Hart (1881) 18 Ch. D. 670 .... *27–050*
Hart v Mills (1846) 15 L.J.Ex. 200 .... *2–005*, *2–030*
Hart v Nash (1835) 2 Cr. M. & R. 337 .... *28–099*
Hart v O'Connor [1985] A.C. 1000; [1985] 3 W.L.R. 214; [1985] 2 All E.R. 880; [1985] 1 N.Z.L.R. 159; (1985) 82 L.S.G. 2658; (1985) 129 S.J. 484, PC (NZ) *7–128*, 7–132, *8–068*, *8–080*
Hart v Prater (1837) 1 Jur. 623 .... *8–016*
Hart v Windsor (1843) 12 M. & W. 68 .... *13–016*
Hart (Inspector of Taxes) v Sangster; sub nom. Sangster v Hart (Inspector of Taxes) [1957] Ch. 329; [1957] 2 W.L.R. 812; [1957] 2 All E.R. 208; 50 R. & I.T. 349; 37 T.C. 231; (1957) 36 A.T.C. 63; [1957] T.R. 73; (1957) 101 S.J. 356, CA *28–039*
Hart (RN) v AR Marshall & Sons (Bulwell) [1977] 1 W.L.R. 1067; [1978] 2 All E.R. 413; [1977] I.C.R. 539; [1977] I.R.L.R. 61; (1977) 12 I.T.R. 190; (1977) 121 S.J. 677, EAT *23–038*
Hartas v Ribbons (1889) L.R. 22 Q.B.D. 254, CA *29–117*
Hartgarten v Australian Gas Light Co (1992) 8 A.C.S.R. 277 .... *20–022*
Hartland v Jukes (1863) 1 H. & C. 667 .... *28–046*
Hartlelid v Sawyer & McClockin Real Estate [1977] 5 W.W.R. 481 .... *6–032*
Hartley v Hymans [1920] 3 K.B. 475, KBD .. *3–100*, *12–037*, *22–042*, *21–013*, *21–014*
Hartley v Pehall (1927) 1 Peake 178 .... *16–125*
Hartley v Ponsonby (1857) 7 E. & B. 872 .... *3–071*
Hartley v Rice (1808) 10 East 22 .... *16–072*
Hartley v Sandholme Iron Co Ltd [1975] Q.B. 600; [1974] 3 W.L.R. 445; [1974] 3 All E.R. 475; [1974] S.T.C. 434; 17 K.I.R. 205; (1974) 118 S.J. 702, QBD *26–162*
Hartog v Colin and Shields [1939] 3 All E.R. 566 .... 5–074, 5–080, 5–083
Hartopp v Hartopp (1855) 21 Beav. 259 .... *7–074*
Hartwells of Oxford v British Motor Trade Association [1951] Ch. 50; [1950] 2 All E.R. 705; 66 T.L.R. (Pt. 2) 483; (1950) 94 S.J. 505, CA *14–138*, *21–020*

Harvela Investments Ltd v Royal Trust Co of Canada (CI) Ltd [1986] A.C. 207; [1985] 3 W.L.R. 276; [1985] 2 All E.R. 966; (1985) 82 L.S.G. 3171; (1985) 135 N.L.J. 730; (1985) 128 S.J. 522, HL; reversing [1985] Ch. 103; [1984] 3 W.L.R. 1280; [1985] 1 All E.R. 261; (1984) 81 L.S.G. 2850; (1984) 128 S.J. 701, CA (Civ Div); reversing [1984] 2 W.L.R. 884; [1984] 2 All E.R. 65; (1984) 81 L.S.G. 1837; (1984) 128 S.J. 348, Ch D *2–009*, *2–022*, *2–039*, 2–040, *2–066*, *2–078*, *2–079*, *2–180*, *3–171*, *27–011*

Harvey v Barnard's Inn (1881) 50 L.J.Ch. 750 .... *2–118*

Harvey v Facey; sub nom. Harvey v Facey [1893] A.C. 552, PC (Jam) 2–007

Harvey v Johnson (1848) 6 C.B. 305 .... *2–030*

Harvey v Pratt [1965] 1 W.L.R. 1025; [1965] 2 All E.R. 786; (1965) 109 S.J. 474, CA; affirming (1964) 109 S.J. 52, Ch D *2–111*

Harvey v Tivoli (Manchester) (1907) 23 T.L.R. 592 .... *20–006*, *23–037*

Harvey Shopfitters Ltd v ADI Ltd [2003] EWCA Civ 1757; [2004] 2 All E.R. 982; [2004] C.P. Rep. 26; 91 Con. L.R. 71; (2004) 20 Const. L.J. 291; (2003) 100(48) L.S.G. 18, CA (Civ Div) *2–116*

Hasan v Willson [1977] 1 Lloyd's Rep. 431, QBD *3–057*, *6–021*, *7–052*

Haseldine v CA Daw & Son [1941] 2 K.B. 343, CA *1–186*, 14–040

Haseldine v Hosken [1933] 1 K.B. 822; (1933) 45 Ll. L. Rep. 59, CA; reversing (1932) 44 Ll. L. Rep. 127, KBD *16–054*, *16–066*, *16–173*

Hasham v Zenab (Executrix of Harji) [1960] A.C. 316; [1960] 2 W.L.R. 374; (1960) 104 S.J. 125, PC (EA) *5–101*, *27–003*, *27–078*, *28–135*

Haslemere Estates v Baker [1982] 1 W.L.R. 1109; [1982] 3 All E.R. 525; (1982) 126 S.J. 463, Ch D *3–163*, *12–028*

Hassanally v Cassim [1960] A.C. 592; [1960] 2 W.L.R. 607; [1960] 2 All E.R. 11; (1960) 104 S.J. 268, PC (Cey) *29–015*

Hasser v Wallis (1708) 1 Salk. 28 .... *29–142*

Hastelow v Jackson (1828) 8 B. & C. 221 .... *16–189*, *16–192*

Hastings (Marquis of) v Thorley (1838) 8 C.P. 573 .... *21–091*

Hatch, Re; sub nom. Public Trustee v Hatch [1948] Ch. 592; [1948] 2 All E.R. 288; [1948] L.J.R. 1393; (1948) 92 S.J. 456, Ch D *16–163*

Hatch v Hale (1850) 15 Q.B. 10 .... *21–094*

Hatch v Hatch (1804) 9 Ves. 292 .... *7–075*, *7–097*

Haugland Tankers AS v RMK Marine Gemi Yapim Sanayii ve Deniz Tasimacilig Isletmesi AS [2005] EWHC 321; [2005] 1 All E.R. (Comm) 679; [2005] 1 Lloyd's Rep. 573; [2005] 1 C.L.C. 271, QBD (Comm) *12–027*, *12–036*, *21–013*

Havenledge Ltd v Graeme John & Partners [2001] Lloyd's Rep. P.N. 223; [2001] P.N.L.R. 17; [2001] N.P.C. 9, CA (Civ Div); reversing [2000] Lloyd's Rep. P.N. 614; [2000] P.N.L.R. 804, QBD *1–167*

Havens v Middleton (1853) 22 L.J. Ch. 746 .... *21–003*

Havering LBC v Stevenson [1970] 1 W.L.R. 1375; [1970] 3 All E.R. 609; [1971] R.T.R. 58; (1970) 114 S.J. 664, QBD *14–065*

Haviland v Long [1952] 2 Q.B. 80; [1952] 1 All E.R. 463; [1952] 1 T.L.R. 576; (1952) 96 S.J. 180, CA *26–117*

Hawke v Cole (1890) 62 L.T. 658 .... *9–073*, *9–078*

Hawkes v Saunders (1782) 1 Cowp. 289 .... *3–032*

Hawkes Bay Milk Corp v Watson [1974] 2 N.Z.L.R. 236 .... *9–012*

Hawkesworth v Chaffey (1886) 55 L.J.Ch. 335 .... *2–118*

Hawkins v Clayton (1988) 164 C.L.R. 539, HC (Aus) *1–126*

Hawkins v Gardiner (1854) 2 Sm. G. 441 .... *21–058*

Hawkins v Maltby (1867–68) L.R. 3 Ch. App. 188, CA in Chancery *27–011*

Hawkins v Northern Marine Management Ltd, 1998 S.L.T. 1107; 1997 G.W.D. 17–760, OH *14–015*

Hawkins v Price [1947] Ch. 645; [1947] 1 All E.R. 689; [1947] L.J.R. 887; 117 L.T. 108; 91 S.J. 263, Ch D *4–026*

Hawksley v Outram [1892] 3 Ch. 359, CA *22–046*

Hay v Carter [1935] Ch. 397; 99 A.L.R. 630, CA *17–028*

Haycock's Policy, Re (1875–76) L.R. 1 Ch. D. 611, Ch D *28–050*

Haycocks v Neville [2007] EWCA Civ 78; [2007] 12 E.G. 156; [2007] 4 E.G. 186 (C.S.), CA (Civ Div) *12–126*

Hayden v Hayden [1992] 1 W.L.R. 986; [1993] 2 F.L.R. 16; [1992] P.I.Q.R. Q111; [1993] Fam. Law 466, CA (Civ Div) *18–076*
Haydon v Lo & Lo [1997] 1 W.L.R. 198; [1997] 1 Lloyd's Rep. 336; [1997] C.L.C. 626; (1997) 147 N.L.J. 125; (1997) 141 S.J.L.B. 35, PC (HK) *12–126*
Haydon v Williams (1830) 7 Bing. 163 .... *28–094*
Hayes v Bristol Plant Hire Ltd [1957] 1 W.L.R. 499; [1957] 1 All E.R. 685, Ch D *27–021*
Hayes v Dodd. *See* Hayes v James & Charles Dodd (A Firm)
Hayes v James & Charles Dodd (A Firm) [1990] 2 All E.R. 815; [1988] E.G. 107 (C.S.); (1988) 138 N.L.J. Rep. 259, CA (Civ Div) *1–123*, 26–079, *26–083*, *26–093*
Hayne v Maltby (1789) 3 Term Rep. 438 .... *1–112*
Haynes v Dorman [1899] 2 Ch. 13, CA *16–092*, *16–097*, *16–104*, *16–108*, *16–110*
Hayton v Irwin (1879–80) L.R. 5 C.P.D. 130, CA *12–057*
Hayward v Pullinger & Partners [1950] 1 All E.R. 581 .... *26–006*
Haywood v Cope (1858) 25 Beav. 140 .... *27–033*
Hazel v Akhtar [2001] EWCA Civ 1883; [2002] 2 P. & C.R. 17; [2002] L. & T.R. 22; [2002] 1 E.G.L.R. 45; [2002] 07 E.G. 124; [2002] 1 E.G. 73 (C.S.); [2002] 1 P. & C.R. DG18, CA (Civ Div) *3–091*, *3–096*
Hazell v Hammersmith and Fulham LBC [1992] 2 A.C. 1; [1991] 2 W.L.R. 372; [1991] 1 All E.R. 545; 89 L.G.R. 271; (1991) 3 Admin. L.R. 549; [1991] R.V.R. 28; (1991) 155 J.P.N. 527; (1991) 155 L.G. Rev. 527; (1991) 88(8) L.S.G. 36; (1991) 141 N.L.J. 127, HL; reversing [1990] 2 W.L.R. 1038; [1990] 3 All E.R. 33; 88 L.G.R. 433; [1990] R.V.R. 140; (1990) 87(20) L.S.G. 36; (1990) 134 S.J. 637, CA (Civ Div); reversing in part [1990] 2 W.L.R. 17; [1989] R.V.R. 188; [1990] C.O.D. 112; (1990) 87(2) L.S.G. 36; (1989) 134 S.J. 21, QBD *9–005*, *9–021*, *10–022*, *29–045*
Hazell v Hammersmith and Fulham LBC. *See* R. v Secretary of State for the Environment Ex p. Hammersmith and Fulham LBC
Head, Re; sub nom. Head v Head (No.2) [1894] 2 Ch. 236, CA *19–087*, *22–031*
Head v Diggon (1828) 3 M. & Ry. 97 .... *3–172*
Head v Tattersall (1871) L.R. 7 Ex. 7 12–030
Heald v O'Connor [1971] 1 W.L.R. 497; [1971] 2 All E.R. 1105; (1970) 115 S.J. 244, QBD *9–038*, *16–165*
Healey v Brown [2002] W.T.L.R. 849; (2001–02) 4 I.T.E.L.R. 894; [2002] 19 E.G. 147 (C.S.); [2002] N.P.C. 59, Ch D *4–063*
Healing Research Trustee Co, Re [1992] 2 All E.R. 481; [1991] B.C.L.C. 716; [1992] 2 E.G.L.R. 231, Ch D *29–106*
Heard v Pilley (1868–69) L.R. 4 Ch. App. 548, CA in Chancery *4–036*
Heath v Chilton (1844) 12 M. & W. 632 .... *20–002*
Heath v Crealock (1874–75) L.R. 10 Ch. App. 22, Lord Chancellor; affirming (1874) L.R. 18 Eq. 215, Ct of Chancery *1–112*
Heath v Tang; Stevens v Peacock [1993] 1 W.L.R. 1421; [1993] 4 All E.R. 694, CA (Civ Div) 20–019, *20–026*, *20–034*
Heathcote v North Stafffordshire Railway Co (1850) 2 Mac. & G. 100 .... *16–025*
Heather Bell, The [1901] P. 272, CA *29–103*
Heaton v Axa Equity & Law Life Assurance Society Plc [2002] UKHL 15; [2002] 2 A.C. 329; [2002] 2 W.L.R. 1081; [2002] 2 All E.R. 961; [2002] C.P. Rep. 52; [2002] C.P.L.R. 475; [2003] 1 C.L.C. 37, HL [2001] Ch. 173; [2000] 3 W.L.R. 1341; [2000] 4 All E.R. 673; [2001] C.P. Rep. 10; [2000] C.P.L.R. 505, CA (Civ Div); reversing, *The Times*, July 19, 1999, Ch D *17–017*, *17–018*, *18–002*, *18–071*
Heaven v Road and Rail Wagons [1965] 2 Q.B. 355; [1965] 2 W.L.R. 1249; [1965] 2 All E.R. 409; (1965) 109 S.J. 335, QBD *28–116*
Heaven and Kesterton v Etablissements Francois Albiac et Cie [1956] 2 Lloyd's Rep. 316, QBD *26–113*

Hebb's Case. *See* National Savings Bank Association, Re
Hebden v Forsey & Son [1973] I.C.R. 607; [1973] I.R.L.R. 344; 15 K.I.R. 161; [1973] I.T.R. 656, NIRC *23–038*
Hector v Lyons (1989) 58 P. & C.R. 156; [1988] E.G. 170 (C.S.), CA (Civ Div) ... *5–095*
Hedley Byrne & Co Ltd v Heller & Partners Ltd [1964] A.C. 465; [1963] 3 W.L.R. 101; [1963] 2 All E.R. 575; [1963] 1 Lloyd's Rep. 485; (1963) 107 S.J. 454, HL; affirming [1962] 1 Q.B. 396; [1961] 3 W.L.R. 1225; [1961] 3 All E.R. 891; (1961) 105 S.J. 910, CA; affirming, *The Times*, December 21, 1960, QBD 1–119, 1–120, 1–126, 1–131, *1–132*, *1–133*, 1–138, 1–139, *1–140*, 1–141, 1–156, 1–158, 1–160, 1–175, 1–179, 1–182, 3–172, *3–179*, *5–047*, 6–005, 6–012, *6–022*, 6–029, 6–040, *6–047*, 6–067, 6–074, *6–077*, 6–078, **6–081**, 6–083, 6–084, 6–085, 6–088, *6–090*, 6–141, *18–022*
Heffield v Meadows (1869) L.R. 4 C.P. 595, CCP *12–123*
Heglibiston Establishments v Heyman (1978) 36 P. & C.R. 351; (1977) 246 E.G. 567; (1977) 121 S.J. 851, CA (Civ Div) *16–068*, *16–069*
Heidberg, The. *See* Partenreederei M/S Heidberg v Grosvenor Grain & Feed Co Ltd; The Heidberg (No.2)
Heifer International Inc v Christiansen [2007] EWHC 3015, [2008] All E.R. (D) 120, QBD (TCC) *15–028*, 15–030, *15–094*
Heilbut Rocca v Nevill (1870) L.R. 5 C.P. 478 .... *29–140*
Heilbut Symons & Co v Buckleton [1913] A.C. 30, HL ...*2–165*, 2–166, 4–076, *6–094*, *12–003*, 12–004, *12–005*, *18–009*
Heindal A/S v Questier (1949) 82 Ll. L. Rep. 452 .... *26–090*
Heinemann v Cooper (1987) 19 H.L.R. 262; (1987) 284 E.G. 1237, CA (Civ Div) *6–069*
Heinrich Hanno & Co BV v Fairlight Shipping Co; The Kostas K; Hanse Schiffahrtskontor GmbH v Andre SA [1985] 1 Lloyd's Rep. 231, QBD (Comm) *3–109*
Heisler v Anglo Dal Ltd [1954] 1 W.L.R. 1273; [1954] 2 All E.R. 770; [1954] 2 Lloyd's Rep. 5; (1954) 98 S.J. 698, CA *24–014*
Helbert Wagg & Co Ltd's Claim, Re. *See* Claim by Helbert Wagg & Co Ltd, Re
Hellenic Steel Co v Svolamar Shipping Co Ltd; The Komninos S [1991] 1 Lloyd's Rep. 370, CA (Civ Div) *30–010*, *30–051*, *30–347*
Helmsing Schiffahrts GmbH v Malta Drydocks Corp [1977] 2 Lloyd's Rep. 444, QBD (Comm) *26–180*, *30–339*
Helmville Ltd v Astilleros Espandes SA; The Jocelyne [1984] 2 Lloyd's Rep. 569, QBD (Admlty) *25–011*, *25–017*, *25–018*
Helps v Clayton (1864) 17 C.B. (N.S.) 553 .... *8–013*
Helps v Winterbottom (1831) 2 B. & Ad. 431 .... *28–052*
Helstan Securities Ltd v Hertfordshire CC [1978] 3 All E.R. 262; 76 L.G.R. 735, QBD *19–043*
Hely-Hutchinson v Brayhead Ltd 39117 [1968] 1 Q.B. 549; [1967] 3 W.L.R. 1408; [1967] 3 All E.R. 98; (1967) 111 S.J., CA (Civ Div); affirming [1967] 2 W.L.R. 1312; [1967] 2 All E.R. 14; (1967) 111 S.J. 329, QBD *9–041*, *9–043*, *9–055*
Hemmens v Wilson Browne (A Firm) [1995] Ch. 223; [1994] 2 W.L.R. 323; [1993] 4 All E.R. 826; [1994] 2 F.L.R. 101; [1994] Fam. Law 669; (1993) 90(45) L.S.G. 45, Ch D *1–177*, *18–037*, *20–003*
Henderson, Re (1916) 12 Tas. L.R. 40 .... *8–047*
Henderson v Arthur [1907] 1 K.B. 10, CA .. *12–096*, *12–100*, *12–103*, *12–112*, *21–076*
Henderson v Folkestone Waterworks Co (1885) 1 T.L.R. 329 .... *29–047*
Henderson v Henderson [1843–60] All E.R. Rep. 378; 67 E.R. 313; (1843) 3 Hare 100, Ct of Chancery *25–013*

Henderson v Merrett Syndicates Ltd (No.1); sub nom. Gooda Walker Ltd v Deeny; McLarnon Deeney v Gooda Walker Ltd; Arbuthnott v Fagan; Hallam-Eames v Merrett Syndicates Ltd; Hughes v Merrett Syndicates Ltd; Feltrim Underwriting Agencies Ltd v Arbuthnott; Deeny v Gooda Walker Ltd (Duty of Care) [1995] 2 A.C. 145; [1994] 3 W.L.R. 761; [1994] 3 All E.R. 506; [1994] 2 Lloyd's Rep. 468; [1994] C.L.C. 918; (1994) 144 N.L.J. 1204, HL; affirming [1994] C.L.C. 55; [1994] E.C.C. 537, CA (Civ Div); affirming [1994] 2 Lloyd's Rep. 193, QBD (Comm) *1–119*, *1–120*, 1–126, 1–127, 1–134, **1–138**, 1–139, 1–140, 1–141, 1–142, 1–143, 1–147, 1–150, 1–152, 1–155, 1–156, 1–157, 1–158, 1–159, 1–160, 1–161, 1–167, **1–180**, 1–181, 1–182, 1–183, *3–179*, *6–083*, *6–088*, *18–013*, *18–023*, *18–031*, *18–059*, 26–005, *26–049*, *28–033*

Henderson v Merrett Syndicates Ltd (No.3); Hallam-Eames v Merrett Syndicates Ltd (No.3); Hughes v Merrett Syndicates Ltd (No.3) [1997] L.R.L.R. 247, QBD *28–011*

Henderson v Stevenson (1870–75) L.R. 2 Sc. 470; (1875) 2 R. (H.L.) 71, HL *12–014*

Henderson v Stobart (1850) 5 Exch. 99 .... *22–015*

Hendry v Chartsearch Ltd [1998] C.L.C. 1382; (2000) 2 T.C.L.R. 115, CA (Civ Div) *19–038*, 19–044, *19–045*

Hendy Lennox (Industrial Engines) Ltd v Grahame Puttick Ltd [1984] 1 W.L.R. 485; [1984] 2 All E.R. 152; [1984] 2 Lloyd's Rep. 422; (1984) 81 L.S.G. 585; (1984) 128 S.J. 220, QBD *29–168*, *29–169*

Henfree v Bromley (1805) 6 East 309 .... *25–020*

Henkel v Pape (1870–71) L.R. 6 Ex. 7, Ex Ct 2–059, *5–071*

Henman v Dickinson (1828) 5 Bing. 183 .... *25–022*

Hennessy v Craigmyle & Co [1986] I.C.R. 461; [1986] I.R.L.R. 300; (1986) 83 L.S.G. 2160; (1986) 130 S.J. 633, CA (Civ Div); affirming [1985] I.C.R. 879; [1985] I.R.L.R. 446, EAT *7–031*, *7–032*, *7–035*, *29–088*

Henniker v Wigg (1843) 4 Q.B. 792 .... *21–066*

Henrich Bjorn, The. *See* Northcote v Owners of the Henrich Bjorn

Henrich Hirdes GmbH v Edmund; Henrich Hirdes GmbH v Peek Puckle (International) Ltd; The Kiel [1991] 2 Lloyd's Rep. 546, QBD (Comm) *12–093*

Henriksens Rederi A/S v Centrala Handlu Zagranicznego (CHZ) Rolimpex; The Brede; sub nom. Henriksens Rederi A/S v THZ Rolimpex; The Brede [1974] Q.B. 233; [1973] 3 W.L.R. 556; [1973] 3 All E.R. 589; [1973] 2 Lloyd's Rep. 333; (1973) 117 S.J. 600, CA (Civ Div) *21–034*, *28–122*, *28–123*

Henry Boot Construction Ltd v Alstom Combined Cycles Ltd [2005] EWCA Civ 814; [2005] 1 W.L.R. 3850; [2005] 3 All E.R. 832; [2005] 2 C.L.C. 63; [2005] B.L.R. 437; 101 Con. L.R. 52; (2005) 102(30) L.S.G. 28, CA (Civ Div) *12–053*

Henry Kendall & Sons v William Lillico & Sons Ltd; sub nom. Hardwick Game Farm v Suffolk Agricultural and Poultry Producers Association Ltd; Holland Colombo Trading Society Ltd v Grimsdale & Sons Ltd; Grimsdale & Sons Ltd v Suffolk Agricultural Poultry Producers Association [1969] 2 A.C. 31; [1968] 3 W.L.R. 110; [1968] 2 All E.R. 444; [1968] 1 Lloyd's Rep. 547, HL; affirming [1966] 1 W.L.R. 287; [1966] 1 All E.R. 309; [1966] 1 Lloyd's Rep. 197; (1966) 110 S.J. 11, CA; affirming in part [1964] 2 Lloyd's Rep. 227, QBD *12–011*, *13–022*, *14–003*, *14–006*, *26–082*

Henry Leetham & Sons Ltd v Johnstone-White [1907] 1 Ch. 322, CA; reversing [1907] 1 Ch. 189, Ch D *16–105*, *16–112*

Henthorn v Fraser [1892] 2 Ch. 27, CA *2–047*, *2–048*, *2–049*, *2–054*, *2–091*

Henwood v Oliver (1841) 1 Q.B. 409 .... *21–092*

Hepburn v A Tomlinson (Hauliers) Ltd; sub nom. A Tomlinson (Hauliers) Ltd v Hepburn [1966] A.C. 451; [1966] 2 W.L.R. 453; [1966] 1 All E.R. 418; [1966] 1 Lloyd's Rep. 309; (1966) 110 S.J. 86, HL; affirming [1966] 1 Q.B. 21; [1965] 2 W.L.R. 634; [1965] 1 All E.R. 284; [1965] 1 Lloyd's Rep. 1; (1965) 109 S.J. 10, CA; affirming [1964] 1 Lloyd's Rep. 416, QBD (Comm) *18–019*, *18–128*, *29–160*

Hepworth Manufacturing Co Ltd v Ryott [1920] Ch. 1 .... *16–087*, *16–106*

Herbert v Sayer (1844) 5 Q.B. 965 .... *20–055*

Herbert Clayton & Jack Waller Ltd v Oliver [1930] A.C. 209; [1930] All E.R. Rep. 414, HL *21–001*, *26–087*
Herbert Morris Ltd v Saxelby [1916] 1 A.C. 688, HL; affirming [1915] 2 Ch. 57, CA *16–095*, *16–104*, *16–105*, *16–108*, *16–113*
Herbert's Trustee v Higgins [1926] Ch. 794 .... *20–020*
Hercy v Birch (1804) 9 Ves. 357 .... *27–038*
Herd v Clyde Helicopters. *See* Fellowes v Clyde Helicopters.
Hereford South Wales Waggon & Engineering Co (1876) 2 Ch. D. 621 ... *9–015*, *9–016*
Heriz v Riera (1840) 11 Sim. 318 .... *16–027*
Herkules Piling Ltd v Tilbury Construction Ltd (1992) 61 Build. L.R. 107; The Times, September 21, 1992 .... *19–016*
Herman v Jeuchner (1884–85) L.R. 15 Q.B.D. 561, CA *16–039*
Herman v Morris (1919) 35 T.L.R. 574; affirming (1919) 35 T.L.R. 328 .... *12–090*
Hermann v Charlesworth [1905] 2 K.B. 123, CA; reversing [1905] 1 K.B. 24, KBD *16–071*, 16–191
Hernaman, Ex p. (1848) 12 Jur. 642 .... *25–001*
Herne Bay Steam Boat Co v Hutton [1903] 2 K.B. 683, CA 23–034
Heron Garage Properties Ltd v Moss [1974] 1 W.L.R. 148; [1974] 1 All E.R. 421; (1974) 28 P. & C.R. 54; (1973) 117 S.J. 697, Ch D *2–157*, *22–046*
Heron II, The. *See* Koufos v C Czarnikow Ltd
Herrick v Leonard and Dingley Ltd [1975] 2 N.Z.L.R. 566 .... *14–042*, *14–048*
Herring v Templeman [1973] 3 All E.R. 569; 72 L.G.R. 162; (1973) 117 S.J. 793, CA (Civ Div); affirming [1973] 2 All E.R. 581; 71 L.G.R. 295; (1973) 117 S.J. 223, Ch D *15–024*
Herschtal v Stewart & Ardern Ltd [1940] 1 K.B. 155, KBD *13–030*
Heskell v Continental Express Ltd [1950] 1 All E.R. 1033; (1949–50) 83 Ll. L. Rep. 438; [1950] W.N. 210; (1950) 94 S.J. 339, KBD *2–021*, *26–041*, *26–070*, *26–078*, *26–089*
Hesketh v Fawcett (1843) 11 M.W. 356 .... *21–095*
Hesketh v Gowing (1804) 5 Esp. 131 .... *8–061*
Heslop v Burns [1974] 1 W.L.R. 1241; [1974] 3 All E.R. 406; (1974) 118 S.J. 581, CA (Civ Div) *2–168*
Hesse v Albert (1828) 3 M. & Ry. 406 .... *12–066*
Hewison v Meridian Shipping Services Pte Ltd; sub nom. Hewison v Meridian Shipping Pte [2002] EWCA Civ 1821; [2002] All E.R. (D) 146; [2003] I.C.R. 766; [2003] P.I.Q.R. P17; (2003) 147 S.J.L.B. 24, CA (Civ Div) *16–001*, *16–167*
Hewlett v LCC (1908) 72 J.P. 136 .... *28–111*
Hewlings v Graham (1901) 70 L.J. Ch. 568 .... *8–016*
Heyman v Darwins Ltd [1942] A.C. 356; [1942] 1 All E.R. 337; (1942) 72 Ll. L. Rep. 65, HL *2–128*, *14–004*, *23–097*, *24–001*, *24–010*, *24–011*, *24–013*, *24–015*, *24–017*, *24–040*, 24–047, *24–048*, *24–050*
Heys (Deceased), Re; sub nom. Heys, In the Estate of; Walker v Gaskill [1914] P. 192, PDAD *4–063*
Heywood v Wellers (A Firm) [1976] Q.B. 446; [1976] 2 W.L.R. 101; [1976] 1 All E.R. 300; [1976] 2 Lloyd's Rep. 88; (1975) 120 S.J. 9, CA (Civ Div) *21–029*, *26–083*, *28–033*
Heywood's Conveyance, Re; sub nom. Cheshire Lines Committee v Liverpool Corp [1938] 2 All E.R. 230, Ch D *10–029*
Hick v Raymond & Reid; sub nom. Hick v Rodocanachi; Pantland Hick v Raymond & Reid [1893] A.C. 22; [1891–4] All E.R. Rep. 491, HL *21–020*
Hickinbotham Developments Pty Ltd v Woods [2005] SASC 215, (2005) 92 S.A.S.R. 52 .... *10–037*
Hickman v Berens [1895] 2 Ch. 638, CA *5–062*, *5–071*
Hickman v Haynes (1874–75) L.R. 10 C.P. 598, CCP *3–081*, *22–043*, *26–064*
Hickman v Kent or Romney Marsh Sheepbreeders Association [1915] 1 Ch. 881, Ch D 9–061, *28–004*
Hickman & Co v Roberts [1913] A.C. 229, HL *1–031*, *13–012*
Hicks v Gregory (1849) 8 C.B. 378 .... *16–067*

Higgins v Hatch & Fielding [1996] 1 E.G.L.R. 133; [1996] 10 E.G. 162; [1995] E.G. 105 (C.S.), CA (Civ Div) *28–011*
Higgins v Hill (1887) 56 L.T. 426 .... *16–006*
Higgins v Scott (1831) 2 B. & Ad. 413 .... *28–133*
Higgins v Senior (1841) 8 M. & W. 834 .... *12–114*
Higgs (Inspector of Taxes) v Olivier [1952] Ch. 311; [1952] 1 T.L.R. 441; 45 R. & I.T. 142; 33 T.C. 136; (1952) 31 A.T.C. 8; [1952] T.R. 57; (1952) 96 S.J. 90, CA; affirming [1951] Ch. 899; [1951] 2 T.L.R. 298; 44 R. & I.T. 509; (1951) 30 A.T.C. 241; [1951] T.R. 213; (1951) 95 S.J. 562, Ch D *16–094*
Higham v Stena Sealink Ltd [1996] 1 W.L.R. 1107; [1996] 3 All E.R. 660; [1996] 2 Lloyd's Rep. 26; [1996] C.L.C. 1193; [1996] P.I.Q.R. P351, CA (Civ Div) *28–023*
Highberry Ltd v Colt Telecom Group Plc (No.2); sub nom. Colt Telecom Group Plc (No.2), Re [2002] EWHC 2815 (Ch); [2003] B.P.I.R. 324, Ch D (Companies Ct) *30–069*, *30–366*
Highlands Insurance Co v Continental Insurance Co [1987] 1 Lloyd's Rep. 109 (Note), QBD (Comm) *6–009*, *6–012*, *6–102*
Highway Properties Ltd v Kelly, Douglas Co (1971) 17 D.L.R. (3d) 710 .... *24–001*
Hilckes Ex p. Muhesa Rubber Plantations Ltd, Re [1917] 1 K.B. 48, CA .. *11–025*, *11–030*
Hill v Alex Lawrie Factors Ltd; sub nom. Burfoot (A Bankrupt), Re [2000] B.P.I.R. 1038, Ch D *20–026*
Hill v Archbold [1968] 1 Q.B. 686; [1967] 3 W.L.R. 1218; [1967] 3 All E.R. 110; 3 K.I.R. 40; (1967) 111 S.J. 543, CA (Civ Div); affirming [1967] 2 Q.B. 418; [1967] 2 W.L.R. 1180; [1967] 1 All E.R. 1038; 2 K.I.R. 138; (1967) 111 S.J. 193, QBD *16–049*, *16–050*, *16–051*, *16–052*
Hill v Barclay (1810) 16 Ves. Jun. 402 .... *27–026*, *27–027*
Hill v CA Parsons & Co [1972] Ch. 305; [1971] 3 W.L.R. 995; [1971] 3 All E.R. 1345; (1971) 115 S.J. 868, CA (Civ Div) *27–008*, 27–023, *27–064*
Hill v Evans (1862) 4 De. G.F. & J. 288 .... *12–046*, *12–057*
Hill v Gomme (1839) 5 My. & Cr. 250 .... *18–079*, *18–081*, *18–087*
Hill v Haines [2007] EWCA Civ 1284; [2008] 2 All E.R. 901 .... *3–002*, *3–014*, 3–047, 3–052
Hill v Harris [1965] 2 Q.B. 601; [1965] 2 W.L.R. 1331; [1965] 2 All E.R. 358; (1965) 109 S.J. 333, CA *12–006*, *13–016*
Hill v Hill [1947] Ch. 231; [1947] 1 All E.R. 54; 176 L.T. 216; (1947) 91 S.J. 55, CA *4–028*, *4–032*, *4–034*
Hill v Kirshenstein [1920] 3 K.B. 556, CA *29–107*
Hill v Manchester and Salford Waterworks Co (1831) 2 B. & Ad. 544 .... *1–112*
Hill v Perrott (1810) 3 Taunt. 274 .... *29–148*
Hill v Secretary of State for the Environment, Food and Rural Affairs [2005] EWHC 696 (Ch); [2006] 1 B.C.L.C. 601; [2005] B.P.I.R. 1330, Ch D 16–005
Hill v Settle [1917] 1 Ch. 319, CA; reversing [1917] 1 Ch. 105, Ch D *20–055*
Hill v Showell (1918) 87 L.J.K.B. 1106 .... *26–115*, *26–118*
Hill v Spread Trustee Co Ltd; sub nom. Nurkowski, Re [2006] EWCA Civ 542; [2007] Bus. L.R. 1213; [2007] 1 W.L.R. 2404; [2007] 1 All E.R. 1106; [2006] B.C.C. 646; [2007] 1 B.C.L.C. 450; [2006] B.P.I.R. 789; [2006] W.T.L.R. 1009, CA (Civ Div) *28–003*
Hill v Van Erp (1997) 142 A.L.R. 687 .... *18–037*
Hill v Walker (1854) 4 K. & J. 166 .... *20–014*, *28–131*
Hill v Wilcox (1831) 1 M. & Rob. 58 .... *12–116*
Hill v William Hill (Park Lane) Ltd [1949] A.C. 530; [1949] 2 All E.R. 452; 65 T.L.R. 471; [1949] L.J.R. 1383; (1949) 93 S.J. 587, HL *16–192*
Hill & Co v Hill (1886) 55 L.T. 769 .... *16–114*
Hill Samuel Bank Ltd v Frederick Brand Partnership, 45 Con. L.R. 141; (1994) 10 Const. L.J. 72, QBD *18–031*
Hillas v Rederiaktiebolaget Aeolus (1926) 32 Com. Cas. 169 .... *12–058*
Hillas & Co Ltd v Arcos Ltd. *See* WN Hillas & Co Ltd v Arcos Ltd
Hillesden Securities Ltd v Ryjack Ltd [1983] 1 W.L.R. 959; [1983] 2 All E.R. 184; [1983] R.T.R. 491; (1983) 80 L.S.G. 2524; (1983) 133 N.L.J. 280; (1983) 127 S.J. 521, QBD *29–144*

Hillingdon Estates Co v Stonefield Estates Ltd [1952] Ch. 627; [1952] 1 All E.R. 853; [1952] 1 T.L.R. 1099; 50 L.G.R. 587; (1951–52) 2 P. & C.R. 415, Ch D *23–057*, *27–007*
Hillingdon LBC v ARC Ltd (No.2) [2001] C.P. Rep. 33; [2000] 3 E.G.L.R. 97; [2000] R.V.R. 283; (2000) 80 P. & C.R. D29, CA (Civ Div) *28–109*
Hillreed Lard v Beautridge [1994] E.G. 55 (C.S.), Ch D *2–112*
Hills v Street (1828) 5 Bing. 37 .... *29–150*
Hills v Sughrue (1846) 15 M.W. 253 .... *23–004*
Hills (Patents) Ltd v University College Hospital Board of Governors [1956] 1 Q.B. 90; [1955] 3 W.L.R. 523; [1955] 3 All E.R. 365; (1955) 99 S.J. 760, CA 10–010, *10–018*,
Hilton v Eckersley, 119 E.R. 781; (1855) 6 El. & Bl. 47, QB *16–137*, *16–200*
Hilton v Sutton Steam Laundry [1946] K.B. 65, CA *20–004*
Hilton v Woods (1867) L.R. 4 Eq. 432, Ct of Chancery *16–055*
Hindcastle Ltd v Barbara Attenborough Associates Ltd [1997] A.C. 70; [1996] 2 W.L.R. 262; [1996] 1 All E.R. 737; [1996] B.C.C. 636; [1996] 2 B.C.L.C. 234; [1996] B.P.I.R. 595; [1996] 1 E.G.L.R. 94; [1996] 15 E.G. 103; [1996] E.G. 32 (C.S.); (1996) 93(12) L.S.G. 29; (1996) 140 S.J.L.B. 84; [1996] N.P.C. 28, HL; affirming [1995] Q.B. 95; [1994] 3 W.L.R. 1100; [1994] 4 All E.R. 129; [1994] B.C.C. 705; [1994] 2 B.C.L.C. 728; (1995) 70 P. & C.R. 29; [1994] 43 E.G. 154; [1994] E.G. 109 (C.S.); [1994] N.P.C. 86, CA (Civ Div) *9–048*, *20–035*
Hinde v Liddell (1874–75) L.R. 10 Q.B. 265, QBD *26–111*
Hines v Birkbeck College (No.2) [1992] Ch. 33; [1991] 3 W.L.R. 557; [1991] 4 All E.R. 450, CA (Civ Div) *25–012*
Hinton v Sparkes (1867–68) L.R. 3 C.P. 161, CCP *29–064*
Hinz v Berry [1970] 2 Q.B. 40; [1970] 2 W.L.R. 684; [1970] 1 All E.R. 1074; (1970) 114 S.J. 111, CA (Civ Div) *26–030*
Hipgrave v Case (1885) L.R. 28 Ch. D. 356; (1885) 54 L.J. Ch. 399, CA *27–084*
Hirachand Punamchand v Temple [1911] 2 K.B. 330, CA 3–126, *18–021*, *19–077*, *22–022*
Hirani v Hirani (1983) 4 F.L.R. 232, CA (Civ Div) *7–010*
Hire Purchase Furnishing Co Ltd v Richens (1888) L.R. 20 Q.B.D. 387, CA *9–048*, *16–204*
Hirji Mulji v Cheong Yue Steamship Co Ltd [1926] A.C. 497; [1926] 1 W.W.R. 917; [1926] W.N. 89, PC (HK) *23–007*, *23–016*, *23–040*, *23–071*, *24–046*
Hirschfeld v London Brighton & South Coast Railway Co (1876–77) L.R. 2 Q.B.D. 1, QBD *6–013*, *22–010*, *22–021*
Hiscox v Outhwaite (No.1) [1992] 1 A.C. 562; [1991] 3 W.L.R. 297; [1991] 3 All E.R. 641; [1991] 2 Lloyd's Rep. 435, HL; affirming [1991] 2 W.L.R. 1321; [1991] 3 All E.R. 124; [1991] 2 Lloyd's Rep. 1, CA (Civ Div); affirming, *The Times*, March 7, 1991, QBD *3–107*, *3–112*
Hiscox v Outhwaite (No.3) [1991] 2 Lloyd's Rep. 524, QBD (Comm) ... *3–090*, *3–099*, *3–100*, *3–109*
Hispanica de Petroles SA v Vencedora Oceanica Navegacion SA; The Kapetan Markos NL (No.2) [1987] 2 Lloyd's Rep. 321, CA (Civ Div); affirming [1986] 1 Lloyd's Rep. 238 (Note), QBD (Comm) *2–111*, *2–160*, *2–166*, *14–040*, *14–054*, *14–055*, *18–022*, 28–022
Hispano Americana Mercantile SA v Central Bank of Nigeria [1979] 2 Lloyd's Rep. 277; (1979) 123 S.J. 336, CA (Civ Div) *11–001*
Hissett v Reading Roofing Co [1969] 1 W.L.R. 1757; [1970] 1 All E.R. 122; (1969) 20 P. & C.R. 924; (1969) 113 S.J. 815, Ch D *25–001*, *25–003*
Hitch v Stone (Inspector of Taxes); sub nom. Stone (Inspector of Taxes) v Hitch [2001] EWCA Civ 63; [2001] S.T.C. 214; 73 T.C. 600; [2001] B.T.C. 78; [2001] S.T.I. 104; [2001] N.P.C. 19, CA (Civ Div); reversing [1999] S.T.C. 431; [1999] B.T.C. 103; [1999] E.G. 44 (C.S.); [1999] N.P.C. 40, Ch D *2–185*
Hitchcock v Coker (1837) 6 A. & E. 438 .... *16–090*, *16–092*
Hitchcock v Giddings (1817) 4 Price 135 .... *5–026*
Hitchcock v Way (1837) 6 A. & E. 943 .... *16–161*

Hitchens v General Guarantee Corp Ltd; sub nom. Hichens v General Guarantee Corp Ltd [2001] EWCA Civ 359, CA (Civ Div) *2–065*
Hitchin v Groom (1848) 5 C.B. 515 .... *12–096*
Hitchings & Coulthurst Co v Northern Leather Co Of America and Doushkess [1914] 3 K.B. 907 .... *12–096*, *12–101*
Hitchman v Crouch Butler Savage Associates (1982) 80 L.S. Gaz. 550 .... *24–049*
Hitchman v Stewart (1855) 3 Drew. 271 .... *17–027*
Hivac Ltd v Park Royal Scientific Instruments Ltd [1946] Ch. 169, CA *16–115*, *27–070*
Hoad v Grace (1861) 7 H. & N. 494 .... *12–108*
Hoare v Graham (1811) 3 Camp. 57 .... *12–101*
Hoare v GW Ry (1877) 37 L.T. 186 .... *14–017*
Hoare v Rennie (1859) 5 H.N. 19 .... *24–044*
Hobbs v London & South Western Railway Co (1874–75) L.R. 10 Q.B. 111, QBD *2–021*, *26–082*
Hoblyn v Hoblyn (1889) 41 Ch. D. 200 .... *7–074*
Hobson v Pattenden & Co (1903) 19 T.L.R. 186 .... *5–025*
Hochster v De La Tour, 118 E.R. 922; (1853) 2 El. & Bl. 678, QB 24–022
Hockley and Papworth v Goldstein (1920) 90 L.J.K.B. 111 .... *19–016*
Hodges v Jones [1935] Ch. 657, Ch D *4–016*
Hodges v Smith (1599) Cro.Eliz. 623 .... *22–006*
Hodgkinson, Ex p. (1815) 19 Ves. 291 .... *17–010*
Hodgkinson & Corby Ltd v Wards Mobility Services Ltd (No.2) [1998] F.S.R. 530, CA (Civ Div) *25–013*
Hodgson v Armstrong [1967] 2 Q.B. 299; [1967] 2 W.L.R. 311; [1967] 1 All E.R. 307; (1966) 110 S.J. 907, CA *28–063*
Hoecheong Products Co Ltd v Cargill Hong Kong Ltd [1995] 1 W.L.R. 404; [1995] 1 Lloyd's Rep. 584; (1995) 92(11) L.S.G. 39; (1995) 139 S.J.L.B. 59, PC (HK) *14–140*, *14–141*, *14–150*
Hoenig v Isaacs [1952] 2 All E.R. 176; [1952] 1 T.L.R. 1360, CA *21–027*, *21–029*, 21–032, *21–033*, *21–035*, *24–043*
Hoes v Bishop [1909] 2 K.B. 390 .... *7–085*
Hoffinghouse & Co v C-Trade SA, Intra Transporter, The [1986] 2 Lloyd's Rep. 132, CA; affirming [1985] 2 Lloyd's Rep. 158 .... *2–029*, *2–116*, *2–129*, *2–139*
Hoffman v Red Owl Stores Inc., 133 N.W. 2d 267 (1965) *2–136*
Hoffman v Sofaer [1982] 1 W.L.R. 1350; (1982) 79 L.S.G. 1291, QBD *30–376*
Hogarth v Wherley (1874–75) L.R. 10 C.P. 630, CCP *21–044*
Hogg v Kirby (1803) 8 Ves. J. 215 .... *29–142*
Hogg Insurance Brokers Ltd v Guardian Insurance Co Inc [1997] 1 Lloyd's Rep. 412, QBD (Comm) *30–077*
Hoggart v Scott (1830) 1 Russ. & My. 293 .... *27–047*
Hoghton v Hoghton (1852) 15 Beav. 278 .... *7–074*
Hohler v Aston [1920] 2 Ch. 420, Ch D *4–047*, *27–050*
Holbeck Hall Hotel Ltd v Scarborough BC [2000] Q.B. 836; [2000] 2 W.L.R. 1396; [2000] 2 All E.R. 705; [2000] B.L.R. 109; (2000) 2 T.C.L.R. 865; 69 Con. L.R. 1; [2000] B.L.G.R. 412; [2000] E.G. 29 (C.S.); (2000) 97(11) L.S.G. 36; (2000) 97(9) L.S.G. 44; (2000) 150 N.L.J. 307; (2000) 144 S.J.L.B. 109; [2000] N.P.C. 17, CA (Civ Div) *23–053*
Holbrow v Wilkins (1822) 1 B.C. 10 .... *21–079*
Holden v Thompson [1907] 2 K.B. 489, KBD *16–052*
Holding v Elliott (1860) 5 H. & N. 117 .... *12–107*
Holding & Barnes Plc v Hill House Hammond Ltd (Preliminary Issue) [2001] EWCA Civ 1334; [2002] 2 P. & C.R. 11; [2002] L. & T.R. 7, CA (Civ Div); affirming in part [2000] L. & T.R. 428, Ch D *12–075*
Holding & Management (Solitaire) Ltd v Ideal Homes North West Ltd (formerly Broseley Estates Ltd) [2005] EWCA Civ 59, CA (Civ Div); affirming [2004] EWHC 2408 (TCC); 96 Con. L.R. 114; [2005] P.N.L.R. 16, QBD (TCC) *13–009*, *18–033*
Hole v Bradbury (1879) L.R. 12 Ch. D. 886, Ch D *19–055*
Hole v Chard Union [1894] 1 Ch. 293, CA *26–015*
Holis Metal Industries Ltd v GMB [2008] I.R.L.R. 187, EAT *30–116*

Holland, Re; sub nom. Gregg v Holland [1902] 2 Ch. 360, CA; reversing [1901] 2 Ch. 145, Ch D *12–108*
Holland v Eyre (1825) 2 Sim. & St. 194 .... *2–032*
Holland v Hall (1817) 1 B. & Ald. 53 .... *16–204*
Holland v Lampen-Wolfe [2000] 1 W.L.R. 1573; [2000] 3 All E.R. 833; [2001] I.L.Pr. 49; [2000] U.K.H.R.R. 734; (2000) 97(32) L.S.G. 37; (2000) 144 S.J.L.B. 223, HL; affirming [1999] 1 W.L.R. 188; (1998) 95(36) L.S.G. 32; (1998) 142 S.J.L.B. 227, CA (Civ Div) *11–002*, 11–003, *11–005*
Holland v Wiltshire (1954) 90 C.L.R. 409 .... *24–013*
Holland Hannen & Cubitts (Northern) Ltd v Welsh Health Technical Services Organisation, 35 B.L.R. 1; 7 Con. L.R. 1; [1985] C.I.L.L. 217, CA (Civ Div) *18–005*
Hollandia, The. *See* Owners of Cargo on Board the Morviken v Owners of the Hollandia
Hollicourt (Contracts) Ltd (In Liquidation) v Bank of Ireland; sub nom. Bank of Ireland v Hollicourt (Contracts) Ltd; Claughton (Liquidator of Hollicourt (Contracts) Ltd) v Bank of Ireland [2001] Ch. 555; [2001] 2 W.L.R. 290; [2001] 1 All E.R. 289; [2001] 1 All E.R. (Comm) 357; [2001] Lloyd's Rep. Bank. 6; [2000] B.C.C. 1210; [2001] 1 B.C.L.C. 233; [2001] B.P.I.R. 47; (2000) 97(45) L.S.G. 41, CA (Civ Div); reversing [2000] 1 W.L.R. 895; [2000] 2 All E.R. 45; [2000] Lloyd's Rep. Bank. 21; [2000] B.C.C. 237; [2000] 1 B.C.L.C. 171; (1999) 96(48) L.S.G. 39; (2000) 144 S.J.L.B. 24, Ch D *9–049*
Holliday v Lockwood [1917] 2 Ch. 47, Ch D *27–030*
Hollier v Rambler Motors (AMC) Ltd [1972] 2 Q.B. 71; [1972] 2 W.L.R. 401; [1972] 1 All E.R. 399; [1972] R.T.R. 190; (1972) 116 S.J. 158, CA (Civ Div) *1–151*, *12–011*, *13–022*, 14–012
Hollingworth v Southern Ferries; The Eagle [1977] 2 Lloyd's Rep. 70, QBD *2–021*, *12–010*, *12–015*, *12–017*
Hollins v Davy (J) [1963] 1 Q.B. 844; [1963] 2 W.L.R. 201; [1963] 1 All E.R. 370; (1962) 106 S.J. 1033, QBD 14–033, *14–036*
Hollins v Russell; Sharratt v London Central Bus Co Ltd (No.3); Worth v McKenna; Pratt v Bull; Dunn v Ward; Tichband v Hurdman [2003] EWCA Civ 718; [2003] 1 W.L.R. 2487; [2003] 4 All E.R. 590; [2003] 3 Costs L.R. 423; (2003) 100(28) L.S.G. 30; (2003) 153 N.L.J. 920; (2003) 147 S.J.L.B. 662, CA (Civ Div) *16–056*
Hollis v Palmer (1836) 2 Bing. N.C. 73 28–038
Hollis & Co v Stocks [2000] U.K.C.L.R. 658; [2000] I.R.L.R. 712, CA (Civ Div) *16–097*, *27–060*
Holloway v Chancery Mead Ltd [2007] EWHC 2495 (TCC); [2008] 1 All E.R. (Comm) 653 2–131
Holman Construction v Delta Timber Co [1972] N.Z.L.R. 1081 .... *3–172*
Holme v Guppy (1838) 3 M. & W. 387 .... *13–012*, *22–038*
Holmes, Re (1885) L.R. 29 Ch. D. 786, CA *19–068*
Holmes v Bell (1841) 3 M.G. 213 .... *25–001*, 25–002
Holmes v Blogg (1818) 8 Taunt. 508 .... *8–033*, *8–040*
Holmes v Cowcher [1970] 1 W.L.R. 834; [1970] 1 All E.R. 1224; (1970) 21 P. & C.R. 766; (1970) 114 S.J. 284, Ch D *28–003*
Holmes v Jones (1907) 4 C.L.R. 1692 .... *6–032*
Holmes v Kerrison (1810) 2 Taunt. 323 .... *28–041*
Holmes v Mitchell (1859) 7 C.B. N.S. 361 .... *12–102*, *12–123*
Holmes v Payne [1930] 2 K.B. 301; (1930) 37 Ll. L. Rep. 41, KBD *29–039*
Holmon v Johnson (1775) 1 Cowp. 341 .... 16–007, *16–014*, *16–205*
Holsworthy Urban DC v Holsworthy Rural DC [1907] 2 Ch. 62, Ch D *3–052*
Holt v Ely, 118 E.R. 634; (1831) 1 El. & Bl. 795, QB *29–147*
Holt v Heatherfield Trust [1942] 2 K.B. 1, KBD *19–017*, *19–019*, 19–033, *19–036*, *19–038*, *19–067*
Holt v Markham [1923] 1 K.B. 504, CA *29–012*, *29–042*, *29–176*, 29–177, *29–178*

Holt v Payne Skillington, 77 B.L.R. 51; 49 Con. L.R. 99; [1996] P.N.L.R. 179; [1995] E.G. 201 (C.S.); (1996) 93(2) L.S.G. 29; (1996) 140 S.J.L.B. 30; [1995] N.P.C. 202, CA (Civ Div) 1–160, *18–023*
Holt v Ward Clarencieux (1732) Stra. 937 .... *3–166*, *8–042*
Holt & Co v Collyer (1880–81) L.R. 16 Ch. D. 718, Ch D *12–052*
Holts' Motors v South East Lancashire Insurance Co (1930) 35 Com. Cas. 281 .... *6–147*
Holwell Securities Ltd v Hughes [1974] 1 W.L.R. 155; [1974] 1 All E.R. 161; (1973) 26 P. & C.R. 544; (1973) 117 S.J. 912, CA (Civ Div); affirming [1973] 1 W.L.R. 757; [1973] 2 All E.R. 476; (1973) 26 P. & C.R. 28; (1973) 117 S.J. 447, Ch D *2–045*, 2–052, *2–053*, *2–065*
Homburg Houtimport BV v Agrosin Private Ltd; The Starsin; sub nom. Owners of Cargo Lately Laden on Board the Starsin v Owners of the Starsin; Hunter Timber Ltd v Agrosin Private Ltd [2003] UKHL 12; [2004] 1 A.C. 715; [2003] 2 W.L.R. 711; [2003] 2 All E.R. 785; [2003] 1 All E.R. (Comm) 625; [2003] 1 Lloyd's Rep. 571; [2003] 1 C.L.C. 921; 2003 A.M.C. 913; (2003) 100(19) L.S.G. 31, HL; reversing [2001] EWCA Civ 56; [2001] 1 All E.R. (Comm) 455; [2001] 1 Lloyd's Rep. 437; [2001] C.L.C. 696, CA (Civ Div); reversing in part [1999] 2 All E.R. (Comm) 591; [2000] 1 Lloyd's Rep. 85; [1999] C.L.C. 1769, QBD (Comm) *1–012*, *2–085*, *12–057*, *12–065*, *12–070*, 12–076, 12–083, *12–114*, *14–005*, 14–009, *14–042*, *14–048*, *14–049*, 14–051, 14–054, 14–055, *18–004*, *18–019*, *18–021*, *18–034*, *18–090*, *18–110*, *18–112*, *18–146*
Home & Colonial Insurance Co Ltd v London Guarantee & Accident Co Ltd (1928) 32 Ll. L. Rep. 267, KBD *29–033*, *29–035*, *29–045*, *29–187*
Home & Overseas Insurance Co v Mentor Insurance Co (UK) [1990] 1 W.L.R. 153; [1989] 3 All E.R. 74; [1989] 1 Lloyd's Rep. 473; (1989) 86(7) L.S.G. 36; (1989) 133 S.J. 44, CA (Civ Div); affirming, *The Times*, August 11, 1988; *Independent*, August 18, 1988; *Financial Times*, August 10, 1988, QBD *2–163*
Home and Colonial Insurance Co Ltd, Re [1930] 1 Ch. 102 .... *29–192*
Home Counties Dairies v Skilton [1970] 1 W.L.R. 526; [1970] 1 All E.R. 1227; 8 K.I.R. 691; (1970) 114 S.J. 107, CA (Civ Div) *16–088*, 16–104, *16–110*, *16–111*, *16–112*, *16–113*
Home Insurance Co and St. Paul Fire and Marine Insurance Co v Administratia Asigurarilor de Stat [1983] 2 Lloyd's Rep. 674 .... *2–163*
Home Office v Ayres [1992] I.C.R. 175; [1992] I.R.L.R. 59, EAT *29–181*
Home Office v Dorset Yacht Co Ltd [1970] A.C. 1004; [1970] 2 W.L.R. 1140; [1970] 2 All E.R. 294; [1970] 1 Lloyd's Rep. 453; (1970) 114 S.J. 375, HL; affirming [1969] 2 Q.B. 412; [1969] 2 W.L.R. 1008; [1969] 2 All E.R. 564; (1969) 113 S.J. 227, CA (Civ Div); affirming (1969) 113 S.J. 57, QBD 1–183
Homer v Ashford (1825) 3 Bing. 322 .... *16–089*
Homfray v Scroope (1849) 13 Q.B. 509 .... *28–064*
Honck v Muller (1880–81) L.R. 7 Q.B.D. 92, CA *21–007*, *24–040*, *24–044*
Hong Guan & Co v R Jumabhoy & Sons [1960] A.C. 684; [1960] 2 W.L.R. 754; [1960] 2 All E.R. 100; [1960] 1 Lloyd's Rep. 405; (1960) 104 S.J. 367, PC (Sing) *14–142*, *14–148*
Hong Kong and Shanghai Banking Corp v Kloeckner & Co AG [1990] 2 Q.B. 514; [1990] 3 W.L.R. 634; [1989] 3 All E.R. 513; [1989] 2 Lloyd's Rep. 323, QBD (Comm) *20–041*
Hong Kong and Shanghai Banking Corp v Lo Lee Shi [1928] A.C. 181; [1928] 1 W.W.R. 593, PC (HK) *25–020*, *25–025*
Hong Kong Shanghai (Shipping) Ltd v The Cavalry [1987] H.K.L.R. 287 .... *30–068*, *30–311*
Hongkong Fir Shipping Co Ltd v Kawasaki Kisen Kaisha Ltd; The Hongkong Fir [1962] 2 Q.B. 26; [1962] 2 W.L.R. 474; [1962] 1 All E.R. 474; [1961] 2 Lloyd's Rep. 478; (1961) 106 S.J. 35, CA; affirming [1961] 2 W.L.R. 716; [1961] 2 All E.R. 257; [1961] 1 Lloyd's Rep. 159; (1961) 105 S.J. 347, QBD (Comm) *12–026*, *12–031*, 12–034, *12–035*, *12–040*, *13–007*, *14–032*, *23–040*, *24–030*, *24–037*, 24–040
Hony v Hony (1824) 1 Sim. & S. 568 .... *28–094*

Hood v Anchor Line (Henderson Bros) Ltd; sub nom. Hood v Anchor Line [1918] A.C. 837; 1918 S.C. (H.L.) 143; (1918) 2 S.L.T. 118, HL; affirming 1916 S.C. 547; 1916 1 S.L.T. 225, IH (2 Div) *12–009*, *12–013*, *12–014*, *14–002*
Hood (Lady) of Avalon v MacKinnon [1909] 1 Ch. 476, Ch D *29–029*, *29–032*, *29–033*
Hookham v Mayle (1906) 22 T.L.R. 241 .... *22–016*
Hoole v Great Western Railway (1867–68) L.R. 3 Ch. App. 262, CA in Chancery *9–020*
Hoop, The (1799) 1 C.Rob. 196 .... *11–024*, *11–027*, *16–026*
Hooper v Exeter Corp (1887) 56 L.J.Q.B. 457 .... *29–043*, *29–084*, *29–094*, *29–095*
Hooper v Fynmores (A Firm) [2002] Lloyd's Rep. P.N. 18; [2001] W.T.L.R. 1019; (2001) 98(26) L.S.G. 45; (2001) 145 S.J.L.B. 156, Ch D *18–025*
Hooper v Keay (1875–76) L.R. 1 Q.B.D. 178; (1875) 24 W.R. 485; (1875) 34 L.T. 574, QBD *21–066*
Hooper v Lane, 10 E.R. 1368; (1857) 6 H.L. Cas. 443, QB *20–020*
Hooper v Sherman [1994] N.P.C. 153, CA (Civ Div) *4–071*
Hooper v Stephens (1835) 4 A. & E. 71 .... *28–099*
Hooper v Woolmer (1850) 10 C.B. 370 .... *21–010*
Hooper & Ashby v Willis (1905) 94 L.T. 624 .... *16–198*
Hooper and Grass' Contract [1949] V.L.R. 269 .... *29–090*
Hop and Malt Exchange and Warehouse Co, Re; sub nom. Hop and Malt Exchange and Warehouse Co Ex p. Briggs, Re (1865–66) L.R. 1 Eq. 483, Ct of Chancery *6–124*
Hope v Hope (1857) 8 De G.M. & G. 731 .... *30–367*
Hopkins v Norcros; sub nom. Norcros v Hopkins [1994] I.C.R. 11; [1994] I.R.L.R. 18, CA (Civ Div) *26–117*
Hopkins v Tanqueray (1854) 15 C.B. 130; 2 C.L.R. 842; 23 L.J.C.P. 162; 23 L.T.O.S. 144; 18 Jur. 608; 2 W.R. 475; 139 E.R. 369, CCP *12–003*
Hopkins v TL Dallas Group Ltd; Hopkins v TL Dallas & Co Ltd [2004] EWHC 1379 (Ch); [2005] 1 B.C.L.C. 543, Ch D *9–031*
Hopkins v Ware (1868–69) L.R. 4 Ex. 268, Ex Ct *21–079*
Hopkinson v Forster (1874) L.R. 19 Eq. 74, Ct of Chancery *19–024*
Hopkinson v Logan (1839) 5 M. & W. 241 .... *3–031*, *3–059*
Hopkinson v Marquis of Exeter (1867–68) L.R. 5 Eq. 63, Ct of Chancery *9–075*
Hoppe v Titman [1996] 1 W.L.R. 841; (1996) 140 S.J.L.B. 58, CA (Civ Div) *25–031*
Hopper v Conyers (1866) L.R. 2 Eq. 549, Ct of Chancery *29–166*
Hopper v Hopper [2008] EWHC 228 (CL), [2008] I F.C.R 557 .... *3–147, 3–154*
Horabin v British Overseas Airways Corp [1952] 2 All E.R. 1016; [1952] 2 Lloyd's Rep. 450; [1952] W.N. 519; (1952) 96 S.J. 803, QBD *14–017*
Horbury v Craig Hall & Rutley [1991] E.G. 81 (C.S.) *28–011*
Horcal Ltd v Gatland; sub nom. Horcal Ltd v Gartland (1984) 1 B.C.C. 99089; [1984] I.R.L.R. 288, CA (Civ Div) *29–031*
Horkulak v Cantor Fitzgerald International; sub nom. Cantor Fitzgerald International v Horkulak [2004] EWCA Civ 1287; [2005] I.C.R. 402; [2004] I.R.L.R. 942; (2004) 148 S.J.L.B. 1218, CA (Civ Div); reversing [2003] EWHC 1918 (QB); [2004] I.C.R. 697; [2003] I.R.L.R. 756, QBD *1–032*, *2–131*, *2–175*, *26–001*
Horlock v Beal; sub nom. Beal v Horlock [1916] 1 A.C. 486, HL *23–011*, 23–038
Horn v Anglo-Australian etc Life Assurance Co (1861) 30 L.J.Ch. 511 .... *16–171*
Horn v Minister of Food [1948] 2 All E.R. 1036; 65 T.L.R. 1906, KBD *23–047*
Horn Linie GmbH & Co v Panamericana Formas e Impresos SA; The Hornbay [2006] EWHC 373; [2006] 2 All E.R. (Comm) 924; [2006] 2 Lloyd's Rep. 44, QBD (Comm) *30–306*
Hornal v Neuberger Products [1957] 1 Q.B. 247; [1956] 3 W.L.R. 1034; [1956] 3 All E.R. 970; (1956) 100 S.J. 915, CA *6–042*
Hornby v Close (1867) L.R. 2 Q.B. 153, QB *16–140*
Horne, Re; sub nom. Wilson v Cox Sinclair [1905] 1 Ch. 76, Ch D *29–043*
Horne v Chester and Fein Property Developments Pty (1986) 11 A.C.L.R. 485 .... *20–025*
Horne v Midland Railway Co (1872–73) L.R. 8 C.P. 131, Ex Chamber *26–062*, *26–070*
Horne v Poland [1922] 2 K.B. 364; (1922) 10 Ll. L. Rep. 275, KBD *6–147*
Horner v Graves (1831) 7 Bing. 735 .... *16–110*

Horner v Walker [1923] 2 Ch. 218, Ch D *4–036*
Horne-Roberts v SmithKline Beecham Plc; sub nom. SmithKline Beecham Plc v H (A Child); H (A Child) v SmithKline Beecham Plc; Smithkline Beecham Plc v Horne-Roberts; H (A Child) v Merck & Co Inc; H (A Child) v Merk & Co Inc; MMR/MR Vaccine Litigation [2001] EWCA Civ 2006; [2002] 1 W.L.R. 1662; [2002] C.P. Rep. 20; (2002) 65 B.M.L.R. 79; (2002) 99(8) L.S.G. 35; (2002) 146 S.J.L.B. 19, CA (Civ Div) *28–118*, *28–119*
Horrocks v Forray [1976] 1 W.L.R. 230; [1976] 1 All E.R. 737; (1975) 6 Fam. Law 15; (1975) 119 S.J. 866, CA (Civ Div) .. *2–169*, *2–171*, *2–183*, *3–022*, *3–039*, *16–067*, *16–068*
Horry v Tate & Lyle Refineries [1982] 2 Lloyd's Rep. 416, QBD *7–082*
Horsefall v Haywards; sub nom. Horsfall v Haywards [1999] 1 F.L.R. 1182; [1999] Lloyd's Rep. P.N. 332; [1999] P.N.L.R. 583; [2000] W.T.L.R. 29; [1999] Fam. Law 383; (1999) 96(10) L.S.G. 31; (1999) 143 S.J.L.B. 66; [1999] N.P.C. 25, CA (Civ Div) *18–037*
Horsey v Graham (1869–70) L.R. 5 C.P. 9, CCP *4–012*
Horsfall v Thomas (1862) 1 H. & C. 90 .... *6–016*, 6–032
Horsford v Bird; sub nom. Horsfold v Bird [2006] UKPC 3; [2006] 1 E.G.L.R. 75; [2006] 15 E.G. 136; (2006) 22 Const. L.J. 187; (2006) 103(6) L.S.G. 34, PC (Ant) *29–142*, *29–144*
Horsler v Zorro [1975] Ch. 302; [1975] 2 W.L.R. 183; [1975] 1 All E.R. 584; (1975) 29 P. & C.R. 180; (1975) 119 S.J. 83, Ch D *6–111*, *6–121*
Horsnell v Boston BC [2005] EWHC 1311 (QB), QBD *10–022*
Horton v Higham. *See* 1 Pump Court Chambers v Horton
Horton v Mead [1913] 1 K.B. 154, KBD *16–111*
Horwood v Millar's Timber & Trading Co Ltd [1917] 1 K.B. 305, CA; affirming [1916] 2 K.B. 44, KBD *16–006*
Hosack v Robins (No.2) [1918] 2 Ch. 339, CA *20–054*
Hosier Bros v Earl of Derby [1918] 2 K.B. 671, CA *10–013*
Hoskins v Woodham [1938] 1 All E.R. 692 .... *13–015*
Hospital for Sick Children (Board of Governors) v Walt Disney Productions Inc [1968] Ch. 52; [1967] 2 W.L.R. 1250; [1967] 1 All E.R. 1005; [1967] F.S.R. 152; (1967) 111 S.J. 150, CA (Civ Div); affirming [1966] 1 W.L.R. 1055; [1966] 2 All E.R. 321; (1966) 110 S.J. 525, Ch D *12–060*
Hospital Products Ltd v United States Surgical Corp, 156 C.L.R. 41, HC (Aus) *26–021*, *29–151*
Hospitality Group Pty Ltd v Australian Rugby Football Union Ltd [2001] F.C.A. 1040 .... *29–152*
Hotel Services Ltd v Hilton International Hotels (UK) Ltd [2000] 1 All E.R. (Comm) 750; [2000] B.L.R. 235, CA (Civ Div) *14–006*
Hotham v East India Co (1787) Doug. 272 .... *12–042*
Hotham v East India Co, 99 E.R. 1295; (1787) 1 Term Rep. 638, KB *24–032*
Hotson v East Berkshire HA; sub nom. Hotson v Fitzgerald [1987] A.C. 750; [1987] 3 W.L.R. 232; [1987] 2 All E.R. 909; [1955–95] P.N.L.R. 330; (1987) 84 L.S.G. 2365; (1987) 131 S.J. 975, HL *26–042*, *26–044*
Hough v May (1836) 4 A.E. 954 .... *21–091*
Houghland v RR Low (Luxury Coaches) Ltd [1962] 1 Q.B. 694; [1962] 2 W.L.R. 1015; [1962] 2 All E.R. 159; (1962) 106 S.J. 243, CA *14–019*
Houghton, Re; sub nom. Hawley v. Blake [1904] 1 Ch. 622, Ch D *20–014*
Houghton v Trafalgar Insurance Co Ltd [1954] 1 Q.B. 247; [1953] 3 W.L.R. 985; [1953] 2 All E.R. 1409; [1953] 2 Lloyd's Rep. 503; (1953) 97 S.J. 831, CA; affirming [1953] 2 Lloyd's Rep. 18, QBD *12–083*, *14–009*
Houghton & Co v Nothard Lowe & Wills. *See* JC Houghton & Co v Nothard Lowe & Wills Ltd
Houghton (Intestacy), Re; sub nom. Houghton v Houghton [1915] 2 Ch. 173, Ch D *16–169*
Houghton Main Colliery Co, Re [1956] 1 W.L.R. 1219; [1956] 3 All E.R. 300; 50 R. & I.T. 189; (1956) 35 A.T.C. 320; [1956] T.R. 333; (1956) 100 S.J. 651, Ch D *26–159*, *26–160*
Houlder, Re [1929] 1 Ch. 205, Ch D *21–065*

Houlder v General Steam Navigation Co (1862) 3 F. & F. 170 .... *13–021*
Houlder v Weir [1905] 2 K.B. 267, KBD *21–022*
Houldsworth v Glasgow City Bank (1879–80) L.R. 5 App. Cas. 317, HL 9–060
Houndsditch Warehouse Co Ltd v Waltex Ltd [1944] K.B. 579, KBD *26–103*, *26–113*
Hounslow LBC v Twickenham Garden Developments Ltd [1971] Ch. 233; [1970] 3 W.L.R. 538; [1970] 3 All E.R. 326; 7 B.L.R. 81; 69 L.G.R. 109; (1970) 114 S.J. 603, Ch D *13–028*, *24–010*, *26–122*, *26–123*, 27–029, *27–070*
House of Spring Gardens Ltd v Waite (No.2) [1991] 1 Q.B. 241; [1990] 3 W.L.R. 347; [1990] 2 All E.R. 990, CA (Civ Div) *25–012*, *25–013*, *25–017*, *25–018*
Household Fire & Carriage Accident Insurance Co Ltd v Grant (1878–79) L.R. 4 Ex. D. 216, CA *1–004*, *1–011*, 2–055, 2–056, *2–058*
Household Machines Ltd v Cosmos Exporters Ltd [1947] K.B. 217; [1946] 2 All E.R. 622; 62 T.L.R. 757; [1947] L.J.R. 578; 176 L.T. 49, KBD *24–018*, *24–044*, *27–008*
Hovenden v Annesley (1806) 2 Sch. & Lef. 607 .... *28–134*
Hovenden & Sons v Millhof (1900) 83 L.T. 41 .... *29–139*, *29–144*
How Engineering Services Ltd v Lindner Ceilings Floors Partitions Plc [1999] 2 All E.R. (Comm) 374; 64 Con. L.R. 67, QBD (TCC) *14–005*
Howard v Chapman (1831) 4 C.P. 508 .... *21–044*
Howard v Fawcetts [2006] UKHL 9 28–012
Howard v Jones [1989] Fam. Law 231, CA (Civ Div) *3–141*
Howard v Odhams Press Ltd [1938] 1 K.B. 1, CA *16–035*, *16–037*
Howard v Patent Ivory Manufacturing Co; sub nom. Patent Ivory Manufacturing Co, Re (1888) L.R. 38 Ch. D. 156, Ch D *9–014*
Howard v Pickford Tool Co [1951] 1 K.B. 417; (1951) 95 S.J. 44; (1951) 95 S.J. 553, CA *24–001*, *24–013*, *24–021*
Howard v Wood (1680) 2 Levinz 245 .... *29–006*, *29–142*
Howard E Perry & Co Ltd v British Railways Board [1980] 1 W.L.R. 1375; [1980] 2 All E.R. 579; [1980] I.C.R. 743; (1980) 124 S.J. 591, Ch D *27–017*, *27–031*, *29–171*
Howard F Hudson Pty v Ronayne (1971) 46 A.L.J.R. 173, HC (Aus) *16–105*
Howard Houlder & Partners and Banchero-Costa & Co SpA v Marine General Transporters Corp and Achille Lauro Lines SRL; The Panaghia P [1983] 2 Lloyd's Rep. 653, QBD (Comm) *18–078*, *18–083*
Howard Houlder & Partners Ltd v Union Marine Insurance Co Ltd (1922) 10 Ll. L. Rep. 627, HL *21–072*
Howard Marine & Dredging Co Ltd v A Ogden & Sons (Excavations) Ltd [1978] Q.B. 574; [1978] 2 W.L.R. 515; [1978] 2 All E.R. 1134; [1978] 1 Lloyd's Rep. 334; 9 B.L.R. 34; (1978) 122 S.J. 48, CA (Civ Div) *1–131*, 6–068, *6–069*, *6–074*, *6–084*, *6–085*, *6–136*, *12–004*, *12–005*, *14–062*, 14–090
Howatson v Webb [1907] 1 Ch. 537, Ch D 5–103, *12–002*
Howatson v Webb [1908] 1 Ch. 1, CA *5–103*, *12–002*
Howcutt v Bonser, 154 E.R. 939; (1849) 3 Ex. 491, Ex Ct *28–094*, *28–095*
Howe v David Brown Tractors (Retail) Ltd [1991] 4 All E.R. 30, CA (Civ Div) ... *28–006*
Howe v Smith (1884) L.R. 27 Ch. D. 89, CA *21–014*, *21–018*, *24–053*, *26–146*, *29–066*
Howe v Synge (1812) 15 East 440 .... *16–195*
Howell v Batt (1833) 2 Nev. M. (K.B.) 381 .... *29–026*
Howell v Coupland (1875–76) L.R. 1 Q.B.D. 258, CA *23–047*, *23–068*, *23–096*
Howell v Falmouth Boat Construction Co Ltd [1951] A.C. 837; [1951] 2 All E.R. 278; [1951] 2 Lloyd's Rep. 45; [1951] 2 T.L.R. 151; (1951) 95 S.J. 413, HL; affirming [1950] 2 K.B. 16; [1950] 1 All E.R. 538; (1949–50) 83 Ll. L. Rep. 320; 66 T.L.R. (Pt. 1) 487; 66 T.L.R. 487, CA; reversing (1948–49) 82 Ll. L. Rep. 904, OR *10–011*, *16–154*
Howell v Young, 108 E.R. 97; (1826) 5 B. & C. 259, KB *28–032*, *27–033*
Howgate and Osborn's Contract, Re [1902] 1 Ch. 451, Ch D *25–023*
Howlett, Re; sub nom. Howlett v Howlett [1949] Ch. 767; [1949] 2 All E.R. 490; 65 T.L.R. 569; [1949] L.J.R. 1632; (1949) 93 S.J. 632, Ch D *28–136*, *28–140*
Howlett v Haswell (1814) 4 Camp. 118 .... *8–043*
Howlett v Tarte, 142 E.R. 673; (1861) 10 C.B. N.S. 813, CCP *25–011*
Howley v Knight (1849) 14 Q.B. 240 .... *9–001*

Hoyle Ex p. Waters, Re (1872–73) L.R. 8 Ch. App. 562, CA in Chancery *20–049*
Hoyle, Re; sub nom. Hoyle v Hoyle [1893] 1 Ch. 84, CA *4–027*
Hoystead v Commissioner of Taxation; sub nom. Hoystead v Taxation Commissioner [1926] A.C. 155; [1925] All E.R. Rep. 62, PC (Aus) .. *25–011*, *25–012*, *25–013*
Hubbard v Vosper [1972] 2 Q.B. 84; [1972] 2 W.L.R. 389; [1972] 1 All E.R. 1023; (1972) 116 S.J. 95, CA (Civ Div) *16–035*
Hubert v Treherne (1842) 3 Man. & G. 743 .... *4–032*
Hucklesby v Hook (1900) 82 L.T. 117 ....*4–032*, *4–034*
Huddersfield Banking Co Ltd v Henry Lister & Son Ltd (No.2) [1895] 2 Ch. 273, CA *5–062*, *29–039*
Hudson, Re (1885) 54 L.J. Ch. 811 .... *3–002*
Hudson v Hill (1874) 43 L.J.C.P. 273 .... *21–021*
Hudson v Revett (1829) 5 Bing. 368 .... *22–036*
Hudson v Temple (1860) 29 Beav. 536 .... *21–013*
Hugall v M'Lean (1885) 53 L.T. 94 .... *21–009*
Huggins v Wiseman (1690) Carth.110 .... *8–013*
Hugh Stephenson & Sons Ltd v Carton Nagen Industrie AG; sub nom. Hugh Stevenson & Sons Ltd v Cartonnagen-Industrie AG [1918] A.C. 239, HL *23–031*
Hughes, Ex p. (1872) 4 Ch. D. 34 .... *25–002*
Hughes v Clewley; The Siben (No.2); sub nom. Hughes v Vail Blyth Clewley; The Siben [1996] 1 Lloyd's Rep. 35, QBD (Admlty) 6–066, *6–111*, *16–176*
Hughes v Greenwich LBC [1994] 1 A.C. 170; [1993] 3 W.L.R. 821; [1993] 4 All E.R. 577; [1994] I.C.R. 48; (1994) 26 H.L.R. 99; 92 L.G.R. 61; (1995) 69 P. & C.R. 487; [1993] E.G. 166 (C.S.); (1993) 90(46) L.S.G. 38; (1993) 137 S.J.L.B. 244; [1993] N.P.C. 137, HL; affirming (1992) 24 H.L.R. 605; (1993) 65 P. & C.R. 12; (1993) 157 L.G. Rev. 41; [1992] E.G. 76 (C.S.); [1992] N.P.C. 73, CA (Civ Div) *13–010*
Hughes v Hall (Gillian) [1981] R.T.R. 430; (1981) 125 S.J. 255, DC *14–063*
Hughes v Lenny (1839) 5 M.W. 183 .... *21–053*
Hughes v Liverpool Victoria Legal Friendly Society [1916] 2 K.B. 482, CA *6–013*, 16–186
Hughes v Lloyd [2007] EWHC 3133 (Ch); [2008] W.T.L.R. 473 .... *18–052*
Hughes v Lord Advocate; sub nom. Hughes v Postmaster General [1963] A.C. 837; [1963] 2 W.L.R. 779; [1963] 1 All E.R. 705; 1963 S.C. (H.L.) 31; 1963 S.L.T. 150; (1963) 107 S.J. 232, HL *26–057*
Hughes v Metropolitan Railway Co (1876–77) L.R. 2 App. Cas. 439, HL; affirming (1875–76) L.R. 1 C.P.D. 120, CA ... 3–085, 3–090, 3–094, 3–096, 3–103, 3–104, 3–128, 3–129, 3–132, *3–133*, 3–135, 3–172, 24–007, *24–008*, 28–109
Hughes v Pump House Hotel Co Ltd (No.1) [1902] 2 K.B. 190, CA ... *19–012*, *19–029*
Hughes v Southwark LBC [1988] I.R.L.R. 55 ....*1–195*, *27–023*
Hughes v Statham (1825) 4 B. & C. 1871 ....*16–023*, *16–024*
Hughes v Thorpe (1839) 5 M.W. 656 .... *29–191*
Hughes & Falconer v Newton [1939] 3 All E.R. 869 .... *3–125*
Hughes-Hallett v Indian Mammoth Gold Mines Co (1883) L.R. 22 Ch. D. 561, Ch D *27–008*
Huguenin v Baseley, 33 E.R. 526; (1807) 14 Ves. Jr. 273, Ct of Chancery *7–057*, *7–077*, *7–082*, *7–125*
Huilerie L'Abeille v Societe des Huileries du Niger; The Kastellon [1978] 2 Lloyd's Rep. 203, QBD (Comm) *14–141*, *14–148*
Hulbert v Avens [2003] EWHC 76 (Ch); [2003] W.T.L.R. 387; (2003) 100(12) L.S.G. 30, Ch D *27–079*
Hulse v Chambers [2001] 1 W.L.R. 2386; [2002] 1 All E.R. (Comm) 812; [2002] R.T.R. 24, QBD *30–337*
Hulthen v Stewart & Co [1903] A.C. 389, HL *21–020*
Hulton v Hulton [1917] 1 K.B. 813, CA; affirming [1916] 2 K.B. 642, KBD *6–114*, 6–117
Humble v Hunter (1848) 12 Q.B. 310 .... *12–114*
Hume v Peploe (1807) 8 East 168 .... *21–090*
Hume v Rundell (1842) 2 S. & S. 174 .... *12–063*

Humfrey v Dale (1857) 7 E. & B. 266 .... *12–128*, *13–023*
Humfrey v Dale (1858) 7 E. & B. 1004 .... *12–133*
Hummingbird Motors Ltd v Hobbs [1986] R.T.R. 276; (1988) 85(1) L.S.G. 28, CA (Civ Div) *6–006*, *6–009*
Humphrey v Chapman (1846) 6 L.T.(O.S.) 413 .... *21–088*
Hungerfords v Walker, 171 C.L.R. 125, HC (Aus) *26–098*
Hunt v Bell (1822) 1 Bing. 1 .... *16–014*
Hunt v Bishop (1853) 8 Exch. 675 .... *13–011*
Hunt v Chamberlain (1896) 12 T.L.R. 186 .... *13–018*
Hunt v Fripp [1898] 1 Ch. 675, Ch D *20–054*
Hunt v Power Resources Ltd [2004] All E.R. (D) 23, EAT *16–166*
Hunt v SE Railway (1875) 45 L.J.Q.B. 87 .... *22–028*
Hunt v Severs; sub nom. Severs v Hunt [1994] 2 A.C. 350; [1994] 2 W.L.R. 602; [1994] 2 All E.R. 385; [1994] 2 Lloyd's Rep. 129; [1994] P.I.Q.R. Q60; (1994) 144 N.L.J. 603; (1994) 138 S.J.L.B. 104, HL *18–052*, *18–076*, *26–030*, *29–133*
Hunt v Silk, 102 E.R. 1142; (1804) 5 East 449, KB *29–057*, *29–058*, *29–061*
Hunt v Wimbledon Local Board (1878–79) L.R. 4 C.P.D. 48, CA; affirming (1877–78) L.R. 3 C.P.D. 208, CPD *9–015*, *9–018*
Hunt & Winterbothom (West of England) v BRS Parcels; sub nom. Hunt & Winterbotham (West of England) v British Road Services (Parcels) [1962] 1 Q.B. 617; [1962] 2 W.L.R. 172; [1962] 1 All E.R. 111; [1961] 2 Lloyd's Rep. 422; (1961) 105 S.J. 1124, CA *14–011*, *14–019*
Hunt, Cox Co v Chamberlain (1896) 12 T.L.R. 186 .... *29–117*
Hunter v Bradford Property Trust Ltd, 1970 S.L.T. 173, HL; affirming, 1977 S.L.T. (Notes) 33, OH *3–052*, *3–057*
Hunter v Chief Constable of the West Midlands; McIlkenny v Chief Constable of the West Midlands; Walker v Chief Constable of the West Midlands; Power v Chief Constable of Lancashire [1982] A.C. 529; [1981] 3 W.L.R. 906; [1981] 3 All E.R. 727; (1981) 125 S.J. 829, HL *25–012*, *25–013*, *25–014*
Hunter v Hunt (1845) 1 C.B. 300 .... *29–105*
Hunter v Young (1878–79) L.R. 4 Ex. D. 256, CA *20–013*
Huntoon Co v Kolynos (Inc) [1930] 1 Ch. 528, CA *24–035*
Hurley v Dyke [1979] R.T.R. 265, HL *6–014*, *14–063*
Hurst v Bryk [2002] 1 A.C. 185; [2000] 2 W.L.R. 740; [2000] 2 All E.R. 193; [2000] 2 B.C.L.C. 117; [2000] E.G. 49 (C.S.); (2000) 97(17) L.S.G. 35; (2000) 150 N.L.J. 511; (2000) 144 S.J.L.B. 189, HL *24–037*, *24–048*, **24–049**, *24–051*, *24–052*
Hurst v Evans [1917] 1 K.B. 352, KBD *14–018*
Hurst v Parker (1817) 1 B. & A. 92 .... *28–061*
Hurst v Picture Theatres [1915] 1 K.B. 1, CA *13–028*
Hurstwood Developments Ltd v Motor & General & Andersley & Co Insurance Services Ltd; sub nom. Hurstwood Developments Ltd v Motor & General & Aldersley & Co Insurance Services Ltd [2001] EWCA Civ 1785; [2002] Lloyd's Rep. I.R. 185; [2002] Lloyd's Rep. P.N. 195; [2002] P.N.L.R. 10, CA (Civ Div) *1–184*, *17–030*
Husband Ex p. Dawes, Re (1874–75) L.R. 19 Eq. 438, Ct of Chancery *20–020*
Husband v Davis (1851) 10 C.B. 645 .... *21–049*
Huscombe v Standing (1607) Cro.Jac.187 .... *7–052*
Hussain v Mehlman [1992] 2 E.G.L.R. 87 .... *24–001*
Hussenabai Hassanally v Mohamed Muheeth Mohamed Cassim. *See* Hassanally v Cassim
Hussey v Eels [1990] 2 Q.B. 227; [1990] 2 W.L.R. 234; [1990] 1 All E.R. 449; [1990] 19 E.G. 77; [1989] E.G. 168 (C.S.); (1990) 140 N.L.J. 53, CA (Civ Div) *26–113*, *26–115*, *26–117*
Hussey v Horne-Payne (1878–79) L.R. 4 App. Cas. 311, HL; affirming (1878) L.R. 8 Ch. D. 670, CA *2–029*
Hussey v Palmer [1972] 1 W.L.R. 1286; [1972] 3 All E.R. 744; (1972) 116 S.J. 567, CA (Civ Div) 2–172, *3–139*, *3–158*, *29–008*, *29–011*
Hutchinson v Bowker (1839) 5 M. & W. 535 .... *12–057*, *12–132*

Hutchinson v Tatham (1872–73) L.R. 8 C.P. 482, CCP *12–133*
Hutley v Hutley (1872–73) L.R. 8 Q.B. 112, QBD *16–052*, *16–054*, *16–055*, *16–066*
Huttman v Boulnois (1826) 2 C.P. 510 .... *21–030*
Hutton v Secretary of State for War (1926) 43 T.L.R. 106 .... *10–019*
Hutton v Warren (1836) 1 M. & W. 466 ....*12–131*, *13–018*
Hutton v Watling [1948] Ch. 398; [1948] 1 All E.R. 803; 64 T.L.R. 326; (1948) 92 S.J. 297, CA; affirming [1948] Ch. 26; [1947] 2 All E.R. 641; 63 T.L.R. 615; [1947] W.N. 292; [1948] L.J.R. 223; (1948) 92 S.J. 55, Ch D *12–096*, *12–107*
Huyton SA v Peter Cremer GmbH & Co [1999] 1 Lloyd's Rep. 620; [1999] C.L.C. 230, QBD (Comm) *3–118*, *3–136*, 7–027, *7–029*, *7–031*, *7–032*, *7–041*
Hvalfangerselskapet Polaris A/S v Unilever Ltd; Hvalfangerselskapet Globus A/S v Unilever Ltd (1933) 46 Ll. L. Rep. 29; (1933) 39 Com. Cas. 1, HL *12–118*
Hyams v Coombes (1912) 28 T.L.R. 413 .... *3–050*
Hybart v Packer (1858) 4 C.B.(N.S.) 209 .... *18–010*
Hyde v Watts (1843) 12 M.W. 254 .... *21–021*
Hyde v Wrench (1840) 3 Beav. 334 2–092
Hydraulic Engineering Co Ltd v McHaffie Goslett & Co (1878–79) L.R. 4 Q.B.D. 670, CA *21–02126–061*, *26–062*, *26–066*, *26–077*
Hyeling v Hastings (1699) 1 Ld.Raym. 389 .... *3–032*
Hyett v Great Western Railway Co (GWR) [1948] 1 K.B. 345; [1947] 2 All E.R. 264; 63 T.L.R. 411; [1947] L.J.R. 1243; 177 L.T. 178; (1947) 91 S.J. 434, CA *29–136*
Hyland v JH Barker (North West) [1985] I.C.R. 861; [1985] I.R.L.R. 403; (1985) 82 L.S.G. 2740, EAT *16–202*
Hyleing v Hastings (1699) 1 Ld. Raym. 389 .... *28–092*
Hylton v Hylton (1754) 2 Ves. Sen. 547 .... *7–075*
Hyman v Hyman; Hughes v Hughes [1929] A.C. 601, HL; affirming [1929] P. 1, CA *16–044*
Hyman v Nye & Sons (1880–81) L.R. 6 Q.B.D. 685, QBD *1–129*
Hyundai Heavy Industries Co Ltd v Papadopoulos [1980] 1 W.L.R. 1129; [1980] 2 All E.R. 29; [1980] 2 Lloyd's Rep. 1; (1980) 124 S.J. 592, HL *24–051*, *24–055*, *26–009*, *26–154*, *29–055*, *29–064*, *29–065*
Hyundai Ltd v Pournouras [1978] 2 Lloyd's Rep. 502 .... *24–001*
Hyundai Merchant Marine Co Ltd v Karander Maritime Inc; The Nizuru [1996] 2 Lloyd's Rep. 66; [1996] C.L.C. 749, QBD (Comm) *18–146*, *21–013*
Hyundai Merchant Marine Co v Gesuri Chartering Co; The Peonia [1991] 1 Lloyd's Rep. 100, CA (Civ Div) *12–043*
Hyundai Shipbuilding & Heavy Industries Co v Pournaras; Hyundai Shipbuilding & Heavy Industries Co v Bouboulina Shipping SA [1978] 2 Lloyd's Rep. 502, CA (Civ Div) *12–118*, *24–051*, *24–055*
I Congreso del Partido, The. *See* Owners of Cargo Lately Laden on Board the Playa Larga v Owners of the I Congreso del Partido
IAC (Leasing) v Humphrey (1972) 126 C.L.R. 131 .... *26–140*
ICI Ltd v Shatwell; sub nom. Shatwell v ICI Ltd. [1965] A.C. 656; [1964] 3 W.L.R. 329; [1964] 2 All E.R. 999; (1964) 108 S.J. 578, HL; reversing, *Guardian*, July 17, 1963, CA *16–001*
IDC Group Ltd v Clark (1993) 65 P. & C.R. 179; [1992] 49 E.G. 103; [1992] E.G. 93 (C.S.); [1992] N.P.C. 88, CA (Civ Div); affirming [1992] 1 E.G.L.R. 187; [1992] 08 E.G. 108, Ch D *12–053*
IFE Fund SA v Goldman Sachs International [2007] EWCA Civ 811; [2007] 2 Lloyd's Rep. 449; [2007] 2 C.L.C. 134; (2007) 104(32) L.S.G. 24, CA (Civ Div); affirming [2006] EWHC 2887 (Comm); [2007] 1 Lloyd's Rep. 264; [2006] 2 C.L.C. 1043, QBD (Comm) *6–006*, *6–009*, *6–018*, *6–083*, *6–138*, *14–062*, *14–063*, *14–098*
IM Properties Plc v Cape & Dalgleish [1999] Q.B. 297; [1998] 3 W.L.R. 457; [1998] 3 All E.R. 203; (1998) 95(24) L.S.G. 34; (1998) 95(31) L.S.G. 34; (1998) 148 N.L.J. 906; (1998) 142 S.J.L.B. 174, CA (Civ Div) *26–174*
IMI Cornelius (UK) Ltd v Alan J Bloor, 57 B.L.R. 108; 35 Con. L.R. 1, QBD *18–053*

ISOFT Group Plc v Misys Holdings Ltd [2003] EWCA Civ 229; [2003] All E.R. (D) 438 (Feb), CA (Civ Div); affirming [2002] EWHC 2094 (Ch), Ch D *2–009*, *2–126*
ISS Machinery Services Ltd v Aeolian Shipping SA; The Aeolian. *See* Aeolian Shipping SA v ISS Machinery Services Ltd; The Aeolian
Ian Stach Ltd v Baker Bosly Ltd; sub nom. Ian Stach Ltd v Baker Bosley Ltd [1958] 2 Q.B. 130; [1958] 2 W.L.R. 419; [1958] 1 All E.R. 542; [1958] 1 Lloyd's Rep. 127; (1958) 102 S.J. 177, QBD *12–037*
Ibberson v Neck (1886) 2 T.L.R. 427 .... *3–119*
Ideal Films Ltd v Richards [1927] 1 K.B. 374, CA *9–068*
Igbo v Johnson, Matthey Chemicals Ltd [1986] I.C.R. 505; 130 S.J. 524; [1986] I.R.L.R. 215; 83 L.S.Gaz. 2089, CA; reversing [1986] I.C.R. 82; [1985] I.R.L.R. 189; 82 L.S.Gaz. 1011, EAT *22–055*
Ignazio Messina & Co v Polskie Linie Oceaniczne [1995] 2 Lloyd's Rep. 566, QBD (Comm) *2–003*, *2–004*, *2–029*, *2–116*, *2–126*, *2–149*, *2–161*, *2–166*
Ikariada, The. *See* Orinoco Navigation Ltd v Ecotrade SpA; The Ikariada
Ikimi v Ikimi (Divorce: Habitual Residence) [2001] EWCA Civ 873; [2002] Fam. 72; [2001] 3 W.L.R. 672; [2001] 2 F.L.R. 1288; [2001] 2 F.C.R. 385; [2001] Fam. Law 660; (2001) 98(27) L.S.G. 38; (2001) 145 S.J.L.B. 163, CA (Civ Div) *30–079*
Ikin v Bradley (1818) 8 Taunt. 250 .... *26–167*
Ilyssia Compania Naviera SA v Ahmed Abdul-Qawi Bamaodah; The Elli 2; Kition Compania Naviera v Ahmed Abdul-Qawi Bamaodah; Lemython Compania Naviera v Ahmed Abdul-Qawi Bamaodah [1985] 1 Lloyd's Rep. 107, CA (Civ Div) *30–010*, *30–011*
Imperial Bank of Canada v Bank of Hamilton [1903] A.C. 49, PC (Can) *25–024*, *29–030*, *29–036*, *29–182*
Imperial Gas Light and Coke Co v Broadbent, 11 E.R. 239; (1859) 7 H.L. Cas. 600, QB *28–135*
Imperial Land Co of Marseilles, Re; sub nom. Harris's Case (1871–72) L.R. 7 Ch. App. 587, CA in Chancery *2–024*, *2–032*, *2–054*
Imperial Loan Co Ltd v Stone [1892] 1 Q.B. 599, CA 8–068, *8–070*, *8–080*
Imperial Mercantile Credit Association (In Liquidation) v Coleman; sub nom. Liquidators of the Imperial Mercantile Credit Association v Edward John Coleman and John Watson Knight; Imperial Mercantile Credit Association (In Liquidation) v Knight (1873) L.R. 6 H.L. 189, HL *9–055*
Imperial Mercantile Credit Association, Re; sub nom. Curtis's Case (1868) L.R. 6 Eq. 455, Ct of Chancery *8–038*
Imperial Tobacco Co Ltd v Parslay [1936] 2 All E.R. 515, CA *26–011*, *26–127*, *26–129*
Impex Transport A/S v Thames Holding AG [1981] 1 W.L.R. 1547; [1982] 1 All E.R. 897; [1981] 2 Lloyd's Rep. 566; [1981] Com. L.R. 153, QBD (Comm) *28–123*
Import Export Metro Ltd v Compania Sud Americana de Vapores SA [2003] EWHC 11; [2003] 1 All E.R. (Comm) 703; [2003] 1 Lloyd's Rep. 405; [2004] 2 C.L.C. 757, QBD (Comm) *30–332*, *30–334*
Imutran Ltd v Uncaged Campaigns Ltd [2001] 2 All E.R. 385; [2001] C.P. Rep. 28; [2001] E.C.D.R. 16; [2001] E.M.L.R. 21; [2001] H.R.L.R. 31; [2002] F.S.R. 2; (2001) 24(5) I.P.D. 24031; (2001) 98(14) L.S.G. 40, Ch D ...*27–010*, *27–061*
Inchbald v Western Neilgherry Coffee, etc., Co (1864) 17 C.B.(N.S.) 733 ....*13–012*, *29–068*
Inche Noriah v Shaik Allie bin Omar [1929] A.C. 127; [1928] All E.R. Rep. 189; (1929) 45 T.L.R. 1; (1928) 98 L.J. P.C. 1, PC (Sing) *7–093*, 7–096
Income Tax Commissioner v Maharajadhiraja of Darbhanga (1933) L.R. 60 I.A. 146 .... *21–067*
Independent Air Travel Ltd, Re [1961] 1 Lloyd's Rep. 604, Ch D *18–082*
Independent Broadcasting Authority v EMI Electronics Ltd; sub nom. IBA v EMI Electronics Ltd and BICC Construction Ltd, 14 B.L.R. 1; [1955–95] P.N.L.R. 179, HL; affirming, 11 B.L.R. 29, CA *2–166*, *6–086*, *12–007*, 18–009
Independent Grocers Ltd v Noble Lowndes Superannuation Consultants Ltd [1993] 60 S.A.S.R. 525 .... *29–021*

Independiente Ltd v Music Trading On-Line (HK) Ltd [2007] EWCA Civ 111; [2008] 1 W.L.R. 608; [2007] 4 All E.R. 736; (2007) 151 S.J.L.B. 159, CA (Civ Div); affirming [2006] EWHC 3081 (Ch); (2006) 103(45) L.S.G. 28, Ch D *18–004*
Indescon Ltd v Ogden [2004] EWHC 2326; [2005] 1 Lloyd's Rep. 31; [2005] B.L.R. 152, QBD *2–006*
India v India Steamship Co Ltd; The Indian Endurance and The Indian Grace (No.1) [1993] A.C. 410; [1993] 2 W.L.R. 461; [1993] 1 All E.R. 998; [1993] 1 Lloyd's Rep. 387; [1994] I.L.Pr. 498, HL *25–011*, *25–012*, 25–016, *30–337*
India v India Steamship Co Ltd; The Indian Endurance and The Indian Grace (No.2) [1998] A.C. 878; [1997] 3 W.L.R. 818; [1997] 4 All E.R. 380; [1998] 1 Lloyd's Rep. 1; [1997] C.L.C. 1581; [1998] I.L.Pr. 511; (1997) 94(43) L.S.G. 29; (1997) 147 N.L.J. 1581; (1997) 141 S.J.L.B. 230, HL; affirming [1997] 2 W.L.R. 538; [1996] 3 All E.R. 641; [1996] 2 Lloyd's Rep. 12; [1996] C.L.C. 1548, CA (Civ Div); reversing [1994] 2 Lloyd's Rep. 331; [1994] C.L.C. 967, QBD (Admlty) .. *3–103*, *3–107*, *3–110*, *5–082*, *25–013*, *25–016*
India v Taylor; sub nom. Delhi Electric Supply & Traction Co Ltd, Re [1955] A.C. 491; [1955] 2 W.L.R. 303; [1955] 1 All E.R. 292; 48 R. & I.T. 98; (1955) 34 A.T.C. 10; [1955] T.R. 9; (1955) 99 S.J. 94, HL; affirming [1954] Ch. 131; [1953] 3 W.L.R. 1085; [1953] 2 All E.R. 1452; 46 R. & I.T. 817; (1953) 32 A.T.C. 413; [1953] T.R. 385; (1953) 97 S.J. 861, CA; affirming (1953) 32 A.T.C. 341; [1953] T.R. 325, Ch D *16–031*, *20–023*, *29–043*
Indian Grace, The. *See* India v India Steamship C
India High Commissioner v Ghosh [1960] 1 Q.B. 134; [1959] 3 W.L.R. 811; [1959] 3 All E.R. 659; (1959) 103 S.J. 939, CA *11–021*
Indian Oil Corp Ltd v Greenstone Shipping Co SA (Panama); The Ypatianna; Greenstone Shipping Co SA v Indian Oil Corp Ltd [1988] Q.B. 345; [1987] 3 All E.R. 893; [1987] 2 Lloyd's Rep. 286; [1987] 2 F.T.L.R. 95; (1987) 84 L.S.G. 2768; (1987) 131 S.J. 1121, QBD (Comm) *29–052*, *29–163*, *29–170*
Indian Oil Corp Ltd v Vanol Inc [1992] 2 Lloyd's Rep. 563, CA (Civ Div); reversing [1991] 2 Lloyd's Rep. 634, QBD (Comm) *12–072*, *28–112*
Industrial Development and Land Co v Goldschmidt (1921) 206 P. 134 .... *23–054*
Industrial Development Consultants Ltd v Cooley [1972] 1 W.L.R. 443; [1972] 2 All E.R. 162; (1972) 116 S.J. 255, Assizes (Birmingham) *9–055*, *29–156*, *29–160*
Industrie Chimiche Italia Centrale and Cerealfin SA v Alexander G Tsavliris & Sons Maritime Co; The Choko Star (1990); Industrie Chimiche Italia Centrale v Pancristo Shipping Co SA; Industrie Chimiche Italia Centrale v Bula Shipping Corp [1990] 1 Lloyd's Rep. 516, CA (Civ Div); reversing [1989] 2 Lloyd's Rep. 42, QBD (Admlty) *13–003*, *13–004*, *13–010*
Industrie Chimiche Italia Centrale v Alexander G Tsavliris & Sons Maritime Co; The Choko Star; Industrie Chimiche Italia Centrale v Pancristo Shipping Co SA; Industrie Chimiche Italia Centrale v Bula Shipping Corp [1996] 1 W.L.R. 774; [1996] 1 All E.R. 114; [1995] 2 Lloyd's Rep. 608; [1995] C.L.C. 1461, QBD (Comm) *28–121*
Industrie Chimiche Italia Centrale v NEA Ninemia Shipping Co SA; The Emmanuel C [1983] 1 All E.R. 686; [1983] 1 Lloyd's Rep. 310; [1983] Com. L.R. 7, QBD (Comm) *14–013*
Industries and General Mortgage Co Ltd v Lewis [1949] 2 All E.R. 573; [1949] W.N. 333; (1949) 93 S.J. 577, KBD *29–139*, *29–156*
Ingall v Moran [1944] K.B. 160, CA *20–004*
Ingham v Emes [1955] 2 Q.B. 366; [1955] 3 W.L.R. 245; [1955] 2 All E.R. 740; (1955) 99 S.J. 490, CA *13–030*
Ingle v Richards (1860) 28 Beav. 366 .... *25–005*
Inglis v Buttery. A&J Inglis v John Buttery & Co
Ingram v Little [1961] 1 Q.B. 31; [1960] 3 W.L.R. 504; [1960] 3 All E.R. 332; (1960) 104 S.J. 704, CA ... *1–082*, *1–170*, *5–009*, *5–089*, *5–091*, 5–093, *5–099*, *6–129*
Initial Services v Putterill [1968] 1 Q.B. 396; [1967] 3 W.L.R. 1032; [1967] 3 All E.R. 145; 2 K.I.R. 863; (1967) 111 S.J. 541, CA (Civ Div) ... *16–004*, *16–005*, *16–035*
IRC v Fry [2001] S.T.C. 1715; [2002] B.T.C. 3; [2001] S.T.I. 1665; (2002) 99(6) L.S.G. 30; (2001) 151 N.L.J. 1820; (2001) 145 S.J.L.B. 279, Ch D *2–027*, *22–022*

IRC v Hashmi; sub nom. Hashmi v Inland Revenue Commissioners [2002] EWCA Civ 981; [2002] B.C.C. 943; [2002] 2 B.C.L.C. 489; [2002] B.P.I.R. 974; [2002] W.T.L.R. 1027, CA (Civ Div); affirming [2002] B.P.I.R. 271; [2002] W.T.L.R. 19; (2001) 98(41) L.S.G. 34, Ch D *20–031*
IRC v Mills (Hayley); sub nom. Mills (Hayley) v Inland Revenue Commissioners [1975] A.C. 38; [1974] 2 W.L.R. 325; [1974] 1 All E.R. 722; [1974] S.T.C. 130; 49 T.C. 367; [1974] T.R. 39; (1974) 118 S.J. 205, HL; reversing [1973] Ch. 225; [1972] 3 W.L.R. 980; [1972] 3 All E.R. 977; [1973] S.T.C. 1; [1972] T.R. 245; (1972) 116 S.J. 802, CA (Civ Div); reversing [1972] 1 W.L.R. 473; [1972] 2 All E.R. 86; [1971] T.R. 501; (1972) 116 S.J. 297, Ch D *8–029*
IRC v Raphael; Inland Revenue Commissioners v Ezra [1935] A.C. 96, HL; affirming [1933] Ch. 858, CA *12–043*, *12–0019*
Inman v Inman (1872–73) L.R. 15 Eq. 260, Ct of Chancery *8–050*, *8–066*
Inman v Stamp (1815) 1 Stark. 12 .... *4–011*
Innes v Stephenson (1831) 1 Moo. Rob. 145 .... *21–049*
Innholders Co v Wainwright (1917) 33 T.L.R. 356 .... *23–049*, *23–066*
Inntrepreneur Pub Co (CPC) Ltd v Sweeney [2002] EWHC 1060 (Ch); [2003] E.C.C. 17; [2002] 2 E.G.L.R. 132; [2002] 25 E.G. 152 (C.S.); (2002) 99(26) L.S.G. 36; (2002) 146 S.J.L.B. 144, Ch D *6–069*
Inntrepreneur Pub Co Ltd v East Crown Ltd; sub nom. Inntrepreneur Pub Co (GL) v East Crown Ltd [2000] 2 Lloyd's Rep. 611; [2000] 3 E.G.L.R. 31; [2000] 41 E.G. 209; [2000] N.P.C. 93, Ch D *2–166*, 4–076, *12–003*, *12–005*, *12–043*, *12–104*, *14–063*
Institution of Mechanical Engineers v Cane; Institution of Mechanical Engineers v Westminster City Council [1961] A.C. 696; [1960] 3 W.L.R. 978; [1960] 3 All E.R. 715; (1961) 125 J.P. 141; 59 L.G.R. 1; 7 R.R.C. 79; 53 R. & I.T. 785; (1960) 104 S.J. 1032, HL; affirming [1960] 1 Q.B. 388; [1960] 2 W.L.R. 48; [1960] 1 All E.R. 129; (1960) 124 J.P. 96; 58 L.G.R. 34; 5 R.R.C. 344; (1960) 104 S.J. 31, CA; reversing 3 R.R.C. 155; 51 R. & I.T. 346; [1958] J.P.L. 370; 108 L.J. 332, Lands Tr *9–004*
Insurance Co of Africa v Scor (UK) Reinsurance Co Ltd [1985] 1 Lloyd's Rep. 312, CA (Civ Div); reversing in part [1983] 1 Lloyd's Rep. 541; [1983] Com. L.R. 81, QBD (Comm) *13–003*
Insurance Co v Lloyd's Syndicate [1995] 1 Lloyd's Rep. 272; [1994] C.L.C. 1303; [1995] 4 Re. L.R. 37, QBD (Comm) *27–031*, *27–060*
Intense Investments Ltd v Development Ventures Ltd [2006] EWHC 1628 (TCC),[2006] All E.R. (D) 346 (Jun), QBD (TCC) *22–025*
Intercontainer Interfrigo (ICF) SC v Balkenende Oosthuizen BV (C–133/08) (pending) [2008] O.J. C158/10 .... *30–019, 30–086, 30–090, 30–188*
Interdesco SA v Nullifire Ltd [1992] 1 Lloyd's Rep. 180; [1992] I.L.Pr. 97, QBD (Comm) *25–017*
Interfoto Picture Library Ltd v Stiletto Visual Programmes Ltd [1989] Q.B. 433; [1988] 2 W.L.R. 615; [1988] 1 All E.R. 348; (1988) 7 Tr. L.R. 187; (1988) 85(9) L.S.G. 45; (1987) 137 N.L.J. 1159; (1988) 132 S.J. 460, CA (Civ Div) ... *1–022*, *2–007*, *2–030*, *2–111*, *12–015*, *14–135*, *15–001*, *15–076*, *26–136*
Interleasing (UK) Ltd v Morris [2003] EWCA Civ 40, CA (Civ Div); affirming [2002] EWHC 1086; [2002] 2 Lloyd's Rep. 563; (2002) 99(30) L.S.G. 37, Ch D *13–010*
International Bulk Shipping and Services Ltd v Minerals and Metals Trading Corp of India; International Bulk Shipping and Services Ltd v President of India; Himoff Maritime Enterprises Ltd v President of India [1996] 1 All E.R. 1017; [1996] 2 Lloyd's Rep. 474, CA (Civ Div) *28–060*, *28–118*
International Consulting Services (UK) Ltd v Hart [2000] I.R.L.R. 227, QBD *16–107*
International Contract Co Re; sub nom. Levita's Case (1867–68) L.R. 3 Ch. App. 36, CA in Chancery *2–045*
International Contract Co, Re; sub nom. Ind's Case (1871–72) L.R. 7 Ch. App. 485, CA in Chancery *5–133*
International Correspondence Schools v Ayres (1912) 106 L.T. 845 .... *24–010*

International Distillers and Vinters Ltd (t/a Percy Fox & Co) v JF Hillebrand (UK) Ltd, *The Times*, January 25, 2000, QBD *28–119*
International Fina Services AG (formerly Finapetro AG) v Katrina Shipping Ltd; The Fina Samco [1995] 2 Lloyd's Rep. 344; [1995] C.L.C. 1335, CA (Civ Div); affirming [1994] 1 Lloyd's Rep. 153, QBD (Comm) ..*12–055*, *12–057*, *12–063*, *12–118*
International General Electric Co of New York v Customs and Excise Commissioners [1962] Ch. 784; [1962] 3 W.L.R. 20; [1962] 2 All E.R. 398; [1962] R.P.C. 235; (1962) 106 S.J. 327, CA *10–017*
International Minerals & Chemical Corp v Karl O Helm AG [1986] 1 Lloyd's Rep. 81, QBD (Comm) *26–098*, *30–340*
International Petroleum Refining & Supply Sociedad LTDA v Caleb Brett & Son Ltd; The Busiris; sub nom. International Petroleum Refining & Supply Sociedad v Caleb Brett & Son, Caleb Brett & Son (Continentaal) BV, Caleb Brett & Son Italia SpA and Petrinspecteur Srl; The Busiris [1980] 1 Lloyd's Rep. 569, CA (Civ Div) *3–039*, *18–008*
International Railway Co v Niagara Parks Commission [1941] A.C. 328, PC (Can); reversing [1940] O.R. 33, CA (Ont) *10–013*
International Sales & Agencies Ltd v Marcus [1982] 3 All E.R. 551; [1982] 2 C.M.L.R. 46, QBD *9–033*, *9–041*, *16–193*, *29–158*
International Sea Tankers Inc of Liberia v Hemisphere Shipping Co of Hong Kong; The Wenjiang [1982] 2 All E.R. 437; [1982] 1 Lloyd's Rep. 128; [1982] Com. L.R. 7; (1982) 126 S.J. 524, CA (Civ Div) *23–015*, *23–035*
International Sea Tankers Inc of Liberia v Hemisphere Shipping Co Ltd of Hong Kong; The Wenjiang (No.2) [1983] 1 Lloyd's Rep. 400; [1983] Com. L.R. 16, QBD (Comm) *23–030*, *23–044*
International Sponge Importers Ltd v Andrew Watt & Sons [1911] A.C. 279; 1911 S.C. (H.L.) 57; 1911 1 S.L.T. 414, HL *21–043*, *21–044*
International Tin Council, Re [1989] Ch. 309; [1988] 3 W.L.R. 1159; [1988] 3 All E.R. 257; (1988) 4 B.C.C. 653; [1989] P.C.C. 90; (1988) 132 S.J. 1494, CA (Civ Div); affirming [1987] Ch. 419; [1987] 2 W.L.R. 1229; [1987] 1 All E.R. 890; (1987) 3 B.C.C. 103; [1987] B.C.L.C. 272; [1987] P.C.C. 283; [1987] 1 F.T.L.R. 305; (1987) 84 L.S.G. 1732; (1987) 131 S.J. 690, Ch D *11–018*
Internationale Guano, v Macandreir & Co [1909] 2 K.B. 360 .... *14–029*
Internaut Shipping GmbH v Fercometal Sarl [2003] EWCA Civ 812; [2003] 2 All E.R. (Comm) 760; [2003] 2 Lloyd's Rep. 430, CA (Civ Div); affirming [2002] EWHC 1230 (Comm), QBD (Comm) *12–075*, *12–114*
Internet Trading Clubs Ltd v Freeserve (Investments) Ltd [2001] E.B.L.R. 142, QBD *24–003*, *27–024*, *27–044*
Interoffice Telephones v Freeman (Robert) Co [1958] 1 Q.B. 190; [1957] 3 W.L.R. 971; [1957] 3 All E.R. 479; (1957) 101 S.J. 958, CA *26–009*, *26–060*, *26–069*, *26–127*
Intertradex SA v Lesieur-Tourteaux Sarl [1978] 2 Lloyd's Rep. 509, CA (Civ Div); affirming [1977] 2 Lloyd's Rep. 146, QBD (Comm) ..*14–148*, *14–150*, *14–151*, *23–035*, *23–064*
Intpro Properties (UK) v Sauvel [1983] 2 W.L.R. 908; [1983] 2 All E.R. 495; (1983) 267 E.G. 515; (1983) 127 S.J. 325, CA (Civ Div); reversing [1983] Q.B. 1019; [1983] 2 W.L.R. 1; [1983] 1 All E.R. 658; (1983) 127 S.J. 16, QBD *11–005*, *11–011*, *11–012*
Introductions Ltd, Re (No.1); sub nom. Introductions Ltd v National Provincial Bank [1970] Ch. 199; [1969] 2 W.L.R. 791; [1969] 1 All E.R. 887; [1969] 1 Lloyd's Rep. 229; (1969) 113 S.J. 122, CA (Civ Div); affirming [1968] 2 All E.R. 1221, Ch D *9–033*
Invercargill City Council v Hamlin [1996] A.C. 624; [1996] 2 W.L.R. 367; [1996] 1 All E.R. 756; 78 B.L.R. 78; 50 Con. L.R. 105; (1996) 146 N.L.J. 246; (1996) 140 S.J.L.B. 86, PC (NZ); affirming, 72 B.L.R. 39; (1995) 11 Const. L.J. 285, CA (NZ) *18–027*

Inverkip Steamship Co Ltd v Bunge & Co [1917] 2 K.B. 193, CA *24–040*
Inverugie Investments Ltd v Hackett [1995] 1 W.L.R. 713; [1995] 3 All E.R. 841; [1996] 1 E.G.L.R. 149; [1996] 19 E.G. 124; [1995] E.G. 37 (C.S.); [1995] N.P.C. 36; (1995) 69 P. & C.R. D48, PC (Bah) *26–022*, *29–142*
Investors Compensation Scheme Ltd v West Bromwich Building Society (No.1); Investors Compensation Scheme Ltd v Hopkin & Sons; Alford v West Bromwich Building Society; Armitage v West Bromwich Building Society [1998] 1 W.L.R. 896; [1998] 1 All E.R. 98; [1998] 1 B.C.L.C. 531; [1997] C.L.C. 1243; [1997] P.N.L.R. 541; (1997) 147 N.L.J. 989, HL; reversing [1998] 1 B.C.L.C. 521; [1997] C.L.C. 348; [1997] P.N.L.R. 166; [1997] N.P.C. 104, CA (Civ Div); affirming [1998] 1 B.C.L.C. 493, Ch D *1–010*, *1–031*, *1–040*, *12–043*, *12–045*, 12–050, 12–055, 12–080, *12–118*, *12–119*, 12–120, 19–010, *22–005*, *22–049*
Investors in Industry Commercial Properties Ltd v South Bedfordshire DC [1986] Q.B. 1034; [1986] 2 W.L.R. 937; [1986] 1 All E.R. 787; 32 B.L.R. 1; 5 Con. L.R. 1; [1986] 1 E.G.L.R. 252; (1986) 2 Const. L.J. 108; (1986) 83 L.S.G. 441; (1986) 136 N.L.J. 118; (1986) 130 S.J. 71, CA (Civ Div) *19–084*
Inwards v Baker [1965] 2 Q.B. 29; [1965] 2 W.L.R. 212; [1965] 1 All E.R. 446; (1965) 109 S.J. 75, CA *3–139*, 3–151, 3–157, *13–028*, *29–161*
Ionides v Pacific Fire & Marine Insurance Co (1871–72) L.R. 7 Q.B. 517, Ex Chamber; affirming (1870–71) L.R. 6 Q.B. 674, QB *2–117*
Ionides v Pender (1873–74) L.R. 9 Q.B. 531, QB *6–146*
Iran Continental Shelf Oil Co v IRI International Corp [2002] EWCA Civ 1024; [2004] 2 C.L.C. 696, CA (Civ Div) *30–020*, *30–024*, *30–051*, *30–077*, *30–078*, *30–090*
Iran Vojdan, The. *See* Dubai Electricity Co v Islamic Republic of Iran Shipping Lines
Irani v Irani [2000] 1 Lloyd's Rep. 412; [2000] C.L.C. 477, CA (Civ Div) *27–032*
Irani v Irani [2006] EWHC 1811 (Ch); [2006] W.T.L.R. 1561, Ch D *2–120*, *15–086*, *15–116*
Irani v Southampton and South West Hampshire HA [1985] I.C.R. 590; [1985] I.R.L.R. 203; (1985) 82 L.S.G. 1167, Ch D *16–102*, *27–023*
Irani Finance Ltd v Singh [1971] Ch. 59; [1970] 3 W.L.R. 330; [1970] 3 All E.R. 199; (1970) 21 P. & C.R. 843; (1970) 114 S.J. 636, CA (Civ Div); affirming [1970] 2 W.L.R. 117; [1969] 3 All E.R. 1455; (1970) 21 P. & C.R. 16; (1969) 113 S.J. 816, Ch D *4–011*, *4–013*
Irish Shell v Elm Motors [1984] I.R. 200, Sup Ct (Irl) *16–085*
Irish Shipping Ltd v Commercial Union Assurance Co Plc; The Irish Rowan [1991] 2 Q.B. 206; [1990] 2 W.L.R. 117; [1989] 3 All E.R. 853; [1989] 2 Lloyd's Rep. 144; (1990) 87(5) L.S.G. 39; (1990) 134 S.J. 426, CA (Civ Div) *9–067*
Iron Trades Mutual Insurance Co Ltd v JK Buckenham Ltd [1990] 1 All E.R. 808; [1989] 2 Lloyd's Rep. 85, QBD (Comm) *1–124*, *1–167*, *28–010*, *28–011*, *28–033*, *28–034*
Irvani v Irvani [2000] 1 Lloyd's Rep. 412; [2000] C.L.C. 477, CA (Civ Div) *7–129*, *7–132*, *7–136*, *8–068*, *8–080*
Irvine v Union Bank of Australia (1876–77) L.R. 2 App. Cas. 366, PC (Ind) *9–035*, *9–040*
Isaac Cooke & Sons v Eshelby (1887) L.R. 12 App. Cas. 271, HL *21–044*
Isaac Naylor & Sons Ltd v New Zealand Co-operative Wool Marketing Association Ltd [1981] 1 N.Z.L.R. 361 .... *30–340*
Isaacs v Green (1866–67) L.R. 2 Ex. 352, Ex Ct *18–122*
Isaacs v Royal Insurance Co (1869–70) L.R. 5 Ex. 296, Ex Ct *12–093*
Isaacs & Sons v Salbstein; sub nom. Salbstein v Isaacs & Son [1916] 2 K.B. 139, CA *25–008*
Isherwood v Whitmore (1843) 11 M.W. 347 .... *21–083*

Islamic Arab Insurance Co v Saudi Egyptian American Reinsurance Co [1987] 1 Lloyd's Rep. 315; [1987] E.C.C. 434, CA (Civ Div) *30–013*
Islamic Republic of Iran v Barakat Galleries Ltd [2007] EWCA Civ 1374; [2008] 1 All E.R. 1177 .... *30–367*
Island Records Ltd v Tring International Plc [1996] 1 W.L.R. 1256; [1995] 3 All E.R. 444; [1995] F.S.R. 560, Ch D *29–146*
Island Tug and Barge Ltd v Owners of the Makedonia [1958] 1 Q.B. 365; [1958] 2 W.L.R. 256; [1958] 1 All E.R. 236; [1957] 2 Lloyd's Rep. 575; (1957) 36 A.T.C. 376; [1958] T.R. 63; 1958 A.M.C. 1300; (1958) 102 S.J. 124, QBD ... *26–164*
Islander Trucking Ltd v Hogg Robinson & Gardner Mountain (Marine) Ltd [1990] 1 All E.R. 826, QBD (Comm) *28–033*, *28–034*
Islander Trucking Ltd (In Liquidation) Ltd v Robinson & Gardner Mountain (Marine) Ltd [1990] 1 All E.R. 826, QBD (Comm) *18–027*
Islington LBC v Uckac [2006] EWCA Civ 340; [2006] 1 W.L.R. 1303; [2006] 1 F.C.R. 668; [2006] H.L.R. 35; [2006] L. & T.R. 10; [2006] N.P.C. 39, CA (Civ Div) *5–058*, *6–111*
Islwyn BC v Newport BC (1994) 6 Admin. L.R. 386; (1994) 158 L.G. Rev. 501, CA (Civ Div) *23–021*, *23–022*
Ispahani v Bank Melli Iran [1998] Lloyd's Rep. Bank. 133, CA (Civ Div) *16–032*, *30–361*, *30–355*, *30–364*, *30–367*
Israel v Douglas (1789) 1 H.Bl. 239 .... *29–194*
Istros, The. *See* Bunge AG v Giuseppe Rocco & Figli; The Istros II
Italmare Shipping Co v Ocean Tanker Co Inc; The Rio Sun (No.2) [1982] 3 All E.R. 273; [1982] 1 Lloyd's Rep. 404; [1982] Com. L.R. 27, QBD (Comm) *3–090*, *21–013*
Italmare Shipping Co v Ocean Tanker Co Inc; The Rio Sun [1982] 1 W.L.R. 158; [1982] 1 All E.R. 517; [1981] 2 Lloyd's Rep. 489; [1981] Com. L.R. 233; (1981) 125 S.J. 859, CA (Civ Div) *3–090*
Item Software (UK) Ltd v Fassihi; sub nom. Fassihi v Item Software (UK) Ltd [2004] EWCA Civ 1244; [2004] B.C.C. 994; [2005] 2 B.C.L.C. 91; [2005] I.C.R. 450; [2004] I.R.L.R. 928; (2004) 101(39) L.S.G. 34; (2004) 148 S.J.L.B. 1153, CA (Civ Div) *21–030*, *29–070*
Itex Itagrani Export SA v Care Shipping Corp; The Cebu (No.2) [1993] Q.B. 1; [1991] 3 W.L.R. 609; [1992] 1 All E.R. 91; [1990] 2 Lloyd's Rep. 316, QBD (Comm) *12–057*
It's a Wrap (UK) Ltd (In Liquidation) v Gula [2006] EWCA Civ 544; [2006] B.C.C. 626; [2006] 2 B.C.L.C. 634; (2006) 103(21) L.S.G. 24, CA (Civ Div) *29–174*
J, Re [1909] 1 Ch. 574, CA *8–011*, *8–074*
J (A Minor) (Abduction: Custody Rights), Re; sub nom. C v S (Minors) (Abduction: Illegitimate Child) [1990] 2 A.C. 562; [1990] 3 W.L.R. 492; [1990] 2 All E.R. 961; [1990] 2 F.L.R. 442; [1991] F.C.R. 129; [1991] Fam. Law 57; (1990) 154 J.P.N. 674; (1990) 87(35) L.S.G. 39; (1990) 140 N.L.J. 1191; (1990) 134 S.J. 1039, HL *30–079*
J&A Developments Ltd v Edina Manufacturing Ltd [2006] N.I. 85; [2007] C.I.L.L. 2417, QBD (NI) 10–037, *10–038*
J&E Kish v Charles Taylor & Sons & Co; sub nom. Kish v Taylor [1912] A.C. 604, HL; reversing [1911] 1 K.B. 625, CA; reversing in part [1910] 2 K.B. 309, KBD *14–032*
J&H Davison Ex p. Chandler, Re (1883–84) L.R. 13 Q.B.D. 50, QBD *17–016*
J&H Ritchie Ltd v Lloyd Ltd; sub nom. JH Ritchie Ltd v Lloyd Ltd [2007] UKHL 9; [2007] Bus. L.R. 944; [2007] 1 W.L.R. 670; [2007] 2 All E.R. 353; [2007] 1 All E.R. (Comm) 987; [2007] 1 Lloyd's Rep. 544; 2007 S.C. (H.L.) 89; 2007 S.L.T. 377; [2007] 1 C.L.C. 208; (2007) 157 N.L.J. 403; (2007) 151 S.J.L.B. 397; 2007 G.W.D. *9–171*, HL; reversing 2005 1 S.C. 155; 2005 S.L.T. 64; 2005 S.C.L.R. 447; 2005 G.W.D. 2–38, IH (Ex Div) *1–032*, *13–006*, *13–007*

J D'Almeida Araujo LDA v Sir Frederick Becker & Co Ltd; sub nom. J D'Almaido Aruajo LDA v Sir Frederick Becker & Co Ltd [1953] 2 Q.B. 329; [1953] 3 W.L.R. 57; [1953] 2 All E.R. 288; [1953] 2 Lloyd's Rep. 30; (1953) 97 S.J. 404, QBD *26–051*, *30–337*

J Defries & Sons Ltd, Re; sub nom. Eichholz v. J Defries & Sons Ltd [1909] 2 Ch. 423, Ch D *21–076*

J Evans & Son (Portsmouth) Ltd v Andrea Merzario Ltd [1976] 1 W.L.R. 1078; [1976] 2 All E.R. 930; [1976] 2 Lloyd's Rep. 165; (1976) 120 S.J. 734, CA (Civ Div); reversing [1975] 1 Lloyd's Rep. 162, QBD 2–187, *12–004*, *12–005*, *12–097*, *12–103*, *14–008*, *14–031*, *14–134*

J Gordon Alison & Co Ltd v Wallsend Shipway and Engineering Co Ltd (1927) 43 T.L.R. 323 14–005

J Jarvis & Sons Ltd v Castle Wharf Developments Ltd; J Jarvis & Sons Ltd v Gleeds Management Services Ltd; J Jarvis & Sons Ltd v Franklin Ellis Architects Ltd; Castle Wharf Developments Ltd v J Jarvis & Sons Ltd [2001] EWCA Civ 19; [2001] Lloyd's Rep. P.N. 308; (2001) 17 Const. L.J. 430; [2001] N.P.C. 15, CA (Civ Div) *18–022*

J Lauritzen AS v Wijsmuller BV; The Super Servant Two [1990] 1 Lloyd's Rep. 1, CA (Civ Div); affirming [1989] 1 Lloyd's Rep. 148, QBD (Comm) *12–082*, *13–004*, *13–008*, *14–137*, *14–138*, *14–146*, *14–148*, *21–007*, 23–007, *23–016*, *23–061*, 23–062, 23–063, 23–064, *23–066*, 23–069, *23–071*

J Leslie Engineers Co Ltd (In Liquidation), Re [1976] 1 W.L.R. 292; [1976] 2 All E.R. 85; (1976) 120 S.J. 146, Ch D *29–163*, *29–166*

J Pereira Fernandes SA v Mehta; sub nom. Metha v J Pereira Fernandes SA [2006] EWHC 813 (Ch); [2006] 1 W.L.R. 1543; [2006] 2 All E.R. 891; [2006] 1 All E.R. (Comm) 885; [2006] 2 Lloyd's Rep. 244; [2006] Info. T.L.R. 203, Ch D *4–006*, *4–027*

J Rosenthal & Sons v Esmail (t/a HMH Esmail & Sons) [1965] 1 W.L.R. 1117; [1965] 2 All E.R. 860; [1965] 2 Lloyd's Rep. 171; (1965) 109 S.J. 553, HL *21–037*, *24–011*, *24–023*, *24–054*

J Sainsbury Ltd v Savage; sub nom. Savage v J Sainsbury Ltd [1981] I.C.R. 1; [1980] I.R.L.R. 109, CA (Civ Div) *24–013*

J Spurling Ltd v Bradshaw [1956] 1 W.L.R. 461; [1956] 2 All E.R. 121; [1956] 1 Lloyd's Rep. 392; (1956) 100 S.J. 317, CA *12–011*, *12–015*, *13–022*, *14–008*, *14–019*, *14–020*, *14–035*

J Vermaas Scheepvaartbedrijf NV v Association Technique De L'Importation Charbonniere; The Laga [1966] 1 Lloyd's Rep. 582; 116 N.L.J. 1034, QBD (Comm) *14–146*

JA Mont (UK) Ltd v Mills [1993] I.R.L.R. 172; [1993] F.S.R. 577, CA (Civ Div) *16–097*, *16–105*, *16–109*

JC Houghton & Co v Nothard Lowe & Wills Ltd [1928] A.C. 1; (1927–28) 29 Ll. L. Rep. 63, HL; affirming [1927] 1 K.B. 246; (1926) 25 Ll. L. Rep. 469, CA; reversing (1926) 24 Ll. L. Rep. 418, KBD *9–041*, *9–042*

JD White v Troups Transport. *See* White (JD) v Troups Transport

JEB Fasteners Ltd v Marks Bloom & Co [1983] 1 All E.R. 583, CA (Civ Div); affirming [1981] 3 All E.R. 289; [1982] Com. L.R. 226, QBD *6–081*

JF Adair & Co Ltd (in Liquidation) v Birnbaum [1939] 2 K.B. 149, CA *26–144*

JFS (UK) Ltd v Dwr Cymru Cyf (No.1) [1999] 1 W.L.R. 231; [1999] B.L.R. 17; (1999) 1 T.C.L.R. 187; (1998) 95(39) L.S.G. 40; (1998) 142 S.J.L.B. 256, CA (Civ Div) *28–122*

JH Rayner (Mincing Lane) Ltd v Bank Fur Gemeinwirtchaft AG [1983] 1 Lloyd's Rep. 462, CA (Civ Div) *25–013*

JH Rayner (Mincing Lane) Ltd v Cafenorte SA Importadora; sub nom. JH Rayner (Mincing Lane) Ltd v Brazil; Citoma Trading Ltd v Brazil [1999] 2 All E.R. (Comm) 577; [1999] 2 Lloyd's Rep. 750; [1999] C.L.C. 1847, CA (Civ Div) *30–345*

JH Rayner (Mincing Lane) Ltd v Department of Trade and Industry; sub nom. Maclaine Watson & Co Ltd v Department of Trade and Industry; Maclaine Watson & Co Ltd v International Tin Council; TSB England and Wales v Department of Trade and Industry; Amalgamated Metal Trading Ltd v International Tin Council [1990] 2 A.C. 418; [1989] 3 W.L.R. 969; [1989] 3 All E.R. 523; (1989) 5 B.C.C. 872; [1990] B.C.L.C. 102; (1990) 87(4) L.S.G. 68; (1989) 139 N.L.J. 1559; (1989) 133 S.J. 1485, HL; affirming [1989] Ch. 72; [1988] 3 W.L.R. 1033; [1988] 3 All E.R. 257; (1988) 4 B.C.C. 563; [1988] B.C.L.C. 404; [1989] P.C.C. 1; [1989] P.C.C. 68; (1988) 132 S.J. 1494, CA (Civ Div); affirming (1987) 3 B.C.C. 413; [1987] B.C.L.C. 667; [1988] P.C.C. 150; [1987] 2 F.T.L.R. 328, QBD (Comm) *9–002*, *11–001*, *11–004*, *11–005*, *11–018*, *11–019*, *18–019*, *30–325*
JH Ritchie Ltd v Lloyd Ltd. *See* J&H Ritchie Ltd v Lloyd Ltd
JIS (1974) Ltd v MCP Investment Nominees I Ltd (Construction of Lease) [2003] EWCA Civ 721; (2003) 100(24) L.S.G. 36, CA (Civ Div); affirming [2002] EWHC 1407 (Ch), Ch D *5–114*
JJ Harrison (Properties) Ltd v Harrison [2001] EWCA Civ 1467; [2002] B.C.C. 729; [2002] 1 B.C.L.C. 162; [2001] W.T.L.R. 1327, CA (Civ Div) *28–019*
JJ Huber (Investments) Ltd v Private DIY Co Ltd [1995] E.G. 112 (C.S.); [1995] N.P.C. 102; (1995) 70 P. & C.R. D33, Ch D *5–112*
JJ Savage & Sons Pty v Blackney (1970) 119 C.L.R. 435 .... *12–003*
JM Allan (Merchandising) v Cloke [1963] 2 Q.B. 340; [1963] 2 W.L.R. 899; [1963] 2 All E.R. 258; 61 L.G.R. 304; (1963) 107 S.J. 213, CA .. *16–008*, *16–010*, *16–012*
JS Bloor (Measham) Ltd v Calcott (No.2) [2002] 1 E.G.L.R. 1; [2002] 09 E.G. 222; (2002) 99(4) L.S.G. 31, Ch D *3–145*
JSC Zestafoni G Nikoladze Ferroalloy Plant v Ronly Holdings Ltd [2004] EWHC 245; [2004] 2 Lloyd's Rep. 335; [2004] 1 C.L.C. 1146, QBD (Comm) *2–051*, *16–031*
JT Developments v Quinn (1991) 62 P. & C.R. 33; [1991] 2 E.G.L.R. 257, CA (Civ Div) *3–139*, *3–143*, *3–151*
JT Stratford & Son Ltd v Lindley (No.1) [1965] A.C. 269; [1964] 3 W.L.R. 541; [1964] 3 All E.R. 102; [1964] 2 Lloyd's Rep. 133; 108 S.J.L.B. 636; (1964) 108 S.J. 636, HL; reversing [1964] 2 W.L.R. 1002; [1964] 2 All E.R. 209; [1964] 1 Lloyd's Rep. 237; 108 S.J.L.B. 298; (1964) 108 S.J. 298, CA; reversing [1964] 1 Lloyd's Rep. 138; (1964) 108 S.J. 636, QBD *7–055*, *29–150*
JT Sydenham & Co v Enichers Elastomers [1989] 1 E.G.L.R. 257 .... *3–130*
JW Taylor & Co v Landauer & Co [1940] 4 All E.R. 335; 1940) 68 Ll. L. Rep. 28[164] L.T. 299; 57 T.L.R. 47; 85 S.J. 119 .... *13–013*, *23–047*
Jabbour v Custodian of Israeli Absentee Property. *See* F&K Jabbour v Custodian of Israeli Absentee Property
Jack v Kipping (1881–82) L.R. 9 Q.B.D. 113, QBD *1–131*, *19–071*, *20–042*
Jackson v Chrysler Acceptances Ltd [1978] R.T.R. 474, CA (Civ Div) 26–083
Jackson v Hayes Candy and Co Ltd [1938] 4 All E.R. 587 26–118
Jackson v Horizon Holidays Ltd [1975] 1 W.L.R. 1468; [1975] 3 All E.R. 92; (1975) 119 S.J. 759, CA (Civ Div) *18–012*, 18–049, 18–050, *18–076*, 26–083
Jackson v North Eastern Railway Co (No.2) (1877–78) L.R. 7 Ch. D. 573, Ch D 13–024
Jackson v Royal Bank of Scotland [2005] UKHL 3; [2005] 1 W.L.R. 377; [2005] 2 All E.R. 71; [2005] 1 All E.R. (Comm) 337; [2005] 1 Lloyd's Rep. 366; (2005) 102(11) L.S.G. 29; (2005) 149 S.J.L.B. 146, HL ... *20–063A*, *26–045*, *26–054*, *26–055*, *26–061*, *26–062*, *26–071*, *26–087*
Jackson v Thakrar [2007] EWHC 271 (TCC); 113 Con. L.R. 58; [2007] B.P.I.R. 367; (2007) 157 N.L.J. 331, QBD (TCC) *2–185*
Jackson v Turquand (1869–70) L.R. 4 H.L. 305, HL *2–024*, *2–032*
Jackson v Union Marine Insurance Co Ltd (1874–75) L.R. 10 C.P. 125, Ex Chamber *5–025*, 23–006, *23–021*, *23–040*, *23–058*, *24–040*, *24–046*
Jackson v Watson & Sons [1909] 2 K.B. 193, CA *26–082*, *26–083*
Jackson Stansfield & Sons v Butterworth [1948] W.N. 315; 64 T.L.R. 481; 112 J.P. 377; 92 S.J. 469;[1948] 2 All E.R. 558; 46 L.G.R. 410 .... *16–154*

Jacobs v Batavia & General Plantations Trust Ltd [1924] 2 Ch. 329, CA; affirming [1924] 1 Ch. 287, Ch D *4–028*, *12–004*, *12–067*, *12–096*
Jacobs v Morris [1902] 1 Ch. 816, CA *29–147*
Jacobs v Revell [1900] 2 Ch. 858, Ch D *27–055*, *27–057*
Jacobs v Richards (1854) 18 Beav. 300 .... *8–068*
Jacobs Marcus & Co v Crédit Lyonnais (1883–84) L.R. 12 Q.B.D. 589, CA *14–147*, *23–028*, *30–005*, *30–011*, *30–012*, *30–363*, *30–332*, *30–334*
Jacobson v Frachon; sub nom. Jacobson v Fraction (1928) 138 L.T. 386 .... *25–018*
Jacobson van den Berg & Co (UK) v Biba (1977) 121 S.J. 333, CA (Civ Div) *22–042*
Jacobus Marler Estates v Marler (1913) L.J.P.C. 167 .... *9–054*
Jacoby v Whitmore (1883) 49 L.T. 335 .... *16–099*
Jacomb v Harwood (1751) 2 Ves. Sen. 265 .... *21–049*
Jacovides v Constantinou, *The Times*, October 27, 1986 .... *6–050*
Jaeger's Sanitary Woollen System Co v Walker & Sons (1897) 77 L.T. 180 .... *19–083*
Jaggard v Sawyer [1995] 1 W.L.R. 269; [1995] 2 All E.R. 189; [1995] 1 E.G.L.R. 146; [1995] 13 E.G. 132; [1994] E.G. 139 (C.S.); [1994] N.P.C. 116, CA (Civ Div) *26–023*, *27–031*, 27–063, *27–079*, *27–080*, *27–084*, *29–139*, *29–144*, *29–151*
Jaglom v Excess Insurance Co Ltd [1972] 2 Q.B. 250; [1971] 3 W.L.R. 594; [1972] 1 All E.R. 267; [1971] 2 Lloyd's Rep. 171; (1971) 115 S.J. 639, QBD (Comm) *3–173*
Jajbhay v Cassim, 1939 A.D. 537 .... *16–179*
Jakeman v Cook (1878–79) L.R. 4 Ex. D. 26, Exchequer Div ...*3–033*, *16–042*, *20–048*
Jaks (UK) Ltd v Cera Investment Bank SA [1998] 2 Lloyd's Rep. 89, QBD (Comm) *24–013*, *24–019*
Jamal v Moolla Dawood Co. *See* AKAS Jamal v Moolla Dawood Sons & Co
James, Ex p. *See* Condon Ex p. James, Re
James, Re; sub nom. James v James [1935] Ch. 449, Ch D *25–005*
James v British General Insurance Co Ltd [1927] 2 K.B. 311; ; 96 L.J.K.B. 729; 137 L.T. 156; 43 T.L.R. 354; 71 S.J. 273; (1927) 27 Ll. L. Rep. 328, KBD *16–173*
James v David (1793) 5 T.R. 141 .... *22–015*
James v Emery (1818) 5 Price 529 .... *3–043*
James v Evans; sub nom. Evans v James (Administratrix of Hopkin's Estate) [2001] C.P. Rep. 36; [2003] C.P.L.R. 163; [2000] 3 E.G.L.R. 1; [2000] 42 E.G. 173; [2000] E.G. 95 (C.S.); [2000] N.P.C. 85; (2000) 80 P. & C.R. D39, CA (Civ Div) 4–080
James v Greenwich LBC [2008] EWCA Civ 35; [2008] I.C.R. 545; [2008] I.R.L.R. 302, CA (Civ Div); affirming [2007] I.C.R. 577; [2007] I.R.L.R. 168, EAT *18–005*
James v Heim Gallery (London) Ltd (1981) 41 P. & C.R. 269; (1980) 256 E.G. 819, CA (Civ Div); reversing (1980) 39 P. & C.R. 155; (1979) 252 E.G. 1017, Ch D *3–089*, *3–090*, *3–094*, *3–098*
James v Hutton [1950] 1 K.B. 9; [1949] 2 All E.R. 243; (1949) 65 T.L.R. 441; (1949) 65 T.L.R. 610; (1949) 93 S.J. 551, CA *26–008*
James v Isaacs (1852) 12 C.B. 791 .... *21–041*
James v Kerr (1889) L.R. 40 Ch. D. 449, Ch D *7–128*, *16–066*
James v Thomas Kent & Co [1951] 1 K.B. 551; [1950] 2 All E.R. 1099; [1951] 1 T.L.R. 552; (1951) 95 S.J. 29, CA *29–080*
James v Vane, 121 E.R. 330; (1860) 2 El. & El. 883, QB *21–085*
James v Williams [2000] Ch. 1; [1999] 3 W.L.R. 451; [1999] 3 All E.R. 309; [1999] 2 F.C.R. 498; (2000) 79 P. & C.R. 421; (1999) 96(15) L.S.G. 30; (1999) 78 P. & C.R. D17, CA (Civ Div) *28–019*, *29–157*
James Archdale & Co Ltd v Comservices Ltd [1954] 1 W.L.R. 459; [1954] 1 All E.R. 210; (1954) 98 S.J. 143, CA *14–011*, *14–015*
James Baird Co v Gimbel Bros, 64 F. 2d. 344 (1933) *3–173*
James Buchanan & Co Ltd v Hay's Transport Services Ltd [1972] 2 Lloyd's Rep. 535, QBD *14–054*
James Burton & Son Ltd, Re [1927] 2 Ch. 132, Ch D *9–060*
James E McCabe Ltd v Scottish Courage Ltd [2006] EWHC 538 (Comm), QBD (Comm) *16–198*

James Finlay & Co Ltd v NV Kwik Hoo Tung Handel Maatschappij; sub nom. James Finlay & Co Ltd v NV Kwik Hoo Tong Handel Maatschappij [1929] 1 K.B. 400; [1928] All E.R. Rep. 110; (1928) 32 Ll. L. Rep. 245, CA *26–104*
James Jones & Sons Ltd v Earl of Tankerville [1909] 2 Ch. 440, Ch D *13–028*, *27–014*, *27–070*
James Laing Son & Co (M/C) v Eastcheap Dried Fruit Co (No.1) [1961] 2 Lloyd's Rep. 277, CA *26–144*
James Lazenby & Co v McNicholas Construction Co Ltd [1995] 1 W.L.R. 615; [1995] 3 All E.R. 820; [1995] 2 Lloyd's Rep. 30, QBD (Comm) *2–006*
James Macara Ltd v Barclay. *See* Macara (James) Ltd v Barclay
James McNaughton Paper Group Ltd v Hicks Anderson & Co [1991] 2 Q.B. 113; [1991] 2 W.L.R. 641; [1991] 1 All E.R. 134; [1990] B.C.C. 891; [1991] B.C.L.C. 235; [1991] E.C.C. 186; [1955–95] P.N.L.R. 574; (1990) 140 N.L.J. 1311, CA (Civ Div) *18–022*
James Miller & Partners Ltd v Whitworth Street Estates (Manchester) Ltd. *See* Whitworth Street Estates (Manchester) Ltd v James Miller & Partners Ltd
James R Rutherford & Sons, Re; sub nom. Lloyds Bank v Winter [1964] 1 W.L.R. 1211; [1964] 3 All E.R. 137; (1964) 108 S.J. 563, Ch D *21–066*
James Roscoe (Bolton) Ltd v Winder [1915] 1 Ch. 62, Ch D *29–167*
James Scott & Sons Ltd v R&N Del Sel; sub nom. Scott & Sons v Del Sel (1923) 14 Ll. L. Rep. 65; 1923 S.C. (H.L.) 37; 1923 S.L.T. 204, HL *23–011*
James Shaffer v Findlay Durham & Brodie. *See* Shaffer (James) v Findlay Durham & Brodie
James Spencer & Co Ltd v Tame Valley Padding Co Ltd, unreported, April 8, 1998, CA (Civ Div) *1–022*
Jameson v Central Electricity Generating Board (No.1) [2000] 1 A.C. 455; [1999] 2 W.L.R. 141; [1999] 1 All E.R. 193; [1999] 1 Lloyd's Rep. 573; [1999] P.I.Q.R. Q81; (1999) 96(5) L.S.G. 37; (1999) 143 S.J.L.B. 29, HL; reversing [1998] Q.B. 323; [1997] 3 W.L.R. 151; [1997] 4 All E.R. 38; [1997] P.I.Q.R. Q89; (1997) 141 S.J.L.B. 55, CA (Civ Div) *2–149*, *3–078*, *17–017*, *17–018*, *22–015*
Jameson v Kinmell Bay Land Co (1931) 47 T.L.R. 410 .... *4–016*, *12–004*
Jameson v Midland Railway (1884) 50 L.T. 426 .... *26–070*
Jameson & Co v Brick & Stone Co Ltd (1878–79) L.R. 4 Q.B.D. 208, CA *20–055*
Jamieson v Jamieson (1898) 15 R.P.C. 169 .... *28–135*
Jamil Line for Trading and Shipping Ltd v Atlanta Handelsgesellschaft Harder & Co; The Marko Polo [1982] 1 Lloyd's Rep. 481, QBD (Comm) *13–007*
Jan Albert (HK) Ltd v Shu Kong Garment Factory Ltd [1990] 1 H.K.L.R. 317 ..... *23–002*
Jananyagam v Commonwealth Secretariat [2007] WL 919439, EAT *11–019*
Janciuk v Winerite [1998] I.R.L.R. 63, EAT *26–001*
Jangmi, The (k/a The Grigorpan) [1989] 2 Lloyd's Rep. 1, CA (Civ Div) *28–118*
Jani-King (GB) Ltd v Pula Enterprises Ltd [2007] EWHC 2433 (QB); [2008] 1 All E.R. (Comm) 451, QBD *1–033*, *2–154*, *2–175*
Janmohamed v Hassam (1976) 241 E.G. 609 .... *2–154*
Janred Properties Ltd v Ente Nazionale Italiano per il Turismo (ENIT) (No.2) [1989] 2 All E.R. 444; [1987] 2 F.T.L.R. 179, CA (Civ Div); affirming [1986] 1 F.T.L.R. 246, Ch D *3–103*, *9–005*, *26–175*, *30–325*
Janson v Driefontein Consolidated Mines Ltd; sub nom. Driefontein Consolidated Gold Mines Ltd v Janson; West Rand Central Gold Mines Co Ltd v De Rougemont [1902] A.C. 484, HL; affirming [1901] 2 K.B. 419, CA; affirming [1900] 2 Q.B. 339, QBD (Comm) *11–024*, *11–025*, *16–003*, *16–004*, *16–026*
Janson v Property Insurance Co (1913) 30 T.L.R. 49 .... *9–065*
Jaques v Lloyd D George & Partners [1968] 1 W.L.R. 625; [1968] 2 All E.R. 187; (1968) 112 S.J. 211, CA (Civ Div) *12–002*, *12–015*, *14–132*
Jaques v Millar (1877) L.R. 6 Ch. D. 153, Ch D *26–092*, *26–175*
Jarl Trä AB v Convoys Ltd [2003] EWHC 1488; [2003] 2 Lloyd's Rep. 459; [2003] 2 C.L.C. 1072, QBD (Comm) *18–135*

Jarrett v Barclays Bank Plc; Jones v First National Bank Plc; First National Bank Plc v Peacock [1999] Q.B. 1; [1997] 3 W.L.R. 654; [1997] 2 All E.R. 484; [1997] 6 Bank. L.R. 66; [1997] C.L.C. 391; [1997] I.L.Pr. 531; [1997] C.C.L.R. 32; (1997) 94(6) L.S.G. 27; (1996) 140 S.J.L.B. 252; [1996] N.P.C. 159, CA (Civ Div) *30–084*
Jarrett v Hunter (1887) L.R. 34 Ch. D. 182, Ch D *4–023*, *12–122*
Jarrott v Ackerley; sub nom. Jarrett v Ackerley (1915) 85 L.J. Ch. 135; (1915) 113 L.T. 371 .... *9–064*
Jarvis, Re; sub nom. Edge v Jarvis [1958] 1 W.L.R. 815; [1958] 2 All E.R. 336; (1958) 102 S.J. 546, Ch D *28–142*
Jarvis v Moy Davies Smith Vandervell & Co [1936] 1 K.B. 399, CA *1–137*
Jarvis v Swans Tours Ltd [1973] Q.B. 233; [1972] 3 W.L.R. 954; [1973] 1 All E.R. 71; (1972) 116 S.J. 822, CA (Civ Div) *1–123*, *6–069*, *26–083*
Jarvis Interiors Ltd v Galliard Homes Ltd; sub nom. Galliard Homes Ltd v J Jarvis & Sons Plc [2000] C.L.C. 411; [2000] B.L.R. 33; 71 Con. L.R. 219, CA *2–116*
Jaura v Ahmed [2002] EWCA Civ 210, CA (Civ Div) *26–178*
Jayaar Impex Ltd v Toaken Group Ltd (t/a Hicks Brothers) [1996] 2 Lloyd's Rep. 437, QBD (Comm) *2–029*, *2–030*, *2–031*, *2–038*, *2–071*
Jayne v Hughes (1854) 10 Exch. 430 .... *12–110*, *28–094*
Jay's Furnishing Co v Brand & Co [1915] 1 K.B. 458, CA; affirming [1914] 2 K.B. 132, KBD *22–055*
Jean Kraut AG v Albany Fabrics Ltd; sub nom. Kraut v Albany Fabrics [1977] Q.B. 182; [1976] 3 W.L.R. 872; [1977] 2 All E.R. 116; [1976] 2 Lloyd's Rep. 350; (1976) 120 S.J. 817, QBD *30–373*, *30–376*
Jeancharm Ltd (t/a Beaver International) v Barnet Football Club Ltd [2003] EWCA Civ 58; 92 Con. L.R. 26, CA (Civ Div) *26–127*
Jeavons Ex p. Mackay, Re; sub nom. Jeavons Ex p. Brown, Re (1872–73) L.R. 8 Ch. App. 643, CA in Chancery *20–025*
Jebco Properties v Mastforce [1992] N.P.C. 42 .... *13–012*
Jebsen v East and West India Dock Co (1874–75) L.R. 10 C.P. 300, CCP *26–117*
Jefferys v Jefferys (1841) Cr. App. R. & Ph. 138 .... *1–108*, *3–021*
Jefford v Gee [1970] 2 Q.B. 130; [1970] 2 W.L.R. 702; [1970] 1 All E.R. 1202; [1970] 1 Lloyd's Rep. 107; (1970) 114 S.J. 206, CA (Civ Div) *26–175*
Jeffreys v Jeffreys (1841) Cr. & Ph. 138 .... *27–034*
Jeffryes v Agra & Masterman's Bank (1866) L.R. 2 Eq. 674, Ct of Chancery *19–070*
Jell v Douglas (1821) 4 B. & Ald. 374 .... *3–042*
Jelson Ltd v Derby City Council [1999] 4 P.L.R. 11; [1999] 3 E.G.L.R. 91; [1999] 39 E.G. 149; [2000] J.P.L. 203; [1999] E.G. 88 (C.S.); (1999) 96(26) L.S.G. 30; [1999] N.P.C. 68, Ch D 4–061, *4–072*
Jenkin v Pharmaceutical Society of Great Britain [1921] 1 Ch. 392, Ch D *9–004*
Jenkins v Jenkins [1928] 2 K.B. 501, KBD *17–023*, *25–005*
Jenkins v Livesey (formerly Jenkins) [1985] A.C. 424; [1985] 2 W.L.R. 47; [1985] 1 All E.R. 106; [1985] Fam. Law 310; (1985) 82 L.S.G. 517; (1985) 134 N.L.J. 55, HL; reversing [1985] Fam. Law 180, CA (Civ Div) ... *6–019*, *6–155*
Jenkins v Morris (1880) L.R. 14 Ch. D. 674, CA *8–070*
Jenkins v Reid. *See* Jenkins Deed of Partnership, Re
Jenkins v Tucker (1788) 1 H.Bl. 90 .... *29–132*
Jenkins v Watford (1918) 87 L.J.K.B. 136 .... *14–138*
Jenkins Deed of Partnership, Re; sub nom. Jenkins v Reid [1948] 1 All E.R. 471; [1948] W.N. 98; (1948) 92 S.J. 142, Ch D *16–097*, *16–098*, *16–105*
Jenner v Jenner (1860) 2 De. G. F. & J. 359 .... *7–074*
Jenner v Walker (1868) 19 L.T. 398 .... *8–016*
Jennings v Broughton (1853) 5 De. G.M. & G. 126 .... *6–032*, *6–037*
Jennings v Brown (1842) 9 M. & W. 496 .... *2–169*, *16–005*, *16–067*
Jennings v Jennings [1898] 1 Ch. 378, Ch D *16–118*
Jennings v Johnson (1872–73) L.R. 8 C.P. 425, CCP *16–056*

Jennings v Rice [2002] EWCA Civ 159; [2003] 1 F.C.R. 501; [2003] 1 P. & C.R. 8; [2002] W.T.L.R. 367; [2002] N.P.C. 28; [2002] 2 P. & C.R. DG2, CA (Civ Div); affirming [2001] W.T.L.R. 871, Ch D ... *3–141*, *3–143*, *3–147*, *3–148*, *3–154*, 3–155, *3–157*, *4–082*
Jennings v Rundall (1799) 8 T.R. 335 ... *1–132*, *8–046*
Jennings v Tavener [1955] 1 W.L.R. 932; [1955] 2 All E.R. 769; (1955) 99 S.J. 543, QBD ... *13–015*
Jennings v Throgmorton (1825) R. & M. 251 ... *16–069*
Jennings' Trustees v King. *See* Jennings (A Bankrupt), Re
Jennings (A Bankrupt), Re; sub nom. Trustee, Ex p. v King [1952] Ch. 899; [1952] 2 All E.R. 608; [1952] 2 T.L.R. 469; (1952) 96 S.J. 648, Ch D ... *20–032*, *24–028*
Jennings and Chapman v Woodman, Matthews & Co [1952] 2 T.L.R. 409; (1952) 96 S.J. 561, CA ... *23–059*
Jersey (Earl of) v Guardians of the Neath Poor Law Union (1889) L.R. 22 Q.B.D. 555, CA ... *12–089*
Jervis v Harris [1996] Ch. 195; [1996] 2 W.L.R. 220; [1996] 1 All E.R. 303; [1996] 1 E.G.L.R. 78; [1996] 10 E.G. 159; [1995] E.G. 177 (C.S.); (1996) 93(3) L.S.G. 30; (1996) 140 S.J.L.B. 13; [1995] N.P.C. 171, CA (Civ Div) ... *21–040*, *26–009*, *26–136*
Jervis v Howle and Talke Colliery Co Ltd [1937] Ch. 67, Ch D ... *5–108*, *5–109*
Jervis v Tomkinson, 156 E.R. 1173; (1856) 1 Hurl. & N. 195, QB ... *23–004*
Jesse v Roy (1834) 1 Cr. M.R. 316 ... *21–029*, *21–030*
Jessmore, The. *See* Owners of the Jessmore v Manchester Ship Canal Co
Jeune v Queen's Cross Properties Ltd [1974] Ch. 97; [1973] 3 W.L.R. 378; [1973] 3 All E.R. 97; (1973) 26 P. & C.R. 98; (1973) 117 S.J. 680, Ch D ... *27–026*, *27–028*
Jewelowski v Propp [1944] K.B. 510, KBD ... *26–104*
Jewson & Son v Arcos (1933) 39 Com. Cas. 59 ... *6–014*, *6–017*, *6–142*
Jiggins v Brisley [2003] EWHC 841 (Ch); [2003] W.T.L.R. 1141, Ch D ... *3–139*, *4–063*
Jimenez v Inland Revenue Commissioners [2004] S.T.C. (S.C.D.) 371; [2004] S.T.I. 1939, Sp Comm ... *11–014*
Jindal Iron & Steel Co Ltd v Islamic Solidarity Shipping Co Jordan Inc; TCI Trans Commodities AG v Islamic Solidarity Shipping Co Jordan Inc [2004] UKHL 49; [2005] 1 W.L.R. 1363; [2005] 1 All E.R. 175; [2005] 1 All E.R. (Comm) 1; [2005] 1 Lloyd's Rep. 57; [2004] 2 C.L.C. 1172; 2005 A.M.C. 1; (2004) 148 S.J.L.B. 1405, HL; affirming [2003] EWCA Civ 144; [2003] 1 All E.R. (Comm) 747; [2003] 2 Lloyd's Rep. 87; [2003] 1 C.L.C. 885, CA (Civ Div); reversing in part [2002] EWHC 1268 (Comm); [2002] 2 All E.R. (Comm) 364, QBD (Comm) ... *14–117*
Joachimson v Swiss Bank Corp. *See* N Joachimson (A Firm) v Swiss Bank Corp (Costs)
Jobson v Johnson [1989] 1 W.L.R. 1026; [1989] 1 All E.R. 621; (1988) 4 B.C.C. 488, CA (Civ Div) ... *26–126*, *26–130*, 26–153, *27–011*
Joel v Law Union & Crown Insurance Co [1908] 2 K.B. 863, CA; reversing [1908] 2 K.B. 431, KBD ... *6–144*, *6–147*, *6–148*, *6–149*
John v Dodwell & Co Ltd [1918] A.C. 563, PC (Cey) ... *29–146*
John v James [1986] S.T.C. 352, Ch D ... *26–161*, *26–165*
John v Matthews [1970] 2 Q.B. 443; [1970] 2 W.L.R. 1246; [1970] 2 All E.R. 643; 68 L.G.R. 581; (1970) 114 S.J. 472, DC ... *9–071*
John v Mendoza [1939] 1 K.B. 141, KBD ... *20–048*
John v Rees; Martin v Davis; Rees v John [1970] Ch. 345; [1969] 2 W.L.R. 1294; [1969] 2 All E.R. 274; (1969) 113 S.J. 487, Ch D ... *9–041*, *9–066*, *9–075*
John Batt & Co (London) Ltd v Brooker Dore & Co Ltd (1942) 72 Ll. L. Rep. 149, KBD ... *14–148*
John Carter (Fine Worsteds) Ltd v Hanson Haulage (Leeds) Ltd [1965] 2 Q.B. 495; [1965] 2 W.L.R. 553; [1965] 1 All E.R. 113; [1965] 1 Lloyd's Rep. 49; (1965) 109 S.J. 47, CA ... *6–134*, *14–011*, *14–016*, *14–032*, *14–036*

John F Hunt Demolition Ltd v ASME Engineering Ltd [2007] EWHC 1507 (TCC); [2008] Bus. L.R. 558; [2008] 1 All E.R. 180; [2008] 1 All E.R. (Comm) 473; [2008] B.L.R. 115; [2007] T.C.L.R. 6; 114 Con. L.R. 105; [2007] C.I.L.L. 2496, QBD (TCC) *1–183*, *1–187*, *18–030*, *26–078*

John Fox (A Firm) v Bannister King & Rigbeys [1988] Q.B. 925; [1987] 3 W.L.R. 480; [1987] 1 All E.R. 737; (1987) 84 L.S.G. 2692; (1987) 137 N.L.J. 122; (1987) 131 S.J. 1063, CA (Civ Div) *2–158*

John H Kilmer v British Columbia Orchard Lands Ltd. *See* Kilmer v British Columbia Orchard Lands Ltd

John Harris Partnership v Groveworld Ltd, 75 Con. L.R. 7; [1999] P.N.L.R. 697, QBD (TCC) *18–056*, *18–076*

John Lee & Son (Grantham) Ltd v Railway Executive [1949] 2 All E.R. 581; 65 T.L.R. 604; [1949] W.N. 373; (1949) 93 S.J. 587, CA; affirming [1949] 2 All E.R. 230, KBD *12–083*, 14–009, *14–135*

John Lewis Properties Plc v Viscount Chelsea (1994) 67 P. & C.R. 120; [1993] 34 E.G. 116; [1993] E.G. 46 (C.S.), Ch D *23–066*, *23–068*

John M Henderson Co Ltd v Montague L Meyer Ltd (1941) 46 Com. Cas. 209 .... *26–078*

John McCann & Co v Pow [1974] 1 W.L.R. 1643; [1975] 1 All E.R. 129; [1974] J.P.L. 720; (1974) 118 S.J. 717, CA (Civ Div) *2–084*

John Michael Design Plc v Cooke [1987] 2 All E.R. 332; [1987] I.C.R. 445; [1987] F.S.R. 402; (1987) 84 L.S.G. 1492; (1987) 131 S.J. 595, CA (Civ Div) *16–110*, *16–111*

John Munroe (Acrylics) Ltd v London Fire and Civil Defence Authority. *See* Capital and Counties Plc v Hampshire CC

John Pfeiffer Pty Ltd v Rogerson, 203 C.L.R. 503, HC (Aus) *30–337*, *30–347*

John Potter & Co v Burrell & Son [1897] 1 Q.B. 97, CA *14–029*

John Shaw & Sons (Salford) Ltd v Shaw [1935] 2 K.B. 113, CA *29–191*

John Snow Co Ltd v DBG Woodcroft Ltd [1985] B.C.L.C. 54 ....*29–158*, *29–168*

John Willmott Homes, Ltd v Read (1986) 51 P. & C.R. 90, Ch D *21–018*

Johns, Re; sub nom. Worrell v Johns [1928] Ch. 737, Ch D *16–042*

Johnsey Estates (1990) Ltd v Newport Marketworld, May 10, 1990, unreported, Ch D *1–090*

Johnsey Estates Ltd v Lewis & Manley (Engineering) Ltd (1987) 54 P. & C.R. 296; (1987) 284 E.G. 1240, CA (Civ Div) *3–004*, *3–008*

Johnson v Agnew [1980] A.C. 367; [1979] 2 W.L.R. 487; [1979] 1 All E.R. 883; (1979) 38 P. & C.R. 424; (1979) 251 E.G. 1167; (1979) 123 S.J. 217, HL; affirming [1978] Ch. 176; [1978] 2 W.L.R. 806; [1978] 3 All E.R. 314; (1979) 38 P. & C.R. 107; (1978) 122 S.J. 230, CA (Civ Div) *6–100*, *6–104*, 6–106, *24–001*, *24–004*, 24–047, *24–051*, *26–001*, *26–064*, *26–091*, *26–092*, 27–079, 27–082, 27–083

Johnson v Boyes [1899] 2 Ch. 73 .... *21–087*

Johnson v Bragge [1901] 1 Ch. 28, Ch D *5–112*, *5–130*, *5–133*

Johnson v Clay (1817) 7 Taunt. 486 .... *21–089*

Johnson v Coventry Churchill International Ltd [1992] 3 All E.R. 14, QBD *30–032*, *30–121*

Johnson v Davies [1999] Ch. 117; [1998] 3 W.L.R. 1299; [1998] 2 All E.R. 649; [1999] B.C.C. 275; [1998] 2 B.C.L.C. 252; [1998] B.P.I.R. 607; (2000) 79 P. & C.R. 14; [1998] L. & T.R. 69; [1998] 3 E.G.L.R. 72; [1998] 49 E.G. 153; (1998) 95(19) L.S.G. 23; (1998) 142 S.J.L.B. 141; [1998] N.P.C. 50, CA (Civ Div); affirming [1997] 1 W.L.R. 1511; [1997] 1 All E.R. 921; [1997] 1 B.C.L.C. 580; [1997] B.P.I.R. 221; [1997] 1 E.G.L.R. 42; [1997] 19 E.G. 157; (1996) 146 N.L.J. 1814, Ch D *3–044*, *3–125*, *3–126*, *17–025*, *18–021*

Johnson v Dodgson (1837) 2 M. & W. 653 .... *4–032*

Johnson v Duke of Marlborough (1818) 2 Stark. 313 ....*25–021*, *25–022*

Johnson v Edgware etc Ry (1866) 35 Beav. 480 .... *12–083*

Johnson v Gore Wood & Co (No.1); sub nom. Johnson v Gore Woods & Co [2002] 2 A.C. 1; [2001] 2 W.L.R. 72; [2001] 1 All E.R. 481; [2001] C.P.L.R. 49; [2001] B.C.C. 820; [2001] 1 B.C.L.C. 313; [2001] P.N.L.R. 18; (2001) 98(1) L.S.G. 24; (2001) 98(8) L.S.G. 46; (2000) 150 N.L.J. 1889; (2001) 145 S.J.L.B. 29, HL; reversing in part [1999] C.P.L.R. 155; [1999] B.C.C. 474; [1999] Lloyd's Rep. P.N. 91; [1999] P.N.L.R. 426; [1998] N.P.C. 151, CA (Civ Div) *3–100*, *3–103*, 3–110, *3–113*, *16–052*, *18–002*, *25–011*, *25–013*, *25–014*, *26–019*, *26–083*
Johnson v Hudson (1809) 11 East 180 .... *16–147*
Johnson v Johnson (1802) 3 B.P. 162 .... *29–057*
Johnson v Jones [1972] N.Z.L.R. 313 .... *29–064*
Johnson v Moreton [1980] A.C. 37; [1978] 3 W.L.R. 538; 122 S.J. 697; [1978] 3 All E.R. 37; 37 P. & C.R. 243; 247 E.G. 895, HL; affirming (1977) 35 P. & C.R. 378; 241 E.G. 759 16–016
Johnson v Pye (1666) 1 Sid. 258; 1 Keb. 913 .... *1–118*, *1–128*, *1–132*, *1–162*, *8–046*, *8–049*, *8–050*
Johnson v Raylton Dixon & Co (1880–81) L.R. 7 Q.B.D. 438, CA 19–082
Johnson v Royal Mail Steam Packet Co (1867–68) L.R. 3 C.P. 38, CCP *29–103*
Johnson v Shrewsbury & Birmingham Railway (1853) 3 D.M. & G. 914 .... *27–021*
Johnson v Skafte (1868–69) L.R. 4 Q.B. 700, QB *29–103*, *29–104*
Johnson v Stear (1863) 33 L.J.C.P. 130 .... *1–133*
Johnson v Unisys Ltd [2001] UKHL 13; [2003] 1 A.C. 518; [2001] 2 W.L.R. 1076; [2001] 2 All E.R. 801; [2001] I.C.R. 480; [2001] I.R.L.R. 279; [2001] Emp. L.R. 469, HL; affirming [1999] 1 All E.R. 854; [1999] I.C.R. 809; [1999] I.R.L.R. 90, CA (Civ Div) *1–032*, *1–063*, *1–123*, 1–155, *26–083*, 26–086, *27–022*
Johnson v Wild (1890) L.R. 44 Ch. D. 146, Ch D *29–105*, 29–122
Johnson Matthey & Co v Constantine Terminals and International Express Co [1976] 2 Lloyd's Rep. 215, QBD (Comm) *1–186*, *14–018*, 14–054
Johnson Matthey Bankers Ltd v State Trading Corp of India Ltd [1984] 1 Lloyd's Rep. 427, QBD (Comm) *2–037*, *12–011*, *14–150*, *23–058*, *26–048*
Johnston v Boyes [1899] 2 Ch. 73, Ch D *2–012*, *3–174*
Johnston v Great Western Railway Co [1904] 2 K.B. 250, CA *26–013*, *26–030*
Johnstone v Bloomsbury HA [1992] Q.B. 333; [1991] 2 W.L.R. 1362; [1991] 2 All E.R. 293; [1991] I.C.R. 269; [1991] I.R.L.R. 118; [1991] 2 Med. L.R. 139; (1991) 141 N.L.J. 271, CA (Civ Div) 1–033, 1–152, *13–003*, *14–062*, *14–071*, *14–108*
Johnstone v Holdway [1963] 1 Q.B. 601; [1963] 2 W.L.R. 147; [1963] 1 All E.R. 432; (1963) 107 S.J. 55, CA *12–117*
Johnstone v Marks (1887) L.R. 19 Q.B.D. 509, QBD *8–008*
Johnstone v Milling; sub nom. Johnston v Milling (1885–86) L.R. 16 Q.B.D. 460, CA *24–001*, *24–003*, 24–022, 24–024
Johnstone v Pedlar [1921] 2 A.C. 262, HL (UK-Irl); affirming [1920] 2 I.R. 450, CA (UK-Irl) *11–007*
Johore (Sultan of) v Abubakar Tunku Aris Bendahar [1952] A.C. 318; [1952] 1 All E.R. 1261; [1952] 1 T.L.R. 1106; (1952) 96 S.J. 325, PC (Sing) *11–020*, *11–021*
Joinery Plus Ltd v Laing Ltd [2003] EWHC 3513 (TCC); [2003] B.L.R. 184; [2003] T.C.L.R. 4; 87 Con. L.R. 87; [2003] B.P.I.R. 890, QBD (TCC) *22–022*
Joint Receivers and Managers of Niltan Carson v Hawthorne (1987) 3 B.C.C. 454; [1988] B.C.L.C. 298, QBD *9–055*
Joliffe v Baker (1882–83) L.R. 11 Q.B.D. 255, QBD *27–055*
Jolley v Carmel Ltd [2000] 3 E.G.L.R. 68; [2000] 43 E.G. 185, CA (Civ Div); affirming [2000] 2 E.G.L.R. 153; [2000] E.G. 72 (C.S.), Ch D *2–155*, *21–020*
Jolliffe v Pitt (1715) 2 Vern. 694 .... *28–031*
Jon Beauforte (London) Ltd, Re; Grainger Smith & Co (Builders) Ltd's Application; John Wright & Son (Veneers) Ltd's Application; Lowell Baldwin Ltd's Application [1953] Ch. 131; [1953] 2 W.L.R. 465; [1953] 1 All E.R. 634; (1953) 97 S.J. 152, Ch D *9–020*, *9–021*
Jonassohn v Young (1863) 4 B.S. 296 .... *24–044*

Jonathan Wren & Co Ltd v Microdec Plc, 65 Con. L.R. 157, QBD (TCC) *12–005*, *13–030*, *13–033*
Jones Ex p. Nichols, Re (1883) L.R. 22 Ch. D. 782, CA *19–061*
Jones, Re (1880–81) L.R. 18 Ch. D. 109, CA *8–017*, *8–018*, *8–051*, *8–052*
Jones, Re [1914] 1 Ir. R. 188 .... *28–058*
Jones, Re; sub nom. Farrington v Forrester [1893] 2 Ch. 461, Ch D *8–041*, *12–005*, *29–118*
Jones v Arthur (1840) 8 Dowl. Pr. Cas. 442 .... *21–087*, *21–093*
Jones v Ashburnham (1804) 4 East 455 .... *3–004*, *3–051*
Jones v Bellgrove Properties [1949] 2 K.B. 700; [1949] 1 All E.R. 498; 65 T.L.R. 451; 99 L.J. 495; (1949) 93 S.J. 512; (1949) 93 S.J. 783, CA *28–094*, *28–095*, *28–101*
Jones v Carter, 153 E.R. 1040; [1846] 15 M. & W. 718, Ex Ct *29–026*
Jones v Commerzbank AG; sub nom. Commerzbank AG v Jones; Commerzbank AG v Price-Jones; Price-Jones v Commerzbank AG [2003] EWCA Civ 1663; (2003) 147 S.J.L.B. 1397; [2004] 1 P. & C.R. DG15, CA (Civ Div) 29–179, *29–180*, 29–181, *29–183*, 29–184
Jones v Daniel [1894] 2 Ch. 332, Ch D *2–032*
Jones v Emerton-Court [1983] C.L.Y. 982 .... *6–061*
Jones v European General Express (1920) 25 Com. Cas. 296 .... *18–013*
Jones v Farrell (1857) 1 D. & J. 208 .... *19–017*, *19–020*
Jones v Gardiner [1902] 1 Ch. 191, Ch D *26–092*
Jones v Gwent CC [1992] I.R.L.R. 521 .... *27–023*
Jones v Herxheimer [1950] 2 K.B. 106; [1950] 1 All E.R. 323; 66 T.L.R. (Pt. 1) 403; (1950) 94 S.J. 97, CA *26–016*
Jones v Humphreys [1902] 1 K.B. 10, KBD *19–008*, *19–014*
Jones v Jones [1970] 2 Q.B. 576; [1970] 3 W.L.R. 20; [1970] 3 All E.R. 47; (1970) 114 S.J. 374, CA (Civ Div) *28–116*
Jones v Jones [1977] 1 W.L.R. 438; (1977) 33 P. & C.R. 147; (1976) 242 E.G. 371; (1976) 120 S.J. 802, CA (Civ Div) *3–137*, *3–139*, *3–151*, *29–161*
Jones v Just (1867–68) L.R. 3 Q.B. 197, QB *1–017*, *1–070*, *1–149*, *26–117*
Jones v Merionethshire Permanent Benefit Building Society [1892] 1 Ch. 173, CA; affirming [1891] 2 Ch. 587, Ch D *7–049*, *7–051*, *16–037*, *16–201*
Jones v Morgan [2001] EWCA Civ 995; [2001] Lloyd's Rep. Bank. 323; [2002] 1 E.G.L.R. 125; [2001] N.P.C. 104; (2001) 82 P. & C.R. DG20, CA (Civ Div) *7–128*
Jones v Morris (1849) 3 Ex. 742 .... *29–105*
Jones v Oceanic Steam Navigation Co Ltd [1924] 2 K.B. 730; (1924) 19 Ll. L. Rep. 348, KBD *12–087*, *30–309*
Jones v Padavatton [1969] 1 W.L.R. 328; [1969] 2 All E.R. 616; (1968) 112 S.J. 965, CA (Civ Div) *2–174*, *2–183*, *3–039*, *3–073*
Jones v Rimmer (1880) L.R. 14 Ch. D. 588, CA *5–077*
Jones v Robinson (1847) 1 Ex. 454 .... *3–036*
Jones v Saudi Arabia; sub nom. Jones v Ministry of the Interior Al-Mamlaka Al-Arabiya AS Saudiya; Mitchell v Al-Dali [2006] UKHL 26; [2007] 1 A.C. 270; [2006] 2 W.L.R. 1424; [2007] 1 All E.R. 113; [2006] H.R.L.R. 32; [2007] U.K.H.R.R. 24; 20 B.H.R.C. 621; (2006) 156 N.L.J. 1025; (2006) 150 S.J.L.B. 811, HL; reversing in part [2004] EWCA Civ 1394; [2005] Q.B. 699; [2005] 2 W.L.R. 808; [2005] U.K.H.R.R. 57; [2005] A.C.D. 50; (2004) 101(44) L.S.G. 31; (2004) 154 N.L.J. 1655; (2004) 148 S.J.L.B. 1286, CA (Civ Div) 11–003, *11–004*
Jones v Sherwood Computer Services Plc [1992] 1 W.L.R. 277; [1992] 2 All E.R. 170; [1989] E.G. 172 (C.S.), CA (Civ Div) *16–047*
Jones v St John's College, Oxford; sub nom. Jones v St John the Baptist's College, Oxford (1870–71) L.R. 6 Q.B. 115, QB *12–055*, *13–007*, *22–038*
Jones v Stones [1999] 1 W.L.R. 1739; (1999) 78 P. & C.R. 293; [1999] 3 E.G.L.R. 81; [1999] 42 E.G. 135; (1999) 96(22) L.S.G. 34, CA (Civ Div) *28–136*
Jones v Tankerville. *See* James Jones & Sons Ltd v Earl of Tankerville
Jones v Trollope Colls Cementation Overseas, *The Times*, January 26, 1990, CA (Civ Div) *30–347*

Jones v Vernons Pools [1938] 2 All E.R. 626 .... *2–162*
Jones v Victoria Graving Dock Co (1876–77) L.R. 2 Q.B.D. 314, CA *4–027*, *4–028*, *4–036*
Jones v Waite (1842) 9 Cl. & F. 101; affirming (1839) 5 Bing.N.C. 341 3–075
Jones (An Infant), Re (1883) 48 L.T. 188 .... *8–013*
Jones Ltd v Waring and Gillow Ltd. *See* RE Jones Ltd v Waring and Gillow Ltd
Jordan Grand Prix Ltd v Vodafone Group Plc [2003] EWHC 1956 (Comm); [2003] 2 All E.R. (Comm) 864; [2003] 2 Lloyd's Rep. 874, QBD (Comm) ... *2–112*
Jordan v Norton (1838) 4 M. & W. 155 .... *2–032*
Jordon v Money (1854) 5 H.L.C. 195 .... *3–103*, *22–004*
Joscelin v Shelton (1557) 3 Leon 4 .... *3–008*
Joscelyne v Nissen [1970] 2 Q.B. 86; [1970] 2 W.L.R. 509; [1970] 1 All E.R. 1213; (1969) 114 S.J. 55, CA (Civ Div) 5–113, 5–114, *5–122*
Joseph v Lyons (1884–85) L.R. 15 Q.B.D. 280, CA *19–032*, *19–068*
Joseph v National Magazine Co [1959] Ch. 14; [1958] 3 W.L.R. 366; [1958] 3 All E.R. 52; (1958) 102 S.J. 602, Ch D *26–087*, *27–025*, *27–042*
Joseph Constantine Steamship Line Ltd v Imperial Smelting Corp Ltd [1942] A.C. 154; [1941] 2 All E.R. 165, HL ... *23–003*, *23–007*, *23–010*, *23–021*, *23–040*, *23–058*, *23–061*, 23–063, 23–065, *23–071*, *30–352*
Joseph Evans & Co v Heathcote [1918] 1 K.B. 418, CA; reversing [1917] 2 K.B. 336, KBD *3–033*, *16–127*, *29–192*
Joseph Pyke & Son (Liverpool) Ltd v Richard Cornelius & Co [1955] 2 Lloyd's Rep. 747, QBD *14–141*
Joseph Thorley Ltd v Orchis Steamship Co Ltd [1907] 1 K.B. 660, CA; affirming [1907] 1 K.B. 243, KBD *14–029*
Joseph Travers & Sons Ltd v Cooper [1915] 1 K.B. 73, CA *14–011*, *14–019*
Josling v Kingsford (1863) 13 C.B.(N.S.) 447 .... *14–027*
Joyce v Rigolli [2004] EWCA Civ 79; (2004) 148 S.J.L.B. 234; [2004] 1 P. & C.R. DG22, CA (Civ Div) 4–057
Joyner v Weeks [1891] 2 Q.B. 31, CA *26–117*
Jubilee Cotton Mills Ltd, Re; sub nom. Jubilee Cotton Mills Ltd (Official Receiver and Liquidator) v Lewis [1924] A.C. 958, HL; reversing [1923] 1 Ch. 1, CA; reversing [1922] 1 Ch. 100, Ch D *9–054*, *9–060*, *16–192*
Judge v Crown Leisure Ltd [2005] EWCA Civ 571; [2005] I.R.L.R. 823, CA (Civ Div) *2–139*, *2–183*
Judgment Summons (No.25 of 1952) Ex p. Henlys Ltd, Re [1953] Ch. 195; [1953] 2 W.L.R. 315; [1953] 1 All E.R. 424; (1953) 97 S.J. 112, CA *29–150*
Jugoslavenska Oceanska Plovidba v Castle Investment Co Inc; The Kozara [1974] Q.B. 292; [1973] 3 W.L.R. 847; [1973] 3 All E.R. 498; [1973] 2 Lloyd's Rep. 1; (1973) 117 S.J. 712, CA (Civ Div) *30–376*, *30–379*
Julian v Mayor of Auckland [1927] N.Z.L.R. 453 .... *29–047*
Julien Praet et Cie SA v HG Poland Ltd. *See* Praet (Julien) et Cie S/A v HG Poland Ltd (Damages)
Junior Books Ltd v Veitchi Co Ltd [1983] 1 A.C. 520; [1982] 3 W.L.R. 477; [1982] 3 All E.R. 201; 1982 S.C. (H.L.) 244; 1982 S.L.T. 492; [1982] Com. L.R. 221; 21 B.L.R. 66; (1982) 79 L.S.G. 1413; (1982) 126 S.J. 538, HL; affirming 1982 S.L.T. 333, IH (2 Div) *1–141*, **1–176**, *14–056*, *14–057*, *18–022*, **18–023**, 18–024, 18–025, 18–027, *18–030*, 18–033, 18–036, 18–093
Justice v Wynne (1861) 12 Ir. Ch. Rep. 289 .... *19–068*
Jyske Bank (Gibraltar) Ltd v Spjeldnaes (No.2), July 29, 1999, CA (Civ Div); reversing in part [2000] B.C.C. 16; [1999] 2 B.C.L.C. 101; [1999] B.P.I.R. 525; (1998) 95(46) L.S.G. 35; (1998) 142 S.J.L.B. 287, Ch D *9–021*
K (Deceased), Re [1986] Ch. 180; [1985] 3 W.L.R. 234; [1985] 2 All E.R. 833; [1986] Fam. Law 19; (1985) 82 L.S.G. 2242; (1985) 135 N.L.J. 655; (1985) 129 S.J. 364, CA (Civ Div); affirming [1985] Ch. 85; [1985] 2 W.L.R. 262; [1985] 1 All E.R. 403; [1986] 1 F.L.R. 79; (1985) 82 L.S.G. 1335, Ch D *16–169*, *16–170*

K Chellaram & Sons (London) v Butlers Warehousing & Distribution [1978] 2 Lloyd's Rep. 412, CA (Civ Div); reversing [1977] 2 Lloyd's Rep. 192, QBD (Comm) *18–135*
K Lokumal & Sons (London) Ltd v Lotte Shipping Co Pte Ltd; The August Leonhardt [1985] 2 Lloyd's Rep. 28, CA (Civ Div); reversing [1984] 1 Lloyd's Rep. 322; (1984) 134 N.L.J. 125, QBD (Comm) *3–092*, *3–109*, *28–109*, 28–136
K Ltd v National Westminster Bank Plc [2006] EWCA Civ 1039; [2007] Bus. L.R. 26; [2007] 1 W.L.R. 311; [2006] 4 All E.R. 907; [2006] 2 All E.R. (Comm) 655; [2006] 2 Lloyd's Rep. 569; [2006] C.P. Rep. 45; (2006) 103(31) L.S.G. 24; (2006) 150 S.J.L.B. 982, CA (Civ Div) 1–047, 1–048
K v P [1993] Ch. 140; [1992] 3 W.L.R. 1015; [1993] 1 All E.R. 521, Ch D *16–164*, *16–175*
KC Sethia (1944) Ltd v Partabmull Rameshwar. *See* Partabmull Rameshar v KC Sethia (1944) Ltd
KH Enterprise v Owners of the Pioneer Container. *See* Pioneer Container, The
KPMG v Network Rail Infrastructure Ltd [2007] EWCA Civ 363; [2007] All E.R. (D) 245; [2007] Bus. L.R. 1336; [2008] 1 P. & C.R. 11; [2007] L. & T.R. 32; (2007) 151 S.J.L.B. 611; [2007] N.P.C. 51, CA (Civ Div); affirming [2006] EWHC 67 (Ch); [2006] All E.R. (D) 247; [2006] 2 P. & C.R. 7; [2006] 6 E.G. 171 (C.S.); [2006] N.P.C. 11, Ch D ...*5–125*, *5–126*, *5–127*, *12–069*, 12–075
K/S Stamar v Seabow Shipping Ltd; The Andreas P [1994] 2 Lloyd's Rep. 183, QBD (Comm) *13–007*
Kabel v Ronald Lyon Espanola SA (1968) 208 E.G. 265 .... *16–192*
Kadel Chajkin & Ce De Ltd v Mitchell Cotts & Co (Middle East) Ltd; The Stensby [1947] 2 All E.R. 786; (1947–48) 81 Ll. L. Rep. 124; 64 T.L.R. 89; [1948] L.J.R. 535; (1948) 92 S.J. 72, KBD *30–051*
Kahan v Pakistan Federation [1951] 2 K.B. 1003; [1951] 2 T.L.R. 697; (1951) 95 S.J. 562, CA *11–001*, *11–020*, *11–022*
Kahler v Midland Bank Ltd [1950] A.C. 24; [1949] 2 All E.R. 621; 65 T.L.R. 663; [1949] L.J.R. 1687, HL; affirming [1948] 1 All E.R. 811, CA ...*16–027*, *16–031*, *23–028*, *30–005*, *30–009*, *30–012*, *30–015*, *30–056*, *30–362*, *30–309*, *30–356*, *30–364*, *30–365*, *30–367*
Kakkar v Szelke [1989] E.P.O.R. 184; [1989] 1 F.S.R. 225, CA (Civ Div) *28–118*
Kaliningrad, The and Nadezhda Krupskaya, The [1997] 2 Lloyd's Rep. 35, QBD (Admlty) *3–008*
Kaliszewska v J Clague & Partners, 5 Con. L.R. 62; [1984] C.I.L.L. 131 ....*28–084*, *28–109*
Kall Kwik Printing (UK) Ltd v Bell [1994] F.S.R. 674, Ch D *27–008*
Kall Kwik Printing (UK) Ltd v Rush [1996] F.S.R. 114, Ch D 16–120
Kallang Shipping SA v AXA Assurances Senegal; The Kallang [2006] EWHC 2825 (Comm); [2007] 1 Lloyd's Rep. 160, QBD (Comm) *13–011*
Kalsep Ltd v X-Flow BV (2001) 24(7) I.P.D. 24044, Ch D *5–016*
Kalwak v Consistent Group Ltd. *See* Consistent Group Ltd v Kalwak
Kammins Ballrooms Co Ltd v Zenith Investments (Torquay) Ltd (No.1) [1971] A.C. 850; [1970] 3 W.L.R. 287; [1970] 2 All E.R. 871; (1971) 22 P. & C.R. 74; (1970) 114 S.J. 590, HL; affirming [1970] 1 Q.B. 673; [1969] 3 W.L.R. 799; [1969] 3 All E.R. 1268; (1969) 20 P. & C.R. 1087; (1969) 113 S.J. 640, CA (Civ Div) *3–081*, *24–003*, *24–007*
Kamouh v Associated Electrical Industries International [1980] Q.B. 199; [1979] 2 W.L.R. 795; (1978) 122 S.J. 714, QBD *28–094*, *28–095*, *28–118*
Kanchenjunga, The. *See* Motor Oil Hellas (Corinth) Refineries SA v Shipping Corp of India
Kanematsu (Hong Kong) Ltd v Eurasia Express Line [1988] 1 C.L. 4404, QBD (Comm) *14–033*
Kanhaya Lal v National Bank of India (1913) 29 T.L.R. 314 ....*29–088*, *29–090*, *29–093*
Kapetan Georgis, The. *See* Virgo Steamship Co SA v Skaarup Shipping Corp

Kapfunde v Abbey National Plc [1998] E.C.C. 440; [1999] I.C.R. 1; [1998] I.R.L.R. 583; [1999] Lloyd's Rep. Med. 48; (1999) 46 B.M.L.R. 176, CA (Civ Div) *18–031*
Kapitan Petko Voivoda, The. *See* Daewoo Heavy Industries Ltd v Klipriver Shipping Ltd
Kapur v Kapur [1985] Fam. Law 22; (1984) 81 L.S.G. 2543, Fam Div *30–079*
Karasiewicz v Eagle Star Insurance Co Ltd; sub nom. Eagle Star Insurance Co Ltd v Karasiewicz [2002] EWCA Civ 940, CA (Civ Div) *29–173*
Karberg's Case. *See* Metropolitan Coal Consumers Association (Karberg's Case), Re
Karflex Ltd v Poole [1933] 2 K.B. 251, KBD *12–023*, *14–028*, *29–057*
Karin Vatis, The. *See* Vagres Compania Maritima SA v Nissho-Iwai American Corp; The Karin Vatis
Karnos Property Co Ltd, Re (1989) 5 B.C.C. 14; [1989] B.C.L.C. 340; 87 L.G.R. 263, Ch D (Companies Ct) *28–070*
Karsales (Harrow) Ltd v Wallis [1956] 1 W.L.R. 936; [1956] 2 All E.R. 866; (1956) 100 S.J. 548, CA *12–021*, *12–023*, *14–020*, *14–028*
Kasumu v Baba-Egbe [1956] A.C. 539; [1956] 3 W.L.R. 575; [1956] 3 All E.R. 266; (1956) 100 S.J. 600, PC (West Africa) *16–185*
Katy, The [1895] P. 56, CA *21–022*
Katzenstein Adler Industries (1975) Ltd v Borchard Lines; The Joanna Borchard [1988] 2 Lloyd's Rep. 274; [1988] 2 F.T.L.R. 1; (1988) 138 N.L.J. Rep. 94, QBD (Comm) *28–118*
Kaufman v Gerson [1904] 1 K.B. 591, CA; reversing [1903] 2 K.B. 114, KBD *7–011*, *7–048*, *7–052*, *16–029*, *29–089*, *30–367*, *30–368*
Kaukomarkkinat O/Y v Elbe Transport-Union GmbH; The Kelo [1985] 2 Lloyd's Rep. 85, QBD (Comm) *16–057*, *19–015*, *19–050*
Kaur v MG Rover Group Ltd [2004] EWCA Civ 1507; [2005] I.C.R. 625; [2005] I.R.L.R. 40, CA (Civ Div); reversing [2004] I.R.L.R. 279, QBD *2–177*
Kaur (Pritam) v S Russell & Sons Ltd [1973] Q.B. 336; [1973] 2 W.L.R. 147; [1973] 1 All E.R. 617; (1972) 117 S.J. 91, CA (Civ Div) *28–062*, *28–063*
Kauri Timber Co Ltd v Taxes Commissioner [1913] A.C. 771, PC (NZ) *4–018*
Kavanagh, Re; sub nom. Bankrupt, Ex p. v Jackson; The Trustee [1950] 1 All E.R. 39 (Note); 66 T.L.R. (Pt. 1) 65; [1950] W.N. 15, CA; affirming [1949] 2 All E.R. 264; (1949) 65 T.L.R. 486; [1949] W.N. 306; (1949) 93 S.J. 465, DC *20–026*, *20–034*
Kawasaki Kisen Kabushiki Kaisha of Kobe v Bantham Steamship Co Ltd (No.2) [1939] 2 K.B. 544; (1939) 63 Ll. L. Rep. 155, CA; affirming (1938) 61 Ll. L. Rep. 131, KBD *14–146*
Kawasaki Steel Corp v Sardoil SpA; The Zuiho Maru [1977] 2 Lloyd's Rep. 552, QBD (Comm) *14–151*, *23–068*
Kay, Re [1939] Ch. 239 .... *27–034*
Kaye v Croydon Tramways Co [1898] 1 Ch. 358, CA *9–055*
Kaye v Waghorn (1809) 1 Taunt. 428 .... *1–115*, *22–030*
Kaye Steam Navigating Co v Barnett (1932) 48 T.L.R. 440 .... *26–048*
Kayford Ltd (In Liquidation), Re [1975] 1 W.L.R. 279; [1975] 1 All E.R. 604; (1974) 118 S.J. 752, Ch D *1–189*
Kay's Leasing Corp Pty v Fletcher, 116 C.L.R. 124 .... *30–007*, *30–068*, *30–311*
Kay's Settlement Trusts, Re; sub nom. Broadbent v MacNab [1939] Ch. 329, Ch D *1–108*
Kazakstan Wool Processors (Europe) Ltd v Nederlandsche Credietverzekering Maatschappij NV [2000] 1 All E.R. (Comm) 708; [2000] C.L.C. 822; [2000] Lloyd's Rep. I.R. 371, CA (Civ Div); affirming [1999] 2 All E.R. (Comm) 445; [1999] Lloyd's Rep. I.R. 596, QBD (Comm) *12–055*
Kearley v Thomson (1890) L.R. 24 Q.B.D. 742, CA *16–042*, 16–189
Kearney v Whitehaven Colliery Co [1893] 1 Q.B. 700, CA *16–194*, *16–201*
Kearon v Pearson (1861) 2 H.N. 386 .... *23–005*
Kearsley v Cole (1846) 16 M. & W. 128 .... *20–052*
Keates v Lord Cadogan (1851) 10 C.B. 591 .... *5–008*, *6–014*

Keeble v Keeble [1956] 1 W.L.R. 94; [1956] 1 All E.R. 100; (1956) 100 S.J. 75, PDAD *12–089*
Keech v Sandford (1726) Cas. King 61 .... *29–160*
Keelwalk Properties Ltd v Waller [2002] EWCA Civ 1076; [2002] 3 E.G.L.R. 79; [2002] 48 E.G. 142; [2002] 33 E.G. 95 (C.S.); [2002] N.P.C. 106; [2003] 1 P. & C.R. DG4, CA (Civ Div) *3–138*
Keen v Commerzbank AG; sub nom. Commerzbank AG v Keen [2006] EWCA Civ 1536; [2006] 2 C.L.C. 844; [2007] I.C.R. 623; [2007] I.R.L.R. 132, CA (Civ Div); reversing [2006] EWHC 785 (Comm), QBD (Comm) *1–032*, *2–175*, *14–074*, *15–046*
Keen v Holland [1984] 1 W.L.R. 251; [1984] 1 All E.R. 75; (1984) 47 P. & C.R. 639; (1984) 269 E.G. 1043; (1983) 80 L.S.G. 3078; (1983) 127 S.J. 764, CA (Civ Div) *3–113*, *3–115*
Keenan v Handley (1864) 10 L.T. 800 .... *27–050*
Keeping v Brown (1895) 11 T.L.R. 595 .... *21–062*
Kehoe v Rutherford (1893) 27 A. 912 .... *29–069*
Keighley Maxsted & Co v Durant (t/a Bryan Durant & Co); sub nom. Durant & Co v Roberts [1901] A.C. 240, HL; reversing [1900] 1 Q.B. 629, CA *18–019*, *21–041*
Keightley v Watson (1849) 3 Ex. 716 .... *3–043*, *3–044*
Keiner v Keiner [1952] 1 All E.R. 643; 45 R. & I.T. 174; 34 T.C. 346; (1952) 31 A.T.C. 87; [1952] T.R. 119; [1952] W.N. 139; (1952) 96 S.J. 213, QBD *30–011*, *30–051*
Keir v Leeman (1846) 9 L.J. Q.B. 371 .... *7–049*
Keith Prowse & Co v National Telephone Co [1894] 2 Ch. 147, Ch D *22–053*
Kekewich v Manning (1851) 1 De. G.M. & G. 176 .....1–108, *18–086*, *19–028*, *19–033*
Kellar v Williams [2004] UKPC 30; [2004] All E.R. (D) 286; [2005] 4 Costs L.R. 559; (2004) 148 S.J.L.B. 821, PC (TCI) 16–049
Kelly v Battershell [1949] 2 All E.R. 830, CA *13–007*
Kelly v Cooper [1993] A.C. 205; [1992] 3 W.L.R. 936; [1994] 1 B.C.L.C. 395; [1992] E.G. 119 (C.S.); (1992) 136 S.J.L.B. 303; [1992] N.P.C. 134, PC (Ber) *29–156*
Kelly v Coote (1856) 5 Ir. C.L.R. 469 .... *8–033*
Kelly v Cornhill Insurance Co Ltd [1964] 1 W.L.R. 158; [1964] 1 All E.R. 321; [1964] 1 Lloyd's Rep. 1; 1964 S.C. (H.L.) 46; 1964 S.L.T. 81; (1964) 108 S.J. 94, HL; reversing, 1963 S.C. 113; 1963 S.L.T. 13; 1962 S.L.T. (Notes) 97, IH (1 Div); affirming, 1962 S.L.T. (Notes) 55, OH *20–007*
Kelly v Liverpool Maritime Terminals Ltd [1988] I.R.L.R. 310, CA (Civ Div) *3–144*
Kelly v Lombard Banking Co [1959] 1 W.L.R. 41; [1958] 3 All E.R. 713; (1959) 103 S.J. 34, CA *29–057*, *29–061*
Kelly v Metropolitan Railway Co [1895] 1 Q.B. 944, CA *1–118*
Kelly v Selwyn [1905] 2 Ch. 117, Ch D *19–068*, *30–125*
Kelly v Solari, 152 E.R. 24; (1841) 9 M. & W. 54, Ex Ct *29–013*, *29–020*, *29–025*, 29–030, *29–033*, 29–036, *29–039*, *29–040*, 29–044, *29–184*, *29–186*
Kelly v Webster (1852) 12 C.B. 283 .... *4–011*
Kelner v Baxter (1866–67) L.R. 2 C.P. 174, CCP *9–012*, *9–014*
Kelo, The *See* Kaukomarkkinat O/Y v Elbe Transport-Union GmbH
Kelsey v Dodd (1883) 52 L.J. Ch. 34 .... *1–109*, *18–125*
Kemble v Farren, 130 E.R. 1234; (1829) 6 Bing. 141, KB *26–127*
Kemp v Baerselman [1906] 2 K.B. 604, CA 19–056
Kemp v Intasun Holidays [1987] 2 F.T.L.R. 234; (1988) 6 Tr. L. 161, CA (Civ Div) *26–063*, *26–083*
Kemp v Neptune Concrete (1989) 57 P. & C.R. 369; [1988] 48 E.G. 71; [1988] E.G. 86 (C.S.), CA (Civ Div) *5–116*
Kemp v Sober (1851) 1 Sim. (N.S) 517 .... *27–060*
Kemp v Tolland. *See* AB Kemp Ltd v Tolland (t/a James Tolland & Co)
Kempson v Ashbee (1874–75) L.R. 10 Ch. App. 15, Lord Chancellor *7–075*

Kenburn Waste Management Ltd v Bergmann [2002] EWCA Civ 98; [2002] C.L.C. 644; [2002] I.L.Pr. 33; [2002] F.S.R. 45, CA (Civ Div) *30–020*, *30–077*, *30–090*
Kendal v Wood (1870–71) L.R. 6 Ex. 243, Ex Chamber *29–099*
Kendall v Hamilton (1878–79) L.R. 4 App. Cas. 504, HL; affirming (1877–78) L.R. 3 C.P.D. 403, CA *17–002*, *17–009*, *17–010*, *17–012*, *17–015*, *24–003*, *25–007*
Keneric Tractor Sales Ltd v Langille (1987) 43 D.L.R. (4d) 171 ..... *22–049*
Kennard v Cory Bros & Co Ltd (No.2) [1922] 2 Ch. 1, CA *27–026*
Kennedy v Brown (1863) 13 C.B. (N.S.) 677 ..... *3–029*, *29–192*
Kennedy v KB Van Emden & Co; Jordan v Gershon Young Finer & Green; Burdge v Jacobs Kane & Blok; sub nom. Kennedy v Emden [1996] P.N.L.R. 409; (1997) 74 P. & C.R. 19; [1997] 2 E.G.L.R. 137; [1997] 44 E.G. 201; (1996) 93(16) L.S.G. 31; (1996) 140 S.J.L.B. 99; [1996] N.P.C. 56, CA (Civ Div) *26–064*
Kennedy v Lee (1817) 3 Mer. 441 ..... *2–028*
Kennedy v Panama New Zealand & Australian Royal Mail Co; sub nom. Lord Gilbert Kennedy v Panama, New Zealand, & Australian Royal Mail Co (Ltd); Panama, New Zealand & Australian Royal Mail Co (Ltd) v Lord Gilbert Kennedy (1866–67) L.R. 2 Q.B. 580, QB **5–022**, 5–052, *6–103*
Kennedy v Thomas [1894] 2 Q.B. 759, CA *28–043*
Kennedy v Thomassen [1929] 1 Ch. 426, Ch D *2–045*, 2–101, *29–074*
Kennet v Brown; sub nom. Kennett v Brown [1988] 1 W.L.R. 582; [1988] 2 All E.R. 600; (1988) 85(19) L.S.G. 43; (1988) 132 S.J. 752, CA (Civ Div) *28–121*
Kenneth Allison Ltd (In Liquidation) v AE Limehouse & Co [1992] 2 A.C. 105; [1991] 3 W.L.R. 671; [1991] 4 All E.R. 500; (1991) 141 N.L.J. 1448; (1991) 135 S.J.L.B. 172, HL; reversing [1990] 2 Q.B. 527; [1990] 3 W.L.R. 216; [1990] 2 All E.R. 723, CA (Civ Div) *3–108*
Kennewell v Dye [1949] Ch. 517; [1949] 1 All E.R. 881; [1949] L.J.R. 1250; (1949) 93 S.J. 250, Ch D *20–005*
Kenney v Wexham (1822) 6 Madd. 355 ..... *27–007*, *27–008*
Kenny v Preen [1963] 1 Q.B. 499; [1962] 3 W.L.R. 1233; [1962] 3 All E.R. 814; (1962) 106 S.J. 854, CA *1–146*, *26–019*
Kenny & Good Pty Ltd v MGICA (1992) Ltd [2000] Lloyd's Rep. P.N. 25, HC (Aus) *26–094*
Kensington and Chelsea BC v Riley [1973] R.T.R. 122; [1973] Crim. L.R. 133, DC *6–012*
Kensington, Chelsea and Westminster AHA v Wettern Composites [1985] 1 All E.R. 346; 31 B.L.R. 57; (1984) 134 N.L.J. 887, DC *28–033*
Kent v Godts (1855) 26 L.T.(O.S.) 88 ..... *24–019*
Kent v Hartley (1966) 200 E.G. 1027 ..... *5–113*, *5–126*
Kent & Sussex Sawmills Ltd, Re [1947] Ch. 177; [1946] 2 All E.R. 638; 62 T.L.R. 747; [1947] L.J.R. 534; 176 L.T. 167; (1947) 91 S.J. 12, Ch D *19–022*, *19–066*
Kenward v Kenward; Way v Way; Rowley v Rowley; Whitehead v Whitehead [1951] P. 124; [1950] 2 All E.R. 297; 66 T.L.R. (Pt. 2) 157; (1950) 94 S.J. 383, CA *23–040*
Kenworthy v Schofield (1824) 2 B. & C. 945 ..... *4–029*, *4–038*
Kenya Railways v Antares Co Pte Ltd; The Antares (No.1) [1987] 1 Lloyd's Rep. 424, CA (Civ Div); affirming [1986] 2 Lloyd's Rep. 626, QBD (Comm) *14–008*, *14–029*, *14–031*
Kenya Railways v Antares Co Pte Ltd; The Antares (No.2) [1986] 2 Lloyd's Rep. 633, QBD (Comm) *28–109*, *28–115*, *28–119*, *28–126*
Kenyon v Darwen Cotton Manufacturing Co Ltd [1936] 2 K.B. 193, CA *16–198*
Kenyon, Son & Craven v Baxter Hoare & Co [1971] 1 W.L.R. 519; [1971] 2 All E.R. 708; [1971] 1 Lloyd's Rep. 232, QBD *14–003*, *14–018*, *14–035*
Kenyon-Brown v Desmond Banks & Co (Undue Influence) (No.1) [2000] Lloyd's Rep. Bank. 80; [2000] Lloyd's Rep. P.N. 338; [2000] P.N.L.R. 266; (1999) 149 N.L.J. 1832; [1999] N.P.C. 140, CA (Civ Div) *7–110*

Kepong Prospecting Ltd v Schmidt; sub nom. Kepong Prospecting Ltd v Jagatheesan [1968] A.C. 810; [1968] 2 W.L.R. 55; (1967) 111 S.J. 909, PC (Mal) 18–017
Kerns v Manning [1935] I.R. 869 .... *4–033*
Kerr v Jeston (1842) 1 Dowl. (N.S.) 538 .... *12–093*
Kerr v Marine Products (1928) 44 T.L.R. 292 .... *9–059*
Kerr v Morris [1987] Ch. 90; [1986] 3 W.L.R. 662; [1986] 3 All E.R. 217; (1986) 83 L.S.G. 2570; (1986) 130 S.J. 665, CA (Civ Div) *16–119*, *27–061*
Kerrison v Glynn Mills Currie Co (1911) 81 L.J.K.B. 465 .....29–031, *29–033*, *29–034*, *29–038*
Kerrison v Smith [1897] 2 Q.B. 445; 66 L.J.K.B. 672; 77 L.T. 344, QBD *13–028*
Kershaw Mechanical Services Ltd v Kendrick Construction Ltd [2006] EWHC 727 (TCC); [2006] 4 All E.R. 79; [2006] 2 All E.R. (Comm) 81; 109 Con. L.R. 42; [2006] C.I.L.L. 2359, QBD (TCC) *12–050*
Kershaw, Re; Whittaker v Kershaw (1890) L.R. 45 Ch. D. 320, CA *12–089*
Kesarmal S/O Letchman Das v NKV Valliappa Chettiar S/O Nagappa Chettiar [1954] 1 W.L.R. 380; (1954) 98 S.J. 126, PC (FMS) *7–052*
Ketsey's Case (1614) Cro.Jac. 320 .... *8–032*
Ketteman v Hansel Properties Ltd [1987] A.C. 189; [1987] 2 W.L.R. 312; [1988] 1 All E.R. 38; 36 B.L.R. 1; [1987] 1 F.T.L.R. 284; 85 L.G.R. 409; [1987] 1 E.G.L.R. 237; (1987) 84 L.S.G. 657; (1987) 137 N.L.J. 100; (1987) 131 S.J. 134, HL; affirming [1984] 1 W.L.R. 1274; [1985] 1 All E.R. 352; 27 B.L.R. 1; (1985) 49 P. & C.R. 257; (1984) 271 E.G. 1099; [1984] C.I.L.L. 109; (1984) 81 L.S.G. 3018; (1984) 128 S.J. 800, CA (Civ Div) *1–124*, *28–119*
Keyes v Elkins (1864) 5 B. & S. 240 .... *22–006*
Keys v Harwood (1846) 2 C.B. 905 .... *24–028*
Khan v Goleccha International [1980] 1 W.L.R. 1482; [1980] 2 All E.R. 259; (1980) 40 P. & C.R. 193; (1980) 124 S.J. 848, CA (Civ Div) *25–012*
Khan v RM Falvey & Co; sub nom. Khan v Falvey [2002] EWCA Civ 400; [2002] Lloyd's Rep. P.N. 369; [2002] P.N.L.R. 28; (2002) 99(19) L.S.G. 30; (2002) 146 S.J.L.B. 108, CA (Civ Div) *28–033*
Khian Captain, The (No.2) *See* Freedom Maritime Corp v International Bulk Carriers SA
Kibble, Ex p. *See* Onslow Ex p. Kibble, Re
Kidd v Boone (1871) L.R. 12 Eq. 89, Ct of Chancery *25–001*
Kidderminster Corp v Hardwick (1873–74) L.R. 9 Ex. 13, Ex Ct *3–167*
Kidner v Keith (1863) 15 C.B. (N.S.) 35 .... *1–105*
Kidner v Stimpson (1918) 35 T.L.R. 63 .... *24–036*
Kiely & Sons v Medcraft (1965) 109 S.J. 829, CA *21–033*
Kijowski v New Capital Properties, 15 Con. L.R. 1, QBD *19–021*, *19–025*, *28–086*
Kilby v Basildon DC; sub nom. R. (on the application of Kilby) v Basildon DC [2007] EWCA Civ 479; [2007] H.L.R. 39; [2007] 22 E.G. 161 (C.S.); (2007) 151 S.J.L.B. 712; [2007] N.P.C. 65, CA (Civ Div); affirming [2006] EWHC 1892 (Admin); [2006] H.L.R. 46; [2006] A.C.D. 94; (2006) 103(37) L.S.G. 34, QBD (Admin) *10–024*
Kilcarne Holdings Ltd v Targetfollow (Birmingham) Ltd [2005] EWCA Civ 1355; [2005] N.P.C. 132; [2006] 1 P. & C.R. DG20, CA (Civ Div); affirming [2004] EWHC 2547 (Ch); [2005] 2 P. & C.R. 8; [2004] N.P.C. 167, Ch D 4–066, *4–067*, *4–077*
Killick v PricewaterhouseCoopers (No.1) [2001] 1 B.C.L.C. 65; [2001] Lloyd's Rep. P.N. 17; [2001] P.N.L.R. 1; [2001] W.T.L.R. 699, Ch D *1–184*, *18–022*
Killick & Co v Price & Co (1896) 12 T.L.R. 263 .... *12–114*
Kilmer v British Columbia Orchard Lands Ltd [1913] A.C. 319, PC (Can) *26–147*
Kimber v William Willett [1947] K.B. 570; [1947] 1 All E.R. 361; 63 T.L.R. 153; [1947] L.J.R. 650; 176 L.T. 566; (1947) 91 S.J. 206, CA *13–032*
Kinane v Mackie-Conteh; Kinane v Almack Marketing Services Ltd [2005] EWCA Civ 45; [2005] W.T.L.R. 345; [2005] 6 E.G. 140 (C.S.); (2005) 149 S.J.L.B. 177; [2005] 2 P. & C.R. DG3, CA (Civ Div); affirming in part [2004] EWHC 998 (Ch); [2004] 19 E.G. 164 (C.S.), Ch D ... *3–115*, *3–140*, *3–144*, *3–147*, *3–151*, 4–077, 4–081

Kinch v Bullard [1999] 1 W.L.R. 423; [1998] 4 All E.R. 650; [1999] 1 F.L.R. 66; [1998] 3 E.G.L.R. 112; [1998] 47 E.G. 140; [1998] Fam. Law 738; [1998] E.G. 126 (C.S.); [1998] N.P.C. 137; (1999) 77 P. & C.R. D1, Ch D *2–060*, *2–061*
Kindlance v Murphy, unreported, unreported, 1997, Ch D (NI) ...*15–019*, *15–020*, *15–098*
King, Re; Ex p. Unity Joint Stock Mutual Banking Association, Re (1858) 3 De. G. & J. 63 .... *8–051*, *8–052*
King v Alston (1848) 12 Q.B. 971 .... *29–142*
King v Brandywine Reinsurance Co (UK) Ltd (formerly Cigna RE Co (UK) Ltd) [2005] EWCA Civ 235; [2005] 2 All E.R. (Comm) 1; [2005] 1 Lloyd's Rep. 655; [2005] 1 C.L.C. 283; [2005] Env. L.R. 33; [2005] Lloyd's Rep. I.R. 509, CA (Civ Div) *30–011*
King v David Allen & Sons Billposting Ltd [1916] 2 A.C. 54, HL (UK-Irl); affirming [1915] 2 I.R. 448, CA (UK-Irl) *9–012*
King v Hoare (1844) 13 M. & W. 494 .... *17–002*, *17–015*, *17–016*
King v Hoare (1844) 13 M.W. 495 .... *25–007*
King v Jackson (t/a Jackson Flower Co) (1998) 30 H.L.R. 541; [1998] 1 E.G.L.R. 30; [1998] 03 E.G. 138; [1997] N.P.C. 116; (1997) 74 P. & C.R. D30, CA (Civ Div) *4–078*
King v King (1981) 41 P. & C.R. 311; (1980) 255 E.G. 1205, Ch D *2–126*, *2–132*
King v Leith (1787) 2 T.R. 141 .... *29–141*
King v Lewis; sub nom. Lewis v King [2004] EWCA Civ 1329; [2005] I.L.Pr. 16; [2005] E.M.L.R. 4; (2004) 148 S.J.L.B. 1248, CA (Civ Div) *30–097*
King v Michael Faraday & Partners Ltd [1939] 2 K.B. 753, KBD *16–006*
King v Parker (1876) 34 L.T. 887 .... *23–035*, *23–047*
King v Smith [1900] 2 Ch. 425, Ch D *21–043*
King v Technology Piling Ltd (Costs) [2003] EWCA Civ 1283, CA (Civ Div) *18–022*
King v Telegraph Group Ltd [2004] EWCA Civ 613; [2005] 1 W.L.R. 2282; [2004] C.P. Rep. 35; [2004] 3 Costs L.R. 449; [2004] E.M.L.R. 23; (2004) 101(25) L.S.G. 27; (2004) 154 N.L.J. 823; (2004) 148 S.J.L.B. 664, CA (Civ Div); affirming [2003] EWHC 1312 (QB), QBD *16–056*
King v Thom (1789) 1 T.R. 487 .... *20–011*
King v Victor Parsons & Co [1973] 1 W.L.R. 29; [1973] 1 All E.R. 206; [1973] 1 Lloyd's Rep. 189; (1972) 116 S.J. 901, CA (Civ Div); affirming [1972] 1 W.L.R. 801; [1972] 2 All E.R. 625; [1972] 1 Lloyd's Rep. 213; (1971) 116 S.J. 239, QBD *13–015*, *28–084*, *28–086*, *28–087*
King v Victoria Insurance Co Ltd [1896] A.C. 250, PC (Aus) *19–008*, *19–011*, *19–049*
King v Zimmerman (1870–71) L.R. 6 C.P. 466, CCP *21–080*
King's Motors (Oxford) v Lax [1970] 1 W.L.R. 426; [1969] 3 All E.R. 665; (1970) 21 P. & C.R. 507; (1970) 114 S.J. 168, Chancery Ct of Lancaster *2–126*
Kings North Trust Ltd v Bell [1986] 1 W.L.R. 119; [1986] 1 All E.R. 423; (1985) 17 H.L.R. 352; [1985] Fam. Law 225; (1985) 82 L.S.G. 1329; (1986) 130 S.J. 88, CA (Civ Div) *6–023*, *7–105*
King's Norton Metal Co v Edridge Merrett & Co (1897) 14 T.L.R. 98 5–096
Kingsbury Collieries and Moore's Contract, Re; sub nom. Kingsbury Collieries Ltd and Moore's Contract, Re [1907] 2 Ch. 259, Ch D *9–022*
Kingscroft Insurance Co v HS Weavers (Underwriting) Agencies [1993] 1 Lloyd's Rep. 187, Ch D *27–008*
Kingscroft Insurance Co Ltd v Nissan Fire & Marine Insurance Co Ltd (No.2) [2000] 1 All E.R. (Comm) 272; [1999] C.L.C. 1875; [1999] Lloyd's Rep. I.R. 603, QBD (Comm) *2–110*
Kingsley v Sterling Industrial Securities Ltd [1967] 2 Q.B. 747; [1966] 2 W.L.R. 1265; [1966] 2 All E.R. 414; (1966) 110 S.J. 267, CA; reversing [1966] 1 All E.R. 37, QBD *16–178*
Kingsley & Keith Ltd v Glynn Bros (Chemicals) Ltd [1953] 1 Lloyd's Rep. 211, QBD *2–139*
Kingsman v Kingsman (1880–81) L.R. 6 Q.B.D. 122, CA *8–036*
Kingston upon Thames RLBC v Prince [1999] 1 F.L.R. 593; (1999) 31 H.L.R. 794; [1999] B.L.G.R. 333; [1999] L. & T.R. 175; [1999] Fam. Law 84; [1998] E.G. 179 (C.S.); (1999) 96(2) L.S.G. 28; (1999) 143 S.J.L.B. 45; [1998] N.P.C. 158, CA (Civ Div) *8–024*, 8–035

Kingston v Ambrian Investment Co [1975] 1 W.L.R. 161; [1975] 1 All E.R. 120; (1974) 119 S.J. 47, CA (Civ Div) *1–105*, *1–106*
Kingston v Preston (1773) 2 Doug. 689 .... *12–026*, *24–037*
Kingston-upon-Hull (Grovernors) v Petch (1854) 10 Ex. 610 .... *2–118*
Kingstreet Investments Ltd v New Brunswick (Department of Finance), 9 I.T.L. Rep. 591, Sup Ct (Can) *29–027*
Kingswood Estate Co v Anderson [1963] 2 Q.B. 169; [1962] 3 W.L.R. 1102; [1962] 3 All E.R. 593; (1962) 106 S.J. 651, CA *2–159*, *4–045*, *4–047*, *4–048*
Kinlen v Ennis [1916] 2 Ir.R. 299 .... *12–118*
Kinnaird v Trollope (No.2) (1889) L.R. 42 Ch. D. 610, Ch D *21–084*
Kinnaird v Webster (1878–79) L.R. 10 Ch. D. 139, Ch D *21–064*
Kinnersley v Orpe (1780) 2 Dougl. K.B. 517 .... *25–012*
Kirby v Duke of Marlborough (1813) 2 M.S. 18 .... *21–064*
Kirby v Leather [1965] 2 Q.B. 367; [1965] 2 W.L.R. 1318; [1965] 2 All E.R. 441; (1965) 109 S.J. 357, CA *28–074*
Kiriri Cotton Co Ltd v Dewani; sub nom. Kiriri Cotton Ct v Dewani [1960] A.C. 192; [1960] 2 W.L.R. 127; [1960] 1 All E.R. 177; (1960) 104 S.J. 49, PC (EA) *16–012*, *16–142*, 16–185, *16–186*, *29–008*, *29–011*, *29–043*
Kirk v Gibbs (1857) 1 H.N. 810 .... *23–004*
Kirk v Todd (1882) L.R. 21 Ch. D. 484, CA *29–144*
Kirkby v Taylor [1910] 1 K.B. 529, KBD *8–023*
Kirklees MBC v Yorkshire Woollen District Transport Co (1978) 77 L.G.R. 448 .... *13–027*, *22–054*, *23–021*
Kirton v Braithwaite (1836) 1 M.W. 310 .... *21–094*
Kirton v Elliott (1614) 2 Bulst. 69 .... *8–032*
Kish v Taylor. *See* J&E Kish v Charles Taylor & Sons & Co
Kissavos Shipping Co SA v Empresa Cubana de Fletes; The Agathon [1982] 2 Lloyd's Rep. 211, CA (Civ Div) *23–044*
Kitchen v Royal Air Force Association [1958] 1 W.L.R. 563; [1958] 2 All E.R. 241; [1955–95] P.N.L.R. 18; (1958) 102 S.J. 363, CA *26–044*, *28–086*
Kitchen Design & Advice Ltd v Lea Valley Water Co [1989] 2 Lloyd's Rep. 221, QBD *22–022*
Kitchen's Trustee v Madders [1950] Ch. 134; [1949] 2 All E.R. 1079, CA; reversing in par; sub nom. [1949] Ch. 588; [1949] 2 All E.R. 54, Ch D *19–071*, *20–042*
Kite, The [1933] P. 154; (1933) 46 Ll. L. Rep. 83, PDAD *14–054*
Kitney v Jones Lang Wootton [1988] 20 E.G. 88 .... *28–054*
Kleen v Commerzbank AG. *See* Commerzbank AG v Keen
Kleinert v Abosso Gold Mining Co (1913) 58 S.J. (P.C.) 45 .... *13–011*, *24–032*
Kleinwort Benson Ltd v Barbrak Ltd; The Myrto; Kleinwort Benson Ltd v Choithram & Sons (London); Kleinwort Benson Ltd v Chemical Importation and Distribution State Enterprises; Kleinwort Benson Ltd v Shell Markets [1987] A.C. 597; [1987] 2 W.L.R. 1053; [1987] 2 All E.R. 289; [1987] 2 Lloyd's Rep. 1; [1987] 1 F.T.L.R. 43; (1987) 84 L.S.G. 1651; (1987) 137 N.L.J. 388; (1987) 131 S.J. 594, HL *28–116*
Kleinwort Benson Ltd v Birmingham City Council [1997] Q.B. 380; [1996] 3 W.L.R. 1139; [1996] 4 All E.R. 733; [1996] C.L.C. 1791, CA (Civ Div) *29–027*, *29–086*
Kleinwort Benson Ltd v Glasgow City Council (No.2) [1999] 1 A.C. 153; [1997] 3 W.L.R. 923; [1997] 4 All E.R. 641; [1998] Lloyd's Rep. Bank. 10; [1997] C.L.C. 1609; [1998] I.L.Pr. 350; (1997) 9 Admin. L.R. 721; (1997) 94(44) L.S.G. 36; (1997) 147 N.L.J. 1617; (1997) 141 S.J.L.B. 237, HL; reversing [1996] Q.B. 678; [1996] 2 W.L.R. 655; [1996] 2 All E.R. 257; [1996] 5 Bank. L.R. 116; [1996] C.L.C. 759; [1996] I.L.Pr. 218, CA (Civ Div) *1–168*, *29–001*, *29–008*, *30–033*, *30–141*

Kleinwort Benson Ltd v Lincoln City Council; Kleinwort Benson Ltd v Birmingham City Council; Kleinwort Benson Ltd v Southwark LBC; Kleinwort Benson Ltd v Kensington and Chelsea RLBC [1999] 2 A.C. 349; [1998] 3 W.L.R. 1095; [1998] 4 All E.R. 513; [1998] Lloyd's Rep. Bank. 387; [1999] C.L.C. 332; (1999) 1 L.G.L.R. 148; (1999) 11 Admin. L.R. 130; [1998] R.V.R. 315; (1998) 148 N.L.J. 1674; (1998) 142 S.J.L.B. 279; [1998] N.P.C. 145, HL *4–041*, 4–086, 5–054, 5–055, 5–056, *6–013*, *8–065*, *23–080*, *23–098*, *28–002*, *28–058*, *28–088*, *29–001*, *29–008*, *29–011*, *29–028*, *29–030*, *29–033*, 29–034, *29–035*, *29–036*, *29–038*, *29–041*, *29–044*, *29–045*, 29–046, 29–047, *29–186*, *29–187*, *29–188*

Kleinwort Benson Ltd v Malaysia Mining Corp Bhd [1989] 1 W.L.R. 379; [1989] 1 All E.R. 785; [1989] 1 Lloyd's Rep. 556; (1989) 5 B.C.C. 337; (1989) 86(16) L.S.G. 35; (1989) 139 N.L.J. 221; (1989) 133 S.J. 262, CA (Civ Div); reversing [1988] 1 W.L.R. 799; [1988] 1 All E.R. 714; [1988] 1 Lloyd's Rep. 556; (1988) 4 B.C.C. 217; [1988] F.T.L.R. 283; (1988) 138 N.L.J. Rep. 21; (1988) 132 S.J. 497, QBD (Comm) *2–125*, *2–183*

Kleinwort Benson Ltd v Sandwell BC (1993) 91 L.G.R. 323 ......*28–002*, *28–123*, *28–128*, *28–135*

Kleinwort Benson Ltd v South Tyneside MBC [1994] 4 All E.R. 972, QBD *9–017*, *28–058*, *28–096*, *29–075*, *29–086*

Kleinwort Benson Ltd v Vaughan and Vaughan [1996] C.L.C. 620; [1995] N.P.C. 195, CA (Civ Div) *29–099*, *29–109*, *29–173*

Kleinwort Sons & Co v Ungarische Baumwolle Industrie AG; sub nom. Kleinwort Sons & Co v Hungarian General Creditbank [1939] 2 K.B. 678, CA *16–031*, *23–028*, *30–364*, *30–365*

Kleinwort Sons Co v Dunlop Rubber Co (1907) 97 L.T. 263 .... *29–178*

Kleovoulos of Rhodes, The. *See* Sunport Shipping Ltd v Tryg Baltica International (UK) Ltd

Kling v Keston Properties Ltd (1985) 49 P. & C.R. 212; (1984) 81 L.S.G. 1683, Ch D *4–013*

Kloepfer Wholesale Hardware & Automotive Co v Roy; sub nom. Roy v Kloepfer Wholesale Hardware and Automotive Co [1952] 3 D.L.R. 705, Sup Ct (Can) *27–003*

Knapp v Ecclesiastical Insurance Group Plc [1998] Lloyd's Rep. I.R. 390; [1998] P.N.L.R. 172, CA (Civ Div) *28–033*, *28–034*

Knibbs v Hall (1794) Peake 276 .... *29–088*

Knight v Bowyer (1858) 2 De G. & J. 421 .... *16–064*

Knight v Burgess (1864) 33 L.J.Ch. 727 .... *20–034*

Knight v Clements (1838) 8 A.E. 215 .... *25–022*

Knight v Crockford (1794) 1 Esp. 190 .... *4–032*

Knight v Gravesend, etc Waterworks Co (1857) 2 H. & N. 6 .... *13–024*

Knight v Lawrence [1991] B.C.C. 411; [1993] B.C.L.C. 215; [1991] 01 E.G. 105; [1990] E.G. 64 (C.S.), Ch D *18–022*

Knight v Rochdale Healthcare NHS Trust [2003] EWHC 1831 (QB); [2004] 1 W.L.R. 371; [2003] 4 All E.R. 416; [2004] C.P. Rep. 6; [2004] P.I.Q.R. P5; (2003) 74 B.M.L.R. 204; (2003) 153 N.L.J. 1203, QBD *28–051*

Knight & Searle v Dove [1964] 2 Q.B. 631; [1964] 3 W.L.R. 50; [1964] 2 All E.R. 307; (1964) 108 S.J. 320, QBD *9–064*

Knight Machinery (Holdings) Ltd v Rennie, 1994 S.C. 338; 1995 S.L.T. 166, IH (Ex Div); affirming, 1993 S.L.T. (Sh Ct) 65, Sh Pr *14–085*

Knight Sugar Co Ltd v Alberta Railway & Irrigation Co [1938] 1 All E.R. 266, PC (Can) *25–003*

Knott v Bolton; sub nom. Knutt v Bolton, 45 Con. L.R. 127; (1995) 11 Const. L.J. 375; [1995] E.G. 59 (C.S.), CA (Civ Div) *1–123*

Knowles v Roberts (1888) L.R. 38 Ch. D. 263, CA *22–013*

Knowles Will Trusts, Re; sub nom. Nelson v Knowles [1948] 1 All E.R. 866; [1948] W.N. 227; (1948) 92 S.J. 322, CA *29–160*

Knox v Gye (1871–72) L.R. 5 H.L. 656, HL *28–031*, *28–057*, *28–134*, *28–135*, *28–139*

Koch Marine Inc v d'Amica Societa di Navigazione arl; The Elena d'Amico [1980] 1 Lloyd's Rep. 75, QBD (Comm) *26–110*, *26–117*

Koch v Dicks [1933] 1 K.B. 307, CA ... *25–022*, *25–023*

Kodros Shipping Corp of Monrovia v Empresa Cubana de Fletes; The Evia [1983] 1 A.C. 736; [1982] 3 W.L.R. 637; [1982] 3 All E.R. 350; [1982] 2 Lloyd's Rep. 307; [1982] Com. L.R. 199; (1982) 126 S.J. 656, HL ... *23–035*, *23–044*, *23–058*, *23–080*, *23–097*, *28–061*

Koenigsblatt v Sweet [1923] 2 Ch. 314, CA ... *4–035*

Kok Hoong v Leong Cheong Kweng Mines [1964] A.C. 993; [1964] 2 W.L.R. 150; [1964] 1 All E.R. 300; (1963) 107 S.J. 1037, PC (FMS) ... *16–013*, *25–011*

Kollerich & Cie SA v State Trading Corp of India Ltd [1980] 2 Lloyd's Rep. 32, CA (Civ Div); affirming [1979] 2 Lloyd's Rep. 442, QBD (Comm) ... *14–136*, *19–082*

Kollman v Watts [1963] V.L.R. 396 ... *26–061*

Komninos, The. *See* Hellenic Steel Co v Svolamar Shipping Co Ltd; The Komninos S

Koninklijke Zwavelzuurfabrieken V/H Ketjen NV v DA and DD Psychoyos, Piraeus; The Metamorphosis; sub nom. Metamorfosis, The [1953] 1 W.L.R. 543; [1953] 1 All E.R. 723; [1953] 1 Lloyd's Rep. 196; (1953) 97 S.J. 230, PDAD ... *30–011*

Koninklijke Bunge v Compagnie Continentale d'Importation [1973] 2 Lloyd's Rep. 44, QBD (Comm) ... *14–141*

Konski v Peet [1915] 1 Ch. 530, Ch D ... *16–100*, *16–111*, *16–198*

Koo Golden East Mongolia v Bank of Nova Scotia [2007] EWCA Civ 1443; [2008] 2 W.L.R. 1160; [2008] Bus. L.R. 744, CA (Civ Div) ... *11–004*, *11–005*

Korbetis v Transgrain Shipping BV [2005] EWHC 1345 (QB), QBD ... *2–051*, 2–058, *2–060*, *2–096*

Kores Manufacturing Co Ltd v Kolok Manufacturing Co Ltd [1959] Ch. 108; [1958] 2 W.L.R. 858; [1958] 2 All E.R. 65; [1958] R.P.C. 200; (1958) 102 S.J. 362, CA; affirming [1957] 1 W.L.R. 1012; [1957] 3 All E.R. 158; [1957] R.P.C. 431; (1957) 101 S.J. 799, Ch D ... *16–095*, *16–137*

Kornatzki v Oppenheimer [1937] 4 All E.R. 133 ... *30–370*

Kosmar Villa Holidays Plc v Trustees of Syndicate 1243 [2008] EWCA Civ 147; [2008] 1 C.L.C. 307; (2008) 105(11) L.S.G. 24, CA (Civ Div); reversing [2007] EWHC 458 (Comm); [2007] 2 All E.R. (Comm) 217; [2007] 1 C.L.C. 642; [2008] Lloyd's Rep. I.R. 43, QBD (Comm) ... *3–081*, *3–090*, *3–094*, *3–096*, *24–005*, *24–007*, *24–009*

Koufos v C Czarnikow Ltd; The Heron II; sub nom. C Czarnikow Ltd v Koufos; The Heron II [1969] 1 A.C. 350; [1967] 3 W.L.R. 1491; [1967] 3 All E.R. 686; [1967] 2 Lloyd's Rep. 457; (1967) 111 S.J. 848, HL; affirming [1966] 2 Q.B. 695; [1966] 2 W.L.R. 1397; [1966] 2 All E.R. 593; [1966] 1 Lloyd's Rep. 595, CA; reversing [1966] 1 Lloyd's Rep. 259; (1966) 110 S.J. 287, QBD (Comm) .. *1–122*, 1–165, *26–001*, 26–054, **26–057**, 26–058, 26–059, *26–060*, *26–062*, *26–070*, *26–089*, 26–100G

Kpohraror v Woolwich Building Society [1996] 4 All E.R. 119; [1996] 5 Bank. L.R. 182; [1996] C.L.C. 510; (1996) 93(1) L.S.G. 22; (1996) 140 S.J.L.B. 28, CA (Civ Div) ... *26–057*, *26–059*

Kralj v McGrath and St Theresa's Hospital [1986] 1 All E.R. 54; (1985) 135 N.L.J. 913, QBD ... *26–019*

Kraut AG v Albany Fabrics Ltd. *See* Jean Kraut AG v Albany Fabrics Ltd

Krawill Machinery Corp v Robert C Herd & Co Inc [1959] 1 Lloyd's Rep. 305, US Ct ... *14–042*

Kreditbank Cassel GmbH v Schenkers Ltd [1927] 1 K.B. 826, CA; reversing [1926] 2 K.B. 450, KBD ... *9–042*, *9–045*

Krell v Henry [1903] 2 K.B. 740, CA ... *5–025*, 23–033, 23–034, *23–052*, 23–080

Kronheim v Johnson (1877–78) L.R. 7 Ch. D. 60, Ch D ... *4–029*, *4–032*

Kruse v Questier & Co [1953] 1 Q.B. 669; [1953] 2 W.L.R. 850; [1953] 1 All E.R. 954; [1953] 1 Lloyd's Rep. 310; (1953) 97 S.J. 281, QBD ... *23–097*

Kuddus v Chief Constable of Leicestershire [2001] UKHL 29; [2002] 2 A.C. 122; [2001] 2 W.L.R. 1789; [2001] 3 All E.R. 193; (2001) 3 L.G.L.R. 45; [2001] Po. L.R. 181; (2001) 98(28) L.S.G. 43; (2001) 151 N.L.J. 936; (2001) 145 S.J.L.B. 166, HL; reversing (2000) 2 L.G.L.R. 822, CA (Civ Div) ... 6–063, *26–019*, *29–145*

Kuenigl v Donnersmarck [1955] 1 Q.B. 515; [1955] 2 W.L.R. 82; [1955] 1 All E.R. 46; (1955) 99 S.J. 60, QBD *11–025*, *16–026*, *16–202*
Kum v Wah Tat Bank Ltd [1971] 1 Lloyd's Rep. 439, PC (Mal) *12–070*, *13–023*
Kumar (A Bankrupt), Re; sub nom. Lewis v Kumar [1993] 1 W.L.R. 224; [1993] 2 All E.R. 700; [1993] B.C.L.C. 548; [1993] 2 F.L.R. 382; [1993] Fam. Law 470, Ch D *2–169*, *3–008*, *3–168*, *18–117*, *20–028*
Kupchak v Dayson Holdings Co (1965) 53 D.L.R. (2d) 482 .... *6–117*, *6–124*
Kuratau Land Co v Kahu Te Kuru [1966] N.Z.L.R. 544 .... *12–094*
Kurt A Becher GmbH & Co KG v Roplak Enterprises SA; The World Navigator; sub nom. World Navigation, Re; Roplak Enterprises SA v Tradax Ocean Transportation SA [1991] 2 Lloyd's Rep. 23, CA (Civ Div); reversing [1991] 1 Lloyd's Rep. 277, QBD (Comm) *13–011*, *26–048*
Kuwait Airways Corp v Iraqi Airways Co (No.2) [2001] 1 W.L.R. 430 .... *11–004*, *11–005*, *11–007*
Kuwait Airways Corp v Iraqi Airways Co (No.6); sub nom. Kuwait Airways Corp v Iraq Airways Co (No.6); Kuwait Airways Corp v Iraqi Airways Co (No.5) [2002] UKHL 19; [2002] 2 A.C. 883; [2002] 2 W.L.R. 1353; [2002] 3 All E.R. 209; [2002] 1 All E.R. (Comm) 843; [2003] 1 C.L.C. 183, HL; affirming [2001] 3 W.L.R. 1117; [2001] 1 All E.R. (Comm) 557; [2001] 1 Lloyd's Rep. 161; [2001] C.L.C. 262; (2000) 97(48) L.S.G. 37; (2001) 145 S.J.L.B. 5, CA (Civ Div); reversing in part [2000] 2 All E.R. (Comm) 360; (2000) 97(23) L.S.G. 44, QBD (Comm) *11–007*, *29–179*, *30–070*, *30–366*
Kuwait Airways Corp v Iraqi Airways Co (No.8) (Petition for Variation of Order) [2001] 1 W.L.R. 429; [2001] 1 Lloyd's Rep. 485; (2001) 98(11) L.S.G. 44; (2001) 145 S.J.L.B. 84, HL *11–005*, *11–006*, *11–002*1
Kuwait Airways Corp v Iraqi Airways Co (No.11) [2003] EWHC 31 (Comm); [2003] 1 Lloyd's Rep. 448, QBD (Comm) *11–004*, *11–005*, *11–006*, *11–007*, *11–021*
Kuwait Airways Corp v Iraqi Airways Corp [1995] 1 W.L.R. 1147; [1995] 3 All E.R. 694; [1995] 2 Lloyd's Rep. 317; (1995) 139 S.J.L.B. 176; (1995) 92(28) L.S.Gaz. 28; The Times, July 25, 1995; The Independent, August 15, 1995, HL, revewrsing [1995] 1 Lloyd's Rep. 24, CA *11–004*, *11–005*, *11–006*, *11–007*, *11–021*
Kuwait Oil Tanker Co SAK v Al-Bader (No.3) [2000] 2 All E.R. (Comm) 271; (2000) 97(23) L.S.G. 44, CA (Civ Div) *30–336*, *30–339*
Kuwait Supply Co v Oyster Marine Management Inc; The Safeer [1994] 1 Lloyd's Rep. 637, QBD (Comm) *23–058*, *23–097*
Kwei Tek Chao (t/a Zung Fu Co) v British Traders & Shippers Ltd [1954] 2 Q.B. 459; [1954] 2 W.L.R. 365; [1954] 1 All E.R. 779; [1954] 1 Lloyd's Rep. 16; (1954) 98 S.J. 163, QBD *24–050*, *24–054*, *29–058*
Kyle Bay Ltd (t/a Astons Nightclub) v Underwriters; sub nom. Kyle Bay Ltd (t/a Astons Nightclub) v Underwriters Subscribing under Policy No.019057/08/01 [2007] EWCA Civ 57; [2007] 1 C.L.C. 164; [2007] Lloyd's Rep. I.R. 460, CA (Civ Div); affirming [2006] EWHC 607 (Comm); [2006] Lloyd's Rep. I.R. 718, QBD (Comm) *5–055*, *6–006*, *6–009*
Kyprianou v Cyprus Textiles Ltd. *See* Phoebus D Kyprianou v Cyprus Textiles
L French & Co Ltd v Leeston Shipping Co Ltd [1922] 1 A.C. 451; (1922) 10 Ll. L. Rep. 448, HL; affirming (1921) 8 Ll. L. Rep. 110, CA; affirming (1921) 6 Ll. L. Rep. 413, KBD *13–007*, *13–012*
L Schuler AG v Wickman Machine Tool Sales Ltd; sub nom. Wickman Machine Tool Sales Ltd v L Schuler AG [1974] A.C. 235; [1973] 2 W.L.R. 683; [1973] 2 All E.R. 39; [1973] 2 Lloyd's Rep. 53; (1973) 117 S.J. 340, HL; affirming [1972] 1 W.L.R. 840; [1972] 2 All E.R. 1173; (1972) 116 S.J. 352, CA (Civ Div) *1–031*, *12–025*, *12–026*, *12–028*, *12–040*, *12–053*, 12–055, *12–118*, *12–119*, *12–121*, *12–123*, *12–126*
L Shaddock & Associates Pty v Parramatta City Council (1981) 55 A.L.J.R. 713 .... *6–084*
L Sutro & Co, and Heilbut, Symons & Co. *See* Arbitration between L Sutro & Co and Heilbut Symons & Co, Re

L v Birmingham City Council; sub nom. R. (on the application of Johnson) v Havering LBC; Johnson v Havering LBC; YL v Birmingham City Council [2007] UKHL 27; [2008] 1 A.C. 95; [2007] 3 W.L.R. 112; [2007] 3 All E.R. 957; [2007] H.R.L.R. 32; [2008] U.K.H.R.R. 346; [2007] H.L.R. 44; [2008] B.L.G.R. 273; (2007) 10 C.C.L. Rep. 505; [2007] LS Law Medical 472; (2007) 96 B.M.L.R. 1; (2007) 104(27) L.S.G. 29; (2007) 157 N.L.J. 938; (2007) 151 S.J.L.B. 860; [2007] N.P.C. 75, HL; affirming [2007] EWCA Civ 26; [2008] Q.B. 1; [2007] 2 W.L.R. 1097; [2007] H.R.L.R. 15; [2007] U.K.H.R.R. 645; [2007] B.L.G.R. 241; (2007) 10 C.C.L. Rep. 7; (2007) 95 B.M.L.R. 33; [2007] M.H.L.R. 69; (2007) 151 S.J.L.B. 199; [2007] N.P.C. 12, CA (Civ Div); affirming [2006] EWHC 1714 (Admin); [2006] B.L.G.R. 631; (2006) 9 C.C.L. Rep. 503; [2006] Lloyd's Rep. Med. 447; [2006] A.C.D. 95, QBD (Admin) *1–050*, *1–051*, 1–052, *1–054*, *1–201*
LD Turner Ltd v RS Hatton (Bradford) Ltd [1952] 1 All E.R. 1286; [1952] 1 T.L.R. 1184, Assizes (Leeds) *4–026*
LE Walwin & Partners Ltd v West Sussex CC [1975] 3 All E.R. 604; 74 L.G.R. 177, Ch D *25–013*
La Banque Internationale de Commerce de Petrograd v Goukassow; sub nom. Banque Internationale de Commerce de Petrograd v Goukassow [1925] A.C. 150; (1924) 20 Ll. L. Rep. 1, HL *30–325*
Labouchere v Dawson (1871–72) L.R. 13 Eq. 322, Ct of Chancery *16–118*, *16–119*
Labouchere v Wharncliffe; sub nom. Labouchere v Earl of Wharncliffe (1879–80) L.R. 13 Ch. D. 346, Ch D *9–075*
Lac Minerals Ltd v International Corona Resources Ltd [1990] F.S.R. 441, Sup Ct (Can) *29–155*
Lacey, Re; sub nom. Howard v Lightfoot [1907] 1 Ch. 330, CA *28–141*
Laceys Footwear (Wholesale) v Bowler International Freight [1997] 2 Lloyd's Rep. 369, CA *12–012*, *12–015*, *14–017*, 14–135
Lacis v Cashmarts [1969] 2 Q.B. 400; [1969] 2 W.L.R. 329; (1968) 112 S.J. 1005, DC *2–014*
Laconia, The. *See* Mardorf Peach & Co v Attica Sea Carriers Corp of Liberia
Ladd v London Road Car Co (1900) 110 L.T. 80 .... *16–052*
Ladd v Marshall [1954] 1 W.L.R. 1489; [1954] 3 All E.R. 745; (1954) 98 S.J. 870, CA *25–014*
Lade v Trill (1842) 11 L.J. Ch. 102 .... *28–108*
Ladywell Mining Co v Brookes; Ladywell Mining Co v Huggons (1887) L.R. 35 Ch. D. 400, CA; affirming (1887) L.R. 34 Ch. D. 398, Ch D *6–128*, *9–054*
Laemthong Glory, The. *See* Laemthong International Lines Co Ltd v Artis
Laemthong International Lines Co Ltd v Artis; The Laemthong Glory (No.2); sub nom. Laemthong International Lines Co Ltd v Abdullah Mohammed Fahem & Co [2005] EWCA Civ 519; [2005] 2 All E.R. (Comm) 167; [2005] 1 Lloyd's Rep. 688; [2005] 1 C.L.C. 739, CA (Civ Div) *18–091*, 18–092, *27–008*
Laemthong International Lines Co Ltd v Artis; The Laemthong Glory (No.3) [2005] EWHC 1595, QBD (Comm) *30–325*, *30–350*
Lafarge (Aggregates) Ltd v Newham LBC [2005] EWHC 1337 (Comm); [2005] 2 Lloyd's Rep. 577, QBD (Comm) *12–075*, *21–022*
Lagden v O'Connor; Clark v Ardington Electrical Services; Dennard v Plant; Sen v Steelform Engineering Co Ltd; Burdis v Livsey; sub nom. Clark v Tull (t/a Ardington Electrical Services) [2003] UKHL 64; [2004] 1 A.C. 1067; [2003] 3 W.L.R. 1571; [2004] 1 All E.R. 277; [2004] R.T.R. 24; [2004] Lloyd's Rep. I.R. 315; (2003) 153 N.L.J. 1869; (2003) 147 S.J.L.B. 1430, HL 26–105
Lagos v Grunwaldt [1910] 1 K.B. 41, CA *29–071*
Lagunas Nitrate Co v Lagunas Syndicate [1899] 2 Ch. 392, CA *6–117*, *6–154*, *9–054*, *9–060*
Lai Wee Lian v Singapore Bus Service [1984] A.C. 729; [1984] 3 W.L.R. 63; (1984) 81 L.S.G. 1597; (1984) 128 S.J. 432, PC (Sing) *26–030*
Laing Management Ltd (formerly Laing Management Contracting Ltd) v Aegon Insurance Co (UK) Ltd, 86 B.L.R. 70; 55 Con. L.R. 1, QBD (OR) 22–049, *24–004*
Laing v Meader (1824) 1 C.P. 257 .... *21–093*

Laing Son & Co (M/C) v Eastcheap Dried Fruit Co Ltd. *See* James Laing Son & Co (M/C) v Eastcheap Dried Fruit Co (No.1)
Lainson v Tremere (1834) 1 Ad. & El. 792 .... *1–112*
Laird v Briggs (1881–82) L.R. 19 Ch. D. 22, CA; reversing (1880–81) L.R. 16 Ch. D. 440, Ch D *12–051*
Laird v Pim (1841) 7 M.W. 474 .... *26–092*
Lake Avery, The. *See* Union de Remorquage et de Sauvetage SA v Lake Avery Inc; The Lake Avery
Lake v Bayliss [1974] 1 W.L.R. 1073; [1974] 2 All E.R. 1114; (1974) 28 P. & C.R. 209; (1974) 118 S.J. 532, Ch D *26–023*, *29–142*, *29–151*, *29–160*
Lake v Lake (1989) [1989] S.T.C. 865, Ch D *5–111*
Lake v Simmons [1927] A.C. 487; (1927) 27 Ll. L. Rep. 377, HL; reversing [1926] 2 K.B. 51; (1926) 24 Ll. L. Rep. 441, CA; reversing [1926] 1 K.B. 366; (1925) 23 Ll. L. Rep. 250, KBD *5–093*, *5–096*, *12–057*
Lakeport Navigation Co Panama SA v Anonima Petroli Italiana SpA; The Olympic Brilliance [1982] 2 Lloyd's Rep. 205, CA (Civ Div); affirming [1981] 2 Lloyd's Rep. 176; [1981] Com. L.R. 203, QBD (Comm) *12–055*, *12–083*
Lakschmijit S/O Bhai Suchit v Sherani; sub nom. Lakshmijit s/o Bhai Suchit v Sherani (Faiz Mohammed Khan) (As Administrator for the Estate of Shahbaz Khan, deceased) [1974] A.C. 605; [1974] 2 W.L.R. 232; [1973] 3 All E.R. 737; (1973) 118 S.J. 35, PC (Fiji) *24–001*
Lamare v Dixon (1873) L.R. 6 H.L. 414, HL *6–103*, *27–030*, *27–035*
Lamb v Vice (1840) 6 M. & W. 467 .... *18–078*
Lambert v Addison (1882) 46 L.T. 20 .... *9–075*
Lambert v Cooperative Insurance Society Ltd [1975] 2 Lloyd's Rep. 485, CA (Civ Div) *6–145*, *6–147*, *6–148*
Lambert v Lewis; sub nom. Lexmead (Basingstoke) Ltd v Lewis [1982] A.C. 225; [1981] 2 W.L.R. 713; [1981] 1 All E.R. 1185; [1981] 2 Lloyd's Rep. 17; [1981] R.T.R. 346; (1981) 125 S.J. 310, HL; reversing [1980] 2 W.L.R. 299; [1980] 1 All E.R. 978; [1980] 1 Lloyd's Rep. 311; [1980] R.T.R. 152; (1980) 124 S.J. 50, CA (Civ Div); reversing in part [1978] 1 Lloyd's Rep. 610; [1979] R.T.R. 61; (1981) 78 L.S.G. 597, QBD *2–018*, 2–165, 6–086, *12–007*, *18–009*, *26–037*, *26–038*, *26–050*, *26–109*
Lambert (Rae) v HTV Cymru (Wales) Ltd [1998] E.M.L.R. 629; [1998] F.S.R. 874; (1998) 21(8) I.P.D. 21086; (1998) 95(15) L.S.G. 30; (1998) 142 S.J.L.B. 1184, CA (Civ Div) *2–138*
Lamberton v Thorpe (1929) 141 L.T. 638 .... *9–075*
Lambeth LBC v O'Kane; Helena Housing Ltd v Pinder [2005] EWCA Civ 1010; [2006] H.L.R. 2; [2005] 32 E.G. 67 (C.S.); [2005] N.P.C. 110, CA (Civ Div) *3–087*
Lamburn v Cruden (1841) 2 Man. & G. 253 .... *22–026*
Lamdon Trust Ltd v Hurrell; sub nom. Landom Trust Ltd v Hurrell [1955] 1 W.L.R. 391; [1955] 1 All E.R. 839; (1955) 99 S.J. 239, QBD *26–131*, *26–136*
Lamine v Dorrell (1705) 2 Ld. Raym. 1216 .... *29–006*, *29–142*
Lampleigh v Brathwait (1615) Hob. 105 .... *3–029*, *16–040*, *29–071*
Lamport & Holt Lines v Coubro & Scrutton (M&I) Ltd; The Raphael [1982] 2 Lloyd's Rep. 42, CA (Civ Div); affirming [1981] 2 Lloyd's Rep. 659; [1982] Com. L.R. 123, QBD (Comm) *12–011*, *12–075*, *13–022*, *14–010*, *14–011*, *14–012*, 14–013
Lamprell v Billericay Union (1849) 3 Exch. 283 .... *21–062*
Lamshed v Lamshed (1963) 37 A.L.J.R. 301 .... *28–142*
Lamson Pneumatic Tube Co v Phillips (1904) 91 L.T. 363 ...... *16–091*, *16–092*, *16–110*
Lancashire & Yorkshire Railway Co v Swann [1916] 1 K.B. 263, KBD *21–022*
Lancashire Loans Ltd v Black [1934] 1 K.B. 380, CA *7–074*
Lancaster v JF Turner & Co Ltd [1924] 2 K.B. 222, CA *26–144*
Lancaster v Walsh (1838) 4 M. & W. 16 .... *2–019*
Land Rover Group Ltd v UPF (UK) Ltd (In Administrative Receivership) [2002] EWHC 3183; [2003] 2 B.C.L.C. 222, QBD (Merc) *27–014*, *27–060*

Landau (A Bankrupt), Re; sub nom. Pointer v Landau; L (A Bankrupt), Re [1998] Ch. 223; [1997] 3 W.L.R. 225; [1997] 3 All E.R. 322; [1997] 2 B.C.L.C. 515; [1997] 2 F.L.R. 660; [1997] B.P.I.R. 229; [1996] O.P.L.R. 371; [1998] Fam. Law 68; (1997) 94(4) L.S.G. 25; (1997) 141 S.J.L.B. 28, Ch D *20–026*
Lane v Dighton (1762) Amb. 409 .... *29–166*
Lane v Hill (1852) 18 Q.B. 252 .... *29–191*
Lane v Holloway [1968] 1 Q.B. 379; [1967] 3 W.L.R. 1003; [1967] 3 All E.R. 129; (1967) 111 S.J. 655, CA (Civ Div) *16–014*
Lane v O'Brien Homes Ltd [2004] EWHC 303 (QB), QBD *29–151*
Langdale v Danby [1982] 1 W.L.R. 1123; [1982] 3 All E.R. 129; (1982) 79 L.S.G. 1258; (1982) 126 S.J. 537, HL; reversing (1981) 125 S.J. 829, CA (Civ Div) *3–014*, *7–139*
Langen & Wind Ltd v Bell [1972] Ch. 685; [1972] 2 W.L.R. 170; [1972] 1 All E.R. 296; (1971) 115 S.J. 966, Ch D *27–011*, *27–048*
Langsdale v Mason (1780) 2 Marshall (2nd ed.) 791 .... *14–146*
Langton v Hughes, 105 E.R. 222; (1813) 1 M. & S. 593, KB *16–014*, *16–143*
Langton v Langton [1995] 2 F.L.R. 890; [1995] 3 F.C.R. 521; [1996] Fam. Law 86, Ch D *7–130*
Lansing Linde Ltd v Kerr [1991] 1 W.L.R. 251; [1991] 1 All E.R. 418; [1991] I.C.R. 428; [1991] I.R.L.R. 80; (1990) 140 N.L.J. 1458, CA (Civ Div) *16–103*, *16–109*, *27–061*
Larios v Gurety (1873–74) L.R. 5 P.C. 346, PC (Gib) *26–098*
Lark v Outhwaite [1991] 2 Lloyd's Rep. 132, QBD (Comm) *2–032*, *2–043*, *2–161*, *3–093*, *3–100*
Larner v London CC [1949] 2 K.B. 683; [1949] 1 All E.R. 964; 65 T.L.R. 316; (1949) 113 J.P. 300; 47 L.G.R. 533; [1949] L.J.R. 1363; (1949) 93 S.J. 371, CA *29–008*, *29–011*, 29–032, *29–179*
Laroche v Spirit of Adventure (UK) Ltd [2008] EWHC 788 (QB); [2008] 2 Lloyd's Rep. 34 .... *3–114*
Larocque v Beauchemin [1897] A.C. 358 .... *21–039*
Larrinaga & Co Ltd v Societe Franco-Americaine des Phosphates de Medulla; sub nom. Larrinaga & Co v Societe Franco-Americaine des Phosphates de Medulla, Paris (1923) 14 Ll. L. Rep. 457, HL *23–021*, *23–034*, *23–040*, *23–058*
Larsen v Sylvester & Co [1908] A.C. 295, HL *12–089*, *14–138*
Lascelles v Rathburn (1919) 35 T.L.R. 347 .... *9–073*, *9–079*
Lasky v Economic Grocery Stores, 319 Mass. 224, 65 N.E. 2d 305 (1946) *2–014*, *2–015*
Last v Hucklesby (1914) 58 S.J. 431 .... *4–028*
Last-Harris v Thompson Bros [1956] N.Z.L.R. 995 .... *26–083*
Latchin (t/a Dinkha Latchin Associates) v General Mediterranean Holdings SA [2002] C.L.C. 330, QBD (Comm) *30–090*
Laurence v Lexcourt Holdings [1978] 1 W.L.R. 1128; [1978] 2 All E.R. 810; (1978) 122 S.J. 681, CA (Civ Div) *5–058*, *5–059*, *6–011*, *6–013*, *6–039*
Laurent v Sale & Co [1963] 1 W.L.R. 829; [1963] 2 All E.R. 63; [1963] 1 Lloyd's Rep. 157; (1963) 107 S.J. 665, QBD *19–049*
Lauri v Renad [1892] 3 Ch. 402, CA *16–161*
LauritzenCool AB v Lady Navigation Inc; sub nom. Lady Navigation Inc v LauritzenCool AB [2005] EWCA Civ 579; [2005] 1 W.L.R. 3686; [2006] 1 All E.R. 866; [2005] 2 All E.R. (Comm) 183; [2005] 2 Lloyd's Rep. 63; [2005] 1 C.L.C. 758, CA (Civ Div) *27–023*, *27–025*, *27–067*, *27–070*, *27–071*
Lavarack v Woods of Colchester [1967] 1 Q.B. 278; [1966] 3 W.L.R. 706; [1966] 3 All E.R. 683; 1 K.I.R. 312; (1966) 110 S.J. 770, CA *26–001*, *26–048*, *26–117*, *26–118*, *26–119*
Lavender v Betts [1942] 2 All E.R. 72, KBD *26–019*
Lavery v Pursell (1888) L.R. 39 Ch. D. 508; (1888) 57 L.J. Ch. 570, Ch D *4–018*, *4–019*, *4–043*, *27–084*
Lavery v Turley (1860) 6 H. & N. 239 .... *22–014*
Law v Coburn; sub nom. Bonar Law v Coburn (Inspector of taxes) [1972] 1 W.L.R. 1238; [1972] 3 All E.R. 1115; [1972] T.R. 133; (1972) 116 S.J. 666, Ch D *19–008*

Law v Dearnley [1950] 1 K.B. 400; [1950] 1 All E.R. 124; 66 T.L.R. (Pt. 1) 156; (1950) 94 S.J. 96, CA *29–192*
Law v Jones [1974] Ch. 112; [1973] 2 W.L.R. 994; [1973] 2 All E.R. 437; (1973) 26 P. & C.R. 42; (1973) 117 S.J. 305, CA (Civ Div) *2–120*, *4–027*, *4–028*
Law v Law [1905] 1 Ch. 140, CA *29–149*
Law v National Greyhound Racing Club; sub nom. Tozer v National Greyhound Racing Club [1983] 1 W.L.R. 1302; [1983] 3 All E.R. 300; (1983) 80 L.S.G. 2367; (1983) 127 S.J. 619, CA (Civ Div) *1–195*
Law v Redditch Local Board [1892] 1 Q.B. 127, CA *26–134*, *26–135*
Law v Robert Roberts & Co [1964] I.R. 292, Sup Ct *4–027*
Law Debenture Trust Corp v Ural Caspian Oil Corp Ltd [1995] Ch. 152; [1994] 3 W.L.R. 1221; [1995] 1 All E.R. 157; [1994] C.L.C. 299, CA (Civ Div); reversing [1993] 1 W.L.R. 138; [1993] 2 All E.R. 355, Ch D *1–171*, *12–007*, *18–009*, *18–019*, *18–140*, *18–141*, *18–143*
Law Society v KPMG Peat Marwick; sub nom. R. v KPMG Peat Marwick McLintock [2000] 1 W.L.R. 1921; [2000] 4 All E.R. 540; [2000] Lloyd's Rep. P.N. 929; [2000] P.N.L.R. 831; (2000) 97(30) L.S.G. 40; (2000) 150 N.L.J. 1017, CA (Civ Div); affirming [2000] 1 All E.R. 515; [2000] E.C.C. 456; [2000] Lloyd's Rep. P.N. 219; [2000] P.N.L.R. 364; (1999) 96(44) L.S.G. 40; (1999) 149 N.L.J. 1698; (1999) 143 S.J.L.B. 269, Ch D *18–022*
Law Society v Sephton & Co [2006] UKHL 22; [2006] 2 A.C. 543; [2006] 2 W.L.R. 1091; [2006] 3 All E.R. 401; [2006] P.N.L.R. 31; (2006) 156 N.L.J. 844; (2006) 150 S.J.L.B. 669; [2006] N.P.C. 56, HL; affirming [2004] EWCA Civ 1627; [2005] Q.B. 1013; [2005] 3 W.L.R. 212; [2005] P.N.L.R. 21; (2005) 102(5) L.S.G. 29; (2005) 149 S.J.L.B. 56, CA (Civ Div); reversing in part [2004] EWHC 544 (Ch); [2004] P.N.L.R. 27, Ch D *1–124*, 28–034
Lawes v Purser (1856) 6 E.B. 930 .... *29–061*
Lawford v Billericay Rural DC [1903] 1 K.B. 772, CA *29–076*
Lawlor v Union of Post Office Workers [1965] Ch. 712; [1965] 2 W.L.R. 579; [1965] 1 All E.R. 353; (1964) 108 S.J. 879, Ch D *9–075*, *9–083*, *27–072*
Lawrence v Cassel [1930] 2 K.B. 83, CA *4–016*, *13–015*, *25–001*, *25–003*
Lawrence v Hayes [1927] 2 K.B. 111, KBD *19–070*, *19–071*
Lawrence v West Somerset Mineral Railway Co [1918] 2 Ch. 250, Ch D *9–020*
Lawrence David Ltd v Ashton [1991] 1 All E.R. 385; [1989] I.C.R. 123; [1989] I.R.L.R. 22; [1989] 1 F.S.R. 87; (1988) 85(42) L.S.G. 48, CA (Civ Div) *16–103*, *27–008*, *27–042*, *27–061*
Laws v London Chronicle (Indicator Newspapers) [1959] 1 W.L.R. 698; [1959] 2 All E.R. 285; 93 I.L.T. 213; (1959) 103 S.J. 462; (1959) 103 S.J. 470, CA *24–018*
Laws v Rand (1857) 3 C.B.(N.S.) 442 .... *28–042*
Laws v Society of Lloyds [2003] EWCA Civ 1887, CA (Civ Div) *1–037*, *6–068*, *28–009*, *28–118*
Lawson (Inspector of Taxes) v Hosemaster Machine Co [1966] 1 W.L.R. 1300; [1966] 2 All E.R. 944; (1966) 110 S.J. 407, CA; reversing [1965] 1 W.L.R. 1399; [1965] 3 All E.R. 401; 43 T.C. 337; (1965) 44 A.T.C. 239; [1965] T.R. 253; (1965) 109 S.J. 902, Ch D *9–051*
Lawson v Serco Ltd; Crofts v Veta Ltd; Botham v Ministry of Defence; sub nom. Serco Ltd v Lawson [2006] UKHL 3; [2006] 1 All E.R. 823; [2006] I.C.R. 250; [2006] I.R.L.R. 289; (2006) 103(6) L.S.G. 36; (2006) 156 N.L.J. 184; (2006) 150 S.J.L.B. 131, HL 30–115, 30–116, *30–282*
Laycock v Pickles (1863) 4 B.S. 497 .... *29–191*
Laythoarp v Bryant (1836) 2 Bing.N.C. 735 .... *3–168*, *4–025*, *4–031*
Layton v Martin [1986] 2 F.L.R. 227; [1986] Fam. Law 212, Ch D *3–148*
Layton v Morris, *The Times*, December 11, 1985 .... *2–183*
Layton v Pearce (1778) 1 Dougl. 15 .... *21–006*
Le Blanche v London & North Western Railway Co (1875–76) L.R. 1 C.P.D. 286, CA *26–103*, *26–120*
Le Bret v Papillon (1804) 4 East 502 .... *11–027*
Le Feuvre v Sullivan (1855) 100 Moo. P.C. 1 .... *30–125*

Leadenhall Residential 2 Ltd v Stirling; sub nom. Stirling v Leadenhall Residential 2 Ltd [2001] EWCA Civ 1011; [2002] 1 W.L.R. 499; [2001] 3 All E.R. 645; [2002] H.L.R. 3; [2002] L. & T.R. 14; (2001) 98(35) L.S.G. 35; (2001) 151 N.L.J. 1005; [2001] N.P.C. 112, CA (Civ Div) *2–185*
Leaf v International Galleries [1950] 2 K.B. 86; [1950] 1 All E.R. 693; (1950) 66 T.L.R. 1031; 66 T.L.R. (Pt. 1) 1031; 25 A.L.J. 443; 101 L.J. 61, CA *6–004*, *6–104*, *6–125*, *6–125*, 6–127, *28–144*
Learoyd Bros & Co and Huddersfield Fine Worsteds v Pope & Sons (Dock Carriers) [1966] 2 Lloyd's Rep. 142, QBD *14–054*
Learoyd v Brook [1891] 1 Q.B. 431, QBD *8–024*
Leather Cloth Co v Hieronimus (1874–75) L.R. 10 Q.B. 140, QBD *3–083*, *22–042*
Leather Cloth Co v Lorsont (1869–70) L.R. 9 Eq. 345, Ct of Chancery *16–091*
Leatherdale v Sweepstone (1828) 3 C.P. 342 .... *21–088*
Lebeaupin v Richard Crispin & Co [1920] 2 K.B. 714; (1920) 4 Ll. L. Rep. 122, KBD 14–148
Lechmere v Fletcher (1833) 1 C. & M. 623 .... *17-016*
Ledingham v Bermejo Estancia Co Ltd; Agar v Bermejo Estancia Co Ltd [1947] 1 All E.R. 749, KBD *3–122*, *28–101*
Leduc & Co v Ward (1888) L.R. 20 Q.B.D. 475, CA *14–007*, *14–029*
Lee v Abdy (1886) L.R. 17 Q.B.D. 309, QBD *30–123*
Lee v Airtours Holidays Ltd [2004] 1 Lloyd's Rep. 683, CC (Central London) *13–034*
Lee v Bissett (1856) 4 W.R. 233 .... *9–073*
Lee v Bullen (1858) 27 L.J.Q.B. 161 .... *20–044*
Lee v Citibank NA [1981] H.K.L.R. 470 .... *25–013*
Lee v Gaskell (1875–76) L.R. 1 Q.B.D. 700, QBD *4–020*
Lee v Jones (1864) 17 C.B. (N.S.) 482 .... *6–159*
Lee v Lancashire and Yorkshire Railway Co (1870–71) L.R. 6 Ch. App. 527, CA in Chancery *12–107*, *21–058*
Lee v Leeds CC. *See* Ratcliffe v Sandwell MBC
Lee v Muggeridge (1813) 5 Taunt. 36 .... *3–032*
Lee v Rayson [1917] 1 Ch. 613, Ch D *27–057*
Lee v Showmen's Guild of Great Britain [1952] 2 Q.B. 329; [1952] 1 All E.R. 1175; [1952] 1 T.L.R. 1115; (1952) 96 S.J. 296, CA *9–071*, 9–074, *9–075*, *9–080*, *9–083*, *16–045*, *18–010*
Lee v Thompson [1989] 40 E.G. 89, CA (Civ Div) *1–124*, *1–167*
Lee Behrens & Co Ltd, Re [1932] 2 Ch. 46, Ch D *9–021*
Lee Chee Wei v Tan Hor Peow Victor [2007] SGCA 22 .... *23–003*
Lee Cooper Ltd v CH Jeakins & Sons Ltd [1967] 2 Q.B. 1; [1965] 3 W.L.R. 753; [1965] 1 All E.R. 280; [1964] 1 Lloyd's Rep. 300; (1965) 109 S.J. 794, QBD *14–054*
Lee Panavision Ltd v Lee Lighting Ltd [1991] B.C.C. 620; [1992] B.C.L.C. 22, CA (Civ Div); affirming [1991] B.C.L.C. 575, Ch D *9–055*
Leeds v Cheetham (1827) 1 Sim. 146 .... *23–004*
Leeds & County Bank Ltd v Walker (1882–83) L.R. 11 Q.B.D. 84, QBD *25–025*
Leeds & Thirsk Ry Co v Fearnley (1849) 4 Exch. 26 ....*8–030*, *8–037*
Leeds and Hanley Theatres of Varieties Ltd (No.1), Re [1902] 2 Ch. 809, CA *6–154*, *9–054*, *9–055*
Leeds Bank, Re (1887) 56 L.J. Ch. 321 .... *6–035*
Leeds (Duke of) v Earl of Amherst (1846) 2 Ph. 117 ....*28–136*, *28–140*
Leeds Rugby Ltd v Harris [2005] EWHC 1591 (QB), [2005] All E.R. (D) 286, QBD *16–104*
Leeman v Stocks [1951] Ch. 941; [1951] 1 All E.R. 1043; [1951] 2 T.L.R. 622; (1951) 95 S.J. 368, Ch D *4–032*
Lee-Parker v Izzet (No.1) [1971] 1 W.L.R. 1688; [1971] 3 All E.R. 1099; (1971) 22 P. & C.R. 1098; (1971) 115 S.J. 641, Ch D *21–038*
Lee-Parker v Izzet (No.2) [1972] 1 W.L.R. 775; [1972] 2 All E.R. 800; 23 P. & C.R. 301; 116 S.J. 446, Ch D *2–154*, *12–103*, *29–161*
Leeson v Leeson [1936] 2 K.B. 156, CA *21–060*
Leetham & Sons Ltd v Johnstone-White. *See* Henry Leetham & Sons Ltd v Johnstone-White

Lefevre v White [1990] 1 Lloyd's Rep. 569, QBD ... *18–131*, *24–013*
Lefkowitz v Great Minneapolis Surplus Stores, 86 N.W. 2d. 689 (1957) ... *2–017*
Legal & General Assurance Society Ltd v Drake Insurance Co (t/a Drake Motor Policies at Lloyd's) [1992] Q.B. 887; [1992] 2 W.L.R. 157; [1992] 1 All E.R. 283; [1991] 2 Lloyd's Rep. 36; [1992] R.T.R. 162; (1992) 89(2) L.S.G. 30, CA (Civ Div); reversing [1989] 3 All E.R. 923, QBD ... *17–028*, *29–128*
Legge v Horlock (1848) 12 Q.B. 1015 ... *22–038*
Legge v Tucker (1856) 1 H. & N. 500 ... *1–118*
Leggott v Barrett; sub nom. Leggett v Barratt (1880) L.R. 15 Ch. D. 306, CA ... *12–066*, *12–096*, *12–103*, *12–119*
Legh v Legh (1930) 143 L.T. 451 ... *28–086*
Legh v Lillie (1860) 6 H.N. 165 ... *21–004*
Legione v Hateley (1983) 46 A.L.R. 1 ... *21–016*, *26–148*
Lehmann v McArthur (1867–68) L.R. 3 Ch. App. 496, CA in Chancery ... *28–143*
Leicester (Earl of) v Wells-next-the-Sea Urban DC [1973] Ch. 110; [1972] 3 W.L.R. 486; [1972] 3 All E.R. 77; (1972) 24 P. & C.R. 72; (1972) 116 S.J. 647, Ch D ... *10–029*
Leicester Wholesale Fruit Market Ltd v Grundy [1990] 1 W.L.R. 107; [1990] 1 All E.R. 442; (1989) 5 Const. L.J. 282; (1990) 134 S.J. 374, CA (Civ Div) ... *28–107*
Leidemann v Schultz (1853) 14 C.B. 38 ... *12–130*
Leif Hoegh & Co A/S v Petrolsea Inc; The World Era [1992] 1 Lloyd's Rep. 45, QBD (Comm) ... *28–126*
Leifchild's Case. *See* British and Foreign Cork Co, Re
Leigh v Dickeson (1884–85) L.R. 15 Q.B.D. 60, CA ... *29–115*, *29–118*
Leigh v National Union of Railwaymen [1970] Ch. 326; [1970] 2 W.L.R. 60; [1969] 3 All E.R. 1249; 8 K.I.R. 629; (1969) 113 S.J. 852, Ch D ... *9–083*, 16–045
Leigh v Paterson (1818) 8 Taunt. 540 ... *24–011*
Leigh & Sillivan Ltd v Aliakmon Shipping Co Ltd; The Aliakmon; sub nom. Leigh & Sillavan Ltd v Aliakmon Shipping Co Ltd; The Aliakmon [1986] A.C. 785; [1986] 2 W.L.R. 902; [1986] 2 All E.R. 145; [1986] 2 Lloyd's Rep. 1; (1986) 136 N.L.J. 415; (1986) 130 S.J. 357, HL; affirming [1985] Q.B. 350; [1985] 2 W.L.R. 289; [1985] 2 All E.R. 44; [1985] 1 Lloyd's Rep. 199; (1985) 82 L.S.G. 203; (1985) 135 N.L.J. 285; (1985) 129 S.J. 69, CA (Civ Div); reversing [1983] 1 Lloyd's Rep. 203, QBD (Comm) ... *1–176*, *14–040*, *14–055*, *14–057*, *18–030*, *18–034*, *18–036*, 18–134, *27–015*
Leighton v Michael; Leighton v Charlambous [1995] I.C.R. 1091; [1996] I.R.L.R. 67, EAT ... *16–167*
Leighton v Wales (1838) 3 M. & W. 545 ... *16–118*
Leiston Gas Co v Leiston-Cum-Sizewell Urban DC [1916] 2 K.B. 428, CA ... *21–034*
Leivers v Barber Walker & CO Ltd [1943] K.B. 385, CA ... *28–003*
Lemenda Trading Co Ltd v African Middle East Petroleum Co Ltd [1988] Q.B. 448; [1988] 2 W.L.R. 735; [1988] 1 All E.R. 513; [1988] 1 Lloyd's Rep. 361; [1988] 1 F.T.L.R. 123; (1988) 132 S.J. 538, QBD (Comm) ...16–028, 16–029, *30–367*
Lemprière v Lange (1879) L.R. 12 Ch. D. 675, Ch D ... 8–049, *8–053*
Lennon v Commissioner of Police of the Metropolis; sub nom. Commissioner of Police of the Metropolis v Lennon [2004] EWCA Civ 130; [2004] 1 W.L.R. 2594; [2004] 2 All E.R. 266; [2004] I.C.R. 1114; [2004] I.R.L.R. 385; [2004] Po. L.R. 134; (2004) 101(11) L.S.G. 36; (2004) 148 S.J.L.B. 264, CA (Civ Div) ... *1–141*, 3–180
Lennon v Napper (1802) 2 Sch. Lef. 682 ... *21–011*
Lens v Devonshire Club, *The Times*, December 4, 1914 ... *2–168*
Leofelis SA v Lonsdale Sports Ltd [2007] EWHC 451 (Ch), Ch D ... *6–138*
Leonidas, The. *See* Bayoil SA v Seawind Tankers Corp
Leonidas D, The. *See* Allied Marine Transport v Vale do Rio Doce Navegacao SA
Leonis Steamship Co Ltd v Rank Ltd [1908] 1 K.B. 499, CA ... *21–022*
Lep Air Services v Rolloswin Investments; *See* Moschi v Lep air Services
Leroux v Brown, 138 E.R. 1119; (1852) 12 C.B. 801, CCP ... *4–041*, *16–030*, *30–311*, *30–354*

Les Affreteurs Réunis SA v Leopold Walford (London) Ltd; sub nom. Leopold Walford (LONDON) Ltd v Les Affreteurs Reunis SA [1919] A.C. 801, HL; affirming [1918] 2 K.B. 498, CA *13–023*, 18–078, *18–083*
Leslie, Re; sub nom. Leslie v French (1883) L.R. 23 Ch. D. 552, Ch D *29–109*
Leslie v Clifford (1884) 50 L.T. 690 .... *5–131*
Leslie v Fitzpatrick (1877–78) L.R. 3 Q.B.D. 229, QBD *8–022*
Leslie v Thompson (1851) 9 Hare 268 .... *27–059*
Leslie Shipping Co v Welstead [1921] 3 K.B. 420; (1921) 7 Ll. L. Rep. 251, KBD *22–049*, *24–051*
Lesotho Highlands Development Authority v Impregilo SpA [2005] UKHL 43; [2006] 1 A.C. 221; [2005] 3 W.L.R. 129; [2005] 3 All E.R. 789; [2005] 2 All E.R. (Comm) 265; [2005] 2 Lloyd's Rep. 310; [2005] 2 C.L.C. 1; [2005] B.L.R. 351; 101 Con. L.R. 1; [2005] 27 E.G. 220 (C.S.); (2005) 155 N.L.J. 1046, HL *30–339*, 30–376, 30–379
Lester v Foxcroft (1701) 1 Colles P.C. 108 .... *4–048*
Lester v Garland, 33 E.R. 748; (1808) 15 Ves. Jr. 248, Ct of Chancery *21–024*
Lester v Garlands (1808) 15 Ves. Jun. 248 .... *12–093*
Lesters Leather & Skin Co Ltd v Home and Overseas Brokers Ltd (1948–49) 82 Ll. L. Rep. 202; 64 T.L.R. 569; [1948] W.N. 437; (1948) 92 S.J. 646, CA *26–104*
L'Estrange v F Graucob Ltd [1934] 2 K.B. 394, KBD *12–002*, *14–001*, *14–027*, *15–076*
Letang v Cooper [1965] 1 Q.B. 232; [1964] 3 W.L.R. 573; [1964] 2 All E.R. 929; [1964] 2 Lloyd's Rep. 339; (1964) 108 S.J. 519, CA *28–031*
Letts v Inland Revenue Commissioners; sub nom. Letts, Re [1957] 1 W.L.R. 201; [1956] 3 All E.R. 588; 49 R. & I.T. 782; (1956) 35 A.T.C. 367; [1956] T.R. 337; (1957) 101 S.J. 130, Ch D *19–025*, *19–033*, *19–034*, *19–058*
Leuty v Hillas, 44 E.R. 929; (1858) 2 De G. & J. 110, QB *5–130*
Levene v Brougham (1909) 25 T.L.R. 265 .... *8–050*
Lever Brothers and Unilever NV v Procurator General; The Unitas [1950] A.C. 536; [1950] 2 All E.R. 219; 66 T.L.R. (Pt. 1) 1130; (1948) Ll. L. Pr. Cas. (N.S.) 277, PC (UK); affirming [1948] P. 205; [1948] 1 All E.R. 421; (1948) Ll. L. Pr. Cas. (N.S.) 247; [1948] L.J.R. 1154, PDAD *7–012*
Lever v Koffler [1901] 1 Ch. 543, Ch D *2–123*, *4–027*, *27–038*
Levermore v Jobey [1956] 1 W.L.R. 697; [1956] 2 All E.R. 362; (1956) 100 S.J. 432; (1956) 100 S.J. 484, CA *12–060*
Levett v Barclays Bank Plc [1995] 1 W.L.R. 1260; [1995] 2 All E.R. 615, QBD 6–159, *12–118*
Levey & Co v Goldberg [1922] 1 K.B. 688, KBD 22–043
Levison v Farin [1978] 2 All E.R. 1149, QBD *26–115*
Levison v Patent Steam Carpet Cleaning Co [1978] Q.B. 69; [1977] 3 W.L.R. 90; [1977] 3 All E.R. 498; (1977) 121 S.J. 406, CA (Civ Div) *7–139*, *14–008*, *14–011*, *14–016*, 14–019, *14–022*, *14–036*, *14–037*, *14–135*
Levita's Case. *See* International Contract Co Re
Levy, Ex p. *See* Walton, Re
Levy v Sale (1877) 37 L.T. 709 .... *17–006*
Levy v Yates (1838) 8 A. & E. 129 16–008
Lewin v Barratt Homes Ltd (2000) 164 J.P. 182; [2000] 1 E.G.L.R. 77; [2000] 03 E.G. 132; [2000] Crim. L.R. 323; (2000) 164 J.P.N. 283; [1999] E.G. 139 (C.S.); (1999) 96(46) L.S.G. 41; (2000) 79 P. & C.R. D20, QBD *6–010*
Lewis v Alleyne (1888) 4 T.L.R. 560 .... *8–020*
Lewis v Averay [1973] 1 W.L.R. 510; 117 S.J. 188; [1973] 2 All E.R. 229; reversing [1972] 1 Q.B. 198 .... *1–082*, *1–170*, 5–093, *5–097*, *5–099*
Lewis v Bond (1853) 18 Beav. 85 .... *27–038*
Lewis v Brass (1877–78) L.R. 3 Q.B.D. 667, CA *2–123*
Lewis v Campbell (1849) 8 C.B. 541 .... *29–113*
Lewis v Clay (1898) 67 L.J.Q.B. 224 .... 5–103, *12–106*
Lewis v Davison (1839) 4 M. & W. 654 .... *12–081*, *16–204*
Lewis v Great Western Railway Co (1877–78) L.R. 3 Q.B.D. 195, CA *14–017*
Lewis v Lechmere (1722) 10 Mod. 503 .... *27–007*
Lewis v Lyster (1835) 2 Cr. M.R. 704 .... *21–077*
Lewis v Pead (1789) 1 Ves. Jun. 19 .... *8–001*

Lewis v Wilson [1949] I.R. 347 .... *2–118*
Lexi Holdings Plc v Stainforth [2006] EWCA Civ 988; (2006) 150 S.J.L.B. 984; [2006] N.P.C. 87, CA (Civ Div) *12–084*
Leyland DAF Ltd v Automotive Products Plc [1993] B.C.C. 389; [1994] 1 B.C.L.C. 245; [1994] E.C.C. 289; (1993) 137 S.J.L.B. 133, CA (Civ Div) *29–088*
Leyvand v Barasch (2000) 97(11) L.S.G. 37; (2000) 144 S.J.L.B. 126, Ch D *30–079*
Lia Oil SA v ERG Petroli SpA [2007] EWHC 505 (Comm); [2007] 2 Lloyd's Rep. 509, QBD (Comm) *3–035*
Libyan Arab Foreign Bank v Bankers Trust Co [1989] Q.B. 728; [1989] 3 W.L.R. 314; [1989] 3 All E.R. 252; [1988] 1 Lloyd's Rep. 259; [1987] 2 F.T.L.R. 509; (1989) 133 S.J. 568, QBD (Comm) ... *16–031*, *16–032*, *21–008*, *21–010*, *21–039*, *23–068*, *30–005*, *30–015*, *30–361*, *30–375*
Libyan Arab Foreign Bank v Manufacturers Hanover Trust (No.1) [1988] 2 Lloyd's Rep. 494, QBD (Comm) *30–015*
Licences Insurance Corp v Lawson (1896) 12 T.L.R. 501 2–183
Liddell v Hopkinson (1974) 233 E.G. 513 .... *4–046*
Liddiard v Skelton (1843) 1 L.T.(O.S.) 143 .... *21–088*
Lido-Savoy Pty Ltd v Paredes [1972] V.R. 297 .... *16–115*
Liebmann, Ex p. *See* R. v Vine Street Police Station Superintendent Ex p. Liebmann
Liesbosch, The; sub nom. Owner of the Liesbosch v Owners of the Edison; Liesbosch Dredger v SS Edison [1933] A.C. 449; [1933] All E.R. Rep. 144; (1933) 45 Ll. L. Rep. 123, HL 26–105
Lievesley v Gilmore (1865–66) L.R. 1 C.P. 570, CCP *22–024*
Life Association of Scotland v Siddall (1861) 3 De G.F. & J. 58 .... *28–136*, *28–140*, 28–142
Lifesavers (Australasia) Ltd v Frigomobile Pty Ltd (1983) 1 N.S.W.R. 431 ...... *14–022*
Liff v Peasley [1980] 1 W.L.R. 781; [1980] 1 All E.R. 623; (1980) 124 S.J. 360, CA (Civ Div) *28–119*
Liggett (Liverpool) Ltd v Barclays Bank Ltd. *See* B Liggett (Liverpool) Ltd v Barclays Bank Ltd
Lightly v Clouston (1808) 1 Taunt. 112 .... *29–142*, *29–144*
Liles v Terry [1895] 2 Q.B. 679, CA *7–076*
Lilley v American Express Europe Ltd [2000] B.P.I.R. 70, Ch D *20–018*
Lilley v Doubleday (1880–81) L.R. 7 Q.B.D. 510, QBD *14–008*, *14–035*
Lilley v Elwin (1848) 11 Q.B. 742 .... *21–030*
Lilley v Hewitt (1822) 11 Price 494 .... *21–009*
Lilly v Hays (1836) 5 A.E. 548 .... *29–194*
Lim Poh Choo v Camden and Islington AHA [1980] A.C. 174; [1979] 3 W.L.R. 44; [1979] 2 All E.R. 910; (1979) 123 S.J. 457, HL; affirming in part [1979] Q.B. 196; [1978] 3 W.L.R. 895; [1979] 1 All E.R. 332; (1978) 122 S.J. 508, CA (Civ Div); affirming (1978) 122 S.J. 82, QBD *1–122*
Lim Teng Huan v Ang Swee Chuan [1992] 1 W.L.R. 113; (1992) 64 P. & C.R. 233; (1992) 89(14) L.S.G. 33; (1992) 136 S.J.L.B. 212; [1992] N.P.C. 129, PC (HK) 3–153
Linaker v Pilcher (1901) 17 T.L.R. 256 .... *9–068*
Linck, Moeller Co v Jameson Co (1885) 2 T.L.R. 206 .... *21–043*
Lincoln National Life Insurance Co v Sun Life Assurance Co of Canada; sub nom. Sun Life Assurance Co of Canada v Lincoln National Life Insurance Co [2004] EWCA Civ 1660; [2006] 1 All E.R. (Comm) 675; [2005] 1 Lloyd's Rep. 606; [2005] 2 C.L.C. 664, CA (Civ Div); reversing [2004] EWHC 343 (Comm); [2004] 1 Lloyd's Rep. 737; [2004] 2 C.L.C. 36; (2004) 154 N.L.J. 352, QBD (Comm) *12–046*
Lincoln v Wright (1859) 4 De. G. & J. 16 .... *4–075*
Lind, Re; sub nom. Industrial Finance Syndicate Ltd v Lind [1915] 2 Ch. 345, CA; affirming [1915] 1 Ch. 744, Ch D 19–032, *20–047*
Linden Gardens Circuit Systems v Zuken-Redac (UK) Ltd. *See* Circuit Systems Ltd (In Liquidation) v Zuken-Redac (UK) Ltd

Linden Gardens Trust Ltd v Lenesta Sludge Disposal Ltd; St Martins Property Corp Ltd v Sir Robert McAlpine & Sons [1994] 1 A.C. 85; [1993] 3 W.L.R. 408; [1993] 3 All E.R. 417; 63 B.L.R. 1; 36 Con. L.R. 1; [1993] E.G. 139 (C.S.); (1993) 143 N.L.J. 1152; (1993) 137 S.J.L.B. 183, HL; reversing in part 57 B.L.R. 57; 30 Con. L.R. 1; (1992) 8 Const. L.J. 180, CA (Civ Div); reversing 52 B.L.R. 93; 25 Con. L.R. 28; [1991] E.G. 11 (C.S.), QBD *18–047*, *18–049*, 18–053, *18–054*, 18–055, 18–056, 18–058, 18–059, 18–060, *18–062*, 18–064, 18–067, *18–068*, *18–076*, 18–093, 19–043, 19–045, *19–075*, *19–076*, *19–077*

Lindenau v Desborough (1828) 8 B. & C. 586 .... *6–147*

Lindley v Lacey (1864) 17 C.B. (N.S.) 578 .... *12–004*, *12–103*, *12–109*

Lindo v Lindo (1839) 1 Beav. 496 .... *22–005*

Lindrea, Re (1913) 109 L.T. 623 .... *4–023*

Lindsay (Sir) Parkinson & Co v Commissioners of Works and Public Buildings [1949] 2 K.B. 632; [1950] 1 All E.R. 208, CA *12–063*

Lindsay Petroleum Co v Hurd; Lindsay Petroleum Co v Farewell; Lindsay Petroleum Co v Kemp (1873–74) L.R. 5 P.C. 221, PC (Can) *6–127*, *28–138*, *28–140*, *28–144*

Lindsey (Earl of) v Great Northern Ry (1853) 10 Hare 664 .... *9–016*

Lindus v Melrose (1858) 3 H. & N. 177 .... *12–083*

Lines Bros (In Liquidation) (No.1), Re [1983] Ch. 1; [1982] 2 W.L.R. 1010; [1982] 2 All E.R. 183; [1982] Com. L.R. 81; (1982) 126 S.J. 197, CA (Civ Div) *30–376*, *30–377*

Lines Bros Ltd (In Liquidation) (No.2), Re [1984] Ch. 438; [1984] 2 W.L.R. 905; (1984) 1 B.C.C. 99007; (1984) 81 L.S.G. 585; (1984) 128 S.J. 261, Ch D *30–376*, *30–377*

Lingen v Simpson (1824) 1 S. & S. 600 .... *27–014*

Linggi Plantations v Jagatheesan [1972] 1 M.L.J. 89 .... *24–053*, *29–064*

Link Stores Ltd v Harrow LBC [2001] 1 W.L.R. 1479; (2001) 165 J.P. 575; (2001) 98(12) L.S.G. 41; (2001) 145 S.J.L.B. 39, QBD (Admin) *2–015*

Linz v Electric Wire Co of Palestine [1948] A.C. 371; [1948] 1 All E.R. 604; [1948] L.J.R. 1836; (1948) 92 S.J. 308, PC (Pal) *29–056*, *29–057*, *29–061*

Linz v Schuck (1907) 67 A. 286 .... *7–041*

Lion Laboratories Ltd v Evans [1985] Q.B. 526; [1984] 3 W.L.R. 539; [1984] 2 All E.R. 417; (1984) 81 L.S.G. 1233; (1984) 81 L.S.G. 2000; (1984) 128 S.J. 533, CA (Civ Div) *16–035*

Lion Nathan Ltd v CC Bottlers Ltd [1996] 1 W.L.R. 1438; [1996] 2 B.C.L.C. 371; (1996) 93(24) L.S.G. 26; (1996) 140 S.J.L.B. 174, PC (NZ) *26–097*

Lipkin Gorman v Karpnale Ltd [1991] 2 A.C. 548; [1991] 3 W.L.R. 10; [1992] 4 All E.R. 512; (1991) 88(26) L.S.G. 31; (1991) 141 N.L.J. 815; (1991) 135 S.J.L.B. 36, HL [1989] 1 W.L.R. 1340; [1992] 4 All E.R. 409; [1989] B.C.L.C. 756; [1989] Fin. L.R. 137; (1990) 87(4) L.S.G. 40; (1989) 139 N.L.J. 76; (1990) 134 S.J. 234, CA (Civ Div); reversing [1987] 1 W.L.R. 987; [1992] 4 All E.R. 331; [1987] B.C.L.C. 159; [1986] F.L.R. 271; (1986) 136 N.L.J. 659; (1987) 131 S.J. 940, QBD 1–189, *1–192*, *3–009*, 3–016, 3–017, *3–132*, 3–169, *9–026*, *23–081*, *29–001*, *29–003*, *29–008*, *29–009*, 29–011, *29–013*, *29–019*, *29–039*, *29–045*, *29–075*, *29–159*, *29–162*, *29–163*, *29–170*, *29–174*, *29–178*, 29–179, 29–180, *29–182*, 29–183, 29–184

Lister v Hooson [1908] 1 K.B. 174, CA *20–044*

Lister v Romford Ice and Cold Storage Co Ltd; sub nom. Romford Ice & Cold Storage Co v Lister [1957] A.C. 555; [1957] 2 W.L.R. 158; [1957] 1 All E.R. 125; [1956] 2 Lloyd's Rep. 505; (1957) 121 J.P. 98; (1957) 101 S.J. 106, HL; affirming [1956] 2 Q.B. 180; [1955] 3 W.L.R. 631; [1955] 3 All E.R. 460; [1955] 2 Lloyd's Rep. 325; (1955) 99 S.J. 794, CA *13–003*, *13–004*, *13–009*, *16–175*

Lister & Co v Stubbs (1890) L.R. 45 Ch. D. 1, CA *29–156*

Liston v Owners of the SS Carpathian [1915] 2 K.B. 42, KBD *3–071*

Litchfield Union v Greene (1857) 1 H.N. 884 .... *21–075*

Little v Courage Ltd [1995] C.L.C. 164; (1995) 70 P. & C.R. 469, CA (Civ Div); reversing (1995) 69 P. & C.R. 447; [1994] N.P.C. 1; (1995) 69 P. & C.R. D14, Ch D ... *1–022*, *2–085*, *2–138*, *3–172*
Little v Poole (1829) 9 B. & C. 192 ... *16–147*
Little Olympian Each Ways Ltd (No.2), Re [1995] 1 W.L.R. 560; [1994] 4 All E.R. 561; [1994] B.C.C. 959; [1995] 1 B.C.L.C. 48, Ch D (Companies Ct) ... *30–080*
Littlefield v Shee (1831) 2 B. & Ad. 811 ... *3–032*
Littlewood v British Overseas Airways Corp. *See* George Wimpey & Co Ltd v British Overseas Airways Corp (BOAC)
Littlewoods Organisation Ltd v Harris [1977] 1 W.L.R. 1472; [1978] 1 All E.R. 1026; (1977) 121 S.J. 727, CA (Civ Div) ... *16–104*, *16–107*, *16–108*, *16–112*, *19–097*
Littman v Aspen Oil (Broking) Ltd [2005] EWCA Civ 1579; [2006] 2 P. & C.R. 2; [2006] L. & T.R. 9; (2006) 103(5) L.S.G. 29; [2005] N.P.C. 150, CA (Civ Div); affirming [2005] EWHC 1369 (Ch); [2005] N.P.C. 88; [2005] 2 P. & C.R. DG19, Ch D ... *5–115*, *5–118*, *12–075*
Littrell v United States (No.2) [1995] 1 W.L.R. 82; [1994] 4 All E.R. 203; [1994] P.I.Q.R. P141; (1993) 137 S.J.L.B. 278, CA (Civ Div) ... *11–001*, *11–002*, *11–005*
Liverpool Adelphi Loan Assoc v Fairhurst (1854) 9 Exch. 422 ... *8–049*, *8–050*
Liverpool and District Hospital for Diseases of the Heart v Attorney General [1981] Ch. 193; [1981] 2 W.L.R. 379; [1981] 1 All E.R. 994; (1981) 125 S.J. 79, Ch D ... *9–006*
Liverpool Borough Bank v Walker (1859) 4 De. G. & J. 24 ... *20–011*
Liverpool City Council v Irwin [1977] A.C. 239; [1976] 2 W.L.R. 562; [1976] 2 All E.R. 39; (1984) 13 H.L.R. 38; 74 L.G.R. 392; (1976) 32 P. & C.R. 43; (1976) 238 E.G. 879; [1976] J.P.L. 427; (1976) 120 S.J. 267, HL; affirming in part [1976] Q.B. 319; [1975] 3 W.L.R. 663; [1975] 3 All E.R. 658; 74 L.G.R. 21; (1976) 31 P. & C.R. 34; (1975) 119 S.J. 612, CA (Civ Div) ... *1–012*, *1–062*, 1–070, *1–158*, *12–126*, *13–003*, *13–004*, *13–005*, *13–007*, 13–008, *13–009*, *13–011*, *13–017*, *13–018*
Liverpool Corp v Wright (1859) 28 L.J.Ch. 868 ... *16–019*
Liverpool Marine Credit Co v Hunter (1867–68) L.R. 3 Ch. App. 479, CA in Chancery; affirming (1867) L.R. 4 Eq. 62, Ct of Chancery ... *7–012*
Liverpool Roman Catholic Archdiocesan Trustees Inc v Goldberg (No.1) [2001] 1 All E.R. 182; [2000] Lloyd's Rep. P.N. 836; [2001] P.N.L.R. 19, Ch D ... *28–085*
Liversidge v Broadbent (1859) 4 H.N. 603 ... *22–031*, *29–194*, *29–195*
Livesey v Jenkins *See* Jenkins v Livesey
Livesley v Clemens Horst Co [1925] 1 D.L.R. 159 ... *30–337*
Livingstone v Rawyards Coal Co (1879–80) L.R. 5 App. Cas. 25, HL ... *1–122*, *26–001*, *29–052*
Livingstone v Whiting (1850) 15 Q.B. 722 ... *21–039*
Llanelec Precision Engineering Co Ltd v Neath Port Talbot CBC [2000] 3 E.G.L.R. 158, Lands Tr ... *28–109*
Llanelly Railway & Dock Co v London & North Western Railway Co; sub nom. Llanelly Railway & Dock Co v LNW Railway (1874–75) L.R. 7 H.L. 550, HL; affirming (1872–73) L.R. 8 Ch. App. 942, CA in Chancery ... *13–027*
Llewellin (A Solicitor), Re [1891] 3 Ch. 145, Ch D ... *29–093*
Llewellyn v Jersey (1843) 11 M. & W. 183 ... *12–075*
Llewellyn v Llewellyn (1854) 3 Dow. L. 318 ... *29–189*
Lloyd v Banks (1867–68) L.R. 3 Ch. App. 488, Lord Chancellor; reversing (1867) L.R. 4 Eq. 222, Ct of Chancery ... *19–068*, *19–069*
Lloyd v Coote & Ball [1915] 1 K.B. 242, KBD ... *28–095*, *28–100*
Lloyd v Dimmack (1877–78) L.R. 7 Ch. D. 398, Ch D ... *27–008*
Lloyd v Dugdale [2001] EWCA Civ 1754; [2002] 2 P. & C.R. 13; [2002] W.T.L.R. 863; [2001] 48 E.G. 129 (C.S.); (2001) 98(47) L.S.G. 28; [2001] N.P.C. 168, CA (Civ Div) ... *3–147*, *18–135*
Lloyd v Grace Smith & Co [1912] A.C. 716, HL; reversing [1911] 2 K.B. 489, CA ... *1–147*, *6–048*
Lloyd v Guibert (1865–66) L.R. 1 Q.B. 115, Ex Chamber ... *30–005*, *30–011*, *30–012*
Lloyd v Johnson (1798) 1 B. & P. 340 ... *16–069*
Lloyd v Lloyd (1837) 2 My. & Cr. App. R.192 ... *12–044*

Lloyd v Nowell [1895] 2 Ch. 744, Ch D *22–046*
Lloyd v Oliver (1852) 18 Q.B. 471 .... *12–085*
Lloyd v Stanbury [1971] 1 W.L.R. 535; [1971] 2 All E.R. 267; (1971) 22 P. & C.R. 432; (1971) 115 S.J. 264, Ch D *5–122*, *26–076*, *26–091*
Lloyd Edwards, Re (1891) 65 L.T. 453 .... *13–022*
Lloyd Royal Belge SA v Stathatos (1917) 34 T.L.R. 70 .... *23–040*
Lloyds & Scottish Finance v Cyril Lord Carpet Sales [1992] B.C.L.C. 609, HL ... *19–066*
Lloyds and Scottish Finance Ltd v Modern Cars and Caravans (Kingston) Ltd [1966] 1 Q.B. 764; [1964] 3 W.L.R. 859; [1964] 2 All E.R. 732; (1964) 108 S.J. 859, QBD *26–120*
Lloyds Bank Ltd, Re; sub nom. Bomze v Bomze; Lederman v Bomze [1931] 1 Ch. 289, Ch D *7–077*
Lloyds Bank Ltd v Bundy [1975] Q.B. 326; [1974] 3 W.L.R. 501; [1974] 3 All E.R. 757; [1974] 2 Lloyd's Rep. 366; (1974) 118 S.J. 714, CA (Civ Div) *1–012*, 1–022, *3–014*, *7–069*, *7–073*, *7–082*, *7–094*, 7–139
Lloyds Bank Ltd v Chartered Bank of India Australia and China [1929] 1 K.B. 40; [1928] All E.R. Rep. 285, CA *29–170*
Lloyds Bank Ltd v EB Savory & Co; sub nom. EB Savory & Co v Lloyds Bank Ltd; Savory & Co v Lloyds Bank Ltd [1933] A.C. 201; (1932) 44 Ll. L. Rep. 231, HL *29–170*
Lloyds Bank Ltd v Margolis [1954] 1 W.L.R. 644; [1954] 1 All E.R. 734; (1954) 98 S.J. 250, Ch D *28–036*, *28–037*, *28–040*
Lloyds Bank Plc v Burd Pearse; sub nom. Lloyds Bank Plc v Crosse & Crosse; Crosse & Crosse v Lloyds Bank Plc [2001] EWCA Civ 366; [2001] Lloyd's Rep. P.N. 452; [2001] P.N.L.R. 34; [2001] 12 E.G. 167 (C.S.); [2001] N.P.C. 59, CA (Civ Div) *28–011*
Lloyds Bank Plc v Carrick [1996] 4 All E.R. 630; [1996] 2 F.L.R. 600; [1996] 2 F.C.R. 771; (1996) 28 H.L.R. 707; (1997) 73 P. & C.R. 314; [1997] 1 E.G.L.R. 160; [1997] 11 E.G. 155; [1997] Fam. Law 94; (1996) 93(14) L.S.G. 30; (1996) 146 N.L.J. 405; (1996) 140 S.J.L.B. 101; [1996] N.P.C. 32, CA (Civ Div) *3–140*, *3–142*, *3–145*, *4–047*
Lloyds Bank Plc v Independent Insurance Co Ltd [2000] Q.B. 110; [1999] 2 W.L.R. 986; [1999] 1 All E.R. (Comm.) 8; [1999] Lloyd's Rep. Bank. 1; [1999] C.L.C. 510; (1999) 96(3) L.S.G. 31, CA (Civ Div) ...*29–018*, *29–034*, *29–037*, *29–038*
Lloyds Bank Plc v Lucken. *See* Royal Bank of Scotland Plc v Etridge (No.2)
Lloyds Bank Plc v Rogers (No.2) [1999] 3 E.G.L.R. 83; [1999] 38 E.G. 187; [1999] E.G. 106 (C.S.); (1999) 96(30) L.S.G. 30, CA (Civ Div) *28–118*
Lloyds Bank Plc v Rosset [1991] 1 A.C. 107; [1990] 2 W.L.R. 867; [1990] 1 All E.R. 1111; [1990] 2 F.L.R. 155; (1990) 22 H.L.R. 349; (1990) 60 P. & C.R. 311; (1990) 140 N.L.J. 478, HL; reversing [1989] Ch. 350; [1988] 3 W.L.R. 1301; [1988] 3 All E.R. 915; [1989] 1 F.L.R. 51; (1989) 57 P. & C.R. 62; [1988] Fam. Law 472; (1989) 86(1) L.S.G. 39; (1988) 138 N.L.J. Rep. 149; (1988) 132 S.J. 1698, CA (Civ Div) *2–169*, *2–171*, *3–138*, *3–147*, 4–077, *13–028*
Lloyds Bank Plc v Voller; sub nom. Voller v Lloyds Bank Plc [2000] 2 All E.R. (Comm) 978; [2001] Lloyd's Rep. Bank. 67, CA (Civ Div) *2–030*
Lloyds Bank Plc v Waterhouse [1993] 2 F.L.R. 97; (1991) 10 Tr. L.R. 161; [1991] Fam. Law 23, CA (Civ Div) *5–080*, *5–086*, 5–102, *5–104*, *14–132*
Lloyds of London v Leigh [1997] CA Transcript 1416 .... *6–117*
Lloyd's v Harper (1880–81) L.R. 16 Ch. D. 290, CA *2–081*, *18–049*, *18–078*
Llynvi Coal & Iron Co Ex p. Hide, Re; sub nom. Hide, Re v Ex p. Llynvi Coal & Iron Co (1871–72) L.R. 7 Ch. App. 28, CA in Chancery *20–049*
Lobb v Vasey Housing Auxiliary (War Widows Guild) [1963] V.R. 239 ....*23–057*, 23–082
Locabail International Finance Ltd v Agroexport and Atlanta (UK) Ltd; The Sea Hawk [1986] 1 W.L.R. 657; [1986] 1 All E.R. 901; [1986] 1 Lloyd's Rep. 317; (1986) 83 L.S.G. 876; (1986) 130 S.J. 245, CA (Civ Div) *27–008*, *27–041*, *27–061*
Lochgelly Iron & Coal Co Ltd v McMullan; sub nom. McMullan v Lochgelly Iron & Coal Co Ltd [1934] A.C. 1; 1933 S.C. (H.L.) 64; 1934 S.L.T. 114, HL *28–061*

Lock International Plc v Beswick [1989] 1 W.L.R. 1268; [1989] 3 All E.R. 373; [1989] I.R.L.R. 481; (1989) 86(39) L.S.G. 36; (1989) 139 N.L.J. 644; (1989) S.J. 1297, Ch D *16–092*, *16–107*, *16–109*, *27–042*, *27–061*
Lock v Bell [1931] 1 Ch. 35, Ch D *21–011*, *21–013*, *21–014*
Lock v Furze (1865–66) L.R. 1 C.P. 441, CCP *26–001*
Locker & Woolf Ltd v Western Australian Insurance Co Ltd [1936] 1 K.B. 408; (1936) 54 Ll. L. Rep. 211, CA; affirming (1935) 52 Ll. L. Rep. 325, KBD *3–169*, *6–037*, 6–145, *6–147*
Lockett v AM Charles [1938] 4 All E.R. 170 .... *18–012*, *18–050*
Lockett v Nicklin (1848) 2 Exch. 93 .... *12–106*
Lockett v Norman-Wright [1925] Ch. 56, Ch D *2–118*
Lockhart v Barnard (1845) 14 M. & W.674 .... *2–019*
Lockie and Craggs, Re (1901) 86 L.T. 388 .... *14–144*
Lockland Builders Ltd v Rickwood, 77 B.L.R. 38; 46 Con. L.R. 92, CA (Civ Div) *22–049*
Lockyer v Jones (1796) Peake 239 .... *21–087*
Lodder v Slowey [1904] A.C. 442, PC (NZ) *29–068*
Lodge v National Union Investment Co Ltd [1907] 1 Ch. 300, Ch D *16–185*
L'Office Cherifien des Phosphates Unitramp SA v Yamashita-Shinnihon Steamship Co Ltd; The Boucraa [1994] 1 A.C. 486; [1994] 2 W.L.R. 39; [1994] 1 All E.R. 20; [1994] 1 Lloyd's Rep. 251; (1994) 138 S.J.L.B. 19, HL; reversing [1993] 3 W.L.R. 266; [1993] 3 All E.R. 686; [1993] 2 Lloyd's Rep. 149; [1993] N.P.C. 64, CA (Civ Div) *2–006*, *23–040*
Loftus, Re. *See* Green v Gaul
Loftus v Roberts (1902) 18 T.L.R. 532 .... *2–129*
Logan v Uttlesford DC (1984) 134 N.L.J. 500, QBD *17–034*
Logicrose Ltd v Southend United Football Club Ltd (No.2) [1988] 1 W.L.R. 1256; [1988] E.G. 114 (C.S.), Ch D *29–149*, *29–156*
Lombank v Excell [1964] 1 Q.B. 415; [1963] 3 W.L.R. 700; [1963] 3 All E.R. 486, CA *26–135*, *26–155*
Lombard Finance v Brookplain Trading [1991] 1 W.L.R. 271; [1991] 2 All E.R. 762, CA (Civ Div) *25–023*
Lombard North Central Plc v Butterworth [1987] Q.B. 527; [1987] 2 W.L.R. 7; [1987] 1 All E.R. 267; (1987) 6 Tr. L.R. 65; (1986) 83 L.S.G. 2750, CA (Civ Div) ... *12–026*, *12–037*, *12–040*, *21–013*, *21–015*, *22–049*, *26–009*, *26–098*, *26–121*, *26–131*, *26–141*
Lombard North Central Plc v Stobart (1990) 9 Tr. L.R. 105; [1990] C.C.L.R. 53, CA (Civ Div) *3–103*
Lombard Tricity Finance v Paton [1989] 1 All E.R. 918; (1989) 8 Tr. L.R. 129; (1988) 138 N.L.J. Rep. 333, CA (Civ Div) *2–131*, *3–071*, *22–039*
London & Clydesbank Properties v HM Investment Co [1993] E.G. 63 (C.S.) *3–091*
London & County Banking Co Ltd v Ratcliffe (1880–81) L.R. 6 App. Cas. 722, HL *21–066*
London & Lancashire Insurance v Bolands Ltd. *See* Bolands Ltd v London & Lancashire Fire Insurance Co Ltd
London & Midland Bank v Mitchell [1899] 2 Ch. 161, Ch D *28–050*
London & North Western Railway Co v Neilson; sub nom. Neilson v London & North Western Railway Co [1922] 2 A.C. 263, HL; affirming [1922] 1 K.B. 192, CA; affirming [1921] 3 K.B. 213, KBD *14–008*, *14–021*, *14–029*
London & Northern Estates Co v Schlesinger [1916] 1 K.B. 20, KBD *23–055*
London & Regional Investments Ltd v TBI Plc [2002] EWCA Civ 355, CA (Civ Div) *2–112*, *2–116*, *2–138*, *3–144*
London & South Western Railway Co v Blackmore (1869–70) L.R. 4 H.L. 610; (1870) 39 L.J. Ch. 713, HL *22–005*
London & South Western Railway Co v Cyril Flower (1875–76) L.R. 1 C.P.D. 77, CPD *21–009*
London & Thames Haven Oil Wharves Ltd v Attwooll (Inspector of Taxes) [1967] Ch. 772; [1967] 2 W.L.R. 743; [1967] 2 All E.R. 124; [1967] 1 Lloyd's Rep. 204; 43 T.C. 491; (1966) 45 A.T.C. 489; [1966] T.R. 411; (1966) 110 S.J. 979, CA *26–163*

London Allied Holdings Ltd v Lee [2007] EWHC 2061 (Ch), Ch D *29–160*
London and Lancashire Fire Insurance Ltd v Bolands. *See* Bolands Ltd v London & Lancashire Fire Insurance Co Ltd
London and New York Investment Corp, Re [1895] 2 Ch. 860, Ch D *9–035*
London and Northern Bank Ex p. Jones, Re [1900] 1 Ch. 220, Ch D *2–048*, *2–054*, *22–051*
London and Overseas Freighters v Timber Shipping Co SA. *See* Timber Shipping Co SA v London and Overseas Freighters
London and River Plate Bank Ltd v Bank of Liverpool Ltd [1896] 1 Q.B. 7, QBD *29–182*
London and South of England Building Society v Stone [1983] 1 W.L.R. 1242; [1983] 3 All E.R. 105; (1983) 267 E.G. 69; (1983) 80 L.S.G. 3048; (1983) 127 S.J. 446, CA (Civ Div) *26–104*
London and Westminster Loan & Discount v Bilton (1911) 27 T.L.R. 184 ...... *7–074*
London Association for the Protection of Trade v Greenlands Ltd; sub nom. Greenlands Ltd v Wilmshurst [1916] 2 A.C. 15, HL; reversing [1913] 3 K.B. 507, CA *9–063*, *9–065*
London Assurance Co v Mansel; sub nom. London Assurance v Mansel (1879) L.R. 11 Ch. D. 363, Ch D *6–144*, *6–147*
London Baggage Co (Charing Cross) Ltd v Railtrack Plc (No.1) [2000] L. & T.R. 439; [2000] E.G. 57 (C.S.); (2000) 80 P. & C.R. D38, Ch D *2–161*
London Borough of Newham v Khatun. *See* R. (on the application of Khatun) v Newham LBC
London Branch of the Nigerian Universities Commission v Bastians. *See* Nigerian Universities Commission (London Branch) v Bastians
London CC v Allen [1914] 3 K.B. 642, CA *18–139*
London CC v Attorney General; sub nom. Attorney General v London CC [1902] A.C. 165, HL; affirming [1901] 1 Ch. 781, CA *9–020*, *10–025*
London CC v Henry Boot & Sons Ltd; sub nom. Henry Boot & Sons Ltd v London CC [1959] 1 W.L.R. 1069; [1959] 3 All E.R. 636; 59 L.G.R. 357; (1959) 103 S.J. 918, HL; reversing [1959] 1 W.L.R. 133; [1959] 1 All E.R. 77; 57 L.G.R. 15; (1959) 103 S.J. 90, CA *1–124*, *5–073*, *5–074*, *5–087*, *12–118*, *12–120*
London Chatham & Dover Railway Arrangement Act, Re; sub nom. Hartridge, Ex p.; Allender, Ex p. (1869–70) L.R. 5 Ch. App. 671, CA in Chancery ... *16–025*
London Chatham & Dover Railway Co v South Eastern Railway Co [1893] A.C. 429, HL *26–098*, 26–167, 26–168, 26–170
London Congregational Union Inc v Harriss & Harriss [1988] 1 All E.R. 15; 35 B.L.R. 58; 8 Con. L.R. 52; [1986] 2 E.G.L.R. 155; (1986) 280 E.G. 1342; (1987) 3 Const. L.J. 37, CA (Civ Div); reversing in part [1985] 1 All E.R. 335; (1984) 1 Const. L.J. 54; [1984] C.I.L.L. 85, QBD *1–124*, *18–031*, *26–018*, *28–033*, 28–061
London County Freehold and Leasehold Properties Ltd v Berkeley Property Investment Co [1936] 2 All E.R. 1039, CA *6–048*
London Drugs Ltd v Kuehne & Nagel International Ltd (1992) 97 (D.L.R.) (4th) 261; [1992] 3 S.C.R. 299, Sup Ct (Can) *14–042*, *18–020*, *18–021*, *18–094*, *18–116*
London Export Corp v Jubilee Coffee Roasting Co [1958] 1 W.L.R. 661; [1958] 2 All E.R. 411; [1958] 1 Lloyd's Rep. 367; (1958) 102 S.J. 452, CA; affirming [1958] 1 W.L.R. 271; [1958] 1 All E.R. 494; [1958] 1 Lloyd's Rep. 197; (1958) 102 S.J. 178, QBD (Comm) *12–128*, *13–023*
London Financial Association v Kelk (1884) L.R. 26 Ch. D. 107, Ch D *9–039*
London Freehold and Leasehold Property Co v Baron Suffield [1897] 2 Ch. 608, CA *1–105*, *12–109*
London General Omnibus Co Ltd v Holloway [1912] 2 K.B. 72, CA *6–159*
London Joint Stock Bank Ltd v Macmillan; sub nom. Macmillan v London Joint Stock Bank Ltd [1918] A.C. 777, HL *25–024*, *26–035*
London Marine Insurance Association, Re; sub nom. Andrews' and Alexander's Case (1869) L.R. 8 Eq. 176, Ct of Chancery *9–073*

London Passenger Transport Board v Moscrop; sub nom. Moscrop v London Passenger Transport Board [1942] A.C. 332, HL; reversing [1941] Ch. 91, CA; reversing [1940] Ch. 755, Ch D *12–027*
London Regional Transport v Mayor of London [2001] EWCA Civ 1491; [2003] E.M.L.R. 4, CA (Civ Div) *1–060*, *1–066*
London Transport Executive v Clarke [1981] I.C.R. 355; [1981] I.R.L.R. 166; (1981) 125 S.J. 306, CA (Civ Div) *24–013*
London Weekend Television v Paris and Griffith (Sued as Representatives of the Test and County Cricket Board) (1969) 113 S.J. 222 5–123
London Wine Co (Shippers), Re [1986] P.C.C. 121 .... *27–015*, *27–017*
London, Brmingham and South Staffordshire Bank, Re (1865) 34 L.J. Ch. 418 .... *21–076*
Long v Lloyd [1958] 1 W.L.R. 753; [1958] 2 All E.R. 402; (1958) 102 S.J. 488, CA *6–125*
Long v Millar (1878–79) L.R. 4 C.P.D. 450, CA *4–028*
Longbottom & Co Ltd v Bass Walker & Co (1922) 12 Ll. L. Rep. 192, CA *24–018*
Longbutt v Amoco Australia Pty (1974) 4 A.L.R. 482 .... *20–005*
Longlands Farm, Re; sub nom. Alford v Superior Developments Ltd [1968] 3 All E.R. 552; (1969) 20 P. & C.R. 25, Ch D *21–020*
Longmate v Ledger, 66 E.R. 67; (1860) 2 Giff. 157, QB *7–128*
Longridge v Dorville (1821) 5 B. & Ad. 117 .... *3–052*, *29–189*
Lonrho Exports Ltd v Export Credits Guarantee Department [1999] Ch. 158; [1998] 3 W.L.R. 394; [1996] 4 All E.R. 673; [1996] 2 Lloyd's Rep. 649; [1997] C.L.C. 259, Ch D *12–086*
Lonrho Plc v Al-Fayed (No.2) [1992] 1 W.L.R. 1; [1991] 4 All E.R. 961, Ch D *29–160*
Lonrho Plc v Tebbit [1992] 4 All E.R. 280; [1992] B.C.C. 779; [1993] B.C.L.C. 96, CA (Civ Div) *29–085*
Lonsdale & Thompson Ltd v Black Arrow Group Plc; sub nom. Lonsdale & Thompson Ltd v Black Arrow Group Plc and American International Underwriters UK Ltd [1993] Ch. 361; [1993] 2 W.L.R. 815; [1993] 3 All E.R. 648; [1993] 2 Lloyd's Rep. 428; (1993) 65 P. & C.R. 392; [1993] 25 E.G. 145; [1992] E.G. 154 (C.S.), Ch D *18–128*, *18–129*
Lonsdale (Earl of) v Attorney General [1982] 1 W.L.R. 887; [1982] 3 All E.R. 579; (1983) 45 P. & C.R. 1; (1982) 126 S.J. 463, Ch D *12–052*, *12–060*, *12–086*, *12–118*, *12–121*
Lonsdale (t/a Lonsdale Agencies) v Howard & Hallam Ltd [2007] UKHL 32; [2007] 1 W.L.R. 2055; [2008] Bus. L.R. 788; [2007] 4 All E.R. 1; [2007] 2 All E.R. (Comm) 621; [2008] 1 Lloyd's Rep. 78; [2007] 2 C.L.C. 1; [2007] Eu. L.R. 799; [2007] I.C.R. 1338; [2007] I.R.L.R. 825; (2007) 151 S.J.L.B. 922, HL *30–042*
Lonsdale Nominee Pty v Southern Cross Airlines [1993] 10 A.C.S.R. 739 .... *9–045*
Looker v Law Union & Rock Insurance Co Ltd [1928] 1 K.B. 554, KBD *2–098*, *2–118*, *6–151*
Lord Strathcona Steamship Co Ltd v Dominion Coal Co Ltd [1926] A.C. 108; (1925) 23 Ll. L. Rep. 145; 1926 A.M.C. 160, PC (Can) *1–188*, 18–139, 18–141, 18–143, 18–146, *27–070*
Lord Strathcona, The (No.2); Old Colony Trust Co v Owners of Lord Strathcona; Dominion Coal Co v Lord Strathcona SS Co Ltd [1925] P. 143; (1925) 22 Ll. L. Rep. 368, PDAD *18–143*
Lordsvale Finance Plc v Bank of Zambia [1996] Q.B. 752; [1996] 3 W.L.R. 688; [1996] 3 All E.R. 156; [1996] C.L.C. 1849, QBD *26–126*, *26–127*, *26–140*
Loring v Warburton (1858) E.B.E. 507 .... *29–091*
Lorna I, The. *See* Compania Naviera General SA v Kerametal; The Lorna I
Losinjska Plovidba v Transco Overseas Ltd; The Orjula [1995] 2 Lloyd's Rep. 395; [1995] C.L.C. 1325, QBD (Comm) *18–027*, *18–033*
Lotus Cars Ltd v Southampton Cargo Handling Plc; The Rigoletto; sub nom. Southampton Cargo Handling Plc v Lotus Cars Ltd; The Rigoletto; Southampton Cargo Handling Plc v Associated British Ports [2000] 2 All E.R. (Comm) 705; [2000] 2 Lloyd's Rep. 532; [2001] C.L.C. 25, CA (Civ Div) *3–074*, *14–049*, *14–054*
Loucks v Standard Oil Co of New York, 120 N.E. 198 .... *30–366*

Louinder v Leis (1982) 149 C.L.R. 509 .... *21–017*
Louis Dreyfus & Cie v Parnaso Cia Naviera SA; The Dominator [1960] 2 Q.B. 49; [1960] 2 W.L.R. 637; [1960] 1 All E.R. 759; [1960] 1 Lloyd's Rep. 117; (1960) 104 S.J. 287, CA; reversing [1959] 1 Q.B. 498; [1959] 2 W.L.R. 405; [1959] 1 All E.R. 502; [1959] 1 Lloyd's Rep. 125; (1959) 103 S.J. 221, QBD (Comm) *12–069*
Louis Dreyfus Trading Ltd v Reliance Trading Ltd [2004] EWHC 525; [2004] 2 Lloyd's Rep. 243, QBD (Comm) *26–060*
Lound v Grimwade (1888) L.R. 39 Ch. D. 605, Ch D *16–039*, *16–201*
Love & Stewart v Instone (S.) & Co (1917) 33 T.L.R. 475 .... *2–032*, *2–141*
Love & Stewart Ltd v Rowtor Steamship Co Ltd; sub nom. Rowtor Steamship Co Ltd v Love & Stewart Ltd [1916] 2 A.C. 527; 1916 S.C. (H.L.) 199; 1916 2 S.L.T. 124, HL; reversing in part 1916 S.C. 223; 1915 2 S.L.T. 386, IH (2 Div); reversing 1915 1 S.L.T. 205, OH *12–078*
Lovell and Christmas v Beauchamp; sub nom. Beauchamp Bros, Re [1894] A.C. 607, HL; affirming in part [1894] 1 Q.B. 1, CA *8–039*, *8–063*, *17–008*
Lovell and Christmas Ltd v Wall (1911) 104 L.T. 85 ...... *5–112*, *5–113*, 5–114, *12–052*, *12–112*, *12–118*, *16–114*
Lovell Projects Ltd v Legg [2003] B.L.R. 452, QBD (TCC) *15–094*
Lovelock v Franklyn (1846) 8 Q.B. 371 .... *21–010*, *24–030*
Lovesy v Palmer; sub nom. Party A evesy [1916] 2 Ch. 233, Ch D *4–036*
Lovesy v Smith (1880) L.R. 15 Ch. D. 655, Ch D *7–077*
Lovett, Re; sub nom. Ambler v Lindsay (1876) L.R. 3 Ch. D. 198; (1876) 45 L.J. Ch. 768 Ch D *28–031*
Lovett v Ambler. *See* Lovett, Re
Low v Bouverie [1891] 3 Ch. 82, CA *3–090*, *3–098*, *3–101*, *3–103*, *3–106*, *3–113*, *6–095*
Low v Fry (1935) 152 L.T. 585 .... *4–041*
Lowe v Bentley (1928) 44 T.L.R. 386 .... *28–122*
Lowe v Fox (1887) L.R. 12 App. Cas. 206, HL *25–021*
Lowe v Griffith (1835) 1 Scott. 458 .... *8–017*
Lowe v Guise [2002] EWCA Civ 197; [2002] Q.B. 1369; [2002] 3 W.L.R. 562; [2002] 3 All E.R. 454; [2002] P.I.Q.R. Q9; (2002) 99(15) L.S.G. 33; (2002) 146 S.J.L.B. 74, CA (Civ Div) *18–076*
Lowe v Hope [1970] Ch. 94; [1969] 3 W.L.R. 582; [1969] 3 All E.R. 605; (1969) 20 P. & C.R. 857; (1969) 113 S.J. 796, Ch D *24–051*, *29–064*
Lowe v Lombank [1960] 1 W.L.R. 196; [1960] 1 All E.R. 611; (1960) 104 S.J. 210, CA *6–135*, 14–133
Lowe v Peers (1768) 4 Burr. 2225; affirmed Wilmot 364 .... *16–072*
Lowe v Peskett (1856) 16 C.B. 500 .... *17–023*
Lowe v Wells Fargo Co Express (1908) 96 P. 74 .... *29–032*
Lowe & Sons v Dixon & Sons (1885–86) L.R. 16 Q.B.D. 455, QBD *17–027*
Lowis v Rumney (1867) L.R. 4 Eq. 451, Ct of Chancery *20–014*, *28–131*
Lowndes v Stamford (1852) 18 Q.B. 425 .... *21–030*
Lowry v Bourdieu, 99 E.R. 299; (1780) 2 Doug. K.B. 468, KB *29–150*
Lowsley v Forbes (t/a LE Design Services) [1999] 1 A.C. 329; [1998] 3 W.L.R. 501; [1998] 3 All E.R. 897; [1998] 2 Lloyd's Rep. 577; (1998) 95(35) L.S.G. 37; (1998) 148 N.L.J. 1268; (1998) 142 S.J.L.B. 247, HL 28–016, *28–084*
Lowther v Heaver (1889) L.R. 41 Ch. D. 248, CA *21–061*
Lowther v Lowther (1806) 3 Ves. 95 .... *27–014*
Lu Shan, The [1991] 2 Lloyd's Rep. 386, QBD (Admlty) *28–118*
Lubbock v Tribe (1838) 3 M.W. 607 .... *29–114*, *29–191*
Lubovsky v Snelling; Cohen v Snelling [1944] K.B. 44; [1943] 2 All E.R. 577; (1944) 77 Ll. L. Rep. 57, CA *28–108*, 28–111
Luby v Warwickshire Miners Association [1912] 2 Ch. 371, Ch D *9–083*
Lucan (Earl of), Re; sub nom. Hardinge v Cobden (1890) L.R. 45 Ch. D. 470, Ch D *19–037*
Lucas v Dixon (1889) L.R. 22 Q.B.D. 357, CA *4–027*
Lucas v Wilkinson (1856) 1 H.N. 420 .... *21–041*
Lucas v Worswick (1833) 1 M.R. 293 .... *29–033*, *29–036*

Lucas & Co Ltd v Mitchell. *See* T Lucas & Co Ltd v Mitchell
Luck v Davenport-Smith (1976) 242 E.G. 455, DC *16–113*
Luck v White (1973) 26 P. & C.R. 89; (1973) 117 S.J. 486, Ch D *21–014*, *22–042*
Lucy v Henley's Telegraph Works; sub nom. Wild v Siemens Bros & Co; Lucy v Henleys (WT) Telegraph Works Co [1970] 1 Q.B. 393; [1969] 3 W.L.R. 588; [1969] 3 All E.R. 456; (1969) 113 S.J. 641, CA (Civ Div) *28–119*
Ludditt v Ginger Coote Airways [1947] A.C. 233; [1947] 1 All E.R. 328; 63 T.L.R. 157; [1947] L.J.R. 1067; 177 L.T. 334, PC (Can) *14–135*
Ludgate Insurance Co Ltd v Citibank NA [1998] Lloyd's Rep. I.R. 221, CA (Civ Div); affirming [1996] L.R.L.R. 247, QBD (Comm) *2–175*
Ludgater v Love (1881) 44 L.T. 694 .... *6–048*
Ludlow Corp v Charlton (1840) 6 M. & W. 815 .... *9–009*
Luganda v Services Hotels [1969] 2 Ch. 209; [1969] 2 W.L.R. 1056; [1969] 2 All E.R. 692; (1969) 20 P. & C.R. 337; (1969) 113 S.J. 165, CA (Civ Div) *27–027*
Luigi Monta of Genoa v Cechofracht Co [1956] 2 Q.B. 552; [1956] 3 W.L.R. 480; [1956] 2 All E.R. 769; [1956] 2 Lloyd's Rep. 97; (1956) 100 S.J. 568, QBD *12–052*
Lumbers (Matthew) v W. Cook Builders Pty Ltd [2008] HCA 27 ....*29–002, 29–015, 29–019, 29–021*
Lumley v Gye, 118 E.R. 749; (1853) 2 El. & Bl. 216, QB *1–019*, *1–171*, 18–135, 18–137
Lumley v Ravenscroft [1895] 1 Q.B. 683, CA *8–042*, *27–046*
Lumley v Wagner, 42 E.R. 687; (1852) 1 De G.M. & G. 604, QB 27–064, *27–065*, 27–066, 27–067, 27–068
Lummus Co v East African Harbours Corp [1978] 1 Lloyd's Rep. 317, HC (Ken) *14–042*, *14–048*
Lumsden's Case. *See* Blakely Ordnance Co, Re
Luna, The; sub nom. Frances & Jane, The v Luna, The [1920] P. 22; (1919) 1 Ll. L. Rep. 475, PDAD *12–002*
Lunn Poly Ltd v Liverpool & Lancashire Properties Ltd [2006] EWCA Civ 430; [2007] L. & T.R. 6; [2006] 2 E.G.L.R. 29; [2006] 25 E.G. 210; [2006] 12 E.G. 222 (C.S.), CA (Civ Div) *27–079*
Lupton v Potts [1969] 1 W.L.R. 1749; [1969] 3 All E.R. 1083; 45 T.C. 643; [1969] T.R. 295; (1969) 113 S.J. 569, Ch D *13–009*
Luttges v Sherwood (1895) 11 T.L.R. 233 .... *21–056*
Luxmore v Clifton (1867) 17 L.T. 460 .... *22–004*
Luxor (Eastbourne) Ltd v Cooper [1941] A.C. 108, HL *1–079*, *2–083*, *13–007*, *13–011*, *13–012*, *24–032*, *29–066*
Lyall v Edwards, 158 E.R. 139; (1861) 6 Hurl. & N. 337, QB *22–005*
Lydney and Wigpool Iron Ore Co v Bird (1886) L.R. 33 Ch. D. 85, CA; reversing (1886) L.R. 31 Ch. D. 328, Ch D *9–054*
Lyle Shipping Co v Cardiff Corp [1900] 2 Q.B. 638, CA *21–020*
Lyme Valley Squash Club Ltd v Newcastle under Lyme BC [1985] 2 All E.R. 405, Ch D *5–130*
Lymington Marina Ltd v Macnamara [2007] EWCA Civ 151; [2007] 2 All E.R. (Comm) 825; [2007] N.P.C. 27; [2007] Bus. L.R. D29, CA (Civ Div); affirming [2006] EWHC 704 (Ch); [2006] 2 All E.R. (Comm) 200; [2006] N.P.C. 43, Ch D 1–033, *2–131*, *2–154*, *13–026*
Lynch v DPP of Northern Ireland. *See* DPP for Northern Ireland v Lynch
Lynch v Halifax Building Society and Royal Bank of Scotland Plc [1995] C.C.L.R. 42, CC *30–084*
Lynch v Thorne [1956] 1 W.L.R. 303; [1956] 1 All E.R. 744, CA *13–007*, *13–015*, *13–032*
Lyndale Fashion Manufacturers v Rich [1973] 1 All E.R. 33, CA (Civ Div) 26–160, *26–163*
Lynde v Anglo Italian Hemp Spinning Co [1896] 1 Ch. 178, Ch D *9–060*
Lyne-Pirkis v Jones [1969] 1 W.L.R. 1293; [1969] 3 All E.R. 738; (1969) 113 S.J. 568, CA (Civ Div) *16–097*, *16–110*, *16–119*
Lynn v Bamber [1930] 2 K.B. 72, KBD *1–124*, *28–033*
Lyon v Home (1868) L.R. 6 Eq. 655, Ct of Chancery *7–064*, *7–077*

Lyons v Thomas [1986] I.R. 666 .... *27–054*
Lyth v Ault (1852) 7 Ex. 669 .... *3–175*, *21–077*
Lythgoe v Vernon (1860) 5 H.N. 180 .... *29–146*
Lyttleton v Blackburne (1875) 45 L.J.Ch. 219 .... *9–080*
Lyus v Prowsa Developments Ltd [1982] 1 W.L.R. 1044; [1982] 2 All E.R. 953; (1982) 44 P. & C.R. 213; (1982) 126 S.J. 102, Ch D *18–080*, *18–125*, *18–135*, *18–143*
M v Home Office [1994] 1 A.C. 377; [1993] 3 W.L.R. 433; [1993] 3 All E.R. 537; (1995) 7 Admin. L.R. 113; (1993) 90(37) L.S.G. 50; (1993) 143 N.L.J. 1099; (1993) 137 S.J.L.B. 199, HL; affirming [1992] Q.B. 270; [1992] 2 W.L.R. 73; [1992] 4 All E.R. 97; [1992] C.O.D. 97; (1991) 141 N.L.J. 1663, CA (Civ Div); reversing [1992] C.O.D. 11, QBD *10–019*
M (Minors) (Residence Order: Jurisdiction), Re [1993] 1 F.L.R. 495; [1993] 1 F.C.R. 718; [1993] Fam. Law 285, CA (Civ Div) *30–79*
M&J Polymers Ltd v Imerys Minerals Ltd [2008] EWHC 344 (Comm), QBD (Comm) *26–137*
M&P Steelcraft Ltd v Ellis [2008] I.R.L.R. 355 .... *2–162*, *2–181*
M&S Drapers (A Firm) v Reynolds [1957] 1 W.L.R. 9; [1956] 3 All E.R. 814; (1957) 101 S.J. 44, CA *16–113*
MA Sassoon & Sons Ltd v International Banking Corp [1927] A.C. 711, PC (Ind) *12–069*
MB Pyramid Sound NV v Briese Schiffahrts GmbH & Co KG MS Sina; The Ines (No.2) [1995] 2 Lloyd's Rep. 144; [1995] C.L.C. 886, QBD (Comm) *14–033*
MC Bacon Ltd (No.1), Re; sub nom. Company (No.005009 of 1987) (No.1), Re [1990] B.C.C. 78; [1990] B.C.L.C. 324, Ch D (Companies Ct) *20–029*
MCI WorldCom International Inc v Primus Telecommunications Inc; sub nom. Primus Telecommunications Inc v MCI Worldcom International Inc [2004] EWCA Civ 957; [2004] 2 All E.R. (Comm) 833; [2004] Info. T.L.R. 250, CA (Civ Div); reversing [2003] EWHC 2182; [2004] 1 All E.R. (Comm) 138; [2004] 1 B.C.L.C. 42, QBD (Comm) *6–021*, *6–037*
MJB Enterprises Ltd v Defence Construction (1951) Ltd (2000) 2 T.C.L.R. 235; (1999) 15 Const. L.J. 455, Sup Ct (Can) *2–022*
MS Fashions Ltd v Bank of Credit and Commerce International SA (In Liquidation); sub nom. MS Fashions Ltd v Bank of Credit and Commerce International SA (No.2); High Street Services v Bank of Credit and Commerce International; Impexbond v Bank of Credit and Commerce International [1993] Ch. 425; [1993] 3 W.L.R. 220; [1993] 3 All E.R. 769; [1993] B.C.C. 360; [1993] B.C.L.C. 1200; (1993) 137 S.J.L.B. 132, CA (Civ Div); affirming [1993] B.C.C. 70, Ch D *20–041*
MSAS Global Logistics Ltd v Power Packaging Inc [2003] EWHC 1393; [2003] All E.R. (D.) 211 (Jun), Ch D *3–096*, *3–104*, *12–037*, *21–013*, *22–041*
M/S Aswan Engineering Establishment Co v Lupdine Ltd; sub nom. Aswan Engineering Establishment Co v Lupdine Ltd [1987] 1 W.L.R. 1; [1987] 1 All E.R. 135; [1986] 2 Lloyd's Rep. 347; (1987) 6 Tr. L.R. 1; (1986) 83 L.S.G. 2661; (1986) 130 S.J. 712, CA (Civ Div) *18–033*, *18–036*
MSC Mediterranean Shipping Co SA v BRE-Metro [1985] 2 Lloyd's Rep. 239, QBD (Comm) *2–006*, *3–092*, *22–027*
MSC Mediterranean Shipping Co SA v Polish Ocean Lines; The Tychy (No.2); sub nom. MSC Mediterranean Shipping Co SA v Owners of the Tychy; Polish Ocean Lines Joint Stock Co (formerly Polish Ocean Lines) v MSC Mediterranean Shipping Co SA [2001] EWCA Civ 1198; [2001] 2 Lloyd's Rep. 403, CA (Civ Div); reversing [2001] 1 Lloyd's Rep. 10, QBD (Admlty) *22–031*
Maas v Pepper; sub nom. Mellor's Trustee v Maas [1905] A.C. 102, HL; affirming [1903] 1 K.B. 226, CA; affirming [1902] 1 K.B. 137, KBD *12–113*
McAlpine Humberoak Ltd v McDermott International Inc (No.1), 58 B.L.R. 1; 28 Con. L.R. 76; (1992) 8 Const. L.J. 383, CA (Civ Div) *23–059*
Macandrew v Chapple (1865–66) L.R. 1 C.P. 643, CCP *12–035*, *24–040*
Macara (James) Ltd v Barclay [1945] K.B. 148, CA *26–152*, *27–007*

McArdle, Re [1951] Ch. 669; [1951] 1 All E.R. 905; (1951) 95 S.J. 284, CA 3–028, *19–031*, *19–033*, *19–037*
Macartney (No.2), Re; sub nom. MacFarlane v Macartney (No.2) [1921] 1 Ch. 522, Ch D *25–017*
Macbeath v Haldimand (1786) 1 T.R. 172 .... *10–013*
McBlain v Cross (1872) 25 L.T. 804 .... *4–034*
MacBryde v Weekes, 52 E.R. 1214; (1856) 22 Beav. 533, Ct of Chancery *21–013*
McCall Bros Ltd v Hargreaves [1932] 2 K.B. 423, KBD *12–113*
McCall v Abelesz [1976] Q.B. 585; [1976] 2 W.L.R. 151; [1976] 1 All E.R. 727; (1976) 31 P. & C.R. 256; (1975) 238 E.G. 335; (1975) 120 S.J. 81, CA (Civ Div) *1–146*, *18–049*, *26–019*
McCallum v Country Residences; sub nom. McCallum v Country Residences [1965] 1 W.L.R. 657; [1965] 2 All E.R. 264; (1965) 109 S.J. 293, CA *22–024*
McCarrick v Liverpool Corp [1947] A.C. 219; [1946] 2 All E.R. 646; 62 T.L.R. 730; (1947) 111 J.P. 6; [1947] L.J.R. 56; 176 L.T. 11; (1947) 91 S.J. 41, HL *21–009*
McCarroll v Statham Gill Davies (A Firm); sub nom. McCarroll v Statham Gill Davis [2003] EWCA Civ 425; [2003] Lloyd's Rep. P.N. 167; [2003] P.N.L.R. 25; (2003) 147 S.J.L.B. 420, CA (Civ Div) *28–011*, *28–033*, *28–034*
McCarthy & Stone (Developments) Ltd v Richmond upon Thames LBC; sub nom. R. v Richmond upon Thames LBC Ex p. McCarthy & Stone (Developments) Ltd [1992] 2 A.C. 48; [1991] 3 W.L.R. 941; [1991] 4 All E.R. 897; 90 L.G.R. 1; (1992) 4 Admin. L.R. 223; (1992) 63 P. & C.R. 234; [1992] 1 P.L.R. 131; [1992] J.P.L. 467; [1991] E.G. 118 (C.S.); (1992) 89(3) L.S.G. 33; (1991) 141 N.L.J. 1589; (1991) 135 S.J.L.B. 206; [1991] N.P.C. 118, HL; reversing [1990] 2 W.L.R. 1294; [1990] 2 All E.R. 852; (1990) 60 P. & C.R. 174; [1990] 1 P.L.R. 109; [1990] C.O.D. 449; (1990) 154 L.G. Rev. 796; [1990] E.G. 30 (C.S.); (1990) 140 N.L.J. 362, CA (Civ Div); affirming (1989) 1 Admin. L.R. 3; (1989) 58 P. & C.R. 434; [1989] 2 P.L.R. 22; [1990] J.P.L. 41; [1989] E.G. 14 (C.S.), QBD *10–023*, 10–026
McCarthy v McCarthy & Stone Plc [2007] EWCA Civ 664; [2008] 1 All E.R. 221, CA (Civ Div); affirming [2006] EWHC 1851 (Ch); [2006] 4 All E.R. 1127, Ch D *2–131*, *29–107*
McCausland v Duncan Lawrie Ltd [1997] 1 W.L.R. 38; [1996] 4 All E.R. 995; (1997) 74 P. & C.R. 343; [1996] E.G. 103 (C.S.); (1996) 93(26) L.S.G. 19; (1996) 146 N.L.J. 1387; [1996] N.P.C. 94, CA (Civ Div); reversing [1995] E.G. 133 (C.S.), Ch D *4–009*, 4–056, 4–078, *4–086*, *22–033*
McCausland v Young [1949] N.I. 49, CA (NI); affirming [1948] N.I. 72 .... *5–115*
McCawley v Furness Railway Co (1872–73) L.R. 8 Q.B. 57, QB *14–014*
McClaren v Home Office; sub nom. McLaren v Secretary of State for the Home Department [1990] I.C.R. 824; [1990] I.R.L.R. 338; (1990) 2 Admin. L.R. 652; [1990] C.O.D. 257; (1990) 87(17) L.S.G. 31; (1990) 134 S.J. 908, CA (Civ Div); reversing [1989] I.C.R. 550, Ch D *2–181*, *27–022*
McClatchiev Haslam (1891) 65 L.T. 691 .... *16–037*
McClelland v Northern Ireland General Health Services Board [1957] 1 W.L.R. 594; [1957] 2 All E.R. 129; [1957] N.I. 100; (1957) 101 S.J. 355, HL (NI); reversing [1956] N.I. 127, CA (NI) *13–027*
Macclesfield Corp v Great Central Railway [1911] 2 K.B. 528, CA *29–107*, *29–110*
McColl's Wholesale Pty Ltd v State Bank of New South Wales [1984] 3 N.S.W.L.R. 365 .... *29–173*
McCollin v Gilpin (1880–81) L.R. 6 Q.B.D. 516; 29 W.R. 408, CA; affirming (1879–80) L.R. 5 Q.B.D. 390, QBD *12–114*, *12–123*
McConnell v Hector (1802) 3 Bros. & P. 113 .... *11–024*
McConnell v Lynch-Robinson Coulter & Son, Third Party [1957] N.I. 70, CA (NI) *29–121*
M'Cormack v M'Cormack (1877) 1 L.R. Ir. 119 .... *28–146*
McCreery v Bennett [1904] 2 Ir.R. 69 .... *16–019*, *16–022*
McCrone v Boots Farm Sales Ltd, 1981 S.C. 68; 1981 S.L.T. 103, OH *12–011*, *14–072*

McCullagh v Lane Fox & Partners Ltd, 49 Con. L.R. 124; [1996] P.N.L.R. 205; [1996] 1 E.G.L.R. 35; [1996] 18 E.G. 104; [1995] E.G. 195 (C.S.); [1995] N.P.C. 203, CA (Civ Div); affirming 38 Con. L.R. 14; [1995] E.C.C. 157; [1994] 08 E.G. 118; [1994] E.G. 2 (C.S.); (1994) 138 S.J.L.B. 54; [1994] N.P.C. 4, QBD *6–029*
McCutcheon v David MacBrayne [1964] 1 W.L.R. 125; 108 S.J. 93; [1964] 1 All E.R. 430; [1964] 1 Lloyd's Rep. 16; 1964 S.C. (H L) 28; 1964 S.L.T. 66; reversing [1963] 1 Lloyd's Rep. 123 .... *12–002*, *12–011*, *12–013*, *12–017*, *13–022*, *14–002*
McDevitt v Stokes, 192 S.W. (1917) *3–073*
McDonald v Coys of Kensington. *See* Cressman v Coys of Kensington (Sales) Ltd
McDonald v Dennys Lascelles, 48 C.L.R. 457 .... *24–048*, *24–051*, *26–154*, *29–065*
Macdonald v Law Union Fire & Life Insurance Co (1873–74) L.R. 9 Q.B. 328; (1874) 38 J.P. 485; (1874) 43 L.J. Q.B. 131; (1874) 30 L.T. 545, QB *6–148*
Macdonald v Longbottom (1860) 1 E. & E. 977 .... *12–123*
Macdonald v Twiname (John) [1953] 2 Q.B. 304; [1953] 3 W.L.R. 347; [1953] 2 All E.R. 589; (1953) 97 S.J. 505, CA *8–023*, *8–024*
Macdonald v Whitfield (1882–83) L.R. 8 App. Cas. 733, PC (Can) *12–113*, *12–116*
M'Dowall v Boyd (1848) 12 Jur. 980 .... *21–081*
Mace v Rutland House Textiles Ltd (1999) 96(46) L.S.G. 37; (2000) 144 S.J.L.B. 7; [1999] N.P.C. 141, Ch D *5–114*
Macedo v Stroud [1922] 2 A.C. 330, PC (Trin) *1–093*, *1–105*
Macedonia Maritime Co, Alcionis Maritime Co, Kozani Maritime Co and Vassiliki Maritime Co v Austin & Pickersgill; The Fayrouz I-IV [1989] 2 Lloyd's Rep. 73, QBD (Comm) *12–053*, *12–055*
McElhinney v Williams [1996] 1 L.L.R.M. 276 .... *11–003*
McEllistrim v Ballymacelligott Cooperative Agricultural & Dairy Society Ltd [1919] A.C. 548, HL (UK-Irl); reversing [1918] 1 I.R. 313, CA (UK-Irl) ... *16–093*, *16–127*
McEvoy v Belfast Banking Co Ltd [1935] A.C. 24, HL 3–044, *18–089*
McFarlane v EE Caledonia Ltd (No.2) [1995] 1 W.L.R. 366; [1995] 1 Lloyd's Rep. 535; 44 Con. L.R. 57, QBD *16–053*
McFarlane v Kent [1965] 1 W.L.R. 1019; [1965] 2 All E.R. 376; (1965) 109 S.J. 497, Ch D *16–110*, *16–113*, *16–119*
McFarlane v Tayside Health Board; sub nom. Macfarlane v Tayside Health Board [2000] 2 A.C. 59; [1999] 3 W.L.R. 1301; [1999] 4 All E.R. 961; 2000 S.C. (H.L.) 1; 2000 S.L.T. 154; 2000 S.C.L.R. 105; [2000] 1 F.C.R. 102; [2000] P.I.Q.R. Q101; [2000] Lloyd's Rep. Med. 1; (2000) 52 B.M.L.R. 1; (1999) 149 N.L.J. 1868; 1999 G.W.D. 39–1888, HL; reversing in part 1998 S.C. 389; 1998 S.L.T. 307; 1998 S.C.L.R. 126; (1998) 44 B.M.L.R. 140; 1998 G.W.D. 4–180, IH (2 Div); reversing 1997 S.L.T. 211; 1996 Rep. L.R. 159, OH *18–039*
McFeetridge v Stewarts & Lloyds Ltd, 1913 S.C. 773; 1913 1 S.L.T. 325, IH (2 Div) *30–324*
McGeown v Direct Travel Insurance; sub nom. Direct Travel Insurance v McGeown [2003] EWCA Civ 1606; [2004] 1 All E.R. (Comm) 609; [2004] Lloyd's Rep. I.R. 599; (2003) 147 S.J.L.B. 1365, CA (Civ Div) *12–083*
McGrath (John) Motors (Canberra) Pty v Applebee, 110 C.L.R. 656, HC (Aus) ... *6–047*
McGrath v Shah (1989) 57 P. & C.R. 452, Ch D *4–017*, *6–137*, *12–104*, *14–063*
McGregor v Michael Taylor & Co [2002] 2 Lloyd's Rep. 468, QBD (Merc) ... *7–065*
McGuffe v Burleigh (1898) 78 L.T. 264 .... *28–094*
McHale v Watson [1966] A.L.R. 513 .... *8–046*
McHenry, Re; sub nom. McDermott v Boyd; Barker's Claim [1894] 3 Ch. 290, CA *28–037*
McIlkenny v Chief Constable of West Midlands [1980] Q.B. 283 .... *25–014*
McIlquham v Taylor [1895] 1 Ch. 53, CA *21–007*
McInerny v Lloyds Bank Ltd [1974] 1 Lloyd's Rep. 246, CA (Civ Div); affirming [1973] 2 Lloyd's Rep. 389, QBD *5–067*, *6–085*
Macintosh v Midland Counties Ry (1845) 14 M. & W. 548 .... *22–038*

MacIntyre v Cleveland Petroleum Co Ltd, 1967 S.L.T. 95, OH *16–087*
McIver v Richardson (1813) 1 M. & S. 557 .... *2–045*
MacJordan Construction Ltd v Brookmount Erostin Ltd [1992] B.C.L.C. 350; [1994] C.L.C. 581; 56 B.L.R. 1, CA (Civ Div) *18–130*
Mack Trucks (Britain) Ltd, Re [1967] 1 W.L.R. 780; [1967] 1 All E.R. 977; (1967) 111 S.J. 435, Ch D *9–050*
Mackay v Attorney General for British Columbia [1922] 1 A.C. 457, PC (Can) ... *10–006*
Mackay v Dick (1880–81) L.R. 6 App. Cas. 251, HL ... 2–153, 2–156, *13–011*, *13–012*, 24–032
Mackay v Wilson, 47 S.R. (N.S.W.) 315; [1947] W.N. (N.S.W.) 103 .... *4–058*
Mackay, Ex p. *See* Jeavons Ex p. Mackay, Re
Mackender v Feldia AG; sub nom. Mackenda v Feldia [1967] 2 Q.B. 590; [1967] 2 W.L.R. 119; [1966] 3 All E.R. 847; [1966] 2 Lloyd's Rep. 449; (1966) 110 S.J. 811, CA *16–027*, *23–029*, *30–006*, *30–305*, *30–308*, *30–364*
McKennitt v Ash; sub nom. Ash v McKennitt [2006] EWCA Civ 1714; [2008] Q.B. 73; [2007] 3 W.L.R. 194; [2007] E.M.L.R. 4; (2007) 151 S.J.L.B. 27, CA (Civ Div); affirming [2005] EWHC 3003 (QB); [2006] E.M.L.R. 10, QBD *1–060*, *1–066*
Mackenzie v Childers (1890) L.R. 43 Ch. D. 265, Ch D *13–024*
Mackenzie v Coulson (1869) L.R. 8 Eq. 368, Ct of Chancery *5–113*
MacKenzie v Royal Bank of Canada [1934] A.C. 468, PC (Can) *6–128*, *7–085*
McKewan v Sanderson (1875) L.R. 20 Eq. 65, Ct of Chancery *16–042*
Mackill v Wright Bros & Co (1889) L.R. 14 App. Cas. 106, HL *12–118*
McKillop v McMullan [1979] N.I. 85 .... *2–157*
Mackinlay v Bathurst (1919) 36 T.L.R. 31 .... *8–022*, *8–027*
Mackley's Case. *See* Tal y Drws Slate Co, Re
Macklin v Dowsett [2004] EWCA Civ 904; 2004] All E.R. (D); [2004] 2 E.G.L.R. 75; [2004] 34 E.G. 68; [2005] W.T.L.R. 1561; [2004] 26 E.G. 193 (C.S.), CA (Civ Div) *7–058*, *7–083*
Maclaine Watson & Co Ltd v International Tin Council (No.2) [1989] Ch. 286; [1988] 3 W.L.R. 1190; [1988] 3 All E.R. 257; (1988) 85(41) L.S.G. 44; (1988) 132 S.J. 1495, CA (Civ Div); affirming [1987] 1 W.L.R. 1711; [1987] 3 All E.R. 886; [1987] B.C.L.C. 653; (1988) 85(2) L.S.G. 36; (1987) 131 S.J. 1659, Ch D *11–005*, *11–018*
McLaren v The Home Office, *See* McClaren v Home Office
McLaughlin v Governor of the Cayman Islands [2007] UKPC 50; [2007] 1 W.L.R. 2839, PC (CI) *27–023*
MacLean v Dummett (1869) 22 L.T. 710 .... *8–051*
McLean v Workers Union [1929] 1 Ch. 602, Ch D *9–075*
McLeish v Amoo-Gottfried & Co, *The Times*, October 13, 1993, DC *1–123*, *26–083*
Maclenan v Segar [1917] 2 K.B. 325, KBD *9–073*
McLeod v Power [1898] 2 Ch. 295, Ch D *17–015*
McLoughlin v Grovers; sub nom. McLoughlin v Jones; McCloughlin v Grovers [2001] EWCA Civ 1743; [2002] Q.B. 1312; [2002] 2 W.L.R. 1279; [2002] P.I.Q.R. P20; [2002] P.N.L.R. 21, CA (Civ Div) *26–083*
McLoughlin v O'Brian [1983] 1 A.C. 410; [1982] 2 W.L.R. 982; [1982] 2 All E.R. 298; [1982] R.T.R. 209; (1982) 79 L.S.G. 922; (1982) 126 S.J. 347, HL; reversing [1981] Q.B. 599; [1981] 2 W.L.R. 1014; [1981] 1 All E.R. 809; (1981) 125 S.J. 169, CA (Civ Div) *1–123*, *16–004*
McManus v Cooke (1887) L.R. 35 Ch. D. 681, Ch D *4–011*, *4–012*, *4–043*
McManus v Fortescue [1907] 2 K.B. 1, CA *2–012*
Mcmanus, Administratrix v Bark (1869–70) L.R. 5 Ex. 65, Ex Ct *3–115*, *12–101*, *22–016*
McMaster University v Wilcher Construction (1971) 22 D.L.R. (3d) 9 .... *5–074*
McMaster v Byrne [1952] 1 All E.R. 1362; [1952] W.N. 239; (1952) 96 S.J. 325, PC (Can); reversing [1951] 1 D.L.R. 593, CA (Ont) *7–076*
M'Meekin v Stevenson [1917] 1 Ir.R. 348 .... *4–029*, *4–038*
Macmillan Inc v Bishopsgate Investment Trust Plc (No.3) [1996] 1 W.L.R. 387; [1996] 1 All E.R. 585; [1996] B.C.C. 453; (1995) 139 S.J.L.B. 225, CA (Civ Div) *29–140*, *30–016*, *30–123*

Macmillan v AW Knott Becker Scott Ltd; Abrahams v Macmillan [1990] 1 Lloyd's Rep. 98, QBD (Comm) *1–177*, *18–027*, *18–131*
McNally v Welltrade International [1978] I.R.L.R. 490 ......*1–122*, 6–012, *6–061*, *6–069*
McNerny v Lambeth LBC (1989) 21 H.L.R. 188; [1989] 19 E.G. 77; (1990) 154 L.G. Rev. 272; [1988] E.G. 169 (C.S.); (1989) 139 N.L.J. 114, CA (Civ Div) *1–154*
McNicholas Construction (Holdings) Ltd v Endemol UK Plc (t/a Initial) [2003] EWHC 2472; [2003] 43 E.G. 136 (C.S.); (2003) 100(40) L.S.G. 32, Ch D *2–007*
Macpherson Train & Co v Howard Ross & Co [1955] 1 W.L.R. 640; [1955] 2 All E.R. 445; [1955] 1 Lloyd's Rep. 518; (1955) 99 S.J. 385, QBD *12–036*
McRae v Commonwealth Disposals Commission (1950) 84 C.L.R. 377; [1951] Argus L.R. 771 ....**5–033**, 5–034, 5–040, 5–045, 5–047, 5–048, *26–074*
Macrae v Swindells (HG) (t/a West View Garage Co) [1954] 1 W.L.R. 597; [1954] 2 All E.R. 260; (1954) 98 S.J. 233, Assizes (Chester) *26–103*
MacRobertson-Miller Airline Services v Commissioner of State Taxation [1975] A.L.R. 131 .... *2–021*
M'Adam v Walker (1813) 1 Dow. 148, HL *8–070*
Maddever, Re; sub nom. Three Towns Banking Co v Maddever (1884) L.R. 27 Ch. D. 523, CA *28–139*
Maddison v Alderson; sub nom. Alderson v Maddison (1882–83) L.R. 8 App. Cas. 467, HL; affirming (1880–81) L.R. 7 Q.B.D. 174, CA; reversing (1879–80) L.R. 5 Ex. D. 293, Exchequer Div *3–103*, *4–041*, *4–043*, *4–044*, 4–045, *4–049*, *4–075*
Maddon v White (1787) 2 Term R. 159 .... *8–032*
Maddox v Miller (1813) 1 M. & S. 738 .... *8–008*
Madell v Thomas & Co [1891] 1 Q.B. 230, CA *12–112*, *12–113*
Maden v Clifford Coppock & Carter [2004] EWCA Civ 1037; [2005] 2 All E.R. 43; [2005] P.N.L.R. 7; (2004) 101(38) L.S.G. 29; (2004) 154 N.L.J. 1218, CA (Civ Div) *26–044*
Madras, The [1898] P. 90, PDAD *21–029*, *21–030*
Maersk Air Ltd v Expeditors International (UK) Ltd [2003] 1 Lloyd's Rep. 491, QBD (Merc) *29–034*, *29–055*, *29–183*
Mafo v Adams [1970] 1 Q.B. 548; [1970] 2 W.L.R. 72; [1969] 3 All E.R. 1404; (1970) 114 S.J. 13, CA (Civ Div) *1–133*, *6–063*
Magdalena Steam Navigation Co, Re (1860) Johns. 690 .... *9–039*
Magee v Atkinson (1837) 2 M. & W. 440 .... *12–114*
Magee v Lavell (1873–74) L.R. 9 C.P. 107, CCP *26–127*
Magee v Pennine Insurance Co [1969] 2 Q.B. 507; [1969] 2 W.L.R. 1278; [1969] 2 All E.R. 891; [1969] 2 Lloyd's Rep. 378; (1969) 113 S.J. 303, CA (Civ Div) 5–058, *5–059*, *22–021*
Magee v UDC Finance [1983] N.Z.L.R. 438 ....*19–016*, *19–020*, 19–036
Magrath v McGeany [1938] Ir.R. 309 .... *12–074*
Maharaj v Chand [1986] A.C. 898; [1986] 3 W.L.R. 440; [1986] 3 All E.R. 107; (1986) 83 L.S.G. 2568; (1986) 130 S.J. 633, PC (Fiji) *3–087*, *3–095*, *3–097*, *3–139*
Mahesan S/O Thambiah v Malaysia Government Officers' Cooperative Housing Society [1979] A.C. 374; [1978] 2 W.L.R. 444; [1978] 2 All E.R. 405; (1978) 122 S.J. 31, PC (Mal) *29–140*, *29–146*, *29–156*
Mahkutai, The [1996] A.C. 650; [1996] 3 W.L.R. 1; [1996] 3 All E.R. 502; [1996] 2 Lloyd's Rep. 1; [1996] C.L.C. 799; (1996) 146 N.L.J. 677; (1996) 140 S.J.L.B. 107, PC (HK) *2–085*, *3–074*, *14–042*, *14–048*, *14–049*, *14–054*, *14–055*, *18–019*, *18–021*, *18–090*
Mahli v Abbey Life Assurance Co Ltd; sub nom. Malhi v Abbey Life Assurance Co [1996] L.R.L.R. 237; [1994] C.L.C. 615; [1995] 4 Re. L.R. 305, CA (Civ Div) *6–033*
Mahmoud and Ispahani, Re; sub nom. Mahmoud v Ispahani; Arbitration between Mahmoud and Ispahani, Re [1921] 2 K.B. 716; (1921) 6 Ll. L. Rep. 344, CA *16–012*, *16–154*, 16–159
Mahmud v Bank of Credit and Commerce International SA. *See* Malik v Bank of Credit and Commerce International SA
Mahon v Ainscough [1952] 1 All E.R. 337; [1952] W.N. 68, CA *12–003*

Mahoney v Purnell [1996] 3 All E.R. 61; [1997] 1 F.L.R. 612; [1997] Fam. Law 169, QBD *6–120*, *7–092*, 7–101
Mahonia Ltd v JP Morgan Chase Bank (No.1) [2003] EWHC 1927 (Comm); [2003] 2 Lloyd's Rep. 911, QBD (Comm) *16–031*, *16–181*
Mahonia Ltd v JP Morgan Chase Bank (No.2); Mahonia Ltd v West LB AG [2004] EWHC 1938 (Comm), QBD (Comm) *16–031*, *16–181*
Mahony v East Holyford Mining Co Ltd (1874–75) L.R. 7 H.L. 869, HL (UK-Irl) *9–040*
Mahse v Ramlal [2003] UKPC 12 .... *21–014*
Maillard v Page (1869–70) L.R. 5 Ex. 312, Ex Ct *12–100*, *12–101*
Mainmet Holdings Plc v Austin [1991] F.S.R. 538, QBD *16–109*
Mainschiffahrts Genossenschaft eG (MSG) v Les Gravieres Rhenanes Sarl (C-106/95) [1997] Q.B. 731; [1997] 3 W.L.R. 179; [1997] All E.R. (EC) 385; [1997] E.C.R. I–911; [1997] I.L.Pr. 411, ECJ *12–011*
Mainwaring v Newman (1800) 2 Bos. & P. 120 .... *17–007*
Mair v Rio Grande Rubber Estates Ltd [1913] A.C. 853; 1913 S.C. (H.L.) 74; (1913) 2 S.L.T.166, HL; reversing 1913 S.C. 183; 1912 2 S.L.T. 398, IH (1 Div) *9–060*
Maira (No.2), The [1985] 1 Lloyd's Rep. 300 .... *23–021*
Majory (A Debtor), Re; sub nom. Debtor (No.757 of 1954), Re; Debtor, Ex p. v FA Dumont Ltd [1955] Ch. 600; [1955] 2 W.L.R. 1035; [1955] 2 All E.R. 65; (1955) 99 S.J. 316, CA *29–150*
Makedonia, The. *See* Island Tug and Barge Ltd v Owners of the Makedonia
Makin v Watkinson (1870–71) L.R. 6 Ex. 25; [1861–73] All E.R. Rep. 281, Ex Ct *21–009*
Malaysian Industrial Development Authority v Jeyasingham [1998] I.C.R. 307, EAT *11–004*, *11–005*, *11–021*
Malcolm v Chancellor, Masters and Scholars of the University of Oxford (t/a Oxford University Press) [1994] E.M.L.R. 17, CA (Civ Div); reversing, *The Times*, March 23, 1990, Ch D *2–116*, *2–126*, *2–142*, 27–024
Male v Roberts (1800) 3 Esp. 163 .... *30–324*
Maleverer v Redshaw (1670) 1 Mod. 35 .... *16–195*
Malhotra v Choudhury [1980] Ch. 52; [1978] 3 W.L.R. 825; [1979] 1 All E.R. 186; (1978) 122 S.J. 681, CA (Civ Div) *26–064*, *26–068*, *26–091*
Malik Co v Central European Trading Agency; Central European Trading Agency v Industrie Chimiche Italia Centrale SpA [1974] 2 Lloyd's Rep. 279, QBD (Comm) *2–155*, *14–141*
Malik v Bank of Credit and Commerce International SA (In Liquidation); sub nom. BCCI SA, Re; Mahmud v Bank of Credit and Commerce International SA (In Liquidation) [1998] A.C. 20; [1997] 3 W.L.R. 95; [1997] 3 All E.R. 1; [1997] I.C.R. 606; [1997] I.R.L.R. 462; (1997) 94(25) L.S.G. 33; (1997) 147 N.L.J. 917, HL; reversing [1995] 3 All E.R. 545; [1996] I.C.R. 406; [1995] I.R.L.R. 375; (1995) 145 N.L.J. 593, CA (Civ Div); affirming [1994] I.R.L.R. 282, Ch D *1–032*, 1–123, *3–048*, *13–003*, *21–030*, *26–019*, *26–032*, 26–083, 26–086, *26–087*, *27–008*
Malins v Freeman (1837) 2 Keen 25 .... *5–077*, *12–082*, *27–032*, *27–033*
Mallalieu v Hodgson (1851) 16 Q.B. 689 .... *16–017*, *16–042*
Mallam v Arden (1833) 10 Bing. 299 .... *21–006*
Mallan v May (1843) 11 M. & W. 653 .... *16–089*, *16–110*, *16–198*
Mallan v May (1844) 12 M. & W. 511 .... *12–051*
Mallet v Great Eastern Railway Co [1899] 1 Q.B. 309, QBD *14–029*
Mallet v Thompson (1804) 5 Esp. 178 .... *17–017*
Malloch v Aberdeen Corp (No.1) [1971] 1 W.L.R. 1578; [1971] 2 All E.R. 1278; 1971 S.C. (H.L.) 85; 1971 S.L.T. 245; (1971) 115 S.J. 756, HL *27–023*
Mallone v BPB Industries Ltd; sub nom. Mallone v BPB Industries Plc [2002] EWCA Civ 126; [2003] B.C.C. 113; [2002] I.C.R. 1045; [2002] I.R.L.R. 452; [2002] Emp. L.R. 919, CA (Civ Div); affirming in part, 1999 M No 0009, QBD *22–039*
Mallozzi v Carapelli SpA [1976] 1 Lloyd's Rep. 407, CA (Civ Div); affirming [1975] 1 Lloyd's Rep. 229, QBD (Comm) *2–136*

Maloco v Littlewoods Organisation Ltd; Smith v Littlewoods Organisation Ltd [1987] A.C. 241; [1987] 2 W.L.R. 480; [1987] 1 All E.R. 710; 1987 S.C. (H.L.) 37; 1987 S.L.T. 425; 1987 S.C.L.R. 489; (1987) 84 L.S.G. 905; (1987) 137 N.L.J. 149; (1987) 131 S.J. 226, HL; affirming 1986 S.L.T. 272, IH (1 Div); reversing 1982 S.L.T. 267, OH *18–036*

Malone v Commissioner of Police of the Metropolis (No.1) [1980] Q.B. 49; [1978] 3 W.L.R. 936; [1979] 1 All E.R. 256; (1979) 69 Cr. App. R. 4; [1978] Crim. L.R. 555; (1978) 122 S.J. 433, CA (Civ Div) *29–138*

Malpas v London & South Western Railway Co (1865–66) L.R. 1 C.P. 336, CCP *12–097*

Malpass (Deceased), Re; sub nom. Lloyds Bank Plc v Malpass [1985] Ch. 42; [1984] 3 W.L.R. 372; [1984] 2 All E.R. 313; (1984) 81 L.S.G. 1916; (1984) 128 S.J. 334, Ch D *2–131*

Malyon v Lawrence Messer and Co; sub nom. Malyon v Lawrance, Messer & Co [1968] 2 Lloyd's Rep. 539; (1968) 112 S.J. 623, QBD *26–044*

Mamidoil-Jetoil Greek Petroleum Co SA v Okta Crude Oil Refinery AD (No.1) [2001] EWCA Civ 406; [2001] 2 All E.R. (Comm) 193; [2001] 2 Lloyd's Rep. 76, CA (Civ Div); reversing [2000] 1 Lloyd's Rep. 554, QBD (Comm) *2–115*, *2–126*, *2–128*, *2–130*, *2–136*, *2–142*, *2–159*

Mamidoil-Jetoil Greek Petroleum Co SA v Okta Crude Oil Refinery AD (No.3); sub nom. Okta Crude Oil Refinery AD v Mamidoil-Jetoil Greek Petroleum Co SA (No.3); Okta Crude Oil Refinery AD v Moil-Coal Trading Co Ltd (No.3) [2003] EWCA Civ 1031; [2003] 2 All E.R. (Comm) 640; [2003] 2 Lloyd's Rep. 635, CA (Civ Div); affirming [2002] EWHC 2210; [2003] 1 Lloyd's Rep. 1, QBD (Comm) *2–128*, *2–130*, *12–039*, *14–140*, *14–141*, *14–150*

Mamidoil-Jetoil Greek Petroleum Co SA v Okta Crude Oil Refinery AD (No.4) [2003] EWCA Civ 617; [2003] 2 Lloyd's Rep. 645, CA (Civ Div) *12–039*

Management Services [1994] C.C.L.R. 127, CA (Civ Div) *14–095*

Manatee Towing Co Ltd v Oceanbulk Maritime SA; The Bay Ridge; Oceanbulk Maritime SA v Manatee Towing Co Ltd; Manatee Towing Co Ltd v McQuilling Brokerage Partners Inc [1999] 2 All E.R. (Comm) 306; [1999] 2 Lloyd's Rep. 227; [1999] C.L.C. 1204, QBD (Comm) *2–028*, *2–116*, *2–161*, *2–185*

Manby v Scott (1659) 1 Sid. 109 .... *8–046*

Manches v Trimborn (1946) 115 L.J. K.B. 305 .... *8–068*, *8–069*

Manches LLP v Freer [2006] EWHC 991; (2007) 151 S.J.L.B. 24, QBD *15–032*

Manchester Airport Plc v Dutton [2000] Q.B. 133; [1999] 3 W.L.R. 524; [1999] 2 All E.R. 675; (2000) 79 P. & C.R. 541; [1999] 1 E.G.L.R. 147; [1999] E.G. 31 (C.S.); (1999) 96(11) L.S.G. 69; (1999) 96(9) L.S.G. 34; (1999) 149 N.L.J. 333; (1999) 143 S.J.L.B. 89; [1999] Env. L.R. D19, CA (Civ Div) *18–147*, *27–007*

Manchester and Oldham Bank v Cook (1884) 49 L.T. 674 .... *26–099*

Manchester Bonded Warehouse Co Ltd v Carr (1879–80) L.R. 5 C.P.D. 507, CPD *12–087*, *13–016*, *21–009*

Manchester Brewery Co v Coombs [1901] 2 Ch. 608, Ch D *19–011*

Manchester College v Trafford (1679) 2 Show 31 .... *12–083*

Manchester Diocesan Council of Education v Commercial & General Investments, Ltd [1970] 1 W.L.R. 241; [1969] 3 All E.R. 1593; (1970) 21 P. & C.R. 38; (1970) 114 S.J. 70, Ch D *2–067*, *2–069*, *2–097*

Manchester Ship Canal Co v Manchester Racecourse Co [1901] 2 Ch. 37, CA *27–070*

Manchester Trust v Furness; sub nom. Manchester Trust Ltd v Furness Withy & Co Ltd [1895] 2 Q.B. 539, CA; affirming [1895] 2 Q.B. 282, QBD *18–139*

Manchester, Sheffield and Lincolnshire Railway Co v Brown; sub nom. Brown v Manchester Sheffield and Lincolnshire Railway Co (1882–83) L.R. 8 App. Cas. 703, HL; reversing (1882–83) L.R. 10 Q.B.D. 250, CA; reversing (1881–82) L.R. 9 Q.B.D. 230, QBD *1–011*, *14–011*

Mangistaumunaigaz Oil Production Association v United World Trading Inc [1995] 1 Lloyd's Rep. 617, QBD (Comm) *5–114*, *12–077*
Mangles v Dixon (1852) 3 H.L.C. 702 .... *19–070*
Manifest Shipping Co Ltd v Uni-Polaris Insurance Co Ltd; The Star Sea; sub nom. Manifest Shipping Co Ltd v Uni-Polaris Shipping Co Ltd; The Star Sea [2001] UKHL 1; [2003] 1 A.C. 469; [2001] 2 W.L.R. 170; [2001] 1 All E.R. 743; [2001] 1 All E.R. (Comm) 193; [2001] 1 Lloyd's Rep. 389; [2001] C.L.C. 608; [2001] Lloyd's Rep. I.R. 247, HL; affirming [1997] 1 Lloyd's Rep. 360; [1997] C.L.C. 481; [1997] 6 Re. L.R. 175, CA (Civ Div); affirming [1995] 1 Lloyd's Rep. 651, QBD (Comm) *6–143*
Manley & Sons Ltd v Berkett [1912] 2 K.B. 329, KBD *21–048*
Mann v Nunn (1874) 30 L.T. 526 .... *12–004*, *12–103*
Mannai Investment Co Ltd v Eagle Star Life Assurance Co Ltd [1997] A.C. 749; [1997] 2 W.L.R. 945; [1997] 3 All E.R. 352; [1997] C.L.C. 1124; [1997] 1 E.G.L.R. 57; [1997] 24 E.G. 122; [1997] 25 E.G. 138; (1997) 16 Tr. L.R. 432; [1997] E.G. 82 (C.S.); (1997) 94(30) L.S.G. 30; (1997) 147 N.L.J. 846; (1997) 141 S.J.L.B. 130; [1997] N.P.C. 81, HL; reversing [1995] 1 W.L.R. 1508; [1996] 1 All E.R. 55; (1996) 71 P. & C.R. 129; [1996] 1 E.G.L.R. 69; [1996] 06 E.G. 140; [1995] E.G. 124 (C.S.); (1995) 139 S.J.L.B. 179; [1995] N.P.C. 117, CA (Civ Div) *5–067*, *12–043*, 12–050, *12–075*, *12–118*, *12–120*, *22–049*
Manners v Pearson & Son [1898] 1 Ch. 581, CA *30–376*
Manning v AIG Europe UK Ltd; sub nom. SSSL Realisations (2002) Ltd (formerly Save Service Stations Ltd) (In Liquidation), Re; Save Group Plc (In Liquidation), Re; Squires v AIG Europe UK Ltd; Robinson v AIG Europe UK Ltd [2006] EWCA Civ 7; [2006] Ch. 610; [2006] 2 W.L.R. 1369; [2006] B.C.C. 233; [2007] 1 B.C.L.C. 29; [2006] B.P.I.R. 457; [2006] W.T.L.R. 705, CA (Civ Div); affirming [2004] EWHC 1760 (Ch); [2005] 1 B.C.L.C. 1; [2004] B.P.I.R. 1334, Ch D (Companies Ct) *20–035*
Manning v Lunn (1845) 2 C.K. 13 .... *21–092*
Manorlike Ltd v Le Vitas Travel Agency and Consultative Services [1986] 1 All E.R. 573; [1986] 1 E.G.L.R. 79; (1986) 278 E.G. 412, CA (Civ Div) *21–025*
Mansell v Robinson [2007] EWHC (QB) 101, [2007] AllE.R. (D) 279 (Jan), QBD *16–057*
Manser v Back (1848) 6 Hare 443 .... *5–077*
Mansouri v Singh [1986] 1 W.L.R. 1393; [1986] 2 All E.R. 619; [1986] F.L.R. 143; (1986) 83 L.S.G. 3508; (1986) 136 N.L.J. 260; (1986) 130 S.J. 801, CA (Civ Div); affirming in part (1984) 134 N.L.J. 991, QBD *16–032*
Mansukhani v Sharkey, (1992) 24 H.L.R. 600; [1992] 33 E.G. 65; [1992] E.G.C.S. 62; [1992] N.P.C. 58; [1992] Gazette, 27 May, 35; The Times, April 17, 1992, CA *3–022*
Mantey's Will Trusts (No.2), Re [1976] 1 All E.R. 673 .... *25–012*
Manwood v Burston (1586) 2 Leon 203 .... *3–008*
Mapes v Sidney (1624) Cro. Jac.83 .... *3–047*
Maple Flock Co Ltd v Universal Furniture Products (Wembley) Ltd [1934] 1 K.B. 148, CA *24–018*, *24–044*
Mapleback Ex p. Caldecott, Re (1876–77) L.R. 4 Ch. D. 150, CA *16–038*
Mapleson v Sears (1911) 105 L.T. 639 .... *21–030*
Maran Road Saw Mill v Austin Taylor Co Ltd. *See* Ng Chee Chong, Ng Weng Chong, Ng Cheng and Ng Yew (A Firm t/a Maran Road Saw Mill) v Austin Taylor & Co
Marathon Electrical Manufacturing Corp v Mashreqbank PSC [1997] 2 B.C.L.C. 460; [1997] C.L.C. 1090, QBD (Comm) *19–070*
Marbe v George Edwardes (Daly's Theatre) Ltd [1928] 1 K.B. 269; 56 A.L.R. 888, CA *1–123*, *26–087*
Marc Rich & Co v Tourloti Compania Naviera SA. *See* Rich (Marc) & Co v Tourloti Compania Naviera SA.

Marc Rich & Co AG v Bishop Rock Marine Co Ltd; The Nicholas H [1996] A.C. 211; [1995] 3 W.L.R. 227; [1995] 3 All E.R. 307; [1995] 2 Lloyd's Rep. 299; [1995] C.L.C. 934; [1996] E.C.C. 120; (1995) 145 N.L.J. 1033; (1995) 139 S.J.L.B. 165, HL; affirming [1994] 1 W.L.R. 1071; [1994] 3 All E.R. 686; [1994] 1 Lloyd's Rep. 492; [1994] C.L.C. 133, CA (Civ Div); reversing [1992] 2 Lloyd's Rep. 481; [1993] E.C.C. 121, QBD (Comm) ..1–142, *1–155*, 1–183, *1–187*, *18–022*, 18–032
Marc Rich & Co AG v Societa Italiana Impianti pA; The Atlantic Emperor (No.1) [1989] 1 Lloyd's Rep. 548; [1991] I.L.Pr. 562, CA (Civ Div) *30–305*
Marc Rich & Co Ltd v Tourloti Compania Naviera SA; The Kalliopi A [1988] 2 Lloyd's Rep. 101; [1988] 2 F.T.L.R. 73, CA (Civ Div); reversing [1987] 2 Lloyd's Rep. 263; [1987] 1 F.T.L.R. 399, QBD (Comm) *12–053*
Marcan Shipping (London) Ltd v Polish Steamship Co; The Manifest Lipkowy [1989] 2 Lloyd's Rep. 138, CA; affirming [1988] 2 Lloyd's Rep. 171 ....*13–004*, *13–006*, *13–007*, *18–078*
March v Culpepper (1628) Cro.Car.70 .... *3–015*
Marchant v Morton Down & Co [1901] 2 K.B. 829, KBD *19–068*
Marchington v Vernon (1787) 1 B. & P. 101 .... *18–019*
Marchioness of Huntly v Gaskell (Indorsement on Writ: Striking Out) [1905] 2 Ch. 656, CA *25–012*
Marcic v Thames Water Utilities Ltd; sub nom. Thames Water Utilities Ltd v Marcic [2003] UKHL 66; [2004] 2 A.C. 42; [2003] 3 W.L.R. 1603; [2004] 1 All E.R. 135; [2004] B.L.R. 1; 91 Con. L.R. 1; [2004] Env. L.R. 25; [2004] H.R.L.R. 10; [2004] U.K.H.R.R. 253; [2003] 50 E.G. 95 (C.S.); (2004) 101(4) L.S.G. 32; (2003) 153 N.L.J. 1869; (2003) 147 S.J.L.B. 1429; [2003] N.P.C. 150, HL *27–063*
Marco Productions Ltd v Pagola [1945] K.B. 111, KBD *27–060*
Marconi Communications International Ltd v PT Pan Indonesia Bank TBK; sub nom. Marconi Communications International Ltd v PT Pan Indonesian Bank Ltd [2005] EWCA Civ 422; [2005] 2 All E.R. (Comm) 325; [2007] 2 Lloyd's Rep. 72, CA (Civ Div) *30–077*, *30–091*, *30–204*
Mardorf Peach & Co Ltd v Attica Sea Carriers Corp of Liberia; The Laconia [1977] A.C. 850; [1977] 2 W.L.R. 286; [1977] 1 All E.R. 545; [1977] 1 Lloyd's Rep. 315; (1977) 121 S.J. 134, HL; reversing [1976] Q.B. 835; [1976] 2 W.L.R. 668; [1976] 2 All E.R. 249; [1976] 1 Lloyd's Rep. 395; (1976) 120 S.J. 231, CA (Civ Div); reversing [1975] 1 Lloyd's Rep. 634, QBD (Comm) *3–081*, *3–090*, *3–091*, *12–037*, *21–013*, *21–046*, *21–053*, *21–088*, *21–089*, *22–048*, *22–049*, *22–051*, *22–053*, *26–148*, *27–014*
Maredelanto Compania Naviera SA v Bergbau-Handel GmbH; The Mihalis Angelos [1971] 1 Q.B. 164; [1970] 3 W.L.R. 601; [1970] 3 All E.R. 125; [1970] 2 Lloyd's Rep. 43; (1970) 114 S.J. 548, CA (Civ Div); reversing [1970] 2 W.L.R. 907; [1970] 1 All E.R. 673; [1970] 1 Lloyd's Rep. 118, QBD (Comm) *12–037*, *22–049*, *24–013*, *24–014*, *24–022*, *24–048*, *26–048*
Margaronis Navigation Agency Ltd v Henry W Peabody & Co of London Ltd [1965] 2 Q.B. 430; [1964] 3 W.L.R. 873; [1964] 3 All E.R. 333; [1964] 2 Lloyd's Rep. 153; (1964) 108 S.J. 562, CA *21–001*, *21–002*
Marginson v Blackburn BC [1939] 2 K.B. 426, CA *25–012*, *25–016*
Mariannina, The. *See* Astro Venturoso Compania Naviera v Hellenic Shipyards SA; The Mariannina
Marifortuna Naviera SA v Government of Ceylon [1970] 1 Lloyd's Rep. 247, QBD (Comm) *14–148*
Marine Blast Ltd v Targe Towing Ltd; sub nom. Targe Towing Ltd v Marine Blast Ltd [2004] EWCA Civ 346; [2004] 1 Lloyd's Rep. 721; [2004] 1 C.L.C. 1082, CA (Civ Div) *14–054*
Marintrans (AB)v Comet Shipping Co Ltd. *See* AB Marintrans v Comet Shipping Co Ltd; The Shinjitsu Maru No.5
Maritime Electric Co Ltd v General Dairies Ltd [1937] A.C. 610, PC (Can) 10–041
Maritime National Fish Ltd v Ocean Trawlers Ltd; sub nom. Ocean Trawlers Ltd v Maritime National Fish Ltd [1935] A.C. 524; (1935) 51 Ll. L. Rep. 299, PC (Can) *23–007*, *23–034*, *23–059*, *23–061*, 23–062, 23–064

Mark v Mark; sub nom. Marks v Marks (Divorce: Jurisdiction) [2005] UKHL 42; [2006] 1 A.C. 98; [2005] 3 W.L.R. 111; [2005] 3 All E.R. 912; [2005] 2 F.L.R. 1193; [2005] 2 F.C.R. 467; [2005] I.N.L.R. 614; [2005] W.T.L.R. 1223; [2005] Fam. Law 857; (2005) 102(28) L.S.G. 32, HL *30–079*
Mark Rowlands Ltd v Berni Inns Ltd [1986] Q.B. 211; [1985] 3 W.L.R. 964; [1985] 3 All E.R. 473; [1985] 2 Lloyd's Rep. 437; [1985] 2 E.G.L.R. 92; (1985) 276 E.G. 191, CA (Civ Div) *18–129*
Markappa Inc v NW Spratt & Son; The Arta [1985] 1 Lloyd's Rep. 534, CA (Civ Div); reversing [1983] 2 Lloyd's Rep. 405, QBD (Comm) *9–067*, *9–068*, *9–069*
Markes v Coodes [1997] P.N.L.R. 252, QBD *28–086*
Markham v Karsten [2007] EWHC 1509 (Ch); [2007] All E.R. (D) 377; [2007] B.P.I.R. 1109; (2007–08) 10 I.T.E.L.R. 475, Ch D *7–076*
Marks & Spencer Plc v Customs and Excise Commissioners (No.5); Sussex University v Customs and Excise Commissioners [2005] UKHL 53; [2005] S.T.C. 1254; [2005] 3 C.M.L.R. 3; [2006] Eu. L.R. 110; [2005] B.T.C. 5472; [2005] B.V.C. 503; [2005] S.T.I. 1338, HL 29–027
Marlborough (Duke of), Re; sub nom. Davis v Whitehead [1894] 2 Ch. 133, Ch D *12–113*
Marles v Philip Trant & Sons Ltd (No.2) [1954] 1 Q.B. 29; [1953] 2 W.L.R. 564; [1953] 1 All E.R. 651; (1953) 97 S.J. 189, CA; reversing [1953] 1 All E.R. 645, Assizes (Hampshire) *16–153*, *16–158*, *16–168*
Marley v Forward Trust Group [1986] I.C.R. 891; [1986] I.R.L.R. 369, CA (Civ Div); reversing [1986] I.C.R. 115; [1986] I.R.L.R. 43, EAT *2–177*
Marley Tile Co v Johnson [1982] I.R.L.R. 75, CA (Civ Div) *16–113*
Marlow v Pitfield (1719) 1 P.Wms. 558 8–020
Marlwood Commercial Inc v Kozeny (Application for Stay of Orders) [2006] EWHC 872, QBD (Comm) *30–355*, *30–358*, *30–367*
Maronier v Larmer [2002] EWCA Civ 774; [2003] Q.B. 620; [2002] 3 W.L.R. 1060; [2003] 3 All E.R. 848; [2003] 1 All E.R. (Comm) 225; [2002] C.L.C. 1281; [2002] I.L.Pr. 39; (2002) 99(28) L.S.G. 30; (2002) 146 S.J.L.B. 161, CA (Civ Div) *30–070*, *30–366*, *30–368*
Marplace (Number 512) Ltd v Chaffe Street (A Firm) [2006] EWHC 1919 (Ch), Ch D *24–023*
Marrache v Ashton [1943] A.C. 311, PC (Gib) *21–068*, *30–370*, *30–375*
Marren v Dawson Bentley & Co [1961] 2 Q.B. 135; [1961] 2 W.L.R. 679; [1961] 2 All E.R. 270; (1961) 105 S.J. 383, Assizes (Leeds) *28–062*
Marriott v Hampton (1797) 7 T.R. 269 ....*29–012*, *29–098*
Marryatts v White (1817) 2 Stark. 101 .... *21–064*
Marsack v Webber (1860) 6 H.N. 1 .... *29–124*
Marsden v Guide Dogs for the Blind Association; sub nom. Burton Marsden Douglas, Re [2004] EWHC 593 (Ch); [2004] 3 All E.R. 222; [2004] 3 Costs L.R. 378; (2004) 154 N.L.J. 618, Ch D 3–176
Marseille Fret SA v D Oltmann Schiffahrts GmbH & Co KG; The Trado [1982] 1 Lloyd's Rep. 157; [1981] Com. L.R. 277, QBD (Comm) *3–077*, *3–095*
Marsh v Jones (1889) L.R. 40 Ch. D. 563, CA *26–175*
Marsh v Keating (1834) 1 Bing N.C. 198 ....*29–142*, *29–147*
Marsh v National Autistic Society [1993] I.C.R. 453, EAT *27–022*
Marsh v Pedder (1815) 4 Camp. 257 .... *21–075*
Marsland, Re; sub nom. Lloyds Bank Ltd v Marsland [1939] Ch. 820, CA *16–073*
Marshall, Re; sub nom. Marshall v Whateley [1920] 1 Ch. 284, Ch D *8–077*
Marshall v Berridge (1881–82) L.R. 19 Ch. D. 233, CA *4–026*
Marshall v Broadhurst (1831 1 Cr. & J. 403 .... *20–002*
Marshall v Glanvill [1917] 2 K.B. 87, KBD *23–023*, *23–039*
Marshall v Green (1875–76) L.R. 1 C.P.D. 35, CPD *4–018*
Marshall v Harland & Wolff Ltd [1972] 1 W.L.R. 899; [1972] 2 All E.R. 715; [1972] 1 R.L.R. 90; [1972] I.C.R. 101; [1972] I.R.L.R. 90; (1972) 7 I.T.R. 150; (1972) 116 S.J. 484, NIRC *23–038*
Marshall v Lynn, 151 E.R. 342; (1840) 6 M. & W. 109, Ex Ct *22–033*
Marshall v Macintosh (1898) 78 L.T. 750 .... *26–092*

Marshall v NM Financial Management Ltd; sub nom. NM Financial Management Ltd v Marshall [1997] 1 W.L.R. 1527; [1997] I.C.R. 1065; [1997] I.R.L.R. 449, CA (Civ Div); affirming [1995] 1 W.L.R. 1461; [1995] 4 All E.R. 785; [1995] I.C.R. 1042; [1996] I.R.L.R. 20, Ch D *16–198*, 16–199
Marshall v Rubypoint Ltd (1997) 29 H.L.R. 850; [1997] 1 E.G.L.R. 69; [1997] 25 E.G. 142; [1997] E.G. 12 (C.S.); (1997) 73 P. & C.R. D42, CA (Civ Div) *26–035*
Marshall & Murray Ltd v Jones (1913) 29 T.L.R. 351 .... *16–114*
Marshall Shipping Co v Board of Trade [1923] 2 K.B. 343 .... *29–094*
Marston Construction Co Ltd v Kigass Ltd, 46 B.L.R. 109; (1990) 15 Con. L.R. 116, QBD *29–021*, *29–071*
Marston Excelsior Ltd v Arbuckle Smith & Co Ltd [1971] 2 Lloyd's Rep. 306; (1971) 115 S.J. 654, CA (Civ Div); reversing [1971] 1 Lloyd's Rep. 70, QBD *14–030*
Martell v Consett Iron Co Ltd [1955] Ch. 363; [1955] 2 W.L.R. 463; [1955] 1 All E.R. 481; (1955) 99 S.J. 148; (1955) 99 S.J. 211, CA; affirming [1954] 3 W.L.R. 648; [1954] 3 All E.R. 339; (1954) 98 S.J. 768, Ch D *16–049*, 16–051, *16–052*, *16–053*
Martin v Andrews (1856) 7 E.B. 1 .... *29–054*
Martin v Brecknell (1813) 2 M.S. 39 .... *21–065*
Martin v Gale (1876–77) L.R. 4 Ch. D. 428, Ch D *8–020*, *8–028*, *8–066*
Martin v Mitchell (1820) 2 J. & W. 413 .... *27–050*
Martin v N Negin Ltd (1945) 172 L.T. 275 .... *21–004*
Martin v Nadel [1906] 2 K.B. 26, CA *21–051*
Martin v Nutkin (1724) 2 P. Wms. 266 .... *27–060*
Martin v Pycroft, 42 E.R. 1079; (1852) 2 De G.M. & G. 785, QB ...*4–026*, *5–124*, *12–112*, *27–037*, *27–047*
Martin v Sitwell (1690) 1 Show. 156 .... *29–006*
Martin v Stout [1925] A.C. 359; [1925] 1 W.W.R. 679, PC (Egy) *24–018*
Martin-Baker Aircraft Co v Canadian Flight Equipment; sub nom. Martin-Baker Aircraft Co v Murison [1955] 2 Q.B. 556; [1955] 3 W.L.R. 212; [1955] 2 All E.R. 722; (1955) 72 R.P.C. 236; (1955) 99 S.J. 472, QBD *13–027*, *22–054*
Martindale v Smith (1841) 1 Q.B. 389 .... *21–011*
Martin-Smith v Williams [1999] E.M.L.R. 571, CA (Civ Div); affirming [1998] E.M.L.R. 334, Ch D *13–012*
Martyn v Hind (1776) 2 Cowp.437 .... *18–019*
Marubeni Corp v Pearlstone Shipping Corp; The Puerto Acevedo [1978] 1 Lloyd's Rep. 38; (1977) 121 S.J. 574, CA (Civ Div) *28–119*
Marubeni Hong Kong & South China Ltd v Mongolia [2005] EWCA Civ 395; [2005] 1 W.L.R. 2497; [2005] 2 All E.R. (Comm) 288; [2005] 2 Lloyd's Rep. 231; [2005] 1 C.L.C. 540, CA (Civ Div); affirming [2004] EWHC 472 (Comm); [2004] 2 Lloyd's Rep. 198, QBD (Comm) *10–011*, *10–012*, *10–043*
Marubeni Hong Kong and South China Ltd v Mongolia (Jurisdiction); sub nom. Marubeni Hong Kong and South China Ltd v Ministry of Finance of Mongolia [2002] 2 All E.R. (Comm) 873, QBD (Comm) *30–051*, *30–173*, *30–325*, *30–324*
Marvin v Marvin (1976) 557 P. (2d)104 .... *16–068*
Marwood v Charter Credit Corp (1971) 20 D.L.R. (3d) 563 .... *5–071*
Mary, Duchess of Sutherland, Re (1915) 31 T.L.R. 248 .... *11–027*
Maryland Casualty Co v Matthews, 209 F.Supp. 822 (1962) *3–062*
Marzetti v Williams (1830) 1 B. & Ad. 415 ....*1–122*, *26–008*
Mascall v Mascall (1985) 50 P. & C.R. 119; (1984) 81 L.S.G. 2218, CA (Civ Div) *19–033*
Maskell v Horner [1915] 3 K.B. 106, CA *3–056*, 7–012, *7–034*, *28–058*, *29–088*, 29–090, *29–092*, *29–094*, *29–098*, *29–111*, *29–186*
Maskell v Ivory [1970] Ch. 502; [1970] 2 W.L.R. 844; [1970] 1 All E.R. 488; (1970) 21 P. & C.R. 360; (1970) 114 S.J. 189, Ch D *27–007*
Maskelyne v Stollery (1899) 16 T.L.R. 97 .... *12–047*
Mason, Re [1929] 1 Ch. 1, CA *28–058*, *28–134*

Mason v Burningham [1949] 2 K.B. 545; [1949] 2 All E.R. 134; 65 T.L.R. 466; [1949] L.J.R. 1430; (1949) 93 S.J. 496, CA *26–074*, *29–059*
Mason v Clarke [1955] A.C. 778; [1955] 2 W.L.R. 853; [1955] 1 All E.R. 914; (1955) 99 S.J. 274, HL; reversing [1954] 1 Q.B. 460; [1954] 2 W.L.R. 48; [1954] 1 All E.R. 189; (1954) 98 S.J. 28, CA *16–011*, *16–167*
Mason v Harman [1972] R.T.R. 1; (1971) 115 S.J. 931, QBD *26–157*
Mason v Mason [1972] Fam. 302; [1972] 3 W.L.R. 405; [1972] 3 All E.R. 315; (1972) 116 S.J. 485, Fam Div *8–069*
Mason v New South Wales (State of), 102 C.L.R. 108 ..*29–027*, *29–084*, *29–086*, *29–094*, *29–095*, *29–186*
Mason v Provident Clothing & Supply Co Ltd. *See* Provident Clothing & Supply Co Ltd v Mason
Masonic and General Life Assurance Co Re (1886) L.R. 32 Ch. D. 373, Ch D *20–004*
Massai Aviation Services v Attorney General [2007] UKPC 12, PC (Bah) *19–050*
Massey v Johnson (1847) 1 Exch. 241 .... *4–011*
Massey v Midland Bank Plc [1995] 1 All E.R. 929; [1994] 2 F.L.R. 342; [1995] 1 F.C.R. 380; (1995) 27 H.L.R. 227; [1994] Fam. Law 562; [1994] N.P.C. 44, CA (Civ Div) *6–024*
Master v Miller (1791) 4 T.R. 320 ...*1–114*, *16–048*, *16–054*, *17–022*, *25–020*, *25–022*, *25–024*
Masters, Re (1835) 4 Dowl. 18 .... *16–055*
Matadeen v Caribbean Insurance Co Ltd [2002] UKPC 69; [2003] 1 W.L.R. 670, PC (Trin) *18–131*, *28–003*
Matalimex Foreign Trade Corp v Eugenie Maritime Ltd [1962] 1 Lloyd's Rep. 378, QBD (Comm) *28–112*
Matanle Ex p. Schulte, Re (1873–74) L.R. 9 Ch. App. 409, CA in Chancery ... *20–020*
Matharu v Matharu [1994] 2 F.L.R. 597; [1994] 3 F.C.R. 216; (1994) 26 H.L.R. 648; (1994) 68 P. & C.R. 93; [1994] Fam. Law 624; [1994] E.G. 87 (C.S.); (1994) 91(25) L.S.G. 31; (1994) 138 S.J.L.B. 111; [1994] N.P.C. 63, CA (Civ Div) *3–138*, *13–028*, *28–136*
Matheson v Smiley [1932] 2 D.L.R. 787 .... *29–019*, *29–022*, *29–132*, *29–134*
Mathew v Blackmore, 156 E.R. 1409; (1857) 1 Hurl. & N. 762, QB *12–092*
Mathew v TM Sutton Ltd [1994] 1 W.L.R. 1455; [1994] 4 All E.R. 793; (1994) 13 Tr. L.R. 461; [1994] C.C.L.R. 140; (1994) 144 N.L.J. 1278, Ch D *26–174*
Mathieson's Trustees v Burrup Mathieson & Co [1927] 1 Ch. 562, Ch D *20–041*
Matrix Securities Ltd v Theodore Goddard [1998] S.T.C. 1; [1998] P.N.L.R. 290; [1997] B.T.C. 578; (1997) 147 N.L.J. 1847, Ch D *13–032*
Matsoukis v Priestman & Co [1915] 1 K.B. 681, KBD *14–144*, *14–148*
Mattei v Vautro (1898) 78 L.T. 682 .... *8–043*, *8–062*
Matthew, Ex p. (1884) 12 Q.B.D. 506 .... *21–074*
Matthews v Baxter (1872–73) L.R. 8 Ex. 132, Ex Ct *8–072*, *8–080*
Matthews v Goodday (1861) 31 L.J.Ch. 282 .... *19–037*
Matthews v Kuwait Bechtel Corp [1959] 2 Q.B. 57; [1959] 2 W.L.R. 702; [1959] 2 All E.R. 345; (1959) 103 S.J. 393, CA *1–152*, *1–168*, *30–032*, *30–121*
Matthews v Ministry of Defence [2003] UKHL 4; [2003] 1 A.C. 1163; [2003] 2 W.L.R. 435; [2003] 1 All E.R. 689; [2003] I.C.R. 247; [2004] H.R.L.R. 2; [2003] U.K.H.R.R. 453; 14 B.H.R.C. 585; [2003] P.I.Q.R. P24; [2003] A.C.D. 42; (2003) 100(13) L.S.G. 26; (2003) 153 N.L.J. 261; (2003) 147 S.J.L.B. 235, HL; affirming [2002] EWCA Civ 773; [2002] 1 W.L.R. 2621; [2002] 3 All E.R. 513; [2002] I.C.R. 1003; [2002] H.R.L.R. 39; 12 B.H.R.C. 652; [2003] P.I.Q.R. P4; [2002] A.C.D. 77; (2002) 99(27) L.S.G. 33; (2002) 152 N.L.J. 879; (2002) 146 S.J.L.B. 144, CA (Civ Div); reversing [2002] EWHC 13 (QB); [2002] C.P. Rep. 26; [2002] P.I.Q.R. P25; [2002] A.C.D. 42, QBD *11–003*
Matthews v Smallwood [1910] 1 Ch. 777, Ch D *12–067*, *24–003*
Matthey v Curling; sub nom. Curling v Matthey [1922] 2 A.C. 180, HL ...*23–055*, *23–066*
Matvieff v Crossfield (1903) 8 Com. Cas. 120 .... *21–044*
Maunsell v Midland GW (Ireland) Ry (1863) 1 Hem. & M. 130 .... *9–020*
Mauritius Oil Refineries Ltd v Stolt-Nielsen Nederlands BV; The Stolt Sydness [1997] 1 Lloyd's Rep. 273; [1997] C.L.C. 417, QBD (Comm) *28–022*, *30–009*

Mavro Vetranic, The. *See* Greenwich Marine Inc v Federal Commerce & Navigation Co Ltd
Maw v Jones (1890) L.R. 25 Q.B.D. 107, QBD *26–019*
Maxim Nordenfelt Guns and Ammunition Co v Nordenfelt. *See* Nordenfelt v Maxim Nordenfelt Guns & Ammunition Co Ltd
Maxwell Communications Corp Plc (No.2), Re; sub nom. Maxwell Communications Corp Plc (No.3), Re [1993] 1 W.L.R. 1402; [1994] 1 All E.R. 737; [1993] B.C.C. 369; [1994] 1 B.C.L.C. 1, Ch D (Companies Ct) *20–025*
Maxwell Fleet and Facilities Management Ltd (In Administration) (No.1), Re [2001] 1 W.L.R. 323; [2000] 1 All E.R. 464; [1999] 2 B.C.L.C. 721; [2000] B.P.I.R. 294, Ch D (Companies Ct) *28–070*
May v Borup [1915] 1 K.B. 830, KBD *22–051*
May v May [1929] 2 K.B. 386, CA *23–040*
May v O'Neill (1875) 44 L.J.Ch. 660 .... *16–110*
May v Platt [1900] 1 Ch. 616, Ch D *5–115*, *5–124*
May v Thompson (1882) 20 Ch. D. 705 .... *2–118*
May & Butcher Ltd v King, The [1934] 2 K.B. 17; [1929] All E.R. Rep. 679, HL ... *2–113*, 2–126, 2–128, *22–039*
Maybury v Atlantic Union Oil Co (1953) 89 C.L.R. 507 .... *12–103*
Maye v Colonial Mutual Life Assurance Society (1924) 35 C.L.R. 14 .... *6–149*
Mayfair Photographic Supplies (London) v Baxter Hoare & Co and Stembridge [1972] 1 Lloyd's Rep. 410, QBD *14–029*, *14–054*, *24–001*
Mayfield Holdings Ltd v Moana Reef Ltd [1973] 1 N.Z.L.R. 309, Sup Ct (Auckland) *13–028*, *27–029*
Maynard v West Midlands RHA; sub nom. Maynard v West Midlands AHA [1984] 1 W.L.R. 634; [1985] 1 All E.R. 635; (1984) 81 L.S.G. 1926; (1983) 133 N.L.J. 641; (1984) 128 S.J. 317, HL *13–032*
Mayor (t/a Granville Coaches) v P&O Ferries Ltd; The Lion [1990] 2 Lloyd's Rep. 144, QBD (Comm) *14–117*
Mayor of Auckland v Alliance Assurance Co Ltd [1937] A.C. 587, PC (NZ) ... *30–370*, *30–374*, *30–375*
Mayson v Clouet [1924] A.C. 980; [1924] 3 W.W.R. 211, PC (Sing) .. *24–051*, *26–150*, *26–154*, *29–061*, *29–065*
Mbasogo v Logo Ltd (No.1) [2006] EWCA Civ 1370; [2007] Q.B. 846; [2007] 2 W.L.R. 1062, CA (Civ Div); affirming [2005] EWHC 2034 (QB); (2005) 102(39) L.S.G. 32, QBD *11–007*
Mead v Babington (formerly Babingtons Estate Agents) [2007] EWCA Civ 518, CA (Civ Div) *6–030*
Mead, Re [1916] 2 I.R. 285 .... *8–016*, *20–049*
Meadow Schama Co v C Mitchel Co (1973) 228 E.G. 1511 .... *29–156*
Meadows v Grand Junction Waterworks Co (1905) 69 J.P. 255 .... *29–043*
Meakin v Morris (1883–84) L.R. 12 Q.B.D. 352, QBD *8–022*, *8–029*
Mears v Safecar Securities [1983] Q.B. 54; [1982] 3 W.L.R. 366; [1982] I.C.R. 626; [1982] 2 All E.R. 865; [1982] I.R.L.R. 183, CA; affirming [1981] I.C.R. 409; [1981] 1 W.L.R. 1214, EAT *1–017*, *12–126*
Measures Bros Ltd v Measures [1910] 2 Ch. 248, CA; affirming [1910] 1 Ch. 336, Ch D *9–047*, *16–100*, *16–102*, *24–028*
Mecca Leisure Ltd v London Residuary Body [1988] Ch. 132; *Daily Telegraph*, September 1, 1988 .... *3–147*
Mecca, The. *See* United Arab Maritime Co v Blue Star Line; The Mecca
Mechelen v Wallace (1837) 7 A. & E. 49 .... *4–011*, *4–016*
Medforth v Blake [1999] N.L.J. 929 .... *18–022*
Medforth v Blake [2000] Ch. 86; [1999] 3 W.L.R. 922; [1999] 3 All E.R. 97; [1999] B.C.C. 771; [1999] 2 B.C.L.C. 221; [1999] B.P.I.R. 712; [1999] Lloyd's Rep. P.N. 844; [1999] P.N.L.R. 920; [1999] 2 E.G.L.R. 75; [1999] 29 E.G. 119; [1999] E.G. 81 (C.S.); (1999) 96(24) L.S.G. 39; (1999) 149 N.L.J. 929, CA (Civ Div) *2–152*
Mediana, The. *See* Owners of the Steamship Mediana v Owners of the Lightship Comet

Medina Housing Association Ltd v Case [2002] EWCA Civ 2001; [2003] 1 All E.R. 1084; [2003] H.L.R. 37, CA (Civ Div) *27–060*
Medusa, The. *See* Mariana Islands Steamship Corp v Marimpex Mineraloel-Handelsgesellschaft m.b.H. & Co K.G.; Medusa, The.
Meek v Kettlewell (1843) 1 Ph. 342 .... *19–028*
Meek v Port of London Authority [1918] 2 Ch. 96, CA; affirming [1918] 1 Ch. 415, Ch D *19–087*
Meggeson v Burns [1972] 1 Lloyd's Rep. 223, MCLC *18–011*
Meher v Dresser (1864) 16 C.B.(N.S.) 646 .... *30–346*
Mehmet v Perry [1977] 2 All E.R. 529, DC *29–133*
Melachrino v Nickoll and Knight [1920] 1 K.B. 693 .... *24–022*, *26–112*
Melanesian Mission Trust Board v Australian Mutual Provident Society [1997] 1 N.Z.L.R. 391 .... *12–050*, *12–051*
Melhado v Porto Alegre, New Hamburgh and Brazilian Railway Co (1873–74) L.R. 9 C.P. 503, CCP *9–014*, *9–061*
Melhuish v Redbridge Citizens Advice Bureau [2005] I.R.L.R. 419, EAT *3–008*
Melles & Co Ltd v Holme [1918] 2 K.B. 100, KBD *21–009*
Melliss v Shirley Local Board of Health; sub nom. Melliss v Shirley and Freemantle Local Board of Health (1885–86) L.R. 16 Q.B.D. 446, CA; reversing (1884–85) L.R. 14 Q.B.D. 911, QBD *16–020*
Mellor v Mellor [1992] 1 W.L.R. 517; [1992] 4 All E.R. 10; [1992] B.C.C. 513; [1993] B.C.L.C. 30, Ch D *9–051*
Mellor v Watkins (1873–74) L.R. 9 Q.B. 400, QB *13–028*
Melville v Grapelodge Developments, ltd (1980) 39 P. & C.R. 179, QBD *21–038*
Menaka v Chum (Lum Kum); sub nom. Menaka, wife of Deivarayan (M) v Chum (Lum Kum) [1977] 1 W.L.R. 267, PC (Mal) *16–147*
Menashe Business Mercantile Ltd v William Hill Organisation Ltd [2002] EWCA Civ 1702; [2003] 1 W.L.R. 1462; [2003] 1 All E.R. 279; [2003] R.P.C. 31; (2003) 26(3) I.P.D. 26013; (2003) 100(5) L.S.G. 32, CA (Civ Div); affirming [2002] EWHC 397 (Pat); [2002] 3 All E.R. 597; [2002] R.P.C. 47; (2002) 25(6) I.P.D. 25041, Ch D (Patents Ct) *12–017*, *12–103*, *14–035*, *14–132*, *14–134*, *30–062*, *30–101*
Mendl & Co v Ropner & Co [1913] 1 K.B. 27, KBD *12–057*
Meng Leong Development Pte v Jip Hong Trading Co Pte [1985] A.C. 511; [1984] 3 W.L.R. 1263; [1985] 1 All E.R. 120; (1984) 81 L.S.G. 3336; (1984) 128 S.J. 852, PC (Sing) *3–094*, *3–096*, *3–130*, *27–007*
Merak, The. *See* TB&S Batchelor & Co Ltd v Owners of the SS Merak
Mercantile Agency Co v Flitwick Chalybeate Co (1897) 14 T.L.R. 90 .... *12–096*
Mercantile Bank of India Ltd v Central Bank of India Ltd [1938] A.C. 287, PC (Ind) *29–176*
Mercantile Bank of London Ltd v Evans [1899] 2 Q.B. 613, CA *19–012*
Mercantile Bank of Sydney v Taylor [1893] A.C. 317, PC (Aus) *12–096*, *12–097*
Mercantile Credit Co Ltd v Hamblin [1965] 2 Q.B. 242; [1964] 3 W.L.R. 798; [1964] 3 All E.R. 592; (1964) 108 S.J. 674, CA; affirming [1964] 1 W.L.R. 423; [1964] 1 All E.R. 680 (Note); (1964) 108 S.J. 180, QBD *5–101*, *5–103*, *5–105*, *5–106*, *16–205*, *29–176*
Mercantile Group (Europe) AG v Aiyela [1994] Q.B. 366; [1993] 3 W.L.R. 1116; [1994] 1 All E.R. 110, CA (Civ Div) *27–078*
Mercantile Investment & General Trust Co v River Plate Trust, Loan & Agency Co (No.2) [1894] 1 Ch. 578, Ch D *25–012*
Mercantile Marine Service Association v Toms [1916] 2 K.B. 243, CA *9–067*
Mercantile Union Guarantee Corp Ltd v Ball [1937] 2 K.B. 498, CA *8–017*, *8–028*, *8–031*
Mercantile Union Guarantee Corp Ltd v Wheatley [1938] 1 K.B. 490, KBD *14–028*
Mercedes Envoy, The. *See* Hanjin Shipping Co v Zenith Chartering Corp
Merchants & Manufacturers Insurance Co Ltd v Hunt (Charles & John (An Infant)) [1941] 1 K.B. 295; (1940) 68 Ll. L. Rep. 117, CA; affirming (1940) 67 Ll. L. Rep. 517, KBD *6–144*

Mercury Communications Ltd v Director General of Telecommunications [1996] 1 W.L.R. 48; [1996] 1 All E.R. 575; [1995] C.L.C. 266; [1998] Masons C.L.R. Rep. 39, HL; reversing [1994] C.L.C. 1125; [1998] Masons C.L.R. Rep. 2; (1994) 91(36) L.S.G. 36; (1994) 138 S.J.L.B. 183, CA (Civ Div) *1–196*
Mercury Machine Importing Corp v City of New York (1957) 144 N.E. 2d 400 ... *29–047*
Meres v Ansell (1771) 3 Wils. 275 ...... *12–096*
Meretz Investments NV v ACP Ltd [2007] EWCA Civ 1303; [2008] 2 W.L.R. 904, CA (Civ Div); affirming in part [2006] EWHC 74 (Ch); [2007] Ch. 197; [2007] 2 W.L.R. 403; [2006] 3 All E.R. 1029; [2006] 2 P. & C.R. 23; [2006] 6 E.G. 170 (C.S.), Ch D *18–135*, *18–145*, *27–078*
Meridian Global Funds Management Asia Ltd v Securities Commission [1995] 2 A.C. 500; [1995] 3 W.L.R. 413; [1995] 3 All E.R. 918; [1995] B.C.C. 942; [1995] 2 B.C.L.C. 116; (1995) 92(28) L.S.G. 39; (1995) 139 S.J.L.B. 152, PC (NZ) 9–007
Meridien BIAO Bank GmbH v Bank of New York [1997] 1 Lloyd's Rep. 437; [1997] I.L.Pr. 155, CA (Civ Div) *30–3450*
Merkur Island Shipping Corp v Laughton; The Hoegh Anapa [1983] 2 A.C. 570; [1983] 2 W.L.R. 778; [1983] 2 All E.R. 189; [1983] 2 Lloyd's Rep. 1; [1983] I.C.R. 490; [1983] I.R.L.R. 218; (1983) 133 N.L.J. 577; (1983) 127 S.J. 306, HL; affirming [1983] 2 W.L.R. 45; [1982] 1 All E.R. 334; [1983] 1 Lloyd's Rep. 154; [1983] I.C.R. 178; [1982] I.R.L.R. 26; (1983) 80 L.S.G. 213; (1983) 133 N.L.J. 186; (1982) 126 S.J. 745, CA (Civ Div) *1–171*
Merrett v Babb [2001] EWCA Civ 214; [2001] Q.B. 1174; [2001] 3 W.L.R. 1; [2001] B.L.R. 483; (2001) 3 T.C.L.R. 15; 80 Con. L.R. 43; [2001] Lloyd's Rep. P.N. 468; [2001] P.N.L.R. 29; [2001] 1 E.G.L.R. 145; [2001] 8 E.G. 167 (C.S.); (2001) 98(13) L.S.G. 41; (2001) 145 S.J.L.B. 75, CA (Civ Div) *1–184*, *18–022*
Merrill Lynch Capital Services Inc v Municipality of Piraeus (No.2); Mitsubishi Bank Ltd v Municipality of Piraeus (No.2) [1997] 6 Bank. L.R. 241; [1997] C.L.C. 1214, QBD (Comm) *30–305*, *30–325*
Merritt v Merritt [1970] 1 W.L.R. 1211; [1970] 2 All E.R. 760; (1970) 114 S.J. 455, CA (Civ Div) *2–169*, *3–008*
Merry v Nickalls. *See* Nickalls v Merry
Mersey Shipping & Transport Co Ltd v Rea Ltd (1925) 21 Ll. L. Rep. 375, KBD; affirming (1924) 20 Ll. L. Rep. 281, CC (Liverpool) *14–046*
Mersey Steel & Iron Co Ltd v Naylor Benzon & Co (1883–84) L.R. 9 App. Cas. 434, HL *24–019*, *24–037*, *24–040*, *24–042*, *24–044*
Merton LBC v Stanley Hugh Leach Ltd, 32 B.L.R. 51; (1986) 2 Const. L.J. 189, Ch D *13–011*, *13–012*
Merwin Pastoral Co Pty v Moolpa Pastoral Co Pty, 48 C.L.R. 565 ...... *30–084*
Messers v Morrison's Export Co [1939] 1 All E.R. 92 ...... *12–036*
Messiniaki Bergen, The. *See* Westfal-Larsen & Co A/S v Ikerigi Compania Naviers SA
Metaalhandel JA Magnus BV v Ardfields Transport [1988] 1 Lloyd's Rep. 197; [1987] 2 F.T.L.R. 319, QBD (Comm) *12–010*, *30–373*
Metal Box Ltd v Currys Ltd [1988] 1 W.L.R. 175; [1988] 1 All E.R. 341; (1987) 84 L.S.G. 3657; (1988) 132 S.J. 52, QBD *26–176*, *26–178*
Metal Scrap Trade Corp Ltd v Kate Shipping Co Ltd; The Gladys (No.2) [1994] 2 Lloyd's Rep. 402, QBD (Comm) *2–126*
Metalfer Corp v Pan Ocean Shipping Co Ltd [1998] 2 Lloyd's Rep. 632; [1997] C.L.C. 1574, QBD (Comm) *12–079*
Metall und Rohstoff AG v Donaldson Lufkin & Jenrette Inc [1990] 1 Q.B. 391; [1989] 3 W.L.R. 563; [1989] 3 All E.R. 14; (1989) 133 S.J. 1200, CA (Civ Div) *29–160*
Metamorphosis, The. *See* Koninklijke Zwavelzuurfabrieken V/H Ketjen NV v DA and DD Psychoyos, Piraeus; The Metamorphosis
Metro Meat v Fares Rural Co Pty [1985] 2 Lloyd's Rep. 13, PC (Aus) *13–011*, *24–019*, *24–032*

Metrolands Investments Ltd v JH Dewhurst Ltd [1986] 3 All E.R. 659; (1986) 52 P. & C.R. 232; [1986] 1 E.G.L.R. 125; (1986) 277 E.G. 1343, CA (Civ Div); reversing [1985] 3 All E.R. 206; (1985) 49 P. & C.R. 334; [1985] 1 E.G.L.R. 105; (1985) 274 E.G. 1388; (1985) 82 L.S.G. 1415, Ch D *2–132*, *21–013*, *21–018*
Metropolitan Coal Consumers Association (Karberg's Case), Re [1892] 3 Ch. 1, CA *6–153*, *9–060*
Metropolitan Electric Supply Co Ltd v Ginder [1901] 2 Ch. 799, Ch D *3–025*, *27–070*
Metropolitan Meat Industry Board v Sheedy [1927] A.C. 899, PC (Aus) *10–010*
Metropolitan Police District Receiver v Croydon Corp; Monmouthshire CC v Smith [1957] 2 Q.B. 154; [1957] 2 W.L.R. 33; [1957] 1 All E.R. 78; (1957) 121 J.P. 63; 55 L.G.R. 18; (1957) 101 S.J. 60, CA *29–101*
Metropolitan Police District Receiver v Tatum; sub nom. Wood v Tatum [1948] 2 K.B. 68; [1948] 1 All E.R. 612; (1948) 112 J.P. 209; 46 L.G.R. 219; [1948] L.J.R. 1171; (1948) 92 S.J. 221, KBD *29–101*
Metropolitan Water Board v Dick Kerr & Co Ltd [1918] A.C. 119, HL *23–012*, 23–024, *23–049*, *23–051*, *23–058*
Meux v Great Eastern Railway Co [1895] 2 Q.B. 387, CA *14–054*
Meyappa Chetty v Supramanian Chetty. *See* Chetty v Chetty
Meyer v Haworth (1838) 8 A.& E. 467 .... *3–032*
Meyrick v Anderson (1850) 14 Q.B. 719 .... *20–012*
Mezey v South West London and St George's Mental Health NHS Trust (Permission to Appeal) [2007] EWCA Civ 106; [2007] I.R.L.R. 244; (2007) 94 B.M.L.R. 25, CA (Civ Div) *27–022*
Michael v Hart & Co [1902] 1 K.B. 482, CA *24–001*, *24–024*, *26–100*
Michael Gerson (Leasing) Ltd v Wilkinson [2001] Q.B. 514; [2000] 3 W.L.R. 1645; [2001] 1 All E.R. 148; [2000] 2 All E.R. (Comm) 890; [2000] C.L.C. 1720; (2000) 97(35) L.S.G. 37, CA (Civ Div) *2–007*, *2–027*
Michael Richards Properties Ltd v Corp of Wardens of St Saviour's Parish (Southwark) [1975] 3 All E.R. 416, Ch D *2–122*, *2–144*, *26–152*
Michael Salliss & Co Ltd v Calil, 13 Con. L.R. 68; (1988) 4 Const. L.J. 125, QBD (OR) *18–031*
Michalinos & Co v Scourfield (1949–50) 83 Ll. L. Rep. 494, KBD *29–061*
Michel Habib Raji Ayoub v Sheikh Suleiman el Taji el Farouqi [1941] A.C. 274, PC (Pal) *26–127*
Michell's Trusts, Re (1878) L.R. 9 Ch. D. 5, CA; reversing (1877) L.R. 6 Ch. D. 618, Ch D *12–066*
Micklefield v SAC Technology Ltd [1990] 1 W.L.R. 1002; [1991] 1 All E.R. 275; [1990] I.R.L.R. 218, Ch D *2–154*, *12–082*, *14–105*, *22–055*
Microfine Minerals & Chemicals Ltd v Transferry Shipping Co Ltd [1991] 2 Lloyd's Rep. 630, QBD (Merc) *28–068*
Middleton v Pollock Ex p. Elliott (1875–76) L.R. 2 Ch. D. 104, Ch D *19–023*
Midgley v Midgley [1893] 3 Ch. 282, CA *20–014*, *28–131*
Mid-Kent Fruit Factory, Re [1896] 1 Ch. 567, Ch D *20–041*
Midland Bank Ltd v Reckitt [1933] A.C. 1, HL *29–170*
Midland Bank Plc v Brown Shipley Co Ltd [1991] 2 All E.R. 690 .... *29–033*, *29–179*
Midland Bank Plc v Cooke [1995] 4 All E.R. 562; [1997] 6 Bank. L.R. 147; [1995] 2 F.L.R. 915; [1996] 1 F.C.R. 442; (1995) 27 H.L.R. 733; [1995] Fam. Law 675; (1995) 145 N.L.J. 1543; (1995) 139 S.J.L.B. 194; [1995] N.P.C. 116, CA (Civ Div) *3–137*
Midland Bank Plc v Greene [1994] 2 F.L.R. 827; [1995] 1 F.C.R. 365; (1995) 27 H.L.R. 350; [1994] Fam. Law 676; [1993] N.P.C. 152, Ch D *6–025*, *7–098*
Midland Bank Plc v Serter [1996] E.C.C. 87; [1995] 1 F.L.R. 1034; [1995] 3 F.C.R. 711; (1995) 27 H.L.R. 647; (1996) 71 P. & C.R. 264; [1995] Fam. Law 481; [1995] E.G. 38 (C.S.); [1995] N.P.C. 38, CA (Civ Div); affirming (1994) 26 H.L.R. 612; [1994] E.G. 45 (C.S.); [1994] N.P.C. 29, Ch D *7–117*
Midland Bank Plc v Shephard; sub nom. Shephard v Midland Bank Plc [1988] 3 All E.R. 17; [1987] 2 F.L.R. 175; [1988] C.C.L.R. 5; [1987] Fam. Law 309, CA (Civ Div) *7–085*

Midland Bank Trust Co Ltd v Green (No.1) [1981] A.C. 513; [1981] 2 W.L.R. 28; [1981] 1 All E.R. 153; (1981) 42 P. & C.R. 201; (1981) 125 S.J. 33, HL 3–020, *25–012*
Midland Bank Trust Co Ltd v Hett Stubbs & Kemp [1979] Ch. 384; [1978] 3 W.L.R. 167; [1978] 3 All E.R. 571; [1955–95] P.N.L.R. 95; (1977) 121 S.J. 830, Ch D *1–124*, *1–129*, *1–167*, *6–080*, *28–033*, *28–035*
Midland Banking Co v Chambers (1868–69) L.R. 4 Ch. App. 398, CA in Chancery *21–065*
Midland Counties District Bank Ltd v Attwood [1905] 1 Ch. 357, Ch D *9–047*
Midland International Trade Services v Sudairy, *Independent*, May 7, 1990; *Financial Times*, May 2, 1990, QBD *30–339*
Midland Silicones v Scruttons. *See* Scruttons v Midland Silicones
Mighell v Sultan of Johore [1894] 1 Q.B. 149, CA *11–020*, *11–022*
Migotti v Colvill (1878–79) L.R. 4 C.P.D. 233, CA *21–026*
Mihalis Angelos, The. *See* Maredelanto Compania Naviera SA v Bergbau-Handel GmbH
Mike Trading and Transport v R Pagnan & Fratelli; The Lisboa [1980] 2 Lloyd's Rep. 546, CA (Civ Div) *27–061*
Mikeover Ltd v Brady [1989] 3 All E.R. 618; (1989) 21 H.L.R. 513; (1990) 59 P. & C.R. 218; [1989] 39 E.G. 92; [1989] E.G. 82 (C.S.); (1989) 139 N.L.J. 1194, CA (Civ Div) *17–001*
Milan Tramways Co Ex p. Theys, Re (1884) L.R. 25 Ch. D. 587, CA; affirming (1883) L.R. 22 Ch. D. 122, Ch D *19–073*
Milburn & Co v Jamaica Fruit Importing & Trading Co of London [1900] 2 Q.B. 540, CA *29–129*
Milburn Services Ltd v United Trading Group (UK) Ltd (1995) C.I.L.L. 1109 ..... *12–104*
Miles v Dell (1821) 3 Stark. 23 ..... *29–149*
Miles v New Zealand Alford Estate Co (1886) L.R. 32 Ch. D. 266, CA *3–051*, *3–053*, 3–057, *29–088*
Miles v Wakefield MDC [1987] A.C. 539; [1987] 2 W.L.R. 795; [1987] 1 All E.R. 1089; [1987] I.C.R. 368; [1987] I.R.L.R. 193; [1987] 1 F.T.L.R. 533; 85 L.G.R. 649; (1987) 84 L.S.G. 1239; (1987) 137 N.L.J. 266; (1987) 131 S.J. 408, HL *18–063*, *29–070*
Miles International Corp v Federal Commerce & Navigation Co Ltd; The Federal Schelde [1978] 1 Lloyd's Rep. 285, Sup Ct (Que) *14–042*
Miliangos v George Frank (Textiles) Ltd [1976] A.C. 443; [1975] 3 W.L.R. 758; [1975] 3 All E.R. 801; [1976] 1 Lloyd's Rep. 201; [1975] 2 C.M.L.R. 585; (1975) 119 S.J. 774, HL *21–068*, *26–064*, *26–080*, *26–180*, *27–002*, *27–005*, *27–007*, *27–051*, 30–376, 30–377
Miliangos v George Frank (Textiles) Ltd [1977] Q.B. 489; [1976] 3 W.L.R. 477; [1976] 3 All E.R. 599; [1976] 2 Lloyd's Rep. 434; (1976) 120 S.J. 450, QBD *30–339*
Millar v Craig (1843) 6 Beav. 433 ..... *5–129*
Millar's Karri and Jarrah Co v Weddel Turner Co (1908) 100 L.T. 128 ..... *24–044*
Millar's Machinery Co v David Way & Son (1934) 40 Com. Cas. 204, CA *14–006*
Millbourn v Lyons [1914] 2 Ch. 231, CA; affirming [1914] 1 Ch. 34, Ch D *12–119*
Millen v Brasch & Co; sub nom. Millen v Brash & Co (1882–83) L.R. 10 Q.B.D. 142, CA *26–089*
Miller v Amalgamated Engineering Union [1938] Ch. 669, Ch D *16–140*
Miller v Bassey [2004] E.M.L.R. 44 ..... *18–135*
Miller v Borner & Co [1900] 1 Q.B. 691, QBD *12–063*
Miller v Cannon Hill Estates Ltd [1931] 2 K.B. 113, KBD *12–003*, *12–004*, *13–015*
Miller v Dell [1891] 1 Q.B. 468, CA *21–010*
Miller v Emcer Products [1956] Ch. 304; [1956] 2 W.L.R. 267; [1956] 1 All E.R. 237; (1956) 100 S.J. 74, CA *12–091*
Miller v FA Sadd & Son [1981] 3 All E.R. 265, DC *2–039*, *2–130*
Miller v Hancock [1893] 2 Q.B. 177, CA *13–017*
Miller v Karlinski (1946) 62 T.L.R. 85, CA 16–012, *16–017*, *16–202*
Miller v Lakefield Estates Ltd (1989) 57 P. & C.R. 104; [1989] 19 E.G. 67; [1988] E.G. 61 (C.S.), CA (Civ Div) *2–127*

Miller v Lawrence and Bardsley [1966] 1 Lloyd's Rep. 90; 116 N.L.J. 585, Ch D *19–055*
Miller v Race (1758) 1 Burr. 452 .... *29–170*
Miller v Travers (1832) 8 Bing. 244 .... *12–096*
Miller & Aldworth Ltd v Sharp [1899] 1 Ch. 622, Ch D *4–048*
Miller Gibb & Co, Re [1957] 1 W.L.R. 703; [1957] 2 All E.R. 266; [1957] 1 Lloyd's Rep. 258; (1957) 101 S.J. 392, Ch D *19–066*
Miller Gibb & Co v Smith & Tyrer Ltd [1917] 2 K.B. 141, CA; reversing [1916] 1 K.B. 419, KBD *12–133*
Miller's Agreement, Re; sub nom. Uniacke v Attorney General [1947] Ch. 615; [1947] 2 All E.R. 78; [1948] L.J.R. 567; 177 L.T. 129, Ch D *18–079*, *18–125*
Miller's Case. *See* European Assurance Society, Re
Millers Ltd v Steadman (1915) 84 L.J.K.B. 2057 .... *16–110*
Millership v Brookes (1860) 5 H. & N. 797 .... *1–105*
Millett v Van Heek & Co (No.2) [1921] 2 K.B. 369, CA *24–022*
Millichamp v Jones [1982] 1 W.L.R. 1422; [1983] 1 All E.R. 267; (1983) 45 P. & C.R. 169; (1983) 80 L.S.G. 35; (1983) 133 N.L.J. 134; (1982) 126 S.J. 726, Ch D *21–013*, *21–018*
Mills v Cooper [1967] 2 Q.B. 459; [1967] 2 W.L.R. 1343; [1967] 2 All E.R. 100; (1967) 131 J.P. 349; 65 L.G.R. 275; (1967) 111 S.J. 273, DC *25–011*, *25–014*
Mills v Dunham [1891] 1 Ch. 576, CA *12–081*, *16–092*, *16–112*, *16–196*,
Mills v Embassy of United States of America, May 9, 2000, CA *11–005*, *11–021*
Mills v Fowkes (1839) 5 Bing N.C. 455 .... *21–063*, *28–128*
Mills v Graham (1804) 1 B. & P.N.R. 140 .... *8–047*
Mills v Haywood (1877) L.R. 6 Ch. D. 196, CA *28–143*
Mills v Northern Railway of Buenos Ayres Co (1869–70) L.R. 5 Ch. App. 621, Lord Chancellor *9–020*
Mills v Stanway Coaches Ltd [1940] 2 K.B. 334, CA *26–030*
Milner, Re (1884–85) L.R. 15 Q.B.D. 605, CA *16–042*
Milner v Harewood, Lord (1810) 18 Ves. 259 .... *8–043*
Milner v Staffordshire Congregational Union Inc [1956] Ch. 275; [1956] 2 W.L.R. 556; [1956] 1 All E.R. 494; (1956) 100 S.J. 170, Ch D *16–179*
Milner (JH) & Son v Bilton (Percy) Ltd; sub nom. JH Milner & Son v Percy Bilton Ltd [1966] 1 W.L.R. 1582; [1966] 2 All E.R. 894; (1966) 110 S.J. 635, QBD *2–183*, *13–027*
Milnes v Duncan (1827) 6 B.C. 671 .... *29–030*
Milroy v Lord, 45 E.R. 1185; (1862) 4 De G.F. & J. 264, QB ... *1–108*, *3–019*, *19–021*, *19–033*, *19–034*
Milton v Farrow (1980) 255 E.G. 449 .... *3–177*
Milward v Earl of Thanet (1801) 5 Ves. 720 .... *28–143*
Mineracoas Brasilieras Reunidas v EF Marine SA; The Freights Queen [1977] 2 Lloyd's Rep. 140, QBD (Comm) *30–011*
Mineral Water Bottle Exchange and Trade Protection Society v Booth (1887) L.R. 36 Ch. D. 465, CA *16–137*
Mineralimportexport v Eastern Mediterranean Maritime Ltd; The Golden Leader [1980] 2 Lloyd's Rep. 573, QBD (Comm) *14–011*
Minister of Agriculture and Fisheries v Matthews [1950] 1 K.B. 148; [1949] 2 All E.R. 724; 65 T.L.R. 655, KBD *10–040*
Minister of Health v Bellotti; Minister of Health v Holliday [1944] K.B. 298; [1944] 1 All E.R. 238, CA *13–028*
Minister of Materials v Steel Brothers & Co [1952] 1 Lloyd's Rep. 87; [1952] 1 T.L.R. 499; [1952] W.N. 114, CA *12–085*
Minister of Supply v British Thompson-Houston Co Ltd [1943] K.B. 478, CA *10–016*
Ministry of Defence v Ashman (1993) 25 H.L.R. 513; (1993) 66 P. & C.R. 195; [1993] 40 E.G. 144; [1993] N.P.C. 70, CA (Civ Div) *29–142*, *29–144*
Ministry of Defence v Thompson (1993) 25 H.L.R. 552; [1993] 40 E.G. 148, CA (Civ Div) *29–142*, *29–144*

Ministry of Defence v Wheeler; Ministry of Defence v Hunt; Ministry of Defence v George; Anderson v Ministry of Defence; Stuart v Ministry of Defence; Ministry of Defence v Donald; Ministry of Defence v Nixon; Ministry of Defence v Joslyn [1998] 1 W.L.R. 637; [1998] 1 All E.R. 790; [1998] I.C.R. 242; [1998] I.R.L.R. 23; (1997) 94(45) L.S.G. 27; (1998) 142 S.J.L.B. 13, CA (Civ Div) *26–044*
Ministry of Health v Simpson; sub nom. Diplock's Estate, Re; Diplock v Wintle; Simpson v Lilburn [1951] A.C. 251; [1950] 2 All E.R. 1137; 66 T.L.R. (Pt. 2) 1015; (1950) 94 S.J. 777, HL; affirming [1948] Ch. 465; [1948] 2 All E.R. 318; [1948] L.J.R. 1670; (1948) 92 S.J. 484, CA; reversing [1947] Ch. 716; [1947] 1 All E.R. 522; [1947] L.J.R. 1158; 177 L.T. 40; (1947) 91 S.J. 248, Ch D ... *5–054*, *9–025*, *28–002*, *28–058*, *28–088*, *28–134*, *29–008*, *29–011*, *29–013*, *29–042*, *29–043*, *29–158*, *29–162*, *29–163*, *29–164*, *29–166*, *29–167*, *29–171*, *29–172*, *29–179*
Ministry of Justice v Prison Officers Association [2008] EWHC 239 (QB); [2008] I.R.L.R. 380 .... *27–036*
Ministry of Sound (Ireland) Ltd v World Online Ltd [2003] EWHC 2178 (Ch); [2003] 2 All E.R. (Comm) 823, Ch D *24–010*, *26–123*, *26–124*
Minories Finance v Afribank Nigeria Ltd [1995] 1 Lloyd's Rep. 134, QBD (Comm) *2–047*, *2–072*, *30–012*, *30–051*
Mint v Good [1951] 1 K.B. 517; [1950] 2 All E.R. 1159; 49 L.G.R. 495; (1950) 94 S.J. 822, CA; reversing, 155 E.G. 409, Ch D *13–016*
Minter v Julius Baer Investment Management Inc London; Minter v Julius Baer Investments Ltd [2004] EWHC 2472; [2005] Pens. L.R. 73, Ch D *2–216*
Minton v Minton [1979] A.C. 593; [1979] 2 W.L.R. 51; [1979] 1 All E.R. 79, HL; affirming (1978) 122 S.J. 31 .... *16–074*
Miraflores v Owners of the George Livanos; The Miraflores, The Abadesa and The Livanos; sub nom. Owners of the Steam Tanker George Livanos v Owners of the Steam Tanker Miraflores [1967] 1 A.C. 826; [1967] 2 W.L.R. 806; [1967] 1 All E.R. 672; [1967] 1 Lloyd's Rep. 191; (1967) 111 S.J. 211, HL *29–121*
Miramar Maritime Corp v Holborn Oil Trading; The Miramar [1984] A.C. 676; [1984] 3 W.L.R. 1; [1984] 2 All E.R. 326; [1984] 2 Lloyd's Rep. 129; (1984) 81 L.S.G. 2000; (1984) 128 S.J. 414, HL; affirming [1984] 1 Lloyd's Rep. 142, CA (Civ Div); affirming [1983] 2 Lloyd's Rep. 319, QBD (Comm) ... *12–055*, *12–057*, *12–075*, *12–079*
Mirams, Re [1891] 1 Q.B. 594, QBD *16–022*, *19–047*
Mirant Asia-Pacific Construction (Hong Kong) Ltd (No.2). *See* Ove Arup & Partners International Ltd v Mirant Asia-Pacific Construction (Hong Kong) Ltd (No.2)
Mirimskaya v Evans [2007] EWHC 2073 (TCC); 114 Con. L.R. 144; (2007) 151 S.J.L.B. 1226, QBD (TCC) *24–053*
Misa v Currie; sub nom. Currie v Misa (1875–76) L.R. 1 App. Cas. 554, HL; affirming (1874–75) L.R. 10 Ex. 153, Ex Chamber *3–034*, *21–074*
Mishara Construction Co Inc v Transit-Mixed Concrete Corp (1974) 310 N.E. 2d 363 .... *23–060*
Missouri Steamship Co, Re (1889) L.R. 42 Ch. D. 321, CA ... *30–005*, *30–011*, *30–012*, *30–309*, *30–365*, *30–367*
Mitas v Hyams [1951] 2 T.L.R. 1215, CA *1–115*
Mitchel v Reynolds (1711) 1 P.Wms. 181 16–075
Mitchell v Al-Dali [2005] EWCA Civ 720, CA (Civ Div) *11–021*
Mitchell v CC Sanitation Co (1968) 430 S.W. 2d. 933 .... *7–045*
Mitchell v Ealing LBC [1979] Q.B. 1; [1978] 2 W.L.R. 999; [1975] 2 All E.R. 779; 76 L.G.R. 703; (1978) 122 S.J. 213, QBD *3–177*
Mitchell v Ede (1840) 11 Ad. & El. 888 .... *18–073*
Mitchell v Harris Engineering Co [1967] 2 Q.B. 703; [1967] 3 W.L.R. 447; [1967] 2 All E.R. 682; (1967) 111 S.J. 355, CA (Civ Div) *28–118*, *28–119*
Mitchell v Homfray (1881–82) L.R. 8 Q.B.D. 587, CA *7–077*, *7–097*
Mitchell v King (1833) 6 C.P. 237 .... *21–091*
Mitchell Cotts & Co (Middle East) Ltd v Hairco Ltd [1943] 2 All E.R. 552 .... *13–013*

Mitchell-Henry v Norwich Union Life Insurance Society Ltd [1918] 2 K.B. 67; 2 A.L.R. 1644, CA *21–056*
Mitsubishi Corp v Alafouzos [1988] 1 Lloyd's Rep. 191; [1988] 1 F.T.L.R. 47, QBD (Comm) *16–176*, *30–012*
Mitsubishi Corp v Castletown Navigation; The Castle Alpha [1989] 2 Lloyd's Rep. 383, QBD (Comm) *28–022*
Mitsubishi Corp v Eastwind Transport Ltd; The Irbenskiy Proliv [2004] EWHC 2924 (Comm); [2005] 1 All E.R. (Comm) 328; [2005] 1 Lloyd's Rep. 383, QBD (Comm) *14–007*
Mitsubishi Heavy Industries Ltd v Gulf Bank KSC [1997] 1 Lloyd's Rep. 343; [1997] C.L.C. 597, CA (Civ Div) *24–019*
Mitsui & Co Ltd v Flota Mercante Grancolombiana SA; The Ciudad de Pasto and The Ciudad de Neiva [1988] 1 W.L.R. 1145; [1989] 1 All E.R. 951; [1988] 2 Lloyd's Rep. 208, CA (Civ Div); reversing [1987] 2 Lloyd's Rep. 392, QBD (Comm) *18–034*
Mitsui & Co Ltd v Novorossiysk Shipping Co; The Gudermes [1993] 1 Lloyd's Rep. 311, CA (Civ Div); reversing [1991] 1 Lloyd's Rep. 456, QBD (Comm) *2–160*, *2–180*, *2–185*, *14–054*, *14–055*, *18–038*
Mitsui Babcock Energy Ltd v John Brown Engineering Ltd, 51 Con. L.R. 129, QBD (OR) *2–128*, *3–113*
Mitsui Construction Co Ltd v Attorney General of Hong Kong, 33 B.L.R. 1; 10 Con. L.R. 1; [1987] H.K.L.R. 1076; (1986) 2 Const. L.J. 133, PC (HK); reversing, 26 B.L.R. 113, CA (HK) 12–056
Mittelholzer v Fullarton (1842) 6 Q.B. 989 .... *16–204*
Mmecen SA v Inter Ro-Ro SA and Gulf Ro-Ro Services SA; The Samah and The Lina V [1981] 1 Lloyd's Rep. 40, QBD (Comm) *2–126*
Mobil North Sea Ltd v PJ Pipe & Valve Co Ltd (t/a PJ Valves or PJ Valve Ltd) [2001] EWCA Civ 741; [2001] 2 All E.R. (Comm) 289, CA (Civ Div) *26–117*
Modahl v British Athletic Federation Ltd (No.2) [2001] EWCA Civ 1447; [2002] 1 W.L.R. 1192; (2001) 98(43) L.S.G. 34; (2001) 145 S.J.L.B. 238, CA (Civ Div) *1–032*, *1–076*, *1–195*, 2–160, *3–004*, *13–004*, *13–007*
Modern Building (Wales) Ltd v Limmer & Trinidad Co Ltd [1975] 1 W.L.R. 1281; [1975] 2 All E.R. 549; [1975] 2 Lloyd's Rep. 318; 14 B.L.R. 101; (1975) 119 S.J. 641, CA (Civ Div) *12–075*, *12–079*
Modern Light Cars Ltd v Seals [1934] 1 K.B. 32, KBD *21–076*
Modiano Bros & Sons v Bailey & Sons Ltd (1933) 47 Ll. L. Rep. 134, KBD *21–071*
Moens v Hayworth (1842) 10 M. & W. 147 .... *6–144*
Moffat v Parsons (1814) 5 Taunt. 307 .... *21–089*, *21–094*
Mogileff, The (No.1); sub nom. Borneo Co v Mogileff , The [1921] P. 236; (1921) 6 Ll. L. Rep. 528, PDAD *8–020*
Mogul Steamship Co Ltd v McGregor Gow & Co [1892] A.C. 25; [1891–4] All E.R. Rep. 263, HL; affirming (1889) L.R. 23 Q.B.D. 598, CA; affirming (1888) L.R. 21 Q.B.D. 544, QBD *16–075*, *16–137*, *16–140*, *16–202*
Mohamed v Alaga & Co; sub nom. Mohammed v Alaga & Co [2000] 1 W.L.R. 1815; [1999] 3 All E.R. 699; [2000] C.P. Rep. 87; [1999] 2 Costs L.R. 169, CA (Civ Div); reversing in part [1998] 2 All E.R. 720; (1998) 95(17) L.S.G. 29; (1998) 142 S.J.L.B. 142, Ch D *16–055*, *29–078*
Mohammad Bin Abdul Rahman Orri v Seawind Navigation Co SA; The Winner [1986] 1 Lloyd's Rep. 36, QBD (Comm) *12–075*
Molling Co v Dean Son Ltd (1902) 18 T.L.R. 216 .... *26–073*, *26–074*
Molloy v Mutual Reserve Life Insurance Co (1906) 94 L.T. 756 .... *28–135*, *28–140*, *28–144*
Molton v Camroux (1849) 4 Exch. 17 .... *8–068*, *8–080*
Molyneux v Hawtrey [1903] 2 K.B. 487, CA *6–157*
Momm v Barclays Bank International Ltd; Delbrueck & Co v Barclays Bank International Ltd; sub nom. Delbrueck & Co v Barclays Bank International Ltd [1977] Q.B. 790; [1977] 2 W.L.R. 407; [1976] 3 All E.R. 588; [1976] 2 Lloyd's Rep. 341; (1976) 120 S.J. 486, QBD (Comm) *21–022*, *21–047*
Mona Oil Equipment & Supply Co Ltd v Rhodesia Railways Ltd [1949] 2 All E.R. 1014; (1949–50) 83 Ll. L. Rep. 178; [1950] W.N. 10, KBD *13–011*

Monaghan CC v Vaughan [1948] I.R. 306 .... *5–113*
Monarch Airlines Ltd v London Luton Airport Ltd [1998] 1 Lloyd's Rep. 403; [1997] C.L.C. 698, QBD (Comm) *13–014*, *14–011*, *14–060*, 14–099
Monarch Steamship Co Ltd v A/B Karlshamns Oljefabriker; sub nom. A/B Karlshamns Oljefabriker v Monarch Steamship Co Ltd [1949] A.C. 196; [1949] 1 All E.R. 1; (1948–49) 82 Ll. L. Rep. 137; 1949 S.C. (H.L.) 1; 1949 S.L.T. 51; 65 T.L.R. 217; [1949] L.J.R. 772; (1949) 93 S.J. 117, HL *26–001*, *26–032*, 26–040, *26–060*, *26–090*, 26–105
Monavon Construction Ltd v Davenport [2006] EWHC 1094 (TCC); 108 Con. L.R. 15, QBD (TCC) *2–183*
Mond v Hammond Suddards (No.1) [1996] 2 B.C.L.C. 470, Ch D *9–049*
Mondel v Steel, 151 E.R. 1288; (1841) 8 M. & W. 858, Ex Ct *21–033*, *28–123*
Money Markets International Stockbrokers Ltd (In Liquidation) v London Stock Exchange Ltd [2002] 1 W.L.R. 1150; [2001] 4 All E.R. 223; [2001] 2 All E.R. (Comm) 344; [2001] 2 B.C.L.C. 347; [2001] B.P.I.R. 1044, Ch D *16–003*, *20–025*
Monk v Redwing Aircraft Co Ltd [1942] 1 K.B. 182, CA *26–160*
Monk Construction v Norwich Union Life Insurance Society, 62 B.L.R. 107, CA (Civ Div) *2–125*
Monkland v Jack Barclay Ltd [1951] 2 K.B. 252; [1951] 1 All E.R. 714; [1951] 1 T.L.R. 763; (1951) 95 S.J. 236, CA; reversing [1950] 2 All E.R. 715; 66 T.L.R. (Pt. 2) 150; [1950] W.N. 387; (1950) 94 S.J. 457, KBD *14–138*, *21–020*
Monmouth BC v Marlog (1995) 27 H.L.R. 30; [1994] 44 E.G. 240; (1994) 158 L.G. Rev. 921; [1994] E.G. 74 (C.S.); (1994) 68 P. & C.R. D4, CA (Civ Div) *2–161*, *2–168*
Monmouthshire CC v Smith [1956] 1 W.L.R. 1132; [1956] 2 All E.R. 800; (1956) 120 J.P. 417; 54 L.G.R. 494; (1956) 100 S.J. 635, Assizes (Monmouthshire) *29–101*
Monnickendam v Leanse (1923) 39 T.L.R. 445 .... *4–041*
Monro v Revenue and Customs Commissioners [2008] EWCA Civ 306; [2008] B.T.C. 188; [2008] S.T.I. 1197; (2008) 105(16) L.S.G. 29, CA (Civ Div) *29–085*
Mont v Mills. *See* JA Mont (UK) Ltd v Mills
Montagu v Flockton (1873) L.R. 16 Eq. 189 .... *27–064*
Montague L Meyer Ltd v Travaru A/B H Cornelius (1930) 46 T.L.R. 553; (1930) 37 Ll. L. Rep. 204, KBD *12–036*
Montague v Perkins (1853) 22 L.J.C.P. 187 .... *28–041*
Monte Video Gas and Dry Dock Co Ltd v Clan Line Steamers Ltd (1921) 37 T.L.R. 866 .... *26–070*
Montedipe SpA v JTP-RO Jugotanker; The Jordan Nicolov [1990] 2 Lloyd's Rep. 11, QBD (Comm) *19–055*
Montefiore v Menday Motor Components Co Ltd [1918] 2 K.B. 241, KBD *16–004*, *16–024*, *16–205*
Monterosso Shipping Co v International Transport Workers' Federation; The Rosso [1982] 3 All E.R. 841; [1982] 2 Lloyd's Rep. 120; [1982] Com. L.R. 152; [1982] I.C.R. 675; [1982] I.R.L.R. 468; (1982) 79 L.S.G. 1175; (1982) 126 S.J. 591, CA (Civ Div) *2–177*, *30–011*, *30–012*, *30–013*, *30–109*, *30–311*
Montgomery Litho Ltd v Maxwell, 2000 S.C. 56; 1999 S.L.T. 1431; 2000 S.C.L.R. 101; 1999 G.W.D. 34–1617, IH (Ex Div); reversing, 1999 S.C.L.R. 115; 1999 G.W.D. 19–869, Sh Pr *12–015*
Montreal Gas Co v Vasey [1900] A.C. 595, PC (Can) *2–139*, *2–183*
Monvia Motorship Corp v Keppel Shipyard (Private) Ltd; The Master Stelios [1983] 1 Lloyd's Rep. 356, PC (Sing) *2–032*
Monypenny v Monypenny (1858) 4 K. & J. 182 .... *12–052*
Moodie v Bannister (1859) 4 Drew. 432 .... *28–131*
Moody v Condor Insurance Ltd [2006] EWHC 100; [2006] 1 W.L.R. 1847; [2006] 1 All E.R. 934; [2006] 1 All E.R. (Comm) 419; [2006] 1 C.L.C. 263, Ch D *1–109*, *18–005*, *18–107*, *18–122*
Moody v Cox [1917] 2 Ch. 71, CA *7–076*
Moon Ex p. Dawes, Re (1886) L.R. 17 Q.B.D. 275, CA *12–066*

Moorcock, The (1889) L.R. 14 P.D. 64; [1886–90] All E.R. Rep. 530, CA; affirming (1888) L.R. 13 P.D. 157, PDAD 13–005, 13–006, *13–007*
Moore v Bushell (1827) 27 L.J. Ex. 3 .... *29–026*
Moore v DER Ltd [1971] 1 W.L.R. 1476; [1971] 3 All E.R. 517; [1971] 2 Lloyd's Rep. 359; [1972] R.T.R. 97; (1971) 115 S.J. 528, CA (Civ Div) *26–104*
Moore v Fulham Vestry [1895] 1 Q.B. 399, CA *29–098*, *29–187*, *29–188*
Moore v Garwood (1849) 4 Exch. 681 .... *12–047*
Moore v Shelley (1882–83) L.R. 8 App. Cas. 285, PC (Aus) *21–053*
Moore v Usher (1835) 7 Sim. 383 .... *16–050*
Moore v Woolsey (1854) 4 E. & B. 243 .... *16–171*
Moore v Yakeley Associates Ltd [2000] C.L.Y. 810 CA (Civ Div); affirming (2000) 2 T.C.L.R. 146; 62 Con. L.R. 76, QBD (TCC) 14–096
Moore & Co And Landauer Co, Re. *See* FW Moore & Co Ltd v Landauer & Co
Moorgate Mercantile Co Ltd v Twitchings [1977] A.C. 890; [1976] 3 W.L.R. 66; [1976] 2 All E.R. 641; [1976] R.T.R. 437; (1976) 120 S.J. 470, HL; reversing [1976] Q.B. 225; [1975] 3 W.L.R. 286; [1975] 3 All E.R. 314; [1975] R.T.R. 528; (1975) 119 S.J. 559, CA (Civ Div) *3–146*, *6–014*, *6–095*, *29–176*
Mora Shipping Inc v Axa Corporate Solutions Assurance SA [2005] EWCA Civ 1069; [2005] 2 Lloyd's Rep. 769; [2005] 2 C.L.C. 349; [2006] I.L.Pr. 10, CA (Civ Div); affirming [2005] EWHC 315; [2005] 1 C.L.C. 339, QBD (Comm) *12–057*, *21–006*
Moran v University College Salford (No.2), *The Times*, November 23, 1993; *Independent*, November 26, 1993, CA (Civ Div) *2–003*, *3–010*
More OG Romsdal Fylkesbatar AS v Demise Charterers of the Jotunheim [2004] EWHC 671; [2005] 1 Lloyd's Rep. 181, QBD (Comm) *22–048*
Morey v Woodfield (No.2) [1964] 1 Q.B. 1; [1963] 3 W.L.R. 486; [1963] 3 All E.R. 584; (1963) 107 S.J. 651, QBD *26–030*
Morgan, Ex p. *See* Simpson Ex p. Morgan, Re
Morgan, Re; sub nom. Pillgrem v Pillgrem (1880–81) L.R. 18 Ch. D. 93, CA *20–010*
Morgan v Ashcroft [1938] 1 K.B. 49, CA ... *29–008*, *29–013*, *29–030*, *29–031*, 29–032, *29–033*, 29–039, 29–075
Morgan v Bain (1874–75) L.R. 10 C.P. 15, CCP *20–032*, *24–018*
Morgan v Fry [1968] 2 Q.B. 710; [1968] 3 W.L.R. 506; [1968] 3 All E.R. 452; [1968] 2 Lloyd's Rep. 82; 5 K.I.R. 275; (1968) 112 S.J. 671, CA (Civ Div); reversing in part [1968] 1 Q.B. 521; [1967] 3 W.L.R. 65; [1967] 2 All E.R. 386; [1967] 1 Lloyd's Rep. 471; 2 K.I.R. 264; (1967) 111 S.J. 397, QBD *1–145*
Morgan v Griffith (1870–71) L.R. 6 Ex. 70; (1871) 40 L.J. Ex. 46, Ex Ct *12–004*, *12–103*
Morgan v Liverpool Corp [1927] 2 K.B. 131, CA *21–009*
Morgan v Manser [1948] 1 K.B. 184; [1947] 2 All E.R. 666, KBD *23–037*, *23–039*
Morgan v Palmer (1824) 2 B. & C. 729 .... *3–062*, *29–094*
Morgan v Rowlands (1871–72) L.R. 7 Q.B. 493, QB *25–009*
Morgan v Russell & Sons [1909] 1 K.B. 357, KBD *4–019*
Morgan & Son v Martin Johnson & Co [1949] 1 K.B. 107; [1948] 2 All E.R. 196; 64 T.L.R. 381; [1948] L.J.R. 1530; (1948) 92 S.J. 391, CA *28–123*
Morgan Crucible Co Plc v Hill Samuel Bank & Co Ltd; sub nom. Morgan Crucible Co Plc v Hill Samuel & Co Ltd [1991] Ch. 295; [1991] 2 W.L.R. 655; [1991] 1 All E.R. 148; [1991] B.C.C. 82; [1991] B.C.L.C. 178; (1990) 140 N.L.J. 1605, CA (Civ Div); reversing [1990] 3 All E.R. 330; [1990] B.C.C. 686; [1991] B.C.L.C. 18; (1990) 140 N.L.J. 1271, Ch D *6–029*, *6–082*, *18–022*
Morgan Grenfell Development Capital Syndications Ltd v Arrows Autosports Ltd (No.2) [2003] EWHC 333, Ch D *2–112*
Morgan Guaranty Trust Co of New York v Lothian RC, 1995 S.C. 151; 1995 S.L.T. 299; 1995 S.C.L.R. 225, IH (Ct of 5 judges) *29–015*, *29–045*
Moriarty v Regent's Garage & Engineering Co Ltd [1921] 2 K.B. 766, CA *21–030*
Morier Ex p., Re; sub nom. Willis, Percival & Co, Re (1879) L.R. 12 Ch. D. 491, CA *20–044*

Morin v Bonhams & Brooks Ltd [2003] EWCA Civ 1802; [2004] 1 All E.R. (Comm) 880; [2004] 1 Lloyd's Rep. 702; [2004] 1 C.L.C. 632; [2004] I.L.Pr. 24, CA (Civ Div) *30–306*, *30–308*
Morison v London County & Westminster Bank Ltd [1914] 3 K.B. 356, CA *29–142*, *29–170*
Morley v Boothby (1825) 3 Bing. 107 .... *1–108*
Morley v Frear (1830) 6 Bing. 547 .... *22–005*
Morley v Loughnan [1893] 1 Ch. 736, Ch D 7–064, *7–093*
Mormaclynx, The [1971] 2 Lloyd's Rep. 476 .... *14–042*
Morphett v Jones (1818) 1 Swanst. 172 .... *4–047*
Morrall v Krause [1994] E.G. 177 (C.S.), CA (Civ Div) 4–015, *4–056*
Morrell v Fisher (1849) 4 Exch. 591 .... *12–075*
Morrell v Studd and Millington [1913] 2 Ch. 648 .... *4–011*, *4–026*, *22–046*
Morris v Bank of India; sub nom. Bank of Credit and Commerce International SA (In Liquidation) (No.15), Re; Bank of India v Morris [2005] EWCA Civ 693; [2005] B.C.C. 739; [2005] 2 B.C.L.C. 328; [2005] B.P.I.R. 1067, CA (Civ Div); affirming [2004] EWHC 528; [2005] 1 All E.R. (Comm) 209; [2004] B.C.C. 404; [2004] 2 B.C.L.C. 279, Ch D (Companies Ct) *9–007*
Morris v Baron & Co [1918] A.C. 1, HL *4–056*, *12–111*, *22–015*, *22–025*, *22–028*, 22–029, 22–030, 22–034
Morris v Breaveglen Ltd (t/a Anzac Construction Co) [1997] C.L.Y. 937, CA (Civ Div) *14–015*
Morris v Burdett (1808) 1 Camp. 218 .... *3–062*
Morris v Colman (1812) 18 Ves. 437 .... *16–119*
Morris v CW Martin & Sons Ltd; sub nom. Morris v Martin [1966] 1 Q.B. 716; [1965] 3 W.L.R. 276; [1965] 2 All E.R. 725; [1965] 2 Lloyd's Rep. 63; (1965) 109 S.J. 451, CA ...*1–071*, *1–186*, *3–177*, *14–054*, *14–057*, *18–022*, *19–084*
Morris v Kanssen; sub nom. Kanssen v Rialto (West End) Ltd [1946] A.C. 459; 115 L.J. Ch. 177; 174 L.T. 353; 62 T.L.R. 306; [1946] 1 All E.R. 596, HL; affirming [1944] Ch. 346, CA; reversing [1944] Ch. 154, Ch D *9–041*, *9–044*
Morris v Redland Bricks. *See* Redland Bricks v Morris
Morris v Richards (1881) 45 L.T. 210 .... *28–063*
Morris v Tarrant [1971] 2 Q.B. 143; [1971] 2 W.L.R. 630; [1971] 2 All E.R. 920; (1970) 115 S.J. 204, QBD *2–169*, *3–087*, *29–011*, *29–142*, *29–144*
Morris v Wentworth-Stanley; sub nom. Morris v Molesworth [1999] Q.B. 1004; [1999] 2 W.L.R. 470; [1999] 1 F.L.R. 83; (1998) 95(39) L.S.G. 34; (1998) 148 N.L.J. 1551; (1998) 142 S.J.L.B. 258, CA (Civ Div) *17–015*, *17–017*, *17–020*
Morrish Ex p. Dyke, Re (1883) L.R. 22 Ch. D. 410, CA *9–048*
Morrison v Coast Finance (1965) 55 D.L.R. (2d) 710 .... *7–136*
Morrison v Thoelke, 155 So. 2d 889 (1963) *2–060*
Morrison v Universal Marine Insurance Co (1872–73) L.R. 8 Ex. 197, Ex Chamber; reversing (1872–73) L.R. 8 Ex. 40, Ex Ct 6–128
Morrison & Co Ltd v Shaw Savill & Albion Co Ltd; sub nom. James Morrison & Co Ltd v Shaw Savill & Albion Co Ltd [1916] 2 K.B. 783, CA; affirming [1916] 1 K.B. 747, KBD *14–029*
Morrison Rose & Partners v Hillman [1961] 2 Q.B. 266; [1961] 3 W.L.R. 301; [1961] 2 All E.R. 891; (1961) 105 S.J. 528, CA *25–013*
Morrison Shipping Co Ltd (In Liquidation) v King, The (1924) 20 Ll. L. Rep. 283, HL; affirming (1923) 16 Ll. L. Rep. 293, CA; reversing (1922) 13 Ll. L. Rep. 273, KBD *2–079*
Morrison Steamship Co Ltd v Owners of Cargo Lately Laden on Board the Greystoke Castle; sub nom. Owners of Cargo Lately Laden on Board The Greystoke Castle v Owners of The Cheldale [1947] A.C. 265; [1946] 2 All E.R. 696; (1947) 80 Ll. L. Rep. 55; 63 T.L.R. 11; [1947] L.J.R. 297; 176 L.T. 66, HL; affirming [1945] P. 10; [1945] 1 All E.R. 177; (1945) 78 Ll. L. Rep. 129, CA; affirming (1944) 77 Ll. L. Rep. 395, PDAD *9–068*
Morse v Royal (1806) 12 Ves. 355 .... *7–097*
Mortgage Corp Plc v Lambert & Co [2000] Lloyd's Rep. Bank. 207; [2000] B.L.R. 265; [2000] Lloyd's Rep. P.N. 624; [2000] P.N.L.R. 820, CA (Civ Div) *28–011*

Mortimer v Bailey [2004] EWCA Civ 1514; [2005] B.L.R. 85; [2005] 2 P. & C.R. 9; [2005] 1 E.G.L.R. 75; [2005] 02 E.G. 102; [2004] N.P.C. 162, CA (Civ Div) *27–060*
Mortimer v Beckett [1920] 1 Ch. 571, Ch D *27–024*, *27–064*, *27–070*
Mortimore v Wright (1840) 6 M. & W. 482 .... *8–061*
Mortlock v Buller (1804) 10 Ves. 292 .... *27–033*, *27–047*
Morton v Burn (1837) 7 A. & E. 19 .... *3–047*
Morton v Lamb (1797) 7 T.R. 125 .... *18–063*
Morton v Morton [1942] 1 All E.R. 273 .... *2–123*, 2–135
Morton Construction v City of Hamilton (1961) 31 D.L.R. (2d) 323 .... *7–047*
Moschi v Lep Air Services Ltd; sub nom. Moschi v Rolloswin Investments Ltd; Lep Air Services v Rolloswin Investments [1973] A.C. 331; [1972] 2 W.L.R. 1175; [1972] 2 All E.R. 393; (1972) 116 S.J. 372, HL; affirming [1971] 1 W.L.R. 934; [1971] 3 All E.R. 45, CA (Civ Div) *12–118*, *12–119*, *17–005*, *24–001*, *24–022*, *24–040*, *24–047*, *24–048*, *24–050*, *24–052*, *24–055*
Moseley v Hanford (1830) 10 B. & C. 729 .... *12–101*
Moseley v Rendell (1870–71) L.R. 6 Q.B. 338, QB *20–002*
Moses v Macferlan, 97 E.R. 676; (1760) 2 Burr. 1005, KB *29–012*, 29–018
Mosley v Virgin (1796) 3 Ves. 184 .... *27–028*
Moss v Hall (1850) 5 Exch. 46 .... *3–014*
Moss Steamship Co Ltd v Whinney; sub nom. Whinney v Moss Steamship Co Ltd [1912] A.C. 254, HL; affirming [1910] 2 K.B. 813, CA *12–107*
Mossop v Mossop [1989] Fam. 77; [1988] 2 W.L.R. 1255; [1988] 2 All E.R. 202; [1988] 2 F.L.R. 173; [1988] Fam. Law 334; (1988) 138 N.L.J. Rep. 86, CA (Civ Div) *16–070*
Mostcash Plc (formerly UK Paper Plc) v Fluor Ltd (No.1) [2002] EWCA Civ 975; [2002] B.L.R. 411; 83 Con. L.R. 1; (2003) 19 Const. L.J. 200, CA (Civ Div); reversing [2002] EWHC 265 (TCC), QBD (TCC) *3–048*, *22–005*
Mostyn v West Mostyn Coal and Iron Co Ltd (1875–76) L.R. 1 C.P.D. 145, CPD *5–131*
Mosvolds Rederi A/S v Food Corp of India; The Damodar General TJ Park and The King Theras [1986] 2 Lloyd's Rep. 68, QBD (Comm) *13–004*
Motis Exports Ltd v Dampskibsselskabet AF 1912 A/S (No.1); sub nom. Dampskibsselskabet AF 1912 A/S v Motis Exports Ltd [2000] 1 All E.R. (Comm) 91; [2000] 1 Lloyd's Rep. 211; [2000] C.L.C. 515; (2000) 97(3) L.S.G. 37, CA (Civ Div); affirming [1999] 1 All E.R. (Comm) 571; [1999] 1 Lloyd's Rep. 837; [1999] C.L.C. 914, QBD (Comm) *14–007*, *14–033*
Motor Oil Hellas (Corinth) Refineries SA v Shipping Corp of India; The Kanchenjunga [1990] 1 Lloyd's Rep. 391, HL; affirming [1989] 1 Lloyd's Rep. 354; (1989) 132 S.J. 19, CA (Civ Div); affirming [1987] 2 Lloyd's Rep. 509, QBD (Comm) *3–081*, *3–096*, *6–126*, *22–040*, *22–044*, *22–047*, *24–002*, *24–003*, *24–004*, *24–005*, *24–007*, *24–008*, *24–013*
Mottram Consultants Ltd v Bernard Sunley & Sons Ltd [1975] 2 Lloyd's Rep. 197; 2 B.L.R. 28; (1974) 118 S.J. 808, HL; affirming (1973) 228 E.G. 723, CA (Civ Div) *12–069*
Mouflet v Cole (1872–73) L.R. 8 Ex. 32, Ex Chamber; affirming (1871–72) L.R. 7 Ex. 70, Ex Ct *16–113*
Moukataff v British Overseas Airways Corp [1967] 1 Lloyd's Rep. 396, QBD *14–054*, *18–022*
Moule v Garrett (1871–72) L.R. 7 Ex. 101, Ex Chamber *29–099*, *29–106*
Moundreas & Co SA v Navimpex Centrala Navala [1985] 2 Lloyd's Rep. 515, QBD (Comm) *2–156*
Mount v Oldham Corp [1973] Q.B. 309; [1973] 2 W.L.R. 22; [1973] 1 All E.R. 26; 71 L.G.R. 105; (1972) 116 S.J. 944, CA (Civ Div) *13–018*, *26–137*
Mount Albert BC v Australasian Temperance & General Mutual Life Assurance Society Ltd [1938] A.C. 224, PC (NZ) *30–005*, *30–012*, *30–332*, *30–339*, *30–345*, *30–374*

Mount Eden Land Ltd v Prudential Assurance Co Ltd; sub nom. Prudential Assurance Co Ltd v Mount Eden Land Ltd (1997) 74 P. & C.R. 377; [1997] 1 E.G.L.R. 37; [1997] 14 E.G. 130; [1996] E.G. 179 (C.S.); [1996] N.P.C. 165; (1997) 73 P. & C.R. D28, CA (Civ Div) *2–116*
Mount I, The. *See* Raiffeisen Zentralbank Österreich A.G. v Five Star General Trading LLC
Mountcashell (Earl of) v Barber (1853) 14 C.B. 53 .... *9–073*
Mountford v Harper (1847) 16 L.J. Ex. 184 .... *21–058*
Mountford v Scott [1975] Ch. 258; [1975] 2 W.L.R. 114; [1975] 1 All E.R. 198; (1975) 29 P. & C.R. 401; (1974) 118 S.J. 755, CA (Civ Div); affirming [1973] 3 W.L.R. 884; [1974] 1 All E.R. 248; (1973) 26 P. & C.R. 497; (1973) 117 S.J. 584, Ch D *1–108*, *27–031*, *27–032*, *27–034*
Mourmand v Le Clair [1903] 2 K.B. 216, KBD *12–076*
Mousaka Inc v Golden Seagull Maritime Inc (Application for Summary Judgment) [2002] 1 Lloyd's Rep. 797, QBD (Comm) *3–052*, *13–009*
Moussavi-Azad v Sky Properties Ltd [2004] EWCA Civ 1211, CA (Civ Div) *25–020*, *25–023*
Mouys v Leake (1799) 8 T.R. 411 .... *16–195*
Movitor Pty Ltd, Re (1996) 19 A.C.S.R. 440 .... *16–063*
Mowatt v Lord Londesburgh (1854) 3 E.B. 307 .... *25–001*
Mowbray v Merryweather [1895] 2 Q.B. 640, CA *26–078*
Möwe, The [1915] P. 1, PDAD *11–029*
Mowlem Plc (t/a Mowlem Marine) v Stena Line Ports Ltd [2004] EWHC 2206 (TCC), QBD (TCC) *29–002*
Moxon v Payne (1872–73) L.R. 8 Ch. App. 881, CA in Chancery *7–097*
Mozley v Tinkler (1835) 1 C.M. & R. 692 .... *2–045*
Mudie v Strick (1909) 100 L.T. 701 .... *12–087*
Muggeridge v Sharp; sub nom. Muggeridge, Re; Bank of London and National Provincial Insurance Association, Ex p. (1870) L.R. 10 Eq. 443, Ct of Chancery *28–004*
Muggeridge, Re. *See* Muggeridge v Sharp
Muhammad Issa El Sheikh Ahmad v Ali [1947] A.C. 414, PC (Pal) *26–063A*, 26–105
Muirhead v Industrial Tank Specialities Ltd; Muirhead v ITT (UK) Ltd; Muirhead v Leroy Somer Electric Motors Ltd [1986] Q.B. 507; [1985] 3 W.L.R. 993; [1985] 3 All E.R. 705; [1986] E.C.C. 225; (1986) 83 L.S.G. 117; (1985) 135 N.L.J. 1106; (1985) 129 S.J. 855, CA (Civ Div) *1–176*, *1–177*, *2–036*, *14–057*, 18–035, 18–036
Mukoro v European Bank for Reconstruction and Development [1994] I.C.R. 897, EAT *11–018*
Mulchrone v Swiss Life (UK) Plc [2005] EWHC 1808; [2006] Lloyd's Rep. I.R. 339, QBD (Comm) *18–002*, *18–089*
Mulholland v Mitchell (No.1) [1971] A.C. 666; [1971] 2 W.L.R. 93; [1971] 1 All E.R. 307; (1971) 115 S.J. 15, HL *26–030*
Mulkerrins v PricewaterhouseCoopers; sub nom. Mulkerrins (formerly Woodward) v Pricewaterhouse Coopers (formerly t/a Coopers & Lybrand) [2003] UKHL 41; [2003] 1 W.L.R. 1937; [2003] 4 All E.R. 1; [2003] B.P.I.R. 1357; [2004] P.N.L.R. 5; (2003) 100(37) L.S.G. 32; (2003) 147 S.J.L.B. 935, HL; reversing [2001] B.P.I.R. 106; (2001) 98(5) L.S.G. 36, CA (Civ Div); reversing [2000] B.P.I.R. 506; (2000) 97(14) L.S.G. 42; (2000) 144 S.J.L.B. 158, Ch D 20–034
Mullen v Conoco Ltd [1998] Q.B. 382; [1997] 3 W.L.R. 1032; (1997) 94(17) L.S.G. 25, CA (Civ Div) *25–012*
Mullett v Hook (1827) M. & M. 89 .... *17–010*
Mulliner v Midland Railway Co; sub nom. Mulliner v Midland Railway (1879) L.R. 11 Ch. D. 611, Ch D *10–027*
Mullins v Laughton [2002] EWHC 2761; [2003] Ch. 250; [2003] 2 W.L.R. 1006; [2003] 4 All E.R. 94; [2003] B.P.I.R. 674; (2003) 100(5) L.S.G. 30; (2003) 147 S.J.L.B. 56, Ch D 24–049
Multi Guarantee Co Ltd (No.3), Re [1987] B.C.L.C. 257, CA (Civ Div) *20–022*, *20–023*, *29–043*

Multinational Gas & Petrochemical Co v Multinational Gas & Petrochemical Services Ltd [1983] Ch. 258; [1983] 3 W.L.R. 492; [1983] 2 All E.R. 563; (1983) 127 S.J. 562, CA (Civ Div) *9–007*
Multiplex Constructions (UK) Ltd v Cleveland Bridge UK Ltd [2007] EWCA Civ 1372, CA (Civ Div); reversing in part [2007] EWHC 145 (TCC); 111 Con. L.R. 48, QBD (TCC) *12–050*
Multiplex Constructions (UK) Ltd v Cleveland Bridge UK Ltd; sub nom. Cleveland Bridge UK Ltd v Multiplex Constructions (UK) Ltd [2007] EWCA Civ 443, CA (Civ Div); affirming [2006] EWHC 1341 (TCC); 107 Con. L.R. 1, QBD (TCC) *2–138*, *12–119*, *13–010*
Multiplex Constructions (UK) Ltd v Honeywell Control Systems Ltd [2007] EWHC 447 (TCC); [2007] B.L.R. 195; 111 Con. L.R. 78; [2007] C.I.L.L. 2458; [2007] Bus. L.R. D109, QBD (TCC) *12–081*, *13–012*
Multiservice Bookbinding Ltd v Marden [1979] Ch. 84; [1978] 2 W.L.R. 535; [1978] 2 All E.R. 489; (1978) 35 P. & C.R. 201; (1978) 122 S.J. 210, Ch D *7–126*, *7–128*, *7–130*, *7–132*, *7–133*, *16–004*, *21–072*
Multitank Holsatia, The. *See* Tankreederei Ahrenkeil GmbH v Frahvil SA
Mulvenna v Royal Bank of Scotland Plc [2003] EWCA Civ 1112; [2004] C.P. Rep. 8, CA (Civ Div) *26–100B*
Mundy v Jolliffe (1839) 5 My. & Cr. App. R. 167 .... *4–042*
Municipal Mutual Insurance v Pontefract Corp (1917) 116 L.T. 671 .... *9–022*
Munir v Jang Publications [1989] I.C.R. 1; [1989] I.R.L.R. 224, CA (Civ Div) *25–012*
Munkenbeck & Marshall v Harold [2005] EWHC 356 (TCC), [2005] All E.R. (D) 227, QBD (TCC) *15–098*, *15–109*
Munn v Baker (1817) 2 Stark. 255 .... *12–085*
Munro v Morrison [1980] V.R. 83 .... *16–179*
Munro v Willmott [1949] 1 K.B. 295; [1948] 2 All E.R. 983; 64 T.L.R. 627; [1949] L.J.R. 471; (1948) 92 S.J. 662, KBD *29–052*, *29–133*
Munro Brice & Co v War Risks Association; Munro Brice & Co v Marten; Munro Brice & Co v King, The [1920] 3 K.B. 94; (1920) 2 Ll. L. Rep. 2, CA; reversing [1918] 2 K.B. 78, KBD *14–018*
Munroe v Butt (1858) 8 E.B. 738 .... *21–029*, *21–031*, *21–035*
Munster, The [1983] 1 Lloyd's Rep. 370, CA (Civ Div) *24–018*
Munt v Beasley [2006] EWCA Civ 370, [2006] All E.R. (D) 29, CA (Civ Div) 5–114
Munton v Greater London Council; sub nom. Munton v Newham LBC [1976] 1 W.L.R. 649; [1976] 2 All E.R. 815; 74 L.G.R. 416; (1976) 32 P. & C.R. 269; (1976) 239 E.G. 43; (1976) 120 S.J. 149, CA (Civ Div); affirming (1975) 29 P. & C.R. 278, Lands Tr *2–122*, *4–014*
Murad v Al-Saraj; Murad v Westwood Business Inc [2005] EWCA Civ 959; [2005] W.T.L.R. 1573; (2005) 102(32) L.S.G. 31, CA (Civ Div); affirming [2004] EWHC 1235 (Ch), Ch D *6–062*, *29–139*, *29–142*, *29–155*, *29–157*
Muray v Parker (1854) 19 Beav. 305 .... *5–108*, 5–112
Murphy v Boese (1874–75) L.R. 10 Ex. 126, Ex Ct *4–038*
Murphy v Brentwood DC [1991] 1 A.C. 398; [1990] 3 W.L.R. 414; [1990] 2 All E.R. 908; [1990] 2 Lloyd's Rep. 467; 50 B.L.R. 1; 21 Con. L.R. 1; (1990) 22 H.L.R. 502; 89 L.G.R. 24; (1991) 3 Admin. L.R. 37; (1990) 6 Const. L.J. 304; (1990) 154 L.G. Rev. 1010; [1990] E.G. 105 (C.S.); (1990) 87(30) L.S.G. 15; (1990) 134 S.J. 1076, HL; reversing [1990] 2 W.L.R. 944; [1990] 2 All E.R. 269; 88 L.G.R. 333; (1990) 87(5) L.S.G. 42; (1990) 134 S.J. 458, CA (Civ Div); affirming 13 Con. L.R. 96, OR *1–176*, 1–180, *14–056*, *18–022*, *18–027*, *18–032*, *18–033*, *18–036*, *28–055*
Murphy v Hurly; sub nom. Murphy v Hurley [1922] 1 A.C. 369, HL (UK-Irl) *21–009*
Murphy v Stone-Wallwork (Charlton) Ltd; sub nom. Murphy v Stong-Wallwork (Charlton) [1969] 1 W.L.R. 1023; [1969] 2 All E.R. 949; 7 K.I.R. 203; (1969) 113 S.J. 546, HL *26–030*
Murphy v Young & Co's Brewery Plc; Murphy v Sun Alliance and London Insurance Plc [1997] 1 W.L.R. 1591; [1997] 1 All E.R. 518; [1997] 1 Lloyd's Rep. 236; [1997] C.L.C. 469; [1998] 1 Costs L.R. 94; [1997] 6 Re. L.R. 113, CA (Civ Div); affirming [1996] L.R.L.R. 60, QBD *16–053*
Murray v Earl of Stair (1823) 2 B.& C. 82 .... *1–105*

Murray v East India Co (1821) 5 B. & Ald. 204 .... *28–031*
Murray v Lloyd [1989] 1 W.L.R. 1060; [1990] 2 All E.R. 92; (1989) 21 H.L.R. 525; [1990] 1 E.G.L.R. 274; (1989) 86(41) L.S.G. 36; (1989) 139 N.L.J. 938; (1989) 133 S.J. 1405, Ch D *1–164*
Murray (Inspector of Taxes) v Goodhews [1978] 1 W.L.R. 499; [1978] 2 All E.R. 40; [1978] S.T.C. 207; [1977] T.R. 255, CA (Civ Div); affirming [1976] 2 All E.R. 296; [1976] S.T.C. 128; 52 T.C. 86; [1976] T.R. 15, Ch D *3–026*
Musawi v RE International (UK) Ltd [2007] EWHC 2981 (Ch); [2008] 1 All E.R. (Comm) 607; [2008] 1 Lloyd's Rep. 326; [2007] N.P.C. 137, Ch D ...*30–005*, *30–016*, *30–022*, *30–048*
Museprime Properties, Ltd v Adhill Properties, Ltd (1991) 61 P. & C.R. 111; [1990] 36 E.G. 114; [1990] E.G. 29 (C.S.), Ch D *6–037*, *6–038*, *6–137*, *14–063*
Musgrave, Re; sub nom. Machell v Parry [1916] 2 Ch. 417, Ch D *29–043*
Musgrave v Forster (1870–71) L.R. 6 Q.B. 590, QB *12–052*
Muskham Finance v Howard [1963] 1 Q.B. 904; [1963] 2 W.L.R. 87; [1963] 1 All E.R. 81; (1962) 106 S.J. 1029, CA *5–103*, *5–106*
Mussen v Van Diemen's Land Co [1938] Ch. 253, Ch D *21–013*, *26–147*
Musurus Bey v Gadban [1894] 2 Q.B. 352, CA; affirming [1894] 1 Q.B. 533, QBD *11–014*, *28–031*
Mutual Finance Ltd v John Wetton & Sons Ltd [1937] 2 K.B. 389, KBD *7–040*, 7–048
Mutual Life & Citizens Assurance Co v Evatt [1971] A.C. 793; [1971] 2 W.L.R. 23; [1971] 1 All E.R. 150; [1970] 2 Lloyd's Rep. 441; (1970) 114 S.J. 932, PC (Aus) 6–084
Mutual Life Assurance Society v Langley (1886) L.R. 32 Ch. D. 460, CA; reversing (1884) L.R. 26 Ch. D. 686, Ch D *19–068*
Mutual Life Insurance Co of New York v The Rank Organisation [1985] B.C.L.C. 11 .... *9–061*
Mutual Pools Staff Pty Ltd v Commonwealth (1994) 179 C.L.R. 155 .... *29–086*
Mutzenbecher v La Aseguradora Espanola [1906] 1 K.B. 254, CA *21–005*
My Kinda Town Ltd (t/a Chicago Pizza Pie Factory) v Soll and Grunts Investments [1983] R.P.C. 407, CA (Civ Div) *29–142*, *29–145*
Myers, Re [1908] 1 K.B. 941, KBD *16–042*
Myers v Sarl, 121 E.R. 457; (1860) 3 El. & El. 306, QB *12–060*, *12–132*
Myrto, The [1978] 1 Lloyd's Rep. 11, CA (Civ Div); reversing [1977] 2 Lloyd's Rep. 243, QBD (Admlty) *18–143*
N Joachimson (A Firm) v Swiss Bank Corp (Costs) [1921] 3 K.B. 110; (1921) 6 Ll. L. Rep. 435, CA *21–010*, *28–039*
NBTY Europe Ltd (formerly Holland & Barrett Europe Ltd) v Nutricia International BV [2005] EWHC 734 (Comm); [2005] 2 Lloyd's Rep. 350, QBD (Comm) *5–071*, *12–050*, *12–119*
NEC Semi-Conductors Ltd v IRC. *See* Boake Allen Ltd v Revenue and Customs Commissioners
NLA Group Ltd v Bowers [1999] 1 Lloyd's Rep. 109, QBD (Comm) *12–118*, *12–120*
NPower Direct Ltd v South of Scotland Power Ltd [2005] EWHC 2123; (2005) 102(43) L.S.G. 29, QBD (Comm) *22–049*
NV Handel My J Smits Import-Export v English Exporters (London) Ltd [1955] 2 Lloyd's Rep. 317, CA *26–051*
NV Kwik Hoo Tong Handel Maatschappij v James Finlay & Co Ltd [1927] A.C. 604, HL *30–005*, *30–010*, *30–011*
NV Slavenburg's Bank v Intercontinental Natural Resources. *See* Slavenburg's Bank NV v Intercontinental Natural Resources
NV Stoomv Maats"De Maas v Nippon Yusen Kaisha. *See* Stoomv Maats De Maas NV v Nippon Yusen Kaisha
Naamlooze, etc. Vulcaan v A/S Ludwig Mowinckel Rederi (1938) 43 Com. Cas. 252 .... *28–125*
Nadreph Ltd v Willmett & Co; sub nom. Nadreth v Willmett & Co [1978] 1 W.L.R. 1537; [1978] 1 All E.R. 746; (1978) 122 S.J. 744, Ch D *26–115*
Naeem (A Bankrupt) (No.18 of 1988), Re [1990] 1 W.L.R. 48; (1989) 86(46) L.S.G. 37, Ch D *20–050*

Nagle v Fielden; sub nom. Nagle v Feilden [1966] 2 Q.B. 633; [1966] 2 W.L.R. 1027; [1966] 1 All E.R. 689; (1966) 110 S.J. 286, CA ...*9–074*, *9–076*, *9–077*, *9–084*, *16–004*, *16–075*, *16–137*, *16–139*, *27–023*, 27–075
Naidoo v Naidu, *The Times*, November 1, 2000, Ch D *7–058*
Nance v British Columbia Electric Railway Co Ltd [1951] A.C. 601; [1951] 2 All E.R. 448; [1951] 2 T.L.R. 137; (1951) 95 S.J. 543, PC (Can) *26–030*
Naoroji v Chartered Bank of India (1867–68) L.R. 3 C.P. 444, CCP *20–041*
Napier v National Business Agency Ltd [1951] 2 All E.R. 264; 44 R. & I.T. 413; (1951) 30 A.T.C. 180; [1951] W.N. 392; (1951) 95 S.J. 528, CA *16–012*, *16–017*, *16–202*
Napier & Ettrick v Hunter. *See* Lord Napier and Ettrick v RF Kershaw Ltd (No.1)
Napier (Lord) and Ettrick v RF Kershaw Ltd (No.1); Lord Napier and Ettrick v Hunter [1993] A.C. 713; [1993] 2 W.L.R. 42; [1993] 1 All E.R. 385; [1993] 1 Lloyd's Rep. 197; (1993) 137 S.J.L.B. 44, HL *27–008*, *29–173*
Napier (Lord) and Ettrick v RF Kershaw Ltd (No.2); sub nom. Society of Lloyd's v Robinson; Society of Lloyd's v Woodard [1999] 1 W.L.R. 756; [1999] 1 All E.R. (Comm.) 545; [1999] C.L.C. 987; [1999] Lloyd's Rep. I.R. 329; (1999) 96(22) L.S.G. 34; (1999) 143 S.J.L.B. 150, HL; affirming in part [1997] L.R.L.R. 1; [1996] C.L.C. 1875, CA (Civ Div) *12–057*
Narbeth v James; The Lady Tahilla [1968] 1 Lloyd's Rep. 168; (1968) 118 N.L.J. 300, CA (Civ Div) *21–006*
Nash v Armstrong (1861) 10 C.B. (N.S.) 259 .... *1–115*
Nash v Eli Lilly & Co [1993] 1 W.L.R. 782; [1993] 4 All E.R. 383; [1992] 3 Med. L.R. 353, CA (Civ Div) *28–011*
Nash v Flyn (1844) 1 Jo. & La.T. 162 .... *1–105*
Nash v Hodgson (1855) 6 De G.M.G. 474 .... *21–060*, *28–128*
Nash v Inman [1908] 2 K.B. 1, CA *8–008*, *8–011*, 8–012, *8–016*
Nash v Stevenson Transport Ltd [1936] 2 K.B. 128, CA; affirming [1935] 2 K.B. 341, KBD *16–011*, *16–012*
Natal Land & Colonization Co Ltd v Pauline Colliery and Development Syndicate Ltd [1904] A.C. 120, PC (Natal) *9–014*, *9–015*
Nathan, Ex p. Stapleton, Re; sub nom. Stapleton, Ex p. (1878–79) L.R. 10 Ch. D. 586, CA *20–032*
Nathan v Ogdens Ltd (1905) 94 L.T. 126 .... *21–058*
Nathan v Smilovitch (No.2) [2002] EWHC 1629, Ch D *1–032*
National Bank of Australasia Ltd v J Falkingham & Sons [1902] A.C. 585, PC (Aus) *12–096*, *12–119*
National Bank of Australia Ltd v Scottish Union and National Insurance Co Ltd [1952] A.C. 493; [1952] 2 T.L.R. 254; (1952) 96 S.J. 529, PC (Aus) *30–012*, *30–372*, *30–375*
National Bank of Commerce v National Westminster Bank Plc [1990] 2 Lloyd's Rep. 514, QBD (Comm) *28–039*
National Bank of Egypt International Ltd v Oman Housing Bank SAOC [2002] EWHC 1760; [2003] 1 All E.R. (Comm) 246, QBD (Comm) *29–020*, *29–074*, *29–179*, *29–182*
National Bank of Greece and Athens SA v Metliss [1958] A.C. 509; [1957] 3 W.L.R. 1056; [1957] 3 All E.R. 608; (1957) 101 S.J. 972, HL *30–325*, *30–345*
National Bank of Greece SA v Pinios Shipping Co No. 1; sub nom. Pinios Shipping Co No. 1 v National Bank of Greece SA [1990] 1 A.C. 637; [1989] 3 W.L.R. 1330; [1990] 1 All E.R. 78; [1990] 1 Lloyd's Rep. 225; [1988] 2 F.T.L.R. 9; [1988] Fin. L.R. 249; [1990] C.C.L.R. 18; (1990) 87(4) L.S.G. 33; (1989) 139 N.L.J. 1711; (1990) 134 S.J. 261, HL; reversing [1989] 3 W.L.R. 185; [1989] 1 All E.R. 213; [1988] 2 Lloyd's Rep. 126; (1989) 133 S.J. 817, CA (Civ Div) *1–126*, 1–158, *13–003*
National Benefit Assurance Co Ltd, Re (No.2); sub nom. National Benefit Assurance Co Ltd, Re [1931] 1 Ch. 46; (1930) 37 Ll. L. Rep. 153, Ch D *16–189*, *20–041*
National Bolivian Navigation Co v Wilson; sub nom. Wilson v Church (1879–80) L.R. 5 App. Cas. 176, HL *29–056*

National Broach & Machine Co v Churchill Gear Machines Ltd; sub nom. Churchill Gear Machines Ltd v National Broach & Machine Co [1967] 1 W.L.R. 384; [1966] 3 All E.R. 923 (Note); [1966] F.S.R. 394; [1967] R.P.C. 99, HL *26–006*
National Car Parks Ltd v Baird (Valuation Officer) [2004] EWCA Civ 967; [2005] 1 All E.R. 53; [2004] R.A. 245; (2004) 148 S.J.L.B. 942; [2004] N.P.C. 126, CA (Civ Div) *21–020*
National Carbonising Co v British Coal Distillation (1936) 54 R.P.C. 41 ..*19–056*, *19–079*
National Carriers Ltd v Panalpina (Northern) Ltd [1981] A.C. 675; [1981] 2 W.L.R. 45; [1981] 1 All E.R. 161; (1982) 43 P. & C.R. 72; (1981) 125 S.J. 46, HL *5–036*, *23–007*, *23–009*, 23–011, *23–012*, 23–013, *23–014*, *23–017*, *23–018*, *23–021*, *23–035*, 23–052, *23–053*, 23–054, 23–055, 23–056, *23–057*, *23–061*, *23–071*, *23–081*
National Coal Board v Galley [1958] 1 W.L.R. 16; [1958] 1 All E.R. 91; (1958) 102 S.J. 31, CA *25–008*, *26–014*, *26–015*
National Coal Board v National Union of Mineworkers [1986] I.C.R. 736; [1986] I.R.L.R. 439, Ch D *2–177*
National Grid Co Plc v Mayes; sub nom. National Grid Co Plc v Laws; Jefferies v Mayes; National Power Plc v Feldon; Laws v National Grid Co Plc; National Grid Co Plc v Lewis; International Power Plc (formerly National Power Plc) v Healy [2001] UKHL 20; [2001] 1 W.L.R. 864; [2001] 2 All E.R. 417; [2001] I.C.R. 544; [2001] I.R.L.R. 394; [2001] O.P.L.R. 15; [2001] Pens. L.R. 121; (2001) 98(23) L.S.G. 38; (2001) 151 N.L.J. 572; (2001) 145 S.J.L.B. 98, HL; reversing [2000] I.C.R. 174; [1999] O.P.L.R. 95; [1999] Pens. L.R. 37; (1999) 96(9) L.S.G. 31, CA (Civ Div); reversing [1997] O.P.L.R. 207, Ch D; reversing [1997] O.P.L.R. 73, Pensions Ombudsman *12–091*
National Motor Mail-Coach Co Ltd, Re [1908] 2 Ch. 515, CA *9–015*, *29–109*
National Mutual Life Association of Australasia v Attorney General of New Zealand [1956] A.C. 369; [1956] 2 W.L.R. 532; [1956] 1 All E.R. 721; (1956) 100 S.J. 149, PC (NZ) *30–370*, *30–375*
National Pari-Mutuel Association Ltd (1930) 47 T.L.R. 110 .... *29–042*
National Permanent Benefit Building Society Ex p. Williamson, Re (1869–70) L.R. 5 Ch. App. 309, CA in Chancery *8–020*
National Power Plc v United Gas Co Ltd, unreported, July 3, 1998 .... *22–048*
National Provincial Bank v Moore, 117 N.L.J. 492; (1967) 111 S.J. 357 .... *4–013*
National Provincial Bank Ltd v Ainsworth; sub nom. National Provincial Bank Ltd v Hastings Car Mart Ltd [1965] A.C. 1175; [1965] 3 W.L.R. 1; [1965] 2 All E.R. 472; (1965) 109 S.J. 415, HL; reversing [1964] Ch. 665; [1964] 2 W.L.R. 751; [1964] 1 All E.R. 688; (1964) 108 S.J. 115, CA; reversing [1964] Ch. 9; [1963] 2 W.L.R. 1015; [1963] 2 All E.R. 204; (1963) 107 S.J. 295, Ch D *2–080*, *19–059*, *20–039*
National Provincial Bank Ltd v Hastings Car Mart. *See* National Provincial Bank v Ainsworth
National Provincial Bank of England Ltd v Glanusk [1913] 3 K.B. 335, KBD *6–159*
National Provincial Bank of England v Jackson (1886) L.R. 33 Ch. D. 1, CA *1–092*, *5–103*
National Provincial Bank of England v Marshall (1889) L.R. 40 Ch. D. 112, CA *16–102*
National Provincial Building Society v British Waterways Board [1992] E.G. 149 (C.S.), CA (Civ Div) *27–048*
National Sales Corp Ltd v Bernardi; Bernardi v National Sales Corp Ltd [1931] 2 K.B. 188, KBD *12–113*
National Savings Bank Association Ltd v Tranah (1866–67) L.R. 2 C.P. 556, CCP *21–073*, *21–074*, *21–079*
National Savings Bank Association, Re; sub nom. Hebb's Case (1867) L.R. 4 Eq. 9, Ct of Chancery *2–024*, *2–045*, *2–088*
National Semiconductors (UK) Ltd v UPS Ltd and Inter City Trucks [1996] 2 Lloyd's Rep. 212, QBD (Comm) *14–017*
National Trust Co v Gleason (1879) 77 N.Y. 400 .... *29–140*

National Trust for Places of Historic Interest or Natural Beauty v Haden Young Ltd, 72 B.L.R. 1, CA (Civ Div); affirming, 66 B.L.R. 88, QBD *14–056*, *18–005*

National Westminster Bank Plc v Kostopoulos [2000] 1 F.L.R. 815; [2000] Fam. Law 403, CA (Civ Div); affirming, 1998 CH 3353, Ch D *6–027*, *7–119*

National Westminster Bank Ltd v Barclays Bank International Ltd [1975] Q.B. 654; [1975] 2 W.L.R. 12; [1974] 3 All E.R. 834; [1974] 2 Lloyd's Rep. 506; (1974) 118 S.J. 627, QBD *29–030*, *29–040*, *29–182*

National Westminster Bank Ltd v Halesowen Presswork and Assemblies Ltd; sub nom. Halesowen Presswork & Assemblies v Westminster Bank Ltd [1972] A.C. 785; [1972] 2 W.L.R. 455; [1972] 1 All E.R. 641; [1972] 1 Lloyd's Rep. 101; (1972) 116 S.J. 138, HL; reversing [1971] 1 Q.B. 1; [1970] 3 W.L.R. 625; [1970] 3 All E.R. 473, CA (Civ Div); reversing [1970] 2 W.L.R. 754; [1970] 1 All E.R. 33; (1969) 113 S.J. 939, QBD *12–096*, *20–041*

National Westminster Bank Plc v Amin [2002] UKHL 9; [2002] 1 F.L.R. 735; [2002] N.P.C. 33; [2002] 2 P. & C.R. DG3, HL; reversing (1999) 77 P. & C.R. D35, CA (Civ Div) *7–115*

National Westminster Bank Plc v Inland Revenue Commissioners; Barclays Bank Plc v Inland Revenue Commissioners [1995] 1 A.C. 119; [1994] 3 W.L.R. 159; [1994] 3 All E.R. 1; [1994] S.T.C. 580; [1994] 2 B.C.L.C. 239; 67 T.C. 38; [1994] S.T.I. 756; (1994) 91(32) L.S.G. 44; (1994) 138 S.J.L.B. 139, HL; affirming [1994] S.T.C. 184; 67 T.C. 15; [1993] S.T.I. 1685; (1994) 91(11) L.S.G. 36; (1994) 138 S.J.L.B. 25, CA (Civ Div); reversing [1993] S.T.C. 639; 67 T.C. 1; [1993] S.T.I. 1144; (1993) 137 S.J.L.B. 204, Ch D *2–024*

National Westminster Bank Plc v Morgan [1985] A.C. 686; [1985] 2 W.L.R. 588; [1985] 1 All E.R. 821; [1985] F.L.R. 266; (1985) 17 H.L.R. 360; (1985) 82 L.S.G. 1485; (1985) 135 N.L.J. 254; (1985) 129 S.J. 205, HL; reversing [1983] 3 All E.R. 85; (1983) 133 N.L.J. 378, CA (Civ Div) *1–012*, *6–027*, 7–060, 7–062, 7–063, 7–067, 7–073, *7–082*, *7–091*, 7–139

National Westminster Bank Plc v Powney [1991] Ch. 339; [1990] 2 W.L.R. 1084; [1990] 2 All E.R. 416; (1990) 60 P. & C.R. 420; (1989) 86(46) L.S.G. 39; (1990) 134 S.J. 285, CA (Civ Div) *28–095*

National Westminster Bank Plc v Rabobank Nederland [2007] EWHC 1742 (Comm); [2008] 1 All E.R. (Comm) 243, QBD (Comm) *26–178*

National Westminster Bank Plc v Somer International (UK) Ltd [2001] EWCA Civ 970; [2002] Q.B. 1286; [2002] 3 W.L.R. 64; [2002] 1 All E.R. 198; [2001] Lloyd's Rep. Bank. 263; [2001] C.L.C. 1579, CA (Civ Div) *3–103*, *29–178*, *29–185*

National Westminster Bank Plc v Utrecht-America Finance Co [2001] EWCA Civ 658; [2001] 3 All E.R. 733; [2001] 2 All E.R. (Comm) 7; [2001] Lloyd's Rep. Bank. 285; [2001] C.L.C. 1372; (2001) 151 N.L.J. 784, CA (Civ Div); affirming [2001] C.L.C. 442, QBD (Comm) *6–137*, *6–139*

Nationwide Building Society v Registry of Friendly Societies [1983] 1 W.L.R. 1226; [1983] 3 All E.R. 296; (1984) 47 P. & C.R. 221; (1983) 80 L.S.G. 3238; (1983) 133 N.L.J. 958; (1983) 127 S.J. 696, Ch D *21–072*

Naughton v O'Callaghan [1990] 3 All E.R. 191, QBD *6–054*

Nautilus Steam Shipping Co Ltd, Re; sub nom. Nautilus Steam Shipping Co Ltd (Application of Gibbs & Co), Re [1936] Ch. 17; (1935) 52 Ll. L. Rep. 183, CA; reversing (1935) 51 Ll. L. Rep. 65, Ch D *16–161*

Naviera Amazonica Peruana SA v Compania Internacional de Seguros de Peru [1988] 1 Lloyd's Rep. 116; [1988] 1 F.T.L.R. 100, CA (Civ Div) *12–070*

Navrom v Callitsis Ship Management SA; The Radauti [1988] 2 Lloyd's Rep. 416, CA (Civ Div); affirming [1987] 2 Lloyd's Rep. 276, QBD (Comm) ...*12–053*, *14–138*, *14–140*, *14–143*, *14–147*, *14–149*

Naylor v Yorkshire Electricity Board. *See* Yorkshire Electricity Board v Naylor

Naylor Benzon & Co Ltd v Krainische Industrie Gesellschaft [1918] 2 K.B. 486, CA *23–030*

Nea Agrex SA v Baltic Shipping Co Ltd; The Agios Lazarus [1976] Q.B. 933; [1976] 2 W.L.R. 925; [1976] 2 All E.R. 842; [1976] 2 Lloyd's Rep. 47; (1976) 120 S.J. 351, CA (Civ Div) *2–140*, *28–022*, *28–115*

Neale v Turton (1827) 4 Bing. 149 .... *17–007*
Nearfield Ltd v Lincoln Nominees Ltd [2006] EWHC 2421 (Ch); [2007] 1 All E.R. (Comm) 441, Ch D *12–115*, *12–119*
Neate v Harding (1851) 6 Exch. 349 .... *29–142*
Nedby v Nedby (1852) 5 De. G. & Sm. 377 .... *7–085*
Nedham's Case (1610) 8 Co. Rep. 135 .... *25–005*, *28–065*
Needler Financial Services Ltd v Taber [2002] 3 All E.R. 501; [2002] Lloyd's Rep. P.N. 32; [2001] Pens. L.R. 253; (2001) 98(37) L.S.G. 39; (2001) 151 N.L.J. 1283; (2001) 145 S.J.L.B. 219, Ch D *26–115*
Neill v Duke of Devonshire (1882–83) L.R. 8 App. Cas. 135, HL (UK-Irl) *12–083*, *12–126*
Neill v Midland Railway (1869) 17 W.R. 871 .... *5–133*
Neilson v Harford (1841) 8 M. & W. 806 .... *12–046*
Neilson v Poole (1969) 20 P. & C.R. 909, Ch D 4–057
Neilson v Stewart, 1991 S.C. (H.L.) 22; 1991 S.L.T. 523; [1991] B.C.C. 713, HL; affirming, 1990 S.L.T. 346, IH (1 Div) 2–129
Nella v Nella, *Independent*, November 1, 1999, Ch D *16–119*
Nelson v Atlantic Power and Gas Ltd, 1995 S.L.T. 102, IH (Ex Div) *14–015*
Nelson v Dahl. *See* Dahl (t/a Dahl & Co) v Nelson
Nelson v Larholt [1948] 1 K.B. 339; [1947] 2 All E.R. 751; 64 T.L.R. 1; [1948] L.J.R. 340, KBD *29–003*, *29–008*, *29–011*, *29–162*
Nelson v Nelson (1995) 132 A.L.R. 133 .... *16–152*, 16–183, 16–184
Nelson v Roberts (1893) 69 L.T. 352 .... *20–044*
Nelson v Rye [1996] 1 W.L.R. 1378; [1996] 2 All E.R. 186; [1996] E.M.L.R. 37; [1996] F.S.R. 313, Ch D *28–138*, *28–140*, 28–141
Nelson v Stocker (1859) 4 De. G. & J. 458 .... *8–051*
Nelson Lines (Liverpool) Ltd v James Nelson & Sons Ltd; sub nom. James Nelson & Sons Ltd v Nelson Line (Liverpool) Ltd (No.2) [1908] A.C. 16, HL; affirming [1907] 1 K.B. 769, CA; affirming [1906] 2 K.B. 804, KBD *12–065*, *14–032*
Nemes v Ata Chaglayam, October 11, 1982 .... *29–021*
Neptune Orient Lines Ltd v JVC (UK) Ltd; The Chevalier Roze [1983] 2 Lloyd's Rep. 438, QBD (Comm) *12–012*, *14–051*, *14–071*, *14–081*, *18–070*
Nerarno, The. *See* Daval Aciers D'Usinor et de Sacilor v Armare Srl
Nereide SpA di Navigazione v Bulk Oil International; The Laura Prima [1981] 3 All E.R. 737; [1982] 1 Lloyd's Rep. 1, HL; reversing [1981] 2 Lloyd's Rep. 24; [1981] Com. L.R. 109; (1981) 125 S.J. 304, CA (Civ Div); reversing [1980] 1 Lloyd's Rep. 466, QBD (Comm) *12–063*
Nerot v Wallace (1789) 3 T.R. 17 .... *3–166*
Nesbitt v Meyer (1818) 1 Swan. 223 .... *27–040*
Nessa v Chief Adjudication Officer [1999] 1 W.L.R. 1937; [1999] 4 All E.R. 677; [1999] 2 F.L.R. 1116; [1999] 3 F.C.R. 538; [2000] Fam. Law 28; (1999) 96(42) L.S.G. 42; (1999) 149 N.L.J. 1619; (1999) 143 S.J.L.B. 250, HL ... *30–079*
Neste Oy v Lloyds Bank Plc; The Tiiskeri, The Nestegas and The Enskeri [1983] 2 Lloyd's Rep. 658; [1983] Com. L.R. 145; (1983) 133 N.L.J. 597, QBD (Comm) *29–059*, *29–160*
Netz v Ede [1946] Ch. 224; [1946] 1 All E.R. 628 174 L.T. 363; 115 L.J. Ch. 197; 90 S.J. 187, Ch D *11–027*
Neville v Dominion of Canada News Co Ltd [1915] 3 K.B. 556, CA *16–005*
Neville v Kelly (1862) 12 C.B. (N.S.) 740 .... *2–041*, *3–062*
Neville v London Express Newspaper Ltd; sub nom. Neville v London Express Newspapers Ltd [1919] A.C. 368, HL; affirming [1917] 2 K.B. 564, CA; affirming [1917] 1 K.B. 402, KBD *16–048*, *16–050*
Neville v Wilson [1997] Ch. 144; [1996] 3 W.L.R. 460; [1996] 3 All E.R. 171; [1996] 2 B.C.L.C. 310, CA (Civ Div) *19–025*
New Brunswick and Canada Ry. And Land Co v Conybeare (1862) 9 H.L.C. 711 ...*6–009*, *6–014*
New Brunswick Railway Co Ltd v British & French Trust Corp Ltd [1939] A.C. 1; [1938] 4 All E.R. 747, HL *21–069*, *21–070*, *25–011*
New Eberhardt Co Ex p. Menzies, Re (1890) L.R. 43 Ch. D. 118, CA *4–027*

New England Reinsurance Corp and First State Insurance Co v Messoghios Insurance Co SA [1992] 2 Lloyd's Rep. 251, CA (Civ Div); reversing [1992] 1 Lloyd's Rep. 201, QBD (Comm) *2–116*
New Finance and Mortgage Co Ltd (In liquidation), Re [1975] Ch. 420; [1975] 2 W.L.R. 443; [1975] 1 All E.R. 684; (1974) 118 S.J. 714, Ch D 9–022
New Hart Builders Ltd v Brindley [1975] Ch. 342; [1975] 2 W.L.R. 595; [1975] 1 All E.R. 1007; (1975) 29 P. & C.R. 476; (1974) 237 E.G. 959; (1974) 119 S.J. 256, Ch D *2–052*, *4–035*, *4–048*, *22–033*
New Islington and Hackney Housing Association Ltd v Pollard Thomas and Edwards Ltd [2001] B.L.R. 74; (2001) 3 T.C.L.R. 25; 85 Con. L.R. 194; [2001] Lloyd's Rep. P.N. 243; [2001] P.N.L.R. 20; (2001) 17 Const. L.J. 55, QBD (TCC) *28–011*, *28–033*
New London Credit Syndicate Ltd v Neale [1898] 2 Q.B. 487, CA *12–101*
New South Wales v Bardolph (1934) 52 C.L.R. 455 .... *10–005*, *10–006*
New System Private Telephones (London) Ltd v Edward Hughes Co [1939] 2 All E.R. 844 .... *23–021*
New Testament Church of God v Stewart [2007] EWCA Civ 1004; [2008] I.C.R. 282; [2008] I.R.L.R. 134; [2008] H.R.L.R. 2, CA (Civ Div); affirming [2007] I.R.L.R. 178, EAT *2–181*
New Zealand Guardian Trust Co Ltd v Brooks [1995] 1 W.L.R. 96; [1995] B.C.C. 407; [1995] 2 B.C.L.C. 242; (1995) 92(1) L.S.G. 36; (1994) 138 S.J.L.B. 240, PC (NZ) *9–007*
New Zealand Netherlands Society "Oranje" v Kuys; sub nom. New Zealand Netherlands Society Oranje Inc v Kuys (Laurentius Cornelis) [1973] 1 W.L.R. 1126; [1973] 2 All E.R. 1222; [1974] R.P.C. 272; (1973) 117 S.J. 565, PC (NZ) *29–160*
New Zealand Payroll Software Systems Ltd v Advanced ManagementSystems Ltd [2003] 3 N.Z.L.R. 1 .... *19–043*
New Zealand Refrigerating Co v Scott [1969] N.Z.L.R. 30, Sup Ct (NZ) *6–049*
New Zealand Shipping Co Ltd v AM Satterthwaite & Co Ltd; The Eurymedon; sub nom. AM Satterthwaite & Co Ltd v New Zealand Shipping Co Ltd [1975] A.C. 154; [1974] 2 W.L.R. 865; [1974] 1 All E.R. 1015; [1974] 1 Lloyd's Rep. 534; (1974) 118 S.J. 387, PC (NZ); affirming [1972] 2 Lloyd's Rep. 544, CA (NZ); reversing [1971] 2 Lloyd's Rep. 399; [1972] N.Z.L.R. 385, Sup Ct (NZ) *1–079*, 1–187, *2–085*, *2–110*, *2–180*, 3–074, *3–075*, *14–042*, 14–048, 14–049, *14–050*, *14–052*, *18–019*, *18–019*, *18–021*, *18–085*
New Zealand Shipping Co Ltd v Société des Ateliers et Chantiers de France; sub nom. Arbitration between New Zealand Shipping Co Ltd and Société des Ateliers et Chantiers de France, Re [1919] A.C. 1; [1918–19] All E.R. Rep. 552, HL; affirming [1917] 2 K.B. 717, CA *12–082*, *14–148*, *22–055*, *23–061*
Newal v Jones (1830) 1 Moo. & M. 449 .... *13–022*
Newark Engineering (NZ) Ltd v Jenkin [1980] N.Z.L.R. 504 .... *6–049*
Newbold v Leicester City Council [1999] I.C.R. 1182; (2000) 2 L.G.L.R. 303; [2000] B.L.G.R. 58; (1999) 96(31) L.S.G. 38; (1999) 143 S.J.L.B. 211, CA (Civ Div) *3–014*
Newborne v Sensolid (Great Britain) Ltd [1954] 1 Q.B. 45; [1953] 2 W.L.R. 596; [1953] 1 All E.R. 708; (1953) 97 S.J. 209, CA *5–096*, *9–012*
Newbould v Smith (1889) L.R. 14 App. Cas. 423, HL *28–100*
Newby v Sharpe (1878) L.R. 8 Ch. D. 39, CA *12–087*, *12–088*
Newdigate v Davy (1701) 1 Ld. Raym. 742 .... *29–098*
Newell v Radford (1867–68) L.R. 3 C.P. 52, CCP *4–023*, *12–122*
Newell v Tarrant [2004] EWHC 772 (Ch); (2004) 148 S.J.L.B. 509, Ch D *4–073*
Newfoundland v Newfoundland Railway Co (1888) L.R. 13 App. Cas. 199, PC (Can) *19–070*, *19–071*
Newington v Levy (1870–71) L.R. 6 C.P. 180, Ex Chamber; affirming (1869–70) L.R. 5 C.P. 607, CCP *22–008*
Newland v Simons & Willer (Hairdressers) [1981] I.C.R. 521; [1981] I.R.L.R. 359, EAT *16–004*, *16–010*, *16–011*, *16–012*
Newman v Gatti (1907) 24 T.L.R. 18 .... *12–004*, *12–096*, *12–103*

Newman v Rogers (1793) 4 Bro. C.C. 391 .... *21–013*
Newmarch v Clay (1811) 14 East 239 .... *21–060*
Newport Association Football Club Ltd v Football Association of Wales Ltd [1995] 2 All E.R. 87; (1994) 144 N.L.J. 1351, Ch D *27–078*
Newry and Enniskillen Ry Co v Coombe (1849) 3 Exch. 565 .... *8–037*, *8–040*
Newsholme Bros v Road Transport & General Insurance Co Ltd [1929] 2 K.B. 356; (1929) 34 Ll. L. Rep. 247, CA; affirming (1928) 32 Ll. L. Rep. 226, KBD *6–149*
Newsome v Graham (1829) 10 B.C. 234 .... *29–042*
Newstead (Inspector of Taxes) v Frost [1980] 1 W.L.R. 135; [1980] 1 All E.R. 363; [1980] S.T.C. 123; [1980] T.R. 1; (1980) 124 S.J. 116, HL; affirming [1978] 1 W.L.R. 1441; [1979] 2 All E.R. 129; [1979] S.T.C. 45; [1978] T.R. 221; (1979) 129 N.L.J. 487; (1978) 122 S.J. 813, CA (Civ Div); affirming [1978] 1 W.L.R. 511; [1978] 2 All E.R. 241; [1978] S.T.C. 239; [1977] T.R. 301; (1978) 122 S.J. 33, Ch D *9–022*
Newton Abbott Cooperative Society Ltd v Williamson & Treadgold Ltd [1952] Ch. 286; [1952] 1 All E.R. 279; [1952] 1 T.L.R. 283, Ch D *16–085*
Newton Woodhouse v Trevor Toys Ltd, Deccember 20, 1991, CA *29–068*
Newtons of Wembley Ltd v Williams [1965] 1 Q.B. 560; [1964] 3 W.L.R. 888; [1964] 3 All E.R. 532; (1964) 108 S.J. 619, CA; affirming [1964] 1 W.L.R. 1028; [1964] 2 All E.R. 135; (1964) 108 S.J. 621, QBD *6–110*
Ng Chee Chong, Ng Weng Chong, Ng Cheng and Ng Yew (A Firm t/a Maran Road Saw Mill) v Austin Taylor & Co [1975] 1 Lloyd's Rep. 156, QBD (Comm) *21–074*
Nichimen Corp v Gatoil Overseas Inc [1987] 2 Lloyd's Rep. 46, CA (Civ Div) *3–082*, *12–037*, *22–042*, *24–003*, *24–008*
Nichol v Godts (1854) 10 Exch. 191 .... *14–027*
Nicholas v Thompson [1924] V.L.R. 554 .... *6–037*
Nichols, Ex p. *See* Jones Ex p. Nichols, Re
Nichols v Haywood (1545) Dyer 59 .... *25–026*
Nichols v Jessup (No.2) [1986] 1 N.Z.L.R. 237 .... *7–132*
Nichols v Marsland (1876–77) L.R. 2 Ex. D. 1, CA; affirming (1874–75) L.R. 10 Ex. 255, Ex Ct *14–146*
Nichols Advance Vehicle Systems Inc v De Angelis, unreported, 1979 .... *27–065*
Nicholson v Chapman (1793) 2 H. Bl. 254 .... *29–136*
Nicholson v Gooch (1856) 5 E. & B. 999 .... *16–192*
Nicholson v Revill, 111 E.R. 941; (1836) 4 Ad. & El. 675, KB *17–017*
Nicholson v Willan (1804) 5 East 507 .... *1–011*, *1–128*, *1–151*, *15–001*
Nicholson and Venn v Smith-Marriott (1947) 177 L.T. 189 5–034
Nickalls v Merry; sub nom. Merry v Nickalls (1874–75) L.R. 7 H.L. 530, HL; affirming (1871–72) L.R. 7 Ch. App. 733, CA in Chancery *8–038*
Nickoll & Knight v Ashton Edridge & Co [1901] 2 K.B. 126, CA *23–047*
Nicolene Ltd v Simmonds [1953] 1 Q.B. 543; [1953] 2 W.L.R. 717; [1953] 1 All E.R. 822; [1953] 1 Lloyd's Rep. 189; (1953) 97 S.J. 247, CA; affirming [1952] 2 Lloyd's Rep. 419, QBD 2–144, *5–071*, *12–077*
Nicoll v Cutts (1985) 1 B.C.C. 99427; [1985] P.C.C. 311, CA (Civ Div) *9–050*
Niell v Morley (1804) 9 Ves. 478 .... *8–068*
Nielsen Co v Waite, James Co (1885) 16 Q.B.D. 67 .... *21–022*
Nigel Upchurch Associates v Aldridge Estates Investment Co [1993] 1 Lloyd's Rep. 535, QBD *18–131*
Nigerian Universities Commission (London Branch) v Bastians [1995] I.C.R. 358, EAT *11–021*
Nike Information Systems Ltd v Avac Systems Ltd (1979) 105 D.L.R. (3d) 455 .... *30–007*, *30–311*
Nikko Hotels (UK) Ltd v MEPC Plc [1991] 2 E.G.L.R. 103; [1991] 28 E.G. 86, Ch D *16–047*
Nile Co for the Export of Agricultural Crops v H&JM Bennett (Commodities) Ltd [1986] 1 Lloyd's Rep. 555, QBD (Comm) *2–136*, *23–027*, *23–059*, *30–365*
Nile Rhapsody, The. *See* Hamed el Chiaty & Co (t/a Travco Nile Cruise Liner) v Thomas Cook Group

Niobe Maritime Corp v Tradax Ocean Transportation SA; The Niobe [1995] 1 Lloyd's Rep. 579; [1995] C.L.C. 371, HL; reversing [1994] 1 Lloyd's Rep. 487; [1994] C.L.C. 163, CA (Civ Div); reversing [1993] 2 Lloyd's Rep. 52, QBD (Comm) *12–055*
Nippon Yusen Kaisha v International Import and Export Co; The Elbe Maru [1978] 1 Lloyd's Rep. 206, QBD (Comm) *14–051*, *18–070*
Nippon Yusen Kaisha v Pacifica Navegacion SA; The Ion [1980] 2 Lloyd's Rep. 245, QBD (Comm) *3–033*, *3–086*, *3–097*, *3–101*, *3–104*
Nippon Yusen Kubishiki Kaisha v Golden Strait Corp; The Golden Victory [2003] EWHC 16; [2003] 2 Lloyd's Rep. 592 .... *12–055*
Niru Battery Manufacturing Co v Milestone Trading Ltd (No.1) [2003] EWCA Civ 1446; [2004] Q.B. 985; [2004] 2 W.L.R. 1415; [2004] 1 All E.R. (Comm) 193; [2004] 1 Lloyd's Rep. 344; [2004] 1 C.L.C. 647; [2004] W.T.L.R. 377; (2003) 100(44) L.S.G. 33, CA (Civ Div); affirming [2002] EWHC 1425 (Comm); [2002] 2 All E.R. (Comm) 705, QBD (Comm) 18–022
Niru Battery Manufacturing Co v Milestone Trading Ltd (No.2) [2004] EWCA Civ 487; [2004] 2 All E.R. (Comm) 289; [2004] 2 Lloyd's Rep. 319; [2004] 1 C.L.C. 882; (2004) 148 S.J.L.B. 538, CA (Civ Div) *29–099*, *29–102*, *29–121*, *29–173*, *29–179*, *29–182*, 29–183, *29–184*
Nissan v Attorney General. *See* Attorney General v Nissan
Nisshin Shipping Co Ltd v Cleaves & Co Ltd [2003] EWHC 2602 (Comm); [2004] 1 All E.R. (Comm) 481; [2004] 1 Lloyd's Rep. 38; [2003] 2 C.L.C. 1097; (2003) 153 N.L.J. 1705, QBD (Comm) *18–002*, *18–078*, *18–091*, *18–096*, *18–116*
Nissho Co Ltd v NG Livanos (1941) 69 Ll. L. Rep. 125, KBD *26–090*
Nissho Iwai Australia v Malaysian International Shipping Corp Bhd (1989) 86 A.L.R. 375, HC (Aus) *14–033*
Nissho Iwai Petroleum Co v Cargill International SA [1993] 1 Lloyd's Rep. 80, QBD (Comm) *2–138*, *13–011*, *13–012*
Nitrate Corp of Chile v Pansuiza Compania de Navegacion SA. *See* Chilean Nitrate Sales Corp v Marine Transportation Co Ltd
Nitrigin Eireann Teoranta v Inco Alloys Ltd [1992] 1 W.L.R. 498; [1992] 1 All E.R. 854; 60 B.L.R. 65; (1992) 89(3) L.S.G. 34; (1991) 141 N.L.J. 1518; [1991] N.P.C. 17, QBD *14–056*, *18–023*, *18–027*, *18–033*, *28–055*
Nittan (UK) v Solent Steel Fabrications [1981] 1 Lloyd's Rep. 633, CA (Civ Div) *12–075*
Nixon v Attorney General 127820 [1931] A.C. 184; 100 L.J. Ch. 70; 144 L.T. 249; 47 T.L.R. 95, HL; affirming [1930] 1 Ch. 566, CA 10–008
Nixon v Furphy (1925) 25 S.R. (N.S.W.) 151 .... *7–015*, *29–088*
Nixon v Loundes [1909] 2 Ir. Rep. 1 .... *25–015*
Nixon v Ward (1867) L.R. 2 Ex. 135 .... *4–056*, *22–033*
Njegos, The [1936] P. 90; (1935) 53 Ll. L. Rep. 286, PDAD *30–012*
Noble v Edwards (1877) 5 Ch. D. 378 .... *26–092*
Nocton v Lord Ashburton [1914] A.C. 932; [1914–15] All E.R. Rep. 45, HL *6–039*, 6–067, *6–078*, **6–079**, *6–080*, 7–101
Nokes v Doncaster Amalgamated Collieries Ltd; Donoghue v Doncaster Amalgamated Collieries Ltd [1940] A.C. 1014, HL; reversing [1939] 2 K.B. 578, CA; affirming [1939] 1 K.B. 70; [1938] W.N. 327, KBD *9–047*, *9–048*, *19–055*, *19–056*, *19–081*
Norden Steamship Co v Dempsey (1875–76) L.R. 1 C.P.D. 654, CPD *12–130*
Nordenfelt v Maxim Nordenfelt Guns & Ammunition Co Ltd; sub nom. Maxim Nordenfelt Guns & Ammunition Co v Nordenfelt [1894] A.C. 535, HL; affirming [1893] 1 Ch. 630, CA .. *16–004*, *16–090*, *16–091*, 16–092, *16–104*, *16–110*, 16–116, 16–117
Nordman v Rayner Sturges (1916) 33 T.L.R. 87 .... *23–039*
Norfolk, Ex p. (1815) 19 Ves. 455 .... *17–010*
Norfolk (Duke of) v Worthy (1808) 1 Camp. 337 .... *27–057*
Norfolk Railway Co v M'Namara (1849) 3 Exch. 628 .... *25–002*

Norglen Ltd (In Liquidation) v Reeds Rains Prudential Ltd; Mayhew-Lewis v Westminster Scaffolding Group Plc; Levy v ABN AMRO Bank NV; Circuit Systems Ltd (In Liquidation) v Zuken-Redac (UK) Ltd [1999] 2 A.C. 1; [1997] 3 W.L.R. 1177; [1998] 1 All E.R. 218; [1998] B.C.C. 44; [1998] 1 B.C.L.C. 176; 87 B.L.R. 1; (1997) 94(48) L.S.G. 29; (1997) 147 N.L.J. 1773; (1998) 142 S.J.L.B. 26; (1998) 75 P. & C.R. D21, HL; affirming [1996] 1 W.L.R. 864; [1996] 1 All E.R. 945; [1996] B.C.C. 532; [1996] 1 B.C.L.C. 690, CA (Civ Div); reversing [1994] E.G. 21 (C.S.), Ch D 16–063, *19–048*, *19–049*

Norman v Cole, 170 E.R. 606; (1800) 3 Esp. 253, KB *16–040*

Norman v Federal Commissioner of Taxation (1963) 109 C.L.R. 9 ...... 19–029, *19–033*

Norman v Ricketts (1886) 3 T.L.R. 182 .... *21–056*

Norman v Strains (1881) L.R. 6 P.D. 219, PDAD *8–062*

Normid Housing Association Ltd v Ralphs & Mansell (Third Party Rights: Mareva Injunction); sub nom. Normid Housing Association Ltd v R John Ralphs; Normid Housing Association Ltd v John S Mansell; Normid Housing Association Ltd v Assicurazioni Generali SpA [1989] 1 Lloyd's Rep. 265; 21 Con. L.R. 98; [1988] E.G. 108 (C.S.), CA (Civ Div) *3–014*, *18–131*

Norreys v Zeffert [1939] 2 All E.R. 187 .... *7–045*, *29–088*

Norseman, The. *See* Owners of the Norseman v British Transport Commission; The Norseman

Norseman, The. *See* Rederi A/S Norseman and Rederi A/S Norse Lady v British Transport Commission

Norsk Hydro ASA v State Property Fund of Ukraine [2002] EWHC 2120, QBD (Admin) *11–006*

North, Ex p. Hasluck, Re [1895] 2 Q.B. 264, CA *12–093*, *21–024*

North v Great Northern Railway (1860) 2 Giff. 64 .... *27–014*

North v Loomes [1919] 1 Ch. 378, Ch D *4–026*, *4–036*, *22–046*

North v Wakefield (1849) 13 Q.B. 536 .... *17–017*, *17–018*

North v Walthamstow UDC (1898) 62 J.P. 836 .... *29–092*, *29–096*

North Atlantic Insurance Co Ltd v Bishopsgate Insurance Ltd [1998] 1 Lloyd's Rep. 459, QBD (Comm) *28–049*

North British & Mercantile Insurance Co v London Liverpool & Globe Insurance Co (1877) L.R. 5 Ch. D. 569, CA *29–128*

North British Insurance Co v Lloyd (1854) 10 Ex. 523 .... *6–159*

North British Railway Co v Budhill Coal & Sandstone Co [1910] A.C. 116; 1910 S.C. (H.L.) 1; 1909 2 S.L.T. 331, HL; reversing in part, 1909 S.C. 504; 1909 1 S.L.T. 121, IH (2 Div) *12–060*

North Central Wagon and Finance Co v Graham *See* North General Wagon and Finance Co v Graham

North Central Wagon Finance Co v Brailsford [1962] 1 W.L.R. 1288; [1962] 1 All E.R. 502; (1962) 106 S.J. 878, Assizes (Nottingham) *29–076*

North Eastern Ry v Hastings [1900] A.C. 260 .... 12–063, *12–126*

North General Wagon and Finance Co Ltd v Graham [1950] 2 K.B. 7; [1950] 1 All E.R. 780; 66 T.L.R. (Pt. 1) 707, CA *14–034*

North Ocean Shipping Co v Hyundai Construction Co; The Atlantic Baron [1979] Q.B. 705; [1979] 3 W.L.R. 419; [1978] 3 All E.R. 1170; [1979] 1 Lloyd's Rep. 89; (1979) 123 S.J. 352, QBD (Comm) ..... *3–066*, *3–067*, *3–069*, *3–070*, *7–005*, *7–012*, *7–013*, 7–015, *7–031*, 7–041 , *7–053*, *7–054*, 7–055, *22–035*, *29–088*, *29–094*

North Sea Energy Holdings NV v Petroleum Authority of Thailand [1999] 1 All E.R. (Comm.) 173; [1999] 1 Lloyd's Rep. 483, CA (Civ Div); affirming [1997] 2 Lloyd's Rep. 418, QBD (Comm) *2–152*, *2–154*, *12–028*, *13–011*, *26–044*, *26–066*

North Staffordshire Railway Co v Edge [1920] A.C. 254; (1919) 1 Ll. L. Rep. 523, HL *29–097*

North Sydney Investment & Tramway Co Ltd (In Liquidation) v Higgins [1899] A.C. 263, PC (Aus) *9–014*, *21–039*

North West Leicestershire DC v East Midlands Housing Association [1981] 1 W.L.R. 1396; [1981] 3 All E.R. 364; 80 L.G.R. 84; (1981) 125 S.J. 513, CA (Civ Div) *2–032*
North West Metropolitan Regional Hospital Board v TA Bickerton & Son; sub nom. Bickerton & Son v North West Metropolitan Regional Hospital Board [1970] 1 W.L.R. 607; [1970] 1 All E.R. 1039; 68 L.G.R. 447; (1970) 114 S.J. 243, HL; affirming [1969] 1 All E.R. 977; 67 L.G.R. 83; (1968) 112 S.J. 922, CA (Civ Div) *12–070*
North West Transportation Co Ltd v Beatty (1887) L.R. 12 App. Cas. 589, PC (Can) *9–055*
North West Water Authority v Binnie [1990] 3 All E.R. 547; 30 Con. L.R. 136, QBD *25–012*, *25–013*
North Western Ry Co v M'Michael (1850) 5 Exch. 114 ....8–030, *8–032*, *8–037*, *8–040*
North Western Salt Co Ltd v Electrolytic Alkali Co Ltd [1914] A.C. 461, HL; reversing [1913] 3 K.B. 422, CA *16–095*, *16–097*, *16–205*
Northcote v Owners of the Henrich Bjorn (1886) L.R. 11 App. Cas. 270, HL *25–019*
Northern & Shell Plc v John Laing Construction Ltd [2003] EWCA Civ 1035; 90 Con. L.R. 26; (2003) 147 S.J.L.B. 902; [2003] N.P.C. 91, CA (Civ Div); affirming [2002] EWHC 2258 (TCC); 85 Con. L.R. 179, QBD (TCC) *12–110*
Northern Bank Finance Corp Ltd v Charlton [1979] E.C.C. 7; [1979] I.R. 149, Sup Ct (Irl) 6–112
Northern Bank Ltd v Laverty [2001] N.I. 315, Ch D (NI) *1–114*
Northern Construction Co v Gloge Heating and Plumbing [1986] 2 W.W.R. 649; (1984) 1 Const. L.J. 144, CA (Alta) *3–173*
Northern Counties Securities, Ltd v Jackson & Steeple, Ltd [1974] 1 W.L.R. 1133; [1974] 2 All E.R. 625; (1974) 118 S.J. 498, Ch D *9–030*
Northern Developments (Cumbria) Ltd v J&J Nichol [2000] B.L.R. 158; (2000) 2 T.C.L.R. 261, QBD (TCC) *24–048*
Northern Foods Plc v Focal Foods Ltd [2003] 2 Lloyd's Rep. 728, QBD (Merc) ...*24–015*, *24–040*, *24–042*
Northern Ireland Human Rights Commission, Re [2002] UKHL 25; [2002] N.I. 236; [2002] H.R.L.R. 35; [2002] A.C.D. 95, HL (NI) *10–024*
Northland Airliners v Dennis Ferranti Meters (1970) 114 S.J. 845, CA (Civ Div) *2–032*
Northside Developments Pty v Registrar-General (1990) 64 A.L.J.R. 427 ....*9–040*, 9–045
Northumberland Ave Hotel Co, Re (1886) L.R. 33 Ch. D. 16, CA *9–014*
Norton v Ellam (1837) 2 M. & W. 461 .... *21–084*, *21–090*, *28–042*
Norton v Relly (1764) 2 Eden. 286 .... *7–064*
Norway (Owners of), The v Ashburner; The Norway. *See* Owners of the Norway v Ashburner; The Norway
Norway's Application (Nos.1 and 2), Re [1990] 1 A.C. 723; [1989] 2 W.L.R. 458; [1989] 1 All E.R. 745; (1989) 133 S.J. 290, HL *25–011*
Norweb Plc v Dixon [1995] 1 W.L.R. 636; [1995] 3 All E.R. 952, DC *1–015*, *15–035*
Norwegian American Cruises A/S v Paul Mundy Ltd; The Vistafjord [1988] 2 Lloyd's Rep. 343, CA (Civ Div) *3–107*, 3–108, *3–109*, *3–110*, *3–111*, 3–113
Norwest Holst Group Administration Ltd v Harrison; sub nom. Harrison v Norwest Holst Group Administration Ltd [1985] I.C.R. 668; [1985] I.R.L.R. 240; (1985) 82 L.S.G. 1410, CA (Civ Div) *24–003*, *24–013*
Norwich City Council v Harvey (Paul Clarke) [1989] 1 W.L.R. 828; [1989] 1 All E.R. 1180; 45 B.L.R. 14; (1989) 5 Const. L.J. 154; (1989) 86(25) L.S.G. 45; (1989) 139 N.L.J. 40; (1989) 133 S.J. 694, CA (Civ Div); affirming, 39 B.L.R. 75; (1988) 4 Const. L.J. 217, QBD *1–183*, 1–187, *14–011*, *14–052*, *14–056*, *18–030*
Norwich City Council v Stringer (2001) 33 H.L.R. 15; (2000) 2 L.G.L.R. 1102, CA (Civ Div) *29–034*, *29–084*
Norwich Provident Insurance Society, Re; sub nom. Bath's Case (1878) L.R. 8 Ch. D. 334, CA *9–022*
Norwich Union Fire Insurance Society Ltd v WMH Price Ltd; sub nom. Norwich Union Fire Insurance Society Ltd v William Price Ltd [1934] A.C. 455; (1934) 49 Ll. L. Rep. 55, PC (Aus) 29–033, *29–043*

Norwich Union Life Insurance Co Ltd v Qureshi; Aldrich v Norwich Union Life Insurance Co Ltd [1999] 2 All E.R. (Comm) 707; [1999] C.L.C. 1963; [2000] Lloyd's Rep. I.R. 1, CA (Civ Div); affirming [1998] C.L.C. 1605; [1999] Lloyd's Rep. I.R. 263, QBD (Comm) ... *6–090*
Norwood v Grype (1599) Cro. Eliz. 727 ... *25–001*
Notcutt v Universal Equipment Co (London) [1986] 1 W.L.R. 641; [1986] 3 All E.R. 582; [1986] I.C.R. 414; [1986] I.R.L.R. 218; (1986) 83 L.S.G. 1314; (1986) 136 N.L.J. 393; (1986) 130 S.J. 392, CA (Civ Div) ... *23–008*, 23–038
Nott and Cardiff Corp, Re. *See* Brodie v Cardiff Corp
Nottidge v Prince (1860) 2 Giff. 246 ... *7–064*
Nottingham Building Society v Eurodynamics Systems Plc [1995] F.S.R. 605, CA (Civ Div) ... *24–018*, *24–019*
Nottingham Permanent Benefit Building Society v Thurstan; sub nom. Thurstan v Nottingham Permanent Benefit Building Society; Thurston v Nottingham Permanent Benefit Building Society [1903] A.C. 6, HL; affirming [1902] 1 Ch. 1, CA; reversing in part [1901] 1 Ch. 88, Ch D ... *8–033*, *8–066*, *29–173*
Nouvion v Freeman; sub nom. Henderson, Re; Henderson's Estate, Re (1890) L.R. 15 App. Cas. 1, HL ... *25–017*
Novorossisk Shipping Co of the USSR v Neopetro Co Ltd; The Ulyanovsk [1990] 1 Lloyd's Rep. 425, QBD (Comm) ... *13–018*
Noyes v Crawley (1878–79) L.R. 10 Ch. D. 31, Ch D ... *28–057*
Nugent v Smith (1875–76) L.R. 1 C.P.D. 423, CA; reversing (1875–76) L.R. 1 C.P.D. 19, CPD ... *14–146*, *14–148*
Nuneaton Borough Association Football Club Ltd (No.1), Re (1989) 5 B.C.C. 792; [1989] B.C.L.C. 454, Ch D (Companies Ct) ... *9–060*
Nunn v Dalrymple (1989) 21 H.L.R. 569; (1990) 59 P. & C.R. 231; [1990] Fam. Law 65, CA (Civ Div) ... *2–172*
Nunn v Fabian (1865–66) L.R. 1 Ch. App. 35, Lord Chancellor ... *4–048*
Nurdin & Peacock Plc v DB Ramsden & Co Ltd [1999] 1 W.L.R. 1249; [1999] 1 All E.R. 941; [1999] 1 E.G.L.R. 15; [1999] 09 E.G. 175; [1999] 10 E.G. 183; [1999] E.G. 19 (C.S.); (1999) 96(8) L.S.G. 29; (1999) 149 N.L.J. 251; [1999] N.P.C. 17, Ch D ... *29–032*, *29–034*, *29–046*
Nutbrown v Thornton (1804) 10 Ves. 159 ... *27–014*
Nutt v Read (2000) 32 H.L.R. 761; (1999) 96(42) L.S.G. 44, CA (Civ Div) ... *5–058*
Nutting v Baldwin [1995] 1 W.L.R. 201; [1995] 2 All E.R. 321, Ch D ... *18–010*, *26–138*
Nwakobi v Nzekwu [1964] 1 W.L.R. 1019; (1964) 108 S.J. 518, PC (Nig) ... *28–138*
Nweze v Nwoko [2004] EWCA Civ 379; [2004] 2 P. & C.R. 33; (2004) 101(17) L.S.G. 30; (2004) 148 S.J.L.B. 472; [2004] N.P.C. 50; [2004] 2 P. & C.R. DG1, CA (Civ Div) ... 4–064, *4–072*
Nyberg v Handelaar [1892] 2 Q.B. 202, CA ... *14–034*
Nye v Moseley (1826) 6 B. & C. 136 ... *16–067*
Nykredit Mortgage Bank Plc v Edward Erdman Group Ltd (Interest on Damages) [1997] 1 W.L.R. 1627; [1998] 1 All E.R. 305; [1998] Lloyd's Rep. Bank. 39; [1998] C.L.C. 116; [1998] 1 Costs L.R. 108; [1998] P.N.L.R. 197; [1998] 1 E.G.L.R. 99; [1998] 05 E.G. 150; (1998) 95(1) L.S.G. 24; (1998) 142 S.J.L.B. 29; [1997] N.P.C. 165; (1998) 75 P. & C.R. D28, HL ... *26–094*, 26–095
OBG Ltd v Allan; sub nom. OBG Ltd v Allen; Douglas v Hello! Ltd; Mainstream Properties Ltd v Young [2007] UKHL 21; [2008] 1 A.C. 1; [2007] 2 W.L.R. 920; [2007] Bus. L.R. 1600; [2007] 4 All E.R. 545; [2008] 1 All E.R. (Comm) 1; [2007] I.R.L.R. 608; [2007] E.M.L.R. 12; [2007] B.P.I.R. 746; (2007) 30(6) I.P.D. 30037; [2007] 19 E.G. 165 (C.S.); (2007) 151 S.J.L.B. 674; [2007] N.P.C. 54, HL; affirming [2005] EWCA Civ 106; [2005] Q.B. 762; [2005] 2 W.L.R. 1174; [2005] 2 All E.R. 602; [2005] 1 All E.R. (Comm) 639; [2005] 1 B.C.L.C. 711; [2005] B.L.R. 245; [2005] B.P.I.R. 928; [2005] P.N.L.R. 27; (2005) 102(14) L.S.G. 27, CA (Civ Div) .. *1–135*, *1–145*, *1–147*, *1–171*, *1–172*, *1–173*, *1–191*, *9–052*, *15–127*, *18–031*, *18–041*, 18–135, 18–141, *18–145*, *29–170*
OEM Plc v Schneider [2005] EWHC 1072, Ch D ... *29–159*, *29–174*
OT Africa Line Ltd v Vickers Plc [1996] 1 Lloyd's Rep. 700; [1996] C.L.C. 722, QBD (Comm) ... *2–003*, *2–004*, 5–075, *30–214*, *30–331*

OTM v Hydranautics [1981] 2 Lloyd's Rep. 211, QBD (Comm) *2–027*, *2–028*, *2–033*, *2–036*, *2–092*
OTV Birwelco Ltd v Technical & General Guarantee Co Ltd [2002] EWHC 2240; [2002] 4 All E.R. 668; [2002] 2 All E.R. (Comm) 1116; [2002] 2 B.C.L.C. 723; 84 Con. L.R. 117; (2002) 152 N.L.J. 1530, QBD (TCC) *1–091*, *1–112*, *12–122*, *18–125*
Oakacre Ltd v Claire Cleaners (Holdings) Ltd [1982] Ch. 197; [1981] 3 W.L.R. 761; [1981] 3 All E.R. 667; (1982) 43 P. & C.R. 48, Ch D *27–078*, *27–081*
Oakdale (Richmond) Ltd v National Westminster Bank Plc [1997] 3 C.M.L.R. 815, CA (Civ Div); affirming [1996] B.C.C. 919; [1997] 1 B.C.L.C. 63; [1997] E.C.C. 130; [1997] Eu. L.R. 27; (1996) 15 Tr. L.R. 541, Ch D *19–043*
Oakdown Ltd v Bernstein & Co (1985) 49 P. & C.R. 282, Ch D *21–014*
Oakes v Hopcroft [2000] Lloyd's Rep. Med. 394; (2000) 56 B.M.L.R. 136; [2000] Lloyd's Rep. P.N. 946, CA (Civ Div) *28–011*
Oakes v Turquand (1867) L.R. 2 H.L. 325 ...... *6–017*, *6–117*, *6–127*, *9–040*, *9–041*, *9–060*
Oakley v Ultra Vehicle Design Ltd (In Liquidation); sub nom. Ultra Motorhomes International Ltd, Re [2005] EWHC 872; [2006] B.C.C. 57; [2005] I.L.Pr. 55; [2006] B.P.I.R. 115, Ch D *30–050*
Oakwell, The. *See* Galaxy Energy International Ltd v Assuranceforeningen Skuld (Ejensidie)
Oasis Merchandising Services Ltd (In Liquidation), Re; sub nom. Ward v Aitken [1998] Ch. 170; [1997] 2 W.L.R. 764; [1996] 1 All E.R. 1009; [1997] B.C.C. 282; [1997] 1 B.C.L.C. 689; (1996) 146 N.L.J. 1513, CA (Civ Div); affirming [1995] B.C.C. 911; [1995] 2 B.C.L.C. 493, Ch D *16–063*, *19–049*
Oates v Hudson (1851) 6 Ex. 346 ....*29–090*, *29–093*, *29–182*
Oatway, Re; sub nom. Hertslet v Oatway [1903] 2 Ch. 356, Ch D *29–166*
Obestain Inc v National Mineral Development Corp Ltd; The Sanix Ace [1987] 1 Lloyd's Rep. 465, QBD (Comm) *18–052*
O'Brien v Associated Fire Alarms [1968] 1 W.L.R. 1916; [1969] 1 All E.R. 93; 3 K.I.R. 223; (1968) 112 S.J. 232, CA (Civ Div) *13–003*
O'Brien v MGN Ltd [2001] EWCA Civ 1279; [2002] C.L.C. 33, CA (Civ Div) ... *12–014*
O'Brien v Robinson [1973] A.C. 912; [1973] 2 W.L.R. 393; [1973] 1 All E.R. 583; (1984) 13 H.L.R. 7; (1973) 25 P. & C.R. 239; (1973) 117 S.J. 187, HL *21–009*
O'Brien Homes Ltd V Lane. *See* Lane v O'Brien Homes Ltd
O'Brien (Inspector of Taxes) v Benson's Hosiery (Holdings) Ltd [1980] A.C. 562; [1979] 3 W.L.R. 572; [1979] 3 All E.R. 652; [1979] S.T.C. 735; 53 T.C. 241; [1979] T.R. 335; (1979) 123 S.J. 752, HL; reversing [1979] Ch. 152; [1978] 3 W.L.R. 609; [1978] 3 All E.R. 1057; [1978] S.T.C. 549; [1978] T.R. 147; (1978) 122 S.J. 439, CA (Civ Div); reversing [1977] Ch. 348; [1977] 3 W.L.R. 206; [1977] 3 All E.R. 352; [1977] S.T.C. 262; (1977) 121 S.J. 376, Ch D *19–055*, *26–166*
O'Byrne v Aventis Pasteur MSD Ltd; sub nom. O'Byrne v Aventis Pasteur SA [2008] UKHL 34; [2008] C.P. Rep. 2; [2008] Eu. L.R. 227; [2008] P.I.Q.R. P3; (2007) 98 B.M.L.R. 160; (2007) 104(41) L.S.G. 27, CA (Civ Div) *28–118*, *28–119*
Occidental Worldwide Investment Corp v Skibs A/S Avanti; The Siboen and The Sibotre [1976] 1 Lloyd's Rep. 293, QBD (Comm) *3–050*, *6–048*, *6–106*, *7–005*, *7–012*, *7–013*, 7–014, 7–021, *7–029*, 7–038, *7–041*, *29–088*, *29–151*
Ocean Chemical Transport Inc v Exnor Craggs Ltd [2000] 1 All E.R. (Comm) 519; [2000] 1 Lloyd's Rep. 446, CA (Civ Div) *12–002*, *12–014*, *12–015*, *14–010*, *30–008*, *30–068*, *30–309*
Ocean Marine Navigation Ltd v Koch Carbon Inc; The Dynamic [2003] EWHC 1936 (Comm); [2003] 2 Lloyd's Rep. 693, QBD (Comm) *28–010*
Ocean Steamship Co v Queensland State Wheat Board [1941] 1 K.B. 402; (1940) 68 Ll. L. Rep. 136, CA *30–009*

Ocean Tramp Tankers Corp v V/O Sovfracht; The Eugenia [1964] 2 Q.B. 226; [1964] 2 W.L.R. 114; [1964] 1 All E.R. 161; [1963] 2 Lloyd's Rep. 381; (1963) 107 S.J. 931, CA *23–008*, 23–044, *23–048*, *23–059*, *23–061*, *23–098*, *24–033*, *29–076*
Oceangas (Gibraltar) v Port of London Authority; The Cavendish [1993] 2 Lloyd's Rep. 292; (1993) 137 S.J.L.B. 159, QBD (Admlty) *1–015*
Oceanic Sun Line Special Shipping Co v Fay (1988) 165 C.L.R. 197, HC (Aus) *2–021*, *30–305*
Oceanografia SA de CV v DSND Subsea AS; The Botnica [2006] EWHC 1360; [2007] 1 All E.R. (Comm) 28; [2007] 1 Lloyd's Rep. 37, QBD (Comm) *2–068*, *2–116*, *3–081*, *3–098*
Ockford v Barelli (1871) 20 W.R. 116 .... *3–052*
O'Connor v BDB Kirby & Co; sub nom. O'Connor v DBD Kirby & Co [1972] 1 Q.B. 90; [1971] 2 W.L.R. 1233; [1971] 2 All E.R. 1415; [1971] 1 Lloyd's Rep. 454; [1971] R.T.R. 440; (1971) 115 S.J. 267, CA (Civ Div) *26–037*
O'Connor v Hume [1954] 1 W.L.R. 824; [1954] 2 All E.R. 301; (1954) 98 S.J. 370, CA *12–096*
O'Connor v Issacs [1956] 2 Q.B. 288; [1956] 3 W.L.R. 172; [1956] 2 All E.R. 417; (1956) 120 J.P. 325; (1956) 100 S.J. 432, CA; affirming [1956] 2 W.L.R. 585; [1956] 1 All E.R. 513; (1956) 120 J.P. 169; (1956) 100 S.J. 171, QBD *28–061*, *29–098*
Ocular Sciences Ltd v Aspect Vision Care Ltd (No.2) [1997] R.P.C. 289; (1997) 20(3) I.P.D. 20022, Ch D (Patents Ct) *21–015*, *21–017*
Oddy v Phoenix Assurance Co [1966] 1 Lloyd's Rep. 134; (1966) 116 N.L.J. 554, Assizes (Cornwall) *14–146*
O'Dea v Allstates Leasing Systems (WA) Party Ltd (1983) 152 C.L.R. 359 ..... *26–140*
Odessa Tramways Co v Mendel (1878) L.R. 8 Ch. D. 235, CA *27–011*, *27–044*
Odfjell Seachem A/S v Continentale des Petroles et d'Investissements; sub nom. Odfjfell Seachem A/S v Continentale des Petroles et d'Investissements [2004] EWHC 2929; [2005] 1 All E.R. (Comm) 421; [2005] 1 Lloyd's Rep. 275, QBD (Comm) *24–051*
Oelkers v Ellis [1914] 2 K.B. 139, KBD *6–127*, *28–135*, *28–140*
Offer-Hoar v Larkstore Ltd; sub nom. Larkstore Ltd v Technotrade Ltd; Technotrade Ltd v Larkstore Ltd [2006] EWCA Civ 1079; [2006] 1 W.L.R. 2926; [2007] 1 All E.R. (Comm) 104; [2006] B.L.R. 345; 109 Con. L.R. 92; [2006] P.N.L.R. 37; [2006] 3 E.G.L.R. 5; [2006] 42 E.G. 246; [2006] C.I.L.L. 2389; [2006] 31 E.G. 89 (C.S.); (2006) 103(32) L.S.G. 20; [2006] N.P.C. 96, CA (Civ Div); affirming [2005] EWHC 2742 (TCC); [2006] P.N.L.R. 17; [2005] 50 E.G. 90 (C.S.), QBD (TCC) *16–061*, 18–057, 18–062, 19–075
Office Angels v Rainer-Thomas [1991] I.R.L.R. 214, CA (Civ Div); reversing, *Independent*, February 4, 1991, QBD *16–083*, *16–092*, *16–094*, *16–108*, *16–113*
Office of Fair Trading v Abbey National Plc [2008] EWHC 875 (Comm); (2008) 105(18) L.S.G. 23; (2008) 158 N.L.J. 633; (2008) 152(18) S.J.L.B. 28, QBD (Comm) *15–009*, *15–014*, *15–031*, *15–043*, 15–052, *15–054*, 15–058, **15–059**, *15–060*, 15–063, *15–098*, *15–110*, *15–112*, *15–130*, *15–134*
Office of Fair Trading v Lloyds TSB Bank Plc [2007] UKHL 48; [2008] 1 A.C. 316; [2007] 3 W.L.R. 733; [2008] Bus. L.R. 450; [2008] 1 All E.R. 205; [2008] 1 All E.R. (Comm) 113; [2008] 1 Lloyd's Rep. 30; (2007) 104(44) L.S.G. 31; (2007) 157 N.L.J. 1614; (2007) 151 S.J.L.B. 1432, HL *30–008*, *30–065*, *30–068*, *30–084*, *30–101*
Office of Fair Trading v MB Designs (Scotland) Ltd, 2005 S.L.T. 691; 2005 S.C.L.R. 894; 2005 G.W.D. *22–393*, OH *15–012*, *15–105*, *15–138*, *15–139*
Official Custodian for Charities v Mackey (No.2) [1985] 1 W.L.R. 1308; [1985] 2 All E.R. 1016; (1986) 51 P. & C.R. 143; [1985] 1 E.G.L.R. 46; (1985) 274 E.G. 398; (1985) 129 S.J. 853, Ch D *29–026*
Offley v Clay (1840) 2 M.G. 172 .... *21–043*
Offord v Davies (1862) 12 C.B. (N.S.) 748 ....*2–081*, *2–085*, *2–088*, *3–010*

Offshore International SA v Banco Central SA; sub nom. Offshore International SA v Banco Central SA and Hijos de J Barreras SA [1977] 1 W.L.R. 399; [1976] 3 All E.R. 749; [1976] 2 Lloyd's Rep. 402; (1977) 121 S.J. 252, QBD (Comm) *30–012*, *30–091*
Ogden v Peele (1826) 8 Dow. & Ry. 1 .... *16–026*
Ogden v Trustees of the RHS Griffiths 2003 Settlement [2008] EWHC 118 (Ch); [2008] 2 All E.R. 655; [2008] S.T.C. 776; [2008] S.T.I. 250, Ch D (Birmingham) *29–043*
Ogdens v Weinberg (1906) 95 L.T. 567 .... *19–049*
Ogdens Ltd v Nelson; Ogdens Ltd v Telford [1905] A.C. 109, HL; affirming [1904] 2 K.B. 410, CA; affirming [1903] 2 K.B. 287, KBD *13–012*, *24–028*
Ogilvie Builders Ltd v Glasgow DC, 1995 S.L.T. 15; 1994 S.C.L.R. 546, OH *26–054*
Ogilvie v Foljambe (1817) 3 Mer. 53 .... *12–123*
Ogilvy v Hope Davies [1976] 1 All E.R. 683; (1976) 31 P. & C.R. 268; (1975) 119 S.J. 826, Ch D *3–097*, *3–103*, *3–104*
Ogilvy & Mather Ltd v Silverado Blue Ltd (formerly Oktobor Ltd) [2007] EWHC 1285 (QB); [2007] All E.R. (D) 383 (May), QBD *22–025*
Ogle v Earl Vane (1867–68) L.R. 3 Q.B. 272, Ex Chamber; affirming (1866–67) L.R. 2 Q.B. 275, QB *22–042*, *26–064*
Ogwr BC v Dykes [1989] 1 W.L.R. 295; [1989] 2 All E.R. 880; (1989) 21 H.L.R. 274; (1989) 58 P. & C.R. 32; (1989) 86(1) L.S.G. 39; (1988) 132 S.J. 1699, CA (Civ Div) *2–161*
O'Hanlan v Great Western Railway (1865) 6 B.S. 484 .... *26–089*
Okura & Co v Navara Shipping Corp SA [1982] 2 Lloyd's Rep. 537, CA (Civ Div); affirming [1981] 1 Lloyd's Rep. 561, QBD (Comm) *2–116*
Okura & Co Ltd v Forsbacka Jernverks AB [1914] 1 K.B. 715, CA *30–081*
Oldershaw v Holt (1840) 12 A.E. 590 .... *26–092*
Oldershaw v King (1857) 2 H. & N. 517 .... *3–047*
Oldfields Ashphalts v Govedale Coolstores (1994) Ltd [1998] 3 N.Z.L.R. 479 .... *5–047*
Olearia Tirrena SpA v NV Algemeene Oliehandel; The Osterbek [1973] 2 Lloyd's Rep. 86, CA (Civ Div); affirming [1972] 2 Lloyd's Rep. 341, QBD (Comm) *12–037*
Olins v Walters [2007] EWHC 3060; affirmed on other grounds [2008] EWCA Civ 782 .... *4–063*
Olivebank A/S v Dansk Svovlsyre Fabrik; sub nom. Aktieselskabet Olivebank v Danck Svovlsyre Fabrik [1919] 2 K.B. 162; 120 L.T. 629; 14 Asp. 426; 88 L.J.K.B. 745; 24 Com. Cas. 178, CA; affirming [1919] 1 K.B. 388, KBD *13–006*
Oliver v Davis [1949] 2 K.B. 727; [1949] 2 All E.R. 353; [1949] L.J.R. 1661; (1949) 93 S.J. 562, CA *3–047*, *21–073*
Oliver v Hunting (1890) L.R. 44 Ch. D. 205, Ch D *4–028*, *4–029*
Oliver v Nautilus Steam Shipping Co Ltd [1903] 2 K.B. 639, CA *21–058*
Oliver Ashworth (Holdings) Ltd v Ballard (Kent) Ltd. *See* Ballard (Kent) Ltd v Oliver Ashworth (Holdings) Ltd
Olley v Fisher (1887) L.R. 34 Ch. D. 367, Ch D *5–124*, *12–112*
Olley v Marlborough Court Ltd [1949] 1 K.B. 532; [1949] 1 All E.R. 127; 65 T.L.R. 95; 9 A.L.R.2d 806; [1949] L.J.R. 360; (1949) 93 S.J. 40, CA; affirming [1948] 1 All E.R. 955, KBD 12–010, *12–017*, *14–013*
Olliver v Woodroffe (1839) 4 M. & W. 650 .... *8–058*
Olsson v Dyson (1969) 120 C.L.R. 365; 43 A.L.J.R. 77, HC (Aus) *19–033*, *19–036*, *19–037*, *19–088*
Olympia & York Canary Wharf Ltd (No.2), Re; sub nom. Bear Stearns International Ltd v Adamson [1993] B.C.C. 159, Ch D (Companies Ct) *12–037*, *12–038*, *21–011*, *21–014*, *21–017*, *24–018*
Olympia Sauna Shipping Co SA v Shinwa Kaiun Kaisha Ltd; The Ypatia Halloussi [1985] 2 Lloyd's Rep. 364, QBD (Comm) *5–108*, *5–116*
Omar v El-Wakil; sub nom. Omar v Wakil [2001] EWCA Civ 1090; [2002] 2 P. & C.R. 3; (2001) 98(30) L.S.G. 40; [2001] N.P.C. 114, CA (Civ Div) *26–152*
O'Mealey v Wilson (1808) 1 Camp. 482 .... *11–024*
Omerri v Uganda High Commission [1973] I.T.R. 14, NIRC *11–009*
Omnium d'Enterprises v Sutherland [1919] 1 K.B. 618, CA *24–030*

Omnium Electric Palaces Ltd v Baines [1914] 1 Ch. 332, CA *9–054*
On Demand Information Plc (In Administrative Receivership) v Michael Gerson (Finance) Plc [2002] UKHL 13; [2003] 1 A.C. 368; [2002] 2 W.L.R. 919; [2002] 2 All E.R. 949; [2002] 1 All E.R. (Comm) 641; [2002] B.C.C. 673; [2002] C.L.C. 1140; (2002) 99(21) L.S.G. 31; (2002) 146 S.J.L.B. 110, HL; reversing [2001] 1 W.L.R. 155; [2000] 4 All E.R. 734; [2000] 2 All E.R. (Comm) 513; [2002] B.C.C. 122; (2000) 150 N.L.J. 1300, CA (Civ Div); affirming [1999] 2 All E.R. 811; [1999] 1 All E.R. (Comm.) 512; [2000] B.C.C. 289, Ch D *22–047*, *26–148*, *26–150*
O'Neil v Armstrong Mitchell & Co [1895] 2 Q.B. 418, CA; affirming [1895] 2 Q.B. 70, QBD *3–071*, *24–028*, *24–048*
O'Neill v Phillips; sub nom. Company (No.000709 of 1992), Re; Pectel Ltd, Re [1999] 1 W.L.R. 1092; [1999] 2 All E.R. 961; [1999] B.C.C. 600; [1999] 2 B.C.L.C. 1; (1999) 96(23) L.S.G. 33; (1999) 149 N.L.J. 805, HL; affirming [1998] B.C.C. 405; [1997] 2 B.C.L.C. 739, CA (Civ Div) *1–023*, *1–027*
Onslow Ex p. Kibble, Re (1874–75) L.R. 10 Ch. App. 373, CA in Chancery *20–049*
Onward Building Society v Smithson [1893] 1 Ch. 1, CA *1–112*
Oom v Bruce (1810) 12 East 225 16–187
Opera Ltd, Re [1891] 3 Ch. 260, CA; reversing [1891] 2 Ch. 154, Ch D *9–049*, *29–043*
Oppenheimer v Cattermole (Inspector of Taxes); sub nom. Nothman v Cooper [1976] A.C. 249; [1975] 2 W.L.R. 347; [1975] 1 All E.R. 538; [1975] S.T.C. 91; 50 T.C. 159; [1975] T.R. 13; (1975) 119 S.J. 169, HL; affirming [1973] Ch. 264; [1972] 3 W.L.R. 815; [1972] 3 All E.R. 1106; (1972) 116 S.J. 802, CA (Civ Div); reversing [1972] Ch. 585; [1972] 2 W.L.R. 1045; [1972] 2 All E.R. 529; [1971] T.R. 507; (1971) 116 S.J. 256, Ch D *12–036*, *30–070*, *30–366*
Opthalmic Innovations International (United Kingdom) Ltd v Opthalmic Innovations International Inc [2004] EWHC 2948 ....*30–020*, *30–075*, *30–077*, *30–090*
Orakpo v Manson Investments Ltd [1978] A.C. 95; [1977] 3 W.L.R. 229; (1978) 35 P. & C.R. 1; (1977) 121 S.J. 632, HL; affirming [1977] 1 W.L.R. 347; [1977] 1 All E.R. 666; (1977) 121 S.J. 256, CA (Civ Div) *8–020*, *9–025*, *29–008*, *29–009*, *29–011*, *29–079*, *29–173*
Oram v Hutt [1914] 1 Ch. 98, CA; affirming [1913] 1 Ch. 259, Ch D *16–052*
Orchis, The (1890) L.R. 15 P.D. 38, CA *29–103*
Ord v Upton [2000] Ch. 352; [2000] 2 W.L.R. 755; [2000] 1 All E.R. 193; [2000] B.P.I.R. 104; [2000] P.I.Q.R. Q150; (2000) 97(1) L.S.G. 22; (1999) 149 N.L.J. 1904; (2000) 144 S.J.L.B. 35, CA (Civ Div); affirming [1999] B.P.I.R. 775, Ch D *20–034*
O'Reilly v Mackman [1983] 2 A.C. 237; [1982] 3 W.L.R. 1096; 126 S.J. 820; [1982] 3 All E.R. 1124, HL; affirming [1982] 3 W.L.R. 604; [1982] 3 All E.R. 680 ....*1–193*, 1–194, 1–196
Oresundsvarvet AB v Lemos; The Angelic Star [1988] 1 Lloyd's Rep. 122; [1988] 1 F.T.L.R. 94, CA (Civ Div) *26–140*
Oriel, Re [1984] B.C.L.C. 241 .... *19–066*
Orient Overseas Management and Finance Ltd v File Shipping Co Ltd; The Energy Progress [1993] 1 Lloyd's Rep. 355, QBD (Comm) *2–156*
Orient Steam Navigation Co Ltd v King, The (1925) 21 Ll. L. Rep. 301, KBD *10–039*
Oriental Bank Corp Ex p. Guillemin, Re (1885) L.R. 28 Ch. D. 634, Ch D *9–049*
Oriental Bank Corp, Re; sub nom. MacDowall's Case (1886) L.R. 32 Ch. D. 366, Ch D *9–047*
Oriental Inland Steam Co Ex p. Scinde Railway Co, Re (1873–74) L.R. 9 Ch. App. 557, CA in Chancery *9–047*
Oriental Inland Steam Co Ltd v Briggs (1861) 4 De G.F. & J. 191 .... *28–143*
Orinoco Navigation Ltd v Ecotrade SpA; The Ikariada [1999] 2 All E.R. (Comm) 257; [1999] 2 Lloyd's Rep. 365; [1999] C.L.C. 1713, QBD (Comm) *30–331*
Orion Finance Ltd v Crown Financial Management Ltd (No.1) [1996] B.C.C. 621; [1996] 2 B.C.L.C. 78, CA (Civ Div); affirming [1994] B.C.C. 897; [1994] 2 B.C.L.C. 607; [1998] Masons C.L.R. Rep. 13, Ch D *19–043*, *19–065*
Orion Finance Ltd v Crown Financial Management Ltd (No.2) [1996] B.C.C. 631; [1996] 2 B.C.L.C. 382, CA (Civ Div) *19–065*
Orion Finance Ltd v Heritable Finance Ltd, unreported, March 10, 1997 .... *24–019*

Orion Finance Ltd v JD Williams & Co Ltd [1998] C.C.L.R. 36, CA (Civ Div) *3–088*
Orion Insurance Co Plc v Sphere Drake Insurance Plc [1992] 1 Lloyd's Rep. 239, CA (Civ Div); affirming [1990] 1 Lloyd's Rep. 465, QBD (Comm) *2–126*, *2–159*, *2–185*, *3–115*, *12–106*, *12–107*
Orman v Saville Sportswear [1960] 1 W.L.R. 1055; [1960] 3 All E.R. 105; (1960) 104 S.J. 212, QBD *13–010*
Ormes v Beadel (1860) 2 De. G.F. & J. 333 .... *6–124*, *7–053*
Orphanos v Queen Mary College [1985] A.C. 761; [1985] 2 W.L.R. 703; [1985] 2 All E.R. 233; [1986] 2 C.M.L.R. 73; [1985] I.R.L.R. 349; (1985) 82 L.S.G. 1787; (1985) 129 S.J. 284, HL *29–042*
Orr v Mitchell [1893] A.C. 238, HL *12–066*
Orton v Butler (1822) 5 B. & Ald. 652 1–128
Orton v Collins [2007] EWHC 803 (Ch); [2007] 1 W.L.R. 2953; [2007] 3 All E.R. 863; (2007) 151 S.J.L.B. 608; [2007] N.P.C. 49, Ch D *3–046*, 4–065
Osborne v Amalgamated Society of Railway Servants (No.1); sub nom. Amalgamated Society of Railway Servants v Osborne (No.1) [1910] A.C. 87, HL; affirming in part [1909] 1 Ch. 163, CA *16–005*
Osborne v Amalgamated Society of Railway Servants. *See* Amalgamated Society of Railway Servants v Osborne (No.2)
Osborne v Williams(1811) 18 Ves. 379 .... *16–019*
Oscar Chess v Williams [1957] 1 W.L.R. 370; [1957] 1 All E.R. 325; (1957) 101 S.J. 186, CA *3–106*, *6–075*, 12–003
Osgood v Nelson (1871–72) L.R. 5 H.L. 636, HL *29–142*
Oshkosh B'Gosh Inc v Dan Marbel Inc Ltd (1988) 4 B.C.C. 795; [1989] B.C.L.C. 507; [1989] P.C.C. 320; [1989] 1 C.M.L.R. 94, CA (Civ Div); reversing (1988) 4 B.C.C. 442; [1988] 3 C.M.L.R. 214; (1988) 85(42) L.S.G. 45; (1988) 132 S.J. 1459, QBD *9–012*
Osman v Moss (J Ralph) [1970] 1 Lloyd's Rep. 313, CA (Civ Div) *16–173*
Osmond v Fitzroy (1731) 3 P.Wms. 129 .... *8–001*
O'Sullivan v Management Agency and Music Ltd [1985] Q.B. 428; [1984] 3 W.L.R. 448; [1985] 3 All E.R. 351, CA (Civ Div) *3–005*, *6–116*, *6–117*, *7–100*, 7–124, *7–125*, *26–165*, *26–171*, *29–157*
O'Sullivan v Thomas [1895] 1 Q.B. 698 .... *29–197*
O'Sullivan v Williams [1992] 3 All E.R. 385; [1992] R.T.R. 402; (1992) 142 N.L.J. 717, CA (Civ Div) *18–076*
Oswald Hickson Collier & Co v Carter-Ruck [1984] A.C. 720; [1984] 2 W.L.R. 847; [1984] 2 All E.R. 15; (1983) 133 N.L.J. 233; (1982) 126 S.J. 120, CA (Civ Div) *16–119*
Other v Iveson (1855) 3 Drew. 177 .... *17–005*
Otter v Church, Adams, Tatham & Co [1953] Ch. 280; [1953] 1 W.L.R. 156; [1953] 1 All E.R. 168; (1953) 97 S.J. 48, Ch D *20–003*, *26–043*
Ottoman Bank of Nicosia v Chakarian [1938] A.C. 260, PC (Cy) *21–068*, *30–370*
Ottoman Bank v Chakarian [1930] A.C. 277; [1930] 2 W.W.R. 82, PC (Cy) *23–039*, *30–373*
Oudaille v Lawson [1922] N.Z.L.R. 259 .... *6–013*
Oughton v Seppings (1830) 1 B. Ad 241 .... *29–140*, *29–142*
Oughtred v Inland Revenue Commissioners [1960] A.C. 206; [1959] 3 W.L.R. 898; [1959] 3 All E.R. 623; (1959) 38 A.T.C. 317; [1959] T.R. 319; (1959) 103 S.J. 896, HL; affirming [1958] Ch. 678; [1958] 3 W.L.R. 64; [1958] 2 All E.R. 443; (1958) 37 A.T.C. 148; [1958] T.R. 177; (1958) 102 S.J. 468, CA; reversing [1958] Ch. 383; [1958] 2 W.L.R. 174; [1958] 1 All E.R. 252; (1957) 36 A.T.C. 291; [1957] T.R. 289; (1958) 102 S.J. 85, Ch D *4–013*
Oun v Ahmad [2008] EWHC 545 (Ch); [2008] 13 E.G. 149 (C.S.); (2008) 152(14) S.J.L.B. 32; [2008] N.P.C. 39; [2008] 2 P. & C.R. DG3, Ch D ...*4–070*, *4–071*
Outram v Academy Plastics Ltd [2001] I.C.R. 367; [2000] I.R.L.R. 499; [2000] O.P.L.R. 321; [2000] Pens. L.R. 283; (2000) 97(20) L.S.G. 46, CA (Civ Div) 1–160, *3–180*
Outram v Homewood (1803) 3 East 346 .... *25–012*

Ove Arup & Partners International Ltd v Mirant Asia-Pacific Construction (Hong Kong) Ltd (No.2); sub nom. Mirant Asia-Pacific Construction (Hong Kong) Ltd (No.2) v Ove Arup & Partners International Ltd [2005] EWCA Civ 1585; [2006] B.L.R. 187; 105 Con. L.R. 1; [2006] C.I.L.L. 2325, CA (Civ Div); affirming [2004] EWHC 1750; 97 Con. L.R. 1; [2005] P.N.L.R. 10, QBD (TCC) *2–076*

Overbrooke Estates Ltd v Glencombe Properties Ltd [1974] 1 W.L.R. 1335; [1974] 3 All E.R. 511; (1974) 118 S.J. 775, Ch D *6–137*, *14–063*

Overend Gurney & Co Ltd (Liquidators) v Oriental Financial Corp Ltd (Liquidators); sub nom. Oriental Financial Corp v Overend Gurney & Co (1874–75) L.R. 7 H.L. 348, HL; affirming (1871–72) L.R. 7 Ch. App. 142, Lord Chancellor *12–116*

Overland Shoes Ltd v Schenkers Ltd; Overland Shoes Ltd v Schenkers International Deutschland GmbH [1998] 1 Lloyd's Rep. 498; (1998) 95(11) L.S.G. 36; (1998) 142 S.J.L.B. 84, CA (Civ Div) *14–062*, *14–085*, 14–095

Overmark Smith Warden Ltd, Re [1982] 1 W.L.R. 1195; [1982] 3 All E.R. 513; (1982) 79 L.S.G. 1025; (1982) 126 S.J. 592, Ch D *3–035*, *28–094*, *28–095*, *28–101*

Overseas Buyers v Granadex SA [1980] 2 Lloyd's Rep. 608, QBD (Comm) *2–155*, *14–141*

Overseas Medical Supplies Ltd v Orient Transport Services Ltd [1999] 1 All E.R. (Comm) 981; [1999] 2 Lloyd's Rep. 273; [1999] C.L.C. 1243, CA (Civ Div) *14–084*, *14–085*, 14–086, *14–087*, 14–094, *14–103*

Overseas Tankship (UK) Ltd v Morts Dock & Engineering Co; The Wagon Mound; sub nom. Morts Dock & Engineering Co v Overseas Tankship (UK) Ltd [1961] A.C. 388; [1961] 2 W.L.R. 126; [1961] 1 All E.R. 404; [1961] 1 Lloyd's Rep. 1; 100 A.L.R.2d 928; 1961 A.M.C. 962; (1961) 105 S.J. 85, PC (Aus); reversing [1959] 2 Lloyd's Rep. 697, CA (NSW); affirming [1958] 1 Lloyd's Rep. 575, Sup Ct (NSW) *1–165*, *26–057*, *26–059*

Overstone v Shipway [1962] 1 W.L.R. 117; [1962] 1 All E.R. 52; (1962) 106 S.J. 14, CA *22–049*, *24–051*, *25–008*, *26–009*

Overton v Bannister (1844) 3 Ha. 503 .... *8–043*, *8–053*

Owen v Homan (1850) 3 Mc.G 378 .... *25–001*

Owen v Sykes [1936] 1 K.B. 192, CA *26–030*

Owen v Tate [1976] Q.B. 402; [1975] 3 W.L.R. 369; [1975] 2 All E.R. 129; (1974) 119 S.J. 575, CA (Civ Div) *21–041*, *29–019*, *29–073*, *29–099*, *29–109*, 29–110, 29–112, *29–115*, *29–119*, *29–131*, *29–133*

Owen v Thomas (1834) My. & K. 353 .... *12–123*

Owen Co v Cronk. *See* D Owen & Co v Cronk

Owens Bank Ltd v Bracco [1992] 2 A.C. 443; [1992] 2 W.L.R. 621; [1992] 2 All E.R. 193; [1993] I.L.Pr. 24, HL *25–017*

Owens Bank Ltd v Etoile Commerciale SA [1995] 1 W.L.R. 44, PC (StV) *25–015*, *25–017*

Owens v Minoprio [1942] 1 K.B. 193, KBD *25–011*

Owners of Cargo Laden on Board the Albacruz v Owners of the Albazero; sub nom. Concord Petroleum Corp v Gosford Marine Panama SA [1977] A.C. 774; [1976] 3 W.L.R. 419; [1976] 3 All E.R. 129; [1976] 2 Lloyd's Rep. 467; (1976) 120 S.J. 570, HL; reversing [1975] 3 W.L.R. 491; [1975] 3 All E.R. 21; [1975] 2 Lloyd's Rep. 295; (1975) 119 S.J. 609, CA (Civ Div); affirming [1974] 2 All E.R. 906; [1974] 2 Lloyd's Rep. 38, QBD (Admlty) *18–049*, 18–052, 18–055, 18–058, *18–068*, *18–076*, *19–076*, *29–160*

Owners of Cargo Lately Laden on Board the Ardennes v Owners of the Ardennes; The Ardennes; sub nom. Torneo v Owners of the Ardennes [1951] 1 K.B. 55; [1950] 2 All E.R. 517; (1950) 84 Ll. L. Rep. 340; (1950) 66 T.L.R. (Pt. 2) 312; (1950) 94 S.J. 458, KBD *12–107*, *26–070*, *26–078*

Owners of Cargo Lately Laden on Board the Deichland v Owners and/or Demise Charterers of the Deichland; The Deichland [1990] 1 Q.B. 361; [1989] 3 W.L.R. 478; [1989] 2 All E.R. 1066; [1989] 2 Lloyd's Rep. 113; [1991] I.L.Pr. 135; (1989) 86(24) L.S.G. 36; (1989) 133 S.J. 596, CA (Civ Div) *30–080*

Owners of Cargo Lately Laden on Board the Playa Larga v Owners of the I Congreso del Partido; sub nom. Owners of Cargo Lately Laden on Board The Marble Islands v Owners of The I Congreso del Partido [1983] 1 A.C. 244; [1981] 3 W.L.R. 328; [1981] 2 All E.R. 1064; [1981] 2 Lloyd's Rep. 367; [1981] Com. L.R. 190; (1981) 125 S.J. 528, HL; reversing [1981] 1 All E.R. 1092; [1980] 1 Lloyd's Rep. 23, CA (Civ Div); affirming [1978] Q.B. 500; [1977] 3 W.L.R. 778; [1978] 1 All E.R. 1169; [1977] 1 Lloyd's Rep. 536, QBD (Admlty) *11–001*, *11–005*

Owners of Cargo Lately Laden on Board the Rewia v Caribbean Liners (Caribtainer) Ltd [1991] 2 Lloyd's Rep. 325; [1993] I.L.Pr. 507, CA (Civ Div) *30–080*

Owners of Cargo Lately Laden on Board the Troilus v Owners, Masters and Crew of the Glenogle; The Troilus and the Glenogle [1951] A.C. 820; [1951] 2 All E.R. 40; [1951] 1 Lloyd's Rep. 467; [1951] 2 T.L.R. 22; (1951) 95 S.J. 465, HL *29–136*

Owners of Cargo Lately on Board the Fehmarn v Owners of the Fehmarn; The Fehmarn [1958] 1 W.L.R. 159; [1958] 1 All E.R. 333; [1957] 2 Lloyd's Rep. 551; (1958) 102 S.J. 123, CA *30–007*

Owners of Cargo on Board the Morviken v Owners of the Hollandia [1983] 1 A.C. 565; [1982] 3 W.L.R. 1111; [1982] 3 All E.R. 1141; [1983] 1 Lloyd's Rep. 1; [1983] Com. L.R. 44; (1982) 126 S.J. 819, HL; affirming [1982] Q.B. 872; [1982] 2 W.L.R. 556; [1982] 1 All E.R. 1076; [1982] 1 Lloyd's Rep. 325; [1982] Com. L.R. 20; (1982) 126 S.J. 115, CA (Civ Div); reversing [1981] 2 Lloyd's Rep. 61, QBD (Admlty) *14–117*, *30–007*, *30–008*, *30–026*, *30–065*, *30–067*, *30–068*, *30–087*, *30–211*, *30–365*

Owners of SS Celia v Owners of SS Volturno [1921] 2 A.C. 544; (1921) 8 Ll. L. Rep. 449; 20 A.L.R. 884, HL *26–080*

Owners of the Andros Springs v Owners of the World Beauty; The Andros Springs and The World Beauty; sub nom. Owners of the Steam Tanker Andros Springs v Owners of the Steam Tanker World Beauty [1970] P. 144; [1969] 3 W.L.R. 110; [1969] 3 All E.R. 158; [1969] 1 Lloyd's Rep. 350; (1969) 113 S.J. 363, CA (Civ Div) *26–115*, *26–120*

Owners of the Borvigilant v Owners of the Romina G; sub nom. Borkan General Trading Ltd v Monsoon Shipping Ltd [2003] EWCA Civ 935; [2003] 2 All E.R. (Comm) 736; [2003] 2 Lloyd's Rep. 520; [2004] 1 C.L.C. 41, CA (Civ Div); affirming [2002] EWHC 1759; [2003] 1 All E.R. (Comm) 129; [2002] 2 Lloyd's Rep. 631, QBD (Admlty) *14–049*

Owners of the Cap Palos v Alder; sub nom. Cap Palos, The v Alder [1921] P. 458; (1921) 8 Ll. L. Rep. 309, CA; reversing (1920) 5 Ll. L. Rep. 442, PDAD *3–025*, *14–016*, *14–021*, *14–030*

Owners of the Eleftherotria v Owners of the Despina R; sub nom. Services Europe Atlantique Sud (SEAS) v Stockholms Rederi AB Svea; The Folias [1979] A.C. 685; [1978] 3 W.L.R. 804; [1979] 1 All E.R. 421; [1979] 1 Lloyd's Rep. 1; (1978) 122 S.J. 758, HL ... *30–370*, *30–372*, *30–373*, *30–376*, *30–377*

Owners of the Jessmore v Manchester Ship Canal Co [1951] 2 Lloyd's Rep. 512, PDAD *14–011*

Owners of the Norseman v British Transport Commission; The Norseman [1957] P. 224; [1957] 3 W.L.R. 263; [1957] 2 All E.R. 660; [1957] 1 Lloyd's Rep. 503; (1957) 36 A.T.C. 173; [1957] T.R. 193; (1957) 101 S.J. 556, PDAD *26–163*

Owners of the Norway v Ashburner; The Norway, 16 E.R. 92; (1865) 3 Moo. P.C. N.S. 245, PC (UK) *21–088*

Owners of the Philippine Admiral v Wallem Shipping (Hong Kong) Ltd; The Philippine Admiral; Telfair Shipping Corp v Owners of the Ship Philippine Admiral [1977] A.C. 373; [1976] 2 W.L.R. 214; [1976] 1 All E.R. 78; [1976] 1 Lloyd's Rep. 234; (1975) 119 S.J. 865, PC (HK); affirming [1974] 2 Lloyd's Rep. 568, CA (HK) *11–001*, *11–020*

Owners of the Sardinia Sulcis v Owners of the Al Tawwab [1991] 1 Lloyd's Rep. 201, CA (Civ Div) *28–118*

Owners of the SS Magnhild v MacIntyre Bros & Co [1921] 2 K.B. 97; (1921) 6 Ll. L. Rep. 190, CA; reversing [1920] 3 K.B. 321; (1920) 4 Ll. L. Rep. 130, KBD *12–088*

Owners of the Steamship Mediana v Owners of the Lightship Comet [1900] A.C. 113, HL *26–008*

Owners of the Tantalus v Owners of the Telemachus [1957] P. 47; [1957] 2 W.L.R. 200; [1957] 1 All E.R. 72; [1956] 2 Lloyd's Rep. 490; 50 R. & I.T. 319; (1956) 35 A.T.C. 497; [1957] T.R. 1; 1957 A.M.C. 2428; (1957) 101 S.J. 112, PDAD *26–164*

Owners of Turbo Electric Bulk Carrier Teh Hu v Nippon Salvage Co Ltd; The Teh Hu [1970] P. 106; [1969] 3 W.L.R. 1135; [1969] 3 All E.R. 1200; [1969] 2 Lloyd's Rep. 365; (1969) 113 S.J. 792, CA (Civ Div) *26–080*, *30–376*

Oxley, Re; sub nom. John Hornby & Sons v Oxley [1914] 1 Ch. 604, CA *20–010*

Ozalid Group (Export) Ltd v African Continental Bank Ltd [1979] 2 Lloyd's Rep. 231, QBD (Comm) *30–340*

P&O Nedlloyd BV v Arab Metals Co; The UB Tiger; sub nom. P&O Nedlloyd BV v Arab Metals Co (No.2) [2006] EWCA Civ 1717; [2007] 1 W.L.R. 2288; [2007] 2 All E.R. (Comm) 401; [2007] 2 Lloyd's Rep. 231; [2006] 2 C.L.C. 985; 116 Con. L.R. 200, CA (Civ Div) *27–013*, *28–134*, 28–135, *28–139*

P&O SS Co v Shand (1865) 3 Moo. P.C.(N.S.) 272 ...*30–005*, *30–011*, *30–012*, *30–309*

P&S Platt Ltd v Crouch [2003] EWCA Civ 1110; [2004] 1 P. & C.R. 18; [2003] 32 E.G. 67 (C.S.); (2003) 147 S.J.L.B. 934; [2003] N.P.C. 97; [2003] 2 P. & C.R. DG19, CA (Civ Div); affirming [2002] EWHC 2195 (Ch); [2002] 45 E.G. 153 (C.S.); [2002] N.P.C. 133, Ch D *12–119*

P, The; sub nom. Motor Vessel P, The [1992] 1 Lloyd's Rep. 470, QBD (Comm) *27–078*

P (Diplomatic Immunity: Jurisdiction), Re; sub nom. P (Child Abduction: State Immunity), Re; P v P (Diplomatic Immunity: Jurisdiction) [1998] 1 F.L.R. 1026; [1998] Fam. Law 384, CA (Civ Div); affirming [1998] 2 F.C.R. 525; [1998] Fam. Law 310; (1998) 95(15) L.S.G. 31; (1998) 142 S.J.L.B. 94, Fam Div *11–011*

P (Minors) (Children Act: Diplomatic Immunity), Re [1998] 1 F.L.R. 624; [1998] 2 F.C.R. 480; [1998] Fam. Law 12, Fam Div *11–015*

P Phipps & Co Ltd v Rogers; sub nom. P Phipps & Co (Northampton and Towcester Breweries) Ltd v Rogers [1925] 1 K.B. 14, CA; affirming in part [1924] 2 K.B. 45, KBD *21–026*, *22–051*

P Samuel & Co Ltd v Dumas; sub nom. P Samuel & Co Ltd v Motor Union Insurance Co Ltd [1924] A.C. 431; (1924) 18 Ll. L. Rep. 211, HL; affirming [1923] 1 K.B. 592; [1926] All E.R. Rep. 66; (1922) 13 Ll. L. Rep. 503, CA; reversing (1922) 12 Ll. L. Rep. 73, KBD *14–146*

PCW Syndicates v PCW Reinsurers [1996] 1 W.L.R. 1136; [1996] 1 All E.R. 774; [1996] 1 Lloyd's Rep. 241; [1995] C.L.C. 1517; [1995] 4 Re. L.R. 373, CA (Civ Div) *6–148*

PJ Van der Zijden Wildhandel NV v Tucker & Cross Ltd (No.1) [1975] 2 Lloyd's Rep. 240, QBD (Comm) *12–089*, *14–138*, *14–140*, *14–141*, *14–142*, *22–050*

PS Chellaram & Co Ltd v China Ocean Shipping Co; The Zhi Jiang Kou [1991] 1 Lloyd's Rep. 493, CA (NSW) *12–014*, *14–033*, *28–109*

PSM International Ltd v Whitehouse; PSM International Ltd v Willenhall Automation; McKechnie v Whitehouse; McKechnie v Willenhall Automation [1992] I.R.L.R. 279; [1992] F.S.R. 489, CA (Civ Div) *18–136*

PT Pan Indonesia Bank Ltd Tbk v Marconi Communications International Ltd. *See* Marconi Communications International Ltd v PT Pan Indonesia Bank TBK

PW & Co v Milton Gate Investments Ltd [2003] EWHC 1994 (Ch); [2004] Ch. 142; [2004] 2 W.L.R. 443; [2004] L. & T.R. 8; [2004] 3 E.G.L.R. 103; (2003) 100(38) L.S.G. 36; (2003) 153 N.L.J. 1347, Ch D 1–038, 1–047

Paal Wilson & Co A/S v Partenreederei Hannah Blumenthal; The Hannah Blumenthal [1983] 1 A.C. 854; [1982] 3 W.L.R. 1149; [1983] 1 All E.R. 34; [1983] 1 Lloyd's Rep. 103; [1983] Com. L.R. 20; (1982) 126 S.J. 835, HL; affirming [1982] 3 W.L.R. 49; [1982] 3 All E.R. 394; [1982] 1 Lloyd's Rep. 582; [1982] Com. L.R. 117; (1982) 126 S.J. 292, CA (Civ Div); affirming [1981] 3 W.L.R. 823; [1982] 1 All E.R. 197; [1981] 2 Lloyd's Rep. 438; [1981] Com. L.R. 231, QBD (Comm) *1–004*, *2–004*, *2–006*, *5–067*, *22–027*, *23–007*, *23–013*, *23–040*, *23–059*, *23–061*, *24–016*
Pacaya Rubber & Produce Co Ltd (Burns Application), Re [1914] 1 Ch. 542, Ch D *9–060*
Pacific & General Insurance Co Ltd v Hazell; Pacific & General Insurance Co Ltd v Home & Overseas Insurance Co Ltd [1997] L.R.L.R. 65; [1997] B.C.C. 400; [1997] 6 Re. L.R. 157, QBD (Comm) *21–041*
Pacific Associates v Baxter [1990] 1 Q.B. 993; [1989] 3 W.L.R. 1150; [1989] 2 All E.R. 159; 44 B.L.R. 33; 16 Con. L.R. 90; (1989) 139 N.L.J. 41; (1989) 133 S.J. 123, CA (Civ Div); affirming 13 Con. L.R. 80, OR *1–176*, *1–177*, *1–186*, *14–056*, *18–030*, *21–041*
Pacific National Investments Ltd v Corp of the City of Victoria [2004] S.C.C. 75 .... *29–015*
Pacific Phosphate Co Ltd v Empire Transport Co Ltd (1920) 4 Ll. L. Rep. 189, KBD *23–058*
Pacol Ltd v Trade Lines Ltd; The Henrik Sif [1982] 1 Lloyd's Rep. 456; [1982] Com. L.R. 92; (1982) 126 S.J. 312, QBD (Comm) *3–088*, *3–098*, *3–101*, *5–082*
Padre Island, The. *See* Socony Mobil Oil Co Inc v West of England Ship Owners Mutual Insurance Association (London) Ltd
Page v Cox (1852) 10 Hare 163 ....*18–079*, *18–080*, *18–086*
Page v Meek (1862) 32 L.J.Q.B. 4 .... *21–042*
Page v Newman (1829) 9 B.C. 378 .... *26–167*
Page v Smith [1996] A.C. 155; [1995] 2 W.L.R. 644; [1995] 2 All E.R. 736; [1995] 2 Lloyd's Rep. 95; [1995] R.T.R. 210; [1995] P.I.Q.R. P329; (1995) 92(23) L.S.G. 33; (1995) 145 N.L.J. 723; (1995) 139 S.J.L.B. 173, HL; reversing [1994] 4 All E.R. 522; [1994] R.T.R. 293; [1995] P.I.Q.R. P58; (1994) 144 N.L.J. 756, CA (Civ Div); reversing [1993] P.I.Q.R. Q55, QBD *1–123*
Page One Records, Ltd v Britton [1968] 1 W.L.R. 157; [1967] 3 All E.R. 822; (1967) 111 S.J. 944, Ch D *13–006*, *16–102*, *27–046*, *27–65*
Paget v Marshall (1885) L.R. 28 Ch. D. 255, Ch D 5–119, *12–112*
Pagnan SpA v Feed Products Ltd [1987] 2 Lloyd's Rep. 601, CA (Civ Div) *2–029*, *2–110*, *2–114*, *2–128*, *2–129*, *2–142*
Pagnan SpA v Granaria BV [1986] 2 Lloyd's Rep. 547, CA (Civ Div); affirming [1985] 2 Lloyd's Rep. 256, QBD (Comm) *2–029*, *2–113*, *2–129*, *2–136*
Pagnan SpA v Tradax Ocean Transportation SA; sub nom. Tradax Ocean Transportation SA v Pagnan [1987] 3 All E.R. 565; [1987] 2 Lloyd's Rep. 342, CA (Civ Div); affirming [1987] 1 All E.R. 81; [1986] 2 Lloyd's Rep. 646, QBD (Comm) *2–155*, *12–078*, *14–137*, *14–148*
Pain, Re; sub nom. Gustavon v Haviland [1919] 1 Ch. 38, Ch D *19–011*, *19–070*
Palace Shipping Co Ltd v Caine; sub nom. Caine v Palace Steam Shipping Co Ltd [1907] A.C. 386, HL; affirming [1907] 1 K.B. 670, CA *3–071*
Palace Theatre Ltd v Clensy (1909) 36 T.L.R. 28 .... *16–102*
Palaniappa Chettiar v Arunsalem Chettiar. *See* Chettiar (ARPL Palaniappa) v Chettiar (PLAR Arunasalam)
Palgrave Brown & Son Ltd v Owners of SS Turid; sub nom. Turid, The v Palgrave, Brown & Son Ltd; Turid, The [1922] 1 A.C. 397; (1922) 10 Ll. L. Rep. 375, HL; affirming [1921] P. 146; (1921) 6 Ll. L. Rep. 44, CA; affirming [1920] P. 370; (1920) 3 Ll. L. Rep. 224, PDAD *12–057*, *12–058*, *12–128*, *13–023*
Pallant v Morgan [1953] Ch. 43; [1952] 2 All E.R. 951; [1952] 2 T.L.R. 813, Ch D 4–077
Pallister v Gravesend Corp (1850) 9 C.B. 774 .... *16–195*

Palmco Shipping Inc v Continental Ore Corp; The Captain George K [1970] 2 Lloyd's Rep. 21, QBD (Comm) *12–031*, *23–021*, *23–044*
Palmer v Bramley [1895] 2 Q.B. 405, CA *21–073*, *21–076*
Palmer v Day & Sons [1895] 2 Q.B. 618, QBD *20–041*
Palmer v East and North Hertfordshire NHS Trust [2006] EWHC 1997 (QB); [2006] Lloyd's Rep. Med. 472, QBD *2–142*, *3–015*
Palmer v Hutchinson (1880–81) L.R. 6 App. Cas. 619, PC (Natal) *10–013*
Palmer v Johnson (1883–84) L.R. 13 Q.B.D. 351, CA *25–003*, *27–058*
Palmer v Mallet (1887) L.R. 36 Ch. D. 411, CA *3–043*, *3–044*, *16–114*
Palmer v Temple (1839) 9 A.E. 508 .... *24–051*, *24–053*, *29–065*
Palmer (Gavin) (Deceased) (A Debtor), Re; sub nom. Gavin Hilary Palmer Estate Trustee v Palmer [1994] Ch. 316; [1994] 3 W.L.R. 420; [1994] 3 All E.R. 835; [1994] 2 F.L.R. 609; [1995] 1 F.C.R. 320; [1994] Fam. Law 566; [1994] E.G. 52 (C.S.); (1994) 138 S.J.L.B. 72; [1994] N.P.C. 41; (1994) 68 P. & C.R. D13, CA (Civ Div); reversing [1993] 3 W.L.R. 877; [1993] 4 All E.R. 812; [1993] 41 E.G. 179; [1993] E.G. 62 (C.S.); [1993] N.P.C. 55, Ch D *20–019*
Palmolive Co (England) Ltd v Freedman [1928] Ch. 264, CA; affirming [1927] 2 Ch. 333, Ch D *16–121*
Pamia, The [1943] 1 All E.R. 269; (1943) 75 Ll. L. Rep. 9, PDAD *11–024*, *11–025*
Pan American World Airways Inc. v Aetna Casualty and Surety Co [1975] 1 Lloyd's Rep. 77, US Ct; affirming [1974] 1 Lloyd's Rep. 207, DC (US) ... *14–146*
Pan Atlantic Insurance Co Ltd v Pine Top Insurance Co Ltd [1989] 1 Lloyd's Rep. 568, CA (Civ Div); affirming [1988] 2 Lloyd's Rep. 505, QBD (Comm) *18–051*, *18–128*
Pan Atlantic Insurance Co Ltd v Pine Top Insurance Co Ltd [1995] 1 A.C. 501; [1994] 3 W.L.R. 677; [1994] 3 All E.R. 581; [1994] 2 Lloyd's Rep. 427; [1994] C.L.C. 868; (1994) 91(36) L.S.G. 36; (1994) 144 N.L.J. 1203; (1994) 138 S.J.L.B. 182, HL; affirming [1993] 1 Lloyd's Rep. 496, CA (Civ Div); affirming [1992] 1 Lloyd's Rep. 101, QBD (Comm) ...*6–035*, *6–036*, *6–037*, 6–145
Pan Ocean Shipping Co Ltd v Creditcorp Ltd; The Trident Beauty [1994] 1 W.L.R. 161; [1994] 1 All E.R. 470; [1994] 1 Lloyd's Rep. 365; [1994] C.L.C. 124; (1994) 144 N.L.J. 1203, HL; affirming [1993] 1 Lloyd's Rep. 443; (1993) 137 S.J.L.B. 53, CA (Civ Div) 19–078, *19–079*, *29–019*, *29–063*
Panalpina International Transport v Densil Underwear [1981] 1 Lloyd's Rep. 187, QBD *26–063*
Panamena Europea Navegacion Compania Limitada v Frederick Leyland & Co Ltd; sub nom. Compania Panamena Europea Navigacion Limitada v Frederick Leyland & Co Ltd; Frederick Leyland & Co Ltd v Compania Panamena Europea Navegacion Limitada [1947] A.C. 428; (1947) 80 Ll. L. Rep. 205; [1947] L.J.R 716; 176 L.T. 524, HL; affirming (1943) 76 Ll. L. Rep. 113, CA; affirming (1942) 74 Ll. L. Rep. 108, KBD *13–011*
Panchaud Frères SA v Etablissements General Grain Co [1970] 1 Lloyd's Rep. 53, CA (Civ Div); reversing [1969] 2 Lloyd's Rep. 109, QBD (Comm) *14–151*, *24–003*, 24–006, *24–007*, *24–008*, *24–014*
Panchaud Freres SA v Pagnan (R) & Fratelli [1974] 1 Lloyd's Rep. 394, CA (Civ Div) *26–175*
Pancommerce SA v Veecheema BV [1983] 2 Lloyd's Rep. 304; [1983] Com. L.R. 230, CA (Civ Div); reversing [1982] 1 Lloyd's Rep. 645, QBD (Comm) *2–126*, *14–140*, *14–141*, *14–151*
Pankhania v Hackney LBC [2002] EWHC 2441 (Ch); [2002] N.P.C. 123, Ch D 6–013
Panorama Developments (Guildford) Ltd v Fidelis Furnishing Fabrics Ltd [1971] 2 Q.B. 711; [1971] 3 W.L.R. 440; [1971] 3 All E.R. 16; (1971) 115 S.J. 483, CA (Civ Div) *9–043*
Panoutsos v Raymond Hadley Corp of New York [1917] 2 K.B. 473, CA; affirming [1917] 1 K.B. 767, KBD *12–027*, *22–042*
Pao On v Lau Yiu Long [1980] A.C. 614; [1979] 3 W.L.R. 435; [1979] 3 All E.R. 65; (1979) 123 S.J. 319, PC (HK) 3–030, *3–066*, *3–067*, 3–075, *3–136*, 7–005, 7–016, 7–021, *7–027*, 7–028, 7–031, 7–033, 7–034, 7–035, 7–038, *7–041*, *7–053*, *7–055*, *12–108*, *27–011*, *29–088*

Papamichael v National Westminster Bank Plc (No.2) [2003] EWHC 164 (Comm); [2003] 1 Lloyd's Rep. 341, QBD (Comm) *29–034*, *29–160*, *29–174*, *29–175*, *29–183*
Pape v Westacott [1894] 1 Q.B. 272, CA *21–044*
Papera Traders Co Ltd v Hyundai Merchant Marine Co Ltd; The Eurasian Dream (No.2) [2002] EWHC 2130 (Comm); [2002] 2 All E.R. (Comm) 1083; [2002] 2 Lloyd's Rep. 692, QBD (Comm) *16–056*
Pappadakis v Pappadakis [2000] W.T.L.R. 719, Ch D *5–122*
Papworth v Battersea Corp (No.2) [1916] 1 K.B. 583; (1915) 84 L.J. K.B. 1881, CA *16–006*
Paquine v Snary [1909] 1 K.B. 688, CA *19–047*
Paradine v Jane (1647) Aleyn 26 .... *1–020*, 23–004
Paragon Finance Plc (formerly National Home Loans Corp) v Nash; sub nom. Nash v Paragon Finance Plc; Staunton v Paragon Finance Plc; Paragon Finance Plc v Staunton [2001] EWCA Civ 1466; [2002] 1 W.L.R. 685; [2002] 2 All E.R. 248; [2001] 2 All E.R. (Comm) 1025; [2002] 2 P. & C.R. 20; (2001) 98(44) L.S.G. 36; (2001) 145 S.J.L.B. 244; [2002] 1 P. & C.R. DG13, CA (Civ Div) 1–033, *2–131*, *13–007*, *13–026*, *14–074*, 22–039, *26–182*
Paragon Finance Plc (formerly National Home Loans Corp) v Pender [2005] EWCA Civ 760; [2005] 1 W.L.R. 3412; [2005] All E.R. (D) 307 (Jun); [2005] N.P.C. 84; [2005] 2 P. & C.R. DG18, CA (Civ Div); affirming [2003] EWHC 2834 (Ch); [2003] 49 E.G. 128 (C.S.), Ch D 1–033, *13–026*, *22–039*
Paragon Finance Plc v DB Thakerar & Co; Paragon Finance Plc v Thimbleby & Co [1999] 1 All E.R. 400; (1998) 95(35) L.S.G. 36; (1998) 142 S.J.L.B. 243, CA (Civ Div) *28–002*, *28–019*, *28–031*, *28–089*, *28–118*, *28–135*, *28–141*
Paragon Finance Plc v Staunton. *See* Paragon Finance Plc (formerly National Home Loans Corp) v Nash
Parana Plantations Ltd, Re (No.1) [1946] 2 All E.R. 214, CA *21–005*, *30–375*
Parana, The (1876–77) L.R. 2 P.D. 118, CA *26–089*
Pardoe (George), Re; sub nom. McLaughlin v Penny [1906] 2 Ch. 340, CA *28–031*
Parfitt v Jepson (1877) 46 L.J.C.P. 529 .... *29–148*
Paris v Machnik (1972) 30 D.L.R. (3d) 723 .... *7–136*
Park, In the Estate of; sub nom. Park v Park [1954] P. 112; [1953] 3 W.L.R. 1012; [1953] 2 All E.R. 1411; (1953) 97 S.J. 830, CA; affirming [1954] P. 89; [1953] 3 W.L.R. 307; [1953] 2 All E.R. 408; (1953) 97 S.J. 491, PDAD *8–069*
Park Air Services Plc, Re; sub nom. Christopher Moran Holdings Ltd v Bairstow [2000] 2 A.C. 172; [1999] 2 W.L.R. 396; [1999] 1 All E.R. 673; [1999] B.C.C. 135; [1999] 1 B.C.L.C. 155; [1999] B.P.I.R. 786; [1999] L. & T.R. 289; [1999] 1 E.G.L.R. 1; [1999] 14 E.G. 149; [1999] E.G. 17 (C.S.); (1999) 149 N.L.J. 195; [1999] N.P.C. 12, HL; reversing [1997] 1 W.L.R. 1376; [1997] 3 All E.R. 193; [1997] B.C.C. 712; [1997] 2 B.C.L.C. 75; (1998) 75 P. & C.R. 161; [1997] 2 E.G.L.R. 36; [1997] 30 E.G. 127; [1997] E.G. 68 (C.S.); (1997) 94(19) L.S.G. 25; (1997) 141 S.J.L.B. 112; [1997] N.P.C. 68; (1997) 74 P. & C.R. D23, CA (Civ Div); reversing [1996] 1 W.L.R. 649; [1996] B.C.C. 556; [1996] 1 B.C.L.C. 547; [1996] B.P.I.R. 377; (1996) 72 P. & C.R. 174; [1996] 2 E.G.L.R. 49; [1996] 40 E.G. 136; [1995] N.P.C. 205, Ch D *9–048*, *20–035*, *26–009*
Park Gate Waggon Works Co, Re (1881) L.R. 17 Ch. D. 234, CA *19–048*
Park Ward & Co Ltd, Re [1926] Ch. 828, Ch D *9–049*
Parke v Daily News (No.2) [1962] Ch. 927; [1962] 3 W.L.R. 566; [1962] 2 All E.R. 929; (1962) 106 S.J. 704, Ch D *9–020*, *9–032*
Parker v Bristol & Exeter Ry. (1851) 6 Exch. 702 .... *7–012*, *29–097*
Parker v Clark [1960] 1 W.L.R. 286; [1960] 1 All E.R. 93; (1960) 104 S.J. 251, Assizes (Exeter) *2–172*, *4–027*
Parker v Great Western Railway (1844) 7 M.G. 253 .... *7–015*, *29–098*
Parker v McKenna (1874–75) L.R. 10 Ch. App. 96, Lord Chancellor *9–055*
Parker v Norton, 101 E.R. 777; (1796) 6 Term Rep. 695, KB *29–141*
Parker v South Eastern Railway Co; Gabell v South Eastern Railway Co (1876–77) L.R. 2 C.P.D. 416, CA; reversing in part (1875–76) L.R. 1 C.P.D. 618, CPD *12–002*, *12–009*, *12–013*, *12–014*, *12–015*, *14–002*, *14–135*

Parker-Tweedale v Dunbar Bank Plc (No.1) [1991] Ch. 12; [1990] 3 W.L.R. 767; [1990] 2 All E.R. 577; (1990) 60 P. & C.R. 83; (1990) 140 N.L.J. 169; (1990) 134 S.J. 886, CA (Civ Div) 1–148, *1–176*, *1–177*, *18–036*
Parkhurst v Smith (1742) Wiles 327 .... *12–074*
Parkin v Thorold (1852) 16 Beav. 59 .... *21–011*, *21–014*, *28–142*
Parkin, Re; sub nom. Hill v Schwarz [1892] 3 Ch. 510, Ch D 27–034
Parkinson v College of Ambulance Ltd [1925] 2 K.B. 1, KBD ...*16–021*, *16–177*, *16–186*, *29–077*
Parkinson v St James and Seacroft University Hospital NHS Trust [2001] EWCA Civ 530; [2002] Q.B. 266; [2001] 3 W.L.R. 376; [2001] 3 All E.R. 97; [2001] 2 F.L.R. 401; [2002] 2 F.C.R. 65; [2001] P.I.Q.R. Q12; [2001] Lloyd's Rep. Med. 309; (2001) 61 B.M.L.R. 100; [2001] P.N.L.R. 43; [2001] Fam. Law 592; (2001) 98(22) L.S.G. 35; (2001) 145 S.J.L.B. 118, CA (Civ Div) *18–031*
Parkinson (Sir Lindsay) Co Ltd v Commissioners of Works. *See* Sir Lindsay Parkinson & Co v Commissioners of Works and Public Buildings
Parlement Belge, The (1879–80) L.R. 5 P.D. 197; [1874–80] All E.R. Rep. 104, CA; reversing (1878–79) L.R. 4 P.D. 129, PDAD *11–004*
Parma v G&S Properties (1969) 5 D.L.r. (3d) 315 .... *6–049*
Parouth, The. *See* Compania Naviera Micro SA v Shipley International Inc; The Parouth
Parrs Banking Co v Yates [1898] 2 Q.B. 460 .... *28–040*, *28–046*
Parry v Great Ship Co Ltd (1864) 4 B.S. 556 .... *21–001*
Parsons v BNM Laboratories Ltd [1964] 1 Q.B. 95; [1963] 2 W.L.R. 1273; [1963] 2 All E.R. 658; (1963) 42 A.T.C. 200; [1963] T.R. 183; (1963) 107 S.J. 294, CA *26–157*, *26–158*, *26–163*, *26–165*
Parsons v George [2004] EWCA Civ 912; [2004] 1 W.L.R. 3264; [2004] 3 All E.R. 633; [2005] C.P. Rep. 3; [2004] 3 E.G.L.R. 49; [2004] 40 E.G. 150; [2004] 31 E.G. 93 (C.S.); (2004) 101(33) L.S.G. 36; (2004) 148 S.J.L.B. 879; [2004] N.P.C. 117; [2005] 1 P. & C.R. DG1, CA (Civ Div) *28–119*
Parsons v Mather & Platt Ltd [1977] 1 W.L.R. 855; [1977] 2 All E.R. 715; (1977) 121 S.J. 204, QBD *26–174*, *26–184*
Parsons v Thompson (1790) 1 H.Bl. 322 .... *16–019*
Parsons Bros v Shea (1965) 53 D.L.R. (2d) 86 .... *23–086*
Parsons Corp v CV Scheepvaartonderneming Happy Ranger [2002] EWCA Civ 694; [2002] 2 All E.R. (Comm) 24; [2002] 2 Lloyd's Rep. 357; [2003] 1 C.L.C. 122, CA (Civ Div); reversing [2002] 1 All E.R. (Comm) 176; [2001] 2 Lloyd's Rep. 530, QBD (Comm) *14–008*, *14–032*
Parsons (Livestock) Ltd v Uttley Ingham & Co Ltd [1978] Q.B. 791; [1977] 3 W.L.R. 990; [1978] 1 All E.R. 525; [1977] 2 Lloyd's Rep. 522; (1977) 121 S.J. 811, CA (Civ Div) 1–165, 1–166, *26–054*, *26–057*, 26–058, *26–059*, *26–066*, *26–082*
Partabmull Rameshar v KC Sethia (1944) Ltd; sub nom. KC Sethia (1944) Ltd v Partabmull Rameshwar [1951] 2 All E.R. 352 (Note); [1951] 2 Lloyd's Rep. 89; [1951] W.N. 389; (1951) 95 S.J. 528, HL; affirming [1950] 1 All E.R. 51; [1950] W.N. 5; (1950) 94 S.J. 112, CA *13–007*, *13–013*, *23–047*
Partenreederei M/S Heidberg v Grosvenor Grain & Feed Co Ltd; The Heidberg (No.2) [1994] 2 Lloyd's Rep. 287, QBD (Comm) *30–305*
Partenreederei MS Karen Oltmann v Scarsdale Shipping Co; The Karen Oltmann [1976] 2 Lloyd's Rep. 708, QBD (Comm) *12–119*
Parton v Crofts (1864) 16 C.B. (N.S.) 11 .... *4–038*
Partridge v Crittenden [1968] 1 W.L.R. 1204; [1968] 2 All E.R. 421; (1968) 132 J.P. 367; (1968) 112 S.J. 582, DC *2–017*
Parway Estates v Inland Revenue Commissioners, 45 T.C. 135; (1958) 37 A.T.C. 164; [1958] T.R. 193, CA; affirming (1957) 36 A.T.C. 310; [1957] T.R. 329, HC *12–028*
Pascoe, Re [1944] Ch. 219, CA *20–054*
Pascoe v Turner [1979] 1 W.L.R. 431; [1979] 2 All E.R. 945; (1978) 9 Fam. Law 82; (1979) 123 S.J. 164, CA (Civ Div) *3–137*, *3–139*, *3–149*, 3–156, 3–157, 3–164, *13–028*, *29–161*
Pasley v Freeman, 100 E.R. 450; (1789) 3 Term Rep. 51, KB *1–131*, *12–003*

Pasmore v North (1811) 13 East. 517 .... *12–110*
Patel v Ali [1984] Ch. 283; [1984] 2 W.L.R. 960; [1984] 1 All E.R. 978; (1984) 48 P. & C.R. 118; (1984) 81 L.S.G. 1285; (1984) 128 S.J. 204, Ch D 27–031
Patel v Hooper & Jackson [1999] 1 W.L.R. 1792; [1999] 1 All E.R. 992; [1999] Lloyd's Rep. P.N. 1; [1998] E.G. 160 (C.S.); (1998) 148 N.L.J. 1751; [1998] N.P.C. 149, CA (Civ Div) *26–093*
Patel (A Debtor), Re; sub nom. Debtor v Dallomo [1986] 1 W.L.R. 221; [1986] 1 All E.R. 522; (1986) 83 L.S.G. 520; (1986) 136 N.L.J. 68; (1986) 130 S.J. 70, DC *20–018*
Pateman v Pay (1974) 232 E.G. 457 .... *2–161*
Paterson v St Andrews Provost; Paterson v Bain (1880–81) L.R. 6 App. Cas. 833, HL *10–030*
Paterson Zochonis & Co Ltd v Elder Dempster & Co Ltd; sub nom. Paterson Zochnois & Co Ltd v Elder Dampster & Co Ltd; Elder Dempster & Co Ltd v Paterson Zochonis & Co Ltd; Griffiths Lewis Steam Navigation Co Ltd v Paterson Zochonis & Co Ltd [1924] A.C. 522; (1924) 18 Ll. L. Rep. 319, HL; reversing [1923] 1 K.B. 420; (1922) 13 Ll. L. Rep. 513, CA; affirming (1922) 12 Ll. L. Rep. 69, KBD *12–014*, *14–045*, *14–046*, *14–047*, *14–054*, *18–021*, *18–022*, *18–094*
Patrick, Re; sub nom. Bills v Tatham [1891] 1 Ch. 82, CA *19–020*, *19–033*
Patrick v Royal London MutualInsurance Socy Ltd. *See* Ronson International Ltd v Patrick; sub nom. Patrick v Royal London Mutual Insurance Society Ltd
Patrick & Co Ltd v Russo-British Grain Export Co Ltd [1927] 2 K.B. 535; (1927) 28 Ll. L. Rep. 358, KBD *26–062*
Patterson v Landeberg & Son (1905) 7 F. 675 .... *6–009*
Pattinson v Luckley (1874–75) L.R. 10 Ex. 330, Ex Ct 25–020
Pattle v Hornibrook [1897] 1 Ch. 25, Ch D *12–106*, *12–109*
Paul v Constance [1977] 1 W.L.R. 527; [1977] 1 All E.R. 195; (1976) 7 Fam. Law 18; (1977) 121 S.J. 320, CA (Civ Div) *16–068*, *18–083*
Paul v Speirway (In Liquidation) [1976] Ch. 220; [1976] 2 W.L.R. 715; [1976] 2 All E.R. 587; (1976) 31 P. & C.R. 353; (1976) 120 S.J. 331, Ch D *29–173*
Paul & Frank v Discount Bank (Overseas) [1967] Ch. 348; [1966] 3 W.L.R. 490; [1966] 2 All E.R. 922; (1966) 110 S.J. 423, Ch D *19–066*, *20–026*
Paul Smith Ltd v H&S International Holding Inc [1991] 2 Lloyd's Rep. 127, QBD (Comm) *2–136*
Paula Lee Ltd v Zehil & Co Ltd [1983] 2 All E.R. 390, QBD *21–006*, *26–048*
Pauling's Settlement Trusts (No.1), Re; sub nom. Younghusband v Coutts & Co (No.1) [1964] Ch. 303; [1963] 3 W.L.R. 742; [1963] 3 All E.R. 1; (1963) 107 S.J. 492, CA; affirming in part [1962] 1 W.L.R. 86; [1961] 3 All E.R. 713; (1962) 106 S.J. 135, Ch D *7–074*, *7–097*, *28–134*, *28–136*, *28–139*
Pavey & Matthews Pty Ltd v Paul (1986–87) 162 C.L.R. 221 .... *16–152*
Pavey and Matthews Proprietary v Paul (1990) 6 Const. L.J. 59, HC (Aus) *29–009*, *29–015*, 29–080
Pavia & Co SpA v Thurmann-Nielsen [1952] 2 Q.B. 84; [1952] 1 T.L.R. 586; 96 S.J.193; (1952) 1 All E.R. 492; 1 Lloyd's Rep. 153, CA *12–037*
Pavlou (A Bankrupt) Re [1993] 1 W.L.R. 1046 .... *20–019*
Pawley v Turnbull (1861) 3 Giff. 70 .... *1–031*
Payabi v Armstel Shipping Corp; The Jay Bola; Baker Rasti Lari v Armstel Shipping Corp; The Jay Bola [1992] Q.B. 907; [1992] 2 W.L.R. 898; [1992] 3 All E.R. 329; [1992] 2 Lloyd's Rep. 62; (1992) 136 S.J.L.B. 52, QBD (Comm) *28–022*, *28–116*, *28–118*, *28–119*, *28–126*
Payne v Barnet LBC (1998) 30 H.L.R. 295; (1998) 10 Admin. L.R. 185; (1998) 76 P. & C.R. 293, CA (Civ Div) *6–014*
Payne v Brecon Corp (1858) 3 H. & N. 572 .... *16–195*
Payne v Cave (1789) 3 T.R. 148 .... *2–011*, *2–088*
Payne v Haine (1847) 16 M. & W. 541 .... *12–060*
Payne v Rogers (1794) 2 H.Bl. 350 .... *1–173*, *1–174*
Payne v Wilson (1827) 7 B. & C. 423 .... *3–047*
Payne v Zafiropoyloy [1994] C.L.Y. 3513 .... *4–064*

Paynter v James (1866–67) L.R. 2 C.P. 348, CCP *12–029*, *12–094*
Payzu Ltd v Saunders [1919] 2 K.B. 581, CA *26–113*, 26–114
Peace v Edinburgh City Council, 1999 S.L.T. 712; 1999 S.C.L.R. 593; [1999] I.R.L.R. 417; 1999 G.W.D. 8–394, OH *27–023*
Peachdart Ltd, Re [1984] Ch. 131; [1983] 3 W.L.R. 878; [1983] 3 All E.R. 204; (1983) 1 B.C.C. 98920; (1984) 81 L.S.G. 204; (1983) 127 S.J. 839, Ch D *29–158*, *29–168*
Peacock v Monk (1748) 1 Ves.Sen. 127 .... *12–108*
Peacock v Pursell (1863) 14 C.B.(N.S.) 728 .... *21–076*, *21–079*
Peacocke (CB) Land Co v Hamilton Milk Producers Co [1963] N.Z.L.R. 576 ......*19–077*, *19–083*
Peak Construction (Liverpool) Ltd v McKinney Foundations Ltd, 1 B.L.R. 111; 69 L.G.R. 1, CA (Civ Div) *26–135*
Pearce v Brain [1929] 2 K.B. 310, KBD *8–065*, *29–081*
Pearce v Brooks (1865–66) L.R. 1 Ex. 213, Ex Ct *16–069*, 16–164
Pearce v Gardner [1897] 1 Q.B. 688, CA *4–028*
Pearce v Merriman [1904] 1 K.B. 80, KBD *2–169*
Pearce v University of Aston (No.2) [1991] 2 All E.R. 469, Visitor (University) *27–023*
Pearks Ltd v Cullen (1912) 28 T.L.R. 371 ....*16–110*, *16–114*
Pearl Carriers Inc v Japan Line Ltd; The Chemical Venture [1993] 1 Lloyd's Rep. 508, QBD (Comm) *3–039*, *3–104*
Pearl v Deacon, 44 E.R. 802; (1857) 1 De G. & J. 461, Ct of Chancery *21–064*
Pearl Mill Co Ltd v Ivy Tannery Co Ltd [1919] 1 K.B. 78, KBD *22–027*
Pearson v Dublin Corp. *See* S Pearson & Son Ltd v Dublin Corp
Pearson v Scott (1878) L.R. 9 Ch. D. 198, Ch D *21–044*
Peat v Jones & Co (1881–82) L.R. 8 Q.B.D. 147, CA *20–042*
Pechell v Watson (1841) 8 M. & W. 691 .... *16–048*
Pecke v Redman (1555) 1 Dyer 113a *3–008*
Peco Arts Inc v Hazlitt Gallery Ltd [1983] 1 W.L.R. 1315; [1983] 3 All E.R. 193; (1984) 81 L.S.G. 203; (1983) 127 S.J. 806, QBD *28–088*, *28–089*
Peek v Derry *See* Derry v Peek
Peek v Gurney; Peek v Birkbeck; Peek v Barclay; Peek v Gordon; Peek v Rennie; Peek v Gibb; Peek v Overend & Gurney Co; Peek v Turquand; Peek v Harding (1873) L.R. 6 H.L. 377; [1861–1873] All E.R. Rep. 116, HL; affirming (1871–72) L.R. 13 Eq. 79, Ct of Chancery *6–017*, 6–028
Peekay Intermark Ltd v Australia & New Zealand Banking Group Ltd [2006] EWCA Civ 386; [2006] All E.R. (D) 70; [2006] 2 Lloyd's Rep. 511; [2006] 1 C.L.C. 582, CA (Civ Div); reversing [2005] EWHC 830 (Comm); [2005] 2 C.L.C. 111; [2005] P.N.L.R. 42, QBD (Comm) ...*6–039*, *6–135*, *12–002*, *14–132*, *14–133*
Peel v London & North Western Railway Co (No.1) [1907] 1 Ch. 5; 76 L.J.Ch. 152; 95 L.T. 897; 23 T.L.R. 85; 14 Manson 30, CA *9–022*
Peel v Peel (1869) 17 W.R. 586 .... *27–050*
Peel (Regional Municipality) v Canada [1992] 3 S.C.R. 762 .... *29–099*
Peer International Corp v Termidor Music Publishers Ltd (No.1); sub nom. Peer International Corp v Termidor Music Publishers Co Inc [2003] EWCA Civ 1156; [2004] Ch. 212; [2004] 2 W.L.R. 849; [2003] E.M.L.R. 34; [2004] R.P.C. 23; (2003) 26(11) I.P.D. 26070; (2003) 100(37) L.S.G. 31, CA (Civ Div) *30–125*, *30–366*
Peffer v Rigg [1977] 1 W.L.R. 285; [1978] 3 All E.R. 745; (1977) 33 P. & C.R. 60; (1976) 242 E.G. 123; (1976) 120 S.J. 332, Ch D *12–108*
Pegler Ltd v Wang (UK) Ltd (No.1) [2000] B.L.R. 218; 70 Con. L.R. 68; [2000] I.T.C.L.R. 617; [2000] Masons C.L.R. 19, QBD (TCC) ...*14–006*, *14–007*, *14–072*, *14–084*, *14–085*, *14–087*, 14–094, *28–054*
Pegler v Railway Executive; sub nom. Pegler v Great Western Railway [1948] A.C. 332; [1948] 1 All E.R. 559; 64 T.L.R. 212; [1948] L.J.R. 939; (1948) 92 S.J. 296, HL *26–013*
Peirce v Corf (1874) L.R. 9 Q.B. 210; 43 L.J.K.B. 52; 29 L.T. 919; 38 J.P. 214; 22 W.R. 299, QBD *4–029*, *4–038*

Pellecat v Angell (1835) 2 Cr.M. & R. 311 .... *16–014*
Pellow v Ivy (1933) 49 T.L.R. 422 .... *16–117*
Pena v Dale [2003] EWHC 1065; [2004] 2 B.C.L.C. 508, Ch D *2–146*, *27–011*, *27–024*
Penarth Dock Engineering Co v Pounds [1963] 1 Lloyd's Rep. 359, QBD *26–022*, *29–151*, *29–139*, *29–144*
Pendelbury v Walker (1841) 4 Y. & C. Ex 424 .... *17–027*
Penelope, The. *See* Cleeves Western Valleys Anthracite Collieries Ltd v Owners of The Penelope
Penn v Bristol and West Building Society; sub nom. Brill & Co v Penn [1997] 1 W.L.R. 1356; [1997] 3 All E.R. 470; [1997] 3 F.C.R. 789; [1997] P.N.L.R. 607; (1997) 74 P. & C.R. 210; [1997] E.G. 54 (C.S.); (1997) 94(18) L.S.G. 32; (1997) 141 S.J.L.B. 105; [1997] N.P.C. 58, CA (Civ Div); affirming [1995] 2 F.L.R. 938; [1996] 2 F.C.R. 729; [1996] Fam. Law 28; (1995) 92(27) L.S.G. 31; (1995) 139 S.J.L.B. 164, Ch D *18–008*
Pennell v Miller (1857) 23 Beav. 172; 26 L.J.Ch. 699; 3 Jur. 850; 5 W.R. 215; 113 R.R. 82 .... *3–021*
Penniall v Harborne (1848) 11 Q.B. 368 .... *21–003*
Pennington v Crossley & Sons (1897) 13 T.L.R. 513 .... *21–056*
Pennington v Waine (No.1); sub nom. Pennington v Crampton (No.1) [2002] EWCA Civ 227; [2002] 1 W.L.R. 2075; [2002] 4 All E.R. 215; [2002] 2 B.C.L.C. 448; [2002] W.T.L.R. 387; (2002) 99(15) L.S.G. 34; (2002) 146 S.J.L.B. 70; [2002] 2 P. & C.R. DG4, CA (Civ Div) *3–021*, 19–035, *27–034*
Pennington & Owen Ltd, Re [1925] Ch. 825; 95 L.J.Ch. 93; 134 L.T. 66; 41 T.L.R. 657; 69 S.J. 759; [1926] B. & C.R. 39, CA *20–044*
Pennsylvania Shipping Co v Compagnie Nationale de Navigation, 42 Com. Cas. 45; 155 L.T. 294; 80 S.J. 722; [1936] 2 All E.R. 1167; 55 Ll. L. Rep. 271 .... *6–004*, *6–104*, *12–112*
Penn-Texas Corp v Anstalt (Murat) [1964] 2 Q.B. 647; [1964] 3 W.L.R. 131; [1964] 2 All E.R. 594; (1964) 108 S.J. 356, CA *25–011*
Pennycook v Shaws (EAL) Ltd; sub nom. Shaws (EAL) Ltd v Pennycook; Pennycook v Shuns (EAL) Ltd [2004] EWCA Civ 100; [2004] Ch. 296; [2004] 2 W.L.R. 1331; [2004] 2 All E.R. 665; [2004] L. & T.R. 34; [2004] 2 E.G.L.R. 55; [2004] 18 E.G. 102; [2004] 8 E.G. 135 (C.S.); (2004) 101(11) L.S.G. 35; (2004) 148 S.J.L.B. 235; [2004] N.P.C. 21; [2004] 1 P. & C.R. DG25, CA (Civ Div); reversing [2002] EWHC 2769 (Ch); [2003] Ch. 399; [2003] 2 W.L.R. 1265; [2003] 3 All E.R. 1316; [2003] 2 P. & C.R. 8; [2003] L. & T.R. 16; [2003] 3 E.G.L.R. 28; [2003] 45 E.G. 176; [2002] 50 E.G. 113 (C.S.); (2002) 99(49) L.S.G. 20; [2002] N.P.C. 157; [2003] 1 P. & C.R. DG24, Ch D 1–047
Pepper & Hope v Daish [1980] I.R.L.R. 13, EAT *3–071*
Pera Shipping Corp v Petroship SA; The Pera [1985] 2 Lloyd's Rep. 103, CA (Civ Div); affirming [1984] 2 Lloyd's Rep. 363, QBD (Comm) ... *12–055*, *12–077*, *12–085*, *14–009*
Percival v Dunn (1885) L.R. 29 Ch. D. 128; 54 L.J.Ch. 570; 52 L.T. 320, Ch D *19–022*
Percival v LCC Asylums etc Committee (1918) 87 L.J.K.B. 677; 82 J.P. 157; 16 L.G.R. 367 .... *2–039*
Percival v Wright [1902] 2 Ch. 421; 71 L.J.Ch. 846; 51 W.R. 31; 18 T.L.R. 697; 18 T.L.R. 697; 46 S.J. 616; 9 Mans. 443, Ch D 6–014
Percy v Church of Scotland Board of National Mission [2005] UKHL 73; [2006] 2 A.C. 28; [2006] 2 W.L.R. 353; [2006] 4 All E.R. 1354; 2006 S.C. (H.L.) 1; 2006 S.L.T. 11; [2006] I.C.R. 134; [2006] I.R.L.R. 195; (2006) 150 S.J.L.B. 30, HL 2–181, *18–004*
Peregrine Systems Ltd v Steria Ltd [2005] EWCA Civ 239; [2005] Info. T.L.R. 294, CA (Civ Div) *21–013*, *21–020*
Perera v Vandiyar [1953] 1 W.L.R. 672; [1953] 1 All E.R. 1109; (1953) 97 S.J. 332, CA *1–123*, *26–019*
Pereria v Inspirations East Ltd (1992) C.A.T. 1048 .... *22–022*
Perestrello e Companhia Limitada v United Paint Co Ltd (No.1) [1969] 1 W.L.R. 570; [1969] 3 All E.R. 479; (1968) 113 S.J. 36, CA (Civ Div) *26–006*

Performing Right Society Ltd v Ciryl Theatrical Syndicate Ltd; sub nom. Performing Right Society Ltd v Ciryl theatrical Syndicate Ltd .The Decision Reported Below Has Since Been Reversed in the Court of Appeal [1924] 1 K.B. 1; 93 L.J.K.B. 33; 130 L.T. 450; 40 T.L.R. 52; 68 S.J. 9, CA; reversing [1923] 2 K.B. 146, KBD *18–083*, *19–038*
Performing Right Society Ltd v Thompson (1918) 34 T.L.R. 351 16–061
Perini Pacific v Greater Vancouver Sewerage and Drainage District (1966) 57 D.L.R.(2d) 307 .... *22–038*
Perls v Saalfeld [1892] 2 Ch. 149; 61 L.J.Ch. 409; 66 L.T. 666; 40 W.R. 548, CA *16–110*, *16–112*
Perrett v Collins [1998] 2 Lloyd's Rep. 255; [1999] P.N.L.R. 77, CA (Civ Div) ... *18–032*
Perrin v Morgan; sub nom. Morgan, Re; Morgan v Morgan [1943] A.C. 399; [1943] 1 All E.R. 187; 112 L.J.Ch. 81; 168 L.T. 177; 59 T.L.R. 134; 87 S.J. 47, HL; reversing [1942] Ch. 345, CA *12–060*
Perring v Hone (1826) 4 Bing. 28; 2 C. & P. 401; 12 Moore C.P. 135; 5 L.J. (O.S.) C.P. 33 .... *17–022*
Perrins v Marine Insurance Society (1859) 2 E. & E. 317; 29 L.J.Q.B. 17; 1 L.T. 27; 6 Jur. (N.S.) 69; 8 W.R. 41 .... *6–147*
Perrott v Perrott (1811) 14 East 423 .... *25–026*
Perry v Attwood (1856) 6 E.B. 691 .... *21–039*
Perry v Davis (1858) 3 C.B.(N.S.) 769 .... *24–003*
Perry v Equitable Life Assurance Society (1929) 45 T.L.R. 468 .... *30–345*
Perry v Jackson (1792) 4 T.R. 416 .... *28–077*
Perry v Moysey [1998] P.N.L.R. 657, QBD *28–011*
Perry v National Provincial Bank; sub nom. Perry v National Provincial Bank of England [1910] 1 Ch. 464; 79 L.J.Ch. 509; 102 L.T. 300; 54 S.J. 233, CA *19–087*
Perry v Sharon Development Co Ltd [1937] 4 All E.R. 390; 81 S.J. 1021, CA *13–015*
Perry v Sidney Phillips & Son [1982] 1 W.L.R. 1297; [1982] 3 All E.R. 705; 22 B.L.R. 120; (1982) 263 E.G. 888; (1982) 79 L.S.G. 1175; (1982) 126 S.J. 626, CA (Civ Div) *26–018*, *26–082*, *26–093*
Perry v Slade (1845) 8 Q.B. 115 .... *29–191*
Perry v Suffields Ltd [1916] 2 Ch. 187; 85 L.J.Ch. 460; 115 L.T. 4; 60 S.J. 494, CA *2–029*, 2–114
Perrylease Ltd v Imecar AG [1988] 1 W.L.R. 463; [1987] 2 All E.R. 373; (1988) 85(17) L.S.G. 32; (1986) 136 N.L.J. 987; (1988) 132 S.J. 536, QBD *4–023*, *4–024*, *12–117*, *12–118*, *12–123*
Personal Service Laundry v National Bank [1964] I.R. 49 .... *9–039*
Persson v London Country Buses [1974] 1 W.L.R. 569; [1974] 1 All E.R. 1251; [1974] 1 Lloyd's Rep. 415; [1974] R.T.R. 346; (1974) 118 S.J. 134, CA (Civ Div) *18–131*
Peruvian Guano Co Ltd v Dreyfus Bros & Co Ltd; sub nom. Dreyfus v Peruvian Guano Co [1892] A.C. 166, HL *29–052*
Peskin v Anderson [2001] B.C.C. 874; [2001] 1 B.C.L.C. 372, CA; affirming [2000] B.C.C. 1110; [2000] 2 B.C.L.C. 1, Ch D *18–010*
Pesquerias y Secaderos de Bacalao de Espana SA v Beer [1949] 1 All E.R. 845 (Note); (1948–49) 82 Ll. L. Rep. 501; [1949] W.N. 189; (1949) 93 S.J. 371, HL; affirming (1947) 80 Ll. L. Rep. 318, CA; reversing (1946) 79 Ll. L. Rep. 417; (1946) 175 L.T. 495, KBD *14–146*
Pesticcio v Huet; sub nom. Niersmans v Pesticcio [2004] EWCA Civ 372; [2004] W.T.L.R. 699; [2004] All E.R. (D) 36; (2004) 154 N.L.J. 653; (2004) 148 S.J.L.B. 420; [2004] N.P.C. 55, CA (Civ Div); affirming [2003] EWHC 2293 (Ch); (2003) 73 B.M.L.R. 57; [2003] W.T.L.R. 1327; [2003] 2 P. & C.R. DG8, Ch D *7–058*
Petch v Lyon (1846) 9 Q.B. 147 .... *29–191*
Petelin v Cullen (1975) 132 C.L.R. 355 .... *5–106*
Peter v Rich (1630) 1 Ch.Rep. 34 .... *17–027*
Peter Cremer GmbH v General Carriers SA; The Dona Mari [1974] 1 W.L.R. 341; [1974] 1 All E.R. 1; [1973] 2 Lloyd's Rep. 366; (1973) 117 S.J. 873, QBD (Comm) *14–055*, *26–178*

Peter Cremer GmbH & Co v Granaria BV; Granaria BV v C Schwarze [1981] 2 Lloyd's Rep. 583, QBD (Comm) *3–091*, *3–103*, *22–044*, *24–004*, *24–008*
Peter Dixon & Sons Ltd v Henderson Craig & Co Ltd [1919] 2 K.B. 778, CA *14–143*, *14–148*
Peter Dumenil & Co Ltd v James Ruddin Ltd [1953] 1 W.L.R. 815; [1953] 2 All E.R. 294; [1953] 2 Lloyd's Rep. 4; (1953) 97 S.J. 437, CA *24–018*, *24–019*
Peter Lind & Co Ltd v Mersey Docks and Harbour Board [1972] 2 Lloyd's Rep. 234, QBD (Comm) 2–027, *2–028*, *2–037*, *29–071*
Peter Pan Manufacturing Corp v Corsets Silhouette Ltd [1964] 1 W.L.R. 96; [1963] 3 All E.R. 402; [1963] R.P.C. 45; (1964) 108 S.J. 97, Ch D *29–145*, *29–151*, *29–155*
Peter Symmons & Co v Cook (1981) 131 N.L.J. 758 .... *14–066*
Peter Turnbull & Co Pty v Mundas Trading Co (Australasia) Pty [1954] 2 Lloyd's Rep. 198, HC (Aus) *24–011*
Peters v Anderson (1814) 5 Taunt. 596 .... *21–059*
Peters v Batchelor (1950) 100 L.J. 718, CA *5–058*
Peters v Fairclough Homes Ltd, unreported, Ch D *4–070*
Peters v Fleming (1840) 6 M. & W. 42 .... *8–004*, *8–007*, *8–008*
Peters v General Accident Fire & Life Assurance Corp Ltd [1938] 2 All E.R. 267; 158 L.T. 476; 54 T.L.R. 663; 82 S.J. 294;; 36 L.G.R. 583 .... *19–055*, *20–007*
Peters American Delicacy Co v Patricia's Chocolates and Candies (1947) 77 C.L.R. 574; 21 A.L.J. 281, HC (Aus) *16–092*
Petersen v Freebody & Co [1895] 2 Q.B. 294; 65 L.J.Q.B. 12; 73 L.T. 163; 14 R. 593; 44 W.R. 5; 8 Asp. M.C. 55, CA *12–130*
Petrofina (Great Britain) Ltd v Martin [1966] Ch. 146; [1966] 2 W.L.R. 318; [1966] 1 All E.R. 126; (1965) 109 S.J. 1009, CA; affirming [1965] Ch. 1073; [1965] 2 W.L.R. 1299; [1965] 2 All E.R. 176; (1965) 109 S.J. 288, Ch D 16–078, *16–083*, *16–098*, *16–121*, *16–199*
Petrofina (UK) Ltd v Magnaload Ltd [1984] Q.B. 127; [1983] 3 W.L.R. 805; [1983] 3 All E.R. 35; [1983] 2 Lloyd's Rep. 91; 25 B.L.R. 37; (1983) 80 L.S.G. 2677; (1983) 127 S.J. 729, QBD (Comm) *18–128*
Petrofina SA of Brussels v Compagnia Italiana Transporto Olii Minerali of Genoa (1937) 57 Ll. L. Rep. 247; (1937) 63 T.L.R. 650; 42 Com. Cas. 286 CA; affirming (1936) 56 Ll. L. Rep. 141; (1937) 53 T.L.R. 650, KBD *14–032*
Petrograde Inc v Stinnes Handel GmbH [1995] 1 Lloyd's Rep. 142, QBD (Comm) *3–092*, *12–036*
Petroleo Brasileiro SA—Petrobras Franto National de Peroleiros—Fronape v Elounda Shipping Co; The Evanthia M [1985] 2 Lloyd's Rep. 154, QBD (Comm) *12–076*
Petroleum Refining & Supply v Caleb Brett & Son. *See* International Petroleum Refining & Supply Sociedad LTDA v Caleb Brett & Son Ltd
Petromec Inc v Petroleo Brasiliero SA Petrobras [2006] EWHC 1443 (Comm); [2007] 1 Lloyd's Rep. 629, QBD (Comm) *2–116*, *18–091*
Petromec Inc v Petroleo Brasileiro SA Petrobras (No.3) [2005] EWCA Civ 891; [2006] 1 Lloyd's Rep. 121, CA (Civ Div); affirming in part [2004] EWHC 1180 (Comm); [2005] 1 Lloyd's Rep. 219, QBD (Comm) 1–029, *2–116*, *2–138*
Petros M Nomikos v Robertson. *See* Robertson v Petros M Nomikos Ltd
Petrotrade Inc v Smith (Vicarious Liability) [2000] 1 Lloyd's Rep. 486; [2000] C.L.C. 916, QBD (Comm) *29–156*
Pettitt v Pettitt; sub nom. P v P [1970] A.C. 777; [1969] 2 W.L.R. 966; [1969] 2 All E.R. 385; (1969) 20 P. & C.R. 991; (1969) 113 S.J. 344, HL; reversing [1968] 1 W.L.R. 443; [1968] 1 All E.R. 1053; (1968) 19 P. & C.R. 245; (1968) 112 S.J. 111, CA (Civ Div) *2–169*, *16–070*
Pettkuss v Becker [1980] 2 S.C.R. 834 .... *29–015*
Peyman v Lanjani [1985] Ch. 457; [1985] 2 W.L.R. 154; [1984] 3 All E.R. 703; (1984) 48 P. & C.R. 398; (1985) 82 L.S.G. 43; (1984) 128 S.J. 853, CA (Civ Div) 6–125, *6–125*, *6–156*, *24–003*, *24–004*, *24–005*, *24–007*, *24–008*, *28–144*
Peytoe's Case (1612) 9 Co.Rep. 79 .... *22–015*
Peyton v Mindham [1972] 1 W.L.R. 8; [1971] 3 All E.R. 1215; (1971) 115 S.J. 912, Ch D *16–097*, *16–110*, *16–119*

Pfizer Corp v Ministry of Health [1965] A.C. 512; [1965] 2 W.L.R. 387; [1965] 1 All E.R. 450; [1965] R.P.C. 261; (1965) 109 S.J. 149, HL; affirming [1964] Ch. 614; [1963] 3 W.L.R. 999; [1963] 3 All E.R. 779; (1963) 107 S.J. 828, CA; reversing [1963] 2 W.L.R. 286; [1963] 1 All E.R. 590; [1963] R.P.C. 173; (1962) 107 S.J. 56, Ch D *3–073*, *3–075*
Pharmaceutical Society of Great Britain v Boots Cash Chemists (Southern) Ltd [1953] 1 Q.B. 401; [1953] 2 W.L.R. 427; [1953] 1 All E.R. 482; (1953) 117 J.P. 132; (1953) 97 S.J. 149, CA; affirming [1952] 2 Q.B. 795; [1952] 2 All E.R. 456; [1952] 2 T.L.R. 340; (1952) 116 J.P. 507; (1952) 96 S.J. 513, QBD *2–014*
Pharmaceutical Society of Great Britain v Dickson; sub nom. Dickson v Pharmaceutical Society of Great Britain [1970] A.C. 403; [1968] 3 W.L.R. 286; [1968] 2 All E.R. 686; (1968) 112 S.J. 601, HL; affirming [1967] Ch. 708; [1967] 2 W.L.R. 718; [1967] 2 All E.R. 558; (1967) 111 S.J. 116, CA (Civ Div); affirming [1966] 1 W.L.R. 1539; [1966] 3 All E.R. 404; (1966) 110 S.J. 685, Ch D *9–004*, *16–096*, *16–139*
Phelps v Spon Smith & Co (Preliminary Issues) [2001] B.P.I.R. 326, Ch D *19–021*, *19–025*
Phibro Energy AG v Nissho Iwai Corp; The Honam Jade [1991] 1 Lloyd's Rep. 38, CA (Civ Div) *12–034*, *12–037*, *12–040*
Philip Alexander Securities & Futures Ltd v Bamberger; Philip Alexander Securities & Futures Ltd v Gilhaus; sub nom. Phillip Alexander Securities & Futures Ltd v Bamberger [1996] C.L.C. 1757; [1997] Eu. L.R. 63; [1997] I.L.Pr. 73, CA (Civ Div) *30–103*
Philip Collins Ltd v Davis [2000] 3 All E.R. 808; [2001] E.C.D.R. 17; [2000] E.M.L.R. 815, Ch D *3–107*, *3–112*, *29–178*, *29–179*, *29–180*, *29–181*, *29–185*
Philipp Brothers v Sierra Leone; sub nom. A Co Ltd v Republic of X and Commission of the European Communities [1995] 1 Lloyd's Rep. 289, CA (Civ Div); affirming [1994] 1 Lloyd's Rep. 111, QBD (Comm) *11–007*
Philips v Ward [1956] 1 W.L.R. 471; [1956] 1 All E.R. 874; (1956) 100 S.J. 317, CA *26–080*, *26–093*
Philips Electronique Grand Public SA v British Sky Broadcasting Ltd [1995] E.M.L.R. 472, CA (Civ Div) *13–004*, *13–012*
Philips Hong Kong Ltd v Attorney General of Hong Kong, 61 B.L.R. 41; (1993) 9 Const. L.J. 202, PC (HK) *26–125*, *26–127*, *26–129*, *26–132*, *26–135*
Philipson-Stow v Inland Revenue Commissioners [1961] A.C. 727; [1960] 3 W.L.R. 1008; [1960] 3 All E.R. 814; (1960) 39 A.T.C. 394; [1960] T.R. 333; (1960) 104 S.J. 1055, HL *30–005*, *30–013*
Phillimore v Barry (1818) 1 Camp. 513; 10 R.R. 742 .... *4–034*
Phillippine Admiral, The. *See* Owners of the Philippine Admiral v Wallem Shipping (Hong Kong) Ltd
Phillips, Ex p., Re Watson. *See* Watson Ex p. Phillips, Re
Phillips, Re [1914] 2 K.B. 689; 83 L.J.K.B. 1364; 110 L.T. 939; 21 Manson 144; 58 S.J. 364, KBD *20–023*
Phillips v Alhambra Palace Co [1901] 1 Q.B. 59; 70 L.J.Q.B. 26; 83 L.T. 431; 17 T.L.R. 40; 45 S.J. 81; 49 W.R. 223, QBD *20–006*, 23–037
Phillips v Brooks [1919] 2 K.B. 243; 88 L.J.K.B. 953; 121 L.T. 249, KBD ...*1–082*, 5–092
Phillips v Butler [1945] Ch. 358; [1945] 2 All E.R. 258 114 L.J.Ch. 327; 173 L.T. 224; 61 T.L.R. 477; 89 S.J. 403, Ch D *4–027*, *4–038*
Phillips v Foxall (1872) L.R. 7 Q.B. 666; 41 L.J.Q.B. 293; 27 L.T. 231, QB ... *6–159*
Phillips v Homfray (No.1); Fothergill v Phillips (1870–71) L.R. 6 Ch. App. 770, Lord Chancellor *20–001*, *26–022*, *29–116*, *29–140*, *29–142*, *29–143*, 29–144
Phillips v Homfray (No.2); sub nom. Phillips v Fothergill (1886) L.R. 11 App. Cas. 466; 49 L.T. 5; 32 W.R. 6, HL; affirming (1883) L.R. 24 Ch. D. 439, CA *20–001*
Phillips v Lamdin [1949] 2 K.B. 33; [1949] 1 All E.R. 770; [1949] L.J.R. 1293; (1949) 93 S.J. 320, KBD *21–018*, *26–092*, *27–015*
Phillips v London & South Western Railway Co; sub nom. Phillips v South Western Railway Co (1879–80) L.R. 5 Q.B.D. 78, CA *26–030*

Phillips (Liquidator of AJ Bekhor & Co) v Brewin Dolphin Bell Lawrie Ltd (formerly Brewin Dolphin & Co Ltd) [2001] UKHL 2; [2001] 1 W.L.R. 143; [2001] 1 All E.R. 673; [2001] B.C.C. 864; [2001] 1 B.C.L.C. 145; [2001] B.P.I.R. 119; (2001) 98(12) L.S.G. 43; (2001) 145 S.J.L.B. 32, HL; affirming [1999] 1 W.L.R. 2052; [1999] 2 All E.R. 844; [1999] B.C.C. 557; [1999] 1 B.C.L.C. 714; [1999] B.P.I.R. 797, CA (Civ Div); affirming [1998] 1 B.C.L.C. 700, Ch D *3–019*
Phillips-Higgins v Harper [1954] 1 Q.B. 411; [1954] 2 W.L.R. 782; [1954] 2 All E.R. 51 (Note); (1954) 98 S.J. 250, CA 28–088
Phillips Petroleum Co (UK) Ltd v Snamprogetti Ltd; sub nom. Snamprogetti Ltd v Phillips Petroleum Co (UK) Ltd [2001] EWCA Civ 889; 79 Con. L.R. 80, CA (Civ Div) *5–122*
Phillips Products v Hyland [1987] 1 W.L.R. 659; [1987] 2 All E.R. 620; (1988) 4 Const. L.J. 53; (1985) 82 L.S.G. 681; (1985) 129 S.J. 47; (1985) 4 Tr. L. 98, CA (Civ Div) *14–003*, *14–062*, *14–063*, *14–071*, *14–087*, 14–092
Phillipson v Kerry (1863) 32 Beav. 628; 11 W.R. 1034; 132 R.R. 871 .... *5–136*
Phillpotts v Clifton (1861) 10 W.R. 135 .... *21–085*
Philpot v Gruninger (1872) 14 Wall. 570 .... *3–010*
Philpott v Jones (1834) 2 A.E. 41 .... *21–063*
Phipps v Boardman. *See* Boardman v Phipps
Phipps v Jackson (1887) 56 L.J. Ch. 550 .... *27–026*
Phipps v Lovegrove; Prosser v Phipps (1873) L.R. 16 Eq. 80; 42 L.J.Ch. 892; 28 L.T. 584; 21 W.R. 590 (1873) L.R. 16 Eq. 80, Ct of Chancery *19–070*
Phipps v Orthodox Unit Trusts [1958] 1 Q.B. 314; [1957] 3 W.L.R. 856; [1957] 3 All E.R. 305; (1957) 36 A.T.C. 267; [1957] T.R. 277; (1957) 101 S.J. 884, CA *13–013*, *26–157*, *26–160*
Phoebus D Kyprianou v Cyprus Textiles [1958] 2 Lloyd's Rep. 60, CA *24–032*
Phoenix Bessemer Steel Co Ex p. Carnforth Haematite Iron Co, Re (1876–77) L.R. 4 Ch. D. 108, CA *24–018*
Phoenix General Insurance Co of Greece SA v Halvanon Insurance Co Ltd; sub nom. Phoenix General Insurance Co of Greece SA v Administratia Asigurarilor de Stat [1988] Q.B. 216; [1987] 2 W.L.R. 512; [1987] 2 All E.R. 152; [1986] 2 Lloyd's Rep. 552; [1987] Fin. L.R. 48; (1987) 84 L.S.G. 1055; (1987) 131 S.J. 257, CA (Civ Div); reversing [1986] 1 All E.R. 908; [1985] 2 Lloyd's Rep. 599; [1985] Fin. L.R. 368; (1985) 135 N.L.J. 1081, QBD (Comm) *16–147*, *16–159*
Phonogram Ltd v Lane [1982] Q.B. 938; [1981] 3 W.L.R. 736; [1981] 3 All E.R. 182; [1981] Com. L.R. 228; [1982] 3 C.M.L.R. 615; (1981) 125 S.J. 527, CA (Civ Div) 9–012
Phonographic Equipment (1958) v Muslu [1961] 1 W.L.R. 1379; [1961] 3 All E.R. 626; (1961) 105 S.J. 947, CA *26–135*, *26–155*
Phosphate Mining Co v Rankin Gilmour & Co (1916) 86 L.J.K.B. 358; 115 L.T. 211; 13 Asp.M.L.C. 418; (1915) 21 Com. Cas. 248 .... *14–143*
Phosphate of Lime Co v Green (1871) L.R. 7 C.P. 43; 25 L.T. 636, CCP *9–039*
Phosphate Sewage Co v Mollison (1879) 4 App. Cas. 801 .... *25–014*
Photo Production Ltd v Securicor Transport Ltd [1980] A.C. 827; [1980] 2 W.L.R. 283; [1980] 1 All E.R. 556; [1980] 1 Lloyd's Rep. 545; (1980) 124 S.J. 147, HL; reversing [1978] 1 W.L.R. 856; [1978] 3 All E.R. 146; [1978] 2 Lloyd's Rep. 172; (1978) 122 S.J. 315, CA (Civ Div) *1–012*, *1–071*, *7–126*, *12–022*, *12–026*, *12–040*, *14–003*, *14–005*, *14–008*, *14–009*, *14–011*, *14–016*, *14–018*, *14–019*, 14–022, 14–024, *14–028*, *14–029*, 14–098, *14–135*, *24–001*, *24–040*, 24–041, 24–047, *24–050*, *24–052*, *26–082*, *26–116*, *26–127*, *26–142*, *26–143*, *27–057*
Picardi (t/a Picardi Architects) v Cuniberti [2002] EWHC 2923 (TCC); [2003] B.L.R. 487; 94 Con. L.R. 81; (2003) 19 Const. L.J. 350, QBD (TCC) *2–030*, 15–094
Pickering v Deacon (t/a JA McConville) [2003] EWCA Civ 554; (2003) 100(21) L.S.G. 29, CA (Civ Div) *16–205*
Pickering v Dowson (1813) 4 Taunt. 779; 128 E.R. 537 .... *12–096*, *12–112*

Pickering v Ilfracombe Ry. (1868) L.R. 3 C.P. 235; 37 L.J.C.P. 118; 17 L.T. 650; 16 W.R. 458 .... *16–195*
Pickering v Sogex Services (UK), 20 B.L.R. 66; (1982) 262 E.G. 770, QBD *16–050*, *16–054*
Pickering v Stephenson (1872) L.R. 14 Eq. 322, Ct of Chancery *30–325*
Pierse v Bowles and Spibey (1816) 1 Stark. 323 .... *21–096*
Pigot's Case; sub nom. Winchcombe v Pigot [1558–1774] All E.R. Rep. 50; 77 E.R. 1177; 80 E.R. 1096; (1614) 2 Bulst. 246; (1614) 11 Co. Rep. 26, KB *1–114*, *17–022*, *25–020*, *25–021*, *25–023*
Pigott v Stratton (1859) 1 D. F. & J. 33; L.J.Ch. 1; 1 L.T. 111; 24 J.P. 69; 6 Jur.(N.S.) 129; 8 W.R. 13; 45 E.R. 271 .... *3–103*
Pike Sons & Co v Ongley (1887) L.R. 18 Q.B.D. 708; 56 L.J.Q.B. 373; 35 W.R. 534, CA *4–038*, *12–133*, *13–018*
Pilkington v Wood [1953] Ch. 770; [1953] 3 W.L.R. 522; [1953] 2 All E.R. 810; (1953) 97 S.J. 572, Ch D *26–103*, *26–104*
Pillans v Van Mierop (1765) 3 Burr. 1663 .... *3–001*
Pilley v Public Trustee [1956] N.Z.L.R. 771 .... *19–033*
Pilling Ex p. Salaman, Re [1906] 2 K.B. 644; 75 L.J.K.B. 739; 95 L.T. 362; 13 Manson 229, KBD *20–032*
Pilmore v Hood (1838) 6 Sco. 827; 8 D.P.C. 21; 1 Arn. 390; 3 Jur. 1153; (1838) 5 Bing. N.C. 97; 8 L.J.P.C. 11; 50 R.R. 622 ....*6–022*, *6–028*
Pinchon's Case (1608) 9 Col.Rep. 86b; 2 Brownl. 137; Cro.Jac. 294; Jenk. 144 ......*1–118*, *20–001*
Pink, Re; sub nom. Pink v Pink [1912] 2 Ch. 528, CA *25–005*
Pinnel's Case (1602) 5 Co.Rep. 117a; Moor. 677 ....3–115, 3–117, *3–122*, 3–129, *22–004*, 22–016, *22–017*
Pinnock Bros v Lewis & Peat Ltd [1923] 1 K.B. 690; (1923) 14 Ll. L. Rep. 277; 92 L.J.K.B. 695; 129 L.T. 320; 39 T.L.R. 212; 28 Com. Cas. 210, KBD ... *14–027*
Pinto Leite and Nephews, Re; sub nom. Visconde des Olivaes, Ex p. [1929] 1 Ch. 221, Ch D *19–070*
Pioneer Container, The; sub nom. Owners of Cargo Lately Laden on Board the KH Enterprise v Owners of the Pioneer Container [1994] 2 A.C. 324; [1994] 3 W.L.R. 1; [1994] 2 All E.R. 250; [1994] 1 Lloyd's Rep. 593; [1994] C.L.C. 332; (1994) 91(18) L.S.G. 37; (1994) 138 S.J.L.B. 85, PC (HK) *1–071*, *1–186*, *14–042*, *14–054*, *18–019*, *18–022*, *19–084*
Pioneer Shipping Ltd v BTP Tioxide Ltd; The Nema (No.2); sub nom. BTP Tioxide Ltd v Pioneer Shipping Ltd; BTP Tioxide Ltd v Armada Marine SA [1982] A.C. 724; [1981] 3 W.L.R. 292; [1981] 2 All E.R. 1030; [1981] 2 Lloyd's Rep. 239; [1981] Com. L.R. 197; (1981) 125 S.J. 542, HL; affirming [1980] Q.B. 547; [1980] 3 W.L.R. 326; [1980] 3 All E.R. 117; [1980] 2 Lloyd's Rep. 339; [1980] E.C.C. 467, CA (Civ Div); reversing [1980] 2 Lloyd's Rep. 83, QBD (Comm) ..*12–053*, *21–001*, *23–003*, *23–007*, *23–012*, *23–013*, *23–014*, *23–015*, *23–034*, 23–035, *23–040*, *23–097*
Pirelli General Cable Works Ltd v Oscar Faber & Partners [1983] 2 A.C. 1; [1983] 2 W.L.R. 6; [1983] 1 All E.R. 65; (1983) 265 E.G. 979, HL; reversing (1982) 262 E.G. 879, CA (Civ Div) *1–124*, *1–167*, *28–033*
Pitman v Woodbury (1848) 3 Exch. 4; R.R. 537 .... *4–040*
Pitt v Coomes (1835) 2 A.E. 459 .... *29–098*
Pitt v PHH Asset Management Ltd [1994] 1 W.L.R. 327; [1993] 4 All E.R. 961; (1994) 68 P. & C.R. 269; [1993] 40 E.G. 149; [1993] E.G. 127 (C.S.); (1993) 143 N.L.J. 1187; [1993] N.P.C. 120A, CA (Civ Div) *2–121*, *3–052*, *3–172*, *4–062*
Pitt v Smith (1811) 3 Camp. 33; 13 R.R. 741 8–080
Pittman v Prudential Deposit Bank (1896) 13 T.L.R. 111; 41 S.J. 129 .... *16–064*
Pitts v Hunt [1991] 1 Q.B. 24; [1990] 3 W.L.R. 542; [1990] 3 All E.R. 344; [1990] R.T.R. 290; (1990) 134 S.J. 834, CA (Civ Div); affirming [1990] 1 Q.B. 302; [1989] 3 W.L.R. 795; [1989] R.T.R. 365, QBD *16–168*
Pitts v Jones [2007] EWCA Civ 1301; [2008] 1 All E.R. 941; [2008] 1 All E.R. (Comm) 548; [2008] 1 B.C.L.C. 613; [2007] 2 C.L.C. 947; (2007) 151 S.J.L.B. 1594, CA (Civ Div) *3–010*, *3–024*
Planche v Colbourn, 131 E.R. 305; (1831) 8 Bing. 14, KB *21–036*, 29–066

Planché v Colburn (1831) 8 Bing. 14; 1 M. & Scott 51; 5 Car. & P. 58 .... *6–120*
Planmount Ltd v Zaire [1981] 1 All E.R. 1110; [1980] 2 Lloyd's Rep. 393, QBD (Comm) *11–001*, *11–002*
Plant v Bourne [1897] 2 Ch. 281; 66 L.J.Ch. 643; 76 L.T. 820; 46 W.R. 59, CA *4–024*, *12–123*
Plasticmoda Societa Per Azioni v Davidsons (Manchester) [1952] 1 Lloyd's Rep. 527, CA *22–042*
Platform Home Loans Ltd v Oyston Shipways Ltd [2000] 2 A.C. 190; [1999] 2 W.L.R. 518; [1999] 1 All E.R. 833; [1999] C.L.C. 867; (1999) 1 T.C.L.R. 18; [1999] P.N.L.R. 469; [1999] 1 E.G.L.R. 77; [1999] 13 E.G. 119; [1999] E.G. 26 (C.S.); (1999) 96(10) L.S.G. 31; (1999) 149 N.L.J. 283; (1999) 143 S.J.L.B. 65; [1999] N.P.C. 21, HL *26–049*, *26–094*
Platt v Bromage (1854) 24 L.J.Ex. 63 .... *29–041*
Playa Larga, The. *See* Empresa Exportadora De Azucar (CUBAZUCAR) v Industria Azucarera Nacional SA (IANSA)
Plevins v Downing (1875–76) L.R. 1 C.P.D. 220; 45 L.J.Q.B. 695; 35 L.T. 263; 40 J.P. 791, CPD *22–033*
Plimley v Westley, 132 E.R. 98; (1835) 2 Bing. N.C. 249, KB *21–073*
Plimmer v Wellington Corp; sub nom. Plimmer v Mayor, Councillors, and Citizens of the City of Wellington (1883–84) L.R. 9 App. Cas. 699; 53 L.J.P.C. 105; 51 L.T. 475, PC (NZ) *3–141*, *3–142*, *3–158*, *29–003*, *29–161*
Plomer v Long (1816) 1 Stark. 153 .... *21–064*
Plowman & Son Ltd v Ash. *See* GW Plowman & Son Ltd v Ash
Plummer v Woodburne (1825) 4 B.C. 625 .... *25–017*
Plumptres Marriage Settlement, Re; sub nom. Underhill v Plumptre [1910] 1 Ch. 609; 79 L.J.Ch. 340; 102 L.T. 315; 26 T.L.R. 321; 54 S.J. 326, Ch D *18–087*
Plymouth Corp v Harvey [1971] 1 W.L.R. 549; [1971] 1 All E.R. 623; 69 L.G.R. 310; (1971) 22 P. & C.R. 475; (1970) 115 S.J. 13, Ch D *1–115*
Podar Trading Co, Bombay v Francois Tagher, Barcelona [1949] 2 K.B. 277; [1949] 2 All E.R. 62; (1948–49) 82 Ll. L. Rep. 705; 65 T.L.R. 433; [1949] L.J.R. 1470; (1949) 93 S.J. 406, KBD *14–147*, *14–148*, *26–144*
Pole v Harrobin (1782) 9 East 416n *7–051*
Polemis and Furness Withy & Co Ltd, Re; sub nom. Polemis v Furness Withy & Co [1921] 3 K.B. 560; (1921) 8 Ll. L. Rep. 351, CA; affirming (1921) 7 Ll. L. Rep. 196, KBD *14–013*
Polglass v Oliver, 149 E.R. 7; (1831) 2 Cr. & J. 15, KB *21–086*
Polhill v Walter (1832) 3 B. & Ad. 114; 1 L.J.K.B. 92 .... *6–046*
Policy of the Equitable Life Assurance of the United States and Mitchell, Re (1911) 27 T.L.R. 213 .... *18–081*
Polish Steamship Co v Atlantic Maritime Co; The Garden City (No.2) [1985] Q.B. 41; [1984] 3 W.L.R. 300; [1984] 3 All E.R. 59; [1984] 2 Lloyd's Rep. 37; (1984) 81 L.S.G. 1367; (1984) 128 S.J. 469, CA (Civ Div) *26–178*
Polkey v AE Dayton Services Ltd; sub nom. Polkey v Edmund Walker (Holdings) Ltd [1988] A.C. 344; [1987] 3 W.L.R. 1153; [1987] 3 All E.R. 974; [1988] I.C.R. 142; [1987] I.R.L.R. 503; (1987) 137 N.L.J. 1109; (1988) 138 N.L.J. Rep. 33; (1987) 131 S.J. 1624, HL *24–014*
Pollard v Bank of England (1870–71) L.R. 6 Q.B. 623, QB *29–038*
Pollard v Clayton (1855) 1 K. & J. 462 .... *27–017*
Pollitt Ex p. Minor, Re [1893] 1 Q.B. 455; 62 L.J.Q.B. 236; 68 L.T. 366; 41 W.R. 276; 4 R. 253, CA; affirming [1893] 1 Q.B. 175, QBD *20–041*
Pollock & Co v Macrae. *See* W&S Pollock & Co v Macrae
Pollway v Abdullah [1974] 1 W.L.R. 493; [1974] 2 All E.R. 381; (1974) 118 S.J. 277, CA (Civ Div) *3–010*, *3–036*, *21–087*
Polly Peck International Plc (In Administration) (No.5), Re; Marangos Hotel Co Ltd v Stone [1998] 3 All E.R. 812; [1998] 2 B.C.L.C. 185, CA (Civ Div) *29–160*
Polsky v S&A Services; sub nom. S&A Services v Polsky [1951] 1 All E.R. 1062 (Note); [1951] W.N. 256; (1951) 95 S.J. 414, CA; affirming [1951] 1 All E.R. 185, KBD *12–113*
Poly Lina Ltd v Finch [1995] F.S.R. 751, QBD *16–108*
Polymasc Pharmaceutical Plc v Charles [1999] F.S.R. 711, Ch D (Patents Ct) *16–108*

Pomeroy v Buckfast (Abbot) (1443) Y.B. 22 Hen. 6; 5 pl 7; (1442) Y.B. 21 Hen.6, p.15; pl 30 ... *16–052*
Pontypridd Union v Drew. *See* Guardians of Pontypridd Union v Drew
Pool Shipping Co Ltd v London Coal Co of Gibraltar Ltd [1939] 2 All E.R. 432; (1939) 63 Ll. L. Rep. 268; 64 W.L.R. 268; 44 Com. Cas. 276, KBD ... *14–151*
Poole Corp v Moody [1945] K.B. 350, CA ... *28–134*
Poole v Middleton (1861) 29 Beav. 646 ... *27–011*
Poole v Poole (1871) L.R. 7 Ch. App. 17 ... *28–130*
Poole v Tunbridge (1837) 2 M.W. 223 ... *21–089*, *21–090*, *21–095*
Poosathurai v Kannappa Chettiar (1919) L.R. 47 Ind. App. 1 ... *7–060*
Pope v Buenos Ayres New Gas Co (1892) 8 T.L.R. 758 ... *5–076*
Pople v Evans [1969] 2 Ch. 255; [1968] 3 W.L.R. 97; [1968] 2 All E.R. 743; (1968) 112 S.J. 441, Ch D ... *25–011*
Poplett v Stockdale (1825) R. & M. 337; 2 C. & P. 198; 31 R.R. 662 ... *16–014*
Popple v Sylvester (1883) L.R. 22 Ch. D. 98; (1883) 52 L.J. Ch. 54, Ch D ... *25–009*
Pordage v Cole (1669) 1 Wms.Saund. 319; 1 Lev. 274; 2 Keb. 542; T.Raym. 183; 1 Sid. 423 ... *12–026*, *24–035*, *24–036*, *24–037*
Port Caledonia, The; Anna, The [1903] P. 184; 72 L.J.P. 60; 80 L.T. 216; 52 W.R. 223; 9 Asp. M.L.C. 479, PDAD ... *7–047*
Port Huron Machinery Co v Wohlers, 207 Iowa 826, 221 N.W. 843 (1928) ... *2–047*
Port Jackson Stevedoring Pty v Salmond & Spraggon (Australia) Pty; The New York Star; Salmond & Spraggon (Australia) Pty v Joint Cargo Services Pty [1981] 1 W.L.R. 138; [1980] 3 All E.R. 257; [1980] 2 Lloyd's Rep. 317; (1980) 124 S.J. 756, PC (Aus) ... *3–074*, *14–033*, *14–042*, 14–048, *18–019*, *18–021*, *18–085*, *24–047*, *24–050*, *24–052*
Port Line v Ben Line Steamers [1958] 2 Q.B. 146; [1958] 2 W.L.R. 551; [1958] 1 All E.R. 787; [1958] 1 Lloyd's Rep. 290; (1958) 102 S.J. 232, QBD ... *1–188*, 18–139, 18–146, 18–147, 23–043
Port Sudan Cotton Co v Govindaswamy Chettiar & Sons [1977] 2 Lloyd's Rep. 5, CA (Civ Div); reversing [1977] 1 Lloyd's Rep. 166, QBD (Comm) ... *2–028*, *2–031*, *2–111*, *12–126*
Port Swettenham Authority v TW Wu & Co Sdn Bhd [1979] A.C. 580; [1978] 3 W.L.R. 530; [1978] 3 All E.R. 337; [1979] 1 Lloyd's Rep. 11; (1978) 122 S.J. 523, PC (Mal) ... *3–177*, *14–018*, *14–019*
Portaria Shipping Co v Gulf Pacific Navigation Co Ltd; The Selene G [1981] 2 Lloyd's Rep. 180; [1981] Com. L.R. 111, QBD (Comm) ... *21–013*
Portavon Cinema Co v Price & Century Co, 161 L.T. 417; 84 S.J. 152; 45 Com. Cas. 93; [1939] 4 All E.R. 601, KBD ... *18–129*
Porter v Addo; sub nom. Porter v Motor Insurers Bureau [1978] 2 Lloyd's Rep. 463; [1978] R.T.R. 503; (1978) 122 S.J. 592, QBD ... *18–131*
Porter v Freudenberg; sub nom. Merten's Patents, Re; Kreglinger v S Samuel & Rosenfeld [1915] 1 K.B. 857; 84 L.J.K.B. 1001; 112 L.T. 313; 31 T.L.R. 162; 20 Com. Cas. 189, CA ... *11–024*, *11–027*, *11–028*, *11–030*
Porter v National Union of Journalists; Pritchard v National Union of Journalists [1980] I.R.L.R. 404, HL; affirming [1979] I.R.L.R. 404, CA (Civ Div) ... *9–083*
Porter v Tottenham Urban DC [1915] 1 K.B. 776; 84 L.J.K.B. 1041; 112 L.T. 711; 31 T.L.R. 97; 79 J.P. 169; 13 L.G.R. 216, CA; affirming [1914] 1 K.B. 663, KBD ... *13–010*
Porter Bristow v Taylor (1817) 6 M.S. 156 ... *21–049*
Portman Building Society v Dusangh [2000] 2 All E.R. (Comm) 221; [2000] Lloyd's Rep. Bank. 197; [2001] W.T.L.R. 117; [2000] N.P.C. 51; (2000) 80 P. & C.R. D20, CA (Civ Div) ... *7–132*
Portman Building Society v Hamlyn Taylor Neck [1998] 4 All E.R. 202; [1998] P.N.L.R. 664; (1999) 77 P. & C.R. 66; [1998] 2 E.G.L.R. 113; [1998] 31 E.G. 102; (1998) 76 P. & C.R. D16, CA (Civ Div) ... *29–018*, *29–019*, *29–034*, *29–182*
Portman Registrars and Nominees v Latif, unreported, April 23, 1987, CC (Willesden) ... *8–035*
Porto Alexandre, The; sub nom. Nora, The v Porto Alexandre, The [1920] P. 30; [1918–19] All E.R. Rep. 615; (1919) 1 Ll. L. Rep. 191, CA; affirming (1919) 1 Ll. L. Rep. 84, PDAD ... *11–001*

Poseidon Freight Forwarding Co Ltd v Davies Turner Southern Ltd [1996] 2 Lloyd's Rep. 388; [1996] C.L.C. 1264, CA (Civ Div) *12–014*
Posner v Scott-Lewis [1987] Ch. 25; [1986] 3 W.L.R. 531; [1986] 3 All E.R. 513; [1986] 1 E.G.L.R. 56; (1985) 277 E.G. 859; (1986) 83 L.S.G. 359; (1986) 130 S.J. 14, Ch D *27–024*, *27–025*, 27–026, *27–044*
Possfund Custodian Trustee Ltd v Diamond; Parr v Diamond [1996] 1 W.L.R. 1351; [1996] 2 B.C.L.C. 665, Ch D *6–082*
Postlethwaite v Freeland (1879–80) L.R. 5 App. Cas. 599, HL *21–020*
Poteliakhoff v Teakle [1938] 2 K.B. 816; 107 L.J.K.B. 678; 54 T.L.R. 1075; 82 S.J. 644; [1938] 3 All E.R. 686, CA *3–050*
Potoi Chau, The. *See* Castle Insurance Co v Hong Kong Islands Shipping Co
Potomek Construction Ltd v Zurich Securities Ltd [2003] EWHC 2827; [2004] 1 All E.R. (Comm) 672, Ch D *21–061*, *21–067*
Pott v Todhunter (1845) 2 Coll. 76; 9 Jur. 589 .... *12–108*
Potter v Burrell. *See* John Potter & Co v Burrell & Son
Potter v Duffield (1874) L.R. 18 Eq. 4; 43 L.J.Ch. 472; 22 W.R. 585, Ct of Chancery *4–023*
Potter v RJ Temple Plc (In Liquidation), *TheTimes*, February 11, 2004, EAT ... *24–013*
Potter v Sanders (1846) 6 Hare 1; 67 E.R. 1057 .... *2–048*, *2–057*
Potters (A Firm) v Loppert [1973] Ch. 399 .... *29–198*
Potters Oils, Re (No.2); sub nom. Potters Oils Ltd (No.2), Re [1986] 1 W.L.R. 201; [1986] 1 All E.R. 890; (1985) 1 B.C.C. 99593; [1986] P.C.C. 185; (1986) 83 L.S.G. 869; (1985) 130 S.J. 166, Ch D (Companies Ct) *20–035*
Potton Ltd v Yorkclose Ltd [1990] F.S.R. 11, Ch D *29–142*
Potts v Bell (1800) 8 T.R. 548; 2 Esp. 612; 5 R.R. 452 .... *16–026*
Potts v Nixon (1870) I.R. 5 C.L. 45 .... *1–112*
Poulton v Moore [1915] 1 K.B. 400; 84 L.J.K.B. 462; 112 L.T. 202, CA *1–112*
Pound & Co v Hardy & Co Inc. *See* AV Pound & Co v MW Hardy & Co Inc
Poussard v Speirs & Pond (1875–76) L.R. 1 Q.B.D. 410, QBD ...*23–038*, *23–068*, *24–040*
Powdrill v Watson; sub nom. Paramount Airways Ltd (No.3), Re; Talbot v Cadge; Talbot v Grundy; Leyland DAF Ltd (No.2), Re; Ferranti International Plc, Re [1995] 2 A.C. 394; [1995] 2 W.L.R. 312; [1995] 2 All E.R. 65; [1995] B.C.C. 319; [1994] 1 B.C.L.C. 386; [1995] I.C.R. 1100; [1995] I.R.L.R. 269; (1995) 92(17) L.S.G. 47; (1995) 145 N.L.J. 449; (1995) 139 S.J.L.B. 110, HL; affirming [1994] 2 All E.R. 513; [1994] B.C.C. 172; [1994] 2 B.C.L.C. 118; [1994] I.C.R. 395; [1994] I.R.L.R. 295; (1994) 91(15) L.S.G. 35; (1994) 91(22) L.S.G. 32; (1994) 144 N.L.J. 389; (1994) 138 S.J.L.B. 76, CA (Civ Div); affirming [1993] B.C.C. 662, Ch D (Companies Ct) *2–030*, 9–050
Powell v Benney [2007] EWCA Civ 1283; (2007) 151 S.J.L.B. 1598; [2008] 1 P. & C.R. DG12, CA (Civ Div) *4–082*
Powell v Braun; sub nom. Powell v Gilmore [1954] 1 W.L.R. 401; [1954] 1 All E.R. 484; (1954) 98 S.J. 144, CA *2–113*, *29–072*
Powell v Brent LBC [1988] I.C.R 176 .... *27–023*
Powell v Brodhurst [1901] 2 Ch. 160, Ch D *21–049*
Powell v Browne [1907] W.N. 228 .... *21–058*
Powell v Hoyland (1851) 6 Exch. 67; 20 L.J.Ex. 82; 16 L.T. 369; 86 R.R. 193 ..... *7–050*
Powell v Lee (1908) 99 L.T. 284; 24 T.L.R. 606; 6 L.G.R. 840; 72 J.P. 353 .... *2–045*
Powell v Marshall Parkes & Co [1899] 1 Q.B. 710, CA *24–028*
Powell v Owners of the Proceeds of Sale of the Halcyon Skies (No.2) [1977] 1 Lloyd's Rep. 22; (1976) 120 S.J. 502, QBD (Admlty) *30–376*
Powell v Powell [1900] 1 Ch. 243; 69 L.J.Ch. 164; 82 L.T. 84, Ch D *7–074*, *7–075*, 7–095
Powell v Rees (1837) 7 A.E. 426 .... *29–142*, *29–143*, *29–144*
Powell v Streatham Manor Nursing Home [1935] A.C. 243, HL *26–030*
Powell Duffryn Steam Coal Co v Taff Vale Railway Co (1873–74) L.R. 9 Ch. App. 331, CA in Chancery *27–026*
Power Co v Gore District Council [1997] N.Z.L.R. 537 .... *13–027*

Power Curber International Ltd v National Bank of Kuwait SAK [1981] 1 W.L.R. 1233; [1981] 3 All E.R. 607; [1981] 2 Lloyd's Rep. 394; [1981] Com. L.R. 224, CA (Civ Div) *30–012*
Pownal v Ferrand (1827) 6 B.C. 439 .... *29–108*, *29–109*
Practice Direction (Fam Div: Ancillary Relief: Payment of School Fees) [1980] 1 W.L.R. 1441; [1980] 3 All E.R. 832, Fam Div *8–027*
Practice Direction (Fam Div: Minors: Maintenance: School Fees); sub nom. Practice Direction (Fam Div: Minor: Payment of School Fees) [1983] 1 W.L.R. 800; [1983] 2 All E.R. 679, Fam Div *8–027*
Practice Note (Ch D: Bankruptcy: Statutory Demands) (No.1/88); sub nom. Practice Note (Ch D: Bankruptcy: Service Abroad) [1988] 1 W.L.R. 461; [1988] 2 All E.R. 126, Ch D *20–018*
Practice Note (Ch D: Bankruptcy: Statutory Demands) (No.2/88) [1988] 1 W.L.R. 557; [1988] 2 All E.R. 127, Ch D *20–018*
Practice Note (Ch D: Bankruptcy: Voluntary Arrangements) (No.1 of 1991) [1992] 1 W.L.R. 120; [1992] 1 All E.R. 678, Ch D *20–050*
Practice Note [1927] W.N. 290 .... *22–024*
Praed v Graham (1890) L.R. 24 Q.B.D. 53, CA *26–030*
Praet (Julien) et Cie S/A v HG Poland Ltd (Damages) [1962] 1 Lloyd's Rep. 566, QBD (Comm) *26–161*, *26–163*, *26–165*
Prater v Cornwall CC. *See* Cornwall CC v Prater
Pratt v Swaine (1828) 8 B. & C. 285 .... *28–031*
Pratt v Vizard (1833) 5 B. Ad. 808 .... *29–093*
Pratt Contractors Ltd v Transit New Zealand [2003] UKPC 83; [2004] B.L.R. 143; 100 Con. L.R. 29, PC (NZ) *10–038*
Prazic v Prazic [2006] EWCA Civ 497; [2007] I.L.Pr. 31; [2006] 2 F.L.R. 1125; [2007] 1 F.C.R. 503; [2006] Fam. Law 745, CA (Civ Div) *30–082*
Precision Dippings Ltd v Precision Dippings Marketing Ltd [1986] Ch. 447; [1985] 3 W.L.R. 812; (1985) 1 B.C.C. 99539; [1986] P.C.C. 105; (1985) 129 S.J. 683, CA (Civ Div) *9–038*
Prees v Coke (1870–71) L.R. 6 Ch. App. 645, Lord Chancellor *7–128*
Prehn v Royal Bank of Liverpool (1869–70) L.R. 5 Ex. 92, Ex Ct *26–098*
Premium Nafta Products Ltd v Fili Shipping Co Ltd. *See* Fiona Trust & Holding Corp v Privalov
Prenn v Simmonds [1971] 1 W.L.R. 1381; [1971] 3 All E.R. 237; (1971) 115 S.J. 654, HL *1–031*, *1–040*, *12–043*, *12–118*, 12–119, *12–120*, *12–126*, *18–091*
Presentaciones Musicales SA v Secunda [1994] Ch. 271; [1994] 2 W.L.R. 660; [1994] 2 All E.R. 737; (1994) 138 S.J.L.B. 4, CA (Civ Div) *28–117*, *30–042*
President of India v La Pintada Compania Navigacion SA; The La Pintada [1985] A.C. 104; [1984] 3 W.L.R. 10; [1984] 2 All E.R. 773; [1984] 2 Lloyd's Rep. 9; [1984] C.I.L.L. 110; (1984) 81 L.S.G. 1999; (1984) 128 S.J. 414, HL; reversing [1983] 1 Lloyd's Rep. 37; [1982] Com. L.R. 250, QBD (Comm) *6–065*, *26–006*, *26–063*, *26–098*, *26–167*, *26–169*, *26–174*, *26–183*
President of India v Lips Maritime Corp; The Lips; sub nom. Lips Maritime Corp v President of India [1988] A.C. 395; [1987] 3 W.L.R. 572; [1987] 3 All E.R. 110; [1987] 2 Lloyd's Rep. 311; [1987] 2 F.T.L.R. 477; [1987] Fin. L.R. 313; (1987) 84 L.S.G. 2765; (1987) 137 N.L.J. 734; (1987) 131 S.J. 1085, HL *26–061*, *26–081*, *26–098*, *26–135*, *26–136*, *26–167*, *26–176*, *30–340*
President of the Methodist Conference v Parfitt [1984] Q.B. 368; [1984] 2 W.L.R. 84; [1983] 3 All E.R. 747; [1984] I.C.R. 176; [1984] I.R.L.R. 141, CA (Civ Div); reversing, *The Times*, November 18, 1982, EAT *2–181*
Preston v Christmas (1759) 2 Wils.K.B. 86 .... *22–003*
Preston v Luck (1884) L.R. 27 Ch. D. 497; 33 W.R. 317, CA *5–077*
Preston v Torfaen BC, 65 B.L.R. 1; 36 Con. L.R. 48; (1994) 26 H.L.R. 149; [1955–95] P.N.L.R. 625; [1993] E.G. 137 (C.S.); [1993] N.P.C. 111, CA (Civ Div); affirming (1991) 7 Const. L.J. 345, QBD (OR) *1–178*, *18–031*
Preston (Ronald) & Partners v Markheath Securities [1988] 2 E.G.L.R. 23; [1988] 31 E.G. 57 .... *2–118*
Prevost v Wood (1905) 21 T.L.R. 694 .... *16–043*, *16–070*

Price v Barker (1855) 4 E. & B. 760; 24 L.J.Q.B. 130; 1 Jur. 775; 3 C.L.R. 927; 25 L.T. 51; 99 R.R. 734 .... *17–018*
Price v Easton (1833) 2 L.J.K.B. 51; 4 B. & Ad. 433; 1 N. & M. 303 .... *18–016*, *18–019*
Price v Green (1847) 16 M.W. 346 .... *26–134*
Price v Jenkins (1877) L.R. 5 Ch. D. 619; 46 L.J.Ch. 805; 37 L.T. 51, CA; reversing (1876–77) L.R. 4 Ch. D. 483, Ch D *3–008*
Price v Macaulay (1852) 2 De G.M. & G. 339 .... *27–055*
Price v Moulton, 138 E.R. 222; (1851) 10 C.B. 561, CCP *25–001*
Price v Neal (1762) 3 Burr. 1354 .... *29–182*
Price v Price (1847) 16 M.W. 232 .... *21–073*
Price v Strange [1978] Ch. 337; [1977] 3 W.L.R. 943; [1977] 3 All E.R. 371; (1978) 36 P. & C.R. 59; (1977) 243 E.G. 295; (1977) 121 S.J. 816, CA (Civ Div) *27–028*, 27–048, *27–078*, *27–084*
Price v Union Lighterage Co [1904] 1 K.B. 412; 73 L.J.K.B. 222; 89 L.T. 731; 20 T.L.R. 177; 52 W.R. 325; 48 S.J. 207; 9 Com. Cas. 120, CA; affirming [1903] 1 K.B. 750, KBD *14–011*
Prickett v Badger (1856) 1 C.B.(N.S.) 296 .... 29–066, *29–068*, *29–069*
Pridean Ltd v Forest Taverns Ltd (1998) 75 P. & C.R. 447, CA (Civ Div) *3–144*
Prideaux v Webber (1661) 1 Lev. 31 .... *28–064*
Priest v Last [1903] 2 K.B. 148 .... *26–082*
Prime Commercial Ltd v Wool Board Disestablishment Co Ltd [2006] N.Z.C.A. 295 .... *10–037*
Primetrade AG v Ythan Ltd [2005] EWHC 2399 (Comm); [2006] 1 All E.R. 367; [2006] 1 All E.R. (Comm) 157; [2006] 1 Lloyd's Rep. 457; [2005] 2 C.L.C. 911, QBD (Comm) *30–066*
Primlake Ltd (In Liquidation) v Matthews Associates [2006] EWHC 1227 (Ch); [2007] 1 B.C.L.C. 666, Ch D *29–016*, *29–075*
Primrose (Builders) Ltd, Re [1950] Ch. 561; [1950] 2 All E.R. 334; 66 T.L.R. (Pt. 2) 99, Ch D *21–066*
Prince of Wales, etc., Association Co v Palmer (1858) 25 Beav. 605; 119 R.R. 567 .... *16–169*
Princess Thurn and Taxis v Moffitt [1915] 1 Ch. 58, Ch D *11–027*
Pring v Clarkson (1822) 1 B.C. 14 .... *21–076*
Pringle of Scotland Ltd v Continental Express Ltd [1962] 2 Lloyd's Rep. 80, QBD (Comm) *14–033*
Print Concept GmbH v GEW (EC) Ltd [2001] EWCA Civ 352; [2002] C.L.C. 352; [2001] E.C.C. 36, CA (Civ Div) *30–020*, *30–076*, *30–077*, *30–090*, *30–200*
Printers & Finishers Ltd v Holloway (No.2) [1965] 1 W.L.R. 1; [1964] 3 All E.R. 731; [1965] R.P.C. 239; (1965) 109 S.J. 47, Ch D *16–107*, *27–070*
Printing and Numerical Registering Co v Sampson (1874–75) L.R. 19 Eq. 462; 44 L.J.Ch. 705; 32 L.T. 354; 23 W.R. 463, Ct of Chancery *1–011*, 16–004
Prior v Hembrow (1841) 8 M. & W. 873; 10 L.J.Ex. 371 .... *17–027*
Pritam Kaur v S Russell & Sons Ltd. *See* Kaur (Pritam) v S Russell & Sons Ltd
Pritchard v Briggs [1980] Ch. 338; [1979] 3 W.L.R. 868; [1980] 1 All E.R. 294; (1980) 40 P. & C.R. 1; (1979) 123 S.J. 705, CA (Civ Div); reversing [1978] 2 W.L.R. 317; [1978] 1 All E.R. 886; (1978) 35 P. & C.R. 266; (1977) 244 E.G. 211, Ch D *2–127*, *4–013*, *4–058*, *18–135*
Pritchard v Merchants' and Tradesmen's Life Assurance Society (1858) 3 C.B. (N.S.) 622; 27 L.J.C.P. 169; 30 L.T. (O.S.) 318; 4 Jur. (N.S.) 307; 6 W.R. 340 .... *5–022*
Pritchard v The Merchant's and Tradesman's Mutual Life Assurance Society (1858) 3 C.B.(N.S.) 622 .... *29–082*
Pritchard's Case, Re; Tavarone Mining Co (1872–73) L.R. 8 Ch. App. 956; 42 L.J.Ch. 768; 29 L.T. 363; 21 W.R. 829, CA in Chancery *9–061*
Procter v Bayley and Son; sub nom. Proctor v Bayley (1889) L.R. 42 Ch. D. 390; (1889) 6 R.P.C. 538, CA *27–084*

Procter & Gamble (Health and Beauty Care) Ltd v Carrier Holdings Ltd; sub nom. Proctor & Gamble (Health and Beauty Care) Ltd v Carrier Holdings Ltd [2003] EWHC 83 (TCC); [2003] B.L.R. 255; [2003] T.C.L.R. 6, QBD (TCC) *12–004*, *24–021*, *24–026*
Procter & Gamble Phillipine Manufacturing Corp v Peter Cremer GmbH & Co; The Manila (No.2) [1988] 3 All E.R. 843, QBD .. *3–104*, *29–022*, *29–110*, *29–115*, *29–133*
Produce Brokers Co Ltd v Olympia Oil & Cake Co Ltd (Reasonableness of Trade Custom) [1917] 1 K.B. 320, CA; affirming [1916] 2 K.B. 296, KBD *12–128*
Produce Brokers Co Ltd v Olympia Oil & Cake Co Ltd; sub nom. Olympia Oil and Cake Co Ltd and the Produce Brokers Co Ltd, Re [1916] 1 A.C. 314, HL *12–133*, *13–018*
Proform Sports Management Ltd v Proactive Sports Management Ltd [2006] EWHC 2903 (Ch); [2007] Bus. L.R. 93; [2007] 1 All E.R. 542; [2007] 1 All E.R. (Comm) 356; (2006) 156 N.L.J. 1723, Ch D (Manchester) *8–005*, *8–028*, *8–045*
Progressive House Party Ltd v Tabali Party Ltd (1985) 157 C.L.R. 17 .... *24–001*
Prole v Allen [1950] 1 All E.R. 476, Assizes (Somerset) *9–073*
Prometheus, The (1948–49) 82 Ll. L. Rep. 859, CA; affirming (1948–49) 82 Ll. L. Rep. 172, PDAD *10–014*
Propend Finance Pty Ltd v Sing, *The Times*, May 2, 1997; 111 Int. L.R. 111, CA (Civ Div) *11–004*, *11–014*, *11–021*, *11–022*
Property & Bloodstock Ltd v Emerton; Bush v Property & Bloodstock Ltd [1968] Ch. 94; [1967] 3 W.L.R. 973; [1967] 3 All E.R. 321; (1967) 111 S.J. 414, CA (Civ Div); affirming [1967] 2 All E.R. 839, Ch D *2–148*, *12–028*
Prosper Homes Ltd v Hambros Bank Executor & Trustee Co Ltd (1980) 39 P. & C.R. 395, Ch D *3–104*
Prosser v Allen (1819) Gow. 117 .... *10–013*
Prosser v Edmunds (1835) 1 Y. & C. Ex. 481; 41 R.R. 322 .... *19–049*
Prosser v Wagner (1856) 1 C.B.(N.S.) 289 .... *21–049*
Prostar Management Ltd v Twaddle, 2003 S.L.T. (Sh Ct) 11; 2002 G.W.D. 28–983, Sh Pr 15–030, *15–036*
Protector Endowment Loan & Annuity Co v Grice; sub nom. Protector Loan Co v Grice (1879–80) L.R. 5 Q.B.D. 592, CA *26–140*
Provident Clothing & Supply Co Ltd v Mason; sub nom. Mason v Provident Clothing & Supply Co Ltd [1913] A.C. 724, HL; reversing [1913] 1 K.B. 65, CA *16–092*, *16–097*, *16–106*, *16–110*, *16–113*, 16–203
Provident Finance Corp Pty v Hammond [1978] V.R. 312 .... *19–070*, *19–071*
Provident Financial Group and Whitegates Estate Agency v Hayward [1989] 3 All E.R. 298; [1989] I.C.R. 160; [1989] I.R.L.R. 84, CA (Civ Div) ... *27–061*, *27–066*, *27–069*
Provimi Hellas AE v Warinco AG [1978] 1 Lloyd's Rep. 373, CA (Civ Div); affirming [1978] 1 Lloyd's Rep. 67, QBD (Comm) *13–013*, *14–141*
Prudential Assurance Co Ltd v Ayres [2008] EWCA Civ 52; [2008] 1 All E.R. 1266; [2008] 16 E.G. 154, CA (Civ Div); reversing [2007] EWHC 775 (Ch); [2007] 3 All E.R. 946; [2007] L. & T.R. 35; [2007] 28 E.G. 122; [2007] 16 E.G. 190 (C.S.); (2007) 151 S.J.L.B. 504, Ch D *18–091*, *18–094*, *18–133*
Prudential Assurance Co Ltd v London Residuary Body [1992] 2 A.C. 386; [1992] 3 W.L.R. 279; [1992] 3 All E.R. 504; (1992) 64 P. & C.R. 193; [1992] 36 E.G. 129; [1992] E.G. 100 (C.S.); (1992) 142 N.L.J. 1087; [1992] N.P.C. 105, HL; reversing (1992) 63 P. & C.R. 386; [1992] 1 E.G.L.R. 47; [1992] 06 E.G. 145; [1991] E.G. 111 (C.S.); (1992) 136 S.J.L.B. 229; [1991] N.P.C. 113, CA (Civ Div) *2–080*, *2–141*, *18–135*, *27–007*
Prudential Assurance Co Ltd v Newman Industries Ltd (No.2) [1982] Ch. 204; [1982] 2 W.L.R. 31; [1982] 1 All E.R. 354, CA (Civ Div); reversing in part [1981] Ch. 257; [1980] 3 W.L.R. 543; [1980] 2 All E.R. 841, Ch D *6–014*, 9–066, *9–067*, *9–068*, 9–069, *9–070*, 16–052
Prudential Assurance Co v Mount Eden Land Co. *See* Mount Eden Land v Prudential Assurance Co

Prudential Staff Union v Hall [1947] K.B. 685; (1947) 80 Ll. L. Rep. 410; 63 T.L.R. 392; [1948] L.J.R. 619, KBD *18–078*, *18–079*
Pryce, Re; sub nom. Nevill v Pryce [1917] 1 Ch. 234, Ch D *27–034*
Pryke v Gibbs Hartley Cooper Ltd; Excess Insurance Co Ltd v Gibbs Hartley Cooper Ltd [1991] 1 Lloyd's Rep. 602, QBD (Comm) *6–161*, *12–129*, *13–018*
Psaltis v Schultz [1948] 2 A.L.R. 502; 22 A.L.J. 328; 76 C.L.R. 547 , HC (Aus) *16–070*
Public Works Commissioners v Hills. *See* Commissioner of Public Works v Hills
Puckett and Smith's Contract, Re [1902] 2 Ch. 258, CA *27–055*, *27–057*
Pugh v Leeds, Duke of, (1777) 2 Cowp. 714 .... *12–093*
Pulbrook v Lawes (1876) (1875–76) L.R. 1 Q.B.D. 284; 45 L.J.Q.B. 178; 34 L.T. 95, QBD *4–016*, *4–041*, *29–080*
Pulbrook v Richmond Consolidated Mining Co (1878) L.R. 9 Ch. D. 610, Ch D *27–021*
Pullen v Gutterridge, Haskins & Davey Party Ltd (1992) Aust. Torts. Rep. 81 ...... *28–061*
Pullin v Stokes (1794) 2 H.Bl. 312 .... *3–047*
Pumfrey, Re; sub nom. Worcester City and County Banking Co v Blick (1883) L.R. 22 Ch. D. 255, Ch D *29–166*
Punjab National Bank v De Boinville [1992] 1 W.L.R. 1138; [1992] 3 All E.R. 104; [1992] 1 Lloyd's Rep. 7; [1992] E.C.C. 348; (1991) 141 N.L.J. 85, CA (Civ Div); affirming, *Financial Times*, February 1, 1991, QBD (Comm) *1–176*, 12–069, *18–022*, *28–033*
Purcell v FC Trigell Ltd (t/a Southern Window & General Cleaning Co) [1971] 1 Q.B. 358; [1970] 3 W.L.R. 884; [1970] 3 All E.R. 671; (1970) 114 S.J. 668, CA (Civ Div) *5–062*, *6–114*
Purcell v Henderson (1885) 16 L.R. Ir. 213 .... *21–041*
Purnell v Roche [1927] 2 Ch. 142, Ch D *28–075*
Purser & Co (Hillingdon) Ltd v Jackson [1977] Q.B. 166; [1976] 3 W.L.R. 700; [1976] 3 All E.R. 641; (1976) 242 E.G. 689; (1976) (1976) 120 S.J. 351, QBD *26–013*
Pusey v Pusey (1684) 1 Vern. 273 .... *27–014*
Pust v Dowie (1863) 5 B.S. 33 .... *24–003*
Putsman v Taylor [1927] 1 K.B. 741, CA; affirming [1927] 1 K.B. 637; 96 L.J.K.B. 315; 136 L.T. 285; 137 L.T. 291; 43 T.L.R. 153, KBD ... *16–110*, *16–198*, *16–201*, *16–203*
Pye v Ambrose [1994] N.P.C. 53 .... *7–128*
Pye v British Automobile Commercial Syndicate Ltd [1906] 1 K.B. 425, KBD *26–127*, *26–132*, *26–146*, *26–150*
Pye Ltd v BG Transport Service Ltd [1966] 2 Lloyd's Rep. 300; 116 N.L.J. 1713, QBD *16–031*, *16–165*
Pym v Campbell (1856) 6 E. & B. 370; 25 L.J.K.B. 277; 2 Jur. 641; 106 R.R. 632 ...*2–131*, 2–151, *12–028*, *12–106*, *12–109*
Pyman Steamship Co v Hull & Barnsley Railway Co [1915] 2 K.B. 729; 84 L.J.K.B. 1235; 112 L.T. 1103; 31 T.L.R. 253; 20 Com. Cas. 259; 13 Asp. 64, CA; affirming [1914] 2 K.B. 788, KBD *14–011*
Pyramid Sound NV v Briese Schiffahrts GmbH & Co. *See* MB Pyramid Sound NV v Briese Schiffahrts GmbH & Co KG MS Sina
Pyrene Co Ltd v Scindia Steam Navigation Co Ltd [1954] 2 Q.B. 402; [1954] 2 W.L.R. 1005; [1954] 2 All E.R. 158; [1954] 1 Lloyd's Rep. 321; (1954) 98 S.J. 354, QBD *2–031*, *2–180*, *14–040*, *18–019*
Pyrmont Ltd v Schott [1939] A.C. 145, PC (Gib) *21–068*, *30–331*, *30–370*
Quadmost Ltd (In Liquidation) v Reprotech (Pebsham) Ltd [2001] B.P.I.R. 349, QBD *19–043*
Quadramian Pty v Sevastapol Investments Pty (1976) 8 A.L.R. 555; (1976) 133 C.L.R. 390, HC (Aus) 16–085
Quadrangle Development and Construction Co v Jenner [1974] 1 W.L.R. 68; [1974] 1 All E.R. 729; (1974) 27 P. & C.R. 441; (1973) 117 S.J. 912, CA (Civ Div) *21–014*

Quadrant Visual Communications v Hutchison Telephone (UK) [1993] B.C.L.C. 442; (1992) 89(3) L.S.G. 31; (1992) 136 S.J.L.B. 32, CA (Civ Div) *1–021*, *27–030*, *27–032*
Quarrier v Colston (1842) 1 Ph. 147; 12 L.J.Ch. 57; 6 Jur. 959; 41 E.R. 587, Ch D *16–030*
Quarter Master UK Ltd (In Liquidation) v Pyke [2004] EWHC 1815; [2005] 1 B.C.L.C. 245, Ch D *29–155*, I29–157
Quebrada Co Ltd, Re (1873) 42 L.J. Ch. 277 .... *21–087*
Queens of the River SS Co Ltd v Conservators of the River Thames (1899) 15 T.L.R. 474 .... *29–084*, *29–095*
Queensbury (Duke) v Cullen (1787) 1 Bro.P.C. 396 .... *9–073*
Queensland Electricity Generating Board v New Hope Collieries [1989] 1 Lloyd's Rep. 205, PC (Aus) *2–128*, *2–131*
Queensland Mines Ltd v Hudson (1978) 18 A.L.R. 1; (1978) 52 A.L.J.R. 399, PC (Aus) *9–055*, *29–160*
Quenerduaine v Coles (1883) 32 W.R. 185 .... *2–049*, *2–096*
Quesnel Forks Gold Mining Co Ltd v Ward [1920] A.C. 222, PC (Can) *12–082*, *22–055*
Quest 4 Finance Ltd v Maxfield [2007] EWHC 2313 (QB); [2007] 2 C.L.C. 706, QBD *6–135*
Quick v Taff Ely BC [1986] Q.B. 809; [1985] 3 W.L.R. 981; [1985] 3 All E.R. 321; (1986) 18 H.L.R. 66; [1985] 2 E.G.L.R. 50; (1985) 276 E.G. 452, CA (Civ Div) *1–049*
Quickmaid Rental Services v Reece (t/a Forge Service Station) (1970) 114 S.J. 372, CA (Civ Div) *12–004*
Quinn v Burch Bros (Builders) Ltd [1966] 2 Q.B. 370; [1966] 2 W.L.R. 1017; [1966] 2 All E.R. 283; 1 K.I.R. 9; (1966) 110 S.J. 214, CA *26–032*, 26–037, *26–049*, *26–120*
Quinn v Leathem [1901] A.C. 495; 70 L.J.P.C. 76; 85 L.T. 289; 17 T.L.R. 749; 50 W.R. 139; 65 J.P. 708, HL (UK-Irl); affirming [1899] 2 I.R. 667, CA (UK-Irl) *7–045*
Quirk v Thomas [1916] 1 K.B. 516, CA *26–019*
R. v AB; R. v Kent [1941] 1 K.B. 454; 110 L.J. K.B. 268, CCA *11–020*
R. v Adams, *The Times*, January 28, 1993, CA *12–046*
R. v Arkwright (1848) 12 Q.B. 960; 18 L.J.Q.B. 26; 13 Jur. 300; 76 R.R. 442 .... *12–094*
R. v Ashwell (1885–86) L.R. 16 Q.B.D. 190, Crown Cases Reserved *29–159*
R. v Attorney General for England and Wales [2002] UKPC 22 ....*29–088*, *29–152*
R. v Attorney General of England and Wales [2003] UKPC 22; [2003] E.M.L.R. 24; (2003) 147 S.J.L.B. 354, PC (NZ) *3–006*, *3–057*, *3–166*, *3–167*, *7–011*, *7–044*, *7–046*, *7–087*
R. v Banaster (Michael) (1979) 68 Cr. App. R. 272; [1979] R.T.R. 113, CA (Crim Div) *6–011*
R. v Barnard (1837) 7 C. & P. 784 .... *6–015*
R. v Barnet LBC Ex p. Shah (Nilish); Akbarali v Brent LBC; Abdullah v Shropshire CC; Shabpar v Barnet LBC; Shah (Jitendra) v Barnet LBC; Ablack v Inner London Education Authority; R. v Shropshire CC Ex p. Abdullah [1983] 2 A.C. 309; [1983] 2 W.L.R. 16; [1983] 1 All E.R. 226; 81 L.G.R. 305; (1983) 133 N.L.J. 61; (1983) 127 S.J. 36, HL *30–079*
R. v Baxter (Robert) [1972] 1 Q.B. 1; [1971] 2 W.L.R. 1138; [1971] 2 All E.R. 359; (1971) 55 Cr. App. R. 214; [1971] Crim. L.R. 281; (1971) 115 S.J. 246, CA (Crim Div) *2–025*
R. v BBC Ex p. Lavelle [1983] 1 W.L.R. 23; [1983] 1 All E.R. 241; [1983] I.C.R. 99; [1982] I.R.L.R. 404; (1983) 133 N.L.J. 133; (1982) 126 S.J.L.B. 836, QBD *1–195*
R. v Berkshire HA Ex p. Walsh. *See* R. v East Berkshire HA Ex p. Walsh
R. v Bhagwan (Dharam Singh); sub nom. DPP v Bhagwan [1972] A.C. 60; [1970] 3 W.L.R. 501; [1970] 3 All E.R. 97; (1970) 54 Cr. App. R. 460; (1970) 114 S.J. 683, HL; affirming [1970] 2 W.L.R. 837; [1970] 1 All E.R. 1129; (1970) 114 S.J. 166, CA (Crim Div) 16–015

R. v Bishirgian (Garabed); R. v Howeson (John Henry); R. v Hardy (Louis) [1936] 1 All E.R. 586; (1936) 25 Cr. App. R. 176; 154 L.T. 499; 30 Cox C.C. 379; 52 T.L.R. 361, CCA *6–017*

R. v Blenkinsop [1892] 1 Q.B. 43, QBD *10–041*

R. v Bottrill Ex p. Kuechenmeister [1947] K.B. 41; [1946] 2 All E.R. 434; 62 T.L.R. 570; 115 L.J. K.B. 500; 175 L.T. 232, CA *11–027*

R. v Bow Street Metropolitan Stipendiary Magistrate Ex p. Pinochet Ugarte (No.3) [2000] 1 A.C. 147; [1999] 2 W.L.R. 827; [1999] 2 All E.R. 97; 6 B.H.R.C. 24; (1999) 96(17) L.S.G. 24; (1999) 149 N.L.J. 497, HL; reversing in part, *The Times*, November 3, 1998; *Independent*, October 30, 1998, DC *11–008*, *11–014*

R. v Braithwaite (Frank Wilson); R. v Girdham (Ralph) [1983] 1 W.L.R. 385; [1983] 2 All E.R. 87; (1983) 77 Cr. App. R. 34; (1983) 147 J.P. 301; [1983] Crim. L.R. 468, CA (Crim Div) *3–004*

R. v Brent LBC Ex p. Risk Management Partners Ltd [2008] EWHC Admin 692 .... *10–026*

R. v Charles. *See* Commissioner of Police of the Metropolis v Charles (Derek Michael)

R. v Chief Constable of North Wales Ex p. Evans; sub nom. Chief Constable of North Wales v Evans [1982] 1 W.L.R. 1155; [1982] 3 All E.R. 141; (1983) 147 J.P. 6; (1982) 79 L.S.G. 1257; (1982) 126 S.J. 549, HL *27–023*

R. v Chief National Insurance Commissioner Ex p. Connor [1981] Q.B. 758; [1981] 2 W.L.R. 412; [1981] 1 All E.R. 769; [1980] Crim. L.R. 579; (1980) 124 S.J. 478, QBD *16–168*, *16–169*, 16–170, *16–173*

R. v Christian. *See* Christian v Queen, The

R. v Church (Peter Leslie) (1971) 55 Cr. App. R. 65; (1970) 114 S.J. 907, CA (Crim Div) *29–138*

R. v Civil Service Appeal Board Ex p. Bruce [1989] 2 All E.R. 907; [1989] I.C.R. 171, CA (Civ Div); affirming [1988] 3 All E.R. 686; [1988] I.C.R. 649, QBD *2–158*, *2–181*, *27–022*

R. v Clarke (1927) 40 C.L.R. 227 .... *2–041*, 2–043

R. v Coney (1881–82) L.R. 8 Q.B.D. 534; 51 L.J.M.C. 66; 46 L.T. 307; 46 J.P. 404; 30 W.R. 678; 15 Cox C.C. 46, QBD *16–014*

R. v Criminal Injuries Compensation Board Ex p. Lain [1967] 2 Q.B. 864; [1967] 3 W.L.R. 348; [1967] 2 All E.R. 770; (1967) 111 S.J. 331, QBD *1–195*

R. v Crown Prosecution Service Ex p. Hogg (1994) 6 Admin. L.R. 778, CA (Civ Div) *1–195*, *27–022*

R. v D (Ian Malcolm) [1984] A.C. 778; [1984] 3 W.L.R. 186; [1984] 2 All E.R. 449; (1984) 79 Cr. App. R. 313; [1984] Crim. L.R. 558; [1984] Fam. Law 311; (1984) 81 L.S.G. 2458, HL; reversing [1984] 2 W.L.R. 112; [1984] 1 All E.R. 574; (1984) 78 Cr. App. R. 219; [1984] Crim. L.R. 103; (1983) 80 L.S.G. 2998; (1984) 128 S.J. 63, CA (Crim Div) *8–011*

R. v Daly (James Joseph) [1974] 1 W.L.R. 133; [1974] 1 All E.R. 290; (1974) 58 Cr. App. R. 333; [1974] Crim. L.R. 263; (1973) 118 S.J. 66, CA (Crim Div) *29–138*

R. v Demers [1900] A.C. 103; 69 L.J.P.C. 5; 81 L.T. 795, PC (Can) *2–039*

R. v Derbyshire CC Ex p. Noble [1990] I.C.R. 808; [1990] I.R.L.R. 332, CA (Civ Div); affirming [1989] C.O.D. 285; (1989) 153 L.G. Rev. 568, QBD *1–196*, *27–022*

R. v Disciplinary Committee of the Jockey Club Ex p. Aga Khan [1993] 1 W.L.R. 909; [1993] 2 All E.R. 853; [1993] C.O.D. 234; (1993) 143 N.L.J. 163, CA (Civ Div); affirming [1992] C.O.D. 51, QBD 1–195, *9–076*, *27–023*, *27–072*, *27–075*

R. v East Berkshire HA Ex p. Walsh [1985] Q.B. 152; [1984] 3 W.L.R. 818; [1984] 3 All E.R. 425; [1984] I.C.R. 743; [1984] I.R.L.R. 278, CA (Civ Div); reversing, *The Times*, November 15, 1983, QBD *1–194*, *1–195*, *1–196*, *27–022*

R. v Feather, 122 E.R. 1191; (1865) 6 B. & S. 257, QB *12–086*
R. v Ferguson (John William) [1970] 1 W.L.R. 1246; [1970] 2 All E.R. 820; (1970) 54 Cr. App. R. 410; (1970) 114 S.J. 472, CA (Crim Div) *29–138*
R. v Fernhill Manor School Ex p. A; R. v Fernhill Manor School Ex p. Brown; R. v Fernhill Manor School Ex p. B [1993] 1 F.L.R. 620; [1994] 1 F.C.R. 146; (1993) 5 Admin. L.R. 159; [1992] C.O.D. 446, QBD *1–195*, *27–024*
R. v Governor of Pentonville Prison Ex p. Osman (No.2); sub nom. Osman (No.2), Re [1989] C.O.D. 446; (1989) 86(7) L.S.G. 36; (1989) 133 S.J. 121, DC *11–014*
R. v Governor of Pentonville Prison Ex p. Teja [1971] 2 Q.B. 274; [1971] 1 W.L.R. 459; [1971] 2 W.L.R. 816; [1971] 2 All E.R. 11; (1971) 115 S.J. 305, QBD *11–014*, *11–015*
R. v Great Wigston (Inhabitants) (1824) 3 B. & C. 484; 5 Dow. & Ry.K.B. 339; 2 Dow. & Ry. M.C. 445; 3 L.J. (O.S.) K.B. 85 ..... *8–024*
R. v Hammersmith and Fulham LBC Ex p. Beddowes [1987] Q.B. 1050; [1987] 2 W.L.R. 263; [1987] 1 All E.R. 369; (1986) 18 H.L.R. 458; 85 L.G.R. 270; [1987] R.V.R. 189; (1986) 83 L.S.G. 3001; (1986) 130 S.J. 696, CA (Civ Div) 10–031, *10–032*
R. v Hartington Middle Quarter (Inhabitants), 119 E.R. 288; (1855) 4 El. & Bl. 780, QB *25–011*
R. v Hull University Visitor Ex p. Page. *See* R. v Lord President of the Privy Council Ex p. Page
R. v Humphery (1839) 10 A. & E. 335 ..... *12–094*
R. v Humphreys [1977] A.C. 1 ..... *25–015*
R. v Incorporated Froebel Educational Institute Ex p. L [1999] E.L.R. 488, QBD *27–024*
R. v Inhabitants of Gresham (1786) 1 Term Rep. 101 ..... *22–026*
R. v Inhabitants of Haslingfield (1814) 2 M. & S. 558 ..... *16–204*
R. v Inhabitants of Leake, 110 E.R. 863; (1833) 5 B. & Ad. 469, KB 10–027
R. v Inhabitants of the Township of Hartington Middle Quarter. *See* R. v Hartington Middle Quarter (Inhabitants)
R. v Inland Revenue Commissioners Ex p. Camacq Corp [1990] 1 W.L.R. 191; [1990] 1 All E.R. 173; [1990] S.T.C. 785; 62 T.C. 651; (1990) 87(5) L.S.G. 41, CA (Civ Div) *11–004*
R. v Inland Revenue Commissioners Ex p. Woolwich Equitable Building Society [1990] 1 W.L.R. 1400; [1991] 4 All E.R. 92; [1990] S.T.C. 682; 63 T.C. 589; (1990) 134 S.J. 1404, HL *29–085*
R. v Insurance Ombudsman Bureau Ex p. Aegon Life Assurance Ltd [1995] L.R.L.R. 101; [1994] C.L.C. 88; [1994] C.O.D. 426, DC *1–195*
R. v International Trustee for the Protection of Bondholders AG; sub nom. International Trustee for the Protection of Bondholders AG v King, The [1937] A.C. 500; (1937) 57 Ll. L. Rep. 145, HL *21–068*, *21–069*, *21–070*, *30–005*, *30–009*, *30–010*, *30–011*, *30–012*, *30–345*, *30–364*
R. v Inwood (Roland Joseph) (1974) 60 Cr. App. R. 70, CA (Crim Div) *29–138*
R. v Ivens (1835) 7 C. & P. 213 ..... *27–074*
R. v Jockey Club Ex p. RAM Racecourses Ltd [1993] 2 All E.R. 225; (1991) 5 Admin. L.R. 265; [1990] C.O.D. 346, QBD *9–074*
R. v Judge Whitehorne [1904] 1 K.B. 827, KBD *5–132*
R. v Kneeshaw (Michael Brian) [1975] Q.B. 57; [1974] 2 W.L.R. 432; [1974] 1 All E.R. 896; (1974) 58 Cr. App. R. 439; [1974] Crim. L.R. 263; (1974) 118 S.J. 218, CA (Crim Div) *29–138*
R. v Kylsant [1932] 1 K.B. 442; 101 L.J.K.B. 97; 146 L.T. 21; 43 T.L.R. 62; 75 S.J. 815; 29 Cox C.C. 379; 23 Cr. App. R. 83, CCA *6–017*
R. v Lambeth Justices Ex p. Yusufu; sub nom. R. v Governor of Brixton Prison Ex p. Yusufu [1985] Crim. L.R. 510, DC *11–014*

R. v Lambie (Shiralee Ann) [1982] A.C. 449; [1981] 3 W.L.R. 88; [1981] 2 All E.R. 776; (1981) 73 Cr. App. R. 294; [1981] E.C.C. 552; [1981] Crim. L.R. 712; (1981) 131 N.L.J. 1041; (1981) 125 S.J. 480, HL; reversing [1981] 1 W.L.R. 78; [1981] 1 All E.R. 332; (1980) 71 Cr. App. R. 350; [1980] Crim. L.R. 725; (1980) 124 S.J. 808, CA (Crim Div) *3–039*, 6–015
R. v Lewisham LBC Ex p. Shell UK [1988] 1 All E.R. 938; (1988) 152 L.G. Rev. 929, DC *1–201*
R. v Lord (1850) 12 Q.B. 757; 17 L.J.M.C. 181; 12 Jur. 101; 76 R.R. 415 ....*8–022*, *8–025*, *8–029*
R. v Lord Chancellor's Department Ex p. Nangle [1992] 1 All E.R. 897; [1991] I.C.R. 743; [1991] I.R.L.R. 343; [1991] C.O.D. 484, QBD *2–161*, *2–163*, *2–181*
R. v Lord President of the Privy Council Ex p. Page; sub nom. Page v Hull University Visitor; R. v Hull University Visitor Ex p. Page; R. v Visitor of the University of Hull Ex p. Page [1993] A.C. 682; [1993] 3 W.L.R. 1112; [1993] 1 All E.R. 97; [1993] I.C.R. 114; (1993) 143 N.L.J. 15; (1993) 137 S.J.L.B. 45, HL *27–023*
R. v Madan (Kanhya Lal) [1961] 2 Q.B. 1; [1961] 2 W.L.R. 231; [1961] 1 All E.R. 588; (1961) 45 Cr. App. R. 80; (1961) 125 J.P. 246; (1961) 105 S.J. 160, CCA *11–020*
R. v McDonald (1884–85) L.R. 15 Q.B.D. 323; 52 L.T. 583; 33 W.R. 735; 49 J.P. 695, CCR *8–046*, *8–047*
R. v Ministry ofDefence Ex p Cookson & Clegg Ltd. *See* Cookson & Clegg Ltd v Ministry of Defence
R. v Miskin Lower, Glamorganshire, Justices Ex p. Young [1953] 1 Q.B. 533; [1953] 2 W.L.R. 409; [1953] 1 All E.R. 495; (1953) 117 J.P. 166; (1953) 97 S.J. 136, DC *21–060*
R. v Morton (Arthur Henry) (1873) L.R. 2 C.C.R. 22; 42 L.J.M.C. 58; 28 L.T. 452; 21 W.R. 629; 12 Cox C.C. 456, CCR *1–085*
R. v Nevill (1846) 8 Q.B. 452; 15 L.J.M.C. 33; 70 R.R. 538 .... *12–087*
R. v North and East Devon HA Ex p. Coughlan [2001] Q.B. 213; [2000] 2 W.L.R. 622; [2000] 3 All E.R. 850; (2000) 2 L.G.L.R. 1; [1999] B.L.G.R. 703; (1999) 2 C.C.L. Rep. 285; [1999] Lloyd's Rep. Med. 306; (2000) 51 B.M.L.R. 1; [1999] C.O.D. 340; (1999) 96(31) L.S.G. 39; (1999) 143 S.J.L.B. 213, CA (Civ Div); affirming (1999) 2 C.C.L. Rep. 27; (1999) 47 B.M.L.R. 27; [1999] C.O.D. 174, QBD *10–003*
R. v Oldham MBC Ex p. Garlick; sub nom. R. v Oldham MBC Ex p. G; R. v Bexley LBC Ex p. B; R. v Bexley LBC Ex p. Bentum; R. v Tower Hamlets LBC Ex p. Begum (Ferdous) [1993] A.C. 509; [1993] 2 W.L.R. 609; [1993] 2 All E.R. 65; [1993] 2 F.L.R. 194; [1993] 2 F.C.R. 133; (1993) 25 H.L.R. 319; 91 L.G.R. 287; (1993) 143 N.L.J. 437; (1993) 137 S.J.L.B. 109, HL; affirming in part [1993] 1 F.L.R. 645; (1992) 24 H.L.R. 726; [1993] Fam. Law 219, CA (Civ Div); affirming [1992] 2 F.C.R. 771; (1992) 24 H.L.R. 501; [1992] C.O.D. 373, QBD 8–003
R. v Paddington and St Marylebone Rent Tribunal Ex p. Bedrock Investments [1948] 2 K.B. 413; [1948] 2 All E.R. 528; 64 T.L.R. 388; (1948) 112 J.P. 367; 46 L.G.R. 367; [1949] L.J.R. 284; (1948) 92 S.J. 408, CA; affirming [1947] K.B. 984; [1947] 2 All E.R. 15; 63 T.L.R. 303; (1947) 111 J.P. 367; 176 L.T. 562; (1947) 91 S.J. 310, DC *13–009*
R. v Panayiotou (Andreas); R. v Antoniades (Agis) [1973] 1 W.L.R. 1032; [1973] 3 All E.R. 112; (1973) 57 Cr. App. R. 762; [1973] Crim. L.R. 445; (1973) 117 S.J. 464, CA (Crim Div) *7–049*, *16–037*
R. v Panel on Takeovers and Mergers Ex p. Datafin Plc [1987] Q.B. 815; [1987] 2 W.L.R. 699; [1987] 1 All E.R. 564; (1987) 3 B.C.C. 10; [1987] B.C.L.C. 104; [1987] 1 F.T.L.R. 181; (1987) 131 S.J. 23, CA (Civ Div) *1–196*
R. v Parker (Harry) [1970] 1 W.L.R. 1003; [1970] 2 All E.R. 458; (1970) 54 Cr. App. R. 339; (1970) 114 S.J. 396, CA (Crim Div) *29–138*
R. v Pembrokeshire CC Ex p. Coker [1999] 4 All E.R. 1007; (2000) 2 L.G.L.R. 625; [1999] N.P.C. 87, QBD *3–019*, *3–022*
R. v Porter [1910] 1 K.B. 369; 79 L.J.K.B. 241; 102 L.T. 255; 26 T.L.R. 200; 74 J.P. 159, CCA *16–039*

R. v Preddy (John Crawford); R. v Slade (Mark); R. v Dhillon (Rajpaul Singh) [1996] A.C. 815; [1996] 3 W.L.R. 255; [1996] 3 All E.R. 481; [1996] 2 Cr. App. R. 524; (1996) 160 J.P. 677; [1996] Crim. L.R. 726; (1996) 160 J.P.N. 936; (1996) 93(31) L.S.G. 29; (1996) 146 N.L.J. 1057; (1996) 140 S.J.L.B. 184, HL *29–164*

R. v Rederiaktiebolaget. *See* Rederiaktiebolaget Amphitrite v R.

R. v Registrar of Companies Ex p. Esal (Commodities) Ltd (In Liquidation); sub nom. R. v Registrar of Companies Ex p. Central Bank of India [1986] Q.B. 1114; [1986] 2 W.L.R. 177; [1986] 1 All E.R. 105; (1985) 1 B.C.C. 99501; [1986] P.C.C. 235; (1985) 129 S.J. 755, CA (Civ Div); reversing [1985] 2 W.L.R. 447; [1985] 2 All E.R. 79; (1985) 1 B.C.C. 99302; (1985) 82 L.S.G. 680; (1985) 129 S.J. 83, QBD *9–046*

R. v Reilly [1934] A.C. 176 23–023

R. v Reilly. *See* Reilly v King, The

R. v Richmond upon Thames LBC Ex p. McCarthy & Stone (Developments) Ltd. *See* McCarthy & Stone (Developments) Ltd v Richmond upon Thames LBC

R. v Riley [1896] 1 Q.B. 309; 65 L.J.M.C. 74; 74 L.T. 254; 44 W.R. 318; 18 Cox C.C. 285; 60 J.P. 519, CCR *4–034*

R. v Ryan (1811) Russ. & Ry. 195 .... *12–125*

R. v Scott (Anthony Peter). *See* Scott (Anthony Peter) v Commissioner of Police of the Metropolis

R. v Secretary of State for Home Affairs Ex p. Dannenberg; sub nom. Dannenberg v Secretary of State for Home Affairs [1984] Q.B. 766; [1984] 2 W.L.R. 855; [1984] 2 All E.R. 481; (1984) 148 J.P. 321; [1984] 2 C.M.L.R. 456; [1984] Imm. A.R. 33; [1984] Crim. L.R. 362; (1984) 128 S.J. 349, CA (Civ Div) *6–028*

R. v Secretary of State for the Environment Ex p. Hammersmith and Fulham LBC [1991] 1 A.C. 521; [1990] 3 W.L.R. 898; [1990] 3 All E.R. 589; 89 L.G.R. 129; [1990] R.V.R. 188; (1991) 155 L.G. Rev. 48; (1990) 140 N.L.J. 1422; (1990) 134 S.J. 1226, HL; affirming [1990] 2 Q.B. 697; [1990] C.O.D. 443, CA (Civ Div) *10–022*, *10–023*, 10–024, *10–025*, *10–026*, *10–032*

R. v Secretary of State for the Home Department Ex p. Bagga [1991] 1 Q.B. 485; [1990] 3 W.L.R. 1013; [1991] 1 All E.R. 777; [1990] Imm. A.R. 413; (1990) 134 S.J. 860, CA (Civ Div); reversing, *The Times*, May 24, 1989, DC *11–014*

R. v Secretary of State for the Home Department Ex p. Benwell [1985] Q.B. 554; [1984] 3 W.L.R. 843; [1984] 3 All E.R. 854; [1984] I.C.R. 723; [1985] I.R.L.R. 6; (1984) 81 L.S.G. 2544; (1984) 128 S.J. 703, QBD 1–195, *27–022*, *27–023*

R. v Secretary of State for the Home Department Ex p. Broom [1986] Q.B. 198; [1985] 3 W.L.R. 778; [1985] I.C.R. 766; (1985) 129 S.J. 737, QBD *27–022*

R. v Secretary of State for the Home Department Ex p. Johnson [1999] Q.B. 1174; [1999] 1 W.L.R. 1375; [1999] 2 W.L.R. 932; [1998] 4 All E.R. 635, DC *11–007*

R. v Secretary of State for the Home Department Ex p. Launder (No.3); Launder v Governor of Brixton Prison [1998] Q.B. 994; [1998] 3 W.L.R. 221; [1998] C.O.D. 301; (1998) 95(11) L.S.G. 36; (1998) 142 S.J.L.B. 101, DC *11–007*

R. v Sevenoaks DC Ex p. Terry [1985] 3 All E.R. 226; [1984] J.P.L. 420, QBD *2–116*

R. v Somerset CC Ex p. Dixon [1998] Env. L.R. 111; (1998) 75 P. & C.R. 175; [1997] J.P.L. 1030; [1997] C.O.D. 323; [1997] N.P.C. 61, QBD *4–061*

R. v Special Commissioners of Income Tax Ex p. Shaftesbury Homes; R. v Special Commissioners of Income Tax Ex p. Arethusa Training Ship [1923] 1 K.B. 393; 92 L.J.K.B. 152; 128 L.T. 463; 39 T.L.R. 99, CA; affirming [1922] 2 K.B. 729, KBD *12–088*

R. v Spens (No.1); sub nom. R. v Lord Spens; R v Rex (Patrick Michael); R v Baron Spens [1991] 1 W.L.R. 624; [1991] 4 All E.R. 421; [1991] B.C.C. 140; (1991) 93 Cr. App. R. 194, CA (Crim Div) *12–046*

R. v Stainer (1870) L.R. 1 C.C.R. 230, CCR *16–202*

R. v Stevens (1804) 5 East. 244 .... *12–064*, *12–092*

R. v Stoke-on-Trent (Inhabitants of) (1843) 8 Q.B. 303 .... *12–133*

R. v Sunair Holidays Ltd [1973] 1 W.L.R. 1105; [1973] 2 All E.R. 1233; (1973) 57 Cr. App. R. 782; [1973] Crim. L.R. 587; (1973) 117 S.J. 429, CA (Crim Div) *6–012*

R. v Surrey County Court Judge [1910] 2 K.B. 410, KBD *4–021*

R. v Thomson Holidays Ltd [1974] Q.B. 592; [1974] 2 W.L.R. 371; [1974] 1 All E.R. 823; (1974) 58 Cr. App. R. 429; [1974] Crim. L.R. 198; (1973) 118 S.J. 96, CA (Crim Div) *2–020*

R. v Tower Hamlets LBC Ex p. Chetnik Developments Ltd [1988] A.C. 858; [1988] 2 W.L.R. 654; [1988] 1 All E.R. 961; 86 L.G.R. 321; [1988] R.A. 45; [1988] E.G. 36 (C.S.); (1988) 138 N.L.J. Rep. 89; (1988) 132 S.J. 4621, HL ..*29–011*, *29–014*, *29–043*, *29–083*, *29–179*

R. v Vine Street Police Station Superintendent Ex p. Liebmann [1916] 1 K.B. 268, KBD *11–027*

R. v Warwickshire CC Ex p. Johnson; sub nom. Warwickshire CC Ex p. Johnson [1993] A.C. 583; [1993] 2 W.L.R. 1; [1993] 1 All E.R. 299; 91 L.G.R. 130; (1993) 12 Tr. L.R. 1; [1993] Crim. L.R. 940; (1993) 157 J.P.N. 201; (1993) 143 N.L.J. 126; (1993) 137 S.J.L.B. 37, HL; reversing (1992) 156 J.P. 577; (1991) 11 Tr. L.R. 76; [1992] Crim. L.R. 644; (1992) 156 J.P.N. 506; (1992) 156 L.G. Rev. 971, DC *2–015*, *2–020*

R. v Whitaker (Charles Hildyard) [1914] 3 K.B. 1283; (1914) 10 Cr. App. R. 245, CCA *16–020*

R. v William Whiteley Ltd (1909) 101 L.T. 741 .... *29–094*, *29–098*, *29–111*

R. v Williams [1980] Crim. L.R. 589, CA (Crim Div) *6–015*

R. (Kilby) v Basildon DC. *See* Kilby v Basildon DC

R. (on the application of Abbasi) v Secretary of State for Foreign and Commonwealth Affairs; sub nom. R. (on the application of Abassi) v Secretary of State for Foreign and Commonwealth Affairs [2002] EWCA Civ 1598; [2003] U.K.H.R.R. 76; (2002) 99(47) L.S.G. 29, CA (Civ Div) *11–007*

R. (on the application of Alamieyeseigha) v Crown Prosecution Service [2005] EWHC 2704; [2006] Crim. L.R. 669, QBD (Admin) *11–006*

R. (on the application of Haggerty) v St Helens BC; sub nom. Haggerty v St Helens Council [2003] EWHC 803; [2003] H.L.R. 69; (2003) 6 C.C.L. Rep. 352; (2003) 74 B.M.L.R. 33; [2003] A.C.D. 73, QBD (Admin) 1–053

R. (on the application of Heather) v Leonard Cheshire Foundation [2002] EWCA Civ 366; [2002] 2 All E.R. 936; [2002] H.R.L.R. 30; [2002] U.K.H.R.R. 883; [2002] H.L.R. 49; (2002) 5 C.C.L. Rep. 317; (2003) 69 B.M.L.R. 22; [2002] A.C.D. 43, CA (Civ Div); affirming [2001] EWHC Admin 429; (2001) 4 C.C.L. Rep. 211; [2002] M.H.L.R. 185; [2001] A.C.D. 75, QBD (Admin) *1–054*, *1–197*

R. (on the application of Kemp) v Denbighshire Local Health Board [2006] EWHC 181 (Admin); [2007] 1 W.L.R. 639; [2006] 3 All E.R. 141; (2006) 9 C.C.L. Rep. 354; [2006] A.C.D. 63, QBD (Admin) *29–085*

R. (on the application of Khatun) v Newham LBC; sub nom. Newham LBC v Khatun; Khatun v Newham LBC; R. (on the application of Zeb) v Newham LBC; R. (on the application of Iqbal) v Newham LBC [2004] EWCA Civ 55; [2005] Q.B. 37; [2004] 3 W.L.R. 417; [2004] Eu. L.R. 628; [2004] H.L.R. 29; [2004] B.L.G.R. 696; [2004] L. & T.R. 18; (2004) 148 S.J.L.B. 268; [2004] N.P.C. 28, CA (Civ Div); reversing in part [2003] EWHC 2326 (Admin); [2004] Eu. L.R. 116; [2004] 1 E.G.L.R. 34; [2004] 08 E.G. 136; [2003] N.P.C. 114, QBD (Admin) *15–017*, 15–019, *15–020*, *15–024*, *27–057*

R. (on the application of L (A Child)) v J School Governors; R. (on the application of W (A Child)) v B School Governors; sub nom. R. v B School Governors Ex p. W; R. v J School Governors Ex p. L; L v J; W v B; L (A Child), Re [2003] UKHL 9; [2003] 2 A.C. 633; [2003] 2 W.L.R. 518; [2003] 1 All E.R. 1012; [2003] 1 F.C.R. 548; [2003] B.L.G.R. 343; [2003] E.L.R. 309; (2003) 100(18) L.S.G. 34, HL *27–024*

R. (on the application of Reprotech (Pebsham) Ltd) v East Sussex CC; sub nom. Reprotech (Pebsham) Ltd v East Sussex CC; R. v East Sussex CC Ex p. Reprotech (Pebsham) Ltd; East Sussex CC v Reprotech (Pebsham) Ltd [2002] UKHL 8; [2003] 1 W.L.R. 348; [2002] 4 All E.R. 58; [2003] 1 P. & C.R. 5; [2002] 2 P.L.R. 60; [2002] J.P.L. 821; [2002] 10 E.G. 158 (C.S.); [2002] N.P.C. 32, HL; reversing [2001] Env. L.R. 14; [2001] 1 P.L.R. 12; [2001] J.P.L. 815; [2000] E.G. 79 (C.S.); [2000] N.P.C. 67, CA (Civ Div); affirming [2000] Env. L.R. 381; [2000] J.P.L. 511; [1999] N.P.C. 109, QBD ...*10–042*, *10–043*

R. (on the application of Rowe) v Vale of White Horse DC; sub nom. Rowe v Vale of White Horse DC [2003] EWHC 388; [2003] 1 Lloyd's Rep. 418; [2003] R.V.R. 170; [2003] 11 E.G. 153 (C.S.); [2003] N.P.C. 34, QBD (Admin) *29–018*, *29–021*, *29–022*, *29–028*

R. (on the application of Structadene Ltd) v Hackney LBC; sub nom. R. v Hackney LBC Ex p. Structadene Ltd; Structadene v Hackney LBC [2001] 2 All E.R. 225; (2001) 3 L.G.L.R. 19; [2001] B.L.G.R. 204; (2001) 82 P. & C.R. 25; [2001] 1 E.G.L.R. 15; [2001] 12 E.G. 168; [2000] E.G. 130 (C.S.); (2001) 98(1) L.S.G. 23; [2000] N.P.C. 119, QBD (Admin) *3–019*

R. (on the application of Supportways Community Services Ltd) v Hampshire CC; sub nom. Hampshire CC v Supportways Community Services Ltd; Supportways Community Services Ltd v Hampshire CC [2006] EWCA Civ 1035; [2006] B.L.G.R. 836; (2006) 9 C.C.L. Rep. 484, CA (Civ Div); reversing [2005] EWHC 3101 (Admin); (2006) 9 C.C.L. Rep. 227, QBD (Admin) *10–003*, *27–038*

R. (on the application of Verner) v Derby City Council; R. (on the application of Sheppard) v Norfolk CC; R. (on the application of Ridley) v St Thomas More Roman Catholic High School [2003] EWHC 2708; [2004] I.C.R. 535; [2004] B.L.G.R. 786; [2003] O.P.L.R. 365; [2004] A.C.D. 39, QBD (Admin) *23–038*, *23–058*

R. (on the application of West) v Lloyd's of London [2004] EWCA Civ 506; [2004] 3 All E.R. 251; [2004] 2 All E.R. (Comm) 1; [2004] 2 C.L.C. 649; [2004] H.R.L.R. 27; [2004] Lloyd's Rep. I.R. 755; (2004) 148 S.J.L.B. 537, CA (Civ Div) 1–051

R. (on the application of Westminster City Council) v National Asylum Support Service; sub nom. R. (on the application of Westminster City Council) v Secretary of State for the Home Department; Westminster City Council v National Asylum Support Services [2002] UKHL 38; [2002] 1 W.L.R. 2956; [2002] 4 All E.R. 654; [2002] H.L.R. 58; [2003] B.L.G.R. 23; (2002) 5 C.C.L. Rep. 511; (2002) 146 S.J.L.B. 241, HL; affirming [2001] EWCA Civ 512; (2001) 33 H.L.R. 83; (2001) 4 C.C.L. Rep. 143, CA (Civ Div); affirming [2001] EWHC Admin 138, QBD (Admin) *12–118*

R. (on theapplication of Wandsworth LBC) v Secretary of State for Transport Local Government and theRegions. *See* Wandsworth LBC v Secretary of State for Transport, Local Government and the Regions (Enforcement Notice)

R&A Kohnstamm Ltd v Ludig Krumm (London) Ltd [1940] 2 K.B. 359, KBD *16–162*

R&B Customs Brokers Co Ltd v United Dominions Trust Ltd [1988] 1 W.L.R. 321; [1988] 1 All E.R. 847; [1988] R.T.R. 134; (1988) 85(11) L.S.G. 42; (1988) 132 S.J. 300, CA (Civ Div) *14–065*, 14–066, 14–095, *15–026*, *15–029*

R&W Paul Ltd v Wheat Commission [1937] A.C. 139; [1936] 2 All E.R. 1243; (1936) 55 Ll. L. Rep. 343, HL *29–094*

R Leslie Ltd v Reliable Advertising & Addressing Agency Ltd [1915] 1 K.B. 652, KBD *16–173*

R Leslie Ltd v Sheill [1914] 3 K.B. 607, CA *8–046*, *8–049*, 8–051, *8–055*, *29–019*, *29–081*

R Pagnan & Fratelli v Corbisa Industrial Agropacuaria Ltd [1970] 1 W.L.R. 1306; [1970] 1 All E.R. 165; [1970] 2 Lloyd's Rep. 14; (1970) 114 S.J. 568, CA (Civ Div) *26–115*, *26–117*

R Pagnan & Fratelli v Finagrain Compagnie Commerciale Agricole et Financiere SA; The Adolf Leonhardt [1986] 2 Lloyd's Rep. 395, QBD (Comm) *14–140*

RA Brierley Investments v Landmark Corp (1966) 40 A.L.J.R. 425 .... *19–042*
RA Cripps (Pharmaceutical) and Son Ltd v Wickenden [1973] 1 W.L.R. 944; [1973] 2 All E.R. 606; (1972) 117 S.J. 446, Ch D *21–053*
RA Securities Ltd v Mercantile Credit Co Ltd [1995] 3 All E.R. 581; [1994] B.C.C. 598; [1994] 2 B.C.L.C. 721; [1994] 44 E.G. 242; [1994] N.P.C. 76, Ch D *17–025*
RB Policies at Lloyd's v Butler [1950] 1 K.B. 76; [1949] 2 All E.R. 226; (1948–49) 82 Ll. L. Rep. 841; 65 T.L.R. 436; (1949) 93 S.J. 553, KBD *28–001*, *28–031*
RBC Dominion Securities Inc v Dawson (1994) 111 D.L.R. (4th) 230 .....*29–036*, *29–180*, *29–185*
RDC Concrete Pte Ltd v Sato Kogyo (S) Pte Ltd [2007] SGCA 39; 115 Con. L.R. 154, CA (Sing) *23–058*
RE Jones Ltd v Waring and Gillow Ltd [1926] A.C. 670; 68 A.L.R. 944, HL ...*29–033*, *29–034*, *29–036*, *29–176*, *29–177*
RF Hill & Associates v Van Erp [1997] 14 A.L.R. 687 .... *1–181*
RG Kensington Management Co Ltd v Hutchinson IDH Ltd [2002] EWHC 1180; [2003] 2 P. & C.R. 13, Ch D *4–072*, *4–074*
RH Green & Silley Weir Ltd v British Railways Board [1985] 1 W.L.R. 570; [1985] 1 All E.R. 237, Ch D *28–049*
RIBA Publications v Customs and Excise Commissioners [1999] B.V.C. 2201; [1999] V. & D.R. 230, V&DTr *29–086*
RM Turton & Co Ltd (In Liquidation) v Kerslake & Partners [2000] Lloyd's Rep. P.N. 967, CA (NZ) 18–032, 18–059
RS Newman Ltd, Re [1916] 2 Ch. 309, CA *9–047*
RSP Architects Planners and Engineers v Ocean Front Pte Ltd (1998) 14 Const. L.J. 139, CA (Sing) *18–027*
RSPCA v Attorney General; sub nom. Royal Society for the Prevention of Cruelty to Animals v Attorney General [2002] 1 W.L.R. 448; [2001] 3 All E.R. 530; [2001] U.K.H.R.R. 905; (2001) 98(11) L.S.G. 43, Ch D *27–023*, *27–072*
RV Ward Ltd v Bignall. *See* Ward (RV) v Bignall
RW Green Ltd v Cade Bros Farms [1978] 1 Lloyd's Rep. 602, QBD *14–085*, *14–085*, 14–090, *14–100*
Raatz, Re [1897] 2 Q.B. 80, QBD *21–074*
Rabin v Gerson Berger Association Ltd [1986] 1 W.L.R. 526; [1986] 1 All E.R. 374; (1986) 130 S.J. 15, CA (Civ Div); affirming [1985] 1 W.L.R. 595; [1985] 1 All E.R. 1041; (1985) 129 S.J. 224, Ch D *12–096*, *12–107*, *12–119*
Racal Communications Ltd, Re; sub nom. Company (No.00996 of 1979), Re [1981] A.C. 374; [1980] 3 W.L.R. 181; [1980] 2 All E.R. 634, HL *29–084*
Racal Group Services Ltd v Ashmore [1995] S.T.C. 1151; 68 T.C. 86, CA (Civ Div); affirming [1994] S.T.C. 416, Ch D *5–111*
Racing Drivers Club Ltd v Hextall Erskine & Co. *See* British Racing Drivers Club Ltd v Hextall Erskine & Co
Radcliffe v Bartholomew [1892] 1 Q.B. 161, QBD *12–093*, *21–024*, *28–062*
Radcliffe v Price (1902) 18 T.L.R. 466 .... *7–077*
Radford v De Froberville [1977] 1 W.L.R. 1262; [1978] 1 All E.R. 33; 7 B.L.R. 35; (1978) 35 P. & C.R. 316; (1977) 121 S.J. 319, Ch D *18–049*, *26–016*, *26–018*, *26–064*, *26–104*, *26–109*, *27–079*
Radford v Smith (1838) 3 M.W. 254 .... *21–010*
Raeburn & Verel v Burness & Son (1895) 1 Com. Cas. 22 .... *2–089*
Raffles v Wichelhaus, 159 E.R. 375; (1864) 2 Hurl. & C. 906, QB 5–071, *12–106*, *12–124*
Rafidain Bank (No.1), Re [1992] B.C.C. 376; [1992] B.C.L.C. 301, Ch D (Companies Ct) *11–004*, *11–005*
Rafsanjan Pistachio Producers Cooperative v Bank Leumi (UK) Ltd [1992] 1 Lloyd's Rep. 513, QBD (Comm) *2–071*, *3–090*
Raggow v Scougall & Co (1915) 31 T.L.R. 564 ....*22–025*, *22–028*

Rahcassi Shipping Co SA v Blue Star Line; The Bede [1969] 1 Q.B. 173; [1967] 3 W.L.R. 1382; [1967] 3 All E.R. 301; [1967] 2 Lloyd's Rep. 261; (1967) 111 S.J. 848, QBD (Comm) *2–140*
Rahman v Sterling Credit Ltd; sub nom. Sterling Credit Ltd v Rahman [2001] 1 W.L.R. 496; (2001) 33 H.L.R. 63; (2000) 97(32) L.S.G. 37; (2000) 144 S.J.L.B. 243; [2000] N.P.C. 84; (2001) 81 P. & C.R. DG4, CA (Civ Div) *28–003*
Raiffeisen Hauptgenossenschaft eG v Louis Dreyfus & Co Ltd; Louis Dreyfus & Co Ltd v Kurt A Becher [1981] 1 Lloyd's Rep. 345; [1980] Com. L.R. 13, QBD (Comm) *3–093*, *14–140*, *14–141*, *14–151*, *22–052*
Raiffeisen Zentralbank Osterreich AG v Crossseas Shipping Ltd [2000] 1 W.L.R. 1135; [2000] 3 All E.R. 274; [2000] 1 All E.R. (Comm) 76; [2000] Lloyd's Rep. Bank. 108; [2000] C.L.C. 553, CA (Civ Div) *25–020*
Raiffeisen Zentralbank Österreich AG v Five Star General Trading LLC; The Mount I; sub nom. Raffeisen Zentralbank Osterreich AG v Five Star General Trading LLC; The Mount I; Raiffeisen Zentral Bank Osterreich AG v An Feng Steel Co Ltd [2001] EWCA Civ 68; [2001] Q.B. 825; [2001] 2 W.L.R. 1344; [2001] 3 All E.R. 257; [2001] 1 All E.R. (Comm) 961; [2001] 1 Lloyd's Rep. 597; [2001] C.L.C. 843; [2001] Lloyd's Rep. I.R. 460; (2001) 98(9) L.S.G. 38; (2001) 145 S.J.L.B. 45, CA (Civ Div); reversing in part [2000] 1 All E.R. (Comm) 897; [2000] 2 Lloyd's Rep. 684; [2000] C.L.C. 1359; (2000) 97(25) L.S.G. 38, QBD (Comm) ...*19–014*, *19–032*, *19–038*, *30–019*, *30–020*, *30–031*, *30–033*, *30–051*, *30–077*, *30–078*, *30–090*, *30–124*, 30–126, *30–346*, *30–350*
Raiffeisen Zentralbank Osterreich AG v National Bank of Greece SA [1999] 1 Lloyd's Rep. 408, QBD (Comm) *1–168*
Raikes v Todd (1838) 8 A.E. 846 .... *21–065*
Railway and Electric Appliances Co, Re (1888) L.R. 38 Ch. D. 597, Ch D *13–010*
Railway Sleepers Supply Co, Re (1885) L.R. 29 Ch. D. 204, Ch D *21–025*
Rainbow Estates Ltd v Tokenhold Ltd; sub nom. Gaynes Park Mansion, Epping, Essex, Re [1999] Ch. 64; [1998] 3 W.L.R. 980; [1998] 2 All E.R. 860; [1998] L. & T.R. 116; [1998] 2 E.G.L.R. 34; [1998] 24 E.G. 123; (1998) 95(15) L.S.G. 30; (1998) 142 S.J.L.B. 116; [1998] N.P.C. 33, Ch D *27–005*, *27–026*, *27–028*, *27–044*, *27–048*
Raineri v Miles [1981] A.C. 1050; [1980] 2 W.L.R. 847; [1980] 2 All E.R. 145; (1981) 41 P. & C.R. 71; (1980) 124 S.J. 328, HL *21–011*, *21–012*, *21–014*, *21–018*, *27–081*
Raingold v Bromley [1931] 2 Ch. 307, Ch D *2–118*, *2–119*
Rainsford v Fenwick (1671) Carter 215 .... *8–018*
Raitt v Mitchell (1815) 4 Camp. 146 .... *13–018*
Raja v Lloyds TSB Bank Plc [2001] EWCA Civ 210; [2001] Lloyd's Rep. Bank. 113; (2001) 82 P. & C.R. 16; (2001) 98(6) L.S.G. 47; (2001) 82 P. & C.R. DG3, CA (Civ Div); affirming [2000] Lloyd's Rep. Bank. 377; [2001] 2 E.G.L.R. 78; [2001] 19 E.G. 143; (2000) 97(21) L.S.G. 40, Ch D *1–148*
Rajas Commercial College v Gian Singh & Co [1977] A.C. 312; [1976] 3 W.L.R. 58; [1976] 2 All E.R. 801; [1976] S.T.C. 282; (1976) 120 S.J. 404, PC (Sing) *26–163*
Rajbenback v Mamon; sub nom. Rajenback v Mamon [1955] 1 Q.B. 283; [1955] 2 W.L.R. 21; [1955] 1 All E.R. 12; (1955) 99 S.J. 29, QBD *2–158*, *3–168*, *16–016*
Raleigh v Goschen [1898] 1 Ch. 73, Ch D *10–019*
Ralli Bros v Compania Naviera Sota y Aznar; sub nom. Compania Naviera Sota Y Aznar v Ralli Bros [1920] 2 K.B. 287; (1920) 2 Ll. L. Rep. 550, CA; affirming [1920] 1 K.B. 614; (1919) 1 Ll. L. Rep. 649, KBD (Comm Ct) *16–032*, *23–004*, *23–027*, *23–028*, *30–012*, 30–358, **30–359**, 30–360, *30–363*
Ralli v Denistown (1851) 6 Ex. 488 .... *30–345*
Ram Narayan s/o Shankar v Rishad Hussain Shah s/o Tusaduq Hussain Shah [1979] 1 W.L.R. 1349; (1979) 123 S.J. 436, PC *4–026*

Rama Corp Ltd v Proved Tin & General Investments Ltd [1952] 2 Q.B. 147; [1952] 1 All E.R. 554; [1952] 1 T.L.R. 709; (1952) 96 S.J. 197, QBD *9–042*

Ramco (UK) Ltd v International Insurance Co of Hanover; sub nom. Ramco (UK) Ltd v International Insurance Co of Hannover Ltd [2004] EWCA Civ 675; [2004] 2 All E.R. (Comm) 866; [2004] 2 Lloyd's Rep. 595; [2004] 1 C.L.C. 1013; [2004] Lloyd's Rep. I.R. 606; (2004) 148 S.J.L.B. 695, CA (Civ Div) *18–002*, *18–049*, *18–128*

Ramoneur & Co v Brixey (1911) 104 L.T. 809 .... *16–114*

Ramsden v Dyson; Ramsden v Thornton (1866) L.R. 1 H.L. 129, HL *3–138*, *3–162*, *3–163*, *29–003*, *29–161*

Ramsey v Hartley [1977] 1 W.L.R. 686; [1977] 2 All E.R. 673; (1977) 121 S.J. 319, CA (Civ Div) *19–049*, *20–026*, *20–032*

Ramsgate Victoria Hotel Co Ltd v Montefiore; Ramsgate Victoria Hotel Co Ltd v Goldsmid (1865–66) L.R. 1 Ex. 109, Ex Ct *2–088*, *2–096*, *9–060*

Ramskill v Edwards (1886) L.R. 31 Ch. D. 100, Ch D *29–126*

Randall v Motor Insurers Bureau [1968] 1 W.L.R. 1900; [1969] 1 All E.R. 21; [1968] 2 Lloyd's Rep. 553; (1968) 112 S.J. 883, QBD *18–131*

Randolph v Tuck [1962] 1 Q.B. 175; [1961] 2 W.L.R. 855; [1961] 1 All E.R. 814; (1961) 105 S.J. 157, QBD *25–012*

Ranelaugh Earl v Hayes (1683) 1 Vern. 189 .... *27–008*

Ranger v Great Western Railway, 10 E.R. 824; (1854) 5 H.L. Cas. 72, QB *1–011*

Rankin v Huskisson (1830) 4 Sim 13 .... *10–016*, *10–019*

Rankin v Shiliday [1927] N.I. 162 .... *21–076*

Rann v Hughes, 101 E.R. 1014; (1778) 7 Term Rep. 350 (Note), KB *1–075*, *3–001*

Rasbora v JCL Marine; sub nom. Atkinson v JCL Marine [1977] 1 Lloyd's Rep. 645, QBD *14–066*, 14–090, *19–086*

Rashdall v Ford (1866) L.R. 2 Eq. 750; 35 L.J.Ch. 769; 14 L.T. 790, Ct of Chancery *6–013*

Ratcliffe v Sandwell MBC; Lee v Leeds City Council [2002] EWCA Civ 6; [2002] 1 W.L.R. 1488; [2002] H.L.R. 17; [2002] B.L.G.R. 305; [2002] 2 P. & C.R. 23; [2002] L. & T.R. 35; [2002] 1 E.G.L.R. 103; (2002) 99(10) L.S.G. 31; (2002) 146 S.J.L.B. 46; [2002] N.P.C. 12; [2003] Env. L.R. D3, CA (Civ Div) *1–049*, 1–055, *1–057*, *1–062*

Rathbone Bros & Co v D Maciver Sons & Co [1903] 2 K.B. 378, CA; reversing (1902) 8 Com. Cas. 1, Assizes (Liverpool) *14–032*

Ratnasingam v Kow Ah Dek alias Kow Lian Poi [1983] 1 W.L.R. 1235; (1983) 80 L.S.G. 2362; (1983) 127 S.J. 521, PC (Mal) *26–030*

Raven, The. *See* Banco Central SA v Lingoss & Falce Ltd

Ravennavi SpA v New Century Shipbuilding Co Ltd [2007] EWCA Civ 58; [2007] 2 All E.R. (Comm) 756; [2007] 2 Lloyd's Rep. 24; [2007] 1 C.L.C. 176, CA (Civ Div); affirming [2006] EWHC 733 (Comm); [2006] 2 Lloyd's Rep. 280, QBD (Comm) *12–104*

Ravenseft Properties Ltd v Director General of Fair Trading; sub nom. Ravenseft Properties Ltd's Application [1978] Q.B. 52; [1977] 2 W.L.R. 432; [1977] 1 All E.R. 47; [1977] I.C.R. 136; (1976) 120 S.J. 834, Ch D (RPC) *16–085*

Rawlings v General Trading Co [1921] 1 K.B. 635; 90 L.J.K.B. 404; 124 L.T. 562; 37 T.L.R. 252; 65 S.J. 220; 26 Com. Cas. 171, CA; reversing [1920] 3 K.B. 30, KBD *16–135*, *16–192*, *27–015*

Rawlins v Wickham (1858) 3 De G.L.J. 304 .... *28–089*

Rawlinson v Ames [1925] Ch. 96; 94 L.J.Ch. 113; 132 L.T. 370, Ch D *4–042*, *4–044*, *4–047*

Rawluk v Rawluk [1990] 1 S.C.R. 70 .... *29–015*

Rawson v Johnson (1801) 1 East 203 .... *21–010*

Ray v Jones (1865) 19 C.B. (N.S.) 416; 34 L.J.C.P. 306; 12 L.T. 737; 11 Jur. (N.S.) 812; 13 W.R. 1018 .... *22–006*

Ray v Sempers. *See* DPP v Ray
Rayfield v Hands [1960] Ch. 1; [1958] 2 W.L.R. 851; [1958] 2 All E.R. 194; (1958) 102 S.J. 348, Ch D *9–061*, *18–019*, *18–113*, *28–004*
Raymond Burke Motors Ltd v Mersey Docks and Harbour Co [1986] 1 Lloyd's Rep. 155, QBD (Comm) *14–008*, *14–011*, *14–042*, *14–049*
Raymond Lyons & Co Ltd v Commissioner of Police of the Metropolis [1975] Q.B. 321; [1975] 2 W.L.R. 197; [1975] 1 All E.R. 335; [1975] Crim. L.R. 92, DC *29–138*
Raymond v Fitch (1835) 2 Cr. M. & R. 588; 1 Gale 377; 5 L.J. Ex. 45 .... *20–001*
Rayner v Davies; sub nom. Davies v Rayner [2002] EWCA Civ 1880; [2003] 1 All E.R. (Comm) 394; [2003] 1 C.L.C. 169; [2003] I.L.Pr. 15, CA (Civ Div) *30–094*
Rayner v Pegler (1964) 189 E.G. 967 .... *16–111*, *16–112*
Rayner vStone (1762) Eden 128 .... *27–026*
Rayner (Mincing Lane) v Department of Trade and Industry. *See* JH Rayner (Mincing Lane) Ltd v Department of Trade and Industry
Read v Astoria Garage (Streatham) Ltd [1952] Ch. 637; [1952] 2 All E.R. 292; [1952] 2 T.L.R. 130, CA; affirming [1952] 1 All E.R. 922; [1952] 1 T.L.R. 1059; [1952] W.N. 185; (1952) 96 S.J. 262, Ch D *9–058*
Read v Brown (1889) L.R. 22 Q.B.D. 128; 59 L.J.Q.B. 120; 60 L.T. 250; 37 W.R. 131, CA *19–073*, *28–031*
Read v Croydon Corp [1938] 4 All E.R. 631; 108 L.J.K.B. 72; 160 L.T. 176; 103 J.P. 25; 55 T.L.R. 212; 82 S.J. 991; 37 L.G.R. 53 .... *1–015*, *15–035*
Read v Goldring (1813) 2 M.S. 86 .... *21–088*, *21–095*
Read v Legard (1851) 6 Exch. 636; 20 L.J.Ex. 309; 15 Jur. 494; 17 L.T. 145; 86 R.R. 118 .... *8–074*
Read v Price [1909] 2 K.B. 724, CA; affirming [1909] 1 K.B. 577, KBD *17–013*, *25–027*, *28–094*
Readhead v Midland Railway Co (1868–69) L.R. 4 Q.B. 379, Ex Chamber; affirming (1866–67) L.R. 2 Q.B. 412, QB *1–147*, *1–149*, *14–032*
Reading v Attorney General; sub nom. Reading v King, The; Reading's Petition of Right, Re [1951] A.C. 507; [1951] 1 All E.R. 617; [1951] 1 T.L.R. 480; (1951) 95 S.J. 155, HL *26–021*, *29–008*, *29–011*, *29–151*, *29–156*, *29–160*
Reading Festival Ltd v West Yorkshire Police Authority; sub nom. West Yorkshire Police Authority v Reading Festival Ltd [2006] EWCA Civ 524; [2006] 1 W.L.R. 2005; [2006] Po. L.R. 91; (2006) 103(20) L.S.G. 28; (2006) 150 S.J.L.B. 607, CA (Civ Div); reversing [2005] Po. L.R. 216, QBD *3–063*
Reading Trust Ltd v Spero; Spero v Reading Trust Ltd [1930] 1 K.B. 492; 99 L.J.K.B. 186; 142 L.T. 361; 46 T.L.R. 117; 74 S.J. 12, CA *4–028*
Read's Trustee in Bankruptcy v Smith (Portman Building Society, Third Party) [1951] Ch. 439; [1951] 1 All E.R. 406; (1951) 95 S.J. 156, Ch D *21–085*
Realisations Industrielles et Commerciales SA v Loescher and Partners [1957] 1 W.L.R. 1026; [1957] 3 All E.R. 241; [1957] 2 Lloyd's Rep. 270; (1957) 101 S.J. 800, QBD *20–019*
Reaney v Co-operative Wholesale Society [1932] W.N. 78 .... *26–030*
Reardon Smith Line v Australian Wheat Board [1956] A.C. 266; [1956] 2 W.L.R. 403; [1956] 1 All E.R. 456; [1956] 1 Lloyd's Rep. 1, PC (Aus); reversing [1953] 1 Lloyd's Rep. 131, Sup Ct (WA) (Full Ct) *12–118*, *26–038*
Reardon Smith Line Ltd v Black Sea & Baltic General Insurance Co Ltd [1939] A.C. 562; (1939) 64 Ll. L. Rep. 229, HL *21–020*
Reardon Smith Line Ltd v Hansen-Tangen; The Diana Prosperity; Hansen-Tangen v Sanko Steamship Co Ltd [1976] 1 W.L.R. 989; [1976] 3 All E.R. 570; [1976] 2 Lloyd's Rep. 621; (1976) 120 S.J. 719, HL; affirming [1976] 2 Lloyd's Rep. 60; (1976) 120 S.J. 329, CA (Civ Div) *12–020*, 12–036, *12–040*, 12–118, *12–119*

Reardon Smith Line Ltd v Ministry of Agriculture, Fisheries and Food; Garibaldi Societa Cooperativa di Navigazione ARL v President of India; Carlton Steamship Co Ltd v Ministry of Agriculture, Fisheries and Food; Cape of Good Hope Motorship Co Ltd v Ministry of Agriculture, Fisheries and Food; Miramar Compania Naviera SA v Government of the Union of South Africa [1963] A.C. 691; [1963] 2 W.L.R. 439; [1963] 1 All E.R. 545; [1963] 1 Lloyd's Rep. 12; (1963) 107 S.J. 133, HL; reversing in part [1962] 1 Q.B. 42; [1961] 3 W.L.R. 110; [1961] 2 All E.R. 577; [1961] 1 Lloyd's Rep. 385; (1961) 105 S.J. 567, CA; affirming [1960] 1 Q.B. 439; [1959] 3 W.L.R. 665; [1959] 3 All E.R. 434; [1959] 2 Lloyd's Rep. 229; (1959) 103 S.J. 920, QBD (Comm) *12–130*, *14–140*, *14–143*, *14–146*, *21–006*, *21–007*, 21–008, *21–022*, *23–045*

Rebecca Elaine, The. *See* Hamble Fisheries Ltd v L Gardner & Sons Ltd

Receiver for the Metropolitan Police District v Croydon Corp. *See* Metropolitan Police District Receiver v Croydon Corp

Receiver for the Metropolitan Police District v Tatum. *See* Metropolitan Police District Receiver v Tatum

Record v Bell [1991] 1 W.L.R. 853; [1991] 4 All E.R. 471; (1991) 62 P. & C.R. 192, Ch D 4–076, *12–004*, *12–033*, *12–103*, *22–036*, *27–014*

Red Raven Ash Coal Co v Bull (1946) 39 S.E. 2d. 231 .... *29–144*

Red Sea Tankers Ltd v Papachristidis; The Hellespont Ardent [1997] 2 Lloyd's Rep. 547, QBD (Comm) *14–017*, *18–023*

Redbridge LBC v Robinson Rentals (1969) 211 E.G. 1125 .... *5–058*

Rede v Farr (1817) 6 M. & S. 121 .... *12–082*, *22–055*

Rederiaktiebolaget Amphitrite v R. [1921] 3 K.B. 500; 91 L.J.K.B. 500; 91 L.J.K.B. 901; 118 L.T. 176; 23 Com. Cas. 133; 14 Asp. 310, KBD *2–179*, 10–008

Rederiaktiebolaget Argonaut v Hani [1918] 2 K.B. 247; 87 L.J.K.B. 901, KBD ... *12–114*

Redgrave v Hurd (1881–82) L.R. 20 Ch. D. 1; 51 L.J.Ch. 118; 45 L.T. 489; 30 W.R. 251, CA *6–039*, *6–041*, *6–103*, *7–132*

Redland Bricks v Morris; sub nom. Morris v Redland Bricks [1970] A.C. 652; [1969] 2 W.L.R. 1437; [1969] 2 All E.R. 576; (1969) 113 S.J. 405, HL *27–031*

Redmond v Dainton [1920] 2 K.B. 256, KBD *23–055*

Redrow Homes Ltd v Bett Brothers Plc [1999] 1 A.C. 197; [1998] 2 W.L.R. 198; [1998] 1 All E.R. 385; 1998 S.C. (H.L.) 64; 1998 S.L.T. 648; 1998 S.C.L.R. 325; [1998] F.S.R. 345; [1998] R.P.C. 793; (1998) 21(4) I.P.D. 21034; (1998) 95(6) L.S.G. 25; (1998) 148 N.L.J. 121; (1998) 142 S.J.L.B. 79; 1998 G.W.D. 4–160, HL *29–140*, *29–142*

Reed v Kilburn Cooperative Society (1874–75) L.R. 10 Q.B. 264, QBD *21–006*

Reed v Madon [1989] Ch. 408; [1989] 2 W.L.R. 553; [1989] 2 All E.R. 431; (1989) 86(15) L.S.G. 42; (1989) 133 S.J. 360, Ch D *27–060*

Reel v Holder [1981] 1 W.L.R. 1226; [1981] 3 All E.R. 321; (1981) 125 S.J. 585, CA (Civ Div); affirming [1979] 1 W.L.R. 1252; [1979] 3 All E.R. 1041; (1979) 123 S.J. 654, QBD *9–071*

Reeman v Department of Transport [1997] 2 Lloyd's Rep. 648; [1997] P.N.L.R. 618, CA (Civ Div) *18–032*

Rees v Darlington Memorial Hospital NHS Trust [2003] UKHL 52; [2004] 1 A.C. 309; [2003] 3 W.L.R. 1091; [2003] 4 All E.R. 987; [2004] 1 F.L.R. 234; [2003] 3 F.C.R. 289; [2004] P.I.Q.R. P14; [2004] Lloyd's Rep. Med. 1; (2004) 75 B.M.L.R. 69; [2004] Fam. Law 22; (2003) 153 N.L.J. 1599, HL; reversing [2002] EWCA Civ 88; [2003] Q.B. 20; [2002] 2 W.L.R. 1483; [2002] 2 All E.R. 177; [2002] 1 F.L.R. 799; [2002] 1 F.C.R. 695; [2002] P.I.Q.R. P26; [2002] Lloyd's Rep. Med. 163; (2002) 65 B.M.L.R. 117; [2002] Fam. Law 348; (2002) 99(12) L.S.G. 32; (2002) 152 N.L.J. 281; (2002) 146 S.J.L.B. 53, CA (Civ Div) *18–031*, *18–037*, 18–039

Rees v De Bernardy (1896) 2 Ch. 437; 65 L.J.Ch. 656; 74 L.T. 585, Ch D *7–128*, *16–065*, *19–049*

Rees v Hughes [1946] K.B. 517; 115 L.J.K.B. 389; 175 L.T. 379; 62 T.L.R. 394; 90 S.J. 394; [1946] 2 All E.R. 47, CA *8–019*, *29–132*

Rees Hough Ltd v Redland Reinforced Plastics Ltd, 27 B.L.R. 136; (1984) 1 Const. L.J. 67; [1984] C.I.L.L. 84; (1984) 134 N.L.J. 706, QBD .. *14–085*, *14–087*, 14–092
Reese River Silver Mining Co Ltd v Smith; sub nom. Reese River Silver Mining Co, Re (1869–70) L.R. 4 H.L. 6; 39 L.J.Ch. 849 4, HL; affirming (1866–67) L.R. 2 Ch. App. 604, CA in Chancery *6–009*, *6–045*, *9–060*
Reeve v Berridge (1888) 20 Q.B.D. 523; 57 L.J.Q.B. 265; 58 L.T. 836; 52 J.P. 549; 36 W.R. 517, CA *6–156*
Reeves v Butcher [1891] 2 Q.B. 509; [1891–94] All E.R. Rep. 943, CA ..*28–031*, *28–035*, *28–037*
Reeves v Hearne (1836) 1 M. & W. 323; 2 Gale 4; 5 L.J.Ex. 156 22–015
Refuge Assurance Co Ltd v Kettlewell; sub nom. Kettlewell v Refuge Assurance Co Ltd [1909] A.C. 243, HL *29–142*, *29–147*
Reg Glass Pty v Rivers Locking Systems Pty (1968) 120 C.L.R. 516, HC (Aus) ... *13–030*
Regal (Hastings) Ltd v Gulliver [1967] 2 A.C. 134; [1942] 1 All E.R. 378, HL *9–055*, *29–155*, *29–156*
Regalian Properties Plc v London Docklands Development Corp [1995] 1 W.L.R. 212; [1995] 1 All E.R. 1005; 45 Con. L.R. 37; (1995) 11 Const. L.J. 127; [1994] E.G. 176 (C.S.); (1995) 92(4) L.S.G. 34; [1994] N.P.C. 139; (1994) 68 P. & C.R. D29, Ch D *2–116*, *3–106*, *29–022*, *29–071*
Regan v Paul Properties Ltd [2006] EWCA Civ 1391; [2007] Ch. 135; [2006] 3 W.L.R. 1131; [2007] 4 All E.R. 48; [2007] B.L.R. 56; [2007] 2 P. & C.R. 14; [2006] 3 E.G.L.R. 94; [2006] 46 E.G. 210; [2007] C.I.L.L. 2411; [2006] 44 E.G. 197 (C.S.); (2006) 103(43) L.S.G. 27; [2007] 2 P. & C.R. DG5, CA (Civ Div) *27–063*
Regazzoni v KC Sethia (1944) Ltd; sub nom. Regazzoni v Sethia (KC) (1944) [1958] A.C. 301; [1957] 3 W.L.R. 752; [1957] 3 All E.R. 286; [1957] 2 Lloyd's Rep. 289; (1957) 101 S.J. 848, HL; affirming [1956] 2 Q.B. 490; [1956] 3 W.L.R. 79; [1956] 2 All E.R. 487; [1956] 1 Lloyd's Rep. 435; (1956) 100 S.J. 417, CA; affirming [1956] 2 W.L.R. 204; [1956] 1 All E.R. 229; [1955] 2 Lloyd's Rep. 766; (1956) 100 S.J. 55, QBD ... 16–031, *16–032*, *30–361*, *30–363*, *30–365*, *30–347*
Regent International Hotels (UK) v Pageguide, *TheTimes*, May 13, 1985, CA (Civ Div) *27–025*
Regent ohG Aisestadt & Barig v Francesco of Jermyn Street Ltd [1981] 3 All E.R. 327; [1981] Com. L.R. 78, QBD *21–029*, *24–044*
Regie Nationale des Usines Renault SA v Zhang (2003) 210 C.L.R. 491 .... *30–337*
Regina and Palacios, Re (1984) 45 O.R. (2d) 269 .... *11–014*
Regis Property Co Ltd v Dudley [1959] A.C. 370; [1958] 3 W.L.R. 647; [1958] 3 All E.R. 491; (1958) 102 S.J. 844, HL *21–038*, *24–036*
Reichman v Beveridge; sub nom. Reichman v Gauntlett [2006] EWCA Civ 1659; [2007] Bus. L.R. 412; [2007] 1 P. & C.R. 20; [2007] L. & T.R. 18; [2007] 8 E.G. 138; [2007] 1 E.G. 92 (C.S.); (2007) 104(4) L.S.G. 35; [2006] N.P.C. 132, CA (Civ Div) *24–010*
Reid v Explosives Co (1887) L.R. 19 Q.B.D. 264; 56 L.J.Q.B. 68; 57 L.T. 439; 35 W.R. 509, CA *9–050*
Reid v Fairbanks (1853) 13 C.B. 692 ....*12–063*, *29–052*
Reid v Rigby & Co [1894] 2 Q.B. 40, QBD *29–170*
Reid v Rush & Tompkins Group [1990] 1 W.L.R. 212; [1989] 3 All E.R. 228; [1989] 2 Lloyd's Rep. 167; 27 Con. L.R. 4; [1990] R.T.R. 144; [1990] I.C.R. 61; [1989] I.R.L.R. 265; (1989) 139 N.L.J. 680, CA (Civ Div) 1–158, *3–180*, *13–003*, *13–010*, *18–033*
Reid Newfoundl & Co v Anglo-American Telegraph Co Ltd [1912] A.C. 555, PC (Can) *26–021*
Reigate v Union Manufacturing Co (Ramsbottom) Ltd [1918] 1 K.B. 592; 87 L.J.K.B. 724; 118 L.T. 479, CA *9–047*, *13–004*, *13–007*, *13–009*
Reilly v King, The [1934] A.C. 176, PC (Can); affirming in part [1932] Ex. C.R. 14, Ex Ct (Can) *10–007*
Rein v Stein [1892] 1 Q.B. 753, CA *21–054*
Reis, Re. *See* Clough v Samuel

Rekstin v Severo Sibirsko Gosudarstvennoe Akcionernoe Obschestvo Komseverputj [1933] 1 K.B. 47; [1932] All E.R. Rep. 534; 102 L.J.K.B. 16; 147 L.T. 231; 48 T.L.R. 578; 76 S.J. 494, CA *19–022*, *19–023*, *19–067*
Reliance Car Facilities v Roding Motors [1952] 2 Q.B. 844; [1952] 1 All E.R. 1355; [1952] 1 T.L.R. 1370; (1952) 96 S.J. 360, CA *22–051*
Reliance Marine Insurance v Duder [1913] 1 K.B. 265; 81 L.J.K.B. 870; 160 L.T. 936; 28 T.L.R. 469; 17 Com. Cas. 227; 12 Asp. M.L.C. 223, CA *12–096*
Rely-a-Bell Burglar & Fire Alarm Co Ltd v Eisler [1926] Ch. 609; 95 L.J.Ch. 345; 135 L.T. 268, Ch D *16–102*, *27–064*
Renault UK Ltd v Fleetpro Technical Services [2007] EWHC 2541 (QB); [2008] Bus. L.R. D17, QBD *6–062*
Rendall v Andreae (1892) 61 L.J.Q.B. 630 .... *20–008*
Rendall v Hills Dry Docks and Engineering Co Ltd [1900] 2 Q.B. 245, CA *28–109*, *28–111*
Rennie v Westbury Homes (Holdings) Ltd [2007] EWCA Civ 1401, CA (Civ Div); affirming [2007] EWHC 164 (Ch); [2007] 2 P. & C.R. 12; [2007] 20 E.G. 296; [2007] N.P.C. 16, Ch D *12–050*, *13–010*
Representative Body for the Church in Wales v Newton [2005] EWHC 631 (QB); [2005] 16 E.G. 145 (C.S.), QBD *4–054*, *4–077*, *4–082*
Republic of India v India Steamship Co Ltd. *See* India v India Steamship Co Ltd; The Indian Endurance and The Indian Grace
Republica de Guatemala v Nunez [1927] 1 K.B. 669, CA *30–123*, *30–125*
Resolute Maritime Inc v Nippon Kaiji Kyokai; The Skopas [1983] 1 W.L.R. 857; [1983] 2 All E.R. 1; [1983] 1 Lloyd's Rep. 431, QBD (Comm) *6–076*
Re-Source America International Ltd v Platt Site Services Ltd (Damages); sub nom. Barkin Construction Ltd v Re-Source America International Ltd [2005] EWCA Civ 97; [2005] 2 Lloyd's Rep. 50; 105 Con. L.R. 30; [2005] N.P.C. 19, CA (Civ Div) *26–116*
Reuss v Picksley (1866) L.R. 1 Ex. 342; 35 L.J.Ex. 218; 12 Jur. 628; 15 L.T. 25; 14 W.R. 924; 4 H. & C. 588; 143 R.R. 797, Ex Chamber *4–027*
Reuter Hufeland & Co v Sala & Co (1878–79) L.R. 4 C.P.D. 239; 48 L.J.C.P. 492; 40 L.T. 476, CA *12–037*, *21–013*
Reuter v Electric Telegraph Co (1856) 6 E. & B. 341; 26 L.J.Q.B. 46; 2 Jur. 1245; 106 R.R. 625 .... *9–039*
Revenue and Customs Commissioners v Total Networks SL [2008] UKHL 19; [2008] 2 All E.R. 143 .... *18–135*
Rewia, The. *See* Owners of Cargo Lately Laden on Board the Rewia v Caribbean Liners (Caribtainer) Ltd
Rex Stewart Jeffries Parker Ginsberg Ltd v Parker [1988] I.R.L.R. 483, CA (Civ Div) *16–110*, *16–197*
Reynard Construction (ME) Pty Ltd v Minister of Public Works (1992) 26 N.S.W.L.R. 234 .... *29–068*
Reynell v Sprye (1852) 1 De. G.M. & G. 660; 21 L.J.Ch. 633; 8 Hare 222; 91 R.R. 228 .... *6–013*, 6–035, *6–039*, *12–112*, *16–186*
Reynolds v Atherton (1922) 127 L.T. 189; 66 S.J. 404 .... *2–096*, 2–101
Reynolds v Boston Deep Sea Fishing & Ice Co Ltd (1921) 38 T.L.R. 22, KBD *14–011*
Reynolds v Bridge (1856) 6 E.B. 528 .... *26–134*
Reynolds v Coleman (1887) L.R. 36 Ch. D. 453, CA *21–005*
Reynolds v General & Finance Facilities (1963) 107 S.J. 889, CA *22–053*
Reynolds v Kinsey [1959] (4) S.A. 50 .... *16–012*
Reynolds v Phoenix Assurance Co Ltd [1978] 2 Lloyd's Rep. 440, QBD *6–147*
Reynolds v Smith (1893) 9 T.L.R. 494 .... *13–018*
Rhoades, Re [1899] 2 Q.B. 347; 68 L.J.Q.B. 804; 80 L.T. 742; 15 T.L.R. 407; 47 W.R. 561; 6 Manson 277, CA; affirming [1899] 1 Q.B. 905, QBD *17–023*
Rhodes, Re; sub nom. Rhodes v Rhodes (1890) L.R. 44 Ch. D. 94; 59 L.J.Ch. 298; 62 L.T. 342; 38 W.R. 385, CA *8–011*, *8–074*, *29–008*, *29–133*
Rhodes v Forwood (1875–76) L.R. 1 App. Cas. 256; 47 L.J.Ex. 396; 34 L.T. 890, HL *13–010*, *13–012*
Rhodes v Smethurst (1840) 6 M. & W. 351 .... *28–064*

Rhodes v Swithenbank (1889) L.R. 22 Q.B.D. 577; 58 L.J.Q.B. 287; 60 L.T. 856; 37 W.R. 457, HL *8–062*
Rhodia International Holdings Ltd v Huntsman International LLC [2007] EWHC 292 (Comm); [2007] 2 All E.R. (Comm) 577; [2007] 2 Lloyd's Rep. 325; [2007] 1 C.L.C. 59; [2007] Bus. L.R. D22, QBD (Comm) *2–138*
Rhodian River Shipping Co SA v Halla Maritime Corp; The Rhodian River and The Rhodian Sailor [1984] 1 Lloyd's Rep. 373, QBD (Comm) *9–042*
Rhondda's (Viscountess) Claim [1922] 2 A.C. 339, HL *12–086*
Rhone v Stephens [1994] 2 A.C. 310; [1994] 2 W.L.R. 429; [1994] 37 E.G. 151; [1994] E.G. 50 (C.S.); (1994) 138 S.J.L.B. 77; [1994] N.P.C. 43, HL; affirming (1994) 67 P. & C.R. 9; [1993] E.G. 3 (C.S.); (1993) 137 S.J.L.B. 46; [1993] N.P.C. 11, CA (Civ Div) *18–019*, 19–080
Rhyl Urban DC v Rhyl Amusements Ltd [1959] 1 W.L.R. 465; [1959] 1 All E.R. 257; 57 L.G.R. 19; (1959) 103 S.J. 327, Ch D 10–040
Rialto, The [1891] P. 175; 60 L.J.P. 71; 64 L.T. 540; 7 Asp. M.L.C. 35, PDAD *7–047*
Ricardo v Garcias (1845) 12 Cl. Fin. 368 .... *25–018*
Rice v Chute (1801) 1 East. 579 .... *10–013*
Rice v Everitt (1801) 1 East 583n *10–013*
Rice v Gordon (1847) 11 Beav. 265 .... *3–014*
Rice v Reed [1900] 1 Q.B. 54, CA *29–146*
Rice (t/a Garden Guardian) v Great Yarmouth [2003] T.C.L.R. 1; (2001) 3 L.G.L.R. 4, CA (Civ Div) *1–031*, *12–040*, *22–048*, *24–040*
Richards v Bluck (1848) 6 C.B. 437; 6 D. & L. 325; 18 L.J.C.P. 15; 12 Jur. 963; 77 R.R. 360 .... *12–063*
Richards v Creighton-Griffiths (Investments) (1972) 225 E.G. 2104 .... *22–033*
Richards v Delbridge (1874) L.R. 18 Eq. 11 .... *1–108*, *18–082*
Richards v Phillips [1969] 1 Ch. 39; [1968] 3 W.L.R. 33; [1968] 2 All E.R. 859; (1968) 112 S.J. 460, CA (Civ Div); affirming [1968] 2 W.L.R. 14; [1967] 3 All E.R. 876; (1967) 111 S.J. 866, Ch D *2–013*
Richard Adler (t/a Argo Rederei) v Sutos (Hellas) Maritime Corp; The Argo Hellas [1984] 1 Lloyd's Rep. 296; (1984) 134 N.L.J. 203, QBD (Comm) *17–005*, *17–015*
Richard and Bartlet's Case (1584) 1 Leon. 19 .... *22–016*
Richard Holden Ltd v Bostock Co Ltd (1902) 18 T.L.R. 317 .... *26–074*, *26–078*
Richard West & Partners (Inverness) Ltd v Dick [1969] 2 Ch. 424; [1969] 2 W.L.R. 1190; [1969] 1 All E.R. 943; 67 L.G.R. 293; (1969) 20 P. & C.R. 293; (1969) 113 S.J. 165, CA (Civ Div); affirming [1969] 2 W.L.R. 383; [1969] 1 All E.R. 289; (1969) 113 S.J. 105, Ch D *2–155*
Richards (t/a Colin Richards & Co) v Hughes; sub nom. Hughes v Richards (t/a Colin Richards & Co) [2004] EWCA Civ 266; [2004] P.N.L.R. 35; (2004) 148 S.J.L.B. 353, CA (Civ Div) *18–012*, *18–037*, *18–038*
Richardson Ex p. Governors of St Thomas Hospital, Re [1911] 2 K.B. 705, CA *28–047*
Richardson Ex p. Harris, Re (1880–81) L.R. 16 Ch. D. 613, Ch D *20–035*
Richardson, Re (1882) 47 L.T. 514 .... *18–079*
Richardson v Jackson (1841) 8 M.W. 298 .... *21–093*
Richardson v Mellish (1824) 2 Bing. 229; 1 C. & P. 241; R. & M. 66; 9 Moore 435; 3 L.J.C.P. 265; 27 R.R. 603 .... *16–003*
Richardson v Silvester (1873) L.R. 9 Q.B. 34; 43 L.J.Q.B. 1; 29 L.T. 395; 22 W.R. 74, QB *6–028*
Richardson-Gardner v Fremantle (1870) 24 L.T. 81; 19 W.R. 56 .... *9–075*
Richardson (Inspector of Taxes) v Worrall; Westall v McDonald (Inspector of Taxes) [1985] S.T.C. 693; 58 T.C. 642; (1985) 82 L.S.G. 2501, Ch D ... *2–014*, *18–007*
Richardson Spence & Co v Rowntree [1894] A.C. 217; 63 L.J.Q.B. 283; 70 L.T. 817; 10 T.L.R. 335; 58 J.P. 493; 7 Asp.M.L.C. 482; 6 R. 95, HL *12–013*, *12–014*, *14–002*
Richardsons and M Samuel & Co's Arbitration, Re [1898] 1 Q.B. 261; 66 L.J.Q.B. 868; 77 L.T. 479; 14 T.L.R. 5; 3 Com. Cas. 7; 8 Asp. M.C. 330, CA *12–087*, *12–088*, *14–0146*
Richco International Ltd v Alfred C Toepfer International GmbH; The Bonde [1991] 1 Lloyd's Rep. 136, QBD (Comm) *12–082*, *13–012*, *22–055*

Richco International Ltd v Bunge & Co Ltd; The New Prosper; sub nom. Bunge & Co v Tradax Ocean Transportation SA [1991] 2 Lloyd's Rep. 93, QBD (Comm) *12–034*
Riches v Westminster Bank Ltd; sub nom. Westminster Bank Ltd v Riches [1947] A.C. 390; [1947] 1 All E.R. 469; 63 T.L.R. 211; 28 T.C. 159; 176 L.T. 405; (1947) 91 S.J. 191, HL *26–163*
Richfield v Udell (1667) Carter 191 .... *11–029*
Richmond Gate Property Co, Re [1965] 1 W.L.R. 335; [1964] 3 All E.R. 936, Ch D *2–175*, *29–071*, 29–076
Rickett, Re; sub nom. Insecticide Activated Products Ltd v Official Receiver [1949] 1 All E.R. 737; 65 T.L.R. 258; [1949] W.N. 151; (1949) 93 S.J. 218, Ch D *26–010*
Rickless v United Artists Corp [1988] Q.B. 40; [1987] 2 W.L.R. 945; [1987] 1 All E.R. 679; [1987] F.S.R. 362, CA (Civ Div); affirming [1986] F.S.R. 502, QBD *18–141*
Rider v Ford [1923] 1 Ch. 541, Ch D *15–014*
Ridge v Baldwin [1964] A.C. 40; [1963] 2 W.L.R. 935; [1963] 2 All E.R. 66; (1963) 127 J.P. 251; (1963) 127 J.P. 295; 61 L.G.R. 369; 37 A.L.J. 140; 234 L.T. 423; 113 L.J. 716; (1963) 107 S.J. 313, HL *27–023*
Ridgeway Motors (Isleworth) Ltd v ALTS Ltd; sub nom. Ridgeway Motors (Isleworth) Ltd v Altis Ltd [2005] EWCA Civ 92; [2005] 1 W.L.R. 2871; [2005] 2 All E.R. 304; [2005] C.P. Rep. 34; [2005] B.C.C. 496; [2005] 2 B.C.L.C. 61; [2005] B.P.I.R. 423; [2005] R.V.R. 173; [2005] N.P.C. 27, CA (Civ Div) 28–016
Ridgway, Re (1889) 6 Morr. 277; 61 L.T. 647; 38 W.R. 432 .... *20–032*
Ridgway v Hungerford Market Co (1853) 3 A.E. 171 .... *21–030*, *24–014*
Ridley v Oster [1939] 1 All E.R. 618 .... *27–055*
Ridout v Bristow (1830) 9 Exch. 48 .... *12–108*
Ridway v Wharton (1857) 6 H.L.C. 238 .... *4–028*
Rigby v Connol 1880) L.R. 14 Ch. D. 482; 49 L.J.Ch. 328; 42 L.T. 139; 28 W.R. 650, Ch D 9–074, *27–021*
Right v Bucknell (1831) 2 B. & Ad. 278 .... *1–112*
Rightside Properties Ltd v Gray [1975] Ch. 72; [1974] 3 W.L.R. 484; [1974] 2 All E.R. 1169; (1974) 28 P. & C.R. 232; (1974) 118 S.J. 698, Ch D ...*21–014*, *21–018*, *21–022*, *21–025*, *24–023*
Rignall Developments Ltd v Halil [1988] Ch. 190; [1987] 3 W.L.R. 394; [1987] 3 All E.R. 170; (1988) 20 H.L.R. 7; (1987) 54 P. & C.R. 245; [1987] 1 E.G.L.R. 193; (1987) 282 E.G. 1414; (1987) 131 S.J. 1039, Ch D *6–157*
Rigoletto, The. *See* Lotus Cars Ltd v Southampton Cargo Handling Plc
Riley v Troll [1953] 1 All E.R. 966, Assizes (Manchester) *2–118*
Riley v William Holland & Sons Ltd [1911] 1 K.B. 1029, CA *21–054*
Rilland, The [1979] 1 Lloyd's Rep. 455, QBD (Admlty) *26–171*
Rimmer v Liverpool City Council [1985] Q.B. 1; [1984] 2 W.L.R. 426; [1984] 1 All E.R. 930; (1984) 12 H.L.R. 23; 82 L.G.R. 424; (1984) 47 P. & C.R. 516; (1984) 269 E.G. 319; (1984) 81 L.S.G. 664, CA (Civ Div) 1–154, *1–174*
Rimmer v Webster [1902] 2 Ch. 163, Ch D *21–058*
Rind v Theodore Goddard [2008] EWHC 459 (Ch); [2008] P.N.L.R. 24 .... *18–022*
Ringway Roadmarking v Adbruf Ltd [1998] 2 B.C.L.C. 625, QBD (OR) *1–031*, *12–118*
Rio Assu, The. *See* C Itoh & Co Ltd v Companhia De Navegacao Lloyd Brasileiro
Rippinghall v Lloyd (1833) 5 B. Ad. 742 .... *21–005*, *21–006*
Risdon Iron & Locomotive Works v Furness [1906] 1 K.B. 49, CA *30–325*
Rishton v Whatmore (1878) L.R. 8 Ch. D. 467; 47 L.J.Ch. 629; 26 W.R. 827, Ch D *4–029*
Ritchie v Atkinson (1808) 10 East 295 .... *24–035*
River Steamer Co, Re; sub nom. Mitchell's Case (1870–71) L.R. 6 Ch. App. 822, CA in Chancery *28–094*
River Wear Commissioners v Adamson (1876–77) L.R. 2 App. Cas. 743, HL; affirming (1875–76) L.R. 1 Q.B.D. 546, CA *12–118*

Riverlate Properties Ltd v Paul [1975] Ch. 133; [1974] 3 W.L.R. 564; [1974] 2 All E.R. 656; (1974) 28 P. & C.R. 220; (1974) 118 S.J. 644, CA (Civ Div) *5–116*, 5–118, 5–120
Riyad Bank v Ahli United Bank (UK) Plc [2006] EWCA Civ 780; [2006] 2 All E.R. (Comm) 777; [2006] 2 Lloyd's Rep. 292; [2006] 1 C.L.C. 1007; [2007] P.N.L.R. 1, CA (Civ Div); affirming [2005] EWHC 279 (Comm); [2005] 2 Lloyd's Rep. 409; [2006] 1 B.C.L.C. 311, QBD (Comm) ... *1–184*, *18–058*, *18–059*
Roadworks (1952) Ltd v Charman [1994] 2 Lloyd's Rep. 99, QBD (Comm) ... *2–148*
Robb v Gow Bros & Gemmell (1905) 8 F. 90; (1905) 13 S.L.T. 609, IH (1 Div) ... *21–056*
Robb v Green [1895] 2 Q.B. 315, CA; affirming [1895] 2 Q.B. 1, QBD *16–107*
Robb v Hammersmith and Fulham LBC [1991] I.C.R. 514; [1991] I.R.L.R. 72, QBD *27–023*
Robbins v Jones (1863) 12 M. & W. 68 .... *13–016*
Robbins of Putney v Meek [1971] R.T.R. 345, QBD *26–107*, 26–110
Robert A Munro & Co v Meyer; sub nom. Robert A Munro & Co Ltd v Meyer [1930] 2 K.B. 312, KBD *14–027*, *24–044*
Robert Leonard (Developments) v Wright. *See* Wright v Robert Leonard (Developments)
Robert Stewart & Sons v Carapanayoti & Co [1962] 1 W.L.R. 34; [1962] 1 All E.R. 418; [1961] 2 Lloyd's Rep. 387; (1962) 106 S.J. 16, QBD (Comm) ... *26–125*, *26–127*, *26–144*
Roberta, The (1937) 58 Ll. L. Rep. 159, PDAD *30–352*
Roberts, Re; Roberts v Roberts [1905] 1 Ch. 704; 74 L.J.Ch. 483; 93 L.T. 253, CA *22–021*
Roberts v Barker (1833) 1 Cr. App. R.. & M. 808; 3 Tyr. 945; 2 L.J.Ex. 268; 28 R.R. 773 .... *12–128*
Roberts v Brett (1865) 11 H.L.C. 337 .... *21–021*
Roberts v Bury Improvement Commissioners (1870) L.R. 5 C.P. 310; 39 L.J.C.P. 129; 22 L.T. 132; 34 J.P. 821; 18 W.R. 702, Ex Chamber; reversing (1868–69) L.R. 4 C.P. 755, CCP *12–082*, *13–011*, *13–012*
Roberts v Elwells Engineers [1972] 2 Q.B. 586; [1972] 3 W.L.R. 1; [1972] 2 All E.R. 890; [1973] 1 Lloyd's Rep. 153; (1972) 116 S.J. 431, CA (Civ Div) *13–022*
Roberts v Gray [1913] 1 K.B. 520; 82 L.J.K.B. 362; 108 L.T. 232; 29 T.L.R. 149, CA *8–004*, *8–011*, 8–013, *8–017*, *8–028*
Roberts v Hardy (1815) 3 M. & S. 533; 2 Rose 457; 16 R.R. 347 .... *11–024*
Roberts v Havelock (1832) 3 B. Ad. 404 .... *21–037*, *21–053*, *29–070*
Roberts v Hayward (1828) 3 C. & P. 432 .... *2–047*, *2–076*
Roberts v J Hampson & Co Ltd [1990] 1 W.L.R. 94; [1989] 2 All E.R. 504; (1988) 20 H.L.R. 615; [1988] 37 E.G. 110; [1988] E.G. 80 (C.S.); (1990) 87(4) L.S.G. 74; (1988) 138 N.L.J. Rep. 166; (1989) 133 S.J. 1234, QBD *14–063*, *18–022*
Roberts v Roberts (1783) 3 P.Wms. 66 .... *16–191*
Roberts v Roberts (1986) [1986] 1 W.L.R. 437; [1986] 2 All E.R. 483; [1986] 2 F.L.R. 152; (1986) 83 L.S.G. 1554; (1986) 130 S.J. 315, Fam Div *16–022*
Roberts v Security Co Ltd [1897] 1 Q.B. 111, CA *12–108*
Roberts v Smith (1859) 28 L.J.Ex. 164; 4 H. & N. 315; 32 L.T. (O.S.) 320; 157 E.R. 861 .... *2–175*
Roberts & Co v Leicestershire CC. *See* A Roberts & Co v Leicestershire CC
Roberts (Deceased), Re [1978] 1 W.L.R. 653; [1978] 3 All E.R. 225; (1978) 122 S.J. 264, CA (Civ Div) *7–010*, *8–069*
Robertson v British Gas Corp [1983] I.C.R. 351; [1983] I.R.L.R. 302, CA (Civ Div) *2–177*
Robertson v Buchanan (1904) 73 L.J.Ch. 408; 90 L.T. 390 .... *16–114*
Robertson v Dicicco [1972] R.T.R. 431; 70 L.G.R. 589; [1972] Crim. L.R. 592; (1972) 116 S.J. 744, DC *6–012*
Robertson v French (1803) 4 East 130; 4 Esp. 246; 7 R.R. 535, KB *12–051*, *12–070*
Robertson v Jackson (1845) 2 C.B. 412 .... *30–334*
Robertson v Minister of Pensions [1949] 1 K.B. 227; [1948] 2 All E.R. 767; 64 T.L.R. 526; [1949] L.J.R. 323; (1948) 92 S.J. 603, KBD *3–087*, *3–103*, 10–008, *10–011*

Robertson v Petros M Nomikos Ltd; sub nom. Petros M Nomikos Ltd v Robertson [1939] A.C. 371; (1939) 64 Ll. L. Rep. 45, HL; affirming [1938] 2 K.B. 603; (1938) 61 Ll. L. Rep. 105, CA; reversing (1937) 59 Ll. L. Rep. 182, KBD *12–085*
Robertson v Ridley [1989] 1 W.L.R. 872; [1989] 2 All E.R. 474; (1989) 133 S.J. 1170, CA (Civ Div) *9–074*
Robertson v Wait (1853) 8 Exch. 299; 22 L.J.Ex. 209; 1 W.R. 132 ..... *18–076*, *18–078*
Robertson v Willmott (1909) 25 T.L.R. 681; 53 S.J. 631 ..... *16–114*
Robertson v Wilson (1958) 75 W.N.(N.S.W.) 503 ..... *23–053*
Robey & Co v Snaefell Mining Co Ltd (1888) L.R. 20 Q.B.D. 152, QBD *21–054*
Robins v Power (1858) 4 C.B.(N.S.) 778 ..... *29–071*
Robinson, Re (1884) 27 Ch. D. 160; 53 L.J.Ch. 986; 51 L.T. 737, CA *19–047*
Robinson, Re; sub nom. McLaren v Public Trustee [1911] 1 Ch. 502, Ch D *28–134*
Robinson v Bland, 97 E.R. 717; (1760) 2 Burr. 1077, KB *30–005*, *30–367*
Robinson v Cook (1815) 6 Taunt. 336 ..... *21–085*
Robinson v Customs and Excise Commissioners [2000] Po. L.R. 112, QBD *2–175*
Robinson v Davison (1870–71) L.R. 6 Ex. 269; 40 L.J.Ex. 172; 24 L.T. 755, Ex Ct *20–006*
Robinson v Ferreday (1839) 8 C.P. 752 ..... *21–092*
Robinson v Golden Chips (Wholesale) [1971] N.Z.L.R. 257, CA (Civ Div) *16–129*
Robinson v Great Western Ry (1865) 35 L.J.C.P. 123; Har. & Ruth. 97; 14 W.R.702 ..... *12–046*
Robinson v Harkin [1896] 2 Ch. 415, Ch D *28–048*, *29–125*
Robinson v Harman (1848) 1 Exch. 850 ..... *1–122*
Robinson v Harman [1843–60] All E.R. Rep. 383; 154 E.R. 363; (1848) 1 Ex. 850, Ex Ct *26–001*, *27–079*
Robinson v Hawksford (1846) 9 Q.B. 52 ..... *28–042*
Robinson v Marsh [1921] 2 K.B. 640, KBD *21–044*
Robinson v Mollett; Robinson v Bull; Robinson v Unsworth (1874–75) L.R. 7 H.L. 802, HL; reversing (1871–72) L.R. 7 C.P. 84, Ex Chamber; affirming (1869–70) L.R. 5 C.P. 646, CCP *12–133*
Robinson v Ommanney (1883) L.R. 23 Ch. D. 285; 52 L.J.Ch. 440; 49 L.T. 19; 31 W.R. 525, CA; affirming (1882) L.R. 21 Ch. D. 780, Ch D *16–073*
Robinson v Page (1826) 3 Russ. 114 ..... *22–032*, *22–033*
Robinson v Read (1829) 9 B.C. 449 ..... *21–075*
Robinson v Rutter, 119 E.R. 355; (1855) 4 El. & Bl. 954, QB *21–048*
Robinson & Co v Continental Insurance Co [1915] 1 K.B. 155, KBD *11–030*
Robinson & Co Ltd v Heuer. *See* William Robinson & Co Ltd v Heuer
Robinson's Motor Vehicles v Graham [1956] N.Z.L.R. 545 ..... *8–047*
Robophone Facilities Ltd v Blank [1966] 1 W.L.R. 1428; [1966] 3 All E.R. 128; (1966) 110 S.J. 544, CA *2–069*, *20–063A*, *26–009*, *26–062*, *26–069*, *26–100B*, *26–125*, *26–126*, *26–129*, *26–155*
Robson and Sharpe v Drummond (1831) 2 B. & Ad. 303 19–083
Robson v Oliver (1847) 10 Q.B. 704 ..... *21–079*
Robson v Premier Oil & Pipe Line Co Ltd [1915] 2 Ch. 124, CA *23–030*, *30–367*
Rocco Giuseppe & Figli v Tradax Export SA [1984] 1 W.L.R. 742; [1983] 3 All E.R. 598; [1983] 2 Lloyd's Rep. 434; (1984) 81 L.S.G. 1518; (1983) 133 N.L.J. 868; (1984) 128 S.J. 243, QBD (Comm) *26–184*
Roche v Sherrington [1982] 1 W.L.R. 599; [1982] 2 All E.R. 426; (1982) 126 S.J. 312, Ch D *9–067*, *9–068*
Rochefoucald v Boustead [1897] 1 Ch. 196 ..... *28–138*
Rock Refrigeration Ltd v Jones [1997] 1 All E.R. 1; [1997] I.C.R. 938; [1996] I.R.L.R. 675; (1996) 93(41) L.S.G. 29; (1996) 140 S.J.L.B. 226, CA (Civ Div) *16–100*, 16–101, *24–036*, *24–047*
Roddy v Fitzgerald (1858) 6 H.L.C. 823; 108 R.R. 327 ..... *12–051*
Roddy v Speyer Brothers [1919] A.C. 59; 88 L.J.K.B. 147; 119 L.T. 409; 62 S.J. 765; 34 T.L.R. 628, HL *11–024*, *11–028*, *11–028*, 11–029, *11–032*
Rodgers v Maw (1846) 15 M.W. 444 ..... *29–142*
Rodocanachi v Milburn; sub nom. Rodocanachi, Sons & Co v Milburn Bros (1887) L.R. 18 Q.B.D. 67, CA *26–001*, *26–089*

Rodriguez v Parker [1967] 1 Q.B. 116; [1966] 3 W.L.R. 546; [1966] 2 All E.R. 349, QBD ... *28–118*
Rodriguez v Speyer Bros. *See* Roddy v Speyer Brothers
Roe v Mutual Loan Association Fund; sub nom. Roe v Mutual Loan Fund, Ltd (1887) L.R. 19 Q.B.D. 347, CA ... *29–146*
Roe v RA Naylor Ltd; sub nom. Roe v Naylor [1917] 1 K.B. 712; (1918) 87 L.J. K.B. 958, KBD ... *12–106*
Roebuck v Mungovin [1994] 2 A.C. 224; [1994] 2 W.L.R. 290; [1994] 1 All E.R. 568; [1994] 1 Lloyd's Rep. 481; [1994] P.I.Q.R. P209; (1994) 91(13) L.S.G. 36; (1994) 144 N.L.J. 197; (1994) 138 S.J.L.B. 59; [1994] J.P.I.L. 164, HL; reversing [1993] P.I.Q.R. P444, CA (Civ Div) ... *3–096*, *3–103*, *3–154*
Roerig v Valiant Trawlers Ltd [2002] EWCA Civ 21; [2002] 1 W.L.R. 2304; [2002] 1 All E.R. 961; [2002] 1 Lloyd's Rep. 681; [2002] C.L.C. 629; [2002] P.I.Q.R. Q8; (2002) 152 N.L.J. 171, CA (Civ Div) ... *30–112*, *30–121*, *30–337*
Roger v Comptoir d'Escompte de Paris (1869) L.R. 2 P.C. 393 ... 3–031
Roger v Davis (1845) 8 Ir.L.R. 399 ... *12–093*
Roger v Drury (1887) 57 L.J.Ch. 504; 36 W.R. 496 ... *16–114*
Roger v Hadley (1863) 2 H. & C. 227; 32 L.J.Ex. 241; 9 Jur. 898; 9 L.T. 292; 11 W.R. 1074; 133 R.R. 652 ... *12–106*
Roger v Ingham (1876) 3 Ch. D. 351; 46 L.J.Ch. 322; 35 L.T. 677; 25 W.R. 338 ... *5–054*
Roger v Maddocks [1892] 3 Ch. 346; 62 L.J.Ch. 219; 67 L.T. 329, CA ... *16–097*, *16–110*
Roger v Snow (1573) Dalison 94 ... *2–078*
Roger Bullivant Ltd v Ellis [1987] I.C.R. 464; [1987] I.R.L.R. 491; [1987] F.S.R. 172, CA (Civ Div) ... *16–107*, *16–109*
Rogers v Challis (1859) 27 Beav. 175 ... *27–012*
Rogers v Head (1610) Cro. Jac. 262 ... *29–006*
Rogers v Ingham (1876) L.R. 3 Ch. D. 351, CA ... *29–042*, *29–043*, *29–098*
Rogers v Louth CC [1981] I.R. 265, Sup Ct (Irl) ... *29–095*
Rogers v Markel Corp (formerly Markel Holdings Inc) (Contractual Construction) [2004] EWHC 1375, QBD ... *30–339*, *30–340*, *30–373*
Rogers v Price (1829) 3 Y. Jer. 28 ... *29–132*
Rogers v Wood (1831) 2 B. Ad. 245 ... *25–015*
Roith (W&M), Re [1967] 1 W.L.R. 432; [1967] 1 All E.R. 427; (1966) 110 S.J. 963, Ch D ... *9–038*
Rolin v Steward (1854) 14 C.B. 595; 2 C.L.R. 959; 23 L.J.C.P. 148; 18 Jur. 536; 2 W.R. 467; 23 L.T. 114; 98 R.R. 774 ... *1–123*, *26–098*
Rolled Steel Products (Holdings) Ltd v British Steel Corp [1986] Ch. 246; [1985] 2 W.L.R. 908; [1985] 3 All E.R. 52; (1984) 1 B.C.C. 99158, CA (Civ Div); affirming [1982] Ch. 478; [1982] 3 W.L.R. 715; [1982] 3 All E.R. 1057, Ch D ... 9–021, *9–022*, *9–023*, *9–033*, *9–038*, *9–039*, *9–040*
Rolling Stock Co of Ireland, Re; sub nom. Shackleford's Case (1865–66) L.R. 1 Ch. App. 567, CA in Chancery ... *2–129*
Rolls Razor Ltd v Cox [1967] 1 Q.B. 552; [1967] 2 W.L.R. 241; [1967] 1 All E.R. 397; (1966) 110 S.J. 943, CA ... *20–041*
Rolls Royce Plc v Heavylift Volga Dnepr Ltd [2000] 1 All E.R. (Comm) 796; [2000] 1 Lloyd's Rep. 653; [2000] C.L.C. 1120; (2000) 97(17) L.S.G. 32; (2000) 144 S.J.L.B. 181, QBD (Comm) ... *14–017*
Rolls Royce Power Engineering Plc v Ricardo Consulting Engineers Ltd [2003] EWHC 2871 (TCC); [2004] 2 All E.R. (Comm) 129; 98 Con. L.R. 169, QBD (TCC) ... *12–014*, *12–114*, *18–051*, *18–052*, *18–062*
Rolls v Miller (1884) L.R. 27 Ch. D. 71, CA; affirming (1884) L.R. 25 Ch. D. 206, Ch D ... *14–065*, *15–027*
Rom Securities v Rogers (Holdings) (1967) 205 E.G. 427 ... *23–053*, *23–057*
Romain and Wolfson v Scuba TV Ltd [1997] Q.B. 887; [1996] 3 W.L.R. 117; [1996] 2 All E.R. 377; (1996) 72 P. & C.R. 39; [1996] 23 E.G. 126; [1995] E.G. 176 (C.S.); (1995) 145 N.L.J. 1850; [1995] N.P.C. 175, CA (Civ Div) ... *28–003*
Romer & Haslam, Re [1893] 2 Q.B. 286, CA ... *21–073*, *21–074*
Romulus Films Ltd v William Dempster Ltd [1952] 2 Lloyd's Rep. 535, QBD ... *26–089*
Ronbar Enterprises Ltd v Green [1954] 1 W.L.R. 815; [1954] 2 All E.R. 266; (1954) 98 S.J. 369, CA ... *16–116*, *16–119*, *16–197*, *16–202*, *16–203*

Rondel v Worsley; sub nom. Rondel v W [1969] 1 A.C. 191; [1967] 1 W.L.R. 142; [1967] 3 W.L.R. 1666; [1967] 3 All E.R. 993; (1967) 111 S.J. 927, HL; affirming [1967] 1 Q.B. 443; [1966] 3 W.L.R. 950; [1966] 3 All E.R. 657; (1966) 110 S.J. 810, CA; affirming [1966] 2 W.L.R. 300; [1966] 1 All E.R. 467; (1966) 110 S.J. 90, QBD *1–142*, *1–154*, *3–029*
Ronex Properties Ltd v John Laing Construction Ltd [1983] Q.B. 398; [1982] 3 W.L.R. 875; [1982] 3 All E.R. 961; (1982) 79 L.S.G. 1413; (1982) 126 S.J. 727, CA (Civ Div) *28–107*
Ronson International Ltd v Patrick; sub nom. Patrick v Royal London Mutual Insurance Society Ltd [2006] EWCA Civ 421; [2006] 2 All E.R. (Comm) 344; [2006] 1 C.L.C. 576; [2007] Lloyd's Rep. I.R. 85, CA (Civ Div); affirming [2005] EWHC 1767 (QB); [2005] 2 All E.R. (Comm) 453; [2006] Lloyd's Rep. I.R. 194, QBD *14–017*
Rooke v Dawson [1895] 1 Ch. 480; 64 L.J.Ch. 301; 72 L.T. 248; 43 W.R. 313; 59 J.P. 231; 13 R. 269, Ch D *2–017*
Rookes v Barnard (No.1) [1964] A.C. 1129; [1964] 2 W.L.R. 269; [1964] 1 All E.R. 367; [1964] 1 Lloyd's Rep. 28; (1964) 108 S.J. 93, HL; reversing [1963] 1 Q.B. 623; [1962] 3 W.L.R. 260; [1962] 2 All E.R. 579; (1962) 106 S.J. 371, CA; reversing [1961] 3 W.L.R. 438; [1961] 2 All E.R. 825; (1961) 105 S.J. 530, QBD *1–123*, *1–135*, *1–145*, 1–172, *1–173*, 6–063, 7–055, *18–019*, 18–040, 26–019, *29–145*, *29–150*
Rooney v Conway [1982] 5 N.I.J.B. *7–132*
Roper v Bunford (1810) 3 Taunt. 76 .... *21–042*
Roper v HM Works and Public Buildings Commissioners [1915] 1 K.B. 45, KBD *10–016*
Roper v Johnson (1872–73) L.R. 8 C.P. 167, CCP *24–022*, *26–103*, *26–112*, *28–062*
Ropeways v Hoyle (1919) 88 L.J. Ch. 446; 120 L.T. 538; 35 T.L.R. 285 .... *16–108*
Ropner v Stoate, Hosegood & Co (1905) 10 Com. Cas. 73; 92 L.T. 328; 21 T.L.R. 245; 49 S.J. 262; 10 Asp. M.L.C. 32 .... *13–018*
Rosa S, The [1989] Q.B. 419; [1989] 2 W.L.R. 162; [1989] 1 All E.R. 489; [1988] 2 Lloyd's Rep. 574; 1989 A.M.C. 912, QBD (Admlty) *21–070*, *21–071*, *30–331*
Roscorla v Thomas (1842) 3 Q.B. 234; 2 G. & D. 508; 11 L.J.Q.B. 214; 6 Jur. 929; 61 R.R. 216 .... *3–026*
Rose, Re [1952] Ch. 499; [1952] 1 T.L.R. 1577; [1952] 1 All E.R. 1217; [1952] T.R. 175; 31 A.T.C. 138 .... *19–033*, *19–034*, *19–058*, *19–059*
Rose, Re; sub nom. Midland Bank Executor & Trustee Co Ltd v Rose [1949] Ch. 78; [1948] 2 All E.R. 971; [1949] L.J.R. 208; (1948) 92 S.J. 661, Ch D *19–033*, *19–034*
Rose v AIB Group (UK) Plc; sub nom. Tain Construction Ltd, Re [2003] EWHC 1737 (Ch); [2003] 1 W.L.R. 2791; [2004] B.C.C. 11; [2003] 2 B.C.L.C. 374; [2003] B.P.I.R. 1188; (2003) 100(30) L.S.G. 31, Ch D (Companies Ct) *9–049*, *29–181*
Rose v Buckett [1901] 2 K.B. 449; 70 L.J.K.B. 736; 84 L.T. 670; 17 T.L.R. 544; 50 W.R. 8; 8 Mans. 259, CA *20–034*
Rose v Savory (1835) 2 Bing. N.C. 145 .... *29–192*
Rose v Stavrou [2000] L. & T.R. 133; (1999) 96(25) L.S.G. 29, Ch D *12–053*, *27–041*
Rose & Frank Co v JR Crompton & Bros Ltd; sub nom. Rose & Frank & Co v Crompton & Bros Ltd & Brittains Ltd; Rose & Frank Co v Brittains Ltd [1925] A.C. 445; (1924) 20 Ll. L. Rep. 249, HL; reversing [1923] 2 K.B. 261; [1924] All E.R. Rep. 245; (1923) 14 Ll. L. Rep. 519, CA 2–162, *2–168*, *22–025*, *22–028*, *22–029*
Rosenbaum v Belson [1900] 2 Ch. 267, Ch D *4–037*
Rosenthal Son Ltd v Esmail. *See* J Rosenthal & Sons v Esmail (t/a HMH Esmail & Sons)
Rosgill Group Ltd v Customs and Excise Commissioners [1997] 3 All E.R. 1012; [1997] S.T.C. 811; [1997] B.T.C. 5261; [1997] B.V.C. 388, CA (Civ Div) *3–012*
Ross v Caunters [1980] Ch. 297; [1979] 3 W.L.R. 605; [1979] 3 All E.R. 580, Ch D *18–022*, *18–037*, *20–003*

Ross River Ltd v Cambridge City Football Club Ltd [2007] EWHC 2115 (Ch); [2008] 1 All E.R. 1004; [2008] 1 All E.R. (Comm) 1028; [2007] 41 E.G. 201 (C.S.); (2007) 157 N.L.J. 1507, Ch D *6–036*, *6–163*

Ross T Smyth & Co (Liverpool) Ltd v WN Lindsay (Leith) Ltd [1953] 1 W.L.R. 1280; [1953] 2 All E.R. 1064; [1953] 2 Lloyd's Rep. 378; (1953) 97 S.J. 744, QBD *14–141*, *23–027*, *23–047*

Ross T Smyth & Co Ltd v TD Bailey & Co; sub nom. TD Bailey Son & Co v Ross T Smyth & Co Ltd [1940] 3 All E.R. 60, HL; reversing [1939] 3 All E.R. 175; (1939) 64 Ll. L. Rep. 95, CA; reversing [1939] 1 All E.R. 115; (1938) 62 Ll. L. Rep. 242, KBD *12–069*, *24–018*, *24–044*

Rossano v Manufacturers Life Insurance Co [1963] 2 Q.B. 352; [1962] 3 W.L.R. 157; [1962] 2 All E.R. 214; [1962] 1 Lloyd's Rep. 187; (1962) 106 S.J. 452, QBD (Comm) *16–031*, *30–009*, *30–011*, *30–013*

Rossdale v Denny [1921] 1 Ch. 57; L.J.Ch. 204; 124 L.T. 294; 37 T.L.R. 45; 65 S.J. 59, CA *2–118*

Rossetti, The [1972] 2 Lloyd's Rep. 116, QBD (Admlty) *14–032*

Rossiter v Miller (1877–78) L.R. 3 App. Cas. 1124; 48 L.J.Ch. 10; 39 L.T. 173, HL; reversing (1877) L.R. 5 Ch. D. 648, CA *2–116*, *2–123*, *4–023*, *12–122*

Roth Schmidt & Co v D Nagase & Co Ltd (1920) 2 Ll. L. Rep. 36, CA *26–144*

Rother Iron Works Ltd v Canterbury Precision Engineers Ltd [1974] Q.B. 1; [1973] 2 W.L.R. 281; [1973] 1 All E.R. 394; (1973) 117 S.J. 122, CA (Civ Div) *9–051*, *19–070*

Rothewell v Pewer (1431) Y.B. 9 Hen. 6, p. 64; pl 713 .... *16–052*

Rothwell v Chemical & Insulating Co Ltd. *See* Grieves v FT Everard & Sons Ltd; Quinn v George Clark & Nem Ltd

Rotterdamsche Bank NV v British Overseas Airways Corp [1953] 1 W.L.R. 493; [1953] 1 All E.R. 675; [1953] 1 Lloyd's Rep. 154; (1953) 97 S.J. 191, QBD *14–029*

Rousillon v Rousillon (1880) L.R. 14 Ch. D. 351; 49 L.J.Ch. 339; 42 L.T. 679, Ch D *16–075*, *16–110*, *30–309*, *30–367*

Routh v Jones [1947] 1 All E.R. 758; [1947] W.N. 205; (1947) 91 S.J. 354, CA; affirming [1947] 1 All E.R. 179, Ch D *16–097*

Routledge v Grant (1828) 4 Bing. 653; 1 M. & P. 717; 3 C. & P. 267; 6 L.J.C.P. 166; 29 R.R. 672 .... 2–088, *3–172*

Routledge v McKay, Nugent (Third Party), Ashgrove (Fourth Party), Mawson (Fifth Party) [1954] 1 W.L.R. 615; [1954] 1 All E.R. 855; 47 R. & I.T. 224; (1954) 98 S.J. 247, CA *12–003*

Rover International Ltd v Cannon Film Sales Ltd [1989] 1 W.L.R. 912; [1989] 3 All E.R. 423; [1988] B.C.L.C. 710, CA (Civ Div); reversing (1987) 3 B.C.C. 369; [1987] B.C.L.C. 540, Ch D *3–107*, *9–012*, 9–014, *9–017*, *26–154*, *27–027*, *27–060*, *27–061*, *29–032*, *29–054*, *29–055*, *29–057*, *29–058*, *29–065*, *29–068*, *29–074*, 29–076, *29–179*, *29–180*

Rowallan Group Ltd v Edgehill Portfolio No 1 Ltd [2007] EWHC 32 (Ch); [2007] All E.R. (D.) 106; [2007] 4 E.G. 187 (C.S.); [2007] N.P.C. 9, Ch D *5–116*

Rowan Companies Inc v Lambert Eggink Offshore Transport Consultants vof; The Gilbert Rowe (No.2) [1999] 2 Lloyd's Rep. 443; [1999] C.L.C. 1461, QBD (Comm) *3–090*, *3–093*, *28–109*

Rowe Ex p. Derenburg & Co, Re [1904] 2 K.B. 483, CA *21–041*

Rowe v Hopwood (1868–69) L.R. 4 Q.B. 1, QB *8–042*

Rowe v Turner Hopkins & Partners [1980] 2 N.Z.L.R. 550, HC (NZ) *26–049*, *28–033*

Rowe v Vale of White Horse DC. *See* R. (on the application of Rowe) v Vale of White Horse DC

Rowett Leakey & Co v Scottish Provident Institution [1927] 1 Ch. 55, CA *12–081*, *16–171*

Rowland v Divall [1923] 2 K.B. 500, CA *12–023*, *14–026*, *29–057*, *29–058*, *29–059*

Rowland v Environment Agency [2003] EWCA Civ 1885; [2005] Ch. 1; [2004] 3 W.L.R. 249; [2004] 2 Lloyd's Rep. 55; (2004) 101(8) L.S.G. 30; [2003] N.P.C. 165, CA (Civ Div); affirming [2002] EWHC 2785 (Ch); [2003] Ch. 581; [2003] 2 W.L.R. 1233; [2003] 1 All E.R. 625; [2003] 1 Lloyd's Rep. 427; (2003) 100(9) L.S.G. 28, Ch D *10–033*
Rowland v Hall (1835) 1 Scott 539 .... *29–142*
Rowling v Takaro Properties Ltd [1988] A.C. 473; [1988] 2 W.L.R. 418; [1988] 1 All E.R. 163, PC (NZ) *26–184*
Rownson, Re; sub nom. Field v White (1885) L.R. 29 Ch. D. 358, CA *20–014*, *28–130*
Rowntree Sons Ltd v Allen Sons (Poplar) Ltd (1936) 41 Com. Cas. 90 .... *26–013*
Roxborough v Rothmans of Pall Mall Australia Ltd (2002) 76 A.L.J.R. 203 .....*29–008*, *29–015*, 29–027, *29–034*, *29–054*, *29–058*, *29–063*, *29–086*
Roxburghe v Cox (1881) L.R. 17 Ch. D. 520; 50 L.J.Ch. 772; 45 L.T. 225; 30 W.R. 74, CA *19–070*
Roy v Kensington and Chelsea and Westminster Family Practitioner Committee [1992] 1 A.C. 624; [1992] 2 W.L.R. 239; [1992] 1 All E.R. 705; [1992] I.R.L.R. 233; (1992) 4 Admin. L.R. 649; [1992] 3 Med. L.R. 177; (1992) 142 N.L.J. 240; (1992) 136 S.J.L.B. 63, HL; affirming (1990) 2 Admin. L.R. 669, CA (Civ Div); reversing (1990) 2 Admin. L.R. 29, QBD *1–017*, 1–196, *27–022*, *29–085*
Roy v Kloepfer Wholesale Hardware and Automotive Co. *See* Kloepfer Wholesale Hardware & Automotive Co v Roy
Roy v Prior [1971] A.C. 470; [1970] 3 W.L.R. 202; [1970] 2 All E.R. 729; (1970) 114 S.J. 552, HL; reversing [1970] 1 Q.B. 283; [1969] 3 W.L.R. 365; [1969] 3 All E.R. 1153; (1969) 113 S.J. 609, CA (Civ Div) *7–050*
Royal Bank of Australia, Re; sub nom. Robinson's Executor's Case, Re, 43 E.R. 1356; (1856) 6 De G.M. & G. 572, Ct of Chancery *29–127*
Royal Bank of Canada v King, The [1913] A.C. 283, PC (Can) *29–056*
Royal Bank of Canada v W Gott Associates Electric Ltd (2000) 178 D.L.R. (4th) 385 .... *26–019*
Royal Bank of Scotland Plc v Etridge (No.2); Kenyon-Brown v Desmond Banks & Co (Undue Influence) (No.2); Bank of Scotland v Bennett; UCB Home Loans Corp Ltd v Moore; National Westminster Bank Plc v Gill; Midland Bank Plc v Wallace; Barclays Bank Plc v Harris; Barclays Bank Plc v Coleman [2001] UKHL 44; [2002] 2 A.C. 773; [2001] 3 W.L.R. 1021; [2001] 4 All E.R. 449; [2001] 2 All E.R. (Comm) 1061; [2002] 1 Lloyd's Rep. 343; [2001] 2 F.L.R. 1364; [2001] 3 F.C.R. 481; [2002] H.L.R. 4; [2001] Fam. Law 880; [2001] 43 E.G. 184 (C.S.); (2001) 151 N.L.J. 1538; [2001] N.P.C. 147; [2002] 1 P. & C.R. DG14, HL; affirming in part [1998] 4 All E.R. 705; [1998] 2 F.L.R. 843; [1998] 3 F.C.R. 675; (1999) 31 H.L.R. 575; [1998] Fam. Law 665; (1998) 95(32) L.S.G. 31; (1998) 148 N.L.J. 1390; (2001) 151 N.L.J. 1538; [1998] N.P.C. 130; (1998) 76 P. & C.R. D39, CA (Civ Div) ...6–023, *6–024*, *6–026*, *7–056*, *7–057*, *7–058*, 7–059, *7–060*, *7–061*, 7–063, *7–064*, 7–065, *7–066*, 7–067, *7–069*, 7–070, 7–072, 7–078, 7–079, 7–080, 7–081, 7–085, *7–086*, 7–087, 7–088, 7–089, *7–090*, 7–091, *7–093*, 7–095, *7–097*, **7–109**, *7–110*, *7–111*, *7–112*, 7–114, 7–115, *7–117*, *7–118*, *7–120*, 7–122
Royal Bank of Scotland Plc v Jennings (1998) 75 P. & C.R. 458; [1997] 1 E.G.L.R. 101; [1997] 19 E.G. 152; [1996] E.G. 168 (C.S.); [1996] N.P.C. 145, CA (Civ Div); affirming (1995) 70 P. & C.R. 459; [1995] 2 E.G.L.R. 87; [1995] 35 E.G. 140, Ch D *2–131*
Royal Bank of Scotland v Greenshields, 1914 S.C. 259; (1914) 1 S.L.T.74, IH (1 Div) *6–159*
Royal Boskalis Westminster NV v Mountain [1999] Q.B. 674; [1998] 2 W.L.R. 538; [1997] 2 All E.R. 929; [1997] L.R.L.R. 523; [1997] C.L.C. 816, CA (Civ Div) *3–081*, *7–011*, *7–037*, *7–051*, *7–053*, *16–032*, *16–144*, *29–088*, *30–355*, *30–364*, *30–366*, *30–367*
Royal Bristol Permanent Building Society v Bomash (1887) L.R. 35 Ch. D. 390, Ch D *26–092*

Royal British Bank v Turquand [1843–60] All E.R. Rep. 435; 119 E.R. 886; (1856) 6 El. & Bl. 327, Ex Chamber **9–040**, *9–041*, 9–042, 9–044, 9–045
Royal Brompton Hospital NHS Trust v Hammond (No.3) [2002] UKHL 14; [2002] 1 W.L.R. 1397; [2002] 2 All E.R. 801; [2002] 1 All E.R. (Comm) 897; [2003] 1 C.L.C. 11; [2002] B.L.R. 255; [2002] T.C.L.R. 14; 81 Con. L.R. 1; [2002] P.N.L.R. 37, HL; affirming, CA (Civ Div); affirming [1999] B.L.R. 385, QBD (TCC) *17–029*, 17–030, *29–121*
Royal Brunei Airlines Sdn Bhd v Tan; sub nom. Royal Brunei Airlines Sdn Bhd v Philip Tan Kok Ming [1995] 2 A.C. 378; [1995] 3 W.L.R. 64; [1995] 3 All E.R. 97; [1995] B.C.C. 899; (1995) 92(27) L.S.G. 33; (1995) 145 N.L.J. 888; [1995] 139 S.J.L.B. 146; (1995) 70 P. & C.R. D12, PC (Bru) *29–174*, *29–183*
Royal Exchange Assurance Corp v Sjoforsakrings AB Vega; sub nom. Royal Exchange Assurance Corp v Sjorforsakrings Aktiebolaget Vega [1902] 2 K.B. 384; 71 L.J.K.B. 739; 87 L.T. 356; 18 T.L.R. 714; 7 Com. Cas. 205; 50 W.R. 694; 9 Asp. 329, CA; affirming [1901] 2 K.B. 567, KBD *16–195*
Royal Exchange Assurance v Hope [1928] Ch. 179; 97 L.J.Ch. 153; [1928] W.C. & Ins. Rep. 213; 138 L.T. 446; 44 T.L.R. 160; 72 S.J. 68, CA *18–079*, *22–028*, *22–032*
Royal Exchange Shipping Co Ltd v WJ Dixon & Co (1887) L.R. 12 App. Cas. 11, HL *14–008*, *14–031*
Royal Greek Government v Minister of Transport; The Ilissos [1949] 1 K.B. 525; [1949] 1 All E.R. 171; (1948–49) 82 Ll. L. Rep. 196; 65 T.L.R. 32; [1949] L.J.R. 670; (1949) 93 S.J. 146, CA; affirming [1949] 1 K.B. 7; [1948] 1 All E.R. 904; (1947–48) 81 Ll. L. Rep. 355; 64 T.L.R. 283; (1948) 92 S.J. 272, KBD *12–051*, *12–077*
Royal Institution of Chartered Surveyors Application, Re [1985] I.C.R. 330, Ch D (RPC) *9–061*
Royal Insurance Co v G&S Assured Investment Co and Growth and Secured Life Assurance Society [1972] 1 Lloyd's Rep. 267, Ch D *12–066*
Royal London Mutual Insurance Society v Barrett [1928] Ch. 411; 97 L.J.Ch. 177; 139 L.T. 208; 44 T.L.R. 363, Ch D *16–171*
Royal Naval School, Re; sub nom. Seymour v Royal Naval School [1910] 1 Ch. 806, Ch D *8–037*
Royal Norwegian Government v Constant & Constant and Calcutta Marine Engineering Co Ltd [1960] 2 Lloyd's Rep. 431, QBD (Comm) *28–126*
Royal Products v Midland Bank [1981] 2 Lloyd's Rep. 194; [1981] Com. L.R. 93, QBD *21–047*
Royscot Trust Ltd v Rogerson; sub nom. Royscott Trust v Maidenhead Honda Centre [1991] 2 Q.B. 297; [1991] 3 W.L.R. 57; [1991] 3 All E.R. 294; [1992] R.T.R. 99; (1992) 11 Tr. L.R. 23; [1991] C.C.L.R. 45; (1991) 141 N.L.J. 493; (1991) 135 S.J. 444, CA (Civ Div) *1–122*, *1–131*, *1–133*, *1–165*, 6–001, 6–070, 6–071, *6–074*, *6–100*, *28–083*
Royse (Deceased), Re; sub nom. Royse v Royse [1985] Ch. 22; [1984] 3 W.L.R. 784; [1984] 3 All E.R. 339; [1985] Fam. Law 156; (1984) 81 L.S.G. 2543, CA (Civ Div) *16–170*
Ruabon Steamship Co Ltd v London Assurance; The Ruabon [1900] A.C. 6, HL *29–019*
Ruben v Great Fingall Consolidated [1906] A.C. 439; 75 L.J.K.B. 843; 95 L.T. 214; 22 T.L.R. 712; 13 Manson 248, HL; affirming [1904] 2 K.B. 712, CA; reversing [1904] 1 K.B. 650, KBD *9–045*
Rubicon Computer Systems Ltd v United Paints Ltd (2000) 2 T.C.L.R. 453, CA (Civ Div) *24–040*, *24–042*
Rucker v Cammeyer (1794) 1 Esp. 105 .... *4–038*
Rudd v Bowles [1912] 2 Ch. 60; 81 L.J.Ch. 277; 105 L.T. 864, Ch D *22–037*
Rudd v Lascelles [1900] 1 Ch. 815, Ch D *27–055*, *27–057*
Rugby Group Ltd v ProForce Recruit Ltd [2006] EWCA Civ 69, CA (Civ Div) [2005] EWHC 70 (QB), QBD *2–124*, *12–104*, *12–119*
Rugg v Weir (1864) 16 C.B.(N.S.) 471 .... *21–006*
Rumball v Ball (1712) 10 Mod. 39 .... *28–036*
Rumbelows v AMK (1982) 19 B.L.R. 25, QBD *14–057*

Rumsey v North Eastern Railway (1863) 14 C.B.(N.S.) 641 .... *29–144*, *29–148*
Runciman v Walker Runciman Plc [1993] B.C.C. 223; [1992] B.C.L.C. 1084, QBD *9–055*
Rural Municipality of Storthoaks v Mobil Oil Canada Ltd [1975] 55 D.L.R. (3d) 1 .... *29–086*, *29–179*, *29–181*
Rushingdale Ltd v Byblos Bank (1985) P.C.C. 342 .... *1–092*
Rushton v Worcester City Council [2001] EWCA Civ 367; [2002] H.L.R. 9; [2003] R.V.R. 129; [2001] 13 E.G. 149 (C.S.); [2001] N.P.C. 65, CA (Civ Div) *1–015*
Russell v Amalgamated Society of Carpenters and Joiners [1912] A.C. 421; 81 L.J.K.B. 619; 106 L.T. 433; 28 T.L.R. 276, HL; affirming [1910] 1 K.B. 506, CA *16–140*, *16–200*
Russell v Duke of Norfolk [1949] 1 All E.R. 109; 65 T.L.R. 225; (1949) 93 S.J. 132, CA; affirming [1948] 1 All E.R. 488, KBD *9–075*, *9–083*, *13–009*
Russell v Niemann (1864) 17 C.B.N.S. 163; 5 New Rep. 190; 34 L.J.C.P. 10; 10 L.T. 786; 13 W.R. 93; 2 Mar.L.C. 72; 144 E.R. 66 .... *14–146*
Russell v Russell (1956) [1956] P. 283; [1956] 2 W.L.R. 544; [1956] 1 All E.R. 466; (1956) 120 J.P. 140; (1956) 100 S.J. 149, CA *16–044*
Russell v Sada Bandeira (1862) 13 C.B. (N.S.) 149 .... *22–038*
Russell v Shenton (1842) 3 Q.B. 449; 2 Gal. & Dav. 573; 11 L.J.Q.B. 289; 6 Jur. 1083; 114 E.R. 579 .... *1–173*
Russell & Co v Austin Fryers (1909) 25 T.L.R. 414 .... *19–055*
Russell Brothers (Paddington) Ltd v John Lelliott Management Ltd (1995) 11 Const. L.J. 377, QBD (OR) *2–113*, *3–113*
Russell-Cooke Trust Co v Prentis (No.1) [2002] EWHC 2227 (Ch); [2003] 2 All E.R. 478; [2003] W.T.L.R. 81; (2002–03) 5 I.T.E.L.R. 532; (2002) 152 N.L.J. 1719, Ch D *29–167*
Russian (Vyksounsky) Ironworks Co, Re; sub nom. Taite's Case (1866–67) L.R. 3 Eq. 795, Ct of Chancery *6–127*, *28–144*
Russian Commercial and Industrial Bank, Re [1955] Ch. 148; [1955] 2 W.L.R. 62; [1955] 1 All E.R. 75; (1955) 99 S.J. 44, Ch D *28–039*
Russo-Asiatic Bank, Re [1934] Ch. 720 .... *28–031*
Rust v Abbey Life Insurance [1979] 2 Lloyd's Rep. 334, CA; affirming [1978] 2 Lloyd's Rep. 386 .... *1–131*, *1–134*, *2–024*, *2–072*, 2–077, *6–085*
Rustenburg Platinum Mines Ltd v South African Airways and Pan American World Airways Inc [1979] 1 Lloyd's Rep. 19, CA (Civ Div); reversing [1977] 1 Lloyd's Rep. 564, QBD (Comm) *3–118*, *3–121*, *14–017*
Rutherford v Acton-Adams [1915] A.C. 866, PC (NZ) *27–055*
Rutherford, Re; sub nom. Brown v Rutherford (1880) L.R. 14 Ch. D. 687, CA *28–042*
Rutland's (Countess of) Case (1602) 5 Co.Rep. 25b *12–096*
Rutter (Inspector of Taxes) v Charles Sharpe & Co Ltd [1979] 1 W.L.R. 1429; [1979] S.T.C. 711; 53 T.C. 163; [1979] T.R. 225; (1979) 123 S.J. 522, Ch D *12–066*
Rutter v Palmer [1922] 2 K.B. 87; 91 L.J.K.B. 657; 127 L.T. 419; 38 T.L.R. 555, CA *14–003*, *14–011*, *14–012*, *14–013*
Ruttinger v Temple (1863) 4 B. & S. 491; 3 New Rep. 34; 33 L.J.Q.B. 1; 9 L.T. 256; 28 J.P. 71; 9 Jur. (N.S.) 1239; 12 W.R. 9 .... *8–061*
Ruxley Electronics & Construction Ltd v Forsyth; Laddingford Enclosures Ltd v Forsyth [1996] A.C. 344; [1995] 3 W.L.R. 118; [1995] 3 All E.R. 268; [1995] C.L.C. 905; 73 B.L.R. 1; 45 Con. L.R. 61; (1995) 14 Tr. L.R. 541; (1995) 11 Const. L.J. 381; [1995] E.G. 11 (C.S.); (1995) 145 N.L.J. 996; (1995) 139 S.J.L.B. 163, HL *18–065*, *26–016*, 26–017, *26–083*, 26–084
Ryan v Mutual Tontine Westminster Chambers Association [1893] 1 Ch. 116, CA 27–026, 27–044
Ryder v Townsend (1825) 7 D. Ry. 119 .... *21–088*
Ryder v Wombwell (1868) L.R. 4 Ex. 32 .... *8–007*, *8–008*, *8–014*, *8–015*, *8–016*
Ryles v Chaudry [1999] Lloyd's Rep. P.N. 454, QBD (Merc) *28–087*

S v S (Ancillary Relief: Consent Order); sub nom. S v S (Divorce: Setting Aside Consent Order) [2002] EWHC 223 (Fam); [2003] Fam. 1; [2002] 3 W.L.R. 1372; [2002] 1 F.L.R. 992; [2002] Fam. Law 422; (2002) 99(15) L.S.G. 34; (2002) 152 N.L.J. 398; (2002) 146 S.J.L.B. 78, Fam Div 5–056, *23–040*
S (A Minor) (Abduction: European Convention), Re; sub nom. S (A Minor) (Abduction: European and Hague Conventions), Re; S (A Minor) (Custody: Habitual Residence), Re [1998] A.C. 750; [1997] 3 W.L.R. 597; [1997] 4 All E.R. 251; [1998] 1 F.L.R. 122; [1997] 3 F.C.R. 293; [1997] Fam. Law 782; (1997) 94(34) L.S.G. 28; (1997) 147 N.L.J. 1310; (1997) 141 S.J.L.B. 205, HL *30–079*
S (David Vincent) v S (now M) (Susan Ann) [2006] EWHC 2892 (Fam); [2007] 1 F.L.R. 1123; [2007] Fam. Law 108, Fam Div *3–140*, *3–145*, *4–077*
S (Deceased) (Forfeiture Rule), Re [1996] 1 W.L.R. 235; [1996] 1 F.L.R. 910; [1996] 3 F.C.R. 357; [1996] Fam. Law 352, Ch D *16–170*
S&M Hotels Ltd v Legal and General Assurance Society Ltd [1972] 1 Lloyd's Rep. 157; (1971) 115 S.J. 888, QBD *14–146*
S&W Process Engineering Ltd v Cauldron Foods Ltd [2005] EWHC 153 (TCC), QBD (TCC) *29–002*, *29–021*
SA&D Wright Ltd, Re; sub nom. Denney v John Hudson & Co Ltd [1992] B.C.C. 503; [1992] B.C.L.C. 901, CA (Civ Div) *9–049*
S Brown & Co, Re. *See* Courts (Emergency Powers) Act 1939, Re
S Instone & Co Ltd v Speedy Marshall & Co (1915) 114 L.T. 370 .... *14–143*
S Nevanas & Co v Walker [1914] 1 Ch. 413, Ch D *16–110*, *16–113*, *16–194*, *16–198*, *16–203*
S Pearson & Son Ltd v Dublin Corp [1907] A.C. 351, HL (UK-Irl); reversing [1907] 2 I.R. 27, CA (UK-Irl) *1–132*, *1–147*, *6–134*, *9–022*, *14–136*, *28–108*
SAM Business Systems Ltd v Hedley & Co [2002] EWHC 2733 (TCC); [2003] 1 All E.R. (Comm) 465; [2003] Masons C.L.R. 11; (2003) 147 S.J.L.B. 57, QBD (TCC) *12–104*, *14–063*, *14–073*, *14–085*, *14–087*, *14–099*
SBJ Stephenson Ltd v Mandy [2000] I.R.L.R. 233; [2000] F.S.R. 286, QBD ... *16–108*
SCF Finance Co Ltd v Masri (No.2) [1987] Q.B. 1002; [1987] 2 W.L.R. 58; [1987] 1 All E.R. 175; [1986] 2 Lloyd's Rep. 366; [1986] Fin. L.R. 309; (1987) 84 L.S.G. 492; (1987) 131 S.J. 74, CA (Civ Div); affirming [1986] 1 All E.R. 40; [1986] 1 Lloyd's Rep. 293; [1986] Fin. L.R. 95; (1985) 135 N.L.J. 914, QBD (Comm) *16–145*, *25–013*, *30–011*
SCI (Sales Curve Interactive) Ltd v Titus Sarl (A Firm) [2001] EWCA Civ 591; [2001] 2 All E.R. (Comm) 416, CA (Civ Div) *24–051*
SHV Gas Supply & Trading SAS v Naftomar Shipping & Trading Co Ltd Inc; The Azur Gaz [2005] EWHC 2528; [2006] 2 All E.R. (Comm) 515; [2006] 1 Lloyd's Rep. 163; [2005] 2 C.L.C. 815, QBD (Comm) *14–140*, *14–150*
SIAT di del Ferro v Tradax Overseas SA [1980] 1 Lloyd's Rep. 53, CA (Civ Div); affirming [1978] 2 Lloyd's Rep. 470, QBD (Comm) *12–011*, *13–022*
SLS Everest, The. *See* Bangladesh Chemical Industries Corp v Henry Stephens Shipping Co and Tex-Bilan Shipping Co; The SLS Everest
SS Ardennes (Cargo Owners) v SS Ardennes (Owners). *See* Owners of Cargo Lately Laden on Board the Ardennes v Owners of the Ardennes; The Ardennes
SS Celia v SS Volturno. *See* Owners of SS Celia v Owners of SS Volturno
SS Knutsford Ltd v Tillmanns & Co; sub nom. Tillmanns & Co v SS Knutsford Ltd [1908] A.C. 406, HL; affirming [1908] 2 K.B. 385, CA; affirming [1908] 1 K.B. 185, KBD (Comm Ct) *12–088*, *12–089*
SS Magnhild v McIntyre Bros & Co. *See* Owners of the SS Magnhild v MacIntyre Bros & Co
SS Pharmaceutical Co Ltd v Qantas Airways Ltd [1991] 1 Lloyd's Rep. 288, CA (NSW) *30–331*
SSL Realisations (2002) Ltd, Re. *See* Manning v AIG Europe UK Ltd
SSQ Europe SA v Johann & Backes OHG [2002] 1 Lloyd's Rep. 465, QBD (Merc) *12–011*

STX Pan Ocean Co Ltd (formerly Pan Ocean Shipping Co Ltd) v Ugland Bulk Transport AS; The Livanita [2007] EWHC 1317 (Comm); [2008] 1 Lloyd's Rep. 86, QBD (Comm) *12–078*
Sabah Flour and Feedmills Sdn Bhd v Comfez Ltd [1988] 2 Lloyd's Rep. 18, CA (Civ Div); affirming [1987] 2 Lloyd's Rep. 647, QBD (Comm) *12–078*, *12–079*
Sabah Shipyard (Pakistan) Ltd v Pakistan [2002] EWCA Civ 1643; [2003] 2 Lloyd's Rep. 571; [2004] 1 C.L.C. 149, CA (Civ Div) *11–005*, *11–021*
Sabah Shipyard (Pakistan) Ltd v Pakistan [2007] EWHC 2602 (Comm); [2008] 1 Lloyd's Rep. 210, QBD (Comm) *12–104*
Sabemo v North Sydney MC [1977] 2 N.S.W.L.R. 880 .... *29–021*, *29–071*
Saccharin Corp Ltd v Chemische Fabrik Von Heyden AG [1911] 2 K.B. 516, CA *30–081*
Sachs v Miklos [1948] 2 K.B. 23; [1948] 1 All E.R. 67; 64 T.L.R. 181; [1948] L.J.R. 1012, CA *29–052*, *29–133*
Sadler v Imperial Life Assurance Co of Canada Ltd [1988] I.R.L.R. 388, QBD *16–087*, *16–104*, *16–196*
Sadler v Smith (1869–70) L.R. 5 Q.B. 40, Ex Ct *16–047*, *29–197*
Safadi v Western Assurance Co (1933) 46 Ll. L. Rep. 140, KBD *14–040*
Safehaven Investments Inc v Springbok Ltd (1996) 71 P. & C.R. 59; [1995] E.G. 96 (C.S.); (1995) 70 P. & C.R. D20, Ch D *24–004*, *24–019*
Sagar v H Ridehalgh & Son Ltd [1931] 1 Ch. 310, CA *21–030*
Saggar v Ministry of Defence; Ministry of Defence v Gandiya; Lucas v Ministry of Defence [2005] EWCA Civ 413; [2005] I.C.R. 1073; [2005] I.R.L.R. 618; (2005) 102(23) L.S.G. 27, CA (Civ Div) *30–115*
Said v Butt [1920] 3 K.B. 497, KBD *5–099*
Saif Ali v Sydney Mitchell & Co [1980] A.C. 198; [1978] 3 W.L.R. 849; [1978] 3 All E.R. 1033; [1955–95] P.N.L.R. 151; (1978) 122 S.J. 761, HL; reversing [1978] Q.B. 95; [1977] 3 W.L.R. 421; [1977] 3 All E.R. 744; (1977) 121 S.J. 336, CA (Civ Div) *1–154*, *13–032*
Saikyo, The. *See* China Shipbuilding Corp v Nippon Yusen Kabukishi Kaisha
Saint Line Ltd v Richardsons Westgarth & Co Ltd [1940] 2 K.B. 99; (1940) 67 Ll. L. Rep. 62, KBD *14–006*, *26–066*, *26–074*, *26–077*
Sainter v Ferguson (1849) 1 Mac. G. 286 .... *26–011*
Sainter v Ferguson (1849) 7 C.B. 716 .... *26–127*
Saipem SpA v Dredging VO2 BV; The Volvox Hollandia (No.2) [1993] 2 Lloyd's Rep. 315, QBD (Comm) *1–176*, *18–023*, *18–027*
Sakkas v Donford Ltd (1983) 46 P. & C.R. 290, Ch D *4–038*
Salaman v Secretary of State in Council of India [1906] 1 K.B. 613, CA *11–007*
Salata v Continental Insurance Co [1948] 2 D.L.R. 663 .... *29–147*
Sale v Lambert (1874) L.R. 18 Eq. 1, Ct of Chancery *4–023*
Saleh v Robinson; sub nom. Robinson v Saleh (1988) 20 H.L.R. 424; [1988] 36 E.G. 180, CA (Civ Div) *16–185*
Salim Nasrallah Khoury (Syndic in Bankruptcy) v Khayat [1943] A.C. 507, PC (Pal) *21–069*, *21–070*, *30–375*
Salmon v Webb (1852) 3 H.L.C. 310 .... *12–101*
Salomon v Salomon & Co Ltd; sub nom. Broderip v Salomon; Salomon & Co Ltd v Salomon [1897] A.C. 22, HL; reversing [1895] 2 Ch. 323, CA *9–054*
Salsi v Jetspeed Air Services [1977] 2 Lloyd's Rep. 57, QBD (Comm) *12–012*, *13–021*
Salt v Marquess of Northampton; Tyler v Marquess of Northampton [1892] A.C. 1, HL *1–011*
Saltoun v Houston (1824) 1 Bing. 433 .... *13–024*
Salvage Association v C.A.P. Financial Services Ltd [1995] F.S.R. 654, QBD *14–072*, *14–087*, 14–093, *14–099*, *14–105*, *29–055*, *29–061*
Salvation Army Trustee Co Ltd v West Yorkshire CC (1981) 41 P. & C.R. 179, QBD *3–145*
Samcrete Egypt Engineers & Contractors SAE v Land Rover Exports Ltd [2001] EWCA Civ 2019; [2002] C.L.C. 533, CA (Civ Div) *30–020*, *30–023*, *30–051*, *30–076*, *30–077*, *30–090*, *30–188*, *30–204*

Samengo-Turner v J&H Marsh & McLennan (Services) Ltd [2007] EWCA Civ 723; [2007] 2 All E.R. (Comm) 813; [2007] C.P. Rep. 45; [2007] 2 C.L.C. 104; [2007] I.L.Pr. 52; [2008] I.C.R. 18; [2008] I.R.L.R. 237, CA (Civ Div) ... *30–110*, *30–111*, *30–278*
Samick Lines Co v Owners of the Antonis P Lemos [1985] A.C. 711; [1985] 2 W.L.R. 468; [1985] 1 All E.R. 695; [1985] 1 Lloyd's Rep. 283; (1985) 82 L.S.G. 1715, HL; affirming [1984] 2 W.L.R. 825; [1984] 2 All E.R. 353; [1984] 1 Lloyd's Rep. 464; (1984) 81 L.S.G. 740; (1984) 129 S.J. 171, CA (Civ Div); affirming [1983] 2 Lloyd's Rep. 310, QBD (Admlty) *18–022*
Samos Shipping Enterprises v Eckhardt and Co KG; The Nissos Samos [1985] 1 Lloyd's Rep. 378, QBD (Comm) *2–116*, *2–139*, *2–154*
Samuel Bros Ltd v Whetherly [1908] 1 K.B. 184, CA; affirming [1907] 1 K.B. 709, KBD *10–013*
Samuel v Wadlow. *See* Wadlow v Samuel
Samuels v Davis [1943] 1 K.B. 526, CA *1–147*, *1–149*, *13–030*, *13–032*
Sandeman Coprimar SA v Transitos y Transportes Integrales SL [2003] EWCA Civ 113; [2003] Q.B. 1270; [2003] 2 W.L.R. 1496; [2003] 3 All E.R. 108; [2003] 1 All E.R. (Comm) 504; [2003] 2 Lloyd's Rep. 172; [2003] 2 C.L.C. 551; [2003] R.T.R. 31, CA (Civ Div) *3–005*, *14–054*, *18–005*
Sanders v Gall, 159 E.G. 397; [1952] C.P.L. 343 .... *6–009*
Sanderson v Bell, 149 E.R. 776; (1834) 2 Cr. & M. 304, KB *21–043*
Sanderson v Graves (1875) L.R. 10 Ex. 234 .... *22–033*
Sanderson v Symonds (1819) 1 B.B. 426 .... *25–021*, *25–023*
Sanderson v Workington Borough Council (1918) 34 T.L.R. 386 .... *3–066*
Sandiford, Re (No.2); sub nom. Italo Canadian Corp Ltd v Sandiford [1935] Ch. 681, Ch D *20–023*, *29–043*
Sandilands, Ex p. (1871) L.R. 6 C.P. 411 .... *1–092*
Sandiman v Breach (1827) 7 B. & C. 96 .... *12–087*
Sandwell Park Colliery Co, Re; sub nom. Field v Sandwell Park Colliery Co [1929] 1 Ch. 277, Ch D *12–028*
Saner v Bilton (No.1) (1877–78) L.R. 7 Ch. D. 815, Ch D *12–087*
Sanko Steamship Co Ltd v Eacom Timber Sales; The Sanko Iris and Sanko Venus [1987] 1 Lloyd's Rep. 487, Sup Ct (BC) *24–019*, *24–029*
Sanko Steamship Co Ltd v Kano Trading Ltd [1978] 1 Lloyd's Rep. 156, CA (Civ Div) *12–036*
Santa Fé Land Co v Forestal Land Co (1910) 26 T.L.R. 534 .... *2–118*, *2–119*
Santay & Co v Cox, McEllen & Co (1921) 10 Ll. L. Rep. 459 .... *12–069*
Santokh Singh v Guru Nanak Gurdwara [1990] I.C.R. 309, CA (Civ Div) *2–181*
Sapsford v Fletcher, 100 E.R. 1147; (1792) 4 Term Rep. 511, KB *29–105*
Sard v Rhodes (1836) 1 M.W. 153 .... *21–077*
Sardinia Sulcis, The. *See* Owners of the Sardinia Sulcis v Owners of the Al Tawwab
Sargant v Cit (England) (t/a Citalia) [1994] C.L.Y. 566, CC (Croydon) *14–085*
Sargood Bros v Commonwealth (1910–11) 11 C.L.R. 258 .... *29–086*
Saris v Westminster Transports SA and Kestral Marine [1994] 1 Lloyd's Rep. 115, QBD (Comm) *28–116*
Saronic Shipping Co Ltd v Huron Liberian Co [1980] 2 Lloyd's Rep. 26, CA (Civ Div) *29–033*, *29–035*
Sarson v Roberts [1895] 2 Q.B. 395, CA *13–016*
Sass Ex p. National Provincial Bank of England Ltd, Re [1896] 2 Q.B. 12, QBD *21–065*
Sassoon v International Banking Corp. *See* MA Sassoon & Sons Ltd v International Banking Corp
Satanita, The. *See* Clarke v Earl of Dunraven
Satef-Huttenes Alberns SpA v Paloma Tercera Shipping Co SA; The Pegase [1981] 1 Lloyd's Rep. 175; [1980] Com. L.R. 9, QBD (Comm) *20–063A*, *26–062*, *26–070*, *26–100B*
Saudi Arabia (Government of Kingdom of) v Nasser, November 14, 2000, CA *11–005*, *11–013*
Saunders v Edwards (1662) Sid. 95 .... *1–124*

Saunders v Edwards [1987] 1 W.L.R. 1116; [1987] 2 All E.R. 651; (1987) 137 N.L.J. 389; (1987) 131 S.J. 1039, CA (Civ Div) *6–066*, *16–017*, *16–165*, 16–176, *16–181*
Saunders v Graham (1819) Gow 121 .... *21–085*
Saunders (Executrix of the Estate of Rose Maud Gallie) v Anglia Building Society (formerly Northampton Town and County Building Society); sub nom. Gallie v Lee [1971] A.C. 1004; [1970] 3 W.L.R. 1078; [1970] 3 All E.R. 961; (1971) 22 P. & C.R. 300; (1970) 114 S.J. 885, HL; affirming [1969] 2 Ch. 17; [1969] 2 W.L.R. 901; [1969] 1 All E.R. 1062; (1969) 20 P. & C.R. 310, CA (Civ Div); reversing [1968] 1 W.L.R. 1190; [1968] 2 All E.R. 322; (1968) 19 P. & C.R. 493, Ch D *5–099*, 5–102, 5–104, 5–106
Saunderson v Jackson (1800) 2 B. & P. 238 .... *4–034*
Saunderson v Piper (1839) 5 Bing.N.C. 425 .... *12–070*
Sauria, The and Trent, The [1957] 1 Lloyd's Rep. 396, CA *28–111*
Sauter Automation Ltd v HC Goodman (Mechanical Services) Ltd (In Liquidation) (1986) 34 B.L.R. 81, Ch D *2–036*
Savage, Re; sub nom. Cull v Howard [1918] 2 Ch. 146, Ch D *28–130*
Savage v Sainsbury Ltd. *See* J Sainsbury Ltd v Savage
Savage v Uwechia [1961] 1 W.L.R. 455; [1961] 1 All E.R. 830; (1961) 105 S.J. 205, PC (Nig) *3–028*
Savill Bros v Langman (1898) 79 L.T. 44 ....*16–023*, *16–024*
Savings & Investment Bank Ltd (In Liquidation) v Fincken (Statement of Claim) [2001] EWCA Civ 1639; (2001) 98(48) L.S.G. 29, CA (Civ Div) *28–118*
Savings Bank of the Russian Federation v Refco Securities LLC [2006] EWHC 857; [2006] 2 All E.R. (Comm) 722, QBD (Comm) *12–050*
Savory v World of Golf. *See* EW Savory Ltd v World of Golf Ltd
Sawyer Vincent v Window Brace Ltd [1943] K.B. 32 ....*29–041*, *29–042*, *29–098*
Saxby v Fulton [1909] 2 K.B. 208, CA *16–030*
Saxty v Wilkin (1843) 11 M.W. 622 .... *21–039*
Say (Lord) and Seal's Case (1711) 10 Mod. 41 .... *12–076*
Sayce v Coupe [1953] 1 Q.B. 1; [1952] 2 All E.R. 715; [1952] 2 T.L.R. 664; (1952) 116 J.P. 552; (1952) 96 S.J. 748, DC *16–159*
Sayer v Wagstaff (1844) 5 Beav. 415 ....*21–074*, *21–077*
Sayers v Harlow Urban DC [1958] 1 W.L.R. 623; [1958] 2 All E.R. 342; (1958) 122 J.P. 351; (1958) 102 S.J. 419, CA *26–049*
Sayers v International Drilling Co NV [1971] 1 W.L.R. 1176; [1971] 3 All E.R. 163; [1971] 2 Lloyd's Rep. 105; 11 K.I.R. 65; (1971) 115 S.J. 466, CA (Civ Div) *1–169*, *16–030*, *30–011*, *30–015*, *30–119*, *30–120*, *30–309*
Scadding v Eyles (1846) 9 Q.B. 858 .... *29–192*
Scally v Southern Health and Social Services Board [1992] 1 A.C. 294; [1991] 3 W.L.R. 778; [1991] 4 All E.R. 563; [1991] I.C.R. 771; [1991] I.R.L.R. 522; (1991) 141 N.L.J. 1482; (1991) 135 S.J. 172, HL *1–017*, 1–032, 1–070, *13–003*, 13–008, *13–009*
Scammell v Dicker. *See* Dicker v Scammell
Scancarriers A/S v Aotearoa International; The Barranduna and The Tarago [1985] 2 Lloyd's Rep. 419; (1985) 135 N.L.J. 799, PC (NZ) *2–007*
Scandinavian Bank Group Plc, Re [1988] Ch. 87; [1987] 2 W.L.R. 752; [1987] 2 All E.R. 70; (1987) 3 B.C.C. 93; [1987] B.C.L.C. 220; [1987] P.C.C. 173; [1987] 1 F.T.L.R. 224; (1987) 84 L.S.G. 979; (1987) 131 S.J. 325, Ch D *30–376*
Scandinavian Trading Co A/B v Zodiac Petroleum SA; The Al Hofuf; sub nom. Scandinavian Trading Co A/B v William Hudson [1981] 1 Lloyd's Rep. 81, QBD (Comm) *12–037*, *24–014*
Scandinavian Trading Tanker Co AB v Flota Petrolera Ecuatoriana; The Scaptrade [1983] 2 A.C. 694; [1983] 3 W.L.R. 203; [1983] 2 All E.R. 763; [1983] 2 Lloyd's Rep. 253, HL; affirming [1983] Q.B. 529; [1983] 2 W.L.R. 248; [1983] 1 All E.R. 301; [1983] 1 Lloyd's Rep. 146; (1983) 133 N.L.J. 133; (1982) 126 S.J. 853, CA (Civ Div); affirming [1981] 2 Lloyd's Rep. 425; [1981] Com. L.R. 214, QBD (Comm) ....*2–136*, *2–138*, *3–081*, *3–090*, *3–091*, *3–093*, *3–104*, *18–146*, , *21–013*, *21–015*, *22–044*, *22–048*, *22–053*, *24–003*, *26–126*, *26–148*, *27–021*, *27–025*, *27–026*, *27–064*, *27–071*

Scaramanga & Co v Stamp (1879–80) L.R. 5 C.P.D. 295, CA; affirming (1878–79) L.R. 4 C.P.D. 316, CPD ... *14–030*
Scarf v Jardine (1881–82) L.R. 7 App. Cas. 345; [1881–5] All E.R. Rep. 651, HL ... *19–087*, *22–025*, *22–031*, *22–051*, *24–013*
Scarfe v Adams [1981] 1 All E.R. 843; (1981) 125 S.J. 32, CA (Civ Div) ... *12–123*
Scarfe v Hallifax (1840) 7 M.W. 288 ... *29–092*
Scarfe v Whittaker (1871) L.R. 7 Q.B. 120 ... *29–090*
Scarisbrick v Parkinson (1869) 20 L.T. 175 ... *29–080*
Schaefer v Schuhmann [1972] A.C. 572; [1972] 2 W.L.R. 481; [1972] 1 All E.R. 621; (1971) 116 S.J. 121, PC (Aus) ... *2–172*
Schaffenius v Goldberg [1916] 1 K.B. 284, CA ... *11–027*
Schawel v Reade [1913] 2 I.R. 64 ... *12–003*
Schebsman (Deceased) Ex p. Official Receiver, Re; sub nom. Trustee v Cargo Supertintendents (London) Ltd [1944] Ch. 83; [1943] 2 All E.R. 768, CA; affirming in part [1943] Ch. 366, Ch D ... *16–114*, *18–042*, *18–079*, *18–080*, *18–081*, *18–086*, *18–099*
Schelde Delta Shipping BV v Astarte Shipping BV; The Pamela; sub nom. Mondial Shipping & Chartering BV v Astarte Shipping BV [1995] 2 Lloyd's Rep. 249; [1995] C.L.C. 1011, QBD (Comm) ... *2–047*, *2–050*, *2–091*, *21–013*, *21–022*
Schenkers v Overland Shoes. *See* Overland Shoes Ltd v Schenkers Ltd
Schering Agrochemicals Ltd v Resibel NV SA, unreported, November 26, 1992, CA (Civ Div) ... *26–050*
Schering Chemicals Ltd v Falkman Ltd [1982] Q.B. 1; [1981] 2 W.L.R. 848; [1981] 2 All E.R. 321; (1981) 125 S.J. 342, CA (Civ Div) ... *16–035*, *16–107*
Schering Ltd v Stockholms Enskilda Bank Aktiebolag [1946] A.C. 219, HL ... *23–031*
Schiffahrtsgesellschaft Detlev von Appen GmbH v Voest Alpine Intertrading GmbH; The Jay Bola; Schiffahrtsgesellschaft Detlev von Appen GmbH v Wiener Allianz Versicherungs AG [1997] 2 Lloyd's Rep. 279; [1997] C.L.C. 993, CA (Civ Div); reversing [1997] 1 Lloyd's Rep. 179; [1996] C.L.C. 1807, QBD (Comm) ... *18–131*
Schiller v Petersen [1924] 1 Ch. 394, CA ... *12–061*
Schindler v Pigault (1975) 30 P. & C.R. 328; (1975) 119 S.J. 273, Ch D ... *13–011*, *26–152*
Schmaltz v Avery (1851) 16 Q.B. 655 ... *12–115*
Schmitz v Van der Veen & Co (1915) 84 L.J.K.B. 861 ... *11–032*
Schnapper, Re [1928] Ch. 420, Ch D ... *30–370*
Schneider v Foster (1857) 2 H.N. 4 ... *21–006*
Schneider v Heath (1813) 3 Camp. 506 ... *6–016*
Schneider v Norris (1814) 2 M. & S. 286 ... *4–032*, *4–034*
Scholefield v Templer (1859) 4 De. G. & J. 429 ... *6–129*
Scholfield v Earl of Londesborough [1896] A.C. 514, HL ... *25–024*
Schorsch Meier GmbH v Hennin [1975] Q.B. 416; [1974] 3 W.L.R. 823; [1975] 1 All E.R. 152; [1975] 1 Lloyd's Rep. 1; [1975] 1 C.M.L.R. 20; (1974) 118 S.J. 881, CA (Civ Div) ... *30–376*
Schroeder v Central Bank of London (1876) 34 L.T. 735 ... *19–015*
Schuldenfrei v Hilton (Inspector of Taxes) [1999] S.T.C. 821; 72 T.C. 167; [1999] B.T.C. 310; (1999) 96(33) L.S.G. 32, CA (Civ Div); affirming [1998] S.T.C. 404; [1998] B.T.C. 156, Ch D ... *2–003*, *2–111*
Schulte, Ex p. *See* Matanle Ex p. Schulte, Re
Schulze & Co v Great Eastern Railway Co (1887) L.R. 19 Q.B.D. 30, CA ... *26–070*, *26–089*
Schwabacher, Re; sub nom. Stern v Schwabacher (1907) 98 L.T. 127 ... *21–013*, *27–002*, *27–011*
Schweppe v Harper [2008] EWCA Civ 442 ... *2–079, 2–086*, *2–140*, *2–142*, *2–150*, *2–154*, *3–170*
Scorer v Seymour Jones [1966] 1 W.L.R. 1419; [1966] 3 All E.R. 347; 1 K.I.R. 303; (1966) 110 S.J. 526, CA ... *16–110*, *16–113*, *16–197*
Scotland v South African Territories (1917) 33 T.L.R. 255 ... *11–024*
Scotson v Peg (1861) 6 H. & N. 295 ... *3–073*
Scott v Avery, 10 E.R. 1121; (1856) 5 H.L. Cas. 811, HL ... *16–045*, 28–059

Scott v Bradley [1971] Ch. 850; [1971] 2 W.L.R. 731; [1971] 1 All E.R. 583; (1971) 22 P. & C.R. 352; (1970) 115 S.J. 172, Ch D *4–025*, *4–026*, *4–028*, *27–037*
Scott v Brown Doering McNab & Co; Slaughter & May v Brown Doering McNab & Co [1892] 2 Q.B. 724, CA *16–014*, *16–176*, *16–205*
Scott v Coulson [1903] 2 Ch. 249, CA; affirming [1903] 1 Ch. 453, Ch D *5–024*, *5–053*
Scott v Frank F Scott (London) Ltd [1940] Ch. 794; [1940] 3 All E.R. 508, CA; affirming [1940] Ch. 217, Ch D *5–135*
Scott v Irving (1830) 1 B. Ad. 605 ...... *21–044*
Scott v Littledale (1858) 8 E. & B. 815 ...... *5–071*
Scott v Lord Ebury (1866–67) L.R. 2 C.P. 255, CCP *9–012*, *9–014*
Scott v Lord Hastings (1858) 4 K. & J. 633 ...... *19–068*
Scott v Musial [1959] 2 Q.B. 429; [1959] 3 W.L.R. 437; [1959] 3 All E.R. 193; (1959) 103 S.J. 634, CA *26–030*
Scott v National Society for the Prevention of Cruelty to Children (1909) 25 T.L.R. 789 ......*16–052*
Scott v Pattison [1923] 2 K.B. 723, KBD *29–080*
Scott v Pilkington (1862) 2 B.S. 11 ......*25–017*, *30–350*
Scott v Rayment (1868–69) L.R. 7 Eq. 112, Ct of Chancery *27–024*
Scott v Scott (1963) 37 A.L.J.R. 345 ...... *29–172*
Scott v Sebright; sub nom. Scott (otherwise Sebright) v Sebright (1887) L.R. 12 P.D. 21, PDAD *7–010*, *7–033*
Scott v Surman (1742) Willes. 400 ......*29–162*, *29–163*, *29–171*
Scott v Uxbridge and Rickmansworth Railway Co (1865–66) L.R. 1 C.P. 596, CCP *21–092*
Scott (Anthony Peter) v Commissioner of Police of the Metropolis; sub nom. R. v Scott (Anthony Peter) [1975] A.C. 819; [1974] 3 W.L.R. 741; [1974] 3 All E.R. 1032; (1974) 60 Cr. App. R. 124; [1975] Crim. L.R. 94; (1974) 118 S.J. 863, HL; affirming [1974] Q.B. 733; [1974] 2 W.L.R. 379; [1974] 2 All E.R. 204; [1974] Crim. L.R. 242; (1974) 118 S.J. 147, CA (Crim Div) *16–017*
Scott and Alvarez's Contract, Re; sub nom. Scott v Alvarez [1895] 2 Ch. 603, CA *26–152*, *27–030*
Scott Lithgow Ltd v Secretary of State for Defence, 1989 S.C. (H.L.) 9; 1989 S.L.T. 236; 45 B.L.R. 1, HL *28–050*
Scottish & Newcastle International Ltd v Othon Ghalanos Ltd [2008] UKHL 11; [2008] Bus. L.R. 583; [2008] 2 All E.R. 768; [2008] 1 Lloyd's Rep. 462; [2008] 1 C.L.C. 186; [2008] I.L.Pr. 30; (2008) 158 N.L.J. 334; (2008) 152(8) S.J.L.B. 32, HL; affirming [2006] EWCA Civ 1750; [2007] 1 All E.R. (Comm) 1027; [2007] 2 Lloyd's Rep. 341; [2006] 2 C.L.C. 1015; [2007] I.L.Pr. 44, CA (Civ Div) *14–055*, *18–034*, *18–052*, *18–133*
Scottish & Newcastle Plc v Lancashire Mortgage Corp Ltd [2007] EWCA Civ 684; [2007] N.P.C. 84, CA (Civ Div) *4–055*, *4–080*, *4–081*, *4–082*
Scottish Equitable Plc v Derby; sub nom. Derby v Scottish Equitable Plc [2001] EWCA Civ 369; [2001] 3 All E.R. 818; [2001] 2 All E.R. (Comm) 274; [2001] O.P.L.R. 181; [2001] Pens. L.R. 163; (2001) 151 N.L.J. 418, CA (Civ Div); affirming [2000] 3 All E.R. 793; [2001] 2 All E.R. (Comm) 119; [2000] Pens. L.R. 1, QBD *3–103*, *29–036*, *29–178*, *29–180*, *29–181*, *29–185*
Scottish Equitable Plc v Thompson [2003] EWCA Civ 225; [2003] H.L.R. 48; [2003] 7 E.G. 137 (C.S.), CA (Civ Div) *28–003*
Scottish Metropolitan Assurance Co v Stewart (1923) 15 Ll. L. Rep. 55, KBD *12–093*
Scottish Petroleum Co (No.2), Re (1883) L.R. 23 Ch. D. 413, CA *6–127*, *28–144*
Scottish Power Plc v Britoil (Exploration) Ltd (1997) 94(47) L.S.G. 30; (1997) 141 S.J.L.B. 246, CA (Civ Div) 12–120
Scottish Power Plc v Kvaerner Construction (Regions) Ltd, 1999 S.L.T. 721; 1998 G.W.D. 14–698, OH *13–011*
Scottish Special Housing Association v Wimpey Construction (UK) Ltd [1986] 1 W.L.R. 995; [1986] 2 All E.R. 957; 1986 S.C. (H.L.) 57; 1986 S.L.T. 559; 34 B.L.R. 1; 9 Con. L.R. 19; (1986) 2 Const. L.J. 149; (1986) 83 L.S.G. 2652; (1986) 130 S.J. 592, HL; reversing 1986 S.L.T. 173; 31 B.L.R. 17, IH (1 Div) *14–011*, *14–015*
Scriven Bros & Co v Hindley & Co [1913] 3 K.B. 564, KBD 5–072

Scrivener v Pask (1865–66) L.R. 1 C.P. 715, Ex Chamber *5–076*
Scruttons Ltd v Midland Silicones Ltd; sub nom. Midland Silicones Ltd v Scruttons Ltd [1962] A.C. 446; [1962] 2 W.L.R. 186; [1962] 1 All E.R. 1; [1961] 2 Lloyd's Rep. 365; (1962) 106 S.J. 34, HL; affirming [1961] 1 Q.B. 106; [1960] 3 W.L.R. 372; [1960] 2 All E.R. 737; [1960] 1 Lloyd's Rep. 571; (1960) 104 S.J. 603, CA; affirming [1959] 2 Q.B. 171; [1959] 2 W.L.R. 761; [1959] 2 All E.R. 289; [1959] 1 Lloyd's Rep. 289; 1962 A.M.C. 2697; (1959) 103 S.J. 415, QBD *14–040*, *14–042*, 14–046, *14–047*, *14–052*, *14–055*, *18–019*, *18–021*, 18–094
Scudamore v Vandenstene (1587) 2 Co.Inst.673 .... *1–109*, *18–122*
Scully UK Ltd v Lee [1998] I.R.L.R. 259, CA (Civ Div) *16–092*, *16–104*, *16–113*
Sea Calm Shipping Co SA v Chantiers Navals de l'Esterel SA sub nom The Uhenbels [1986] 2 Lloyd's Rep. 294, QBD (Comm) *24–003*, *24–004*, *24–007*
Seacrystal Shipping v Bulk Transport Group Shipping Co. *See* Bulk Transport Group Shipping Co Ltd v Seacrystal Shipping Ltd
Seaflower, The. *See* BS&N Ltd (BVI) v Micado Shipping Ltd (Malta)
Seager, Re (1889) 60 L.T. 665 .... *8–047*
Seager v Copydex Ltd (No.2) [1969] 1 W.L.R. 809; [1969] 2 All E.R. 718; [1969] F.S.R. 261; [1969] R.P.C. 250; (1969) 113 S.J. 281, CA (Civ Div) *29–139*, *29–145*
Seagram v Knight (1866–67) L.R. 2 Ch. App. 628, Lord Chancellor ... *25–005*, *28–065*
Seaman Ex p. Furness Finance Co Ltd, Re [1896] 1 Q.B. 412, QBD *20–021*
Searles v Sadgrave (1855) 5 E.B. 639 .... *21–085*
Sears v Tanenbaum. *See* Tanenbaum v Sears
Seaton v Burnand; sub nom. Seaton v Heath [1900] A.C. 135, HL; reversing [1899] 1 Q.B. 782, CA 6–158
Sebel Products v Customs and Excise Commissioners [1949] Ch. 409; [1949] All E.R. 729; 65 T.L.R. 107; 65 T.L.R. 207; [1949] L.J.R. 925; (1949) 93 S.J. 198, Ch D *29–094*
Secretary of State for Employment v Globe Elastic Thread Co Ltd [1980] A.C. 506; [1979] 3 W.L.R. 143; [1979] 2 All E.R. 1077; [1979] I.C.R. 706; [1979] I.R.L.R. 327; (1979) 123 S.J. 504, HL; reversing [1979] Q.B. 183; [1978] 3 W.L.R. 679; [1978] 3 All E.R. 954; [1978] I.C.R. 1041; [1978] I.R.L.R. 417; (1978) 13 I.T.R. 540; (1978) 122 S.J. 661, CA (Civ Div); affirming [1978] Q.B. 86; [1977] 3 W.L.R. 293; [1978] 1 All E.R. 987; [1978] I.C.R. 473; [1977] I.R.L.R. 233; (1977) 12 I.T.R. 402; (1977) 121 S.J. 407, EAT *3–088*, *3–098*, *12–103*
Secretary of State for the Home Department v Wainwright. *See* Wainwright v Home Office
Secretary of State for Trade and Industry v Frid; sub nom. West End Networks Ltd (In Liquidation), Re [2004] UKHL 24; [2004] 2 A.C. 506; [2004] 2 W.L.R. 1279; [2004] 2 All E.R. 1042; [2004] B.C.C. 525; [2004] 2 B.C.L.C. 1; [2004] B.P.I.R. 841; (2004) 154 N.L.J. 770; (2004) 148 S.J.L.B. 631, HL; reversing [2002] EWHC 3194 (Ch); [2003] 2 B.C.L.C. 284; [2003] B.P.I.R. 496, Ch D (Companies Ct) *20–041*
Secretary of State for Transport v Christos [2003] EWCA Civ 1073; (2004) 1 P.&C.R. 17 .... *3–137*
Secretary of State in Council of India v Kamachee Boye Sahaba (1859) 13 Moo.P.C. 22 .... *11–007*
Secretary of State v Bank of India Ltd [1938] 2 All E.R. 797 .... *29–113*, *29–120*
Securities and Investments Board v Pantell SA (No.2) [1993] Ch. 256; [1992] 3 W.L.R. 896; [1993] 1 All E.R. 134; [1993] B.C.L.C. 146; (1992) 142 N.L.J. 931; (1992) 136 S.J.L.B. 198; [1992] N.P.C. 79, CA (Civ Div); affirming [1991] 3 W.L.R. 857; [1991] 4 All E.R. 883; [1992] B.C.L.C. 58; (1991) 141 N.L.J. 1333; (1992) 136 S.J.L.B. 198, Ch D *6–090*
Seddon v North Eastern Salt Co Ltd [1905] 1 Ch. 326, Ch D *6–124*, 6–133
Seddon v Senate (1810) 13 East. 63 .... *12–042*
Seddon v Tutop (1796) 6 T.R. 607 .... *25–007*
Sedgewick v Daniell (1857) 2 H.N. 319 .... *29–127*
Seear v Cohen (1881) 45 L.T. 589 .... *7–051*

Seear v Lawson (No.1) (1880) L.R. 15 Ch. D. 426, CA *16–063*, *20–032*
Seeberg v Russian Wood Agency Ltd (1934) 50 Ll. L. Rep. 146, KBD *14–146*
Seechurn v Ace Insurance SA NV; sub nom. Ace Insurance SA NV v Seechurn [2002] EWCA Civ 67; [2002] 2 Lloyd's Rep. 390; [2002] Lloyd's Rep. I.R. 489, CA (Civ Div) *3–091*, *28–109*
Sefton (Earl of) v Tophams Ltd (No.2); sub nom. Earl of Sefton v Capital and Counties Property Co Ltd [1967] 1 A.C. 50; [1966] 2 W.L.R. 814; [1966] 1 All E.R. 1039; (1966) 110 S.J. 271, HL; reversing [1965] Ch. 1140; [1965] W.L.R. 523; [1965] 3 All E.R. 1; (1965) 109 S.J. 456, CA; affirming [1964] 1 W.L.R. 1408; [1964] 3 All E.R. 876; (1964) 108 S.J. 880, Ch D *18–141*
Segal Securities Ltd v Thoseby [1963] 1 Q.B. 887; [1963] 2 W.L.R. 403; [1963] 1 All E.R. 500; (1962) 106 S.J. 1053, QBD *24–004*
Segap Garages v Gulf Oil (Great Britain), The Times, October 24, 1988, CA (Civ Div) *24–011*, 24–025
Selangor United Rubber Estates Ltd v Cradock [1965] Ch. 896; [1965] 2 W.L.R. 67; [1964] 3 All E.R. 709; (1965) 109 S.J. 111, Ch D *6–078*
Selangor United Rubber Estates Ltd v Cradock (No.3) [1968] 1 W.L.R. 1555; [1968] 2 All E.R. 1073; [1968] 2 Lloyd's Rep. 289; (1968) 112 S.J. 744, Ch D 16–193, *29–160*
Selby v Jackson (1844) 6 Beav. 192 .... *8–070*
Selda, The. *See* Bem Dis A Turk Ticaret S/A TR v International Agri Trade Co Ltd
Select Commodities Ltd v Valdo SA; The Florida [2006] EWHC 1137 (Comm); [2006] 2 All E.R. (Comm) 493; [2007] 1 Lloyd's Rep. 1, QBD (Comm) *23–058*
Selectmove Ltd, Re [1995] 1 W.L.R. 474; [1995] 2 All E.R. 531; [1995] S.T.C. 406; [1994] B.C.C. 349; 66 T.C. 552, CA (Civ Div) *2–072*, *3–117*, *3–136*, *22–016*
Self v Hove Commissioners [1895] 1 Q.B. 685, QBD *29–098*
Selkirk v Romar Investments [1963] 1 W.L.R. 1415; [1963] 3 All E.R. 994; (1963) 107 S.J. 907, PC (Bah) *2–176*
Sellin v Price (1866–67) L.R. 2 Ex. 189, Ex Ct *25–020*, *25–023*
Sellin v Scott (1901) 1 S.R.(N.S.W.) Eq.64 .... *8–028*
Selwin v Brown (1735) 3 Brown P.C. 607 .... *25–005*
Semco Salvage & Marine Pte Ltd v Lancer Navigation Co Ltd; The Nagasaki Spirit [1997] A.C. 455; [1997] 2 W.L.R. 298; [1997] 1 All E.R. 502; [1997] 1 Lloyd's Rep. 323; [1997] C.L.C. 507; [1997] 6 Re. L.R. 305; 1997 A.M.C. 1989; (1997) 141 S.J.L.B. 43, HL *29–136*
Sempra Metals Ltd (formerly Metallgesellschaft Ltd) v Inland Revenue Commissioners [2007] UKHL 34; [2008] 1 A.C. 561; [2007] 3 W.L.R. 354; [2008] Bus. L.R. 49; [2007] 4 All E.R. 657; [2007] S.T.C. 1559; [2008] Eu. L.R. 1; [2007] B.T.C. 509; [2007] S.T.I. 1865; (2007) 104(31) L.S.G. 25; (2007) 157 N.L.J. 1082; (2007) 151 S.J.L.B. 985, HL; affirming in part [2005] EWCA Civ 389; [2006] Q.B. 37; [2005] 3 W.L.R. 521; [2005] S.T.C. 687; [2005] 2 C.M.L.R. 30; [2005] Eu. L.R. 773; [2005] B.T.C. 202; [2005] S.T.I. 831; [2005] N.P.C. 52, CA (Civ Div); affirming [2004] EWHC 2387 (Ch); [2004] S.T.C. 1178; [2004] Eu. L.R. 939; [2004] B.T.C. 358; [2004] S.T.I. 1495, Ch D *6–065*, 26–098, *26–167*, 26–170, *26–171*, 29–024, *29–085*
Sen v Headley [1991] Ch. 425; [1991] 2 W.L.R. 1308; [1991] 2 All E.R. 636; [1996] 1 F.C.R. 692; (1991) 62 P. & C.R. 277; [1991] Fam. Law 373; [1991] E.G. 23 (C.S.); (1991) 88(16) L.S.G. 32; (1991) 141 N.L.J. 384; (1991) 135 S.J. 384, CA (Civ Div); reversing [1990] Ch. 728; [1990] 2 W.L.R. 620; [1990] 1 All E.R. 898; [1990] 1 F.L.R. 449; (1990) 87(7) L.S.G. 32; (1990) 140 N.L.J. 133; (1990) 134 S.J. 342, Ch D *3–140*
Senanayake v Cheng [1966] A.C. 63; [1965] 3 W.L.R. 715; [1965] 3 All E.R. 296; (1965) 109 S.J. 756, PC (Sing) *6–124*, *6–133*
Sengupta v India [1983] I.C.R. 221; (1982) 126 S.J. 855, EAT *11–001*, *11–002*, *11–005*, *11–009*
Sepoong Engineering Construction Co Ltd v Formula One Management Ltd (formerly Formula One Administration Ltd) [2000] 1 Lloyd's Rep. 602, QBD (Comm) *3–015*, *3–167*
Serco Ltd v Lawson. *See* Lawson v Serco Ltd

Sercombe v Sanders (1865) 34 Beav. 382 .... *7–075*
Series 5 Software Ltd v Clarke [1996] 1 All E.R. 853; [1996] C.L.C. 631; [1996] F.S.R. 273; (1996) 19(3) I.P.D. 19024, Ch D *27–061*
Services Europe Atlantique Sud (SEAS) v Stockholms Rederi AB Svea; The Folias. *See* Owners of the Eleftherotria v Owners of the Despina R
Seton v Slade (1802) 7 Ves. 265 .... *27–047*
Seton Laing & Co v Lafone (1887) L.R. 19 Q.B.D. 68; (1887) 3 T.L.R. 624; (1887) 56 L.J. Q.B. 415; (1887) 57 L.T. 547, CA; affirming (1887) L.R. 18 Q.B.D. 139, QBD *6–095*
Seven Pioneer, The [2001] 2 Lloyd's Rep. 57, HC (NZ) *18–034*
Seven Seas Properties Ltd v Al-Essa (No.2) [1993] 1 W.L.R. 1083; [1993] 3 All E.R. 577, Ch D *20–063A*, *26–091*
Seven Seas Transportation Ltd v Pacifico Union Marina Corp; The Satya Kailash and The Oceanic Amity [1984] 2 All E.R. 140; [1984] 1 Lloyd's Rep. 588, CA (Civ Div); affirming [1983] 1 All E.R. 672; [1982] 2 Lloyd's Rep. 465; [1982] Com. L.R. 236, QBD (Comm) *14–013*
Seven Utility Services Ltd v Rosekey Ltd. *See* 24 Seven Utility Services Ltd v Rosekey Ltd (t/a Atwasl Builders)
Severn Trent Water Ltd v Barnes [2004] EWCA Civ 570; [2004] 2 E.G.L.R. 95; [2004] 26 E.G. 194; [2005] R.V.R. 181; (2004) 148 S.J.L.B. 693; [2004] N.P.C. 76, CA (Civ Div) *29–144*
Sevin v Deslandes (1860) 30 L.J. (Ch.) 457 .... *27–070*
Seymour, Re; sub nom. Fielding v Seymour [1913] 1 Ch. 475, CA *1–093*
Seymour v Pickett [1905] 1 K.B. 715, CA *21–061*, *21–063*
Seymour v Royal Naval School. *See* Seymour v Royal Naval School
Sforza v Ottoman Bank of Nicosia [1938] A.C. 282, PC (Cy) *21–068*
Shackell v Rosier (1836) 3 Scott 59 .... *16–201*, *16–202*
Shackleford, The. *See* Surrey Shipping Co v Compagnie Continentale (France) SA
Shackleford's Case. *See* Rolling Stock Co of Ireland, Re
Shackleton Ex p. Whittaker, Re (1874–75) L.R. 10 Ch. App. 446, CA in Chancery *6–010*, *6–015*
Shade v Compton Partnership [2000] Lloyd's Rep. P.N. 81; [2000] P.N.L.R. 218, CA (Civ Div) *28–118*
Shadwell v Shadwell (1860) 9 C.B. (N.S.) 159 .... *2–174*, *3–010*, 3–073
Shaffer (James) v Findlay Durham & Brodie [1953] 1 W.L.R. 106; (1953) 97 S.J. 26, CA *24–019*
Shah v Shah [2001] EWCA Civ 527; [2002] Q.B. 35; [2001] 3 W.L.R. 31; [2001] 4 All E.R. 138, CA (Civ Div) 1–104, *3–101*, *3–115*, *4–004*
Shahabina v Gyachi, unreported, 1989 .... *7–138*
Shallcross v Wright (1850) 12 Beav. 558 .... *2–175*, *29–134*
Shalson v Russo; sub nom. Mimran v Russo [2003] EWHC 1637 (Ch); [2005] Ch. 281; [2005] 2 W.L.R. 1213; [2003] W.T.L.R. 1165; (2005–06) 8 I.T.E.L.R. 435; (2003) 100(35) L.S.G. 37, Ch D *6–130*, *29–162*
Shamia v Joory [1958] 1 Q.B. 448; [1958] 2 W.L.R. 84; [1958] 1 All E.R. 111; (1958) 102 S.J. 70, QBD 19–089, *29–194*, 29–195, 29–196
Shamil Bank of Bahrain EC v Beximco Pharmaceuticals Ltd (No.1); sub nom. Beximco Pharmaceuticals Ltd v Shamil Bank of Bahrain EC [2004] EWCA Civ 19; [2004] 1 W.L.R. 1784; [2004] 4 All E.R. 1072; [2004] 2 All E.R. (Comm) 312; [2004] 2 Lloyd's Rep. 1; [2004] 1 C.L.C. 216; (2004) 101(8) L.S.G. 29, CA (Civ Div) *30–009*, *30–022*, *30–029*, *30–048*
Shamji v Johnson Matthey Bankers Ltd [1986] B.C.L.C. 278; (1986) 2 B.C.C. 98910, CA (Civ Div) *1–148*
Shamrock SS Co v Storey & Co (1899) 81 L.T. 413 .... *2–141*
Shamsher Jute Mills v Sethia London [1987] 1 Lloyd's Rep. 388, QBD (Comm) *3–081*
Shand v Du Buisson (1874) L.R. 18 Eq. 283, Ct of Chancery *19–024*
Shanklin Pier Ltd v Detel Products Ltd [1951] 2 K.B. 854; [1951] 2 All E.R. 471; [1951] 2 Lloyd's Rep. 187; (1951) 95 S.J. 563, KBD *6–086*, 12–007, 18–005, 18–008

Shannon, The v Venner [1965] Ch. 682; [1965] 2 W.L.R. 718; [1965] 1 All E.R. 590; (1965) 109 S.J. 12, CA *12–117*
Shannon v Bradstreet (1803) 1 Sch. & Lef. 52 .... *8–042*
Shanshal v Al-Kishtaini. *See* Al-Kishtaini v Shanshal
Shardlow v Cotterell (1881–82) L.R. 20 Ch. D. 90, CA; reversing (1880–81) L.R. 18 Ch. D. 280, Ch D *4–010*, *4–029*, *12–123*
Sharif v Azad [1967] 1 Q.B. 605; [1966] 3 W.L.R. 1285; [1966] 3 All E.R. 785; (1966) 110 S.J. 791, CA *16–031*, *16–033*
Sharman v Brandt (1870–71) L.R. 6 Q.B. 720, Ex Chamber *4–039*, *12–115*
Sharneyford Supplies Ltd (formerly Flinthall Farms) v Edge [1987] Ch. 305; [1987] 2 W.L.R. 363; [1987] 1 All E.R. 588; (1987) 53 P. & C.R. 320, CA (Civ Div); reversing [1986] Ch. 128; [1985] 3 W.L.R. 1; [1985] 1 All E.R. 976; (1985) 50 P. & C.R. 343; (1985) 82 L.S.G. 2081; (1985) 35 N.L.J. 288; (1985) 129 S.J. 316, Ch D *1–122*, *6–052*
Sharp v Christmas (1892) 8 T.L.R. 687 .... *21–013*
Sharp v Ellis (1971) 20 F.L.R. 199, Sup Ct (Vic) *3–033*
Sharp v Harrison [1922] 1 Ch. 502, Ch D *27–060*
Sharp Bros & Knight v Chant [1917] 1 K.B. 771, CA *29–042*, *29–043*
Sharpe Ex p. Trustee of the Bankrupt's Property, Re; sub nom. Sharpe Re, Ex p. Trustee of the Bankrupt v Sharpe [1980] 1 W.L.R. 219; [1980] 1 All E.R. 198; (1980) 39 P. & C.R. 459; (1980) 124 S.J. 147, Ch D *1–188*, *2–172*, *3–137*, *3–142*, *3–144*, *3–151*, *3–157*, *13–028*, *18–135*
Sharpe, Re; Bennett, Re; sub nom. Masonic and General Life Assurance Co v Sharpe [1892] 1 Ch. 154, CA *28–138*, *28–141*
Sharpe v Gibbs (1864) 16 C.B.(N.S.) 527 .... *25–001*
Sharpley v Louth and East Coast Railway Co (1875–76) L.R. 2 Ch. D. 663, CA *6–124*, *6–127*, *28–144*
Sharratt v London Central Bus Co Ltd. *See* Hollins v Russell
Shave v Lees (JW) (Brewers) [1954] 1 W.L.R. 1300; [1954] 3 All E.R. 249; (1954) 98 S.J. 717, CA *26–030*
Shaw v Applegate [1977] 1 W.L.R. 970; [1978] 1 All E.R. 123; (1978) 35 P. & C.R. 181; (1977) 121 S.J. 424, CA (Civ Div) *28–135*, *28–136*, *28–141*
Shaw v DPP; sub nom. R. v Shaw (Frederick Charles) [1962] A.C. 220; [1961] 2 W.L.R. 897; [1961] 2 All E.R. 446; (1961) 45 Cr. App. R. 113; (1961) 125 J.P. 437; (1961) 105 S.J. 421, HL; affirming [1961] 1 All E.R. 330, CCA *16–014*, *16–069*
Shaw v Groom [1970] 2 Q.B. 504; [1970] 2 W.L.R. 299; [1970] 1 All E.R. 702; (1970) 21 P. & C.R. 137; (1969) 114 S.J. 14, CA (Civ Div) ...*4–003*, *16–004*, *16–012*, *16–146*, 16–150, *16–151*, *16–152* , *16–157*
Shaw v Holland (1846) 15 M.W. 136 .... *26–100*
Shaw v Moss' Empires and Boston (1909) 25 T.L.R. 191 .... *19–055*
Shaw v Picton (1825) 4 B.C. 715 .... *21–060*
Shaw v Shaw [1954] 2 Q.B. 429; [1954] 3 W.L.R. 265; [1954] 2 All E.R. 638; (1954) 98 S.J. 509, CA *1–124*, *20–006*, *28–086*
Shaw v Shaw [1965] 1 W.L.R. 537; [1965] 1 All E.R. 638; (1965) 109 S.J. 233, CA *16–014*, *16–177*
Shaw v Shaw [1979] Fam. 62; [1979] 3 W.L.R. 24; [1979] 3 All E.R. 1; (1979) 9 Fam. Law 187; (1979) 123 S.J. 142, Fam Div *11–011*, *11–014*
Shaw v Woodcock (1827) 7 B.C. 73 .... *29–079*, *29–092*
Shawton Engineering Ltd v DGP International Ltd (t/a Design Group Partnership) [2005] EWCA Civ 1359; [2006] B.L.R. 1; (2006) 22 Const. L.J. 129, CA (Civ Div) *12–038*, *21–014*
Shayler v Woolf [1946] Ch. 320; [1946] 2 All E.R. 54; [1947] L.J.R. 71; 175 L.T. 170; (1946) 90 S.J. 357, CA *19–055*
Shears v Mendeloff (1914) 30 T.L.R. 342 .... *8–004*, *8–017*, *8–028*
Shearson Lehman Brothers Inc v Maclaine Watson & Co Ltd [1988] 1 W.L.R. 16; [1988] 1 All E.R. 116; [1988] F.T.L.R. 225; (1988) 85(2) L.S.G. 35; (1987) 131 S.J. 1658, HL; reversing, *Independent*, August 12, 1987*; Financial Times*, August 5, 1987, CA (Civ Div) *11–018*

Shearson Lehman Hutton Inc v Maclaine Watson & Co Ltd [1989] 2 Lloyd's Rep. 570; [1989] 3 C.M.L.R. 429; (1990) 140 N.L.J. 247, QBD (Comm) *3–088, 3–107, 3–110, 3–113, 12–014, 12–015, 12–118, 14–073, 14–084, 14–152*
Shearson Lehman Hutton Inc v Maclaine Watson & Co Ltd (Damages and Interest) [1990] 3 All E.R. 723; [1990] 1 Lloyd's Rep. 441, QBD (Comm) *26–178*
Sheers v Thimbleby & Son (1897) 76 L.T. 709 .... *4–028*, *12–102*
Sheeskin v, Giant Food Inc, 318 A 2d 874 (1974) *2–015*
Sheffield v Conrad (1988) 22 Con. L.R. 108 .... *24–014*
Sheffield v Pickfords Ltd [1997] C.L.C. 648; (1997) 16 Tr. L.R. 337, CA (Civ Div) *14–088*
Sheffield Building Society, Re (1889) 22 Q.B.D. 470 .... *9–001*
Sheffield Corp v Barclay [1905] A.C. 392, HL *29–120*
Sheffield Corp v Sheffield Electric Light Co [1898] 1 Ch. 203, Ch D *12–093*
Sheffield Gas Co v Harrison (1853) 17 Beav. 294 .... *27–038*
Sheffield Nickel Co v Unwin (1877) 2 Q.B.D. 214 .... *6–117*
Sheikh Bros v Ochsner (Arnold Julius) [1957] A.C. 136; [1957] 2 W.L.R. 254; (1957) 101 S.J. 128, PC (EA) 5–034
Sheldon v RHM Outhwaite (Underwriting Agencies) Ltd [1996] A.C. 102; [1995] 2 W.L.R. 570; [1995] 2 All E.R. 558; [1995] 2 Lloyd's Rep. 197; [1995] C.L.C. 655; [1995] 4 Re. L.R. 168; (1995) 92(22) L.S.G. 41; (1995) 145 N.L.J. 687; (1995) 139 S.J.L.B. 119, HL 28–082
Shelfer v City of London Electric Lighting Co (No.1); Meux's Brewery Co v City of London Electric Lighting Co [1895] 1 Ch. 287, CA *27–063*
Shell (UK) Ltd v Lostock Garage Ltd [1976] 1 W.L.R. 1187; [1977] 1 All E.R. 481; (1976) 120 S.J. 523, CA (Civ Div) *13–003*, *13–007*, *13–009*, *16–088*, *27–036*
Shell Chemicals UK Ltd v P&O Roadtanks Ltd [1995] 1 Lloyd's Rep. 297, CA (Civ Div); affirming [1993] 1 Lloyd's Rep. 114, QBD (Comm) ... *14–011*, *14–013*, *14–015*
Shell Tankers (UK) Ltd v Astro Comino Armadora SA; The Pacific Colocotronis [1981] 2 Lloyd's Rep. 40, CA (Civ Div); affirming [1980] 1 Lloyd's Rep. 366, QBD (Comm) *12–062*, *12–118*
Shelley v Paddock [1980] Q.B. 348; [1980] 2 W.L.R. 647; [1980] 1 All E.R. 1009; (1979) 123 S.J. 706, CA (Civ Div); affirming [1979] Q.B. 120; [1978] 2 W.L.R. 877; [1978] 3 All E.R. 129; (1978) 122 S.J. 317, QBD *6–061*, *7–049*, 16–176, *29–043*
Shell-Mex Ltd v Elton Coop Dyeing Co (1928) 34 Com. Cas. 39 .... *27–013*
Shelton v Springett, 138 E.R. 549; (1851) 11 C.B. 452, CCP *8–061*
Shephard v Cartwright; sub nom. Shephard, Re [1955] A.C. 431; [1954] 3 W.L.R. 967; [1954] 3 All E.R. 649; (1954) 98 S.J. 868, HL; reversing [1953] Ch. 728; [1953] 3 W.L.R. 378; [1953] 2 All E.R. 608; (1953) 97 S.J. 524, CA; affirming [1953] 1 W.L.R. 460; [1953] 1 All E.R. 569; (1953) 97 S.J. 151, Ch D *8–058*
Shepheard v Walker (1875) L.R. 20 Eq. 659, Ct of Chancery *28–143*
Shepherd v Croft [1911] 1 Ch. 521, Ch D *27–054*, *27–055*, *27–057*
Shepherd v Federal Commissioner of Taxation (1965) 113 C.L.R. 385; 39 A.L.J.R. 351 ....*19–028*, *19–029*, *19–033*
Shepherd v Kain (1821) 5 B. & Ald. 240 .... *14–027*
Shepherd Homes Ltd v Encia Remediation Ltd [2007] EWHC 70 (TCC); [2007] B.L.R. 135; 110 Con. L.R. 90, QBD (TCC) *12–013*, *12–015*, *14–002*, *14–085*, *14–087*
Shepherd Homes Ltd v Sandham (No.1) [1971] Ch. 340; [1970] 3 W.L.R. 348; [1970] 3 All E.R. 402; (1970) 21 P. & C.R. 863; (1970) 114 S.J. 636, Ch D ... *27–060*
Shepherds Investments Ltd v Walters [2006] EWHC 836 (Ch); [2007] 2 B.C.L.C. 202; [2007] I.R.L.R. 110; [2007] F.S.R. 15; (2006) 150 S.J.L.B. 536, Ch D ... *16–107*
Sherbrooke v Dipple (1981) 41 P. & C.R. 173; (1980) 255 E.G. 1203; (1980) 124 S.J. 345, CA (Civ Div) *4–027*

Sherdley v Sherdley [1988] A.C. 213; [1987] 2 W.L.R. 1071; [1987] 2 All E.R. 54; [1987] S.T.C. 217; (1987) 151 J.P. 715; [1987] 2 F.L.R. 242; [1987] F.C.R. 149; [1987] F.T.L.R. 60; [1987] Fam. Law 385; (1987) 151 J.P.N. 333; (1987) 84 L.S.G. 1492; (1987) 137 N.L.J. 363; (1987) 131 S.J. 504, HL; reversing [1986] 1 W.L.R. 732; [1986] 2 All E.R. 202; [1986] S.T.C. 266; (1986) 150 J.P. 305; [1986] 2 F.L.R. 326; [1986] Fam. Law 272; (1986) 150 J.P.N. 366; (1986) 83 L.S.G. 1636; (1986) 136 N.L.J. 464; (1986) 130 S.J. 356, CA (Civ Div) *8–027*

Sherk v Horwitz [1973] 1 O.R. 160; affirming [1972] 2 O.R. 451 .... *16–095*

Sherry, Re; sub nom. London and County Banking Co v Terry (1884) L.R. 25 Ch. D. 692, CA *21–066*

Shewen v Vanderhorst (1831) 1 R. & M. 347 .... *28–131*

Shiell's Trustees v Scottish Property Investment Building Society (In Liquidation); sub nom. Small v Smith (1884–85) L.R. 10 App. Cas. 119; (1884) 12 R. (H.L.) 14, HL *10–023*, 10–027

Shilena Hosiery Co Ltd, Re [1980] Ch. 219; [1979] 3 W.L.R. 332; [1979] 2 All E.R. 6; (1979) 123 S.J. 568, Ch D *20–031*

Shilliday v Smith, 1998 S.C. 725; 1998 S.L.T. 976; 1998 S.C.L.R. 502; 1998 G.W.D. 16–821, IH (1 Div) *29–015*

Shiloh Spinners Ltd v Harding [1973] A.C. 691; [1973] 2 W.L.R. 28; [1973] 1 All E.R. 90; (1973) 25 P. & C.R. 48; (1972) 117 S.J. 34, HL .... *7–126, 21–016*, , *22–047, 26–148*, *27–027*

Shindler v Northern Raincoat Co [1960] 1 W.L.R. 1038; [1960] 2 All E.R. 239; (1960) 104 S.J. 806, Assizes (Manchester) .. *9–058*, *13–012*, *24–010*, *26–103*, *26–113*

Shipbuilders v Benson [1992] 3 N.Z.L.R. 349 .... *12–012*

Shipley Urban DC v Bradford Corp [1936] Ch. 375, Ch D 5–113

Shipley v Marshall (1863) 14 C.B. (N.S.) 566 .... *20–026*

Shipping Corp of India v Gamlen Chemical Co (Australia) Pty (1980) 147 C.L.R. 142, HC (Aus) *14–019*

Shipping Corp of India v Naviera Letasa, SA [1976] 1 Lloyd's Rep. 132, QBD (Comm) *2–153*

Shipping Corp of India Ltd v NBB Niederelbe Schifffahrtsgesellschaft GmbH; The Black Falcon [1991] 1 Lloyd's Rep. 77, QBD (Comm) *12–057*

Shipton, Re; sub nom. Arbitration between Anderson & Co and Harrison Brothers & Co, Re [1915] 3 K.B. 676, KBD 23–026, *23–047*

Shipton v Cardiff Corp (1917) 87 L.J.K.B. 51 .... *2–047*

Shipton v Casson (1826) 5 B.C. 378 .... *21–035*

Shipwright v Clements (1871) 19 W.R. 599 .... *16–118*

Shires v Brock (1977) 247 E.G. 127, CA (Civ Div) *2–155*

Shizelle, The [1992] 2 Lloyd's Rep. 444, QBD (Admlty) *18–138*

Shogun Finance Ltd v Hudson; sub nom. Hudson v Shogun Finance Ltd [2003] UKHL 62; [2004] 1 A.C. 919; [2003] 3 W.L.R. 1371; [2004] 1 All E.R. 215; [2004] 1 All E.R. (Comm) 332; [2004] 1 Lloyd's Rep. 532; [2004] R.T.R. 12; (2003) 100(46) L.S.G. 25; (2003) 153 N.L.J. 1790; (2003) 147 S.J.L.B. 1368, HL; affirming [2001] EWCA Civ 1000; [2002] Q.B. 834; [2002] 2 W.L.R. 867; [2002] 4 All E.R. 572; [2002] R.T.R. 17, CA (Civ Div) *1–082*, *1–170*, *5–090*, *5–091*, *5–092*, 5–093, 5–094, 5–095, 5–096, *5–097*, *12–122*

Shore v Ministry of Works [1950] 2 All E.R. 228, CA *9–073*

Shore v Wilson (1842) 9 Cl. & F. 355 .... *12–051*, *12–060*, 12–118, *12–121*

Short v M'Carthy (1820) 3 B. & Ald. 626 .... *28–032*, *28–033*

Short v Stone (1846) 8 Q.B. 358 .... *21–010*, *24–028*

Shoubridge v Clark (1852) 12 C.B. 335 .... *29–142*

Shove v Downs Surgical Plc [1984] 1 All E.R. 7; [1984] I.C.R. 532; [1984] I.R.L.R. 17; (1984) 81 L.S.G. 893; (1983) 133 N.L.J. 938; (1984) 128 S.J. 221, QBD *26–158*

Showlag v Mansour [1995] 1 A.C. 431; [1994] 2 W.L.R. 615; [1994] 2 All E.R. 129; [1994] C.L.C. 314; [1995] I.L.Pr. 157, PC (Jer) *25–016*, *25–017*

Shrewsbury (Earl of) v North Staffordshire Railway Co (1865–66) L.R. 1 Eq. 593, Ct of Chancery *9–016*, *16–025*

Shrewsbury and Birmingham Ry Co v London and NW Ry Co (1851) 17 Q.B. 652 .... *16–025*
Shuey v U.S. (1875) 92 U.S. 73 .... *2–091*
Shurey, Re; sub nom. Savory v Shurey [1918] 1 Ch. 263, Ch D *8–002*
Shuttleworth v Clews [1910] 1 Ch. 176, Ch D *29–064*
Shuttleworth v Garnett (1688) 3 Mod. 240 .... *29–006*
Shyam Jewellers Ltd v Cheeseman [2001] EWCA Civ 1818, CA (Civ Div) *24–018*
Sibree v Tripp (1846) 15 M.W. 23 .... *21–077*
Sichel v Mosenthal (1862) 30 Beav. 371 .... *27–012*
Sick and Funeral Society of St John's Sunday School, Golcar, Re [1973] Ch. 51; [1972] 2 W.L.R. 962; [1972] 2 All E.R. 439; (1972) 116 S.J. 355, Ch D *9–074*, *9–078*
Sicklemore v Thistleton (1817) 6 M.S. 9 .... *21–009*
Sidaway v Board of Governors of the Bethlem Royal Hospital [1985] A.C. 871; [1985] 2 W.L.R. 480; [1985] 1 All E.R. 643; (1985) 82 L.S.G. 1256; (1985) 135 N.L.J. 203; (1985) 129 S.J. 154, HL; affirming [1984] Q.B. 493; [1984] 2 W.L.R. 778; [1984] 1 All E.R. 1018; (1984) 81 L.S.G. 899; (1984) 128 S.J. 301, CA (Civ Div) *1–119*, *1–153*
Siddell v Smith Cooper & Partners; Follows v Smith Cooper & Partners [1999] Lloyd's Rep. P.N. 79; [1999] P.N.L.R. 511, CA (Civ Div) *1–184*
Sidebotham v Holland [1895] 1 Q.B. 378, CA *4–041*
Sidhu v British Airways Plc. *See* Abnett v British Airways Plc
Sierra Leone v Davenport [2003] EWHC 2769, Ch D *4–074*
Sierra Leone v Marmaro Shipping Co; The Amazona and The Yayamaria; Sierra Leone v Margaritis Marine Co [1989] 2 Lloyd's Rep. 130, CA (Civ Div) *28–022*
Sierra Leone Telecommunications Co Ltd v Barclays Bank Plc; sub nom. Sierratel v Barclays Bank Plc [1998] 2 All E.R. 820; [1998] C.L.C. 501; (1998) 95(17) L.S.G. 32, QBD (Comm) *30–077*, *30–081*, *30–325*
Siew Soon Wah (alias Siew Pooi Yong) v Yong Tong Hong [1973] A.C. 836; [1973] 2 W.L.R. 713; (1973) 117 S.J. 341, PC (Mal) *2–143*, *29–161*
Sig Bergesen DY & Co v Mobil Shipping and Transportation Co; The Berge Sund [1993] 2 Lloyd's Rep. 453, CA (Civ Div); reversing [1992] 1 Lloyd's Rep. 460, QBD (Comm) *14–018*
Silles v Fulham BC [1903] 1 K.B. 829, CA *29–107*
Silverman v Imperial London Hotels Ltd (1927) 137 L.T. 57; 43 T.L.R. 260 .... *13–006*
Silverman (George) v Silverman (1969) 113 S.J. 563, CA (Civ Div) *16–113*
Silvertone Records Ltd v Mountfield; Zomba Music Publishers Ltd v Mountfield [1993] E.M.L.R. 152, QBD *16–198*
Silvester, Re [1895] 1 Ch. 573 .... *2–100*
Sim v Rotherham MBC; Townend v Doncaster MBC; Barnfield v Solihull MBC; Rathbone v Croydon LBC [1987] Ch. 216; [1986] 3 W.L.R. 851; [1986] 3 All E.R. 387; [1986] I.C.R. 897; [1986] I.R.L.R. 391; 85 L.G.R. 128; (1986) 83 L.S.G. 3746; (1986) 130 S.J. 839, Ch D 1–070, 13–008, *21–032*
Simaan General Contracting Co v Pilkington Glass Ltd [1988] Q.B. 758; [1988] 2 W.L.R. 761; [1988] 1 All E.R. 791; 40 B.L.R. 28; [1988] F.T.L.R. 469; [1988] E.G. 16 (C.S.); (1988) 138 N.L.J. Rep. 53; (1988) 132 S.J. 463, CA (Civ Div) *1–176*, 1–177, *14–056*, *14–057*, *18–005*, *18–027*, 18–031, 18–032, *18–034*, *18–036*
Simmonds, Ex p. *See* Carnac Ex p. Simmonds, Re
Simmonds v Heffer [1983] B.C.L.C. 298, Ch D *9–032*
Simmons v Simmons [1996] C.L.Y. 2874 .... *4–011*, *4–064*, *4–067*
Simms Ex p. Trustee, Re [1934] Ch. 1, CA *29–142*, *29–145*, *29–146*
Simms, Re [1930] 2 Ch. 22, Ch D *20–019*
Simon v Pawsons & Leafs Ltd (1932) 38 Com. Cas. 151 .... *16–173*
Simon Container Machinery Ltd v Emba Machinery AB [1998] 2 Lloyd's Rep. 429, QBD (Comm) *3–068*, *12–118*, *18–128*, *22–035*
Simoco Digital UK Ltd: Thunderbird Industries LLC v Simoco Digital UK Ltd. *See* Thunderbird Industries LLC v Simoco Digital UK Ltd
Simona, The. *See* Fercometal Sarl v MSC Mediterranean Shipping Co SA
Simond v Boydell (1779) 1 Dougl. 268 .... *12–065*

Simonin v Mallac, 164 E.R. 917; (1860) 2 Sw. & Tr. 67, Ct of Probate *30–324*
Simper v Coombs [1948] 1 All E.R. 306; 64 T.L.R. 131; [1948] W.N. 74; [1948] L.J.R. 1080; (1948) 92 S.J. 85, KBD *23–055*
Simpkins v Pays [1955] 1 W.L.R. 975; [1955] 3 All E.R. 10; (1955) 99 S.J. 563, Assizes (Chester) *2–158*, 2–173
Simpson, Ex p. Morgan, Re (1875–76) L.R. 2 Ch. D. 72, CA *1–115*
Simpson v Connolly [1953] 1 W.L.R. 911; [1953] 2 All E.R. 474; (1953) 97 S.J. 490, QBD *4–010*
Simpson v Crippin (1872–73) L.R. 8 Q.B. 14, QB *24–044*
Simpson v Eggington, 156 E.R. 683; (1855) 10 Ex. 845, Ex Ct *21–041*, *29–099*
Simpson v Hughes (1897) 66 L.J.Ch. 334 .... *2–032*
Simpson v John Reynolds & Co (Insurances) Ltd [1975] 1 W.L.R. 617; [1975] 2 All E.R. 88; [1975] 1 Lloyd's Rep. 512; [1975] S.T.C. 271; 49 T.C. 693; [1975] T.R. 33; (1975) 119 S.J. 287, CA (Civ Div); affirming [1974] 1 W.L.R. 1411; [1974] 2 All E.R. 545; [1974] 2 Lloyd's Rep. 334; [1974] S.T.C. 277; [1974] T.R. 129; (1974) 118 S.J. 701, Ch D *3–026*
Simpson v Lamb (1857) 7 E. & B. 84 .... *16–064*
Simpson v London & North Western Railway Co (1875–76) L.R. 1 Q.B.D. 274, QBD *26–007*, *26–070*
Simpson v Lord Howden (1842) 9 Cl. & Fin. 61 .... *16–025*
Simpson v Margitson (1847) 11 Q.B. 23 .... *12–046*
Sims v Landray [1894] 2 Ch. 318, Ch D *4–038*
Simson v Ingham (1823) 2 B.C. 65 .... *21–059*, *21–061*, *21–066*
Sinason-Teicher Inter-American Grain Corp v Oilcakes and Oilseeds Trading Co [1954] 1 W.L.R. 1394; [1954] 3 All E.R. 468; [1954] 2 Lloyd's Rep. 327; (1954) 98 S.J. 804, CA *24–024*
Sinclair Investment Holdings SA v Versailles Trade Finance Ltd (In Administrative Receivership) [2007] EWHC 915 (Ch); [2007] 2 All E.R. (Comm) 993; (2007–08) 10 I.T.E.L.R. 58, Ch D *29–160*, *29–174*
Sinclair v Bowles (1829) 9 B.C. 92 .... *21–029*, *21–030*, *21–031*
Sinclair v British Telecommunications Plc [2001] 1 W.L.R. 38; [2000] 2 All E.R. 461; [2001] 1 Costs L.R. 40, CA (Civ Div) *19–048*, *19–070*
Sinclair v Brougham; sub nom. Birkbeck Permanent Benefit Building Society, Re [1914] A.C. 398; [1914–15] All E.R. Rep. 622, HL; reversing in part [1912] 2 Ch. 183, CA ... *9–025*, 29–007, 29–008, *29–012*, *29–013*, *29–043*, I29–158, *29–162*, *29–163*, *29–164*, *29–165*, *29–166*, *29–172*
Sinclair's Life Policy, Re [1938] Ch. 799, Ch D *18–042*, *18–073*, *18–079*, *18–081*, *18–086*, *18–125*
Sindel v Georgio (1984) 154 C.L.R. 661, HC (Aus) *2–119*
Sindh, The [1975] 1 Lloyd's Rep. 372 .... *30–010*
Singer Co (UK) Ltd v Tees & Hartlepool Port Authority [1988] 2 Lloyd's Rep. 164; [1988] 1 F.T.L.R. 442, QBD (Comm) *14–054*, *14–084*, *14–085*, *14–087*, 14–095, *18–019*
Singh v Ali [1960] A.C. 167; [1960] 2 W.L.R. 180; [1960] 1 All E.R. 269; (1960) 104 S.J. 84, PC (FMS) *16–178*, *16–180*
Singh v Beggs (1996) 71 P. & C.R. 120, CA (Civ Div) *4–054*, 4–075
Singh v Sardar Investments Ltd [2002] EWCA Civ 1706; [2002] N.P.C. 134, CA (Civ Div) *24–023*
Singh v Singh [1971] P. 226; [1971] 2 W.L.R. 963; [1971] 2 All E.R. 828; (1971) 115 S.J. 205, CA (Civ Div) *7–010*
Singh (Sudagar) v Nazeer [1979] Ch. 474; [1978] 3 W.L.R. 785; [1978] 3 All E.R. 817; (1978) 36 P. & C.R. 407, Ch D *27–082*
Sinochem International Oil (London) Co Ltd v Mobil Sales and Supply Corp (No.1) [2000] 1 All E.R. (Comm) 474; [2000] 1 Lloyd's Rep. 339; [2000] C.L.C. 878, CA (Civ Div); reversing [1999] 2 All E.R. (Comm) 522; [1999] 2 Lloyd's Rep. 769; [2000] C.L.C. 186, QBD (Comm) ... *12–050*, *12–055*, *12–057*, *12–072*, *12–083*
Sion v Hampstead HA [1994] 5 Med. L.R. 170; [1994] J.P.I.L. 241, CA (Civ Div) *28–118*

Siporex Trade SA v Banque Indosuez [1986] 2 Lloyd's Rep. 146, QBD (Comm) *13–011*
Siqueira v Noronha [1934] A.C. 332; [1934] All E.R. Rep. 78; [1934] 2 W.W.R. 117, PC (EA) *29–190*
Sir Anthony Main's Case (1596) 5 Co. Rep. 21 .... *24–028*
Sir Lindsay Parkinson & Co v Commissioners of Works and Public Buildings [1949] 2 K.B. 632; [1950] 1 All E.R. 208, CA *23–012*, *23–051*, *29–072*
Sirius International Insurance Co (Publ) v FAI General Insurance Ltd; sub nom. Sirius International Insurance Corp Ltd v FAI General Insurance Co Ltd [2004] UKHL 54; [2004] 1 W.L.R. 3251; [2005] 1 All E.R. 191; [2005] 1 All E.R. (Comm) 117; [2005] 1 Lloyd's Rep. 461; [2005] 1 C.L.C. 451; [2005] Lloyd's Rep. I.R. 294; (2004) 101(48) L.S.G. 25; (2004) 148 S.J.L.B. 1435, HL; reversing [2003] EWCA Civ 470; [2003] 1 W.L.R. 2214; [2004] 1 All E.R. 308; [2003] 1 All E.R. (Comm) 865; [2003] 1 C.L.C. 1124; [2004] Lloyd's Rep. I.R. 47; (2003) 147 S.J.L.B. 477, CA (Civ Div); reversing in part [2002] EWHC 1611 (Ch); [2003] 1 W.L.R. 87; [2002] 2 All E.R. (Comm) 745; (2002) 99(39) L.S.G. 37, Ch D (Companies Ct) *12–050*, *12–057*, *12–118*
Sirius International Insurance Corp v Oriental Assurance Corp [1999] 1 All E.R. (Comm.) 699; [1999] Lloyd's Rep. I.R. 343, QBD (Comm) *6–012*
Siu Yin Kwan v Eastern Insurance Co Ltd [1994] 2 A.C. 199; [1994] 2 W.L.R. 370; [1994] 1 All E.R. 213; [1994] 1 Lloyd's Rep. 616; [1994] C.L.C. 31; (1994) 144 N.L.J. 87; (1994) 138 S.J.L.B. 26, PC (HK) ... *12–114*, *18–019*, *18–051*
Sivanandan v Enfield LBC; sub nom. Enfield LBC v Sivanandan [2005] EWCA Civ 10; (2005) 102(8) L.S.G. 30, CA (Civ Div) *24–013*
Siveyer v Allison [1935] 2 K.B. 403, KBD *16–070*
Skaife v Jackson (1824) 3 B.C. 421 .... *21–058*
Skeate v Beale (1840) 11 A. & E. 983 .... *7–01*, *229–088*, *29–092*
Skidmore v Dartford and Gravesham NHS Trust [2003] UKHL 27; [2003] 3 All E.R. 292; [2003] I.C.R. 721; [2003] I.R.L.R. 445; [2003] Lloyd's Rep. Med. 369; (2003) 73 B.M.L.R. 209; (2003) 100(27) L.S.G. 35; (2003) 153 N.L.J. 881; (2003) 147 S.J.L.B. 624, HL; affirming [2002] EWCA Civ 18; [2002] I.C.R. 403; [2002] Lloyd's Rep. Med. 299; (2003) 69 B.M.L.R. 13; (2002) 99(10) L.S.G. 29; (2002) 146 S.J.L.B. 31, CA (Civ Div); reversing [2001] I.C.R. 911; [2001] Lloyd's Rep. Med. 175, EAT *1–031*
Skinner v Trustee of the Property of Reed (A Bankrupt); sub nom. Skinner v Vick & Partners [1967] Ch. 1194; [1967] 3 W.L.R. 871; [1967] 2 All E.R. 1286; (1967) 111 S.J. 477, Ch D *29–198*
Skipper & Tucker v Holloway [1910] 2 K.B. 635 (Note), CA; reversing [1910] 2 K.B. 630, KBD *19–014*
Skips A/S Nordheim v Syrian Petroleum Co and Petrofina SA; The Varenna [1984] Q.B. 599; [1984] 2 W.L.R. 156; [1983] 3 All E.R. 645; [1983] 2 Lloyd's Rep. 592, CA (Civ Div); affirming [1983] 1 Lloyd's Rep. 416, QBD (Comm) *2–147*, *12–025*, *12–053*, *12–079*
Skipskredittforeningen v Emperor Navigation [1998] 1 Lloyd's Rep. 66; [1997] 2 B.C.L.C. 398; [1997] C.L.C. 1151, QBD (Comm) ..*6–136*, *6–139*, *14–010*, *14–062*, *14–095*, *14–100*, *14–114*
Skrine & Co v Euromoney Publications Plc [2001] EWCA Civ 1479; [2002] E.M.L.R. 15, CA (Civ Div); reversing in part [2002] I.L.Pr. 22; [2001] E.M.L.R. 16; (2000) 97(45) L.S.G. 40; (2000) 144 S.J.L.B. 274, QBD *11–007*
Sky Petroleum v VIP Petroleum [1974] 1 W.L.R. 576; [1974] 1 All E.R. 954; (1973) 118 S.J. 311, Ch D *27–017*
Skyring v Greenwood (1825) 4 B.C. 281 .... *29–029*, 29–177, *29–178*, *29–184*
Slade v Metrodent [1953] 2 Q.B. 112; [1953] 2 W.L.R. 1202; [1953] 2 All E.R. 336; (1953) 97 S.J. 389, QBD *8–025*, *8–029*, *8–043*
Slater v Hoyle & Smith Ltd [1920] 2 K.B. 11, CA *26–089*, *26–117*
Slater v Jones (1873) L.R. 8 Ex. 186 .... *22–008*
Slater v Raw, *The Times*, October 15, 1977, CA (Civ Div) *2–144*, *27–042*
Slavenburg's Bank NV v Intercontinental Natural Resources [1980] 1 W.L.R. 1076; [1980] 1 All E.R. 955; (1980) 124 S.J. 374, QBD *9–046*, *19–065*, *19–066*

Sleafer v Lambeth BC [1960] 1 Q.B. 43; [1959] 3 W.L.R. 485; [1959] 3 All E.R. 378; 57 L.G.R. 212; (1959) 103 S.J. 599, CA *13–016*
Sleap v Newman (1862) 12 C.B. (N.S.) 116 .... *20–008*
Sledmore v Dalby (1996) 72 P. & C.R. 196; [1996] N.P.C. 16, CA (Civ Div) 3–159
Sleigh v Sleigh (1850) 5 Ex. 514 .... *29–109*, *29–115*
Slingsby v District Bank Ltd (Manchester) [1932] 1 K.B. 544; (1931) 41 Ll. L. Rep. 138, CA *25–023*, *25–025*
Slingsby v Westminster Bank Ltd [1931] 1 K.B. 173; [1931] 2 K.B. 583; (1930) 38 Ll. L. Rep. 14, KBD *25–025*
Slingsby's Case (1588) 5 Co.Rep. 186 .... *3–044*
Smackman v General Steam Navigation Co (1908) 98 L.T. 396 .... *14–033*
Small v Smith. *See* Shiell's Trustees v Scottish Property Investment Building Society
Small Sons Ltd v Middlesex Real Estates Ltd [1921] W.N. 245 .... *21–029*, *21–035*
Smallman v Smallman [1972] Fam. 25; [1971] 3 W.L.R. 588; [1971] 3 All E.R. 717; (1971) 115 S.J. 527, CA (Civ Div) *2–155*, *12–028*
Smally v Smally (1700) 1 Eq.Cas.Abr. 283 .... *8–059*
Smeaton Hanscomb & Co v Sassoon I Setty Son & Co (No.1) [1953] 1 W.L.R. 1468; [1953] 2 All E.R. 1471; [1953] 2 Lloyd's Rep. 580; (1953) 97 S.J. 862, QBD *12–021*, *14–004*, *14–020*, *14–027*, *24–041*
Smedvig Ltd v Elf Exploration UK Plc; The Super Scorpio II [1998] 2 Lloyd's Rep. 659, QBD (Comm) *14–015*
Smelter Corp v O'Driscoll [1977] I.R. 305, Sup Ct (Irl) *6–010*
Smidt v Tiden (1873–74) L.R. 9 Q.B. 446, QB *5–071*
Smit International Singapore Pte Ltd v Kurnia Dewi Shipping SA; The Kurnia Dewi [1997] 1 Lloyd's Rep. 552, QBD (Admlty) *2–030*, *2–047*, *2–085*, *2–116*
Smit Tak International Zeesleepen Bergingsbedrijf BV v Selco Salvage [1988] 2 Lloyd's Rep. 398, Ch D *30–376*
Smith Ex p. Brown (No.2), Re (1888) L.R. 20 Q.B.D. 321, CA *29–098*
Smith, Re (1892) 67 L.T. 64 .... *1–092*
Smith v Algar (1830) 1 B.&Ad.603 .... *3–047*
Smith v Anderson (1880) L.R. 15 Ch. D. 247, CA *14–065*
Smith v Baker (1873) L.R. 8 C.P. 350 .... *29–146*
Smith v Bank of Scotland; Mumford v Bank of Scotland, 1997 S.C. (H.L.) 111; 1997 S.L.T. 1061; 1997 S.C.L.R. 765; [1998] Lloyd's Rep. Bank. 62; [1997] 2 F.L.R. 862; (1997) Hous. L.R. 89; [1997] Fam. Law 791; [1997] N.P.C. 94; 1997 G.W.D. 21–1004, HL; reversing 1996 S.L.T. 392; 1995 S.C.L.R. 839; [1996] 1 F.L.R. 344; [1996] Fam. Law 149, IH (1 Div); affirming 1994 S.C. 613; 1994 S.L.T. 1288; 1994 S.C.L.R. 856, OH *7–107*
Smith v Battams (1857) 26 L.J. Ex 232 .... *21–039*
Smith v Betty [1903] 2 K.B. 317, CA *21–061*, *21–063*
Smith v Bromley, 99 E.R. 441; (1760) 2 Doug. K.B. 696, KB *29–043*
Smith v Butler [1900] 1 Q.B. 694, CA 2–152, *12–028*, *29–064*
Smith v Chadwick (1883–84) L.R. 9 App. Cas. 187, HL; affirming (1881–82) L.R. 20 Ch. D. 27, CA *6–032*, *6–036*, *6–037*, *6–047*, *12–067*
Smith v Chalick (William) (1924) 34 C.L.R. 38 .... *7–015*, *7–047*
Smith v Charles Baker & Sons [1891] A.C. 325, HL *1–157*
Smith v Claremont Haynes & Co, *The Times*, September 3, 1991, QBD *18–022*
Smith v Clay (1767) 3 Bro. C.C. 639 .... *28–134*
Smith v Clinton (1908) 99 L.T. 840 .... *16–175*
Smith v Cork and Bandon Railway (1870) I.R. 5 Eq. 65 .... *28–004*
Smith v Cox [1940] 2 K.B. 558, KBD *21–041*, *29–099*
Smith v Croft (No.2) [1988] Ch. 114; [1987] 3 W.L.R. 405; [1987] 3 All E.R. 909; (1987) 3 B.C.C. 207; [1987] B.C.L.C. 206; [1986] P.C.C. 209; [1987] 1 F.T.L.R. 319; (1987) 84 L.S.G. 2449; (1987) 131 S.J. 1038, Ch D *9–020*
Smith v Cuff (1813) 6 M. & S. 160 .... *7–049*, *16–186*
Smith v Doe d. Jersey (1821) 2 Brod. & Bing. 473 .... *12–060*, *12–096*

Smith v Eric S Bush (A Firm); Harris v Wyre Forest DC [1990] 1 A.C. 831; [1989] 2 W.L.R. 790; [1989] 2 All E.R. 514; (1989) 21 H.L.R. 424; 87 L.G.R. 685; [1955–95] P.N.L.R. 467; [1989] 17 E.G. 68; [1989] 18 E.G. 99; (1990) 9 Tr. L.R. 1; (1989) 153 L.G. Rev. 984; (1989) 139 N.L.J. 576; (1989) 133 S.J. 597, HL; affirming [1988] Q.B. 743; [1987] 3 W.L.R. 889; [1987] 3 All E.R. 179; (1987) 19 H.L.R. 287; [1987] 1 E.G.L.R. 157; (1987) 283 E.G. 56; (1987) 84 L.S.G. 3260; (1987) 137 N.L.J. 362; (1987) 131 S.J. 1423, CA (Civ Div) *1–119*, *1–131*, *1–141*, 1–178, *1–186*, 6–029, *6–039*, *6–081*, 6–083, *6–141*, *14–003*, 14–063, *14–087*, 14–092, *18–014*, *18–022*
Smith v Ferrand (1827) 7 B.C. 19 .... *21–075*, *21–077*
Smith v Goodwin (1833) 4 B. Ad. 413 .... *21–094*
Smith v Hamilton [1951] Ch. 174; [1950] 2 All E.R. 928; 66 T.L.R. (Pt. 2) 937; (1950) 94 S.J. 724, Ch D *21–014*
Smith v Hancock [1894] 2 Ch. 377, CA; affirming [1894] 1 Ch. 209, Ch D *16–114*
Smith v Harrison (1857) 26 L.J. Ch. 412 .... *3–023*
Smith v Henniker-Major & Co [2002] EWCA Civ 762; [2003] Ch. 182; [2002] 3 W.L.R. 1848; [2002] B.C.C. 768; [2002] 2 B.C.L.C. 655; (2002) 99(37) L.S.G. 36, CA (Civ Div); affirming [2002] B.C.C. 544, Ch D ... 9–032, *9–041*, *28–118*
Smith v Hodson (1791) 4 T.R. 211 .... *29–146*
Smith v Hughes (1870–71) L.R. 6 Q.B. 597; [1861–73] All E.R. Rep. 632; (1871) 19 W.R. 1059, QB *2–002*, *5–008*, 5–052, *5–067*, *5–071*, 5–076, 5–080, *6–014*, *6–032*
Smith v Hull Glass Co (1852) 11 C.B. 897 .... *9–039*
Smith v Jefferys (1846) 15 M. & W. 561 .... *12–096*
Smith v Johnson (1899) 15 T.L.R. 179 .... *26–078*
Smith v Jones [1954] 1 W.L.R. 1089; [1954] 2 All E.R. 823; (1954) 98 S.J. 540, Ch D *5–130*
Smith v Kay (1859) 7 H.L.C. 750 .... *6–037*, *7–057*, *7–064*, *7–082*
Smith v Land & House Property Corp (1885) L.R. 28 Ch. D. 7, CA *6–008*, *6–009*
Smith v Law Guarantee & Trust Society Ltd [1904] 2 Ch. 569, CA *21–067*
Smith v Lawson (1998) 75 P. & C.R. 466; [1997] E.G. 85 (C.S.); [1997] N.P.C. 87; (1997) 74 P. & C.R. D34, CA (Civ Div) *3–085*, *3–096*, 3–102
Smith v Littlewoods Organisation. *See* Maloco v Littlewoods Organisation Ltd
Smith v Lucas (1880–81) L.R. 18 Ch. D. 531, Ch D *12–043*
Smith v M'Guire (1858) 3 H.N. 554 .... *26–090*
Smith v MacGowan [1938] 3 All E.R. 447; (1938) 159 L.T. 278 .... *4–026*, 4–036
Smith v Mansi [1963] 1 W.L.R. 26; [1962] 3 All E.R. 857; (1962) 106 S.J. 876, CA *2–120*, *4–036*, *12–109*
Smith v Mapleback (1786) 1 T.R. 441 .... *22–006*
Smith v Marrable (1843) 11 M. & W. 5 .... *13–016*
Smith v Mawood (1845) 14 M. & W. 452 .... *16–147*
Smith v Mercer (1867–68) L.R. 3 Ex. 51, Ex Ct *21–079*
Smith v Monteith (1844) 13 M. & W. 427 .... *7–048*, *7–051*
Smith v Moore (1845) 1 C.B. 438 .... *2–043*, *3–062*
Smith v Morgan [1971] 1 W.L.R. 803; [1971] 2 All E.R. 1500; (1971) 22 P. & C.R. 618; (1971) 115 S.J. 288, Ch D *2–127*, *2–128*
Smith v Neale (1857) 2 C.B. (N.S.) 67 .... *4–027*
Smith v Nicolls (1839) 5 Bing. N.C. 208 .... *25–016*
Smith v Osborn (1858) 1 F. & F. 267 .... *20–020*
Smith v Owners of the SS Zigurds [1934] A.C. 209; (1933) 47 Ll. L. Rep. 267, HL; affirming [1933] P. 87; (1933) 45 Ll. L. Rep. 1, CA; reversing [1932] P. 113; (1932) 43 Ll. L. Rep. 387, PDAD *19–069*
Smith v Packhurst (1742) 3 Atk. 135 .... *12–044*, *12–063*, *12–077*
Smith v River Douglas Catchment Board [1949] 2 K.B. 500; [1949] 2 All E.R. 179; 65 T.L.R. 628; (1949) 113 J.P. 388; 47 L.G.R. 627; (1949) 93 S.J. 525, CA *18–019*
Smith v Roche (1859) 6 C.B. (N.S.) 223 .... *16–067*
Smith v Schilling [1928] 1 K.B. 429, CA *26–030*
Smith v Shirley & Baylis (1875) 32 L.T. 234 .... *22–015*
Smith v Sleap (1844) 12 M.W. 585 .... *29–093*

Smith v Smith (1832) 3 B. & Ad. 728 .... *12–058*, *12–130*
Smith v South Wales Switchgear Co. *See* Smith v UMB Chrysler (Scotland) Ltd
Smith v Spurling Motor Bodies (1961) 105 S.J. 967, CA *12–007*
Smith v Surman (1829) 9 B. & C. 561 .... *4–018*
Smith v Taylor [1966] 2 Lloyd's Rep. 231; 116 N.L.J. 1518, QBD *12–017*
Smith v Thompson (1849) 8 C.B. 44 .... *12–118*
Smith v UMB Chrysler (Scotland) Ltd; sub nom. Smith v South Wales Switchgear Co Ltd [1978] 1 W.L.R. 165; [1978] 1 All E.R. 18; 1978 S.C. (H.L.) 1; 1978 S.L.T. 21; 8 B.L.R. 1; (1978) 122 S.J. 61, HL; reversing 1977 S.C. 93; 1977 S.L.T. (Notes) 37, IH (2 Div); affirming 1976 S.L.T. (Notes) 42, OH *14–010*, *14–011*, *14–012*, *14–013*, *14–015*
Smith v Webster (1876) L.R. 3 Ch. D. 49, CA *4–036*
Smith v Wheatcroft (1878) L.R. 9 Ch. D. 223, Ch D *5–089*
Smith v White (1865–66) L.R. 1 Eq. 626, Ct of Chancery *16–069*
Smith v White Knight Laundry Ltd [2001] EWCA Civ 660; [2002] 1 W.L.R. 616; [2001] 3 All E.R. 862; [2001] C.P. Rep. 88; [2003] B.C.C. 319; [2001] 2 B.C.L.C. 206; [2001] P.I.Q.R. P30, CA (Civ Div) *28–070*
Smith v Wilson (1807) 8 East 437 .... *24–032*, *24–037*
Smith-Bird v Blower [1939] 2 All E.R. 406, Ch D *4–028*
Smith Glaziers (Dunfermline) Ltd v Customs and Excise Commissioners. *See* CR Smith Glaziers (Dunfermline) Ltd v Customs and Excise Commissioners
Smith Hogg & Co Ltd v Louis Bamberger & Sons [1929] 1 K.B. 150; (1928) 31 Ll. L. Rep. 203, CA; reversing in part (1928) 30 Ll. L. Rep. 148, KBD *12–058*, *12–128*
Smith Kline & French Laboratories Ltd v Long [1989] 1 W.L.R. 1; [1988] 3 All E.R. 887; (1988) 132 S.J. 1553, CA (Civ Div) *6–049*, *6–052*
Smith New Court Securities Ltd v Citibank NA; sub nom. Smith New Court Securities Ltd v Scrimgeour Vickers (Asset Management) Ltd [1997] A.C. 254; [1996] 3 W.L.R. 1051; [1996] 4 All E.R. 769; [1997] 1 B.C.L.C. 350; [1996] C.L.C. 1958; (1996) 93(46) L.S.G. 28; (1996) 146 N.L.J. 1722; (1997) 141 S.J.L.B. 5, HL; reversing [1994] 1 W.L.R. 1271; [1994] 4 All E.R. 225; [1994] 2 B.C.L.C. 212; [1994] C.L.C. 203; (1994) 91(15) L.S.G. 35; (1994) 91(22) L.S.G. 32; (1994) 138 S.J.L.B. 77, CA (Civ Div); reversing [1992] B.C.L.C. 1104, Ch D *1–122*, *6–035*, 6–051, *6–052*, *6–053*, *6–054*, 6–055, 6–056, 6–057, 6–058, 6–059, 6–070, *6–100*, *6–116*, *26–079*
Smith New Court Securities v Scrimgeour Vickers (Asset Management). *See* Smith New Court Securities Ltd v Citibank NA
Smithies v National Association of Operative Plasterers [1909] 1 K.B. 310, CA *18–145*
SmithKline Beecham Plc v Apotex Europe Ltd [2006] EWCA Civ 658; [2007] Ch. 71; [2006] 3 W.L.R. 1146; [2006] 4 All E.R. 1078; [2006] C.P. Rep. 39; [2007] F.S.R. 6; (2006) 29(10) I.P.D. 29072; (2006) 103(23) L.S.G. 32; (2006) 156 N.L.J. 952, CA (Civ Div) *3–107*, *3–113*, *18–049*, *18–058*, *18–059*, 18–067
Smith's Trusts, Re (1890) 25 L.R. Ir. 439 .... *8–042*
Smyth, Re [1970] Argus L.R. 919 .... *19–037*
Snamprogetti Ltd v Phillips Petroleum Co (UK) Ltd. *See* Phillips Petroleum Co (UK) Ltd v Snamprogetti
Sneezum Ex p. Davis, Re (1876) L.R. 3 Ch. D. 463, CA *20–032*
Snell v Unity Finance Co Ltd [1964] 2 Q.B. 203; [1963] 3 W.L.R. 559; [1963] 3 All E.R. 50; (1963) 107 S.J. 533, CA *16–205*
Snelling v John G Snelling Ltd [1973] Q.B. 87; [1972] 2 W.L.R. 588; [1972] 1 All E.R. 79; (1972) 116 S.J. 217, QBD ... *2–125*, *2–126*, *2–127*, *2–128*, *2–183*, *3–125*, *3–126*, *14–051*, 18–071
Snepp v United States (1980) 444 U.S. 507 .... *26–021*
Sneyd Ex p. Fewings, Re (1884) L.R. 25 Ch. D. 338, CA *25–009*
Snowball, Ex p. *See* Douglas Ex p. Snowball, Re

Snowdon, Re; sub nom. Ex p. Snowdon, Re (1881) L.R. 17 Ch. D. 44, CA *17–028, 28–048*
Soames v Edge (1860) Johns. 669 .... *27–081*
Soames, Re (1897) 13 T.L.R. 439 3–012
Sociedad Financiera de Bienes Raices SA v Agrimpex Hungarian Trading Co for Agricultural Products; The Aello; sub nom. Agrimpex Hungarian Trading Co for Agricultural Products v Sociedad Financiera de Bienes Raices SA [1961] A.C. 135; [1960] 3 W.L.R. 145; [1960] 2 All E.R. 578; [1960] 1 Lloyd's Rep. 623; (1960) 104 S.J. 543, HL; affirming [1958] 2 Q.B. 385; [1958] 3 W.L.R. 152; [1958] 2 All E.R. 695; [1958] 2 Lloyd's Rep. 65; (1958) 102 S.J. 527, CA; affirming [1957] 1 W.L.R. 1228; [1957] 3 All E.R. 626; [1957] 2 Lloyd's Rep. 423; (1957) 101 S.J. 975, QBD *13–011*
Sociedad Iberica de Molturacion SA v Tradax Export SA [1978] 2 Lloyd's Rep. 545, QBD (Comm) *14–141*
Societa Esplosivi Industriali SpA v Ordnance Technologies (UK) Ltd (formerly SEI (UK) Ltd) [2004] EWHC 48 (Ch); [2004] 1 All E.R. (Comm) 619, Ch D *13–026, 16–084*
Societe Anonyme Maritime et Commerciale of Geneva v Anglo-Iranian Oil Co Ltd [1954] 1 W.L.R. 492; [1954] 1 All E.R. 529; [1954] 1 Lloyd's Rep. 1; (1954) 98 S.J. 178, CA; affirming [1953] 1 W.L.R. 1379; [1953] 2 All E.R. 1325; [1953] 2 Lloyd's Rep. 466; (1953) 97 S.J. 797, QBD *12–044*
Societe Commerciale de Reassurance v Eras International Ltd (formerly Eras (UK)); sub nom. Eras EIL Actions, Re [1992] 2 All E.R. 82 (Note); [1992] 1 Lloyd's Rep. 570, CA (Civ Div) *18–027, 28–010, 28–033*
Societe Cooperative Suisse des Cereales et Matieres Fourrageres v La Plata Cereal Co SA (1947) 80 Ll. L. Rep. 530, KBD *12–078, 23–047, 30–364*
Société d'Avances Commerciales (London) Ltd v A Besse & Co (London) Ltd [1952] 1 Lloyd's Rep. 242; [1952] 1 T.L.R. 644, QBD *12–070, 13–013*
Societe des Hotels le Touquet Paris-Plage v Cummings; sub nom. Societe des Hotels le Touquet Paris-Plage v Cumming [1922] 1 K.B. 451, CA *21–086, 30–370*
Societe des Industries Metallurgiques SA v Bronx Engineering Co [1975] 1 Lloyd's Rep. 465, CA (Civ Div) *27–008, 27–014*
Société Dunkerquoise de Remorquage et de Sauvetage v Owners of the ship Atlantic Scout; The Atlantic Scout [1950] P. 266; (1950) 84 Ll. L. Rep. 22; (1950) 94 S.J. 438, PDAD *11–031, 16–163*
Société Eram Shipping Co Ltd v Compagnie Internationale de Navigation [2003] UKHL 30; [2004] 1 A.C. 260; [2003] 3 W.L.R. 21; [2003] 3 All E.R. 465; [2003] 2 All E.R. (Comm) 65; [2003] 2 Lloyd's Rep. 405; [2003] 1 C.L.C. 1163; [2003] I.L.Pr. 36; (2003) 100(28) L.S.G. 31; (2003) 153 N.L.J. 948; (2003) 147 S.J.L.B. 749, HL *21–051*
Societe Francaise Bunge SA v Belcan NV; The Federal Huron [1985] 3 All E.R. 378; [1985] 2 Lloyd's Rep. 189; [1985] Fin. L.R. 282, QBD (Comm) *30–373, 30–376*
Societe Franco-Tunisienne d'Armement-Tunis v Sidermar SpA [1961] 2 Q.B. 278; [1960] 3 W.L.R. 701; [1960] 2 All E.R. 529; [1960] 1 Lloyd's Rep. 594; (1960) 104 S.J. 850, QBD (Comm) *23–098, 29–076*
Societe Generale de Paris v Dreyfus Bros (1888) L.R. 37 Ch. D. 215, CA *25–018*
Société Italo-Belge Pour le Commerce et L'Industrie SA (Antwerp) v Palm and Vegetable Oils (Malaysia) Sdn Bhd; The Post Chaser [1982] 1 All E.R. 19; [1981] 2 Lloyd's Rep. 695; [1981] Com. L.R. 249, QBD (Comm) ... *3–090, 3–091, 3–094, 3–095, 3–096, 3–103, 12–037, 21–013, 22–044, 24–008*
Societe Nouvelle des Papeteries de l'Aa SA v BV Machinefabrik BOA [1992] N.J. 750 ....*30–077, 30–090, 30–188*
Society of Lloyd's v Robinson. *See* Napier (Lord) and Ettrick v RF Kershaw Ltd (No.2)
Society of Lloyd's v Fraser [1998] C.L.C. 1630 ....*30–003, 30–305, 30–310, 30–364, 30–367*
Society of Lloyd's v Khan; sub nom. Lloyd's of London v Khan [1999] 1 F.L.R. 246; [1998] 3 F.C.R. 93; [1999] Fam. Law 92; (1998) 162 J.P.N. 321, QBD (Comm) *6–117, 6–129, 7–085, 7–113*

Society of Lloyd's v Lyon, unreported, August 11, 1997 .... *6–119*, *6–129*
Society of Lloyd's v Twinn (Geoffrey George); Society of Lloyd's v Twinn (Gail Sally) (2000) 97(15) L.S.G. 40, CA (Civ Div) *2–032*
Society of Lloyd's v Wilkinson (No.2) [1997] C.L.C. 1012; [1997] 6 Re. L.R. 214, QBD (Comm) *6–136*
Society of Medical Officers of Health v Hope (Valuation Officer) [1960] A.C. 551; [1960] 2 W.L.R. 404; [1960] 1 All E.R. 317; (1960) 124 J.P. 128; 58 L.G.R. 165; 5 R.R.C. 388; 53 R. & I.T. 102; (1960) 104 S.J. 147, HL *25–012*
Socimer International Bank Ltd v Standard Bank London Ltd [2008] EWCA Civ 116; [2008] 1 Lloyd's Rep. 558 .... *2–131*, *13–009*, *13–026*
Socony Mobil Oil Co Inc v West of England Ship Owners Mutual Insurance Association (London) Ltd; The Padre Island (No.1); Mobil Oil Co Inc v West of England Ship Owners Mutual Insurance Association (London) Ltd [1984] 2 Lloyd's Rep. 408, QBD (Comm) *18–131*
Soden v British & Commonwealth Holdings Plc (In Administration) [1998] A.C. 298; [1997] 3 W.L.R. 840; [1997] 4 All E.R. 353; [1997] B.C.C. 952; [1997] 2 B.C.L.C. 501; (1997) 94(41) L.S.G. 28; (1997) 147 N.L.J. 1546, HL; affirming [1997] 2 W.L.R. 206; [1996] 3 All E.R. 951; [1997] B.C.C. 249; [1996] 2 B.C.L.C. 207; (1996) 140 S.J.L.B. 141, CA (Civ Div); affirming [1995] B.C.C. 531; [1995] 1 B.C.L.C. 686, Ch D *9–060*, *8–010*, *18–113*
Sole v WJ Hallt Ltd [1973] Q.B. 574; [1973] 2 W.L.R. 171; [1973] 1 All E.R. 1032; (1972) 14 K.I.R. 116; (1972) 117 S.J. 110, QBD *26–037*
Soleh Boneh International v Government of the Republic of Uganda and National Housing Corp [1993] 2 Lloyd's Rep. 208; The Times, March 18, 1993, CA *11–006*
Soleimany v Soleimany [1999] Q.B. 785; [1998] 3 W.L.R. 811; [1999] 3 All E.R. 847; [1998] C.L.C. 779; The Times, March 4, 1998, CA *16–031*, *30–355*, *30–367*
Solholt, The. *See* Sotiros Shipping Inc v Sameiet Solholt; The Solholt
Solicitor Ex p. Law Society, Re [1912] 1 K.B. 302, KBD *16–055*
Solicitor, Re a (1913) 29 T.LR. 354 .... *16–055*
Solicitor's Arbitration, Re [1962] 1 W.L.R. 353; 106 S.J. 221; [1962] 1 All E.R. 772 .... *12–061*
Solle v Butcher [1950] 1 K.B. 671; 66 T.L.R. (Pt.1) 448; [1949] 2 All E.R. 1107 ..... *1–083*, 5–34, 5–040, *5–054*, 5–057, 5–058, 5–059, 5–060, 5–061, *5–099*, *6–013*
Solley v Forbes (1820) 2 Brod. & B 28 .... *1–031*, *12–081*, *17–018*, *22–005*
Solly v Hinde (1834) 2 Cr. & M. 516 .... *12–108*
Solon, The. *See* Cero Navigation Corp v Jean Lion & Cie
Soltykoff Ex p. Margrett, Re [1891] 1 Q.B. 413, CA *8–020*
Somers v Erskine [1944] Ir. R. 368 .... *28–033*
Somerset v Cookson (1735) 3 P. Wms. 390 .... *27–014*
Somerset, Re; sub nom. Somerset v Earl Poulett [1894] 1 Ch. 231, CA *28–057*
Somes (Joseph) v Director of British Empire Shipping Co, 11 E.R. 459; (1860) 8 H.L. Cas. 338, HL *29–088*, *29–090*
Sommerfelds v Freeman [1967] 1 W.L.R. 489; [1967] 2 All E.R. 143; 44 T.C. 43; (1966) 45 A.T.C. 457; [1966] T.R. 381; (1966) 110 S.J. 949, Ch D *26–163*
Sommerville v National Coal Board, 1963 S.C. 666; 1963 S.L.T. 334, IH (1 Div); reversing, 1963 S.L.T. (Notes) 46, OH *2–101*
Sonat Offshore SA v Amerada Hess Development and Texaco (Britain) [1988] 1 Lloyd's Rep. 145; 39 B.L.R. 1; [1987] 2 F.T.L.R. 220, CA (Civ Div) *14–010*, *14–011*, *14–013*, *14–015*, *14–138*, *14–148*, *18–023*
Sondes (Lord) v Fletcher (1822) 5 B. Ald. 835 .... *26–019*
Sonicare International Ltd v East Anglia Freight Terminal Ltd; Sonicare International Ltd v Neptune Orient Lines Ltd [1997] 2 Lloyd's Rep. 48, CC (Central London) *14–054*, *14–055*, 14–095, *18–022*
Sookraj v Samaroo [2004] UKPC 50; (2004) 148 S.J.L.B. 1244; [2005] 1 P. & C.R. DG11, PC (Trin) *22–028*, *24–013*
Soon Hua Seng Co Ltd v Glencore Grain Ltd, LTA 96/5656/B, CA (Civ Div); affirming [1996] 1 Lloyd's Rep. 398; [1996] C.L.C. 729, QBD (Comm) ... *12–036*

Sorrell v Finch [1977] A.C. 728; [1976] 2 W.L.R. 833; [1976] 2 All E.R. 371; 19 Man. Law 4; (1976) 120 S.J. 353, HL; reversing [1975] J.P.L. 474; 18 Man. Law 45; (1975) 119 S.J. 475, CA (Civ Div) *29–198*
Sorrell v Paget [1950] 1 K.B. 252; [1949] 2 All E.R. 609; 65 T.L.R. 595; (1949) 93 S.J. 631, CA *29–115*, *29–136*
Sorrell v Smith [1925] A.C. 700, HL *29–088*
Sorsbie v Park (1843) 12 M. & W.146 .... *3–042*
Sotiros Shipping Inc v Sameiet Solholt; The Solholt [1983] 1 Lloyd's Rep. 605; [1983] Com. L.R. 114; (1983) 127 S.J. 305, CA (Civ Div) .. *26–020*, *26–103*, *26–113*, *26–121*, *26–141*
Sottomayor (otherwise De Barros) v De Barros (No.1) (1877–78) L.R. 3 P.D. 1; (1877) 26 W.R. 455, CA *30–324*
Sottomayor (otherwise De Barros) v De Barros (No.2) (1879–80) L.R. 5 P.D. 94; [1874–80] All E.R. Rep. 97, PDAD *30–324*
Soulsbury v Soulsbury [2007] EWCA Civ 969; [2008] 2 W.L.R. 834; [2008] 1 F.L.R. 90; [2007] 3 F.C.R. 811; [2007] W.T.L.R. 1841; [2008] Fam. Law 13, CA (Civ Div) 2–080, *2–148*, *2–149*, *2–155*
Source Ltd v TUV Rheinland Holding AG [1998] Q.B. 54; [1997] 3 W.L.R. 365; [1997] I.L.Pr. 514; [1998] I.L.Pr. 432, CA (Civ Div) 1–168, *30–287*
South African Breweries Ltd v King [1900] 1 Ch. 273, CA *30–011*, *30–120*
South African Territories Ltd v Wallington [1898] A.C. 309, HL *26–099*, *27–012*
South Australia Asset Management Corp v York Montague Ltd; United Bank of Kuwait Plc v Prudential Property Services Ltd; Nykredit Mortgage Bank Plc v Edward Erdman Group Ltd [1997] A.C. 191; [1996] 3 W.L.R. 87; [1996] 3 All E.R. 365; [1996] 5 Bank. L.R. 211; [1996] C.L.C. 1179; 80 B.L.R. 1; 50 Con. L.R. 153; [1996] P.N.L.R. 455; [1996] 2 E.G.L.R. 93; [1996] 27 E.G. 125; [1996] E.G. 107 (C.S.); (1996) 93(32) L.S.G. 33; (1996) 146 N.L.J. 956; (1996) 140 S.J.L.B. 156; [1996] N.P.C. 100, HL; affirming [1995] E.G. 71 (C.S.); [1995] N.P.C. 66, QBD (Comm) *1–164*, *1–165*, 6–057, 6–059, 6–089, *6–101*, *13–002*, *26–059*, *26–061*, 26–079, *26–093*, 26–094, **26–096**, *26–097*, *26–100B*, 26–100D, *26–100E*, *26–100F*, *26–120*, *26–184*, *28–034*
South Australia Cold Stores Ltd v Electricity Trust of South Australia (1957) 98 C.L.R. 65 .... *29–188*
South Bedfordshire Electrical Finance Ltd v Bryant [1938] 3 All E.R. 580 .... *25–008*
South Buckinghamshire DC v Flanagan; sub nom. Flanagan v South Bucks DC [2002] EWCA Civ 690; [2002] 1 W.L.R. 2601; [2002] 3 P.L.R. 47; [2002] J.P.L. 1465; (2002) 99(25) L.S.G. 35; (2002) 146 S.J.L.B. 136; [2002] N.P.C. 71, CA (Civ Div); affirming [2001] 4 P.L.R. 110; (2001) 98(30) L.S.G. 40, QBD *10–043*
South Caribbean Trading Ltd v Trafigura Beheer BV [2004] EWHC 2676; [2005] 1 Lloyd's Rep. 128, QBD (Comm) *3–066*, *3–069*, *3–076*, *3–079*, *3–095*, *7–019*, *24–013*, *24–014*
South East Thames RHA v YJ Lovell (London) Ltd, 32 B.L.R. 127; 9 Con. L.R. 36, QBD *19–050*
South East Windscreens Ltd v Jamshidi [2005] EWHC 3078; [2005] All ER (D) 317, QBD *5–071*
South Eastern Railway Co v Cooper [1924] 1 Ch. 211, CA *10–027*, *10–030*
South India Shipping Corp v Export-Import Bank of Korea [1985] 1 W.L.R. 585; [1985] 2 All E.R. 219; [1985] 1 Lloyd's Rep. 413; (1985) 1 B.C.C. 99350; [1985] P.C.C. 125; [1985] Fin. L.R. 106; (1985) 82 L.S.G. 1005; (1985) 129 S.J. 268, CA (Civ Div) *30–081*
South London Greyhound Racecourses Ltd v Wake [1931] 1 Ch. 496, Ch D *9–041*, *9–042*, *9–045*
South of Scotland Electricity Board v British Oxygen Co Ltd. *See* British Oxygen Co Ltd v South of Scotland Electricity Board (No.2)
South Staffordshire Tramways Co Ltd v Sickness & Accident Assurance Association Ltd [1891] 1 Q.B. 402, CA *12–093*, *21–026*
South Tyneside MBC v Svenska International Plc [1995] 1 All E.R. 545, QBD *29–180*

South Wales Miners Federation v Glamorgan Coal Co Ltd; sub nom. Glamorgan Coal Co Ltd v South Wales Miners Federation [1905] A.C. 239, HL; affirming [1903] 2 K.B. 545, CA; reversing [1903] 1 K.B. 118, KBD *18–145*
South West Trains Ltd v Wightman [1997] O.P.L.R. 249, Ch D *2–153*
South West Water Authority v Palmer (1982) 263 E.G. 438 .... *2–159*
South West Water Services Ltd v International Computers Ltd [1999] B.L.R. 420; [1998–99] Info. T.L.R. 154; [1999–2000] Info. T.L.R. 1; [1999] I.T.C.L.R. 439; [2001] Lloyd's Rep. P.N. 353; [1999] Masons C.L.R. 400, QBD (TCC) *12–104*, *14–063*, *14–072*
South Western General Property Co v Marton (1982) 263 E.G. 1090; (1983) 2 Tr. L. 14, QBD *6–139*, *14–092*, *27–058*
South Western Mineral Water Co Ltd v Ashmore [1967] 1 W.L.R. 1110; [1967] 2 All E.R. 953; (1967) 111 S.J. 453, Ch D *9–038*, *16–179*, 16–201
Southampton Container Terminals Ltd v Hansa Schiffahrts GmbH; The Maersk Colombo; sub nom. Southampton Container Terminals Ltd v Schiffahrtsgesellschaft "Hansa Australia" MGH & Co [2001] EWCA Civ 717; [2001] 2 Lloyd's Rep. 275; (2001) 98(24) L.S.G. 43; (2001) 145 S.J.L.B. 149, CA (Civ Div) *26–017*
Southampton v Brown (1827) 6 B. & C. 718 .... *18–122*
Southend on Sea Corp v Hodgson (Wickford) [1962] 1 Q.B. 416; [1961] 2 W.L.R. 806; [1961] 2 All E.R. 46; (1961) 125 J.P. 348; 59 L.G.R. 193; (1961) 12 P. & C.R. 165; (1961) 105 S.J. 181, DC 10–042
Southern British National Trust v Pither (1937) 57 C.L.R. 89 .... *19–072*
Southern Foundries (1926) Ltd v Shirlaw [1940] A.C. 701; [1940] 2 All E.R. 445, HL; affirming [1939] 2 K.B. 206; [1939] 2 All E.R. 113, CA *9–058*, *13–007*, *13–012*
Southern Industrial Trust v Brooke House Motors (t/a Starnes Motors) (1968) 112 S.J. 798, CA (Civ Div) *16–176*
Southern Portland Cement v Cooper (Rodney John) (An Infant by his next friend Peter Alphonsus Cooper) [1974] A.C. 623; [1974] 2 W.L.R. 152; [1974] 1 All E.R. 87; (1974) 118 S.J. 99, PC (Aus) *26–058*
Southern Water Authority v Carey [1985] 2 All E.R. 1077, QBD *1–176*, *14–047*, *14–049*, *14–050*, *14–056*, *18–019*, *18–030*, *18–085*, *18–125*
Southern Water Authority v Lewis and Duvivier (No.1); sub nom. Southern Water Authority v Duvivier, 27 B.L.R. 111; (1984) 1 Const. L.J. 70; [1984] C.I.L.L. 90, QBD *14–056*
Southerton v Whitlock (1762) 2 Str. 690 .... *8–044*
Southland Frozen Meat & Produce Export Co Ltd v Nelson Bros Ltd [1898] A.C. 442, PC (NZ) *12–057*
Southwark LBC v Logan (1997) 29 H.L.R. 40; (1996) 8 Admin. L.R. 315; [1995] E.G. 165 (C.S.); [1995] N.P.C. 166, CA (Civ Div) *2–113*, *3–029*, *3–095*
Southway Group Ltd v Wolff, 57 B.L.R. 33; 28 Con. L.R. 109; [1991] E.G. 82 (C.S.), CA (Civ Div) *19–082*
Southwell v Bowditch (1875–76) L.R. 1 C.P.D. 374, CA; reversing (1875–76) L.R. 1 C.P.D. 100, CPD *12–057*
Sovereign Finance Ltd v Silver Crest Furniture Ltd (1997) 16 Tr. L.R. 370; [1997] C.C.L.R. 76, QBD *14–095*
Sovfracht (V/O) v Van Udens Scheepvaart en Agentuur Maatschappij (NV Gebr); sub nom. NV Gerb Van Udens Scheepvaart en Agentuur Maatschappij v V/O Sovfracht [1943] A.C. 203; (1942) 74 Ll. L. Rep. 59; 1943 A.M.C. 445, HL; reversing [1942] 1 K.B. 222; (1941) 71 Ll. L. Rep. 61, CA *11–024*, *11–025*, *11–026*, *11–027*, *11–028*, *11–029*
Soward v Palmer (1818) 8 Taunt. 277 .... *21–079*
Sowler v Potter [1940] 1 K.B. 271, KBD *5–099*
Sowman v Samuel (David) Trust Ltd (In Liquidation) [1978] 1 W.L.R. 22; [1978] 1 All E.R. 616; (1978) 36 P. & C.R. 123; (1977) 121 S.J. 757, Ch D *9–051*
Space Investments Ltd v Canadian Imperial Bank of Commerce Trust Co (Bahamas) Ltd [1986] 1 W.L.R. 1072; [1986] 3 All E.R. 75; (1986) 2 B.C.C. 99302; (1986) 83 L.S.G. 2567; (1986) 130 S.J. 612, PC (Bah) *29–164*
Spafax (1965) v Dommett (1972) 116 S.J. 711, CA (Civ Div) *16–108*, *16–110*

Spain v Arnott (1817) 2 Stark. M.P.C. 256 .... *21–030*
Spalding v Crocker (1897) 2 Com. Cas. 189 .... *5–133*
Spalding v Tarmac Civil Engineering Ltd. *See* Arthur White (Contractors) Ltd v Tarmac Civil Engineering Ltd
Spanish Government v North of England SS (1938) 54 T.L.R. 852 .... *7–012*
Sparenburgh v Bannatyne (1797) 1 Bos. & P. 163 .... *11–027*
Sparham-Souter v Town & Country Developments (Essex) Ltd [1976] Q.B. 858; [1976] 2 W.L.R. 493; [1976] 2 All E.R. 65; 3 B.L.R. 70; 74 L.G.R. 355; (1976) 241 E.G. 309; (1976) 120 S.J. 216, CA (Civ Div) *1–124*
Spartali v Benecke (1850) 10 C.B. 212 .... *12–128*
Spears v Hartly (1800) 3 Esp. 81 .... *28–133*
Speciality Shops Ltd v Yorkshire & Metropolitan Estates Ltd [2002] EWHC 2969; [2003] 2 P. & C.R. 31, Ch D *2–127*
Spector v Ageda [1973] Ch. 30; [1971] 3 W.L.R. 498; [1971] 3 All E.R. 417; (1971) 22 P. & C.R. 1002; (1971) 115 S.J. 426, Ch D 16–165, *16–194*
Spectra International Plc v Hayesoak Ltd [1998] 1 Lloyd's Rep. 162, CA (Civ Div); reversing [1997] 1 Lloyd's Rep. 153, CC (Central London) *14–054*, *18–022*
Spectra International Plc v Tiscali UK Ltd (formerly World Online UK Ltd) [2002] EWHC 2084; [2002] Masons C.L.R. 62, QBD (Comm) *2–112*, *2–152*
Spectrum Plus Ltd (In Liquidation), Re; sub nom. National Westminster Bank Plc v Spectrum Plus Ltd (In Creditors Voluntary Liquidation) [2005] UKHL 41; [2005] 2 A.C. 680; [2005] 3 W.L.R. 58; [2005] 4 All E.R. 209; [2005] 2 Lloyd's Rep. 275; [2005] B.C.C. 694; [2005] 2 B.C.L.C. 269; (2005) 155 N.L.J. 1045, HL *29–047*
Speed Seal Products Ltd v Paddington [1985] 1 W.L.R. 1327; [1986] 1 All E.R. 91; [1986] F.S.R. 309; (1985) 135 N.L.J. 935, CA (Civ Div); reversing in part [1984] F.S.R. 77, Ch D *16–107*
Speedlink Vanguard, The and European Gateway, The [1987] Q.B. 206; [1986] 3 W.L.R. 756; [1986] 3 All E.R. 554; [1986] 2 Lloyd's Rep. 265; (1986) 83 L.S.G. 3253; (1986) 130 S.J. 748, QBD (Admlty) *25–012*, *25–013*
Spellman v Spellman [1961] 1 W.L.R. 921; [1961] 2 All E.R. 498; (1961) 105 S.J. 405, CA *2–169*, *19–025*, *19–046*
Spenborough Urban DC's Agreement, Re; sub nom. Stenborough Corp v Cooke Sons & Co [1968] Ch. 139; [1967] 2 W.L.R. 1403; [1967] 1 All E.R. 959; 56 L.G.R. 300; (1967) 111 S.J. 253, Ch D *13–027*, *22–054*
Spence v Chadwick (1847) 10 Q.B. 5 .... *14–146*
Spence v Crawford [1939] 3 All E.R. 271; 1939 S.C. (H.L.) 52; 1939 S.L.T. 305, HL *6–109*, *6–117*
Spence v Shell UK (1980) 256 E.G. 55, CA (Civ Div) *3–089*, *3–090*, *3–103*
Spence v Union Marine Insurance Co Ltd (1867–68) L.R. 3 C.P. 427, CCP *29–052*
Spencer v Harding (1869–70) L.R. 5 C.P. 561, CCP *2–009*, *2–022*
Spencer v Hemmerde [1922] 2 A.C. 507, HL *28–092*, *28–095*
Spencer v Marchington [1988] I.R.L.R. 392, Ch D *16–113*
Spencer v Parry (1835) 3 A.E. 331 .... *29–114*
Spettabile Consorzio Veneziano di Armamento e Navigazione v Northumberland Shipbuilding Co (1919) 121 L.T. 628 .... *24–019*
Sphinx Export Co Ltd v Specialist Shippers Ltd [1954] 1 Lloyd's Rep. 407, QBD *16–206*
Spice Girls Ltd v Aprilia World Service BV; sub nom. Spice Girls Ltd v Aprilla World Service BV [2002] EWCA Civ 15; [2002] E.M.L.R. 27; (2002) 25(4) I.P.D. 25024, CA (Civ Div); reversing in part [2000] E.M.L.R. 478, Ch D ...6–011, *6–014*, *6–015*
Spicer v Cooper (1841) 1 Q.B. 424 .... *12–132*
Spicer v Martin; sub nom. Martin v Spicer (1889) L.R. 14 App. Cas. 12, HL; affirming (1887) L.R. 34 Ch. D. 1, CA; affirming (1886) L.R. 32 Ch. D. 592, Ch D *12–004*
Spidad Holding v Popovic (1995) 19 A.C.S.R. 108 .... *9–050*

Spiers v Hunt [1908] 1 K.B. 720, KBD *16–070*
Spiliada Maritime Corp v Louis Dreyfus Corp [1983] Com. L.R. 268; (1983) 133 N.L.J. 1102 .... *26–048*
Spiller v Paris Skating Rink Co (1877–78) L.R. 7 Ch. D. 368, Ch D *9–015*
Spink, Re (1913) 108 L.T. 572 .... *20–032*
Spink (Bournemouth) Ltd v Spink [1936] Ch. 544, Ch D *16–203*
Spinney's (1948) Ltd v Royal Insurance Co Ltd [1980] 1 Lloyd's Rep. 406, QBD (Comm) *14–146*
Spiro v Glencrown Properties Ltd [1991] Ch. 537; [1991] 2 W.L.R. 931; [1991] 1 All E.R. 600; (1991) 62 P. & C.R. 402; [1991] 02 E.G. 167; [1990] E.G. 148 (C.S.); (1991) 141 N.L.J. 124; (1990) 134 S.J. 1479, Ch D *3–172*, 4–058
Spiro v Lintern [1973] 1 W.L.R. 1002; [1973] 3 All E.R. 319; (1973) 117 S.J. 584, CA (Civ Div) 2–073
Spiros C, The. *See* Tradigrain SA v King Diamond Marine Ltd
Spoor v Green (1873–74) L.R. 9 Ex. 99, Ex Ct *28–035*
Sporle v Whayman (1855) 20 Beav. 607 .... *27–008*
Sport International Bussum BV v Inter-Footwear [1984] 1 W.L.R. 776; [1984] 2 All E.R. 321; (1984) 81 L.S.G. 1992; (1984) 134 N.L.J. 568; (1984) 128 S.J. 383, HL *21–013*, *22–048*, *26–148*, *29–061*
Spottiswoode's Case (1855) 6 De G.M.G. 345 .... *29–009*, *29–122*, *29–126*
Spragg v Hammond (1820) 2 Brod. B. 59 .... *29–111*
Sprague v Booth [1909] A.C. 576, PC (Can) *13–011*, *21–013*
Spriggs v Sotheby Parke Bernet & Co [1986] 1 Lloyd's Rep. 487; [1986] 1 E.G.L.R. 13; (1986) 278 E.G. 969, CA (Civ Div) *14–011*
Spring v Guardian Assurance Plc [1995] 2 A.C. 296; [1994] 3 W.L.R. 354; [1994] 3 All E.R. 129; [1994] C.L.C. 766; [1994] I.C.R. 596; [1994] I.R.L.R. 460; (1994) 91(40) L.S.G. 36; (1994) 144 N.L.J. 971; (1994) 138 S.J.L.B. 183, HL; reversing [1993] 2 All E.R. 273; [1993] I.C.R. 412; [1993] I.R.L.R. 122; (1993) 12 Tr. L.R. 33; (1993) 143 N.L.J. 365; (1993) 137 S.J.L.B. 47, CA (Civ Div); reversing [1992] I.R.L.R. 173; (1992) 11 Tr. L.R. 100, QBD *1–119*, *1–141*, *1–179*, *13–003*, *26–045*
Spring v National Amalgamated Stevedores and Dockers Society (No.2) [1956] 1 W.L.R. 585; [1956] 2 All E.R. 221; [1956] 1 Lloyd's Rep. 331; (1956) 100 S.J. 401, Chancery Ct of Lancaster *13–007*
Sprye v Porter (1856) 7 E. & B. 58 .... *16–065*
Spurrier v La Cloche [1902] A.C. 446, PC (Jer) *30–005*, *30–010*, *30–012*
Sri Lanka Omnibus Co v Perera [1952] A.C. 76; [1951] 2 T.L.R. 1184, PC (Cey) *26–100*, *27–011*
Stabilad Ltd v Stephens & Carter Ltd (No.2) [1999] 2 All E.R. (Comm) 651, CA (Civ Div) *2–139*, *2–154*, *2–175*, *2–176*, *3–025*
Stacey v Hill [1901] 1 K.B. 660, CA; affirming (1900) 69 L.J.Q.B. 796 .... *20–035*
Stack v Dowden; sub nom. Dowden v Stack [2007] UKHL 17; [2007] 2 A.C. 432; [2007] 2 W.L.R. 831; [2007] 2 All E.R. 929; [2007] 1 F.L.R. 1858; [2007] 2 F.C.R. 280; [2007] B.P.I.R. 913; [2008] 2 P. & C.R. 4; [2007] W.T.L.R. 1053; (2006–07) 9 I.T.E.L.R. 815; [2007] Fam. Law 593; [2007] 18 E.G. 153 (C.S.); (2007) 157 N.L.J. 634; (2007) 151 S.J.L.B. 575; [2007] N.P.C. 47; [2007] 2 P. & C.R. DG11, HL; affirming [2005] EWCA Civ 857; [2006] 1 F.L.R. 254; [2005] 2 F.C.R. 739; [2006] 1 P. & C.R. 15; [2006] W.T.L.R. 511; (2005–06) 8 I.T.E.L.R. 174; [2005] Fam. Law 864; [2005] N.P.C. 93; [2006] 1 P. & C.R. DG3, CA (Civ Div) *3–140*, *4–081*, *29–160*
Stackhouse v Barnston (1805) 10 Ves. 453 .... *22–004*
Stafford v Stafford, 44 E.R. 697; (1857) 1 De G. & J. 193, QB *28–140*
Staffordshire AHA v South Staffordshire Waterworks Co [1978] 1 W.L.R. 1387; [1978] 3 All E.R. 769; 77 L.G.R. 17; (1978) 122 S.J. 331, CA (Civ Div) *12–051*, *12–118*, *13–027*, *22–054*, *23–008*, *23–021*, *26–080*

Stag Line Ltd v Foscolo Mango & Co Ltd; sub nom. Foscolo Mango & Co Ltd v Stag Line Ltd; Foscolo, Mango & Co Ltd, and HC Vivian Ltd v Stag Line Ltd; Foscolo, Mango & Co Ltd, and HC Vivian Ltd v Stag Line Ltd; Foscolo, Mango & Co Ltd, v Stag Line Ltd [1932] A.C. 328; (1931) 41 Ll. L. Rep. 165, HL; affirming [1931] 2 K.B. 48; (1931) 39 Ll. L. Rep. 101, CA; affirming (1930) 38 Ll. L. Rep. 271, KBD *14–029*
Stag Line Ltd v Tyne Ship Repair Group Ltd; The Zinnia [1984] 2 Lloyd's Rep. 211; (1985) 4 Tr. L. 33, QBD (Comm) *14–011*, *14–047*, *14–085*, 14–092, *18–004*
Stage Club v Millers Hotels Proprietary, 150 C.L.R. 535, HC (Aus) *28–101*
Stahlschmidt v Lett (1853) 1 Sm. & G. 415 .... *20–014*, *28–131*
Stahlwerk Becker AG's Patent (1918) 36 R.P.C. 13, HL [1917] 2 Ch. 272, Ch D *11–030*
Staines v Wainwright (1839) 6 Bing.N.C. 174 .... *16–042*
St Albans City and District Council v International Computers Ltd [1996] 4 All E.R. 481; [1997–98] Info. T.L.R. 58; [1997] F.S.R. 251; (1996) 15 Tr. L.R. 444; [1998] Masons C.L.R. Rep. 98; (1997) 20(2) I.P.D. 20020, CA (Civ Div); reversing in part [1997–98] Info. T.L.R. 25; [1995] F.S.R. 686; [1998] Masons C.L.R. Rep. 19, QBD *13–032*, *14–066*, *14–072*, *14–073*, *14–085*, *14–087*, 14–093, *14–103*, *18–051*, *26–142*
St Anne's Well Brewery Co v Roberts (1929) 140 L.T. 1 .... *1–173*
St George Soccer Football Association Inc v Soccer NSW Ltd [2005] N.S.W.S.C. 1288 10–036
St James' Club, Re (1852) 2 De. G.M. & G. 383 .... *9–073*
St John Shipping Corp v Joseph Rank Ltd [1957] 1 Q.B. 267; [1956] 3 W.L.R. 870; [1956] 3 All E.R. 683; [1956] 2 Lloyd's Rep. 413; (1956) 100 S.J. 841, QBD *4–003*, 16–010, *16–142*, *16–147*, 16–148, 16–149, *16–151*, *16*-153, 16–157, 16–168, 16-*171*, *29–082*
St Mary, Islington v Hornsey Urban DC [1900] 1 Ch. 695; 69 L.J. Ch. 324; 82 L.T. 580; 48 W.R. 401; 16 T.L.R. 286, CA *9–024*
St Paul Fire & Marine Insurance Co (UK) Ltd v McConnell Dowell Constructors Ltd; sub nom. St Paul Fire & Marine Insurance Co (UK) Ltd v McDonnell Dowell Constructors Ltd [1996] 1 All E.R. 96; [1995] 2 Lloyd's Rep. 116; [1995] C.L.C. 818; 74 B.L.R. 112; 45 Con. L.R. 89; [1995] 4 Re. L.R. 293, CA (Civ Div); affirming [1993] 2 Lloyd's Rep. 503; 67 B.L.R. 72; 37 Con. L.R. 96, QBD (Comm) *6–036*, 6–145
St Pierre v South American Stores (Garth & Chaves) Ltd [1936] 1 K.B. 382, CA *21–071*, *30–011*, *30–331*
Stait v Fenner [1912] 2 Ch. 504, Ch D *5–122*
Stamford Banking Co v Smith. *See* Stamford Spalding & Boston Banking Co v Smith
Stamford Spalding & Boston Banking Co v Smith [1892] 1 Q.B. 765, CA *28–100*
Stancliffe Stone Co Ltd v Peak District National Park Authority [2005] EWCA Civ 747; [2006] Env. L.R. 7; [2005] 4 P.L.R. 35; [2006] J.P.L. 247; [2005] A.C.D. 104; [2005] N.P.C. 78, CA (Civ Div); affirming [2004] EWHC 1475 (QB); [2005] Env. L.R. 4; [2004] N.P.C. 101, QBD *10–043*
Standard Bank London Ltd v Apostolakis (No.1) [2002] C.L.C. 933; [2000] I.L.Pr. 766, QBD (Comm) 15–030, 15–095, *30–240*
Standard Bank London Ltd v Apostolakis (No.2) [2001] Lloyd's Rep. Bank. 240; [2002] C.L.C. 939, QBD (Comm) *15–030*, *15–088*, *15–095*, *30–094*, *30–103*, *30–240*
Standard Bank Plc v Agrinvest International Inc [2007] EWHC 2595 (Comm); [2008] 1 Lloyd's Rep. 532 QBD (Comm) *30–031*, *30–075*, *30–077*
Standard Chartered Bank v Banque Marocaine du Commerce Exterieur [2006] EWHC (Comm) 413; [2006] All E.R. (D) 213, Ch D *5–016*, *5–039*
Standard Chartered Bank v Pakistan National Shipping Corp (Assessment of Damages) [2001] EWCA Civ 55; [2001] 1 All E.R. (Comm) 822; [2001] C.L.C. 825, CA (Civ Div); affirming [1999] 1 All E.R. (Comm.) 417; [1999] 1 Lloyd's Rep. 747; [1999] C.L.C. 761, QBD (Comm) *6–051*

Standard Chartered Bank v Pakistan National Shipping Corp (No.1) [1998] 1 Lloyd's Rep. 656, CA (Civ Div); reversing [1995] 2 Lloyd's Rep. 365; [1995] C.L.C. 1293, QBD (Admlty) *6–046*
Standard Chartered Bank v Pakistan National Shipping Corp (No.2); Standard Chartered Bank v Mehra [2002] UKHL 43; [2003] 1 A.C. 959; [2002] 3 W.L.R. 1547; [2003] 1 All E.R. 173; [2002] 2 All E.R. (Comm) 931; [2003] 1 Lloyd's Rep. 227; [2002] B.C.C. 846; [2003] 1 B.C.L.C. 244; [2002] C.L.C. 1330; (2003) 100(1) L.S.G. 26; (2002) 146 S.J.L.B. 258, HL; reversing in part [2000] 1 All E.R. (Comm) 1; [2000] 1 Lloyd's Rep. 218; [2000] Lloyd's Rep. Bank. 40; [2000] C.L.C. 133, CA (Civ Div); reversing in part [1998] 1 Lloyd's Rep. 684, QBD (Comm) *6–037*, *6–064*, *6–074*, *16–007*, *26–049*, *26–103*
Standard Chartered Bank Ltd v International Tin Council [1987] 1 W.L.R. 641; [1986] 3 All E.R. 257; (1987) 84 L.S.G. 1881; (1987) 131 S.J. 595, QBD *11–018*, *11–023*
Standing v Bowring (1886) L.R. 31 Ch. D. 282, CA; affirming (1884) L.R. 27 Ch. D. 341, Ch D *19–023*
Stanley v English Fibres Industries (1899) 68 L.J. Q.B. 839 .... *19–016*
Stanley v Jones (1831) 7 Bing. 369 .... *16–065*
Stanley Bros Ltd v Nuneaton Corp (1913) 108 L.T. 986 ....*29–036*, *29–043*
Stansbie v Troman [1948] 2 K.B. 48; [1948] 1 All E.R. 599; 64 T.L.R. 226; 46 L.G.R. 349; [1948] L.J.R. 1206; (1948) 92 S.J. 167, CA *26–035*
Stansfield v Levy (1820) 3 Stark. 8 .... *17–010*
Stanton v Callaghan [2000] Q.B. 75; [1999] 2 W.L.R. 745; [1998] 4 All E.R. 961; [1999] C.P.L.R. 31; [1999] B.L.R. 172; (1999) 1 T.C.L.R. 50; 62 Con. L.R. 1; [1999] P.N.L.R. 116; [1998] 3 E.G.L.R. 165; (1999) 15 Const. L.J. 50; [1998] E.G. 115 (C.S.); (1998) 95(28) L.S.G. 32; (1998) 95(33) L.S.G. 33; (1998) 148 N.L.J. 1355; (1998) 142 S.J.L.B. 220; [1998] N.P.C. 113, CA (Civ Div) *1–142*
Stanton v Richardson; Richardson v Stanton (1873–74) L.R. 9 C.P. 390, Ex Chamber; affirming (1871–72) L.R. 7 C.P. 421, CCP *12–069*, *24–040*
Stanwell Park Hotel Co v Leslie, 85 C.L.R. 189 .... *21–072*
Stapleton, Ex p. *See* Nathan Ex p. Stapleton, Re
Stapleton-Bretherton, Re; sub nom. Weld-Blundell v Stapleton-Bretherton [1941] Ch. 482, Ch D *18–073*, *18–079*, *18–082*
Stapylton Fletcher Ltd (In Administrative Receivership), Re; Ellis Son & Vidler Ltd (In Administrative Receivership), Re [1994] 1 W.L.R. 1181; [1995] 1 All E.R. 192; [1994] B.C.C. 532; [1994] 2 B.C.L.C. 681, Ch D (Companies Ct) *27–015*
Star Rider Ltd v Inntrepreneur Pub Co [1998] 1 E.G.L.R. 53; [1998] 16 E.G. 140, Ch D *14–105*
Star Shipping AG v China National Foreign Trade Transportation Corp; The Star Texas [1993] 2 Lloyd's Rep. 445, CA (Civ Div) *2–131*, *2–140*, *2–144*, *30–005*, *30–006*, *30–010*, *30–051*
Star Steamship Society v Beogradska Plovidba; The Junior K [1988] 2 Lloyd's Rep. 583, QBD (Comm) *2–116*, *2–136*, *2–138*, *2–154*
Stark, Ex p. *See* Consort Deep Level Gold Mines Ltd
Starside Properties v Mustapha [1974] 1 W.L.R. 816; [1974] 2 All E.R. 567; (1974) 28 P. & C.R. 95; (1974) 118 S.J. 388, CA (Civ Div) *22–048*, *26–147*
Starsin, The. *See* Homburg Houtimport BV v Agrosin Private Ltd
Startup v Macdonald, 134 E.R. 1029; (1843) 6 Man. & G. 593, QB *12–093*, *21–083*
State Bank of New South Wales Ltd v Swiss Bank Corp [1997] 6 Bank. L.R. 34, CA (NSW) *29–180*
State of Norway's Application (No.2).*See* Norway's Application (Nos.1 and 2), Re
State Rail Authority of New South Wales v Heath Outdoor Pty (1986) 7 N.S.W.L.R. 170 .... *12–098*, *12–099*, *12–100*, *12–103*
State Securities Plc v Initial Industry Ltd [2004] All E.R. (D) 317 (Jan) ...22–045, *21–015*, *24–003*

State Trading Corp of India Ltd v Cie Francaise d'Importation et de Distribution [1983] 2 Lloyd's Rep. 679, QBD (Comm) *3–082*, *22–042*
State Trading Corp of India Ltd v M Golodetz & Co Inc Ltd [1989] 2 Lloyd's Rep. 277, CA (Civ Div); reversing [1988] 2 Lloyd's Rep. 182, QBD (Comm) *12–026*, *12–037*, *12–040*, *14–029*, *24–001*, *24–013*, *24–014*, 24–015
Stathlorne SS Co Ltd v Andrew Weir Co (1934) 40 Com. Cas. 168 .... *29–120*
Static Control Components (Europe) Ltd v Egan; sub nom. Egan v Static Control Components (Europe) Ltd [2004] EWCA Civ 392; [2004] 2 Lloyd's Rep. 429; (2004) 148 S.J.L.B. 507, CA (Civ Div) *12–050*, *12–055*, *12–080*, *12–083*
Staunton v Wood (1851) 16 Q.B. 638 .... *21–021*
Stavers v Curling (1836) 3 Bing. N.C. 355 .... *24–035*
Stavers v Curling (1836) 3 Scott. 740 .... *12–063*
Stead Hazel & Co v Cooper [1933] 1 K.B. 840, KBD *9–048*
Stead v Dawber, 113 E.R. 22; (1839) 10 Ad. & El. 57, QB *3–079*, *3–084*, *22–032*, *22–033*
Steadman v Steadman [1976] A.C. 536; [1974] 3 W.L.R. 56; [1974] 2 All E.R. 977; (1975) 29 P. & C.R. 46; (1974) 118 S.J. 480, HL; affirming [1974] Q.B. 161; [1973] 3 W.L.R. 695; [1973] 3 All E.R. 977; (1973) 26 P. & C.R. 249; (1973) 117 S.J. 794, CA (Civ Div) *4–045*, 4–046, *4–049*, 4–052
Steam Herring Fleet v Richards (1901) 17 T.L.R. 731 .... *26–066*, *26–074*
Steam Saw Mills Co Ltd v Baring Bros & Co Ltd; Archangel Saw Mills Co v Baring Bros & Co Ltd [1922] 1 Ch. 244; (1921) 9 Ll. L. Rep. 460, CA *29–030*, *29–038*
Steam Stoker Co, Re (1874–75) L.R. 19 Eq. 416, Ct of Chancery *21–087*, *21–090*
Steamship Induna Co Ltd v British Phosphate Commissioners; The Loch Dee [1949] 2 K.B. 430; [1949] 1 All E.R. 522; (1948–49) 82 Ll. L. Rep. 430; 65 T.L.R. 149; [1949] L.J.R. 1058; (1949) 93 S.J. 237, KBD *14–140*
Steamship Mutual Underwriting Association Ltd v Trollope & Colls (City) Ltd, 33 B.L.R. 77; 6 Con. L.R. 11; (1986) 2 Const. L.J. 224, CA (Civ Div) *28–118*
Steane's (Bournemouth) Ltd, Re [1950] 1 All E.R. 21; 66 T.L.R. (Pt. 1) 71; [1949] W.N. 490, Ch D *9–049*
Stearn v Twitchell [1985] 1 All E.R. 631; (1985) 135 N.L.J. 128, Ch D *2–049*
Stebbing v Spicer (1849) 8 C.B. 827 .... *12–124*
Stedman v Swan's Tours (1951) 95 S.J. 727, CA *26–082*
Steedman v Drinkle [1916] 1 A.C. 275, PC (Can) *12–037*, *21–013*, *21–016*, *26–147*
Steeds v Steeds (1889) L.R. 22 Q.B.D. 537, QBD *1–115*, *22–012*, *22–014*
Steel v State Line Steamship Co (1877–78) L.R. 3 App. Cas. 72, HL *14–032*
Steel Authority of India Ltd v Hind Metals Inc; Hind Metals Inc v Sail International Ltd; Hind Metals inc v Steel Authority of India Ltd [1984] 1 Lloyd's Rep. 405; (1984) 134 N.L.J. 204, QBD (Comm) *30–007*, *30–010*
Steel Wing Co Ltd, Re [1921] 1 Ch. 349, Ch D *19–014*
Steele v Gourley (1887) 3 T.L.R. 772, affirming (1886) 3 T.L.R. 118 .... *9–064*, *9–073*
Steele v Hoe (1849) 14 Q.B. 431 .... *12–081*
Steele v McKinlay (1879–80) L.R. 5 App. Cas. 754, HL *12–113*
Steele v McMahon (1990) 22 H.L.R. 479; [1990] 44 E.G. 65; [1990] E.G. 73 (C.S.), CA (Civ Div) *16–185*
Steele v Williams (1853) 8 Ex. 625 .... *29–043*, *29–084*, *29–094*, *29–095*
Steeples v Lea [1998] 1 F.L.R. 138; [1998] 2 F.C.R. 144; (1998) 76 P. & C.R. 157; [1998] Fam. Law 75, CA (Civ Div) *7–091*
Stein v Blake (No.1) [1996] A.C. 243; [1995] 2 W.L.R. 710; [1995] 2 All E.R. 961; [1995] B.C.C. 543; [1995] 2 B.C.L.C. 94; (1995) 145 N.L.J. 760, HL; affirming [1994] Ch. 16; [1993] 3 W.L.R. 718; [1993] 4 All E.R. 225; [1993] B.C.C. 587; [1993] B.C.L.C. 1478, CA (Civ Div) *16–063*, 19–009, *20–026*, *20–032*, *20–040*
Steinberg v Scala (Leeds) Ltd [1923] 2 Ch. 452, CA *8–033*, *8–038*, *8–040*, *8–065*, *29–061*, *29–081*
Stella, The [1900] P. 161, PDAD *14–011*
Stenhouse Australia v Phillips [1974] A.C. 391; [1974] 2 W.L.R. 134; [1974] 1 All E.R. 117; [1974] 1 Lloyd's Rep. 1; (1973) 117 S.J. 875, PC (Aus) *16–087*, *16–097*, *16–104*, *16–108*, *16–112*, *16–203*

Stenning, Re; sub nom. Wood v Stenning [1895] 2 Ch. 433, Ch D *29–167*
Stensby, The. *See* Kadel Chajkin & Ce De Ltd v Mitchell Cotts & Co (Middle East) Ltd; The Stensby
Stent Foundations Ltd v MJ Gleeson Group Plc [2001] B.L.R. 134; (2001) 17 Const. L.J. 186, QBD (TCC) *14–005*, *14–010*, *14–013*, *14–015*
Stephens v Badcock (1832) 3 B. Ad. 354 .... *29–026*
Stephens v Dudbridge Ironworks Co Ltd [1904] 2 K.B. 225, CA *8–029*
Stephens v Gulf Oil Canada Ltd (1976) 11 O.L.R. (2D) 229 ....*16–085*, *16–129*
Stephens v The Queen (1978) 139 C.L.R. 315 .... *12–046*
Stepney Corp v Osofsky [1937] 3 All E.R. 289 ....*21–060*, *21–063*
Stepps Investment v Security Capital Corp (1976) 73 D.L.R. (3d) 351, HC (Ont) *5–120*
Sterling Hydraulics Ltd v Dichtomatik Ltd [2006] EWHC 2004 (QB); [2007] 1 Lloyd's Rep. 8, QBD *2–037*, *2–092*, *14–092*, 14–096
Stern v McArthur (1988) 165 C.L.R. 489 .... *21–016*, *26–148*
Sterry v Clifton (1850) 9 C.B. 110 .... *16–022*
Steven v Bromley & Son [1919] 2 K.B. 722, CA *2–005*, *2–030*, *2–031*, 29–073
Stevens v Benning (1855) 6 De G.M. & G. 223 .... *19–055*
Stevens v Head, 176 C.L.R. 433, HC (Aus) *30–337*
Stevens v Hill (1805) 5 Esp. 247 .... *29–194*
Stevens v Webb (1835) 7 C.P. 60 .... *21–007*
Stevenson v Rogers [1999] Q.B. 1028; [1999] 2 W.L.R. 1064; [1999] 1 All E.R. 613; (1999) 96(2) L.S.G. 29; (1999) 149 N.L.J. 16; (1999) 143 S.J.L.B. 21, CA (Civ Div) *15–026*
Stevenson v United Road Transport Union [1977] 2 All E.R. 941; [1977] I.C.R. 893, CA (Civ Div) *27–022*
Stevenson Jaques & Co v McLean (1879–80) L.R. 5 Q.B.D. 346, QBD *2–048*, *2–089*, 2–093
Stevenson Jordan & Harrison v McDonnell & Evans [1952] 1 T.L.R. 101; (1952) 69 R.P.C. 10, CA *16–106*
Stewart v Aberdein (1838) 4 M.W. 211 .... *21–044*
Stewart v Chapman [1951] 2 K.B. 792; [1951] 2 All E.R. 613; [1951] 2 T.L.R. 640; (1951) 35 Cr. App. R. 102; (1951) 115 J.P. 473; 49 L.G.R. 816; (1951) 95 S.J. 641, DC *12–093*, *21–024*
Stewart v Eddowes; Hudson v Stewart (1873–74) L.R. 9 C.P. 311, CCP *4–035*
Stewart v Engel (Permission to Amend) [2000] 1 W.L.R. 2268; [2000] 3 All E.R. 518; [2001] C.P. Rep. 9; [2001] E.C.D.R. 25, CA (Civ Div) *28–118*
Stewart v Glentaggart Ltd, 1963 S.C. 300; 1963 S.L.T. 119; (1963) 42 A.T.C. 318; [1963] T.R. 345, OH *26–158*, *26–165*
Stewart v Kennedy (No.1) (1890) L.R. 15 App. Cas. 75, HL *5–077*
Stewart v Oriental Fire & Marine Insurance Co Ltd [1985] Q.B. 988; [1984] 3 W.L.R. 741; [1984] 3 All E.R. 777; [1984] 2 Lloyd's Rep. 109; (1984) 1 B.C.C. 99127; [1984] E.C.C. 564; [1985] Fin. L.R. 64; (1984) 81 L.S.G. 1915; (1984) 134 N.L.J. 584; (1984) 128 S.J. 645, QBD (Comm) *16–147*
Stewart v Reavell's Garage [1952] 2 Q.B. 545; [1952] 1 All E.R. 1191; [1952] 1 T.L.R. 1266; (1952) 96 S.J. 314, QBD *13–030*, *19–081*, *19–084*
Stewart v Todd (1846) 9 Q.B. 759 .... *25–007*
Stewart Gill Ltd v Horatio Myer & Co Ltd [1992] Q.B. 600; [1992] 2 W.L.R. 721; [1992] 2 All E.R. 257; 31 Con. L.R. 1; (1991) 11 Tr. L.R. 86; (1992) 142 N.L.J. 241, CA (Civ Div) ...*6–139*, *14–062*, *14–063*, *14–084*, *14–085*, 14–092, *14–100*, *14–101*, *15–072*
Stickney v Keeble [1915] A.C. 386, HL *21–011*, *21–014*, *21–018*, *27–029*
Stiftung v Lewis [2004] EWHC 2589, Ch D *30–075*, *30–077*, *30–090*, *30–124*, *30–125*
Stikeman v Dawson (1847) 1 De. G. & Sm. 90 .... *8–046*, *8–051*
Stiles v Cooper (1748) 3 Atk. 692 .... *29–116*
Stilk v Myrick (1809) 2 Camp. 317 .... 3–066, 3–067, *3–068*, 3–069, *3–071*, 3–074, 3–076, 3–099, *22–035*
Stimson v Gray [1929] 1 Ch. 629, Ch D *4–043*
Stirling v Burdett [1911] 2 Ch. 418, Ch D *17–028*
Stirling v Maitland, 122 E.R. 1043; (1864) 5 B. & S. 840, QB *13–012*

Stirling v Norwest Holst Ltd (No.1), 1997 S.L.T. 973, OH *14–015*
Stockloser v Johnson [1954] 1 Q.B. 476; [1954] 2 W.L.R. 439; [1954] 1 All E.R. 630; (1954) 98 S.J. 178, CA *22–048*, *26–146*, 26–148, 26–150, *26–154*, *29–061*, 29–064
Stockport Ragged Industrial and Reformatory Schools, Re [1898] 2 Ch. 687, CA; affirming in part [1898] 1 Ch. 610, Ch D *12–087*
Stocks v Dobson (1853) 4 De G.M. & G. 11 .... *19–020*
Stocks v Wilson [1913] 2 K.B. 235, KBD *8–015*, *8–016*, *8–047*, *8–051*, *8–052*, *8–055*
Stockwell v Niven (1889) 61 L.T. 18 .... *4–023*
Stockwell v Southgate Corp [1936] 2 All E.R. 1343 .... *10–042*
Stocznia Gdanska SA v Latreefers Inc; sub nom. Latreefers Inc, Re; Stocznia Gdanska SA v Latvian Shipping Co (Abuse of Process) [2000] C.P.L.R. 65; [2001] B.C.C. 174; [2001] 2 B.C.L.C. 116; [2001] C.L.C. 1267, CA (Civ Div); affirming [1999] 1 B.C.L.C. 271, Ch D *16–066*
Stocznia Gdanska SA v Latvian Shipping Co (Repudiation) [2002] EWCA Civ 889; [2002] 2 All E.R. (Comm) 768; [2002] 2 Lloyd's Rep. 436; [2003] 1 C.L.C. 282, CA (Civ Div) 24–002, *24–004*, *24–010*, *24–011*, *24–013*, *24–021*
Stocznia Gdanska SA v Latvian Shipping Co; sub nom. Stocznia Gdanska SA v Latreefers Inc [1998] 1 W.L.R. 574; [1998] 1 All E.R. 883; [1998] 1 Lloyd's Rep. 609; [1998] C.L.C. 540; (1998) 95(15) L.S.G. 33; (1998) 148 N.L.J. 330; (1998) 142 S.J.L.B. 118, HL; reversing in part [1996] 2 Lloyd's Rep. 132; [1996] C.L.C. 1410, CA (Civ Div); affirming in part [1995] 2 Lloyd's Rep. 592; [1995] C.L.C. 956, QBD (Comm) *4–085*, *26–009*, *26–154*, 29–054, *29–055*, 29–063, *29–064*, *29–065*
Stoddart v Union Trust Ltd [1912] 1 K.B. 181, CA *19–070*, 19–071
Stoke on Trent City Council v W&J Wass Ltd (No.1) [1988] 1 W.L.R. 1406; [1988] 3 All E.R. 394; 87 L.G.R. 129; (1989) 153 L.G. Rev. 586; [1988] E.G. 121 (C.S.); (1988) 85(40) L.S.G. 44; (1988) 132 S.J. 1458, CA (Civ Div) *29–008*, *29–011*, *29–142*, *29–144*
Stoke on Trent City Council v Wood Mitchell & Co Ltd; sub nom. Wood Mitchell & Co Ltd v Stoke on Trent City Council [1980] 1 W.L.R. 254; [1979] 2 All E.R. 65; [1979] S.T.C. 197; (1979) 38 P. & C.R. 126; (1978) 248 E.G. 871; [1978] T.R. 471; [1979] J.P.L. 230; (1980) 124 S.J. 168, CA (Civ Div) *26–157*, *26–163*
Stokes v Lewis (1785) 1 T.R. 20 .... *29–109*, *29–115*
Stokes v Whicher [1920] 1 Ch. 411, Ch D *4–023*, 4–028, *12–122*
Stokes (Deceased), Re; sub nom. Mellish, Ex p. [1919] 2 K.B. 256, KBD *20–023*, *20–054*
Stolt Loyalty, The [1995] 1 Lloyd's Rep. 598, CA (Civ Div); affirming [1993] 2 Lloyd's Rep. 281, QBD (Admlty) *2–073*, *3–088*, *3–092*, *5–082*
Stone v Godfrey (1854) 5 De G.M.G. 76 ....*5–054*, *29–043*
Stone v Marsh (1826) Ry. M. 364 .... *21–049*
Stone v Reliance Mutual Insurance Society [1972] 1 Lloyd's Rep. 469, CA (Civ Div) *6–149*
Stone v Wythipol (1588) Cro.Eliz. 126 .... *3–051*
Stone v Yeovil Corp (1876–77) L.R. 2 C.P.D. 99, CA; affirming (1875–76) L.R. 1 C.P.D. 691, CPD *12–077*
Stone Vickers Ltd v Appledore Ferguson Shipbuilders Ltd [1992] 2 Lloyd's Rep. 578, CA (Civ Div); reversing [1991] 2 Lloyd's Rep. 288, QBD (Comm) ...*14–049*, *18–128*
Stone and Rolls Ltd (In Liquidation) v Moore Stephens (A Firm) [2007] EWHC 1826 (Comm); [2008] Bus. L.R. 304; [2008] P.N.L.R. 4; (2007) 157 N.L.J. 1154, QBD (Comm) *16–164*
Stone and Saville's Contract, Re [1963] 1 W.L.R. 163; [1963] 1 All E.R. 353; (1962) 106 S.J. 1030, CA *21–014*
Stoneleigh Finance v Phillips [1965] 2 Q.B. 537; [1965] 2 W.L.R. 508; [1965] 1 All E.R. 513; (1965) 109 S.J. 68, CA *16–010*
Stoomv Maats De Maas NV v Nippon Yusen Kaisha; The Pendrecht [1980] 2 Lloyd's Rep. 56, QBD (Comm) *2–050*, *2–091*, *28–061*
Storer v Gordon (1814) 3 M. & S. 308 .... *18–122*

Storer v Great Western Railway (1842) 2 Y. & C.C.C. 48 .... *27–026*
Storer v Manchester City Council [1974] 1 W.L.R. 1403; [1974] 3 All E.R. 824; 73 L.G.R. 1; (1974) 118 S.J. 599, CA (Civ Div) ...*2–003*, *2–114*, *2–118*, *2–123*, *2–161*
Storey v Fulham Steel Works (1907) 24 T.L.R. 89 .... *23–038*
Storey v Waddle (1878–79) L.R. 4 Q.B.D. 289, CA *5–131*
Stornvaart Maatschappij Sophie H v Merchants' Marine Insurance Co (1919) 89 L.J.K.B. 834 .... *12–090*
Storthoaks v Mobil Oil of Canada Ltd (1975) 55 D.L.R. (3d) 1 .... *23–081*
Stoss v Fairlamb (1883) 52 L.J.Q.B. 420 .... *12–101*
Stott v Shaw & Lee Ltd [1928] 2 K.B. 26, CA *12–067*
Stott (Baltic) Steamers Ltd v Marten [1916] 1 A.C. 304, HL; affirming [1914] 3 K.B. 1262, CA; affirming [1914] 1 K.B. 442, KBD *12–087*
Stour Valley Builders v Stuart [2003] T.C.L.R. 8, CA (Civ Div) *22–022*
Stourcliffe Estate Co Ltd v Bournemouth Corp [1910] 2 Ch. 12, CA 10–029
Stovin v Wise [1996] A.C. 923; [1996] 3 W.L.R. 388; [1996] 3 All E.R. 801; [1996] R.T.R. 354; (1996) 93(35) L.S.G. 33; (1996) 146 N.L.J. 1185; (1996) 140 S.J.L.B. 201, HL; reversing [1994] 1 W.L.R. 1124; [1994] 3 All E.R. 467; [1994] R.T.R. 225; 92 L.G.R. 577; 159 J.P.N. 722; (1994) 91(14) L.S.G. 48; (1994) 138 S.J.L.B. 60, CA (Civ Div) *18–027*
Stovold v Barlows [1996] C.L.C. 228; [1996] E.C.C. 101; [1996] P.N.L.R. 91; [1995] E.G. 155 (C.S.); (1995) 92(40) L.S.G. 22; [1995] N.P.C. 154; (1996) 71 P. & C.R. D3, CA (Civ Div) *26–045*
Strachan v Brander (1759) 1 Eden 303 ....*16–064*, *16–065*
Strachan & Henshaw Ltd v Stein Industrie (UK) Ltd (No.1), 63 Con. L.R. 132; (1997) 13 Const. L.J. 418, QBD (OR) *6–036*
Strachan & Henshaw Ltd v Stein Industrie (UK) Ltd (No.2), 87 B.L.R. 52; 63 Con. L.R. 160; (1998) 14 Const. L.J. 370, CA (Civ Div) *6–006*, *6–134*
Strand Electric and Engineering Co Ltd v Brisford Entertainments Ltd [1952] 2 Q.B. 246; [1952] 1 All E.R. 796; [1952] 1 T.L.R. 939; (1952) 96 S.J. 260, CA *26–022*, *29–139*, *29–144*, *29–145*
Strand Music Hall Co, Re (1865) 35 Beav. 153 .... *12–063*
Strange v Brennan (1846) 15 Sim. 346 .... *16–055*
Strange (SW) v Mann [1965] 1 W.L.R. 629; [1965] 1 All E.R. 1069; (1965) 109 S.J. 352, Ch D *16–100*, *16–108*, *16–110*, *16–113*
Stratford-upon-Avon Corp v Parker [1914] 2 K.B. 562, KBD *20–012*
Strathford East Kilbride Ltd v HLM Design Ltd, 1999 S.L.T. 121; 1997 S.C.L.R. 877; 1997 Rep. L.R. 112; 1997 G.W.D. 31–1554, OH *18–027*
Straton v Rastall (1788) 2 T.R. 366 .... *21–058*
Stray v Russell (1859) 1 E. & E. 888 .... *27–011*
Street v Mountford [1985] A.C. 809; [1985] 2 W.L.R. 877; [1985] 2 All E.R. 289; (1985) 17 H.L.R. 402; (1985) 50 P. & C.R. 258; [1985] 1 E.G.L.R. 128; (1985) 274 E.G. 821; [2008] B.T.C. 7094; (1985) 82 L.S.G. 2087; (1985) 135 N.L.J. 460; (1985) 129 S.J. 348, HL; reversing (1984) 16 H.L.R. 27; (1985) 49 P. & C.R. 324; (1984) 271 E.G. 1153; (1984) 271 E.G. 1261; (1984) 81 L.S.G. 1844; (1984) 128 S.J. 483, CA (Civ Div) *1–069*, *2–161*
Stretford v Football Association Ltd [2007] EWCA Civ 238; [2007] Bus. L.R. 1052; [2007] 2 All E.R. (Comm) 1; [2007] 2 Lloyd's Rep. 31; [2007] 1 C.L.C. 256; (2007) 151 S.J.L.B. 437, CA (Civ Div); affirming [2006] EWHC 479 (Ch), Ch D *1–049*
Strickland v Symons (1884) L.R. 26 Ch. D. 245, CA; affirming (1883) L.R. 22 Ch. D. 666, Ch D *20–010*
Strickland v Turner (1852) 7 Exch. 208 ....5–019, *5–022*, *29–074*
Stromdale & Ball Ltd v Burden [1952] Ch. 223; [1952] 1 All E.R. 59; [1951] 2 T.L.R. 1192, Ch D *1–092*, *18–125*
Stroms Bruks AB v John & Peter Hutchison (A Firm); sub nom. Stroms Bruk Aktie Bolag v John & Peter Hutchison [1905] A.C. 515; (1905) 7 F. (H.L.) 131; (1905) 13 S.L.T. 376, HL *26–070*, *26–090*
Strong v Bird (1874) L.R. 18 Eq. 315, Ct of Chancery *17–023*, *25–005*
Strong v Hart (1827) 6 B.C. 160 .... *21–075*
Strong v Harvey (1825) 3 Bing. 304 ....*21–085*, *21–090*

Strongman (1945) v Sincock [1955] 2 Q.B. 525; [1955] 3 W.L.R. 360; [1955] 3 All E.R. 90; (1955) 99 S.J. 540, CA 16–176
Stroude v Beazer Homes Ltd [2005] EWCA Civ 265; [2005] N.P.C. 45, CA (Civ Div); affirming [2004] EWHC 676 (Ch), Ch D *12–119*
Stroughill v Buck (1850) 14 Q.B. 781 .... *1–112*
Strover v Harrington [1988] Ch. 390; [1988] 2 W.L.R. 572; [1988] 1 All E.R. 769; (1988) 56 P. & C.R. 302; [1988] 09 E.G. 61; (1988) 132 S.J. 416, Ch D *2–166*, *6–033*
Strover v Strover [2005] EWHC 860; [2005] W.T.L.R. 1245; [2005] N.P.C. 64, Ch D *3–146*
Strutt v Whitnell [1975] 1 W.L.R. 870; [1975] 2 All E.R. 510; (1975) 29 P. & C.R. 488; (1975) 119 S.J. 236, CA (Civ Div) *26–103*, *26–113*, *26–121*
Stubbs, Administrator v Holywell Railway Co (1866–67) L.R. 2 Ex. 311, Ex Ct ...*20–006*, *23–037*, *23–091*
Studds v Watson (1885) L.R. 28 Ch. D. 305, Ch D *4–010*, *4–028*, *4–029*
Studdy v Sanders (1826) 5 B. & C. 628 .... *12–058*
Studholme v Mandell (1698) 1 Ld. Raym. 279 .... *21–007*
Studholme v South Western Gas Board [1954] 1 W.L.R. 313; [1954] 1 All E.R. 462; (1955) 99 S.J. 112, QBD *23–023*
Sturke v SW Edwards Ltd (1971) 23 P.C.R. 185 .... *23–068*
Sturlyn v Albany (1587) Cro.Eliz. 67 .... *3–015*
Style Financial Services Ltd v Bank of Scotland (No.1), 1996 S.L.T. 421; [1996] 5 Bank. L.R. 15; [1995] B.C.C. 785, IH (2 Div) *29–164*
Styles v Smith [2005] EWHC 3224; [2005] All ER (D) 167, QBD *4–057*
Suarez (No.1), Re; sub nom. Suarez v Suarez [1918] 1 Ch. 176, CA *11–020*, *11–021*
Sucre Export SA v Northern River Shipping Ltd; The Sormovskiy 3068 [1994] 2 Lloyd's Rep. 266; [1994] C.L.C. 433, QBD (Admlty) ...*12–129*, *13–018*, *14–033*
Sudan Import and Export Co (Khartoum) v Societe Generale de Compensation [1958] 1 Lloyd's Rep. 310, CA *24–022*
Sudatlantic Navegacion SA v Devamar Shipping Corp; The Ionio [1985] 2 Lloyd's Rep. 271, QBD (Comm) *12–073*, *12–078*, *12–119*
Sudbrook Trading Estate Ltd v Eggleton [1983] 1 A.C. 444; [1982] 3 W.L.R. 315; [1982] 3 All E.R. 1; (1982) 44 P. & C.R. 153; (1983) 265 E.G. 215; (1982) 79 L.S.G. 1175; (1982) 126 S.J. 512, HL; reversing [1981] 3 W.L.R. 361; [1981] 3 All E.R. 105; (1981) 260 E.G. 1033; (1981) 125 S.J. 513, CA (Civ Div) 2–131, *2–140*, *4–025*, *12–073*
Suffell v Bank of England (1881–82) L.R. 9 Q.B.D. 555, CA *25–023*, *25–025*
Sugar v London Midland & Scottish Railway Co [1941] 1 All E.R. 172; 105 J.P. 100, KBD *12–014*
Suisse Atlantique Societe d'Armement SA v NV Rotterdamsche Kolen Centrale [1967] 1 A.C. 361; [1966] 2 W.L.R. 944; [1966] 2 All E.R. 61; [1966] 1 Lloyd's Rep. 529; (1966) 110 S.J. 367, HL; affirming [1965] 1 Lloyd's Rep. 533, CA; affirming [1965] 1 Lloyd's Rep. 166, QBD (Comm) *1–012*, *3–025*, *12–022*, 12–024, *14–003*, *14–004*, *14–005*, *14–007*, *14–008*, 14–016, *14–020*, **14–021**, 14–022, *14–024*, *14–027*, *14–028*, *14–029*, *14–030*, *14–033*, *14–035*, *14–036*, *24–001*, *24–003*, *24–008*, *24–010*, *24–011*, *24–018*, *24–040*, 24–041, *24–042*, *26–142*, *26–143*
Suleman v Shahsavari [1988] 1 W.L.R. 1181; [1989] 2 All E.R. 460; (1989) 57 P. & C.R. 465; [1989] 09 E.G. 69; (1988) 85(32) L.S.G. 38; (1988) 138 N.L.J. Rep. 241; (1988) 132 S.J. 1243, Ch D *26–091*, *26–092*, *27–079*
Suleyman Stalskiy, The [1976] 2 Lloyd's Rep. 609, Sup Ct (BC) *14–042*, *14–048*, *14–049*
Sullivan v Henderson [1973] 1 W.L.R. 333; [1973] 1 All E.R. 48; (1972) 116 S.J. 969, Ch D *27–011*, *27–031*, *27–041*
Sullivan v Lee (1995) 95 B.C.L.R. (2d) 195 .... *29–184*
Suma, The. *See* China Shipbuilding Corp v Nippon Yusen Kabukishi Kaisha
Sumitomo Bank Ltd v Banque Bruxelles Lambert SA [1997] 1 Lloyd's Rep. 487; [1996] E.G. 150 (C.S.), QBD (Comm) *1–160*, *18–023*, *18–128*
Summers v Salford Corp [1943] A.C. 283, HL *26–082*

Sumpter v Hedges [1898] 1 Q.B. 673, CA .. *21–029*, *21–030*, *21–031*, *21–033*, *21–035*, *23–074*, *29–021*, *29–053*, *29–073*, *29–080*
Sumukan Ltd v Commonwealth Secretariat [2007] EWCA Civ 1148; [2008] 1 Lloyd's Rep. 40; [2007] 2 C.L.C. 821; 116 Con. L.R. 17; (2007) 104(46) L.S.G. 26, CA (Civ Div); reversing [2007] EWHC 188 (Comm); [2007] 1 Lloyd's Rep. 370, QBD (Comm) *12–015*
Sumukan Ltd v Commonwealth Secretariat; sub nom. Sukuman Ltd v Commonwealth Secretariat [2007] EWCA Civ 243; [2007] Bus. L.R. 1075; [2007] 3 All E.R. 342; [2007] 2 All E.R. (Comm) 23; [2007] 2 Lloyd's Rep. 87; [2007] 1 C.L.C. 282; (2007) 157 N.L.J. 482; (2007) 151 S.J.L.B. 430, CA (Civ Div); affirming [2006] EWHC 304 (Comm); [2006] 1 All E.R. (Comm) 621; [2006] 2 Lloyd's Rep. 53; [2006] 1 C.L.C. 394, QBD (Comm) ...*1–049*, *12–014*
Sun Alliance Pensions Life & Investments Services Ltd v RJL; Sun Alliance Pensions Life & Investments Services Ltd v Anthony Webster [1991] 2 Lloyd's Rep. 410, QBD *12–116*
Sun Fire Office v Hart (1889) L.R. 14 App. Cas. 98, PC (Wind) *12–087*
Sun Life Assurance Co of Canada v CX Reinsurance Co Ltd (formerly CNA Reinsurance Co Ltd) [2003] EWCA Civ 283; [2004] Lloyd's Rep. I.R. 58, CA (Civ Div) *2–116*
Sun Life Assurance Co of Canada v Lincoln National Life Insurance Co. *See* Lincoln National Life Insurance Co v Sun Life Assurance Co of Canada
Sun Life Assurance Society Plc v Tantofex (Engineers) Ltd [1999] L. & T.R. 568; [1999] 2 E.G.L.R. 135; [1999] E.G. 50 (C.S.), Ch D *17–018*, *17–020*
Sunbeam Shipping Co Ltd v President of India; The Atlantic Sunbeam [1973] 1 Lloyd's Rep. 482, QBD (Comm) *13–011*
Sundell Sons v Emm Yannoulatos (Overseas) Pty Ltd (1956) 56 S.R.(N.S.W.) 323 .... *29–088*
Sunderland Corp v Priestman [1927] 2 Ch. 107, Ch D 10–042
Sunderland Marine Insurance Co v Kearney, 117 E.R. 1136; (1851) 16 Q.B. 925, QB *18–122*
Sunley & Co Ltd v Cunard White Star Line Ltd. *See* B Sunley & Co Ltd v Cunard White Star Ltd
Sunny Metal and Engineering Pte Ltd v Ng Khim Ming Eric [2007] SGCA 36; 113 Con. L.R. 112, CA (Sing); reversing [2006] SGHC 222; 110 Con. L.R. 115, HC (Sing) *18–023*
Sunport Shipping Ltd v Tryg Baltica International (UK) Ltd; The Kleovoulos of Rhodes; sub nom. Sunport Shipping Ltd v Atkin; The Kleovoulos of Rhodes [2003] EWCA Civ 12; [2003] 1 All E.R. (Comm) 586; [2003] 1 Lloyd's Rep. 138; [2003] 1 C.L.C. 772; [2003] Lloyd's Rep. I.R. 349; (2003) 100(11) L.S.G. 33, CA (Civ Div); affirming [2002] EWHC 235; [2002] 2 All E.R. (Comm) 350; [2002] 2 Lloyd's Rep. 277; [2002] C.L.C. 808; [2003] Lloyd's Rep. I.R. 27; (2002) 99(16) L.S.G. 38, QBD (Comm) *12–053*
Sunrock Aircraft Corp Ltd v Scandinavian Airlines System Denmark-Norway-Sweden [2007] EWCA Civ 882; [2007] 2 Lloyd's Rep. 612; (2007) 104(35) L.S.G. 39, CA (Civ Div) *26–017*
Super Chem Products Ltd v American Life & General Insurance Co Ltd [2004] UKPC 2; [2004] 2 All E.R. 358; [2004] 1 All E.R. (Comm) 713; [2004] 1 C.L.C. 1041; [2004] Lloyd's Rep. I.R. 446; (2004) 148 S.J.L.B. 113, PC (Trin) *3–090*, *28–109*
Super Servant Two, The. *See* J Lauritzen A/S v Wijsmuller BV
Surf City, The [1995] 2 Lloyd's Rep. 242, QBD (Admlty) *29–173*
Suriya & Douglas v Midland Bank Plc [1999] 1 All E.R. (Comm.) 612; [1999] Lloyd's Rep. Bank. 103; (1999) 96(12) L.S.G. 33, CA (Civ Div) *13–010*
Surrendra Overseas Ltd v Sri Lanka; The Apj Akash [1977] 1 W.L.R. 565; [1977] 2 All E.R. 481; [1977] 1 Lloyd's Rep. 653; (1977) 121 S.J. 13, QBD (Comm) *3–035*, *28–095*, *28–096*

Surrey CC and Mole DC v Bredero Homes Ltd [1993] 1 W.L.R. 1361; [1993] 3 All E.R. 705; [1993] 25 E.G. 141; [1993] E.G. 77 (C.S.); (1993) 137 S.J.L.B. 135; [1993] N.P.C. 63, CA (Civ Div); affirming [1992] 3 All E.R. 302; (1992) 64 P. & C.R. 57; [1993] 03 E.G. 112; [1991] E.G. 127 (C.S.); [1991] N.P.C. 125, Ch D .. *1–123*, *2–136*, *26–008*, *26–023*, *27–079*, *27–084*, *29–139*, *29–151*

Surrey Shipping Co v Cie Continentale (France) SA. *See* Shackleford, The

Surrey Shipping Co v Compagnie Continentale (France) SA; The Shackleford [1978] 1 W.L.R. 1080; [1978] 2 Lloyd's Rep. 154; (1978) 122 S.J. 555, CA (Civ Div); affirming [1978] 1 Lloyd's Rep. 191, QBD (Comm) *3–090*, *24–006*

Surzur Overseas Ltd v Ocean Reliance Shipping Co Ltd [1997] C.L. 318 ....*30–008*, *30–068*, *30–077*, *30–309*

Surzur Overseas Ltd v Ocean Reliance Shipping Co Ltd [1997] C.L.Y. 906, QBD (Comm) *14–062*, *14–095*, *14–113*

Suse & Sibeth Ex p. Dever, Re (1887) L.R. 18 Q.B.D. 660, CA *30–009*

Susquehanna, The. *See* Admiralty Commissioners v Owners of the SS Susquehanna

Sussex Caravan Parks v Richardson [1961] 1 W.L.R. 561; [1961] 1 All E.R. 731; (1961) 125 J.P. 237; 59 L.G.R. 175; [1961] R.V.R. 134; 8 R.R.C. 26; (1961) 105 S.J. 253, CA; reversing 175 E.G. 1287; 7 R.R.C. 247; 53 R. & I.T. 427; [1960] J.P.L. 574, Lands Tr *12–126*

Sutherland Shire Council v Heyman [1955–95] P.N.L.R. 238; 157 C.L.R. 424; (1985) 60 A.L.R. 1; (1985) 59 A.L.J.R. 564; (1986) 2 Const. L.J. 161, HC (Aus); reversing [1982] 2 N.S.W.L.R. 618, CA (NSW) *1–184*

Sutherland v Briggs (1841) 1 Hare 26 .... *4–050*

Sutradhar v Natural Environment Research Council [2006] UKHL 33; [2006] 4 All E.R. 490; [2007] Env. L.R. 10; [2006] P.N.L.R. 36; (2006) 150 S.J.L.B. 922, HL; affirming [2004] EWCA Civ 175; [2004] P.N.L.R. 30; (2004) 101(13) L.S.G. 36; [2004] Env. L.R. D8, CA (Civ Div); reversing [2003] EWHC 1046 (QB); [2003] P.I.Q.R. P34; [2003] N.P.C. 61, QBD *18–032*

Sutton v Hawkins (1838) 8 C.P. 259 .... *21–091*

Sutton v Hutchinson [2005] EWCA Civ 1773, CA (Civ Div) *16–167*

Sutton v Mishcon de Reya [2003] EWHC 3166 (Ch); [2004] 1 F.L.R. 837; [2004] 3 F.C.R. 142; [2004] Fam. Law 247, Ch D *2–184*

Sutton v Sutton [1984] Ch. 184; [1984] 2 W.L.R. 146; [1984] 1 All E.R. 168; [1984] Fam. Law 205; (1984) 81 L.S.G. 591; (1984) 128 S.J. 80, Ch D *4–046*, 16–043, *16–044*, *27–048*

Sutton v Tatham (1839) 10 A. & E. 27 .... *13–018*

Sutton v Temple (1843) 12 M. & W. 52 .... *13–016*

Sutton Housing Trust v Lawrence (1987) 19 H.L.R. 520; (1988) 55 P. & C.R. 320, CA (Civ Div) *27–027*, *27–060*

Sutton's Hospital Case (1612) 10 CoRep. 23a *9–004*

Sutton LBC v Morgan Grenfell & Co Ltd [1997] 6 Bank. L.R. 156; (1997) 29 H.L.R. 608; (1997) 9 Admin. L.R. 145, CA (Civ Div) *10–024*

Svanosio v McNamara (1956) 96 C.L.R. 186 .... *5–048*, *5–058*

Svenska Petroleum Exploration AB v Lithuania (No.1) [2005] EWHC 9; [2005] 1 All E.R. (Comm) 515; [2005] 1 Lloyd's Rep. 515, QBD (Comm) *11–005*

Svenska Petroleum Exploration AB v Lithuania (No.2) [2006] EWCA Civ 1529; [2007] Q.B. 886; [2007] 2 W.L.R. 876; [2007] 1 All E.R. (Comm) 909; [2007] 1 Lloyd's Rep. 193; [2006] 2 C.L.C. 797, CA (Civ Div); affirming [2005] EWHC 2437 (Comm); [2006] 1 All E.R. (Comm) 731; [2006] 1 Lloyd's Rep. 181; [2005] 2 C.L.C. 965; (2005) 102(47) L.S.G. 26, QBD (Comm) *11–005*, *11–021*

Svenssons Travaruaktiebolag v Cliffe Steamship Co. *See* C Wilh Svenssons Travarnaktiebolag v Cliffe Steamship Co

Swain, Re; sub nom. Swain v Bringeman [1891] 3 Ch. 233, Ch D *28–057*

Swain v Law Society [1983] 1 A.C. 598; [1982] 3 W.L.R. 261; [1982] 2 All E.R. 827; (1982) 79 L.S.G. 887; (1982) 126 S.J. 464, HL; reversing [1982] 1 W.L.R. 17; [1981] 3 All E.R. 797; (1981) 125 S.J. 542, CA (Civ Div); reversing in part [1980] 1 W.L.R. 1335; [1980] 3 All E.R. 615; (1980) 124 S.J. 220, Ch D *1–189*, 1–201, *18–020*, *18–079*, *18–082*, *18–130*

Swain v West (Butchers) [1936] 1 All E.R. 224, KBD *3–066*
Swaine v Wilson (1890) L.R. 24 Q.B.D. 252, CA *16–200*
Swan v Bank of Scotland, 6 E.R. 231; (1836) 10 Bli. N.S. 627, HL *16–165*
Swan Hunter & Wigham Richardson Ltd v France Fenwick Tyne & Wear Co Ltd; The Albion (No.2) [1953] 1 W.L.R. 1026; [1953] 2 All E.R. 679; [1953] 2 Lloyd's Rep. 82; (1953) 97 S.J. 524, CA *14–015*, *14–016*
Swaziland Central Transport Administration and Alfko Aussenhandels GmbH v Leila Maritime Co Ltd and Mediterranean Shipping Co SA; The Leila [1985] 2 Lloyd's Rep. 172, QBD (Comm) *3–108*, *3–109*
Sweeney v Astle [1923] N.Z.L.R. 1198 .... *16–114*
Sweet v Lee (1841) 3 Man. & G. 452 .... *4–034*, *29–079*
Sweet & Maxwell v Universal News Services [1964] 2 Q.B. 699; [1964] 3 W.L.R. 356; [1964] 3 All E.R. 30; (1964) 108 S.J. 478, CA *2–142*, *24–019*, *27–042*
Sweeting v Fowler (1815) 1 Stark. 106 .... *12–124*
Sweeting v Pearce (1861) 9 C.B.(N.S.) 534 .... *21–044*
Sweetman v Nathan [2003] EWCA Civ 1115; [2004] C.P. Rep. 7; [2004] P.N.L.R. 7, CA (Civ Div); reversing [2002] EWHC 2458, QBD *16–167*
Swift v Jewsbury; sub nom. Swift v Winterbotham (1873–74) L.R. 9 Q.B. 301, Ex Chamber; reversing in part (1872–73) L.R. 8 Q.B. 244, QBD *6–028*
Swift v MacBean [1942] 1 K.B. 375, KBD *23–055*
Swift v Swift (1841) 3 Ir. Eq. R. 267 .... *27–008*
Swift v Winterbotham. *See* Swift v Jewsbury
Swindle v Harrison [1997] 4 All E.R. 705; [1997] P.N.L.R. 641; [1997] N.P.C. 50, CA (Civ Div) *6–059*
Swingcastle Ltd v Alastair Gibson (A Firm) [1991] 2 A.C. 223; [1991] 2 W.L.R. 1091; [1991] 2 All E.R. 353; [1955–95] P.N.L.R. 590; [1991] 17 E.G. 83; [1991] C.C.L.R. 55; [1991] E.G. 46 (C.S.); (1991) 141 N.L.J. 563; (1991) 135 S.J. 542, HL; reversing [1990] 1 W.L.R. 1223; [1990] 3 All E.R. 463; [1990] 34 E.G. 49; [1990] C.C.L.R. 127; (1990) 140 N.L.J. 818, CA (Civ Div) *1–164*, *26–094*, *26–095*
Swinyard v Bowes (1816) 5 M.S. 62 .... *21–079*
Swire v Redman (1875–76) L.R. 1 Q.B.D. 536, QBD *17–021*
Swiss Bank Corp v Boehmische Industrial Bank [1923] 1 K.B. 673, CA *21–051*
Swiss Bank Corp v Brink's-MAT Ltd (Interest) [1986] Q.B. 853; [1986] 3 W.L.R. 12; [1986] 2 All E.R. 188; [1986] 2 Lloyd's Rep. 99 (Note); (1986) 130 S.J. 446, QBD (Comm) *14–007*, *14–011*, *14–055*, *18–019*
Swiss Bank Corp v Lloyds Bank Ltd [1982] A.C. 584; [1981] 2 W.L.R. 893; [1981] 2 All E.R. 449; (1981) 125 S.J. 495, HL; affirming [1980] 3 W.L.R. 457; [1980] 2 All E.R. 419; (1980) 124 S.J. 741, CA (Civ Div); reversing [1979] Ch. 548; [1979] 3 W.L.R. 201; [1979] 2 All E.R. 853; (1979) 123 S.J. 536, Ch D *1–188*, *18–138*, *18–140*, *18–141*, *18–145*, *27–008*
Swiss Bank Corp v State of New South Wales (1993–94) 33 N.S.W.L.R. 63 ... *30–339*
Swithenbank Foods Ltd v Bowers [2002] EWHC 2257 (QB); [2002] 2 All E.R. (Comm) 974, QBD (Merc) *30–110*
Swordheath Properties Ltd v Tabet [1979] 1 W.L.R. 285; [1979] 1 All E.R. 240; (1979) 37 P. & C.R. 327; (1978) 249 E.G. 439; (1978) 122 S.J. 862, CA (Civ Div) *26–022*, *29–144*
Sybron Corp v Rochem Ltd [1984] Ch. 112; [1983] 3 W.L.R. 713; [1983] 2 All E.R. 707; [1983] I.C.R. 801; [1983] I.R.L.R. 253; (1983) 127 S.J. 391, CA (Civ Div) *3–066*, 29–031, *29–043*
Sydall v Castings [1967] 1 Q.B. 302; [1966] 3 W.L.R. 1126; [1966] 3 All E.R. 770; (1966) 110 S.J. 790, CA *12–060*
Sydney City Council v West, 114 C.L.R. 481; (1965) 39 A.L.J.R. 323, HC (Aus) *14–005*, *14–033*, *14–036*
Syers v Jonas (1848) 2 Exch. 111 .... *12–133*
Sykes v Beadon (1879) L.R. 11 Ch. D. 170, Ch D *16–192*
Sykes v Dixon (1839) 9 Ad. & El. 693 .... *2–158*
Sykes v Giles (1839) 5 M.W. 645 .... *21–044*, *29–198*

Sykes v Midland Bank Executor & Trustee Co Ltd [1971] 1 Q.B. 113; [1970] 3 W.L.R. 273; [1970] 2 All E.R. 471; (1970) 114 S.J. 225, CA (Civ Div) *26–008, 26–032, 26–043, 26–157*
Sykes (Basil Landon) v DPP; sub nom. R. v Sykes (Basil Landon) [1962] A.C. 528; [1961] 3 W.L.R. 371; [1961] 3 All E.R. 33; (1961) 45 Cr. App. R. 230; (1961) 125 J.P. 523; (1961) 105 S.J. 566, HL; affirming [1961] 2 Q.B. 9; [1961] 2 W.L.R. 392; [1961] 1 All E.R. 702; (1961) 105 S.J. 183, CCA ... *3–062*
Sylvan Crest Sand & Gravel Co v U.S., 150 F. 2d 642 (1945) ... *2–039*
Symbian Ltd v Christensen [2000] U.K.C.L.R. 879; [2001] I.R.L.R. 77; [2001] Masons C.L.R. 75, CA (Civ Div) ... *16–103, 16–115, 27–066, 27–068, 27–069*
Symes v Hughes; Symes v Hughes (1869–70) L.R. 9 Eq. 475, Ct of Chancery *16–189*
Syndic for Khoury v Khayat. *See* Salim Nasrallah Khoury (Syndic in Bankruptcy) v Khayat
Synge v Synge [1894] 1 Q.B. 466, CA ... *2–169, 16–073, 24–022, 24–030*
Syrett v Egerton [1957] 1 W.L.R. 1130; [1957] 3 All E.R. 331; (1957) 101 S.J. 869, DC ... *19–032*
Syros Shipping Co SA v Elaghill Trading Co; The Proodos C [1981] 3 All E.R. 189; [1980] 2 Lloyd's Rep. 390; [1981] Com. L.R. 80, QBD (Comm) ... *3–053, 3–066, 3–098, 3–099, 3–100, 7–005, 22–035*
Systems Reliability Holdings v Smith [1990] I.R.L.R. 377, Ch D ... *16–104*, 16–109, *16–117*
Sze Hai Tong Bank v Rambler Cycle Co [1959] A.C. 576; [1959] 3 W.L.R. 214; [1959] 3 All E.R. 182; [1959] 2 Lloyd's Rep. 114; (1959) 103 S.J. 561, PC (Sing) ... *14–007, 14–016, 14–020*, 14–033, *14–036*
Szechter v Szechter [1971] P. 286; [1971] 2 W.L.R. 170; [1970] 3 All E.R. 905, PDAD ... *7–010*
T&N Ltd, Re [2005] EWHC 2870 (Ch); [2006] 1 W.L.R. 1728; [2006] 3 All E.R. 697; [2006] 2 B.C.L.C. 374; [2006] B.P.I.R. 532, Ch D (Companies Ct) ... *1–047*
T&N Ltd, Re [2006] EWHC 1447 (Ch); [2007] Bus. L.R. 1411; [2007] 1 All E.R. 851; [2007] 1 B.C.L.C. 563; [2006] B.P.I.R. 1283; [2006] Lloyd's Rep. I.R. 817, Ch D (Companies Ct) ... *18–131*
T (Adult: Medical Treatment), Re. *See* T (Adult: Refusal of Treatment), Re
T (Adult: Refusal of Treatment), Re; sub nom. T (Consent to Medical Treatment) (Adult Patient), Re [1993] Fam. 95; [1992] 3 W.L.R. 782; [1992] 4 All E.R. 649; [1992] 2 F.L.R. 458; [1992] 2 F.C.R. 861; [1992] 3 Med. L.R. 306; [1993] Fam. Law 27; (1992) 142 N.L.J. 1125, CA (Civ Div) ... *29–133*
T Choithram International SA v Pagarani; sub nom. Pagarani, Re [2001] 1 W.L.R. 1; [2001] 2 All E.R. 492; [2001] W.T.L.R. 277; (2000–01) 3 I.T.E.L.R. 254; (2001) 145 S.J.L.B. 8, PC (BVI); reversing (1998) 2 O.F.L.R. 1, CA (BVI) ... *3–021, 27–034*
T Comedy (UK) Ltd v Easy Managed Transport Ltd [2007] EWHC 611 (Comm); [2007] 2 All E.R. (Comm) 242; [2007] 2 Lloyd's Rep. 397; [2007] 1 C.L.C. 503, QBD (Comm) ... *18–022, 18–135, 22–032*
T Lucas & Co Ltd v Mitchell [1974] Ch. 129; [1972] 3 W.L.R. 934; [1972] 3 All E.R. 689; (1972) 116 S.J. 711, CA (Civ Div); reversing [1972] 1 W.L.R. 938; [1972] 2 All E.R. 1035; (1972) 116 S.J. 506, Ch D ... *16–108, 16–110, 16–113, 16–203*
TA Sundell & Sons Pty v Emm Yannoulatos (Overseas) Pty [1956] 56 S.R. (N.S.W.) 323 ... *3–067, 7–012, 7–019*
TB&S Batchelor & Co Ltd v Owners of the SS Merak; The Merak [1965] P. 223; [1965] 2 W.L.R. 250; [1965] 1 All E.R. 230; [1964] 2 Lloyd's Rep. 527; (1964) 108 S.J. 1012, CA; affirming [1964] 3 All E.R. 638; [1964] 2 Lloyd's Rep. 283, PDAD ... *12–077, 28–022, 28–115*
TC Industrial Plant Pty Ltd v Robert's Queensland Pty Ltd (1964) 37 A.L.J.R. 239, HC (Aus) ... *26–077*
TCB Ltd v Gray [1987] Ch. 458; [1987] 3 W.L.R. 1144; [1988] 1 All E.R. 108; (1987) 3 B.C.C. 503; [1988] B.C.L.C. 281; [1988] Fin. L.R. 116, CA (Civ Div); affirming [1986] Ch. 621; [1986] 2 W.L.R. 517; [1986] 1 All E.R. 587; (1986) 2 B.C.C. 99044; [1986] 3 C.M.L.R. 439; (1986) 83 L.S.G. 520; (1986) 130 S.J. 224, Ch D ... *1–092, 3–103, 3–108*

TD Keegan Ltd v Palmer [1961] 2 Lloyd's Rep. 449, QBD *29–090*, *29–092*
TFS Derivatives Ltd v Morgan [2004] EWHC 3181 (QB); [2005] I.R.L.R. 246, QBD *16–115*
TH Knitwear (Wholesale) Ltd, Re; sub nom. Customs and Excise Commissioners v TH Knitwear (Wholesale) Ltd [1988] Ch. 275; [1988] 2 W.L.R. 276; [1988] 1 All E.R. 860; [1988] S.T.C. 79; (1988) 4 B.C.C. 102; [1987] B.C.L.C. 195; [1988] P.C.C. 281; (1988) 85(4) L.S.G. 35; (1987) 131 S.J. 1696, CA (Civ Div); affirming [1987] 1 W.L.R. 371; [1986] S.T.C. 572; (1986) 2 B.C.C. 99544; [1987] B.C.L.C. 86; [1987] P.C.C. 112; (1987) 84 L.S.G. 188; (1987) 131 S.J. 46, Ch D *29–043*, *29–173*, *20–022*
TNT Global SpA v Denfleet International Ltd; sub nom. Denfleet International Ltd v TNT Global SpA [2007] EWCA Civ 405; [2008] 1 All E.R. (Comm) 97; [2007] 2 Lloyd's Rep. 504; [2007] 1 C.L.C. 710; [2007] R.T.R. 41; (2007) 104(20) L.S.G. 27, CA (Civ Div) *14–017*
TS Havprins, The. *See* Chevron International Oil Co Ltd v A/S Sea Team; The TS Havprins
TSB Bank Plc v Camfield [1995] 1 W.L.R. 430; [1995] 1 All E.R. 951; [1995] 1 F.L.R. 751; [1995] 2 F.C.R. 254; (1995) 27 H.L.R. 205; (1995) 92(3) L.S.G. 37; (1995) 145 N.L.J. 215; (1995) 139 S.J.L.B. 15, CA (Civ Div) 6–025, 6–026, *6–102*, *6–111*, 6–118, *7–097*, *7–120*
TSB Bank Plc v Connell, 1997 S.L.T. 1254, OH *16–109*
TSC Europe (UK) Ltd v Massey [1999] I.R.L.R. 22, Ch D *16–120*
TW Construction, Re [1954] 1 W.L.R. 540; [1954] 1 All E.R. 744; (1954) 98 S.J. 216, Ch D *9–049*
TW Thomas & Co Ltd v Portsea Steamship Co Ltd; The Portsmouth [1912] A.C. 1, HL; affirming [1911] P. 54, CA; reversing [1910] P. 293, PDAD *12–070*
Tackey v Mcbain [1912] A.C. 186, PC (Shanghai) 6–030
Tadcaster Tower Brewery Co v Wilson [1897] 1 Ch. 705, Ch D *21–013*
Taff Vale Railway Co v Amalgamated Society of Railway Servants [1901] A.C. 426, HL; reversing [1901] 1 Q.B. 170, CA *9–068*, 9–081
Tai Hing Cotton Mill Ltd v Kamsing Knitting Factory [1979] A.C. 91; [1978] 2 W.L.R. 62; [1978] 1 All E.R. 515; (1977) 121 S.J. 662, PC (HK) *24–001*, *24–004*, *24–011*, *24–022*, *26–007*, *26–008*, *29–176*
Tai Hing Cotton Mill Ltd v Liu Chong Hing Bank Ltd (No.1) [1986] A.C. 80; [1985] 3 W.L.R. 317; [1985] 2 All E.R. 947; [1985] 2 Lloyd's Rep. 313; [1986] F.L.R. 14; (1985) 82 L.S.G. 2995; (1985) 135 N.L.J. 680; (1985) 129 S.J. 503, PC (HK); reversing [1984] 1 Lloyd's Rep. 555, CA (HK) *1–012*, 1–126, 1–147, *1–150*, 1–152, *1–154*, 1–155, 1–158, *13–005*, *13–009*, *13–010*
Tailby v Official Receiver; sub nom. Official Receiver as Trustee of the Estate of Izon (A Bankrupt) v Tailby (1888) L.R. 13 App. Cas. 523, HL; reversing (1887) L.R. 18 Q.B.D. 25, CA; reversing (1886) L.R. 17 Q.B.D. 88, QBD *19–032*, *27–015*
Tain Construction Ltd, Re. *See* Rose v AIB Group (UK) Plc
Taite's Case. *See* Russian (Vyksounsky) Ironworks Co, Re
Taittinger SA v Allbev Ltd [1994] 4 All E.R. 75; [1993] 2 C.M.L.R. 741; [1993] F.S.R. 641; (1993) 12 Tr. L.R. 165, CA (Civ Div); reversing [1993] 1 C.M.L.R. 597, Ch D *6–016*
Tajik Aluminium Plant v Ermatov (No.4); sub nom. Ansol Ltd v Tajik Aluminium Plant [2006] EWHC 2374, QBD (Comm) *11–007*
Take Harvest v Liu [1993] A.C. 532; [1993] 2 All E.R. 459, PC *4–041*
Tal y Drws Slate Co, Re; sub nom. Mackley's Case (1875–76) L.R. 1 Ch. D. 247, Ch D *9–060*
Talbot v Berkshire CC [1994] Q.B. 290; [1993] 3 W.L.R. 708; [1993] 4 All E.R. 9; [1993] R.T.R. 406; [1993] P.I.Q.R. P319; (1993) 157 L.G. Rev. 1004; (1993) 143 N.L.J. 402, CA (Civ Div) *25–012*, *25–013*
Talbot v Von Boris [1911] 1 K.B. 854, CA *7–052*

Talbot Underwriting Ltd v Nausch Hogan & Murray Inc; The Jascon 5 [2006] EWCA Civ 889; [2006] 2 All E.R. (Comm) 751; [2006] 2 Lloyd's Rep. 195; [2006] 1 C.L.C. 1138; [2006] Lloyd's Rep. I.R. 531, CA (Civ Div); affirming [2005] EWHC 2359 (Comm); [2005] 2 C.L.C. 868, QBD (Comm) *12–114*, *18–080*
Talcott v Lewis [1940] 3 All E.R. 592 ...... *19–016*, *19–022*, *19–025*
Tam Wing Chuen v Bank of Credit and Commerce Hong Kong Ltd [1996] B.C.C. 388; [1996] 2 B.C.L.C. 69, PC (HK) *12–084*, *12–085*
Tameside MBC v Barlow Securities Group Services Ltd [2001] EWCA Civ 1; [2001] B.L.R. 113; 75 Con. L.R. 112, CA (Civ Div) *3–090*, *24–008*, *28–109*
Tamil Nadu Electricity Board v ST-CMS Electric Co Private Ltd [2007] EWHC 1713 (Comm); [2007] 2 All E.R. (Comm) 701; [2008] 1 Lloyd's Rep. 93, QBD (Comm) *3–107*, *3–109*, *3–112*, *23–027*, *30–040*, *30–061*, *30–358*
Tamlin v Hannaford [1950] 1 K.B. 18; [1949] 2 All E.R. 327; (1949) 65 T.L.R. 422; (1949) 93 S.J. 465, CA; reversing (1948) 98 L.J. 660, CC *10–010*
Tamplin Steamship Co Ltd v Anglo Mexican Petroleum Products Co Ltd. *See* FA Tamplin Steamship Co Ltd v Anglo Mexican Petroleum Products Co Ltd
Tamplin v James (1880) L.R. 15 Ch. D. 215; [1874–80] All E.R. Rep. 562, CA *5–063*, *5–077*
Tancred v Delagoa Bay & East Africa Railway (1889) L.R. 23 Q.B.D. 239, QBD *19–012*
Tanenbaum v Sears (1971) 18 D.L.R. (3d) 709, Sup Ct (Can) *27–052*
Tankexpress A/S v Compagnie Financiere Belge des Petroles SA. *See* A/S Tankexpress v Compagnie Financiere Belge des Petroles SA
Tankreederei Ahrenkeil GmbH v Frahuil SA; The Multitank Holsatia [1988] 2 Lloyd's Rep. 486, QBD (Comm) *2–004*, *2–006*, *2–076*, *2–111*, *3–092*, *3–093*, *22–027*
Tanner v Moore (1846) 9 Q.B. 1 ...... *3–027*
Tanner v Smart (1827) 6 B. & C. 603 ...... *28–092*
Tanner v Tanner (No.1) [1975] 1 W.L.R. 1346; [1975] 3 All E.R. 776; (1975) 5 Fam. Law 193; (1975) 119 S.J. 391, CA (Civ Div) *2–169*, *2–171*, *2–172*, *3–039*, *3–141*, *3–142*, *3–151*, *3–158*, *13–028*, 16–068
Tappenden (t/a English & American Autos) v Artus [1964] 2 Q.B. 185; [1963] 3 W.L.R. 685; [1963] 3 All E.R. 213; (1963) 107 S.J. 572, CA *13–006*, *18–135*
Tapster v Ward (1909) 101 L.T. 503 ...... *20–023*
Targe Towing Ltd v Marine Blast Ltd. *See* Marine Blast Ltd v Targe Towing Ltd
Target Holdings Ltd v Priestley [1999] Lloyd's Rep. Bank. 175; (2000) 79 P. & C.R. 305; (1999) 96(14) L.S.G. 33; (1999) 96(18) L.S.G. 34; (1999) 143 S.J.L.B. 121; [1999] N.P.C. 51, Ch D 4–055
Target Holdings Ltd v Redferns [1996] A.C. 421; [1995] 3 W.L.R. 352; [1995] 3 All E.R. 785; [1995] C.L.C. 1052; (1995) 139 S.J.L.B. 195; [1995] N.P.C. 136, HL; reversing [1994] 1 W.L.R. 1089; [1994] 2 All E.R. 337, CA (Civ Div) *1–189*
Tarleton v Allhusen (1834) 2 A.E. 32 ...... *21–074*
Tarn v Commercial Banking Co of Sydney (1883–84) L.R. 12 Q.B.D. 294, QBD *20–004*
Tarrabochcia v Hickie (1856) 1 H.N. 183 ...... *24–040*
Tasarruf Mevduati Sigorta Fonu v Demirel; sub nom. Tasarruff Mevduati Sigorta Fonu (A Firm) v Demirel (Application to Set Aside); Demirel v Tasarruff Mevduati Sigorta Fonu [2007] EWCA Civ 799; [2007] 1 W.L.R. 2508; [2007] 4 All E.R. 1014; [2007] 2 All E.R. (Comm) 925; [2007] 2 Lloyd's Rep. 440; [2007] C.P. Rep. 47, CA (Civ Div); affirming [2006] EWHC 3354 (Ch); [2007] 2 All E.R. 815; [2007] 1 All E.R. (Comm) 649; [2007] 1 Lloyd's Rep. 223; [2007] I.L.Pr. 8; (2007) 104(5) L.S.G. 30, Ch D *11–007*
Tasman Discoverer, The. *See* Dairy Containers Ltd v Tasman Orient Line CV; The Tasman Discoverer
Tate v Crowdson [1938] Ch. 869 ...... *28–036*
Tate v Williamson (1866–67) L.R. 2 Ch. App. 55, Lord Chancellor; affirming (1865–66) L.R. 1 Eq. 528, Ct of Chancery 6–080, *7–056*, 7–082, *7–084*, 7–101

Tate & Lyle Food & Distribution Ltd v Greater London Council. *See* Tate & Lyle Industries Ltd v Greater London Council
Tate & Lyle Industries Ltd v CIA Usina Bulhoes and Cargill Inc [1997] 1 Lloyd's Rep. 355, CA (Civ Div) *27–061*
Tate & Lyle Industries Ltd v Greater London Council; sub nom. Tate & Lyle Food & Distribution Ltd v Greater London Council [1983] 2 A.C. 509; [1983] 2 W.L.R. 649; [1983] 1 All E.R. 1159; [1983] 2 Lloyd's Rep. 117; 81 L.G.R. 4434; (1983) 46 P. & C.R. 243, HL; reversing [1982] 1 W.L.R. 971; [1982] 2 All E.R. 854; 80 L.G.R. 753, CA (Civ Div); reversing [1982] 1 W.L.R. 149; [1981] 3 All E.R. 716; (1981) 125 S.J. 865, QBD *18–031*, *18–036*, *26–178*
Tate & Lyle Ltd v Hain Steamship Co Ltd; sub nom. Hain Steamship Co v Tate & Lyle Ltd [1936] 2 All E.R. 597; (1936) 55 Ll. L. Rep. 159; 52 T.L.R. 617; 41 Com. Cas. 350; [1936] W.N. 210, HL; reversing (1934) 49 Ll. L. Rep. 123; 50 T.L.R. 415; 39 Com. Cas. 259; 151 L.T. 249, CA; reversing (1933) 47 Ll. L. Rep. 297, KBD *12–023*, *14–029*, *24–001*, *24–003*, *24–004*, *24–010*, *29–070*
Tatem Ltd v Gamboa. *See* WJ Tatem Ltd v Gamboa
Tatlock v Harris (1789) 3 T.R. 174 .... *19–088*
Tattersall v Drysdale [1935] 2 K.B. 174; (1935) 52 Ll. L. Rep. 21, KBD *18–127*
Tattersall v National Steamship Co Ltd (1883–84) L.R. 12 Q.B.D. 297, QBD *14–032*
Tatung (UK) Ltd v Galex Telesure Ltd (1989) 5 B.C.C. 325, QBD (Comm) *19–066*
Taubman v Pacific Steam Navigation Co (1872) 26 L.T. 704 .... *14–011*
Taunton, Delmard Lane & Co, Re. *See* Christie v Taunton Delmard Lane & Co
Taylor Ex p. Norvell, Re [1910] 1 K.B. 562, CA *20–041*
Taylor, Re; sub nom. Taylor v Wade [1894] 1 Ch. 671, Ch D *28–130*
Taylor v Allon [1966] 1 Q.B. 304; [1965] 2 W.L.R. 598; [1965] 1 All E.R. 557; [1965] 1 Lloyd's Rep. 155; (1965) 109 S.J. 78, DC *2–030*
Taylor v Ashton (1843) 11 M. & W. 401 .... *6–045*
Taylor v Beal, 78 E.R. 478; (1591) Cro. Eliz. 222, QB *21–038*
Taylor v Best (1854) 14 C.B. 487 .... *11–020*
Taylor v Bhail [1996] C.L.C. 377; 50 Con. L.R. 70, CA (Civ Div) *16–176*, *29–008*
Taylor v Blakelock (1886) L.R. 32 Ch. D. 560; (1886) 56 L.J. Ch. 390; (1886) 55 L.T. 8, CA *19–068*, *29–164*
Taylor v Bowers (1875–76) L.R. 1 Q.B.D. 291, CA *16–167*, 16–189
Taylor v Brewer (1813) 1 M. & S. 290 2–175
Taylor v Caldwell (1863) 32 L.J. Q.B. 164; (1863) 3 B. & S. 826 ...*1–020*, 5–025, 23–003, 23–004, 23–005, 23–006, 23–010, *23–021*, 23–033, 23–034, *23–052*, *23–053*
Taylor v Chester (1868–69) L.R. 4 Q.B. 309, QB *16–165*, 16–177, *16–178*
Taylor v Chichester and Midhurst Railway Co (1869–70) L.R. 4 H.L. 628, HL; reversing (1866–67) L.R. 2 Ex. 356, Ex Chamber *16–025*
Taylor v Crowland Gas & Coke Co (1854) 9 B.& C. 192 .... *16–147*
Taylor v Davies [1920] A.C. 636, PC (Can) *28–019*
Taylor v Dickens [1998] 1 F.L.R. 806; [1998] 3 F.C.R. 455; [1998] Fam. Law 191, Ch D *2–111*, *2–171*, *2–183*, *3–015*, *3–144*
Taylor v Glasgow Corp, 1952 S.C. 440; 1952 S.L.T. 399, IH (2 Div) *12–009*
Taylor v Hare (1805) 1 B.P.N.R. 260 .... *29–061*
Taylor v Hilary (1835) 1 Cr.M. & R. 741 .... *22–029*
Taylor v Holland [1902] 1 K.B. 676 .... *25–018*
Taylor v John Lewis Ltd (1927) 28 Ll. L. Rep. 329; 1927 S.C. 891; 1927 S.L.T. 625, IH (2 Div); affirming (1927) 27 Ll. L. Rep. 250, OH *14–140*
Taylor v Johnson (1983) 151 C.L.R. 422; 45 A.L.R. 265; 45 H.L.R. 265, HC (Aus) *5–074*, *5–078*, *5–085*, 5–117
Taylor v Johnston (1881–82) L.R. 19 Ch. D. 603, Ch D *7–075*, *8–065*
Taylor v Jones (1875–76) L.R. 1 C.P.D. 87, CPD *2–025*
Taylor v Laird (1856) 1 H.N. 266 .... *21–037*
Taylor v Laird, 1952 S.L.T. (Sh. Ct.) 74; (1952) 68 Sh. Ct. Rep. 207, Sh Ct (Glasgow) *29–070*, *29–073*

Taylor v Motability Finance Ltd [2004] EWHC 2619, QBD (Comm) *29–002*, *29–054*, 29–067, 29–068
Taylor v National Union of Mineworkers (Derbyshire Area) [1985] B.C.L.C. 237 .... *9–082*
Taylor v National Union of Seamen [1967] 1 W.L.R. 532; [1967] 1 All E.R. 767; [1966] 2 Lloyd's Rep. 504; 1 K.I.R. 702; (1967) 111 S.J. 192, Ch D *9–083*, *27–021*
Taylor v Oakes Roncoroni & Co (1922) 127 L.T. 267 .... *24–011*, *24–014*, *24–023*, *24–044*
Taylor v Oil and Ozokerite Co (1913) 29 T.L.R. 515 .... *6–127*, *28–144*
Taylor v Plumer (1815) 3 M.S. 562 .... *29–162*, *29–163*
Taylor v Rive Droite Music Ltd [2005] EWCA Civ 1300; [2006] E.M.L.R. 4, CA (Civ Div); reversing in part [2004] EWHC 1605, Ch D *12–078*, *13–012*
Taylor v St Helens Corp; sub nom. Taylor v Corp of St Helens (1877) L.R. 6 Ch. D. 264, CA *12–083*
Taylor v Vectapike Ltd [1990] 2 E.G.L.R. 12 .... *25–012*
Taylor v Water (1816) 7 Taunt. 374 .... *3–143*
Taylor v Webb [1937] 2 K.B. 283, CA *21–038*, *24–036*
Taylor v Wilsons Trustees (1975) S.C. 146 .... *29–036*, *29–043*
Taylor Fashions Ltd v Liverpool Victoria Trustees Co Ltd; Old & Campbell Ltd v Liverpool Victoria Friendly Society [1982] Q.B. 133; [1981] 2 W.L.R. 576; [1981] 1 All E.R. 897; [1981] Com. L.R. 34; (1979) 251 E.G. 159, Ch D *3–098*, *3–138*, *3–147*, *3–162*, *3–163*, *28–136*
Taylor Barnard v Tozer (1984) 269 E.G. 225 .... *5–117*
Taylor & Sons v Bank of Athens; Pennoid Bros v Bank of Athens (1922) 10 Ll. L. Rep. 88; (1922) 27 Com. Cas. 142, KBD *26–008*
Taylor's, Re [1972] 2 Q.B. 369; [1972] 2 W.L.R. 1337; [1972] 2 All E.R. 873; (1972) 116 S.J. 314, CA (Civ Div) 8–62
Teacher v Calder [1899] A.C. 451; (1899) 1 F. (H.L.) 39; (1899) 7 S.L.T.153, HL; reversing (1898) 25 R. 661; (1898) 5 S.L.T. 353, IH (1 Div) *1–123*, *29–151*
Team Services v Keir Management, 63 B.L.R. 76; 36 Con. L.R. 32, CA (Civ Div); reversing, 61 B.L.R. 99; 31 Con. L.R. 9; [1992] N.P.C. 128, QBD (OR) *12–069*
Technotrade Ltd v Larkstore Ltd. *See* Offer-Hoar v Larkstore Ltd
Teh Hu, The. *See* Owners of Turbo Electric Bulk Carrier Teh Hu v Nippon Salvage Co Ltd; The Teh Hu
Tekron Resources Ltd v Guinea Investment Co Ltd [2003] EWHC 2577; [2004] 2 Lloyd's Rep. 26, QBD *16–028*, *30–069*, *30–355*, *30–358*, *30–367*
Tektrol Ltd (formerly Atto Power Controls Ltd) v International Insurance Co of Hanover Ltd [2005] EWCA Civ 845; [2006] 1 All E.R. (Comm) 780; [2005] 2 Lloyd's Rep. 701; [2005] 2 C.L.C. 339; [2006] Lloyd's Rep. I.R. 38, CA (Civ Div); reversing [2004] EWHC 2473; [2005] 1 All E.R. (Comm) 132; [2005] Info. T.L.R. 130; [2005] Lloyd's Rep. I.R. 358, QBD (Comm) *12–083*, *12–085*
Telemachus, The. *See* Owners of the Tantalus v Owners of the Telemachus
Telephone Rentals v Burgess Salmon & Co, *Independent*, April 22, 1987, CA (Civ Div) *24–010*
Telewest Communications Plc (No.1), Re [2004] EWCA Civ 728; [2005] B.C.C. 29; [2005] 1 B.C.L.C. 752, CA (Civ Div) *30–376*
Telfair Shipping Corp v Athos Shipping Co SA; The Athos [1983] 1 Lloyd's Rep. 127, CA (Civ Div); affirming in part [1981] 2 Lloyd's Rep. 74; [1981] Com. L.R. 105, QBD (Comm) *3–081*, *3–090*, *3–091*, *22–051*, *24–004*, *24–007*, *24–008*, *24–019*
Telfair Shipping Corp v Inersea Carriers SA; The Caroline P [1985] 1 W.L.R. 553; [1985] 1 All E.R. 243; [1984] 2 Lloyd's Rep. 466; (1985) 82 L.S.G. 1781; (1985) 129 S.J. 283, QBD (Comm) *28–049*
Telfair Shipping Corp v Inersea Carriers SA; The Caroline P (Injunction); sub nom. Carolina P, The (Injunction) [1983] 2 Lloyd's Rep. 351, QBD (Comm) *25–008*
Tempest v Kilner (1845) 3 C.B. 249 .... *26–100*

Temple Steamship Co Ltd v V/O Sorfracht; sub nom. Vsesojuznoje Objediheni Sovfracht of Moscow v Temple Steamship Co Ltd (1946) 79 Ll. L. Rep. 1; (1945) 62 T.L.R. 43; 173 L.T. 373, HL; affirming (1944) 77 Ll. L. Rep. 257, CA; reversing (1943) 76 Ll. L. Rep. 182, KBD *14–029*, *24–003*
Templiss Properties Ltd v Hyams [1999] E.G. 60 (C.S.), Ch D *5–116*
Tempus Shipping Co Ltd v Louis Dreyfus & Co; sub nom. Louis Dreyfus & Co v Tempus Shipping Co Ltd [1931] A.C. 726; (1931) 40 Ll. L. Rep. 217, HL; affirming [1931] 1 K.B. 195; (1930) 37 Ll. L. Rep. 273, CA; reversing in part [1930] 1 K.B. 699; (1930) 36 Ll. L. Rep. 159, KBD *14–146*
Tenax Steamship Co v Owners of the Motor Vessel Brimnes; The Brimnes; sub nom. Tenax Steamship Co v Reinante Transoceanica Navegacion SA; The Brimnes [1975] Q.B. 929; [1974] 3 W.L.R. 613; [1974] 3 All E.R. 88; [1974] 2 Lloyd's Rep. 241; (1974) 118 S.J. 808, CA (Civ Div); affirming [1973] 1 W.L.R. 386; [1973] 1 All E.R. 769; [1972] 2 Lloyd's Rep. 465; (1973) 117 S.J. 244, QBD (Admlty) *2–047*, *2–091*, *21–013*, *21–022*, *21–045*, *21–047*, *21–088*, *22–051*
Tennant Radiant Heat v Warrington Development Corp [1988] 1 E.G.L.R. 41; [1988] 11 E.G. 71; (1988) 4 Const. L.J. 321, CA (Civ Div) ...*26–039*, *26–049*, *26–050*
Tennant v Elliott (1791) 1 B. & P. 3 .... *16–192*
Tennants (Lancashire) Ltd v CS Wilson & Co Ltd; sub nom. Wilson & Co Ltd v Tennants (Lancashire) Ltd [1917] A.C. 495, HL; reversing [1917] 1 K.B. 208, CA *14–141*, *14–143*, *14–151*, *23–064*
Tennaro Ltd v Majorarch Ltd; sub nom. Tennero Ltd v Majorarch Ltd [2003] EWHC 2601 (Ch); [2003] 47 E.G. 154 (C.S.); [2004] 1 P. & C.R. DG13, Ch D *21–013*, *26–152*
Tennent v Tennents (1870) L.R. 2 Sc. & Div. 6 .... *3–014*, *3–021*
Tergeste, The [1903] P. 26, PDAD *21–053*
Terkol Rederierne v Petroleo Brasileiro SA and Frota Nacional de Petroleiros; The Badagry [1985] 1 Lloyd's Rep. 395, CA (Civ Div) *13–009*
Termes de la Leys v Fait, Co.Litt. 171b *1–093*
Terrapin International Ltd v Inland Revenue Commissioners [1976] 1 W.L.R. 665; [1976] 2 All E.R. 461; [1976] S.T.C. 197; [1976] T.R. 57; (1976) 120 S.J. 302, Ch D *1–105*, *1–107*
Terry and White's Contract, Re (1886) L.R. 32 Ch. D. 14, CA *12–042*, *27–057*
Tesco Stores v Gibson (William) & Son (1970) 214 E.G. 835 .... *2–155*
Tesco Stores Ltd v Norman Hitchcox Partnership Ltd; Clark Care Group Ltd v Norman Hitchcox Partnership Ltd; Maidstone Grove Ltd v Norman Hitchcox Partnership Ltd, 56 Con. L.R. 42, QBD (OR) *1–160*
Tessler Bros (BC) v Italpacific Line and Matson Terminals Inc [1975] 1 Lloyd's Rep. 210, US Ct *14–042*
Tester v Bisley (1948) 64 T.L.R. 184; [1948] W.N. 83 .... *12–052*
Tetley v Wanless (1866–67) L.R. 2 Ex. 275, Ex Chamber; affirming (1866–67) L.R. 2 Ex. 21, Ex Ct *22–003*, *22–005*
Tew v Newbold-on-Avon United District School Board (1884) 1 Cab. & E. 260 .... *22–038*
Tewkesbury Gas Co, Re; sub nom. Tysoe v Tewkesbury Gas Co [1912] 1 Ch. 1, CA; affirming [1911] 2 Ch. 279, Ch D *12–078*
Texaco v Mulberry Filling Station [1972] 1 W.L.R. 814; [1972] 1 All E.R. 513; (1971) 116 S.J. 119, Ch D 16–096, *16–096*, *16–102*, *16–122*, *27–061*
Texaco Ltd v Eurogulf Shipping Co Ltd [1987] 2 Lloyd's Rep. 541, QBD (Comm) *24–018*
Texaco Melbourne, The. *See* Attorney General of Ghana v Texaco Overseas Tankships Ltd; The Texaco Melbourne
Thackwell v Barclays Bank Plc [1986] 1 All E.R. 676, QBD *16–181*
Thai Trading Co v Taylor [1998] Q.B. 781; [1998] 2 W.L.R. 893; [1998] 3 All E.R. 65; [1998] 1 Costs L.R. 122; [1998] 2 F.L.R. 430; [1998] 3 F.C.R. 606; [1998] P.N.L.R. 698; [1998] Fam. Law 586; (1998) 95(15) L.S.G. 30; (1998) 142 S.J.L.B. 125, CA (Civ Div) *16–049*, *16–054*, 16–055, *16–066*

Thai-Europe Tapioca Service Ltd v Pakistan Directorate of Agricultural Supplies; The Harmattan; sub nom. Thai-Europe Tapioca Service Ltd v Pakistan, Ministry of Food and Agriculture; The Harmattan [1975] 1 W.L.R. 1485; [1975] 3 All E.R. 961; [1976] 1 Lloyd's Rep. 1; (1975) 119 S.J. 745, CA (Civ Div) *11–001*
Thai-Europe Tapioca Service Ltd v Seine Navigation Co Inc; The Maritime Winner [1989] 2 Lloyd's Rep. 506, QBD (Comm) *2–004*, *2–006*, *2–111*, *22–027*
Thairlwall v Great Northern Railway Co [1910] 2 K.B. 509, KBD *21–056*
Thake v Maurice [1986] Q.B. 644; [1986] 2 W.L.R. 337; [1986] 1 All E.R. 479; (1986) 83 L.S.G. 123; (1986) 136 N.L.J. 92, CA (Civ Div); affirming [1985] 2 W.L.R. 215; [1984] 2 All E.R. 513; (1985) 82 L.S.G. 871; (1985) 129 S.J. 86, QBD *1–147*, 1–149, 1–164, *13–032*
Thames & Mersey Marine Insurance Co Ltd v Gunford Ship Co Ltd; sub nom. Gunford Steamship Co Ltd (in Liquidation) v Thames & Mersey Marine Insurance Co Ltd,; Gunford Steamship Co Ltd and Liquidator v Thames & Mersey Marine Insurance Co; Gunford Ship Co Ltd (in Liquidation) and Liquidator v Thames & Mersey Marine Insurance Co Ltd; Southern Marine Mutual Insurance Association Ltd v Gunford Ship Co Ltd [1911] A.C. 529; 1911 S.C. (H.L.) 84; 1911 2 S.L.T. 185, HL; reversing 1910 S.C. 1072; 1910 2 S.L.T. 154, IH (1 Div); affirming 1909 2 S.L.T. 240, OH *6–147*
Thames and Mersey Marine Insurance Co Ltd v Hamilton Fraser & Co; sub nom. Hamilton, Fraser & Co v Thames & Mersey Marine Insurance Co Ltd (1887) L.R. 12 App. Cas. 484, HL; reversing (1886) L.R. 17 Q.B.D. 195, CA *12–053*, *12–062*, *12–087*, *14–146*
Thames Sack & Bag Co Ltd v Knowles (1918) 88 L.J.K.B. 585 .... *27–016*
Thames Tideway Properties Ltd v Serfaty & Partners [1999] 2 Lloyd's Rep. 110, CC (Central London) *3–025*, *14–085*, 14–097
Thames Valley Power Ltd v Total Gas & Power Ltd [2005] EWHC 2208; [2006] 1 Lloyd's Rep. 441; (2006) 22 Const. L.J. 591, QBD (Comm) *12–051*, *14–141*, *27–008*, 27–018, *27–026*
Thames Water Utilities Ltd v Reynolds [1996] I.R.L.R. 186, EAT *21–030*
Thamesmead Town Ltd v Allotey (1998) 30 H.L.R. 1052; (2000) 79 P. & C.R. 557; [1998] 3 E.G.L.R. 97; [1998] 37 E.G. 161; (1998) 95(3) L.S.G. 26; (1998) 76 P. & C.R. D20, CA (Civ Div) *19–080*
Thavorn v Bank of Credit and Commerce International SA [1985] 1 Lloyd's Rep. 259, QBD (Comm) 3–044, *8–049*, *18–074*, *29–039*, *29–049*, *29–081*, 29–158
Thelluson v Rendlesham (1859) 7 H.L.C. 429 .... *12–055*
Thellusson Ex p. Abdy, Re [1919] 2 K.B. 735, CA *20–023*, *29–043*
Thellusson v Viscount Valentia [1907] 2 Ch. 1, CA; affirming [1906] 1 Ch. 480, Ch D *9–074*
Themehelp Ltd v West [1996] Q.B. 84; [1995] 3 W.L.R. 751; [1995] 4 All E.R. 215; [1995] C.L.C. 703, CA (Civ Div) *27–008*, *27–061*
Theodohos, The [1977] 2 Lloyd's Rep. 428, QBD (Admlty) *30–081*
Thiis v Byers (1875–76) L.R. 1 Q.B.D. 244, QBD 23–045
Thimbleby v Barron (1838) 3 M. & W. 210 .... *22–006*
Thirkell v Cambi [1919] 2 K.B. 590, CA *4–027*, *4–036*
Thistle Hotels v Sir Robert McAlpine, *The Times*, April 11, 1989, CA (Civ Div) *28–118*
Thoday v Thoday [1964] P. 181; [1964] 2 W.L.R. 371; [1964] 1 All E.R. 341; (1964) 108 S.J. 15, CA *25–011*
Thomas v Brown (1875–76) L.R. 1 Q.B.D. 714, QBD *4–023*, *4–041*, *4–084*, *29–079*
Thomas v Cambi (1655) Sty.461 .... *18–019*
Thomas v Davis (1757) 1 Dick. 301 .... *5–124*
Thomas v Evans (1808) 10 East 101 .... *21–088*
Thomas v Farr Plc [2007] EWCA Civ 118; [2007] I.C.R. 932; [2007] I.R.L.R. 419; (2007) 151 S.J.L.B. 296, CA (Civ Div) *16–107*, *16–108*
Thomas v Fredricks (1847) 10 Q.B. 775 .... *24–032*
Thomas v Harris [1947] 1 All E.R. 444, CA *19–025*
Thomas v Houston Corbett & Co [1969] N.Z.L.R. 151, CA (Civ Div) *29–026*, *29–184*

Thomas v Ken Thomas Ltd [2006] EWCA Civ 1504; [2007] Bus. L.R. 429; [2007] B.P.I.R. 959; [2007] L. & T.R. 21; [2007] 1 E.G. 94; [2006] 42 E.G. 244 (C.S.); (2006) 150 S.J.L.B. 1396, CA (Civ Div) *21–059*, *21–060*, *21–061*
Thomas v Poole (1655) Sty. 461 .... *18–019*
Thomas v Sorrell (1673) Vaughan 330 .... *13–028*
Thomas v Thomas (1842) 2 Q.B. 851 ....*3–002*, *3–003*, *3–004*, *3–008*, 3–011, 3–012, 3–022, *3–036*, *3–061*
Thomas v Todd [1926] 2 K.B. 511, KBD *9–051*
Thomas v University of Bradford; sub nom. Thomas v Bradford University [1987] A.C. 795; [1987] 2 W.L.R. 677; [1987] 1 All E.R. 834; [1987] I.C.R. 245; (1987) 84 L.S.G. 980; (1987) 137 N.L.J. 220; (1987) 131 S.J. 296, HL *27–023*
Thomas Bates & Son Ltd v Wyndham's (Lingerie) Ltd [1981] 1 W.L.R. 505; [1981] 1 All E.R. 1077; (1981) 41 P. & C.R. 345; (1980) 257 E.G. 381; (1981) 125 S.J. 32, CA (Civ Div); affirming (1980) 39 P. & C.R. 517, Ch D *2–128*, *2–132*, 5–115, *5–118*, *5–122*
Thomas Borthwick (Glasgow) Ltd v Bunge & Co Ltd [1969] 1 Lloyd's Rep. 17, QBD (Comm) *12–069*, *14–147*, *14–148*
Thomas Brown & Sons v Fazal Deen (1962) 108 C.L.R. 391 .... *16–180*
Thomas Cook Group Ltd v Air Malta Co Ltd (t/a Air Malta) [1997] 2 Lloyd's Rep. 399, QBD (Comm) *14–017*
Thomas Feather & Co (Bradford) v Keighley Corp, 52 L.G.R. 30 .... *27–003*
Thomas Marshall (Exports) Ltd v Guinle [1979] Ch. 227; [1978] 3 W.L.R. 116; [1978] 3 All E.R. 193; [1978] I.C.R. 905; [1978] I.R.L.R. 174; [1979] F.S.R. 208; (1978) 122 S.J. 295, Ch D *16–107*, *24–001*, *24–013*
Thomas National Transport (Melbourne) Pty Ltd and Pay v May & Baker (Australia) Pty Ltd [1966] 2 Lloyd's Rep. 347; 40 A.L.J.R. 189; 116 N.L.J. 1544, HC (Aus) *14–008*, *14–030*
Thomas P Gonzalez Corp v Muller's Muhle Muller GmbH & Co KG (No.2) [1980] 1 Lloyd's Rep. 445, QBD (Comm) *14–140*
Thomas Wilson Sons & Co v Owners of Cargo of the Xantho; The Xantho (1887) L.R. 12 App.Cas. 503, HL; reversing (1886) 11 L.R. P.D. 170, CA *14–146*
Thomas Witter Ltd v TBP Industries Ltd [1996] 2 All E.R. 573, Ch D ... *6–018*, 6–098, *6–138*, *6–139*, *12–104*, *14–063*
Thompson v ASDA-MFI Group Plc [1988] Ch. 241; [1988] 2 W.L.R. 1093; [1988] 2 All E.R. 722; [1988] I.R.L.R. 340; (1988) 132 S.J. 497, Ch D *2–153*, *2–156*, *13–012*, *22–055*
Thompson v Australian Capital Television Pty (1996) 186 C.L.R. 574 .... *17–020*
Thompson v Cohen (1871–72) L.R. 7 Q.B. 527; (1872) 41 L.J. Q.B. 221; (1872) 26 L.T. 693, QB *20–047*
Thompson v Corroon (1993) 66 P. & C.R. 445; [1993] N.P.C. 54, PC (WI) *24–018*, *24–019*, *24–047*, *24–050*, *24–051*, *24–053*
Thompson v Gardiner (1875–76) L.R. 1 C.P.D. 777, CPD *4–038*
Thompson v Hakewill (1865) 9 C.B. (N.S.) 713 ....*3–042*, *3–044*
Thompson v Hickman [1907] 1 Ch. 550, Ch D *5–112*
Thompson v Hudson (Appropriation of Payments) (1870–71) L.R. 6 Ch. App. 320, CA in Chancery *21–065*
Thompson v Lack (1846) 3 C.B. 540 .... *17–018*
Thompson v London Midland & Scottish Railway Co [1930] 1 K.B. 41, CA *2–021*, *12–009*, *12–014*, *12–016*, *12–017*, *14–135*
Thompson v McCullough [1947] K.B. 447; [1947] 1 All E.R. 265; 63 T.L.R. 95; 176 L.T. 493; (1947) 91 S.J. 147, CA *1–105*
Thompson v Palmer [1893] 2 Q.B. 80, CA *21–054*
Thompson v Park [1944] K.B. 408, CA *13–028*
Thompson v Percival (1834) 5 B. & Ad. 925 ....*3–175*, *21–077*
Thompson v Reynolds (1872) 3 C. & P. 123 .... *20–004*
Thompson v Stimpson [1961] 1 Q.B. 195; [1960] 3 W.L.R. 818; [1960] 3 All E.R. 500; (1960) 104 S.J. 912, DC *12–093*

Thompson v T Lohan (Plant Hire) and Hurdiss (JW) [1987] 1 W.L.R. 649; [1987] 2 All E.R. 631; [1987] I.R.L.R. 148; (1987) 84 L.S.G. 979; (1987) 131 S.J. 358, CA (Civ Div) *14–015*, *14–071*, *14–076*, *14–092*
Thompson and Norris Manufacturing Co Ltd v Hawes (1895) 73 L.T. 369 .... *29–096*
Thomson v Clanmore [1900] 1 Ch. 718 .... *28–031*
Thomson v Clydesdale Bank Ltd; sub nom. Dunlop's Trustees v Clydesdale Bank Ltd [1893] A.C. 282; (1893) 20 R. (H.L.) 50; (1893) 1 S.L.T.111, HL *29–164*
Thomson v Weems (1883–84) L.R. 9 App. Cas. 671, HL; reversing (1884) 11 R. 658, IH (2 Div) *12–031*
Thor Navigation Inc v Ingosstrakh Insurance Co Ltd [2005] EWHC 19; [2005] 1 Lloyd's Rep. 547; [2005] 1 C.L.C. 12; [2005] Lloyd's Rep. I.R. 490, QBD (Comm) *3–107*, *3–109*, *12–079*
Thorensen Car Ferries v Weymouth Portland BC [1977] 2 Lloyd's Rep. 614, QBD (Comm) *2–002*, *2–028*, *3–008*, *3–062*, *3–063*, *12–118*
Thoresen & Co (Bangkok) Ltd v Fathom Marine Co Ltd [2004] EWHC 167; [2004] 1 All E.R. (Comm) 935; [2004] 1 Lloyd's Rep. 622, QBD (Comm) *2–116*
Thorman v Dowgate Steamship Co Ltd [1910] 1 K.B. 410, KBD *12–087*, *12–088*, *14–138*
Thorn v City Rice Mills (1889) L.R. 40 Ch. D. 357, Ch D *21–006*, *21–054*
Thorn v Commissioners of Her Majesty's Works and Public Buildings (1863) 32 Beav. 490 .... *10–016*
Thorn v Deas (1809) 4 Johns. 84 .... *3–178*
Thornbury v Bevill (1842) 1 Y. & C.C.C. 554 .... *27–043*
Thorndike v Hunt (1859) 3 De G.J. 563 .... *29–164*
Thorne, Re. *See* HE Thorne & Son Ltd, Re
Thorne v Heard & Marsh [1895] A.C. 495, HL *28–057*
Thorne v Motor Trade Association [1937] A.C. 797; (1938) 26 Cr. App. R. 51, HL *7–045*, *7–046*, *29–088*
Thorne v Silverleaf [1994] B.C.C. 109; [1994] 2 B.C.L.C. 637, CA (Civ Div) *16–168*
Thorne v Smith (1851) 10 C.B. 659 .... *21–074*
Thorner v Curtis [2007] EWHC 2422 (Ch); [2008] W.T.L.R. 155; [2007] N.P.C. 112, Ch D (Bristol) *3–154*
Thorner v Feild (1612) 1 Bulst. 120 .... *3–026*
Thornett and Fehr v Yuills Ltd. *See* Thornett v Yuills Ltd
Thornett v Haines (1846) 15 M.W. 367 .... *29–148*
Thornett v Yuills Ltd; sub nom. Arbitration between Thornett and Fehr & Yuills Ltd, Re [1921] 1 K.B. 219; (1920) 5 Ll. L. Rep. 47, KBD *23–047*, *26–048*
Thornhill v Neats (1860) 8 C.B. (N.S.) 831 .... *22–028*
Thornton Springer v NEM Insurance Co Ltd [2000] 2 All E.R. 489; [2000] 1 All E.R. (Comm) 486; [2000] C.L.C. 975; [2000] Lloyd's Rep. I.R. 590; (2000) 97(13) L.S.G. 42; (2000) 144 S.J.L.B. 147, QBD (Comm) *3–057*, *3–098*, *3–108*, *3–113*
Thornton v Jenkyns (1840) 1 M. & G.166 .... *3–027*
Thornton v Kempster (1814) 5 Taunt. 786 .... *5–071*
Thornton v Sherratt (1818) 8 Taunt. 529 .... *16–126*
Thornton v Shoe Lane Parking [1971] 2 Q.B. 163; [1971] 2 W.L.R. 585; [1971] 1 All E.R. 686; [1971] 1 Lloyd's Rep. 289; [1971] R.T.R. 79; (1970) 115 S.J. 75, CA (Civ Div) .. *2–016*, *2–021*, *12–009*, *12–010*, *12–013*, *12–015*, *12–017*, *14–002*
Thoroughgood's Case (1584) 2 Co Rep. 9a *1–111*, *5–101*
Thorpe v Booth (1826) Ry. & M. 388 .... *28–042*
Thorpe v Brumfitt (1872–73) L.R. 8 Ch. App. 650, CA in Chancery *12–117*
Thorpe v Fasey [1949] Ch. 649; [1949] 2 All E.R. 393; 65 T.L.R. 561; [1949] L.J.R. 1613; (1949) 93 S.J. 552, Ch D *6–117*, *21–014*, *24–018*, *24–026*
Thos P Gonzales Corp v FR Waring (International) Party Ltd [1986] 2 Lloyd's Rep. 160 .... *26–127*

Thrasyvoulou v Secretary of State for the Environment; Oliver v Secretary of State for the Environment [1990] 2 A.C. 273; [1990] 2 W.L.R. 1; [1990] 1 All E.R. 65; 88 L.G.R. 217; (1990) 2 Admin. L.R. 289; (1990) 59 P. & C.R. 326; [1990] 1 P.L.R. 69; [1990] 13 E.G. 69; (1990) 154 L.G. Rev. 192; [1989] E.G. 178 (C.S.), HL *25–011*, *25–012*
Three Rivers DC v Bank of England (No.1) [1996] Q.B. 292; [1995] 3 W.L.R. 650; [1995] 4 All E.R. 312; [1995] C.L.C. 99, CA (Civ Div) *19–005*, *19–038*
Three Rivers Trading Co v Gwinear & District Farmers (1967) 111 S.J. 831, CA (Civ Div) *12–129*
Three Spanish Sailors, The (1779) 2 W.Bl. 1324 .... *11–027*
Throcmerton v Tracey (1585) 1 Plow. 145 .... *12–063*
Thunderbird Industries LLC v Simoco Digital UK Ltd; sub nom. Simoco Digital UK Ltd, Re [2004] EWHC 209 (Ch); [2004] 1 B.C.L.C. 541, Ch D (Companies Ct) *21–013*, *24–030*
Thursby v Eccles (1900) 17 T.L.R. 130 .... *4–011*
Thurstan Hoskin & Partners v Allbright (formely t/a Jewill Hill & Bennett); sub nom. Thurstan Hoskin & Partners v Jewill Hill & Bennett [2002] EWCA Civ 249, Ch D; affirming, TR710841, CC (Truro) *16–119*
Thwaite v Thwaite [1982] Fam. 1; [1981] 3 W.L.R. 96; [1981] 2 All E.R. 789; (1981) 125 S.J. 307, CA (Civ Div) *5–062*
Thyssen Inc v Calypso Shipping Corp SA [2000] 2 All E.R. (Comm) 97; [2000] 2 Lloyd's Rep. 243; [2001] C.L.C. 805; 2001 A.M.C. 198; (2000) 97(27) L.S.G. 37, QBD (Comm) *28–022*
Tielens v Hooper (1850) 5 Exch. 830 .... *12–051*
Tiernan v Magen Insurance Co Ltd [2000] I.L.Pr. 517, QBD (Comm) *30–011*, *30–023*, *30–051*, *30–055*, *30–077*
Tiessen v Henderson [1899] 1 Ch. 861, Ch D *9–055*
Tiffany Investments Ltd v Bircham & Co Nominees (No.2) Ltd [2003] EWCA Civ 1759; [2004] 2 P. & C.R. 10; [2004] L. & T.R. 22; [2004] 2 E.G.L.R. 31; [2004] 21 E.G. 152, CA (Civ Div); affirming [2003] EWHC 143; [2003] 2 P. & C.R. 29; [2003] L. & T.R. 29; [2003] 12 E.G. 127 (C.S.); [2003] N.P.C. 18, Ch D *2–127*
Tilden Rent-a-Car Co v Clendenning (1978) 83 D.L.R. (3d) 400 ... *5–079*, *12–002*, *12–015*
Tilley v Bowman Ltd [1910] 1 K.B. 745, KBD *1–131*, *19–071*, *20–033*, *20–039*, *20–041*, *20–042*
Tilley v Thomas (1867–68) L.R. 3 Ch. App. 61, CA in Chancery *21–013*
Tilley's Will Trusts, Re; sub nom. Burgin v Croad [1967] Ch. 1179; [1967] 2 W.L.R. 1533; [1967] 2 All E.R. 303; (1967) 111 S.J. 237, Ch D ... *29–158*, *29–172*
Tillmanns v SS Knutsford. *See* SS Knutsford Ltd v Tillmanns & Co
Tilly Russ (MS), The. *See* Partenreederei M.S. Tilly Russ v Haven & Vervoerbedrijf Nova
Tilney Engineering v Admods Knitting Machinery [1987] C.L.Y. 412 .... *3–115*
Tilt, Re (1896) 74 L.T. 163 .... *19–028*
Timber Shipping Co SA v London and Overseas Freighters; sub nom. London & Overseas Freighters Ltdv Timber Shipping Co SA [1972] A.C. 1; [1971] 2 W.L.R. 1360; [1971] 2 All E.R. 599; [1971] 1 Lloyd's Rep. 523; (1971) 115 S.J. 404, HL; affirming in part [1971] 1 Q.B. 268; [1970] 3 W.L.R. 784; [1970] 3 All E.R. 756; [1970] 2 Lloyd's Rep. 207; (1970) 114 S.J. 785, CA (Civ Div) *12–069*, *12–093*
Timeload Ltd v British Telecommunications Plc [1995] E.M.L.R. 459, CA (Civ Div) *14–073*, *14–074*, 14–093, *14–112*
Times Newspapers Ltd v Burstein (Costs: Champertous Retainer); sub nom. Burstein v Times Newspapers Ltd (No.2) [2002] EWCA Civ 1739; [2003] 1 Costs L.R. 111; (2003) 100(3) L.S.G. 31; (2002) 146 S.J.L.B. 277, CA (Civ Div) *16–056*
Times Newspapers Ltd v Chohan (Limitation Periods); sub nom. Chohan v Times Newspapers Ltd (Limitation Periods) [2001] EWCA Civ 964; [2001] 1 W.L.R. 1859; [2001] C.P. Rep. 100; [2002] 1 Costs L.R. 1; [2001] B.P.I.R. 943; (2001) 98(30) L.S.G. 38; (2001) 145 S.J.L.B. 165, CA (Civ Div) *28–016*

Times Newspapers Ltd v George Weidenfeld & Nicolson Ltd [2002] F.S.R. 29, QBD *13–007*, *13–009*, *13–012*
Timmins v Moreland Street Property Co Ltd [1958] Ch. 110; [1957] 3 W.L.R. 678; [1957] 3 All E.R. 265; (1957) 101 S.J. 815, CA *4–024*, *4–028*, 4–029, *12–102*
Timothy v Simpson (1834) 6 C. & P. 499 .... *2–014*
Timpson's Executors v Yerbury (Inspector of Taxes) [1936] 1 K.B. 645, CA ... *19–023*
Tiney Engineering v Amods Knitting Machinery, unreported, May 15, 1986, CA (Civ Div) *22–016*
Tinker v Wandsworth DSW (1858) 2 De.G & J. 261 .... *9–023*
Tinline v White Cross Insurance Association Ltd [1921] 3 K.B. 327, KBD *16–173*
Tinn v Hoffman (1873) 29 L.T. 271 .... *2–032*, *2–044*, *2–067*, *2–092*, *2–093*
Tinsley v Milligan [1994] 1 A.C. 340; [1993] 3 W.L.R. 126; [1993] 3 All E.R. 65; [1993] 2 F.L.R. 963; (1994) 68 P. & C.R. 412; [1993] E.G. 118 (C.S.); [1993] N.P.C. 97, HL; affirming [1992] Ch. 310; [1992] 2 W.L.R. 508; [1992] 2 All E.R. 391; (1992) 63 P. & C.R. 152; (1991) 88(33) L.S.G. 32; (1991) 135 S.J.L.B. 108; [1991] N.P.C. 100, CA (Civ Div) *1–188*, *1–189*, *16–001*, *16–007*, *16–167*, 16–176, *16–178*, *16–180*, 16–181, 16–182, 16–183
Tipping v Eckersley (1855) 2 K. & J. 264 .... *27–060*
Tippins v Coates (1853) 18 Beav. 401*17–006*
Tito v Waddell (No.2); Tito v Attorney General [1977] Ch. 106; [1977] 2 W.L.R. 496; [1977] 3 W.L.R. 972; [1977] 3 All E.R. 129 (Note), Ch D *2–131*, *2–140*, *18–139*, *19–079*, 19–080, *25–003*, 26–016, *27–005*, *27–027*, *27–031*, *27–042*, *28–002*, *28–019*, *28–058*, *29–151*
Tiverton Estates Ltd v Wearwell Ltd [1975] Ch. 146; [1974] 2 W.L.R. 176; [1974] 1 All E.R. 209; (1974) 27 P. & C.R. 24; (1978) 117 S.J. 913, CA (Civ Div) *2–120*, *4–027*, *4–028*
Tivoli Freeholds, Re [1972] V.R. 445 .... *9–022*
Tivoli (Manchester) v Colley (1904) 20 T.L.R. 437 .... *16–110*, *27–064*
Tod v Barton. *See* Barton (Deceased), Re
Todd v British Midland Airways Ltd [1978] I.C.R. 959; [1978] I.R.L.R. 370; (1978) 13 I.T.R. 553; (1978) 122 S.J. 661, CA (Civ Div) *12–126*
Todd v Emly (1841) 7 M. & W. 427 .... *9–073*
Toepfer v Schwarze [1980] 1 Lloyd's Rep. 385, CA (Civ Div); affirming [1977] 2 Lloyd's Rep. 380, QBD (Comm) *12–039*, *14–140*, *14–141*, *14–150*, *22–052*
Toepfer v Warinco AG [1978] 2 Lloyd's Rep. 569, QBD (Comm) *3–083*, *22–042*, *24–008*, *26–109*
Toepfer (Hamburg) v Lenersan-Poortman NV (Rotterdam); Toepfer (Hamburg) v Verheijdens Veervoeder Commissiehandel (Rotterdam) [1980] 1 Lloyd's Rep. 143, CA (Civ Div); affirming [1978] 2 Lloyd's Rep. 555; (1978) 122 S.J. 417, QBD (Comm) *12–037*, *21–013*
Tolhurst v Associated Portland Cement Manufacturers (1900) Ltd; Associated Portland Cement Manufacturers (1900) Ltd v Tolhurst [1903] A.C. 414, HL; affirming [1902] 2 K.B. 660, CA; reversing [1901] 2 K.B. 811, KBD *9–048*, *19–042*, *19–054*, 19–056, 19–057, 19–077, 19–079, *19–082*
Tollit v Sherstone (1839) 5 M. & W. 283 .... *1–174*
Tolnay v Criterion Film Production Ltd [1936] 2 All E.R. 1625 .... *26–087*
Tom Shaw & Co v Moss Empires (1908) 25 T.L.R. 190 .... *19–045*
Tomkins v Tomkins [1948] P. 170; [1948] 1 All E.R. 237; 64 T.L.R. 106; [1948] L.J.R. 1028; (1948) 92 S.J. 111, CA *23–040*
Tomkinson v First Pennsylvania Banking and Trust Co [1961] A.C. 1007 ....*26–080*, *30–005*, *30–010*, *30–012*, *30–013*, *30–346*, *30–376*
Tomkyns v Barnet (1693) Skin. 411 .... *29–006*
Tomlinson v Dick Evans U Drive Ltd [1978] I.C.R. 639; [1978] I.R.L.R. 77, EAT *16–012*
Tomlinson v Gill (1756) Amb. 330 .... *18–078*
Tommey v Finextra (1962) 106 S.J. 1012 .... *5–033*
Toms v Wilson, 122 E.R. 524; (1862) 4 B. & S. 442, QB *21–053*

Tonicstar Ltd (t/a Lloyds Syndicate 1861) v American Home Assurance Co [2004] EWHC 1234 (Comm); [2005] Lloyd's Rep. I.R. 32, QBD (Comm) *30–051*, *30–077*
Tony Cox (Dismantlers) Ltd v Jim 5 Ltd (1997) 13 Const. L.J. 209, QBD (OR) ... *13–018*
Tool Metal Manufacture Co Ltd v Tungsten Electric Co Ltd. *See* Tungsten Electric Co Ltd v Tool Metal Manufacturing Co Ltd
Toomey v Eagle Star Insurance Co Ltd (No.2) [1995] 2 Lloyd's Rep. 88; [1995] 4 Re. L.R. 314, QBD (Comm) *6–134*, *14–013*
Tootal Clothing Ltd v Guinea Properties Management Ltd (1992) 64 P. & C.R. 452; [1992] 41 E.G. 117; [1992] E.G. 80 (C.S.); [1992] N.P.C. 75, CA (Civ Div) *4–056*, *4–064*, 4–067, 4–086
Topham v Braddick (1809) 1 Taunt. 572 .... *21–010*
Toppenden v Randall (1801) 2 B. & P. 467 .... *16–188*
Toppin v Lomas (1855) 16 C.B. 145 .... *4–012*
Toprak Enerji Sanayi AS v Sale Tilney Technology Plc [1994] 1 W.L.R. 840; [1994] 3 All E.R. 483; [1994] 1 Lloyd's Rep. 303, QBD (Comm) *28–034*
Toprak Mahsulleri Ofisi v Finagrain Compagnie Commerciale Agricole et Financière SA [1979] 2 Lloyd's Rep. 98, CA (Civ Div) ...*16–031*, *16–032*, 30–365
Tor Line A/B v Alltrans Group of Canada Ltd; The TFL Prosperity; sub nom. Investment AB Torman v Alltrans Group of Canada Ltd; The TFL Prosperity [1984] 1 W.L.R. 48; [1984] 1 All E.R. 103; [1984] 1 Lloyd's Rep. 123; (1984) 81 L.S.G. 435; (1984) 134 N.L.J. 34; (1984) 128 S.J. 18, HL; reversing [1983] 2 Lloyd's Rep. 18; (1983) 127 S.J. 409, CA (Civ Div); reversing [1982] 1 Lloyd's Rep. 617; [1982] Com. L.R. 66, QBD (Comm) *12–022*, 14–007, *14–011*
Torkington v Magee [1903] 1 K.B. 644, CA; reversing [1902] 2 K.B. 427, KBD ...*19–001*, *19–007*, *19–008*, *19–011*, *19–042*, *19–049*
Torni, The [1932] P. 78; (1932) 43 Ll. L. Rep. 78; 48 T.L.R. 471; 101 L.J. P. 44; 147 L.T. 208, CA *30–050*, *30–365*
Torquay Hotel Co Ltd v Cousins [1969] 2 Ch. 106; [1969] 2 W.L.R. 289; [1969] 1 All E.R. 522; 6 K.I.R. 15; (1968) 113 S.J. 52, CA (Civ Div); affirming [1968] 3 W.L.R. 540; [1968] 3 All E.R. 43; 4 K.I.R. 635; (1968) 112 S.J. 688, Ch D *1–019*, *1–171*, *14–148*
Torrens Aloha Pty Co v Citybank NA [1997] 72 F.C.R. 581 .... *29–047*
Torrens v Walker [1906] 2 Ch. 166, Ch D *21–009*
Torva Exploring Syndicate Ltd v Kelly [1900] A.C. 612, PC (Cape) *9–054*
Torvald Klaveness A/S v Arni Maritime Corp; The Gregos [1994] 1 W.L.R. 1465; [1994] 4 All E.R. 998; [1995] 1 Lloyd's Rep. 1; [1994] C.L.C. 1188; (1994) 144 N.L.J. 1550, HL; reversing [1993] 2 Lloyd's Rep. 335, CA (Civ Div); reversing [1992] 2 Lloyd's Rep. 40, QBD (Comm) *12–026*, *12–037*, *21–013*, *24–018*
Total E&P Soudan SA v Edmonds [2007] EWCA Civ 50; [2007] C.P. Rep. 20; (2007) 104(9) L.S.G. 30; (2007) 151 S.J.L.B. 195, CA (Civ Div); reversing in part [2006] EWHC 1136 (Comm), QBD (Comm) *11–007*
Total Gas Marketing Ltd v Arco British Ltd [1998] 2 Lloyd's Rep. 209; [1998] C.L.C. 1275, HL; affirming (1998) 95(5) L.S.G. 28; (1998) 142 S.J.L.B. 47, CA (Civ Div) *2–148*, *2–152*, *12–027*, *12–028*, *12–030*, *23–003*, *23–035*
Total Graphics Ltd v AGF Insurance Ltd [1997] 1 Lloyd's Rep. 599, QBD (Comm) *18–131*
Total International Ltd v Addax BV (t/a Addax BV Geneva Branch) [1996] 2 Lloyd's Rep. 333, QBD (Comm) *12–036*
Total Liban SA v Vitol Energy SA [2001] Q.B. 643; [2000] 3 W.L.R. 1142; [2000] 1 All E.R. 267; [1999] 2 All E.R. (Comm) 65; [1999] 2 Lloyd's Rep. 700; [1999] C.L.C. 1301, QBD (Comm) *26–013*, *26–078*, *28–049*
Total Oil Great Britain Ltd v Thompson Garages (Biggin Hill) Ltd [1972] 1 Q.B. 318; [1971] 3 W.L.R. 979; [1971] 3 All E.R. 1226; (1971) 115 S.J. 848, CA (Civ Div) *24–001*, *27–017*

Total Transport Corp v Arcadia Petroleum Ltd; The Eurus [1998] 1 Lloyd's Rep. 351; [1998] C.L.C. 90; (1998) 95(1) L.S.G. 24; (1998) 142 S.J.L.B. 22, CA (Civ Div); affirming [1996] 2 Lloyd's Rep. 408; [1996] C.L.C. 1084, QBD (Comm) *12–042*, *12–077*
Total Transport Corp of Panama v Amoco Transport Co; The Altus [1985] 1 Lloyd's Rep. 423, QBD (Comm) *12–082*
Touche Ross & Co v Baker (Colin) [1992] 2 Lloyd's Rep. 207; (1992) 89(28) L.S.G. 31; (1992) 136 S.J.L.B. 190, HL; affirming [1991] 2 Lloyd's Rep. 230, CA (Civ Div) *18–010*
Touche v Metropolitan Railway Warehousing Co (1870–71) L.R. 6 Ch. App. 671, Lord Chancellor *9–015*
Tourret v Cripps (1879) 48 L.J. Ch. 567 .... *4–034*
Tout and Finch Ltd, Re [1954] 1 W.L.R. 178; [1954] 1 All E.R. 127; 52 L.G.R. 70; (1954) 98 S.J. 62, Ch D *19–025*
Tower Hamlets LBC v British Gas Corp, *The Times*, March 23, 1982, CA (Civ Div) *13–027*
Towers v Barratt (1786) 1 Term Rep. 133 .... *22–026*, *29–012*, *29–058*
Town Investments Ltd v Department of the Environment; sub nom. London County Freehold and Leasehold Properties v Department of the Environment; HEPC (Mayfair Properties) v Department of the Environment [1978] A.C. 359; [1977] 2 W.L.R. 450; [1977] 1 All E.R. 813; (1977) 34 P. & C.R. 48; (1977) 121 S.J. 203, HL; reversing [1976] 1 W.L.R. 1126; [1976] 3 All E.R. 479; (1976) 120 S.J. 435, CA (Civ Div) *14–065*, *15–027*
Towne v Eisner (1918) 245 U.S. 416 .... *12–050*
Townend v Toker (1865–66) L.R. 1 Ch. App. 446, CA in Chancery *3–021*, *12–108*
Townends Group Ltd v Cobb; sub nom. Townends Grove Ltd v Cobb [2004] EWHC 3432; [2004] All E.R. (D) 421; (2005) 102(4) L.S.G. 30, Ch D *16–105*
Townsend v Bishop [1939] 1 All E.R. 805 .... *25–012*
Townsend v Crowdy (1860) 8 C.B.(N.S.) 477 .... *29–036*
Townsend v Jarman [1900] 2 Ch. 698, Ch D *16–099*
Townsend (Builders) v Cinema News & Property Management [1959] 1 W.L.R. 119; [1959] 1 All E.R. 7; (1959) 123 J.P. 115; 57 L.G.R. 174; (1959) 103 S.J. 74, CA *16–011*
Townsend's Case (1871) L.R. 13 Eq. 148 .... *2–058*
Townshend v Stangroom (1801) 6 Ves. 328 .... *5–063*
Tozer Kemsley & Millbourn (A/Asia) Pty v Collier's Interstate Transport Service (1956) 94 C.L.R. 384 .... *14–036*
Tracomin SA v Anton C Neilson A/S [1984] 2 Lloyd's Rep. 195; (1984) 134 N.L.J. 705, QBD (Comm) *2–006*, *2–042*, *2–043*, *2–076*, *22–027*
Tracomin SA v Sudan Oil Seeds (No.1) [1983] 1 W.L.R. 1026; [1983] 3 All E.R. 137; [1983] 2 Lloyd's Rep. 384; [1983] Com. L.R. 269; [1984] E.C.C. 165, CA (Civ Div) *25–017*
Tradax Export SA v Andr'e et Cie [1976] 1 Lloyd's Rep. 916 .... *14–150*
Tradax Export SA v André & Cie SA [1977] 2 Lloyd's Rep. 484, QBD (Comm) *14–141*
Tradax Export SA v André et Cie [1976] 1 Lloyd's Rep. 109 .... *14–148*
Tradax Export SA v Andre et Cie SA; sub nom. Andre et Cie SA v Tradax Export SA [1976] 1 Lloyd's Rep. 416, CA (Civ Div); reversing [1975] 2 Lloyd's Rep. 516, QBD (Comm) *12–039*, *14–140*, *14–141*, *14–144*, *14–150*, *14–151*
Tradax Export SA v Carapelli SpA [1977] 2 Lloyd's Rep. 157, QBD (Comm) *14–141*
Tradax Export SA v Cook Industries Inc [1982] 1 Lloyd's Rep. 385, CA (Civ Div); reversing [1981] 1 Lloyd's Rep. 236, QBD (Comm) *14–141*, *14–151*, *22–052*
Tradax Export SA v Dorada Compania Naviera SA of Panama; The Lutetian [1982] 2 Lloyd's Rep. 140; [1982] Com. L.R. 130, QBD (Comm) *3–092*, *22–051*
Tradax Export SA v European Grain & Shipping Ltd [1983] 2 Lloyd's Rep. 100, QBD (Comm) *12–036*
Tradax Export SA v Volkswagenwerk AG [1970] 1 Q.B. 537; [1970] 2 W.L.R. 339; [1970] 1 All E.R. 420; [1970] 1 Lloyd's Rep. 62; (1969) 113 S.J. 978, CA (Civ Div); affirming [1969] 2 Q.B. 599; [1969] 2 W.L.R. 498; [1969] 2 All E.R. 144; [1969] 1 Lloyd's Rep. 494, QBD (Comm) *12–069*

Tradax Internacional SA v Goldschmidt SA [1977] 2 Lloyd's Rep. 604, QBD (Comm) *12–036*
Tradax Internacional SA v Pagnan (R) and Fratelli [1968] 1 Lloyd's Rep. 244; (1968) 118 N.L.J. 373, QBD (Comm) *12–078*
Trade and Transport Inc v Iino Kaiun Kaisha Ltd; The Angelia [1973] 1 W.L.R. 210; [1973] 2 All E.R. 144; [1972] 2 Lloyd's Rep. 154; (1972) 117 S.J. 123, QBD *1–147*, *14–003*, *14–029*, *14–137*, 14–140, *23–035*, *24–030*, *24–033*, *24–040*, *24–046*
Trade Indemnity Plc v Forsakringsaktiebolaget Njord [1995] 1 All E.R. 796; [1995] L.R.L.R. 367, QBD (Comm) *30–011*, *30–031*
Tradigrain SA v King Diamond Marine Ltd; The Spiros C; sub nom. Tradigrain SA v King Diamond Shipping SA; The Spiros C [2000] 2 All E.R. (Comm) 542; [2000] 2 Lloyd's Rep. 319; [2000] C.L.C. 1503, CA (Civ Div); reversing [1999] 1 All E.R. 837; [1999] 2 Lloyd's Rep. 91; [1999] C.L.C. 1136, QBD (Comm) *18–046*, *18–073*
Trading in Compliance Ltd v Dewse (t/a Data Research Co) [2004] EWHC 3094 (QB), [2004] All ER (D) 377 (Dec), QBD *1–032*
Trafigura Beheer BV v Kookmin Bank Co (Preliminary Issue) [2006] EWHC 1450; [2006] 2 All E.R. (Comm) 1008; [2006] 2 Lloyd's Rep. 455; [2006] 1 C.L.C. 1049, QBD (Comm) *30–032*, *30–077*, *30–078*
Trafigura Beheer BV v Mediterranean Shipping Co SA [2007] EWCA Civ 794; [2008] 1 All E.R. (Comm) 385; [2007] 2 Lloyd's Rep. 622; [2007] 2 C.L.C. 379, CA (Civ Div) *26–175*, *27–079*, *30–065*, *30–087*
Traherne v Gardner (1856) 5 E.B.913 .... *29–094*
Traill v Baring (1864) 33 L.J. Ch. 521 .... *6–018*
Tramp Shipping Corp v Greenwich Marine Inc; The New Horizon [1975] 1 W.L.R. 1042; [1975] 2 All E.R. 989; [1975] 2 Lloyd's Rep. 314; [1975] I.C.R. 261; (1975) 119 S.J. 300, CA (Civ Div); affirming [1974] 2 Lloyd's Rep. 210, QBD (Comm) *14–146*
Tramway Building & Construction Co Ltd, Re [1988] Ch. 293; [1988] 2 W.L.R. 640; (1987) 3 B.C.C. 443; [1987] B.C.L.C. 632; [1988] P.C.C. 85; (1988) 132 S.J. 460, Ch D *9–049*
Trans Trust SPRL v Danubian Trading Co Ltd [1952] 2 Q.B. 297; [1952] 1 All E.R. 970; [1952] 1 Lloyd's Rep. 348; [1952] 1 T.L.R. 1066; (1952) 96 S.J. 312, CA; reversing in part [1952] 1 K.B. 285; [1952] 1 All E.R. 89; [1951] 2 Lloyd's Rep. 644; [1952] 1 T.L.R. 13, KBD ...12–027, *21–040*, *26–060*, *26–098*, 26–107
Transag Haulage Ltd (IAR) v Leyland DAF Finance Plc [1994] B.C.C. 356; [1994] 2 B.C.L.C. 88; (1994) 13 Tr. L.R. 361, Ch D *22–048*
Transcatalana de Commercio SA v Incobrasa Industrial e Commercial Brazileira SA; The Vera [1995] 1 Lloyd's Rep. 215; [1994] C.L.C. 400, QBD (Comm) *3–095*
Transcontainer Express v Custodian Security [1988] 1 Lloyd's Rep. 128; [1988] 1 F.T.L.R. 54, CA (Civ Div) *18–034*
Transfield Shipping Inc v Mercator Shipping Inc (The Achilleas) [2007] EWCA [2008] UKHL 48, [2008] 3 W.L.R. 345; [2008] All E.R. (Comm) 685; [2007] 2 Lloyd's Rep. 555; [2007] 2 C.L.C. 400, CA (Civ Div) 26–001A, 26–051, *26–058*, *26–061*, *26–062*, 26–066, 26–070, *26–088*, *26–089*, 26–100A, 26–100B, 26–100C, 26–100E, 26–100G, *26–170*
Transmotors v Robertson, Buckley & Co [1970] 1 Lloyd's Rep. 224, QBD *12–011*, *13–022*
Transoceanica Francesca, The and Nicos V, The [1987] 2 Lloyd's Rep. 155, QBD (Admlty) *30–376*
Transpetrol Ltd v Ekali Shipping Co Ltd; The Aghia Marina [1989] 1 Lloyd's Rep. 62, QBD (Comm) *28–125*
Transpetrol Ltd v Transol Olieprodukten BV [1989] 1 Lloyd's Rep. 309, QBD (Comm) *12–037*
Transplanters (Holding Co), Re [1958] 1 W.L.R. 822; [1958] 2 All E.R. 711; (1958) 102 S.J. 547, Ch D *28–101*

Transvaal & Delagoa Bay Investment Co Ltd v Atkinson [1944] 1 All E.R. 579, KBD *29–008*, *29–176*
Transvaal Lands Co v New Belgium (Transvaal) Land & Development Co [1914] 2 Ch. 488, CA *9–055*
Transworld Oil (USA) Inc v Minos Compania Naviera SA; The Leni [1992] 2 Lloyd's Rep. 48, QBD (Comm) *28–022*, *28–118*
Trasimex Holding SA v Addax BV; The Red Sea [1999] 1 Lloyd's Rep. 28, CA (Civ Div); affirming [1997] 1 Lloyd's Rep. 610, QBD (Comm) *12–069*
Travelers Casualty & Surety Co of Europe Ltd v Sun Life Assurance Co of Canada (UK) Ltd [2004] EWHC 1704; [2004] I.L.Pr. 50; [2004] Lloyd's Rep. I.R. 846, QBD (Comm) *30–051*, *30–053*, *30–055*, *30–056*, *30–071*
Travers v Gloucester Corp [1947] K.B. 71; [1946] 2 All E.R. 506; 62 T.L.R. 723; (1946) 110 J.P. 364; 115 L.J. K.B. 517; 175 L.T. 360; (1946) 90 S.J. 556, KBD *1–154*
Trawnik v Gordon Lennox; sub nom. Trawnik v Ministry of Defence [1985] 1 W.L.R. 532; [1985] 2 All E.R. 368, CA (Civ Div); reversing [1984] 2 All E.R. 791; (1984) 81 L.S.G. 2929, Ch D *10–015*
Treacy v DPP; sub nom. R. v Treacy (Eugene Anthony) [1971] A.C. 537; [1971] 2 W.L.R. 112; [1971] 1 All E.R. 110; (1971) 55 Cr. App. R. 113; (1971) 115 S.J. 12, HL; affirming [1970] 3 W.L.R. 592; [1970] 3 All E.R. 205; (1970) 114 S.J. 604, CA (Crim Div) *2–025*
Tredegar Iron and Coal Co v Hawthorne & Co (1902) 18 T.L.R. 716 .... *24–001*, *24–010*, *24–011*, *26–121*
Tredway v Machin (1904) 91 L.T. 310 .... *21–009*
Trego v Hunt [1896] A.C. 7, HL; reversing [1895] 1 Ch. 462, CA *1–032*, 16–118, 16–119, *27–043*
Tremeere v Morrison (1834) 1 Bing. N. C. 89 .... *20–008*
Trenchard v Hoskins (1625) Winch. 93 .... *12–063*
Trendtex Trading Corp v Central Bank of Nigeria [1977] Q.B. 529; [1977] 2 W.L.R. 356; [1977] 1 All E.R. 881; [1977] 1 Lloyd's Rep. 581; [1977] 2 C.M.L.R. 465; (1977) 121 S.J. 85, CA (Civ Div); reversing [1976] 1 W.L.R. 868; [1976] 3 All E.R. 437; [1976] 2 C.M.L.R. 668; (1976) 120 S.J. 554, QBD *11–001*
Trendtex Trading Corp v Credit Suisse [1982] A.C. 679; [1981] 3 W.L.R. 766; [1981] 3 All E.R. 520; [1981] Com. L.R. 262; (1981) 125 S.J. 761, HL; affirming [1980] Q.B. 629; [1980] 3 W.L.R. 367; [1980] 3 All E.R. 721; (1980) 124 S.J. 396, CA (Civ Div) 16–049, *16–050*, *16–051*, 16–052, *16–053*, *16–054*, *16–055*, 16–057, *16–058*, 16–059, 16–060, *16–064*, 19–049, 19–050, *19–051*, 19–053, *30–123*, *30–125*, *30–366*
Trent and Humber Co Ex p. Cambrian Steam Packet Co, Re (1868–69) L.R. 4 Ch. App. 112, Lord Chancellor *26–066*
Trepca Mines Ltd (No.2), Re; sub nom. Radomir Nicola Pachitch (Pasic)'s Application, Re [1963] Ch. 199; [1962] 3 W.L.R. 955; [1962] 3 All E.R. 351; (1962) 106 S.J. 649, CA; affirming [1962] Ch. 511; [1962] 2 W.L.R. 800; [1962] 1 All E.R. 755; (1962) 106 S.J. 175, Ch D ... *16–012*, *16–048*, *16–050*, *16–054*, *16–055*
Treseder-Griffin v Cooperative Insurance Society Ltd [1956] 2 Q.B. 127; [1956] 2 W.L.R. 866; [1956] 2 All E.R. 33; [1956] 1 Lloyd's Rep. 377; (1956) 100 S.J. 283, CA *21–068*, *21–070*, *21–071*, *26–080*, *30–331*
Trevor v Whitworth (1887) L.R. 12 App. Cas. 409, HL *9–038*
Triad Shipping Co v Stellar Chartering & Brokerage Inc; The Island Archon [1995] 1 All E.R. 595; [1994] 2 Lloyd's Rep. 227; [1994] C.L.C. 734, CA (Civ Div); affirming [1993] 2 Lloyd's Rep. 388, QBD (Comm) *13–006*
Triangle Steel & Supply Co v Korean United Lines Inc (1985) 63 B.C.L.R. 66, Sup Ct (BC) *18–034*
Tribe v Tribe [1996] Ch. 107; [1995] 3 W.L.R. 913; [1995] 4 All E.R. 236; [1995] C.L.C. 1474; [1995] 2 F.L.R. 966; [1996] 1 F.C.R. 338; (1996) 71 P. & C.R. 503; [1996] Fam. Law 29; (1995) 92(28) L.S.G. 30; (1995) 145 N.L.J. 1445; (1995) 139 S.J.L.B. 203; [1995] N.P.C. 151; (1995) 70 P. & C.R. D38, CA (Civ Div) 16–182, *16–189*, *16–190*, *29–003*

Tricks, Re (1885) 3 Morr. 15 .... *20–023*
Trident General Insurance Co v McNiece Bros Pty (1988) 165 C.L.R. 107, HC (Aus) *18–020*, *18–042*, *18–079*
Triggs v Staines Urban DC; sub nom. Staines Urban DC's Agreement, Re [1969] 1 Ch. 10; [1968] 2 W.L.R. 1433; [1968] 2 All E.R. 1; (1968) 132 J.P. 255; 66 L.G.R. 618; (1968) 19 P. & C.R. 450; (1968) 112 S.J. 171, Ch D ...*10–020*, *10–029*
Trinidad Asphalte Co v Coryat [1896] A.C. 587, PC (Trin) *1–112*
Triodos Bank NV v Dobbs; sub nom. Triodosbank NV v Dobbs [2005] EWCA Civ 630; [2005] 2 Lloyd's Rep. 588; [2005] 2 C.L.C. 95, CA (Civ Div) ... *3–107*
Tristate Roofing Co Of Uniontown v Simon (1958) 142 A. (2d) 333 .... *7–031*
Tristram v Harte (1841) 3 Ir. Eq. R. 386 .... *28–094*
Troilus, The. *See* Owners of Cargo Lately Laden on Board the Troilus v Owners
Trollope v Martyn. *See* George Trollope & Sons v Martyn Bros
Trollope & Colls Ltd v North West Metropolitan Regional Hospital Board [1973] 1 W.L.R. 601; [1973] 2 All E.R. 260; 9 B.L.R. 60; (1973) 117 S.J. 355, HL *12–126*, *13–007*, *13–009*, *22–038*
Trollope & Colls Ltd (t/a Nuclear Civil Constructions) v Atomic Power Constructions Ltd [1963] 1 W.L.R. 333; [1962] 3 All E.R. 1035; (1963) 107 S.J. 254, QBD *2–124*
Troop v Gibson [1986] 1 E.G.L.R. 1; (1986) 277 E.G. 1134, CA (Civ Div) ... *3–107*, *3–111*
Tropical Traders v Goonan, 111 C.L.R. 41, HC (Aus) *21–019*
Tropwood AG of Zug v Jade Enterprises Ltd [1982] 1 Lloyd's Rep. 232; [1982] Com. L.R. 17, CA (Civ Div); reversing [1981] 1 Lloyd's Rep. 45, QBD (Comm) *2–128*, *2–140*, *2–144*, *12–076*, *12–077*
Trow v Ind Coope (West Midlands) Ltd [1967] 2 Q.B. 899; [1967] 3 W.L.R. 633; [1967] 2 All E.R. 900; (1967) 111 S.J. 375, CA (Civ Div); affirming [1966] 3 W.L.R. 1300; [1967] 1 All E.R. 19; (1966) 110 S.J. 964, QBD *12–093*, *21–024*, *28–116*
Trueman v Fenton (1777) 2 Cowp. 544 .... *3–032*
Trueman v Loder (1840) 11 A. & E. 589 .... *4–038*, *12–133*
Trufort, Re; sub nom. Trafford v Blanc (1887) L.R. 36 Ch. D. 600, Ch D *1–175*, *25–019*
Trustee of the Property of FC Jones & Sons (A Firm) v Jones [1997] Ch. 159; [1996] 3 W.L.R. 703; [1997] 1 W.L.R. 51; [1996] 4 All E.R. 721; [1996] B.P.I.R. 644; (1996) 93(19) L.S.G. 29; (1996) 140 S.J.L.B. 123, CA (Civ Div) *29–162*, *29–163*, *29–170*, *29–171*
Trustee Solutions Ltd v Dubery; sub nom. Cripps v Trustee Solutions Ltd [2007] EWCA Civ 771; [2008] 1 All E.R. 826; [2008] 1 C.M.L.R. 45; [2008] I.C.R. 101; [2007] Pens. L.R. 237; (2007) 157 N.L.J. 1354; (2007) 151 S.J.L.B. 1024, CA (Civ Div); reversing [2006] EWHC 1426 (Ch); [2007] 1 All E.R. 308; [2007] I.C.R. 412; [2006] Pens. L.R. 177, Ch D *3–107*
Try Build Ltd v Blue Star Garages Ltd, 66 Con. L.R. 90, QBD (TCC) *14–013*
Tryg Baltica International (UK) Ltd v Boston Compania de Seguros SA [2004] EWHC 1186; [2005] Lloyd's Rep. I.R. 40, QBD (Comm) *30–051*, *30–055*
Trytel, Re; sub nom. Trustee of the Property of the Bankrupt, Ex p. v Performing Right Society and Soundtrac Film Co [1952] 2 T.L.R. 32; [1952] W.N. 355 ....*19–020*, *19–032*, *19–061*, *20–026*
Tsakiroglou & Co Ltd v Noblee Thorl GmbH; Albert D Gaon & Co v Societe Interprofessionelle des Oleagineux Fluides Alimentaires [1962] A.C. 93; [1961] 2 W.L.R. 633; [1961] 2 All E.R. 179; [1961] 1 Lloyd's Rep. 329; (1961) 105 S.J. 346, HL; affirming [1960] 2 Q.B. 318; [1960] 2 W.L.R. 869; [1960] 2 All E.R. 160; [1960] 1 Lloyd's Rep. 349; (1960) 104 S.J. 426, CA; affirming [1959] 2 W.L.R. 179; [1959] 1 All E.R. 45; [1958] 2 Lloyd's Rep. 515; (1959) 103 S.J. 112, QBD (Comm) *1–020*, *14–141*, *14–148*, *21–001*, *21–002*, *21–020*, *23–012*, *23–014*, *23–015*, *23–047*, 23–048, *24–033*
Tsang Chuen v Li Po Kwai [1932] A.C. 713 .... *12–096*, *21–058*
Tsavliris Salvage (International) Ltd v Grain Board of Iraq [2008] EWHC 612 (Comm), QBD (Comm) *11–004*, *11–005*, *11–021*
Tuberville v Whitehouse (1823) 1 C. & P. 94 .... *8–017*

Tuck v Baker [1990] 32 E.G. 46; [1990] E.G. 20 (C.S.), CA (Civ Div); affirming [1989] E.G. 70 (C.S.), Ch D *2–088*
Tucker v Barrow (1828) 7 B.C. 623 .... *29–191*
Tucker v Bennett (1888) L.R. 38 Ch. D. 1, CA; reversing (1887) L.R. 34 Ch. D. 754, Ch D *5–122*, *5–134*
Tucker v British Museum Trustees; sub nom. Tucker v Trustees of the British Museum (1967)112 S.J. 70, CA (Civ Div) *27–023*
Tucker v Linger (1882–83) L.R. 8 App. Cas. 508, HL; affirming (1882) L.R. 21 Ch. D. 18, CA *13–018*, *13–023*, *26–103*
Tucker v Trustees of the British Museum. *See* Tucker v British Museum Trustees
Tudor Grange Holdings Ltd v Citibank NA [1992] Ch. 53; [1991] 3 W.L.R. 750; [1991] 4 All E.R. 1; [1991] B.C.L.C. 1009; (1991) 135 S.J.L.B. 3, Ch D ...*14–064*, *14–081*
Tufnell v Constable (1836) 8 Sim. 69 .... *22–004*
Tufton v Sperni [1952] 2 T.L.R. 516; [1952] W.N. 439, CA ...*7–056*, *7–065*, *7–069*, *7–084*
Tugwell v Heyman (1812) 3 Camp. 298 .... *29–132*
Tulk v Moxhay, 41 E.R. 1143; (1848) 2 Ph. 774; (1848) 18 L.J. Ch. 83, Ch D ...1–071, 16–082, 16–085, 18–139, 18–146
Tullis v Jacson [1892] 3 Ch. 441, Ch D *14–136*
Tunbridge v Buss Murton & Co, *The Times*, April 8, 1997, Ch D *28–086*
Tungsten Electric Co Ltd v Tool Metal Manufacturing Co Ltd (No.3); sub nom. Tool Metal Manufacture Co Ltd v Tungsten Electric Co Ltd [1955] 1 W.L.R. 761; [1955] 2 All E.R. 657; (1955) 72 R.P.C. 209; (1955) 99 S.J. 470, HL; reversing [1954] 1 W.L.R. 862; [1954] 2 All E.R. 28; (1954) 71 R.P.C. 201; (1954) 98 S.J. 389, CA *3–096*, *3–098*, *3–130*, 3–131, *3–132*, *3–135*, *13–028*
Tupper v Foulkes, 142 E.R. 314; (1861) 9 C.B. N.S. 797, CCP *1–093*
Turcan, Re (1889) L.R. 40 Ch. D. 5, CA *19–021*, *19–045*
Turiddu, The. *See* Cil v Owners of the Turiddu
Turkey v Awadh [2005] EWCA Civ 382; [2005] 2 F.C.R. 7; [2005] 2 P. & C.R. 29; [2006] W.T.L.R. 553, CA (Civ Div) *7–058*, *7–083*, 7–088
Turkiye Is Bankasi AS v Bank of China (1994) [1993] 1 Lloyd's Rep. 132; [1994] 3 Bank. L.R. 34, QBD (Comm) *30–011*, *30–012*
Turnbull v Robertson (1878) 47 L.J.C.P. 294 .... *21–051*
Turnbull & Co v Duval [1902] A.C. 429, PC (Jam) *7–106*, *7–107*
Turner, Re; sub nom. Skelton, Re (1879–80) L.R. 13 Ch. D. 130, Ch D *27–058*
Turner v Anquetil [1953] N.Z.L.R. 952 .... *12–003*
Turner v Barclays Bank Plc [1998] 1 F.L.R. 276; [1997] 2 F.C.R. 151; [1997] Fam. Law 791, Ch D *7–089*
Turner v Camerons Coalbrook Steam Coal Co (1850) 5 Ex. 932 .... *29–140*
Turner v Civil Service Supply Association Ltd [1926] 1 K.B. 50, KBD *14–012*
Turner v Collins (1871–72) L.R. 7 Ch. App. 329, Lord Chancellor; affirming in part (1871) L.R. 12 Eq. 438, Ct of Chancery *7–074*, *7–097*, *28–141*, *28–145*, *28–146*
Turner v Commonwealth & British Minerals Ltd [2000] I.R.L.R. 114, CA (Civ Div) *16–113*
Turner v Deane (1849) 3 Ex. 836 .... *29–093*
Turner v Evans (1853) 2 E. & B. 512 .... *12–063*
Turner v Forwood [1951] 1 All E.R. 746; [1951] W.N. 189, CA *3–020*, *12–098*, *12–108*
Turner v General Motors (Australia) Pty Ltd, 42 C.L.R. 352 .... *28–141*
Turner v Goldsmith [1891] 1 Q.B. 544, CA *13–012*, *23–021*
Turner v Green [1895] 2 Ch. 205, Ch D *5–008*, *6–014*
Turner v Hatton. *See* LD Turner Ltd v RS Hatton (Bradford) Ltd
Turner v Jones (1857) 1 H.N. 878 .... *21–051*
Turner v London Transport Executive [1977] I.C.R. 952; [1977] I.R.L.R. 441; (1977) 121 S.J. 829, CA (Civ Div) *25–012*
Turner v Owen (1862) 3 F. & F. 176 .... *3–070*, *3–074*
Turner v Robinson (1833) 5 B. Ad. 789 .... *21–030*
Turner v Trisby (1719) 1 Stra. 168 .... *8–018*
Turner v Vaughan (1767) 2 Wils.K.B. 339 .... *16–067*

Turnley v Hartley (1848) 3 New Pr. Cas. 96 .... *4–028*
Turrell v Bank of London (1862) 10 H.L.C. 26 .... *7–076*
Turriddu, The. *See* Cil v Owners of the Turiddu
Turriff Construction Ltd v Regalia Knitting Mills Ltd, 9 B.L.R. 20; (1971) 222 E.G. 169, QBD *2–125*, *2–183*
Turul, The [1919] A.C. 515, PC (Aus) *14–148*
Turvey v Dentons (1923) Ltd [1953] 1 Q.B. 218; [1952] 2 All E.R. 1025; [1952] 2 T.L.R. 996; 45 R. & I.T. 772; (1952) 31 A.T.C. 470; [1952] T.R. 471; (1952) 96 S.J. 852, QBD *29–031*, *29–036*
Tustian v Johnston (Note) [1993] 3 All E.R. 534; [1993] 47 E.G. 139, CA (Civ Div) *27–028*
Tutova, The. *See* Almatrans SA v Steamship Mutual Underwriting Association (Bermuda) Ltd
Tweddell v Henderson [1975] 1 W.L.R. 1496; [1975] 2 All E.R. 1096; (1975) 30 P. & C.R. 201; (1975) 119 S.J. 776, Ch D *2–118*, *2–123*, *2–161*, *4–026*
Tweddle v Atkinson, 121 E.R. 762; (1861) 1 B. & S. 393, QB *1–188*, *3–022*, *3–036*, *18–016*, 18–019, *18–021*
Twins Transport Ltd v Patrick & Brocklehurst (t/a HV&C Patrick Estates Developers), 25 B.L.R. 65, QBD *14–057*
Twinsectra Ltd v Yardley [2002] UKHL 12; [2002] 2 A.C. 164; [2002] 2 W.L.R. 802; [2002] 2 All E.R. 377; [2002] P.N.L.R. 30; [2002] W.T.L.R. 423; [2002] 38 E.G. 204 (C.S.); (2002) 99(19) L.S.G. 32; (2002) 152 N.L.J. 469; (2002) 146 S.J.L.B. 84; [2002] N.P.C. 47, HL; reversing [1999] Lloyd's Rep. Bank. 438; [2000] Lloyd's Rep. P.N. 239; [2000] W.T.L.R. 527, CA (Civ Div) *1–189*, *6–130*, *29–159*, *29–174*, *29–183*
Twopenny v Young, 107 E.R. 711; (1824) 3 B. & C. 208, KB *25–001*, *25–002*
Twycross v Grant (No.1) (1876–77) L.R. 2 C.P.D. 469, CA 6–056, 6–058
Twyford v Manchester Corp [1946] Ch. 236; [1946] 1 All E.R. 621; 62 T.L.R. 367; (1946) 110 J.P. 196; [1946] W.N. 70; [1947] L.J.R. 12; 175 L.T. 124; (1946) 90 S.J. 164, Ch D *29–088*, *29–094*, *29–111*
Tychy (No.2), The. *See* MSC Mediterranean Shipping Co SA v Polish Ocean Lines
Tye v House (1998) 76 P. & C.R. 188; [1997] 2 E.G.L.R. 171; [1997] 41 E.G. 160, Ch D *2–121*, *2–127*, *3–172*, *27–007*
Tyers v Rosedale and Ferryhill Iron Co Ltd (1874–75) L.R. 10 Ex. 195, Ex Chamber; reversing (1872–73) L.R. 8 Ex. 305, Ex Ct *22–027*, *22–042*
Tyler Ex p. Official Receiver, Re [1907] 1 K.B. 865, CA *20–022*, *20–023*, *29–043*
Tynan v Bridges (1612) Cro.Jac. 301 .... *22–005*
Tyne Tugs v Owners of the MV Aldora; The MV Aldora [1975] Q.B. 748; [1975] 2 W.L.R. 791; [1975] 2 All E.R. 69; [1975] 1 Lloyd's Rep. 617; (1974) 119 S.J. 253, QBD (Admlty) *26–171*
Tyrie v Fletcher, 98 E.R. 1297; (1777) 2 Cowp. 666, KB *23–096*, *29–054*, *29–082*
Tyso v Petitt (1879) 40 L.T. 132 .... *20–044*
Tzortzis v Monark Line A/B [1968] 1 W.L.R. 406; [1968] 1 All E.R. 949; [1968] 1 Lloyd's Rep. 337; (1968) 112 S.J. 108, CA (Civ Div) *30–010*
UBAF Ltd v European American Banking Corp; The Pacific Colocotronis [1984] Q.B. 713; [1984] 2 W.L.R. 508; [1984] 2 All E.R. 226; [1984] 1 Lloyd's Rep. 258; (1984) 81 L.S.G. 429; (1984) 128 S.J. 243, CA (Civ Div) *6–021*, *6–041*, *28–034*, *30–339*
UCB Bank Plc v Hepherd Winstanley & Pugh [1999] Lloyd's Rep. P.N. 963; (1999) 96(34) L.S.G. 34, CA (Civ Div) *1–166*, *26–049*
UCB Corporate Services Ltd v Kohli [2004] EWHC 1126; [2004] 2 All E.R. (Comm) 422, Ch D *28–100*, *28–103*
UCB Corporate Services Ltd v Thomason [2005] EWCA Civ 225; [2005] 1 All E.R. (Comm) 601, CA (Civ Div); affirming [2004] EWHC 1164 (Ch); [2004] 2 All E.R. (Comm) 774, Ch D *6–101*, *6–102*, *12–118*
UCB Corporate Services Ltd v Williams; sub nom. Williams v UCB Corporate Services [2002] EWCA Civ 555; [2002] 3 F.C.R. 448; [2003] 1 P. & C.R. 12; [2002] 19 E.G. 149 (C.S.); (2002) 99(24) L.S.G. 34; (2002) 146 S.J.L.B. 151; [2002] N.P.C. 63; [2002] 2 P. & C.R. DG17, CA (Civ Div) *6–035*, 7–068

UCB Home Loans Corp Ltd v Carr [2000] Lloyd's Rep. P.N. 754, QBD *28–089*
UCM v Royal Bank of Canada. *See* United City Merchants (Instruments) and Glass Fibres and Equipments v Royal Bank of Canada
UGS Finance v National Mortgage Bank of Greece and National Bank of Greece SA [1964] 1 Lloyd's Rep. 446; (1963) 107 S.J. 552, CA 14–021, *24–003*, *24–008*
UK Safety Group Ltd v Heane [1998] 2 B.C.L.C. 208, Ch D *2–031*
US Shipping Board v Bunge y Born (1925) 31 Com. Cas. 118 .... *14–029*
Uddin v Ahmed [2001] EWCA Civ 204; [2001] 3 F.C.R. 300, CA (Civ Div) ...*18–004*, *18–016*
Ugland Trailer, The. *See* Welsh Irish Ferries Ltd , Re
Ultraframe (UK) Ltd v Tailored Roofing Systems Ltd [2004] EWCA Civ 585; [2004] 2 All E.R. (Comm) 692; [2004] B.L.R. 341, CA (Civ Div) *13–010*
Ulysses Compania Naviera SA v Huntingdon Petroleum Services; The Ermoupolis [1990] 1 Lloyd's Rep. 160, QBD (Comm) *2–006*
Unchained Growth III Plc v Granby Village (Manchester) Management Co Ltd; Granby Village (Manchester) Management Co Ltd v Unchained Growth III Plc [2000] 1 W.L.R. 739; [2000] L. & T.R. 186; [1999] E.G. 116 (C.S.); (1999) 96(45) L.S.G. 33, CA (Civ Div) *14–105*
Uncle Ben's Tartan Holdings v North West Sport Enterprises (1974) 46 D.L.R. (3d) 280 .... *6–052*
Under Water Welders & Repairers Ltd v Street; sub nom. SBC v Street; SBC v Longthorne; Under Water Welders & Repairers Ltd v Longthorne [1967] 1 Lloyd's Rep. 364; [1967] F.S.R. 194; [1968] R.P.C. 498; 117 N.L.J. 547, Ch D *16–107*
Underhay v Read (1888) L.R. 20 Q.B.D. 209, CA *29–105*
Underhill v Ministry of Food [1950] 1 All E.R. 591; 66 T.L.R. (Pt. 1) 730; [1950] W.N. 133; (1950) 94 S.J. 194, Ch D *10–017*
Underwood v Nicholls (1855) 17 C.B. 239 .... *21–044*
Underwood v Underwood [1894] P. 204, CA *3–115*, *22–016*
Underwood & Son v Barker. *See* E Underwood & Son Ltd v Barker
Unger v Preston Corp [1942] 1 All E.R. 200 .... *23–039*
Ungley v Ungley (1877) L.R. 5 Ch. D. 887, CA; affirming (1876–77) L.R. 4 Ch. D. 73, Ch D *4–042*, *4–047*
Ungurian v Lesnoff [1990] Ch. 206; [1989] 3 W.L.R. 840; [1990] 2 F.L.R. 299; [1990] F.C.R. 719; [1990] Fam. Law 93; (1989) 133 S.J. 948, Ch D *3–139*
Union Carbide Corp v BP Chemicals Ltd [1999] R.P.C. 409; (1999) 22(2) I.P.D. 22012, CA (Civ Div) *29–142*, *29–143*
Union de Remorquage et de Sauvetage SA v Lake Avery Inc; The Lake Avery [1997] 1 Lloyd's Rep. 540; [1997] C.L.C. 683, QBD (Admlty) *30–305*, *30–308*
Union Eagle Ltd v Golden Achievement Ltd [1997] A.C. 514; [1997] 2 W.L.R. 341; [1997] 2 All E.R. 215; (1997) 141 S.J.L.B. 56; [1997] N.P.C. 16, PC (HK) 1–023, *3–104*, *21–016*, *22–048*, *26–147*, *26–148*
Union Pacific Ry Co v Public Service Commission of Missouri (1918) 248 U.S. 67 .... *7–004*
Union Steamships v Barnes (1956) 5 D.L.R. (2d) 535 .... *12–014*
Union Transport Finance v British Car Auctions [1978] 2 All E.R. 385; (1977) 246 E.G. 131, CA (Civ Div) *22–051*
Union Transport v Continental Lines SA; sub nom. Cross AM Lines [1992] 1 W.L.R. 15; [1992] 1 All E.R. 161; [1992] 1 Lloyd's Rep. 229; [1992] I.L.Pr. 385; (1992) 89(2) L.S.G. 30; (1992) 136 S.J.L.B. 18, HL *30–306*
Uniproducts (Manchester) Ltd v Rose Furnishers Ltd [1956] 1 W.L.R. 45; [1956] 1 All E.R. 146; (1956) 100 S.J. 15, Assizes (Manchester) *21–009*
Unique Mariner, The (No.2) [1979] 1 Lloyd's Rep. 37, QBD (Admlty) *2–085*, *13–012*
Unique Pub Properties Ltd v Beer Barrels & Minerals (Wales) Ltd [2004] EWCA Civ 586; [2005] 1 All E.R. (Comm) 181; [2004] N.P.C. 77, CA (Civ Div) *18–135*
Unisys International Services Ltd (formerly Sperry Rand) v Eastern Counties Newspapers Ltd; Unisys International Services Ltd (formerly Sperry Rand) v Eastern Counties Newspapers Group [1991] 1 Lloyd's Rep. 538, CA (Civ Div); reversing, *Independent*, April 30, 1990, QBD *2–006*
Unit Construction Co v Liverpool Corp (1972) 221 E.G. 459 .... *2–166*

Unitas, The. *See* Lever Bros & Unilever NV v HM Procurator General
United Arab Emirates v Abdelghafar [1995] I.C.R. 65; [1995] I.R.L.R. 243, EAT *11–004*, *11–005*
United Arab Maritime Co v Blue Star Line; The Mecca [1968] P. 665; [1968] 3 W.L.R. 497; [1968] 2 All E.R. 731; [1968] 2 Lloyd's Rep. 17; (1968) 112 S.J. 670, PDAD *26–178*
United Australia Ltd v Barclays Bank Ltd [1941] A.C. 1; [1940] 4 All E.R. 20, HL; reversing [1939] 2 K.B. 53, CA *7–045*, *29–007*, *29–008*, *29–011*, *29–140*, *29–141*, *29–146*, *29–156*
United Bank of Kuwait Plc v Sahib [1997] Ch. 107; [1996] 3 W.L.R. 372; [1996] 3 All E.R. 215; [1996] 2 F.L.R. 666; (1997) 73 P. & C.R. 177; [1997] Fam. Law 17; [1996] E.G. 19 (C.S.); [1996] N.P.C. 12; (1996) 72 P. & C.R. D17, CA (Civ Div); affirming [1995] 2 W.L.R. 94; [1995] 2 All E.R. 973; [1996] 1 F.L.R. 379; [1996] Fam. Law 87, Ch D 4–044, *4–055*, 4–059
United City Merchants (Investments) Ltd v Royal Bank of Canada; The American Accord [1983] 1 A.C. 168; [1982] 2 W.L.R. 1039; [1982] 2 All E.R. 720; [1982] 2 Lloyd's Rep. 1; [1982] Com. L.R. 142, HL; reversing [1982] Q.B. 208; [1981] 3 W.L.R. 242; [1981] 3 All E.R. 142; [1981] 1 Lloyd's Rep. 604; [1981] Com. L.R. 98; (1981) 125 S.J. 413, CA (Civ Div); affirming [1979] 1 Lloyd's Rep. 267, QBD (Comm) *1–084*, *3–182*, *16–032*, *16–159*, *16–195*, *16–196*, *16–205*
United Dominions Corp (Jamaica) v Shoucair (Michael Mitri) [1969] 1 A.C. 340; [1968] 3 W.L.R. 893; [1968] 2 All E.R. 904; (1968) 112 S.J. 482, PC (Jam) ...*22–028*, *22–030*, *22–033*
United Dominions Trust (Commercial) Ltd v Parkway Motors Ltd [1955] 1 W.L.R. 719; [1955] 2 All E.R. 557; (1955) 99 S.J. 436, QBD *19–043*
United Dominions Trust (Commercial) v Eagle Aircraft Services; sub nom. United Dominions Trust (Commercial) v Eagle Aviation [1968] 1 W.L.R. 74; [1968] 1 All E.R. 104; (1967) 111 S.J. 849, CA (Civ Div) *12–028*
United Dominions Trust (Commercial) v Ennis [1968] 1 Q.B. 54; [1967] 3 W.L.R. 1; [1967] 2 All E.R. 345; (1967) 111 S.J. 191, CA (Civ Div) *22–049*, *26–131*, *26–141*
United Dominions Trust v Western [1976] Q.B. 513; [1976] 2 W.L.R. 64; [1975] 3 All E.R. 1017; (1975) 119 S.J. 792, CA (Civ Div) 5–102, *5–105*, *18–006*
United International Pictures v Cine Bes Filmcilik ve Yapimcilik AS; sub nom. Cine Bes Filmcheck ve Yapimcilik AS v United International Pictures [2003] EWCA Civ 1669; [2004] 1 C.L.C. 401; (2003) 147 S.J.L.B. 1396, CA (Civ Div) *23–021*, *23–048*
United Kingdom Shipowning Co Ltd (1865) 2 De G.J. Sm. 456 .... *25–023*
United Overseas Bank Ltd v Jiwani [1976] 1 W.L.R. 964; [1977] 1 All E.R. 733; (1976) 120 S.J. 329, QBD *29–176*, *29–178*, *29–180*
United Railways of Havana and Regla Warehouses Ltd, Re [1961] A.C. 1007; [1960] 2 W.L.R. 969; [1960] 2 All E.R. 332; (1960) 104 S.J. 466, HL; reversing in part [1960] Ch. 52; [1959] 2 W.L.R. 251; [1959] 1 All E.R. 214; (1959) 103 S.J. 155, CA; affirming [1958] Ch. 724; [1958] 2 W.L.R. 229; [1957] 3 All E.R. 641; (1958) 102 S.J. 106, Ch D ...*22–031*, *30–005*, *30–010*, *30–012*, *30–015*, *30–051*, *30–346*
United Scientific Holdings Ltd v Burnley BC; Cheapside Land Development Co Ltd v Messels Service Co [1978] A.C. 904; [1977] 2 W.L.R. 806; [1977] 2 All E.R. 62; 75 L.G.R. 407; (1977) 33 P. & C.R. 220; (1977) 243 E.G. 43; (1977) 121 S.J. 223, HL; reversing [1976] Ch. 128; [1976] 2 W.L.R. 686; [1976] 2 All E.R. 220; 74 L.G.R. 316; (1976) 32 P. & C.R. 183; (1976) 238 E.G. 487; (1976) 120 S.J. 183, CA (Civ Div); affirming (1974) 231 E.G. 1543, Ch D *3–172*, 12–037, *12–040*, *21–011*, *21–012*, *21–013*, *21–014*, *21–017*, *21–018*, *24–037*, *24–040*
United Shoe Machinery Co of Canada v Brunet [1909] A.C. 330, PC (Can) 16–130
United States v Braunstein (1948) 168 F. 2d 749 .... *5–074*
United States v Motor Trucks Ltd [1924] A.C. 196, PC (Can) *5–112*, *5–113*, *5–124*
United States of American and Republic of France v Dollfus Mieg et Cie SA. *See* Dollfus Mieg et Compagnie SA v Bank of England

Unity Finance v Hammond (1962) 106 S.J. 327 .... *14–028*
Unity Finance v Hammond (1965) 109 S.J. 70, CA *5–105*
Unity Joint Stock Mutual Banking Association v King, 53 E.R. 563; (1858) 25 Beav. 72, Ct of Chancery *29–116*
Universal Banking Corp, Re; sub nom. Gunn's Case (1867–68) L.R. 3 Ch. App. 40; 37 L.J. Ch. 40; 17 L.T. 365; 16 W.R. 97, CA in Chancery *2–045*
Universal Bulk Carriers Pte Ltd v Andre et Cie SA; sub nom. Andre et Cie SA v Universal Bulk Carriers Ltd [2001] EWCA Civ 588; [2001] 2 All E.R. (Comm) 510; [2001] 2 Lloyd's Rep. 65; [2001] C.L.C. 1179, CA (Civ Div); affirming [2000] 1 Lloyd's Rep. 459, QBD (Comm) *12–037*
Universal Cargo Carriers Corp v Citati (No.1) [1957] 1 W.L.R. 979; [1957] 3 All E.R. 234; [1957] 2 Lloyd's Rep. 191; (1957) 101 S.J. 762, CA *24–014*, *24–017*, *24–018*, *24–021*, *24–026*, *24–028*, *24–029*, 24–030
Universal Corp v Five Ways Properties [1979] 1 All E.R. 552; (1979) 38 P. & C.R. 687; (1978) 250 E.G. 447; (1979) 123 S.J. 33, CA (Civ Div) *26–152*
Universe Tankships Inc of Monrovia v International Transport Workers Federation; The Universe Sentinel [1983] 1 A.C. 366; [1982] 2 W.L.R. 803; [1982] 2 All E.R. 67; [1982] 1 Lloyd's Rep. 537; [1982] Com. L.R. 149; [1982] I.C.R. 262; [1982] I.R.L.R. 200, HL; affirming [1980] 2 Lloyd's Rep. 523; [1981] I.C.R. 129; [1980] I.R.L.R. 363, CA (Civ Div); reversing in part [1980] I.R.L.R. 239, HC *1–135*, *2–177*, *3–067*, *3–071*, 7–005, *7–007*, *7–012*, 7–017, 7–031, *7–045*, 7–055, *29–088*, *29–140*, *29–143*, *29–150*
Universities Superannuation Scheme Ltd v Royal Insurance (UK) Ltd [2000] 1 All E.R. (Comm) 266; [2000] Lloyd's Rep. I.R. 524, QBD (Comm) *28–050*
University Council of the Vidyodaya University of Ceylon v Silva; sub nom. Vidyodaya University of Ceylon v Silva [1965] 1 W.L.R. 77; [1964] 3 All E.R. 865; (1964) 108 S.J. 896, PC (Cey) *27–022*, *27–023*
University of Edinburgh v Onifade, 2005 S.L.T. (Sh Ct) 63; 2005 G.W.D. 5–60, Sh Pr 2–016, *2–027*, *2–030*
University of Nottingham v Eyett (No.2) [1999] 1 W.L.R. 594; [1999] 2 All E.R. 445; [1999] I.C.R. 730; [1999] Pens. L.R. 25, Ch D *1–032*, *13–008*
University of Nottingham v Fishel [2000] I.C.R. 1462; [2000] I.R.L.R. 471; [2001] R.P.C. 22; [2000] Ed. C.R. 505; [2000] E.L.R. 385; (2001) 24(2) I.P.D. 24009, QBD *6–142*, *29–151*, *29–157*
Unwin v Wolseley (1787) 1 T.R. 674 .... *10–013*
Upfill v Wright [1911] 1 K.B. 506, KBD *16–069*
Upjohn v Hitchens; Upjohn v Ford [1918] 2 K.B. 48, CA; affirming [1918] 1 K.B. 171, KBD *12–057*
Upton v Henderson (1912) 28 T.L.R. 398 .... *26–011*
Upton-on-Severn Rural DC v Powell [1942] 1 All E.R. 220, CA 2–042, *5–090*, *29–073*
Uren v First National Home Finance Ltd [2005] EWHC 2529, Ch D 29–015, *29–018*, *29–025*, *29–026*
Urmston v Newcomen (1836) 4 A. & E. 899 .... *8–061*
Urmston v Whitelegg Bros. (1890) 63 L.T. 455 .... *16–134*
V Berg & Son v Vanden Avenne-Izegem PVBA [1977] 1 Lloyd's Rep. 499, CA (Civ Div); reversing [1976] 1 Lloyd's Rep. 348, QBD (Comm) *3–091*, *12–039*, *14–150*, *22–052*, *24–004*, *24–008*
VAI Industries (UK) Ltd v Bostock & Bramley; sub nom. Vai Industries (UK) Ltd v Bostock & Bromley Transmissions Ltd [2003] EWCA Civ 1069; [2003] B.L.R. 359, CA (Civ Div) *28–035*
VOS of Moscow v Temple SS Co Ltd. *See* Temple Steamship Co Ltd v V/O Sorfracht
VSH v BKS Air Transport and Stevens [1964] 1 Lloyd's Rep. 460, QBD *12–116*
Vacwell Engineering Co Ltd v BDH Chemicals Ltd; sub nom. Vacwell Engineering Co v British Drug House Chemicals [1971] 1 Q.B. 111; [1970] 3 W.L.R. 67; [1970] 3 All E.R. 553 (Note); (1970) 114 S.J. 472, CA (Civ Div) *26–059*
Vadala v Lawes (1890) L.R. 25 Q.B.D. 310, CA *25–015*
Vadasz v Pioneer Concrete (SA) Pty (1995) 184 C.L.R. 102 .... *6–111*, 6–118, *29–149*
Vagliano Bros v Bank of England. *See* Bank of England v Vagliano Bros

Vagres Compania Maritima SA v Nissho-Iwai American Corp; The Karin Vatis [1988] 2 Lloyd's Rep. 330, CA (Civ Div) *23–072*
Vainqueur Jose, The. *See* CVG Siderurgicia del Orinoco SA v London Steamship Owners Mutual Insurance Association Ltd; The Vainqueur Jose
Vakante v Addey and Stanhope School Governing Body; sub nom. Addey and Stanhope School v Vakante; V v Addet & Stanhope School [2004] EWCA Civ 1065; [2004] 4 All E.R. 1056; [2005] 1 C.M.L.R. 3; [2005] I.C.R. 231; (2004) 101(36) L.S.G. 33, CA (Civ Div); affirming [2004] I.C.R. 279, EAT *16–166*
Valentini v Canali (1890) L.R. 24 Q.B.D. 166, QBD *8–065*, *29–081*
Vallance, Re; Vallance v Blagden (1884) L.R. 26 Ch. D. 353, Ch D *16–067*
Valpy v Manley (1845) 1 C.B. 594 .... *29–090*
Vamvakas v Custodian of Enemy Property [1952] 2 Q.B. 183; [1952] 1 All E.R. 629; [1952] 1 T.L.R. 638; (1952) 96 S.J. 213, QBD *16–163*
Van den Derb v Giles [1979] 2 N.Z.L.R. 111 .... *29–116*, *29–161*
Van Den Hurk v R Martens & Co Ltd (In Liquidation) [1920] 1 K.B. 850; (1920) 2 Ll. L. Rep. 281, KBD (Comm Ct) *26–064*, *26–109*
Van der Linde v Van der Linde [1947] Ch. 306; [1947] L.J.R. 592; 176 L.T. 297; (1947) 91 S.J. 131, Ch D *5–136*
Van Diemen's Land Co v Table Cape Marine Board [1906] A.C. 92, PC (Aus) *12–126*
Van Grutten v Digby (1862) 31 Beav. 561 .... *30–310*
Van Laethem v Brooker [2005] EWHC 1478; [2006] 2 F.L.R. 495; [2006] 1 F.C.R. 697; [2006] Fam. Law 537; [2005] N.P.C. 91, Ch D *3–139*, *3–147*
Van Laun Ex p. Chatterton, Re; sub nom. Van Laun Ex p. Pattullo [1907] 2 K.B. 23, CA; affirming [1907] 1 K.B. 155, KBD *20–049*
Van Lynn Developments v Pelias Construction Co (formerly Jason Construction Co) [1969] 1 Q.B. 607; [1968] 3 W.L.R. 1141; [1968] 3 All E.R. 824; (1968) 112 S.J. 819, CA (Civ Div) *19–016*
Van Oppen v Bedford Charity Trustees; sub nom. Van Oppen v Clerk to the Trustees of the Bedford Charity; Van Oppen v Bedford School Trustees [1990] 1 W.L.R. 235; [1989] 3 All E.R. 389; (1989) 139 N.L.J. 900, CA (Civ Div); affirming [1989] 1 All E.R. 273; (1988) 138 N.L.J. Rep. 221, QBD *1–158*, *3–180*, *18–022*, *18–027*
Van Praagh v Everidge [1903] 1 Ch. 434, CA; reversing [1902] 2 Ch. 266, Ch D *4–038*, *5–071*, *5–077*
Van Sandau v Corsbie (1819) 3 B. & Ald. 13 .... *20–047*
Van Toll v SE Ry (1862) 12 C.B.(N.S.) 75 .... *14–135*
Vanbergen v St Edmunds Properties Ltd [1933] 2 K.B. 223, CA; reversing [1933] 1 K.B. 345, KBD *3–066*, *3–079*, *22–017*, *22–035*
Vance v Lowther (1875–76) L.R. 1 Ex. D. 176, Exchequer Div 25–022
Vancouver Malt & Sake Brewing Co Ltd v Vancouver Breweries Ltd [1934] A.C. 181, PC (Can); reversing, 47 B.C.L.R. 89, CA (BC) *16–091*, *16–092*, *16–117*, *16–132*
Vandenbergh v Spooner (1865–66) L.R. 1 Ex. 316, Ex Ct *4–023*
Vandepitte v Preferred Accident Insurance Corp of New York; sub nom. Vandepitte v Preferred Accident Insurance Co of New York [1933] A.C. 70; (1932) 44 Ll. L. Rep. 41, PC (Can) *18–079*, *18–080*, 19–046
Vandervell v Inland Revenue Commissioners [1967] 2 A.C. 291; [1967] 2 W.L.R. 87; [1967] 1 All E.R. 1; 43 T.C. 519; (1966) 45 A.T.C. 394; [1966] T.R. 315; (1966) 110 S.J. 910, HL; affirming [1966] Ch. 261; [1965] 2 W.L.R. 1085; [1965] 2 All E.R. 37; (1965) 44 A.T.C. 46; [1965] T.R. 45; (1965) 109 S.J. 235, CA; affirming (1964) 43 A.T.C. 74; [1964] T.R. 93; (1964) 108 S.J. 279, Ch D *19–026*, *19–058*
Vandervell Products v McLeod [1957] R.P.C. 185, CA *16–112*
Vandervell's Trusts (No.2), Re; sub nom. White v Vandervell Trustees [1974] Ch. 269; [1974] 3 W.L.R. 256; [1974] 3 All E.R. 205; (1974) 118 S.J. 566, CA (Civ Div); reversing [1973] 3 W.L.R. 744; [1974] 1 All E.R. 47; (1973) 117 S.J. 856, Ch D *19–026*
Vandyke v Adams [1942] Ch. 155, Ch D *11–024*, *16–163*
Vane v Vane (1873) L.R. 8 Ch. App. 383 .... *28–089*

Vantage Navigation Corp v Suhail and Saud Bahwan Building Materials; The Alev [1989] 1 Lloyd's Rep. 138, QBD (Comm) *3–010*, *3–066*, *3–067*, *7–005*, *7–013*, *7–018*, *7–031*, *29–088*, *29–092*
Vardon's Trusts, Re (1886) L.R. 31 Ch. D. 275, CA; reversing (1885) L.R. 28 Ch. D. 124, Ch D *8–036*
Varverakis v Compagnia de Navegacion Artico SA; The Merak [1976] 2 Lloyd's Rep. 250, CA (Civ Div) *2–154*
Vaswani v Italian Motors (Sales and Services) Ltd [1996] 1 W.L.R. 270; [1996] R.T.R. 115; (1996) 93(2) L.S.G. 27; (1996) 140 S.J.L.B. 27, PC (HK) *24–019*
Vaughan v Hancock (1846) 3 C.B. 766 .... *4–011*
Vaughan v Matthews (1849) 13 Q.B. 187 .... *29–147*
Vaughan v Vaughan [1953] 1 Q.B. 762; [1953] 1 W.L.R. 236; [1953] 1 All E.R. 209; (1953) 97 S.J. 65, CA *2–169*, *2–183*, *3–098*
Vedatech Corp v Crystal Decisions (UK) Ltd (formerly Seagate Software IMG Ltd) [2002] EWHC 818, Ch D *29–080*
Vellino v Chief Constable of Greater Manchester [2001] EWCA Civ 1249; [2002] 1 W.L.R. 218; [2002] 3 All E.R. 78; [2002] P.I.Q.R. P10; [2001] Po. L.R. 295; (2001) 151 N.L.J. 1441, CA (Civ Div) *16–007*
Venezuela Central Railway Co v Kisch (1867) L.R. 2 H.L. 99, HL *6–039*, *6–153*
Venning, Re; sub nom. Halifax Building Society Appeal, Re, 63 T.L.R. 394; [1947] W.N. 196, CA *3–129*
Veracruz Transportation v VC Shipping Co Inc (Veracruz, The) [1992] 1 Lloyd's Rep. 353, CA (Civ Div) *27–078*
Verderame v Commercial Union Assurance Co Plc, The Times, April 2, 1992, CA *1–177*, *18–031*
Verlest v Motor Union Insurance Co Ltd [1925] 2 K.B. 137 .... *21–021*
Verrall v Farnes [1966] 1 W.L.R. 1254; [1966] 2 All E.R. 808; (1966) 110 S.J. 406, Ch D *3–177*
Verrall v Great Yarmouth BC [1981] Q.B. 202; [1980] 3 W.L.R. 258; [1980] 1 All E.R. 839, CA (Civ Div) *13–028*, *27–007*, *27–010*
Verren v Anglo-Dutch Brick Co (1927) Ltd (1929) 34 Ll. L. Rep. 210, CA *21–022*
Verschures Creameries Ltd v Hull and Netherlands Steamship Co Ltd [1921] 2 K.B. 608, CA *29–146*
Vertex Data Science Ltd v Powergen Retail Ltd [2006] EWHC 1340 (Comm); [2006] 2 Lloyd's Rep. 591, QBD (Comm) *27–025*, *27–026*, *27–042*
Vervaeke v Smith [1983] 1 A.C. 145; [1982] 2 W.L.R. 855; [1982] 2 All E.R. 144; (1982) 126 S.J. 293, HL *25–011*, *25–013*
Vesta v Butcher. *See* Forsikringsaktieselskapet Vesta v Butcher
Vic Mill Ltd, Re [1913] 1 Ch. 465, CA *26–069*, *26–111*
Victor Battery Co Ltd v Curry's Ltd [1946] Ch. 242, Ch D *9–038*
Victoria Fur Traders Ltd v Roadline (UK) Ltd [1981] 1 Lloyd's Rep. 570, QBD (Comm) *14–019*, *14–054*
Victoria Laundry (Windsor) v Newman Industries [1949] 2 K.B. 528; [1949] 1 All E.R. 997; 65 T.L.R. 274; (1949) 93 S.J. 371, CA *26–052*, 26–054, *26–055*, **26–056**, 26–057, *26–058*, *26–059*, *26–060*, *26–061*, *26–062*, *26–063*, 26–066, 26–067, *26–070*
Victorian Daylesford Syndicate Ltd v Dott [1905] 2 Ch. 624, Ch D *16–147*
Viditz v O'Hagan [1900] 2 Ch. 87, CA *30–310*, *30–324*
Vidyodaya University Council v Silva. *See* University Council of the Vidyodaya University of Ceylon v Silva
Vigers v Cook [1919] 2 K.B. 475, CA *21–001*, *21–030*, *21–031*, *24–043*
Vigers v Pike (1842) 8 Cl. & F. 562 .... *6–033*, *6–117*
Villa v Dimock (1694) Skin. 370 .... *11–029*
Vinall v Howard [1954] 1 Q.B. 375; [1954] 2 W.L.R. 314; [1954] 1 All E.R. 458; (1954) 98 S.J. 143, CA; reversing [1953] 1 W.L.R. 987; [1953] 2 All E.R. 515; (1953) 97 S.J. 508, QBD *16–147*
Vinava Shipping Co Ltd v Fineluet AG; The Chrysalis. *See* Finelvet AG v Vinava Shipping Co Ltd; The Chrysalis

Vincent v Premo Enterprises (Voucher Sales) [1969] 2 Q.B. 609; [1969] 2 W.L.R. 1256; [1969] 2 All E.R. 941; (1969) 20 P. & C.R. 591; (1969) 113 S.J. 266, CA (Civ Div) *1–093*, *1–105*
Vincents of Reading v Fogden (1932) 48 T.L.R. 613 .... *16–110*
Vines v Arnold (1849) 8 C.B. 632 .... *25–010*
Virani Ltd v Manuel Revert y Cia SA [2003] EWCA Civ 1651; [2004] 2 Lloyd's Rep. 14, CA (Civ Div) *30–373*
Virgo Steamship Co SA v Skaarup Shipping Corp; The Kapetan Georgis [1988] 1 Lloyd's Rep. 352; [1988] F.T.L.R. 180, QBD (Comm) *18–034*
Virk v Gan Life Holdings Plc [2000] Lloyd's Rep. I.R. 159; (2000) 52 B.M.L.R. 207, CA (Civ Div) *28–050*
Vita Food Products Inc v Unus Shipping Co Ltd (In Liquidation) [1939] A.C. 277; (1939) 63 Ll. L. Rep. 21, PC (Can) *16–147*, *30–007*, *30–009*, *30–050*, *30–365*
Vita, The [1990] 1 Lloyd's Rep. 528, QBD (Admlty) *28–116*
Vitesse Yacht Charters SL v Spiers'he Deverne II [2003] EWHC 2426; [2004] 1 Lloyd's Rep. 179, QBD (Admlty) *18–012*
Vitol BV (formerly t/a Vitol Trading BV) v Compagnie Europeene des Petroles [1988] 1 Lloyd's Rep. 574, QBD (Comm) *12–118*
Vitol SA v Norelf Ltd; The Santa Clara [1996] A.C. 800; [1996] 3 W.L.R. 105; [1996] 3 All E.R. 193; [1996] 2 Lloyd's Rep. 225; [1996] C.L.C. 1159; (1996) 15 Tr. L.R. 347; (1996) 93(26) L.S.G. 19; (1996) 146 N.L.J. 957; (1996) 140 S.J.L.B. 147, HL; reversing [1996] Q.B. 108; [1995] 3 W.L.R. 549; [1995] 3 All E.R. 971; [1995] 2 Lloyd's Rep. 128; [1995] C.L.C. 1018; (1995) 14 Tr. L.R. 451, CA (Civ Div); reversing [1994] 1 W.L.R. 1390; [1994] 4 All E.R. 109; [1993] 2 Lloyd's Rep. 301; (1993) 90(30) L.S.G. 36; (1993) 137 S.J.L.B. 146, QBD (Comm) *2–071*, *2–072*, *2–077*, *24–001*, *24–013*
Vitol SA v Phibro Energy AG; The Mathraki [1990] 2 Lloyd's Rep. 84, QBD (Comm) *12–129*, *13–018*
Voaden v Voaden, unreported, February 21, 1997, Ch D *16–108*
Voest Alpine Intertrading GmbH v Chevron International Oil Co Ltd [1987] 2 Lloyd's Rep. 547, QBD (Comm) *2–128*, *2–129*, *3–097*
Vogeman v Bisley (1897) 13 T.L.R. 172 .... *12–029*
Vokl v Rotuna Hospital [1914] 2 I.R. 549 .... *11–027*
Von Goetz v Rogers. *See* Goetz v Rogers
Von Hatzfeldt Wildenburg v Alexander [1912] 1 Ch. 284, Ch D *2–032*, *2–116*, *2–118*, *2–134*, *2–136*
Vosper Thornycroft v Ministry of Defence [1976] 1 Lloyd's Rep. 58, QBD (Comm) *2–128*
Voyce v Voyce (1991) 62 P. & C.R. 290, CA (Civ Div) *3–139*, *3–152*
Voyle v Hughes (1854) 2 Sm. & G.18 .... *19–033*
Vyse v Wakefield (1840) 6 M.W. 442 .... *21–006*, *21–009*
W v Commissioner of Police of the Metropolis [2000] 1 W.L.R. 1607; [2000] 4 All E.R. 934; [2000] I.C.R. 1064; [2000] I.R.L.R. 720; [2001] P.I.Q.R. P6; [2000] Po. L.R. 322; (2000) 97(39) L.S.G. 42; (2000) 144 S.J.L.B. 248, HL; reversing [1997] I.C.R. 1073; [1997] I.R.L.R. 589, CA (Civ Div); affirming [1995] I.C.R. 510; [1995] I.R.L.R. 531, EAT *2–181*
W&S Pollock & Co v Macrae; Macrae v W&S Pollock & Co (1922) 12 Ll. L. Rep. 299; 1922 S.C. (H.L.) 192; 1922 S.L.T. 510, HL *14–027*
W Cook Builders Pty Ltd v Matthew Lumbers [2007] S.A.S.C. 20 .... *29–022*
W Cory Son Ltd v Lambton and Hetton Collieries Ltd (1916) 86 L.J.K.B. 401 ..... *29–120*
W Devis & Sons Ltd v Atkins [1977] A.C. 931; [1977] 3 W.L.R. 214; [1977] 3 All E.R. 40; 8 B.L.R. 57; [1977] I.C.R. 662; [1977] I.R.L.R. 314; (1978) 13 I.T.R. 71; (1977) 121 S.J. 512, HL *24–014*
W Higgins Ltd v Northampton Corp [1927] 1 Ch. 128, Ch D *5–113*, *5–122*
W Photoprint v Forward Trust Group (1993) 12 Tr.L.R. 146 QBD *14–095*
WB Anderson & Sons Ltd v Rhodes (Liverpool) Ltd [1967] 2 All E.R. 850, Assizes (Liverpool) *6–071*, *6–081*, *6–084*
WC Leng & Co Ltd v Andrews [1909] 1 Ch. 763, CA *8–026*, *16–106*
WE Cox Toner (International) Ltd v Crook [1981] I.C.R. 823; [1981] I.R.L.R. 443, EAT *24–002*

WEA (A Debtor), Re [1901] 2 K.B. 642, CA *17–005*, *17–017*, *17–018*, *17–020*
WF Harrison & Co v Burke [1956] 1 W.L.R. 419; [1956] 2 All E.R. 169; (1956) 100 S.J. 300, CA *19–016*
WH Martin Ltd v Feldbinder Spezialfahrzeugwerke GmbH; sub nom. WH Martin Ltd v Spezialfahrzeugwerke GmbH [1998] I.L.Pr. 794, CA (Civ Div) *30–077*, *30–090*
WJ Alan & Co Ltd v El Nasr Export & Import Co [1972] 2 Q.B. 189; [1972] 2 W.L.R. 800; [1972] 2 All E.R. 127; [1972] 1 Lloyd's Rep. 313; (1972) 116 S.J. 139, CA (Civ Div); reversing [1971] 1 Lloyd's Rep. 401, QBD (Comm) ...*3–079*, *3–094*, *3–097*, *3–104*, *3–129*, *3–130*, *21–074*, *22–035*, *22–042*, *22–044*, *30–331*, *30–372*
WJ Investments Ltd v Bunting [1984] 1 N.S.W.L.R. 331 .... *26–143*
WJ Tatem Ltd v Gamboa [1939] 1 K.B. 132; (1938) 61 Ll. L. Rep. 149, KBD 23–017, *23–021*, 23–044, *23–059*
WL Thompson Ltd v R Robinson (Gunmakers) Ltd [1955] Ch. 177; [1955] 2 W.L.R. 185; [1955] 1 All E.R. 154; (1955) 99 S.J. 76, Ch D *26–069*
WN Hillas & Co Ltd v Arcos Ltd; WN Hillas & Co Ltd v Arcos Ltd (Quantum) (1932) 43 Ll. L. Rep. 359; (1932) 147 L.T. 503, HL; reversing (1931) 40 Ll. L. Rep. 307, CA; reversing in part (1931) 40 Ll. L. Rep. 106, KBD 2–130, *2–136*, 2–140, 2–142, *12–065*
WPP Holdings Italy Srl v Benatti; sub nom. Benatti v WPP Holdings Italy Srl [2007] EWCA Civ 263; [2007] 1 W.L.R. 2316; [2007] 2 All E.R. (Comm) 525; [2008] 1 Lloyd's Rep. 396; [2007] 1 C.L.C. 324; [2007] I.L.Pr. 33; (2007) 104(15) L.S.G. 21, CA (Civ Div) *18–117*, *30–110*, *30–278*
WRM Group Ltd v Wood [1998] C.L.C. 189, CA (Civ Div) *6–136*, *14–062*, *14–095*
WW Duncan & Co, Re [1905] 1 Ch. 307, Ch D *21–058*, *26–167*
WWF World Wide Fund for Nature (formerly World Wildlife Fund) v World Wrestling Federation Entertainment Inc [2007] EWCA Civ 286; [2007] Bus. L.R. 1252; [2008] 1 W.L.R. 445; [2008] 1 All E.R. 74; [2008] 1 All E.R. (Comm) 129, CA (Civ Div) *26–023*, 26–027, 29–154
WX Investments Ltd v Begg; sub nom. WX Investments Ltd v Beg [2002] EWHC 925 (Ch); [2002] 1 W.L.R. 2849; [2002] L. & T.R. 39; [2002] 3 E.G.L.R. 47; [2002] 50 E.G. 115; (2002) 99(24) L.S.G. 36; (2002) 146 S.J.L.B. 135; [2002] N.P.C. 69; [2002] 2 P. & C.R. DG18, Ch D .. *12–082*, *13–009*
Wace v Pan Atlantic Group Inc [1981] 2 Lloyd's Rep. 339, QBD (Comm) *12–055*, *12–118*
Waddon v Whitecroft-Scovill Ltd [1988] 1 W.L.R. 309; [1988] 1 All E.R. 996; (1988) 85(11) L.S.G. 43; (1988) 132 S.J. 263, HL *28–116*
Wade v Simeon (1846) 2 C.B. 548 .... *3–047*, 3–050, *7–041*
Wade's Case (1601) 5 Co. Rep. 114 .... *21–085*
Wadham Stringer Finance Ltd v Meaney [1981] 1 W.L.R. 39; [1980] 3 All E.R. 789; [1980] Com. L.R. 7; [1981] R.T.R. 152; (1980) 124 S.J. 807, QBD *26–140*
Wadlow v Samuel (aka Seal) [2007] EWCA Civ 155; (2007) 151 S.J.L.B. 331, CA (Civ Div); affirming [2006] EWHC 1492, QBD *7–121*, *22–001*, *22–028*, *22–034*
Wadsworth v Lydell [1981] 1 W.L.R. 598; [1981] 2 All E.R. 401; (1981) 125 S.J. 309, CA (Civ Div) *21–040*, *26–063*, *26–098*, 26–107, *26–167*, *26–169*
Wahda Bank v Arab Bank Plc (Conflict of Law) [1996] 1 Lloyd's Rep. 470; [1996] 5 Bank. L.R. 128; [1996] C.L.C. 408, CA (Civ Div) *30–011*, *30–012*, *30–051*
Waikato Regional Airport Ltd v Attorney General (on behalf of the Director General of Agriculture and Forestry) [2003] UKPC 50, PC (NZ) *29–084*
Wainwright v Home Office; sub nom. Secretary of State for the Home Department v Wainwright; Wainwright v Secretary of State for the Home Department [2003] UKHL 53; [2004] 2 A.C. 406; [2003] 3 W.L.R. 1137; [2003] 4 All E.R. 969; [2004] U.K.H.R.R. 154; 15 B.H.R.C. 387; [2004] Prison L.R. 130; (2003) 100(45) L.S.G. 30; (2003) 147 S.J.L.B. 1208, HL; affirming [2001] EWCA Civ 2081; [2002] Q.B. 1334; [2002] 3 W.L.R. 405; [2003] 3 All E.R. 943; [2002] Po. L.R. 133; (2002) 99(9) L.S.G. 31; (2002) 146 S.J.L.B. 18, CA (Civ Div) *1–060*

Walley v Holt (1876) 35 L.T. 631 .... *8–047*
Wallingford v Mutual Society (1879–80) L.R. 5 App. Cas. 685, HL *26–140*
Wallis v Littell (1861) 11 C.B.(N.S.) 369 .... *12–109*
Wallis v Smith (1882) L.R. 21 Ch. D. 243, CA *26–098*, *26–127*, *26–132*
Wallis Son & Wells v Pratt & Haynes [1911] A.C. 394, HL; reversing [1910] 2 K.B. 1003, CA *12–026*, *12–033*, *14–006*, *14–027*, *24–001*, *24–005*, *24–040*
Wall's Case (1872) 42 L.J. Ch. 372 .... *2–024*
Walmsley v Acid Jazz Records Ltd [2001] E.C.D.R. 4, Ch D *3–101*
Walsh v Lonsdale (1882) L.R. 21 Ch. D. 9, CA *13–028*
Walsh v Trevanion (1850) 15 Q.B. 733 .... *12–066*
Walter v Everard [1891] 2 Q.B. 369, CA *8–004*, *8–006*, *8–013*, *8–020*
Walter v Haynes (1824) Ry. M. 149 .... *21–056*
Walter v James (1871) L.R. 6 Ex. 124 .... *21–041*
Walter & Sullivan v J Murphy & Sons [1955] 2 Q.B. 584; [1955] 2 W.L.R. 919; [1955] 1 All E.R. 843; (1955) 99 S.J. 290, CA *19–014*, *19–038*
Walter (Deceased), Re; sub nom. Slocock v Official Receiver [1929] 1 Ch. 647, Ch D *20–023*
Walters v Morgan (1861) 3 De. G. F. & J. 718 ....*6–015*, 27–032
Walters v Northern Coal Mining Co (1855) 5 De G.M. & G. 629 .... *27–040*
Walters v Whessoe Ltd; Walters v Shell Refining Co Ltd [1968] 2 All E.R. 816 (Note); 6 B.L.R. 23, CA *14–015*
Walton, Ex p.; sub nom. Levy Ex p Walton, Re; Levy, Re (1881) L.R. 17 Ch. D. 746; (1881) 50 L.J. Ch. 657; (1881) 45 L.T. 1, CA *12–055*
Walton v Bank of Nova Scotia (1965) 52 D.L.R. (2d) 506 .... *9–039*
Walton v Mascall (1844) 13 M.W. 452 .... *21–010*
Walton (Grain and Shipping) Ltd v British Italian Trading Co Ltd [1959] 1 Lloyd's Rep. 223, QBD (Comm) *12–078*, *14–148*, *23–027*, *30–364*
Walton Harvey Ltd v Walker & Homfrays Ltd [1931] 1 Ch. 274, CA *23–026*, *23–059*
Walton's Settlement, Re; Walton v Peirson [1922] 2 Ch. 509, Ch D *5–122*
Waltons Stores (Interstate) v Maher (1988) 164 C.L.R. 387; (1988) 62 A.L.J.R. 110 ....*3–088*, 3–106, *3–141*, *3–144*
Wandsworth LBC v Secretary of State for Transport, Local Government and the Regions (Enforcement Notice); sub nom. R. (on the application of Wandsworth LBC) v Secretary of State for Transport, Local Government and the Regions [2003] EWHC 622 (Admin); [2004] 1 P. & C.R. 32; [2004] J.P.L. 291; [2003] N.P.C. 11, QBD (Admin) *10–043*
Wandsworth LBC v Winder (No.1) [1985] A.C. 461; [1984] 3 W.L.R. 1254; [1984] 3 All E.R. 976; (1985) 17 H.L.R. 196; 83 L.G.R. 143; (1985) 82 L.S.G. 201; (1985) 135 N.L.J. 381; (1984) 128 S.J. 838, HL; affirming [1984] 3 W.L.R. 563; [1984] 3 All E.R. 83; (1984) 15 H.L.R. 1; 82 L.G.R. 509; (1984) 81 L.S.G. 1684; (1984) 128 S.J. 384, CA (Civ Div) *1–196*, *10–032*
Wankford v Wankford (1704) 1 Salk. 299 .... *25–005*
Warbrook v Griffin (1609) 2 Brownlow 254 .... *29–006*
Ward v British Oak Insurance Co Ltd [1932] 1 K.B. 392; (1931) 41 Ll. L. Rep. 42, CA; affirming [1931] 2 K.B. 637; (1931) 40 Ll. L. Rep. 172, KBD *16–161*
Ward v Byham [1956] 1 W.L.R. 496; [1956] 2 All E.R. 318; (1956) 100 S.J. 341, CA 3–022, *3–061*, 3–064, *16–067*
Ward v Hobbs (1878–79) L.R. 4 App. Cas. 13, HL; affirming (1877–78) L.R. 3 Q.B.D. 150, CA; reversing (1876–77) L.R. 2 Q.B.D. 331, QBD *6–014*
Ward v James (No.2) [1966] 1 Q.B. 273; [1965] 2 W.L.R. 455; [1965] 1 All E.R. 563; [1965] 1 Lloyd's Rep. 145; (1965) 109 S.J. 111, CA *26–030*
Ward v Kirkland [1967] Ch. 194; [1966] 1 W.L.R. 601; [1966] 1 All E.R. 609; (1966) 110 S.J. 289, Ch D *29–161*
Ward & Co v Wallis [1900] 1 Q.B. 675, QBD *21–058*, *29–029*, *29–043*, *29–098*
Ward (RV) v Bignall [1967] 1 Q.B. 534; [1967] 2 W.L.R. 1050; [1967] 2 All E.R. 449; (1967) 111 S.J. 190, CA (Civ Div) *24–001*, *26–154*, *29–064*
Warde v Feedex International [1985] 2 Lloyd's Rep. 289; [1984] 1 Lloyd's Rep. 310; (1984) 81 L.S.Gaz. 36 .... *12–037*
Wardley Australia Ltd v Western Australia, 175 C.L.R. 514, HC (Aus) *28–034*
Ware v Grand Junction Waterworks Co (1831) 2 Russ. & My. 470 .... *16–025*

Ware & De Freville Ltd v Motor Trade Association [1921] 3 K.B. 40; 19 A.L.R. 893, CA *7–045*
Waren Import Gesellschaft Krohn & Co v Alfred C Toepfer; The Vladimir Ilich [1975] 1 Lloyd's Rep. 322, QBD (Comm) *24–006*
Warinco v Mauthner (Fritz) [1978] 1 Lloyd's Rep. 151, CA (Civ Div); reversing [1977] 1 Lloyd's Rep. 277, QBD (Comm) *14–141*
Warinco v Samor SpA [1979] 1 Lloyd's Rep. 450, CA (Civ Div) *24–019*, *24–044*
Waring & Gillow v Thompson (1912) 29 T.L.R. 154 .... *27–042*
Warlow v Harrison (1859) 1 E. & E. 309 .... *2–012*, *3–174*
Warlow v Harrison, 120 E.R. 920; (1858) 1 El. & El. 295, QB *29–113*
Warman v Southern Counties Car Finance Corp Ltd [1949] 2 K.B. 576; [1949] 1 All E.R. 711; [1949] L.J.R. 1182; (1949) 93 S.J. 319, KBD *12–023*, *14–028*, *29–057*, *29–059*, *29–061*
Warmings Used Cars v Tucker [1956] S.A.S.R. 249 .... *14–026*
Warmington v Miller [1973] Q.B. 877; [1973] 2 W.L.R. 654; [1973] 2 All E.R. 372; (1973) 25 P. & C.R. 340; (1973) 117 S.J. 166, CA (Civ Div) *27–041*
Warnborough Ltd v Garmite Ltd [2006] EWHC 10 (Ch); [2007] 1 P. & C.R. 2; [2006] 3 E.G. 121 (C.S.); [2006] 2 P. & C.R. DG8, Ch D *21–056*
Warner Bros Pictures Inc v Nelson [1937] 1 K.B. 209, KBD *16–102*, *16–115*, *27–060*, *27–064*, *27–065*, *27–068*, 27–069, *30–338*
Warner Bros Records Inc v Rollgreen Ltd [1976] Q.B. 430; [1975] 2 W.L.R. 816; [1975] 2 All E.R. 105; (1974) 119 S.J. 253, CA (Civ Div) *19–005*, *19–016*, *19–020*, *19–036*, *19–042*
Warner Engineering Co v Brennan (1913) 30 T.L.R. 191 .... *20–007*
Warner v Basildon Development Corp (1991) 7 Const. L.J. 146, CA (Civ Div) *14–056*, *18–033*
Warnford Investments Ltd v Duckworth [1979] Ch. 127; [1978] 2 W.L.R. 741; [1978] 2 All E.R. 517; (1978) 36 P. & C.R. 295; (1978) 122 S.J. 63, Ch D *9–048*
Warren, Re (1884) 53 L.J.Ch. 101 .... *3–118*, *3–129*
Warren v Agdeshman (1922) 38 T.L.R. 588 .... *13–012*
Warren v Keen [1954] 1 Q.B. 15; [1953] 3 W.L.R. 702; [1953] 2 All E.R. 1118; (1953) 97 S.J. 742, CA *13–016*
Warren v King [1964] 1 W.L.R. 122 (Note); [1963] 3 All E.R. 993 (Note); (1964) 108 S.J. 114, CA *26–030*
Warren v Mendy [1989] 1 W.L.R. 853; [1989] 3 All E.R. 103; [1989] I.C.R. 525; [1989] I.R.L.R. 210; (1989) 133 S.J. 1261, CA (Civ Div) *16–102*, *27–046*, *27–065*
Warwick v Bruce (1813) 2 M. & S. 205 .... *8–042*
Warwick v Warwick (1918) 34 T.L.R. 475 .... *29–191*
Washbourn v Burrows (1847) 1 Exch. 107 .... *4–018*
Wason v Waring (1852) 15 Beav. 151 .... *29–187*
Watcham v Attorney General of East Africa Protectorate [1919] A.C. 533; [1918–19] All E.R. Rep. 455, PC (EA) *12–125*, *12–126*
Waterman v Fryer [1922] 1 K.B. 499, KBD *8–024*
Waterpark (Lord) v Fennell (1859) 7 H.L.C. 650 .... *12–126*
Waters, Ex p. *See* Hoyle Ex p.
Waters v Commissioner of Police of the Metropolis. *See* W v Commissioner of Police of the Metropolis
Waters v Earl of Thanet (1842) 2 Q.B. 757 .... *28–110*
Waters v Monarch Fire and Life Assurance Co (1856) 5 E. & B. 870 .... *18–079*, *18–128*
Waters v Weigall (1795) 2 Anst. 575 .... *29–136*
Waters Trading Co v Dalgety & Co [1951] 2 Lloyd's Rep. 385, Sup Ct (NSW) *14–046*
Wates Construction (London) v Franthom Property (1991) 7 Const. L.J. 243, CA (Civ Div) *12–069*
Wates Ltd v Greater London Council, 25 B.L.R. 1, CA (Civ Div) *23–050*, *23–058*
Watford BC v Watford Rural DC, 86 L.G.R. 524 .... *23–021*

Watford Electronics Ltd v Sanderson CFL Ltd [2001] EWCA Civ 317; [2001] 1 All E.R. (Comm) 696; [2001] B.L.R. 143; (2001) 3 T.C.L.R. 14; [2002] F.S.R. 19; [2001] Masons C.L.R. 57; (2001) 98(18) L.S.G. 44, CA (Civ Div); reversing [2000] 2 All E.R. (Comm) 984, QBD (TCC) *2–138*, *6–135*, *6–138*, *6–139*, *12–104*, *14–006*, *14–063*, *14–085*, 14–099, *14–103*, *14–133*
Wathen v Sandys (1811) 2 Camp. 640 .... *3–062*
Wathes (Western) Ltd v Austins (Menswear) Ltd [1976] 1 Lloyd's Rep. 14; 9 B.L.R. 113; (1975) 119 S.J. 527, CA (Civ Div) *14–020*, *14–022*
Watkin v Watson-Smith, *The Times*, July 3, 1986 .... *5–074*, *7–128*, *7–130*
Watkins v Carrig, 21 A. 2d 591 (1941) *3–069*
Watkins v Nash (1878) L.R. 20 Eq. 262, Ct of Chancery *1–105*
Watkins v Rymill (1882–83) L.R. 10 Q.B.D. 178, QBD *12–017*, *14–135*
Watkins v Vince (1818) 2 Stark. 368 .... *8–059*
Watkins v Watkins [1896] P. 222, CA *19–047*
Watling v Lewis [1911] 1 Ch. 414, Ch D *12–078*
Watson, Ex p.; Phillips, Re (1887) L.R. 19 Q.B.D. 234, CA; affirming (1887) L.R. 18 Q.B.D. 116, QBD *20–009*
Watson, Ex p.; sub nom. Companies Acts, Re (1888) L.R. 21 Q.B.D. 301, QBD *9–024*
Watson v British Boxing Board of Control Ltd [2001] Q.B. 1134; [2001] 2 W.L.R. 1256; [2001] P.I.Q.R. P16; 98(12) L.S.G. 44; 145 S.J.L.B. 31, CA *18–032*
Watson v Burton [1957] 1 W.L.R. 19; [1956] 3 All E.R. 929; (1957) 101 S.J. 45, Ch D *27–055*, *27–057*
Watson v Croft Promosport Ltd [2008] EWHC 759 (QB); [2008] 3 All E.R. 1171 .... *27–063*
Watson v Duff, Morgan & Vermont (Holdings) [1974] 1 W.L.R. 450; [1974] 1 All E.R. 794; (1973) 117 S.J. 910, Ch D *19–070*
Watson v Gray (1900) 16 T.L.R. 308 .... *26–078*
Watson v Haggitt [1928] A.C. 127, PC (NZ) *12–055*
Watson v Healey Lands [1965] N.Z.L.R. 511 .... *22–041*
Watson v Hetherington (1843) 1 C.K. 36 .... *21–094*
Watson v Mid Wales Railway Co (1866–67) L.R. 2 C.P. 593, CCP *19–070*
Watson v Prager [1991] 1 W.L.R. 726; [1991] 3 All E.R. 487; [1991] I.C.R. 603; [1993] E.M.L.R. 275, Ch D *16–083*, *16–086*, *16–088*
Watson v Winget Ltd (1960) S.C. 92 .... *1–124*
Watson, Laidlow & Co Ltd v Potts, Cassels and Williamson (1914) 31 R.P.C 104 .... *26–022*, *26–029*
Watt v Mortlock [1964] Ch. 84; [1963] 2 W.L.R. 626; [1963] 1 All E.R. 388; (1963) 107 S.J. 235, Ch D *29–119*
Watteau v Fenwick [1893] 1 Q.B. 346, QBD *10–012*
Watters v Smith (1831) 2 B. & Ad. 889 .... *17–018*
Watts v Adlington; Tolstoy v Aldington, *The Times*, December 16, 1993; *Independent*, January 25, 1994, CA *17–018*, *17–020*
Watts v Assets Co [1905] A.C. 317 .... *28–141*
Watts v Morrow [1991] 1 W.L.R. 1421; [1991] 4 All E.R. 937; 54 B.L.R. 86; 26 Con. L.R. 98; (1991) 23 H.L.R. 608; [1991] 2 E.G.L.R. 152; [1991] 43 E.G. 121; (1992) 8 Const. L.J. 73; [1991] E.G. 88 (C.S.); (1992) 89(14) L.S.G. 33; (1991) 141 N.L.J. 1331; [1991] N.P.C. 98, CA (Civ Div); reversing 24 Con. L.R. 125; [1991] 14 E.G. 111; [1991] 15 E.G. 113, QBD (OR) *1–123*, *26–082*, *26–083*, *26–085*, *26–093*, *26–178*
Watts v Spence [1976] Ch. 165; [1975] 2 W.L.R. 1039; [1975] 2 All E.R. 528; (1975) 29 P. & C.R. 501; (1975) 119 S.J. 168, Ch D *1–122*, *6–052*, *6–069*, *27–031*, *27–041*
Watts Watts & Co Ltd v Mitsui & Co Ltd; sub nom. Mitsui & Co Ltd v Watts, Watts & Co Ltd [1917] A.C. 227, HL *23–035*, *26–001*, *26–090*, *26–143*
Waugh v Bussell (1814) 5 Taunt. 707 .... *12–077*, *25–023*
Waugh v Middleton (1853) 8 Exch. 352 .... *12–080*
Waugh v Morris (1873) L.R. 8 Q.B. 202 .... *16–012*
Wauthier v Wilson (1912) 28 T.L.R. 239 .... *8–063*

Wauton v Coppard [1899] 1 Ch. 92, Ch D *6–006*
Way v Bishop [1928] Ch. 647, CA *16–114*
Way v Latilla [1937] 3 All E.R. 759, HL *29–071*
Wayling v Jones [1995] 2 F.L.R. 1029; [1996] 2 F.C.R. 41; (1995) 69 P. & C.R. 170; [1996] Fam. Law 88; [1993] E.G. 153 (C.S.), CA (Civ Div) *1–006*, *3–141*, *3–147*, 4–080
Wayman v Hilliard (1830) 7 Bing. 101 .... *29–191*
Waymell v Reed (1794) 5 Term Rep. 599 .... *16–014*
Weary v Alderson (1837) 2 M. Rob. 127 .... *21–043*
Weatherby v Banham (1832) 5 C. & P. 228 .... *2–030*, *2–047*
Weaver v Commercial Process Co (1947) 63 T.L.R. 466 .... *29–121*
Webb, Re [1941] Ch. 225, Ch D *18–079*, *18–080*
Webb v Adkins (1854) 14 C.B. 401 .... *20–004*
Webb v Chief Constable of Merseyside; sub nom. Porter v Chief Constable of Merseyside; Chief Constable of Merseyside v Porter [2000] Q.B. 427; [2000] 2 W.L.R. 546; [2000] 1 All E.R. 209; (1999) 96(47) L.S.G. 33; (2000) 144 S.J.L.B. 9, CA (Civ Div) *16–180*
Webb v Fairmaner (1838) 3 M.W. 473 .... *21–026*
Webb v Hewitt (1857) 3 K. & J. 438 .... *1–115*
Webb v Spicer (1849) 13 Q.B. 886 .... *22–006*
Webb Electrical, Re (1988) 4 B.C.C. 230; [1988] P.C.C. 230; [1989] P.C.C. 379, Ch D (Companies Ct) *9–049*
Webber v Cecil (1861) 30 Beav. 62 .... *5–077*, *12–112*
Webber v Higgin [1948] 2 All E.R. 127; 92 S.J. 454, CA *12–004*, *12–103*, *14–009*, 14–134
Webber v Lee (1881–82) L.R. 9 Q.B.D. 315, CA *4–021*
Webster, Ex p. Official Receiver, Re [1907] 1 K.B. 623, KBD *21–051*
Webster v Armstrong (1885) 54 L.J.Q.B. 236 .... *25–010*
Webster v Bosanquet [1912] A.C. 394, PC (Cey) *26–127*
Webster v Higgin. *See* Webber v Higgin
Webster v Kirk (1852) 17 Q.B. 944 .... *28–044*
Webster v Webster (1804) 10 Ves. Jun. 93 .... *28–031*
Weddell v JA Pearce & Major (A Firm) [1988] Ch. 26; [1987] 3 W.L.R. 592; [1987] 3 All E.R. 624; (1988) 85(32) L.S.G. 33; (1987) 131 S.J. 1120, Ch D *16–063*, *19–016*, *19–020*, *19–038*, *19–039*, *20–024*, *28–117*
Wedgerfield v De Bernardy (1908) 25 T.L.R. 21 .... *16–065*
Wedgewood v Adams (1843) 6 Beav. 600 .... *27–031*
Weeds v Blaney (1977) 247 E.G. 211; (1977) 121 S.J. 794, CA (Civ Div) *5–126*
Weeks v Bradshaw [1993] E.G. 65 (C.S.), CA (Civ Div) *24–018*
Weeks v Tybald (1605) Noy. 11 2–165
Weg Motors v Hales [1962] Ch. 49; [1961] 3 W.L.R. 558; [1961] 3 All E.R. 181; (1961) 105 S.J. 610, CA; affirming [1961] Ch. 176; [1960] 3 W.L.R. 964; [1960] 3 All E.R. 762; (1960) 104 S.J. 1057, Ch D *13–007*
Wegg Prosser v Evans [1895] 1 Q.B. 108, CA; affirming [1894] 2 Q.B. 101, QBD *17–015*, *25–007*
Wehner v Dene Steam Shipping Co [1905] 2 K.B. 92, KBD *24–051*
Weinberger v Inglis [1919] A.C. 606, HL; affirming [1918] 1 Ch. 517, CA *9–077*
Weir (Andrew) & Co v Dobell & Co. *See* Andrew Weir & Co v Dobell & Co
Welby v Drake (1825) 1 C. & P. 557 .... *3–126*
Welch v Bank of England [1955] Ch. 508; [1955] 2 W.L.R. 757; [1955] 1 All E.R. 811; (1955) 99 S.J. 236, Ch D *21–049*
Weld v Petre [1929] 1 Ch. 33, CA *28–138*, *28–141*, *28–142*
Weld-Blundell v Stephens [1920] A.C. 956, HL; affirming [1919] 1 K.B. 520, CA; reversing [1918] 2 K.B. 742, KBD *1–173*, *26–008*, 26–036
Weld-Blundell v Synott [1940] 2 K.B. 107, KBD *29–030*, *29–033*, *29–036*, *29–176*, *29–177*
Weldon v GRE Linked Life Assurance Ltd [2000] 2 All E.R. (Comm) 914, QBD *1–184*, *13–007*, *18–023*
Weldtech Equipment Ltd, Re [1991] B.C.C. 16; [1991] B.C.L.C. 393, Ch D (Companies Ct) *19–099*, *29–168*

Welex AG v Rosa Maritime Ltd; The Epsilon Rosa (No.2) [2003] EWCA Civ 938; [2003] 2 Lloyd's Rep. 509; [2003] 2 C.L.C. 207, CA (Civ Div) *30–306*, *30–308*
Well Barn Farming Ltd v Backhouse [2005] EWHC 1520; [2005] 3 E.G.L.R. 109, Ch D *3–015*, *3–024*
Weller v Akehurst [1981] 3 All E.R. 411; (1981) 42 P. & C.R. 320; (1980) 257 E.G. 1259, Ch D *2–132*
Wells v Minister of Housing and Local Government [1967] 1 W.L.R. 1000; [1967] 2 All E.R. 1041; (1967) 131 J.P. 431; 65 L.G.R. 408; (1967) 18 P. & C.R. 401; (1967) 111 S.J. 519, CA (Civ Div); affirming, 65 L.G.R. 43; (1966) 110 S.J. 889, DC *10–042*
Wells v Wells; Thomas v Brighton HA; Page v Sheerness Steel Co Plc [1999] 1 A.C. 345; [1998] 3 W.L.R. 329; [1998] 3 All E.R. 481; [1998] I.R.L.R. 536; [1998] 2 F.L.R. 507; [1998] P.I.Q.R. Q56; (1998) 43 B.M.L.R. 99; [1998] Fam. Law 593; (1998) 95(35) L.S.G. 35; (1998) 148 N.L.J. 1087; (1998) 142 S.J.L.B. 245, HL *26–001*
Wells v Wiliams (1697) 1 Ld.Raym. 282 .... *11–027*
Wells (Merstham) v Buckland Sand and Silica Co [1965] 2 Q.B. 170; [1964] 2 W.L.R. 453; [1964] 1 All E.R. 41; (1964) 108 S.J. 177, QBD *6–022*, *6–077*, *6–086*, *12–007*, *18–005*
Wellworth Cash & Carry (North Shields) Ltd v North Eastern Electricity Board (1986) 2 B.C.C. 99265, Ch D *20–056*
Welsh Development Agency v Export Finance Co Ltd [1992] B.C.C. 270; [1992] B.C.L.C. 148, CA (Civ Div); reversing in part [1990] B.C.C. 393; [1991] B.C.L.C. 936, Ch D *2–133*, *9–052*, *16–085*
Welsh Development Agency v Redpath Dorman Long Ltd [1994] 1 W.L.R. 1409; [1994] 4 All E.R. 10; 67 B.L.R. 1; 38 Con. L.R. 106; (1994) 10 Const. L.J. 325; (1994) 91(21) L.S.G. 42; (1994) 138 S.J.L.B. 87, CA (Civ Div) *28–121*
Welsh Health Technical Services Organisation v Haden Young Ltd, 37 B.L.R. 130, QBD *14–056*, *18–005*, *18–023*
Welsh Irish Ferries Ltd , Re; The Ugland Trailer [1986] Ch. 471; [1985] 3 W.L.R. 610; [1985] 2 Lloyd's Rep. 372; (1985) 1 B.C.C. 99430; [1985] P.C.C. 303; (1985) 129 S.J. 683, Ch D (Companies Ct) *19–032*, *19–066*
Welstead v Hadley (1904) 21 T.L.R. 165 .... *16–099*
Welton v North Cornwall DC [1997] 1 W.L.R. 570; (1997) 161 J.P. 114; (1997) 9 Admin. L.R. 45; [1997] P.N.L.R. 108; (1996) 93(34) L.S.G. 34; (1996) 140 S.J.L.B. 186, CA (Civ Div) *1–142*
Wenham, Re; sub nom. Hunt v Wenham [1892] 3 Ch. 59, Ch D *28–131*
Wenkheim v Arndt (1873) (N.Z.) 1 J.R. 73 .... *2–060*
Wenlock v Moloney, 117 N.L.J. 295; (1967) 111 S.J. 437, CA (Civ Div) *20–034*
Wenlock (Baroness) v River Dee Co (No.3) (1888) L.R. 38 Ch. D. 534, CA; affirming (1887) L.R. 36 Ch. D. 674, Ch D *9–004*, *9–005*, *9–020*, *9–025*
Wentworth v Bullen (1829) 9 B. & C. 840 .... *22–024*
Wentworth v Wiltshire CC [1993] Q.B. 654; [1993] 2 W.L.R. 175; [1993] 2 All E.R. 256; 90 L.G.R. 625; (1993) 5 Admin. L.R. 189; (1992) 89(27) L.S.G. 36; (1992) 142 N.L.J. 1376; (1992) 136 S.J.L.B. 198; [1992] N.P.C. 72, CA (Civ Div) *26–174*
Werderman v Societe Generale d'Electricite (1881–82) L.R. 19 Ch. D. 246, CA *19–079*
Werner v Humphreys (1841) 2 M. & G. 853 .... *20–002*
Wertheim v Chicoutimi Pulp Co [1911] A.C. 301, PC (Can) *26–001*, *26–117*
Wessex Reserve Forces and Cadets Association v White [2005] EWCA Civ 1744; [2006] 2 P. & C.R. 3; [2006] L. & T.R. 15; [2006] 1 E.G.L.R. 55; [2006] 13 E.G. 142; [2005] 49 E.G. 89 (C.S.), CA (Civ Div); affirming [2005] EWHC 983 (QB); [2006] 1 P. & C.R. 22; [2005] 3 E.G.L.R. 127; [2005] 22 E.G. 132 (C.S.); [2005] 2 P. & C.R. DG17, QBD *22–046*
Wessex RHA v HLM Design Ltd, 71 B.L.R. 32; (1994) 10 Const. L.J. 165, QBD *28–033*
West v Blakeway (1841) 2 M. & G. 729 .... *22–030*
West v Downes (1778) 1 Doug. K.B. 23 .... *22–026*

West v Gwynne [1911] 2 Ch. 1, CA *1–040*
West v Houghton (1878–79) L.R. 4 C.P.D. 197, CPD *18–080*
West v London & North Western Railway Co (1853) 11 C.B. 327 .... *12–062*
West Bromwich Albion Football Club Ltd v El-Safty [2006] EWCA Civ 1299; [2007] P.I.Q.R. P7; [2007] LS Law Medical 50; (2006) 92 B.M.L.R. 179; (2006) 103(41) L.S.G. 34; (2006) 150 S.J.L.B. 1428, CA (Civ Div); affirming [2005] EWHC 2866 (QB); [2006] Lloyd's Rep. Med. 139; (2006) 88 B.M.L.R. 196; [2006] P.N.L.R. 18, QBD *2–160*, *18–004*, *18–008*, *18–031*
West Bromwich Building Society v Crammer [2002] EWHC 2618; [2003] B.P.I.R. 783; (2003) 147 S.J.L.B. 58; [2002] N.P.C. 131, Ch D *21–059*, *21–063*, *21–067*
West Bromwich Building Society v Mander Hadley & Co [1998] C.L.C. 814; [1998] N.P.C. 30, CA (Civ Div) *28–010*
West Bromwich Building Society v Wilkinson; sub nom. Wilkinson v West Bromwich Building Society [2005] UKHL 44; [2005] 1 W.L.R. 2303; [2005] 4 All E.R. 97; [2005] 27 E.G. 221 (C.S.); (2005) 102(28) L.S.G. 32; [2005] 2 P. & C.R. DG20, HL *28–003*
West London Commercial Bank Ltd v Kitson; West London Commercial Bank Ltd v Porter; West London Commercial Bank Ltd v Woodward (1883–84) L.R. 13 Q.B.D. 360, CA; affirming (1883–84) L.R. 12 Q.B.D. 157, QBD *6–013*, *29–041*, *29–043*
West Tankers Inc v RAS Riunione Adriatica di Sicurta SpA; The Front Comor [2007] UKHL 4; [2007] 1 All E.R. (Comm) 794; [2007] 1 Lloyd's Rep. 391; [2007] I.L.Pr. 20; (2007) 23 Const. L.J. 458; (2007) 104(10) L.S.G. 30; (2007) 151 S.J.L.B. 294, HL *30–127*, *30–129*
West of England Shipowners Mutual Insurance Association (Luxembourg) v Cristal Ltd; The Glacier Bay [1996] 1 Lloyd's Rep. 370; [1996] C.L.C. 240, CA (Civ Div); reversing [1995] 1 Lloyd's Rep. 560; [1995] C.L.C. 242, QBD (Comm) *16–047*, *18–021*
West Sussex Properties Ltd v Chichester DC; sub nom. Chichester DC v West Sussex Properties Ltd [2000] N.P.C. 74; [2000] All E.R. (D) 887, CA (Civ Div) 5–058, *6–110*
West Yorkshire Darracq Agency Ltd (In Liquidation) v Coleridge [1911] 2 K.B. 326, KBD *3–037*, *3–125*
West Yorkshire MCC v MFI Furniture Centres Ltd [1983] 1 W.L.R. 1175; [1983] 3 All E.R. 234; 82 L.G.R. 214; [1983] Crim. L.R. 631; (1983) 127 S.J. 389, QBD *6–006*
Westacott v Hahn [1918] 1 K.B. 495, CA; affirming [1917] 1 K.B. 605, KBD *12–057*, *12–128*, *13–023*
Westacre Investments Inc v Jugoimport SPDR Holding Co Ltd [2000] Q.B. 288; [1999] 3 W.L.R. 811; [1999] 3 All E.R. 864; [1999] 1 All E.R. (Comm) 865; [1999] 2 Lloyd's Rep. 65; [1999] C.L.C. 1176; [1999] B.L.R. 279, CA (Civ Div) *25–015*, *30–355*, *30–367*
Westcott v John Jenner (JH) (Plasterers) [1962] 1 Lloyd's Rep. 309; (1962) 106 S.J. 281, CA *14–015*
Westdeutsche Landesbank Girozentrale v Islington LBC; sub nom. Islington LBC v Westdeutsche Landesbank Girozentrale; Kleinwort Benson Ltd v Sandwell BC [1996] A.C. 669; [1996] 2 W.L.R. 802; [1996] 2 All E.R. 961; [1996] 5 Bank. L.R. 341; [1996] C.L.C. 990; 95 L.G.R. 1; (1996) 160 J.P. Rep. 1130; (1996) 146 N.L.J. 877; (1996) 140 S.J.L.B. 136, HL; reversing [1994] 1 W.L.R. 938; [1994] 4 All E.R. 890; [1994] C.L.C. 96; 92 L.G.R. 405; (1994) 158 L.G. Rev. 981; (1994) 91(8) L.S.G. 29; (1994) 138 S.J.L.B. 26, CA (Civ Div); affirming 91 L.G.R. 323, QBD *4–085*, *6–065*, 9–017, *9–021*, *9–025*, *9–026*, *18–139*, *26–171*, *26–174*, *28–058*, *29–001*, *29–003*, 29–008, *29–011*, *29–013*, 29–024, *29–036*, *29–041*, *29–043*, *29–049*, *29–056*, *29–057*, *29–058*, 29–063, *29–074*, *29–075*, *29–076*, *29–160*, *29–164*, *29–165*, *29–181*, *29–187*, *29–188*
Western v Russell (1814) 3 V. & B. 187 .... *27–033*
Western Bank of Scotland v Addie (1867) L.R. 1 Sc. & Div. 145 .... *6–034*, *6–117*, *9–060*

Western Broadcasting Services v Seaga [2007] UKPC 19; [2007] E.M.L.R. 18, PC (Jam) *2–112*
Western Digital Corp v British Airways Plc [2001] Q.B. 733; [2000] 3 W.L.R. 1855; [2001] 1 All E.R. 109; [2000] 2 All E.R. (Comm) 647; [2000] 2 Lloyd's Rep. 142; [2000] C.L.C. 1276; (2000) 144 S.J.L.B. 273, CA (Civ Div); reversing in part [1999] 2 All E.R. (Comm) 270; [1999] 2 Lloyd's Rep. 380; [1999] C.L.C. 1681, QBD (Comm) *18–034*
Western Fish Products Ltd v Penwith DC [1981] 2 All E.R. 204; 77 L.G.R. 185; (1979) 38 P. & C.R. 7; [1978] J.P.L. 627; (1978) 122 S.J. 471, CA (Civ Div) *3–145*, *3–146*, *3–147*
Western Front Ltd v Vestron Inc [1987] F.S.R. 66, Ch D *19–025*
Western Power Investment Ltd v Teeside Power Ltd, unreported February 18, 2005 .... *16–205*
Westerngeco Ltd v ATP Oil & Gas (UK) Ltd [2006] EWHC 1164 (Comm); [2006] 2 All E.R. (Comm) 637; [2006] 2 Lloyd's Rep. 535; 115 Con. L.R. 84, QBD (Comm) *12–050*
Westerton, Re; sub nom. Public Trustee v Gray [1919] 2 Ch. 104, Ch D ...*19–015*, *19–016*, *19–019*, *19–020*, *19–025*, *19–033*, *19–034*, *19–036*, *19–046*, *19–059*
Westfalische Central-Genossenschaft v Seabright Chemicals, unreported, 1979 ... *14–151*
Westfal-Larsen & Co A/S v Ikerigi Compania Naviers SA; The Messiniaki Bergen [1983] 1 All E.R. 382; [1983] 1 Lloyd's Rep. 424; (1983) 133 N.L.J. 125, QBD (Comm) *2–135*, *25–017*
Westhead v Sproson (1861) 6 H.& N. 728 .... *2–158*
Westhoughton Urban DC v Wigan Coal & Iron Co Ltd [1919] 1 Ch. 159, CA *18–125*
Westlake v Adams (1858) 5 C.B. (N.S.) 248 .... *3–014*, *3–015*
Westland Helicopters Ltd v Arab Organisation for Industrialisation [1995] Q.B. 282; [1995] 2 W.L.R. 126; [1995] 2 All E.R. 387; [1994] 2 Lloyd's Rep. 608, QBD (Comm) *11–007*
Westminster (Duke of) v Guild [1985] Q.B. 688; [1984] 3 W.L.R. 630; [1984] 3 All E.R. 144; (1984) 48 P. & C.R. 42; (1983) 267 E.G. 762; (1984) 128 S.J. 581, CA (Civ Div) *13–009*, *13–010*, *13–016*
Westminster Building Co Ltd v Beckingham [2004] EWHC 138 (TCC); [2004] B.L.R. 163; [2004] B.L.R. 265; [2004] T.C.L.R. 8; 94 Con. L.R. 107, QBD (TCC) *2–076*, 15–094
Westminster City Council v Duke of Westminster (1992) 24 H.L.R. 572, CA (Civ Div); reversing [1991] 4 All E.R. 136; (1991) 23 H.L.R. 174; [1990] E.G. 146 (C.S.), Ch D *3–008*, *3–011*, *3–020*, *3–027*
Westminster City Council v Iran [1986] 1 W.L.R. 979; [1986] 3 All E.R. 284; (1986) 83 L.S.G. 1636; (1986) 130 S.J. 393, Ch D *11–006*, *11–012*
Westoby v Day (1853) 2 E.B. 605 .... *21–051*
Weston, Re; sub nom. Davies v Tagart [1900] 2 Ch. 164, Ch D *13–024*
Weston v Downes, 99 E.R. 19; (1778) 1 Doug. K.B. 23, KB *29–012*, *29–058*, *29–066*
Westpac Banking Corp v Paterson [2001] FCA 1630; [2001] 187 A.L.R. 168, Fed Ct (Aus) *7–132*, *7–136*
Westropp v Solomon (1849) 8 C.B. 345 .... *29–117*
Westway Homes Ltd v Moores (1992) 63 P. & C.R. 480; [1991] 2 E.G.L.R. 193; [1991] 31 E.G. 57, CA (Civ Div) *2–122*
Westwood v Secretary of State for Employment [1985] A.C. 20; [1984] 2 W.L.R. 418; [1984] 1 All E.R. 874; [1985] I.C.R. 209; [1984] I.R.L.R. 209; (1984) 81 L.S.G. 1443; (1984) 134 N.L.J. 359; (1984) 128 S.J. 221, HL *26–001*, *26–103*, *26–115*, *26–120*
Wettern Electric Ltd v Welsh Development Agency [1983] Q.B. 796; [1983] 2 W.L.R. 897; [1983] 2 All E.R. 629; (1984) 47 P. & C.R. 113, QBD *2–066*, *2–076*, *13–016*
Wharton v Mackenzie (1844) 5 Q.B. 606 .... *8–004*, *8–016*
Wharton v Walker (1825) 4 B. & C. 163 .... *19–088*
Wheatley v Westminster Brymbo Coal Co (1869–70) L.R. 9 Eq. 538, Ct of Chancery *27–026*
Wheeler, Re [1938] Ch. 725 .... *19–025*

Wheeler v Leicester City Council [1985] A.C. 1054; [1985] 3 W.L.R. 335; [1985] 2 All E.R. 1106; 83 L.G.R. 725; (1985) 129 S.J. 558, HL; reversing [1985] 2 All E.R. 151; (1985) 82 L.S.G. 1710; (1985) 135 N.L.J. 413, CA (Civ Div) *1–201*
Wheeler v Quality Deep Ltd (t/a Thai Royale Restaurant); sub nom. Wheeler v Qualitydeep Ltd (t/a Thai Royale Restaurant) [2004] EWCA Civ 1085; [2005] I.C.R. 265; (2004) 101(35) L.S.G. 33, CA (Civ Div) *16–166*
Wheeler v Stratton (1911) 105 L.T. 786 .... *21–035*
Wheeler v Trotter (1737) 3 Swan. 174 .... *27–038*
Wheelton v Hardisty (1857) 8 E. & B. 232 .... *6–148*
Whincup v Hughes (1870–71) L.R. 6 C.P. 78, CCP ...*23–073*, *29–054*, *29–060*, *29–182*
Whitbread v Smith (1854) 3 De. G.M. & G. 727 .... *12–067*
White v Bijou Mansions Ltd [1938] Ch. 351, CA; affirming [1937] Ch. 610, Ch D *18–125*
White v Blackmore [1972] 2 Q.B. 651; [1972] 3 W.L.R. 296; [1972] 3 All E.R. 158; (1972) 116 S.J. 547, CA (Civ Div) *2–168*, *12–014*, *12–017*, *13–014*, *14–011*, *15–001*, *18–011*
White v Bluett (1853) 23 L.J.Ex.36 3–022
White v Bristol Rugby Ltd [2002] I.R.L.R. 204, QBD (Merc) *2–166*
White v British Empire Mutual Life Assurance Co (1868–69) L.R. 7 Eq. 394, Ct of Chancery *16–171*
White v Chief Constable of South Yorkshire; Frost v Chief Constable of South Yorkshire; Duncan v British Coal Corp [1999] 2 A.C. 455; [1998] 3 W.L.R. 1509; [1999] 1 All E.R. 1; [1999] I.C.R. 216; [1999] I.R.L.R. 110; (1999) 45 B.M.L.R. 1; (1999) 96(2) L.S.G. 28; (1998) 148 N.L.J. 1844; (1999) 143 S.J.L.B. 51, HL; reversing [1998] Q.B. 254; [1997] 3 W.L.R. 1194; [1997] 1 All E.R. 540; [1997] I.R.L.R. 173; (1997) 33 B.M.L.R. 108; (1996) 146 N.L.J. 1651, CA (Civ Div); reversing, *The Times*, July 3, 1995, QBD *1–123*, *2–182A*
White v Garden (1851) 10 C.B. 919 .... *6–129*
White v John Warwick & Co [1953] 1 W.L.R. 1285; [1953] 2 All E.R. 1021; (1953) 97 S.J. 740, CA *1–151*, *14–013*
White v Jones [1995] 2 A.C. 207; [1995] 2 W.L.R. 187; [1995] 1 All E.R. 691; [1995] 3 F.C.R. 51; (1995) 145 N.L.J. 251; (1995) 139 S.J.L.B. 83; [1995] N.P.C. 31, HL; affirming [1993] 3 W.L.R. 730; [1993] 3 All E.R. 481; (1993) 90(23) L.S.G. 43; (1993) 143 N.L.J. 473; [1993] N.P.C. 37, CA (Civ Div) *1–141*, **1–181**, *1–186*, *3–180*, *6–083*, *18–019*, *18–022*, *18–024*, 18–025, *18–031*, *18–034*, 18–037, 18–038, 18–039, *18–049*, 18–093, *18–116*, *20–003*, *26–044*
White v Kuzych; sub nom. Kuzych v White [1951] A.C. 585; [1951] 2 All E.R. 435; [1951] 2 T.L.R. 277; (1951) 95 S.J. 527, PC (Can); reversing [1950] 4 D.L.R. 187, CA (BC); affirming [1949] 4 D.L.R. 662, Sup Ct (BC) *9–083*
White v London Transport Executive [1971] 2 Q.B. 721; [1971] 3 W.L.R. 169; [1971] 3 All E.R. 1; [1971] 2 Lloyd's Rep. 256; [1971] R.T.R. 326; (1971) 115 S.J. 368, CA (Civ Div) *18–131*
White v Procter (1811) 4 Taunt. 209 .... *4–038*
White v Tyndall (1888) L.R. 13 App. Cas. 263, HL *17–005*, *17–006*, *17–012*
White & Carter (Councils) Ltd v McGregor [1962] A.C. 413; [1962] 2 W.L.R. 17; [1961] 3 All E.R. 1178; 1962 S.C. (H.L.) 1; 1962 S.L.T. 9; (1961) 105 S.J. 1104, HL; reversing, 1960 S.C. 276; 1961 S.L.T. 144; 1960 S.L.T. (Notes) 96, IH (2 Div) *2–086*, *24–001*, 24–010, *26–009*, 26–112, 26–121, 26–122, 26–123, 26–124, *26–136*
White (Brian) v White; Mighell v Reading; Evans v Motor Insurers Bureau [2001] UKHL 9; [2001] 1 W.L.R. 481; [2001] 2 All E.R. 43; [2001] 1 All E.R. (Comm) 1105; [2001] 1 Lloyd's Rep. 679; [2001] R.T.R. 25; [2001] 2 C.M.L.R. 1; [2001] Lloyd's Rep. I.R. 493; [2001] P.I.Q.R. P20; (2001) 98(15) L.S.G. 33; (2001) 151 N.L.J. 350; (2001) 145 S.J.L.B. 67, HL; reversing [1999] 1 C.M.L.R. 1251; [1999] Eu. L.R. 389; [1999] Lloyd's Rep. I.R. 30; [1999] P.I.Q.R. P101, CA (Civ Div); affirming [1997] 3 C.M.L.R. 1218, QBD (Comm) *12–054*, *18–131*

White (JD) v Troups Transport, unreported, October 6, 1976, CC (Stockton on Tees) *29–134*, *29–136*
White (Marion) v Francis [1972] 1 W.L.R. 1423; [1972] 3 All E.R. 857; (1972) 116 S.J. 822, CA (Civ Div) *16–108*
White Arrow Express Ltd v Lamey's Distribution Ltd [1995] C.L.C. 1251; (1996) 15 Tr. L.R. 69; (1995) 145 N.L.J. 1504, CA (Civ Div) *29–063*
White Carter Ltd v Carbis Bay Garage Ltd [1941] 2 All E.R. 633 .... *23–024*
White Cross Equipment v Farrell (1983) 2 Tr. L.R. 21, DC *6–139*
Whitecomb v Jacob (1710) Salk 160 .... *29–163*
Whitehall Court Ltd v Ettlinger [1920] 1 K.B. 680, KBD *23–055*
Whitehead v Palmer [1908] 1 K.B. 151, KBD *20–008*
Whitehead v Walker (1842) 9 M. & W. 506 .... *28–043*
Whitehill v Bradford [1952] Ch. 236; [1952] 1 All E.R. 115; [1952] 1 T.L.R. 66; (1952) 96 S.J. 42, CA; affirming [1951] 2 T.L.R. 946, Ch D *16–110*, *16–119*
Whitehouse v Jordan [1981] 1 W.L.R. 246; [1981] 1 All E.R. 267; (1981) 125 S.J. 167, HL; affirming [1980] 1 All E.R. 650, CA (Civ Div) *13–032*
Whiteley Ltd v Hilt [1918] 2 K.B. 808, CA; reversing [1918] 2 K.B. 115, KBD *19–042*, *27–002*
Whiteley v Delaney; sub nom. Manks v Whiteley [1914] A.C. 132, HL; reversing [1912] 1 Ch. 735, CA; reversing [1911] 2 Ch. 448, Ch D *12–067*
Whiten v Pilot Insurance Co (2002) 209 D.L.R. (4th) 257 .... *26–019*
Whiteside v Whiteside [1950] Ch. 65; [1949] 2 All E.R. 913; 66 T.L.R. (Pt. 1) 126; [1949] T.R. 457, CA; affirming [1949] Ch. 448; [1949] 1 All E.R. 755, Ch D *5–054*, *5–111*
Whitham v Bullock [1939] 2 K.B. 81, CA *29–102*, *29–121*
Whitmore v Farley (1881) 45 L.T. 99 .... *16–037*
Whitmore v King (1918) 87 L.J. Ch. 647 .... *16–109*
Whittaker v Campbell [1984] Q.B. 318; [1983] 3 W.L.R. 676; [1983] 3 All E.R. 582; (1983) 77 Cr. App. R. 267; [1984] R.T.R. 220; [1983] Crim. L.R. 812; (1983) 127 S.J. 714, DC *2–003*, *5–091*, *5–097*, *29–011*, *29–149*
Whittaker v Howe (1841) 3 Beav. 383 .... *16–110*
Whittall Builders Co Ltd v Chester-le-Street DC (1986) 11 Const. L.R. 40 .... *28–003*
Whittam v WJ Daniel & Co (Amendment to Writ) [1962] 1 Q.B. 271; [1961] 3 W.L.R. 1123; [1961] 3 All E.R. 796; (1961) 105 S.J. 886, CA *12–075*
Whittingham v Murdy (1889) 60 L.T. 956 .... *8–033*
Whittington v Seale-Hayne (1900) 82 L.T. 49 .... *6–100*, *6–121*, 6–122
Whitwham v Westminster Brymbo Coal & Coke Co [1896] 2 Ch. 538; (1896) 65 L.J. Ch. 741, CA *26–022*
Whitwood Chemical Co v Hardman [1891] 2 Ch. 416, CA *16–102*, *27–021*, *27–064*, *27–071*
Whitworth Street Estates (Manchester) Ltd v James Miller & Partners Ltd; sub nom. James Miller & Partners Ltd v Whitworth Street Estates (Manchester) Ltd [1970] A.C. 583; [1970] 2 W.L.R. 728; [1970] 1 All E.R. 796; [1970] 1 Lloyd's Rep. 269; (1970) 114 S.J. 225, HL; reversing [1969] 1 W.L.R. 377; [1969] 2 All E.R. 210; (1969) 113 S.J. 126, CA (Civ Div) ...*12–126*, *30–005*, *30–010*, *30–011*, *30–012*, *30–013*, *30–024*, *30–054*
Wholesale Distributors Ltd v Gibbons Holdings Ltd [2007] N.Z. S.C. 37 .... *12–126*
Wibau Maschinefabrik Hartman SA v Mackinnon Mackenzie; The Chanda [1989] 2 Lloyd's Rep. 494, QBD (Comm) *14–004*, *18–052*
Wickham & Burton Coal Co v Farmer's Lumber Co (1923) 189 Iowa 1183 .... *3–025*
Wickham Holdings v Brooke House Motors [1967] 1 W.L.R. 295; [1967] 1 All E.R. 117, CA *19–043*
Wiebe v Butchart's Motors [1949] 4 D.L.R. 838 .... *6–117*
Wieler v Schilizzi (1856) 17 C.B. 619 .... *14–027*
Wigan v English and Scottish Law Life Assurance Association [1909] 1 Ch. 291, Ch D 3–031, 3–059, *3–170*
Wigg v Shuttleworth (1810) 13 East 87 .... *16–195*
Wiggins v Lavy (1928) 44 T.L.R. 721 .... *16–052*, *16–055*

Wight v Eckhardt Marine GmbH; sub nom. Wight v Eckhardt GmbH [2003] UKPC 37; [2004] 1 A.C. 147; [2003] 3 W.L.R. 414; [2003] B.C.C. 702; [2004] 2 B.C.L.C. 539, PC (CI) *30–346*
Wigzell Ex p. Hart, Re [1921] 2 K.B. 835, CA *20–022*, *20–023*, *29–043*
Wilbeam v Ashton (1807) 1 Camp. 78 .... *26–143*
Wilby v Henman (1834) 2 C. & M. 658 .... *28–061*
Wild v Civil Aviation, unreported September 25, 1987, CA *12–098*, *12–099*
Wild v Simpson [1919] 2 K.B. 544, CA *16–055*
Wild v Tucker [1914] 3 K.B. 36, KBD *3–014*, *3–033*, *16–042*, *20–048*
Wild v Williams (1840) 6 M. & W. 490 .... *22–010*
Wildes v Russell (1865–66) L.R. 1 C.P. 722, CCP *29–142*
Wilding v Sanderson [1897] 2 Ch. 534, CA *5–062*, *5–077*
Wilensko v Fenwick [1938] 3 All E.R. 429 .... *14–027*
Wiles v Maddison [1943] 1 All E.R. 315, KBD *2–014*
Wiles v Woodward (1850) 5 Exch. 557 .... *1–112*
Wilhem, The (1866) 14 L.T. 636 .... *26–040*
Wilkie v Inland Revenue Commissioners [1952] Ch. 153; [1952] 1 All E.R. 92; [1952] 1 T.L.R. 22; 45 R. & I.T. 29; 32 T.C. 495; (1952) 31 A.T.C. 442; [1951] T.R. 371; (1951) 95 S.J. 817, Ch D *12–061*
Wilkie v London Passenger Transport Board [1947] 1 All E.R. 258; 63 T.L.R. 115; (1947) 111 J.P. 98; [1947] L.J.R. 864; 177 L.T. 71, CA *2–021*, 2–178
Wilkinson v Ancliff (BLT) Ltd [1986] 1 W.L.R. 1352; [1986] 3 All E.R. 427; (1986) 83 L.S.G. 3248; (1986) 130 S.J. 766, CA (Civ Div) *28–116*
Wilkinson v Byers (1834) 1 A. & E. 106 .... *3–119*, *22–012*
Wilkinson v Clements (1872–73) L.R. 8 Ch. App. 96, CA in Chancery *24–018*, *27–047*
Wilkinson v Coverdale (1793) 1 Esp. 75 .... *3–179*
Wilkinson v Evans (1865–66) L.R. 1 C.P. 407, CCP *4–027*
Wilkinson v Gaston (1846) 9 Q.B. 137 .... *12–064*, *12–093*
Wilkinson v Godefroy (1839) 9 A.E. 536 .... *29–197*
Wilkinson v Johnson (1824) 3 B.C. 428 .... *25–020*
Wilkinson v Lloyd (1845) 7 Q.B. 27 .... *29–056*
Wilkinson v Verity (1870–71) L.R. 6 C.P. 206, CCP *28–043*
Willatts v Kennedy (1831) 8 Bing. 5 .... *3–047*
William v Stern (1879) 5 Q.B. 409 .... 3–095, 3–100
William Brandt's Sons & Co v Dunlop Rubber Co Ltd [1905] A.C. 454, HL; reversing [1904] 1 K.B. 387, CA *18–083*, *19–004*, *19–021*, *19–025*, *19–038*, *19–039*
William Cory & Son Ltd v Harrison; sub nom. William Cory & Son Ltd v CW Harrison [1906] A.C. 274, HL *16–114*
William Cory & Son Ltd v Inland Revenue Commissioners [1965] A.C. 1088; [1965] 2 W.L.R. 924; [1965] 1 All E.R. 917; [1965] 1 Lloyd's Rep. 313; (1965) 44 A.T.C. 61; [1965] T.R. 77; (1965) 109 S.J. 254, HL; reversing [1964] 1 W.L.R. 1332; [1964] 3 All E.R. 66; [1964] 2 Lloyd's Rep. 43; (1964) 43 A.T.C. 215; [1964] T.R. 231; (1964) 108 S.J. 579, CA; affirming [1964] 1 W.L.R. 529; [1964] 1 All E.R. 509; [1963] 2 Lloyd's Rep. 446; (1963) 42 A.T.C. 475; [1963] T.R. 441; (1964) 108 S.J. 443, Ch D *12–028*, *12–094*, *19–025*
William Cory & Son Ltd v London Corp [1951] 2 K.B. 476; [1951] 2 All E.R. 85; [1951] 1 Lloyd's Rep. 475; [1951] 2 T.L.R. 174; (1951) 115 J.P. 371; (1951) 95 S.J. 465, CA; affirming [1951] 1 K.B. 8; [1950] 2 All E.R. 584; (1950) 84 Ll. L. Rep. 278; 66 T.L.R. (Pt. 2) 265; (1950) 114 J.P. 422, KBD *10–007*, *10–030*, *13–012*
William Hall Ltd (Contractors) (In Liquidation), Re [1967] 1 W.L.R. 948; [1967] 2 All E.R. 1150; (1967) 111 S.J. 472, Ch D *21–061*
William Hill Organisation Ltd v Tucker [1999] I.C.R. 291; [1998] I.R.L.R. 313; (1998) 95(20) L.S.G. 33; (1998) 142 S.J.L.B. 140, CA (Civ Div) *27–066*, *27–068*
William Lacey (Hounslow) Ltd v Davis [1957] 1 W.L.R. 932; [1957] 2 All E.R. 712; (1957) 101 S.J. 629, QBD *2–022*, *3–106*, *29–021*, *29–071*, *29–116*
William Morton & Co v Muir Bros & Co, 1907 S.C. 1211; (1907) 15 S.L.T. 252; (1907) 44 S.L.R. 885, IH (Ex Div) *13–007*

William Pickersgill & Sons Ltd v London and Provincial Marine & General Insurance Co Ltd [1912] 3 K.B. 614; 82 L.J.K.B. 130; 107 L.T. 305; 28 T.L.R. 591; 18 Com. Cas. 1; 57 S.J. 11, KBD *6–144*, *19–070*, *19–072*
William Porter & Co Ltd, Re [1937] 2 All E.R. 361, Ch D *3–122*, *21–030*, *22–035*
William Robinson & Co Ltd v Heuer [1898] 2 Ch. 451, CA *27–064*, *27–069*
William Sindall Plc v Cambridgeshire CC [1994] 1 W.L.R. 1016; [1994] 3 All E.R. 932; 92 L.G.R. 121; [1993] E.G. 105 (C.S.); [1993] N.P.C. 82, CA (Civ Div) *5–016*, *5–039*, 5–059, *6–100*, 6–101, *6–102*, *23–012*
William Thomas & Co Ltd, Re; sub nom. William Thomas & Co Ltd v Sully [1915] 1 Ch. 325, Ch D *9–022*
William Thomas & Sons v Harrowing Steamship Co; sub nom. Harrowing Steamship Co v Thomas [1915] A.C. 58, HL *21–034*
Williams, Re; sub nom. Williams v Ball [1917] 1 Ch. 1, CA *19–022*, *19–025*, *19–033*
Williams v Atlantic Assurance Co Ltd [1933] 1 K.B. 81; (1932) 43 Ll. L. Rep. 177, CA; affirming (1932) 42 Ll. L. Rep. 206, KBD *19–014*, *19–038*
Williams v Baltic Insurance Association of London Ltd [1924] 2 K.B. 282; (1924) 19 Ll. L. Rep. 126, KBD *18–079*, *18–080*
Williams v Bayley (1866) L.R. 1 H.L. 200, HL *7–011*, *7–040*, 7–048, *7–049*, *7–052*, *16–037*, *29–089*
Williams v Burrell (1845) 1 C.B. 402 .... *20–005*
Williams v Carwardine (1833) 5 C. & P. 566 .... *2–019*, *2–043*
Williams v Commissioner of Inland Revenue. *See* Williams v IRC
Williams v Evans (1865–66) L.R. 1 Q.B. 352, QB *21–044*
Williams v Evans (1874–75) L.R. 19 Eq. 547, Ct of Chancery *4–048*
Williams v Everett (1811) 14 East. 582 .... *29–026*
Williams v Fanshaw Porter & Hazelhurst [2004] EWCA Civ 157; [2004] 1 W.L.R. 3185; [2004] 2 All E.R. 616; [2004] Lloyd's Rep. I.R. 800; [2004] P.N.L.R. 29; (2004) 101(12) L.S.G. 36, CA (Civ Div) *28–086*
Williams v Greatrex [1957] 1 W.L.R. 31; [1956] 3 All E.R. 705; (1957) 101 S.J. 43, CA *21–011*, *21–018*, *28–135*, *28–143*
Williams v Harrison (1691) Carth. 160 .... *8–043*
Williams v Hathaway (1877) L.R. 6 Ch. D. 544, Ch D *12–078*
Williams v Heales (1873–74) L.R. 9 C.P. 177; [1874–80] All E.R. Rep. 364; (1874) 22 W.R. 317; (1874) 43 L.J. C.P. 80; (1874) 30 L.T. 20, CCP *20–012*
Williams v IRC [1965] N.Z.L.R. 395 .... *19–030*
Williams v Jordan (1877) L.R. 6 Ch. D. 517, Ch D *4–023*
Williams v Mercer [1940] 3 All E.R. 292 .... *23–067*
Williams v Millington, 126 E.R. 49; (1788) 1 H. Bl. 81, KB *21–048*, *29–198*
Williams v Moor (1843) 11 M. & W. 256 .... *8–005*, *8–020*, *8–042*, *8–044*
Williams v Moss Empires Ltd [1915] 3 K.B. 242, KBD *22–030*
Williams v Naamlooze (1915) 21 Com. Cas. 253 .... *14–146*
Williams v Natural Life Health Foods Ltd [1998] 1 W.L.R. 830; [1998] 2 All E.R. 577; [1998] B.C.C. 428; [1998] 1 B.C.L.C. 689; (1998) 17 Tr. L.R. 152; (1998) 95(21) L.S.G. 37; (1998) 148 N.L.J. 657; (1998) 142 S.J.L.B. 166, HL; reversing [1997] B.C.C. 605; [1997] 1 B.C.L.C. 131, CA (Civ Div); affirming [1996] B.C.C. 376; [1996] 1 B.C.L.C. 288; (1996) 140 S.J.L.B. 43, QBD *1–119*, *1–120*, *1–141*, *1–181*, **1–182**, 1–183, *6–076*, *6–083*, *18–020*, *18–039*
Williams v Protheroe (1829) 3 Y. & J. 129 16–061
Williams v Rawlinson (1825) 3 Bing. 71 .... *21–064*
Williams v Roffey Bros & Nicholls (Contractors) Ltd [1991] 1 Q.B. 1; [1990] 2 W.L.R. 1153; [1990] 1 All E.R. 512; 48 B.L.R. 69; (1991) 10 Tr. L.R. 12; (1990) 87(12) L.S.G. 36; (1989) 139 N.L.J. 1712, CA (Civ Div) 1–002, *3–002*, *3–006*, *3–007*, *3–037*, *3–064*, *3–067*, 3–068, 3–069, 3–076, *3–080*, 3–099, *3–111*, *3–113*, *3–117*, *3–123*, 7–019, 7–040, *7–041*, *21–032*, *22–035*, *24–043*
Williams v Staite [1979] Ch. 291; [1978] 2 W.L.R. 825; [1978] 2 All E.R. 928; (1978) 36 P. & C.R. 103; (1978) 122 S.J. 333, CA (Civ Div) *13–028*
Williams v University of Nottingham [2007] I.R.L.R. 660, EAT *30–115*, *30–116*
Williams v Walker Thomas Furniture Co, 121 U.S. App.D.C. 315, 350 F. 2d 445 (1965) *7–137*

Williams v Williams (Enforcability of Agreement) [1957] 1 W.L.R. 148; [1957] 1 All E.R. 305; (1957) 121 J.P. 93; (1957) 101 S.J. 108, CA *3–061*
Williams v Williams, 1980 S.L.T. (Sh. Ct.) 25, Sh Pr *19–015*
Williams Bros v Ed T Agius Ltd [1914] A.C. 510, HL *22–028*
Williamson v Governor of the Bank of Scotland [2006] EWHC 1289; [2006] B.P.I.R. 1085, Ch D *15–032*
Willins v Smith (1854) 4 E. & B. 180 .... *28–102*
Willion v Berkley (1562) 1 Plow. 223 .... *12–086*
Willis v Baggs and Salt (1925) 41 T.L.R. 453 .... *2–123*
Willis v Baldwin (1780) 2 Doug. K.B. 450 .... *16–017*
Willis v Barrett (1816) 2 Stark. 29 .... *12–122*
Willis v Barron; sub nom. Barron v Willis [1902] A.C. 271, HL; affirming [1900] 2 Ch. 121, CA; reversing [1899] 2 Ch. 578, Ch D *7–076*, *7–085*, *7–095*
Willis v De Castro (1858) 4 C.B.(N.S.) 216 .... *17–018*
Willis v Earl Howe [1893] 2 Ch. 545, CA *28–089*
Willis v Peckham (1820) 1 Br. & B. 515 .... *3–062*
Willis Faber Enthoven (Pty) v Receiver of Revenue, 1992 (4) S.A. 202, Sup Ct (SA) *29–015*, *29–045*
Willis Management (Isle of Man) Ltd v Cable & Wireless Plc; sub nom. Cable & Wireless Plc v Valentine [2005] EWCA Civ 806; [2005] 2 Lloyd's Rep. 597, CA (Civ Div) *2–126*, *2–130*, *2–136*, *2–142*
Willmott v Barber (1881) L.R. 17 Ch. D. 772, CA; affirming in part (1880) L.R. 15 Ch. D. 96, Ch D *3–138*, *3–162*, *27–041*, *27–055*, 28–136, *29–161*
Wills v Murray (1850) 4 Exch. 843 .... *20–005*
Wills v Stradling (1797) 3 Ves. 378 .... *4–048*
Wills v Wright (1677) 2 Mod. 285 .... *12–080*
Wills, Percival & Co, Re. *See* Morier Ex p.
Willson v Love [1896] 1 Q.B. 626, CA *26–127*
Wilmer v Currey (1848) 2 De G & Sm. 347 .... *17–006*, *17–007*
Wilmot v Alton [1897] 1 Q.B. 17, CA; affirming [1896] 2 Q.B. 254, QBD *19–061*, *20–026*
Wilmott v Smith (1828) Moo. M. 238 .... *21–043*, *21–094*
Wilson, Ex p. Salaman, Re [1926] Ch. 21, Ch D *20–023*
Wilson, Re; sub nom. Wilson v Trustee of a Deed of Arrangement [1937] Ch. 675 .... *28–099*
Wilson v Avec Audio-Visual Equipment [1974] 1 Lloyd's Rep. 81, CA (Civ Div) *29–109*, *29–117*
Wilson v Best Travel Ltd [1993] 1 All E.R. 353, QBD *13–032*, *18–012*
Wilson v Carnley [1908] 1 K.B. 729, CA *16–004*, *16–070*
Wilson v Darling Island Stevedoring and Lighterage Co Ltd [1956] 1 Lloyd's Rep. 346, HC (Aus) *14–042*
Wilson v First County Trust Ltd (No.2); sub nom. Wilson v Secretary of State for Trade and Industry [2003] UKHL 40; [2004] 1 A.C. 816; [2003] 3 W.L.R. 568; [2003] 4 All E.R. 97; [2003] 2 All E.R. (Comm) 491; [2003] H.R.L.R. 33; [2003] U.K.H.R.R. 1085; (2003) 100(35) L.S.G. 39; (2003) 147 S.J.L.B. 872, HL; reversing [2001] EWCA Civ 633; [2002] Q.B. 74; [2001] 3 W.L.R. 42; [2001] 3 All E.R. 229; [2001] 2 All E.R. (Comm) 134; [2001] E.C.C. 37; [2001] H.R.L.R. 44; [2001] U.K.H.R.R. 1175; (2001) 98(24) L.S.G. 44; (2001) 145 S.J.L.B. 125, CA (Civ Div) ... 1–037, 1–038, 1–039, 1–040, 1–043, 1–044, 1–045, 1–047, 1–048, *1–060*, *1–110*
Wilson v General Iron Screw Colliery Co Ltd (1877) 47 L.J.Q.B. 239 .... *26–066*
Wilson v Harper [1908] 2 Ch. 370, Ch D *20–006*
Wilson v Hodson (1871–72) L.R. 7 Ex. 84, Ex Ct *20–012*
Wilson v Kearse (1800) Peake.Add.Cas. 196 .... *8–065*
Wilson v Keating (1859) 27 Beav. 121 .... *21–058*
Wilson v Lancs Yorks Railway (1861) 9 C.B.(N.S.) 632 .... *26–089*
Wilson v Le Fevre Wood & Royle, 66 Con. L.R. 74; [1996] P.N.L.R. 107, CA (Civ Div) *28–011*
Wilson v Lloyd (1873) L.R. 16 Eq. 60, Ct of Chancery *19–087*

Wilson v Maynard Shipbuilding Consultants AB [1978] Q.B. 665; [1978] 2 W.L.R. 466; [1978] 2 All E.R. 78; [1978] I.C.R. 376; [1977] I.R.L.R. 491; (1978) 13 I.T.R. 23; (1977) 121 S.J. 792, CA (Civ Div); reversing [1977] I.C.R. 112; [1976] I.R.L.R. 384; (1976) 11 I.T.R. 303, EAT *12–126*
Wilson v Northampton and Banbury Junction Railway Co (1873–74) L.R. 9 Ch. App. 279, CA in Chancery *27–042*
Wilson v Robertsons (London) Ltd [2005] EWHC 1425 (Ch); [2006] 1 W.L.R. 1248; [2005] 3 All E.R. 873; (2005) 102(30) L.S.G. 29, Ch D *14–126*
Wilson v St Helens BC; Meade v British Fuels Ltd; Baxendale v British Fuels Ltd; sub nom. British Fuels Ltd v Baxendale [1999] 2 A.C. 52; [1998] 3 W.L.R. 1070; [1998] 4 All E.R. 609; [1999] 1 C.M.L.R. 918; [1998] I.C.R. 1141; [1998] I.R.L.R. 706; (1999) 1 L.G.L.R. 123; [1999] B.L.G.R. 255, HL *27–021*
Wilson v Truelove [2003] EWHC 750 (Ch); [2003] 2 E.G.L.R. 63; [2003] 23 E.G. 136; [2003] W.T.L.R. 609; [2003] 10 E.G. 164 (C.S.); (2003) 100(10) L.S.G. 31; (2003) 100(14) L.S.G. 28, Ch D *3–115*
Wilson v United Counties Bank Ltd [1920] A.C. 102, HL *1–123*, *20–026*, *20–034*, *26–098*, *26–120*
Wilson v Vysar (1812) 4 Taunt. 288 .... *21–078*
Wilson v Wallani (1879–80) L.R. 5 Ex. D. 155, Exchequer Div *19–006*
Wilson v West Hartlepool Ry (1865) 2 De. G.J. & S. 475 .... *9–015*
Wilson v Williams (1857) 3 Jur. (N.S.) 810 .... *27–047*
Wilson v Wilson (1854) 14 C.B. 616 .... *29–191*
Wilson v Wilson (Rectification of Deed) [1969] 1 W.L.R. 1470; [1969] 3 All E.R. 945; (1969) 20 P. & C.R. 780; (1969) 113 S.J. 625, Ch D *1–112*
Wilson & Co v Baker, Lees & Co (1901) 17 T.L.R. 473 .... *9–012*
Wilson & Sons v Pike [1949] 1 K.B. 176; [1948] 2 All E.R. 267; 64 T.L.R. 566; [1949] L.J.R. 17; (1948) 92 S.J. 513, CA *4–038*, *4–039*
Wilson and Meeson v Pickering [1946] K.B. 422; [1946] 1 All E.R. 394; [1947] L.J.R. 18; 175 L.T. 65, CA *5–106*
Wilson and Wilson Ex p. Marum, Re (1915) 84 L.J.K.B. 1893 .... *11–030*
Wilson Bowden Properties Ltd v Milner [1997] N.P.C. 187, CA (Civ Div); affirming [1995] N.P.C. 182, QBD *3–113*
Wilson Smithett & Cape (Sugar) v Bangladesh Sugar and Food Industries Corp [1986] 1 Lloyd's Rep. 378, QBD (Comm) *2–125*, *2–183*
Wilson, Smithett & Cope Ltd v Terruzzi [1976] Q.B. 683; [1976] 2 W.L.R. 418; [1976] 1 All E.R. 817; [1976] 1 Lloyd's Rep. 509; (1976) 120 S.J. 116, CA (Civ Div); affirming [1975] 2 W.L.R. 1009; [1975] 2 All E.R. 649; [1975] 1 Lloyd's Rep. 642; (1975) 119 S.J. 318, QBD (Comm) *16–011*, *16–014*, *16–159*
Wilson Sons & Co v Balcarres Brook Steamship Co Ltd [1893] 1 Q.B. 422, CA *17–010*
Wilson's Music & General Printing Co v Finsbury BC [1908] 1 K.B. 563, KBD *29–096*
Wilton Group Plc v Abrams; Abrams v Samuelson [1990] B.C.C. 310; [1991] B.C.L.C. 315, Ch D *27–035*
Wiltshire Iron Co, Re; sub nom. Ex p. Pearson (1867–68) L.R. 3 Ch. App. 443, CA in Chancery *9–049*
Wiltshire v Marshall (1866) 14 L.T. (N.S.) 396 .... *8–080*
Wiluszynski v Tower Hamlets LBC [1989] I.C.R. 493; [1989] I.R.L.R. 259; 88 L.G.R. 14; (1989) 133 S.J. 628, CA (Civ Div) *21–032*, *29–021*, *29–070*, *29–080*
Wimble v Lillico (1922) 38 T.L.R. 296 .... *14–027*
Wimbledon and Putney Commons Conservators v Tuely [1931] 1 Ch. 190, Ch D *9–022*
Wimpey Construction UK v Scottish Special Housing Association. *See* Scottish Special Housing Association v Wimpey Construction UK.
Wincanton Ltd v Cranny [2000] I.R.L.R. 716, CA (Civ Div) *16–106*
Windeler v Whitehall (1990) 154 J.P. 29; [1990] 2 F.L.R. 505; [1990] F.C.R. 268, CA (Civ Div) *2–171*, *2–183*
Windhill Local Board of Health v Vint (1890) L.R. 45 Ch. D. 351, CA *7–049*, *16–039*

Windle (A Bankrupt), Re; sub nom. Trustee Ex p. v Windle [1975] 1 W.L.R. 1628; [1975] 3 All E.R. 987; (1975) 119 S.J. 808, Ch D *2–169*, *4–047*, *4–048*, *4–049*, *18–125*
Windschuegl (Charles H) v Alexander Pickering & Co (1950) 84 Ll. L. Rep. 89, KBD *2–155*, *13–013*
Wing v Burn (1928) 44 T.L.R. 258 .... *9–068*
Winkfield, The [1902] P. 42; [1900–03] All E.R. Rep. 346, CA *2–118*, *18–076*
Winn v Bull (1877–78) L.R. 7 Ch. D. 29, Ch D 2–118
Winnipeg (City of) v Canadian Pacific Railway Co [1953] A.C. 618; [1953] 3 W.L.R. 438; [1953] 2 All E.R. 988; (1953) 97 S.J. 536, PC (Can) *9–022*
Winnipeg Condominium Corp v Bird Construction Co (1995) 121 D.L.R. (4th) 193 .... *18–027*
Winslow Hall Estates Co and United Glass Bottle Manufacturers Ltd's Contract, Re [1941] Ch. 503, Ch D *27–007*
Winstone v Linn (1823) 1 B.C. 460 .... *24–036*
Winter Ex p. Bolland, Re (1878) L.R. 8 Ch. D. 225, Ch D *20–041*
Winter Garden Theatre (London) Ltd v Millennium Productions Ltd; sub nom. Millennium Productions Ltd v Winter Garden Theatre (London) Ltd [1948] A.C. 173; [1947] 2 All E.R. 331; 63 T.L.R. 529; [1947] L.J.R. 1422; 177 L.T. 349; (1947) 91 S.J. 504, HL; reversing [1946] W.N. 151; (1946) 115 L.J. Ch. 297, CA; reversing (1946) 115 L.J. Ch. 185, Ch D *9–080*, *13–027*, *13–028*, *22–054*
Winterbottom v Wright (1842) 10 M. & W. 109 .... *1–173*, 1–174
Wintle v Nye; sub nom. Wells, In the Estate of [1959] 1 W.L.R. 284; [1959] 1 All E.R. 552, HL; reversing, Times, December 17, 1957, CA; reversing, *The Times*, May 21, 1957, PDAD *7–076*
Wise v Perpetual Trustee Co Ltd [1903] A.C. 139, PC (Aus) *9–073*
Wishart v National Association of Citizens Advice Bureaux [1990] I.C.R. 794; [1990] I.R.L.R. 393, CA (Civ Div) *2–154*, *27–021*
With v O'Flanagan [1936] Ch. 575, CA *6–018*
Withers v Bircham (1824) 3 B. & C. 254 .... *3–043*
Withers v General Theatre Co Ltd; sub nom. Withers v General Theatre Corp Ltd [1933] 2 K.B. 536, CA *1–123*, *26–048*, *26–087*
Withers v Reynolds, 109 E.R. 1370; (1831) 2 B. & Ad. 882, KB *24–018*, *24–027*
Wollaston v Hakewill (1841) 3 M. & G. 297 .... *20–008*
Wollaston v Tribe (1869–70) L.R. 9 Eq. 44, Ct of Chancery *5–122*
Wolmershausen v Gullick [1893] 2 Ch. 514, Ch D *17–027*, *17–028*, *28–047*, *28–048*
Wolmershausen, Re (1890) 62 L.T. 541 .... *17–018*
Wolterbeek v Barrow (1857) 23 Beav. 423 .... *28–146*
Wolverhampton Corp v Emmons [1901] 1 Q.B. 515, CA *27–028*
Wong Lai Ying v Chinachem Investment Co Ltd, 13 B.L.R. 81, PC (HK) *23–057*
Wong Mee Wan v Kwan Kin Travel Services Ltd [1996] 1 W.L.R. 38; [1995] 4 All E.R. 745; [1995] C.L.C. 1593; (1996) 93(3) L.S.G. 28; (1995) 139 S.J.L.B. 246, PC (HK) 1–149, *13–006*, *19–081*
Wood v Abrey (1818) 3 Madd. 417 .... *7–128*
Wood v Downes (1811) 18 Ves. 120 .... *16–064*
Wood v Dunn (1866–67) L.R. 2 Q.B. 73, Ex Chamber *21–051*
Wood v Jones (1889) 61 L.T. 551 .... *28–033*
Wood v Leadbitter (1845) 13 M. & W. 838 .... *4–018*, *13–028*
Wood v Lucy, Lady Duff-Gordon (1917) 222 N.Y. 88 .... *2–084*
Wood v Luscombe [1966] 1 Q.B. 169; [1965] 3 W.L.R. 998; [1964] 3 All E.R. 972; (1965) 109 S.J. 833, Assizes (Bristol) *25–012*
Wood v McCarthy [1893] 1 Q.B. 775, QBD *9–068*
Wood v Roberts (1818) 2 Stark. 417 .... *3–125*
Wood v Rowcliffe (1851) 6 Exch. 407 .... *12–091*
Wood v Scarth (1855) 2 K. & J. 33; (1855) 1 F. & F. 293 .... *5–011*, *5–071*, *5–115*, *12–123*
Wood v Slack (1867–68) L.R. 3 Q.B. 379, QB *25–023*
Wood Preservation v Prior [1969] 1 W.L.R. 1077; [1969] 1 All E.R. 364; 45 T.C. 112; [1968] T.R. 353; (1968) 112 S.J. 927, CA; affirming [1968] 2 All E.R. 849; [1968] T.R. 37; (1968) 112 S.J. 275, Ch D *2–157*, *12–028*

Woodar Investment Development Ltd v Wimpey Construction UK Ltd [1980] 1 W.L.R. 277; [1980] 1 All E.R. 571; (1980) 124 S.J. 184, HL *18–019*, *18–020*, 18–050, 18–051, 18–062, *18–068*, *18–076*, *24–019*
Woodbridge v Spooner (1819) 3 B. & Ald. 233 .... *12–101*
Woodbridge & Sons v Bellamy [1911] 1 Ch. 326, CA *16–114*
Woodford v Smith [1970] 1 W.L.R. 806; [1970] 1 All E.R. 1091 (Note); (1970) 114 S.J. 245, Ch D *9–074*
Woodhouse AC Israel Cocoa SA v Nigerian Produce Marketing Co Ltd; sub nom. Woodhouse v Nigerian Produce Marketing Co Ltd [1972] A.C. 741; [1972] 2 W.L.R. 1090; [1972] 2 All E.R. 271; [1972] 1 Lloyd's Rep. 439; (1972) 116 S.J. 329, HL; affirming [1971] 2 Q.B. 23; [1971] 2 W.L.R. 272; [1971] 1 All E.R. 665; [1971] 1 Lloyd's Rep. 25; (1970) 115 S.J. 56, CA (Civ Div); reversing [1970] 2 All E.R. 124; [1970] 1 Lloyd's Rep. 295, QBD (Comm) *3–079*, *3–090*, *3–103*, 3–104, *3–129*, *5–067*, *6–095*, *22–035*, *22–044*, *24–006*, *24–008*, *30–374*
Woods v Mackenzie Hill Ltd [1975] 1 W.L.R. 613; [1975] 2 All E.R. 170; (1975) 29 P. & C.R. 306; (1975) 119 S.J. 187, Ch D *21–014*
Woods v Pickersgill (1859) 1 F. & F. 710 .... *22–015*
Woods v Wise [1955] 2 Q.B. 29; [1955] 2 W.L.R. 734; [1955] 1 All E.R. 767; (1955) 119 J.P. 254; (1955) 99 S.J. 234, CA *12–108*, *12–112*
Woodward v Wolferstans [1997] N.P.C. 51, Ch D *18–028*
Wookey v Pole (1820) 4 B. Ald. 1 .... *29–170*
Woolcott v Sun Alliance and London Insurance Ltd [1978] 1 W.L.R. 493; [1978] 1 All E.R. 1253; [1978] 1 Lloyd's Rep. 629; (1977) 121 S.J. 744, QBD ... *6–147*
Wooley v Clarke (1822) 5 B. & Ald. 744 .... *20–004*
Woolf v Collis Removal Service [1948] 1 K.B. 11; [1947] 2 All E.R. 260; 63 T.L.R. 540; 3 A.L.R.2d 378; [1947] L.J.R. 1377; 177 L.T. 405, CA *14–004*, *14–008*
Woolf v Woolf [1899] 1 Ch. 343, Ch D *8–053*
Woolfe v Horne (1876–77) L.R. 2 Q.B.D. 355, QBD *21–011*
Woolfe v Wexler [1951] 2 K.B. 154; [1951] 1 All E.R. 635; [1951] 1 T.L.R. 794; (1951) 115 J.P. 202; 49 L.G.R. 307; (1951) 95 S.J. 171, CA *16–154*
Woollam v Hearn (1802) 7 Ves. 211 .... *5–124*
Woollatt v Stanley (1928) 138 L.T. 620 .... *25–024*
Woolmer v Delmer Price [1955] 1 Q.B. 291; [1955] 2 W.L.R. 329; [1955] 1 All E.R. 377; (1955) 99 S.J. 112, QBD *14–011*, *14–019*
Woolton Isaacson, Re (1904) 21 T.L.R. 89 .... *16–067*
Woolwich Equitable Building Society v Inland Revenue Commissioners [1993] A.C. 70; [1992] 3 W.L.R. 366; [1992] 3 All E.R. 737; [1992] S.T.C. 657; (1993) 5 Admin. L.R. 265; 65 T.C. 265; (1992) 142 N.L.J. 1196; (1992) 136 S.J.L.B. 230, HL; affirming [1991] 3 W.L.R. 790; [1991] 4 All E.R. 577; [1991] S.T.C. 364; (1991) 135 S.J.L.B. 46, CA (Civ Div); reversing [1989] 1 W.L.R. 137; [1989] S.T.C. 111; (1989) 133 S.J. 291, QBD *1–192*, *3–056*, *3–062*, *29–001*, *29–008*, *29–011*, *29–013*, *29–015*, *29–018*, *29–034*, *29–036*, *29–043*, *29–048*, *29–075*, 29–083, 29–084, *29–085*, *29–086*, 29–094, 29–095, *29–098*, *29–111*, *29–188*
Wootton Trucks Ltd v Man ERF UK Ltd [2006] EWCA Civ 1042; [2007] R.T.R. 19; [2006] Eu. L.R. 1217, CA (Civ Div); reversing [2006] EWHC 943 (Ch); [2006] Eu. L.R. 967, Ch D *13–009*
Worboys v Carter [1987] 2 E.G.L.R. 1; (1987) 283 E.G. 307, CA (Civ Div) ... *4–037*
Worby v Rosser [1999] Lloyd's Rep. P.N. 972; [2000] P.N.L.R. 140; (1999–2000) 2 I.T.E.L.R. 59; (1999) 96(24) L.S.G. 39, CA (Civ Div) *18–022*
Worcester Ex p. Agra Bank, Re (1867–68) L.R. 3 Ch. App. 555, CA in Chancery *19–069*
Workers Trust & Merchant Bank Ltd v Dojap Investments Ltd [1993] A.C. 573; [1993] 2 W.L.R. 702; [1993] 2 All E.R. 370; (1993) 66 P. & C.R. 15; [1993] 1 E.G.L.R. 203; [1993] E.G. 38 (C.S.); (1993) 143 N.L.J. 616; (1993) 137 S.J.L.B. 83; [1993] N.P.C. 33, PC (Jam) ...*26–126*, *26–127*, *26–130*, 26–146, 26–151, *29–064*
World Beauty, The. *See* Owners of the Andros Springs v Owners of the World Beauty; The Andros Springs and The World Beauty

World Online Telecom Ltd v I-Way Ltd [2002] EWCA Civ 413, CA (Civ Div) *22–045*
World Wide Fund for Nature (formerly World Wildlife Fund) v World Wrestling Federation Entertainment Inc; sub nom. WWF v World Wrestling Federation Entertainment Inc [2002] EWCA Civ 196; [2002] U.K.C.L.R. 388; [2002] E.T.M.R. 53; [2002] F.S.R. 33; (2002) 25(4) I.P.D. 25023; (2002) 99(15) L.S.G. 33; (2002) 152 N.L.J. 363; (2002) 146 S.J.L.B. 70, CA (Civ Div); affirming [2002] F.S.R. 32; (2001) 24(12) I.P.D. 24079, Ch D *16–085*, *26–025*, *26–029*
Worsley v Wood (1796) 6 Term Rep. 710 .... *12–028*
Worthington Re [1914] 2 K.B. 299 .... *20–007*, *20–034*
Worthington v Wigley, 132 E.R. 485; (1837) 3 Bing. N.C. 454, KB *21–076*
Wragg v Lovett [1948] 2 All E.R. 968; [1948] W.N. 455, CA *4–037*
Wren v Holt [1903] 1 K.B. 610, CA *26–082*
Wrexham Associated Football Club Ltd (In Administration) v Crucialmove Ltd [2006] EWCA Civ 237; [2007] B.C.C. 139; [2008] 1 B.C.L.C. 508, CA (Civ Div) *9–033*
Wrexham Mold & Connah's Quay Railway Co, Re [1899] 1 Ch. 440, CA; affirming [1899] 1 Ch. 205, Ch D *9–025*, *29–173*
Wright v Carter [1903] 1 Ch. 27, CA *7–056*, *7–076*, *7–095*, *7–125*
Wright v Colls (1849) 8 C.B. 150 .... *29–057*
Wright v Dean [1948] Ch. 686; [1948] 2 All E.R. 415; 64 T.L.R. 467; [1948] L.J.R. 1571; (1948) 92 S.J. 393, Ch D *24–022*, *26–068*
Wright v Horton (1887) L.R. 12 App. Cas. 371, HL *16–156*
Wright v John Bagnall & Sons Ltd [1900] 2 Q.B. 240, CA *28–109*, 28–111
Wright v Laing (1824) 3 B.C. 165 .... *21–062*
Wright v New Zealand Farmers Cooperative Association of Canterbury Ltd [1939] A.C. 439, PC (NZ) *28–046*
Wright v Newton, 150 E.R. 53; (1835) 2 Cr. M & R. 124, Ex Ct *29–064*
Wright v Pepin [1954] 1 W.L.R. 635; [1954] 2 All E.R. 52; (1954) 98 S.J. 252, Ch D *28–094*, *28–100*
Wright v Robert Leonard (Developments) [1994] E.G. 69 (C.S.); [1994] N.P.C. 49, CA (Civ Div) 4–070
Wright v Stavert (1860) 2 E. & E. 721 .... *3–143*, *4–013*
Wright v Vanderplank (1855) 2 K. & J. 1 .... *7–074*, *7–097*
Wright v Vanderplank (1856) 8 De G.M. & G. 133 .... *28–145*
Wringe v Cohen [1940] 1 K.B. 229, CA *1–173*
Wroth v Tyler [1974] Ch. 30; [1973] 2 W.L.R. 405; [1973] 1 All E.R. 897; (1973) 25 P. & C.R. 138; (1972) 117 S.J. 90, Ch D *26–051*, *26–059*, *26–061*, *26–091*, 26–107, *26–109*, *26–110*, *27–031*, 27–079, *27–084*
Wrotham Park Estate Co Ltd v Parkside Homes Ltd [1974] 1 W.L.R. 798; [1974] 2 All E.R. 321; (1974) 27 P. & C.R. 296; (1973) 118 S.J. 420, Ch D 26–023, 26–024, 26–025, 26–026, **26–027**, *29–151*, 29–154
Wu Koon Tai v Wu Yau Loi [1997] A.C. 179; [1996] 3 W.L.R. 778; (1996) 140 S.J.L.B. 221; [1996] N.P.C. 139, PC (HK) *27–039*
Wuchter v Fitzgerald (1917) 163 P.819 .... *29–069*
Wyatt, Re; sub nom. Ward v Duncombe; White v Ellis [1893] A.C. 369, HL; affirming [1892] 1 Ch. 188, CA *19–068*
Wyatt v Kreglinger [1933] 1 K.B. 793, CA *2–168*, *3–026*, *3–166*, *3–167*, *16–094*, 16–105
Wycherley v Wycherley (1763) 2 Eden 175 .... *1–108*
Wylson v Dunn (1887) L.R. 34 Ch. D. 569, Ch D *4–028*, *27–047*
Wyndham Rather Ltd v Eagle Star & British Dominions Insurance Co Ltd (1925) 21 Ll. L. Rep. 214, CA *12–017*
Wyvern Developments, Re [1974] 1 W.L.R. 1097; [1974] 2 All E.R. 535; (1974) 118 S.J. 531, Ch D *3–039*, *3–057*, *3–098*, *6–095*, *29–043*

X (Minors) v Bedfordshire CC; M (A Minor) v Newham LBC; E (A Minor) v Dorset CC (Appeal); Christmas v Hampshire CC (Duty of Care); Keating v Bromley LBC (No.2) [1995] 2 A.C. 633; [1995] 3 W.L.R. 152; [1995] 3 All E.R. 353; [1995] 2 F.L.R. 276; [1995] 3 F.C.R. 337; 94 L.G.R. 313; (1995) 7 Admin. L.R. 705; [1995] Fam. Law 537; (1996) 160 L.G. Rev. 103; (1996) 160 L.G. Rev. 123; (1995) 145 N.L.J. 993, HL; affirming [1994] 2 W.L.R. 554; [1994] 4 All E.R. 602; [1994] 1 F.L.R. 431; 92 L.G.R. 427; [1994] Fam. Law 434; (1994) 144 N.L.J. 357, CA (Civ Div); affirming [1993] 2 F.L.R. 575; [1994] P.I.Q.R. P515; [1993] Fam. Law 575; (1993) 143 N.L.J. 1783, QBD *18–032*
XL Insurance Ltd v Owens Corning [2001] 1 All E.R. (Comm) 530; [2000] 2 Lloyd's Rep. 500; [2001] C.P. Rep. 22; [2001] C.L.C. 914, QBD (Comm) *30–005*, *30–010*, *30–015*, *30–046*, *30–052*, *30–056*, *30–071*
Xantho, The. *See* Thomas Wilson Sons & Co v Owners of Cargo of the Xantho
Xenos v Danube, etc. Railway (1863) 13 C.B.(N.S.) 825 .... *24–022*
Xenos v Wickham (1867) L.R. 2 H.L. 296, HL; reversing, 143 E.R. 515; (1863) 13 C.B. N.S. 435, Ex Chamber *1–003*, *1–093*, *1–105*
Xydhias v Xydhias [1999] 2 All E.R. 386; [1999] 1 F.L.R. 683; [1999] 1 F.C.R. 289; [1999] Fam. Law 301; (1999) 96(6) L.S.G. 34; (1999) 149 N.L.J. 52, CA (Civ Div) *2–158*
YL v Birmingham City Council. *See* L v Birmingham City Council
Yager v Guardian Assurance Co (1912) 29 T.L.R. 53 .... *6–147*
Yango Pastoral Co Ltd v First Chicago Australia Ltd (1978) 139 C.L.R. 410 ... *16–152*
Yani Haryanto v ED&F Man (Sugar). *See* ED&F Man (Sugar) Ltd v Haryanto (No.1)
Yarborough v Bank of England (1812) 16 East 6 .... *9–009*
Yarm Road Ltd (formerly Kvaerner Cleveland Bridge UK Ltd) v Hewden Tower Cranes Ltd; sub nom. Hewden Tower Cranes Ltd v Yarm Road Ltd [2003] EWCA Civ 1127; 90 Con. L.R. 1; (2004) 20 Const. L.J. 137; (2003) 147 S.J.L.B. 994, CA (Civ Div); affirming [2002] EWHC 2265 (TCC); 85 Con. L.R. 142, QBD (TCC) *13–003*, *13–028*
Yarmouth (Isle of Wight) Harbour Commissioners v Harold Hayles (Yarmouth Isle of Wight) Ltd [2004] EWHC 3375 (Ch); [2004] All E.R. (D) 66, Ch D ... *10–043*
Yasuda Fire & Marine Insurance Co of Europe Ltd v Orion Marine Insurance Underwriting Agency Ltd [1995] Q.B. 174; [1995] 2 W.L.R. 49; [1995] 3 All E.R. 211; [1995] 1 Lloyd's Rep. 525; [1994] C.L.C. 1212; [1995] 4 Re. L.R. 217, QBD (Comm) *24–047*
Yat Tung Investment Co Ltd v Dao Heng Bank Ltd [1975] A.C. 581; [1975] 2 W.L.R. 690; (1975) 119 S.J. 273, PC (HK) *25–013*, *25–014*
Yates v Aston (1843) 4 Q.B. 182 .... *25–002*
Yates v Freckleton (1781) 2 Dougl. 623 .... *21–043*
Yates v Pym (1816) 6 Taunt. 446 .... *12–126*, *13–018*
Yaxley v Gotts; sub nom. Yaxley v Gott [2000] Ch. 162; [1999] 3 W.L.R. 1217; [2000] 1 All E.R. 711; [1999] 2 F.L.R. 941; (2000) 32 H.L.R. 547; (2000) 79 P. & C.R. 91; [1999] 2 E.G.L.R. 181; [1999] Fam. Law 700; [1999] E.G. 92 (C.S.); (1999) 96(28) L.S.G. 25; (1999) 143 S.J.L.B. 198; [1999] N.P.C. 76; (1999) 78 P. & C.R. D33, CA (Civ Div) *1–006*, 1–104, *3–115*, *3–140*, *3–142*, *3–151*, *4–075*, 4–077, 4–078, *4–079*, 4–081, *29–160*
Yeoman Credit v Apps [1962] 2 Q.B. 508; [1961] 3 W.L.R. 94; [1961] 2 All E.R. 281; (1961) 105 S.J. 567, CA *12–021*, *14–020*, *14–028*, *29–057*, *29–061*
Yeoman Credit v Odgers Vospers Motor House (Plymouth) (Third Party) [1962] 1 W.L.R. 215; [1962] 1 All E.R. 789; (1962) 106 S.J. 75, CA *12–007*, *18–006*
Yeoman Credit v Waragowski [1961] 1 W.L.R. 1124; [1961] 3 All E.R. 145; (1961) 105 S.J. 588, CA *22–049*, *26–098*
Yeoman Credit Ltd v Gregory [1963] 1 W.L.R. 343; [1963] 1 All E.R. 245; [1962] 2 Lloyd's Rep. 302; (1963) 107 S.J. 315, QBD (Comm) *12–113*
Yeoman's Executrix v Ferries; sub nom. Yeoman v Ferries, 1967 S.C. 255; 1917 2 S.L.T. 261; 1967 S.L.T. 332, OH *26–044*

Yeoman's Row Management Ltd v Cobbe [2008] UKHL 55 ......*29–021, 29–071, 29–160, 29–161*
Yeovil Glove Co, Re [1965] Ch. 148; [1964] 3 W.L.R. 406; [1964] 2 All E.R. 849; (1964) 108 S.J. 499, CA *21–066*
Yetton v Eastwood Froy Ltd [1967] 1 W.L.R. 104; [1966] 3 All E.R. 353; 1 K.I.R. 469; (1967) 111 S.J. 32, QBD *26–103*
Yeung Kai Yung v Hong Kong and Shanghai Banking Corp [1981] A.C. 787; [1980] 3 W.L.R. 950; [1980] 2 All E.R. 599; (1980) 124 S.J. 591, PC (HK) ... *29–120*
Yianni v Edwin Evans & Sons [1982] Q.B. 438; [1981] 3 W.L.R. 843; [1981] 3 All E.R. 592; (1981) 259 E.G. 969; (1981) 125 S.J. 694, QBD *6–028, 18–022*
Yin (Chai Sau) v Sam (Liew Kwee) [1962] A.C. 304; [1962] 2 W.L.R. 765; (1962) 106 S.J. 217, PC (FMS) *16–147*, 16–159
Yona International Ltd v La Réunion Francaise SA D'Assurances et de Reassurances [1996] 2 Lloyd's Rep. 84, QBD (Comm) *2–072, 2–073, 2–077*
Yonge v Toynbee [1910] 1 K.B. 215, CA *8–076*
York Corp v Henry Leetham & Sons Ltd [1924] 1 Ch. 557, Ch D *9–020, 9–024*, 10–030
York Estates v Wareham 1950 (1) S.A. 125 .... *16–161*
York Glass Co v Jubb (1925) 42 T.L.R. 1 .... *8–068*
York Glass Co v Jubb (1926) 134 L.T. 36 .... *26–092*
York Products Pty v Gilchrist Watt & Sanderson Pty [1970] 1 W.L.R. 1262; [1970] 3 All E.R. 825; [1970] 2 Lloyd's Rep. 1; (1970) 114 S.J. 571, PC (Aus) *14–054*
York Trailer Co v Sparkes [1973] I.C.R. 518; [1973] I.R.L.R. 348; [1973] I.T.R. 491, EAT *26–001*
Yorkshire Bank Plc v Hall; Hall v Yorkshire Bank Plc [1999] 1 W.L.R. 1713; [1999] 1 All E.R. 879; (1999) 78 P. & C.R. 136, CA (Civ Div) *1–148*
Yorkshire Bank Plc v Lloyds Bank Plc [1999] 1 All E.R. (Comm) 154; [1999] Lloyd's Rep. Bank. 191, QBD *1–184*
Yorkshire Bank Plc v Tinsley [2004] EWCA Civ 816; [2004] 1 W.L.R. 2380; [2004] 3 All E.R. 463; [2004] 2 F.L.R. 1079; [2004] Fam. Law 719; [2004] 28 E.G. 176 (C.S.); (2004) 101(27) L.S.G. 32; (2004) 148 S.J.L.B. 822; [2004] 2 P. & C.R. DG19, CA (Civ Div) *7–121, 29–137*
Yorkshire Electricity Board v Naylor [1968] A.C. 529; [1967] 2 W.L.R. 1114; [1967] 2 All E.R. 1; 6 K.I.R. 259; (1967) 111 S.J. 278, HL *26–030*
Yorkshire RHA v Fairclough Building Ltd; Yorkshire RHA v Percy Thomas Partnership [1996] 1 W.L.R. 210; [1996] 1 All E.R. 519; [1996] C.L.C. 366; 78 B.L.R. 59; 47 Con. L.R. 120; (1995) 139 S.J.L.B. 247, CA (Civ Div) *28–121*
Yorkshire Water Services Ltd v Sun Alliance and London Insurance Plc (No.1) [1997] 2 Lloyd's Rep. 21; [1997] C.L.C. 213; (1996) 93(34) L.S.G. 34; (1996) 140 S.J.L.B. 193; [1997] Env. L.R. D4, CA (Civ Div) *13–009, 13–010*
Youell v Bland Welch & Co Ltd (No.1) [1992] 2 Lloyd's Rep. 127, CA (Civ Div); affirming [1990] 2 Lloyd's Rep. 423, QBD (Comm) *2–117, 12–085, 12–096, 12–099, 12–117, 12–119, 14–009*
Youell v Bland Welch & Co Ltd (No.2) [1990] 2 Lloyd's Rep. 431, QBD (Comm) *1–166, 3–090, 3–092, 3–094, 3–104, 26–109*
Yougmin v Heath [1974] 1 W.L.R. 135 .... *23–055*
Young v Austen (1868–69) L.R. 4 C.P. 553, CCP *12–100, 12–101, 12–108*
Young v Buckles [1952] 1 K.B. 220; [1952] 1 All E.R. 354; [1952] 1 T.L.R. 271; (1952) 116 J.P. 96; (1952) 96 S.J. 120, CA *16–154*
Young v English (1843) 7 Beav. 10 .... *21–060*
Young v Higgon, 151 E.R. 317; (1840) 6 M. & W. 49, Ex Ct *12–093*
Young v Kitchin; sub nom. Young v Kitchen (1877–78) L.R. 3 Ex. D. 127, Exchequer Div *19–070, 19–071*
Young v Ladies Imperial Club Ltd [1920] 2 K.B. 523, CA; reversing [1920] 1 K.B. 81, KBD *9–075, 27–023, 27–072*
Young v Lauretani [2007] EWHC 1244 (Ch); [2007] 2 F.L.R. 1211; [2008] 1 F.C.R. 669; [2007] Fam. Law 906; [2007] 2 P. & C.R. DG12, Ch D *4–064*
Young v Marshall (1831) 8 Bing. 43 .... *29–140*
Young v Peachy (1741) 2 Atk. 254 .... *7–074*

Young v Purdy [1996] 2 F.L.R. 795; [1997] 1 F.C.R. 632; [1997] P.N.L.R. 130; [1997] Fam. Law 93, CA (Civ Div) *26–037*
Young v Raincock (1849) 7 C.B. 310 .... *1–112*
Young v Robson Rhodes (A Firm) [1999] 3 All E.R. 524; [1999] Lloyd's Rep. P.N. 641, Ch D *27–022*, *27–023*, *27–066*
Young v Schuler (1882–83) L.R. 11 Q.B.D. 651, CA *12–114*, *12–116*
Young v Smith (1865–66) L.R. 1 Eq. 180, Ct of Chancery *12–066*
Young v Sun Alliance and London Insurance Ltd [1977] 1 W.L.R. 104; [1976] 3 All E.R. 561; [1976] 2 Lloyd's Rep. 189; (1976) 120 S.J. 469, CA (Civ Div) *14–146*
Young v Timmins (1831) 1 Cr. & J. 331 .... *16–115*, *27–068*
Young & Marten Ltd v McManus Childs Ltd; sub nom. Prior v McManus Childs Ltd [1969] 1 A.C. 454; [1968] 3 W.L.R. 630; [1968] 2 All E.R. 1169; 67 L.G.R. 1; (1968) 112 S.J. 744, HL; affirming [1967] 3 All E.R. 451, CA (Civ Div) *13–009*, *13–030*
Youngmin v Heath [1974] 1 W.L.R. 135; [1974] 1 All E.R. 461; (1973) 26 P. & C.R. 570; (1973) 117 S.J. 795, CA (Civ Div) *20–005*, *20–008*, *23–037*
Yrazu v Astral Shipping Co (1904) 20 T.L.R. 153 .... *14–148*
Yuen Kun Yeu v Attorney General of Hong Kong [1988] A.C. 175; [1987] 3 W.L.R. 776; [1987] 2 All E.R. 705; [1987] F.L.R. 291; (1987) 84 L.S.G. 2049; (1987) 137 N.L.J. 566; (1987) 131 S.J. 1185, PC (HK) *1–176*, *18–036*
Yukong Line Ltd of Korea v Rendsburg Investments Corp of Liberia; The Rialto (Preliminary Issues) [1996] 2 Lloyd's Rep. 604, QBD (Comm) *24–003*, *24–004*, *24–007*, *24–008*
Zakhem International Construction Ltd v Nippon Kokkan KK (No.1) [1987] 2 Lloyd's Rep. 596, CA (Civ Div); affirming, *The Times*, May 12, 1987, QBD *2–158*, *2–186*
Zambia Steel & Building Supplies Ltd v James Clark & Eaton Ltd [1986] 2 Lloyd's Rep. 225, CA (Civ Div) *2–037*
Zamet v Hyman [1961] 1 W.L.R. 1442; [1961] 3 All E.R. 933; (1961) 105 S.J. 911, CA *7–077*
Zamir v Secretary of State for the Home Department; sub nom. R. v Secretary of State for the Home Department Ex p. Zamir [1980] A.C. 930; [1980] 3 W.L.R. 249; [1980] 2 All E.R. 768; [1980] Crim. L.R. 647; (1980) 124 S.J. 527, HL; affirming [1980] Q.B. 378; [1980] 2 W.L.R. 357; [1980] 1 All E.R. 1041; (1980) 124 S.J. 204, CA (Civ Div); affirming [1979] Q.B. 688; [1979] 3 W.L.R. 89; [1979] 2 All E.R. 849; [1979] Crim. L.R. 391; (1979) 123 S.J. 455, QBD *16–015*
Zanzibar v British Aerospace (Lancaster House) Ltd [2000] 1 W.L.R. 2333; [2000] C.L.C. 735, QBD (Comm) 6–098, *6–138*, *12–104*
Zealander v Laing Homes Ltd (2000) 2 T.C.L.R. 724, QBD (TCC) 15–020, 15–094
Zebrarise Ltd v De Nieffe [2004] EWHC 1842; [2005] 2 All E.R. (Comm) 816; [2005] 1 Lloyd's Rep. 154, QBD (Comm) *30–012*, *30–038*, *30–339*, *30–347*
Zeus Tradition Marine Ltd v Bell; The Zeus V [2000] 2 All E.R. (Comm) 769; [2000] 2 Lloyd's Rep. 587; [2000] C.L.C. 1705, CA (Civ Div); reversing [1999] 1 Lloyd's Rep. 703; [1999] C.L.C. 391, QBD (Comm) *12–050*, *12–055*, *12–060*, *12–118*, *12–121*, *12–125*
Zim Israel Navigation Co Ltd v Effy Shipping Corp [1972] 1 Lloyd's Rep. 18, QBD (Comm) *21–056*
Zim Properties Ltd v Procter (Inspector of Taxes); sub nom. Procter (Inspector of Taxes) v Zim Properties [1985] S.T.C. 90; 58 T.C. 371; (1985) 82 L.S.G. 124; (1985) 129 S.J. 323; (1985) 129 S.J. 68, Ch D *26–166*
Zinc Corp Ltd v Hirsch [1916] 1 K.B. 541, CA *14–148*
Zivnostenska Banka National Corp v Frankman; sub nom. Frankman v Prague Credit Bank [1950] A.C. 57; [1949] 2 All E.R. 671, HL; reversing [1949] 1 K.B. 199; [1948] 2 All E.R. 1025; (1948) 92 S.J. 705, CA; reversing [1948] 1 K.B. 730, KBD *16–027*, *23–029*, *30–009*, *30–012*, *30–015*, *30–356*, *30–364*, *30–365*, *30–367*
Zoan v Rouamba [2000] 1 W.L.R. 1509; [2000] 2 All E.R. 620; [2000] C.C.L.R. 18; (2000) 150 N.L.J. 99, CA (Civ Div) *5–117*, *12–093*

Zockoll Group Ltd v Mercury Communications Ltd (No.2) [1999] E.M.L.R. 385; [1998] I.T.C.L.R. 104, CA (Civ Div) *14–073*, *14–093*
Zoernsch v Waldock [1964] 1 W.L.R. 675; [1964] 2 All E.R. 256; (1964) 108 S.J. 278, CA *11–014*
Zouch d Abbot and Hallet v Parsons, 97 E.R. 1103; (1765) 3 Burr. 1794, KB *8–058*, *8–066*, *8–067*
Zucker v Tyndall Holdings Plc [1992] 1 W.L.R. 1127; [1993] 1 All E.R. 124; [1993] I.L.Pr. 434, CA (Civ Div) *27–078*
Zuhal K, The and Selin, The [1987] 1 Lloyd's Rep. 151; [1987] 1 F.T.L.R. 76, QBD (Admlty) *29–099*, *29–112*, *29–119*, *29–131*
Zuiho Maru, The. *See* Kawasaki Steel Corp v Sardoil SpA

TABLE OF EUROPEAN COMMUNITY CASES

Where a reference indicates significant discussion of the legislation in the text, it is in **bold**. Where a reference is to a footnote, it is *italic*.

Al-Adsani v United Kingdom (2002) 34 E.H.R.R. 273, ECHR *11–003*
Alrosa Co Ltd v Commission of the European Communities (T–170/06) [2007] 5 C.M.L.R. 7, CFI *1–013*, *1–018*
Amministrazione delle Finanze dello Stato v San Giorgio SpA (199/82) [1983] E.C.R. 3595; [1985] 2 C.M.L.R. 658, ECJ *29–083*, *29–086*
Arblade. *See* Criminal Proceedings against Arblade (C–369/96)
Arcado SPRL v Haviland SA (9/87) [1988] E.C.R. 1539; [1989] E.C.C. 1, ECJ *15–034*, *30–031*, *30–336*
Bamberski v Krombach (C–7/98); sub nom. Krombach v Bamberski (C–7/98) [2001] Q.B. 709; [2001] 3 W.L.R. 488; [2001] All E.R. (EC) 584; [2000] E.C.R. I–1935; [2001] I.L.Pr. 36, ECJ *15–081*, *30–070*, *30–366*, *30–368*
Benincasa v Dentalkit Srl (C–269/95) [1998] All E.R. (EC) 135; [1997] E.C.R. I–3767; [1997] E.T.M.R. 447; [1997] I.L.Pr. 559, ECJ 15–029, 15–030, *30–093*, *30–240*
Beyeler v Italy (2001) 33 E.H.R.R. 1224, ECHR *10–033*
Blanckaert and Willems PVBA v Trost (C–139/80) [1981] E.C.R. 819; [1982] 2 C.M.L.R. 1, ECJ *30–242*
Brenner v Dean Witter Reynolds Inc (C–318/93) [1995] All E.R. (E.C.) 278; [1994] E.C.R. I–4275; [1994] I.L.Pr. 720, ECJ *30–093*
Cape SNC v Idealservice Srl (C–541/99); Idealservice MN RE SAS v OMAI Srl (C–542/99) [2002] All E.R. (EC) 657; [2001] E.C.R. I–9049; [2003] 1 C.M.L.R. 42, ECJ *15–028*, *15–029*
Chacon Navas v Eurest Colectividades SA (C–13/05) [2007] All E.R. (EC) 59; [2006] E.C.R. I–6467; [2006] 3 C.M.L.R. 40; [2007] I.C.R. 1; [2006] I.R.L.R. 706, ECJ *27–074*
Cie Europeene des Petroles SA v Sensor Nederland BV. *See* Compagnie Europeene des Petroles SA v Sensor Nederland BV
Cofidis SA v Fredout (C–473/2000) [2002] E.C.R. I–10875 ...... *15–114*, 15–117, *15–120*, *15–126*
Commission of the European Communities v Spain (C–70/03) [2004] E.C.R. I–0799 .... *15–110*, *15–113*, *15–114*, *15–132*, *15–134*, *30–103*
Commission of the European Communities v Sweden (C–478/99) [2002] E.C.R. I–4147, ECJ *15–091*
Commission of the European Communities v United Kingdom (165/82); sub nom. Equal Treatment, Re (165/82) [1984] 1 All E.R. 353; [1983] E.C.R. 3431; [1984] 1 C.M.L.R. 44; [1984] I.C.R. 192; [1984] I.R.L.R. 29, ECJ *2–177*
Compagnie Europeene des Petroles SA v Sensor Nederland BV [1983] E.C.C. 532, RB (Den Haag) *30–361*
Concrete Reinforcement Bars, Re (154/78, 205/78, 206/78, 226/78, 227/78, 228/78, 263/78, 264/78, 31/79, 39/79, 83/79, 85/79); Forges de Thy-Marcinelle et Monceau SA v Commission of the European Communities (26/79 and 86/79); sub nom. Ferriera Valsabbia SpA v Commission of the European Communities (154/78) [1981] E.C.R. 907; [1980] E.C.R. 907; [1981] 1 C.M.L.R. 613, ECJ *14–149*
Cooperatieve Rabobank "Vecht en Plassengebied" BA v Minderhoud (C–104/96) [1998] 1 W.L.R. 1025; [1997] E.C.R. I–7211; [1998] 2 B.C.L.C. 507; [1998] 2 C.M.L.R. 270, ECJ *9–029*, *9–033*

Copland v United Kingdom (App. No.62617/00) (2007) 45 E.H.R.R. 37, ECHR *1–055*

Criminal Proceedings against Arblade (C–369/96); Criminal Proceedings against Leloup (C–376/96) [1999] E.C.R. I–8453; [2001] I.C.R. 434, ECJ *30–063*

Criminal Proceedings against Mazzoleni (C–165/98) [2001] E.C.R. I–2189; [2003] 2 C.M.L.R. 10, ECJ *30–108*

Dansommer A/S v Gotz (C–8/98) [2001] 1 W.L.R. 1069; [2000] E.C.R. I–393; [2001] I.L.Pr. 28, ECJ *30–084*

De Jong Verenigde v VIB. *See* NV de Jong Verenigde et Cooperatieve Melkprodukten Bedrijven domo-bedum ga v Voedselvoorzienings In- en Verkoopbureau (Vib) (20/84)

De Landtsheer Emmanuel SA v Comite Interprofessionnel du Vin de Champagne (C–381/05) [2007] Bus. L.R. 1484; [2007] 2 C.M.L.R. 43; [2007] E.T.M.R. 69-, ECJ *15–031*

Decker v Caisse de Maladie des Employes Prives (C–120/95); Kohll v Union des Caisses de Maladie (C–158/96) [1998] All E.R. (E.C.) 673; [1998] E.C.R. I–1831; [1998] 2 C.M.L.R. 879; (1999) 48 B.M.L.R. 32, ECJ *15–081*

Denkavit International BV v Bundesamt fur Finanzen (C–283/94) [1996] S.T.C. 1445; [1996] E.C.R. I–5063, ECJ *15–036*

Easycar (UK) Ltd v Office of Fair Trading (C–336/03) [2005] All E.R. (EC) 834; [2005] E.C.R. I–1947; [2005] 2 C.M.L.R. 2; [2005] C.E.C. 577, ECJ *15–048*, *15–056*

Eco Swiss China Time Ltd v Benetton International NV (C–126/97) [1999] 2 All E.R. (Comm) 44; [1999] E.C.R. I–3055; [1999] U.K.C.L.R. 183; [2000] 5 C.M.L.R. 816, ECJ *15–118*

Edwards v Malta (App. No. 17647/04), 2000 .... *1–013*

Engler v Janus Versand GmbH (C–27/02) [2005] E.C.R. I–481; [2005] C.E.C. 187; [2005] I.L.Pr. 8, ECJ *30–093*

Estee Lauder Cosmetics GmbH & Co OHG v Lancaster Group GmbH (C–220/98) [2000] All E.R. (EC) 122; [2000] E.C.R. I–117; [2000] 1 C.M.L.R. 515; [2000] C.E.C. 317, ECJ *15–031*

Eurofood IFSC Ltd, Re (C–341/04); sub nom. Bondi v Bank of America NA (C–341/04) [2006] Ch. 508; [2006] 3 W.L.R. 309; [2006] All E.R. (EC) 1078; [2006] E.C.R. I–3813; [2006] B.C.C. 397; [2007] 2 B.C.L.C. 151; [2006] I.L.Pr. 23; [2006] B.P.I.R. 661, ECJ *30–070*, *30–366*, *30–368*

Faccini Dori v Recreb Srl (C–91/92) [1995] All E.R. (E.C.) 1; [1994] E.C.R. I–3325; [1995] 1 C.M.L.R. 665, ECJ *15–014*

Finalarte Sociedade de Construcao Civil Lda v Urlaubs- und Lohnausgleichskasse der Bauwirtschaft (C–49/98); Portugaia Construcoes Lda v Urlaubs- und Lohnausgleichskasse der Bauwirtschaft (C–70/98); Engil Sociedade de Construcao Civil SA v Urlaubs- und Lohnausgleichskasse der Bauwirtschaft (C–71/98); Urlaubs- und Lohnausgleichskasse der Bauwirtschaft v Amilcar Oliveira Rocha (C–50/98); Urlaubs- und Lohnausgleichskasse der Bauwirtschaft v Tudor Stone Ltd (C–52/98); Urlaubs- und Lohnausgleichskasse der Bauwirtschaft v Tecnamb-Tecnologia do Ambiante Lda (C–53/98); Urlaubs- und Lohnausgleichskasse der Bauwirtschaft v Turiprata Construcoes Civil SA (C–54/98); Urlaubs- und Lohnausgleichskasse der Bauwirtschaft v Duarte dos Santos Sousa (C–68/98); Urlaubs- und Lohnausgleichskasse der Bauwirtschaft v Santos & Kewitz Construcoes Lda (C–69/98) [2001] E.C.R. I–7831; [2003] 2 C.M.L.R. 11, ECJ *30–108*

Fogarty v United Kingdom (2002) 34 E.H.R.R. 302, ECHR *11–003*, *11–005*

Fonderie Officine Meccaniche Tacconi SpA v Heinrich Wagner Sinto Maschinenfabrik GmbH (HWS) (C–334/00) [2002] E.C.R. I–7357, ECJ *30–031*

Foster v British Gas Plc (C–188/89) [1991] 1 Q.B. 405; [1991] 2 W.L.R. 258; [1990] 3 All E.R. 897; [1990] E.C.R. I–3313; [1990] 2 C.M.L.R. 833; [1991] I.C.R. 84; [1990] I.R.L.R. 353, ECJ *15–014*

France v Di Pinto (C–361/89) [1991] E.C.R. I–1189; [1993] 1 C.M.L.R. 399, ECJ 15–029, 15–030

Freiburger Kommunalbauten GmbH Baugesellschaft & Co KG v Hofstetter (C–237/02) [2004] E.C.R. I–3403; [2004] 2 C.M.L.R. 13, ECJ 15–019, 15–115

Gabriel v Schlank & Schick GmbH (C–96/00); sub nom. Gabriel, Re (C–96/00); Gabriel v Schlanck & Schick GmbH (C–96/00) [2002] E.C.R. I–6367; [2002] I.L.Pr. 36, ECJ *30–093*, *30–094*, *30–240*
Gaillard v Chekili (C–518/99) [2001] E.C.R. I–2771; [2001] I.L.Pr. 33, ECJ ... *30–082*
Greek Refineries & Stratis Andreadis v Greece (App. No.13427/87). *See* Stran Greek Refineries v Greece (A/301-B)
Gruber v Bay Wa AG (C–464/01) [2006] Q.B. 204; [2006] 2 W.L.R. 205; [2005] E.C.R. I–439; [2005] I.L.Pr. 12, ECJ 15–029, *30–093*, *30–240*
Gut Springenheide GmbH v Oberkreisdirektor des Kreises Steinfurt - Amt fur Lebensmitteluberwachung (C–210/96) [1998] E.C.R. I–4657; [1999] 1 C.M.L.R. 1383, ECJ *15–031*
Halford v United Kingdom (App. No.20605/92) [1997] I.R.L.R. 471; (1997) 24 E.H.R.R. 523; 3 B.H.R.C. 31; [1998] Crim. L.R. 753; (1997) 94(27) L.S.G. 24, ECHR *1–055*
Hamilton v Volksbank Filder eG (412/06) *15–014*, *15–126*
Hoekstra (née Unger) v Bestuur der Bedrijfsvereniging voor Detailhandel en Ambachten (C–75/63). *See* Unger v Bestuur der Bedrijfsvereniging voor Detailhandel en Ambachten (75/63)
Hutten-Czapska v Poland (35014/97) (2006) 42 E.H.R.R. 15; 19 B.H.R.C. 373, ECHR *1–013*
Ingmar GB Ltd v Eaton Leonard Technologies Inc (C–381/98) [2001] All E.R. (EC) 57; [2001] 1 All E.R. (Comm) 329; [2000] E.C.R. I–9305; [2001] 1 C.M.L.R. 9, ECJ *30–042*, *30–065*, *30–068*, *30–179*, *30–242*
Internationale Handelsgesellschaft mbH v Einfuhr- und Vorratsstelle fur Getreide und Futtermittel (11/70); Einfuhr und Vorratsstelle fur Getreide und Futtermittel v Firma Koster, Berodt & Co (25/70); Einfuhr und Vorratsstelle fur Getreide und Futtermittel v Firma Gunther Henck (26/70); Firma Ottoscheer v Einfuhr und Vorratsstelle fur Getreide und Futtermittel (30/70) [1970] E.C.R. 1125; [1972] C.M.L.R. 255, ECJ *14–149*
Ivenel v Schwab (133/81) [1982] E.C.R. 1891; [1983] 1 C.M.L.R. 538, ECJ *30–019*, *30–110*
JA Pye (Oxford) Ltd v United Kingdom (App. No.44302/02) (2006) 43 E.H.R.R. 3; 19 B.H.R.C. 705; [2005] 3 E.G.L.R. 1; [2005] 49 E.G. 90; [2006] R.V.R. 188; [2005] 47 E.G. 145 (C.S.); [2005] N.P.C. 135, ECHR *1–047*
Jakob Handte & Co GmbH v Societe Traitments Mecano-Chimiques des Surfaces (TMCS) (C–26/91) [1992] E.C.R. I–3967; [1993] I.L.Pr. 5, ECJ *1–007*, *1–168*, *15–034*, *15–035*
Kalfelis v Bankhaus Schröder Munchmeyer Hengst & Co (t/a HEMA Beteiligungsgesellschaft mbH) (189/87) [1988] E.C.R. 5565; [1989] E.C.C. 407, ECJ *1–007*, 1–168, *30–032*, *30–287*
Kapniki Michailidis AE v Idrima Kinonikon Asphaliseon (IKA) (C–441/98); sub nom. Kapniki Mikhailidis AE v Idrima Kinonikon Asphaliseon (IKA) (C–441/98) [2000] E.C.R. I–7145; [2001] 1 C.M.L.R. 13, ECJ *29–086*
Klein v Rhodos Management Ltd (C–73/04) [2005] E.C.R. I–8667; [2006] I.L.Pr. 2, ECJ *30–084*
Kleinwort Benson Ltd v Glasgow City Council (C–346/93); sub nom. Kleinwort Benson Ltd v City of Glasgow DC (C–346/93) [1996] Q.B. 57; [1995] 3 W.L.R. 866; [1995] All E.R. (E.C.) 514; [1995] E.C.R. I–615; [1996] 5 Bank. L.R. 140; [1995] I.L.Pr. 393, ECJ *30–025*
Krombach v Bamberski (C–7/98). *See* Bamberski v Krombach (C–7/98)
Kyocera Electronics GmbH v Hauptzollamt Krefeld (C–152/01) [2003] E.C.R. I–13821, ECJ *15–007*
Lechouritou v Germany (C–292/05); sub nom. Lechouritou v Dimosio tis Omospondiakis Dimokratias tis Germanias (C–292/05) [2007] All E.R. (EC) 1177; [2007] 2 All E.R. (Comm) 57; [2007] I.L.Pr. 14; [2007] I.L.Pr. 216, ECJ *11–003*
Leloup. *See* Criminal Proceedings against Arblade (C–369/96)
Lidl Belgium GmbH & Co KG v Etablissementen Franz Colruyt NV (C–356/04) [2007] Bus. L.R. 492; [2006] E.C.R. I–8501; [2007] 1 C.M.L.R. 9; [2007] C.E.C. 3; [2007] E.T.M.R. 28, ECJ *15–031*

Marks & Spencer Plc v Customs and Excise Commissioners (C–309/06) [2008] S.T.I. 1194, ECJ *29–014*, *29–086*
Marleasing SA v La Comercial Internacional de Alimentacion SA (C–106/89) [1990] E.C.R. I–4135; [1993] B.C.C. 421; [1992] 1 C.M.L.R. 305, ECJ *15–007*, 15–013
Marshall v Southampton and South West Hampshire AHA (152/84) [1986] Q.B. 401; [1986] 2 W.L.R. 780; [1986] 2 All E.R. 584; [1986] E.C.R. 723; [1986] 1 C.M.L.R. 688; [1986] I.C.R. 335; [1986] I.R.L.R. 140; (1986) 83 L.S.G. 1720; (1986) 130 S.J. 340, ECJ *15–014*
Martin Peters Bauunternehmung GmbH v Zuid Nederlandse Aannemers Vereniging (C–34/82) [1983] E.C.R. 987; [1984] 2 C.M.L.R. 605, ECJ *15–034*, *30–031*
Masdar (UK) Ltd v Commission of the European Communities (T–333/03) [2007] 2 All E.R. (Comm) 261, CFI *15–014*
Mazzoleni and Inter Surveillance Assistance SARL. *See* Criminal Proceedings against Mazzoleni (C–165/98)
McElhinney v Ireland (2002) 34 E.H.R.R. 322, ECHR *11–003*
Metallgesellschaft Ltd v Inland Revenue Commissioners (C–397/98); Hoechst AG v Inland Revenue Commissioners (C–410/98) [2001] Ch. 620; [2001] 2 W.L.R. 1497; [2001] All E.R. (EC) 496; [2001] S.T.C. 452; [2001] E.C.R. I–1727; [2001] 2 C.M.L.R. 32; [2001] B.T.C. 99; 3 I.T.L. Rep. 385; [2001] S.T.I. 498, ECJ *29–083*
Mietz v Intership Yachting Sneek BV (C–99/96) [1999] E.C.R. I–2277; [1999] I.L.Pr. 541, ECJ *30–093*
Mostaza Claro v Centro Movil Milenium SL (C–168/05) [2007] Bus. L.R. 60; [2006] E.C.R. I–10421; [2007] 1 C.M.L.R. 22; [2007] C.E.C. 290, ECJ 15–081, *15–094*, *15–114*, *15–115*, 15–117, *15–118*, *15–120*, *15–126*, *30–103*
Mulox IBC Ltd v Geels (C–125/92) [1993] E.C.R. I–4075; [1993] I.L.Pr. 668; [1994] I.R.L.R. 422, ECJ *30–107*, *30–112*
Netherlands v Ruffer (C–814/79) [1980] E.C.R. 3807; [1981] 3 C.M.L.R. 293, ECJ *1–168*
NV de Jong Verenigde et Cooperatieve Melkprodukten Bedrijven domo-bedum ga v Voedselvoorzienings In- en Verkoopbureau (Vib) (20/84) [1985] E.C.R. 2061, ECJ *14–149*
Océano Grupo Editorial SA v Quintero (C–240/98); Salvat Editores SA v Prades (C–241/98); Salvat Editores SA v Badillo (C–242/98); Salvat Editores SA v Berroane (C–243/98); Salvat Editores SA v Feliu (C–244/98) [2000] E.C.R. I–4941; [2002] 1 C.M.L.R. 43, ECJ *15–095*, *15–114*, 15–115, 15–117, *15–118*, *15–120*, *15–126*, *30–103*
Parking Brixen GmbH v Gemeinde Brixen (C–458/03) [2006] All E.R. (EC) 779; [2005] E.C.R. I–8612; [2006] 1 C.M.L.R. 3; [2006] C.E.C. 144, ECJ *1–069*
Partenreederei M/S Tilly Russ v Haven & Vervoerbedrijf Nova (71/83) [1985] Q.B. 931; [1985] 3 W.L.R. 179; [1984] E.C.R. 2417; [1984] 3 C.M.L.R. 499; (1985) 82 L.S.G. 2905; (1985) 129 S.J. 483, ECJ *12–011*
Peters v ZNAV. *See* Martin Peters Bauunternehmung GmbH v Zuid Nederlandse Aannemers Vereniging (C–34/82)
Pine Valley Developments v Ireland (A/222) (1992) 14 E.H.R.R. 319, ECHR *10–033*
Pippig Augenoptik GmbH & Co KG v Hartlauer Handelsgesellschaft mbH (C–44/01) [2004] All E.R. (EC) 1156; [2003] E.C.R. I–3095; [2004] 1 C.M.L.R. 39; [2004] E.T.M.R. 5, ECJ *15–031*
Portugaia Construcoes Lda, Re (C–164/99) [2002] E.C.R. I–787; [2003] 2 C.M.L.R. 35, ECJ *30–108*
Pugliese v Finmeccanica SpA (C–437/00) [2004] All E.R. (EC) 154; [2003] E.C.R. I–3573; [2003] C.E.C. 310; [2003] I.L.Pr. 21, ECJ *30–110*, *30–119*
Regie Nationale des Usines Renault SA v Maxicar SpA (C–38/98) [2000] E.C.R. I–2973; [2000] E.C.D.R. 415; (2000) 23(7) I.P.D. 23050, ECJ *30–070*, *30–366*, *30–368*
Remia BV and Verenigde Bedrijven Nutricia NV v Commission of the European Communities (C–42/84) [1985] E.C.R. 2545; [1987] 1 C.M.L.R. 1; [1987] F.S.R. 190, ECJ *16–116*

Rewe-Zentral AG v Bundesmonopolverwaltung fur Branntwein (120/78); sub nom. Cassis de Dijon (120/78), Re [1979] E.C.R. 649; [1979] 3 C.M.L.R. 494, ECJ *15–040*
Rutten v Cross Medical Ltd (C–383/95) [1997] All E.R. (EC) 121; [1997] E.C.R. I–57; [1997] I.L.Pr. 199; [1997] I.C.R. 715; [1997] I.R.L.R. 249, ECJ *30–110*, *30–119*
Sanders v Van der Putte (73/77) [1977] E.C.R. 2383; [1978] 1 C.M.L.R. 331, ECJ *30–084*
Schulte v Deutsche Bausparkasse Badenia AG (C–350/03) [2006] All E.R. (EC) 420; [2005] E.C.R. I–9215; [2006] 1 C.M.L.R. 11; [2006] C.E.C. 115, ECJ *30–103*
Schwarzwaldmilch GmbH v Einfuhr- und Vorratsstelle fur Fette (4/68) [1968] E.C.R. 377; [1969] C.M.L.R. 406, ECJ *14–149*
Shearson Lehmann Hutton Inc v TVB Treithandgesellschaft fur Vermogensverwaltung und Beteiligungen mbH (C–89/91) [1993] E.C.R. I–139; [1993] I.L.Pr. 199, ECJ *15–029, 30–093*, *30–240*
Shenavai v Kreischer (266/85) [1987] E.C.R. 239; [1987] 3 C.M.L.R. 782, ECJ *30–110*, *30–201*
Soc Handte et Cie GmbH v TMCS [1992] E.C.R. I–3967 .... *30–031*
Societe Bertrand v Paul Ott KG (C–150/77) [1978] E.C.R. 1431; [1978] 3 C.M.L.R. 499, ECJ *30–093*
Société thermale d'Eugénie-les-Bains v Ministère de l'Economie, des Finances et de l'Industrie (C–277/05) [2007] E.C.R. I–6415 .... *1–013*
Spain v Commission of the European Communities (C–240/97) [1999] E.C.R. I–6571, ECJ *1–013*
Sporrong & Lönnroth v Sweden (A/52) (1983) 5 E.H.R.R. 35, ECHR *1–047*
Stran Greek Refineries v Greece (A/301-B) (1995) 19 E.H.R.R. 293, ECHR *1–045*
Stretch v United Kingdom (App. No.44277/98) (2004) 38 E.H.R.R. 12; [2004] B.L.G.R. 401; [2004] 1 E.G.L.R. 11; [2004] 03 E.G. 100; [2003] 29 E.G. 118 (C.S.); [2003] N.P.C. 125, ECHR *1–045*, 1–046, *1–047*, *10–033*
Swaddling v Adjudication Officer (C–90/97) [1999] All E.R. (EC) 217; [1999] E.C.R. I–1075; [1999] 2 C.M.L.R. 679; [1999] C.E.C. 184; [1999] 2 F.L.R. 184; [1999] Fam. Law 382, ECJ *30–078*
Travel Vac SL v Sanchis (C–423/97) .....[1999] All E.R. (EC) 656; [1999] E.C.R. I–2195; [1999] 2 C.M.L.R. 1111; (1999) 96(31) L.S.G. 43, ECJ *30–103*
Unger v Bestuur der Bedrijfsvereniging voor Detailhandel en Ambachten (75/63) [1964] E.C.R. 177; [1964] C.M.L.R. 319, ECJ *1–008*
Van der Weerd v Minister van Landbouw, Natuur en Voedselkwaliteit (C–222/05) [2007] 3 C.M.L.R. 7, ECJ *15–118*
Veedfald v Århus Amtskommune (C–203/99) [2001] E.C.R. I–3569; [2003] 1 C.M.L.R. 41; (2002) 66 B.M.L.R. 1, ECJ 15–024, *15–025, 15–048, 15–056, 15–126*
Verein fur Konsumenteninformation v Henkel (C–167/00) [2003] All E.R. (EC) 311; [2003] 1 All E.R. (Comm) 606; [2002] E.C.R. I–8111; [2003] I.L.Pr. 1, ECJ *30–240*
Von Colson v Land Nordrhein-Westfahlen (C–14/83); Harz v Deutsche Tradax GmbH (C–79/83) [1984] E.C.R. 1891; [1986] 2 C.M.L.R. 430, ECJ *15–007*
Waite v Germany (App No.26083/94) (2000) 30 E.H.R.R. 261; 6 B.H.R.C. 499, ECHR *11–018*
Weber v Universal Ogden Services Ltd (C–37/00) [2002] Q.B. 1189; [2002] 3 W.L.R. 931; [2002] All E.R. (EC) 397; [2002] E.C.R. I–2013; [2002] I.L.Pr. 23; [2002] I.C.R. 979; [2002] I.R.L.R. 365, ECJ *30–110*, *30–119*
Weber's Wine World Handels GmbH v Abgabenberufungskommission Wien (C–147/01) [2005] All E.R. (EC) 224; [2003] E.C.R. I–11365; [2004] 1 C.M.L.R. 7; [2003] C.E.C. 501; [2004] B.T.C. 8019, ECJ *29–086*

Part One
INTRODUCTION

CHAPTER 1

INTRODUCTORY

	PARA.
1. Definitions of contract	1–001
2. Fundamental principles of contract law	1–010
(a) Freedom of contract	1–011
(b) The binding force of contract	1–019
(c) A principle of good faith or contractual fairness?	1–022
3. The Human Rights Act 1998 and contracts	1–035
(a) Contracts made before October 2, 2000	1–037
(i) The construction and review of legislation governing contracts	1–037
(ii) Contracts made by "public authorities"	1–039
(iii) The duty of courts as "public authorities" in relation to contracts	1–043
(b) Contracts made on or after October 2, 2000	1–044
(i) The construction and review of legislation governing contracts	1–044
(ii) Contracts made by "public authorities"	1–050
(iii) The duty of courts as "public authorities" in relation to contracts	1–058
(iv) Contractual confidentiality and section 12 of the 1998 Act	1–065
4. Classification of contracts	1–067
(a) Classification of contracts according to their subject matter	1–068
(b) Classification of contracts according to their parties	1–073
(c) Classification of contracts according to their form or means of formation	1–074
(d) Classification of contracts according to their effect	1–078
5. Contracts contained in deeds	1–085
(a) General	1–085
(b) Intention, form and delivery	1–089
(i) deeds executed on or after July 31, 1989 and before or on September 14, 2005	1–090
(ii) deeds executed on or after September 15, 2005	1–095
(iii) common aspects	1–102
(c) Consideration	1–108
(c) Other aspects	1–109
6. The relationship between contract and tort	1–117
(a) The classification of the forms of action at common law	1–118
(b) Differences of substance between contract and tort	1–119
(c) Concurrence of actions in contract and tort	1–126
(i) Pre-contractual liability	1–131
(ii) Torts committed in the course of performance of a contract	1–137
(d) The influence of contract on tort beyond privity	1–170
7. Contract and other legal categories	1–188

1. DEFINITIONS OF CONTRACT

1–001 **Competing definitions of contract.** There are two main competing definitions of a contract in the common law. The first, which was adopted by the 26th edn of this work, defines a contract as a promise or set of promises which the law will enforce.[1] The competing view, which was taken by the 2nd edn of this work,[2] is that a "contract is an agreement giving rise to obligations which are enforced or recognised by law".[3]

There are two main arguments in favour of the definition of contract in terms of promise. First, the idea of contracts as being based on agreement was introduced into English legal discussions only in the nineteenth century, in particular under the influence of Pothier's *Treatise on Obligations*[4] and does not accord with the raw material of the common law, in particular in relation to the requirement of consideration.[5] For English law does not in general enforce gratuitous promises, the element of non-gratuity being expressed technically by the requirement that some consideration must move from the promisee and in lay terms that it enforces bargains rather than agreements.[6] Moreover, it is in relation to the requirement of consideration that modern usage most readily relies on the language of promise: what is required is consideration for a party's *promise*, not consideration for the parties' *agreement*.[7] Finally, one of the justifications for the enforcement of contracts is said to lie in the moral obligation of a party to perform his promise.[8]

1–002 **Difficulties with "contract as promise".** However, analysis of contracts in terms of an enforceable promise or sets of enforceable promises is not entirely satisfactory. First, outside the context of consideration, in general neither courts

---

[1] *Chitty on Contracts*, 26th edn (1989), Vol.I, para.1; Pollock, *Principles of Contract*, 13th edn (1950), p.1; cf. Pollock, *Principles*, 1st edn (1876), p.5. The American Law Institute's *Restatement of Contracts*, 2nd edn, para.1, adopts substantially the same definition.

[2] Chitty, *A Practical Treatise on the Law of Contracts* (1834), pp.1–2.

[3] Treitel, *The Law of Contract*, 12th edn (2007 by Peel), para.1–001.

[4] Pothier, *Treatise on Obligations* (trans. Evans, 1806) and see Simpson (1975) 91 L.Q.R. 247, 257–262; Atiyah, *The Rise and Fall of Freedom of Contract* (1979), p.399; Gordley, *The Philosophical Origins of Modern Contract Doctrine* (1991), Ch.6.

[5] cf. Nicholas, *The French Law of Contract*, 2nd edn (1992), p.144.

[6] According to the *Restatement of Contracts* at para.3, a bargain is an agreement, whereby two or more persons exchange promises, or exchange a promise for a performance. However, the word "bargain" is seldom used in any technical sense in the law of contract: Atiyah, *Essays on Contract* (1986), Essay 8, p.207; and see Eisenberg (1982) 95 H.L.R. 741. It is sometimes said that the requirement of consideration means that contracts are *exchanges*. This suggests some element of reciprocity between the parties to the contract and while this is often the case, a promise by A to do work for B can support a promise by C of payment for it: see below, para.3–005 According to Gordley at pp.137–139, the systematisation of the doctrine of consideration took place at the same time as the acceptance of civilian theories of contract and was intended to act as a control device on the ambit of contract.

[7] See below, para.3–001.

[8] Goodhart, *English Law and the Moral Law* (1953), p.101; Fried, *Contract as Promise* (1983); Harris (1983) 3 Int. Rev. Law & Econ. 69; Burrows (1985) C.L.P. 141. cf. Atiyah (1978) 94 L.Q.R. 193; *Promises, Morals and Law* (1981); *Essays on Contract* (1986), Essays 2 and 6; Raz in Hacker and Raz (eds), *Law, Morality and Society* (1977), Ch.12; Smith, *Contract Theory* (2004), Chs 2–4.

nor parties to contracts describe the relationships which they create in terms of promises, but rather in terms of agreements, and for the courts this is clearest in the context of the rules as to offer and acceptance which when satisfied form that agreement.[9] Moreover, as will be described later, the doctrine of consideration to which the "promise theory" is so closely related, is somewhat under siege: from the legislature, since the enactment of the Contracts (Rights of Third Parties) Act 1999 has limited its traditional domain,[10] and from the courts, notably in the decision in *Williams v Roffey Bros & Nicholls (Contractors) Ltd*.[11] Secondly, definition of contracts in terms of sets of promises does not give full force to the interrelationship of the obligations of the parties which exists in many contracts,[12] an interrelationship which can be seen particularly in the availability of the remedy of termination for substantial failure in performance, by which an injured party may terminate his own obligations by reason of the failure of the other party to perform his side of the bargain.[13]

Difficulties with "contract as agreement". However, an understanding of modern contracts as agreements does not fit easily with two recognised types of contract. First, in the case of a unilateral contract[14] where A promises to do something if B does something else, the performance by B of the condition is enough for A to be bound. Here, analysis in terms of doing something of value in return for a promise fits more naturally than does the construction of an acceptance by B's performance of the condition of A's promise.[15] Secondly, promises contained in deeds[16] are enforceable by the person in whose favour they are made, whether or not that person is aware of them[17] and so while a deed may give contractual force to an agreement, agreement is unnecessary for the enforcement of the promises which it contains. And, for Pollock, writing in 1885, the position of contracts under seal made it difficult for him to accept that "proposal 1–003

[9] See below, Ch.2.

[10] And see The Law Commission, *Privity of Contract: Contracts for the Benefit of Third Parties*, Law Com. No.242 (1996), para.6.8 and below, Ch.18.

[11] *William v Roffey Bros Nicholls (Contractors) Ltd* [1991] 1 Q.B. 1 and see below, para.3–068.

[12] cf. Atiyah, *An Introduction to the Law of Contract*, 5th edn (1995), pp.38–39.

[13] See below, paras 24–034—24–046. This is not to say that the availability of this remedy cannot be expressed in terms of independent or dependent promises, but the term "promise" here is used synonymously with that of obligation and can apply to obligations imposed on a contractor by law, which are not a matter of "promise" at all. Thus, a buyer of goods can terminate the contract, and thereby extinguish his own obligation to pay the price, for breach of the term that they are of satisfactory quality, a term imposed by s.14 of the Sale of Goods Act 1979 on sellers selling goods in the course of business (and not capable of exclusion as against a buyer dealing as consumer: Unfair Contract Terms Act 1977 s.6(2)) and see Vol.II, paras 43–104 et seq.

[14] See below, para.1–079.

[15] There is some doubt as to whether an offeree of a unilateral offer must be aware of that offer on performance of the condition for a contract to arise: see below, para.2–039. If the offeree need not be so aware, then no agreement can be constructed from performance of the condition. It is clear that the offeree of a unilateral offer does not in general have to communicate his acceptance to the offeror before he fulfills the condition and the contract arises: *Carlill v Carbolic Smoke Ball Co* [1893] 1 Q.B. 256, and see below, para.2–045.

[16] After the abolition by the Law of Property (Miscellaneous Provisions) Act 1989 s.1(1) of the requirement of sealing for the validity of deeds made by individuals, it is more appropriate to refer to promises in deeds rather than the former "promises under seal": see below, paras 1–085 et seq.

[17] *Xenos v Wickham* (1866) L.R. 2 H.L. 296, 312; *Macedo v Stroud* [1922] 2 A.C. 330.

and acceptance [form] part of the general conception of contract".[18] For other writers, however, it has led instead to a denial that the binding force of a promise in a deed depends on contract at all.[19] Certainly, although it is true that the action to enforce promises made under seal, the action of covenant, was traditionally classified as arising *ex contractu*,[20] this classification cannot be treated as conclusive as to whether promises in deeds should be considered contractual, given that at the time other actions which are clearly not so considered were also included within this category (notably, actions for money had and received, which would now be understood as restitutionary[21] and actions for detinue whose function before their abolition was clearly proprietary).[22]

1–004 **Actual agreement not required.** Moreover, even though it is true that the existence of an agreement is in the vast majority of cases a condition for the existence of a contract not contained in a deed, this statement ought to be treated with some caution. First, the existence of an agreement is not an issue merely of fact, to be found by a psychological investigation of the parties at the time of its alleged origin: English law takes an "objective" rather than a "subjective" view of the existence of agreement[23] and so its starting-point is the manifestation of mutual assent by two or more persons to one another[24]:

> "Agreement is not a mental state but an act, and, as an act, is a matter of inference from conduct. The parties are to be judged, not by what is in their minds, but by what they have said or written or done."[25]

Moreover, for reasons of commercial convenience, the common law regulates what is to be treated as a manifestation of assent capable of giving rise to a contract in its rules relating to offer and acceptance.[26] For example, a posted acceptance of an offer is said to conclude a contract on posting, rather than on communication to the offeror, and so an acceptance lost in the post will bind the offeror.[27] Similarly, if A sends an offer to B by post, and then changes his mind and sends a letter revoking his offer, but B posts an acceptance of the offer after A posted his letter of revocation, but before B received it, there may be a

---

[18] Pollock, *Principles of Contract at Law and in Equity*, 4th edn (1885), p.9 and cf. p.5.

[19] Treitel, *The Law of Contract*, 12th edn (2007 by Peel), para.3–164.

[20] Bacon, *A New Abridgment of the Law*, 7th edn (1832), Vol.I, p.55 included debt, detinue, account, covenant, assumpsit, quantum meruit, *quantum valebat* and annuity in his treatment of actions *ex contractu*. cf. Chitty and Chitty, *A Treatise on the Parties to Actions and on Pleading*, 6th edn (1836), pp.98–125.

[21] See below, para.29–006; Birks, *An Introduction to the Law of Restitution* (1985), pp.29–39.

[22] Technically, detinue protected the plaintiff's right to possession of personal property. For further discussion of the classification of actions at common law, see below, para.1–118. Detinue was abolished by the Torts (Interference with Goods) Act 1977 s.2.

[23] Howarth (1984) 100 L.Q.R. 265 and 528; Vorster (1987) 103 L.Q.R. 274; Goddard (1987) 7 L.S. 263; de Moor (1990) 106 L.Q.R. 632 and see *The Hannah Blumenthal* [1983] 1 A.C. 854; *The Leonidas D.* [1985] 1 W.L.R. 925; Beatson (1986) 102 L.Q.R. 19; Atiyah (1986) 102 L.Q.R. 363 and below, para.2–002.

[24] *Restatement of Contracts* at para.3.

[25] Furmston, *Cheshire, Fifoot and Furmston's Law of Contract*, 15th edn (2007), p.38.

[26] See below, paras 2–002 et seq.

[27] *Household Fire Insurance Co v Grant* (1879) 3 Ex. D. 216, overruling *British and American Telegraph Co Ltd v Colson* (1871) L.R. 6 Ex. 108. See below, para.2–046.

contract, though the parties were never *ad idem*.[28] Another example of common law regulation of what constitutes an agreement may be found in the general rule that silence in an offeree cannot be treated as acceptance.[29]

Agreement and consideration not sufficient. Secondly, the presence of an agreement supported by consideration is not always sufficient to establish the existence of a contract. This is notably the case where the parties agree in circumstances in which it is considered inappropriate for the law to impose legal obligations, for example, in a social or domestic context, and is justified on the basis that the parties cannot be considered to have intended to create a legal relationship.[30] However, the courts have used the requirement that the parties must possess an intention to create legal relations to exclude other types of non-gratuitous agreement from the domain of contract.[31] Furthermore, even if a transaction fulfils these three conditions of agreement, consideration and an intention to create legal relations, it may be defeated by the presence of other factors such as the absence of a particular form,[32] mistake,[33] misrepresentation,[34] duress,[35] undue influence,[36] incapacity[37] or illegality.[38] Some of these factors will render the contract void,[39] others voidable,[40] and others still will render it unenforceable against one or both contracting parties.[41] 1–005

Enforcement of agreements under other rules. Thirdly, even though contracts are in general to be defined as agreements, this does not mean that all enforceable agreements (or enforceable promises) are contracts. This is particularly noticeable in relation to promissory and proprietary estoppel and constructive trust. In the case of promissory estoppel, A may be prevented from going back on a promise not to rely on his legal rights against B, subject to the condition that B has relied on A's promise (possibly, to B's detriment).[42] B does not need to furnish consideration for A's promise for it to be enforceable under this doctrine and although the requirement of reliance by B suggests some element of acceptance on the latter's part of the benefit of the promise, there is no need for this to be communicated to or known by A.[43] The doctrines of proprietary estoppel and constructive trust may also enforce promises or agreements, even though these elements form merely part of the factual circumstances 1–006

[28] *Byrne v Van Tienhoven* (1880) 5 C.P.D. 344; below, para.2–089.
[29] *Felthouse v Bindley* (1862) 11 C.B. (N.S.) 869, affirmed (1863) 1 N.R. 401 and see below, paras 2–068 et seq.
[30] See below, paras 2–168—2–174.
[31] See below, paras 2–178—2–188.
[32] See below, Ch.4.
[33] See below, Ch.5.
[34] See below, Ch.6.
[35] See below, paras 7–001—7–055.
[36] See below, paras 7–056—7–125.
[37] See below, Chs 8 and 9.
[38] See below, Ch.17.
[39] See below, para.1–080.
[40] See below, para.1–082.
[41] See below, para.1–084.
[42] See below, paras 3–128 et seq.
[43] See below, para.3–093.

which attract their application. For example, in *Crabb v Arun DC*,[44] A made an assurance to B that it would grant a right of way to B over its land to and from B's land and B acted in reliance on this assurance. B's claim for a declaration that he was entitled to the right of access succeeded by way of estoppel, even though apparently B could not have established the existence of a contract on the ground of its uncertainty.[45] So too, as will be seen, both constructive trust and proprietary estoppel are used by the courts to give some legal effect to agreements for the sale or other disposition of an interest in land which do not constitute contracts for lack of the proper form.[46] On the other hand, sometimes constructive trust is used not so as to allow an agreement not counting as a contract to be enforced between its parties but rather so as to allow it to affect the position of third parties. For example, in *Binions v Evans*,[47] A had been given permission by B to occupy a cottage on B's land for the rest of her life. B sold the land to C expressly subject to A's tenancy of the cottage, but a few months later C gave A notice to quit. It was accepted by the majority of the Court of Appeal[48] that the agreement between A and B had contractual force, but for Lord Denning, M.R. in the circumstances of the case it would also give rise to a constructive trust so as to bind C.[49]

1–007 **European definitions of contract.** The definitions which we have so far discussed have been those which have arisen from analysis of the common law, equitable and statutory material native to English law or the legal systems which have developed from it. However, modern English courts are sometimes required to look to other definitions or understandings of what is meant by a contract. For legislation of the European Union has now had a very considerable effect on the law governing English contracts. This may be seen in three main areas, though others have also been affected[50]: first, the rules of private international law regarding both jurisdiction and choice of law; secondly, contracts of employment; and, thirdly, consumer contracts. In all these areas, the relevant EU legislation, at times, makes the application of legislation contingent on the existence of a contract, but the question arises whether this notion should be interpreted according to the understanding of the various Member States or instead on the basis of an "autonomous" definition to be formulated by the European Court of Justice. It is submitted that there is not likely to be any single answer to be given to this question. Different answers may be given according to the context of the legislation in question, these turning on a variety of considerations, but particularly on the degree of juristic integration which the European Court of Justice thinks desirable and practicable in that context. Of those areas which have already been mentioned, the European Court itself has had occasion

---

[44] [1976] Ch. 179 and see below, para.3–163.

[45] [1976] Ch. 179, 195 and see below, paras 3–163, 4–080.

[46] e.g. *Yaxley v Gotts* [2000] Ch. 162 (constructive trust), below, para.4–078; *Wayling v Jones* [1995] 2 F.L.R. 1029 (proprietary estoppel), below, para.4–080.

[47] [1972] Ch. 359.

[48] [1972] Ch. 359 at 367, 371.

[49] [1972] Ch. 359 at 367–368. Megaw and Stephenson L.JJ. preferred to protect A's position by holding her to be a tenant for life within the meaning of the Settled Land Act 1925.

[50] See also the impact of EU legislation on public procurement contracts (below, paras 10–044 et seq.) and contracts made by electronic means (below, para.4–005).

to hold that a European and "autonomous" view should be taken of the understanding of what constitutes a contractual as opposed to an extra-contractual action for the purposes of jurisdictional rules under the Brussels Convention,[51] and this has meant that an action classified in one Member State (France) as contractual has been held extra-contractual for these purposes.[52] The European Court decided that:

> " . . . the phrase 'matters relating to a contract' within the meaning of Article 5(1) of the Convention should not be understood to cover a situation where there is no obligation freely entered into by one party to another. Where a sub-buyer of goods which are bought from an intermediate seller brings an action against a manufacturer for damages on the sole ground that the goods are not in conformity, it is important to observe that there is no contractual link between the sub-buyer and the manufacturer because the latter has not undertaken a contractual obligation of any kind to the former."[53]

European definition of "worker". As to the various legislative provisions governing contracts of employment and contracts under which "workers" act, clearly their concern is not with "contract", but rather with "employment contract" or "worker", but in this respect some of the EU legislation clearly invites the courts of the Member States to refer to a conception of contract drawn from their own legal system, while other provisions have attracted a European conception. So, for example, Directive 91/533 which makes certain requirements as to the information to be given by employers to their employees as to the conditions of employment expressly provides that it shall apply "to every paid employee having a contract or employment relationship defined by the law in force in a Member State".[54] On the other hand, the European Court of Justice had occasion to make clear as early as 1964 that "worker" for the purposes of the principle of freedom of movement of workers contained in art.48 (new art.39) of the EC Treaty must be given a European understanding[55] the fleshing out of this being the matter for a series of subsequent judgments.[56] 1–008

"Consumer contract". Finally, while it is clear that certain aspects of the notion of "consumer contract" for the purposes of the Directive on Unfair Terms in Consumer Contracts 1993[57] are to be interpreted "autonomously", it is less clear whether the notion of "contract" itself will also be so interpreted by the European Court of Justice or will instead fall to be governed by the legislation or case law of the Member States.[58] If it were interpreted autonomously, then the 1–009

[51] *Kalfelis v Schröder* (C-189/87) [1988] E.C.R. 5565 especially at 5577 (A.G. Darmon), 5585. The Brussels Convention was replaced as from March 1, 2002 by the Council Regulation 44/2001 on jurisdiction and the recognition and enforcement of judgments in civil and commercial matters [2001] OJ L012/1. And see below, para.1–168.

[52] *Jakob Handte & Co GmbH v Société Traitements Mécano-chimiques des Surfaces* (TMCS) (C-26/91) [1993] I.L.Pr. 5 and see below, para.1–168.

[53] [1993] I.L.Pr. 5 at 22.

[54] Directive 91/533 on an employer's obligation to inform employees of the conditions applicable to the contract or employment relationship [1991] OJ L288/32.

[55] *Hoekstra (née Unger) v Bestuur der Bedrijfsvereniging voor Detailhandel en Ambachten* (C-75/63) [1964] E.C.R. 177.

[56] See Craig and de Búrca, *EU Law*, 4th edn (2008), pp.746 et seq.

[57] See below, paras 15–004 et seq.

[58] Whittaker (2000) 116 L.Q.R. 95 and see below, paras 15–034—15–035.

significance of "contract" may well differ from that given by English law, notably as regards the latter's requirement of consideration, a requirement which is not shared by the other Member States except the Republic of Ireland. Furthermore, in coming to a view as to what constitutes "a contract" for this purpose, the European Court of Justice is likely to be inspired by the work of those who have formulated a pan-European definition of contract, such as the authors of the *Draft Common Frame of Reference*,[59] who define a contract as:

> "An agreement which gives rise to, or is intended to give rise to, a binding legal relationship or which has, or is intended to have, some other legal effect."[60]

2. FUNDAMENTAL PRINCIPLES OF CONTRACT LAW

1–010 There are a number of norms of the English law of contract of a generality, pervasiveness and importance to have attracted the designation of principle, though such a designation does not have a technical legal significance. A number of legal norms could be advanced as included within such a category of principle, including the principle of privity of contract,[61] the principle of "objectivity" in agreement,[62] and principles of contractual interpretation.[63] However, two linked principles remain of fundamental importance, viz the principles of freedom of contract and of the binding force of contract.[64] By these two principles, English law has expressed its attachment to a general vision of contract as the free expression of the choices of the parties which will then be given effect by the law. However, while the modern law still takes these principles as the starting point of its approach to contracts, it also recognises a host of qualifications to them, some recognised at common law and some created by legislation.[65] Moreover, some commentators have argued that these various qualifications should not be seen merely as the expression of particular reasons or considerations of policy special to their context, but should instead be seen as themselves reflecting a further, central principle, sometimes put in terms of a principle of good faith in contract or a principle of contractual fairness.[66]

(a) *Freedom of contract*

1–011 **Freedom of contract in the nineteenth century.** In the nineteenth century, freedom of contract was regarded by many philosophers, economists and judges

---

[59] Study Group on a European Civil Code and Research Group on EC Private Law (Acquis Group), *Principles, Definitions and Model Rules of European Private Law*, Interim Outline edn (Sellier, 2008) ("Draft Common Frame of Reference" or "DCFR"). This work is likely to form the basis of an instrument (to be known as the "Common Frame of Reference") to be used on a voluntary basis by the European legislator as a "tool for better lawmaking targeted at Community lawmakers": 2863 EU Council Meeting, *Justice and Home Affairs* (April 18, 2008), Press Release, p.18.

[60] Draft Common Frame of Reference, above para.II.-1:101(1).

[61] See below, Ch.18, para.18–003.

[62] See below, para.2–001.

[63] See below, paras 12–041 et seq. and especially *Investors Compensation Scheme Ltd v West Bromwich Building Society Ltd* [1998] 1 W.L.R. 896 at 912–913, per Lord Hoffmann.

[64] See below, paras 1–011—1–018, 1–019—1–021.

[65] See below, paras 1–012, 1–014 et seq.

[66] See below, paras 1–022 et seq.

as an end in itself, finding its philosophical justification in the "will theory" of contract and its economic justification in laissez faire liberalism.[67] Thus, the parties were to be the best judges of their own interests, and if they freely and voluntarily entered into a contract, the only function of the law was to enforce it. In particular, its validity should not be challenged on the ground that its effect was unfair or socially undesirable (as long as it was not actually illegal or immoral, the latter of which was understood in a restrictive sense)[68] and it was immaterial that one party was economically in a stronger bargaining position than the other. Nowhere can this attitude be seen more clearly than in the attitude of the courts to clauses which attempted to regulate the damages payable on breach of contract. For, the courts held that parties to a contract were able to limit or exclude liability in damages not merely for breach of contract, but also in tort.[69] The courts' attitude to freedom of contract can also be seen in their treatment of an exception to it, for while they accepted that penalty clauses were ineffective even if agreed by the parties, they did so only owing to the force of established precedent to this effect and with considerable reluctance.[70]

Freedom of contract in the modern common law. Freedom of contract as a general principle of the common law retains considerable support. For example, in 1966, Lord Reid rejected the idea that the doctrine of fundamental breach was a substantive rule of law, negativing any agreement to the contrary (and capable of being used to strike down an exemption clause)[71] on the ground, inter alia, that this would restrict "the general principle of English law that parties are free to contract as they may think fit".[72] In 1980, in the same context, Lord Diplock observed[73] that: 1–012

> "A basic principle of the common law of contract . . . is that parties to a contract are free to determine for themselves what primary obligations they will accept."[74]

---

[67] See Dicey, *Law and Opinion in England*, 2nd edn (1914), pp.150–158; *Printing and Numerical Registering Co v Sampson* (1875) L.R. 19 Eq. 462 at [465] per Jessel M.R.; *Manchester, Sheffield and Lincolnshire Ry v Brown* (1883) 8 App. Cas. 703 at [716]–[720], per Lord Bramwell; *Salt v Marquis of Northampton* [1892] A.C. at 1 [18]–[19], per Lord Bramwell. It is instructive to observe that Lord Bramwell, who was one of the foremost judicial champions of freedom of contract, also believed in the necessity for a real as opposed to an apparent consent: see his judgment in *British and American Telegraph Co Ltd v Colson* (1871) L.R. 6 Ex. 108, and his dissenting judgment in *Household Fire Insurance Co v Grant* (1879) 4 Ex. D. 216, 232. See further, Atiyah, *The Rise and Fall of Freedom of Contract* (1979) and cf. Gordley at pp.214–217.

[68] See below, paras 16–003 et seq.

[69] *Nicholson v Willan* (1804) 5 East 507. Lord Ellenborough C.J., at 513, rejected the plaintiff's argument that the attempt of the defendant, a common carrier, to exclude his liability for the loss of goods carried beyond the value of £5 was: "contrary to the policy of the common law, which has made common carriers responsible to an indefinite extent for losses not occasioned by . . . act of God [or] the King's enemies."

[70] *Ranger v G.W. Ry Co* (1854) 5 H.L.C. 72, 94–95, 118–119; Atiyah, *The Rise and Fall of Freedom of Contract* (1979), pp.414–415.

[71] See *Suisse Atlantique Société d'Armement Maritime SA v N.V. Rotterdamsche Kolen Centrale* [1967] 1 A.C. 361.

[72] [1967] 1 A.C. 361 at 399.

[73] *Photo Production Ltd v Securicor Transport Ltd* [1980] A.C. 827 at 848.

[74] And see *Eurico SpA v Philipp Brothers* [1987] 2 Lloyd's Rep. 215, 218 (term to do the impossible valid).

This support remains particularly strong in commercial contexts. So Lord Bingham of Cornhill has stated that "[l]egal policy favours the furtherance of international trade. Commercial men must be given the utmost liberty of contracting".[75] Moreover, English courts have proved unwilling to strike down contracts on the ground simply that one of the parties suffered from an "inequality of bargaining power".[76] Conversely, the House of Lords has made clear that it will not *add* to the agreement which the parties have made by implying a term merely because it would be reasonable to do so, but only where it is "necessary",[77] nor will the courts put a meaning on the words of a contract different from that which they clearly express.[78]

1–013 **Freedom of contract in European law.** Freedom of contract has also been recognised as a "general principle of civil law" by the European Court of Justice,[79] has been seen as protected by art.16 of the EU Charter of Fundamental Rights ("freedom to conduct business")[80] and has been set by the EC Commission as a fundamental point of reference for the future development of European contract law.[81] Furthermore, while the European Convention on Human Rights does not refer to freedom of contract, the European Court of Human Rights has held that the extent to which a State interferes with an owner of property's freedom of contract relating to the property is relevant to the assessment of its compliance with its duties in respect of the right to property under art.1 of the First Protocol.[82]

1–014 **Qualifications on freedom of contract.** However, the principle of freedom of contract is subject to many qualifications in the modern law. These qualifications may affect a person's decision as to whether and with whom to contract; the parties' choice as to the terms on which their contractual relations are to be governed and more generally as to their legal consequences. Furthermore, even where it does not bear directly on the mutual rights and duties of the contracting parties, modern legislation has also regulated the contractual environment in

---

[75] *Homburg Houtimport B.V. v Agrosin Private Ltd (The Starsin)* [2003] UKHL 12, [2003] 3 W.L.R. 711 at [57].

[76] *National Westminster Bank Plc v Morgan* [1985] 1 A.C. 686, 708, disapproving the dictum of Lord Denning M.R. in *Lloyds Bank Ltd v Bundy* [1975] Q.B. 326, 339; and see below, para.7–139. cf. 7–126 et seq. (unconscionable bargains).

[77] *Liverpool City Council v Irwin* [1977] A.C. 239, 254; *Tai Hing Cotton Mill Ltd v Liu Chong Hing Bank Ltd* [1986] A.C. 80, 104–105; and see below, para.13–009.

[78] See below, paras 12–041 et seq.

[79] *Spain v European Commission* (C-240/9) [1999] E.C.R. I-6571 at [99] (common agricultural policy); *Société thermale d'Eugénie-les-Bains v Ministère de l'Economie, des Finances et de l'Industrie* (C-277/05) [2007] E.C.R. I-6415 at [21], [24], [28] and [49] (VAT); *Alrosa Co Ltd v Commission of the European Communities* (T-170/06) [2007] 5 C.M.L.R. 7 at [108] implicitly referring to "the fundamental economic freedoms guaranteed by the Treaty" (competition law).

[80] EC Commission, *Explanations relating to the Charter of Fundamental Rights* [2007] OJ C303/17, 23.

[81] EC Commission, *First Annual Progress Report on European Contract Law and the Acquis Review* COM (2005) 456 final para.2.6.3. See further *Draft Common Frame of Reference*, para.II.-1:102(1) which qualifies the principle by reference to "rules on good faith and fair dealing."

[82] *Hutten-Czapska v Poland* (2006) 42 E.H.R.R. 15 at [151]; App. no.17647/04 *Edwards v Malta* at [69]–[71].

which the parties to some types of contract negotiate, conclude and perform their contracts.

1–015 **(i) Refusal to enter contracts.** Even at common law, an innkeeper or common carrier was not entitled to refuse to accommodate a would-be customer without sufficient excuse.[83] Companies which supply what used to be called public utilities, such as water, gas and electricity, in some circumstances are under a statutory duty to supply the commodity in question,[84] though in this type of case the existence of the duty has led the courts to hold that the relationship so created is not contractual.[85]

1–016 **(ii) The law of discrimination.** Moreover, modern discrimination law has forbidden a person to refuse to contract in certain situations and has provided more widely for the prevention of discrimination. This is the case as regards discrimination on the grounds of the sex,[86] racial group,[87] or disability[88] of the would-be contractor, and to these have been added in the context of employment prohibitions on discrimination on the ground of a person's sexual orientation,[89] religious belief,[90] and age.[91]

1–017 **(iii) Restricted freedom as to terms.** Moreover, even where, as in the majority of cases, a person is free to decide whether to enter a particular contract, he is not free to determine on what terms to do so. First, many contracts, whether between two commercial parties or between such a party and a consumer, are made on the written standard terms of one of the parties in such circumstances that it is all but impossible for them to be varied,[92] a phenomenon which led French commentators to refer to such transactions as *contrats d'adhésion*. Similarly, the terms of an employee's contract of employment may be determined by agreement between his trade union and his employer,[93] or by a statutory scheme

[83] *Clarke v West Ham Corp* [1909] 2 K.B. 858, 879, 882. See Vol.II para.36–008 on the ways by which a carrier could "abdicate" this status by giving notice that he would not accept custom from the public.

[84] Gas Act 1986 s.10; Electricity Act 1989 s.16 (as substituted by Utilities Act 2000 s.44); Electricity Act 1989 Sch.6 para.3 (as substituted by Utilities Act 2000 s.51 and Sch.4) (deemed contracts in respect of the supply of electricity in certain cases).

[85] *Read v Croydon Corp* [1938] 4 All E.R. 631; *Norweb Plc v Dixon* [1995] 1 W.L.R. 637, cf. *Oceangas (Gibraltar) Ltd v Port of London Authority* [1993] 2 Lloyd's Rep. 292 (no contract in respect of compulsory pilotage services); cf. *Rushton v Worcester City Council* [2001] EWCA Civ 367; [2002] H.L.R. 9 (no contract between council and tenant exercising "right to buy" under scheme created by Pt V of the Housing Act 1985).

[86] Sex Discrimination Act 1975 s.6(1)(c).

[87] Race Relations Act 1976 ss.4(1)(c), 17, 20 and 21 (as amended).

[88] Disability Discrimination Act 2005; Disability Discrimination Act (Amendment) Regulations 2003 (SI 2003/1673).

[89] Employment Equality (Sexual Orientation) Regulations 2003 (SI 2003/1661).

[90] Employment Equality (Religion or Belief) Regulations 2003 (SI 2003/1660).

[91] Employment Equality (Age) Regulations 2006 (SI 2006/1031).

[92] Sales (1953) 16 M.L.R. 318; Law Commissions, *UnfairTerms in Contracts,* Law Com no.292 (2005), esp. parts 4 and 5. Where both parties to the contract are in business, each may attempt to impose its own conditions on the other, and this sometimes gives rise to what is known as a "battle of forms": see below, paras 2–034—2–037.

[93] See Vol.II, paras 39–043 et seq.

of employment.[94] However, in both the latter situations, despite the lack of real freedom of the parties to do other than accept or reject the whole package as it is offered to them, these types of transactions are still treated as contracts.[95] Secondly, although, as has been said, the courts formally state the need for a term to be "necessary" before it will be implied into a contract,[96] in fact the courts have over the years found many such implied terms, often in situations where it is difficult to see how this test is fulfilled,[97] thereby creating for many types of contracts the "legal incidents of those . . . kinds of contractual relationship".[98] According to one author:

> "Faced with a problem in contract, the Common lawyer is as likely as not to try to solve it with an implied term. [In contrast,] the Civil lawyer will probably resort to a rule, whether it be a broad and fundamental precept such as the German requirement of good faith[99] . . . or one derived from the nature of obligation or contract . . . or, finally, one derived from the nature of the particular contract in question."[100]

While some judicially implied terms have been recognised by statute,[101] many remain a matter of common law, where they constitute an important part of the regulation of many contractors' relations.[102] Thirdly, the effects of many modern contracts are regulated by statute, sometimes by way of statutory insertion of an implied term,[103] but sometimes by attaching a legal consequence directly to the conclusion of a particular type of contract. This is particularly noticeable as regards some types of contracts made by consumers, notably contracts for the sale of goods, hire purchase and consumer credit,[104] where the protection which the law thereby ensures is often not capable of avoidance by an expression of contrary intention.[105] Contracts of employment and between a landlord and tenant have also been subjected to considerable legislative regulation, to the

---

[94] cf. *Barber v Manchester Regional Hospital Board* [1958] 1 W.L.R. 181, 196; *Roy v Kensington & Chelsea and Westminster Family Practitioner Committee* [1992] 1 A.C. 624; *Scally v Southern Health and Social Services Board* [1992] 1 A.C. 294, 304.

[95] cf. below, paras 1–196 et seq. on the question of the availability of public law remedies in this sort of case.

[96] See above, para.1–012.

[97] cf. Treitel, *The Law of Contract*, 12th edn (2007 by Peel), para.6–042 on the different significance of the test of necessity in terms implied in law.

[98] *Mears v Safecar Securities Ltd* [1983] Q.B. 54, 78 per Stephenson L.J. The learned Lord Justice specifically accepted, however, that "the obligation must be a *necessary* term; that is, required by their relationship".

[99] cf. below, paras 1–022 et seq.

[100] Nicholas (1974) 48 Tulane L.R. 946, 950.

[101] See, e.g. *Jones v Just* (1868) L.R. 3 Q.B. 197 and Sale of Goods Act 1893 s.14 (now Sale of Goods Act 1979).

[102] See, below, Ch.13. The contract of employment has proved particularly fertile ground for the implication of terms: see Vol.II, paras 39–054—39–065, 39–067—39–068.

[103] See Sale of Goods Act 1979 ss.12–15; Supply of Goods (Implied Terms) Act 1973 ss.8–11; Equal Pay Act 1970 s.1(1) as amended by the Sex Discrimination Act 1975 and the Equal Pay (Amendment) Regulations 1983 (SI 1983/1794).

[104] See Vol.II, Chs 38 and 43.

[105] Other contracts made with consumers, for example contracts of insurance and guarantee, were for long left unregulated in this way, but important changes were made in this respect by the Unfair Terms in Consumer Contracts Regulations 1994 (SI 1994/3159); revoked and replaced by the Unfair Terms in Consumer Contracts Regulations 1999 (SI 1999/2083): see below, paras 15–004 et seq., Vol.II, Chs 41, 44.

extent that the voluntary aspect of the contract appears only to be whether or not to enter the contract, a decision which then triggers a set of obligations which are determined by the law.[106]

(iv) Regulation of the contractual environment. Other statutory techniques for the regulation of contracts are less direct. For example, one aim of modern competition law is to help ensure that no company is able to impose what terms it likes on those with whom it deals because of its "dominant position" in the market.[107] This can be seen either as an intervention in the market (and therefore as interfering with the principle of freedom of contract[108]) or as a mechanism for ensuring that the market functions properly (and therefore as promoting freedom of contract). Another modern technique is for legislation to set up a system of regulation for a particular type of business with an element of "self-regulation." For example, under the Financial Services and Markets Act 2000, there is a general prohibition on the carrying on without authorisation or exemption of a regulated investment activity,[109] and doing so may constitute an offence and give rise to civil liability.[110] The Act gives to the Financial Services Authority very considerable rule-making powers for the conduct of investment business,[111] and breach of a rule so made is actionable at the suit of a private person who suffers loss as a result, though it will not constitute a criminal offence.[112] Clearly, this system of regulation affects the way in which contracts relating to investment business are concluded, even though breach of the rules does not affect the validity of any such contract.[113] A further example of the regulation of contractual behaviour is to be found in the regulations which give effect in English law to the EC Directive on Unfair Commercial Practices 2005.[114] While art.3(2) of this Directive explicitly provides that it is "without prejudice to contract law and, in particular, to the rules on the validity, formation or effect of a contract",[115] it then sets a very broad standard of commercial behaviour in relation to consumers in a "general clause" which prohibits practices which contrary to "professional diligence", "materially distort the economic behaviour" of an 1–018

[106] Hepple (1986–1987) 36 *King's Counsel* 11.

[107] See arts 81, 82 EC; Vol.II, Ch.41, especially paras 42–004 et seq.

[108] See, e.g. *Alrosa* (T-170/06) [2007] 5 C.M.L.R. 7 at [108].

[109] Financial Services and Markets Act 2000 s.19(1). "Regulated activities" are defined by s.22.

[110] ss.23, 20(3), respectively.

[111] s.138.

[112] ss.150, 151(1).

[113] s.151(2).

[114] Consumer Protection from Unfair Trading Regulations 2008 SI 1277 (due in force on May 26, 2008) implementing Directive 2005/29 of the European Parliament and of the Council concerning unfair business-to-consumer commercial practices in the internal market, on which see Collins (ed.), *The Forthcoming EC Directive on Unfair Commercial Practices* (2004); Weatherill and Bernitz (eds), *The Regulation of Unfair Commercial Practices under EC Directive 2005/29, New Rules and New Techniques* (2007).

[115] On which see Whittaker in Weatherill and Bernitz at Ch.8. The Consumer Protection from Unfair Trading Regulations 2008 reg.29 provides explicitly that "an agreement shall not be void or unenforceable by reason only of a breach of these regulations" but says no more as to the wider lack of effect of the Regulations on the "law of contract", apparently on the basis that they set out the consequences of the new controls and do not need to set out other non-consequences.

average consumer.[116] This general standard frames particular protections given to consumers by existing EC directives and is fleshed out by the 2005 Directive itself by the setting of two main examples of unfair commercial practices: misleading actions and omissions and aggressive commercial practices.[117] The Directive also provides a black list of particular commercial practices which "are in all circumstances [to be] considered unfair".[118]

(b) *The binding force of contract*

1–019 **General significance.** A concomitant of the doctrine of freedom of contract is the binding force of contracts,[119] a force which the French Civil Code compares to the binding force of the law itself.[120] English law has long recognised this principle, which suits the needs of commerce as well as the expectations of parties to contracts more generally. However, care must be taken in interpreting what is meant by the "binding force" of contracts. Some authors argue that "[g]enerally speaking the law does not actually compel the performance of a contract, it merely gives a remedy, normally damages, for the breach,"[121] an approach which echoes Oliver Wendell Holmes' famous statement that the law leaves a contractor "free from interference until the time for fulfilment has gone by, and therefore free to break his contract if he chooses".[122] However, four arguments can counter such an approach. First, the courts sometimes do enforce the primary obligations of a contract: apart from the equitable remedies of specific performance and injunction,[123] this is clearest in relation to the action for the agreed contract price, a remedy available at common law and as of right which enforces a party's primary contractual obligation to pay money.[124] Secondly, the purpose of many awards of damages for breach of contract, and the one which is particular to it,[125] is to put the injured party in the position as though the contract had been performed.[126] While this approach to damages is not

[116] Unfair Commercial Practices Directive art.5; Consumer Protection from Unfair Trading Regulations 2008 reg.3(3).

[117] Unfair Commercial Practices Directive arts 6 and 7; Consumer Protection from Unfair Trading Regulations 2008 regs 5, 6, 7.

[118] Unfair Commerical Practices Directive art.5(5) referring to Annex I; Consumer Protection from Unfair Trading Regulations 2008 reg.3(4)(d) Sch.1.

[119] This has been termed the "sanctity of contracts": see Hughes Parry, *The Sanctity of Contracts in English Law* (1959).

[120] French Civil Code art.1134.1 (inspired by D. 16.3.1.6; D. 50.17.23 (both attributed to Ulpian)). Logically, this Code recognised the effectiveness of penalty clauses, whose purpose is to ensure the performance of a contract: arts 1152, 1226. The law relating to penalty clauses was changed in 1975, when the courts were given a discretion to modify them where otherwise their effect would be "manifestly excessive or derisory": see new art.1152.1, C. civ.

[121] Atiyah, *An Introduction to the Law of Contract*, 5th edn (1995), p.37.

[122] *The Common Law* (1881), p.301.

[123] See below, Ch.27.

[124] See below, para.26–009.

[125] In particular, a contrast is drawn here with the basis of awards of damages in tort: see below, paras 1–163—1–164.

[126] See below, para.26–002. Such an award is sometimes said to be made to protect the injured party's expectation interest or performance interest. An award of damages may be made on other bases, in particular in order to protect what is known as the reliance interest of the injured party: below, paras 26–002—26–003.

without its restrictions[127] (notably, those imposed by the rules as to remoteness[128] and mitigation of damage),[129] where an award of damages is made on this basis, it can be seen as reflecting the idea that the obligations created by the contract *should* have been performed. Thirdly, a concern with the apparent injustice of allowing a party to break his contract without sanction where the breach has occasioned no loss but has allowed him to make a profit can be seen to lie behind the recognition of the remedy of an "account of profits" on breach based on the principle of unjustified enrichment.[130] Fourthly, English law recognises the binding force of contracts in another way, it being a tort for a third party knowingly[131] to induce a party to a contract to break his obligations to his co-contractor.[132] While a third party may be liable in damages for such a tort of interference with a contractual relationship, its commission may also be prevented by injunction in an appropriate case.[133] And finally, and at a much more general level, the argument that English law does not recognise the truly obligational character of contracts often rests on the absence of a particular form of sanction for a breach of contract—viz the threat of punishment for contempt of court, a sanction which exists in the contractual context only in relation to a failure to conform to a judicial order for specific performance or injunction. However, to this it may be countered that there is no reason to tie the question of the truly binding character of a contract to the presence of a particular type of any sanction for its breach and that many English lawyers are content to use the language of obligation to describe the consequences of contracts, which suggests that they see contract terms as set up and to be used as guides for the conduct of the contracting parties.[134]

However, rather than alluding to the variety of sanctions which are available if a contract is broken, the notion of the binding force of contracts is often used instead to draw attention to the general refusal of the courts to deny them effect on the ground of unfairness or inequality, for example where an inadequate price has been stipulated for the sale of property.[135] This refusal is also reflected in the development of the law of frustration. Until 1863, the general rule was that a party who contracted in absolute terms remained liable, notwithstanding a change of circumstances between the time of making the contract and the time for performance,[136] but in that year this harsh rule was mitigated by the doctrine of frustration,[137] which for many years was reconciled with principle by the **1–020**

[127] A practical as opposed to a legal restriction is that a claim for damages on the basis of an injured party's performance interest may be difficult to show: see below, para.26–073.

[128] See below, paras 26–051 et seq.

[129] See below, paras 26–101 et seq.

[130] See *A.G. v Blake* [2001] 1 A.C. 268 and below, paras 29–152—29–154.

[131] See Deakin, Johnston and Markesinis, *Markesinis' and Deakin's, Tort Law*, 6th edn (2008), pp.576–577.

[132] See *Lumley v Gye* (1853) 2 E.B. 216 and below, para.1–171.

[133] e.g. *Torquay Hotel Co Ltd v Cousins* [1969] 2 Ch. 106.

[134] cf. Hart, *The Concept of Law* (1961), pp.79–88, who distinguishes the situation where a person is under an *obligation* and where a person is *obliged*.

[135] This can be seen in those cases which hold that the consideration for a promise need not be adequate: below, paras 3–014—3–021.

[136] *Paradine v Jane* (1647) *Aleyn* 26.

[137] *Taylor v Caldwell* (1863) 3 B.S. 826; see below, Ch.23.

device of implying a term into the contract, to which both parties could be supposed to have agreed, and which provided for its discharge in the event of a given thing or state of things ceasing to exist. However, the doctrine came to be applied in circumstances where it was obvious that both parties would never have agreed to any such term and in *Davis Contractors Ltd v Fareham Urban DC*,[138] this basis for relief on frustration was firmly rejected. While some judges had relied simply on the notion of justice to justify the doctrine,[139] this decision of the House of Lords also made clear that its proper basis is the construction of the contract.[140] By so doing, reliance is again placed on what the parties agreed or rather on what they did not agree, viz to perform the contract in such radically different circumstances from those which obtained when it was made. However, even if the view were taken that the rationale for the doctrine of frustration is simply that in the circumstances the law decides that it would be unfair to keep the parties to the terms of their agreement, this does not mean that simple unfairness is the test of frustration. Again, in *Davis Contractors Ltd*[141] Lord Radcliffe made clear that the proper test for frustration is whether performance of the contract is radically different from that which was undertaken by the contract[142] and this test has been consistently upheld,[143] the courts refusing to grant relief for frustration merely because performance of the contract is more onerous than was envisaged by the parties on contract.[144]

1–021 **Limits on binding force of contracts.** Nevertheless, recognition of the principle of the binding force of contracts does not mean that contracts, or particular terms of contracts, will always be enforced. This is clearest in cases of illegal contracts,[145] but another exception to the principle exists at common law in the case of penalty clauses.[146] Furthermore, very important changes have taken place in this respect as a result of modern legislative intervention, of which the Unfair Contract Terms Act 1977 and the Unfair Terms in Consumer Contracts Regulations 1999[147] are particularly prominent.[148] First, the Unfair Contract Terms Act 1977 declares exemption clauses totally ineffective in certain situations, notably where they attempt to exclude business liability for death or personal injuries

---

138 [1956] A.C. 696, 720–729.

139 e.g. *Denny, Mott & Dickson Ltd v James B. Fraser & Co Ltd* [1944] A.C. 265, 275; *British Movietonews Ltd v London and District Cinemas Ltd* [1951] 1 K.B. 190, 202 (reversed [1952] A.C. 166).

140 [1956] A.C. 696, 720–721; and see below, para.23–012.

141 [1956] A.C. 696.

142 [1956] A.C. 696, 729; and see below, para.23–012.

143 See below, para.23–013.

144 *British Movietonews Ltd v London and District Cinemas Ltd* [1952] A.C. 166, 185; *Davis Contractors Ltd v Fareham Urban DC Ltd* [1956] A.C. 696; *Tsakiroglou & Co Ltd v Noblee Thorl GmbH* [1962] A.C. 93.

145 See below, Ch.17.

146 See below, paras 26–125 et seq. Another exception is to be found in the inability of the parties to a contract to fetter the discretion of the court in deciding whether to grant the remedy of specific performance: *Quadrant Visual Communications Ltd v Hutchison Telephone (UK) Ltd* [1993] B.C.L.C. 442, 451, 452.

147 SI 1999/2083. The 1999 Regulations revoked and replaced the Unfair Terms in Consumer Contracts Regulations 1994 (SI 1994/3159). Both sets of Regulations seek to implement Directive 93/13 on unfair terms in consumer contracts.

148 See below, paras 14–059 et seq. and Ch.15.

caused by negligence[149] and where they attempt to exclude or limit liability for breach of the terms as to quality and fitness for purpose implied by s.14 of the Sale of Goods Act 1979 as against someone dealing as consumer.[150] Furthermore, it gives to the courts a discretion in a wide category of other cases to deny effectiveness to an exemption clause unless it is proven to be "fair and reasonable" by the person who seeks to rely upon it.[151] Secondly, the Unfair Terms in Consumer Contracts Regulations 1999 impose a system of control of the terms of consumer contracts on the ground of unfairness which is not restricted to exemption, limitation and indemnity clauses, but extends to any "non-core" term[152] which has not been individually negotiated and:

> ". . . which contrary to the requirement of good faith causes a significant imbalance in the parties' rights and obligations under the contract to the detriment of the consumer."[153]

Another very striking inroad into the binding force of contracts may be found in provisions of the Consumer Credit Act 2006 which replaced earlier provisions governing extortionate credit bargains in the Consumer Credit Act 1974 with very broad provisions concerning "unfair relationships" arising from a consumer credit agreement.[154] The new provisions empower a court to make a range of orders (including requiring the creditor to repay any sums paid by the debtor, to reduce or discharge any sum payable by the debtor and to alter the terms of the agreement)[155] in connection with a consumer credit agreement:

> ". . . if it determines that the relationship between the creditor and the debtor arising out of the agreement (or the agreement taken with any related agreement) is unfair to the debtor"

in one or more of a number of ways.[156]

(c) *A principle of good faith or of contractual fairness?*

No general principle of good faith. Use by EC legislation of the notion of good faith has made more prominent the question whether English law requires that a party to a contract exercise his rights in good faith, whether the right in question concerns the creation of a contract, its performance or its non-performance. Such a question may be expressed in different ways and may use a variety of language: put negatively, it may be asked whether a party's *bad faith* should affect his exercise of rights or whether his "unconscionable conduct" in the 1–022

[149] Unfair Contract Terms Act 1977 s.2(1).
[150] s.6(2).
[151] Unfair Contract Terms Act 1977 ss.2(2), 3, 6(3) and 11; and see below, paras 14–084 et seq.
[152] "Non-core" term refers to the exclusion from the ambit of controls found in reg.6(2) of the 1999 Regulations; below, paras 15–049—15–063.
[153] Unfair Terms in Consumer Contracts Regulations 1999 reg.5(1).
[154] Consumer Credit Act 1974 ss.140A–140D as inserted by Consumer Credit Act 2006 ss.19–22. See paras 38–198—38–215 below.
[155] Consumer Credit Act 1974 s.140(B)(1) as inserted by Consumer Credit Act 2006 s.20.
[156] Consumer Credit Act 1974 s.140(A)(1) as inserted by Consumer Credit Act 2006 s.19.

creation or performance of a contract should affect its validity.[157] Put at its most general and more positively, the question may be posed in terms of a general requirement or series of more particular requirements that a person act in good faith, reasonably and fairly.[158] In 1766, in the context of recognising the duty of disclosure in contracts of insurance,[159] Lord Mansfield C.J. stated that:

> "The governing principle is applicable to all contracts and dealings. Good faith forbids either party by concealing what he privately knows, to draw the other into a bargain, from his ignorance of that fact, and his believing the contrary. But either party may be innocently silent, as to grounds open to both, to exercise their judgment upon."[160]

Nevertheless, the modern view is that, in keeping with the principles of freedom of contract and the binding force of contracts, in English contract law there is no principle of good faith of general application, although some authors have argued that there should be.[161] As Bingham L.J. has stated:

> "In many civil law systems, and perhaps in most legal systems outside the common law world, the law of obligations recognises and enforces an overriding principle that in making and carrying out contracts parties should act in good faith. This does not simply mean that they should not deceive each other, a principle which any legal system must recognise; its effect is perhaps most aptly conveyed by such metaphorical colloquialisms as 'playing fair', 'coming clean' or 'putting one's cards face upwards on the table.' It is in essence a principle of fair open dealing . . . English law has, characteristically, committed itself to no such overriding principle but has developed piecemeal solutions in response to demonstrated problems of unfairness."[162]

The fact that at least some English judges have not been attracted by the idea of a general ground for relief for unfairness is also clear from judicial treatment of the attempt of Lord Denning M.R. to construct a general principle of "inequality

---

[157] See below, paras 7–126 et seq.

[158] Art.1:201(1) of the *Principles of European Contract Law* provides that "[e]ach party must act in accordance with good faith and fair dealing." cf. *Draft Common Frame of Reference*, para. II.-1:102(1): "Parties are free to make a contract or other juridical act and to determine its contents, subject to the rules on good faith and fair dealing and any other applicable mandatory rules."

[159] See Vol.II, paras 41–030 et seq.

[160] *Carter v Boehm* (1766) 3 Burr. 1905, 1910.

[161] Bridge (1984) 9 Can. Bus. L.J. 385; Collins, *The Law of Contract*, 4th edn (2003), Chs 13 and 15; Finn in Finn (ed.), *Essays on Contract Law* (1987), p.104; Lücke in Finn (ed.), *Essays on Contract Law* p.155; Steyn (1991) Denning L.J. 131; Carter and Furmston (1994) 8 J.C.L. 1; Brownsword (1994) 7 J.C.L. 197; Staughton (1994) 7 J.C.L. 193; Beatson and Friedmann (eds), *Good Faith and Fault in Contract Law* (1995), especially the essays by Beatson and Friedmann, p.3; Cohen, p.25; McKendrick, p.305; Friedmann, p.399; Brownsword in Deakin and Michie (eds), *Contracts, Co-operation and Competition* (1997), p.255; Stein (1997) 113 L.Q.R. 433; Teubner (1998) 6 M.L.R. 11; Brownsword [1997] C.L.P. 111; McKendrick, *Contract Law*, 3rd edn (2005), Ch.15; Smith, *Atiyah's Introduction to the Law of Contract*, 6th edn (2006), pp.164–166.

[162] *Interfoto Picture Library Ltd v Stilletto Visual Programmes Ltd* [1989] 1 Q.B. 433, 439. Bingham L.J. gave as illustrations of these solutions equity's striking down of unconscionable bargains (see below, paras 7–126 et seq.), statutory control of exemption clauses (see below, paras 14–059 et seq.) and hire-purchase (see Vol.II, paras 38–336 et seq.) and the ineffectiveness of penalty clauses (see below, paras 26–125 et seq.). See similarly, *Director General of Fair Trading v First National Bank* [2001] UKHL 52, [2002] 1 A.C. 507 at [17] (Lord Bingham of Cornhill), below, para.15–069.

of bargaining power" in *Lloyds Bank Ltd v Bundy*[163] and the House of Lords' refusal in *Walford v Miles*[164] to imply a term in a "lock-out" agreement that a party to it be obliged to continue to negotiate in good faith. Indeed, in that case, Lord Ackner stated that:

> "... the concept of a duty to carry on negotiations in good faith is inherently repugnant to the adversarial position of the parties when involved in negotiations[165] ... [and] ... unworkable in practice."[166]

Similarly, Potter L.J. has observed in denying relevance to a injured party's motive in termination of a contract, that:

> "There is no general doctrine of good faith in the English law of contract. The [injured parties] are free to act as they wish, provided that they do not act in breach of a term of the contract."[167]

A very stark example of the preference of English judges for the strict application of the terms of a contract rather than tempering their effect on the grounds of fairness may be found in *Union Eagle Ltd v Golden Achievement Ltd.*[168] There, the Privy Council refused specific performance of a contract for the sale of land to its purchaser who had paid the price 10 minutes late, time having been made expressly of the essence for performance of this obligation. It rejected the argument that the courts enjoyed a discretion to relieve a party from the contractual consequences of late performance (stemming from its jurisdiction to relieve from forfeitures in equity). According to Lord Hoffmann: **1–023**

> "The principle that equity will restrain the enforcement of legal rights when it would be unconscionable to insist upon them has an attractive breadth. But the reasons why the courts have rejected such generalisations are founded not merely upon authority ... but also upon considerations of business. These are, in summary, that in many forms of transaction it is of great importance that if something happens for which the contract has made express provision, the parties should know with certainty that the terms of the contract will be enforced. The existence of an undefined discretion to refuse to enforce the contract on the ground that this would be 'unconscionable' is sufficient to create uncertainty."[169]

---

[163] [1975] Q.B. 326, 339; and see below, para.7–139.

[164] *Walford v Miles* [1992] 2 A.C. 128, 138. cf. *Little v Courage Ltd, The Times*, January 19, 1994.

[165] [1992] 2 A.C. 128, 138. The agreement was held unenforceable on the grounds of uncertainty, and see below, paras 2–136—2–138.

[166] [1992] 2 A.C. 128, 138. In *Banque Keyser Ullmann SA v Skandia (UK) Insurance Co Ltd* [1990] 1 Q.B. 665, 772 (affirmed on other grounds [1990] 2 All E.R. 947), Slade L.J. rejected Steyn J.'s formulation of the content of the ambit of the duty of disclosure on insurers based simply on the question "did good faith and fair dealing require a disclosure?" on the ground that: "[I]n the case of commercial contracts, broad concepts of honesty and fair dealing, however laudable, are a somewhat uncertain guide when determining the existence or otherwise of an obligation which may arise even in the absence of any dishonest or unfair intent."

[167] *James Spencer & Co Ltd v Tame Valley Padding Co Ltd* Unreported April 8, 1998 CA (Civ Div). See similarly *Bernhard Schulte GmbH & Co KG v Nile Holdings Ltd* [2004] EWHC 977, [2004] 2 Lloyd's Rep. 352 at [113].

[168] [1997] A.C. 514.

[169] [1997] A.C. 514 at [218].

It is to be noted, though, that Lord Hoffmann recognised that "the same need for certainty is not present in all transactions".[170]

Moreover, the House of Lords has had occasion to hold that a party is not prevented from relying on the formal invalidity of a contract on the ground merely that it would be "unconscionable" to do so, in the absence of an unambiguous representation of the contract's validity (not being the promise to be enforced itself) on which to base an estoppel.[171] In the words of Lord Clyde:

> "Without entering into questions of categorisation of different classes of estoppel, it seems to me that some recognisable structural framework must be established before recourse is had to the underlying idea of unconscionable conduct in the particular circumstances."[172]

1–024 **Good faith in other common law systems.** As Lord Brown-Wilkinson has observed:

> " . . . throughout the common law world it is a matter of controversy to what extent obligations of good faith are to be found in contractual relationships",[173]

and other common law systems have taken varying positions as to the relevance of good faith in the creation or the performance of contracts.[174] Perhaps the most extensive use is taken by lawyers in the United States, the Restatement (Second) of Contracts requiring that "[e]very contract imposes upon each party a duty of good faith and fair dealing in its performance and enforcement".[175] In Australia too, courts and writers are generally quite open to the use of good faith, holding that an agreement to negotiate in good faith may be contractually enforceable,[176] and willing to find implied terms requiring co-operation in performance, if not always good faith, between the parties.[177] In Canada, however, there is no duty to negotiate a contract in good faith and it is yet uncertain whether there is any legal requirement that a party must perform his obligations in good faith.[178]

---

[170] [1987] A.C. 574 at [219]. cf. *O'Neill v Phillips* [1999] 1 W.L.R. 1092, 1098 where Lord Hoffmann observed in the context of contracts of partnership and a company's duty not to engage in conduct "unfairly prejudicial" to its members that: "One of the traditional roles of equity, as a separate jurisdiction, was to restrain the exercise of strict legal rights in certain relationships in which it considered that this would be contrary to good faith."

[171] *Actionstrength Ltd v International Glass Engineering IN.GL.EN SpA* [2003] UKHL 17; [2003] 2 All E.R. 615 especially at [16]–[20], [51].

[172] [2003] 2 All E.R. 615 at [34].

[173] *Dymocks Franchise Systems (NSW) Pty Ltd v Todd* [2002] 2 All E.R. (Comm) 849 (PC) at [54].

[174] See also works noted above, at n.161.

[175] Restatement (Second) of Contracts para.205. cf. Uniform Commercial Code s.1–203 and see for a general introduction Summers in Zimmermann and Whittaker (eds), *Good Faith in European Contract Law* (2000), Ch.4; White and Summers, *Uniform Commercial Code*, 5th edn (2000), Vol.1, Ch.4.

[176] *Coal Cliff Collieries Pty Ltd v Sijehama Pty Ltd* (1991) 24 N.S.W.L.R. 1 at 21–27 especially.

[177] Carter and Harland, *Contract Law in Australia*, 4th edn (2002), paras 270–272, 1809 and 1842 and see Carter and Peden (2003) 19 J.C.L. 155.

[178] Fridman, *The Law of Contract in Canada*, 4th edn (1999), pp.85–87, 555–556.

Good faith in civil law systems. As Bingham L.J.'s observations quoted above illustrate,[179] in modern discussions of the English position contrasts are often drawn with use of the concept of good faith in civil law systems, i.e. those whose private law has derived substantially from doctrines and rules of Roman law. The practical interest of this use is hightened by the increasing reference to good faith in European legislation in the area of contract law and the possibility of the European Court of Justice drawing on its existing significance in the laws of the Member States in interpreting its significance there.[180] In this respect, though, it is helpful to note that, even restricting the discussion to the legal systems of western Europe, there are very considerable divergences in both the significances given to "good faith" and its supposed linguistic equivalents and in the uses to which they are put within each legal system. So, in some (but not in all) systems, good faith has provided the basis of some pre-contractual grounds of relief or compensation (notably, as regards duties of disclosure and information and breaking-off from negotiations); the addition of "supplementary" obligations to those expressly provided either by the parties or by legislation; the control of unfair contract terms; the toughening of the sanction of deliberate breaches of contract; the control of the exercise of a party's contractual right; and relief on account of supervening circumstances or the substantively unfair nature of the contract as a whole.[181] In the result: 1–025

> ". . . the notion of good faith (or its equivalents in the various languages . . .) actually means different things both *within* a particular legal system and *between* the legal systems."[182]

And while in those legal systems which possess a general requirement of good faith:

> ". . . good faith is not devoid of meaning, a pious hope or incantation or simply a super-technique waiting to be put to whatever legal end a legal system wishes (though it may act as a super-technique if required, . . . even where a particular meaning of good faith is accepted in two systems, this does not entail that they will take the same view of what it in fact requires in any given situation."[183]

---

[179] Above, para.1–022.

[180] Apart from the reference to the "requirement of good faith" in Directive 93/13 on unfair terms in consumer contracts art.3(1), now implemented by the Unfair Terms in Consumer Contracts Regulations (SI 1999/2083) reg.5(1) (on the significance of which see below, paras 15–066 et seq.), good faith is used by Directive 86/653 on the coordination of the laws of the Member States relating to self-employed commercial agents art.3(1), implemented in English law by Commercial Agents (Council Directive) Regulations 1993 (SI 1993/3053) reg.3(1) ("agent must . . . act dutifully and in good faith"), Vol.2, para.31–017 and Directive 2002/65 concerning the distance marketing of consumer financial services art.3.2 (referring to the "principles of good faith in commercial transactions") implemented by the Distance Contracts (Financial Services) Regulations 2004 (SI 2004/2095); Directive 2005/29 concerning unfair business-to-consumer commercial practices in the internal market art.5 implemented by the Consumer Protection from Unfair Trading Regulations 2008 SI no. 1277 regs 3(3) and 2(1) "professional diligence".

[181] For an overview see Whittaker and Zimmermann in Zimmermann and Whittaker (eds), *Good Faith in European Contract Law* (2000), Ch.1.

[182] Whittaker and Zimmermann at p.690 and cf. *Director General of Fair Trading v First National Bank* [2001] UKHL 52, [2002] 1 A.C. 507 at [17] per Lord Bingham of Cornhill (Member States "have no common concept of . . . good faith").

[183] Whittaker and Zimmermann at p.699.

Moreover, the extent of the use to which a legal system puts a potentially corrective principle such as good faith depends on the extent to which it is dissatisfied with its more particular, established laws of contract, on the availability of other legal techniques which have a similar corrective possibility and on the perceived appropriateness of judicial as opposed to legislative intervention in the area in question. For English law, the difference between resort to the "piecemeal solutions" mentioned by Bingham L.J. and recognition of a *principle* of good faith in contract is likely to be that the latter would tend not merely to give a juridical unity to existing examples of situations in which good faith or fairness is considered relevant, but also to invite future courts to add further examples in new situations by way of application of the principle.[184] Given the remarkably open-textured nature of good faith, this would lead to a very considerable degree of legal uncertainty, and could be seen as trespassing too far into the legislative domain.

1–026 **Good faith, fairness or reasonableness relevant exceptionally in English law.** The following paragraphs set out a number of ways by which English law takes into account considerations of fairness which qualify the position established either by the general law or by a contract to govern the creation or the regulation of contractual relationships. Some of these refer explicitly to the notion of good faith, as is the case in contracts of insurance, contracts arising from fiduciary relations, contracts of partnership and of employment, though they do so sometimes by way of application of an exceptional rule and sometimes by the implication of a term. However, other qualifications on the strictness of the express terms of the contract or on contract law itself do not refer explicitly to good faith, preferring rather to use the language of fairness, equitableness or reasonableness.

1–027 **(i) Duties to consider other party's interest.** First, some particular types of contract attract rules (usually considered to be of law, though sometimes justified by reference to the implied intentions of the parties) which impose duties on one party to act other than in their own interest. This is most clearly the case in contracts under which a person assumes fiduciary duties, as is notably the case as regards agents, for a fiduciary must act honestly and must not allow his own interests to conflict with those of his principal.[185] Indeed, the Commercial Agents (Council Directive) Regulations 1993, echoing the EC Directive that they implement, put the duties of agents to their principals expressly in terms of good faith.[186] So too, it has been said that partnership is a "contract of good faith"[187] and held that this means that prospective partners owe each other a duty to disclose all material facts of which each has knowledge and of which the other negotiating parties may not be aware.[188] Another example may be found in relation to mortgages. Thus, the Privy Council has recognised that a mortgagee

---

[184] Whittaker and Zimmermann at pp.687–690.
[185] See Vol.II, paras 31–016, 31–119 et seq.
[186] SI 1993/3053 reg.3(1), implementing Directive 86/653 art.3(1).
[187] *O'Neill v Phillips* [1999] 1 W.L.R. 1092, 1098, per Lord Hoffmann and see *Blisset v Daniel* (1853) 10 Hare 493; *Floydd v Cheney, Cheney, & Floydd* [1970] Ch. 602, 608.
[188] *Conlon v Simms* [2006] EWCA Civ 1749, [2007] 3 All E.R. 802 at [127].

of property must exercise his powers in good faith and for the purpose of obtaining repayment of the debt, though given this purpose these powers may be exercised in such a way that disadvantageous consequences accrue to the borrower.[189] And of course the parties to contracts of insurance owe each other duties of "the utmost good faith", the most important consequence of which is the imposition of extensive obligations of disclosure.[190]

(ii) Express terms as to good faith or fairness. Sometimes, the express terms of a contract require one or both of the parties to act fairly or in good faith towards the other in a particular context or respect. 1–028

Express term to negotiate in good faith. In the case of good faith, the validity of such a term remains doubtful owing to the view expressed by Lord Ackner in *Walford v Miles* that a duty to negotiate in good faith is "'unworkable in practice.'"[191] However, a rather more liberal approach was taken to this question in *Petromec Inc v Petroleo Brasileiro SA Petrobras (No.3).*[192] In that case the Court of Appeal considered that Lord Ackner's observations were not appropriate (nor binding on it[193]) to determine the validity of an express obligation to negotiate in good faith contained in a complex concluded contract which had been drafted by City of London solicitors. The term in question formed part of a contract supplementing a complex series of contractual arrangements relating to the purchase, "upgrading" and hire of an oil production platform, and provided for the negotiation in good faith of the cost of the upgrading of the platform for use on a particular oil-field. On the loss by fire of the platform, the question arose, inter alia, of the applicability and enforceability of the term as to negotiation in good faith. Having held it inapplicable as a matter of construction,[194] Longmore L.J. nevertheless considered whether the term would have been enforceable. In this respect, he noted that there were three traditional objections to enforcing an obligation to negotiate in good faith: 1–029

> "(1) . . . that the obligation is an agreement to agree and thus too uncertain to enforce, (2) that it is difficult, if not impossible, to say where, if negotiations are brought to an end, the termination is brought about in good or in bad faith, and (3) that, since it can never be known whether good faith negotiations would have produced an agreement at all or what the terms of any agreement would have been if it would have been reached, it is impossible to assess any loss caused by breach of the obligation."[195]

---

[189] *Downsview Ltd v First City Corp Ltd* [1993] A.C. 295, 312 and see also *Albany Home Loans Ltd v Massey* [1997] 2 All E.R. 609, 612–613.

[190] See Vol.II, paras 41–030 et seq.

[191] [1992] 2 A.C. 128. In *Banque Keyser Ullmann SA v Skandia (UK) Insurance Co Ltd* [1990] 1 Q.B. 665, 772 (affirmed on other grounds [1990] 2 All E.R. 947), Slade L.J. rejected Steyn J.'s formulation of the content of the ambit of the duty of disclosure on insurers based simply on the question "did good faith and fair dealing require a disclosure?" on the ground that: "[I]n the case of commercial contracts, broad concepts of honesty and fair dealing, however laudable, are a somewhat uncertain guide when determining the existence or otherwise of an obligation which may arise even in the absence of any dishonest or unfair intent."

[192] [2005] EWCA Civ 891, [2006] 1 Lloyd's Rep. 121.

[193] [2005] EWCA Civ 891 at [121].

[194] [2005] EWCA Civ 891 at [45], [112]–[113] and [124].

[195] [2005] EWCA Civ 891 at [117].

In the view of the learned Lord Justice, the first of these objections carried little weight in the context as the express obligation to negotiate in good faith was contained in a contract which it was accepted was generally enforceable; and the third objection could be overcome as the obligation to negotiate in question related to a limited aspect of the extra costs involved in the upgrade of the platform and so, if agreement were not reached, the court could itself ascertain the losses arising, these being likely to be the same as the reasonable cost of the upgrade.[196] Rather:

> "It is the second objection that is likely to give rise to the greatest problem viz that the concept of bringing negotiations to an end in bad faith is somewhat elusive. But the difficulty of a problem should not be an excuse for the court to withhold relevant assistance from the parties by declaring a blanket unenforceability of the obligation."

However, he added that in the absence of fraud, it would be unlikely that there would be a finding of bad faith.[197] Overall, therefore, given the inclusion of a term of "comparatively narrow scope" which had been "deliberately and expressly" entered by the parties to a professionally drafted commercial contract, Longmore L.J. concluded that it would be "a strong thing to declare [it] unenforceable" as this would "defeat the reasonable expectations of honest men".[198]

1–030 **Express term to act fairly.** In a very different context, in *Gray v Marlborough College*[199] the Court of Appeal considered the significance of an express term in the standard contract between an independent school and the parent of one of its pupils which required the headmaster of the school to consult the pupil's parents and generally to act fairly before requiring the pupil's removal from the school. For this purpose, in the view of Auld L.J.:

> " . . . fairness is a flexible principle and highly fact-sensitive in its application. That is so whether a duty to act fairly is one of public law or contractual in nature. Much depends on the context of and procedural framework in which a decision is made, the nature of the decision, who made it, how it was made, what is at stake and the contribution, if any, by those affected by it to the chain of events leading to it."[200]

As will be seen, the courts have sometimes also seen some *implied* contractual duties to act fairly as analogous to public law duties, though sometimes this analogy has been rejected.[201]

1–031 **(iii) Contractual interpretation.** Considerations of fairness and reasonableness are more generally relevant to the way in which English courts treat the

---

[196] [2005] EWCA Civ 891 at [117].
[197] [2005] EWCA Civ 891 at [119].
[198] [2005] EWCA Civ 891 at [121] echoing Steyn (1997) 113 L.Q.R. 433.
[199] [2006] EWCA Civ 1262, [2006] E.L.R. 516. See also *Berkley Community Villages Ltd v Pullen* [2007] EWHC 1130 (Ch) especially at [86]–[97]; [2007] 3 E.G.L.R. 101 (express term requiring "utmost good faith" interpreted as requiring the "observance of reasonable commercial standards of fair dealing").
[200] [2006] EWCA Civ 1262 at [54].
[201] Below, para.1–033.

consequences of making contracts in several different ways. First, the fairness or reasonableness of the result reached is clearly relevant to the interpretation of the express terms which the parties have made. The courts have long made clear that, in general, they should look to the intention of the parties rather than the strict letter of a contract's stipulations[202] and in interpreting their intention, the courts look at the factual matrix of the contract:

> " . . . modern principles of construction require the court to have regard to the commercial background, the context of the contract and the circumstances of the parties, and to consider whether, against that background and in that context, to give the words a particular or restricted meaning would lead to an apparently unreasonable and unfair result."[203]

As Lord Reid earlier observed, "[t]he more unreasonable the result the more unlikely it is that the parties can have intended it."[204] Furthermore, other principles governing the relationship of the parties also find their formal source in the construction of the contract: so, for example, the courts accept that, in general, a party in default under a contract cannot take advantage of his own wrong,[205] an idea which in some other systems is put in terms of the adage *nemo auditur turpitudinem suam allegans.* Another example of English law's occasional imposition of a requirement of fairness may be found in the situation where a contract on its terms provides that a particular act of one of its parties (or their agent) will result in or affect a liability in the other: here, the courts have held that this act must be made fairly to have this effect. This result has been long established in the context of the issuing of certificates by an owner's agent (for example, his architect) in respect of building work having been properly executed: here, the certification holds good only if the agent acts fairly as between the two parties to the contract.[206] Similarly, where a charterparty provided that the ship's master's "notice of readiness" to receive cargo would, after a delay, start "notice time" running so as to allow its owner to claim demurrage, it was observed that:

> " . . . a notice of readiness proved to be given by the master or chief officer with knowledge that it was untrue, that is to say in the knowledge that the vessel was not then

---

[202] e.g. *Solley v Forbes* (1820) 2 Brod. & B. 28, 48, per Dallas C.J.

[203] *Cargill International SA v Bangladesh Sugar and Food Industries Corp* [1998] 1 W.L.R. 461, 468, per Potter L.J. and see the important speech of Lord Hoffmann in *Investors Compensation Scheme Ltd v West Bromwich Building Society Ltd* [1998] 1 W.L.R. 896, 912–913, explaining *Prenn v Simmonds* [1971] 1 W.L.R. 1381 especially at 1383–1384 and *Charter Reinsurance Co Ltd v Fagan* [1997] A.C. 313 especially at 387–388. See further below, paras 12–041 et seq.

[204] *Wickman Machine Tool Sales Ltd v Schuler A.G.* [1974] A.C. 235, 251. For examples of this sort of approach in the context of rights of termination of a contract see *Ringway Roadmarking v Adbruf Ltd* [1998] 2 B.C.L.C. 625; *Rice (t/a The Garden Guardian) v Great Yarmouth BC* (2001) 3 L.G.L.R. 4, CA.

[205] *Alghussein Establishment v Eton College* [1988] 1 W.L.R. 587.

[206] *Pawley v Turnbull* (1861) 3 Giff. 70; *Hickman & Co v Roberts* [1913] A.C. 229. cf. *Skidmore v Dartford & Gravesham NHS Trust* [2003] UKHL 27, [2003] 3 All E.R. 292 at [15]–[16] (power to decide on disciplinary procedure in employment).

ready would be ineffective to start time running. There must by implication be a requirement of good faith."[207]

1–032 **(iv) Implied terms.** As has been indicated,[208] the common law often resorts to the implication of a term in a contract in a case which could otherwise be considered to be a matter of "good faith in the performance of a contract". Thus, for example, the House of Lords has accepted that a term is to be implied in contracts of employment to the effect that the:

> "... employer [will] not, without reasonable and proper cause, conduct itself in a manner likely to destroy or seriously damage the relationship of confidence and trust between employer and employee."[209]

The courts sometimes refer to this as an implied term requiring good faith and loyalty in both employer and employee.[210] Sometimes, indeed, an implied term imposes a duty on an employer to act positively in the interests of the employee. So, for example, in *Scally v Southern Health and Social Services Board*,[211] the House of Lords held that an employer who knew that its employees had a valuable right under the terms of their contracts of employment (here, relating to the enhancement of their pension rights), in a situation where it was reasonable for the employee to be unaware of that right (as it stemmed from a collective agreement), was under a duty to take reasonable steps to inform those employees of their rights. And again in the context of employment, it has been accepted that where an employee bonus scheme gives the employer a very wide discretion as to the payment and size of bonus, this discretion must nevertheless be exercised bona fide, rationally and not perversely.[212] An example drawn from another context may be found in the courts' implication of a term in a contract of sale of the goodwill of a business that the seller is not entitled to solicit the business's former customers, it being "not an honest thing to pocket the price and then to recapture the subject of sale",[213] though the courts do not go further and accept

---

[207] *Colbelfret N.V. v Cylclades Shipping Co Ltd (The Linardos)* [1994] 1 Lloyd's Rep. 28, 32, per Colman J.

[208] See above, para.1–017.

[209] *Malik v Bank of Credit and Commerce International SA (In Liquidation)* [1998] A.C. 20 but see *Johnson v Unisys Ltd* [2001] UKHL 13, [2003] 1 A.C. 518 (no term to be implied not to dismiss employee without good cause or in an unfair manner as inconsistent with the statutory system of unfair dismissal and see below, Vol.II, para.39–196) and cf. *Modahl v British Athletic Federation* [2001] EWCA Civ 1447, [2002] 1 W.L.R. 1192 (implied term in contract of membership of British Athletic Federation under which Federation agreed to provide a disciplinary hearing to provide a fair result overall). Outside the context of employment see *Nathan v Smilovitch (No.2)* [2002] EWHC 1629 (Ch) at [9]; *Training in Compliance Ltd v Dewse* [2004] EWHC 3094 (QB), [2004] All ER (D) 377 (Dec) (implied terms of honesty and good faith in contracts for joint business venture); *Dymocks Franchise Systems (NSW) Pty Ltd v Todd* [2002] 2 All E.R. (Comm) 849 at [57] (PC not ruling out implied obligation of good faith in franchise contract). But cf. *Bedfordshire CC v Fitzpatrick Contractors Ltd* (1999) 62 Con. L.R. 64 (no implied term of mutual trust and confidence in the "purely commercial contract" between a local authority and highway maintenance contractor).

[210] *Johnson v Unisys Ltd* [2001] UKHL 13, [2003] 1 A.C. 518 at [24]. *Eastwood v Magnox Electric Plc* [2004] UKHL 35, [2005] 1 A.C. 503 at [4]–[6], [51].

[211] [1992] 1 A.C. 294. cf. *University of Nottingham v Eyett* [1999] 1 W.L.R. 594.

[212] *Horkulak v Cantor Fitzgerald* [2004] EWCA Civ 1287, [2005] I.C.R. 402 at [46]–[47]; *Commerzbank AG v Keen* [2006] EWCA Civ 1536, [2007] I.C.R. 623 at [53]–[59].

[213] *Trego v Hunt* [1896] A.C. 7 at 25, per Lord Macnaghten.

that the seller is not entitled to compete with his purchaser in the absence of express provision.[214] And where a buyer has returned defective goods to their seller for inspection and, if possible, repair (it not being clear as to the nature of the problem), and the seller has repaired them, the latter has been held to bear an implied obligation to inform the buyer about the nature of the defect and what has been done to repair it, as this information was necessary in the circumstances of the case for the buyer to make a properly informed choice between accepting and rejecting the goods as it was entitled to do under the contract of sale.[215] On the other hand, it has been said that a court should not imply a term requiring good faith in a party to a contract where it would be "inconsistent with the express terms which set out the parties' mutual obligations", though this leaves a duty of honesty.[216]

Implied restrictions on broad contractual powers. The courts have also sometimes used the implication of a term to restrict the ambit of a unilateral discretionary power conferred on one of the parties by the contract.[217] In *Paragon Finance Plc v Nash*[218] a mortgage company possessed a power expressed in very general terms to vary the interest rates in a contract of consumer credit. Drawing on analogies from public law, the Court of Appeal held that this power was "not completely unfettered"[219] and implied a term that "it should not be exercised dishonestly, for an improper purpose, capriciously or arbitrarily".[220] While the court was prepared to imply a term that the interest rate would not be set in a way that "no reasonable lender, acting reasonably, would do", this was not the same as saying that the lender could not impose unreasonable rates.[221] On the other hand, in *Paragon Finance Plc v Plender*[222] it was held that this approach should not mean: 1–033

> "... that a lender may not, *for a genuine commercial reason*, adopt a policy of raising interest rates to levels at which its borrows generally, or a particular category of its borrowers, may be expected to consider refinancing their borrowings at more favourable rates of interest offered by other commercial lenders. Save as otherwise expressly agreed with its borrowers, a commercial lender is ... free to conduct its business in what it genuinely believes to be its best commercial interest."[223]

In a different context, in *Lymington Marina Ltd v MacNamara*[224] the Court of Appeal accepted that it should imply some limitations on the exercise of a contractual power in one of the parties drawn in very broad terms, but it

[214] [1896] A.C. 7 at 20.
[215] *J.H. Ritchie Ltd v Lloyd Ltd* [2007] UKHL 9, [2007] 1 W.L.R. 670 especially at [18], [36]–[37] (on appeal from Ct. of Sess).
[216] *Bernhard Schulte GmbH & Co K.G. v Nile Holdings Ltd* [2004] EWHC 977 (Comm), [2004] 2 Lloyd's Rep. 352 at [113]–[114].
[217] cf. *Johnstone v Bloomsbury Health Authority* [1992] Q.B. 334 (express discretionary power in employer read subject to duty not to harm employee's health), below, para.1–152.
[218] [2001] EWCA Civ 1466, [2002] 1 W.L.R. 685.
[219] [2002] 1 W.L.R. 685 at [30], per Dyson L.J.
[220] [2002] 1 W.L.R. 685 at [32].
[221] [2002] 1 W.L.R. 685 at [40].
[222] [2005] EWCA Civ 760, [2005] 1 W.L.R. 3412.
[223] [2005] EWCA Civ 760 at [120].
[224] [2007] EWCA Civ 151, [2007] Bus. L.R. D29.

considered that the standard to be applied should not be too onerous, nor should it rest on public law principle.[225] The case concerned a contractual licence to berth a yacht at a marina, express terms of which provided that the licensee was entitled to authorise a third party to exercise his rights for a period of between one month and one year "provided that such party first be approved" by the licensor who operated the marina. In these circumstances, the Court of Appeal was clear that the grounds on which approval of the sub-licence might be withheld were limited to those relating to the sub-licensee himself and his proposed use, and more generally could not be "wholly unreasonable" or be made "arbitrarily", "capriciously" or "in bad faith".[226] However, it refused to imply a term in the contract that the approval should be "objectively justifiable" as this was neither so obvious that the parties would not have thought it necessary to mention nor necessary to give the contract business efficacy.[227]

1–034 **(v) Equitable and statutory discretions.** General considerations of fairness are also relevant to the availability of certain equitable doctrines which are significant in the contractual context, notably promissory estoppel,[228] as well as to the equitable remedies of specific performance and injunction which are sometimes available on breach.[229] To these, modern statutes have added discretions given to the courts to act according to the dictates of justice, equity or reasonableness (as the case may be) in relation to the exercise of other remedies by parties to contracts, notably, in relation to rescission for misrepresentation[230] and termination for breach in contracts of sale of goods[231] and also in relation to contracts which have been frustrated.[232]

3. THE HUMAN RIGHTS ACT 1998 AND CONTRACTS

1–035 **Introduction.** The Human Rights Act 1998 ("the 1998 Act") was enacted in order to "bring home" the human rights declared by the European Convention on Human Rights ("the Convention") into the domestic legal systems of the United Kingdom.[233] In order to do so, it put in place two main mechanisms. First, there are controls on legislation. So, under s.3 of the 1998 Act it is provided that:

> "So far as it is possible to do so, primary legislation and subordinate legislation must be read and given effect in a way which is compatible with Convention rights."[234]

---

[225] [2007] EWCA Civ 151 at [36]–[37].

[226] [2007] EWCA Civ 151 at [42]–[44].

[227] [2007] EWCA Civ 151 at [43], per Arden L.J. (with whom Pill L.J. and Sir Martin Nourse agreed). See similarly *Jani-King (GB) Ltd v Pula Enterprises Ltd* [2007] EWHC 2433 (QBD) at [33]–[34].

[228] See below, paras 3–128 et seq.

[229] See below, paras 27–030 et seq.

[230] Misrepresentation Act 1967 s.2(2) (damages in lieu of rescission) on which see below, paras 6–096—6–102.

[231] Sale of Goods Act 1979 s.15A.

[232] Law Reform (Frustrated Contracts) Act 1943 s.1(2) and (3).

[233] Not all the rights contained in the European Convention and its protocols were included in this process, but only those defined by the Act as "Convention rights": Human Rights Act 1998 s.1.

[234] Human Rights Act 1998 s.3(1).

And under s.4 of the 1998 Act, where a court is unable to "read down" primary legislation in this way, and where a court[235] is satisfied that the legislation is incompatible with Convention rights, it may make a "declaration of incompatibility".[236] As a result, the duty of compatible interpretation and the possibility of a declaration of incompatibility may arise in any proceedings in which the compatibility of primary legislation is challenged, whether or not a "public authority" is party. Secondly, the Act declares it unlawful for "public authorities" to act in a way which is incompatible with a "Convention right," and for this purpose "public authority" includes a court or tribunal and may include any person certain of whose functions are functions of a public nature.[237]

Temporal impact of the Human Rights Act on contracts. In determining the impact of these provisions on contracts and, indeed, also upon the *law* of contract itself, a distinction must be drawn between contracts made before and after the coming into force of the operative provisions of the 1998 Act—October 2, 2000.[238] 1–036

(a) *Contracts made before October 2, 2000*

(i) *The construction and review of legislation governing contracts*

The impact of sections 3 and 4 of the 1998 Act on accrued contractual rights. In *Wilson v First County Trust Ltd (No.2)*,[239] the question arose whether provisions in the Consumer Credit Act 1974 which have the effect of denying the enforceability of a creditor's rights under the contract and its accompanying security for lack of fulfilment of some of its requirements as to proper execution[240] were "incompatible" with the creditor's "Convention rights". The effect of the relevant provisions of the 1974 Act is to deprive the court of any power to enforce a regulated agreement from which a prescribed term has been omitted for the benefit of the creditor, notwithstanding that no prejudice has been caused to anyone by that omission.[241] The Court of Appeal held that a court, as itself a "public authority,"[242] must not act in a way which is incompatible with Convention rights.[243] In its view, the provisions in the 1974 Act in question which required a court to deny any possibility of enforcement for the benefit of the creditor infringed to a disproportionate and unexplained extent its right to a fair and public hearing under art.6(1) of the Convention.[244] The Court of Appeal therefore exercised its discretion in favour of declaring the relevant provision of 1–037

---

235 The courts which are so entitled are listed in s.4(5).

236 Human Rights Act 1998 s.4(1) and (2).

237 Human Rights Act 1998 s.6(1) and (3). Section 6(5) further provides that "[i]n relation to a particular act, a person is not a public authority by virtue only of subs.3(b) if the nature of the act is private" and see below, paras 1–050—1–052.

238 The Human Rights Act 1998 (Commencement No.2) Order 2000 (SI 2000/1851).

239 [2003] UKHL 40, [2003] 3 W.L.R. 568, reversing [2001] EWCA Civ 633, [2002] 2 Q.B. 74.

240 Consumer Credit Act 1974 ss.65(1) and 127(3).

241 [2001] EWCA Civ 633 at [9].

242 Human Rights Act 1998 s.6(3)(a).

243 [2001] EWCA Civ 633 at [17]–[18].

244 [2001] EWCA Civ 633 at [28]–[29].

the 1974 Act incompatible with the Convention.[245] However, this decision was reversed by the House of Lords in a ruling of fundamental importance for the temporal application of the Human Rights Act to private transactions, including contracts.[246] Unlike the Court of Appeal, whose starting point was the duty of a court under s.6 of the 1998 Act, the House of Lords started by asking whether ss.3 and 4 of the 1998 Act apply retrospectively to the facts before them, the contract of consumer credit having been made and having been due to have been performed before the coming into force of the operative provisions of the 1998 Act on December 2, 2000. The House of Lords held unanimously that in the circumstances of the case ss.3 and 4 should not be held to apply to a contract made and to be performed before the coming into force of the 1998 Act. For a majority of their lordships this position was reached by holding that while ss.2–4 of the 1998 Act may clearly apply to enactments made before its coming into force,[247] they should not be interpreted so as to allow the challenge of primary legislation affecting "transactions that have created rights and obligations which the parties seek to enforce against each other".[248] In the words of Lord Scott of Foscote:

> "The legal consequences under the civil law of a transaction or of events ought to be established by reference to the law at the time they take place. They cannot do so if subsequent legislation may add to or diminish those rights or obligations."[249]

Given their lordships' view of the lack of impact of ss.3 and 4 on the contract before them, it followed that the Court of Appeal's reliance on s.6 of the 1998 Act was misplaced, since s.6 can not make unlawful a court's lawful action in giving effect to pre-Act rights and obligations.[250] As a result, the Court of Appeal should not have considered the question of the compatibility with Convention rights of the Consumer Credit Act's provisions which denied the enforceability of the contract for the benefit of the creditor.[251] While Lord Rodger of Earlsferry agreed with this decision on the facts before the House, he did so explicitly on the narrower ground that ss.3 and 4 of the 1998 Act did not apply to pending proceedings so as to protect the Convention rights enshrined in art.1 of the First Protocol to the Convention protecting a person's right to the peaceful enjoyment of his possessions.[252]

1–038 On the other hand, in *PW & Co v Milton Gate Investments Ltd*[253] Neuberger J. was prepared to accept that s.3 of the Human Rights Act could apply to an

---

245 Human Rights Act 1998 s.4(2).

246 [2003] UKHL 40, [2003] 3 W.L.R. 568.

247 [2003] 3 W.L.R. 568 at [17], per Lord Nicholls.

248 [2003] 3 W.L.R. 568 at [98] and see at [101]–[102] (Lord Hope of Craighead); [26] (Lord Nicholls of Birkenhead); [145] (Lord Hobhouse of Woodborough); [161]–[162] (Lord Scott of Foscote).

249 [2003] 3 W.L.R. 568 at [161].

250 [2003] 3 W.L.R. 568 at [157] (Lord Hope of Craighead).

251 See below, paras 1–044—1–045 on the substantive issues of compatibility of the provisions of the Consumer Credit Act 1974 with the Human Rights Act 1998, putting aside the issue of retroactivity.

252 [2003] UKHL 40, [2003] 3 W.L.R. 568 at [215]–[220]. For a straightforward application of the HL's approach see *Laws v Society of Lloyd's* [2003] EWCA Civ 1887 at [32]–[33] (Lloyd's enjoyed statutory immunity barring bad faith prior to coming into force of 1998 Act).

253 [2003] EWHC 1994 (Ch), [2003] All E.R. (D) 58 (Aug).

issue arising from a lease made before its coming into force. There, the learned judge had held that, apart from the operation of s.3, the exercise of a "break clause" in a head-tenancy did not determine the sub-tenancies entered into by the tenant as permitted under the head-lease even though the head-landlord was unable to recover rent under the sub-tenancy covenants.[254] Having referred to a number of passages in the speeches of their lordships in *Wilson v First County Trust (No.2)*,[255] Neuberger J. concluded that their reasoning did not preclude the application of ss.3 or 4 of the 1998 Act to issues arising out of contracts made before its coming into force as long as this did not impair "vested rights" or otherwise create unfairness.[256] In particular, he noted as "very much in point" Lord Scott of Foscote's reference in *Wilson's* case to the example of the impact of legislation intervening between the creation of a lease and its expiry where the legislation could affect the rights and obligations arising under the transaction.[257] On the facts before him, Neuberger J. considered that:

> " . . . the earliest that any 'vested rights' could be said to have arisen under [the break clause in the head-lease], was the date of the service of the Notice under that clause. Unless and until [the break clause] was operated, the rights and obligations of any of the parties as a result of the exercise were merely contingent and not vested."[258]

Since this notice had been served after the coming into force of s.3 of the 1998 Act there were no vested rights at the relevant time so as to prevent its operation on the legislative provisions whose application allegedly prejudiced the head-landlord's right to property under art.1 of the First Protocol of the European Convention. Moreover, in the learned judge's view, it was not more generally unfair to apply s.3 in this way even though the notice had been served only four days after its coming into force given, in particular, that the 1998 Act had been on the Statute Book for around two years before it came into force.[259]

(ii) *Contracts made by "public authorities"*

Section 6 and accrued contractual rights. The making of a contract by a person or body may sometimes constitute an "act" by a "public authority" within the meaning of s.6 of the 1998 Act.[260] While the decision in *Wilson v First County Trust Ltd (No.2)*[261] was directly concerned with the application of ss.3 and 4 of the 1998 Act to transactions which created rights accruing before its coming into force, it is submitted that a similar approach would be taken so as to deny the application of s.6 of the 1998 Act to contracts made by "public authorities" before its coming into force. As Lord Nicholls observed in setting out the general framework of the 1998 Act: 1–039

[254] [2003] EWHC 1994 (Ch) at [103]–[104].
[255] [2003] UKHL 40, [2004] 1 A.C. 816, above, para.1–037.
[256] [2003] EWHC 1994 (Ch) at [107]–[115].
[257] [2003] UKHL 40 at [161]; [2003] EWHC 1994 (Ch) at [110] and [114].
[258] [2003] EWHC 1994 (Ch) at [114].
[259] [2003] EWHC 1994 (Ch) at [115].
[260] On the application of the definition of "public authority" under ss.6(3) and (5) of the 1998 Act to the making of contracts, see below, para.1–044—1–045.
[261] [2003] 3 W.L.R. 568, (2003) 3 W.L.R. 568.

> "On a natural reading [s.6] is directed at post-Act conduct. The context powerfully supports this interpretation. One would not expect a statute promoting human rights values to render unlawful acts which were lawful when done."[262]

Lord Scott of Foscote agreed, observing that:

> "It is plain that section 6 is looking to the future. It is not purporting to make unlawful a pre 2 October 2000 act of a public authority."[263]

The approach of the majority of the House of Lords in *Wilson v First County Trust Ltd (No.2)* therefore clearly indicates that s.6 of the 1998 Act will not be applied so as to make unlawful the making of contracts by public authorities before its coming into force on December 2, 2000. And while Lord Rodger of Earlsferry took a more nuanced approach to the distinct types of "retroactivity" which he identified according to the different Convention rights protected by the 1998 Act,[264] he also proceeded on the basis that:

> "Parliament must have intended all the operative provisions [which include s.6] of this particular statute to take effect in the same way in respect of any given Convention right."[265]

1–040 **The later performance of contracts made by "public authorities."** A further question relating to contracts made before the coming into effect of s.6 of the 1998 Act concerns a public authority's "act" of performance of a contract rather than its "act" in making one.[266] For if a public authority has made a contract before the coming into effect of the 1998 Act, but *after* its coming into effect performs one of its obligations in a way required by the contract but incompatible with a Convention right, such a performance could be thought itself to constitute an "act" made unlawful by s.6 of the 1998 Act. On the other hand, against this line of reasoning it could be contended that s.6 of the 1998 Act should not be interpreted so as to render illegal the performance of existing contractual obligations since this would have the correlative effect of prejudicing the existing rights of the other party under the contract. In resolving these arguments, observations made in *Wilson v First County Trust Ltd (No.2)* concerning the retroactive effect of legislation in general and the 1998 Act in particular may be helpful, even though that decision was concerned with the incompatibility with Convention rights of primary legislation as applied to facts occurring before the 1998 Act's coming into force.[267] In this respect, Lord Rodger of Earlsferry noted that:

---

[262] [2003] 3 W.L.R. 568 at [12].

[263] [2003] 3 W.L.R. 568 at [156].

[264] See above, para.1–037.

[265] [2003] UKHL 40, [2003] 3 W.L.R. 568 at [156].

[266] For the purposes of the present discussion, it will be assumed that the public authority fulfils the criteria required by the 1998 Act s.6(3) and (4), on which see below, paras 1–044—1–045.

[267] [2003] UKHL 40, [2003] 3 W.L.R. 568. Lord Rodger of Earlsferry explicitly stated that ss.3–9 of the 1998 Act should be interpreted so as to apply retroactively or only from commencement as a whole: at [204], [206].

"Retroactive provisions alter the existing rights and duties of those whom they affect. But not all provisions which alter existing rights and duties are retroactive. The statute book contains many statutes which are not retroactive but alter existing rights and duties—only prospectively, with effect from the date of commencement."[268]

While Lord Rodger quoted with approval the words of Dickson J. to the effect that "[n]o-one has a vested right to continuance of the law as it stood in the past",[269] he observed that:

". . . often . . . a sudden change in existing rights would be so unfair to certain individuals or businesses in their particular predicament that it is to be presumed that Parliament did not intend the new legislation to affect them in that respect."[270]

Although he added that "in practice the presumption against legislation altering vested rights is regarded as weaker than the presumption against legislation having retroactive effect".[271] What these observations suggest is that s.6 of the 1998 Act should be interpreted so as not to make unlawful the "acts of performance" of public authorities of contractual obligations created before its coming into force even if these acts are incompatible with Convention rights, since such an illegality would prejudice the existing rights of other parties under those contracts. However, a future court could prefer to follow also the more nuanced approach adopted by Lord Rodger for this purpose, distinguishing between the various Convention rights[272] in assessing the effect of the operative provisions of the 1998 Act.[273]

Effect of any unlawful performance by a public authority. If a court were to hold that a public authority would act unlawfully within the meaning of s.6 of the 1998 Act by performing an obligation arising under a contract made before the coming into force of that Act, then either the performance of the contractual obligation in question would be excused or the contract as a whole would be 1–041

[268] [2003] 3 W.L.R. 568 at [188]. On the restricted basis for Lord Rodger's decision, see above, para.1–037. Lord Rodger drew on the discussion in P.-A. Coté, *The Interpretation of Legislation in Canada*, 3rd edn (2000), Ch.2, s.1 and referred to *West v Gwynne* [1911] 2 Ch. 1. Lord Hobhouse adopted Lord Rodger's observations on the various usages of the word "retrospective": [2003] UKHL 40, [2003] 3 W.L.R. 568 at [145]. See also the observations of Lord Scott of Foscote at [161], who noted that: "Where transactions calculated to continue for some considerable period are entered into, intervening legislation may in some respect or other affect the rights or obligations that accrue after the legislation has come into force." He illustrated this by reference to contracts of lease and landlord and tenant legislation.

[269] [2003] UKHL 40; [2003] 3 W.L.R. 568 at [192]; *Gustavson Drilling (1964) Ltd v Minister of National Revenue* [1977] 1 S.C.R. 271, 282–283.

[270] [2003] UKHL 40; [2003] 3 W.L.R. 568 at [193].

[271] [2003] 3 W.L.R. 568 at [195].

[272] [2003] 3 W.L.R. 568 at [209]–[210]. He distinguished in particular between the procedural rights protected by art.6 of the Convention and other, substantive rights. For Lord Rodger the proper question was therefore whether the 1998 Act gave effect to art.1 of the First Protocol to the Convention so as to affect vested rights or pending proceedings: [2003] 3 W.L.R. 568 at [215].

[273] i.e. Human Rights Act 1998 ss.3–9.

frustrated by this supervening illegality, this depending on the illegality's significance for the main purpose of the contract as a whole.[274]

1–042 **Unlawful manner of performance by public authority.** Different considerations apply where a public authority's action in performing an obligation arising under a contract made before the coming into force of the 1998 Act is incompatible with a Convention right, but where this incompatibility is not required by the obligation itself, but rather reflects the chosen manner of its performance by the public authority. In these circumstances, the arguments as to the effect of s.6 of the 1998 Act would differ from those exposed earlier,[275] as *ex hypothesi* the other party to the contract would not have any accrued rights to the action of the public authority in purported performance of the contract. It is submitted, therefore, that in these circumstances a public authority could be held to act unlawfully within the meaning of s.6, even though the contract predated the 1998 Act's coming into force. Where this is the case, then the courts are likely to look to their general approach to illegality in performance to determine the effects of this "unlawful act" on the contractual rights of the parties *inter se*.[276]

(iii) *The duty of courts as "public authorities" in relation to contracts*

1–043 **The construction of contracts.** In *Biggin Hill Airport Ltd v Bromley LBC*[277] (which concerned a contract made between a local authority and a private company), it was held that the 1998 Act did not require a court as itself a public authority[278] to interpret a contract made *before* the coming into effect of the same Act in such a way as to be compatible with the Convention rights of third parties to the contract, since common law authority established that a court should look to the factual circumstances at the time of a contract's conclusion for the resolution of issues of its construction.[279] This decision may be seen as reflecting in the context of the control and application of the common law a similar principle of non-retroactivity as was applied by the House of Lords in its later decision in *Wilson v First County Trust Ltd (No.2)* for the purposes of the control and application of primary legislation.[280] On the other hand, in *Biggin Hill Airport* it was accepted that even in respect of a contract made before the coming into force of the 1998 Act, where the contract was *made by* a public authority the protection of people's Convention rights might form an element in its decision-making process, although on the facts the court found that it had not done so.[281] If a court were to find such an element to have been the case, then its decision

---

[274] cf. Treitel, *The Law of Contract*, 12th edn (2007 by Peel), paras 19–049—19–050 and see below, paras 23–066—23–069.

[275] Above, paras 1–040—1–041.

[276] See below, paras 16–189 et seq.

[277] *The Times*, January 9, 2001, (2001) 98(3) L.S.G. 42 reversed on other grounds [2001] EWCA Civ 1089, *The Times*, August 13, 2001, (2001) 98(33) L.S.G. 30.

[278] Human Rights Act 1998 s.6(3)(a).

[279] *Prenn v Simmonds* [1971] 1 W.L.R. 1381; *Investors Compensation Scheme Ltd v West Bromwich Building Society* [1998] 1 W.L.R. 896.

[280] Above, para.1–037.

[281] *Biggin Hill Airport Ltd v Bromley LBC*, *The Times*, January 9, 2001, (2001) 98(3) L.S.G. 42 at [173], reversed on other grounds [2001] EWCA Civ 1089, *The Times*, August 13, 2001, (2001) 98(33) L.S.G. 30.

protecting the Convention right would not have any true retroactive impact: it would merely be giving effect to the existing common law principle of interpretation of a contract by reference to the common intentions of the parties as construed in their factual matrix.[282]

(b) *Contracts made on or after October 2, 2000*

(i) *The construction and review of legislation governing contracts*

1–044 **Sections 3 and 4 of the 1998 Act: primary or secondary legislation governing the contract and Convention rights.** While it was not necessary for its decision in *Wilson v First County Trust Ltd (No.2)*,[283] four members of the House of Lords considered there the substantive questions of compatibility with Convention rights of the provisions of the Consumer Credit Act 1974 (putting aside the retroactive element found on the facts), and this makes clear their general view that questions of compatibility with Convention rights of legislation governing contracts made *on or after* the date of their coming into force, viz October 2, 2000, would arise for the purposes of ss.3 and 4 of the 1998 Act. The substantive questions raised in *Wilson (No.2)* itself were whether the denial of any possibility of enforcement of the contract of consumer credit or its attendant security by the creditor against the consumer was incompatible either with the creditor's right to a fair trial under art.6 of the European Convention or with the creditor's right to the peaceful enjoyment of his possessions under art.1 of the First Protocol to the Convention. The issue of compatibility with art.6 was fairly quickly dealt with by the House of Lords as art.6(1) is concerned to ensure a fair civil process and "does not itself guarantee any particular content for civil rights and obligations in the substantive law of the contracting states".[284] The effect of the Consumer Credit Act was to deny the creditor any substantive legal rights under the contract or in relation to the security and did not concern its procedural rights.[285] While their lordships also agreed that (putting aside the question of the temporal application of the 1998 Act) the creditor's right to its possessions was not denied by the relevant provisions of Consumer Credit Act 1974,[286] their reasons for coming to this conclusion differed. Here, there were two issues: (i) did the facts of the case engage the application of art.1 of the First Protocol; (ii) if so, did the provisions of the Consumer Credit Act put in place a legitimate, proportionate and sufficiently certain restriction on the creditor's rights? The following paragraphs will examine the treatment of these issues in *Wilson v First County Trust Ltd (No.2)* itself and in the subsequent case law.

1–045 **Unenforceable contractual rights and engaging article 1 of the First Protocol.** The four members of the House of Lords who expressed their views

---

[282] See below, paras 12–050, 12–117 et seq.

[283] [2003] UKHL 40, [2003] 3 W.L.R. 568. These observations were obiter given their decision on the non-retroactive impact of ss.3 and 4 of the 1998 Act: see above, paras 1–037—1–038. Lord Rodger expressed no views on these hypothetical issues: [2003] 3 W.L.R. 568 at [220].

[284] [2003] UKHL 40, [2003] 3 W.L.R. 568 at [33], per Lord Nicholls.

[285] [2003] 3 W.L.R. 568 at [104]–[105] (Lord Hope); [132] (Lord Hobhouse); [165]–[166] (Lord Scott); [215] (Lord Rodger agreeing with Lord Nicholls).

[286] Consumer Credit Act 1974 ss.106, 113 and especially 127(3).

were divided in their response to the question whether the facts of *Wilson v First County Trust Ltd (No.2)*[287] engaged the application of art.1 of the First Protocol.[288] For Lord Nicholls, " 'possessions' in Article 1 is apt to embrace contractual rights",[289] and the provisions of the 1974 Act which deny any rights of enforcement of the contract to the creditor would engage art.1 as they are:

> " . . . more readily and appropriately to be characterised as a statutory deprivation of the lender's rights of property in the broadest sense of that expression than as a mere delimitation of the extent of the rights granted by a transaction."[290]

Lord Hobhouse of Woodborough agreed that art.1 could be engaged, but on the narrower ground that the 1974 Act could operate so as to deprive the creditor of its special title to possession of the security under a contract of pledge; conversely, if a creditor had not taken possession of any security, art.1 would not be engaged as the creditor would be left merely with "the purported enforcement of a claimed contractual right which the lenders had never in truth validly acquired".[291] By contrast, Lords Hope and Scott agreed that art.1 would not be engaged on the facts before them: art.1 of the First Protocol is directed to interference with existing possessions or property rights, whereas the creditor never had any rights of enforcement or possession against the borrower owing to the application of the provisions of the 1974 Act.[292] In the words of Lord Hope, art.1:

> " . . . does not confer a right of property as such nor does it guarantee the content of any rights of property. What it does is to guarantee the peaceful enjoyment of the possessions that a person already owns . . . [I]t is a matter for domestic law to define the nature and extent of any rights which a party acquires from time to time as a result of the transactions which he or she enters into."[293]

According to Lord Scott:

> "No authority has been cited . . . for the proposition that a statutory provision which prevents a transaction from having the quality of legal enforceability can be regarded an interference for Article 1 purposes with the possessions of the party who would have benefited if the transaction had had that quality."[294]

Implicit in Lord Nicholls' view is an understanding that even in a context such as consumer credit where statute defines the circumstances in which the parties'

---

[287] [2003] UKHL 40, [2003] 3 W.L.R. 568. These observations were obiter given their decision on the non-retroactive impact of ss.3 and 4 of the 1998 Act: see above, para.1–037.

[288] As has been noted, Lord Rodger of Earlsferry did not decide the point: [2003] 3 W.L.R. 568 at [220].

[289] [2003] UKHL 40, [2003] 3 W.L.R. 568 at [39]. This view may be supported from the Strasbourg case law, e.g. *Stran Greek Refineries & Stratis Andreadis v Greece* (1995) E.H.R.R. 293 at [60]–[62] (right under arbitration award); *Stretch v UK* (2004) 38 E.H.R.R. 12 especially at [32] (option to renew lease later considered void as ultra vires the public authority lessor's power).

[290] [2003] 3 W.L.R. 568 at [44].

[291] [2003] 3 W.L.R. 568 at [137].

[292] [2003] 3 W.L.R. 568 at [107] (Lord Hope) and [168] (Lord Scott).

[293] [2003] 3 W.L.R. 568 at [106].

[294] [2003] 3 W.L.R. 568 at [168].

rights arise, it is the parties' agreement (possibly as recognised by the common law) which forms the source of their contractual rights, which are then eligible for protection under art.1. For Lords Hope and Scott, it is the statute itself which defines the circumstances when the parties' agreement will or will not give rise to rights in them: the law creates the parties' rights, it does not curtail pre-existing rights.[295]

It is submitted, that whatever the general theoretical validity of either view of the nature and origin of contractual rights in the modern law, the approach of Lord Nicholls is to be preferred for the purposes of art.1 of the First Protocol.[296] For the overall function of art.1 is to prevent states from depriving persons of their possessions illegitimately and for this purpose legislation which denies a right which would otherwise arise (i.e. under the general law) can be seen to have such a depriving effect. This approach may be supported by reference to the case law of the European Court of Human Rights[297] and especially its later decision in *Stretch v UK*[298] in which it held that art.1 of the First Protocol was engaged where a person's option to renew a lease was subsequently found to be void as ultra vires the lessor public authority's powers, the Court observing that: 1–046

> "... according to the established case law of the Convention organs, 'possessions' can be 'existing possessions' or assets, including claims, in respect of which the applicant can argue that he has at least a 'legitimate expectation' of obtaining effect enjoyment of a property right."[299]

This decision is therefore incompatible with an approach to art.1 which views the existence of a property right as contingent on its recognition by the national law of contract unmitigated by the influence of Convention rights.

Subsequent cases. In subsequent English decisions, Lord Nicholls' distinction in *Wilson v First County Trust Ltd (No.2)* between an Act's deprivation of a person's contractual rights and its mere delimitation of them has sometimes been taken up and applied.[300] So, for example, in *Pennycook v Shaws (EAL) Ltd*,[301] the Court of Appeal considered whether a tenant's statutory right to renew a business tenancy conferred by Pt II of the Landlord and Tenant Act 1954 is a "possession" for the purposes of art.1. Arden L.J. (with whom Thorpe L.J. and Sir Martin Nourse agreed) found "the most detailed guidance" as to how to 1–047

---

[295] While the context of this discussion was the application of s.4 of the 1998 Act to primary legislation, similar questions would arise in relation to any review or development of the common law undertaken by the courts as "public authorities" under s.6 of the 1998 Act. On this see below, para.1–060.

[296] See further McMeel, *The Construction of Contracts: Interpretation, Implication and Rectification* (2007), pp.205 et seq.; Allen, *Property and the Human Rights Act 1998* (2005), Ch.8.

[297] See cases cited at fn. 289, above.

[298] (2004) 38 E.H.R.R. 12.

[299] (2004) 38 E.H.R.R. 12 at [32], and see also [34] and [35].

[300] [2003] UKHL 40, [2004] 1 A.C. 816 at [137].

[301] [2004] EWCA Civ 100, [2004] Ch. 296 at [30]–[42]. See also *C A Webber (Transport) Ltd v Railtrack Plc* [2003] EWCA Civ 1167, [2004] 1 W.L.R. 320 at [59]–[61]; *Re T & N Ltd* [2005] EWHC 2870 (Ch), [2006] 1 W.L.R. 1728 at [171]; *JA Pye (Oxford) Ltd v United Kingdom* (2006) 43 E.H.R.R. 3 at [52].

approach this question in Lord Nicholls's speech in the *Wilson* case,[302] with the result that the court needing to look:

> ". . . at the substance of the claimed right to see whether the bar to the exercise of the tenant's right is a delimitation of the right or whether it represents a deprivation of right."[303]

On the facts before her, Arden L.J. held that the 1954 Act deprived the tenant of a right.[304] By the time of *PW & Co Ltd v Milton Gate Investments Ltd*,[305] however, Neuberger J. was able to take into account the decision of the European Court of Human Rights in *Stretch v UK*[306] in deciding whether art.1 was engaged. Neuberger J. there accepted that the Human Rights Act required ss.139 or 141 of the Law of Property Act 1925 to be interpreted so as to prevent a head-landlord from being deprived of rent under the covenants of sub-tenancies which had not determined by the exercise of a "break clause" by the head-tenant. In these circumstances, art.1 of the First Protocol to the European Convention was engaged: if the underleases would survive the determination of the head-lease without the tenant's covenants being enforceable, the head-landlord would be kept out of the premises in question for the remainder of the sub-leases without being able to recover any rent whatever: "[t]hat is scarcely 'peaceful enjoyment of [its] possessions' ".[307] On the other hand, in *K Ltd v National Westminster Bank Plc*[308] Longmore L.J. (with whom Ward and Laws L.JJ. agreed) doubted whether the exception creation by ss.328, 333, 335 and 338 of the Proceeds of Crime Act 2002 to a bank's customer's right to have the contract of mandate performed is "the kind of possession which art.1 [of the First Protocol] contemplates will be peaceably enjoyed" as the legislation did not cancel the debt but merely deferred performance of the contract for a number of days during which the bank's suspicion of money-laundering was investigated.[309]

1–048 **The legitimacy, certainty, and proportionality of the legislative interference with a person's property.** If a court decides that art.1 of the First Protocol is engaged, it must then address the question whether the law's interference with the right of property is legitimate, sufficiently certain and proportionate.[310] In this respect, in *Wilson v First County Trust Ltd (No.2)*[311] those judges who expressed a view on the matter considered that if the provisions of the Consumer Credit Act 1974 were properly held to interfere with the creditor's right of property, then this interference was both "legitimate" and "proportionate" given the importance of the social policy of protection of borrowers

---

302 [2004] EWCA Civ 100 at [34].
303 [2004] EWCA Civ 100 at [35].
304 [2004] EWCA Civ 100 at [38].
305 [2003] EWHC 1994 (Ch), [2004] Ch. 142.
306 (2004) 38 E.H.R.R. 12 especially at [32].
307 [2003] EWHC 1994 (Ch) at [126], per Neuberger J.
308 [2006] EWCA Civ 1039, [2007] 1 W.L.R. 311.
309 [2006] EWCA Civ 1039 at [25].
310 *Sporrong and Lönnroth v Sweden* (1983) 5 E.H.R.R. 35 at [69]–[73].
311 [2003] UKHL 40, [2003] 3 W.L.R. 568.

which lay behind them.[312] And while Lord Nicholls expressed some hesitation on the issue of certainty, he concluded that he was "not persuaded [that] the degree of uncertainty involved . . . [was] unacceptably high."[313] Therefore, there was no incompatibility between the relevant provisions of the Consumer Credit Act 1974 and creditors' Convention rights. Similarly, in *K Ltd v National Westminster Bank Plc*[314] the Court of Appeal held that even if the exception created by the Proceeds of Crime Act 2002 to a bank's customer's right to have the contract of mandate performed attracted the application of art.1, any interference with the customer's common law rights under the mandate did not impair its right of access to the courts in anything more than a short suspensory manner and, given the purposes of the 2002 Act, did so in pursuance of a legitimate aim in a proportionate manner.[315]

Examples of other Convention rights. Examples of the application of ss.3 and 4 of the 1998 Act may arise in relation to other Convention rights.[316] So, it has been argued that s.11(1)(a) of the Landlord and Tenant Act 1985 imposing an obligation "to keep in repair the structure" of the dwelling house must be construed by operation of s.3(1) of the 1998 Act so as to give effect to the tenant's rights under Art.8 of the European Convention and thereby must be read as imposing an obligation "to put and keep [the structure] in good habitable repair".[317] However, this argument was rejected by the Court of Appeal on the basis that this was not a possible reading of the relevant provisions of the Landlord and Tenant Act 1985, given the interpretation to them previously established by the Court of Appeal.[318] It has also been argued that the system of adjudication set up by the Housing Grants Construction and Regeneration Act 1996, s.108(2) is incompatible with art.6 of the European Convention.[319] Furthermore, in *Ghaidan v Godin Mendoza*[320] a majority of the House of Lords relied on s.3 of the Human Rights Act 1998 to "read and give effect" to the provisions of the Rent Act 1977[321] which grants a statutory tenancy to "[t]he surviving spouse (if any) of the original tenant if residing in the dwelling-house immediately before the death of the original tenant" so as to include homosexual 1–049

---

312 [2003] UKHL 40, [2003] 3 W.L.R. 568 at [62], [74]–[75] (Lord Nicholls, with whom Lord Hope agreed at [109]); [138] (Lord Hobhouse of Woolborough); [169]–[170] (Lord Scott).

313 [2003] UKHL 40 at [77].

314 [2006] EWCA Civ 1039 [2007] 1 W.L.R. 311.

315 [2006] EWCA Civ 1039 at [24].

316 On the possible impact of the Human Rights Act on arbitral proceedings see Vol.II, paras 32–015—32–018 referring to *Stretford v Football Association Ltd* [2007] EWCA Civ 238, [2007] 2 Lloyd's Rep. 31 (where it was held that an arbitration clause and any arbitration made under it which was subject to the provisions of the Arbitration Act 1996 did not constitute an infringement of a person's rights under art.6 of the European Convention); *Sumukan Ltd v The Commonwealth Secretariat* [2007] EWCA Civ 243, [2007] 2 Lloyd's Rep. 87 at [53]–[62] (where it was held that an agreement not to appeal an arbitration award under s.69 of the Arbitration Act 1996 did not constitute an infringement of a person's rights under art.6 of the European Convention).

317 *Lee v Leeds City Council* [2002] EWCA Civ 6, [2002] 1 W.L.R. 1488 at [56].

318 [2002] 1 W.L.R. 1488 at [56]–[59], referring to *Quick v Taff Ely BC* [1986] Q.B. 809.

319 *Austin Hall Building Ltd v Buckland Securities Ltd* [2001] B.L.R. 272 at [18]. No determination was made under s.4 of the Act as no notice had been given to the Crown pursuant to s.5 of the Human Rights Act 1998.

320 [2004] UKHL 30, [2004] 2 A.C. 557.

321 Rent Act 1977 Sch.I paras 2 and 3 (as amended).

cohabitees, so as to give effect to their Convention right not to be discriminated against on the ground of sexual orientation in respect of their right to respect for a person's home.[322]

(ii) *Contracts made by "public authorities"*

1–050 **"Public authorities" within the meaning of section 6 of the 1998 Act.** An important preliminary question is whether, when or to what extent contracts made (or not made)[323] by public authorities or by other persons attract the application of s.6 of the 1998 Act. According to s.6(1) "[i]t is unlawful for a public authority to act in a way which is incompatible with a Convention right". Section 6(3) provides for this purpose that "public authority includes (a) a court or tribunal, and (b) any person certain of whose functions are functions of a public nature"; s.6(5) then explains that:

> "In relation to a particular act, a person is not a public authority by virtue only of subsection 3(b) if the nature of the act is private."

This provision therefore recognises two categories of person: "core public authorities" (sometimes termed "pure public authorities"), that is, those persons or bodies which are public authorities for all purposes, such as government ministers, local authorities, and the police)[324]; and "hybrid" bodies which may act either publicly or privately depending on the nature of the act or omission.[325] As regards "core public authorities," *all* their "acts" (including apparently their acts in making, performing or breaking their contracts) are subject to the test of illegality found in s.6, however "private" they may appear.[326] As regards "hybrid" bodies, it is a much more difficult question whether their conclusion of a contract constitutes an act "the nature of [which] is private," rather than public.

1–051 **"Hybrid bodies"and "functions of a public nature."** The way in which s.6 applies to "hybrid bodies" has arisen in three important decisions.[327] In *Aston*

---

[322] European Convention on Human Rights arts 8 and 14.

[323] See below, para.1–043.

[324] For the HL in *Aston Cantlow and Wilmcote with Billesley Parochial Church Council v Wallbank* [2003] UKHL 37, [2004] 1 A.C. 546 at [6]–[7], [52], [88], [171] the purpose of s.6(1) is that those bodies for whose acts the state is answerable before the European Court of Human Rights shall be subject to a domestic law obligation not to act incompatibly with Convention rights and the phrase "a public authority" for the purpose of s.6(1) is therefore "essentially a reference to a body whose nature is governmental in the broad sense of the expression".

[325] *Aston Cantlow and Wilmcote with Billesley Parochial Church Council v Wallbank* [2003] UKHL 37, [2004] 1 A.C. 546 at [8]–[11], [35], [85]. Craig, *Administrative Law*, 6th edn (2008), para.18–017 et seq. (who notes that this categorisation reflects the parliamentary debates of the Human Rights Act and accords with the approach adopted by the European Court of Human Rights).

[326] *YL v Birmingham City Council* [2007] UKHL 27, [2007] 3 W.L.R. 112 at [131] (Lord Neuberger).

[327] See further HL & HC Joint Committee on Human Rights, *The Meaning of Public Authority under the Human Rights Act 2006–2007* (2007) (published before the decision in *YL v Birmingham City Council* [2007] UKHL 27, [2007] 3 W.L.R. 112); Craig, *Administrative Law*, paras 18–017—18–025.

Cantlow and Wilmcote with Billesley Parochial Church Council v Wallbank[328] the House of Lords considered that there is no single test to determine whether or not a particular function exercised by a "hybrid body" is "public" within the meaning of s.6(3)(b), though factors to be taken into account include:

> "... the extent to which in carrying out the relevant function the body is publicly funded, or is exercising statutory powers, or is taking the place of central government or local authorities, or is providing a public service."[329]

In this respect, although the domestic case law on judicial review may provide some assistance as to what does and does not constitute a "function of a public nature" within the meaning of s.6(3)(b), this case law must be examined in the light of the jurisprudence of the European Court of Human Rights as to those bodies which engage the responsibility of the state for the purposes of the Convention.[330]

Subsequently in *R. (West) v Lloyd's of London*[331] the Court of Appeal held that decisions by Lloyd's of London under powers contained in its byelaws to approve minority buy-outs of four syndicates of which the applicant was a member (and which he complained were prejudicial to his rights of due process and of possession of this property under art.6 of the Convention and under art.1 to its First Protocol) were not subject to challenge by way of judicial review, whether by virtue of s.6 of the 1998 Act or more generally. In the view of the Court of Appeal, the relationship between Lloyd's and its members was entirely voluntary and contractual and their rights to participate in a syndicate governed exclusively by the terms of their contracts with their managing agents.[332] Applying the approach of the House of Lords in *Aston Cantlow*, the Court of Appeal held that for the purposes of s.6 of the 1998 Act the objectives of Lloyd's were "wholly commercial" and "not governmental even in the broad sense of that expression": it was rather the Financial Services Authority acting under the Financial Services and Markets Act 2000 "which is the governmental organisation which will be answerable to the Strasbourg court".[333]

Thirdly, in the important and controversial decision in *YL v Birmingham City Council*[334] a majority of the House of Lords held that a commercial company providing residential and nursing care to a person under a contract was not acting as someone "certain of whose functions are functions of a public nature" within the meaning of s.6(3)(b) of the 1998 Act, even though in so doing the company acted under a contract with a local authority which concluded it in furtherance of its statutory duties to make arrangements for providing residential accommodation for persons in need of care and attention not otherwise available to them. The grounds of their lordships' decisions were complex, but of key significance for the majority were the nature of the body providing the care ("a private, profit- 1–052

[328] [2003] UKHL 37, [2004] 1 A.C. 546.
[329] [2003] UKHL 37 at [12]
[330] [2003] UKHL 37 at [52].
[331] [2004] EWCA Civ 506, [2004] 3 All E.R. 251.
[332] [2004] EWCA Civ 506 at [8]–[9].
[333] [2004] EWCA Civ 506, at [38], per Brooke L.J.
[334] [2007] UKHL 27, [2007] 3 W.L.R. 112 noted by Landu (2007) P.L. 630.

earning company"[335]); the nature of the obligation which the person in receipt of nursing care was seeking to enforce, namely "a private law contract"[336]; and, more widely, a concern for the widespread effect of the opposite decision, which was seen as requiring any commercial company (and its employees) which carried on an operation of a similar nature to an operation carried on by a local authority under statutory powers also to be covered by the 1998 Act.[337] For the minority (Baroness Hale of Richmond, with whom Lord Bingham of Cornhill agreed) the meaning of s.6 had to be seen in the context of the case law of the European Court of Human Rights which has sometimes placed responsibility on a state for the acts of a private body, notably imposing positive obligations on it to prevent violations of an individual's human rights.[338] So, for the purposes of s.6 of the 1998 Act in Baroness Hale's view:

> "The contrast is between what is 'public' in the sense of being done for or by or on behalf of people as a whole and what is 'private' in the sense of being done for one's own purposes."[339]

and:

> ". . . while there cannot be a single litmus test of what is a function of a public nature, the underlying rationale must be that it is a task for which the public, in the shape of the state, have assumed responsibility, at public expense if need be, and in the public interest."[340]

This led the minority to hold that the company undertook functions "of a public nature" in providing residential care to persons in need under a contract with the local authority which discharged thereby its statutory duty to make arrangements for this purpose.[341] The minority's position has been cogently supported by Professor Craig on the basis that: "If it is decided that a core public authority is performing a public function pursuant to a statutory duty or power cast upon it, then that should be decisive,"[342] of the question of its performing a public function and so there should be no assessment of factors (as undertaken by the majority):

---

[335] [2007] UKHL 27, per Lord Mance at [115] with whom Lord Neuberger of Abbotsbury agreed at [126].

[336] [2007] UKHL 27, per Lord Scott of Foscote at [34], although cf. Lord Mance at [117]–[118] and Lord Neuberger at [151] who saw the absence of any relevant difference between a resident staying privately under a contract with the company and one staying under an arrangement between the company and a local authority as a reason for treating both as unable to rely on Convention rights against the company.

[337] [2007] UKHL 27 at [30] and [82] (Lord Mance using the example of private contractors cleaning the windows of premises let to council tenants).

[338] [2007] UKHL 27 at [56]–[57], per Baroness Hale of Richmond.

[339] [2007] UKHL 27 at [62], per Baroness Hale of Richmond.

[340] [2007] UKHL 27 at [66] and see also [7]–[12] (Lord Bingham of Cornhill).

[341] A private Members' Bill has been introduced to Parliament, the Human Rights Act 1998 (Meaning of Public Authority) Bill 2007 cl.1 of which provides that: "[F]or the purposes of section 6(3)(b) of the Human Rights Act 1998 (c.42), a function of a public nature includes a function performed pursuant to a contract or other arrangement with a public authority which is under a duty to perform that function."

[342] Craig, *Administrative Law*, 6th edn (2008) para.18–024.

"... the nature of the function does not change if the task is contracted out to a body that is nominally private.[343] It cannot be correct as a matter of principle for the availability of Convention rights to be dependent upon the fortuitous incidence as to how the core public authority chooses to discharge its functions."[344]

However, he acknowledges that legislative intervention may be required to reform the law on the question.[345]

Unlawful refusal to contract by public authority. Section 6(6) of the 1998 Act provides that " '[a]n act' includes a failure to act". In *R. (Haggerty) v St. Helen's BC*[346] Silber J. was prepared to assume that a local authority's decision not to enter a new contract with a private sector provider for the provision of places in a nursing home in fulfilment of a statutory duty,[347] did fall within s.6 so as to require its effects to be assessed as to their compatibility with the Convention rights of the existing residents of the home (who had to move to other accommodation provided by the local authority as a result of its decision not to enter the contract).[348] However, on the facts the learned judge held that this act of the local authority did not infringe any of their Convention rights. **1–053**

Unlawful conclusion of contract. Where a "public authority",[349] concludes a contract after the coming into force of the operative provisions of the 1998 Act, then the "act" of so doing would engage s.6 of the 1998 Act. Where this "act" is itself incompatible with a Convention right (either of the other party and of a third party) then it is rendered "unlawful". So, for example, it has been said that a local authority must bear in mind the Convention rights of the residents of accommodation to be provided in performance of its functions under the National Assistance Act 1948 s.21 in making their contracts with private sector providers.[350] Similarly, where a "public authority" concludes a contract of employment, it should bear in mind its employees' Convention rights, notably, to freedom of expression and privacy.[351] **1–054**

Unlawful manner of performance of contract. Section 6 of the 1998 Act may also affect the way in which "public authority" ought to act in performance of, or in relation to a situation created by, a contract. So, for example, in *Lee v Leeds City Council*,[352] the Court of Appeal proceeded on the basis that a local authority acted as a "public authority" in relation to the provision of public sector housing and that this therefore imposed on it a statutory duty to take steps to ensure that the condition of the houses which they provided was such that their **1–055**

---

343 Craig at para.18–024.
344 Craig at para.18–024 (with other arguments to the same effect).
345 Craig para.18–025 noting the Human Rights Act (Meaning of Public Authority) Bill 2007.
346 [2003] EWHC 803 (Admin), *The Times*, April 30, 2003.
347 National Assistance Act 1948 s.21.
348 [2003] EWHC 803 (Admin) at [25]–[26].
349 Above, paras 1–051—1–052.
350 *R. (Heather) v Leonard Cheshire Foundation* [2002] EWCA Civ 366, [2002] H.R.L.R. 30 at [34]. Cf. *YL v Birmingham City Council* [2007] UKHL 27, [2007] 3 W.L.R. 112 in relation to the position of the private sector providers themselves: above, para.1–052.
351 See further Morris (1998) I.L.J. 293 and Palmer [2000] C.L.J. 168.
352 [2002] EWCA Civ 6; [2002] 1 W.L.R. 1488 at [26].

tenants' rights to respect of their private and family life under Art.8 of the European Convention were not infringed.[353] However, according to the Court of Appeal:

> "The steps which a public authority will be required to take in order to ensure compliance with Article 8 . . . must be determined, in each case, by having due regard to the needs and resources of the community and of individuals, [having regard to the fact that] [t]he allocation of resources to meet the needs of social housing is very much a matter for democratically determined priorities".[354]

In relation to the cases before it, the Court of Appeal held that no breach of the statutory duty which it had identified had been established, in part owing to the proceedings being by way of preliminary issues without any determination of the relevant facts.[355] A further example may be found in the actions of a public employer, which must not act inconsistently with the Convention rights of its employees, for instance, as regards the secret monitoring of their telephone conversations.[356]

1–056 **Effect on the contract.** Where s.6 of the 1998 Act renders the making or performance of a contract unlawful as incompatible with Convention rights it creates a new head of contractual illegality. In the absence of special provision on this issue in the 1998 Act, the contractual and restitutionary consequences for the parties to the contract of this "unlawfulness" fall to be governed by the common law's approach to illegality exposed and analysed in Ch.16. In this respect, difficult questions may arise as to whether the "unlawful act" of the public authority renders the whole contract illegal (and with what effects for its parties) or whether it merely renders a term or terms illegal by application of the doctrine of severance.[357]

1–057 **Construction of contracts made by a "public authority".** In *Biggin Hill Airport Ltd v Bromley LBC*[358] it was held that the 1998 Act did not require a court as itself a public authority[359] to interpret a contract made *before* the coming into effect of the same Act in such a way as to be compatible with the Convention rights of third parties to the contract.[360] On the other hand, where a contract is made after the coming into force of the 1998 Act by a "public authority"[361] and another person (whether or not a public authority), it may be argued that there is a presumption that such a public authority intends in making and performing the contract to avoid acting unlawfully under s.6 of the 1998 Act, without any need for reliance on the position of courts as themselves "public authorities." For such a presumption could be supported by reference to the maxim *ut res magis valeat*

---

[353] [2002] 1 W.L.R. 1488 at [48].
[354] [2002] 1 W.L.R. 1488 at [49] per Chadwick L.J.
[355] [2002] 1 W.L.R. 1488 at [51].
[356] *Halford v UK* (1997) 24 E.H.R.R. 523; *Copland v UK* (2007) 45 E.H.R.R. 37.
[357] See below, Ch.17 and especially paras 16–188 et seq.
[358] *The Times*, January 9, 2001, (2001) 98(3) L.S.G. 42 at [171]; reversed on other grounds [2001] EWCA Civ 1089; *The Times*, January 9, 2001; (2001) 98(3) L.S.G. 42.
[359] Human Rights Act 1998 s.6(3)(a) and see below, para.1–060.
[360] See above, para.1–043.
[361] See above, paras 1–051—1–052.

quam pereat, since a construction of compatibility with Convention rights in these circumstances would avoid the threat of contractual illegality. Moreover, as regards "terms implied in law" it may be argued that a court should imply terms in a contract so as allow a public authority to perform its duty to act consistently with Convention rights, as "necessary" for the efficacy of the particular type of contract in question (viz a contract made by a public authority whose performance would have otherwise potentially prejudicial effect on a person's Convention rights).[362]

(iii) *The duty of courts as "public authorities" in relation to contracts*

Introduction. The way in which the terms of s.6 of the 1998 Act are drafted demonstrate that actions by public authorities are the primary focus of its protection of Convention rights. However, "courts and tribunals" are specifically included as "public authorities" for these purposes[363] and as a result a number of questions arise as to how their duty as "public authorities" may affect their functions in relation to disputes concerning contracts where neither party is itself a "public authority". A very clear application of this duty is found in relation to issues arising from the courts' supervision and management of the civil process, applicable to proceedings arising from contracts as to other civil proceedings. However, other questions arising from the application of s.6 in this way are less straightforward. 1–058

The exercise of judicial discretions. Where the law in certain circumstances grants a true discretion to a court then its exercise of that discretion can be seen as an "act" so as to engage s.6 of the 1998 Act, with the result that the court must exercise the discretion in a way which is compatible with Convention rights. Both statute and common law confer discretions on courts in a number of situations affecting the relationship between parties to a contract. Examples of such statutory discretions may be found in the power to award damages in lieu of rescission for misrepresentation[364] or the determination of the "just sum" for the purposes of relief on frustration.[365] Rather more likely to involve the consideration of Convention rights, though, are the discretions enjoyed by courts in relation to the equitable remedies of specific performance and injunction.[366] 1–059

The development of the common law. The question has arisen whether the courts as "public authorities" have a duty to protect Convention rights in their work in the development of the substantive common law as between two persons neither of whom are themselves "public authorities" within the meaning of the 1998 Act.[367] This "highly controversial topic" is often referred to as the possible 1–060

---

[362] cf. *Lee v Leeds City Council* [2002] EWCA Civ 6, [2002] 1 W.L.R. 1488 at [62]–[63] (no implied term in public sector residential tenancy inconsistent with limited express terms). On the general law as to the implication of terms, see below, Ch.13.

[363] Human Rights Act 1998 s.6(3)(a).

[364] Misrepresentation Act 1967 s.2(2) and see below, paras 6–096, 6–102.

[365] Law Reform (Frustrated Contracts) Act 1943 s.1(3) and see below, para.23–090.

[366] See below, paras 27–030 et seq. and 27–060 et seq.

[367] For discussion of these other "public authorities," see above, paras 1–050—1–051.

"indirect horizontal effect" of s.6 of the 1998 Act.[368] An important context in which this question has arisen has been the development of the law of breach of confidence so as to reflect the Convention rights to a private life and to freedom of expression, this having proved possible owing to the relative flexibility of the established law of breach of confidence.[369] It remains to be seen how far the courts will be willing to mould existing common law rules or principles or, more radically, to create entirely new legal remedies so as to give effect to Convention rights.[370] In the context of the law of contract, the general question is particularly likely to arise in the following contexts.

1–061 **The construction of contracts.** As regards contracts made after the coming into force of the Human Rights Act, ought courts *as* "public authorities" to interpret contracts (where neither party is a "public authority"),[371] so as to be compatible with Convention rights, either of the parties or of third parties? While there is no provision in the 1998 Act requiring courts to construe *contracts* so as not to be incompatible with Conventions rights,[372] in contrast to the position as regards legislation which must be so read "in so far as it is possible",[373] this silence may not rule out such a duty arising from s.6 and stemming from the courts' functions either in finding of facts or in the development of the common law. As to the former, it is established at common law that the purpose of construction of the contract is to give effect to the parties' intentions as objectively determined, this involving issues both of fact and law, and that, at least where the express terms of the contract are ambiguous, the court should look to the factual matrix of the contract for guidance.[374] It may be argued that a court should "interpret" the contract so as to ensure that performance of its obligations is compatible with Convention rights, at least, perhaps, where such an interpretation is possible on the natural meaning of the words used. On the other hand, it may be countered that if it appears either from the terms of the contract on their natural meaning or from the factual matrix of the contract that the parties

[368] *Wilson v First County Trust Ltd (No.2)* [2003] UKHL 40; [2003] 3 W.L.R. 568 at [25], per Lord Nicholls and see similarly at [174] (Lord Rodger). See for an introduction to this question: Craig at paras 18–027—18–028 and see further Hunt [1998] P.L. 423; Markesinis (1998) 114 L.Q.R. 47; Bamforth [1999] C.L.J. 159; Buxton (2000) 116 L.Q.R. 48; Wade (2000) 116 L.Q.R. 217; Morgan (2002) L.S. 259; Phillipson (2003) 66 M.L.R. 726.

[369] *Douglas v Hello! Ltd (No.1)* [2001] Q.B. 967; *A v B Plc* [2002] EWCA Civ 337, [2003] Q.B. 195; *London Regional Transport v Mayor of London* [2001] EWCA Civ 1491, [2003] E.M.L.R. 4; *Douglas v Hello Ltd (No.6)* [2003] EWHC 786, (2003) 153 N.L.J. 595; *Lady Archer v Williams* [2003] EWHC 1670, [2003] E.M.L.R. 38; *Douglas v Hello! Ltd (No.3)* [2005] EWCA Civ 595, [2006] Q.B. 125; *Campbell v MGN Ltd* [2004] UKHL 22, [2004] 2 A.C. 457; *McKennit v Ash* [2006] EWCA Civ 1714, [2007] 3 W.L.R. 194 and see below, para.1–066.

[370] cf. the observations on the creation of an independent tort of privacy in *Douglas v Hello! Ltd (No.1)* [2001] Q.B. 967, 997 et seq. (Sedley L.J.) and the denial of any general tort of invasion of privacy at common law by the House of Lords in *Wainwright v Home Office* [2003] UKHL 53, [2003] 3 W.L.R. 1137 (though on facts preceding the coming into effect of the 1998 Act and involving a claim against a public authority).

[371] For discussion of how the 1998 Act may affect construction of contracts made by a "public authority," see above, para.1–057.

[372] *Biggin Hill Airport Ltd v Bromley LBC* (2001) 98(3) L.S.G. 42, *The Times*, January 9, 2001 [171], reversed on other grounds [2001] EWCA Civ 1089, *The Times*, August 13, 2001; (2001) 98(33) L.S.G. 30.

[373] Human Rights Act 1998 s.3(1).

[374] See below, paras 12–050, 12–117 et seq.

intended to agree to something which *would* be incompatible with a person's Convention rights, then the courts should hold to this interpretation, rather than impose on the parties something to which they did not agree. Indeed, for the courts to do otherwise in such a situation could be thought to be a misuse of their powers of "fact-finding" in a way itself vulnerable under art.6(1) of the Convention, for the court would be imposing its view of what should have been agreed by the parties and deliberately "mistaking" the facts of a case as generally understood and determined in order to do so. A similar set of arguments would apply to the implication of terms "in fact".[375] A more robust argument would be that the courts should develop the common law governing the construction of the express terms of contracts so that it builds within it a requirement of interpretation "whenever possible" which makes performance compatible with Convention rights, this being an example of the "horizontal effect" of s.6. However, such a development would fly in the face of existing contractual principles of construction which have been established in the interests of commercial certainty and fairness to the parties: this would not be an example of Convention rights suffusing existing common law principles, but rather of their subverting them.[376]

New implied terms. Similar lines of argument may be developed for the implication of terms "in law" as have been just exposed in relation to the construction of express terms, so as to contend that a court should imply a term in a contract so as to give protection to the Convention rights of parties or of non-parties.[377] However, the established test for the implication of such terms is that they are necessary as well as reasonable,[378] and where neither party to the contract is a public authority[379] it is difficult to see the genuine necessity of the implication of such a term. Again, though, if the courts as themselves "public authorities" have a duty under the 1998 Act to adapt and develop the common law so as to protect Convention rights, then this test of the implication of terms could itself fall to be interpreted or adapted so as to promote the protection of Convention rights.[380] In support of this, it may be argued that the courts have historically taken a more or a less liberal approach to the test of necessity so as to give effect to their own views of the proper balance of interest between the parties and to create thereby the incidents of particular types of contract.[381] At least as regards the protection of the Convention rights of the parties to the contract, use of an implied term to achieve compatibility may not be alien to the spirit of the common law technique. On the other hand, the technique of implication of terms does have its limits, given that they must be fitted around the express terms and legal regulation of the contract in question. So, for example, it has been held that no term to maintain the dwelling in good condition should be implied in a residential tenancy which contains only an express term to keep the *structure* in good repair or which contains no express repairing obligation on 1–062

[375] See below, para.13–007.
[376] cf. below, para.1–066 concerning the law of confidentiality.
[377] On implied terms generally, see below, Ch.13.
[378] *Liverpool City Council v Irwin* [1977] A.C. 239.
[379] For the position where one of the parties *is* a public authority, see above, 1–057.
[380] On this wider question, see above, para.1–058.
[381] See above, para.1–017 and below, para.13–003.

the landlord as this would "invite the criticism that the court is seeking to make for the parties a bargain which they have not themselves made".[382]

1–063 **Open-textured norms governing the contract.** The courts may also protect or promote Convention rights in the process of the interpretation and application of broad or "open-textured" norms applicable to particular types of contract, whether these norms are expressed as implied terms or as common law rules,[383] even where neither party is a "public authority" so as to be caught directly by s.6 of the 1998 Act.[384] So, for example, at common law it has been held that contracts of employment contain as their incident an implied term of mutual trust and confidence between the parties.[385] Such a term could be used by a court as a vehicle for the protection of an employee's rights under the Convention, for example, his right to privacy or freedom of expression, by treating a disregard by an employer of his employee's rights as a breach of his obligation of trust and confidence.[386] Such a development could be seen as reflecting a positive, indirect impact of the Human Rights Act on contractual relations, positive in that it would increase the practical duties of employer or employee, even if under the cover of an existing general implied term.

1–064 **Open-textured controls on express contract terms.** Rather differently, and "negatively" as it could lead to the striking down of contract terms, it may be argued that the judicial control of the fairness of terms in consumer contracts under the Unfair Terms in Consumer Contracts Regulations 1999 may properly take into account in determining whether a term: "contrary to the requirement of good faith, . . . causes a significant imbalance in the parties rights and obligations arising under the contract, to the detriment of the consumer,"[387] whether or not that term is incompatible with Convention rights.[388] In this respect, it should be noted that the preamble to the EC Directive which the 1999 Regulations implement suggests that the function of the "requirement of good faith" is to ensure that a court makes "an overall evaluation of the different interests involved", and it then refers to matters which appear to relate to the public interest.[389] So, for example, where rules governing the legal relationship between a university and

---

[382] *Lee v Leeds City Council* [2002] EWCA Civ 6, [2002] 1 W.L.R. 1488 at [62], per Chadwick L.J. The context of this decision was a claim that the existing interpretation of a "public authority" landlord's obligations to his residential tenants was incompatible with their Convention rights, on which see above, para.1–057.

[383] Where an open-textured rule which governs a contract is legislative, then courts are under a duty to interpret the legislation itself "so far as it is possible to do so" in a way which is compatible with Convention rights: Human Rights Act 1998 s.3(1) and see above, para.1–035.

[384] On which see above, paras 1–050—1–052.

[385] See Vol.II, paras 39–057—39–060; 39–143—39–146 and *Johnson v Unisys Ltd* [2001] 2 W.L.R. 1076.

[386] Hepple, *Amicus Curiae* (June 8, 1998), pp.19–23; Palmer [2000] C.L.J. 168, 181. cf. the moulding of the existing law of breach of confidence rather than the direct creation of a law of privacy so as to give effect to Convention rights of privacy noted, below, paras 1–065—1–066.

[387] Unfair Terms in Consumer Contracts Regulations 1999 (SI 1999/2083) reg.5(1).

[388] A similar argument could be run as regards the application of the "reasonableness test" under the Unfair Contract Terms Act 1977 s.11(1), though this test does not explicitly draw attention to the relevance of issues of public interest for its assessment.

[389] Directive 93/13 on unfair terms in consumer contracts, preamble, recital 16 and see below, paras 15–066—15–069, 15–081.

its students find their basis in terms of the contract between them, the question of the fairness of these rules within the meaning of the 1999 Regulations could take into account their impact on the student's Convention rights (for example, their rights to privacy or freedom of expression).[390]

(iv) *Contractual confidentiality and section 12 of the 1998 Act*

Section 12 and "horizontal effect". Section 12 of the 1998 Act makes special provision for the protection of freedom of expression after the general coming into effect of the Act, on the basis that otherwise this right (which is itself found in art.10 of the Convention) may be unduly curtailed as the result of developments giving effect to the right to a private life contained in art.8 of the Convention. Section 12 therefore constrains in certain ways the granting by a court of relief which, if granted, might affect the exercise of the Convention right to freedom of expression. In this respect, s.12(4) provides that: 1–065

> "The court must have particular regard to the importance of the Convention right to freedom of expression and, where the proceedings relate to material which the respondent claims, or which appears to the court, to be journalistic, literary or artistic material (or to conduct connected with such material), to—
> (a) the extent to which
> (i) the material has, or is about to, become available to the public; or
> (ii) it is, or would be, in the public interest for the material to be published;
> (b) any relevant privacy code."

According to Sedley L.J., this provision:

> "... puts beyond question the direct applicability of at least one Article of the Convention as between one private party to litigation and another—in the jargon, its horizontal effect."[391]

Its impact on duties of confidentiality. Before the coming into force of the Human Rights Act, English law recognised the existence of duties of confidentiality arising from express or implied contractual agreement or from the nature of a non-contractual relationship between the parties and saw the basis of these duties in very broad concepts of good faith, loyalty and fair dealing.[392] The application of s.12 of the 1998 Act has arisen in the context of both contractual and non-contractual duties of confidentiality in a number of cases since its coming into force.[393] It has been observed that "these cases . . . represent a fusion between the pre-existing law of confidence and rights and duties arising under the 1–066

[390] Whittaker (2001) 21 O.J.L.S. 193, 210–213.

[391] *Douglas v Hello! Ltd (No.1)* [2001] Q.B. 967 at [133].

[392] *Fraser v Evans* [1969] 1 Q.B. 349, 361; *A.G. v Guardian Newspaper (No.2)* [1990] 1 A.C. 109, 269; *Douglas v Hello! Ltd (No.6)* [2003] EWHC 786, (2003) 153 N.L.J. 595 at [181].

[393] *Douglas v Hello! Ltd (No.1)* [2001] Q.B. 967; *A v B Plc* [2002] EWCA Civ 337, [2003] Q.B. 195; *London Regional Transport v Mayor of London* [2001] EWCA Civ 1491, [2003] E.M.L.R. 4; *Douglas v Hello! Ltd (No.6)* [2003] EWHC 786, (2003) 153 N.L.J. 595; *Lady Archer v Williams* [2003] EWHC 1670, [2003] E.M.L.R. 38; *Campbell v MGN Ltd* [2004] UKHL 22, [2004] 2 A.C. 457; *Douglas v Hello! Ltd (No.3)* [2005] EWCA Civ 595, [2006] Q.B. 125; *McKennit v Ash* [2006] EWCA Civ 1714, [2007] 3 W.L.R. 194.

Human Rights Act".[394] In the result, "the values enshrined in articles 8 and 10 are now part of the cause of action for breach of confidence".[395] In applying s.12, the court evaluates and weighs up duties of confidentiality, competing rights of privacy and of free expression and more general considerations of the public interest.[396] In this respect, it has been observed that:

> "... it is arguable that a duty of confidentiality that has been expressly assumed under contract carries more weight, when balanced against the restriction of the right of freedom of expression, than a duty of confidentiality not buttressed by express agreement."[397]

4. CLASSIFICATION OF CONTRACTS

1–067 **The different types of classification.** Contracts may be classified in a variety of ways: according to their subject-matter[398]; according to their parties[399]; according to their form (whether contained in deeds[400] or in writing,[401] whether express or implied[402]) or according to their effect (whether bilateral or unilateral,[403] whether valid, void, voidable or unenforceable[404]).

(a) *Classification of Contracts according to their Subject-matter*

1–068 **General.** Despite the generality of approach of English contract law,[405] the most prominent classification of contracts in the modern law divides them according to their subject-matter: thus, there are contracts of sale of goods and of

---

394 *Douglas v Hello! Ltd (No.6)* above at [186], per Lindsay J.

395 *Campbell v MGN Ltd* [2004] UKHL 22, [2004] 2 A.C. 457 at [17], per Lord Nicholls of Birkenhead.

396 *A v B Plc* [2002] EWCA Civ 337, [2003] Q.B. 195 at [6]; *Douglas v Hello! Ltd (No.1)* [2001] Q.B. 967 at [135]; *Lady Archer v Williams* [2003] E.M.L.R. 38 at [59] and note s.12(4)(a)(ii)'s reference to the significance of the public interest.

397 *Campbell v Frisbee* [2002] EWCA Civ 1374, [2003] I.C.R. 141 at [22], per Lord Phillips M.R. (who noted, however, conflicting dicta on this point in *London Regional Transport v The Mayor of London* [2003] E.M.L.R. 4 at [46]; *A.G. v Barker* [1990] 3 All E.R. 257, 260–261) (No comment was made by members of the HL on appeal in *Campbell v MGN Ltd* [2004] UKHL 22, [2004] 2 A.C. 457). cf. *McKennit v Ash* [2006] EWCA Civ 1714, [2007] 3 W.L.R. 194 at [43], where in the circumstances Buxton L.J. considered that: "the provision of the written contract did not add much to the obligations that the first defendant owed in equity by reason of the closeness of her personal relationship with the first claimant".

398 See below, paras 1–068—1–072.

399 See below, para.1–073.

400 See below, paras 1–075, 1–085—1–116.

401 See below, Ch.4.

402 See below, para.1–076.

403 See below, para.1–079.

404 See below, paras 1–080—1–085.

405 Nicholas (1974) 48 Tulane L.R. 946, 948–949. This approach in English law is to be contrasted with, for example, French law. In that legal system, while the Civil Code contains provisions describing the conditions for and effects of contracts in general, it also contains much more extensive sections relating to particular *types* of contract, e.g. sale, hire, mandate, etc. Thus, some of the "nominate contracts" of Roman law survived into the, Civil Code, though as particular examples of a general principle of contract based on agreement: art.1101, C. civ.

land, insurance, suretyship, employment, hire, etc., and some of the more prominent of these special contracts are discussed in the second volume of this work.

Classification for statutory purposes. Some types of contract are statutorily defined, for example, contracts of sale of goods,[406] for the carriage of goods by sea,[407] of marine insurance,[408] and of consumer credit,[409] and the purpose of these definitions is made clear by the statute in which they are contained. However, in other cases, even where important statutory regulation applies to a particular type of contract, its definition is left to the common law, examples of this being the contracts of employment,[410] tenancy[411] or insurance.[412] Further, in the case of the classification of a contract for the purposes of EC legislation, the European Court of Justice has held that "it is not for [itself] to classify specifically the transactions at issue" in the main proceedings from which a reference has been made, this being: 1–069

> ". . . within the jurisdiction of the national court alone. The [European] Court's role is confined to providing the national court with an interpretation of Community law which will be useful for the decision which it has to take in the dispute before it."[413]

For this purpose, the European Court has explained, for example, the distinction between "public service contracts" and "service concession" contracts found in the European law of public procurement.[414]

Classification for common law purposes. Classification of the parties' agreement as a particular type of contract may also need to be undertaken for the purposes of the common law. First, the courts have over the years found many implied terms in contracts which are not special to the particular agreement of the parties,[415] but are considered incidental to the *type* of agreement in question.[416] By attaching an implied term to a particular set of facts in this way, a court thereby either recognises an existing category of contract or creates a new one. In this respect, there is a certain tendency for the broader categories of contracts to be subdivided into smaller ones. For example, the contract of employment 1–070

[406] Sale of Goods Act 1979 s.2(1) and see below, Vol.II, para.43–008.

[407] Carriage of Goods by Sea Act 1971 s.1 and Schedule to the Act art.I(b).

[408] Marine Insurance Act 1906 s.1.

[409] Consumer Credit Act 1974 s.8 and see below, Vol.II, para.38–014.

[410] See Vol.II, paras 39–010 et seq., where it is noted that there is no comprehensive definition of the contract, the cases instead relying on a number of factors relevant to finding whether a particular contract is of service.

[411] There has been particular difficulty in distinguishing between leases and contractual licences: see *Street v Mountford* [1985] A.C. 809; *A.G. Securities v Vaughan* [1990] 1 A.C. 417.

[412] See Vol.II, para.41–001. For an example of the statutory significance of a contract being classified as one of insurance, see the Financial Services and Markets Act 2000 s.141 (power in Financial Services Authority to make insurance business rules).

[413] *Parking Brixen GmbH v Gemeinde Brixen* (C-458/03) [2006] 1 C.M.L.R. 3 at [32].

[414] [2006] 1 C.M.L.R. 3 at [38]–[43].

[415] cf. *Ashmore v Corp of Lloyd's* [1992] 2 Lloyd's Rep. 620, 630–631.

[416] See above, para.1–032 and below, para.13–003.

attracts many implied terms which are of general application,[417] but in *Sim v Rotherham MBC*,[418] the court implied a term into a contract of employment between a local authority and a school teacher that the latter would cover for her fellow teachers in their absence if reasonably requested to do so, a term which would apply to similar contracts but not necessarily to contracts of employment beyond that context.[419] In *Scally v Southern Health and Social Services Board*,[420] Lord Bridge felt able to imply a term in the contracts of employment between a hospital board and its employees to take reasonable steps to inform the latter of their valuable right to opt to make payments into their pension schemes. His Lordship rejected the argument that the formulation of an implied term must necessarily be too wide, holding that "this difficulty is surmounted if the category of contractual relationship in which the implication will arise is defined with sufficient precision".[421] Similarly, while some terms are implied into leases in general,[422] others apply only to particular types of lease. Thus, in *Liverpool City Council v Irwin*[423] the House of Lords implied a term into a contract of lease, but their Lordships' speeches suggest that this term was considered incidental to a much more specific contract, namely one made by a local authority for the lease of a flat in a high-rise block.[424]

1–071 **Exceptional rules.** Secondly, the courts sometimes make a formal exception to a rule of common law which applies only to a particular type of contract. For example, although in general a breach of contract, however fundamental, does not terminate it so as to prevent the application of any exemption clause which it may contain,[425] in a contract of carriage of goods by sea, any unnecessary deviation from the agreed or customary route constitutes a breach of the contract which gives rise in the owner to a right to treat himself as discharged and this right, if exercised, does have the effect of disapplying any exemption clause from the deviating journey.[426] Similarly, although in general a person is not bound by an exemption clause in a contract to which he is not party, if for example, A sends goods for repair to B with permission to send the work out to a sub-contractor, C, A may be bound by any exemption clause in this contract of sub-bailment.[427] Again, while in general there is no pre-contractual duty of disclosure, such a duty does rest on both parties to a contract of insurance, this being said to arise from

[417] For example, it is an implied term in every contract of employment that the employee will not disclose any confidential information which he learns by reason of his employment: see Vol.II, para.39–061.

[418] [1987] Ch. 216.

[419] cf. [1987] Ch. 216 at [248].

[420] [1992] 1 A.C. 294.

[421] [1992] 1 A.C. 294 at [307]. Lord Bridge defined the category by reference to three special circumstances.

[422] e.g. a landlord's implied covenant for quiet enjoyment: see Gray and Gray, *Elements of Land Law*, 4th edn (2005), pp.1438–1443.

[423] [1977] A.C. 239.

[424] See [1977] A.C. 239 at 254, 258, 261. This subdivision of large categories for the purposes of the implication of terms can be seen in *Jones v Just* (1868) L.R. 3 Q.B. 197, 202–203 in relation to sale before the Sale of Goods Act 1893.

[425] *Photo Production Ltd v Securicor Transport Ltd* [1980] A.C. 827.

[426] See below, para.14–029.

[427] *Morris v C. W. Martin & Sons Ltd* [1966] 1 Q.B. 716; *The Pioneer Container* [1994] 2 A.C. 324 and see below, paras 14–054, 33–026.

the nature of the contract itself.[428] A final example may be found in relation to restrictive covenants concerning land. These started life as a particular type of contract, or rather a particular type of contractual obligation, as they were stipulated as part of the sale of land,[429] but after *Tulk v Moxhay*[430] in 1848, they were held capable of binding a successor in title of the purchaser of the land, despite the principle of privity of contract. While technically this is justified by saying that the making of the covenant creates an equitable (proprietary) interest in land,[431] it can equally be seen as an example of the law creating an exception to the rules of privity of contract for a particular type of term in a particular type of contract.

Commercial practice. Other types of contract arise from commercial practice rather than from the regulation of either statute or common law, though the practical homogeneity on which they are based easily attracts particular treatment by the courts. Very clear examples of this can be found in an area like the building industry, in which the industry offers standard forms for the conclusion of the many contracts which modern construction requires.[432] Moreover, new types of contracts in this sense are constantly arising, for example, for the supply and maintenance of information technology.[433] 1–072

(b) *Classification of Contracts according to their Parties*

General. Contracts are sometimes classified according to their parties and this type of classification sometimes cuts across those other types which have already been mentioned. Perhaps the most important of this type of division is between commercial and non-commercial contracts. Commercial contracts can be described as those which are made between two or more parties who are in business for the purposes of trade. "Non-commercial contracts" is a residual category and would include transactions as disparate as contracts on the dissolution of marriage, contracts under which legal claims are settled, sales between private individuals other than in the course of business as well as "consumer contracts". The latter is in the modern law an important category and may be defined as those contracts which are made between one party who is in business and one who is contracting other than for trade purposes.[434] However, the common law of contract does not recognise the categories of commercial[435] or consumer contracts and the latter category has only really become prominent as 1–073

[428] *Carter v Boehm* (1766) 3 Burr. 1905, 1909 and see Vol.II, paras 41–030 et seq.

[429] Lawson and Rudden, *The Law of Property*, 3rd edn (2002), p.157.

[430] (1848) 2 Ph. 774.

[431] Gray and Gray, *Elements of Land and Law*, 4th edn (2005), pp.804–805.

[432] These are known as "RIBA/JCT standard forms": see Vol.II, paras 37–021 et seq.

[433] See Morgan and Burden, *Morgan and Burden on Computer Contracts*, 7th edn (2005).

[434] cf. Unfair Contract Terms Act 1977 s.12.

[435] cf. Goode, *Commercial Law*, 3rd edn (2004), p.141. Some legal systems possess a commercial law code to govern at least in part the relationships of traders and which is distinct from the civil code which is of more general application: see Zekoll and Reimann, *Introduction to German Law*, 2nd edn (2005), Ch.4; Bell in Bell, Boyron and Whittaker, *Principles of French Law*, 2nd edn (2008), Ch.11.

a result of modern legislation passed for the protection of consumers, in particular concerning credit agreements[436] and the effectiveness of exemption clauses[437] and other unfair contract terms.[438]

Another important distinction in the modern law is between contracts made between private persons and those where one or both parties are public bodies. This distinction has been discussed for the purposes of the Human Rights Act 1998[439] and will be discussed generally later.[440]

(c) *Classification of Contracts according to their Form or Means of Formation*

1–074 **Introduction.** Contracts can also be classified according to their form or means of formation and for this purpose, distinctions can be drawn between formal and informal contracts, and express and implied contracts, and contracts which are and which are not made at a distance.

1–075 **Formal and informal contracts.** Contracts may be either formal or informal. Apart from the so-called contracts of record, comprising judgments and recognisances, which are not properly speaking contracts at all, the only formal contract in English law is the contract contained in a deed or specialty contract. All others are informal contracts, or simple contracts as they are more often termed. Such contracts may in principle be oral or in writing,[441] though particular contracts possess different requirements as to writing.[442] The requirements of a valid contract contained in a deed are discussed in the next section of this chapter. The chief respect in which they differ from simple contracts is that, for historical reasons, they are valid without the necessity for consideration.

1–076 **Express and implied contracts.** Contracts may be either express or implied. The difference is not one of legal effect but simply of the way in which the consent of the parties is manifested. Contracts are express when their terms are stated in words by the parties. They are often said to be implied when their terms are not so stated, as, for example, when a passenger is permitted to board a bus: from the conduct of the parties the law implies a promise by the passenger to pay the fare, and a promise by the operator of the bus to carry him safely to his destination.[443] There may also be an implied contract when the parties make an express contract to last for a fixed term, and continue to act as though the contract still bound them after the term has expired. In such a case the court may infer that the parties have agreed to renew the express contract for another term. Express and implied contracts are both contracts in the true sense of the term, for they

---

[436] Consumer Credit Act 1974 and see Vol.II, Ch.38.

[437] Unfair Contract Terms Act 1977, see below, para.14–066.

[438] Unfair Terms in Consumer Contracts Regulations 1999 (SI 1999/2083) on which see below, paras 15–004 et seq.

[439] See above, paras 1–039—1–042, 1–050—1–051.

[440] See below, Ch.10.

[441] *Rann v Hughes* (1778) 7 T.R. 350n.

[442] See below, Ch.4.

[443] *Modahl v British Athletic Federation* [2001] EWCA Civ 1447, [2002] 1 W.L.R. 1192 at [100].

both arise from the agreement of the parties, though in one case the agreement is manifested in words and in the other case by conduct. Since, as we have seen,[444] agreement is not a mental state but an act, an inference from conduct, and since many of the terms of an express contract are often implied, it follows that the distinction between express and implied contracts has little importance. However:

> "One distinction exists . . . in relation to the ease with which an express or implied contract may be established. Where there is an express agreement on essentials of sufficient certainty to be enforceable, an intention to create legal relations may commonly be assumed. It is otherwise when the case is that a contract should be implied from the parties' conduct. It is then for the party asserting a contract to show the necessity for implying it."[445]

"Distance contracts". The Consumer Protection (Distance Selling) Regulations 2000[446] introduced into English law a distinction between those consumer contracts which are made at a distance and other contracts. For this purpose, a "distance contract": 1–077

> " . . . means any contract concerning goods or services concluded between a supplier and a consumer under an organised distance sales or service provision scheme run by the supplier who, for the purpose of the contract, makes exclusive use of one or more means of distance communication up to and including the moment at which the contract is concluded."[447]

These Regulations introduced, inter alia, rights of information, of cancellation and to performance within a maximum of 30 days for the benefit of the consumers who make "distance contracts".[448]

(d) *Classification of Contracts according to their Effect*

Introduction. Contracts are sometimes classified according to their effect and so distinctions can be drawn between unilateral and bilateral contracts and valid, void, voidable and unenforceable contracts. The last three terms denote varying degrees of imperfection and are in constant use in the law of contract. 1–078

Unilateral and bilateral contracts. Contracts may be either unilateral or bilateral.[449] By a unilateral contract is meant a contract under which only one 1–079

---

[444] Above, para.1–004.

[445] *Modahl v British Athletic Federation* [2001] EWCA Civ 1447, [2002] 1 W.L.R. 1192 at [102], per Mance L.J. and see below, paras 2–160—2–162.

[446] SI 2000/2334 implementing Directive 97/7 on the protection of consumers in respect of distance contracts. Directive 2002/65 concerning the distance marketing of consumer financial services, whose art.2(1) sets out an equivalent definition of "distance contract" as is found in Directive 97/7 art.2(a) for the purposes of the distance marketing of financial services, is being implemented partly by the Financial Services (Distance Marketing) Regulations 2004 (SI 2004/2095) and partly by the amendment of rules by the Financial Services Authority.

[447] SI 2000/2334 reg.3(1). Certain contracts are excluded wholly or in part by regs 5 and 6. "Means of distance communication" is defined by reg.3 and illustrated by Sch.2.

[448] SI 2000/2334 regs 7–8, 10–18 and 19 respectively.

[449] *Restatement of Contracts* (1932), para.12. The *Restatement of Contracts*, 2nd edn (1981), para.45 abandons this distinction and substitutes for unilateral contracts "option contracts".

party undertakes an obligation.[450] Bilateral (or synallagmatic) contracts, on the other hand, are those under which both parties undertake obligations. It is to be noted, though, that the unilateral nature of the contract does not (in the ordinary case) mean that there is only one party, nor that there is no need for an acceptance or the provision of consideration by the other party.[451] An example of a unilateral contract may be found in the case of an offer for a reward for the return of lost property: here, a contract is formed (at the latest) on the return of the property, this constituting the offeree's acceptance of the offer and the furnishing of consideration for the creation of the contract.[452] Bilateral contracts comprise the exchange of a promise for a promise, e.g. if you promise to pay me £1,000, I promise to sell you my car.

1–080 **Void contracts.** A void contract is strictly a contradiction in terms, because if an agreement is truly void it is not a contract; but the term is a useful one and well understood by lawyers. Properly speaking, a void contract should produce no legal effects whatsoever. Neither party should be able to sue the other on the contract. If goods have been delivered, they or their value should be recoverable by an action in tort, because the property will not pass. If money has been paid, it should be recoverable by an action in restitution, because the money was not due. In one situation, i.e. where a contract is void for mistake, these consequences would appear to follow from the fact that the contract is void.[453] But it is by no means true that all contracts termed "void" by the law necessarily produce this effect.

1–081 **"Void" contract may have effects.** For example, a contract may be void for illegality. But, although in many cases, neither party can sue on it, in other cases a party who is innocent of any illegal design may have a right of action.[454] Property may pass under an illegal contract[455] and money paid in pursuance of it is often irrecoverable.[456] Moreover, where A and B have paid money to C under an agreement under which C is empowered to pay some of the money to B, the court will not at A's request restrain C from so doing, even though the agreement is illegal and void as an unreasonable restraint of trade.[457] Other difficult questions arise in relation to the relative positions of the parties to a contract for the sale or other disposition of an interest in land which is a nullity

---

[450] See *New Zealand Shipping Co Ltd v A.M. Satterthwaite & Co Ltd* [1975] A.C. 154, 167–168, 171, 177. *Quaere* whether the engagement of an estate agent is a unilateral contract: *Luxor (Eastbourne) Ltd v Cooper* [1941] A.C. 108, 124; Murdoch (1975) 91 L.Q.R. 357; McConnell (1983) 265 E.G. 547.

[451] See *Carlill v Carbolic Smoke Ball Co* [1893] 1 Q.B. 256. In certain situations, a contract under which only one party undertakes an obligation may be truly one-sided, in that the other party may be dispensed from the need to provide consideration. Thus, an agreement contained in a deed under which A covenants to pay B a sum of money may be considered a unilateral contract as only A undertakes an obligation (see below, para.1–108).

[452] On the issue of when such a contract is formed see below, paras 2–078 et seq.

[453] See below, Ch.5.

[454] See below, para.16–011.

[455] See below, para.16–178.

[456] See below, para.16–177.

[457] *Boddington v Lawton* [1994] I.C.R. 478.

as a result of not having been made in writing as is required by s.2 of the Law of Property (Miscellaneous Provisions) Act 1989.[458]

Voidable contracts. A voidable contract is one where one or more of its parties have the power, by a manifestation of election to do so, to avoid the legal relations created by the contract; or by affirmation of the contract to extinguish the power of avoidance.[459] In English law, contracts may be voidable, e.g. for misrepresentation,[460] duress,[461] undue influence,[462] minority,[463] lack of mental capacity,[464] drunkenness[465] or under statute.[466] If the contract is wholly executory, the party entitled to avoid the contract can plead its voidability in an action against him. If it has been wholly or partly executed, he can claim to have set it aside and to be restored to his original position. But until the right of avoidance is exercised, the contract is valid. Thus if a contract for the sale of goods is voidable for fraud (but has not been avoided), the fraudulent party acquires a good title to the goods which he can transfer to an innocent purchaser for value.[467] The right of avoidance must also be exercised promptly in most cases. It is theoretically possible for a contract to be avoidable by both parties thereto, e.g. if each defrauds the other, or both are drunk; but naturally instances of this are rare. 1–082

Power to set aside on terms. In the case of contracts said to be voidable for common mistake in equity, this description refers not to a power in one or other of the parties to avoid the contract, but to a power in the court to set aside the contract on terms.[468] However, the existence of such a distinct equitable jurisdiction has been denied on the ground of its being irreconcilable with the leading, higher common law authority.[469] 1–083

Unenforceable contracts. Unenforceable contracts are valid in all respects except that one or both parties cannot be sued on the contract. Instances of unenforceable contracts in English law are afforded by certain contracts which 1–084

---

[458] See below, paras 4–075 et seq.

[459] See *Restatement of Contracts*, 2nd edn, para.7.

[460] See below, Ch.6.

[461] See below, paras 7–001—7–055.

[462] See below, paras 7–056—7–125.

[463] See below, paras 8–002—8–067.

[464] See below, paras 8–068 et seq.

[465] See below, paras 8–080—8–081.

[466] e.g. Auctions (Bidding Agreements) Act 1969 s.3(1) replacing Auctions (Bidding Agreements) Act 1927 s.2 (as amended). Consumer Credit Act 1974 ss.67–73 (cancellation of consumer credit agreements) and see below, Vol.II, paras 38–085 et seq.

[467] See *Phillips v Brooks Ltd* [1919] 2 K.B. 243; *Lewis v Averay* [1972] 1 Q.B. 198; Sale of Goods Act 1979 s.23. Contrast *Cundy v Lindsay* (1878) 3 App. Cas. 459 and *Ingram v Little* [1961] 1 Q.B. 31, where the contract was void for mistake (though see *Shogun Finance Ltd v Hudson* [2003] UKHL 62, [2004] 1 A.C. 919). See below, para.5–095 and Vol.II, para.43–237.

[468] See *Solle v Butcher* [1950] 1 K.B. 671, 696–697.

[469] *Great Peace Shipping Ltd v Tsavliris Salvage Ltd* [2002] EWCA Civ 1407, [2003] Q.B. 679; *Bell v Lever Bros* [1932] A.C. 161 and see below, paras 5–057—5–062.

are not evidenced by a signed writing as required by statute[470]; contracts in respect of which the right of action is barred by the Limitation Act 1980[471]; and certain contracts with a foreign sovereign[472] or in breach of foreign exchange control regulations.[473] In some cases the defect of unenforceability is curable. Thus, if written evidence of a contract of guarantee comes into existence, the contract becomes enforceable, though it was made orally[474]; a current period of limitation may be repeatedly extended if the defendant makes a written acknowledgment of his indebtedness, or a part payment[475]; a foreign sovereign may waive his immunity.[476] An unenforceable contract may be indirectly enforceable by means other than bringing an action. Thus a statute-barred debt may be recoverable indirectly if the creditor has a lien on goods of the debtor which are in his possession.[477] Frequently the contract is enforceable by one party but not by the other. For example, under the Race Relations Act 1976 s.72(1), a term of a contract is "void" on the ground, inter alia, that its inclusion renders the making of the contract unlawful by virtue of that Act, but this sub-section:

> "... does not apply to a term the inclusion of which constitutes . . . unlawful discrimination against a party to the contract, but the term shall be unenforceable against that party."[478]

5. CONTRACTS CONTAINED IN DEEDS

(a) *General*

1–085 **Preliminary.** At common law, contracts under seal, or specialties, were an important example of deeds and at common law a deed was an instrument which was not merely in writing, but which was sealed by the party bound thereby, and delivered by him to or for the benefit of the person to whom the liability was incurred.[479] In no other way than by the use of this form could validity be given to executory contracts at common law in early times. At common law, all deeds were documents under seal, but not all documents under seal were and are deeds. A deed must either:

(a) effect the transference of an interest, right or property;

---

[470] e.g. contracts of guarantee: Statute of Frauds 1677 s.4 (see Vol.II, 44–038—44–053, Ch.32). Cf. consumer credit agreements whose failure to satisfy certain requirements of form render them in principle enforceable only on order of the court: Consumer Credit Act 1974 ss.60, 61, 65 and see Vol.II, paras 38–071, 38–082—38–083.

[471] See below, Ch.28.

[472] See below, Ch.11.

[473] *United City Merchants (Investments) Ltd v Royal Bank of Canada* [1983] 1 A.C. 168, 189–190.

[474] See below, Vol.II, Ch.44.

[475] Limitation Act 1980 s.29 and see below, paras 28–092 et seq.

[476] See below, paras 11–020 et seq.

[477] See below, para.28–133.

[478] Race Relations Act 1976 s.72(2). See also Unfair Terms in Consumer Contracts Regulations 1999 (SI 1999/2083) reg.8 (unfair terms "not binding" on consumer).

[479] Compare above, para.1–003 on the question of agreement in relation to deeds.

(b) create an obligation binding on some person or persons;

(c) confirm some act whereby an interest, right or property has already passed.

Some documents under seal are not deeds, for instance a certificate of admission to a learned society or probate of a will.[480]

General abolition of the requirement of sealing. In 1989, legislation was enacted which abolished the ancient requirement of sealing for the execution of the deeds in many situations.[481] As regards deeds executed by an individual, s.1 of the Law of Property (Miscellaneous Provisions) Act 1989 (the "1989 Act") replaced the requirement of sealing with requirements that the intention of the party making a deed should make this intention clear on its face, of signature by that party[482] and of attestation.[483] As regards companies incorporated under the Companies Acts ("companies"), the requirement of sealing for the execution of *documents*[484] was supplemented by an alternative method of execution of a document which required signature by a director and the secretary of the company or by two directors and the expression "in whatever form of words" that it was executed by the company; and it was further provided that where a document made clear on its face that it was intended to be a *deed*, it should take effect on delivery as a deed, delivery being rebuttably presumed where it was so executed.[485] Similar provisions were enacted in 1993 to govern the position of charities incorporated under the Charities Act 1993.[486] In the case of deeds executed by other persons (including other corporations aggregate[487] and corporations sole[488]), the common law requirement of sealing was left unaffected. 1–086

Further amendment of the law governing the execution of instruments. In 2005 further amendments were made to the law governing the execution of deeds and some other instruments by an order ("the 2005 Order") made under the 1–087

---

[480] *R. v Morton* (1873) L.R. 2 C.C.R. 22, 27.

[481] On the ancient requirement see Sheppard's *Touchstone of Common Assurances*, 7th edn (1820), p.56.

[482] This requirement had been imposed by the Law of Property Act 1925 s.73.

[483] Law of Property (Miscellaneous Provisions) Act 1989 s.1.

[484] Companies Act 1985 s.36A(2) (as inserted by s.36A inserted by Companies Act 1989 (c.40) ss.130(2), 213(2)). This provision has been superseded as explained at para.1–100 below.

[485] Companies Act 1985 s.36A(4) and (5) (as inserted by s.36A inserted by Companies Act 1989 (c.40) ss.130(2), 213(2)). This provision has been superceded as explained at para.1–100 below.

[486] Charities Act 1993 ss.50 and 60.

[487] A corporation aggregate may be defined as consisting of: "[A] body of persons which is recognised by the law as having a personality which is distinct from the separate personalities of the members of the body or the personality of the individual holder of the office in question for the time being": Law Com. No.253 para.4.1, fn.1 referring to *Halsbury's Laws of England*, 4th edn (reissue, 1998), Vol.9(2), para.1005.

[488] A corporation sole may be defined as consisting of: "[O]ne person and his or her successors in some particular office or status, who are incorporated in law in order to give them certain legal capacities and advantages which they would not have in their natural person": Law Com. No.253 para.4.23 referring to *Halsbury's Laws of England*, 4th edn, Vol.9(2), para.1007 and giving as examples a government minister or Church of England bishop.

Regulatory Reform Act 2001,[489] so as to give effect to the principal recommendations of a report of the Law Commission.[490] The main changes introduced in 2005 concern the creation of standard requirements for companies incorporated under the Companies Act 1985 and corporations aggregate (but not corporations sole) for the due execution of instruments in general and of deeds in particular; the making of specific provision for the execution of documents by persons (including companies and corporations aggregate) by or on behalf of another person (whether the latter is an individual, a company within the meaning of the Companies Act or a corporation); and the clarification that the mere sealing of a document by a person (whether an individual or another corporate body) does not in itself satisfy the so-called "face-value requirement" that: "an instrument shall not be a deed unless . . . it makes clear on its face that it is intended to be a deed by the person making it."[491] The changes introduced by the 2005 Order came into force as regards "instruments executed" on or after September 15, 2005, but leave unaffected any instrument executed before this date.[492]

1–088 **Electronic documents and deeds.** Following the recommendations of the Law Commission,[493] the Land Registration Act 2002 made provision for the creation of a framework in which it will be possible to transfer and create interests in registered land by electronic means through a network controlled by the Land Registry. In order to permit this, Pt 8 of the Act makes provision for the fulfilment of formality requirements by the transactions in question. Accordingly, by s.91(4) and (5) of the 2002 Act:

> ". . . a document to which this section applies is to be regarded as: (a) in writing; and (b) signed by each individual, and sealed by each corporation, whose electronic signature it has. [And such a document] is to be regarded for the purposes of any enactment as a deed."[494]

Section 91 applies to "documents in electronic form" of certain types dealing with registered interests in land[495] as long as: (a) the document makes provision for the time and date when it takes effect; (b) the document has the electronic signature of each person by whom it purports to be authenticated; (c) each electronic signature is certified; and (d) such other conditions as rules may provide are met. This provision does not, therefore, create a new type of deed capable of being made electronically; rather it assimilates certain qualifying electronic documents to deeds for the purposes of any enactment requiring the

---

[489] Regulatory Reform (Execution of Deeds and Documents) Order 2005 (SI 2005/1906).

[490] *The Execution of Deeds and Documents by or on behalf of Bodies Corporate*, Law Com. No.253 (1998).

[491] Law of Property (Miscellaneous Provisions) Act 1989 s.1(2)(a) and see below.

[492] 2005 Order art.1(2). The 2005 Order art.1(1) (this being 12 weeks from June 23, 2005, the day on which the Order was made).

[493] Law Commission, *Land Registration for the Twenty-First Century* (2001) Law Com. No.271.

[494] Land Registration Act 2002 (Commencement No.4) Order 2003 (SI 2003/1725) brought this provision into force on October 13, 2003.

[495] These are defined by the Land Registration Act 2002 s.92(1).

dispositions to which those documents relate to use a deed.[496] At the time of writing, this new system has not yet been brought into operation.[497]

(b) *Intention, form, and delivery*

Introduction. The following paragraphs will explain first the law as amended by the legislation in 1989 and then explain how this position was affected by the 2005 Order, though it is to be noted that the position of charitable corporations differs again as the relevant legisltion took effect from August 1, 1993 and remains in force.[498] There will then follow a discussion of certain aspects of the requirements of form and of delivery which apply to deeds whenever executed. 1–089

(i) *Deeds executed on or after July 31, 1989 and before or on September 14, 2005*

Deeds executed by an individual. The law introduced by the Law of Property (Miscellaneous Provisions) Act 1989 s.1 requires that for an instrument made by an individual to be a deed, it must make: 1–090

> "... clear on its face that it is intended to be a deed by the person making it or, as the case may be, by the parties to it (whether by describing itself as a deed or expressing itself to be executed or signed as a deed or otherwise)."[499]

It has been observed that:

> "... the Act provides that documents can be deeds without using the word 'deed'; but ... that a document is only to be held to be a deed if it is clear from the wording of the document itself ('on its face') that it was intended to be a deed."[500]

And so, words which indicate an intention by the parties that a document should be legally binding are not enough: "what is needed is something showing that the parties intended the document to have the extra status of being a deed".[501] The 1989 Act also introduced other requirements for the execution of a deed by an

---

[496] Land Registration Act 2002 s.91(3).

[497] For developments see *http://wwwl.landregistry.gov.uk/e-conveyancing* [Accessed June 10, 2008].

[498] Below, para.1–092. It is also to be noted that the relevant provisions of the Companies Act 1989 which were amended in 2005 were then replaced by the Companies Act 2006, though without substantive changes. The notes to the following paragraphs will explain these sets of legislative changes.

[499] s.1(2)(a). Section 1(11) of the 1989 Act provided that "nothing in this section applies in relation to instruments *delivered* as deeds before this section comes into force" i.e. July 31, 1989. This appears to mean that an *instrument* made before this date but delivered after it remains governed by the earlier law.

[500] *HSBC Trust Co v Quinn* [2007] EWHC 1543 (Ch), [2007] All E.R. (D) 125 (Jul) at [50], per Christopher Nugee Q.C. Cf. *Johnsey Estates (1900) Ltd v Newport Marketworld Ltd* Unreported May 10, 1996 (noted and criticised by Law Com. No.253, paras 2.17–2.18) where it was held that the mere fact that a document was made under seal is sufficient to make it clear that it was executed as a deed.

[501] [2007] EWHC 1543 (Ch) at [51].

individual and preserved an existing one. For an instrument to be validly executed as a deed, it must be:

> "... signed (i) by him in the presence of a witness who attests the signature; or (ii) at his direction and in his presence and the presence of two witnesses who each attest the signature."[502]

"Signature" is defined later in the section to include making one's mark.[503] The Act specifically preserved the common law requirement that for an instrument to be validly executed as a deed it must be "delivered" as a deed by him or a person authorised to do so on his behalf.[504]

1–091 **Deeds executed by companies incorporated under the Companies Acts.** In 1989, the law governing the execution of documents and deeds by companies incorporated under the Companies Acts was amended so as to create a "dual system".[505] So, while it preserved the possibility for a company to execute a document (including a deed) by the affixing of its common seal,[506] it also provided that a document signed by a director and secretary, or by two directors, of a company incorporated under the Act and expressed to be executed by the company has the same effect as if executed under the common seal of the company and notwithstanding that the company has no common seal.[507] In either case, it is provided that a:

> "... document executed by a company which makes clear on its face that it is intended by the person or persons making it to be a deed has effect, upon delivery, as a deed."[508]

The deeds of a company must be executed in accordance with its articles of association but, in favour of a purchaser, s.74(1) of the Law of Property Act 1925 provides that a deed is deemed to have been duly executed if its seal is affixed thereto in the presence of and attested by its secretary and a member of the board of directors[509] and a similar deeming provision applies to documents not made under the company seal, but where the document makes clear on its face that it is intended by the person or persons making it to be a deed.[510] There is no statutory requirement that the name used in the body of a deed should be the company's registered name rather than its trading name and the common law rule

---

502 Law of Property (Miscellaneous Provisions) Act 1989 s.1(3) (as enacted).

503 Law of Property (Miscellaneous Provisions) Act 1989 s.1(4).

504 1989 Act s.1(3)(b).

505 Law Commission, *The Execution of Deeds and Documents by or on behalf of Bodies Corporate*, Law Com. No.253 (1998), para.3.3.

506 Companies Act 1985 s.36A(4) as inserted by Companies Act 1989 s.130(2).

507 Companies Act 1985 s.36A(3) as inserted by Companies Act 1989 s.130(2).

508 Companies Act 1985 s.36A(5) as inserted by Companies Act 1989 s.130(2).

509 This provision was amended by the 2005 Order for instruments executed on or after September 14, 2005, below, para.1–100.

510 Companies Act 1985 s.36A(6) and cf. s.36C, also inserted by Companies Act 1989 s.130(1) (pre-incorporation contracts, deeds and obligations).

therefore applies so that extraneous evidence is admissible to identify a contracting party when its identity is not clear from the face of the deed.[511]

Deeds executed by other persons. Where a deed is executed by a person other than a private individual, a company incorporated under the Companies Acts, or a charity incorporated under the Charities Act 1993,[512] the common law requirement of sealing still applies. This would apply to corporations aggregate and to corporations sole.[513] However, the requirement of sealing has been interpreted by the courts very liberally: "to constitute a sealing neither wax nor wafer nor a piece of paper nor even an impression is necessary".[514] Pieces of green ribbon[515] or a circle printed on the document containing the letters "L.S." (*locus sigilli*)[516] or even a document bearing no indication of a seal at all[517] will suffice, if there is evidence (e.g. attestation) that the document was intended to be executed as a deed.[518] In the absence of such evidence, a signatory of a document expressed to have been "signed, sealed and delivered" by him may be estopped from denying that it was sealed.[519] 1–092

Delivery. It remains the case after the 1989 legislation that "[w]here a contract is to be by deed, there must be a delivery to perfect it".[520] "Delivered", however, in this connection does not mean "handed over" to the other party. It means delivered in the old legal sense,[521] namely, an act done so as to evince an intention to be bound.[522] Any act of the party which shows that he intended to deliver the deed as an instrument binding on him is enough. He must make it his deed[523] and recognise it as presently binding on him.[524] Delivery is effective even though the grantor retains the deed in his own possession. There need be no actual transfer of possession to the other party: 1–093

---

511 *OTV Birwelco Ltd v Technical & General Guarantee Company Ltd* [2002] 4 All E.R. 668.

512 Charities Act 1993 ss.50, 60. These provisions apply to instruments made on or after August 1, 1993 and remain in force.

513 Law of Property (Miscellaneous Provisions) Act 1989 s.1(10). On "corporations aggregate" and "corporations sole" see above, fn.487 and 488. Note also s.1(9) which specifically reserves the requirement of sealing at common law in relation to deeds required or authorised to be made under the seals of the County Palatine of Lancaster, the Duchy of Lancaster or the Duchy of Cornwall.

514 *Ex p. Sandilands* (1871) L.R. 6 C.P. 411, 413.

515 *Ex p. Sandilands* (1871) L.R. 6 C.P. 411; See also *Stromdale & Ball Ltd v Burden* [1952] Ch. 233, 230.

516 *First National Securities Ltd v Jones* [1978] Ch. 109; Hoath (1980) 43 M.L.R. 415.

517 *First National Securities Ltd v Jones* [1978] Ch. 109; *Commercial Credit Services v Knowles* [1978] 6 C.L. 64.

518 cf. *National Provincial Bank v Jackson* (1886) 33 Ch D 1; *Re Balkis Consolidated Ltd* (1888) 58 L.T. 300; *Re Smith* (1892) 67 L.T. 64 (these cases were explained in *First National Securities Ltd v Jones* [1978] Ch. 109): cf. *TCB v Gray* [1986] 1 Ch. 621, 633.

519 *TCB v Gray* [1986] 1 Ch. 621. cf. *Rushingdale Ltd v Byblos Bank* (1985) P.C.C. 342, 346–347.

520 *Xenos v Wickham* (1863) 14 C.B.(N.S.) 435, 473; *Termes de la Ley*, s.v. Fait; Co Litt. 171b; Law of Property (Miscellaneous Provisions) Act 1989 s.1(3)(b).

521 But see Yale [1970] C.L.J. 52.

522 *Vincent v Premo Enterprises Ltd* [1969] 2 Q.B. 609, 619.

523 *Tupper v Foulkes* (1861) 9 C.B.(N.S.) 797; *Xenos v Wickham* (1867) L.R. 2 H.L. 296, 312; *Re Seymour* [1913] 1 Ch. 475.

524 *Xenos v Wickham* (1867) L.R. 2 H.L. 296.

"... the efficacy of a deed depends on its being sealed[525] and delivered by the maker of it, not on his ceasing to retain possession of it."[526]

Where a solicitor or licensed conveyancer in the course of a transaction involving the disposition or creation of an interest in land, purports to deliver an instrument as a deed on behalf of a party to the instrument, it shall be conclusively presumed in favour of a purchaser that he is authorised so to deliver the instrument.[527]

1–094 **Delivery and corporate bodies.** In *Bolton Metropolitan BC v Torkington*[528] the Court of Appeal held that while s.74(1) of the Law of Property Act 1925 deemed a deed "duly executed" where a corporation's seal is affixed in the presence of and attested by its designated officers, it created no presumption as to its delivery.[529] Moreover, while strictly obiter, Peter Gibson L.J. expressed the view that at common law:

"... to describe the sealing by a corporation as giving rise to a rebuttable presumption may go too far, implying, as that does, that the burden is on the corporation affixing the seal."[530]

As a result, where, as on the facts before the court, negotiations were undertaken towards a lease expressly subject to contract, a court should not infer an intention to be bound from the mere sealing of a deed of execution of a lease.[531] On the other hand, in the case of a company incorporated under the Companies Act 1985, where a document makes it clear on its face that:

"[I]t is intended by the person or persons making it to be a deed ... it shall be presumed, unless a contrary intention is proved, to be delivered upon its being so executed".[532]

(ii) *Documents executed on or after September 15, 2005*

1–095 **"Instruments executed".** The 2005 Order[533] refers to "instruments executed" and this raises the question as to how the changes it introduced apply in relation to the making of deeds.[534] It could be thought that a deed (the "instrument") is "executed" only after its delivery, and not merely after the making of

[525] But see above, para.1–086.

[526] *Xenos v Wickham* (1867) L.R. 2 H.L. 296, per Lord Cranworth at 323; cf. per Pigott B. at 309; *Doe d. Garnons v Knight* (1826) 5 B. & C. 671; *Macedo v Stroud* [1922] 2 A.C. 330; *Beesly v Hallwood Estates Ltd* [1960] 1 W.L.R. 549, affirmed [1961] Ch. 105; *Vincent v Premo Enterprises Ltd* [1969] 2 Q.B. 609.

[527] Law of Property (Miscellaneous Provisions) Act 1989 s.1(5).

[528] [2003] EWCA Civ 1634, [2004] Ch. 66. The decision concerned the effect of s.74(1) as in force before its amendment by the 2005 Order, on which see below, para.1–100.

[529] [2003] EWCA Civ 1634 at [22], [45].

[530] [2003] EWCA Civ 1634 at [46].

[531] [2003] EWCA Civ 1634 at [53].

[532] Companies Act 1985 s.36A(5) as inserted by the Companies Act 1989 s.130(2). On the new law, see below, para.1–100.

[533] Regulatory Reform (Execution of Deeds and Documents) Order 2005 (SI 2005/1906).

[534] cf. the discussion in Law Com. No.253, paras 3.6–3.12 as to the confusion over whether the term "executed" in the Companies Act 1985 s.36A (as amended in 1989), the Law of Property Act 1925 s.74 and the Law of Property (Miscellaneous Provisions) Act 1989 s.1 included "delivery".

the document, as only on delivery is the deed a valid instrument. However, the 2005 Order (following the Law Commission's recommendation[535]) distinguishes clearly between the formal requirements required for the execution of an instrument (or document) and the further requirement of delivery for the execution of an instrument *as a deed*[536] and this argues that the changes in the Order apply only to *documents executed* on or after September 15, 2005, and not also to documents executed as deeds on or before September 14, 2005, but delivered as deeds only after this date. This interpretation also has the practical advantage of not applying the changes contained in the Order retrospectively.

The new general requirements for deeds after the 2005 Order. Under s.1(2) of the Law of Property (Miscellaneous Provisions) Act 1989 (as amended by the 2005 Order[537]), an instrument shall not be a deed unless— 1–096

(a) it makes clear on its face that it is intended to be a deed by the person making it or, as the case may be, by the parties to it (whether by describing itself as a deed or expressing itself to be executed to be signed as a deed or otherwise); and

(b) it is validly executed as a deed:

   (i) by that person or a person authorised to execute it in the name or on behalf of that person; or

   (ii) by one or more of those parties or a person authorised to execute it in the name or on behalf of one or more of those parties.

These requirements apply to instruments executed by an individual, by a company incorporated under the Companies Act 1985, by a corporation aggregate or by a corporate sole.[538] However, even after the reforms of 2005, the significance and impact of these provisions differ somewhat according to these different categories of person. In this respect, a distinction is to be drawn between the condition contained in s.1(2)(a) of the 1989 Act as amended (the so-called "face-value requirement") and the condition in s.1(2)(b) of the 1989 Act as amended (the condition of "valid execution").

The "face-value requirement" for deeds. The reforms of 1989 introduced the idea that an instrument should qualify as a deed by reference to the intention of the party or parties to it as made clear on its face,[539] this reflecting earlier developments in judicial attitudes to the common law requirement of sealing.[540] Following the Law Commission's recommendations,[541] this face-value requirement was retained in 2005, though its formulation was clarified and standardised 1–097

[535] Law Com. No.253, para.3.12.

[536] See notably, the 2005 Order arts 4, 6 and below, paras 1–099—1–100.

[537] 2005 Order art.7(3).

[538] For the position as regards charitable corporations, see above, para.1–092.

[539] Above, para.1–000.

[540] *First National Securities v Jones* [1978] Ch. 109 and *Chitty on Contracts*, 26th edn (1989), para.23.

[541] Law Com. No.253, paras 2.29–2.34.

for instruments executed by individuals and companies.[542] In particular, it is expressly provided that:

> "... an instrument shall not be taken to make it clear on its face that it is intended to be a deed merely because it is executed under seal."[543]

1–098 **Execution on behalf of one or more of the parties to the instrument.** Following the Law Commission's recommendations,[544] the 2005 Order introduced new clarifying provisions so as to provide expressly for execution in the name or on behalf of another person. So, it is provided that as regards individuals, a document may be executed by a person on behalf of another, and that it is the person who executes the document (whether or not on behalf of the other) who must comply with the formalities[545]; as regards companies, the legislative provisions which state how a company may execute a document and provide for deemed execution in favour of a purchaser apply where a company executes a document on behalf of another person[546]; and as regards corporations aggregate, the Law of Property Act 1925 was amended so as to provide that deemed execution in favour of a purchaser applies where the corporation executes an instrument on behalf of another person.[547]

1–099 **"Valid execution": individuals.** After amendment by the 2005 Order, the 1989 Act provides that for an instrument to be validly executed as a deed by an individual, it must be:

> "... signed
> (i) by him in the presence of a witness who attests the signature; or
> (ii) at his direction and in his presence and the presence of two witnesses who each attest the signature."

"Signature" is defined later in the section to include making one's mark.[548] The 2005 Order preserved the further common law requirement that for an instrument to be validly executed as a deed it must be "delivered" as a deed.[549]

1–100 **"Valid execution": companies and corporations aggregate.** One of the purpose of the 2005 Order was to harmonise the law governing the execution of

---

542 2005 Order art.7(3) (individuals); Sch.2, repealing Companies Act 1985 s.36A(5) (companies); Law Com. No.253, paras 2.50, 2.54. cf. above.

543 Law of Property (Miscellaneous Provisions) Act 1989 s.1(2A) as inserted by the 2005 Order art.8.

544 Law Com. No.253, Pt 7.

545 Law of Property (Miscellaneous Provisions) Act 1989 s.1(2)(b) and (4A), as amended and inserted by the 2005 Order art.7(3) and 7(4) respectively.

546 Companies Act 1985 s.36A(7) as inserted by the 2005 Order art.7(2) and replaced by Companies Act 2006 s.44(8).

547 Law of Property Act 1925 s.74(1A) as inserted by the 2005 Order art.7(1).

548 Law of Property (Miscellaneous Provisions) Act 1989 s.1(4)(b) as amended by the 2005 Order Sch.1 para.14.

549 Law of Property (Miscellaneous Provisions) Act 1989 s.1(3)(b).

instruments as deeds by corporate bodies.[550] So, it is now provided that a document is validly executed *as a deed* by both companies and corporations aggregate so as to satisfy the general requirements imposed by the 1989 Act[551] "if and only if" it is "duly executed" by the corporate body *and* if it is delivered as a deed.[552] As regards delivery, it is provided for both types of corporate body that an instrument shall be presumed to be delivered for these purposes "upon its being executed, unless a contrary intention is proved".[553] As regards companies, this provision marked a change from the previous law where the presumption of delivery was irrebuttable in these circumstances[554]; as regards corporations aggregate, it clarified the position given that the existence of a rebuttable presumption at common law had been recently judicially questioned.[555] However, the conditions for the "due execution" of a document still differ somewhat as between companies and corporations aggregate. In the case of companies, there are alternative requirements: a document may be executed either by the affixing of its common seal or by being signed "by two authorised signatories or by a directory of the company in the presence of a witness who attests the signature."[556] Where a document is to be signed by a person as a director or the secretary of more than one company, it shall not be taken to be duly signed by that person for these purposes unless the person signs it separately in each capacity.[557] In the case of corporations aggregate, the common law requirement of affixing the corporation's seal still applies in principle,[558] but it is provided that:

> ". . . in favour of a purchaser an instrument shall be deemed to have been duly executed . . . if a seal purporting to be the corporation's seal purports to be affixed to the instrument in the presence of and attested by (a) two members of the board of directors, council or other governing body of the corporation, or (b) one such member and the clerk, secretary or other permanent officer of the corporation or his deputy."[559]

---

[550] Law Com. No.153, Pt 4.

[551] Law of Property (Miscellaneous Provisions) Act 1989 s.1(2)(b) (as amended); see above, para.1–096.

[552] Law of Property Act 1925 s.74A(1) as inserted by the 2005 Order art.4 (corporations aggregate); Companies Act 1985 s.36AA(1) as inserted by the 2005 Order art.6 replaced by Companies Act 2006 s.46(1).

[553] Law of Property Act 1925 s.74A(2) as inserted by the 2005 Order art.4 (corporations aggregate); Companies Act 1985 s.36AA(2) (companies) as inserted by 2005 Order art.6 and replaced by Companies Act 2006 s.46(2).

[554] As a result, the 2005 Order art.5 amended the Companies Act 1985 s.36A(6) and see Law Com. No.253 paras 6.37–6.43.

[555] *Bolton Metropolitan BC v Torkington* [2003] EWCA Civ 1634, [2004] Ch. 66 at [46], above, para.1–094.

[556] Companies Act 2006 s.44(2) replacing Companies Act 1985 s.36A(1), (4) as inserted by the Companies Act 1989 s.130(2).

[557] Companies Act 2006 s.44(6) replacing Companies Act 1985 s.36A(4A) as inserted by 2005 Order art.10(1) Sch.1 para.10.

[558] Law Com. No.253 para.4.5.

[559] Law of Property Act 1925 s.74(1) as substituted by the 2005 Order art.3. Section 74(1B) of the 1925 Act as inserted by the 2005 Order art.10(1) Sch.1 para.2 provides that for these purposes: "a seal purports to be affixed in the presence of and attested by an officer of the corporation, in the case of an officer which is not an individual, if it is affixed in the presence of and attested by an individual authorised by the officer to attest on its behalf." And see Law Com. No.253 paras 4.6–4.9.

1–101 **"Valid execution": corporations sole.** Where a deed is executed by a corporation sole, the common law requirement of sealing which has already been explained still applies.[560]

(iii) *Common Aspects*

1–102 **Introduction.** There remain certain aspects of the law governing deeds which apply irrespective of the nature of the person making them or the date on which they are executed.

1–103 **Date.** A date is not essential to the validity of a deed.[561] A deed takes effect on the date of its delivery.[562]

1–104 **Estoppel preventing reliance on formal invalidity.** In *Shah v Shah*[563] the Court of Appeal held in relation to an instrument governed by the 1989 Act as enacted[564] that where an individual has signed an instrument which on its face purports to be a deed and has delivered it apparently attested by the signature of a witness, he may be estopped from denying the validity of this "deed" on the ground that the apparently attesting signatory was not present at the time of that individual's signature.[565] The Court of Appeal expressed its approval in this respect for Beldam L.J.'s earlier statement in *Yaxley v Gotts* to the effect that the:

> " . . . general principle that a party cannot rely on an estoppel in the face of a statute depends upon the nature of the enactment, the purpose of the provision and the social policy behind it."[566]

While it was accepted before the Court of Appeal in *Shah v Shah* that no estoppel could operate in the case of the absence of a signature by the person allegedly executing a deed, there was no social policy requiring a person attesting such a signature to be present so as to prevent an estoppel from arising in respect of a defect in attestation.[567] However, as the House of Lords subsequently made clear in *Actionstrength Ltd v International Glass Engineering IN.GL.EN SpA* (which concerned s.4 of the Statute of Frauds[568]), an estoppel cannot arise to prevent a person relying on formal invalidity unless there is an unambiguous representation that the transaction in question was enforceable.[569] This was the case in *Shah v*

---

[560] See above, fn.488, for a definition of corporations sole and see also Law. Com. No.253 para.4.23. On the common law requirements see above, para.1–092.

[561] Bacon, *Abridgment Obligation* (C); Comyns Digest *Fait* (B3); *Goddard's Case* (1584) 2 Co Rep. 4b.

[562] See also below, para.1–105 (escrow).

[563] [2001] EWCA Civ 527, [2002] Q.B. 35

[564] Above, para.1–090.

[565] The 1989 Act s.1(3) requires that the instrument is signed in the presence the attending witness or witnesses.

[566] [2001] EWCA Civ 527, [2002] Q.B. 35 at 44 (Pill L.J. with whom Tuckley L.J. and Sir Christopher Slade agreed): *Yaxley v Gotts* [2000] Ch. 162, 191.

[567] [2001] EWCA Civ 527, [2002] Q.B. 35 at 47.

[568] See Vol.II, para.44–054.

[569] [2003] UKHL 17, [2003] 2 All E.R. 615 at [51].

Shah where "the delivery of an apparently valid deed constituted an unambiguous representation of its nature".[570]

Delivery of deed as an escrow. A party may deliver a deed as an escrow, that is, so that it shall take effect or be his deed on certain conditions. It is in other words a limited or conditional delivery. Such delivery need not be accompanied by express words; if from all the facts attending the transaction it can reasonably be inferred that the writing was delivered so as not to take effect as a deed until a certain condition should be satisfied, it will operate as an escrow.[571] To constitute a delivery as an escrow, however, it was at one time necessary that the deed should not have been handed over to the grantee or covenantee.[572] But nowadays a deed may be delivered as an escrow by handing it to a solicitor who is acting for all the parties to it[573]; or even to the solicitor of the grantee or covenantee himself, provided it is clear upon the whole transaction that such handing over was not intended to be a delivery at that time to such grantee or covenantee.[574] In other words, evidence is admissible to show the character in which and the terms upon which the deed was delivered.[575] It is a question of fact, and depends on what the parties intended. Their intention may be ascertained either from their statements or from the surrounding circumstances prior to or simultaneous with (but not subsequent to) the delivery of the instrument.[576] 1–105

Conveyance as an escrow. Where a conveyance is executed by the vendor and entrusted to his solicitor with a view to its being handed over to the purchaser on completion, then, in the absence of special circumstances, it is to be inferred that the conveyance is executed as an escrow conditional upon payment of the purchase price and (where appropriate) execution by the purchaser.[577] In such a case, there must be a time limit within which the implied condition of the escrow is to be performed.[578] So if the vendor by notice makes time of the essence of the contract, and the purchaser does not within the time specified in the notice perform the condition, it is no longer possible for the condition of the escrow to 1–106

570 [2003] UKHL 17 at [51], per Lord Walker of Gestingthorpe.

571 *Murray v Earl of Stair* (1823) 2 B. & C. 82; *Xenos v Wickham* (1867) L.R. 2 H.L. 296 at [323]; *Macedo v Stroud* [1922] 2 A.C. 330 at [337]; *Beesly v Hallwood Estates Ltd* [1961] Ch. 105; *Vincent v Premo Enterprises Ltd* [1969] 2 Q.B. 609; *D'Silva v Lister House Development Ltd* [1971] Ch. 17; *Kingston v Ambrian Investment Co Ltd* [1975] 1 W.L.R. 161; *Glessing v Green* [1975] 1 W.L.R. 863; *Terrapin International Ltd v IRC* [1976] 1 W.L.R. 665.

572 Co.Litt. 36a; Sheppard's *Touchstone of Common Assurances*, 7th edn (1820), p.59.

573 *Millership v Brookes* (1860) 5 H. & N. 797; *Kidner v Keith* (1863) 15 C.B.(N.S.) 35; 42. *Glessing v Green* [1975] 1 W.L.R. 863.

574 *Watkins v Nash* (1875) L.R. 20 Eq. 262, 266; *Nash v Flyn* (1844) 1 Jo. & La.T. 162, 177.

575 *London Freehold and Leasehold Property Co v Suffield* [1897] 2 Ch. 608, 621–622. See below, para.12–106.

576 *Bowker v Burdekin* (1843) 11 M.W. 128, 147; *Davis v Jones* (1856) 17 C.B. 625, 634; *Governors, etc., of Foundling Hospital v Crane* [1911] 2 K.B. 367, 374. *Thompson v McCullough* [1947] K.B. 447.

577 *Kingston v Ambrian Investment Co Ltd* [1975] 1 W.L.R. 161; *Glessing v Green* [1975] 1 W.L.R. 863.

578 *Glessing v Green* [1975] 1 W.L.R. 863. cf. *Kingston v Ambrian Investment Co Ltd* [1975] 1 W.L.R. 161 at [168]–[169].

be performed.[579] However, the inference as to delivery as an escrow arising from non payment of the price can be rebutted by other circumstances attending the delivery.[580]

1–107 **Retrospective effect.** A deed delivered as an escrow takes effect as between grantor and grantee retrospectively from the date of its delivery, and not on the date on which the relevant conditions are satisfied.[581]

(c) *Consideration*

1–108 **No consideration required.** Generally speaking, as will be seen later in detail,[582] the law does not enforce gratuitous promises but instead requires a certain reciprocity for the creation of a "simple" contract, this requirement being expressed through the rules gathered under the heading of the doctrine of consideration. However, in contracts contained in a deed no such reciprocity is ordinarily required, the rule being that a contract contained in a deed is good even against a party standing to derive no advantage from it.[583] This means that the common law actions of debt (for a promised sum of money) or damages (for failure to perform promises more generally) are available to the person for whose benefit they are expressed. On the other hand equity never favoured voluntary transactions even if they were contained in a deed, and refused to grant its special remedies in cases where these were without consideration. So it has been laid down that specific performance will not be decreed of a contract contained in a deed which is entirely without consideration.[584] Knight-Bruce L.J. in *Kekewich v Manning*[585] said:

> "In equity, where at least the covenantor is living, or where specific performance of such a (voluntary) covenant is sought, it stands scarcely, or not at all, on a better footing than if it were contained in an instrument unsealed."[586]

And an imperfect conveyance, if voluntary, is not binding, and equity will not execute it in favour of volunteers if anything remains to be done.[587] A contract contained in a deed, if made without consideration, may be impeached by third

---

[579] *Glessing v Green* [1975] 1 W.L.R. 863. cf. *Beesly v Hallwood Estates Ltd* [1961] Ch. 105, 118, 120; *Kingston v Ambrian Investment Co Ltd* [1975] 1 W.L.R. 161 at 166.

[580] *Bank of Scotland Plc v King* [2007] EWHC 2747 (Ch), [2007] All E.R. (D) 376 (Nov) at [51].

[581] *Alan Estates Ltd v W.G. Stores Ltd* [1982] Ch. 511, not following *Terrapin International Ltd v IRC* [1976] 1 W.L.R. 665; *Bank of Scotland Plc v King* [2007] EWHC 2747 (Ch), [2007] All E.R. (D) 376 (Nov) at [51]; Kenny (1982) Conv. 409.

[582] See below, Ch.3.

[583] See Plowd. 308; *Morley v Boothby* (1825) 3 Bing. 107, 111–112.

[584] *Wycherley v Wycherley* (1763) 2 Eden 175, 177; *Groves v Groves* (1829) 3 Y. & J. 163; *Jefferys v Jefferys* (1841) Cr. & Ph. 138. See *Fry on Specific Performance*, 6th edn (1921), p.53; Jones and Goodhart, *Specific Performance*, 2nd edn (1996), p.24. Contrast *Mountford v Scott* [1975] Ch. 258 (token payment for grant of option). See also below, paras 3–021, 27–033.

[585] (1851) 1 De G.M. & G. 176, 188.

[586] But see above, para.1–086.

[587] As in *Milroy v Lord* (1862) 4 De G.F. & J. 264; *Richards v Delbridge* (1874) L.R. 18 Eq. 11; *Re Kay's Settlement* [1939] Ch. 329; *Re Fry* [1946] Ch. 312. See also Law of Property Act 1925 s.173, replacing Voluntary Conveyances Act 1893.

parties on similar grounds to those on which voluntary settlements can be impeached as being fraudulent as against creditors or purchasers.[588]

(c) *Other Aspects*

Benefit of person not a party. According to an ancient rule of the common law, no one could take an immediate interest as grantee nor the benefit of a covenant as covenantee under an indenture inter partes (as opposed to a deed poll) unless he was named as a party thereto.[589] This was altered by s.5 of the Real Property Act 1845, which provided that under an indenture, an immediate estate or interest in any tenements or hereditaments, and the benefit of a condition or covenant respecting any tenements or hereditaments, might be taken, although the taker was not named a party to the same indenture.[590] This section was re-enacted with modifications by s.56(1) of the Law of Property Act 1925, which provides that a person may take the benefit of any covenant *or agreement* over or respecting land *or other property*, although he may not be named as a party to the conveyance or other instrument.[591] The determination of the exact scope of this provision is a matter of considerable difficulty[592]; but it is clear that it does not effect any general abrogation of the doctrine of privity of contract.[593] In *Beswick v Beswick*,[594] a majority of the House of Lords was of the opinion that a limited meaning should be given to the word "property". Lord Guest thought it meant real property. Lord Upjohn, however, was not prepared to accept this limitation, although he considered that the application of the section was restricted to covenants contained in documents strictly inter partes and under seal.[595] 1–109

Contract (Rights of Third Parties) Act 1999. It is not entirely clear how the position described in the preceding paragraph is affected by the coming into force of the Contract (Rights of Third Parties) Act 1999, which creates a new exception to privity of contract where the contract expressly provides that a third party may in his own right enforce a term of the contract, or where a term purports to confer 1–110

[588] See Law of Property Act 1925 ss.172, 173.

[589] *Scudamore v Vandenstene* (1587) 2 Co.Inst. 673; *Berkeley v Hardy* (1826) 5 B. & C. 355; *Forster v Elvet Colliery Co Ltd* [1908] 1 K.B. 629, 639, affirmed sub nom. *Dyson v Forster* [1909] A.C. 98. (An "indenture" is a deed executed by more than one party, whereas a "deed poll" is one executed by only one party). cf. *Moody v Condor Insurance Ltd* [2006] EWHC 100, [2006] 1 W.L.R. 1847, where it was held that the mere fact that a deed was executed by a guarantor and a principal debtor and expressed as being made "between" them did not conclude the issue whether the document was a deed poll or a deed inter partes, as it was "necessary to examine what the parties ... set out to do by it": at [18], per Park J.

[590] *Kelsey v Dodd* (1881) 52 L.J.Ch. 34, 39; *Forster v Elvet Colliery Co Ltd* [1908] 1 K.B. 629.

[591] "Property" is defined in s.205(1)(xx). See also Law of Property Act s.78, re-enacting with modifications Conveyancing Act 1881 s.58.

[592] *Beswick v Beswick* [1968] A.C. 58; Elliott (1956) 20 Conv.(N.S.) 43, 114; Andrews (1959) 23 Conv.(N.S.) 179; Ellinger (1963) 26 M.L.R. 396; below, para.18–020.

[593] *Beswick v Beswick* [1968] A.C. 58.

[594] [1968] A.C. 58, 77, 81, 87.

[595] [1968] A.C. 58 at [105]–[107]. See also Lord Pearce at [94]. The reference to sealing must be read in the light of the effect of the Law of Property (Miscellaneous Provisions) Act 1989 s.1, above, para.1–086.

a benefit on him unless on a proper construction of the contract it appears that the parties did not intend the term to be enforceable by the third party.[596] Where a contract in the ordinary sense of an agreement supported by consideration is contained in a deed, there is nothing in the 1999 Act which suggests that its provisions should not apply to contracts owing to the use of this formality. More difficult, however, is the question whether an agreement contained in a deed is itself "a contract" for the purposes of the 1999 Act even in the absence of any supporting consideration. As has been noted,[597] there is no agreement as to whether in general a promise or an agreement contained in a deed takes effect as a "contract". In the case of the 1999 Act, though, its own provisions do make clear that the contracts with which it is concerned must consist of an agreement between two or more persons for the benefit (as defined) of a third party.[598] Moreover, the Law Commission's report on whose recommendations the 1999 Act was based took the view that its proposed reform would restrict the ambit of the doctrine of consideration so as to prevent the rule that "consideration must move from a promisee" from denying a right in a third party to a contract otherwise fulfilling the requisite conditions.[599] In the course of exposing its views of the future position, however, the Law Commission observed that:

> "... provided there is a contract supported by consideration (*or made by deed*), it may then be enforceable by a third party beneficiary who has not provided consideration."[600]

Given that the courts refer to Law Commission reports for guidance in the interpretation of resulting legislation,[601] this suggests that an agreement contained in a deed should count as a "contract" for the purposes of the 1999 Act, even if it is unsupported by consideration.

1–111 ***Non est factum.*** There was an ancient common law defence to actions on specialties known as *non est factum*: if an illiterate man, to whom the provisions of a deed had been wrongly read, executed it under a mistake as to its contents, he could say that it was not his deed.[602] In modern times this doctrine has undergone modification[603] and has been extended to cases other than those of illiteracy and to simple contracts in writing,[604] so that there is now no difference between specialty and other written contracts in this respect.

---

[596] Contract (Rights of Third Parties) Act 1999 s.1 and see generally, below, paras 18–088 et seq.

[597] See above, para.1–003.

[598] Contract (Rights of Third Parties) Act 1999 s.1(2) which refers to the intention of the *parties*.

[599] Law Commission, *Privity of Contract: Contracts for the Benefit of Third Parties*, Law Com. No.242 (1996) Pt VI.

[600] *Privity of Contract*, Law Com. No.242, para.6.4 (emphasis added).

[601] *Wilson v First County Trust Ltd (No.2)* [2003] UKHL 40, [2003] 3 W.L.R. 568 at [56].

[602] *Thoroughgood's Case* (1584) 2 Co.Rep. 9a. But the doctrine was much older than that case: see Holdsworth, *History of English Law*, Vol.8, p.50.

[603] See below, paras 5–101 et seq.

[604] See below, para.5–101.

Estoppel and facts stated in the deed. 1–112

> "A party who executes a deed is estopped in a Court of Law from saying that the facts stated in the deed are not truly stated."[605]

The principle has been extended to statements in recitals in a deed.[606] It is a question of the construction of the deed as a whole as to which parties are estopped by a recital. When a recital is intended to be a statement which all the parties to the deed have mutually agreed to admit as true, it is an estoppel upon all. But when it is intended to be the statement of one party only, the estoppel is confined to that party: and the intention is to be gathered by construing the instrument.[607] The scope of the doctrine is extremely limited in modern law. First, it only applies between the parties to the deed and those claiming through them.[608] Secondly, it only applies when an action is brought to enforce rights arising out of the deed and not collateral to it.[609] Thirdly, it only applies if the statement is clear and unambiguous.[610] Fourthly, it does not prevent a party from relying on defences such as *non est factum*, fraud, illegality or incapacity. In such cases the facts may be pleaded in order to defeat the deed, even though they may contradict statements made on the face of the deed.[611] And so, although a party to a deed may be estopped from denying facts which are stated in it, he is not estopped from saying that, on the facts so stated, the deed is void in law.[612] Fifthly, where a deed is rectifiable (that is to say, ought to be rectified), the doctrine of estoppel by deed will not bind the parties to it.[613] In view of these limitations, there seems little point in preserving any separate category of estoppels by deed, since the basis of the estoppel appears now to be covered by estoppel by representation or by convention.[614]

Merger. A deed is an instrument of a higher nature than a simple contract. A security created by simple contract will be merged in and extinguished by a 1–113

---

[605] *Baker v Dewey* (1823) 1 B. & C. 704, 707. See also *Hayne v Maltby* (1789) 3 Term Rep. 438, 441; *Potts v Nixon* (1870) I.R. 5 C.L. 45.

[606] *Lainson v Tremere* (1834) 1 Ad. & El. 792; *Bowman v Taylor* (1834) 2 Ad. & El. 278; *Young v Raincock* (1849) 7 C.B. 310, 338.

[607] *Stroughill v Buck* (1850) 14 Q.B. 781, 787; cf. *Greer v Kettle* [1938] A.C. 156, 168–171.

[608] *Carpenter v Buller* (1841) 8 M. & W. 209, 212.

[609] *Carpenter v Buller* (1841) 8 M. & W. 209 at [213]; *Wiles v Woodward* (1850) 5 Exch. 557, 563; *Ex p. Morgan* (1875) 2 Ch D 72.

[610] *Bensley v Burdon* (1830) 8 L.J.(O.S.) Ch. 85, 87; *Right v Bucknell* (1831) 2 B. & Ad. 278, 282; *Heath v Crealock* (1874) L.R. 10 Ch.App. 22; *General Finance, etc., Co v Liberator, etc., Building Society* (1879) 10 Ch D 15; *Onward Building Society v Smithson* [1893] 1 Ch. 1; *Poulton v Moore* [1915] 1 K.B. 400; cf. *Trinidad Asphalte Co v Coryat* [1896] A.C. 587.

[611] *Collins v Blantern* (1767) 2 Wils.K.B. 341; *Hayne v Maltby* (1789) 3 Term Rep. 438; *Hill v Manchester and Salford Waterworks Co* (1831) 2 B. & Ad. 544.

[612] *Doe d. Preece v Howells* (1831) 2 B. & Ad. 744, and see *Re A Bankruptcy Notice* [1924] 2 Ch. 76.

[613] *Greer v Kettle* [1938] A.C. 156, 171; *Wilson v Wilson* [1969] 1 W.L.R. 1470; *OTV Birwelco Ltd v Technical & General Guarantee Co Ltd* [2002] 4 All E.R. 668.

[614] cf. *Amalgamated Investment and Property Co Ltd v Texas Commercial International Bank Ltd* [1982] Q.B. 84.

specialty security if it secures the same obligation.[615] A simple contract may also be merged in a deed, e.g. a conveyance, if so intended by the parties.[616]

1–114 **Alteration of deeds.** Where a deed is altered in a material way either by a party in whose custody it is kept or by a stranger to the transaction, it becomes void, but where the alteration is not material it does not become void.[617] This rule applicable to deeds was extended in 1791 to contracts in written instruments generally[618] and is discussed further in Ch.25.[619]

1–115 **Variation or discharge.** At common law, an attribute of a contract contained in a deed was that it could only be varied or discharged by another contract contained in a deed, and not by a contract under hand or by word of mouth[620]; but in equity such contracts could be varied or discharged by parol,[621] and the rule of equity now prevails.[622]

1–116 **Period of limitation.** The period of limitation for an action for a breach of contract is 12 years if the contract is contained in a deed, whereas it is only six years in the case of a simple contract.[623]

6. THE RELATIONSHIP BETWEEN CONTRACT AND TORT

1–117 **Introduction.** The proper relationship between contract and tort has caused considerable difficulty and justifies some discussion of its history as well as an examination of the modern law.[624] As a matter of history, the first problem for the common law was to decide whether a particular form of action which it granted ought to be considered as founded on tort or on contract, a problem of the

---

[615] See below, paras 25–001 et seq.

[616] See below, para.25–003.

[617] *Pigot's Case* (1614) 11 Co. Rep. 26B, 27A; *Aldous's Case* (1868) L.R. 3 Q.B. 753; *Northern Bank Ltd v Laverty* [2001] N.I. 315.

[618] *Master v Millar* (1791) 14 T.R. 320.

[619] See below, paras 25–020 et seq.

[620] *Kaye v Waghorn* (1809) 1 Taunt. 428; cf. *Ex p. Morgan* (1875) 2 Ch D 72 at 89 and see the rule recognised but infringed in *Nash v Armstrong* (1861) 10 C.B.(N.S.) 259.

[621] *Webb v Hewitt* (1857) 3 K. & J. 438.

[622] Supreme Court Act 1981 s.49; *Steeds v Steeds* (1889) 22 QBD 537; *Berry v Berry* [1929] 2 K.B. 316; *Mitas v Hyams* [1951] 2 T.L.R. 1215; *Plymouth Corp v Harvey* [1971] 1 W.L.R. 549.

[623] Limitation Act 1980 s.8(1) (but subject to s.8(2)). See, e.g. *Aiken v Stewart Wrightson Members Agency Ltd* [1995] 1 W.L.R. 1281, 1292. See below, paras 28–002, 28–003.

[624] See Prosser, *Selected Topics on the Law of Torts* (1953), p.380; Guest (1961) 3 Univ. Malaya L.R. 191; Poulton (1966) 82 L.Q.R. 346; Fridman (1977) 93 L.Q.R. 422; Duncan Wallace (1978) L.Q.R. 60; Burrows (1983) 99 L.Q.R. 217; Smith (1984) U.B.C.L. Rev. 95; Jaffey (1985) 5 L.S. 77; Reynolds (1985) 11 N.Z. Univ. Law Rev. 215; Atiyah (1986) *Law & Contemporary Problems* 287; Cane, in Furmston (ed.), *The Law of Torts* (1986), Ch.6; Cane, *Tort Law and Economic Interests*, 2nd edn (1996), pp.129–149, 307–343; McLaren (1989) 68 Can. Bar Rev. 30; Adams and Brownsword (1991) 55 Sask. L. Rev. 441; Burrows (1995) C.L.P. 103; Cane in Rose (ed.), *Consensus ad Idem* (1996), p.96; Whittaker (1996) 16 O.J.L.S. 191; Whittaker (1997) 17 Legal Studies 169. For an economic analysis see Bishop (1983) 12 L.S. 241. For comparative studies see Weir, *International Encyclopedia of Comparative Law* (1976), Vol.XI, "Torts" Ch.12; Markesinis (1987) 103 L.Q.R. 354.

classification of actions.[625] Secondly, it is clear that there are considerable differences between the typical cases of liability in tort and contract: contractual obligations are voluntary and particular to the parties, whereas liability in tort is imposed by law as a matter of policy and affects persons generally.[626] Moreover, the distinction between the two liabilities is reflected in differences of rule which govern not merely their existence but also their incidents.[627] Thirdly, given these differences of regime between contract and tort, the question arises whether a party to a contract may choose to sue the other party in tort where the constituent elements of a tort can be made out and, if so, with what effects.[628] Again, where the existence of liability in tort is doubtful, the question arises whether the existence of a contract between the parties is a reason in favour of the recognition of such a tortious duty or a reason against it, a question which has arisen in particular in the context of recovery of pure economic loss in the tort of negligence.[629] Finally, the question is posed whether or to what extent the existence of a contractual obligation owed by A to B under a contract affects any liability in A to C, who is not party to that contract or, conversely, liability in C to A: do contracts affect torts beyond privity?[630]

(a) *The Classification of the Forms of Action at Common Law*

Forms of action. For a long time, the common law did not require formally to distinguish between actions in contract and in tort.[631] Until the late seventeenth century, only Bracton used a Roman legal framework for the treating of common law material, including the distinction between actions *ex delicto* and *ex contractu*, and even he did not make this distinction central to his exposition.[632] Moreover, while some early decisions appear to turn on such a distinction, care should be taken not to read into these cases, which turned on differences of individual writs, disputes as to a classification unfamiliar and irrelevant to contemporary legal thought[633]: indeed, the action which became the main sanction of breach of contract (*assumpsit*) and the modern torts both grew out of the action of trespass.[634] However, from the late seventeenth century, the courts did distinguish between actions in contract (*assumpsit*, covenant and account) and actions in tort (which included trespass, trover and nuisance). They did so for the purposes of rules governing transmissibility of actions on death[635] and capacity,[636] but the principal purposes were procedural and in particular the rules 1–118

[625] See below, para.1–118.
[626] See below, paras 1–119—1–121.
[627] See below, paras 1–122—1–125.
[628] See below, paras 1–126 et seq.
[629] See below, paras 1–138 et seq.
[630] See below, paras 1–170 et seq.
[631] Maitland, Appendix A to Pollock, *The Law of Torts*, 1st edn, p.467, p.468.
[632] Maitland, Appendix A to Pollock, *The Law of Torts*, p.468.
[633] Prosser at pp.380–381.
[634] Simpson, *A History of the Common Law of Contracts* (1975), p.199; Milsom, *Historical Foundations of the Common Law*, 2nd edn (1981), Ch.12; Fridman (1977) 93 L.Q.R. 422.
[635] *Pinchon's Case* (1608) 9 Col. Rep. 86b; *Hambly v Trott* (1776) 1 Cowp. 371.
[636] *Johnson v Pye* (1666) 1 Sid. 258, 1 Keb. 913; *Bristow v Eastman* (1794) 1 Esp. 172.

as to joinder of actions in the same declaration and joinder of parties to proceedings were said to turn on whether the action was in a form *ex contractu* or a form *ex delicto*.[637] Even so, it was not until the nineteenth century that this distinction was used as a general basis of exposition of the common law material,[638] though it had been mentioned in earlier works.[639] However, since the abolition in the mid-nineteenth century of many of the procedural differences between the two types of action,[640] these disputes could be seen as "useless, and worse than useless learning".[641] Where, therefore, after these reforms a court has had to classify a particular *type* of claim by a claimant as contractual or tortious, for example for the purposes of the jurisdiction of a court of limited jurisdiction, it has done so on the basis of what it considered was the substance rather than the form of action.[642]

(b) *Differences of Substance between Contract and Tort*

1–119 **General.** Publication in the mid-nineteenth century of the great systematising textbooks of Addison,[643] Underhill,[644] and Pollock[645] saw a change in understanding of the distinction between contract and tort from one of form to one of substance. This change resulted, not only from the sweeping away of the old procedural differences between the two types of action, but also from the

[637] *Denison v Ralphson* (1682) 1 Vent. 365; *Bosun v Sandford* (1691) 2 Salk. 440. In this respect, there was something of a dispute as to the form in which the action of detinue was properly to be classified: see Chitty, *A Practical Treatise on Pleading* (1809), Vol.2, p.399; *Cooper v Chitty* (1756) 1 Burr. 20, 31; *Gledstane v Hewitt* (1831) 1 C. & J. 566; Manning, note to *Walker v Needham* (1841) 3 Man. & Gr. 561. This dispute appears particularly strange given the clearly proprietary function of the action.

[638] Chitty at Vol.I, Chs 1 and 2.

[639] Bracton, Fol. 102; Bacon, *A New Abridgement of the Law* (1736) "Actions in General (A) Of the different Kinds of Actions"; Comyns, *A Digest of the Laws of England*, 1st edn (1762–67), Vol.1, p.120; Blackstone, *Commentaries*, III, Ch.VIII.

[640] Common Law Procedure Act 1852 ss.34, 35, 41, 74.

[641] *Bryant v Herbert* (1878) 3 C.P.D. 389, 392, per Bramwell L.J., referring to the problem of the classification of detinue, on which see above fn.499.

[642] *Bryant v Herbert* (1878) 3 C.P.D. 389; *Legge v Tucker* (1856) 1 H. & N. 500. In theory, this issue of the classification of a particular type of claim is distinct from the issue whether in cases of concurrence of actions the claimant may choose the basis of his claim. Thus, in *Att-Gen v Canter* [1939] 1 K.B. 318 the question arose whether a claim by the Crown for a penalty imposed on a taxpayer for fraud transmitted against the latter's estate under s.1 of the Law Reform (Miscellaneous Provisions) Act 1934, and if so, whether it ought to be considered a "cause of action in tort" for the purposes of s.1(3) of the same Act which imposed time restrictions as to the accrual of such a transmitted claim. At first instance, Lawrence J. held that the claim was "one for a debt created by the statute" under which the penalty was imposed and did transmit against the estate, but was not a "cause of action in tort": at 321. The Court of Appeal confirmed this decision, though only the principle of transmissibility was addressed. However, the courts have also looked to the substance of a plaintiff's claim as being contract rather than tort in cases of concurrence, to prevent the plaintiff's choice of form of action from governing the procedural rule applicable: see *Legge v Tucker*, above, though the court denied the "independence" of the tort from the contractual duty: at 502; *Kelly v Metropolitan Ry Co* [1895] 1 Q.B. 944; *Edwards v Mallen* [1908] 1 K.B. 1002.

[643] Addison, *Contracts*, 1st edn (1845).

[644] Underhill, *A Summary of the Law of Torts or Wrongs Independent of Contract*, 1st edn (1873).

[645] Pollack, *Principles of Contract at Law and in Equity*, 1st edn (1876); *The Law of Torts*, 1st edn (1887).

acceptance by English lawyers of the "will theory" of contractual obligation,[646] a theory which pointed to the special voluntary nature of contractual obligations, in contrast to duties in tort which were not.[647] This contrast lies behind part of the generally accepted modern distinction between contract and tort. Thus, according to Winfield,[648] liability for breach of contract is distinguished from liability in tort in that:

(i) the duties in tort are primarily fixed by the law while in contract they are fixed by the parties themselves; and

(ii) in tort the duty is towards persons generally while in contract it is towards a specific person or persons.

Both propositions still hold good, at least as a starting point. Moreover, there is a further real, general distinction: for torts can be said to make the claimant's (existing) position worse, whereas a breach of contract often consists of failing to make the claimant's position better, better, that is, from the claimant's pre-contractual position and as defined by the other party's obligations under the contract.[649] However, developments in the modern law have blurred these contrasts. First, as has already been remarked, many of the incidents of modern contracts are not fixed by the parties: the courts[650] and the legislature have regulated the relationships of many contractors. Moreover, even where this regulation is effected by the implication of a term, some terms are not susceptible to express exclusion or alteration by the parties.[651] Indeed, in some types of contracts legislative regulation has reached a level where the "voluntary element" is reduced to a simple choice whether or not to enter the relationship.[652] Furthermore, in general common law or statute, rather than the parties, specify what legal consequences arise on the failure to perform a contract, whether this is considered a matter of breach[653] or frustration.[654] It is the law itself which provides and delineates the remedies of damages, termination for major breach of contract or specific performance, and the role of the parties' agreement here is not to create but at most to modify the rules already provided by the law.[655] Conversely, "voluntariness" can be relevant to the imposition of liability in tort: positively, where "voluntariness" or consent on the part of the *defendant* is a factor in the imposition of liability, for example, in relation to occupier's

[646] See Gordley, *The Philosophical Origins of Modern Contract Doctrine* (1991), Ch.6.
[647] Atiyah, *The Rise and Fall of Freedom of Contract* (1979), p.408.
[648] Winfield, *Province of the Law of Tort* (1931), p.380.
[649] cf. Weir, *International Encyclopedia of Comparative Law* (1976), Vol.XI, "Torts", Ch.12, p.5; Whittaker (1996) 16 O.J.L.S. 191, 207 et seq. cf. below, para.1–122.
[650] See above, para.1–017; below, Ch.13.
[651] See, e.g. Sex Discrimination Act 1975 s.8; Sale of Goods Act 1979 s.14; Unfair Contract Terms Act 1977 s.6.
[652] Hepple (1986–1987) 36 *King's Counsel* 11 and see above, para.1–017.
[653] See below, Chs 24, 26, 27.
[654] See below, Ch.23.
[655] For example, the law specifies what losses may be compensated by an action for damages for breach of contract: see below, paras 26–082—26–087. In principle, the parties may specify the circumstances in which a right to terminate a contract on the ground of breach will arise (below, paras 12–019, 24–038) or can exclude or limit a party's liability in damages, but they cannot resort to the use of "penalties": below, paras 26–125 et seq.

liability,[656] liability for omissions[657] or under the principle established by *Hedley Byrne & Co Ltd v Heller & Partners Ltd*.[658] Negatively, however, the consent of a *claimant* may prevent liability from arising in tort: thus, consent to medical treatment[659] or to a risk of injury in sport[660] may exclude liability in tort by operation of the maxim volenti non fit injuria, as may a contractual agreement by the parties excluding liability, whether in tort or in contract.[661]

1–120 Some writers have stressed the special protection of expectations created by a contract, reflected in the nature of the damages awarded on its breach and the lack of protection of expectations by the law of torts.[662] Others have disagreed,[663] arguing that this obscures the importance of awards of damages in contract based on the claimant's "reliance interest," which is similar to that protected generally in tort.[664] Conversely, damages in tort can compensate the injured party's disappointed expectations, for example, his expectation to be able to earn a living,[665] although it has been pointed out that this expectation is general, unlike contractual expectations which are induced by making the contract.[666] On the other hand, while traditionally it could be said that recovery for non-intentional pure economic loss was generally irrecoverable in tort, while being recoverable in contract, this position has been significantly qualified by the House of Lords' application of the principle of "assumption of responsibility" of *Hedley Byrne & Co Ltd v Heller & Partners*[667] to cases of the negligent performance of services.[668]

1–121 More radical criticism of the division between contract and tort argues that it, together with other broad conceptual distinctions in the law, at times helps to obscure similarities of factual situation which cut across it and at others to group

---

[656] The liability of an occupier to someone on the premises for injury depends, inter alia on whether that person had permission to be there: see Occupiers' Liability Act 1957 s.1(2) (visitors) and Occupiers' Liability Act 1984 s.1(1) (trespassers).

[657] Thus, liability in the tort of negligence will be imposed for a negligent "pure omission" where the defendant has voluntarily accepted a duty: *Clerk & Lindsell on Torts*, 19th edn (2006), paras 8–50—8–52.

[658] [1964] A.C. 465. See *Spring v Guardian Assurance Co Ltd* [1995] 2 A.C. 296; *Henderson v Merrett Syndicates Ltd* [1995] 2 A.C. 145; *Williams v Natural Life Health Foods Ltd and Mistlin* [1998] 1 W.L.R. 830. cf. *Smith v Eric S Bush* [1990] 1 A.C. 831; *Harris v Wyre Forest District Council* [1990] 1 A.C. 831 at 862 and see below, paras 1–120 et seq. See also Barker (1993) 109 L.Q.R. 461; Whittaker (1997) 17 *Legal Studies* 169.

[659] See *Sidaway v Board of Governors of the Bethlem Royal Hospital* [1985] A.C. 871.

[660] *Condon v Basi* [1985] 1 W.L.R. 866.

[661] See below, para.1–151.

[662] Burrows (1983) 99 L.Q.R. 217; Taylor (1982) 45 M.L.R. 139; Friedmann (1995) 111 L.Q.R. 628; Whittaker (1996) 16 O.J.L.S. 191, 207 et seq. cf. Stapleton (1997) 113 L.Q.R. 257.

[663] Atiyah, *Essays on Contract* (1986), Essay 2; Hedley (1988) 9 L.S. 137.

[664] Fuller & Purdue (1936–1937) 46 Yale L.J. 52 and 373.

[665] Atiyah, *The Rise and Fall of Freedom of Contract* (1979), pp.762–763.

[666] Treitel, *The Law of Contract*, 12th edn (2007 by Peel), paras 20–017—20–018.

[667] [1964] A.C. 465.

[668] See *Henderson v Merrett Syndicates Ltd* [1995] 2 A.C. 145; *Williams v Natural Life Health Foods Ltd and Mistlin* [1998] 1 W.L.R. 830 and below, paras 1–138—1–144.

together situations which have practically nothing in common.[669] Instead, it has been suggested, private law should be reclassified according to the nature of the interest of the claimant to be protected.[670] However, this type of suggestion has not been generally accepted and the distinction between contract and tort remains fundamental.

Differences of regime between contract and tort: damages. Some legal incidents of liability differ according to whether the claimant's claim is based on a breach of contract or a tort. Thus, there are important differences between the damages recoverable in contract and in tort.[671] As has been noted, the most basic difference remains that the function of damages in contract is primarily to put the injured party as far as possible in the position in which he would have been had the contract been performed,[672] whereas the function of damages in tort is to put the injured party in the position in which he would have been if the tort had not been committed.[673] Thus, damages for breach of warranty may give the claimant his lost bargain,[674] whereas damages in the tort of deceit,[675] negligent misstatement[676] and under s.2 of the Misrepresentation Act 1967[677] may not, being instead restricted to what has been termed compensation of his "status quo interest".[678] The tests of remoteness of damage in contract and in tort are apparently different[679] and in general the defence of contributory negligence does not apply to claims in contract, though it is now established that the court may reduce a claimant's damages for breach of contract on this ground if his claim is 1–122

---

669 Atiyah, *Essays on Contract* (1986), pp.53–55. cf. Burrows (1983) 99 L.Q.R. 217.

670 Atiyah at Essay 2; Hedley (1988) 8 L.S. 137.

671 *McGregor on Damages*, 17th edn (2003), paras 19–001 et seq.; Burrows, *Remedies for Torts and Breach of Contract*, 3rd edn (2004), Ch.2.

672 *Robinson v Harman* (1848) 1 Exch. 850, 855; Burrows (1983) 99 L.Q.R. 217. cf. Atiyah (1978) 94 L.Q.R. 193 and *Essays on Contract* (1986), Ch.2; Owen (1984) 4 O.J.L.S. 393; Waddams (1983–84) 8 Can.Bus.L.J. 2; Friedmann (1995) 111 L.Q.R. 628.

673 *Livingstone v Raywards Coal Co* (1880) 5 App.Cas. 25, 39; *Lim Poh Choo v Camden and Islington Area Health Authority* [1980] A.C. 174, 186 et seq.; *Gates v City Mutual Life Assurance Society Ltd* (1986) C.L.R. 1, 11–12.

674 e.g. Sale of Goods Act 1979 s.53(3).

675 *Peek v Derry* (1887) 37 Ch D 541, 578; *Doyle v Olby (Ironmongers) Ltd* [1969] 2 Q.B. 158, 167 and see *Smith New Court Securities v Scrimgeour Vickers (Asset Management) Ltd* [1997] A.C. 254; cf. *Davidson v Tullock* (1860) 3 Macq. 783; *East v Maurer* [1991] 1 W.L.R. 461 and see below, para.6–049.

676 *Esso Petroleum Co Ltd v Mardon* [1976] Q.B. 801, 820–821; *Box v Midland Bank Ltd* [1979] 2 Lloyd's Rep. 391.

677 *André & Cie SA v Ets Michel Blanc et Fils* [1977] 2 Lloyd's Rep. 166, 181; *McNally v Welltrade International Ltd* [1978] I.R.L.R. 497, 499; Taylor (1982) 45 M.L.R. 139; Cartwright (1987) 51 Conv. 423; *Sharneyford Supplies Ltd v Edge Barrington & Black* [1986] Ch. 128, [1987] Ch. 305, not following *Watts v Spence* [1976] Ch. 16; *Royscot Trust Ltd v Rogerson* [1991] 2 Q.B. 297 and see below, para.6–070.

678 Burrows (1983) 99 L.Q.R. 217, 219–221. Damages in tort may include compensation for wasted expenditure and lost opportunities: *East v Maurer* [1991] 1 W.L.R. 461 and see below, para.6–052.

679 *Koufos v Czarnikow Ltd* [1969] 1 A.C. 350 and see below, para.26–051. The principles of causation, e.g. in relation to the effect of supervening causes, are said sometimes to be the same in contract as in tort: *Beoco Ltd v Alfa Laval Co Ltd* [1995] Q.B. 137; cf. *Galoo Ltd v Bright Grahame Murray* [1994] 1 W.L.R. 1360.

based on breach of a contractual duty to take reasonable care, concurrent with liability in the tort of negligence.[680]

1–123 Other differences in the heads of damages available in contract and in tort are often to be based on circumstances other than the mere classification of the liability in issue. Thus, whereas nominal damages are always possible in an award in contract, it would appear that they are only available in tort if it is actionable per se.[681] Punitive or exemplary damages are sometimes said to be possible in tort, but not in contract,[682] though the exceptional circumstances in which they are permitted in tort are usually inapplicable to the contractual context.[683] Similarly, damages for injured feelings or mental distress not consequential on the claimant's own physical injury are very closely, if differently, circumscribed both in tort[684] and in contract,[685] though there remains some authority which excludes them entirely from liability in contract.[686] Traditionally, it was sometimes said that damages for loss of reputation are not available in contract in contrast to tort,[687] but there were conflicting decisions on this point,[688] and some cases clearly recognised such a recovery in contract in appropriate cases, such as injury to a trader whose business reputation is affected by the breach[689] and where the contract can be said to be for the maintenance or

---

[680] Law Reform (Contributory Negligence) Act 1945; *Forsikringsaktieselskapet Vesta v Butcher* [1989] A.C. 852; *Barclays Bank Plc v Fairclough Building Ltd* [1995] Q.B. 21; *Barclays Bank Plc v Fairclough Building Ltd (No.2)* [1995] I.R.L.R. 605 and see below, para.26–049.

[681] Ogus, *The Law of Damages* (1973), pp.22 et seq. cf. *Marzetti v Williams* (1830) 1 B. & Ad. 415.

[682] *Addis v Gramophone Co Ltd* [1909] A.C. 488; *Perera v Vandiyar* [1953] 1 W.L.R. 672, see below, para.26–019.

[683] *Rookes v Barnard* [1964] A.C. 1129; *Cassell & Co Ltd v Broome* [1972] A.C. 1027. cf. below, para.6–063 (fraud). The exception to this is where "the defendant's conduct had been calculated by him to make a profit for himself which may well exceed the compensation payable to the plaintiff" *Rookes v Barnard* [1964] A.C. 1129, 1126–1127. The traditional and general rule is that a party injured by a breach of contract cannot on this ground alone recover against the party in breach for profits made as a consequence of that breach as distinct from losses caused by that breach: *Teacher v Calder* [1899] A.C. 451; *Surrey CC v Bredero Homes Ltd* [1993] 3 W.L.R. 1361. However, in *Att-Gen v Blake* [2001] 1 A.C. 268, the House of Lords held that exceptionally the courts possess a discretion to award an account of profits against a party in breach of contract, even where the injured party has suffered no loss and see below, paras 26–001, 26–020—26–026.

[684] *McGregor on Damages*, 17th edn (2003), para.3–011. cf. *McLoughlin v O'Brien* [1983] 1 A.C. 785; *Alcock v Chief Constable of South Yorkshire Police* [1992] 1 A.C. 310; *Page v Smith* [1995] 2 W.L.R. 644; *White v Chief Constable of South Yorkshire* [1998] 3 W.L.R. 1509.

[685] Below, para.26–074 and see *McGregor on Damages*, 17th edn (2003) paras 13–018—13–30; *Cook v Swinfen* [1967] 1 W.L.R. 457; *Jarvis v Swann Tours Ltd* [1973] 1 Q.B. 233; *Bliss v S.E. Thames Regional Health Authority* [1985] I.R.L.R. 308; *Hayes v James & Charles Dodd (A Firm)* [1990] 2 All E.R. 815, 824; *McLeish v Amoo-Gottfried & Co, The Times*, October 13, 1993; *Watts v Morrow* [1991] 1 W.L.R. 1421; *Knott v Bolton* [1995] E.G.C.S. 59; *Mahmud v Bank of Credit and Commerce International SA (In Liquidation)* [1998] A.C. 20; *Johnson v Unisys Ltd* [2001] UKHL 13, [2001] 2 W.L.R. 1076.

[686] *Addis v Gramophone Co Ltd* [1909] A.C. 488.

[687] *Addis v Gramophone Co Ltd* [1909] A.C. 488; *Withers v General Theatre Corp Ltd* [1933] 2 K.B. 536.

[688] cf. *Withers v General Theatre Corp Ltd* [1933] 2 K.B. 536 with *Marbe v George Edwardes (Daly's Theatre) Ltd* [1928] 1 K.B. 269.

[689] *Wilson v United Counties Bank Ltd* [1920] A.C. 102.

promotion of the claimant's reputation.[690] Moreover, in *Mahmud v Bank of Credit and Commerce International SA (In Liquidation.)*,[691] the House of Lords allowed recovery by two former employees for damage to their employment prospects by breach of their employer's obligation not to damage the relationship of trust between employer and employee, seeing this as an example of the general rule allowing recovery for financial harm caused by breach of contract (as opposed to caused by the manner in which the contract was breached).[692]

Limitation of actions. Although the Limitation Act 1980,[693] provides an identical period of six years[694] for actions founded on simple contract or on tort, the period begins to run "from the date on which the cause of action accrued".[695] This may vary according to whether the action is framed in tort, contract or restitution.[696] For example, in contract the cause of action accrues when the breach of contract takes place, not when the damage occurs or is discovered.[697] But, in the tort of negligence, the cause of action accrues when damage occurs, and not at the time of the act or default giving rise to the claim.[698] However, the practical effect of this rule was reduced by the provision of the Latent Damage Act 1986, which provides[699] that: 1–124

> "... actions for damages for negligence in respect of latent damage not involving personal injuries may be brought for a period of three years after the discovery of the

[690] *Rolin v Steward* (1854) 14 C.B. 595; *Aerial Advertising Co v Batchelors Peas (Manchester) Ltd* [1938] 2 All E.R. 788.

[691] [1998] A.C. 20.

[692] [1998] A.C. 20, 51. But see *Johnson v Unisys Ltd* [2001] UKHL 13, [2003] 1 A.C. 518; *Eastwood v Magnox Electric Plc* [2004] UKHL 35, [2005] 1 A.C. 503 and below, paras 26–083—26–086.

[693] ss.2, 5.

[694] But see s.11 (three years for actions in respect of personal injuries): below, paras 28–006 et seq. This provision specifically applies to actions in contract as well as in tort.

[695] A similar phrase is used in the Supreme Court Act 1981 s.35A (interest on debt and damages) which by the Administration of Justice Act 1982 s.15(1) Sch.1 Pt 1 replaced s.3 of the Law Reform (Miscellaneous Provisions) Act 1934.

[696] *Battley v Faulkner* (1820) 3 B. & Ald. 288; *Beaman v A.R.T.S. Ltd* [1948] 2 All E.R. 89, 92 (revd. on other grounds [1949] 1 K.B. 550); *Bagot v Stevens, Scanlan & Co Ltd* [1966] 1 Q.B. 197; *Midland Bank Trust Co Ltd v Hett, Stubbs & Kemp* [1979] Ch. 384. See below, paras 28–031—28–061. *Saunders v Edwards* (1662) Sid. 95; *Bonomi v Backhouse* (1859) E., B. & E. 646; *Gibbs v Guild* (1881) 8 QBD 296, 302; *Chesworth v Farrar* [1967] 1 Q.B. 407; *Pirelli General Cable Works Ltd v Oscar Faber & Partners* [1983] 2 A.C. 1.

[697] *Battley v Faulkner* (1820) 3 B. Ald. 288; *Walker v Milner* (1866) 4 F. & F. 745; *Lynn v Bamber* [1930] 2 K.B. 72; *Bagot v Stevens, Scanlan & Co Ltd* [1966] 1 Q.B. 197. cf. *Shaw v Shaw* [1954] 2 Q.B. 429; *Midland Bank Trust Co Ltd v Hett, Stubbs Kemp* [1979] Ch. 384; *Forster v Outred & Co* [1982] 1 W.L.R. 86.

[698] *Watson v Winget Ltd* (1960) S.C. 92; *Cartledge v L. Jopling & Sons Ltd* [1963] A.C. 758 (now modified by ss.11(4), 14 of the Limitation Act 1980); *Sparham-Souter v Town and Country Developments Ltd* [1976] 1 Q.B. 858; *Anns v Merton London BC* [1978] A.C. 728; *Midland Bank Trust Co Ltd v Hett, Stubbs & Kemp* [1979] Ch. 384; *Pirelli General Cable Works Ltd v Oscar Faber & Partners* [1983] 2 A.C. 1; *Ketterman v Hansel Properties Ltd* [1987] 1 A.C. 189; *London Congregational Union Inc v Harriss and Harriss (A Firm)* [1988] 1 All E.R. 15; *D. W. Moore & Co Ltd v Ferrier* [1988] 1 W.L.R. 267; *Lee v Thompson* [1989] 40 E.G. 89; McGee (1988) 104 L.Q.R. 376; *Law Society v Sephton & Co* [2006] UKHL 22, [2006] 2 W.L.R. 1091.

[699] Creating new s.14A of the Limitation Act 1980.

damage by the plaintiff even if this is after six years after accrual of the cause of action."

This provision has created its own distinction between claims in contract and in tort, as it has been held that the term "negligence actions" for this purpose does not include actions for breach of a contractual obligation to take reasonable care, even where this is concurrent with an action for tortious negligence.[700]

1–125 **Other differences.** A contractual right, for example, to a certain sum due under a contract, can generally be assigned, but a right of action in tort generally cannot.[701] The rules of the conflict of laws governing both jurisdiction[702] and applicable law are different in matters relating to tort and to contract.[703] The law governing the capacity of parties may be different: so, for example, a minor is in principle liable for his torts, but only to a limited extent on his contracts.[704] Statutory provisions sometimes distinguish according to rights arising out of a contract, and other rights (which would include tort) though this appears to be a diminishing practice.[705]

(c) *Concurrence of Actions in Contract and Tort*

1–126 **General.** Where the constituent elements of a claimant's case are capable of being put either in terms of a claim in tort or for breach of contract, the general rule is that the claimant may choose on which basis to proceed, though this rule is subject to a number of qualifications, notably where to do so would be inconsistent with the terms of the contract. This traditional position was clearly affirmed by the House of Lords in the important decision *Henderson v Merrett*

---

[700] *Iron Trades Mutual Insurance Co Ltd v J.K. Buckenham Ltd* [1990] 1 All E.R. 808 and see below, para.28–033. cf. Consumer Protection Act 1987 s.5(5) which sets a different time of accrual for actions for damage to property against a supplier or producer under Pt I of the Act from that which would exist against a contractor under the general law of limitation.

[701] See below, para.19–049.

[702] Council Regulation 44/2001 of 2001 on jurisdiction and the recognition and enforcement of judgments in civil and commercial matters art.5(1) ("matters relating to a contract") and (3) ("matters relating to tort, delict or quasi-delict") replacing Convention on Jurisdiction and the Enforcement of Judgments in Civil and Commercial Matters 1968 (the "Brussels Convention").

[703] As to contract, see Contracts (Applicable Law) Act 1990 implementing the Rome Convention on the law applicable to contractual obligations 1980. The Rome Convention is to be replaced by Regulation (EC) No.593 of the European Parliament and of the Council on the law applicable to contractual obligations ("Rome I") [2008] OJ L 177/6. The UK has announced its intention of applying to the Council and Commission for their consent to the UK's participation in the Regulation. As to tort, the choice of law rules are at present contained in the Private International Law (Miscellaneous Provisions) Act 1995 ss.9, 14, but these will be changed as a result of an EC Regulation: see Regulation 864/2007 of the European Parliament and of the Council law applicable to non-contractual obligations ("Rome II Regulation") [2007] OJ L199/40 which will apply to all Member States from January 11, 2009. And see further *Dicey, Morris and Collins on The Conflict of Laws*, 14th edn (2006), First Supplement, paras 35–165 et seq.

[704] See below, paras 8–046—8–047. See also below, para.9–085 (trade unions).

[705] An example may be found in ss.4 and 5 of the Business Names Act 1985. The former distinction in the Bankruptcy Act 1914 s.30(1) between demands arising by reason of contract which were provable in bankruptcy and others which were not normally so provable, is not found in the provisions which replaced it in the Insolvency Act 1985 (ss.163, 211(1), (2) and (3)).

Syndicates Ltd,[706] which drew to a close the uncertainty on this point caused by a dictum of Lord Scarman in the Privy Council in 1985 in *Tai Hing Cotton Mill Ltd v Liu Chong Hing Bank Ltd*, to the effect that:

> "... their Lordships do not believe that there is anything to the advantage of the law's development in searching for a liability in tort where the parties are in a contractual relationship."[707]

This dictum appeared to favour the exclusion of claims in tort where the parties were in a contractual relationship, though the context of its acceptance by later courts was typically the denial of liability of recovery of pure economic loss in the tort of negligence.[708] However, paradoxically, the House of Lords' decision on the nature and ambit of the tortious liability to be found on the facts before it in *Henderson v Merrett Syndicates Ltd* created new and very considerable uncertainty as regards the relationship of contractual and tortious claims between parties to a contract. For, it accepted that its own earlier decision in *Hedley Byrne & Co Ltd v Heller & Partners Ltd*[709] should be interpreted as establishing a "broad principle" of liability in tortious negligence based on the defendant's assumption of responsibility, an assumption which would appear to be satisfied whenever a party to a contract either possessing or holding himself out as possessing a special skill agrees to perform a service for the other party. In this respect, the courts have apparently returned to an approach similar to one taken in the earlier nineteenth century, though subsequently superseded.[710]

The present discussion will start by looking briefly at the older authorities which governed the issue of concurrence of actions in contract and tort; it will then state the modern law allowing an option, first as regards pre-contractual liability and then as regards liability for torts committed in the course of performance of a contract; as to the latter, it will discuss the breadth of the principle of "assumption of responsibility" recognised in *Henderson v Merrett Syndicates Ltd* and the nature and ambit of the qualifications on the option and on the effects which its exercise will entail. 1–127

Older authorities. Disputes as to the availability of an action in tort against one's fellow contractor are not new and before the reforms of common law procedure of the mid-nineteenth century three positions can be detected in the cases. The first was that a plaintiff could neither join a claim in tort with one in contract in the same action nor opt whether to sue in tort when there was a 1–128

---

706 [1995] 2 A.C. 145. This position is also taken in Canada: *Central Trust Co v Rafuse* (1987) D.L.R. (4th) 481 SCC; *Canadian Pacific Hotels Ltd v Bank of Montreal* (1988) 40 D.L.R. (4th) 385; *B.C. Checo International Ltd v British Colombia Hydro & Power Authority* (1993) 99 D.L.R. (4th) 477. Although there was Australian authority against concurrence (*Hawkins v Clayton* (1988) 164 C.L.R. 539), the approach of the Canadian Supreme Court in *Central Trust Co v Rafuse* was followed in *Bryan v Maloney* (1995) 182 C.L.R. 609, 620–622.

707 [1986] A.C. 80, 107.

708 See, e.g. *Banque Keyser Ullmann SA v Skandia (UK) Co Insurance Ltd* [1990] 1 Q.B. 665, [1991] 2 A.C. 249 (affirmed on other grounds; *National Bank of Greece SA v Pinios Shipping (No.1)* [1990] 1 A.C. 637).

709 [1964] A.C. 465.

710 See below, para.1–129.

contract between the parties. For example, in *Orton v Butler*,[711] Best J. refused to allow the joining of actions in trover (tort) and money had and received (contract), stating that:

> "There is a broad distinction between actions ex contractu and ex delicto. Here, it arises out of breach of a contract, and the party ought not to be allowed to proceed in the present mode of framing his count [*sci.* claim] ex delicto."[712]

Other cases distinguished between the rules against joinder of counts in contract and tort and the question whether a plaintiff was entitled to opt on which of the two bases to put his claim,[713] some expressly recognising the validity of the option. Moreover, where they did it was acknowledged that the plaintiff's choice would affect the rules applicable to his claim. As Abbott J. observed:

> "There is nothing to compel a plaintiff to elect that form which may be most convenient to the defendant. The very notion of election imports that the plaintiff may exercise it for his own benefit."[714]

At the time, those courts which allowed an option between contract and tort thereby enabled a plaintiff to avoid in particular the rules against transmissibility of actions on death which applied to actions in tort[715] or the rules of joinder of parties to litigation which applied to actions in contract.[716] However, the courts did not allow the plaintiff's option to avoid certain other rules which applied to contract, notably, those as to capacity,[717] nor the express terms of a contract, notably, limitation clauses.[718]

1–129 The third approach to the relationship between actions in contract and tort can be seen in the decision in *Brown v Boorman*.[719] The plaintiffs retained the defendant as broker to sell their linseed oil on commission. This he did, but in breach of contract delivered it without payment and to the wrong (and later insolvent) person. The plaintiffs sued in case (i.e. tort), contending that the broker owed them a duty at common law to take reasonable care based on his trade or calling. The defendant countered that their proper form of action should have been *assumpsit* (i.e. contract). The House of Lords upheld Tindal C.J.'s judgment for the plaintiffs, Lord Campbell stating that:

> " . . . wherever there is a contract, and something to be done in the course of the employment which is the subject of that contract, if there is a breach of a duty in the course of that employment, the plaintiff may either recover in tort or in contract."[720]

---

[711] (1822) 5 B. & Ald. 652.
[712] (1822) 5 B. Ald. 652 at [656].
[713] e.g. *Brown v Dixon* (1786) 1 T.R. 274, 276–277.
[714] *Ansell v Waterhouse* (1817) 6 M. & S. 385, 392.
[715] *Hambly v Trott* (1776) 1 Cowp. 371.
[716] *Govett v Radnidge* (1802) 3 East 62.
[717] *Johnson v Pye* (1666) 1 Sid. 258, 1 Keb. 913.
[718] *Nicholson v Willan* (1804) 5 East 507.
[719] (1842) 3 Q.B. 511, (1844) 11 Cl. Fin. 1, HL.
[720] (1844) 11 Cl. Fin. 1, 44.

It is difficult not to agree with the defendant's contention that such an approach "would altogether destroy the distinction between *assumpsit* [i.e. contract] and tort",[721] as it suggests that the option to plead in tort or contract exists in *all* situations of breach of contract and not merely in those where an independent cause of action exists in tort. However, this was not the fate of *Brown v Boorman*. As Pollock stated[722]:

> " . . . notwithstanding the verbal laxity of one or two passages, the House of Lords did not authorize the parties to treat the mere non-performance of a promise as a substantive tort."

Instead, the decision was relied on as authority for the existence of an option for the plaintiff as to whether to sue in tort as long as a distinct and independent action in tort exists.[723]

1–130 **The modern law.** In the modern law, a distinction can usefully be drawn between a claim by a party to a contract on the basis of a pre-contractual liability to be imposed on the other party and one based on a liability arising in the course of performance of the contract.

(i) *Pre-contractual Liability*

1–131 **Representations.** Even at the time when it was doubtful whether a party to a contract could claim in tort against the other party in respect of matters relating to the performance of the contract, it was established that such a party could rely on established liabilities in tort arising from facts which occur in the course of the dealings of the parties before contract. A party to a contract can therefore claim damages for a pre-contractual statement which induced him to contract under various headings: in the tort of deceit, where the statement was made fraudulently[724]; in the tort of negligence,[725] if the claimant can establish the conditions for the existence of a duty of care under *Hedley Byrne & Co Ltd v Heller & Partners Ltd*[726] or under the provisions of the Misrepresentation Act 1967.[727] It is also clear that these rights to damages in tort may exist whether or not the misrepresentation has been incorporated into the contract, thereby giving rise to

---

[721] (1844) 11 Cl. Fin. 1, 12.

[722] Pollock, *Torts*, 1st edn (1887), p.434.

[723] *Hyman v Nye* (1881) 6 QBD 685; *Baylis v Lintott* (1873) L.R. 8 C.P. 345; *Esso Petroleum Co Ltd v Mardon* [1976] Q.B. 801; *Midland Bank Trust Co Ltd v Hett, Stubbs & Kemp* [1979] Ch. 384.

[724] *Pasley v Freeman* (1789) 3 T.R. 51; *Peek v Derry* (1887) 37 Ch D 541 (reversed on other grounds (1889) 14 App.Cas. 337); *Doyle v Olby (Ironmongers) Ltd* [1969] 2 Q.B. 158; *Archer v Brown* [1985] 1 Q.B. 401. cf. *Jack v Kipping* (1882) 9 QBD 113; *Tilley v Bowman Ltd* [1910] 1 K.B. 745.

[725] *Esso Petroleum Co Ltd v Mardon* [1976] Q.B. 801; *Howard Marine & Dredging Co Ltd v A. Ogden & Sons (Excavations) Ltd* [1978] Q.B. 574; *Rust v Abbey Life Insurance Co Ltd* [1978] 2 Lloyd's Rep. 386; *Banque Financière de la Cité SA v Westgate Insurance Co Ltd* [1991] 2 A.C. 249, 275. cf. *Cemp Properties (UK) Ltd v Dentsply Research & Development Corp (No.1)* (1989) 35 E.G. 99, 104.

[726] [1964] A.C. 465.

[727] See below, paras 6–068—6–076. Liability in damages under s.2(1) is treated as tortious: see *André & Cie SA v Ets. Michel Blanc et Fils* [1977] 2 Lloyd's Rep. 166; *Royscott Trust Ltd v Rogerson* [1991] 2 Q.B. 297 and see below, para.6–069.

a claim for breach of contractual warranty,[728] and whether or not the claimant chooses to exercise any right of rescission of the contract on the grounds of misrepresentation.[729]

1–132 More complex, however, is the question whether the claimant's option to rely on one of these liabilities in tort enables him to avoid restrictions which exist on any claim in contract. While it is clear that a party can by contract exclude liability for negligent misstatement at common law or liability in damages for misrepresentation under the 1967 Act to the extent to which such a term satisfies the requirements of reasonableness,[730] a party to a contract cannot exclude liability in damages for his own fraud.[731] On the other hand, a party to a contract with a minor cannot avoid a defence of infancy by claiming damages in the tort of deceit against the minor on the ground that the latter fraudulently misrepresented his age, even though in general, an infant is liable for his torts,[732] because:

> "If it were in the power of a plaintiff to convert that which arises out of a contract into a tort, there would be an end of that protection which the law affords to infants."[733]

1–133 **Damages for misrepresentation.** Finally, although there are considerable differences between damages in tort and for breach of contract,[734] not all of these are significant in the context of pre-contractual statements. In general, an injured party can claim damages for the loss of an expectation or performance interest in contract but not in tort, and in the context of pre-contractual representation the latter rule means that a claimant can recover damages for misrepresentation in tort only so as to put him in a position as though the representation (and, therefore, it is assumed, the contract) had not been made and not damages as though the representation had been true.[735] By contrast, if a court finds that a party made a contractual promise or warranty that his pre-contractual statement was true, then he can recover damages for breach of contract to put him in the position as thought the statement had been true.[736] On the other hand, in some cases where a claim is based on breach of a term which has resulted from the

---

[728] *Esso Petroleum Co Ltd v Mardon* [1976] Q.B. 801.

[729] *Archer v Brown* [1985] 1 Q.B. 401, 415 and see below, para.6–072. After the Misrepresentation Act 1967 s.1(a) a representee's right to rescind is not barred merely by the incorporation of a representation as a term of the contract. cf. the power of the court under s.2(2) of the Misrepresentation Act 1967 to refuse rescission of the contract and award damages in lieu; and see below, para.6–096.

[730] See *Hedley Byrne & Co Ltd v Heller & Partners Ltd* [1964] A.C. 465; *Smith v Eric S. Bush* [1990] 1 A.C. 831; Unfair Contract Terms Act 1977 s.2(2); Misrepresentation Act 1967 s.3 as replaced by Unfair Contract Terms Act 1977 s.8 and see below, paras 6–136 et seq.

[731] *S. Pearson & Son Ltd v Dublin Corp* [1907] A.C. 351, 353–354, 362.

[732] *Johnson v Pye* (1666) 1 Sid. 258 and see below, para.8–046.

[733] *Jennings v Rundall* (1799) 8 T.R. 335, 336, per Lord Kenyon C.J. and see below, para.8–046.

[734] See above, paras 1–122—1–123.

[735] *Doyle v Olby (Ironmongers) Ltd* [1969] 2 Q.B. 158; *André & Cie SA v Ets Michel Blanc et Fils* [1977] 2 Lloyd's Rep. 166; *East v Maurer* [1991] 1 W.L.R. 461; *Clef Aquitaine SARL v Laporte Materials (Barrow) Ltd* [2001] Q.B. 488; and see below, paras 6–069—6–071.

[736] Cartwright, *Misrepresentation, Mistake, and Non-disclosure* (2007), paras 8.024–8.025 referring to *Brown v Sheen and Richmond Car Sales Ltd* [1950] 1 All E.R. 1102 at 1104.

incorporation of a pre-contractual statement,[737] there will be no difference on this ground between the contractual and tortious measures of damages. In *Esso Petroleum Co Ltd v Mardon*,[738] the Court of Appeal accepted that a representation of "throughput" of petrol of a garage by Esso which later proved false, was incorporated into the contract as a warranty. However, the ability of the representee to claim for breach of contract did not affect the damages which he could recover, in particular it did not allow him to claim for the loss of profits he expected to make from taking a lease of the garage with the throughput represented, despite such claims for lost profits being typical of contract. This refusal resulted from the court's decision as to the *content* of the warranty: it was construed not as a promise that the throughput would be a certain amount, but rather that Esso had taken reasonable care in making the estimate of throughput.[739] A claim in contract can indeed put an injured party in the position as though the contract had been performed, but if Esso had performed this contractual warranty, and as a result Mardon had been given a true estimate of the throughput of the garage, then Mardon would not have entered into the contract.[740] In this way, damages in contract and in tort[741] are based on the same measure, viz to put the claimant in the position as though the contract had not been made.[742] On the other hand, while it has been stated that a claimant will not recover more damages in tort than he would in contract,[743] it is clear that a claimant may indeed recover more damages where his claim is based on fraud or for negligent misrepresentation under the 1967 Act,[744] as the test of remoteness of damage applicable to these claims is more generous than the test which applies to claims for breach of contract.[745] Furthermore, it is possible (if unlikely) that someone suing for fraud may be able to recover punitive damages,[746] whereas these are not available for claims for breach of contract.[747]

---

[737] Treitel, *The Law of Contract*, 12th edn (2007 by Peel), paras 9–042—9–050 and Atiyah, *Essays on Contract* (1986), Essay 10.

[738] [1976] 1 Q.B. 801.

[739] [1976] 1 Q.B. 801 at 818, 823–824.

[740] [1976] 1 Q.B. 801 at 820 (Lord Denning M.R.) and [834] (Shaw L.J.). This reasoning is based on two assumptions: first, that if Esso had taken reasonable care in making its statement as to throughput it would have made an accurate estimate and, secondly, that if Mardon had been given an accurate estimate he would not have entered the contract or perhaps, would not have entered it on the same terms. Ormrod L.J. expressed no view on the claim for loss of profits as it was "virtually incapable of proof": at 829.

[741] The Court of Appeal based its decision in tort on *Hedley Byrne & Co Ltd v Heller & Partners Ltd* [1964] A.C. 465.

[742] The Court of Appeal did allow Mardon damages for loss of his "general expectations", i.e. what he would have expected to have earned if he had not spent his time running the garage: [1976] 1 Q.B. 801, 821.

[743] *Chinery v Viall* (1860) 5 H. & N. 28, 29 L.J. Ex. 180; *Johnson v Stear* (1863) 33 L.J.C.P. 130 (both conversion).

[744] *Royscott Trust Ltd v Rogerson* [1991] 2 Q.B. 297, in which the Court of Appeal rejected the proposition that a claim for damages under s.2(1) of the Misrepresentation Act 1967 possesses the same test of remoteness of damage as applies generally to claims in the tort of negligence; and see below, para.6–070.

[745] See below, paras 26–051 et seq.

[746] *Mafo v Adams* [1970] 1 Q.B. 548; *Cassell & Co Ltd v Broome* [1972] A.C. 1027, 1076; *Archer v Brown* [1985] 1 Q.B. 401, 418–421 and see below, para.6–063.

[747] See below, para.26–019.

1–134 **Liability for non-disclosure.** As will be seen, the courts draw a clear line between cases of misrepresentation and of non-disclosure for the purposes of deciding the availability of rescission for the other party.[748] While in general the courts have echoed this distinction in the context of liability in damages, they have accepted that in principle a contractor may be liable in the tort of negligence for a failure to speak,[749] but the modern approach has been to restrict liability in these circumstances to cases where the defendant has "voluntarily accepted responsibility".[750] Indeed, even in a case where the law exceptionally imposes a duty of pre-contractual disclosure on a party to a contract, the courts have refused to impose liability in damages in tort to sanction its breach.[751] While this result was reached before the House of Lords in *Henderson v Merrett Syndicates Ltd*[752] had disapproved the idea that the existence of a contract between the parties is in itself a reason for denying a claim in tort, it may well be that a future court would hold that a person cannot be said to "assume responsibility" for a matter in relation to which he owes a legal duty. Moreover, the idea that the law of tort should not be allowed to "cut across the principles of contract law" could be considered as a consideration of policy arguing against the existence of a duty of care in the tort of negligence, even where this was based on an "assumption of responsibility".[753]

1–135 **Duress.** Duress, whether by means of physical or economic threats, exercised by A against B with the view to making B enter a contract with A, may in certain circumstances give rise to a right in B to avoid that contract.[754] While the circumstances which give rise to this right of avoidance will not necessarily give rise to a right to damages,[755] in contrast to the position as regards fraud,[756] they may give rise to the conditions of liability under the tort of intimidation (or tort of causing loss by unlawful means).[757] This tort is usually applied to cases where

[748] See below, paras 6–014 et seq.

[749] *Rust v Abbey Life Assurance Co Ltd* [1978] 2 Lloyd's Rep. 386; *Cornish v Midland Bank Plc* [1985] 3 All E.R. 513, 522–523; *Al-Kandari v J.R. Brown & Co* [1988] Q.B. 665, 672; *Banque Keyser Ullmann SA v Skandia (UK) Co Insurance Ltd* [1990] 1 Q.B. 665, 794. cf. *Argy Trading Developments Ltd v Lapid Developments Ltd* [1977] 1 W.L.R. 444, 461; *Barclays Bank Plc v Khaira* [1992] 1 W.L.R. 623; *Ashmore v Corp of Lloyd's* [1992] 2 Lloyd's Rep. 1, 5 (and see [1992] 2 Lloyd's Rep. 620). See also Cartwright, *Misrepresentation, Mistake, and Non-disclosure* (2007), para.17.37

[750] *Banque Keyser Ullmann SA v Skandia (UK) Insurance Co Ltd* [1990] 1 Q.B. 665 at 794, per Slade L.J. cf. below, paras 1–138—1–141 concerning the significance more generally of a "voluntary assumption of responsibility" for liability for pure economic loss in the tort of negligence.

[751] *Banque Keyser Ullmann SA v Skandia (UK) Insurance Co Ltd* [1990] 1 Q.B. 665.

[752] [1995] 1 A.C. 145.

[753] For the relevance of considerations of policy in this context, see below, paras 1–142 et seq.

[754] See below, paras 7–001 et seq.

[755] *Universe Tankships Inc of Monrovia v International Transport Workers Federation* [1983] 1 A.C. 366, 385, cf. 400; *Banque Keyser Ullmann SA v Skandia (UK) Insurance Co Ltd* [1990] 1 Q.B. 665 at 780; and see below, para.7–055.

[756] See above, para.1–131 and below, para.6–042.

[757] See *Clerk & Lindsell on Torts*, 19th edn (2006), paras 25–65—25–87. In *OGB Ltd v Allan, Douglas v Hello! Ltd, Mainstream Properties Ltd v Young* [2007] UKHL 21, [2008] 1 A.C. 1 the HL prefered to refer to the "tort of causing loss by unlawful means" rather than to "intimidation", seeing threats as only one example of "unlawful means" for this purpose: see below, paras 1–045—1–146. Where the defendant's conduct threatens physical injury to the claimant, the latter may possess an action of assault: *Clerk & Lindsell on Torts*, paras 15–13—15–14.

A forces B to do or to refrain from doing something to the prejudice of C ("three-party intimidation"), but there is high authority for the proposition that it also applies to cases where A forces B to do something for A's intended benefit ("two-party intimidation").[758] In circumstances where the conditions for the existence of the tort exist, it would seem that it can be relied on by one party to a contract as against the other, although it is more controversial whether this right remains after the coerced party has affirmed the contract.[759] While the ambit of the doctrine of economic duress as a vitiating element in contract remains somewhat uncertain,[760] some argue that its ambit should be coterminous and not wider than any liability which would exist under the tort of intimidation.[761]

"Culpa in contrahendo". Some legal systems consider that cases of fraud or duress are merely examples of a wider category of "fault in the formation of contract," a category famously termed *culpa in contrahendo* by the German jurist, Ihering.[762] In French law, despite its general rule against allowing delict to intrude between contractors (a rule known as *non-cumul*),[763] pre-contractual fault can give rise to a claim for damages in delict,[764] there being a very general principle of delictual liability based on fault.[765] However, English law possesses no such general principle and so no claims for damages in tort based on a party's "pre-contractual fault" can be brought in the absence of proof of an established tort. This had led to an occasional temptation in the courts to resort to the law of contract to found a claim for damages in this type of situation. This was clearest in relation to claims for damages for innocent (i.e. non-fraudulent) misrepresentation before the Misrepresentation Act 1967, where the courts allowed some claims for damages for false pre-contractual statements by way of contractual warranty.[766] More recently, in *Blackpool and Fylde Aero Club v Blackpool BC*,[767] the defendant local authority had invited sealed tenders from a limited number of persons for licences to use a local airport, to arrive at their premises by a certain date. The plaintiff delivered such a tender by the stipulated time, but owing to the failure of the defendant's staff, it did not consider the plaintiff's tender and failed therefore to award it a licence. The plaintiff's claim for damages for breach of contract was upheld by the Court of Appeal[768] on the basis that the defendant local authority's express request for tenders to be made 1–136

[758] *Rookes v Barnard* [1964] A.C. 1129, 1205, 1209 and see *Clerk and Lindsell* at paras 25–85—25–86.

[759] See below, para.7–055.

[760] See below, paras 7–014 et seq.

[761] *Clerk and Lindsell* at paras 25–85—25–86.

[762] On the German position see Markesinis, *The German Law of Obligations*, Vol.I; Markesinis, Lorenz and Dannemann, *The Law of Contracts and Restitution: a Comparative Introduction* (1997), pp.64 et seq.

[763] *Bell v Peter Browne & Co* [1990] 2 Q.B. 495, 511. The full term for the rule is *non-cumul des responsabilités contractuelle et délictuelle* and see Whittaker in Bell, Boyron and Whittaker, *Principles of French Law* 2nd edn (2008), pp.328–9.

[764] Whittaker at pp.308–309.

[765] i.e. arts 1382–1383 C. civ. and see Whittaker at pp.364 et seq.

[766] *Esso Petroleum Co Ltd v Mardon* [1976] Q.B. 801, 817.

[767] [1990] 1 W.L.R. 1195.

[768] The case came to the court by way of a preliminary issue as to the existence of liability.

in a particular form by a particular date,[769] coupled with the limited number of persons invited to tender,[770] gave rise to an implied contract to consider conforming tenders[771] and therefore the court found it unnecessary to consider whether the plaintiff could have succeeded in the tort of negligence.[772] Overall, however, it cannot be said that English courts evince any desire to develop a general principle of liability in damages for pre-contractual fault, whether this is put in terms of tort or contract, any more than they wish to recognise a general principle of pre-contractual good faith to which such a liability would be closely related.[773]

(ii) *Torts Committed in the Course of Performance of a Contract*

1–137 **General.** As Greer L.J. observed in 1936:

> "... where the breach of duty alleged arises out of a liability independent of the personal obligation undertaken by contract, it is tort, and it may be tort even though there may happen to be a contract between the parties, if the duty in fact arises independently of the contract."[774]

In the modern law, it may be stated that a party to a contract may choose to base his claim on an established and independent tort against the other party, but this choice will not be allowed to subvert the contract's express[775] or implied terms[776] nor any legal immunity attaching to the other party *qua* contractor.[777] On the other hand, where the contract is silent as to the issue to which a tort relates, in principle this is no reason for denying the existence of that tort, though an exception may properly be made where the tort is based on the defendant's "assumption of responsibility".[778] In general,[779] though, the choice whether to sue in tort or contract does allow a claimant to gain the benefit of any incidental rules of the regime of liability applicable,[780] though the modern tendency has been to reduce the differences between these two regimes in cases of concurrence.[781]

1–138 ***Henderson v Merrett Syndicates Ltd.*** As has been noted, in *Henderson v Merrett Syndicates Ltd*[782] (*Henderson*) the House of Lords held that a party to a

[769] [1990] 1 W.L.R. 1195 at 1204.
[770] [1990] 1 W.L.R. 1195 at 1202.
[771] The public character of the defendant was also relied on by the plaintiff as support for the existence of the contract as it had as a matter of public law a duty to comply with its standing orders (to consider tenders) and a fiduciary duty to ratepayers to act with reasonable prudence in managing its financial affairs: [1990] 1 W.L.R. 1195 at 1201.
[772] [1990] 1 W.L.R. 1195 at 1204.
[773] See above, paras 1–022 et seq.
[774] *Jarvis v Moy, Davies, Smith, Vandervell & Co* [1936] 1 K.B. 399, 405.
[775] See below, paras 1–147, 1–151—1–153.
[776] See below, para.1–147.
[777] See below, para.1–154.
[778] See below, paras 1–156—1–160.
[779] The notable exception is in the case of contractual capacity.
[780] See below, para.1–161.
[781] See above, paras 1–122 et seq.
[782] [1995] 2 A.C. 145.

contract may rely on a tort committed by the other party, as long as doing so is not inconsistent with the express or implied terms of the contract. However, in finding a duty of care on which to base the plaintiffs' claim in tort, Lord Goff of Chieveley relied on *Hedley Byrne* as establishing a very broad principle of liability based on an "assumption of responsibility" and this principle suggests a very considerable overlap between the tort of negligence and liability in contract between parties to contracts.[783] As will be seen, moreover, the basis of a finding of an "assumption of responsibility" is so closely related to the finding of an agreement in respect of the same matter that the claim to true independence of the tortious liability thereby established is open to question.

In *Henderson*, the plaintiffs were all Lloyd's "Names" who had agreed to take unlimited liability in respect of certain proportions of risks to be underwritten in the insurance market, but who had done so through different forms of arrangement. In the case of "direct Names",[784] those persons who acted as their members' agents also acted as their managing agents (being known sometimes as "combined agents", though being termed "managing agents" here) and therefore any claim for negligence in respect of their claims was within privity of contract. The issue which came before the House of Lords was whether the "direct Names" could opt to sue their managing agents in the tort of negligence in respect of the management of the underwriting, the limitation period for their action for breach of contract having expired. In this respect, Lord Goff of Chieveley, who gave the leading speech and with whom Lords Keith of Kinkel, Browne-Wilkinson, Mustill and Nolan concurred, held that prima facie the managing agents did owe a duty of care in the tort of negligence to the "Names". Such a duty was, according to Lord Goff, to be based on a broad principle found in *Hedley Byrne & Co Ltd v Heller & Partners Ltd*,[785] according to which a person possessed of special skill or knowledge may owe a duty of care in tort by assuming a responsibility to another person within a relationship (whether special or particular to a transaction and whether contractual or not): the principle was not, therefore, restricted to cases of statements.[786] The House of Lords further held that, on the facts of the case, there was no reason why the "Names" should not opt to sue on the breach of such a duty of care in the tort of negligence rather than for breach of an implied term in their contract with the managing agents. Lord Goff considered that there was "no sound basis for a rule which automatically restricts the claimant to either a tortious or a contractual remedy",[787] though he added that this general right of option was: 1–139

> "... subject only to ascertaining whether the tortious duty is so inconsistent with the applicable contract that, in accordance with ordinary principle, the parties must be taken to have agreed that the tortious remedy is to be limited or excluded".[788]

---

[783] Burrows (1995) C.L.P. 103, 118 et seq.; Whittaker (1997) 17 Legal Studies 169.
[784] For the position of "indirect Names" see below, para.1–180.
[785] [1964] A.C. 465.
[786] [1995] 2 A.C. 145 at 180–181.
[787] [1995] 2 A.C. 145 at 193–194.
[788] [1995] 2 A.C. 145 at 194.

1–140 **Contract inconsistent with liability in tort.** This decision therefore affirms the general availability of an option to sue in either tort or contract where the constituent elements allow, the exception being where the contract is inconsistent with a claim in tort. While Lord Goff's discussion of the "inconsistency of the contract" did not go beyond reference to its express or implied terms (on the facts there was no reason for it to do so), it is submitted that neither the decision itself in *Henderson* nor Lord Goff's speech casts doubt on the proposition that such an "inconsistency" may be found in other features of the contract, notably the existence of a certain contractual immunity enjoyed by the party to the contract against whom the claim in tort is brought.[789]

1–141 **Assumption of responsibility.** However, with respect, Lord Goff's approach in *Henderson* to the existence of a duty of care in tort on which a party to a contract may choose to rely is more problematic. As has been noted, this approach rested on a broad principle of assumption of responsibility drawn from the speeches of the members of the House of Lords in *Hedley Byrne*.[790] While the notion of "assumption of responsibility" is clearly present in those speeches, they also contained various other elements on which the imposition of a duty of care was to be based, including the special skill and knowledge of the defendant and his or her "special relationship" with the plaintiff. During the period from its decision in 1963 to the mid-1990s,[791] the courts either combined these various elements or emphasised one or more of them as the facts of the case or their own preference suggested,[792] but *Hedley Byrne* was not, in general, used to expand liability for pure economic loss beyond the situation of liability for negligent *misstatements*.[793] This restriction on the ambit of the "broad principle of assumption of responsibility" was, however, firmly rejected by Lord Goff in *Henderson*[794] and it seems that the principle will apply where: (i) the defendant has agreed to perform a service or otherwise to do something for the claimant, whether under a contract or not[795]; (ii) the defendant possessed or held himself out as possessing special skill or knowledge in relation to these services or this task[796]; and (iii) some evidence of reliance by the claimant can be made out. As regards the last of these conditions, in cases of negligent misstatement the claimant's reliance provides the causal link between the defendant's statement and the claimant's loss.[797] However, outside this type of case and as between

[789] See below, paras 1–147 et seq.

[790] *Hedley Byrne & Co Ltd v Heller & Partners Ltd* [1964] A.C. 465.

[791] It would seem that the speech of Lord Goff in *Spring v Guardian Assurance Plc* [1995] 2 A.C. 296 marked the turning-point.

[792] e.g. *Caparo Industries v Dickman* [1990] 2 A.C. 605; *Smith v Eric S. Bush* [1990] 1 A.C. 831.

[793] An exception could be found in the decision of the House of Lords in *Junior Books Ltd v Veitchi Co Ltd* [1983] 1 A.C. 520, but this decision has not been followed but has been distinguished on various grounds: see below, paras 1–176 et seq.

[794] [1995] 2 A.C. 145 at 178–181.

[795] See especially *White v Jones* [1995] 2 A.C. 207, 273–274 (Lord Browne-Wilkinson, referring to "assumption of responsibility for the task not the assumption of legal liability"), 280, 288 (Lord Mustill). See also *Barclays Bank Plc v Fairclough Building Ltd (No.2)* [1995] I.R.L.R. 605; below, para.1–143.

[796] *Henderson v Merrett Syndicates Ltd* [1995] 2 A.C. 145, 180, per Lord Goff of Chieveley.

[797] *Henderson v Merrett Syndicates Ltd* [1995] 2 A.C. 145, 180.

parties to a contract, the element of "reliance" by the claimant may be found in the claimant's entering the contract under which the services, etc. are agreed to be done by the defendant.[798] This basis of liability in tort is not merely "equivalent to contract"; it is likely in very many cases to be parasitic on it.[799]

Fair, just and reasonable. Finally, according to Lord Goff in *Henderson*, where an alleged duty of care is based on the doctrine of assumption of responsiblity there is no need to enter the question of whether it is "fair, just and reasonable" to impose such a duty, even in cases where the claimant's loss is purely economic: 1–142

> "... the concept [of assumption of responsibility] provides its own explanation why there is no problem in cases of this kind about liability for economic loss; for if a person assumes responsibility to another in respect of certain services, there is no reason why he should not be liable in damages for [*sic*, to] that other in respect of economic loss which flows from the negligent performance of those services."[800]

It may be argued in support of this proposition that where a claimant has satisfied the conditions for the application of the "broad principle", there is no need for an inquiry as to the desirability as a matter of policy of the imposition of liability *for pure economic loss* as the principle itself contains the requisite factors—such as "special skill or knowledge" and "reliance"—which balance the justice of its imposition.[801] However, in the dictum quoted above Lord Goff may be thought to go further: for it appears to suggest, if not that a person who "assumes responsibility" does so *for* economic loss (a position which gives to "assumption of responsibility" the meaning of agreeing *to be liable* which was clearly rejected by the House of Lords), then at least that such a person is to be held liable for a type of loss which flows from the nature of his agreement (to perform a certain type of service) which he has made. If so, this surely expresses no more than the idea that in these circumstances pure economic loss is a natural and probable (or indeed forseeable) type of harm arising from the breach of his agreement. And if this is so, then it is at most an argument in favour of recovery for pure economic loss, rather than a unanswerable reason for it. With the greatest respect, Lord Goff's suggestion that there "should be no need" to inquire into the "fairness, justice and reasonableness" of imposition of a duty of care should not be interpreted to mean that, apart from the issue of liability for pure economic loss, questions of policy are incapable of acting to negative a prima facie duty arising from an assumption of responsibility. Such an interpretation would, it is submitted, be inconsistent with the careful enquiry undertaken by members of the

798 *Henderson v Merrett Syndicates Ltd* [1995] 2 A.C. 145, 180, 182.

799 cf. *Lennon v Metropolitan Police Commissioner* [2004] EWCA Civ 130, [2004] 1 W.L.R. 2594 where the principle in *Henderson v Merrett Syndicates* [1995] 2 A.C. 145 was applied so as to impose liability on a police authority vicariously in respect of its agent's express assumption of responsibility towards one of its constables (technically not being a contractual employee) in respect of the task of transferring him without loss of allowance to another police force.

800 [1995] 2 A.C. 145, 181. This proposition was treated as established by *Henderson* by Lord Steyn in *Williams v Natural Life Health Foods Ltd and Mistlin* [1998] 1 W.L.R. 830, 834.

801 cf. the approach of Lord Steyn to the question of "justice and reasonableness" in *Marc Rich & Co AG v Bishop Rock Marine Co* [1996] 1 A.C. 221 at 236 et seq., where he weighs various factors for and against the imposition of a duty of care on the facts.

House of Lords in *Arthur J.S. Hall v Simons*[802] into the considerations of policy relevant to the question whether barristers and other advocates should enjoy a degree of immunity from liability in respect of the conduct and management of litigation. Moreover, in *Marc Rich & Co AG v Bishop Rock Marine Co*,[803] the House of Lords confirmed that the mere fact that a defendant's conduct has caused damage to property of a forseeable type does not rule out an inquiry as to the "justice and reasonableness" of the imposition of a duty of care in the tort of negligence. It would be indeed a paradox if the courts were to inquire into the justice and reasonableness of imposing liability for forseeable damage to property caused by negligence, but not into the justice and reasonableness of imposing liability for albeit forseeable pure economic loss.

1–143 **Effect of broad liability in tort.** One effect of judicial acceptance of such a very broad principle of "assumption of responsibility" may be seen to be the creation of a very wide means of circumventing the doctrine of consideration: for as long as a defendant is possessed of special skill or knowledge, his agreement with the claimant to perform a service within that skill or pertaining to that knowledge will give rise to a cause of action in tort based on the negligent performance of those services, whether they were to be paid for or not. A second type of effect may be the disapplication of other established rules of contract law. For example, in *Barclays Bank Plc v Fairclough Building Ltd (No.2)*,[804] building sub-contractors had engaged cleaning contractors to clean an asbestos cement roof, but in doing so negligently the cleaners created a danger from the asbestos which required considerable expenditure by the owner of the building to make it safe.[805] The Court of Appeal upheld the builders' claim for an indemnity against the cleaners in respect of their own liabilities, but reduced the award on the basis of their contributory negligence in failing to take steps to inform themselves of the problems involved in the cleaning of the asbestos cement in the way intended. The Court of Appeal accepted that contributory negligence is a defence to a claim for breach of contract only where it is concurrent with the existence of a liability in tort based on negligence,[806] but found such a liability in the cleaners in their breach of a duty of care based on their "assumption of responsibility", the latter arising simply from their contractual undertaking to do a job which required special skill and which they held themselves out as capable of doing, coupled with the roofing contractors' reliance on this, as evidenced by their entering into the same contract. In the result, the cleaners were entitled to rely on their own duty of care in tort to allow them to reduce by one half their own liability for breach of contract. Clearly, then, while in some cases, notably those turning on issues of limitation of actions such as *Henderson* itself, judicial acceptance of

[802] [2002] 1 A.C. 615 and see especially 688 et seq. (Lord Hoffmann), the HL not following its earlier decision in *Rondel v Worsley* [1969] 1 A.C. 191. In *Stanton v Callaghan* [1998] 4 All E.R. 961, the CA upheld a certain immunity from liability in negligence for expert witnesses on the grounds of public policy. cf. the differences of approach to the relevance of considerations of policy in *Welton v North Cornwall DC* [1997] 1 W.L.R. 570, 583 and 580–581.

[803] [1996] 1 A.C. 211.

[804] [1995] I.R.L.R. 605.

[805] cf. *Barclays Bank Plc v Fairclough Building Ltd* [1995] Q.B. 214 which concerned the claim by the owner of the buildings against the main building contractors.

[806] *Forsikringsaktieselskapet Vesta v Butcher* [1989] A.C. 852 and see below, para.26–049.

such a wide basis for establishing a duty of care in tort will benefit claimants, allowing them to avoid disadvantageous incidental rules applicable to actions in contract, paradoxically in others, it will instead benefit defendants.

The following discussion will look first at the question whether a threatened breach of contract gives rise to liability in the tort of intimidation, before turning to examine the qualifications on the general rule allowing a claimant to opt whether to sue in contract or in tort and at how such an option affects the regime of liability applicable to the plaintiff's claim. 1–144

Threatened breach of contract as a tort. While some dicta in *Brown v Boorman*[807] suggest that any breach of contract gives rise to liability in tort,[808] such a broad interpretation of that case does not reflect the modern law: a breach of contract may be linked historically to tort, but does not itself constitute one.[809] However, it would seem that what has often been called the tort of intimidation (and is now likely to be known as the tort of causing loss by unlawful means[810]) could allow at least *threatened* breaches of contract to give rise to liability in tort. The tort is committed, inter alia, where A uses "unlawful means" to force B to do something to his prejudice and it is clear that it includes a threatened breach of contract[811] and it appears that this applies to "two-party" intimidation as much as to "three-party" intimidation.[812] Thus, according to *Clerk & Lindsell on Torts*, the tort of intimidation extends to a threat of breach of contract or at least to a threat of *some* breaches of contract,[813] despite the fact that the victim of such a threat may also have an action for anticipatory breach of contract.[814] 1–145

If so, then it would appear that rules which govern claims in contract, for example ruling out punitive damages or relating to remoteness of damage, could be avoided.[815] Indeed, the same authors add that it is not clear whether a party who has affirmed the contract after a threatened breach is thereby prevented from relying on the tort of intimidation.[816] However, if a claimant who was the victim of such a threat were allowed to rely on this tort rather than on the contract, it 1–146

---

[807] (1842) 3 Q.B. 511, (1844) 11 Cl. & Fin. 1 HL.

[808] See above, para.1–129.

[809] But compare para.1–141 above.

[810] *OGB Ltd v Allan, Douglas v Hello! Ltd, Mainstream Properties Ltd v Young* [2007] UKHL 21, [2008] 1 A.C. 1 especially at [6]–[8].

[811] *Rookes v Barnard* [1964] A.C. 1129.

[812] For example, where A threatens B, his creditor, that he will not pay a debt owed unless B accepts a smaller sum in full satisfaction, A may be liable to B in the tort of intimidation: *D.&C. Builders Ltd v Rees* [1966] 2 Q.B. 617, 625.

[813] *Clerk & Lindsell on Torts*, 19th edn (2006), paras 25–80—25–82. In *Morgan v Fry* [1968] 2 Q.B. 710, 737, Russell L.J.'s judgment suggests that not every threat to break a contract of employment would be sufficient to constitute the tort of intimidation. *Clerk & Lindsell on Torts*, para.25–81, text at fn.56, suggest that this view: " . . . may depend upon absence of proof that the threat of a minor breach could cause damage. For damage is, of course, essential to the cause of action and the plaintiff must prove that his damage was caused by the coercive threat."

[814] See below, para.24–021.

[815] *Clerk & Lindsell on Torts* at para.25–86, especially at fn.87, referring to *Kenny v Preen* [1963] 1 Q.B. 499 in which the Court of Appeal refused to award punitive damages where the claim was only for breach of contract and see above, para.1–123.

[816] *Clerk & Lindsell on Torts* at para.25–86, fn.91.

would be odd to deny him the same option where the other party had not merely threatened to break the contract, but had carried out this threat.[817] If this situation were allowed to give rise to liability in the tort of intimidation, then the law would be fast approaching the recognition of a distinction based on whether or not a defendant's breach of contract was "wilful" or "intended to injure" and there is no reason to think that English courts are inclined to do so.[818] It is submitted that there is no convincing reason for allowing a party to a contract to avoid the restrictions which the law already has decided should apply to that party's claim simply by claiming in tort. For this reason, the view that "two-party" and "three-party" intimidation should be treated differently where breach of contract is relied on as the unlawful means is to be preferred.[819] Thus, while a threatened breach of contract may constitute the tort of intimidation/tort of causing harm by unlawful means, as between parties to a contract a threatened breach should not in itself be considered sufficient "unlawful means" for the purposes of that tort; other *independent* "unlawful" elements should be required, for example, tortious means.[820]

1–147 **Contractual standards of care: can tort be stricter?** It is clear that where either the express or implied terms of the contract or the law itself governs the standard of care owed by the defendant to the claimant, the latter cannot seek to impose a higher standard by claiming in tort, notably the tort of negligence.[821] Where a contract expressly restricts a party's standard of care, it would seem that ordinary principles of construction apply, rather than construction *contra proferentum* which applies to exemption clauses proper, i.e. those clauses which intend to restrict or exclude a party's *liability*.[822] In the case of implied terms, those which relate to the safety of a person or of his property often impose either

[817] Cane, *Tort Law and Economic Interests*, 2nd edn (1996), p.130.

[818] cf. *Kenny v Preen* [1963] 1 Q.B. 499; *McCall v Abelesz* [1976] Q.B. 585, 594 and see below, para.26–019 and cf. the refusal of English courts to distinguish between deliberate and other breaches of contract for the purposes of the validity of exemption clauses, below, para.14–016 and see Unfair Contract Terms Act 1977 s.1(4). In *Bank of Nova Scotia v Hellenic Mutual War Risks Association (Bermuda) Ltd* [1990] 1 Q.B. 818, 894, May L.J. observed that "a deliberate contract breaker is guilty of no more than breach of contract". For a useful discussion of the US position see Farnsworth, *Contracts*, 3rd edn (2004), paras 12.8, 12.17a.

[819] *Winfield and Jolowicz on Tort*, 17th edn (2006), paras 18–21—18–23.

[820] In *OGB Ltd v Allan, Douglas v Hello! Ltd, Mainstream Properties Ltd v Young, Douglas v Hello! Ltd, Mainstream Properties Ltd v Young* [2007] UKHL 21, [2008] 1 A.C. 1 at [61] Lord Hoffmann was careful to put aside the question of possible recovery by a claimant who has been compelled by unlawful intimidation to act to his own detriment: "[s]uch a case of 'two party intimidation' raises altogether different issues".

[821] An exception to this rule is found in the case of personal fraud in a contractor liability for which cannot be excluded by contract: *S. Pearson & Son Ltd v Dublin Corp* [1907] A.C. 351, 353–354, 362. Fraud may occur in the course of performance of a contract as well at the pre-contractual stage, for example, where a solicitor's clerk acts fraudulently in relation to his commission: see *Lloyd v Grace, Smith & Co* [1912] A.C. 716, where a solicitor's employee's fraud was held to give rise to liability in both tort and contract in the solicitor. Of course, in many situations the standard of care owed by a contractor is the same in tort and in contract, notably where the tort is one of negligence and the relevant contractual obligation is one of reasonable care: see below, paras 13–014, 13–032.

[822] cf. *Trade and Transport Inc v Ilno Kaiun Kaisha Ltd* [1973] 1 W.L.R. 210, 230–231 and see below, para.14–009 but cf. Unfair Contract Terms Act 1977 s.13(1), below, para.14–062.

reasonable care[823] or some stricter duty on the contractor,[824] and so any liability in tort in the latter would not impose any higher standard than in contract. However, implied terms whose breach gives rise to economic loss in the other party sometimes impose a more restricted standard of care than that imposed by the general law, and here the courts have refused to allow the other party to circumvent this contractual standard by claiming in tort. This was the particular issue in *Tai Hing Cotton Mill Ltd v Liu Chong Hing Bank Ltd*[825] which gave rise to Lord Scarman's dictum advising against the intervention of tort between parties to a contract,[826] and this was the basis on which the decision of the Privy Council in that case which denied a claim in tort was explained by the House of Lords in *Henderson v Merrett Syndicates Ltd*.[827] *Tai Hing Cotton Mill Ltd* itself concerned a claim by a bank against its customer for economic loss caused by the latter's alleged negligence in the running of its own account. The Privy Council held that as a matter of authority a bank customer owed only a duty to act honestly in relation to the conduct of his own account under the contract with the bank and should not, therefore, be held to a duty to take reasonable care whether by way of implied term or of breach of an alleged duty of care in the tort of negligence.[828]

Contractual standards and equitable principles. The courts have taken a similar approach where the relationship between the parties is contractual, but where it has traditionally been subject to regulation by equitable principle. Thus, in *Parker-Tweedale v Dunbar Bank Plc*[829] Nourse L.J. stated that any duty of a mortgagee to a mortgagor or of a creditor to a guarantor in respect of the property or debt respectively arose in equity out of that particular relationship, it being: 1–148

> "... both unnecessary and confusing for the duties owed by a mortgagee to the mortgagor and the surety, if there is one, to be expressed in terms of the tort of negligence."[830]

Similarly, according to Lord Templeman, giving judgment on behalf of the Privy Council, where a creditor was "not obliged to do anything" for the benefit of a surety under these equitable principles, for example in relation to the recovery of

---

823 e.g. *Readhead v Midland Ry Co* (1867) L.R. 2 Q.B. 412, (1869) L.R. 4 Q.B. 379 (carriage of persons); *Davie v New Merton Board Mills* [1959] A.C. 604 (employment); Occupiers' Liability Act 1957 s.5(1); *Thake v Maurice* [1986] 1 Q.B. 644 (medical liability).

824 e.g. *Samuels v Davis* [1943] 1 K.B. 526 (dentist who designed and constructed prothesis liable strictly to patient) and see Sale of Goods Act 1979 s.14.

825 [1986] A.C. 80.

826 [1986] A.C. 80, 107.

827 [1995] 2 A.C. 145 see especially at 186.

828 cf. *Blackwood v Robertson* 1984 S.L.T. 68 (lesser standard of care between partners).

829 [1991] Ch. 12 (and see *Shamji v Johnson Matthey Bankers Ltd* [1986] B.C.L.C. 278).

830 [1991] Ch. 12 at 18 (and cf. at 24–25, Purchas L.J.), thereby disapproving Salmon L.J.'s dictum in *Cuckmere Brick Co Ltd v Mutual Finance Ltd* [1971] Ch. 949, 966 which talks of a duty of care in the context of the liability of a mortgagee; and see *Downsview Nominees Ltd v First City Corp Ltd* [1993] A.C. 295, 315 and *AIB Finance Ltd v Debtors* [1998] 2 All E.R. 929, 937; *Yorkshire Bank Plc v Hall* [1999] 1 W.L.R. 1713, 1728; *Raja v Lloyds TSB Bank Plc* [2001] EWCA Civ 210, [2001] Lloyd's Rep. Bank. 113; and see Megarry and Wade, *The Law of Real Property*, 6th edn (2000), paras 19–061—19–062.

the debt, no duty of care in the tort of negligence can arise.[831] Indeed, it has been said that "the duty arises in equity, not in contract or tort".[832]

1–149 **Contractual standard stricter.** In certain types of case, the courts have refused to construe a contract or imply a term in it so as to circumvent the traditional standard of care or scope of liability applied to the type of case in question, even where this has usually been put as a matter of tort. For example, in *Thake v Maurice*,[833] a majority of the Court of Appeal refused to interpret a contract to perform a vasectomy as importing an obligation that the patient would be rendered sterile as a result, holding that it contained only one of reasonable care in warning the latter of the possibility of future fertility. Although not put in these terms by the court, it could be said that the established standard of care in tort was applied to the claim in contract despite persuasive factual considerations which could have lead in a different direction.[834] However, in many other situations the courts have accepted that the standard of care owed by a defendant in contract by reason of an implied term is higher than the reasonable care which would be imposed in the tort of negligence.[835] An example may be found in the decision of the Privy Council in *Wong Mee Wan v Kwan Kin Travel Services Ltd*.[836] There a travel agent was held liable for the death of one of its customers on the basis of the negligence of one of its agents, even though there was no negligence on its own part, on the basis that the contract included an obligation that the services which the travel agent had engaged to perform *would be carried out* with reasonable care.

1–150 **Stricter contractual standard does not affect tort.** Finally, in *Aiken v Stewart Wrightson Members Agency Ltd*[837] the question arose whether the fact that the defendant owed a contractual duty *more onerous* than one of reasonable care could and should affect the standard of care owed in the tort of negligence. The case concerned a claim by Lloyd's "indirect Names" against their "members' agents", i.e. the agents who had contracted with them to advise them on their choice of syndicates and to place them on any syndicate once chosen, leaving the placing of the insurance to "managing agents". It was conceded by the members' agents that they owed the plaintiff "Names" a contractual duty that:

---

831 *China and South Seas Bank v Tan* [1990] 1 A.C. 536, 543–544.

832 *Raja v Lloyds TSB Bank Plc* [2001] EWCA Civ 210 at [31], per Mance L.J.

833 [1986] 1 Q.B. 644. Peter Pain J. at first instance and Kerr L.J. on appeal took the opposite view on this issue from the majority in the Court of Appeal and see below, para.1–164.

834 cf. *Readhead v Midland Ry Co* (1867) L.R. 2 Q.B. 412, (1869) L.R. 4 Q.B. 379, in which the court held that a passenger injured while travelling on a railway could sue the company only on the basis of breach of a duty to take reasonable care, rejecting the plaintiff's contention that the company owed an obligation to provide a carriage fit for its purpose, by analogy with cases on sale of goods.

835 The stricter type of contractual term was implied by the courts in the context of sale of goods: *Jones v Just* (1868) L.R. 3 Q.B. 197 (see now Sale of Goods Act 1979 s.14). See further, *Samuels v Davis* [1943] 1 K.B. 526 (liability of dentist in respect of manufacture and supply of dental prothesis); Supply of Goods and Services Act 1982 s.4 and below, para.13–029.

836 [1996] 1 W.L.R. 38.

837 [1995] 1 W.L.R. 1281.

> " . . . the actual underwriting would be carried out with reasonable care and skill so that the members' agent remains directly responsible to its Names for any failure to exercise reasonable care and skill by the managing agent of any syndicate to whom such underwriting has been delegated."[838]

The "Names" contended that the members' agents also owed them a duty of care in the tort of negligence of the same content, a "parallel and *co-extensive* duty of care in tort", arguing that it was inherent in Lord Goff's view expressed in *Henderson v Merrett Syndicates Ltd*[839] that any liability in tort should not be inconsistent with the terms of the contract that the latter "ought in logic and in law to be definitive also of the nature and extent of their duty in tort".[840] However, Potter J rejected this argument both as a matter of authority[841] and principle. The latter he considered well expressed in a dictum of Le Dain J. in *Central Trust Co v Refuse*[842]:

> "A claim cannot be said to be in tort if it depends for the nature and scope of the asserted duty of care on the manner in which an obligation or duty has been expressly and specifically defined by a contract."

Potter J. therefore concluded that on the facts before him the:

> " . . . common law duty of care . . . falls short of the specific obligation or duty imposed by the express terms of the contract, unless that common law duty of care can be shown to be non-delegable in character for the purposes of the law of tort,"

a proviso which was not satisfied in the case itself.[843]

Contractual exclusion of liability in tort. The law has taken a similar but not identical approach to cases where a contract term excludes or limits *liability* of one contractor to another. Since at least the early nineteenth century, exemption clauses have been held capable of excluding or limiting liability in tort,[844] though it should be noted that where the clause limits liability, a (limited) claim in tort may still exist.[845] While at times the interpretation of exemption clauses *contra proferentum* has led to the courts distinguishing between the two types of liability, holding that a particular clause covered a strict contractual liability but did not cover liability for negligence in tort,[846] there would appear to be no real reason to characterise a contractor's liability for negligence in these circumstances as tortious rather than contractual and in other cases the courts have simply inquired whether a particular clause should be construed to cover cases of 1–151

---

[838] [1995] 1 W.L.R. 1281 at 1290.
[839] [1995] 2 A.C. 145, 194 and see above, paras 1–138—1–139.
[840] [1995] 1 W.L.R. 1281 at 1294.
[841] [1995] 1 W.L.R. 1281 at 1295. Notably, *Tai Hing Cotton Mill Ltd v Liu Chong Hing Bank Ltd* [1986] A.C. 80.
[842] (1986) 31 D.L.R. (4th) 481, 521–522.
[843] [1995] 1 W.L.R. 1281, 1301, 1305.
[844] *Nicholson v Willan* (1804) 5 East 507 and see below, paras 14–001 et seq.
[845] *White v John Warwick & Co Ltd* [1953] 1 W.L.R. 1285.
[846] *White v John Warwick & Co Ltd* [1953] 1 W.L.R. 1285 at 1294 where Denning L.J. held that the plaintiff "can avoid the exemption clause by framing his claim in tort".

negligence as well as any stricter liability.[847] Of course, in many situations, the effectiveness of such a term will be subject to the provisions of s.2 of the Unfair Contract Terms Act 1977, which applies to cases of tortious as well as to contractual negligence.[848]

1–152 **Incompatibility of express term and liability in tort.** *Johnstone v Bloomsbury Health Authority*[849] concerned an alleged incompatibility between an express term of a contract and the existence of an established liability in the tort of negligence in a rather unusual way. The plaintiff was a junior hospital doctor who worked under a contract of employment which stipulated a working week of 40 hours and provided for a possible 48 additional hours availability for work. He claimed that in compliance with this contract he had sometimes worked in excess of 88 hours per week and had become ill as a result. The issue before the Court of Appeal was whether his claim for a declaration that he should not be required to work more than a 72-hour week should be struck out. The plaintiff relied on his employer's duty, which exists both as a matter of contract and the tort of negligence,[850] to take reasonable care as to his health at work, but the defendant countered that the express provision in the contract as to his hours of work limited the impact of this implied term and that no wider tortious duty could be imposed, relying on Lord Scarman's dictum in *Tai Hing Cotton Mill Ltd v Liu Chong Hing Bank Ltd.*[851] The majority of the Court of Appeal refused to strike out the plaintiff's claim, but for different reasons. Stuart-Smith L.J. considered that while it was quite possible for an express term to exclude an implied one, the express term in question had not attempted to do so.[852] Sir Nicolas Browne-Wilkinson V.C. agreed with Stuart-Smith L.J.'s decision on this point, but on more restricted grounds. The Vice-Chancellor considered that the approach of the Privy Council in *Tai Hing Cotton Mill Ltd*:

> "... shows that where there is a contractual relationship between the parties their respective rights and duties have to be analysed wholly in contractual terms and not a mixture of duties in tort and contract. It necessarily follows that the scope of the duties owed by one party to the other will be defined by the terms of the contract between them."[853]

However, the Vice-Chancellor held that the clause in question did not on its terms impose an absolute obligation on the doctor to work the extra hours, but merely gave the defendant a discretion as to the number of hours extra that were to be worked and that this right should be considered subject to their ordinary duty not to injure the plaintiff.[854] Leggatt L.J., dissenting, considered that the express term

---

[847] e.g. *Hollier v Rambler Motors (A.M.C.) Ltd* [1972] 2 Q.B. 71.

[848] Unfair Contract Terms Act 1977 s.1(1) and see below, para.14–060. Such an attempted exclusion may also fall within the controls of the Unfair Terms in Consumer Contracts Regulations 1999 (SI 1999/2083), below, paras 15–004 et seq.

[849] [1992] Q.B. 334.

[850] See *Davie v New Merton Board Mills* [1959] A.C. 604 (negligence); *Matthews v Kuwait Bechtel Corp* [1959] 2 Q.B. 57 (contract).

[851] [1986] A.C. 80, 107; see above, para.1–147.

[852] [1986] A.C. 80.

[853] [1986] A.C. 80 at 350.

[854] [1986] A.C. 80 at 350–351.

on the facts did indeed cut down the impact of the employer's implied term as to the safety of its employee and, following *Tai Hing Cotton Mill Ltd*, no tortious obligation could be any greater.[855] It is submitted that the approach of all members of the Court of Appeal in *Johnstone v Bloomsbury Health Authority* to these issues is consistent with that adopted subsequently by the House of Lords in *Henderson v Merrett Syndicates Ltd*,[856] since the latter confirmed that no concurrent liability in tort would be allowed where this would be inconsistent with the terms of the contract between the parties.[857] However, the decisions of the majority in *Johnstone* also shows that judges will be slow to interpret a contract as incompatible with an established liability in tort, perhaps particularly where this relates to personal injuries.

Contract removing condition of or giving rise to a defence to liability in tort. A contract's terms can affect liability in tort in another way as it may remove one of the conditions for its existence or give rise to the existence of a defence, and this is particularly clear where the consent of an injured party excludes liability. Thus, in cases concerning medical treatment involving physical contact with the patient, the contact is prima facie a battery unless the claimant has consented to the treatment,[858] but where a person is able to and has consented, this will exclude liability in tort as well as contract.[859] Similarly, a contractual licence given by an owner of land prevents any liability arising in the licensee in the tort of trespass as long as the latter does not act beyond the permission.[860] A contractual consent can also allow the application of the defence of volenti non fit injuria. For example, in *Chapman v Ellesmere*,[861] a racing steward who acted under a licence from the Jockey Club was held unable to sue members of a committee appointed under that club's rules in the tort of defamation in respect of the publication of a report on his role in a particular race, because on accepting his licence he had agreed to rules under which publication of such a report was specifically permitted. 1–153

Legal immunities for contractors. Where the law itself rather than a contractual term grants a party to a contract a certain immunity from liability, the courts have looked to the reason for this immunity and decided whether it applies equally to a claim in tort as to the one in contract. For example, while the courts recognised that a solicitor enjoyed a certain immunity from liability in negligence in relation to the conduct and management of a case for reasons of policy, this 1–154

---

855 [1986] A.C. 80 at 349.

856 [1995] 2 A.C. 145.

857 See above, paras 1–138—1–139.

858 *Chatterton v Gerson* [1981] 1 Q.B. 432, 442–443. For the extent to which the consent needs to be "informed" see *Sidaway v Governors of the Bethlem Royal Hospital* [1985] A.C. 871. That the consent of the claimant goes to the existence of the tort of battery rather than being merely an example of *volenti non fit injuria* is supported by the fact that the claimant must show his own lack of consent: *Freeman v Home Office (No.2)* [1984] Q.B. 524, 539.

859 [1985] A.C. 871 at 904–905.

860 There is no need for such a licence to be contractual for the defence to arise. See *Clerk & Lindsell on Torts*, 19th edn (2006), para.19–45.

861 [1932] 2 K.B. 431.

immunity applied both to tort and to contract.[862] However, the approach of the courts to the very wide[863] immunity from liability at common law[864] of landlords to their tenants has been very different. In *Rimmer v Liverpool City Council*,[865] while the Court of Appeal did not consider itself able as a matter of authority to impose a duty of care in the tort of negligence on a landlord as to the safety of the premises at the time of letting, it did impose a duty of care on a landlord *qua* designer of the premises let as to the reasonable safety of their design to the tenant *qua* person who might reasonably be expected to be affected.[866] As Stephenson L.J. noted, *Cavalier v Pope*,[867] the leading authority which supported the landlord's immunity, should be restrictively interpreted[868] for at the time it was decided:

> "... contractual duties were regarded as excluding delictual duties and a contractual relationship determined completely the rights and obligations of the related parties, as well as the rights of third parties."[869]

In this context, and as regards liability for personal injuries, the courts showed themselves willing to allow the tort of negligence to develop in order to circumvent an immunity attaching to a particular contract where that immunity was no longer considered justified as a matter of policy, but which was supported by superior authority.[870]

The decision of the Court of Appeal in *Bank of Nova Scotia v Hellenic Mutual War Risks Association (Bermuda) Ltd (The Good Luck)*[871] concerned a situation in which a legal rule (as opposed to the terms of the contract) provided one party to a contract with a remedy based on breach of a duty in the other, but where that breach of duty had not previously been held to give rise to liability in damages. One issue before the court was whether breach by an insurer of its duty to disclose matters to the assured during the course of the contract could give rise to liability in damages as well as the possibility of rescission of the contract by the assured.[872] Having held that it should not imply a relevant term as to disclosure into the contract either on the basis of the "bystander test"[873] or the

---

[862] *Saif Ali v Sydney Mitchell & Co* [1980] A.C. 198 applying to solicitors *Rondel v Worsley* [1969] A.C. 191; Courts and Legal Services Act 1990 s.62. In *Arthur J.S. Hall v Simons* [2002] 1 A.C. 615 this immunity was rejected and these earlier decisions not followed.

[863] The immunity extended to positive acts of malfeasance as well as to non-feasance and to claims for personal injuries: *Travers v Gloucester Corp* [1947] 1 K.B. 71.

[864] *Cavalier v Pope* [1906] A.C. 428. See now Defective Premises Act 1972 ss.3, 4.

[865] [1985] 1 Q.B. 1.

[866] [1985] 1 Q.B. 1 at 13.

[867] [1906] A.C. 428.

[868] *Rimmer v Liverpool City Council* [1985] 1 Q.B. 1 at 9.

[869] [1985] 1 Q.B. 1 at 11.

[870] cf. *McNerny v Lambeth LBC* (1988) 21 H.L.R. 188 (no liability in tort of negligence in landlord to tenant for condensation damage and illness) and *Baxter v Camden LBC (No.2)* [2001] Q.B. 1 (no liability in tort of nuisance in landlord to tenant owing to noise from neighbouring property also owned by landlord) in both of which the rule in *Cavalier v Pope* [1906] A.C. 428 was applied.

[871] [1990] 1 Q.B. 818 (reversed on other grounds [1992] 1 A.C. 233).

[872] cf. *Banque Keyser Ullmann SA v Skandia (UK) Co Insurance Ltd* [1990] 1 Q.B. 655 (affirmed on other grounds [1991] 2 A.C. 249).

[873] [1990] 1 Q.B. 818; [1990] 1 Q.B. 655 at 897–898 and see below, para.13–007.

"test of necessity,"[874] the court considered that, whatever the degree of proximity of the parties or the fairness and reasonableness of recognising a duty of care in tort, it should still apply the "principle established in *Tai Hing Cotton Mill Ltd v Lui Chong Hing Bank Ltd*".[875] According to May L.J.:

> ". . . the [insurer] was entitled . . . to look to the contract between the parties to discover what was the obligation of the [insurer] with regard to reporting to the [assured]."[876]

Thus, legal recognition of a *limited* remedy for a party to a contract for breach of a particular legal duty imposed on the other party, was seen by the court as a reason for refusing to impose a duty of care in the tort of negligence so as to give an *additional* remedy.

It should be noted, however, that *Bank of Nova Scotia* was decided before the decision of the House of Lords in *Henderson v Merrett Syndicates Ltd*[877] and therefore at a time when *Tai Hing Cotton Mill Ltd v Liu Chong Hing Bank Ltd*[878] was still seen as an authority against allowing a liability in tort (at least for economic loss) to be relied on by one party to a contract against the other and some of these dicta should be seen in this light.[879] While it would be open to a future court simply to distinguish the decision on this basis, it is submitted that it is more likely that the latter will be interpreted as an illustration of the proposition that new or doubtful liabilities in tort should not be imposed between parties to a contract where to do so would subvert the policy of the law of contract as reflected in its grant of a more limited remedy than recognition of the tort would entail. Such a proposition could be seen as the reflection of the idea that any liability in tort between the parties to a contract should not be inconsistent with that contract or, more directly, as constituting a consideration of policy arguing for the rejection of a duty of care in tort.[880] So, for example, in *Johnson v Unisys Ltd*[881] a majority of the House of Lords held that a claim for damages by an employee for breach of contract for the manner of his dismissal by his employer had rightly been struck out as disclosing no reasonable cause of action on the basis that any implied term concerning the manner of dismissal would be inconsistent with the statutory scheme of unfair dismissal put in place by Parliament. Lord Hoffmann considered that the same reasoning precluded any imposition of a duty of care in the tort of negligence and observed that: 1–155

> "It is of course true that a duty of care can exist independently of the contractual relationship. But the grounds upon which . . . it would be wrong to impose an implied

[874] [1990] 1 Q.B. 818 at 898–899 and see below, paras 13–003, 13–009.
[875] [1990] 1 Q.B. 818, at 901, per May L.J.
[876] [1990] 1 Q.B. 818 at 902.
[877] [1995] 2 A.C. 145.
[878] [1986] A.C. 80.
[879] See above, para.1–126.
[880] On this role of policy in recognition of the duty of care in the tort of negligence, see especially *Marc Rich & Co AG v Bishop Rock Marine Co* [1996] 1 A.C. 211. For the significance of considerations of policy in relation to liability in the tort of negligence based on an "assumption of responsibility", see above, paras 1–138—1–139.
[881] [2001] 2 W.L.R. 1076 and see *Eastwood v Magnox Plc* [2004] UKHL 35, [2005] 1 A.C. 503.

contractual duty would make it equally wrong to achieve the same result by the imposition of a duty of care."[882]

1–156 **Contractual silence.** In the preceding situations, either the contract's terms or the law itself has regulated the obligation or liability imposed on the defendant. More difficult has been the case where the contract is silent as to an issue which is allegedly governed by a tort, for silence is ambiguous: where the parties have not provided for a certain issue, this can mean either that they did not address that issue, even implicitly, or it can mean that they consciously chose *not* to provide for that issue.[883] The typical case in which this problem has arisen has been where a contract has been held not to contain a relevant implied term and so the claimant has sued instead in the tort of negligence. Clearly, the choice for a court is whether to hold that the contract's silence excludes the recognition of any liability in tort, or, conversely, that it has no effect on the recognition of any liability in tort, which arises or does not arise according to its own rules. The acceptance by the House of Lords in *Henderson v Merrett Syndicates Ltd* of the general rule that a party to a contract may rely on a tort committed by the other party even in the course of performance of the contract would appear at first sight to have settled this question in favour of the latter position, but, as been already noted, that same decision's acceptance of the "broad principle" of assumption of responsibility drawn from *Hedley Byrne* reintroduces the question in this particular context. The following will, therefore, look first at the general position and then at the approach taken by the courts to the question of tortious "assumptions of responsibility" between parties to a contract which is silent as to the issue on which the assumption is alleged to have been made.

1–157 **The general position.** In *Henderson v Merrett Syndicates Ltd* it was held, inter alia, that a party to a contract may rely on a tort committed by the other party, as long as doing so is not inconsistent with its express or implied terms: contract does not necessarily exclude tort. While *Henderson* itself concerned a case where the defendant owed a contractual duty *concurrent* with the alleged tortious duty, it could be argued that a contract's silence is by its nature not inconsistent with the existence of any liability in tort. In support of this interpretation, it can be noted that to allow a person's mere entering into a contract with another to have the effect of excluding the latter's liability in tort would mean that the law allowed by *implication* (the implication that by their silence the parties had intended that the issue in question should not be regulated) what it traditionally allowed only by a very clear contractual *expression*,[884] a paradox which would only be heightened by the fact that such an express exemption clause would, in many cases, be subject to legislative control.[885] In general,

---

[882] [2001] 2 W.L.R. 1076 at 1097 and see also at 1122, per Lord Millett.

[883] cf. *Ali v Christian Salvesen Food Services Ltd* [1997] 1 All E.R. 721, especially at 726 in which the Court of Appeal refused to imply a term in a collective agreement which represented "a carefully negotiated compromise between two potentially conflicting objectives" and which was "wholly silent" as to the issue about which it was argued a term should be implied.

[884] See below, paras 14–005 et seq. and cf. *Smith v Charles Baker & Sons* [1891] A.C. 325 (mere entry of contract with knowledge of risk not sufficient for defence of volenti non fit injuria).

[885] This would be the case notably as regards "business liability for negligence" under the Unfair Contract Terms Act 1977 s.2.

therefore, a contract's silence should not be interpreted as a choice to oust the general law of tort.

1–158 **Contractual silence and "assumption of responsibility".** However, more difficulty arises in relation to cases of recovery of pure economic loss in the tort of negligence based on the idea of "assumption of responsibility" drawn from the speeches of the members of the House of Lords in *Hedley Byrne*. Certainly, until the decision of the House of Lords in *Henderson v Merrett Syndicates Ltd*[886] the courts on more than one occasion refused to recognise a duty of care in the tort of negligence in respect of pure economic loss based on an "assumption of responsibility" of one party to a contract to the other where that contract was silent as to the issue in question. For example, in *Reid v Rush & Tompkins Group Plc*[887] the plaintiff was injured in a car accident in Ethiopia in the course of his employment for his English employer, but as he could not recover compensation there from the person responsible, he sued his employer, arguing that the latter owed him an obligation either to insure him against this type of accident or to advise him that he ought himself to take out appropriate insurance. However, having refused to find an implied term in his contract of employment either as to insurance or advising him of his position,[888] the Court of Appeal rejected his claim for pure economic loss in the tort of negligence, refusing to accept his argument that the defendant had voluntarily accepted this responsibility. According to Ralph Gibson L.J.:

> "Where there is a contract between the parties, and any 'voluntary assumption of responsibility' occurred, if at all, at the time of making and by reason of the contract, it seems unreal to me to try to separate a duty of care arising from the relationship created by the contract from one 'voluntarily assumed' but not specifically assumed by a term of the contract itself."[889]

Having cited with approval Lord Scarman's dictum in *Tai Hing Cotton Ltd v Liu Chong Hing Bank Ltd*[890] the learned Lord Justice added that:

> " . . . it is not open to this court to extend the duty of care owed by this defendant to the plaintiff by imposing a duty in tort which . . . is not contained in any express or implied term of the contract,"[891]

Similarly, in *National Bank of Greece SA v Pinios Shipping Co (No.1), The Maira*,[892] while Lloyd L.J. accepted that "in a large class of cases it was always, and maybe still is, possible for the plaintiff to sue either in contract or in tort"[893] he considered that:

---

886 [1995] 2 A.C. 145 and see above, paras 1–138—1–139.
887 [1990] 1 W.L.R. 212 and see also *Van Oppen v Clerk to the Bedford Charity Trustees* [1990] 1 W.L.R. 235.
888 Relying on *Liverpool City Council v Irwin* [1977] A.C. 239 and see below, para.13–009.
889 [1990] 1 W.L.R. 212 at 229.
890 [1986] A.C. 80, 107.
891 [1990] 1 W.L.R. 212, 232.
892 [1990] 1 A.C. 637.
893 [1990] 1 A.C. 637 at 650.

> "... it has never been the law that a plaintiff who has the choice of suing in contract or tort can fail in contract yet nevertheless succeed in tort; and if it ever was the law, it has ceased to be the law since *Tai Hing Cotton Ltd.*"[894]

Here, again, therefore, the silence of the contract prevented the imposition of a duty of care in tort.[895]

1–159 However, as this brief discussion makes clear, this approach to the imposition of a duty of care based on an assumption of responsibility in the context of contractual silence was heavily influenced by the general judicial disfavour with which *any* liability in tort between the parties to a contract was viewed, and such an approach was thoroughly disapproved by the House of Lords in *Henderson v Merrett Syndicates Ltd.*[896] However, even after the latter decision a logical difficulty remains with the imposition of liability in tort based on an assumption of responsibility where the contract is silent. As has been seen, the current meaning given to the notion of "assumption of responsibility" by the courts is that the defendant agreed to undertake a task or perform some service for the claimant. In cases of "contractual silence", *ex hypothesi*,[897] the court has already decided that a defendant did not make any relevant agreement (as a matter of the express or implied construction of the contract). How then can a court hold that a defendant did not agree for one legal purpose, but did do so for another? It would be understandable if a court should consider it illogical to find the existence of such a duty of care owed by one contractor to another having already decided that there has been no *contractual* assumption of responsibility.

1–160 However, in *Holt v Payne Skillington*,[898] the Court of Appeal took a rather different view of this matter. In this case, the plaintiffs had indicated to the defendant estate agents that they wished to purchase a property in London with the view to letting it on "holiday lets", a use which they made clear they required so as to benefit from tax relief in respect of a capital gain they had already made.[899] One of the estate agents' employees had, at some time before any retainer, assured them that he knew about the local planning requirements which would need to be satisfied to allow the plaintiffs to use whatever property they bought for this purpose. In the result, however, the property which the estate agents put forward and which the plaintiffs bought could not be used for holiday lets under the relevant planning rules. At first instance, the judge held the estate agents liable in the tort of negligence, but *not* liable for breach of contract on the basis that there was no express term of the retainer agreement (nor of a second "valuation agreement") between the parties that the agents should investigate the

[894] [1990] 1 A.C. 637. If given a general application, this statement would clearly prevent a claimant from suing in tort after the expiry of a limitation period applicable to a contractual action, on which see below, para.1–167.

[895] See similarly, *Bank of Nova Scotia v Hellenic War Risks Association (Bermuda) Ltd* [1990] 1 Q.B. 818 and see above, para.1–154 and *Greater Nottingham Co-Operative Society Ltd v Cementation Piling & Foundations Ltd* [1989] Q.B. 71.

[896] Above, paras 1–138 et seq.

[897] On the assumption that the implied term is put before the court for its consideration.

[898] [1995] 49 Con. L.R. 99.

[899] The plaintiffs also claimed against their solicitors, but no issue relating to the latters' liability arose before the Court of Appeal.

planning issue. The estate agents appealed against this decision as to their liability in tort, but no appeal was made by the plaintiffs on the decision made against them in contract. Before the Court of Appeal, therefore, the estate agents argued that any duty of care in tort which they might have owed to the plaintiffs could not be wider than the express and implied terms of the contract between them and contended that the judge's decision on the terms of their contracts meant that they could not be liable in tort. Hirst L.J., however, rejected this argument, relying on a passage of Lord Goff of Chieveley's speech in *Henderson v Merrett Syndicates Ltd*[900] and stating that:

> "... there is no reason in principle why a *Hedley Byrne* type of duty of care cannot arise in an overall set of circumstances where, by reference to certain limited aspects of those circumstances, the same parties enter into a contractual relationship involving more limited obligations than those imposed by the duty of care in tort. In such circumstances, the duty of care in tort and the duties imposed by the contract will be concurrent but not coextensive."[901]

The Court of Appeal held, therefore, that the judge below was entitled to rely on a factual context wider than the contractual agreements between the parties to establish a duty of care in tort.[902] This approach clearly accords with the general position taken in *Henderson v Merrett Syndicates Ltd* in favour of allowing tort to apply between parties to a contract, but it appears to ignore the thrust of the "logical argument" outlined in the previous paragraph against finding a tortious assumption of responsibility in a case of contractual silence. In this regard, however, there is, with respect, a particular difficulty with the decision in *Holt*: for while Hirst L.J. based the estate agents' liability in tort on the principle of assumption of responsibility,[903] he found (as he had been invited to by *both* parties) the: "... essential characteristics of a situation giving rise to a cause of action in negligence based on a duty of case of the *Hedley Byrne* type," in a passage of Lord Oliver's speech in *Caparo Industries Plc v Dickman*,[904] which looks to the defendant's giving of advice to a person who he knows is likely to rely on it, rather than to any agreement to do a task by the defendant.[905] This approach to the *Hedley Byrne* principle was entirely understandable on the facts, since it was clearly the bad or inadequate advice which the plaintiffs were given by the estate agents' employee which formed the basis of any imposition of liability in tort. Certainly, where liability under *Hedley Byrne* is put in terms of a negligent misstatement given by a person who can foresee that it will be relied on rather than in the broader terms of an "assumption of responsibility" in the sense of an agreement to perform a service for the other party, then there is nothing inconsistent in finding a duty of care under *Hedley Byrne* but no express or implied duty of care in contract. By contrast, however, to the extent to which

---

900 [1995] 2 A.C. 145, 193.

901 [1995] 49 Con. L.R. 99, 114.

902 This approach was followed by the HC in *Sumitomo Bank Ltd v Banque Bruxelles Lambert SA* [1997] 1 Lloyd's Rep. 487 (duty of care arising from failure in carrying out pre-contractual disclosure).

903 This can be seen Hirst L.J.'s reliance on passages from Lord Goff's speech in *Henderson v Merrett Syndicates Ltd* [1995] 2 A.C. 145, 178 and 193–194, notably.

904 [1990] 2 A.C. 605, 638.

905 [1995] 49 Con. L.R. 99, 114.

a defendant's having "assumed responsibility" for doing something is to mean that he "agreed to do it", then it is submitted that it is much more difficult to hold that a party "agreed to do it" for the purposes of the tort but did not "agree to do it" for the purposes of the contract.[906] So, in *Outram v Academy Plastics Ltd*[907] the Court of Appeal held that where a contract of employment did not contain an express or implied term imposing on the employer a duty to inform his employee of a right arising from the contract, no duty of care in the tort of negligence would be imposed to the same effect based on an assumption of responsibility or otherwise.

1–161 **The contractual regime.** Both common law and legislation attach particular legal consequences to the classification of a claim as contractual and together these consequences can be considered to form the "contractual regime". As has been noted, some rules of this regime are significantly different from their counterparts in the law of torts, particularly in the context of rules as to the capacity of minors, damages, limitation of actions and the conflict of laws.[908] It is clear from the decision of the House of Lords in *Henderson v Merrett Syndicates Ltd*[909] that, in principle, the option of a party to a contract to sue in tort rather than in contract attracts the application to his claim of those rules incidental to tort, since on the facts of that case proceeding in tort allowed the plaintiffs to avoid the expiry of the limitation period for their action for breach of contract. However, the general terms of the acceptance by the House of Lords of a party's option to sue in tort (if one is established on the facts) rather than in contract supports the converse of this proposition, so that a party who could sue in tort, but chooses instead to sue in contract, thereby gains whatever advantages may be had from those rules which are incidental to claims in contract. However, it is submitted that these general effects of an option will not be universally followed by the courts (as the example of contractual capacity of minors will show) and, perhaps more importantly, where (even before *Henderson v Merrett Syndicates Ltd*) the courts have accepted a claimant's option, they have sometimes reduced the practical differences between the rules incidental to one or other basis of liability, so that the choice of legal basis does not affect the outcome of the case.

1–162 **Capacity of minors.** A minor's capacity to make a contract and to commit a tort are very different.[910] However, as has been seen, a party to a contract with a minor cannot in general avoid a minor's contractual incapacity by suing in tort where to do so would subvert the policy of the common law in protecting minors from making unfavourable contracts.[911] This approach is particularly clear in the context of a fraudulent misrepresentation by a minor as to his age,[912] but has been

[906] cf. *Tesco Stores Ltd v The Norman Hitchcox Partnership Ltd* [1998] 56 Con. L.R. 52, 163–165.
[907] [2000] I.R.L.R. 499 at [21]–[23].
[908] See above, paras 1–122—1–125.
[909] [1995] 2 A.C. 145.
[910] See below, paras 8–046—8–047.
[911] See above, para.1–125.
[912] *Johnson v Pye* (1665) 1 Sid. 258.

applied to other torts.[913] However, the courts have allowed a person who has contracted with a minor to sue the latter in tort, but only if the minor's tort can be considered as arising *independently* of the contract.[914] For example, in one case a minor who hired a mare "merely for a ride" and was warned at the hiring that she was unfit for jumping, having lent her to a friend who killed her by that act, was held liable in the tort of trespass which was "wholly independent of any contract".[915] Here, it cannot be said that the tort was unrelated to the contract: the tort consisted in permitting something to be done which the minor had been expressly forbidden by the contract to do.[916] In this type of case, the courts are concerned to limit the protection which the rules of contractual capacity give to a minor where this policy is considered to be outweighed by the tort's appeal for sanction and this is the case where a contractual permission for use of property by the minor is exceeded.[917]

Damages. There are important differences in the rules under which damages are awarded for breach of contract and in tort.[918] However, in cases of concurrence of liability in contract and tort, in many cases the courts have found means to prevent a claimant recovering more damages merely by the way in which his claim is put. Thus, although a claim for breach of contract can compensate the claimant for loss of his expectation or performance interest, whereas a claim in tort can compensate only his status quo interest,[919] in cases of concurrence of liability the courts are slow to allow the claimant to recover damages based on the former measure merely because the claim can be classified as contractual, and instead award damages for loss of his "general expectations".[920] In this type of case, indeed, the significant distinction appears to be between cases where the content of the contractual obligation is to take reasonable care and where it is stricter, a "guarantee" that something is the case or will occur.[921] 1–163

This has already been seen in relation to pre-contractual statements which are held to have been incorporated into the contract,[922] but that the proper distinction in these cases turns on the content of the defendant's obligation, rather than on the mere classification of his liability can be supported by other cases which concern professional negligence, whether contractual or tortious. In *Ford v White & Co*[923] a firm of solicitors was sued for contractual[924] negligence by the plaintiffs who had been advised that a particular restrictive covenant did not 1–164

---

913 See below, para.8–046.

914 See below, para.8–047.

915 *Burnard v Haggis* (1863) 32 L.J.N.S. 189, 191, per Keating J. This passage does not appear in the other report at (1863) 14 C.B.(N.S.) 45.

916 (1863) 14 C.B. (N.S.) 45, 53, (1863) 32 L.J.N.S. 189, 191.

917 See also *Ballett v Mingay* [1943] K.B. 281.

918 See above, paras 1–122—1–123.

919 See above, para.1–122 and below, paras 6–051, 26–002.

920 See above, para.1–122.

921 And cf. Cane, *Tort Law and Economic Interests*, 2nd edn (1996), pp.142–145 and Whittaker (1996) 16 O.J.L.S. 191, 207 et seq.

922 See above, para.1–133.

923 [1964] 1 W.L.R. 885.

924 [1964] 1 W.L.R. 885 at 891.

affect a plot of land which they were intending to purchase (whereas it did).[925] The plaintiffs' claim for the difference between the value of the property with and without the restriction was rejected by the court. Although Pennycuick J. accepted that in general damages for breach of contract should put the injured party in "as good a situation as if the contract had been performed",[926] this did not mean that the plaintiffs should be put in a better position than if the defendant solicitors had performed their duty, as though the latter had warranted that their view of the restrictive covenant was right.[927] A similar view was taken by the House of Lords in relation to a claim by a finance company against a valuer of a house intended as security for a loan.[928] Their Lordships held that the finance company could recover damages for the negligence of the valuer representing the difference in what the secured property could make if sold (less the expenses of this) and the amount which they had lent in reliance on the valuation. The House of Lords rejected the finance company's claim that it could recover the interest which it had hoped to charge the borrower on the transaction (but had not been able to), accepting the valuer's argument that this would put them in a position as if he had warranted performance of the loan contract by the borrower,[929] rather than the proper damages for the valuer's negligence.[930] *Thake v Maurice*[931] supplies an example of this difference in the context of medical negligence. At first instance, Peter Pain J. had found on the facts that the defendant surgeon had warranted to his patient that a vasectomy operation would be successful,[932] but the majority of the Court of Appeal disagreed,[933] holding that the defendant could be held bound only to take reasonable care in the giving of information as to the effect of the operation and finding it unnecessary to distinguish for this purpose between claims of contractual or tortious negligence, referring to this as the "negligence claim".[934] However, Kerr L.J. disagreed with the majority's interpretation of the contract and would have upheld the existence of a contractual warranty as to the success of the operation (the "contractual claim").[935] If this approach had been accepted, he considered that it would affect the

[925] And cf. *County Personnel (Employment Agency) Ltd v Alan R. Pulver & Co* [1987] 1 W.L.R. 916, where the court did not generally feel it necessary to classify the claim beyond that it was for negligence, though the test of remoteness applied was found in *Hadley v Baxendale* (1854) 9 Exch. 341: *County Personnel (Employment Agency) Ltd v Alan R. Pulver & Co* [1987] 1 W.L.R. 916 at 926.

[926] [1964] 1 W.L.R. 885, 887, citing Lord Haldane in *British Westinghouse Electric & Manufacturing Co Ltd v Underground Electric Rlys Co of London Ltd* [1912] A.C. 673, 689.

[927] [1964] 1 W.L.R. 885 at 888. As the property with the restriction was worth the price which they paid, the plaintiffs' loss was held to be nil: at [891]. cf. *Murray v Lloyd* [1989] 1 W.L.R. 1260.

[928] *Swingcastle Ltd v Alistair Gibson* [1991] 2 A.C. 223. cf. *Banque Bruxelles Lambert SA v Eagle Star Insurance Co Ltd; sub nom. South Australia Asset Management Corp v York Montague Ltd* [1997] A.C. 191 especially at 216–217, and see below, para.26–079.

[929] *Swingcastle Ltd v Alistair Gibson* [1991] 2 A.C. 223, 225.

[930] *Swingcastle Ltd v Alistair Gibson* [1991] 2 A.C. 223 at 238. While the House of Lords noted that the action before it was founded in tort, it did not consider the principles applicable to be any different from those in contract.

[931] [1986] 1 Q.B. 644.

[932] [1986] 1 Q.B. 644 at 658.

[933] [1986] 1 Q.B. 644 at 685, 688.

[934] [1986] 1 Q.B. 644 at 679 (Kerr L.J.), with whom Neill and Nourse L.JJ. agreed on this point: at 684, 685.

[935] [1986] 1 Q.B. 644 at 678.

damages recoverable by the plaintiffs, as damages in tort (i.e. the negligence claim) would be lower than those in contract.[936] In tort, damages for pain and suffering caused by the pregnancy should be reduced to take into account the distress of having to undergo an abortion (which *would* have been the case even if the patient had been properly advised as to the risk of pregnancy after the operation), but this was not the case in contract,[937] where if the defendant's warranty had not been broken the plaintiff's wife would not have become pregnant and so would not have suffered either proceeding. It is clear, however, that though put in terms of a contrast between tort and contract, the contrast which Kerr L.J. was intending to draw was between a duty to take reasonable care whether in tort or contract and a contractual duty to see that a particular result occurs.

Remoteness of damage. Another important difference between claims in tort and contract is said to be found in relation to the applicable tests of remoteness of damage.[938] In contract, the court asks whether the kind of loss is within the reasonable contemplation of the parties,[939] whereas in the tort of negligence, it asks whether the type of harm is reasonably foreseeable.[940] Although the difference between these has been termed "semantic, not substantial",[941] members of the House of Lords in *The Heron II*[942] considered, and some authors agree,[943] that a real difference in the two tests exists in relation to the degree of probability required, the position in contract being less generous than that in tort. However, where a case concerns concurrent liability in tort and contract, the courts are unwilling to allow the way in which the claimant puts his claim to affect the quantum of damages recoverable. Thus, in the Court of Appeal's decision in *H. Parsons (Livestock) Ltd v Uttley Ingham & Co Ltd*[944] which was such a case, Scarman L.J., with whom Orr L.J. agreed, assimilated the tests of remoteness in tort and in contract.[945] On the other hand, the "foreseeability test" of remoteness 1–165

936 [1986] 1 Q.B. 644 at 683. This point had been agreed by the parties.

937 [1986] 1 Q.B. 644.

938 Cartwright (1996) 55 C.L.J. 488 and see Cane at pp.145–147, for a discussion of the different treatment in tort and contract of damages for "lost chances."

939 See below, paras 26–051 et seq.

940 *Overseas Tankship (UK) Ltd v Morts Dock & Engineering Co Ltd, The Wagon Mound (No.1)* [1961] A.C. 388.

941 *H. Parsons (Livestock) Ltd v Uttley Ingham & Co Ltd* [1978] Q.B. 791, 807. See similarly *Banque Bruxelles Lambert SA v Eagle Star Insurance Co Ltd* [1995] Q.B. 375, 405, per Sir Thomas Bingham M.R. (though the decision of the Court of Appeal was reversed on other grounds *sub nom. South Australia Asset Management Corp v York Montague Ltd* [1997] A.C. 191).

942 *Koufos v C. Czarnikow Ltd* [1969] 1 A.C. 350, 385–386, 422–423 and cf. at 413 and see below, para.26–057.

943 See Harris, Campbell and Halson, *Remedies in Contract and Tort*, 2nd edn (2002), pp.331–333.

944 [1978] Q.B. 791.

945 [1978] Q.B. 791 at 806–807. Lord Denning, M.R. agreed with the result of the majority, but justified it by drawing a distinction between claims for physical damage and ones for economic loss: at 802–804. For further discussion of this decision, see Burrows, *Remedies for Torts and Breach of Contract*, 3rd edn (2004), pp.88 et seq.; Cane at pp.146–147. cf. *Galoo Ltd v Bright Grahame Murray* [1994] 1 W.L.R. 1360, 1369 where Glidewell L.J. adopted an approach to causation which he considered applicable to a claim for breach of contract and to one in "tort in a situation analogous to a breach of contract".

of damage[946] does not apply to claims for damages in the tort of deceit, where the claimant can recover all the damage directly flowing from the tortious act,[947] and the Court of Appeal has made clear that the latter test also applies to claims for damages under s.2(1) of the Misrepresentation Act 1967, whose imposition rests on a fiction of fraud.[948] This suggests that in some cases a representee will have an advantage in claiming damages for misrepresentation, rather than for breach of a contractual warranty which results from the incorporation of a statement into the contract,[949] as the former allows recovery of all losses flowing from the misrepresentation even if unforeseeable, "provided that they [are] not otherwise too remote".[950]

1–166 **Contributory negligence.** In *Forsikringsaktieselskapet Vesta v Butcher*,[951] the Court of Appeal took a very similar approach to the defence of contributory negligence as it had done in *H. Parsons (Livestock) Ltd v Uttley Ingham & Co Ltd*[952] to remoteness of damage, and held that while s.1 of the Law Reform (Contributory Negligence) Act 1945 does not in general apply to claims for breach of contract so as to allow a court to reduce any award of damages on the ground of contributory negligence, it does apply to claims based on the breach of a contractual obligation to take reasonable care ("contractual negligence") as long as this is concurrent with liability for breach of a duty of care in tort.[953] This approach leads to the paradox that a court's recognition of a duty of care in the tort of negligence in *addition* to and concurrent with a contractual obligation to take reasonable care owed to a claimant may lead to the *reduction* of the latter's damages on the ground of contributory negligence, whereas its refusal to do so would rule out such a reduction.[954]

1–167 **Limitation of actions.** As has been seen, differences as to the rules of limitation of actions exist according to whether the claim is brought in tort or contract[955] and this has often been a reason for a claimant to put a claim in tort rather for breach of contract. Traditionally, the courts allowed a claimant's choice whether to sue for breach of contract or in tort to determine which of the two regimes of limitation will apply and this practice was confirmed in *Henderson v*

---

[946] *The Wagon Mound (No.1)* [1961] A.C. 388.

[947] *Doyle v Olby (Ironmongers) Ltd* [1969] 2 Q.B. 158.

[948] *Royscott Trust Ltd v Rogerson* [1991] 2 Q.B. 297; and see below, paras 6–070—6–071.

[949] See above, para.1–133.

[950] *Royscott Trust Ltd v Rogerson* [1991] 2 Q.B. 297 at 307, per Balcombe L.J.

[951] [1989] A.C. 852, 858.

[952] [1978] Q.B. 791.

[953] And see *Gran Gelato Ltd v Richcliff (Group) Ltd* [1992] Ch. 560; *Youell v Bland Welch & Co Ltd (No.2)* [1990] 2 Lloyd's Rep. 431; *Barclays Bank Plc v Fairclough Building Ltd* [1995] Q.B. 214; *Barclays Bank Plc v Fairclough Building Ltd (No.2)* [1995] I.R.L.R. 605; *UCB Bank Plc v Hepherd Winstandley & Pugh* [1999] Lloyd's Rep. P.N. 963, and see below, para.26–049.

[954] *Barclays Bank Plc v Fairclough Building Ltd (No.2)* [1995] I.R.L.R. 605.

[955] In particular, in principle, accrual of actions for breach of contract occurs on breach, whereas accrual for actions in tort occurs when the damage is suffered. The latter rule has caused not inconsiderable difficulty in cases for negligently caused economic loss: see *D.W. Moore & Co Ltd v Ferrier* [1988] 1 W.L.R. 267, 279–280; *Iron Trades Mutual Insurance Co Ltd v J.K. Buckenham Ltd* [1990] 1 All E.R. 808; *Bell v Peter Browne & Co* [1990] 2 Q.B. 495; *F.G. Whitley & Sons & Co Ltd v Thomas Bickerton* (1993) 07 E.G. 100 and see above, para.1–124.

Merrett Syndicates Ltd.[956] However, although the general rule is that an action in contract accrues on its breach, whereas an action in tort accrues only on damage being suffered by the claimant,[957] in those cases where the courts accept that the claimant would have had[958] a claim for pure economic loss in the tort of negligence concurrent with a claim in contract, their approach has been to assimilate the two rules as to accrual, by finding that the claimant suffered damage for the purposes of the rule in tort at the same date as the breach of contract.[959] On the other hand, rather than reducing differences of rule as to limitation of actions in contract and in tort, the Latent Damage Act 1986 added a further one, as its provision according to which "negligence actions" for latent damage can accrue on the latter's discovery rather than on its occurrence, has been held to apply only to actions based on negligence in *tort*.[960]

The conflict of laws: jurisdiction. It was clearly established at common law that in cases with a foreign element where English law allows a person alternative claims in contract and in tort, his election between them brings with it the appropriate rules both of jurisdiction and choice of law.[961] However, Council Regulation of 2001 on jurisdiction and the recognition and enforcement of judgments in civil and commercial matters now governs jurisdiction both in "matters relating to a contract" and "matters relating to tort".[962] In a case where English substantive law would in principle allow a claimant to choose whether to put his claim in terms of contract or of tort, it would appear instead that the European Court of Justice would regard the claim as "relating to a contract" for this purpose and so outside the scope of the jurisdictional rule for tort.[963] 1–168

[956] [1995] 2 A.C. 145. In *Midland Bank Trust Co Ltd v Hett, Stubbs & Kemp* [1979] Ch. 384, it was held that a claim in tort could exist even if the claim in contract was statute-barred, though the contract claim still existed on the facts. In *Pirelli General Cable Works Ltd v Oscar Faber & Partners* [1983] 2 A.C. 1, a case in which the plaintiff's claim in contract was statute-barred, the House of Lords had to decide when a claim in tort accrued, on the plaintiff's suffering of the damage or on its discovery: at 12. This discussion would have been pointless if the expiry of the contractual limitation period had been thought to have prevented any concurrent claim in tort even if the latter's limitation period had not expired.

[957] *Pirelli General Cable Works Ltd v Oscar Faber & Partners* [1983] 2 A.C. 1 at 19 and see above para.1–124.

[958] i.e. apart from the question whether the claim is statute-barred.

[959] See *D.W. Moore & Co Ltd v Ferrier* [1988] 1 W.L.R. 267, 280; *Iron Trades Mutual Insurance Co Ltd v J.K. Buckenham Ltd* [1990] 1 All E.R. 808, 820–821; *Bell v Peter Browne & Co* [1990] 2 Q.B. 495, 501–504; *Lee v Thompson* [1989] 40 E.G. 89; *Havenledge Ltd v Graeme John & Partners* [2001] Lloyd's Rep. P.N. 223 at [35] et seq. cf. *Forster v Outred & Co* [1982] 1 W.L.R. 86; *F.G. Whitley & Sons Co Ltd v Thomas Bickerton* (1993) 07 E.G. 100 at 108 and see Cane at pp.134–136.

[960] *Iron Trades Mutual Insurance Co Ltd v J.K.Buckenham* [1990] 1 All E.R. 808, see above, para.1–124.

[961] *Matthews v Kuwait Bechtel Corp* [1959] 2 Q.B. 57; *Coupland v Arabian Gulf Oil Co* [1983] 1 W.L.R. 1136 and see *Dicey and Morris on The Conflict of Laws*, 11th edn (1987), Vol.1, pp.328, 329, 345.

[962] Regulation 44/2001 arts 5(1) and 5(3). This Regulation (which came into force on March 1, 2002) replaced the Convention on Jurisdiction and the Enforcement of Judgments in Civil and Commercial Matters 1968 ("the Brussels Convention") and see Dicey, *Morris and Collins on The Conflict of Laws*, 14th edn (2006), paras 11–013—11–018.

[963] *Kalfelis v Schröder* (189/87) [1988] E.C.R. 5565, 5577 (A.G. Darmon), 5585 and see Dicey, *Morris and Collins on the Conflict of Laws*, 14th edn (2006), paras 11–284, 11–299.

Moreover, the classification of a claim as contractual or tortious for these purposes is in principle a matter for European Community law as these concepts should have an "autonomous" interpretation.[964] This view of the position was taken by the Court of Appeal in *Source Ltd v TUV Rheinland Holding AG.*[965] In that case, the plaintiffs claimed that the English courts had jurisdiction to hear their claim in tortious negligence against the defendants, a claim which arose out of and was concurrent with a claim against them for breach of their contractual obligation to exercise reasonable care and skill in presenting a report following the inspection of goods which they (the plaintiffs) had wished to import from China and Taiwan. The Court of Appeal noticed that the European Court of Justice in *Kalfelis v Schröder*,[966] had held that the phrase "matters relating to tort" in art.5(3) of the Brussels Convention (the predecessor to the Council Regulation of 2001) refers to:

> "... all actions which seek to establish the liability of a defendant and which are not related to a 'contract' within the meaning of Article 5(1)."[967]

For Staughton L.J., with whom Waite and Aldous L.JJ. agreed, this means that a claim which may be brought under a contract or independently of a contract on the same facts, save that a contract does not need to be established, is excluded from art.5(3) by the European Court's words "which are not related to a 'contract' within the meaning of Art.5(1)".[968] In the result, therefore, both the contractual and tortious claims of the plaintiffs "related to a contract" and they could not by relying on art.5(3) bring the tortious claim before the English courts.[969]

1–169 **Conflict of laws: applicable law.** By contrast, although the matter is not free from doubt, it would seem that there is nothing in the Rome Convention on the Law Applicable to Contractual Obligations[970] to prevent such a person from framing his claim in tort so as to attract the choice of law rules applicable to that

---

[964] *Netherlands State v Rüffer* (814/79) [1980] E.C.R. 3807, 3832–3833, 3836; *Kalfelis v Schröder* (C-189/87) [1998] E.C.R. 5565; *Jakob Handte & Co GmbH v Société Traitements Mécano-chimiques des Surfaces (TMCS)* (C-26/91) [1993] I.L.Pr. 5 and see *Dicey and Morris and Collins*, 14th edn (2006), paras 11–284, 11–299.

[965] [1998] Q.B. 54.

[966] *Kalfelis v Schröder* (189/87) [1988] E.C.R. 5565.

[967] [1988] E.C.R. 5565 at [5585].

[968] [1998] Q.B. 54, 63.

[969] The decision of the Court of Appeal in *Source Ltd v TUV Rheinland Holding A.G.* [1998] Q.B. 54 is held to represent the law by *Dicey & Morris and Collins on the Conflict of Laws*, 14th edn (2006), para.11–299 but its authority was doubted by Tuckey J. in *Raiffeisen Zentralbank Osterreich Aktiengesellschaft v National Bank of Greece S.A.* [1999] 1 Lloyd's Rep. 408, 411 on the basis that its wide approach to art.5(1) is inconsistent with the restrictive approach taken by the HL in *Kleinwort Benson Ltd v Glasgow City Council* [1999] 1 A.C. 153. See also *Domicrest Ltd v Swiss Bank Corp* [1999] Q.B. 548, 561.

[970] Introduced into English law by the Contracts (Applicable Law) Act 1990 and see generally, below, paras 30–017 et seq. The Rome Convention is to be replaced by Regulation (EC) No.593 of the European Parliament and of the Council on the law applicable to contractual obligations ("Rome I") [2008] OJ L 177/6. The UK has announced its intention of applying to the Council and Commission for their consent to the UK's participation in the Regulation.

basis of liability, rather than in contract whose applicable law would be determined by that Convention.[971] And the notion of contract for the purposes of the Rome Convention is likely to be given an autonomous interpretation and follow in this respect the interpretation given to "matters relating to contract" for the purposes of the Brussels Convention (and therefore the Council Regulation of 2001).[972] But even if a claimant is allowed to claim in tort rather than in contract so as generally to avoid the law applicable to the contract, the latter may be relevant, for example, if its contract law grants a defence to the defendant.[973] However, the law governing *non-contractual* obligations is set to change on the coming into force of the Regulation of the European Parliament and of the Council on the law applicable to non-contractual obligations ("Rome II Regulation") which will apply to all Member States from January 11, 2009.[974] This Regulation makes specific provision for the law applicable to some situations which in many national domestic laws exist at the borderline of contract and tort, notably pre-contractual liability[975] and product liability.[976] Moreover, the general rule applicable to a non-contractual obligation[977] arising from a tort/delict ("the law of the country in which the damage occurs"[978]) has an exception where: ". . . it is clear from all the circumstances of the case that the tort/delict is manifestly more closely connected with a country other than," this law; and for this purpose it is provided that:

> "A manifestly closer connection with another country might be based in particular on a preexisting relationship between the parties, *such as a contract*, that is closely connected with the tort/delict in question."[979]

Finally, the Rome II Regulation permits in principle the parties to agree to submit their non-contractual obligations to the law of their choice (subject to certain conditions)[980]: here, therefore, the contract can change the law otherwise applicable to the tort.

(d) *The Influence of Contract on Tort beyond Privity*

Introduction. One of the most basic characteristics of liability in tort is that it can exist in the absence of any contractual relationship existing between the parties: there is in general no need for any voluntary element on the part of 1–170

---

[971] *Dicey, Morris and Collins on the Conflict of Laws*, 14th edn (2006), paras 32R–061 et seq.

[972] *Dicey, Morris and Collins* at paras 32–023—32–024.and see below, para.30–031.

[973] *Dicey, Morris and Collins* at paras 33–085, 35–048—35–049 referring to *Sayers v International Drilling Co* [1971] 1 W.L.R. 1176; *Coupland v Arabian Gulf Oil Co* [1983] 1 W.L.R. 1136.

[974] Regulation 864/2007 and see *Dicey, Morris and Collins on The Conflict of Laws*, First Supplement, paras 35–165 et seq.

[975] Regulation 864/2007 art.12 ("culpa in contrahendo" on which see above, para.1–136).

[976] Regulation 864/2007 art.5.

[977] "Non-contractual obligation" is to be given an "autonomous" interpretation: Regulation 864/2007 recital 11.

[978] Regulation 864/2007 art.4(1).

[979] Regulation 864/2007 art.4(3) (emphasis added).

[980] Regulation 864/2007 art.14.

someone on whom duties or liabilities in tort are imposed.[981] However, a contract may affect liabilities in tort beyond its parties either positively or negatively. Positively, in certain circumstances someone not party to a contract, C, may be liable in tort for behaviour which induces breach of B's contract with A (the tort of inducing breach of contract)[982] and, secondly, A may be liable to C for threatening B that he will break his contract with B (so-called "three-party" intimidation).[983] A contract may have a negative effect on torts involving third parties in two ways. First, in certain circumstances the fact that A and B are parties to a contract has sometimes been seen as a reason for refusing to impose or for modifying any liability in tort in A to C. This idea, long derided as the "contract fallacy", enjoyed during the later 1980s and early 1990s a resurgence of judicial popularity in the context of liability for pure economic loss in the tort of negligence, and to a much lesser extent, in the context of liability in the same tort for damage to property.[984] However, since 1994 the courts have taken rather different approaches to these questions, in general coralling liability in negligence for pure economic loss within the doctrine of "assumption of responsibility" and treating the disruption of contractual arrangements as a possible reason of policy for refusing to accept a novel duty of care. Secondly, the existence of a contract between A and B may be a reason for refusing to impose liability on C to either A or B, depending on the terms of the contract between A and B. This issue arises clearly in the context of the question whether A and B can by contract ensure that a third party, C, enjoys the benefit of an exemption clause so as to be protected from liability to A or B, whether or not C is in privity of contract with that person. These situations will be examined in turn.

1–171 **The tort of inducing breach of contract.** It was clearly established by *Lumley v Gye*[985] in 1853 that if A intentionally induces B to break her contract with C, then A can be liable in damages for any harmful consequences that this causes C[986] or restrained by injunction from continuing to prejudice C's contractual rights in this way.[987] The courts accept that in this way C may be able to recover more damages against A than he would be able to against B, this being seen as a reason for imposing the liability in tort, rather than for denying it.[988] While at one time this liability in tort was held to extend to cases where A's interference with C's rights does not constitute a breach of contract by reason, for

---

[981] See above, para.1–119. cf. below, paras 1–179—1–184 on liability in the tort of negligence beyond privity on the basis of an "assumption of responsibility".

[982] See below, para.1–171.

[983] See below, para.1–171. Contracts may have other consequences for the incidence of liability in tort. For example, where A has sold goods to B, who has resold them to C, the question whether the contract between A and B is void for mistake or merely voidable for fraud determines whether title to the property has passed to B and therefore whether C is liable to A in the tort of conversion: see *Ingram v Little* [1961] 1 Q.B. 31; *Lewis v Averay* [1973] 1 W.L.R. 510; *Shogun Finance Ltd v Hudson* [2003] UKHL 62, [2004] 1 A.C. 919 and below, paras 5–078 et seq.

[984] See below, paras 1–174, 1–177 et seq.

[985] (1853) 2 E.B. 216.

[986] As was the case in *Lumley v Gye* (1853) 2 E.B. 216 itself.

[987] As was the case in *Torquay Hotel Co Ltd v Cousins* [1969] 2 Ch. 106 (though as explained in the text the extended view of the tort in this case will not be followed after *OGB Ltd v Allan, Douglas v Hello! Ltd, Mainstream Properties Ltd v Young* [2007] UKHL 21, [2008] 1 A.C.).

[988] *Lumley v Gye* (1853) 2 E.B. 216 at 234.

example, of the presence of a force majeure clause, the House of Lords has since held that it may not arise in the absence of a breach of contract: the tort liability is accessory to the breach of contract.[989] Moreover, liability under this tort does not extend to interference with remedies arising out of a broken contract. Thus, where A has received shares from B in breach of B's contractual obligations to C, while A may be ordered to retransfer the shares to B and may be restrained by injunction from retransferring them to D, it is no *tort* in A to retransfer them nor in D to receive them.[990]

The tort of causing loss by unlawful means: "three-party intimidation." The tort of causing loss by unlawful means is committed, inter alia,[991] where A threatens B that he will commit an act, or use means, unlawful as against B, as a result of which B does or refrains from doing some act which he is entitled to do, thereby causing damage to C,[992] an instance of tortious liability often called "three-party intimidation".[993] In *Rookes v Barnard*,[994] the House of Lords recognised the existence of this liability in tort and further held that a threatened breach of contract by A can constitute unlawful means for this purpose.[995] In the Court of Appeal the view had been expressed that to extend the tort to threats of breach of contract "would overturn or outflank some elementary principles of contract law",[996] notably, privity of contract.[997] However, for the House of Lords the two causes of action (for breach of contract and for the "tort of intimidation") are "quite independent",[998] "the vice of [C's] argument is the threat to break and not the breach itself".[999] Thus, it is the independence of liability in tort which allows its extension into what had previously been an exclusively contractual domain.[1000] 1–172

A contractor's liability beyond privity and independent torts. At common law, in principle privity of contract prevents any breach by A of a term of a contract made with B from giving rise to any contractual liability in A to C, a third party to the contract. This position has been qualified significantly by the 1–173

[989] *OGB Ltd v Allan, Douglas v Hello! Ltd, Mainstream Properties Ltd v Young* [2007] UKHL 21, [2008] 1 A.C. 1 especially at [44] and [189] not following *Torquay Hotel Co Ltd v Cousins* [1969] 2 Ch. 106; *Merkur Island Shipping Corp v Laughton* [1983] 2 A.C. 570, 607–610 and cf. Deakin, Johnston and Markesinis, *Markesinis's and Deakin's Tort Law*, 6th edn (2008), pp.582–585.

[990] *Law Debenture Trust Corp Plc v Ural Caspian Oil Corp Ltd* [1994] 3 W.L.R. 1221 especially at 1231–1232.

[991] For "two-party" intimidation see above, and *Clerk & Lindsell on Torts*, 19th edn (2006) paras 25–85—25–86.

[992] *Clerk & Lindsell on Torts*, para.24–65.

[993] See, though, *OGB Ltd v Allan, Douglas v Hello! Ltd, Mainstream Properties Ltd v Young* [2007] UKHL 21, [2008] 1 A.C. 1 at [6]–[10] where the terminiology of "tort of intimidation" was criticised.

[994] [1964] A.C. 1129.

[995] This position is consistent with the interpretation of "unlawful means" in *OGB Ltd v Allan, Douglas v Hello! Ltd, Mainstream Properties Ltd v Young* [2007] UKHL 21 at [49]–[51], [162], [266]–[270], [302], [320].

[996] *Rookes v Barnard* [1963] 1 Q.B. 623, 695, per Pearson L.J.

[997] *Rookes v Barnard* [1963] 1 Q.B. 623.

[998] [1964] A.C. 1129, 1207, per Lord Devlin.

[999] [1964] A.C. 1129, 1200–1201, per Lord Hodson and see also 1168, 1234–1235.

[1000] cf. Wedderburn (1964) 27 M.L.R. 257 at 263–267.

Contract (Rights of Third Parties) Act 1999, which allows parties to a contract to create rights in third parties (not being party to the contract) in certain circumstances.[1001] But can C sue A in tort instead? First, it is clear that the mere breach of a contract by A does not in itself give rise to liability in tort to C. As Pollock stated in 1887[1002]:

> "... there is a certain tendency to hold that facts which constitute a contract cannot have any other legal effect. We think we have shown that such is not really the law . . . the authorities commonly relied on for this proposition[1003] really prove something different and much more rational, namely that if A breaks his contract with B ... that is not of itself sufficient to make A liable to C, a stranger to the contract, for consequential damage."

Secondly, therefore, where the facts which constitute a breach of contract in A to B also constitute the grounds of an *independent* liability in tort in A to C, the existence of that contract does not in itself prevent liability in A to C.[1004] Thus, as has been seen, where A *threatens* to break his contract with B, this may give rise to an action in C in the tort of causing loss by unlawful means[1005] and this tort may also apply to cases of actual as opposed to threatened breach of contract.[1006] Similarly, where a tenant, A, commits an act which constitutes a breach of the terms of his lease with his landlord, B, this does not prevent his neighbour, C, from suing A in private nuisance for any harm which he suffers as a result as long as the conditions for the existence of that tort are fulfilled.[1007]

> "If it is the tenant who has undertaken the repair [*sci.* of the premises], of course he is liable, but his liability is based on the fact that he is the occupier of the premises; any additional obligation which he may have undertaken by contract with the landlord cannot affect his liability in tort to third parties."[1008]

On the other hand, where the landlord has undertaken to the tenant to repair, he can be liable in nuisance to a third party based on the control which this gives him despite not being an occupier[1009] in addition to his liability to the tenant.[1010] Finally, where an agent publishes defamatory material concerning the claimant, the fact that this publication also constitutes a breach of his contract actionable

[1001] See below, paras 18–088 et seq.
[1002] Pollock, *The Law of Torts*, 1st edn, pp.448–449.
[1003] Notably *Winterbottom v Wright* (1842) 10 M.W. 109 and see below, para.1–174.
[1004] Pollock at p.450.
[1005] See above, para.1–172.
[1006] cf. above, para.1–145. In either case, this tort is clearly restricted to situations where A has acted intentionally to injure C: *Rookes v Barnard* [1964] A.C. 1129, 1183; *OGB Ltd v Allan, Douglas v Hello! Ltd., Mainstream Properties Ltd v Young* [2007] UKHL 21, [2008] 1 A.C. 1 and see *Clerk & Lindsell on Torts* at para.25–65.
[1007] *Winfield and Jolowicz on Tort*, 13th edn (1989), pp.404–405.
[1008] *Winfield and Jolowicz* at pp.404–405 and see *Russell v Shenton* (1842) 3 Q.B. 449, 457.
[1009] *Payne v Rogers* (1794) 2 H.Bl. 350, 351; *Wringe v Cohen* [1940] 1 K.B. 229.
[1010] *St. Anne's Well Brewery Co v Roberts* (1929) 140 L.T. 1, 8. cf. Defective Premises Act 1972 ss.1, 4; and see Spencer (1974) C.L.J. 307, (1975) C.L.J. 48 and *Andrews v Schooling* [1991] 1 W.L.R. 783.

at the suit of his principal[1011] does not prevent the claimant from suing the agent in the tort of defamation.[1012]

Privity of contract and the tort of negligence.[1013] At two stages in the development of the tort of negligence, it has been argued that A's breach of contract to B should not be considered capable of giving rise to liability in this tort for harm caused to C. The leading nineteenth century authority was *Winterbottom v Wright*,[1014] in which the plaintiff was employed to drive a mail-coach by one Atkinson, who had been engaged to carry mail by the Postmaster-General. The latter had hired a coach from the defendant, who had undertaken to him that it would be kept in a fit, proper, safe and secure state. The plaintiff's claim for damages in respect of injuries suffered when the coach broke down on a journey owing to its dangerous state was rejected by the court, which accepted the defendant's contention that: 1–174

> "... wherever a wrong arises merely out of the breach of a contract ... whether the form in which the action is conceived be *ex contractu* or *ex delicto*, the party who made the contract alone can sue."[1015]

However, this approach[1016] was of course rejected by the House of Lords in *Donoghue v Stevenson*.[1017] As Lord Macmillan put it:

> "... there is no reason why the same set of facts should not give one person a right of action in contract and another person a right of action in tort."[1018]

The approach in *Winterbottom v Wright*[1019] came to be derided as the "contract fallacy".[1020]

[1011] It has been held to be a breach of contract for an agent to disclose a document which is libellous: *Weld-Blundell v Stephens* [1920] A.C. 956.

[1012] In *Weld-Blundell v Stephens* [1920] A.C. 956 the principal had been held liable in libel personally for publishing the defamatory statement, which had then been republished by the agent.

[1013] See also below, paras 18–022 et seq.

[1014] (1842) 10 M.W. 109.

[1015] (1842) 10 M.W. 109, 111, 114. See also *Tollit v Sherstone* (1839) 5 M.W. 283, 289 where Maule B. considered it: "[C]lear that an action of contract cannot be maintained by a person who is not a party to the contract; and the same principle extends to an action of tort arising out of a contract." Pollock, *Law of Torts*, p.449 supported the *decision* in *Winterbottom v Wright* (1842) 10 M.W. 109 on the ground that no bad faith or negligence in the defendant had been shown and cf. *Donoghue v Stevenson* [1932] A.C. 562, 589. cf. also Atiyah, *The Rise and Fall of Freedom of Contract* (1979), pp.501–505.

[1016] The approach was not universal: see *Payne v Rogers* (1794) 2 H.Bl. 350 (landlord liable to third party injured on highway owing to poor state of repair of premises as long as landlord had covenanted to repair) and *Gladwell v Steggall* (1839) 5 Bing. (N.C.) 733 (medical practitioner liable to patient where fees had been paid by patient's father).

[1017] [1932] A.C. 562. cf. the dissent of Lord Buckmaster on this ground at 568, 577–578 and see *Grant v Australian Knitting Mills Ltd* [1936] A.C. 85, 101–102.

[1018] [1932] A.C. 562, 610.

[1019] (1842) 10 M.W. 109.

[1020] See *Greene v Chelsea BC* [1954] 2 Q.B. 127, 138 and as late as 1983, *Rimmer v Liverpool City Council* [1985] Q.B. 1, 11.

1–175 **Liability for pure economic loss.** While the courts were still willing to extend liability in the tort of negligence, the "contractual environment" of a claim in the tort of negligence was even considered a ground for the imposition of a duty of care, rather than a reason for rejecting one. Thus, in *Hedley Byrne & Co Ltd v Heller & Partners Ltd*[1021] one of the circumstances on which the House of Lords relied for finding the existence of a "special relationship" so as to give rise to liability for pure economic loss caused by a negligent misstatement was that the relationship of the parties was "equivalent to contract".[1022] While Lord Devlin considered that the reason that the plaintiff's claim could not be considered contractual was the absence of consideration for the defendants' undertaking,[1023] on the facts there was also no obvious privity between the parties.[1024]

1–176 **The *Junior Books* case.** The courts' recognition of liability for negligently caused pure economic loss was taken one stage further in 1982 by the decision of the House of Lords in *Junior Books Ltd v Veitchi Co Ltd*,[1025] where it held that a specialist flooring sub-contractor who had built a defective but not dangerous floor could owe a duty of care to the owner of the building who had to replace it as a result.[1026] Clearly, there was no privity of contract between the parties, but the majority of their Lordships found that there was a "special relationship" between them, which again rested on a variety of factors, of which one was the fact that it fell "only just short of a direct contractual relationship".[1027] At the time of its decision, *Junior Books* appeared to mark a radical departure, for it allowed recovery of pure economic loss beyond privity of contract other than where it was consequential on the defendant's negligent misstatement. However, the fate of *Junior Books* was not a happy one, its approach to liability for pure economic loss not being followed by subsequent courts.[1028] While the courts gave many reasons in the many cases in which recovery for pure economic loss in the tort of negligence has been denied,[1029] in some cases the presence of a

---

[1021] [1964] A.C. 465.

[1022] [1964] at 525–526, 529 and cf. at 538.

[1023] [1964] A.C. 465 at 529.

[1024] The statement in question had been made by A (the defendants) to B at the latter's request (who had in turn been asked to do so by C), A knowing that the statement would be passed on to B's customer, C (the plaintiff). In these circumstances, A could only be considered in privity with C if B were treated as C's agent for this purpose.

[1025] [1983] 1 A.C. 520 and see below, paras 18–023.

[1026] As the case came to the House of Lords by way of a preliminary issue, it was not necessary to consider what damages would be recoverable nor whether the sub-contractor was negligent.

[1027] [1983] 1 A.C. 520, 533, per Lord Fraser of Tullybelton and cf. 542.

[1028] See *Governors of the Peabody Donation Fund v Sir Lindsay Parkinson & Co Ltd* [1985] A.C. 210; *Leigh & Sillavan Ltd v Aliakmon Shipping Co Ltd* [1986] A.C. 785; *Candlewood Navigation Corp Ltd v Mitsui O.S.K. Lines Ltd* [1986] A.C. 1; *Muirhead v Industrial Tank Specialities Ltd* [1986] Q.B. 507; *D. & F. Estates Ltd v Church Commissioners for England* [1989] A.C. 177; *Simaan General Contracting Co v Pilkington Glass Ltd (No.2)* [1988] Q.B. 758; *Yuen Kun Yeu v Att-Gen of Hong Kong* [1988] A.C. 175; *Business Computers International Ltd v Registrar of Companies and Alex Lawrie Factors* [1988] Ch. 229; *Pacific Associates v Baxter* [1990] 1 Q.B. 993; *Parker-Tweedale v Dunbar Bank Plc* [1991] Ch. 12; *Murphy v Brentwood DC* [1991] 1 A.C. 398; *Department of Environment v Thomas Bates & Son Ltd* [1991] 1 A.C. 499; *Punjab National Bank v De Boinville* [1992] 3 All E.R. 104; *Saipem SpA v Dredging VO2 BV* [1993] 2 Lloyd's Rep. 315.

[1029] See Stapleton (1991) 107 L.Q.R. 249.

contract or contracts has proven particularly important. In *Junior Books* itself, Lord Roskill noted that any exclusion clause in the main contract[1030] may exclude or modify the liability in the sub-contractor directly to the building owner,[1031] and Lord Fraser of Tullybelton considered that the terms of the sub-contract may have a similar effect.[1032] However, later courts considered the *possibility* that the imposition of a duty of care will upset contractual standards or allocations of risk as itself a reason for refusing to impose one, thereby preferring Lord Brandon's approach in his dissenting speech in *Junior Books*.[1033]

"Contractual structure" and liability in tort. Thus, the existence of a "contractual structure" of which the parties to the litigation are members but according to which they are not in privity of contract was relied on as a reason for refusing to impose liability for economic loss in the tort of negligence. For example, in *Balsamo v Medici*[1034] Walton J. refused to allow a claim in the tort of negligence by a principal against an unauthorised sub-agent on the ground that otherwise the *Anns* principle[1035] of the tort of negligence "will come perilously close to abrogating completely the concept of privity of contract".[1036] In 1987 in *Simaan General Contracting Co v Pilkington Glass Ltd (No.2)*,[1037] there was a chain of contracts, consisting of a building owner (A), a main building contractor (B), a sub-contractor (C) and a manufacturer of glass which had been incorporated into a building (D). The glass had failed to come up to specification and B, who had settled with A, claimed damages in the tort of negligence against D for the economic loss which it had thereby been caused. The Court of Appeal rejected this claim. According to Bingham L.J.: 1–177

> "Just as equity remedied the inadequacies of the common law, so has the law of torts filled gaps left by other causes of action where the interests of justice so required. I see no such gap here, because there is no reason why the claims beginning with [A] should not be pursued down the contractual chain."[1038]

1030 The relevant terms of neither this contract nor the subcontract were presented to the House of Lords: [1983] 1 A.C. 520, 538.

1031 [1983] 1 A.C. 520 at 546.

1032 [1983] 1 A.C. 520 at 533–534.

1033 [1983] A.C. 520, 550–552 and see *Greater Nottingham Co-operative Society Ltd v Cementation Piling & Foundations Ltd* [1989] Q.B. 71, 96 where Purchas L.J. noted that Lord Brandon's speech had subsequently achieved greater significance. This approach avoids the difficult question whether *liability* arising on breach of a recognised duty of care in respect of pure economic loss may be modified or excluded by either: (i) an exemption clause in A's contract with B restricting A's liability to C (*Simaan General Contracting Co v Pilkington Glass Ltd (No.2)* [1988] Q.B. 758, 782–783; 785–786); or (ii) an exemption clause in A's contract with B which attempts to exclude C's liability to A (*Southern Water Authority v Carey* [1985] 2 All E.R. 1077, 1093–1094) and see below, para.1–185 et seq.

1034 [1984] 1 W.L.R. 951 and see Whittaker (1985) 48 M.L.R. 86.

1035 This is to be found in Lord Wilberforce's speech in *Anns v Merton London BC* [1978] A.C. 728, 751–752. This principle itself has been subject to considerable judicial reservation: see *Governors of the Peabody Donation Fund v Sir Lindsay Parkinson & Co Ltd* [1985] A.C. 210 at 240–241; *Caparo Industries Plc v Dickman* [1990] 2 A.C. 605, 618.

1036 [1984] 1 W.L.R. 951, 959–960.

1037 [1988] Q.B. 758. cf. *Muirhead v Industrial Tank Specialities Ltd* [1986] Q.B. 507.

1038 [1988] Q.B. 758, 782 and cf. *Greater Nottingham Co-operative Society Ltd v Cementation Piling & Foundations Ltd* [1989] Q.B. 7, 99 and *Pacific Associates v Baxter* [1990] 1 Q.B. 993.

Thus the courts treated the fact that A owes a duty under a contract to B to be an important factor in denying liability to C for negligently caused pure economic loss[1039] and considered that where B owes a contractual duty to C, there is no good reason for adding an additional duty of care in A for C's benefit.[1040]

1–178 Nevertheless, at least in some situations the existence of a contractual duty in A to B was not allowed to rule out the existence of a duty of care in respect of pure economic loss owed by A to C concerning the same issue. This was the position in the decision of the House of Lords in *Smith v Eric S. Bush*,[1041] in which a valuer had been engaged by a mortgagee to report on a property of modest value to be bought by the plaintiff. The plaintiff bought the property in reliance on the report and suffered economic loss as a result. The House of Lords unanimously held that the valuer owed the plaintiff a duty of care in the circumstances, which included the fact that the valuer knew that the plaintiff would be told of their advice and that he would act in reliance on it. The House of Lords further held that a contractual disclaimer under which the valuer worked did not prevent the duty of care in tort from arising on the basis that it was incompatible with any "voluntary assumption of responsibility", but was to be treated as an exemption clause and subjected to the reasonableness test imposed by the Unfair Contract Terms Act 1977.[1042] Moreover, Lord Griffiths disapproved the notion of "assumption of responsibility" as a test for the imposition of a duty of care in the tort of negligence, considering it "not a helpful or realistic test of liability".[1043]

1–179 **Assumption of responsibility.** However, since 1994 the House of Lords has taken a very different approach to the imposition of liability for pure economic loss in the tort of negligence and by so doing has allowed liability to be imposed on one party to a contract beyond privity. The basis on which it has tended to choose to rely for the imposition of liability has been an "assumption of responsibility" in the defendant to the claimant, this idea being drawn from the Lords' earlier decision in *Hedley Byrne & Co Ltd v Heller & Partners Ltd*[1044] but

---

1039 *Pacific Associates v Baxter* [1990] 1 Q.B. 993 at 1023. And see *Macmillan v AW Knott Becker Scott* [1990] 1 Lloyd's Rep. 98 at 110–111; *Parker-Tweedale v Dunbar Bank Plc (No.1)* [1991] Ch. 12 (no duty of care in tort owed by mortgagor to beneficiary under trust of property subject to mortgage); *Verderame v Commercial Union Assurance Co Plc, The Times*, April 2, 1992 (no duty of care owed by insurance brokers employed by a company to the directors of that company); *Hemmens v Wilson Browne* [1994] 2 W.L.R. 323, 334–335 (no duty of care owed by solicitor to beneficiary of ineffective *inter vivos* transaction where the situation was not irremediable).

1040 *Gran Gelato Ltd v Richcliff (Group) Ltd* [1992] Ch. 560, 570–571, in which the court held that there is in normal conveyancing transactions no duty of care in the solicitor of a vendor of land to the buyer in respect of misstatements. On the facts, the court accepted that the duty owed by A, the vendor, to B, the buyer could be put equally in terms of contract or the tort of negligence: at 569, relying on *Esso Petroleum Co Ltd v Mardon* [1976] Q.B. 801.

1041 Joined with the decision in *Harris v Wyre Forest DC* [1990] 1 A.C. 831. cf. *Preston v Torfaen BC* [1993] N.P.C. 111.

1042 s.2(2).

1043 [1990] 1 A.C. 831 at 862. cf. at 846, per Lord Templeman.

1044 [1964] A.C. 465.

its application being extended beyond the context of negligent misstatement.[1045] This "broad principle of *Hedley Byrne*" or of "assumption of responsibility" has already been seen in relation to liability in the tort of negligence between the parties to a contract, but now its impact beyond the parties will be assessed. In this respect, three cases are of particular importance.[1046]

Henderson v Merrett Syndicates Ltd. The first and most important is *Henderson v Merrett Syndicates Ltd.*[1047] This case concerned claims in the tort of negligence by various underwriting members of Lloyd's ("Names") against the underwriting agents who had acted for them. In the case of the "indirect Names", with whom we are now concerned, they had entered agreements with underwriting agents, known as "members' agents", who advised "Names", inter alia, on their choice of syndicates and placed them on a syndicate once chosen, but who entrusted the placing of the insurance to others, "managing agents" for the syndicate which they had chosen. The claims of the "indirect Names" therefore bypassed two contracts: the first being the agency contract between themselves and the members' agents and the second being the sub-agency contract between the members' agents and the managing agents. Despite this, however, the House of Lords found no difficulty in finding a duty of care owed by the managing agents directly to the "indirect Names". Lord Goff of Chieveley, who gave the leading speech and with whom Lords Keith of Kinkel, Browne-Wilkinson, Mustill and Nolan concurred, based this decision on a finding of an assumption of responsibility by the managing agents to the "indirect Names", this being found in the managing agents' agreement to undertake the commission for the indirect Names, coupled with the formers' special skill. However, the wider significance of this decision was far from clear. Lord Goff: 1–180

> "... strongly suspect[ed] that the situation . . . [was] most unusual; and that in many cases in which a contractual chain comparable to that in the present case is constructed it may well prove to be inconsistent with an assumption of responsibility which has the effect of, so to speak, short circuiting the contractual structure so put in place by the parties."[1048]

With respect, no very clear indication was given as to what was special about the facts of *Henderson* for this purpose: the managing agents had agreed to take on their commission and were aware of the position of their ultimate principals, but then so are many other sub-agents. Clearly, the context of the Lloyd's insurance market may have played some part, but the precise nature of its role does not appear from the speeches. On the other hand, Lord Goff did see the case of a

---

[1045] Some courts have chosen rather to treat the various approaches to the imposition of a duty of care as alternative routes, to be tried in turn in relation to the facts before them: see *Bank of Credit and Commerce International (Overseas) Ltd (In Liquidation) v Price Waterhouse* [1998] P.N.L.R. 564, 583–586, per Sir Brian Neill; *Briscoe v Lubrizol* [2000] P.I.Q.R. P39.

[1046] The doctrine of "assumption of responsibility" had been relied on by Lord Goff in *Spring v Guardian Assurance Plc* [1995] 2 A.C. 296, 324 but it had not been argued before the House and his fellow judges chose to rely on other grounds for their decisions. For cases discussing "assumption of responsibility" between parties to a contract, see above, paras 1–141 et seq.

[1047] [1995] 2 A.C. 145 and see Whittaker (1996) 16 O.J.L.S. 191, especially 204–205, 219 et seq.

[1048] [1995] 2 A.C. 145 at 195.

claim by a building owner against his sub-contractor in respect of a failure to conform to the required standard as an example of where "ordinarily" such an assumption of responsibility would be inconsistent with a contractual structure.[1049] Clearly, then, it was not intended that any doubt should be thrown on the decision of the House in *Murphy v Brentwood DC.*[1050]

1–181 ***White v Jones.*** The second important decision is *White v Jones*,[1051] in which a majority of the House of Lords held that a solicitor who had negligently failed to execute a testament before the decease of the testator owed a duty of care in the tort of negligence to the would-be legatee under that testament. The House of Lords considered whether the legatee should be able to sue in contract, rather than in tort, the contract in question being between the testator and the defendant solicitor. While Lord Goff of Chieveley considered this attractive, he thought that it "would be open to criticism as an illegitimate circumvention of [the] long-established doctrines" of privity and consideration.[1052] Instead, he preferred to hold the defendant liable in tort on the basis that his "assumption of responsibility . . . should be held in law to extend" to the plaintiff, though the contract between the testator and the solicitor remained significant in that its terms set the content of the duty of care in tort.[1053] Lord Nolan also relied on the defendant's "assumption of responsibility", though apparently seeing this as real rather than (as with Lord Goff) deemed.[1054] Lord Browne-Wilkinson preferred to consider the facts before him as justifying the imposition of a duty of care as a matter of "justice and reasonableness" as an "extension of the principle of assumption of responsibility".[1055] By contrast, Lords Mustill and Keith of Kinkel dissented, finding no special reason why a special exception should be made in the circumstances, the latter expressing the view that the principle of privity of contract should not be circumvented by extending the law of tort.[1056] This decision of the majority is clearly a remarkable example of the willingness of our judges to find legal justifications for the imposition of a duty where they find it necessary in the interests of justice and, as both their own and the minority's speeches make clear, despite established principle, whether tortious or contractual. However, the speeches of their lordships in the case itself and subsequent judicial discussions of it have made clear that the situation in *White v Jones* was exceptional[1057] and the decision has not been as influential on subsequent judicial developments as has *Henderson v Merrett Syndicates Ltd.*[1058]

1–182 ***Williams v Natural Life Health Foods Ltd and Mistlin.*** The importance of *Henderson v Merrett Syndicates Ltd*, and more particularly, the significance of

[1049] [1995] 2 A.C. 145 at 196.
[1050] [1991] 1 A.C. 398.
[1051] [1995] 2 A.C. 207.
[1052] [1995] 2 A.C. 207 at 266.
[1053] [1995] 2 A.C. 207 at 268.
[1054] [1995] 2 A.C. 207 at 294.
[1055] [1995] 2 A.C. 207 at 270, 275–276.
[1056] [1995] 2 A.C. 207 at 251.
[1057] See, notably, *Williams v Natural Life Health Foods Ltd and Mistlin* [1998] 1 W.L.R. 830, 837, per Lord Steyn.
[1058] cf. the approach of the High Court of Australia in *R.F. Hill & Associates v Van Erp* [1997] 14 A.L.R. 687.

Lord Goff's exposition there of the principle of "assumption of responsibility" can be seen in the decision of the House of Lords in 1998 in *Williams v Natural Life Health Foods Ltd and Mistlin.*[1059] In that case, the second defendant, M, who had worked in the health food trade for several years, formed a company, the first defendant, to franchise the concept of health food shops. M was the company's managing director and principal shareholder, having only two employees. The plaintiffs approached the company with the view to acquiring a franchise, dealing with one of the employees, but also relying on a brochure produced by the company which advertised M's experience in the trade. The plaintiffs entered a franchise agreement with the company, but the turnover of the shop was substantially less than predicted by the company and they traded for only 18 months and at a loss. The question before the House of Lords was whether M owed the plaintiffs a duty of care so as to allow him to be liable personally in damages for the loss caused by their entering the contract of franchise. According to Lord Steyn, who gave judgment on behalf of the House, the governing principles for the case were to be found in the "extended *Hedley Byrne* principle" to be found in Lord Goff's speech in *Henderson v Merrett Syndicates Ltd*, which Lord Steyn saw as a:

> "... rationalisation or technique adopted by English law to provide a remedy for the recovery of damages in respect of economic loss caused by the negligent performance of services."[1060]

He noted that the test of "assumption of responsibility" is an objective one and this means that the primary focus of the courts should be on what was said or done by the defendant or on his behalf in dealings with the plaintiff. This meant that the question for the House was:

> "... whether the director, or anybody on his behalf, conveyed directly or indirectly to the prospective franchisees that the director assumed personal responsibility towards the prospective franchisees."[1061]

However, applying this principle to the facts, Lord Steyn held that there was not enough to show a personal assumption of responsibility in M to the plaintiffs: while the brochure produced by the company made clear that its expertise came from M's experience, in the absence of more and in particular of personal dealings with the plaintiffs, no duty of care arose.[1062]

Lord Steyn in *Williams v Natural Life Health Foods Ltd and Mistlin* accepted the view expressed by Lord Goff in *Henderson* that once a court finds that a defendant has "accepted responsibility" towards the plaintiff in the relevant sense, there is no need to investigate whether it is "just, fair and reasonable" to impose liability for pure economic loss.[1063] This aspect of Lord Goff's views has 1–183

[1059] [1998] 1 W.L.R. 830.
[1060] [1998] 1 W.L.R. 830 at 834.
[1061] [1998] 1 W.L.R. 830 at 836.
[1062] [1998] 1 W.L.R. 830 at 837–838.
[1063] [1998] 1 W.L.R. 830, 834.

already been discussed,[1064] but here a striking contrast can be noted with Lord Steyn's own approach to the imposition of a duty of care *not* based on an "assumption of responsibility" taken earlier in *Marc Rich & Co AG v Bishop Rock Marine Co.*[1065] In the latter case, the plaintiffs were cargo owners whose property was lost when the vessel in which it was carried sank. They claimed damages against the shipowners on the basis that the sinking had been caused by the latters' failure to act with due diligence in relation to the seaworthiness of the vessel at the beginning of the voyage, but they also claimed damages from a classification society, one of whose surveyors had inspected the vessel during its voyage and had recommended that its voyage should continue. Lord Steyn,[1066] considered that since *Dorset Yacht Co Ltd v Home Office*[1067] it had been settled law that considerations of fairness, justice and reasonableness as well as the elements of foreseeability and proximity are relevant to the imposition of a duty of care in the tort of negligence, whatever the nature of the harm sustained by the plaintiff and, therefore, including the situation where the plaintiff has sustained damage to property.[1068] On the facts before the House in *Marc Rich*, Lord Steyn considered that the property damage suffered by the cargo owners was only indirect as it was the shipowners rather than the classification society which were primary responsible for the vessel's sailing in an seaworthy condition nor was there any direct contact between the plaintiffs and the classification society and therefore no element of reliance so as to give rise to an assumption of responsibility in the sense explained by Lord Goff in *Henderson v Merrett Syndicates Ltd.*[1069] Even so, Lord Steyn was prepared to assume that there was sufficient proximity between the cargo owners and the classification society, but considered that it was not "fair, just and reasonable" to impose a duty of care. First, such a duty would outflank the bargain between the shipowners and the cargo-owners. He stated:

> "The dealings between shipowners and cargo owners are based on a contractual structure, the Hague Rules, and tonnage limitation on which the insurance of international trade depends . . . Underlying it is the system of double or overlapping insurance of the cargo. Shipowners take out liability risks insurance in respect of breaches of their duties of care in respect of the cargo. The insurance system is structured on the basis that the potential liability of shipowners to cargo owners is limited under the Hague Rules and by virtue of tonnage limitation provisions. And insurance premiums payable by owners obviously reflect such limitations on the shipowners' exposure."[1070]

While Lord Steyn found various other policy factors which argued against imposing a duty of care, including the non-profit-making nature of the defendant, the scale of the classification society's potential liability and the added complication to the settlement of proceedings concerning lost or damaged cargo of such

[1064] See above, para.1–142.
[1065] [1996] 1 A.C. 211.
[1066] Lords Keith of Kinkel, Jauncey of Tullichettle and Browne-Wilkinson agreed; Lord Lloyd of Berwick dissented.
[1067] [1970] A.C. 1004.
[1068] [1996] 1 A.C. 211, 235.
[1069] [1996] 1 A.C. 211 at 237–238.
[1070] [1996] 1 A.C. 211, 239.

societies' involvement, clearly the limited nature of the rights of A (the cargo owners) under a contract with B (the shipowners) was significant in the House of Lords' decision not to impose a duty of care in the tort of negligence on C to A, even in respect of damage to property.[1071]

Subsequent cases. There have been many subsequent cases determining whether or not liability based (in part) on an assumption of responsibility may establish liability in the tort of negligence beyond privity of contract.[1072] Of these *Briscoe v Lubrizol*[1073] is a good example of the way in which the contractual structure of the parties' relations may still argue for the rejection of an "assumption of responsibility" in the tort of negligence. In that case, under the terms of a contract of employment, L, the employer, undertook to B, their employee, to arrange a disability insurance scheme, subject to "acceptance by insurers". B was registered under the scheme, and later became incapable of work, but L's claim in respect of B's disability was rejected by their insurer, P. B then claimed, inter alia, damages in the tort of negligence against P on the basis that they were negligent in rejection of the claim (it being accepted that there was no privity of contract between these parties). The insurer's contention that this claim should be struck out was accepted both at first instance and by the Court of Appeal. Giving judgment, Roch L.J. denied the existence of a duty of care on the facts before him, by whichever legal approach this was canvassed, whether in terms of the three-fold test of forseeability, proximity and "justice and reasonableness", an assumption of responsibility or taking an "incremental approach".[1074] Roch L.J. agreed with the court below that the contractual provisions between the employer and insurer showed completely the reverse of any "assumption of responsibility": "[t]here was a very carefully structured contractual framework . . . [which] imposed a curtain between the [employee] and the [insurer]".[1075] While Roch L.J. accepted that: 1–184

[1071] See similarly *Norwich City Council v Harvey* [1989] 1 W.L.R. 828 below para.1–187; *John F Hunt Demolition Ltd v ASME Engineering Ltd* [2007] EWHC 1507 (TCC), [2008] 1 All E.R. 180 at [38]–[42].

[1072] These include *Siddell v Smith Cooper & Partners* [1999] P.N.L.R. 511; *Barex Brothers Ltd v Morris Dean & Co* [1999] P.N.L.R. 344, 349; *A.J. Fabrication (Batley) Ltd v Grant Thornton* [1999] B.C.C. 807; *Electra Private Equity Partners v KPMG Peat Marwick* [1999] 1 Lloyd's Rep. P.N. 670; *Connolly-Martin v Davis, The Times*, June 8, 1999; *Yorkshire Bank Plc v Lloyds Bank Plc* [1999] 2 All E.R. (Comm.) 153; *Hamble Fisheries Ltd v L. Gardner and Sons Ltd* [1999] 2 Lloyd's Rep. 1; *Gorham v British Telecommunications Plc* [2000] 1 W.L.R. 2129; *B.D.G. Roof-Bond v Douglas* [2000] 1 B.C.L.C. 401; *European Gas Turbines Ltd v MSAS Cargo International Inc* [2002] C.L.C. 880; *Killick v PricewaterhouseCoopers (A Firm)* [2001] 1 B.C.L.C. 65; *Merrett v Babb* [2001] 3 W.L.R. 1; *Weldon v GRE Linked Life Assurance Ltd* [2000] 2 All E.R. (Comm.) 914; *Dean v Allin and Watts* [2001] EWCA Civ 758; [2001] 2 Lloyd's Rep. 249; *Niru Battery Manufacturing Co v Milestone Trading Ltd* [2002] EWHC 1425 (Comm.), [2002] All E.R. (D) 206; *European International Reinsurance Co Ltd v Curzon Insurance Ltd* [2003] EWCA Civ 1074; [2003] Lloyd's Rep. I.R. 793; *BP Plc v Aon Ltd* [2006] EWHC 424 (Comm), [2006] 1 All E.R. (Comm.) 789; *Riyad Bank Plc v Ahli United Bank Plc* [2006] EWCA Civ 780, [2006] 2 Lloyd's Rep. 292.

[1073] [2000] P.I.Q.R. P39.

[1074] He accepted the description of the three approaches to the finding of a duty of care in the tort of negligence found in the judgment of Sir Brian Neill in *Bank of Credit and Commerce International (Overseas) Ltd (In Liquidation) v Price Waterhouse* [1998] P.N.L.R. 564, 583–586. The "incremental approach" was famously advocated by Brennan J. in *Sutherland Shire Council v Heyman* (1985) 157 C.L.R. 424 at 481.

[1075] [2000] P.I.Q.R. P39 at P44.

> "the existence of a contractual regime is not necessarily fatal to a claim such as the [employee's]; . . . it is nevertheless a powerful indication against the existence of a duty."[1076]

The assumption of responsibility by the insurer was to the employer, not to the employees under the scheme: a finding of a duty of care would therefore (in the words of counsel for the insurer) "spell the end of the doctrine of privity of contract".[1077] Nor did the Court of Appeal consider that recognition of a duty of care was required as a matter of justice and reasonableness or appropriate as an incremental development. Moreover, the more eclectic approach to deciding whether or not a duty of care should be imposed in the tort of negligence (especially as regards pure economic loss) seen in *Briscoe v Lubrizol,* and which looks in turn at "assumption of responsibility", the "three-fold test" in *Caparo Industries Plc v Dickman*[1078] and the "incremental approach", was taken by the House of Lords in *Customs and Excise Commissioners v Barclays Bank Plc*[1079] though the third approach was seen as "of little value as a test in itself" and as "an important cross-check."[1080] In that case, the House of Lords unanimously held that a third party (here, the bank) with notice of a "freezing order" (formerly known as a *Mareva* injunction) who nevertheless released the property subject to the order did not owe a duty of care to the person for whose benefit the order had been made (here, the Customs and Excise). While the grounds of the decisions of the five members of the House differed, the principal points can be summarised as follows. First, the involuntary nature of the position of the bank as recipient of the order was inconsistent with any assumption of responsibility, even if this were understood to mean the undertaking of a task for another person.[1081] Secondly, the courts had developed a very powerful means for protecting those who fear that their legitimate claims are to be thwarted by disposal of available assets by the development of freezing orders and these are buttressed by the sanction of contempt of court. In this respect, a distinction is drawn between the strict liability of the person against whom an order has been made, and the requirement that a third party with notice of an order is liable for contempt only if he knowingly takes a step to frustrate the court's purpose. It would be inconsistent with this to impose the higher standard of reasonable care by means of a duty of care in tort.[1082] Thirdly, their Lordships were concerned with the practical effects of the imposition of liability in damages for negligence by third parties with notice of a freezing order. While it may appear reasonable in this respect to impose liability for negligence in a business such as a bank, the new duty of care would also apply to any non-business with notice of such an order which would be unreasonable.[1083]

1–185 **The effect of contractual terms on established torts beyond privity.** In general, a term in a contract between A and B will not affect liability in A to C

[1076] [2000] P.I.Q.R. P39 at P48.
[1077] [2000] P.I.Q.R. P39 at P50.
[1078] [1990] 2 A.C. 605 at 618.
[1079] [2006] UKHL 28, [2006] 3 W.L.R. 1.
[1080] [2006] UKHL 28 at [7] and [93].
[1081] [2006] UKHL 28 at [14], [65], [74].
[1082] [2006] UKHL 28 at [61]–[64].
[1083] [2006] UKHL 28 at [23], [61], [77] and [102].

under an established tort since to allow it to do so would contravene the principle of privity of contract.[1084] However, the courts have allowed exceptions to be developed to this general rule and these are particularly clear where the term in question expressly allocates the risk of some event, often by way of an exemption clause. Two situations ought to be distinguished.

Clauses in contract between tortfeasor and another. First, although in general A's contractual exclusion of liability to B will not affect A's liability to C,[1085] it has been held to do so in certain circumstances. Thus, where a court relies on a defendant's "voluntary assumption of responsibility" for the imposition of a duty of care, any disclaimer of liability will apparently affect any third party who wishes to rely on breach of that duty,[1086] though in the case of liability for negligent misstatements, it appears that such a clause will only be effective if notice of it has come to the third party.[1087] So too, where an owner of property entrusts it to a bailee and expressly or implicitly consents to the latter sub-contracting work to a sub-bailee subject to certain exemption conditions, the owner will not be able to sue that sub-bailee in tort except subject to these conditions.[1088] 1–186

Clauses in contract between injured party and another. Secondly, if A contracts with B on terms that A will not be able to sue C, the courts found various ways to give effect to this agreement despite privity of contract, even before this was made overtly possible by the Contracts (Rights of Third Parties) Act 1999.[1089] In *New Zealand Shipping Co Ltd v A.M. Satterthwaite & Co Ltd (The Eurymedon)*[1090] the Privy Council found that a stevedore engaged to unload goods by a carrier was protected from liability to their shipper in the tort of negligence for damage to the goods by a clause in the contract between the shipper and the carrier which was expressed to exempt the stevedore from liability and to be made by the carrier as his agent. Here, then, an exemption clause was given effect by the finding of a collateral contract between A and C, through the agency of B. However, on occasion the courts have instead refused to recognise the existence of a duty of care in the tort of negligence where to do so would disrupt the 'contractual structure' in which the parties worked, not only in the context of pure economic loss,[1091] but also in one of physical damage to 1–187

[1084] Below, paras 14–039 et seq.
[1085] See *Haseldine v C.A. Daw & Son Ltd* [1941] 2 K.B. 343, 397 and see below, para.14–040.
[1086] *Pacific Associates v Baxter* [1990] 1 Q.B. 993, 1022–1023, 1033; *White v Jones* [1995] 2 A.C. 207, 268.
[1087] In *Smith v Eric S. Bush, Harris v Wyre Forest DC* [1990] 1 A.C. 831, the House of Lords considered the validity of such a clause under the Unfair Contract Terms Act 1977 s.2(2) which concerns the effect of contract terms and *notices*.
[1088] *Morris v C.W. Martin & Sons Ltd* [1966] 1 Q.B. 716, 729 and see also *Johnson Matthey Co Ltd v Constantine Terminals Ltd* [1976] 2 Lloyd's Rep. 215; *The Pioneer Container* [1994] 2 A.C. 324 and below, para.14–054.
[1089] s.1(6) and see below, paras 14–043—14–044.
[1090] [1975] A.C. 154 and see below, paras 14–049—14–049.
[1091] Above, paras 1–177—1–178.

the claimant's property. In *Norwich City Council v Harvey*,[1092] the plaintiff owned a building, which it wished to have extended and it employed building contractors to do so on standard terms according to which the "existing structures" should be at its own risk as regards loss or damage by fire while the works were in progress and should be insured against these risks. The building contractors engaged sub-contractors to undertake the roofing of the extension on this basis and owing to the negligence of one of the latter's employees, a fire was started which spread to and damaged the plaintiff's existing building. The Court of Appeal rejected the plaintiff's claim for this damage to its property, refusing to recognise the existence of a duty of care in these circumstances. "On the basis of what is just and reasonable"[1093] May L.J. did not think that:

> "... the mere fact that there is no strict privity between the employer and the subcontractor should prevent the latter from relying on the clear basis on which all the parties contracted in relation to damage to the employer's building caused by fire, even when due to the negligence of the contractors or sub-contractors."[1094]

However, after the Contracts (Rights of Third Parties) Act 1999, parties to a contract may make provision for the protection from liability of third parties in tort, subject to that Act's requirements as to the necessary intention and more generally.[1095]

7. CONTRACT AND OTHER LEGAL CATEGORIES

1–188 **Contract and trust.** It is sometimes important to distinguish a contract, which creates rights *in personam*, from a trust which creates equitable rights indistinguishable in practice from rights in rem.[1096] Until the Contracts (Rights of Third Parties) Act 1999, a crucial difference lay in the possibility or otherwise of creating rights in third parties to an agreement. So, it used to be the case that if A agreed with B to pay money to C in return for valuable consideration furnished by B, C could not in his own right sue A for failure to pay the money, owing to the application of privity of contract[1097]; but he could do so if he established that

[1092] [1989] 1 W.L.R. 828 and see similarly *John F Hunt Demolition Ltd v ASME Engineering Ltd* [2007] EWHC 1507 (TCC), [2008] 1 All E.R. 180 at [38]–[42] and (in a different context) *Marc Rich & Co AG v Bishop Rock Marine Co* [1996] 1 A.C. 211, above, para.1–183. But cf. *British Telecommunications Plc v James Thomson & Sons (Engineers) Ltd* [1999] 1 W.L.R. 9.

[1093] The phrase "just and reasonable" is a reference to the approach recommended to the finding of a duty of care by Lord Keith of Kinkel in *Governors of Peabody Donation Fund v Sir Lindsay Parkinson & Co Ltd* [1985] A.C. 210, 240–241, which May L.J. had previously quoted.

[1094] [1989] 1 W.L.R. 828, 837, per May L.J. and cf. the approach of the House of Lords in *Marc Rich & Co AG v Bishop Rock Marine Co* [1996] 1 A.C. 211, above, para.1–183.

[1095] s.1(1) and (6) and see below, paras 14–043—14–044.

[1096] This is the generally accepted view, despite Maitland's opinion to the contrary: *Equity* (1909), Lect. IX. See Scott (1917) 17 Col.L.R. 269; Winfield, *Province of the Law of Tort* (1931), pp.108–112. See also *Binions v Evans* [1972] Ch. 359; *Re Sharpe* [1980] 1 W.L.R. 219; *Tinsley v Milligan* [1993] 3 W.L.R. 126, 147–148. See also the cases cited in para.13–028, fn.148, below.

[1097] *Tweddle v Atkinson* (1861) 1 B. & S. 393; *Dunlop Pneumatic Tyre Co Ltd v Selfridge & Co Ltd* [1915] A.C. 847 (although B can obtain an order for specific performance in favour of C: *Beswick v Beswick* [1968] A.C. 58); and see below, Ch.19.

a trust had been created in his favour.[1098] While this difference has been considerably eroded by the Contracts (Rights of Third Parties) Act 1999, which allows parties to a contract to make provision for the existence of a right of enforcement of a term of their contract in a third party, the third party's right so created is subject to the conditions of that Act and these differ from those applicable to the creation of a right under a trust.[1099] Again, if A, the owner of a chattel, first agrees that B shall have the right to use it, and then, during the currency of the agreement, sells or charges it to C, who takes with notice of B's rights, B can sue A for breach of contract if C refuses to honour the agreement, and he may be able to recover damages from C for the tort of knowingly inducing a breach of contract. The question whether B is able to restrain C by injunction from using the chattel in such a way as to prevent A from performing his contractual obligations is more difficult. The better view appears to be that there are three bases on which to ground such an injunction. The first is found in the equitable doctrine in *De Mattos v Gibson*,[1100] and the second in the tort of inducing breach of contract.[1101] The third basis is for B to establish an equitable interest in or charge over the chattel or that C is in the position of constructive trustee.[1102]

Moreover, in some cases the courts have found a trust relationship between the parties in parallel to their established contractual one.[1103] Thus, for example, in *Barclays Bank Ltd v Quistclose Investments Ltd*,[1104] A Ltd loaned a sum of money to B Ltd on condition that it would be used to pay the latter's share dividends. The money was paid into a separate account specially opened for this purpose with and to the knowledge of a bank, C Ltd. On B Ltd's voluntary liquidation, the House of Lords held A Ltd entitled to the money held by C Ltd and not paid out as dividend: the loan arrangements showed a clear intention "to create a secondary trust for the benefit of the lender, to arise if the primary trust, to pay the dividend could not be carried out."[1105] On the other hand, in *Lipkin* 1–189

[1098] See below, paras 18–078 et seq.

[1099] For example, the power of the parties to a contract to vary or rescind the contract so as to extinguish or alter the third party's rights are subject to the conditions provided the Contracts (Rights of Third Parties) Act 1999 by s.2; the variation of a trust is governed by different rules: Martin, *Hanbury and Martin*'s, *Modern Equity*, 17th edn (2005), Ch.22.

[1100] (1858) 4 De G. & J. 276, 282; and see *Lord Strathcona S.S. Co Ltd v Dominion Coal Co Ltd* [1926] A.C. 108; *Port Line Ltd v Ben Line Steamers Ltd* [1958] 2 Q.B. 146; *Swiss Bank Corp v Lloyds Bank Ltd* [1979] Ch. 548; [1982] A.C. 584. See also below, paras 18–139—18–140.

[1101] Gardner (1982) 98 L.Q.R. 279; Tettenborn (1982) 41 C.L.J. 58, 82. cf. *Swiss Bank Corp v Lloyds Bank Ltd* [1979] Ch. 548, 573 where the court considered that the law in *De Mattos v Gibson* (1858) 4 De G. & J. is to be understood merely as the "equitable counterpart of the tort of interference with contract".

[1102] *Swiss Bank Corp v Lloyds Bank Ltd* [1979] Ch. 548.

[1103] For example, where a solicitor is employed by a mortgagee lending a sum to a mortgagor for the purchase of property and pays the mortgage money which he has received before his authority to do so, he is liable for breach of trust in respect of that money unless he can justify this action: *Target Holdings Ltd v Redferns* [1996] 1 A.C. 421; cf. also *Tinsley v Milligan* [1993] 3 W.L.R. 126 and see generally McKendrick (ed.), *Commercial Aspects of Trusts and Fiduciary Obligations* (1992).

[1104] [1970] A.C. 567. cf. *Re E. Dibbens & Sons Ltd* [1990] B.C.L.C. 577.

[1105] [1970] A.C. 567, 582. See also *Re Kayford* [1975] 1 W.L.R. 279; Goodhart and Jones (1980) 43 M.L.R. 489; *Swiss Bank Corp v Lloyds Bank Ltd* [1974] Ch. 548; *Twinsectra v Yardley* [2002] 2 A.C. 164 and cf. *Clough Mill Ltd v Martin* [1985] 1 W.L.R. 111, 120 and *Swain v The Law Society* [1983] 1 A.C. 598.

Gorman v Karpnale Ltd[1106] the Court of Appeal accepted an approach to the relationship between contract and trust which echoes that already examined in relation to contract and tort.[1107] In that case a partner in a firm of solicitors drew cheques on a client account and then gambled away the proceeds. The solicitors sued, inter alia,[1108] the bank, claiming that the latter was liable under a constructive trust. The Court of Appeal took the view that a bank would be subject to a constructive trust to its customer in respect of the running of an account only in circumstances where the bank would also be in breach of its contractual duty of care.[1109] Moreover, the content of this duty had to be set in the context of the bank's primary contractual duty which was to honour its customer's cheques in accordance with its mandate[1110] and so should be limited to cases where there is a "serious or real possibility, albeit not amounting to a probability, that its customer might be being defrauded".[1111] *Lipkin Gorman v Karpnale Ltd* therefore concerned the requisite degree of knowledge for liability in a third party "accessory" to a breach of trust and is to be distinguished from *Barclays Bank Ltd v Quistclose Investments Ltd* where the bank (C Ltd) had *received* the money in respect of which the constructive trust was imposed and had actual notice of the purpose for which it was intended.[1112]

1–190 **Contract and conveyance.** A contract, which creates rights *in personam*, must be distinguished from a conveyance of property, which creates rights in rem. Yet sometimes a contract operates, to some extent at any rate, as a conveyance of property. For instance, a specifically enforceable contract for the sale of land constitutes the vendor a trustee of the property for the purchaser, and thus conveys equitable rights which are scarcely distinguishable in practice from rights in rem. Again, a contract for the sale of goods passes the property in the goods to the buyer under s.18 of the Sale of Goods Act 1979. But in both cases the vendor has a lien on the property for unpaid purchase-money; and in the case of goods, as the rubric to the group of sections containing s.18 indicates, the property passes only as between the seller and the buyer: as regards third parties the seller in possession has powers of disposition which may defeat the buyer's title, notwithstanding the maxim *nemo dat quod non habet*.[1113]

1–191 **Contractual rights as property.** Although contracts create only rights in personam, these rights are treated by the law as themselves items of property, an example of things in action or choses in action.[1114] So, a right under a contract

[1106] [1989] 1 W.L.R. 1340. The claim against the bank was not pursued in the House of Lords: [1991] 2 A.C. 548.

[1107] See above, paras 1–126 et seq.

[1108] The solicitors also claimed against the casino where the money was lost: see *Lipkin Gorman v Karpnale Ltd* [1991] 2 A.C. 548.

[1109] [1989] 1 W.L.R. 1340, 1373. This point had been conceded by the solicitors early in argument: at 1349.

[1110] [1989] 1 W.L.R. 1340 at 1356.

[1111] [1989] 1 W.L.R. 1340 at 1378, per Parker L.J. and cf. at [1356] and see Birks (1989) 105 L.Q.R. 352, 355; Martin, *Hanbury and Martin*'s *Modern Equity*, 17th edn (2005), pp.249–252.

[1112] On this distinction see *Hanbury and Martin's Modern Equity*, pp.252–253.

[1113] See Vol.II, paras 43–221 et seq.

[1114] See also Insolvency Act 1986 s.436 including thing in action within its definition of "property".

may be assigned, subject to the conditions which are explained in Ch.19. And a person may constitute himself trustee of a contractual promise, giving rise to a trust of the right under the contract: the conditions for such a constitution (in particular relating to the person's intention) are explained in Ch.18 in the context of privity of contract.[1115] More generally, it has earlier been explained that a party to a contract may invoke the Human Rights Act 1998 so as to claim the protection of property rights under art.1 of the First Protocol to the European Convention on Human Rights.[1116] However, while not rejecting the proprietary character of contractual rights, a majority of the House of Lords has recently refused to assimilate them to chattels (things or choses in possession) for the purpose of the tort of conversion[1117]; for the minority, by contrast, "once the law recognises something [here, a contractual right] as property, the law should extend a proprietary remedy to protect it".[1118]

Contract and restitution. 1–192

> "The law of restitution is the law relating to all claims, quasi-contractual or otherwise, which are founded upon the principle of unjust enrichment."[1119]

Such claims are not dependent upon the existence of any contract, express or implied, between the person enriched and the person at whose expense the enrichment has occurred. From the seventeenth century, the same form of action, *indebitatus assumpsit*, was used to remedy breaches of contract and to enforce claims which we would nowadays consider to be claims in restitution, e.g. for money had and received, for money paid to the use of another, and on a quantum meruit. In these cases the obligation to make restitution was deemed to arise on an implied promise or implied contract (*quasi ex contractu*) in order to render them enforceable by a court in *indebitatus assumpsit*. This fiction has long been discredited. Further, although the boundaries of the law of restitution are not, and have no need to be, settled, restitutionary claims extend beyond those previously classified as "quasi-contractual". The nature of restitutionary recovery and its significance for contracts will be discussed in Ch.29.

Contract and public law. Contracts have often been seen as the expression of individual and private autonomy and therefore to be contrasted with the expressions of public powers.[1120] Since the rise in prominence of the distinction between public and private law since the early 1980s, spurred on first by the House of Lords in its separation of the procedures for judicial review under RSC 1–193

1115 Below, paras 18–078—18–087.

1116 Above, paras 1–044—1–045.

1117 *OGB Ltd v Allan, Douglas v Hello! Ltd, Mainstream Properties Ltd v Young* [2007] UKHL 21, [2008] 1 A.C. 1 especially at [95]–[106].

1118 [2007] UKHL 21 at [310], per Baroness Hale of Richmond, and see also [220]–[240] (Lord Nicholls of Birkenhead).

1119 Goff and Jones, *The Law of Restitution*, 7th edn (2007), p.3. See *Lipkin Gorman v Karpnale Ltd* [1991] 2 A.C. 548, 578; *Woolwich Equitable Building Society v IRC* [1993] A.C. 70; Birks, *An Introduction to the Law of Restitution* (1985), pp.44–48; [1983] C.L.P. 141; cf. Atiyah, *The Rise and Fall of Freedom of Contract* (1979), p.768; *Essays on Contract* (1986), pp.47–52. See also below, Ch.30.

1120 Whittaker (2001) 21 O.J.L.S. 103, 193.

O.53 and for ordinary claims based on private rights,[1121] the presence of a contract has often been seen as a significant element in, if not the touchstone of, the private nature of a person's activity. At the same time, though, there has been an increasing awareness of the importance of contract as a basis for governmental action, leading to calls for the development of the adaptation of the ordinary and private law principles of the law of contract so as to take into account public law considerations[1122]: a need for a public law of contract, rather than a law of public contracts. In the following paragraphs, some of the issues arising from these significances of contract for the borderline between public and private law will be identified.

1–194 **RSC Order 53 and CPR Part 54.** In 1982 in *O'Reilly v Mackman* the House of Lords held that the procedure for judicial review under RSC O.53 was an exclusive one.[1123] Thus, if a plaintiff's case was a matter of "private right" he could not proceed by way of judicial review,[1124] whereas if it was a matter of "public right" this was the only appropriate way of commencing proceedings.[1125] While there were good reasons for the protection of the special features of the public law procedure, this led to a good deal of waste of time and of money in purely procedural disputes. In the words of Wade and Forsyth, the decision in *O'Reilly v Mackman* "turned the law in the wrong direction, away from flexibility of procedure and towards the rigidity reminiscent of the bad old days".[1126] However, since the early 1990s, judges have made clear that a more flexible approach should be taken to the line between proceeding by way of an application for judicial review and an action in private law. This process has been given support by the replacement of O.53 by Pt 54 of the Civil Procedure Rules, which are to be interpreted by the courts according to their "overriding objective" of dealing with cases justly, as part of which a court is to consider in its duties of case management considerations of time and cost.[1127]

1–195 **Caselaw under RSC Order 53.** It was clear that the mere existence of a contractual relationship between an applicant for judicial review and the respondent does not make the case a matter of private law, nor conversely are all issues arising from a public authority's contracts matters of public law,[1128] and the courts used a range of criteria to determine where to draw the line between private and public law for the purposes of O.53.[1129] However, in the employment context, the source of the power or duty challenged was for some time prominent. Thus, in *Ex p. Walsh* the applicant was a nurse who had been dismissed on

---

[1121] *O'Reilly v Mackman* [1983] 2 A.C. 237; *Cocks v Thanet DC* [1983] 2 A.C. 286.

[1122] Leyland and Woods, *Textbook on Administrative Law*, 5th edn (2005), p.499.

[1123] [1983] 2 A.C. 237; *Cocks v Thanet DC* [1983] 2 A.C. 286.

[1124] *R. v East Berkshire Health Authority, Ex p. Walsh* [1985] Q.B. 152. In *Council of Civil Service Trade Unions v Minister for the Civil Service* [1985] A.C. 374, Crown service was held susceptible to judicial review, although the contractual issues involved were not argued before the House of Lords: see Wade (1985) 101 L.Q.R. 180, 194–197 and cf. Fredman and Morris (1988) P.L. 58.

[1125] *O'Reilly v Mackman* [1983] 2 A.C. 237.

[1126] Wade and Forsyth, *Administrative Law*, 9th edn (2004), p.676.

[1127] CPR Pt 1.

[1128] cf. Wade and Forsyth at pp.668–70; Beatson (1987) 103 L.Q.R. 34, 48.

[1129] Beatson (1987) 103 L.Q.R. 34.

grounds of misconduct.[1130] His claim under O.53 argued that his dismissal was ultra vires and decided upon in breach of natural justice. To support this, he alleged a breach of particular conditions of his employment which had been incorporated into his contract in compliance with regulations made under statute. However, this statutory background was not enough to give him "public law rights". According to the Court of Appeal, these would only arise if Parliament had directly restricted his employer's freedom to dismiss him, rather than requiring his employer to contract on particular terms, otherwise his claim was purely contractual.[1131] The applicant was therefore left to his private law remedies for unfair dismissal and breach of contract.[1132] By contrast, in *Ex p. Benwell* the applicant, who had been a prison officer, based his application for the judicial review of his dismissal on the failure to observe a code of discipline of prison officers in the Prison Rules, themselves made under a statutory power.[1133] The court held that this basis gave his claim "sufficient statutory under-pinning" for it to be properly a matter of public law,[1134] although the lack of any other remedy in the context appeared to weigh in the applicant's favour.[1135] The courts also refused to allow the use of the public law procedure to challenge the decisions of certain types of domestic tribunal, in part on the ground that the relationship between the association and its members was "wholly contractual".[1136] However, a decision of the Take-Over and Mergers Panel has been held susceptible to judicial review despite the self-regulatory and private form of its control, because inter alia it operated as an integral part of a governmental framework for the regulation of financial activity.[1137]

A more flexible approach. On the other hand, by 1992 a more flexible approach was taken to the resolution of this type of procedural dispute by the House of Lords in *Roy v Kensington & Chelsea and Westminster Family Practitioner Committee*.[1138] In that case, a doctor who worked for the defendant committee as a general practitioner under a statutory scheme claimed by writ sums allegedly owing to him which had been denied him because the Committee 1–196

[1130] *R. v East Berkshire Health Authority Ex p. Walsh* [1985] Q.B. 152.

[1131] [1985] Q.B. 152 at 165. cf. *R. v Crown Prosecution Service Ex p. Hogg* (1994) 6 Admin. L.R. 778.

[1132] Employment Rights Act 1996 Pt X, as amended. In some employment cases the courts have considered issues typical of public law, such as the reasonableness of the exercise of a discretion and relating to observance of natural justice, as a matter of contract law and in the course of private law proceedings: *R. v British Broadcasting Corp, Ex p. Lavelle* [1983] 1 W.L.R. 23; *Dietman v Brent LBC* [1987] I.C.R. 737, 752; *Hughes v Southwark LBC* [1988] I.R.L.R. 55.

[1133] *R. v Secretary of State for the Home Department Ex p. Benwell* [1984] 3 All E.R. 854.

[1134] [1984] 3 All E.R. 854, 867.

[1135] [1984] 3 All E.R. 854, 866, 868.

[1136] *Law v National Greyhound Racing Club Ltd* [1983] 1 W.L.R. 1302, following *R. v Criminal Injuries Compensation Board Ex p. Lain* [1967] 2 Q.B. 864; *R. v BBC Ex p. Lavelle* [1983] 1 W.L.R. 23; *R. v Fernhill Manor School Ex p. A.* [1993] 1 F.L.R. 620; *R. v Disciplinary Committee of the Jockey Club Ex p. Aga Khan* [1993] 2 All E.R. 853; *R. v Insurance Ombudsman Bureau Ex p. Aegon Life Assurance Ltd* [1995] L.R.L.R. 101. cf. *Modahl v British Athletic Federation* [2001] EWCA 1447, [2002] 1 W.L.R. 1192.

[1137] *R. v Panel of Take-Overs and Mergers, Ex p Datafin Plc* [1987] 1 Q.B. 815 and see *R. v East Berkshire Authority Ex p. Walsh* [1985] Q.B. 152 and *Wandsworth LBC v Winder* [1985] A.C. 461.

[1138] [1992] 1 A.C. 624 and see Cane (1992) P.L. 193.

had come to the view that he had not devoted a "substantial amount of time to general practice" within the meaning of the relevant regulations. The Committee claimed that his action should be struck out as an abuse of the process of the court, arguing that his proper recourse was by judicial review alone. The House of Lords rejected this argument, holding that, whether or not the doctor worked under a contract for the committee, his claim for payment was a matter of "private right." According to Lord Bridge:

> ". . . where a litigant asserts his entitlement to a subsisting right in private law, whether by way of claim or defence,[1139] the circumstance that the existence and extent of the private right asserted may incidentally involve the examination of a public law issue cannot prevent the litigant from seeking to establish his right by action commenced by writ or originating summons, any more than it can prevent him from setting up his private right in proceedings brought against him."[1140]

Moreover, Lord Lowry noticed that Lord Diplock in *O'Reilly v Mackman*[1141] had acknowledged that there may be exceptions to the principle that cases involving public law issues should proceed only by way of judicial review, "particularly where the invalidity of the decision arises as a collateral issue in a claim for infringement of a right of the plaintiff arising under private law".[1142] Lord Lowry recommended that a "liberal attitude" be taken to the ambit of such exceptions,[1143] and approved a broad approach according to which judicial review would be reserved for cases where private rights were not at stake.[1144] Clearly, the House of Lords intended to mould the distinction between private and public law according to the appropriateness of the different procedures in a particular case (for example, whether the case required oral evidence and discovery[1145]), rather than according to the formal source of the plaintiff's claim.[1146]

1–197 **CPR Part 54.** In 2000, O.53 was revoked and replaced by Pt 54 of the CPR.[1147] Under Pt 54, a claim for judicial review is defined as a claim to:

> ". . . review the lawfulness of: (i) an enactment; or (ii) a decision, action or failure to act in relation to the exercise of a public function."[1148]

It is provided that the judicial review procedure must be used for applications for certain types of order (mandatory orders, prohibiting orders, quashing orders, and

---

[1139] See *Wandsworth LBC v Winder* [1985] A.C. 461.

[1140] [1992] 1 A.C. 624, 628–629.

[1141] [1983] 2 A.C. 237.

[1142] [1983] 2 A.C. 237, 285, quoted in *Roy* [1992] 1 A.C. 624, 642.

[1143] [1992] 1 A.C. 624, 654.

[1144] [1992] 1 A.C. 624, 653.

[1145] [1992] 1 A.C. 624, 647, per Lord Lowry, approving the approach of Woolf L.J. in *R. v Derbyshire CC Ex p. Noble* [1990] I.C.R. 808, 813.

[1146] This approach was followed by the Court of Appeal in *Trustees of the Dennis Rye Pension Fund v Sheffield City Council* [1997] 4 All E.R. 747. The need for flexibility in approach to the distinction between the public and private procedures was noted by the HL in *Mercury Communications Ltd v Director General of Telecommunications* [1996] 1 W.L.R. 48 and by the CA in *Clark v The University of Lincolnshire and Humberside* [2000] 1 W.L.R. 1988.

[1147] The Civil Procedure (Amendment No.4) Rules 2000 (SI 2000/2092) rr.1, 22 Pt 54 came into force on October 2, 2000.

[1148] CPR Pt 54.1(2).

injunctions under s.30 of the Supreme Court Act 1981),[1149] and may be used in certain other cases, though not as regards claims solely for damages.[1150] The court has power to order a claim to continue as if it had not been started by way of judicial review and, where it does so, to give directions about the future management of the claim.[1151] In common with applications under RSC O.53, the court's permission to proceed is required in a claim for judicial review[1152] and applications for leave must be made promptly and in any event within three months of when the grounds arose, unless time is enlarged by agreement or by the court.[1153] These features of claims for judicial review remain distinctive and this means that the courts still need to resolve whether a claim is sufficiently public to be appropriately dealt with under Pt 54 or whether it is private and to be dealt with by ordinary action.[1154] In deciding this, the courts sometimes still see claims based on the contract as being appropriate for ordinary action. So, for example, as regards disputes between students and their Universities it has been said that the normal procedure will be judicial review, but where claims are based on the contract between them, then ordinary action is appropriate.[1155] But the courts have made clear that their approach to the differences in procedure and the exercise of their power to transfer claims between the two routes will be flexible and subject to the overriding objective of the CPR.[1156] As Lord Woolf C.J. has observed, Pt 54 was intended to avoid wholly unproductive disputes as to when judicial review is or is not appropriate.[1157] So:

> "... in a case ... where a bona fide contention is being advanced (although incorrect) that [a private sector provider of services for a local authority] was performing a public function, that is an appropriate issue to be brought to the court by way of judicial review."[1158]

The Court of Appeal wished:

> "... to make clear that the CPR provide a framework which is sufficiently flexible to enable all the issues between the parties to be determined."[1159]

Contracts made by public bodies: capacity. The nature and limits of the capacity of the Crown and of public authorities is treated at length in Ch.10.[1160] 1–198

[1149] CPR r.54.2.
[1150] CPR r.54.3.
[1151] CPR r.54.20.
[1152] CPR r.54.4.
[1153] CPR r.54.5.
[1154] It has been noticed that under the CPR delay is also relevant to claims by ordinary action—CPR Pt 24; *Clark v The University of Lincolnshire and Humberside* [2000] 1 W.L.R. 1988, 1997.
[1155] [2000] 1 W.L.R. 1988, 1996.
[1156] [2000] 1 W.L.R. 1988, 1997.
[1157] *R. (Heather) v Leonard Cheshire Foundation* [2002] EWCA Civ 366, [2002] 2 All E.R. 936 at [38].
[1158] [2002] 2 All E.R. 936 at [38].
[1159] [2002] 2 All E.R. 936 at [39].
[1160] Paras 10–004, 10–015 et seq.

1–199 **Contracts made by "public authorities" and the Human Rights Acts 1998.** The Human Rights Act 1998 has had important effects on the law of contract itself as well as on the law governing contracts made by "public authorities." These effects have been discussed together earlier.[1161]

1–200 **Public contractors and the Human Rights Act 1998.** The question has been discussed earlier whether a commercial company providing a service to a person under a contract was acting as someone "certain of whose functions are functions of a public nature" within the meaning of s.6 of the 1998 Act where it did so under a contract with a public authority made by it in furtherance of its statutory duties.[1162]

1–201 **Contracts made by public bodies: other differences in rule.** There are also circumstances in which the public nature of a party's contractual capacity (or contract-making power) affects the substantive rules applicable.[1163] For example, the general rule, based on the principle of freedom of contract, is that a person can choose with whom to contract and with whom not to contract.[1164] However, a local authority's decision not to contract with a company which had indirect trading links with South Africa was successfully challenged by way of judicial review: although the policy was not itself unreasonable, it had been adopted partly in order to penalise the company in question and not solely in order to further racial harmony within the borough.[1165] Moreover, a public authority must not discriminate against the nationals or products of the Member States of the European Union in awarding major contracts.[1166] Another example of difference in substantive rule may be found in *Swain v The Law Society*[1167] in which the rules as to accountability of an agent were held inapplicable to the Society's arrangement of liability insurance on behalf of its members. The insurance scheme was made under statutory powers and the Society and its Council acted thereby "in a public capacity and what they do in that capacity is governed by public law".[1168]

[1161] See above, paras 1–035 et seq.

[1162] See above, para.1–052 concerning *YL v Birmingham City Council* [2007] UKHL 27, [2007] 3 W.L.R. 112.

[1163] And see Freedland (1994) P.L. 86.

[1164] See above, paras 1–010 et seq.

[1165] *R. v Lewisham London Borough Council Ex p. Shell UK Ltd* [1988] 1 All E.R. 938, applying *Wheeler v Leicester City Council* [1985] A.C. 1054 and see Local Government Act 1988 ss.17–23.

[1166] See Public Works Contracts Regulations 1991 (SI 1991/2680); Public Supply Contracts Regulations 1995 (SI 1995/201); Utility Supply and Works Contracts Regulations 1992 (SI 1992/3279); Utilities Contracts Regulations 1996 (SI 1996/2911).

[1167] [1983] 1 A.C. 598.

[1168] [1983] 1 A.C. 598 at [608].

Part Two

FORMATION OF CONTRACT

CHAPTER 2

THE AGREEMENT

		PARA.
1.	Preliminary	2–001
2.	The offer	2–003
3.	The acceptance	2–027
	(a) Definition	2–027
	(b) Communication of acceptance	2–045
	(c) Posted acceptance	2–048
	(d) Prescribed mode of acceptance	2–065
	(e) Silence	2–070
	(f) Unilateral contracts	2–078
4.	Termination of the offer	2–087
	(a) Withdrawal	2–088
	(b) Rejection	2–092
	(c) Lapse of time	2–095
	(d) Occurrence of condition	2–098
	(e) Death	2–099
	(f) Supervening personal incapacity	2–102
	(g) Supervening corporate incapacity	2–103
5.	Special cases	2–110
6.	Incomplete agreement	2–112
7.	Certainty of terms	2–139
8.	Conditional agreements	2–147
	(a) Classification	2–147
	(b) Degrees of obligation	2–150
9.	Contractual intention	2–158

1. PRELIMINARY

Introduction. The first requirement for the formation of a contract is that the parties should have reached agreement. Generally speaking,[1] agreement is reached when an offer made by one of the parties (the offeror) is accepted by the other (the offeree or acceptor). Such an agreement may, however, lack contractual force because it is incomplete,[2] because its terms are not sufficiently certain,[3] because its operation is subject to a condition which fails to occur[4] or **2–001**

---

[1] The analysis of the process of reaching agreement into the steps of offer and acceptance gives rise to difficulties in a number of situations to be discussed in paras 2–110 to 2–111 below.

[2] Below, paras 2–112 to 2–138.

[3] Below, paras 2–139 to 2–145.

[4] Below, paras 2–147 to 2–157.

because it was made without any intention to create legal relations.[5] An agreement may also lack contractual force on the ground of want of consideration. The requirement of consideration is discussed in Chapter 3.

2–002 **The objective test.** In deciding whether the parties have reached agreement, the courts normally apply the objective test,[6] which is further discussed at para.2–003 below. Under this test, once the parties have to all outward appearances agreed in the same terms on the same subject-matter,[7] then neither can, generally,[8] rely on some unexpressed qualification or reservation to show that he had not in fact agreed to the terms to which he had appeared to agree. Such subjective reservations of one party therefore do not prevent the formation of a contract.[9]

2. THE OFFER

2–003 **Offer defined.** An offer is an expression of willingness to contract on specified terms made with the intention (actual or apparent) that it is to become binding as soon as it is accepted by the person to whom it is addressed.[10] Under the objective test of agreement,[11] an apparent intention to be bound may suffice, *i.e.* the alleged offeror (A) may be bound if his words or conduct[12] are such as to induce a reasonable person to believe that he intends to be bound, even though in fact he has no such intention. This was, for example, held to be the case where a university had made an offer of a place to an intending student as a result of a clerical error[13]; and where a solicitor who had been instructed by his client to

---

[5] Below, paras 2–158 to 2–188.

[6] Howarth (1984) 100 L.Q.R. 265; Vorster (1987) 103 L.Q.R. 247; Howarth, *ibid.*, 547; De Moor (1990) 106 L.Q.R. 632; *Smith v Hughes* (1871) L.R. 6 Q.B. 597, 607; below, para.5–067.

[7] See *Falck v Williams* [1900] A.C. 176; *cf. Thake v Maurice* [1986] Q.B. 644 and *Eyre v Measday* [1986] 1 All E.R. 488 (applying the objective test for the purpose of determining the contents of an admitted contract).

[8] The rule stated in the text does not apply in favour of a party who knows that the other does not assent to the terms proposed: *e.g.* where an offer is expressed in a language which the offeree, to the offeror's knowledge, does not understand: *Geier v Kujawa, Weston and Warne Bros (Transport) Ltd* [1970] 1 Lloyd's Rep. 364. See also below, para.2–004 at n.19. *cf.*, in cases of mistake, below, para.5–074.

[9] See, *e.g. Thoresen Car Ferries Ltd v Weymouth Portland BC* [1977] 2 Lloyd's Rep. 614.

[10] *e.g. Storer v Manchester City Council* [1974] 1 W.L.R. 1403; *First Energy (UK) Ltd v Hungarian International Bank Ltd* [1993] 2 Lloyd's Rep. 195, 201; contrast *André & Cie v Cook Industries Inc* [1987] 2 Lloyd's Rep. 463; *Schuldenfrei v Hilton (Inspector of Taxes* [1998] S.T.C. 404 (statement that something *had* been done not an offer).

[11] Above, para.2–002; *Ignazio Messina & Co v Polskie Linie Oceaniczne* [1995] 2 Lloyd's Rep. 566, 571; *Bowerman v ABTA Ltd* [1995] N.L.J. 1815; *Covington Marine Corporation v Xiamen Shipbuilding Industry Co Ltd* [2005] EWHC 2912 (Comm), [2006] 1 Lloyd's Rep. 748 at [43].

[12] For offers made by conduct, see below, para.2–005; *The Aramis* [1989] 1 Lloyd's Rep. 213 (where the objective test was not satisfied); *G. Percy Trentham Ltd v Archital Luxfer Ltd* [1993] 1 Lloyd's Rep. 25, 27.

[13] *Moran v University College Salford (No.2), The Times*, November 23, 1993.

settle a claim for $155,000 by mistake offered to settle it for the higher sum of £150,000.[14] Similarly, if A offers to sell a book to B for £10 and B accepts the offer, A cannot escape liability merely by showing that his actual intention was to offer the book to B for £20, or that he intended the offer to relate to a book other than that specified in the offer.[15]

State of mind of alleged offeree. Whether A is actually bound by an acceptance of his apparent offer depends on the state of mind of the alleged offeree (B); to this extent, the test of agreement is not purely objective.[16] With regard to B's state of mind, there are three possibilities. First, B actually and reasonably believes that A has the requisite intention: here the objective test is satisfied so that B can hold A to his apparent offer even though A did not, subjectively, have the requisite intention.[17] The general view is that there is no further requirement that A must also be aware of B's state of mind.[18] Secondly, B knows that, in spite of the objective appearance, A does not have the requisite intention: here A is not bound; the objective test does not apply in favour of B as he knows the truth about A's actual intention.[19] Thirdly, B has simply formed no view on the question of A's intention, so that B neither believes that A has the requisite intention nor knows that A does not have this intention. This third situation has given rise to a conflict of judicial opinion. One view is that A is not bound: in other words, the objective test is satisfied only if A's conduct is such as to induce a reasonable person to believe that A had the requisite intention *and* if B actually held that belief.[20] The opposing view is that (in our third situation) A is bound: in other words, the objective test is satisfied if A's words or conduct would induce a reasonable person to believe that A had the requisite intention, so long 2–004

[14] *O.T. Africa Line Ltd v Vickers plc* [1996] 1 Lloyd's Rep. 700.

[15] *cf. Centrovincial Estates plc v Merchant Investors Assurance Co Ltd* [1983] Com.L.R. 158; cited with approval in *Whittaker v Campbell* [1984] Q.B. 318, 327, in *Food Corp. of India v Antclizo Shipping Corp* (*The Antclizo*) [1987] 2 Lloyd's Rep. 130, 146, affirmed [1988] 1 W.L.R. 603 and in *O.T. Africa Line Ltd v Vickers plc* [1996] 1 Lloyd's Rep. 700, 702.

[16] *Paal Wilson & Co A/S v Partenreederei Hannah Blumenthal* (*The Hannah Blumenthal*) [1983] 1 A.C. 854, 924.

[17] *André & Cie SA v Marine Transocean Ltd* (*The Splendid Sun*) [1981] 1 Q.B. 694, as explained in *The Hannah Blumenthal*, above; *Challoner v Bower* (1984) 269 E.G. 725; *Tankrederei Ahrenkeil GmbH v Frahuil SA* (*The Multibank Holsatia*) 2 Lloyd's Rep. 486, 493 ("subjective understanding").

[18] The suggestion that A must be aware of B's state of mind was made by Lord Diplock in *The Hannah Blumenthal* [1983] 1 A.C. 854, 916, but Lord Brightman's contrary view, expressed at 924 has been generally preferred: see *The Multibank Holsatia*, above, 492.

[19] *Ignazio Messina & Co v Polskie Linie Oceaniczne* [1995] 2 Lloyd's Rep. 566, 571; *O.T. Africa Line Ltd v Vickers plc* [1996] 1 Lloyd's Rep. 700, 703; *Covington Marine Corporation v Xiamen Shipbuilding Industry Co Ltd* [2005] EWHC 2912 (Comm), [2006] 1 Lloyd's Rep. 748 at [45] ("Subject only to actual knowledge on the part of the buyer [the offeree] that no offer was intended") and see the authorities cited in n.21, below.

[20] *The Hannah Blumenthal*, above, as interpreted in *Allied Marine Transport v Vale de Rio Doce Navegaçeo SA (The Leonidas D.)* [1985] 1 W.L.R. 925; Beatson (1986) 102 L.Q.R. 1; Atiyah, *ibid.* 363; *Gebr. van Weelde Sheepvaart Kantoor BV v Homeric Marine Services (The Agrabele)* [1987] 2 Lloyd's Rep. 223, especially at 235; *cf. Cie Française d'Importation, etc., SA v Deutsche Continental Handelsgesellschaft* [1985] 2 Lloyd's Rep. 592, 597; *Amherst v James Walker Goldsmith and Silversmith Ltd* [1983] Ch.305.

as B does not actually know that A does *not* have any such intention.[21] This latter view no doubt facilitates proof of agreement, but it is hard to see why B should be protected in the situation to which it refers. Where B has no positive belief in A's (apparent) intention to be bound, he cannot be prejudiced by acting in reliance on it; and the purpose of the objective test is simply to protect B from the risk of suffering such prejudice. The test embodies a principle of convenience; it is not based on any inherent superiority of objective over subjective criteria. It is therefore submitted that the objective test should not apply to our third situation since in it there is, by reason of B's state of mind, no risk of his suffering any prejudice as a result of the objective appearance of A's intention. For this purpose, it should make no difference whether B's state of mind amounts to knowledge of, or merely to indifference to, the truth.

2–005 **Conduct as offer.** An offer may be addressed either to a specified person or to a specified group of persons or to the world at large; and it may be made expressly (by words) or by conduct. At common law, a person who had contracted to sell goods and tendered different goods (or a different quantity) might be considered to make an offer by conduct to sell the goods which he had tendered.[22] It seems that an offer to sell can still be made in this way, though by legislation against "inertia selling" the dispatch of goods "without any prior request" may amount to a gift to the recipient, rather than to an offer to sell.[23]

2–006 **Inactivity as an offer.** A number of cases raise the further question whether the "conduct" from which an offer may be inferred can take the form of inactivity. The issue in these cases was whether an agreement to submit a dispute to arbitration could be said to have been "abandoned" by long delay, where, over a long period of time, neither party had taken any steps in the arbitration

---

[21] *Excomm Ltd v Guan Guan Shipping (Pte) Ltd (The Golden Bear)* [1987] 1 Lloyd's Rep. 330, 341 (doubted on another point in para.2–070, n.307 below, and see para.2–006, n.32); this view was approved in *The Antclizo* [1987] 2 Lloyd's Rep. 130, 143 but doubted *ibid.* 147 (affirmed [1988] 1 W.L.R. 603 without reference to the point); and *semble* in *Floating Dock Ltd v Hong Kong and Shanghai Bank Ltd* [1986] 1 Lloyd's Rep. 65, 77; *The Multibank Holsatia* [1988] 2 Lloyd's Rep. 486, 492 ("at least did not conflict with [B's] subjective understanding"); *Thai-Europe Tapioca Service Ltd v Seine Navigation Inc (The Maritime Winner)* [1989] 2 Lloyd's Rep. 506, 515 (using similar language). A dictum in *Furness Withy (Australia) Pty Ltd v Metal Distribution (UK) Ltd (The Amazonia)* [1990] 1 Lloyd's Rep. 236, 242 goes even further in suggesting that there may be a contract even though "*neither* [party] intended to make a contract."

[22] *Hart v Mills* (1846) 15 L.J.Ex. 200; *cf. Steven v Bromley & Son* [1919] 2 K.B. 722; *Greenmast Shipping Co S.A. v Jean Lion et Cie. SA (The Saronikos)* [1986] 2 Lloyd's Rep. 277; *Confetti Records v Warner Music UK Ltd* [2003] EWHC 1274 (Ch); [2003] E.M.L.R. 35.

[23] Consumer Protection (Distance Selling) Regulations 2000, (SI 2000/2334) (implementing Dir. 97/7/EC), regs 22 (amending Unsolicited Goods and Services Act 1971) and 24 (as amended by Consumer Protection from Unfair Trading Regulations 2008 (SI 2008/1277) reg.30(1) and Sched. 2, para.96) see also reg.3(4)(d) and Sched. 1, para.29 of the 2008 Regulations, above). For further amendments of the 1971 Act, see Regulatory Reform (Unsolicited Goods and Services Act 1971) (Directory Entries and Demand for Payment) Order 2005 (SI 2005/55) and Unsolicited Goods and Services Act 1971 (Electronic Commerce) (Amendment) Regulations 2005 (SI 2005/148). Normally, these provisions against "intertia selling" would not apply where goods were dispatched in response to the buyer's order, even if they were not in accordance with the order; but they might apply where the qualitative or quantitative difference between what was ordered and what was sent was extreme.

proceedings. In cases of "inordinate and inexcusable delay" of this kind, arbitrators now have a statutory power to dismiss the claim for want of prosecution[24] and it is also open to the parties expressly to provide for "lapse" of the claim if steps in the proceedings are not taken within a specified period.[25] Conversely, however, the statutory power to dismiss the claim for want of prosecution may be excluded by agreement,[26] and where it is so excluded the question of abandonment can still arise in the present context. Such a question could also arise in the context of the alleged abandonment of some other type of right or remedy,[27] to which no similar legislative provision extends. The arbitration cases indicate that, on the objective test,[28] inactivity may amount to an offer of abandonment when combined with other circumstances (such as the destruction of relevant files),[29] even though those circumstances would not, of themselves, constitute sufficient evidence from which an offer could be inferred. But mere inactivity by one party is unlikely,[30] when standing alone, to have this effect, for it is equivocal and generally explicable on other grounds, such as inertia or forgetfulness, or the tactical consideration that the party alleged to have made the offer does not wish to reactivate his opponent's counter-claims.[31] Consequently, it will not normally suffice to induce a reasonable person in the position of the other party to believe that an offer is being made[32]; and the mere fact that the other party nevertheless

---

[24] Arbitration Act 1996, s.41(3), replacing Arbitration Act 1950, s.13A. Under s.13A, it had been held that the court could take into account delay occurring before the section came into force: *Yamashita-Shinnihon SS. Co Ltd v L'Office Cherifien des Phosphate (The Boucraa)* [1994] 1 A.C. 486, and that the court would (*mutatis mutandis*) apply the same principles to the power to dismiss arbitration proceedings as those which govern the dismissal of an action for want of prosecution: *James Lazenby & Co v McNicholas Construction Co Ltd* [1995] 1 W.L.R. 615.

[25] See the GAFTA arbitration rules referred to in *Cargill SpA v Kadinopoulos SA* [1992] 1 Lloyd's Rep. 1.

[26] Arbitration Act 1996, s.41(2) so provides.

[27] *cf. Amherst Ltd v James Walker Goldsmith & Silversmith Ltd* [1983] Ch.305; *Collin v Duke of Westminster* [1985] Q.B. 581; *M.S.C. Mediterranean Shipping SA v B.R.E. Metro Ltd* [1985] 2 Lloyd's Rep. 239; *Fenton Inns. Ltd v Gothaer Versicherungsbank VVaG* [1991] 1 Lloyd's Rep. 172, 180; *Indescon Ltd v Ogden* [2004] EWHC 2326 (TCC), [2005] 1 Lloyd's Rep. 31 (right to appoint arbitrator not lost by lapse of time).

[28] Above, paras 2–003, 2–004.

[29] *The Splendid Sun* [1981] Q.B. 694, as explained in *The Hannah Blumenthal* [1983] 1 A.C. 854 (though this explanation was doubted in *Cie Française d'Importation, etc., SA v Deutsche Conti Handelsgesellschaft* [1985] 2 Lloyd's Rep. 592, 599); *Tracomin SA v Anton C. Nielsen* [1984] 2 Lloyd's Rep. 195 (as to which see below, para.2–076, n.339); *The Multibank Holsatia* [1988] 2 Lloyd's Rep. 486; for the question whether such an offer can be *accepted* by inactivity, see below, para.2–070.

[30] *Unisys International Services Ltd v Eastern Countries Newspaper Group Ltd* [1991] 1 Lloyd's Rep. 538, 553 suggests that the possibility cannot be wholly ruled out; *cf. The Boucraa* [1994] 1 A.C. 486, 521 (describing the "abandonment" approach as "largely useless in practice").

[31] *Unisys* case, above, n.30 at 553.

[32] *The Leonidas D.* [1985] 1 W.L.R. 925; *Cie Française d'Importation, etc., SA v Deutsche Conti Handelsgesellschaft* [1985] 2 Lloyd's Rep. 592; *The Antclizo* [1988] 1 W.L.R. 603; *The Agrabele* [1987] 2 Lloyd's Rep. 223; *The Maritime Winner* [1989] 2 Lloyd's Rep. 506; *contra, The Golden Bear* [1987] 1 Lloyd's Rep. 330 (*sed quaere*: the decision was in part based on the decision at first instance in *The Agrabele* [1985] 2 Lloyd's Rep. 496, but this was reversed on appeal: [1987] 2 Lloyd's Rep. 223); *Ulysses Compania Naviera SA v Huntington Petroleum Services (The Ermoupolis)* [1990] 1 Lloyd's Rep. 161, 166 see also below, para.2–071, n.307); *Unisys* case, above, n.30.

had this belief cannot suffice to turn the former party's inactivity into such an offer.[33]

2–007 **Offer and invitation to treat.** When parties negotiate with a view to making a contract, many preliminary communications may pass between them before a definite offer is made. One party may simply ask, or respond to, a request for information, or he may invite the other to make an offer. For example, in *Harvey v Facey*[34] the claimants telegraphed to the defendants, "Will you sell us Bumper Hall Pen? Telegraph lowest cash price." The defendants replied, "Lowest cash price for Bumper Hall Pen £900." The claimants then telegraphed, "We agree to buy Bumper Hall Pen for £900 asked for by you." The Judicial Committee of the Privy Council held that the defendants' telegram was not an offer but merely a statement as to the price for which they might be prepared to sell; that the claimants' second telegram was an offer to buy but that, as this had never been accepted by the defendants, there was no contract. Similarly, in *Gibson v Manchester City Council*[35] it was held that a letter in which a local authority stated (in reply to an enquiry from the tenant of a council house) that it "may be prepared to sell" the house to him at a specified price was not an offer to sell the house: its purpose was simply to invite the making of a "formal application," amounting to an offer, from the tenant. On the same principle, it has been held that a telephoned request for the supply of goods suitable for a prospective customer's purpose was only a "preliminary enquiry,"[36] the offer being made by conduct, when the supplier subsequently despatched the goods; and that a draft document, sent in the course of contractual negotiations with the clear intention of eliciting further comment from the recipient, was not an offer.[37] In electronic trading (*e.g.* on a website) an " 'order' may be, but need not be, the contractual offer . . . " for certain purposes specified in Regulations which apply to such trading.[38]

2–008 A communication by which a party is invited to make an offer is commonly called an invitation to treat. It is distinguishable from an offer primarily on the ground that it is not made with the intention that it is to become binding as soon as the person to whom it is addressed simply communicates his assent to its terms. A statement is clearly not an offer if it expressly provides that the person who makes it is *not* to be bound merely by the other party's notification of assent

[33] *The Antclizo*, above; Davenport (1988) 104 L.Q.R. 493.

[34] [1893] A.C. 552. See also *Clifton v Palumbo* [1944] 2 All E.R. 497; *Scancarriers A/S v Aotearoa International Ltd (The Barranduna)* [1985] 2 Lloyd's Rep. 419 (quotation of freight rates not an offer). But see *Philip & Co v Knoblauch*, 1907 S.C. 994 (*Harvey v Facey* distinguished).

[35] [1979] 1 W.L.R. 294. *cf. Michael Gerson (Leasing) Ltd v Wilkinson* [2000] Q.B. 514 at 540 ("I am willing to make an outright sale [of specified machinery] for £319,000 . . . ") not an offer and, even if it was, it had not been accepted: below, para.2–027.

[36] *Interfoto Picture Library Ltd v Stiletto Visual Programmes Ltd* [1989] 1 Q.B. 433, 436.

[37] *McNicolas Construction Holdings v Endemol UK plc* [2003] EWHC 2472, [2003] E.G.C.S. 136.

[38] Electronic Commerce (EC Directive) Regulations 2002 (SI 2002/2013) (partly implementing Dir.2000/31/EC), reg.12.

but only when he himself has signed the document in which the statement is contained.[39]

Wording not conclusive. Apart from cases of the kind just described, the wording of a statement does not conclusively determine the distinction between an offer and an invitation to treat. Thus a statement may be an invitation to treat although it contains the word "offer"[40]; while a statement may *be* an offer although it is expressed as an "acceptance,"[41] or although it requests the person to whom it is addressed to make an "offer."[42] The point that use of the word "offer" in a document does not conclusively determine its legal nature is further illustrated by *Datec Electronic Holdings Ltd v United Parcels Ltd*[43] where carriers of goods had issued standard terms, clause 3 of which stated that the carriers did not "offer carriage of goods" except subject to specified restrictions, one of which was that the value of any package was not to exceed $50,000. After the shippers had indicated their acceptance of these terms, they "booked" a number of packages; these were then collected from their premises by an employee of the carriers who was unaware of the fact that each package was worth more than $50,000. The argument that there was no contract because the carriers' "offer" to carry could not be accepted by tendering packages which were not in conformity with that offer[44] was rejected. Lord Mance said that the contract had been made at one of two points: "either when a shipment was booked or at latest when it was collected pursuant to such a booking."[45] At first instance, Andrew Smith J. had said that, in the phrase from clause 3 quoted above, "offer" had not been used in its technical legal sense.[46] This view was approved both in the Court of Appeal[47] and in the House of Lords.[48] The fact that the packages were not in conformity with clause 3 did not prevent the conclusion of a contract at one of the two stages described above.[49] In the words of Lord Mance, "the more natural inference" was that "the whole of clause 3 provides a contractual regime governing the carriage of non-conforming goods."[50] Where the contract is made in the second of the two ways described above[51] (i.e. by the carriers' collecting the goods) the restrictions in clause 3 could, in spite of the use of the word "offer," be regarded as part of an invitation to treat, while the shippers' tender of non-conforming goods could be regarded as an offer to enter into a contract for the carriage of those goods which was then accepted by the carriers' conduct. The view that a contract was made at this stage was also supported by other provisions of clause 3: in particular, those entitling the carrier 2–009

[39] *Financings Ltd v Stimson* [1962] 1 W.L.R. 1184.
[40] *Spencer v Harding* (1870) L.R. 5 C.P. 561; *Clifton v Palumbo*, above, para.2–007, n.34; *iSoft Group plc v Misys Holdings Ltd* [2003] EWCA Civ 229; [2003] All E.R. (D) 438 (Feb).
[41] *Bigg v Boyd Gibbins Ltd* [1971] 1 W.L.R. 913; (1987) 87 L.Q.R. 307.
[42] *Harvela Investments Ltd v Royal Trust Co of Canada (C.I.) Ltd* [1986] A.C. 207.
[43] [2007] UKHL 23, [2007] 1 W.L.R. 1325.
[44] See below, para. 2–032.
[45] At [23].
[46] [2005] EWHC 239, [2005] 1 Lloyd's Rep. 470 at [118].
[47] [2005] EWCA Civ 1418, [2006] 1 Lloyd's Rep. 279 at [15].
[48] Above, n.43 at [24].
[49] Above, at n.45.
[50] Above, n.43, at [25]; *cf.* [2005] EWCA Civ 1481, [2006] 1 Lloyd's Rep. 279 at [16].
[51] Above, at n.45.

to "suspend" the carriage of non-confirming goods and making the shippers liable for charges in respect of such goods. There would, on the other hand, have been no such acceptance by the carriers' conduct if, knowing of the non-conformity of the goods, they had refused to collect them. This point accounts for Lord Hope's statement that, in that event, there would have been "no contract."[52] At first sight, this view may seem to be inconsistent with that expressed by Andrew Smith J. in the passage referred to above,[53] and approved by Lord Mance,[54] that "unless and until [the carriers] exercise their right [to refuse to carry, conferred by clause 3] there is a contract that they will carry the package." The apparent conflict can be resolved on the ground that Andrew Smith J's view refers to the first of the two ways described above[55] in which the contract is alleged to have been made (i.e., "when the shipment was booked") while Lord Hope's view refers to the second of those two ways (i.e. "when [the shipment was collected pursuant to such a booking").[56] The distinction between the two ways of making the contract would raise an issue of contractual intention. The outcome would depend on whether, when the booking was made, the parties intended it to have contractual force; and it may, in particular, be doubtful whether the carriers had such an intention.[57]

2–010 **Distinction between offer and invitation to treat.** As the discussion in para.2–009 above shows, the distinction between offer and invitation to treat is often hard to draw, as it depends primarily on the elusive criterion of the intention of the person making the statement in question. But it does not depend entirely on this criterion. In certain stereotyped situations, the distinction is determined, at least *prima facie*, by rules of law. It may be that such rules can be displaced by evidence of contrary intention; but in the absence of such evidence they will determine the distinction between offer and invitation to treat, and they will do so without reference to the intention (actual or even objectively ascertained) of the maker of the statement. This is true, for example, in the cases of auction sales and shop window displays. These and other illustrations of the distinction will be discussed in paras 2–011—2–024 below.

2–011 **Auctions.** At an auction sale the general rule is that the auctioneer's request for bids is not an offer which can be accepted by the highest bidder.[58] Instead it is a bid that constitutes an offer, which the auctioneer may, but generally[59] is not bound to, accept. Accordingly s.57(2) of the Sale of Goods Act 1979 provides that a sale by auction is completed when the auctioneer announces its completion by the fall of the hammer, or in other customary manner; and that until then the bidder may retract his bid. Similarly, the auctioneer can generally[60] withdraw the

---

[52] Above, n.43, at [9].
[53] Above, at n.46.
[54] Above, n.43 at [24].
[55] Above, at n.45.
[56] *ibid.*
[57] See *Carver on Bills of Lading*, 2nd ed (2005) para. 3–002.
[58] *Payne v Cave* (1789) 3 T.R. 148; *British Car Auctions v Wright* [1972] 1 W.L.R. 1519; (1973) 89 L.Q.R. 7.
[59] For the position where the auction is "without reserve", see below, para. 2–012.
[60] Subject to the qualification stated in n.59 above.

lot before he accepts the bid. It seems, moreover, that the offer made by each bidder lapses[61] as soon as a higher bid is made. Thus if a higher bid is made and then withdrawn, the auctioneer can no longer accept the next highest.

Auctions with and without reserve. When property is put up for auction subject to a reserve price, there is no contract if the auctioneer by mistake purports to accept a bid lower than the reserve price.[62] Where the auction is without reserve, there is no contract *of sale* between the highest bidder and the *owner* of the property if the auctioneer refuses to accept the highest bid. But it has been held that the *auctioneer* is in such a case liable on a separate or collateral contract between him and the highest bidder that the sale will be without reserve.[63] Although a mere advertisement of an auction is not an offer to hold it,[64] the actual request for bids at the auction itself seems to be an offer by the auctioneer that he will (on the owner's behalf) accept the highest bid; and this offer is accepted by bidding. The question whether there is any consideration for the auctioneer's promise to highest bidder is discussed in Chapter 3.[65] 2–012

Provision for resale in case of dispute. An auction sale may be conducted subject to the express stipulation that, "if any dispute[66] arises between two or more bidders, the lot in dispute shall be immediately put up again and resold." If the dispute arises after the lot has been knocked down to one bidder, it seems that there is a contract with him, subject to the condition subsequent that the sale may be annulled if a dispute immediately breaks out between two or more bidders. 2–013

Display of goods for sale: general rule. As a general rule, a display of goods at a fixed price in a shop window[67] or on a shelf in a self-service store[68] is an invitation to treat and not an offer. The display is an invitation to the customer to make an offer which the retailer may then accept or reject. Similar principles 2–014

---

[61] Below, para.2–096.

[62] *McManus v Fortescue* [1907] 2 K.B. 1; on a sale of land, it must be expressly stated whether the sale is with reserve or not: Sale of Land by Auction Act 1867, s.5.

[63] *Warlow v Harrison* (1859) 1 E. & E. 309; *cf. Johnston v Boyes* [1899] 2 Ch.73, 77; *Barry v Davies* [2000] 1 W.L.R. 1962, 1967, citing a previous edition of this book with approval. *Contra, Fenwick v Macdonald, Fraser & Co Ltd* (1904) 6 F. (Ct. of Sess.) 850; Slade (1952) 68 L.Q.R. 238; Gower, *ibid.* 457; Slade (1953) 69 L.Q.R. 21. Under the American Uniform Commercial Code (hereinafter referred to as U.C.C.) the goods may not be withdrawn once they have been put up, if the auction is without reserve: s.2–328(3). This position is restated, though in different terminology, in s.2–328(3) of the American Law Institute's proposed revisions of Art.2 of the U.C.C. (2003, not yet in force).

[64] *Harris v Nickerson* (1873) L.R. 8 Q.B. 286.

[65] Below, para.3–174.

[66] See *Richards v Phillips* [1969] 1 Ch.39.

[67] *Timothy v Simpson* (1834) 6 C. & P. 499, 500; *Fisher v Bell* [1961] 1 Q.B. 394 (actual decision reversed by Restriction of Offensive Weapons Act 1961, s.1; contrast Criminal Justice Act 1988, s.14A(1), as inserted by Offensive Weapons Act 1996, s.6: this refers only to selling). Dicta in *Wiles v Maddison* [1943] 1 All E.R. 315, 317 may perhaps suggest that a shop window display is an offer. See also Winfield (1939) 55 L.Q.R. 499, 516–518.

[68] *Pharmaceutical Society of Great Britain v Boots Cash Chemists (Southern) Ltd* [1953] 1 Q.B. 410; *cf. Lacis v Cashmarts Ltd* [1969] 2 Q.B. 400; *Davies v Leighton* [1978] Crim.L.R. 575. For the contrary view, see Ellison Kahn (1955) 72 S.A.L.J. 246, 250–253; *Lasky v Economic Grocery Stores*, 319 Mass. 224; 65 N.E. 2d 305 (1946).

would seem to apply where a supplier of goods or services indicates their availability on a website: that is, the offer would seem to come from the customer (*e.g.* when he clicks the appropriate "button") and it is then open to the supplier to accept or reject that offer.[69] There is judicial support for the view that an indication of the price at which petrol is to be sold at a filling station is likewise an invitation to treat,[70] the offer to buy being made by the customer and accepted by the seller's conduct in putting the petrol into the tank.[71] But this analysis hardly fits the now more common situation in which the station operates a self-service system[72]; for once the customer has put petrol into his tank, the seller has no effective choice of refusing to deal with him.

2–015 **Display of goods for sale: exceptional cases.** The general rule relating to shop and similar displays is well established; but it seems that it can be excluded by special circumstances: *e.g.* if the retailer has stated unequivocally that he will sell to the first customer who tenders the specified price. The distinction between an offer and an invitation to treat depends, in the last resort, on the intention of the maker of the statement; and where his intention to be bound immediately on acceptance is sufficiently clear it is submitted that a shop window or shelf display may be an offer. For example, a notice in a shop window stating that "We will beat any TV . . . price by £20 on the spot" has been described as "a continuing offer."[73] The customer may, indeed, still lose his bargain since the offer can be withdrawn at any time before it is accepted[74]; but if it is so withdrawn the person displaying the notice may incur criminal liability under legislation passed for the protection of consumers.[75] In the case of a self-service shop, acceptance of any offer which might be made by the terms of the display would normally take place, not when the customer took the goods off the shelf, but only when he did some less equivocal act, such as presenting them for payment.[76]

2–016 **Other displays.** The principles stated in paras 2–014 and 2–015 above can also apply to other displays. Thus where a menu is displayed outside a restaurant,

---

[69] *See* below, para.2–027 for what *constitutes* an acceptance, and below, para.2–051 n.243 for the *time* of acceptance, in such cases.

[70] *Esso Petroleum Ltd v Commissioners of Customs & Excise* [1976] 1 W.L.R. 1, 5, 6, 11; *Richardson v Worrall* [1985] S.T.C. 693, 717.

[71] *Re Charge Card Services* [1989] Ch.417, 512; for acceptance by conduct, see below, para.2–030.

[72] *cf.* below, para.2–016 at n.78.

[73] *R. v Warwickshire CC, Ex p. Johnson* [1993] A.C. 583, 588.

[74] Below, para.2–088.

[75] Under the Consumer Protection from Unfair Trading Regulations 2008 (SI 2008/1277) reg.3(4)(d) and Sched 1 para.6, a trader (as defined in reg.2) commits an offence if he "makes an invitation to purchase products at a specified price" and then refuses to show the advertised item to consumers or refuses to take orders for it, though only if he does so "with the intention of promoting a different product (bait and switch)." A misleading price indication could also conceivably amount to deceit. And see below, para.2–020.

[76] See *Lasky v Economic Grocery Stores*, above, n.68. An alternative possibility is that the acceptance may take place before such presentation of the goods but be subject until then to the customer's power to cancel: see *Gillespie v Great Atlantic & Pacific Stores*, 187 S.E. 3d 441 (1972); *Sheeskin v Giant Food Inc*, 318 A 2d 874 (1974). *cf. R. v Morris* [1984] A.C. 320 where taking goods off the shelf of a self-service store *and changing the price-labels* was held to be an "appropriation" within Theft Act 1968, s.3(1); but it does not follow that at this stage there would for the purpose of the law of contract be an acceptance even if the shelf-display amounted to an offer: see *ibid.* 334.

or handed to a customer, it seems that the proprietor only makes an invitation to treat,[77] the offer coming from the customer. On the other hand, a notice at the entrance to an automatic car-park may be an offer which can be accepted by driving in[78]; and a display of deck-chairs for *hire* has been held to be an offer.[79] There is no perfectly general answer to the question whether such displays are offers or invitations to treat; the answer depends in each case on the intention with which the display was made.[80] In *University of Edinburgh v Onifade*[81] a notice displayed by a landowner on its land stated that any persons parking their cars there without permit would be liable to a "fine" of £30 per day. A motorist who had so parked his car was held liable for the specified amount as his conduct amounted to an acceptance[82]; so that it must have been assumed that the notice was an offer. It is, however, with respect, open to question whether the landowner had any intention (even objectively ascertained) to enter into a contract with persons parking without permit. The landowner's intention seems to have been to deter unauthorised parking, rather than to invite it with a view to earning the specified amount. The point could be significant if an action had been brought against the landowner, e.g. in respect of loss or damage to the car.

Advertisements: bilateral contracts. Advertisements intended to lead to the making of bilateral contracts are not often held to be offers. Thus a newspaper advertisement that goods are for sale is not generally an offer[83]; an advertisement that a scholarship examination will be held is not an offer to a candidate[84]; and the circulation of a price-list by a wine merchant has been held only to be an invitation to treat.[85] It has been said that, if such statements were offers, a merchant could be liable to everyone who purported to accept his offer even though his stocks were insufficient to meet the requirements of all the "acceptors."[86] But this result would not necessarily follow even if the advertisement were an offer; for it could be construed as one which expired as soon as the merchant's stock was exhausted. There is, again, no absolute rule determining the character of advertisements of bilateral contracts: they are normally invitations to treat, but they may be offers if the advertiser's intention to be bound immediately on acceptance is sufficiently clear.[87] 2–017

Advertisements: unilateral contracts. There are probably two reasons why advertisements intended to lead to the making of bilateral contracts are not commonly regarded as offers. First, such advertisements often lead to further bargaining, *e.g.* where a house is advertised for sale. Secondly, the advertiser may legitimately wish, before becoming bound, to assure himself that the other party 2–018

[77] *cf. Guildford v Lockyer* [1975] Crim.L.R. 235.
[78] *Thornton v Shoe Lane Parking Ltd* [1971] 2 Q.B. 163, 169.
[79] *Chapelton v Barry UDC* [1940] 1 K.B. 532.
[80] *cf.* the cases discussed below, para.2–021.
[81] 2005 SLT (Sh Ct) 63.
[82] See below, para. 2–027.
[83] *Partridge v Crittenden* [1968] 1 W.L.R. 1204; contrast *Lefkowitz v Great Minneapolis Surplus Stores*, 86 N.W. 2d. 689 (1957).
[84] *Rooke v Dawson* [1895] 1 Ch.480.
[85] *Grainger & Son v Gough* [1896] A.C. 325.
[86] *ibid.* at 334.
[87] *cf.* the cases discussed below, para.2–021.

is able (financially or otherwise) to perform his obligations under any contract which may result. Neither of these reasons applies in the case of a unilateral contract[88]; and advertisements of such contracts are therefore commonly held to be offers. In the leading case of *Carlill v Carbolic Smoke Ball Co Ltd*,[89] for example, the defendants issued an advertisement promising to pay £100 to any person who, in accordance with certain directions, used a carbolic smoke ball made by them and then caught influenza. This was held to be an offer, the defendants' intention to be bound[90] being made particularly clear by their statement that they had deposited £1,000 with their bankers "shewing our sincerity in the matter." A case nearer the borderline was *Bowerman v Association of British Travel Agents Ltd*[91] where a package holiday had been booked with a tour operator who was a member of the defendant association (ABTA). A notice displayed on the tour operator's premises stated, *inter alia*, that in the event of the financial failure of an ABTA member before commencement of the holiday, "ABTA arranges for you to be reimbursed the money you have paid for your holiday." A majority of the Court of Appeal held that these words constituted an offer since, on the objective test,[92] they would reasonably be regarded as such by a member of the public booking a holiday with an ABTA member.

2–019 **Rewards.** Advertisements of rewards for the return of lost or stolen property, or for information leading to the capture or conviction of a criminal, are commonly regarded as offers.[93] Some difficulty arises if, in cases of this kind, the information is given by several persons in succession. In one case it was held that the first person to give the information was alone entitled to the reward[94] as the offeror did not intend to pay more than once. This is no doubt the most likely construction; but an advertisement could be so worded as to impose a more extensive liability. The defendants' liability in *Carlill's* case would not have been limited to 10 persons merely because the advertisement stated that they had deposited only £1,000.

2–020 **Other liability in connection with advertisements.** A person who issues an advertisement may be under some form of liability even though the advertisement does not amount to an offer. For example, a person who indicates by such an advertisement that he intends to sell goods when he in fact has no such intention might be liable in deceit to someone who suffered loss by acting in reliance on the statement; and he might incur criminal liability under legislation passed for the protection of consumers,[95] or even of traders who are misled by

[88] For the distinction between unilateral and bilateral contracts, see below, para.2–078.
[89] [1893] 1 Q.B. 256.
[90] Contrast *Lambert v Lewis* [1982] A.C. 225, 262, *per* Stephenson L.J., affirmed without reference to the point [1982] A.C. 271, below, para.2–165.
[91] [1995] N.L.J. 1815.
[92] Above, paras 2–002, 2–003.
[93] *e.g. Gibbons v Proctor* (1891) 64 L.T. 594; *Williams v Carwardine* (1833) 5 C. & P. 566; 4 B. & Ad. 621.
[94] *Lancaster v Walsh* (1838) 4 M. & W. 16. Where two persons *together* supply the information, they may share a single reward: *Lockhart v Barnard* (1845) 14 M. & W. 674.
[95] *e.g.* under Consumer Protection from Unfair Trading Regulations 2008 (SI 2008/1277) reg.3(4)(d) and Sched.1 para 6, above, para.2–015 n. 75. See also Consumer Credit Act 1974, s.45.

statements made by their suppliers in the course of marketing.[95a] He may also be liable for false statements in advertisements relating to the characteristics of the subject-matter, or to the terms on which it is to be supplied.[96] Two further possibilities arise where the advertisement leads to the making of a contract for the sale or supply of goods to a consumer. First, the advertisement may amount to a "consumer guarantee" and so take effect as a "contractual obligation" owed by the guarantor by virtue of the Sale and Supply of Goods to Consumers Regulations 2002.[97] Secondly, public statements on the specific characteristics of the goods made "in advertising" may be a "relevant circumstance" for the purpose of determining whether the goods are of satisfactory quality and so whether the seller is in breach of the statutorily implied term that the goods are of such quality.[98]

Timetables and passenger tickets. There is a remarkable diversity of views on the question just when a contract of carriage is concluded between a carrier and an intending passenger. It has been said that railway carriers made offers by issuing advertisements stating the times at and conditions under which trains would run[99]; and that a road carrier made offers to intending passengers by the act of running buses.[100] Such offers could be accepted by an indication on the part of the passenger that he wished to travel: *e.g.* by applying for a ticket or getting on the bus. Another view is that the carrier makes the offer at a later stage, by issuing the ticket; and that this offer is accepted by the passenger's retention of the ticket without objection,[101] or even later, when he claims the accommodation offered in the ticket.[102] On this view, the passenger makes no more than an invitation to treat when he asks for a ticket to be issued to him; and the offer contained in the ticket may be made to, and accepted by, the passenger even though the fare is paid by a third party (*e.g.* the passenger's employer).[103] Where the booking is made in advance, e.g., through a travel agent, yet a third view has been expressed: that the contract is concluded when the carrier indicates, even 2–021

[95a] Business Protection from Misleading Marketing Regulations 2009, SI 2008/1276.

[96] Below, Ch.6.

[97] SI 2002/3045, reg.15 (as amended by Consumer Protection from Unfair Trading Regulations 2008 (SI 2008/1277) reg.30(1) and Sched. 2, para.97); for definition of "consumer" and "consumer guarantee", see reg.2.

[98] Sale of Goods Act 1979, s.14(2D), as inserted by SI 2002/3045, reg.3. See also Supply of Goods and Services Act 1982, s.11D(3A) and Supply of Goods (Implied Terms) Act 1973, s.10(2D), as inserted by regs 8 and 13 of SI 2002/3045.

[99] *Denton v G.N. Ry* (1856) 5 E. & B. 860; *Thompson v L.M.S. Ry* [1930] 1 K.B. 41, 47; perhaps because such companies could not refuse to carry? See now Railways Act 1993, s.123.

[100] *Wilkie v L.P.T.B.* [1947] 1 All E.R. 258, 259.

[101] *Thornton v Shoe Lane Parking Ltd* [1971] 2 Q.B. 163, 169; *Cockerton v Naviera Aznar SA* [1960] 2 Lloyd's Rep. 450; the acceptance in such cases would be by conduct rather than by "silence": *cf.* below, para.2–076.

[102] *MacRobertson-Miller Airline Services v Commissioner of State Taxation* [1975] A.L.R. 131; the principle resembles that stated in *Heskell v Continental Express Ltd* [1950] 1 All E.R. 1033, 1037 in relation to the time of formation of a contract for the carriage of goods by sea; *Carver on Bills of Lading* (2nd ed 2005), para.3–001 n.80.

[103] *Hobbs v L. & S.W. Ry* (1875) L.R. 10 Q.B. 111, 119, as explained in the *MacRobertson-Miller* case, above, at 147; consideration for the promises of both parties would be provided on the principle of *Gore v Van der Lann* [1967] 2 Q.B. 31, below, para.3–181.

before issuing the ticket, that he "accepts" the booking,[104] or when he issues the ticket[105]: on this view, it is the passenger who makes the offer. The authorities yield no single rule; one can only say that the exact time of contracting depends in each case on the wording of the relevant document and on the circumstances in which it was issued.

2–022 **Tenders.** At common law, a statement that goods are to be sold by tender is not normally an offer to sell to the person making the highest tender[106]; it merely indicates a readiness to receive offers. Similarly, an invitation for tenders for the supply of goods or for the execution of works is, generally, not an offer,[107] even though the preparation of the tender may involve very considerable expense. The offer comes from the person who submits the tender and there is no contract until the person asking for the tenders accepts one of them. These rules may, however, be excluded by evidence of contrary intention: *e.g.* where the person who invites the tenders states in the invitation that he binds himself to accept the highest offer to buy[108] (or, as the case may be, the lowest offer to sell or to provide the specified services).[109] In such cases, the invitation for tenders may be regarded *either* as itself an offer *or* as an invitation to submit offers coupled with an undertaking to accept the highest (or, as the case may be, the lowest) offer; and the contract is concluded as soon as the highest offer to buy (or lowest offer to sell, etc.) is communicated.[110] There is also an intermediate possibility. This is illustrated by a case[111] in which an invitation to submit tenders was sent by a local authority to seven selected parties; the invitation stated that tenders submitted after a specified deadline would not be considered. It was held that the authority was contractually bound to consider (though not to accept) a tender submitted before the deadline.

2–023 **Public procurement.** The common law position stated in para.2–022 above is modified by legislation, for example, by Regulations[112] which give effect to European Community Directives, the object of which is to prevent discrimination in the award of major contracts for public works, supplies and services in one

---

[104] *Hollingworth v Southern Ferries Ltd (The Eagle)* [1977] 2 Lloyd's Rep. 70; *Daly v Gen. Steam Navigation Co Ltd (The Dragon)* [1980] 2 Lloyd's Rep. 415; affirming [1979] 1 Lloyd's Rep. 257; *Oceanic Sun Line Special Shipping Co v Fay* (1988) 165 C.L.R. 97; *cf.* (in cases of carriage of goods by sea) *Gulf Steel Co Ltd v Al Khalifa Shipping Co (The Anwar al Sabar)* [1980] 2 Lloyd's Rep. 261, 263. See also *British Airways Board v Taylor* [1976] 1 W.L.R. 13.

[105] *Dillon v Baltic Shipping Co (The Mikhail Lermontov)* [1991] 2 Lloyd's Rep. 155, 159; reversed on other grounds (1993) 176 C.L.R. 344.

[106] *Spencer v Harding* (1870) L.R. 5 C.P. 561.

[107] *ibid.* at 564.

[108] *ibid.* at 563.

[109] See *William Lacey (Hounslow) Ltd v Davis* [1957] 1 W.L.R. 932, 939. See also *MJB Enterprises Ltd v Defence Construction Ltd* (1999) 15 Const. L.J. 455: promise to accept lowest *compliant* tender broken by accepting lowest non-compliant one (Supreme Court of Canada).

[110] *Harvela Investments Ltd v Royal Trust of Canada (C.I.) Ltd* [1986] A.C. 207, 224–225.

[111] *Blackpool and Fylde Aero Club Ltd v Blackpool BC* [1990] 1 W.L.R. 25. No decision was reached on the quantum of damages. See also *Fairclough Building v Port Talbot BC* (1992) 62 B.L.R. 82.

[112] See below, para.10–044; Craig in (ed. Rose) *Consensus ad Idem, Essays in the Law of Contract in Honour of Guenter Treitel*, 148–151; and Environmental Protection Act 1990, Sch.2, Pt II, applied in *R. v Avon C., Ex p. Terry Adams Ltd, The Times*, January 20, 1994.

member state against nationals of another member state. These Regulations restrict the freedom of the body seeking tenders to decide which tender it will accept and they provide a remedy in damages for a person who has made a tender and is prejudiced by breach of the Regulations. A fuller account of the topic is given in Chapter 10.[113]

Share offers. A company which, in commercial language,[114] makes an "offer to the public" of new shares does not in law "offer" to allot the shares. It invites members of the public to apply for them, reserving the right to decide how many, if any, to allot to any particular applicant.[115] On the other hand a letter informing an existing shareholder of his entitlement under a "rights" issue of new shares is regarded as an offer.[116] This type of communication will set out the precise rights of the persons to whom it is addressed, so that it may be inferred that the company intends to be bound in relation to any shareholder who takes up his rights. 2–024

Place of making an offer. It may, for a variety of purposes, be important to know exactly *where* an offer has been made: for example, in order to determine whether a contract can be sued on in a particular court.[117] For this purpose it has been held that an offer sent through the post had been made where it was posted.[118] Since requirements of this kind are generally imposed by legislation, it is unsafe to lay down any general rule. The question where an offer was made must, in the last resort, turn on the construction of the relevant legislation. 2–025

Time of making an offer. Since an offer may expire by lapse of time,[119] the question *when* it was made may also arise, especially if there has been some delay in its transmission. In *Adams v Lindsell*[120] an offer to sell wool was made in a letter which was misdirected by the offerors and consequently delayed by two days. On receipt of the letter, the offeree immediately posted an acceptance. It was held that there was a binding contract as the delay arose "entirely from the mistake of the" offerors. On the other hand, if the delay had been of such length as to make it clear to the offeree that the offer was "stale," it seems unlikely that the offeree could still have accepted; *a fortiori*, he could not have done so if the offer had reached him only after an expiry date specified in it. The emphasis placed in *Adams v Lindsell* on the fault of the offerors also makes it possible to argue that a different result might have been reached in that case if the delay had 2–026

[113] Below, para.10–044.

[114] And indeed in the language of Financial Services and Markets Act 2000, s.103(4) and of Companies Act 2006, ss.551(17), 578 and 756 (not yet in force).

[115] *e.g. Hebb's Case* (1867) L.R. 4 Eq. 9; *Harris' Case* (1872) L.R. 7 Ch.App. 587; *Wall's Case* (1872) 42 L.J.Ch. 372; *cf. Wallace's Case* [1900] 2 Ch.671; *National Westminster Bank plc v I.R.C.* [1995] 1 A.C. 119, 126; *cf. Rust v Abbey Life Ins. Co* [1979] 2 Lloyd's Rep. 335 (property bonds).

[116] *Jackson v Turquand* (1869) L.R. 4 H.L. 305.

[117] *Taylor v Jones* (1875) 1 C.P.D. 87; *cf.* in criminal law, *Treacy v D.P.P.* [1971] A.C. 537 (blackmail); contrast *R. v Baxter* [1972] 1 Q.B. 1 (attempt to obtain by deception).

[118] *Taylor v Jones*, above n.117.

[119] Below, paras 2–095—2–097.

[120] (1818) 1 B. & Ald. 681; Winfield (1939) 55 L.Q.R. at 499, 503–504.

been due to some other factor, such as an accident in the post. The time within which the offer could be accepted might then have run, not from the time of the offeree's receipt of the offer, but from the time at which the offer would, but for the accident, have been communicated[121] to the offeree.

3. THE ACCEPTANCE

(a) *Definition*

2–027 **Acceptance defined.** An acceptance is a final and unqualified expression of assent to the terms of an offer. The objective test of agreement applies to an acceptance no less than to an offer.[122] On this test, a mere acknowledgement of an offer would not be an acceptance; nor would a person to whom an offer to sell goods had been made accept it merely by replying that it was his "intention to place an order"[123] or by asking for an invoice.[124] The mere acknowledgement of an offer, in the sense of a communication stating simply that the offer had been received, would likewise not be an acceptance. But an "acknowledgement" may by its express terms or, in a particular context by implication, contain a statement that the sender had agreed to the terms of the offer and that he was therefore accepting it. In website trading, for example, a customer's order may amount to an offer,[125] and where this is the case an "acknowledgement" of the order may indicate the supplier's intention to accept that offer.[126] Where the offer makes alternative proposals, the acceptance must make it clear to which set of terms the assent is directed. In *Peter Lind & Co Ltd v Mersey Docks & Harbour Board*[127] an offer to build a freight terminal was made by a tender quoting in the alternative a fixed, and a "cost-plus," price. The offeree purported to accept "your tender," and it was held that there was no contract.

2–028 **Continuing negotiations.** When parties carry on lengthy negotiations, it may be hard to say exactly when an offer has been made and accepted. As negotiations progress, each party may make concessions or new demands and the parties

---

[121] As to the meaning of "communicated" *cf.* below, paras 2–046, 2–089.

[122] Above, para.2–003; *Inland Revenue Commissioners v Fry* [2001] S.T.C. 1715 at [6], [7]. For an application of the objective test to an acceptance, see *University of Edinburgh v Onifade* 2005 SLT (Sh Ct 63), above para. 2–016. The motorist was there held to have accepted the landowner's offer by parking his car on the owner's land and it was "nothing to the purpose that he did not intend to pay" (at 6) the "fine" specified in the offer.

[123] *O.T.M. Ltd v Hydranautics* [1981] 2 Lloyd's Rep. 211, 214.

[124] *Michael Gerson (Leasing) Ltd v Wilkinson* [2000] Q.B. 514 at 530 (where there was probably no offer: see above, para.2–007, n.35).

[125] Above, para.2–007.

[126] In the Electronic Commerce (EC Directive) Regulations 2002, (SI 2002/2013, partly implementing Dir.2000/31/EC), reg.11, the words "acknowledge" and "acknowledgement" seem to be used in this sense.

[127] [1972] 2 Lloyd's Rep. 234.

may in the end disagree as to whether they had ever agreed at all. The court must then look at the whole correspondence and decide whether, on its true construction, the parties had agreed to the same terms. If so, there is a contract even though both parties, or one of them, had reservations not expressed in the correspondence.[128] The court will be particularly anxious to hold that continuing negotiations have resulted in a contract where the performance which was the subject-matter of the negotiations has actually been rendered. In one such case a building sub-contract was held to have come into existence (even though agreement had not yet been reached when the contractor began work) as during its progress outstanding matters were resolved by further negotiations.[129] The contract may then be given retrospective effect, so as to cover work done before the final agreement was reached.[130]

Negotiation after apparent agreement. Businessmen do not, any more than the courts, find it easy to say precisely when they have reached agreement, and may continue to negotiate after they appear to have agreed to the same terms. The court will then look at the entire course of negotiations to decide whether an apparently unqualified acceptance did in fact conclude the agreement.[131] If it did, the fact that the parties continued negotiations after this point does not affect the existence of the contract between them,[132] unless the continued correspondence can be construed as an agreement to rescind the contract. *A fortiori*, the binding force of an oral contract is not affected or altered merely by the fact that, after its conclusion, one party sends to the other a document containing terms significantly different from those which had been orally agreed.[133] 2–029

[128] *Kennedy v Lee* (1817) 3 Mer. 441; *cf. Cie de Commerce, etc. v Parkinson Stove Co* [1953] 2 Lloyd's Rep. 487; B.S.E., 17 M.L.R. 476; *Port Sudan Cotton Co v Govindaswamy Chettiar & Sons* [1977] 2 Lloyd's Rep. 5; *Thoresen Car Ferries Ltd v Weymouth Portland BC* [1977] 2 Lloyd's Rep. 614; *O.T.M. Ltd v Hydranautics* [1981] 2 Lloyd's Rep. 211, 215; *Manatee Towing Co v Oceanbulk Maritime S.A. (The Bay Ridge)* [1999] 2 All E.R. (Comm) 306; *David de Jongh Weill v Mean Fiddler Holdings* [2003] EWCA Civ 1058.

[129] *G. Percy Trentham Ltd v Archital Luxfer Ltd* [1993] 1 Lloyd's Rep. 25. *Peter Lind's* case (above, para.2–127) shows that the factor of performance of work is not decisive, though it may (as in that case) give the performing party a restitutionary claim.

[130] *G. Percy Trentham Ltd v Archital Luxfer Ltd*, above at n.129.

[131] *Hussey v Horne-Payne* (1878) 4 App.Cas. 311; *Bristol, Cardiff & Swansea Aerated Bread Co v Maggs* (1890) 44 Ch.D. 616; *British Guiana Credit Corp. v Da Silva* [1965] 1 W.L.R. 248; *Container Transport International Inc v Oceanus Mutual, etc., Association* [1984] 1 Lloyd's Rep. 476; *Asty Maritime Co Ltd v Rocco Guiseppe & Figli (The Astyanax)* [1985] 2 Lloyd's Rep. 109, 112; *Hofflinghouse & Co Ltd v C. Trade SA (The Intra Transporter)* [1986] 2 Lloyd's Rep. 132; *Pagnan SpA v Granaria B.V.* [1986] 1 Lloyd's Rep. 547; *Pagnan SpA v Feed Products Ltd* [1987] 2 Lloyd's Rep. 601, 619; *Ignazio Messina & Co v Polskie Linie Oceaniczne* [1995] 2 Lloyd's Rep. 566 (no contract); *Frota Oceanica Brasilieira SA v Steamship Mutual Underwriting Association (The Frotanorte)* [1996] 2 Lloyd's Rep. 461 (no contract as matters of substance remained unresolved). The same principle has been applied in the context of the question whether a contract had been rescinded: *Drake Insurance plc v Provident Insurance plc* [2003] EWCA Civ 1834, [2004] Q.B. 601 at [100].

[132] *Perry v Suffields Ltd* [1916] 2 Ch.187; *Davies v Sweet* [1962] 2 Q.B. 300; *Cranleigh Precision Engineering Ltd v Bryant* [1965] 1 W.L.R. 1293; *Harmony Shipping Co SA v Saudi-Europe Line Ltd (The Good Helmsman)* [1981] 1 Lloyd's Rep. 377, 409, 416.

[133] *Jayaar Impex Ltd v Toaken Group Ltd* [1996] 2 Lloyd's Rep. 437.

2–030 **Acceptance by conduct.** An offer may be accepted by conduct. For example, an offer to buy goods can be accepted by supplying them[134]; an offer to sell goods, made by sending them to the offeree, can be accepted by using them,[135] and an offer contained in a request for services can be accepted by beginning to render them,[136] where a customer of a bank draws a cheque which will, if honoured, cause his account to be overdrawn, the bank, by deciding to honour the cheque, impliedly accepts the customer's implied request for an overdraft on the bank's usual terms.[137] But conduct will amount to acceptance only if it is clear that the offeree did the act of alleged acceptance with the intention (ascertained in accordance with the objective principle[138]) of accepting the offer. Thus a buyer's taking delivery of goods after the conclusion of an oral contract of sale will not amount to his acceptance of written terms which differ significantly from those orally agreed and which are sent to him by the seller after the making of the oral contract but before taking delivery.[139] That conduct is then referable to the oral contract rather than to the attempted later variation. Nor is a company's offer to insure a car accepted by taking the car out on the road, if there is evidence that the driver intended to insure with another company.[140] *A fortiori*, there is no acceptance where the offeree's conduct clearly indicates an intention to reject the offer. This was the position in a Scottish case where a notice on a package containing computer software stated that opening the package would indicate acceptance of the terms on which the supply was made, and the customer returned the package unopened.[141]

---

[134] *Harvey v Johnson* (1848) 6 C.B. 305; *cf. Steven v Bromley & Son* [1919] 2 K.B. 722, 728; *Greenmast Shipping Co SA v Jean Lion et Cie (The Saronikos)* [1986] 2 Lloyd's Rep. 277; *cf. Interfoto Picture Library Ltd v Stiletto Visual Programmes Ltd* [1989] Q.B. 433, 436; *Re Charge Card Services* [1989] Ch.417 (above, para.2–014); *Carlyle Finance Ltd v Pallas Industrial Finance Ltd* [1999] 1 All E.R. (Comm) 659 at 670; and see below, para.2–076; contrast *Capital Finance Co Ltd v Bray* [1964] 1 W.L.R. 323. As to counter-offers, see below, paras 2–092, 2–093.

[135] *Weatherby v Banham* (1832) 5 C. & P. 228; *Brogden v Metropolitan Ry* (1877) 2 App.Cas. 666, below, at n.145; *cf. Hart v Mills* (1846) 15 L.J.Ex. 200; *Confetti Records v Warner Music UK Ltd* [2003] EWHC 1274, *The Times*, June 12, 2003. It is assumed that the goods are not "unsolicited" within the legislation against "inertia selling" (above, para.2–005).

[136] *Smit International Singapore Pte Ltd v Kurnia Dewi Shipping SA (The Kurnia Dewi)* [1997] 1 Lloyd's Rep. 553; *cf. Datec Electronics Holdings Ltd v United Parcels Ltd* [2007] UKHL 23, [2007] 1 W.L.R. 1325 at [23]: contract for the carriage of goods "would come into being either when the shipment was booked [by the shipper] . . . or at the latest when it was collected [by the carrier] pursuant to the booking." Such collection would amount to an acceptance by the carrier's conduct of the shipper's offer contained in the booking. See also above, para.2–009.

[137] *Lloyds Bank v Voller* [2000] 2 All E.R. (Comm) 978.

[138] Above, paras 2–002, 2–003. For the application of the objective principle to an acceptance by conduct, see *University of Edinburgh v Onifade* 2005 S.L.T. (Sh Ct) 63, above para. 2–027 n.122.

[139] *Jayaar Impex Ltd v Toaken Group Ltd* [1996] 2 Lloyd's Rep. 437.

[140] *Taylor v Allon* [1966] 1 Q.B. 304. The objective principle (above, paras 2–002, 2–003) could not apply in this case, as the conduct alleged to constitute the acceptance had never come to the notice of the offeror. *cf. Picardi v Cuniberti* [2002] EWHC 2933; (2003) 19 Const. L.J. 350: payments made under another contract held not to amount to acceptance of an offer to enter into the alleged new contract; and see, in another context, *Re Leyland Daf Ltd* [1994] 4 All E.R. 300, affirmed sub nom. *Powdrill v Watson* [1995] 2 A.C. 394.

[141] *Beta Computers (Europe) v Adobe Systems (Europe)* 1996 S.L.T. 604; even opening the package would not necessarily be an acceptance so as to incorporate the printed terms: see Tapper in (ed. Rose) *Consensus ad Idem, Essays in the Law of Contract in Honour of Guenter Treitel*, 287–288.

Establishing the terms of contracts made by conduct. Where an offer or an acceptance or both are alleged to have been made by conduct, the terms of the agreement are obviously more difficult to ascertain than where the agreement was negotiated by express words. The difficulty may be so great as to force the court to conclude that no agreement was reached at all.[142] But sometimes the court can resolve the uncertainty by applying the standard of reasonableness[143] or by reference to another contract (whether between the same parties or between one of them and a third party[144]), or even to a draft agreement between them which had never matured into a contract. For example, in *Brogden v Metropolitan Ry*[145] a railway company submitted to a merchant a draft agreement for the supply of coal. He returned it marked "approved" but also made a number of alterations to it, to which the railway company did not expressly assent; but the company accepted deliveries of coal under the draft agreement for two years. It was held that once the company began to accept these deliveries there was a contract on the terms of the draft agreement.[146] 2–031

Correspondence between acceptance and offer. A communication may fail to take effect as an acceptance because it attempts to vary the terms of the offer. Thus an offer to sell 1,200 tons of iron is not accepted by a reply asking for 800 tons[147]; an offer to pay a *fixed* price for building work cannot be accepted by a promise to do the work for a *variable* price[148]; and an offer to *supply* goods cannot be accepted by an "order" for their "*supply and installation.*"[149] Nor, generally, can an offer be accepted by a reply which varies one of its other terms (*e.g.* that specifying the time of performance),[150] or by a reply which introduces an entirely new term.[151] Such a reply is not an acceptance; but it may, on the contrary, be a counter-offer,[152] which the original offeror can then accept or reject. On the other hand, statements which are not intended to vary the terms of the offer, or to add new terms, do not vitiate the acceptance, even where they do 2–032

---

[142] *Capital Finance Co Ltd v Bray* [1964] 1 W.L.R. 323.

[143] Sale of Goods Act 1979, s.8(2); Supply of Goods and Services Act 1982, s.15(1); below, para.2–113 *cf. Steven v Bromley & Son* [1919] 2 K.B. 722.

[144] *e.g. Pyrene Co Ltd v Scindia Navigation Co Ltd* [1954] 2 Q.B. 402.

[145] (1877) 2 App.Cas. 666; see also *Jones v Daniel* [1894] 2 Ch.332; *Port Sudan Cotton Co v Govindaswamy Chettiar & Sons* [1977] 2 Lloyd's Rep. 5; *cf. D. & M. Trailers (Halifax) Ltd v Stirling* [1978] R.T.R. 468. *UK Safety Group Ltd v Heane* [1998] 2 B.C.L.C. 208.

[146] Contrast *Jayaar Impex Ltd v Toaken Group Ltd* [1996] 2 Lloyd's Rep. 437, where the conduct of the buyer was referable, not to the draft sent by the seller, but to the earlier oral agreement (above at n.139) between the parties; and *UK Safety Group Ltd v Heane* [1998] 2 B.C.L.C. 208 (company director not bound by terms of a draft agreement which was under the company's Articles required to be, but had not been, authorised by the board).

[147] *Tinn v Hoffman & Co* (1873) 29 L.T. 271; *cf. Holland v Eyre* (1825) 2 Sim. & St. 194; *Jordan v Norton* (1838) 4 M. & W. 155; *Harrison v Battye* [1975] 1 W.L.R. 58.

[148] *North West Leicestershire DC v East Midlands Housing Association* [1981] 1 W.L.R. 1396.

[149] *Butler Machine Tool Co Ltd v Ex-Cell-O Corp. (England) Ltd* [1979] 1 W.L.R. 401.

[150] *ibid.*; *North West Leicestershire DC v East Midlands Housing Association* [1981] 1 W.L.R. 1396; *cf. Brinkibon Ltd v Stahag Stahl und Stahlwarenhandelsgesellschaft mbH* [1983] 2 A.C. 34.

[151] *Jackson v Turquand* (1869) L.R. 4 H.L. 305; *Jones v Daniel* [1894] 2 Ch.332; *Von Hatzfeldt-Wildenburg v Alexander* [1912] 1 Ch.284; *Love & Stewart Ltd v S. Instone & Co Ltd* (1917) 33 T.L.R. 475; *Northland Airliners v Dennis Ferranti Meters Ltd* (1970) 114 S.J. 845; *Lark v Outhwaite* [1991] 2 Lloyd's Rep. 132, 139; *Bircham & Co Nominees (No.2) v Worrell Holdings Ltd* [2001] EWCA Civ 775, (2001) 82 P. & C.R. 427 at [11].

[152] Below, para.2–092.

not precisely match the words of the offer.[153] It is, moreover, submitted that, if the new term merely makes express what would otherwise be implied, it does not destroy the effectiveness of the acceptance.[154] Nor will the new term have this effect if it is merely a declaration by the acceptor that he is prepared to grant some indulgence to the offeror, *e.g.* to condone late payment in return for specified interest.[155] Similarly, it is submitted, that an acceptance which asks for some indulgence to the offeree is, nevertheless, effective, so long as it is clear that the offeree is prepared to perform even if the indulgence is not granted: *e.g.* to buy for cash if his request for credit is refused. The test in each case is whether the offeror reasonably regarded the purported acceptance "as introducing a new term into the bargain and not as a clear acceptance of the offer."[156] It is also possible for a communication which contains new terms to amount at the same time: (1) to a firm acceptance of the offer; and (2) to a new offer to enter into a further contract. In such a case, there will be a contract on the terms of the original offer, but none on the terms of the new offer, unless that, in turn, is accepted.[157]

2–033 **Subsequent formal document inaccurate.** After parties have reached agreement, the offer and acceptance may be set out in formal documents. The purpose of such documents may be merely to record the agreed terms[158]; and where one of the documents performs this function accurately while the other fails to do so, the discrepancy between them will not prevent the formation of a contract. In such a case, the court can rectify the document which fails to record the agreed terms, and the contract will be on those agreed terms.[159]

2–034 **The "battle of forms."** The rule that offer and acceptance must correspond gives rise to problems where one or both of the parties wish to contract by reference to a "standard form" contractual document. Two situations call for discussion.

2–035 **One party's "usual conditions".** First, A may make an offer to B by asking for a supply of goods or services. B may reply that he is willing to supply the goods or services on his "usual conditions." Prima facie, B's statement is a counter-offer which A is free to accept or reject, and he may accept it by accepting the goods or services. If he does so, there is a contract between A and B, though the question whether B's "usual conditions" actually form part of it

---

[153] *Clive v Beaumont* (1847) 1 De G. & Sm. 397; *Simpson v Hughes* (1897) 66 L.J.Ch. 334; *Butler Machine Tool Co Ltd v Ex-Cell-O Corp. (England) Ltd* [1979] 1 W.L.R. 401.

[154] *Lark v Outhwaite* [1991] 2 Lloyd's Rep. 132, 139. For another qualification of the requirement of exact correspondence between offer and acceptance, see Vienna Convention on Contracts for the International Sale of Goods (below, para.2–063), Art.19(2).

[155] *Harris's Case* (1872) L.R. 7 Ch.App. 587.

[156] *Global Tankers Inc v Amercoat Europa N.V.* [1975] 1 Lloyd's Rep. 666, 671; *cf. G. Percy Trentham Ltd v Archital Luxfer Ltd* [1993] 1 Lloyd's Rep. 25, 28.

[157] *Monrovia Motorship Corp v Keppel Shipyard (Private) Ltd (The Master Stelios)* [1983] 1 Lloyd's Rep. 356; *Society of Lloyd's v Twinn, The Times*, April 4, 2000.

[158] *e.g. O.T.M. Ltd v Hydranautics* [1981] 2 Lloyd's Rep. 211, 215; *cf.* below, para.2–116.

[159] *Domb v Isoz* [1980] Ch. 548, 559.

may depend on a number of further factors which will be discussed in Chapter 12.[160]

Each party refers to own conditions. Secondly, *each* party may purport to contract with reference to his own set of standard terms and these terms may conflict. In *B.R.S. v Arthur V. Crutchley Ltd*[161] the claimants delivered a consignment of whisky to the defendants for storage. Their driver handed the defendants a delivery note purporting to incorporate the claimants' "conditions of carriage." The note was stamped by the defendants: "Received under [the defendants'] conditions." It was held that this amounted to a counter-offer which the claimants had accepted by handing over the goods, and that the contract therefore incorporated the defendants' and not the claimants' conditions. 2–036

"Last shot" doctrine. This case gave some support to the so-called "last shot" doctrine: *i.e.* to the view that, where conflicting communications are exchanged, each is a counter-offer, so that if a contract results at all (*e.g.* from an acceptance by conduct) it must be on the terms of the final document in the series leading to the conclusion of the contract.[162] But the authorities show that this is not necessarily the outcome in cases of this kind. In one case,[163] for example, a buyer placed a purchase order subject to its own conditions, and the seller acknowledged the order by a fax containing the words "Delivery based on our general conditions of sale." These were not attached and, mainly for this reason, it was held that the seller's acknowledgement was not a counter-offer but an acceptance, so that the resulting contract was on the buyer's conditions even though the seller's acknowledgement was the last shot in the exchange of messages. A more complex situation arose in *Butler Machine Tool Co Ltd v Ex-Cell-O Corp. (England) Ltd*,[164] where sellers had offered to supply a machine for a specified sum. The offer was expressed to be subject to certain terms and conditions, including a "price escalation clause" by which the amount actually payable by the buyers was to depend on "prices ruling upon date of delivery." In reply the buyers placed an order for the machinery on a form setting out their own terms and conditions, which differed from those of the sellers in containing no price-escalation clause and also in various other respects.[165] It also contained a tear-off slip to be signed by the sellers and returned to the buyers, stating that the sellers accepted the buyers' order "on the terms and conditions stated therein." The sellers did sign the slip and returned it with a letter saying that they were "entering" the order "in accordance with" their offer. This communication 2–037

---

[160] Below, paras 12–008—12–018. If the test of reasonable notice or signature is satisfied, the contract will be on B's conditions.

[161] [1968] 1 All E.R. 811; *cf. A. Davies & Co (Shopfitters) v William Old* (1969) 113 S.J. 262; *O.T.M. Ltd v Hydranautics* [1981] 2 Lloyd's Rep. 211; *Muirhead v Industrial Tank Specialities Ltd* [1986] Q.B. 507, 530; *Souter Automation v Goodman Mechanical Services* (1984) 34 Build.L.R. 81.

[162] As in *Zambia Steel & Building Supplies v James Clark & Eaton Ltd* [1986] 2 Lloyd's Rep. 225.

[163] *Sterling Hydraulics Ltd v Dictomatic Ltd* [2006] EWHC 2004 (Q.B.), [2007] 1 Lloyd's Rep. 8.

[164] [1979] 1 W.L.R. 401, especially at 405; Adams (1979) 94 L.Q.R. 481; Rawlings (1979) 42 M.L.R. 715.

[165] Above, para.2–032 at nn.149 and 150.

from the sellers was held to be an acceptance of the buyers' counter-offer[166] so that the resulting contract was on the buyers' terms, and the sellers were not entitled to the benefit of the price escalation clause. The sellers' reply to the buyers' order did not prevail (though it was the "last shot" in the series) because the reference in it to the sellers' original offer was made, not for the purpose of re-iterating all its terms, but only for the purpose of identifying the subject-matter. It would, however, have been possible for the sellers to have turned their final communication into a counter-offer by explicitly referring in it not only to the subject-matter of the original offer, but also to all its other terms. In that case no contract would have been concluded, since the buyers had made it clear before the machine was delivered that they did not agree to the "price escalation" clause.[167] Thus it is possible by careful draftsmanship to avoid losing the battle of forms, but not (if the other party is equally careful) to win it. In the *Butler Machine Tool* case, for example, sellers' conditions included one by which their terms were to "prevail over any terms and conditions in Buyer's order"; but this failed (in consequence of the terms of the buyers' counter-offer) to produce the effect desired by the sellers.[168] The most that the draftsman can be certain of achieving is the stalemate situation in which there is no contract at all. Such a conclusion will often be inconvenient,[169] though where the goods are nevertheless delivered it may lead to a liability on the part of the buyers to pay a reasonable price.[170]

2–038 **Documents sent after contract made.** The discussion in para.2–037 above is concerned with the effect of the submission of a document or documents containing terms *before* the alleged contract is made. The submission of such a document by one party *after* the making of the contract will not affect the existence of the contract[171]; nor will the terms of the document form part of the contract unless they are, in turn, accepted as variations of the contract, either expressly or by conduct.

2–039 **Acceptance of tenders.** The submission of a tender normally amounts to an offer[172]; and the effect of an "acceptance" of such a tender turns on the construction of the acceptance and the tender in each case. Where a tender is submitted, *e.g.* for the erection of a building, a binding contract will normally arise from acceptance of the tender, unless it is expressly stipulated that there is to be no contract until certain formal documents have been executed.[173] But

---

[166] *Per* Lawton and Buckley L.JJ.; Lord Denning, M.R. also uses this analysis, but prefers the alternative approach of considering "the documents . . . as a whole": see 405 and *cf.* above, para.2–028.

[167] At 406, *per* Lawton L.J.

[168] *cf. Matter of Doughboy Industries Inc*, 233 N.Y.S. 2d 488, 490 (1962): "The buyer and seller accomplished a legal equivalent to the irresistible force colliding with the immoveable object."

[169] It seems to have been rejected for this reason in *Johnson Matthey Bankers Ltd v State Trading Corp. of India* [1984] 1 Lloyd's Rep. 427.

[170] *cf. Peter Lind & Co Ltd v Mersey Docks & Harbour Board* [1972] 2 Lloyd's Rep. 234, above, para.2–027; McKendrick (1988) 8 O.J.L.S. 197.

[171] *Jayaar Impex Ltd v Toaken Group Ltd* [1996] 2 Lloyd's Rep. 437; *cf.* below, para.2–116.

[172] Above, para.2–022.

[173] Below, para.2–116.

greater difficulty arises in construing an "acceptance" of a tender for an indefinite amount for example, of one to supply "such quantities (not exceeding a specified amount) as you may order." The person to whom such a tender is submitted does not incur any liability merely by "accepting" it: he becomes liable only when he places an order for goods,[174] and he would not be bound to place any order at all[175] unless he had (expressly or by necessary implication[176]) indicated in his invitation for tenders that he would do so.[177] The party submitting the tender also becomes bound, once a definite order has been placed, to fulfil it.[178] Whether he can withdraw before this point, or avoid liability with respect to future orders, depends on the interpretation of the tender. He can do so if the tender means: "I will supply such quantities as you may order."[179] But he will not be entitled to withdraw if the tender means "I hereby bind myself to execute orders which you may place," and if this promise is supported by some consideration.[180]

Acceptance by tender. An invitation for tenders may, exceptionally, amount to an offer, *e.g.* where the person issuing the invitation binds himself to accept the highest or, as the case may be, the lowest tender.[181] The acceptance then takes the form of the submission of a tender; but difficulties can arise where several tenders are made and one (or more) of them takes the form of a so-called "referential bid." In *Harvela Investments Ltd v Royal Trust Co of Canada (C.I.) Ltd*[182] an invitation for the submission of "offers" to buy shares was addressed to two persons; it stated that the prospective sellers bound themselves to accept the "highest offer." One of the persons to whom the invitation was addressed made a bid of a fixed sum while the other submitted a "referential bid" undertaking to pay either a fixed sum or a specified amount in excess of the bid made by the other, whichever was the higher amount. It was held that the "referential bid" was ineffective and that the submission of the other bid had concluded the contract for the sale of the shares. In reaching this conclusion, the House of Lords stressed that the bids were, by the terms of the invitation, to be confidential, so that neither bidder would know the amount bid by the other. In these circumstances the object of the invitation, which was to ascertain the highest amount that each of the persons to whom it was addressed was willing to pay, would have been defeated by allowing it to be accepted by a "referential bid." 2–040

[174] *Percival Ltd v L.C.C. Asylums, etc., Committee* (1918) 87 L.J.K.B. 677.

[175] *cf. Churchward v R.* (1865) L.R. 1 Q.B. 173; *R. v Demers* [1900] A.C. 103.

[176] *e.g. Sylvan Crest Sand & Gravel Co v U.S.*, 150 F.2d 642 (1945).

[177] *cf. Harvela Investments Ltd v Royal Trust Co of Canada (C.I.) Ltd* [1986] A.C. 207.

[178] *Great Northern Ry v Witham* (1873) L.R. 9 C.P. 16; *cf.* the similar rule applied to "declarations" under an "open cover" insurance in *Citadel Insurance Co v Atlantic Union Insurance Co* [1982] 2 Lloyd's Rep. 543.

[179] *G.N. Ry v Witham* (1873) L.R. C.P. 16, 19.

[180] *Percival Ltd v L.C.C. Asylums, etc., Committee* (1918) 87 L.J.K.B. 677, 678; *Miller v F. A. Sadd & Son Ltd* [1981] 3 All E.R. 265. For an exception to the requirement of consideration in the law of insurance, see the *Citadel* case, above, n.178 at 546; below, para.3–173.

[181] Above, para.2–022.

[182] [1986] A.C. 207.

2–041 **Acceptance in ignorance of offer: unilateral contracts.** In some jurisdictions it has been held that a person who gives information for which a reward has been offered cannot claim the reward unless he knew of the offer at the time of giving the information[183]; and the position has been said to be the same where that person once knew of the offer but had, at the time of the alleged acceptance, forgotten it.[184] The English case of *Gibbons v Proctor*[185] is sometimes thought to support the contrary view, but the actual decision can probably be explained on the ground that the claimant did know of the offer of reward by the time the information was given on his behalf to the person named in the advertisement.[186] To allow recovery where the claimant did *not* know of the offer when he gave the information may raise the doctrinal difficulty that, in such cases, the parties have not *reached* any agreement; the position is simply that their wishes coincide. But in the case of a unilateral contract it is hard to see what legitimate interest of the promisor is prejudiced by holding him liable to a party who has in fact complied with the terms of the offer, though without being aware of it.

2–042 **Acceptance in ignorance of offer: bilateral contracts.** Different considerations may apply where a person who does acts alleged to amount to acceptance of an offer of a bilateral contract does these acts in ignorance of the offer. For in that case the actor may (if the acts amount to an acceptance) not only acquire rights but also incur liabilities under the contract, and it may be unfair to subject him to these if at the time of the alleged acceptance he was not aware of the fact that an offer had been made to him, and thus had no intention of entering into a contract. In *Upton RDC v Powell*[187] the defendant, whose house was on fire, telephoned the Upton police and asked for "the fire brigade." He was entitled to the services of the Pershore fire brigade free of charge as he lived in its district; but the police called the Upton fire brigade, in the belief that the defendant lived in that district. The Upton fire brigade for a time shared this belief and thought "that they were rendering gratuitous services in their own area."[188] It was held that the defendant was contractually bound to pay for these services. But even if the defendant's telephone call was an offer, it is hard to see how the Upton fire brigade's services, given with no thought of reward, could be an acceptance. It would have been better to have given the claimants a restitutionary remedy than to hold that there was a contract. The case was concerned only with the rights of the fire brigade, but, if there was a contract, the fire brigade also owed more extensive duties than they would have owed, had they been volunteers. It may well be hard to subject a person who thinks he is a volunteer to the more stringent

---

[183] *Bloom v American Swiss Watch Co* (1915) App.Div. 100 (S. Afr.); American authorities are divided: see Corbin, *Contracts*, para.59.

[184] *R. v Clarke* (1927) 40 C.L.R. 277, 241.

[185] (1891) 64 L.T. 594; 55 J.P. 616; *cf. Neville v Kelly* (1862) 12 C.B.(N.S.) 740.

[186] "The information ultimately reached Penn at a time when the plaintiff knew that the reward had been offered": 55 J.P. 616.

[187] [1942] 1 All E.R. 220; Mitchell, (1997) 12 J.C.L. 78; for the extent of the fire brigade's duty apart from contract, see *John Monroe (Acrylics) Ltd v London Fire & Civil Defence Authority* [1997] 2 Lloyd's Rep. 161.

[188] At 221.

duties of a contractor.[189] Similar reasoning applies where the effect of an alleged bilateral contract is not to impose liabilities on a party but simply to deprive him of rights. It has accordingly been held that an alleged offer to abandon arbitration proceedings cannot be accepted unless the persons claiming to have accepted it understood or believed at the time of the alleged acceptance that such an offer was being made.[190]

Motive for the acceptance. A person who knows of the offer may do the act required for acceptance with some motive other than that of accepting the offer. In *Williams v Carwardine*[191] the defendant offered a reward of £20 to anyone who gave information leading to the conviction of the murderers of Walter Carwardine. The plaintiff knew of the offer, and, thinking that she had not long to live, signed a "voluntary statement to ease my conscience, and in hopes of forgiveness hereafter." This statement resulted in the conviction of the murderers. It was held that the plaintiff had brought herself within the terms of the offer and was entitled to the reward. Patteson J. added: "We cannot go into the plaintiff's motives."[192] Similarly, in *Carlill v Carbolic Smoke Ball Co*,[193] the claimant recovered the £100, although her predominant motive in using the smoke ball was (presumably) to avoid catching influenza. But in the Australian case of *R. v Clarke*[194] a reward had been offered for information leading to the arrest and conviction of the murderers of two police officers. Clarke, who knew of the offer and was himself suspected of the crime, gave information leading to the conviction of the culprits. He admitted that he gave the information to clear himself of the charge, and with no thought of claiming the reward. His claim for the reward failed as he had not given the information "in exchange for the offer."[195] It seems that an act which is *wholly* motivated by factors other than the existence of the offer cannot amount to an acceptance[196]; but if the existence of the offer plays some part, however small, in inducing a person to do the required act, there is a valid acceptance of the offer. 2–043

Cross-offers. It seems that there is generally no contract if two persons make identical cross-offers, neither knowing of the other's offer when he made his own: *e.g.* if A writes to B offering to sell B his car for £5,000 and B simultaneously writes to A offering to buy the car for £5,000. The most natural reaction 2–044

[189] *cf. B.S.C. v Cleveland Bridge & Engineering Co Ltd* [1984] 1 All E.R. 504, 510. *Quaere* what the position should be where one party thinks that he is giving or getting a gratuitous service while the other thinks that he is contracting; *i.e.* if the fire brigade had intended from the beginning to charge for their services.

[190] *Tracomin SA v Anton C. Nielsen* [1984] 2 Lloyd's Rep. 195, 203; and see above, para.2–006, below, para.2–071.

[191] (1833) 5 C. & P. 566; 4 B. & Ad. 621; it must be assumed that the claimant knew of the offer; *Carlill v Carbolic Smoke Ball Co Ltd* [1892] 2 Q.B. 484, 489, n.2. See also *England v Davidson* (1840) 11 A. & E. 856; *Smith v Moore* (1845) 1 C.B. 438; and *cf. Bent v Wakefield Bank* (1878) 4 C.P.D. 1; *Fallick v Barber* (1813) 1 M. & S. 108. See also Theft Act 1968, s.23, penalising advertisements of rewards for stolen goods which state that no questions will be asked, etc.

[192] (1833) 4 B. & Ad. at 623.

[193] [1893] 1 Q.B. 256; above, para.2–018.

[194] (1927) 40 C.L.R. 227; contrast *Simonds v U.S.*, 308 F. 2d 160 (1962).

[195] (1927) 40 C.L.R. 227, 233; *Tracomin SA v Anton C. Nielsen* [1984] 2 Lloyd's Rep. 195, 203.

[196] *Lark v Outhwaite* [1991] 2 Lloyd's Rep. 132, 140.

to letters which cross in this way would be for one of the parties to communicate with the other to make sure that there was indeed an agreement between them. To hold that there was a contract without some such further communication might cause considerable surprise to one of the parties, or possibly to both. The view that "cross-offers are not an acceptance of each other"[197] can therefore be supported not only on the theoretical ground that the requirements of offer and acceptance are not satisfied, but also on the practical grounds that it accords with normal commercial expectations and that it promotes certainty.

(b) *Communication of Acceptance*

2–045 **General requirement of communication.** The general rule is that an acceptance has no legal effect until it is communicated to the offeror.[198] Accordingly, there is no contract where a person writes an acceptance on a piece of paper which he simply keeps[199]; where a company resolves to accept an application for shares but does not communicate the resolution to the applicant[200]; where a person decides to accept an offer to sell goods to him and instructs his bank to pay the offeror but neither he nor the bank gives notice of this fact to the offeror[201]; and where a person communicates the acceptance only to his own agent.[202] The main reason for the rule is that it could cause hardship to the offeror to be bound without knowing that his offer had been accepted. It follows that, so long as the offeror knows of the acceptance, there can be a contract even though the acceptance was not brought to his notice *by the offeree*.[203] However, there will be no contract if the communication is made by a third party without the authority of the offeree in circumstances indicating that the offeree's decision to accept was not yet regarded by him as irrevocable.[204]

2–046 **What amounts to communication.** For an acceptance to be "communicated" it must normally be brought to the notice of the offeror. Thus there is no contract if the words of acceptance are "drowned by an aircraft flying overhead"; or if they are spoken into a telephone after the line has gone dead or become so indistinct that the offeror does not hear them.[205] The requirement of "communication" may, however, in some circumstances be satisfied even though the acceptance has not actually come to the notice of the offeror: *e.g.* where a written notice of acceptance is left by the offeree at the offeror's address.[206]

---

[197] *Tinn v Hoffman & Co* (1873) 29 L.T. 271, 278.

[198] *McIver v Richardson* (1813) 1 M. & S. 557; *Mozley v Tinkler* (1835) 1 C.M. & R. 692; *Ex p. Stark* [1897] 1 Ch. 575; *Holwell Securities Ltd v Hughes* [1974] 1 W.L.R. 155, 157; *Allied Marine Transport Ltd v Vale do Rio Doce Navegaçao SA (The Leonidas D.)* [1985] 1 W.L.R. 925, 937.

[199] *Kennedy v Thomassen* [1929] 1 Ch. 426; *Brogden v Metropolitan Ry* (1877) 2 App. Cas. 666, 692.

[200] *Best's Case* (1865) 2 D.J. & S. 650; *cf. Gunn's Case* (1867) L.R. 3 Ch.App. 40.

[201] *Brinkibon Ltd v Stahag Stahl und Stahlwarenhandelsgesellschaft mbH* [1983] 2 A.C. 34.

[202] *Hebb's Case* (1867) L.R. 4 Eq. 9; *Kennedy v Thomassen* [1929] 1 Ch. 426.

[203] *Bloxham's Case* (1864) 33 Beav. 529; (1864) 4 D.J. & S. 447; *Levita's Case* (1867) L.R. 3 Ch.App. 36.

[204] This appears to be the best explanation of *Powell v Lee* (1908) 99 L.T. 284.

[205] *Entores Ltd v Miles Far East Corp.* [1955] 2 Q.B. 327, 332.

[206] *cf.* below, para.2–091.

Exceptions to requirement of communication of acceptance. In the following situations an acceptance is, or may be, effective although it is not communicated to the offeror. 2–047

(1) Terms of the offer. The offer may expressly or impliedly waive the requirement of communication of acceptance. One situation in which this may be the case is that in which an offer invites acceptance by conduct. For example, where an offer to supply goods is made by sending them to the offeree it may be accepted by simply using them[207]; and where an offer to buy goods is made by ordering them, it may sometimes be accepted by simply despatching them.[208] Similarly a tenant can accept an offer of a new tenancy by simply staying on the premises.[209]

(2) Unilateral contracts. In the case of a unilateral contract,[210] the requirement of communication of acceptance is almost always waived. For this reason, performance of the required act or abstention normally suffices, without any previous intimation of acceptance.[211] Thus in *Carlill v Carbolic Smoke Ball Co*[212] the court rejected the argument that the claimant should have notified the defendants of her acceptance of their offer. The contract which arises[213] between a bank which has issued a credit card to one of its customers and the retailer to whom the customer presents the card has similarly been described as unilateral,[214] so that the bank's offer can be accepted by the retailer's dealing with the customer without any need for the retailer's acceptance to be communicated to the bank.[215] Another situation in which notification of acceptance was said to be unnecessary in the case of a unilateral contract arose in *Argo Fund Ltd v Esser Steel Ltd*[216] where an arrangement between a debtor and its creditor banks empowered each creditor to transfer its rights by delivery of a transfer certificate to an "agent." This arrangement was said to be a unilateral contract[217] by which the debtor made a standing offer (a) to the creditor, to terminate the original contract and (b) to the transferee to enter into a new one.[218] The former offer was accepted by the creditor's delivery of the transfer certificate to the agent[219] and the latter by the transferee's agreeing to the transfer with the transferor on the

---

207 *Weatherby v Banham* (1832) 5 C. & P. 228; *cf. Minories Finance Ltd v Afribank Nigeria Ltd* [1995] 1 Lloyd's Rep. 134, 140; it is assumed that the goods are not "unsolicited" within the legislation against "inertia selling" (above, para.2–005).

208 *Port Huron Machinery Co v Wohlers*, 207 Iowa 826, 221 N.W. 843 (1928); *cf.* U.C.C., s.2–206(1)(b); *Smit International Singapore Pte Ltd v Kurnia Dewi Shipping SA (The Kurnia Dewi)* [1997] 1 Lloyd's Rep. 553, 559.

209 *Roberts v Hayward* (1828) 3 C. & P. 432; but not if the tenant disclaims the intention to accept: *Glossop v Ashley* [1921] 2 K.B. 451.

210 See above, para.1–079; below para.2–078.

211 *Shipton v Cardiff Corp.* (1917) 87 L.J.K.B. 51; *Davies v Rhondda UDC* (1917) 87 L.J.K.B. 166.

212 [1893] 1 Q.B. 256, above, para.2–018.

213 Below, paras 3–039, 18–007.

214 *First Sport Ltd v Barclays Bank plc* [1993] 1 W.L.R. 1228, 1234 (where the card had been stolen and been presented to the retailer by the thief).

215 *ibid.* at 1234–1235.

216 [2005] EWHC 600 (Comm), [2006] 1 All E.R. (Comm) 56; affd on other grounds [2006] EWCA Civ 241, [2006] 2 All E.R. (Comm) 104.

217 [2005] EWHC 600 (Comm), [2006] 1 All E.R. (Comm) 56 at [51].

218 *ibid.*; the effect of the new contract was said at [50], [51] to be to novate the original one.

219 *ibid.*

terms of the agreement, as set out in the certificate.[220] Notification of these acts of acceptance was not necessary since no such requirement was stated in the original loan agreement and this fact was apparently regarded as a waiver of the requirement of communication of acceptance.[221]

(3) "Fault" of offeror. The offeror may be precluded from denying that the acceptance was communicated if it was "his own fault that he did not get it"; *e.g.* "if the listener on the telephone does not catch the words of acceptance but nevertheless does not . . . ask for them to be repeated."[222] If an acceptance is sent and duly received during business hours by telex or fax but is simply not read by anyone in the offeror's office when it is there transcribed or printed out on his machine, it is probably taken to have been communicated at that time[223]; if such a message is received out of business hours, it probably takes effect at the beginning of the next business day.[224] Similar rules probably apply *(mutatis mutandis)* to determine when an acceptance sent by email and duly received, but not read by the offeror or anyone in his office, is, or is taken to be, communicated to the offeror.[225]

(4) Communication to offeror's agent. The acceptance may be communicated, not to the offeror personally, but to his agent. The effect of such a communication depends on the agent's authority.[226] It concludes a contract if the agent is authorised to *receive* the acceptance, but not if he is authorised only to *transmit* it to the offeror: *e.g.* if a written acceptance is handed to a messenger sent to the offeree by the offeror. In the latter case the acceptance takes effect only when it is communicated to the offeror (unless the case falls within one of the other exceptions to the general rule requiring the acceptance to be communicated to the offeror).

(5) Acceptance sent by post. An acceptance sent by post often takes effect before it is communicated. The exact effects of such an acceptance are discussed in paragraphs 2–048 to 2–060 below.

(c) *Posted Acceptance*

2–048 **The posting rule.**[227] An acceptance sent by post could take effect when it is actually communicated to the offeror, when it arrives at his address, when it would in the ordinary course of post have reached him, or when it is posted. Each of these solutions could cause inconvenience or injustice to one of the parties,

[220] *ibid.*, at [52].

[221] *ibid.*, at [53] ("perhaps this is the right analysis").

[222] *Entores Ltd v Miles Far East Corp.* [1955] 2 Q.B. 327, 333.

[223] *cf. Tenax Steamship Co Ltd v The Brimnes (Owners) (The Brimnes)* [1975] Q.B. 929; and see below, para.2–091.

[224] *Schelde Delta Shipping BV v Astarte Shipping Ltd (The Pamela)* [1995] 2 Lloyd's Rep. 249, 252; *Galaxy Energy International Ltd v Novorossiyk Shipping Co (The Peter Schmidt)* [1998] 2 Lloyd's Rep. 1.

[225] Our concern here is whether the requirement of communication is satisfied. For the question whether, in cases of emailed acceptances, there is an *exception* to the requirement of communication, see below, para.2–051.

[226] *Henthorn v Fraser* [1892] 2 Ch.27, 33.

[227] Winfield (1939) 55 L.Q.R. 499; Nussbaum (1926) 36 Col.L.Rev. 920; Ellison Kahn (1955) 72 S.A.L.J. 246; Evans (1966) 15 I.C.L.Q. 553; Gardner (1992) 12 O.J.L.S. 170.

especially when the acceptance is lost or delayed in the post. In English law, what is usually regarded as the general rule[228] is that a postal acceptance takes effect when the letter of acceptance is posted.[229] A letter is "posted" for this purpose when it is put in the control of the Post Office[230] or of one of its employees authorised to *receive* letters. Handing letters to a postman authorised to *deliver* letters is not posting.[231] The same principle applies to the now uncommon case of an acceptance by telegram: such an acceptance takes effect when the telegram is communicated to a person authorised to receive it for transmission to the addressee[232]; and it seems that this rule would apply to telemessages, which have replaced inland telegrams. The "posting" rule is probably best explained as one of convenience; it generally favours the offeree for the reasons stated in paras 2–053 to 2–057 below.

Conditions of applicability. The posting rule applies only if it is reasonable to use the post. This will normally be the case if the offer itself is made by post. It may be reasonable to use the post even though the offer was made orally if immediate acceptance was not contemplated and the parties lived at a distance.[233] On the other hand it would not normally be reasonable to attempt to reply by a posted letter of acceptance to an offer made by telex[234] or by telephone, fax or e-mail. Nor would it be reasonable to accept by post if the postal service was, to the acceptor's knowledge, disrupted.[235] 2–049

Instantaneous communications. The posting rule does not apply to acceptances made by some "instantaneous" mode of communication, *e.g.* by telephone or by telex.[236] The reason why the rule does not apply in such cases is that the acceptor will often know at once that his attempt to communicate was unsuccessful, so that he has the opportunity of making a proper communication.[237] A person who accepts by a letter which goes astray, on the other hand, may not know of the loss or delay until it is too late to make another communication. Such 2–050

---

[228] But see below, paras 2–053 *et seq.*

[229] *Henthorn v Fraser* [1892] 2 Ch.27, 33; *Adams v Lindsell* (1818) 1 B. & Ald. 681; *Potter v Sanders* (1846) 6 Hare 1; *Harris' Case* (1872) L.R. 7 Ch.App. 587.

[230] *Brinkibon Ltd v Stahag Stahl and Stahlwarenhandelsgesellschaft mbH* [1983] 2 A.C. 34, 41; the "Post Office" here refers to the provider of the universal postal service under the Postal Services Act 2000, by whatever name that provider may from time to time be known.

[231] *Re London & Northern Bank* [1900] 1 Ch. 220.

[232] *Bruner v Moore* [1904] 1 Ch.305; *cf. Stevenson Jacques & Co v McLean* (1880) 5 Q.B.D. 346. See also *Cowan v O'Connor* (1888) 20 Q.B.D. 640 (place of acceptance).

[233] *e.g.* in *Henthorn v Fraser* [1892] 2 Ch. 27. Such a written acceptance of an oral offer does not, however, create a "contract by correspondence" within Law of Property Act 1925, s.46: *Stearn v Twitchell* [1985] 1 All E.R. 631.

[234] *cf. Quenerduaine v Cole* (1883) 32 W.R. 185 (telegram).

[235] *Bal v Van Staden* [1902] T.S. 128.

[236] *Entores Ltd v Miles Far East Corp.* [1955] 2 Q.B. 327; *Brinkibon Ltd v Stahag Stahl und Stahlwarengesellschaft mbH* [1983] 2 A.C. 34; *cf. N.V. Stoomv Maats "De Maas" v Nippon Yusen Kaisha (The Pendrecht)* [1980] 2 Lloyd's Rep. 56, 66; *Gill & Duffus Landauer Ltd v London Export Corp GmbH* [1982] 2 Lloyd's Rep. 627; *cf. Schelde Delta Shipping B.V. v Astarte Shipping Ltd (The Pamela)* [1995] 2 Lloyd's Rep. 249, 252 (telexed notice withdrawing ship from charterparty); and (in tort) *Diamond v Bank of London & Montreal* [1979] Q.B. 333.

[237] See the *Entores* case, above n.236, at 333 and the *Brinkibon* case, above n.236, at 43.

instantaneous communications are therefore governed by the general rule[238] that an acceptance must be actually communicated, subject to the other exceptions to that rule stated in para.2–047 above.

2–051 **Dictated telegrams, faxes, emails and web-site trading.** It is now uncommon for acceptances to be made by telegram or telemessage dictated over the telephone and there is no authority on the question whether such an acceptance takes effect when the message is dictated by the sender or when it is communicated to the addressee. It is submitted that such an acceptance should, in accordance with the above reasoning,[239] take effect as soon as it is dictated[240]; for if it later goes astray, the acceptor is unlikely to have any means of knowing this fact until it is too late to make a further communication. Fax messages seem to occupy an intermediate position between postal and instantaneous communications. The sender will know at once if his message has not been received at all, or if it has been received only in part, and in such situations the mere sending of the message should not amount to an effective acceptance.[241] It is also possible for the entire message to have been received, but in such a form as to be wholly or partly illegible.[242] Since the sender is unlikely to know, or to have means of knowing, this at once, it is suggested that an acceptance sent by fax might well be effective in such circumstances. The same reasoning should apply to messages sent by electronic means, *e.g.* by email[243] or in the course of website trading[244]: here again the effects of unsuccessful attempts to communicate should depend on whether the sender of the message knows (or has the means of knowing) at once of any failure in communication.

---

238 Above, para.2–045.

239 At n.237, above.

240 *Contra* Winfield (1939) 55 L.Q.R. 499, 515.

241 *JSC Zestafoni Nikoladze Ferroalloy Plant v Ronly Holdings Ltd* [2004] EWHC 245 (Comm), [2004] 2 Lloyd's Rep. 335, where a fax message was classified at [75] as an "instantaneous communication" and to take effect only on full receipt as the sender's machine would usually indicate whether the message had been received "effectively" (as distinct from having been received only in part). *Cf.* also *Korbetis v Transgrain Shipping BV* [2005] EWHC 1345 (QB) (misdirected fax acceptance, below, para.2–058).

242 This possibility is not considered (as it did not arise) in the *JSC Zestafoni* case, above n.241.

243 For various possible times at which an email can be said to have been *received,* see Law Commission, *Electronic Commerce: formal Requirements in Electronic Communications* (December 2001), para.3.56; the present question is whether such a message may be effective *before* it is received. The Electronic Commerce (EC Directive) Regulations 2002, (SI 2002/2013) which implement most of the EC Directive on Electronic Commerce (2000/31/EC), provide that the formal requirements contained in regs 9 and 11 do not apply to "contracts concluded exclusively by electronic mail or by equivalent individual communications": regs 9(4) and 11(3). *cf. Bermuth Lines Ltd v High Seas Shipping Ltd (The Eastern Navigator)* [2005] EWHC 3020 (Comm), [2006] 1 Lloyd's Rep. 537 at [21]–[31] (email notice of arbitration effective on receipt).

244 The Law Commission paper (above, n.243) para.3.37 regards "clicking on a website button" as satisfying the requirement of *signature* but does not state whether it is an offer or an acceptance, or specify *when* it takes effect. Art.11.1 of the Directive on Electronic Commerce (above) states that "the order and acknowledgement are deemed to be received when the parties to whom they are addressed are able to access them"; and almost identical language is used in reg.11(2)(a) of the Regulations cited in n.243, above. But this form of words does not of itself answer the question whether the contract may not be concluded even before that time.

Terms of the offer. The posting rule can be excluded by the terms of the offer. For this purpose, it is not necessary to say expressly that the acceptance will take effect only when it has been actually communicated. In *Holwell Securities Ltd v Hughes*[245] an offer to sell a house was made in the form of an option "to be exercisable by notice in writing to the Intending Vendor." Such a notice was posted but did not arrive. It was held that there was no contract of sale as the offer, on its true construction, required actual communication of acceptance. 2–052

Operation of the posting rule. The posting rule is essentially one of convenience.[246] The English authorities support its application in three situations discussed in paras 2–054 to 2–057 below. It should not, however, be thought that the rule will be mechanically applied to all situations which it might, by a process of apparently logical deduction, be thought to govern. It has been said that the rule will not be applied where it would lead to "manifest inconvenience and absurdity"[247]; so that the question of its application to a further group of situations discussed in paras 2–058 to 2–061 below depends on practical considerations and on the balance of convenience. 2–053

Posted acceptance preceded by uncommunicated withdrawal. A posted acceptance prevails over a withdrawal of an offer which was posted before the acceptance but which had not yet reached the offeree when the acceptance was posted.[248] In practice, this is probably the most important application of the rule. It can be justified on the ground that, if the acceptance did not prevail, reliance could not be placed on a posted offer. It also operates as a restriction on the otherwise unfettered power[249] of the offeror to withdraw his offer. 2–054

Acceptance lost or delayed in the post. A posted acceptance takes effect even though it never reaches the offeror because it is lost through an accident in the post[250]; and the same rule probably applies where the acceptance is merely delayed through an accident in the post,[251] *i.e.* the contract is concluded at the time of posting of the acceptance. In *Household Fire Insurance Co Ltd v Grant*,[252] for example, the defendant had applied for shares in a company: this application amounted to an offer by him to subscribe for the shares.[253] An acceptance, in the form of a letter of allotment, was posted to him but never received. Some three years later, the company went into liquidation, and it was held that the defendant was a shareholder and so liable for calls on the shares. The case has certain unusual features: namely that the initial deposit on application for the shares was not actually paid, the defendant being instead credited 2–055

---

[245] [1974] 1 W.L.R. 155; *cf. New Hart Builders Ltd v Brindley* [1975] Ch. 342.

[246] *Brinkibon* case (above, n.236) at 41; *Gill & Duffus Landauer* case (above, n.236) at 631.

[247] *Holwell Securities Ltd v Hughes* [1974] 1 W.L.R. 157, 161.

[248] *Harris' Case* (1872) L.R. 7 Ch.App. 587; *Byrne & Co v Leon van Tienhoven* (1880) 5 C.P.D. 344; *Henthorn v Fraser* [1892] 2 Ch. 27; *Re London & Northern Bank* [1900] 1 Ch.200.

[249] Below, paras 2–088, 3–172.

[250] *Household Fire Insurance Co Ltd v Grant* (1879) 4 Ex.D. 216.

[251] See *Dunlop v Higgins* (1848) 1 H.L.C. 381, which would probably be followed in England though it is expressly restricted (at 402) to Scots law.

[252] (1879) 4 Ex.D. 216.

[253] Above, para.2–024.

with an equivalent sum due to him from the company; and that dividends declared by the company were not actually paid out to the defendant but simply credited to his account with the company. But for these circumstances the defendant would necessarily have become aware (long before the end of the three years) of the fact that he was regarded by the company as a shareholder.

2–056 The decision in *Household Fire Insurance Co Ltd v Grant* was reached only by a majority and involved the overruling of a previous contrary decision.[254] This indicates that the arguments of convenience for and against applying the posting rule to such a situation are finely balanced. On the one hand, it may be hard to hold an offeror liable on an acceptance which, through no fault of his own, was never received by him; on the other it may be equally hard to deprive the offeree of the benefit of an acceptance if he had taken all reasonable steps to communicate it. Moreover, each party may act in reliance on his (perfectly reasonable) view of the situation: the offeror may enter into other contracts, believing that his offer had not been accepted, while the offeree may refrain from doing so, believing that he had effectively accepted the offer. In this situation, English law favours the offeree on the grounds that it is the offeror who "trusts to the post"[255] and that the offeror can safeguard himself by stipulating in the offer that the acceptance must be actually communicated to him.[256] These arguments may be generally valid but they are not wholly convincing. The offer may be a counter-offer, in which case it will be the ultimate offeree who originally "trust[ed] to the post." Or the offer may be made on a form prepared by the offeree,[256a] in which case he and not the offeror will, for practical purposes, be in control of its terms.

2–057 **Priorities.** A contract is taken to be made at the time when the acceptance was posted, so as to take priority over another contract affecting the same subject-matter made after the posting of the first acceptance.[257] This application of the posting rule can perhaps be explained as a reward for the superior diligence of the first acceptor.

2–058 **Misdirected letter of acceptance.** A letter of acceptance may be lost or delayed because it bears a wrong or an incomplete address, or because it is not properly stamped. Normally such defects will be due to the carelessness of the offeree; and, although there is no English authority precisely in point,[258] it is submitted that the posting rule should not apply to such cases. Although an offeror may have to take the risk of accidents in the post, it would be unreasonable to impose on him the further risk of the acceptor's carelessness. These arguments do not apply where the misdirection is due to the fault of the *offeror—e.g.* where his own address is incompletely or illegibly given in the offer

[254] *British & American Telegraph Co v Colson* (1871) L.R. 6 Ex. 108.
[255] *Household Insurance* case, (1879) 4 Ex.D. 216, 223.
[256] *ibid.*
[256a] Below, para.2–069.
[257] *Potter v Sanders* (1846) 6 Hare 1.
[258] See, by way of analogy, *Getreide-Import Gesellschaft v Contimar* [1953] 1 W.L.R. 207 and 793.

itself.[259] In such a case, the offeror should not be allowed to rely on the fact that the acceptance was misdirected (except perhaps where his error in stating his own address was obvious to the offeree; for in such a case the offeror's fault would not be the effective cause of the misdirection of the acceptance). It is submitted that a misdirected acceptance should take effect (if at all) at the time which is least favourable to the party responsible for the misdirection.

In *L.J. Korbetis v Transgrain Shipping BV* Toulson J. said that he agreed with the above "general approach" to the problem of misdirected acceptances "because it seems to me to correspond with principle and justice."[260] The question in that case was whether shipowners and charterers had agreed on the nomination of a sole arbitrator to whom a dispute which had arisen under a charterparty between them was to be referred. In reply to a fax from the charterers inviting the shipowners to choose one of three names, the shipowners sent a fax from their office in Piraeus, agreeing to one of those names. This fax was intended for the charterers in the Netherlands, but it never reached them because the appropriate international dialling code had not been entered. It was held that the misdirected acceptance was not effective to conclude an agreement between shipowners and charterers for the appointment of the arbitrator.

Garbled messages. A message may be garbled as a result of some inaccuracy in transmission for which the sender is not responsible. This problem used to arise in the case of telegraphed messages and could still arise from the use of now more common modes of communication: *e.g.* where a telex or electronic message was corrupted in transmission without any fault on the part of the sender; and the discussion of garbled telegraphic messages in (and arising from) the older authorities may provide some guidance to the solution of such problems. In *Henkel v Pape*[261] the claimant invited the defendant to make an offer to buy 50 rifles; and the defendant, not wanting this number, telegraphed "send *three* rifles." The telegram reached the claimant in the form "send *the* rifles" and the claimant despatched 50. It was held that the defendant was not bound to accept more than three. Here the garbled telegram was an offer, but such a communication could also be an acceptance: for example where, in response to an offer to sell 50, the buyer sent a telegraphed message in the form "send *the* rifles." It is submitted that this would be a valid acceptance (so long as it was reasonable for the buyer to accept by this medium) even if the message arrived in the form "send *three* rifles." If the offeror has to take the risk of loss or delay in the post, there seems to be no good reason why he should not also take the risk of errors in the transmission of a telegraphed message; for in each case the offeree will have no means of knowing that something has gone wrong until it is too late to make another, proper, communication.[262] 2–059

Revocation of posted acceptance. There is no English authority on the question whether a posted acceptance can be revoked by a later communication 2–060

[259] *cf. Townsend's Case* (1871) L.R. 13 Eq. 148 (the actual reasoning of which is obsolete since *Household Fire Insurance Co Ltd v Grant* (1879) 4 Ex.D. 216).
[260] [2005] EWHC 1345 (QB) at [15].
[261] (1870) 6 Ex. 7.
[262] *cf.* above, para.2–050.

(such as a telex or an email message) which reaches the offeror before, or at the same time as, the acceptance. One view is that the revocation has no effect since, once a contract has been concluded by the posting of the acceptance, it cannot be dissolved by the act of one party.[263] But this apparently "logical" deduction from the "posting rule" overlooks the fundamental point that that rule is only one of convenience.[264] Hence the issue is whether the offeror could be unjustly prejudiced by allowing the offeree to rely on the subsequent revocation. On the one hand, it can be argued that the offeror cannot be prejudiced since he was not entitled to have his offer accepted and cannot have relied on its having been accepted if he did not yet know of the acceptance. On the other hand it can be argued that, once the acceptance has been posted, the offeror can no longer withdraw his offer,[265] and that reciprocity demands that the offeree should likewise not be allowed to withdraw his acceptance.[266] For if the offeree were allowed to do this he could speculate, without risk to himself, at the offeror's expense. He could post an acceptance and hold the offeror bound if the market moved in his own favour, but retract the acceptance by an overtaking communication if the market moved against him, while the offeror had no similar freedom of action. It has been suggested that the offeror should take the risk of such a revocation, just as he takes the risk of loss or delay[267]; but while the offeror may take the risks of accidents in the post, it is submitted that he should not have to bear risks due entirely to the conduct of the offeree.[268]

2–061 So far it has been assumed that the offeror wants to hold the offeree to the contract notwithstanding the revocation. But to hold an acceptance binding as soon as it was posted, in spite of an overtaking communication purporting to revoke it, might also cause hardship to the offeror, particularly where he had acted in reliance on the revocation; *e.g.* by selling the subject-matter of the original offer to a third party. In such a case it is submitted that the offeree should not be entitled to change his mind yet again and rely on his letter of acceptance with the object of claiming damages from the offeror. The offeree's subsequent purported revocation could in such a case be regarded as an offer to rescind the contract, accepted by the offeror's conduct in relation to subject-matter; communication of such acceptance could be deemed to have been waived. Alternatively,

---

[263] This view is sometimes said to be supported by *Wenkheim v Arndt* (N.Z.) 1 J.R. 73 (1873), where the defendant had by letter accepted an offer of marriage: *her mother* then sent a telegram purporting to cancel the acceptance. The actual decision was that the mother had no authority to act on behalf of her daughter in this way, so that the claimant recovered damages (of no more than one farthing). The view stated in the text is supported by *Morrison v Thoelke*, 155 So. 2d 889 (1963) and by *A to Z Bazaars (Pty) Ltd v Minister of Agriculture* (1974) (4) S.A. 392 (c) (discussed by Turpin [1975] C.L.J. 25); but contradicted by *Dick v U.S.*, 82 F.Supp. 326 (1949). It is also sometimes said to be contradicted by *Dunmore v Alexander* (1830) 9 Shaw 190, but there the first letter was probably an offer; only the dissenting judge regarded it as an acceptance. See generally Hudson (1966) 82 L.Q.R. 169. *cf. Kinch v Bullard* [1999] 1 W.L.R. 423 (notice which, by virtue of Law of Property Act 1925 s.196(3), had taken effect on being left at a person's place of abode, but without having been actually communicated to him, could not thereafter be withdrawn by sender).

[264] Above, para.2–048.

[265] Above, para.2–054.

[266] For similar reasoning in the case of a misdirected acceptance (above, para.2–058) see *L.J. Korbetis v Transgrain Shipping BV* [2005] EWHC 1345 (QB) at [11].

[267] Hudson, above, n.263.

[268] *cf.* above, para.2–058.

the purported revocation could be regarded as repudiation in breach of contract, giving the offeror the power to put an end to his obligations under the contract by "accepting" the breach.[269] The latter view is preferable from the offeror's point of view if the sale to the third party was for a price below that to be paid by the original offeree, for it would enable the offeror to claim the difference from the offeree as damages.[270]

Revocation distinguished from "right to cancel". An offeree who is bound by a contract made by an exchange of letters under the common law rules stated in paras 2–048 and 2–060 above may nevertheless have the "right to cancel" the contract under the Consumer Protection (Distance Selling) Regulations 2000 in circumstances to be more fully described below.[271] The legal consequences of the exercise of this right to cancel are, however, not entirely the same as those that would follow at common law if legal effect were given to the revocation of a posted acceptance.[272] For the purpose of the argument put forward in para.2–060 above (that, if the revocation were effective, the offeree could speculate without risk to himself at the offeror's expense), it is also significant that the "right to cancel" under the Regulations does not (unless otherwise agreed) extend to contracts "for the supply of goods or services the price of which is dependent on fluctuations in the financial market which cannot be controlled by the supplier."[273] 2–062

International sales. The Vienna Convention on Contracts for the International Sale of Goods[274] (which has not been ratified by the United Kingdom) governs not only the rights and duties of the parties to, but also the formation of, such contracts. Under the Convention an offer takes effect when it "reaches" the offeree[275] and an acceptance when it "reaches" the offeror,[276] *i.e.* (in both cases) when it is communicated to the addressee or delivered to his address.[277] Thus there is no contract if the acceptance is lost in the post; but if the acceptance is delayed in transmission, it is effective, unless the offeror informs the offeree promptly on its receipt that he regards the offer as having lapsed.[278] Once an offer has become effective, it cannot be revoked after the offeree has dispatched his acceptance[279]: this again preserves the English position that a posted acceptance prevails over a previously posted withdrawal (referred to in the Convention as a revocation). An acceptance may be withdrawn by a communication which 2–063

[269] Below, para.24–001.

[270] *cf. Kinch v Ballard* [1999] 1 W.L.R. 423, 430 (purported withdrawal by sender of a notice after it had taken effect ineffective against addressee (above, n.263) but said at 430–431 to be effective against sender).

[271] Below, para.2–064.

[272] See below, para.2–064 after n.286.

[273] Consumer Protection (Distance Selling) Regulations 2000, (SI 2000/2334), reg.13(1)(b).

[274] Below, Vol.II, para.43–004.

[275] Art.15(1).

[276] Art.18(2).

[277] Art.24.

[278] Art.21(2).

[279] Art.16(1); "dispatch" is not defined.

reaches the offeror before (or at the same time as) the acceptance would have become effective[280] if there had been no such withdrawal.

2–064 **Consumer's right to cancel distance contracts.** A contract made by (for example) exchange of letters, faxes or emails or website trading falls within the definition of a "distance contract" within the Consumer Protection (Distance Selling) Regulations 2000 if it is one for the supply of goods or services by a commercial supplier to a consumer.[281] The Regulations do not specify when such a contract is made,[282] but if it has been made, they give the consumer the right to cancel it[283] by notice within a cancellation period specified in the Regulations (*e.g.* of seven working days from the consumer's receipt of the goods which have been supplied under the contract).[284] The contract, if so cancelled, is as a general rule "treated as if it had not been made"[285] but this general rule is qualified in various ways.[286] The effect of the exercise of the right to cancel is therefore not the same as the effect of saying that no contract has been concluded by (*e.g.*) exchange of letters under the common law rules of offer and acceptance discussed in paras 2–048 to 2–061 above; on the contrary, the very concept of the consumer's "right to cancel" is based on the assumption that, as a matter of common law, a contract has come into the existence. Moreover, *the supplier* has no right to cancel under the Regulations, so that the question whether he has entered into the contract continues to be governed by the common law rules.

(d) *Prescribed Mode of Acceptance*

2–065 **Method must generally be complied with.** An offer which requires the acceptance to be expressed or communicated in a specified way can generally be accepted only in that way. Thus if the offeror asks for the acceptance to be sent to a particular place one sent elsewhere will not bind him[287]; nor will he be bound

[280] Art.22.

[281] SI 2000/2334 (implementing Dir.97/7/EC); for definitions of "distance contract", "consumer" and "supplier", see reg.3; for a list of methods of communication by which such a contract may be made, see *ibid.* Sch.1. For contracts to which only part of the Regulations apply see reg.6. For amendments to SI 2000/2334, see Financial Services (Distance Marketing) Regulations 2004 (SI 2004/2095 as amended by Consumer Protection from Unfair Trading Regulation 2008 (SI 2008/1277) reg.30(1) and Sched.2, para.110) and Consumer Protection (Distance Selling) Regulations 2005 (SI 2005/689).

[282] This is also true of the Electronic Commerce (EC Directive) Regulations 2002 (SI 2002/2013) (implementing Dir.2000/31/EC) which merely provide that in the case of, for example, a contract made on a web-site, "the order and the acknowledgement of receipt [of the order] will be deemed to be received when the parties to whom they are addressed are able to access them" (reg.11(2)(a)). The effect of acknowledgement of receipt of an order falls to be determined as a matter of common law: see the definition of acceptance in para.2–027 above. The provision of reg.11(2)(a) quoted in this note does *not*, in any event apply to "contracts concluded exclusively by exchange of electronic mail or by equivalent individual communications:" reg.11(3).

[283] reg.10.

[284] reg.11(12).

[285] reg.10(2).

[286] See, *e.g.* reg.13 (exceptions to right to cancel); reg.17 (dealing with restoration of goods to the supplier after cancellation).

[287] *Frank v Knight* (1937) O.P.D. 113; *cf. Eliason v Henshaw* 4 Wheat. 225 (1819); *Walker v Glass* [1979] N.I. 129.

by an oral acceptance if he has asked for one to be expressed in writing.[288] This rule is particularly strict where the offer is contained in an option.[289]

Purported acceptance as counter-offer. It is sometimes possible for a purported acceptance which does not comply with the prescribed method to be regarded as a counter-offer and for a contract to come into existence when that counter-offer is in turn accepted.[290] Since such acceptance may be effected by conduct,[291] the contract may be concluded without any further communication between the parties after the original, ineffective, acceptance. 2–066

Other equally efficacious mode. Stipulations as to the mode of acceptance are usually made by the offeror with some particular object in view, *e.g.* to obtain a speedy acceptance, or one expressed (for the sake of certainty) in a particular form. It seems that an acceptance which accomplishes that object just as well as, or better than, the stipulated method may bind the offeror. For this purpose, the court must first decide, as a matter of construction, what object it was that the offeror had in view. For example, a requirement that the acceptance must be sent by letter by return of post may "fix the time for acceptance and not the manner of accepting."[292] An acceptance by telex could then suffice. But such an acceptance would not be effective if the offeror's object (on the true construction of the offer) was to have a full, accurate and signed record of the acceptance. 2–067

Method of acceptance waived. Even if the prescribed method of acceptance is not complied with, the offeror would no doubt be bound by, and apparently entitled to enforce,[293] the contract if he had acquiesced in a different mode of acceptance and had so waived the stipulated mode. 2–068

Terms of offer drawn up by offeree. The rules relating to failure to use a prescribed mode of acceptence are traditionally based on two assumptions: that the offer was drawn up by the offeror; and that stipulations as to the mode of acceptance were made by him for his own benefit. It is, however, also possible for the offer to be made on a form drawn up by the offeree: *e.g.* where a customer submits a proposal to enter into a hire-purchase agreement; or where an offer is made by tender on a form of tender issued by the offeree. Stipulations as to the mode of acceptance in such documents are usually intended for the benefit and protection of the *offeree*. If the offeree accepts in some other way, this will often 2–069

---

[288] *Financings Ltd v Stimson* [1962] 1 W.L.R. 1184, 1186. Contrast *Hitchens v General Guarantee Corp* [2001] EWCA Civ 359, *The Times*, March 13, 2001 (where there was *no* requirement that the acceptance must be in writing).

[289] *Holwell Securities Ltd v Hughes* [1974] 1 W.L.R. 157.

[290] *Wettern Electricity Ltd v Welsh Development Agency* [1983] Q.B. 796.

[291] As in the *Wettern Electricity* case, above; provided, however, that such conduct is accompanied by the requisite contractual intention: see *Harvela Investments Ltd v Royal Trust Co of Canada (C.I.) Ltd* [1986] A.C. 207 and below, para.2–159; for counter-offers, see above para.2–032; below, para.2–092.

[292] *Tinn v Hoffmann & Co* (1873) 29 L.T. 271, 278; *cf. Manchester Diocesan Council for Education v Commercial & General Investments Ltd* [1970] 1 W.L.R. 242; *Edmund Murray v B.S.P. International Foundations* (1994) 33 Con.L.R. 1.

[293] On the analogy of the reasoning of *Oceanografia SA de CV v DSND Subsea AS (The Botnica)* [2006] EWHC 1300 (Comm), [2007] 1 All E.R. (Comm) 28, below paras 2–116, 3–081.

be evidence that he has waived the stipulation; and it is submitted that the acceptance ought to be treated as effective unless it can be shown that failure to use the stipulated mode has prejudiced the offeror.[294] In one case,[295] for example, an offer to enter into a conditional sale agreement was made by the buyer on a form provided by the offeree (a finance company). It was held that the offer had been accepted by delivery of the subject-matter in spite of a provision in the offer to the effect that this was *not* to constitute acceptance, that provision having been waived by the offeree.

(e) *Silence*

2–070 **Offeree generally not bound.** As a general rule, an offeree who does nothing in response to an offer is not bound by its terms. This is so even though the offer provides that it can be accepted by silence. Thus in *Felthouse v Bindley*[296] an uncle offered to buy a horse from his nephew for £30 15s., adding "If I hear no more about him I shall consider the horse is mine at £30 15s." The uncle brought an action for conversion against an auctioneer who had by mistake included the horse in a sale of the nephew's property. It was held that, the auctioneer was not liable because "The uncle had no right to impose upon the nephew the sale of his horse . . . unless he chose to comply with the condition of writing to repudiate the offer . . . ."[297] The reason for the rule is that it is, in general, undesirable to impose on an offeree the trouble and expense of rejecting an offer which he does not wish to accept. But in *Felthouse v Bindley* this was not the position. The nephew had, before the auction, told the auctioneer that he "intended to reserve" the horse for his uncle, and later correspondence showed that the nephew did at the time of the auction intend to sell the horse to the uncle. In spite of this, it was held that there was no contract because the nephew "had not communicated his intention to the uncle."[298] But the need to communicate an acceptance can be waived by the terms of the offer[299] and it seems clear that the uncle's letter did waive that need. The actual decision is, in view of these facts, hard to support, but this is no criticism of the general rule laid down in the case.

2–071 **Silence generally equivocal.** The question whether silence may amount to an acceptance binding the offeree has also arisen in the arbitration cases (discussed in para.2–006 above) in which the issue was whether an agreement to abandon an earlier agreement to submit a claim to arbitration could be inferred from inactivity in the form of long delay in prosecuting the claim. Such a delay is now in certain circumstances a statutory ground for dismissing the claim for want of

---

[294] See *Robophone Facilities v Blank* [1966] 1 W.L.R. 1428 and *cf.* the *Manchester Diocesan* case, above, n.292; from this point of view these cases are, it is submitted, to be preferred to *Financings Ltd v Stimson* [1962] 1 W.L.R. 1184.

[295] *Carlyle Finance Ltd v Pallas Industrial Finance Ltd* [1999] All E.R. (Comm) 659, approving the reasoning now contained in para.2–069 above.

[296] (1862) 11 C.B.(N.S.) 869; affirmed (1863) 1 N.R. 401; Miller (1972) 35 M.L.R. 489; *cf. Financial Techniques (Planning Services) v Hughes* [1981] I.R.L.R. 32.

[297] (1862) 11 C.B.(N.S.) 869 at 875.

[298] *ibid.* at 876.

[299] Above, para.2–047.

prosecution[300]; but the statutory power to dismiss claims on this ground can be excluded by contrary agreement[301]; and similar questions of agreement to abandon *other* types of claim could still be governed by the common law principles developed in the arbitration cases. In these cases, it had been held that, even if one party's inactivity could be regarded as an offer to abandon the arbitration,[302] the mere silence or inactivity of the other did not normally amount to an acceptance. For one thing, such inactivity was often[303] equivocal,[304] being explicable on other grounds (such as forgetfulness or delay on the part of the offeree's solicitors).[305] For another, acceptance could not, as a matter of law, be inferred from silence alone[306] "save in the most exceptional circumstances."[307]

Can offeree exceptionally be bound? As the above reference to "exceptional circumstances" suggests, there may be exceptions to the general rule that an offeree is not bound by silence. If the offer has been solicited by the offeree, the argument that he should not be put to the trouble of rejecting it[308] loses much of its force,[309] especially if the offer is made on a form provided by the offeree[310] and that form stipulates that silence may amount to acceptance.[311] Again, if there is a course of dealing between the parties, the offeror may be led to suppose that silence amounts to acceptance: *e.g.* where his offers to buy goods have in the past been accepted as a matter of course by the despatch of the goods in question.[312] In such a case it may not be unreasonable to impose on the offeree an obligation to give notice of his rejection of the offer, especially if the offeror, in reliance on his belief that the goods would be delivered in the usual way, had forborne from 2–072

300 Arbitration Act 1996 s.41(3).
301 *ibid.* s.41(2).
302 Above, para.2–006.
303 But not always: see para.2–072 at n.313.
304 *e.g. Jayaar Impex Ltd v Toaken Group Ltd* [1996] 2 Lloyd's Rep. 437, 445.
305 For acceptance by silence and conduct, see below, para.2–076.
306 *Allied Marine Transport Ltd v Vale do Rio Doce Navegaçao SA (The Leonidas D.)* [1985] 1 W.L.R. 925, 927; *Rafsanjan Pistachio Producers Co-operative v Bank Leumi (U.K.) plc* [1992] 1 Lloyd's Rep. 513, 542; *Exmar N.V. v BP Shipping Ltd (The Gas Enterprise)* [1993] 2 Lloyd's Rep. 352, 357, affirmed without reference to this point *ibid.* at 364; *Vitol SA v Norelf Ltd* [1996] A.C. 800, 812; *Front Carriers Ltd v Atlantic and Orient Shipping Corporation (The Archimidis)* [2007] EWHC 421; [2007] 2 Lloyd's Rep. 131 at [45]–[46].
307 *The Leonidas D.*, above, n.306, at 927; *Cie Française d'Importation, etc. v Deutsche Continental Handelsgesellschaft* [1985] 2 Lloyd's Rep. 592, 598; *Gebr. van Weelde Sheepvaartkantoor B.V. v Compania Naviera Orient SA (The Agrabele)* [1987] 2 Lloyd's Rep. 223, 234–235. *Excomm Ltd v Guan Guan Shipping (Pte) Ltd (The Golden Bear)* [1987] 1 Lloyd's Rep. 330 is hard to reconcile with these cases and was apparently doubted in *The Antclizo*, above n.306, [1987] 2 Lloyd's Rep. at 147. Such "exceptional circumstances" may be illustrated by *André & Cie SA v Marine Transocean Ltd (The Splendid Sun)* [1981] Q.B. 694 (where the acceptance may have been by conduct: below, para.2–076, n.339), though it has been said that this case is hard to reconcile with *The Leonidas D*, above: see *Food Corp of India v Antclizo Shipping Corp (The Antclizo)* [1987] 2 Lloyd's Rep. 130, 149, affirmed [1988] 1 W.L.R. 607.
308 Above, para.2–070.
309 *cf. Rust v Abbey Life Ins. Co* [1979] 2 Lloyd's Rep. 335, below, para.2–077.
310 *cf.* above, para.2–069.
311 As in *Alexander Hamilton Institute v Jones* 234 Ill.App. 444 (1924).
312 As in *Cole-McIntyre-Norfleet Co v Holloway* 141 Tenn. 679, 214 S.W. 87 (1919).

seeking an alternative supply. It has been held that one party's wrongful repudiation of a contract may be accepted by the other party's failure to take such further steps in the performance of that contract as he would have been expected to take, if he were treating the contract as still in force[313]; and similar reasoning might be applied in the present context. There may also be "an express undertaking or implied obligation to speak"[314] arising out of the course of negotiations between the parties, *e.g.* "where the offeree himself indicates that an offer is to be taken as accepted if he does not indicate the contrary by an ascertainable time."[315] The offeree's failure to perform such an "obligation to speak" could thus be treated by the *offeror* as an acceptance by silence. But it is not normally open to the *offeree* in such cases to treat his own silence (in breach of his duty to speak) as an acceptance.[316] This course would be open to him only in situations such as that in *Felthouse v Bindley*,[317] in which the offeror had indicated (usually in the terms of the offer) that he would treat silence as an acceptance. There is finally the possibility that silence may constitute an acceptance by virtue of a custom of the trade or business in question.[318]

2–073 **Liability of offeree based on estoppel?** Even where silence of the offeree does not amount to an acceptance, it is arguable that he might be liable on a different basis. In *Spiro v Lintern* it was said that: "If A sees B acting in the mistaken belief that A is under some binding obligation to him and in a manner consistent only with such an obligation, which would be to B's disadvantage if A were thereafter to deny the obligation, A is under a duty to B to disclose the non-existence of the supposed obligation."[319] Although this statement was made with reference to wholly different circumstances, it could also be applied to certain cases in which an offeror had, to the offeree's knowledge,[320] acted in reliance on the belief that his offer had been accepted by silence. The liability of the offeree would then be based on a kind of estoppel.[321] But the application of this doctrine to cases of alleged acceptance by silence gives rise to the difficulty that such an estoppel can arise only out of a "clear and unequivocal"[322] representation. For this purpose, mere inactivity is not generally sufficient,[323] so that

[313] *Vitol S.A. v Norelf Ltd* [1996] A.C. 800.

[314] *Gebr. van Weelde Scheepvaartkantor B.V. v Compania Naviera Orient SA (The Agrabele)* [1985] 2 Lloyd's Rep. 496, 509, *per* Evans J., whose statement of the relevant principles was approved on appeal though the actual decision was reversed on the facts: [1987] 2 Lloyd's Rep. 223, 225. The case concerned an alleged "abandonment" by delay of an agreement to submit a claim to arbitration and would now be governed by Arbitration Act 1996 s.41(3) (above, para.2–006).

[315] *Re Selectmove* [1995] 1 W.L.R. 474, 478 (where the point was left open).

[316] *Yona International Ltd v La Réunion Française, etc.* [1996] 2 Lloyd's Rep. 84, 110.

[317] Above, para.2–070; further discussed in para.2–075 below.

[318] *Minories Finance Ltd v Afribank Nigeria Ltd* [1995] 1 Lloyd's Rep. 134 (where a contract between two banks for the collection of drafts and remittance of their proceeds arose in this way).

[319] [1973] 1 W.L.R. 1002, 1011.

[320] See *Yona International Ltd v Law Réunion Française, etc.* [1996] 2 Lloyd's Rep. 84, 107 (where this requirement of knowledge was not satisfied).

[321] Below, para.3–103; and *cf. The Stolt Loyalty* [1993] 2 Lloyd's Rep. 281, 289–291; affirmed, without reference to this point, [1995] 1 Lloyd's Rep. 598. The case put in the text above would not be one of estoppel by convention (below, para.3–107); for such estoppel is based on an *agreed* assumption, while in cases of the present kind the question is whether there was any agreement.

[322] Below, para.3–090.

[323] Below, para.3–092.

silence in response to an offer will not normally give rise to an estoppel. It is likely to do so only in cases of the kind discussed above,[324] in which there are special circumstances which give rise to a "duty to speak," and in which it would be unconscionable for the party under that duty to deny that a contract had come into existence.[325]

Performance by offeror benefiting offeree. It is finally possible that the offeree may be bound by silence if the offeror to the offeree's knowledge actually performs in accordance with his offer and so confers a benefit on the offeree; though the better solution in this type of case would be to make the offeree restore the benefit rather than to hold him to an obligation to perform his part of a contract to which he had never agreed. 2–074

Can offeror be bound? There is some authority for saying that the offeror cannot, any more than the offeree, be bound where the offeree simply remains silent in response to an offer,[326] and the case is not one of the exceptional ones, discussed in para.2–072 above, in which an offer can be accepted by silence.[327] But it is submitted that the general rule in *Felthouse v Bindley*[328] does not lead invariably to such a conclusion. For the object of this rule is to protect the *offeree* from having to incur the trouble and expense of rejecting the offer so as to avoid being bound. No similar argument can be advanced for protecting the offeror. He may, indeed, be left in doubt on the point whether his offer has been accepted; but this is a matter about which he cannot legitimately complain where he has drawn his offer so as to permit (and even to encourage) acceptance by silence.[329] Thus it is submitted that the uncle in *Felthouse v Bindley* might have been bound if the nephew had resolved to accept the offer and had, in reliance on its terms, forborne from attempting to dispose of the horse elsewhere. This possibility has, indeed, been doubted[330]; but in the case in which the doubt was expressed there was no express stipulation in the offer that silence would be regarded as acceptance. Where the offer does contain such a stipulation, it is submitted that silence in response to it by the offeree should be capable of binding the offeror. 2–075

Silence and conduct. The general rule that there can be no acceptance by silence does not mean that an acceptance always has to be given in so many words. An offer can be accepted by conduct; and this is never thought to give rise to any difficulty where the conduct takes the form of a positive act.[331] In principle, conduct can also take the form of a forbearance: for example, a 2–076

---

[324] Above, at n.314.

[325] See *AC Yule & Son Ltd v Speedwell Roofing & Cladding Ltd* [2007] EWHC 1360 (TCC), [2007] B.L.R. 499.

[326] *Fairline Shipping Corp. v Anderson* [1975] Q.B. 180, 189.

[327] Even in such exceptional cases, the offeror is not *invariably* bound by the offeree's silence: see above, at n.316.

[328] Above, para.2–070.

[329] This argument would, however, not apply where the terms of the offer had been drafted by the offeree: *cf.* above, para.2–069.

[330] *Fairline Shipping Corp. v Anderson*, above, n.326.

[331] *cf.* above, para.2–030.

debtor's offer to give additional security for a debt can be accepted by the creditor's forbearing to sue for the debt.[332] Similarly, a tenant can accept an offer of a new tenancy by simply not vacating the premises. In one such case it was said that the offer had been accepted by "silence"[333]; but it seems better to say that it was accepted by conduct and that the landlord had waived notice of acceptance. Similarly an offer made *to* a landowner to occupy land under a licence containing specified terms may be accepted by the landowner's permitting the offeror to occupy the land.[334] An offer by a contractor to carry out building work on the offeree's land may also sometimes be accepted by the offeree's allowing the work to proceed.[335] The possibility of acceptance by conduct is, yet again, illustrated by the arbitration cases already mentioned, in which an agreement to abandon the proceedings was alleged to have arisen from delay in prosecuting them. As already noted, legislation has now dealt with the practical problems which used to arise from delay in the pursuit of arbitration claims,[336] but the reasoning of the arbitration cases could still apply where the legislative provisions have been excluded by agreement[337] or where it was alleged that some other type of claim or remedy had been abandoned by tacit agreement. According to those cases, an offer of abandonment can be accepted by reacting to it, not merely by inactivity,[338] but also by some further conduct: *e.g.* by closing, or disposing of, the relevant files.[339] On the same principle, the wrongful repudiation of an arbitration agreement (by repeatedly denying its existence) can be accepted by starting court proceedings to enforce the injured party's substantive claim.[340]

2–077 In *Rust v Abbey Life Ins Co*[341] the plaintiff applied and paid for a "property bond" which was allocated to her on the terms of the defendants' usual policy of insurance. After having retained this document for some seven months, she

[332] Below, para.3–057.

[333] *Roberts v Hayward* (1828) 3 C. & P. 432.

[334] *Wettern Electric Ltd v Welsh Development Agency* [1983] Q.B. 796. For acceptance by conduct (as opposed to mere silence) see also *Aspinall's Club Ltd v Al Zayat* [2007] EWCA Civ 1001 at [19], [30] (acceptance of alleged terms on which a cheque was given by the recipient's accepting the cheque and returning "scrip" cheques previously given in respect of gambling losses).

[335] See *Westminster Building Co Ltd v Buckingham* [2004] EWHC 138, [2004] B.L.R. 163; contrast *Mirant Asia-Pacific Construction (Hong Kong) Ltd v Ove Arup & Partners International OAPIL (No. 2)* [2004] EWHC 1750, 97 Con. L.R. 1. In these cases the point at issue related to the terms, rather than to the existence, of the contract.

[336] Arbitration Act 1996 s.41(3); above, para.2–006.

[337] Arbitration Act 1996 s.41(2).

[338] *cf. Collin v Duke of Westminster* [1985] Q.B. 581.

[339] See *André & Cie v Marine Transocean Ltd (The Splendid Sun)* [1981] Q.B. 694, 712, 713 ("closed their file"); *cf. ibid.* 706 ("did so act"). *Tracomin SA v Anton C. Nielsen A/S* [1984] 2 Lloyd's Rep. 195 can be supported on the same ground even though it was in part based on the decision at first instance in *Allied Marine Transport Ltd v Vale do Rio Doce Navegaçao SA (The Leonidas D.)* which was reversed on appeal [1985] 1 W.L.R. 925; above para.2–052; *cf. Tankrederei Ahrenkeil GmbH v Frahuil SA (The Multibank Holsatia)* [1988] 2 Lloyd's Rep. 486, 493 (where the offeree had destroyed relevant files, so that the case was not one of mere inaction). There seems to have been no "conduct" amounting to an acceptance in *Excomm Ltd v Guan Guan Shipping (Pte) Ltd (The Golden Bear)* [1988] 1 Lloyd's Rep. 330.

[340] *Downing v Al Tameer Establishment* [2002] EWCA Civ 545; [2002] 2 All E.R. (Comm) 545.

[341] [1979] 2 Lloyd's Rep. 355.

claimed the return of her payment, alleging that no contract had been concluded. The claim was rejected on the ground that her application was an offer which had been accepted by issue of the policy.[342] But it was further held that, even if the policy constituted a counter-offer, that counter-offer had been accepted by "the conduct of the plaintiff in doing and saying nothing for seven months . . . ".[343] Thus mere inaction was said to be sufficient to constitute acceptance; but it is submitted that this conclusion may be justified by reference to the special circumstances of the case. The negotiations had been started by the plaintiff (the counter-offeree)[344] and, in view of this fact, it was reasonable for the defendants to infer from her silence over a long period that she had accepted the terms of the policy which had been sent to her and which she must be "taken to have examined."[345] The case thus falls within one of the suggested exceptions[346] to the general rule that an offeree is not bound by silence where this alone is alleged to amount to an acceptance.

(f) *Unilateral Contracts*

Introduction. An offer of a unilateral contract is made when one party promises to pay the other a sum of money (or to do some other act, or to forbear from doing something) if the other will do (or forbear from doing) something without making any promise to that effect: for example where A promises to pay B £100 if B will walk from London to York[347] or find and return A's lost dog or give up smoking for a year.[348] The contract in these cases is called "unilateral" because it arises without B's having made any counter-promise to perform the stipulated act or forbearance; it is contrasted with a bilateral contract under which each party undertakes an obligation. The distinction between the two types of contract is not always clear-cut[349]; but once a promise is classified as an offer of a unilateral contract, a number of rules apply to the acceptance of such an offer. First, the offer can be accepted by fully performing the required act or forbearance.[350] Secondly, there is no need to give advance notice of such acceptance to the offeror.[351] Thirdly, it is probable that the offer can be accepted *only* by some performance and not by a counter-promise, since such a counter-promise would not be what the promisor had bargained for. And fourthly, the offer can, like all offers, be withdrawn before it is accepted.[352] It is the application of this 2–078

---

[342] *cf.* above, para.2–024.

[343] [1979] 2 Lloyd's Rep. 335, 340; affirming [1978] 2 Lloyd's Rep. 386, 393. For another illustration of acceptance by silence and conduct, see *AC Yule & Son Ltd v Speedwell Roofing and Cladding Ltd* [2007] EWHC 1360 (TCC), [2007] B.L.R. 499.

[344] *cf.* above, para.2–069 and *Vitol S.A. v Norelf Ltd* [1996] A.C. 800 (above, para.2–072).

[345] *Yona International Ltd v La Réunion Française, etc.* [1996] 2 Lloyd's Rep. 84, 110 (where no inference of assent was drawn from silence).

[346] Above, para.2–072.

[347] *Rogers v Snow* (1573) Dalison 94; *Great Northern Ry v Witham* (1873) L.R. 9 C.P. 16, 19.

[348] *cf. Hamer v Sidway* 124 N.Y. 538 (1881).

[349] See below, para.2–085.

[350] See *Daulia Ltd v Four Millbank Nominees Ltd* [1978] Ch. 231, 238; *Harvela Investments Ltd v Royal Trust of Canada (C.I.) Ltd* [1986] A.C. 207, 229.

[351] *Carlill v Carbolic Smoke Ball Co* [1893] 1 Q.B. 256; *Bowerman v Association of British Travel Agents* [1995] N.L.J. 1815.

[352] Below, para.2–088.

fourth rule which gives rise to the greatest difficulty, for it raises the question of exactly when acceptance of such an offer can be said to have occurred.

2–079 **Acceptance by part performance.** It is disputed whether an offer of a unilateral contract can be withdrawn after the offeree has *partly* performed the stipulated act or forbearance. The first question (to be discussed here) is whether at this stage the offeree has accepted the offer; the second (to be discussed in Chapter 3) is whether (before full performance) he has provided any consideration for the offeror's promise.[353] With regard to the first question, one possible view is that there is no acceptance until the stipulated act or forbearance has been completely performed. This may, indeed, be the position where it is the intention of both parties that, until then, the offeror should have a *locus poenitentiae*. But in most cases the offeree will not intend to expose himself to the risk of withdrawal when he has partly performed,[354] intends to complete performance and is able to do so.[355] In such cases, his position can be protected by distinguishing between two stages: (1) that at which the offer is accepted and (2) that at which the offeree has satisfied the conditions which must be satisfied before he can enforce the offeror's promise.[356] Where the contract is unilateral, the second stage is not reached until performance of the stipulated act has been completed.[357] But the first stage (of acceptance) can be reached as soon as the offeree has unequivocally begun performance of the stipulated act or abstention. If so, the part performance can amount to an acceptance so that the offer can no longer be withdrawn. Of course it may be difficult in fact to tell when performance has begun, particularly where the offer amounts to a promise in return for an abstention. But once the conduct of the offeree has gone beyond mere preparation to perform, and amounts to actual part performance, then it can amount to an acceptance, so that as a general rule[358] the offer can no longer be withdrawn.[359]

---

[353] Below, para.3–170.

[354] Lord Diplock in *Harvela Investments Ltd v Royal Trust of Canada (C.I.) Ltd* [1986] A.C. 207, 224 can be read as depriving the offeror of the power to withdraw as soon as his offer is *communicated* (*i.e.* before any performance by the offeree); but in that case the offeree had completely performed the required act by making the requested bid.

[355] See note 358 below.

[356] Pollock, *Principles of Contract* (13th ed) p.19.

[357] For a quasi-exception, see para.2–086 below.

[358] i.e., so long as no *locus poenitentiae* has been reserved and so long as performance remains within the offeree's power: see *Morrison SS. Co v The Crown* (1924) 20 Ll.L.Rep. 283 (where the House of Lords held that the offer could be withdrawn, in spite of the fact that the offeree had taken steps towards performance, as the acts of foreign governments had made it impossible for the offeree to complete performance).

[359] The corresponding paragraph of the above text in the previous edition of this book is (among others) cited with approval in *Schweppe v Harper* [2008] EWCA Civ 442 at [41] by Waller L.J. in a dissenting judgment, but the issue on which he dissented was the different one, whether the agreement lacked contractual force for want of certainty: see below, para.2–142 note 650. Dyson L.J. at [62] treated the alleged contract as bilateral, while Sir Robin Auld at [77] left open the question whether, if it had come into existence, the contract would have been "bilateral or unilateral". See also the American Law Institute's *Restatement of the Law*, Contracts (hereinafter called Restatement, *Contracts*), § 45, and *Restatement of the Law*, 2d, Contracts (hereinafter called Restatement, 2d, *Contracts*), § 45. The Restatement, 2d, *Contracts*, § 12 abandons the distinction between bilateral and unilateral contracts, and in § 45 substitutes "option contract" where formerly "unilateral contract" had been used. See also below, para.3–011.

Support for this view is to be found in *Errington v Errington*,[360] where a father bought a house, subject to a mortgage, allowed his son and daughter-in-law to live in it, and told them that if they paid the mortgage instalments the house would be theirs when the mortgage was paid off. The couple started to live in the house and paid some of the mortgage instalments; but they did not bind themselves to go on making the payments. It was held that the arrangement amounted to a contract which could not, after the father's death, be revoked by his personal representatives. Denning L.J. said: "The father's promise was a unilateral contract—a promise of the house in return for their act of paying the instalments. It could not be revoked by him once the couple entered on the performance of the act, but it would cease to bind him if they left it incomplete and unperformed."[361] This dictum was cited with approval in *Soulsbury v Soulsbury*[362] where a husband (H) promised his former wife (W) to leave her £100,000 in his will if (1) during their joint lives, she did not enforce or seek to enforce a maintenance order which she had obtained against him in divorce proceedings and (2) she survived him.[363] Longmore L.J. described this promise as "a classic unilateral contract" and said that, in the case of such a contract, [o]nce the promisee acts on the promise by inhaling the smoke ball, by starting the walk to York or (as here) by not suing for the maintenance to which she was entitled, the promisor cannot revoke or withdraw his offer."[364] He added that the present case was "stronger than *Errington* since on [H's] death [W] had completed all possible performance of the act required for the enforcement of [H's] promise."[365] 2–080

Continuing guarantees. The view that the offeree's part performance of a unilateral contract can amount to an acceptance, and so deprive the offeror of the power to withdraw, is also supported by the law relating to continuing guarantees. These may be divisible, where each advance constitutes a separate transaction; or indivisible, *e.g.* where, on A's admission to an association, B guarantees all liabilities which A may incur as a member of the association.[366] If the guarantee is divisible, it can be revoked at any time with regard to future advances,[367] but an indivisible guarantee cannot be revoked once the creditor has begun to act on it by giving credit to the principal debtor.[368] This rule applies even though the contract of guarantee is unilateral, in the sense that the creditor has not made any promise to the guarantor (in return for the guarantee) to give credit to the principal debtor. 2–081

[360] [1952] 1 K.B. 290; doubted on other points in *National Provincial Bank Ltd v Ainsworth* [1965] A.C. 1175, 1239–1240, 1251–1252 and in *Ashburn Anstalt v Arnold* [1989] Ch. 1, 17 (overruled on another ground in *Prudential Assurance Co Ltd v London Residuary Body* [1992] A.C. 386). For another possible illustration, see *Beaton v McDivitt* (1988) 13 N.S.W.L.R. 162, 175.

[361] [1952] 1 K.B. 290, 295. *cf. Daulia Ltd v Four Millbank Nominees Ltd* [1978] Ch. 231, 239.

[362] [2007] EWCA Civ 969 at [50].

[363] *ibid.*, at [10]; *cf.* at [22], where the condition of survivorship is not expressly stated.

[364] *ibid.*, at [49].

[365] *ibid.*, at [50].

[366] As in *Lloyd's v Harper* (1880) 16 Ch.D. 290.

[367] As in *Offord v Davies* (1862) 12 C.B.(N.S.) 748. An obscure passage in the argument at 753 is inconclusive on the general question of acceptance in unilateral contracts; *cf.* below, n.379.

[368] *Lloyd's v Harper* (1880) 16 Ch.D. 290.

2–082 **Bankers' irrevocable credits.** The issue (or confirmation) by a bank of an irrevocable credit amounts to a promise to pay to the beneficiary a sum of money on certain conditions, usually if the beneficiary will present specified documents to the bank.[369] Often the beneficiary is a seller of goods who will have done some act of part performance, *e.g.* in manufacturing or shipping the goods. As he makes no promise *to the bank*, its liability to him might at first sight seem to be based on a unilateral contract between them. But the bank's promise is regarded as binding as soon as it is communicated to the seller, *i.e.* before he has done any act of part performance or indeed done any other act of acceptance. The binding force of the promise is therefore not explicable in terms of acceptance of an offer of a unilateral contract.[370]

2–083 **Estate agents' contracts.** A unilateral contract may arise where an estate agent is engaged to negotiate the sale of a house. In one case of this kind it was said that "No obligation is imposed on the agent to do anything."[371] If he succeeds in negotiating a sale, his claim for the agreed commission could be regarded as a claim based on a unilateral contract. However, it is well settled that the client may revoke his instructions, or sell through another agent, or without any agent, in spite of the fact that the first agent has made considerable efforts to find a purchaser.[372] It could be argued that this line of cases supports the view that, where a contract is unilateral, the offeror (*i.e.* in cases of the present kind, the client) can withdraw after part performance by the offeree (the agent); but the better explanation is that this is one of the exceptional types of case in which, on the true construction of the promise, a *locus poenitentiae* is intended to be reserved to the client even after part performance by the agent.

2–084 **Estate agents appointed "sole agents".** There is a further group of cases in which persons appointed "sole agents" have been held entitled to damages when the client sold through another agent.[373] However, these have been treated as cases of bilateral contracts, on the ground that the agents promised to use their best endeavours to effect a sale,[374] or to bear advertising expenses.[375] Such promises may be (and, it seems, commonly are) made by agents who are not sole agents at all, though the question whether a promise to use best endeavours is sufficiently certain to have any legal effect may still be an open one.[376] The rules

[369] See below, Vol.II, para.34–424.

[370] Vol.II para.34–485.

[371] *Luxor (Eastbourne) Ltd v Cooper* [1941] A.C. 108, 124. But in fact he may promise to do something: see below, at nn.374 and 375; *cf.* Murdoch (1975) 91 L.Q.R. 357. "Obligation" in the dictum quoted in the text above refers to obligations under any contract between agent and client (as distinct from obligations that may be imposed on the agent by legislation).

[372] Below, Vol.II, paras 31–138, 31–148.

[373] *Hampton & Sons v George* [1939] 3 All E.R. 627; *Christopher v Essig* [1958] W.N. 461; and see below, Vol.II, para.31–148.

[374] *Christopher v Essig*, above, n.311; *John McCann & Co v Pow* [1974] 1 W.L.R. 1643, 1647. In *Wood v Lucy, Lady Duff-Gordon* 222 N.Y. 88; 118 N.E. 214 (1917) it was held that such a promise could be implied.

[375] *cf. Bentall, Horsley & Baldry v Vicary* [1931] 1 K.B. 253 (where it was held that the owner committed no breach of a "sole agency" agreement by selling it without the intervention of a second agent).

[376] Below, para.2–136.

as to the revocability of the client's promise would, it seems, apply whether the contract is regarded as a unilateral or as a bilateral one and accordingly it is doubtful whether the estate agency cases shed any light on the problems of acceptance in unilateral contracts.

Unilateral contract becoming bilateral. A contract may be in its inception unilateral but become bilateral in the course of its performance.[377] In the examples given in para.2–078 above, a bilateral contract would not indeed arise merely because the promisee had promised to perform the stipulated act or abstention (*e.g.* to walk to York). This is because the promisor has not bargained for a counter-promise, so that his offer cannot be accepted by promising to perform but only by actually performing (or by beginning to do so). But if A promises to pay B a sum of money in return for some service to be rendered by B (such as repainting A's house) it is possible that B may, by beginning to render the service (*e.g.*, by stripping off the old paint), impliedly promise[378] to complete it.[379] In such a case, the contract would at this stage become bilateral, so that neither party could withdraw with impunity. 2–085

Extent of liability. It is generally assumed that, where a unilateral contract takes the form of a promise to pay money, an offeror who purports to withdraw after part performance by the offeree must either be liable in full or not be liable at all. There, is, however, also an intermediate possibility. If, for example, the offer is withdrawn after the offeree has walked half-way to York, it is arguable that, on being notified of the withdrawal, he should desist and recover damages[380] amounting to his expenses, or to the value of the chance of completing the walk,[380a] less the expenses saved by not completing it. 2–086

---

[377] *New Zealand Shipping Co Ltd v A.N. Satterthwaite Ltd (The Eurymedon)* [1975] A.C. 154, 167–168 ("a bargain initially unilateral but capable of becoming mutual"); *cf. The Mahkutai* [1996] 2 A.C. 650, 664, treating the contract in *The Eurymedon* as "nowadays bilateral"; but this description should not be understood as meaning that the contract imposed on the offeree any executory obligations to the offeror: *Hombourg Houtimport BV v Agrosin Private Ltd (The Starsin)* [2003] UKHL 13; [2004] 1 A.C. 715 at [34], [59], [93], [153] and [196], where the contract is described as "unilateral". See also *Carver on Bills of Lading* (2nd ed., 2005) para.7–052.

[378] It has, indeed, been suggested that it is "impossible to imply terms . . . which impose legal obligations . . . into a unilateral contract" (*Little v Courage* (1995) 70 P. & C.R. 469, 474). The reason for this view seems to be that such an implication would destroy the unilateral character of the contract by imposing an obligation on the promisee. But there is, it is submitted, no good reason why an intention to undertake such an obligation should not be inferred from the conduct of the promisee *after* the unilateral contract has come into existence. This possibility is recognised in the dictum from *The Eurymedon* cited in n.377 above and by the example given in the text to this note.

[379] See *The Unique Mariner* [1979] 2 Lloyd's Rep. 37, 51–2; *Smit International Singapore Pte Ltd v Kurnia Dewi Shipping SA (The Kurnia Dewi)* [1997] 1 Lloyd's Rep. 553, 559; contrast *B.S.C. v Cleveland Bridge & Engineering Co Ltd* [1984] 1 All E.R. 504, 510–511, where such an implied promise was negatived by the fact that the terms of a bilateral contract were still under negotiation and were never agreed. It is not clear whether the situation discussed in *Offord v Davies* (1862) 12 C.B.N.S. 748, 753 falls into the category of a unilateral or into that of a bilateral contract.

[380] Unless the offeree has a "substantial or legitimate interest" in completing the walk, this may be the law under the principles laid down in *White & Carter (Councils) Ltd v McGregor* [1962] A.C. 413, below, para.26–124.

[380a] The suggestion made in the text above is adopted in *Schweppe v Harper* [2008] EWCA Civ 442 at [51]–[54] by Waller L.J. who dissented on the different issue, whether the agreement was sufficiently certain to have contractual force: see below, para.2–142 n.650.

4. TERMINATION OF THE OFFER

2–087 **Introductory.** An offer may be terminated by withdrawal, rejection, lapse of time, occurrence of a condition, death and supervening incapacity. These methods of termination will be discussed in the paragraphs that follow.

(a) *Withdrawal*

2–088 **General rule.** The general rule is that an offer may be withdrawn at any time before it is accepted.[381] The rule applies even though the offeror has promised to keep the offer open for a specified time,[382] for such a promise is unsupported by consideration[383] and is therefore not binding. Thus in *Routledge v Grant*[384] the defendant offered to buy a house, giving the offeree six weeks for a definite answer; and it was held that the defendant was free to withdraw at any time before acceptance even though the six weeks had not expired. Conversely, in *Dickinson v Dodds*[385] the defendant offered to sell land to the offeree and said that the offer was to be "left over till Friday." It was held that he could nevertheless withdraw before Friday.

2–089 **Communication of withdrawal generally required.** An offer cannot be withdrawn merely by acting inconsistently with it: for example, an offer to sell goods to A is not withdrawn by selling them to B.[386] If A accepts the offer before he has notice of the subsequent sale, he will be entitled to damages (though not to the goods themselves). To be effective in law, a withdrawal must, in general, be communicated to the offeree: that is, notice of the withdrawal must actually reach the offeree.[387] This requirement of communication applies to withdrawals sent through the post and by telegram as well as to those sent by other methods. In *Byrne & Co. v Van Tienhoven*[388] an offer to sell tinplates was posted in Cardiff on October 1 and reached the offerees in New York on October 11; on the same

[381] See, *e.g.* *Payne v Cave* (1789) 3 T.R. 148; *Routledge v Grant* (1828) 4 Bing. 653; *Offord v Davies* (1862) 12 C.B.(N.S.) 748; *Hebb's Case* (1867) L.R. 4 Eq. 9; *Tuck v Baker* [1990] 2 E.G.L.R. 195; *Scammel v Dicker* [2001] 1 W.L.R. 631, applying the principle to an offer to settle an action under CPR, Pt 36 (for further proceedings in this case, see [2005] EWCA Civ 405, [2005] 3 All E.R. 838, below para. 2–145); *Bircham Nominees (No.2) Ltd v Worrell Holdings Ltd* [2001] EWCA Civ 775; (2001) 82 P. & C.R. 472 at [24], [35]; *cf.* Defamation Act 1996, s.2(6). Contrast Vienna Convention on Contracts for the International Sale of Goods (above, para.2–063), Art.16(2).

[382] An offer is assumed to be open for a reasonable time if no time limit is expressed in it: see *Ramsgate Victoria Hotel Co Ltd v Montefiore* (1866) L.R. 1 Ex. 109; below, para.2–096.

[383] Below, para.3–172.

[384] (1828) 4 Bing. 653. See also *Cooke v Oxley* (1790) 3 T.R. 653.

[385] (1876) 2 Ch.D. 463.

[386] *Adams v Lindsell* (1818) 1 B. & Ald. 681; *Stevenson, Jacques & Co v Maclean* (1880) 5 Q.B.D. 346; it is submitted that contrary dicta in *Dickinson v Dodds* (1876) 2 Ch.D. 463, 472 would no longer be followed.

[387] For a statutory exception to the rule stated in the text, see Consumer Credit Act 1974, s.69(1)(ii) and (7), as substituted by Consumer Credit Act 1974 (Electronic Communications) Order 2004 (SI 2004/3236) art.2(5).

[388] (1880) 5 C.P.D. 44. See also *Stevenson Jacques & Co v McLean* (1880) 5 Q.B.D. 346; *Henthorn v Fraser* [1892] 2 Ch. 27; *Raeburn & Verel v Burness & Son* (1895) 1 Com.Cas. 22.

day, they accepted the offer by a telegram, which they confirmed by a letter posted on October 15. Meanwhile, however, the offerors had on October 8 posted a letter withdrawing their offer; this letter reached the offerees on the October 20. It was held that this withdrawal did not take effect on posting: it took effect only when it reached the offerees. As the acceptance had been posted before this happened, there was a binding contract.[389] The result was that a contract came into existence even though the parties were demonstrably never in agreement; for when the offerees first learnt (on October 11) of the defendants' offer the defendants had already (on October 8) ceased to intend to deal with the offerees. The rule is based on convenience; for no reliance could be placed on a posted offer if it could be effectively withdrawn by a letter posted by the offeror but not yet received by the offeree.

Communication need not come from offeror. Although the withdrawal of an offer must, in general, be communicated *to the offeree*, the communication need not come *from the offeror*: it is sufficient if the offeree knows from any reliable source that the offeror no longer intends to deal with him. In *Dickinson v Dodds*[390] it was accordingly held that an offer to sell land could not be accepted after the offeror had, to the offeree's knowledge, decided to sell the land to a third party. The judgments stress the fact that there is, in such circumstances, no agreement between the parties; but this would also be true if the offeree had accepted the offer when he had no knowledge at all of the offeror's change of mind. Yet where this is the case there can be a contract, as *Byrne & Co v Van Tienhoven*[391] shows. The rule that communication of withdrawal need not come from the offeror can be a source of uncertainty, making it hard for the offeree to tell exactly when it becomes impossible for him to accept the offer. For example, in *Dickinson v Dodds* it is not clear whether such acceptance was precluded when the offeree knew that the offeror had (a) sold the land to a third party or (b) started negotiations for its sale to a third party or (c) had simply decided not to sell it to the offeree. 2–090

Exceptions to the requirement of communication. If the general rule means that notice of withdrawal must actually be "brought to the mind of"[392] the offeree, convenience requires its qualification in a number of situations. 2–091

(1) Letter to commercial organisation. Where the offer has been made to a commercial organisation, the requirement cannot be taken quite literally in the sense of requiring the withdrawal to be brought to the actual notice of the officer responsible for the matter. It seems probable that the offer would be withdrawn when the letter of withdrawal "was opened in the ordinary course of business or

[389] The same result would be reached under Vienna Convention on Contracts for the International Sale of Goods, Art.16(1) (see above, para.2–063), even though under Arts 18(2) and 24 the contract would not be made until the acceptance was communicated to the offeror or delivered to his address.
[390] (1876) 2 Ch.D. 463; *cf. Cartwright v Hoogstoel* (1911) 105 L.T. 628.
[391] (1880) 5 C.P.D. 344; above, para.2–089.
[392] *Henthorn v Fraser* [1892] 2 Ch. 27, 32.

would have been so opened if the ordinary course of business was followed."[393]

(2) Offeree's conduct displacing general rule. The concluding words of the passage just quoted suggest that the general rule may be displaced by the conduct of the offeree. For example, a withdrawal which was delivered to the offeree's last known address could be effective if he had moved without notifying the offeror. Similarly, a withdrawal which had reached the offeree could be effective even though he had simply failed to read it after it had reached him: this would be the position where a withdrawal by telex or fax arrived in the offeree's office during business hours[394] even though it was not actually read by the offeree or by any of his staff till the next day.[395] But the withdrawal would not be effective, in such a case, if it had been sent to the offeree at a time when he and all responsible members of his staff were, to the offeror's knowledge, away on holiday or on other business.[396]

(3) Offers made to the public. The requirement that a withdrawal must be actually communicated finally does not apply to offers made to the public, *e.g.* of rewards for information leading to the arrest of the perpetrator of a crime. As it is impossible for the offeror to ensure that the notice of withdrawal comes to the attention of everyone who knew of the offer, it seems to be enough for him to take reasonable steps to bring the withdrawal to the attention of such persons, even though it does not in fact come to the attention of them all.[397]

(b) *Rejection*

2–092 **What amounts to rejection; counter-offers.** A rejection terminates an offer, so that it can no longer be accepted.[398] For this purpose, an attempt to accept an offer on new terms (not contained in the offer) may be a rejection accompanied by a counter-offer.[399] Thus in *Hyde v Wrench*[400] the defendant offered to sell a farm for £1,000. The offeree replied offering to buy for £950, and when that counter-offer was rejected, purported to accept the defendant's original offer to

[393] *Eaglehill Ltd v J. Needham (Builders) Ltd* [1973] A.C. 992, 1011, discussing notice of dishonour of a cheque; *cf. Curtice v London, etc., Bank* [1908] 1 K.B. 291, 300–301 (notice to countermand a cheque); *Schelde Delta Shipping BV v Astarte Shipping Ltd (The Pamela)* [1995] 2 Lloyd's Rep. 249, 252; *N.V. Stoomv Maats "De Maas" v Nippon Yusen Kaisha (The Pendrecht)* [1980] 2 Lloyd's Rep. 56, 66 (telex notice of arbitration) and *Bernuth Lines Ltd v High Seas Shipping Ltd (The Eastern Navigator)* [2005] EWHC 3020 (Comm), [2006] 1 Lloyd's Rep. 537 at [30], [37]; according to these passages, it is not necessary for such notices to arrive during business hours. *Quaere* whether a notice withdrawing an offer must so arrive; there seems to be no good reason for distinguishing between such a notice and an acceptance by telex, as to which see above, para.2–047 at nn.223, 224.

[394] For the effect of such messages when sent *out* of business hours, see above, para.2–047 (acceptance received out of business hours).

[395] *cf. Tenax Steamship Co Ltd v Brimnes (Owners), (The Brimnes)* [1975] 5 Q.B. 929 (notice withdrawing ship from charterparty) and the last two cases cited in n.393 above.

[396] *Brinkibon Ltd v Stahag Stahl und Stahlwarenhandelsgesellschaft mbH* [1983] 2 A.C. 34, 42.

[397] *Shuey v U.S.* 92 U.S. 73 (1875).

[398] *Tinn v Hoffmann & Co* (1873) 29 L.T. 271, 278.

[399] Above, para.2–032; for an exception see Vienna Convention on Contracts for the International Sale of Goods (above, para.2–063), Art.19(2).

[400] (1840) 3 Beav. 334; *cf. O.T.M. Ltd v Hydranautics* [1981] 2 Lloyd's Rep. 211, 214; *Sterling Hydraulics Ltd v Dichtomatic Ltd* [2006] EWHC 2004 (QB); [2007] 1 Lloyd's Rep. 8 at [17].

sell for £1,000. It was held that there was no contract as the offeree had, by making a counter-offer of £950, rejected, and so terminated, the original offer.

Inquiries and requests for information. A communication from the offeree *may* be construed as a counter-offer (and hence as a rejection) even though it takes the form of a question as to the offeror's willingness to vary the terms of the offer.[401] But such a communication is not *necessarily* a counter-offer: it may be a mere inquiry or request for information made without any intention of rejecting the terms of the offer.[402] Whether the communication is a counter-offer or a request for information depends on the intention, objectively ascertained,[403] with which it was made. In *Stevenson, Jacques & Co v McLean*[404] an offer was made to sell iron to offerees who asked by telegram whether they might take delivery over a period of four months. It was held that this telegram was not a counter-offer but only a request for information as it was "meant . . . only as an inquiry" and as the offeror "ought to have regarded it" in that sense.[405] Similarly, if an offer is made to sell a house at a specified price, an inquiry whether the intending vendor is prepared to reduce that price will not amount to a rejection of the offer if the inquiry is "merely exploratory."[406] 2–093

Rejection must be communicated. A rejection takes effect when it is communicated to the offeree. There is no ground of convenience for holding that it should terminate the offer as soon as it is posted. The offeree will not act in reliance on it as he derives no rights or liabilities from it; and the offeror will not know that he is free from the offer until the rejection is actually communicated to him. Hence if the rejection is overtaken by a subsequently despatched acceptance which reaches the offeror first, the latter should take effect so long as the offeree has made his intention to accept (inspite of his original rejection) clear to the offeror. If, however, the rejection has reached the offeror, it is submitted that he would not be bound by an acceptance posted after the rejection and also reaching him after the rejection. To apply the "posted acceptance" rule[407] here merely because at the time of posting the rejection had not reached the offeror could expose him to hardship particularly where he had acted on the rejection, *e.g.* by disposing of the subject-matter elsewhere. An offeree who has posted a rejection and then wishes, after all, to accept the offer should ensure that the subsequently posted acceptance comes to the notice of the offeror before the latter has received the rejection. 2–094

(c) *Lapse of time*

Specified time. An offer which expressly states that it will last only for a specified time cannot be accepted after that time. The most common application 2–095

[401] See the treatment in *Tinn v Hoffmann* (1873) 29 L.T. 271, 278 of the claimant's letter of November 27.
[402] *cf.* above, para.2–032.
[403] Above, paras 2–002, 2–003.
[404] (1880) 5 Q.B.D. 346.
[405] *ibid.* at 349–350; in fact the offeror did not so regard it but sold the iron to a third party.
[406] *Gibson v Manchester City Council* [1979] 1 W.L.R. 294, 302.
[407] Above, para.2–048.

of this rule is to offers taking the form of options,[408] which obviously cannot be accepted after the expiry of the period during which the option is expressed to be exercisable. On a similar principle, an offer which stipulates for acceptance "by return of post" must be accepted either in the specified way or by some other no less expeditious method.[409]

2–096 **Reasonable time.** Where the duration of an offer is not limited by its express terms, the offer comes to an end after the lapse of a reasonable time.[410] What is a reasonable time depends on all the circumstances: for example on the nature of the subject-matter and on the means used to communicate the offer. An offer to sell a perishable thing, or a thing subject to sudden price fluctuations, would terminate after a relatively short time; and this would often also be true of an offer made by telegram[411] or by other equally speedy means of communication such as telex or fax.

2–097 **Effect of conduct of offeree known to offeror.** The period which would normally constitute a reasonable time for acceptance may be extended if the conduct of the offeree within that period indicates an intention to accept and this is known to the offeror. Often on such facts there would be an acceptance by conduct, but this possibility may be ruled out by the terms of the offer, which may require the acceptance to be by written notice sent to a specified address.[412] In such a case the offeree's conduct, though it could not *amount* to an acceptance, could nevertheless prolong the time for giving a proper notice of acceptance. For the offeree's conduct to have this effect, it must be known to the offeror; for if this were not the case the offeror might reasonably suppose that the offer had not been accepted within the normal period of lapse, and act in reliance on that belief: *e.g.* by disposing elsewhere of the subject-matter.

(d) *Occurrence of Condition*

2–098 **Provision for termination of offer.** An offer which expressly provides that it is to determine on the occurrence of some condition cannot be accepted after that condition has occurred; and a similar provision for determination may be implied. If an offer to buy, or hire-purchase, goods is made after the offeror has examined them, it may be subject to the implied condition that they should, at the time of the acceptance, still be in substantially the same state as that in which they were when the offer was made. Such an offer could not be accepted after the

[408] For the legal nature of an enforceable option, see below, para.3–172, n.943.

[409] *cf.* above, paras 2–065, 2–067.

[410] *Ramsgate Victoria Hotel Co v Montefiore* (1866) L.R. 1 Ex. 109; see also *Reynolds v Atherton* (1922) 127 L.T. 189; *Chem Co Leasing SpA v Rediffusion* [1987] 1 F.T.L.R. 201. And *cf. L.J. Korbetis v Transgrain Shipping BV* [2005] EWHC 1345 (QB) (offer to appoint an arbitrator to whom disputes under a charterparty were to be referred held to have lapsed after eight months; the fact that the charterparty required agreement on the appointment to be made "forthwith" was said at [18] to connote "some urgency"). *Semble*, the offeror could waive the delay. See also Vienna Convention on Contracts for the International Sale of Goods (above, para.2–063), Art.21(1).

[411] *Quenerduaine v Cole* (1883) 32 W.R. 185.

[412] As in *Manchester Diocesan Council for Education v Commercial and General Investments Ltd* [1970] 1 W.L.R. 241.

goods had been seriously damaged.[413] Similarly, an offer to insure the life of a person cannot be accepted after he has suffered serious injuries by falling over a cliff.[414] On the same principle, it is submitted that the offer which is made by bidding at an auction impliedly provides that it is to lapse as soon as a higher bid is made.[415]

(e) *Death*

In general. It has been suggested that the death of either party terminates the offer as it makes it impossible for the parties to reach agreement.[416] But there may be a contract in spite of a demonstrable lack of agreement, if this result is required by considerations of convenience[417]; and such considerations might in some circumstances support the view that an offer should be capable of acceptance after the death of one party. This would, in particular, be the case where one party was ignorant of the other's death at the relevant time; or where a person who had validly contracted not to revoke an offer for a fixed period died during that time. More generally, it may be doubted whether there are any grounds of convenience for holding that the death of either party should of itself terminate an offer, except where the offer is one to enter into a contract which, because of its "personal" nature, would be terminated by the death of either party.[418] **2–099**

Death of the offeror. The effect of the death of the offeror has been considered in a number of cases concerning continuing guarantees. Such a guarantee (*e.g.* of a bank overdraft) is, in general, divisible: it is a continuing offer, accepted from time to time as the bank makes further loans to its customer. It seems that a guarantee of this kind is not terminated merely by the death of the guarantor.[419] But it is terminated if the creditor knows that the guarantor is dead and that his personal representatives have no power under his will to continue the guarantee[420]; or if for some other reason it is inequitable to charge the guarantor's estate.[421] If the guarantee expressly provides that it can be terminated only by notice given by the guarantor or his personal representatives, the death of the guarantor (even if known to the creditor) will not terminate the guarantee; only **2–100**

---

[413] *Financings Ltd v Stimson* [1962] 1 W.L.R. 1184.

[414] *Canning v Farquhar* (1885) 16 Q.B.D. 727; *Looker v Law Union Insurance Co. Ltd* [1928] 1 K.B. 554.

[415] Above, para.2–011.

[416] *Dickinson v Dodds* (1876) 2 Ch.D. 463, 475.

[417] As, for example, in *Byrne & Co v Van Tienhoven* (1880) 5 C.P.D. 344 (above, para.2–089), where the offeree did not know that the offeror intended to contract with him until after the offeror had ceased to have any such intention.

[418] Below, para.23–037. Even in such cases the legal effects of saying that the offer was determined, so that there was never any contract, would be likely to differ from those of saying that there had been a contract which had been terminated: *e.g.* the Law Reform (Frustrated Contracts) Act 1943 could apply to the latter, but not to the former, situation.

[419] *Bradbury v Morgan* (1862) 1 H. & C. 249; *Harriss v Fawcett* (1873) L.R. 8 Ch.App. 866, 869; *Coulthart v Clementson* (1879) 5 Q.B.D. 42, 46.

[420] *Coulthart v Clementson*, above.

[421] *Harriss v Fawcett* (1873) L.R. 8 Ch.App. 866.

express notice will have this effect.[422] In so far as any general statement can be based on this special group of cases, it seems that the death of the offeror determines an offer only if the offer on its true construction so provides.

2–101 **Death of the offeree.** Two cases have some bearing on the effect of the death of the offeree. In *Reynolds v Atherton*[423] an offer to sell shares was made in 1911 to "the directors of" a company. An attempt to accept the offer was made in 1919 by the survivors of the persons who were directors in 1911 and by the personal representatives of those who had since died. The purported acceptance was held to be ineffective; and Warrington L.J. said: "The offer having been made to a living person who ceases to be a living person before the offer is accepted, there is no longer an offer at all. The offer is not intended to be made to a dead person or to his executors, and the offer ceases to be an offer capable of acceptance." The actual ground for the decision, however, was that the offer had, on its true construction, been made to the directors of the company for the time being, and not to those who had happened to hold office in 1911. In *Kennedy v Thomassen*[424] acceptance by solicitors of the offeree in ignorance of her death was held ineffective on the grounds that their authority to act on her behalf had been revoked by her death[425] and that they had acted under a mistake. Neither case supports the view that an offer can never be accepted after the death of the offeree. It is submitted that, where an offer related to a contract which was not "personal,"[426] it might, on its true construction, be held to have been made to the offeree or to his executors, and that such an offer could be accepted after the death of the original offeree.

(f) *Supervening Personal Incapacity*

2–102 **Mental incapacity.** If, after making an offer, the offeror suffers from "an impairment of, or a disturbance in the functioning of, the mind or brain"[427] and for that reason "lacks capacity",[428] then he will not be bound by an acceptance made after this fact has become known to the offeree, or after the offeror's property has been made subject to the control of the court. But the offeror could hold the other party to the acceptance; and an offer made to a person who later became so incapacitated could be accepted so as to bind the other party. These rules can readily be deduced from the law as to contracts with persons who lack mental capacity.[429]

---

422 *Re Silvester* [1895] 1 Ch. 573.

423 (1921) 125 L.T. 690, 695; affirmed (1922) 127 L.T. 189; *cf. Somerville v N.C.B.*, 1963 S.L.T. 334.

424 [1929] 1 Ch. 426.

425 Vol.II, para.31–164.

426 "Personal" is here used in the same sense as in the law relating to termination of a contract by the death of a party: see n.418, above.

427 Mental Capacity Act 2005, s.2.

428 *ibid.*

429 Below, paras 8–068, 8–079.

(g) *Supervening Corporate Incapacity*

2–103 **Supervening corporate incapacity.** In discussing the effect on an offer of supervening corporate incapacity, a distinction must be drawn between companies incorporated under the Companies Acts (and now governed by the Companies Act 2006[430]) and other corporations.

2–104 **Companies incorporated under the Companies Acts.** In these Acts, the expression "company" generally means a company formed and registered under the Companies Act 2006 or under earlier Companies Acts.[431] The legal capacity of such a company depends on the company's constitution, an expression which includes the company's articles[432]; and, in particular, on any statement of the company's objects in the articles,[433] which may be amended by special resolution.[434] Unless the articles specifically restrict the objects of a company, its objects are (in general) unrestricted[435]; but our present concern is with cases in which a special resolution amends the articles by either restricting originally unrestricted objects or imposing further restrictions on originally restricted objects. If the company nevertheless entered into a transaction which fell within the newly imposed restrictions on its objects, that transactions would formerly have been *ultra vires* and void.[436] The Companies Act 2006 does not abolish this *ultra vires* doctrine but it contains a number of provisions which significantly restrict its operation. Of these, the following are of particular importance for the purposes of the discussion that follows in paragraphs 2–105 to 2–107 below. First, section 31(3) provides that, in general,[437] "Any such amendment does not affect any rights or obligations of the company"; the phrase "such amendments" here refers to an amendment of the company's "articles so as to add, remove or alter a statement of the company's objects."[438] Secondly, section 39(1) provides that, in general,[439] "the validity of an act done by a company shall not be called into question on the ground of lack of capacity by reason of anything in the company's constitution."[440] Further problems can, however, arise from the fact that a contract which violated a restriction on the company's objects would on that ground be beyond the power of its directors. Section 40(1) therefore provides, thirdly, that, in general,[441] "In favour of a person dealing with the company in good faith, the power of the directors to bind the company, or

[430] At the time of writing, the Companies Act 2006 is only partly in force: see below, para. 9–003.
[431] Companies Act 2006, s.1.
[432] *ibid*., s.17(a).
[433] See *ibid*., s.31.
[434] *ibid*., s.21; such a resolution is also part of the company's constitution: see ss.17(b), 29.
[435] *ibid*., s.31(1); for special rules applicable to companies that are charities, see s.31(4); Charities Act 1993, s.64.
[436] See below, para.9–020.
[437] For the position of charitable companies, see above, n.435.
[438] Companies Act 2006, s.31(2).
[439] For special rules applicable to companies that are charities, see Companies Act 2006, ss.39(2), 42.
[440] *ibid*., s.39(1).
[441] *i.e.*, subject to s.40(6)(a) (certain transactions with directors: see s.41) and 40(6)(b) (companies that are charitable: see s.42).

authorise others to do so, is deemed to be free of any limitations under the company's constitution." Section 40(4), however, provides that, in general,[442] section 40 "does not affect any right of a member of the company to bring proceedings to restrain the doing of an action that is beyond the powers of the directors"; but that "no such proceedings lie in respect of an act to be done in fulfilment of a legal obligation arising from a previous act of the company." Our concern here is with the effect of these provisions where an offer is made either to or by a company which then changes its articles by restricting its objects so as to deprive itself of the power of entering into the contract that would, but for such changes, have resulted from an acceptance of the offer.[443]

2–105 **Company as offeree.** A company may receive an offer to enter into a contract and then amend its articles so as to restrict its objects in such a way as to deprive itself of its capacity to enter into that contract. If the company nevertheless then (whether by oversight or for good commercial reasons) accepts the offer, two provisions of the Companies Act 2006 referred to in paragraph 2–104 above may determine the effect of the acceptance. The first is section 31(3), by which "any such amendment does not affect the rights or obligations of the company." The second is section 40(1), by which "in favour of a person dealing with the company in good faith, the power of the directors to bind the company . . . is deemed to be free of any limitation under the company's constitution."[444] Both these provisions can lead to the conclusion that the acceptance is effective; but they give rise, in the present context, to the problem that the scope of section 40(1) differs in several respects from that of section 31(3). First, the requirement in section 40(1) of "dealing . . . in good faith" has no counterpart in section 31(3). Secondly, section 40(1) applies only "in favour of a person dealing with the company" while section 31(3) can apply also in favour of the company itself; this view is reinforced by the reference in section 31(3) to "the *rights or* obligations of the company." Thirdly, section 40(4) provides that "*this section* does not affect any right of a member of a company to bring proceedings to restrain the doing of an action that is beyond the powers of the directors . . ."; and this subsection of section 40 (further provisions of which are discussed in paragraph 2–106 below) has no counterpart in section 31. Fourthly, sections 31(3) and 40(1) lay down general rules but the qualifications to which these rules are subject are not the same. Section 31 is subject only to one qualification, which applies where the company is a charity[445]; section 40 is subject to two qualifications which apply to certain transactions with directors and where the company is a charity.[446] The scope of section 40(1) is in all these respects narrower than that of section 31(3) and it is by no means obvious which subsection would, in case of a conflict between them, prevail. One possible view is that, in the present context, section 31(3) should prevail since it deals specifically with the effect of an *amendment* of the articles. But section 40(1) is

---

[442] *i.e.*, subject to the restrictions referred to in n.441 above.

[443] The text will be concerned only with the effect of the general rules stated in this paragraph. It will not deal with the exceptional cases referred to in nn.437, 439, 441 and 442 above.

[444] The company's constitution includes its articles and any resolution amending them: see Companies Act 2006, ss.17, 29.

[445] *ibid.*, s.31(4).

[446] *ibid.* s.40(6), referring to ss.41 and 42.

expressed to apply to limitations on the directors' powers deriving "from a resolution of the company . . . "[447] and "from any agreement between the members of the company . . . "; and such resolutions and agreements can form part of the company's "constitution",[448] to which section 40(1) applies. A second possible view is that the words "rights or obligations of the company" in section 31(3) refer to rights already in existence at the time of the amendment of the articles, and not to rights which are alleged to have come into existence after that time. It is submitted, though not without hesitation, that this second view is to be preferred as it avoids what would be a conflict between the two subsections; and that accordingly the rights of the offeror would, in the situation discussed in this paragraph, be governed, not by section 31(3), but by section 40. The rights of the company itself would be governed by the general principle, stated in section 39(1), that the validity of an act done by it was not to be "called into question by reason of anything in the company's constitution." At the relevant time (*i.e.*, that of the acceptance) the "constitution" would include the amendment of the articles.[449] Hence the company would be able to enforce the contract by virtue of section 39(1) and its right to do so would not be subject to the restrictions placed by section 40 on the rights of the offeror to do so.

Company as offeror. A company may make an offer to enter into a contract, amend its articles so as to restrict its objects in such a way as to deprive itself of the capacity to enter into that contract, and the offeree may then (perhaps in ignorance of the amendment) accept the offer. If the reasoning in paragraph 2–105 is correct, such a case would not be governed by section 31(3) of the Companies Act 2006 since at the time of the amendment of the articles the company would not have acquired any rights or been subjected to any liabilities by reason of the then unaccepted offer. Nor (subject to a possible argument to be discussed below) would the case be governed by section 40 since, when the offer was made, there was no relevant "limitation under the company's constitution" on "the power of the directors to bind the company" within section 40(1); or by section 39(1) since, when the offer was made, the company suffered from no "lack of capacity [to make it] by reason of anything in the company's constitution." It is, however, arguable that holding the offer open was a continuing act; and if that argument were accepted two consequences could follow. First, the offeree could acquire rights against the company by virtue of section 40(1) if he accepted the offer in good faith, *i.e.* (presumably) in ignorance of the amendment of the articles. But, secondly, it would appear to be open to a member of the company to bring proceedings to "restrain the doing of an action that is beyond the powers of the directors" (*i.e.*, the continued making of the offer) at any time before the offer had been accepted. The company could also normally withdraw the offer at any time before it had been accepted[450] and would be likely to do so in pursuance of the policy which had led it to amend its articles in the way described at the beginning of this paragraph. But this possibility would not be open to the company where it had bound itself not to withdraw the offer, *i.e.* 2–106

[447] *ibid.*, s.40(3)(a).
[448] *ibid.*, ss.17, 29.
[449] *ibid.*
[450] See above, para.2–088.

where it had granted a legally enforceable option.[451] In such a case, it is clear that a member of the company could not take proceedings to prevent the conclusion of the contract since "no such proceedings lie in respect of an act to be done in fulfilment of a legal obligation arising from a previous act of the company"[452]: *i.e.*, in the case put, from the grant of the option.

2–107 A further problem that arises in the situation described in paragraph 2–106 above is whether, if the company's offer were accepted when the company no longer had the capacity to enter into the contract, and were accepted by the offeree in good faith so as to confer rights under it on the offeree, the company would also be entitled to enforce the contract. No doubt, if the offeree sought to enforce the contract, then he could normally do so only on condition of performing his own obligations under it. But there is also the possibility that, having accepted the offer, the offeree might nevertheless refuse to perform its part and that the company might then seek to enforce the contract (*e.g.* by claiming damages for its breach) even though by the time of the acceptance of its offer it no longer had the capacity to enter into the contract. Section 40(1) of the Companies Act 2006 would not support such a claim since it applies only "in favour of a person dealing with the company . . . " and not in favour of the company itself; nor could the claim be brought under section 31(3) if, as has been suggested in paragraph 2–105 above, that section refers only to rights and obligations already in existence when the company amended its constitution. An attempt by the company to enforce the contract under section 39(1) would run into a difficulty similar to that discussed in paragraph 2–106 above. The difficulty arises because section 39(1) provides that "The validity of an *act done by the company* shall not be called into question" by reason of anything in the company's constitution. If the "act done by the company" were the making of the offer, then section 39(1) would, at first sight, be irrelevant since, when the offer was made, it was, *ex hypothesi*, within the company's capacity. It would be the validity of an act done by the offeree (*i.e.*, the acceptance), rather than any act by the company, that would be in question. The outcome would depend on section 39(1) only if a suggestion similar to that put forward in paragraph 2–106 were accepted: *i.e.*, if the making of the offer were regarded as a continuous act. If that argument failed, the company would be driven back on argument that a contract outside its capacity was *at common law*[453] enforceable *by*, even though not *against* it. This argument would not prevail if, as is sometimes said, *ultra vires* contracts were at common law "wholly void"[454], but the authorities give no clear guidance on the point.[455]

2–108 **Other corporations.** Companies may also be incorporated by Royal Charter or by special legislation. Charter corporations have the legal capacity of a natural person so that an alteration of the charter would not affect the validity of an offer

---

[451] For the nature of legally enforceable options, see below, para.3–172 n.943.
[452] Companies Act 2006, s.40(4).
[453] *i.e.*, apart from s.39(1); no doubt in a case *within* s.39(1), the contract could be enforced by the company.
[454] See below, para.9–021.
[455] For a discussion of policy considerations which should govern the outcome in such cases, see Treitel, *The Law of Contract* (12th ed. by Peel, 2007), para.12–080.

or acceptance made by the corporation.[456] The legal capacity of corporations incorporated by special statute is governed by the statute, and acts not within that capacity are *ultra vires* and void.[457] An alteration of the statute could therefore prevent the corporation from accepting an offer made to it, and from being bound by the acceptance of an offer made by it, where the offer was made before the alteration came into effect. In practice, the problem is likely to be dealt with in the statute which changes the capacity of the corporation.

Limited liability partnerships. Limited liability partnerships incorporated under the Limited Liability Partnerships Act 2000[458] are bodies corporate[459] but problems of the kind discussed in paras 2–103 to 2–107 above cannot arise with regard to them as they have "unlimited capacity."[460] 2–109

5. SPECIAL CASES

Difficulty of offer and acceptance analysis in certain cases. The analysis of the process of reaching agreement into the elements of offer and acceptance gives rise, in a number of situations,[461] to considerable difficulties. 2–110

(1) Multilateral contracts. One such situation arises where participants in a competition address their entries to the organiser. It is then hard to say whether a particular entry constitutes an offer or an acceptance (or both), or whether two entry forms put into the post by different competitors at the same time constituted cross-offers. Yet in spite of such difficulties it has been held that the competitors enter into multilateral contracts binding each to the others to observe the rules of the competition.[462] Similar reasoning would seem to apply to the multilateral contract which governs the legal relations between members of an unincorporated association.[463] Such decisions are based on the assumption that all the parties to the alleged multilateral contract were willing to agree to the same terms. Where one of the negotiating parties had refused to accept one of the terms

---

456 Below, para.9–004; but a member of the corporation could bring proceedings to restrain the conclusion of the contract: *ibid.*

457 Subject to mitigations provided for, in the case of contracts with "local authorities", by Local Government Contracts Act 1996.

458 See ss.2 and 3 of that Act.

459 *ibid.*, s.1(2).

460 *ibid.*, s.1(3).

461 See, in addition to the situations discussed in para.2–110, *e.g. A. N. Satterthwaite & Co Ltd v New Zealand Shipping Co Ltd (The Eurymedon)* [1975] A.C. 154, 167; *Commission for the New Towns v Cooper (G.B.) Ltd* [1995] Ch. 259 (below, para.2–119) and see below at nn.471 and 472.

462 *The Satanita* [1895] P. 248, affirmed *sub nom. Clarke v Dunraven* [1897] A.C. 59; Phillips, 92 L.Q.R. 499. *cf. Kingscroft Insurance Co Ltd v Nissan Fire and Marine Insurance Co Ltd* [2000] 1 All E.R. (Comm) 272 at 291 (admission of new members to an existing insurance pool analysed in terms of offer and acceptance).

463 See *Artistic Upholstery Ltd v Art Forma (Furniture) Ltd* [1999] 4 All E.R. 277, 285; though breach of the rules by one member may not, on their true construction, be actionable in damages at the suit of another: *Anderton v Rowland, The Times*, November 5, 1999.

of the proposed contract, no multilateral contract would arise between that party and any of the others, unless the others agreed to be bound to that party on terms excluding the one rejected by him.[464]

(2) Reference to third party. It is, secondly, hard to apply the analysis of offer and acceptance where negotiations have reached deadlock and the parties simultaneously agree to a solution proposed by a third party whom they have asked to resolve their differences.[465] The same is true where parties negotiate through a single broker acting for both parties who eventually obtains their consent to the same terms.[466]

(3) Sale of land. There is, thirdly, some difficulty, in applying the offer and acceptance analysis to transactions such as sales of land where parties agree "subject to contract", so that they are not bound until formal contracts are exchanged.[467] Strictly, an "offer" subject to contract does not satisfy the legal definition of an offer,[468] since the person making such an "offer" has *no* intention to be bound immediately on its acceptance.[469] However, the *agreement* is generally made by the usual, process; the reason why the parties to it are not bound until they exchange formal contracts is that the terms of the agreement negative, until then, the intention to enter into legal relations. Alternatively, a party could be regarded as making an offer when he submits a signed contract for exchange,[470] and this would be accepted when the exchange took place.

2–111 The difficulties described in para.2–110 above have given rise to the view that the analysis of the process of reaching agreement in terms of offer and acceptance is "out of date"[471] and that "you should look at the correspondence as a whole and at the conduct of the parties and see therefrom whether the parties have come to an agreement."[472] But such an outright rejection of the traditional analysis is open to the objection that it provides too little guidance for the courts (or for the parties or for their legal advisers) in determining whether an agreement has been reached. For this reason the cases described above are best regarded as exceptions[473] to a general requirement of offer and acceptance. This approach is supported by cases in which it has been held that there was no

---

[464] *Azov Shipping Co v Baltic Shipping Co* [1999] 2 Lloyd's Rep. 159 at 165.

[465] See Pollock, *Principles of Contract* (13th ed.), p.5.

[466] *Pagnan SpA v Feed Products Ltd* [1987] 2 Lloyd's Rep. 601, 616.

[467] Below, paras 2–118, 2–119.

[468] Above, para.2–003.

[469] Below, para.2–119.

[470] See *Christie Owen & Davies v Rapacioli* [1974] Q.B. 781; *cf. Commission for the New Towns Ltd v Cooper (Great Britain) Ltd* [1995] Ch. 259 at 285.

[471] *Butler Machine Tool Co Ltd v Ex-Cell-O Corp. (England) Ltd* [1979] 1 W.L.R. 401, 404; *cf. Port Sudan Cotton Co v Govindaswamy Chettiar & Sons* [1977] 2 Lloyd's Rep. 5, 10; *Tankrederei Ahrenkeil GmbH v Frahuil SA (The Multibank Holsatia)* [1988] 2 Lloyd's Rep. 486, 491–492; *Interfoto Picture Library Ltd v Stiletto Visual Programmes Ltd* [1989] Ch. 433, 443.

[472] *Gibson v Manchester City Council* [1978] 1 W.L.R. 520, 523; reversed [1979] 1 W.L.R. 294.

[473] *Gibson v Manchester City Council* [1979] 1 W.L.R. 294, 297; *cf. Harmony Shipping Co SA v Saudi-Europe Line Ltd (The Good Helmsman)* [1981] 1 Lloyd's Rep. 377, 409; *G. Percy Trentham Ltd v Archital Luxfer Ltd* [1993] 1 Lloyd's Rep. 27, 29–30.

contract precisely because there was no offer and acceptance[474]; and by those in which the terms of the contact have been held to depend on the analysis of the negotiations into offer, counter-offer and acceptance.[475]

6. INCOMPLETE AGREEMENT

Agreement in principle only.[476] Parties may reach agreement on essential matters of principle, but leave important points unsettled so that their agreement is incomplete.[477] It has, for example, been held that there was no contract where an agreement for a lease failed to specify the date on which the term was to commence[478]; that an agreement "in principle" for the redevelopment and disposal of residential property, which specified core terms but left important matters, such as the timing of the project, for future discussion was an "incomplete agreement" and so did not amount to a binding contract[478a]; that an agreement for sale of land by instalments was not a binding contract where it provided for conveyance of "a proportionate part" as each instalment of the price was paid, but failed to specify which part is to be conveyed on each payment[479]; and that where, though agreement had been reached "covering some significant matters",[480] there was no contract because "many fundamental matters remained to be resolved."[481] An agreement is also incomplete if it expressly provides that it is "subject to" specified points; there is no contract in such a case until either those points are resolved or the parties agree that their resolution is no longer necessary for the agreement to enter into contractual force.[482] 2–112

---

474 *Hispanica de Petroleos SA v Vencedora Oceanica Navegacion SA (The Kapetan Markos N.L.)* [1987] 2 Lloyd's Rep. 323, 331 ("What was the mechanism of offer and acceptance?"); *The Aramis* [1989] 1 Lloyd's Rep. 213; Treitel [1989] L.M.C.L.Q. 162; *Taylor v Dickens* [1998] F.L.R. 806, 818 (doubted on another point in *Gillett v Holt* [2001] Ch. 210); *Schuldenfrei v Hilton* [1999] S.T.C. 821. The "offer and acceptance" analysis is also used in many of the arbitration cases discussed above, paras 2–006, 2–076 though it is viewed with scepticism in *The Multibank Holsatia*, above n.471, at 491 and in *Thai-Europe Tapioca Service Ltd v Seine Navigation Inc (The Maritime Winner)* [1989] 2 Lloyd's Rep. 506, 515.

475 *e.g.* the "battle of forms" cases discussed above, para.2–034.

476 Lücke (1967) 3 Adelaide L.Rev. 46.

477 Referred to with apparent approval in *Western Broadcasting Services v Seaga* [2007] UKPC 19, [2007] E.M.L.R. 18 at [19].

478 *Harvey v Pratt* [1965] 1 W.L.R. 1025; and see *Re Day's Will Trusts* [1962] 1 W.L.R. 1419.

478a *Cobbe v Yeoman's Row Management Ltd* [2008] UKHL 55, [2008] 1 W.L.R. 1752 at [15]; see also at [7], [88].

479 *Bushwall Properties Ltd v Vortex Properties* [1976] 1 W.L.R. 591; *cf. Hillreed Land v Beautridge* [1994] E.G.C.S. 55; *Avintar v Avill*, 1995 S.C.L.R. 1012; *Hadley v Kemp* [1999] E.M.L.R. 589 at 628; *London & Regional Development v TBI plc* [2002] EWCA Civ 355; *Spectra International plc v Tiscali Ltd* [2002] EWHC 2084 (Comm); [2002] All E.R. (D) 2009 (Oct); *Morgan Grenfell Development v Arrows Autosport Ltd* [2003] EWHC 333 (Ch); [2003] All E.R. (D) 417 (Feb); *Jordan Grand Prix Ltd v Vodafone Group plc* [2003] EWHC 1956 (Comm); [2003] 2 All E.R. (Comm) 864; *Compagnie Nogar D'Importation et D'Exportation SA v Abacha* [2003] EWCA Civ 1100; [2003] 2 All E.R. (Comm) 915.

480 *Bols Distilleries BV v Superior Yacht Services Ltd* [2006] UKPC 45, [2007] 1 W.L.R. 12 at [32].

481 *ibid.*, at [35].

482 *Electrosteel Castings Ltd v Scan-Trans Shipping & Chartering Co* [2002] EWHC 1993 (Comm); [2002] 2 All E.R. (Comm) 1064 at [24].

2–113 **Agreement complete despite lack of detail.** On the other hand, an agreement may be complete although it is not worked out in meticulous detail.[483] Thus an agreement for the sale of goods may be complete as soon as the parties have agreed to buy and sell, where the remaining details can be determined by the standard of reasonableness or by law.[484] Even failure to agree the price is not necessarily fatal in such a case. Section 8(2) of the Sale of Goods Act 1979 provides that, if no price is determined by the contract, a reasonable price must be paid. Under s.15(1) of the Supply of Goods and Services Act 1982, a reasonable sum must similarly be paid where a contract for the supply of services fails to fix the remuneration to be paid for them.[485] These statutory provisions assume that the agreement amounts to a contract in spite of its failure to fix the price or remuneration. The very fact that the parties have not reached agreement on this vital point may indicate that there is *no* contract, *e.g.* because the price or remuneration is to be fixed by further agreement.[486] In such a case, the statutory provisions for payment of a reasonable sum do not apply. There may, however, be a claim for payment of such a sum at common law: for example, where work is done in the belief that there was a contract or in the expectation that the negotiations between the parties would result in the conclusion of a contract.[487] Such liability is based on the need to deprive the recipient of the services of unjust enrichment that may result from his having benefited from the services without being required to pay for them[487a]; and it arises in spite of the fact that there was *no* contract. It follows that the party doing the work, though he is entitled to a reasonable sum, is not liable in damages, *e.g.* for failing to do the work within a reasonable time.[488] If the claim arose under a contract by virtue of s.15(1) of the 1982 Act, the party doing the work would be both entitled and liable.

2–114 Even an agreement for sale of land dealing only with the barest essentials may be regarded as complete if that was the clear intention of the parties. Thus in *Perry v Suffields Ltd*[489] an offer to sell a public-house with vacant possession for £7,000 was accepted without qualification. It was held that there was a binding

---

[483] *First Energy (UK) Ltd v Hungarian International Bank Ltd* [1993] 2 Lloyd's Rep. 195, 205; *cf. de Jongh Weill v Mean Fiddler Holdings Ltd* [2003] EWCA Civ 1058.

[484] See *Bear Stearns Bank plc v Forum Global Equity Ltd* [2007] EWHC (below, para.2–114), where the fact that no settlement date had been agreed did not prevent the conclusion of a contract since, in the absence of express agreement on this point, there was "an implied term of the agreement that the parties would execute it within a reasonable time" (at [164]; *cf.* at [169]).

[485] *cf.*, at common law, *Way v Latilla* [1937] 3 All E.R. 759; and see, as to agents' commissions, *British Bank of Foreign Trade v Novinex* [1949] 1 K.B. 623; *Powell v Braun* [1954] 1 W.L.R. 401.

[486] *e.g. May & Butcher v R.* [1934] 2 K.B. 17n, below, para.2–126; *Courtney & Fairbairn Ltd v Tolaini Bros. (Hotels) Ltd* [1975] 1 W.L.R. 297; Dugdale and Lowe [1976] J.B.L. 312; *Chamberlain v Boodle & King* [1982] 1 W.L.R. 1443n; *Pagnan SpA v Granaria B.V.* [1986] 2 Lloyd's Rep. 547; *Russell Bros. (Paddington) Ltd v John Elliott Management Ltd* (1995) 11 Const. L.J. 377; *Southwark LBC v Logan* (1996) 8 Admin. L.R. 315.

[487] Below, para.29–071.

[487a] *Cobbe v Yeoman's Row Management Ltd* [2008] UKHL 55, [2008] 1 W.L.R. 1752 at [40]–[45], [93].

[488] *B.S.C. v Cleveland Bridge & Engineering Co Ltd* [1984] 1 All E.R. 504.

[489] [1916] 2 Ch. 187; *cf. Elias v George Sahely & Co (Barbados) Ltd* [1982] 3 All E.R. 801.

contract even though many important points, *e.g.* the date for completion[490] and the question of paying a deposit, were left open. In another case[491] a buyer and seller of corn feed pellets had reached agreement on the "cardinal terms of the deal: product, price, quantity, period of shipment, range of loading ports and governing contract terms."[492] The agreement was held to have contractual force even though the parties had not yet reached agreement on a number of other important points, such as the loading port,[493] the rate of loading and certain payments (other than the price) which might in certain events become payable under the contract. An even more striking illustration of this approach is provided by a case[494] in which parties had reached an oral agreement by telephone for the sale of notes evidencing "distressed debt" of a company which was in liquidation. The agreement identified the subject-matter and specified the price; and it was held to be contractually binding even though it did not specify the settlement date and left many other important points to be resolved by further agreement. In all these cases, the courts took the view that the parties intended to be bound at once in spite of the fact that further significant terms were to be agreed later and that even their failure to reach such agreement would not invalidate the contract unless without such agreement it was unworkable or too uncertain[495] to be enforced.

Agreement required for continued operation of contract. A distinction must finally be drawn between cases in which agreement on such matters as the price is required for the making, and those in which it is required for the *continued operation*, of a contract. The latter possibility is illustrated by a case[496] in which an agreement for the supply of services for 10 years fixed the fee to be paid only for the first two of those years. On the parties' failure to fix the fee in later years, it was held that they had intended to enter into a 10-year contract and that a term was to be implied into that contract for payment of a reasonable fee in those later years. 2–115

Stipulation for the execution of a formal document. The effect of a stipulation that an agreement is to be embodied in a formal written document depends on its purpose.[497] One possibility is that the agreement is regarded by the parties as incomplete, or as not intended to be legally binding,[498] until the terms of the formal document are agreed and the document is duly executed in accordance 2–116

---

[490] *cf. Storer v Manchester City Council* [1974] 1 W.L.R. 1403.

[491] *Pagnan SpA v Feed Products Ltd* [1987] 2 Lloyd's Rep. 601.

[492] *ibid.* at 611.

[493] *cf.* below, para.2–142.

[494] *Bear Stearns Bank plc v Forum Global Equity Ltd* [2007] EWHC 1576.

[495] Below, para.2–139.

[496] *Mamidoil-Jetoil Arab Petroleum Co SA v Okta Crude Oil Refinery AD* [2001] EWCA Civ 406; [2001] 2 Lloyd's Rep. 76; for further proceedings in this case, see [2003] EWCA Civ 1031; [2003] 2 All E.R. (Comm) 640, below, para.2–130. *Cf. Scammell v Dicker* [2005] EWCA 405, [2005] 3 All E.R. 838 at [40] per Rix L.J. ("The world is full of perfectly sound contracts which require further agreement for the purpose of their implementation").

[497] *Von Hatzfeldt-Wildenburg v Alexander* [1912] 1 Ch. 284, 288–289.

[498] *B.S.C. v Cleveland Bridge & Engineering Co. Ltd* [1984] 1 All E.R. 504; *Manatee Towing Co v Oceanbulk Maritime S.A.* (*The Bay Ridge*) [1999] 2 All E.R. (Comm) 306 at 329 ("no intention to create legal relations"); *Eurodata Systems plc v Michael Gershon plc, The Times*, March 25, 2003; *Emcor Drake & Scull Ltd v Sir Robert McAlpine Ltd* [2004] EWCA Civ 1733, 98 Con.L.R. 1; *cf.* the

with the terms of the preliminary agreement (*e.g.* by signature).[499] This is generally the position where "solicitors are involved on both sides, formal written agreements are to be produced and arrangements are made for their execution."[500] The normal inference will then be that "the parties are not bound unless and until both of them sign the agreement."[501] A second possibility is that such a document is intended only as a solemn record of an already complete and binding agreement.[502] Yet a third possibility is that the main agreement lacks contractual force for want of execution of the formal document but that nevertheless a separate preliminary contract comes into existence at an earlier stage, *e.g.* when one party begins to render services requested by the other, so that under this contract the former party will be entitled to a reasonable remuneration for

---

wording of the "Total Price Box" in *Smith Glaziers (Dunfermline) v Customs & Excise Commissioners* [2003] UKHL 7; [2003] 1 W.L.R. 656.

[499] *Okura & Co Ltd v Navara Shipping Corp. SA* [1982] 2 Lloyd's Rep. 537; *cf. R. v Sevenoaks DC Ex p. Terry* [1985] 3 All E.R. 226; *Samos Shipping Enterprises Ltd v Eckhart & Co KG (The Nissos Samos)* [1985] 1 Lloyd's Rep. 378; *Hofflinghouse & Co Ltd v C. Trade SA (The Intra Transporter)* [1985] 2 Lloyd's Rep. 159, 163; affirmed [1986] 2 Lloyd's Rep. 132; Debattista [1985] L.M.C.L.Q. 241; *Star Steamship Society v Beogradska Plovidba (The Junior K.)* [1988] 2 Lloyd's Rep. 583; Debattista [1988] L.M.C.L.Q. 441; *Atlantic Marine Transport Corp. v Coscol Petroleum Corp. (The Pina)* [1992] 2 Lloyd's Rep. 103, 107; *New England Reinsurance Corp. v Messaghios Insurance Co SA* [1992] 2 Lloyd's Rep. 251; *CPC Consolidated Pool Carriers GmbH v CTM Cia Transmediterranea SA (The CPC Gallia)* [1994] 1 Lloyd's Rep. 68; *Ignazio Messina & Co v Polskie Linie Oceaniczne* [1995] 2 Lloyd's Rep. 566; *Drake Scull Engineering Ltd v Higgs & Hill (Northern) Ltd* (1995) 11 Const. L.J. 214; *Regalian Properties plc v London Dockland Development Corp.* [1995] 1 W.L.R. 212; *Enfield LBC v Arajah* [1995] E.G.C.S. 164; *Galliard Homes Ltd v Jarvis Interiors Ltd* [2000] C.L.C. 411; *Britvic Soft Drinks Ltd v Messer UK Ltd* [2001] 1 Lloyd's Rep. 20 at [64]; affirmed on other grounds [2002] EWCA Civ 548; [2002] 2 All E.R. (Comm) 321; *Sun Life Assurance Co of Canada v CX Reinsurance Co Ltd* [2003] EWCA Civ 283; *Thoreson & Co (Bangkok) Ltd v Fathom Marine Co* [2004] EWHC 167 (Comm), [2004] 1 All E.R. (Comm) 935 (agreement for sale of ship "sub details" not a binding contract); *Petromec Inc v Petroleo Brasileiro SA Petrobas* [2005] EWCA Civ 891, [2006] 1 Lloyd's Rep. 121 at [74]–[77] (MOA to be governed by later Transaction Documents not a binding contract; for further proceedings, see [2006] EWHC 1443 (Comm), [2007] 1 Lloyd's Rep. 629); *Oceonografia SA de CV v DSND Subsea AS (The Botnica)* [2006] EWHC 1300 (Comm), [2007] 1 All E.R. (Comm) 28 (charter "subject to the signing of mutually agreeable terms and condition" not a binding contract); *cf. Prudential Assurance Co Ltd v Mount Eden Land Co Ltd* [1997] 1 E.G.L.R. 37 (consent to alterations given by landlord "subject to licence" held effective as the consent was a unilateral act, so that no question of agreement arose).

[500] *Cheverny Consulting Ltd v Whitehead Mann Ltd* [2006] EWCA Civ 1303; [2007] 1 All E.R. (Comm) 124 at [45], *per* Sir Andrew Morritt C; the above statement was accepted at [81] by Carnwath L.J., who dissented in the result.

[501] *ibid.*, at [45].

[502] *Rossiter v Miller* (1878) 3 App.Cas. 1124 (below, para.2–123); *Filby v Hounsell* [1896] 2 Ch. 737; *Branca v Cobarro* [1947] K.B. 854 (below, para.2–123); *E.R. Ives Investments Ltd v High* [1967] 2 Q.B. 379; *Elias v George Sahely & Co (Barbados) Ltd* [1982] 3 All E.R. 801; *Damon Cie Naviera SA v Hapag-Lloyd International SA (The Blankenstein)* [1985] 1 W.L.R. 435; *Clipper Maritime Ltd v Shirlstar Container Transport Ltd (The Anemone)* [1987] 1 Lloyd's Rep. 547; *Malcolm v Chancellor, Masters and Scholars of the University of Oxford, The Times*, December 19, 1990; *Ateni Maritime Corp v Great Marine Ltd (The Great Marine) (No.2)* [1990] 2 Lloyd's Rep. 250; affirmed (without reference to this point) [1991] 1 Lloyd's Rep. 421; *Jayaar Impex Ltd v Toaken Group Ltd* [1996] 2 Lloyd's Rep. 437; *The Kurnia Dewi*, below n.503, at 559; *Harvey Shopfitters Ltd v ADI Ltd* [2004] EWCA Civ 1752, [2004] 2 All E.R. 982; *Bryen & Langley Ltd v Boston* [2005] EWCA Civ 973, [2005] B.L.R. 508; *cf. Crowden v Aldridge* [1993] 1 W.L.R. 433, applying the same principle to a document which was not a contract but a direction by beneficiaries to executors.

those services.[503] Conversely, an agreement which originally lacked contractual force for want of execution of the formal document may acquire such force by reason of supervening events. This could, for example, be the position where "it can be objectively ascertained that the continuing intention [sc. not to be bound until execution of the document] has changed or . . . subsequent events have occurred whereby the non-executing party is estopped by replying on his non-execution."[504] Where an agreement for the joint acquisition of property lacks contractual force for want of execution of a formal document and one of the parties then acquires the property for himself, he may also be liable to hold a share of that property for the other party by virtue of a constructive trust.[505] The first two of the above possibilities are further illustrated in the following paragraphs.

Insurance. A contract of insurance is generally regarded as complete as soon as the insurer initials a slip setting out the main terms of the contract. This is so even though the execution of a formal policy is contemplated[506] and even though the contract, if it is one of marine insurance, is "inadmissible in evidence" unless it is embodied in a policy signed by the insurer and containing particulars specified by statute.[507] 2–117

Agreement "subject to contract." Agreements for the sale of land by private treaty are usually[508] made "subject to contract." Such agreements are normally[509] regarded as incomplete until the terms of a formal contract have been settled and approved by the parties. Thus, in *Winn v Bull*[510] the defendant agreed 2–118

[503] *Smit International Singapore Pte Ltd v Kurnia Dewi Shipping SA (The Kurnia Dewi)* [1997] 1 Lloyd's Rep. 553. *Galliard Homes Ltd v Jarvis Interiors Ltd* [2000] C.L.C. 411, where an incomplete agreement expressly provided for a reasonable remuneration to be paid in the events which happened.

[504] *Cheverney Consulting Ltd v Whitehead Mann Ltd* [2006] EWCA Civ 1303, [2007] 1 All E.R. (Comm) 124 at [46]. This dictum envisages that the non-executing party may be *bound* by the "estoppel." *The Botnica* [2006] EWHC 1300 (Comm), [2007] 1 All E.R. (Comm) 28 (above, n.499) envisages the further possibility that the non-executing party may, by "waiver" or "a kind of election" (at [90]) *acquire rights* under the unexecuted document. For this possibility, see further para.3–081 below.

[505] *Banner Homes Group plc v Luff Developments Ltd* [2000] Ch. 372; contrast *London & Regional Investments Ltd v TBI plc* [2000] EWCA Civ 355, where the joint venture agreement was expressly "subject to contract" (below, para.2–118), thus reserving a right to withdraw.

[506] *Ionides v Pacific Insurance Co* (1871) L.R. 6 Q.B. 674, 684; *Cory v Patton* (1872) L.R. 7 Q.B. 304; *General Reinsurance Corp. v Forsakringsaktiebolaget Fennia Patria* [1983] Q.B. 856; *Hadenfayre Ltd v British National Insurance Soc. Ltd* [1984] 2 Lloyd's Rep. 393; *G.A.F.L.A.C. v Tanter (The Zephyr)* [1984] 1 Lloyd's Rep. 56, 69–70; reversed in part on other grounds [1985] 2 Lloyd's Rep. 529; *Youell v Bland Welch & Co. Ltd* [1992] 2 Lloyd's Rep. 127, 140–141; *HIH Casualty & General Insurance v New Hampshire Insurance* [2001] EWCA Civ 735; [2001] 2 All E.R. (Comm) 39 at [86], [87]. Under an "open cover" arrangement, it is not the initialling of the slip but the declaration of the insured, which creates the obligation of the insurer: *Citadel Insurance Co v Atlantic Union Insurance Co* [1985] 2 Lloyd's Rep. 543.

[507] See Marine Insurance Act 1906, ss.22, 23 and 24.

[508] Not always: see *Storer v Manchester City Council* [1974] 1 W.L.R. 1403; *Tweddell v Henderson* [1975] 1 W.L.R. 1496, 1501–1502; *Elias v Group Sahely & Co (Barbados) Ltd* [1982] 3 All E.R. 801.

[509] See below at n.518.

[510] (1877) 7 Ch.D. 29. See also *Santa Fé Land Co v Forestal Land Co* (1910) 26 T.L.R. 534.

to take a lease of a house for a specified time at a stated rent, "subject to the preparation and approval of a formal contract." It was held that there was no enforceable contract and Jessel, M.R. said,[511] "It comes, therefore, to this, that where you have a proposal or agreement made in writing expressed to be subject to a formal contract being prepared, it means what it says; it is subject to and is dependent upon a formal contract being prepared." Other examples where it has been held that the parties have made the operation of their contract conditional on the execution of a further document are an agreement to purchase freehold land "subject to a proper contract to be prepared by the vendor's solicitors"[512]; an agreement to take a flat "subject to suitable agreements being arranged between your solicitors and mine"[513]; an agreement to grant a lease "subject to the terms of a lease" (because this meant "subject to the terms to be contained in a lease executed by the lessor"[514]); and an agreement to purchase a house "subject to formal contract to be prepared by the vendors' solicitors if the vendors shall so require."[515] In each of these cases the court held that the agreement gave rise to no legal liability.[516] On the same principle, it has been held that an agreement to pay a fee to an estate agent was not legally binding where it was expressed to be "subject to contract."[517]

2–119 **General requirement of "exchange of contracts."** Even after the terms of the formal contract have been agreed, there is, where the agreement is "subject to contract", no binding contract until there has been an "exchange of contracts."[518] It is also necessary (though not sufficient) for the formal requirements for contracts for the sale of land (which are described in Chapter 4) to be satisfied.[519] The formal requirement in cases of the present kind is that each party must sign a document containing all the terms which have been expressly

[511] (1877) 7 Ch.D. 29, 32.

[512] *Chillingworth v Esche* [1924] 1 Ch. 97.

[513] *Lockett v Norman-Wright* [1925] Ch. 56.

[514] *Raingold v Bromley* [1931] 2 Ch. 307. See also *Berry Ltd v Brighton and Sussex Building Society* [1939] 3 All E.R. 217.

[515] *Riley v Troll* [1953] 1 All E.R. 966.

[516] See also *Kingston-upon-Hull (Governors) v Petch* (1854) 10 Ex. 610; *Chinnock v Marchioness of Ely* (1865) 4 De G.J. & S. 638; *Harvey v Barnard's Inn* (1881) 50 L.J.Ch. 750; *May v Thomson* (1882) 20 Ch.D. 705; *Hawkesworth v Chaffey* (1886) 55 L.J.Ch. 335; *Von Hatzfeldt-Wildenburg v Alexander* [1912] 1 Ch. 284 (disapproving *North v Percival* [1898] 2 Ch.128); *Rossdale v Denny* [1921] 1 Ch. 57; *Looker v Law Union Insurance Co Ltd* [1928] 1 K.B. 554; *Brilliant v Michaels* [1945] 1 All E.R. 121; *Lowis v Wilson* [1949] Ir.R. 347; *Graham & Scott (Southgate) Ltd v Oxlade* [1950] 2 K.B. 257; *Bennett, Walden & Co v Wood* [1950] 2 All E.R. 134; *Christie, Owen and Davies Ltd v Stockton* [1953] 1 W.L.R. 1353.

[517] *Ronald Preston & Partners v Markheath Securities* [1988] 2 E.G.L.R. 23.

[518] *Eccles v Bryant & Pollock* [1948] Ch. 93; *Sante Fé Land Co Ltd v Forestal Land Co Ltd* (1910) 26 T.L.R. 534; *cf. Coope v Ridout* [1921] 1 Ch. 291; *Chillingworth v Esche* [1924] 1 Ch. 97; *Raingold v Bromley* [1931] 2 Ch. 307; *Cohen v Nessdale* [1982] 2 All E.R. 97; *Secretary of State for Transport v Christos* [2003] EWCA Civ 1073, [2004] 1 P. & C.R. 17; *Bolton MBC v Torkington* [2003] EWCA Civ 1634, [2004] Ch. 66 at [53], where mere sealing (without delivery) of a counterpart lease by a local authority was held not to give rise to a contract binding the authority.

[519] Below, para.4–052. A document setting out all the terms expressly agreed and signed by both parties would satisfy the *formal* requirements; but if it were expressed to be "subject to contract" it would not give rise to a contract till "exchange" had taken place.

agreed[520]; and the requirement of exchange traditionally refers to the handing over by each party to the other of one of these documents, or to their despatch by post; if the latter method is adopted, the process is completed on the receipt of the second of the posted documents.[521] Such an exchange may be effected by telephone or by telex.[522] It has been held in Australia that, once an exchange has taken place, there can be a binding contract even though the two parts do not match precisely (unless it is clear that the parties only intended to be bound by an exchange of precisely corresponding parts).[523] The discrepancy can then be remedied by rectification. No doubt the mechanics of "exchange" will be suitably modified when the proposed system of electronic conveyancing is brought into operation.[524] Before "exchange" (or whatever requirement may be substituted for it under that system), there is no uncertainty as to the terms of the agreement, but the agreement has no contractual force because, at this stage, neither party intends to be legally bound.[525]

Mitigations of the requirement of "exchange of contracts." The rules stated in paras 2–118 to 2–119 above enable either party to a concluded agreement to go back on it with impunity. This position has been described as "a social and moral blot on our law"[526] and there are indications that the courts are prepared to mitigate the former strictness of the requirement of "exchange of contracts." Thus it has been held that certain technical slips in the process of exchange may be disregarded[527]; and that exchange is not necessary where both parties use the same solicitor.[528] The parties may also create a binding contract by a subsequent agreement to remove the effect of the words "subject to contract," thus indicating their intention henceforth to be legally bound.[529] Subsequent conduct may also give rise to liability on other grounds: where one 2–120

[520] Law of Property (Miscellaneous Provisions) Act 1989, ss.2(1), (3).

[521] See *Commission for the New Towns v Cooper (Great Britain) Ltd* [1995] Ch. 259, 285, 289; *cf. ibid.* at 293, 295.

[522] *Domb v Izoz* [1980] Ch. 548. This relaxation refers only to the process of exchange; the formal requirements referred to at n.520 above must also be satisfied.

[523] *Sindel v Georgiou* (1984) 154 C.L.R. 661.

[524] On the making of orders under the Land Registration Act 2002.

[525] Below, para.2–162.

[526] *Cohen v Nessdale* [1981] 3 All E.R. 118, 128; affirmed [1982] 2 All E.R. 97; *cf.* Law Commission Paper No.65.

[527] *Harrison v Battye* [1975] 1 W.L.R. 53.

[528] *Smith v Mansi* [1963] 1 W.L.R. 26; exchange is also unnecessary in the case of a deed which takes effect on execution and delivery: see above, paras 1–085 *et seq.*; *Vincent v Premo Enterprises Ltd* [1969] 2 Q.B. 609.

[529] *Law v Jones* [1974] Ch. 112, as explained in *Daulia v Four Millbank Nominees* [1978] Ch. 231, 250; *Cohen v Nessdale* [1981] 3 All E.R. 118, 127; [1982] 2 All E.R. 97, 104; see also *Tiverton Estates Ltd v Wearwell* [1975] Ch. 146, followed in *Irani v Irani* [2006] EWHC 1811, [2006] W.T.L.R. 1561; *cf. Secretary of State for Transport v Christos* [2003] EWCA Civ 1073, [2004] 1 P. & C.R. 17 at [36]–[37] (statement that a party would "not renege" insufficient). Any subsequent agreement would now have to satisfy more stringent requirements, imposed by Law of Property (Miscellaneous Provisions) Act 1989, s.2 (below, para.4–052) than those which were in force at the time of the first four of the decisions cited in this note, though these requirements would not apply if the subsequent agreement could take effect as a collateral contract.

party to the agreement encourages the other to believe that he will not withdraw, and the other acts to his detriment in reliance on that belief, the former may be liable on the basis of "proprietary estoppel."[530] In "a very strong and exceptional context"[531] the court may infer that the parties had an intention to be legally bound by the original document, even though it is expressed to be "subject to contract." This was held to be the position where a document containing these words laid down an elaborate timetable, imposed a duty on the purchaser to approve the draft contract (subject only to reasonable amendments) and required him then to exchange contracts.[532] In these exceptional circumstances, the words "subject to contract" were taken merely to mean that the parties had not yet settled all the details of the transaction and therefore not to negative the intention to be bound.

2–121 **Collateral contracts; "lock out" agreements.** There is also the possibility that the freedom of action of the parties may be restricted by a collateral contract. For example a vendor who has agreed to sell land "subject to contract" may, either at the same time or subsequently, undertake not to negotiate for the sale of the land with a third party. Such a collateral agreement (sometimes called a "lock-out" agreement) must itself satisfy the requirement of certainty[533] and in *Walford v Miles*[534] it was held that this requirement had not been satisfied where the agreement failed to specify the time for which the vendor's freedom to negotiate with third parties was to be restricted. But in a later case[535] it was held that a vendor's promise not to negotiate with third parties *for two weeks* was sufficiently certain, and that the purchaser had provided consideration for it by in turn promising to complete within that time.

2–122 **Exceptions to requirement of execution and exchange of formal contracts.** Agreements for the sale of land by auction or by tender are not normally made "subject to contract." The intention of the parties in such cases is to enter into a binding contract as soon as an offer has been accepted; and the terms of that contract are usually set out, or referred to, in a document signed to provide a written record of the fact of agreement. In one case of this kind,[536] however, the words "subject to contract" were, by a clerical error, added to the acceptance. It

---

[530] See the discussion at para.3–144 below of *Att.-Gen. of Hong Kong v Humphreys Estate (Queen's Gardens) Ltd* [1987] A.C. 114. In *Cobbe v Yeoman's Row Management Ltd* [2008] UKHL 55, [2008] 1 W.L.R. 1752 Lord Scott said that in a "subject to contract" case proprietary estoppel "cannot ordinarily arise" (at [25]) and that in such a case it would be "very difficult" (at [26]) to establish a proprietary estoppel. These statements do not wholly rule out the possibility of establishing such an estoppel in such cases.

[531] *Alpenstow Ltd v Regalian Properties Ltd* [1985] 1 W.L.R. 721, 730; Harpum [1986] C.L.J. at 356.

[532] *Alpenstow Ltd v Regalian Properties Ltd*, above.

[533] Below, para.2–138.

[534] [1992] 2 A.C. 128. See further para.2–136.

[535] *Pitt v PHH Asset Management Ltd* [1994] 1 W.L.R. 327; *cf. Tye v House* [1997] 2 E.G.L.R. 171.

[536] *Michael Richards Properties Ltd v St. Saviour's* [1975] 3 All E.R. 416; Emery [1976] C.L.J. 28.

was held that there was nevertheless a binding contract since the tender documents set out in full the description of the property and the terms of the transaction. In these highly exceptional[537] circumstances, the words "subject to contract" were treated as meaningless and disregarded.[538] Presumably this reasoning could also apply where the sale was by auction. The same reasoning has also been applied where a notice exercising an option to purchase land was expressed to be "subject to contract": this phrase was again held to be meaningless as the notice was clearly intended to give rise to a binding contract.[539]

Binding provisional agreements. Even in the case of an ordinary sale of land by private treaty, the agreement is not invariably made "subject to contract,"[540] and the court may on construction find that the parties have made an immediately binding agreement, even though this is later to be superseded by a formal contract. Thus in *Rossiter v Miller*[541] the defendant offered to purchase land and was informed that he must purchase subject to certain conditions; his offer remained open and was accepted "subject to the conditions and stipulations printed on the plan." It was held that the acceptance gave rise to a binding contract and Lord Blackburn said,[542] " . . . the mere fact that the parties have expressly stipulated that there shall be a formal agreement prepared . . . does not, by itself, show that they continue merely in negotiation." And in *Branca v Cobarro*[543] an agreement for the sale of a farm provided that it was "a provisional agreement until a fully legalised agreement, drawn up by a solicitor and embodying all the conditions herewith stated, is signed." It was held that the provisional agreement was binding until it was superseded when the formal agreement was drawn up and signed; execution of the formal agreement was not a condition which had to be fulfilled before the parties were bound. 2–123

Acting on agreement subsequently completed. The parties may begin to act on the terms of an agreement before it has contractual force. When it is later given such force, the resulting contract may then, if it expressly or by implication so provides, have retrospective effect so as to apply to work done or goods supplied before it was actually made.[544] Similarly, where an agreement for the supply of services provided that specified terms should "subject to contract" apply and the parties acted on that agreement without executing any further 2–124

537 See *Munton v G.L.C.* [1976] 1 W.L.R. 649.

538 *cf.* below, para.2–144.

539 *Westway Homes v Moore* (1991) 63 P. & C.R. 480.

540 *Storer v Manchester City Council* [1974] 1 W.L.R. 1403; *Tweddell v Henderson* [1975] 1 W.L.R. 1496, 1501–1502; *Elias v George Sahely & Co (Barbados) Ltd* [1982] 3 All E.R. 801.

541 (1878) 3 App.Cas. 1124. For other examples of a completed agreement, see *Lewis v Brass* (1877) 3 Q.B.D. 667; *Bonnewell v Jenkins* (1878) 8 Ch.D. 70; *Bolton Partners v Lambert* (1888) 41 Ch.D. 295; *Gray v Smith* (1889) 43 Ch.D. 208; *Filby v Hounsell* [1896] 2 Ch. 737; *Lever v Koffler* [1901] 1 Ch. 543; *E.R. Ives Investments Ltd v High* [1967] 2 Q.B. 379; *cf. Willis v Baggs and Salt* (1925) 41 T.L.R. 453; *Morton v Morton* [1942] 1 All E.R. 273; *Cranleigh Precision Engineering Ltd v Bryant* [1965] 1 W.L.R. 1293.

542 (1878) 3 App. Cas. 1124, 1151.

543 [1947] K.B. 854.

544 *Trollope & Colls Ltd v Atomic Power Construction Ltd* [1963] 1 W.L.R. 333.

document, it was held that an implied binding contract on those terms had come into being between the parties.[545]

2–125 **Letters of intent; letters of comfort.**[546] Issues of contractual intention have arisen in a number of cases concerned with the legal effects of the commercial practice whereby parties to a transaction issue or exchange "letters of intent" on which they act pending the preparation of formal contracts. One possibility is that such letters may, by their express terms or on their true construction, negative contractual intention.[547] This possibility is illustrated by a case[548] in which a company issued a "letter of comfort" to a lender in respect of a loan to one of the company's subsidiaries. The letter stated that "it is our policy that [the subsidiary] is at all times in a position to meet its liabilities." This was held to be no more than a statement of the present policy of the company: it was not an undertaking that the policy would not be changed since the parties had not intended it to take effect as a contractually binding promise. On the other hand, where the language of such a document does not negative contractual intention, it is open to the courts to hold the parties bound by the document; and they will, in particular, be inclined to do so where the parties have acted on the document for a long period of time or have expended considerable sums of money in reliance on it.[549] The fact that the parties envisage that the letter is to be superseded by a later, more formal, contractual document does not, of itself, prevent the letter from taking effect as a contract.[550]

2–126 **Terms "to be agreed."** The parties to an agreement may be reluctant to commit themselves to a rigid long-term arrangement, particularly when prices and other circumstances affecting performance are likely to fluctuate. They sometimes attempt to introduce an element of flexibility by providing that certain terms are to be agreed later, or from time to time. The result of such a provision may be to make the agreement so uncertain that it cannot be enforced. In *May & Butcher v R.*[551] an agreement for the sale of tentage provided that the price, dates

---

[545] *Rugby Group Ltd v Pro Force Recruit Ltd* [2006] EWCA Civ 69.

[546] Lake and Draetta, *Letters of Intent* (2d ed., 1994); Furmston, Poole and Norinado, *Contract Formation and Letters of Intent* (1997).

[547] Below, para.2–183; *cf. Snelling v John G. Snelling Ltd* [1973] 1 Q.B. 87.

[548] *Kleinwort Benson Ltd v Malaysian Mining Corp* [1989] 1 All E.R. 785; Reynolds 104 L.Q.R. 353 (1988); Davenport [1988] L.M.C.L.Q. 290; Prentice (1989) 105 L.Q.R. 346; Ayres and Moore [1989] L.M.C.L.Q. 281; Tyree (1989) 2 J.C.L. 279, *cf. Chemco Leasing SpA v Rediffusion* [1987] 1 F.T.L.R. 201 (where such a letter was held to be an offer but to have lapsed before acceptance); *Monk Construction v Norwich Union Life Insurance Society* (1992) 62 B.L.R. 107.

[549] *cf. Turriff Construction Ltd v Regalia Knitting Mills* (1971) 22 E.G. 169 (letter of intent held to be a collateral contract for preliminary work); *Wilson Smithett & Cape (Sugar) Ltd v Bangladesh Sugar Industries Ltd* [1986] 1 Lloyd's Rep. 378 (letter of intent held to be an acceptance); *Chemco Leasing SpA v Rediffusion* [1987] 1 F.T.L.R. 201 (letter of intent held to be an offer but to have lapsed before acceptance).

[550] Above, para.2–116.

[551] [1934] 2 K.B. 17n.; *cf. British Homophone Ltd v Kunz* (1935) 152 L.T. 589; *Mmecen SA v Inter Ro-Ro SA (The Shamah)* [1981] 1 Lloyd's Rep. 40, 43; *Harmony Shipping Co SA v Saudi-Europe Line Ltd (The Good Helmsman)* [1981] 1 Lloyd's Rep. 377, 409; *Pancommerce SA v Veecheema BV* [1983] 2 Lloyd's Rep. 304, 307; *Cedar Trading Co Ltd v Transworld Oil Ltd (The Gudermes)* [1985] 2 Lloyd's Rep. 623; *iSoft Group plc v Misys Holdings Ltd* [2003] EWCA Civ 229; [2003] All E.R. (D) 438 (Feb); *Minter v Julius Baer Investments Ltd* [2004] EWHC 2472, [2005] Pens. L.R. 73.

of payment and manner of delivery should be agreed from time to time. The House of Lords held that the agreement was incomplete as it left vital matters to be settled. Had the agreement simply been silent on these points, they could perhaps have been settled in accordance with the provisions of the Sale of Goods Act 1979[552] or by the standard of reasonableness[553]; but the parties showed that this was not their intention by providing that such points were to be settled by further agreement between them.[554] Similarly, a lease at "a rent to be agreed" is not a binding contract.[555] In the above cases, the most natural inference to be drawn from the fact that the parties left such an important matter as the price to be settled by further agreement was that they did not intend to be bound until they had agreed on the price. Even where the points left outstanding are of relatively minor importance, there will be no contract if it appears from the words used or other circumstances that the parties did not intend to be bound until agreement on these points had been reached.[556] *A fortiori* parties are not bound by a term requiring outstanding points to be agreed if that term forms part of an agreement which is itself not binding because it was made without any intention of entering into contractual relations.[557]

Options and rights of pre-emption. It follows from the principle stated in para.2–126 above that an option to sell land "at a price to be agreed" is not a binding contract[558]; but such an option must be distinguished from a "right of pre-emption" by which a landowner agrees to give the purchaser the right to buy "at a figure to be agreed" should the landowner wish to sell.[559] An *option* has at least some of the characteristics of an offer[560] in that it can become a contract of sale when the purchaser accepts it by exercising the option[561]; and it cannot have this effect where it fails to specify the price. A *right of pre-emption*, on the other 2–127

[552] Above, para.2–113; *cf.* Supply of Goods and Services Act 1982, s.15(1).

[553] *cf. Mamidoil-Jetoil Greek Petroleum S.A. v Okta Crude Oil Refinery AD* [2001] EWCA Civ 406; [2001] 2 Lloyd's Rep. 76, especially at [73]; *Malcolm v Chancellor, Masters & Scholars of the University of Oxford, The Times*, December 19, 1990.

[554] *cf. Willis Management (Isle of Man) Ltd v Cable & Wireless plc* [2005] EWCA Civ 806, [2005] 2 Lloyd's Rep. 597 at [33].

[555] *King's Motors (Oxford) Ltd v Lax* [1970] 1 W.L.R. 426; *cf. King v King* (1981) 41 P. & C.R. 311 (rent review clause).

[556] *Metal Scrap Trade Corporation v Kate Shipping Co Ltd (The Gladys)* [1994] 2 Lloyd's Rep. 402; *Ignazio Messina & Co v Polskie Linie Oceaniczne* [1995] 2 Lloyd's Rep. 566.

[557] *Orion Insurance plc v Sphere Drake Insurance plc* [1992] 1 Lloyd's Rep. 239.

[558] This is assumed in *Brown v Gould* [1972] Ch. 53, where, however, the option was upheld as it specified criteria for determining the price: see below, para.2–130.

[559] *Pritchard v Briggs* [1980] Ch. 339. For the purposes of Landlord and Tenant (Covenants) Act 1995, "option" includes "a right of first refusal": s.1(6).

[560] Below, para.3–172, n.943. See also *Bircham & Co Nominees (No.2) Ltd v Worrell Holdings Ltd* [2001] EWCA Civ 775; (2001) 82 P. & C.R. 427 at [41]; *Re Gray* [2004] EWHC 1538 (Ch), [2005] 1 W.L.R. 815 at [25]. On the exercise of a right of pre-emption, the right may acquire characteristics of an option; see *Cottrell v King* [2004] EWHC 397, [2004] B.C.C. 309.

[561] See *Coaten v PBS Corporation* [2006] EWHC 1781, (2006) 44 E.G. 198 (agreement held to be an option, not a right of pre-emption, as the exercise of the right conferred by it on the grantee imposed on the grantor an "immediate obligation to sell . . . if [the grantee] wished that to happen" (at [35]).

hand, is not itself an offer[562] but an undertaking to make an offer in certain specified future circumstances.[563] An agreement conferring such a right is, therefore, not void for uncertainty merely because it fails to specify the price. It obliges the landowner to offer the land to the purchaser at a price at which he is in fact prepared to sell; and if the purchaser accepts that offer there is no uncertainty as to price.[564] This is so even though the parties have described the right as an "option" when its true legal nature is that of a right of pre-emption.[565]

2–128 **Agreement not incomplete merely because further agreement is required.** Because the courts are "reluctant to hold void for uncertainty any provision that was intended to have legal effect,"[566] they may sometimes give effect even to an agreement which provides for further terms "to be agreed." This was the position in *Foley v Classique Coaches Ltd.*[567] The claimant owned a petrol-filling station and adjoining land. He sold the land to the defendants on condition that they should enter into an agreement to buy petrol for the purpose of their motor-coach business exclusively from him. This agreement was duly executed, but the defendants broke it, and argued that it was incomplete because it provided that the petrol should be bought "at a price to be agreed by the parties from time to time." The Court of Appeal rejected this argument and held that, in default of agreement, a reasonable price must be paid.[568] *May & Butcher v R*[569] was distinguished on a number of grounds: the agreement in *Foley's* case was contained in a stamped document; it was believed by both parties to be binding and had been acted upon for a number of years[570]; it contained an arbitration

---

[562] *ibid.*, at [16], [23]; *Speciality Shops Ltd v Yorkshire & Metropolitan Estates Ltd* [2002] EWHC 2969; [2003] 2 P. & C.R. 410 at [28]; for other types of rights of pre-emption, in which the offer comes from the grantee, see *ibid.*, at [26], [27]. For the distinction between options and rights of pre-emption, see also *Tiffinany Investments Ltd v Bircham & Co Nominees (No.2)* [2003] EWCA Civ 1759, [2002] 2 P. & C.R. 10 and *Coaten v PBS Corporation* [2006] EWHC 1781, [2006] 44 E.G. 198 (above, n. 561).

[563] Similarly, a "lock-out" agreement (above, para.2–121) does not bind the promisor to sell to the promisee; it merely restricts his freedom to sell to someone else: see *Tye v House* [1997] 2 E.G.L.R. 171.

[564] *Smith v Morgan* [1971] 1 W.L.R. 803; *cf. Snelling v John G. Snelling Ltd* [1973] 1 Q.B. 87, 93; *Fraser v Thames Television Ltd* [1984] Q.B. 44, 57; *Miller v Lakefield Estates Ltd*, *The Times*, May 16, 1988.

[565] See *Fraser v Thames Television Ltd* [1984] Q.B. 44.

[566] *Brown v Gould* [1972] Ch. 53, 57–58; *cf. Smith v Morgan* [1971] 1 W.L.R. 803, 807; *Snelling v John G. Snelling Ltd* [1973] 1 Q.B. 87, 93; *Queensland Electricity Generating Board v New Hope Collieries Pty Ltd* [1989] 1 Lloyd's Rep. 205, 210; *Global Container Lines Ltd v State Black Sea Shipping Co* [1999] 1 Lloyd's Rep. 127, 155; *Scammell v Dicker* [2005] EWCA Civ 405, [2005] 3 All E.R. 838 at [31], [40].

[567] [1934] 2 K.B. 1.

[568] *cf. British Bank for Foreign Trade v Novinex* [1949] 1 K.B. 623; *Beer v Bowden* [1981] 1 W.L.R. 522; *Thomas Bates & Son Ltd v Wyndham's (Lingerie) Ltd* [1981] 1 W.L.R. 505; 518–519; *Tropwood A.G. of Zug v Jade Enterprises (The Tropwind)* [1982] 2 Lloyd's Rep. 233, 236; *Pagnan SpA v Feed Products Ltd* [1987] 2 Lloyd's Rep. 601; *Granit SA v Benship International SA* [1994] 1 Lloyd's Rep. 526; *Mitsui Babcock Engineering Ltd v John Brown Engineering Ltd* (1996) 51 Const. L.R. 129; *Mamidoil-Jetoil Greek Petroleum S.A. v Okta Crude Oil Refinery AD* [2001] EWCA Civ 406; [2001] 2 Lloyd's Rep. 76; for further proceedings, see n.570 below.

[569] Above, para.2–126.

[570] *cf. Mamidoil-Jetoil Greek Petroleum SA v Okta Crude Oil Refinery AD (No.3)* [2003] EWCA Civ 1031; [2003] 2 All E.R. (Comm) 640 at [38].

clause in a somewhat unusual form which was construed to apply "to any failure to agree as to the price"[571]; and it formed part of a larger bargain under which the defendants had acquired the land at a price which was no doubt based on the assumption that they would be bound to buy all their petrol from the claimant.[572] While none of these factors is in itself conclusive,[573] their cumulative effect seems to be sufficient to distinguish the two cases.[574]

Thus an agreement is not incomplete *merely* because it calls for some further agreement between the parties. Even the parties' later failure to agree on the matters left outstanding will vitiate the contract only if it makes it "unworkable or void for uncertainty."[575] Often, the failure will not have this effect, for it may be possible to resolve the uncertainty in one of the ways already discussed, *e.g.* by applying the standard of reasonableness[576]; or the matter to be negotiated may be of such subsidiary importance[577] as not to negative the intention of the parties to be bound by the more significant terms to which they have agreed. Thus in *Neilson v Stewart*[578] a contract for the sale of shares provided that part of the price payable by the buyer was to be lent back to him and to a third party on repayment terms to be negotiated after one year. The House of Lords held that there was nevertheless a binding contract for the sale of the shares as the parties had not intended the validity of this contract to depend on the outcome of the negotiations as to the repayment of the loan. There can be no doubt as to the commercial convenience of the judicial approach described in this paragraph. Commercial agreements are often intended to be binding in principle even though the parties are not at the time able or willing to settle all the details. For example, contracts of insurance may be made "at a premium to be arranged" when immediate cover is required but there is no time to go into all the details at once: such agreements are perfectly valid and a reasonable premium must be paid.[579] All this is not to say that the courts will hold parties bound when they 2–129

[571] [1934] 2 K.B. 1, 10; the clause covered disputes as to "the *subject-matter or* construction of this agreement," while the arbitration clause in *May & Butcher v R* covered "disputes with reference to or arising out of this agreement." For the distinction between the two forms of clause, see *Heyman v Darwins* [1942] A.C. 356, 385, 392. *cf.* also *Sykes (Wessex) Ltd v Fine Fare Ltd* [1967] 1 Lloyd's Rep. 53; *Voest Alpine Intertrading GmbH v Chevron International Oil Co Ltd* [1985] 2 Lloyd's Rep. 547; and see *Vosper Thorneycroft Ltd v Ministry of Defence* [1976] 1 Lloyd's Rep. 58 where the existence of a contract was admitted and the arbitration clause referred to "any dispute *or difference....*"

[572] Scrutton L.J. said at 7 that he was glad to decide in favour of the claimant "because I do not regard the appellants' [defendants'] contention as an honest one."

[573] R.S.T.C. (1933) 49 L.Q.R. at 316.

[574] *Foley's* case was approved by the House of Lords in *G. Scammell & Nephew Ltd v Ouston* [1941] A.C. 251.

[575] *Pagnan SpA v Feed Products Ltd* [1987] 2 Lloyd's Rep. 601, 619.

[576] Above, para.2–113; below, para.2–142; or by imposing on one party the duty to resolve the uncertainty: below, para.2–140; *Pagnan SpA v Feed Products Ltd*, above n.575.

[577] Though this point is not decisive: see above, para.2–126 at n.556.

[578] (1991) S.L.T. 523.

[579] *Glicksten & Son Ltd v State Assurance Co* (1922) 10 Ll.L.Rep. 604; *cf.* Marine Insurance Act 1906, s.31(2); and *American Airline Inc. v Hope* [1973] 1 Lloyd's Rep. 233; affirmed [1974] 2 Lloyd's Rep. 301 ("at an additional premium *and geographical area* to be agreed").

have not yet reached substantial agreement,[580] but once they have reached such agreement it is not fatal that some points (even important ones) remain to be settled by further negotiation.[581]

2–130 **Criteria laid down in the agreement.** The courts have less difficulty in upholding agreements which lay down *criteria* for determining matters which are left open. For example, in *Hillas & Co Ltd v Arcos Ltd*[582] an option to buy timber was held binding even though it did not specify the price, since it provided for the price to be calculated by reference to the official price list. Similarly, an option to renew a lease "at a rent to be fixed having regard to the market value of the premises" has been held binding as it provided a criterion (though not a very precise one) for resolving the uncertainty.[583] Even a provision that hire under a charterparty was in certain specified events to be "equitably decreased by an amount to be mutually agreed" has been held (by reason of its reference to what was equitable) "to provide a sufficient criterion to enable the appropriate reduction . . . to be determined."[584] It was said that "equitably" meant "fairly and reasonably" and that "a purely objective standard has been prescribed."[585] Where, on the other hand, an agreement provided for payment of a fixed percentage of the "open market value" of shares in a *private* company, it was held that these words did not provide a sufficiently precise criterion since there was more than one formula for calculating the market value of shares in such a company.[586] An agreement may also lack contractual force where, though it lays down a criterion for resolving matters which are left open, it goes on to provide that the principles for determining the application of that criterion are to be settled by further negotiations between the parties.[587]

2–131 **Machinery laid down in the agreement.** An agreement is not incomplete where it provides *machinery* for resolving matters originally left open.[588] Perhaps the most striking illustration of this possibility is provided by cases in which such

---

[580] *e.g. Shakleford's Case* (1866) L.R. 1 Ch.App. 567; *Bertel v Neveux* (1878) 39 L.T. 257; *Loftus v Roberts* (1902) 18 T.L.R. 532; *Hofflinghouse SpA v C-Trade SA (The Intra Transporter)* [1986] 2 Lloyd's Rep. 132; *Pagnan SpA v Granaria B.V.* [1986] 2 Lloyd's Rep. 547; *Alfred McAlpine Construction Ltd v Panatown Ltd* [2001] EWCA Civ 485, (2001) 76 Con.L.R. 224 at [35].

[581] *Voest Alpine Intertrading GmbH v Chevron International Oil Co Ltd* [1987] 2 Lloyd's Rep. 547.

[582] (1932) 147 L.T. 503; *cf. Miller v F.A. Sadd & Son Ltd* [1981] 3 All E.R. 265; *Mamidoil-Jetoil Greek Petroleum S.A. v Okta Crude Oil Refinery AD (No.3)* [2003] 1 Lloyd's Rep. 1 at [161]–[165]; affirmed [2003] EWCA Civ 1031; [2003] 2 All E.R. (Comm) 640 at [36]–[41].

[583] *Brown v Gould* [1972] Ch. 53.

[584] *Didymi Corp. v Atlantic Lines & Navigation Co Inc.* [1987] 2 Lloyd's Rep. 166, 169; Reynolds (1988) 104 L.Q.R. 353; affirmed [1988] 2 Lloyd's Rep. 108; *cf.* below, para.2–141.

[585] At p.117.

[586] *Gillatt v Sky Television Ltd* [2000] 1 All E.R. (Comm) 461.

[587] *Willis Management (Isle of Man) Ltd v Cable and Wireless plc* [2005] EWCA Civ 1287, [2005] 2 Lloyd's Rep. 597; below para.2–142.

[588] *Machinery* for resolving matters left open must be distinguished from *mechanism* in the sense of an agreed formula for determining the price (or other matters): e.g., where work is done on a "cost plus" basis. The purpose of such a "mechanism" is not to resolve matters originally left open. The already agreed mechanism merely has to be *applied* to determine the matter governed by it. It is in this sense that the word "mechanism" is used in *Coaten v PBX Corporation* [2006] EWHC 1781 (Ch), (2006) 44 E.G. 198 at [13].

matters are to be resolved by the decision of one party: for example a term, by which interest rates are expressed to be variable on notification by the creditor, is in principle valid,[589] though the creditor's power to set interest rates under such a contract is limited by an implied term that he must not exercise it "dishonestly, for an improper purpose, capriciously or arbitrarily."[590] Similarly, an arbitration clause can validly provide for the arbitration to take place at one of two or more places to be selected by one of the parties[591]; and a compromise agreement can provide that one party is to have the right to choose which assets are to be transferred under it.[592] Agreements are *a fortiori* not incomplete merely because they provide that outstanding points shall be determined by arbitration[593] or other dispute resolution procedure,[594] or by the decision or valuation[595] of a third party; though the Sale of Goods Act 1979 provides that if the third party "cannot or does not make the valuation, the agreement is avoided."[596] An agreement is not, however, ineffective merely because such machinery fails to work. Thus, in *Sudbrook Trading Estate Ltd v Eggleton*[597] a lease gave a tenant an option to purchase the premises "at such price as may be agreed upon by two valuers, one to be nominated by" each party. The landlord having refused to appoint a valuer, the House of Lords held that the option did not fail for uncertainty. It amounted, on its true construction, to an agreement to sell at a reasonable price to be determined by valuers. The stipulation that each party should nominate one of the valuers was merely "subsidiary and inessential"[598]; and where the agreed machinery (which fails to operate) is of this character,[599] the court can, on its

---

[589] *Lombard Tricity Finance Ltd v Paton* [1989] 1 All E.R. 918. This position is preserved by Unfair Terms in Consumer Contracts Regulations 1999, (SI 1999/2083) reg.5(5) and Sch.2, para.2(b).

[590] *Paragon Finance Ltd v Staunton* [2001] EWCA Civ 1466; [2001] 1 W.L.R. 685 at [36]; the power (to maintain interest rates at a level above that charged by other lenders) had in that case been validly exercised. For similar restrictions on the exercise of contractually reserved discretions, see also *Horkulak v Cantor Fitzgerald International* [2004] EWCA Civ 1287, [2005] I.C.R. 402 at [48] (below, para. 2–175); *cf. Lymington Marina Ltd v Macnamara* [2007] EWCA Civ 151, [2007] 2 All E.R. (Comm) 825; *McCarthy v McCarthy & Stone plc* [2007] EWCA Civ 664, [2008] 1 All E.R. (Comm) 221 at [54]; *Socimer International Bank Ltd v Standard Bank (London) Ltd* [2008] EWCA Civ 116, [2008] 1 Lloyd's Rep. 558 at [60], [66].

[591] *Star Shipping AS v China National Foreign Trade Transportation Corp. (The Star Texas)* [1993] 2 Lloyd's Rep. 445.

[592] *Halpern v Halpern* [2007] EWCA Civ 291, [2007] 3 All E.R. 478 at [50].

[593] *Arcos Ltd v Aronson* (1930) 36 Ll.L.Rep. 108; *cf. Campbell v Edwards* [1976] 1 W.L.R. 403; *Buber v Kenwood Mfg Co Ltd* [1978] 1 Lloyd's Rep. 175; *Queensland Electricity Generating Board v New Hope Collieries Pty Ltd* [1989] 1 Lloyd's Rep. 205.

[594] *Cable & Wireless plc v IBM United Kingdom Ltd* [2002] EWHC 2059 (Comm); [2002] 2 All E.R. (Comm) 1041; *Alstom Signalling Ltd v Jarvis Facilities Ltd* [2004] EWHC 1232, 95 Con. L.R. 55; *Holloway v Chancery Mead Ltd* [2007] EWHC 2495 (TCC), [2008] 1 All E.R. (Comm) 653 at [66]–[85].

[595] *Halpern v Halpern* [2007] EWCA Civ 291, [2007] 3 All E.R. 478 at [50] ("machinery for valuation").

[596] Sale of Goods Act 1979, s.9(1); *cf. Pym v Campbell* (1856) 6 E. & B. 370.

[597] [1982] 1 A.C. 493; Robertshaw (1982) 46 M.L.R. at 493.

[598] *Re Malpas* [1985] Ch. 42, 50; *cf. Tito v Waddell (No.2)* [1877] Ch. 106, 314; *Didymi Corp. v Atlantic Lines & Navigation Co Ltd* [1988] 2 Lloyd's Rep. 108, 115.

[599] *i.e.* not if it is "an integral and essential part of the definition of the payments to be made": *Gillatt v Sky Television Ltd* [2000] 1 All E.R. (Comm) 461 at 419. In that case, the machinery was of this kind so that, neither party having taken any steps to bring it into operation, it was held that the court could not intervene by making its own valuation.

failure to operate, substitute other machinery: for example, the court can itself fix the price with the aid of expert evidence. This is so not only where the agreed machinery fails because of one party's refusal to operate it,[600] but also where it fails for some other reason, such as the refusal of a designated valuer to make the valuation.[601]

2–132 **Rent review clauses.** Problems of the kind discussed in paras 2–126 to 2–131 have in a number of cases arisen in connection with rent review clauses in leases. A provision in a lease that, after an initial period for which the rent is specified, the tenant shall pay "such rent as may be agreed" is *prima facie* ineffective.[602] It does not follow that the lease is, or becomes, void on failure to agree the new rent; indeed, it is unlikely that the court would so hold where the parties had acted during the initial period in the belief that the lease was binding for its full term; nor is it likely that the court would hold that, in default of agreement, no rent at all need be paid.[603] Failure to agree a new rent will therefore lead to one of two results: that the old rent continues[604] or that a reasonable rent must be paid. The first of these conclusions is open to the objection that it makes the rent review clause inoperative since under it the party in whose interest it was to maintain the old rent would have no incentive to agree to a new one.[605] The better view, therefore, is that a reasonable rent must be paid.[606] The lease may, of course, contain an express provision to this effect,[607] or provide for the rent to be determined by arbitration or by a valuer.[608] The original rent may, however, continue to govern for some *other* reason than the fact that the clause provides that the new rent is to be agreed or to be fixed by a third party: for example, because the party who wishes to vary it has not complied with the conditions laid down by the contract as a prerequisite to the operation of the rent review clause.[609]

2–133 **Facts to be ascertained.** An agreement is not ineffective for uncertainty merely because the facts on which its operation is to depend are not known when it is made. The requirement of certainty will be satisfied if those facts become ascertainable and are ascertained, without the need for further negotiation, after the making of the agreement. Thus a finance agreement which depended on the merchantability of goods dealt with under it was held not to be invalid for

---

[600] As in *Sudbrook Trading Estate Ltd v Eggleton* [1982] 1 A.C. 493.
[601] As in *Re Malpas*, above; *cf. Royal Bank of Scotland v Jennings* [1996] E.G.C.S. 168.
[602] *King v King* (1981) 41 P. & C.R. 311.
[603] See *Beer v Bowden* [1981] 1 W.L.R. 522, 525.
[604] *King v King*, above.
[605] *Beer v Bowden*, above.
[606] *Beer v Bowden*, above; *Thomas Bates & Son Ltd v Wyndham's (Lingerie) Ltd* [1981] 1 W.L.R. 505; *cf.* above, para.2–115.
[607] See *Brown v Gould* [1972] Ch. 53.
[608] In *Thomas Bates & Sons Ltd v Wyndham's (Lingerie) Ltd*, above, the lease was rectified to include such a term.
[609] *Weller v Akehurst* [1981] 3 All E.R. 411 (where the rent review clause was invoked too late and time was expressly made of the essence of the contract); contrast *Metrolands Investment Ltd v J.H. Dewhurst Ltd* [1986] 3 All E.R. 659 (where time was not of the essence).

uncertainty merely because it was not known, when the agreement was made, whether the goods were in fact merchantable.[610]

Contract to make a contract. In some cases of incomplete agreements it is said that there is a "contract to make a contract."[611] This expression may refer to a number of different situations. 2–134

Contract to execute a document incorporating terms previously agreed. One possibility is that the parties may agree to execute a formal document incorporating terms on which they have previously agreed. Such a provision does not deprive the agreement of contractual force.[612] For example, in *Morton v Morton*[613] an agreement to "enter into a separation deed containing the following clauses" (of which a summary was then given) was held to be a binding contract. The grant of an option to purchase can similarly be described as a contract by which one party binds himself to enter into a further contract if the other so elects; and neither of these contracts is (on this ground) void for uncertainty.[614] 2–135

Agreement to negotiate. A further possibility is that the parties have simply agreed to negotiate. In spite of dicta to the contrary,[615] it has been held that an express agreement merely to negotiate is not a contract "because it is too uncertain to have any binding force."[616] It therefore does not impose any obligations to negotiate, or to use best endeavours to reach agreement[617] or to accept proposals that "with hindsight appear to be reasonable."[618] Nor, where an agreement fails to satisfy the requirement of certainty, can this defect be cured by *implying* into it a term to the effect that the parties must continue to negotiate in 2–136

610 *Welsh Development Agency v Export Finance Co Ltd,* [1992] B.C.L.C. 148.

611 *Von Hatzfeld-Wildenburg v Alexander* [1912] 1 Ch. 284, 284, 288–289 ("contract to enter into a contract").

612 Subject to statutory exceptions: see Consumer Credit Act 1974, s.59.

613 [1942] 1 All E.R. 273.

614 See *The Messiniaki Bergen* [1983] 1 Lloyd's Rep. 424, 426. *cf.* below, para.3–172, n.943 for the nature of an option.

615 *Chillingworth v Esche* [1924] 1 Ch. 91, 113; *Hillas & Co Ltd v Arcos Ltd* (1932) 147 L.T. 503, 515. See F.P. (1932) 48 L.Q.R. 141; F.W.M.C. *ibid.* 310; Williams (1943) 6 M.L.R. 81.

616 *Courtney & Fairbairn Ltd v Tolaini Bros (Hotels) Ltd* [1975] 1 W.L.R. 297, 301; *cf. Von Hatzfeldt-Wildenburg v Alexander* [1912] 1 Ch. 284, 249; *Malozzi v Carapelli SpA* [1976] 1 Lloyd's Rep. 407; *Scandinavian Trading Tanker Co A.B. v Flota Petrolera Ecuatoriana (The Scaptrade)* [1981] 2 Lloyd's Rep. 425, 432; affirmed without reference to this point [1983] 2 A.C. 694; *Nile Co for the Export of Agricultural Crops v H. & J. M. Bennett (Commodities) Ltd* [1986] 1 Lloyd's Rep. 555, 587; *Paul Smith Ltd v H. & S. International Holdings* [1991] 2 Lloyd's Rep. 127, 131; *Mamidoil-Jetoil Greek Petroleum S.A. v Okta Crude Oil Refinery AD* [2001] EWCA Civ 406; [2001] 2 Lloyd's Rep. 76 at [53], [59]; *Willis Management (Isle of Man) Ltd v Cable and Wireless plc* [2005] EWCA Civ 806, [2005] 2 Lloyd's Rep. 597 at [24], [26]; *Covington Marine Corp. v Xiamen Shipbuilding Co Ltd* [2005] EWHC 2912 (Comm), [2006] 1 Lloyd's Rep. 278 at [52].

617 *The Scaptrade*, above, at 616; *Star Steamship Society v Beogradska Plovidba (The Junior K.)* [1988] 2 Lloyd's Rep. 583. *cf.*, in the United States, *Hoffman v Red Owl Stores Inc.*, 133 N.W. 2d 267 (1965).

618 *Pagnan SpA v Granaria B.V.* [1985] 1 Lloyd's Rep. 256, 270; affirmed [1986] 2 Lloyd's Rep. 547.

good faith. In *Walford v Miles*,[619] a "lock-out" agreement collateral to negotiations for the sale of a business lacked sufficient certainty because it failed to specify the time during which the vendors were not to negotiate with third parties[620]; and the House of Lords unanimously rejected the argument that a term should be implied requiring the vendors to continue to negotiate in good faith with the purchaser for as long as the vendors continued to desire to sell, since such a term was itself too uncertain to be enforced. The uncertainty lay in the fact that the alleged duty was "inherently inconsistent with the position of a negotiating party"[621] who must normally[622] be free to advance his own interests during the negotiations. The point is well illustrated by the facts of *Walford v Miles* itself, where the defendants had agreed subject to contract to sell a property to the purchasers for £2m and had (in breach of the ineffective "lock-out" agreement) sold it to a third party for exactly that sum, and the purchasers then claimed damages of £1m on the basis that the property was (by reason of facts known to them but not to the defendants) worth £3m. If a duty to negotiate in good faith exists, it must be equally incumbent on both parties, so that it can hardly require a vendor to agree to sell a valuable property for only two thirds of its true value when the facts affecting that value are known to the purchaser and not disclosed (as good faith would seem to require) to the vendor. The actual result in *Walford v Miles* (in which the purchasers recovered the sum of £700 in respect of their wasted expenses as damages for misrepresentation,[623] but not the £1m which they claimed as damages for breach of contract[624]) seems, with respect, to be entirely appropriate on the facts, especially because the vendors reasonably believed themselves to be protected from liability in the principal negotiation by the phrase "subject to contract."

2–137 In *Cobbe v Yeomans Row Management Ltd*[625] Mummery L.J. said that "Under English law there is no general duty to negotiate in good faith"; but he added that there were "plenty of other ways of dealing with particular problems of unacceptable conduct occurring in the course of negotiations without unduly hampering the ability of the parties to negotiate their own bargains without the intervention of the courts."[626] In the *Cobbe* case itself, Court of Appeal had relied on the doctrine of proprietary estoppel to this end; and although on further

---

[619] [1992] 2 A.C. 128; Neill (1992) 108 L.Q.R. 405.

[620] Above, para.2–121.

[621] [1992] 2 A.C. 128, 138; *cf. Surrey C.C. v Bredero Homes Ltd* [1993] 1 W.L.R. 1361, 1368 (doubted on other grounds in *Att.-Gen. v Blake* [2001] 1 A.C. 268 at 283); *Halifax Financial Services Ltd v Intuitive Systems Ltd* [1999] 1 All E.R. (Comm) 303 at 311; *Baird Textile Holdings Ltd v Marks & Spencer plc* [2001] EWCA Civ 274; [2002] 1 All E.R. (Comm) 737 (below, para.2–142) where an alleged duty to deal with the claimants in good faith was held to be insufficiently certain to form a basis for an implied contract.

[622] For an exception, see *Re Debtors (Nos 4449 and 4450 of 1998)* [1999] 1 All E.R. (Comm) 149 at 158 (Lloyd's bound to negotiate in good faith with its "names" on the terms of a "hardship agreement" since for this purpose it was "performing functions in the public interest within a statutory framework, so that its freedom of action was restricted).

[623] See [1992] 2 A.C. 128, 136.

[624] *ibid.* at 135.

[625] [2006] EWCA Civ 1139, [2006] 1 W.L.R. 2964.

[626] *ibid.*, at [4].

appeal this doctrine was held not to apply on the facts of the case,[627] the House of Lords did provide other relief, by way of *quantum meruit*, to the party prejudiced by the other party's "unattractive"[627a] conduct in withdrawing from the agreement which required further negotiations to acquire contractual force; and in *Walford v Miles* the award of damages for misrepresentation may illustrate the same point.[628] It should be emphasised that, in neither of these cases, did the claimant recover the full damages for loss of his bargain to which he would have been entitled, if the defendant's failure to negotiate in good faith had amounted to a breach of contract.

In *Walford v Miles* Lord Ackner, with whom all the other members of the House agreed, described as "unsustainable" the view expressed in an American case[629] "that an agreement to negotiate in good faith is synonymous with an agreement to use best endeavours and, as the latter is enforceable so is the former."[630] He went on to say that "the reason why an agreement to negotiate, like an agreement to agree, is unenforceable is simply because it lacks the necessary certainty. The same does not apply to an agreement to use best endeavours."[631] If (as appears to be the case) the reference in this passage is to an agreement to use best endeavours to reach agreement, then the passage gives rise to a number of difficulties. The first arises from dictum in an English case[632] (which is cited with approval in *Walford v Miles*[633]) to the effect that an agreement to negotiate does not impose any obligation to use best endeavours to reach agreement; and this dictum certainly supports the view that an agreement to negotiate contains no *implied* term to use such endeavours. It may be that Lord Ackner's reference was to an *express* term to use best endeavours to reach agreement, or that he was simply prepared to assume (without deciding) that an agreement (express or implied) to use such endeavours might be legally enforceable and that he was concerned only to make the point that, even on that assumption, the same was not true of an agreement to negotiate in good faith. That explanation of Lord Ackner's statement in turn gives rise to the difficulty of distinguishing between the two types of agreement. One possibility is that an agreement to negotiate in good faith refers to the *formation* and one to use best endeavours to the *performance* of a contract, *e.g.* where an admitted contract between A and B requires A to use his best endeavours to make a computer software system work, or to procure C to enter into a contract with B. There is 2–138

[627] [2008] UKHL 55; [2008] 1 W.L.R. 1752, below paras 3–148A to 3–148C.

[627a] [2008] UKHL 55, [2008] 1 W.L.R. 1752 at [93].

[628] See above, at n.623. The misrepresentation was to the effect, not that the defendants *would* negotiate with the claimants, but that they *would not* go on negotiating with third parties (to whom they proceeded to sell the property).

[629] *Channel Home Centers Division of Grace Retail Corp. v Grossman* 795 F. 2d 291 (1986).

[630] [1992] 2 A.C. 128, 138.

[631] *ibid.*

[632] *Scandanavian Trading Co A.B. v Flota Petrolera Ecuatoriana (The Scaptrade)* [1981] 2 Lloyd's Rep. 425, 432 (and see above n.616); *cf. Star Steamships Society v Beogradska Plovidba (The Junior K.)* [1988] 2 Lloyd's Rep. 583. See also *Covington Marine Corp v Xiamen Shipping Co Ltd* [2005] EWHC 2912 (Comm), [2006] 1 Lloyd's Rep. 745 at [52], where it was not argued that an agreement to use best endeavours to reach agreement had any greater legal effect than an agreement to agree.

[633] [1992] 2 A.C. 128, 137.

no doubt that a term of this kind can impose a legal obligation on A.[634] But such cases are not concerned with the legal effect (if any) of an agreement to use best endeavours *to reach agreement*; and where the question is whether, in consequence of such an agreement, any contract has come into existence, later decisions support the view that an express agreement to use best or reasonable endeavours to agree on the terms of a contract is no more than an agreement to negotiate, lacking contractual force.[635] An alternative explanation of Lord Ackner's statement may be that, while an agreement to use best endeavours to reach agreement could be interpreted as referring to the *machinery* of negotiation, one to negotiate in good faith is more plausibly interpreted as referring to its *substance*. A promise to use such endeavours might, for example, oblige a party to make himself available for negotiations, or at least not (*e.g.* by deliberately failing to pick up his telephone) to prevent the other from communicating with him.[636] A promise to negotiate in good faith, on the other hand, would oblige a party not to take unreasonable or exorbitant positions during the negotiations; and it is the difficulty of giving precise content to this obligation, while maintaining each party's freedom to pursue his own interests, that makes such a promise too uncertain to be enforced.

In *Walford v Miles* the principal agreement was not legally binding because it was subject to contract, and the lock-out agreement was not legally binding because it specified no dates.[637] The case does not exclude the possibility that a different conclusion may be reached where the parties have reached agreement on all essential points so as to show that they do intend to be legally bound by the agreement, but have left other points open. The court may then imply a term that they are to negotiate in good faith so as to settle outstanding details which are to be incorporated in the formal document setting out the full terms of the contract between them.[638] An express term in an agreement that is intended to be legally binding to negotiate outstanding matters in good faith may likewise have contractual force.[639]

---

[634] See *Watford Electronics Ltd v Sanderson Ltd* [2001] EWCA Civ 317, [2001] 1 All E.R. (Comm) 696 at [45], and the cases discussed above, para.2–130; *cf. Lambert v HTV Cymru (Wales) Ltd, The Times*, March 17, 1998.

[635] See *Little v Courage* (1995) 70 P. & C.R. 469 at 475; *London & Regional Investments Ltd v TBI plc* [2002] EWCA Civ 355 at [39]; *Multiplex Construction (UK) Ltd v Cleveland Bridge (UK) Ltd* [2006] EWHC 1341; 107 Con. L.R. 1. For the distinction between an undertaking to use "best" and one to use "reasonable" endeavours, see *Rhodia International Holdings Ltd v Huntsman International* LLC [2007] EWHC 292 (Comm), [2007] 2 Lloyd's Rep. 325, at [33]–[35].

[636] Example based on *Nissho Iwai Petroleum Co Inc v Cargill International SA* [1993] 1 Lloyd's Rep. 80, where such conduct was held to amount to a breach of a party's duty to co-operate in the *performance* (not in the *formation*) of a contract. *cf. Re Debtors (Nos 4449 and 4450 of 1998)* [1999] 1 All E.R. (Comm) 49 at 158 (implied obligation to use "best endeavours" to conclude an agreement requires the party "not unreasonably to frustrate" its conclusion); for the basis of the duty to negotiate in this case, see above, n.622).

[637] Above, para.2–138.

[638] *Donwin Productions Ltd v E.M.I. Films Ltd, The Times*, March 9, 1984 (not cited in *Walford v Miles* [1992] 2 A.C. 128).

[639] *Petromec Inc v Petroleo Brasileiro SA Petrobas* [2005] EWCA Civ 891, [2006] 1 Lloyd's Rep. 121 at [115]–[125], distinguishing *Walford v Miles*, above para.2–136, on the ground that, in the latter case, there was "no concluded agreement since everything was subject to contract" and that there was "no express agreement to negotiate in good faith" (at [120]). In the *Petromec* case, the point was "not essential to the disposition of the appeal" (at [115]). For further proceedings in the *Petromec* case, see above, para.2–116 n.499.

7. CERTAINTY OF TERMS

Requirement of certainty. An agreement may lack contractual force because it is so vague or uncertain that no definite meaning can be given to it without adding further terms. For example, in *G. Scammell & Nephew Ltd v Ouston,*[640] the House of Lords held that an agreement to acquire goods "on hire-purchase" was too vague to be enforced since there were many kinds of hire-purchase agreements in widely different terms, so that it was impossible to specify the terms on which the parties had agreed. Similar reasoning is sometimes applied where the agreement is expressed so as to be subject to a condition depending on the satisfaction of one of the parties.[641] The problems arising from such provisions are discussed in para.2–154, below. 2–139

Qualifications of the requirement of certainty. The courts do not expect commercial documents to be drafted with strict legal precision. The cases provide many examples of judicial awareness of the danger that too strict an application of the requirement of certainty could result in the striking down of agreements intended by the parties to have binding force. The courts are reluctant to reach such a conclusion, particularly where the parties have acted on the agreement.[642] As Lord Wright said in *Hillas & Co Ltd v Arcos Ltd*[643]: 2–140

> "Businessmen often record the most important agreements in crude and summary fashion; modes of expression sufficient and clear to them in the course of their business

[640] [1941] A.C. 251, described as "a rare case of uncertainty" in *Scammell v Dicker* [2005] EWCA Civ 405, [2005] 3 All E.R. 838 at [41]. See also *Davies v Davies* (1887) 36 Ch.D. 359; *Kingsley & Keith Ltd v Glynn Bros. (Chemicals) Ltd* [1953] 1 Lloyd's Rep. 211; *Judge v Crown Leisure Ltd* [2005] EWCA Civ 571, [2005] I.R.L.R. 823 at [23]; and below, para.2–141 at nn.646–648.

[641] *e.g. Montreal Gas Co v Vasey* [1900] A.C. 595; *Hofflinghouse & Co Ltd v C. Trade SA (The Intra Transporter)* [1986] 2 Lloyd's Rep. 132; *Shipping Enterprises Ltd v Eckhart & Co K G (The Nissos Samos)* [1985] 1 Lloyd's Rep. 378, 385; *Stabilad Ltd v Stephens & Carter Ltd (No.2)* [1999] 2 All E.R. (Comm) 651, 659 ("void for uncertainty").

[642] *Brown v Gould* [1977] Ch. 53, 57–58; *Tito v Waddell (No.2)* [1977] Ch. 106, 314; *Sudbrook Trading Estate Ltd v Eggleton* [1983] 1 A.C. 444; *Clement v Gibb* [1996] C.L.Y. 1209; *Hanjin Shipping Co Ltd v Zenith Chartering Corp. (The Mercedes Envoy)* [1995] 2 Lloyd's Rep. 559, 564; *Hackney L.B.C. v Thompson* [2001] L. & T. Rep. 7; *Alstom Signalling Ltd v Jarvis Facilities Ltd* [2004] EWHC 1232, 95 Con.L.R. 55. The reluctance referred to in the text above may account for the lack of "enthusiasm" with which Dyson L.J. and Sir Robin Auld in *Schweppe v Harper* [2008] EWCA Civ 442 at [75] and [82] concluded that the agreement in that case was too uncertain to be enforced; and for Ward L.J.'s dissent in that case.

[643] (1932) 147 L.T. 503, 514; *cf. Rahcassi Shipping Co v Blue Star Line* [1969] 1 Q.B. 176 (agreement for arbitration "by commercial men and not lawyers" upheld); *Nea Agrex SA v Baltic Shipping Co Ltd* [1976] Q.B. 933; *Tropwood AG of Zug v Jade Enterprises Inc (The Tropwind)* [1981] 1 Lloyd's Rep. 232; *Deutsche Schachtbau und Tiefbohrgesellschaft mbH v Ras Al Khaimah National Oil Co* [1990] 1 A.C. 295, 306; reversed on other grounds, at 329 *et seq.*; *Grace Shipping Inc. v C.F. Sharpe (Malaysia) Pte* [1987] 1 Lloyd's Rep. 207; *Didymi Corp. v Atlantic Lines & Navigation Co Inc.* [1987] 2 Lloyd's Rep. 166; affirmed [1988] 2 Lloyd's Rep. 108 (above, para.2–130); *Anangel Atlas Compania Naviera SA v Ishikawajima Harima Heavy Industries Corp. (No.2)* [1990] 2 Lloyd's Rep. 526, 546; *Star Shipping AS v China National Foreign Trade Transportation Corp. (The Star Texas)* [1993] 2 Lloyd's Rep. 445, 455; *Scammell v Dicker* [2005] EWCA Civ 405, [2005] 3 All E.R. 838 at [31]; *Halpern v Halpern* [2006] EWHC 603 (Comm), [2006] 2 Lloyd's Rep. 83 at [115], affirmed on this point [2007] EWCA Civ 291, [2007] 3 All E.R. 478 at [50]. See also Fridman (1960) 76 L.Q.R. 521.

may appear to those unfamiliar with the business far from complete or precise. It is accordingly the duty of the court to construe such documents fairly and broadly, without being too astute or subtle in finding defects; but, on the contrary, the court should seek to apply the old maxim of English law, *verba ita sunt intelligenda ut res magis valeat quam pereat.* That maxim, however, does not mean that the court is to make a contract for the parties, or to go outside the words they have used, except in so far as they are appropriate implications of law."

In accordance with these principles, the courts have developed a number of qualifications to the requirement of certainty; these qualifications are stated in paras 2–141 to 2–146, below.

2–141 **Custom and trade usage.** Apparent vagueness may be resolved by custom. For example, a contract to load coal at Grimsby "on the terms of the usual colliery guarantee" was upheld on proof of the terms usually contained in such guarantees at Grimsby.[644] It has similarly been held that undertaking to grant a lease of a shop "in prime position" was not too uncertain to be enforced since the phrase was commonly used by persons dealing with shop property, so that its meaning could be determined by expert evidence.[645] On the other hand, agreements "subject to war clause,"[646] "subject to strike and lock-out clause,"[647] and "subject to *force majeure* conditions,"[648] have been held too vague, as there was no evidence in any of the cases of any customary or usual form of such clauses or conditions.

2–142 **Reasonableness.** In *Hillas & Co Ltd v Arcos Ltd*[649] an agreement for the sale of timber "of fair specification" was made between persons well acquainted with the timber trade. The agreement was held binding on the grounds that, in these circumstances, the standard of reasonableness could be applied to give sufficient certainty to an otherwise vague phrase, since that phrase imported an objective standard for assessing the quality of the goods to be supplied. The case should be

---

[644] *Shamrock SS. Co v Storey & Co* (1899) 81 L.T. 413; *cf. Hart v Hart* (1881) 18 Ch.D. 670; *Bayham v Phillips Electronics (UK) Ltd, The Times*, July 19, 1995 where uncertainty in a long-term health insurance agreement was resolved by reference to circumstances existing at the time of its formation.

[645] *Ashburn Anstalt v Arnold* [1989] Ch. 1, 27, overruled, on another ground, in *Prudential Assurance Co Ltd v London Residuary Body* [1992] A.C. 386.

[646] *Bishop & Baxter Ltd v Anglo-Eastern Trading Co* [1944] K.B. 12.

[647] *Love & Stewart Ltd v S. Instone Ltd* (1917) 33 T.L.R. 475.

[648] *British Electrical, etc., Industries v Patley Pressings Ltd* [1953] 1 W.L.R. 280.

[649] (1932) 147 L.T. 503 (and see above, para.2–130); *Sweet & Maxwell Ltd v Universal News Services Ltd* [1964] 2 Q.B. 699; *cf. G.L.C. v Connolly* [1970] 2 Q.B. 100; *Finchbourne v Rodriguez* [1976] 3 All E.R. 581; *Pagnan SpA v Feed Products Ltd* [1987] 2 Lloyd's Rep. 601; *Malcolm v Chancellor, Masters and Scholars of the University of Oxford, The Times*, December 19, 1990; *Hackney LBC v Thompson* [2001] L.&T. Rep. 7 (agreement to pay "the due proportion of the reasonably estimated amount" held to impose an obligation to pay a "fair and reasonable" proportion); *Mamidoil-Jetoil Greek Petroleum Co SA v Okta Crude Oil Refinery AD* [2001] EWCA Civ 406; [2001] 2 Lloyd's Rep. 76 (above, para.2–115); *Scammell v Dicker* [2005] EWCA Civ 405, [2005] All E.R. 838 at [42] ("reasonably certain"); *Bear Stearns Bank plc v Forum Global Equity Ltd* [2007] EWHC 1576, at [64], above paras 2–113, 2–114, where the standard of reasonableness was invoked to deal with the failure of an agreement to specify the *time* of performance. *cf.* the position where the terms of the agreement are such as to negative contractual intention: below, para.2–175.

contrasted with one in which a supplier of clothing to a retail chain alleged that there was an implied contract between them not to terminate their long-standing relationship except on reasonable notice. One ground for rejecting the claim was that there were "no objective criteria by which the court could assess what would be reasonable either as to quantity or price"[650]: hence none of the essential terms governing the supply of the goods could be determined by such criteria. An agreement to pay a "fair" sum may also lack contractual force where it states that the principles for determining what amounts to such a sum are to be settled by further negotiations between the parties. In one such case,[651] a compromise agreement provided that A was to pay to B a "fair" share of certain losses suffered by B and that the parties were to draw up a list of principles by which that "fair" share was to be determined. The description of the share as a "fair" one was said to be "simply the label which the parties put on the outcome which they hoped to achieve. There was no unqualified commitment to pay a fair share."[652] The compromise agreement was therefore merely an agreement to agree and had no contractual force.[653]

Duty to resolve uncertainty. An agreement containing a vague phrase may be binding because one party is under a duty to resolve the uncertainty. In one case an agreement to sell goods provided for delivery "free on board . . . good Danish port." It was held that the agreement was not too vague: it amounted to a contract under which the buyer was bound to select the port of shipment.[654] Where delivery of goods was to be made "free on truck" in the country of destination and no place for delivery in that country was specified in the contract, it was again held that one of the parties was under a duty to specify that place; though in this case the duty was held to be on the seller since it was he who had made all the necessary arrangements with the ship on which the goods were to be carried to that country.[655] 2–143

650 *Baird Textile Holdings Ltd v Marks & Spencer plc* [2001] EWCA Civ 274; [2002] 1 All E.R. (Comm) 737 at [30]; *cf. Schweppe v Harper* [2008] EWCA Civ 442 at [72] ("the concept of reasonable finance is too uncertain to be given any practical meaning"); and *ibid.* at [66], [80], [81]. In that case, C had agreed with D to obtain an annulment of D's bankruptcy in return for a fee of £50,000 to be paid by D. It was a "fundamental element" (at [59]) of the agreement that C should obtain the necessary finance from a third party. It was held by a majority that the agreement was too uncertain to have contractual force as the agreement did not specify the amount of the loan or the terms of repayment; and it was impossible for the court to determine these matters by applying the standard of reasonable-ness; and see below, para.2–164.

651 *Willis Management (Isle of Man) Ltd v Cable and Wireless plc* [2005] EWCA Civ 806, [2005] 2 Lloyd's Rep. 597.

652 *ibid.*, at [24].

653 See above, para.2–126.

654 *David T. Boyd & Co v Louis Louca* [1973] 1 Lloyd's Rep. 209; *cf. Siew Soon Wah v Yong Tong Hong* [1973] A.C. 836; *Bushwall Properties Ltd v Vortex Properties Ltd* [1976] 1 W.L.R. 591, above, para.2–112; *Palmer v East and North Herefordshire NHS Trust* [2006] EWHC 1997, [2006] Lloyd's Rep. Med. 427 where an agreement between a consultant surgeon and the defendant Trust provided for his being found a "suitable medical attachment" at another hospital. Failure to identify that hospital in the agreement did not deprive it of contractual force since the identification was a contingency to be satisfied in the performance of the contract.

655 *Bulk Trading Corp. Ltd v Zenziper Grains & Feedstuffs* [2001] 1 Lloyd's Rep. 357.

2–144 **Meaningless and self-contradictory phrases.** The court will make considerable efforts to give meaning to an apparently meaningless phrase[656]; but even where these efforts fail, the presence of such phrases does not necessarily vitiate the agreement. In *Nicolene Ltd v Simmonds*[657] steel bars were bought on terms which were perfectly clear except for a clause which provided that the sale was subject to "the usual conditions of acceptance." There being no such usual conditions, it was held that the phrase was meaningless, but that this did not vitiate the whole contract: the phrase was severable and could be ignored. A self-contradictory clause can be treated in the same way. Thus where an arbitration clause provided for arbitration of "any dispute" in London and of "any other dispute" in Moscow the court disregarded the clause and determined the dispute itself.[658] Such cases show that the question whether the inclusion of a meaningless clause vitiates the contract, or can be ignored, depends on the importance which the parties may be considered to have attached to it. If it is simply verbiage, not intended to add anything to an otherwise complete agreement, or if it relates to a matter of relatively minor importance, it can be ignored. But if the parties intend it to govern some vital aspect of their relationship its vagueness will vitiate the entire agreement.

2–145 **Conflicting provisions.** An agreement is not too uncertain to have contractual force merely because of a conflict between two of its terms if, as is often the case, the conflict can be resolved in the course of the normal adjudication of a contractual dispute. In *Scammell v Dicker*,[659] a consent order relating to a boundary dispute was alleged to be ineffective by reason of a conflict between the words of the order and a plan annexed to it. The Court of Appeal held that the order was not vitiated by uncertainty since it was "for the parties to resolve any disagreement as to interpretation" and if they failed to do so they would "go to tribunals and find the answer."[660] The uncertainty can in such cases be resolved by the ordinary processes of construction.

2–146 **Vagueness in a subsidiary term.** It has been held that vagueness in one of the terms of an agreement did not of itself vitiate the agreement as a whole.[661] The underlying assumption appears to be that the vague term related only to a subsidiary point[662] so that there was no practical difficulty in enforcing the rest of the agreement.

---

[656] *Tropwood A.G. of Zug v Jade Enterprises Inc (The Tropwind)* [1982] 1 Lloyd's Rep. 232.

[657] [1953] 1 Q.B. 543; discussed in *Heisler v Anglo-Dal Ltd* [1954] 1 W.L.R. 1273 and applied in *Michael Richards Properties Ltd v St. Saviour's* [1975] 3 All E.R. 416; see also *Slater v Raw*, *The Times*, October 15, 1977.

[658] *E. J. R. Lovelock v Exportles* [1968] 1 Lloyd's Rep. 163. *cf. Star Shipping A/S v China National Foreign Trade Transportation Corp. (The Star Texas)* [1993] 2 Lloyd's Rep. 445 where a clause for "arbitration in Beijing or London *in defendant's option*" was upheld.

[659] [2005] EWCA Civ 405, [2005] 3 All E.R. 838.

[660] *ibid.*, at [31].

[661] *Pena v Dale* [2003] EWHC 3166 (Ch), [2004] 2 B.C.L.C. at 508 at [96].

[662] In *Pena v Dale*, above n.661, an option agreement which was otherwise clear provided that the grantor would "endeavour to issue these options . . . in the most tax efficient manner." The vagueness of this term was held to be no bar to the enforcement of the agreement.

8. CONDITIONAL AGREEMENTS

(a) *Classification*

Introductory. An agreement is conditional if its operation depends on an event which is not certain to occur. Discussions of this topic are made difficult by the fact that in the law of contract the word "condition" bears many senses: it is "a chameleon-like word which takes on its meaning from its surroundings."[663] At this stage, we are concerned with only one of these meanings; but to clear the ground it is necessary to draw a number of preliminary distinctions. 2–147

Contingent and promissory conditions. The word "condition" may refer either to an *event*, or to a *term* of a contract (as in the phrase "conditions of sale"[664]). Where "condition" refers to an event, that event may be either an occurrence which neither party undertakes to bring about, or the performance by one party of his undertaking. The first possibility is illustrated by a contract by which A is to work for B, and B is to pay A £50, "if it rains tomorrow." Here the obligations of both parties are contingent on the happening of the specified event which may therefore be described as a *contingent* condition. The second possibility is illustrated by the ordinary case in which A agrees to work for B at a weekly wage payable at the end of the week. Here the contract is immediately binding on both parties, but B is not liable to pay until A has performed his promise to work. Such performance is a condition of B's liability, and, as A has promised to render it, the condition may be described as *promissory.*[665] An intermediate situation arises in the case of a unilateral contract, in which performance by the promisor becomes due on the performance by the promisee of the stipulated act (such as walking to York) or abstention (such as not smoking for a year).[666] Since it follows from the nature of such a contract that the promisee has not promised to render the stipulated performance, the condition on which his entitlement depends[667] is properly classified as contingent. Our concern here is with contingent conditions. 2–148

Conditions precedent and subsequent. Contingent conditions may be precedent or subsequent.[668] A condition is precedent if it provides that the contract is not to be binding until the specified event occurs. It is subsequent if it provides 2–149

[663] *Skips A/S Nordheim v Petrofina SA (The Varenna)* [1984] Q.B. 599, 618.

[664] *Property and Bloodstock Ltd v Emerton* [1968] Ch. 94, 118.

[665] For the distinction between *promissory* and *contingent* condition see Chalmers, *Sale of Goods* (18th ed.) Appendix 2, Note A; *Roadworks (1952) Ltd v Charman* [1994] 2 Lloyd's Rep. 99, 103. *Total Gas Marketing Ltd v Arco British Ltd* [1998] 2 Lloyd's Rep. 209, 215, 218.

[666] See above, para.2–078.

[667] *e.g., Soulsbury v Soulsbury* [2007] EWCA Civ 969 at [50]; above, para.2–080; below n.669.

[668] Conditions precedent are also sometimes called "suspensive," and conditions subsequent "resolutive," conditions: see Treitel, *Remedies for Breach of Contract*, (1988) 262–263. In *Ignazio Messina & Co v Polskie Linie Oceaniczne* [1995] 2 Lloyd's Rep. 566, 580 a condition there under discussion was said to be "a true condition subsequent or suspensive condition." "Subsequent" here seems to be a misprint for "precedent". Conversely, in *Golden Strait Corporation v Nippon Yusen Kubishika Kaisha (The Golden Victory)* [2007] UKHL 1, [2007] 2 A.C. 353 a time charter contained a war clause by which each party was to have a right to cancel if war broke out between specified countries. This clause was described at [59], [74] and [82] as a "suspensive" condition. With great respect, it is submitted that a clause of this kind (entitling parties to bring contractual obligations to

that a previously binding contract is to determine on the occurrence of the event: *e.g.* where A contracts to pay an allowance to B until B marries.[669]

(b) *Degrees of obligation*

2–150 **Effects of agreements subject to contingent conditions precedent: in general.** Where an agreement is subject to a contingent condition precedent, there is, before the occurrence of the condition, no duty on either party to render the principal performance promised by him[669a]: for example, a seller is not bound to deliver and a buyer is not bound to pay. Nor, in such a case, does either party undertake that the condition will occur. But an agreement subject to such a condition may impose some degree of obligation on the parties or on one of them. Whether it has this effect, and if so what degree of obligation is imposed, depends on the true construction of the term specifying condition.[670] Various possible degrees of obligation are discussed in paras 2–151 to 2–155 below.

2–151 **Unrestricted right to withdraw.** One possibility is that, before the event occurs, each party is free to withdraw from the agreement. In *Pym v Campbell*[671] an agreement for the sale of a patent was executed, but the parties at the same

an end) is more properly described as resolutive. For difficulties in drawing the distinction between the two types of condition, see below nn.669 and 678 and para.2–152 at nn.676, 677.

[669] *cf. Brown v Knowsley B.C.* [1986] I.R.L.R. 102 (appointment to "last only as long as sufficient funds were provided" from specified sources); (*semble*) *Gyllenhammar & Partners International v Sour Brodogradevna Industria* [1989] 2 Lloyd's Rep. 403 (contract to "become null and void" if certain consents were not obtained) and *Jameson v CEGB* [2000] 1 A.C. 455 at 477 (settlement of tort claim immediately binding but subject to implied resolutive condition that it was to become void if the agreed amount was not paid); *Covington Marine Corp v Xiamen Shipbuilding Industry Corp* [2005] EWHC 2912 (Comm), [2006] 1 Lloyd's Rep. 748 at [49] (contract to be "automatically rescinded" if parties to a shipbuilding contract could not reach agreement within 20 days as to the supplier of the main engine). The distinction between conditions precedent and subsequent was criticised by Holmes (*The Common Law* (1881), 371); for discussion of this criticism, see Treitel, *Remedies for Breach of Contract* (1988), 263–264. English authority recognises that the distinction is by no means always clear cut: see below at n.677. In *Soulsbury v Soulsbury* [2007] EWCA Civ 969, above, para.2–080, H promised W to leave her £100,000 if W (1) did not enforce or seek to enforce a maintenance order (obtained in divorce proceedings) against him during their joint lives and (2) she survived H (at [10]). These conditions were described as "subsequent" (at [22], where the second is said simply to be the death of H, without any reference to W's surviving H). Since H's estate did not become liable for the £100,000 until both conditions had been satisfied, it might seem that they should more properly have been classified as *precedent*. Their description as "subsequent" may reflect the facts that, once W had begun the stipulated forbearance, H could no longer revoke his promise (above, para.2–080) and that, if W had, after having begun to forbear, *then* sought to enforce the order, she would have lost any right to *damages* in respect of any purported revocation by H which she might have had (before her change of course) by virtue of her earlier forbearance (see above, para.2–086). But her right *to payment of the £100,000* as an agreed sum would not have accrued until both of the above conditions had been fully satisfied. The starting point for assessing damages would no doubt be the £100,000; but that sum would have to be discounted: e.g. (if the action were brought during the parties' joint lives), by the risk of W's not surviving H and by the factor of accelerated payment.

[669a] In *Schweppe v Harper* [2008] EWCA Civ 442 Dyson L.J. at [64] referred to the text above (in a previous edition of this book) with apparent approval.

[670] For special difficulties where the condition precedent is implied, see *Bentworth Finance Ltd v Lubert* [1968] 1 Q.B. 680; Carnegie 31 M.L.R. 78.

[671] (1856) 6 E. & B. 370.

time agreed that it should not "be the agreement" unless a third party approved of the invention. He did not approve, and it was held that the buyer was not liable for refusing to perform. The written agreement was "not an agreement at all."[672] If this is taken literally, either party could have withdrawn even before the third party had given his opinion.

Restricted right to withdraw. A second possibility is that, before the event occurs, the main obligations have not accrued; but that, so long as the event can still occur, one (or both) of the parties cannot withdraw. Thus in *Smith v Butler*[673] A bought land from B on condition that a loan to B (secured by a mortgage on the premises) would be transferred to A.[674] It was held that A could not withdraw before the time fixed for completion: he was bound to wait until then to see whether B could arrange the transfer. However, if it becomes clear that the condition has not occurred, or that it can no longer occur, within the time specified in the contract, the parties will be under no further obligations under the contract. In such a case, the effect of the non-occurrence of the condition is that the parties are "no longer bound"[675] by the contract, or that the contract is "discharged."[676] What the parties have called a "condition precedent" can thus operate as, or have the effect of, a condition subsequent.[677] 2–152

Duty not to prevent occurrence of the event. A third possibility is that, before the event occurs, the main obligations have not accrued; but that in the meantime neither party must do anything to prevent the occurrence of that event. Thus in *Mackay v Dick*[678] an excavating machine was sold on condition that it could excavate at a specified rate on the buyer's property. The buyer's refusal to provide facilities for a proper trial was held to be a breach. Similarly, the seller would have been in breach, had he refused to subject the machine to the proper test. The same principle is illustrated by a case[679] in which a professional footballer was transferred for a fee, part of which was to be paid only after he had 2–153

---

[672] *ibid.* at 374.

[673] [1900] 1 Q.B. 694, *cf. Felixstowe Dock & Ry Co v British Transport Docks Bd.* [1976] 2 Lloyd's Rep. 656; *Alan Estates Ltd v W. G. Stores Ltd* [1982] Ch. 511, 520; *Spectra International plc v Tiscali UK Ltd* [2002] EWHC 2084 (Comm) at [119].

[674] On agreements "subject to finance," see Coote, 40 Conv. (N.S.) 37; Furmston, 3 O.J.L.S. 438, discussing *Meehan v Jones* (1982) 149 C.L.R. 571.

[675] *North Sea Energy Holdings NV v Petroleum Authority of Thailand* [1997] 2 Lloyd's Rep. 418, 428–429; affirmed on other grounds [1999] 1 Lloyd's Rep. 483. *Total Gas Marketing Ltd v Arco British Ltd* [1998] 2 Lloyd's Rep. 209, 215.

[676] *ibid.* at 218.

[677] *ibid.* at 221, 224. And see n.678 below.

[678] (1881) 6 App. Cas. 251. The condition is described as subsequent in *Colley v Overseas Exporters* [1921] 3 K.B. 302, 308. *cf.* also *Shipping Corp. of India v Naviera Letasa* [1976] 1 Lloyd's Rep. 132 and *C.I.A. Barca de Panama SA v George Wimpey & Co Ltd* [1980] 1 Lloyd's Rep. 598; *South West Trains Ltd v Wightman, The Times*, January 14, 1998. The "principle in *Mackay v Dick*" would not apply if the parties had not reached agreement on the matter alleged to have been prevented: see *Covington Marine Corp v Xiamen Shipbuilding Industry Co* [2005] EWHC 2912 (Comm), [2006] 1 Lloyd's Rep. 748 at [56] (where the actual decision was that such agreement had been reached). For exclusion of the duty by express contrary provision, see below, para.2–154.

[679] *Bournemouth & Boscombe Athletic F.C. v Manchester United F.C., The Times*, May 22, 1980. *cf. CEL Group Ltd v Nedlloyd Lines UK Ltd* [2003] EWCA Civ 1716, [2004] 1 All E.R. (Comm) 689, where the contract was not in terms conditional but the court applied a similar principle to that stated in the text above by virtue of the rule stated in para.13–102 below.

scored 20 goals. Before he had done so, the new club dropped him from their first team, and they were held to be in breach as they had not given the player a reasonable opportunity to score the 20 goals. The duty not to prevent the occurrence of the condition has been explained as resting on an implied term and this explanation limits the scope of the duty in a number of ways. For example, the implied term may be only to the effect that a party will not *deliberately* prevent the occurrence of the condition[680]; or (even more narrowly) that he will not *wrongfully* do so.[681] The latter type of implication may allow a party to engage in certain kinds of deliberate prevention but not in others: for example, it may allow a company which has promised an employee the opportunity of earning a bonus to deprive him of that opportunity by going out of business, but not by simply dismissing him, before the bonus has become due.[682]

2–154 **Condition of "satisfaction".** The implied term can also be excluded by an express contrary provision[683] and, in particular, by a provision making the operation of a contract depend on the "satisfaction" of one of the parties with the subject-matter or other aspects relating to the other's performance.[682a] Thus it has been held that there was no contract where a house was bought "subject to satisfactory mortgage"[684]; and where a boat was bought "subject to satisfactory survey"[685] it was held that the buyer was not bound if he expressed his dissatisfaction,[686] in spite of the fact that such expression was a deliberate act on his part which prevented the occurrence of the condition. The same is true where goods are bought on approval and the buyer does not approve them,[687] and where an offer of employment is made "subject to satisfactory references," and the prospective employer does not regard the references as satisfactory.[688] There is some apparent conflict in the authorities on the question whether the law imposes any restriction on the freedom of action of the party on whose satisfaction the operation of the contract depends. In one case[689] a proposed royalty agreement relating to the use by a manufacturer of an invention was "subject to detailed evaluation of production and marketing feasibility" by the manufacturer. It was held that his discretion whether to enter into the contract was "unfettered by any

---

[680] See *Blake & Co v Sohn* [1969] 1 W.L.R. 1412.

[681] See *Thompson v ASDA-MFI Group plc* [1988] Ch. 241. A party would not act "wrongfully" for the present purpose merely by reason of having failed to use its best endeavours to reach agreement on matters left outstanding: see the *Covington* case, above n.678, at [56].

[682] Example based on *Thompson v ASDA-MFI Group plc*, above.

[682a] This sentence (in a previous edition of this book) is cited with approval in *Schweppe v Harper* [2008] EWCA Civ 442 at [70].

[683] See *Micklefield v S.A.C. Technology Ltd* [1990] 1 W.L.R. 1002; *cf. North Sea Energy Holdings NV v Petroleum Authority of Thailand* [1999] 1 Lloyd's Rep. 483. *cf.* below, para.2–175.

[684] *Lee-Parker v Izett (No.2)* [1975] 1 W.L.R. 775; distinguished in *Janmohammed v Hassam, The Times*, June 10, 1976.

[685] *Astra Trust Ltd v Adams & Wiliams* [1969] 1 Lloyd's Rep. 81 doubted in *Varverakis v Compagnia de Navegacion Artico SA (The Merak)* [1976] 2 Lloyd's Rep. 250, 254 and in *Ee v Kahar* (1979) 40 P. & C.R. 223 (as to which see below, n.694).

[686] But if the buyer declared his satisfaction the seller would be bound even though the survey was not objectively satisfactory: *Graham v Pitkin* [1992] 1 W.L.R. 403, 405.

[687] *cf.* Sale of Goods Act 1979, s.18, r.4.

[688] *Wishart v National Association of Citizens' Advice Bureaux* [1990] I.C.R. 794.

[689] *Stabilad Ltd v Stephens & Carter (No.2)* [1999] 2 All E.R. (Comm) 651.

obligation to act reasonably or in good faith"[690] and that, as his satisfaction had not been communicated[691] to the other party, the agreement had not acquired contractual force. On the other hand, where a ship was sold "subject to satisfactory completion of two trial voyages" it was said that such a stipulation was to be construed as "subject to bona fides".[692] The distinction between the two lines of cases turns, ultimately, on the construction of the agreement. Even if this requires the discretion to be exercised in good faith, it does not follow that it must be exercised reasonably; the matter may be left to the relevant party's "subjective decision."[693] It has also been held that the party on whose satisfaction the operation of the contract depends must at least provide facilities for, or not impede, the inspection referred to in the agreement.[694] Of course if the result of the inspection is unsatisfactory, the principal obligation of the contract will not take effect.[695]

Duty of reasonable diligence to bring about the event. A fourth possibility is that, before the event occurs, the main obligations do not accrue but that one of the parties undertakes to use reasonable efforts to bring the event about (without absolutely undertaking that his efforts will succeed). This construction was applied, for instance, where land was sold subject to the condition that the purchaser should obtain planning permission to use the land as a transport depot: he was bound to make reasonable efforts to obtain the permission, but he was free from liability when those efforts failed.[696] Similarly, where goods are sold "subject to export (or import) licence," the party whose duty it is to obtain the 2–155

[690] *ibid.*, p.662.

[691] For the requirement of communication see *ibid.*, p.660; the requirement may be satisfied by conduct from which satisfaction can be inferred, *e.g.* where a buyer of goods on approval retains them without notifying rejection for more than the stipulated or a reasonable time: Sale of Goods Act 1979, s.18, r.4(b).

[692] *Albion Sugar Co v William Tankers (The John S. Darbyshire)* [1977] 2 Lloyd's Rep. 457, 464; *cf. BV Oliehandel Jongkind v Coastal International Ltd* [1983] 2 Lloyd's Rep. 463; *The Nissos Samos* [1985] 1 Lloyd's Rep. 378, 385; *cf. Star Steamship Society v Beogradska Plovidba (The Junior K)* [1988] 2 Lloyd's Rep. 583, 589 (where the words were held to negative contractual intention). See also *El Awadi v Bank of Credit & Commerce International SA* [1990] 1 Q.B. 606, 619; and, in an analogous context, *Abu Dhabi National Tanker Co v Product Star Shipping Co (The Product Star (No.2))* [1993] 1 Lloyd's Rep. 397, 404; *Lymington Marina Ltd v Macnamara* [2007] EWCA Civ 151, [2007] 2 All E.R. (Comm) 825 at [42]–[45], [70].

[693] *Stabilad Ltd v Stephens & Carter Ltd (No.2)* [1999] 2 All E.R. (Comm) 651 at 659; *Jani-King (GB) Ltd v Pula Enterprises* [2007] EWHC 2433 (QB), [2008] 1 All E.R. (Comm) 457 at [35]–[36]; *cf. Schweppe v Harper* [2008] EWCA Civ 442 at [71]–[72].

[694] *Varverakis v Compagnia de Navegacion Artico SA (The Merak)* [1976] 2 Lloyd's Rep. 250; *cf. Ee v Kahar* (1979) 40 P. & C.R. 223 (where the sale was simply "subject to survey"—omitting the word "satisfactory"—thus falling, it is submitted, within the principle of *Mackay v Dick*, above n.678).

[695] As in *Albion Sugar Co v Williams Tankers (The John S. Darbyshire)* [1977] 2 Lloyd's Rep. 457.

[696] *Hargreaves Transport Ltd v Lynch* [1969] 1 W.L.R. 215 (condition not satisfied); *Richard West & Partners (Inverness) Ltd v Dick* [1969] 2 Ch. 424 (similar condition satisfied); *cf. Fisher v Tomatousos* [1991] 2 E.G.L.R. 204; *Jolley v Carmel Ltd* [2000] 2 E.G.L.R. 153 (buyer who was required by the contract to make reasonable efforts to get planning permission under no duty to get it within a reasonable time). *cf. Tesco Stores Ltd v Gibson* (1970) 214 E.G. 835 (no obligation on purchaser to apply for planning permission).

licence[697] does not prima facie promise absolutely that a licence will be obtained[698]; but only undertakes to make reasonable efforts to that end.[699] The principal obligations to buy and sell will not take effect if no licence is obtained[700]; but if the party who should have made reasonable efforts has failed to do so he will be liable in damages,[701] unless he can show that any such efforts, which he should have made would (if made) have necessarily been unsuccessful.[702] The same principles have been applied where an agreement was made "subject to the approval of the court"; and where an agreement was made to assign a lease which could be assigned only with the consent of the landlord. In such cases the requisite approval or consent must be sought; but the main obligations do not accrue until the approval or consent is given,[703] and if it is refused the principal obligation will not take effect.[704]

2–156 **Principal and subsidiary obligations.** It will be seen that, in cases falling within the categories discussed in paras 2–152 to 2–155 above, a distinction must be drawn between two types of obligation: the principal obligation of each party (*e.g.* to buy and sell) and a subsidiary obligation, *i.e.* one not to withdraw, not to prevent occurrence of the condition, or to make reasonable efforts to bring it about. One view is that the party who fails to perform the subsidiary obligation

---

[697] As to which party has this duty, see *H. O. Brandt & Co v H. N. Morris & Co* [1917] 2 K.B. 784; *AV Pound & Co v M. W. Hardy & Co* [1956] A.C. 588; *Benjamin's Sale of Goods* (7th ed., 2006) paras 18–209—18–311.

[698] The *prima facie* rule may be excluded by express words which, on their true construction, impose an absolute duty; *e.g. Peter Cassidy Seed Co Ltd v Osuustukkukauppa* [1957] 1 W.L.R. 273; *C. Czarnikow Ltd v Centrale Handlu Zagranicznego "Rolimpex"* [1979] A.C. 351, 371; *Congimex Companhia Geral, etc., S.A.R.L. v Tradax Export SA* [1983] 1 Lloyd's Rep. 250; *Pagnan S.p.A. v Tradax Ocean Transport SA* [1987] 3 All E.R. 565; Yates and Carter, 1 J.C.L. 57. See also *B.S. & N. Ltd (BVI) v Micado Shipping Ltd (The Seaflower)* [2000] 2 Lloyd's Rep. 37, a charterparty case in which the issue was whether failure to perform a "guarantee" that the shipowner would obtain a third party's approval amounted to a repudiation. A negative answer was given to this question, but it was held in further proceedings that the "guarantee" was a promissory condition, so that failure by the shipowner to obtain the approval justified rescission by the charterer: [2001] 1 Lloyd's Rep. 341. There was no issue as to the standard of the owner's duty, but it seems to have been assumed that the duty was strict (*i.e.* not merely one of diligence).

[699] *Re Anglo-Russian Merchant Traders and John Batt & Co (London) Ltd* [1917] 2 K.B. 679; *Coloniale Import-Export v Loumidis & Sons* [1978] 2 Lloyd's Rep. 560; *Overseas Buyers Ltd v Granadex S.A.* [1980] 2 Lloyd's Rep. 608; *Gamerco SA v I.C.M./Fair Warning (Agency) Ltd* [1995] 1 W.L.R. 1226, 1231. Where the contract is expressly subject to the approval of a public authority, there may not even be a duty to make reasonable efforts to secure that approval: see *Gyllenhammar Partners International v Sour Brodegradevna Industria* [1989] 2 Lloyd's Rep. 403. For the standard of duty, see generally *Benjamin's Sale of Goods* (7th ed., 2006), paras 18–313—18–348.

[700] *Charles H. Windschuegl Ltd v Alexander Pickering & Co Ltd* (1950) 84 Ll.L.Rep. 89, 92–93; *Brauer & Co (Great Britain) Ltd v James Clark (Brush Materials) Ltd* [1952] 2 All E.R. 497, 501; *cf.* the cases on sales of goods "to arrive" discussed in *Benjamin's Sale of Goods* (7th ed., 2006), paras 21–022—21–027.

[701] *e.g. Malik v C.E.T.A.* [1974] 1 Lloyd's Rep. 279; *Agroexport v Cie. Européenne de Céréales* [1974] 1 Lloyd's Rep. 499.

[702] See *Benjamin's Sale of Goods* (7th ed., 2006), para.18–328; *Overseas Buyers Ltd v Granadex SA*, above, n.604 at 612.

[703] *Smallman v Smallman* [1972] Fam. 25. Contrast *Soulsbury v Soulsbury* [2007] EWCA Civ 969, where the agreement, though subject to the conditions described in para.2–149 n.669 above, was not subject to any further condition of approval by the court, and so became enforceable when "the events upon which payment depended came to be fulfilled" (at [46]).

[704] *Shires v Brock* (1977) 247 E.G. 127.

is to be treated as if the condition had occurred; and that he is then liable on the principal obligation. Thus in *Mackay v Dick*[705] the buyer was held liable *for the price*; but there was no discussion as to the remedy. In principle it seems wrong to hold him so liable, for such a result ignores the possibility that, in that case, the machine might have failed to come up to the standard required by the contract, even if proper facilities for trial had been provided. It is submitted that the correct result in cases of this kind is to award *damages* for breach of the subsidiary obligation: in assessing such damages, the court can take into account the possibility that the condition might not have occurred, even if there had been no such breach.[706] To hold the party in breach liable for the full performance promised by him, on the fiction that the condition had occurred, seems to introduce into this branch of the law a punitive element that is inappropriate to a contractual action. The most recent authority rightly holds that such a doctrine of "fictional fulfilment" of a condition does not form part of English law.[707]

Waiver of condition. Where a condition is inserted entirely for the benefit of one party, that party may waive the condition. If he does so, he can then sue[708] and be sued[709] on the contract as if the condition had occurred. Obviously this rule does not apply to cases falling within the first of the categories discussed above, in which there is no contract at all before the condition occurs. 2–157

9. CONTRACTUAL INTENTION

General. In a number of situations to be discussed in paras 2–159 to 2–186 below, it has been held that an agreement, though supported by consideration,[710] was not binding as a contract[711] because it was made without any intention of creating legal relations.[712] 2–158

---

705 (1881) 6 App. Cas. 251, above, para.2–153.

706 *Bournemouth & Boscombe Athletic F.C. v Manchester United F.C.*, *The Times*, May 22, 1980; *cf. The Blankenstein* [1985] 1 W.L.R. 435; *Alpha Trading Ltd v Dunshaw-Patten Ltd* [1981] Q.B. 290; *George Moundreas & Co SA v Navimpex Centrala Navala* [1985] 2 Lloyd's Rep. 515; *Orient Overseas Management & Finance Ltd v File Shipping Co Ltd (The Energy Progress)* [1993] 1 Lloyd's Rep. 355, 358.

707 *Thompson v ASDA-MFI Group plc* [1988] Ch. 241, 266 (where the condition was said at 251 to be subsequent); and see *Little v Courage Ltd* (1995) 70 P. & C.R. 469, 474.

708 *Wood Preservation Ltd v Prior* [1969] 1 W.L.R. 1077; *cf. Heron Garages Properties Ltd v Moss* [1974] 1 W.L.R. 148.

709 *McKillop v McMullan* [1979] N.I. 85.

710 *R. v Civil Service Appeal Board Ex p. Bruce* [1988] 3 All E.R. 686, 693, 698; *cf. Re Beaumont* [1980] Ch. 444, 453: consideration may be provided "under a contract *or otherwise*."

711 For enforcement on other grounds, see *John Fox v Bannister King & Rigbeys* [1988] Q.B. 925, 928 (court's jurisdiction to enforce honourable conduct on the part of solicitors); *Xydhias v Xydhias* [1999] 2 All E.R. 386, 394 (compromise of claim for ancillary relief in divorce proceedings).

712 For recent statements of the requirement to create legal relations, see *Baird Textile Holdings Ltd v Marks & Spencer plc* [2001] EWCA Civ 274; [2002] 1 All E.R. (Comm) 737 at [30], [59]; below, para.2–164. See also *Zakhem International Construction Ltd v Nippon Kohan KK* [1987] 2 Lloyd's Rep. 596. For a denial of the requirement, see Williston, *Contracts*, para.21; *cf.* Tuck, 21 Can. Bar Rev. 123 (1943); Shatwell (1954) 1 Sydney L.R. at 293; Unger (1956) 19 M.L.R. 96; Hepple [1970] C.L.J. 122; Hedley (1985) 50 J.L.S. 391. There is also said to be a requirement of "mutuality": see *Simpkins v Pays* [1955] 1 W.L.R. 975, 979; *Rajbenback v Mamon* [1955] 1 Q.B. 283, 286; but this expression here refers to consideration rather than to contractual intention: see *Lees v Whitcombe*

2–159 **Burden of proof: express agreements.** In the case of ordinary commercial transactions it is not normally necessary to prove that the parties to an express agreement in fact intended to create legal relations.[713] The onus of proving that there was no such intention "is on the party who asserts that no legal effect is intended, and the onus is a heavy one."[714] In deciding whether the onus has been discharged, the courts will be influenced by the importance of the agreement to the parties, and by the fact that one of them acted in reliance on it.[715]

2–160 **Burden of proof: agreements inferred from conduct.** The rule as to burden of proof stated in paragraph 2–159 above applies where the parties had entered into an *express* agreement; but claims or defences are sometimes based on the allegation that parties between whom there was no express agreement had so conducted themselves in relation to each other that an implied contract was to be inferred from their conduct; and in a number of cases of this kind the allegation has been rejected on the ground that there was no contractual intention.[716] Such cases illustrate the judicial attitude that "contracts are not lightly to be implied" and that the courts must (in cases of this kind) be able "to conclude with confidence that . . . the parties intended to create contractual relations."[717] The burden of proof on this issue appears, in cases of this kind, to be on the proponent

(1828) 5 Bing. 34; *Sykes v Dixon* (1839) 9 Ad. & El. 693; *Westhead v Sproson* (1861) 6 H. & N. 728; Treitel (1961) 77 L.Q.R. 83.

[713] Certain regulated agreements under the Consumer Credit Act 1974 must contain a signature in a "signature box" warning the signer to sign the agreement "only if you want to be legally bound by its terms": Consumer Credit (Agreements) Regulations 1983, (SI 1983/1553), as amended by Consumer Credit (Agreements) (Amendment) Regulations 2004 (SI 2004/1482) reg.2. For amendment of the definition of a "regulated" consumer credit agreement, see Consumer Credit Act 2006, s.2.

[714] *Edwards v Skyways Ltd* [1964] 1 W.L.R. 349, 355; *Bahamas Oil Refining Co v Kristiansands Tankrederei A/S (The Polyduke)* [1978] 1 Lloyd's Rep. 211; *Financial Techniques (Planning Services) Ltd v Hughes* [1981] I.R.L.R. 32; *G.A.F.L.A.C. v Tanter (The Zephyr)* [1985] 2 Lloyd's Rep. 529, 537 (disapproving [1984] 1 Lloyd's Rep. 58, 63–64); *Yani Haryanto v E.D. & F. Man (Sugar) Ltd* [1986] 2 Lloyd's Rep. 44; *Orion Insurance plc v Sphere Drake Insurance plc* [1992] 1 Lloyd's Rep. 239 at 263, where the burden was discharged; *Mamidoil-Jetoil Greek Petroleum Co SA v Okta Crude Oil Refinery AD* [2003] 1 Lloyd's Rep. 1 at [159]; *cf. Coastal Bermuda Petroleum Ltd v VTT Vulcan Petroleum SA (The Marine Star) (No.2)* [1994] 2 Lloyd's Rep. 629, 632, reversed on other grounds [1996] 2 Lloyd's Rep. 383.

[715] *cf.* above, para.2–140; *Kingswood Estate Co v Anderson* [1963] 2 Q.B. 169; *South West Water Authority v Palmer* (1982) 263 E.G. 438.

[716] *Hispanica de Petroleos SA v Vencedora Oceana Navegaceon SA (The Kapetan Markos N.L.) (No.2)* [1987] 2 Lloyd's Rep. 323; *The Aramis* [1989] 1 Lloyd's Rep. 213; *Mitsui & Co Ltd v Novorossiysk Shipping Co (The Gudermes)* [1993] 1 Lloyd's Rep. 311; in some of these cases rights and liabilities under the shipping documents would now arise by virtue of Carriage of Goods by Sea Act 1992, ss.2 and 3.

[717] *Blackpool and Fylde Aero Club v Blackpool BC* [1990] 1 W.L.R. 1195, 1202; *cf. Baird Textile Holdings Ltd v Marks & Spencer plc* [2001] EWCA Civ 274; [2002] 1 All E.R. (Comm) 737 at [20], [21], [30], [62] where the argument that there was an implied contract was rejected for the reasons given in para.2–164 below. The argument was likewise rejected in *West Bromwich Albion Football Club v El Safty* [2006] EWCA Civ 1299, (2006) 92 B.M.L.R. 179 at [43], [48] (below, para.18–004) and *Cairns v Visteon UK Ltd* [2007] I.R.L.R. 175 at [18], [23] on the ground that in these two cases there was no "necessity" for any such implication; and see below, para.18–005. Contrast *Goshaw Dedicated Ltd v Tyser & Co Ltd* [2006] EWCA Civ 54, [2006] 1 All E.R. (Comm) 501 at [66], apparently rejecting the argument that there was no implied contract.

of the contract, contrary to the rule which applies to express agreements regulating commercial relationships. The view that the burden of proof on the issue of contractual intention in the case of an implied contract rests on the proponent of the contract was accepted in *Modahl v British Athletics Federation*.[718] In that case, the burden was held to have been discharged so that a contract came into existence between an athlete and the Federation, under whose rules the athlete had for a long time competed. The rules of the Federation had contractual force by reason of the "continuous long-term relationship based on a programme and rules couched in language of a contractual character and purporting to impose mutual rights and obligations."[719]

Intention judged objectively. In deciding issues of contractual intention, the courts normally apply an objective test[720]: for example, where the sale of a house is *not* "subject to contract,"[721] both parties are likely to be bound even though one of them subjectively believed that he would not be bound until the usual exchange of contracts had taken place.[722] In *Edmonds v Lawson*,[723] the Court of Appeal similarly applied the objective test to hold that the requirement of contractual intention was satisfied where a pupil barrister accepted an offer of pupillage with a set of chambers. The resulting contract[724] was between the pupil and all the members of the chambers—not between the pupil and the individual members of the chambers who acted as her pupil masters. The objective test is, however, here (as elsewhere)[725] subject to the limitation that it does not apply in favour of a party who knows the truth. Thus, in the house sale example given above, the party who did not intend to be bound would not be bound if his state of mind was actually known to the other party.[726] Nor could a party who did not in fact intend to be bound invoke the objective test so as to hold the other party 2–161

---

[718] [2001] EWCA Civ 1447; [2002] 1 W.L.R. 1192; *cf.* recognition of the distinction, for the purpose of burden of proof, between express and implied agreements, drawn in paras 2–159 and 2–160 above, in *Baird Textile Holdings Ltd v Marks & Spencer plc* [2001] EWCA Civ 274; [2002] 1 All E.R. (Comm) 737 at [61].

[719] *Modahl's* case, above n.718, at [109]; *cf. ibid.* at [52]. Jonathan Parker L.J. dissented on this point.

[720] See *Carlill v Carbolic Smoke Ball Co* [1893] 1 Q.B. 256; *Ignazio Messina & Co v Polskie Linie Oceaniczne* [1995] 2 Lloyd's Rep. 566, 579; *Bowerman v Association of British Travel Agents* [1995] N.L.J. 1815; *Manatee Towing Co v Oceanbulk Maritime SA (The Bay Ridge)* [1999] 2 All E.R. (Comm) 306 at 327; *London Baggage (Charing Cross v Railtrack plc)* [2000] E.G.C.S. 57; *Baird Textile Holdings Ltd v Marks & Spencer plc* [2001] EWCA Civ 274; [2002] 1 All E.R. (Comm) 737. For a statement of the objective test of contractual intention, see also *Bear Stearns Bank plc v Forum Global Equity Ltd* [2007] EWHC 1576, above para.2–114, where an oral acceptance of a "firm" offer (also made orally) was held to give rise to a contract although at the stage of that acceptance many important points remained unresolved. *cf. Crowden v Aldridge* [1993] 1 W.L.R. 433, applying the objective test of intention to produce legal consequences to a non-contractual direction to executors in favour of a third party. *Quaere* whether, in the absence of reliance on the direction, the policy which justifies the objective test in a contractual context extends to the situation which arose in this case.

[721] Above, para.2–118.

[722] *Tweddell v Henderson* [1975] 1 W.L.R. 1496; *Storer v Manchester City Council* [1974] 1 W.L.R. 1403, 1408.

[723] [2000] Q.B. 501.

[724] For the consideration moving from the pupil, see below, para.3–038.

[725] Above, para.2–004.

[726] *Pateman v Pay* (1974) 263 E.G. 467.

to the contract[727]: to apply that test in such a case would pervert its purpose, which is to protect a party who has relied on the objective appearance of consent from the prejudice which he would suffer if the *other* party could escape liability on the ground that he had no real intention to be bound. The objective test, moreover, merely prevents a party from relying on his *uncommunicated* belief as to the binding force of the agreement. The test therefore does not apply where the parties have expressed their actual intention in the document alleged to constitute the contract: the question whether they intended the document to have contractual force then becomes one "of construction of the documents as a whole what effect is to be given to such a statement."[728] In the absence of such an expression of intention, however, the legal *effect* of an agreement which is clearly intended to give rise to some legal relations is not determined by the subjective intentions of the parties or of one of them: for example, an agreement may take effect as a lease even though it is intended by the lessor to take effect only as a licence.[729]

2–162 **Intention expressly negatived.** The clearest illustration of the requirement of contractual intention is to be found in cases where the agreement contains an express provision negativing the intention.[730] For example, in *Rose & Frank Co v J.R. Crompton & Bros Ltd*[731] an agency agreement provided: "This arrangement is not entered into, nor is this memorandum written, as a formal or legal agreement . . . but it is only a definite expression and record of the purpose and intention of the . . . parties concerned, to which they each honourably pledge themselves." It was held that this "honour clause" negatived contractual intention. Similarly agreements for the sale of land are generally made "subject to contract." These words negative contractual intention,[732] so that the parties are not normally bound until formal contracts are exchanged.[733] It is a crucial part of this process of "exchange" that the parties should intend by it to bring a legally binding contract into existence.[734] Football pool coupons also commonly contain words expressly negativing contractual intention.[735]

---

[727] *Lark v Outhwaite* [1991] 2 Lloyd's Rep. 132, 141.

[728] *R. v Lord Chancellor's Department Ex p. Nangle* [1991] I.C.R. 743, 751.

[729] *Street v Mountford* [1985] A.C. 809; *A. G. Securities v Vaughan* [1990 1 A.C. 417; contrast *Ogwr BC v Dykes* [1989] 1 W.L.R. 295; *Monmouth BC v Marlog*, *The Times*, May 4, 1994 (where there was no intention to enter into *any* legal relationship); *Bruton v Quadrant Housing Trust* [1997] N.L.J. 1385.

[730] *e.g. Broadwick Financial Services Ltd v Spencer* [2002] EWCA Civ 35; [2002] 1 All E.R. (Comm) 446 at [27].

[731] [1925] A.C. 445; affirming [1923] 2 K.B. 261; *County Ltd v Girozentrale Securities* [1996] 3 All E.R. 834; *M&P Steelcraft Ltd v Ellis* [2008] I.R.L.R. 355, below, para.2–181.

[732] They can have the same effect in other types of agreement: see *Confetti Records v Warner Music UK Ltd* [2003] EWHC 1274, *The Times*, June 12, 2003.

[733] Above, paras 2–118, 2–119; *Rose & Frank Co v J.R. Crompton & Bros Ltd* [1923] 2 K.B. 261, 294; *Ali v Ahmed* (1996) 71 P. & C.R. D39.

[734] *Commission for the New Towns v Cooper (G.B.) Ltd* [1995] Ch. 259, 295.

[735] See *Jones v Vernons Pools Ltd* [1938] 2 All E.R. 626; *Appleson v Littlewood Ltd* [1939] 1 All E.R. 464; *Guest v Empire Pools* (1964) 108 S.J. 98. In Scotland, it has been argued that such honour clauses in football coupons may be unreasonable and hence ineffective: *Ferguson v Littlewoods Pools* 1997, S.L.T. 309, 314–315.

Whether a particular phrase has this effect is a question of construction.[736] In *Edwards v Skyways Ltd*[737] employers promised to make a dismissed employee an "*ex gratia* payment." It was held that these words did not negative contractual intention but amounted merely to a denial of a pre-existing legal liability to make the payment.[738] Contractual intention was, similarly, not negatived where an arbitration clause in a reinsurance contract provided that "this treaty shall be *interpreted as* an honourable engagement rather than as a legal obligation . . ." The contract as a whole was clearly intended to be binding; and the purpose of the words quoted was merely to free the arbitrator "to some extent from strict legal rules"[739] in interpreting the agreement. Again, in *The Mercedes Envoy*[740] a shipowner during negotiations for a charterparty said: "we are fixed in good faith." It was held that the words "in good faith" did not negative contractual intention: if they had any effect, it amounted merely to a "collateral understanding"[741] that account should be taken of damage to the vessel, of which both shipowner and charterer were aware. 2–163

Intention impliedly negatived. This possibility is illustrated by *Baird Textile Holdings Ltd v Marks & Spencer plc*[742] where the claimants had for some 30 years been a principal supplier of clothing to the defendants, a leading retail chain. When the defendants terminated the arrangement with effect from the end of the then current production season, the claimants sought damages, basing their claim on, *inter alia*,[743] an alleged implied contract not to terminate the arrangement except on reasonable notice of three years. The claim was rejected on account of "the absence of any intention to create legal relations".[744] One factor[745] on which this conclusion was based was that the defendants had (as the claimants themselves had alleged in their points of claim)[746] deliberately abstained from entering into a long-term contractual relationship with the claimants in order to maintain the flexibility of the *de facto* long-term commercial relationship between the parties.[747] It followed that the claimants must be taken to have accepted the risk inherent in such a relationship "without specific contractual protection."[748] Contractual retention was, again, impliedly negatived 2–164

[736] *R. v Lord Chancellor's Department Ex p. Nangle* [1991] I.C.R. 743; above, para.2–161.

[737] [1964] 1 W.L.R. 349. It was admitted that there was consideration moving from the employee.

[738] *cf. Glaxosmithkline UK Ltd v Department of Health* [2007] EWHC 1470, [2007] 2 All E.R. (Comm) 1140, where a "voluntary" scheme agreed between the Department and members of the pharmaceutical industry, containing "mandatory provisions" (at [13]), was held to have contractual force.

[739] *Home Insurance Co Ltd v Administratia Asigurarilor* [1983] 2 Lloyd's Rep. 674, 677; *Home and Overseas Insurance Co Ltd v Mentor Insurance Co (UK) Ltd* [1989] 1 Lloyd's Rep. 473.

[740] *Hanjin Shipping Co Ltd v Zenith Chartering Corp. (The Mercedes Envoy)* [1995] 2 Lloyd's Rep. 559.

[741] *ibid.* at 564.

[742] [2001] EWCA Civ 274; [2002] 1 All E.R. (Comm) 737.

[743] For the alternative basis of the claim on the ground of estoppel, see below, para.3–098.

[744] *Baird* case, above n.742, at [30], [47], [69].

[745] For another such factor, see below, para.2–183.

[746] *Baird* case, above n.742, at [10], [46], [73].

[747] *ibid.*, at [30], [47], [73], [74].

[748] *ibid.*, at [76].

in *Cobbe v Yeoman's Row Management Ltd*[748a] where an agreement "in principle" for the redevelopment and disposal of residential property left other aspects of the scheme to be settled by further negotiations between the parties. It was held that the agreement "in principle" lacked contractual force since, until those outstanding matters had been settled and embodied in a formal agreement between the parties, each regarded the other as bound in honour only.[748b]

2–165 **Statements inducing a contract.** A statement inducing a contract may be a "mere puff" if the court considers that it was not seriously meant and that this should have been obvious to the person to whom it was made. In *Weeks v Tybald*,[749] for example, the defendant "affirmed and published that he would give £100 to him that should marry his daughter with his consent." The court held that it was "not reasonable that the defendant should be bound by such general words spoken to excite suitors." Similarly, in *Lambert v Lewis*,[750] a manufacturer stated in promotional literature that his product was "foolproof" and that it "required no maintenance." These statements did not give rise to a contract between the manufacturer and a dealer (who had bought the product from an intermediary) as they were "not intended to be, nor were they, acted on as being express warranties."[751]

2–166 Other statements which induce persons to enter into contracts have some effect in law, but exactly what that effect is often turns on whether they are "mere representations" or have contractual force. The distinction between these categories turns on the test of contractual intention. In cases concerning the effect of such statements, the test of intention generally determines the *contents* of a contract, the *existence* of which is not in doubt. But where the inducing statement for some reason cannot take effect as a term of the main contract it may, nevertheless, amount to a collateral contract; and whether it has this effect again depends on the test of contractual intention. For example, in *Heilbut, Symons & Co v Buckleton*[752] the claimant applied for shares in a company after a conversation with the defendants' manager, which led the claimant to believe that the

[748a] [2008] UKHL 55, [2008] 1 W.L.R. 1752.

[748b] *ibid.* at [7], [71].

[749] (1605) Noy 11; *cf. Dalrymple v Dalrymple* (1811) 2 Hag.Con. 54, 105.

[750] [1982] A.C. 225 affirmed so far as the manufacturer's liability was concerned, but on other grounds at 271.

[751] [1982] A.C. 225, 262; contrast *Carlill v Carbolic Smoke Ball Co Ltd* [1893] 1 Q.B. 256 and *Bowerman v Association of British Travel Agents* [1995] N.L.J. 1815, above, para.2–018. Under s.14(2D) of the Sale of Goods Act 1979, as inserted by the Sale and Supply of Goods to Consumers Regulations 2002, (SI 2002/3045), reg.3, implementing Dir.1999/44/EC, a commercial seller of goods to a buyer who deals as consumer may be liable if the goods lack a quality claimed for them in "public statements on the *specific* characteristics of the goods made about them by the seller, the producer or his representative in advertising or labelling." Statements such as those made in *Lambert v Lewis*, above, would probably not be sufficiently "specific" for this purpose. Similar provisions apply to contracts for the supply of goods other than contracts of sale: see Supply of Goods and Services Act 1982, s.4(2B), as inserted by reg.7 of the Regulations cited above and Supply of Goods (Implied Terms) Act 1973, s.10(2D) as inserted by reg.13 of those Regulations.

[752] [1913] A.C. 30 criticised by Atiyah in *The Rise and Fall of Freedom of Contract*, p.772; but followed by the House of Lords in *I.B.A. v E.M.I. Electronics Ltd* (1980) 14 Build.L.R. 1; *cf. Strover v Harrington* [1988] Ch. 390, 410; *Ignazio Messina & Co v Polskie Linie Oceaniczne* [1995] 2 Lloyd's Rep. 566, 581. The Regulations referred to in n.751 above and in para.2–167 below would not apply on facts such as those of any of the cases cited in this note.

company (which the defendants were "bringing out") was a rubber company. It was not a rubber company, and the claimant alleged that the defendants had warranted that it was a rubber company. It was held that nothing said by the manager was intended to have the effect of a collateral contract. Lord Moulton said: "Not only the terms of such contracts but the existence of an *animus contrahendi* on the part of all the parties to them must be clearly shewn."[753] It follows that an oral statement made in the course of negotiations will not take effect as collateral contract where the terms of the main contract show that the parties did *not* intend the statement to have such effect. This was, for example, the position where the main contract contained an "entire agreement" clause: this showed that statements made in the course of negotiations were to "have no contractual force."[754] Similarly, where a party during negotiations for a lease made a statement as to its intention as to its future conduct under the lease, but the negotiations were then continued and the final agreement was inconsistent with the statement, it was held that these circumstances negatived contractual intention with respect to the statement, so that it could not take effect as a collateral contract.[755]

Consumer guarantees. The Sale and Supply of Goods to Consumers Regulations 2002[756] provide that, where goods are sold or supplied to a consumer and are offered with a "consumer guarantee", that guarantee "takes effect as a contractual obligation owed by the guarantor."[757] It seems to take effect by virtue of the Regulations, without any separate requirement of contractual intention. 2–167

Social agreements. Many social arrangements do not amount to contracts because they are not intended to be legally binding. "The ordinary example is where two parties agree to take a walk together, or where there is an offer and an acceptance of hospitality."[758] Similarly it has been held that the winner of a competition held by a golf club could not sue for his prize where "no one concerned with that competition ever intended that there should be any legal results flowing from the conditions posted and the acceptance by the competitor of those conditions"[759]; that the rules of a competition organised by a "jalopy club" for charitable purposes did not have contractual force[760]; that "car pool" 2–168

753 [1913] A.C. 30, 47; *Unit Construction Co Ltd v Liverpool Corp.* (1972) 221 E.G. 459; *Hispanica de Petroleos SA v Vencedora Oceanica Navegacion SA (The Kapetan Markos NL)* [1987] 2 Lloyd's Rep. 323, 332.

754 *Inntrepreneur Pub Co (GL) v East Crown Ltd* [2000] 2 Lloyd's Rep. 611 at 614; *cf. White v Bristol Rugby Club Ltd* [2002] I.R.L.R. 2004.

755 *Business Environment Bow Lane Ltd v Deanwater Estates Ltd* [2007] EWCA Civ 622, [2007] NLJ 1263.

756 SI 2002/3045.

757 *ibid.*, reg.15(1); for the definition of "consumer guarantee" see *ibid.*, reg.2. In the present context, it is significant that this definition refers to such a guarantee as an "*undertaking*"; *cf.* the reference, *ibid.*, in the definition in reg.2 of "consumer" to "*contracts* governed by these Regulations".

758 *Balfour v Balfour* [1919] 2 K.B. 571, 578; *Rose & Frank Co v J.R. Crompton & Bros Ltd* [1923] 2 K.B. 261, 293; *Wyatt v Kreglinger & Fernau* [1933] 1 K.B. 793, 806.

759 *Lens v Devonshire Club, The Times*, December 4, 1914; referred to in *Wyatt's* case, above n.758 from which the quotation in the text is taken.

760 *White v Blackmore* [1972] 2 Q.B. 651.

and similar arrangements between friends or neighbours did not amount to contracts even though one party contributed to the running costs of the other's vehicle[761]; that an agreement between members of a group of friends relating to musical performances by the group was not intended to have contractual effect,[762] and that the provision of free residential accommodation for close friends did not amount to a contract as it was an act of bounty, done without any intention to enter into legal relations.[763]

2–169 **Domestic agreements between spouses.** For the same reason, many domestic arrangements between spouses lack contractual force. In *Balfour v Balfour*[764] a husband who worked abroad promised to pay an allowance of £30 per month to his wife, who had to stay in England on medical grounds. The wife's attempt to enforce this promise by action failed for two reasons: she had not provided any consideration, and the parties did not intend the arrangement to be legally binding. On the second ground alone, most domestic arrangements between husband and wife are not contracts. Atkin L.J. said: "Those agreements, or many of them, do not result in contracts at all . . . even though there may be what as between other parties would constitute consideration for the agreement . . . They are not contracts . . . because the parties did not intend that they should be attended by legal consequences . . . Agreements such as these are outside the realm of contracts altogether."[765] It has been said that the facts of *Balfour v Balfour* "stretched the doctrine to its limits"[766]; but the doctrine itself has not been judicially questioned and the cases provide many other instances of its application.[767] The doctrine does not, of course, prevent a husband from making a binding contract with his wife. For example, a husband can be his wife's tenant.[768] Binding separation agreements are often made when husband and wife agree to live apart.[769] And where a man before marriage promised his future wife

---

[761] *Coward v M.I.B.* [1963] 1 Q.B. 259; overruled, but not on the issue of contractual intention, in *Albert v M.I.B.* [1972] A.C. 301; *Buckpitt v Oates* [1968] 1 All E.R. 1145, criticised on this point by Karsten (1969) 32 M.L.R. 88. The actual decisions are obsolete by reason of Road Traffic Act 1988, ss.145, 149; *cf.* also s.150; but an issue of contractual intention might still arise if one party to such an arrangement simply failed to turn up at the agreed time. For another context in which sharing of expenses did not give rise to an inference of contractual intention, see *Monmouth C. v Marlog*, *The Times*, May 4, 1994.

[762] *Hadley v Kemp* [1999] E.M.L.R. 589 at 623.

[763] *Heslop v Burns* [1974] 1 W.L.R. 1241; *cf. Horrocks v Forray* [1976] 1 W.L.R. 230.

[764] [1919] 2 K.B. 571. *cf. Gould v Gould* [1970] 1 Q.B. 275, where there was a division of opinion on the issue of contractual intention, the majority holding that there was no such intention where a husband on leaving his wife promised to pay her £15 per week so long as he could manage it. And see generally Ingman [1970] J.B.L. 109.

[765] *Balfour v Balfour*, above n.764 at 578: it would clearly be undesirable to enforce such agreements in accordance with their original terms, however much the position of the parties had changed.

[766] *Pettitt v Pettitt* [1970] A.C. 777, 816.

[767] *e.g. Gage v King* [1961] 1 Q.B. 188; *Spellman v Spellman* [1961] 1 W.L.R. 921; *cf. Re Beaumont (dec'd.)* [1980] Ch. 444, 453; *cf. Lloyds Bank plc v Rosset* [1991] A.C. 107.

[768] *Pearce v Merriman* [1904] 1 K.B. 80; *cf. Morris v Tarrant* [1971] 2 Q.B. 143.

[769] *e.g. Merritt v Merritt* [1970] 1 W.L.R. 1211; *cf. Tanner v Tanner* [1975] 1 W.L.R. 1346 as explained in *Horrocks v Forray* [1976] 1 W.L.R. 230; *Re Windle* [1975] 1 W.L.R. 1628 (doubted in *Re Kumar* [1993] 1 W.L.R. 224); contrast *Vaughan v Vaughan* [1953] 1 Q.B. 762 (below, para.2–183).

to leave her a house if she married him she was able to enforce the promise although it was made informally and in affectionate terms.[770]

Domestic agreements between civil partners. The authorities relating to the effects of domestic agreements between spouses, discussed in paragraph 2–169 above, could, it is submitted, be applied by analogy to such agreements between persons of the same sex who had entered into a civil partnership under the Civil Partnership Act 2004.[771] The Act is silent on the point but present submission derives support from the fact that it treats civil partnerships as analogous to marriages for many legal purposes, including (in particular) statutory provisions relating to the legal effects of agreements between the parties[772] or for the benefit of one of them.[773] **2–170**

Domestic agreements between other cohabitants. Issues of contractual intention can similarly arise where a couple make an agreement with regard to a house in which they live together in a quasi-marital relationship without being married or having entered into a civil partnership.[774] Where, for example, a man and a woman so cohabited, it was said to be "part of the bargain between the parties expressed or to be implied that the [woman] should contribute her labour towards the reparation of the house in which she was to have some beneficial interest."[775] This "bargain" was enforceable, either by way of contract[776] or by way of constructive trust.[777] Formal requirements (imposed in 1989) for contracts for the creation of interests in land[778] make it unlikely[779] that such an arrangement could now take effect as such a contract, but they would not prevent it from taking effect by way of constructive trust[780] or of proprietary estoppel.[781] Even where (in a case of this kind) the woman did nothing to increase the value of the house (and so had no "proprietary interest in the property"[782]) the man's promise that the house should continue to be available for her and the couple's children was held to be enforceable as a contractual licence as she had moved out **2–171**

---

770 *Synge v Synge* [1894] 1 Q.B. 466, *cf. Jennings v Brown* (1842) 9 M. & W. 496 (promise to discarded mistress).

771 Civil Partnership Act 2004, s.1.

772 *ibid.*, s.73.

773 *ibid.*, s.70.

774 Either because they have chosen not to enter into such a partnership or because, not being of the same sex, they were not eligible to do so: see Civil Partnership Act 2004, s.1(1).

775 *Eves v Eves* [1975] 1 W.L.R. 1338, 1345.

776 *ibid. per* Browne L.J. and Brightman J.

777 *ibid.* at 1342, *per* Lord Denning, M.R.; for this basis of liability, see *Grant v Edwards* [1986] Ch. 638; *cf. Lloyds Bank plc v Rosset* [1991] A.C. 107, 129, *Burns v Burns* [1984] Ch. 317; Lowe and Smith (1984) 47 M.L.R. 341; Dewar, 735.

778 Law of Property (Miscellaneous Provisions) Act 1989, s.2; below, para.4–052.

779 *cf. Taylor v Dickens* [1998] F.L.R. 806, 819; the reasoning of this case was doubted, but not on the issue of contractual intention, in *Gillett v Holt* [2001] Ch. 210, 227; s.2(1) of the 1989 Act (above, n.778) requires the contract to be made in writing incorporating all its "expressly agreed" terms in a document (or documents, where contracts are exchanged), and if the promise in *Eves v Eves* (above, at n.775) was indeed implied, it could be argued that there were no "expressly agreed" terms.

780 The formal requirements imposed by the 1989 Act (above n.778) do not apply to "the creation or operation of . . . constructive trusts": s.2(5).

781 See below, para.3–114 n.592.

782 *Tanner v Tanner* [1975] 1 W.L.R. 1346, 1351.

of her rent-controlled flat in reliance on the promise.[783] But in another case,[784] in which there was no such element of reliance, it was held that the provision by a married man of a house for his mistress did not give rise to a legally binding promise that she should be allowed to stay in the house. Even when such a promise can be established, it would (whether or not the parties were spouses or civil partners) be more difficult to show that some less important promise, *e.g.* as to the amount of money to be provided by way of a dress or housekeeping allowance, was intended to have contractual effect.

2–172 **Other shared households.** Where adult members of a family (other than husband and wife, persons living together as such or civil partners) share a common household, the financial terms on which they do so may well be intended to have contractual effect. This was for example held to be the position where a young couple were induced to sell their house, and to move in with their elderly relations, by the latters' promise to leave them a share of the proposed joint home. The argument that this promise was not intended to be legally binding was rejected as the young people would not have taken the important step of selling their own house on the faith of a merely social arrangement.[785] But while the common household was a going concern the parties must have made many arrangements about its day-to-day management which were not intended to be legally binding. In cases of this kind, it may often be clear that there is some contract, but the terms of the arrangement may be so imprecise that it is hard to say just what obligation it imposes. For example, in *Hussey v Palmer*[786] a lady spent £600 on having a room added to her son-in-law's house, on the understanding that she could live there for the rest of her life. When she left voluntarily, about a year later, it was held that there was no contract of loan in respect of the £600[787]; but it seems likely that there was a contract to allow her to live in the room for the rest of her life.

2–173 An agreement between persons who share a common household may be a contract if it has nothing to do with the routine management of the household. Thus in *Simpkins v Pays*[788] three ladies who lived in the same house took part in a fashion competition run by a newspaper. They agreed to send in their entries on one coupon and to share the prize which any entry might win; and the agreement to share was held to be legally binding.

2–174 **Parents and children.** Similar issues of contractual intention can arise from promises between parents and children. An informal promise by a parent to pay

---

[783] *Tanner v Tanner*, above.

[784] *Horrocks v Forray* [1976] 1 W.L.R. 320; *cf. Coombes v Smith* [1986] 1 W.L.R. 808; *Windeler v Whitehall* [1990] 2 F.L.R. 505.

[785] *Parker v Clark* [1960] 1 W.L.R. 286; *cf. Schaefer v Schuhman* [1972] A.C. 572; Lee (1972) 88 L.Q.R. 320; *Tanner v Tanner* [1975] 1 W.L.R. 1346; *Nunn v Dalrymple*, *The Times*, August 3, 1989.

[786] [1972] 1 W.L.R. 1286.

[787] But she recovered the £600 on equitable grounds; below, para.3–139; *cf. Re Sharpe* [1980] 1 W.L.R. 219, where there was both a loan and an equitable right in the lender; *Briggs v Rowan* [1991] E.G.C.S. 6.

[788] [1955] 1 W.L.R. 975.

a child an allowance during study is not normally a contract, though it may become one if, for example, it is part of a bargain made to induce the child to give up some occupation so as to enter on some particular course of study.[789] Similarly, there is not normally a contract where a mother agrees to nurse her child who has fallen ill or been injured, even though she has to give up her work to do so.[790] Conversely, it has been held that the gift of a flat by a mother to her daughter on condition that the daughter should look after the mother there did not amount to a contract because it was not intended to have contractual force.[791] On the other hand, where a mother bought a house as a residence for her son and daughter-in-law on the terms that they should pay her £7 per week to pay off the purchase price, this was held to amount to a contractual licence which the mother could not revoke so long as either of the young couple kept up the payments.[792]

Agreements giving discretion to one party whether to perform. An agreement may consist of mutual promises one of which gives a very wide discretion to one party. In such a case the discretionary promise may be too vague to constitute consideration for the other party's promise which may therefore be unenforceable.[793] But if the other party has actually performed (so that there can be no question that *he* has provided consideration), the further question may arise whether the discretionary promise can be enforced; and this raises an issue of contractual intention. In *Taylor v Brewer*[794] the claimant agreed to do work for a committee who resolved that he should receive "such remuneration . . . as should be deemed right." His claim for a reasonable remuneration for work done failed: the promise to pay was "merely an engagement of honour."[795] This case is now more often distinguished than followed,[796] but its reasoning would still be applied if the wording made it clear that the promise was not intended to be legally binding.[797] *A fortiori*, there is no contract where performance by *each* party was left to that party's discretion.[798] Where, however, an agreement is clearly intended to have contractual effect, there is judicial support for the view that a discretion conferred by it on one party cannot "however widely worded . . . be exercised for purposes contrary to those of the instrument by which it is 2–175

[789] See *Jones v Padavatton* [1969] 1 W.L.R. 328, 333; *cf. Shadwell v Shadwell* (1860) 9 C.B.(N.S.) 159; below, para.3–073.

[790] If there is very clear evidence of contractual intention there may be a binding contract, as in *Haggar v de Placido* [1972] 1 W.L.R. 716. But in practice such "contracts" were made only as devices to enable the value of the mother's services to be recovered from a tortfeasor who had injured the child, and for this purpose they are now unnecessary: *Donelly v Joyce* [1974] Q.B. 454.

[791] *Ellis v Chief Adjudication Officer* [1998] 1 F.L.R. 184, 188.

[792] *Hardwick v Johnson* [1978] 1 W.L.R. 683, *per* Roskill and Browne L.JJ.; Lord Denning, M.R. thought that there was no contract but reached the same conclusion on other grounds; *cf. Collier v Hollingshead* (1984) 272 E.G. 941.

[793] Below, para.3–025; *Stabilad Ltd v Stephens & Carter (No.2)* [1999] 2 All E.R. (Comm) 651 at 659–660.

[794] (1813) 1 M. & S. 290; *cf. Shallcross v Wright* (1850) 12 Beav. 558; *Roberts v Smith* (1859) 28 L.J.Ex. 164; *Robinson & Commissioners of Customs & Excise*, *The Times*, April 28, 2000.

[795] (1813) 1 M. & S. 290, 291.

[796] Vol.II, para.39–074; *cf. Re Brand's Estate* [1936] 3 All E.R. 374.

[797] *cf. Re Richmond Gate Property Co Ltd* [1965] 1 W.L.R. 335.

[798] *Carmichael v National Power plc* [1999] 1 W.L.R. 2042; contrast *Franks v Reuters Ltd* [2003] EWCA Civ 417; *The Times*, April 23, 2003.

conferred."[799] The court may also be able to control the exercise of such a contractual discretion by holding that it must be exercised "rationally and in good faith"[800]; but, if these requirements are satisfied, there is no further requirement that the exercise of the discretion must be reasonable.[801]

Even where an agreement does not, from its inception, impose any contractual obligation on either party, such obligations may arise from the subsequent conduct of the parties in pursuance of it. This was the position where a local authority engaged the claimant as home tutor for pupils who were unable to attend school.[802] The arrangement did not bind the claimant to accept, or the authority to offer, any pupil but once the claimant had agreed to accept a particular pupil, she was obliged to fulfil her commitment to that pupil and the authority was bound to provide work in relation to that pupil until the engagement in relation to him had run its course. Thus a series of contracts arose in relation to each pupil offered to, and accepted by, the claimant, even though the original arrangement in pursuance of which the pupils were sent had no contractual force.

2–176 **Agreements giving discretion to rescind.** An agreement may give one party a discretion to rescind. That party will not be bound if his promise means "I will only perform if I do not change my mind." But the power to rescind may only be inserted as a safeguard in certain eventualities which are not exhaustively stated, for example, where a contract for the sale of land entitles the vendor to rescind if the purchaser persists in some requisition or objection which the vendor is "unable *or unwilling* to satisfy." In such a case there is a contract and the court will control the exercise of the power to rescind by insisting that the vendor must not rescind "arbitrarily, or capriciously, or unreasonably. Much less, can he act in bad faith."[803]

---

[799] *Equitable Life Assurance Society v Hyman* [2002] 1 A.C. 408 at 460, *per* Lord Cooke, giving this as an alternative ground for the decision while also accepting the "implied term" reasoning of the majority.

[800] *Horkulak v Cantor Fitzgerald Ltd* [2004] EWCA Civ 1287, [2005] I.C.R. 402 at [48] (discretionary bonus on dismissal); *cf. ibid.*, at [46]; contrast *Keen v Commerzbank AG* [2006] EWCA Civ 1536, [2007] I.C.R. 623, where an employer's "very wide discretion" in relation to a bonus had not "been exercised irrationally" (at [59], [60]).

[801] *Ludgate Insurance Co Ltd v Citibank NA* [1998] Lloyd's Rep. IR 221 at [35]–[36]; *Jani-King (GB) Ltd v Pula Enterprises Ltd* [2007] EWHC 2433 (QB), [2008] 1 All E.R. (Comm) 457 at [33]–[34].

[802] *Prater v Cornwall CC* [2006] EWCA Civ 102, [2006] I.C.R. 731.

[803] *Selkirk v Romar Investments Ltd* [1963] 1 W.L.R. 1415, 1422; *cf.* the authorities on agreements subject to a condition depending on the "satisfaction" of one party, discussed above, para.2–154. A contract term giving a wide discretion to one party may be subject to the requirement of reasonableness under Unfair Contract Terms Act 1977, s.3(2)(b)(ii), or may not be binding on a consumer under Unfair Terms in Consumer Contracts Regulations 1999, (SI 1999/2083), especially Sch.2, para.1(c). In the cases of agreements subject to the "satisfaction" of one party, there is *no* general rule requiring that party to act in good faith or reasonably: see *Stabilad Ltd v Stephens & Carter Ltd* [1999] 2 All E.R. (Comm) 651 at 622, above, para.2–154 such agreements can be distinguished from contracts which give one party a discretion to rescind since the exercise of such a discretion deprives the other party of rights under an existing contract, while in the "satisfaction" cases there is no such contract unless the party's satisfaction is communicated to the other. Similar reasoning serves to distinguish a contractual discretion to rescind (here under discussion) from a contractual discretion of the kind discussed in para.2–175 above at n.801.

Collective agreements. The terms of collective agreements between trade unions and employers (or employers' associations) may be incorporated in individual employment contracts and so become binding on the parties to those contracts.[804] But the general common law view was that such collective agreements were not legally binding between the parties to them[805]; and in 1969 this view was upheld in *Ford Motor Co Ltd v A.E.F.*[806] The Trade Union and Labour Relations (Consolidation) Act 1992 goes further in providing that a collective agreement[807] is "conclusively presumed not to have been intended by the parties to be a legally enforceable contract" unless it is in writing and expressly provides the contrary (in which case the agreement is conclusively presumed to have been intended by the parties to be a legally enforceable contract).[808] To displace the presumption that a collective agreement is not intended to be a legally binding contract, the agreement must provide that it was intended to be *legally* binding. The presumption is not displaced by a statement that the parties shall be "bound by the agreement" for this may mean that they are bound in honour only.[809] 2–177

Free travel passes. There are conflicting decisions on the question whether the issue and acceptance of a free travel pass amounts to a contract. In *Wilkie v L.P.T.B.*[810] it was held that such a pass issued by a transport undertaking to one of its own employees did not amount to a contract. But the contrary conclusion was reached in *Gore v Van der Lann*[811] where the pass was issued to an old age pensioner. This conclusion was based on the ground that an application for the pass had been made on a form couched in contractual language; and *Wilkie's* case was distinguished on the ground that the pass there was issued to the employee "as a matter of course . . . as one of the privileges attaching to his employment."[812] But as the pass in *Gore's* case was issued expressly on the "understanding" that it constituted only a licence subject to conditions, the distinction seems, with respect, to be a tenuous one. 2–178

---

[804] *Robertson v British Gas Corp.* [1983] I.C.R. 351; *Marley v Forward Trust Group* [1986] I.C.R. 891; *cf. N.C.B. v N.U.M.* [1986] I.C.R. 736; contrast *Kaur v MG Rover Group Ltd* [2004] EWCA Civ 1507, [2005] I.C.R. 625, where a term to the effect that there would be no compulsory redundancies was held not to have been incorporated in individual employment contracts as it was not intended to constitute a binding contractual commitment. And see below, para.13–019, Vol.II, para.39–045.

[805] Kahn-Freund in Flanders and Clegg (eds.), *The System of Industrial Relations in Great Britain*, Ch.2; and in Ginsberg (ed.), *Law and Opinion in England in the 20th Century*, p.215; Grunfeld, *Modern Trade Union Law*, pp.219–220; Wedderburn, *The Worker and the Law* (3rd ed.), pp.318–322; Report of the Royal Commission on Trade Unions and Employers Associations, Cmnd. 3623 (1968), paras 470–471.

[806] [1969] 2 Q.B. 303; Selwyn (1969) 32 M.L.R. 377; Hepple [1970] C.L.J. 122.

[807] As defined by s.178(1) and (2) of the 1992 Act.

[808] s.179(1) and (2); *Universe Tankships Inc. v International Transport Workers' Federation (The Universe Sentinel)* [1983] A.C. 366, 380; *Monterosso Shipping Co Ltd v International Transport Workers' Federation (The Rosso)* [1982] 2 Lloyd's Rep. 120; *N.C.B. v N.U.M.* [1986] I.C.R. 736; *cf. Cheall v A.P.E.X.* [1983] A.C. 180, 189 (inter-union agreement). Provisions making collective agreements legally binding seem to be very rare: see *Commission of the European Communities v United Kingdom* [1984] I.C.R. 192, 195.

[809] *N.C.B. v N.U.M.* [1986] I.C.R. 736.

[810] [1947] 1 All E.R. 258.

[811] [1967] 2 Q.B. 31; Odgers (1970) 86 L.Q.R. 69.

[812] [1967] 2 Q.B. at 41.

2–179 **Statements of governmental policy.** In a case[813] arising out of the First World War a statement was made, during the war, on behalf of the Government, to the effect that a certain neutral ship would be allowed to leave a British port if specified conditions were met. It was held that the statement did not amount to a contract: it was "merely an expression of intention to act in a particular way in a certain event."[814]

2–180 **Agreements giving effect to pre-existing rights.** A number of cases support the view that an arrangement which is believed simply to give effect to pre-existing contractual rights is not a contract because the parties had no intention to enter into a *new* contract[815]; this may be true even where the contract giving rise to those rights had been discharged, so long as the parties believed that it was still in existence.[816] But other cases show that contractual intention is not negatived where the conduct of the parties makes it clear that they intended not merely to give effect to their earlier contract but also to enter into a new contract containing additional terms[817]; or merely because the conduct of one party to the alleged new contract consisted of his performance of a contract between him and a third party.[818]

2–181 **Nature of relationship between the parties: clergy.** Contractual intention may sometimes be negatived by the nature of the relationship between the parties.[818a] This view was, for example, taken in a number of cases in which it was held that there was no contract between a minister of the church (or between a person holding a corresponding appointment in a similar religious institution) and the church (or other similar institution) because the relationship was not one "in which the parties intended to create legal relations between themselves so as

---

[813] *Rederiaktiebolaget Amphitrite v R.* [1921] 3 K.B. 500.

[814] *ibid.* at 503; see further below, paras 10–007—10–008.

[815] *Beesly v Hallwood Estates Ltd* [1960] 1 W.L.R. 549, 558; the actual decision was affirmed on other grounds [1961] Ch. 105, while dicta in the decision at first instance were disapproved, on a point not here under discussion, in *Bolton MBC v Torrington* [2003] EWCA Civ 1634, [2004] Ch. 66; *cf. Harvela Investments Ltd v Royal Trust of Canada (C.I.) Ltd* [1986] A.C. 207; *The Aramis* [1989] 1 Lloyd's Rep. 213; Treitel; [1989] L.M.C.L.Q. 162; *Mitsui & Co Ltd v Novorossiysk Shipping Co (The Gudermes)* [1993] 1 Lloyd's Rep. 311; *Glencore Grain Ltd v Flacker Shipping Ltd (The Happy Day)* [2002] EWCA Civ 1068, [2002] 2 Lloyd's Rep. 487 at [63].

[816] *G.F. Sharp & Co v McMillan* [1998] I.R.L.R. 632.

[817] *Furness Withy (Australia) Pty Ltd v Metal Distributors (UK) Ltd (The Amazonia)* [1990] 1 Lloyd's Rep. 238, 241–242; *cf.* the *Stirling* case, below para.2–186 n.851, where it was accepted that a new contract was created by virtue of a subsequent agreement increasing the monthly rent.

[818] *Pyrene v Scindia Navigation Co Ltd* [1954] 2 Q.B. 402; *A.M. Satterthwaite & Co Ltd v New Zealand Shipping Co Ltd (The Eurymedon)* [1975] A.C. 514; *Companie Portorafti Commerciale SA v Ultramar Panama Inc (The Captain Gregos) (No.2)* [1990] 2 Lloyd's Rep. 395 (so far as it relates to BP's claim). *cf. Halifax Building Society v Edell* [1992] Ch. 436, discussed below, para.18–014.

[818a] See, in addition to the cases discussed in this and the two following paragraphs, *M&P Steelcraft Ltd v Ellis* [2008] I.RL.R 355 (relationship between a prisoner and a company for which he had worked under a work placement scheme organised by the Prison Service and recorded in a tripartite agreement stating that the agreement was not intended to create legally enforceable rights *held* not to have contractual force).

to make the agreement enforceable in the courts."[819] But in *Percy v Board of National Mission of the Church of Scotland*,[820] the House of Lords held that the appointment of Ms Percy as an associate minister of the Church of Scotland had given rise to a "contract of employment"[821] for the purpose of the statutory prohibition against sex discrimination in such a contract. One possibility is that this case can be distinguished from earlier authorities on the ground that these were concerned with claims for unfair dismissal, the statutory requirements for which were expressed in different terms from those applicable to sex discrimination claims.[822] But the better view is that *Percy's* case marks a change in the judicial approach to the question of contractual intention in cases of this kind. This view is supported by statements of Lord Nicholls in that case that "in this regard there seems to be no cogent reason today to draw a distinction between a post whose duties are primarily religious and a post within the church where this is not so"[823]; and that in the context of statutory protection of employees it was "time to recognise that employment arrangements between the church and its ministers should not lightly be taken as intended to have no legal effect."[824] It has been said that the case has reversed the former presumption that, in such a relationship, the parties are unlikely to have intended to have entered into a legally binding contract.[825] It was accepted in *Percy's* case that "many arrangements . . . in church matters" were such that "viewed objectively . . . the parties [could] not be taken to have intended to enter into a legally binding contract" because of the "breadth and looseness [of the arrangements] and the circumstances in which they were undertaken".[826] But this principle "could not be carried into arrangements which on their face were intended to give rise to legal obligations"[827] such as the offer and acceptance of employment, specifying in some detail the rights and obligations of the parties.[828]

Civil Servants. A development similar to that described in paragraph 2–181 above has occurred in the judicial approach to the legal relationship between the Crown and its civil servants. At one time, it was thought that this relationship was not contractual because the Crown did not, when the relationship was entered into, have the necessary contractual intention.[829] But in one of the cases which supported that view it was said that there was evidence that the Crown was 2–182

819 *President of the Methodist Conference v Parfit* [1984] Q.B. 368 at 378; approved in *Davies v Presbyterian Church of Wales* [1986] 1 W.L.R. 323 (no contract of employment between pastor and Presbyterian church); Woolman (1986) 102 L.Q.R. at 356; *Santok Sing v Guru Nanak Gurdwara* [1990] I.C.R. 309; *Birmingham Mosque Trust v Alawi* [1992] I.C.R. 435; *Diocese of Southwark v Coker* [1998] I.C.R. 140.

820 [2005] UKHL 73, [2006] 2 A.C. 28.

821 Within Sex Discrimination Act 1975, s.82(1).

822 Employment Rights Act 1996, ss.94(1), 230(1) and (2).

823 *Percy's* case, above n.819, at [26]; *cf. ibid.*, at [152].

824 *ibid.*, at [26].

825 *New Testament Church of God v Stewart* [2007] I.R.L.R. 168 (EAT).

826 *Percy's* case, above n.819, at [23].

827 *ibid.*, at [23].

828 *ibid.*, at [24]; *cf.* at [112], [137].

829 *R. v Civil Service Appeal Board Ex p. Bruce* [1988] I.C.R. 649; affirmed on other grounds [1989] I.C.R. 171; *Mclaren v Home Office, The Times*, May 18, 1989.

reconsidering its position on the point[830]; and more recently it has been held[831] that the requirement of contractual intention was satisfied in spite of the fact that the terms of appointment stated that "a civil servant does not have a contract of employment" but had rather "a letter of appointment." These words were not sufficient to turn a relationship which, apart from them, had all the characteristics of a contract into one which was binding in honour only.

2–182A **Police constables.** It has been said that a police constable is a person who "holds an office and is not therefore strictly an employee;"[832] and that there is "no contract between a police officer and a chief constable."[833] But it does not follow that the relationship is binding in honour only: the resulting relationship is "closely analogous to a contract of employment"[834] so that duties analogous to those arising out of such a contract may be owed to the constable.

2–183 **Vague agreements.** Another relevant factor is the degree of precision with which the agreement is expressed. In one case it was held that a husband's promise to let his deserted wife stay in the matrimonial home had no contractual force because it was not "intended by him, or understood by her, to have any contractual basis or effect."[835] The promise was too vague: it did not state for how long or on what terms the wife could stay in the house.[836] So, too, the use of deliberately vague language was held to negative contractual intention where a property developer reached an "understanding" with a firm of solicitors to employ them in connection with a proposed development, but neither side entered into a definite commitment.[837] For the same reason, "letters of intent"[838] may lack the force of legally binding contracts.[839] The assumption in all these cases was that the parties had reached agreement, and in them lack of contractual intention prevented that agreement from having legal effect. Vagueness may also be a ground for concluding that the parties had never reached agreement at all.[840] This issue is separate from that of contractual intention, which strictly speaking

---

[830] *R. v Civil Service Appeal Board Ex p. Bruce*, above, at 659.

[831] *R. v Lord Chancellor's Department Ex p. Nangle* [1991] I.C.R. 743; *cf.* Trade Union and Labour Relations (Consolidation) Act 1992, ss.62(7), 245: "deemed [for certain purposes] to constitute a contract."

[832] *White v Chief Constable of the South Yorkshire Police* [1999] A.C. 455 at 481. *cf. Essex Strategic Health Authority v David-John* [2003] Lloyd's Rep. Med. 586 (relationship between general practitioner and Health Authority not contractual).

[833] *White's* case, above n.832 at p.497.

[834] *ibid.*, see also *Waters v Commissioner of Police to the Metropolis* [2000] 1 W.L.R. 1607, 1616.

[835] *Vaughan v Vaughan* [1953] 1 Q.B. 762, 765; *cf. Booker v Palmer* [1942] 2 All E.R. 674; *Horrocks v Forray* [1976] 1 W.L.R. 230; *Windeler v Whitehall* [1990] 2 F.L.R. 505.

[836] *cf. Jones v Padavatton* [1969] 1 W.L.R. 328; and see *Gould v Gould* [1970] 1 Q.B. 275; *Layton v Morris*, *The Times*, December 11, 1985.

[837] *J.H. Milner & Son v Percy Bilton Ltd* [1966] 1 W.L.R. 1582.

[838] Above, para.2–125.

[839] *cf. Snelling v John G. Snelling Ltd* [1973] 1 Q.B. 87, 93; *Montreal Gas Co v Vasey* [1900] A.C. 595; *B.S.C. v Cleveland Bridge & Engineering Co Ltd* [1984] 1 All E.R. 504; *cf. Turiff Construction Ltd v Regalia Knitting Mills* (1971) 222 E.G. 169 (letter of intent held to be a collateral contract to pay for preliminary work); *Wilson Smithett & Cope (Sugar) Ltd v Bangladesh Sugar Industries Ltd* [1986] 1 Lloyd's Rep. 378 (letter of intent held to be an acceptance); *Kleinwort Benson Ltd v Malaysian Mining Corp.* [1989] 1 W.L.R. 379 ("letters of comfort").

[840] Above, para.2–139.

concerns only the *effect* of an agreement which is first shown to exist.[841] But the two issues are related in borderline cases[842] in which the question whether an agreement exists depends on the degree of vagueness or on whether the vagueness can be resolved, *e.g.* by applying the standard of reasonableness; for in such cases "the absence of any intention to create legal relations"[843] may be a ground for holding that no agreement ever came into existence. Vagueness is, *a fortiori*, a ground on which contractual intention may be negatived where the claim is based, not on an express agreement, but on one alleged to be implied from conduct.[844]

Statements made in jest or anger. Contractual intention may be negatived by the fact that the statement is made in jest or anger, at least if this fact is obvious to the person to whom the statement is made.[845] Thus in *Licences Insurance Corporation v Lawson*[846] the defendant was a director of Company A and of Company B. Company A held shares in Company B and resolved, in the defendant's absence, to sell them. At a later meeting this resolution was rescinded after a heated discussion, during which the defendant said that he would make good any loss which Company A might suffer if it kept the shares. It was held that the defendant was not liable on this undertaking. Nobody at the meeting regarded it as a contract; it was not recorded as such in the minute book; and the defendant's fellow-directors at most thought that he was bound in honour. **2–184**

Other cases. The cases in which there is no intention to create legal relations cannot be exhaustively classified. Contractual intention may, for example, be negatived by evidence that "the agreement was a goodwill agreement . . . made without any intention of creating legal relations,"[847] that it was a sham, made with "no intention . . . to create bona fide legal relations,"[848] that it formed part **2–185**

[841] See *Re Goodchild* [1997] 1 W.L.R. 1216 where it is said at 1226 that one of the parties to alleged mutual wills "regarded the arrangement as irrevocable, but . . . [the other] did not"; *cf. Taylor v Dickens* [1998] 1 F.L.R. 806 (the reasoning of this case is doubted, but not on the issue of contractual intention, in *Gillett v Holt* [2001] Ch. 210). See also *Judge v Crown Leisure Ltd* [2005] EWCA Civ 571, [2005] I.R.L.R. 823 (above, para.2–139) at [23], distinguishing between the two issues; and *Bear Stearns Bank plc v Forum Global Equity Ltd* [2007] EWHC 1576 at [152], [170] and [171], where certainty and intention to create legal relations were treated as separate requirements, both of which were satisfied.

[842] This view is supported by passages in *Judge v Crown Leisure Ltd*, above n.841 at [9] and [24]. For another borderline case, see *Monovan Construction Ltd v Davenport* [2006] EWHC 1094, 108 Con. L.R. 15 where an agreement to do building work for a "provisional guide price" of £100,000 failed to specify the exact scope of the work and was said not to be legally enforceable as it was not intended to have contractual effect (at [17]).

[843] *Baird Textile Holdings Ltd v Marks & Spencer plc* [2001] EWCA Civ 274; [2002] 1 All E.R. (Comm) 737 at [30]; and see above, paras 2–142—2–164.

[844] As in the *Baird* case, above.

[845] So that he cannot rely on the objective test: see above, para.2–161.

[846] (1896) 12 T.L.R. 501.

[847] *Orion Ins. Co plc v Sphere Drake Ins. plc* [1990] 1 Lloyd's Rep. 465, 505; affirmed (by a majority) [1990] 1 Lloyd's Rep. 239; *Mitsui & Co Ltd v Novorossiysk Shipping Co (The Gudermes)* [1993] 1 Lloyd's Rep. 311; *cf. County Ltd v Girozentrale Securities Ltd* [1996] 3 All E.R. 834, 837; *Clarke v Nationwide Anglia Building Society* (1998) 76 P. & C.R. D5.

[848] *Glatzer & Warwick Shipping Co v Bradstone Ltd (The Ocean Enterprise)* [1997] 1 Lloyd's Rep. 449, 484; *Hitch v Stone* [2001] EWCA Civ 63; [2001] S.T.C. 214.

of a course of conduct that was "just an act or a role-play",[849] and that the parties had not yet completed the contractual negotiations.[850] Many other disparate factors can lead to the same conclusion: for example, where an agreement was made that a landlord would not enforce an order for possession against a tenant who had fallen into arrears with her rent, it was held that this agreement did not create a new tenancy as the parties "plainly did not [so] intend"[851]: the agreement merely had the effect of turning the tenant into a "tolerated trespasser."[852]

2–186 The cases on this topic,[853] and in particular those discussed in paras 2–176 to 2–178 above, show that the question of contractual intention is, in the last resort, one of fact[854]; and in doubtful cases its resolution depends, in particular, on the incidence of the burden of proof and on the objective test which generally determines the issue. These points have already been discussed[855]; they help to explain two controversial decisions, in each of which there was a difference of judicial opinion on the issue of contractual intention.

2–187 The first is *Esso Petroleum Ltd v Commissioners of Customs and Excise*.[856] Esso supplied garages with tokens called "World Cup coins," instructing them to give away one coin with every four gallons of petrol sold. The scheme was advertised by Esso and also on posters displayed by garages. By a majority of four to one, the House of Lords held that there was no "sale" of the coins; but that majority was equally divided on the question whether there was any contract at all with regard to the coins. Those who thought that there was a contract[857] relied on the incidence of the burden of proof, and on the argument that "Esso envisaged a bargain of some sort between the garage proprietor and the motorist."[858] But this reasoning relates rather to the intention of Esso than to that of the alleged contracting parties. With regard to their intention, it is submitted that the more realistic view is that of Lords Dilhorne and Russell, who relied on the language of the advertisements (in which the coins were said to be "going free"), and on the minimal value of the coins, as negativing contractual intention.

2–188 The second case is *J. Evans & Son (Portsmouth) Ltd v Andrea Merzario Ltd.*[859] The representative of a firm of forwarding agents told a customer (with whom the firm had long dealt) that his goods would henceforth be packed in containers, and

---

[849] *Sutton v Mishcon Reya* [2003] EWHC 3166 (Ch), [2004] Fam. Law 247 at [26].

[850] *Manatee Towing Co v Oceanbulk Maritime SA (The Bay Ridge)* [1999] 2 All E.R. (Comm) 306, 329; *Jackson v Thakrar* [2007] EWHC 271 (TCC), [2007] B.P.I.R. 167.

[851] *Burrows v Brent LBC* [1996] 1 W.L.R. 1448, 1454; *cf. Stirling v Leadenhall Residential 2 Ltd* [2001] EWCA Civ 1011; [2001] 3 All E.R. 645: agreement as to *rate* at which payments under a court order for rent arrears were to be made held not to give rise to a new tenancy.

[852] *Burrows* case, above n.851, at 1455.

[853] Above, paras 2–162 *et seq.*

[854] See *Zakhem International Construction Ltd v Nippon Kohan KK* [1987] 2 Lloyd's Rep. 596.

[855] Above, paras 2–159—2–161.

[856] [1976] 1 W.L.R. 1; Atiyah (1976) 39 M.L.R. 335.

[857] Lords Simon and Wilberforce. Lord Fraser, who dissented on the main issue, took the same view.

[858] [1976] 1 W.L.R. 1, 6.

[859] [1976] 1 W.L.R. 1078; Adams (1977) 40 M.L.R. 227.

that these would be carried under deck. About a year later, one such container was carried on deck and lost. At first instance,[860] Kerr J. held that the promise was not intended to be legally binding since it was made in the course of a courtesy call, not related to any particular transaction, and indefinite with regard to its future duration. The Court of Appeal, however, held[861] that the promise did have contractual force, relying principally on the importance attached by the customer to the carriage of his goods under deck, and on the fact that he would not have agreed to the new mode of carriage but for the promise. The case is no doubt a borderline one, but it is submitted that Kerr J.'s view accords more closely with the objective test of contractual intention. In most cases, that test prevents the promisor from relying on his subjective intention not to enter into a contractual undertaking; but it should equally prevent the promisee's subjective intention (if not known to the promisor) from being decisive. The Court of Appeal appears with respect to have attached too much weight to the customer's subjective intention, and too little weight to the circumstances in which the promise was made.

[860] [1975] 1 Lloyd's Rep. 162.

[861] [1976] 1 W.L.R. 1078; cited with apparent approval of the outcome in *Daewoo Heavy Industries Ltd v Klipriver Shipping Ltd (The Kapitan Petko Voivoda)* [2003] EWCA Civ 451; [2003] 1 All E.R. (Comm) 801 at [19], [40].

CHAPTER 3

CONSIDERATION[1]

		PARA.
1.	Introduction	3–001
2.	Definitions	3–004
3.	Adequacy of consideration	3–014
4.	The concept of "valuable" consideration	3–022
5.	Past consideration	3–026
6.	Consideration must move from the promisee	3–036
7.	Compromise and forbearance to sue	3–046
	(a) Valid claims	3–047
	(b) Invalid or doubtful claims	3–050
	(c) Actual forbearance	3–057
8.	Existing duties as consideration	3–061
	(a) Public duty	3–062
	(b) Duty imposed by contract with promisor	3–065
	(c) Duty imposed by contract with a third party	3–072
9.	Discharge and variation of contractual duties	3–076
	(a) Rescission	3–077
	(b) Variation	3–079
	(i) Requirement of consideration	3–079
	(ii) Common law mitigations	3–081
	(iii) Equitable mitigations	3–085
10.	Part payment of a debt	3–115
	(a) General rule	3–115
	(b) Limitations at common law	3–118
	(c) Limitations in equity	3–128
11.	Proprietary estoppel	3–137
	(a) Nature of the doctrine	3–137
	(b) Bases of liability	3–139
	(c) Conditions giving rise to liability	3–144
	(d) Effects of the doctrine	3–149
	(e) Comparison with other doctrines	3–160
12.	Special cases	3–165

1. INTRODUCTION

General. In English law, a promise is not, as a general rule, binding as a contract unless it is either made in a deed or supported by some "consideration." The purpose of the doctrine of consideration is to put some legal limits on the enforceability of agreements even where they are intended to be legally binding and are not vitiated by some factor such as mistake, misrepresentation, duress or illegality. The existence of such limits is not a peculiarity of English law: for example, in some civil law countries certain promises which in England are not **3–001**

[1] Sutton, *Consideration Reconsidered* (1974); Shatwell (1955) 1 *Sydney Law Review* 289.

binding for "want of consideration" cannot be enforced unless they are made in some special form, *e.g.* by a notarised writing.[2] The view was, indeed, at one time put forward in England that consideration was only evidence of the intention of the parties to be bound, and that (at any rate in the case of certain commercial contracts), such evidence could equally well be furnished by writing.[3] But the view that agreements (other than those contained in deeds) were binding without consideration merely because they were in writing was rejected over 200 years ago,[4] though it has been revived as a proposal for law reform.[5] The present position therefore is that English law limits the enforceability of agreements (other than those contained in deeds) by reference to a complex and multifarious body of rules known as "the doctrine of consideration."

3–002 **Informal gratuitous promises.** The doctrine of consideration is based on the idea of reciprocity: that "something of value in the eye of the law"[6] must be given for a promise in order to make it enforceable as a contract. It follows that an informal gratuitous promise does not amount to a contract.[7] A person or body to whom a promise of a gift is made from purely charitable or sentimental motives gives nothing for the promise; and the claims of such a promisee are regarded as less compelling than those of a person who has provided (or promised) some return for the promise.[8] The invalidity of informal gratuitous promises of this kind can also be supported on the ground that their enforcement could prejudice third parties such as creditors of the promisor.[9] Such promises, too, may be rashly made[10]; and the requirements of executing a deed or giving value provide at least some protection against this danger.

3–003 **Other promises without consideration.** The doctrine of consideration, however, also struck at many promises which were not "gratuitous" in any ordinary or commercial sense. These applications of the doctrine were brought within its scope by stressing that consideration must be not merely "something of value," but "something of value *in the eye of the law.*"[11] The law in certain cases refused to recognise the "value" of acts or promises even though they would, or might, be regarded as valuable by a lay person. This refusal was based on many disparate policies; so that "promises without consideration" included many

---

[2] See generally, von Mehren (1959) 72 Harv.L.Rev. 1009.

[3] *Pillans v Van Mierop* (1765) 3 Burr. 1663.

[4] *Rann v Hughes* (1778) 7 T.R. 350n; 4 Bro.P.C. 27.

[5] Law Revision Committee, 6th Interim Report, Cmnd. 5449 (1937), para.29; for comments on this and other proposals in the Report, see Lord Wright, *Legal Essays and Addresses*, p.287; Hamson (1938) 54 L.Q.R. 233; Hays (1941) 41 Col.L.Rev. 849; Chloros (1968) 17 I.C.L.Q. 137; Beatson [1992] C.L.P. 1. In many of the United States, writing is (at least for some purposes) regarded as a substitute for consideration: *Farnsworth on Contracts*, (4th ed.) para.2.18.

[6] *Thomas v Thomas* (1842) 2 Q.B. 851, 859; *Hill v Haines* [2007] EWCA Civ 1284, [2008] 2 All E.R. 901 at [79], citing para.3–002 of this book (in its 29th edition) with apparent approval.

[7] *Re Hudson* (1885) 54 L.J. Ch. 811; *Re Cory* (1912) 29 T.L.R. 18; *Williams v Roffey Bros & Nicholls (Contractors) Ltd* [1991] 1 Q.B. 1, 19.

[8] *cf.* Eisenberg, 85 Cal.L.Rev. 821 (1997).

[9] *Eastwood v Kenyon* (1840) 11 Ad. & E. 438, 451.

[10] *Beaton v McDivitt* (1988) 13 N.S.W.L.R. 162 at 170. It is often easier to promise to make a gift than actually to make one.

[11] See above, at n.6.

different kinds of transactions which, at first sight, had little in common.[12] It is this fact which is the cause of the very great complexity of the doctrine; and which has also led to its occasional unwarranted extensions and hence to demands for reform of the law.[13]

2. DEFINITIONS

Benefit and detriment. The traditional definition of consideration concentrates on the requirement that "something of value" must be given and accordingly states that consideration is either some detriment to the promisee (in that he may give value) or some benefit to the promisor (in that he may receive value).[14] Usually, this detriment and benefit are merely the same thing looked at from different points of view. Thus payment by a buyer is consideration for the seller's promise to deliver and can be described either as a detriment to the buyer or as a benefit to the seller; and conversely delivery by a seller is consideration for the buyer's promise to pay and can be described either as a detriment to the seller or as a benefit to the buyer. It should be emphasised that these statements relate to the consideration *for each promise* looked at separately. For example, the seller suffers a "detriment" when he delivers the goods and this enables him to enforce the buyer's promise to pay the price. It is quite irrelevant that the seller has made a good bargain and so gets a benefit from the performance of the contract. What the law is concerned with is the consideration *for a promise*—not the consideration *for a contract*. 3–004

Either sufficient. Under the traditional definition, it is sufficient if there is either a detriment to the promisee or a benefit to the promisor. Thus detriment to the promisee suffices even though the promisor does not benefit[15]: for example if A guarantees B's bank overdraft and the promisee bank suffers detriment by advancing money to B, then A is bound by his promise, even though he gets no benefit from the advance to B.[16] One view, indeed, was that "Detriment to the promisee is of the essence of the doctrine, and benefit to the promisor is, when it exists, merely an accident."[17] But in a number of cases promises have been 3–005

---

[12] *cf.* Corbin, *Contracts*, Vol.I, p.489: "The doctrine of consideration is many doctrines."

[13] See above, n.5.

[14] *Currie v Misa* (1875) L.R. 10 Ex. 153, 162. See also *Barber v Fox* (1670) 2 Wms.Saund. 134, n.(e); *Cooke v Oxley* (1790) 3 T.R. 653, 654; *Jones v Ashburnham* (1804) 4 East 455; *Bainbridge v Firmstone* (1838) 8 A. & E. 743, 744; *Thomas v Thomas* (1842) 2 Q.B. 851, 859; *Bolton v Madden* (1873) L.R. 9 Q.B. 55, 56; *Gore v Van der Lann* [1967] 2 Q.B. 31, 42; *Argy Trading Development Co Ltd v Lapid Developments Ltd* [1977] Lloyd's Rep. 67, 75; *Midland Bank & Trust Co Ltd v Green* [1981] A.C. 513, 531; *R. v Braithwaite* [1983] 1 W.L.R. 383, 391; *Johnsey Estates Ltd v Lewis Manley (Engineering) Ltd* [1987] 2 E.G.L.R. 69, 70; *Guiness Mahon & Co Ltd v Kensington & Chelsea Royal B.C.* [1999] Q.B. 215 at 236; *Modahl v British Athletics Federation Ltd* [2001] EWCA Civ. 1447, [2002] 1 W.L.R. 1192 at [50]; *cf.* at [103].

[15] *O'Sullivan v Management Agency & Music Ltd* [1985] Q.B. 428, 459; *Re Dale* [1994] Ch. 31, 38. *cf. Gill & Duffus SA v Rionda Futures* [1994] 2 Lloyd's Rep. 67 at 82.

[16] *cf.* below, para.3–039.

[17] Holdsworth, *History of English Law*, Vol.8, p.11.

enforced in spite of the fact that there was no apparent detriment to the promisee[18]; and these cases support the view that benefit to the promisor is (even without detriment to the promisee) sufficient to satisfy the requirement of consideration.[19]

3–006 **Benefit and detriment may be factual or legal.** The traditional definition of consideration lacks precision because the key notions of "benefit" and "detriment" are used in at least two senses. They may mean, first any act,[20] which is of some value, or secondly, only such acts, the performance of which is not already legally due from the promisee. In the first sense, there is consideration if a benefit or detriment is *in fact* obtained or suffered. When the words are used in the second sense this factual benefit or detriment is disregarded, and a notion of what may be called legal benefit or detriment is substituted. Under this notion, the promisee may provide consideration by doing anything that he was not legally bound to do, whether or not it actually occasions a detriment to him or confers a benefit on the promisor; while conversely he may provide no consideration by doing only what he was legally bound to do, however much this may in fact occasion a detriment to him or confer a benefit on the promisor. The English courts have not consistently adopted either of these senses of the words "benefit" and "detriment." In some of the cases to be discussed in this chapter, factual benefit is stressed[21] even though legal detriment may also have been present; while in others the absence of legal detriment or benefit has in the past been regarded as decisive.[22] One modern authority[23] regards factual benefit to the promisor as sufficient, even in the absence of a legal benefit to him or of a legal detriment to the promisee; and it is possible (though far from certain) that this approach may spread to at least some[24] of the situations in which the courts have in the past insisted on legal benefit or detriment.

3–007 **Other definitions.** The traditional definition of consideration in terms of benefit and detriment is sometimes felt to be unsatisfactory. One cause of dissatisfaction is that it is thought to be wrong to talk of benefit and detriment when both parties expect to, and actually may, benefit from the contract. But this reasoning falls, with respect, into the error of looking at the subject-matter of the definition as the consideration *for a contract*,[25] when the definition is actually concerned with the consideration *for a promise*.[26] Another cause of dissatisfaction is the artificial reasoning that is sometimes necessary to accommodate the

---

[18] *e.g.* below, paras 3–037—3–040, 3–068, 3–125.

[19] *cf. Sandeman Coprimar SA v Transitos y Transportes Integrales SL* [2003] EWCA Civ. 113; [2003] 3 All E.R. 108 at [63], referring only to "benefit" (and not to detriment).

[20] Or forbearance, or promise to do or to forbear. For the sake of simplicity, references in the text are confined to the doing of an act.

[21] *e.g.* in *Bolton v Madden* (1873) L.R. 9 Q.B. 55, below, para.3–040; *cf. R v Att-Gen for England and Wales* [2003] UKPC 22, [2003] E.M.L.R. 24, at [32] ("practical benefit" to promisor).

[22] *e.g.* in some of the existing duty cases discussed in paras 3–068, 3–073, 3–075, below.

[23] *Williams v Roffey Bros & Nicholls (Contractors) Ltd* [1991] 1 Q.B. 1.

[24] *e.g.* to the variation cases discussed in paras 3–079—3–080; but probably not to the forebearance to sue cases discussed in paras 3–050—3–053.

[25] There are traces of this approach in *Williams v Roffey Bros. & Nicholls (Contractors) Ltd* [1991] 1 Q.B. 1, 23: "If both parties benefit from an agreement it is not necessary that each also suffered a detriment."

[26] Above, para.3–004.

cases within the traditional definition. Sir Frederick Pollock has, accordingly, described consideration simply as "the price for which the promise is bought."[27] This statement has been approved in the House of Lords[28]; but if it is to be regarded as a definition of consideration it is defective in being so vague as to give no help in determining whether consideration exists on any given set of facts. A view which leads to even more uncertainty is that consideration "*means* a reason for the enforcement of promises"[29]—that reason being simply "the justice of the case."[30] But "the justice of the case" is in almost all the decided cases highly debatable, so that the suggested definition provides no basis at all for formulating a coherent legal doctrine.[31] A modification of the suggested definition, describing consideration as "a reason for the recognition of an obligation"[32] is open to the same objection. Of course the traditional definition does not provide complete (or even a very high degree of) certainty. But it does state the doctrine in a way that is broadly consistent with the case law on the subject and that gives some basis for predicting the course of future decisions. The traditional definition also has more support in the authorities than any other definition. For these reasons it will be used in this chapter.

Performances and promises as consideration. The consideration for a promise may consist either of a performance rendered by the promisee or by a promise to render a performance. The first possibility is illustrated by cases of unilateral contracts[33] where performance by the promisee of the stipulated act or forbearance (*e.g.* walking from London to York) constitutes the consideration for the promise (usually) to pay a sum of money to the promisee.[34] The second possibility is illustrated by cases in which each party makes a promise to the other, but neither party has yet rendered any performance. The rule that, in such a case, the parties' mutual promises can amount to consideration for each other has long been settled.[35] Hence if a seller promises to deliver goods in six months' time and the buyer to pay for them on delivery, there is an immediately binding 3–008

---

27 *Principles of Contract* (13th ed.), p.133.

28 *Dunlop Pneumatic Tyre Co Ltd v Selfridge Ltd* [1915] A.C. 847, 855.

29 Atiyah, *Consideration in Contracts: A Fundamental Restatement*, Canberra, 1971, p.60. For an earlier, similar statement, see Llewellyn (1931) 40 Yale L.J. at p.741—"any sufficient justification for court enforcement"; but no attempt is there made to suggest that this actually is the law. For further criticism of Atiyah's views, see Treitel (1976) 50 A.L.J. 439. *cf. Colonia Versicherung A.G. v Amoco Oil Co* [1995] 1 Lloyd's Rep. 570, 577 (affirmed without reference to this point [1997] 1 Lloyd's Rep. 261) where the words "(a) the reason for and (b) ample consideration for" a payment clearly treat these concepts as distinct.

30 Atiyah, *loc. cit.* pp.52, 58.

31 *cf.* the description of a similar concept as "potentially very confusing": *Guinness Mahon & Co Ltd v Kensington & Chelsea Royal B.C.* [1999] Q.B. 215 at 216.

32 Atiyah, *Essays on Contract*, pp.179, 183.

33 Above, para.2–078. See also *Carlill v Carbolic Smoke Ball Co* [1892] 2 Q.B. 484; *Budgett v Stratford Co-operative and Industrial Society Ltd* (1916) 32 T.L.R. 378; *Melhuish v Redbridge Citizens Advice Bureau* [2005] I.R.L.R. 415 at [18].

34 The promisee may accept and provide consideration at an earlier stage: see above, para.2–079 and below, para.3–170.

35 See, *e.g. Pecke v Redman* (1555) 1 Dyer 113a; *Joscelin v Shelton* (1557) 3 Leon. 4; *Manwood v Burston* (1586) 2 Leon. 203; *Harrison v Cage* (1698) 12 Mod. 214; Simpson, *A History of the Common Law of Contract*, pp.459–470; Baker (1980) 43 M.L.R. 467, 468 (reviewing Atiyah, *The Rise and Fall of Freedom of Contract*). But a mere proposal falling short of a promise does not suffice: *The Kaliningrad and Nadezhda Krupskaya* [1997] 2 Lloyd's Rep. 35, 39.

contract from which neither party can withdraw, though, of course, performance cannot be claimed till the appointed time. An implied, no less than an express, promise is capable of constituting consideration.[36] A promise can, however, only be regarded as consideration for a counter-promise if the performance of the promise would have been so regarded.[37] It is, for example, settled that part payment of a debt by the debtor on or after the due day does not amount to consideration for a promise by the creditor to forgo the balance,[38] and the position would be exactly the same if the debtor, instead of actually making such a payment, simply promised to do so. Similarly, a promise to make a gift of £100 could not be made binding by a counter-promise to accept it since performance of the counter-promise could not conceivably amount to a benefit to the original promisor or to a detriment to the original promisee. Such benefit or detriment can (in such a case) arise only if the subject-matter of the promised gift is onerous property and the donee makes a counter-promise to discharge the obligations attached to it: *e.g.* to perform the covenants in a lease,[39] or to pay outstanding mortgage instalments[40] or to pay calls on shares.[41] Of course if the property is worth more than the obligations attached to it there will be an element of gift in such a transaction; and special safeguards are provided by law to ensure that certain categories of third parties (such as creditors of the promisor) are not prejudiced by this aspect of the transaction.[42]

3–009 **Mutual promises as consideration for each other.** Some difficulty has been felt in explaining the rule that mutual promises can be consideration for each other. At first sight, it might seem that the mere giving of a promise was not a detriment, nor its receipt a benefit, so as to make the counter-promise binding. It will not do to say that the person making the promise suffers a detriment because he is legally bound to perform it; for if this assumption is made about one of the promises, it must also be made of the other, so that the "explanation" assumes the very point in issue. Probably the reason for the rule is simpler. A person who makes a commercial promise expects to have to perform it (and is in fact under considerable pressure to do so). Correspondingly, one who receives such a promise expects it to be kept. These expectations, which can exist even where the promise is not legally enforceable,[43] are based on commercial morality, and

[36] *Thoresen Car Ferries Ltd v Weymouth Portland BC* [1977] 2 Lloyd's Rep. 614, 619; *The Aramis* [1989] 2 Lloyd's Rep. 213 at 225 (where the claim failed for want of contractual intention).

[37] *Re Dale* [1994] Ch. 31, 38.

[38] Below, para.3–115.

[39] *Price v Jenkins* (1877) 5 Ch.D. 619. In so far as *Thomas v Thomas* (1842) 2 Q.B. 851 (above, para.3–010) is *contra*, it seems to be inconsistent with *Price v Jenkins* (where the "case which is not reported" mentioned at p.620 closely resembles *Thomas v Thomas*); *cf. Johnsey Estates v Lewis & Manley* [1987] 2 E.G.L.R. 69; *Westminster City Council v Duke of Westminster* [1991] 4 All E.R. 136 (reversed in part on other grounds (1992) 24 H.L.R. 572).

[40] *Merritt v Merritt* [1970] 1 W.L.R. 1211.

[41] *Cheale v Kenward* (1858) 3 D. & J. 27.

[42] Insolvency Act 1986, ss.238, 339; and see below, para.3–018 n.99; *Re Kumar* [1993] 1 W.L.R. 224.

[43] *cf. Lipkin Gorman v Karpnale Ltd* [1991] 2 A.C. 548 at 581; the promise under consideration in this case would now be legally enforceable by virtue of Gambling Act 2005, s.335(1); Vol II, para 40–093.

can properly be called a detriment and a benefit; hence they satisfy the requirement of consideration in the case of mutual promises.

Invented consideration. Normally, a party enters into a contract with a view to obtaining the consideration promised by the other: for example, the buyer wants the goods and the seller the price. In the United States it has been said that this is essential, and that "Nothing is consideration that is not regarded as such by both parties."[44] But English courts do not insist on this requirement and may regard an act or forbearance as consideration even though the promisee "did not consciously realise that [he was] subjecting himself to a detriment and [was] giving consideration for the [promisor's] undertaking"[45] or even though it was not the object of the promisor to secure it.[46] They may also treat the possibility of some prejudice to the promisee as a detriment without regard to the question whether it has in fact been suffered.[47] These practices may be called "inventing" consideration,[48] and the temptation to adopt one or the other of them is particularly strong when the act or forbearance which was actually bargained for cannot be regarded as consideration for some reason which is thought to be technical and without merit. In such cases the practice of inventing consideration may help to make the operation of the doctrine of consideration more acceptable; but the practice may also be criticised[49] on the ground that it gives the courts a wide discretion to hold promises binding or not as they please. Thus the argument that the promisee *might* have suffered prejudice by acting in reliance on a promise is in some cases made a basis of decision,[50] while in others precisely the 3–010

---

[44] *Philpot v Gruninger* (1872) 14 Wall. 570, 577; Restatement, *Contracts*, §75(1): "bargained for and given in exchange for the promise"; Restatement 2d, *Contracts*, §75(1) and (2); Williston, *Contracts* (rev.ed.), Vol.1, p.320; Corbin, *Contracts*, §172, is more sceptical. The Restatement 2d, §72 also supports the converse proposition that "any performance which is bargained for is consideration," even though there may be no element of benefit or detriment; but this is subject to important exceptions, especially where the performance bargained for is the settlement of an invalid claim and the performance of an existing duty: see §§73 and 74; as to these topics, see below, paras 3–050—3–075.

[45] *Pitts v Jones* [2007] EWCA Civ. 1301, [2008] Q.B. 76 at [18].

[46] See, for example, below, paras 3–013, 3–016, 3–073, 3–174 and below at n.50; and *cf. Pollwaty Ltd v Abdullah* [1974] 1 W.L.R. 493, discussed by Zuckerman (1975) 38 M.L.R. 384 and Thornely [1975] C.L.J. 26; *cf. Vantage Navigation Corp. v. Sahail and Saud Building Materials Co LLC (The Alev)* [1989] 1 Lloyd's Rep. 138, 147; *Moran v University College Salford (No.2)*, *The Times*, November 23, 1993.

[47] *e.g.* below, n.50.

[48] Atiyah, *loc. cit.* n.29 above, accuses the present editor of having "invented the concept of invented consideration;" but all that the editor can claim to have invented is a phrase for describing what the courts sometimes actually do. The phrase does not imply approval of the practice: see below after n.49. Nor does the phrase necessarily imply inconsistency between decisions, as Atiyah suggests *ibid.*: courts could *consistently* hold that an act or forbearance was consideration although it was not the promisor's object to secure it. In fact, the decisions on the point are not perfectly consistent with each other: see below at nn.50 and 51; but that is hardly unusual in a common law system.

[49] For criticism, see Holmes, *The Common Law*, p.292. In the United States there is less need for "inventing" consideration because of the existence of a broad doctrine of promissory estoppel: see Restatement, *Contracts*, §90, and Restatement 2d, *Contracts*, §90 and below para.3–106.

[50] *Shadwell v Shadwell* (1860) 9 C.B.(N.S.) 159, 174: the consideration was said by Erle C.J. to consist of the possibility that the promisor "*may* have made a most material change in his position . . . " (italics supplied).

same argument is rejected.[51] The practice of "inventing" consideration is, therefore, a source of considerable uncertainty in this branch of the law.

3–011 **Motive and consideration.** In *Thomas v Thomas*[52] a testator shortly before his death expressed a desire that his widow should during her life have the house in which he lived, or £100. After his death, his executors "in consideration of such desire" promised to convey the house to the widow during her life or for so long as she should continue a widow, "provided nevertheless and it is hereby further agreed" that she should pay £1 per annum towards the ground rent, and keep the house in repair. In an action by the widow for breach of this promise, the consideration for it was stated to be the widow's promise to pay and repair. An objection that the declaration omitted to state part of the consideration, *viz.* the testator's desire, was rejected. Patteson J. said: "Motive is not the same thing with consideration. Consideration means something which is of value in the eye of the law moving from the plaintiff."[53] This remark should not be misunderstood: a common motive for making a promise is the desire to obtain the consideration; and an act or forbearance on the part of the promisee may (unless the court is prepared to "invent"[54] a consideration) fail to constitute consideration precisely because it was not the promisor's motive to secure it. What Patteson J. meant was that a motive for promising did not amount to consideration unless two further requirements were satisfied, *viz.*: (i) that the thing secured in exchange for the promise was "of some value in the eye of the law"; and (ii) that it moved from the plaintiff.[55] Consideration and motive are not opposites; the former concept is a subdivision of the latter. The consideration for a promise is (unless the consideration is nominal or invented)[56] always a motive for promising; but a motive for making a promise is not necessarily consideration for it in law. Thus the testator's desire in *Thomas v Thomas* was a motive for the executors' promise but not part of the consideration for it. The widow's promise to pay and repair was another motive for the executors' promise and did constitute the consideration for that promise.

3–012 **Consideration and condition.** *Thomas v Thomas*[57] also illustrates the difference between consideration and condition: the plaintiff's remaining a widow was not part of the consideration but a condition of her entitlement to enforce the executor's promise. On the other hand, in *Re Soames*[58] A promised £3,000 to B if B would set up a school in the running of which A was to have an active part.

---

[51] In *Offord v Davies* (1862) 12 C.B.(N.S.) 748: the argument of counsel (at 750) that "the plaintiff *might* have altered his position in consequence of the guarantie" (italics supplied) was rejected, Erle C.J. being again a member of the court. *cf.* also *Collier v P & M.J. Wright (Holdings)* [2007] EWCA Civ. 1329, [2008] 1 W.L.R. 643 at [27(ii)]; and see below, para.3–015 n.79 and para.3–016 at n.89 for refusal to "invent" consideration.

[52] (1842) 2 Q.B. 851.

[53] At 859; *cf. Hadley v Kemp* [1999] E.M.L.R. 589 at 625.

[54] Above, para.3–010.

[55] Discussion of these requirements forms the bulk of this chapter.

[56] In *Thomas v Thomas* the consideration may not have been adequate, but it was not nominal; *cf. Westminster City Council v Duke of Westminster* [1991] 4 All E.R. 136 (reversed in part on other grounds (1992) 24 H.L.R. 572); below, para.3–020.

[57] Above, para.3–011 at n.52.

[58] (1897) 13 T.L.R. 439; *cf.* below, para.3–170.

It was held that, by establishing the school, B had provided consideration for A's promise. It seems that the distinction between consideration and condition depends, in such cases, on whether "a reasonable man would or would not understand that the performance of the condition was requested as the price or exchange for the promise."[59] In *Thomas v Thomas* the executors had not requested the plaintiff to remain a widow; while in *Re Soames* a request that B should establish the school could be inferred from A's expressed intention to participate in its management. The distinction is further illustrated by *Carlill v Carbolic Smoke Ball Co*[60] where the claimant provided consideration for the defendants' promise by using the smoke-ball; but her catching influenza was a condition of her entitlement to enforce that promise.[61]

Certain limited effects of promises without consideration. A promise that is not supported by consideration may nevertheless give rise to certain legal effects. In particular, English law places certain restrictions on the revocability of a promise where the promisee has acted on it in a way that was intended and could have been anticipated (without having been requested) by the promisor; and it may give a remedy against a promisor who would be unjustly enriched (or otherwise act unconscionably) if he were allowed freely to revoke and did revoke his promise after such action in reliance on it by the promisee. These limited legal effects of promises without consideration are discussed later in this chapter.[62] Here it is only necessary to emphasise that these legal effects do not give such promises the full consequences of a binding contract. Thus the restriction on revocability may be only temporary[63]; breach of the promise may not entitle the injured party to the full loss of bargain damages normally awarded for breach of contract,[64] or may not entitle him to them as of right.[65] Only a promise supported by consideration or made in a deed has these full contractual effects. "Contract" does not exhaust the category of promises having *some* legal effect; it refers, more narrowly, to those promises or agreements leading to the full degree of enforceability accorded by the law to contractual promises.[66] Moreover, while promises without consideration may have some legal effects, the promisee can still gain a number of important practical advantages by showing that he provided consideration. If the promise was supported by consideration, the promisee will 3–013

[59] Williston, *Contracts* (3rd ed.), §112; *cf. Dickinson v Abel* [1969] 1 W.L.R. 295 (where A had promised to pay £10,000 to B if A succeeded (as he did) in buying Blackacre from X. This was said to be "nothing but a conditional promise without consideration" because B had not been requested to do anything to promote the sale by X to A); see also *Ellis v Chief Adjudication Officer* [1998] 1 FLR 184 where performance of the condition was no doubt requested but the actual decision was that an executed gift of a flat failed because the condition (that the donee should look after her mother there) had not been performed. The agreement in that case lacked contractual force for want of contractual intention: above, para.2–173.

[60] [1893] 1 Q.B. 256; stated above, para.2–018.

[61] For the purpose of assessing VAT, a wider test (laid down by European Community Law), requiring only a "direct link" between performance and counterperformance, suffices: see *Rosgill Group Ltd v Customs & Excise Commissioners* [1997] 3 All E.R. 1012, though in that case the English test for what constitutes consideration was also said at 1020 to have been satisfied.

[62] Below, paras 3–081—3–106, 3–128—3–164.

[63] Below, paras 3–096, 3–129, 3–149.

[64] Below, para.3–153—3–159.

[65] Below, para.3–154.

[66] See below, Chs 26 and 27.

not need to show that he had acted in reliance on the promise or that the promisor would be unjustly enriched or would otherwise be acting unconscionably if he went back on the promise; the promise will not be revocable but enforceable according to its terms; and the promisee will be entitled to full loss of bargain damages as of right. The limited legal effects of promises without consideration may have mitigated some of the rigours of the strict doctrine; but they have not eliminated consideration as an essential requirement of a binding contract.[67]

3. ADEQUACY OF CONSIDERATION

3–014 **Courts generally will not judge adequacy.** Under the doctrine of consideration, a promise has no contractual force unless *some* value has been given for it. But as a general rule[68] the courts do not concern themselves with the question whether "adequate" value has been given,[69] or whether the agreement is harsh or one-sided.[70] The fact that a person pays "too much" or "too little" for a thing may be evidence of fraud[71] or mistake, or it may induce the court to imply a term as to the quality of the subject-matter or be relevant to the question whether a contract has been frustrated. But it does not of itself affect the validity of the contract, so that (for example) a promise by a local authority to make "irrationally generous"[72] redeployment payments to certain employees has been enforced.

The present rule is subject to a number of exceptions discussed elsewhere in this book.[73] These indicate that the courts are (even where the legislature has not

[67] See further, below, paras 3–105, 3–164.

[68] For exceptional cases, see below, paras 3–018, 7–126, 7–138, 27–033. See also *Bankway Properties Ltd v Penfold Dunsford* [2001] EWCA Civ. 538; [2001] 1 W.L.R. 1369, where a provision for rent increase in a shorthold tenancy far beyond the amount which (as the landlord knew) the tenant could possibly pay was held to be unenforceable as being inconsistent with the intention of the parties to create an assured tenancy.

[69] *Haigh v Brooks* (1839) 10 A. & E. 309, 320; *Moss v Hall* (1850) 5 Exch. 46, 49–50; *Westlake v Adams* (1858) 5 C.B.(N.S.) 248, 265; *Gravely v Barnard* (1874) L.R. 18 Eq. 518; *Wild v Tucker* [1914] 3 K.B. 36, 39; *Midland Bank & Trust Co Ltd v Green* [1981] A.C. 513, 532; *cf. Ball v National and Grindley's Bank* [1973] Ch. 127, 139; *Langdale v Danby* [1982] 1 W.L.R. 1123; *CCC Films (London) Ltd v Impact Quadrant Films Ltd* [1985] Q.B. 16, 27; *Brady v Brady* [1989] A.C. 755, 775; *Normid Housing Association Ltd v R. John Ralphs* [1989] 1 Lloyd's Rep. 265, 272; *Hill v Haines* [2007] EWCA Civ 1284, [2008] 2 All E.R. 901 at [79], referring to para.3–014 of this book (in it's 29th edition) with apparent approval. *cf.* Barton (1987) 103 L.Q.R. 118. The principle is recognised and preserved by Unfair Terms in Consumer Contracts Regulations 1999 (SI 1999/2033) reg.6(2)(b), giving effect to the EC Directive on Unfair Terms in Consumer Contracts (93/13/EEC), Art.4(2): see *Director General of Fair Trading v First National Bank plc* [2001] UKHL 52; [2002] 1 A.C. 481 at [12], *per* Lord Bingham, with whose reasoning all the other members of the House of Lords agreed. Lord Roger at [64] expresses "no concluded view" on the present point, relying on the reference in Recital 19 of the Directive to "the price/quality ratio." The Recital is not easy to interpret, but at least one possible view is that this "ratio" is *not* relevant to the fairness of the *price* term (first sentence) though it may be relevant to the fairness of *other* terms of the contract.

[70] *Gaumont-British Pictures Corp. v Alexander* [1936] 2 All E.R. 1686. On such facts, the Regulations cited in the previous note would not apply: see Dir.93/13/EEC, Recital 10 and below, paras 15–006 and 15–036.

[71] *Tennent v Tennents* (1870) L.R. 2 Sc. & Div. 6, 9. See also *Rice v Gordon* (1847) 11 Beav. 265; *Cockell v Taylor* (1851) 15 Beav. 103.

[72] *Newbold v Leicester CC* [1999] I.C.R. 1182, 1185.

[73] See above, n.68; Waddams (1976) 39 M.L.R. 393; Tiplady (1983) 46 M.L.R. 601.

intervened) by no means insensitive to the problems raised by unequal or unfair bargains; but in none of them is a promise held invalid merely because adequate value for it has not been given. Some additional factor is required to bring a case within one of the exceptions: for example, the existence of a relationship in which one party is able to take an unfair advantage of the other. In the absence of some such factor, the general rule applies that the courts will enforce a promise so long as *some* value for it has been given: "no bargain will be upset which is the result of the ordinary interplay of forces."[74]

Illustrations. It follows from the principles stated in para.3–014 above that acts or omissions of very small value can be consideration. Thus it has been said that there was consideration for a promise to give a man £50 "if you will come to my house"[75]; that the act of executing a deed could be consideration for a promise to pay money although the deed was void[76]; that the execution of a will can be consideration (for a promise to make, and not to revoke, a similar will) even though the will is in its nature revocable[77]; that to give up a piece of paper without reference to its contents was consideration,[78] and even that to show a person a document was consideration.[79] The mere act of conducting negotiations can similarly satisfy the requirement of consideration, even though the act does not commit the promisee to bringing the negotiations to a successful conclusion.[80] Further illustrations of the principle are provided by a case in which a promise to cut back undergrowth was regarded as consideration for the grant of a contractual licence to occupy land[81] and by one in which an employee's agreement to submit to a temporary change of workplace and to take part in an assessment of his professional competence was held (though it had no easily quantifiable value) to amount to consideration for his employer's promise not to take disciplinary proceedings against him.[82] 3–015

Objects of trifling value. In *Chappell & Co Ltd v Nestlé Co Ltd*,[83] chocolate manufacturers sold gramophone records for 1s. 6d. plus three wrappers of their 3–016

---

[74] *Lloyd's Bank Ltd v Bundy* [1975] Q.B. 326, 336, *per* Lord Denning, M.R.

[75] *Gilbert v Ruddeard* (1608) 3 Dy. 272b (n); *cf. Denton v G.N. Ry.* (1856) 5 E. & B. 860.

[76] *Westlake v Adams* (1858) 5 C.B.(N.S.) 248; perhaps there was also an element of compromise in this case.

[77] *Re Dale* [1994] Ch. 31. *cf. Re Goodchild* [1997] 1 W.L.R. 1216 where a mere "common understanding" (as opposed to definite mutual promises) did not suffice to make B's promise irrevocable, but some effect to it was given by an order in favour of the intended beneficiary under the Inheritance (Provision for Dependants) Act 1975; *Taylor v Dickens* [1998] 1 F.L.R. 806, the reasoning of which was doubted on other grounds in *Gillett v Holt* [2001] Ch. 210.

[78] *Haigh v Brooks* (1839) 10 A. & E. 309, 334; *cf. Foster v Dawber* (1861) 6 Ex. 839; *Aspinall's Club Ltd v Al Zayat* [2007] EWCA Civ 1001 at [30].

[79] *Sturlyn v Albany* (1587) Cro.Eliz. 67; *March v Culpepper* (1628) Cro.Car.70; contrast *Re Charge Card Services* [1987] Ch. 150, 164, affirmed [1989] Ch. 487 (production of charge card and signature of voucher not consideration for a supply of goods, evidently because such "consideration" would be blatantly "invented": *cf.* above, para.3–010).

[80] *Sepoong Engineering Construction Co Ltd v Formula One Management Ltd* [2000] 1 Lloyd's Rep. 602, 611.

[81] *Well Barn Farming Ltd v Backhouse* [2005] EWHC 1520, [2005] 3 E.G.L.R. 109 at [45].

[82] *Palmer v East & North Herefordshire NHS Trust* [2006] EWHC 1997, [2006] Lloyd's Rep. Med 472.

[83] [1960] A.C. 87.

6d. bars of chocolate. It was held that the delivery of the wrappers formed part of the consideration, though the wrappers were of little value to the buyer and were in fact thrown away by the seller. If the delivery of the wrappers formed part of the consideration it could, presumably, have formed the whole of the consideration, so that a promise to deliver records for wrappers alone would have been binding. This case should be contrasted with *Lipkin Gorman v Karpnale Ltd*,[84] where gaming chips supplied by a gaming club to one of its members (and then lost by the member in the course of the gaming) were held not to constitute consideration for the money which the member had paid for them. One reason for this view appears to have been that "the chips themselves were worthless"[85]; but this is equally true of the wrappers in the *Chappell* case. Another seems to have been that the chips "remained the property of the club"[86]; but this again would not of itself be decisive, for the transfer of possession (no less than that of ownership) can constitute consideration.[87] A third reason for the view that the chips were not consideration for the money may be that the parties did not so regard the transaction: they regarded the chips as merely "a convenient mechanism for facilitating gambling,"[88] and the case may be one in which the court refused to "invent" consideration[89] (by regarding something as consideration which was not so regarded by the parties) even though this course was technically open to it. This refusal appears to have been based on the context in which the question arose. The issue was not whether the club could sue the member on any promise made by him: it arose because the money paid by the member to the club had been stolen; and the club, which had received the money in good faith, argued that it had given valuable consideration for it, so as to defeat the true owner's claim for the return of the money. This explanation of the case derives some support from Lord Goff's discussion of a hypothetical case of tokens supplied by a department store in exchange for cash: he said that "by receiving the money in these circumstances the store does not *for present purposes* give valuable consideration for it."[90] Yet he also accepted that (in the store example) "an independent contract is made for the chips when the customer originally obtains them at the cash desk."[91] The question whether a party has provided consideration may thus receive one answer when it arises for the purpose of determining the enforceability of a promise, and a different and narrower one when it arises for the purpose of determining whether a transaction has adversely affected the rights of an innocent third party.[92] It was the desire to protect the victim of the theft which led the House of Lords in the *Lipkin Gorman* case to

---

[84] [1991] 2 A.C. 548. On facts such as those of this case, consideration for the money paid by the member to the club would now be provided by reason of the fact that the club's promise to the member would be legally enforceable by virtue of s.335(1) of the Gambling Act 2005: Vol II, para.40–093. But the question whether tokens of very small intrinsic value can constitute consideration can still arise in other contexts, not connected with gambling: see below at n.90.

[85] [1991] 2 A.C. 548 at 561.

[86] *ibid.*; and see 575.

[87] *Bainbridge v Firmstone* (1838) 8 A. & E. 743; below, para.3–177.

[88] *Lipkin Gorman* case at 575.

[89] Above, para.3–010.

[90] *Lipkin Gorman* case at 577; italics supplied; *cf.* below, para.3–031.

[91] *Lipkin Gorman* case at 576.

[92] Above, para.3–002.

reject the, no doubt somewhat technical, argument that the chips constituted consideration for the money.

3–017 The *Lipkin Gorman* case gives rise to further difficulty because the chips were supplied on the terms that they could be used, not only for gaming, but also to purchase refreshments at the club. There was no evidence of their having been used for this purpose,[93] but Lord Templeman said that "neither the power to buy refreshments nor the exercise of that power could constitute consideration for the receipt [by the club] of £154,693."[94] One possible interpretation of this passage is that the supply of refreshments could not constitute consideration for £154,693 (the sum lost by the member of the club) since the disparity in value was too great; but this would be inconsistent with the principle that consideration need not be adequate. It is submitted that the preferable explanation of Lord Templeman's statement is that the chips were simply "treated as currency"[95] in the club and could be used for a variety of transactions. The reason why the supply of refreshments was no consideration for the face value of the chips lost at play was simply that these transactions were entirely separate ones.

3–018 **Nominal consideration.** The rule that consideration need not be adequate makes it possible to evade the doctrine of consideration in the sense that a gratuitous promise can be made binding by giving a nominal consideration, *e.g.* £1 for the promise of valuable property, or a peppercorn for a substantial sum of money. Such cases are merely extreme examples of the rule that the courts will not judge the adequacy of consideration.[96] If, however, it appears on the face of the agreement that the consideration must as a matter of arithmetic be worth less than the performance of the counter-promise, there would seem to be no contract: for example, if A promised to pay B £100 in return for £1 to be simultaneously paid by B to A. It is assumed in the example that both sums are simply to be paid in legal tender. An agreement to exchange a specific coin or coins of a particular description for a sum of money greater than their face value (*e.g.* 20 shilling pieces bearing the date 1900 for £100) would be a good contract. The same would be true of an agreement to pay a sum in one currency in exchange for one payable in another, and of an agreement to pay a larger sum tomorrow in exchange for a smaller sum paid today.

3–019 Where an agreement is legally binding on the ground that it is supported by nominal consideration, the doctrine of consideration does not serve its main purpose, of distinguishing between gratuitous and onerous promises. But the law has no settled policy against enforcing all gratuitous promises. It refuses to

[93] *Lipkin Gorman* case at 569.

[94] *ibid.* at 567. For the effect of s.335(1) of the Gambling Act 2005 on the reasoning of the *Lipkin Gorman* case, see above, para.3–016 n.84.

[95] *Lipkin Gorman* case at 561.

[96] Atiyah, *Essays on Contracts*, p.194 argues that there is no logical connection between the two rules, relying on the fact that in many of the United States the courts recognise the principle that consideration need not be adequate, while rejecting the device of nominal consideration. The answer to this argument lies in Holmes' aphorism (*The Common Law*, p.1) that "life of the law has not been logic: it has been experience:" American courts which reject the device of nominal consideration do so on policy grounds which have nothing to do with logic.

enforce only *informal* gratuitous promises[97]; and the deliberate use of a nominal consideration can be regarded as a form to make a gratuitous promise binding. In some cases it may, indeed, be undesirable to give promises supported by nominal consideration the same legal effect as promises supported by substantial consideration; but these cases are best dealt with by special rules.[98] Such rules are particularly necessary where the promise can cause prejudice to third parties. For example, the danger that company promoters might use the device of nominal consideration to the prejudice of shareholders is avoided by imposing fiduciary duties on the promoters.[99]

3–020 **Nominal distinguished from inadequate consideration.** It is not normally necessary to distinguish between "nominal" and "inadequate" consideration, since both equally suffice to make a promise binding. The need to draw the distinction may, however, arise where rules of law treat promises or conveyances supported only by nominal consideration differently from those supported by consideration which is substantial or "valuable" even though it may be inadequate.[100] One view is that a nominal consideration is one that is of only token value,[101] while an inadequate consideration is one that has substantial value even though it is manifestly less than that of the performance promised or rendered in return. A second view is that "'Nominal consideration' and 'nominal sum' appear . . . , as terms of art, to refer to a sum or consideration which can be mentioned as consideration but is not necessarily paid."[102] This view was expressed by Lord Wilberforce (in a speech with which all the other members of the House of Lords concurred) in *Midland Bank & Trust Co Ltd v Green*.[103] In that case a husband sold a farm, said to be worth £40,000, to his wife for £500. It was held that the wife was, for the purposes of s.13(2) of the Land Charges Act 1925, a "purchaser for money or money's worth" so that the sale to her prevailed over an unregistered option to purchase the land, which had been granted to one

---

[97] See above, para.3–002.

[98] Thus a nominal consideration was disregarded in *Milroy v Lord* (1862) 4 D.F. & J. 264, discussed below, para.19–034; specific performance will not be ordered of a promise supported by only nominal consideration (below, para.27–034) and for the purposes of the Law of Property Act 1925, "valuable consideration does not include a nominal consideration in money": s.205(1)(xxi).

[99] Below, para.9–054. For other ways of protecting third parties from being prejudiced by promises made for inadequate consideration, see Trustee Act 1925, s.13; Law of Property Act 1925, ss.172, 173; Local Government Act 1972, s.123, considered in *R. v Pembrokeshire CC Ex p. Coker* [1999] 4 All E.R. 1007 and *Structadene Ltd v Hackney LBC* [2001] 2 All E.R. 225, discussing s.123(2) of the 1972 Act, restricting disposals by local authorities "for a consideration less than the best that can reasonably be obtained"; Inheritance (Provision for Family and Dependants) Act 1975, ss.10(2)(b), 10(5)(b), 11(2)(c); Insolvency Act 1986, ss.238, 239, 423 (applied in *Barclays Bank plc v Eustice* [1995] 1 W.L.R. 1238; *Agricultural Mortgage Corp. plc v Woodward* [1995] B.C.L.C. 1); *Phillips v Brewin Dolphin Bell Lawrie Ltd* [2001] U.K.H.L. 2, [2001] 1 W.L.R. 143; *cf.* Companies Act 2006, ss.190, 593 (not yet in force). See also Charities Act 1993, s.65(1)(a), requiring "full consideration in money or money's worth" (a requirement not satisfied in *Bayoumi v Women's Total Abstinence Educational Union Ltd* [2003] EWCA Civ. 1548 [2004] Ch. 40 at [46]–[47]).

[100] Above, para.3–018 at nn.97 and 98.

[101] This seems to be the sense in which 10 shillings was described as "nominal" consideration (for the assignment of a debt) in *Turner v Forwood* [1951] 1 All E.R. 746.

[102] *Midland Bank & Trustee Co Ltd v Green* [1981] A.C. 513, 532.

[103] above.

of the couple's children.[104] It was not necessary to decide whether the consideration for the sale was nominal but Lord Wilberforce said that he would have had "great difficulty" in so holding; and that "To equate 'nominal' with 'inadequate' or even 'grossly inadequate' consideration would embark the law on inquiries which I cannot think were ever intended by Parliament."[105] On the facts of the case the £500 was paid and was more than a mere token, so that the consideration was not nominal on either of the two views stated above. But if the stated consideration had been only £1, or a peppercorn, it is submitted that it would have been nominal even if it had been paid, or delivered, in accordance with the intention of the parties. So to hold would not lead to inquiries as to the adequacy of consideration; for the distinction between a consideration that is a mere token and one that is inadequate (or even grossly inadequate) is, it is submitted, clear as a matter of common sense. Thus where the question was whether a lease amounted to a "disposition . . . for a nominal consideration"[106] it was said that "Any substantial value—that is, a value of more than, say, £5 . . . will prevent [the] disposition from being for a nominal consideration."[107] Such an approach gives rise to no more difficulty than the concept of a consideration which is "mentioned as a consideration but . . . not necessarily paid." This test would presumably make the question whether consideration was nominal turn on the intention of the parties; and in the present context this would be an even more than usually elusive criterion since no guidance could be obtained from the terms of the contract, those terms being in cases of this kind often deliberately drafted so as to conceal the true nature of the transaction.

Attitude of equity. Even in equity the validity of a contract could not generally be challenged on the ground that the consideration provided for one party's promise was inadequate.[108] But the equitable remedy of specific performance may be refused on this ground[109] (at least if coupled with certain other factors); and in exceptional cases gross undervalue may even be a ground for more radical forms of equitable relief, such as setting a contract aside or reopening it.[110] Equity also refuses to aid a "volunteer"—so that its remedy of specific performance is not available to a person who has given no substantial consideration but who can nevertheless bring an action on the promise because it is in a deed or supported by nominal consideration.[111] But while the equitable 3–021

[104] For later successful proceedings by that child against the parents for conspiracy, see [1982] Ch. 529.

[105] [1981] A.C. 513, 532. In other legislative contexts such an inquiry may be intended: *e.g.* by use of the phrase "full and valuable consideration" in the Inheritance (Provisions for Family and Dependants) Act 1975, s.1(3); *cf.* Charities Act 1993, s.65(1)(a), above n.99.

[106] Within Law of Property Act 1925, s.84(7).

[107] *Westminster City Council v Duke of Westminster* [1991] 4 All E.R. 136, 146 (reversed in part on another ground (1992) 24 H.L.R. 572).

[108] See, *e.g. Cheale v Kenward* (1858) 3 De G. & J. 27; *Townsend v Toker* (1866) L.R. 1 Ch. App. 446.

[109] Below, para.27–033.

[110] Below; para.7–126; *Pennell v Miller* (1857) 23 Beav. 172; *Butler v Miller* (1867) L.R. 1 Eq. 195, 210; *Tennent v Tennents* (1870) L.R. 2 Sc. & Div. 6, 9.

[111] *Jefferys v Jefferys* (1841) Cr. & Ph. 138; below, para.27–034.

principle restricts the enforceability of gratuitous *promises*, it does not affect the validity of a *completed gift*.[112]

4. THE CONCEPT OF "VALUABLE" CONSIDERATION

3–022 **"Value in the eye of the law".** Although consideration need not be adequate, it must be "of some value in the eye of the law,"[113] that is, it must be capable of estimation in terms of economic or monetary value,[114] even though there may be no very precise way of quantifying that value. This is one reason why there is no consideration for a promise made "in consideration of natural love and affection,"[115] and why in *Thomas v Thomas*[116] the testator's desire that his widow should live in his house was not part of the consideration for the executors' promise that she might do so. The same reasoning may explain the decision in *White v Bluett*[117] that a son had not provided consideration for his father's promise not to sue him on a promissory note by promising in return not to bore his father with complaints. But in *Ward v Byham*[118] a promise by the mother of an illegitimate child to make it happy appears to have been regarded as part of the consideration for the father's promise to pay her an allowance. It is by no means clear why the mother's promise in the latter case was, while the son's promise in the former was not, thought to have "value in the eye of the law."[119]

3–023 **Impossible and illusory consideration.** A contract may be void for mistake if at the time of the agreement its performance is, unknown to either party, physically impossible.[120] In such a case there may nevertheless be consideration, *e.g.* in the mutual promises of the parties. But if the performance of one party's promise is known by both to be impossible to perform, it is arguable that the consideration is only illusory and therefore to be disregarded. For example, a promise by A to pay B £100 for all the wine in B's cellar would probably be regarded as gratuitous if at the time when it was made both A and B knew[121] that

---

[112] *T. Choithram International S.A. v Pagarani* [2001] 1 W.L.R. 1; *Pennington v Waine* [2002] EWCA Civ. 227; [2002] 1 W.L.R. 2075.

[113] *Thomas v Thomas* (1842) 2 Q.B. 851, 859.

[114] See *R. v Pembrokeshire CC Ex p. Coker* [1999] 4 All E.R. 1007 where it was held that, for the purpose of Local Government Act 1972, s.123(2), only "those elements of commercial or monetary value to the local authority" (at 1013) were to be taken into account for the purpose of determining whether a disposal by the authority had been made for "a consideration less than the best that could reasonably be obtained."

[115] *Bret v J.S.* (1600) Cr.Eliz. 755; *Tweddle v Atkinson* (1861) 1 B. & S. 393, disapproving of *Dutton v Poole* (1677) 2 Lev. 211; *cf. Horrocks v Forray* [1976] 1 W.L.R. 230; *Mansukhani v Sharkey* [1992] 2 E.G.L.R. 125.

[116] (1842) 2 Q.B. 851; above, para.3–011.

[117] (1853) 23 L.J.Ex. 36.

[118] [1956] 1 W.L.R. 496; below, para.3–064.

[119] *White v Bluett*, above, can perhaps be explained on the ground that the father, in spite of his promise, retained the note.

[120] Below, Ch.5.

[121] There could be a good contract if the parties were in doubt on this point: see *Smith v Harrison* (1857) 26 L.J.Ch. 412.

there was no wine in the cellar. The position would be different if B's promise was to deliver the *future* contents of the cellar. In that case, A would be buying the chance of the cellar's containing wine[122]; and the value of that chance would be illusory only if the question whether any wine was put into the cellar had been left entirely to B's discretion.[123]

Promisee would have performed anyway. Consideration may also be said to be illusory where it is clear that the promisee would have accomplished the act of forbearance anyway, even if the promise had not been made. This would be the position if A promised B, who had religious objections to smoking, £10 if B did not smoke for a week. Since "it is no consideration to refrain from a course of conduct which it was never intended to pursue,"[124] B's forbearance from smoking would not constitute consideration for A's promise. The burden of proof on this issue is on the promisor.[125] To discharge it, the promisor must show that the promisee would (even if the promise had not been made) definitely have accomplished the act or forbearance in question; the burden would not be discharged by the promisor's showing no more than that the promisee had simply not given any thought to the question whether or not to accomplish it.[126] Moreover, where the promise provided *an* inducement for the act or forbearance, the requirement of consideration is satisfied even though there were also other inducements operating on the promisee's mind.[127] 3–024

Discretionary promise. Consideration would again be illusory where it was alleged to consist of a promise the terms of which left performance entirely to the discretion of the promisor.[128] A person does not provide consideration by promising to do something "if I feel like it," or "unless I change my mind." Promises are not often made in this form; but the same principle may apply in analogous cases. Thus a promise may be illusory if it is accompanied by a clause effectively[129] excluding all liability of the promisor for breach.[130] And a promise to pay for "so much coal as I may decide to order" would be an illusory consideration for the seller's counter-promise to deliver, which would therefore not be 3–025

---

[122] *cf. Brady v Brady* [1989] A.C. 755, 774 ("at the date of the promise").

[123] Below, para.3–025.

[124] *Arrale v Costain Civil Engineering Ltd* [1976] 1 Lloyd's Rep. 98, 106; *cf. Colchester BC v Smith* [1991] Ch. 448, 489, affirmed without reference to this point [1992] Ch. 421; *Beaton v McDivitt* (1988) 13 N.S.W.L.R. 162.

[125] *Well Barn Farming Ltd v Backhouse* [2005] EWHC 1520, [2005] E.G.L.R. 109, where the promisor failed to discharge this burden (at [47], [48]); *cf.* below, para.3–147.

[126] *Pitts v Jones* [2007] EWCA Civ. 1301, [2008] Q.B. 706 at [15]–[18].

[127] *Brikom Investments Ltd v Carr* [1979] Q.B. 467, 490.

[128] For another problem arising out of such promises, see above, para.2–175; *Stabilad Ltd v Stephens & Carter (No.2)* [1999] 2 All E.R. (Comm), 651, 659 (citing a previous edition of this book).

[129] See below, Ch.14. If the clause were ineffective (*e.g.* under Unfair Terms in Consumer Contracts Regulations 1999, SI 1999/2083, Sch.2, paras 1(c) or 1(f)), this fact would give reality to an otherwise illusory promise.

[130] *Firestone Tyre & Rubber Co Ltd v Vokins* [1951] 1 Lloyd's Rep. 32, 39; *cf.* the discussion of *The Cap Palos* [1921] p.458, in the *Suisse Atlantique* case [1967] 1 A.C. 361, 432.

enforced.[131] On the other hand, if the promise were one to buy "so much of the coal that I require as I may order from you," the court could give reality to the promise by implying a term into it to the effect that at least a reasonable part of any requirements which the promisor actually turned out to have must be ordered from the promisee. Equally the buyer would provide consideration by promising to buy "*all* the coal I require"; for in such a case, even if the buyer does not promise to have any requirements, he does at least give a definite undertaking not to deal with anybody else.[132] This promise may, it is true, be illegal as being in restraint of trade; but if this makes the whole contract invalid, such invalidity probably rests on grounds of public policy and not on lack of consideration.[133] Similarly, a promise which is subject to cancellation by A may nevertheless constitute consideration for a counter-promise from B where A's power to cancel is limited by the express terms of the promise: *e.g.* where it can be exercised only within a specified time. Such a limitation on the power to cancel may also be implied, so that (for example) A could not cancel after B had begun to perform his counter-promise. A's promise would then constitute consideration, so that B would be liable if he failed to complete the performance. Finally, the objection that a promise amounts, on the grounds here discussed, only to an illusory consideration can be removed if the promise is performed. Such actual performance can constitute consideration even though the person who has rendered it was not legally obliged to render it.[134]

5. PAST CONSIDERATION

3–026 **Past consideration is no consideration.** The consideration for a promise must be given in return for the promise. If the act or forbearance alleged to constitute the consideration has already been done before, and independently of, the giving of the promise, it is said to amount to "past consideration"; and such past acts or forbearances do not in law amount to consideration for the promise.[135] If, for example, a thing is guaranteed by a seller *after* it has been sold the guarantee is not contractually binding on the seller as the consideration for his promise is past.[136] Similarly a promise to make a payment in respect of past

---

[131] See *Wickham & Burton Coal Co v Farmer's Lumber Co* 189 Iowa 1183, 179 N.W. 417 (1923); *cf.* the discussion in *Cotswold Development Construction Ltd v Williams* [2006] I.R.L.R. 181 of the status of a casual worker. For an exception, see *Citadel Insurance Co v Atlantic Union Insurance Co* [1982] 2 Lloyd's Rep. 543, below para.3–173.

[132] The validity of "requirement" contracts is assumed in such cases as *Metropolitan Electric Supply Co v Ginder* [1901] 2 Ch. 799 and *Dominion Coal Co Ltd v Dominion Steel & Iron Co Ltd* [1901] A.C. 293. Similarly, a contract by a manufacturer to sell his entire output to a particular buyer is binding even though he does not bind himself to have any output: see, *e.g.*, *Donnell v Bennett* (1883) 22 Ch.D. 835 and *cf. Thames Tideway Properties Ltd v Serfaty* [1999] 2 Lloyd's Rep. 110, 127; Howard (1967) 2 U. of Tas.L.R. 446; Adams (1978) 94 L.Q.R. 173.

[133] Below, para.3–165.

[134] *Cambridge Nutrition Ltd v BBC* [1990] 3 All E.R. 523, 528; *Stabilad Ltd v Stephens & Carter (No.2)* [1999] 2 All E.R. (Comm), 651, 660.

[135] *Dent v Bennett* (1839) 4 My. & Cr. 269; *Eastwood v Kenyon* (1840) 11 A. & E. 438.

[136] *Thorner v Field* (1612) 1 Bulst. 120; *Roscorla v Thomas* (1842) 3 Q.B. 234. In the latter case an oral warranty was given at the time of sale (see (1842) 11 L.J.Q.B. 214 and 6 Jur. 929) but this was presumably considered at the time to be "void" for want of written evidence: *cf.* below, para.4–041.

services is not contractually binding unless the conditions specified in para.3–029 below are satisfied or some other consideration is provided. For example, a promise to pay money may be made to an employee after his retirement or to an agent after the termination of the agency. If the sole consideration for the promise is the service previously rendered by the former employee or agent, it will be past consideration, so that the promise will not be contractually binding.[137] It will be so binding only if some consideration other than the past service has been provided by the promisee. Such other consideration may consist in his giving up rights which are outstanding (or are in good faith believed to be outstanding) under the original contract,[138] or in his promising to perform or actually performing some other act or forbearance not due from him under the original contract: for example, in his validly promising not to compete with the promisor.[139]

When consideration is past. In determining whether consideration is past, the courts are not, it is submitted, bound to apply a strictly chronological test. If the giving of the consideration and the making of the promise are substantially one transaction, the exact order in which these events occur is not decisive.[140] Where, for example, a contract to erect buildings on land and to grant a lease of that land are substantially one transaction, the expenditure of money on the buildings would not be past consideration for the execution of the lease, even though the lease was not executed until after completion of the buildings.[141] Similarly, a manufacturer's "guarantee" may be given to a customer after he has bought the goods. But it is submitted that the consideration for such a guarantee is not, merely on that ground, past, for the sale and the giving of the "guarantee" will often in substance be a single transaction. Where the guarantee is a "consumer guarantee" within the Sale and Supply of Goods to Consumers Regulations 2002,[142] it "takes effect as a contractual obligation owed by the guarantor" by force of this legislation. For this purpose, the consumer need not show that he has provided consideration for the guarantor's promise; but the requirement of consideration continues to apply to guarantees which are *not* "consumer guarantees" within the Regulations.[143] 3–027

[137] See the facts of *Simpson v John Reynolds* [1975] 1 W.L.R. 617, where such a payment was held to be voluntary for tax purposes and *cf. Murray v Goodhews* [1978] 1 W.L.R. 499.

[138] *e.g. Bell v Lever Bros. Ltd* [1932] A.C. 1616 (where the value of the rights given up in return for the payment was uncertain in amount since it included not only future salary but also possible future commission).

[139] *cf. Wyatt v Kreglinger and Fernau* [1933] 1 K.B. 793—where the ex-employee's claim would have succeeded if the restraint undertaken by him had not been invalid (below, para.16–105).

[140] *Thornton v Jenkyns* (1840) 1 M. & G. 166; *Tanner v Moore* (1846) 9 Q.B. 1; *cf.* the discussion of *Halifax B.S. v Edell* [1992] Ch. 436, below, para.18–014.

[141] *Westminster City Council v Duke of Westminster* [1991] 4 All E.R. 136, 145 (reversed in part on another ground (1992) 24 H.L.R. 572).

[142] SI 2002/3045, reg.15, implementing Directive 1999/44/EC Art.7. For definitions, of "consumer", "consumer guarantee" and "guarantor", see reg.2. Reg.15(1) requires the goods to be "offered with" the guarantee and these words would seem not to cover the case where no mention is made of the guarantee until *after* the supply contract has been made, as in the situation described above, para.3–026 at n.136. For an amendment of reg.15, see Consumer Protection from Unfair Trading Regulation 2008, SI 2008/1277 reg. 30 (1) Sched. 2, para.97.

[143] *e.g.* where the buyer is not a "natural person" and so does no fall within the definition of "consumer" in reg.2.

3–028 **Wording of promise not decisive.** The question whether consideration is past is one of fact: the wording of the promise is not decisive. Thus in *Re McArdle*[144] a promise made "in consideration of your carrying out" certain work was held to be gratuitous on the ground that the work had already been done. Conversely, a promise made "in consideration of your having today advanced . . . £750" has been held to be binding on proof that the advance was made at the same time as the promise.[145]

3–029 **Past act done at promisor's request.** An act done before the promise was made can be consideration for the promise if three conditions are satisfied. First, the act must have been done at the request of the promisor[146]; secondly, it must have been understood that payment would be made; and thirdly, the payment, if it had been promised in advance, must have been legally recoverable.[147] In such a case the promisee is, quite apart from the subsequent promise, entitled to a *quantum meruit* for his services. The promise can be regarded either as fixing the amount of that *quantum meruit*[148] or as being given in consideration of the promisee's releasing his *quantum meruit* claim. On the other hand, a past service for which payment was not expected, or one for which payment, though expected, is not legally recoverable, is no consideration for a subsequent promise to pay for it.[149]

3–030 **Past promise given at promisor's request.** The principle stated in para. 3–029 above can apply not only where the consideration for A's promise consists of a past *act* done by B at A's request, but also where it consists of an earlier *promise* made by B at A's request. Thus in *Pao On v Lau Yiu Long*[150] the claimants had entered into a contract with the X Co for the sale to that company of their shares in another company. Under that contract, the claimants were to be paid by an allotment of shares in the X Co, and they also promised not to sell 60 per cent of these shares for one year. This promise had been made at the request of the defendants, who held most of the shares in the X Co and who were anxious that the value of their holding should not be depressed by a sudden sale of all the shares allotted to the claimants. Later, the defendants gave the claimants a guarantee in which they promised to indemnify the claimants against any loss

---

[144] [1951] Ch. 669.

[145] *Goldshede v Swan* (1847) 1 Ex. 154. In such cases, the burden of proving that the consideration is not past lies on the person seeking to enforce the promise: *Savage v. Uwechia* [1961] 1 W.L.R. 455.

[146] See *Southwark LBC v Logan* (1996) 8 Admin.L.R. 292 (where this requirement was not satisfied).

[147] *Re Casey's Patents* [1892] 1 Ch. 104, 115–116; *cf. Lampleigh v Brathwait* (1615) Hob. 105.

[148] *Kennedy v Brown* (1863) 13 C.B.(N.S.) 677, 740; *Rondel v Worsley* [1969] 1 A.C. 191, 236, 278, 287, as to which, see n.149 below.

[149] See the authorities cited in the preceding note: promise to pay barrister for past professional services not binding since he could not sue for his fees; see now Courts and Legal Services Act 1990, s.61. In *Arthur J.S. Hall Ltd v Simons* [2002] 1 A.C. 615 the House of Lords disapproved the reasoning of *Rondel v Worsley* so far as it relates to an advocate's immunity from liability for negligence in the conduct of civil or (by a majority) criminal proceeding. This disapproval does not affect the point for which *Rondel v Worsley* is cited in n.149 above *i.e.* the common law rule that a barrister cannot sue for his fees. Reference to this point is made, perhaps with some scepticism, in the *Arthur J.S. Hall* case at pp.676 and 685.

[150] [1980] A.C. 614.

which they might suffer as a result of a fall in the value during the year of the shares in the X Co[151] The Privy Council rejected the argument that the consideration for the guarantee was past.[152] The claimants' promise not to sell the shares in the X Co was good consideration for the guarantee; for although that promise had been made before the guarantee was given, it had been made at the defendants' request and on the understanding that the claimants were, in return for making it, to receive some form of protection against the risk (to which the promise exposed them) of a fall in the value of the X Co's shares.

Antecedent debt. In a number of cases it has been held that the mere existence of an antecedent debt does not constitute "value" for a transfer since it amounts only to past consideration. Accordingly, in *Roger v Comptoir d'Escompte de Paris*[153] it was held that a transfer of a bill of lading by a buyer in consideration of a debt already due from him to the transferee did not deprive the seller of his right of stoppage *in transit*[154]; in *Re Barker's Estate*[155] a mortgage executed as security for an antecedent debt and not communicated to the creditor was held to be voluntary and hence a fraudulent conveyance in bankruptcy; and in *Wigan v English & Scottish Law Life Assurance Society*[156] an assignment of an insurance policy which was made as security for an antecedent debt and had not been communicated to the creditor was held not to have been made (to him as assignee) "for valuable consideration" within a clause of the policy protecting the rights of such an assignee on the death of the assured by his own hand. These cases are not directly concerned with the question of whether such an antecedent debt can constitute consideration for a later *promise* by the debtor: indeed, in *Wigan's* case such enforceability at common law could hardly have been disputed since the assignment was under seal. The cases may, however, be relevant by analogy to the enforceability of a promise made by the debtor to the creditor (*e.g.* of one to pay higher interest or to pay early); and, in principle, it seems that where the only possible consideration for such a promise is an antecedent debt owed by the promisor to the promisee, then such consideration is past, so that the promise is not contractually binding.[157] In practice, however, the creditor (*i.e.* the promisee) will often be held to have provided consideration for such a promise if, on the strength of it, he forbears to sue for the debt.[158] 3–031

"Moral" obligation. In the eighteenth and early nineteenth centuries, an attempt was made (originally by Lord Mansfield) to define consideration so as to include certain pre-existing "moral" obligations. In accordance with this theory it was held that an executor was personally liable on a promise to pay a legacy if he had sufficient assets of the deceased in his hands to pay the deceased's debts 3–032

---

[151] This guarantee replaced an earlier agreement (made at the time of the principal sale but subsidiary to it) which was less favourable to the claimants.

[152] For the further argument that the consideration was no more than the promise to perform an existing contractual duty, see below, para.3–075.

[153] (1869) L.R. 2 P.C. 393.

[154] Below, Vol.II, para.43–357.

[155] (1875) 44 L.J.Ch. 487.

[156] [1909] 1 Ch. 291.

[157] *e.g. Hopkinson v Logan* (1839) 5 M. & W. 241 (promise fixing date of payment).

[158] Below, paras 3–057, 3–059.

and legacies[159]; that a promise by a discharged bankrupt to pay a debt contracted before the discharge was binding[160]; and that a promise to pay a statute-barred debt[161] or one contracted during minority[162] was binding. In some of these cases, the consideration for the promise was said to be the "moral" obligation of the promisor to pay the debt. In this context, the term "moral obligation" was used in a narrow sense. It was restricted to cases in which the promisor's previous obligation was not legally enforceable (or not enforceable in the particular court in which the action on the promise was brought[163]) because it suffered from some specific legal defect. It did not follow that any "moral obligation," such as one which might be said to arise from the receipt of a past benefit, constituted consideration. Thus in *Eastwood v Kenyon*[164] the guardian of a young girl had raised a loan to pay for her maintenance and education, and to improve her estate. After she had come of age and married, her husband promised the guardian to pay the amount of the loan. In dismissing the guardian's action on this promise, the court rejected the argument that the defendant's promise was binding merely because he was under a moral obligation to perform it. Lord Denman C.J. said that this argument would "annihilate the necessity for any consideration at all, inasmuch as the mere fact of giving a promise creates a moral obligation to perform it."[165] The case also shows that the mere existence of an antecedent moral obligation (in the ordinary sense of the phrase) to reimburse the guardian did not amount to consideration for the husband's promise. From this point of view, the case provides the classic illustration of the requirement that the consideration for a promise must not be past.

3–033 **Defective obligations as consideration: present position.** Many of the cases in which promises were held binding under the old "moral obligation" theory would now go the other way. For example, an executor who has assets of the deceased in his hands is no longer personally liable on a promise to pay legacies[166]; a promise by a discharged bankrupt to pay in full debts incurred before his discharge is binding only if supported by fresh consideration[167]; and the same is true of a promise to pay a debt after it has become statute-barred.[168] There is Australian authority in favour of the same rule where a company renewed a note that was originally *ultra vires* after it had been validated by

---

[159] *Atkins v Hill* (1775) 1 Cowp. 284; *Hawkes v Saunders* (1782) 1 Cowp. 289; an alternative ground for the decision given by Buller J. was that the defendant's equitable (as opposed to "moral") obligation to pay the legacy was consideration for the promise.

[160] *Trueman v Fenton* (1777) 2 Cowp. 544.

[161] *Hyeling v Hastings* (1699) 1 Ld.Raym. 389.

[162] Below, para.8–044, *cf. Lee v Muggeridge* (1813) 5 Taunt. 36 (promise by a woman after her husband's death to pay debt incurred during marriage); for attempts to restrict or define the doctrine, see *Littlefield v Shee* (1831) 2 B. & Ad. 811; *Meyer v Haworth* (1838) 8 A. & E. 467.

[163] As in *Hawkes v Saunders*, above, n.159.

[164] (1840) 11 A. & E. 438.

[165] *ibid.* at 450.

[166] *Williams, Mortimer and Sunnucks on Executors, Administrators and Probate* (19th ed., 2007), para.55–80.

[167] *Jakeman v Cook* (1878) 4 Ex.D. 26; *Re Bonacina* [1912] 2 Ch. 394; *Wild v Tucker* [1914] 3 K.B. 36.

[168] Limitation Act 1980, s.29(7) (below para.3–035); *cf.*, as to time bars imposed by contract, *Nippon Yusen Kaisha v Pacifica Navegaceon SA (The Ion)* [1980] 2 Lloyd's Rep. 245, 249.

subsequent legislation.[169] On the other hand, a promise by an adult to pay a debt (or to perform some other obligation) contracted during minority is enforceable[170]; and *Eastwood v Kenyon*[171] did not purport to overrule the "moral obligation" theory in its original narrow sense, that a promise to discharge an earlier obligation which suffered from some specific legal defect might be binding. In this sense the theory was again recognised in *Flight v Reed*.[172] That case supports the view that a promise made after the repeal of the legislation against usury was not invalid for want of consideration merely because the original loan was usurious. Of course an action on such a promise might, under the modern view of past consideration, fail because the loan was an antecedent debt; but this objection would be overcome if the promisee's forbearance to enforce the loan could be regarded as consideration for the promise in accordance with the requirements stated in paras 3–057 and 3–059, below.

Bills of exchange. Under s.27(1)(b) of the Bills of Exchange Act 1882, an "antecedent debt or liability" constitutes valuable consideration for a bill of exchange.[173] In many cases, such a consideration would not be past: it could be said to consist in the forbearance of the creditor to sue for the debt or in his treating the bill as conditional payment.[174] But the provision would apply even though, for some reason, this analysis were not possible; and in such cases it would constitute an exception to the rule that past consideration is no consideration. 3–034

Acknowledgments of statute-barred debts. A further qualification of the past consideration rule is contained in s.29(5) of the Limitation Act 1980. This provides (*inter alia*) that, where a debtor in a writing signed by him[175] "acknowledges" a debt, it shall be deemed to have accrued on and not before the date of the acknowledgment. An "acknowledgment" need not take the form of a promise[176]; but if it does take this form the promise can extend the period of limitation even though the only consideration for it was the antecedent debt, and thus past. Further acknowledgments made within such an extended period or periods have the same effect.[177] But once the debt has become statute-barred the right to sue 3–035

[169] *Sharp v Ellis* (1971) 20 F.L.R. 199.

[170] Minors' Contracts Act 1987, ss.1 and 4, repealing Infants Relief Act 1874, s.2 and Betting and Loans (Infants) Act 1892, s.5.

[171] (1840) 11 A. & E. 438.

[172] (1863) 1 H. & C. 703; mentioned with approval in *J. Evans & Co v Heathcote* [1918] 1 K.B. 418, 437.

[173] Below, Vol.II, para.34–063.

[174] See *Currie v Misa* (1875) L.R. 10 Ex. 153 and *cf.* below, paras 3–057—3–060.

[175] Limitation Act 1980, s.30(1). An inscription of a person's name, typed on a telex document, is a sufficient signature for the present purpose: *Good Challenger Navegante SA v Metalexportimport SA (The Good Challenger)* [2003] EWCA Civ 1668, [2004] 1 Lloyd's Rep. 67 at [20]–[28].

[176] *Lia Oil SA v ERG Petroli* [2007] EWHC 505 (Comm), [2007] 2 Lloyd's Rep. 509; an admission of liability suffices: *Surrendra Overseas Ltd v Government of Sri Lanka* [1977] 1 W.L.R. 481; see further *Bradford & Bingley plc v Rashid* [2006] UKHL 37, [2006] 1 W.L.R. 2066, where a debtor's statement that he was not in a position to pay "the outstanding amount due to you" was held to amount to an "acknowledgement within s.29(5) even though it contained no admission of the amount (or undisputed amount) of the debt; *cf. Re Overmark Smith Warden Ltd* [1982] 1 W.L.R. 1195 ("statement of affairs" by insolvent company).

[177] Limitation Act 1980, s.29(7).

for it cannot be revived by any subsequent acknowledgment[178]: to this extent, the old "moral obligation" theory as applied to statute-barred debts[179] has been reversed.

6. CONSIDERATION MUST MOVE FROM THE PROMISEE

3–036 **Promisee must provide consideration.** The rule that "consideration must move from the promisee"[180] means that a person can enforce a promise only if he himself provided consideration for it. Thus if A promises B to pay a sum of money to B if C will paint A's house and C does so, B cannot enforce the promise (unless, of course, he procured, or expressly or impliedly undertook to procure, C to do the work). It is, however, not necessary for the promisee to provide the whole consideration for the promise: thus he can enforce a promise part of the consideration for which was provided by his agent or partner or by some other co-promisee.[181]

3–037 **Benefit to promisor sufficient.** The requirement that consideration must move from the promisee is most generally satisfied where some detriment is suffered by him: *e.g.* where he parts with money or goods, or renders services, in exchange for the promise. But the requirement may equally well be satisfied where the promisee confers a benefit on the promisor without suffering any detriment. This point is illustrated by two rules to be discussed later in this chapter. The first is that performance of an existing contractual duty (or a promise to perform such a duty) can constitute consideration if it benefits the promisor[182]: this benefit is conferred by, and so "moves" from, the promisee in that it is conferred by him, even though it may cause him no detriment[183] in the sense that he was already bound to do the acts in question. The second is that a composition agreement between a debtor and his creditors is binding[184] because it benefits the creditors; and this benefit can be said to "move" from the debtor in that his co-operation is essential to the making and performance of the composition agreement. It could be said that the debtor suffers a legal detriment by signing the agreement when he is not bound to do so. But the rule in question is not in fact

---

[178] *ibid.*

[179] Above, para.3–032.

[180] *Barber v Fox* (1670) 2 Wms.Saund. 134, n.(*e*); *Thomas v Thomas* (1842) 2 Q.B. 851, 859; *Tweddle v Atkinson* (1861) 1 B. & S. 393, 399; *Pollway v Abdullah* [1974] 1 W.L.R. 493, 497; *cf. Dickinson v Abel* [1969] 1 W.L.R. 295, and (for VAT purposes) *Customs and Excise Commissioners v Telemed* [1992] S,T.C. 89. For criticism of a possibly contrary dictum, see below, para.3–044 at n.215.

[181] *Jones v Robinson* (1847) 1 Ex.454; *Fleming v Bank of New Zealand* [1900] A.C. 577. For the position where the *whole* consideration is provided by a co-promisee, see below, paras 3–041—3–044.

[182] Below, para.3–068.

[183] *Williams v Roffey Bros. & Nicholls (Contractors) Ltd* [1991] 1 Q.B. 1, 16.

[184] Below, para.3–125; the application of this rule in *West York Darracq Agency Ltd v Coleridge* [1911] 2 K.B. 326 is hard to support, since there the creditors got nothing and so received no benefit. The consideration was said at 329 to be benefit to the debtor, but he was the person *to* whom the promise was made, and benefit to the promisee is obviously no consideration. If it were, there would be consideration for every gratuitous promise.

based on this invented consideration.[185] It is based on benefit to the promisors.[186]

3–038 **Bar pupillage contracts.** The possibility that consideration may consist in benefit to the promisor is further illustrated by *Edmonds v Lawson*,[187] where the relationship between a pupil barrister and the members of the chambers at which she had accepted an offer of pupillage was held to be contractual even though she had paid no pupillage fee.[188] The requirement of consideration was satisfied in that her (and other pupils') agreement to accept pupillage "provided a pool of selected candidates who can be expected to compete with each other for recruitment as tenants;"[189] and in that "chambers may see an advantage in developing close relationships with pupils who plan to practise as employed barristers or overseas."[190] Both these factors stress the benefit to the promisors (the members of the chambers), moving from the promisee (the pupil barrister) even though no detriment was suffered by her.

3–039 **Consideration need not move to the promisor.** While consideration must move from the promisee, it need not move to the promisor.[191] It follows that the requirement of consideration may be satisfied where the promisee suffers some detriment at the promisor's request, but confers no corresponding benefit on the promisor. Thus the promisee may provide consideration by giving up a job[192] or the tenancy of a flat,[193] even though no direct benefit results to the promisor from these acts. It also follows that the promisee may provide consideration by conferring a benefit on a third party at the promisor's request: *e.g.* by entering into a contract with the third party.[194] This possibility is illustrated by the case in which goods are bought and paid for by the use of a cheque card or credit card. The issuer of the card makes a promise to the supplier of the goods that the cheque will be honoured or that the supplier will be paid; and the supplier

---

[185] Above, para.3–010. The creditors do not bargain for the debtor's signature but for a dividend. If the debtor's signature were regarded as the consideration it could equally well be so regarded in a composition with a single creditor, *i.e.* in a case such as *Foakes v Beer* (1884) 9 App. Cas. 605, below, para.3–115, where it was held that the agreement was not binding.

[186] Below, para.3–125.

[187] [2000] Q.B. 501; see also above, para.2–161.

[188] But an application for pupillage is not one for "membership" of chambers within Disability Discrimination Act 1995, s.13(1)(c): *Horton v Higham* [2004] EWCA Civ. 941, [2005] I.C.R. 292, where *Edmonds v Lawson*, above n.187 is cited at [2].

[189] [2000] Q.B., at 515.

[190] *ibid.*

[191] *Re Wyvern Developments Ltd* [1974] 1 W.L.R. 1097; *cf. International Petroleum Refining & Supply Ltd v Caleb Brett & Sons Ltd* [1980] 1 Lloyd's Rep. 569, 594 (below, para.18–008); *Barclays Bank plc v Weeks, Legg & Dean* [1998] 3 All E.R. 213, 220–221.

[192] *Jones v Padavatton* [1969] 1 W.L.R. 628.

[193] *Tanner v Tanner* [1975] 1 W.L.R. 1346; contrast *Horrocks v Forray* [1976] 1 W.L.R. 230 where there was no such (nor any other) consideration and no contract, partly for this reason and partly for lack of contractual intention: above, para.2–168; and see *Coombes v Smith* [1986] 1 W.L.R. 808.

[194] See *International Petroleum Refining Supply Ltd v Caleb Brett & Son Ltd* [1980] 1 Lloyd's Rep. 569, 594, where the promisor benefited indirectly since promisor and third party were associated companies. *cf. Pearl Carriers Inc. v Japan Lines Ltd (The Chemical Venture)* [1993] 1 Lloyd's Rep. 509, 522 (payments made by charterers of ship to the crew regarded as consideration for promise by shipowners to charterers).

provides consideration for this promise by supplying the goods to the customer.[195] In the case of a credit card transaction there is also consideration in the form of the discount allowed by the supplier of the goods or services to the issuer of the card[196]: this is both a detriment to the supplier and a benefit to the issuer of the card.

3–040 In the last example, there was detriment to the supplier; but the rule that consideration need not move to the promisor equally applies where the consideration consists simply in a benefit conferred by the promisee without loss to himself. Here the requirement of consideration is satisfied if a benefit is conferred either on the promisor or on a third person at his request. For example, in *Bolton v Madden*[197] the claimant and defendant were subscribers to a charity and entitled to vote on the disposition of its funds. The claimant promised to vote at one meeting for a person whom the defendant wished to benefit, and the defendant promised in return to vote at the next meeting for a person whom the claimant wished to benefit. In an action to enforce the defendant's promise, it was argued that there was no consideration for it as the claimant "incurred neither trouble nor prejudice,"[198] but the court rejected this argument and held the agreement binding. Consideration moved from the claimant when he had at the defendant's request conferred a benefit on a third party. It could, of course, be argued that the claimant had suffered a legal detriment[199] by voting in accordance with his promise as he was not previously bound to do so. But this was not the basis of the decision.

3–041 **More than one promisee.**[200] Where a promise is made to more than one person, it is clear that it can be enforced by any of the promisees even by one who provided only *part* of the consideration.[201] But the further question may arise whether the promise can be enforced by one of the promisees even though he provided no part of the consideration, the *whole* being provided by the other or others. There is no clear answer in the present law to this question; but it is submitted that the position depends on the following distinctions.

3–042 **Joint promisees.** Where a promise is made to A and B *jointly*, it can be enforced by both of them, even though the whole consideration was provided by A.[202] If this were not so, the promise could not be enforced at all; for, if A tried to sue alone, he would be defeated by the rule that all the creditors must be parties to the action.[203] It follows from the doctrine of survivorship (which

---

[195] *R. v Lambie* [1982] A.C. 449; *Re Charge Card Services* [1987] Ch. 150, affirmed [1989] Ch. 497.
[196] *Customs & Excise Commissioners v Diners Club Ltd* [1989] 1 W.L.R. 1196, 1207.
[197] (1873) L.R. 9 Q.B. 55.
[198] At 57.
[199] Above, para.3–006.
[200] Cullity (1969) 85 L.Q.R. 530; Winterton (1970) 47 Can.Bar Rev. 483.
[201] Above, para.3–036, at n.181.
[202] This proposition seems to have been accepted in *Coulls v Bagot's Executor and Trustee Co Ltd* [1967] A.L.R. 385; though the majority of the court held that no joint promise had in fact been made: below, para.18–074.
[203] *Jell v Douglas* (1821) 4 B. & Ald. 374; *Sorsbie v Park* (1843) 12 M. & W. 146; *Thompson v Hakewill* (1865) 9 C.B.(N.S.) 713.

applies between joint promisees)[204] that B would be entitled to the entire benefit of the promise after A's death.

3–043 **Several promisees.** None of the above reasoning applies where a promise is made to A and B *severally.*[205] Hence it seems that each promisee must provide consideration for what is in theory a separate promise to him.

3–044 **Joint and several promisees.** It is, however, uncertain which of the rules stated in paragraphs 3–042 and 3–043 above applies to the intermediate case of a promise made to two persons *jointly and severally.* Such a promise may be made under s.81 of the Law of Property Act 1925[206]; but that section appears to contemplate only promises under seal,[207] so that no question of consideration can arise. The common law originally did not recognise the possibility that a promise *to* a number of persons[208] could be joint and several[209]; but the possibility came to be recognised late in the nineteenth century.[210] It may be illustrated by *McEvoy v Belfast Banking Co*,[211] where a father, A, deposited £10,000 in a bank and the deposit receipt stated that this amount had been received from him and his son, B, and that it was payable "to either or the survivor." With reference to these facts, Lord Atkin said *obiter* that the contract was not by the bank with A for the benefit of B but "with A and B,[212] and I think with them jointly and severally. A purports to make the contract on behalf of B as well as himself and the consideration supports such a contract."[213] Of course after A's death (which in *McEvoy's* case had occurred) B would be entitled to sue on any joint promise under the doctrine of survivorship.[214] But it is harder to see how he could sue on any several promise, for this is *ex hypothesi* an independent promise and on the facts stated no consideration for it moved from B.[215] Indeed, the more probable view of such facts is that the bank makes no promise at all to B but only has authority to pay him. Hence the bank is discharged by paying B but it is not liable to him.[216] The bank would not, however, be discharged by such payment if it

---

204 *Anderson v Martindale* (1801) 1 East 497.

205 In such cases it is not necessary to join all the creditors to the action: *James v Emery* (1818) 5 Price 529; *Keightley v Watson* (1849) 3 Ex. 716; *Palmer v Mallett* (1887) 36 Ch.D. 411; nor did the doctrine of survivorship apply: *Withers v Bircham* (1824) 3 B. & C. 254.

206 Re-enacting, with some changes, the Conveyancing Act 1881, s.60. Section 81 of the 1925 Act does not affect the law relating to joint *debtors*: *Johnson v Davies* [1999] Ch. 117, 127; but our present concern is with the case in which there is more than one *creditor.*

207 See now Law of Property (Miscellaneous Provisions) Act 1989, s.1(7).

208 For promises made *by* a number of persons, see Ch.17, below.

209 *Slingsby's Case* (1588) 5 Co.Rep. 186; *Anderson v Martindale* (1801) 1 East 487; *Bradburne v Batfield* (1845) 14 M. & W. 559, 573; *Keighley v Watson* (1849) 3 Ex. 716, 723 (criticising the rule).

210 *Thompson v Hakewill* (1865) 19 C.B.(N.S.) 713, 726; *Palmer v Mallett* (1887) 36 Ch.D. 410, 421.

211 [1935] A.C. 24.

212 Hence B would not be a "third party" within s.1(1) of the Contracts (Rights of Third Parties) Act 1999 (below, paras 18–088 *et seq*).

213 At 43.

214 *cf. Aroso v Coutts & Co* [2002] 1 All E.R. (Comm) 241, where the contract expressly so provided.

215 S.J.B. (1935) 51 L.Q.R. 419.

216 See *Coulls v Bagot's Executor and Trustee Co Ltd* [1967] A.L.R. 385; below, para.18–074.

were *not* authorised by its contract with A to pay B. This possibility is illustrated by *Thavorn v Bank of Credit & Commerce SA*[217] where A opened a bank account in the name of her nephew B (who was under age), stipulating that only A should operate the account. It was held that B was a mere nominee and that the bank was not discharged by (or was liable in damages to A for) paying B at the sole request of B and without any instructions from A. There were two reasons why B could not have sued the bank: no promise by the bank had been made to him, and no consideration had moved from him.

3–045 **Contracts (Rights of Third Parties) Act 1999.** Under this Act, a term in a contract between A (the promisor) and B (the promisee) is, in specified conditions, enforceable by a third party, C, against A. The Act is more fully discussed in Chapter 18[218]; the only points to be made here are that C is not prevented from enforcing the term by the fact that no consideration for A's promise moved from him,[219] and that C's right to enforce that promise can be described as a quasi-exception to the rule that consideration must move from the promisee.[220] It is not a true exception to the rule since in the case put the promisee is B, who must provide consideration for A's promise.

7. COMPROMISE AND FORBEARANCE TO SUE

3–046 **Introductory.** Three situations call for discussion: in the first a person promises not to enforce a *valid* claim (or performs such a promise); in the second the claim which is the subject-matter of such a promise is *invalid* or *doubtful*; and in the third the person in question simply *forbears in fact* from enforcing a claim, without making any *promise* to forbear. The question in all these cases is whether the promise to forbear (or its performance), or the actual forbearance (without any promise), can constitute consideration for a (counter-) promise made by the other party.[221]

(a) *Valid Claims*

3–047 **Promise not to sue on a valid claim.** A creditor's promise not to enforce a valid claim is normally good consideration for a promise given in return.[222] For

---

[217] [1985] 1 Lloyd's Rep. 529. The Contracts (Rights of Third Parties) Act 1999 would not apply to such a case as it was not the intention of the contracting parties that B should be entitled to enforce the contract: see s.1(2) of the Act, below, para.18–091.

[218] Below, paras 18–088 *et seq.*

[219] Law Com. No.242 (on which the Act is based), para.6.8.

[220] Below, para.18–097.

[221] Our concern in the ensuing discussion is with compromises made otherwise than in legal proceedings. Where legal proceedings have been brought, acceptance of an offer to settle the proceedings under CPR Pt. 36 "may well create a contract and probably does so in the vast majority of cases": *Orton v Collins* [2007] EWHC 803 (Ch), [2007] 1 W.L.R. 2953 at [60]. But the obligation that arises from a Pt. 36 settlement agreement "is not primarily contractual. It is *sui generis*. It is part of the court's inherent jurisdiction . . . " (*ibid.*, at [62]). It may therefore be binding even though it lacks contractual force, e.g. for failure to comply with formal requirements (as in *Orton v Collins*, above) or, presumably, for want of consideration.

[222] See *Pullin v Stokes* (1794) 2 H.Bl. 312; *Smith v Algar* (1830) 1 B. & Ad. 603; *Morton v Burn* (1837) 7 A. & E. 19; *Coles v Pack* (1869) L.R. 5 C.P. 65; *Crears v Hunter* (1887) 19 Q.B.D. 341; *Greene v Church Commissioners for England* [1974] Ch. 467. See also *Oliver v Davis* [1949] 2 K.B.

example, a creditor to whom a sum of money has become due may promise to give the debtor extra time to pay, in return for the debtor's promise to give additional security or to pay higher interest. In such a case, there is good consideration for the debtor's promise: the creditor suffers a detriment in that he is, at least for a time, kept out of his money, while the debtor benefits by getting extra time to pay.[223] In the case put (of a creditor giving his debtor extra time to pay) there is such detriment and benefit even though the creditor has promised to forbear only for a limited time[224]; if no time is specified in the promise, the court will infer that the creditor undertook to forbear for a reasonable time.[225] *A fortiori*, the creditor will provide consideration where he promises absolutely not to sue on the claim[226]: this is the position where a valid claim is settled by agreement between the parties. The principles just stated apply not only to a promise not to enforce a claim but also to one to abandon a good defence[227]; and to one to abandon a particular remedy: *e.g.* to one to abandon arbitration proceedings.[228] Analogous reasoning has been used to support the view that, where a husband is ordered to transfer property to his former wife by way of ancillary relief in divorce proceedings, then the wife provides consideration for the transfer in the sense that the transfer wholly or in part satisfies her claim for an ancillary relief.[228a]

Construction of releases: Although a promise to release a valid claim is thus supported by consideration, the court may protect the party granting the release on other grounds. This possibility is illustrated by *Bank of Credit and Commerce International S.A. v Ali*[229] where an employee, on being dismissed for redundancy, promised, in return for certain payments, to release all claims against the employers "of whatever nature that exist or may exist." At the time of the release, claims for "stigma damages" were believed not to be available to employees for breach of their employment contracts, but the availability of such claims was established by a later decision of the House of Lords.[230] It was held 3–048

727, especially at 743; *Centrovincial Estates plc v Merchant Investors Assurance Co Ltd, The Times*, March 8, 1983 (as to which see above para.2–003, n.15); *G.N. Angelakis Co SA v Cie Algérienne de Navigation (The Attika Hope)* [1988] 1 Lloyd's Rep. 439; *Hill v Haines* [2007] EWCA Civ 1284, [2008] 2 All E.R. 901 at [79].

[223] *Crowther v Farrer* (1850) 15 Q.B. 677. It seems to be immaterial whether the proceedings have been commenced or not: see *Wade v Simeon* (1846) 2 C.B. 548, 565, 567.

[224] *Willatts v Kennedy* (1831) 8 Bing. 5; *Morton v Burn* (1837) A. & E. 19; *Board v Hoey* (1949) 65 T.L.R. 43.

[225] *Payne v Wilson* (1827) 7 B. & C. 423; *Oldershaw v King* (1857) 2 H. & N.517; *Fullerton v Provincial Bank of Ireland* [1903] A.C. 309, 313.

[226] *Mapes v Sidney* (1624) Cro.Jac. 683.

[227] See *Banque de l'Indochine v J. H. Rayner (Mincing Lane) Ltd* [1983] Q.B. 711; *Hill v Haines* [2007] EWCA Civ 1284, [2008] 2 All E.R. 901 at [30].

[228] *Allied Marine Transport Ltd v Vale do Rio Doce Navegaçao SA (The Leonidas D.)* [1985] 1 W.L.R. 925, 933.

[228a] *Hill v Haines* [2007] EWCA Civ 1284, [2008] 2 All E.R. 901 at [39]; the issue in this case was not whether there was any consideration for a *promise* but whether there was consideration for a *transfer* (*cf.* above, paras 3–016, 3–031). The wife was held to have provided such consideration even though her original claim depended for its quantification on the discretion of the court: *Hill v Haines*, above, at [39], approving the judgment of District Judge Cooke, described at [53] as "a model of lucid erudition".

[229] [2001] UKHL 8; [2002] 1 A.C. 251.

[230] *Malik v Bank of Credit and Commerce International* [1998] A.C. 20, below, para.26–086.

by the House of Lords in the present case that the general words of the release (quoted above) were not sufficiently clear to show "that the parties intended to provide for the release of rights and surrender of claims which they could never have had in contemplation at all."[231] It is implicit in this reasoning that the possibility of releasing such a claim is not ruled out as a matter of law: the court is simply "slow to infer that a party intended to surrender rights and claims of which he was unaware and could not have been aware."[232]

3–049 **Other grounds for relief.** The crucial point in *Ali's* case (above, para.3–048) seems to have been that *neither* party could have been aware of the possibility that the employee might, in law, have had a claim for stigma damages. If the *employer* had been aware of this possibility, it is far from clear that the employee would have succeeded on the issue of *construction*. There is, however, the further possibility that the amount of a settlement may be affected by the fact that "the party to whom the release was given [B] knew that the other party [A] had or might have a claim [beyond the one he thought he was releasing] *and knew also* that the other party was ignorant of this."[233] B's taking the release "without disclosing the existence of the claim or possible claim" would then be "unacceptable sharp practice"[234] and there is judicial support for the view that the law should on this ground grant relief to A,[235] *i.e.* allow him to pursue the claim which he had unwittingly abandoned.

(b) *Invalid or Doubtful Claims*

3–050 **Claims known to be invalid.** A compromise of a claim which is legally invalid and which is either known by the party asserting it to be invalid or not believed by that party to be valid is not contractually binding. This rule can be explained either on the ground that merely making or performing a promise to give up a worthless claim cannot constitute consideration for the counter-promise,[236] or (preferably) on grounds of public policy. As Tindal C.J. said in *Wade v Simeon*[237]: "It is almost *contra bonos mores* and certainly contrary to all

[231] [2002] 1 A.C. 251 at [19]. This reasoning does not apply to an arbitration clause in a contract since the very purpose of such a clause is "to provide machinery for the resolution of disputes which may arise in the future": *Capital Trust Investment Ltd v Radio Design TJAB* [2002] EWCA Civ. 135; [2002] 2 All E.R. 159, at [50]; *cf.* on the issue of construction, *Mostcash plc v Fluor Ltd* [2002] EWCA Civ. 975, [2002] B.L.R. 411.

[232] [2002] 1 A.C. 251 at [10]. Lord Hoffmann dissented.

[233] *ibid.*, at [32], italics supplied.

[234] *ibid.*, at [32]. In *Ali's* case there was no such knowledge on B's part.

[235] *ibid.*, *per* Lord Nicholls. Lord Bingham left the point open: *ibid.*, at [20].

[236] The position is different if there is also *other* consideration for the promise; see *The Siboen and the Sibotre* [1976] 1 Lloyd's Rep. 293, 334.

[237] (1846) 2 C.B. 548, 564. See also *Edwards v Baugh* (1843) 11 M. & W. 641, especially at 646; *Callisher v Bischoffsheim* (1870) L.R. 5 Q.B. 449 at 452 ("fraudulent"). It followed that a promise by a bookmaker not to sue his client for lost bets was formerly no consideration for a promise made in return by the client: was hard to support. Now that the bookmaker can enforce the client's promise by virtue of Gambling Act 2005, s.335(1) (Vol. II, para.40–000) the bookmaker's promise not to sue the client for the amount of the lost bet will generally constitute good consideration for a promise made in return by the client: *Hyams v Coombes* (1912) 28 T.L.R. 413; *Burrell & Son v Leven* (1926) 42 T.L.R. 407; *Poteliakhoff v Teakle* [1938] 2 K.B. 816; *Goodson v Baker* (1908) 98 L.T. 415 (*contra*).

the principles of natural justice that a man should institute proceedings against another when he is conscious that he has no good cause of action."

Claims which are doubtful in law. The compromise of a claim which is doubtful in law is binding as a contract. Making or performing a promise to give up a doubtful claim can constitute consideration for a counter-promise since it involves the possibility of detriment to the person to whom the latter promise is made and that of benefit to the person making it. In *Haigh v Brooks*, for example,[238] it was held that the promisee had provided consideration by giving up a guarantee containing "an ambiguity that might be explained . . . so as to make it a valid contract."[239] **3–051**

Claims in law invalid but made in good faith. The rule stated in para.3–051 above applies also if the forbearing party's claim is *clearly invalid* in law, so long as it was a "reasonable claim"[240] (*i.e.* one made on reasonable grounds) which was in good faith believed by the party forbearing to have at any rate a fair chance of success.[241] Since the claimant would, if he did not forbear, in such a case lose both his action and the costs, it is not easy to see what detriment he suffers by forbearing; one possible argument is that the delay in bringing the action (induced by the other party's promise) will increase the difficulty and costs of bringing it,[242] even though it was bound to fail. It is also arguable that the other party (the promisor) benefits since "instead of being annoyed with the action, he escapes from the vexations incident to it."[243] This may, indeed, also be true where the claim is *known* to be invalid; but the rule that a compromise of such a claim is not binding is, as has been suggested in para.3–050 above, more appropriately based on grounds of public policy than on want of consideration. **3–052**

Two further conditions must be satisfied by a party who relies on his forbearance to enforce an invalid claim as the consideration for a promise made to him. He must not deliberately conceal from the other party (*i.e.* the promisor) **3–053**

[238] (1839) 10 A. & E. 309; for the earlier, contrary view see *Stone v Wythipol* (1588) Cro.Eliz. 126; *Jones v Ashburnham* (1804) 4 East 455 and dicta in *Ex p. Banner* (1881) 17 Ch.D. 480, 490 (these dicta being disapproved in *Miles v New Zealand Alford Estate Co* (1885) 32 Ch.D. 266).

[239] (1839) 10 A. & E. 309, 334; *cf. Colchester BC v Smith* [1992] Ch. 421; *Colonia Versicherung A.G. v Amoco Oil Co* [1995] 1 Lloyd's Rep. 570, 577 (affirmed without reference to this point [1997] 1 Lloyd's Rep. 261).

[240] *Cook v Wright* (1861) 1 B. & S. 559, 569.

[241] *Callisher v Bischoffsheim* (1870) L.R. 5 Q.B. 449. See also *Longridge v Dorville* (1821) 5 B. & Ad. 117; *Cooper v Parker* (1855) 15 C.B. 822; *Cook v Wright* (1861) 1 B. & S. 559; *Ockford v Barelli* (1871) 20 W.R. 116; *Holsworthy UDC v Holsworthy RDC* [1907] 2 Ch. 62; *Re Cole* [1931] 2 Ch. 174; *Freedman v Union Group plc* [1997] E.G.C.S. 28; *Moussaka Inc. v Golden Seagull Maritime Inc.* [2002] 1 Lloyd's Rep. 797 at [14]; *Hill v Haines* [2007] EWCA Civ 1284, [2008] 2 All E.R. 901 at [79]. For a discussion of the English decisions on a Scottish appeal, see *Hunter v Bradford Property Trust*, 1970 S.L.T. 173. Scots law does not require promises to be supported by consideration but distinguishes for certain purposes between gratuitous and onerous promises.

[242] *Cook v Wright* (1861) 1 B.& S. 559, 569.

[243] *Callisher v Bischoffsheim*, above n.233, at 452; *cf. Pitt v P.H.H. Asset Management Ltd* [1994] 1 W.L.R. 327 at 322, but in that case it is not clear that the party forbearing in fact believed in the validity of his claim; *Moussaka Inc v Golden Seagull Maritime Inc* [2002] 1 Lloyd's Rep. 797 at [14] ("commercial benefit").

facts which, if known to the latter, would enable him to defeat the claim.[244] And he must show that he seriously intended to pursue the claim.[245]

3–054 **Claims on disputed facts.** The cases considered in paras 3–051 and 3–052 concern claims the validity of which is doubtful in law. It seems that the same principles can apply where the validity of a claim is in doubt because of a dispute about the facts. A settlement based on a simple *mistake* of fact shared by both parties may be void for mistake.[246] But this would not be the case where both parties knowingly took the risk that the facts might turn out to be different from the facts as they were alleged or supposed to be. A negotiation of a settlement on disputed facts always takes such an element of risk into account.

3–055 **Void forbearances.** The forbearance itself (as opposed to the claim forborne) may be void on grounds of public policy, or by statute: for example, where a wife promises her husband not to apply for maintenance in matrimonial proceedings.[247] In such cases the promise to forbear cannot of course be enforced; but, unless the promise is illegal, it may nevertheless constitute consideration for a counter-promise to make a payment in return for it.[248] *A fortiori* the performance of the promise to forbear may (if the promise was not illegal) be good consideration for a counter-promise[249] even though the promise could not have been enforced.

3–056 **Executed compromises.** The discussion in paras 3–050 to 3–055 is concerned with the enforceability of an agreement to compromise a claim. Different problems can arise after such an agreement has been *performed*, generally by payment of the amount which one party agreed to pay under the compromise. Even if there was, under the rules discussed above, no consideration for that party's promise, he will not be entitled to the return of the payment if it was made "to close the transaction"[250]; in such a case the payment is treated as if it were an executed gift.[251] To give rise to a claim for repayment, it will be necessary to establish other circumstances, such as that the payment was made under duress.[252]

---

[244] *Miles v New Zealand Alford Estate Co*, above n.238, at 284; *Colchester BC v Smith* [1992] Ch. 421, 435. The discussion in para.3–049, above, is concerned with the different problem of non-disclosure by the party *against* whom a valid claim is made of facts affecting the extent of that party's liability.

[245] *Cook v Wright* (1861) 1 B. & S. 559, 569; *Syros Shipping Co SA v Elaghill Trading Co (The Proodos C)* [1980] 2 Lloyd's Rep. 390, 392.

[246] *e.g. Gloyne v Richardson* [2001] EWCA Civ. 716; [2002] 2 B.C.L.C. 669 at [39]; *cf. Grains & Fourrages SA v Huyton* [1997] 1 Lloyd's Rep. 628, where there was no compromise since both parties wished from the start to achieve the same result but were mistaken only as to the effect of the steps they had taken to achieve it.

[247] Matrimonial Causes Act 1973, s.34, re-enacting Maintenance Agreements Act 1957, s.1, below, para.16–044.

[248] Below, para.3–166.

[249] Below, para.3–167.

[250] *Woolwich Equitable B.S. v IRC* [1993] A.C. 70, 165.

[251] *ibid.* citing *Maskell v Horner* [1915] 3 K.B. 106, 120.

[252] Below, Ch.7.

(c) *Actual Forbearance*

Actual forbearance may be consideration. A creditor who, without making any express promise, simply forbears from enforcing a debt or other claim may be held to have impliedly promised to forbear.[253] For example, the acceptance of a cheque in payment of a debt may be evidence of a promise not to sue the debtor so long as the cheque is not dishonoured, or at least for a reasonable time.[254] Where the claim is of such a kind that a promise to forbear (or the performance of it) would constitute consideration for a counter-promise,[255] an actual forbearance may also constitute consideration even though the creditor has not made any express or implied promise to forbear. In *Alliance Bank v Broom*[256] the defendant owed £22,000 to his bank, who pressed him to give security. He promised to do so but the bank made no counter-promise not to sue him. It was held that there was consideration for the defendant's promise as the bank had given, and the defendant received, "some degree of forbearance."[257] On the other hand, in *Miles v New Zealand Alford Estate Co*[258] a company had bought land and then became dissatisfied with the purchase. The vendor later promised to make certain payments to the company, and it was alleged that the consideration for this promise was the company's forbearance to take proceedings to rescind the contract. A majority of the Court of Appeal held that there was no consideration for the vendor's promise as no proceedings to rescind were ever intended; and Cotton L.J. added that "it must be shown that there was something which would bind the company not to institute proceedings."[259] Bowen L.J. dissented from his proposition,[260] relying on *Alliance Bank v Broom*; but it may be possible to reconcile the cases by reference to the types of claim forborne. A bank to which £22,000 is owed is virtually certain to take steps to enforce its claim, but a dissatisfied purchaser of land is much less certain to take proceedings for rescission. It may, therefore, be reasonable to say that mere forbearance will amount to consideration in relation to the former type of claim, but that a promise to forbear is necessary where it is problematical whether the claim will ever be enforced. A promise to forbear is also, of course, necessary where that is what the debtor bargains for. 3–057

Time for which creditor must forbear. Where the consideration consists of a promise to forbear which specifies no time the creditor must forbear for a 3–058

[253] *Re Wyvern Developments Ltd* [1974] 1 W.L.R. 1097; *Thornton Springer v NEM Insurance Co Ltd* [2000] 2 All E.R. 489 at 516.

[254] *Baker v Walker* (1845) 14 M. & W. 465; *Elkington v Cooke-Hill* (1914) 30 T.L.R. 670; contrast *Hasan v Wilson* [1977] 1 Lloyd's Rep. 431, where the debt in respect of which the cheque was given was that of a third party.

[255] *i.e.* not if the claim is known to be invalid: above, para.3–050.

[256] (1864) 2 Dr. & Sm. 289; *R v Att-Gen for England and Wales* [2003] UKPC 22, [2003] E.M.L.R. 24 at [31].

[257] At 292.

[258] (1886) 32 Ch.D. 267; *cf. Hunter v Bradford Property Trust Ltd*, 1970 S.L.T. 173.

[259] (1886) 32 Ch.D. 267, 285.

[260] *ibid.* at 291; his view was approved by Lord Macnaghten in *Fullerton v Provincial Bank of Ireland* [1903] A.C. 309, 314.

reasonable time.[261] There is no such requirement where the consideration consists of actual forbearance: here it is enough that the debtor had "a certain amount of forbearance."[262]

3–059 **Relation between actual forbearance and the promise made in return for it.** Where the consideration is alleged to consist of an actual forbearance, that forbearance must be causally connected with the debtor's promise. A creditor does not give consideration[263] merely by forbearing to enforce an antecedent debt.[264] In *Wigan v English & Scottish Law Life Assurance Society*[265] a debtor executed an assignment of an insurance policy by way of mortgage in favour of his creditor. Parker J. held that the creditor, who knew nothing of the mortgage, had given no consideration for it[266]; but he added that the creditor would have provided consideration if he had been told of the mortgage and if, "on the strength of" it, he had actually forborne to sue for the debt.

3–060 **Express or implied request of debtor necessary.** The crucial question, therefore, is whether the creditor has forborne "on the strength of" the debtor's promise. He will clearly have done so where the debtor has *expressly* requested the forbearance.[267] But such an express request is not necessary. In *Alliance Bank v Broom*[268] the bank's forbearance was held to constitute consideration even though the defendant had not expressly requested it. Lord Macnaghten later explained the case on the ground that the debtor had impliedly requested forbearance.[269] It seems that an actual forbearance which is not induced by either the express or the implied request of the debtor is no consideration. In *Combe v Combe*[270] a husband during divorce proceedings promised to pay his wife an annual allowance. In an action to enforce this promise, the wife argued, *inter alia*, that she had given consideration for it by forbearing to apply to the court for a maintenance order. But it was held that there was no consideration as the wife had not forborne at the husband's request.[271]

8. EXISTING DUTIES AS CONSIDERATION[272]

3–061 **General.** Much difficulty arises in determining whether a person who does, or promises to do, what he is already in law bound to do thereby provides consideration for a promise made to him. One possible view is that, as he was already

[261] Above, para.3–047.
[262] *Alliance Bank v Broom* (1864) 2 Dr. & Sm. 289, 292.
[263] Or, which comes to the same thing, gives only past consideration.
[264] Above, para.3–031.
[265] [1909] 1 Ch. 291; *cf. Hopkins v Logan* (1839) 5 M. & W. 241.
[266] Above, para.3–031.
[267] *Crears v Hunter* (1887) 19 Q.B.D. 341, 344.
[268] (1864) 2 Dr. & Sm. 289; above, para.3–057.
[269] *Fullerton v Provincial Bank of Ireland* [1903] A.C. 309, 313.
[270] [1951] 2 K.B. 215.
[271] *Quaere* whether such a request should not have been implied. On the question whether a "request" is necessary, see A.L.G. (1951) 67 L.Q.R. 456; Smith (1953) 69 L.Q.R. 99. It seems that in the present type of case, involving a forbearance to sue, a request is necessary, whether or not this is true of unilateral contracts generally. As to this, see *Australian Woollen Mills Pty Ltd v The Commonwealth* (1954) 92 C.L.R. 424, especially at 457–460.
[272] Reynolds and Treitel (1965) 7 Malaya L.Rev. 1; Aivazian, Trebilcock & Penny (1984) 22 Osgoode Hall L.J. 173; Hooley [1991] J.B.L. 195; Halson (1991) 107 L.Q.R. 649.

bound to do the thing in question, his doing, or promising to do, it has no "value in the eye of the law"[273]: hence it cannot amount to a legal detriment to him, or to a legal benefit[274] to the person already entitled to performance. On the other hand the actual performance of the legal duty may amount to a factual detriment or benefit: it may be a detriment to the party performing the duty since actual performance may be more troublesome to him than the payment of (or the risk of being sued for) damages; while the other party may benefit in the sense of finding his legal remedy for breach of the duty less beneficial than its actual performance. Denning L.J. has therefore said that the performance of an existing duty, or the promise to perform it, was always good consideration.[275] This radical view has not been accepted; but the requirement of consideration in this group of cases has been mitigated by recognising that it can be satisfied where the promisee has conferred a factual (as opposed to a legal) benefit on the promisor.[276]

(a) *Public Duty*

Where the promisee is under a public duty. It has been held that a person cannot recover money promised to him in return for his performance of, or promise to perform, a duty imposed by law. In *Collins v Godefroy*,[277] an attorney had been subpoenaed to give evidence on the defendant's behalf and alleged that the defendant had promised to pay him a guinea a day for his loss of time incurred in such attendance. It was held that, as the promisee was under a duty imposed by law to attend, the defendant's promise was given "without consideration." But this reasoning is hard to reconcile with some of the cases to be discussed below,[278] holding that promises of rewards for information leading to the arrest of criminals could be enforced; and other "public duty" cases are more readily explained on grounds of public policy: it has, for example, been held that a public officer cannot enforce a promise by a private citizen to pay him money for doing his public duty[279] and that a person cannot enforce a promise made in consideration of his forbearing to engage in a course of conduct that is criminal.[280] To uphold such promises would encourage undesirable forms of extortion; and this, rather than want of consideration, accounts for most of the authorities which establish the present rule. It is arguable that, when there are no such grounds of public policy against enforcing the promise, an action on it will not fail for want of consideration merely because the performance rendered in return 3–062

[273] *Thomas v Thomas* (1842) 2 Q.B. 851 at 859.

[274] Above, para.3–006.

[275] *Ward v Byham* [1956] 1 W.L.R. 496, 498; *Williams v Williams* [1957] 1 W.L.R. 148, 151.

[276] Below, para.3–068.

[277] (1831) 1 B. & Ad. 950. See also *Willis v Peckham* (1820) 1 Br. & B. 515; *Thoresen Car Ferries Ltd v Weymouth Portland BC* [1977] 2 Lloyd's Rep. 614, 619. For contracts to pay fees to expert witnesses, see *Goulden v Wilson Barca* [2000] 1 W.L.R. 167.

[278] below, at n.282.

[279] *Wathen v Sandys* (1811) 2 Camp. 640; *Morris v Burdett* (1808) 1 Camp. 218; *Bilke v Havelock* (1813) 3 Camp. 374; *cf. Morgan v Palmer* (1824) 2 B. & C. 729, 736 (where the actual decision was that money paid to the official was recoverable by the payee as having been extorted from him *colore officii*: see *Woolwich Equitable B.S. v I.R.C.* [1993] A.C. 70, 155, 165, 181, 198).

[280] *Brown v Brine* (1875) L.R. 1 Ex.D. 5 (forbearance to commit criminal libel).

was already due under a public duty from the promisee. Before 1968 a person who knew that a felony had been committed and had information which might lead to the arrest of the felon was bound to communicate the information to the police: if he failed to do so he was guilty of misprision of felony.[281] Yet promises to pay rewards for such information could be enforced, even by police officers giving the information.[282] Public policy was not offended by such offers, as they might induce people to look for the information and so promote the interests of justice. The term "felony" is now obsolete[283] and the mere failure to disclose information which might lead to the arrest of a criminal is no longer an offence[284] or a breach of a duty imposed by law. But the old reward cases show that an act may constitute consideration even though there is a public duty to do it.

3–063 **Promisee doing more than public duty.** A person who is under a public duty can provide consideration for a promise by doing (or promising to do) more than he was by law obliged to do. In *Glasbrook Brothers Ltd v Glamorgan County Council*[285] the owners of a coal mine, who feared violence from strikers, asked, and promised to pay, the police for a greater degree of protection than the police reasonably thought necessary. It was held that the police had provided consideration for this promise by providing the extra protection, and that accordingly the promise was enforceable. The position in cases of this kind is now regulated by statute. Section 25(1) of the Police Act 1996 provides that payment can be claimed for "special police services" rendered at the "request" of the person requiring them. Such a request can be implied from conduct: *e.g.* where a person organises an event which cannot safely take place without such services. On this reasoning, a football club has been held liable to the police authority for the cost of policing matches played on its ground.[286] Such liability arises irrespective of contract.[287]

---

281 *Sykes v D.P.P.* [1962] A.C. 528.

282 *England v Davidson* (1840) 11 A. & E. 856; *Smith v Moore* (1845) 1 C.B. 438; *Neville v Kelly* (1862) 12 C.B.(N.S.) 740; *Bent v Wakefield and Barnsley Union Bank* (1878) 4 C.P.D. 1. Contrast *Maryland Casualty Co v Matthews* 209 F.Supp. 822 (1962) where a similar claim by a detective failed on grounds of public policy.

283 Criminal Law Act 1967, s.1.

284 The offence of concealing an arrestable offence created by s.5(1) of the Criminal Law Act 1967 is much narrower in scope than the former offence of misprision of felony; the statutory offence is committed only if the person withholding the information accepts or agrees to accept some consideration (other than making good the loss) for not disclosing it. For the definition of "arrestable offence," see now Police and Criminal Evidence Act 1984, s.24; as amended by Police Reform Act 2002, s.48.

285 [1925] A.C. 270. *cf. Thoresen Car Ferries v Weymouth Portland BC* [1997] 2 Lloyd's Rep. 614 (A's promise to *make use* of B's services for which he was under a legal duty to *pay* held to constitute consideration for B's counterpromise).

286 *Harris v Sheffield United F.C. Ltd* [1988] Q.B. 77. Contrast *Reading Festival Ltd v West Yorkshire Police Authority* [2006] EWCA Civ. 524, [2006] 1 W.L.R. 2005 where a similar claim against the promoters of a music festival failed, principally on the ground that they had not made any "request" for the police services in respect of which the claim was made.

287 Dicta in the *Reading Festival* case, above n.286, emphasise that a claim under subsection 25(1) can succeed only if there has been a "meeting of the minds" between the police authority and the promoter (at [54]) and add (at [20]) that the subsection had not "added to or altered the common law position" as stated in the *Glasbrook* case, above n.285. But it was also said that the police "had the last word on charges" (at [20]) and that "how the police provide the services must always be a matter for them" (at [21]). It is respectfully submitted that an agreement for services which left such a broad

In *Ward v Byham*[288] the father of an illegitimate child wrote to its mother, from whom he was separated, saying that she could have the child and an allowance of £1 a week if she proved that the child was "well looked after and happy and also that she is allowed to decide for herself whether or not she wishes to come and live with you." The father refused to continue the payments after the marriage of the mother to another man. It was held that the mother was entitled to enforce the father's promise even though she was under a statutory duty to maintain the child. One ground for the decision is that the mother had provided consideration by showing that she had made the child happy, etc.: in this way, she could be said to have done more than she was required by law to do,[289] and to have conferred a factual benefit on the father[290] or on the child,[291] even though she may not have suffered any detriment. But if a son's promise not to bore his father is not good consideration, it is hard to see why a mother's promise to make her child happy should, for the present purpose, stand on a different footing.[292] There is, with respect, force in Denning L.J.'s view that the mother provided consideration by merely performing her legal duty to support the child. There was certainly no ground of public policy for refusing to enforce the promise. 3–064

(b) *Duty Imposed by Contract with Promisor*

Contractual duty to promisor. When A was bound by contract with B to do, or to forbear from doing, something, the law at one time took the view that A's performance of that duty (or his promise to perform it) was no consideration for a new promise by B. Later authority has qualified that view, but the extent of the qualification is uncertain. The cases fall into three groups. 3–065

Cases in which there was no consideration. The view that there was no consideration for B's new promise is usually traced back to *Stilk Myrick*.[293] In that case two of the crew of a ship had deserted during the voyage for which they had contracted to serve and the master promised to divide the wages of the deserters amongst the other nine if replacements for the deserters could not be found (as turned out to be the case). The court rejected a claim brought by one of the promisees against the master for a share of the extra wages promised by the master. According to one of the reports,[294] the claim was rejected on grounds of public policy stated in an earlier similar case,[295] *viz*. that the enforcement of such promises might lead sailors to refuse to perform their contracts unless they 3–066

---

discretion to the provider of the services as to what services were to be provided and what the recipient of the services was to pay for them would not normally be sufficiently certain to give rise to a binding contract (see above, para.2–112).

[288] [1956] 1 W.L.R. 496.

[289] This may be what Morris and Parker L.JJ. had in mind when saying at 499 that the mother had provided "ample consideration" for the promise.

[290] See *Williams v Roffey Bros. & Nicholls (Contractors) Ltd* [1991] 1 Q.B. 1, 13.

[291] Consideration need not move to the promisor: above para.3–039.

[292] Above, para.3–022.

[293] (1809) 2 Camp. 317; 6 Esp. 129. See also *Harris v Carter* (1854) 3 E. & B. 559; *Sanderson v Workington BC* (1918) 34 T.L.R. 386; *Swain v West (Butchers) Ltd* [1936] 1 All E.R. 224.

[294] (1809) 6 Esp. 129.

[295] *Harris v Watson* (1791) Peake 102.

were promised extra pay. But according to the other report[296] (which has been said to have "the better reputation")[297] the court doubted that reasoning and based its decision instead on the ground that the nine crew members had provided no consideration by doing what they were already bound by their contracts to do; and it is on this ground that the case is now generally explained.[298] On the same principle, a promise to pay more than the originally agreed freight for the carriage of goods to the agreed destination cannot be enforced by the carrier[299]; and, where a debt is already due in full, a promise by the debtor to pay it in stated instalments is no consideration for the creditor's promise not to take bankruptcy proceedings in respect of the debt.[300]

3–067 **Bases of the rule: public policy or want of consideration?** The public policy explanation of the rule, stated in para.3–066 above,[301] was always open to the objection that it was based on a danger that was no more than hypothetical: in the cases on seamen's wages,[302] for example, there was no evidence of any refusal on the men's part to perform their original contracts. Even where there is such evidence, the public policy argument is much reduced in importance now that the law has come to recognise that such a refusal may amount to economic duress.[303] Where the refusal *does* amount to duress, a promise induced by it can be avoided (and money paid in pursuance of it be recovered back) on that ground.[304] This is true even where the promise *is* supported by consideration: for example, where the promisee has undertaken not merely to perform his duties under the original contract, but also to render some relatively small additional service.[305] If, on the other hand, the promisee's refusal to perform the original contract does *not* amount to duress, the promise cannot be impugned merely on

[296] (1809) 2 Camp. 317; in *Harris v Carter* (1854) 3 E. & B. 559, both public policy and want of consideration are relied on to explain the rule.

[297] *North Ocean Shipping Co Ltd v Hyundai Construction Co Ltd (The Atlantic Baron)* [1979] Q.B. 705, 712, where the rule in *Stilk v Myrick* was recognised as being still good law, though held inapplicable for reasons stated in para.3–067, below; Coote [1980] C.L.J. 40; *South Caribbean Trading Ltd v Trafigura Beheer BV* [2004] EWHC 2676, [2005] 1 Lloyd's Rep. 128 at [107], as to which case see also below, paras 3–069, 3–079.

[298] *Harrison v Dodd* (1914) 111 L.T. 47; *Swain v West (Butchers) Ltd* [1936] 3 All E.R. 261; *North Ocean Shipping Co Ltd v Hyundai Construction Co Ltd (The Atlantic Baron)* [1979] Q.B. 705, 712; *Pao On v Lau Yiu Long* [1980] A.C. 614, 633; *Sybron Corp. v Rochem Ltd* [1983] I.C.R. 801, 817; *Vantage Navigation Corp. v Suhail and Saud Building Materials LLC (The Alev)* [1989] 1 Lloyd's Rep. 138, 147; *Hadley v Kemp* [1999] E.M.L.R. 586, 626.

[299] *Syros Shipping Co SA v Elaghill Trading Co Ltd (The Proodos C)* [1980] 2 Lloyd's Rep. 390; *Atlas Express Ltd v Kafco (Importers and Distributors) Ltd* [1989] 1 Q.B. 833.

[300] *Vanbergen v St. Edmunds Properties Ltd* [1933] 2 K.B. 223.

[301] above, at n.295.

[302] above, at nn.293–295.

[303] Below, Ch.7; *Atlas Express Ltd v Kafco (Importers and Distributors) Ltd* [1989] 1 Q.B. 833.

[304] This would have been the result in *North Ocean Shipping Co Ltd v Hyundai Construction Co Ltd (The Atlantic Baron)*, above, n.297, if the victim of the duress had not affirmed the contract. For cases in which recovery was allowed on this ground, see *Universe Tankships Inc v International Transport Workers' Federation (The Universe Sentinel)* [1983] 1 A.C. 366; *B. & S. Contracts & Designs v Victor Green Publications Ltd* [1984] I.C.R. 449; and *T. A. Sundell & Sons Pty Ltd v Emm Yannoulatos (Overseas) Pty Ltd* [1956] 56 S.R. (N.S.W.) 323.

[305] *e.g. North Ocean Shipping Co Ltd v Hyundai Construction Co Ltd (The Atlantic Baron)* [1979] Q.B. 705; below, para.3–070; *Vantage Navigation Corp. v. Sahail and Saud Building Materials LLC (The Alev)* [1989] 1 Lloyd's Rep. 138, 147.

the ground that the refusal amounted to an abuse by the promisee of a dominant bargaining position.[306] To allow a promise to be invalidated on this ground even though there was *no* duress would introduce an intermediate category of promises unfairly obtained; and this would (in the words of Lord Scarman) "be unhelpful because it would render the law uncertain."[307] The now more generally held view is that the new promises in the present group of cases are unenforceable for want of consideration; and the reason for this view seems to have been that the promisee suffered no legal detriment[308] in performing what was already due from him, nor did the promisor receive any legal benefit in receiving what was already due to him. But this reasoning takes no account of the fact that the promisee may in fact suffer a detriment: for example, the wages which a seaman could earn elsewhere might exceed those due to him under the original contract together with the damages which he would have to pay for breaking it. Conversely the promisor may in fact benefit from the performance which he receives in consequence of the new promise: in *Stilk v Myrick* the master got the ship home, and this may well have been worth more to him than any damages that he could have recovered from the crew.

Factual benefit to promisor. The forgoing discussion shows that a new promise by B in consideration of A's performing his duty to B under an earlier contract between them is not necessarily obtained by duress; and that A's performance of the duty may in fact benefit B. Where both these conditions are satisfied, it has been held that A can enforce B's new promise. In *Williams v Roffey Bros. & Nicholls (Contractors) Ltd*[309] B had engaged A as carpentry subcontractor, for the purpose of performing a contract between B and X to refurbish a number of flats. The amount payable by B to A under the subcontract was £20,000 but B later promised to make extra payments to A, who undertook no additional obligation in return.[310] B made this new promise because B's own surveyor recognised that the originally agreed sum of £20,000 was too low, and because B feared that A (who was in financial difficulties) would not be able to complete his work on time, and so expose B to penalties for delay under his contract with X. It was held that B's promise to make the extra payments to A was supported by consideration in the shape of the "practical benefits"[311] obtained by B from A's performance of his duties under the original contract 3–068

[306] *Pao On v Lau Yiu Long* [1980] A.C. 614, 632.

[307] *ibid.* at 634. This statement was made in a case involving three parties, but is of general application: *Williams v Roffey Bros. & Nicholls (Contractors) Ltd* [1991] 1 Q.B. 1, 15.

[308] Above, para.3–006.

[309] [1991] 1 Q.B. 1; Adams and Brownsword (1991) 53 M.L.R. 536; Chen-Wishart (1991) 14 N.Z.U.L.R. 270; Hird and Blair, [1996] J.B.L. 254.

[310] The payments under the original contract were found to be due in unspecified instalments while those under the new promise were due as each flat was completed, but no attempt was made to argue that this change in the times when payment was due *might* have been to A's disadvantage and therefore provided consideration. There is perhaps a hint to this effect in Russell L.J.'s judgment at 19.

[311] [1991] 1 Q.B. at 11; *cf. ibid.* at 19, 23, followed in *Anangel Atlas Compania Naviera SA v Ishikawajima Harima Heavy Industries Co Ltd (No.2)* [1990] 2 Lloyd's Rep. 526, where "promisor" and "promisee" appear to have been transposed in a passage at 545; *Simon Container Machinery Ltd v Emba Machinery Ltd* [1998] 2 Lloyd's Rep. 428 at 435.

between them.[312] Since no allegation of duress on A's part had been made by B, the new promise by B to pay extra could not be avoided on this ground. There had been no threat by A to break his original contract; indeed, the initiative for the agreement containing the promise of extra pay seems to have come from B.

3–069 The consideration for B's promise in the *Williams* case appears to have been the factual benefit obtained by B from A's actual performance of his earlier contract with B. This element of factual benefit has been regarded as consideration where a person performs or (promises to perform) a contractual duty owed to a third party[313]; and the *Williams* case is to be welcomed in bringing the two-party cases in line with those involving three parties.[314] But it is by no means clear how the case is, from this point of view, to be reconciled with *Stilk v Myrick* and the line of more recent decisions which have followed that case.[315] As has been suggested above, the master in *Stilk v Myrick* also obtained a factual benefit (in getting the ship home); and such a factual benefit will very often be obtained by B where he secures actual performance from A (as opposed to having to sue him for non-performance of the original contract). In the *Williams* case, *Stilk v Myrick* was not overruled; indeed Purchas L.J. described it as a "pillarstone of the law of contract."[316] But he added that the case might be differently decided today[317]; while Glidewell L.J. said that the present decision did not "contravene" but did "refine and limit"[318] the principle of the earlier case; and Russell L.J. said that the "rigid approach" to consideration in *Stilk v Myrick* was "no longer necessary or desirable."[319] The conclusion which may tentatively be drawn from these statements is that the factual benefit to B in securing A's performance of the earlier contract normally suffices to constitute consideration. The insistence in

[312] In fact, B did not secure the whole of this benefit, but this was because B's wrongful failure to make the extra payments justified A's refusal to continue with the work.
[313] Below, para.3–075.
[314] See below, para.3–074.
[315] Above, para.3–066. The difficulty of reconciling the *Williams* case with *Stilk v Myrick* and the cases which have followed it is discussed in *South Caribbean Trading Ltd v Trafigura Beheer BV* [2004] EWHC 2676 (Comm), [2005] 1 Lloyd's Rep. 128 at [107]–[109]. Colman J, although accepting that the *Williams* case appeared to have introduced "some amelioration", said that he would not have followed it, if it had not been a decision of the Court of Appeal. He regarded the decision as "inconsistent with the . . . rule that consideration must move from the promisee" (at [108]); but it is respectfully submitted that this requirement can be (and in the *Williams* case was) satisfied by the promisee's conferring a benefit on the promisor even though the promisee, in doing so, suffers no detriment (see above, para.3–037).
[316] [1991] 1 Q.B. 1, 20.
[317] *ibid.* at 21. But he was not prepared to accept *Watkins v Carrig* 21 A. 2d 591 (1941), where a contractor who had agreed to do excavating work unexpectedly struck hard rock and was held entitled to enforce a promise to pay nine times the originally agreed sum. The case was said not to represent English law in *North Ocean Shipping Co Ltd v Hyundai Construction Co Ltd* (*The Atlantic Baron*) [1979] Q.B. 705, 714. It was cited with apparent approval in *Compagnie Noga D'Importation et D'Exportation SA v Abacha* [2003] EWCA Civ. 1100; [2003] 2 All E.R. (Comm) 915 at [54] but on the point that the requirement of consideration was satisfied by rescission of the original contract, followed by the making of a new one: below, paras 3–071, 3–079. No mention was made in the *Compagnie Noga* case, above, of the more sceptical references to *Watkins v Carrig* in the *Williams* case and in *The Atlantic Baron*, cited earlier in this note.
[318] [1991] 1 Q.B. 1, 16.
[319] *ibid.* at 18.

the earlier cases on the stricter requirement of legal benefit or detriment is no longer justified (if it ever was) by the need to protect B from the undue pressure that A might exert by refusing to perform his original contract; for this need can now be met by the expanding concept of duress.[320] This provides a more satisfactory solution of the present problem since it invalidates promises only where actual duress is established. Where this is not the case, and the promisee has in fact conferred a benefit on the promisor by performing the original contract, then the requirement of consideration is satisfied and there seems to be no good reason for refusing to enforce the new promise.

Other consideration. The promisee may provide other consideration for the new promise by doing, or promising, more than he was bound by the original contract to do. Thus in one case[321] a seaman was promoted during the course of the voyage and undertook additional duties: these were held to constitute consideration for a promise to pay him extra wages. The same principle was applied where shipbuilders claimed an increase in the agreed price for a supertanker on the ground that the currency in which that price was to be paid had been devalued. The contract provided for the giving by the builders of a performance guarantee, and it was held that they had provided consideration for the prospective owners' promise to pay the price-increase by making corresponding increase in their performance guarantee.[322] 3–070

The promisee similarly provides other consideration where, before the new promise was made, circumstances have arisen which justify the promisee's refusal to perform the original contract. Thus the crew of a ship may be justified in refusing to complete the contractual voyage because so many of their fellows have deserted that its completion will involve hazards not originally contemplated. If they are induced to go on by a promise of extra pay, they do something which they were not bound by the original contract to do and so provide consideration for that promise.[323] The same principle applies if the original contract is determined for other reasons: for example, by lapse of time or by notice or by mutual consent. Thus the parties to a contract could rescind it and then make a new agreement providing for the payment of higher wages. Factual difficulties can no doubt arise in distinguishing between: (1) a rescission followed by a new agreement; and (2) a mere variation. But in principle the distinction is clear[324]: in the first of these situations, the original contract is 3–071

[320] The actual decision in the *South Caribbean* case (above n.315) seems to be explicable on the ground that the promisee's "threat of non-compliance" with the original contract was "analogous to economic duress" (at [108]); though the words "analogous to" give rise to some difficulty insofar as they suggest that there was no actual duress: see above, para.3–067 at n.307.

[321] *Hanson v Royden* (1867) L.R. 3 C.P. 47; *cf. Turner v Owen* (1862) 3 F. & F. 176. *Semble*, such extra pay is recoverable notwithstanding failure to comply with the formal requirements now prescribed by Merchant Shipping Act 1995, s.25.

[322] *North Ocean Shipping Co Ltd v Hyundai Construction Co Ltd (The Atlantic Baron)* [1979] Q.B. 705.

[323] *Hartley v Ponsonby* (1857) 7 E. & B. 872. See also *O'Neil v Armstrong Mitchell & Co* [1895] 2 Q.B. 418; *Palace Shipping Co v Caine* [1907] A.C. 386; *Liston v SS. Carpathian (Owners)* [1915] 2 K.B. 42.

[324] *Compagnie Noga D'Importation et D'Exportation SA v Abacha* [2003] EWCA Civ. 1100; [2003] 2 All E.R. (Comm) 915 at [57].

brought to an end and replaced by a new one in respect of which the requirement of consideration is satisfied,[325] while in the second the original contract continues, so that each party is still bound by it and the promisee who seeks to enforce the variation of it provides no consideration merely by performing his obligations under it.[326] This reasoning would not apply where the original contract was void, or voidable at the option of the promisee, or unenforceable against him, so that in such cases performance by him of the work specified in it would, it seems, be consideration for a promise of extra pay; and if the original contract was in fact good but was believed to be defective, the new promise might still be binding on the analogy of the rule that forbearance to litigate an invalid claim may amount to consideration.[327] A further possibility is that the original contract might, expressly or impliedly, provide for revision of pay scales[328]; in which case a promise to pay higher wages made during the currency of the contract would be binding at common law even if it was not matched by a promise of higher productivity.[329]

(c) *Duty imposed by Contract with a Third Party*

3–072 **Introductory.**[330] Two problems arise under this heading. The first is whether, if A is under a contractual duty to B, the *performance* of this duty can constitute consideration for a promise made to A by C. The second is whether A's *promise* to perform his contractual duty to B can constitute consideration for a counter-promise made to A by C.

3–073 **Performance of the duty.** It is now generally accepted that actual performance of a contractual duty owed to a third party can constitute consideration.[331] Two mid-nineteenth century cases which support this view are not wholly conclusive, since in each of them the promisee did, or may have done, more than he was bound under the earlier contract to do, and so have provided additional consideration.[332] But it is harder to find any such additional consideration in

---

[325] *ibid.* at [44–61]; below, para.3–079.

[326] Below, para.3–079; this was the reasoning of *Stilk v Myrick* (1809) 2 Camp. 317.

[327] Above, para.3–052; *E. Hulton & Co v Chadwick Taylor Ltd* (1918) 34 T.L.R. 230, 231.

[328] *cf. Finland SS. Co Ltd v Felixstowe Dock & Railway Co* [1980] 2 Lloyd's Rep 287; *Lombard Tricity Finance Ltd v Paton* [1989] 1 All E.R. 918 (contract providing for increase in interest rates to be made by lender).

[329] *e.g. Pepper & Hope v Daish* [1980] I.R.L.R. 13. Perhaps it was for this reason that the argument of want of consideration was not raised in *Universe Tankships Inc v International Transport Workers' Federation (The Universe Sentinel)* [1983] 1 A.C. 366.

[330] See A. G. Davis (1937) 6 Camb.L.J. 202.

[331] For the contrary view, see *McDevitt v Stokes* 192 S.W. (1917). In *Pfizer Corp. v Ministry of Health* [1965] A.C. 512 Lord Reid said that there was no contract where a chemist supplied drugs to a patient under the National Health Service in return for a prescription charge, because the chemist is "bound by his contract with the appropriate authority to supply the drug . . . " (at 536). But it seems from the context that Lord Reid was considering whether the relationship was consensual and was not thinking of the problem of consideration.

[332] *Scotson v Peg* (1861) 6 H. & N. 295; *Chichester v Cobb* (1866) 14 L.T. 433. The question in these cases was whether A provided consideration for C's promise by performing a contractual duty owed by A to B. There is no doubt that C's promise to perform a duty owed by B to A (or the performance of such a promise) can constitute consideration for a promise (express or implied) by A to C: see, *e.g. Brandt v Liverpool, etc. S.N. Co* [1924] 1 K.B. 575; *The Aramis* [1989] 1 Lloyd's Rep. 213, 225 (where C's claim failed for want of contractual intention: above para.2–180).

Shadwell v Shadwell.[333] An uncle wrote to his nephew: "I am glad to hear of your intended marriage with Ellen Nicholl; and as I promised to assist you at starting, I am happy to tell you that I will pay you £150 yearly during my life . . . " A majority of the Court of Common Pleas held that the nephew had provided consideration for the uncle's promise by marrying Ellen Nicholl. It was said that there was a detriment to the nephew in that he "may have made a most material change in his position, and induced the object of his affection to do the same, and may have incurred pecuniary liabilities resulting in embarrassments"[334]; and that there was a benefit to the uncle in that the marriage was "an object of interest to a near relative."[335] This reasoning simply ignores the nephew's previous contractual obligation to marry Ellen Nicholl,[336] under which he was legally bound to suffer the alleged detriment. It could perhaps be argued that he forbore from trying to persuade his fiancée to postpone the wedding or to put an end to the engagement[337]; but it is doubtful whether his forbearance to attempt to persuade her to do this can be regarded as consideration in the absence of any suggestion that he contemplated the possibility.[338] The argument that the uncle benefited fares little better, for the benefit described by the court was a purely sentimental one. It is, moreover, very doubtful whether, on the true construction of the uncle's letter, the nephew's marriage to Ellen Nicholl was intended to be the consideration for the uncle's promise, or only a condition.[339] Byles J., who dissented, treated it as a condition and also thought that the uncle's promise was not made with any contractual intent. His view was subsequently approved,[340] so that the correctness of the actual decision in *Shadwell v Shadwell* is very much in doubt. But for what the decision is worth, it does support the view that the performance of a contractual duty owed to a third party can be good consideration for a promise. More recent authorities also support that view.

In *The Eurymedon*,[341] A (a firm of stevedores) had unloaded goods from B's ship. Some of these belonged to C who, for present purposes,[342] may be taken to have promised A not to sue him for damaging the goods. It was held that A had provided consideration for this promise by unloading the goods[343] even if he was already bound by a contract with B to unload them. This conclusion seems to be 3–074

---

[333] (1860) 9 C.B.(N.S.) 159.

[334] *ibid.* at 174.

[335] *ibid.*

[336] If the facts recurred now, such a promise would no longer give rise to a contractual obligation: Law Reform (Miscellaneous Provisions) Act 1970, s.1. A "civil partnership agreement" likewise has no contractual force: Civil Partnership Act 2004, s.73.

[337] *cf. De Cicco v Schweitzer* 221 N.Y. 413, 117 N.E. 807 (1917).

[338] Above, para.3–024.

[339] *cf.* above, para.3–012.

[340] *Jones v Padavatton* [1969] 1 W.L.R. 328, 333.

[341] *New Zealand Shipping Co Ltd v A.M. Satterthwaite & Co Ltd (The Eurymedon)* [1975] A.C. 154, 168; followed in *Port Jackson Stevedoring Pty Ltd v Salmond and Spraggon (Australia) Pty Ltd (The New York Star)* [1981] 1 W.L.R. 138 and *Glebe Island Terminals Pty Ltd v Continental Seagram Pty Ltd (The Antwerpen)* [1994] 1 Lloyd's Rep. 213; *The Mahkutai* [1996] A.C. 650, 664.

[342] See further para.14–048, below.

[343] A question may arise as to whether A has indeed performed or begun to perform his contract with B: see *Lotus Cars Ltd v Southampton Cargo Handling plc (The Rigoletto)* [2000] 2 Lloyd's Rep. 532, 542–545, where it was assumed that performance of a contract with a third party would constitute consideration.

based on the fact that such performance conferred a benefit on C[344]; and the benefit may be regarded either as factual (in the sense that C secured the actual delivery of his goods) or as legal (in the sense that C was not legally entitled to the performance of A's duty to unload, this duty being owed only to B). It would, of course, be open to C to avoid liability if he could show that his promise had been obtained by duress.[345] It is arguable that this defence is less likely to succeed in a three-party than in a two-party case[346]; but this is not invariably the case. Sailors in a case like *Stilk v Myrick*[347] could exert economic duress on the captain whether their original contract was with him or with a third party.[348] In both types of cases, it is now recognised that performance of a prior contractual duty can constitute consideration for a subsequent promise if that performance amounts to a benefit to the promisor.[349] The promise is therefore binding in the absence of a legally recognised vitiating factor, such as duress.

3–075 **Promise of performance.** There was formerly some support for the view that a promise to perform a contractual duty owed to a third party (as opposed to the actual performance of the duty) could not constitute consideration for a counter-promise. Thus in *Jones v Waite*[350] it was said that a promise by A to C that A would pay a debt which A owed to B was no consideration for a promise made by C to A. This view seems to be based on the idea that A suffers no (legal) detriment by promising to pay a debt that he was already bound to pay; nor did it appear that C gained any benefit as a result of the promise. But C may gain such a benefit: for example, where B is a company in which C has an interest. This was the position in *Pao On v Lau Yiu Long*[351] where the claimants, having entered into a contract with a company, refused to perform it unless the defendants, who were shareholders in the company, guaranteed them against loss which might be incurred as a result of the performance of one of the terms of that contract. The guarantee was given in consideration of the claimants' promise to perform their pre-existing contractual obligations to the company; and was held binding[352] on the ground that "A promise to perform, or the performance of, a pre-existing contractual obligation to a third party can be valid consideration."[353]

---

[344] *The Eurymedon*, above, n.341 at 168 ("for the benefit of the shipper", *i.e.* of C).

[345] *cf.* above, para.3–067.

[346] Goodhart, (1956) 72 L.Q.R. 490.

[347] Above, para.3–066.

[348] In *Stilk v Myrick* the distinction between two- and three-party cases was ignored; no one asked whether the original contract was with the captain (the promisor) or the shipowner, if these were separate persons. The report in 6 Esp. 129 makes it clear that the *action* was against the captain. *cf.* also *Turner v Owen* (1862) 3 F. & F. 176, where improper pressure may have been the ground for the jury's verdict even before the law recognised the concept of economic duress; and *B. & S. Contractors & Designs v Victor Green Publications Ltd* [1984] I.C.R. 419.

[349] Above, para.3–068; above, n.344; *cf.* below, para.3–075 (in the case of a *promise* to perform a duty to a third party).

[350] (1839) 5 Bing.N.C. 341 affirmed without reference to this point (1842) 9 Cl. & F. 101. A dictum in *Pfizer Corp. v Ministry of Health* [1965] A.C. 512, 536 could be interpreted to support the same view but appears (from the context) to be based on lack of contractual intention: see above, para.3–073, n.331.

[351] [1980] A.C. 614.

[352] For rejection of the argument that the consideration was past, see above, para.3–030.

[353] [1980] A.C. 614, 632. In *The Eurymedon*, above, n.341, it was said at 168 that a promise to perform a contractual duty owed by a third party was consideration because it was a *benefit to the promisee*. This is at first sight puzzling, since consideration must be a detriment to the promisee or

This view seems, with respect, to be preferable to that expressed in *Jones v Waite*; for, where a shareholder makes a promise to induce a person to perform a contract with the company, the promise is certainly not gratuitous in a commercial sense. It will, of course, be open to the promisor to avoid liability if he can show that the promisee's refusal to perform the contract with the company amounted to duress[354] not merely with regard to the company, but also with regard to the promisor himself.

9. DISCHARGE AND VARIATION OF CONTRACTUAL DUTIES

Introduction. The parties to a contract may agree to rescind it or to vary its terms. This subject is discussed in Chapter 22, but it is necessary in the present chapter to say something of the problems of consideration to which such agreements give rise. Indeed one aspect of the matter has already been discussed, for cases such as *Stilk v Myrick*[355] and *Williams v Roffey Bros. & Nicholls (Contractors) Ltd*[356] raise a problem of consideration arising from the variation of an existing contract. In those cases, the question was whether the performance by A of his obligations under the old contract could be consideration for a new promise from B. Our present problem is whether there is consideration for a promise by B to accept, in discharge of A's obligations, some performance other than that originally undertaken by A,[357] or to grant A a total release from his obligations under the original contract. Even if there is no such consideration, B's subsequent promise may, nevertheless, have some limited legal effect.[358] 3–076

(a) *Rescission*

Agreements to rescind where each party has outstanding rights. The parties to a contract may agree to rescind it at a time when each has outstanding rights under the contract against the other. They most obviously have such rights where the contract is wholly executory and neither party is in breach: for example, where a contract for the sale of goods to be delivered and paid for on a future day is rescinded before that day by mutual consent. They equally have such rights where both parties are, at the time of rescission, in breach; and where the contract is partly executed and obligations remain outstanding on both sides: for example, where a lease for seven years is rescinded by mutual consent after three years of the term have expired. In all such cases, each party generally 3–077

a benefit to the promisor. The reference, however, was to a case in which A's promise to C was said to be consideration for C's *counter-promise* to A and it was the consideration for that counter-promise which was in issue. In relation to that counter-promise, C was the promisor and the benefit that C got from A's promise satisfied the orthodox test of consideration for C's counter-promise. *cf.* above para.3–074.

354 *cf.* above, para.3–067.

355 (1809) 2 Camp. 317; 6 Esp. 129; above, para.3–066.

356 [1991] 1 Q.B. 1, above, para.3–068.

357 The issue discussed in *South Caribbean Trading Ltd v Trafigura Beheer BV* [2004] EWHC 2676 (Comm), [2005] 1 Lloyd's Rep. 128 at [107]–[112] seems to have been of this kind: see below, para.3–079.

358 Below, paras 3–081—3–100, 3–128—3–136.

provides consideration for the other's promise to release him by promising to give up his own rights under the contract.[359] It is, of course, essential that *each* party should make such a promise. If only one party does so, the other making no counter-promise, the former party's promise will be "entirely unilateral and unsupported by any consideration."[360]

3–078 **Agreements to rescind where only one party has outstanding rights.** An agreement to rescind a contract may also be unsupported by consideration (and so lack contractual force) where only one party has outstanding rights under the contract. This will often be the position where the contract has been wholly executed by that party (A) alone and he then promises to release the other party (B) from his obligations. In such a case there is *prima facie* no consideration for A's promise since A gets no benefit and B suffers no detriment from the arrangement. The same is true where A is ready and willing to perform but B is not: B is then liable in damages and "rescission" of the contract at this stage would be gratuitous if it merely released B from liability. This is what is meant by the statement that rescission after breach requires separate consideration.[361] Whenever the rescinding agreement does not generate its own consideration, such separate consideration must be provided by B (usually in the form of some additional performance rendered or promise made by B) to make A's promise binding. There must, in the traditional terminology, be not merely accord but also satisfaction. The "accord" here refers to the agreement and the "satisfaction" to the consideration for it.[362]

(b) *Variation*

(i) *Requirement of Consideration*

3–079 **Agreements to vary contracts.** Four situations call for discussion.

(1) Rescission followed by new contract. First, the parties may agree to rescind an existing contract and to enter into a new one, on different terms, in relation to the same subject-matter. The question whether there is consideration for the rescission then depends on the tests stated in paras 3–077—3–078. If these are satisfied, there will also generally be consideration for the promises of both parties made under the new contract. "The same consideration which existed for the old agreement is imported into the new agreement which is substituted for it."[363]

---

359 *Foster v Dawber* (1851) 6 Ex.839, 850; *cf. Marseille Fret SA v D. Oltman Schiffahrts GmbH & Co (The Trado)* [1982] 1 Lloyd's Rep. 157; *Argo Fund Ltd v Essar Steel Ltd* [2005] EWHC 600 (Comm), [2006] 1 All E.R. (Comm) at [51]; affd. on other grounds [2006] EWCA Civ. 241, [2006] 2 All E.R. (Comm) 104.

360 *Collin v Duke of Westminster* [1985] Q.B. 581, 588.

361 *Atlantic Shipping & Trading Ltd v Louis Dreyfus & Co* [1922] 2 A.C. 250 at 262.

362 Below, para.3–115. For an exception to the requirement, see Bills of Exchange Act 1882, s.62, below, Vol.II, para.34–139. The release *prima facie* takes effect at the time of the accord: see *Jameson v CEGB* [2000] 1 A.C. 455 at 477 (where the original liability arose in tort).

363 *Stead v Dawber* (1839) 10 A. & E. 57, 66; *Compagnie Nogar D'Importation et D'Exportation SA v Abacha* [2003] EWCA Civ. 1100; [2003] 2 All E.R. (Comm) 915 *per* Tuckey L.J., with whose judgment on this point the other members of the court agreed.

(2) Variation which can prejudice or benefit either party. Secondly, the parties may agree to vary the contract in a way that can prejudice or benefit either party. Here the *possible* detriment or benefit suffices to provide consideration for the promise of each party. This situation may be illustrated by an agreement to vary the currency in which a future payment under a contract of sale is to be made.[364] The seller's promise to accept payment in the new currency is supported by consideration since it *may* benefit him and prejudice the buyer as it is possible for the new currency to appreciate in relation to the old between the time of the variation and the time of payment. This possibility of benefit and detriment is sufficient. It is immaterial for the purpose of the requirement of consideration that the new currency in fact depreciates in relation to the old, or even that at the time of the variation it was highly probable that it would so depreciate. On the same principle, an agreement for the sale of goods can effectively be varied by mutual promises (made before the delivery date originally specified) on the part of the buyer to accept delivery and by the seller to perform his obligations with respect to delivery on a different (later) date. In one such case, it was said that such a variation amounted to "a new agreement supported by mutual promises" and that "sufficient consideration [for the buyer's promise] moved from the promisee."[365] (i.e., the seller). If a variation is, taken as a whole, capable of benefiting either party, the requirement of consideration will be satisfied even though a particular term of the variation is for the sole benefit of one.[366] However, it has been held that there is no consideration for a variation which, though capable of benefiting either party, is in fact made wholly for the benefit of one. For example, a variation as to the place at which a debt is to be paid is capable of benefiting either party; but where such a variation was introduced solely for the benefit of the debtor there was held to be no consideration for a promise by the creditor: *e.g.* for one to accept part payment in full settlement if the debtor made such payment at the different place.[367]

(3) Variation which can benefit only one party. Thirdly, the parties may agree to vary the contract in a way that is considered to be capable of conferring a legal benefit on one party only: *e.g.* where one party agrees to pay more for the performance of the other party's original obligation, or to accept less than the other party had originally undertaken without any corresponding variation (that could benefit him) of his own obligation. In some situations of this kind, it is settled that there is no consideration. Where, for example, after a debt has fallen due, the creditor promises to accept part payment of it in full settlement, the mere part payment does not constitute consideration for the variation,[368] though the 3–080

[364] *W. J. Alan & Co Ltd v El Nasr Export & Import Co* [1972] 2 Q.B. 189; *Woodhouse A.C. Israel Cocoa Ltd SA v Nigerian Produce Marketing Co* [1972] A.C. 741.

[365] *South Caribbean Trading Ltd v Trafigura Beheer BV* [2004] EWHC 2676 (Comm), [2005] 1 Lloyd's Rep. at [105]. The seller's "apparently insuperable" difficulties in meeting the originally agreed delivery dates appear not to have been treated by the buyer as breaches of the original contract.

[366] *Ficom SA v Sociedad Cadex Ltd* [1980] 2 Lloyd's Rep. 118, 132.

[367] *Vanbergen v St. Edmunds Properties Ltd* [1933] 2 K.B. 233; *cf. Continental Grain Export Corp. v S.T.M. Grain Ltd* [1979] 2 Lloyd's Rep. 460, 476.

[368] Below, para.3–115.

creditor's promise may have a limited effect as a waiver, or in equity.[369] Consideration for the creditor's promise could be provided by some further variation which could benefit the creditor: *e.g.* by the debtor's promise to make the payment *before* the day when the debt becomes due. In other situations falling within the present group, it is arguable[370] that the variation may be supported by consideration if, though capable of conferring a legal benefit on only one party, it can also confer a factual benefit[371] on the other: *e.g.* where a buyer's promise to pay more than the originally agreed price secures eventual delivery of goods when strict insistence on the original contract would have led to nothing but litigation.

(4) "Variation" before conclusion of contract. Fourthly, there is the apparently paradoxical possibility that the parties may agree to vary a contract even before that contract has been concluded. This may be the position where A and B negotiate on the basis of formal documents and A represents that the proposed contract will be on terms less favourable to himself than those set out in the documents. If the documents are nevertheless executed without alteration, the representation may then be enforceable as a collateral contract. The consideration for the promise contained in A's representation is provided by B when he executes the documents, and so enters into the principal contract, at the request of A and in reliance on the representation. This was the position in *Brikom Investments Ltd v Carr*,[372] where the landlords of blocks of flats negotiated with their tenants for the sale of long leases of the flats on terms requiring the tenants to contribute to the cost of (*inter alia*) roof maintenance. At the time of the negotiations, the roof was in need of repairs, and the landlords promised to execute these "at our own cost." It was held that one of the tenants had provided consideration for this promise by executing the agreement for the lease, and the lease itself; and that the promise was accordingly binding as a collateral contract.[373] It followed that the landlords could not enforce the term in the lease under which the tenant would (but for the collateral contract) have been liable to contribute to the cost of the roof repair.[374] Greater difficulty would have arisen if the tenant had already entered into the agreement to take the lease *before* the landlord's promise had been made,[375] for in that case the execution of the documents would have been past consideration.[376] The tenants could, however,

[369] Below, paras 3–128—3–136.

[370] On the analogy of the reasoning of *Williams v Roffey Bros. & Nicholls (Contractors) Ltd* [1991] 1 Q.B. 1, above, para.3–068.

[371] Above, para.3–006.

[372] [1979] Q.B. 467.

[373] Contrast, on the issue of the contractual intention necessary to establish such a contract, *Business Environment Bow Lane Ltd v Deanwater Estates Ltd* [2007] EWCA Civ. 622, [2007] NLJ 1263, above para.2–166.

[374] This was agreed by all members of the Court of Appeal. For other grounds for the decision, see below, paras 3–127, 3–133.

[375] From the grounds of appeal as stated on pp.472–473 of the report, it seems that reliance was placed on pre-contract promises or representations; *cf.* the statement at 490 that the landlord's promise was made "at the time when the leases were granted." According to Lord Denning, M.R. at 480 "some of the tenants" had *already* signed agreements for leases when the representations were made; but that does not seem to have been the position with regard to any of the cases before the court.

[376] Above, para.3–026.

have succeeded, even in such a case, on an alternative ground. The landlords had been guilty of unreasonable delay in executing the repairs, and the tenants would, by forbearing to take proceedings in respect of that breach,[377] have provided consideration for the landlords' promise to bear the cost of the repairs.

(ii) *Common Law Mitigations*

Waiver[378] or forbearance at common law. A variation which is not contractually binding (*e.g.* for want of consideration) may nevertheless have certain limited legal effects. These are sometimes said to arise because the promise by a party to relinquish some or all of his rights under a contract amounts to a "waiver" of those rights. Unfortunately, however, "the word 'waiver' . . . covers a variety of situations different in their legal nature . . . "[379] It is, for example, sometimes used to refer to the variation of a contract which is supported by consideration and therefore binding as a contract.[380] To distinguish between such variations and those which are not supported by consideration, the latter will in the following discussion be referred to as "forbearances." A forbearance in this sense may in certain circumstances limit the right of the party granting it to enforce his rights under the contract.[381] The exact effects of such a forbearance are discussed in Chapter 22; but something must be said here about the distinction between a forbearance and a variation. 3–081

Forbearance generally revocable. The effect of a forbearance of the kind mentioned in the preceding paragraph differs from that of a contractually binding variation which is supported by consideration in that it does not *irrevocably* alter the rights of the parties under the original contract. The party granting the forbearance *can generally retract it*, provided that he gives reasonable notice of 3–082

---

[377] See [1979] Q.B. 467, 490; *cf.* above, para.3–057. Delay in *executing* the repairs was a breach irrespective of the question of who was to *pay* for them.

[378] Ewart, *Waiver Distributed*; Wilkins and Villiers, *Waiver, Variation and Estoppel*; Spence, *Protecting Reliance*; Cheshire and Fifoot (1947) 63 L.Q.R. 283; Stoljar (1958) 35 Can. Bar Rev. 485; Dugdale and Yates (1976) 39 M.L.R. 680.

[379] *Mardorf Peach & Co Ltd v Attica Sea Carriers Corp. of Liberia (The Laconia)* [1977] A.C. 850, 871; *cf. Kammins Ballrooms Co Ltd v Zenith Investments (Torquay) Ltd* [1971] A.C. 850, 882–883; *Telfair Shipping Corp. v Athos Shipping Corp. (The Athos)* [1981] 2 Lloyd's Rep. 74, 87 (a passage approved on appeal: [1983] 1 Lloyd's Rep. 127, 134); *Scandinavian Trading Tanker Co A.B. v Flota Petrolera Ecuatoriana (The Scaptrade)* [1981] 2 Lloyd's Rep. 425, 430, affirmed [1983] 2 A.C. 694; *Motor Oil Hellas (Corinth) Refineries SA v Shipping Corp. of India (The Kanchenjunga)* [1990] 1 Lloyd's Rep. 391, 397; *Oliver Ashworth (Holdings) Ltd v Ballard (Kent) Ltd* [2000] Ch. 12 at 28; *Glencore Grain Ltd v Flacker Shipping Ltd (The Happy Day)* [2002] EWCA Civ. 1068; [2002] 2 Lloyd's Rep. 487 at [64]; *Oceanografia SA de CV v DSND Subsea AS (The Botnica)* [2006] EWHC 1300 (Comm), [2007] 1 All E.R. (Comm) 28 at [89], [90]; *Kosmar Villa Holidays plc v Trustees of Syndicate 1243* [2008] EWCA Civ. 147, [2008] 2 All E.R. (Comm) 14 at [1], [36]–[37].

[380] *e.g.* in *Hickman v Haynes* (1875) L.R. 10 C.P. 598, 604; and (*semble*) by Roskill and Cumming-Bruce L.JJ. in *Brikom Investments Ltd v Carr* [1979] Q.B. 467; *cf. Shamsher Jute Mills v Sethia (London) Ltd* [1987] 1 Lloyd's Rep. 388, 392. In *Royal Boskalis Westminster NV v Mountain* [1997] 2 All E.R. 929 "waiver" is similarly used to refer to a variation which would have been contractually binding if it had not been vitiated by duress and illegality. Only Phillips L.J. took the view that there was no "meaningful" consideration. "Meaningful" here seems to mean no more than "adequate;" for it appears from the facts stated at 934 and 958–959 that in the subsequent agreement each party gave up rights existing under the original contract.

[381] Phillips, (2007) 123 L.Q.R. 286.

his intention to do so to the other party.[382] Thus in *Charles Rickards Ltd v Oppenhaim*[383] a contract for the sale of a car provided for delivery on March 20. The car was not delivered on that day but the buyer continued to press for delivery and finally told the seller on June 29 that he must have the car by July 25 at the latest. It was held that the buyer could not have refused peremptorily to accept the car merely because the original delivery date had gone by, as he had continued to press for delivery; but that he could refuse on the seller's failure to comply with a notice to deliver within a reasonable time. As the notice had given the seller a reasonable time to deliver, the buyer was justified in refusing to take the car after July 25. *A fortiori*, the buyer could have refused to take delivery if the original delivery date had been extended only for a fixed time and if delivery had not been made by the end of that time.[384]

3–083 **Forbearance may become irrevocable.** A forbearance may, however, become irrevocable as a result of subsequent events: for example if a buyer indicates that he is willing to accept goods of a different quality from those contracted for, and the seller, in reliance on that assurance, so conducts himself as to put it out of his power to supply goods of the contract quality within the contract period.[385]

3–084 **Basis of distinction between variation and forbearance.** The question whether a subsequent agreement amounted to a contractually binding variation or to a forbearance is sometimes said to depend on the intention of the parties.[386] It seems that a statement should be a forbearance if the party making it intended to reserve a power to retract, and a variation if he intended it permanently to affect his rights. In practice, however, neither this nor any other explanation of the distinction provides any very sound basis for distinguishing between the authorities on this subject. The explanation is also open to the objection that it leads to the paradoxical result that, the more a party tried to bind himself by a subsequent agreement, the less he was likely to be bound. An attempt to abandon a right altogether would be classified as a variation, and so be invalid without consideration; while an attempt merely to suspend a right would have at least a limited effect as a waiver. The courts were, however anxious to avoid the injustice which could result from holding that a variation was not binding for want of consideration. Accordingly, they were inclined to interpret the subsequent agreement as a forbearance, so as to give it at least some legal effects.

(iii) *Equitable Mitigations*

3–085 **Forbearance in equity.** Equity developed a more satisfactory approach to the problem discussed in para.3–084 above by concentrating, not on the intention of

---

[382] *Banning v Wright* [1972] 1 W.L.R. 972, 981; *Ficom SA v Sociedad Cadex Ltda.* [1980] 2 Lloyd's Rep. 118, 131.

[383] [1950] 1 K.B. 616; *cf. State Trading Corp. of India v Cie Française d'Importation et de Distribution* [1983] 2 Lloyd's Rep. 679, 681.

[384] *cf. Nichimen Corp. v Gatoil Overseas Inc* [1987] 2 Lloyd's Rep. 46, where similar fixed-term extensions were granted by a seller.

[385] *Toepfer v Warinco A.G.* [1978] 2 Lloyd's Rep. 569, 576; *cf. Leather Cloth Co v Hieronimus* (1875) L.R. 10 Q.B. 140 (goods lost while on altered route); *Bottiglieri di Navigazione SpA v Cosco Quindao Shipping Co (The Bunge Saga Lima)* [2005] EWHC 244 (Comm), [2005] 2 Lloyd's Rep. 1 at [31], below para.3–097.

[386] *Stead v Dawber* (1839) 10 A. & E. 57, 64.

the party granting the forbearance, but on the conduct of that party and on its effect on the position of the other party. The leading case is *Hughes v Metropolitan Ry*[387] where a landlord had given his tenant notice requiring him to do repairs within six months. During the six months he began to negotiate with the tenant for the purchase of his lease. When the negotiations broke down, he immediately claimed to forfeit the lease on the ground that the tenant had not done the repairs. The claim was rejected, Lord Cairns saying that if one party leads the other "to suppose that the strict rights arising under the contract will not be enforced, or will be kept in suspense, or held in abeyance, the person who otherwise might have enforced those rights will not be allowed to enforce them where it would be inequitable having regard to the dealings which have thus taken place between the parties."[388] The landlord had by his conduct during the negotiations led the tenant to suppose that he would not enforce his right to forfeit. Hence he could not forfeit immediately the negotiations broke down; he was bound to give the tenant a reasonable time from that date to do the repairs. This equitable doctrine can now be applied to arrangements which might formerly have been regarded as variations ineffective at common law for want of consideration.[389] For reasons to be discussed in para.3–103 below, the doctrine is often (if rather misleadingly) referred to as "promissory" or "equitable" estoppel.

Requirements. For the equitable doctrine to operate there must be a legal relationship giving rise to rights and duties between the parties; a promise or a representation by one party that he will not enforce against the other his strict legal rights arising out of that relationship; an intention on the part of the former party that the latter will rely on the representation; and such reliance by the latter party.[390] Even if these requirements are satisfied, the operation of the doctrine may be excluded if it is, nevertheless, not "inequitable" for the first party to go back on his promise. The doctrine most commonly applies to promises not to enforce contractual rights, but it also extends to certain other relationships. These points will be discussed in the following paragraphs. 3–086

Relationships within the doctrine. The legal rights which the promisor or representor is prevented by the equitable doctrine from enforcing normally arise out of a contract between him and the other party. But the doctrine can also apply where the relationship giving rise to rights and correlative duties is non-contractual: *e.g.* to prevent the enforcement of a liability imposed by statute on a 3–087

---

[387] (1877) 2 App. Cas. 439.

[388] *ibid.* at 448; *cf. Smith v Lawson* (1998) 75 P.&C.R. 466: landlord who had told tenant that he would not ask her to continue to pay rent could not have recovered possession for non-payment of rent. See further para.3–102, below.

[389] *e.g. Charles Rickards Ltd v Oppenhaim* [1950] K.B. 616 (where both common law and equitable principles were applied). The principle in *Hughes v Metropolitan Ry* was said in *Brikom Investments Ltd v Carr* [1979] Q.B. 467, 489 to be "an illustration of *contractual* variation of strict contractual rights." This description was apt on the facts of that case, where the promise not to enforce such rights was supported by consideration: above, para.3–080. But the principle stated in *Hughes v Metropolitan Ry* applies even in the absence of such consideration: *cf.* below, para.3–132.

[390] *B.P. Exploration (Libya) v Hunt (No.2)* [1979] 1 W.L.R. 783, 812, affirmed (without reference to the point) [1983] 2 A.C. 352; *Nippon Yusen Kaisha v Pacifica Navegacion SA (The Ion)* [1980] 2 Lloyd's Rep. 245, 250.

company director for signing a bill of exchange on which the company's name is not correctly given[391]; or to prevent a man from ejecting a woman, with whom he has been cohabitating, from the family home.[392] On the other hand, it has been said that the doctrine has "no application as between landlord and trespasser."[393] Hence the mere fact that a landowner has for some time failed or neglected to enforce his rights against a trespasser does not prevent him from subsequently doing so without notice.[394] The doctrine may also be excluded in some situations by statute. Thus it has been held[395] that estoppel or waiver could not preclude a man from withdrawing his consent to the use by a woman of his genetic material since the right to withdraw such consent was expressly given by statute[396] and since the application of waiver or estoppel to limit that right "would conflict with the Parliamentary scheme."[397]

3–088 **Requirement of pre-existing legal relationship.** It has, indeed, been suggested that the doctrine can apply where, before the making of the promise or representation, there is no legal relationship giving rise to rights and duties between the parties,[398] or where there is only a putative contract between them: *e.g.* where the promisee is induced to believe that a contract into which he had undoubtedly entered was between him and the promisor, when in fact it was between the promisee and another person.[399] But it is submitted that these suggestions mistake the nature of the doctrine, which is to restrict the enforcement by the promisor of previously existing rights against the promisee. Such rights can arise only out of a legal relationship existing between these parties

---

[391] *Durham Fancy Goods Ltd v Michael Jackson (Fancy Goods) Ltd* [1968] 2 Q.B. 839. A statement may also prevent the representor from denying the existence of a statutory liability, as in *Robertson v Minister of Pensions* [1949] 1 K.B. 227, as to which see also para.3–103, n.503 below.

[392] *Maharaj v Chand* [1986] A.C. 898.

[393] *Morris v Tarrant* [1971] 2 Q.B. 143, 160; *cf. Burrows v Brent LBC* [1996] 1 W.L.R. 1448, 1455, where no attempt was made to invoke the doctrine in favour of a "tolerated trespasser".

[394] *Lambeth LBC v O'Kane Holdings Ltd* [2005] EWCA Civ. 1010; [2006] H.L.R. 2.

[395] *Evans v Amicus Healthcare Ltd* [2004] EWCA Civ. 727, [2005] Fam. 1.

[396] Human Fertilisation and Embryology Act 1990, Sch.3 para.4(1).

[397] *Evans v Amicus Healthcare Ltd*, above n.395, at [37]; see also at [36] and [120].

[398] *Evenden v Guildford City F.C.* [1975] Q.B. 917, 924, 926 (actual decision overruled in *Secretary of State for Employment v Globe Elastic Thread Co Ltd* [1980] A.C. 506). The view stated in the text above was expressed at first instance in *Evans v Amicus Healthcare Ltd* [2003] EWHC 2161 (Fam), [2003] 4 All E.R. 903 at [304], [305], but the only authority there cited for this view was one of *proprietary* estoppel, to which the present requirement does not apply as this kind of estoppel can give rise to a cause of action: see below, para.3–162. The *Evans* case was affirmed on other grounds [2004] EWCA Civ. 727, [2005] Fam. 1, above para.3–087. For the position in Australia, see *Waltons Stores (Interstate) Ltd v Maher* (1988) 164 C.L.R. 387; below, para.3–106.

[399] *Pacol Ltd v Trade Lines Ltd (The Henrik Sif)* [1982] 1 Lloyd's Rep. 456, 466. Some doubt as to the correctness of this case is expressed by Webster J. (who decided it) in *Shearson Lehman Hutton Inc v MacLaine Watson & Co Ltd* [1989] 2 Lloyd's Rep. 570, 596, 604 though the decision was approved on another point in *The Stolt Loyalty* [1993] 2 Lloyd's Rep. 281, 289–290, 291, affirmed without reference to this point [1995] 1 Lloyd's Rep. 599; see also *Orion Finance Ltd v J. D. Williams & Co Ltd* [1997] C.L.Y. 986, where no estoppel arose in the absence of a previous legal relationship; *Baird Textile Holdings Ltd v Marks & Spencer plc* [2001] EWCA Civ. 274; [2002] 1 All E.R. (Comm) 737, at [89] apparently doubting some of the reasoning in *The Henrik Sif*, but not the outcome since there was undoubtedly "a legal relationship . . . whoever were the parties thereto" (though the difficulty remains that the first defendants, against whom the doctrine was said to operate, were not parties to that relationship).

before the making of the promise or representation. To apply doctrine where there was no such relationship would contravene the rule (to be discussed in para.3–098 below) that the doctrine creates no new rights.

A promise or representation. There must, next, be a promise (or an assurance or representation in the nature of a promise[400]) which is intended to affect the legal relationship between the parties[401] and which indicates that the promisor will not insist on his strict legal rights,[402] arising out of that relationship, against the promisee. Here, as elsewhere, the law applies an objective test. It is enough if the promise induces the promisee reasonably to believe that the other party will not insist on his strict legal rights.[403] A mere threat to do something is not sufficient, nor, probably, is a representation or promise by a person that he *will* enforce a legal right: thus the doctrine does not apply where A tells B that he will exercise his right to cancel a contract between them unless by a specified date B has paid sums due under the contract to A.[404] 3–089

The promise or representation must be "clear" or "unequivocal". The promise or representation must be "clear" or "unequivocal," or "precise and unambiguous." This requirement seems to have originated in the law relating to estoppel by representation[405]; and it is now frequently stated in relation to "waiver"[406] and "promissory estoppel."[407] It does not mean that the promise or 3–090

[400] *James v Heim Galleries* (1980) 256 E.G. 819, 821; *Collin v Duke of Westminster* [1985] Q.B. 581, 595.

[401] *Central London Property Trust Ltd v High Trees House Ltd* [1947] K.B. 130 at 134; *Spence v Shell* (1980) 256 E.G. 55, 63; *Baird Textile* case, above n.399, at [92].

[402] Or that he will not rely on an available defence: below para.3–101.

[403] *Bremer Handelsgesellschaft mbH v Vanden Avenne-Izegem P.V.B.A.* [1978] 2 Lloyd's Rep. 109, 126; *Bremer Handelsgesellschaft mbH v C. Mackprang Jr.* [1979] 1 Lloyd's Rep. 221 (both these cases concerned "waiver"); *cf.* below, n.406.

[404] *Drexel Burnham Lambert International NV v El Nasr* [1986] 1 Lloyd's Rep. 357.

[405] *Low v Bouverie* [1891] 3 Ch. 82, 106; *Woodhouse A.C. Israel Cocoa Ltd SA v Nigerian Produce Marketing Co Ltd* [1972] A.C. 741; *The Shackleford* [1978] 2 Lloyd's Rep. 155, 159; *Channel Island Ferries Ltd v Sealink UK Ltd* [1987] 1 Lloyd's Rep. 559, 580, affirmed without reference to this point [1988] 1 Lloyd's Rep. 323.

[406] *Finagrain SA Geneva v P. Kruse Hamburg* [1976] 2 Lloyd's Rep. 508, 534; *Mardorf Peach & Co Ltd v Attica Sea Carriers Corp. of Liberia (The Laconia)* [1977] A.C. 850, 871; *Bremer Handelsgesellschaft mbH v Vanden Avenne-Izegem P.V.B.A.* [1978] 2 Lloyd's Rep. 109, 126; *China National Foreign Trade Transportation Corp. v Evoglia Shipping Co of Panama SA (The Mihalios Xilas)* [1979] 1 W.L.R. 1018, 1024; *Avimex SA v Dewulf & Cie.* [1979] 2 Lloyd's Rep. 57, 67; *Bremer Handelsgesellschaft mbH v Westzucker GmbH* [1981] 1 Lloyd's Rep. 207, 212; *Bremer Handelsgesellschaft mbH v Finagrain Cie. Commercial Agricole & Financière SA* [1981] 2 Lloyd's Rep, 259, 266; *Scandinavian Tanker Co A.B. v Flota Petrolera Ecuatoriana (The Scaptrade)* [1981] 2 Lloyd's Rep. 425, 431; (affirmed [1983] 2 A.C. 694) *Italmare Shipping Co v Ocean Tanker Co Inc (The Rio Sun)* [1981] 2 Lloyd's Rep. 489 and [1982] 1 Lloyd's Rep. 404; *Telfair Shipping Corp. v Athos Shipping Corp. (The Athos)* [1983] 1 Lloyd's Rep. 127, 134–135; *Bremer Handelsgesellschaft mbH v Deutsche-Conti Handelsgesellschaft mbH* [1983] 1 Lloyd's Rep. 689; *Super Chem Products Ltd v American Life & General Insurance Co Ltd* [2004] UKPC 2, [2004] 2 All E.R. 358 at [23], where the present requirement was not satisfied; *Fortisbank SA v Trenwick International* [2005] EWHC 339, [2005] Lloyd's Rep. I.R. 464 at [32], [35]; *Kosmar Villa Holidays plc v Trustees of Syndicate 1243* [2008] EWCA Civ. 147, [2008] 2 All E.R. (Comm) 14 at [84] ("waiver by estoppel" ; the reference is to "promissory estoppel": see below para 3–094 note 443). For the analogy between waiver and the equitable doctrine here under discussion, see above, para.3–085; below, para.3–104.

[407] *B.P. Exploration Co (Libya) Ltd v Hunt (No.2)* [1979] 1 W.L.R. 783, 812 (affirmed without reference to this point [1983] 2 A.C. 352.); *Spence v Shell* (1980) 256 E.G. 55, 63; *James v Heim Galleries* (1980) 256 E.G. 819, 821; *Société Italo-Belge pour le Commerce et l'Industrie v Palm &*

representation must be express[408]; it may equally well be implied. For example, in *Hughes v Metropolitan Ry.*[409] itself the landlord made no express promise that he would not enforce his right to forfeit the lease; but an implication of such a promise fairly arose from the course of the negotiations between the parties. There is some support for the view that the promise must have the same degree of certainty as would be needed to give it contractual effect if it were supported by consideration.[410] Thus if the statement could not have had contractual force because it was too vague,[411] or if it was insufficiently precise to amount to an offer,[412] or if it did not amount to an unqualified acceptance,[413] it will not bring the equitable doctrine into operation.[414]

3–091 The purpose of the requirement that the promise or representation must be "clear" or "unequivocal" is to prevent a party from losing his legal rights under a contract merely because he has granted some indulgence by failing to insist throughout on strict performance of the contract[415]; or merely because he has

Vegetable Oils (Malaysia) Sdn. Bhd. (The Post Chaser) [1981] 2 Lloyd's Rep. 695, 700; *Goldsworthy v Brickell* [1987] Ch. 378, 410; *Hiscox v Outhwaite (No.3)* [1991] 2 Lloyd's Rep. 523, 524, 535; *Rowan Companies Inc v Lambert Eggink Offshore Transport Consultants* [1999] 2 Lloyd's Rep. 443 at 448, *Thameside MBC v Barlow Securities Group Services Ltd* [2001] EWCA Civ. 1; [2001] B.L.R. 113 and *Evans v Amicus Healthcare Ltd* [2003] EWHC 2161 (Fam), [2003] 4 All E.R. 903 at [303]–[306] (where this requirement was not satisfied), affirmed on other grounds [2004] EWCA Civ. 727; [2005] Fam. 1 (see above, para.3–088).

[408] *Spence v Shell* (1980) 256 E.G. 55, 63.

[409] (1877) 2 App. Cas. 439; *cf. The Post Chaser*, above, n.407, at 700.

[410] *China-Pacific SA v The Food Corp. of India (The Winson)* [1980] 2 Lloyd's Rep. 213, 222; reversed on other grounds [1982] A.C. 939; *Food Corp. of India v Antclizo Shipping Corp. (The Antclizo)* [1988] 2 Lloyd's Rep. 130, 142, affirmed [1988] 1 W.L.R. 603; *Youell v Bland Welch & Co Ltd (The Superhulls Cover Case) (No.2)* [1990] 2 Lloyd's Rep. 431, 452; *Rafsanjan Pistachio Producers Co-operative v Bank Leumi (UK) plc* [1992] 1 Lloyd's Rep. 513, 542.

[411] Above, paras 2–139—2–144; *cf. Baird Textile Holdings Ltd v Marks & Spencer plc* [2001] EWCA Civ. 274; [2002] 1 All E.R. (Comm) 737 at [38], [54], where one reason why the claim based on estoppel failed was that the implied agreement on which it was based was not sufficiently certain to have contractual force: see above, para.2–183 and below, para.3–098. The difficulty arising from lack of certainty was said, at [54], to "extend to the estoppel as well as the contractual issue."

[412] Above, para.2–003.

[413] *Azov Shipping Co v Baltic Shipping Co* [1999] 2 Lloyd's Rep. 159, 173, a case of estoppel by representation, to which the requirement of a clear and unequivocal representation also applies: see *Low v Bouverie* [1891] 3 Ch. 82; *Woodhouse A.C. Israel Cocoa Ltd v Nigerian Produce Marketing Co* [1972] A.C. 741. For the requirement of an "unqualified" acceptance, see above, para.2–032.

[414] *China-Pacific SA v The Food Corp. of India (The Winson)* [1980] 2 Lloyd's Rep. 213, 223; reversed on other grounds [1982] A.C. 939; *Drexel Burnham Lambert International NV v El Nasr* [1986] 1 Lloyd's Rep. 357. A promise which lacks contractual force can give rise to a *proprietary* estoppel even though by reason of its uncertainty or incompleteness it lacks contractual force (see below, para.3–143); but in *Cobbe v Yeoman's Row Management Ltd* [2008] UKHL 55, [2008] 1 W.L.R. 1752 (below paras 3–148A to 3–148D) it was held that no such estoppel arose in favour of a party who *knew* that the promise was binding only in honour.

[415] *Scandinavian Trading Tanker Co A.B. v Flora Petrolera Ecuatoriana (The Scaptrade)* [1981] 2 Lloyd's Rep. 425, 431, distinguishing *Tankexpress AS v Cie. Financière Belge des Petroles SA* [1949] A.C. 76 on the ground that there the creditor's conduct had resulted in a change in the "accepted method of payments"; *The Scaptrade*, above was affirmed without reference to the present point [1983] 2 A.C. 694; *cf. Cape Asbestos Ltd v Lloyd's Bank Ltd* [1921] W.N. 274, 276; *Bunge SA v Compagnie Européenne de Céréales* [1982] 1 Lloyd's Rep. 306; *Bremer Handelsgesellschaft mbH v Raiffeisen Hauptgenossenschaft E.G.* [1982] 2 Lloyd's Rep. 599; *Bremer Handelsgesellschaft mbH v Bunge Corp.* [1983] 1 Lloyd's Rep. 476.

offered some concession in the course of negotiations for the settlement of a dispute arising out of the contract[416] or merely because he has declared his willingness to continue such negotiations.[417] Thus the requirement was not satisfied where one of the parties to such a negotiation throughout insisted on strict compliance with the terms of the contract[418]; where he accepted less than that to which he was entitled but did so subject to an express reservation of his rights[419]; and where an admission that he was liable for certain expenses was made by his solicitor, expressly "without prejudice."[420] Failure, in the course of negotiations of this kind, to object to a defect or deficiency in performance is likewise insufficient if the injured party did not know and could not reasonably have known of it[421] or if full performance remained possible and continued to be demanded by that party.[422] On the other hand, failure to object to a known defect or deficiency within a reasonable time of its discovery[423] may be regarded as an unequivocal indication of the injured party's intention not to insist on his strict legal rights.[424] The position seems to be the same where the defect or deficiency, though not actually known to the injured party, was obvious or could have been discovered by him, if he had taken reasonable steps.[425] But where more than one matter is in dispute between the parties, "emphatic reliance upon some important disputed point does not by itself . . . imply any unequivocal representation that compliance with other parts of the bargain is thereby waived."[426]

Inactivity. Although a promise or representation may be made by conduct, mere inactivity will not normally suffice for the present purpose since "it is difficult to imagine how silence and inaction can be anything but equivocal."[427] Unless the law took this view, mere failure to assert a contractual right 3–092

---

[416] *cf. London & Clydebank Properties v H.M. Investment Co* [1993] E.G.C.S. 63.

[417] *Seechurn v Ace Insurance SA* [2002] EWCA Civ. 67; [2002] 2 Lloyd's Rep. 390, esp. at [55].

[418] *V. Berg & Son Ltd v Vanden Avenne-Izegem P.V.B.A.* [1977] 1 Lloyd's Rep. 500; *cf. Edm. J. M. Mertens & Co P.V.B.A. v Veevoeder Import Export Vimex B.V.* [1979] 2 Lloyd's Rep. 372.

[419] *Finagrain SA Geneva v P. Kruse Hamburg* [1976] 2 Lloyd's Rep. 508; *cf. Cook Industries Inc v Meunerie Liegeois SA* [1981] 1 Lloyd's Rep. 359, 368; *Peter Cremer v Granaria B.V.* [1981] 2 Lloyd's Rep. 583; *Bremer Handelsgesellschaft mbH v Deutsche Conti-Handelsgesellschaft mbH* [1983] 2 Lloyd's Rep. 476.

[420] *China-Pacific SA v The Food Corp. of India (The Winson)* [1980] 2 Lloyd's Rep. 213 (reversed on other grounds [1982] A.C. 399).

[421] *Avimex SA v Dewulf & Cie* [1979] 2 Lloyd's Rep. 57.

[422] *China National Foreign Trade Transportation Corp. v Evoglia Shipping Co SA of Panama (The Mihalios Xilas)* [1979] 1 W.L.R. 1018; *Bremer Handelsgesellschaft mbH v Westzucker GmbH* [1981] 1 Lloyd's Rep. 207, 212–213; *Bremer Handelsgesellschaft mbH v C. Mackprang Jr.* [1981] 1 Lloyd's Rep. 292, 299; *Peter Cremer v Granaria B.V.* [1981] 2 Lloyd's Rep. 583; *The Post Chaser*, above, n.407 at 700.

[423] See *Mardorf Peach & Co Ltd v Attica Sea Carriers Corp. of Liberia (The Laconia)* [1977] A.C. 850 (where retention of an underpayment accepted without authority by the payee's bank was held not to amount to a waiver).

[424] *e.g. Bremer Handelsgesellschaft mbH v Vanden Avenne-Izegem P.V.B.A.* [1978] 2 Lloyd's Rep. 109; *Hazel v Akhtar* [2001] EWCA Civ. 1883; [2002] 2 P. & C.R. 17 (landlord tolerating habitually late payment of rent).

[425] See *Bremer Handelsgesellschaft mbH v C. Mackprang Jr.* [1979] 1 Lloyd's Rep. 221, where there was a division of opinion on the point in the Court of Appeal.

[426] *Telfair Shipping Corp. v Athos Shipping Corp. (The Athos)* [1983] 1 Lloyd's Rep. 127, 135.

[427] *Allied Marine Transport v Vale do Rio Doce Navegaçao SA (The Leonidas D.)* [1985] 1 W.L.R. 925, 937; *cf. Cook Industries v Tradax Export SA* [1983] 1 Lloyd's Rep. 327, 332 ([1985] 2 Lloyd's

could lead to its loss; and the courts have on a number of occasions rejected this clearly undesirable conclusion. Thus it has been held that there is "no ground for saying that mere delay, however lengthy, destroys the contractual rights"[428]; and that the mere failure to prosecute a claim regarded by both parties as hopeless did not amount to a promise to abandon it.[429] The only circumstances in which "silence and inaction" can have this effect are the exceptional ones (discussed elsewhere in this book[430]) in which the law imposes a duty to disclose facts or to clarify a legal relationship and the party under the duty fails to perform it.

3–093 **Reliance.** The first requirement to be discussed under this heading is that the promise or representation must in some way have influenced the conduct of the party to whom it was made. Although the promise need not form the sole inducement,[431] it must (it is submitted) be *some* inducement. Hence the present requirement would not be satisfied if it could be shown that the other party's conduct was not influenced by the promise[432] so that he was not in any way prejudiced by it.[433] But if this is a matter of "mere speculation,"[434] or if the promise or representation "was one of the factors. . . relied upon,"[435] it would

---

Rep. 454); *K. Lokumal & Sons (London) Ltd v Lotte Shipping Co Pte Ltd (The August P. Leonhardt)* [1985] 2 Lloyd's Rep. 28, 33; *M.S.C. Mediterranean Shipping Co SA v B.R.E. Metro Ltd* [1985] 2 Lloyd's Rep. 239; *Cie Française d'Importation, etc., SA v Deutsche Continental Handelsgesellschaft* [1985] 2 Lloyd's Rep. 592, 598; *Food Corp. of India v Antclizo Shipping Corp. (The Antclizo)* [1986] 1 Lloyd's Rep. 181, 187, affirmed 1 W.L.R. 603; *Youell v Bland Welch & Co Ltd (The Superhulls Cover Case) (No.2)* [1990] 2 Lloyd's Rep. 431, 452; *HIH Casualty & General Insurance v Axa Corporate Solutions* [2002] EWCA Civ. 1253; [2002] 2 All E.R. (Comm) 1053 at [26] (where there was no action in reliance); *Front Carriers Ltd v Atlantic Orient Shipping Corporation (The Archimidis)* [2007] EWHC 421 (Comm), [2007] 2 Lloyd's Rep. 131 at [45]–[46]; *cf. Tankerederei Ahrenkeil GmbH v Frahuil SA (The Multibank Holstia)* [1988] 2 Lloyd's Rep. 486, 493 (no estoppel as no action in reliance).

[428] *Amherst v James Walker Goldsmith & Silversmith Ltd* [1983] Ch. 305, 315; *cf.*, in another context, *Agip SpA v Navigazione Alta Italia SpA (The Nai Genova)* [1984] 1 Lloyd's Rep. 353, 365.

[429] *Collin v Duke of Westminster* [1985] Q.B. 581.

[430] Above, para.2–072; below, paras 6–142—6–164; see, *e.g. Tradax Export SA v Dorada Compania Naviera SA (The Lutetian)* [1982] 2 Lloyd's Rep. 140, 158; *The Stolt Loyalty* [1993] 2 Lloyd's Rep. 281, 289–291, affirmed (without reference to the point here under discussion) [1995] 1 Lloyd's Rep. 559; and see *Petrotrade Inc v Stinnes Handel GmbH* [1995] 1 Lloyd's Rep. 142, 151, where the statement that there may be a representation by "conduct (including silence)" evidently refers to the exceptional situations described in the text above.

[431] *cf.* below, para.6–034.

[432] See *Fontana N.V. v Mautner* (1979] 254 E.G. 199; *Raiffeisen Hauptgenossenschaft v Louis Dreyfus & Co* [1981] 1 Lloyd's Rep. 345, 352; *Cook Industries Ltd v Meunerie Liegeois SA* [1981] 1 Lloyd's Rep. 359, 368; *Scandinavian Trading Tanker Co A.B. v Flota Petrolera Ecuatoriana (The Scaptrade)* [1983] 1 All E.R. 301, affirmed without reference to this point [1983] 2 A.C. 694; *Bremer Handelsgesellschaft mbH v Bunge Corp.* [1983] 1 Lloyd's Rep. 476; *Bremer Handelsgesellschaft mbH v Deutsche Conti-Handelsgesellschaft mbH* [1983] 1 Lloyd's Rep. 689; *Lark v Outhwaite* [1991] 2 Lloyd's Rep. 132, 142; *The Nerano* [1996] 1 Lloyd's Rep. 1; *Rowan Companies Inc v Lambert Eggink Offshore Transport Ltd* [1999] 2 Lloyd's Rep. 443 at 449.

[433] *Ets. Soules & Cie v International Trade Development Co Ltd* [1980] 1 Lloyd's Rep. 129; *Tankrederei Ahrenkeil GmbH v Frahuil SA (The Multibank Holsatia)* [1988] 2 Lloyd's Rep. 486, 493.

[434] *Brikom Investments Ltd v Carr* [1979] Q.B. 467, 482.

[435] *ibid.* at 490 (*per* Cumming-Bruce L.J., whose decision was based on the different ground discussed in para.3–080, above).

form a sufficient inducement. Where the promisee has, after the promise, conducted himself in the way intended by the promisor, it will be up to the promisor to establish that the conduct was not induced by the promise.[436]

Whether "detriment" required. There is sometimes said to be a further requirement, namely that the promisee must have suffered "detriment" by acting in reliance on the promise.[437] This may mean that the promisee must have done something that he was not previously bound to do and as a result suffered loss: for example, by incurring some expenditure in reliance on the promise. This alleged requirement of "detriment" is based on the analogy of the doctrine of estoppel by representation.[438] But that analogy is (as we shall see)[439] inexact, and the equitable doctrine may be applied even though there is no "detriment" in this sense.[440] It is enough if the promisee has altered his position in reliance on the promise so that it would be inequitable to allow the promisor to act inconsistently with it[441]: for example, if the promisee has forborne from taking steps that he would otherwise have taken to safeguard his legal position (as in *Hughes v Metropolitan Ry.*[442] itself); or if he has performed, or made efforts to perform the altered obligation (for example, where a seller after being promised extra time for delivery has continued his efforts to perform after the originally agreed delivery date had gone by). On the other hand, the fact that the promisee has not suffered any prejudice by acting in reliance on the promise may be relevant for the purpose of the requirement to be discussed in para.3–095 below; for in such circumstances it may not be "inequitable" for the promisor to go back on his promise.[443] 3–094

---

436 *cf.* the similar rule in cases of "proprietary estoppel" stated in para.3–147, below.

437 *e.g.* in *Fontana N.V. v Mautner* (1979] 254 E.G. 199; *Meng Long Development Pte Ltd v Jip Hong Trading Co Pte Ltd* [1985] A.C. 511, 524; *cf.* Wilson (1951) 67 L.Q.R. 344.

438 For the requirement of detriment in cases of such estoppel, see *Carr v L. & N.W. Ry* (1875) L.R. 10 C.P. 310, 317. In *Aker Oil & Gas Technology UK plc v Sovereign Corporate Ltd* [2002] C.L.C. 557 benefit to the representor (as opposed to the more usually stated factor of detriment of the promisee) is said to suffice for the purpose of giving rise to this type of estoppel.

439 Below, para.3–103.

440 *W.J. Alan & Co Ltd v El Nasr Export & Import Co* [1972] 2 Q.B. 189 at 213.

441 *James v Heim Galleries* (1980) 256 E.G. 819, 825; *Société Italo-Belge pour le Commerce et l'Industrie v Palm & Vegetable Oils (Malaysia) Sdn. Bhd. (The Post Chaser)* [1981] 2 Lloyd's Rep. 695, 701. *Youell v Bland Welch & Co Ltd (The Superhulls Cover Case) (No.2)* [1990] 2 Lloyd's Rep. 431, 454; *Fortisbank SA v Trenwick International Ltd* [2005] EWHC 339; [2005] 2 Lloyd's Rep. I.R. 464 at [13].

442 (1877) 2 App. Cas. 439; *cf. Bottiglieri di Navigazione SpA v Quindao Ocean Shipping Co (The Bunge Saga Lima)* [2005] EWHC 244, [2005] 2 Lloyd's Rep. 1 at [31] ("some conduct [including "a failure to act"] which differs from that which would have occurred in the absence of the representation").

443 *Société Italo-Belge pour le Commerce et l'Industrie v Palm & Vegetable Oils (Malaysia) Sdn. Bhd. (The Post Chaser)* [1981] 2 Lloyd's Rep. 695. The point made in the text above may account for Rix L.J.'s statement in *Kosmar Villa Holidays plc v Trustees of Syndicate 1243* [2008] EWCA Civ. 147, [2008] 2 All E.R. (Comm) 14 at [38] that detriment is "probably" a requirement of the operation of this type of "estoppel". (For the use of "estoppel" to describe the equitable doctrine , see above, para.3–090 and below para.3–103.) The description in [2008] EWCA Civ. 147 at [38] of the "estoppel" in question as "a promise supported not by consideration but by reliance" indicates that the reference is to the type of "estoppel" here under discussion.

3–095 **Inequitable.** It must be "inequitable" for the promisor to go back on the promise. This requirement cannot be defined with anything approaching precision, but the underlying idea is that the promisee must have acted in reliance on the promise in one of the ways just described, so that he can no longer be restored to the position in which he was before he took such action.[444] If the promisee can be restored to that position, it will not be inequitable for the promisor to go back on the promise. In one case[445] the promisor reasserted his strict legal rights only two days after the promise had been made. It was held that this was not "inequitable" since the promisee had not, in this short period, suffered any prejudice by acting in reliance on the promise: he could be, and was, restored to exactly the position in which he had been before the promise was made. Sometimes, moreover, extraneous circumstances may justify the promisor in going back on the promise even without giving reasonable notice of his intention to do so.[446] In *Williams v Stern*[447] the plaintiff gave the defendant a bill of sale of furniture as security for a loan; the bill entitled the defendant to seize the furniture if the plaintiff defaulted in making payments under it. When the fourteenth instalment became due, the plaintiff asked for extra time, and the defendant said that he "would not look to a week." Three days later he seized the furniture because he had heard that the plaintiff's landlord intended to distrain it for arrears of rent. It was held that the defendant's seizure was justified. The defendant's promise to give time was not binding contractually as the plaintiff had given no consideration for it; nor did it, in the circumstances, bring the equitable doctrine into operation. Brett L.J. said: "Has there been any misconduct on the part of the defendant? I think not: it appears that a distress by the plaintiff's landlord has been threatened; and under these circumstances I do not blame the defendant for changing his mind."[448] The conduct of the promisee in obtaining the promise may also be relevant to the issue whether the promisor has acted "inequitably" in going back on it.[449]

3–096 **Effect of the doctrine generally suspensive.** The equitable doctrine, like the common law doctrine of waiver, generally does not extinguish, but only suspends rights. The landlord in *Hughes v Metropolitan Ry*[450] was not permanently debarred from enforcing the covenant to repair. He could have enforced it by

---

[444] *Maharaj v Chand* [1986] A.C. 898; *The Bunge Saga Lima*, above n.482, at [31] (quoted in para.3–097 n.458 below).

[445] *Société Italo-Belge pour le Commerce et l'Industrie v Vegetable Oils (Malaysia) Sdn. Bhd. (The Post Chaser)* [1981] 2 Lloyd's Rep. 695; *cf. Bremer Handelsgesellschaft mbH v Bunge Corp.* [1983] 1 Lloyd's Rep. 476, 484; *Marseille Fret SA v D. Oltman Schiffahrts GmbH & Co K.G. (The Trado)* [1982] 1 Lloyd's Rep. 157, 160; *Bremer Handelsgesellschaft mbH v Deutsche Conti-Handelsgesellschaft mbH* [1983] 1 Lloyd's Rep. 689; *Banner Industrial & Commercial Properties Ltd v Clark Paterson Ltd* [1990] 2 E.G.L.R. 139; *Transatlantica de Commercio SA v Incrobasa Industrial & Commercio Brazileira SA* [1995] 1 Lloyd's Rep. 214, 219.

[446] See below, para.3–096 and *cf.* above, para.3–082 for the requirement of such notice.

[447] (1879) 5 Q.B.D. 409.

[448] *ibid.* at 413; *cf.* also *Southwark LBC v Logan* (1996) 8 Admin.L.R. 315; *Evans v Amicus Healthcare Ltd* [2003] EWHC 2161 (Fam), [2003] 4 All E.R. 903 at [309], affirmed [2004] EWCA Civ. 727, [2005] Fam. 1 on the ground stated in para.3–088 above.

[449] See *D. & C. Builders Ltd v Rees* [1966] 2 Q.B. 167, below, paras 3–116, 3–136 and *South Caribbean Trading Ltd v Trafigura Beheer BV* [2004] EWHC 2676 (Comm), [2005] 1 Lloyd's Rep. 128 at [112] (promise obtained by economic duress).

[450] (1877) 2 App. Cas. 439.

giving reasonable notice to the tenant requiring him to repair.[451] The reason for the general rule is that, in equity, the effect of the representation is to give the court a discretion to give such relief as is just and equitable in all the circumstances[452]; and in cases such as *Hughes v Metropolitan Ry* it would be neither equitable nor in accordance with the intention of the parties to treat the promisor's rights as having been wholly extinguished.[453]

3–097 **Extinctive effect in exceptional cases.** Subsequent events may, however, give the doctrine an extinctive effect, by way of exception to the general rule stated in para.3–096 above.[454] They can most obviously lead to this result where they make it impossible for the promisee to perform his original obligation. For example, in *Birmingham & District Land Co v L. & N.W. Ry*[455] a building lease bound the tenant to build by 1885. The lessor agreed to suspend this obligation; but in 1886, while the suspension was still in force, the land was compulsorily acquired by a railway company, so that performance of the tenant's obligation became impossible. The tenant recovered statutory compensation from the railway company on the footing that the building lease was still binding; but clearly his obligation to build was utterly extinguished. Even where performance of the original obligation has not literally become impossible, the doctrine may sometimes have an extinctive effect. For example, where a vendor of land on August 15 indicated that he would not insist on the contractual completion date of August 30, it was held that no question of reinstating that date could arise "because the time was far too short."[456] And where a shipowner represented to a charterer that he would not rely, by way of defence to claims under the charterparty, on a one-year time bar (which had expired) it was held that he could not, after nearly another year had gone by, go back on the representation, since it would by then have been too late to restore the charterer to his original position.[457] In all these cases the doctrine has an extinctive effect because

[451] *cf. Tool Metal Manufacturing Co Ltd v Tungsten Electric Co Ltd* [1955] 1 W.L.R. 761; (below, para.3–131) *Banning v Wright* [1972] 1 W.L.R. 972, 981; *Brikom Investments Ltd v Seaford* [1981] 1 W.L.R. 863, 869; *Société Italo-Belge v Palm & Vegetable Oils (The Post Chaser)* [1981] 2 Lloyd's Rep. 695, 701; *Meng Long Development Pte Ltd v Jip Hong Trading Co Ltd* [1985] A.C. 511, 524; *Motor Oil Hellas (Corinth) Refineries SA v Shipping Corp. of India (The Kanchenjunga)* [1987] 2 Lloyd's Rep. 509, 518 affirmed [1989] 1 Lloyd's Rep. 354; *MSAS Global Logistics Ltd v Power Packaging Inc* [2003] EWHC 1391, *The Times*, June 26, 2003; *Kosmar Villa Holidays plc v Trustees of Syndicate 1243* [2008] EWCA Civ. 147, [2008] 2 All E.R. (Comm) 14 at [38] ("may be suspensory"; the reference appears to be to "promissory estoppel": see above, para 3–094 note 443); and see *Hazel v Akhtar* [2001] EWCA Civ. 1883; [2002] 2 P. & C.R. 17 at [43]. No reference to the suspensive nature of the doctrine was made in *Smith v Lawson* (1999) 75 P.&C.R. 466 (below, para.3–102), probably because no attempt was made by the promisor to give reasonable notice of any intention to resume enforcement of his legal rights.

[452] *Roebuck v Mungovin* [1994] A.C. 224, 234.

[453] This is also true of cases such as *Tool Metal Manufacturing Co Ltd v Tungsten Electric Co Ltd* [1955] 1 W.L.R. 761 and *Ajayi v R. T. Briscoe (Nig.) Ltd* [1964] 1 W.L.R. 1236, discussed in paras 3–130 and 3–131 below.

[454] *cf.* below, para.3–132.

[455] (1888) 40 Ch.D. 268; *cf. W. J. Alan & Co Ltd v El Nasr Export & Import Co* [1972] 2 Q.B. 189, where the actual decision was that there was a contractually binding variation: see above, para.3–079.

[456] *Ogilvie v Hope-Davies* [1976] 1 All E.R. 683, 696; *cf. Voest Alpine International GmbH v Chevron International Oil Co Ltd* [1987] 2 Lloyd's Rep. 547, 560.

[457] *Nippon Yusen Kaisha v Pacifica Navegacion SA (The Ion)* [1980] 2 Lloyd's Rep. 245.

subsequent events or the passage of time, though not making performance of the original obligation impossible, have made it highly inequitable to require such performance, even after reasonable notice.[458]

3–098 **Defensive nature of the doctrine.** The equitable doctrine prevents the enforcement of existing rights; but it does not "create new causes of action where none existed before."[459] The point was decided in *Combe v Combe*[460] where a husband, during divorce proceedings, promised to pay £100 per annum to his wife, who in reliance on the husband's promise, forbore from applying to the court for maintenance; and this forbearance did not constitute consideration for the husband's promise.[461] It was held that the equitable doctrine did not entitle the wife to recover the promised payments; nor is there any support in English cases for the view that it could create a cause of action in the narrower sense of creating a new right but "limiting recovery to reliance loss."[462] The view that the doctrine gave rise to no new rights came to be associated with its description as a kind of estoppel (known as "promissory estoppel"[463]) and hence with the rule, established in relation to another kind of estoppel (known as "estoppel by representation"[464]), that "you cannot found a cause of action on an estoppel."[465] It will be submitted below[466] that the analogy between the two kinds of estoppel is (to say the least) imperfect and that it does not satisfactorily account for the rule that the equitable doctrine (or "promissory estoppel") gives rise to no new rights. The more plausible explanation for this restriction on the scope of the equitable doctrine is that the restriction is needed to prevent that doctrine from coming into head-on collision with the rules which lay down the requirements for the creation of a binding contract. The significant point in the present context is that the restriction preserves consistency between the equitable doctrine and the rule that a promise is not binding as a contract unless it is supported by consideration or made in a deed.[467] *Combe v Combe* has likewise been relied on in support of the view that the equitable doctrine could not give rise to a cause

---

[458] See *Maharaj v Chand* [1986] A.C. 898; *cf. W. J. Alan & Co Ltd v El Nasr Export & Import Co* [1972] 2 Q.B. 189 (where the actual decision was that there was a variation supported by consideration); *Bottiglieri di Navigazione SpA v Cosco Quindao Ocean Shipping Co (The Bunge Saga Lima)* [2005] EWHC 244 (Comm), [2005] 2 Lloyd's Rep. 1 at [31]. The further statement in this passage that "no revocation can be retrospective" is, with respect, open to question; in a sense, any reassertion of the original obligation has "retrospective" effect. The crucial limitation on the effectiveness of a revocation is its inequitable, rather than its merely retrospective, operation.

[459] *Combe v Combe* [1951] 2 K.B. 215 at 219; the point had been foreshadowed in *Central London Property Trust Ltd v High Trees House Ltd* [1947] K.B. 130 at 134.

[460] [1951] 2 K.B. 215.

[461] Above, para.3–060.

[462] *Baird Textile Holdings Ltd v Marks & Spencer plc* [2001] EWCA Civ. 274; [2002] 1 All E.R. (Comm) 737 at [91]; for the difficulty of distinguishing in that case between reliance and expectation loss, see *ibid*, at [81], [82].

[463] Above, para.3–085, below, para.3–103.

[464] Below, para.3–103.

[465] *Low v Bouverie* [1891] 3 Ch. 82 at 101; *cf. ibid.* at 105.

[466] Below, para.3–103, especially n.509.

[467] This appears to be the point that Denning L.J. had in mind in *Combe v Combe* [1951] 2 K.B. 215 at 219 when he said that he did not want the equitable principle to be "stretched too far lest it be endangered." *cf. Brikom Investments Ltd v Carr* [1979] Q.B. 467, 486; *Tool Metal Manufacturing Co Ltd v Tungsten Electric Co Ltd* [1955] 1 W.L.R. 761, 764; *Beesly v Hallwood Estates Ltd* [1960]

of action on a promise which lacked contractual force for want, not of consideration, but of certainty and contractual intention.[468] There seems, with respect, to be no reason in principle for distinguishing for the present purpose between promises which lack contractual effect for want of consideration and those which lack such effect for some other reason: the danger of collision between the equitable doctrine and the requirements for the creation of a contract exist, whatever the reason may be why a particular promise lacks contractual force.[469] The view that the equitable doctrine does not create new causes of action seems, indeed, to have been doubted[470] or ignored[471] by dicta in later cases; but the promises in these cases created new rights on the perfectly orthodox ground that they were, in fact, supported by consideration.[472] *Combe v Combe* therefore still stands as the leading English[473] authority for the proposition that the equitable doctrine creates no new rights[474]; and this proposition has been reaffirmed in a number of later cases.[475]

---

1 W.L.R. 549, 561; *Drexel Burnham Lambert International NV v El Nasr* [1986] 1 Lloyd's Rep. 357, 365. Contrast *Vaughan v Vaughan* [1953] 1 Q.B. 762, 768; Denning (1952) 15 M.L.R. 1.

[468] *Baird Textile Holdings Ltd v Marks & Spencer plc*, above, n.462, where *Combe v Combe* is cited at [34], and [87] in support of the view stated in the text above; though an alternative explanation for the result in the *Baird* case may be that, in the absence of certainty or contractual intention, the requirements for the operation of the equitable doctrine are simply not satisfied (above, paras 2–142, 3–090), so that no question can arise as to its effects.

[469] In *Azov Shipping Co v Baltic Shipping Co* [1999] 2 Lloyd's Rep. 159, 175 it is suggested that the rule that promissory estoppel gives rise to no cause of action "is limited to the protection of consideration" and has "no general application in the field of estoppel." The estoppel there under discussion was estoppel by representation, and the suggestion is, with respect, hard to reconcile with the statements in *Low v Bouverie* [1891] 3 Ch. 82 at 101, 105 cited at n.465 above. Similar difficulty arises from the more tentative suggestion in *Thornton Springer v NEM Insurance Ltd* [2000] 2 All E.R. 489 at 519 that estoppel could lead to the "enforcement of the promise" where no contract was concluded for want of acceptance of an offer, though not where there was no contract for want of consideration. The former situation is one of estoppel by convention (as to which see below, para.3–107); and it is also, with respect, hard to see why one answer should be given to the question whether rule in *Combe v Combe* applies where the promise lacks contractual force for want of consideration and a different one where it lacks such force for want of an effective acceptance. Such a distinction seems also to be inconsistent with the readiness of the Court of Appeal in the *Baird* case (above at n.468) to apply the rule in *Combe v Combe* to an alleged promise which lacked contractual force for some reason other than want of consideration. See also *Oceanografia SA de CV v DSND Subsea AS (The Botnica)* [2006] EWHC 1300 (Comm), [2007] 1 All E.R. (Comm) 1 where "waiver" was invoked (at [89]) in the context of failure to comply with one of the requirements of contract formation, in that case the execution of a formal document (above, para.2–116). The normal effect of such a waiver is that the party granting it is *bound* by the contract (e.g., above paras 2–047, 2–068); but in *The Botnica* it resulted in that party's entitlement to *enforce* a term of the contract. No reference was made to the equitable doctrine or to the normally defensive nature of waiver.

[470] *Re Wyvern Developments Ltd* [1974] 1 W.L.R. 1097, 1104–1105; Atiyah (1974) 38 M.L.R. 65; and see Allan (1963) 79 L.Q.R. 238; the point was left open in *Pacol Ltd v Trade Lines Ltd (The Henrik Sif)* [1982] 1 Lloyd's Rep. 456, 466–468 (as to which see above para.3–088, n.399).

[471] *Evenden v Guildford City F.C.* [1975] Q.B. 917, 924, 926; Napier [1976] C.L.J. 38; and see next note.

[472] See *Secretary of State for Employment v Globe Elastic Thread Co Ltd* [1980] A.C. 506, overruling *Evenden's* case, above. Lord Wilberforce remarked at 518 that "To convert this [contract] into an estoppel is to turn the doctrine of promissory estoppel . . . upside down."

[473] For the position in other common law jurisdictions, see para.3–106, below.

[474] *cf.* the position in cases of estoppel by representation, below, para.3–103 n.509.

[475] *Argy Trading Development Co Ltd v Lapid Developments Ltd* [1977] 1 W.L.R. 444, 457; *Aquaflite Ltd v Jaymar International Freight Consultants Ltd* [1980] 1 Lloyd's Rep. 36; *Syros Shipping Co SA v Elaghill Trading Co (The Proodos C)* [1980] 2 Lloyd's Rep. 390, 391; *James v*

3–099 **Modifications increasing a party's obligation.** It appears to follow from the proposition stated at the end of para.3–098 above that the equitable doctrine would not enable employees in a case like *Stilk v Myrick*[476] to recover the extra pay which they had been promised. It could, indeed, be argued[477] that in such a case the cause of action was the original contract of employment and that the subsequent agreement fell within the principle stated by Denning L.J. in *Combe v Combe* that consideration was not necessary for the "modification or discharge"[478] of a contract where the conditions required for the operation of the equitable doctrine were otherwise satisfied. This argument may derive some judicial support from a dictum that promissory estoppel "may enlarge the effect of an agreement"[479]; for this could mean that a promise of extra pay on facts such as those of *Stilk v Myrick* could create a cause of action even though it was not supported by consideration. This view is, however, hard to reconcile with the treatment of *Stilk v Myrick* in *Williams v Roffey Bros*[480] and with the fact that the decision in the latter case was based, not on estoppel,[481] but on the ground that the promise of extra pay there was supported by consideration. It is submitted that, when in *Combe v Combe* Denning L.J. used the phrase "modification or discharge", he had in mind a modification which *reduced* a party's obligations[482]; for to apply it to a case in which it had the effect of *increasing* them necessarily amounts to giving the other party new rights of action as a result of a promise for which he has not provided any consideration; and *Combe v Combe* decides that this is not the effect of the equitable doctrine here under discussion.[483] A cause of action on a promise unsupported by consideration may, however, arise under other equitable doctrines: *e.g.* under the doctrine of "proprietary estoppel," discussed later in this chapter.[484]

3–100 **"Shield and not a sword".** The essentially defensive nature of the equitable doctrine here under discussion is sometimes expressed by saying that it operates as a shield and not as a sword.[485] This is true in most cases: usually it protects

Heim Galleries (1980) 256 E.G. 819, 821; *Brikom Investments Ltd v Seaford* [1981] 1 W.L.R. 863; *cf. Taylors Fashions Ltd v Liverpool Victoria Trustee Co Ltd* [1982] Q.B. 133, 152; *Baird Textile Holdings Ltd v Marks & Spencer plc* [2001] EWCA Civ. 274; [2002] 1 All E.R. (Comm) 737, above, n.468.

[476] (1809) 2 Camp. 317; 6 Esp. 129; above, para.3–066.

[477] See *Hiscox v Outhwaite (No.3)* [1991] 2 Lloyd's Rep. 524, 535.

[478] [1951] 2 K.B. 215, 219.

[479] *Baird Textile Holdings Ltd v Marks & Spencer plc* [2001] EWCA Civ. 274; [2002] 1 All E.R. (Comm) 737, at [88].

[480] [1991] 1 Q.B. 1, above, para.3–068.

[481] Though there are references to estoppel in that case at pp.13 ("not yet fully developed") and 17–18 (this reference seems to be estoppel by convention, the relevance of which to the case is doubted in para.3–111 n.572 below).

[482] As in *Central London Property Trust Ltd v High Trees House Ltd* [1947] K.B. 130, below para.3–128, this being the case under discussion in *Combe v Combe*, above.

[483] *Syros Shipping Co SA v Elaghill Trading Co (The Proodos C)* [1980] 2 Lloyd's Rep. 390.

[484] Below, paras 3–137—3–164, especially para.3–151.

[485] *Combe v Combe* [1951] 2 K.B. 215, 224; The *Proodos C*, above n.483 at 391 ("time honoured phrase"); *Lark v Outhwaite* [1991] 2 Lloyd's Rep. 132, 142; *Hiscox v Outhwaite (No.3)* [1991] 2 Lloyd's Rep. 524, 535.

a promisee against enforcement of his original obligation. But the metaphor is apt to mislead[486]: the essential point is that the doctrine excuses (at least temporarily) the performance of the original obligation; and such an excuse may benefit a claimant no less than a defendant. For example, if the creditor's conduct in *Williams v Stern*[487] (discussed in para.3–095 above) had been "inequitable" the debtor could no doubt have obtained an injunction against a *threatened* seizure of his property. Similarly, a seller may tender delivery after the originally agreed date in reliance on the buyer's promise to accept such delivery. If the buyer then refuses to accept the delivery, the seller can claim damages.[488]

Doctrine may deprive promisor of certain defences. The equitable doctrine can also assist the promisee as claimant in that it may prevent the promisor from relying on a defence that would, but for the promise, have been available to him: *e.g.* the defence that a claim which the promisee has made against him is time-barred,[489] or that the claim has been satisfied[490] or that the contractual document suffers from some minor formal defect, the effect of which on the validity of the contract is not specified by the statute imposing the formal requirement.[491] In such cases, the doctrine will, once again, enable the promisee to win an action which, but for the doctrine, he would have lost.[492] But it must be stressed that, in cases of this kind, the promisee's cause of action will have arisen independently of the promise which brought the equitable doctrine into operation: the effect of the doctrine is merely to prevent the promisor from relying on some circumstance which would, if the promise had not been made, *have destroyed the promisee's original cause of action*. This situation must be distinguished from that in which the promisor's "defence" is that (apart from the promise) the promisee's alleged *cause of action never existed at all*. It is submitted that the equitable doctrine should not prevent the promisor from relying on a "defence" of this kind. To allow the doctrine to operate in this way would amount to giving 3–101

[486] *Azov Shipping Co v Baltic Shipping Co* [1999] 2 Lloyd's Rep. 159 at 175 ("largely inaccurate"); *Baird Textile Holdings Ltd v Marks & Spencer plc* [2001] EWCA Civ. 274; [2002] 1 All E.R. (Comm) 737, at [54] ("misleading aphorism").

[487] (1879) 5 Q.B.D. 409.

[488] *cf. Hartley v Hymans* [1920] 3 K.B. 475, applying the corresponding common law doctrine: above, para.3–081; *Johnson v Gore Wood* [2002] 2 A.C. 1 at [40]. And see Jackson (1965) 81 L.Q.R. 223.

[489] See *Nippon Yusen Kaisha v Pacifica Navegacion SA (The Ion)* [1980] 2 Lloyd's Rep. 245, above, para.3–097; the Australian case of *Commonwealth of Australia v Verwayen* (1990) 170 C.L.R. 394 (discussed by Spence (1991) 107 L.Q.R. 221) could, in England, be decided on the same ground (*Baird Textile Holdings Ltd v Marks & Spencers plc* [2001] EWCA Civ. 274; [2002] 1 All E.R. (Comm) 737 at [98]) though it was actually based on the wider Australian principle referred to in para.3–106, below.

[490] *cf.* in cases of estoppel by representation, *Burrowes v Lock* (1805) Ves. 470, as explained in *Low v Bouverie* [1891] 3 Ch. 82.

[491] *Shah v Shah* [2001] EWCA Civ. 527; [2002] Q.B. 35 at [31] (a case of estoppel by representation).

[492] This may be the force of the statement in *Evans v Amicus Healthcare Ltd* [2003] EWHC 2161 (Fam); [2003] 4 All E.R. 903 at [303] that promissary estoppel "is not, of itself, the cause of action, although it may be an element in it"; affirmed, without reference to this point, [2004] EWCA Civ. 727, [2005] Fam. 1 (above, para.3–088).

the promisee a new cause of action based on the promise though it was unsupported by consideration; and such a result would be inconsistent with the essentially defensive nature of the equitable doctrine.[493]

3–102 **Doctrine may deprive promisee of a defence.** The doctrine may also, somewhat paradoxically, deprive a *promisee* of a defence. This was the position in *Smith v Lawson*[494] where a lessor told the lessee that he would not trouble to collect the small rent which the lessee had previously paid. It was held that the lessee's rent-free occupation did not amount to adverse possession since the lessor was precluded by the doctrine of promissory estoppel from obtaining possession on the ground of non-payment of rent. It followed that the lessee could not rely on her occupation to defeat the lessor's claim for the declaration that he remained freehold owner of the land.

3–103 **Analogy with estoppel.** The equitable doctrine is sometimes compared with the doctrine of estoppel by representation and the two have, indeed, certain features in common. Each is based on a representation followed by reliance, and the nature of each is defensive in the sense that neither is capable of giving rise to new rights. On the other hand, there are many significant differences between the two, even though the word "estoppel" is now often used to refer to the equitable doctrine.[495] These differences are reflected in the statement of Millett L.J. that "the attempt . . . to demonstrate that all estoppels . . . are now subsumed in the single and all-embracing estoppel by representation and that they are all governed by the same principle"[496] has "never won general acceptance."[497] The various kinds of estoppel discussed in this book[498] are linked only by the broadest of general principles, that a person's taking of inconsistent positions is in some situations to be discouraged by law: in this sense it can be said that "unconscionability . . . provides the link between them."[499] But they nevertheless have

[493] *cf.* the criticism (above, para.3–088) of *Pacol Ltd v Trade Lines Ltd (The Henrik Sif)* [1982] 1 Lloyd's Rep. 456. For the position in relation to estoppel by convention see below, para.3–137.

[494] (1998) 75 P. & C.R. 466.

[495] Below, n.504.

[496] The reference seems to be to Lord Denning, M.R.'s statement in *Amalgamated Investment & Property Co Ltd v Texas Commerce International Bank Ltd* [1982] 2 Q.B. 73 at 122 ("one general principle shorn of limitations"). The passage containing these words is cited with apparent approval by Lord Bingham in *Johnson v Gore Wood & Co* [2002] 2 A.C. 1 at 33 but it is not clear whether (a) this citation is part of Lord Bingham's *ratio* in that case; or (b) the apparent approval is shared by Lords Hutton and Cooke who agree generally with the part of Lord Bingham's speech in which it occurs. *cf.* also the reference, in another context, to a possible "move to a more uniform doctrine of estoppel" in *Scottish Equitable plc v Derby* [2001] EWCA Civ. 369; [2001] 2 All E.R. 818 at [48].

[497] *First National Bank plc v Thomson* [1996] Ch. 231, 236; *cf. Republic of India v India S.S. Co Ltd (The Indian Endurance) (No.2)* [1998] A.C. 878 at 913; *National Westminster Bank plc v Somer* [2001] EWCA Civ. 970; [2002] 1 All E.R. 198 at [38], [39]; dicta in *Baird Textile Holdings Ltd v Marks & Spencer plc* [2001] EWCA Civ. 274; [2002] 1 All E.R. (Comm) 737 at [38], [50], [83], [84] perhaps incline in the other direction but cannot be regarded as conclusive.

[498] *i.e.* estoppel by representation (below, para.6–095) promissory estoppel (discussed here), estoppel by convention (below, paras 3–107 *et seq.*) and proprietary estoppel (below paras 3–137 *et seq.*).

[499] *Johnson v Gore Wood & Co* [2002] 2 A.C. 1 at 41. In *Cobbe v Yeoman's Row Management Ltd* [2008] UKHL 55, [2008] 1 W.L.R. 1752 at [59] Lord Walker refers with apparent approval to a "broad or unified approach to equitable estoppel". But in this speech he uses "equitable estoppel" to mean *proprietary* estoppel: see below, para.3–137 n. 720; so that his approval is of a "unified

"separate requirements and different terrains of application"[500] and therefore "cannot be accommodated within a single principle."[501] An important difference between the two types of estoppel at this stage under discussion[502] relates to the types of representations required to bring them into operation. For the purpose of true estoppel by representation, there must be representation of *existing fact*.[503] The equitable doctrine, by contrast, can apply where there is no such representation, but only one of intention as to the promisor's future conduct, or a promise. For this reason, and because the doctrine was developed in equity, the doctrine is sometimes called "promissory" or "equitable" estoppel.[504] The latter description is, however, misleading as the requirement of a representation of existing fact for the purposes of estoppel by representation was recognised in equity[505] no

---

approach" to the various situations within *this* kind of estoppel (below, para.3–138): not to such an approach to all of the *other* kinds of estoppel discussed in this chapter.

[500] *Republic of India v India S.S. Co Ltd (The Indian Endurance) (No.2)* [1998] A.C. 878 at 914, distinguishing between estoppels by convention and by acquiescence. See also *Donegal International Ltd v Zambia* [2007] EWHC 197 (Comm), [2007] 1 Lloyd's Rep. 397, distinguishing between estoppels by convention and by representation and referring with apparent approval to the text above in a previous edition of this book.

[501] *Johnson v Gore Wood & Co* [2000] 2 A.C. 1 at 41.

[502] *i.e.* estoppel by representation and promissory estoppel.

[503] *Jordan v Money* (1854) 5 H.L.C. 195, criticised by Jackson (1965) 81 L.Q.R. 84; *cf.* Halliwell, 5 L.S. 15. Atiyah (*op. cit.*, above, para.3–007, n.29, pp.53–57) suggests that the case does not support the proposition for which it is usually cited, but that there *was* a contract, which was unenforceable for want of written evidence. But the claimant alleged no such contract: as Lord Cranworth said at p.215, "it is put entirely on the ground of misrepresentation." The orthodox view is also supported by Lord Selborne (who was counsel in *Jordan v Money*) in his speech in *Maddison v Alderson* (1883) 8 App. Cas. 467, 473. For recent statements of the rule that estoppel can be based only on a representation of *existing fact*, see *Argy Trading Development Co Ltd v Lapid Developments Ltd* [1977] 1 Lloyd's Rep. 67, 76; *China-Pacific SA v The Food Corp. of India (The Winson)* [1980] 2 Lloyd's Rep. 213, 222 (reversed on other grounds [1982] A.C. 939); *Spence v Shell* (1980) 256 E.G. 55, 63; *T.C.B. Ltd v Gray* [1986] Ch. 621, 634 (affirmed [1987] Ch. 458); *Roebuck v Mungovin* [1994] 2 A.C. 224, 235; *cf. Janred Properties v Ente Nazionale per il Turismo* [1987] F.L.R. 179 (implied representation that approval *had* been given). So-called "estoppel by convention" is similarly based on a common assumption of *fact* or (at least to some extent) on one of "law": see below, para.3–110. In *Robertson v Minister of Pensions* [1949] 1 K.B. 227, the equitable doctrine was mentioned though the representation was a statement of fact rather than a promise.

[504] *e.g. Woodhouse A.C. Israel Cocoa Ltd v Nigerian Produce Marketing Co Ltd* [1972] A.C. 741, 758; *Ogilvy v Hope-Davies* [1976] 1 All E.R. 683, 689; *B.P. Exploration Co (Libya) Ltd v Hunt (No. 2)* [1979] 1 W.L.R. 783, 812 (affirmed [1983] 2 A.C. 352, without reference to this point); *China-Pacific SA v The Food Corp. Of India (The Winson)* [1980] 2 Lloyd's Rep. 213, 222 (reversed on other grounds [1982] A.C. 939); *Ets. Soules & Cie v International Trade Development Co Ltd* [1980] 1 Lloyd's Rep. 129, 133; *Nippon Yusen Kaisha v Pacifica Navegacion SA (The Ion)* [1980] 1 Lloyd's Rep. 245, 259; *Peter Cremer v Granaria B.V.* [1981] 2 Lloyd's Rep. 583, 587; *Société Italo-Belge pour le Commerce et l'Industrie v Palm & Vegetable Oils (Malaysia) Sdn. Bhd. (The Post Chaser)* [1981] 2 Lloyd's Rep. 695, 700; *Roebuck v Mungovin* [1994] 2 A.C. 224, 235; *cf. Brikom Investments Ltd v Carr* [1979] Q.B. 467, 485, 489, where Roskill L.J. prefers to refer simply to the principle of *Hughes v Metropolitan Ry* (1877) 2 App. Cas. 439. *Amherst v James Walker Goldsmiths & Silversmiths Ltd* [1983] Ch. 305, 316 somewhat puzzlingly seems to distinguish between "promissory" and "equitable" estoppel. Terminological difficulty is compounded by occasional use of the phrase "equitable estoppel" to refer to true estoppel by representation: see below n.506.

[505] *Jordan v Money*, above, was itself an appeal from the Court of Appeal in Chancery. See also *Pigott v Stratton* (1859) 1 D.F. & J. 33, 51; *Citizens' Bank of Louisiana v First National Bank of New Orleans* (1873) L.R. 6 H.L. 352, 360; *Maddison v Alderson* (1883) 8 App. Cas. 467, 473; *Chadwick v Manning* [1896] A.C. 231, 238.

less than at common law.[506] There are, moreover, other significant differences between the two doctrines. One relates to the requirements of the two doctrines; the equitable doctrine can operate even though there is no such "detriment" as is required to bring the doctrine of estoppel by representation into play.[507] A second relates to their effects: in general, the equitable doctrine only suspends rights,[508] while estoppel by representation, where it operates, has a permanent effect. And thirdly there is a difference in the legal nature of the two doctrines. Estoppel by representation prevents a party from establishing *facts*: *i.e.* from alleging that the facts represented by him are untrue, even where that is actually the case.[509] The equitable doctrine, by contrast, has nothing to do with proof of facts; it is concerned with the *legal effects* of a promise. There was, for example, no dispute about facts in *Hughes v Metropolitan Ry*[510]: the issue was not whether the repairs had been done or whether the landlord had promised or represented that he would not forfeit the lease; it was simply whether he was (to some extent, at least) bound by that undoubted promise.

3–104 **Analogy with waiver.** It is submitted that the characteristics of the equitable doctrine described in para.3–103, above indicate that the equitable doctrine is not truly analogous to estoppel by representation. As Denning J. (a leading proponent of the modern equitable doctrine) has pointed out, the authorities which support that doctrine, "although they are said to be cases of estoppel, are not really such".[511] The doctrine has closer affinities with the common law rules of waiver, in the sense of forbearance[512]: both are based on promises, or representations of intention; both are suspensive (rather than extinctive) in nature and both are concerned with the legal effects of promises rather than with proof of disputed facts. The main difference between them is that the equitable doctrine avoids the difficulties encountered at common law in distinguishing between a variation and a forbearance.[513]

There is now much judicial support for these submissions. Thus Lord Pearson in *Woodhouse A.C. Israel Cocoa Ltd v Nigerian Produce Marketing Co Ltd* said

---

[506] Estoppel by representation of fact was recognised at common law at least as long ago as *Freeman v Cooke* (1848) 2 Ex. 654; but sometimes this form of estoppel is (confusingly) referred to as "equitable estoppel:" *e.g.* in *Lombard North Central plc v Stobart* [1990] Tr.L.R. 105, 107. In that case, an estoppel arose from a finance company's statement that no more than £1,003 was due under a conditional sale, when the actual sum due was nearly five times as much. This statement was clearly a representation of *fact* rather than a *promise*.

[507] Above, para.3–094.

[508] Above, para.3–096.

[509] This point accounts for the rule that estoppel by *representation* does not give rise to a cause of action: *Low v Bouverie* [1891] 3 Ch. 82 at 101, 105. If, for example, there are two warehousemen, A and B, and A represents to C that goods which have been bought by C are in B's warehouse when they are not, then the fact that A is estopped from denying the truth of the representation does not make A liable to C as a bailee of those goods. The rule that *promissory* estoppel does not give rise to a cause of action is based on different grounds explained in para.3–098 above.

[510] (1877) 2 App. Cas. 439, above, para.3–085. The application of the principle of this case in *Central London Property Trust Ltd v High Trees House Ltd* [1947] K.B. 130 (below para.3–128) likewise did not give rise to any dispute about facts.

[511] *Central London Property Trust v High Trees House Ltd* [1947] K.B. 130, 134.

[512] Above, para.3–081. For other senses of "waiver" see above, para.3–098 below, paras 22–040—22–047.

[513] Above para.3–084.

that "promissory estoppel" was "far removed from the familiar estoppel by representation of fact and seems, at any rate in a case of this kind, to be more like a waiver of contractual rights."[514] In a number of later cases, "waiver" and "promissory estoppel" (or the rule in *Hughes v Metropolitan Ry*)[515] are treated as substantially similar doctrines,[516] the requirements and effects of the one being stated in terms equally applicable to the other.[517] Indeed, the expressions "waiver" and "promissory estoppel" have been judicially described as "two ways of saying exactly the same thing,"[518] and the courts often use them interchangeably when discussing situations in which it is alleged that one party to a legal relationship has indicated that he will not enforce his strict legal rights against the other.[519] This usage further supports the view that the equitable

---

514 [1972] A.C. 741, 762.

515 (1877) 2 App. Cas. 439; above, para.3–085.

516 *e.g. Ogilvy v Hope-Davies* [1976] 1 All E.R. 683, 688–689; *Finagrain SA Geneva v P. Kruse Hamburg* [1976] 2 Lloyd's Rep. 508, 534; *Bremer Handelsgesellschaft mbH v C. Mackprang Jr.* [1979] 1 Lloyd's Rep. 221, 226; *Prosper Homes v Hambro's Bank Executor & Trustee Co* (1979) 39 R. & C.R. 395, 401; *Brikom Investments Ltd v Carr* [1979] Q.B. 467, 488, 489, 490; *Scandinavian Trading Tanker Co A.B. v Flota Petrolera Ecuatoriana (The Scaptrade)* [1981] 2 Lloyd's Rep. 425, 430 (affirmed without reference to this point [1983] 2 A.C. 694) *Procter & Gamble Philippine Manufacturing Corp. v Peter Cremer GmbH & Co (The Manila)* [1988] 3 All E.R. 843, 853; *MSAS Global Logistics Ltd v Power Packaging Inc* [2003] EWHC 1393, *The Times*, June 25, 2003; *Fortisbank SA v Trenwick International Ltd* [2005] EWHC 339; [2005] Lloyd's Rep. I.R. 464 at [29]; *cf. Bremer Handelsgesellschaft mbH v Finagrain Cie. Commercial Agricole & Financière* [1981] 2 Lloyd's Rep. 259, where Lord Denning, M.R. refers at 263 to "the principle . . . in *Hughes v Metropolitan Railway*" while Fox L.J. refers at 266 to "waiver"; *Bremer Handelsgesellschaft mbH v C. Mackprang Jr.* [1981] 1 Lloyd's Rep. 292, 298; *Bremer Handelsgesellschaft mbH v Bunge Corp.* [1983] 1 Lloyd's Rep. 476, 484; *BICC Ltd v Burndy Corp.* [1985] Ch. 232, 253; *Pearl Carriers Inc v Japan Lines Ltd (The Chemical Venture)* [1993] 1 Lloyd's Rep. 509, 521; *cf. Oliver Ashworth (Holdings) Ltd v Ballard (Kent) Ltd* [2000] Ch. 12 at 27, 28, where the issue was whether there had been a "waiver" in the sense of election between remedies, rather than in the sense (here under discussion) of giving up rights. In *W. J. Alan & Co Ltd v El Nasr Export & Import Co* [1972] 2 Q.B. 189, 212 waiver is described as an instance of the principle of *Hughes v Metropolitan Ry* (above), which, however, is said to be of "wider" scope; *cf. Nippon Yusen Kaisha v Pacifica Navegacion SA (The Ion)* [1980] 2 Lloyd's Rep. 245 where an agreement not to plead a contractual time bar was held not to take effect as a "waiver" (at 249) but to give rise to an "equitable or promissory estoppel" (at 250). In *Brikom Investments Ltd v Carr* [1979] Q.B. 467, 485, 489 the principle of *Hughes v Metropolitan Ry* (above) is, unusually, regarded as distinct from "promissory estoppel" but rather as an illustration of "waiver," thus suggesting a difference between these two concepts—perhaps because in the *Brikom* case the waiver amounted to a contractual variation supported by consideration: *cf.* below, para.3–133. In *Youell v Bland Welch & Co Ltd* (*The Superhulls Cover Case*) (*No.2*) [1990] 2 Lloyd's Rep. 431, 449 "waiver" is distinguished from "equitable estoppel" on the ground that the former doctrine requires the party who is alleged to have lost his rights to know the material facts, while the latter is not subject to any such requirements. But when "waiver" is said to be subject to this requirement, the reference is to "waiver" in the sense of election between remedies (below, para.24–007) and not to the "waiver" in the sense of relinquishing rights; and it is this latter type of waiver which is here under discussion. The reference in *Union Eagle Ltd v Golden Achievement Ltd* [1997] A.C. 514, 518 to "waiver or estoppel" is likewise to election between remedies rather than to the relinquishing of rights which is under discussion in the present chapter. This was also the type of waiver under discussion in the *Oliver Ashworth* case, above, and in *Glencore Grain Ltd v Flacker Shipping Ltd (The Happy Day)* [2002] EWCA Civ. 1068; [2002] 2 Lloyd's Rep. 487 at [64].

517 *e.g. Bremer Handelsgesellschaft mbH v Westzucker GmbH* [1981] 1 Lloyd's Rep. 207, 212–213.

518 *Prosper Homes v Hambro's Bank Executor Trustee Co* (1979) P. & C.R. 395, 401; *cf. The Nerano* [1996] 1 Lloyd's Rep. 1, 6 ("really one and the same thing").

519 See the authorities cited in nn.516 and 517, above.

doctrine is more closely akin to waiver (in the sense of forbearance) than to true estoppel by representation of fact.

3–105 **Distinguished from promises supported by consideration.** Under the equitable doctrine, certain limited effects are given to a promise without consideration. But it is nevertheless in the interests of the promisee to show, if he can, that he did provide consideration so that the promise amounted to a contractually binding variation. Such proof will free him from the many rules that restrict the scope of the equitable doctrine: he need not then show that he has in any way "relied" on the promise, or that it would be "inequitable" for the other party to go back on it; the variation will permanently affect the rights of the promisor and not merely suspend them (unless it is expressed so as to have only a temporary effect); and a contractual variation can not only reduce or extinguish existing rights but also create new ones. Where parties agree to modify an existing contract, the equitable doctrine and its common law counterpart may have reduced, but they have by no means eliminated, the practical importance of the doctrine of consideration.

3–106 **Other jurisdictions.** The English view that the doctrine of promissory estoppel gives rise to no cause of action has not been followed in other common law jurisdictions. In the United States, a similar doctrine has long been regarded as being capable of creating new rights, though both the existence and the content of the resulting rights are matters for the discretion of the courts.[520] A line of Australian cases likewise supports the view that promises or representations which, for want of consideration or of contractual intention, lack contractual force may nevertheless (by virtue of an estoppel) be enforceable as if they were binding contracts. The leading Australian case is *Waltons Stores (Interstate) Ltd v Maher*,[521] where A, a prospective lessor of business premises, did demolition and building work on the premises while the agreement for the lease lacked contractual force because it was still subject to contract[522]; he had done so to meet the prospective lessee's (B's) requirements and on the assumption, of which B must have known, that a binding contract would be brought into existence. B withdrew from the agreement (relying on his solicitor's advice that he was not bound by it); and it was held that he was estopped from denying that a contract had come into existence and that the agreement for the lease was therefore specifically enforceable against him. The reasoning of the High Court is complex, but the basis of the decision appears to be that B had knowingly induced A to believe that a binding contract would be brought into existence by exchange of contracts[523] and to act in reasonable reliance on that belief. In English law, such reliance is, in appropriate circumstances, capable of giving rise to a variety of remedies, even where the promise or representation which induces it lacks contractual force. Sometimes the remedy may be the enforcement of the promise

---

[520] *Restatement, Contracts* §90 and *Restatement 2d, Contracts* §90. In English law, the need to use the doctrine to give rise to a cause of action is less acute than in the United States, where the courts are less ready than the English courts to "invent" consideration (above para.3–010).

[521] (1988) 164 C.L.R. 387; Duthie 104 L.Q.R. 362; Sutton 1 J.C.L. 205.

[522] Above, para.2–118.

[523] For this requirement, see above, para.2–119.

according to its terms, as in cases of proprietary estoppel (to be discussed later in this Chapter)[524]; sometimes it may be an award of the reasonable value of work done in the belief that a contract had, or would, come into existence.[525] Neither of these remedies would have been available in the *Waltons Stores* case since proprietary estoppel does not arise where work is done on the promisee's (rather than on the promisor's) land[526] and a claim for the reasonable value of the claimant's work is not available where the promisor is not unjustly enriched by the promisee's work[526a] and the promisee is aware of the fact that no binding agreement has come into existence and so takes the risk that the negotiations may fail.[527] Even where the second of these objections can be overcome (*e.g.* on the ground that the work was done at the request of the promisor and as a result of his assurance that an exchange of contracts would take place) it does not follow that the appropriate remedy is enforcement of the supposed or anticipated contract in its terms[527a]: if the basis of "Australian estoppel"[528] is reliance induced by the promisor, compensation for reliance loss would appear to be the more appropriate remedy. The Australian doctrine also gives rise to the difficulties that there appear to be no clear limits to its scope, and that this lack of clarity is a regrettable source of uncertainty. The doctrine is, moreover, hard to reconcile with a number of fundamental principles of English law, such as the non-enforceability of informal gratuitous promises (even if relied on)[529] and the rule that there is no right to damages for a wholly innocent non-contractual misrepresentation.[530] While on the facts of some of the cases in which the Australian doctrine has been applied the same conclusions would probably be reached in English law on other grounds,[531] the broad doctrine remains, in the present context, inconsistent with the view that the English doctrine of promissory estoppel (like that of estoppel by representation)[532] does not give rise to a cause

---

524 *e.g.* in *Dillwyn v Llewelyn* (1862) 4 D.F. & G. 517 below, paras 3–139, 3–151.

525 *e.g.* in *William Lacey (Hounslow) Ltd v Davis* [1954] 1 Q.B. 428; *Countrywide Communications Ltd v ICL Pathways Ltd* [2002] C.L.C. 325; *Cobbe v Yeoman's Row Management Ltd* [2008] UKHL 55, [2008] 1 W.L.R. 1752, as to which see n.526a below.

526 Below, para.3–145; proprietary estoppel would also probably have been excluded on the ground that A had no belief that a right had been or would be created in his favour while the agreement remained "subject to contract": see *Att.-Gen. of Hong Kong v Humphreys Estates (Queens Gardens)* [1987] 1 A.C. 114; this obstacle can be overcome if one party induces the other to believe that he will not withdraw: see *ibid.* at 124; but this qualification can scarcely enable the party *by* whom the interest in property is to be created to rely on proprietary estoppel.

526a Such enrichment was the crucial factor leading to the award of a *quantum meruit* in *Cobbe v Yeoman's Row Management Ltd* [2008] UKHL 55, [2008] 1 W.L.R. 1752 (below, para.3–148 D) even though the claimant knew that the anticipated contract was binding in honour only and so took the risk of its never becoming legally binding.

527 *Regalian Properties plc v London Dockland Development Corp.* [1995] 1 W.L.R. 212.

527a There was no such enforcement in *Cobbe v Yeoman's Row Management Ltd* [2008] UKHL 55, [2008] 1 W.L.R. 1752, as to which see above, n.526a.

528 A phrase borrowed from the title of a thesis for the degree of D.Phil. at Oxford University by M. J. Spence, in which the Australian cases are fully discussed and compared with English and other common law authorities.

529 Above, para.3–002.

530 *e.g. Oscar Chess Ltd v Williams* [1957] 1 W.L.R. 370.

531 See, *e.g.*, *Commonwealth of Australia v Verwayen* (1990) 179 C.L.R. 394, which could be explained in English law on the ground stated in para.3–101 at n.489.

532 *Low v Bouverie* [1891] 3 Ch. 82; *Clipper Maritime Ltd v Shirlstar Container Transport Ltd (The Anemone)* [1987] 1 Lloyd's Rep. 547, 557.

of action in the sense of entitling the promisee to enforce a promise in its terms, even though it was unsupported by consideration. It is true that other forms of estoppel, such as proprietary estoppel, may produce this result; but the scope of that doctrine is limited in many important ways[533] and the law would present an incongruous appearance if those limits could be outflanked simply by invoking the broader doctrine of "Australian estoppel."

3–107 **Distinguished from estoppel by convention.** Estoppel by convention may arise where both[534] parties to a transaction "act on assumed state of facts or law,[535] the assumption being either shared by both or made by one and acquiesced in by the other."[536] The parties are then precluded from denying the truth of that assumption, if it would be unjust or unconscionable[537] to allow them (or one of them) to go back on it.[538] Such an estoppel differs from estoppel by

[533] *e.g.* by the requirements that the promisee must believe that legal rights have been, or will be, created in his favour, and that these are rights in or over the promisor's land: see below, para.3–145; and by the further requirements stated in *Cobbe v Yeoman's Row Management Ltd* [2008] UKHL 55, [2008] 1 W.L.R. 1752 and discussed in paras 3–148A to 3–148C below.

[534] There can be no such estoppel where one party is not yet in existence: see *Rover International Ltd v Cannon Film Sales Ltd* (1987) 3 B.C.C. 369, reversed in part on other grounds [1989] 1 W.L.R. 912 (company not yet formed).

[535] See below, para.3–110.

[536] *Republic of India v India Steamship Co (The Indian Endurance) (No.2)* [1998] A.C. 878, 913; and see *Norwegian American Cruises A/S v Paul Mundy Ltd (The Vistafjord)* [1988] 2 Lloyd's Rep. 343, 351; *Shearson Lehman Hutton Inc v Maclaine Watson & Co Ltd* [1989] 2 Lloyd's Rep. 570, 596; *Phillip Collins Ltd v Davis* [2000] 3 All E.R. 808 at 823 (where there was no common assumption or acquiescence): *Thor Navigation Inc v Ingosstrakh Insurance* [2005] EWHC 19 (Comm), [2005] 1 Lloyd's Rep. 547 at [66], [70]; *Triodos Bank NV v Dobbs* [2005] EWCA Civ. 630, [2005] 2 Lloyd's Rep. 588 at [2]; *Canmer International Insurance v UK Mutual Assurance* [2005] EWHC 1694, [2005] 2 Lloyd's Rep. 479 at [41], where there was no common assumption and hence no estoppel by convention; *Tamil Nadu Electricity Board v ST-CMS Electricity Company Private Ltd* [2007] EWHC 1713 (Comm), [2007] 2 All E.R. (Comm) 701 at [104], where again there was no evidence of the alleged shared assumption (at [115]); *Kosmar Villa Holidays plc v Trustees of Syndicate 1243* [2007] EWHC 458 (Comm), [2007] 2 All E.R. (Comm) 215 at [53], where reliance on estoppel by convention failed on the same ground. On appeal this aspect of the decision at first instance in the *Kosmar* case was affirmed ([2008] EWCA Civ. 147, [2008] 2 All E.R. (Comm) 14 at [85]) even though the actual decision was reversed on the ground that the principle of "estoppel by election" (*c.f.* below para.24–003) did not there apply; or , if it did apply , the requirement of an "unequivocal communication" (at [71]) needed to give rise to such an estoppel had not been satisfied (at [79]). Spencer Bower and Turner, *Estoppel by Representation*, (3rd ed., 1977) p.157; Dawson (1989) L.S. 16.

[537] *Crédit Suisse v Borough Council of Allerdale* [1995] 2 Lloyd's Rep. 315, 367–370 (where this requirement was not satisfied); affirmed on other grounds [1997] Q.B. 362; *Thor Navigation* case, above n.536 at [66] and *Ease Faith Ltd v Leonis Marine Management* [2006] EWHC 232 (Comm), [2006] 1 Lloyd's Rep. 673 at [171], where the requirements of estoppel by convention were not satisfied.

[538] *Norwegian American Cruises A/S v Paul Mundy Ltd (The Vistafjord)* [1988] 2 Lloyd's Rep. 343, 352; *Hiscox v Outhwaite (No.1)* [1992] 1 A.C. 562, affirmed on other grounds at 585; *The Indian Endurance (No.2)*, above, n.536 at 913. For the difficulties of applying estoppel by convention so as to bind members of a company pension scheme, see *Trustee Solutions v Dubery* [2006] EWHC 1426 (Ch), [2007] I.C.R. 412. They arise mainly from the need to show that "the general body of members" (at [50]) had all put the same interpretation on the scheme and had acted on the assumption. Here "the evidence was simply too exiguous" to support such a conclusion. The decision was reversed on other grounds: [2007] EWCA Civ. 771, [2008] I.C.R. 101; there was no appeal on the estoppel point: see [2007] EWCA Civ. 771 at [12].

representation and from promissory estoppel[539] in that it does not depend on any representation or promise.[540] It can arise by virtue of a common assumption which was not induced by the party alleged to be estopped but which was based on a mistake spontaneously made by the party relying on it and acquiesced in by the other party. It seems, however, that the assumption resembles the representation required to give rise to other forms of estoppel to the extent that it must be "unambiguous and unequivocal".[541] Estoppel by convention has also been said to arise out of an express agreement by which the parties had compromised a disputed claim[542]; but where such a compromise is supported by consideration (in accordance with the principles discussed earlier in this Chapter[543]) it is binding as a contract,[544] so that there is, it is submitted, no need to rely on estoppel by convention.

Further requirements of estoppel by convention. This kind of estoppel was discussed in *Amalgamated Investment & Property Co Ltd v Texas Commerce International Bank Ltd.*[545] In that case, A had negotiated with the X Bank for a loan to B (one of A's subsidiaries) for the purpose of acquiring and developing a property in the Bahamas. It was agreed that the loan was to be secured by a mortgage on that property and also by a guarantee from A. In the guarantee, A promised the X Bank, in consideration of the Bank's giving credit to B, to "pay you . . . all moneys . . . due *to you*" from B. This was an inappropriate form of words since the loan to B was not made directly by the X Bank but by one of its subsidiaries, the Y Bank, with money provided by the X Bank: hence, if the guarantee were read literally, it would not apply to the loan since no money was due from B to the X Bank. The Court of Appeal, however, took the view that this literal interpretation would defeat the intention of the parties, and held that, on its true construction, the guarantee applied to the loan made by the Y Bank.[546] But even if the guarantee did not, on its true construction, produce this result, A was estopped from denying that the guarantee covered the loan by the Y Bank, since, when negotiating the loan, both A and the X Bank had assumed that the guarantee did cover it; and since the X Bank continued subsequently to act on 3–108

[539] *cf.* the discussion of the distinction between various kinds of estoppel in para.3–103, above.

[540] *Amalgamated Investment & Property Co Ltd v Texas Commerce International Bank Ltd* [1982] Q.B. 84, 131–132 below, para.3–109.

[541] *Smithkline Beecham plc v Apotex Europe Ltd* [2006] EWCA Civ. 658, [2007] Ch.71 at [102], where this point was "not disputed" and the concession was evidently approved by the Court; *cf. Commercial Union Assurance plc v Sun Alliance Group plc* [1992] 1 Lloyd's Rep. 474, 481 where the argument based on estoppel by convention failed as the evidence did not "clearly and equivocally establish the agreement of the parties on the conventional interpretation." A passage from *Troop v Gibson* [1986] 1 E.G.L.R. 1 cited in *Baird Textile Holdings Ltd v Marks & Spencer plc* [2001] EWCA 274, [2002] 1 All E.R. (Comm) 734 at [84] must be read as denying the requirement of a representation rather than the quality of clarity of the common assumption: see the reference there to "sufficient clarity and certainty of the common assumption"; *cf. ibid.*, at [38].

[542] *Colchester BC v Smith* [1992] Ch. 421, 434.

[543] Above, paras 3–047 *et seq.*

[544] *Colchester BC v Smith*, above, at 435.

[545] [1982] Q.B. 84. See also *Astilleros Canarios SA v Cape Hatteras Shipping Co SA* [1982] 1 Lloyd's Rep. 518, 527.

[546] *cf.* on the issue of construction, *TCB Ltd v Gray* [1987] Ch. 458; *Bank of Scotland v Wright* [1990] B.C.C. 663.

that assumption[547] in granting various indulgences to A in respect of the loan to B and of another loan made directly by the X Bank to A. It made no difference that the assumption was not induced by any representation[548] made by A but originated in the X Bank's own mistake: the estoppel was not one by representation but by convention.[549] The same principle was applied in *The Vistafjord*[550] where an agreement for the charter of a cruise ship had been negotiated by agents on behalf of the owners. Both the agents and the owners believed throughout that commission on this transaction would be payable under an earlier agreement, but on its true construction this agreement gave no such rights to the agents. It was held that estoppel by convention precluded the owners from relying on the true construction of the earlier agreement, so that the agents were justified in retaining the amount of the commission out of sums received by them from the charterers.

3–109 **"Communication" passing "across the line".** To give rise to an estoppel by convention, the mistaken assumption of the party claiming the benefit of the estoppel must, however, have been shared or acquiesced in by the party alleged to be estopped; and both parties must have conducted themselves on the basis of such a shared assumption[551]: the estoppel "requires communications to pass across the line between the parties. It is not enough that each of two parties acts on an assumption not communicated to the other."[552] Such communication may

---

[547] Contrast *Crédit Suisse v Allerdale BC* [1996] 2 Lloyd's Rep. 315, 367, where this requirement was not satisfied as the conduct of the party alleged to be estopped had not "influenced the mind" of the other party; the decision was affirmed on other grounds [1997] Q.B. 362.

[548] A dictum in the *Crédit Suisse* case, above n.547 at 367 which appears to treat representation as a requirement of estoppel by convention is, with respect, inconsistent with the treatment of that doctrine in the *Amalgamated Investment* case.

[549] *cf. Government of Swaziland Central Transport Administration v Leila Maritime Co Ltd (The Leila)* [1985] 2 Lloyd's Rep. 172; as to which see below, n.554; *Thornton Springer v NEM Insurance Co Ltd* [2000] 2 All E.R. 489 at 516–518.

[550] *Norwegian American Cruises A/S v Paul Mundy Ltd* (*The Vistafjord*) [1988] 2 Lloyd's Rep. 343. *cf.* also *Kenneth Allison Ltd v A. E. Limehouse & Co* [1992] 2 A.C. 105, 127 *per* Lord Goff. The other members of the House of Lords took the view that there was an actual agreement (to accept service of a writ) which was legally effective even though the requirements of the Rules of the Supreme Court (with regard to personal service) had not been complied with.

[551] *Empresa Lineas Maritimas Argentinas v The Oceanus Mutual Underwriting Association (Bermuda) Ltd* [1984] 2 Lloyd's Rep. 517 (where neither of these requirements was satisfied); *Astilleros Canarios SA v Cape Hatteras Shipping Co SA* [1982] 1 Lloyd's Rep. 518, 527; *Heinrich Hanno & Co B.V. v Fairlight Shipping Co (The Kostas K.)* [1985] 1 Lloyd's Rep. 231, 237; *The Vistafjord*, above n.550; *Thor Navigation Inc v Ingosstrakh Insurance* [2005] EWHC 19 (Comm), [2005] 1 Lloyd's Rep. 547 at [66]; *Fortisbank SA v Trenwick International* [2005] EWHC 339, [2005] Lloyd's Rep. I.R. 464 at [43], where the present requirement was not satisfied; *Tamil Nadu Electricity Board v ST-CMS Electricity Company Private Ltd* [2007] EWHC 1713 (Comm), [2007] 2 All E.R. (Comm) 701 at [125], where again this requirement was not satisfied; *Bear Stearns plc v Forum Global Equities Ltf* [2007] EWHC 1576 at [192], where again the present requirement was not satisfied but the actual decision was that the communications between the parties had given rise to a contract: see above, para.2–114.

[552] *Compania Portorafti Commerciale SA v Ultramar Panama Inc (The Captain Gregos) (No.2)* [1990] 2 Lloyd's Rep. 395, 405, following *K. Lokumal & Sons (London) Ltd v Lotte Shipping Co Pty Ltd (The August P. Leonhardt)* [1985] 2 Lloyd's Rep. 28, 35; *Hiscox v Outhwaite (No.3)* [1991] 2 Lloyd's Rep. 524, 533; *The Indian Endurance*, above n.536, at 913.

be effected by the conduct of one party, known to the other.[553] But no estoppel by convention arose where each party spontaneously made a different mistake and there was no subsequent conduct by the party alleged to be estopped from which any acquiescence in the other party's mistaken assumption could be inferred.[554] An estoppel by convention likewise cannot arise where neither party was aware of the facts on which the alleged common assumption is said to have been based.[555] Nor can a party (A) invoke such an estoppel to prevent the other (B) from denying facts alleged to have been agreed between A and B if A has later withdrawn from that agreement; for in the light of A's withdrawal it is no longer unjust to allow B to rely on the true state of affairs.[556]

Assumption of law. It is often said that the assumption giving rise to an estoppel by convention can be one of "fact or law."[557] The point of the reference to "law" in this formulation appears to be to include within the scope of the doctrine assumptions about the construction of a contract[558]; for, since the construction of a contract is often said to be a matter of "law,"[559] all such assumptions would be excluded from the scope of the doctrine (and its scope be unduly narrowed) if it did not include at least assumptions of this kind. The question whether estoppel by convention could be based on assumptions of "law" in a wider sense was the subject of conflicting views in *Johnson v Gore Wood & Co*[560] In that case, a company had brought a claim for professional negligence against a firm of solicitors who were told that a further claim based on the same negligence would be made against them by the company's managing director. The company's claim was settled on terms which limited *some* of the director's personal claims against the solicitors and when the director later brought *other* claims against the solicitors, it was held that this was not an abuse of process. Lord Bingham based this conclusion in part[561] on estoppel by convention: in his view, the terms of the settlement were based on the common assumption that it would not be an abuse of process for the director to pursue the 3–110

---

553 As in *The Vistafjord* [1988] 2 Lloyd's Rep. 343, 351 ("very clear conduct crossing the line . . . of which the other party was fully cognisant").

554 *K. Lokumal & Sons (London) Ltd v Lotte Shipping Co Pty Ltd (The August P. Leonhardt)* [1985] 2 Lloyd's Rep. 28, reversing [1984] 1 Lloyd's Rep. 332, which had been followed in *The Leila*, above n.549. The present status of *The Leila* therefore remains in some doubt but the two cases can be reconciled on the ground that in *The Leila* there was, while in *The August P. Leonhardt* there was not, conduct by the party alleged to be estopped from which acquiescence in the other party's mistaken belief could be inferred.

555 *HIH Casualty & General Insurance v Axa Corporate Solutions* [2002] EWCA Civ. 1253; [2002] 2 All E.R. (Comm) 1053 at [32].

556 *Gloyne v Richardson* [2001] EWCA Civ. 716; [2001] 2 B.C.L.C. 669 at [41].

557 *Amalgamated Investment* case [1982] 2 Q.B. 84 at 122, 126; *The Vistafjord* [1988] 2 Lloyd's Rep. 343 at 351; *Shearson Lehman Hutton Inc v Maclaine Watson & Co Ltd* [1989] 2 Lloyd's Rep. 570 at 596; *Republic of India v India Steamship co. (The Indian Endurance) (No.2)* [1998] A.C. 878 at 913.

558 Such an assumption could also be called one of "private rights" and hence of fact: below, para.6–013.

559 *e.g. Carmichael v National Power plc* [1992] 1 W.L.R. 2042 at 2049.

560 [2002] 2 A.C. 1.

561 See *ibid.* at p.34 for an alternative ground for Lord Bingham's decision. Lords Cooke and Hutton agreed with Lord Bingham on the "abuse of process" point but without referring to estoppel by convention.

claims which he had in fact brought; and it would be unfair to allow the solicitors to go back on this assumption. All members of the House of Lords agreed with Lord Bingham's conclusion that there was no abuse of process; but Lord Goff was "reluctant to proceed on estoppel by convention"[562] as the common assumption was one of law, a type of assumption which in his view did not give rise to this form of estoppel; while Lord Millett was equally reluctant to "put it on the ground of estoppel by convention" as he had "some difficulty in discerning a common assumption."[563] Lord Millet's difficulty is an entirely factual one but Lord Goff's raises a more difficult issue of principle. Support for the view that estoppel by convention can be based on a common assumption of law is admittedly based only on dicta[564]; but it is arguable that those dicta gain support from cases concerned with mistakes and misrepresentations of law. In these fields, the distinction between matters of "law" and of "fact" has proved hard to draw and is now discredited.[565] On the other hand, the extension of estoppel by convention to *all* common assumptions of "law" could undermine the security of commercial transactions by allowing a party to resist enforcement merely on account of an assumption as to the *legal effect* of a contract, the terms or meaning of which were not in dispute; and this is a type of assumption which, on the authorities, does not give rise to such an estoppel.[566]

3–111 **Effect of estoppel by convention.** The effect of this form of estoppel is to preclude a party from denying the agreed or common assumption of fact or, at least to the extent suggested in para.3–110, above, of law.[567] One such assumption may be that a particular promise has been made[568]: thus it is possible to describe the result in *Amalgamated Investment & Property Co Ltd v Texas Commerce International Bank Ltd*[569] by saying that A was estopped from denying that it had promised the X Bank to repay any sum left unpaid by B to the Y Bank. But, although estoppel by convention may thus take effect in relation to a promise, it is quite different in its legal nature[570] from promissory estoppel. In cases of promissory estoppel, the promisor or representor is not estopped from denying that the promise or representation *has been made*: on the contrary, this must be proved to establish that kind of estoppel. The doctrine of promissory estoppel is concerned with the *legal effects* of a promise that has been shown to exist. Where, on the other hand, the requirements of estoppel by convention are satisfied, then this type of estoppel normally operates to prevent a party from denying a *fact*,[571] *i.e.* that the assumed promise *has been made*, or that a promise contains the assumed term: it does not specify the *legal effects* of the assumed

[562] *ibid.* at p.40.
[563] *ibid.* at p.61.
[564] Above, n.557.
[565] Below, para.5–044, 29–045.
[566] Below para.3–114.
[567] *Amalgamated Investment & Property* case [1982] Q.B. 84, 126, 130.
[568] Such an assumption is one of fact (and not as to the future): below, para.6–012.
[569] Above, para.3–108.
[570] Above, para.3–103.
[571] In this respect its legal nature resembles that of estoppel by representation: see above, para.3–103.

promise or term.[572] In *Amalgamated Investment & Property Co Ltd v Texas Commerce International Bank Ltd*, once A was estopped from denying the *existence* of the promise described above, no question arose as to its legal *validity*. There could be no doubt that that promise was supported by consideration[573]: this was provided by the X Bank in making funds available to the Y Bank to enable it to make a loan to B, and in inducing the Y Bank to make that loan.[574] Where the assumed promise is one that would, if actually made, have been unsupported by consideration, both types of estoppel can, however, operate in the same case: estoppel by convention to establish the existence of the promise, and promissory estoppel to determine its legal effect.[575]

Estoppel by convention does not operate prospectively. Estoppel for convention does not operate prospectively, so that "once the common assumption is revealed to be erroneous the estoppel will not apply to future dealings."[576] 3–112

Whether estoppel by convention creates new rights. We have seen that promissory estoppel does not "create new causes of action where none existed before"[577]; and we shall see that the same principle applies to estoppel by representation.[578] Estoppel by convention resembles estoppel by representation in that it can prevent a party from denying *existing facts*, and one would therefore expect estoppel by convention to further to resemble estoppel by representation in operating only where its effect was defensive in substance. The question whether estoppel by convention is so limited was discussed in the *Amalgamated Investment & Property* case[579] where, however, it was not necessary to decide the point. This action was brought because the X Bank had sought to apply money due from it to A under another transaction in discharge of A's alleged liability under its guarantee of B's debt. Hence the effect of the estoppel was to provide the X Bank with a defence to A's claim for a declaration that the bank was not entitled to apply the money in that way. Eveleigh L.J. said: "I do not think that the bank could have succeeded in a claim on the guarantee itself."[580] Brandon L.J. seems to have taken the view that the bank could have sued on the guarantee, but to have based that view on the ground that the loan agreement between A and the X Bank imposed an obligation on A to give the guarantee: hence it was that agreement, and not the estoppel, which would have given rise to the X Bank's 3–113

---

572 *The Vistafjord* [1988] 2 Lloyd's Rep. 343, 351 ("not dependent on contract but on common assumption"). For this reason the citation in *Williams v Roffey Bros & Nicholls (Contractors) Ltd* [1991] 1 Q.B. 1, 17–18 of the *Amalgamated Investment & Property case* (above, para.3–108) seems, with respect, to be of doubtful relevance. In the *Williams* case there was no doubt that the promise had been made; and the actual decision was that it was supported by consideration and thus binding contractually: above, para.3–068.

573 This was also true in *The Vistafjord*, above, para.3–108.

574 It is enough for consideration to move from the promisee (the X bank); it need not move to the hypothetical promisor (A): above paras 3–036 *et seq.*

575 *e.g.* (apparently) *Troop v Gibson* [1986] 1 E.G.L.R. 1.

576 *Hiscox v Outhwaite* [1992] A.C. 562 at 575, *per* Lord Donaldson, M.R. (affirmed *ibid.* p.585 on other grounds); *Phillip Collins Ltd v Davis* [2000] 3 All E.R. 808 at 823. *Tamil Nadu Electricity Board v ST-CMS Electricity Company Private Ltd* [2007] EWHC 1713 (Comm), [2007] 2 All E.R. (Comm) 701 at [105], [128].

577 *Combe v Combe* [1951] 2 K.B. 215, 219; above, para.3–098.

578 Below, para.6–095.

579 [1982] Q.B. 84; above, para.3–108.

580 [1982] Q.B. 84, 126.

cause of action, if it had sued on the guarantee.[581] Lord Denning, M.R. seems to have expressed the principle of estoppel by convention in such a way as to enable it to give rise to a cause of action[582] but he was alone in stating the principle so broadly.[583] In *The Vistafjord*[584] the estoppel similarly operated defensively. This factor was not stressed in the judgments, but there is no suggestion in them that in this respect estoppel by convention differs from estoppel by representation, which does not, of itself, give rise to a cause of action.[585] It is indeed, possible for estoppel by convention (as it is for promissory estoppel[586] and estoppel by representation[587]) to deprive the defendant of a *defence*, and so to enable the claimant to win an action which otherwise he would have lost[588]; but even in such cases the estoppel does not create the cause of action, for the *facts giving rise to the cause of action* exist independently of the estoppel.[589] No other authority squarely supports the view that estoppel by convention can, of itself, create a new cause of action; and the present position seems to be that it cannot, any more than promissory estoppel or estoppel by representation, produce this effect.[590]

---

[581] *ibid.* at 132; *cf. Dumford Trading A-G v OAO Atlantrybflot* [2005] EWCA Civ. 24, [2005] 1 Lloyd's Rep. 289 at [39], where Rix L.J. referred to Brandon L.J.'s view in the *Amalgamated Investment* case [1982] Q.B. 84, 131–132 as the likely answer to the argument that the estoppel was being used "as a sword rather than a shield." In *Baird Textile Holdings Ltd v Marks & Spencer plc* [2001] EWHC 274, [2002] 1 All E.R. (Comm) 737 at [88] Mance L.J. said that he "would prefer" the view of Brandon L.J. to that of Lord Denning M.R. The alleged estoppel in the *Baird* case was regarded at first instance as one "by convention" (at [20]) but it is far from clear whether the Court of Appeal so regarded it.

[582] [1982] Q.B. 84 at 122. A similar view may be hinted at in *Williams v Roffey Bros. & Nicholls (Contractors) Ltd* [1999] Q.B. 1 at 17–18; but as to this see above, para.3–111 n.572.

[583] *Keen v Holland* [1984] 1 W.L.R. 251, 261–262; and see n.581 above. In *Wilson Bowden Properties Ltd v Milner and Bardon* [1996] C.L.Y. 1229 the cause of action arose out of the undisputed contract and not out of the estoppel.

[584] [1988] 2 Lloyd's Rep. 343; above, para.3–108. In *Shearson Lehman Hutton Inc v Maclaine Watson & Co Ltd* [1989] 2 Lloyd's Rep. 570, the estoppel would likewise (if supported on the facts) have operated defensively; *cf.* also *Mitsui Babcock Energy Ltd v John Brown Energy Ltd* (1996) 51 Const. L.R. 129, 185–186 where the effect of the estoppel would (if the contract in question had not existed) again have been to *restrict* the plaintiff's rights by reference to the terms of the (in that event non-existent) contract.

[585] Below, para.6–095.

[586] Above, para.3–101.

[587] *Burrowes v Lock* (1805) 10 Ves. 470, as explained in *Low v Bouverie* [1891] 3 Ch. 82.

[588] This was the effect of the estoppel in *Furness Withy (Australia) Ltd v Metal Distrubutors (UK) Ltd, (The Amazonia)* [1990] 1 Lloyd's Rep. 238, where it operated to prevent a party from relying on facts giving rise to a mistake of both parties alleged to make the contract void (below, para.5–074) and where the effect of allowing him to rely on those facts would have been to bar the other party's claim by lapse of time. For the possibility that estoppel by convention may deprive a party of a defence, see also *Azov Shipping Co v Baltic Shipping Co* [1999] 1 Lloyd's Rep. 159 at 175–176; *semble* this is subject to the limitation discussed with regard to promissory estoppel at para.3–101 above.

[589] *cf. Johnson v Gore Wood & Co* [2002] 2 A.C. 1 (above, para.3–110) where the estoppel likewise did not create the cause of action, which was based on the alleged negligence of the defendant solicitors; it merely helped to dispose of the defendants' objection that the action to enforce that claim was an abuse of process.

[590] *cf. Russell Brothers (Paddington) Ltd v John Elliott Management Ltd* (1995) 1 Const. L.J. 377, denying that estoppel by convention can be used as a sword. Contrast dicta in *Thornton Springer v NEM Insurance Co Ltd* [2000] 2 All E.R. 489 at 516–518, which seem to assume that estoppel by convention can give rise to new rights. This aspect of the case gives rise to the same difficulty as that

Invalidity of assumed term. A party is not liable on the basis of estoppel by convention where the alleged agreement would, if concluded, have been ineffective for want of contractual intention,[591] or on account of a formal defect[592] (other than a minor one)[593] or unenforceable for want of written evidence of it,[594] or where the term in respect of which such an estoppel is alleged to operate would, if actually incorporated in the contract, have been invalid (*e.g.* because it amounted to an attempt to deprive a tenant of statutory security of tenure which could not be excluded by contract)[595]; nor does such an estoppel prevent a party from relying on the true legal effect (as opposed to the meaning[596]) of an admitted contract merely because the parties have entered into it under a mistaken view as to that effect.[597] 3–114

10. PART PAYMENT OF A DEBT

(a) *General Rule*

General common law rule. At common law, the general rule is that a creditor is not bound by a promise to accept part payment in full settlement of a debt. An 3–115

---

discussed in relation to promissory estoppel at para.3–098 n.469, above. The actual decision in the *Thornton Springer* case was that there was a contract supported by consideration in the form of "an implied promise not to take proceedings" (at p.516): see above, para.3–047. The view that estoppel by convention cannot create new rights is also supported by *Smithkline Beecham plc v Apotex Europe Ltd* [2006] EWCA Civ. 658, [2007] Ch. 71 at [103], [107] and [110]. The claim in that case was based on estoppel by representation and by convention: at [102].

[591] *Orion Insurance plc v Sphere Drake Insurance* [1922] 1 Lloyd's Rep. 239.

[592] *Yaxley v Gotts* [2000] Ch. 162 at 182. A party may, however, be liable on an agreement which does not comply with the formal requirements of s.2(1) of the Law of Property (Miscellaneous Provisions) Act 1989 on the basis of a *proprietary* estoppel amounting, or giving rise also, to a constructive trust: see *Kinane v Mackie Conteh* [2005] EWCA Civ. 45, [2005] W.T.L.R. 345, below paras 3–139, 4–077. Such liability arises by virtue of s.2(5) of the 1989 Act. On the question whether a defendant would be so liable, if his conduct gave rise to a proprietary estoppel but *not* to a constructive trust, there may be a difference of judicial opinion in the *Kinane* case when Arden L.J. at [28] can be read as taking the view that the s.2(5) exception to s.2(1) would apply in such a case, while Neuberger L.J. at [46] takes the opposite view. In *Cobbe v Yeoman's Row Management Ltd* [2008] UKHL 55, [2008] 1 W.L.R. 1752, the latter view is also supported by Lord Scott at [29] (with whose speech Lords Hoffman, Brown and Mance agreed) who added that it was not necessary to resolve the question since in that case the agreement was not specifically enforceable (quite apart from s. 2) as it "remained incomplete" (above, para.2–112). Probably for this reason, Lord Walker in the *Cobbe* case [2008] UKHL 55, [2008] 1 W.L.R. 1752 at [93] said that it was "not necessary to consider the issue in section 2". For the relationship between proprietary estoppel and constructive trusts, see below, para.3–140. The requirements of proprietary estoppel (below, paras 3–144 to 3–148C) differ widely from those of estoppel by convention (above, paras 3–107 to 3–110).

[593] *cf. Shah v Shah* [2001] EWCA Civ. 527; [2001] 4 All E.R. 138 at [31] (deed signed and witnessed but not signed in presence of attesting witness); contrast *ibid.* at [28] (deed not signed at all). The case was one of estoppel by representation.

[594] *Actionstrength Ltd v International Glass Engineering SpA* [2003] UKHL 17; [2003] 2 A.C. 541.

[595] See *Keen v Holland* [1984] 1 W.L.R. 251; *cf. Wilson v Truelove* [2003] EWHC 750, [2003] W.T.L.R. 609; *Laroche v Spirit of Adventure (UK) Ltd* [2008] EWHC 788 (QB), [2008] 2 Lloyd's Rep. 34 at [73]; contrast *Furness Withy (Australia) Pty Ltd v Metal Distributors (UK) Ltd (The Amazonia)* [1989] 1 Lloyd's Rep. 403 (illegality under foreign statute); *Godden v Merthyr Tydfil Housing Association* (1997) 74 P. & C.R. D1.

[596] above, para.3–110.

[597] *Keen v Holland*, above, n.595; *Hamed El Chiaty & Co (T/A Travco Nile Cruise Lines) v Thomas Cook Group (The Nile Rhapsody)* [1992] 2 Lloyd's Rep. 399, 408, where, however, the court treated

accrued debt can be discharged by the creditor's promise only if the promise amounts, or gives rise, to an effective accord and satisfaction.[598] A counter-promise by the debtor to pay only part of the debt provides no consideration for the accord, as it is merely a promise to perform part of an existing duty owed to the creditor. And the actual payment is no satisfaction under the rule in *Pinnel's Case* that "Payment of a lesser sum on the day in satisfaction of a greater sum cannot be any satisfaction for the whole."[599] This rule was approved by the House of Lords in *Foakes v Beer*.[600] Mrs Beer had obtained a judgment against Dr Foakes for £2,090 19s. Sixteen months later, Dr Foakes asked for time to pay. A written agreement[601] was made under which Mrs Beer undertook not to take "any proceedings whatsoever" on the judgment, in consideration of an immediate payment by Dr Foakes of £500 and on condition[602] of his paying specified instalments "until the whole of the said sum of £2,090 19s. shall have been paid and satisfied." Some five years later, when Dr Foakes had paid £2,090 19s., Mrs Beer claimed £360[603] for interest on the judgment debt. The House of Lords upheld her claim and the actual result does not appear to be unjust; for it seems that in making the agreement Mrs Beer intended only to give Dr Foakes time to pay and not to forgive interest.[604]

3–116 **Effects of the rule.** The rule established in *Foakes v Beer* may sometimes have performed the useful function of protecting a creditor against a debtor who too ruthlessly exploited the tactical advantage of being a potential defendant in litigation. This point is well illustrated by *D. & C. Builders Ltd v Rees*.[605] The defendant owed £482 to a firm of builders. Six months after payment had first been demanded, the defendant's wife (acting on his behalf) offered the builders £300 in full settlement. The builders accepted this offer as they were in desperate straits financially and there was some evidence that the defendant's wife knew this.[606] It was held that they were nevertheless entitled to the balance; and the

---

the contract as rectified so as to correct the mistake; affirmed [1994] 1 Lloyd's Rep. 382, without reference to estoppel by convention.

[598] *Commissioners of Stamp Duties v Bone* [1977] A.C. 511, 519 ("A debt can only be truly released by agreement for valuable consideration or under seal.") This principle appears to have been overlooked in a dictum in *Brikom Investments Ltd v Carr* [1979] Q.B. 467, 488, according to which a "waiver" of instalments of rent would bind the landlord. The actual promise of the landlord in that case was supported by consideration: above, para.3–080; below, para.3–133.

[599] (1602) 5 CoRep. 117a; *Cumber v Wane* (1721) 1 Stra. 426; *McManus v Bark* (1870) L.R. 5 Ex. 65; *Underwood v Underwood* [1894] P. 204; *Re Broderick* [1986] N.I.J.B. 36, 49–55; *Tilney Engineering v Admods Knitting Machinery* [1987] C.L.Y. 412; *cf. Bagge v Slade* (1616) 3 Bulst. 162.

[600] (1884) 9 App. Cas. 605.

[601] Drawn up by Dr Foakes' solicitor: (1884) 9 App. Cas. at 625.

[602] Dr Foakes made no *promise* to pay the instalments.

[603] *Beer v Foakes* (1883) 11 Q.B.D. 221, 222.

[604] Lords Fitzgerald and Watson thought that the agreement did not, on its true construction, cover interest. Lords Selborne and Blackburn sympathised with this view but felt unable to adopt it as the operative part of the document was too "clear" to be controlled by the recitals. See (1884) 9 App. Cas. at 610, 614, 615.

[605] [1966] 2 Q.B. 617; Chorley (1966) 29 M.L.R. 165; Cornish (1966) 29 M.L.R. 428; and see below, para.3–136.

[606] [1966] 2 Q.B. at 625.

majority[607] of the Court of Appeal based their decision to this effect on the rule in *Foakes v Beer*.

On the other hand, it is arguable that the function of protecting the creditor in such a situation is now more satisfactorily performed by the expanding concept of economic duress[608] than by the rule in *Pinnel's Case*; and that the rule therefore no longer serves any useful purpose. In some circumstances, an agreement to accept part payment of a debt in full settlement may be a perfectly fair and reasonable transaction.[609] Moreover, in *Foakes v Beer* the rule was criticised[610] on the ground that part payment was often in fact more beneficial to the creditor than strict insistence on his legal rights. A factual benefit[611] of a similar kind has been accepted as sufficient consideration for a promise to make an extra payment for the performance of an existing contractual duty owed by the promisee to the promisor[612]; and the law would be more consistent, as well as more satisfactory in its practical operation, if it adopted the same approach to cases of part payment of a debt. Agreements of the kind here under discussion would then be binding unless they had been made under duress. But the rule in *Foakes v Beer* is open to challenge only in the House of Lords.[613] In the meantime, its operation is mitigated by limitations on its scope at common law[614] and in equity. These are discussed in the following paragraphs. 3–117

(b) *Limitations at Common Law*

Disputed claims. The rule stated in para.3–115 above does not apply where the creditor's claim (or its amount) is disputed in good faith.[615] In such a case, 3–118

[607] Lord Denning, M.R. based his decision on a different ground: below, para.3–136.

[608] *cf.* above, para.3–067.

[609] *e.g.* on the facts of *Central London Property Trust Ltd v High Trees House Ltd* [1947] K.B. 130; below, para.3–128.

[610] Especially by Lord Blackburn: (1884) 9 App. Cas. at 617–622; see also Lord Selborne at 613 and *Couldery v Bartrum* (1881) 19 Ch.D. 394, 399, where Jessel, M.R. called the rule "a most extraordinary peculiarity of English law."

[611] Above, para.3–004.

[612] *Williams v Roffey Bros. & Nicholls (Contractors) Ltd* [1991] 1 Q.B. 1, above para.3–068.

[613] *Re Selectmove* [1995] 1 W.L.R. 474, where the Court of Appeal refused to apply the principle of the *Williams* case, above n.612, in the present context; Peel, (1994) 110 L.Q.R. 353; *Collier v P & M.J. Wright (Holdings) Ltd* [2007] EWCA Civ. 1329, [2008] 1 W.L.R. 643 at [27(i)], [44].

[614] In *Collier v P & M.J. Wright (Holdings) Ltd* above, n.613 Arden L.J. said at [3] that "the rule does not apply where the debt arises from the provision of services : *Williams v Roffey* [1991] 1 Q.B. 1" ; but that *Re Selectmove* [1995] 1 W.L.R 474 had "confirmed that a promise to pay part of the money to which the creditor is already entitled is not good consideration ." The reference to "the rule" in the first part of this statement appears to be to "the rule in *Pinnel's* case" (at [3]) (1603) 5 Co. Rep. 117a, (above, para.3–115) but it is respectfully submitted that this rule was not under consideration in the *Williams* case. The issue in that case was not whether payment of *less* than the amount due could be good consideration for the creditor's promise to forgo the balance. It was whether performance (in full) of the agreed services could be consideration for a promise by the recipient of the services (the debtor) to pay *more* than the originally agreed sum: see above, para.3–068. In the *Collier* case, the actual decision was that the debtor had an arguable case based on the doctrine of promissory estoppel: see below, para.3–132.

[615] *Cooper v Parker* (1855) 15 C.B. 822; *Re Warren* (1884) 53 L.J.Ch. 1016; *Anangel Atlas Compania Naviera SA v Ishikawajima Harima Heavy Industries Co Ltd (No.2)* [1990] 2 Lloyd's Rep. 526, 544; for other consideration in this case, see *ibid.* at 545 and below, para.3–123; *Huyton SA v Peter Cremer GmbH* [1999] 1 Lloyd's Rep. 620 at 629.

the value of the creditor's claim is doubtful and the debtor therefore provides consideration by paying something, even though it is less than the amount claimed. It is irrelevant that the amount paid is small in relation to the amount claimed, or that the creditor has a good chance of succeeding on the claim; for the law will not generally investigate the adequacy of consideration.[616] However, where the defendant admits liability for a sum less than that claimed, payment of that smaller sum is no consideration for the claimant's promise to accept payment of that sum in full settlement of the larger claim. The rule in *Foakes v Beer* applies since, once a binding admission has been made to pay the smaller sum, the payment of it amounts to no more than the performance of what, at that stage, is legally due from the defendant.[617]

3–119 **Unliquidated claims.** For reasons similar to those given in para.3–118 above, the general rule applies only if the original claim is a "liquidated" one, *i.e.* a claim for a fixed sum of money, such as one for money lent or for the agreed price of goods[618] or services. It does not apply where the creditor's claim is an unliquidated one,[619] such as a claim for damages or for a reasonable remuneration (where none is fixed by the contract). The value of such a claim is again uncertain; and even if the overwhelming probability is that it is worth more than the sum paid, the possibility that it may be worth less suffices to satisfy the requirement of consideration.

3–120 **Unliquidated claims becoming liquidated.** An originally unliquidated claim may subsequently become liquidated by act of the parties. This appears to have happened in *D. & C. Builders v Rees*,[620] where it does not seem that the contract specified the amount to be paid to the builders. When they presented their account they had only an unliquidated claim; and if they had at this stage accepted the £300 in full settlement they would not have been protected by the rule in *Foakes v Beer*.[621] That rule became applicable only because the defendant had, by retaining the account without objection, impliedly agreed that it correctly stated the sum due, and so turned the builders' claim into a liquidated one.[622]

3–121 **Claim partly liquidated and partly unliquidated.** A creditor may have two claims against the same debtor, one of them liquidated and the other unliquidated; or a single claim which is partly liquidated and partly unliquidated. If the

[616] Above, para.3–014. But the fact that the sum received is much smaller than that claimed may be evidence that the recipient has not accepted it in full settlement: *Rustenburg Platinum Mines Ltd v Pan Am* [1979] 1 Lloyd's Rep. 19.

[617] *Ferguson v Davies* [1997] 1 All E.R. 315 *per* Henry L.J.; Evans L.J.'s judgment is based on the ground that, as a matter of construction, the claimant had not accepted the smaller sum in full settlement. Aldous L.J. agreed with both the other judgments.

[618] A claim may be "liquidated" even though it is disputed and even though the dispute relates to its amount: *e.g.* where it is for the price of goods and the buyer alleges short delivery: *Aectra Refining and Manufacturing Inc v Exmar N.V. (The New Vanguard)* [1994] 1 W.L.R. 1634.

[619] *Wilkinson v Byers* (1834) 1 A. & E. 106; *Ibberson v Neck* (1886) 2 T.L.R. 427.

[620] [1966] 2 Q.B. 617; above, para.3–116.

[621] (1884) 9 App. Cas. 605; above, para.3–115.

[622] *cf. Amantilla v Telefusion* (1987) 9 Con.L.R. 139, where a builder's *quantum meruit* claim, which had not been disputed, was treated as "liquidated" for the purpose of Limitation Act 1980, s.29(5)(a).

debtor pays no more than the liquidated amount, and if his liability to pay this amount was undisputed, the payment of it will not constitute consideration for a promise by the creditor to accept that payment in full settlement of the *whole* of the claim or claims in question. In *Arrale v Costain Civil Engineering Ltd*[623] an employee was injured at work. Legislation in force at the place of work gave him a right against the employers to a fixed lump sum of £490, for which the employers did not dispute liability; and it was assumed that he also had a common law right to sue the employers in tort for unliquidated damages. It was held that any promise which he might have made not to pursue the common law claim was not made binding by the employers' payment of the £490. The employers had provided no consideration for such a promise since in making the payment, they merely did what they were already bound to do.[624]

Variation in the debtor's performance. Consideration for a creditor's promise to accept part payment of a debt in full settlement can be provided by the debtor's doing some act that he was not previously bound by the contract to do.[625] For example, payment of a smaller sum at the creditor's request before the due day is good consideration for a promise to forgo the balance, since it is a benefit to the creditor to be paid before he was entitled to payment, and a corresponding detriment to the debtor to pay early.[626] The same rule applies, *mutatis mutandis*, where payment of a smaller sum is made at the creditor's request at a place different from that originally fixed for payment,[627] or in a different currency.[628] Again, payment of a smaller sum accompanied at the creditor's request by the delivery of a chattel is good consideration for a promise to forgo the balance: "The gift of a horse, hawk or robe, etc. in satisfaction is goods. For it shall be intended that a horse, hawk or robe, etc., might be more beneficial than the money. . . ."[629] 3–122

Other benefit to creditor. We have seen that a promise to pay a supplier of services more than the agreed sum for performing his part of the contract can be supported by consideration in the form of a benefit in fact obtained by the other party as a result of that party's obtaining the promised performance.[630] Conversely, a promise by the supplier to accept less than the agreed sum may be supported by a similar consideration. The mere receipt of the smaller sum cannot, indeed, constitute the consideration: that possibility is precluded by *Foakes v Beer*.[631] But the performance by the debtor of *other* obligations under the 3–123

---

623 [1976] 1 Lloyd's Rep. 98; *cf. Rustenburg Platinum Mines Ltd v Pan Am* [1979] 1 Lloyd's Rep. 19, 24.

624 *Per* Stephenson and Geoffrey Lane L.JJ.; Lord Denning, M.R. based his decision on a different ground: below, para.3–136, n.715.

625 *e.g. Re William Porter & Co* [1937] 2 All E.R. 261; *Ledingham v Bermejo Estancia Co Ltd* [1947] 2 All E.R. 748.

626 *Pinnel's Case,* above, para.3–115.

627 *ibid.*

628 *cf.* above, para.3–079.

629 *Pinnel's Case,* above, para.3–115. Cases which formerly supported the view that part payment by a negotiable instrument, made at the request of the creditor and accepted by him in full settlement, discharged the debt so were overruled in *D. & C. Builders Ltd v Rees* [1966] 2 Q.B. 617.

630 *Williams v Roffey Bros & Nicholls (Contractors) Ltd* [1991] 1 Q.B. 1, above, para.3–068.

631 (1884) 9 App. Cas. 605, above, para.3–120.

contract may confer such a benefit on the creditor and so satisfy the requirement of consideration. This possibility is illustrated by the *Anangel Atlas*[632] case, where a shipbuilder's promise to reduce the price which the buyers had agreed to pay was held to have been supported by consideration, and one way in which the buyers to whom the reduction was promised had provided consideration was by accepting delivery on the day fixed for such acceptance. Even if the buyers were already bound to take delivery on that day, they had conferred a benefit on the shipbuilder by so doing since they were "core customers"[633] and their refusal to take delivery might have led other actual or potential customers to cancel (or not to place) orders.

3–124 **Forbearance to enforce cross-claims.** A debtor may provide consideration for the creditor's promise not only by doing an *act* that he was not previously bound to do, but also by a *forbearance*. Thus, where the debtor has a claim against the creditor, the debtor's forbearance to enforce that claim can constitute consideration for the creditor's promise not to claim part of the debt. For example, where a landlord promises to accept part payment of rent in full settlement, the tenant may provide consideration for this promise by forbearing to sue the landlord for breach of the latter's obligation to keep the premises in repair.[634]

3–125 **Composition with creditors.** The doctrine of consideration gives rise to some difficulty in relation to composition agreements by which a debtor who cannot pay all his creditors in full induces them to agree with himself and with each other to accept part payment in full settlement of their claims.[635] The binding force of such agreements is well established,[636] in spite of the rule in *Foakes v Beer*.[637] One possible reason for the validity of such agreements is that it would be a fraud on the other parties for a creditor who had accepted a composition to claim the balance of his original debt.[638] An alternative view is that the consideration for the creditor's promise is to be found in the promise of every other creditor to forgo part of his own debt[639]; but this consideration does not move

[632] *Anangel Atlas Compania Naviera SA v Ishikawajima Harima Heavy Industries Co Ltd (No.2)* [1990] 2 Lloyd's Rep. 526. For other consideration in that case, in the form of reducing "a previously ill-defined understanding to 'precise terms,' and so settling a potential dispute", see *ibid.* 544.

[633] *ibid.* at 544.

[634] *Brikom Investments Ltd v Carr* [1979] Q.B. 467, as explained in para.3–080, above.

[635] Provision for publicity and substantial agreement among creditors is made by Deeds of Arrangement Act 1914 (repealed in part by Insolvency Act 1985, s.235 and Sch.10, Pt III, and amended by Insolvency Act 1986, s.439(2)). *Oral* agreements are not caught by the 1914 Act: *Hughes & Falconer v Newton* [1939] 3 All E.R. 869. "Voluntary arrangements" under Insolvency Act 1986, Pts. I and VIII can, by virtue of ss.5(2) and 260(2), bind even a creditor who did not attend the meeting, or dissented from the proposal, "as if he were a party to the arrangement:" see *Johnson v Davies* [1999] Ch. 117 at 138; *cf. Re Cancol Ltd* [1996] 1 All E.R. 37. *Re a Debtor* (*No.259 of 1990*) [1992] 1 W.L.R. 226.

[636] *Good v Cheesman* (1831) 2 B. & Ad. 328; *Boyd v Hind* (1857) 1 H. & N. 938; an *agreement* to pay a dividend may, if the parties so intend, operate as satisfaction: *Bradley v Gregory* (1810) 2 Camp. 383.

[637] (1894) 9 App. Cas. 605; above, para.3–115.

[638] *Wood v Roberts* (1818) 2 Stark. 417; *Cook v Lister* (1863) 13 C.B.(N.S.) 543, 595.

[639] *Boothbey v Snowden* (1812) 3 Camp. 175.

from the promisee (*i.e.* the debtor) unless he also joins in the agreement.[640] In that event there may be consideration in the shape of a benefit to each creditor[641]: he is certain of some payment, while in the scramble for priorities which might take place if there were no composition agreement he might get nothing at all.

Part payment of debt by a third party. Part payment by a third party, if accepted by the creditor in full settlement of the debtor's liability, is a good defence to a later claim by the creditor for the balance.[642] This rule seems not to depend on any contract between debtor and creditor, so that it can apply even though no promise has been made to the debtor and even though no consideration has moved from him.[643] The rule has therefore been explained on other grounds. One such ground is that it would be a fraud[644] on the third party to allow the creditor, in disregard of his promise to the third party, to sue the debtor for the balance of the debt. The difficulty with this reasoning is that the mere breach of a promise does not amount to fraud at common law: it has this effect only if the promisor had no intention of performing his promise when he made it.[645] A second reason for the rule is that the court will not help the creditor to break his contract with the third party by allowing him to obtain a judgment against the debtor. On the contrary, it has been held that where A (the creditor) expressly contracts with B (the third party) not to sue C (the debtor) and A nevertheless does sue C, then B can intervene so as to obtain a stay of the action.[646] This possibility would extend to the case where the consideration provided by B was a *promise* by B to pay A: it thus goes beyond the cases in which B had *actually paid* A. A third explanation is suggested by *Hirachand Punamchand v Temple*[647] where the defendant was indebted on a promissory note to the claimant, who accepted a smaller sum from the defendant's father in full settlement. It was held that the claimant could not later recover the balance of the debt from the defendant because the promissory note was extinct: the position was the same as if the note had been cancelled.[648] This reasoning again does not depend on any contract between the claimant and the defendant, for the cancellation of a promissory note can release a party liable on it irrespective of contract and 3–126

[640] As in *Good v Cheesman* (1831) 2 B. & Ad. 328 where the debtor also made an assignment for the benefit of his creditors.

[641] In *West Yorkshire Darracq Agency Ltd v Coleridge* [1911] 2 K.B. 326, the same principle was applied although the creditors got nothing; but it is hard to see how this application of the rule can be justified: above, para.3–037, n.184. Even in such a case, the debtor may get the benefit of the agreement if, when he is sued by one creditor, the other (or others) can intervene to stay the action: see *Snelling v John G. Snelling* [1973] 1 Q.B. 87, below, para.18–071. The debtor will not, however, be able to avoid the requirement of consideration by relying on the Contracts (Rights of Third Parties) Act 1999 since this applies only in favour of "a person who is *not* a party" to the contract (s.1(1)); and in the case of a composition agreement the debtor typically *will* be a party.

[642] *Welby v Drake* (1825) 1 C.&P. 557; *Cook v Lister* (1863) 13 C.B.N.S. 543 at 595; *Bracken v Billingshurst* [2003] EWHC 1333 (TCC); [2003] All E.R. (D) 488 (Jul).

[643] As in *Hirachand Punamehand v Temple* [1911] 2 K.B. 339, below at n.622.

[644] See the authorities cited in n.617, above.

[645] Below, para.6–008.

[646] See *Snelling v John G. Snelling Ltd* [1973] 1 Q.B. 87 (below, para.18–070), distinguishing *Gore v Van der Lann* [1967] 2 Q.B. 31 where no promise was made not to sue C.

[647] [1911] 2 K.B. 330.

[648] *Ibid.* at 336; *cf.*, in the case of joint debts, *Johnson v Davies* [1999] Ch. 117, 130.

without considertion.[649] After the coming into force of the Contracts (Rights of Third Parties) Act 1999, the debtor may also, if the requirements of the Act are satisfied,[650] be able to take the benefit of any term in the contract between the creditor and the person making the payment, which may exclude the debtor's liability for the balance; and he will be able to do so without having to show that he provided any consideration for the creditor's promise to accept the part payment in full settlement.[651]

3–127 **Collateral contract.** An agreement to accept part payment of a debt may take effect as a collateral contract if the requirements of contractual intention and consideration are satisfied. This was the position in *Brikom Investments Ltd v Carr*[652] where a tenant's liability to contribute to the maintenance costs of a block of flats was held to have been reduced by a collateral contract under which the landlord undertook to execute certain roof repairs at his own expense.[653] The landlord's claim for contribution in this case was probably unliquidated; but the principle seems to be equally applicable where a creditor enters into a collateral contract to accept part payment in full settlement of a liquidated claim.

(c) *Limitations in Equity*

3–128 **Equitable forbearance.** Under the equitable doctrine of *Hughes v Metropolitan Ry*[654] a promise by a contracting party not to enforce his strict legal rights has (even where it is not supported by consideration) at least a limited effect in equity. Before 1947, this doctrine had not been applied where a creditor's promise to accept part payment of a debt in full settlement was not supported by any consideration moving from the debtor.[655] Such an extension of the rule seemed to be barred by *Foakes v Beer.*[656] The possibility of making the extension was, however, suggested in 1947 in *Central London Property Trust Ltd v High Trees House Ltd.*[657] In that case a block of flats had been let for 99 years to the defendants in 1937 at a rent of £2,500 a year. In January 1940 the landlords agreed to reduce this rent to £1,250 a year because of wartime conditions as a result of which only a few of the flats were let. After the end of the war, when

---

[649] Bills of Exchange Act 1882, s.62; below, paras 22–020 Vol.II, 34–139.

[650] Below, para.18–088 *et seq.*

[651] Above, para.3–045, below para.18–097. For the purposes of the Act it is the debtor who, in the example given above, is the "third party".

[652] [1979] Q.B. 467. Contrast, on the issue of contractual intention necessary to establish a collateral contract, *Business Environment Bow Lane Ltd v Deanwater Estates Ltd* [2007] EWCA Civ. 622, [2007] NLJ 1263, above para.2–166.

[653] For the consideration supporting this promise, see above, para.3–080; for other grounds for the decision, see below, para.3–133.

[654] (1877) 2 App. Cas. 439; above, para.3–085.

[655] The doctrine had been applied in *Buttery v Pickard* (1946) 62 T.L.R. 241 to a landlord's promise to accept payment of part of the rent in full settlement, but in that case consideration did move from the tenant in the shape of her forbearance to exercise her contractual right to terminate the lease (though this was not the *ratio decidendi* to the case).

[656] (1884) 9 App. Cas. 605, above, para.3–115.

[657] [1947] K.B. 130; Denning (1952) 15 M.L.R. 1; Wilson (1951) 67 L.Q.R. 330; Sheridan (1952) 15 M.L.R. 325; Bennion (1953) 16 M.L.R. 441; Guest (1955) 30 A.L.J. 187; Turner (1964) 1 N.Z.U.L.Rev. 185; Campbell, *ibid.* 232.

the flats were fully let, the landlords claimed the full rent, and tested their claim by suing for rent at the original rate for the last two quarters of 1945. Denning J. upheld the claim on the ground that, as a matter of construction, the agreement of 1940 was intended to apply only while the war-time difficulties of sub-letting lasted, and that it had therefore ceased to operate in the early part of 1945, when the difficulties had come to an end. But he also said that the landlords would have been precluded by the equitable doctrine of *Hughes v Metropolitan Ry*[658] from recovering the full rent for a period which *was* covered by the agreement of 1940. He added: "The logical consequence no doubt is that a promise to accept a smaller sum in discharge of a larger sum, if acted upon, is binding notwithstanding the absence of consideration."[659] The requirements of the equitable doctrine have already been discussed.[660] A number of further points give rise to difficulty in its application to promises to accept part payment in full settlement of a debt; these points are considered in paras 3–129 to 3–136 below.

Suspensive nature of the doctrine. The first difficulty is to reconcile Denning J.'s statement in the *High Trees* case, quoted in para.3–128 above,[661] with the actual decision in *Foakes v Beer*.[662] If Mrs Beer could go back on her promise not to claim interest, why could not the landlords in the *High Trees* case go back on their promise not to ask for the full rent in (say) 1941, when the war-time difficulties of subletting still prevailed? One possibility is to say that "That aspect was not considered in *Foakes v Beer*"[663] which was decided on purely common law principles, without reference to equity,[664] and is therefore "no longer valid"[665]; but this reasoning is open to the objection that the rule in *Pinnel's Case*[666] (on which *Foakes v Beer* was based) was recognised in equity no less than at common law.[667] Another possibility, and the one which does least violence to the authorities, is to say that the creditor's right to the balance of his debt is (save in exceptional cases[668]) not extinguished but only suspended.[669] This is generally the sole effect of the rule in *Hughes v Metropolitan Ry.*[670] and in the present context it would give effect to the intention of the parties where the 3–129

[658] (1877) 2 App. Cas. 439; above, para.3–085.

[659] [1947] K.B. 130, 134; *cf. Combe v Combe* [1951] 2 K.B. 215, 220.

[660] Above, paras 3–085 *et seq.*

[661] At n.659.

[662] (1884) 9 App. Cas. 605; above para.3–115.

[663] *High Trees* case, above, at p.135; this sentence does not occur in any of the other reports of the case ([1947] L.J.R. 77, (1946) 175 L.T. 333, (1946) 62 T.L.R. 557, [1956] 1 All E.R. 256n.); see also *Arrale v Costain Civil Engineering Ltd* [1976] 1 Lloyd's Rep. 98, 102. The argument, with respect, lacks plausibility since *Hughes v Metropolitan Ry*, above, n.658 had been decided only seven years before *Foakes v Beer* and Lords Selborne and Blackburn heard the appeals in both cases.

[664] *High Trees* case, above, at 133.

[665] *Arrale v Costain Civil Engineering Ltd* [1976] 1 Lloyd's Rep. 98 at 102.

[666] (1602) Co.Rep. 117a; above, para.3–115.

[667] *Re Warren* (1884) 53 L.J.Ch. 1016; *Bidder v Bridges* (1887) 37 Ch.D. 406.

[668] Below, para.3–132.

[669] *Ajayi v R.T. Briscoe (Nig.) Ltd* [1964] 1 W.L.R. 1326, 1330; Unger (1965) 28 M.L.R. 231; *cf. Re Venning* [1947] W.N. 196. Gordon [1963] C.L.J. 222 objects to giving the creditors' promise even this limited effect, arguing that the equitable principle is limited to relief against forfeiture. But though *Hughes v Metropolitan Ry* was a case of this kind, the equitable principle had developed since 1877 and is no longer restricted to such cases: see Wilson [1965] C.L.J. 93.

[670] Above, para.3–096.

purpose of the arrangement was merely to give the debtor extra time to pay,[671] rather than to extinguish the debt. Of course where the intention is to extinguish, and not merely to suspend, the creditor's right to the balance, the suggestion that he is permanently bound by his promise to accept part payment in full settlement[672] may seem to be an attractive one.[673] But such an extension of the principle of *Hughes v Metropolitan Ry* would require the overruling of *Foakes v Beer*. It is, no doubt, with such difficulties in mind that Lord Hailsham L.C. has said that the *High Trees* principle "may need to be reviewed and reduced to a coherent body of doctrine by the courts."[674]

3–130 **Continuing obligations.** For the present, the better view is that the principle only suspends rights; but the meaning of this statement is not entirely clear where the promisee is under a continuing obligation to make a series of payments, *e.g.* of rent under a lease,[675] of royalties under a licence to use a patent,[676] or of instalments under a hire-purchase agreement.[677] In such cases the statement may mean one of two things: first, that the creditor is entitled to payment in full only of amounts which fall due after the expiry of a reasonable notice of the retraction of the promise,[678] or, secondly, that he is then entitled, not only to future payments in full, but also to the balance of past ones. Of course the latter interpretation of the rule might sometimes be at variance with the intention of the parties at the time of the promise.[679] On the other hand it is hard to see why a debtor whose liability accrues from time to time should, for the purpose of the present rule, be in a more favourable position than one whose liability is to pay a single lump sum; nor is it clear which of the two possible rules should apply where a debtor who owed a lump sum promised to pay it off in instalments and the creditor first made, and then gave reasonable notice revoking, a promise to accept reduced instalments. In such a case, it is at least arguable that the intention

---

671 *e.g.* in *Ajayi v R.T. Briscoe (Nig.) Ltd* [1964] 1 W.L.R. 1326: see below, para.3–130, n.652. This seems also to have been the position in *Foakes v Beer*: see above, para.3–115, esp. at n.604.

672 Originally made by Lord Denning in the *High Trees* case at 134 and repeated by him in *D. & C. Builders Ltd v Rees* [1966] 2 Q.B. 617, 624; *cf. W.J. Alan & Co Ltd v El Nasr Export & Import Co* [1972] 2 Q.B. 189, 213; *cf. ibid.* at 218, 220; but in that case there was consideration: above, para.3–079.

673 Provided, at any rate, that there was no duress: *cf.* above, para.3–116.

674 *Woodhouse A.C. Israel Cocoa Ltd v Nigerian Produce Marketing Co* [1972] A.C. 741, 758; *cf. Baird Textile Holdings Ltd v Marks & Spencer plc* [2001] EWCA Civ. 274; [2002] 1 All E.R. (Comm) 737 at [49] ("not yet . . . fully developed").

675 As in the *High Trees* case, above, para.3–128.

676 As in the *Tool Metal* case [1955] 1 W.L.R. 761, discussed in para.3–131, below.

677 As in *Ajayi v R.T. Briscoe (Nig.) Ltd* [1964] 1 W.L.R. 1326.

678 *Banning v Wright* [1972] 1 W.L.R. 972, 981; *cf. W.J. Alan & Co Ltd v El Nasr Export & Import Co* [1972] 2 Q.B. 189, 213; the statement in *Bottiglieri di Navigazione v Cosco Quindao Ocean Shipping Co (The Bunge Saga Lima)* [2005] EWHC 244 (Comm), [2005] 1 Lloyd's Rep. 1 at [31] that "no revocation can be retrospective"; but this statement is, with respect, open to question for the reason given in para.3–097 n.458.

679 This would be so in cases like the *High Trees* case and the *Tool Metal* case (below, para.3–131) but probably not in a case like *Ajayi v R.T. Briscoe (Nig.) Ltd* [1964] 1 W.L.R. 1326, as the promise there "was not intended to be irrevocable:" *Meng Long Development Pte Ltd v Jip Hong Trading Pte Ltd* [1985] A.C. 511, 524. *J.T. Sydenham & Co Ltd v Enichem Elastometers Ltd* [1989] E.G.L.R. 257, 260 (discussed by Cartwright [1990] C.L.J. 13) purports to give the "estoppel" an extinctive effect; but the amount of rent due in that case was in dispute, so that the actual decision is explicable on the ground stated in para.3–118, above.

of the creditor is only to give extra time for payment. Hence the total debt remains due, and the only effect of the promise is to extend the period over which it is to be repaid.[680]

In *Tool Metal Manufacturing Co Ltd v Tungsten Electric Co Ltd*[681] a licence for the use of a patent provided that the licensees should pay "compensation" if they manufactured more than a stated number of articles incorporating the patent. The owners of the patent agreed in 1942 to suspend the obligation to pay compensation until a new agreement was made. No such agreement had been made by 1944, when disputes arose between the parties. In 1945 the owners claimed to have revoked their suspension and to be entitled to the "compensation" as from June 1, 1945. This claim failed, the Court of Appeal holding that the arrangement to suspend claims for compensation was binding until proper notice of its termination had been given; and that no such notice had been given. The owners then brought the present action claiming compensation as from January 1, 1947. The House of Lords upheld the claim on the ground that, by then, a sufficient notice had been given of the ending of the suspension period. It seems to have been assumed that the defendants were no longer liable to pay the sums which would, under the original contract, have fallen due during the suspension period. But this point was not directly considered by the House of Lords; so that the case does not conclusively determine the precise results that flow, in cases of continuing obligations, from the suspensive nature of the doctrine. 3–131

Extinctive effects in exceptional cases. There may, moreover, be exceptional situations in which the creditor's promise can wholly extinguish his rights. We have seen that, under the rule in *Hughes v Metropolitan Ry*,[682] a promise cannot be retracted where subsequent events make it impossible to perform the original obligation.[683] That principle cannot, as such, be applied to cases of part payment of a debt, since performance of the original obligation, being one to pay money, can never become literally impossible. But there is also support for the view that a forbearance cannot be retracted where it would, even after reasonable notice, be highly inequitable to require performance of the original obligation[684]; and this aspect of the principle could be applied to cases of the present kind, with the result that the promise becomes "final and irrevocable if the promisee cannot resume his position."[685] Thus the creditor's right to the balance of a debt might be extinguished if in reliance on his promise the debtor had undertaken new commitments in relation to the subject-matter: if, for example, the tenant in the 3–132

680 *Hardwick v Johnson* [1978] 1 W.L.R. 683 (where the creditor was said at 691 to have agreed to "postpone" the debtor's obligation to pay instalments).

681 [1955] 1 W.L.R. 761; Smith (1955) 18 M.L.R. 609.

682 (1877) 2 App. Cas. 439; above para.3–097.

683 Above para.3–097.

684 *ibid.*

685 *Ajayi v R.T. Briscoe (Nig.) Ltd* [1964] 1 W.L.R. 1326, 1330; in *The Bunge Saga Lima*, above para.3–130 n.678: it was said at [31] that it would there have been "inequitable to permit retraction." The case was not concerned with "waiver" of an obligation to pay money.

High Trees case had used the rebate to modernise the flats.[686] There is some support in the authorities for the view that the creditor's right may be extinguished (as opposed to being suspended) even where the debtor's reliance on the creditor's promise goes no further than merely paying the part of the debt which the creditor had agreed to accept in full settlement. This had been the view of Lord Denning MR in *D & C Buildings Ltd v Rees*.[687] His actual decision there was that it was not "inequitable" for the creditor to go back on his promise to accept part payment of the debt in full settlement as there had been no "true accord" to this effect.[688] But he went on to say that "where there has been a *true accord*" and "the debtor *acts upon* that accord by paying the lesser sum, then it is inequitable for the creditor afterwards to insist on the balance."[689] In *Collier v P & M.J. Wright (Holdings) Ltd*[690] Arden LJ relied on this dictum in support of the view that, if a creditor promised to accept part payment in full settlement of a debt, and the debtor relied on that promise by making the stipulated payment, then the debtor's defence on the ground of promissory estoppel was one which had a real prospect of success.[691] She accepted that "the effect of promissory estoppel is usually suspensory only" but added that "if the effect of resiling is sufficiently inequitable, a debtor may be able to show that the right to recover the debt is not merely postponed but extinguished."[692] There may, indeed, as is pointed out in para.3–136 below, be special circumstances in which promissory estoppel may, exceptionally, have such an extinctive effect; but the difficulty to which the *Collier* case gives rise is that the judgments do not identify any such circumstances beyond (a) the creditor's promise to accept part payment in full settlement and (b) the debtor's making the stipulated part payment. If these circumstances were sufficient for the application of promissory estoppel with extinctive effect, the difficulty mentioned in the discussion of the *High Trees* case[693] in para.3–129 above would again arise: that is, there would be a direct conflict between such an application and the outcome in *Foakes v Beer*.[694] No doubt, the law as laid down in that case may, for reasons given in para.3–117, be defective, at least in its operation in some situations. But any such defect would be more satisfactorily dealt with by a reconsideration by the House of Lords of *Foakes v Beer* than by continuing to regard that case as good law while seeking to bypass its consequences by invoking the doctrine of promissory estoppel. The

[686] *cf.* Mitchell (1951) Univ. of W. Australia Law Rev. 245, 251. The principle is somewhat similar to that which underlies the defence of "change of position" in an action for the recovery of money paid; for recognition of this defence, see *Lipkin Gorman v Karpnale Ltd* [1991] 2 A.C. 548; below paras 29–179, Vol.II, 40–087.

[687] [1967] 2 Q.B. 617; above, para.3–116.

[688] At 625.

[689] At 625; and see below, para.3–136.

[690] [2007] EWCA Civ. 1329, [2008] 1 W.L.R. 643; Trukhtanov, (2008) 124 L.Q.R. 364.

[691] [2007] EWCA Civ. 1329 at [21], [37]–[40], [50]; Longmore L.J. was more sceptical: see [2007] EWCA Civ. 1329 at [45]–[49].

[692] [2007] EWCA Civ. 1329 at [37].

[693] [1947] K.B. 130, stated above in para.3–128.

[694] The citation of the *High Trees* case in the *Collier* case [2007] EWCA 1329 at [37] does not help to resolve the difficulty discussed in the text below, i.e. that of reconciling what is described in the latter case (at [42]) as "the brilliant obiter dictum of Denning J, as he then was, in the *High Trees* case "with the outcome in *Foakes v Beer* (above, para.3–115): see above, para.3–129. Nor does the citation in the *Collier* case at [37] of "the *Tool Metal* case" [1955] 1 W.L.R. 761 help to resolve this difficulty: see the discussion of that case in para.3–131 above.

latter course would provide no clear guidance as to which of the two conflicting principles would apply in any particular situation and so be a source of undesirable uncertainty. The point is well illustrated by the *D & C Builders* case itself where the judgment of Lord Denning was based on the doctrine of promissory estoppel,[695] while those of Danckwerts and Winn L.JJ. were based on the rule in *Foakes v Beer*[696] and conflict between these two approaches was avoided in the *D & C Builders* case only by Lord Denning's conclusion that promissory estoppel was of no avail by reason of the debtor's conduct in securing the creditor's promise.[697] In the *Collier* case, it was assumed that there was no such objectionable conduct on the debtor's part. The conflict between the two approaches was thus a real one and the judgments do not provide any principled basis for its resolution.

In *Brikom Investments Ltd v Carr*[698] long leases of flats obliged the tenants to pay, not only rent and a maintenance charge, but also contributions in respect of certain "excess expenses" incurred by the landlords in keeping the structure in repair. In the course of the negotiations leading to the execution of the leases, the landlords had promised to put the roof into repair "at our own cost." This was held to amount to a collateral contract[699] with one of the original tenants, precluding the landlords from enforcing against her the provision in the lease requiring her to contribute to the cost of the roof repairs. It was further held that claims for contributions to the cost of those repairs could not be made against assignees and sub-assignees of original tenants, even though there was no collateral contract with these persons. Lord Denning, M.R. based this conclusion on the *High Trees* principle which, in his view, was available not only between the original parties, but also in favour of and against their assigns.[700] The extinctive effect of the principle in these circumstances can perhaps be supported on the ground that the original tenants, the assignees and the sub-assignees had all, in reliance on the landlords' promise, undertaken fresh commitments by entering into long leases of the flats. Roskill and Cumming-Bruce L.JJ., on the other hand, treated the case, not as one of "promissory estoppel,"[701] but as one of "waiver."[702] It seems that the latter expression here refers to a variation supported by consideration,[703] for the consideration provided by the tenants[704] **3–133**

[695] See para.3–136 below.

[696] See para.3–116 above. Danckwerts L.J. did indeed begin his judgment by saying ([1962] 2 Q.B. 617 at 625–626): "I agree with the judgment of the Master of the Rolls." But his own reasoning is entirely concerned with the rule in *Foakes v Beer* and his conclusion (at 627) is that "the county court judge was right in applying the rule in *Foakes v Beer*."

[697] Above at n.688; below, para.3–136.

[698] [1979] Q.B. 467.

[699] Above, para.3–080; contrast *ibid.*, n.373.

[700] [1979] Q.B. 467, 484–485.

[701] *ibid.* at 485, 490.

[702] *ibid.* at 488, 490.

[703] *cf.* above, para.3–081.

[704] Above, para.3–080. Roskill L.J. at 489 refers to *Hughes v Metropolitan Ry* (1877) 2 App. Cas. 439 (above, para.3–085) as stating a principle of "contractual variation of strict contractual rights." It is respectfully submitted that this phrase should be interpreted to refer simply to *variations of contracts*, rather than to *contractually binding variations*; for the principle clearly applies to variations which are not contractually binding (but revocable on reasonable notice) because they are not supported by consideration.

could equally support the landlords' promise whether that promise was regarded as a collateral contract or as a variation. On this interpretation of the case, there is no difficulty in accounting for the extinctive effect of the landlords' promise. It amounted to a variation supported by consideration, so that the liability of the original tenants to contribute to the cost of the repairs in question was extinguished; and once it had been so extinguished it was not revived on assignment of the leases.

3–134 **Requirements.** Granted that the equitable principle can apply to cases of part payment of a debt, it is in this context subject to the usual requirements on which its operation depends. These have already been considered[705] but two of them call for further discussion at this point.

3–135 **Whether detriment necessary.** The equitable principle is sometimes said to be analogous to the doctrine of estoppel by representation.[706] According to this analogy, the principle would operate only in favour of a person who had suffered some "detriment" in the sense in which that word is used in that branch of the law.[707] Where, as in the *High Trees* case, a tenant pays only half the agreed rent he suffers no such "detriment"; and although ingenious attempts have been made to find some other "detriment" in the *High Trees* case,[708] the better view is that "detriment" of the kind required for the purpose of estoppel by representation is not an essential requirement of the operation of the equitable principle.[709] This is the position under the rule in *Hughes v Metropolitan Ry*[710] on which the *High Trees* case is based; and no such requirement of "detriment" is mentioned by Denning J. in the *High Trees* case itself or in his later statements of the principle.[711] All that is necessary is that the promisee should have acted in reliance on the promise in such a way as to make it inequitable to allow the promisor to act inconsistently with it.[712] This requirement was satisfied on the facts of the *High Trees* case, no less than on those of *Hughes v Metropolitan Ry.*

3–136 **Inequitable.** By making the part payment, the debtor acts in reliance on the creditor's promise, and so makes it *prima facie* "inequitable" for the creditor peremptorily to go back on his promise. But other circumstances may lead to the conclusion that it would not be "inequitable" for the creditor to reassert his claim for the full amount[713]: this would, for example, be the position where the debtor

[705] Above, paras 3–086 *et seq.*
[706] Above, para.3–103.
[707] *cf.* above, para.3–094.
[708] Wilson (1951) 67 L.Q.R. 330, 344.
[709] *cf.* Denning (1952) 15 M.L.R. 1, 6–8.
[710] (1877) 2 App. Cas. 439.
[711] *e.g.* in *Combe v Combe* [1951] 2 K.B. 215 at 220.
[712] Above, para.3–095; *Tool Metal* case [1955] 1 W.L.R. 761, 764; *Beesly v Hallwood Estates Ltd* [1960] 1 W.L.R. 548, 560; affirmed [1961] Ch. 105, as to which see above, para.2–180 n.815; *Ajayi v R.T. Briscoe (Nig.) Ltd* [1964] 1 W.L.R. 1326, 1330.
[713] *cf.* above, para.3–097.

had failed to perform his promise to pay the smaller amount.[714] Another such circumstance may be the conduct of the debtor in obtaining the creditor's promise. This possibility may be illustrated by further reference to *D. & C. Builders Ltd v Rees*.[715] Lord Denning, M.R. there stressed the fact that the builders' promise to accept £300 in full settlement of their claim for £482 had been obtained by taking undue advantage of their desperate financial position. In these circumstances it was not "inequitable" for the builders to go back on their promise, so that the *High Trees* principle did not apply. The difficulty with this reasoning is that most debtors who offer part payment in full settlement try to exert some kind of "pressure" against their creditors. The law now recognises that it is possible for such "pressure" to amount to duress,[716] and where it has this effect, a promise obtained as a result of it should clearly not bring the *High Trees* principle into effect.[717] Where, on the other hand, there is no duress, the *High Trees* principle should not be excluded merely because it could be said that the promise has been "improperly obtained." Such an intermediate category between promises obtained by duress and those not so obtained should here, as elsewhere,[718] be rejected as "unhelpful because it would render the law uncertain."[719]

11. Proprietary Estoppel

(a) *Nature of the Doctrine*

Introductory. Proprietary estoppel is said to arise in certain situations in which a person has done acts in reliance on the belief that he has, or that he will acquire, rights in or over another's land. Usually, but not invariably, these acts consist of erecting buildings on, or making other improvements to, the land in question. Where the requirements of proprietary estoppel are satisfied, the landowner is precluded from denying the existence of the rights in question, and may 3–137

[714] *Re Selectmove* [1995] 1 W.L.R. 474, 481, where the debtor's promise was not to pay *less* but to pay *late*; *cf. Burrows v Brent LBC* [1996] 1 W.L.R. 1448, where decision was based on lack of contractual intention so that neither the requirement of consideration nor the equitable doctrine was discussed.

[715] [1966] 2 Q.B. 617; above para.3–116; Winder (1966) 82 L.Q.R. 165; *cf. Arrale v Costain Civil Engineering Ltd* [1976] 1 Lloyd's Rep. 98, 102.

[716] Below, paras 7–014, 7–019.

[717] The same would be true where the creditor's promise had been obtained by misrepresentation, e.g. as to the debtor's ability to pay. In the *D & C Builders* case, above, Danckwerts L.J. at 626 suggested that there had been such a misrepresentation by the defendant's wife on his behalf, while Winn L.J. said that there was no finding to this effect. If such a false representation were now made dishonestly and induced the creditor to accept part payment in full settlement, the representor could be criminally liable under s.2 of the Fraud Act, 2006.

[718] Above, para.3–067.

[719] *Pao On v Lau Yiu Long* [1980] A.C. 614, 634. *cf. Huyton SA v Peter Cremer GmbH* [1999] 1 Lloyd's Rep. 620, where the requirement of consideration was satisfied (above para.3–118); and there was no duress (below para.7–022). It was said at 629 that "the submissions relating to consideration and duress inter-relate". No separate argument seems to have been advanced that, in the absence of duress, the agreement might be open to attack on the ground that it had been "improperly obtained".

indeed be compelled to grant them. Because the estoppel precludes him from denying the existence of rights in property, it has come to be known as "proprietary estoppel."[720] It is distinct[721] from promissory estoppel, both in the conditions which must be satisfied before it comes into operation and in its effects. But under both doctrines some legal effects can be given to promises which are not contractually binding for want of consideration; and it is this aspect[722] of proprietary estoppel which calls for discussion in the present chapter.

3–138 **Scope of proprietary estoppel.** Proprietary estoppel operates in a variety of cases so disparate that it has been described as "an amalgam of doubtful utility."[723] The cases can be divided broadly into two categories. In the first, one person acts under a mistake as to the existence or as to the extent of his rights in or over another's land. Even though the mistake was in no way induced by the landowner, he might be prevented from taking advantage of it, particularly if he "stood by" knowing of the mistake, or actively encouraged the mistaken party to act in reliance on his mistaken belief.[724] These cases of so-called "acquiescence"[725] do not raise any questions as to the enforceability of promises and therefore do not call for further discussion in this chapter.[726] In the second situation, there is not merely "acquiescence" by the landowner, but "encouragement"[727] in the sense of conduct by the landowner, or a representation by him, from which a promise to the other party (the promisee) can be inferred[728] to the

[720] *Jones v Jones* [1977] 1 W.L.R. 438, 442; *Pascoe v Turner* [1979] 1 W.L.R. 431, 436; *Re Sharpe* [1980] 1 W.L.R. 219, 233; *Greasley v Cooke* [1980] 1 W.L.R. 1306, 1311; *cf. Midland Bank plc v Cooke* [1995] 4 All E.R. 564, 573 ("equities in the nature of an estoppel"). In *Cobbe v Yeoman's Row Management Ltd* [2008] UKHL 55, [2008] 1 W.L.R. 1752 at [3] and [14]–[29] Lord Scott uses the expression "proprietary estoppel" to refer to the doctrine, while Lord Walker generally refers to the doctrine simply as "equitable estoppel". He uses the expression "proprietary estoppel" only when quoting from or summarising other sources in which it occurs (e.g., at [48], [67], [73] and [78]); and where he so uses it he does without disapproval. For the use of "equitable estoppel" to mean "proprietary estoppel," see also *Secretary of State for Transport v Christos* [2003] EWCA Civ 1073, (2004) 1 P.&C.R. 17, e.g. at [42].

[721] *Fontana N.V. v Mautner* (1980) 254 E.G. 199, 207; and see below, paras 3–160—3–163.

[722] For wider discussions see Davies (1979) 8 Sydney L.Rev. 200 and (1980) 7 Adelaide L.Rev. 200; Moriarty (1984) 100 L.Q.R. 376; Smith in (ed. Rose) *Consensus ad Idem: Essays in the Law of Contract in Honour of Guenter Treitel*, p.235 (1996).

[723] *Amalgamated Investment & Property Co Ltd v Texas Commerce International Bank Ltd* [1982] Q.B. 84, 103.

[724] *Wilmott v Barber* (1880) 15 Ch.D. 96; *cf. Taylors Fashions Ltd v Liverpool Victoria Trustee Co Ltd* [1982] Q.B. 133 note; *Coombes v Smith* [1986] 1 W.L.R. 808; *Matharu v Matharu, The Times*, May 13, 1994.

[725] *Wilmott v Barber* (1880) 15 Ch.D. 96, 105; in *Blue Haven Enterprises Ltd v Tully* [2006] UKPC 17 the alleged estoppel was likewise based on acquiescence, so that no question arose as to the enforceability of any promise. The claim failed as the defendant had drawn the claimant's attention to his (the defendant's) interest in good time and so had not acted unconscionably in asserting that interest against the claimant.

[726] See below, para.29–161.

[727] *Ramsden v Dyson* (1866) L.R. 1 H.L. 129, 170; *cf. Att.-Gen. of Hong Kong v Humphreys Estates (Queen's Gardens)* [1987] 1 A.C. 114 (where this requirement was not satisfied: below, para.3–144).

[728] See *Lloyd's Bank plc v Rosset* [1991] 1 A.C. 107 and *Keelwalk Properties Ltd v Walker* [2002] EWCA Civ. 1076 at [63] (where this requirement was not satisfied).

effect that the promisee has a legally enforceable[729] interest in the land or that one will be created in his favour. If the other party acts in reliance on such a promise, the question will arise to what extent the promise can be enforced, even though it may not be supported by consideration, or fail to satisfy the other requirements (such as those of certainty or form[730]) of a binding contract.

(b) *Bases of Liability*

Expenditure on another's land in reliance on a promise. In *Dillwyn v Llewelyn*[731] a father executed a memorandum "presenting" a named estate to his son "for the purpose of furnishing himself with a dwelling house." The son spent £14,000 in building a house on the land; and it was held (after the father's death) that he was entitled to have the fee simple of the estate conveyed to him. Many later cases similarly give some degree of legal enforceability to a promise by a landowner in reliance on which the promisee has spent money on making improvements to the promisor's land: for example, where A built a bungalow on B's land in reliance on B's promise that A could stay there for the rest of his life[732]; where B purported to make a gift of a cottage to her son A "provided he did it up" and A incurred considerable expense in doing so[733]; where A spent money on extending or improving B's house in reliance on a similar promise by B[734]; where, in reliance on such a promise, A actually did the work of improvement him- or herself [735]; and where a tenant, whose lease had been terminated, spent money on improving the premises in reliance on the landlord's promise to grant him a new lease.[736] Cases of this kind can be explained on the basis of unjust enrichment: in all of them, the landowner would benefit unjustly if he were allowed to disregard his promise and to take back the land after he had induced the promisee to make improvements to it. But the unjust enrichment explanation will not account for cases in which the doctrine has been applied even though the promisee's expenditure on another's land did not result in any benefit to the owner of that land.[737] It follows that, although unjust enrichment of the promisor may be the most obvious basis of proprietary estoppel, it cannot provide complete explanation of the doctrine. 3–139

[729] *Coombes v Smith* [1986] 1 W.L.R. 808 (where there was no belief in the existence of a *legally enforceable* right); and *cf. Brinand v Ewens* (1987) 19 H.L.R. 415.

[730] See, *e.g.* below, para.3–140, n.739.

[731] (1862) 4 D.F. & G. 517.

[732] *Inwards v Baker* [1965] 2 Q.B. 507.

[733] *Voyce v Voyce* (1991) 62 P. & C.R. 290.

[734] *Hussey v Palmer* [1972] 1 W.L.R. 1286; *Pascoe v Turner* [1979] 1 W.L.R. 431; *Durrant v Heritage* [1994] E.G.C.S. 134; *semble* spending money on mere maintenance would not suffice: *Griffiths v Williams* [1978] E.G.D. 919. *cf. Maharaj v Chand* [1986] A.C. 898 (where, because of local legislation, proprietary estoppel was not argued).

[735] *Eves v Eves* [1975] 1 W.L.R. 1338; *Jones v Jones* [1977] 1 W.L.R. 438; *Ungurian v Lesnoff* [1990] Ch. 206; *Clough v Kelly* (1996) 72 P. & C.R. D22 (where the claimant had also spent money on the premises); *cf. Jiggins v Brisley* [2003] EWHC 841; [2003] 1 W.T.L.R. 1141 (provision of purchase money and money to pay for improvements); see also *Van Leathen v Brooker* [2006] EWHC 1478, [2006] 1 F.C.R. 697, below para.3–147.

[736] *J.T. Developments v Quinn* (1991) 62 P. & C.R. 33.

[737] *Canadian Pacific Railway v The King* [1931] A.C. 414; *Armstrong v Sheppard & Short* [1959] 2 Q.B. 384.

3–140 **Proprietary estoppel and constructive trust.** The explanation of proprietary estoppel as a mechanism for preventing unjust enrichment[738] perhaps accounts for the view that liability, where such an estoppel operates, is based on "an implied or constructive trust."[739] While this view does not assert that the two concepts "can or should be completely assimilated",[740] it recognises that there is a significant area of overlap between them.[741] Many of the cases in which the relationship between the two concepts was considered were concerned, not with want of consideration, but with the question whether proprietary estoppel could be a ground on which a person could be held liable on a transaction which failed to comply with formal requirements, such as those imposed by section 2 of the Law of Property (Miscellaneous Provisions) Act 1989.[742] This question is discussed in Chapter 4 below[743]; here it suffices to say that the relation between the two concepts depends on a distinction between two types of cases. The first is that in which one of the elements capable of giving rise[744] to proprietary estoppel is an "agreement, or at least an expression of common understanding, exchanged between the parties as to the existence, or intended existence, of a proprietary interest . . . "[745] The second type of case is that in which proprietary estoppel can arise without any such element of agreement: e.g., where "a landowner stands by while his neighbour mistakenly builds on the former's land."[746] In cases of the first kind, the two concepts overlap in the sense that the same facts can give rise, not only to a proprietary estoppel, but also to a constructive trust.[747] In cases of the second kind, there is no such overlap, so that, even if the requirements of

[738] See above, after n.736.

[739] *Sen v Headley* [1991] Ch. 425, 440; *Re Dale* [1994] Ch. 31, 47; *Lloyd's Bank plc v Carrick* [1996] 4 All E.R. 632, 640; *cf. Drake v Whipp* (1996) 28 H.L.R. 531; *Yaxley v Gotts* [2000] Ch. 162 at 176, 193; *Banner Homes Group plc v Luff Developments Ltd* [2000] Ch. 372 at 382 where the agreement (if any) lacked contractual force, not for want of consideration, but on account of its incompleteness (above, para.2–116).

[740] *Stack v Dowden* [2007] UKHL 17, [2007] 2 A.C. 432 at [13]; in this passage, Lord Walker is reported as having referred to "common interest constructive trust." *Quaere* whether "interest" is not here a misprint for "intention": *cf.* the reference to "common intention" *ibid.* at [17], [18], [25], [30] and [37]. In *Cobbe v Yeoman's Row Management Ltd* [2008] UKHL 55, [2008] 1 W.L.R. 1752 there was neither a proprietary estoppel (see below, paras 3–148A to 3–148C) nor a constructive trust but it is significant that Lord Scott treats these issues in separate parts of his speech, paras [14]–[29] being devoted to proprietary estoppel and paras [30]–[38] to constructive trust. Lord Walker at [93] briefly dismisses the constructive trust claim, having devoted the bulk of his speech to proprietary (or "equitable": see above, para.3–137 n. 720) estoppel. For the recognition of the distinction between the two doctrines, see also the *Cobbe* case [2008] UKHL 55 at [24] and [29].

[741] *Kinane v Mackie-Conteh* [2005] EWCA Civ. 45, [2005] W.T.L.R. 45 at [24]; *cf. Stack v Dowden* [2007] UKHL 17, [2007] 2 A.C. 432 at [128].

[742] e.g., *Yaxley v Gotts* [2000] Ch.162; *Kinane v Mackie-Conteh*, above n.741.

[743] See above, para.2–171 n.780; and paras 4–077, 4–081 below.

[744] i.e., if the conditions specified in paras 3–143 to 3–147 below are satisfied.

[745] *Kinane v Mackie-Conteh*, above n.741 at [51]; *cf. ibid.*, at [50], citing *Yaxley v Gotts*, above n.742, at 180.

[746] *ibid.*, at [176], cited in *Kinnane v Mackie-Conteh*, above n.741 at [47].

[747] *ibid.*, at [51]; *S v S* [2006] EWHC 2892 (Fam), [2007] F.L.R. 1123 at [59]; but even in such cases it should be emphasised the two concepts cannot be "completely assimilated" (above at n.740); in particular, their legal effects may differ: *Stack v Dowden* above n.740 at [37]; Lord Neuberger *ibid.*, at [128] more cautiously says that "it may well be that facts which may justify a proprietary estoppel . . . would give rise to a constructive trust."

proprietary estoppel are satisfied, there will not, for this reason alone, be a constructive trust.[748]

3–141 **Other acts done in reliance on the promise.** The operation of proprietary estoppel is not confined to cases in which the promisee has incurred expenditure on, or done work to, the promisor's land. It can also apply where the promisee has conferred some other benefit on the promisor[749]; and even where no work has been done on the promisor's land and he has not received any other benefit. This indeed appears from one of the illustrations given by Lord Westbury in *Dillwyn v Llewelyn*: if "A gives a house to B, but makes no formal conveyance, and the house is afterwards included, with the knowledge of A, in the marriage settlement of B, A would be bound to complete the title of the parties claiming under the settlement."[750] Similarly, the doctrine operated in the absence of any expenditure on the promisor's land in *Crabb v Arun DC*.[751] In that case A (a local authority) by its conduct represented to B that B had a right of way from his land over adjoining land owned by A. In reliance on that representation, B sold part of his own land, so that the only access from the remainder to the nearest public highway was by means of the right of way across A's land. It was held that B had a right to cross A's land for the purpose of access to his retained land. Detrimental reliance by the promisee here gave rise to a proprietary estoppel even though no benefit was conferred on the promisor.[752]

3–142 **Alternative explanation: contract.** In *Dillwyn v Llewelyn* Lord Westbury, while referring to the parties of the transaction as "donor" and "donee" also said that the son's expenditure "supplied a valuable consideration originally wanting"[753]; and in discussing a hypothetical example similar to the facts of the case before him he concluded "that the donee acquires a right from the subsequent

---

[748] This follows from the reasoning of *Kinane v Mackie-Conteh*, above n.741 at [51] and of *S v S*, above n.747 above at [59].

[749] *e.g. Tanner v Tanner* [1975] 1 W.L.R. 1346 (services rendered to promisor in managing his property); *Greasley v Cooke* [1980] 1 W.L.R. 1306 (personal and nursing services); *Wayling v Jones* (1993) 69 P. & C.R. 170 (services rendered to promisor for virtually no pay); *Campbell v Griffin* [2001] EWCA Civ. 999; [2001] W.T.L.R. 981 (lodger caring for elderly couple); *Jennings v Rice* [2002] EWCA Civ. 159; [2002] W.T.L.R. 367 (gardener-handyman caring for childless widow, below, para.3–144); *cf. Plimmer v Mayor of Wellington* (1884) 9 App. Cas. 699 and *E.R. Ives Investments Ltd v High* [1967] 2 Q.B. 379 (where the landowner benefited from improvements to his land but also—and more significantly—in other ways); *Grant v Edwards* [1986] Ch. 638, 657; contrast *Howard v Jones* (1988) 19 Fam. Law 231 (contribution to running costs of *another* property insufficient).

[750] (1862) 4 D.F. & G. 517, 521.

[751] [1976] Ch. 179. The case was described in *Amalgamated Investment & Property Co Ltd v Texas Commerce International Bank Ltd* [1982] Q.B. 84, 121 as one of "estoppel by convention"; but this would require a dealing between A and B on the basis of a common assumption (above, paras 3–108, 3–109) while in *Crabb's* case the dealing was between B and the purchaser from him. In *Waltons Stores (Interstate) Ltd v Maher* (1988) 164 C.L.R. 387, 403, *Crabb's* case was described as one of "promissory estoppel" (see above, para.3–085); but the requirements of that doctrine (in particular, the requirement of a pre-existing legal relationship: above, para.3–088) were not satisfied in *Crabb's* case, and the effect of the estoppel differed from promissory estoppel in giving rise to a new right: *cf.* above, para.3–098.

[752] *cf. Hammersmith & Fulham BC v Top Shop Centres Ltd* [1990] Ch. 237 and *Evans v HSBC Trust Co (UK) Ltd* [2005] W.T.L.R. 1289 (as to which see also para.3–148 below, n.802).

[753] (1862) 4 D. F. & G. 517, 521.

transaction to call upon the donor to perform that contract and to complete the imperfect donation."[754] These passages may suggest that he regarded the memorandum as a kind of unilateral contract[755] by which the father promised to convey the land if the son built a house on it. The terms of the memorandum make it improbable that a modern court would so regard it; it is more likely that these terms would now be regarded as negativing contractual intention.[756] However, in a number of later cases the rights of a person who has expended money on the property of another have been explained as being based on contract[757]; and often such an explanation is sufficiently plausible to make reliance on a doctrine of proprietary estoppel unnecessary.[758] A unilateral contract to transfer an interest in land has been held to arise out of a promise to make the transfer if the promisee would pay instalments due under a mortgage on the house[759]; it can equally arise out of a promise to make the transfer if the promisee will make improvements to the land, or indeed do any other act.[760]

3–143 But there are, it is submitted, obstacles to treating all cases of proprietary estoppel as depending on contract. One is that the promises in cases of this kind are often made in a family context, without contractual intention. Another is that the promise may lack consideration because the party relying on the estoppel made no counter-promise and so incurred no obligation, and that the arrangement was one in which it would not be in accordance with the intention of the parties to treat it as a unilateral contract.[761] A third is that the terms of the alleged contract are often too vague to satisfy the requirement of certainty.[762] This difficulty accounts for the view of the Court of Appeal that there was no contract

---

[754] *ibid.* at 522.

[755] Above, para.2–078.

[756] Above, para.2–170.

[757] *e.g. Plimmer v Mayor of Wellington* (1884) 9 App. Cas. 699 as explained in *Canadian Pacific Railway v The King* [1931] A.C. 414, 428; *Eves v Eves* [1975] 1 W.L.R. 1338; *Tanner v Tanner* [1975] 1 W.L.R. 1346; *cf. Re Sharpe* [1980] 1 W.L.R. 219, 224; and see *E.R. Ives Investments Ltd v High* [1967] 2 Q.B. 379 (where there was a contract between the defendant and the claimant's predecessor in title).

[758] See *Lloyd's Bank plc v Carrick* [1996] 4 All E.R. 632, where the existence of a contract of sale precluded reliance by the purchaser on proprietary estoppel, even though that contract was, as against a bank to which the property had been charged as security, void for non-registration. Contract *Yaxley v Gotts* [2000] Ch. 162 at 179, when thee was *no* such contract but, at most, an agreement lacking contractual force. See also *Oxley v Hiscock* [2004] EWCA Civ. 546, [2005] Fam. 211 at [35]–[36], distinguishing between cases of proprietary estoppel and those in which parties, *before* acquiring property, reach "an agreement, arrangement or understanding . . . that each is to have a beneficial share in the property."

[759] *Errington v Errington* [1952] 1 Q.B. 290; above, para.2–078.

[760] *e.g. Tanner v Tanner* [1975] 1 W.L.R. 1346; merely to maintain the house in repair could be sufficient for the present purpose, even if it did not suffice to raise a proprietary estoppel: see above, para.3–139, n.734.

[761] *J.T. Developments v Quinn* (1991) 62 P. & C.R. 33.

[762] Above, para.2–138. See *Gillet v Holt* [2001] Ch. 210 at 230; *Banner Homes Group plc v Luff Developments Ltd* [2000] Ch. 372; *Jennings v Rice* [2002] EWCA Civ. 159; [2002] W.T.L.R. 367, at [10], [49], [50]; if the party claiming the benefit of a proprietary estoppel *knows* that the agreement has no contractual force because it lacks certainty or is incomplete, this fact may prevent the estoppel from arising, as in *Cobbe v Yeoman's Row Management Ltd* [2008] UKHL 55, [2008] 1 W.L.R. 1752, below, paras 3–148A to 3–148D.

in *Crabb v Arun DC* [763]: there may have been an implied promise to grant the claimant some right of way across the defendant's land, but no financial or other terms were specified in that promise, so that it would not (even if supported by consideration) have been sufficiently certain to give rise to a contract. A fourth is that many arrangements which can give rise to proprietary estoppel are made without any attempt to comply with the stringent formal requirements now imposed on the making of contracts for the disposition of interests in land.[764] Failure to comply with these requirements does not prevent such arrangements from giving rise in certain circumstances to a proprietary estoppel,[765] but it does prevent them from taking effect as contracts. The possibility of explaining proprietary estoppel on the basis of contract is therefore in practice likely to be restricted to cases where the arrangement does *not* purport to dispose of an interest in land.[766] Finally, the explanation of proprietary estoppel as based on contract also fails to take account of the fact that the promisee's remedy in cases of proprietary estoppel may fall short of awarding him the full amount of the expectation interest to which he is in principle entitled for breach of contract, at least where the value of that interest can be established with sufficient certainty. In cases of proprietary estoppel the court may, under the principles discussed in paragraph 3–154 below, award less than the value of his expectations. This fact (among others),[767–768] supports the view that remedies based on proprietary estoppel are distinct from those for breach of contract.

(c) *Conditions giving rise to Liability*

Kinds of promises capable of giving rise to a proprietary estoppel. A promise may give rise to a proprietary estoppel even though it is not express but is implied: for example, from the fact that the parties acted on the common assumption that one of them was to have the right to reside on the other's property.[769] The promise must be of such a kind that it is reasonable for the promisee to rely on it; the promisor must have been aware of the fact that the 3–144

---

[763] [1976] Ch. 179; Atiyah (1974) 92 L.Q.R. 174 criticises the view that there was no contract but the argument is based on the fallacy that, merely because a promise has *some* legal effects, it must necessarily have *all* the effects of a contract: *cf.* above, paras 3–013, 3–105 and below, para.3–164. The alleged contract in *Crabb's* case would, quite apart from lacking consideration, be impossibly vague: see above, para.2–139 and *cf.* Millett (1976) 92 L.Q.R. 342; Duncanson (1976) 39 M.L.R. 268.

[764] Law of Property (Miscellaneous Provisions) Act 1989, s.2(1)–(3). Previously the contract could be *made* informally, but Law of Property Act 1925, s.40 (replacing part of Statute of Frauds 1677, s.4, and now repealed) had required either a note or memorandum in writing as evidence of the contract, or "part performance" of the contract. The latter requirement could be satisfied by the conduct of the promisee giving rise to proprietary estoppel. *cf.* the reference to "part performance" in *Dillwyn v Llewelyn* (1862) 4 D.F. & G. 517, 521.

[765] See above, para.3–114 n.592. *cf.* Law Com. No.164 (1987) para.5.5.

[766] For the view that proprietary estoppel can apply where the subject-matter of the promise is property other than land, see below, para.3–146. For the definition of "interest in land" within s.2 of the Law of Property (Miscellaneous Provisions) Act 1989 s. 2, see *ibid*, s.2(6). An irrevocable licence can be a sufficiently certain "interest in land" for the purpose of satisfying the second of the requirements of proprietary estoppel stated in para.3–148B below: see *Cobbe v Yeoman's Row Management Ltd* [2008] UKHL 55, [2008] 1 W.L.R. 1752 at [21], [22], per Lord Scott.

[767–768] Such as the discretionary nature of the remedy: below, paras 3–154, 3–164.

[769] *e.g. Re Sharpe* [1980] 1 W.L.R. 219.

promisee would so rely on it and the promisor must have intended that the promisee would so rely on it.[770] The promise must also induce the promisee to believe that a legal right has been, or will be, created in his favour.[771] There can normally be no such belief, and hence no proprietary estoppel, if the promise expressly disclaims legal effect: for example, in one case[772] it was held that no proprietary estoppel arose out of an agreement for the transfer of a number of flats "subject to contract," it being well known that the effect of these words was to negative the intention to be legally bound.[773] The promisee may have formed "the confident and not unreasonable hope"[774] that the promise would not be withdrawn; but no *belief* to this effect had been encouraged[775] by the promisor or relied on by the promisee. It seems that a proprietary estoppel could arise out of such an agreement if one of the parties *did* encourage such a belief in the other and the other acted to his detriment in reliance on that belief.[776] Similar reasoning applies where the promise in terms reserves a right to the promisor wholly to revoke the promise. Thus where a landowner promised her part-time gardener to leave him her house in her will but told him "not to count his chickens before they were hatched", it was held that no proprietary estoppel arose when, after having made a will in his favour, she then revoked it and made another leaving the property to someone else: in these circumstances it was not unconscionable for the landowner to revoke the promise.[777] The position is the same where the promise, even though it does not in terms reserve a power to revoke, is in its nature revocable and this is a matter of common knowledge so that the promisee must be taken to have been aware of the risk of its being revoked. This will often be the position where the promise is one to make a will in favour of the promisee;

---

[770] *Gillett v Holt* [2001] Ch. 210, 229.

[771] See *Kinane v Mackie-Conteh* [2005] EWCA Civ. 45, [2005] W.T.L.R. 345 at [29] (requirement of a representation "that the agreement created an enforceable obligation").

[772] *Att.-Gen. of Hong Kong v Humphreys Estates (Queen's Gardens)* [1987] 1 A.C. 114; the case was said in *Waltons Stores (Interstate) Ltd v Maher* (1988) 164 C.L.R. 387, 404 to be "not a case of proprietary estoppel" but (apparently) one of *promissory* estoppel. But most of the authorities relied on in the *Humphreys Estates* case were cases of proprietary estoppel; the leading cases on promissory estoppel were not cited; and if the requirements of encouragement and reliance had been satisfied the estoppel would have created a new right, which in English law is not the effect of promissory estoppel: above para.3–100. *cf. Saloman v Akiens* [1993] 1 E.G.L.R. 101 (no proprietary estoppel arising from agreement "subject to lease"); *Pridean Ltd v Forest Taverns* (1998) 75 P. & C.R. 447 (no proprietary estoppel arising from work done during negotiations which failed to lead to a contract); *Edwin Shirley Productions v Workspace Management Ltd* [2001] 23 E.G. 158 (negotiations "subject to contract" and "without prejudice" held not to give rise to proprietary estoppel); *London & Regional Investments Ltd v TBI plc* [2002] EWCA Civ. 355, [2002] All E.R.(D) 360 (Mar) (no estoppel or constructive trust where agreement was "subject to contract"); *Secretary of State for Transport v Christos* [2003] EWCA Civ. 1073, [2004] 1 P. & C.R. 17 where "equitable estoppel" is used (*e.g.* at [42]) to refer to proprietary estoppel. *Cf.* above, para.3–137 n. 720 and see the discussion of *Cobbe v Yeoman's Row Management Ltd* [2008] UKHL 55, [2008] 1 W.L.R. 1752 in paras 3–148B and 3–148C below.

[773] Above, para.2–162.

[774] [1987] 1 A.C. 114, 124.

[775] *cf.* above para.3–138; *Brinnand v Ewens* (1987) 19 H.L.R. 415; and (in a different context) *Kelly v Liverpool Maritime Terminals* [1988] I.R.L.R. 310, where authorities on proprietary estoppel are cited in a case unconnected with property.

[776] This is assumed in *Att-Gen of Hong Kong v Humphreys Estates (Queen's Gardens)*, n.721, above, where the Privy Council at 124 stresses that there had been *no* such encouragement.

[777] *Taylor v Dickens* [1998] F.L.R. 806, as explained in *Gillett v Holt* [2001] Ch. 210 at 227.

but it does not follow as a matter of law that such a promise cannot give rise to proprietary estoppel. In *Gillett v Holt*[778] the claimant had worked for nearly 40 years in the defendant's farming business in reliance on the defendant's frequently repeated promises to leave him the bulk of his estate; the claimant had also in various other ways relied on those promises. It was held that the promises were "more than a statement of revocable intention[779]; and that they were capable of giving rise, and did give rise to a proprietary estoppel.

Promise must generally be to create rights in or over promisor's property. The rights which the promisee believes to have been created must, as a general rule, be rights in or over the property of the promisor. Thus a representation by a planning authority to the effect that a landowner does not need permission to carry out development on his *own* land is not capable of giving rise to a proprietary estoppel.[780] The promisor may, however, make two promises, of which the first relates to the promisor's land while the second relates to that of the promisee; and the two promises may be so closely linked as to form in substance a single transaction. If the doctrine of proprietary estoppel applies to that transaction as a whole, then it can provide the promisee with a remedy in respect of the second promise even though that promise, standing alone, could not have given rise to proprietary estoppel because it related only to the promisee's land. In one case,[781] for example, A promised B (1) to sell Blackacre to B to enable B to build on it, and (2) to buy Whiteacre from B so that B could pay for the building operations on Blackacre. B carried out the building work envisaged in the first of A's promises and it was held that the doctrine of proprietary estoppel provided B with a remedy in respect of the second promise (which had no contractual force), even though that promise related only to B's land. But it was recognised that the doctrine could not have applied to the second promise if it had stood alone and not formed part of a transaction also relating to A's land.[782] It could not, for example, have applied if A had simply made a non-contractual promise to B to buy Whiteacre from B, knowing that B intended to use the proceeds of the sale to buy shares from C, and if B had then entered into a contract to that effect with C. Normally, the doctrine applies to promises to *grant* rights in land *to* the promisee; it only applies to promises to *acquire* such rights *from* him where they are inextricably linked with promises of the former kind. The doctrine has also been invoked to prevent the promisor from asserting rights against the promisee in land which the latter had acquired from a third party[783]; and from enforcing a charge which had been created in the promisor's favour over the promisee's land.[784] 3–145

[778] [2001] Ch. 210.

[779] *ibid.* p.228.

[780] *Western Fish Products Ltd v Penwith DC* [1981] 2 All E.R. 204 (decided in 1978); *cf. Lloyd's Bank plc v Carrick* [1996] 4 All E.R. 632 (no proprietary estoppel in favour of a purchaser of land as by virtue of the contract he had become equitable owner of the land).

[781] *Salvation Army Trustee Co v West Yorks Metropolitan CC* (1981) 41 P. & C.R. 179.

[782] *ibid.* at 191; the case was approved but distinguished in *Att.-Gen. of Hong Kong v Humphreys Estates (Queen's Gardens)* [1987] A.C. 114, 126–127.

[783] *J.S. Bloor (Meacham) Ltd v Calcott (No.2), The Times*, December 12, 2001.

[784] *S v S* [2006] EWHC 2892 (Fam), [2007] F.L.R. 1123.

3–146 **Subject-matter of the promise.** In the cases to which the doctrine has so far been applied, the subject-matter of the promise has almost always been[785] (or at least included[786]) land. There has been some conflict of judicial opinion on the question whether a promise can give rise to a proprietary estoppel where its subject-matter is property of some other kind.[787] The view that it can apply is supported by a dictum in the House of Lords[787a]; but even if the doctrine is extended to such promises, its scope will in one respect remain narrower than that of so-called promissory estoppel[788]: the promise must relate to the acquisition of an interest in the property that is the subject-matter of the promise. It is not enough that the promise should merely (in some other way) relate to property: for example, the doctrine of proprietary estoppel would not apply on the facts of *Central London Property Trust v High Trees House Ltd.*[789]

3–147 **Detrimental reliance.** The promisee must have relied on the promise or representation to his detriment.[790] The requirement has been doubted[791]; but in the absence of any such reliance it is hard to see why failure to perform a merely gratuitous promise should be regarded as giving rise to any legal liability. The element of detrimental reliance is necessary to satisfy "the essential test of unconscionability"[792] which is a necessary condition for the operation of proprietary estoppel; and the existence of the requirement is further supported by the

---

[785] See below, n.787.

[786] *Re Basham* [1987] 1 W.L.R. 1498.

[787] *Western Fish* case, above, n.780 at 217; *cf.* the reference *ibid.* at 218, and in *Crabb v Arun DC* [1976] Ch. 179, 187, to the decision of the Court of Appeal in *Moorgate Mercantile Co v Twitchings* [1976] Q.B. 225; that decision was reversed by the House of Lords: [1977] A.C. 890. For the view that proprietary estoppel is limited to cases in which the subject-matter of the promise is land, see *ibid*, at *Baird Textile Holdings Ltd v Marks & Spencer plc* [2001] EWCA Civ. 274; [2002] 1 All E.R. (Comm) 737, at [97]. In *Strover v Strover* [2005] EWHC 860, [2005] W.T.L.R. 1245 "proprietary estoppel" (at [39]) operated in relation to an insurance policy. The case was one in which the estoppel arose from a mistake and so was one of "acquiescence" as opposed to one of "assurance" or "encouragement"; and it is with cases of the latter kind that the discussion of proprietary estoppel in this chapter is concerned (see above, para.3–138).

[787a] *Cobbe v Yeoman's Row Management Ltd* [2008] UKHL 55, [2008] 1 W.L.R. 1752 at [14] per Lord Scott ("in principle equally available in relation to chattels or choses in action").

[788] See above, paras 3–085, 3–101, 3–128.

[789] [1947] K.B. 130; above, para.3–128.

[790] This was the view of the majority of the Court of Appeal in *Greasley v Cooke* [1980] 1 W.L.R. 1306; the requirement is assumed to exist in *Taylors Fashions Ltd v Liverpool Victoria Trustee Co Ltd* [1982] Q.B. 133n, and stated in *Grant v Edwards* [1986] Ch. 638, 657; *Jennings v Rice* [2002] EWCA Civ. 159; [2002] W.T.L.R. 367 at [21], [42]; *cf. Lloyds Bank plc v Rosset* [1991] 1 A.C. 107, 132; *Hammond v Mitchell* [1991] 1 W.L.R. 1127; *Van Leathem v Booker* [2005] EWCA Civ. 1478, [2006] F.C.R. 697. The fact that there was no such reliance was one reason why the claim based on proprietary estoppel failed in *Western Fish Products Ltd v Penwith DC* [1981] 2 All E.R. 204, see *ibid.*, at 217; in *Coombes v Smith* [1986] 1 W.L.R. 808; in *Att.-Gen. of Hong Kong v Humphreys Estates (Queen's Gardens)* [1987] A.C. 114; and in *H v M (Property Occupied by Wife's Parents* [2004] EWHC 625, [2004] F.L.R. 16. *cf. Mecca Leisure v The London Residuary Body* [1988] C.L.Y. 1375; *Jones v Stones* [1999] 1 W.L.R. 1739. See also *Lloyd v Dugdale* [2001] EWCA Civ. 1754; [2001] 48 E.G.C.S. 129, where the detrimental reliance was mainly by a company controlled by the promisee but also by the promisee himself and the actual result was that the promisee's claim failed against a third party to whom the land had been transferred and who had become registered proprietors of it.

[791] By Lord Denning M.R. in *Greasley v Cooke*, above n.790 at 1311.

[792] *Gillett v Holt* [2001] Ch. 210 at 232; *Jennings v Rice* [2002] EWCA Civ. 159; [2002] W.T.L.R. 367 at [21], [42]; *Kinane v Mackie-Conteh* [2005] EWCA Civ. 45, [2005] W.T.L.R. 345 at [29];

rules (to be discussed below) as to the revocability of the promise.[793] The detriment must be "substantial," *i.e.* such as to make it "unjust or inequitable to allow the assurance to be disregarded"[794]; and the question whether it has this character is to be judged "as at the moment when the person who has given the assurance seeks to go back on it."[795] Where a promise has been made which is capable of inducing detrimental reliance, and which is in fact followed by such reliance, the question may arise whether the reliance was actually induced by the promise. The burden on this issue is on the promisor: that is, it is up to the promisor, in order to escape liability, to show that the promisee would have done the acts in question anyway (even if the promise had not been made).[796] The position appears to be different where a proprietary estoppel arises because both parties have acted under a mistake as to their rights in the land.[797] Here it seems to be up to the party relying on the proprietary estoppel to show that his conduct in relation to the property was in fact induced by his belief that he had an interest in it.[798]

Whether reliance must relate to specific property. The authorities are divided on the further question whether, to give rise to a proprietary estoppel, the reliance must relate to identifiable property. According to one case, the promisee's conduct must relate to "some specific asset" in which an interest is claimed; so that proprietary estoppel did not arise merely because B rendered services to A in the expectation of receiving some indeterminate benefit under A's will.[799] But in another case reliance on a similar expectation (induced by A's promise) was held to be sufficient even though it did not relate to any "particular property."[800] The latter case can perhaps be explained on the ground that the promise did to some extent identify the property.[801] It is submitted that the view that the promise must relate to identified or identifiable property is to be preferred[801a]; for without some such limitation on the scope of proprietary estoppel the doctrine could extend to any gift promise on which the promisee had 3–148

Hopper v Hopper [2008] EWHC 228 (CL), [2008] I F.C.R 557 at [111]; "unconscionability" is a necessary, but not a sufficient condition for the operation of proprietary estoppel: see the discussion of *Cobbe v Yeoman's Row Management Ltd* [2008] UKHL 55, [2008] 1 W.L.R. 1752 in para.3–148B below.

[793] Below, para.3–149.

[794] *Gillett v Holt*, above n.792, at 232.

[795] *ibid.*

[796] *Greasley v Cooke*, above; *Grant v Edwards* [1986] Ch. 638, 657; *Re Basham* [1986] 1 W.L.R. 1498; *Hammersmith & Fulham BC v Top Shop Centres Ltd* [1990] Ch. 237; *Wayling v Jones* (1993) 69 P. & C.R. 170, 172.

[797] Above, para.3–138.

[798] *Taylors Fashions Ltd v Liverpool Victoria Trustee Co Ltd* [1982] Q.B. 133 note; *cf. Coombes v Smith* [1986] 1 W.L.R. 808.

[799] *Layton v Martin* [1986] 2 F.L.R. 277.

[800] *Re Basham* [1986] 1 W.L.R. 1498, 1508.

[801] By referring to the promisor's cottage. In *Gillett v Holt* [2001] Ch. 210 the property was likewise identified, if not very precisely; *cf. Jennings v Rice* [2002] EWCA Civ. 159; [2002] W.T.L.R. 367, at [50], where the promise again related in part to the promisor's house.

[801a] This view is supported, though perhaps not conclusively, by repeated references in Lord Scott's speech in *Cobbe v Yeoman's Row Management Ltd* [2008] UKHL 55, [2008] 1 W.L.R. 1752 at [18], [19], [20] to a "certain interest in land" and at [28] to "clarity as to the interest in the property". If there is no certainty or clarity in "the property" it is unlikely for this requirement to be satisfied with regard to the "interest" in it.

relied to his detriment. Such a very broad doctrine would be fundamentally inconsistent with the doctrine of consideration[802] and, indeed, with the rule that the doctrine of *promissory* estoppel gives rise to no new rights.[803]

3–148A **Further requirements.** Further requirements for the operation of proprietary estoppel were laid down in the decision of the House of Lords in *Cobbe v Yeoman's Row Management Ltd.*[803a] In that case an oral agreement "in principle" had been reached between a landowner (D) and a property developer (C). The purpose of the agreement was to secure the redevelopment and disposal of residential property owned by D, but the agreement lacked contractual force as it left significant aspects of the scheme to be settled by further negotiation,[803b] and then to be embodied in a formal agreement, between the parties, each of whom regarded the agreement at this stage as binding in honour only. C made considerable efforts and incurred considerable expense in securing the necessary planning permission; but on the day when the planning authority resolved to grant the permission D withdrew from the agreement. In the lower courts,[803c] this conduct on D's part was, by reason of its unconscionableness, regarded as "sufficient to justify the creation of a 'proprietary estoppel equity' " in favour of C.[803d] Their decision was reversed by the House of Lords which held that C had no such proprietary claim.

3–148B In discussing the proprietary estoppel claim,[803e] Lord Scott said that "to treat a 'proprietary estoppel equity' as requiring . . . simply unconscionable behaviour" was a "recipe for confusion"[803f] and he listed two further "ingredients for a proprietary estoppel . . . These ingredients should include, in principle, a proprietary claim made by a claimant and an answer to that claim based on some fact, or some point of mixed fact and law, that the person against whom the claim is made can be estopped from asserting".[803g] He in substance repeated these points in a later passage: "Proprietary estoppel requires . . . clarity as to what it is that the object of the estoppel [*i.e.*, the defendant] is to be estopped from denying, or asserting, and clarity as to the interest in the property in question that that denial, or assertion, would otherwise defeat. If these requirements are not

[802] *e.g.* above, paras 3–002, 3–026. For this reason, *Evans v HSBC Trust Co (UK) Ltd* [2005] W.T.L.R. 1298 may, with respect, be doubted. The promise which was held there to have given rise to a proprietary estoppel was one that the promisee would inherit the whole of promisor's estate. This did indeed, at least in general terms, identify the relevant property. But the acts done in reliance on the promise did not in any way either relate to the property or benefit the promisor. While the latter factor is not decisive (see above, para.3–141) the combination of both of them seems to reduce the case to one of mere action in reliance on a gratuitous promise. The judgment recognises that mere change of position does not suffice to give rise to proprietary estoppel (at [73]) but does not explain what additional factors in the case justified the application of the doctrine.

[803] Above, para.3–098.

[803a] [2008] UKHL 55, [2008] 1 W.L.R. 1752.

[803b] Above, para.2–110.

[803c] [2005] EWHC 266 (Ch), [2005] W.T.L.R. 625; [2006] EWCA Civ 1139, [2006] 1 W.L.R. 2964.

[803d] [2008] UKHL 55, [2008] 1 W.L.R. 1752 at [28].

[803e] With whose speech Lord Hoffman; Brown and (except on a point relating to the amount of the *quantum meruit* claim: see at [44], [96] Lord Mance agreed.

[803f] [2008] UKHL 55, [2008] 1 W.L.R. 1752 at [16].

[803g] *ibid.* at [16].

recognised, proprietary estoppel will . . . risk becoming unprincipled and therefore unpredictable, if it has not already done so."[803h] In the *Cobbe* case, neither requirement was satisfied since the "agreement in principle", was, as C knew, incomplete and binding in honour only, so that C could not allege that D was bound by it; and since, at the time of D's withdrawal, C was not asserting any expectation that he would acquire a proprietary right.[803i] His expectation was "the wrong sort of expectation"[803j]; namely one that further negotiations between him and D would fill the gaps in the "agreement in principle" and that the agreement, thus completed, would be embodied in a formal written agreement and so become a binding contract. He was expecting to get a contractual, rather than a proprietary, right.[803k]

Lord Walker[803l] also rejected the claim based on proprietary estoppel (which he calls "equitable estoppel").[803m] His policy reasons for so doing seem to resemble (though they are not expressed in the same language as) Lord Scott's. While accepting the flexibility of the doctrine, Lord Walker starts with the point that it is "not a sort of joker or wild card to be used whenever the Court disapproves of the conduct of a litigant who seems to have the law on his side"[803n] since, if it were so used, it would impair the certainty which was important in property transactions, especially in those of a commercial nature.[803o] This reasoning can be said to resemble Lord Scott's view that such a broad application of proprietary estoppel would be a "recipe for confusion"[803p]; but Lord Walker's reasons for rejecting the proprietary estoppel claim seem to differ in a number of important respects from those given in support of the same conclusion by Lord Scott. First, Lord Scott's two "ingredients for a proprietary estoppel" (discussed in paragraph 3–148B above) have no counterpart in Lord Walker's speech. Secondly (and conversely) Lord Walker's main ground for dismissing the proprietary estoppel claim has no counterpart in Lord Scott's speech. That ground was stated by Lord Walker to be that C's proprietary estoppel claim "seems to me to fail on the simple but fundamental point that, as persons experienced in the property world, both parties knew that there was no legally binding contract, and that either was free to discontinue the negotiations without legal liability, that is liability in equity as well as at law. [C] was therefore running a risk . . He ran a commercial risk with his eyes open,"[803q] 3–148C

[803h] *ibid.* at [26]. The concluding words of this passage may contain an implied criticism of recent decisions but it is not clear at which, if any, such decisions that criticism is directed. Lord Walker at [66] cites a number of such cases without adverse comment.

[803i] [2008] UKHL 55, [2008] 1 W.L.R. 1752 at [15]. C's constructive trust claim also failed (at [30]–[38]) for reasons beyond the scope of this chapter.

[803j] [2008] UKHL 55, [2008] 1 W.L.R. 1752 at [20].

[803k] C's claim for specific performance of the "agreement in principle" had been abandoned as that agreement was not enforceable: [2008] UKHL 55, [2008] 1 W.L.R. 1752 at [9], so that it was not open to him to argue that he had, by virtue of that agreement, become owner in equity of the property.

[803l] With whose speech Lord Brown agreed.

[803m] See above, para.3–137 n.720.

[803n] [2008] UKHL 55, [2008] 1 W.L.R. 1752 at [46].

[803o] *ibid.* at [81].

[803p] *ibid.* at [16]; above para.3–148A at n. 803f.

[803q] [2008] UKHL 55, [2008] 1 W.L.R. 1752 at [91].

Lord Scott makes no express reference to *this* risk, though it may be reflected in his discussion of the reasons why the first of the "ingredients" of proprietary estoppel (discussed in paragraph 3–148B above) had not been established. The only "risks" to which Lord Scott expressly refers as having been taken by C were the different risks "that planning permission might be refused" and that the enterprise "might leave him with an inadequate profit or even none at all."[803r] Thirdly, Lord Scott rejects the proprietary estoppel claim in spite of the fact that D's conduct was "unconscionable", regarding that circumstance as not "sufficient to justify the creation of a 'proprietary estoppel equity' ".[803s] Lord Walker, by contrast, rejects that claim on the further [803t] ground that C "knew that [D] was bound in honour only, and so in the eyes of equity her [D's] conduct, although unattractive, was not unconscionable".[803u] It may be that this difference between the two speeches can be explained on the ground that Lord Scott was concerned to deny that unconscionable conduct was a *sufficient*, while Lord Walker's point was that such conduct was a *necessary*, condition for the operation of proprietary estoppel; or perhaps on the ground that Lord Scott was concerned with conduct that was actually unconscionable while Lord Walker's reference was to conduct that was unconscionable by virtue of a legal fiction.[803v]

3–148D **Quantum meruit.** Although in *Cobbe v Yeoman's Row Management Ltd*[803w] C's proprietary estoppel claim failed for the reasons given in paragraphs 3–148B and 3–148C above, C was not sent away empty handed. Such an outcome would have had the effect of leaving D with an enrichment in the form of the enhanced value of D's property as a result of the planning permission; and this enrichment, having been obtained at the expense of C, would have been unjust.[803x] C was therefore entitled to a *quantum meruit* on the basis of having rendered services in pursuance of a contract which was expected to materialise but never came into existence.[803y] This *quantum meruit* was to cover, not only the value of C's services, but also his expenses reasonably incurred in making and prosecuting the planning application (those expenses being necessary to secure the planning permission which had enhanced the value of the property); it was, on the other hand, subject to C's making the architect's plans used to secure that permission available to D.[803z] Some care is, however, needed in defining the limits of such a remedy in cases of this kind. Such a *quantum meruit* might not be available where a party to an anticipated contract which failed to materialise had taken the risk of events that turned out to his disadvantage. In the *Cobbe* case, C took two such risks: that planning permission might be refused[803aa] and that no binding

---

[803r] *ibid.* at [6].

[803s] *ibid.* at [28].

[803t] *i.e.* in addition to the ground stated by him at [91], above at n.803q.

[803u] [2008] UKHL 55, [2008] 1 W.L.R. 1752 at [92].

[803v] *ibid.* at [92] ("in the eyes of equity").

[803w] [2008] UKHL 55, [2008] 1 W.L.R. 1752

[803x] *ibid.* at [40] and see below at nn.803ac and 803ad.

[803y] [2008] UKHL 55, [2008] 1 W.L.R. 1752 at [42].

[803z] *ibid.* at [45] and [93].

[803aa] *ibid.* at [6].

contract might come into existence.[803ab] In the first of those situations, D would not be enriched so that there would seem to be no basis for the *quantum meruit* claim. In the second situation, there was such anenrichment and the enrichment was unjust on account of either the unconscionable[803ac] or at least the unattractive[803ad] conduct of D. It was this combination of circumstances that justified the remedy by way of a *quantum meruit* in the *Cobbe* case.

(d) *Effects of the Doctrine*

Revocability. We have seen that proprietary estoppel will not arise at all where the promise to confer a benefit on the promisee is revocable in the sense that it reserves a power to the promisor wholly to deprive the promisee of that benefit.[804] But even where the promise does not allow the promisor do this, and so is capable of giving rise to a proprietary estoppel, the extent of the promisee's rights under the estoppel may be limited by terms of the promise giving the promisor a power of putting an end to those rights. Thus if the landowner promises to allow the promisee to stay on the land "until I decide to sell," then the promisee cannot, merely by spending money on improvements to the land, acquire any right to stay there for a longer period.[805] Even where the promise is not expressed to be revocable, it can be revoked before the promisee has acted on it. Thus in *Dillwyn v Llewelyn*[806] it seems that the father could have revoked his promise before the son had started to build on the land[807]; and in *Crabb v Arun DC*[808] the promise to grant a right of way could have been revoked before the promisee, by selling off part of his land, had made it impossible for himself to obtain access to the retained land except by means of the promised right of way. In this respect proprietary estoppel resembles so-called promissory estoppel (under which promises are similarly revocable[809]) and differs from contractually binding promises which are not revocable unless they expressly, or impliedly, so provide. The cases on proprietary estoppel assume that, once the requisite action in reliance on the representation has taken place, the promisee cannot be restored to his original position. Where he has made improvements to land, this will generally be the case. Where a restoration of the status quo is physically possible, it seems that a promise giving rise to a proprietary estoppel could be revoked, even after the promisee had acted on it, provided that the promisor in fact restored the promisee to the position in which he was before he had acted in reliance on the promise. 3–149

A promise which has given rise to proprietary estoppel may also be none the less revocable, because the court considers it appropriate in this way to limit the

---

[803ab] *ibid.* at [91]; above, para.3–147C.

[803ac] [2008] UKHL 55, [2008] 1 W.L.R. 1752 at [40], where "the circumstances that I need not again rehearse" (per Lord Scott) seem to refer back to [13] and [16].

[803ad] *ibid.* at [92] (per Lord Walker).

[804] Above, para.3–144.

[805] *E. & L. Berg Homes v Gray* (1979) 253 E.G. 473.

[806] (1862) D. F. & G. 517; above, para.3–139.

[807] *cf. Pascoe v Turner* [1979] 1 W.L.R. 431, 435 (where before the promisee's action in reliance on the promise she was said to have been only a licensee at will).

[808] [1976] Ch. 179; above, para.3–140.

[809] Above, para.3–096.

effect to be given to the promise. This situation is discussed in para.3–151 below.[810]

3–150 **Operation of a proprietary estoppel.** Where the conditions required to give rise to a proprietary estoppel have been satisfied, the effect of the doctrine is said to be to confer an "equity" on the promisee. Two further questions then arise: namely, what is the extent of that "equity," and what are the remedies for its enforcement.[811] In practice these questions tend to merge into each other; but an attempt to discuss them in turn will be made in paras 3–151 to 3–153 and 3–154—3–159 below.

3–151 **Extent of the equity.** At one extreme, the promisee may be entitled to conveyance of the fee simple in the property which is the subject-matter of the promise, as in *Dillwyn v Llewelyn*.[812] On the other hand, in *Inwards v Baker*,[813] where a son had also built a house for himself at his father's suggestion on the latter's land, the result of the estoppel was only to entitle the son to occupy the house for life. Similar results were reached in a number of later cases in which the promisee made improvements to the promisor's property (or otherwise acted to his detriment) in reliance on a promise, or common understanding, that the promisee would be able to reside in the property for as long as he or she wished to do so[814]; or for some shorter period: *e.g.* until her children had left school[815]; or that a lease of the premises would be granted to him[816]; or that he was entitled to an equitable charge on the land.[817] Such cases can be reconciled with *Dillwyn v Llewelyn* by reference to the terms of the respective promises[818]: in the former case, the promise was expressed in terms of a gift of the property, while in the latter cases it amounted to no more than an assurance that the promisee would be entitled to reside in the property for the specified period. Another way of giving effect to a promise of the latter kind is by the grant of a long, non-assignable lease at a nominal rent, on terms that ensured that the right of occupation was personal to the promisee.[819] In other cases, not concerned with rights of personal occupation but with the right to keep and use structures on promisor's land, the promisee has been held entitled only to a revocable licence.[820]

---

[810] At n.820.

[811] *Crabb v Arun DC* [1976] Ch. 179, 193, *per* Scarman L.J.

[812] (1862) D. F. & G. 517; above, para.3–139; *Durant v Heritage* [1994] E.G.C.S. 134; or, in the exceptional cases discussed in para.3–145, nn.781–783, to orders enforcing the promises in those cases.

[813] [1965] 2 Q.B. 507; above, para.3–139, n.732.

[814] *Jones v Jones* [1977] 1 W.L.R. 438; *Re Sharpe* [1980] 1 W.L.R. 219; *Greasley v Cooke* [1980] 1 W.L.R. 1306.

[815] *Tanner v Tanner* [1975] 1 W.L.R. 1346 (where there was a contract: *cf.* above, para.3–142); *Yaxley v Gotts* [2000] Ch. 162 (where the remedy was based on constructive trust).

[816] *J.T. Developments v Quinn* (1991) 62 P. & C.R. 33.

[817] As in *Kinane v Mackie-Conteh* [2005] EWCA Civ. 45, [2005] W.T.L.R. 345: see at [1], [36].

[818] *cf. Kinane v Mackie-Conteh* [2005] EWCA Civ. 45, [2005] W.T.L.R. 345 at [33] ("a remedy appropriate to the expectations that the defendant has indeed"; the last word of this phrase appears to be a misprint, probably for "induced").

[819] *Griffiths v Williams* [1978] E.G.D. 919; *cf. Jones v Jones* [1977] 1 W.L.R. 438.

[820] *Canadian Pacific Railway v The King* [1931] A.C. 414; *Armstrong v Sheppard & Short* [1959] Q.B. 384; *cf. Clark v Clark* [2006] EWHC 275, [2006] 1 F.C.R. 421 (proprietary estoppel held to give

Estoppel available against third party donee. Where the circumstances are such as to give rise to an estoppel against the landowner, the estoppel is equally available against a third party who claims later to have obtained title to the land by way of gift from the landowner.[821] 3–152

Estoppel may operate conditionally. The estoppel may operate conditionally where the promisee has acted in reliance on the promise but the terms of the promise show that the promisor did not intend to give up his title to the land gratuitously. This was the position in *Lim Teng Huan v Ang Swee Chuan*[822] where A built a house on land jointly owned by him and L, who had agreed that he was to have no title to the house and would exchange his share in the land for other land. The arrangement had no contractual force as the other land was not identified with sufficient certainty; and it was held that L was estopped from asserting title to the house but that he was entitled to be compensated for the loss of his share in the land. Similarly, where the promise is one to allow the promisee access to his own land over that of the promisor, the effect of the proprietary estoppel will be to entitle the promisee to an easement or licence on terms.[823] Such terms, if not agreed between the parties, may be imposed by the court: they can specify the extent of the permitted user as well as any payment that the promisee may be required to make for the exercise of the right.[824] However, an order for such payment may not be appropriate where the promisor has already obtained other benefits under the agreement.[825] It may also be inappropriate for other reasons to be discussed in para.3–156 below. 3–153

Remedy: principled discretion. The remedy in cases of proprietary estoppel is "extremely flexible", its object being "to do what is equitable in all the circumstances."[826] Although the court thus has a considerable discretion with regard to the remedy in cases of proprietary estoppel, that discretion is not a "completely unfettered"[827] one and a "principled approach"[828] must be taken to its exercise. In giving effect to the "equity"[829] account must be taken, not only of the claimant's expectations "but also of the extent of his detrimental reliance"[830–831]; and there must also be "proportionality between the expectation and the detriment."[832] For the purpose of achieving such "proportionality" 3–154

rise to temporary right of access to land for so long as it continued to be used by one party for the purpose of a business originally carried on by both parties jointly).

[821] *Voyce v Voyce* (1991) 62 P. & C.R. 290.

[822] [1991] 1 W.L.R. 113.

[823] *E.R. Ives Investments Ltd v High* [1967] 2 Q.B. 379; *Crabb v Arun DC* [1976] Ch. 179.

[824] *Crabb v Arun DC*, above n.823, at 199.

[825] As in *E.R. Ives Investments Ltd v High* [1967] 2 Q.B. 379.

[826] *Roebuck v Mungovin* [1994] 2 A.C. 224 at 235; *cf.* the remedy granted in *Gillett v Holt* [2001] Ch. 210, below, para.3–158. Gardner, (1999) 115 L.Q.R. 348. For the flexibility of the remedy in cases of proprietary estoppel, see also *Gillett v Holt* [2001] Ch. 210, below para.3–158; *Clark v Clark* [2006] EWHC 725, [2006] 1 F.C.R. 421, above, para.3–151; and *Thorner v Curtis* [2007] EWHC 2422 (Ch), [2008] W.T.L.R. 155; *Hopper v Hopper* [2008] EWHC 228 (Ch), [2008] I F.C.R. 557.

[827] *Jennings v Rice* [2002] EWCA Civ. 159; [2002] W.T.L.R. 367 at [43].

[828] *ibid.*

[829] See above, para.3–151.

[830–831] *Jennings v Rice*, above, n.827 at [49].

[832] *Jennings v Rice*, above n.827 at [36]; *cf. ibid.* at [56] ("proportionality (between remedy and detriment)"). For the relevance of the promisor's conduct *after* the facts giving rise to the estoppel, see below, para.3–156.

regard must be had to the degree of precision of the promise giving rise to the expectation. Where this amounts to an assurance that an interest in specific property will be transferred in return for specified acts, then an order for the specific enforcement of that promise (once the acts have been done) may be the appropriate remedy.[833] Where, on the other hand, the terms of the promise are less precise, amounting only to an assurance that some indeterminate benefit will be conferred on the promisee, so that the expectations reasonably arising from it are, at least objectively, uncertain, then the court will not give effect in full to expectations which the promisee may in fact have formed if they are "uncertain or extravagant or out of all proportion to the detriment which the claimant has suffered."[834] In such cases, compensation in money is likely to be the more appropriate remedy. That compensation must be proportionate to the detriment, but need not be its precise equivalent[835]: the fact that the detriment was incurred in response to a promise indicating (though in vague terms) some higher level of recompense is also to be taken into account.

3–155 **Illustrations of exercise of the discretion.** The balancing of the factors discussed in paragraph 3–154 above is well illustrated by *Jennings v Rice*[836] where for some 17 years the claimant had worked as gardener-handyman for an elderly widow without pay and had also provided personal care for her in the years of increasing frailty towards the end of her life. He had done so in response to her statements that "he would be alright" and that "all this will be yours one day".[837] The latter statement referred to her house and its contents, valued on her death at £435,000 out of a total estate of £1.285 million. The Court of Appeal upheld an award of £200,000 as being properly proportionate to the detriment suffered by the claimant in reliance on the assurances given to him. In cases of this kind, the amount recoverable may be further reduced by the amount of lifetime gifts made by the promisor to the promisee.[838–848]

3–156 **Conduct of promisor.** Apart from the factors discussed in paras 3–154 and 3–155 above the court may also take into account the conduct of the promisor after the facts giving rise to the estoppel. Thus in *Crabb v Arun DC*[849] the defendants had acted without warning in blocking the claimant's access to his land. In view of this "high-handedness"[850] and the resulting loss to the claimant, he was not required to make the payment that would otherwise have been a

[833] *ibid.* at [45].
[834] *ibid.* at [50].
[835] *ibid.* at [51].
[836] [2002] EWCA Civ. 159, [2005] W.T.L.R. 367. For the flexibility of the remedy, see also the decision of the Court of Appeal in *Cobbe v Yeoman's Row Management Ltd* [2006] EWCA 1139, 2006 1 W.L.R. 2964. This decision was reversed by the House of Lords ([2008] UKHL 55, [2008] 1 W.L.R. 1752, above paras 3–148A to 3–148D) on the ground that, on the facts, no proprietary estoppel arose. The speeches in the House of Lords therefore contain no discussion of what remedy might have been appropriate if a proprietary estoppel had arisen.
[837] At [9].
[838–848] *Evans v HSBC Trust Co (UK) Ltd* [2005] W.T.L.R. 1289, as to which see above, para.3–148 n.802.
[849] [1976] Ch. 179; above, para.3–141.
[850] [1976] Ch. at 199; *cf. ibid.* at 189.

condition of the exercise of the right of way. Similarly, in *Pascoe v Turner*[851] a proprietary estoppel arose when a man told a woman with whom he had formerly cohabited that the house in which they had lived was hers, and she later spent some £230 of her limited resources on repairs and improvements to it. The Court of Appeal relied on the man's "ruthlessness"[852] in seeking to evict the promisee as a ground for ordering him to convey the fee simple to her. The submission that she should have no more than a licence to occupy the house was rejected since this would not protect her against a bona fide purchaser from the promisor. The result seems, with respect, unduly punitive; and intermediate possibilities (such as granting the promisee a long lease[853]) were not put before the court.

Compensation in money. *Pascoe v Turner* illustrates the possibility that the grant of an irrevocable licence to remain on the property may constitute an unsatisfactory remedy because it will not adequately secure the promisee's possession. It may also be unsatisfactory on account of its inflexibility: thus in *Inwards v Baker*[854] this remedy would have been of no use to the promisee, had he wanted to move elsewhere; nor would his dependants have had any remedy, had he died shortly after completing the house. In such cases a remedy by way of compensation in money would be more satisfactory for the promisee; and it would also have the advantage for the promisor that he would not be impeded in dealing with the property for an indefinite time.[855] Such a remedy was granted in *Dodsworth v Dodsworth*[856] where the promisees spent £700 on improvements to the promisor's bungalow in reliance on an implied promise (not intended to have contractual force) that they could live there as if it were their home. The Court of Appeal held that to give the promisees a right of occupation for an indefinite time would confer on them a greater interest than had been contemplated by the parties; and that the most appropriate remedy was to repay them their outlay on improvements. Compensation in money will also be the more appropriate remedy where, as a practical matter, the promise which gave rise to the estoppel cannot be specifically enforced: for example, where its performance would involve joint occupation of premises by, and co-operation between, members of a family who later quarrel,[857] or between a couple whose relationship has broken down.[858] Where there is evidence that the improved property has increased in 3–157

[851] [1979] 1 W.L.R. 431.

[852] *ibid.* at 439. *cf.* the reference in *Gillett v Holt* [2001] Ch. 210 at 235 to the promisee's "bitter humiliation" on being summarily dismissed and made the subject of a police investigation for allegations of dishonesty which the promisor made no attempt to justify at the trial of the civil action.

[853] As in *Griffiths v Williams* [1978] E.G. 919; above, para.3–151.

[854] [1965] 2 Q.B. 507; above, para.3–139.

[855] *cf.* criticisms of the law by Browne-Wilkinson J. in *Re Sharpe* [1980] 1 W.L.R. 219, 226.

[856] [1973] E.G.D. 233; to the extent that the reasoning is based on the provisions of Settled Land Act 1925, s.1, it is criticised in *Griffiths v Williams* [1978] E.G.D. 919. *cf. Campbell v Griffin* [2001] EWCA Civ. 990, [2001] W.T.L.R. 981; *Jennings v Rice* [2002] EWCA Civ. 159; [2002] W.T.L.R. 367, above para.3–155; *Evans v HSBC Trust (UK) Ltd* [2005] W.T.L.R. 1299, above, para.3–148.

[857] *Burrows and Burrows v Sharp* (1991) 23 H.L.R. 82; *cf. Baker v Baker* (1993) 25 H.L.R. 408 (where the action was for damages).

[858] *Clough v Kelly* (1996) 72 P. & C.R. D22.

value by reason of market fluctuations, it is submitted that the amount recoverable by the promisee should be increased correspondingly; conversely, it should be reduced where the market value of the property has declined.[859]

3–158 In *Dodsworth v Dodsworth*[860] the court awarded compensation even though, when the action was brought, the promisee was still in possession of the improved property. More commonly this form of remedy is granted where the promisee is no longer in possession, having either left voluntarily[861] or been lawfully ejected as a result of legal proceedings.[862] Where the promisee has been wrongly ordered to give up possession, compensation in money is similarly available,[863] though in such a case the court may alternatively order the promisee to be put back into possession of the premises.[864] The compensation has been assessed in a variety of ways: at the cost of improvements made with the promisee's money[865]; at a proportionate interest in the property[866]; at the reasonable value of the right of occupation, based (presumably) on the cost to the promisee of equivalent alternative accommodation[867]; or by applying the more general principle that the remedy in cases of proprietary estoppel must reflect the reasonable expectations of the promisee and be proportionate to the detriment suffered by him in reliance on the promise.[868] The flexibility of the remedy also enables the court to combine monetary compensation with specific relief: for example, in *Gillett v Holt*[869] the promisee was awarded part of the property to which the promise referred, together with a cash payment to compensate him for his exclusion from the farming business on that property.

3–159 **Balance of hardship.** The court may deny the promisee a remedy where, on balance, greater hardship would be produced by giving effect to the promise than by allowing the promisor to go back on it. This was the position in *Sledmore v Dalby*,[870] where the promisee had contributed to major improvements to the property but at the time of the proceedings had already enjoyed 20 years' rent-free occupation and was gainfully employed, while the promisor was a widow living on social security benefits. The promisee's claim to be entitled to a licence for life to stay in the house was in these circumstances rejected and the promisor was held entitled to possession. In deciding on the amount of monetary compensation, the court can also take account of the interests of third parties, such as blood relatives of the promisor with whom the latter had been on close terms.[871]

---

[859] *cf.*, in a case of undue influence. *Cheese v Thomas* [1994] 1 W.L.R. 129.
[860] above, n.856.
[861] As in *Hussey v Palmer* [1972] 1 W.L.R. 1286 and *Eves v Eves* [1975] 1 W.L.R. 1328.
[862] As in *Plimmer v Mayor of Wellington* (1884) 9 App. Cas. 699.
[863] *Tanner v Tanner* [1975] 1 W.L.R. 1346 (where there was a contract).
[864] *ibid.*
[865] *Hussey v Palmer* [1972] 1 W.L.R. 1286; *Burrows and Burrows v Sharp* (1991) 23 H.L.R. 82.
[866] *Eves v Eves* [1975] 1 W.L.R. 1338.
[867] *Tanner v Tanner* [1975] 1 W.L.R. 1346; *Baker v Baker* (1993) 25 H.L.R. 408.
[868] Above, paras 3–154, 3–155.
[869] [2001] Ch. 210; above, para.3–144.
[870] (1996) 72 P. & C.R. 196.
[871] *Evans v HSBC Trust Co (UK) Ltd* [2005] W.T.L.R. 1299, above para.3–148.

(e) *Comparison with other Doctrines*

3–160 **Proprietary and promissory estoppels.** Proprietary and promissory estoppels have a number of points in common. Both can arise from promises[872]; consideration is not, while action in reliance is, a necessary condition for their operation[873]; and both are, within limits, revocable.[874] Perhaps for this reason, Lord Scott has described "proprietary" estoppel as "a sub-species of 'promissory' estoppel—if the right claimed is a proprietary right".[874a] But there are also important differences between the two doctrines.

3–161 **Proprietary estoppel in some respects narrower than promissory estoppel.** The scope of proprietary is in two respects narrower than that of promissory estoppel. First, proprietary estoppel is restricted to situations in which one party acts under the belief that he has or will be granted an interest in or over the property (generally the land) of another. A promissory estoppel may, on the other hand, arise out of *any* promise that strict legal rights will not be enforced: there is no need for those rights to relate to land or other property. Secondly, proprietary estoppel requires the promisee to have acted to his detriment,[875] while promissory estoppel may operate even though the promisee merely performs a pre-existing duty and so suffers no detriment in the sense of doing something that he was not previously bound to do.[876] This difference between the two doctrines follows from the fact that promissory estoppel is (unlike proprietary estoppel) concerned only with the variation or abandonment of rights arising out of a pre-existing legal relationship between promisor and promisee.

3–162 **Proprietary estoppel in other respects wider than promissory estoppel.** On the other hand, the scope of proprietary is in two other respects wider than that of promissory estoppel. First, promissory estoppel arises only out of a representation or promise that is "clear" or "precise and unambiguous."[877] There is no such requirement in the case of a proprietary estoppel[878]: this can arise where there is no actual promise: for example, where one party makes improvements to another's land under a mistake and the other either knows of the mistake[879] or seeks to take unconscionable advantage of it.[880] Secondly (and

---

[872] Above, paras 3–089, 3–138. For use of the expression "promissory estoppel" see above, para.3–103.

[873] Above, paras 3–093, 3–139.

[874] Above, paras 3–096, 3–149.

[874a] *Cobbe v Yeoman's Row Management Ltd* [2008] UKHL 55, [2008] 1 W.L.R. 1752 at [14]; the dictum does not go on to consider the differences between the two doctrines discussed in paras 3–161 and 3–162 below.

[875] Above, para.3–147.

[876] Above, para.3–094.

[877] Above, para.3–090.

[878] See above, para.3–142; but in *Cobbe v Yeoman's Row Management Ltd* [2008] UKHL 55, [2008] 1 W.L.R. 1752 (above, paras 3–148A to 3–148D) it was held that no such estoppel arose out of an agreement which lacked contractual force as it was incomplete and *known* by the party claiming the benefit of the estoppel to be binding in honour only.

[879] *Wilmott v Barber* (1880) 15 Ch.D. 96, 105 (the claim in that case failed as the party against whom it was made did not know of the extent of his own rights or of the other party's mistake).

[880] *Taylors Fashions Ltd v Liverpool Victoria Trustee Co Ltd* [1982] Q.B. 133.

most significantly), while promissory estoppel is essentially defensive in nature,[881] proprietary estoppel can give rise to a cause of action.[882] The promisee is not merely entitled to raise the estoppel as a defence to an action of trespass or to a claim for possession: the court can make an order for the land to be conveyed to him,[883] or for compensation[884] or for such other remedy as it regards as appropriate in the exercise of its "principled discretion".[885] Although the authorities support this second distinction between the two kinds of estoppel, they do not make any attempt to explain or justify it. It is submitted that the explanation is in part historical and terminological. In the early cases, proprietary estoppel was explained in terms of *acquiescence*[886] or *encouragement*.[887] Hence no conflict with the requirement that *promises* must be supported by consideration was perceived; or where it was perceived the facts were said to give rise to a contract.[888] Promissory estoppel, on the other hand, dealt principally with the renegotiation of contracts; it obviously depended on giving binding effect to promises, and did so in the context of releases and variations, in which the common law requirement of consideration had long been established.[889] The rule that promissory estoppel gives rise to no cause of action was evolved to prevent what would otherwise have been an obvious conflict between promissory estoppel and consideration.[890] In cases of proprietary estoppel there was no such conflict where liability was based on "acquiescence"; and where it was based on "encouragement" the conflict, though sometimes real enough, was at least less obvious. There are, moreover, two aspects of proprietary estoppel which help to justify the distinction. These are that the acts done by the promisee are not ones which he was under any previous legal obligation to perform; and that generally their effect would be unjustly to enrich the promisor if he were allowed to go back on his promise.[891] In these respects, the facts on which proprietary estoppel is based provide more compelling grounds for relief[892] than those commonly found in cases of promissory estoppel.

3–163 **Common basis of proprietary and promissory estoppel?** While the two doctrines are in the above respects distinct it can also be argued that they have a common basis, *viz.* that it would be unconscionable for the promisor to go back on his promise after the promisee has acted in reliance on it; and that the precise

---

[881] Above, para.3–098.

[882] *Crabb v Arun DC* [1976] Ch. 179, 187; *Taylors Fashions Ltd v Liverpool Victoria Trustee Co Ltd* [1982] Q.B. 133, 148.

[883] *e.g. Dillwyn v Llewelyn* (1862) 4 D. F. & G. 517.

[884] *e.g. Eves v Eves* [1975] 1 W.L.R. 1338.

[885] See above, paras 3–154, 3–155.

[886] *Wilmott v Barber* (1880) 15 Ch.D. 96, 105.

[887] *Ramsden v Dyson* (1866) L.R. 1 H.L. 129, 170.

[888] *Dillwyn v Llewelyn* (1862) 4 D. F. & G. 517, 522; above, para.3–142.

[889] Above, paras 3–077—3–080.

[890] See above, para.3–098.

[891] See the reference to the landowner's "profit" in *Ramsden v Dyson* (1866) L.R. 1 H.L. 129, 141 and *cf.* above, para.3–139.

[892] See Fuller and Eisenberg, *Basic Contract Law* (3rd ed.), p.70; "Unjust enrichment presents a more urgent case for judicial intervention than losses through reliance which do not benefit the defendant." *cf.* Fuller and Perdue (1936) 46 Yale L.J. 52, 56.

labels to be attached to them are "immaterial."[893] It is perhaps for these reasons that the distinction between the two kinds of estoppel was described as "not . . . helpful" by Scarman L.J. in *Crabb v Arun DC*.[894] That decision was, in a later case, said to illustrate "a virtual equation of promissory and proprietary estoppel,"[895] perhaps because it extended the operation of proprietary estoppel beyond the situations originally within its scope, *viz.* those in which the promisor would be unjustly enriched by the work done by the promisee on the promisor's land unless some legal effect were given to the promise. Nevertheless it is submitted that the doctrines are distinct in the respects stated above.[896] Attempts to unite them by posing "simply" the question whether it would be "unconscionable"[897] for the promisor to go back on his promise are, for reasons given earlier in this chapter,[898] unhelpful,[899] insofar as they detract attention from the other conditions which must also be satisfied to bring the two doctrines into operation[900] and from the differences in their respective legal effects.[901]

Proprietary estoppel and contract contrasted. We have seen that some cases which have been said to support the doctrine of proprietary estoppel have been explained on the alternative basis that there was a contract between the parties.[902] But often no such explanation is possible; for proprietary estoppel can operate even though the conditions required for the creation of a contract are not satisfied. The need to discuss the doctrine in this chapter arises precisely because a promise may give rise to a proprietary estoppel even though it is not supported by consideration; and it can also have this effect even though it cannot take effect as a contract because it is not sufficiently certain, because there is no contractual intention or (sometimes) because it fails to comply with formal requirements. 3–164

[893] *Taylors Fashions Ltd v Liverpool Victoria Trustee Co Ltd* [1982] Q.B. 133, 153, *cf.* above, para.3–160 at n.874a; where, however, a distinction is also drawn between "promissory estoppel" and the principle in *Ramsden v Dyson* (1866) L.R. 1 H.L. 129 (*i.e.* proprietary estoppel).

[894] [1976] Ch. 179, 193.

[895] *Taylors Fashions Ltd v Liverpool Victoria Trustee Co Ltd* [1982] Q.B. 133, 153; *cf.* above, para.3–160 at n.874a; the use of "promissory estoppel" to describe a typical proprietary estoppel situation in *Griffiths v Williams* [1978] E.G.D. 919, 921 may be a misprint.

[896] At paras 3–161 and 3–162; *cf.* above, para.3–147. Lord Scott's dictum in *Cobbe v Yeoman's Row Management Ltd* [2008] UKHL 55, [2008] 1 W.L.R. 1752 at [14] (quoted in para.3–160 above) falls short of stating that the requirements and effects of the two doctrines are identical.

[897] *Taylors Fashions Ltd v Liverpool Victoria Trustee Co Ltd* [1982] Q.B. 133, 155; *cf. Amalgamated Investment & Property Co Ltd v Texas Commerce International Bank* [1982] Q.B. 84, 104, 122. *cf.* also the reference in *Gillett v Holt* [2001] Ch. 210 at 232 to "the essential test of unconscionability" in cases of proprietary estoppel (above, para.3–147).

[898] Above, para.3–103.

[899] *cf.*, *Haslemere Estates Ltd v Baker* [1982] 1 W.L.R. 1109, 1119 where Megarry V.-C., rejecting the argument that proprietary estoppel arises "whenever justice and good conscience requires it," said "I do not think that the subject is as wide and indefinite as that." See also *Cobbe v Yeoman's Row Management Ltd* [2008] UKHL 55, [2008] 1 W.L.R. 1752 at [16], [17], [28] and [46], emphasising that unconscionability (or judicial disapproval) of the conduct of the party alleged to be estopped is not a sufficient (though it may be a necessary) condition of the operation of proprietary estoppel. Dicta emphasising the flexibility of the *remedy* (above, para.3–154) must be read subject to the requirement of adopting a "principled approach" (*ibid.*) to this aspect of the doctrine and not be taken to refer to *conditions of liability.*

[900] See above, paras 3–080 to 3–095, 3–144 to 3–148C.

[901] See above, paras 3–096 to 3–102, 3–149 to 3–159.

[902] Above, para.3–142.

Moreover, the effect of a proprietary estoppel differs from that of a contract. Sometimes, indeed, the result of a proprietary estoppel is to give effect to the promise in the terms in which it was made[903]; but such a result does not follow as of right. We have seen that the promisee's remedy may depend, not only on the terms of the promise, but also on other factors, such as the extent of the promisee's detrimental reliance on it and the proportionality of that reliance to his reasonable expectations induced by the promise and as the conduct of the promisor after the facts giving rise to the estoppel. Thus in *Crabb v Arun DC* the promisee would have had to make some payment for the right of way but for the "high-handedness"[904] of the promisor; and in *Pascoe v Turner* the promisee would not have been entitled to the fee simple of the house (but only to an irrevocable licence for life) if the promisor had not shown a "ruthless"[905] determination to evict her. The rights arising under a binding contract are fixed at its formation and not subject to such variation in the light of the court's approval or disapproval of the subsequent conduct of one of the parties. For this reason, and because proprietary estoppel may be revocable,[906] it will generally be more advantageous to a party to show (if he can) the existence of a binding contract than to rely on a proprietary estoppel.

12. SPECIAL CASES

3–165 **Defective promises.**[907] Mutual promises are generally consideration for each other,[908] but difficulty is sometimes felt in treating a promise as consideration for another if the former suffers from some defect, by reason of which it is not legally binding. The law on this topic is based on expediency rather than on any supposedly logical deductions which might be drawn from the doctrine of consideration. The question whether a defective promise can constitute consideration for a counter-promise depends on the policy of the rule of law making the former promise defective.

3–166 **Policy considerations.** One group of cases concerns contracts made between persons, one of whom lacks contractual capacity. A minor can enforce a promise made to him under such a contract even though the only consideration for it is his own promise, which does not bind him by reason of his minority.[909] The same rule applies to contracts with mental patients.[910] The reason for these rules is that it is the policy of the law to protect the person under the incapacity, and not the other party, who is therefore not allowed to rely on that incapacity. It has, on the other hand, been said that a promise by which the Crown purported to fetter its discretion would not constitute consideration where that promise did not bind the

---

903 *e.g. Dillwyn v Llewelyn* (1862) 4 D. F. & G. 517.
904 [1976] Ch. 179, 199.
905 [1979] 1 W.L.R. 431, 438.
906 Above, para.3–149.
907 Treitel (1961) 77 L.Q.R. 83.
908 Above, para.3–009.
909 *Holt v Ward Clarencieux* (1732) Stra. 937; below para.8–042.
910 Below, para.8–068.

Crown[911] under the principles discussed in Chapter 10 below.[912] A contrasting group of cases concerns contracts which are illegal. Obviously the illegal promise cannot be enforced and if both promises are illegal the consequence that neither can be enforced follows from the policy of the invalidating rule or rules rather than from the fact that an illegal promise cannot constitute consideration.[913] But in some cases of illegal contracts only one of the promises is illegal: this is, for example, often the position where the contract is in restraint of trade. In such a case, the party who makes the illegal promise (*e.g.* not to compete) cannot enforce the counter-promise (*e.g.* to pay a sum of money) if the illegal promise constitutes the sole consideration for the counter-promise.[914] Indeed, where one of the two promises is illegal, the counter-promise cannot be enforced even if there was *some* other consideration for it, but the *main* consideration for it was the illegal promise. The reason for this rule lies in the policy of the law to discourage illegal bargains.[915]

Performance of defective promises. Where a defective *promise* does not constitute consideration, the *performance* of it can nevertheless sometimes provide consideration for the counter-promise. For example a mere promise to negotiate has no contractual force[916] and so cannot constitute consideration for a counter-promise; but actually carrying on the negotiations can satisfy the requirement of consideration.[917] Likewise, where a promise would not bind the Crown because it purported to fetter the Crown's discretion, the actual performance of the promise can nevertheless constitute consideration for a counter-promise.[918] A similar principle applies where a victim of fraud, misrepresentation, duress or undue influence can sue but not be sued: by suing, he affirms the contract, makes his own promise binding, and so supplies consideration. But where the promise of one party is illegal even its performance does not entitle that party to enforce the counter-promise,[919] for the law must not give him any incentive to perform the illegal promise. 3–167

Promise defective by statute. Where one of the promises is defective by statute, the statute may expressly solve the problem whether the person giving 3–168

[911] *R. v Att.-Gen. for England and Wales* [2003] UKPC 22, [2002] E.M.L.R. 24 at [31]. There seems to be no strong policy reason for allowing enforcement by the Crown of the other party's promise where the contract remains executory.

[912] Below para.10–008.

[913] As suggested in *Nerot v Wallace* (1789) 3 T.R. 17, 23.

[914] *e.g. Wyatt v Kreglinger & Fernau* [1933] 1 K.B. 793.

[915] See *Goodinson v Goodinson* [1954] 2 Q.B. 118 (the actual decision is obsolete in view of Matrimonial Causes Act 1973, s.34, below, para.3–168).

[916] Above, para.2–136.

[917] *Sepong Engineering Construction Co Ltd v Formula One Management Ltd* [2000] 1 Lloyd's Rep. 602 at 611, where it was also said that damages for breach of the resulting contract would be no more than nominal. The same reasoning applied when, before the Corporate Bodies Contracts Act 1960, unsealed promises made by a corporation did not bind it: see *Fishmonger's Corp. v Robinson* (1843) 5 Man. & G. 131; *Kidderminster Corp. v Hardwick* (1873) L.R. 9 Ex. 13; *Re Dale* [1994] Ch. 31, 38.

[918] *R. v Att.-Gen. for England and Wales* [2003] UKPC 22, [2003] EMLR 24 at [31]; and see para.3–166 at nn.911 and 912.

[919] *e.g. Wyatt v Kreglinger & Fernau* [1933] 1 K.B. 793.

the defective promise can sue on the counter-promise.[920] Thus a party who gives a promise which is defective under s.4 of the Statute of Frauds 1677, or under s.34 of the Matrimonial Causes Act 1973 may, in spite of not being bound by that promise, be entitled to enforce the counter-promise,[921] and this may be so even though for other purposes (such as the validity of a disposition) his or her promise, precisely because it is void, cannot constitute consideration.[922] Where a statute invalidates a promise but does not provide for the effect of its invalidity on the other party's counter-promise, the general rule seems to be that the invalid promise is not good consideration[923]; but, unless that promise is illegal, the party giving it can sue on the counter-promise if he actually performs his promise.[924]

3–169 **Both promises defective by statute.** A statute may also invalidate *both* promises. Formerly, this was the position with regard to contracts "by way of gaming or wagering", which were "null and void" under section 18 of the Gaming Act 1845. This section has been repealed by the Gambling Act 2005,[925] section 335(1) of which provides that, as a general rule, "[t]he fact that a contract relates to gambling shall not prevent its enforcement." This subsection does not prejudice "any rule of law preventing the enforcement of a contract on the ground of unlawfulness . . . "[926] so that where (for example) a party had, in relation to the gambling contract committed an offence under the 2006 Act,[927] then that party would not be able to enforce the other party's promise; and where both parties had committed such an offence, then neither party's promise would be enforceable.[928] This would also be the position where the Gambling Commission was satisfied that a bet was "substantially unfair" and on that ground made an order by virtue of which "any contract . . . in relation to the bet [was] void."[929] It is also possible for the promises of both parties to be void under other legislation: for example, under section 4 of the Marine Insurance Act 1906, by which a contract of marine insurance is void where the assured has no "insurable interest", as defined by the Act.[930] In such cases, the making or performance of one of the promises would clearly not make the other promise enforceable. This conclusion follows simply from the fact that both promises are void by statute, so that there is no need to enquire whether the making or performance of one of

---

[920] See *Laythoarp v Bryant* (1836) 2 Bing.N.C. 735.

[921] Below, para.16–044. For more elaborate provisions of this kind, see Financial Services and Markets Act 2000, ss.20, 26–30.

[922] *Re Kumar* [1993] 1 W.L.R. 224, where the void promise was held not to constitute consideration for the purpose of Insolvency Act 1986, s.339.

[923] *Clayton v Jennings* (1760) 2 W.Bl. 706.

[924] *Rajbenback v Mamon* [1955] 1 Q.B. 283 as explained in (1961) 77 L.Q.R. 83, 95; *cf.* Unger (1956) 19 M.L.R. 99.

[925] 2005 Act, ss.334(1), 356(3), 356(1) and Sch.16. The 2005 Act is discussed in Volume II, paras 40–089 *et seq.*

[926] 2005 Act, s.335(2), below, Vol. II para.40–099.

[927] See below, Vol. II, paras 40–100, 40–101.

[928] e.g. where one party has provided facilities for commercial gambling without the requisite licence, and the other has cheated: ss.2, 33(2), and 42.

[929] Ss.336(2) and (3).

[930] In spite of its title, the Act applies (where appropriate) to contracts of insurance generally: see *Locker & Woolf Ltd v W. Australian Insurance Co Ltd* [1936] 1 K.B. 408 at 416.

the promises can constitute consideration for the other. The question whether the making or performance of such a void promise could constitute consideration might, however, arise in the context other than that of the enforceability of the counter-promise: for example, in the context of the question whether the performance could constitute consideration for the purpose of a rule of law by which a transfer or disposition of property was effective only if made for valuable consideration. This was the question which arose in *Lipkin Gorman v Karpnale Ltd*[931] where stolen money had been used by a thief for gambling at a club of which he was a member and it was held that the club had not received the money for valuable consideration so as to be entitled, as against the victim of the theft, to retain it. We have noted that the club had not provided consideration for the member's payment by exchanging the money for gaming chips.[932] The present point is that the club had not provided consideration for the payments made to it by the member and received by it in good faith by allowing him to gamble in the club or by promising to pay, or actually paying him, in respect of any bets won by him. This aspect of the decision was based on section 18 of the Gaming Act 1845 and is undermined by the repeal of that section by the Gambling Act 2005 and by the general rule, laid down in that Act, that contracts relating to gambling are legally enforceable. Under that rule, the club's promises to its members, or the performance of those promises, would clearly constitute good consideration for the club's receipt of the member's payments. A number of other problems which could arise under the 2005 Act on facts such as those of the *Lipkin Gorman* case are discussed in Volume II, paragraphs 40–130 to 40–132.

Unilateral contracts. In the case of a unilateral contract,[933] the promisee clearly provides consideration if he completes the stipulated act or forbearance (such as walking to York, or not smoking for a year).[934] This amounts in law to a detriment to the promisee; and the promisor may also obtain a benefit: *e.g.* where he promises a reward for the return of lost property and it is actually returned to him. It was suggested in Chapter 2 that commencement of performance can amount to acceptance of an offer of a unilateral contract,[935] and it is here submitted that such commencement can also amount to consideration; for it may in law be a detriment to the promisee to walk only part of the way to York, or to refrain from smoking for part of the year. Difficult questions of fact may, indeed, arise in determining whether performance has actually begun and whether such a beginning was made "on the strength of"[936] the promise. This is particularly true where the stipulated performance is a forbearance; but if an actual forbearance to sue can constitute good consideration,[937] it must in principle be possible to tell when a forbearance has begun. Thus commencement of performance (whether of an act or of a forbearance) may provide both an acceptance and consideration, and may accordingly deprive the promisor of his right to withdraw 3–170

[931] [1991] 2 A.C. 548.
[932] Above, para.3–016.
[933] Above, paras 2–078 *et seq.*
[934] See *Daulia Ltd v Four Millbank Nominees Ltd* [1978] Ch. 231, 238.
[935] Above, para.2–078.
[936] *Wigan v English & Scottish Law Life Assurance Association* [1909] 1 Ch. 291, 298; above, para.3–059.
[937] See above, para.3–057.

the promise.[938] Of course, the promisor's liability to pay the amount promised (*e.g.* the £100 for walking to York) does not accrue before the promisee has fully performed the required act or forbearance. The present point is merely that, after part performance by the promisee, the promisor cannot withdraw with impunity.[938a]

3–171 The further suggestion has been made that a unilateral contract may be made as soon as the offer is received by the offeree[939]; and this could be interpreted to mean that the contract was binding even before the offeree had acted on it in any way. But at this stage the offeree has clearly not provided any consideration, and in the case in which the suggestion was made no problem of consideration arose as the offeree had in fact completed the required act[940] before any attempt to withdraw the offer was made. Except in the case of bankers' irrevocable credits,[941] the better view is that an offer of a unilateral contract is not binding on receipt of the offer, but only when the offeree has begun to render the required performance.

3–172 **Firm offers.** A "firm" offer is one containing a promise not to withdraw it for a specified time. Such a promise does not prevent the offeror from withdrawing the offer within that period since normally the promise will be unsupported by consideration.[942] Consideration for such a promise is most obviously provided if the offeree pays (or promises to pay) a sum of money for the promise and so buys an option.[943] Consideration may also be provided by some other promise: for example, in the case of an offer to sell a house, the offeree may provide consideration for the offeror's promise to hold the offer open by promising to apply for a mortgage on the house; and, in the case of an offer to buy shares, the

[938] For the contrary view see Wormser in *Selected Readings on the Law of Contracts*, p.307—but he recanted in (1956) 3 *Journal of Legal Education* 146.

[938a] The above passage (para.3–168 in the 29th edition of this book) is cited with apparent approval in *Schweppe v Harper* [2008] EWCA Civ 444 at [42] by Waller L.J. who there dissented on the different issue, whether the agreement was sufficiently certain to have contractual force: see above, para.2–142 note 650.

[939] *Harvela Investments Ltd v Royal Trust Co of Canada (C.I.) Ltd* [1986] 1 A.C. 207, 224 ("when the invitation was received").

[940] By submitting the requested bid: *cf.* above para.2–040.

[941] Below, para.3–182.

[942] *Cooke v Oxley* (1790) 3 T.R. 653; *Routledge v Grant* (1828) 4 Bing. 653; *Head v Diggon* (1828) 3 M. & Ry 97; *Dickinson v Dodds* (1876) 2 Ch.D. 463; above, para.2–088.

[943] The legal characteristics of such an option have been variously described: (1) as a contract: *Greene v Church Commissioners for England* [1947] Ch. 467, 476, 478 (disapproving a dictum in *Beesly v Hallwood Estates Ltd* [1960] 1 W.L.R. 549, 555, actual decision affirmed [1961] Ch. 549 but dicta at first instance are disapproved on a point not here under discussion in *Bolton MBC v Torrington* [2003] EWCA Civ. 1634, [2004] Ch. 66); though not one of sale: *Chippenham Golf Club v North Wilts. RDC* (1992) 64 P. & C.R. 527; (2) as a transaction which, even though it is not a contract, gives rise to an interest in property: *Re Button's Lease* [1964] Ch. 263, 270–271; *Armstrong & Holmes Ltd v Holmes* [1994] 1 All E.R. 826; (3) as a unilateral contract: *United Scientific Holdings Ltd v Burnley BC* [1978] A.C. 904, 945; *Little v Courage* (1995) 70 P. & C.R. 469, 474; (4) as a conditional contract: *Bircham & Co Nominees (No.2) Ltd v Worrell Holdings Ltd* [2001] EWCA Civ. 773; (2001) 82 P. & C.R. 427 at [45]; *Coaten v PBS Corporation* [2006] EWHC 1781, [2007] 1 P. & C.R. DG 11 at [33]; (5) as an irrevocable offer: *Re Gray* [2004] EWHC 1538, [2005] 1 W.L.R. 815 at [25]; contrast the *Coaten* case, above; and (6) as being *sui generis*: *Spiro v Glencrown Properties* [1991] Ch. 537. And see Mowbray, 74 L.Q.R. 242; Lücke, 3 Adelaide L.Rev. 200.

offeree may provide consideration for the offeror's promise not to withdraw the offer for a specified time by promising not to dispose of those shares elsewhere during that time. The performance of the offeree's promise in such cases could likewise provide consideration for the offeror's promise to keep the offer open. In one case a vendor of land entered into a so-called "lock-out" agreement[944] by which he promised a prospective purchaser not to consider other offers if that purchaser would exchange contracts within two weeks; and it was said that "the promise by the [purchaser] to get on by limiting himself to just two weeks"[945] constituted consideration for the vendor's promise not to consider other offers. The case is not strictly one of a firm offer since the vendor's promise would not in terms have prevented him from simply deciding not to sell at all; but the practical effect of a binding "lock-out" agreement may be to prevent the vendor from withdrawing his offer; and the reasoning quoted above[946] could apply to the case of a firm offer. On the facts of the case from which it is taken, the reasoning gives rise to some difficulty since it does not appear that the purchaser made any promise to exchange contracts within two weeks. It seems more plausible to say that the vendor's promise had become binding as a unilateral contract under which the purchaser had provided consideration by actually making efforts to meet the deadline, even though he had not promised to do so. Similar reasoning can apply if a seller of land promises to keep an offer open for a month, asking the buyer during that period to make efforts to raise the necessary money. If the buyer makes such efforts (without promising to do so), it is arguable that he has by part performance accepted the seller's offer of a unilateral contract to keep the principal offer open. Similarly, it is possible for a person, to whom a promise not to revoke an offer for the sale of a house has been made, to provide consideration for that promise by incurring the expense of a survey.[947] On the other hand, the equitable doctrine of *Hughes v Metropolitan Ry*[948] and of the *High Trees* case[949] will not avail the offeree since it does not create new causes of action where none existed before.[950] Nor does it seem probable that the offeree will be able to claim damages in tort[951] under the principles laid down in *Hedley Byrne & Co Ltd v Heller & Partners Ltd.*[952]

Exceptions. The general rule that a promise to keep an offer open is not binding has been criticised[953]; indeed, there are some situations in which it has 3–173

[944] Above, para.2–121.
[945] *Pitt v P.H.H. Asset Management Ltd* [1994] 1 W.L.R. 327, 332; for other consideration in this case, see above. para.3–052; *Tye v House* [1997] 2 E.G.L.R. 171.
[946] At n.945.
[947] *cf. Ee v Kakar* (1979) 40 P. & C.R. 223 (a case not concerned with a "firm" offer).
[948] (1877) 2 App. Cas. 439; above, para.3–085.
[949] [1947] K.B. 130; above, para.3–128.
[950] Above, para.3–098.
[951] *cf. Holman Construction Ltd v Delta Timber Co Ltd* [1972] N.Z.L.R. 1081; and see *Blackpool and Fylde Aero Club v Blackpool BC* [1990] 1 W.L.R. 1195, 1202.
[952] [1964] A.C. 465; below, para.6–081.
[953] Law Revision Committee, 6th Interim Report, Cmd. 5449 (1937), para.38; Law Commission Working Paper No.60 (1975).

been said that "the market would disdain to take"[954] the point that such a promise was not binding. The rule does not, of course, apply if the promise is made in a deed; and it is rejected by the Vienna Convention on Contracts for the International Sale of Goods.[955] It is also subject to a common law exception in the law of insurance where an underwriter who initials a slip under an "open cover" arrangement is regarded as making a "standing offer" which the insured can accept from time to time by making "declarations" under it. The underwriter's commitment is regarded as binding even though there is no consideration for his implied promise not to revoke the "standing offer."[956] But even with these mitigations, the rule can still cause hardship to an offeree who has acted in reliance on the promise to keep the offer open.[957] On the other hand, the rule does sometimes provide necessary protection for the offeror: *e.g.* when an offer is made by a customer on a form provided by a supplier and expressed to be irrevocable; or when the period of irrevocability is not specified, so that the offeror is left subject to an indefinite obligation without acquiring any corresponding right. Any further development of the law on the point will require a balancing of these conflicting factors.[958]

3–174 **Auction sales without reserve.** Where goods are put up for auction without reserve, there is no contract *of sale* if the auctioneer refuses to knock the goods down to the highest bidder; but the auctioneer is liable to the highest bidder on a separate promise that the auction will be without reserve.[959] It can be argued that there is no consideration for this promise as the bidder is not bound by his unaccepted bid.[960] But it has been held that there is both a detriment to the bidder, since he runs the risk of being bound, and a benefit to the auctioneer, as the bidding is driven up.[961] Hence there is consideration for the auctioneer's separate promise, and it makes no difference to the auctioneer's liability *on this promise* that he would not be liable if he did not put the goods up for sale at all (since an

---

954 *Jaglom v Excess Insurance Ltd* [1972] 2 Q.B. 250, 258; *cf. County Ltd v Girozentrale Securities* [1996] 3 All E.R. 834 where an "offer to subscribe" for shares was described at 837 as "not legally binding but regarded by City convention as binding in honour unless some unforeseen exceptional circumstances supervened." It seems that the "commitment" (below, before n.956) was given not to the company but to the underwriter, or by prospective investors to each other, so that the principles discussed in para.2–024 above did not apply. For the view that the statement in question in the *Jaglom* case was not an offer at all, but an acceptance (and binding as such) see *General Reinsurance Corporation v Forsakringsaktiebolaget Fennia Patria* [1983] Q.B. 856, 863–864.

955 Above, para.2–063; Art. 16(2).

956 *Citadel Insurance Co v Atlantic Union Insurance Co* [1982] 2 Lloyd's Rep. 543, 546.

957 *e.g.* where a builder enters into a contract in reliance of offers from sub-contractors to supply services or materials and expressed to be "firm" for a fixed period. For conflicting American authorities, see *James Baird Co v Gimbel Bros.*, 64 F. 2d. 344 (1933); *Drennan v Star Paving Co* 51 Cal. 2d. 409, 333 P. 2d. 757 (1958); for a review of Canadian authorities, see *Northern Construction Co v Gloge Heating & Plumbing* (1984) 6 D.L.R. (4th) 450 (holding the sub-contractor bound by his offer).

958 See Law Com. Work Paper 60 (1975).

959 *Warlow v Harrison* (1859) 1 E. & E. 309; *Harris v Nickerson* (1873) L.R. 8 Q.B. 286, 288; *Johnson v Boyes* [1899] 2 Ch. 73, 77.

960 See Slade (1952) 68 L.Q.R. 238; Gower, *ibid.* at 457; Slade (1953) 69 L.Q.R. 21.

961 *Barry v Davies* [2000] 1 W.L.R. 1962 at 1967.

advertisement of an auction is not an offer to hold it),[962] or that there was no contract *of sale* because of his refusal to accept the highest bid.[963]

3–175 **Novation of partnership debts.** When the composition of a partnership changes, it is usual to arrange that liability for the debts owed by the existing partners should be transferred by novation[964] to the new partners. Two situations call for discussion.

(1) A and B are in partnership; A retires and C is admitted as a new partner; it is agreed between A, B and C, and the creditors of the old firm of A and B, that A shall cease to be liable for the firm's debts, and that C shall undertake such liability. The result is that the creditors can sue C and can no longer sue A. They provide good consideration for C's promise to pay by abandoning their claim against A; and A provides good consideration for their promise to release him by procuring a substitute debtor, C.

(2) A and B are in partnership; A retires; it is agreed between A, B and the creditors of the firm that A shall cease to be liable and that B shall be solely liable. It seems that the creditors cannot sue A, but it is hard to see what consideration moves from him. In one case it was said that there was consideration in that a remedy against a single debtor might be easier to enforce than one against several, all of whom were solvent[965]; thus the creditors benefit by the release of A. This is a possible, if invented,[966] consideration.

3–176 The second of the situations discussed in para.3–175 above should be distinguished from that in which the original liability is incurred by an individual who then enters into a partnership. This was the position in *Re Burton Marsden Douglas*[967] where A, a solicitor, incurred liabilities to a client (X) and then entered into partnership with B and C. It was held that B and C were not liable for the liabilities incurred by A to X before A had entered into the partnership with B and C. There had been no novation of those liabilities since (a) there had been no agreement to novate them and (b) if there had been such an agreement, there would have been no consideration for any promise by B and C to X to discharge those liabilities since there had been no promise by X to release A.

3–177 **Gratuitous bailments.** A gratuitous bailment may be for the benefit of the bailee or for the benefit of the bailor.

(1) For benefit of bailee. The first possibility is illustrated by *Bainbridge v Firmstone*[968] where the defendant asked for and received permission from the

---

[962] *Harris v Nickerson* (1873) L.R. 8 Q.B. 286; above para.2–012.

[963] *ibid.*

[964] Below, para.19–086; Partnership Act 1890, s.17(3). Problems of the kind here discussed do not arise in the same form in the case of limited liability partnership incorporated under the Limited Liability Partnerships Act 2000 since the liabilities of the partnership are those of the body corporate incorporated under ss.1–3 of that Act; these are not affected by a change in the membership of the body. Section 6(3) of the Act deals with the different question of the extent to which acts of a person who has ceased to be a member can still impose liability on the partnership.

[965] *Lyth v Ault* (1852) 7 Ex. 669; *Thompson v Percival* (1834) 5 B. & Ad. 925 is based on reasoning which is obsolete after *D. & C. Builders Ltd v Rees* [1967] 2 Q.B. 617; above, para.3–122, n.629.

[966] Above, para.3–009.

[967] [2004] EWHC 593 (Ch), [2004] 3 All E.R. 222.

[968] (1838) 8 A. & E. 743.

plaintiff to weigh two boilers belonging to the plaintiff. In performing this operation, the defendant damaged the boilers, and the plaintiff claimed damages for breach of the defendant's promise to return the boilers in good condition. The defendant argued that, as he was not paid to weigh or look after the boilers, no consideration for his promise had been provided by the plaintiff; but the court rejected this argument. Patteson J. said: "I suppose the defendant thought he had some benefit; at any rate, there is a detriment to the plaintiff from his parting with the possession for even so short a time."[969] This consideration would also support some other promise by the defendant, *e.g.* a promise to repair the boilers. It is more doubtful whether there would be any consideration moving from the defendant for any promise by the plaintiff to allow the defendant to have possession of the boilers. A mere promise to return the boilers might not suffice on the ground that it was no more than a promise to perform a duty imposed by law on all bailees; but a promise to repair the boilers or to improve them in some way, or one to look after them for a fixed time, would probably be regarded as consideration moving from the defendant.[970]

(2) For benefit of bailor. The second possibility would, for example, arise where a thing was deposited by A with B, not for use but for safe-keeping, without reward. In such a case, A's parting with the possession is hardly a detriment to him; and B's duty to look after the thing[971] does not arise out of a contractual promise but is imposed by the general law.[972] It follows that B's *only* duty is that imposed by law. Thus B is under no obligation before he actually receives the thing; and if he promised to do anything which went beyond the duty imposed by law (for example, to keep the thing in repair) he would be bound by his promise only if A had provided some consideration for it apart from the delivery of the chattel.[973] To constitute such consideration, it is not necessary to show that B obtained any benefit from the bailment: thus it is enough if A reimburses (or promises to reimburse) B for any expenses that B has incurred for the purpose of performing his promise.[974] This follows from the principle that consideration may consist *either* in a benefit to the promisor (B) *or* in a detriment to the promisee (A).[975]

3–178 **Gratuitous services.** Normally a promise to render services without reward is not supported by consideration and is therefore not binding contractually. For example, where A gratuitously promises to insure B's property but fails to do so, A is not liable to B for breach of contract if the property is destroyed or damaged.[976] Occasionally, it may be possible to find consideration in the indirect

---

[969] At 744.

[970] *cf. Verral v Farnes* [1966] 1 W.L.R. 1254, a case relating to land; followed in *Milton v Farrow* (1980) 255 E.G. 449.

[971] For this duty, see *Coggs v Bernard* (1703) 2 Ld. Raym. 909; *Mitchell v Ealing LBC* [1979] Q.B. 1; *Port Swettenham Authority v T.W. Wu & Co* [1979] A.C. 580, 590.

[972] *Morris v C.W. Martin Ltd* [1966] 1 Q.B. 716, 731; *Compania Continental del Peru v Evelpis Shipping Corp. (The Agia Skepi)* [1992] 2 Lloyd's Rep. 467, 472.

[973] *cf. Charnock v Liverpool Corporation* [1968] 1 W.L.R. 1498; below, para.18–008.

[974] *CCC Films (London) Ltd v Impact Quadrant Films Ltd* [1985] Q.B. 16, 27.

[975] Above, para.3–014.

[976] *Argy Trading & Development Co Ltd v Lapid Developments Ltd* [1977] 1 W.L.R. 444; *cf.* the New York case of *Thorn v Deas*, 4 Johns. 84 (1809); later American authorities are divided: Corbin, *Contracts*, para.205, n.54.

financial benefit which the promisor obtains from the arrangement, *e.g.* in the form of favourable publicity.[977]

Liability in tort for negligent performance. Even where the promise is not supported by consideration, the promisor may be liable in tort for negligence if he actually renders the gratuitous services but fails to perform a duty to exercise due care in rendering them and so causes loss. A banker giving a negligent reference or an accountant giving a negligent report on the financial position of a company could be liable on this ground, even though he made no charge to the person to whom the information was given.[978] Similarly, where A gratuitously promised to insure B's property but did so negligently, with the result that the policy did not cover the loss which occurred, A was held liable to B in tort.[979] In one case, a person was even held liable in damages for negligently giving free advice to a friend in connection with the purchase of a second-hand car which turned out to be seriously defective.[980] 3–179

Non-feasance and misfeasance. The most important distinction between the two groups of cases discussed in paras 3–178 and 3–179 is that between non-feasance and misfeasance in the performance of a promise to render gratuitous service. For this purpose, non-feasance means complete failure to pursue a *promised course of action*, while misfeasance means carelessness in the pursuit of that course of action, leading to failure to achieve a *promised result*. The first group of cases shows that non-feasance does not (in the absence of consideration[981]) make the promisor liable in contract, while the second shows that misfeasance can make him liable in tort. There is no liability in tort for simply doing nothing after having promised to render services gratuitously; for to impose such liability would amount to holding "that the law of England recognises the enforceability of a gratuitous promise. On the face of it, this would be inconsistent with fundamental principle."[982] In cases of pure non-feasance, the 3–180

[977] *cf. De la Bere v Pearson* [1908] 1 K.B. 280, 287.

[978] *Hedley Byrne & Co Ltd v Heller & Partners Ltd* [1964] A.C. 465; *cf.* below, para.6–081.

[979] *Wilkinson v Coverdale* (1793) 1 Esp. 75.

[980] *Chaudhry v Prabhakar* [1989] 1 W.L.R. 29; the defendant conceded that he owed a duty of care to the claimant and two members of the Court of Appeal seem to have regarded this concession as correct; Brown [1989] L.M.C.L.Q. 148. Contrast *Henderson v Merrett Syndicates Ltd* [1995] 2 A.C. 145, 181, suggesting that there may be no liability in respect of services rendered on "an informal occasion."

[981] Or of privity of contract: see *Hamble Fisheries Ltd v L. Gardner & Son Ltd (The Rebecca Elaine)* [1999] 2 Lloyd's Rep. 1 at 5.

[982] *G.A.F.L.A.C. v Tanter (The Zephyr)* [1985] 2 Lloyd's Rep. 529, 538, disapproving the contrary view expressed at first instance [1984] 1 Lloyd's Rep. 58, 85 and there based on authorities which were all cases of misfeasance. *The Zephyr* itself was also such a case: [1984] 1 Lloyd's Rep. at 79, 86 ("he was making the position steadily worse"). *A fortiori*, there is no liability in tort for pure omission where *no* promise has been made: see *Reid v Rush & Tompkins Group plc* [1990] 1 W.L.R. 212 and *Van Oppen v Clerk to the Bedford Charity Trustees* [1990] 1 W.L.R. 235 though in the latter case it was said at 260 that a voluntary assumption of responsibility by one party followed by reliance on it by the other might in exceptional cases give rise to such liability. The scope of the exceptions is not clear; in the last two cases it was held that there was *no* duty on respectively an employer and a school to advise an employee or the parents of a pupil to insure against foreseeable risks of injury *cf. Outram v Academy Plastics Ltd* [2001] I.C.R. 367 at 372: generally no liability in tort "for pure omission", the omission taking the form of an employer's failure, without breach of contract, to advise as employee as to his membership of the employer's pension scheme. Liability in tort for pure omission may exceptionally arise where there is a "duty to act": see *White v Jones* [1995] 2 A.C. at

promisee will therefore have a remedy only if he can show that he provided consideration for the promise. If he can show this he may also be in a better position with regard to damages even in cases of misfeasance.[983] There may be an exception to the general rule that there is no liability in tort for pure omissions. This exception was said to apply *in Lennon v Metropolitan Police Commissioner*,[984] where A represented to B that A would take steps to safeguard some specified financial interest of B's (in that case B's housing allowance as a police officer on his transfer from one force to another) and that representation amounted to an "express assumption of responsibility for a particular matter."[985] A's failure to exercise due care in discharging that responsibility could then make him liable to B in tort, and such liability was said to cover "acts of omission."[986] It may, however, be respectfully doubted whether A's allegedly wrongful conduct in this case did not amount to misfeasance in the sense in which this expression has been used in this paragraph, i.e. to failure to achieve a *promised result*.

3–181 In *Gore v Van der Lann*[987] a corporation issued a free travel pass to the claimant who "in consideration of my being granted a free pass" undertook that the use of the pass by her should be subject to certain conditions. One of these was that she would not sue the corporation or its servants for loss or injury suffered while she was boarding, alighting from, or being carried in, the corporation's vehicles. The claimant was injured while boarding a corporation bus; and it was held that the issue and acceptance of the free pass amounted to a contract.[988] Willmer L.J. said that "Each party gave good consideration by accepting a detriment in return for the advantages gained."[989] The parties were, as a result of the issue of the pass, brought into a relationship of passenger and carrier which gave rise to duties quite independently of contract; and it was the promise not to enforce these obligations which constituted the consideration moving from the claimant. In the absence of such a relationship, the person to whom the gratuitous service was promised would not provide consideration for that promise merely by making a counter-promise not to sue for loss or damage caused by the defective performance of the services. It follows that, if in *Gore v Van der Lann* the pass had been issued for a specified period but had been withdrawn before the end of that period, then the holder would have had no claim in contract in respect of that premature withdrawal. Similarly, if A promised to carry B's goods to London free of charge and B promised not to sue A for negligently damaging them in the course of that operation, then A would not be under any contractual liability for failing to pick up the goods. But he might be

---

261, 268, 295 below, para.18–037); but it is submitted that no such duty would be imposed by merely making gratuitous promise. For a further possible exception, see below, after n.984.

[983] Because he will then be able to recover damages for loss of bargain.

[984] [2004] EWCA Civ. 130, [2004] 1 W.L.R. 2594 at [34].

[985] *ibid.*, at [34].

[986] *ibid.*, at [20].

[987] [1967] 2 Q.B. 31; Harris (1967) 30 M.L.R. 584; Odgers (1970) 86 L.Q.R. 69; and see above, para.2–178 on the issue of contractual intention.

[988] This contract was void, so far as it purported to exclude liability for personal injury, by virtue of s.151 of the Road Traffic Act 1960 (now Public Passenger Vehicles Act 1981, s.29); below, para.14–116.

[989] [1967] 2 Q.B. 31, 42.

liable if he did pick them up and then unloaded them short of the agreed destination.

Bankers' irrevocable credits. Where a banker issues (or confirms) an irrevocable credit, the generally held commercial view is that the banker's promise to the beneficiary is binding as soon as it is communicated to the beneficiary, and before the latter has acted on it in any way.[990] If, as seems probable, this view also represents the law, it constitutes a clear exception to the doctrine of consideration.[991] 3–182

[990] Below, Vol.II, para.34–485.

[991] For explicit recognition of such an exception in the United States, see UCC, s.5–105; *cf. United City Merchants Ltd v Royal Bank of Canada (The American Accord)* [1982] Q.B. 208, 225, reversed on other grounds [1983] 1 A.C. 168. Under the Contracts (Rights of Third Parties) Act 1999 (below, paras 19–088 *et seq.*) the beneficiary might have a claim against the bank as a third party identified in the contract between the bank and its customer; there is no requirement, in such cases, of consideration moving from the third party: above, para.3–045. But his rights under the Act would be less secure than his common law rights in two respects. First, they would be subject under subs.3(2) to any defences which the bank might have against its customer. And, secondly they could be defeated or diminished by recission or variation of the contract by subsequent agreement between the bank and its customer before the seller had *either* communicated his assent to the bank *or* relied on the credit, and the bank either was aware of, or reasonably should have foreseen such reliance: see subs.2(1) and paras 18–100 and 18–101 below.

CHAPTER 4

FORM

	PARA.
1. In general	4–001
2. Contracts for the sale or other disposition of an interest in land	4–009
(a) The old law: contracts made on or before September 26, 1989	4–010
(i) Contracts within section 40 of the Law of Property Act 1925	4–011
(ii) Formal requirements	4–022
(iii) The effect of failure to comply with the formal requirements	4–041
(b) The new law: contracts made on or after September 27, 1989	4–052
(i) Contracts within section 2 of the Law of Property (Miscellaneous Provisions) Act 1989	4–054
(ii) Formal requirements	4–069
(iii) The effect of failure to comply with the formal requirements	4–075

1. IN GENERAL

The general rule. The general rule of English law is that contracts can be made quite informally: no writing or other form is necessary. At common law there was only one exception to this rule: a corporation had to contract under seal until the last vestiges of this rule were abolished in 1960.[1] At present, all formal requirements in the law of contract are contained in legislation which deals with specific contracts. There are four main purposes for making such formal requirements.[2] First, they may serve as clear evidence of a transaction and of its terms. Secondly, they may have a cautionary effect, thereby deterring hasty, premature or ill-considered contracts being made. Thirdly, they may have a "channelling" function, offering "a legal framework into which a party may fit his actions".[3] Thus, formalities may mark off transactions from one another and create a standardised form of transaction.[4] Fourthly, formal requirements may be used as a device to protect the weaker parties to contracts. There has been an increasing 4–001

---

[1] Corporate Bodies' Contracts Act 1960.

[2] Fuller (1941) 41 Col. L. Rev. 799; Law Commission No.164 (1987), pp.6–7; Whittaker in Birks and Pretto (eds), *Themes in Comparative Law in Honour of Bernard Rudden* (2002), p.199.

[3] Fuller (1941) 41 Col. L. Rev. 799, 801.

[4] Law Com. No.164 (1987), p.7.

tendency to impose such requirements with this last purpose in view: for example, in the cases of tenants, employees, debtors and sureties under consumer credit agreements[5] and consumers of certain classes of services, such as package holidays[6] or "timeshare" accommodation.[7]

Formal requirements are discussed in relation to a number of specific contracts in Vol.II of this work.[8] In the present Volume, which deals with general principles, there would be no point in attempting to make an exhaustive list of contracts for which formal requirements are imposed by statute. But four general matters may usefully be discussed here: types of formal requirement; the effects of non-compliance; the impact of estoppel; and contracts made by electronic communications.

4–002 **Types of formal requirement.** Legislative requirements of form differ widely from one another. In a few cases, contracts are required to be made by deed: this is true, for example, of a lease for more than three years.[9] More frequently the requirement is that certain contracts must be in, or evidenced in, writing; but even requirements of this kind vary a good deal in stringency. Some statutes simply require, in general terms, that the contract must be in writing, or that there must be a note or memorandum in writing.[10] Others set out the formal requirements in great detail and even specify the size of the lettering and the colour of the print and paper.[11] Yet others do not require the contract to be, or to be evidenced in, writing at all, but only require one party to give the other written notice of specified terms of the contract.[12] A further type of formal requirement may be found in the Timeshare Act 1992 which requires that those offering timeshare rights in respect of immovable property inform their would-be customers in writing of various matters relating to the contract, such as the services to which the customer would have access and the common facilities.[13] The form of a contract may also affect the regulation which it attracts, rather than going to its validity. Thus, for example, the scheme of rules governing "construction contracts" under Pt II of the Housing Grants, Construction and Regeneration Act 1996 applies only "where the construction contract is in writing", any other

---

[5] Landlord and Tenant Act 1985 s.4; Consumer Credit Act 1974 ss.60, 61, 105; Consumer Credit (Agreements) Regulations (SI 1983/1553) Sch.5 as amended by SI 1984/1600, SI 1985/666, SI 1988/2047.

[6] The Package Travel, Package Holidays and Package Tours Regulations 1992 (SI 1992/3288) reg.9.

[7] The Timeshare Regulations 1997 (SI 1997/1081) reg.6, amending the Timeshare Act 1992.

[8] See Vol.II, Chs 34, 38, 39, and 44.

[9] Law of Property Act 1925 ss.52, 54, as amended by Law of Property (Miscellaneous Provisions) Act 1989 s.1(8) Sch.1 para.2.

[10] e.g. Law of Property Act 1925 s.40, discussed below, paras 4–010 et seq.

[11] e.g. Regulations made or to be made by the Secretary of State under the Hire-Purchase Act 1965, under the Consumer Credit Act 1974 s.60, or under the Unsolicited Goods and Services Act 1971 s.3A (inserted by the Unsolicited Goods and Services (Amendment) Act 1975 s.1). See SI 1965/1646, SI 1975/731, SI 1975/732, and see Consumer Credit (Agreements) Regulations 1983.

[12] e.g. Landlord and Tenant Act 1985 s.4; Employment Rights Act 1996 ss.1–2, 4–6 (as amended); Estate Agents Act 1979 s.18.

[13] Timeshare Act 1992 s.1A(1) and Sch.1 as inserted by Timeshare Regulations 1997 (SI 1997/1081) reg.3; and see the Consumer Protection (Distance Selling) Regulations 2000 (SI 2000/2334).

agreement between the parties being "effective for the purposes of this Part only if in writing".[14]

Effect of non-compliance. Non-compliance with such statutory requirements may produce various effects. It may make the contract void,[15] or unenforceable,[16] or unenforceable by one party[17] or enforceable only on an order of the court.[18] It may simply deprive the transaction of certain effects which it would have had, if the formal requirement had been observed, without generally impairing its validity or enforceability; this would be the case, for example, if a lease for more than three years were not made by deed[19]; if an assignment of a chose in action were made orally[20]; or if the sort of promise which is normally contained in a bill of exchange or promissory note were made orally. Failure to comply with formal requirements may also be a criminal offence, and in some cases this is the sole consequence of failure which is actually specified in the relevant statute.[21] The civil consequences of failure to comply with a statutory requirement of form in such a case would presumably depend on the court's view of the objects which the legislature sought to achieve in imposing the requirement. If the requirement was imposed to protect one of the parties to a contract, that party would probably be able to enforce the contract notwithstanding the formal defect; whether the other party could enforce it would depend on principles discussed elsewhere in this book.[22] 4–003

Requirements of form and estoppel. As will be described in more detail below in relation to contracts for the sale or other disposition of an interest in land, the application of the various doctrines of estoppel have sometimes caused difficulty in relation to contracts invalid for want of the applicable formality.[23] In this regard, the House of Lords in *Actionstrength Ltd v International Glass Engineering IN.GL.EN SpA*[24] in the context of s.4 of the Statute of Frauds made clear that while in an appropriate case where there had been a clear representation by a party that the contract was valid (despite any want of formality),[25] the courts 4–004

[14] Housing Grants, Construction and Regeneration Act 1996 s.107 (which defines what is meant by agreement in writing for this purpose).

[15] Bills of Sale Act (1878) Amendment Act 1882 s.9; Law of Property (Miscellaneous Provisions) Act 1989 s.2.

[16] e.g. Law of Property Act 1925 s.40: for the distinction between "void" and "unenforceable" contracts, see above, paras 1–080, 1–084.

[17] Consumer Credit Act 1974 s.65; Timeshare Act 1992 ss.5(2), 5A (as inserted by Timeshare Regulations 1997 (SI 1997/1081) reg.9).

[18] Consumer Credit Act 1974 s.127.

[19] Law of Property Act 1925 s.52 ("void for the purpose of conveying or creating a legal estate"); and see s.54, as amended by the Law of Property (Miscellaneous Provisions) Act 1989 s.1 and Sch.1 para.2.

[20] Below, paras 19–006, 19–015, 19–034.

[21] e.g. Landlord and Tenant Act 1962 s.1, repealed and replaced by Landlord and Tenant Act 1985 s.4; *Shaw v Groom* [1970] 2 Q.B. 504.

[22] i.e. on the principles stated in *St John Shipping Corp v Joseph Rank Ltd* [1957] 1 Q.B. 267; below, paras 16–146 et seq.

[23] See below, paras 4–078—4–083.

[24] [2003] UKHL 17, [2003] 2 A.C. 541.

[25] e.g. *Shah v Shah* [2001] EWCA Civ 527, [2001] 4 All E.R. 138.

should not found an estoppel simply on the informal agreement itself.[26] As Lord Hoffmann observed:

> "The terms of the Statute of Frauds therefore show that Parliament, although obviously conscious that it would allow some people to break their promises, thought that this injustice was outweighed by the need to protect people from being held liable on the basis of oral utterances which were ill-considered, ambiguous or completely fictitious. This means that while normally one would approach the construction of a statute on the basis that Parliament was unlikely to have intended to cause injustice by allowing people to break promises which had been relied upon, no such assumption can be made about the statute . . . [I]t must not be construed in a way which would undermine its purpose."[27]

4–005 **Contracts made by electronic communications.** The Electronic Communications Act 2000 created a power in the appropriate Minister to issue statutory instruments in order to modify provisions of: " . . . any enactment or subordinate legislation . . . in such manner as he may think fit for the purpose of authorising or facilitating the use of electronic communications" for a number of purposes, including the making of contracts.[28] Moreover, art.9(1) of the European Directive on Electronic Commerce 2000[29] provides that:

> "Member States *shall* ensure that their legal system allows contracts to be concluded by electronic means. Member States shall in particular ensure that the legal requirements applicable to the contractual process neither create obstacles for the use of electronic contracts nor result in such contracts being deprived of legal effectiveness and validity on account of their being made by electronic means."[30]

Article 9 continues by allowing Member States to provide for exceptions to this principle notably in "contracts that create or transfer rights in real estate, except for rental rights"[31] and "contracts of suretyship granted and on collateral securities furnished by persons acting outside their trade, business or profession".[32] Where it applies, this obligation on Member States is not limited to the conclusion of the contract, but extends to all aspects of the contractual process.[33]

4–006 **Impact on formality requirements.** At first sight, art.9 of this Directive might appear to have required the United Kingdom to revise a good deal of its law of contractual formalities, much of which requires a contract to be contained or evidenced in writing and/or signed, neither of these appearing to be able to be achieved by electronic means. However, the Law Commission advised the Government that in general requirements of "writing" and of "signature" can be

[26] [2003] UKHL 17 at [9], [25].
[27] [2003] UKHL 17 at [20]. On the Statute of Frauds s.4, see Vol.II, paras 44–038—44–054.
[28] Electronic Communications Act 2000 s.8(1).
[29] Directive 2000/31 on certain legal aspects of information society services, in particular electronic commerce, in the Internal Market [2000] OJ L178/1.
[30] Emphasis added.
[31] Directive 2000/31 art.9(2)(a).
[32] Directive 2000/31 art.9(2)(d).
[33] Directive 2000/31, Recital 34; Beale and Griffiths (2002) L.M.C.L.Q. 467, 468.

fulfilled via some electronic means without any changes being made to the law.[34] So, as to "writing" this requirement can be fulfilled by electronic mail and website trading, but not by electronic data interchange as this does not involve any visible text so as to satisfy s.5 of the Interpretation Act 1978's definition of writing.[35] Its view is that "writing" does not need any "physical memorial," such as paper.[36] Secondly, the Law Commission's view was that requirements of signature can generally be interpreted in a functional way, by asking whether or not the conduct of a would-be signatory indicates an authenticating intention to a reasonable person, though each requirement must be considered in its own statutory context.[37] Following this approach, a requirement of signature can be fulfilled in a number of ways: by "electronic signature" using a dual-key encryption system and a certification authority[38]; by use of a manuscript signature scanned into a computer and incorporated into an email or other document; by a person typing their name or initials or by setting up a system by which this occurs automatically[39]; and even by a purchaser on a website "clicking" a button after entering onto the web details of the goods that they wish to purchase, confirming payment and personal details.[40] The Law Commission concluded that:

> ". . . there is no need for general legislative reform, because we consider that legislation is not only unnecessary but also risky. It is difficult to envisage a simple global reform that would be effective in all eventualities. . . . [So], it is only in very rare cases that the statute book will conflict with Article 9 of the Electronic Commerce Directive."[41]

Where legislative change is needed, it can be effected by exercise of the power contained in s.8 of the Electronic Communications Act 2000. One particular context in which this may need to be the case is s.2 of the Law of Property (Miscellaneous) Provisions Act 1989. For, as will be explained, in this context it

---

[34] Law Commission, *Electronic Commerce: Formal Requirements in Commercial* Transactions (2001), available in full at *http://www.lawcom.gov.uk* [Accessed June 11, 2008] and see a shorter version in Beale and Griffiths (2002) L.M.C.L.Q. 467 to which the following references will relate.

[35] Beale and Griffiths, (2002) L.M.C.L.Q. 467, 471–472. The Interpretation Act 1978 s.5 states that: "'Writing' includes typing, printing, lithography, photography and other modes of representing or reproducing words in a visible form, and expressions referring to writing are construed accordingly."

[36] Beale and Griffiths (2002) L.M.C.L.Q. 467, 472.

[37] Beale and Griffiths (2002) L.M.C.L.Q. 467, 473.

[38] And see below, para.4–007.

[39] In *J Pereira Fernandes SA v Mehta* [2006] EWHC 813 (Ch), [2006] 2 All E.R. 881 at [25]–[30], it was held that the automatic insertion of an email address in a message by an internet service provider did not constitute a signature by the writer of the message as it did not represent any intention to authenticate the message by the writer. However, Judge Pelling Q.C. accepted that: "[I]f a party or a party's agent sending an e-mail types his or her or his or her principal's name to the extent required or permitted by existing case law in the body of an e-mail, then . . . that would be sufficient signature for the purposes of section 4 [of the Statute of Frauds]" (at [31]), the learned judge noting the position of the Law Commission to this effect.

[40] Beale and Griffiths (2002) L.M.C.L.Q. 467, 473–474.

[41] Beale and Griffiths (2002) L.M.C.L.Q. 467, 473.

has been said that "signature" must be given its ordinary linguistic meaning, so as to require each of the parties to contracts for the sale or other disposition of an interest in land to write their names with their own hands upon the document.[42] However, some or all of the contracts contained within this category may come within one of the exceptions to art.9 of the EC Directive so as to allow English law to retain a formal requirement which is inconsistent with the effectiveness of a contract made by electronic means.[43] Moreover, the courts may well consider that in some other statutory contexts (for example, contracts of guarantee under s.4 of the Statute of Frauds) either "writing" or "signature" should not be interpreted as broadly as the Law Commission generally propose, in the interests of the protection of the person to be bound thereby.[44] Here, without legislative intervention, a conflict may arise between the interpretation of the English courts and the requirements of art.9 of the Electronic Commerce Directive, which does allow a Member State to make an exception for contracts of suretyship but only where undertaken by persons "acting outside their trade, business or profession".[45]

4–007 **Electronic signatures.** The United Kingdom implemented the Electronic Signatures Directive 1999 by two instruments.[46] First, s.7 of the Electronic Communications Act 2000 provides for the admissibility in legal proceedings of electronic signatures and related digital signatures (although this appears to do little more than state the existing common law position). Secondly, the Electronic Signatures Regulations 2002 provide for the supervision and liability of "certification-service-providers", (i.e. persons who issue certificates or provide other services related to electronic signatures) and for consequential matters relating to data protection.[47]

4–008 **Electronic documents and deeds.** Following the recommendations of the Law Commission,[48] the Land Registration Act 2002 made provision for the creation of a framework in which it will be possible to transfer and create interests in registered land by electronic means through a network controlled by the Land Registry.[49] In order to permit this, Pt 8 of the Act makes provision for the fulfilment electronically of formality requirements by the transactions in question, doing so by assimilating certain qualifying electronic documents to deeds for the purposes of any enactment requiring the dispositions to which those documents relate to use a deed.

---

[42] *Firstpost Homes Ltd v Johnson* [1995] 1 W.L.R. 1567, 1574–1577 and see below, para.4–073.

[43] Directive 2000/31 art.9(2)(a), above, para.4–005.

[44] cf. *J Pereira Fernandes SA v Mehta* [2006] EWHC 813 (Ch), [2006] 2 All E.R. 881 at [31], where the Law Commission's broad approach was approved (and see above, fn.39).

[45] Directive 2000/31 art.9(2)(d), above, para.4–005.

[46] Directive 1999/93 on a Community framework for electronic signatures [2000] OJ 13/12.

[47] SI 2002/318.

[48] Law Commission, *Land Registration for the Twenty-First Century a Conveyancing Revolution* (2001), Law Com. No.271 and see above, para.1–088.

[49] See further *http://www.landreg.gov.uk/e-conveyancing/* [Accessed June 11, 2008].

2. CONTRACTS FOR THE SALE OR OTHER DISPOSITION OF AN INTEREST IN LAND

Legislative history. The Statute of Frauds was passed in 1677 and in ss.4 and 17 it required that six classes of contracts must be supported by written evidence. Its object was to prevent fraudulent claims based on false evidence; but in practice it worked badly as it enabled contracting parties to rely on what were considered to be technical defences. Hence the statute was, whenever possible, whittled down by judicial construction; and it was largely repealed by the Law Reform (Enforcement of Contracts) Act 1954. Nevertheless, the statute still applies to contracts of guarantee[50] and its provisions were re-enacted in s.40 of the Law of Property Act 1925, which applies to contracts for the disposition of interests in land made on or before September 26, 1989.[51] However, by the Law of Property (Miscellaneous Provisions) Act 1989 s.2, the Law of Property Act 1925 s.40 was itself repealed and new requirements were enacted which apply to all contracts for the sale or other disposition of interests in land made on or after September 27, 1989. The present edition of this work retains discussion of the old law (in the present tense) as it still governs contracts made before that date. While the old law may at times be of help in interpreting the new, this may not always be appropriate. As Peter Gibson L.J. observed in *Firstpost Homes Ltd v Johnson*[52]: 4–009

> "... the Act of 1989 seems to me to have a new and different philosophy from that which the Statute of Frauds 1677 and s.40 of the Act of 1925 had. Oral contracts are no longer permitted. To my mind it is clear that Parliament intended that questions as to whether there was a contract, and what were the terms of the contract, should be readily ascertained by looking at the single document said to constitute the contract."

(a) *The Old Law: Contracts made on or before September 26, 1989*

Law of Property Act 1925 section 40. By s.40(1) of the Law of Property Act 1925: 4–010

> "No action may be brought upon any contract for the sale[53] or other disposition of land or any interest in land, unless the agreement upon which such action is brought, or some memorandum or note thereof, is in writing, and signed by the party to be charged or by some other person thereunto by him lawfully authorised."[54]

---

[50] See Vol.II, Ch.44.

[51] See below, paras 4–010—4–051.

[52] [1995] 1 W.L.R. 1567 at 1576 and see *McCausland v Duncan Lawrie Ltd* [1996] 4 All E.R. 995, 1001.

[53] A "sale" means the exchanging of property for money. An agreement to extinguish an existing debt if land is transferred is not a sale; see *Simpson v Connolly* [1953] 1 W.L.R. 911.

[54] As to the contents and signature of the memorandum or note in writing, see below, paras 4–022 et seq.; and see *Shardlow v Cotterell* (1881) 20 Ch D 90; *Studds v Watson* (1884) 28 Ch D 305; *Auerbach v Nelson* [1919] 2 Ch. 383; *Lord Cloncurry v Laffan* [1924] 1 Ir.R. 78.

The section replaced, and was intended to give effect to the construction judicially placed upon, that portion of s.4 of the Statute of Frauds which related to interests in land. The section applies to contracts whether made before or after the commencement of the year 1926[55] and on or before September 26, 1989[56] and does not affect the law relating to part performance and sales by the court.[57]

(i) *Contracts within section 40 of the Law of Property Act 1925*

4–011 **Contracts within the section.** The words "or other disposition" are widely defined[58] and include, inter alia, a mortgage, charge, lease, release and disclaimer; and an "interest in land" includes an undivided share, although this is converted into an equivalent share in the proceeds of sale.[59] Similarly, s.4 of the Statute of Frauds applied to many contracts that concerned land although they were not contracts of sale.[60] Thus an agreement to convey an equity of redemption in land was within the statute, for a court of equity treated the equity of redemption as the land itself, or at all events as an interest in land.[61] Contracts for the disposition of an interest in land within the meaning of the statute have been held to include the following: an agreement that if the plaintiff, the tenant of a farm, would surrender her tenancy to her landlord, and would prevail on her landlord to accept the defendant as his tenant in place of the plaintiff, the defendant would pay the plaintiff £100[62]; an agreement by the defendant, the landlord of a house, to put certain furniture into the house in consideration that the plaintiff would become tenant thereof[63]; an agreement to grant a lease of furnished premises[64]; and an agreement by the plaintiff to let a house to the defendant, to sell him furniture and fixtures therein, and to make alterations and improvements in the house, the defendant agreeing to take the house, and to pay for the furniture, fixtures and alterations.[65] An agreement to extend the time for acceptance, or an agreement that an acceptance which is out of time shall be treated as valid so as to create a contract, is not an agreement which the statute requires to be evidenced in writing, provided that the note or memorandum contained in the signed offer is otherwise sufficient.[66] Furthermore, it has been held that an agreement which compromised an action arising out of claims for

[55] The date at which the Law of Property Act 1925 came into operation.

[56] The day before the Law of Property (Miscellaneous Provisions) Act 1989 s.2 came into operation.

[57] s.40(2); below, paras 4–042—4–050.

[58] s.205(1)(ii).

[59] See *Cooper v Critchley* [1955] Ch. 431, 439. cf. *Irani Finance Ltd v Singh* [1971] 1 Ch. 59, 79.

[60] *McManus v Cooke* (1887) 35 Ch D 681, 687–690, and cases there cited.

[61] *Massey v Johnson* (1847) 1 Exch. 241, 255.

[62] *Cocking v Ward* (1845) 1 C.B. 858, 867; followed in *Kelly v Webster* (1852) 12 C.B. 283. (In both these cases there was a "part performance," but this could not assist the plaintiffs in courts of common law before the Judicature Acts.)

[63] *Mechelen v Wallace* (1837) 7 A. & E. 49.

[64] *Inman v Stamp* (1815) 1 Stark. 12; *Edge v Strafford* (1831) 1 Cr. & J. 391; *Thursby v Eccles* (1900) 17 T.L.R. 130.

[65] *Vaughan v Hancock* (1846) 3 C.B. 766.

[66] *Morrell v Studd and Millington* [1913] 2 Ch. 648, 658.

land between cohabitants was not a contract for the disposition of land, but rather related to accounting for the proceeds of sale of the properties.[67]

An agreement to sell a debt, secured by bond and also by a mortgage of land,[68] or to sell debentures of a company possessed of land charging all its property whatsoever and wheresoever,[69] is within the section. So is an agreement between two persons to become partners in working a colliery owned by one of them[70]; but a contract for a partnership is not within the section merely because the acquisition of land is necessary for carrying on the business.[71] An agreement by A, who had borrowed a sum of money from his bankers in July, to repay the loan out of the rent of a farm to become due to him at the Michaelmas following,[72] has been held within the section; so also has an agreement for regulating the height of a party wall, which was to be pulled down and rebuilt, and the position and shape of skylights on either side of it.[73] It seems that the contract may be within the section although the party agreeing to confer the interest does not, at the time, possess any interest in the land in question, as was held in an action against a public-house broker for breach of a contract to procure a lease of a public-house to be transferred by the lessee to the plaintiff.[74] 4–012

It has been held that a right of option in respect of land, as opposed to a mere right of pre-emption, is an interest in land for the purposes of binding third parties.[75] It is not settled, however, whether this distinction holds good in the context of the requirements of s.40.[76] Similarly, licences to occupy land may create "interests in land" in order to bind third parties, sometimes by way of proprietory estoppel and sometimes by way of imposing a constructive trust.[77] There is no requirement of written evidence in the case of the *creation* of a constructive trust,[78] but it appears that any *disposition* of an interest arising 4–013

---

[67] *Simmons v Simmons* [1996] C.L.Y. 2874 (decided under Law of Property (Miscellaneous Provisions) Act s.2 which specifies that "disposition" bears the same meaning as under the Law of Property Act 1925 s.40).

[68] *Toppin v Lomas* (1855) 16 C.B. 145.

[69] *Driver v Broad* [1893] 1 Q.B. 744.

[70] *Caddick v Skidmore* (1857) 2 De G. & J. 52.

[71] *Forster v Hale* (1800) 5 Ves. 308; *Dale v Hamilton* (1846) 5 Hare 369; *Gray v Smith* (1890) 43 Ch D 208; cf. *Re De Nicols (No.2)* [1900] 2 Ch. 410.

[72] *Ex p. Hall* (1879) 10 Ch D 615.

[73] *McManus v Cooke* (1887) 35 Ch D 681.

[74] *Horsey v Graham* (1869) L.R. 5 C.P. 9.

[75] *Pritchard v Briggs* [1980] Ch. 388, 418 (for the purposes of the Land Charges Act 1925 s.10), followed in *Kling v Keston Properties Ltd* [1985] P. & C.R. 212 (for the purposes of s.70(1) Land Registration Act 1925). For rights of pre-emption in relation to registered land see Land Registration Act 2002 s.115. cf. below, para.4–058 relating to s.2 of the Law of Property (Miscellaneous Provisions) Act 1989.

[76] *Emmet on Title* (1993), para.2.039 citing *National Provincial Bank Ltd v Moore* (1967) 111 S.J. 357 and cf. *Cooper v Critchley* [1955] Ch. 431 and *Irani Finance Ltd v Singh* [1971] 1 Ch. 59 which establish that an undivided share in land is an "interest in land" for the purposes of s.40 Law of Property Act 1925 but *not* for the purposes of registration under the Land Charges Act 1925 or Land Registration Act 1925.

[77] Megarry and Wade, *The Law of Real Property*, 6th edn (2000), Ch.17; cf. *Wright v Stavert* (1860) 3 E. & E. 721 where a "mere contractual licence" was held not subject to the Statute of Frauds s.4.

[78] Law of Property Act 1925 s.53(2).

thereby would fall within s.53(1)(c) of the Law of Property Act 1925.[79] A similar distinction may well apply to any interest arising under the doctrine of proprietary estoppel.

4–014 It is established that any transfer of an interest occurring as a result of compulsory purchase does not require the observance of s.40.[80] And where an equitable mortgage secures a guarantee, it appears that it is subject to the formal requirements of s.4 of the Statute of Frauds which applies to guarantees[81] rather than those of s.40 of the Law of Property Act 1925.[82]

4–015 **Variations.** In *Morall v Krause*[83] the Court of Appeal held that any variation of a contract for the sale or other disposition of land must also satisfy the formal requirements of s.40 of the Law of Property Act 1925. In the absence of either a written memorandum or of part performance, any oral variation of such a contract can have no effect.

4–016 **Collateral agreements.**[84] If a collateral agreement, not involving the acquisition of land, is entered into at or before the time of making a written contract concerning land, the collateral agreement does not require to be evidenced in writing.[85] So, on the purchase of land an oral promise by the vendor to make up the road leading to the premises sold is not a contract for an interest in land apart from a conveyance of the highway.[86] Any such collateral agreement must be clearly proved.[87] Where, however, a collateral agreement is established, damages for breach of it can be recovered after conveyance of the land, as, for example, where the contract was to complete the building of a house on the land conveyed.[88]

4–017 **Entire agreement clauses.** No oral collateral agreement may arise if the written contract, for example, of sale of an interest in land, is expressed to constitute the entire contract between the parties, variable only in writing.[89]

---

[79] Martin, *Hanbury and Martin's Modern Equity*, 17th edn (2005), pp.82 et seq.; *Oughtred v IRC* [1960] A.C. 206. It could be argued that the transfer of such an interest is part of the *operation* of a constructive trust within s.53(2) but cf. Law Com. No.164 (1987), para.4.4 which recommended that the disposition of equitable interests in land, even those created informally, should be subject to formal requirements and see below, para.4–075.

[80] *Munton v G.L.C.* [1976] 1 W.L.R. 649, 653.

[81] See Vol.II, paras 44–038 et seq.

[82] *Deutsche Bank A.G. v Ibrahim, Financial Times*, December 13, 1991 and January 15, 1992; Baughen [1992] Conv. 330; and see below, para.4–058.

[83] [1994] E.G.C.S. 177.

[84] Wedderburn [1959] Camb.L.J. 58, cf. Law Com. No.164 (1987), pp.20–21; and see below, para.4–076.

[85] *Angell v Duke* (1875) L.R. 10 Q.B. 174 (in which *Cocking v Ward* (1845) 1 C.B. 858 and *Mechelen v Wallace* (1837) 7 A. & E. 49 were distinguished); *Boston v Boston* [1904] 1 K.B. 124. See also *Pullbrook v Laws* (1876) 1 QBD 284.

[86] *Jameson v Kinmell Bay Land Co Ltd* (1931) 47 T.L.R. 593; following *Erskine v Adeane* (1873) L.R. 8 Ch.App. 756.

[87] *Hodges v Jones* [1935] Ch. 657.

[88] *Lawrence v Cassell* [1930] 2 K.B. 83.

[89] *McGrath v Shah, The Times*, October 22, 1987 and see *Britain v Rossiter* (1883) 11 QBD 123, 127.

Sale of growing crops. A contract conferring an exclusive right to enter land in order to mow and take away a crop of grass has been held to be within the statute.[90] It is difficult to reconcile all the decisions and dicta on the subject of simple sales of growing crops (conferring no right to enter the land).[91] A distinction is commonly drawn between *fructus industriales* and *fructus naturales*. The former are crops which are produced by annual cultivation and are not within the section. The latter are things which grow without any or with very little cultivation, trees being *fructus naturales* because "the labour employed in their planting bears so small a proportion to their natural growth".[92] It seems that a contract for the sale of *fructus naturales*, such as trees, is a contract for the sale of an interest in land if the trees are to remain in the land; but if they are to be immediately severed by the vendor[93] or if the contract requires the purchaser to sever them at once, the contract is not one for the sale of an interest in land.[94] 4–018

Other things to be detached from land. The section has been applied to other things to be detached from land, such as gravel[95] and the building materials to accrue on the demolition of a house.[96] Such things are within the definition of "goods" given in s.61 of the Sale of Goods Act 1979; but it may equally well be that such things are goods for the purpose of the Sale of Goods Act and land or interests in land for the purpose of s.40 of the Law of Property Act 1925.[97] 4–019

Fixtures. Fixtures are normally an interest in land. But a sale by a tenant of fixtures which he is entitled to remove is not within the section. He is considered to have sold neither goods nor an interest in land but to have assigned his right to sever.[98] 4–020

Shooting rights. A grant of a right to shoot over land and to take away a part of the game killed is a grant of an interest in land, and consequently within the statute.[99] 4–021

(ii) *Formal Requirements*

General. Section 40 does not specify the matters which the memorandum is to contain. These have been left to judicial interpretation and the courts have laid down the following rules as to the contents and nature of the memorandum. 4–022

---

[90] *Crosby v Wadsworth* (1805) 6 East 602; and see *Wood v Leadbitter* (1845) 13 M. & W. 838.

[91] See, e.g. *Marshall v Green* (1875) 1 C.P.D. 35, 38 et seq.; and *Lavery v Pursell* (1888) 39 Ch D 508.

[92] *Marshall v Green* (1875) 1 C.P.D. 35, 40.

[93] *Smith v Surman* (1829) 9 B. & C. 561; *Washbourn v Burrows* (1847) 1 Exch. 107, 115.

[94] *Marshall v Green* (1875) 1 C.P.D. 35; *Kauri Timber Co Ltd v Commissioner of Taxes* [1913] A.C. 771, 778.

[95] *Morgan v Russell & Sons* [1909] 1 K.B. 357, 365.

[96] *Lavery v Pursell* (1888) 39 Ch D 508.

[97] *Benjamin's Sale of Goods*, 7th edn (2006), para.1–092. See also Blackburn, *Contract of Sale*, 3rd edn (1910), pp.7–16.

[98] *Hallen v Runder* (1834) 1 Cr.M. & R. 266; *Lee v Gaskell* (1876) 1 QBD 700.

[99] *Webber v Lee* (1882) 9 QBD 315; *R. v Surrey County Court Judge* [1910] 2 K.B. 410.

4–023 **Parties.** The memorandum must identify the parties and the capacity in which each of them contracts: it must name or describe them[100] and state which is (for example) buyer and which is seller.[101] It may sufficiently describe the parties without actually naming them. Thus a vendor of land may be adequately described as "proprietor",[102] or as "trustee selling under a trust for sale"[103] or even as "legal personal representative".[104] But it is not sufficient to describe a party as "vendor"[105] or "landlord".[106] A pronoun may be sufficient if there is evidence to show to whom it refers.[107]

4–024 **Subject matter.** The memorandum must describe the subject-matter,[108] but may sufficiently describe it even though the description has to be supplemented by extrinsic evidence. Thus a memorandum recording the sale of "24 acres of land, freehold . . . at Totmonslow" was held sufficient on proof that the vendor had no other land there.[109] If the land is subject to incumbrances the memorandum need not state them all.[110]

4–025 **Consideration.** The memorandum of a contract for the disposition of an interest in land must state the consideration provided by the purchaser.[111]

4–026 **Terms.** The memorandum must contain a statement of the material[112] terms of the contract. Thus the memorandum of an agreement for a lease must state the beginning and duration of the term.[113] If on a sale separate prices are to be paid for separate lots,[114] or if the price is agreed to be paid by instalments,[115] or if chattels are to be included as well as land for an indivisible price,[116] the

---

[100] See *Williams v Jordan* (1877) 6 Ch D 517 ("Sir" insufficient); *Re Lindrea* (1913) 109 L.T. 623 (Christian name sufficient); *E. Goldsmith (Sicklesmere) Ltd v Baxter* [1970] Ch. 85 (company misdescribed but identifiable) and see *Perrylease Ltd v Imecar A.G.* [1988] 1 W.L.R. 463, 468–469.

[101] *Vandenbergh v Spooner* (1866) L.R. 1 Ex. 316; *Newell v Radford* (1867) L.R. 3 C.P. 52; *Stockwell v Niven* (1889) 61 L.T. 18; *Dewar v Mintoft* [1912] 2 K.B. 373.

[102] *Sale v Lambert* (1874) L.R. 18 Eq. 1; *Rossiter v Miller* (1878) 3 App. Cas. 1125, 1140–1141.

[103] *Catling v King* (1877) 5 Ch D 660, 664.

[104] *Fay v Miller, Wilkins & Co* [1941] Ch. 360.

[105] *Potter v Duffield* (1874) L.R. 18 Eq. 4; *Thomas v Brown* (1876) 1 QBD 714; cf. *Jarrett v Hunter* (1886) 34 Ch D 182.

[106] *Coombs v Wilks* [1891] 3 Ch. 77.

[107] *Carr v Lynch* [1900] 1 Ch. 613; cf. *Stokes v Whicher* [1920] 1 Ch. 411, 419–422.

[108] Description of part is insufficient: *Burgess v Cox* [1951] Ch. 383.

[109] *Plant v Bourne* [1897] 2 Ch. 281 and see *Perrylease Ltd v Imecar A.G.* [1988] 1 W.L.R. 463, 469–473.

[110] *Timmins v Moreland Street Property Co* [1958] Ch. 110.

[111] *Blagden v Bradbear* (1806) 12 Ves. 466, 471; *Laythoarp v Bryant* (1836) 2 Bing.N.C. 735, 742; *Burgess v Cox* [1951] Ch. 383 (disapproved on other grounds in *Scott v Bradley* [1971] Ch. 850). cf. *Sudbrook Trading Estate Ltd v Eggleton* [1983] 1 A.C. 444.

[112] *Hawkins v Price* [1947] Ch. 645; cf. *Beckett v Nurse* [1948] 1 K.B. 535.

[113] *Marshall v Berridge* (1881) 19 Ch D 233; *Edwards v Jones* (1921) 124 L.T. 740.

[114] *Smith v MacGowan* (1938) 159 L.T. 278.

[115] *Tweddell v Henderson* [1975] 1 W.L.R. 1496.

[116] *Ram Narayan s/o Shankar v Rishad Hussain Shah s/o Tusaduq Hussain Shah* [1979] 1 W.L.R. 1349.

memorandum must not omit such terms, otherwise it will not satisfy the statute. The reason for these rules is that:

> "... the very object of the Statute of Frauds was to prevent parol evidence being gone into to elucidate that which the parties failed to make distinct by reducing it into writing."[117]

There is, however, authority[118] for the view that if a material term has been omitted from the memorandum, the claimant may waive such a term where it is solely for his benefit[119] and not of a major importance, and enforce the contract without the term in question. Conversely, a party may cure the omission of a term to his detriment by consenting to perform it.[120] Finally, an express term which is identical to a term implied by law, for example, a term that vacant possession is to be given on completion, need not be included in the memorandum.[121]

Memorandum need not be prepared as such. The memorandum need not be prepared for the purpose of satisfying the statutory requirement of written evidence. Any writing which contains the requisite particulars will suffice so long as it comes into existence before an action is brought on the contract.[122] Thus a recital in a will,[123] a receipt given by an auctioneer before receiving the purchaser's deposit,[124] a letter written by one of the parties to his own agent,[125] an entry in the minute book of a company[126] and pleadings in a previous action between different parties[127] have been held sufficient. A letter repudiating liability is sufficient if it admits the terms of the contract but disputes the construction put upon them by the other party; but not if it denies that a contract was ever made on the terms alleged.[128] Apart from the exceptional case of a written offer signed by one party and accepted orally by the other,[129] the writing must acknowledge the existence of a contract. It is now settled, after some hesitation, 4–027

[117] *Caddick v Skidmore* (1857) 2 De G. & J. 52, 56.

[118] *Morrell v Studd and Millington* [1913] 2 Ch. 648, 660; *North v Loomes* [1919] 1 Ch. 378, 385–386; *Beckett v Nurse* [1948] 1 K.B. 535; *Turner v Hatton* [1952] 1 T.L.R. 1184; *Ram Narayan s/o Shankar v Rishad Hussain Shah s/o Tusaduq Hussain Shah* [1979] 1 W.L.R. 1349, 1351.

[119] cf. *Hawkins v Price* [1947] Ch. 645, 657–658.

[120] *Martin v Pycroft* (1852) 2 De G.M. & G. 785; Megarry (1951) 67 L.Q.R. 300; *Scott v Bradley* [1971] Ch. 850. Contrast *Burgess v Cox* [1951] Ch. 383, 391.

[121] *Farrell v Green* (1974) 232 E.G. 587.

[122] See *Lucas v Dixon* (1889) 22 QBD 357; cf. *Farr, Smith & Co Ltd v Messers Ltd* [1928] 1 K.B. 397; *Daniels v Trefusis* [1914] 1 K.B. 788.

[123] *Re Hoyle* [1893] 1 Ch. 84.

[124] *Phillips v Butler* [1945] Ch. 358.

[125] *Gibson v Holland* (1865) L.R. 1 C.P. 1; *Law v Robert Roberts & Co* [1964] I.R. 292.

[126] *Jones v Victoria Graving Dock Co* (1877) 2 QBD 314.

[127] *Grindell v Bass* [1920] 2 Ch. 487; cf. *Hardy v Elphick* [1974] Ch. 65 (action between same parties).

[128] *Dobell v Hutchinson* (1835) 3 A. & E. 355; *Bailey v Sweeting* (1861) 9 C.B.(N.S.) 843; *Wilkinson v Evans* (1866) L.R. 1 C.P. 407; *Buxton v Rust* (1872) L.R. 7 Ex. 279; *Thirkell v Cambi* [1919] 2 K.B. 591.

[129] *Smith v Neale* (1857) 2 C.B.(N.S.) 67, 88; *Reuss v Picksley* (1866) L.R. 1 Ex. 342; *Lever v Koffler* [1901] 1 Ch. 543; *Parker v Clark* [1960] 1 W.L.R. 286; *J Pereira Fernandes SA v Mehta* [2006] EWHC 813 (Ch), [2006] 2 All E.R. 881 at [11]–[17] (s.4 of the Statute of Frauds 1677). But cf. *Re New Eberhardt Co* (1889) 43 Ch D 118, 129.

that a letter expressed to be "subject to contract" is not in itself a sufficient memorandum to satisfy the statute.[130]

4–028 **Agreement contained in several documents.** Where no single document fully records the transaction, it may be possible to produce a sufficient memorandum by joining together two or more documents. This may be done where the document which is signed by the party to be charged expressly or by implication refers to another existing document.[131] Thus where a signed document, which does not contain the terms of the agreement, refers to an unsigned document which does, parol evidence may be given for the purpose of identifying the latter as being the document referred to in the former.[132] But such express reference is not absolutely necessary: it is enough if "you can spell out of the document a reference in it to some other transaction".[133] So, in *Stokes v Whicher*[134] the defendant's agent signed for him, as "vendor", a carbon copy of a typewritten contract not containing a purchaser's name. The plaintiff had signed the original document, of which the carbon copy was a duplicate, and had given a cheque for the deposit, a receipt for it signed by the defendant's agent being put on the carbon copy. The court held that a sufficient memorandum had been constituted by: (a) incorporating the cheque into the carbon copy; (b) connecting the carbon copy with the original; and (c) identifying the person who paid the deposit as the plaintiff. A similar decision was reached where a house was sold by auction and the name of the vendor did not appear in the memorandum signed by the purchaser. The latter, however, by the memorandum acknowledged that she bought the property "subject to the conditions of sale", the contents of which sufficiently identified the vendor. The memorandum was therefore sufficient to satisfy the statute.[135] Similarly, a letter which admits the existence of an oral agreement may be joined with an earlier letter written "subject to contract", to

---

130 *Tiverton Estates Ltd v Wearwell Ltd* [1975] Ch. 146; *Sherbrooke v Dipple* (1980) 255 E.G. 1203; *Cohen v Nessdale Ltd* [1981] 3 All E.R. 118, [1982] 2 All E.R. 97; *Clipper Maritime Ltd v Shirlstar Container Transport Ltd* [1987] 1 Lloyd's Rep. 546 (guarantee). cf. *Griffiths v Young* [1970] Ch. 675. *Law v Jones* [1974] Ch. 112 was not followed in *Tiverton Estates Ltd v Wearwell Ltd*: cf. *Daulia Ltd v Four Millbank Nominees Ltd* [1978] Ch. 231, 249–251 and cf. Law Com. No.164 (1987), para.1.4.

131 *Ridgway v Wharton* (1857) 6 H.L.C. 238; *Long v Millar* (1879) 4 C.P.D. 450; *Studds v Watson* (1884) 28 Ch D 305; *Wylson v Dunn* (1887) 34 Ch D 569; cf. *Reading Trust Ltd v Spero* [1930] 1 K.B. 492; *Hill v Hill* [1947] Ch. 231; *Fowler v Bratt* [1950] 2 K.B. 96; *Burgess v Cox* [1951] Ch. 383; *Timmins v Moreland Street Property Co Ltd* [1958] Ch. 110, 130; *Elias v George Sahely & Co (Barbados) Ltd* [1983] 1 A.C. 646. See also *Re Danish Bacon Co Ltd Staff Pension Fund Trusts* [1971] 1 W.L.R. 248 (on s.53(1)(c) of the Law of Property Act 1925; below, para.19–025). The document must be in existence: *Turnley v Hartley* (1848) 3 New Pr. Cas. 96; *Timmins v Moreland Street Property Co Ltd* at 123, 133.

132 See *Ridgway v Wharton* (1857) 6 H.L.C. 238, 257; *Jones v Victoria Graving Dock Co* (1877) 2 QBD 314; *Oliver v Hunting* (1890) 44 Ch D 205; *Smith-Bird v Blower* [1939] 2 All E.R. 406; *Re Danish Bacon Co Ltd Staff Pension Fund Trusts* [1971] 1 W.L.R. 248.

133 *Stokes v Whicher* [1920] 1 Ch. 411, 418.

134 [1920] 1 Ch. 411. cf. *Cave v Hastings* (1881) 7 QBD 125; *Franco-British Ship Store Co v Compagnie des Chargeurs Française* (1926) 42 T.L.R. 735; *Jacobs v Batavia & General Plantations Trust Ltd* [1924] 1 Ch. 287 (a case not involving the statute); contrast *Coombs v Quinney* (1916) 142 L.T.J. 23.

135 *Fay v Miller, Wilkins & Co* [1941] Ch. 360. See also *Albert (Men's Wear) v Prevezer* (1949) 154 E.G. 424.

which the latter letter refers, for the purpose of ascertaining the terms of the admitted agreement.[136] Also a letter beginning "Dear Sir" and signed by the defendant can be joined with the envelope in which it was sent (so as to identify the addressee)[137] since "the existence of a letter sent by post presupposes the existence of an envelope containing it".[138] And it has been held that two documents can be joined (even if they do not refer to each other) if on placing them side by side it becomes obvious without the aid of parol evidence that they are connected.[139]

Documents which cannot be connected by parol evidence. Parol evidence to identify references has been frequently admitted.[140] But parol evidence cannot be admitted to connect two or more writings which contain no reference express or implied to each other. Thus, where the defendant signed a book, headed "Shakespeare Subscribers, their Signatures", and a printed prospectus which contained the terms of the agreement was delivered to him at the time, but this prospectus was not referred to in the book signed by the defendant, the contract was unenforceable because the connection between the book containing the signature and the prospectus could be established only by parol evidence.[141] So where, at a sale of goods by auction, the auctioneer signed the purchaser's name in the catalogue, but the conditions of sale were not annexed to the catalogue or referred to therein, it was held that there was not a sufficient memorandum of the contract within s.40.[142] An entry in the auctioneer's book cannot be used to prove a contract within the statute, unless the entry comprises such a reference to the conditions of sale as will identify them upon production as being the conditions mentioned in the entry.[143] In *Timmins v Moreland Street Property Co Ltd*,[144] prospective purchasers gave a cheque payable to the vendors' solicitors as the deposit on the purchase and the vendors in return gave a receipt incorporating the terms of the contract. It was held that there could not be spelled out of the cheque any reference, express or implied, to any other document or to any transaction other than the order to pay a sum of money constituted by the cheque itself. 4–029

[136] *Griffiths v Young* [1970] Ch. 675, as interpreted in *Tiverton Estates Ltd v Wearwell Ltd* [1975] Ch. 146. See also *Law v Jones* [1974] Ch. 112 as interpreted in *Daulia Ltd v Four Millbank Nominees Ltd* [1978] Ch. 231; *Elias v George Sahely & Co (Barbados) Ltd* [1983] 1 A.C. 646, at 655.

[137] *Pearce v Gardner* [1897] 1 Q.B. 688.

[138] *Stokes v Whicher* [1920] 1 Ch. 411, 418. See also *Last v Hucklesby* (1914) 58 S.J. 431 (lost envelope).

[139] *Studds v Watson* [1884] 28 Ch D 305, 308–309; *Sheers v Thimbleby* (1897) 13 T.L.R. 451; *Stokes v Whicher* [1920] 1 Ch. 411, 419. cf. *Burgess v Cox* [1951] Ch. 383 (disapproved on other grounds by *Scott v Bradley* [1971] Ch. 850).

[140] See *Cave v Hastings* (1881) 7 QBD 125, 128, and the cases there cited; *Oliver v Hunting* (1890) L.R. 44 Ch D 205; *Shardlow v Cottrell* (1881) 20 Ch D 90; *Studds v Watson* (1884) 28 Ch D 305; *Filby v Hounsell* (1896) 2 Ch. 737; *Auerbach v Nelson* [1919] 2 Ch. 383; *Elliott v Pierson* [1948] Ch. 452, 455.

[141] *Boydell v Drummond* (1809) 11 East 142, 158; cf. *Peirce v Corf* (1874) L.R. 9 Q.B. 210; *Kronheim v Johnson* (1877) 7 Ch D 60.

[142] *Kenworthy v Schofield* (1824) 2 B. & C. 945; *Rishton v Whatmore* (1878) 8 Ch D 467.

[143] *Rishton v Whatmore* (1878) 8 Ch D 467 at 468; *M'Meekin v Stevenson* [1917] 1 Ir.R. 348.

[144] [1958] Ch. 110. See Megarry (1958) 74 L.Q.R. 22.

4–030 **Lost memorandum.** If it is proved that the memorandum has been lost or destroyed a copy not signed by the party to be charged may be admitted as secondary evidence.[145]

4–031 **Signature.** The Law of Property Act 1925 s.40, requires that the document should be "signed by the party to be charged", and it is sufficient if it is signed by the party to be charged without being signed by the other party.[146] The interpretation of this provision well illustrates the reluctance of the courts to enforce the full rigour of the statute, as will be seen from the following paragraphs.

4–032 **Position of signature.** The signature need not be at the foot of the matter written, but may be either in the body or at the beginning of it[147]; it may be in any part of the document provided that it authenticates every material clause.[148] If it is at the foot of the matter written, it is to be taken to apply to the whole, unless there is something expressly to rebut that presumption: and if it is not at the foot it may apply to the whole if upon the evidence it is found that the party signing so intended.[149] Accordingly it has been held that if a party draws up an agreement in his own handwriting, beginning, "I, AB, agree, etc.", this is a sufficient signature, although he does not subscribe his name at the bottom.[150] So, a memorandum in the buyer's handwriting beginning, "[s]old J.D." (i.e. to him) and signed by the seller's agent, was held to bind the buyer.[151] But if a memorandum is headed "[a]rticles of Agreement between A and B" and concludes "[a]s witness our hands" the parties must actually subscribe: the mention of their names at the beginning is clearly not intended as a signature.[152] And it is clear that, if the memorandum which contains the name of the party to be charged is written by someone else, the fact of his name being written in the body of it will not avail as a signature within the statute unless there is evidence that the person who wrote the instrument had the authority of that party to do so.[153] When an auctioneer filled in the defendant's name as vendor in a document purporting to be an agreement for sale and presented it to the plaintiff purchaser for signature, the document was a valid memorandum, although neither auctioneer nor vendor had signed it in the ordinary sense of the word.[154]

---

[145] *Barber v Rowe* [1948] 2 All E.R. 1050.

[146] *Laythoarp v Bryant* (1836) 2 Bing. N.C. 735; *Buxton v Rust* (1872) L.R. 7 Ex. 279. cf. below, para.4–072.

[147] *Schneider v Norris* (1814) 2 M. & S. 286 (bill-head); *Caton v Caton* (1867) L.R. 2 H.L. 127; *Evans v Hoare* [1892] 1 Q.B. 593.

[148] *Caton v Caton* (1867) L.R. 2 H.L. 127; *Kronheim v Johnson* (1877) 7 Ch D 60, 67; *Cohen v Roche* [1927] 1 K.B. 169, 174–176; *Behnke v Bede Shipping Co Ltd* [1927] 1 K.B. 649, 660; *Hill v Hill* [1947] 1 Ch. 231, 240.

[149] *Foster v Mentor Life Assurance Co* (1854) 3 E. & B. 48, 71; and see *Lobb v Stanley* (1844) 5 Q.B. 574.

[150] *Knight v Crockford* (1794) 1 Esp. 190.

[151] *Johnson v Dodgson* (1837) 2 M. & W. 653; *Durrell v Evans* (1862) 1 H. & C. 174.

[152] *Hubert v Treherne* (1842) 3 Man. & G. 743, 754.

[153] *Hubert v Treherne* (1842) 3 Man. & G. 743, 754; *Hucklesbury v Hook* (1900) 82 L.T. 117, 118.

[154] *Leeman v Stocks* [1951] Ch. 941, applying *Schneider v Norris* (1814) 2 M. & S. 286 and *Evans v Hoare* [1892] 1 Q.B. 593; distinguishing *Hubert v Treherne* (1842) 3 Man. & G. 743.

Signature intended to authenticate document. The signature must be affixed with the intention of authenticating the whole document. Thus where one party or his agent merely adds his signature to the document as witness of the signature of the other, the former is not bound by the signature.[155] But the use of the term "witness" is not conclusive to show that the signature was added for the purpose of witnessing, especially if the document did not require attestation.[156] 4–033

Form of signature. Where the name of the vendor was printed in the heading of an invoice sent by him to the buyer, and which contained the particulars, quantities and prices of the goods sold, the printed name was held to be a sufficient signature to bind the vendor.[157] But there must be circumstances which show a recognition of the printed signature as his own by the party to be charged in order that the document to which it is affixed may bind him. Where a purchaser took up a sheet of paper bearing the printed name and address of the vendor, wrote in his own address and the name of the vendor, but the paper was not signed by the latter or dictated by him, it was held not to be a sufficient memorandum to bind the vendor.[158] 4–034

Signature by pencil is clearly sufficient,[159] and so is the signature on a telegraph form,[160] or by mark,[161] or by initials.[162]

Alteration in memorandum. Where a memorandum is altered after it has been signed either in order to correct a mistake in the written statement of an existing contract[163] or before the parties are contractually bound at all,[164] parol evidence is admissible to show that the signature was intended to apply to the memorandum as altered.[165] But such signature cannot authenticate subsequent alterations which effect a variation of a contract concluded and binding on the parties at some time previous to the alterations.[166] And an alteration of the memorandum in a material particular subsequent to the signature without the 4–035

---

155 *Gosbell v Archer* (1835) 2 A. & E. 500; *Kerns v Manning* [1935] I.R. 869.

156 *Wallace v Roe* [1903] 1 I.R. 32.

157 *Saunderson v Jackson* (1800) 2 B. & P. 238; *Schneider v Norris* (1814) 2 M. & S. 286; *Sweet v Lee* (1841) 3 Man. & G. 452; and see *Durrell v Evans* (1862) 1 H. & C. 174; *Tourret v Cripps* (1879) 48 L.J.Ch. 567; *Cohen v Roche* [1927] 1 K.B. 169.

158 *Hucklesby v Hook* (1900) 82 L.T. 117; *Cohen v Roche* [1927] 1 K.B. 169; cf. *Evans v Hoare* [1892] 1 Q.B. 593; *Behnke v Bede Shipping Co Ltd* [1927] 1 K.B. 649, 660; *Decouvreur v Jordan*, *The Times*, May 25, 1987.

159 See *Geary v Physic* (1826) 5 B. & C. 234 (indorsement of promissory note).

160 *Godwin v Francis* (1870) L.R. 5 C.P. 295; *McBlain v Cross* (1872) 25 L.T. 804; *R. v Riley* [1896] 1 Q.B. 309, 313.

161 See *Baker v Dening* (1838) 8 A. & E. 94 (signature of will); *Dyas v Stafford* (1881) 7 L.R. Ir. 590.

162 *In the Goods of Blewitt* (1879) 5 P.D. 116 (signature of will); see *Phillimore v Barry* (1818) 1 Camp. 513; *Chichester v Cobb* (1866) 14 L.T. 433; *Hill v Hill* [1947] Ch. 231, 240.

163 *Black v Gompertz* (1852) 7 Exch. 862.

164 *Stewart v Eddowes* (1874) L.R. 9 C.P. 311; *Koenigsblatt v Sweet* [1923] 2 Ch. 314.

165 *New Hart Builders Ltd v Brindley* [1975] Ch. 342.

166 *New Hart Builders Ltd v Brindley* [1975] Ch. 342 although the court considered that there was no logical ground for this distinction, 352.

consent of both parties destroys the rights of the party making such alteration.[167]

4–036 **Signature by agent.** A memorandum in writing within the statute may be signed by the party to be charged or "by some other person thereunto by him lawfully authorised". The authority of the agent need not be in writing[168]; and the principal may be undisclosed[169] or unnamed.[170] In order to satisfy the statute the memorandum so signed need not be one which the principal has authorised the agent to sign for the purpose of a contract: thus where the chairman of a limited company signed minutes containing the contract there was a sufficient memorandum.[171] Any letter written by an agent within the scope of his authority which refers to and recognises an unsigned document as containing the terms of a contract made by his principal is a sufficient memorandum and it is not necessary that the principal should have authorised the agent to sign the letter as a record of the contract.[172] A solicitor who is employed to prepare a draft contract has no authority to state the heads of the agreement to be embodied in the formal contract in such a way as to bind his client,[173] nor, if he is instructed by his client to deny the existence of a contract, has he any authority to admit it[174]; but counsel employed to draft pleadings in an action[175] and a solicitor authorised to complete a contract[176] have been held to be lawfully authorised to sign a memorandum.[177] In *Smith v MacGowan*[178] the defendant's solicitors purchased on his account three lots of freehold land at an auction. The three lots were combined in one memorandum, but the solicitors had no authority so to combine the lots; there ought to have been a separate memorandum for each lot. In an action for specific performance, it was held that the memorandum was not a proper memorandum of any of the contracts shown to have been entered into and did not satisfy the statute.

4–037 **Estate agents.** In general, the function of an estate agent is to introduce a purchaser for property which it is desired to sell to a would-be vendor. Ordinarily,

---

[167] *Davidson v Cooper* (1844) M. & W. 343 (guarantee). As to what is a material particular see *Adsetts v Hives* (1863) 33 Beav. 52; and see below, para.25–020.

[168] *Emmerson v Heelis* (1809) 2 Taunt. 38, 46; *Graham v Musson* (1839) 5 Bing. N.C. 603; *Heard v Pilley* (1869) L.R. 4 Ch.App. 548; *Daniels v Trefusis* [1914] 1 Ch. 788.

[169] *Filby v Hounsell* [1896] 2 Ch. 737.

[170] *Davies v Sweet* [1962] 2 Q.B. 300. cf. *Lovesy v Palmer* [1916] 2 Ch. 233 (signature of disclosed agent not himself liable under the agreement not enough to bind principal unnamed and unidentifiable from memorandum) and see *Bowstead and Reynolds on Agency*, 18th edn (2006) para.8–003.

[171] *Jones v Victoria Graving Dock Co* (1877) 2 QBD 314; cf. *John Griffiths Cycle Corp Ltd v Humber & Co Ltd* [1899] 2 Q.B. 414, 417; *Daniels v Trefusis* [1914] 1 Ch. 788; *North v Loomes* [1919] 1 Ch. 378.

[172] *John Griffiths Cycle Corp Ltd v Humber & Co Ltd* [1899] 2 Q.B. 414; *Horner v Walker* [1923] 2 Ch. 218.

[173] *Smith v Webster* (1876) 3 Ch D 49.

[174] *Thirkell v Cambi* [1919] 2 K.B. 590. cf. *Daniels v Trefusis* [1914] 1 Ch. 788.

[175] *Grindell v Bass* [1920] 2 Ch. 487; *Farr, Smith & Co Ltd v Messers Ltd* [1928] 1 K.B. 397.

[176] *North v Loomes* [1919] 1 Ch. 378; *Gavaghan v Edwards* [1961] 2 Q.B. 220; *Smith v Mansi* [1963] 1 W.L.R. 26, 34.

[177] Legal professional privilege may attach to such documents so as to prevent disclosure of a memorandum for the purposes of s.40: *Balabel v Air India* [1988] Ch. 317, 330.

[178] [1938] 3 All E.R. 447.

therefore, he has no authority to enter into or sign a contract on behalf of the vendor, although this may be conferred upon him expressly.[179] A vendor may, however, be estopped from asserting the want of authority of his agent.[180]

Agent for both parties. The same person may be agent for both parties.[181] Thus, by the usage of a business, a broker may be the agent of both buyer and seller, so that his signature of the contract binds both parties within the statute.[182] A sale by auction is within the section and the auctioneer, who is primarily the agent of the vendor, becomes at the fall of the hammer the agent of the highest bidder also; he is authorised to sign the highest bidder's name as purchaser and so may sign the contract for both parties.[183] Thus he is entitled to sign in the name and on behalf of the purchaser a memorandum sufficient to satisfy the provisions of the statute,[184] provided that he does so at the time of the auction.[185] The authority of the auctioneer does not extend to his clerk[186] unless the bidder by word or sign or otherwise confers such authority on the clerk[187] but a licensed auctioneer employed by a firm of auctioneers to conduct the auction can sign on behalf of the buyer even though the buyer has not specifically conferred authority on him.[188] **4–038**

Agent must be a third person. The memorandum cannot be signed by one contracting party as agent of the other.[189] Nor, generally speaking, will one contracting party be bound by the signature of an employee of the other party[190]; but he may be bound by such signature if the employee in question has, for the purpose of the transaction, authority to sign on behalf of both parties.[191] **4–039**

Deeds. It was formerly doubtful whether the requirement of writing applied to deeds, the subject matter of which was within the statute, so as to require them, **4–040**

---

[179] *Davies v Sweet* [1962] 2 Q.B. 300, 305; *Wragg v Lovett* [1948] 2 All E.R. 968, 969. cf. *Rosenbaum v Belson* [1900] 2 Ch. 267.

[180] *Worboys v Carter* (1987) 283 E.G. 307.

[181] *Durrell v Evans* (1862) 1 H. & C. 174; *Murphy v Boese* (1875) L.R. 10 Ex. 126; *Gavaghan v Edwards* [1961] 2 Q.B. 220.

[182] *Rucker v Cammeyer* (1794) 1 Esp. 105; *Parton v Crofts* (1864) 16 C.B.(N.S.) 11; *Trueman v Loder* (1840) 11 A. & E. 589; and see *Pike Sons & Co v Ongley* (1887) 18 QBD 708; *Thompson v Gardiner* (1876) 1 C.P.D. 777.

[183] *Kenworthy v Schofield* (1824) 2 B. & C. 945, 947; *Bartlett v Purnell* (1836) 4 A. & E. 792; *Phillips v Butler* [1945] Ch. 358.

[184] *Emmerson v Heelis* (1809) 2 Taunt. 38; *White v Procter* (1811) 4 Taunt. 209; *Sims v Landray* [1894] 2 Ch. 318, 320; see *Van Praagh v Everidge* [1903] 1 Ch. 434; *Dewar v Mintoft* [1912] 2 K.B. 373, doubted in *Cohen v Roche* [1927] 1 K.B. 169; *Phillips v Butler* [1945] Ch. 358; Fry, *Specific Performance*, 6th edn (1921), paras 529–531.

[185] *Peirce v Corf* (1874) L.R. 9 Q.B. 210; *Chaney v Maclow* [1929] 1 Ch. 461; the auctioneer's signature need not be appended before he leaves the saleroom but must fairly form "part of the transaction of sale". *M'Meekin v Stevenson* [1917] 1 Ir.R. 348, 354; *Sakhas v Donford Ltd* (1983) 46 P. & C.R. 290.

[186] *Bell v Balls* [1897] 1 Ch. 663.

[187] As in *Bird v Boulter* (1833) 4 B. & Ad. 443; *Sims v Landray* [1894] 2 Ch. 318, 320.

[188] *Wilson & Sons v Pike* [1949] 1 K.B. 176. The distinctions drawn in the text above are supported by authority but appear to have little (if any) merit.

[189] *Farebrother v Simmons* (1822) 5 B. & Ad. 333; *Sharman v Brandt* (1871) L.R. 6 Q.B. 720.

[190] *Dixon v Broomfield* (1814) 2 Chit. 205 (guarantee); cf. *Graham v Musson* (1839) 5 Bing. N.C. 603.

[191] *Wilson & Sons v Pike* [1949] 1 K.B. 176.

as was usual and desirable, to be signed as well as sealed[192]; but in the case of deeds executed on or after January 1, 1926, it was provided by s.73 of the Law of Property Act 1925 that where an individual executes a deed he shall either sign or place his mark upon the same and sealing alone shall not be deemed sufficient.[193] Moreover, with effect from July 31, 1990, the requirement of sealing for deeds executed by individuals[194] and by companies within the meaning of the Companies Act 1985[195] has been abolished and replaced with new requirements of intention, signature and attestation.[196]

(iii) *The Effect of Failure to Comply with the Formal Requirements*

4–041 **At law: contract unenforceable.** A contract which fails to comply with the statutory formalities imposed by s.40 is not void but only unenforceable.[197] No action can be brought to enforce it directly. Nor can it be indirectly enforced by suing on some other cause of action. Thus if A orally agrees to allow B to dig for gravel on A's land and later turns B and his machinery off the land, B cannot sue A in trespass.[198] But as the contract is not void, it can sometimes be relied upon as a defence.[199] Thus in the above example B does not commit a trespass by entering on the land and digging for the gravel: the oral contract operates as a licence and excuses the trespass.[200] Once, however, A withdraws the licence B will become a trespasser if he does not leave within a reasonable time; and if A then sues B for possession B cannot, in this action, rely on the oral contract as a defence.[201] *A fortiori* A is entitled to turn B out or to sue for possession if he withdraws the licence before B enters but B nonetheless makes a clandestine entry.[202] As the contract is not void, money or property transferred under it cannot be recovered back: thus, if a purchaser pays a deposit under an oral contract, the vendor can retain the deposit if the purchaser defaults.[203] And a security given for the performance of the oral contract is not void for want of

[192] See *Aveline v Whisson* (1842) 4 Man. & G. 801; *Cooch v Goodman* (1842) 2 Q.B. 580; *Cherry v Hemming* (1849) 4 Exch. 631, 636; but see *Pitman v Woodbury* (1848) 3 Exch. 4, 11; Black.Com.ii. 306.

[193] See above, para.1–086.

[194] Law of Property (Miscellaneous Provisions) Act 1989 s.1.

[195] Companies Act 1985 s.36A (as inserted by Companies Act 1989 s.130(1)).

[196] See above, paras 1–085 et seq.

[197] *Leroux v Brown* (1852) 12 C.B. 801; *Elias v George Sahely & Co (Barbados) Ltd* [1983] A.C. 646, at 650.

[198] *Carrington v Roots* (1837) 2 M. & W. 248; the actual decision is still law though dicta at 255, 257 that failure to comply with the statute makes the contract void are not.

[199] Williams (1934) 50 L.Q.R. 532. cf. *Take Harvest Ltd v Liu* [1993] A.C. 532.

[200] *Carrington v Roots* (1837) 2 M. & W. 248, 255.

[201] cf. *Sidebotham v Holland* [1895] 1 Q.B. 378. It is assumed that the licence is revocable.

[202] *Delany v T. P. Smith Ltd* [1946] K.B. 393; cf. *Maddison v Alderson* (1883) 8 App. Cas. 467 (title deeds wrongfully obtained).

[203] *Thomas v Brown* (1876) 1 QBD 714; *Monnickendam v Leanse* (1923) 39 T.L.R. 445. After the decision of the House of Lords in *Kleinwort Benson v Lincoln City Council* [1998] 3 W.L.R. 1095 a person who has paid money under a contract of sale etc. of an interest in land thought by that person to be valid, but in law unenforceable for want of formality, may be able to recover it on the ground of this mistake of law, see below, paras 4–086 and 29–041 et seq. Of course, if the vendor repudiates, the purchaser can recover the deposit on the ground of failure of consideration: *Pulbrook v Lawes* (1876) 1 QBD 284. See also Law of Property Act 1925 s.49(2) and Goff and Jones, *The Law of Restitution*, 7th edn (2007) para.21–006.

consideration merely because the oral contract is unenforceable: thus an action can be brought on a cheque given in payment of a deposit under the oral contract.[204]

In equity: the doctrine of part performance. Where the claimant has partly performed an oral contract required by the statute to be evidenced in writing, in the expectation that the defendant would perform the rest of the contract, the court will not allow the defendant to escape from his contract upon the strength of the statute,[205] but may order specific performance of the oral contract. The principle is that the defendant may not set up the statute where the claimant has been induced, or allowed, by the defendant to alter his position on the faith of the contract, so that it would be fraud on the part of the defendant to rely on the statute.[206] The doctrine of part performance was expressly preserved by ss.40(2) and 55(d) of the Law of Property Act 1925. 4–042

Scope of the doctrine. There was formerly some conflict of judicial opinion as to the types of contract within the doctrine,[207] but it is now applicable only to contracts affecting interests in land within the meaning of s.40(1) of the Law of Property Act 1925. There must, however, be a definite contract in existence of which the court would order specific performance, since part performance cannot of itself determine material terms of the contract.[208] Nor will part performance substantiate a claim for damages unless the contract is specifically enforceable, in which case damages may be awarded in lieu of specific performance.[209] 4–043

Acts by the person seeking to enforce the contract. The acts of part performance relied on must have been done by the person seeking to enforce the contract, or on his behalf.[210] It is not therefore in general possible to rely on acts done by the person against whom the contract is sought to be enforced. However, in *United Bank of Kuwait Plc v Sahib*[211] the court accepted that, by way of exception to this rule, a deposit of deeds with the intention of creating an equitable mortgage avoids the need to satisfy the formal requirements of s.40, even though the deposit (and therefore the act of part performance) is made by the mortgagor and, therefore, not by the person seeking to enforce the contract. 4–044

Acts must point to the existence of a contract. The acts of part performance relied on must be such as to be referable to some contract, and may be referred 4–045

---

204 *Low v Fry* (1935) 152 L.T. 585.

205 *Mundy v Jolliffe* (1839) 5 My. & Cr. 167, 177; *Ungley v Ungley* (1877) 5 Ch D 887; *Dickinson v Barrow* [1904] 2 Ch. 339; *Rawlinson v Ames* [1925] Ch. 96.

206 See *Caton v Caton* (1865) L.R. 1 Ch.App. 137, 148, affirmed (1867) L.R. 2 H.L. 127.

207 See *Britain v Rossiter* (1879) 11 QBD 123, 129; *Maddison v Alderson* (1883) 8 App. Cas. 467 at 474; *McManus v Cooke* (1887) 35 Ch D 681. cf. Spry, *Equitable Remedies*, 7th edn (2007), pp.254 et seq.

208 *Stimson v Gray* [1929] 1 Ch. 629, 643–644.

209 *Britain v Rossiter* (1879) 11 QBD 123; *Lavery v Pursell* (1888) 39 Ch D 508; *Stimson v Gray* [1929] 1 Ch. 629.

210 *Caton v Caton* (1865) L.R. 1 Ch. App. 137, 148, affirmed (1867) L.R. 2 H.L. 127; *Maddison v Alderson* (1883) 8 App. Cas. 467, 475; *Rawlinson v Ames* [1925] Ch. 96, 108.

211 [1995] 2 W.L.R. 94, 108, 110. cf. the position under the 1989 Act, below, para.4–059.

to the alleged one; they must prove the existence of some contract, and be consistent with the contract alleged.[212] In *Maddison v Alderson*,[213] the House of Lords held that an oral contract between an intestate and a woman, that he should devise to her a life estate in land, in return for her promise to serve him as his housekeeper without wages, could not be enforced merely because the woman had served without wages for many years up to his death, since her service might have been for reasons other than the alleged contract. In his work on specific performance Fry L.J. further stated that the acts of part performance must be referable to "no other title" than the alleged contract[214]; but this view "has long been exploded".[215] If the obvious explanation of the acts is that they were done with reference to a contract, the doctrine of part performance applies although some ingenious alternative explanation for them can be suggested.[216] It is only necessary that the acts relied on should, on the balance of probabilities, point to their having been done in pursuance of[217] some contract, and either show the nature of or be consistent with the oral contract alleged.[218] It is not necessary for the acts of part performance to show the precise terms of the oral contract.[219]

4–046 **Act relating to land.** It is not clear from the decision of the House of Lords in *Steadman v Steadman*[220] whether the acts of part performance need to be referable to the disposition of an interest in land. In that case, the payment by a husband to his wife of £100 arrears of maintenance was held to be on the facts a sufficient act of part performance of an oral agreement for the transfer by the wife of an interest in the matrimonial home. Lord Reid and Viscount Dilhorne considered that the acts of part performance need not relate to land, whereas Lord Salmon and Lord Morris of Borth-y-Gest (dissenting) considered that they should.[221] Lord Simon of Glaisdale found it unnecessary to determine the issue as he found a sufficient act relating to land on the facts.[222] Walton J. subsequently considered that he was entitled to follow the traditional view which requires that the act relates to land.[223] It has been suggested, however, that acts of part performance which have reference to any term of an indivisible contract will be acceptable as sufficient to allow the doctrine to be applied when this is necessary to prevent injustice.[224] Such a suggestion may be supported by reference to Lord

---

[212] Fry, *Specific Performance*, 6th edn (1921), p.278, cited with approval in *Kingswood Estate Co Ltd v Anderson* [1963] 2 Q.B. 169, 189; *Wakeham v Mackenzie* [1968] 1 W.L.R. 1175, 1181; *Steadman v Steadman* [1976] A.C. 536.

[213] (1883) 8 App.Cas. 467. See also *Re Gonin* [1979] Ch. 16. cf. *Wakeham v Mackenzie* [1968] 1 W.L.R. 1175.

[214] Fry at p.277.

[215] *Kingswood Estate Co Ltd v Anderson* [1963] 2 Q.B. 169, 189.

[216] *Broughton v Snook* [1938] Ch. 505, 515.

[217] *Elsden v Pick* [1980] 1 W.L.R. 898, 905.

[218] *Steadman v Steadman* [1976] A.C. 536.

[219] *Kingswood Estate Co Ltd v Anderson* [1963] 2 Q.B. 169, cited with approval in *Steadman v Steadman* [1976] A.C. 536, 542, 546.

[220] [1976] A.C. 536. See also *Liddell v Hopkinson* (1974) 233 E.G. 513, and Wade (1974) 90 L.Q.R. 433.

[221] [1976] A.C. 536, 542, 554, 568–570 and 547, respectively.

[222] [1976] A.C. 536, 563.

[223] *Re Gonin* [1979] Ch. 16, 31 and see *Sutton v Sutton* [1984] Ch. 184; Thompson (1984) 48 Conv. 152.

[224] Hanbury and Maudsley, *Modern Equity*, 12th edn (1985), p.669.

Reid's observation in *Steadman v Steadman* that the doctrine of part performance is:

> " . . . an invention of the Court of Chancery and in deciding any case not clearly covered by authority . . . the equitable nature of the remedy must be kept in mind."[225]

Acts held sufficient. A sufficient act of part performance has been found where one party (previously a stranger to the possession) has taken possession of premises with the consent of the other party[226]; where one party has instructed solicitors to prepare a transfer, paid costs and disbursements including those of mortgagees, and entered into covenants with mortgagees[227]; where alterations have been done on the premises by one party at the request of and under the supervision of the other (the purchaser)[228]; where one party has given notice to weekly tenants at the other's (the purchaser's) request[229]; and where a third party was let into possession, it appearing that the contract was made for that party's benefit.[230] Where an oral agreement for a lease provided for an option to purchase and the proposed lessee took possession, it was held that the lessee could exercise the option.[231] 4–047

On the other hand, acts in contemplation of or preparatory to performance,[232] such as viewing the land or having it valued,[233] are not sufficient, nor is the attendance of one party at the other party's premises at an appointed time with a banker's draft for the deposit, and his part of the written contract of sale duly signed and engrossed, which is then and there tendered.[234] The mere continued possession of a tenant at will, or from year to year, in expectation of a lease is not part performance,[235] for possession is not sufficient if it is explicable without reference to a contract.[236] The payment of one quarter's rent at an increased figure orally stipulated for has been held to be such part performance of a contract for a lease by a tenant as to entitle him to enforce the contract.[237] Any act which is referable to the grant of a new tenancy is sufficient. Thus, while 4–048

---

225 [1976] A.C. 536, 540.

226 *Morphett v Jones* (1818) 1 Swanst. 172; *Ungley v Ungley* (1877) 5 Ch D 887; *Brough v Nettleton* [1921] 2 Ch. 25; *Kingswood Estate Co Ltd v Anderson* [1963] 2 Q.B. 169; *Lloyds Bank Plc v Carrick*, *The Times*, March 13, 1996.

227 *Re Windle* [1975] 1 W.L.R. 1628, 1635–1636.

228 *Dickinson v Barrow* [1904] 2 Ch. 339; *Rawlinson v Ames* [1925] Ch. 96; *Broughton v Snook* [1938] Ch. 505.

229 *Daniels v Trefusis* [1914] 1 Ch. 788, 799.

230 *Hohler v Aston* [1920] 2 Ch. 420.

231 *Brough v Nettleton* [1921] 2 Ch. 25.

232 Fry, *Specific Performance*, 6th edn (1921), p.295.

233 *Clerk v Wright* (1737) 1 Atk. 12, 13; *Cooth v Jackson* (1801) 6 Ves. 12, 41; *Elsden v Pick* [1980] 1 W.L.R. 898, 905. cf., *Re Windle* [1975] 1 W.L.R. 1628.

234 *Daulia Ltd v Four Millbank Nominees Ltd* [1978] Ch. 231.

235 *Faulkner v Llewellin* (1862) 31 L.J.Ch. 549.

236 *Wills v Stradling* (1797) 3 Ves. 378; *Kingswood Estate Co Ltd v Anderson* [1963] 2 Q.B. 169, 181.

237 *Nunn v Fabian* (1865) L.R. 1 Ch.App. 35; *Miller and Aldworth Ltd v Sharp* [1899] 1 Ch. 622.

expenditure on a farm in the ordinary course of husbandry will not suffice,[238] expenditure on such things as alterations, new buildings, or repairs, will entitle the tenant to a decree.[239] An application for planning permission has been held insufficient.[240]

4–049 **Payment of money.** It was previously believed that part payment of the purchase price[241] or of rent in advance[242] was not part performance, for "the payment of money is an equivocal act, not (in itself) . . . indicative of a contract concerning land".[243] But since the decision of the House of Lords in *Steadman v Steadman*,[244] there is no general rule that the payment of money cannot constitute an act of part performance.[245]

4–050 **Effect of an act of part performance.** The effect of a sufficient act of part performance is to enable evidence to be given of all the terms of the contract and not only of the terms related to the act of part performance.[246] It does not, however, enable evidence to be given of independent contracts, even though made between the same parties and on the same occasion.[247]

4–051 **Proprietary estoppel.** A substantive equitable right of property may also be conferred by the operation of "proprietary estoppel"[248] in cases of acquiescence or encouragement, without any need for a written memorandum or agreement.

(b) *The New Law: Contracts made on or after September 27, 1989*

4–052 **Law of Property (Miscellaneous Provisions) Act 1989 section 2.** The law relating to the formal requirements of contracts for the sale or other disposition of an interest in land was significantly changed by the Law of Property (Miscellaneous Provisions) Act 1989 s.2. This provision, which put into law the recommendations of the Law Commission in its report, *Formalities for Contracts for Sale etc. of Land*[249] supersedes s.40 of the Law of Property Act 1925[250] in relation to contracts made on or after September 27, 1989.[251] Section 2(1) states:

---

[238] *Brennan v Bolton* (1842) 2 Dr. & War. 349; *Conner v Fitzgerald* (1883) 11 L.R. Ir. 106, 113.

[239] *Lester v Foxcroft* (1701) 1 Colles PC 108; *Williams v Evans* (1875) L.R. 19 Eq. 547; *Broughton v Snook* [1938] Ch. 505.

[240] *New Hart Builders Ltd v Brindley* [1975] Ch. 342.

[241] *Britain v Rossiter* (1879) 11 QBD 123, 130.

[242] *Chapronière v Lambert* [1917] 2 Ch. 356.

[243] *Maddison v Alderson* (1883) 8 App. Cas. 467, 479.

[244] [1976] A.C. 536.

[245] *Steadman v Steadman* [1976] A.C. 536; *Re Gonin* [1979] Ch. 16, 30; *Cohen v Nessdale Ltd* [1981] 3 All E.R. 118 affirmed on other grounds [1982] 2 All E.R. 97. cf., *Re Windle* [1975] 1 W.L.R. 1628, 1635.

[246] *Sutherland v Briggs* (1841) 1 Hare 26, 32; *Brough v Nettleton* [1921] 2 Ch. 25.

[247] *Buckmaster v Harrop* (1807) 13 Ves. 456, 474.

[248] See above, paras 3–137 et seq.

[249] Law Commission, *Formalities for Contracts for Sale etc. of Land* Law Com. No.164 (1987).

[250] Law of Property (Miscellaneous Provisions) Act 1989 s.2(8).

[251] Law of Property (Miscellaneous Provisions) Act s.5(3), (4).

"A contract for the sale or other disposition of an interest in land can only be made in writing and only by incorporating all the terms which the parties have expressly agreed in one document or, where contracts are exchanged, in each."

This change was prompted by a concern to settle the uncertainty surrounding s.40, in particular as regards the status of letters made "subject to contract" as memoranda for the purposes of that section[252] and the ambit of the doctrine of part performance after the decision of the House of Lords in *Steadman v Steadman*.[253] Section 2 makes a strict formal requirement whose effect is to preclude the existence of any contract for the sale or other disposition of land unless it is *made* in writing. Unlike the position under the old law, written evidence by way of a memorandum or note of the contract is clearly not enough. Moreover, the doctrine of part performance, at least in its normal form, is abolished.[254] On the other hand:

" . . . the demise of the doctrine of part performance has not brought about such wide-ranging effects as might at first have been supposed . . . and has simply thrown a heightened emphasis upon the application of alternative equitable doctrines,"[255]

notably, constructive trust and proprietary estoppel.[256]

Agreements made "subject to contract". In *Enfield LBC v Arajah*[257] the Court of Appeal held that, quite apart from the question whether the formal requirements contained in s.2 of the 1989 Act had been satisfied, a letter which was headed "subject to contract" and which was relied on by a tenant as creating a new tenancy, clearly envisaged that a new lease would be completed before the parties were bound, with the result that, while this qualification was in force, the relationship did not become binding on either party unless and until there was an exchange of lease and counterpart. 4–053

(i) *Contracts within section 2 of the Law of Property (Miscellaneous Provisions) Act 1989*

General. The new formal requirements apply to contracts[258] for the "sale or other disposition of an interest in land".[259] Section 2(6) of the 1989 Act specifies that "disposition" has the same meaning for this purpose as for the Law of Property Act 1925 and reference should be made to the earlier discussion of this 4–054

[252] Law Com. No.164 (1987), paras 1.4–1.6 and cf. above, para.4–027 fn.127.

[253] [1976] A.C. 563 and see Law Com. No.164, para.1.9 and cf. above, para.4–046.

[254] This part of para.4–052 was quoted with approval by Simon Brown L.J. in *Godden v Merthyr Tydfil Housing Association* [1997] 1 N.P.C. 1.

[255] Gray and Gray, *Elements of Land Law*, 4th edn (London, 2005), para.12.35.

[256] Below, paras 4–077—4–083.

[257] [1995] E.G.C.S. 164.

[258] Jenkins [1993] Conv. 13, 18 et seq. contends that the term "contract" for the purposes of s.2 of the 1989 Act does not include "arrangements" effected by deed. However, it is difficult to see why a court should wish to allow avoidance of the special formal requirements imposed on contracts for the sale, etc. of interests in land contained in s.2, simply because such a contract is contained in a deed. The historical differences between covenant and *assumpsit* on which Jenkins relies should not be permitted to defeat the clear purpose of s.2 which was to make one set of clear requirements in relation to this type of contract in the interests of certainty.

[259] Law of Property (Miscellaneous Provisions) Act 1989 s.2(1).

term in that context.[260] The 1989 Act, however, itself defines the term "interest in land" for the purposes of these new formal requirements as "any estate, interest or charge in or over land or in or over the proceeds of sale of land".[261] It has been held that s.2 of the 1989 Act applies equally to an executory agreement, that is in this context, an agreement which was made at a time when neither of its parties possessed any proprietary interest in the property in question,[262] and to an agreement contingent on another event, such as the giving of consent by a landlord to the assignment of a lease.[263]

4–055 **"Contracts for the disposition of an interest" and "contracts of disposition".** The formal requirements created by s.2 apply to "contracts *for* the sale or other disposition of an interest in land".[264] This raises the question whether they apply to contracts *of* sale or other disposition of an interest in land, i.e. contracts by which the contract itself transfers the interest as opposed to imposing an obligation on the party (transferor) to do so. In *Target Holdings Ltd v Priestley*[265] an oral agreement to vary the terms of repayment of a loan under an executed second mortgage contract was held to fall outside the terms of s.2 of the 1989 Act. According to Judge Hicks Q.C., the legislative history of s.2 and ss.51 to 55 of the Law of Property Act 1925 (which concern the *disposition* of interests as opposed to contracts *for* the disposition of interests) disclose that a distinction had been consistently drawn between contracts *for* the disposition of land and contracts *of* disposition of land. According to the learned judge, the second mortgage fell into the latter category and so outside the ambit of s.2: this provision should not be applied to instruments for which the formal or evidential requirements are governed by ss.51–55 of the 1925 Act. As a result, in his view, any variation of the second mortgage also fell outside the ambit of s.2. A similar approach was taken by the Court of Appeal in *Eagle Star Insurance Co Ltd v Green*,[266] where it held that a mortgage executed by deed must fulfil the formal requirements for a deed (contained in s.1 of the Law of Property (Miscellaneous Provisions) Act 1989) rather than the formal requirements for a contract for the disposition of an interest in land (contained in s.2 of the same Act). So, a mortgage executed by deed does not have to comply with the formal requirements of s.2 of the 1989 Act, but a contract to create a mortgage would have to do so, as would an equitable mortgage or charge arising out of the deposit of documents which have been held to find their basis in an implied contract.[267]

---

[260] See above, paras 4–011 et seq.

[261] Law of Property (Miscellaneous Provisions) Act 1989 s.2(6).

[262] *Singh v Beggs* (1996) 71 P. & C.R. 120.

[263] *Representative Body of the Church in Wales v Newton* [2005] EWHC 631 (QB), [2005] All ER (D) 163 (Apr).

[264] A variation in the beneficial interests of the parties in the net proceeds of sale of a house has been held not to constitute the disposition of an interest in the house: *Lancashire Mortgage Corp Ltd v Scottish and Newcastle Plc* [2007] EWCA Civ 684, [2007] All ER (D) 68 (Jul) at [54].

[265] [1999] Lloyd's Rep. Bank. 175.

[266] [2001] EWCA Civ 1389.

[267] *United Bank of Kuwait Plc v Sahib* [1997] Ch. 107 on which see below, para.4–059. cf. *Clark v Chandler* [2002] EWCA Civ 1249, [2003] 1 P. & C.R. 15 at [13]–[17]; where the document could not be construed as an immediate and unconditional disposition so as to fall outside the requirements of s.2 of the 1989 Act and within s.53(1)(c) of the Law of Property Act 1925.

Variations. In *McCausland v Duncan Lawrie Ltd*[268] the Court of Appeal held that material variations of contracts of sale, etc. of an interest in land also have to fulfill the formal requirements contained in s.2 of the 1989 Act. According to the court this means that the contract as varied has to be in writing and incorporated in one document, or each document if contracts were exchanged, and signed by or on behalf of each party to the contract.[269] On the facts of *McCausland*, the variation was held to be material as it attempted to advance the contractual date for completion and therefore the time when either party might make time of the essence by service of a notice to complete.[270] On the other hand, the Court of Appeal has held that s.2 does not apply to an agreement by a party to a contract to waive a term inserted for his benefit as such an agreement does not vary the contract.[271] **4–056**

Boundary agreements between neighbours. In *Joyce v Rigolli*[272] the Court of Appeal considered whether a boundary agreement between neighbouring landowners constituted "a contract for the sale or other disposition of an interest in land" within the meaning of s.2 of the 1989 Act. In this respect, the court adopted the distinction drawn by Megarry J. in *Neilson v Poole*,[273] in the context of the requirement of registration of such an agreement as an "estate contract" within s.10(1) of the Land Charges Act 1925, between agreements which constitute an exchange of land and those by which the parties merely intend to "demarcate" an unclear boundary referred to in title documents, "a contract merely to demarcate and confirm [not being] a contract to convey".[274] According to the Court of Appeal, for a contract to be one "for" selling or disposing of land within the meaning of s.2: **4–057**

> "... it must have been part of the parties' purposes, or the purposes to be attributed to them, in entering into such a contract that the contract should achieve a sale or other disposition of land. The fact that the effect of their contract is that land or an interest in land is actually conveyed, when that effect was neither foreseen nor intended nor was it something which ought to have been foreseen or intended, is not the acid test."[275]

Moreover, s.2 remains inapplicable even if (as on the facts) one of the parties to a demarcation agreement consciously thought that he was giving up a small amount of land[276]: the important public policy in upholding informal boundary

---

268 [1997] 1 W.L.R. 38; *Eyestorm Ltd v Hoptonacre Homes Ltd* [2007] EWCA Civ 1366, [2007] All ER (D) 284 (Dec). cf. *Morall v Krause* [1994] E.G.C.S. 177 (decided under the Law of Property Act 1925 s.40) above, para.4–015.

269 The Court of Appeal thereby followed the approach of the House of Lords in *Morris v Baron & Co* [1918] A.C. 1, 31 and 29 and Willes J. in *Noble v Ward* (1867) L.R. 2 Ex. 135, 137, though in relation to different formal requirements. cf. *H.L. Estates Ltd v Parker-Lake Homes Ltd* [2003] EWHC 604, [2003] All E.R. (D) 245.

270 cf. *HL Estates Ltd v Parker-Lake Homes Ltd* [2003] EWHC 604 (Ch).

271 *Glen Courtney v Corp Ltd* [2006] EWCA Civ 518 at [12]–[14].

272 [2004] EWCA Civ 79, [2004] All E.R. (D) 203 (Feb) applied in *Styles v Smith* [2005] EWHC 3224 (QB), [2005] All ER (D) 167 (Dec).

273 (1969) 20 P. & C.R. 909.

274 *Neilson v Poole* (1969) 20 P. & C.R. 909, 918–920.

275 *Joyce v Rigolli* [2004] EWCA Civ 79 at [31], per Arden L.J.

276 *Joyce v Rigolli* [2004] EWCA Civ 79 at [30], [32].

agreements which are "act[s] of peace, quieting strife and averting litigation"[277] means that Parliament could not have intended s.2 to apply to transfers of land pursuant to demarcating boundary agreements simply because a trivial transfer or transfers of land were consciously involved. It should, moreover, be presumed, until the contrary is shown, that any transfer of land effected by such an agreement is trivial for this purpose.[278]

4–058 **Options and rights of pre-emption.** In *Spiro v Glencrown Properties Ltd*[279] the question arose whether an option granted by a vendor of land is a "contract for the sale or other disposition of an interest in land" within the meaning of s.2(1) of the 1989 Act.[280] Hoffmann J. held that it was, but that the notice by which the option was exercised was not: the section

> "... was intended to prevent disputes over whether the parties had entered into a binding agreement or over what terms they had agreed. It prescribes the formalities for recording their mutual consent. But only the grant of the option depends upon consent. The exercise of the option is a unilateral act. It would destroy the very purpose of the option if the purchaser had to obtain the vendor's countersignature to the notice by which it was exercised."[281]

As Scott L.J. observed in a later case, the alternative view which Hoffmann J. rejected, and according to which the exercise of options are subject to the section's formal requirements, would mean that it "had by an unintended side wind destroyed the enforceability of options".[282] The approach of Hoffmann J. has been held to apply equally to a "put option" in a lease (i.e. one where it is the potential grantor or lessor who is to exercise it), as well as to a "call option" (as in *Spiro v Glencrown Properties Ltd*,[283] where it is the potential grantee or purchaser who can exercise the option).[284] On the other hand, the position of a right of pre-emption (under which a person holding an interest grants another person a right to acquire it if he chooses to sell) is less clear.[285] As regards registered land, a right of pre-emption is deemed by statute to have effect "from the time of creation as an interest capable of binding successors in title" and this strongly suggests that it should included be regarded as an "interest in land" for the purposes of s.2[286]; but as regards unregistered land a right of pre-emption has been held to confer:

---

[277] *Nielson v Poole* (1969) 20 P. & C.R. 909, 919, per Megarry J.

[278] [2004] EWCA Civ 79 at [32]–[34]. cf., at [45] Sir Martin Nourse referring to the "de minimis principle".

[279] [1991] Ch. 537; and see Jenkins [1993] Conv. 13.

[280] As Scott L.J. remarked in a later case "[i]t is evident that the draftsman of this section did not take account of options": *Trustees of the Chippenham Golf Club v North Wiltshire DC* (1991) 64 P. & C.R. 527, 530.

[281] [1991] Ch. 537, 541, per Hoffmann J.; *Bircham & Co, Nominees Ltd v Worrell Holdings Ltd* [2001] EWCA Civ 775, (2001) 82 P. & C.R. 34 at [39]–[45].

[282] *Trustees of the Chippenham Golf Club v North Wiltshire DC* (1991) 64 P. & C.R. 527, 530; and see further *Tootal Clothing Ltd v Guinea Properties Ltd* (1991) 64 P. & C.R. 452, 455.

[283] [1991] Ch. 537.

[284] *Active Estates Ltd v Parness* [2002] EWHC 893, [2002] B.P.I.R. 865.

[285] Smith, *Property Law*, 5th edn (2006), pp.92–93.

[286] Land Registration Act 2002 s.115.

"... no immediate right upon the prospective purchaser. It imposes a negative obligation on the possible vendor requiring him to refrain from selling the land to any other person without giving to the holder of the right of first refusal the opportunity of purchasing in preference to any other buyer."[287]

For this reason, the 1989 Act is said not to apply to any contract which creates a right of pre-emption over unregistered land.[288] However, this leaves the question as to the application of s.2 to any subsequent agreement arising from the right of pre-emption. In *Bircham & Co, Nominees Ltd v Worrell Holdings Ltd*,[289] a clause in a lease was held to have created a mere right of pre-emption (as opposed to an option) in a landlord in respect of its tenant's interest in the land and the tenant notified the landlord of the circumstances giving rise to the latter's opportunity to acquire this interest in exercise of this right. In these circumstances, the Court of Appeal held that any "acceptance" by the landlord of this offer by the tenant in its notice could take effect only by contract and had therefore to conform to the formal requirements of s.2 of the 1989 Act.

Equitable mortgages. In *United Bank of Kuwait Plc v Sahib*,[290] the Court of Appeal held that equitable mortgages or charges arising out of a deposit of documents of title found their basis in an implied contract and that such a contract could exist only if the rigorous formal requirements of s.2 of the Law of Property (Miscellaneous Provisions) Act 1989 are satisfied.[291] But it is less clear whether this provision applies where the equitable mortgage secures a guarantee which would attract the less rigorous requirements of s.4 of the Statute of Frauds.[292] In *Deutsche Bank A.G. v Ibrahim*,[293] which was decided under the old law,[294] the plaintiff bank sought a declaration that a deposit of documents of title by the defendants created an enforceable equitable mortgage in its favour. However, the court accepted the defendants' argument that where a third party pledges property with a creditor for the purposes of providing security for the liability of a debtor, that third party is a guarantor up to the value of the pledged property and the transaction is therefore governed by the formal requirements contained in s.4 of the Statute of Frauds rather than s.40 of the Law of Property Act 1925, and therefore held that the doctrine of part performance was inapplicable.[295] However, as one commentator has noted, there was no clear reason given 4–059

[287] *Mackay v Wilson* (1947) 47 S.R. (NSW) 315, 325 per Street J. quoted with approval by Goff and Stephenson L.JJ. in *Pritchard v Briggs* [1980] Ch. 338, 390 and 423 respectively.

[288] Farrand, *Emmet on Title*, 19th edn (looseleaf updated to 2007), para.2.083.

[289] [2001] EWCA Civ 775, (2001) 82 P. & C.R. 34.

[290] [1997] Ch. 107; *Dean v Allin and Watts* [2001] EWCA Civ 758, [2001] 2 Lloyd's Rep. 249 at [43].

[291] cf. *De Serville v Argee Ltd* (2001) P. & C. R. D12 where it was observed that *United Bank of Kuwait v Sahib* [1997] Ch. 107 did not hold that all liens were contract-based, but merely that any lien created by deposit of title deeds alone was contract-based. This leaves the possibility of a document which intends to make an immediately effective disposition of an interest in land taking effect as long as it conforms to the formal requirements contained in the Law of Property Act 1925 s.53(1)(a) and see, above, para.4–055.

[292] See below, Vol.II, paras 44–038 et seq.

[293] *Financial Times*, December 13, 1991 and January 15, 1992, noted by Baughen [1992] Conv. 330.

[294] See above, paras 4–010—4–051.

[295] cf. above, paras 4–042 et seq.

by the court for giving priority to s.4 of the Statute of Frauds in this way, particularly given that the plaintiff had relied on the equitable mortgage rather than on the guarantee.[296] It may be thought instead that where two analyses of a transaction exist in parallel, each with their own formal requirements, the more demanding set of requirements should prevail, and, if this were accepted, then s.2 of the 1989 Act would apply to cases like *Deutsche Bank A.G. v Ibrahim*. It is submitted, however, that a better view would be to apply those formal requirements which apply to the analysis of the transaction on which the claimant is relying before the court. Thus, where a claimant seeks a remedy such as foreclosure which can only be justified by treating the transaction as an equitable mortgage, s.2 of the 1989 Act should apply.[297]

4–060 **Equitable leases.** Under the old law, a lease which was required to be made by deed[298] but which had been merely put in writing could take effect in equity as a contract to create a legal lease as the writing would satisfy the formal requirements of s.40 of the Law of Property Act 1925.[299] However, this equitable relief depended on the availability of specific enforcement of a contract to create the lease and this would clearly not be available if this contract were a nullity owing to its failure to comply with the formal requirements of s.2.[300] While under the old law a purely oral contract to create a lease could be enforceable as long as there existed sufficient part performance, with the exception of short leases,[301] such an oral contract for a lease would also fall foul of s.2.

4–061 **Conditions in planning agreements.** In *Jelson Ltd v Derby City Council*[302] it was held that a planning agreement made between a developer and a local authority under s.106 of the Town and Country Planning Act 1990 was a contract for the purposes of the formal requirements contained in s.2 of the Law of Property (Miscellaneous Provisions) Act 1989. As a result, a clause in the planning agreement which obliged the developer to convey property to a hitherto unidentified purchaser (a housing association) was held to have failed the formal requirements of the 1989 Act for lack of the purchaser's signature. However, the court further held, (though "with some hesitation" as only two decisions were cited to it[303]), that it could apply a "blue pencil" test and uphold the remainder of the agreement. With respect, this last decision is difficult to reconcile with the approach to "composite agreements" taken by the Court of Appeal in *Godden v Merthyr Tydfil Housing Association*, according to which one single agreement which includes an element governed by s.2 of the 1989 Act and which fails its

---

296 Baughen p.332.

297 Baughen p.332.

298 The Law of Property (Miscellaneous Provisions) Act 1989 s.1 changed the law relating to the formal requirements for deeds, abolishing the requirement of sealing and replacing it with requirements of a clear intention as to the making of a deed, of signature and of attestation: see above, paras 1–085 et seq.

299 Gray, *Elements of Land Law*, 2nd edn (1993), p.744.

300 Howell [1990] Conv. 441, 443.

301 See below, para.4–068.

302 [1999] E.G.C.S. 88.

303 The two decisions were *Director of Public Prosecutions v Hutchinson* [1990] 2 A.C. 783 and *R. v Somerset CC, Ex p. Dixon* (1997) 75 P. & C.R. 175, neither of which were decided in the context of the requirements of s.2 of the 1989 Act.

requirements is void in its entirety: only if the composite agreement is capable of being divided into two discrete agreements (one subject to s.2 and the other not) can part of that "contract" be enforced, part held a nullity for want of formality.[304]

"Lock-out agreements". Where a prospective vendor of land agrees with a prospective purchaser for a clear specified period not to deal with any other purchaser and this agreement is supported by consideration,[305] this agreement is in principle enforceable and is commonly known as a "lock-out agreement".[306] Although such an agreement clearly relates to the sale of land, the Court of Appeal has confirmed that its negative nature means that it is not a contract for the sale of any interest in land and is not therefore subject to the requirements of s.2 of the 1989 Act.[307] 4–062

Mutual wills. Where two testators, such as a husband and wife, make mutual non-revocable wills, in principle a court will enforce the underlying contract against the estate of the survivor.[308] Where such a contract is for the sale or disposition of an interest in land, then it must conform to the formal requirements of s.2 of the 1989 Act: "an undertaking not to revoke a testamentary disposition is the same in effect as a promise to make that disposition".[309] So, for example, where two persons with a joint interest in real property execute mutual wills in identical form, it has been held that there is no contract since their underlying agreement is void for failing to comply with these requirements.[310] For, "if the mutual will compact falls to be regarded as one agreement, it is clear that there is no single document signed by both parties", nor is it possible to construe the handing over of the parties' respective wills to the same solicitor for safe-keeping as "an exchange of contracts" within the meaning of s.2(3) of the 1989 Act.[311] If, on the other hand, the mutual will compact is analysed as two contracts, one by each party in mirror image terms, then neither will fulfils the formal requirements of s.2 as neither is signed by both parties nor do either of them contain any terms as to the consideration for the undertaking (and the precondition for its becoming binding upon each of them), namely that the other shall maintain his or her will unrevoked until death. As a result, neither will incorporates all the terms or even the essential terms as s.2(1) requires.[312] Despite this, a court may 4–063

304 *R. v Somerset CC, Ex p. Dixon* (1997) 74 P. & C.R. D1 and see below, para.4–067.

305 Such an agreement would be valid in the absence of consideration if contained in a deed, but this would possess its own formal requirements: see above, paras 1–085 et seq.

306 *Walford v Miles* [1992] 2 A.C. 128, 139.

307 *Pitt v P.H.H. Asset Management Ltd* [1994] 1 W.L.R. 327.

308 *Re Goodchild* [1997] 1 W.L.R. 1216 CA. Even where a will is stated to be revocable or where, the testator has agreed contractually with another person not to revoke it, a subsequent testament will be admitted to probate, even though its making constitutes a breach of contract: e.g. *Re Heys (Deceased)* [1914] P 192.

309 *Healey v Brown* [2002] 19 E.G.C.S. 147, transcript at [19], per David Donaldson Q.C. and see *Jiggins v Brisley* [2003] EWHC 841, [2003] W.T.L.R. 1141 at [66].

310 *Healey v Brown* [2002] 19 E.G.C.S. 147. cf. *Olins v Walters* [2007] EWHC 3060 (Ch) at [31] (affirmed on other grounds), [2008] EWCA Cw. 782.

311 *Healey v Brown* [2002] 19 E.G.C.S. 147 at [20], per David Donaldson Q.C. On these aspects of the formal requirements, see below, para.4–071.

312 *Healey v Brown* [2002] 19 E.G.C.S. 147.

give the underlying agreement represented by mutual wills some effect in equity by way of constructive trust,[313] as it may be judged inequitable after the death of one of the parties to frustrate that person's expectations by the other seeking to pass on property received otherwise than in accordance with its terms.[314]

4–064 **Contracts relating to proceeds of sale of land.** Section 2(6) defines "interest in land" as "any estate, interest or charge in or over land or in or over the proceeds of sale of land". This definition makes clear that "interest in land" includes an undivided share in land, that is a share in the proceeds of sale of land subject to a trust for sale, although this has become unnecessary since the amendments made by the Trusts of Land and Appointment of Trustees Act 1996.[315] However, the question arises whether the formal requirements of s.2 apply to all contracts relating to the proceeds of sale of land, for example, where an owner is contemplating selling his land or has entered a binding contract to do so and then contracts to assign his right to the proceeds of sale or charge them in favour of an agent. The inclusion of such contracts within s.2 has been described as "surprising", but the language of s.2 appears to be broad enough to cover them.[316] On the other hand, some contracts relating to the proceeds of sale of land will not be caught by the Act. In *Nweze v Nwoko*[317] the Court of Appeal held that a compromise agreement between two parties to an executed contract of sale of land under which, inter alia, the buyer agreed to sell the property with vacant possession at the best price available on the open market (so as to be in a position to pay the price of the earlier purchase to the sellers) was not a contract *for* the sale or other disposition of an interest in land within the meaning of s.2. In doing so, Waller L.J. relied on the Law Commission's Report, *Formalities for Contracts for Sale, etc. of Land*,[318] which "is clearly concerned with contracts or dispositions under which land or an interest in land is actually sold or disposed of".[319] While the compromise agreement required the buyer to sell the property (to a third party), it did not itself effect a sale of the property.[320]

4–065 **Part 36 settlements.** In *Orton v Collins* the question arose whether a settlement that is alleged to arise under CPR Pt 36 which, if implemented, would require the sale or other disposition of an interest in land falls within s.2 of the 1989 Act, so as to require in particular that the settlement is contained in one document rather than two for it to be enforced.[321] It was held that while "a Pt 36 offer may well create a contract and probably does so in the vast majority of cases", it can be enforced by the court even where for some reason there is no

[313] This is expressly preserved by s.2(5) of the 1989 Act and see below, para.4–077.
[314] *Healey v Brown* [2002] 19 E.G.C.S. 147 at [26], [27].
[315] Farrand, *Emmet on Title*, 19th edn (looseleaf updated to 2007), para.2–033; Smith, *Property Law*, 5th edn (2006), p.92.
[316] Smith, *Property Law* p.92.
[317] [2004] EWCA Civ 379, [2004] 2 P. & C.R. 33. See similarly *Payne v Zafiropoyloy* [1994] C.L.Y. 3513. (Eastboune C.Ct.) and cf. *Simmons v Simmons* [1996] C.L.Y. 2874. See also *Young v Lauretani* [2007] EWHC 1244 (Ch), [2007] 2 F.L.R. 1211 (agreement to apply proceeds of sale of property to the reduction of the mortgage of another property not within s.2).
[318] (1987) No.164.
[319] *Nweze v Nwoko* [2004] EWCA Civ 379 at [25].
[320] *Nweze v Nwoko* [2004] EWCA Civ 379 at [31].
[321] [2007] EWHC 803 (Ch), [2007] 3 All ER 863 especially at [53].

contract as 'the regime of Pt 36 . . . does not depend upon contract law"[322]; the parties' obligation to perform such a settlement is sui generis and rests on the court's jurisdiction to administer "justice according to law in a regular, orderly and effective manner".[323]

Partnerships. In *Kilcarne Holdings Ltd v Targetfollow (Birmingham) Ltd*[324] it was held that an overall bargain for the creation of a joint venture involving the development of premises which consisted of a number of individual contracts could include contracts falling within and attracting the formal requirements of s.2 of the 1989 Act and that this remained the case even though the contract was expressed as a partnership. In so holding, the court rejected the argument, based on nineteenth century authority,[325] that an oral partnership agreement can be validly made but that if the partnership assets include land, then the land is held on a constructive trust for the partnership[326]: unlike the Statute of Frauds, the 1989 Act created a "substantive rule of law which prohibits the making of an oral contract for the sale or disposition of an interest in land" even if "it is wrapped up in an alleged partnership".[327] 4–066

Composite agreements. Where a larger agreed arrangement between two parties includes within it an agreement relating to the sale or other disposition of an interest in land, the formal requirements of s.2 apply only to that part of their composite agreement. So, according to Scott L.J. in *Tootal Clothing Ltd v Guinea Properties Ltd*: 4–067

> "... if parties choose to hive off part of the terms of their composite bargain into a separate contract distinct from the written land contract that incorporates the rest of the terms, I can see nothing in s.2 that provides an answer to an action for enforcement of the land contract, on the one hand, or of the separate contract on the other hand. Each has become, by the contractual choice of the parties, a separate contract."[328]

Where the land contract otherwise fulfils the formal requirements of s.2, it will not fail to do so simply because it does not incorporate other elements from the composite agreement.[329] On the other hand, in *Godden v Merthyr Tydfil Housing Association*[330] the parties had made an agreement under which the defendants undertook to purchase from the plaintiff land which he was to acquire, prepare and develop to their order. The Court of Appeal held that this agreement constituted a single scheme and could not be divided into two discrete agreements, one involving the disposition of land and another not. However, in

---

[322] *Orton v Collins* [2007] EWHC 803 (Ch) at [60] and [62], per Peter Prescott Q.C.
[323] [2007] EWHC 803 (Ch) at [62] referring to the overriding objective found in CPR Pt 1.
[324] [2004] EWHC 2547 at [193]–[195], [200]–[204].
[325] *Forster v Hale* (1800) 5 Ves. Jr. 308; *Dale v Hamilton* (1846) 5 Hare 369.
[326] [2004] EWHC 2547 at [200]–[204].
[327] [2004] EWHC 2547 at [203], per Lewison J.
[328] (1992) 64 P. & C.R. 452, 456; *Simmons v Simmons* [1996] C.L.Y. 2874.
[329] cf. below, para.4–070.
[330] [1997] 1 N.P.C. 1. See similarly *Dolphin Quays Development Ltd v Mills* [2006] EWHC 931, [2007] 1 P. & C.R. 12 (side-letter provided that purchase price be supplied by seller by way of reduction of its existing indebtedness to buyer).

Grossman v Hooper[331] the appropriateness of the approach of Scott L.J. in *Tootal Clothing Ltd v Guinea Properties Ltd*[332] to the question of composite agreements was questioned. For Chadwick L.J. in *Grossman v Hooper* the relevant inquiry is:

> "(i) . . . upon what terms did the parties agree that the land (or interest in land) was to be sold, and (ii) are all these terms incorporated in the document which the parties have signed."[333]

Whether an agreement for the disposition of an interest in land does or does not contain other terms is not to be answered by asking whether or not these terms formed a:

> "'. . . collateral contract,' unless by that term, it is intended to refer only to a contract the existence of which has no effect upon the efficacy of the principal contract."[334]

Moreover, Sir Christopher Staughton cast doubt on whether the parties can simply choose to hive off parts of the terms of their composite bargain:

> ". . . if the parties are allowed by a simple device to avoid the effects of section 2 of [the 1989 Act], what was the point of Parliament enacting it?"[335]

4–068 **Excluded contracts.** Section 2(5) of the 1989 Act excludes from its formal requirements contracts to grant short leases,[336] contracts regulated under the Financial Services and Markets Act 2000, other than regulated mortgage contracts,[337] and those made in the course of a public auction. The last of these exclusions represents a change, as such contracts were subject to a requirement of a written memorandum under the previous law.[338] The Law Commission considered that the retention of this requirement fulfilled no cautionary or protective purpose as the practice is that the auctioneer may sign as agent for both the purchaser and vendor.[339]

(ii) *Formal Requirements*

4–069 **"Made in writing".** As has been noted, the most important change is that contracts for the sale, etc. of an interest in land:

---

[331] [2001] EWCA Civ 615; [2001] E.G. 135; [2001] 3 F.C.R. 662.

[332] (1991) 64 P. & C.R. 452, 456.

[333] [2001] EWCA Civ 615 at [20].

[334] [2001] EWCA Civ 615 at [22].

[335] [2001] EWCA Civ 615 at [35]. See also the criticisms of the approach of Scott L.J. in *Tootal Clothing Ltd v Guinea Properties Ltd* (1992) 64 P. & C.R. 3513 in *Kilcarne Holdings Ltd v Targetfollow (Birmingham) Ltd* [2004] EWHC 2547 at [197]–[198]; itself followed by *Dolphin Quays Development Ltd v Mills* [2006] EWHC 931, [2007] 1 P. & C.R. 12 at [45]–[46].

[336] Under the Law of Property Act 1925 s.54(2).

[337] "Regulated mortgage contract" must be read with s.22 of the Financial Services and Markets Act 2000, any relevant order under that section, and Sch.2 to that Act: 1989 Act s.2(6) (as amended).

[338] See above, para.4–038.

[339] Law Com. No.164 (1987), para.4.11. For another exclusion from the ambit of s.2, see Channel Tunnel Rail Link Act 1996 ss.41(1) and 56(1).

"... can only be made in writing and only by incorporating all the terms which the parties have expressly agreed in one document, or where contracts are exchanged, in each."[340]

So, for example, where it was held that a single contract was contained partly in a letter between the parties and partly in signed writing (which made no express reference to the earlier agreement in the letter), then the requirements of s.2 were not fulfilled as all the express terms of the contract were not contained in "one document" as is required.[341] On the other hand, s.2(3) explains that:

"The terms may be incorporated in a document either by being set out in it or by reference to some other document."[342]

No longer is a note or memorandum which may serve as evidence of the contract enough.

"All the terms which the parties have expressly agreed in one document" and rectification. At first sight, the omission of an express term of an oral agreement would seem to have the effect of rendering the whole contract a nullity as one can "only be made... by incorporating all the terms... expressly agreed".[343] However, s.2(4) of the Act recognises the power of the court to order the rectification of a written document so as to conform with the express terms of the oral agreement which it records and provides that where a written document relating to the sale of land has been so rectified, "the contract shall come into being, or be deemed to have come into being, at such a time as may be specified in the order". In *Firstpost Homes Ltd v Johnson*,[344] the Court of Appeal explained what is meant by the requirement that the contract be made in one document. There, an owner of certain farm property had agreed orally with a director of a company to sell the property to it at a cost of £1,000 per acre. The director had then typed a letter purporting to come from the owner agreeing to sell the land at this price, with a place for her signature and with an enclosed plan, which showed the land in question outlined in colour and which was signed by the director. The Court of Appeal held that, on these facts, the requirements of s.2 of the 1989 Act had not been fulfilled, as the letter and the plan constituted two documents (the former referring to the latter as being enclosed with it), but the letter (which allegedly contained the contract) had not been signed by the director on behalf of the company as was required.[345] However, the court also noted that while on its terms the letter contained no commitment by the company to purchase the property, the company could have applied to the court to rectify the letter so as to reflect the oral agreement.[346] In *Robert Leonard (Developments)* 4–070

[340] Law of Property (Miscellaneous Provisions) Act 1989 s.2(1).
[341] *Dolphin Quays Development Ltd v Mills* [2006] EWHC 931, [2007] 1 P. & C.R. 12.
[342] e.g. *Glen Courtney v Corp Ltd* [2006] EWCA Civ 518 at [11], [30].
[343] Law of Property (Miscellaneous Provisions) Act 1989 s.2(1).
[344] [1995] 1 W.L.R. 1567.
[345] See below, para.4–072.
[346] *Firstpost Homes Ltd v Johnson* [1995] 1 W.L.R. 1567, 1576, 1577.

Ltd v Wright,[347] the Court of Appeal exercised its power to order rectification of the terms of documents exchanged by the parties' solicitors by telephone so as to include reference to the sale of the chattels which had been included in the parties' previous oral contract, and the court also ordered that this rectified contract should be deemed to come into being from the date of the exchange of documents. The Court of Appeal recognised that allowing rectification detracted from the legislative purpose of s.2 which was to prevent disputes either as to whether the parties had entered into a binding agreement or as to what terms they had agreed, but the availability of rectification showed that:

> ". . . it was clearly the intention of the Act that the all terms requirement should not be so inflexible as to cause hardship or unfairness where there has been a mistake resulting in a venial non-compliance with the Act."[348]

However, in *Oun v Ahmad*[349] it was held that the court could not order rectification of a document so as to include all the terms of the would-be contract where there was an express agreement to omit a term or terms from the written record of the agreement since in these circumstances there was no mistake in the recording of the agreement.[350] For this purpose, it was held that a court should apply the conventional rules governing rectification of written instruments applicable generally,[351] even though the effect of rectification in the context of the 1989 Act is to rescue an otherwise invalid agreement.[352]

4–071 **"Exchange of contracts".** In *Commission for the New Towns v Cooper (Great Britain) Ltd*,[353] the Court of Appeal explained the significance of the alternative formal requirement in s.2 of the Law of Property (Miscellaneous Provisions) Act 1989 that all the terms of the contract which the parties have expressly agreed be incorporated "where contracts are exchanged, in each [document]". According to Stuart-Smith L.J.[354] the expression "exchange of contracts", even if not a term of art, possesses the following features:

> "1. Each party draws up or is given a document which incorporates all the terms which they have agreed, and which is intended to record their proposed contract. The terms that have been agreed may have been agreed either orally or in writing or partly orally or [sic: and] partly in writing.
>
> 2. The documents are referred to as 'contracts' or 'parts of contract', although they need not be so entitled. They are intended to take effect as formal documents of

[347] [1994] N.P.C. 49. See also *Peters v Fairclough Homes Ltd* Unreported December 20, 2002 Ch D at [26]–[27] (contractual document rectified so as to include longstop date included in correspondence between solicitors). cf. *Enfield LBC v Arajah* [1995] E.G.C.S. 164 (where apparently the possibility of rectification was not raised).
[348] [1994] N.P.C. 49 at [10], per Henry L.J.
[349] [2008] EWHC 545 (Ch), [2008] All E.R. (D) 270.
[350] [2008] EWHC 545 (Ch) at [42]–[48].
[351] [2008] EWHC 545 (Ch) at [55].
[352] [2008] EWHC 545 (Ch) at [36] referring to 1989 Act s.2(4) which states that after rectification "the contract shall come into being, or be deemed to have come into being".
[353] [1995] Ch. 259.
[354] [1995] Ch. 259, 285.

title and must be capable on their face of being fairly described as contracts having that effect.

3. Each party signs his part in the expectation that the other party has also executed or will execute a corresponding part incorporating the same terms.
4. At the time of execution neither party is bound by the terms of the document which he has executed, it being their mutual intention that neither will be bound until the executed parts are exchanged.
5. The act of exchange is a formal delivery by each party of its part into the actual or constructive possession of the other with the intention that the parties will become actually bound when exchange occurs, but not before.
6. The manner of exchange may be agreed and determined by the parties."

As a result, the Court of Appeal held (through strictly obiter) that this requirement was not satisfied by the mere exchange of a signed letter of offer and a signed letter of acceptance, even if each had contained the (same) express terms of the contract as alleged.[355] Moreover, as a result of the requirement of the third feature of an "exchange of contracts" as set out by Stuart-Smith L.J., there can be no "exchange of contracts" within the meaning of s.2(1) where the documents in question contain substantial differences.[356]

Signature. Section 2(3) requires that: 4–072

"The document incorporating the terms or, where contracts are exchanged, one of the documents incorporating them (but not necessarily the same one) must be signed by or on behalf of each party to the contract."

This provision requires both parties to the contract to sign,[357] though it recognises the possibility of valid signature by the agent of either vendor or purchaser.[358]

Meaning of "signature". In *Firstpost Homes Ltd v Johnson*,[359] the Court of Appeal held that "signature" in s.2 of the 1989 Act should be given its ordinary linguistic meaning, with the result that the section requires that the parties must write their names with their own hands upon the document. The court thereby rejected the applicability of earlier authorities on the meaning of "signature" for the purposes of the Statute of Frauds 1677 and s.40 of the Law of Property Act 925.[360] As Balcombe L.J. observed: 4–073

---

355 The Court of Appeal distinguished its earlier unreported decision in *Hooper v Sherman* November 30, 1994 which took a different position adding that it had been made on the basis of a wrong concession by counsel: [1995] Ch. 259, 289, 295.

356 *De Serville v Argee Ltd* (2001) 82 P. & C.R. D12. See also, above, para.4–063 (mutual wills).

357 Under s.40 of the Law of Property Act 1925, signature is necessary only for "the party to be charged": see above, para.4–031. A third party who is intended as transferee of the interest in property need not sign: *RG Kensington Management Co Ltd v Hutchinson IDH Ltd* [2002] EWHC 1180, [2003] 2 P. & C.R. 13 at [57] not following *Jolson Ltd v Derby CC* [1999] 3 E.G.L.R. 1991; *Nweze v Nwoko* [2004] EWCA Civ 399, (2004) 2 P. & C.R. 33 at [21].

358 See below, para.4–074.

359 [1995] 1 W.L.R. 1567.

360 Notably *Evans v Hoare* [1892] 1 Q.B. 550, 561 and cf. above, para.4–034: see [1995] 1 W.L.R. 1567, 1574–1577.

> "... the clear policy of [section 2] is to avoid the possibility that one or other party may be able to go behind the document and introduce extrinsic evidence to establish a contract, which was undoubtedly a problem under the old law".[361]

However, it has been held that a party can sign a document by writing only his initials, provided that it is clear that he intended to authenticate the full terms of the document.[362] On the other hand, in *Firstpost Homes Ltd*, Peter Gibson L.J. accepted that the principle laid down by the House of Lords in *Caton v Caton*[363] in relation to the Statute of Frauds 1677 to the effect that the party's signature must be inserted in such a way as to authenticate the whole instrument[364] applies equally to the requirement of signature made by s.2 of the 1989 Act. Thus, where a letter in which A agrees to sell a piece of land to B refers to a plan of the land in question and the court considers that the letter and the plans constitute a single document, B's signature of the plan may well not constitute authentication of the whole.[365] Similarly, while a manuscript initialling of a document may constitute its "signature", the mere initialling of corrections at the margins of a document does not constitute its signing for the purposes of s.2 of the 1989 Act, as it does not evidence assent to the whole document.[366]

4–074 **Signature by agent.** Section 2(3) requires signature "by or on behalf of each party to the contract".[367] Clearly, no difficulty arises where an authorised agent signs on behalf of a principal who is named in the document otherwise satisfying the section.[368] On the other hand, a signature made without authority clearly does not satisfy the section (as not made *on behalf of* the would-be party) and it is to be noted that a solicitor is not necessarily authorised to sign the writing on behalf of his client merely as a result of the solicitor-client relationship.[369] However, where a person with authority to sign does so "as agent only" and no principal is named or identifiable from the document, it has been said that the section is presumably not satisfied as one of its parties is not named,[370] this view apparently resting on the proposition that the identity of the contracting party is a term of the contract, all the terms of the contract being required to be incorporated in the document by s.2(1).[371] A similar argument can be put as regards the significance

---

[361] [1995] 1 W.L.R. 1567, 1577.

[362] *Newell v Tarrant* [2004] EWHC 772, (2004) 148 S.J.L.B. 509 at [47].

[363] (1867) L.R. 2 H.L. 127.

[364] See above, para.4–033.

[365] *Firstpost Homes Ltd v Johnson* [1995] 1 W.L.R. 1567, 1573 (though on the facts the Court of Appeal held that the letter and plan before them constituted *two* documents: see above, para.4–071).

[366] *Newell v Tarrant* [2004] EWHC 772 , (2004) 148 S.J.L.B. 509 at [48].

[367] Signature is required by each party to the contract, not each party to the prospective conveyance or transfer: *RG Kensington Management Co v Hutchinson* [2002] EWHC 1180, [2003] 2 P. & C.R. 13.

[368] *Bowstead and Reynolds on Agency*, 18th edn (2006), para.8–004. cf. *Braymist Ltd v Wise Finance Co Ltd* [2002] EWCA Civ 127, [2002] 3 W.L.R. 322 (a person who signs a contract for the purchase of land as agent of a company not yet incorporated and who can, therefore, sue on the contract by virtue of s.36C(1) of the Companies Act 1985, is properly to be treated as having signed the agreement on its own behalf for the purposes of s.2 of the Act 1989).

[369] *Emmet on Title*, 19th edn (looseleaf updated to 2007), para.2–042.

[370] *Bowstead and Reynolds on Agency*, para.8–004.

[371] Above, para.4–070.

of signature by the agent of an undisclosed principal[372] and in both cases this strict approach can be supported from the purpose of the section in terms of certainty.[373] On the other hand, the Law Commission's Working Paper which led to the Act intended to "let the ordinary principles of agency operate"[374] and it can be argued that an agent:

> "... signs 'on behalf of' the principal whenever he signs with authority to do so and intending to act for his principal, which would allow both unnamed and undisclosed principals to enforce or be liable under the contract."[375]

It would certainly be a surprising (and practically very inconvenient) effect of the 1989 Act if signature by the agent of an undisclosed principal were held insufficient to satisfy its formal requirements and would mark a significant change from the old law[376] apparently not envisaged in course of the preparation of the Act.[377]

(iii) *The Effect of Failure to Comply with the Formal Requirements*

Effect of non-compliance. Unlike s.40 of the Law of Property Act 1925, which makes unenforceable those contracts which do not comply with its requirements,[378] any agreement not complying with the requirements contained in s.2 of the 1989 Act is a nullity,[379] as a contract governed by the section "can only be made in writing". The Law Commission considered that the principal effect of this would be to exclude the operation of the doctrine of part performance[380]: "[w]ithout writing there will be no contract for either party to perform".[381] Certainly, the courts could hardly use the doctrine of part performance as such to enforce an oral agreement. However, the doctrine is itself merely part of a wider equitable principle, viz that equity will not allow a statute to be used as an engine of fraud[382] and this principle is left untouched by the Act: indeed, it is difficult to see how the operation of such a principle could be excluded by the legislature.[383] In *Singh v Beggs*[384] Neill L.J. doubted the view that s.2 of the 1989 Act had "abolished" the doctrine of part performance, observing (if obiter) that: 4–075

> "It is true that it is provided by s.2(8) of the 1989 Act, that section 40 of the Law of Property Act 1925 will cease to have effect, but the doctrine [of part performance] is an

---

[372] *Bowstead and Reynolds on Agency*, para.8–004.
[373] Above, para.4–052.
[374] Law Com.Working Paper No. 92 (1985), s.5.16.
[375] *Bowstead and Reynolds on Agency*, para.8–004.
[376] See above, para.4–036.
[377] cf. *Government of Sierra Leone v Davenport* [2003] EWHC 2769, [2003] All ER (D) 99 (Nov.) at [69] where some of these difficulties were noted.
[378] See above, para.4–041.
[379] Gray and Gray, *Elements of Land Law*, 4th edn (2005), pp.1171 ("utterly void and ineffective").
[380] See above, paras 4–042 et seq.
[381] Law Com. No.164 (1987), para.4.13.
[382] *Lincoln v Wright* (1859) 4 De G. & J. 16; *Maddison v Alderson* (1883) 8 App. Cas. 467.
[383] See Goff & Jones, *The Law of Restitution*, 5th edn (1998), p.580.
[384] (1996) 71 P. & C.R. 120.

equitable doctrine, and it may be that in certain circumstances the doctrine could be relied on.[385]

The Law Commission itself recognised that circumstances may arise in which justice would be denied if a strict requirement of writing were universally upheld. Its view, reflected in s.2(5) of the 1989 Act,[386] was that any potential injustice could be avoided by judicial use of the techniques of collateral contracts, constructive trust or equitable estoppel. This has indeed occurred.[387] However, in determining the circumstances in which it will be appropriate to rely on any of these techniques, the courts are likely to bear in mind the general considerations outlined by the House of Lords in *Actionstrength Ltd v International Glass Engineering IN.GL.EN SpA*[388] as to the proper limits of equitable qualifications on or supplements to statutory rules entailing the formal invalidity of a contract, notably, the importance of not frustrating the purpose of the statutory provisions by simply enforcing invalid executory agreements by another, equitable name.[389] In this respect, while in common with its predecessor, s.40 of the Law of Property Act 1925, s.2 of the 1989 Act can be seen as based on a perceived need to protect people from being liable on the basis of oral utterances which are ill-considered, ambiguous or completely fictitious,[390] it was intended to go further and to introduce a greater certainty into the law and stricter formal requirements.[391]

4–076 **Collateral contracts.** Although s.2(1) of the 1989 Act makes clear that "*all* the terms which the parties have expressly agreed" must be incorporated in one document or, "where contracts are exchanged, in each" it has been held that this does not prevent the existence of a valid contract (which does not satisfy s.2's formal requirements) *collateral to* the main contract for the sale or other disposition of an interest in land (which does).[392] So, for example, in *Record v Bell*[393] the question arose whether the formal requirements contained in s.2 had been satisfied where a contract in two parts had been duly signed by the respective parties and was awaiting exchange and then some term was orally agreed immediately prior to exchange and was confirmed by the exchange of letters. On the facts, the vendor had made an undertaking as to the state of his title in order to induce the buyer to exchange contracts.[394] The court held that it resulted from s.2 of the 1989 Act that such a term would only be incorporated into the contract of sale if the latter referred to it,[395] but it felt able to construe the oral agreement

[385] (1996) 71 P. & C.R. 120, 122.

[386] "[N]othing in this section affects the creation or operation of resulting, implied or constructive trusts".

[387] Below, paras 4–077—4–083.

[388] [2003] UKHL 17, [2003] 2 A.C. 541 (in the context of the Statute of Frauds 1677 s.4) and see above, para.4–004 and Vol.II, para.44–054.

[389] [2003] UKHL 17 at [8]–[9], [20]–[26], [35], [52]. See further *Yaxley v Gotts* [2000] Ch. 162, 164, below, para.4–077.

[390] cf. in similar terms, [2003] UKHL 17 at [20], per Lord Hoffmann concerning the Statute of Frauds generally.

[391] See above, para.4–052.

[392] cf. above, para.4–067.

[393] [1991] 1 W.L.R. 853. See Harpum [1991] C.L.J. 399.

[394] *Record v Bell* [1991] 1 W.L.R. 853 at [862].

[395] [1991] 1 W.L.R. 853 at [860].

as to the new term as an independent collateral contract, which was valid so long as it was not itself a sale of an interest in land.[396] In this way, the requirements of s.2 had been fulfilled. However, in *Business Environment Bow Lane Ltd v Deanwater Estates Ltd* the Court of Appeal took a more restrictive approach to the recognition of such a collateral agreement, though s. 2 had not been relied on.[397] There the parties entered discussions and exchanged correspondence (all "subject to contract") towards the renewal of a lease, the negotiations concerning provision in the draft lease concerning the lessee's repairing covenants. The lease was executed with the provision in question amended, but (according to the lessee) not in the way which had earlier been agreed. The lessee therefore contended that this agreement in the course of negotiations could take effect as a collateral contract. For this purpose, the Court of Appeal agreed[398] with Lightman J in *Inntrepreneur Pub Co Ltd v East Crown Ltd*[399] that the question whether a pre-contractual statement made in the course of negotiations should be treated as having contractual force rested on a finding of the parties' objective intention based on the totality of the evidence and that for this purpose:

> "... one important consideration will be whether the statement is followed by further negotiations and a written contract not containing any term corresponding to the statement"

as there "the prima facie assumption will be that the written contract includes all the terms the parties wanted to be binding between them"; another consideration will be any lapse of time between the statement and the making of the contract; and, finally, "a representation of fact is much more likely intended to have contractual effect than a statement of future fact or future forecast". More generally, the Chancellor of the High Court, Sir Andrew Morritt, recognised that:

> "... the law relating to collateral contracts is well-established but in connection with sales or leases of land needs to be applied with caution if not the suspicion to which Lord Moulton referred in *Heilbut Symons v Buckleton.*[400] Thus, if the promise said to be binding as a collateral contract is in truth one of the terms for the sale or other disposition of land it will be unenforceable unless it is contained in the written contract required by s. 2. ... In a normal conveyancing transaction in a commercial context with both parties represented by experienced solicitors the usual course of dealing is to ensure that all agreed terms are put into the contract and the conveyance, transfer or lease. Accordingly those who assert a collateral contract in relation to a term not so contained must show that it was intended to have contractual effect separate from the normal conveyancing documents."[401]

---

396 [1991] 1 W.L.R. 853.

397 [2007] EWCA Civ 622, [2007] L. & T.R. 26.

398 [2007] EWCA Civ 622 at [46], [60]–[61]. The CA also relied on the leading general authority on collateral warranty, *Heilbut Symons & Co v Buckleton* [1913] A.C. 30. *Record v Bell* [1991] 1 W.L.R. 853 was not discussed.

399 [2000] 2 Lloyd's Rep. 611 at 615.

400 [1913] A.C. 30 at 47.

401 *Business Environment Bow Lane Ltd v Dean Water Estates Ltd* [2007] EWCA Civ 622 at [42], [43].

On the facts, the Court of Appeal found that on executing the lease[402] the parties had not intended to conclude a collateral contract relating to the tenant's covenants, this view being supported by the fact that the representation relied on related to "future events in unforeseeable circumstances", a commitment which would be "wholly uncommercial"[403]; that the statement in question was followed by further negotiations[404]; and that these negotiations were followed by the actual amendment of the lease which was executed, which "is to be seen as the parties' considered agreed conclusion of the negotiations".[405]

4–077 **Constructive trust.** Section 2(5) of the Law of Property (Miscellaneous Provisions) Act 1989 specifically precluded that section's requirements from affecting "the creation or operation of . . . constructive trusts". In *Yaxley v Gotts*[406] Robert Walker L.J. considered that the relevant "species of constructive" trust for this purpose is one based on "common intention" and is to be found where, in the words of Lord Bridge in *Lloyds Bank Plc v Rossett*[407] there is an:

> "'. . . agreement, arrangement or understanding' actually reached between the parties, and relied on and acted on by the claimant. . . . Equity enforces it because it would be unconscionable for the other party to disregard the claimant's rights."[408]

In *Yaxley v Gotts* itself, A made an oral agreement to give B the ground floor of a house which he (A) was proposing to buy in exchange for B's supplying labour and materials to convert the house into flats and managing the letting of the property. The house was purchased in the name of A's son, C, who subsequently refused to grant B any interest in the property. At first instance, it was held that C had adopted the oral agreement between A and B and that B and C were bound by proprietary estoppel to grant a 99-year lease of the ground floor to B. The Court of Appeal upheld this result, rejecting A and C's argument based on s.2 of the 1989 Act, but preferring to rely on the ground of constructive trust rather than proprietary estoppel, though seeing these as running together on the facts.[409] While the oral agreement between A and B was void by reason of the 1989 Act, which had abolished the doctrine of part performance and required all contracts for the sale or disposal of land to be in writing, the agreement could be enforced on the basis of a constructive trust in circumstances where, previously, the

[402] It was held that this was the relevant time owing to the negotiations being "subject to contract": [2007] EWCA Civ 622 at [45].

[403] [2007] EWCA Civ 622 at [47] (Sir Andrew Moritt).

[404] [2007] EWCA Civ 622 at [60] (Lloyd L.J.).

[405] [2007] EWCA Civ 622 at [57] (May L.J.)

[406] [2000] Ch. 162.

[407] [1991] 1 A.C. 107, 132.

[408] [2000] Ch. 162 at 180. See similarly *David Vincent S v Susan Ann S (now M)* [2006] EWHC 2892 (Fam), [2007] 1 F.L.R. 1123 at [56]. It has been held that where an agreement for the disposition of an interest in land is made subject to a condition, then no constructive trust can arise until the condition is fulfilled so as to allow the "beneficiary" under the would-be trust (the would-be transferee) to require the would-be "trustee" (the would-be transferor) to transfer the beneficial interest (the interest in land in question): *Representative Body of the Church in Wales v Newton* [2005] EWHC 631 (QB), [2005] All ER (D) 163 (Apr) especially at [64].

[409] [2000] Ch. 162 at 180, 181 & 193.

doctrine of part performance might have been relied upon.[410] Similarly, in *Kinane v Mackie-Conteh*[411] the claimant had loaned money to a company of which one of the defendants was managing director, this loan being intended to be secured by a charge on a house in the form of a "security agreement" signed by himself and his wife. The question arose whether the security agreement came within the formal requirements found in s.2 of the 1989 Act. The Court of Appeal held that on the facts "an estoppel overlapping with a constructive trust" was established so as to come within the exception found in s.2(5) of the 1989 Act, in that the defendants had encouraged the claimant in his erroneous belief that the agreement created an enforceable obligation. A further illustration of the way in which a constructive trust may avoid the formal requirements imposed by s.2 of the 1989 Act may be found in the application of the so-called *Pallant v Morgan* equity.[412] Where A and B agree that A will acquire some specific property for the joint benefit of A and B, and B, in reliance on A's agreement, refrains from attempting to acquire the property, then equity will not permit A, when he acquires the property, to keep it for his own benefit, to the exclusion of B. It has been said that because this equity is in the nature of a constructive trust, it is unaffected by s.2(1) the 1989 Act.[413]

Estoppel generally. Despite the absence of any express saving provision in s.2 as is provided for constructive trusts, in *McCausland v Duncan Lawrie Ltd*[414] Neill L.J. considered that the "doctrine of estoppel" (without further specification) was "plainly arguable" to give some effect to the agreement underlying a fairly trivial variation of a contract for the sale etc. of an interest in land, the variation itself being void for informality.[415] Morritt L.J. observed that: 4–078

> "Section 2 does not give rise to any illegality if its terms are not observed and the need for an estoppel arises in just those circumstances where there is no enforceable contract. For my part I would not place weight on the contention that an estoppel such as the vendor would advance is impossible as a matter of law but it still has to be made out as a matter of fact."[416]

The issue could not, therefore, be determined in an application to strike out a plaintiff's claim. In *Yaxley v Gotts*,[417] Robert Walker L.J. had:

> "... no hesitation in agreeing ... that the doctrine of estoppel may operate to modify (and sometimes perhaps even to counteract) the effect of section 2 of the Act of 1989. The circumstances in which section 2 has to be complied with are so various, and the scope of the doctrine of estoppel is so flexible, that any general assertion that section 2 as a 'no-go area' would be unsustainable."[418]

---

410 *Yaxley v Gotts* [2000] Ch. 162 at 179–181.
411 [2005] EWCA Civ 45, [2005] W.T.L.R. 345.
412 *Pallant v Morgan* [1953] Ch. 43; *Banner Homes Group Plc v Luff Developments Ltd* [2000] Ch. 372.
413 *Kilcarne Holdings Ltd v Targetfollow (Birmingham) Ltd* [2004] EWHC 2547 at [219] (where it was held inapplicable on the facts).
414 [1997] 1 W.L.R. 38.
415 [1997] 1 W.L.R. 38 at 45.
416 [1997] 1 W.L.R. 38 at 50. Tucker L.J. agreed. cf. *King v Jackson* [1998] 03 E.G. 138.
417 [2000] Ch. 162.
418 [2000] Ch. 162 at 174.

Nevertheless, in deciding whether or how it may apply, the courts must take into account the Act's policy of the need for certainty as to the formation of bargains of this type in the general public interest.[419]

4–079 **Estoppel by convention.** It is fairly clear that the courts will not allow the application of estoppel by convention so as simply to give effect to an agreement rendered a nullity by s.2 of the 1989 Act. In *Godden v Merthyr Tydfil Housing Association*[420] a building contractor claimed damages for breach of an oral agreement with a Housing Association, under which he had agreed to purchase a particular site, obtain planning permission for the building of seven houses and prepare the site for development, the Housing Association agreeing to reimburse him for the costs of this acquisition and work and that it would enter a contract with him for the construction of the houses. In response to the Housing Association's claim that this agreement failed the formal requirements of s.2 of the 1989 Act, the builder argued that since both parties had contracted in ignorance of this provision, the Housing Association was precluded by the doctrine of estoppel by convention from relying on this provision so as to deny that there was indeed an agreement reached between the parties. According to Simon Brown L.J., with whom Thorpe L.J. and Sir John Balcombe agreed, this submission:

> "... necessarily involves saying that, although Parliament has dictated that a contract involving the disposition of land made otherwise than in compliance with s.2 is void, the defendants are not allowed to say so. That, to my mind, is an impossible argument ... [I]f it were soundly made, it is difficult to see why it should not operate to escape the intended constraints of s.2 in virtually all cases."[421]

In Simon Brown L.J.'s view, the doctrine of estoppel may not be invoked to render valid a transaction which the legislature has, on grounds of general public policy, enacted is to be invalid.[422]

4–080 **Proprietary estoppel.**[423] In its work towards the 1989 Act the Law Commission saw proprietary estoppel as a particularly attractive technique for the avoidance of injustice caused by a rigid adherence to the new formality rules because, unlike the doctrine of part performance, it does not simply enforce the underlying agreement but allows a flexible remedy which can vary according to the particular circumstances.[424] While somewhat elusive of definition,[425] for one author:

---

[419] [2000] Ch. 162 at 174–175 and cf. the approach of the HL in *Actionstrength Ltd v International Glass Engineering IN.GL.EN SpA* [2003] UKHL 17, [2003] 2 A.C. 541, above, para.4–004 and below, para.4–081.

[420] (1997) 74 P. & C.R. D1. On estoppel by convention generally, see above, paras 3-107—3-114.

[421] (1997) 74 P. & C.R. DI, D3. Simon Brown L.J. thereby approved the statement found in *Halsbury's Laws of England*, 4th edn, Vol.16, para.962.

[422] In *Yaxley v Gotts* [2000] Ch. 162, 174 Robert Walker L.J. agreed that estoppel by convention in the context of s.2 of the 1989 Act was "impossible"; Clarke L.J. considered it "likely to fail": at 182.

[423] See above, paras 3–137 et seq.

[424] Law Com. No.164 (1987), para.5.5.

[425] Gray and Gray *Elements of Land Law* 4th edn (2005) at para.10.173.

> "... the doctrine of proprietary estoppel is applicable where some action is taken by a person ... in reliance on a mistaken belief as to his rights in or over land, or in reliance on expectations relating to land, where the landowner stands by or encourages the action in such circumstances that it would be unconscionable for him later to seek to enforce his strict legal rights."[426]

Thus, even if adopted by a court in a case where an agreement for the sale of land did not satisfy the formal requirements of s.2, it would apply only so as to give a remedy to a would-be purchaser[427]: any claim by a would-be vendor would not be for a right to land nor indeed for a specific asset, but for a sum of money, a simple claim for a debt.[428] An example of the application of proprietary estoppel in this context may be found in *Wayling v Jones*.[429] In that case, A had promised his companion of some ten years, B, that he would bequeath B the business in which he worked at very low wages, but died without having done so. The Court of Appeal held that B was entitled to rely on a proprietary estoppel against A's executors and therefore ordered them to pay the proceeds of sale of the business to B. If, by contrast, B had alleged that he had *contracted* with A that the latter would bequeath him the business in return for working for low wages, his claim would have failed for lack of fulfilling the formal requirements in s.2 of the 1989 Act. On the other hand, in *James v Evans*[430] the Court of Appeal rejected a defence of proprietary estoppel to a claim for possession of land. There, an owner of property and its would-be tenant had carried on negotiations towards the conclusion of a 10-year lease of land for the raising of sheep. These negotiations were carried on through their respective solicitors and "subject to contract", even though with the permission of the owner the would-be tenant had entered possession and treated the sheep as his own. In these circumstances, the Court of Appeal held that it was clear that the parties did not intend to be bound until the execution of the documents necessary to give legal effect to the transaction, and no estoppel operated to prevent the vendor from exercising his legal right to refuse to execute the documents and withdraw from the transaction unless it could be shown that it was unfair, unjust or unconscionable for him to refuse to proceed.

Proprietary estoppel and constructive trust. In *Yaxley v Gotts*,[431] Robert Walker L.J. considered that where a constructive trust is based on "common intention", then it is "closely akin to, if not indistinguishable from, proprietary estoppel".[432] While the Court of Appeal substituted constructive trust for proprietary estoppel (on which the trial judge had relied) as the basis for its decision, this case has been seen as authority for the proposition that: 4–081

---

[426] Davis (1993) 13 O.J.L.S. 101, 103. cf. *Lancashire Mortage Corp Ltd v Scottish & Newcastle Plc* [2007] EWCA Civ 684, [2007] All ER (D) 68 (Jul) at [44]–[45].

[427] Davis (1993) 13 O.J.L.S. 101, 103.

[428] (1993) 13 O.J.L.S. 101, 104 and see *Godden v Merthyr Tydfil Housing Association* (1997) 74 P. & C.R. D1.

[429] [1995] 2 F.L.R. 1029.

[430] [2000] 42 E.G. 173.

[431] [2000] Ch. 162, above, 4–077.

[432] [2000] Ch. 162 at 180. cf. Lord Walker's "lesser enthusiasm" for the complete assimilation of "common intention" constructive trust and proprietory estoppel in *Stack v Dowden* [2007] UKHL 17, [2007] 2 A.C. 432 at [37].

"... the doctrine of estoppel may operate to modify and counteract the effect of section 2(2) [of the 1989 Act]; and that section 2(5) can cover cases of the equitable intervention of proprietary estoppel *which coincide with or overlap* the concept of a constructive trust, even though section 2(5) does not expressly refer to proprietary estoppel."[433]

On the other hand, in *Kinane v Mackie-Conteh*[434] Arden L.J. and Neuberger L.J. expressed contrasting views as to whether a proprietary estoppel "unassociated with a constructive trust" would avoid the formal requirements found in s.2. According to Neuberger L.J.:

"... one must ... avoid regarding [subsection 2(5)] as an automatically available statutory escape route from the rigours of section 2(1) of the 1989 Act, simply because fairness appears to demand it. A provision such as section 2 ... was enacted for policy reasons which, no doubt, appeared sensible to the legislature ... the Court should not allow its desire to avoid what might appear a rather harsh result in a particular case to undermine the statutory policy."[435]

He concluded, therefore, that a "mere estoppel, unassociated with a constructive trust" might not avoid the formal requirements of s.2, especially given the decision of the House of Lords in *Actionstrength Ltd v International Glass Engineering SpA*.[436] However, here Arden L.J. did not agree, and emphasised that the latter decision was concerned with s.4 of the Statute of Frauds 1677 which contains no exception to its formal requirements equivalent to s.2(5) of the 1989 Act. In her view, proprietary estoppel could form the basis of disapplying s.2(1):

"... the cause of action in proprietary estoppel is ... not founded on the unenforceable agreement but upon the defendant's conduct which, when viewed in all relevant aspects, is unconscionable".[437]

4–082 **Remedies.** One important aspect of the difference between proprietary estoppel and constructive trust lies in the former's greater flexibility of remedial response.[438] For:

"... if there is a constructive trust the court must usually give effect to it, often by ordering a transfer of the relevant proprietary interest, whereas if there is an estoppel the court will give a remedy that reflects the value of the equity in question."[439]

---

[433] *Lancashire Mortgage Corp Ltd v Scottish and Newcastle Plc* [2007] EWCA Civ 684, [2007] All ER (D) 68 (Jul) at [55], per Mummery L.J. (emphasis added).

[434] [2005] EWCA Civ 45, [2005] W.T.L.R. 345.

[435] [2005] EWCA Civ 45 at [40].

[436] [2003] UKHL 17, [2003] 2 A.C. 541.

[437] [2005] EWCA Civ 45 at [29].

[438] Goff and Jones, *The Law of Restitution*, 7th edn (2007), p.579–580.

[439] *Representative Body of the Church in Wales v Newton* [2005] EWHC 631 (QB), [2005] All E.R. (D) 163 (Apr) at [62], per Antony Edwards-Stuart Q.C. For general discussions of the remedial flexibility of proprietary estoppel see *Jennings v Rice* [2002] EWCA Civ 159, [2002] All ER (D) 324 (Feb); *Powell v Benny* [2007] EWCA Civ 1283, [2007] All ER (D) 71 (Dec); Gardner (1999) 115 L.Q.R. 438 & (2006) 122 L.Q.R. 492.

Sometimes, the effect of the application of the two doctrines will be the same,[440] but the remedial flexibility of proprietary estoppel was of central importance to the decision of the Court of Appeal in *Cobbe v Yeoman's Row Management Ltd.*[441] There a company which owned a building had orally agreed in principle with a property developer that it would sell the building to him if he obtained planning permission for its redevelopment, this agreement fixing a price and specifying an "overage" payment if the gross resale of the building exceeded a certain sum. The director of the company encouraged the developer to expect that her company would fulfil this agreement even after she had decided not to do so but to renegotiate for more money, and then (acting for the company) reneged on the agreement on the same day on which planning permission was granted. Mummery L.J. (with whom Dyson L.J. and Sir Martin Nourse agreed) held that s.2 of the 1989 did not prevent the application of proprietary estoppel.[442] He observed that its availability:

> "... does not infringe the public policy underlying section 2(1) of the 1989 Act by either directly or indirectly enforcing the [agreement] so as to frustrate the purpose of section 2. The estoppel here did not rest merely on the existence of the [agreement]. It was founded on the fact that [the developer] was induced and encouraged to believe that [the company] regarded the [agreement] as binding in honour and would not withdraw from its terms if [he] obtained planning permission; that [he] relied on that inducement and encouragement; and that it was unconscionable for [the company] to rely on its strict legal rights."[443]

Rather than making an award for a reasonable sum to cover the cost of the work done by the developer towards winning planning permission (which would not have done justice to the developer's equity as it would not have reflected his expectation of profit from the increased value of the property with planning permission[444]), the Court of Appeal confirmed the judge's award at first instance which had given the developer a half interest in the increase in value of the property after planning permission.[445] In this respect, Dyson L.J. observed that:

> "... the fundamental question for the court in each case is to decide what relief justice requires to satisfy the equity. Relevant factors include the nature of the expectation created by the defendant's conduct; the detriment suffered by the claimant in reliance on the defendant's representations; the degree to which the defendant's conduct can properly be said to be unconscionable; and the need for some proportionality between the claimant's expectation and his or her detriment."[446]

---

440 e.g. *Lancashire Mortgage Corp Ltd v Scottish and Newcastle plc* [2007] EWCA Civ 684, [2007] All ER (D) 68 (Jul) at [56] (defendant prevented from asserting a prior beneficial interest in proceeds of sale of security ahead of repayment to claimant under their legal charge).

441 [2006] EWCA Civ 1139, [2006] 1 W.L.R. 2964.

442 [2006] EWCA Civ 1139 at [62]–[68], [120], [141].

443 [2006] EWCA Civ 1139 at [66]–[67].

444 [2006] EWCA Civ 1139 at [90], [132].

445 [2006] EWCA Civ 1139 at [90]–[95] (Mummery L.J. seeing this as the "least unsatisfactory" solution); [135]–[138].

446 [2006] EWCA Civ 1139 at [126].

4–083 **Promissory estoppel ("forbearance in equity").** The Law Commission considered that "promissory estoppel" might apply to qualify the strictness of the formal requirements of s.2 of the 1989 Act.[447] In the present context, however, the so-called doctrine of promissory or equitable estoppel, sometimes known as "forbearance in equity", would not improve a vendor's position owing to its essentially defensive nature, for promissory estoppel cannot create a new cause of action in substitution for the contractual action denied for want of formality.[448]

4–084 **Restitution: recovery of money paid by purchaser on a failure of consideration.** The availability of restitution of money paid under an agreement which fails to comply with s.40 of the Law of Property Act 1925 and therefore renders the contract unenforceable depends on whether the vendor or purchaser defaults. The general rule is that if the vendor defaults, the purchaser may recover his deposit on the ground of total failure of consideration.[449] It is, however, possible that, even here, consideration for the payment will not have failed if the vendor has done acts of part performance of the contract and these acts benefited the purchaser.[450] If, on the other hand, the purchaser defaults, he may not recover a deposit paid on the ground of failure of consideration as the consideration for the payment cannot be said to have failed.[451] This position remains unaltered under the new law.[452]

4–085 Nevertheless, failure to fulfil the requirements of s.2 of the 1989 Act may lead to different restitutionary effects. In the case of a vendor in default, if the notion of consideration were understood as the basis on which the payment was made,[453] then this basis would be the existence of the contract of sale. Under the new requirements, failure to comply with the formalities nullifies the contract rather than simply making it unenforceable: thus, consideration for the payment will always fail if the formal requirements are not fulfilled. If, on the other hand, the receipt of any promised benefit by the purchaser (such as, for example, by entering possession) were to be taken as preventing the failure of consideration even under this non-existent contract, then recovery would be denied. The former interpretation of the notion of failure of consideration has the attraction in the present context of tending to further the protective purpose of the new formal requirements: a purchaser who pays a deposit under an informal sale of land should not be discouraged from claiming the benefit of the statutory invalidity by the threat of losing his deposit, even if he can be said to have benefited in some way from the transaction. However, where a buyer has paid the full price and entered into possession of the land for a period, it is submitted that it would be

[447] Law Commission, Working Paper No.92, para.5.8.

[448] cf. above, paras 3–085 et seq. especially para.3–098.

[449] See above, para.4–041 and below, paras 29–054 et seq.

[450] cf. Goff and Jones, *The Law of Restitution*, 7th edn (2007), paras 1.054–1.055. Of course, if the acts of part performance are sufficient to satisfy the doctrine of part performance, then the contract may be enforced in equity: see above, paras 4–042 et seq.

[451] *Thomas v Brown* [1878] 1 QBD 714, subject to the discretion granted to the court under the Law of Property Act 1925 s.49(2).

[452] cf. Burrows, *The Law of Restitution*, 2nd edn (2002) pp.331, 386–388.

[453] Birks, *An Introduction to the Law of Restitution* (1985), pp.219–221.

unjust to allow him to rely on the statutory invalidity in order to claim back the price, leaving the seller to any possible counterclaim in restitution on the ground of the buyer's unjust enrichment in enjoying the property during the period. Therefore, this type of case makes more attractive an understanding of the notion of failure of consideration in terms, not of the existence of the underlying contract, but of the absence of any promised benefit received under it by the party claiming restitution.[454]

Restitution: recovery of money paid by purchaser under a mistake of law. As the previous paragraph indicates, the traditional ground for recovery of money paid under a contract for the sale, etc. of an interest of land has been a total failure of consideration. However, in *Kleinwort Benson v Lincoln City Council*[455] the House of Lords allowed a party to a contract void under the ultra vires doctrine to recover payments made under it on the ground that at the time of payment it laboured under a mistake of law as to the validity of the contract: restitution for mistaken payments applies in principle to mistakes of law as to mistakes of fact.[456] While, therefore, this decision was not made in the context of a contract which failed to comply with the formal requirements of s.2 of the 1989 Act, the abolition of the mistake of law rule was put in very general terms and it could well be argued that where a purchaser of land pays money under an agreement for the sale etc. of an interest in land thinking it to be a valid contract, but which as a matter of law is void for want of formality, then that purchaser should be able to recover the money on the ground of this mistake of law, whether or not consideration for the payment can be said to have failed. However, such a reopening of executed *land* transactions may be thought undesirable by future courts. In this respect, it is to be recalled that in *Tootal Clothing Ltd v Guinea Properties Ltd* (which was not cited to the House of Lords in *Kleinwort Benson v Lincoln City Council*), Scott L.J. expressed the view that: 4–086

> "... section 2 [of the 1989 Act] is of relevance only to executory contracts. It has no relevance to contracts which have been completed. If parties choose to complete an oral land contract or a land contract that does not in some respect or other comply with section 2, they are at liberty to do so. Once they have done so, it becomes irrelevant that the contract they have completed may not have been in accordance with section 2."[457]

While in *Kleinwort Benson v Lincoln City Council* Lord Goff of Chieveley (with whom Lord Browne-Wilkinson, Lord Lloyd of Berwick, Lord Hoffmann and Lord Hope of Craighead agreed on this point) rejected a restriction on the ambit of restitution on the ground of mistake of law for the case where a transaction is

---

[454] cf. Burrows at pp.333–336 who argues that the law ought to recognise a partial failure of consideration as a ground of restitutionary liability and see *Westdeutsche Landesbank Girozentrale v Islington LBC* [1996] A.C. 669; *Goss v Chilcott* [1996] A.C. 788; *Stocznia Gdanska SA v Latvian S.S. Co* [1998] 1 W.L.R. 574, 590; Goff and Jones at paras 19–007 et seq. and below, paras 29–054 et seq.

[455] [1998] 2 A.C. 349. See also *Deutsche Morgan Grenfell Group Plc v IRC* [2006] UKHL 49, [2007] 1 A.C. 558.

[456] See further, below, paras 29–046 et seq.

[457] (1991) 64 P. & C.R. 452, 455.

completed,[458] he did so by reference to the cause of the voidness of the contracts before him, i.e. interest rate swap transactions. These had been held void on the ground that they were ultra vires the local authorities which had entered them and, as Lord Goff concluded:

> "... it is incompatible with the ultra vires rule that an ultra vires transaction should become binding on a local authority simply on the ground that it has been completed."[459]

According to Lord Hope, "the purpose of the ultra vires doctrine is to protect the public" and therefore "it would be unsatisfactory if restitution were to be possible only in the case of uncompleted transactions",[460] though he put his rejection of the restriction in very general terms.[461] It is submitted that a future court could take the view that the policy underlying the invalidity of informal transactions relating to land would not be defeated by a rule which prevented the restitution of monies paid under them where they are wholly executed.[462] For, while the formalities required by the 1989 Act may to a degree serve a protective purpose of would-be purchasers, the main reason for the requirements is the need for certainty in transactions and where a transaction had been completed there should be no concern on this ground.[463] On the other hand, a court could instead take a position similar to that taken by the Court of Appeal in *Godden v Merthyr Tydfil Housing Association* in relation to the application of the doctrine of estoppel by convention to a land transaction void for informality, where it held that a court should not uphold a transaction declared invalid on grounds of general public policy.[464] If it did, or if the full force of restitution on the ground of mistake of law is not otherwise restrained, then any payments made under a transaction which was thought valid by the payer, but was void for informality may be recovered.

4–087 **Restitution: benefits conferred other than money.** Under the Law of Property Act 1925, s.40, a *purchaser* of an interest in land under a contract unenforceable under that provision may recover on a quantum meruit for improvements to the land if the vendor has allowed him to go on to effect them, but then repudiates the contract, as the permission to enter may be taken as acquiescence in the work being done.[465] Similarly, in *Deglman v Guaranty Trust Co of Canada and Constantineau*,[466] the defendants' predecessor in title had promised to bequeath

---

458 [1998] 2 A.C. 349, 385–387. Lord Goff thereby rejected an argument to this effect found in Birks (1993) 23 U.W.A.L.R. 195, 230.

459 [1998] 2 A.C. 349, 387.

460 [1998] 2 A.C. 349, 415.

461 [1998] 2 A.C. 349, 415–416 and see Burrows [1995] R.L.R. 15, 18–19.

462 cf. *Deutsche Morgan Grenfell Group Plc v IRC* [2006] UKHL 49, [2007] 1 A.C. 558 where the HL considered whether the statutory tax regime under which the payments in question were paid was incompatible as a matter of policy with restitutionary recovery on the ground of mistake of law and found that it was not.

463 See *Firstpost Homes Ltd v Johnson* [1995] 1 W.L.R. 1567, 1576, per Peter Gibson L.J., quoted above, para.4–009.

464 (1997) 74 P. & C.R. D1 at D3. cf. *McCausland v Duncan Lawrie Ltd* [1997] 1 W.L.R. 38, 45, 50 and see above, para.4–079.

465 Goff and Jones, *The Law of Restitution*, 7th edn (2007), p.582.

466 [1954] 3 D.L.R. 78 and cf. below, para.29–080.

a house to the plaintiff, her nephew, if he performed various household tasks. He performed the tasks, but she did not leave the house to him in her will. The Supreme Court of Canada held his acts were not sufficient to satisfy the doctrine of part performance and thus to avoid the effect of the Statute of Frauds, but further held that the plaintiff was entitled to recover on a quantum meruit for the work he had done in the expectation of some remuneration and at his aunt's request. This law would also apply under s.2 of the 1989 Act.[467]

On the other hand, if the *vendor* of an interest in land improves it at the request of the purchaser and in anticipation of the contract going ahead, it is not clear whether the purchaser will be liable on a quantum meruit in respect of the work, because although he has requested the work done, he has not benefited from its execution.[468] Dicta in the decision of the Court of Appeal in *Brewer Street Investments Ltd v Barclays Woollen Co Ltd*[469] suggest that a vendor should not recover where a contract has failed to materialise owing to his own fault, but should do so only where it is owing to the purchaser's fault, or perhaps, circumstances beyond either's control. However, the case concerned an agreement made expressly "subject to contract" which failed to proceed further and it is submitted that, whatever the position under s.40 of the Law of Property Act 1925, a distinction based on the respective fault of the parties is inappropriate to recovery in respect of benefits conferred under a contract nullified under the 1989 Act: a party could not be described as "at fault" merely by relying on the statutory invalidity of an agreement which he has made—an invalidity part of whose purpose was his own protection.[470] On the other hand, if a purchaser is allowed to enter possession under a contract void for failing to fulfill the requirements of s.2 of the 1989 Act, a vendor should be able to recover on a quantum meruit for the purchaser's enjoyment of the property, this clearly counting as a benefit for this purpose.[471] 4–088

[467] cf. Bentley & Coughlan [1989] 10 L.S. 325.
[468] cf. Goff and Jones at pp.664 et seq.
[469] [1954] 1 Q.B. 428, 434, 437, 438.
[470] See Law Com. No.164 (1987), para.2.9.
[471] Goff and Jones, *The Law of Restitution*, 5th edn (1998), p.581. This passage does not appear in the 7th edn.

Chapter 5

MISTAKE[1]

		PARA.
1.	Introduction	5–001
2.	Common mistake	5–017
	(a) Introduction	5–017
	(b) Different approaches before *Bell v Lever Bros*	5–019
	(c) Mistake at common law	5–028
	(i) *Bell v Lever Bros*	5–028
	(ii) The Modern Doctrine	5–033
	(d) Mistakes of Law	5–054
	(e) No separate Rule in Equity	5–057
	(f) Mistake and Construction	5–064
3.	Mistakes in "communication"	5–066
	(a) Underlying principles	5–066
	(b) Mutual misunderstanding	5–071
	(c) Unilateral mistake as to terms	5–074
	(i) When mistake will affect contract	5–074
	(ii) Effect on Contract	5–080
	(d) Mistaken identity	5–088
4.	*Non est factum*	5–101
5.	Rectification of written agreements	5–107
	(a) Common mistake	5–108
	(b) Unilateral mistake	5–115
	(c) General principles	5–122

1. Introduction

Types of mistake. The doctrine of mistake in the law of contract deals with two rather different situations. In the first, the parties are agreed on the terms of the contract but have entered it under a shared and fundamental misapprehension as to the facts or the law.[2] Cases in this category are now usually referred to as "common" mistake, for normally the mistake is legally relevant only if both parties have contracted under the same misapprehension.[3] In the second, there is 5–001

---

[1] See generally Cheshire (1944) 60 L.Q.R. 175; Tylor (1948) 11 M.L.R. 257; Slade (1954) 70 L.Q.R. 385; Stoljar (1965) 28 M.L.R. 265; Stoljar, *Mistake and Misrepresentation: A Study in Contractual Principles* (1968); Smith (1994) 110 L.Q.R. 400; Friedmann (2003) 119 L.Q.R. 68; Cartwright, *Misrepresentation, Mistake and Non-disclosure* (2007).

[2] On mistakes as to the law, see below, para.5–054.

[3] Earlier editions of this work used the phrase "mutual mistake", following the terminology used by Lord Atkin in *Bell v Lever Bros* [1932] A.C. 161, and some works adhere to this usage: e.g. *Anson's Law of Contract*, 28th edn (by Beatson, 2002), Ch.8. Other works refer to this type of mistake as "common mistake" (e.g. Cheshire, Fifoot and Furmston, *Law of Contract*, 15th edn (2007), Ch.8); and more recently the courts have also referred to common mistake: e.g. *Great Peace Shipping Ltd v Tsavliris Salvage (International) Ltd (The Great Peace)* [2002] EWCA Civ 1407, [2003] Q.B. 679. One reason for using the phrase "common mistake" is to reduce the risk of confusion with what is

some mistake or misunderstanding in the communications between the parties which prevents there being an effective agreement (for instance, if the parties misunderstand each other) or at least means that there is no agreement on the terms apparently stated (for instance, if one party in an offer states terms which the other party knows the first party does not intend, but nonetheless the other purports to accept). This second category of mistake, which can generally be referred to as "mistake in communication", includes "mutual misunderstanding", where each is mistaken as to the terms intended by the other,[4] and "unilateral mistake", where only one of the parties is mistaken, over the terms of the contract[5] or the identity of the other party.[6]

5–002 **Non est factum.** There is, however, a third type of mistake which might be seen as a variant of unilateral mistake, but which for convenience will be placed in a separate category. It is peculiar to the law of written contracts, and it allows a party who has executed a document under a fundamental misapprehension as to its nature to plead that it is "not his deed". This is the defence of non est factum.[7]

5–003 **Rectification of written documents.** This chapter also deals separately with the remedy of rectification, which may be available when the parties have signed a written document that does not state accurately the terms that were agreed between them.[8]

5–004 **Money paid under mistake of fact.** Mistake may also entitle a party who has paid money under the mistake to recover it back in an action for money had and received to his use.[9] The subject of the recovery of money paid under a mistake is principally dealt with in Chapter 29 of this work.

5–005 **Mistakes as to facts and mistakes as to terms.** The categorisation of the situations in which the doctrine of mistake affects a contract[10] into cases of "common mistake", "unilateral mistake" or "mutual misunderstanding"[11] is useful, but it highlights only one of the distinctions between the cases. For the purposes of the law, there is a second and vital distinction between common mistake on the one hand and unilateral mistake or mutual misunderstanding on the other. This is that the doctrine of mistake takes account of a mistake as to the factual circumstances[12] in which the contract is made only if the mistake was common, i.e. both parties made substantially the same mistake—for example,

---

termed here "mutual misunderstanding" (where the parties are at cross-purposes as to the terms of the contract): see below, para.5–071.

[4] See below, para.5–071.

[5] Below, paras 5–005 and 5–074 et seq.

[6] Below, paras 5–088 et seq. The phrase "mistake in communication" is perhaps not wholly apt to cover the "mistake of identity" cases (though it can be said there is a mistake over whom the communication is with) but it is hard to find a better phrase to describe the category.

[7] See below, paras 5–101—5–106.

[8] See below, paras 5–107—5–136.

[9] See below, paras 29–029 et seq.

[10] Compare those cases in which the mistake is not legally relevant, below, para.5–007.

[11] Above, para.5–001.

[12] Or possibly as to the law: see below, para.5–054.

when an agreement was made to rent a room overlooking the route of a coronation procession, that both parties believed that the procession was scheduled to take place on the date concerned when in fact it had been cancelled.[13] Common mistake cases are ones:

> "... in which the parties, though genuinely agreed, have both contracted in the mistaken belief that some fact which lies at the root of the contract is true."[14]

(As will be seen, the mistake must also be fundamental.[15]) In contrast, where only one of the parties is mistaken as to the facts—a "unilateral" mistake as to the facts—there is no basis for relief under the doctrine of mistake. A unilateral mistake or a mutual misunderstanding will only operate where the mistake or misunderstanding is about the terms of the contract—for example, the price or the contractual description of what is being sold.[16] This category includes cases of mistaken identity, when one party thinks he is dealing with someone different to the person with whom he actually is dealing. We shall see that mistaken identity cases also seem to depend on the distinction between the terms of the contract and the surrounding facts. If the mistaken party's offer was, by its express or implied terms, not made to anyone other than the person with whom the mistaken party thought he was dealing, no other person can accept it and no contract will result from a purported acceptance by anyone else. If however the offer or acceptance was not so confined, it will result in a contract with the other person, whoever he is, and the first party's mistake is treated as merely being to the surrounding facts.[17]

"Mistake" implies a positive belief. Further, it seems that relief will only be granted under the doctrine of mistake if one or both parties entered the contract under a positive belief which was incorrect, rather than merely not having thought about a particular issue.[18] Thus in all the cases in which a contract has been held to be void[19] for common mistake, it seems that the parties had a positive belief that X was the case when it was not, rather than merely making no assumptions about whether X was so or not. Similarly, in the cases of unilateral mistake over the terms, one party has positively thought the terms he has offered, or has been offered, are Y when Y is not what in fact was said or written. It is very doubtful whether relief can be given on the ground of mistake when the party was simply unaware that the terms on offer included a particular clause, as opposed to positively believing that they were Y when they were not.[20] However, it seems that the positive belief may be that something is not the case, 5–006

[13] *Griffith v Brymer* (1903) 19 T.L.R. 434.

[14] *Anson's Law of Contract*, 28th edn (by Beatson, 2002), p.311.

[15] Below, para.5–017.

[16] See below, para.5–076.

[17] See below, paras 5–088—5–100.

[18] cf. Cartwright, *Misrepresentation, Mistake and Non-disclosure* (2007), para.12.03.

[19] Or voidable in equity, under a line of cases no longer accepted as good law: see below, para.5–057.

[20] See below, para.5–079.

e.g. that the terms on offer do not include a particular clause or that the other party is not Z.[21]

5–007 **Mistakes that are not legally relevant.** Thus there are many situations that may loosely be called cases of "mistake" in which the contract will nonetheless be binding. One example is the case considered earlier, in which one party enters the contract under a mistake as to the facts which the other party does not share.[22] Suppose I buy a ring mistakenly thinking it is a gold ring. Nothing is said by the vendor as to what the ring is made of[23]; but he knows that it is not gold. Even if he knows that I think the ring to be made of gold, I cannot avoid the contract on the ground of mistake, though I would never have entered into it had I known the true position. The mistake does not relate to the terms of the contract, which are simply to sell and buy the specific ring, so neither mutual not unilateral mistake is relevant. Nor does the doctrine of common mistake apply: though the mistake may be fundamental, it is not shared.[24] A second example of a mistake that is not legally relevant is where the mistake is shared by both parties[25] but it is not sufficiently fundamental to render the contract void.[26]

5–008 **Underlying policy.** There are, of course, in modern contract law many circumstances in which liability may be imposed on a party for the consequences of facts that are unknown to one of (or both) the parties. This may be the result of the implication of appropriate terms by statute[27] or at common law, or by the normal process of construction, or as the result of doctrines that have a limited application, such as misrepresentation[28] or the duty of disclosure that applies to insurance contracts.[29] But subject to this, a mistake about the facts surrounding the contract which is made by both parties is relevant only if it is fundamental. A mistake as to the facts made by one party only is legally irrelevant, even if the other party knows of it. Mere silence as regards a material fact which the one party is not bound to disclose to the other is not a ground of invalidity, for the principle that in relation to sale is referred to as caveat emptor ("let the buyer beware") is still the starting point of the English law of contract.[30] This sets English law apart from many of the continental systems, which seem to give relief in cases of shared mistake more readily than does English law and which

---

[21] See below, para.5–099.

[22] See above, para.5–005.

[23] Therefore there is no misrepresentation: compare below, para.5–014.

[24] Compare Anson's famous "Dresden china" example: *Anson's Law of Contract*, 28th edn, p.324 (second senario). Friedmann (2003) 119 L.Q.R. 68, 79–81 argues that in such a case relief should be given, by analogy of cases of innocent misrepresentation.

[25] Again it is assumed that neither party has stated what he believes to be the facts. If he had, the other might have a remedy for misrepresentation. See below, para.5–014.

[26] See below, para.5–017.

[27] For example, the terms as to fitness for purpose that are implied into a contract for the sale of goods where the goods are sold in the course of a business: see Sale of Goods Act 1979 s.14, below, Vol.II, paras 43–081—43–100.

[28] See below, para.5–014 and generally Ch.6.

[29] See below, para.6–144.

[30] *Bell v Lever Brothers Ltd* [1932] A.C. 161, 227; *Keates v Lord Cadogan* (1851) 10 C.B. 591; *Smith v Hughes* (1871) L.R. 6 Q.B. 597, 603; *Turner v Green* [1895] 2 Ch. 203.

may allow a party who has made a unilateral mistake about the subject matter to avoid the contract provided the mistake was sufficiently serious.[31] The restrictive approach to mistake seems to represent a strong policy underlying English contract law. As Lord Atkin said[32]:

> "It is of paramount importance that contracts should be observed, and that if parties honestly comply with the essentials of the formation of contracts—i.e. agree in the same terms on the same subject-matter—they are bound, and must rely on the stipulations of the contract for protection from the effect of facts unknown to them".[33]

Effects of mistake. The first type of mistake (termed above "common mistake") is sometimes said to operate so as to nullify consent, the second (termed above "mistake in communication") so as to negative it.[34] In other words, in the first case, the mistake renders the agreement ineffective as a contract; in the second, the parties have not in fact reached an agreement. In either case, if the mistake is operative the contract is said to be void ab initio. This is correct in cases of common mistake; although until very recently there was authority for the proposition that some common mistakes that would not make the contract void would nonetheless give either party the right to avoid it, the Court of Appeal has now disapproved this line of cases.[35] The proposition that in cases of unilateral mistake and of mutual misunderstanding the contract is also void ab initio must be treated with more reservation. It is certainly correct in cases of mutual misunderstanding[36] and in some cases of unilateral mistake. Thus a unilateral mistake as to the identity of the other party may prevent the formation of a contract, so that if the subject matter of the contract consists of goods, no property in the goods will pass under the contract, and they may be recovered by the true owner even from a bona fide purchaser for value.[37] In other cases of unilateral mistake, however, it seems more accurate to say that there is no contract on the terms apparently agreed.[38] If one party made a mistake in his offer and the other knew what the offer was meant to be but purported to "snap up" the apparent offer, the result may be that there is a contract on the terms the first 5–009

---

[31] For French and German Law see Beale, Hartkamp, Kötz and Tallon (eds), *Casebooks on the Common Law of Europe: Contract Law* (2002), Ch.3, section 2; and for a broader survey of the European legal systems, Sefton-Green, *Mistake, Fraud and Duties to Inform in European Contract Law* (2004). See also Friedmann (2003) 119 L.Q.R. 68, who demonstrates the links between the English doctrine of mistake and the "objective" principle in contract (on which see above, para.2–003).

[32] *Bell v Lever Bros Ltd* [1932] A.C. 161, 224 (referring to common mistake, but the policy appears to be a general one).

[33] The reasons for this narrow approach in cases of common mistake are explored in MacMillan (2003) 119 L.Q.R. 625, 657–658. In cases of mistaken identity, the courts have often been reluctant to find the contract void because of a desire to protect subsequent innocent purchasers of goods who, if the initial contract were void, would receive no title: see below, para.5–088.

[34] *Bell v Lever Bros Ltd* [1932] A.C. 161, 217.

[35] See below, paras 5–057 et seq.

[36] Below, para.5–071.

[37] *Hardman v Booth* (1863) 1 H. & C. 803; *Cundy v Lindsay* (1878) 3 App. Cas. 459; *Ingram v Little* [1961] 1 Q.B. 31. See below, paras 5–088 et seq.

[38] See below, paras 5–080 et seq.

party intended.[39] If necessary the terms of any contractual document may then be "rectified" to correspond to this contract.[40]

5–010 **Common law and equity.** Until recently it could be argued that what has been said above about the circumstances in which the law takes account of a mistake by one party, or both parties, to a contract represented the position at common law; and that the rules of equity "cut across this distinction".[41] This referred to the line of cases to the effect that in some circumstances a common mistake would give either party the right to avoid a contract that was not void for mistake at common law[42] based on a rule of equity. Now that these cases have been disapproved,[43] and if the interpretation of certain cases of unilateral mistake that will be offered in this chapter[44] is accepted, it seems that there is no inconsistency between common law and equity. Equity will on occasion supplement the remedies available at common law: for example, a mistake may entitle a party to a contract that has been reduced to writing to have the document rectified if it is not expressed in accordance with the parties' true intentions, or does not reflect the terms that the claimant intended and the other party knew him to intend.[45]

5–011 The only apparent "divergence" between the treatment of mistake cases in common law and in equity is that the hardship that would be caused by granting specific performance of a contract made under either type of mistake may lead to the court refusing specific performance as a matter of discretion even though the mistake does not render the contract void or have any other effect at common law.[46] As this is merely the denial of a particular remedy, and the contract remains binding in other respects (e.g. the claimant would still be entitled to damages if the contract were not performed[47]) this is not a contradiction of the common law rules.[48] Thus in cases of contractual mistake, common law and equity are consistent and equity plays only a minor role. Thus in this edition of this work there is no separate treatment of "Mistake in Equity".[49]

5–012 **Is there a separate doctrine of mistake?** Any "doctrine" of mistake in English contract law seems to have emerged only in the late nineteenth or even the twentieth century,[50] and from time to time commentators have argued that the

---

39 See below, paras 5–080 et seq.
40 See below, paras 5–115 et seq.
41 See the 28th edition of this work, para.5–001.
42 Above, para.5–001.
43 See below, paras 5–057 et seq.
44 Below, paras 5–080—5–086.
45 See below, paras 5–107—5–113. Equity may also prevent a mistaken party from relying on the "true" terms of a contract if a third party has relied on a document that stated the terms differently: see below, para.5–130.
46 See below, para.5–063.
47 See, e.g. *Wood v Scarth* (1855) 2 K. & J. 33 (equity); (1858) 1 F. & F. 293 (law).
48 cf. cases in which specific performance may be refused because of the hardship that would result because of a subsequent change of circumstances: see below, para.5–063 and para.27–031.
49 cf. *Chitty*, 28th edn, paras 5–060 et seq.
50 See below, paras 5–019 et seq.

doctrine is redundant or that the cases are better explained on some other basis.[51] Thus it has been said that cases of common mistake may be explained as resting on the construction of the contract, and in particular on an implied condition precedent[52]; while cases of unilateral and mutual mistake may be no more than an application of the rules of offer and acceptance.[53] From a conceptual point of view there is force in these arguments, and it is certainly hard to discern a single "doctrine" of mistake when the two categories of case described above are subject to quite different rules. However in this Work it is assumed that there are distinct rules on mistake dealing with each category. This is partly because the courts have recognised distinct rules of mistake[54] and partly because mistake is what may be called a "functional category". In factual terms, a party may claim that he, or both he and the other party, made the contract under a misapprehension of some kind, whether it be as to some fact bearing on the contract, as to the terms he has included in his offer or as to the other party's intentions or identity, when the mistake was self-induced.[55] We need to know what self-induced "mistakes" or (to use a word that does not have legal connotations) "misapprehensions", the law will take account of and what the parties' rights will be. Whether the rules that are applied are simply applications of more general rules, such as the doctrine of implied conditions or the rules of offer and acceptance, is from a functional viewpoint irrelevant; they are the rules that govern these types of mistake.

Mistake and unconscionability. Facts that bring a case within the category covered by the rules on "mistake" may, in an extreme case, give one party the right to avoid the contract on the ground of unconscionability.[56] Broadly speaking, if one party is suffering from what is sometimes termed a "special disability",[57] such as "poverty, or ignorance, or lack of advice",[58] and the other party consciously takes advantage of the disability, the first party may be entitled to avoid the contract. In many unconscionability cases the first party was in fact making the contract under a misapprehension as to the facts, typically as to the value of the property he was selling.[59] There is some suggestion that the doctrine may sometimes be used more broadly to prevent one party taking unconscientious advantage of the other's mistake. In *Bank of Credit and Commerce International SA (In Liquidation) v Ali (No.1)*[60] Lord Nicholls said that where the 5–013

[51] e.g. Slade (1954) 70 L.Q.R. 385.

[52] Smith (1994) 110 L.Q.R. 400. See below, para.5–016.

[53] e.g. Slade (1954) 70 L.Q.R. 385; Atiyah, *Essays in Contract* (1986), Ch.9.

[54] e.g. *Bell v Lever Bros* [1932] A.C. 161; *Associated Japanese Bank International Ltd v Crédit du Nord SA* [1989] 1 W.L.R. 255; *Great Peace Shipping Ltd v Tsavliris Salvage (International) Ltd (The Great Peace)* [2002] EWCA Civ 1407, [2003] Q.B. 679.

[55] Or when it resulted from a misrepresentation but the right to rescind for misrepresentation has been lost. See below, para.5–014.

[56] See below, paras 7–126 et seq.

[57] A phrase used by Deane J. in *Commercial Bank of Australia v Amadio* (1983) 151 C.L.R. 447, 474; see below, para.7–131.

[58] *Alec Lobb Ltd v Total Oil (Great Britain) Ltd* [1983] 1 W.L.R. 87, 94–95, per Peter Millett Q.C. sitting as a Deputy High Court Judge (reversed in part [1985] 1 W.L.R. 173); below, para.7–113.

[59] e.g. *Boustany v Piggott* (1995) 69 P. & C.R. 298 (PC); below, para.7–130.

[60] [2001] UKHL 8; [2002] 1 A.C. 251, in which the House of Lords held that a general release was not effective to release a claim for "stigma" damages that neither party could have known about (see above, para.3–048).

party to whom a general release was given knew that the other party has or might have a claim and knew that the other party was ignorant of this, to take the release without disclosing the existence of the claim or possible claim could be unacceptable sharp practice. The law would be defective if it did not provide a remedy, and while the case did not raise the issue, he had no doubt that the law would provide a remedy.[61] It is obvious that the unconscionability doctrine has the potential to undermine the principle that a mistake as to the factual circumstances is irrelevant unless it is a common mistake, and the courts will no doubt restrict it to cases of "special disability".

5–014 **Mistake and misrepresentation.** In earlier paragraphs the factual situation to which the rules on mistake apply was described as one in which one party, or both he and the other party, have entered the contract under a "self-induced" misapprehension. This is to differentiate it from a closely similar situation that the law treats in a different fashion, under the rubric of misrepresentation. If one party has entered the contract relying on a statement made by the other party about some fact that is material to the contract, and the statement was untrue, the first party will normally have a remedy for misrepresentation. At least if he acts promptly he will normally be entitled[62] to avoid the contract for misrepresentation, and this is so whether the misrepresentor, when he made the untrue statement, was acting fraudulently, negligently or wholly innocently.[63] In one sense, all cases of misrepresentation are also cases of "misapprehension", as the result is that at least one party entered the contract believing the facts to be different to what they were. Because one party has misled the other, the law gives relief even though the misapprehension is about the facts surrounding the contract[64] and is not of the seriousness that we will see is required for relief to be given on the ground of mistake. However, if the right to rescind has been lost, for example because an innocent third party has acquired rights over the property sold,[65] the misrepresentee may have an effective remedy only if he can show that the contract was void for mistake.[66]

5–015 **Misrepresentation and common mistake.** Relief may be given on the ground of misrepresentation whether the resulting misapprehension was only on the part of the misrepresentee, as when he is the victim of a fraudulent misrepresentation by the other, or whether both parties were under the same misapprehension, as in cases of "innocent" misrepresentation. The misrepresentation cases are treated differently simply because one party chose to

---

[61] [2001] UKHL 8 at [32]–[33]. Lord Bingham preferred not to address this question (at [20]), and so it seems did Lord Clyde (at [87]).

[62] Subject in some cases to a statutory discretion in the court: see below, para.6–107.

[63] The law on misrepresentation is described in Ch.6.

[64] One party might also make a misrepresentation as to the terms of the contract, for example as to the contents of a written contract that the other party is being asked to sign. Where the statement is that a particular term is or is not in the document, the result will normally be determined by the rules that determine the content of the contract: see Ch.12 (Express terms), in particular paras 12–096 et seq. (parol evidence rule) and Ch.14 (Exemption Clauses). Where the misrepresentation is as to the meaning of a clause in the contract the courts have also fashioned a remedy: below, paras 6–017 and 14–132.

[65] See below, para.6–129.

[66] See below, para.5–088.

make a statement of fact on which the other party relied when he entered the contract.[67] It probably happens far more frequently that one party states the facts as he believes them, and the other party enters the contract relying to some extent on that statement,[68] than that each enters the contract relying on his own, equally mistaken view of the facts. This goes some way to explain why there are relatively few cases in which a party seeks to escape from a contract on the ground of common mistake: he will often be able to rescind the contract for misrepresentation, while it seems that the other party, the misrepresentor, will be precluded from arguing that the contract is void for common mistake.[69] Nonetheless, shared "self-induced" mistake over the facts does happen, and the rules that apply in this type of case form part of the subject matter of the present chapter.

Common mistake and construction of the contract. The question of the effect of common mistake in the law of contract is basically one of the allocation of risk as to the facts being as assumed.[70] In most situations one or other of the parties will be considered to have assumed the risk of the ordinary uncertainties which exist when an agreement is concluded. Where contracts of sale of goods are concerned, for example, the seller will normally be held to have assumed the risk that the goods do not correspond to their description, or that they may be defective, under express or implied terms, except insofar as the usual conditions are validly excluded, or may in the particular circumstances be inapplicable.[71] The risk that for other reasons the goods will be less useful than the parties envisaged will be borne by the buyer. Thus it has been said that one must first determine whether the contract itself, by express or implied condition (promissory or non-promissory) or otherwise, provides who bears the risk of the relevant mistake. Only if the contract is silent on the point is there scope for invoking the rules or "doctrine" of mistake.[72] It has been pointed out that if the enquiry whether the construction of the contract is only as to "whether either party has given an undertaking as to the matter at issue (i.e. if that is what is meant by a provision as to 'who bears the risk of the relevant mistake'), and the answer is that neither has", that does not preclude a second enquiry as to the effect of the 5–016

---

[67] One justification given for granting a remedy even when the misrepresentor was acting wholly innocently is that the statement may put the other party off from making further enquires that might have revealed the truth: see below, para.6–039.

[68] See below, para.6–034.

[69] See below, para.5–042.

[70] *Amalgamated Investment & Property Co Ltd v John Walker & Sons Ltd* [1977] 1 W.L.R. 164; McTurnan (1963) 41 Can. Bar Rev. 1; Swan, "The Allocation of Risk in the Analysis of Mistake and Frustration" in Reiter and Swan, *Studies in Contract Law* (1980); American Law Institute's *Restatement of Contracts* (2d), para.152.

[71] e.g. *Gloucestershire CC v Richardson* [1969] 1 A.C. 480 (normal implied term did not apply when contractor had no right to object to supplier nominated by employer).

[72] *Associated Japanese Bank International Ltd v Credit du Nord SA* [1989] 1 W.L.R. 255, 268. See also *William Sindall Plc v Cambridgeshire CC* [1994] 1 W.L.R. 1016, 1035; *Grains & Fourriers SA v Huyton* [1997] 1 Lloyd's Rep. 628. Thus, in *Kalsep Ltd v X-Flow BV*, *The Times*, May 3, 2001 it was held that the risk of the mistake which had been made was allocated to one party by an express clause of the agreement. In *Standard Chartered Bank v Banque Marocaine De Commerce Exterieur* [2006] EWHC 413 (Comm), [2006] All E.R. (D) 213 (Feb) the contract was held to be binding on the alternative grounds that the mistake did not make the agreement essentially different and that the risk was clearly allocated to one party.

mistake; but if it includes asking whether, if neither bears the risk, the contract is as a matter of construction subject to an implied condition precedent that the facts assumed existed, there seems to be no scope for asking whether the contract is void for mistake.[73] In other words, if it does include asking whether the contract is subject to such a condition, there is no room for an independent doctrine of common mistake.[74] Although the courts have held that there is a separate doctrine of mistake,[75] this is a formidable argument. It will be submitted that it can really be met only by admitting that, in cases which involve the kind of facts to which the doctrine of common mistake might apply, the process of construction and the application of the rules of mistake are really merely alternative ways of formulating the same thing and reaching the same result.[76] We will see later, however, that sometimes courts have held a contract to be ineffective because as a matter of construction it was subject to an implied condition which has not been fulfilled, in circumstances in which the requirements of common mistake do not seem to have been met.[77]

2. Common Mistake[78]

(a) *Introduction*

5–017 **Common mistake.** Where the mistake is common, that is shared by both parties, there is *consensus ad idem*, but the law may nullify this consent if the parties are mistaken as to some fact or point of law[79] which lies at the basis of the contract. In summary, if: (i) the parties have entered a contract under a shared and self-induced[80] mistake as to the facts or law[81] affecting the contract; (ii) under the express or implied terms of the contract neither party is treated as taking the risk of the situation being as it really is[82]; (iii) neither party was responsible for or should have known of the true state of affairs[83]; and (iv) the mistake is so fundamental that it makes the "contractual adventure" impossible,

[73] Smith (1994) 110 L.Q.R. 400, 407.

[74] Smith (1994) 110 L.Q.R. 400, 419.

[75] *Great Peace Shipping Ltd v Tsavliris Salvage (International) Ltd (The Great Peace)* [2002] EWCA Civ 1407, [2003] Q.B. 679 at [73] and [82], discussed below, para.5–036.

[76] See below, paras 5–031 and 5–064—5–065.

[77] See *Graves v Graves* [2007] EWCA Civ 660, [2007] All E.R. (D) 32 (Jul), discussed below, para.5–065.

[78] See Cheshire (1944) 60 L.Q.R. 175, 177; Tylor (1948) 11 M.L.R. 257, 262; Slade (1954) 70 L.Q.R. 385, 396; Bamford (1955) 32 S.A.L.J. 166; Atiyah (1957) 73 L.Q.R. 340; Atiyah and Bennion (1961) 24 M.L.R. 421; McTurnan (1963) 41 Can. Bar Rev. 1; Stoljar (1965) 28 M.L.R. 265, 275; Cartwright, *Misrepresentation, Mistake and Non-disclosure* (2007), Part II.

[79] On mistake of law see below, para.5–054.

[80] In other words, it is not a case where one party's mistaken belief was induced by a repesentation by the other party; cf. para.5–015 above. If it was, the first party will normally have a remedy for misrepresentation, see Ch.6 below.

[81] See below, para.5–054.

[82] See below, paras 5–039—5–042.

[83] In such cases the relevant party will normally be treated as bearing the risk of the mistake: see below, para.5–042.

or makes performance essentially different to what the parties anticipated,[84] the contract will be void.

Different conceptual bases. While it is clear on the authorities that a doctrine of common mistake exists in English law, the situation is complicated by the fact that there are three possible conceptual routes which have been employed in considering whether a fundamental mistake has prevented the formation of an effective contract: (1) that there has been a total failure of consideration; (2) that the contract is subject to an express or implied condition that the facts were as the parties believed them to be, or (to use a modern formulation derived from the same argument) that it would be invalid if, on the true construction of the contract, the essence of the obligations are impossible to perform; and (3) that there is a separate doctrine of mistake. We will see that these grounds were not always kept distinct and the leading cases seem to combine the three in a way that makes it hard to state the rules in a simple form. A further issue is whether there is, or was, a separate rule for mistake in equity under which the contract would be treated as voidable rather than void. The Court of Appeal[85] has now made it clear that no such doctrine can have survived the decision of the House of Lords in the leading case of common mistake, *Bell v Lever Bros.*[86] 5–018

(b) *Different approaches before* Bell v Lever Bros

Total failure of consideration. There are a number of early cases in which the parties had bought and sold something which, unknown to either of them, was very different to what they thought or even did not exist at all; but the seller tried to claim the price or to retain the price paid. Thus in *Strickland v Turner*[87] the purchaser of an annuity on the life of a man who was, unknown to both parties, already dead, was able to recover the purchase price from the vendor on the basis of total failure of consideration, as the annuity had ceased to exist at the time of the contract for sale. In *Gompertz v Bartlett*[88] an unstamped bill of exchange was sold by the defendant to the plaintiff on a non-recourse basis. The parties believed that it was a foreign bill but it was shown in fact to have been drawn in England and it was therefore unenforceable for want of a stamp. The buyer sued to recover the price paid. The Court of Queen's Bench held that this was not merely a case of the bill being of poor quality, when the seller would have been liable only if he had given an express warranty or had been fraudulent. The bill did not meet the description of "a foreign bill" by which it was sold and the buyer was entitled to recover the price. 5–019

Couturier v Hastie. In *Couturier v Hastie*[89] there was a sale of a cargo of corn which was believed to be in transit from Salonica to the United Kingdom. 5–020

---

[84] See below, paras 5–043—5–053.
[85] *Great Peace Shipping Ltd v Tsavliris Salvage (International) Ltd (The Great Peace)* [2002] EWCA Civ 1407, [2003] Q.B. 679. See below, para.5–057.
[86] [1932] A.C. 161.
[87] (1852) 7 Exch. 208, 155 E.R. 919.
[88] (1853) 2 El. & Bl. 849, 118 E.R. 985.
[89] (1856) 5 H.L.C. 673, HL; (1853) 9 Exch. 102 (Ex.Ch.); (1852) 8 Exch. 40.

Unknown to either party the cargo had deteriorated and had already been sold by the master of the ship. The liability of the purchaser to pay the price depended upon the construction of the contract. If the contract was a contract for the sale of that specific cargo of corn, then the consideration for the contract had totally failed and the seller was not entitled to the price. If, however, as the seller contended, it was a contract for the sale of the adventure, the seller had performed his side of the contract by offering to deliver the shipping documents and the purchaser was liable to pay the purchase price. The House of Lords, confirming the decision of the Exchequer Chamber that had reversed a contrary decision by the Court of Exchequer, held that the contract was for the sale of a cargo and therefore the purchaser was not bound to pay.

5–021 **Seller liable for non-delivery.** Neither *Couturier v Hastie* nor *Gompertz v Bartlett* was decided on the ground of mistake invalidating the contract. In each case there was what would later be termed a total failure of consideration.[90] For the purposes of the decision it did not matter whether the contract was valid or void; the purchaser could not be compelled to pay for what he had never received. It seems more likely that the court thought that the contract was valid and that the seller would have been liable, had he been sued, for damages for failure to deliver the subject matter of the contract. Certainly this seems to have been the view of Parke B. In *Barr v Gibson*[91] the parties had bought and sold a ship that, unknown to either of them, had already become stranded on rocks in the Gulf of St Lawrence. Parke B. said that the sale as a "ship" implied a contract that the subject of the transfer did exist in the character of a ship. In *Couturier v Hastie* in the Court of Exchequer, he said that where there is a sale of a specific chattel, there is an implied undertaking that it exists.[92]

5–022 ***Kennedy's* case.** In *Kennedy v Panama, New Zealand and Australian Royal Mail Co*[93] the prospectus of a company offering shares stated that fresh capital was required in order to fulfil a lucrative mail contract with the Postmaster of New Zealand. The contract proved to be beyond the Postmaster's authority to make and the plaintiff, who had purchased shares in reliance on the prospectus, claimed to repudiate the transaction on the ground that there had been a total failure of consideration. The Court of Queen's Bench refused to allow him to do so. In deciding whether or not that had been a total failure of consideration so as to entitle the buyer to get his money back, Blackburn J. referred to the Roman

---

[90] In *Gompertz v Bartlett* (1853) 2 El. & Bl. 849, 854; 118 E.R. 985, 987 Lord Campbell C.J. said that the money paid for the bill could be recovered as it was paid in mistake of the facts. See Lord Atkin's comment in *Bell v Lever Bros* [1932] A.C. 161, 222, on *Gompertz v Bartlett* and *Gurney v Wormesley* (1854) 3 El & Bl 133: "In these cases I am inclined to think that the true analysis is that there is a contract, but that the one party is not able to supply the very thing whether goods or services that the other party contracted to take; and therefore the contract is unenforceable by the one if executory, while if executed the other can recover back money paid on the ground of failure of the consideration."

[91] (1838) 3 M. & W. 390; 150 E.R. 1196.

[92] 8 Ex. 40, 55; 155 E.R. 1250, 1257.

[93] (1867) L.R. 2 Q.B. 580.

law on mistake and its distinction between mistakes as to substance, which in Roman law would invalidate the contract,[94] and mistakes as to quality, which would not; and held that as the misunderstanding about the shares went only to quality, there was no total failure of consideration. It is easy to see how this might be interpreted as saying that a mistake as to substance might make the contract void in English law. It is not clear that this was what was meant[95]; and in any event, the fact that a mistake has led to there being a total failure of consideration cannot lead straight to the conclusion that the contract is void, since it might be that the seller is liable for non-performance. In other words, total failure is not an independent ground on which a contract may be held void: rather, it is a possible basis for an action for the recovery of money when the contract is void.[96] There will equally be a total failure of consideration when one party has simply failed to perform.[97] Even in cases in which at the time of sale the goods might have been said no longer to exist[98] (when in Roman law there could be no contract for want of an object[99]), in English law there might be an implied promise that the thing existed, so that the seller would be liable for failing to deliver.

Development of an independent doctrine of common mistake. The cases of total failure of consideration seem to have played a central role in the development of a doctrine of mistake in English law, but one that involved their being given a rather different interpretation. The great work of Pothier was very influential.[100] His statement, derived from the Roman law, that if there was no object (because, for example, the thing sold had ceased to exist before the contract was made) there could be no contract of sale, was cited by counsel for the seller[101] in *Couturier v Hastie*[102] and may have formed the basis for s.6 of the Sale of Goods Act 1893.[103] This stated: 5–023

[94] Lawson (1936) 52 L.Q.R. 79 argued that the Roman texts were not wholly clear on the effect of such a mistake. If the thing did not exist at all, there would be no object and therefore no contract; that did not depend on a doctrine of mistake but on the lack of an object.

[95] In *Great Peace Shipping Ltd v Tsavliris Salvage (International) Ltd (The Great Peace)* [2002] EWCA Civ 1407, [2003] Q.B. 679 at [59] the Court of Appeal agreed with this comment.

[96] Although when a contract is void for common mistake either party will be able to obtain restitution (see, e.g. Treitel, *Law of Contract*, 12th edn (by Peel, 2007), paras 22–013), there is some uncertainty as to the basis of the restitutionary remedy. One possibility is that restitution is permitted simply because the contract is void: Treitel at paras 22–014—22–015. When a contract is void for mistake there will usually be a total failure of consideration, as was held to be the case in *Strickland v Turner* (1852) 7 Exch. 208, but it has been argued that this does not necessarily follow from the fact that the contract is void, as it might nonetheless have been completely executed: Burrows, *Law of Restitution*, 2nd edn (2002), p.387. But even in such a case it seems that either party would be able to recover on the basis that he had performed under a mistake. Mistake appears to have been the basis of recovery in *Pritchard v Merchant's and Tradesman's Mutual Life Assurance Society* (1858) 3 C.B. (N.S.) 622, 645. See Treitel at para.22–017; Burrows at pp.388–389.

[97] See below, paras 29–054 et seq.

[98] As in *Barr v Gibson* (1838) 3 M. & W. 390; 150 E.R. 1196.

[99] See above, fn.94.

[100] See Simpson (1975) 91 L.Q.R. 247, 266–269.

[101] Who argued that this was not a case of a sale of something that had ceased to exist but a sale of an expectation. Counsel for the defendant was not called upon.

[102] (1856) 5 H.L.C. 673.

[103] See now Sale of Goods Act 1979 s.6, which is identical.

> "Where there is a contract for the sale of specific goods, and the goods without the knowledge of the seller have perished at the time when the contract was made, the contract is void.

The draftsman stated that the rule might be based on mutual mistake or impossibility of performance, and cited *Couturier v Hastie*.[104]

5–024 The notion that a contract might be void for mistake may also have been influenced by the development of the idea that a contract depends upon agreement. It has been said that with the emergence of the theory of *consensus ad idem*, "it became possible to treat misrepresentation, undue influence and mistake as factors vitiating consent".[105] At any event, in the early years of the last century there were a few cases in which contracts entered on the basis of a common mistake were held to be void.[106]

5–025 **Express or implied condition.** Meanwhile situations of "common mistake" were also sometimes approached on the basis of that the contract might be subject to a condition that the facts were as the parties believed them to be, just as "frustration" cases were explained on the basis that there was an implied condition that the facts would remain as they were. The foundations of the doctrine of frustration were laid in 1863 in the judgment of Blackburn J. in *Taylor v Caldwell*.[107] In that case the subject-matter of the contract had been destroyed by fire after the contract had been made and before the date for its performance. The Court of Queen's Bench held that performance of the contract was excused by reason of an implied term:

> "... in contracts in which the performance depends on the continued existence of a given person or thing, a condition is implied that the impossibility of performance arising from the perishing of the person or thing shall excuse the performance".[108]

The same approach was applied when subsequent events made the contract a completely different venture from that which the parties had contemplated.[109] The courts would later abandon the notion that the doctrine of frustration rests on an implied term.[110] Though in 1916 Earl Loreburn was still basing frustration on an implied condition of the contract,[111] in the "coronation cases" that arose out

---

[104] See Chalmers, *The Sale of Goods Act 1893* (1894), p.17, cited in *Great Peace Shipping Ltd v Tsavliris Salvage (International) Ltd (The Great Peace)* [2002] EWCA Civ 1407, [2003] Q.B. 679 at [52].

[105] Steyn J. in *Associated Japanese Bank International Ltd v Credit du Nord SA* [1989] 1 W.L.R. 255, 264.

[106] *Scott v Coulson* [1903] 2 Ch. 249 (contract for sale of life assurance policy when person whose life was assured was already dead. Vaughan Williams L.J. at p.252, said the contract was void at law); *Galloway v Galloway* (1914) 30 T.L.R. 531 (separation deed between parties who incorrectly thought they were married held void).

[107] (1863) 3 B. & S. 826, 122 E.R. 309.

[108] (1863) 3 B. & S. 826, 833–834.

[109] *Jackson v Union Marine Insurance Co Ltd* (1874) L.R. 10 C.P. 125.

[110] See below, Ch.23.

[111] *F.A. Tamplin Steamship Co Ltd v Anglo-Mexican Products Co Ltd* [1916] 2 A.C. 397, 403–404.

of the sudden cancellation of the coronation of King Edward VII[112] the question was said to be whether the parties must have contemplated a particular state of affairs as forming the foundation of the contract. If, because of some event for which neither party was responsible, the contract becomes impossible because the state of things assumed by the parties as the foundation of the contract ceases to exist, the contract will be frustrated.[113] In *Griffith v Brymer*[114] Wright J. applied the same principle to a case of common mistake, one in which the contract had been made after the announcement of the cancellation of the procession, and held that the agreement was void because it was made on a missupposition that went to the whole root of the matter. Thus common mistake cases were sometimes dealt with by analogy to frustration, which was derived from the notion of an implied condition.

Cases in equity. In the eighteenth and nineteenth centuries there were many cases in the courts of equity in which it was held that relief could be given where an agreement had been made under a mistake. It is not easy to discern the basis for relief. Some cases were based on a wide notion of fraud in equity[115] which has probably not survived the decision of the House of Lords in *Derry v Peek*.[116] Others seem to have involved undue influence.[117] Yet others give no real hint of the basis of relief but their facts were similar to those involving total failure of consideration.[118] While some cases suggest that equity might grant rescission on the basis of a common mistake that was not induced by one of the parties, "no coherent equitable doctrine of mistake can be spelt from them".[119] 5–026

It appears that rescission was granted in *Cooper v Phibbs*.[120] A had agreed to take a lease of a fishery in Ireland from B, though contrary to the belief of both parties at the time A was himself tenant in tail of the fishery. The proceedings were brought in equity[121] and the House of Lords ordered that the agreement should be set aside. However the respondents had a lien on the fishery for the money they had spent on its improvement. Lord Westbury said that if parties contract under a mutual mistake and misapprehension as to their relative and 5–027

---

[112] See below, paras 23–033—23–034.

[113] See the judgments of Lord Alverstone C.J. in *Hobson v Pattenden & Co* (1903) 19 T.L.R. 186 and *Clark v Lindsay* (1903) 19 T.L.R. 202; and of Vaughan Williams L.J. in *Krell v Henry* [1903] 2 K.B. 740, 749.

[114] (1903) 19 T.L.R. 434.

[115] e.g. *Hitchcock v Giddings* (1817) 4 Price 135; 146 E.R. 418 (fraud in equity for a party to bargain and sell as if he had title to the property when he had none).

[116] (1889) 14 App. Cas. 337: below, para.6–043.

[117] e.g. *Cocking v Pratt* (1750) 1 Ves. Snr. 400; 27 E.R. 1150. On undue influence, see below, paras 7–056 et seq.

[118] e.g. *Bingham v Bingham* (1748) 1 Ves. Snr. 126; 27 E.R. 934 (purchaser bought an estate which later was found already to have belonged to him; "a plain mistake such as the court was warranted to give relief against"). In *Cochrane v Willis* (1865) L.R. 1 Ch. 58 an agreement was made on the basis that a tenant for life was alive when in fact he had died. The Court of Appeal held that it would be contrary to all the rules of equity and common law to enforce it or hold a party bound by it.

[119] *Great Peace Shipping Ltd v Tsavliris Salvage (International) Ltd (The Great Peace)* [2002] EWCA Civ 1407, [2003] Q.B. 679 at [100], quoting Goff & Jones, *Law of Restitution*, 5th edn (1998), 288 (see now 7th edn (2007) para.9–044).

[120] (1867) L.R. 2 H.L. 149.

[121] See Matthews (1989) 105 L.Q.R. 599.

respective rights, the result is that the agreement is liable to be set aside as proceeding upon a common mistake.[122]

(c) *Mistake at Common Law*

(i) Bell v Lever Bros

5–028 ***Bell v Lever Bros.*** The law on common mistake was extensively reviewed by the House of Lords in *Bell v Lever Brothers Ltd.*[123] There an action was brought by Lever Brothers for the recovery of money paid to the two defendants under the following circumstances. Lever Brothers had large interests in Africa and set up a subsidiary company, called the Niger Company, to control them there. The defendants were members of the board of the Niger Company and received large salaries in respect of their service agreements with Lever Brothers. One of the conditions of their service agreements was that they were not to make any private profit for themselves by doing business on their own account while serving the company. The defendants did in fact make such profits, unknown to Lever Brothers and undisclosed by the defendants. Lever Brothers, having made other arrangements for their interests in Africa, desired to terminate the service agreements with the defendants before their expiry, and accordingly entered into compensation agreements with them whereby the defendants consented to terminate their service agreements in consideration of the payment to them of large sums of money. After the money had been paid, Lever Brothers discovered the breaches of their service agreements committed by the defendants, which would have entitled the company to dismiss them summarily without notice or compensation. They therefore claimed to recover the sums which they had paid on the ground, inter alia, that they had entered into the compensation agreements under the mistaken assumption that the service contracts could only have been determined by them with the consent of the defendants.

5–029 At the trial of the action, the jury found that there was no evidence of fraud on the part of the defendants, and that when they entered into the compensation agreements they had not directed their minds to their previous breaches of duty. The case was therefore one of common (or as their Lordships described it, mutual)[124] mistake, as both parties had made the same mistaken assumption. Wright J. held that this assumption that a state of facts existed which entitled the defendants to compensation was essential to the agreement; consequently there could be no binding contract, and Lever Brothers were therefore entitled to recover the money paid. This decision was unanimously affirmed by the Court of Appeal. Scrutton and Greer L.JJ. both held that if the contract is made on the basis of a state of facts which is fundamental to the contract, and which turns out not to exist, the contract is void. Greer L.J. based this on an implied condition,[125]

[122] See also *Earl of Beauchamp v Winn* (1873) L.R. 6 H.L. 223, 233. Lord Westbury's suggestion that the contract is merely "liable to be set aside" has been criticised in the House of Lords: see below, para.5–058.

[123] [1932] A.C. 161. The background to the case and its progress through the courts are explored in MacMillan (2003) 119 L.Q.R. 625.

[124] See above, para.5–001 fn.3.

[125] [1931] 1 K.B. 577, 595.

Scrutton L.J. on either an implied term or mutual mistake as to the assumed foundation of the contract, which he regarded as "only another way of putting the proposition".[126] In the House of Lords an appeal by the defendants was allowed by a majority of three to two. Lord Blanesburgh,[127] one of the majority, based his opinion largely on the fact that mutual mistake had not been originally pleaded. The other two majority opinions, those of Lord Atkin[128] and Lord Thankerton,[129] both rested on the ground that the mistake was not sufficiently fundamental to avoid the contract, although they reached this conclusion by somewhat different paths. Lord Warrington of Clyffe (with whom Lord Hailsham agreed) dissented, not on the law but on its application to the facts.[130]

Lord Atkin's analysis. In his speech Lord Atkin gave a number of instances in which a common mistake would nullify the parties' consent. He accepted that there is indeed a separate doctrine of mistake that, when the mistake is shared, may "nullify consent".[131] First, he said that when there is a sale of a thing that has ceased to exist, or that already belongs to the buyer, the contract will be void. Then he stated that: 5–030

> "... mistake as to quality of the thing contracted for raises more difficult questions. In such a case a mistake will not affect assent unless it is the mistake of both parties, and is as to the existence of some quality which makes the thing without the quality essentially different from the thing as it was believed to be."[132]

Applying this test to the facts of the case, Lord Atkin concluded that the contracts to terminate the defendants' service agreements were not void merely because it turned out that the agreements had already been broken and could have been terminated otherwise.

> "The contract released is the identical contract in both cases, and the party paying for the release gets exactly what he bargains for."[133]

Lastly, Lord Atkin turned to what he calls "an alternative way of expressing the result of a mutual mistake". He accepted a proposition formulated by counsel for the respondents: 5–031

> "Whenever it is to be inferred from the terms of a contract or its surrounding circumstances that the consensus has been reached upon the basis of a particular

---

[126] [1931] 1 K.B. 577, 585.

[127] [1932] A.C. 161, 167. Lord Blanesburgh also held that the payments were irrecoverable as: (i) the defendants' service contracts were made with the Niger Company and not with the plaintiffs; and (ii) the payments were in part voluntary, since they greatly exceeded in value the unexpired portion of the service agreements.

[128] [1932] A.C. 161, 210.

[129] [1932] A.C. 161, 229.

[130] [1932] A.C. 161, 200. On the difference between the majority and minority views see below, fn.133.

[131] [1932] A.C. 161, 217.

[132] [1932] A.C. 161 at 218.

[133] [1932] A.C. 161, 223–224. In contrast, it seems the minority considered the subject-matter to be not just a contract of employment but a binding contract of employment: see [1932] A.C. 161 at 208–209.

contractual assumption, and that assumption is not true, the contract is avoided; i.e. it is void *ab initio* if the assumption is of present fact and it ceases to bind if the assumption is of future fact."[134]

However, Lord Atkin seemed to think this alternative way of expressing the result of a mutual mistake as one that gives little guidance as to when a condition should be implied that the facts are as the parties believed them to be:

> "... [if] the contract expressly or impliedly contains a term that a particular assumption is a condition of the contract, the contract is avoided if the assumption is not true. But we have not advanced far on the inquiry whether the contract does contain such a condition ... The implications to be made are to be no more than are 'necessary' for giving business efficacy to the transaction; and it appears to me that as to both existing and future facts a condition should not be implied unless the new state of facts makes the contract something different in kind from the contract in the original state of facts [Lord Atkin referred to a number of cases on frustration] ... We therefore get a common standard for mutual mistake and implied conditions, whether as to existing or as to future facts."[135]

Thus it seems that Lord Atkin viewed saying that the contract was subject to an implied condition precedent and saying that it was void for mutual mistake as different ways of putting the same thing, and that he regarded the latter as having more explanatory power as to when the contract will fail. The last sentence of the passage quoted also suggests that he thought there is a direct parallel between common mistake and frustration. Lord Thankerton, in contrast, rejected the implied term approach: the frustration cases had "no bearing on the question of error or mistake as rendering a contract void owing to failure of consideration".[136]

5–032 **A separate doctrine.** Thus *Bell v Lever Bros* seemed to establish the existence in English law of a doctrine of common mistake which is separate from the effect of an implied condition, though often it will lead to the same results.

(ii) *The modern doctrine*

Analysis after Bell v Lever Bros

5–033 ***McRae's* case.** This conclusion was not accepted throughout the common law world. In *McRae v Commonwealth Disposals Commission*[137] the defendants sold to the plaintiffs an oil tanker said to be lying on a certain reef off New Guinea. The plaintiffs thereupon fitted out a salvage expedition, but found that there was no tanker at the place indicated, nor even any such reef. They brought an action against the defendants claiming damages for breach of contract. The High Court of Australia held that the plaintiffs were entitled to succeed. The principal ground was that the Commission had promised that the tanker existed. They should have known that it had never existed, whereas the plaintiffs knew nothing except what the defendants told them. It followed that no condition could be implied into the

---

[134] [1932] A.C. 161, 225.
[135] [1932] A.C. 161, 225–226.
[136] [1932] A.C. 237.
[137] (1951) 84 C.L.R. 377; *Tommey v Finextra* (1962) 106 S.J. 1012.

contract that it was to be void if the tanker was not in existence. Dixon and Fullagar JJ., giving the leading judgment, doubted whether there was a doctrine of common mistake in contract. They thought that in cases such as *Couturier v Hastie*, the fundamental question is:

> "What did the promisor really promise? Did he promise to perform his part in all events, or only subject to the mutually contemplated original or continued existence of a particular subject matter? . . . the problem is fundamentally one of construction".[138]

However they said that if there is a doctrine of common mistake, a party cannot rely on a mistake consisting "of a belief which is entertained without any reasonable ground, and . . . deliberately induced by him in the mind of the other party".[139]

Subsequent cases. Notwithstanding the views expressed in *McRae's* case, the doctrine was applied by the Privy Council in *Sheikh Bros Ltd v Ochsner,*[140] where the parties' mistake had led them to make a contract that was impossible to perform. The case was decided under the Indian Contract Act 1872 s.20, which enacts that where both the parties to an agreement are under a mistake as to a matter of fact essential to the agreement, the agreement is void, but the English authorities on the law of mistake were expressly cited to the Board. The contract was for the production of a stated amount of sisal on a piece of land and was held to be void when the land turned out to be incapable of producing the quantity contracted for. In *Nicholson and Venn v Smith-Marriott*[141] the buyer could have avoided a contract for the sale of table linen which the parties believed to have been the property of Charles I when it was in fact Georgian. 5–034

The *Associated Japanese Bank* case. In *Associated Japanese Bank International Ltd v Crédit du Nord SA*[142] Steyn J. gave a detailed account of the doctrine. The plaintiffs had entered a sale and lease-back agreement with B and the defendants had guaranteed the performance of B's obligations under the lease. It was then discovered that the machines purportedly sold and leased back did not exist and the arrangement was a fraud perpetrated by B. Steyn J. held that the defendants were not liable on the guarantee, which was expressly or by necessary implication subject to a condition precedent that the leases related to machines that existed.[143] He went on to say that in his view the guarantee was also void for common mistake. Steyn J. said that *Bell v Lever Bros* had decided that a mistake might render a contract void provided it rendered the subject- 5–035

---

[138] (1951) 84 C.L.R. 377, 407–408.
[139] (1951) 84 C.L.R. 377, 408.
[140] [1957] A.C. 136.
[141] See (1947) 177 L.T. 189. The case was said to have been wrongly decided on this point in *Solle v Butcher* [1950] 1 K.B. 671, 692, but that case itself has been disapproved: see below, para.5–060.
[142] [1989] 1 W.L.R. 255.
[143] [1989] 1 W.L.R. 255, 263. On this point see below, para.5–039.

matter essentially different from what the parties believed to exist.[144] The doctrine was subsequently applied in a number of other cases.[145]

5–036 ***The Great Peace.*** In *Great Peace Shipping Ltd v Tsavliris Salvage (International) Ltd (The Great Peace)*[146] the principal point was the rejection of the equitable doctrine that had been developed by earlier decisions of the same court. However, the judgment contains a valuable discussion of the doctrine of mistake at common law. The Court of Appeal also were quite clear that there is a separate doctrine of common mistake, which will apply "where that which is expressly defined as the subject matter of a contract does not exist".[147] But as to mistakes in relation to the quality of the subject matter of the contract, the Court favoured a different approach to Lord Atkin's. It preferred to approach the question of common mistake as a parallel to the doctrine of frustration. Although originally frustration was based on an implied condition, and that approach was still favoured in some twentieth-century cases,[148] it has since been rejected as unrealistic. The modern approach is to say that frustration takes place whenever a supervening event that occurs without the fault of either party and is not provided for in the contract so changes the nature of the outstanding obligations from what the parties could reasonably have contemplated that it would be unjust to hold them to the literal terms of the contract.[149] Equally the Court of Appeal were quite clear that the doctrine of common mistake is a rule of law, not based on an implied term.[150] However:

> "... the implication of a term of the same nature as that which was applied under the doctrine of frustration, as it was then understood ... was a more solid jurisprudential basis for the test of common mistake that Lord Atkin was proposing."[151]

A mistake, including one as to some quality of the subject-matter, will render a contract void only if the non-existence of the state of affairs assumed by the parties rendered the contract or the contractual adventure impossible.[152]

5–037 **Elements of common mistake.** According to the Court of Appeal:

> "... the following elements must be present if common mistake is to avoid a contract: (i) there must be a common assumption as to the existence of a state of affairs; (ii) there

---

[144] [1989] 1 W.L.R. 255, 266.

[145] In *Re Cleveland Trust Plc* [1991] B.C.L.C. 424 the common law of mistake was applied to a bonus issue of shares which was held to be void when a subsidiary's dividend, which was to pay for the issue, was held to be ultra vires. In *Grains & Fourriers SA v Huyton* [1997] 1 Lloyd's Rep. 628 the parties believed the results in two certificates of analysis to have been transposed. An agreement to rectify them was void when it was discovered that there had been no transposition, so the rectification would produce the very result it was supposed to avoid.

[146] *Great Peace Shipping Ltd v Tsavliris Salvage (International) Ltd (The Great Peace)* [2002] EWCA Civ 1407, [2003] Q.B. 679.

[147] [2002] EWCA Civ 1407 at [55].

[148] See the cases in para.23–010 fn.21, below.

[149] *Great Peace Shipping Ltd v Tsavliris Salvage (International) Ltd (The Great Peace)* [2002] EWCA Civ 1407, [2003] Q.B. 679 at [70], quoting *National Carriers Ltd v Panalpina (Northern) Ltd* [1981) A.C. 675, 700. See further below, para.23–013.

[150] [2002] EWCA Civ 1407 at [73] and [82].

[151] [2002] EWCA Civ 1407 at [61].

[152] [2002] EWCA Civ 1407 at [76].

must be no warranty by either party that that state of affairs exists; (iii) the non-existence of the state of affairs must not be attributable to the fault of either party; (iv) the non-existence of the state of affairs must render contractual performance impossible; (v) the state of affairs may be the existence, or a vital attribute, of the consideration to be provided or circumstances which must subsist if performance of the contractual adventure is to be possible."[153]

In what follows we will discuss these elements in more detail, and consider how the doctrine may apply in particular fact situations.

Conditions for common mistake to render contract void

Common assumption as to the existence of a state of affairs. We saw earlier that mistake requires that the parties have a positive belief in something which is not in fact true[154]; and that where the mistake is as to the nature of the subject matter or the factual circumstances, relief on the ground of mistake is possible only where the parties made the same mistake.[155] They may not have to believe precisely the same thing but they must make "substantially" the same mistake.[156] 5–038

Risk not allocated to the other party. It is evident that to decide whether the subject matter has turned out to be essentially different or the contractual adventure has turned out to be impossible, and therefore the contract is void for "mistake", the court must construe the contract and, in particular, consider the contractual allocation of risk. In *The Great Peace*[157] the Court of Appeal quoted Steyn J.'s words in the *Associated Japanese Bank* case: 5–039

"Logically, before one can turn to the rules as to mistake, whether at common law or in equity, one must first determine whether the contract itself, by express or implied condition precedent or otherwise, provides who bears the risk of the relevant mistake. It is at this hurdle that many pleas of mistake will either fail or prove to have been unnecessary. Only if the contract is silent on the point, is there scope for invoking mistake."[158]

In the summary of the rules of mistake from *The Great Peace* quoted above,[159] the court refers to a warranty by one party or the other that the state of affairs exists. That may be the case either because the law allocates a particular risk to one party (e.g. where the goods do not conform to the contract)[160] or because that is the correct interpretation of the facts.[161] But the Court points out that relief on

153 [2002] EWCA Civ 1407 at [76].
154 Above, para.5–006.
155 Above, para.5–007.
156 *Associated Japanese Bank (International) Ltd v Crédit du Nord* [1989] 1 W.L.R. 255, 268.
157 [2002] EWCA Civ 1407, [2003] Q.B. 679 at [80].
158 *Associated Japanese Bank (International) Ltd v Crédit du Nord* [1989] 1 W.L.R. 255, 268.
159 See para.5–037.
160 See above, para.5–016.
161 In *Standard Chartered Bank v Banque Marocaine De Commerce Exterieur* [2006] EWHC 413 (Comm), [2006] All E.R. (D) 213 (Feb) the contract was held to be binding on the alternative grounds that the mistake did not make the agreement essentially different and that the risk was clearly allocated to one party.

the ground of mistake may also be precluded because the risk is allocated under the contract in other ways than by a warranty, for example when the correct interpretation is that the buyer takes the risk that the property sold is less valuable than the parties suppose, or that each party takes the risk that the facts will turn out to be less favourable than he hopes.[162] We will see a particular application of an allocation of the risk of this kind when we come to consider compromise agreements which turn out to have been made on a mistaken assumption about the law.[163]

5–040 **Non-existence of the state of affairs must not be attributable to the fault of either party.** The most obvious meaning of this is that the contract will not be void if one party should have known the truth, since he could have prevented the parties from making the mistake they did.[164] The rule that a party who should have known the truth cannot rely on common mistake at common law was first stated by Steyn J. in the *Associated Japanese Bank* case[165]: he derived it from *McRae's* case, in which the High Court of Australia had said that a party cannot rely on a mistake consisting:

> " . . . of a belief which is entertained without any reasonable ground, and . . . deliberately induced by him in the mind of the other party."[166]

Steyn J. also referred to a similar requirement stated in *Solle v Butcher*,[167] one of the "equitable mistake cases which is no longer treated as good law".[168] It has been pointed out that Steyn J.'s principle goes further than what is stated in *McRae's* case, since the latter refers only to cases in which one party should have known the truth and (by a promise or representation) induced the other party to share the same mistaken belief.[169] In those circumstances the party who induced the other's belief will almost invariably have committed at least a negligent misstatement if not (as in *McRae's* case) a breach of warranty, and he should not be permitted to avoid liability by arguing that the resulting contract was void. But it is submitted that relief on the ground of mistake should be denied in at least two further cases.[170]

---

[162] See [2002] EWCA Civ 1407 at [81], referring to the judgment of Hoffmann LJ in *William Sindall Plc v Cambridgeshire CC* [1994] 1 W.L.R. 1016 at 1035, that: "Such allocation of risk can come about by rules of general law applicable to contract, such as 'caveat emptor' in the law of sale of goods or the rule that a lessor or vendor of land does not impliedly warrant that the premises are fit for any particular purpose, so that this risk is allocated by the contract to the lessee or purchaser."

[163] Below, para.5–055.

[164] It is possible that there is an exception to this when s.6 of the Sale of Goods Act 1979 applies, since that section seems at first sight to state an absolute rule that the contract is void: but it will be submitted that this is not the correct interpretation of the section, which should be interpreted as stating the prima facie position. See below, para.5–047.

[165] *Associated Japanese Bank (International) Ltd v Crédit du Nord* [1989] 1 W.L.R. 255, 268.

[166] (1951) 84 C.L.R. 377, 408.

[167] [1950] 1 KB 671, 693. Steyn J. also noted that the civilian doctrine of error in substantia is qualified by the principles governing culpa in contrahendo: [1989] 1 W.L.R 255, 269.

[168] See below, para.5–060.

[169] Cartwright, *Misrepresentation, Mistake and Non-disclosure* (2007), para.15.20; Treitel, *Law of Contract*, 12th edn (by Peel, 2007), para.8–005.

[170] The second is considered in para.5–042.

The first is the situation encompassed by Steyn J.'s wider principle. If a party entered the contract relying on his own self-induced mistake rather than any misrepresentation by the other, he will only wish to argue that the contract is void for common mistake if otherwise he would bear the risk of the facts being as in truth they are. Thus in *Griffith v Brymer*, [171] had the contract not been void the hirer would have had to pay the agreed fee even though there would be no procession to watch. If he could have discovered the true situation and have prevented either party from being mistaken, it seems appropriate to place the risk on him by preventing him from arguing that the contract was void. The rule will give parties who have reasonable means to discover the truth an incentive to do so. It is submitted that Steyn J.'s wider principle should be followed. 5–041

Misrepresentor cannot rely on common mistake. The second situation is where the party who is claiming that the contract is void induced the other party's mistake, and the other party to enter the contract, by an innocent, non-negligent misrepresentation. Although the issue is unlikely to arise in practice, it is submitted that in principle the misrepresentor should not be able to raise common mistake as a defence to a claim for remedies for misrepresentation—for example, if the other party were to seek an indemnity for costs or liabilities incurred as part of the process of rescission.[172] 5–042

Non-existence of the state of affairs must render contractual performance impossible. In *The Great Peace* the Court of Appeal appears to assume that where the subject matter of the contract does not exist, the contract will necessarily be one that cannot be performed.[173] In other cases, even if performance in a literal sense is impossible, the mistake may be such that the contractual venture is impossible and the contract will again be void. Each of these propositions needs examination. We will consider first cases in which it turns out that property "sold" no longer exists, or already belongs to the buyer.[174] We will then turn to cases in which the subject matter differs in quality from what the parties believed and the Court of Appeal's preferred explanation in terms of the impossibility of the contractual venture.[175] 5–043

Sale of thing that has ceased to exist. Lord Atkin said[176]: 5–044

"So the agreement of A and B to purchase a specific article is void if in fact the article had perished before the date of sale. In this case, though the parties in fact were agreed about the subject-matter, yet a consent to transfer or take delivery of something not existent is deemed useless, the consent is nullified. As codified in the Sale of Goods Act the contract is expressed to be void if the seller was in ignorance of the destruction of the specific chattel. I apprehend that if the seller with knowledge that a chattel was destroyed purported to sell it to a purchaser, the latter might sue for damages for non-

---

[171] (1903) 19 T.L.R. 434. See above, para.5–023.
[172] See below, para.6–121.
[173] [2002] EWCA Civ 1407 at [55].
[174] Below, paras 5–044—5–049.
[175] Below, para.5–050.
[176] *Bell v Lever Bros Ltd* [1932] A.C. 161, 217.

> delivery though the former could not sue for non-acceptance, though I know of so case where the seller has so committed himself."

Although we have seen that the nineteenth century cases of sales of a non-existent thing were unclear as to whether the contract was void or merely not enforceable by the seller,[177] there are cases that apply s.6 and hold the contract to be void.[178] There are two questions that remain unclear, however. One is posed by the fact that Lord Atkin's statement and s.6 refer strictly to those cases where the subject matter of the contract has once been in existence, but has subsequently perished before the contract is made. The question is whether the same principles apply where the subject matter of the contract has never been in existence at all. The second is whether the fact that the subject matter of the contract has perished always renders the contract void, particularly if the seller should have known the truth. These questions will be considered in the following paragraphs.

5–045 **Sale of goods that have never existed.** Although such a case is outside both s.6 of the Sale of Goods Act 1979 and Lord Atkin's dictum, there seems no reason why in an appropriate case the same principle should not apply, with the result that (subject to what is said in the next paragraph) the contract will be void. Such facts did arise in the Australian case of *McRae v Commonwealth Disposals Commission*[179] though, as we have seen, the High Court held that the contract was not void for other reasons.[180]

5–046 **Seller responsible if should have known that goods have ceased to exist.** Although Lord Atkin appears to refer to an absolute rule that if the subject matter has ceased to exist, the sale must be void, it is submitted that this is not the case except perhaps in cases to which s.6 of the Sale of Goods Act applies.[181] We have seen that earlier cases sometimes based the doctrine of common mistake on an implied condition, in parallel with the doctrine of frustration. This made it clear that the condition would not occur, and thus the contract would not be void, unless the mistake came about without the fault of either party. In other words, the court may refuse to imply such a condition where it would be inappropriate, and it would normally be inappropriate to do so when one of the parties should have known the true situation and therefore could have prevented the mistake.[182] Lord Atkin's acceptance of the "alternative way of formulating the effect of a

---

[177] Above, paras 5–019—5–021.

[178] e.g. *Barrow, Lane & Ballard Ltd v Phillip Phillips & Co* [1929] 1 K.B. 574, in which A agreed to buy and B to sell 700 specific bags of nuts lying in a particular warehouse. Unknown to both parties, 109 bags had been stolen prior to the sale. The contract was held void. However it should be noted that the surviving bags were delivered and paid for; the action was brought by the sellers for the price of the missing bags.

[179] (1950) 84 C.L.R. 377.

[180] Above, para.5–033.

[181] On this point see below, para.5–047.

[182] cf. *The Great Peace* [2002] EWCA Civ 1407, [2003] Q.B. 679 at [84] (". . . whether . . . one or other party has taken responsibility . . . is another way of asking whether one or other party has taken the risk . . . and the answer to this question may well be the same as the answer to the question of whether the impossibility of performance is attributable to the fault of one party or the other.").

mutual mistake" seems to accept that whether the contract will be nullified will depend on its construction. This is reflected also in the summary found in the judgment in *The Great Peace*.[183] If the seller should have known that the goods no longer exist, he will be treated as warranting that the goods do exist and this will exclude the doctrine of common mistake.

Section 6 cases. Where, however, the case is one of the sale of goods which have perished before the contract was made, s.6 of the Sale of Goods Act 1979 may preclude such a result, since it provides that the contract will be void.[184] It has been argued that the parties are unable to vary this rule by contrary agreement.[185] In the light of *McRae*'s case and the fact that under s.6 a seller who knows that the goods no longer exist may nonetheless commit himself to deliver, it seems unlikely that a modern court would accept that s.6 necessarily has the effect that a seller who ought to have known that the goods no longer exist will escape liability. It is submitted that even though s.6 is not expressly stated to apply only if the parties have not agreed otherwise, it is a statement of the "default position" which will apply unless in the circumstances the contract should be construed otherwise.[186] 5–047

Sale of non-existent goods: a question of construction. In reliance upon the *McRae* decision, it has been suggested that a contract concerning non-existent subject-matter is always valid and binding unless a condition can be implied to the contrary.[187] It is submitted that the question is really one of the construction of the contract. Normally, the parties will be taken to have contracted on the basis that the subject-matter of their agreement was in existence: the inference is that neither party assumed the risk of such mischance.[188] Prima facie, therefore, the contract will be void. But if (as was argued in *Couturier v Hastie*[189]) one of the parties contracts to purchase an adventure, he binds himself to pay in any event. Conversely, if the seller either expressly or impliedly assumes responsibility that the subject-matter of the contract is in existence, he will be liable in damages if 5–048

---

183 See above, para.5–037.

184 cf. Atiyah (1957) 83 L.Q.R. 340, 348; Sale of Goods Act 1979 s.55. An extensive discussion of the meaning of "perish", in the context of the New Zealand equivalent of s.7, will be found in *Oldfields Asphalts v Govedale Coolstores (1994) Ltd* [1998] 3 N.Z.L.R. 479.

185 See Treitel, *The Law of Contract*, 12th edn (by Peel, 2007), para.8–010.

186 cf. Atiyah, *Sale of Goods*, 11th edn (2005), pp.106–107; Benjamin, *Sale of Goods*, 7th edn (2006), para.1–132. Alternatively, it might be held that the seller was liable for breach of a collateral warranty (see below, para.12–004) or in tort for damages for negligent misstatement, if such should exist, under the principle stated in *Hedley Byrne & Co v Heller & Partners* [1964] A.C. 465. It is doubtful whether he could be liable under Misrepresentation Act 1967 s.2(1), as that subsection applies "where a person has entered a contract" and thus may not apply when the contract is void for mistake. See further, below, paras 6–068—6–077.

187 *Svanosio v McNamara* (1956) 96 C.L.R. 186; Slade (1954) 70 L.Q.R. 385; Shatwell (1955) 33 Can. Bar Rev. 164; Atiyah (1957) 73 L.Q.R. 340.

188 *Couturier v Hastie* (1856) 5 H.L.C. 673, 681; *Barrow, Lane & Ballard Ltd v Phillip Phillips & Co* [1929] 1 K.B. 574, 582; Corbin, *Contracts* (1960) Vol.3, para.600; American Law Institute's *Restatement of Contracts* (1932), paras 456, 460 and *Restatement of Contracts* (2d), para.263; Uniform Commercial Code s.2–613.

189 (1856) 5 H.L.C. 673; see above, para.5–020.

in fact it is non-existent. As we have seen, a seller will be normally be taken to have assumed responsibility for facts about which he should have known.

5–049 **Sale of property already belonging to the buyer.** Lord Atkin said:

> "Corresponding to mistake as to the existence of the subject-matter is mistake as to title in cases where, unknown to the parties, the buyer is already the owner of that which the seller purports to sell to him. The parties intend to effect a transfer of ownership; such a transfer is impossible; the stipulation is *naturali ratione inutilis.*"[190]

In support, he cited the case of *Cooper v Phibbs*[191] and Lord Westbury's statement that if parties contract under a mutual mistake and misapprehension as to their relative and respective rights, the result is that the agreement is liable to be set aside as proceeding upon a common mistake. Lord Atkin said that the only criticism that could be made of this statement was that the agreement "would appear to be void rather than voidable". We will consider the last point below.[192] It is submitted that the position with sales of property that belong to the buyer is directly parallel to that of sales of goods that do not exist. The question is again one of the construction of the contract. Normally the parties will be taken to have contracted on the basis that the subject-matter did not already belong to the buyer. Prima facie, therefore, if that turns out to be the case the contract will be void. However, if the seller should have known the truth the contract will be binding on him; he will be taken to have assumed responsibility.[193]

5–050 **Mistakes as to quality of subject matter.** On mistakes as to the quality of the subject matter, Lord Atkin said:

> " . . . mistake as to quality of the thing contracted for raises more difficult questions. In such a case a mistake will not affect assent unless it is the mistake of both parties, and is as to the existence of some quality which makes the thing without the quality essentially different from the thing as it was believed to be."[194]

Lord Thankerton, though phrasing his view in a negative sense, seems to have agreed with Lord Atkin: he said that a common mistake would not avoid the contract unless it related "to something which both must necessarily have accepted in their minds as an essential and integral part of the subject matter".[195] Lord Blanesburgh, who would not have allowed the plea of mistake to be put forward at such a late stage, nonetheless said that he was in "entire accord" with what Lord Atkin said.[196]

---

[190] *Bell v Lever Bros* [1932] A.C. 161, 218.

[191] (1867) L.R. 2 H.L. 149. See above, para.5–027.

[192] Below, para.5–058.

[193] The practical difference in this case will be slight or nil, as the buyer will recover the money he has paid on either supposition; and by definition he has the property. It is conceivable that the buyer might be held to have agreed to pay in any event (compare the argument in *Couturier v Hastie* (1856) 5 H.L.C. 673, above, para.5–018) but this seems very unlikely.

[194] [1932] A.C. 161, 218.

[195] *Bell v Lever Bros* [1932] A.C. 161, 236.

[196] [1932] A.C. 161, 198–199.

In the light of Lord Atkin's statement it has been suggested that a distinction should be drawn between a mistake as to the substance of the thing contracted for, which will avoid the contract, and mistake as to its qualities, which will be without effect.[197] Moreover, all the examples given by Lord Atkin were aimed at supporting his conclusion that the contracts in question in *Bell v Lever Bros* were not void, and are ones in which he said that the contract would not be void because the mistake did not make the thing essentially different: 5–051

"A buys B's horse; he thinks the horse is sound and he pays the price of a sound horse; he would certainly not have bought the horse if he had known as the fact is that the horse is unsound. If B has made no representation as to soundness and has not contracted that the horse is sound, A is bound and cannot recover back the price. A buys a picture from B; both A and B believe it to be the work of an old master, and a high price is paid. It turns out to be a modern copy. A has no remedy in the absence of representation or warranty. A agrees to take on lease or to buy from B an unfurnished dwelling-house. The house is in fact uninhabitable. A would never have entered into the bargain if he had known the fact. A has no remedy."[198]

There is thus some doubt whether a common mistake as to the quality of the subject matter will ever render a contract void for mistake.

Impossibility of the contractual venture. In *The Great Peace* the Court said that the cases cited by Lord Atkin in support of his statement "form an insubstantial basis for his formulation".[199] One was *Kennedy v Panama, New Zealand and Australian Royal Mail Co*,[200] in which, as we saw earlier, it is not clear that Blackburn J. was intending to say that a mistake as to substance would make a contract void at English law. The other was *Smith v Hughes*,[201] which does not appear to be relevant.[202] However, the Court said that just as a contract may be frustrated if subsequent events make the contractual adventure impossible, so a contract may be void for common mistake if the mistake is as to: 5–052

"... the existence, or a vital attribute, of the consideration to be provided or circumstances which must subsist if performance of the contractual adventure is to be possible."[203]

Where it is possible to perform the letter of the contract but it is alleged that there was a common mistake in relation to a fundamental assumption which renders performance of the essence of the obligation impossible it is a matter of construction to decide whether this is the case.[204]

"... it is necessary to identify what it is that the parties agreed would be performed. This involves looking not only at the express terms, but at any implications that may

---

[197] Tylor (1948) 11 M.L.R. 257.
[198] [1932] A.C. 161, 224.
[199] *Great Peace Shipping Ltd v Tsavliris Salvage (International) Ltd (The Great Peace)* [2002] EWCA Civ 1407, [2003] Q.B. 679 at [61].
[200] (1867) L.R. 2 Q.B. 580.
[201] (1871) L.R. 6 Q.B. 597. See below, para.5–068.
[202] See *The Great Peace* [2002] EWCA Civ 1407, [2003] Q.B. 679 at [59]–[60].
[203] [2002] EWCA Civ 1407 at [76].
[204] [2002] EWCA Civ 1407 at [82].

arise out of the surrounding circumstances. In some cases it will be possible to identify details of the 'contractual adventure' which go beyond the terms that are expressly spelt out, in others it will not."[205]

5–053 **What mistakes may frustrate contractual venture?** Clearly a contract which turns out to be literally impossible to perform may be void for mistake, provided the other conditions set out above are met. But what other kinds of case may fall within the phrase, "frustration of the contractual venture"—or, for that matter, following Lord Atkin's formulation, make the subject matter "essentially different from the thing it was believed to be"?[206] The cases give examples: a contract for "a room with a view" when in fact there was no procession to look at[207]; a guarantee of a lease of machines when in fact no machines existed[208]; possibly the sale of a life insurance policy on someone the parties did not know was already dead.[209] Beyond this it is not easy to generalise. However it has been argued that an appropriate test for determining whether a mistake is fundamental is to ask the parties "what are you contracting about"? If they would both identify the subject matter in terms that are correct (e.g. in *Bell v Lever Bros* they would have answered, "[w]e are contracting about a service agreement") the mistake is not fundamental. If they would identify the subject matter in terms that in fact are not correct, the mistake is fundamental.[210] This argument is attractive but it presupposes that the correct test is one of the identity of the subject matter. That fits Lord Atkin's analysis but not necessarily that in *The Great Peace*.

(d) *Mistakes of law*

5–054 **Mistakes as to law.** Until recently, it was established that, for a common mistake to be operative at common law,[211] and (when it was thought that there might be a separate equitable right to rescind)[212] in equity,[213] it must be a mistake as to fact and not one as to law. This did not apply when an error as to the meaning of a document resulted in a mistake as to private rights which led to a party attempting to buy his own property.[214] Moreover, a question of foreign law

205 [2002] EWCA Civ 1407 at [74].

206 See above, para.5–050.

207 *Griffiths v Brymer* (1903) 19 T.L.R. 434, above, para.5–025.

208 *Associated Japanese Bank (International) Ltd v Crédit du Nord* [1989] 1 W.L.R. 255, cited with apparent approval in *The Great Peace* [2002] EWCA Civ 1407 at [93].

209 *Scott v Coulson* [1903] 2 Ch. 249. In *The Great Peace* [2002] EWCA Civ 1407 the Court seems to have had some difficulty in explaining this decision but did not say it was wrong (at [87]–[88]).

210 Treitel, *Law of Contract*, 12th edn (by Peel, 2007), para.8–019.

211 *Beesley v Hallwood Estates Ltd* [1960] 1 W.L.R. 549, 563, affirmed [1961] Ch. 105.

212 See above, para.5–510.

213 *Stone v Godfrey* (1854) 5 De G.M. & G. 76, 90; *Rogers v Ingham* (1876) 3 Ch D 351, 357; *Alcard v Walker* [1896] 2 Ch. 369, 375; *Re Diplock* [1948] Ch. 465 (affirmed *sub nom. Ministry of Health v Simpson* [1951] A.C. 251); *Whiteside v Whiteside* [1950] Ch. 65, 74; see below, para. 29–043. However in *Solle v Butcher* [1950] 1 K.B. 671 the Court of Appeal assumed that no relief could be given where the mistake was purely one of law.

214 *Cooper v Phibbs* (1867) L.R. 2 H.L. 149. As we have seen, on the facts of this case the contract would now to be regarded as void: above, para.5–049.

is a question of fact.[215] The rule that a mistake of pure law could not invalidate a contract seems to have been based on the rule that only a mistake of fact would entitle a party to claim restitution on the grounds of mistake.[216] In *Kleinwort Benson Ltd v Lincoln City Council* the House of Lords held that the latter rule is not part of English law.[217] It was not immediately clear whether this would affect the law of common mistake. The grounds on which a payment made by mistake may be recovered are wider than those on which a contract may be void for common mistake.[218] This is said to be because of the policy favouring finality of contracts.[219] Thus a mistaken payment may be recovered without showing that the mistake was fundamental or that the recipient shared the payer's mistake.[220] However, it has been accepted by the Court of Appeal that in principle a fundamental common mistake as to law may render a contract void; the principle underlying the decision in the *Kleinwort Benson* case[221] is not confined to restitution. However, on the facts (which involved a compromise agreement) the agreement was not void for common mistake.[222]

Mistake of law and compromise agreements. In *Brennan v Bolt Burdon*[223] the Court of Appeal accepted that a mistake of law may render a contract void. However, there is not a mistake of law if the relevant law was merely in doubt, as the majority held it was in this case; the parties could have discovered that the relevant decision was under appeal. In addition, when combined with the "declaratory theory of law" espoused in the *Kleinwort Benson* case, that when a decision is overturned the previous view of the law was mistaken,[224] the mistake of law rule would threaten the finality of compromise agreements. In the view of Maurice Kay L.J. and Bodey J., a compromise agreement is one under which each party should be treated as accepting the risk that their view of the law might subsequently turn out to be mistaken.[225] The court left open the question whether a mistake of law could ever invalidate a compromise agreement if, as a matter of construction, the compromise applies.[226] To exempt compromises altogether from the mistake of law rule might not be inconsistent with the *Kleinwort* case, as Lord Goff[227] and Lord Hope[228] had suggested that in a restitution case there 5–055

[215] *Furness Withy (Australia) Pty Ltd v Metal Distributors (UK) Ltd (The Amazonia)* [1990] 1 Lloyd's Rep. 236.

[216] *Bilbie v Lumley* (1802) 2 East 469: see below, paras 29–041 et seq.

[217] *Kleinwort Benson Ltd v Lincoln City Council* [1999] 2 A.C. 349; below, para.29–045.

[218] Below, para.29–033.

[219] See the authors cited in para.30–030, fn.1597.

[220] See below, para.30–030 fnn.159–163.

[221] [1999] 2 A.C. 349.

[222] [2004] EWCA Civ 1017, [2005] Q.B. 303.

[223] [2004] EWCA Civ 1017, [2005] Q.B. 303.

[224] [1999] 2 A.C. 349, e.g. 378–379 (Lord Goff), 399 (Lord Hoffmann), cf. 410 (Lord Hope).

[225] [2004] EWCA Civ 1017 at [31] and [39]; cf. above, para.5–039. Bodey J. would imply a term to that effect (at [42]). Sedley L.J. reached the same result by considering the agreement in its factual matrix (at [64]).

[226] cf. *Bank of Credit and Commerce International SA (In Liquidation) v Ali (No.1)* [2001] UKHL 8, [2002] 1 A.C. 251, in which the House of Lords held that a general release was not effective to release a claim for "stigma" damages that neither party could have known about: see above, para.5–013.

[227] [1999] 2 A.C. 349, 382G.

[228] [1999] 2 A.C. 349, 412F–G.

might be a defence of "settlement of an honest claim". Maurice Kay L.J. doubted if a mistake of law would ever render performance impossible.[229] Sedley L.J. considered that in mistake of law cases the test of impossibility was too narrow; he would apply a test of whether the mistake destroyed the subject matter.[230] Subsequently the Court of Appeal[231] has said that in practice it makes little difference which approach is followed: on Sedley L.J.'s approach the contract would be void only if the mistake renders "the subject matter of the contract essentially and radically different from the subject matter which the parties believed to exist".[232] On the facts before the court, this test was not satisfied.

5–056 **Mistake of law and consent orders.** In *S v S*[233] it was held that a mistake of law was not a sufficient ground to set aside a consent order[234] made in ancillary relief proceedings, though there was no such mistake on the facts. One ground for the decision, that the *Kleinwort* principle was confined to restitution cases, was later rejected in *Brennan v Bolt Burdon*[235] but Maurice Kay L.J. expressed sympathy with the other ground, that public policy favouring an end to litigation must prevail.[236]

(e) *No Separate Rule in Equity*

5–057 **No separate doctrine of common mistake in equity.** In *The Great Peace*[237] the Court of Appeal held that there is no separate jurisdiction in equity to set aside a contract on the ground of common mistake if the contract is not void at common law. This decision, it is to be hoped, ends years of uncertainty following the earlier decision of the Court of Appeal in *Solle v Butcher*.[238]

5–058 **Previous authority on common mistake in equity.**[239] We saw earlier that before *Bell v Lever Bros Ltd*[240] no coherent equitable doctrine of mistake had developed.[241] In that case Lord Atkin did not advert to a separate equitable doctrine; he approved Lord Westbury's words in *Cooper v Phibbs*[242] subject to

---

[229] [2004] EWCA Civ 1017 at [22].
[230] [2004] EWCA Civ 1017 at [60].
[231] *Kyle Bay Ltd (t/a Astons Nightclub) v Underwriters Subscribing under Policy No.019057/08/01* [2007] EWCA Civ 57, [2007] 1 C.L.C. 164 at [24]–[26].
[232] Steyn J. in *Associated Japanese Bank (International) Ltd v Crédit du Nord SA* [1989] 1 W.L.R. 255, 268.
[233] [2003] Fam. 1.
[234] On consent orders see below, para.5–062, fn.277.
[235] [2004] EWCA Civ 1017, [2005] Q.B. 303.
[236] [2004] EWCA Civ 1017 at [12].
[237] *The Great Peace* [2002] EWCA Civ 1407, [2003] Q.B. 679.
[238] [1950] 1 K.B. 671. The Court of Appeal in Singapore has hinted that it might not follow *The Great Peace* [2002] EWCA Civ 1407. See *Chwee Kin Keong v Digilandmall.com Pte Ltd* [2005] SGCA 2, [2005] 1 S.L.R. 502 at [66]–[73]. The case was one of unilateral mistake (see below, para.5–064). It is noted by Yeo in (2005) 121 L.Q.R. 393.
[239] See Cartwright (1987) 103 L.Q.R. 594; Slade (1954) 70 L.Q.R. 385.
[240] [1932] A.C. 161.
[241] See above, paras 5–019—5–026.
[242] (1867) L.R. 2 H.L. 149, quoted above, para.5–026.

the remark that "the agreement would appear to be void rather than voidable".[243] At least so far as common mistake is concerned, the modern equitable principle of rescission was developed by the Court of Appeal in the case of *Solle v Butcher*.[244] Drawing upon the various cases in which contracts have been set aside on the ground of mistake, together with those in which the defendant has been given the option to rescind or accept rectification,[245] the Court of Appeal enunciated a new doctrine of mistake in equity: that the courts have a discretionary jurisdiction to grant such relief as in the circumstances seems just, including setting aside the contract on terms. In that case, the defendant leased to the plaintiff a dwelling-house which both parties erroneously believed to have been so altered in structure that it had become a "new" dwelling-house and fell outside the restrictions imposed by the Rent Acts. The controlled rent of the house was £140 per annum, but the rent inserted in the lease was £250 per annum. The plaintiff claimed to recover the money overpaid, and, in his defence, the defendant counter-claimed for rescission of the lease on the ground of mutual mistake. The majority of the Court of Appeal[246] considered that there had been a mutual mistake of fact. They ordered that the lease should be rescinded, but on the terms that the plaintiff should choose whether to accept the rescission or claim a new lease at the full rent of £250 per annum. In his judgment Denning L.J. said[247]:

> "It is now clear that a contract will be set aside if the mistake of one party has been induced by the material misrepresentation of the other, even though it was not fraudulent or fundamental; or if one party, knowing that the other is mistaken about the terms of an offer, or the identity of the person by whom it is made, lets him remain under his delusion and concludes a contract on the mistaken terms instead of pointing out the mistake . . . . A contract is also liable in equity to be set aside if the parties were under a common misapprehension either as to facts or as to their relative or respective rights, provided that the misapprehension was fundamental, and that the party seeking to set it aside was not himself at fault."

Denning L.J said that the correct interpretation of *Bell v Lever Bros* was that:

> " . . . if the parties have agreed in the same terms on the same subject matter, the contract is good unless and until it is set aside for failure of some condition on which the existence of the contract depends, or for fraud, or on some equitable ground."[248]

Lord Denning M.R. (as he by then was) applied this doctrine again in the Court of Appeal case of *Magee v Pennine Insurance*.[249] In this case the court held by a majority[250] that an agreement by an insurance company to pay £385 on the

[243] [1932] A.C. 161, 218.
[244] [1950] 1 K.B. 671.
[245] See below, paras 5–119—5–120.
[246] Denning and Bucknill L.JJ. (Jenkins L.J. dissenting).
[247] [1950] 1 K.B. 671, 692.
[248] [1950] 1 K.B. 571, 691. In *Associated Japanese Bank International Ltd v Crédit du Nord SA* [1989] 1 W.L.R. 255, 267 Steyn J. said that Lord Denning's "interpretation of *Bell v Lever Bros Ltd* does not do justice to the speeches of the majority".
[249] [1969] 2 Q.B. 507.
[250] Winn L.J. dissented on the ground that the case was indistinguishable from *Bell v Lever Bros Ltd* [1932] A.C. 161.

occurrence of the risk insured against was invalidated because the policy was voidable, though this was only discovered later, but the second member of the majority, Fenton Atkinson L.J., did not make it clear whether he regarded the contract as void or voidable.[251] The supposed equitable rule was applied in a number of cases at first instance.[252] In *Associated Japanese Bank International Ltd v Crédit du Nord SA* Steyn J. said that he would have been prepared to set the contract aside even if he had not found it to be void at common law.[253] And in *West Sussex Properties Ltd v Chichester DC*[254] the Court of Appeal had considered itself bound by the decision, but apparently without argument because counsel had accepted that it was good law unless and until overturned by the House of Lords.[255]

5–059 **Scope of supposed equitable jurisdiction.** Even if it was accepted that there was an equitable jurisdiction to set aside a contract on terms on the ground of a mutual mistake, there remained doubt about how the jurisdiction was to be exercised. First, it was suggested above that the common law doctrine will not apply if the risk is one which the contract expressly or by implication puts on one of the parties.[256] Given the general importance of upholding agreements and the agreed allocation of risk,[257] it would have been surprising if relief were given in equity in these circumstances. However, the only explicit limitation upon the equitable doctrine was that the party seeking relief should not be at fault, and it has to be said that relief was sometimes given when the normal allocation of risk would suggest that it should be denied. In *Grist v Bailey*[258] a vendor sold property subject to an existing tenancy which both parties thought was protected, when in fact both the protected tenant and her husband were dead. Although neither the vendor nor her solicitor were personally at fault, it seems more natural to put the risk of this kind of mistake occurring on the vendor; yet the contract was set aside.[259] Perhaps it was relevant that if it had been upheld the purchaser

---

[251] [1969] 2 Q.B. 507, 517; see *The Great Peace* [2002] EWCA Civ 1407, [2003] Q.B. 679 at [139]–[140]. The equitable doctrine seems to have been applied by the Court of Appeal in *Nutt v Read* (2000) 32 H.L.R. 761, but "the proceedings had been beset by muddle and confusion" (see *The Great Peace* [2002] EWCA Civ 1407, [2003] Q.B. 679 at [148]; *Islington London BC v UCKAC* [2006] EWCA Civ 340, [2006] 1 W.L.R. 1303 at [19]–[21]) and it seems that the point was not argued.

[252] See *Peters v Batchelor* (1950) 100 L.J. News. 718; *Grist v Bailey* [1967] Ch. 532; *Laurence v Lexcourt Holdings Ltd* [1978] 1 W.L.R. 1128; *London Borough of Redbridge v Robinson Rentals* (1969) 211 E.G. 1125. (Contrast *Svanosio v McNamara* (1956) 96 C.L.R. 186; Slade (1954) 70 L.Q.R. 385, 407; Shatwell (1955) 33 Can. Bar Rev. 164; Atiyah and Bennion (1961) 24 M.L.R. 421, 439.) In *Clarion Ltd v National Provident Institution* [2000] 1 W.L.R 1888 Rimer J. held that the grounds for rescission were not made out.

[253] [1989] 1 W.L.R. 255, 270. See above, para.5–038.

[254] [2000] All E.R. (D) 887.

[255] In the court below junior counsel had sought to challenge the correctness of *Solle v Butcher*: see *The Great Peace* [2002] EWCA Civ 1407, [2003] Q.B. 679 at [160].

[256] See above, para.5–039.

[257] See above, para.5–008.

[258] [1967] Ch. 532.

[259] In *William Sindall Plc v Cambridgeshire CC* [1994] 1 W.L.R. 1016, 1035, Hoffmann L.J. suggested that this case and *Laurence v Lexcourt Holdings Ltd* [1978] 1 W.L.R. 1128 might have been decided differently if the judges at first instance had adverted to the question of the contractual allocation of risk. *Magee v Pennine Insurance* [1969] 2 Q.B. 507 was also criticised on this ground: Atiyah, *Introduction to the Law of Contract*, 5th edn, p.226.

would have received a considerable windfall at the vendor's expense. Secondly, it seemed that there must be some difference between common law and equity in the seriousness of the mistake which was necessary for the doctrine to operate, or it would be hard to see why the contract in *Solle v Butcher* was not void at common law. However, it is not easy to see the difference between a mistake rendering the thing contracted for essentially different from what it was believed to be (or rendering the contractual adventure impossible) and a fundamental mistake (the test in equity).[260] In the *Associated Japanese Bank case*[261] Steyn J. merely remarked that the equitable doctrine "will give relief against mistake in cases where the common law will not." In *William Sindall Plc v Cambridgeshire CC*[262] Evans L.J. said:

> "... the difference may be that the common law rule is limited to mistakes with regard to the subject matter, whilst equity can have regard to a wider and perhaps unlimited category of 'fundamental' mistake."

Rejection of the equitable doctrine. In *The Great Peace* case, the contract for salvage services to be provided by *The Great Peace* to *The Cape Providence* was made on a shared assumption that *The Great Peace* was the nearest available ship to *The Cape Providence*, being some 35 miles away. It was then discovered that in fact she was 410 miles away and the defendants, after finding a nearer vessel that could render assistance, purported to cancel the contract. At first instance,[263] Toulson J. rejected the argument that the contract was void for mistake at common law. The contract did involve the necessary implication that *The Great Peace* was capable of providing the services contracted for. Had she been far away from *The Cape Providence*, there would have been a failure of an implied condition precedent. As *The Great Peace*, though not as the parties thought the nearest vessel, could have reached *The Cape Providence* within 22 hours, the mistake did not turn the contract into something essentially different from that for which the parties bargained.[264] The contract was therefore not void at law.[265] He then turned to the supposed equitable doctrine, noting the unanswered problems, the small number of decided cases and the unsatisfactory nature of them. He held, first, that there is no *right* to rescind in equity on grounds of common mistake a contract which is valid and enforceable at common law.[266] Secondly, to hold that the court has a *discretion* to set aside a contract entered into under a fundamental mistake if the court considers that the general justice of the case merits it "puts palm tree justice in place of party autonomy".[267] He appeared to favour a third view, that Lord Denning's statement in *Solle v Butcher* 5–060

[260] See above, para.5–058.

[261] [1989] 1 W.L.R. 255, 270.

[262] [1994] 1 W.L.R. 1016, 1035.

[263] (2001) 151 N.L.J. 1696, [2001] All E.R. (D) 152.

[264] [2001] All E.R. (D) 152 (Nov) at [56].

[265] [2001] All E.R. (D) 152 (Nov) at [62].

[266] [2001] All E.R. (D) 152 (Nov) at [118]. He added that, if he was wrong, that he did not know what is the test for determining the nature of the fundamental mistake necessary to give birth to such a right.

[267] [2001] All E.R. (D) 152 (Nov) at [119]–[120].

that the court has jurisdiction to set aside a contract on grounds of mutual mistake was "over broad".[268]

5–061 In the Court of Appeal, both the judge's decision on the facts and his view that there is no separate equitable jurisdiction were upheld. Delivering the judgment of the court, Lord Phillips M.R. examined at length the decision in *Cooper v Phibbs*,[269] and concluded that though "the House of Lords . . . approached the case on the basis that in equity alone did the agreement fail", and the speeches did not define the nature of the mistake that would justify the intervention of equity, there was nothing to indicate that the House intended to go beyond those cases in which a party agrees to purchase a title he already owns.[270] He then turned to *Bell v Lever Bros* and pointed out that counsel for the appellants had cited *Cooper v Phibbs*, but in support of the submission, not that equity might provide relief where the common law would not, but that a common mistake had to be as to the subject matter of the contract if it was to render the contract void.[271] He concluded that the House did not overlook a separate right to rescind; they considered that the intervention of equity "took place in circumstances where the common law would have ruled the contract void for mistake".[272] There is no separate right in equity to set aside a contract on the ground of common mistake if the contract is not void at common law. None of the cases that follow *Solle v Butcher*:

> " . . . defines the test of mistake that gives rise to the [supposed] equitable jurisdiction to rescind in a manner that distinguishes this from a test of mistake that renders a contract void in law."[273]

Nor is it possible "to define satisfactorily two different qualities of mistake, one operating in law and one in equity".[274] Coherence can be restored only:

> " . . . by declaring that there is no jurisdiction to grant rescission of a contract on the ground of common mistake where the contract is valid and enforceable on ordinary principles of contract law."[275]

As this was the first occasion on which the Court of Appeal had heard full argument on the relation between *Bell v Lever Bros* and *Solle v Butcher*, it was open to the court to hold that *Solle v Butcher* cannot stand with the earlier decision of the House of Lords.[276]

5–062 **Mistake and equity after *The Great Peace*.** The decision of the Court of Appeal rejects emphatically the notion that there is any separate equitable

---

[268] [2001] All E.R. (D) 152 (Nov) at [121]. Toulson J. continued that, if he was wrong and there were a discretion to set aside for common mistake which is valid on ordinary principles of contract law, he declined to exercise the discretion on the facts of the case (at [123]).

[269] (1867) L.R. 7 H.L. 149.

[270] [2002] EWCA Civ 1407, [2003] Q.B. 679 at [110].

[271] [2002] EWCA Civ 1407 at [113].

[272] [2002] EWCA Civ 1407 at [118].

[273] [2002] EWCA Civ 1407 at [153].

[274] [2002] EWCA Civ 1407.

[275] [2002] EWCA Civ 1407 at [157].

[276] [2002] EWCA Civ 1407 at [160]. cf. Midwinter (2003) 119 L.Q.R. 180.

jurisdiction to rescind a contract on the ground of common mistake: the contract will be either fully binding or void.[277] If it is void there is no scope for the court to impose terms on either party, as the previous decisions of the Court of Appeal had done.[278] This does not prevent the court requiring a party to make payments to the other on general principles of restitution. This happened in *Cooper v Phibbs*,[279] where payments were ordered in respect of improvements.

Refusal of specific performance. The decision in *The Great Peace* does not prevent a common mistake that is not sufficient to make the contract void being used as a defence to an action for specific performance. Specific performance is a discretionary remedy, and, in the exercise of its discretion, a court may refuse an order for specific performance on the ground of a mistake by the defendant.[280] Although the cases are nearly all ones in which the defendant unilaterally misunderstood the terms,[281] it is submitted that the same approach should apply in a case in which the contract has been made under a common mistake that was not sufficient to invalidate the contract at common law, if to enforce the contract specifically would cause particular hardship to the defendant.[282] 5–063

(f) *Mistake and construction*

Construction: an alternative route. It must now be taken as established that there is at common law a doctrine of common mistake, a rule of law distinct from any question of implying a condition on the facts of the case. However, as was suggested earlier,[283] construction of the contract, without reference to "mistake", 5–064

---

[277] This does not appear to affect the jurisdiction to set aside a consent order. Except in matrimonial cases (as to which see *de Lasala v de Lasala* [1980] A.C. 546, 560 and *Thwaite v Thwaite* [1982] Fam. 1, 7–8), a judgment given or an order made by consent, being founded on the agreement of the parties, may be set aside if it was entered into under a mutual mistake of fact or in ignorance of a material fact if the mistake would justify the setting aside of an agreement on the same grounds (*Att-Gen v Tomline* (1877) 7 Ch D 388. See also *Hickman v Berens* [1895] 2 Ch. 638; *Allcard v Walker* [1896] 2 Ch. 369; *Wilding v Sanderson* [1897] 2 Ch. 534). In *Huddersfield Banking Co Ltd v Henry Lister & Son Ltd* [1895] 2 Ch. 273 the mortgagees of certain factory premises allowed the defendants to sell, under a consent order, trade machinery on the premises in the belief, shared by both parties, that the machinery was affixed to the realty. It subsequently appeared that it had been unlawfully detached, and so properly belonged to the mortgagees. The order was set aside. (See also *Furnival v Bogle* (1827) 4 Russ. 142; *Wilding v Sanderson* [1897] 2 Ch. 534; *Dietz v Lennig Chemicals Ltd* [1969] 1 A.C. 170.) But a consent order cannot be set aside on the ground of a mistake where the mistake would not suffice to impeach the agreement on which the order was based: *Purcell v F.C. Trigell Ltd* [1971] 1 Q.B. 358; cf. *Chanel Ltd v F.W. Woolworth & Co Ltd* [1981] 1 W.L.R. 485.

[278] See above, para.5–058. In *The Great Peace* [2002] EWCA Civ 1407, at [161], Lord Phillips, M.R. said: "Just as the Law Reform (Frustrated Contracts) Act 1943 was needed to temper the effect of the common law doctrine of frustration, so there is scope for legislation to give greater flexibility to our law of mistake than the common law allows."

[279] (1867) L.R. 7 H.L. 149.

[280] *Townshend v Stangroom* (1801) 6 Ves. 328. See further below, para.5–077.

[281] See below, para.5–077.

[282] "It would be dangerous to attempt an exhaustive definition of the cass in which the court will refuse specific performance": Brett L.J. in *Tamplin v James* (1879) 15 Ch D 215, 221.

[283] Above, para.5–016.

remains an alternative route by which the courts may reach its conclusion.[284] This is likely to cause some confusion unless the courts accept that when they apply the process of construction to a case in which, factually speaking, the parties have entered the contract under a shared misapprehension as to the surrounding facts, they are normally merely applying "an alternative formulation" of the doctrine of common mistake. Normally the outcome will be the same whichever approach is applied.[285]

5–065 **Contract void as a matter of construction where no common mistake.** In exceptional circumstances the outcomes may differ according to whether the case is analysed in terms of common mistake or as a matter of construction. On occasion the courts have held that a contract is ineffective because on the facts it was subject to an implied condition precedent which has failed, even though the conditions for common mistake were not met—in particular because the contract or contractual venture may not have been impossible to perform. One example is *Financings Ltd v Stimson*.[286] The defendant offered to take a car on hire-purchase, his offer acknowledging that he had examined the car and had satisfied himself that it was in good condition. Before his offer had been accepted the car was stolen and damaged. It was held that his offer was subject to the implied condition that the car remained in substantially the same condition as when he saw it, so that the offer could no longer be accepted.[287] However, in that case the court emphasised that the condition was as to the offer, rather than the contract once formed.[288] The same does not apply however to *Graves v Graves*.[289] In that case divorcees had agreed that the wife would rent a property from the husband; they had assumed that the wife would be eligible for housing benefit which would pay 90 per cent of the rent. It turned out that the wife was not eligible. Thomas L.J., delivering the only full judgment, referred to Steyn J.'s words in the *Associated Japanese Bank* case that one must first determine whether the contract itself, by express or implied condition precedent or otherwise, provides who bears the risk of the relevant mistake.[290] Following this approach, he held that it was necessary to imply a condition in the agreement that if housing benefit was not payable, the tenancy would come to an end, and it was not necessary to consider either mistake or frustration.[291]

---

[284] See, e.g. *Associated Japanese Bank International Ltd v Crédit du Nord SA* [1989] 1 W.L.R. 255. Chandler, Deveney and Poole [2004] J.B.L. 34 argue that as the result of the abolition of the equitable jurisdiction, courts may resort more frequently to the construction technique, which may give them more flexibility.

[285] e.g. in *Standard Chartered Bank v Banque Marocaine De Commerce Exterieur* [2006] EWHC 413 (Comm), [2006] All E.R. (D) 213 (Feb) the contract was held to be binding on the alternative grounds that the mistake did not make the agreement essentially different and that the risk was clearly allocated to one party.

[286] [1962] 1 W.L.R. 1184, CA.

[287] See further Atiyah, *Essays in Contract* (1986), Ch.10.

[288] Treitel, *Law of Contract*, 12th edn (by Peel, 2007), para.2–066.

[289] [2007] EWCA Civ 660, [2007] All E.R. (D) 32 (Jul).

[290] *Associated Japanese Bank (International) Ltd v Crédit du Nord* [1989] 1 W.L.R. 255, 268, quoted above, para.5–039.

[291] [2007] EWCA Civ 660 at [38]–[42].

3. MISTAKES IN "COMMUNICATION"[292]

(a) *Underlying principles*

Underlying basis of law. It is arguable that the cases in which a "mistake in communication" between the parties will have some legal effect are no more than an application of general rules of contract formation and interpretation.[293] They fall into three groups, each seeming to depend on a particular application of those rules. 5–066

Mistake may prevent agreement. No contract can be formed if there is no correspondence between the offer and the acceptance,[294] or if the agreement is not sufficiently certain.[295] The starting point must be whether the parties have reached an agreement that there is a contract between them on the same terms, so that subjectively they are agreed on the same thing. If so there will be a contract on the agreed terms.[296] If, however, one party claims that he did not intend to contract at all, or did not intend to contract on the terms which the other party claims were agreed, then the question is whether, there is a contract (or, as it is often put, whether or not the "contract is void"). The intention of the parties is, as a general rule, to be construed objectively: the language used by one party, whatever his real intention may be, is to be construed in the sense in which it would be reasonably understood by the other.[297] Thus: 5–067

> "... if one party (O) so acts that his conduct, objectively considered, constitutes an offer, and the other party (A), believing that the conduct of O represents his actual intention, accepts O's offer, then a contract will come into existence, and on those facts it will make no difference if O did not in fact intend to make an offer, or if he misunderstood A's acceptance, so that O's state of mind is, in such circumstances, irrelevant.[298]

---

[292] On this phrase see above, para.5–001, fn.6. On the kinds of mistake dealt with in this section, see Cheshire (1944) 60 L.Q.R. 175, 178, 180; Tylor (1948) 11 M.L.R. 257, 259; Slade (1954) 70 L.Q.R. 385, 386; Stoljar (1965) 28 M.L.R. 265, 266.

[293] See above, para.5–012.

[294] See above, para.2–032.

[295] See above, para.2–139.

[296] Cartwright *Misrepresentation, Mistake and Non-disclosure* (2007), para.13.10, citing Lord Macnaghten in *Falcke v Williams* [1900] A.C. 176 at 178–179, PC.

[297] *Cornish v Abington* (1859) 4 H. & N. 549, 556; *Fowkes v Manchester and London Assurance Association* (1863) 3 B. & S. 917, 929; *Smith v Hughes* (1871) L.R. 6 Q.B. 597, 607; *Woodhouse A.C. Israel Cocoa Ltd SA v Nigerian Products Marketing Co Ltd* [1972] A.C. 741; *McInerny v Lloyds Bank* [1974] 1 Lloyd's Rep. 246. Compare the effect of a mistake in a contractual notice. In *Mannai Investment Co Ltd v Eagle Star Life Assurance Co Ltd* [1997] A.C. 749 (above, para.12–050) the House of Lords held that a contractual notice to determine a lease was effective although it did not comply exactly with the break clause in the contract, provided that the notice given would convey the lessee's intention to exercise its rights under the clause unambiguously to a reasonable recipient.

[298] Goff L.J. in *Allied Marine Transport Ltd v Vale do Rio Navegacao SA, The Leonidas D* [1985] 1 W.L.R. 925, summarising the approach of Lord Brightman in *Paal Wilson & Co A/S v Partenreederi Hannah Blumenthal, The Hannah Blumenthal* [1983] 1 A.C. 854, 924. The Court of Appeal in *The Leonidas D* preferred Lord Brightman's formulation of the objective principal to those of Lords Brandon and Diplock ([1985] 1 W.L.R. 925, 936). See above, para.2–004.

Nevertheless cases may occur in which the terms of the offer and acceptance do not match or suffer from such latent ambiguity that it is impossible reasonably to impute any agreement between the parties. Thus "mutual misunderstanding" may prevent the formation of a contract,[299] and arguably this is no more than an application of the requirements of offer and acceptance and certainty.

5–068 **Known mistake may prevent party holding other to words used.** The "objective principle" just referred to means that normally a party is bound by what he said or wrote: he cannot escape by simply saying that he did not mean what the other reasonably understood, in the circumstances, by the words used. It may happen, however, that one party accepts a promise knowing that the terms stated by the other differed from what the other party intended. In such circumstances, the mistake may prevent the party's acceptance being effective at face value: either the contract will be on the terms the other party actually intended or, possibly, the "mistake" will render the contract void.[300] This explains the cases on "unilateral mistake as to the terms of the contract".[301]

5–069 **Offer limited to particular person cannot be accepted by another.** If an offer is by its express or implied terms open only to one person, or to a defined group of persons, no one else can accept the offer; and if they purport to do so, no contract will result. This underlies the cases of "mistaken identity".[302]

5–070 **Older "subjective" notions.** The modern "objective principle" referred to in the previous paragraphs was not firmly established in the nineteenth century, and some cases seem to depend on an older theory, probably derived from continental thinking, that "subjective agreement" or *consensus ad idem* was necessary for a contract.[303] Some of the earlier authorities may thus require re-interpretation in the light of the modern principle.[304]

(b) *Mutual Misunderstanding*

5–071 **Parties at cross-purposes.** In most cases the application of the objective test will preclude a party who has entered into a contract under a mistake from setting up his mistake as a defence to an action against him for breach of contract. If a reasonable person would have understood the contract in a certain sense but a party "mistakenly" understood it in another, then, despite his mistake, the court will hold that the mistaken party is bound by the meaning that the reasonable person would have understood.[305] But where parties are genuinely at cross-purposes as to the subject-matter of the contract, the result may be that there is

---

[299] See below, para.5–071.
[300] See below, paras 5–080—5–086.
[301] See below, paras 5–074 et seq.
[302] See below, paras 5–088 et seq.
[303] See *Anson's Law of Contract*, 28th edn (by Beatson, 2002), p.308.
[304] For examples, see below, paras 5–071, 5–094.
[305] *Scott v Littledale* (1858) 8 E. & B. 815; *Wood v Scarth* (1855) 1 F. & F. 293; *Smith v Hughes* (1871) L.R. 6 Q.B. 597.

no offer and acceptance of the same terms because neither party can show that the other party should reasonably have understood his version.[306] Alternatively, the terms of the offer and acceptance may be so ambiguous that it is not possible to point to one or other of the interpretations as the more probable, and the court must necessarily hold that no contract exists.[307] The best-known example is of some antiquity. In *Raffles v Wichelhaus*[308] the defendants contracted to buy a cargo of cotton to arrive "*ex Peerless* from Bombay." There were two ships of that name and both sailed from Bombay, but one left in October and the other in December. The description of the goods pointed equally to either cargo. To an action for refusal to accept goods from the December shipment, the defendant pleaded that the agreement referred to the other one. The plaintiff demurred, but the court gave judgment for the defendants, apparently taking the view that it was open to the latter to adduce parol evidence as to which ship was meant. The judgment does not indicate what the position would be if the parol evidence failed to point to one cargo rather than the other, but the court did not express any disagreement with counsel's proposition that, if the defendant meant one *Peerless* and the plaintiff the other, there would be no contract. At that time it is likely that it was thought that there would be no contract without subjective agreement, *consensus ad idem*. In a modern case of a similar character it would have to be shown that each party's interpretation was as reasonable as the other's,[309] and it is unlikely that the facts proved would be so sparse as not to give some ground for adopting one interpretation of the contract rather than the other.[310]

Reasonable meaning of A's offer may depend on B's conduct. If one party has misled the other, even unintentionally, he may be precluded from relying on the normal interpretation of the other's words or conduct, with the result that even on an objective criterion no agreement results. In the case of *Scriven v Hindley*,[311] an auctioneer acting for the plaintiff put up for sale lots of hemp and tow from a single ship. It was very unusual for both hemp and tow to be shipped 5–072

[306] e.g. *South East Windscreens Ltd v Jamshidi* [2005] EWHC 3322 (QB), [2005] All ER (D) 317 (Dec) (parties put forward different versions of the agreement as to price; ". . . it is a question of trying to decide objectively what was agreed . . . neither party has discharged the burden of proving, on the balance of probabilities, that their version of the agreement is correct." (at [84]).

[307] *Thornton v Kempster* (1814) 5 Taunt. 786; *Henkel v Pape* (1870) L.R. 6 Ex. 7; *Smidt v Tiden* (1874) L.R. 9 Q.B. 446; *Hickman v Berens* [1895] 2 Ch. 638; *Falck v Williams* [1900] A.C. 176; *Van Praagh v Everidge* [1903] 1 Ch. 434; cf. *Marwood v Charter Credit Corp* (1971) 20 D.L.R. (3d) 563. However, it seems possible that the mistake must relate to a point which is of some importance. If the misunderstanding is as to some unimportant point the court might simply disregard the relevant term and uphold the rest of the contract. cf. *Nicolene Ltd v Simmonds* [1953] 1 Q.B. 543.

[308] (1864) 2 H. & C. 906. See further as to this case, Grant Gilmore, *The Death of Contract* (1974), pp.35–41; Simpson (1975) 91 L.Q.R. 247, 268.

[309] Thus *Hickman v Berens* [1895] Ch. 638 would not be followed today: a compromise agreement was set aside for want of consensus even though the document apparently expressed exactly what one of the parties meant.

[310] This paragraph in the 29th edn was cited in *NBTY Europe Ltd (formerly Holland & Barrett Europe Ltd) v Nutricia International BV* [2005] EWHC 734, [2005] 2 Lloyd's Rep. 350, but it was held on the facts that there was no ambiguity in the agreement, nor indeed were the parties at cross-purposes.

[311] [1913] 3 K.B. 564.

together. The auction catalogue did not indicate the difference in the contents of the lots. A lot of tow was put up, and the defendant bid for it thinking it was hemp. The bid was accepted. The jury found that the auctioneer intended to sell tow, while the defendant intended to bid for hemp, and that the former had merely thought that an overvalue had been placed by the defendant on the tow. It was held that, as the parties were never *ad idem* as to the subject-matter of the contract, there was no binding contract of sale. In the ordinary way an auctioneer is entitled to assume that a bidder knows what he is bidding for, and acceptance of a bid will create a binding contract; the decision in this case seems to have turned on the misleading nature of the catalogue.[312]

5–073 **Parties aware of disagreement over meaning of clause.** The case of mutual misunderstanding should be distinguished from the case in which the parties are aware that they disagree over the meaning of a term of the contract. It has been held that there may be a valid contract despite the fact that the parties know that they are not agreed as to the meaning of one of its terms. Provided there is evidence that the parties intended to make a binding agreement, the contract will be valid and the parties are treated as having left it to the court to determine its correct meaning.[313]

(c) *Unilateral Mistake as to Terms*

(i) *When mistake will affect contract*

5–074 **Mistake known to the other party.** A mistake as to the terms of the contract,[314] *if known to the other party*, may affect the contract. In this case, the normal rule of objective interpretation is displaced in favour of admitting evidence of subjective intention.[315] In *Hartog v Colin and Shields*[316] the defendants offered for sale to the plaintiffs some Argentine hare skins, but by mistake offered them at so much per pound instead of so much per piece. The previous negotiations between the parties had proceeded on the basis that the price was to be assessed at so much per piece as was usual in the trade. But the plaintiffs purported to accept the offer and sued for damages for non-delivery. The court held that the plaintiffs must have known that the offer did not express the true

[312] Although the jury found the parties were not *ad idem*, this does not mean that the court thought subjective agreement was necessary. A.T Lawrence J. discussed whether the defendants were "estopped", which seems to be equivalent to asking whether they were bound by the normal meaning of their conduct in bidding, and held that, because of the auctioneer's behaviour, they were not. It is conceivable that, had the question arisen, the court might have held, not that there was no contract, but that the lot was sold as hemp. Compare below, para.5–080.

[313] *LCC v Henry Boot & Sons Ltd* [1959] 1 W.L.R. 1069.

[314] On the application of this to cases of mistaken identity, see above, para.5–005 and below, paras 5–088 et seq.

[315] Contrast *LCC v Henry Boot & Sons Ltd* [1959] 1 W.L.R. 1069, criticised by Goodhart (1960) 76 L.Q.R. 32.

[316] [1939] 3 All E.R. 566, followed in *McMaster University v Wilcher Construction Ltd* (1971) 22 D.L.R. (3d) 9.

intention of the defendants and that the apparent contract[317] was therefore void.[318] On the same principle, it has been held in Canada[319] that an offer contained in a tender cannot be accepted when it is apparent that the tender is based upon a serious mistake in calculating the totals.[320]

Mistakes which ought to have been apparent. It is not clear whether for the mistake to be operative it must actually be known to the other party, or whether it is enough that it ought to have been apparent to any reasonable man. In Canada the latter suffices,[321] but the Singapore Court of Appeal has held that the common law doctrine of mistake applies only when the non-mistaken party had actual knowledge of the other's mistake.[322] In England there is no clear authority, but two cases suggest that if the other party ought to have known of the mistake, he will not be able to hold the mistaken party to the literal meaning of his offer. In *Centrovincial Estates Plc v Merchant Investors Assurance Co Ltd*[323] the Court of Appeal appeared to consider that the plaintiff might be able to negate any binding agreement by showing that the defendant ought to have known that the plaintiff's offer contained an error; and in *O.T. Africa Line Ltd v Vickers Plc*[324] Mance J. said that the objective principle would be displaced if a party knew or ought to have known of the mistake. The latter situation would include cases in which the party refrained from making enquiries or failed to make enquiries when these were reasonably called for,[325] but first there must be a real reason to suspect a mistake. However, below it will be submitted that the effects of the mistake may differ according to whether the party knew not only that the offer contained a 5–075

[317] The question whether there was no contract at all, or one on the terms in fact intended by the defendants, is discussed below, para.5–080.

[318] See also *Watkin v Watson-Smith, The Times*, July 3, 1986. In *Taylor v Johnson* (1983) 151 C.L.R. 422, 45 A.L.R. 265 the High Court held that where one party knew that the other was mistaken as to a term in a formal written contract, the contract was voidable rather than void; *sed quaere*. Part of the majority judgment of the High Court was adopted by the Court of Appeal in *Commission for New Towns v Cooper (Great Britain) Ltd* [1995] 2 Ch. 259, a case of rectification, without discussion of the majority's view on this point. See further, below, para.5–171. In *Deputy Commissioner of Taxation (N.S.W.) v Chamberlain* (1990) 93 A.L.R. 729 (Federal Court General Division) a taxpayer was not permitted to take advantage of a typing error he had noticed in a writ issued against him.

[319] *Belle River Community Arena Inc v Kaufmann Co Ltd* (1978) 87 D.L.R. (3d) 761 (see Fridman, *Law of Contract*, 4th edn (1999), 261–262); to the same effect is *U.S. v Braunstein* (1948) 168 F. 2d 749.

[320] See also *Chwee Kin Keong v Digilandmall.com Pte Ltd* [2005] SGCA 2, [2005] 1 S.L.R. 502 (buyers tried to take advantage of offer on Internet to sell goods at mistakenly low price). The case is noted by Yeo in (2005) 121 L.Q.R. 393.

[321] See cases cited in fn.319 above.

[322] *Chwee Kin Keong v Digilandmall.com Pte Ltd* [2005] SGCA 2, [2005] 1 S.L.R. 502 at [53]. It appears that actual knowledge would include cases of "'Nelsonian knowledge', namely, wilful blindness or shutting one's eyes to the obvious" (at [42]). The court considered that there is also an equitable jurisdiction to set aside a contract for unilateral mistake in cases in which there is "sharp practice" or "unconscionable conduct" (at [76]–[77]) but this does not seem to represent English law, see below, para.5–078.

[323] [1983] Com.L.R. 158. In this case it was said that if the other party did not know and had no reason to know of the mistake, he is entitled to hold the mistaken party to the terms of the contract in their objective sense; it is immaterial that he has not changed his position or relied upon the contract.

[324] [1996] 1 Lloyd's Rep. 700.

[325] See below para.5–116.

mistake but what the mistake was, and where he merely knew or should have known that it contained a mistake.[326]

5–076 **Mistake as to the terms of the contract.** It is not sufficient that one party knows the other has entered the contract under a mistake of some kind. The mistake must relate to the terms of the contract.[327] If it relates, for example, to what is the subject-matter that is being bought and sold, the mistake is to the terms and may prevent there being a contract; but if the mistake is merely to the quality or the substance of the thing contracted for, it will be a mistake as to the facts (or "an error in motive") and it is well established that an error in motive will not avoid a contract.[328] In *Smith v Hughes*[329] the defendant purchased from the plaintiff a quantity of oats in the belief that they were old oats, whereas in fact they were new oats and quite unsuitable for the purpose for which he wanted them. On discovering his mistake, he refused to accept them and was sued by the plaintiff for the price. The judge asked the jury whether the plaintiff believed the defendant to believe, or to be under the impression, that he was contracting for the purchase of old oats. If so, they were to return a verdict for the defendant. On a motion for a new trial, the Court of Queen's Bench considered that this direction would not sufficiently distinguish between a mistake on the part of the defendant that the oats were old oats, and a mistake that they were being offered to him as old oats. In the former case, the contract would be valid, as the error would be one of motive; in the latter, the mistake would be as to the terms of the contract, and, if known to the plaintiff, would provide a defence to the action. A new trial was ordered. It is not clear whether the defendant would, on the latter hypothesis, have been free from liability on the ground that the contract was void, or on the ground that the seller was in breach by delivering new oats.[330] As the buyer had been given a sample of the oats it is difficult to see how, on similar facts occurring today, any sort of a defence could be made out.

5–077 **Refusal of specific performance for unilateral mistakes not known to the other party or not as to terms.** Even though a mistake by one party has no effect at common law, for example because the other party neither knew nor had reason to know of it,[331] or because it is not a mistake as to the terms of the

[326] See below, paras 5–080—5–086.

[327] Or, where the mistake is over one party's identity, must prevent effective offer and acceptance: above, para.5–005 and below, paras 5–088 et seq.

[328] *Balfour v Sea Fire and Life Assurance Co* (1857) 3 C.B.(N.S.) 300; *Scrivener v Pask* (1866) L.R. 1 C.P. 715; *Pope v Buenos Ayres New Gas Co* (1892) 8 T.L.R. 758; cf. *Gill v M'Dowell* [1903] 2 Ir.Rep. 463. In *G & S Fashions v B&Q Plc* [1995] 1 W.L.R. 1088 it was held that, if a landlord purports to forfeit a lease in the mistaken belief that the tenant is in breach of covenant, the fact that the tenant knows of the landlord's mistake does not prevent it accepting the forfeiture. See also *Bank of Credit and Commerce International SA (In Liquidation) v Ali* [1999] 2 All E.R. 1005, 1019. See further above, para.5–005. A contract will not be invalidated by a unilateral mistake over a separate document that was itself of no legal effect: *Donegal International Ltd v Zambia* [2007] EWHC 197, [2007] 1 Lloyd's Rep. 397 at [471], referring to this paragraph.

[329] (1871) L.R. 6 Q.B. 597.

[330] See *Roberts & Co Ltd v Leicestershire CC* [1961] Ch. 555 (rectification).

[331] See above, paras 5–074—5–075.

contract,[332] it may be a ground on which the court will refuse to order specific performance when it would otherwise have done so. In *Barrow v Scammell*[333] Bacon V.C. said:

> "It cannot be disputed that courts of equity have at all times relieved against honest mistakes in contracts, where the literal effect and the specific performance of them would be to impose a burden not contemplated, and which it would be against all reason and justice to fix, upon the person who, without the imputation of fraud, has inadvertently committed an accidental mistake; and also where not to correct the mistake would be to give an unconscionable advantage to the other party."

It has been held that specific performance may be refused if it would cause the defendant "a hardship amounting to injustice"[334] although he may still be liable to an action for damages at law.[335] It has also been held that mistake may also be a defence if the plaintiff has in some way contributed, even unwittingly, to the mistake.[336] But a mistake which is entirely the product of the defendant's own carelessness will afford no ground for relief[337] unless (perhaps) the case is one of considerable harshness or hardship.[338] Most of the cases are ones in which one party made a mistake about the terms and the other party did not know of the mistake,[339] but there is no reason in principle why the mistake might not have been one as to the surrounding facts rather than the terms of the contract and at least one case involved that.[340] However, most of the cases on refusal of specific performance are old. It is not clear whether the modern tendency to cut down defences of unilateral mistake as grounds for rectifying a contract, or allowing it to be rescinded as an alternative,[341] will extend also to cases where the defendant seeks to be excused from specific performance.

No equitable power to set aside contract. It appears that if one party enters a contract under a mistake as to the terms, and what was really intended is known to the other who nonetheless purports to agree, the contract will be on the terms actually intended by the first party,[342] and if necessary the document may be rectified to bring it into line with the contract.[343] In other cases (where the other party knows there has been a mistake but not what it is, or where he should know 5–078

[332] See previous paragraph.

[333] (1881) 19 Ch D 175, 182. See also *Preston v Luck* (1884) 27 Ch D 497, 506; *Stewart v Kennedy* (1890) 15 App. Cas. 75, 105.

[334] *Tamplin v James* (1880) 15 Ch D 215, 221.

[335] *Webster v Cecil* (1861) 30 Beav. 62, 64.

[336] *Baskomb v Beckwith* (1869) L.R. 8 Eq. 100; *Denny v Hancock* (1870) L.R. 6 Ch. App. 1; *Wilding v Sanderson* [1897] 2 Ch. 534.

[337] *Tamplin v James* (1880) 15 Ch D 215.

[338] *Manser v Back* (1848) 6 Hare 443; *Malins v Freeman* (1837) 2 Keen 25; *Van Praagh v Everidge* [1903] 1 Ch. 434.

[339] If the other party did know of the mistake, it would have the effects described in the next section.

[340] *Jones v Rimmer* (1880) 14 Ch D 588 (though the omission of any mention of the ground rent in otherwise very detailed particulars makes the case very close to one of misrepresentation by a misleading half-truth: see below, para.6–017.)

[341] See below, paras 5–119—5–120.

[342] See below, para.5–080.

[343] See below, para.5–115.

there is a mistake) the mistake seems to render the contract void, as some of the authorities suggest.[344] In neither situation is there a separate equitable jurisdiction to set aside the contract for unilateral mistake.[345]

5–079 **Positive mistake necessary.** It is submitted that there will not be an effective mistake as to the terms unless the "mistaken" party has a positive belief that the terms are X when the contract in fact says Y, or at least that the contract does not include term Y, and the other party knows or ought to know of the mistake.[346] It will not suffice that the "mistaken" party simply did not know that the contract contained a particular term, for example because he had not read it before signing it.[347]

(ii) *Effect on Contract*

5–080 **Effect of mistake as to terms: mistaken party's intention known to other.** In both *Hartog v Colin and Shields*[348] and *Smith v Hughes*[349] it was suggested that the effect of a mistake by one party as to the terms of the contract would, if it were known to the other party, make the contract void. However in both cases the only question was whether the party who had made the mistake could be held to the objective meaning of his words. The *apparent* contract was void, but it was not decided that neither party had any contractual rights against the other. Further, although a contract entered under an operative mistake is often said to be void, it appears that this cannot be raised by the mistaken party against a third party who in good faith and without notice of the mistake has relied on the signed document. The signer is estopped and can only succeed against the third party if he can show non est factum.[350] When the actual intentions of the mistaken party are known to the other, it is possible that the mistaken party can enforce the contract in those terms. Thus it may be that in *Hartog v Colin and Shields* the seller could have enforced the contract at so much per piece (the

---

[344] See below, paras 5–083—5–084.

[345] In *Taylor v Johnson* (1983) 151 C.L.R. 422, 45 A.L.R. 265 the Australian High Court held that where one party knew that the other was probably mistaken as to the terms of a formal written contract, and tried to prevent her discovering the mistake, the contract was voidable rather than void. Part of the majority judgment of the High Court was adopted by the Court of Appeal in *Commission for New Towns v Cooper (Great Britain) Ltd* [1995] 2 Ch. 259, a case of rectification, without discussion of the majority's view on this point. In *Deputy Commissioner of Taxation (NSW) v Chamberlain* (1990) 93 A.L.R. 729 (Federal Court General Division) a taxpayer was not permitted to take advantage of a typing error he had noticed in a writ issued against him. The dictum of Rimer J. in *Clarion Ltd v National Provident Institution* [2000] 2 All E.R. 265, 276, that there are "plenty of examples of equity permitting either rescission or rectification where one party has, to the knowledge of the other, made the contract under a mistake as to its subject matter or terms" must, with respect, be doubted as regards rescission.

[346] See above, para.5–006.

[347] Compare Spencer [1973] C.L.J 103, 114–116, cited in *Tilden Rent-a-Car Co v Clendenning* (1978) 83 D.L.R. (3d) 400 CA Ont. (signature does not show assent to provision which company "had no reason to believe were being assented to by the other contracting party").

[348] [1939] 3 All E.R. 566; above, para.5–074.

[349] (1871) L.R. 6 Q.B. 597; above, para.5–076.

[350] See the judgment of Sir Edward Eveleigh in *Lloyds Bank Plc v Waterhouse* (1991) 10 Tr.L.R. 161. Contrast the "mistaken identity" cases, below, para.5–088, where the mistaken party is not estopped simply by entrusting possession of his property to the rogue who sells it to the third party. On non est factum see below, para.5–101.

figure the seller actually intended) against the buyer.[351] The buyer, having accepted an offer which he knew was meant to read so much per piece, could be said to be bound by it.

Rectification cases. This interpretation is consistent with the cases granting rectification in cases of unilateral mistake.[352] There it is said that if the party against whom rectification is sought knew that the documents did not represent the true intention of the party seeking relief, the documents will be rectified to show what the party seeking relief actually intended. This presupposes the existence of a valid contract despite the mistake, on the terms actually intended by the mistaken party and known by the other to be so intended. 5–081

Estoppel. To hold the party to the terms actually intended by the mistaken party is also consistent with cases on estoppel. There it has been said that if one party knows the other has made a mistake and fails to point it out when the reasonable person would expect him to do so were he acting honestly and reasonably, an estoppel by silence or acquiescence may arise and result in liability where there would otherwise be none.[353] 5–082

Mistake should have been known to the other party; or true intention not known. It was submitted earlier that, at present, English law gives relief for a unilateral mistake if the mistake was known to the other party; but there are suggestions in some of the cases that relief should also be given if the other party ought to have known of it.[354] If it were decided to give relief in these circumstances, what should the effect on the contract be? A similar question arises when the other party knows that the first party has made a mistake over the terms but (unlike in *Hartog v Colin and Shields*,[355] for example) does not know what the first party actually intended. 5–083

In this situation it might be argued that if the first party were to purport to accept the apparent offer, he was estopped from denying that he had accepted whatever the offeror can prove he actually meant. But this would at the very least leave the first party in some uncertainty, and might involve holding him to a contract to which he would never have agreed. In a recent rectification case it was said that: 5–084

"The effect of a successful rectification claim based on unilateral mistake is always that it imposes a contract upon the defendant which he did not intend to make. It is the unconscionable conduct involved in staying silent when aware of the claimant's

[351] See also Anson, *Law of Contract*, 28th edn (by Beatson, 2002), p.326; compare Treitel, *Law of Contract*, 12th edn (by Peel, 2007), para.8–053 (possibly seller could have held buyer to contract on the *stated* terms had he wished to do so).

[352] See below, para.5–115.

[353] *Pacol Ltd v Trade Lines Ltd, The Henryk Sif* [1982] 1 Lloyd's Rep. 456, 465; *The Stolt Loyalty* [1993] 2 Lloyd's Rep. 281, 290; *Republic of India v Indian Steamship Co, The Indian Grace (No.2)* [1994] 2 Lloyd's Rep. 331, 344. See above, para.2–073.

[354] See above, para.5–075.

[355] [1939] 3 All E.R. 566; above, para.5–074.

mistake that makes it just to impose a different contract upon him from that by which he intended to be bound."[356]

When the first party's mistake was not actually known to the second party, or what the first party actually meant when that was unknown to the second party, it seems inappropriate to hold the second party to the terms intended by the first. It is more appropriate to hold that there is no contract.[357]

5–085 **Oral and written contracts.** It may be noted that there is at least one difference between the treatment of oral and written contracts which have been entered into as the result of a mistake as to the terms by one party which was known to the other. If the submissions above are correct, with an oral contract or one made by exchange of written communications, where the mistaken party's real intentions are known to the other, there will be a contract on those terms[358]; and for the most part the result when the contract has been reduced to writing is parallel. As was just mentioned,[359] a party who has signed a written agreement under a mistake may, if the mistake was known to the other party, claim to have the document rectified. However, the right to rectification may be lost, so in that case it is the ostensible agreement which will stand.[360]

5–086 It is possible that there is a second difference between the treatment of oral and written contracts, in the case where the mistaken party's intentions are not known to the other party, but either the other knows that there was a mistake but not what it is or he should have known that there was a mistake. In these cases it is suggested that if the contract was oral, or formed simply by an exchange of correspondence, it is void.[361] What is not wholly clear is whether the same applies when the parties have reduced their agreement to writing. If oral and written contracts were to be treated identically, the contract should be void. As we will see below, in very limited circumstances a party who has signed a deed or other document under a misapprehension can claim that it is not binding on him under the doctrine of non est factum. The circumstances are very limited because a plea of non est factum can operate to prejudice third parties who have relied on the contract. It may be thought that this is the only ground on which the mistaken party can escape from a written contract. But it has been pointed out that when the dispute is between the original parties, there is no need to rely on

---

[356] *Chartbrook Ltd v Persimmon Homes Ltd* [2007] EWHC 409 (Ch), [2007] 2 P. & C.R. 9 at [137].

[357] In Canada, in the analogous situation in which the mistaken party seeks rectification, the other party is given the option of submitting to rectification or to rescission, see below, para.5–120. It does not seem easy to reach a parallel conclusion in the case of an oral agreement if it is the law that the effect of a mistake is to make the contract void rather than voidable.

[358] See above, para.5–080.

[359] See above, para.5–081.

[360] See below, para.5–127. In *Taylor v Johnson* (1983) 151 C.L.R. 422, 45 A.L.R. 265 the Australian High Court held that where one party knew that the other was probably mistaken as to the terms of a formal written contract, and tried to prevent her discovering the mistake, the contract was voidable rather than void. This is an attractive solution but seems to go beyond English authority in allowing recission for unilateral mistake: see below, para.5–120.

[361] See above, para.5–084.

this defence: the contract may be void for mistake.[362] It is submitted that, if necessary, the court should cancel the document.[363]

Parties aware of disagreement over meaning of clause. It has been held that there may be a valid contract despite the fact that the parties know that they are not agreed as to the meaning of one of its terms. Provided there is evidence that the parties intended to make a binding agreement, the contract will be valid and the parties are treated as having left it to the court to determine its correct meaning.[364] 5–087

(d) *Mistaken Identity*

Mistaken identity. A number of cases have raised the question whether a mistake by one party as to the identity of the person with whom he appears to be contracting will render the contract void. The question arises in a recurrent situation typified by the facts of *Cundy v Lindsay.*[365] A fraudulent person named Blenkarn wrote to the plaintiffs offering to buy certain goods, and so contrived his signature to resemble that of Blenkiron & Co, a prosperous firm carrying on business in the same street and with whom the plaintiffs had previously dealt. The plaintiffs despatched the goods in the belief that they were dealing with Blenkiron & Co and the goods eventually came into the hands of an innocent purchaser, the defendant. If the contract between the plaintiffs and Blenkarn was void for mistake, no property in the goods had passed under the contract, and the plaintiffs were entitled to recover them. But otherwise the contract was merely voidable for fraud, and the defendant would have acquired a good title.[366] 5–088

Mistake as to the person.[367] The identity of the person with whom one is contracting or proposing to contract is often immaterial. It is usually of no importance to a shopkeeper to whom he sells goods across the counter for cash[368]; and an auctioneer who accepts a bid at a public auction is not normally concerned with the identity of the person who makes the bid.[369] Sometimes, however, and for special reasons, the identity of the person is material. In such circumstances, if one party mistakenly believes that he is dealing with person A 5–089

---

[362] See the judgment of Sir Edward Eveleigh in *Lloyds Bank Plc v Waterhouse* (1991) 10 Tr.L.R. 161, discussed further below, para.5–102.

[363] On cancellation of documents see *Halsbury's Laws of England* Vol.16(2) (reissue), paras 485–486.

[364] *LCC v Henry Boot & Sons Ltd* [1959] 1 W.L.R. 1069.

[365] (1878) 3 App. Cas. 459; see further below, para.5–094.

[366] The owner who has parted with possession of the goods to the rogue is not estopped from reclaiming them from the innocent third party to whom the rogue sells them; contrast the case where a party has mistakenly signed a document which is relied on by an innocent third party, below, para.5–102.

[367] See Goodhart (1941) 57 L.Q.R. 228; Cheshire (1944) 60 L.Q.R. 175, 183; Williams (1945) 23 Can. Bar Rev. 271; Tylor (1948) 11 M.L.R. 257, 259; Slade (1954) 70 L.Q.R. 385, 390; Wilson (1954) 17 M.L.R. 515; Unger (1955) 18 M.L.R. 259; Hall [1961] Camb.L.J. 86; Stoljar (1965) 28 M.L.R. 265, 280.

[368] *Ingram v Little* [1961] 1 Q.B. 31, 57.

[369] *Dennant v Skinner* [1948] 2 K.B. 164. See also *Smith v Wheatcroft* (1878) 9 Ch D 223.

when he is in fact dealing with B, and he communicates to B an offer that is intended only for A, the mistake as to identity may prevent a contract coming into existence. The same may apply if the mistaken party purports to accept an offer that he believes to have been made by A but that was in fact made by B.[370]

5–090 **Offer to B cannot be accepted by C.** Assuming the identity of the other party to be material, we may start with the general proposition that, if A offers to make a contract with B, C cannot give himself any rights under the offer:

> "A person cannot constitute himself a contracting party with one whom he knows or ought to know has no intention of contracting with him. An offer can be accepted only by the person to whom it is addressed."[371]

Equally, if a party makes an offer to another and the other addresses his acceptance to a third person with whom the other intends to deal, there will be no contract.[372] In *Boulton v Jones*[373] the defendant had been used to deal with one Brocklehurst, against whom he had a set-off. He sent Brocklehurst a written order for some goods. On the very day that the order was sent, Brocklehurst had transferred his business to his foreman, the plaintiff. The plaintiff thereupon dispatched the goods without informing the defendant of the change of ownership. The defendant refused to pay for the goods, and the court held that he was not liable to do so as the plaintiff could not accept an offer which was not addressed to him. Nevertheless the test is not entirely a subjective one. The question is not simply "[w]ith whom did the offeror intend to contract?" but also "[h]ow would the offer have been understood by a reasonable man in the position of the offeree"? If A makes an offer to B in mistake for C, and B accepts the offer reasonably believing it to have been intended for him, A will be bound despite the mistake.[374] In *Boulton v Jones* the circumstances were such that a reasonable man would not have believed the offer to have been addressed to him. The business had only just changed hands, and the plaintiff either knew of[375] or could easily have discovered the existence of the set-off. But where such knowledge or means of knowledge is lacking, the offeror will be bound. Moreover, the growth of companies and the increasing depersonalisation of commerce may mean that nineteenth-century cases on questions of this kind are not very reliable as authorities. In 1857 a buyer of goods from a shop may well have regarded the

---

[370] The same may occasionally apply when the mistake is one as attributes rather than identity: see below, para.5–097.

[371] Anson, *Law of Contract*, 28th edn (by Beatson, 2002), p.326; see *Shogun Finance Ltd v Hudson* [2003] UKHL 62, [2004] 1 A.C. 919 at [63], [125] and [184].

[372] *Shogun Finance Ltd v Hudson* [2003] UKHL 62, [2004] 1 A.C. 919, per Lord Phillips at [125].

[373] (1857) 2 H. & N. 564, 6 L.R. 107.

[374] Goodhart (1941) 57 L.Q.R. 228, 241–244; Cheshire (1944) 60 L.Q.R. 175, 186–187. See also *Upton-on-Severn RDC v Powell* [1942] 1 All E.R. 220; *Shogun Finance Ltd v Hudson* [2003] UKHL 62, [2004] 1 A.C. 919 at [65], [123] and [183].

[375] See the report in (1857) 6 W.R. 107.

identity of the seller as a matter of importance; in the day of the supermarket this is less likely to be the case.

Offer may be accepted only by person to whom it was made. Thus the question is, to whom was the offer[376] made: to the actual recipient to whom it was addressed or sent, or to the person with whom the offeror thought he was dealing? There will be no contract if it is shown that: 5–091

> " . . . there was no objective agreement, *e.g.* that the offer was, objectively speaking, made to one person and (perhaps as the result of fraud) objectively speaking, accepted by another."[377]

In the typical case[378] in which a rogue (R) has fraudulently induced the innocent party (S) to believe that R is in fact a third person (X), R is of course aware of S's mistake and it makes no sense to ask whether S intended to deal with R or X: to him they were the same person.[379] Nonetheless the question is whether the offer must in the circumstances be interpreted as made to, or intended for, only X or as made to the person with whom S was actually dealing, whom he merely thought to be X. In practice the answer will depend on whether the parties were dealing face-to-face or by correspondence.

Face-to-face dealings. When the parties are dealing with each other face to face[380] there is a strong presumption that the mistaken party "intends" to deal with the person physically present or, to put it in other words, there is a presumption that the offer is made to him.[381] Thus, in *Phillips v Brooks*[382] one North entered the plaintiff's shop and selected several pieces of jewellery. He then wrote out a cheque for the price, saying "I am Sir George Bullough"—a person known by reputation to the plaintiff. He took away some of the jewellery and pledged it with the defendant who received it in good faith. In an action by the plaintiff to recover the jewellery pledged, it was held that the plaintiff intended to contract with the person in the shop. There was therefore no operative mistake and the property in the jewellery passed. 5–092

---

[376] For convenience it is assumed that it is the offeror who is the mistaken party. The same principle will apply when the mistaken party purportedly accepts an offer that he believes came from X but was in fact made by R. See fn.372, above.

[377] Robert Goff L.J. in *Whittaker v Campbell* [1984] Q.B. 318, 327.

[378] See above, para.5–076.

[379] See the judgment of Devlin L.J. in *Ingram v Little* [1961] Q.B. 31, 65 and the speeches of Lords Millett, Phillips and Walker in *Shogun Finance Ltd v Hudson* [2003] UKHL 62, [2004] 1 A.C. 919 at [64], [138], and [125], respectively.

[380] Or probably where they negotiate over the telephone or by other means involving inter-personal contact other than in writing: *Shogun Finance Ltd v Hudson* [2003] UKHL 62, [2004] 1 A.C. 919 at [153].

[381] See the speech of Lord Walker in *Shogun Finance Ltd v Hudson* [2003] UKHL 62 at [184].

[382] [1919] 2 K.B. 243, criticised by Goodhart (1941) 57 L.Q.R. 228 at 241, and by Gresson P. in *Fawcett v Star Car Sales* [1960] N.Z.L.R. 406. See also *Dennant v Skinner* [1948] 2 K.B. 164; *Barclays Bank Ltd v Okenarhe* [1966] 2 Lloyd's Rep. 87.

5–093 The cases have not been wholly consistent in their outcomes.[383] In *Ingram v Little*[384] the plaintiffs advertised their car for sale. A rogue who called himself Hutchinson offered to buy the car and to pay for it with a cheque. This offer was rejected. "Hutchinson" then gave his initials and address, describing himself as a respectable business man living in Caterham. The plaintiffs had never heard of this man but one of the plaintiffs ascertained from the telephone directory that such a person lived at that address. Relying on this information, they accepted the cheque, which was dishonoured on presentation. The rogue sold the car, which subsequently came into the hands of the defendant, a bona fide purchaser for value. In an action by the plaintiffs to recover the car, or its value, from the defendant, the Court of Appeal by a majority held that the contract between the plaintiffs and the rogue was void for mistake as to identity, and that they were entitled to judgment since the car was still their property. The circumstances (particularly the investigation of the telephone directory) indicated that it was with Hutchinson that the plaintiffs intended to deal and not with the rogue who was physically present before them. Devlin L.J. dissented: there was a presumption that the person intended to contract with the person to whom she was addressing her words and that the presumption had not been rebutted. It did not suffice to show that S would not have contracted with R unless she thought he was X. The decision in *Ingram v Little* was criticised and not followed in *Lewis v Averay*[385] where the facts were very similar but judgment was given for the bona fide purchaser. Phillimore L.J. emphasised that each of these cases must be decided on its own facts but that there is a strong presumption against holding a contract to be totally void where it is entered into *inter praesentes*. Megaw L.J. held that it had not been shown that the seller considered the identity of the buyer to be of vital importance. Denning L.J. expressed the view that a mistake of identity would never make a contract void. In the recent House of Lords case of *Shogun Finance Ltd v Hudson*[386] (a case of a contract in writing) it seems to have been accepted by all their lordships who discussed the point that, in face-to-face dealings, there is a strong presumption that the offer is made to the person physically present.[387] Indeed, two of their lordships doubted whether the presumption could be rebutted.[388] The tenor of their lordships' speeches was that the

[383] *Phillips v Brooks* [1919] 2 K.B. 243 was distinguished by Viscount Haldane in *Lake v Simmons* [1927] A.C. 487, 502, who pointed out that the misrepresentation of his identity by North had not occurred until after the sale had been concluded and the property had passed. But in *Lake v Simmons* the question was whether the loss was covered by an insurance policy and Viscount Haldane's approach was not adopted by the other Lords: see Devlin L.J. in *Ingram v Little* [1961] 1 Q.B. 31, 69–73 and Lord Phillips in *Shogun Finance Ltd v Hudson* [2003] UKHL 62, [2004] 1 A.C. 919 at [141].

[384] [1961] 1 Q.B. 31 (Devlin L.J. dissenting).

[385] [1972] 1 Q.B. 198.

[386] [2003] UKHL 62, [2004] 1 A.C. 919. See below, para.5–095.

[387] [2003] UKHL 62. See the speeches of Lord Nicholls at [22] and [37], of Lord Millett at [69], of Lord Phillips at [170] and of Lord Walker at [187]. Lord Hobhouse did not address the question.

[388] Lord Nicholls, [2003] UKHL 62 at [37] and Lord Millett, who at [67] suggested that perhaps the presumption should be conclusive. Both were dissenting. Of the majority, Lord Walker said at [187] that exceptions to the presumption would be very rare but might occur in, e.g. cases of impersonation of someone actually known to a mistaken party whose senses are impaired.

dissenting approach of Devlin L.J. in *Ingram v Little*[389] was to be preferred; Lord Walker said that the case was wrongly decided.[390]

Contracts in writing. Where the contract is in writing, in contrast, only the persons named in the writing can be parties to the contract, and it seems that the same applies when the negotiations for the contract were conducted in writing evn if there was no formal written agreement. In *Cundy v Lindsay*[391] (the facts of which were given in para.5–076, above) it was held that the mistake was one as to the identity of the contracting party and the contract was void. Lord Cairns remarked: 5–094

> "... how is it possible to imagine that in the that state of things any contract could have arisen between the Respondents and Blenkarn, the dishonest man? Of him they knew nothing, and of him they never thought. With him they never intended to deal. Their minds never, even for an instant of time, rested on him, and as between him and them there was no consensus of mind which could lead to any agreement or contract whatever."[392]

This decision does not seem at the time to have rested on the distinction between face-to-face negotiations and a written contract; rather it seems to reflect the subjective approach to intention that was widely adopted in the nineteenth century.[393] However the decision has been upheld on the basis that the negotiations were by correspondence and therefore the respondent's offer was made only to the person identified in the writing, i.e. the respectable firm of Blenkirons to whom the respondents dispatched the goods. This is the effect of the recent House of Lords decision in *Shogun Finance Ltd v Hudson*.[394]

In *Shogun Finance Ltd v Hudson* a rogue wanted to acquire a vehicle displayed by a car dealer and showed the dealer a driving licence in the name of a Mr Patel. The dealer contacted the claimants and, after the claimants had checked Mr Patel's credit details, a financing agreement with the claimants was arranged in the name of Mr Patel. After the rogue had paid a deposit partly in cash and partly by cheque (which was later dishonoured), the dealer allowed the rogue to take the vehicle. The defendant bought the vehicle in good faith. The defendant claimed that he was protected by Hire Purchase Act 1964 s.27. This provides that when a motor vehicle has been bailed under a hire-purchase agreement or agreed to be sold under a conditional sale agreement, and before the property has vested in the debtor he disposes of it to a private purchaser who buys it in good faith, the purchaser will obtain good title. The Court of Appeal,[395] by a majority, held that the defendant had not acquired the vehicle from a "debtor" under a hire-purchase agreement as there was no valid agreement. Mr Patel was not bound by any 5–095

[389] [1961] 1 Q.B. 31.
[390] [2003] UKHL 62, [2004] 1 A.C. 919 at [185].
[391] (1878) 3 App. Cas. 459.
[392] (1878) 3 App. Cas. 459 at 465. See also the speeches of Lord Hatherly at 469 and Lord Penzance at 471.
[393] For a useful discussion see Simpson (1975) 91 L.Q.R. 247, 266 et seq. and MacMillan in Lewis and Lobban (eds), *Law and History Current Legal Issues* (2004) Vol.6, pp.285–315.
[394] [2003] UKHL 62, [2004] 1 A.C. 919.
[395] [2001] EWCA Civ 100, [2002] Q.B. 834.

agreement and there was no valid agreement with the rogue. By a majority this decision was affirmed in the House of Lords. A minority of their lordships argued powerfully that there was a contract between the finance company and the rogue; the effect of the fraudulently induced belief by the company that it was dealing with Mr Patel merely rendered the contract voidable. Lord Millett accepted that A cannot accept an offer that is made to B but argued that, whether the parties are dealing with each other face-to-face or in writing, there should be a presumption that the mistaken party intends to deal with the person with whom he is physically dealing—the person present or the writer of the letter. A contract should come into existence whenever there is sufficient correlation between the offer and the acceptance to make it possible to say that the imposter's offer has been accepted by the person to whom it was addressed.[396] Lord Millett said that *Cundy v Lindsay* was wrongly decided.[397] Lord Nicholls agreed that *Cundy v Lindsay* should not be followed.[398] A person should be presumed to intend to contract with the person with whom he is actually dealing, whatever the mode of communication.[399] But the majority held that when the dealings are carried out in writing, and certainly when the contract is reduced to a writing,[400] the identification of the parties to the agreement is a question of the construction of the putative contract. If an individual is unequivocally identified by the description in the writing, that precludes any finding that the party to the agreement is anyone other than the person so described.[401] On the facts, the finance company was willing to do business only with the person who appeared to have identified himself in the written document, i.e. Mr Patel[402]; and where the party is specifically identified in the document, oral or other extrinsic evidence is not admissible to show that the party is someone else.[403] There was therefore no contract between the rogue and the finance company.

5–096 **Non-existent person.** It seems that if the rogue purports to be not another individual who exists but a non-existent person, then even when the contract is in writing it will normally be between the mistaken party and the rogue. In *King's*

---

396 [2003] UKHL 62, [2004] 1 A.C. 919 at [81].

397 [2003] UKHL 62 at [93]. The minority were in part driven by the desire to protect innocent third parties who might purchase the property: see Lord Nichols at [35] and Lord Millett at [60] and [84].

398 [2003] UKHL 62 at [34].

399 [2003] UKHL 62 at [36].

400 Lord Hobhouse appears to state this as the rule when the contract is reduced to writing (at [46]) and then gives as a separate ground that the finance company only accepted the written offer apparently made on the form by Mr Patel. Lord Walker agreed with Lord Hobhouse and in his further remarks he appears to say that where there is an alleged contract reached by correspondence, again the identity of the parties will normally be determined by the writing; but he seemed to envisage that in such a case there might be room for argument, for example if in *Cundy v Lindsay* the respondents had never heard of Blenkiron & Co (at [188]). Lord Phillips does not seem to distinguish the two situations (see at [170] and [178]).

401 See the speeches of Lord Hobhouse, especially at [47]–[50]; Lord Phillips, especially at [154], [161] and [170]; and Lord Walker especially at [180] and [188]. The decision in *Hector v Lyons* (1989) 58 P. & C.R. 156 was said to be correct in principle though the reason for the decision on the facts was not wholly clear: see [2003] UKHL 62 at [49], [166] and [192].

402 See the speech of Lord Hobhouse at [48].

403 [2003] UKHL 62 at [49]. It could of course be shown that the party named was acting as agent.

Norton Metal Co v Edridge, Merrett & Co Ltd[404] the plaintiffs had despatched goods to one Wallis, who had written to them posing as a member of a mythical firm named "Hallam & Co". Wallis subsequently sold the goods so obtained to the defendants, who took in good faith and for value. The Court of Appeal held that the plaintiffs had intended to contract with the writer of the letter, although they had invested him with the attributes of solvency and respectability. A.L. Smith L.J. said[405] that if there had been a separate entity called Hallam & Co the case might have been within *Cundy v Lindsay.*[406] In the *Shogun* case, Lord Phillips said that in the *King's Norton* case:

> "... the plaintiffs intended to deal with whoever was using the name Hallam & Co. Extrinsic evidence was needed to identify who that was but, once identified as the user of that name, the party with whom the plaintiffs had contracted was established. They could not demonstrate that their acceptance of the offer was intended for anyone other than Wallis."[407]

The *King's Norton* decision does not completely preclude a finding that the mistaken party intended to contract only with a person who does not in fact exist[408] but, as Lord Hobhouse pointed out in the *Shogun* case, in a credit agreement it would be useless to use a pseudonym as there would be no actual person against whom a credit check could be run.[409]

Identity and attributes. It used often to be said that only a mistake as to the identity of the other party could ever prevent the formation of a contract; a mistake as to attributes could never do so.[410] While it is clear that a mistake as to an attribute of the other party such as whether he is credit-worthy will not prevent the formation of a contract,[411] the distinction has been criticised.[412] It is possible that in exceptional circumstances a mistake as to attribute may prevent a contract coming into existence, if a person is for the purpose identified by some attribute. An offer made only to members of the University of Warwick could not be accepted by someone who was not a member of the University.[413] 5–097

Mistake and third parties. It is not clear whether a person can intervene and allege that a contract is void for mistake as to the person when the contracting parties themselves are unwilling to assert its invalidity. In *Fawcett v Saint Merat* 5–098

---

[404] (1897) 14 T.L.R. 98.
[405] (1897) 14 T.L.R. 98, 99.
[406] (1878) 3 App. Cas. 459; above, paras 5–076 and 5–081.
[407] [2003] UKHL 62 at [135]. See also the speech of Lord Walker at [189].
[408] *Lake v Simmons* [1927] A.C. 487; cf. *Newborne v Sensolid (Great Britain) Ltd* [1954] 1 Q.B. 45.
[409] [2003] UKHL 62, [2004] 1 A.C. 919 at [48].
[410] e.g. in *Lewis v Averay* [1972] 1 Q.B. 198, 215 Megaw L.J. decided the case on the ground that the mistake was merely as to attributes. See also *Whittaker v Campbell* [1984] Q.B. 318, 324. A mistake as to whether a person is contracting as agent for another or as principal may be relevant, as in *Hardman v Booth* (1863) 1 H. & C. 803; but not a mistake as to the identity of a mere messenger: *Midland Bank Plc v Brown Shipley & Co Ltd* [1991] 1 Lloyd's Rep. 576.
[411] *Midland Bank Plc* [1991] 1 Lloyd's Rep. 576.
[412] See *Shogun Finance Ltd v Hudson* [2003] UKHL 62, [2004] 1 A.C. 919 at [5].
[413] See Treitel, *Law of Contract*, 12th edn (by Peel, 2007), para.8–037.

(Star Car Sales Ltd, Claimant)[414] Hardie Boys J. in the Supreme Court of New Zealand held that a third party could not raise "in the name of one of the contracting parties" the question of mistake as to the person; but his view did not form part of the reasoning of the decision on appeal.[415] At first sight it might seem that a third party should be allowed to rely on the invalidity of the transaction for the contract is not voidable at the parties' option but void ab initio. But in practice some strange consequences would follow from permitting such intervention. If the buyer in *Boulton v Jones*[416] had waived his objections to the identity of the seller and paid for the goods could it really be contended by a third party that the property did not thereby pass to the buyer?

5–099 **A believes B is not B.** Suppose that A makes an offer to B merely in the belief that B is not B? The offer has been made to B even though A would never have made it had he known B's true identity. B can therefore accept the offer whether or not he knows of the mistake. The contract may be voidable for fraud, but it is not a nullity from the beginning.[417] It is only if a term can be implied into the contract that B is not B, and it is proved that this was known to the other party, that the contract will be void ab initio.[418] In such a case there is a mistake as to the terms of the contract known to the other party, and, as we have seen,[419] this may invalidate the agreement.

5–100 **Proposal for reform.** In its Twelfth Report,[420] the Law Reform Committee recommended that, in the case of mistake as to the person, the distinction between void and voidable contracts should be abrogated so far as the acquisition of title by innocent parties is concerned. However, the Report was never implemented.

4. NON EST FACTUM

5–101 **Definition.** This category of mistake is derived from a small group of cases most of them of modern times, although the doctrine existed at least as early as 1584.[421] The general rule is that a person is estopped by his or her deed, and although there is no such estoppel in the case of ordinary signed documents, a party of full age and understanding is normally bound by his signature to a

---

[414] [1959] N.Z.L.R. 952.

[415] sub nom. *Fawcett v Star Car Sales* [1960] N.Z.L.R. 406. The majority of the court make no reference to this point, and Gresson P. (dissenting) expressly rejects it.

[416] (1857) 2 H. & N. 564, above, para.5–090.

[417] *Ingram v Little* [1961] 1 Q.B. 31, 54; Goodhart (1941) 57 L.Q.R. 228; Unger (1955) 18 M.L.R. 259. See also *Dyster v Randall & Sons* [1926] Ch. 932. Contrast *Gordon v Street* [1899] 2 Q.B. 641; *Sowler v Potter* [1940] 1 K.B. 271, which may perhaps now be taken to have been overruled, see *Solle v Butcher* [1950] 1 K.B. 671, 691; *Gallie v Lee* [1969] 2 Ch. 17, 33, 41, 45, affirmed sub nom. *Saunders v Anglia Building Society* [1971] A.C. 1004; *Lewis v Averay* [1972] 1 Q.B. 198, 206; and Wilson (1954) 17 M.L.R. 515.

[418] *Said v Butt* [1920] 3 K.B. 497 (a case of agency); see Vol.II, para.31–068.

[419] See above, para.5–080.

[420] Cmnd.2958 (1966), para.15.

[421] *Thoroughgood's Case* (1584) 2 Co.Rep. 9a. The doctrine was probably much older than that case: see Holdsworth, *History of English Law*, Vol.8, p.50.

document, whether he reads or understands it or not. If, however, a party has been misled into executing a deed or signing a document essentially different from that which he intended to execute or sign, he can plead non est factum in an action against him. The deed or writing is completely void in whosesoever hands it may come. In most of the cases in which non est factum has been successfully pleaded, the mistake has been induced by fraud. But the presence of fraud is probably not a necessary factor. As Byles J. said in *Foster v Mackinnon*[422]:

> "... it is invalid not merely on the ground of fraud, where fraud exists, but on the ground that the mind of the signor did not accompany the signature; in other words, that he never intended to sign, and therefore in contemplation of law never did sign, the contract to which his name is appended."

Importance of doctrine. The defence of non est factum is most obviously important in two situations. The first is where a party has signed the supposed contract as the result of the fraud of a third party and the other party to it has no actual knowledge or reason to know of, the fraud.[423] For example, in *United Dominions Trust Ltd v Western*[424] the defendant signed a blank hire-purchase proposal form and the dealer filled in incorrect figures before dispatching it to the finance company. The second is where the fraud has been committed by the other party to the alleged contract or deed and a third party has then relied on the document. In *Saunders v Anglia Building Society*[425] an elderly lady signed what she believed to be a deed of gift to her house to her nephew but which was in fact an assignment on sale to a third party who mortgaged the house to the defendants and kept the proceeds. If the case is one of fraud or misrepresentation by the other party to the contract, with no third party involved, the majority in the Court of Appeal in *Lloyds Bank Plc v Waterhouse*[426] said that the case should be dealt with as one of misrepresentation. Alternatively, where the other party knew that the document did not represent the intention of the party signing it, the latter may have a remedy for unilateral mistake.[427] 5–102

Nature of mistake necessary to invalidate transaction. The plea of non est factum was formerly held to be available only if the mistake was as to the very nature of the transaction. In *Foster v Mackinnon*[428] the defendant was induced to 5–103

---

422 (1869) L.R. 4 C.P. 704, 711. See also *Bank of Ireland v M'Manamy* [1916] 2 I.R. 161. cf. *Hasham v Zenab* [1960] A.C. 316; *Mercantile Credit Co Ltd v Hamblin* [1965] 2 Q.B. 242, 268, 280 (misrepresentation).

423 On notice of fraud or misrepresentation by a third party, see below, paras 6–021—6–027.

424 [1976] Q.B. 513.

425 [1971] A.C. 1004.

426 (1991) 10 Tr.L.R. 161.

427 See the judgment of Sir Edward Eveleigh in *Lloyds Bank Plc v Waterhouse* (1991) 10 Tr.L.R. 161. Although a contract entered under an operative mistake is often said to be void, above, para.5–080, it appears that this cannot be raised by the mistaken party against a third party who in good faith and without notice of the mistake has relied on the signed document. The signer is estopped and can only succeed against the third party if he can show non est factum: Contrast the "mistaken identity" cases, above, para.5–088, where the mistaken party is not estopped simply by entrusting possession of his property to the rogue who sells it to the third party.

428 (1869) L.R. 4 C.P. 704; cf. *National Provincial Bank of England v Jackson* (1886) 33 Ch D 1; *Carlisle and Cumberland Banking Co v Bragg* [1911] 1 K.B. 489; *Muskham Finance Ltd v Howard* [1963] 1 Q.B. 904. See also *Bagot v Chapman* [1907] 2 Ch. 222.

indorse a bill of exchange on the false representation that it was a guarantee similar to one he had signed on a previous occasion. He was held not liable when sued by an innocent indorsee of the bill. In *Lewis v Clay*[429] the result was the same. The defendant was induced by a friend of long standing to sign a document, which was covered by a paper with four openings in it, under the representation that he was witnessing it. The defendant had in fact signed two promissory notes and two letters authorising the plaintiff to pay the proceeds of the notes to the friend. The defendant was held not liable because his mind never went with the transaction. On the other hand, mistake as to the contents of a deed or document was held not sufficient. An extreme case was that of *Howatson v Webb*,[430] where the defendant was fraudulently induced by one Hooper to execute a mortgage relating to certain property. The defendant executed the mortgage without reading the deed; he knew that it disposed in some way of the land in question, but was induced to believe that it was a conveyance rather than a mortgage. The plaintiff became transferee of the mortgage in good faith and sued the defendant on a covenant therein to repay £1,000. The defendant's plea of non est factum did not succeed as the deed in question was not of a wholly different class and character from that which the defendant believed it to be. It purported to be a transfer of property, and the defendant was merely mistaken as to its contents.

5–104 **Distinction between nature and contents of document rejected.** The law on this subject was completely reviewed and restated by the House of Lords in *Saunders v Anglia Building Society*[431] and the distinction between the character and nature of a document and the contents of the document was rejected as unsatisfactory. It was stressed that the defence of non est factum was not lightly to be allowed where a person of full age and capacity had signed a written document embodying contractual terms. But it was nevertheless held that in exceptional circumstances the plea was available so long as the person signing the document had made a fundamental mistake as to the character or effect of the document. Their Lordships appear to have concentrated on the disparity between the effect of the document actually signed, and the document as it was believed to be (rather than on the nature of the mistake) stressing that the disparity must be "radical", "essential", "fundamental", or "very substantial".[432]

5–105 **Documents signed in blank.** The plea of non est factum is likewise potentially applicable where one person signs a document in blank and hands it to another, leaving him to fill in the details and complete the transaction.[433] However, where erroneous details are inserted which are not in accord with the

[429] (1898) 67 L.J.Q.B. 224.

[430] [1907] 1 Ch. 537, affirmed [1908] 1 Ch. 1; cf. *Mercantile Credit Co Ltd v Hamblin* [1965] 2 Q.B. 242.

[431] [1971] A.C. 1004; see Stone (1972) 88 L.Q.R. 190.

[432] [1971] A.C. 1004, at 1017, 1022, 1026. In *Lloyds Bank Plc v Waterhouse* (1991) 10 Tr.L.R. 161 it was held that an "all monies" guarantee was fundamentally different to one of liability under a particular transaction for the purchase of land. cf. *Hambros Bank Ltd v British Historic Buildings Trust and Din* [1995] N.P.C. 179.

[433] *United Dominions Trust v Western* [1976] Q.B. 513. cf. *Mercantile Credit Co Ltd v Hamblin* [1965] 2 Q.B. 242 at [279]–[280].

instructions of the person executing the document, he may yet be liable if the transaction which the document purports to effect is not essentially different in substance or in kind from the transaction intended.[434] Moreover, the onus is on the person signing the document to show that he has acted carefully,[435] and if he fails to discharge that onus he will be bound.[436]

Negligence. A person who signs a document may not be permitted to raise the defence of non est factum where he has been guilty of negligence in appending his signature. It was formerly held in a number of cases, of which the leading one was *Carlisle and Cumberland Banking Co v Bragg*[437] that negligence was only material where the document actually signed was a negotiable instrument, for there was not otherwise any duty of care owed by the person executing the document to an innocent third party who acted in reliance on it. But these cases were much criticised, both by the courts[438] and by writers,[439] and they were eventually reconsidered by the House of Lords in *Saunders v Anglia Building Society*, above. *Bragg's* case was overruled, and it was held that no matter what class of document was in question, negligence or carelessness on the part of the person signing the document would exclude the defence of non est factum. This does not depend on the principle of estoppel but on the principle that no man can take advantage of his own wrong.[440] 5–106

5. RECTIFICATION OF WRITTEN AGREEMENTS

Rectification of document to match contract. Rectification only applies to contracts which have been reduced to writing. It is a process by which the document is made to conform to what was actually agreed between the parties. 5–107

> "... the remedy of rectification is one permitted by the Court, not for the purpose of altering the terms of an agreement entered into between two or more parties, but for that

[434] *United Dominions Trust Ltd v Western* [1976] Q.B. 513 disapproving *Campbell Discount Ltd v Gall* [1961] 1 Q.B. 431; see also Bills of Exchange Act 1882 s.20. cf. *Unity Finance Ltd v Hammond* (1965) 109 S.J. 70.

[435] See below, para.5–091 (same principles applicable).

[436] See also *British Ry Traffic and Electric Co Ltd v Roper* (1939) 162 L.T. 217; *Eastern Distributors Ltd v Goldring* [1957] 2 Q.B. 600.

[437] [1911] 1 K.B. 489; *Campbell Discount Co Ltd v Gall* [1961] 1 Q.B. 431, *Wilson and Meeson v Pickering* [1946] K.B. 422, 425.

[438] *Muskham Finance Ltd v Howard* [1963] 1 Q.B. 904, 913; *Mercantile Credit Co Ltd v Hamblin* [1965] 2 Q.B. 242 at [278].

[439] Anson (1912) 28 L.Q.R. 190; Guest (1963) 79 L.Q.R. 346.

[440] [1971] A.C. 1004, at 1019, 1038. In the Australian case of *Petelin v Cullen* (1975) 132 C.L.R. 355 the High Court held that where no innocent third party is involved the question of negligence is not relevant. But in England it has been held that such a case should be dealt with as one of misrepresentation or unilateral mistake, not as non est factum, above, para.5–087. Negligence was one ground for failure of the plea in *Hambros Bank Ltd v British Historic Buildings Trust and Din* [1995] N.P.C. 179.

of correcting a written instrument which, by a mistake in verbal expression, does not accurately reflect their true agreement."[441]

Most of the cases involve what has been agreed by the parties having been wrongly recorded in the document without either party being aware of the mistake. These cases involve what may be termed rectification to correct a common mistake. Rectification may also be available when one party signed a written document which did not record his intentions correctly, and the other party knew of the first party's intentions. In this case the court may rectify the document so that it reflects the first party's intentions. This may be termed a case of rectification to correct a unilateral mistake. There are some general principles which apply in both situations.

(a) *Common mistake*

5–108 **Common mistake.** It has long been an established rule of equity that where a contract has by reason of a mistake common[442] to the contracting parties been drawn up so as to militate against the terms intended by both as revealed in their previous oral understanding, the court will rectify the document so as to carry out such intentions.[443] Rectification will not be ordered if a written agreement fails to mention a matter because the parties simply overlooked it, having no intention on the point at all,[444–446] nor if they decided deliberately to omit the issue. In such cases the written agreement must be construed as it stands.

5–109 **Mistake in recording of terms or as to legal effect.** Rectification may be ordered where the document did not record correctly what the parties had agreed, or where the legal effect of the words used was not what the parties had agreed on: for example, if the document states that £*x* is to be paid "free of tax" when what was meant was that the payment would be of such sum that after deduction of tax would amount to £*x*.[447]

5–110 **Issue may be solved by construction.** Reference is made elsewhere to a series of cases in which the courts of common law have corrected clerical errors[448]; and also to cases in which parol evidence has been admitted to explain latent ambiguities.[449] Where a mistake is obvious, for example because the literal

---

[441] *Agip SpA v Navigazione Alta Italia SpA (The Nai Genova and the Nai Superba)* [1984] 1 Lloyd's Rep. 353, 359.

[442] *Murray v Parker* (1854) 19 Beav. 305.

[443] *Burroughs v Abbott* [1922] 1 Ch. 86; *Constantinidi v Ralli* [1935] Ch. 427; *Jervis v Howle and Talke Colliery Co Ltd* [1937] Ch. 67. As regards past transactions, the court may give effect to a "defence" of rectification without actually ordering rectification: *The Nile Rhapsody* [1992] 2 Lloyd's Rep. 399, 408. A claimant may also invoke rectification on the same basis; [1992] 2 Lloyd's Rep. 399, 409.

[444–446] *Harlow Development Corp v Kingsgate (Clothing Productions)* (1973) 226 E.G. 1960; *Olympia Sauna Shipping Co SA v Shinwa Kaiun Kaisha Ltd (The Ypatia Halcoussi)* [1985] 2 Lloyd's Rep. 364.

[447] See *Burroughs v Abbott* [1922] 1 Ch. 86; *Jervis v Howle and Talke Colliery Co Ltd* [1937] Ch. 67.

[448] See below, paras 12–072—12–080.

[449] See below, paras 12–117—12–126.

meaning of the words would be absurd,[450] and it is clear what is meant, rectification is not necessary; the matter will be dealt with as one of construction. As Brightman L.J. said in *East v Pantiles Plant Hire Ltd*[451]:

> "It is clear on the authorities that a mistake in a written instrument can, in limited circumstances, be corrected as a matter of construction without obtaining a decree in an action for rectification. Two conditions must be satisfied: first, there must be a clear mistake on the face of the instrument; secondly, it must be clear what correction ought to be made in order to cure the mistake. If those conditions are satisfied, then the correction is made as a matter of construction. If they are not satisfied, then either the Claimant must pursue an action for rectification or he must leave it to a court of construction to reach what answer it can on the basis that the uncorrected wording represents the manner in which the parties decided to express their intention."

Live issue required. Rectification will only be ordered so long as there is an issue between the parties as to their legal rights inter se. If there is no such issue or if no substantive relief is sought and no practical purpose will be achieved rectification may be refused.[452] 5–111

Parol evidence. Where it is sought to construe a document, parol evidence may not be admissible to add to or vary the terms of the written agreement.[453] But where it is sought to rectify a document, this rule does not apply.[454] In *Murray v Parker*[455] Lord Romilly, M.R. said: 5–112

> "In matters of mistake the court undoubtedly has jurisdiction, and though this jurisdiction is to be exercised with great caution and care, still it is to be exercised, in all cases, where a deed, as executed, is not according to the real agreement between the parties. In all cases the real agreement must be established by evidence, whether parol or written . . . If there be a previous agreement in writing which is unambiguous, the deed will be reformed accordingly: if ambiguous, parol evidence may be used to explain it, in the same manner as in other cases where parol evidence is admitted to explain ambiguities in a written instrument."

Even where the contract is one which is required to be in writing under s.2(1) of the Law of Property (Miscellaneous Provisions) Act 1989[456] or under s.4 of the

---

[450] See para.12–055.

[451] [1982] 2 E.G.L.R. 111, 112, quoted in *Dalkia Utilities Services Plc v Celtech International Ltd* [2006] EWHC 63, [2006] 1 Lloyd's Rep. 599, at [109].

[452] *Whiteside v Whiteside* [1950] Ch. 65; cf. *Re Colebrook's Conveyances* [1972] 1 W.L.R. 1397; *Etablissements Georges et Paul Levy v Adderley Navigation Co SA* [1980] 2 Lloyd's Rep. 67. Provided that there is an issue capable of being contested by the parties it is no bar to rectification that both sides wish the document to be rectified so as to reduce one party's tax liability: *Lake v Lake* [1989] S.T.C. 895; *Racal v Ashmore* [1995] S.T.C. 1151.

[453] See below, paras 12–095 et seq.

[454] *Lovell and Christmas Ltd v Wall* (1911) 104 L.T. 85. In *J.J. Huber (Investments) Ltd v Private DIY Co Ltd* [1995] N.P.C. 102, Ch D it was held that the presence on an "entire agreement" clause in the contract does not prevent rectification.

[455] (1854) 19 Beav. 305, 308.

[456] See above, paras 4–052 et seq.

Statute of Frauds 1677[457] parol evidence is admissible, for the jurisdiction of the court to rectify is outside the prohibition of the statute.[458]

5–113 **Concluded agreement.** It was formerly thought that a plaintiff must show that there was an antecedent concluded contract, which was inaccurately represented by the instrument purporting to be made in pursuance of it:

> "Courts of equity do not rectify contracts; they may and do rectify instruments purporting to have been made in pursuance of the terms of contracts."[459]

Where, therefore, a builder entered into a contract with an urban authority, the contract being sealed in accordance with s.174 of the Public Health Act 1875, it was held that it could not subsequently be rectified, for until the seal was affixed to the formal contract (i.e. the instrument sought to be rectified) there was no contract at all between the parties, and also because the effect of rectification, if allowed, would have been to bind the corporation to a contract which required a seal for its validity but which they had never sealed.[460] But although there was a strong body of judicial opinion in favour of this view,[461] Clauson J. in *Shipley UDC v Bradford Corp*[462] refused to accept that:

> "... the jurisdiction of the court cannot be exercised even in cases of clear mutual mistakes in the attempt to embody in the instrument the concurrent intentions of the parties existing at the moment of the execution of the instrument unless a previously existing contract can be proved."

This view was confirmed by a unanimous Court of Appeal in *Joscelyne v Nissen*.[463] The parties had negotiated an agreement but no concluded contract was made until execution of a formal legal document. It was held that the court had power to rectify the agreement so long as there was a continuing common intention in regard to a particular provision down to the execution of the written contract.

5–114 **Outward expression of accord.** Although it is unnecessary to show that there was a binding agreement prior to the execution of the written document, in *Joscelyne v Nissen* it was said that there must have been an "outward expression of accord".[464] The Court of Appeal cited with approval its previous decision,

---

[457] See Vol.II, Ch.44 (contracts of suretyship).

[458] *Cowen v Truefitt Ltd* [1899] 2 Ch. 309; *Johnson v Bragge* [1901] 1 Ch. 28; *Thompson v Hickman* [1907] 1 Ch. 550; *Craddock Bros v Hunt* [1923] Ch. 136; *USA v Motor Trucks Ltd* [1924] A.C. 196. cf. para.4–070.

[459] *Mackenzie v Coulson* (1869) L.R. 8 Eq. 368, 375.

[460] *W. Higgins Ltd v Northampton Cpn* [1927] 1 Ch. 128.

[461] *Mackenzie v Coulson* (1869) L.R. 8 Eq. 368; *Faraday v Tamworth Union* (1916) 86 L.J.Ch. 436, 438; *W. Higgins Ltd v Northampton Corp* [1927] 1 Ch. 128, 136; *USA v Motor Trucks Ltd* [1924] A.C. 196, 200; *Lovell Christmas Ltd v Wall* (1911) 104 L.T. 85.

[462] [1936] Ch. 375. See also *Frederick E. Rose (London) Ltd v William H. Pim Jnr. & Co Ltd* [1953] 2 Q.B. 450, 461; *Crane v Hegemann-Harris Co Inc* [1939] 1 All E.R. 662, affirmed [1939] 4 All E.R. 68, [1971] 1 W.L.R. 1390n.; *Monaghan CC v Vaughan* [1948] Ir.R. 306; *Carlton Contractors v Bexley Corp* (1962) 106 S.J. 391; *Kent v Hartley* (1966) 200 E.G. 1027.

[463] [1970] 2 Q.B. 86.

[464] [1970] 2 Q.B. 86, 98. Use of this phrase is criticised by Bromley in (1971) 87 L.Q.R. 532.

Lovell and Christmas Ltd v Wall[465] and, in particular, the following passage from the judgment of Buckley L.J.:

> "In ordering rectification the court does not rectify contracts, but what it rectifies is the erroneous expression of contracts in documents. For rectification it is not enough to set about to find out what one or even both of the parties to the contract intended. What you have got to find out is what intention was communicated by one side to the other, and with what common intention and common agreement they made their bargain."

It is not necessary, however, that the parties had formulated their intention into words at the time provided they had a common intention as to the substance, but there must have been some outward agreement.[466] Recently it has been said that the requirement of an "outward expression of accord" is not an absolute one, but one of evidence that the parties shared a common intention even if they had not put it into words. The requirement of outward accord was first relaxed in a series of cases involving pension schemes[467] but in *Munt v Beasley*, which involved rectification of a lease, Mummery L.J., with whom the other members of the court agreed, said:

> "I would also accept . . . that the recorder was wrong to treat 'an outward expression of accord' as a strict legal requirement for rectification in a case such as this, where the party resisting rectification has in fact admitted . . . that his true state of belief when he entered into the transaction was the same as that of the other party and there was therefore a continuing common intention which, by mistake, was not given effect in the relevant legal document. I agree with the trend in recent cases to treat the expression 'outward expression of accord' more as an evidential factor rather than a strict legal requirement in all cases of rectification."[468]

It is submitted that the "recent trend" does not mean that rectification can be based on intentions that were never expressed to the other party in any form, even if the unexpressed intentions of each party happened to coincide.[469] Rectification is to make the document conform to the agreement and in English law some outward manifestation is required for there to be an agreement. However, it might cover understandings that the parties thought so obvious as to go without saying, or that were reached without being spelled out in so many words.[470]

---

[465] (1911) 104 L.T. 85.

[466] *Grand Metropolitan Plc v William Hill Group Ltd* [1997] 1 B.C.L.C. 390. In *Mangistaumunaigaz Oil Production Association v United World Trading Inc* [1995] 1 Lloyd's Rep. 617 no prior agreement was shown and rectification was refused. In *Mace v Rutland House Textiles Ltd (In Administrative Receivership), The Times*, January 11, 2000 rectification was permitted when the text of the agreement had been prepared by a person instructed by both parties and did not represent their common intention although that had not been expressed in a settled form of words.

[467] In particular *AMP v Barker* [2001] P.L.R. 77 and *Gallaher v Gallaher Pensions Ltd* [2005] EWHC 42 (Ch), [2005] All E.R. (D) 177 (Jan).

[468] [2006] EWCA Civ 370, [2006] All E.R. (D) 29 (Apr), at [36].

[469] cf. Smith (2007) 123 L.Q.R. 116.

[470] Carnwath L.J. in *JIS (1974) Ltd v MCP Investment Nominees Ltd* [2003] EWCA Civ 721 at [33]–[34]; see also *Cambridge Antibody Technology v Abbott Biotechnology Ltd* [2004] EWHC 2974 (Pat), [2005] F.S.R. 27 at [105]–[112].

(b) *Unilateral mistake*

5–115 **Unilateral mistake.** Where the mistake is unilateral, that is of one party only, it was formerly thought that rectification would not be granted unless a case of fraud or misrepresentation,[471] or unfair dealing,[472] or perhaps sharp practice, could be shown. In *Roberts & Co Ltd v Leicestershire CC*[473] it was said that the doctrine might be based on either fraud or estoppel, when:

> "... it is not an essential ingredient of the right of action to establish any particular degree of obliquity to be attributed to the defendants in such circumstances."[474]

But in *Thomas Bates Son v Wyndhams Ltd* the Court of Appeal rejected these limits on the availability of the remedy of rectification.[475] Where one party is mistaken as to the incorporation of the agreement in the document, and the other knows of the mistake, and does not draw it to the attention of the first party, it suffices that it would be inequitable to allow the second party to insist on the binding force of the document either because this would benefit him or because it would be detrimental to the mistaken party.[476] Buckley L.J. said:

> "For this doctrine—that is to say the doctrine of *A. Roberts & Co. Ltd. v. Leicestershire County Council*—to apply I think it must be shown: first, that one party A erroneously believed that the document sought to be rectified contained a particular term or provision, or possibly did not contain a particular term or provision which, mistakenly, it did contain; secondly, that the other party B was aware of the omission or the inclusion and that it was due to a mistake on the part of A; thirdly, that B has omitted to draw the mistake to the notice of A. And I think there must be a fourth element involved, namely, that the mistake must be one calculated to benefit B. If these requirements are satisfied, the court may regard it as inequitable to allow B to resist rectification to give effect to A's intention on the ground that the mistake was not, at the time of execution of the document, a mutual mistake."[477]

There are at least two issues which require discussion: the degree of knowledge required and the "fourth element", which may be put as whether in addition to knowing of the mistake the defendant must be guilty of some inequity.

5–116 **Knowledge of the mistake**. Even though sharp practice may not be required, unilateral mistake is not by itself a ground for rescinding or rectifying a contract

---

[471] *Wood v Scarth* (1855) 2 K. & J. 33, 41; *May v Platt* [1900] 1 Ch. 616.

[472] *McCausland v Young* [1949] N.I. 49.

[473] *Roberts & Co Ltd v Leicestershire CC* [1961] Ch. 555.

[474] Pennycuick J. at 570.

[475] *Thomas Bates & Son v Wyndhams Ltd* [1981] 1 W.L.R. 505.

[476] Differing views were expressed by the members of the Court of Appeal in *Thomas Bates & Son v Wyndhams Ltd* [1981] 1 W.L.R. 505 on this fourth element. See below, para.5–118.

[477] [1981] 1 W.L.R. 505, 516. In unilateral mistake cases, it may be said that rectification can be granted without there having been an antecedent agreement between the parties: *Littman v Aspen Oil (Broking) Ltd* [2005] EWCA Civ 1579; but as Jacobs L.J noted at [24], a party who accepts a clause knowing full well what the other party (mistakenly) thinks it means or says is in effect agreeing to the other party's version.

unless the other party knew of the mistake.[478] It appears that the knowledge must be actual knowledge.[479] It is not enough that the party against whom rectification is sought may have suspected that a mistake had been made[480]; but if a party wilfully shuts its eyes to the obvious, or wilfully and recklessly fails to make such inquiries as an honest and reasonable man would make, that will count as actual knowledge.[481] The nature of the knowledge that A must be shown to have of B's mistake if rectification is to be granted was discussed in detail by the Court of Appeal in *George Wimpey UK Ltd v VI Construction Ltd*.[482] Using the analysis of the various forms of knowledge made by Peter Gibson J. in *Baden v Société Générale pour Favoriser le Développement du Commerce et de l'Industrie en France SA*,[483] it must be: (i) actual knowledge; (ii) wilfully shutting one's eyes to the obvious; or (iii) wilfully and recklessly failing to make such inquiries as an honest and reasonable man would make. In *Agip (Africa) Ltd v Jackson*[484] Millett J. said that the true distinction is between honesty and dishonesty. In cases within (i)–(iii) A would not be acting honestly. The implication is that the same would not be true if A had merely (again using the categories of Peter Gibson J.); (iv) knowledge of circumstances which would indicate the facts to an honest and reasonable man; or (v) knowledge of circumstances which would put an honest and reasonable man on inquiry:

> "The remedy of rectification for unilateral mistake is a drastic remedy, for it has the result of imposing on the defendant to the claim a contract which he did not, and did not intend to, make. Accordingly the conditions for the grant of such relief must be strictly satisfied."[485]

However, what amounts to sharp practice may depend on the comparative competence and resources of the parties.[485a]

Conduct contributing to the mistake. It seems that rectification will be 5–117
granted even if the defendant did not have positive knowledge of the claimant's

---

[478] *Riverlate Properties Ltd v Paul* [1975] Ch. 133, below, para.5–120; *Kemp v Neptune Concrete* (1989) 57 P. & C.R. 369. In the latter case Purchas L.J. (at 377) said that it must have been unconscionable for the non-mistaken party to execute the deed or to stand by while the other does so; but it seems that the requirement of unconscionability will be satisfied if the non-mistaken party seeks to take advantage of the other's mistake: *Templiss Properties Ltd v Hyams* [1999] E.G.C.S. 60.

[479] *Agip SpA v Navigazione Alta Italia SpA (The Nai Genova and the Nai Superba)* [1984] 1 Lloyd's Rep. 353; *Commission for New Towns v Cooper (Great Britain)* [1995] Ch. 259. cf. above, para.5–076.

[480] *Olympia Sauna Shipping Co SA v Shinwa Kaiun Kaisha Ltd (The Ypatia Halcoussi)* [1985] 2 Lloyd's Rep. 364, 371.

[481] cf. *Commission for New Towns v Cooper (Great Britain) Ltd* [1995] Ch. 259, applying the analysis of various forms of knowledge made by Peter Gibson J. in *Baden v Société Générale pour Favouriser le Développement du Commerce et de l'Industrie en France SA* [1993] 1 W.L.R. 509 and adopted by Millett J. in *Agip (Africa) Ltd v Jackson* [1990] Ch. 265, see further, Vol.II, paras 34–297 et seq.

[482] [2005] EWCA Civ 77, [2005] B.L.R. 135.

[483] [1993] 1 W.L.R. 509.

[484] [1990] Ch. 265 at 293.

[485] See the judgment of Sedley L.J. in the *George Wimpey* case, [2005] EWCA Civ 77 at [65]).

[485a] *Rowallan Group Ltd v Edgehill Portfolio No.1 Ltd* [2007] EWHC (Ch) 32, [2007] All E.R. (D) 106 (Jan), at [14].

mistake if the defendant deliberately sought to prevent the claimant from discovering that what was written in the document did not accord with his intentions. Although it has been suggested that it is not sufficient that the defendant contributed to the mistake unless he did so knowingly,[486] if a party puts forward a draft document in such a way that he makes a representation that it is in accordance with an earlier accord of the parties, and the other party foreseeably relies on this, an estoppel may arise.[487] Further, in *Commission for New Towns v Cooper* Stuart Smith L.J. said:

> "... were it necessary to do so in this case, I would hold that where A intends B to be mistaken as to the construction of the agreement, so conducts himself that he diverts B's attention from discovering the mistake by making false and misleading statements, and B in fact makes the very mistake that A intends, then notwithstanding that A does not actually know, but merely suspects, that B is mistaken, and it cannot be shown that the mistake was induced by any misrepresentation, rectification may be granted. A's conduct is unconscionable and he cannot insist on performance in accordance to the strict letter of the contract; that is sufficient."[488]

This type of conduct would clearly not be honest. In the Australian case of *Taylor v Johnson*[489] the High Court had held that this sort of unconscionable conduct on A's part would suffice for the contract to be rescinded on the ground of mistake.[490] The same principle does not necessarily apply to cases of rectification, since the court is not simply undoing the bargain but also imposing a different bargain on A. However, it is not unjust to insist that the contract be performed according to B's understanding where that was the very meaning that A intended B to put on it, and rectification may be granted.[491] If it is reasonable to expect the other party to check the draft, there will be no relief.[492] In cases of pure unilateral mistake unknown to the other party the remedy (if any, and there will often be none), is refusal of an order of specific performance[493] but not, it appears, rescission.[494]

5–118 **Inequity.** In *Riverlate Properties Ltd v Paul*[495] it was suggested that in a case of unilateral mistake the defendant must not only have known of the mistake but be guilty of sharp practice. In *Thomas Bates Son v Wyndhams Ltd* Buckley L.J. rejected this,[496] saying:

---

486 *Agip SpA v Navigazione Alta Italia SpA (The Nai Genova and the Nai Superba)* [1983] 2 Lloyd's Rep. 333, 344. The point was not discussed directly on appeal but appears to be consistent with the Court of Appeal's insistence on actual knowledge: [1984] 1 Lloyd's Rep. 353.

487 [1984] 1 Lloyd's Rep. 353, 365.

488 [1995] Ch. 259 at 280.

489 (1983) 151 C.L.R. 422, 45 A.L.R. 265; see above, para.5–074, fn.318.

490 See above, para.5–078.

491 *Commission for New Towns v Cooper (Great Britain) Ltd* [1995] 2 Ch. 259.

492 *Taylor Barnard v Tozer* (1984) 269 E.G. 225.

493 See above, para.5–077.

494 See above, para.5–078. Nor will a document be interpreted in a way one party contends merely because the other party knew or suspected, at the time, that that was what the first party was hoping to achieve: *Zoan v Rouamba* [2000] 2 All E.R. 620, 633.

495 [1955] Ch 133, 140.

496 [1981] 1 W.L.R. 505 at 515; see similarly Brightman L.J. at 522.

"Undoubtedly I think in any such case the conduct of the defendant must be such as to make it inequitable that he should be allowed to object to the rectification of the document. If this necessarily implies some measure of "sharp practice", so be it; but for my part I think that the doctrine is one which depends more upon the equity of the position. The graver the character of the conduct involved, no doubt the heavier the burden of proof may be; but, in my view, the conduct must be such as to affect the conscience of the party who has suppressed the fact that he has recognised the presence of a mistake."

He went on to say that for this requirement[497] to be satisfied, the mistake must be one "calculated to benefit B". In contrast, Eveleigh L.J. said that this was not necessary: it was enough that there would be a detriment to the claimant.[498] It is submitted that either should suffice. In practice, if the claimant's mistake was known to the defendant, or the defendant deliberately induced the mistake in the way described earlier,[499] and the terms of the written document are less favourable to the claimant than those the defendant knew that the claimant actually intended, it will be inequitable for the defendant to insist on the terms stated in the document and the grounds for rectification will be satisfied.[500]

Cancellation with option of rectification. In a small group of cases, however, a middle course between refusing and granting rectification was adopted. 5–119
These cases are *Garrard v Frankel*,[501] *Harris v Pepperell*,[502] *Bloomer v Spittle*[503] and *Paget v Marshall*.[504] The course adopted was to order cancellation with an option to the defendant to accept rectification instead. They are all cases of unilateral mistake. In *Garrard v Frankel*[505] the defendant agreed to take from the plaintiff a lease of a house at the rent of £230, and in the lease drawn up in pursuance of the agreement the rent was stated to be £130. Lord Romilly M.R. considered that the error was the plaintiff's but that the defendant must have perceived it, and held that though the plaintiff was not entitled to have the lease rectified, the lessee ought to be put to his election whether to have the lease rectified or to reject it. In *Harris v Pepperell*[506] the vendor had executed a conveyance including a piece of land he had not intended to sell but which the defendant alleged he had intended to buy. Lord Romilly, following his previous decision in *Garrard v Frankel*, gave the defendant the option "of having the whole contract annulled or else of taking it in the form which the plaintiff intended". In *Bloomer v Spittle*[507] a conveyance of land reserved to the vendor

[497] The "fourth element": see para.5–115 above.
[498] [1981] 1 W.L.R. 505 at 521.
[499] Above, para.5–117.
[500] In *Littman v Aspen Oil (Broking) Ltd* [2005] EWCA Civ 1579 at [23]–[24] Jacobs L.J. said that it would be sufficiently inequitable for one party to take deliberate advantage of a drafting error by the other.
[501] (1862) 30 Beav. 445.
[502] (1867) L.R. 5 Eq. 1.
[503] (1872) L.R. 13 Eq. 427.
[504] (1884) 28 Ch D 255.
[505] Above, fn.501.
[506] Above, fn.502.
[507] Above, fn.503. This decision was said by Neville J. in *Beale v Kyte* [1907] 1 Ch. 564, 565 to be "unintelligible as reported".

the right to minerals. The purchaser alleged that the reservation had been inserted by mistake, but the vendor denied that this was so. The vendor died before he could be cross-examined on this point. In an action by the purchaser for rectification of the conveyance, it was held that this relief could not be granted after a long lapse of time and in the face of the vendor's denial. Nevertheless the personal representatives of the vendor were to choose whether to have the conveyance set aside or rectified. In *Paget v Marshall*[508] the plaintiff by mistake had offered and demised to the defendant four floors of three houses, whereas he had intended to reserve for his own use the first floor of one of the houses. Again the defendant had to elect whether to submit to rectification or have the lease cancelled.

5–120 This group of cases has, however, been critically re-examined by the Court of Appeal. In *Riverlate Properties Ltd v Paul*[509] the court expressed serious doubts about the authority of these cases and was specially critical of *Garrard v Frankel*.[510] Although they did not expressly overrule this case they left little doubt that in their view it was wrongly decided. They emphasised that if the defendant neither knows of, nor contributes to nor shares the mistake, but bona fide assumes that the written document correctly represents the common intention, there is no ground for rescission or rectification. If, on the other hand, the defendant does know of the claimant's mistake, and what his intention was, the claimant is today entitled to rectification, and there is no reason why the defendant should be offered the option of rescission. It seems that the cases referred to in para.5–119 must be explained on the ground that they were decided before it became clear that rectification could be ordered even for a unilateral mistake if known to (or, perhaps, if contributed to) by the defendant.[511]

5–121 **Rescission when known that claimant had made some mistake.** There may be cases in which the claimant has made a mistake, and the defendant is aware of that but does not know what the mistake is. It is submitted that in such a case the contract should not be rectified to accord with what the claimant shows his true intention to have been; that would force the defendant into a contract to which he had never agreed. However in such a case it seems appropriate to allow rescission. This seems to have been recognised by Stuart Smith L.J. in *Commission for New Towns v Cooper*.[512] The passage quoted in para.5–117 above in fact ends: "... that is sufficient for *rescission*". (Emphasis supplied.) If necessary the document should be cancelled.[513]

---

[508] (1884) 28 Ch D 255.

[509] [1975] Ch. 133.

[510] Above, fn.501.

[511] In *Stepps Investments Ltd v Security Capital Corp Ltd* (1976) 73 D.L.R. (3d) 351 the Ontario High Court held that an order for rectification or rescission at the defendant's option could be granted where the defendant did not actually know of the mistake but should have known of it.

[512] [1995] Ch. 259, 280.

[513] On cancellation of documents see *Halsbury's Laws of England*, Vol.16(2) (reissue), para.485.

(c) *General principles*

Proof of mistake. The burden of proof is on the party seeking rectification.[514] He must produce "convincing proof"[515] not only that the document to be rectified was not in accordance with the parties' true intentions at the time of its execution, but also that the document in its proposed form does accord with their intentions.[516] It is essential that the extent of the rectification should be clearly ascertained and defined by evidence contemporaneous with or anterior to the contract.[517] The denial of one of the parties that the deed as it stands is contrary to his intention ought to have considerable weight,[518] and unless the other party can convince the court that the document does not represent both parties' intentions at the time of execution, rectification will only exceptionally be ordered.[519] Indeed, it has been said that it is not sufficient that the written contract does not represent the true intention of the parties; it must be shown that the written contract was actually *contrary* to the intention of the parties.[520] Where it is sought to rectify a document in accordance with a prior agreement between the parties, it must be shown that the intention of the parties continued unaltered up to the time of the execution of the document.[521] 5–122

Literal disparity. There must be a literal disparity between the terms of the prior agreement and those of the document which it is sought to rectify. In *Frederick E. Rose (London) Ltd v William H. Pim Junior & Co Ltd*,[522] Denning L.J. said: 5–123

> "Rectification is concerned with contracts and documents, not with intentions. In order to get rectification it is necessary to show that the parties were in complete agreement on the terms of their contract, but by an error wrote them down wrongly; and in this

514 *Tucker v Bennett* (1887) 38 Ch D 1, 9.

515 This was the expression preferred by the Court of Appeal in *Joscelyne v Nissen* [1970] 2 Q.B. 86. See also *Ernest Scragg & Sons Ltd v Perseverance Banking and Trust Co Ltd* [1973] 2 Lloyd's Rep. 101; *Thomas Bates & Son v Wyndhams Ltd* [1981] 1 W.L.R. 505; compare *Atlantic Maritime Transport Corp v Coscol Petroleum Corp, The Pina* [1991] 1 Lloyd's Rep. 246, 250 ("proof to the criminal standard").

516 *Fowler v Fowler* (1859) 4 De G. & J. 250, 265; *Constantinidi v Ralli* [1935] Ch. 427. But provided that the true agreement is clear, it is sufficient if it is merely doubtful whether the document accurately records this agreement: *Re Walton's Settlement* [1922] 2 Ch. 509.

517 *Earl of Bradford v Earl of Romney* (1862) 30 Beav. 431; *Harris v Pepperell* (1867) L.R. 5 Eq. 1, 4; *Stait v Fenner* [1912] 2 Ch. 504. Where lengthy negotiations have taken place between experienced negotiators, there must be a strong presumption that the parties intended to be bound by precisely the words they used, not some earlier understanding which might be derived from earlier, less carefully drafted documents: *Snamprogetti Ltd v Phillips Petroleum Co UK Ltd* [2001] EWCA Civ 889 at [33].

518 *Fowler v Fowler* (1859) 4 De G. & J. 250, 265; *Wollaston v Tribe* (1869) L.R. 9 Eq. 44; *Cook v Fearn* (1878) 48 L.J. Ch. 63; *Hanley v Pearson* (1879) 13 Ch D 545. cf. *Tucker v Bennett* (1887) 38 Ch D 1; *Bonhote v Henderson* [1895] 1 Ch. 742, affirmed [1895] 2 Ch. 202; *Re Walton's Settlement* [1922] 2 Ch. 509.

519 *W. Higgins Ltd v Northampton Corp* [1927] 1 Ch. 128. See above, para.5–115.

520 *Lloyd v Stanbury* [1971] 1 W.L.R. 535; *Pappadakis v Pappadakis, The Times*, January 19, 2000. It is not enough that there has been confusion between the parties as to what was being agreed: *Cambro Contractors Ltd v John Kennelly Sales Ltd, The Times*, April 14, 1994.

521 *Fowler v Fowler* (1859) 4 De G. & J. 250.

522 [1953] 2 Q.B. 450, 461.

regard, in order to ascertain the terms of the contract, you do not look into the inner minds of the parties—into their intentions—any more than you do in the formation of any other contract."

In this case, the parties entered into an oral agreement for the purchase of horsebeans, in the belief that they were "feveroles," and a subsequent written agreement embodied the same terms. The Court of Appeal refused rectification as both the oral and written contracts were for horse-beans; there was no literal disparity between them. However, in *London Weekend Television v Paris and Griffith*[523] Megaw J. held that, where two persons expressly agree with one another what is the meaning of a particular phrase used in a written contract, the contract can be rectified to make it clear that the phrase bears the meaning agreed.

5–124 **Specific performance.** Before the Judicature Act 1873, it was generally held that the court would not grant rectification of the contract to comply with its proper terms and then grant specific performance of the contract so rectified, at least in the same action.[524] But the Judicature Act 1925, s.43, requires the court to grant to the parties in one action all the relief to which they are entitled, and this has been held to confer upon the court the power to order rectification and specific performance in the same action, even though the mistake has been proved by parol evidence.[525]

5–125 **A discretionary remedy.** As with other equitable remedies, the court has a residual discretion to refuse to grant rectification.[526]

5–126 **Effect of negligence.** The fact that one party's negligence has caused the mistake appears to be irrelevant where rectification is sought on the ground of a mistake common to both parties[527]:

> "If it were, many a claim to rectification for mutual mistake would fail since, ex hypothesi, the instrument as executed has failed accurately to express the parties' common intention and this will very often have been as a result of carelessness for which, in part at least, the claimant for relief must share responsibility."[528]

Equally in cases of unilateral mistake, provided the claimant's mistake was known to the defendant or the defendant had deliberately sought to distract the

[523] (1969) 113 S.J. 222; see also *Re Butlin's Settlement Trusts* [1976] Ch. 251.

[524] *Woollam v Hearn* (1802) 7 Ves. 211; *Martin v Pycroft* (1852) 3 De G.M. & G. 785; cf. *Thomas v Davis* (1757) 1 Dick. 301.

[525] *Olley v Fisher* (1886) 34 Ch D 367; *Craddock Bros v Hunt* [1923] 2 Ch. 136; *USA v Motor Trucks Ltd* [1924] A.C. 196, not following *May v Platt* [1900] 1 Ch. 616. See now Supreme Court Act 1981 s.49.

[526] *KPMG LLP v Network Rail Infrastructure Ltd* [2006] EWHC 67 (Ch), [2006] All E.R. (D) 247 (Jan) at [193] et seq. (party not disentitled by sending a clean copy of a draft rather than one showing the amendments which were proposed, and stating that none of the amendments were of any substance, even when it was known that some were. The other party in fact spotted the changes); rev'd without reference to this point [2007] EWCA Civ 363, [2007] All E.R. (D) 245 (Apr).

[527] *Kent v Hartley* (1966) 200 E.G. 1027; *Weeds v Blaney*, *The Times*, March 18, 1976.

[528] Blackburne J. in *KPMG LLP v Network Rail Infrastructure Ltd* [2006] EWHC 67 (Ch), [2006] All E.R. (D) 247 (Jan) at [195]; rev'd without reference to this point [2007] EWCA Civ 363, [2007] All E.R. (D) 245 (Apr).

claimant from discovering that the document did not reflect what he intended,[529] it seems to be irrelevant that the claimant might have discovered the mistake had he used more care.

Delay. A claimant who has discovered the mistake but delayed in seeking rectification may be denied it. Mere lapse of time is no bar if the mistake is clearly proved,[530] but as Blackburne J. has put it[530a]: 5–127

> "... it is well established that the doctrine does not come into play before the person against whom it is raised as a defence has discovered the material facts, in this case the mistake. It must be shown that the subsequent delay in pursuing the claim renders it 'practically unjust to give a remedy, either because the party has, by his conduct, done that which might fairly be regarded as a waiver of it, or where by his conduct and neglect he has, though perhaps not waiving that remedy, yet put the other party in a situation in which it would not be reasonable to place him if the remedy were otherwise to be asserted'. See Lindsay Petroleum Company v Hurd (1873) 5 App Cas 221 at 239 (per Lord Selborne). As Lord Selborne went on (at 240) to observe:
>
> > 'Two circumstances, always important in such cases, are the length of the delay and the nature of the acts done during the interval, which might affect either party and cause a balance of justice or injustice in taking one course or the other, so far as relates to the remedy.'"

Parties must be restored to former position. Rectification will be refused if the parties cannot be restored to the same position which they occupied prior to the contract sought to be rectified; but this rule will not be applied so strictly as to require an exact restoration where such is difficult or impossible.[531] 5–128

Payment of money under judgment. After money had been paid under a judgment founded on the construction of an agreement, an action to rectify the agreement on the ground that this construction was contrary to the intention of all parties was refused by the Court of Appeal. There was no question of res judicata, but the agreement had been worked out and a fund distributed on that footing.[532] 5–129

Third parties. Rectification may be granted against third parties[533] but a conveyance will not be rectified as against a purchaser for value of a legal or equitable interest claiming under the deed in good faith and without notice of the mistake.[534] It may, however, be granted after the death of one of the parties.[535] 5–130

---

529 See above, para.5–117.

530 *Millar v Craig* (1843) 6 Beav. 433; *Re Garnett* (1885) 31 Ch D 1; cf. *Beale v Kyte* [1907] 1 Ch. 564 (laches).

530a *KPMG LLP v Network Rail Infrastructure Ltd* [2006] EWHC 67 (Ch), [2006] All E.R. (D) 247 (Jan), reversed without reference to this point [2007] EWCA Civ 363, [2007] All E.R. (D) 245 (Apr).

531 *Earl of Beauchamp v Winn* (1873) L.R. 6 H.L. 223.

532 *Caird v Moss* (1886) 33 Ch D 22.

533 *Leuty v Hillas* (1858) 2 De & G. J. 110; *Craddock Bros v Hunt* [1923] 2 Ch. 136.

534 *Bell v Cundall* (1750) Amb. 101; *Smith v Jones* [1954] 1 W.L.R. 1089; *Lyme Valley Squash Club Ltd v Newcastle-under-Lyme BC* [1985] 2 All E.R. 405, 413.

535 *Johnson v Bragge* [1901] 1 Ch. 28.

5–131 **Procedure.** Actions for rectification, setting aside or cancellation of deeds or other written instruments are by s.61 of and Sch.1 to the Supreme Court Act 1981 assigned to the Chancery Division of the High Court, but a counterclaim for rectification or cancellation is not infrequently entertained by the Queen's Bench Division.[536]

5–132 **Jurisdiction of the county court.** By ss.23 and 147(1) of the County Courts Act 1984,[537] a county court may exercise all the powers of the High Court in proceedings for the rectification, delivery up or cancellation of any agreement for the sale, purchase or lease of any property where, in the case of a sale or purchase, the purchase money, or, in the case of a lease, the value of the property, does not exceed £30,000 and also in proceedings for relief against fraud or mistake, where the damage sustained or the estate or fund in respect of which relief is sought does not exceed in amount or value £30,000.[538] The same limit applies to actions for the specific performance of such contracts.[539]

5–133 **Other instances of rectification.** The court has rectified a bill of exchange,[540] a marine insurance policy,[541] a transfer of shares wrongly numbered,[542] a bill of quantities,[543] and bought and sold notes by inserting therein a clause customary in a particular trade,[544] and very frequently conveyances of land.[545]

5–134 **Marriage settlements.** The court has used its jurisdiction in order to rectify marriage settlements.[546] If both the marriage articles and the settlement are executed before the marriage takes place, rectification will not be ordered so as to bring the settlement into line with the articles unless the settlement is expressly or impliedly executed in pursuance of the articles. But if the settlement is made after the marriage, it will be rectified so as to make it correspond with the articles.[547] It also seems that the court will readily admit evidence on behalf of the settlor alone that the settlement does not conform with his intention.[548]

5–135 **Articles of association.** The court has no jurisdiction to rectify the articles of association of a company on the ground that they do not accord with the proved intention of the signatories at the moment of signature. Any power of alteration

---

[536] *Mostyn v West Mostyn Coal & Iron Co Ltd* (1876) 1 C.P.D. 145; *Storey v Waddle* (1879) 4 QBD 289; but see *Leslie v Clifford* (1884) 50 L.T. 690 (partnership accounts transferred to Chancery Division).

[537] See County Courts Jurisdiction Order 1981 (SI 1981/1123).

[538] *R. v Judge Whitethorne* [1904] 1 K.B. 827 and *Angel v Jay* [1911] 1 K.B. 666.

[539] See below, Ch.27; but see also *Bourne v Macdonald* [1950] 2 K.B. 422 and ss.21 and 38 of the Act.

[540] *Druiff v Lord Parker* (1868) L.R. 5 Eq. 131.

[541] *Spalding v Crocker* (1897) 2 Com. Cas. 189.

[542] *Re International Contract Co* (1872) L.R. 7 Ch. App. 485.

[543] *Neill v Midland Ry* (1869) 17 W.R. 871.

[544] *Caraman Rowley & May v Aperghis* (1923) 40 T.L.R. 124.

[545] *Beale v Kyte* [1907] 1 Ch. 564; *Craddock Bros v Hunt* [1923] 2 Ch. 136.

[546] *Johnson v Bragge* [1901] 1 Ch. 28.

[547] *Cogan v Duffield* (1876) 2 Ch D 44.

[548] *Hanley v Pearson* (1879) 13 Ch D 545; cf. *Tucker v Bennett* (1887) 38 Ch D 1.

in this respect is purely statutory and there is no hint in the Companies Act of any power in the court to rectify.[549]

Voluntary settlements. A voluntary deed cannot be rectified except with the consent of the donor,[550] and the court will hesitate to rectify such a deed at the suit of the settlor merely on his own evidence as to his intention unsupported by other evidence such as written instructions.[551] Nevertheless, the unilateral mistake of the settlor will suffice, in certain circumstances, to justify rectification of a settlement.[552] If it is clearly shown that the settlement as executed does not express the true intentions of the settlor, and if the settlement was not executed by trustees or other parties as the result of a contract or bargain, rectification can be ordered. If the trustees object, however, the court may, in its discretion, refuse an order for rectification.[553] **5–136**

549 *Evans v Chapman* (1902) 86 L.T. 381; *Scott v Frank F. Scott (London) Ltd* [1940] Ch. 217, 794.

550 *Phillipson v Kerry* (1863) 32 Beav. 628.

551 *Bonhote v Henderson* [1895] 1 Ch. 742, affirmed [1895] 2 Ch. 202; *Van der Linde v Van der Linde* [1947] Ch. 306, 311.

552 *Re Butlin's Settlement Trusts* [1976] Ch. 251.

553 [1976] Ch. 251.

in this respect is purely statutory and there is no hint in the Companies Act of any power in the court to rectify.[94]

5-136 **Voluntary settlements.** A voluntary deed cannot be rectified except with the consent of the donor,[95] and the court will hesitate to rectify such a deed at the suit of the settlor merely on his own evidence as to his intention unsupported by other evidence such as written instructions.[96] Nevertheless, the unilateral mistake of the settlor will suffice, in certain circumstances, to justify rectification of a settlement.[97] If it is clearly shown that the settlement as executed does not express the true intentions of the settlor, and if the settlement was not executed by trustees or other parties as the result of a contract or bargain, rectification can be ordered. If the trustees object, however, the court may, in its discretion, refuse an order for rectification.

94 [illegible] (1902) 86 L.T. 33; [illegible] Scott [illegible] [1940] Ch. 217 [illegible].

95 Phillipson v Kerry (1863) 32 Beav. 628.

96 [illegible] [1895] 1 Ch. [illegible] affirmed [1895] 2 Ch. 21; [illegible] [1942] Ch. 95, 111.

97 Re [illegible] Settlement Trusts [1970] Ch. [illegible]; [illegible] [1970] Ch. 251 [illegible].

Chapter 6

MISREPRESENTATION[1]

		PARA.
1.	In general	6–001
2.	What constitutes effective misrepresentation	6–006
	(a) False statement of fact	6–006
	(b) Statement by or known to other party	6–021
	(c) Other requirements	6–028
3.	Damages for misrepresentation	6–041
	(a) Fraudulent misrepresentation	6–042
	(b) Negligent misrepresentation	6–067
	(c) Innocent misrepresentation	6–094
4.	Rescission for misrepresentation	6–103
	(a) General	6–103
	(b) *Restitutio in integrum*	6–115
	(c) Other bars to remedy of rescission	6–123
5.	Exclusion of liability for misrepresentation	6–134
6.	Contracts *uberrimae fidei*	6–142
	(a) Insurance	6–144
	(b) Contracts to take shares in companies	6–153
	(c) Family settlements	6–155
	(d) Contracts for the sale of land	6–156
	(e) Contracts of suretyship	6–158
	(f) Partnership agreements	6–162
	(g) General releases	6–164

1. In General

Preliminary. The modern law relating to misrepresentation is a somewhat complex amalgam of rules of common law, equity and (since the coming into force of the Misrepresentation Act 1967)[2] statute law. It is also complicated by the fact that misrepresentation may constitute an actionable tort in certain circumstances, as well as providing grounds for relief in the law of contract. Prior to the enactment of the Misrepresentation Act 1967, the position broadly speaking was that a misrepresentation which induced a person to enter into a contract gave the representee the right to rescind the contract, subject to certain conditions, but generally gave him no right to damages unless the misrepresentation was fraudulent, or, in some cases, negligent, or unless the misrepresentation had contractual force. Since the coming into force of the Misrepresentation Act the **6–001**

[1] See Allen, *Misrepresentation* (1988); Cartwright, *Unequal Bargaining* (1991), Ch.3; Cartwright, *Misrepresentation, Mistake and Non-disclosure* (2007).

[2] The Act was based on the recommendations in the Law Reform Committee's Tenth Report, Cmnd.1782, (1962) but with one important change, as to which see below, para.6–133. For a full appraisal of the Act, see Atiyah and Treitel, "Misrepresentation Act 1967" (1967) 30 M.L.R. 369.

representee will always be able to claim damages for negligent misrepresentation in circumstances in which he could have recovered damages had the misrepresentation been fraudulent. In addition the Act gives the court a discretion to refuse to permit a representee to rescind a contract, but to award him damages in lieu of rescission, if the misrepresentation is negligent or wholly innocent; but it leaves the representee with an absolute right to rescind where the misrepresentation is fraudulent. The Act of 1967 does not, however, alter the rules as to what constitutes an effective misrepresentation. It has been said that the rules on misrepresentation have developed piecemeal, and that some of the rules, which were developed when the remedies for misrepresentation were narrower than they now are, may not now operate well. Given the present state of the law, especially in the light of the decision in *Royscot Trust Ltd v Rogerson*[3] that the rules of fraud attach to liability for "negligent" misrepresentation under Misrepresentation Act 1967 s.2(1), the court should not be too ready to find that a misrepresentation has been made.[4]

6–002 **Prohibitions on misrepresentations in consumer cases.** The Unfair Commercial Practices Directive[5] requires Member States to prohibit, and to provide "adequate and effective" means to combat, unfair commercial practices. These are defined so as to include misleading actions[6] and misleading omissions.[7] However unfair commercial practices within the meaning of the Directive will not give rise to civil remedies for individual consumers, as the Directive is "without prejudice to contract law and, in particular, to the rules of validity, formation or effect of a contract".[8] Accordingly the Regulations passed to implement the Directive prohibit unfair commercial practices, but provide that an agreement shall not be void or unenforceable by reason only of a breach of the Regulations.[9]

6–003 **Criminal fraud.** Fraudulent misrepresentation may also be an offence under the Fraud Act 2006. The definition of fraud for the purposes of the criminal law is different from the civil law definition.[10]

6–004 **Misrepresentation and contractual terms.** Before the Misrepresentation Act was passed, the law relating to misrepresentation was generally concerned solely with misrepresentations made before the contract was entered into, and not to misrepresentations which actually constituted contractual terms. Although the word "misrepresentation" is literally applicable to a contractual term which consists of a false statement of fact (as opposed to a promise of future conduct), the term was commonly confined to misrepresentations which did not constitute

---

[3] [1991] 2 Q.B. 297; see below, para.6–070.

[4] *Avon Insurance v Swire* [2000] 1 All E.R. (Comm) 573, 633, Rix J.

[5] Directive 2005/29 on unfair commercial practices [2005] OJ L149/22. A useful summary of the Directive and its likely impact will be found in Twigg-Flesner (2005) 121 L.Q.R. 386.

[6] Directive 2005/29 art.6.

[7] Directive 2005/29 art.7.

[8] Directive 2005/29 art.3(1).

[9] Consumer Protection from Unfair Trading Regulations 2008 (SI 2008/1277) reg.29; Business Protection from Misleading Marketing Regulations 2008 (SI 2008/1276) reg.29.

[10] See below, para.6–046.

contractual terms, simply because the law relating to contractual terms (whether promises as to future conduct or misrepresentations of fact) differed from the law relating to misrepresentations which were not contractual terms. Moreover, there was also some authority for the proposition that if a misrepresentation was made before a contract was entered into, and the misrepresentation was subsequently incorporated into the contract as a contractual term, the law relating to misrepresentation was not applicable, and the case had to be dealt with as one involving a contractual term and nothing else.[11] Since the passing of the Act of 1967 this is no longer the case, and it will often be necessary in any one situation to inquire carefully as to the effect of a misrepresentation both as a pre-contractual statement, *and* as a contractual term. Where these effects differ (as they often do) it is in some cases a matter of considerable difficulty to determine with any certainty the effect of the Misrepresentation Act on the law relating to contractual misstatement.[12]

Terminology. For many years it was usual to divide misrepresentations into two categories, fraudulent and innocent misrepresentation. The latter category included negligent misrepresentations, for, at least until the decision of the House of Lords in *Hedley Byrne & Co Ltd v Heller and Partners Ltd*[13] it was thought that there was generally no difference between a negligent and a completely innocent misrepresentation. But since that decision, and the passing of the Misrepresentation Act, which also distinguishes in some respects between negligent and completely innocent misrepresentations, it has clearly become necessary to recognise that there are now three categories of misrepresentations. It seems better, therefore, to reserve the term "innocent misrepresentation" for representations which are neither fraudulent nor negligent, though it must be appreciated that there are many cases in which the term has been used to include negligent misrepresentation. 6–005

2. WHAT CONSTITUTES EFFECTIVE MISREPRESENTATION

(a) *False statement of Fact*

Statements of opinion and intention. The traditional rule is that a misrepresentation must be a false statement of fact,[14] past or present, as distinct from a statement of opinion, or of intention or mere commendatory statements. Mere "puffs" do not amount to representations.[15] A mere statement of opinion which proves to have been unfounded, will not be treated as a misrepresentation,[16] nor 6–006

[11] *Pennsylvania Shipping Co v Compagnie Nationale de Navigation* [1936] 2 All E.R. 1167, 1171; *Leaf v International Galleries* [1950] 2 K.B. 86.

[12] Below, paras 6–108 and 6–140.

[13] [1964] A.C. 465.

[14] Traditionally relief was only given for misrepresentations of fact, not of law. But see now below, para.6–013.

[15] *Dimmock v Hallett* (1866) L.R. 7 Ch.App. 21, 27. See also, for an analogous criminal law case, *West Yorkshire Metropolitan CC v MFI Furniture Centre* [1983] 1 W.L.R. 1175; *Chartered Trust v Davies* [1997] 2 E.G.L.R. 83, 86 ("prestigious retail development").

[16] This passage was cited with approval in *Hummingbird Motors Ltd v Hobbs* [1986] R.T.R. 276.

will a simple statement of intention which is not put into effect; for as a general rule these cannot be regarded as representations of fact, except in so far as they show that the opinion or intention is held by the person expressing it.[17] Moreover, statements must be construed as they would reasonably be understood by the recipient in the context in which the statement was made.[18] Thus a statement as to the nature of a policy made to an experienced loss adjuster who had a copy of the policy schedule that described it correctly, and was thought to have a copy of the policy itself, was regarded as "a contention, not as a representation"[19] —in other words, it was merely an expression of opinion.

6–007 **Statement of opinion may amount to statement of fact.** However, in certain circumstances a statement of opinion or of intention may be regarded as a statement of fact, and therefore as a ground for avoiding a contract if the statement is false. Thus, if it can be proved that the person who expressed the opinion did not hold it, or could not, as a reasonable man having his knowledge of the facts, honestly have held it, the statement may be regarded as a statement of fact.[20]

6–008 **Opinion not honestly held.** If a person states as his opinion something which he does not in fact believe, or which given the facts known to him, he could not honestly hold, he makes a false statement of fact. So where, at a sale of property, the vendor described the occupier as "a most desirable tenant", while in fact he knew that the rent was considerably in arrear, this was held to entitle the purchaser to rescind the contract.[21]

6–009 **Statement of opinion may carry implication that grounds for belief.** In *Brown v Raphael*,[22] the purchaser of an absolute reversion in a trust fund expectant on the death of an annuitant was likewise held entitled to rescind: the particulars of sale stated that estate duty would be payable on the death of the

[17] See *Strachan & Henshaw Ltd v Stein Industrie (UK) Ltd (No.2)* (1997) 87 B.L.R. 52.

[18] *IFE Fund SA v Goldman Sachs International* [2006] EWHC 2887 (Comm), [2007] 1 Lloyd's Rep. 264 at [50]; affirmed without comment on this point [2007] EWCA Civ 811, [2007] 2 Lloyd's Rep. 449.

[19] *Kyle Bay Ltd (t/a Astons Nightclub) v Underwriters Subscribing under Policy No. 019057/08/01* [2007] EWCA Civ 57, [2007] 1 C.L.C. 164 at [33]–[35]; distinguishing *Wauton v Coppard* [1899] 1 Ch. 92. In that case the statement was by a vendor's agent as to the effect of a restrictive covenant to a lay person who, as a prospective purchaser, did not (to the knowledge of the vendor's agent) have a copy of the covenant.

[20] *Connolly Ltd v Bellway Homes Ltd* [2007] EWHC 895, [2007] All E.R. (D.) 182 (Apr). The sentences in this paragraph were cited with approval in *Economides v Commercial Union Assurance Co Plc* [1998] Q.B. 587, by Simon Brown L.J. at 645 (who considered that *Brown v Raphael* [1958] Ch. 636, below, para.6–007, rested on a different principle) and Sir Iain Glidewell (who considered that the statement summarised that case accurately also), 655. Another way to put the same point is that if a person states that he holds an opinion that in fact he does not hold, or that he has an intention that in fact he does not have, he makes a false statement of fact. See Cartwright, *Misrepresentation, Mistake and Non-disclosure* (2007), para.3.17.

[21] *Smith v Land and House Property Corp* (1884) 28 Ch D 7.

[22] [1958] Ch. 636; *Crédit Lyonnais Bank Nederland v Export Credit Guarantee Department* [1996] 1 Lloyd's Rep. 200 (bank's statement that a management was "respectable and trustworthy" a misrepresentation as it was contrary to the bank's actual experience of the management). See also *Patterson v Landsberg & Son* (1905) 7 F. 675.

annuitant, "who is believed to have no aggregable estate"; the vendor's solicitors honestly believed this to be true but had no reasonable grounds for this belief. The Court of Appeal held that as the vendor was in a far stronger position than the purchaser to ascertain the facts, there must be implied a further representation that the former had reasonable grounds for his belief.[23] If, on the other hand, it is clear that the person who expressed the opinion had no real way of knowing whether or not it was correct, no such implication can be made.[24] In *Economides v Commercial Union Assurance Co Plc*[25] it was held that a statement by an insured, a private person with no specialist knowledge, of the value of the contents of a flat which contained his parents' belongings as well as his own, did not carry an implication that he had an objectively reasonable basis for the value stated. Thus a statement of the value which the insured made honestly was not a misrepresentation even though it was inaccurate. Equally, propositions put forward by parties engaged in negotiating the settlement of a dispute are likely to be treated as mere statements of opinion and, at least when the negotiations are conducted by experienced professionals in good faith, are unlikely to be treated as including a representation that they are based on reasonable grounds.[26] Subject to the principle illustrated by *Brown v Raphael*,[27] an opinion expressed in good faith is not to be held to be a misrepresentation merely because it turns out to be incorrect.[28] But a statement of opinion which is published as if it were a fact may be regarded as a statement of fact.[29]

---

[23] It is possible that *Smith v Land House Property Corp.*(1889) 28 Ch D 7 was also decided on the basis that the vendor was impliedly representing that he had reasonable grounds for his belief, or at least that he knew of nothing which might be inconsistent with it: Bennett (1998) 61 M.L.R. 886, 888. See also *Highland Insurance Co v Continental Insurance Co* [1987] 1 Lloyd's Rep. 109; *Crédit Lyonnais Bank Nederland v Export Credit Guarantee Department* [1996] 1 Lloyd's Rep. 200; *Barings Plc (In Liquidation) v Coopers & Lybrand* [2002] EWHC 461 (Ch), [2002] 2 B.C.L.C. 410 at [50]–[51].

[24] *Bisset v Wilkinson* [1927] A.C. 177; *Hummingbird Motors Ltd v Hobbs* [1986] R.T.R. 276.

[25] [1998] Q.B. 587. Simon Brown and Peter Gibson L.JJ. expressed the view that under the Marine Insurance Act 1906 s.20(5), which states that a representation as to a matter of expectation or belief is true if it be made in good faith, there is no room for such an implication, doubting a dictum to the contrary by Steyn J. in *Highlands Insurance Co v Continental Insurance Co* [1987] 1 Lloyd's Rep. 109, 112–113. Sir Iain Glidewell preferred to leave the matter open. But see Bennett (1998) 61 M.L.R. 886; Cartwright, *Misrepresentation, Mistake and Non-disclosure* (2007), para.3.16. See further below, paras 6–012 and 41–035.

[26] *Kyle Bay Ltd (trading as Astons Nightclub) v Underwriters subscribing under policy 019057/08/01* [2006] EWHC 607 (Comm), [2006] All E.R. (D) 433 (Mar), Jonathan Hirst Q.C. at [45]–[47], [52]–[54]. On appeal, this was accepted as the correct approach in principle: [2007] EWCA Civ 57, [2007] 1 C.L.C. 164 at [31]; see above, para.6–006. Likewise, when a party had expressly stated that it was giving no representation as to the accuracy of the information provided, there was no implication that it had no further information suggesting that what was stated might not be correct. The question is what would the reasonable person in the context have inferred was being implicitly represented: *IFE Fund SA v Goldman Sachs International* [2006] EWHC 2887 (Comm), [2007] 1 Lloyd's Rep. 264 at [50] ; affirmed [2007] EWCA Civ 811, [2007] 2 Lloyd's Rep. 449. There might be an implied representation that the information was supplied in good faith, but not one that the party knew of nothing that might possibly cast doubt on it: [2006] EWCA 2887 at [60].

[27] [1958] Ch. 636; above.

[28] *New Brunswick and Canada Ry and Land Co v Conybeare* (1862) 9 H.L.C. 711; *Anderson v Pacific Insurance Co* (1872) L.R. 7 C.P. 65; *Bisset v Wilkinson* [1927] A.C. 177; *Sanders v Gall* [1952] *Current Property Law* 343.

[29] See *Reese River Silver Mining Co Ltd v Smith* (1869) L.R. 4 H.L. 64.

6–010 **Statement of intention not honestly held.** With regard to a statement of intention, this may be looked upon as a misrepresentation of existing fact if, at the time when it was made, the person making the statement did not in fact intend to do what he said or knew that he did not have the ability to put the intention into effect; for the promisor's state of mind was not what he led the other party to believe it to be.[30] Thus, where a man ordered goods having at the time the intention not to pay for them, he was held to have made a fraudulent misrepresentation.[31] Equally, if a person makes a statement of an intention that he should have known he was not able to carry out, in appropriate circumstances he may be held to have made an implied representation that he did have that ability.[32] There is no doubt that a statement as to the intentions of a third party is a statement of fact and can constitute a misrepresentation in the ordinary way.[33]

6–011 **Implied representations.** *Brown v Raphael* could be regarded as a case of an implied representation; there are a number of other cases which can also be regarded as instances of implied representations, though this category overlaps with that of representations by conduct.[34] Thus in *Spice Girls Ltd v Aprilia World Service BV*[35] it was held that a pop group had made an implied misrepresentation when they continued with arrangements to publicise the defendant's products when they knew that one member of the group was intending to leave the group shortly, which would prevent the contract being carried out and the defendants deriving any benefit from the arrangement. It has been held that a description of premises as "offices" may amount to an implied representation as to the availability of the appropriate planning consents.[36] The essential issue is whether in all the circumstances it has been impliedly represented that there exists some state of facts different from the truth. In evaluating the effects of the statement or conduct in such circumstances, a helpful test is whether a reasonable representee would naturally assume that the true state of facts did not exist and that, had it existed, he would in all circumstances necessarily have been informed of it.[37]

6–012 **Reasonable reliance on statements of opinion or statements as to the future.** It is submitted that no simple distinction between statements of fact and statements of opinion or intention will sufficiently take account of the different

[30] See *Edgington v Fitzmaurice* (1885) 29 Ch D 459; *Angus v Clifford* [1891] 2 Ch. 449, 470; *Goff v Gauthier* (1991) P. & C.R. 388. cf. *Lewin v Barratt Homes Ltd* [2000] Crim. L.R. 323 (a case under Property Misdescriptions Act 1991 s.1).

[31] *Re Shackleton Ex p. Whittaker* (1875) L.R. 10 Ch.App. 446; *Ray v Sempers* [1974] A.C. 370; *Re Gerald Cooper Chemicals Ltd* [1978] Ch. 262.

[32] cf. *Brown v Raphael* [1958] Ch. 636 above, para.6–009.

[33] *Smelter Corp of Ireland Ltd v O'Driscoll* [1977] I.R. 305.

[34] See below, para.6–015.

[35] *The Times*, April 5, 2000 Ch D (reversed in part on other grounds [2002] EWCA Civ 15.)

[36] *Laurence v Lexcourt Holdings Ltd* [1978] 1 W.L.R. 1128. In the criminal law the concept of an implied representation is widely relied upon in prosecutions under the Theft Act; for instance, it has been held that a minicab driver who solicited a customer at a London airport, saying, "yes, I am an airport taxi", and subsequently assured the customer that £27.50 was the "correct fare" was guilty of representing that he was an officially licensed taxi driver and that the fare was somehow at an officially approved rate: *R. v Banaster* [1979] R.T.R 113. See also below, para.6–015.

[37] *Geest Plc v Fyffes Plc* [1999] 1 All E.R. (Comm) 672, 683.

varieties of possible statements which may be made in pre-contractual negotiations. For example, statements as to the future are not always mere statements of intention; and statements of opinion may range from casual, unconsidered remarks to considered judgments, based on well-studied evidence. Cases have occurred, for instance, which suggest the need for a more careful differentiation between types of statements of opinion, and statements as to the future. These are principally where an action in tort lies for negligent advice. This form of liability is considered later,[38] but it is mentioned here in order to stress that in an action in tort it is not necessary to show that the statement complained of was a representation in the sense which this term has traditionally borne in the law of contract. Thus, where there is a sufficient "special relationship" to give rise to liability in tort under *Hedley Byrne & Co Ltd v Heller & Partners Ltd*,[39] it would seem immaterial that the statement consists of mere opinion or even of a proposition of abstract law.[40] Certainly the distinction between statements of existing facts and predictions seems less important in tort cases. For instance, in *Esso Petroleum Co v Mardon*[41] an action for damages for negligent misrepresentation succeeded where a petrol company, negotiating with a prospective tenant about a lease of a filling station, had offered a forecast of the probable sales potential of the filling station. In *McNally v Welltrade International Ltd*[42] an employment agency was held liable to an employee for implied representations as to the plaintiff's suitability for a job from which he was dismissed. And in *Box v Midland Bank Ltd*[43] it was said that the distinction between fact and opinion had become much less important since *Esso Petroleum Ltd v Mardon*. It is suggested that the fundamental principle which underlies all the cases of misrepresentation, whether in tort or otherwise, is not so much that statements as to the future, or statements of opinion, cannot be misrepresentations; but rather that statements are not to be treated as representations where, having regard to all the circumstances, it is unreasonable of the representee to rely on the representor's statements rather than on his own judgment.[44] In general this seems to be the reason why statements as to the future and statements of opinion have been held not to ground relief; in dealing with statements of this nature it has usually been felt that the representee ought not to have relied on the representor. It has been recognised that sometimes a statement which was on its face a statement of fact was really only one of opinion because it was apparent that the maker had no real knowledge or was simply passing on information for what it was worth.[45] On the other hand there are circumstances in which it is perfectly reasonable for the representee to rely on the representor's statements even where those statements are matters of opinion, or statements as to the future, and where this is the case,

---

[38] Below, paras 6–078—6–089.
[39] [1964] A.C. 465; below, para.6–081.
[40] On statements of law, see below, para.6–013.
[41] [1976] Q.B. 801, below, para.6–085.
[42] [1978] I.R.L.R. 497.
[43] [1979] 2 Lloyd's Rep. 391; in the Court of Appeal (on costs only) [1981] 1 Lloyd's Rep. 434.
[44] cf. *Harlingdon and Leinster Enterprises Ltd v Christopher Hull Fine Art Ltd* [1991] 1 Q.B. 564, Vol.II, para.43–074.
[45] *Bisset v Wilkinson* [1927] A.C. 177; *Highland Insurance Co v Continental Insurance Co* [1987] 1 Lloyd's Rep. 109; and the cases cited in para.6–009, above. But see *Sirius International Insurance Corp v Oriental Insurance Corp* [1999] 1 All E.R. (Comm) 699.

it is thought that the statement should be treated as a representation in the relevant sense.[46]

6–013 **Statements of law.** It used commonly to be said that a statement of law cannot be treated as a misrepresentation.[47] But the proposition was always in need of qualification and it is now more accurate to say that a statement of law will amount to a misrepresentation unless, in the circumstances, it reasonably appeared that the statement was put forward as nothing more than an opinion on which it would not be reasonable to rely. First, a statement of law may be regarded as a statement of opinion, but just as a statement of opinion may be a representation of fact, so too a statement of law may amount to a representation, or misrepresentation, as the case may be. So a wilful misstatement of law would always amount to a misrepresentation[48] and even an innocent misstatement of law may do so where it carries an implication of fact which is itself untrue. Secondly, the question whether a statement is one of law or fact gives rise to no small difficulty,[49] especially as statements of law and of fact are so frequently intermingled. It has been said that the dichotomy between statements of fact and statements of law is too neat, and is apt to mislead.[50] It seems that the courts tend to regard statements of mixed law and fact, and statements capable of having either meaning, as statements of fact,[51] and therefore as representations; that they also regard statements as to the purport, effect and objects of documents as representations[52]; and in *Cooper v Phibbs*,[53] a statement as to private rights, as distinct from the general law, was regarded as a statement of fact.[54] So a representation that planning permission exists for a particular use is a representation of fact, and not of law[55]; similarly with a representation by a landlord that he accepts liability for repairs under a lease.[56] On the other hand a statement of law made separately from a statement of fact was held not to be a misrepresentation.[57] This seems to rest on a distinction between a statement of an abstract proposition of law, which was not regarded as a misrepresentation, and a

---

[46] However, there are some cases under the Trade Descriptions Act in which the courts have continued to apply the traditional distinctions drawn in the contractual cases between statements as to the future and statements of fact: *R. v Sunair Holidays Ltd* [1973] 1 W.L.R. 1105; *Kensington and Chelsea BC v Riley* [1973] R.T.R. 122; *Robertson v Diciccio* [1972] R.T.R. 431; *Beckett v Cohen* [1972] 1 W.L.R. 1593; *British Airways Board v Taylor* [1976] 1 W.L.R. 13.

[47] *Beattie v Ebury* (1872) L.R. 7 Ch. App. 777, 802; *Beesly v Hallwood Estates Ltd* [1960] 1 W.L.R. 549, 560.

[48] *West London Commercial Bank v Kitson* (1884) 13 QBD 360, 362–363; *Oudaille v Lawson* [1922] N.Z.L.R. 259.

[49] See *Solle v Butcher* [1950] 1 K.B. 671.

[50] *Brikom Investments Ltd v Seaford* [1981] 1 W.L.R. 863.

[51] *Reynell v Sprye* (1852) 1 De G.M. & G. 660; *West London Commercial Bank v Kitson* (1884) 13 QBD 360; *Hughes v Liverpool Victoria Legal Friendly Society* [1916] 2 K.B. 482.

[52] *Hirshfeld v L.B. & S.C. Ry* (1876) 2 QBD 1; *De Tchihatchef v Salerni Coupling Ltd* [1932] 1 Ch. 330; *Curtis v Chemical Cleaning & Dyeing Co* [1951] 1 K.B. 805.

[53] (1867) L.R. 2 H.L. 149.

[54] (1867) L.R. 2 H.L. 149 at 170.

[55] *Laurence v Lexcourt Holdings Ltd* [1977] 1 W.L.R. 1128.

[56] *Brikom Investments Ltd v Seaford* [1981] 1 W.L.R. 863. But cf. *China Pacific SA v Food Corp of India* [1981] Q.B. 403, 429 (reversed on different grounds [1982] A.C. 939) where an admission of liability was said to be a representation of law.

[57] *Rashdall v Ford* (1866) L.R. 2 Eq. 750; *Harse v Pearl Life Assurance Co* [1904] 1 K.B. 558.

statement applying the law to the facts of a particular situation which, at least in some circumstances, may constitute a misrepresentation.[58] But thirdly, in the law of restitution the distinction between a payment made under a mistake of fact and one made under a mistake of law has recently been held by the House of Lords not to be part of English law,[59] and, in the light of this, it was held in *Pankhania v Hackney LBC*[60] that the "misrepresentation of law" rule is no longer good law. Thus, for the purposes of the law of misrepresentation, the distinction between statements of law and statements of fact is no longer maintainable and that even an incorrect statement of an abstract proposition of law may amount to a misrepresentation unless it is apparent that all that is being offered is an opinion without implication that the speaker has reasonable grounds for that opinion.[61] It is submitted that the underlying principle here is the same as that suggested in the previous paragraph, viz that even a statement as to the law may be a misrepresentation if it was reasonable, in all the circumstances, for the representee to rely upon it. In any event a statement of foreign law is here (as elsewhere in the law) treated as a statement of fact.[62]

Non-disclosure. The general rule is that mere non-disclosure does not constitute misrepresentation, for there is, in general, no duty on the parties to a contract to disclose material facts to each other, however dishonest such non-disclosure may be in particular circumstances.[63] So, for example, in *Percival v Wright*,[64] a company director who had inside information about certain facts likely to enhance the value of the company's shares was held to be under no duty to disclose this fact to a shareholder from whom he bought some shares. For the same reason it is not possible to set up an estoppel on the basis of an omission to disclose unless a duty to disclose can be established in the particular circumstances of the case.[65] Tacit acquiescence in another's self-deception does not itself amount to a misrepresentation, provided that it has not previously been caused by a positive misrepresentation.[66] But there are exceptions to the general 6–014

[58] See also, below, paras 29–041—29–046.

[59] *Kleinwort Benson Ltd v Lincoln City Council* [1999] 2 A.C. 349. See below, para.29–045.

[60] [2002] EWHC 2441(Ch). See also above, para.5–054.

[61] cf. above, para.6–006. It has rightly been remarked that the reasons often given for refusing relief on the grounds of a mistake of law—for example, that it would be easy to claim a mistaken belief in the law and hard to disprove it—have much less weight when the mistake was the result of a misrepresentation by the other party: Cartwright, *Misrepresentation, Mistake and Non-disclosure* (2007), para.3.30.

[62] *André & Cie SA v Ets Michel Blanc & Fils* [1977] 2 Lloyd's Rep. 166.

[63] *Ward v Hobbs* (1878) 4 App. Cas. 13, but doubts have been cast on this case by the House of Lords in *Hurley v Dyke* [1979] R.T.R. 265. Certain statutes may impose duties of disclosure in particular circumstances: e.g. Housing Act 1985 (as amended) s.125(4A): see *Payne v Barnet LBC* (1998) 30 H.L.R. 295 (no duty at common law should be superimposed on statutory scheme).

[64] [1902] 2 Ch. 421; cf. *Coleman v Myers* [1977] 2 N.Z.L.R. 225, and see also *Gething v Kilner* [1972] 1 W.L.R. 237; *Prudential Insurance Co Ltd v Newman Industries Ltd* [1981] Ch. 257, 295. Such conduct could constitute an offence under the Criminal Justice Act 1993 s.52, but s.63(2) provides that no contract shall be void or unenforceable by reason only of s.52.

[65] *Moorgate Mercantile Co Ltd v Twitchings* [1977] A.C. 890.

[66] See *Keates v Cadogan* (1851) 10 C.B. 591; *New Brunswick and Canada Ry and Land Co v Conybeare* (1862) 9 H.L.C. 711; *Smith v Hughes* (1871) L.R. 6 Q.B. 597; *Turner v Green* [1895] 2 Ch. 205; see also *Jewson & Son Ltd v Arcos Ltd* (1933) 39 Com.Cas. 59; *Wales v Wadham* [1977] 1 W.L.R. 199. This sentence of the text was cited with approval in *Donegal International Ltd v Zambia* [2007] EWHC 197 (Comm), [2007] 1 Lloyd's Rep. 397 at [465].

rule that there is no duty to disclose. First, there are many statutory exceptions.[67] Second, there are exceptions at common law where the contract is within the class of contracts uberrimae fidei,[68] where there is a fiduciary relationship between the parties,[69] and where failure to disclose some fact distorts a positive representation. It is also possible for a person to be guilty of misrepresentation by conduct.[70] The first two exceptions at common law are dealt with later.[71] Misrepresentation by conduct and cases in which a failure to disclose a fact distorts a positive misrepresentation are dealt with in the following paragraphs.

6–015 **Misrepresentation by conduct.** As previously mentioned, a person may be guilty of misrepresentation by conduct.[72] It is sometimes hard to distinguish misrepresentation by conduct from implied representation, but normally it is unnecessary to do so.[73] In the simplest case, conduct may be intended to convey information in precisely the same way as the written or spoken word. Thus a person who goes into a shop in a university town wearing cap and gown may (if such costume is still customary) be representing that he is an undergraduate,[74] a person who sits down in a restaurant and orders a meal impliedly represents that he has the means to pay,[75] and more generally it has been said in a well-known dictum that "a nod or a wink or a shake of the head or a smile"[76] may amount to a representation if it is intended to induce the other party to believe in a certain state of facts. It is well established that a mere ordering of goods in the course of business carries a representation that the buyer is not aware that he will be unable to pay for them[77]; a mere payment of money by A to B may in appropriate circumstances (e.g. where A is B's employer) amount to a representation by A that B is entitled to the money so paid[78]; and it has been held in a criminal case that tendering of obsolete foreign bank notes to a currency dealer is a representation that the notes are current tender of some value.[79] Other important criminal cases concerning representations by conduct relate to the use of bank (cheque)

---

[67] See e.g. below, para.6–153.

[68] See below, paras 6–153 et seq.

[69] See below, paras 6–079—6–080.

[70] In certain circumstances failing to disclose information may be a criminal offence, e.g. Timeshare Act 1992 s.1A (inserted by Timeshare Regulations 1997 (SI 1997/1081)).

[71] See below, paras 6–080 and 6–142.

[72] See above, para.6–010. The representation in *Spice Girls Ltd v Aprilia World Service BV, The Times*, April 5, 2000 (Ch D) (reversed in part on other grounds [2002] EWCA Civ 15), referred to in that paragraph, may equally well be interpreted as one of representation by conduct.

[73] But it was necessary where the question was whether there is a representation in writing sufficient to satisfy the Statute of Frauds (Amendment) Act 1828 (Lord Tenterden's Act) (see below, para.6–041): *Contex Drouzhba v Wiseman* [2007] EWCA Civ 1201, [2007] All E.R. (D) 293 (Nov) (representation implied by a written statement would suffice but representation by conduct would not).

[74] *R. v Barnard* (1837) 7 C. & P. 784.

[75] *Ray v Sempers* [1974] A.C. 370.

[76] *Walters v Morgan* (1861) 3 De G.F. & J. 718, 723. See also *Gill v M'Dowel* [1903] 2 Ir.R. 463.

[77] *Re Shackleton Ex p. Whittaker* (1875) L.R. 10 Ch.App. 446; *Re Gerald Cooper Chemicals Ltd* [1978] Ch. 262; *Ray v Sempers* [1974] A.C. 370.

[78] *Avon CC v Howlett* [1981] I.R.L.R. 447.

[79] *R. v Williams* [1980] Crim. L.R. 589.

cards and credit cards. In *R. v Charles*[80] the House of Lords held that use of a cheque card amounts to a representation that the user has authority, as between himself and his bank, to use his card. Thus, even though payment of the cheque may be guaranteed by the bank, and may in fact be made by the bank, the use of the card will amount to a false representation if it is, in the circumstances, unauthorised by the bank. In *R. v Lambie*[81] the House of Lords likewise held that use of a credit card to purchase goods amounts to a representation that the user has the authority of the credit card company to use the card. So even if the credit card company has a previous contract with the seller whereby it undertakes to pay for goods acquired with the use of the card, irrespective of amount, there will be a false representation if the user exceeds the limits agreed between him and the credit card company. The importance of these decisions for the civil law is that they justify the seller or supplier in rescinding the contract of sale and reclaiming the goods in the event of the fraud being discovered while the goods are still in the possession of the buyer.

Conduct intended to conceal facts. But there is also another class of case where conduct may amount to a representation, and that is where the conduct is not so much intended to convey information as to conceal facts from the other party. There does not appear to be any modern authority illustrating this type of misrepresentation, but there are some nineteenth-century cases in which a seller of goods was held guilty of misrepresentation where it was shown that he had deliberately concealed defects in the goods being sold, as, for instance, by nailing down planks and closing the seams of a rotten ship,[82] or by plugging a hole in a gun with soft metal.[83] This principle has not been fully developed by the courts, and it is uncertain whether it would extend to conduct which is not intended solely to conceal defects; it is, for instance, not clear whether the vendor of a house could be held guilty of misrepresentation if he papered a room, partly to hide the defective state of the plaster, but partly because it needed decorating in any event. 6–016

Partial non-disclosure.[84] Although total non-disclosure does not amount to a misrepresentation, a partial non-disclosure may do so. This may happen in a number of different ways. Thus a statement may be a misrepresentation even though it is literally true if it implies certain additional facts which are themselves false. A striking instance of this possibility is *Goldsmith v Rodger*[85] in which the defendant who was negotiating for the purchase of the plaintiff's yacht informed the plaintiff, after paying a visit to the yacht, that she had rot in her keel. The Court of Appeal held that this statement implied that the defendant had actually 6–017

[80] [1977] A.C. 177.
[81] [1982] A.C. 449.
[82] *Baglehole v Walters* (1811) 3 Camp. 154; *Schneider v Heath* (1813) 3 Camp. 506. For a case under the Trade Descriptions Act 1968, see *Cottee v Douglas Seaton (Used Cars) Ltd* [1972] 1 W.L.R. 1408. In *Taittinger v Allbev* (1993) 12 Tr.L.R. 165, a passing-off case, it was held that the labelling and "get-up" of a bottle constituted a false representation.
[83] *Horsfall v Thomas* (1862) 1 H. & C. 90, but it was held in this case that as the buyer had not examined the gun he had not been influenced by the misrepresentation. See below, para.6–032.
[84] See Hudson (1969) 85 L.Q.R. 524.
[85] [1962] 2 Lloyd's Rep. 249.

examined the keel, and as he had not done so, this was itself a misrepresentation, whether or not the yacht did have rot in her keel. Again, a statement may amount to a misrepresentation if facts are omitted which render that which has actually been stated false or misleading in the context in which it is made.[86] So, for example, where a shop assistant told a customer that a receipt for the cleaning of a dress which she was required to sign excluded liability for damage to beads and sequins, and in fact the receipt excluded all liability, this was held to be a misrepresentation.[87] It will be observed that these cases of partial non-disclosure can either be explained as cases of actual misrepresentation, or as cases in which there is a duty to disclose certain facts by reason of the facts actually stated. Until the passing of the Misrepresentation Act 1967, it was immaterial which explanation was adopted since the effect of an actual misrepresentation and the breach of a duty to disclose (where such a duty exists) were generally the same. But since the passing of this Act this is no longer the case as the Act applies to misrepresentations, but not to the breach of duties of disclosure. It is thought that cases of partial non-disclosure will normally be treated as cases of actual misrepresentation falling within the Act, but it has been held that cases of complete non-disclosure will not.[88]

6–018 **Representation ceases to be true.** A statement may be made which is true at that time but which subsequently ceases to be true to the knowledge of the representor before the contract is entered into. In such circumstances a failure to inform the representee of the change in circumstances will itself amount to a misrepresentation,[89] unless in the context it is quite clear to the reasonable recipient of the information that the party who gives it accepts no responsibility for its accuracy or for reviewing it.[90]

6–019 **Continuity of representations.** Representations are treated for many purposes as continuing in their effect until the contract between the parties is actually concluded. This is one reason why a statement which is true when made,

[86] *Oakes v Turquand* (1867) L.R. 2 H.L. 325; *Barwick v English Joint Stock Bank* (1867) L.R. 2 Ex. 259; *Peek v Gurney* (1873) L.R. 6 H.L. 377, 403; *Arkwright v Newbold* (1881) 17 Ch D 301, 318; *R. v Kylsant* [1932] 1 K.B. 442; *Jewson & Sons Ltd v Arcos Ltd* (1933) 39 Com.Cas. 59; *R. v Bishirgian* [1936] 1 All E.R. 586.

[87] *Curtis v Chemical Cleaning and Dyeing Co Ltd* [1951] 1 K.B. 805; see below, para.14–132.

[88] *Banque Keyser Ullman SA v Skandia (UK) Insurance Co Ltd* [1990] 1 Q.B. 665, 787–789, affirmed on other grounds [1991] 2 A.C. 249; cf. Hudson (1969) 85 L.Q.R. 524.

[89] *Traill v Baring* (1864) 33 L.J.Ch. 521; *With v O'Flanagan* [1936] Ch. 575; *Ray v Sempers* [1974] A.C. 370; cf. *Wales v Wadham* [1977] 1 W.L.R. 199 (see below, para.6–155). It has been said that if a person who has made a representation of fact which, before the contract is made, he discovers to be untrue, he is not fraudulent in failing to correct the representation, as he will not be dishonest: *Thomas Witter Ltd v TBP Industries Ltd* [1994] Tr.L.R. 145. It is submitted that there may still be fraud if the person knows that he should tell the other party but fails to do so; see (1995) 111 L.Q.R. 385. Where statements in listing particulars or in a prospectus become incorrect, supplementary particulars or a supplementary prospectus may have to be issued: Financial Services and Markets Act 2000 ss.81, 87G. Section 87G applies to both listed and unlisted securities.. See further below, para.6–090.

[90] *IFE Fund SA v Goldman Sachs International* [2006] EWHC 2887 (Comm), [2007] 1 Lloyd's Rep. 26 at [60]; [2007] EWCA Civ 811, [2007] 2 Lloyd's Rep. 449, see at [35], [38] and [74]. See above, para.6–009.

but which ceases to be true to the knowledge of the representor before the contract is concluded, is treated as a misrepresentation unless the representor informs the representee of the change in circumstances.[91] This principle may have other effects as well. First, as we have just seen, if a representation is made innocently but falsely, and facts later come to the knowledge of the representor which show that the statement was false, a failure to inform the representee of the truth may convert what was originally an innocent misrepresentation into a fraudulent one.[92] Again, if a man truthfully states that he intends to do something but changes his mind at a later stage he may come under a duty to disclose that change.[93] The principle is also recognised by s.2(1) of the Misrepresentation Act which extends the right to damages for negligent misrepresentation,[94] for a misrepresentation falls within this subsection unless the representor had reasonable grounds to believe and did believe *up to the time the contract was made* that the facts represented were true.[95] Another consequence of the principle that representations are continuous in their effect is that if a representation is made by an agent who is acting without authority, and he subsequently obtains the authority of his principal to continue the negotiations, the principal will become responsible for the representations previously made by the agent.[96] There are some circumstances in which a contract may be treated as commercially binding before it becomes legally binding, and in such a case it seems that the principle of continuity of representations does not operate beyond the time when the contract becomes commercially binding. So, for instance, an insured was held not to be obliged (despite the general duty of disclosure in insurance contracts)[97] to disclose facts coming to his notice after the insurer had initialled a slip indicating that he was at risk, although there was no binding legal contract until a policy was issued later.[98]

Statement must be false. It is an obvious requirement of misrepresentation that the statement relied on be false. As to what amounts to falsity, in *Avon Insurance v Swire*[99] Rix J. adopted as representing the common law the test laid down in Marine Insurance Act 1906 s.20(4), so that a statement will be treated as true if it is substantially correct and the difference would not have induced a reasonable person to enter the contract. The last phrase reflects the requirement of materiality discussed below.[100] 6–020

---

[91] Above, para.6–018.

[92] *Davies v London Provincial Marine Insurance Co* (1878) 8 Ch D 469.

[93] *Ray v Sempers* [1974] A.C. 370. But contrast *Wales v Wadham* [1977] 1 W.L.R. 199, 211 (wife not obliged to reveal change of intention not to marry; overruled on another ground but apparent approval given to the decision on this point, *Livesey v Jenkins* [1985] A.C. 424, 439); see Cartwright, *Unequal Bargaining*, pp.84–88.

[94] This is dealt with fully, below, paras 6–068 et seq.

[95] *Corner v Munday* [1987] C.L.Y. 479.

[96] *Briess v Woolley* [1954] A.C. 333.

[97] Below, para.6–144.

[98] *Cory v Patton* (1872) L.R. 7 Q.B. 304; cf. *Berger and Light Diffusers Pty Ltd v Pollock* [1973] 2 Lloyd's Rep. 442, 460–461.

[99] [2000] 1 All E.R. (Comm) 573.

[100] See para.6–037.

(b) *Statement By or Known to Other Party*

6–021 **The representor.** In order to ground relief to a person who has entered into a contract as a result of a misrepresentation, it is normally necessary that the misrepresentation should have been made either by the other party to the contract,[101] or by his agent acting within the scope of his authority,[102] or that the other party had notice of the misrepresentation.[103] A person who has been induced to enter into a contract with A as a result of a misrepresentation made to him by B and of which A had no notice has no ground of relief against A unless B were A's agent.[104] It is, however, not necessary to show that the misrepresentor was the agent of the other contracting party for the purpose of concluding the contract, or even for the purpose of conducting negotiations; it is sufficient if the misrepresentor was the agent of the other contracting party simply for the purpose of passing on the misrepresentation to the misrepresentee.[105]

6–022 **Third party representor may be liable in damages.** Although, apart from cases of notice or of agency, a misrepresentation made by one person will not found relief against another, nevertheless where the representee has been induced to enter into a contract with a third party, the representor may himself be liable in damages to the representee, either in tort, if the misrepresentation was fraudulent or, in some cases, negligent[106] or on the grounds of a collateral contract between the representor and the representee.[107]

6–023 **Sureties and misrepresentation by debtor.** In a number of cases a recurring situation has arisen. A husband has wanted to borrow money from a creditor who has refused to proceed without having a guarantee secured by a charge over the matrimonial home, or similarly a charge without a guarantee, from the wife. The wife's consent has been secured by misrepresentation[108] or undue influence[109] by the husband. Can the creditor enforce the guarantee? In a number of cases it was held that if the creditor had "left it to the husband" to get the wife's signature,

---

[101] *Hasan v Willson* [1977] 1 Lloyd's Rep. 431.

[102] But an agent who seeks to enforce in his own name a contract made by him as such is affected by a misrepresentation made by his principal: *Garnac Grain Co Inc v H.M. Faure & Fairclough Ltd* [1966] 1 Q.B. 650, reversed on the facts [1966] 1 Q.B. 658 and [1968] A.C. 1130n. See also *U.B.A.F. Ltd v European American Banking Corp* [1984] Q.B. 713. An agent may have authority to make representations in relation to a particular transaction even though he has no authority to conclude the transaction: *First Energy v HIB* [1993] 2 Lloyd's Rep. 194, 204; *MCI Worldcom International Inc v Primus Telecommunications Plc* [2004] EWCA Civ 957, [2004] 2 All E.R. (Comm) 833 at [25]. For examples see Vol.II, para.31–012.

[103] *Barclays Bank Plc v O'Brien* [1994] 1 A.C. 180; *Bank of Credit and Commerce International SA v Aboody* [1990] 1 Q.B. 923, 973 (undue influence: see below, para.7–104).

[104] For an extreme example, see *Foote v Hayne* (1824) 1 C. & P. 545 (defendant liable for breach of promise of marriage despite fraud of plaintiff's father with respect to plaintiff's illegitimate child).

[105] *Pilmore v Hood* (1838) 5 Bing. N.C. 97.

[106] That is, if the case falls within the principle in *Hedley Byrne & Co Ltd v Heller & Partners Ltd* [1964] A.C. 465, below, para.6–081.

[107] See, e.g. *Wells (Merstham) Ltd v Buckland Sand & Silica Co Ltd* [1965] 2 Q.B. 170, below, para.12–007.

[108] e.g. *Kings North Trust Ltd v Bell* [1961] 1 W.L.R. 119.

[109] e.g. *CIBC Mortgages Plc v Pitt* [1994] 1 A.C. 200.

the husband was acting as agent for the creditor[110] and it was therefore responsible for his misconduct. In *Barclays Bank Plc v O'Brien*,[111] a case where the husband had by misrepresentation secured his wife's signature to a charge over the matrimonial home to secure the debts of his business, this approach was rejected as artificial. However, the bank was prevented from enforcing the charge on the ground that it had constructive notice of the husband's misrepresentation even though it had no actual knowledge of it. Lord Browne-Wilkinson, delivering the only full speech in the House of Lords, pointed out that there is a substantial risk that the wife may act as surety when the transaction is not to her advantage because of some legal or equitable wrong by the husband. Where the creditor is aware that the debtor and the surety are husband and wife, and the transaction is on its face not to the financial advantage of the surety as well as of the debtor, the creditor will be fixed with constructive notice of any undue influence, misrepresentation or other legal wrong by the debtor unless it has taken reasonable steps to satisfy itself that the surety has entered into the obligation freely and with knowledge of the true facts.[112] The decision in *Barclays Bank v O'Brien*, and many other decisions that followed it, must be read in the light of the subsequent decision of the House of Lords in *Royal Bank of Scotland v Etridge (No.2)*.[113] That case applied a similar approach wherever "the relationship between the surety and the debtor is non-commercial", and considered in detail the steps that the lender should take if, instead of itself ensuring that the wife was not the victim of misrepresentation or undue influence, it chooses to rely on a confirmation from a solicitor that the wife has received advice.[114] Since *Etridge* and most of the decisions following *O'Brien* were cases of alleged undue influence rather than misrepresentation, the topic is treated in detail in Ch.7.[115]

Application to cases of misrepresentation. As far as cases of misrepresentation by the debtor are concerned, the bank cannot rely on a solicitor to give advice if it has material information which is not made available to the solicitor. Lord Nicholls said: 6–024

> "... the solicitor should obtain from the bank any information he needs. If the bank fails for any reason to provide information requested by the solicitor, the solicitor should decline to provide the confirmation sought by the bank ... [116] It should become routine practice for banks, if relying on confirmation from a solicitor for their protection, to send to the solicitor the necessary financial information. What is required must depend on the facts of the case. Ordinarily this will include information on the purpose for which the proposed new facility has been requested, the amount of the husband's indebtedness, the amount of his current overdraft facility, and the amount and terms of any new facility. If the banks' request for security arose from a written application by the husband for a facility, a copy of the application should be sent to the solicitor...

[110] See *Coldunell Ltd v Gallon* [1986] Q.B. 1184.

[111] [1994] 1 A.C. 180.

[112] [1994] 1 A.C. 180, at 196.

[113] [2001] UKHL 44, [2002] 2 A.C. 773. This case and seven other appeals were heard together.

[114] [2001] UKHL 44 at [87].

[115] See below, paras 7–104 et seq.

[116] *Royal Bank of Scotland v Etridge (No.2)* [2001] UKHL 44, [2002] 2 A.C. 773, at [67], per Lord Nicholls, with whose speech the rest of the House concurred: see below, para.7–109.

> Exceptionally there may be a case where the bank believes or suspects that the wife has been misled by her husband . . . If such a case occurs the bank must inform the wife's solicitor of the facts giving rise to its belief or suspicion."[117]

Where there has been a misrepresentation by the husband of the kind which occurred in *O'Brien*'s case (as to the extent and duration of the guarantee), there should be no problem, as the solicitor will always be informed of the terms of the guarantee or charge. What might be more problematic is if there has been some misrepresentation by the husband as to some other matter, such as the state of his business affairs,[118] but it is submitted that the information required of the bank should reveal many such misrepresentations. Lord Nicholls said that the protection of sureties wives did not require a review of the rule that a creditor does not normally have any duty to disclose to a surety any unusual risks relating to the debtor,[119] let alone normal ones. The possibility that the husband has lied to both the bank and his wife will remain.

6–025 **Effect of constructive notice.** After *O'Brien*'s case there was some uncertainty as to the position when, as in that case, the husband had misrepresented the extent of the charge and the bank had constructive notice of the misrepresentation. Is the charge completely unenforceable against the wife or enforceable to the extent she was given to believe? (In *O'Brien*'s case it seems that £60,000, the sum which the wife had been led to believe was the limit of her liability, had been paid before the final decision, which did not discuss its fate.) In *TSB Bank Plc v Camfield*[120] the Court of Appeal held on similar facts that the charge was completely unenforceable. As against the husband the wife would have the right to set aside the whole charge.[121] The bank took subject to the equity in favour of the wife and could not be in a better position. However, in that case the wife had not received any benefit under the agreement. If she had done so, her right to rescind would have been conditional on her making counter-restitution of the benefit received.[122] Where a later security is unenforceable by reason of undue influence, that may still leave an earlier, untainted one in force.[123]

6–026 **Need the party who made the misrepresentation be a party to the transaction?** In *TSB Bank Plc v Camfield*[124] the bank was treated as having constructive notice of the wife's right to set aside the charge as against the husband.

---

[117] [2001] UKHL 44 at [79]. Lord Nicholls pointed out that the bank may need to get the customer's consent to the circulation of this confidential information and, if consent is not forthcoming, the transaction will not be able to proceed. The steps described were said to be applicable to future transactions: at [80].

[118] cf. *Massey v Midland Bank Plc* [1995] 1 All E.R. 929.

[119] *Crédit Lyonnais Bank Nederland v Export Credit Guarantee Department* [1996] 1 Lloyd's Rep. 200; *Royal Bank of Scotland v Etridge (No.2)* [2001] UKHL 44, [2002] 2 A.C. 773 at [81]; below, para.6–158.

[120] [1995] 1 W.L.R. 430. See further below, para.6–118.

[121] This was said to be implicit in Misrepresentation Act 1967 s.2(2), which also implies that the court had no discretion save under that subsection. The subsection does not apply as between a misrepresentee and a third party.

[122] *Dunbar Bank Plc v Nadeem* [1998] 3 All E.R. 876; *Midland Bank Plc v Greene* (1995) 27 H.L.R. 350. See further below, paras 6–118 and 7–120.

[123] *Barclays Bank Plc v Caplan* [1998] 1 F.L.R. 532.

[124] [1995] 1 W.L.R. 430.

What would be the position if the husband were not a party to the charge? As a matter of principle, it seems that a party to a contract who has actual notice that the other party has entered the contract as the result of a misrepresentation by a third party should be unable to enforce it, and it is submitted that the same should apply in cases of constructive notice. In *Banco Exterior Internacional SA v Thomas*[125] (a case of alleged undue influence) Sir Richard Scott V.C. expressed the view that it could not have made a difference if in *O'Brien*'s case the wife had been sole owner of the home, but the case was decided on other grounds, Roch L.J. reserving this question. More recent authority treats the two situations in the same way.[126]

Procedure. It will be for the wife or other surety to show that the bank had notice of the non-commercial relationship between her and the debtor, and that the transaction was, on its face, not to her advantage. The burden will then be on the bank or other lender to show that it has taken sufficient steps to prevent it being fixed with constructive notice.[127] **6–027**

(c) *Other Requirements*

The representee or person intended to act on the representation. In order to be entitled to relief in respect of misrepresentation, the person seeking relief must be able to demonstrate that he is a representee; for, subject to the transmission by operation of law of claims on death, bankruptcy and assignment, the person or persons who in law come within the category of representees are alone entitled to a remedy. To put the matter another way, the claimant must show that it was intended that he was intended to act on the representation, rather than it being aimed solely at someone else.[128] There may be said to be three types of representees[129]: first, persons to whom the representation is directly made and their principals; secondly, persons to whom the representor intended or expected the representation to be passed on[130]; and thirdly, members of a class at which the **6–028**

---

[125] [1997] 1 W.L.R. 221.

[126] *Royal Bank of Scotland v Etridge (No.2)* [1998] 4 All E.R. 705 (CA), [2001] UKHL 44 at [39] 717–718. See also Proksch [1997] R.L.R. 71 and below, para.7–120.

[127] *Barclays Bank Plc v Boulter* [1999] 1 W.L.R. 1919. Lord Hoffmann, delivering the only full judgment, said that enough facts must be pleaded to give rise to the presumption of constructive notice; but it would not be adequate to rely on inferences derived from statements tucked away in documents that were pleaded. However, the Court of Appeal should be slow to intervene in the decision that an arguable defence had been raised: *National Westminster Bank Plc v Kostopoulos, The Times*, March 2, 2000.

[128] Compare below, para.6–030.

[129] See *Swift v Winterbotham* (1873) L.R. 8 Q.B. 244, 253; the rule there stated was applied in *Richardson v Silvester* (1873) L.R. 9 Q.B. 34, 36; see also *Commercial Banking Co of Sydney Ltd v R.H. Brown & Co* (1972) 126 C.L.R. 13, below, para.6–029.

[130] This category includes third persons to whom the original representee passes on the representation to the knowledge of the representor (see *Pilmore v Hood* (1838) 5 Bing.N.C. 97 which was applied in *Clef Aquitaine SARL v Laporte Materials (Barrow) Ltd* [2001] Q.B. 488 CA; *Yianni v Edwin Evans & Sons* [1982] Q.B. 438), but excludes persons to whom the representor does not intend any communication to be made (see *Peek v Gurney* (1873) L.R. 6 H.L. 377), unless (semble) he ought to foresee such communication, see below.

representation was directed.[131] But if the representation is directed at a particular class of persons, the alleged representee must be able to bring himself within that class. *Peek v Gurney*[132] illustrates this point: the plaintiffs bought shares in the market in reliance on the terms of a fraudulent prospectus issued by the promoters. The House of Lords held that the plaintiffs could not recover from the promoters: the purpose of issuing a prospectus was said to be to induce people to apply for shares, and not to induce them to buy in the market shares already issued; therefore the function of the prospectus was exhausted with the allotment, and the plaintiffs could not show that they came within the class of persons at which it was directed.[133] Similarly, in *Gross v Lewis Hillman Ltd*[134] it was held that the right of a purchaser of certain land to rescind the contract for misrepresentation did not "run with the land" so as to be available to a subsequent purchaser; the subsequent purchaser was not himself a representee of the original vendor. On the other hand, where a person makes a false statement in a document (such as a bill of lading) which he knows is going to be passed on to other people and relied on by them, any person who does in fact rely on the document will be a representee.[135] Nor is it always necessary that the actual representation should reach the representee. If a person asks an agent to find some property for him, and the agent, relying on the fraudulent inducements of the vendor, recommends the vendor's property, the buyer will be entitled to relief for misrepresentation even though the agent did not actually pass on the fraudulent statements.[136]

6–029 **Tort actions for misrepresentation.** In tort actions based on negligent misrepresentation, there seems to be a tendency to apply rules which may be somewhat more favourable to a party claiming to be a representee. This is because in such actions the defendant's liability turns on whether he owed a duty of care to the claimant, and that in turn may depend largely upon whether he ought to have foreseen that the statement would be acted upon by the claimant. In *Hedley Byrne & Co Ltd v Heller & Partners Ltd*[137] a case of negligent misrepresentation in tort, the plaintiffs asked their bankers to obtain a reference from the defendants, who were also bankers, about a client with whom the plaintiffs were proposing to do business. Although the action failed on other

[131] The class may amount to the public at large (cf. *R. v Silverlock* [1984] 2 Q.B. 766), for if a representation is made to the public generally with the intention that it should be acted upon, any member of the public may be a representee, though it does not follow that a legal remedy exists in respect of it. This is particularly so in cases of negligence, where (even if any member of the public is a representee) the absence of a duty of care may be fatal to a claim for damages, below, paras 6–081—6–083.

[132] (1873) L.R. 6 H.L. 377.

[133] It might be thought that the actual decision in this case would no longer be the common law because a prospectus today is intended to be addressed to would-be purchasers in the market just as much as to purchasers from the company, but in *Al Nakib Investments Ltd v Longcroft* [1990] 1 W.L.R. 1390 it was applied in a case of alleged negligent misstatement. Now, however, under Financial Services and Markets Act 2000 s.90, compensation is payable to any person who has acquired securities relying on incorrect or incomplete statements in the prospectus or listing particulars. See Gower and Davies, *Principles of Modern Company Law*, 7th edn (2003), pp.672–673 and below, para.6–090.

[134] [1970] Ch. 445.

[135] See, e.g. *Brown, Jenkinson & Co Ltd v Percy Dalton (London) Ltd* [1957] 2 Q.B. 621.

[136] *Gross v Hillman Ltd* [1970] Ch. 445, 461.

[137] [1964] A.C. 465.

grounds, it was held that it was no defence that the defendants did not know anything about the plaintiffs personally, for it was enough that they must have realised that the reference was wanted by some customer of the bank who would most probably act upon it. The Australian High Court has held that a bank giving a reference to another bank must have known that the reference would be passed on to the second bank's client even though it was prefaced with the words "[t]his opinion is confidential and for your private use".[138] In *Smith v Eric S. Bush*[139] a surveyor instructed by a building society to value a house for mortgage purposes knew that the prospective purchaser, who had in effect paid for the valuation, would probably rely on it in deciding whether or not to purchase. The surveyor was liable in tort to the purchaser even though the purchaser's application form for the mortgage contained a disclaimer of responsibility on the part of the surveyor towards the purchaser; the clause was held not to be fair and reasonable under the Unfair Contract Terms Act 1977.[140] It would seem, therefore, that it is sufficient if the representor either intends the representee to act on the statement or at least should have realised that he would probably do so.[141] On the other hand, in *Caparo Industries Plc v Dickman*[142] it was held that there will be no liability in tort for negligent misrepresentation unless the maker of the statement knew that the statement would be communicated to the person relying on it, either as an individual or as a member of a specified class, specifically in connection with a particular transaction or a transaction of a particular kind.[143] In relation to misrepresentation as between contracting parties, the second requirement appears to mean that the misrepresentation must have been made in connection with the contract in respect of which relief is sought, or at least that reliance on the representation in connection with the contract was likely.

Intention. It is also sometimes said that a misrepresentation will not be effective to ground relief unless it was intended to be acted on by the representee.[144] If this means no more than that the representee cannot complain unless the misrepresentation was addressed to him, or to a class of persons to whom he was one, the statement is doubtless correct. This point has been dealt with earlier.[145] But if the statement that the representor must have intended the representee to act on the representation means that the representor will not be liable if he did not intend that the person to whom he was deliberately giving the false information should act on it at all, or not in the way he did, the proposition must be treated with some caution. First, it seems that the requirement of 6–030

---

[138] *Commercial Banking Co of Sydney Ltd v R.H. Brown & Co* (1972) 126 C.L.R. 13.

[139] [1990] 1 A.C. 831.

[140] s.2(2); see below, para.14–071.

[141] cf. *McCullagh v Lane Fox and Partners Ltd* [1996] 1 E.G.L.R. 35, where at the time the information was given the surveyor did not know that the purchaser would act without getting his own survey, and by the time the surveyor did know he had issued a disclaimer.

[142] [1990] 2 A.C. 605, below, para.6–082.

[143] cf. *Morgan Crucible Co Plc v Hill Samuel Bank Ltd* [1991] Ch. 295; *Galoo Ltd (In Liquidation) v Bright Grahame Murray* [1994] 1 W.L.R. 1360.

[144] Cartwright, *Misrepresentation, Mistake and Non-disclosure* (2007), para.5.19; *Clerk & Lindsell on Torts*, 19th edn (2006), para.18–28.

[145] See above, paras 6–028—6–029.

intention applies only to cases of fraud[146] and perhaps (because of the "fiction of fraud") to cases in which it is claimed that the misrepresentor is liable in damages under Misrepresentation Act 1967 s.2(1).[147] In cases of liability in tort for negligence, the test is one of reasonable foreseeability.[148] It is submitted in cases in which the claimant seeks to rescind on the grounds of a non-fraudulent misrepresentation it will suffice that it was foreseeable that the misrepresentee will act on the representation, and it is not clear that even this is required. Secondly, even in fraud cases the authorities are not clear on whether it suffices that it must have been obvious that the claimant or someone in his position might rely on the statement. In *Cullen v Thomson*[149] three company directors were responsible for reading a report to a shareholders' meeting which contained a completely fraudulent account of the company's financial condition. It seems probable that the report was merely intended to conceal the company's financial condition from the shareholders, but the plaintiff, himself a shareholder, purchased additional shares in reliance on this report. It was held that the directors were liable for their fraudulent misrepresentations if they were made:

> "... with the real intent to cause the [representee] to act on that representation, or under such circumstances as they must have supposed would probably induce a person in the situation of the [representee] to act upon it."[150]

In *Tackey v McBain*[151] it was held that a manager of a company who said that he had no information to a broker about an important find of oil when in fact he did was not liable to a party who as a result sold his shares at a low price, whether or not the plaintiff was within the class to whom the statement was addressed, because the manager did not intend anyone to act as the plaintiff did and therefore had no fraudulent intent.[152] The likelihood of reliance was not discussed.

6–031 Given that fraud is a tort of intention, it is possible that a representor might escape liability for damages by proving that he genuinely had no intention that the representee should act on the statement, for example if a vendor says something untrue about a property honestly believing that the purchaser will not rely on it at all but will get his own survey and inevitably discover the truth. But we will see that the law seems to take a harsh approach to fraud, not even requiring that the fraud be a "but for" cause of the representee entering the contract.[153] In the light of that, it is doubtful whether a court would allow a party

---

146 Cartwright, *Misrepresentation, Mistake and Non-disclosure* (2007), para.3.49. In a case of fraud it is necessary only that the representor intended the representation to be acted on: *Goose v Wilson Sandford (No.2)* [2000] All E.R. (D.) 324 at [48]; *Mead v Babington (formerly t/a Babington Estate Agents)* [2007] EWCA Civ 518 at [16].

147 See below, para.6–070; *Banque Keyser Ullman SA v Skandia (UK) Insurance Ltd* [1990] 1 Q.B. 665, 790 (affirmed on other grounds [1991] 2 A.C. 249).

148 See above, para.6–029.

149 (1862) 6 L.T. 870.

150 (1862) 6 L.T. 870, 874.

151 [1912] A.C. 186 PC.

152 Rather similarly, see *Banque Keyser Ullman SA v Skandia (UK) Insurance Ltd* [1990] 1 Q.B. 665, 790 (affirmed on other grounds [1991] 2 A.C. 249).

153 Below, para.6–035.

who had knowingly made a false statement to another to rely on a defence that the representee was not meant to act on the statement unless the representee's action was quite unforeseeable. When the claimant is seeking to rescind on the basis of fraudulent misrepresentation,[154] it is unclear whether "intention" in the sense discussed needs to be shown.

Inducement. It is essential if the misrepresentation is to have legal effect that it should have operated on the mind of the representee. It follows that if the misrepresentation did not affect the representee's mind, because he was unaware that it had been made,[155] or because he was not influenced by it,[156] or because he knew that it was false,[157] he has no remedy. Thus in *Horsfall v Thomas*[158] a seller delivered to a buyer a gun which was defective, for after being fired it exploded, and the buyer was injured; the buyer had not examined the gun, but he alleged that the sale had been procured by fraudulent misrepresentation and that the defect had been concealed. The court rejected his claim because, as the buyer had never examined the gun, an attempt to conceal the defect, if such an attempt had been made, had had no effect on his mind. An action for breach of the implied terms as to quality and fitness would probably lie in such circumstances today.[159] Where an estate agent's particulars misrepresented the size of a garage, and the buyer had examined the whole property thoroughly on two separate occasions, it was held that the misrepresentation had had no effect.[160] **6–032**

Burden of proof. The burden of proving that the claimant had actual knowledge of the truth, and therefore was not deceived by the misrepresentation, lies on the defendant; if established, knowledge on the part of the representee is of course a complete defence, because he is then unable to show that he was misled by the misrepresentation.[161] It has also been held that a defence is made out if the truth was known to the agent of the claimant, at least where the facts had deliberately been communicated to the agent.[162] **6–033**

Need not be sole inducement. It is not necessary that the misrepresentation should be the sole cause which induced the representee to make the contract. It is sufficient if it can be shown to have been one of the inducing causes.[163] Thus **6–034**

---

[154] It may matter whether the misrepresentation was fraudulent or innocent for the purposes of Misrepresentation Act 1967 s.2(2): below, para.6–096.

[155] *Horsfall v Thomas* (1862) 1 H. & C. 90.

[156] *Attwood v Small* (1838) 6 Cl. & F. 232; *Jennings v Broughton* (1853) 5 De G.M. & G. 126; *Smith v Chadwick* (1884) 9 App. Cas. 187; *Holmes v Jones* (1907) 4 C.L.R. 1692.

[157] *Cooper v Tamms* [1988] 1 E.G.L.R. 257.

[158] (1862) 1 H. & C. 90. The judgment of Bramwell B. was criticised in *Smith v Hughes* (1871) L.R. 6 Q.B. 597, 605 by Cockburn C.J.

[159] See Vol.II, paras 43–081—43–100.

[160] *Hartlelid v Sawyer & McClockin Real Estate Ltd* [1977] 5 W.W.R. 481.

[161] *Dyer v Hargrave* (1805) 10 Ves. 505; *Attwood v Small* (1838) 6 Cl. & F. 232; *Vigers v Pike* (1842) 8 Cl. & F. 562, 650.

[162] *Strover v Harrington* [1988] Ch. 390; compare *Markappa Inc v N.W. Spratt & Son Ltd* [1985] 1 Lloyd's Rep. 534. However, the information must be received by a person authorised and able to appreciate its significance: *Malhi v Abbey Life Assurance Co Ltd* [1996] L.R.L.R. 237.

[163] *Western Bank of Scotland v Addie* (1867) L.R. 1 Sc. & Div. 145, 158; *Geest Plc v Fyffes Plc* [1999] 1 All E.R. (Comm) 672.

in *Edgington v Fitzmaurice*[164] the plaintiff was induced to take debentures in a company partly because of a misrepresentation in the prospectus, but also because of a mistaken belief of his own that the debentures conferred a charge on the company's property. He was held to be entitled to have the contract rescinded, and Cotton L.J. said, "[i]t is not necessary to show that the misstatement was the sole cause of his acting as he did".[165]

6–035 **"But for" causation not required for rescission for fraud.** It seems to be the normal rule that, where a party has entered a contract after a misrepresentation has been made to him, he will not have a remedy if it is shown that he would have entered the contract in any event. Certainly this seems to be the case when the misrepresentee claims damages in tort for negligent misstatement; and it seems also to be required if damages are claimed for fraud.[166] It seems likely that the same rule applies if he seeks to rescind on the ground of an innocent or negligent misrepresentation.[167] In cases of fraud, however, if the representee seeks to rescind, it is no defence for the representor to show that if the misrepresentation had not been made, the misrepresentee would still have made the contract.[168] It is sufficient if there is evidence to show that he was materially influenced by the misrepresentation merely in the sense that it had some impact on his thinking, "was actively present to his mind".[169] As Lord Cross put it in a case of duress to the person[170]:

> ". . . [i]n this field the court does not allow an examination into the relative importance of contributory causes.
>
> 'Once make out that there has been anything like deception, and no contract resting in any degree on that foundation can stand':
>
> per Lord Cranworth L.J. in *Reynell v Sprye*."[171]

The Privy Council applied this "fraud rule" when B had entered a contract with A after A had made threats against B's life. It held that B was entitled to relief

[164] (1885) 29 Ch D 459.

[165] (1885) 29 Ch D 459, 481.

[166] *Barings Plc (In Liquidation) v Coopers & Lybrand* [2002] EWHC 461 (Ch), [2002] 2 B.C.L.C. 410 at [127]–[130], relying on statements from the speech of Lord Steyn in *Smith New Court v Scrimgeour Vickers (Asset Management) Ltd* [1997] A.C. 254, 284. (For the *Smith New Court* case see below, para.6–055.) Thus there would be no inducement if the representee would have gone ahead even if he had been told the truth: *Dadourian Group International v Simms* [2006] EWHC 2973 (Ch), [2006] All E.R. (D) 351 (Nov) at [548].

[167] In *Pan Atlantic Insurance Co Ltd v Pine Top Insurance Co Ltd* [1995] 1 A.C. 501, a case of non-disclosure in insurance (see below, para.6–145), Lord Mustill spoke of inducement both "in the sense in which that expression is used in the general law of misrepresentation" and (549) "in the sense in which it is used in the general law of contract" without apparently seeing any difference between the two. As the "but for" test is applied generally to breach of contract, his statements and an overall reading of his speech suggest that he thought that the insurer's decision as to whether to enter the contract or at what premium must have been influenced by the non-disclosure in the sense that "but for" causation is required. cf. *Bennett* (1996) 112 L.Q.R. 405, 408.

[168] See *Re Leeds Bank* (1887) 56 L.J. Ch. 321.

[169] Bowen L.J. in *Edgington v Fitzmaurice* (1885) 29 Ch D 459, 483.

[170] *Barton v Armstrong* [1976] A.C. 104 PC at 118–119.

[171] (1852) 1 De G.M. & G. 660, 708. See also *Arnison v Smith* (1889) 41 Ch D 348, 369, where Lord Halsbury L.C. said, "[y]ou cannot weight the elements by ounces").

even though he might well have entered into the contract if A had uttered no threats. It was only if it were shown that B did not allow the threat to affect his judgment at all that relief would be denied.[172] This does not seem to be merely a reversal of the usual burden of proof[173] but a special rule that in fraud cases that, provided the misrepresentation had some influence, it is no defence that the misrepresentee would have entered the contract even if the statement had not been made. The rule is intended to deter fraud.[174] The same approach has been applied by the Court of Appeal in a case of "actual" undue influence,[175] which is seen as a "species of fraud."[176] The rule applies only to rescission, however. The victim of fraud cannot recover damages unless the fraud caused the loss for which damages are claimed.[177]

Material misrepresentation and a presumption of inducement. Once it is proved that a false statement was made which is "material" in the sense that it was likely to induce the contract, and that the representee entered the contract, it is a fair inference of fact (though not an inference of law) that he was influenced by the statement,[178] and the inference is particularly strong where the misrepresentation was fraudulent.[179] There is no set list of matters that might rebut the presumption which arises from a fraudulent statement. One is to show that the misrepresentee had already firmly made up his mind, but even then the misrepresentation might have induced him not to change his mind.[180] 6–036

Materiality. It is sometimes said that a misrepresentation will not be effective to ground relief in law unless it was material, in the sense that a reasonable man would have been influenced by it in deciding whether to enter into the contract.[181] It is true that courts have sometimes used language which would support 6–037

---

[172] [1976] A.C. 104 PC at 118–119.

[173] But see Burrows, *Law of Restitution*, 2nd edn (2002), pp.46–47.

[174] cf. below, para.6–057.

[175] *UCB Corporate Services Ltd v Williams* [2002] EWCA Civ 555 at [86].

[176] See below, para.7–068.

[177] See above, fn.166.

[178] *Smith v Chadwick* (1884) 9 App. Cas. 187, 196; also (1882) 20 Ch D 27, 44–45; *Pan Atlantic Insurance Co Ltd v Pine Top Insurance Co Ltd* [1992] 1 Lloyd's Rep. 101, 112–113 (affirmed without reference to this point, [1993] 1 Lloyd's Rep. 496, and by the House of Lords, where Lord Mustill refers to the "presumption of inducement" in the case of fraud, but he does not deny that there may be a similar presumption in other cases of positive misrepresentation: [1995] 1 A.C. 501, 542.) There is not unanimity as to the weight of any presumption. The following passage from *Halsbury's Laws of England*, 4th edn, Vol.3, para.1067): "Inducement cannot be inferred in law from proved materiality, although there may be cases where the materiality is so obvious as to justify an inference of fact that the representee was actually induced, but, even in such exceptional cases, the inference is only a prima facie one and may be rebutted by counter-evidence," was approved in *St Paul Fire and Marine Insurance Co Ltd v McConnell Dowell Constructors Ltd* [1996] 1 All E.R. 96, 112; but the same case refers simply to a "presumption". See Bennett (1996) 112 L.Q.R. 405. A material representation was said to create a presumption in *Strachan & Henshaw Ltd v Stein Industrie (UK) Ltd* (1997) 13 Const.L.J. 418.

[179] *Ross River Ltd v Cambridge City Football Club Ltd* [2007] EWHC 2115 (Ch), [2008] 1 All E.R. 1004 at [241] (Briggs J.).

[180] *County Natwest Bank Ltd v Barton*, *The Times*, July 29, 1999.

[181] Treitel, *The Law of Contract*, 12th edn (by Peel), para.9–013.

this contention[182] and it is also true that if the representation is not material in this sense, the representee may have considerable difficulty in satisfying the court that he was in fact influenced by it. There is no clear authority denying relief to a representee who has in fact been influenced by a misrepresentation which would not have influenced a reasonable man,[183] but this may be one reason why a mere "puff" or sales talk does not ground relief.[184] It is submitted that a remedy will be given where the representor knows or ought to know that the representee is likely to act on the misrepresentation.[185] In contrast, save in cases of fraud, [186] if the representor has no reason to know that the representee regards as relevant some fact which the reasonable person would think was immaterial, there will be no remedy for misrepresentation.

> "... whether there is a representation and what its nature is must be judged objectively according to the impact that whatever is said may be expected to have on a reasonable representee in the position and with the known characteristics of the actual representee ... The position in the case of a fraudulent misrepresentation may of course be different."[187]

6–038 **Unforeseeable reliance.** The question may arise whether relief may be given when the in the circumstances the representee was unlikely to act on the representation, even though it was a statement that was material in the sense that objectively speaking it was relevant: in other words, a question of whether reliance has to be reasonable or at least foreseeable. This, it is respectfully

---

[182] *Jennings v Broughton* (1854) 5 De G.M. & G. 126, 130; *Smith v Chadwick* (1884) 9 App.Cas. 187. The Marine Insurance Act 1906 s.20(2), incorporates the requirement of materiality, and it has been said that this represents the general law: *Locker & Woolf Ltd v Western Australian Insurance Co Ltd* [1936] 1 K.B. 408, 414. But a requirement of materiality is a necessary part of a rule requiring disclosure; it is not a necessary part of a rule affording relief for active misrepresentation. Note the current definition of materiality in relation to non-disclosure in insurance: *Pan Atlantic Insurance Co Ltd v Pine Top Insurance Co Ltd* [1995] 1 A.C. 501, below, para.6–145.

[183] In *Avon Insurance v Swire* [2000] 1 All E.R. (Comm) 573 Rix J. held that a statement will be treated as true if it is substantially correct and the difference would not have induced a reasonable person to enter the contract. This might seem to support the requirement of materiality.

[184] Above, para.6–006.

[185] It has been so held in Australia: *Nicholas v Thompson* [1924] V.L.R. 554. In *Cuthbertson v Friends' Provident Life Office* (2006) S.L.T. 567, (2006) S.C.L.R. 697 Lord Eassie pointed out that the materiality test in insurance (set out in s.20(2) of the Marine Insurance Act) would be satisfied if the proposer actually appreciated that the fact stated would be relevant to the insurer. In *Museprime Properties Ltd v Adhill Properties Ltd* [1990] 2 E.G.L.R. 196 it was said that materiality was really a question of the burden of proof: if the statement would not have influenced a reasonable person, the burden of proving that it did induce the contract will be on the representee, but relief may still be obtained if the burden is discharged. However, the case did not involve materiality in the sense discussed here, see next paragraph.

[186] The rule does not apply in cases of fraud: *Smith v Kay* (1859) 7 H.L.C. 750. It is no defence that the maker of a fraudulent statement thought that it was irrelevant or unimportant: *Standard Chartered Bank v Pakistan National Shipping Corp (No.2)* [2001] 1 Lloyd's Rep. 218, 225 (reversed in part on other grounds, [2002] UKHL 43, [2002] 3 W.L.R. 1547: see below, para.6–063).

[187] Mance L.J. in *MCI Worldcom International Inc v Primus Telecommunications Plc* [2004] EWCA Civ 957, [2004] All E.R. (Comm) 833 at [30]. He said that the version of this paragraph in the 29th edn "appears ... to put the position too cautiously".

submitted, is a different question from whether the statement is material.[188] A person who has entered a contract as a result of a fraudulent misrepresentation may be entitled to rescind even though one would not have expected a reasonable person to enter the contract at that stage because, for example, he has not yet secured finance for the transaction[189] or because he was expected to take the opportunity to check the facts for himself. It is not clear whether the same would apply if the party unforeseeably entered into a transaction as the result of an innocent or negligent misrepresentation, rather than a fraudulent one which was intended to induce the other to act quickly. It depends to some extent on the cases to be discussed in the next paragraph. We will see that the misrepresentee may be permitted to rescind even though he passed up an opportunity to discover the truth for himself, but it is not quite clear whether that applies if it was unforeseeable (as opposed to being merely unreasonable) that he would do so.

Representee could have discovered truth: rescission. If the representee did not know that the representation was false, it is no defence to an action for rescission that the representee might have discovered its falsity by the exercise of reasonable care.[190] Thus it is irrelevant that the true position is stated in the contract signed by the misrepresentee unless he was actually aware of the "correction" in the contract document.[191] It has been argued that the rule that a misrepresentee's failure to take advantage of an opportunity to discover the truth is no bar to rescission may require re-consideration in the light of indications in cases of claims for damages for negligent misstatement to the effect that buyers of expensive or commercial properties would be expected to have their own survey done, and thus would fail in a claim for negligent misrepresentation against a surveyor employed by the lender[192]; it is suggested that the rule should be limited to cases in which it was reasonable not to take the opportunity.[193] It is not clear, however, that the same approach should apply as between contracting parties when the misrepresentee is seeking to rescind, as is taken when a party claims damages for a negligent misstatement by a person with whom he is not in a contractual relationship. When the misstatement leads to a contract with the misrepresentor, there is at least the possibility that the misrepresentor will have benefited from his mistatement, for example by obtaining a better price for the 6–039

---

[188] It is submitted that this was the question in *Goff v Gauthier* (1991) 62 P. & C.R. 388, although the court referred to an earlier version of the *previous* paragraph of this work. It was also the question in *Museprime Properties Ltd v Adhill Properties Ltd* [1990] 2 E.G.L.R. 196 (representee did not take opportunity to check accuracy.) cf. Treitel, *The Law of Contract*, 12th edn (by Peel, 2007), para.9–016.

[189] *Goff v Gauthier* (1991) 62 P. & C.R. 388.

[190] *Dyer v Hargrave* (1805) 10 Ves. 505; *Dobell v Stevens* (1825) 3 B. & C. 623; *Reynell v Sprye* (1852) 1 De G.M. & G. 660; *Central Ry of Venezuela v Kisch* (1867) L.R. 2 H.L. 99, 120; *Redgrave v Hurd* (1881) 20 Ch D 1; *Nocton v Ashburton* [1914] A.C. 932, 962; *Laurence v Lexcourt Holdings Ltd* [1977] 1 W.L.R. 1128.

[191] *Peekay Intermark Ltd v Australia & New Zealand Banking Group Ltd* [2006] EWCA Civ 386, [2006] All E.R. (D) 70 (Apr). However, the misrepresentee must still prove inducement and if the misrepresentation was in very "rough and ready terms", while the contract was a detailed financial instrument which the investor would be expected to read in order to discover the details which he claimed were of importance to him, but the investor signed the contract without reading it, he may be held not to have relied on the misrepresentation.

[192] *Smith v Eric S. Bush* [1990] 1 A.C. 831, 854, 872.

[193] Treitel, *The Law of Contract*, 12th edn (by Peel, 2007), para.9–020.

property he is selling. The fact that he was innocent, and the other party careless of his own interests, does not necessarily justify allowing the misrepresentor to retain the advantage gained.[194] It is possible, however, that relief might be denied if it was unforeseeable that the victim of an non-fraudulent misrepresentation would not check the accuracy of the statement for himself before entering the contract. It was submitted earlier that when a misrepresentee seeks to rescind on the ground of a non-fraudulent misrepresentation, there may be a requirement that his reliance on it was at least foreseeable.[195] If there is such a requirement, it would not be fulfilled if it was unforeseeable that the misrepresentee would act without checking first.

6–040 **Representee could have discovered truth: damages.** As will be seen later, the victim of a fraudulent or negligent misrepresentation may have a claim for damages. Can these be reduced on the ground that the representee might have discovered the truth? Contributory negligence is not a defence to an action of deceit and the Law Reform (Contributory Negligence) Act 1945[196] does not apply.[197] It has been held that damages for negligent misrepresentation under the Misrepresentation Act 1967 s.2(1)[198] may be reduced if the loss was partly the fault of the representee, at least when there is concurrent liability under that section and in tort for negligent misrepresentation under the principle of *Hedley Byrne v Heller*[199]; but it would not be just and equitable to reduce the damages when the representor had intended, or should be taken as having intended, that the representee should act in reliance on the answers which had been given to his questions.[200]

3. DAMAGES FOR MISREPRESENTATION

6–041 **Preliminary.** Damages are always recoverable for a fraudulent misrepresentation.[201] Under s.2(1) of the Misrepresentation Act 1967 damages are now always

---

[194] See Jessel, M.R. in *Redgrave v Hurd* (1881) 20 Ch D 1, 13.

[195] Above, para.6–028.

[196] See below, para.6–064.

[197] *Alliance and Leicester Building Society v Edgestop Ltd* [1994] 1 All E.R. 38.

[198] See below, para.6–068.

[199] See below, para.6–081.

[200] *Gran Gelato Ltd v Richcliff (Group) Ltd* [1992] Ch. 560. See further below, para.6–074. In *Smith v Eric S. Bush* [1990] 1 A.C. 831 (where there was no contract between plaintiff and defendant) the plaintiff recovered although she might have had her own survey of the house she bought; but it was not reasonable to expect her to have her own survey of a modest property. Had the property been more expensive it might have been different and a disclaimer of liability might have been reasonable: *Smith* [1990] 1 A.C. 831, 854, 872. See above, para.6–029 and below, para.14–092.

[201] Below, paras 6–042—6–065. Exceptionally, no action may be brought on a fraudulent misrepresentation as to a person's credit unless the representation is in writing and signed by the representor: Statute of Frauds Amendment Act 1828 (Lord Tenterden's Act) s.6. This applies only to fraud, *Banbury v Bank of Montreal* [1918] A.C. 626 HL, and possibly to claims under Misrepresentation Act 1967 s.2(1): *UBAF Ltd v European American Banking Corp* [1984] Q.B. 713 CA. On the latter point see further below, para.6–070. The Act may be satisfied by a representation implied by a signed writing but a representation by conduct would not suffice: *Contex Drouzhba v Wiseman* [2007] EWCA Civ 1201, [2007] All E.R. (D) 293 (Nov).

recoverable for a negligent misrepresentation if they would have been so recoverable in fraud, where the representee enters into a contract with the representor as a result of the misrepresentation.[202] Damages for negligent misrepresentation are also recoverable in some circumstances at common law, quite apart from the Act of 1967.[203] Damages are not generally recoverable for innocent misrepresentation unless the representation is, or becomes, a contractual term, but there are a number of important exceptions to this principle.[204]

(a) *Fraudulent Misrepresentation*

Claims for damages for fraud. Where a person has been induced to enter into a contract as a result of a fraudulent misrepresentation by the other contracting party, he may rescind the contract, or claim damages, or both.[205] Rescission is dealt with in the next section.[206] It should be noted here that, as a result of the Misrepresentation Act 1967, claims for damages by a person who has been induced to enter into a contract by the misrepresentation of another party thereto may now be based either on fraud or on negligence. As will be seen in detail below,[207] s.2(1) of this Act allows a person who has been induced to enter into a contract by a misrepresentation to make a claim for damages as of right, as though the representation had been fraudulent, unless the representor "proves that he had reasonable ground to believe and did believe up to the time the contract was made that the facts represented were true". In an action under this subsection, it is for the representor to disprove negligence, whereas in an action in fraud it is for the representee affirmatively to prove the fraud—and the burden is no light one.[208] However, claims for damages against a representor who does not subsequently enter into a contract with the representee may have to be brought in fraud, for although even here negligence may sometimes suffice, it will not always do so.[209] Further, as will be seen below, the Misrepresentation Act has created a new distinction of some importance between fraudulent and other misrepresentations in connection with rescission.[210] 6–042

Definition of fraud. The common law relating to fraud was established by the House of Lords in *Derry v Peek*.[211] It was there decided that in order for fraud to be established, it is necessary to prove the absence of an honest belief in the truth of that which has been stated. In the words of Lord Herschell: 6–043

---

[202] Below, paras 6–068—6–077. Whether it is strictly correct to refer to the statutory liability as a liability for negligent misrepresentation may be open to argument, see below, para.6–068.

[203] Below, paras 6–078—6–089.

[204] Below, paras 6–094—6–098.

[205] *Archer v Brown* [1985] Q.B. 401; cf. Companies Act 2006 s.655, replacing Companies Act 1985 s.111A.

[206] Below, paras 6–103—6–133.

[207] Below, paras 6–068 et seq.

[208] Strictly, the burden is the same as that in other civil proceedings, namely, proof on the balance of probabilities (*Hornal v Neuberger Properties Ltd* [1957] 1 Q.B. 247), but it is well known that the burden of proof of fraud is not easily discharged in practice.

[209] Below, para.6–087.

[210] Below, para.6–096.

[211] (1889) 14 App. Cas. 337.

"... fraud is proved when it is shown that a false representation has been made: (1) knowingly; or (2) without belief in its truth; or (3) recklessly, careless whether it be true or false."[212]

The converse of this is that however negligent a person may be, he cannot be liable for fraud, provided that his belief is honest; mere carelessness is not sufficient, although gross carelessness may justify an inference that he was not honest.

6–044 **Absence of honest belief.** That the claimant who alleges fraud must prove the absence of an honest belief is demonstrated by *Derry v Peek* itself. A company issued a prospectus stating that it was entitled to use steam power to run trams; the respondents obtained shares on the strength of this representation, which was in fact false, although at the time the company had reason to believe that permission would be granted by the Board of Trade as a matter of course. Permission to use steam power was, however, not granted and the company was wound up. In an action for deceit the House of Lords held that the directors were not liable in damages for fraudulent misrepresentation. The decisive factor, in Lord Herschell's words, was that "they honestly believed that what they asserted was true".[213]

6–045 **Defendant's knowledge of falsity of statement.** The requirement of proof of the absence of honest belief does not, however, mean that the claimant must prove the defendant's knowledge of the falsity of the statement. It is enough to establish that the latter suspected that his statement might be inaccurate, or that he neglected to inquire into its accuracy, without proving that he actually knew that it was false. Thus where directors issued a prospectus setting out the advantages of working a particular mine, without having ascertained the truth of these representations, they were held to have committed a fraud.[214] Lord Cairns expressed the principle as follows:

"... if persons take upon themselves to make assertions as to which they are ignorant whether they are true or untrue, they must, in a civil point of view, be held as responsible as if they had asserted that which they know to be untrue."[215]

6–046 **Motive irrelevant.** Further, it is not necessary to establish that the defendant's motive was dishonest.[216]

---

[212] (1889) 14 App. Cas. 37, 374.

[213] (1889) 14 App. Cas. 37, 379.

[214] *Reese River Silver Mining Co Ltd v Smith* (1869) L.R. 4 H.L. 64. See also *Taylor v Ashton* (1843) 11 M. & W. 401, 415; *Evans v Edmonds* (1853) 13 C.B. 777, 786.

[215] (1869) L.R. 4 H.L. 64, 79–80.

[216] See *Polhill v Walter* (1832) 3 B. & Ad. 114; *Denton v G.N. Ry* (1856) 5 E. & B. 860; *Brown Jenkinson & Co Ltd v Percy Dalton (London) Ltd* [1957] 2 Q.B. 621; *Standard Chartered Bank v Pakistan National Shipping Corp* [1995] 2 Lloyd's Rep. 365; *Standard Chartered Bank v Pakistan National Shipping Corp (No.2)* [2000] 1 Lloyd's Rep. 218, 224. The definition of criminal fraud under the Fraud Act 2006 is different. Section 2 requires both dishonesty and an intention, by making the representation, either to make a gain for oneself or to cause loss to another or to expose another to the risk of loss.

Ambiguity. If the statement is ambiguous, the representee must first prove that he understood the statement in a sense in which it is in fact false.[217] If the representor intended the statement to be understood in that sense, he will be guilty of fraud. But a person who makes a statement honestly believing it to be true in the sense which he understands it to bear is not guilty of fraud merely because the representee understands it in a different sense which is false to the knowledge of the representor.[218] And this is still the case even though the court may agree that the sense in which the representee understands the statement is the meaning which, on its true construction, it ought to bear.[219] To hold a person guilty of fraud it must be shown that he intended, or at least was willing, that the representation should be understood in a sense which is false.[220] 6–047

Principal and agent. Much difficulty has arisen in dealing with cases where responsibility for a statement is divided between principal and agent, or between several agents of one principal. It has been held that the law does not recognise any conception of "composite fraud", i.e. an action in fraud will not lie where a statement is made by an agent who honestly believes it to be true, merely because the principal, or another agent, knew the statement to be false.[221] But a principal is vicariously liable for the fraud of an agent, so that if an agent makes a statement in the scope of his authority, and the agent is himself fraudulent, the principal will be liable.[222] And if one agent makes a fraudulent statement to another agent, intending the latter to pass the statement on to a third party, and this is done, the principal will again be liable; for in these circumstances, the first agent is guilty of the complete tort of fraudulent misrepresentation, the second agent being his innocent agent.[223] Again, if one agent makes a statement honestly believing it to be true, but another agent or the principal himself knows that it is not true, knows that the statement will be or has been made, and deliberately abstains from intervening, the principal will be liable.[224] In these circumstances the party with the guilty knowledge can himself be treated as being guilty of fraud. 6–048

Measure of damages for fraudulent misrepresentation. The proper measure of damages for fraudulent misrepresentation was discussed by the Court of Appeal in *Doyle v Olby (Ironmongers) Ltd.*[225] It was here held that damages for 6–049

[217] *Smith v Chadwick* (1884) 9 App.Cas. 187.

[218] *Akerhielm v De Mare* [1959] A.C. 789; *John McGrath Motors (Canberra) Pty Ltd v Applebee* (1964) 110 C.L.R. 656.

[219] *Akerhielm v De Mare* [1959] A.C. 789.

[220] *Gross v Lewis Hillman Ltd* [1970] Ch. 445.

[221] *Cornfoot v Fowke* (1840) 6 M. & W. 358; *Armstrong v Strain* [1952] 1 K.B. 232.

[222] *Lloyd v Grace, Smith & Co* [1912] A.C. 716; *Briess v Woolley* [1954] A.C. 333. The position of a junior employee, for instance one who passes on information given to him by a more senior officer and, though he has doubts about its accuracy, puts his name to it because he does not like to question it, is discussed by Tugendhat J. in *GE Commercial Finance Ltd v Gee* [2006] 1 Lloyd's Rep. 337 at [96]–[112].

[223] *London County Freehold & Leasehold Properties Ltd v Berkeley Property & Investment Co Ltd* [1936] 2 All E.R. 1039, as explained in *Armstrong v Strain* [1952] 1 K.B. 232.

[224] *Ludgater v Love* (1881) 44 L.T. 694; *Occidental Worldwide Investment Corp v Skibs A/S Avanti* [1976] 1 Lloyd's Rep. 293, 320–321 (where this sentence in the text was cited with approval).

[225] [1969] 2 Q.B. 158, noted (1969) in 32 M.L.R. 556; see also *New Zealand Refrigerating Co v Scott* [1969] N.Z.L.R. 30; *Parma v G. & S. Properties* (1969) 5 D.L.R. (3d) 315.

fraud were not the same as damages for breach of contract in that they were not designed to place the innocent party in the position he would have been in if the representation had been true, but to put him in the position he would have been in if the representation had not been made. The presumption seems to be that if the misrepresentation had not been made, the claimant would not have entered into the contract.[226] So the plaintiff ought to be awarded such damages as will put him back in the financial position he was in before the contract was made. This means that where a person is induced by fraud to buy some property, the proper measure of damages is *prima facie* the difference between the price paid and the fair value of the property.[227]

6–050 **Unforeseeable losses.** In *Doyle v Olby (Ironmongers) Ltd*, it was held that in cases of fraud the plaintiff was entitled to damages for any such loss which flowed from the defendants' fraud, even if the loss could not have been foreseen by the latter. Thus the claimant may recover not only the difference between the price paid and the value of what he received[228] but also expenditure wasted in reliance on the contract and compensation for other opportunities passed over in reliance on it.

6–051 In *Smith New Court Securities Ltd v Scrimgeour Vickers (Asset Management) Ltd*[229] Lord Browne-Wilkinson described *Doyle v Olby (Ironmongers) Ltd* as re-stating the law correctly. He stated the principles applicable in assessing damages where a party has been induced by a fraudulent misrepresentation to buy property as follows:

"(1) The defendant is bound to make reparation for all the damage directly flowing from the transaction;

(2) although such damage need not have been foreseeable, it must have been directly caused by the transaction;

(3) in assessing such damage, the plaintiff is entitled to recover by way of damages the full price paid by him, but he must give credit for any benefits which he has received as a result of the transaction;

(4) as a general rule, the benefits received by him include the market value of the property acquired at the date of the transaction; but such general rule is not to be inflexibly applied where to do so would prevent him obtaining full compensation for the wrong suffered;

(5) although the circumstances in which the general rule should not apply cannot be comprehensively stated, it will normally not apply where either (a) the misrepresentation has continued to operate after the date of the acquisition of the asset so as to induce the plaintiff to retain the asset or (b) the circumstances of

---

[226] See *Esso Petroleum Ltd v Mardon* [1976] Q.B. 801, 820, 828, 833.

[227] *Newark Engineering (N.Z.) Ltd v Jenkin* [1980] N.Z.L.R. 504; *Smith Kline & French Laboratories Ltd v Long* [1989] 1 W.L.R. 1.

[228] When there is no evidence as to values, the cost of making good the representation may be taken to represent the difference in value: *Jacovides v Constantinou, The Times*, October 27, 1986.

[229] [1997] A.C. 254, 263.

the case are such that the plaintiff is, by reason of the fraud, locked into the property;

(6) in addition, the plaintiff is entitled to recover consequential losses caused by the transaction;

(7) the plaintiff must take all reasonable steps to mitigate his loss once he has discovered the fraud."[230]

Lost opportunity but not loss of bargain. The points that damages for fraud will not compensate the claimant for loss of bargain but may cover loss caused by passing up other profitable opportunities are well illustrated by *East v Maurer*.[231] The plaintiffs bought a hairdressing business in reliance on a false representation that the defendant had no intention of working regularly at a second hairdressing business he owned in the same town. In fact he continued to work at the second business and the plaintiffs were forced to resell the business they had bought at a substantial loss. They were awarded damages for the difference between the price they had paid and the price they received on resale, plus expenditure wasted in attempting to improve the business and in other ways. They were also awarded the sum they could have expected to make as profit had they bought another similar business in the same area.[232] However they were not entitled to the higher amount they might have earned from the actual business bought had the defendant kept to his stated intention; he had not warranted that they would keep all his old customers or that he would not compete. Thus in many cases the measure of damages for breach of contract will be higher, as it will include the profit that would have been made on the contract in question had the representation been true. If as a result of a fraudulent misrepresentation the claimant has bought a property, but the property appears to be worth the price paid for it and there is no wasted expenditure or loss of a more valuable 6–052

[230] [1997] A.C. 254, 267. Lord Mustill said that the judgment of Lord Denning in *Doyle v Olby (Ironmongers) Ltd* [1969] 2 Q.B. 158 was in some respects too broad-brush; the case had not been fully argued (apparently a reference to the fact mentioned by Lord Browne-Wilkinson that certain nineteenth century cases on the date of valuation had not been cited). He considered that, in future, courts would do well to be guided by Lord Browne-Wilkinson's seven propositions: 269. On the duty to mitigate, see *Standard Chartered Bank v Pakistan National Shipping Corp* [1999] 1 All E.R. (Comm) 417, affirmed [2001] EWCA Civ 55, [2001] 1 All E.R. (Comm) 822.

[231] *East v Maurer* [1991] 1 W.L.R. 461; *Clef Aquitaine SARL v Laporte Materials (Barrow) Ltd* [2001] Q.B. 488 (claimants had agreed to buy goods from defendants at prices which defendants had fraudulently stated to be those charged to the defendants' UK customers. Although claimants had been able to resell the goods profitably, they were still entitled to the difference between the prices they had paid and those they would probably have been able to negotiate had the misrepresentation not been made). Similar damages for wasted expenditure and loss of other opportunities were awarded in *Esso Petroleum Ltd v Mardon* [1976] Q.B. 801. But cf. *Davis v Churchward* (unreported May 6, 1993) noted in (1994) 110 L.Q.R. 35. See also *Smith Kline & French Laboratories Ltd v Long* [1989] 1 W.L.R. 1, in which sellers, who had been tricked into supplying goods to a buyer who was unable to pay, recovered the normal wholesale price of the goods, not just the cost of producing them.

[232] The award in *East v Maurer* [1991] 1 W.L.R. 461 based on a hypothetical profitable business in which the plaintiff would have engaged but for the deceit has been described by Lord Steyn as "classic consequential loss": *Smith New Court Securities Ltd v Scrimgeour Vickers (Asset Management) Ltd* [1997] A.C. 254, 282.

opportunity, the claimant damages according to the tort measure would appear to be nil.[233]

6–053 **Property worth less than paid for it.** While the claimant in an action for fraud cannot claim to be put into the position he would have been in if the fact represented were true, a claimant who has made a bad bargain, in the sense that even if what he had been told were true, at the time the contract is made the property he is induced to buy would have been worth less than he has agreed to pay for it, he will be better off under the tortious measure than the contractual one.[234]

6–054 **Subsequent falls in value of property.** As Lord Browne-Wilkinson's fourth proposition indicates, the damages are normally to be calculated according to the difference between the contract price and the value of the property at the time of the contract.[235] This seems to follow from the rule that the loss must flow directly from the transaction.[236] But this is only a prima facie rule; as Lord Steyn put it,[237] the date of transaction rule is simply a second-order rule applicable only if the valuation method is followed, and the court is entitled to assess the loss flowing directly from the fraud without any reference to the date of the transaction or indeed any particular date. In some situations, the claimant may recover the difference between the contract price and the value of the property at a later date. This is so when the fall in value is due to the discovery of the defendant's fraud, which has also deceived others in the market.[238] However, it may also apply even if the reduction of value is not the result of the fraud.

6–055 **"Already flawed assets".** One such case is where, as the result of the fraud, the claimant has bought an "already flawed asset", the value of which falls when

[233] In the United States, some jurisdictions allow recovery of damages for loss of bargain in actions for fraud, e.g. *Beardmore v T.D. Burgess Co* (1967) 226 A. 2d 329; cf. *Uncle Ben's Tartan Holdings Ltd v North West Sport Enterprises Ltd* (1974) 46 D.L.R. (3d) 280. Loss of bargain damages did appear to be recoverable in English law where there had been fraud by a vendor of land who knew that he had no good title and would be unable to make one, with the result that the rule in *Bain v Fothergill* (1874) L.R. 7 H.L. 158, below, para.26–091 did not apply; but this was not a true exception: the fraud simply lifted a restriction on recovery of damages for breach of contract that would otherwise apply. Mere negligence was not enough: see the disapproval of *Watts v Spence* [1976] Ch. 165 in *Sharneyford Supplies Ltd v Edge* at first instance [1986] Ch. 128, 149 and by Balcombe L.J. in the Court of Appeal [1987] Ch. 305, 323. In any event the rule has been abolished as regards all contracts made after September 27, 1989: Law of Property (Miscellaneous Provisions) Act 1989 s.3.

[234] *Smith New Court Securities Ltd v Scrimgeour Vickers (Asset Management) Ltd* [1997] A.C. 254, 281–282, per Lord Steyn, approving the statement by Treitel (1969) 32 M.L.R. 558–559.

[235] See the speech of Lord Steyn in *Smith New Court Securities Ltd v Scrimgeour Vickers (Asset Management) Ltd* [1997] A.C. 254, 284; *Great Future International Ltd v Sealand Housing Corp* [2002] All E.R. (D.) 28; *McGregor on Damages*, 17th edn (2003), para.41–011.

[236] See the speech of Lord Steyn at 281–284.

[237] [1997] A.C. 254, 284.

[238] [1997] A.C. 254, 262 and 265; *McGregor on Damages*, 17th edn (2003), para.41–012. A rather similar explanation may underlie *Naughton v O'Callaghan* [1990] 3 All E.R. 191, a case under Misrepresentation Act s.2(1), in which the purchaser did not realise that the pedigree of the horse had been misrepresented until it had been very unsuccessful, by which time its value had fallen. Alternatively, the case may be one of a "flawed asset": see, para.6–055 and *McGregor on Damages*, 17th edn (2003), para.41–049.

the flaw is discovered, but the fraud did not relate to the flaw. In *Smith New Court Securities Ltd v Scrimgeour Vickers (Asset Management) Ltd*,[239] SNC had bought shares in Ferranti as the result of fraudulent misrepresentations by the defendants. SNC intended to keep the shares for a period of time. Their value fell drastically when it was discovered that Ferranti had been the victim of another fraud by a third party. The House of Lords, reversing the Court of Appeal,[240] held that SNC were not limited to recovering the difference between the contract price and the market value of the shares at the date of the transaction; they could recover the difference between the contract price and the prices obtained for the shares when they were sold after the discovery of the fraud. As stated in the fourth and fifth propositions of Lord Browne-Wilkinson quoted above (see para.6–051), the date of transaction rule will not be applied if it would prevent the claimant obtaining full compensation, for example if the claimant is locked into the transaction. In this case, as SNC had intended to keep the shares and it was not commercially feasible to resell them immediately, it was locked into the property.

It is not wholly clear whether the purchaser who has bought a "flawed asset", which falls in value after the date of the transaction because the flaw is discovered, can recover for this further loss if it was not clearly the purchaser's purpose to retain the property. In *Twycross v Grant*,[241] Cockburn C.J. gave the example of a person who is induced by fraud to buy a racehorse. If the horse has already contracted some disease from which it dies when he gets it home, the buyer may recover the entire price paid. In the *Smith New Court Securities* case Lord Steyn refers to this example with apparent approval.[242] It may suffice that it was to be expected that the claimant would keep the property for at least the time that it took for the flaw to emerge. 6–056

Loss caused by fall in market. Secondly, as the result of the fraud, the claimant may have acquired a property which, had it known the truth, it would not have acquired, and that property may have fallen because of a subsequent fall in the general value of property of the kind in question. It is possible that in an appropriate case, damages for fraud may include such losses. In *South Australia Asset Management Corp v York Montague Ltd*[243] the House of Lords held that in a case of negligent valuation, recovery of such losses may be "capped" at the difference between the valuation given and a correct one, but it left open the question in cases of fraud.[244] In *Downs v Chappell*[245] the plaintiffs had bought a business as the result of the defendant's fraudulent statements; they recovered the difference between the price paid and the value of the business when the fraud was discovered, even though the difference may have been increased by a general fall in property prices. In that case, Hobhouse L.J. said that only losses flowing from the tort would be recoverable, and as a means of testing whether the loss 6–057

---

[239] [1997] A.C. 254.
[240] [1994] 1 W.L.R. 1271.
[241] (1877) 2 C.P.D. 469, 544–545.
[242] [1997] A.C. 254, 279.
[243] [1997] A.C. 191, [1997] A.C. 191. See below, para.26–094.
[244] [1997] A.C. 191, 215.
[245] [1997] 1 W.L.R. 426.

was caused by the tort and of preventing over-compensation, proposed comparing:

> "The loss consequent upon entering the transaction with that which what would have been the position had the represented, or supposed, state of affairs actually existed."

This last aspect of the case was disapproved by the House of Lords in *Smith New Court Securities Ltd v Scrimgeour Vickers (Asset Management) Ltd*.[246] Thus it appears that in a fraud case the claimant can recover the full fall in value of the property, at least up to the date of discovery of the fraud, where the claimant was "locked into the transaction". Lord Steyn justified a special rule for cases of deceit by considerations of morality and deterrence.[247]

6–058 **Other cases.** Where the asset bought is not "already flawed" and the claimant is not locked into the transaction, nor is the fraud continuing to operate to induce him to retain the property (so that Lord Browne-Wilkinson's fifth proposition does not apply), it appears that the damages will still be assessed by the value of the property at the date of the transaction. In *Twycross v Grant*,[248] Cockburn C.J. also gave the example of a person who is induced by fraud to buy a racehorse which subsequently catches a disease and dies; the buyer may only recover the difference between the price paid and the real value at the time of the transaction. In *Smith New Court Securities Ltd v Scrimgeour Vickers (Asset Management) Ltd* Lord Steyn gave this as an example of a case in which there would not be a sufficient causal link between the fraud and the loss.[249] But it seems that the claimant will be treated as locked into the transaction where the other party knew that the claimant was purchasing the property for a purpose that would require him to retain it.

6–059 **Claimant would have entered another losing transaction.** As mentioned earlier, in fraud cases it is presumed that had it not been for the fraud, the claimant would not have entered the contract.[250] In *Downs v Chappell*[251] it was said that a party who has been induced to enter a contract by fraud and who seeks damages need not show that, had he known the truth, he would not have entered the transaction. He need only show that he was induced to enter the contract by a material misrepresentation and the loss that flowed from entering it. Where the misrepresentee claims to rescind the contract, it is irrelevant that he might have entered a contract with the misrepresentor even if the fraudulent misrepresentation had not been made: it need only have been one of the factors which influenced him.[252] But what the misrepresentee would have done will normally be relevant to a claim for damages, since he must show a causal connection

---

246 [1997] A.C. 254.

247 [1997] A.C. 254, 280.

248 (1877) 2 C.P.D. 469.

249 [1997] A.C. 254, 285. *McGregor on Damages*, 17th edn (2003), para.41–015 appears to take the view that the plaintiff may only be compensated for a subsequent fall in value when the asset was already flawed.

250 See above, para.6–049.

251 [1997] 1 W.L.R. 426.

252 See para.6–035, above.

between the misrepresentation and the loss claimed. Thus in *South Australia Asset Management Corp v York Montague Ltd* Lord Hoffmann pointed out that it might be shown that, had the valuer not been negligent, the lender would have lent a lesser amount to the same borrower on the same security, or "would have used his money in some altogether different, but equally disastrous venture".[253] But it seems that this may not apply in cases of fraud. Here, according to Lord Steyn's speech in the *Smith New Court Securities* case, the rules of causation are applied differently[254] and:

> "... it is not necessary for the judge to embark on a hypothetical reconstruction of what the parties would have agreed had the deceit not occurred."[255]

Mitigation. Finally it should be noted that Lord Browne-Wilkinson's final proposition is that once the fraud is discovered, the plaintiff must take all reasonable steps to mitigate his loss.[256] 6–060

Damages for non-pecuniary losses. Damages for worry and inconvenience[257] and for mental and physical suffering[258] have been awarded in actions based on fraud. 6–061

No account of profits. The victim of fraud may not obtain an account of profits made by the fraudulent party, at least where the victim has affirmed the contract and has suffered no loss.[259] The House of Lords in *A.G. v Blake*[260] held that, in certain circumstances, the victim of a breach of contract may obtain an account of the profit made by the other party through his breach. This is undoubtedly a relaxation of the rule in cases of breach of contract and it may be asked whether the rule that an account of profits is not available in case of fraud will continue to be applied. However, the conditions which the House of Lords laid down for an account of profits in breach of contract cases—broadly, that the claimant has a legitimate interest in the promised performance which an award of damages will not satisfy because the breach will not necessarily cause a loss—are less likely to occur in cases of fraud, since damages for fraud by definition do not include the gain the claimant would have made (the "expectation") had the statement made been true. Thus the claimant is entitled only to be 6–062

253 [1997] A.C. 191, 218.

254 [1997] A.C. 254, 284–285.

255 [1997] A.C. 254, 283. The decision in *Downs v Chappell* [1997] 1 W.L.R. 426, as far as the vendor's accountants were concerned, may have been interpreted in *Bristol and West Building Society v Mothew* [1998] Ch. 1 as applying the same measure in cases of negligence, but Hobhouse L.J., who delivered the only full judgment in *Downs*, has said that this is not an accurate account of the decision: *Swindle v Harrison* [1997] 4 All E.R. 705, 728. But a different view is taken by *McGregor on Damages*, 17th edn (2003), para.41–010.

256 For an application of the mitigation rule in a fraud case see *Downs v Chappell* [1997] 1 W.L.R. 426.

257 *McNally v Welltrade International Ltd* [1978] I.R.L.R. 497; *Jones v Emerton-Court* [1983] C.L.Y. 982.

258 *Shelley v Paddock* [1980] Q.B. 348; *Archer v Brown* [1985] Q.B. 401.

259 *Halifax B.S. v Thomas* [1996] Ch. 217; see also *Murad v Al-Saraj* [2005] EWCA Civ 959, [2005] W.T.L.R. 1573; *Renault UK Ltd v Fleetpro Techincal Services Ltd* [2007] EWHC 2541 (QB), [2007] All E.R. (D) 208 (Nov) at [153]–[158]; and below, para.29–147.

260 [2001] A.C. 268; see below, para.26–024.

put into the position he would have been in had the misrepresentation not been made,[261] and it is suggested that damages will normally be adequate for this purpose. To award the victim of a fraud an account of profit would be to allow him a fully restitutionary claim, and in *Halifax Building Society v Thomas* that was held by the Court of Appeal not to be available.[262]

6–063 **Exemplary damages.** It is not yet wholly clear if exemplary damages can be awarded for fraud.[263] Until recently it seemed very unlikely. Even if fraud could be brought within the first or second of Lord Devlin's three categories in *Rookes v Barnard*,[264] namely, first, oppressive, arbitrary or unconstitutional action by the servants of government or, secondly, cases in which the defendant's conduct has been calculated to make a profit for himself which may well exceed the compensation payable to the plaintiff,[265] the interpretation of those categories by the House of Lords in *Cassell & Co Ltd v Broome*[266] and by the Court of Appeal in *AB v South West Water Services Ltd*[267] required that for exemplary damages to be awarded the tort must be one in respect of which such an award had been made prior to 1964, and deceit is not such a tort.[268] However in *Kuddus v Chief Constable of Leicestershire Constabulary*[269] the House of Lords held that the power to award exemplary damages is not limited to those cases in which such awards had been made before 1964. *AB v South West Water Services Ltd* was overruled. This seems to open the way for awards of exemplary damages in cases of deceit which fall into Lord Devlin's first two categories. However both Lord Nicholls[270] and Lord Scott[271] remarked that the growth of remedies for unjust enrichment may make Lord Devlin's second category of less importance as the defendant's profit may be removed without an award of exemplary damages.[272] Even if it is still open to a court to hold that exemplary damages may be awarded in an action for deceit (even if the defendant has not succeeded in making any

---

[261] See above, para.6–049.

[262] [1996] Ch. 217. The Law Commission has recommended that restitutionary damages should be available if the defendant has committed a tort and his conduct shows a deliberate and outrageous disregard for the claimant's rights, but that was thought to require legislation: Report on *Aggravated, Exemplary and Restitutionary Damages* (No.247, 1997), para.3.51.

[263] See *Mafo v Adams* [1970] 1 Q.B. 548; *Cassell & Co Ltd v Broome* [1972] A.C. 1027 and *Archer v Brown* [1985] 1 Q.B. 401, 418–421.

[264] [1964] A.C. 1129.

[265] *Rookes v Barnard* [1964] A.C. 1129, 1225–1226.

[266] *Cassell Co Ltd v Broome* [1972] A.C. 1072, *Mafo v Adams* [1970] 1 Q.B. 548 was criticised.

[267] [1993] Q.B. 507.

[268] *Cassell & Co Ltd v Broome* [1972] A.C. 1027, 1076, per Lord Hailsham L.C. See also Law Commission, *Aggravated, Exemplary and Restitutionary Damages* (Report No.247, 1997), para.4.25.

[269] [2001] UKHL 29, [2002] 2 A.C. 122.

[270] [2001] UKHL 29 at [67]. Lord Nicholls considered that Lord Devlin's second category should be expanded to include cases in which the defendant had acted with a malicious motive.

[271] [2001] UKHL 29 at [109]. Lord Scott thought that if exemplary damages were to be retained (which he personally regretted), deceit practised by a government or local authority official, or by a police officer, would be a suitable case for their award (at [122]).

[272] See above, para.6–062 and below, para.26–019. The Law Commission, in its Report on *Aggravated, Exemplary and Restitutionary Damages* (No.247, 1997) had recommended that punitive damages be available when, in committing a wrong or in subsequent conduct, the defendant deliberately disregarded the claimant's rights.

profit from his deceit) it is wrong to do so where the defendant has already been convicted and imprisoned for the same fraud.[273] This would infringe the basic principle that a man should not be punished twice for the same offence.

Contributory negligence. Contributory negligence is not a defence to an action of deceit and the Law Reform (Contributory Negligence) Act 1945[274] does not apply. Section 1(1) of the Law Reform (Contributory Negligence) Act 1945 applies "[w]hen any person suffers damage as the result partly of his own fault and partly of the fault of any other person". Section 4 defines "fault" as: **6–064**

> "... negligence, breach of statutory duty or other act or omission which gives rise to liability in tort or would, apart from this Act, give rise to the defence of contributory negligence."

Thus for the Act to apply, the claimant's conduct must either be an act giving rise to liability to the defendant in tort or be one which at common law would have given rise to the defence of contributory negligence.[275] It has been held that at common law contributory negligence is not a defence to fraud and that therefore the Law Reform (Contributory Negligence) Act does not apply to fraud.[276]

Compound interest. In *Black v Davies*[277] the Court of Appeal held that compound interest cannot be awarded on damages for fraud. Waller L.J., giving the judgment of the court, said that compound interest will be awarded in equity in the two cases: **6–065**

> "[1] ... where money had been obtained and retained by fraud, or [2] where it had been withheld or misapplied by a trustee or anyone else in a fiduciary position."[278]

However, the House of Lords has recently said that the rule that lost interest may not be recovered by way of damages should be confined to those cases in which the loss is not pleaded or proved.[279] Loss of interest at compound rates can be recovered if that is the loss pleaded and proven.[280] This presumably applies to damages for fraud as much as to damages for any other common law claim.

Illegality. It has been held that payments made under a contract which was illegal (though not to the knowledge of the plaintiff) could be recovered in an **6–066**

---

[273] *Archer v Brown* [1985] Q.B. 401.

[274] See below, para.26–049.

[275] *Forsikringaktieselskapet Vesta v Butcher (No.1)* [1989] A.C. 852, 862 et seq.

[276] *Alliance and Leicester Building Society v Edgestop Ltd* [1993] 1 W.L.R. 1462; *Standard Chartered Bank v Pakistan National Shipping Corp (No.2)* [2002] UKHL 43, [2003] 1 A.C. 959; see also *Corp Nacional del Cobre de Chile v Sogemin Metals Ltd* [1997] 2 All E.R. 917, 921–923.

[277] [2005] EWCA Civ 531, [2005] All E.R. (D) 78 (May). The question had been left open in *Clef Aquitaine SARL v Laporte Materials (Barrow) Ltd* [2001] Q.B. 488.

[278] The categories given by Lord Brandon in *President of India v LaPintada Compania Navigacion SA* [1985] A.C. 104 at 116A HL. This was the view of the majority in *Westdeutsche Landesbank Girozentrale v Islington LBC* [1996] A.C. 669 HL.

[279] *Sempra Metals Ltd v Commissioners of Inland Revenue* [2007] UKHL 34, [2007] 3 W.L.R. 354 at [96]. See below, para.26–170.

[280] [2007] UKHL 34 at [16]–[17], [94]. [100], [132], and [154].

action of fraud,[281] though the contract itself could not be sued upon because of the illegality. Further, damages for fraud may be recovered even where the contract was known by the plaintiffs to be illegal, if the fraud and the illegality were quite unconnected.[282] In *Hughes v Clewley, The Siben (No.2)*[283] the misrepresentee was permitted to claim damages for fraud although part of the business transferred to him was used for immoral purposes, as it was said that he did not have to rely on the illegal contract. Moreover, in calculating the value of what he had received for the purposes of damages, the value of this part of the business was disregarded.

(b) *Negligent Misrepresentation*

6–067 **Preliminary.** A negligent misrepresentation is one which is made carelessly, or without reasonable grounds for believing it to be true. Apart from statute, a misrepresentation could not be regarded as negligent unless the representor owed a duty to be careful to the representee, and the law relating to the existence of such a duty of care has undergone some quite remarkable fluctuations since the case of *Derry v Peek*.[284] That case was at one time thought to lay down that there could never be a duty to take care in the making of statements unless the duty arose out of a contract itself, but the House of Lords has rejected this view in two leading cases in this country. In *Nocton v Ashburton*[285] it was decided that such a duty to take care could arise out of a fiduciary relationship, and in *Hedley Byrne & Co Ltd v Heller and Partners Ltd*[286] the law was greatly widened by the decision that a duty to take care in making statements could arise out of many other "special relationships". But the enactment of the Misrepresentation Act 1967 has somewhat reduced the importance of these cases so far as the law of contract is concerned.

6–068 **Misrepresentation Act section 2(1).** This subsection reads as follows:

> "Where a person has entered into a contract after a misrepresentation has been made to him by another party thereto and as a result thereof he has suffered loss, then, if the person making the misrepresentation would be liable to damages in respect thereof had the misrepresentation been made fraudulently, that person shall be so liable notwithstanding that the misrepresentation was not made fraudulently, unless he proves that he had reasonable ground to believe and did believe up to the time the contract was made that the facts represented were true."

Thus, where a person is induced to enter into a contract as a result of a misrepresentation, this subsection does away with the need to establish any duty of care as between the representor and the representee. In any circumstances in which this section applies, the representee will have an action for damages under

[281] *Saunders v Edwards* [1987] 1 W.L.R. 1116.
[282] [1987] 1 W.L.R. 1116.
[283] [1996] 1 Lloyd's Rep. 35.
[284] (1889) 14 App.Cas. 337; above, paras 6–043—6–044.
[285] [1914] A.C. 932.
[286] [1964] A.C. 465.

the Act. In *Howard Marine and Dredging Co Ltd v A. Ogden & Sons (Excavations) Ltd*[287] the plaintiffs misrepresented to the defendants the carrying capacity of two barges which the defendants wished to hire for carrying large quantities of clay out to sea and dumping them. The defendants entered into the contract in reliance on this misrepresentation and used the barges for some time, after which they discovered the true facts and returned the barges. It was said by a majority of the Court of Appeal that the plaintiffs were probably not under a duty of care at common law, but a differently-constituted majority held that the defendants were entitled to damages for a breach of s.2(1) of the 1967 Act. It was also stressed that the question was, strictly speaking, not one of negligence, but that the Act imposed an absolute obligation not to state facts which the representor cannot prove he had reasonable grounds to believe. No doubt it is correct to say that it is not a question of negligence, as at common law, where a duty of care is in issue[288]; and it is possible that circumstances may exist in which a person may make a statement without having reasonable ground to believe it, yet in which it would be held that he was not (having regard to all the circumstances) negligent. Nevertheless, for explanatory purposes it is sufficient to equate liability under s.2(1) of the Act with liability for negligence, and the statutory liability is referred to in this chapter, for the sake of convenience, as a liability for negligence.

Effect of section 2(1). It will be noted that the gist of the subsection is to confer a right to damages for negligent misrepresentation in circumstances in which such a right would exist if the misrepresentation has been fraudulent.[289] A number of consequences seem to follow from this. First, the rules relating to what constitutes a misrepresentation,[290] and the principle that the representation must have been one of the inducements influencing the mind of the representee,[291] will apply to an action under the subsection as they apply to an action in fraud. Secondly, it is now settled that the basic measure of damages under the subsection is the same as the measure of damages for fraud.[292] This follows from the wording of the subsection.[293] In any event it would be highly anomalous if the basic measure of damages for negligent misrepresentation under the Act were 6–069

[287] [1978] Q.B. 574, noted (1978) 94 L.Q.R. 334.

[288] An action under s.2(1) is not an action for negligence within the meaning of the Limitation Act 1980 s.14A, since it is not necessary for the claimant to aver any negligent act or omission: *Laws v Society of Lloyd's* [2003] EWCA Civ 1887, *The Times*, January 23, 2004 at [91]. Whether it is an action in tort within s.2 of that Act was left open (see at [92]).

[289] s.2(1) only gives rise to a right to damages and cannot be relied on as a defence to a claim for injunctive relief by a misrepresentee who does not wish to avoid the contract as a whole but to repudiate just one of its terms: *Inntrepreneur Pub Company (CPC) v Sweeney*, *The Times*, June 26, 2002.

[290] Above, paras 6–006 et seq.

[291] Above, paras 6–032 et seq. See the *Howard Marine* case [1978] Q.B. 574.

[292] *Royscot Trust Ltd v Rogerson* [1991] 2 Q.B. 297. See also *F. & H. Entertainments Ltd v Leisure Enterprises Ltd* (1976) 120 S.J. 331; *André & Cie SA v Ets Michel Blanc & Fils* [1977] 2 Lloyd's Rep. 166; *McNally v Welltrade International Ltd* [1978] I.R.L.R. 497; *Chesnau v Interhomes* (1983) 134 New.L.J. 341; *Heineman v Cooper* (1987) 19 H.L.R. 262 (apparently an action under s.2(1)); *Cooper v Tamms* [1988] 1 E.G.L.R. 257.

[293] *Royscot Trust Ltd v Rogerson* [1991] 2 Q.B. 297. Note that actual fraud still has to be proved if it becomes relevant for other purposes: *Garden Neptune Shipping Ltd v Occidental World Wide Investment Ltd* [1990] 1 Lloyd's Rep. 330.

different from the normal measure of damages for common law negligent misrepresentation. This means that generally damages will be awarded to put the representee in the position in which he would have been if he had never entered into the contract, and not to put him in the position in which he would have been if the misrepresentation had been true.[294]

6–070 **Application of rules on damages for fraud.** It has been shown that damages for fraud are governed by somewhat different rules to damages for negligent misrepresentation at common law: losses may be recoverable even though they were not of a foreseeable kind[295] and, in some circumstances, consequential losses may include compensation for falls in the value of the property acquired which were unrelated to the fraudulent statement.[296] It is not clear whether these rules, which appear to be justified by considerations of morality and deterrence,[297] are applicable to damages claimed under s.2(1). In the 26th edn of this work it was suggested[298] that the first rule did not apply, but this was rejected by the Court of Appeal in *Royscot Trust Ltd v Rogerson*[299] on the ground that this interpretation "is to ignore the plain words of the subsection".[300] In *Smith New Court Securities Ltd v Scrimgeour Vickers (Asset Management) Ltd*[301] both Lords Browne-Wilkinson and Steyn declined to comment on the correctness of the *Royscot* case. If the interpretation of s.2(1) taken in *Royscot* is correct, however, it would presumably follow that damages under s.2(1) can also include compensation for loss of value caused by a fall in the market, at least where the claimant has acquired an "already flawed asset",[302] and that contributory negligence will not necessarily be a defence or lead to a reduction in the claimant's damages.[303] Whether it is necessary to interpret s.2(1) in this way may, with respect, be doubted. It does not seem appropriate to apply the special rules governing damages for fraud, which are justified by considerations of morality and deterrence,[304] to cases in which there was, by definition, no fraud.[305]

6–071 **Fraud rules on knowledge.** Further, a possible consequence of the decision in *Royscot Trust Ltd v Rogerson*[306] is that the difficulties which arise in cases of

---

[294] Though see the contrary suggestion in *Jarvis v Swan Tours Ltd* [1973] Q.B. 233, 237. See also *Davis & Co (Wines) Ltd v Afa-Minerva (EMI) Ltd* [1974] 2 Lloyd's Rep. 27; *Esso Petroleum Co Ltd v Mardon* [1976] Q.B. 801. *Watts v Spence* [1976] Ch. 165, which suggested that damages under s.2(1) might be on a loss of bargain basis, has been disapproved: see above, fn.233.

[295] Above, para.6–050.

[296] Above, paras 6–054—6–059.

[297] See the words of Lord Steyn in *Smith New Court Securities Ltd v Scrimgeour Vickers (Asset Management) Ltd* [1997] A.C. 254, 280, referred to earlier, para.6–057.

[298] *Chitty*, 26th edn, Ch.6, para.439, referring to Treitel, *Law of Contract*, 7th edn, p.278.

[299] [1991] 2 Q.B. 297. See the criticisms of that case in (1991) 107 L.Q.R. 547.

[300] [1991] 2 Q.B. 297 at 307 and 309.

[301] [1997] A.C. 254 at 267 and 283. In *Avon Insurance v Swire* [2000] 1 All E.R. (Comm) 573 the defendants reserved the right to argue the correctness of the *Royscot* case in a higher court.

[302] Above, paras 6–054—6–059.

[303] See above, para.6–064 and below, para.6–074. Lord Tenterden's Act may also apply: see above, para.6–041 fn.201.

[304] See above, para.6–057.

[305] cf. *McGregor on Damages*, 17th edn (2003), para.41–046; Treitel, *Law of Contract*, 12th edn (by Peel, 2007), para.9–063.

[306] [1991] 2 Q.B. 297.

fraud where the misrepresentation is made by one person, but the guilty knowledge is that of another, seem to apply equally to an action for negligence under the subsection.[307] If, for example, the representee contracts with a company as a result of a misrepresentation made to him by one of the company's employees or agents, and that employee or agent did have reasonable grounds for believing the statement to be true, the representee will have no action under the subsection merely because another employee or agent of the company knew that the representation was untrue, or knew that there were no reasonable grounds for believing it to be true.[308] However, in practice this type of case may not prove so troublesome in cases of negligence as it has been in cases of fraud. Although a court will not impute fraud to an employee or agent merely because his principal (or another employee or agent) knows that the statement he has made is untrue, a court might be much more ready to hold that the person making the statement in these circumstances did not have reasonable grounds for believing that the facts stated were true; and it would also be possible to find negligence at common law as a result of a failure of one employee to inform another of the true facts.[309] Damages have been awarded under this subsection against a vendor of land because of the misrepresentations of his estate agent.[310]

Rescission and damages. There is nothing in the subsection to prevent the representee from both rescinding the contract and claiming damages,[311] though (as will be seen below)[312] the court now has a discretion to refuse to allow rescission, except in cases of fraud, under s.2(2) of the Act. If the representee does rescind he was, even before the passing of the Act, entitled to an "indemnity"[313] against liabilities incurred as a result of the contract, and it seems clear that he cannot claim both an indemnity and damages under s.2(1) in respect of the same loss. 6–072

The section does not give rise to liability in damages for failure to disclose, even when there is a duty to disclose material facts.[314] Silence as to material facts which should be disclosed is not an implicit representation that there is nothing to be disclosed, nor does it constitute a "misrepresentation made" within s.2(1).[315] 6–073

Contributory negligence. It was held in *Gran Gelato Ltd v Richcliff (Group) Ltd*[316] that damages for negligent misrepresentation under s.2(1) of the Misrepresentation Act 1967 may be reduced under s.1 of the Law Reform (Contributory Negligence) Act 1945[317] if the loss was partly the fault of the representee. 6–074

307 Above, para.6–048.
308 cf. *Armstrong v Strain* [1952] 1 K.B. 232.
309 See, e.g. *W.B. Anderson & Sons Ltd v Rhodes (Liverpool) Ltd* [1967] 2 All E.R. 850.
310 *Gosling v Anderson* [1972] C.L.Y. 492.
311 See *F. & H. Entertainments Ltd v Leisure Enterprises Ltd* (1976) 120 S.J. 331.
312 Below, paras 6–096 and 6–107.
313 Below, paras 6–121—6–122.
314 See below, paras 6–142 et seq.
315 *Banque Keyser Ullman SA v Skandia (UK) Insurance Co Ltd* [1990] 1 Q.B. 665, 787–789, approved by the House of Lords [1991] 2 A.C. 249, 268, 280, 281.
316 [1992] Ch. 560.
317 See below, para.26–049.

Liability under s.2(1) applies unless the representor "had reasonable grounds to believe and did believe . . . that the facts represented were true" and thus is "essentially founded on negligence". However it would not be just and equitable to reduce the damages when the representor had intended, or should be taken as having intended, that the representee should act in reliance on the answers which had been given to his questions.[318] The decision was based on the fact that there was concurrent liability under s.2(1) and in tort for negligent misrepresentation under the principle of *Hedley Byrne & Co Ltd v Heller & Partners Ltd.*[319] It may happen that a defendant is liable under s.2(1) without being concurrently liable in tort for negligent misrepresentation, for instance because the court considers that there was on the facts no undertaking of responsibility towards the claimant.[320] In such a case it seems that the claimant's damages could not be reduced on account of any contributory negligence. This is because s.2(1) makes the misrepresentor who cannot prove reasonable grounds liable as if the statement had been fraudulent. It has been held that at common law contributory negligence is not a defence to fraud and that therefore the Law Reform (Contributory Negligence) Act does not apply to fraud.[321] Because the misrepresentor is to be liable under the Misrepresentation Act 1967 s.2(1), "as if the representation had been fraudulent",[322] the Law Reform (Contributory Negligence) Act seems not to apply to claims under s.2(1) where there is no concurrent liability in tort for negligent misrepresentation.

6–075 **Burden of proof.** Once the representee proves that the statement was in fact false, the burden under the subsection shifts to the representor to prove that he had reasonable ground to believe and did believe up to the time the contract was made that the facts represented were true. Where the negotiations for a contract have continued over a substantial time, and the misrepresentation was made some while before the contract was finally entered into, this burden may indeed prove a heavy one. It will not be sufficient for the representor to prove that he had reasonable grounds to believe the statement was true when made; he will have to go on to prove that he had reasonable grounds to believe and did believe the statement was true when the contract was made.[323]

6–076 **Parties liable under the subsection.** The subsection only applies where the representee has entered into a contract after a misrepresentation was made to him by another party to the contract. Presumably, ordinary principles of agency will still apply, so that an action will lie under the subsection where the misrepresentation has been made by an agent of the other contracting party, acting within the scope of his authority.[324] But an agent who makes a misrepresentation which is

---

[318] [1992] Ch. 560, 574.

[319] [1964] A.C. 465.

[320] See the views of the majority in the *Howard Marine* case [1978] Q.B. 574, below, para.6–085 fn.361.

[321] *Alliance and Leicester Building Society v Edgestop Ltd* [1993] 1 W.L.R. 1462; *Standard Chartered Bank v Pakistan National Shipping Corp (No.2)* [2002] UKHL 43, [2002] 3 W.L.R. 1547, above, para.6–064.

[322] *Royscot Trust Ltd v Rogerson* [1991] 2 Q.B. 297, above, para.6–070.

[323] *Cooper v Tamms* [1988] 1 E.G.L.R. 257. Perhaps the burden would also have been discharged in *Oscar Chess Ltd v Williams* [1957] 1 W.L.R. 370.

[324] See *Gosling v Anderson* [1972] C.L.Y. 492.

within his actual or ostensible authority is not personally liable under the subsection, despite the fact that the subsection, having referred to a misrepresentation having been made by a *party* to the contract (i.e. the principal via the agent) then goes on to refer to the liability of the *person* making the representation.[325] The agent may, of course, be liable for negligence at common law but only if he has assumed personal responsibility towards the claimant.[326] If the agent seeks to enforce the contract in his own name, the misrepresentation may be set up as a defence against him whether or not it is attributable to him rather than his principal.[327]

Misrepresentation by third person. The subsection has no application where the representor is neither himself the other contracting party nor the agent of the other contracting party. Thus where B is induced to enter into a contract with C as a result of a misrepresentation made by A, and A is not C's agent,[328] B will have no right of action against A under the subsection. He may, however, have a remedy in damages against A on some other ground. There is, of course, no doubt that A would be liable to B in tort for fraud if fraud were proved, and in these circumstances, he might also be liable on the ground of a collateral contract or warranty (which requires neither fraud nor negligence to support it).[329] Further, an action may lie for negligent misrepresentation quite apart from s.2(1) of the Misrepresentation Act. 6–077

Liability for negligence at common law. It would be beyond the scope of this work to examine this kind of liability in detail[330] since it is not strictly contractual in its nature, and in any event, its importance has been greatly diminished by s.2(1) of the Misrepresentation Act which has been discussed in the preceding paragraphs.[331] But some account of this kind of liability is not out of place even in a work on the law of contract, since cases may arise in which a person is induced to enter into a contract as a result of a misrepresentation by a third party, and in these circumstances it is obviously desirable to consider the remedies available to the representee as a whole. This kind of liability may sometimes also arise where parties are negotiating for a contract but no contract is ever concluded, and loss is caused to one party as a result of a negligent statement by the other. Since the decisions in *Nocton v Ashburton*[332] and *Hedley Byrne & Co Ltd v Heller & Partners Ltd*[333] it is clear that an action will lie in tort 6–078

[325] *Resolute Maritime Inc v Nippon Kaiji Kyokai (The Skopas)* [1983] 1 W.L.R. 857, disapproving a suggestion in earlier editions of this work.

[326] *Williams v Natural Life Health Foods Ltd* [1998] 1 W.L.R. 830; see further below, para.6–083.

[327] *Garnac Grain Co v H.M. Faure & Fairclough Ltd* [1966] 1 Q.B. 650, reversed on facts, 658 and [1968] A.C. 1130n.

[328] As happened, e.g. in *Hedley Byrne & Co Ltd v Heller and Partners Ltd* [1964] A.C. 465. For rescission in such circumstances see above, paras 6–021 et seq.

[329] See *Wells (Merstham) Ltd v Buckland Sand & Silica Co Ltd* [1965] 2 Q.B. 170; below, para.12–007.

[330] For a full account see *Clerk & Lindsell on Torts*, 19th edn (2006), paras 8–83—8–107, and especially 8–102—8–104.

[331] But the existence of concurrent liability under s.2(1) and at common law may be important if a question of contributory negligence arises; see above, para.6–074.

[332] [1914] A.C. 932.

[333] [1964] A.C. 465.

for negligent misrepresentation causing loss to the representee where the relationship of the parties is such as to give rise to a duty of care. The former case establishes that such a duty may arise (even apart from contract) out of a fiduciary relationship, such as that of solicitor and client, principal and agent, or trustee and beneficiary; the latter case establishes that such a duty may also arise in other circumstances.[334]

6–079 ***Nocton v Ashburton.*** In this case a mortgagee sued his solicitor, alleging that by improper advice the latter had induced him to release part of his security, whereby the security had become insufficient; it was further alleged that the solicitor knew that the security would be rendered insufficient, and that his advice was given in order that he himself might benefit. The House of Lords held that fraud in the sense of *Derry v Peek*[335] had not been proved, but that the mortgagee was entitled to relief for the breach of a duty imposed on the solicitor by the relationship in which he stood to his client.

6–080 **What is a fiduciary relationship.** The fiduciary or confidential relationship necessary to bring this doctrine into operation extends to certain obvious ties, such as those between trustee and cestui que trust, solicitor and client, and parent and child. But the courts have not fettered their jurisdiction by defining its limits, and are ready to interfere in order to protect the person who is under the influence of another. The principle was stated in *Tate v Williamson*[336]:

> "Wherever two persons stand in such a relation that, while it continues, confidence is necessarily reposed by one, and the influence which naturally grows out of that confidence is possessed by the other, and this confidence is abused, or the influence is exerted to obtain an advantage at the expense of the confiding party, the person so availing himself of his position will not be permitted to retain the advantage, although the transaction could not have been impeached if no such confidential relation had existed."[337]

Cases relating to fiduciary relationships are generally dealt with as part of the doctrine of "undue influence",[338] but it is not wholly clear whether every relationship which would justify rescission of a contract for undue influence would also give rise to a duty of care which would support an action for damages for negligence.[339]

---

[334] The plaintiff may be required to specify the nature of the duty in his pleadings: *Selangor United Rubber Estates Co Ltd v Cradock* [1965] Ch. 896.

[335] (1889) 14 App. Cas. 337; above, para.6–043.

[336] (1866) L.R. 2 Ch. App. 55.

[337] (1866) L.R. 2 Ch. App. 55, 61.

[338] Below, paras 7–056 et seq.

[339] It is perhaps not strictly accurate to refer to an action for "damages" for negligence in breach of a fiduciary relationship, for this was an equitable remedy and equity did not award damages. In *Nocton v Ashburton* [1914] A.C. 932 the House of Lords spoke of an action for "compensation" and it may be that the measure of damages which they had in mind as appropriate in that case would have been lower than the usual tort measure. But today it is at least clear that a fiduciary relationship arising out of a professional relationship will ordinarily support a duty of care in tort for which ordinary tort damages will be recoverable, see, e.g. *Arenson v Arenson* [1977] A.C. 405; *Midland Bank v Hett, Stubbs and Kemp* [1979] Ch. 384.

Hedley Byrne & Co Ltd v Heller & Partners Ltd. Until the decision of the House of Lords in the *Hedley Byrne*[340] case in 1964, it was thought that a duty to take care in the making of statements could only arise in the case of fiduciary (or, of course, contractual) relationships, but that decision has shown that the law is very much wider than this. Although the House made it clear that misrepresentations made in the course of a mere social relationship would not ground liability in tort, they also made it clear that many "special relationships" would suffice. In particular, it is clear that professional relationships, even where there is no contract between the parties, will often give rise to a duty of care if it can be said that the representor knew or ought reasonably to have known that the representee was likely to act on the representation.[341] So, for example, if a company's auditor gives negligent advice to a person who invests money in the company on the strength of the advice, and it can be shown that the auditor ought to have realised that the representee would act on the advice, an action for negligent misrepresentation will lie against the auditor.[342] Again advice given "in a business connection" about the creditworthiness of a third party may give rise to a duty of care even where the adviser is not acting in a professional capacity,[343] provided he has some financial interest in the transaction.[344] On the other hand, the question whether a banker owes a duty to take care in giving references about his customers was left open by the House of Lords in the *Hedley Byrne* case, since it was thought that such a liability might be too onerous. It was, however, said that a "duty to be honest" is at least owed in such circumstances, though it is far from clear whether this is the same thing as the duty merely to abstain from fraud.[345] If the "duty to be honest" goes beyond liability in fraud, it would seem necessary to recognise a new form of liability midway between fraud and negligence, but it is submitted that this is a confusing and unnecessary conception. Since the duty of care means a duty to take such care as is reasonable in all circumstances of the case, the law of negligence is already sufficiently flexible to cater for different degrees of care. There is, for instance, no reason why a court should not hold that a banker giving references about a customer does owe a duty of care to the representee, while at the same time recognising that this duty does not require the banker to compile an exhaustive dossier on the customer's activities over a period of many years.[346] 6–081

[340] [1964] A.C. 465. On the facts the defendants could not be liable because they had coupled their statement with a disclaimer of responsibility. Such a disclaimer is subject to Unfair Contract Terms Act 1977 s.2(2): *Smith v Eric S. Bush* and *Harris v Wyre Forest DC* [1990] 1 A.C. 831.

[341] It seems that an explicit voluntary assumption of responsibility by the defendant may not always be needed, at least when the defendant should know that the plaintiff will reasonably rely on the defendant's statement: see further below, para.6–083.

[342] See, e.g. *Candler v Crane, Christmas & Co* [1951] 2 K.B. 164, the majority decision in which was overruled in the *Hedley Byrne* case [1964] A.C. 465; *J.E.B. Fasteners Ltd v Marks, Bloom & Co* [1981] 3 All E.R. 289, [1983] 1 All E.R. 583. But note the restriction described in para.6–082, below.

[343] *W.B. Anderson & Sons Ltd v Rhodes (Liverpool) Ltd* [1967] 2 All E.R. 850.

[344] See below, para.6–084.

[345] Honoré, "Hedley Byrne & Co Ltd v Heller and Partners Ltd" (1965) 8 *Journal of the Society of Public Teachers of Law* (N.S.) 284.

[346] For UK and Commonwealth cases on the *Hedley Byrne* principle, see *Clerk & Lindsell on Torts*, 19th edn (2006), paras 8–83—8–101.

6–082 **Statement in connection with particular transaction.** In *Caparo Industries Plc v Dickman*[347] it was held that there will be no liability in tort for negligent misrepresentation unless the maker of the statement knew that the statement would be communicated to the person relying on it specifically in connection with a particular transaction or a transaction of a particular kind. In relation to misrepresentation as between contracting parties,[348] this appears to mean that the misrepresentation must have been made in connection with the contract in respect of which relief is sought, or at least that reliance on the representation in connection with the contract was likely.

6–083 **Voluntary assumption of responsibility.** In *Hedley Byrne*, considerable emphasis was placed on whether the defendants had voluntarily assumed responsibility towards the plaintiffs[349]; and the defendants' disclaimer of responsibility prevented them from being liable in that case. The meaning of assumption of responsibility is not wholly clear. In *Smith v Eric S. Bush*,[350] in which the plaintiff had purchased a house on the strength of a valuation made by surveyors employed by the building society from whom the plaintiff borrowed to finance the purchase, the application form signed by the plaintiff stated that the defendant valuer's report would be "supplied without acceptance of responsibility on their part to me". Similarly, in the joined case of *Harris v Wyre Forest DC*, in which the survey was carried out by an employee of the lender, the application form stated that the lender took "no responsibility . . . for the value or condition of the property". It was held by the House of Lords that the defendants were responsible nonetheless; the clauses were subject to Unfair Contract Terms Act 1977 s.2(2) and had not been shown to be reasonable. Lord Griffiths stated that he did not find that "voluntary assumption of responsibility is a helpful or realistic test for liability".[351] However, subsequent authority in the House of Lords again stressed that liability for economic loss, including in cases of negligent misstatement, is based on an "assumption of responsibility".[352] Lord Goff has explained that:

> " . . . especially in a context concerned with a liability which may arise under a contract or in a situation 'equivalent to contract', it must be expected that an objective test will

[347] [1990] 2 A.C. 605. cf. *Morgan Crucible Co Plc v Hill Samuel Bank Ltd* [1991] Ch. 295. In *Galoo Ltd (In Liquidation) v Bright Grahame Murray* [1994] 1 W.L.R. 1360, it was held that an auditor of a company's accounts may owe a duty of care to a take-over bidder if he has expressly been informed that the bidder will rely on the accounts for the purpose of deciding whether to make an increased bid and intends that the bidder should so rely. See also *Possfund Custodian Trustee Ltd v Diamond* [1996] 1 W.L.R. 1351.

[348] See below, para.6–085.

[349] e.g. by Lord Reid and Lord Devlin in *Hedley Byrne* [1964] A.C. 465 at 487 and 529, respectively. There was no assumption of responsibility or duty of care in *IFE Fund SA v Goldman Sachs International* [2007] EWCA Civ 811, [2007] 2 Lloyd's Rep. 449.

[350] [1990] 1 A.C. 831.

[351] [1990] 1 A.C. 831, 862.

[352] See *Henderson v Merrett Syndicates Ltd* [1995] 2 A.C. 145; *White v Jones* [1995] 2 A.C. 207; *Williams v Natural Life Health Foods Ltd* [1998] 1 W.L.R. 830. All three cases are discussed in more detail above, paras 1–138—1–142.

be applied when asking the question whether, in a particular case, responsibility should be held to have been assumed by the defendant to the plaintiff."[353]

Thus the existence of a disclaimer will not necessarily negate an assumption of liability if the defendant knows that there is a strong probability that the plaintiff will nonetheless rely on the information given.[354] The defendant will be protected only if he shows that the disclaimer satisfies the requirement of reasonableness under the Unfair Contract Terms Act 1977.[355]

Statements not made in course of business. The principle of the *Hedley Byrne* case was somewhat limited by the majority decision of the Privy Council in *Mutual Life and Citizen's Assurance Co Ltd v Evatt*[356] where it was held that in general there is no duty to take care in the making of statements unless the maker has held himself out as having some special skill or competence in the matter in question. In general, it was held, the duty will only arise where the statement is made in the course of a business though in some cases other factors may be sufficient to impose a duty, for example that the person making the statement has a financial interest in the transaction on which he has given advice.[357] However, it seems unlikely that this decision will now be followed. It was decided by a bare majority and several judges have felt free to indicate their preference for the minority judgments of Lord Reid and Lord Morris.[358] 6–084

Special relationship between parties negotiating contract. It has now become clear that a special relationship, giving rise to a duty of care, may subsist between parties negotiating a contract if information is given in connection with the contract.[359] In *Esso Petroleum Co Ltd v Mardon*[360] it was held that a petroleum company, negotiating a lease of a filling station, was liable to the tenant for negligently giving him over-optimistic estimates of the sales potential of the filling station. It should be noted that this was not a casual observation made between parties each of whom was in the same position to judge the accuracy of the estimate. The information was based on a detailed evaluation of the position by the petroleum company and the tenant was clearly not in as good a position as they were to make such an estimate.[361] Similarly, it has been held that a special relationship existed between a landlord and a tenant as a result of 6–085

[353] *Henderson v Merrett Syndicates Ltd* [1995] 2 A.C. 145, 181. See also the speech of Lord Steyn in *Williams v Natural Life Health Foods Ltd* [1998] 1 W.L.R. 830.

[354] See, e.g. the judgments of Lords Templeman and Griffiths in *Smith v Eric S. Bush* [1990] 1 A.C. 831, at 852 and 865, respectively.

[355] ss.2(2), 11(5) and 13.

[356] [1971] A.C. 793, noted (1971) 87 L.Q.R. 147.

[357] See *W.B. Anderson & Sons Ltd v Rhodes (Liverpool) Ltd* [1967] 2 All E.R. 850.

[358] In *Esso Petroleum Co Ltd v Mardon* [1975] Q.B. 819 and [1976] Q.B. 801, below, para.6–085, and also in the *Howard Marine* case [1978] Q.B. 574, above, para.6–068. The Australian High Court has also refused to follow the majority judgments in the *Evatt* case: see *L. Shaddock & Associates Pty Ltd v Parramatta City Council* (1981) 55 A.L.J.R. 713.

[359] See above, para.6–082.

[360] [1976] Q.B. 801; also *McInerny v Lloyds Bank Ltd* [1974] 2 Lloyd's Rep. 246, 253–254; *Cornish v Midland Bank Plc* [1985] 3 All E.R. 513; *Gran Gelato Ltd v Richcliff (Group) Ltd* [1992] Ch. 560.

[361] Contrast the *Howard Marine* case [1978] Q.B. 574, where the majority seems to have considered that the casual nature of the answer precluded a duty of care.

pre-contractual discussion during which the landlord assured the tenant that he would keep the premises insured[362]; but it was also held in this case that the duty was only a duty not to give misleading information, and did not extend to requiring the landlord to exercise care not to allow the insurance to expire unrenewed without informing the tenant.[363] On the other hand, it has been held that a special relationship existed between an astute and experienced business woman and an insurance company with whom she was contemplating investing over £90,000 in a property bond; and in this case it was held that the consequential duty of care required the defendants' agent to give the plaintiff an adequate explanation of the nature of property bonds, and was not merely a duty to avoid misrepresentation.[364] An estate agent may be liable to a customer who purchases a house in reliance on a negligent misrepresentation.[365] A Canadian case has held that a builder who provided an estimate as to the cost of building a house was under a duty to take care to see that the client realised that his estimate did not include his 15 per cent mark-up.[366] Sometimes even a failure to disclose may give rise to liability, but this will only be so if there has been a voluntary assumption of responsibility to disclose and the claimant has relied on it. There is no liability under the *Hedley Byrne* principle simply because the contract was uberrimae fidei and thus could be avoided for non-disclosure of a material fact.[367]

6–086 **Relationship between manufacturer and purchaser of goods.** In *Lambert v Lewis*[368] it was held by the Court of Appeal that a person who purchases goods in reliance on statements in a manufacturer's promotional literature is not, for that reason alone, entitled to claim that a special relationship exists as a result of which the manufacturer may be held liable for negligent statements in the literature. The mere making of a serious statement with the intent that it should be relied upon was not enough, said the court, to create a special relationship. It may seem regrettable that a manufacturer is under no duty of care with respect to statements made in his brochures and advertising leaflets which are plainly designed to influence buyers. However, the decision itself seems consistent with the later decision in *Caparo Industries Plc v Dickman*[369] that there will be no liability in tort for negligent misrepresentation unless the maker of the statement knew that the statement would be communicated to the person relying on it either as an individual or as a member of a specified class, specifically in connection with a particular transaction or a transaction of a particular kind. In most cases a manufacturer will not know the purchaser's identity other than as a member of

---

362 *Argy Trading Development Co Ltd v Lapid Developments Ltd* [1977] 1 W.L.R. 444.
363 [1977] 1 W.L.R. 444.
364 *Rust v Abbey Life Insurance Co Ltd* [1978] 2 Lloyd's Rep. 386.
365 *Computastaff Ltd v Ingledew Brown Bennison & Garrett* (1983) 268 E.G. 598.
366 *A.L. Gullison & Sons Ltd v Corey* (1980) 29 N.B.R. (2d) 86.
367 *La Banque Financière de la Cité SA v Westgate Insurance Co Ltd Banque Keyser Ullman SA v Skandia (UK) Insurance Co Ltd* [1990] 1 Q.B. 665, 791, 794–795, 799, 802–803, affirmed on other grounds [1991] 2 A.C. 249. On contracts uberrimae fidei see below, paras 6–142 et seq. It is possible that there might be an implicit assumption of responsibility if the defendant should have known that the plaintiff was reasonably relying on the defendant to disclose certain facts: cf. *Smith v Eric S. Bush* [1990] 1 A.C. 831, above, para.6–083.
368 [1982] A.C. 225; this issue was not discussed on appeal to the House of Lords.
369 [1990] 2 A.C. 605, above, para.6–082.

a very broad class and will know the purchaser's purposes only in general terms. If the manufacturer knows both the purchaser's identity and his purposes it is submitted that there may be a special relationship.[370] There is authority for saying that in such circumstances information given by the manufacturer may constitute a contractual warranty.[371] There is some ground for suggesting that even in the absence of direct contact between manufacturer and purchaser, statements in the manufacturer's literature should be treated as warranties, rendering the manufacturer strictly liable, and not merely liable for negligence: this is certainly the position in American law,[372] but in English law such statements are said not to be warranties unless there is an intent to warrant.[373] However, where goods are sold or supplied to a consumer with a "consumer guarantee", under the Sale and Supply of Goods to Consumers Regulations 2002[374] the consumer guarantee "takes effect . . . as a contractual obligation owed by the guarantor under the conditions set out in the guarantee statement and associated advertising".[375]

Where negotiations do not lead to contract. In principle there seems no reason why a special relationship should not be held to exist between parties negotiating a contract even where the negotiations break down so that no contract is ultimately made. Indeed, this seems to have been the basis of the decision in *Box v Midland Bank Ltd*[376] where the plaintiff sought a large loan from his bankers. His bank manager told him that the loan would need approval from head office but gave the plaintiff to think that this was a formality; in the meantime, the plaintiff was permitted overdraft facilities. The loan application was refused by head office and the plaintiff claimed that he had suffered loss through being led to believe that the loan would be forthcoming. This claim was, in part, upheld by Lloyd J. on the basis that the bank manager owed a duty not to mislead the plaintiff by careless advice as to the probable outcome of his loan application. 6–087

Special relationship between parties already in contractual relationship. It is now clear that one party to a contractual relationship may owe duties in tort to the other; these duties may overlap with contractual duties, and where this is the case the claimant may have alternative causes of action in contract and in tort.[377] It has also been held that damages may be obtainable for misrepresentations made in the course of renegotiating a contract already in existence, under the Misrepresentation Act,[378] and there seems no reason to doubt 6–088

[370] cf. *Independent Broadcasting Authority v EMI Electronics and BICC Construction Ltd* (1980) 14 Build. L.R. 1, a case of a post-contractual representation.
[371] *Shanklin Pier v Detel Products Ltd* [1951] 2 K.B. 854; *Wells (Merstham) Ltd v Buckland Sand and Silica Co Ltd* [1965] 2 Q.B. 170.
[372] See, e.g. *Greenman v Yuba Power Products* (1963) 377 P. 2d 897, and many other cases cited in White & Summers, *Uniform Commercial Code*, 5th edn (2000), para.11–2.
[373] See *Lambert v Lewis* [1982] A.C. 225 itself, and see also below, paras 12–003—12–007.
[374] SI 2002/3045. See further below, para.43–155.
[375] 2002 Regulations reg.15(1).
[376] [1979] 2 Lloyd's Rep. 391, on appeal (as to costs only) [1981] 1 Lloyd's Rep. 434.
[377] *Henderson v Merrett Syndicates Ltd* [1995] 2 A.C. 145; above, paras 1–126 et seq.
[378] *André & Cie SA v Ets Michel Blanc & Fils* [1977] 2 Lloyd's Rep. 166.

that in an appropriate case liability could also arise under the *Hedley Byrne* principle in such a situation.

6–089 **Damages at common law.** Damages for negligent misrepresentation at common law will naturally be on the tortious measure[379]; but the usual rules on remoteness[380] and contributory negligence[381] will apply. So will the restrictions on a negligent valuer's liability for subsequent falls in the value of the property set down in *South Australia Asset Management Corp v York Montague Ltd.*[382]

6–090 **Other legislative provisions creating liability for negligent misrepresentations: financial services.** There are a number of legislative provisions that in effect create liability for negligent misrepresentation in particular circumstances.[383] For example, Financial Services and Markets Act 2000 Pt VI imposes stringent duties on persons responsible for listing particulars of securities for admission to the Official List, and prospectuses.[384] The legislation makes the person responsible liable to pay compensation to a person who has acquired securities to which the legislation applies,[385] and who has suffered loss as the result of any untrue or misleading statement in the prospectus or, in the case of listing particulars, the particulars.[386] It then provides a number of exceptions, one of which is that liability for the loss will not be incurred if the person responsible satisfies the court that, at the time when the particulars were submitted to the relevant authority or delivered for registration, he reasonably believed that the statement was true and not misleading.[387] There is also liability for failure to publish a supplementary prospectus when necessary.[388]

---

[379] See above, para.6–049.

[380] Compare above, para.6–050.

[381] Above, para.6–074.

[382] [1997] A.C. 191; above, para.6–057 and below, para.26–094.

[383] Financial Services and Markets Act 2000 s.397 imposes criminal liability for knowingly or recklessly making a false or deceptive statement, promise or forecast to induce another to make an investment or other specified agreement; but it does not appear that there will be civil liability. This section replaced Financial Services Act 1986 s.47, which was held not to confer any right to damages or other civil remedy: *Norwich Union Life Insurance Society v Qureshi* [1999] 2 All E.R. (Comm) 707 CA. See further Cartwright, *Misrepresentation, Mistake and Non-disclosure* (2007), para.7.71. For the possibility of a restitution order on the basis that the conduct may constitute market abuse within s.118 of the Act see Gower & Davies, *Principles of Modern Company Law*, 7th edn (2003), pp.789–790, and cf. *Securities and Investments Board Ltd v Pantell SA (No.2)* [1993] Ch. 256, decided under Financial Services Act 1986.

[384] See generally, Gower & Davies, *Principles of Modern Company Law*, 7th edn (2003), pp.649 et seq. For the duties of disclosure imposed by these provisions see below, para.6–153.

[385] Thus investors who have bought on the market after dealing has commenced are now protected.

[386] Financial Services and Markets Act 2000 ss.86(1), 90(1). Note that the section is without prejudice to any liability which may be incurred apart from the section or regulation: s.90(6). These provisions stem ultimately from the Directors Liability Act 1890, which was passed to reverse the effect of *Derry v Peek* (1889) 14 App.Cas. 337, so far as it applied to prospectuses.

[387] Financial Services and Markets Act 2000 Sch.10 para.1(2). For the possible application of the *Hedley Byrne* principle (above, para.6–081) and of Misrepresentation Act 1967 to misstatements in prospectuses and particulars, see Gower & Davies, *Principles of Modern Company Law*, 7th edn (2003), pp.675–679.

[388] See further below, para.6–153.

Property Misdescriptions Act. Under s.1 of the Property Misdescriptions Act 1991, the making of a false or misleading statement about a prescribed matter[389] in the course of an estate agency business or a property development business may constitute a criminal offence, unless all reasonable steps and due diligence had been used to avoid committing the offence.[390] However no contract is void or unenforceable and no right of action in civil proceedings will arise by reason only of the commission of an offence under the section.[391] 6–091

Package travel, etc. Under the Package Travel, Package Holidays and Package Tours Regulations 1992,[392] organisers or retailers of such packages must not supply any descriptive matter concerning a package, the price of a package or any other conditions applying to the contract which contains misleading information. If a consumer suffers loss as a result of a breach of this requirement the organiser or retailer is liable to pay compensation.[393] As liability appears to be strict it might be regarded as contractual than for misrepresentation; but it has been pointed out that the relevant regulation differs from others which imply terms into the contract.[394] The measure of damages is not stated, but it seems likely that a tort measure would be applied.[395] 6–092

Home Information Packs. It had been intended that vendors (or their estate agents) of larger types of residential property would be required to provide on request a "Home Information Pack" including a "home condition report" prepared by a home inspector.[396] However, the relevant Regulations were revoked before coming into force[397] and a home condition report is now optional.[398] If a report is provided, the home inspector must use reasonable care and skill and the terms of the contract under which the report is prepared must provide that, if he does not, the seller, the purchaser or a mortgagee of the property will have a direct right of action against him.[399] 6–093

(c) *Innocent Misrepresentation*

No damages for innocent misrepresentation. The term "innocent misrepresentation" is here used to mean a representation which is neither fraudulent nor 6–094

---

[389] See Property Misdescriptions (Specified Matters) Order (SI 1992/2834).
[390] Property Misdescriptions Act 1991 s.2. See *Enfield LBC v Castles Estate Agents Ltd* (1997) 73 P. & C.R. 343.
[391] s.1(4).
[392] SI 1992/3288 implementing Directive 90/314. See below, para.13–034.
[393] 1992 Regulations reg.4.
[394] Cartwright, *Misrepresentation, Mistake and Non-disclosure* (2007), para.7.69.
[395] Cartwright at para.7.89.
[396] See the Housing Act 2004 Pt 5 and the Home Information Pack Regulations 2006 (SI 2006/1503) reg.8.
[397] By SI 2007/1525.
[398] See Home Information Pack (No.2) Regulations 2007 (SI 2007/1667) reg.9.
[399] Sch.9 arts 2 and 3.

negligent, and the general rule remains what it has always been, namely, that no action for damages lies for a mere innocent misrepresentation in this sense.[400] Damages in respect of the misrepresentation will be recoverable, however, if the court exercises its discretion under the Misrepresentation Act 1967 s.2(2), to declare the contract subsisting, and awards damages in lieu of rescission.[401] Also it must be stressed that a misrepresentation will found a claim for damages if it can be construed as a contractual promise, and is either part of a wider contract, or is itself supported by consideration. This may happen in two principal types of case. First, where the representor and representee themselves enter into a contract after the misrepresentation was made. Here, if the misrepresentation becomes a term of the contract, an action for damages will lie, whether the misrepresentation was fraudulent, negligent or innocent.[402] Secondly, the representee may enter into a contract with a third party as a result of the misrepresentation. Even in this situation, it is often possible to construe the misrepresentation as a collateral contract, the consideration for which is supplied by the fact that the representee enters into the contract with the third party.[403] A familiar illustration of the principle of the collateral contract can be seen in an agent's liability for breach of warranty of authority.[404]

6–095 **Estoppel.** Circumstances may arise in which damages are recoverable for a completely innocent misrepresentation, through the assistance of the doctrine of estoppel. For example, if a person agrees to buy shares in a company on the strength of a share certificate issued to the seller stating that he is the registered owner of the shares, the company may be estopped from denying that the seller was in truth the owner of the shares. The purchaser is, in these circumstances, entitled to demand that the company register him as the owner of the shares, or to claim damages in lieu.[405] The purchaser does not claim damages directly for the misrepresentation, but the net effect is very much the same. For the doctrine of estoppel to apply the usual requirements of an estoppel must be satisfied; in particular the statement relied on must be precise, unambiguous and unqualified.[406] An estoppel may in exceptional circumstances arise out of non-disclosure, but a duty to disclose must then be shown.[407] It is also necessary that some independent cause of action be shown, apart from the misrepresentation

[400] *Heilbut, Symonds & Co v Buckleton* [1913] A.C. 30; *Gilchester Properties Ltd v Gomm* [1948] 1 All E.R. 493.

[401] See below, para.6–107.

[402] See, e.g. *Dick Bentley Productions Ltd v Harold Smith (Motors) Ltd* [1965] 1 W.L.R. 623, below, para.12–003.

[403] Below, para.12–007.

[404] See Vol.II, paras 31–101—31–108.

[405] *Re Bahia and San Francisco Ry* (1868) L.R. 3 Q.B. 584; *Balkis Consolidated Co v Tomkinson* [1893] A.C. 396.

[406] *Low v Bouverie* [1891] 3 Ch. 82; *Woodhouse A.C. Israel Cocoa Ltd v Nigerian Produce Marketing Co Ltd* [1972] A.C. 741; *China-Pacific SA v Food Corp of India* [1981] Q.B. 403, reversed on different grounds [1982] A.C. 939.

[407] *Greenwood v Martin's Bank* [1933] A.C. 51; *Moorgate Mercantile Co Ltd v Twitchings* [1977] A.C. 890; *Banque Keyser Ullman SA v Skandia (UK) Insurance Co Ltd* [1990] 1 Q.B. 665, affirmed on other grounds [1991] 2 A.C. 249.

itself.[408] This cause of action will normally be a claim to some form of property to which the representee would be entitled if the representation were true, and the truth of which the representor is not entitled to deny, e.g., money which would be due to the representee as assignee,[409] or goods which the representor has acknowledged that he holds on behalf of the representee.[410]

Misrepresentation Act section 2(2). This subsection reads as follows: 6–096

> "Where a person has entered into a contract after a misrepresentation has been made to him otherwise than fraudulently, and he would be entitled, by reason of the misrepresentation, to rescind the contract, then, if it is claimed, in any proceedings arising out of the contract, that the contract ought to be or has been rescinded, the court or arbitrator may declare the contract subsisting and award damages in lieu of rescission, if of opinion that it would be equitable to do so, having regard to the nature of the misrepresentation and the loss that would be caused by it if the contract were upheld, as well as to the loss that rescission would cause to the other party."

It will be seen that this subsection does not give a representee any *right* to claim damages, but it enables the court, in its discretion, to grant damages to the representee in lieu of rescinding the contract.[411] It seems probable that the subsection was intended principally for the benefit of the representor, so that a contract need not be rescinded where the court feels that the representee can be adequately compensated in damages.[412] But cases may well occur in which damages would be the preferable remedy for the representee. In this event there seems nothing to prevent the representee from claiming the right to rescind but then inviting the court to award damages in lieu. Nor does there seem to be anything which would prevent the court from taking this course over the protests of the representor, who may prefer rescission to an award of damages.

Damages only in lieu of rescission. But it is important to note two limitations on the power to award damages under this subsection. First, damages can only be awarded *in lieu* of rescission. In the case of a fraudulent misrepresentation, to which the subsection does not apply, the representee can both rescind and claim damages as of right.[413] Rescission for fraud is rescission ab initio, and damages for breach of contract cannot be recovered after such rescission, but damages for fraud are recovered in tort and there is no reason why this remedy should not 6–097

[408] [1990] 1 Q.B. 665. But cf. *Brikom Investments Ltd v Seaford* [1981] 1 W.L.R. 863; *Re Wyvern Developments Ltd* [1974] 1 W.L.R. 1097. In cases based on "proprietary estoppel" it seems that no independent cause of action need be shown, but the authorities in this area of the law are still developing. See above, paras 3–098—3–105 and 3–137—3–164.

[409] *Burrows v Lock* (1805) 10 Ves. 470.

[410] *Seton, Laing & Co v Lafone* (1887) 19 QBD 68.

[411] It is apparent from subs.(3) that this subsection also applies where the misrepresentation was negligent, but clearly the victim of such a misrepresentation who wants damages rather than rescission will claim under subs.(1).

[412] See paras 11 and 12 of the Tenth Report of the Law Reform Committee, Cmnd.1782 (1962) on which s.2 was based.

[413] *Attwood v Small* (1838) 6 Cl. & F. 232, 444; *Newbigging v Adam* (1886) 34 Ch D 582, 592. There is nothing inconsistent with this in *Johnson v Agnew* [1980] A.C. 367. See below, paras 6–106 and 24–047.

survive rescission of the contract. In the case of a negligent misrepresentation, the representee can claim both rescission and damages, but whereas his claim to damages is as of right under s.2(1) his claim to rescission is now subject to the discretion of the court under s.2(2).[414] But in the case of an innocent misrepresentation, the representee cannot get both rescission and damages,[415] nor can he claim either remedy as of right.

6–098 **Rescission barred.** A second limitation on the subsection is that the power to grant damages is, on the balance of authority, available only where the remedy of rescission would still be available at the time of the court's order. The court may award damages in lieu of rescission wherever the representee "would be entitled . . . to rescind the contract". The question is whether this means: "would be entitled at the time of the court's order", or: "would have been entitled after the representation was made". Purely linguistic considerations suggest that the former meaning is the correct one and in *Atlantic Lines & Navigation Co Inc v Hallam Ltd (The Lucy)*[416] Mustill J. accepted it. Nonetheless earlier editions of this Work suggested that the wording was ambiguous. In *Thomas Witter Ltd v TBP Industries Ltd*[417] Jacob J. also considered the section to be ambiguous[418] and referred to a statement of the Solicitor-General during a debate on the Misrepresentation Bill.[419] Jacob J. expressed the view that damages could have been awarded under s.2(2) even though the misrepresentee had lost the right to rescind. But the suggestion that the words were unclear was disapproved in *Zanzibar v British Aerospace (Lancaster House) Ltd*,[420] in which Judge Jack Q.C. held that the power to award damages is an alternative to damages and no longer existed when the right to rescission had been lost. The same conclusion had been reached earlier by Judge Humphrey Lloyd Q.C. in *Floods of Queensferry Ltd v Shand Construction Ltd*,[421] who refused to follow the decision in the *Thomas Witter* case. It is submitted that after all the power to award damages ends if the claimant loses the right (subject to s.2(2)) to rescind.

6–099 **Measure of damages under section 2(2).** Section 2(2) does not state the measure of damages to be awarded. It is possible that the measure of damages which may be awarded under subs.(2) is intended to be lower than the measure of damages for fraudulent misrepresentation which, as seen above, is now also

[414] For a case in which damages and rescission were permitted under the Act, see *F. & H. Entertainments Ltd v Leisure Enterprises Ltd* (1976) 120 S.J. 331.

[415] Except in those exceptional cases in which damages are recoverable for innocent misrepresentation, above, para.6–094. Note also that, on rescission, the representee is entitled to an indemnity for burdens assumed under the contract, but this is much narrower than the right to damages, below, paras 6–121—6–122.

[416] [1983] 1 Lloyd's Rep. 188.

[417] See (1995) 111 L.Q.R. 385.

[418] As was argued in previous editions of this work.

[419] The statement itself lends some support to this view but further investigation of the legislative history throws some doubt on it: see (1995) 111 L.Q.R. 385.

[420] [2000] 1 W.L.R. 2333.

[421] [2000] Building L.R. 81.

applicable to negligent misrepresentation under s.2(1). This possibility is suggested by subs.(3) of the same section which provides that damages may be awarded under subs.(2) whether or not the representor is liable to damages under subs.(1) (i.e. whether or not he has been negligent), but goes on to provide that any damages awarded under subs.(2) shall be taken into account in assessing liability under subs.(1). This seems to indicate that the damages awarded under subs.(2) may be lower than the damages awarded under subs.(1), and there might be something to be said for this since the representor may be wholly innocent in a case under subs.(2). But the Act gives little clue as to how damages are to be assessed under this subsection if they are not to be assessed in the same way as under subs.(1). It has already been seen that damages under subs.(1) are tortious rather than contractual.[422] It would seem a fortiori that damages under subs.(2) would not be at the contractual level. The alternatives then would seem to be to award either the tort measure or a special measure designed to compensate the representee for the loss resulting from his inability to obtain rescission. There seem to be two reasons to interpret s.2(2) as applying a special measure. The first relates to consequential loss, the second to bad bargains.

Section 2(2) and consequential loss. Suppose the vendor of a house has made an innocent misrepresentation about the state of the drains and as a result the purchaser has suffered personal injury and property damage. Rescission, even with an indemnity, would not compensate the purchaser for these losses[423] and it is arguable that they should not be compensated under s.2(2), which refers to damages "in lieu of rescission".[424] But it has been held that consequential damages may be recovered under this subsection,[425] though without averting to these questions. 6–100

Section 2(2) and bad bargains. The second relates to cases where the misrepresentee has made a bad bargain in the sense that, quite apart from the misrepresentation, the property is worth less than he has paid for it. In such a case the court might well exercise its discretion to declare the contract subsisting if it thinks the misrepresentee is less concerned about the effect of the misrepresentation than to escape from the contract. Were the damages in lieu of rescission to be on the tortious measure as applied in actions for fraud,[426] or were the damages 6–101

[422] Above, para.6–069.

[423] *Whittington v Seale-Hayne* (1900) 82 L.T. 49, below, para.6–122.

[424] In favour of this alternative is the literal interpretation given to s.2(1) by the Court of Appeal in *Royscott Trust Ltd v Rogerson* [1991] 2 Q.B. 297. Against it is the analogy of damages under Lord Cairns' Act 1858 *in lieu* of an award of specific performance where (it seems) the damages are to be assessed as at common law, and not in accordance with some special measure: *Johnson v Agnew* [1980] A.C. 367, 400.

[425] *Davis & Co (Wines) Ltd v Afa-Minerva (EMI) Ltd* [1974] 2 Lloyd's Rep. 27. In *William Sindall Plc v Cambridgeshire CC* [1994] 1 W.L.R. 1016, 1044 Evans L.J. said that in his view a plaintiff under s.2(2) should recover the same additional compensation as was permitted in *Cemp Properties (UK) Ltd v Dentsply Research and Development Corp* [1991] 2 E.G.L.R. 197, a case under s.2(1) in which the plaintiffs recovered for wasted expenditure. See generally, *McGregor on Damages*, 17th edn (2003), paras 41–057 et seq.

[426] See above, paras 6–054 et seq. It would have to be shown that the misrepresentee would not have entered the contract but for the fraud.

to be calculated so as to indemnify the misrepresentee fully against the consequences of rescission being refused, the damages might include loss suffered by the misrepresentor through the general fall in value of the property. The Court of Appeal in *William Sindall Plc v Cambridgeshire CC*[427] said that this would not be appropriate in a case like the one outlined since the result would be to defeat the object of declaring the contract subsisting; the loss caused by the general fall in value would once again be put onto the misrepresentor. Evans L.J.[428] said that in such a case the contract measure—the difference in value between the property with and without the "defect" to which the misrepresentation related, or the cost of correcting the defect—would be appropriate. With respect, it seems to be contrary to principle to award the contractual measure when the claim was to rescind because of a misrepresentation. Moreover, the solution will not always be attractive. Even without the defect, the property might be worth as much as the misrepresentee had paid for it. In such circumstances and provided that there is no consequential loss, damages for misrepresentation will normally be nil.[429] It would not be logical for an award under s.2(2) to include the additional value the property would have had if the representation had been true, which would be included were the contractual measure to apply.[430] Nor should the amount recoverable under the contractual measure be used to "cap" recovery for misrepresentation.[431] However, since the *Sindall* case was decided it has become clear that in a claim at common law against a negligent valuer, the valuer will not necessarily be liable for the losses caused by the fall in property prices generally, even though the lender would not have taken the property as security had a correct valuation been given. The damages are limited to the difference between the valuation negligently provided and the correct property value at the time.[432] By analogy, it is submitted that in a case where property has been bought as the result of a misrepresentation, damages under Misrepresentation Act 1967 s.2(2) should be limited to any difference between the contract price and the actual value of the property taking account the misrepresentation but not taking into account the general fall in the value of the property. This was canvassed as an alternative approach by Evans L.J. in *Sindall*'s case[433] and it does not seem inconsistent with the words of the statute. It would, in effect, reverse any unjust enrichment of the defendant.[434] Where as the result of the misrepresentation the

[427] [1994] 1 W.L.R. 1016: held that there were no grounds for rescission.

[428] [1994] 1 W.L.R. 1016, 1045. At 1037 Hoffmann L.J. remarked that while s.2(1) is concerned with damage flowing from the plaintiff having entered the contract, s.2(2) is concerned with damage caused by the property not being what it was supposed to be.

[429] See *McGregor on Damages*, 17th edn (2003), paras 41–063 et seq.

[430] cf. above, para.6–049.

[431] *Smith New Court Securities Ltd v Scrimgeour Vickers (Asset Management) Ltd* [1997] A.C. 254, disapproving on this point *Downs v Chappell* [1997] 1 W.L.R. 426; see above, para.6–057. (Both cases were ones of fraud but it is not clear that disapproval of this form of "cap" is limited to cases of fraud.)

[432] *South Australia Asset Management Corp v York Montague Ltd* [1997] A.C. 191; see below, para.26–094.

[433] [1994] 1 W.L.R. 1016, 1046. It is, with respect, preferred to the explanation given by McGregor at paras 41–065—41–066, for reasons given below, para.6–116, fn.491.

[434] See Birks [1997] R.L.R. 72, who argues that this is what Parliament intended despite use of the word "damages".

misrepresentee has given up some other right, the damages should be the value of that other right.[435]

Exercise of court's discretion. The court's discretion under s.2(2) is a wide one. In particular, it is to be noted that the court is not confined to a consideration of whether damages would be an adequate remedy to the representee. The court is also required to consider the loss that would be caused to the representor by rescission. Thus even where damages would not be an adequate remedy for the representee, the court may feel that it would be more equitable to award damages where it is shown that great loss would be caused to the representor by rescinding the whole contract, for instance because the market value of the services to be rendered has fallen dramatically.[436] The court may also exercise its discretion where to permit rescission would expose the misrepresentor to a large liability, even if that might in practice not be enforceable, whereas to maintain it would result in little additional loss to the misrepresentee.[437] A court is unlikely to exercise its power to declare the contract subsisting under s.2(2) when an award of damages against the misrepresentor will be an empty remedy.[438] However, it has been said that it would not be appropriate to refuse rescission of a reinsurance contract for misrepresentation by the reinsured, as avoidance of the contract performs an important policing function.[439] The burden of persuading the court to exercise its discretion is on the party seeking its exercise.[440] 6–102

4. RESCISSION FOR MISREPRESENTATION

(a) *General*

Preliminary. Before the passing of the Misrepresentation Act 1967, the position with regard to rescission was, broadly speaking, as follows: where a person was induced to enter into a contract as a result of a misrepresentation by the other party to the contract, and the misrepresentation never became incorporated as a contractual term, the representee was entitled to rescind the contract, whether the misrepresentation was fraudulent, negligent or wholly innocent. At 6–103

---

[435] In *UCB Corporate Services Ltd v Thomason* [2005] EWCA Civ 225, [2005] 1 All E.R. (Comm) 601 the respondents were liable for large sums under two guarantees. As the result of misrepresentation, the appellants entered an agreement to waive their rights under the guarantees in exchange for payment of a much smaller sum. The damages that might be awarded to the appellants under s.2(2) were not the full sums due under the guarantees but only compensation for any loss of the chance to recover more than the appellants gave up when they entered the waiver agreement (at [38] and [51]).

[436] *Atlantic Lines & Navigation Co Inc v Hallam Ltd* [1983] 1 Lloyd's Rep. 188; and see *William Sindell Plc v Cambridgeshire CC* [1994] 1 W.L.R. 1016, discussed in the previous paragraph.

[437] *UCB Corporate Services Ltd v Thomason* [2005] EWCA Civ 225, [2005] 1 All E.R. (Comm) 601. It was said that "loss" in s.2(2) includes financial loss and "what may loosely be described as detriment" (Latham L.J. at [37]).

[438] *TSB Bank Plc v Camfield* [1995] 1 W.L.R. 430, 439.

[439] *Highland Insurance Co v Continental Insurance Co* [1987] 1 Lloyd's Rep. 109.

[440] *British & Commonwealth Holdings Plc v Quadrex Holdings Inc* (unreported April 10, 1985) CA.

common law, the right to rescind was confined to cases in which the misrepresentation was fraudulent or in which there was a total failure of consideration,[441] but in equity there was a right to rescind even for innocent misrepresentation.[442] Since the Act of 1967 this right of rescission is qualified (except in cases of fraud) by the court's power to refuse rescission and award damages in lieu,[443] and there remain certain bars to rescission in all cases, which are discussed below.[444–445] But it still remains a general proposition that the remedy for misrepresentation is rescission of the contract.

6–104 **Misrepresentation incorporated as contractual term.** Where the misrepresentation was later incorporated into the contract as a contractual term, the position was in some respects uncertain before the Act of 1967. In cases of fraud, the subsequent incorporation of the misrepresentation into the contract made no difference to the representee's right to rescind, but in cases of innocent misrepresentation (including, for this purpose, negligent misrepresentation) the position was different. For in this case there was some authority for saying that the equitable right to rescind did not arise, and the representee's right to rescind (if any) depended entirely on the effect of the misrepresentation as a contractual term.[446] That is to say, if the term was a condition or an innominate term, breach might justify rescission (or, as it would now be more appropriately put,[447] termination of the representee's outstanding obligations) whereas if the term was a warranty, breach would not justify rescission at all.[448] Thus the somewhat strange result followed that a misrepresentation which would have justified rescission as of right by the representee if it had remained a representation pure and simple, might cease to have this effect if it later became incorporated into the contract as a warranty.[449]

6–105 **Misrepresentation Act section 1(a).** Section 1(a) of the Act of 1967 provides that a person is not to be deprived of the right to rescind for misrepresentation merely because the representation has become a term of the contract. Thus a misrepresentation which is subsequently incorporated into the contract as a warranty will now remain a ground for rescission, whereas breach of a warranty which has never been a misrepresentation will never ground rescission. But it is not easy to see how, in fact, a misrepresentation could ever be a term of the

---

[441] *Kennedy v Panama, etc., Royal Mail Co Ltd* (1867) L.R. 2 Q.B. 580.

[442] *Lamare v Dixon* (1873) L.R. 6 H.L. 414. The generalisation of this remedy was largely a post-Judicature Act development, stemming principally from *Redgrave v Hurd* (1881) 20 Ch D 1 and *Adam v Newbigging* (1888) 13 App. Cas. 308.

[443] Above, paras 6–096 et seq.

[444–445] Below, paras 6–115—6–133.

[446] *Pennsylvania Shipping Co v Compagnie Nationale de Navigation* [1936] 2 All E.R. 1167, 1171; *Leaf v International Galleries* [1950] 2 K.B. 86; cf. *Compagnie Française de Chemins de Fer Paris-Orleans v Leeston Shipping Co Ltd* (1919) 1 Ll.L.Rep. 235, 237–238.

[447] See *Johnson v Agnew* [1980] A.C. 367.

[448] See below, paras 12–031—12–032.

[449] However, this "somewhat strange result" was held not to be law in *Academy of Health and Fitness Pty Ltd v Power* [1973] V.R. 254, a case arising in a jurisdiction not governed by the Misrepresentation Act 1967.

contract except where the term had previously been a representation,[450] though a warranty might, of course, be a promise as to future conduct which would not be a misrepresentation in any event (unless fraudulent).

Rescission and termination. Since the decision of the House of Lords in *Johnson v Agnew*[451] a much clearer and sharper distinction has been drawn between rescission of a contract ab initio and termination of the contract for subsequent breach. The former generally has retrospective effect, while the latter does not; indeed, termination usually affects only some of the obligations under the contract and it is strictly incorrect to speak of the contract ceasing to exist through termination. It is clear from *Johnson v Agnew* itself that rescission for fraud is rescission ab initio, and will therefore prima facie have retrospective effect, though it has already been submitted[452] that such rescission will not deprive the representee of a right to damages for fraud, because that right arises in tort, and not out of the contract. Where s.1(a) of the Act of 1967 applies, it seems that the representee retains his right to rescind ab initio, but may in addition have a right to terminate for breach of the one-time representation, now become a term of the contract. Problems may well arise in deciding whether a refusal to continue with the contract in such circumstances amounts to a rescission or only a termination. It has been held that where a variation of a contract has been induced by fraud, the innocent party may rescind the variation ab initio, with the effect that the original contract is retrospectively revived.[453] 6–106

Present position. The right to rescind for fraudulent misrepresentation is unimpaired by the Misrepresentation Act, but there is no longer any absolute right to rescind for negligent or innocent misrepresentation. Section 2(2) of the Act (which has been set out above)[454] provides that the court now has a discretion to award damages in lieu of rescission wherever it is of the opinion that it would be equitable to do so, having regard to the nature of the misrepresentation and the loss that would be caused by it if the contract were upheld, as well as to the loss that rescission would cause the other party. It has already been observed that this is a wide discretion, and the court is not confined to a consideration of whether damages would be an adequate remedy to the representee.[455] 6–107

Effect on right to terminate for breach. There is one point of possible difficulty on the construction of s.2(2) of the Act. As mentioned above, it is clear from s.1(a) of the Act that (subject to the court's discretion under s.2(2)) there is now a right to rescind for any misrepresentation made before the contract was entered into, notwithstanding that the misrepresentation has become a term of the 6–108

---

[450] If the representee did not know of the representation before the contract was made (as, e.g. where he simply signed a written agreement) it would not in any event be an effective misrepresentation, above, para.6–032. But it is possible, though in practice unlikely, for a person to warrant the truth of a fact without making any representation at all, e.g. where he expressly agrees to take the risk, however the facts may turn out.

[451] [1980] A.C. 367.

[452] See above, para.6–072.

[453] *Occidental Worldwide Investment Corp v Skibs A/S Avanti* [1976] 1 Lloyd's Rep. 293.

[454] Above, para.6–096.

[455] Above, para.6–102.

contract. But what is not wholly clear is whether, when this happens, any right to terminate for breach of contract also becomes subject to the discretion of the court under subs.(2). There are many circumstances in which a person has a right to terminate a contract for breach of condition, in which no loss has in fact been incurred by him, and a case could be made for saying that, where the term is a representation of fact, the court now has a discretion to refuse to permit repudiation, but to award damages in lieu—indeed, the damages might well be nominal.[456] On the other hand, it is unlikely that the subsection was intended to have this effect, and it is submitted that the words: "[w]here a person . . . would be entitled by reason of the misrepresentation, to rescind the contract" would exclude the case under discussion since the right to rescind then arises from breach of the contractual term.[457] But whatever the answer to this point may be, it is at least clear that subs.(2) would not affect a right to treat the contract as terminated for breach of a contractual term which was a promise of future conduct; nor for a breach of a contractual term which was an undertaking as to fact but which was never made before the contract was entered into.

6–109 **Misrepresentation as defence to proceedings.** There is no doubt that a misrepresentation which would justify rescission of a contract may also be used as a defence to an action brought by the representor against the representee. The use of misrepresentation as a defence has sometimes been distinguished from its use as a ground for rescission,[458] and it is possible that the principles governing the two situations are not in all respects identical[459] but generally speaking they appear to be the same. Indeed, the courts have sometimes treated the setting up of a misrepresentation as a defence as though this were in itself one way of rescinding the contract.[460] Accordingly, it is thought that although s.2(2) of the 1967 Act speaks of rescission, its provisions would apply equally to a case in which the misrepresentation is set up by way of defence. However, fraud may be used as a defence to a claim for specific performance (which is a discretionary remedy[461]) even where the right to rescind has been lost (save by affirmation, when the inconsistency of affirming and then resisting specific performance would be unconscionable).[462] It was said that impossibility of restoring the

---

456 See, e.g. *Re Moore & Co Ltd and Landauer Co* [1921] 2 K.B. 519 (although the term here may well have been a promise rather than a statement of fact). This argument is also applicable to insurance contracts in which the insured may warrant some fact which is untrue, but the fact in question may have no bearing on the risk which occurs. Hitherto, it has always been clear that the insurer may repudiate liability in these circumstances, below, para.6–149.

457 Yet the term is, *ex hypothesi*, a misrepresentation itself.

458 Treitel, *The Law of Contract*, 12th edn (by Peel, 2007), para.9–086.

459 Treitel points to the rule that an insurer who uses fraud as a defence may repudiate liability and keep the premiums: see below, Vol.II, para.41–057. Further, he suggests that in cases of criminal fraud a representee who sets the fraud up by way of defence need not return money received under the contract (*Berg v Sadler & Moore* [1937] 2 K.B. 158), whereas if he sues for rescission he must do so (*Spence v Crawford* [1939] 3 All E.R. 271). *Berg v Sadler Moore* is contrary to dicta of the Exchequer Chamber in *Clough v L. & N.W. Ry* (1871) L.R. 7 Ex. 26, 37 which do not seem to have been cited, and the refusal of the claim for return of the money may be better explained on the basis of illegality: see below, para.16–177.

460 *Clough v L. & N.W. Ry* (1871) L.R. 7 Ex. 26; *Academy of Health and Fitness Pty Ltd v Power* [1973] V.R. 254.

461 See below, para.27–030.

462 *Geest Plc v Fyffes Plc* [1999] 1 All E.R. (Comm) 627, 694 et seq.

parties to their original position will not necessarily prevent the use of fraud as a defence; it will depend on the impact that enforcement would have on the representee, and especially on whether it would cause hardship, whether on the facts any estoppel had arisen and the importance of the term to be enforced and the breach of it. The fact that there would be a claim for damages for deceit should be taken into account.[463]

Rescission normally requires notice. The general rule is that, in order to rescind the contract, the representee must communicate his intention to do so to the representor.[464] But in *Car & Universal Finance Co Ltd v Caldwell*[465] it was held by the Court of Appeal that this was not an inflexible rule. In this case a person was induced to sell his car by fraud to a purchaser who paid with a bad cheque, and promptly disappeared. When the seller discovered the fraud he informed the police and the Automobile Association, but was, of course, unable to notify the fraudulent purchaser. It was held that the seller had done sufficient to rescind the contract, and that accordingly a subsequent purchaser from the fraudulent party had acquired no title to the car, as the title had revested in the seller on rescission. The actual ratio of the decision seems confined to circumstances in which communication of the representee's desire to rescind is not possible because the representor is deliberately keeping out of the way, and the court left open the question whether the decision would apply to a case where the impossibility of communication did not arise from the representor's deliberate fraud. 6–110

Court order not required. Although it is common to speak of a court "setting aside" or rescinding a contract for misrepresentation, it seems clear from this and other cases[466] that the remedy is not necessarily a judicial one.[467] A representee is entitled to rescind for misrepresentation without invoking the assistance of the court at all, although the court now has (as seen above) a 6–111

[463] [1999] 1 All E.R. 627. On the facts of the case, restitutio was impossible. To refuse specific performance altogether of the undertaking to provide security for an indemnity that the defendant had given the plaintiff would expose the plaintiff to very different risks. Specific performance would be granted but limited to the excess of the claim over any counterclaim for damages.

[464] *Car & Universal Finance Co Ltd v Caldwell* [1961] 1 Q.B. 525. It was accepted that the misrepresentee could also rescind by retaking the goods, even without the misrepresentor's knowledge: 555, 558. There is no principle that rescission (in the case concerned, for repayment on the ground of mistake) is unavailable unless sought by a notice given before an action is brought: *West Sussex Properties Ltd v Chichester DC* [2000] N.P.C. 74 CA, at [12].

[465] [1961] 1 Q.B. 525; see also *Newtons of Wembley Ltd v Williams* [1965] 1 Q.B. 560.

[466] *Abram S.S. Co Ltd v Westville Shipping Co Ltd* [1923] A.C. 773. In Australia, the High Court has taken a different approach, holding that even in a case of fraud equity does more than recognise rescission effected by the action of the innocent party. It may impose terms to achieve observance of the requirements of good conscience and practical justice and this enables it to grant partial rescission. Thus it could set aside the part of a contract of guarantee to which the fraud related (previous supplies) but leave the rest (as to future supplies) intact: *Vadasz v Pioneer Concrete (S.A.) Pty Ltd* (1995) 184 C.L.R. 102, noted (1997) 113 L.Q.R. 16; Proksch [1996] R.L.R. 71. On the *Vadasz* case see further below, para.6–118.

[467] See however O'Sullivan [2000] C.L.J. 509.

discretion to refuse to allow rescission in some cases.[468] It may well be, as a purely practical matter, that the representee will require the assistance of the court in some cases, e.g. where rescission of an executed conveyance is sought[469]; but "the process of rescission is essentially the act of the party rescinding, and not of the court".[470]

6–112 **Rescission not available except against contracting party.** It seems clear that rescission is prima facie a remedy which is only available against the other party to the contract. In *Northern Bank Finance Corp Ltd v Charlton*[471] this principle was affirmed by a bare majority of the Supreme Court of Eire in a case in which the plaintiff had been induced by the fraud of a bank to pay various sums to the bank in order that these sums should be used by the bank to purchase various properties on behalf of the plaintiff. The properties were in fact so purchased from third parties. The plaintiff claimed rescission of the contracts of purchase but the majority of the court held that rescission was not available as against the bank since the properties were not bought from the bank itself. Rescission would in fact have amounted to a sort of compulsory subrogation under which the bank would have taken over the properties and refunded the purchase price to the plaintiff.

6–113 **Misrepresentation inducing consent order.** Where proceedings are compromised by agreement, and the compromise is made the subject of a consent order, the court may set aside the consent order if it is shown to have been based on an agreement induced by misrepresentation.[472]

6–114 **Effect of rescission.** When a contract is rescinded it has the effect of revesting any property transferred in the transferor, so far as no formal steps are required

[468] Thus the court may, in effect, annul a rescission previously effected by self-help: see *Atlantic Lines & Navigation Co Inc v Hallam Ltd* [1983] 1 Lloyd's Rep. 188, 202. The conferral of a discretion on the court by s.2(2) has been said to imply that, apart from that section, there is no power to declare the contract subsisting; the right to rescind is that of the representee, not that of the court, which merely has to decide whether the rescission was lawful: *TSB Bank Plc v Camfield* [1995] 1 W.L.R. 430, 439.

[469] In *Hughes v Clewley, The Siben (No.2)* [1996] 1 Lloyd's Rep. 35 it was held that rescission will not be ordered [sic] if the effect would be to transfer a business being used for unlawful purposes from one party to the other. The case was one of fraud, so there was no power to declare the contract subsisting under s.2(2).

[470] *Horsler v Zorro* [1975] Ch. 302, 310. In *Islington London BC v UCKAC* [2006] EWCA Civ 340, [2006] 1 W.L.R. 1303, it was held that a tenancy to which the Act applies can be brought to an end only on the grounds stated in the Act on which the landlord may obtain possession, which include a false statement made knowingly or recklessly by the tenant (s.84 and Sch.2, ground 5). In reaching this conclusion, Dyson L.J. adopted the opposing theory that a contract is only rescinded for misrepresentation by a court order (at [26]). But the court's conclusion that, as Mummery L.J. put it: "[T]he relevant provisions of the 1985 Act provide a complete code for the termination of a secure tenancy, the private law remedy of rescission of the tenancy for fraudulent representation is not available to the council" (at [46]), can be supported as a matter of statutory construction without resorting to the notion that a court order is needed for rescission.

[471] [1979] I.R. 149.

[472] *Dietz v Lennig Chemicals Ltd* [1969] 1 A.C. 170. The consent order had not been drawn up in this case, but that seems immaterial. Except in matrimonial cases, a consent order derives its force and effect from the contract underlying it, and if the contract can be set aside, so can the order: *Purcell v F.C. Trigell Ltd* [1971] 1 Q.B. 358. See further above, para.5–062, fn.277.

for the retransfer.[473] Thus property in goods will revest in the victim of fraud without more.[474] If land has been conveyed, rescission will have the effect that the representor holds the title on constructive trust for the representee.[475] Although the contract is avoided retrospectively, some clauses that are regarded as "separable" may continue to have effect. Thus unless otherwise agreed an arbitration agreement is unaffected by the invalidity of the substantive contract of which it forms part[476]; and an exclusive jurisdiction clause will survive rescission.[477]

(b) *Restitutio in Integrum*

Restitutio in integrum. The purpose of rescission is to restore the status quo ante, and it was said by Bowen L.J. in *Newbigging v Adam*[478] that "there ought . . . to be a giving back and a taking back on both sides". Thus the traditional view is that the remedy will not lie if the parties are not in a position to make restitutio in integrum. In *Clarke v Dickson*[479] Crompton J. said that when a party: 6–115

> " . . . exercises his option to rescind the contract, he must be in a state to rescind; that is he must be in such a situation as to be able to put the parties into their original state before the contract."

Common law and equity. Common law put a strict interpretation on the requirement of restitution, and consequently restricted the field within which rescission could operate. Further, there was no machinery for taking accounts, or for balancing set-offs against each other, or for making allowances. As a result the injured party was often relegated to his remedy in damages, if any. In contrast equity offered two advantages to the litigant.[480] As at common law the parties to an action for rescission were required to make restitution, but equity did not insist that this should be precise. It was content to do practical justice between the parties. Secondly, the greater flexibility of the machinery at its disposal enabled equity to direct accounts to be taken and balances to be struck and adjustments to be made which were impossible at common law. Both of these points were emphasised by Lord Blackburn in *Erlanger v New Sombrero Phosphate Co*[481]: 6–116

---

[473] Until the contract is rescinded, the accepted view is that the misrepresentee has no proprietary right in the property transferred but only a "mere equity": below, para.6–130.

[474] *Car & Universal Finance Co Ltd v Caldwell* [1961] 1 Q.B. 525.

[475] Megarry & Wade, *The Law of Real Property*, 6th edn (by Harpum, 2000), paras 5.078–5.079. Note that completion of the contract is no longer a bar to rescission: Misrepresentation Act 1967 s.1(b), below, para.6–130.

[476] Arbitration Act 1996 s.7; Vol.II, para.32–024.

[477] *FAI General Insurance Co Ltd v Ocean Marine Mutual Protection and Indemnity Association* [1998] L.R.L.R. 24, 28; Vol.II, para.32–024.

[478] (1886) 34 Ch D 582, 595.

[479] (1858) E.B. & E. 148, 154.

[480] But note that fraud may be used as a defence to specific performance even when restitutio in integrum is impossible: *Geest Plc v Fyffes Plc* [1999] 1 All E.R. (Comm) 672. See above, para.6–109.

[481] (1878) 3 App. Cas. 1218, 1278–1279. See also *O'Sullivan v Management Agency Ltd* [1985] Q.B. 428, below, para.7–100.

> "It [a court of equity] can take account of profits and make allowance for deterioration. And I think the practice has always been for a court of equity to give this relief whenever, by the exercise of its powers, it can do what is practically just, though it cannot restore the parties precisely to the state they were in before the contract."

The present position seems to be that in contracts where the benefits received are in their nature returnable, such as contracts of sale, while an ability to make restitution is an essential to an action for rescission, the courts require that this should be substantial rather than precise.[482] In other words, the equitable approach to this requirement has prevailed over that of the common law. Further, it has been suggested that a contract for services, which in their nature cannot be restored, may be rescinded despite part performance of the services by the misrepresentor.[483]

6–117 **Alteration of subject matter.** Clearly, it is impossible to make substantial restitution of property transferred under the contract if it has altered its character. Thus in *Clarke v Dickson*[484] rescission was refused where a partnership, in which the representee had been induced to take shares, had been converted into a limited liability company, for the existing shares were wholly different from those which he originally received. Other examples of alteration in the subject-matter of the contract sufficient to disentitle the representee to rescission are the working out of mines[485]; the conversion of an unincorporated banking company into an incorporated joint stock company[486]; a material change in the position of both parties in relation to the patents and business in question[487]; the commencement of winding-up proceedings[488] and, when completion was a bar to rescission of a contract for the sale of land,[489] part performance of a single contract.[490] On the other hand, if property has retained its substantial identity, restitution may be ordered even though it has deteriorated or depreciated or cannot be restored in its

[482] In *Smith New Court Securities Ltd v Scrimgeour Vickers (Asset Management) Ltd* in the Court of Appeal it had been accepted that rescission was no longer possible because the plaintiffs had disposed of the shares they had brought. Nourse L.J. referred to this rule as harsh in relation to fungible assets: [1994] 1 W.L.R. 1271, 1280. In the House of Lords, Lord Browne-Wilkinson remarked that, if a sale of shares cannot be rescinded once the specific shares purchased have been sold, "the law will need to be looked at closely hereafter": [1997] A.C. 254, 262. See Halson [1997] R.L.R. 89.

[483] *Atlantic Lines & Navigation Co Inc v Hallam Ltd* [1983] 1 Lloyd's Rep. 188, 202. See further below, para.6–119.

[484] (1858) E.B. & E. 148. Some dicta in this case were disapproved in *Armstrong v Jackson* [1917] 2 K.B. 822, 829. A Name at Lloyd's cannot rescind membership because the benefits received are not in their nature returnable: *Lloyd's of London v Leigh* [1997] CA Transcript 1416; *Society of Lloyd's v Khan* [1998] 3 F.C.R. 93.

[485] *Vigers v Pike* (1842) 8 Cl. & F. 562.

[486] *Western Bank of Scotland v Addie* (1867) L.R. 1 Sc. & Div. 145, 159–160.

[487] *Sheffield Nickel Co v Unwin* (1877) 2 QBD 214; see also *Lagunas Nitrate Co v Lagunas Syndicate* [1899] 2 Ch. 392.

[488] *Oakes v Turquand* (1867) L.R. 2 H.L. 325.

[489] See now below, para.6–133.

[490] *Thorpe v Fasey* [1949] Ch. 649; cf. *Kupchak v Dayson Holdings Co Ltd* (1965) 53 D.L.R. (2d) 482.

original state.[491] Thus in *Adam v Newbigging*[492] the respondent was induced by an innocent misrepresentation to become a partner in a business which was insolvent and which subsequently failed. He was held to be entitled to rescind and to have his capital repaid although the business to be restored was worthless. Two further comments may be useful: first, in appropriate cases the court may order the plaintiff to pay compensation on account of any deterioration that has occurred, in accordance with the principle that this is preferable to allowing the defendant to retain all the advantages of property transferred under the contract.[493] The point was put by Roche J. as follows:

> "The principle of *restitutio in integrum* did not require that a person should be put back into the same position as before; it meant that he should be put into as good a position as before."[494]

Secondly, it seems that the courts are more willing to exercise their discretionary powers and to order restitution in a case of fraud than in a case of innocent misrepresentation.[495] Thus in *Hulton v Hulton*[496] the court rescinded a separation deed obtained by the husband by fraudulent misrepresentation, and refused to order the wife to repay the sums that she had received under the deed because the husband had received corresponding benefits, such as freedom from molestation and from proceedings by the wife for restitution of conjugal rights.

Partial rescission not allowed. The more flexible approach advocated in the previous paragraph would not necessarily be inconsistent with what appears to be the current rule that the misrepresentee may only rescind the whole contract and not part of it. In *Vadasz v Pioneer Concrete (S.A.) Pty*[497] the High Court of Australia had held that in a case of fraud the court has power to set aside the contract on terms and thus could set aside the part of the contract of guarantee to which the fraud related (previous supplies) but leave the rest (as to future supplies) intact. This should be contrasted with the decision of the English Court of Appeal in *TSB Bank Plc v Camfield*,[498] in which a wife was held to have the right to set aside a charge in its entirety when she had entered it as the result of 6–118

[491] *Armstrong v Jackson* [1917] 2 K.B. 822. The contrary suggestion in *McGregor on Damages*, 17th edn (2003), para.41–065 is, with respect, doubtful.

[492] (1888) 13 App. Cas. 308.

[493] *Lagunas Nitrate Co v Lagunas Syndicate* [1899] 2 Ch. 392, 456, 457. See also *O'Sullivan v Management Agency Ltd* [1985] Q.B. 428, below, para.7–100.

[494] *Compagnie Chemin de Fer Paris-Orleans v Leeston Shipping Co* (1919) 36 T.L.R. 68, 69; cf. *Wiebe v Butchart's Motors* [1949] 4 D.L.R. 838 (contract for sale of car rescinded subject to allowance for depreciation during use).

[495] *Spence v Crawford* [1939] 3 All E.R. 271, 288. The effect of negligent misrepresentation in this respect is an open question.

[496] [1917] 1 K.B. 813.

[497] (1995) 184 C.L.R. 102, noted in (1997) 113 L.Q.R. 16.

[498] [1995] 1 W.L.R. 430. The case, and *De Molestina v Ponton* [2002] EWHC 2413, are criticised by Poole and Keyser (2005) 121 L.Q.R. 273, who argue that in cases of non-fraudulent misrepresentation, where rescission is allowed under equity's auxiliary jurisdiction, if the misrepresentation is as to the terms, partial rescission can be ordered to bring the contract into line with the misrepresentee's expectation. This seems doubtful on the authorities, which seem to recognise that even rescission for non-fraudulent misrepresentation is the act of the party not of the court. See above, para.6–111.

the husband's misrepresentation that it was limited to £15,000. In *Scales Trading Ltd v Far Eastern Shipping Plc*[499] the Privy Council had left open the question of whether the approach in *Vadasz* should be preferred to that in *TSB Bank Plc v Camfield*. However, in *De Molestina v Ponton*[500] Colman J. held that it was not even arguable that partial rescission may be awarded. That there cannot be partial rescission is part of a wider principle that there cannot be rescission unless there can be restitutio in integrum.[501] Thus:

> "... if a representee is induced to enter separate contracts A and B by the same misrepresentation, it may be that performance of contract B depends on the prior performance of contract A. In that case one cannot rescind contract A without also rescinding contract B ... But there may be cases where, although both contracts were induced by the same misrepresentation, either can be performed without performance of the other. In that case the misrepresentee may rescind unless the contract not sought to be rescinded would never have been entered without also entering the other."[502]

6–119 **Services.** The suggestion[503] that a partly performed contract for services may be rescinded is attractive but raises difficulties. One view might be that the contract is rescinded for the future, leaving the services already rendered unaffected, but this would be inconsistent with the normal view that rescission for misrepresentation is rescission ab initio.[504] It might also result in the party who had rendered the services going without payment for them if the contract were entire and the payment due on completion.[505] Rather the suggestion seems to be that the contract is rescinded ab initio but the misrepresentee must make an allowance for the services received.[506] That seems a workable proposition but it would leave an anomaly when the services had been performed by the misrepresentee: it would be rather hard if he were permitted to rescind only at the price of forgoing payment for what he had done, but unless the contract was severable it is not clear what remedy he would have to claim payment. The adjustments and allowances which a court may make in a claim for rescission may not include the allowance of a quantum meruit. This is suggested by *Boyd and Forrest v Glasgow Ry.*[507] During the negotiations for a contract for constructing a railway, an innocent misrepresentation was made about the nature of the subsoil; the contractors claimed to rescind the contract, and sued on a quantum meruit for the difference between the contract price, which they had received, and the increased cost of the work which was due to the misrepresentation. The House of Lords, reversing the Scottish courts, rejected the claim on the ground

499 [2001] 1 All E.R. (Comm) 319.
500 [2002] 1 Lloyd's Rep. 271.
501 [2002] 1 Lloyd's Rep. 271 at [6.2].
502 [2002] 1 Lloyd's Rep. 271 at [6.9].
503 Above, para.6–116 fn.483.
504 Above, para.6–115. These two sentences were endorsed by the Court of Appeal in *Society of Lloyds v Lyon* (unreported August 11, 1997).
505 See below, para.24–054.
506 [1983] 1 Lloyd's Rep. 188, 202.
507 (1915) S.C. (HL) 20.

that, if allowed, it would be equivalent to an award of damages to the contractors.

A more flexible approach? In the *Boyd and Forrest* case[508] the work had actually been completed, so it was clearly too late for the contractor to "rescind", and it is to be hoped that a modern court might see its way to granting a quantum meruit to the misrepresentee in a case in which he only discovers that an innocent misrepresentation has been made after he has performed some of the services required of him.[509] It has been argued that the courts should adopt a still more flexible approach to the requirement of restitutio in integrum where third party rights are not in question,[510] allowing restitution to be made in the form of money.[511] This, despite recent endorsement by the Court of Appeal of the difficulties alluded to earlier,[512] seems a sensible development and one which is in line with the decision in a case of undue influence to award "equitable compensation" when the property transferred could no longer be returned.[513] A recent decision of the Court of Appeal in a duress case suggests that the courts are now adopting this approach.[514] 6–120

Indemnity distinguished from damages. Assuming that a claimant who wishes to rescind is in a position to make restitutio in integrum, the present position seems to be that he may expect the restoration of benefits and resumption of burdens which have passed under the contract. Thus, if property has been delivered, it must be restored, and the claimant likewise must make restitution of any property delivered to him; and if obligations have passed to the claimant, these must be resumed by the defendant so that the restoration of the status quo ante may be achieved. In practical terms this means that the defendant must indemnify the claimant against obligations which he has discharged or will become liable to discharge. One problem arises: how is the rule requiring the defendant to indemnify the claimant for obligations assumed by him reconciled with the rule that damages cannot be recovered for an innocent misrepresentation which has not become a term of the contract? The traditional answer has been that the defendant must indemnify the claimant against obligations necessarily created by the contract, i.e. against liabilities to third parties which the contract required the claimant to incur or payments to third parties which it required him 6–121

---

508 Above, para.6–119.

509 If the misrepresentation had been fraudulent or negligent the problem could be avoided since the victim could claim the cost of performing as part of the damages. In the loosely analogous situation where a contract is terminated for breach after the victim has performed part of the services required, the victim may opt to abandon his remedies on the contract and claim a quantum meruit: *Planché v Colburn* (1831) 8 Bing. 14; see below, para.29–066.

510 cf. below, paras 7–099 et seq.

511 Burrows, *Law of Restitution*, 2nd edn (2002) pp.176–179, arguing that the requirement of restitution is best rationalised as a form of the "change of position" defence; Birks [1997] R.L.R. 72.

512 See above, fn.504.

513 *Mahoney v Purnell* [1996] 3 All E.R. 61, discussed below, para.7–101.

514 See *Halpern v Halpern (No.2)* [2007] EWCA Civ 291, [2007] 3 All E.R. 478 at [70]–[73]; below, para.7–054.

to make, but against these only. Thus the court is enabled to stop short of making an award which could be classified as damages.[515]

6–122 The practical operation of the distinction between indemnity and damages is illustrated by *Whittington v Seale-Hayne*.[516] The plaintiffs took a lease of certain premises on the strength of the defendant's innocent misrepresentation that they were in a sanitary condition and they erected certain poultry sheds thereon. As a result of the insanitary state of the premises the manager of the plaintiffs' poultry farm became ill, and the poultry died; the local council ordered the plaintiffs to renew the drains, and the plaintiffs were obliged to remove their sheds. In an action for rescission and for an indemnity against the consequences of having entered into the contract, it was held that the plaintiffs were entitled to an indemnity against the obligations to pay rates and to effect repairs, for these were necessarily assumed under the contract. But they were not entitled to recover anything in respect of medical expenses or loss of poultry, or the removal of the sheds, for these were in effect claims for damages, and therefore not admissible in an action based on innocent misrepresentation.

(c) *Other Bars to Remedy of Rescission*

6–123 **Restrictions on the right to rescind.** The ability to make restitution is an essential to the rescission of a contract, but it does not follow that because restitution is possible, rescission must result. For (apart altogether from the court's discretionary power to refuse rescission in cases of innocent or negligent misrepresentation)[517] the plaintiff may find his claim barred by one of three restrictions on the right to rescind, namely, affirmation of the contract, lapse of time or the acquisition by a third party of rights in the subject-matter of the contract. Until the passing of the Misrepresentation Act there was also a fourth bar to rescission in cases of innocent misrepresentation, namely, the execution of the contract; this has now been abrogated.

6–124 **Affirmation of the contract.** If the representee, having discovered the misrepresentation, either expressly declares his intention to proceed with the contract, or does some act inconsistent with an intention to rescind the contract, he is bound by his affirmation.[518] Thus a shareholder's right to claim rescission of a contract to take shares, made on the strength of a misrepresentation in the prospectus, may be lost if, after discovering the facts, he carries on the business

---

[515] *Newbigging v Adam* (1886) 34 Ch D 582, 594, per Bowen L.J. Cotton and Fry L.JJ. interpreted "indemnity" more widely, but their view was not followed in *Whittington v Seale-Hayne* (1900) 82 L.T. 49, below, para.6–122. cf. *Horsler v Zorro* [1975] Ch. 302 where it was held that, on termination for *breach of contract* the innocent party was entitled to recover expenses thrown away.

[516] (1900) 82 L.T. 49.

[517] Above, paras 6–061 et seq.

[518] *Ormes v Beadel* (1860) 2 De G.F. & J. 333; *Clough v L. & N.W. Ry* (1871) L.R. 7 Ex. 26, 34; *Sharpley v Louth and East Coast Ry* (1876) 2 Ch D 663.

of which the shares give him control,[519] or if he attends a shareholders' meeting[520] or tries to sell the shares[521]; for by such acts he is taken to have affirmed the contract. But, where rescission cannot in fact be made without the co-operation of the representor, affirmation is not to be inferred merely because the representee continues to enjoy the fruits of the contract. So where purchasers of shares in a motel company continued to occupy the motel and manage the company after discovering that they had been induced to buy by fraud, this was held insufficient evidence of affirmation[522]; the purchasers in fact took prompt proceedings for rescission, and they could not have rescinded out of court without the co-operation of the vendors. And a representee who became suspicious of the truth of representations which induced her to buy a share in a partnership was held not to have affirmed merely because she continued to act as a partner while she took steps to verify her suspicions.[523] Each case is decided on its own facts, and the courts pay particular attention to the nature of the contract, to any lapse of time which may have occurred, and to the question whether the representor has changed his position in reliance on the absence of a protest by the representee, or whether third parties have been affected by this.[524]

Affirmation requires knowledge. In contracts for the sale of goods, it has been said that the right to rescind for innocent misrepresentation will be lost when, had the statement been a condition, the right to reject for breach of condition would have been lost.[525] In most circumstances an act which constitutes an acceptance of the goods within s.35 of the Sale of Goods Act, and so bars the right to reject the goods for breach of condition, would doubtless also constitute an affirmation of the contract and would also bar the right to rescind. But there may be some cases in which this is not so, because a person can "accept" goods within s.35 without knowing of his right to reject them,[526] whereas there can be no affirmation without knowledge of the facts. In *Peyman v Lanjani*,[527] after a full review of the authorities, the Court of Appeal concluded that a party entitled to rescind or avoid a contract will not be held to have affirmed it unless he knows the facts, and also is aware that he has a right to rescind or avoid.[528] Such an affirmation, where there is such knowledge, is 6–125

519 *Seddon v North Eastern Salt Co* [1905] 1 Ch. 326. As to the wider grounds for this decision, see below, para.6–133.

520 *Sharpley v Louth and East Coast Ry* (1876) 2 Ch D 663.

521 *Re Hop and Malt Exchange and Warehouse Co Ex p. Briggs* (1866) L.R. 1 Eq. 483.

522 *Kupchak v Dayson Holdings Co Ltd* (1965) 53 D.L.R. (2d) 482.

523 *Senenayake v Cheng* [1966] A.C. 63.

524 See *Clough v L. & N.W. Ry* (1871) L.R. 7 Ex. 26, 34, 35; *Bank of Credit and Commerce International SA (In Liquidation) v Ali* [1999] 2 All E.R. 1005, 1023.

525 *Leaf v International Galleries* [1950] 2 K.B. 86 (lapse of time). See also *Long v Lloyd* [1958] 1 W.L.R. 753. Sale and delivery to a sub-purchaser also amounts to acceptance (though only after he has had a reasonable opportunity to examine the goods: Sale of Goods Act 1979 (as amended) s.35), but if the sub-purchaser rejects the goods the right to rescind for misrepresentation can probably still be exercised, cf. below, para.6–132. It should make no difference to the right to rescind for misrepresentation that the representation has become a term of the contract: Misrepresentation Act 1967 s.1(a). On loss of the right to reject, see Vol.II, paras 43–309 et seq.

526 e.g. *Leaf v International Galleries* [1950] 2 K.B. 86.

527 [1985] Ch. 457.

528 For a case where any right to rescind would have been lost, see *Donegal International Ltd v Zambia* [2007] EWHC 197 (Apr), [2007] 1 Lloyd's Rep. 397 at [467].

conclusive evidence of the party's election, whether or not it is acted upon, and whether or not there is any change of position by the other party.

6–126 **Estoppel.** A party may, however, be held estopped from rescinding or avoiding the contract even where he does not know the facts or his rights,[529] but in this event, he must have led the other to believe, by unequivocal statements or actions, that he does intend to affirm the contract, and the other party must show that he has acted on the statement or conduct to his prejudice.[530]

6–127 **Lapse of time.** Lapse of time after discovery that there has been a misrepresentation may be evidence of affirmation.[531] In *Clough v L. & N.W. Ry*[532] it was said that "when the lapse of time is great it probably would be treated in practice as conclusive evidence" of a decision to proceed with the contract. This is especially true of contracts for the sale or allotment of shares in companies, where the utmost promptness is required.[533] In such a case a delay of even a few weeks after discovery of the misrepresentation is usually fatal, and there cannot, in any event, be rescission of an allotment after the company has gone into liquidation.[534] But there can normally be no affirmation where the representee is ignorant of the truth and therefore of his right to rescind,[535] and the inference of affirmation from lapse of time should therefore be rebuttable by proof of lack of knowledge of the untruth. In *Leaf v International Galleries*[536] the right to rescind a contract for the sale of goods was held barred by five years' delay despite the fact that the representee only discovered the truth shortly before the proceedings but that was a case in which the delay would have amounted to acceptance of the

---

[529] In *Habib Bank Ltd v Tufail* [2006] EWCA Civ 374, [2006] All E.R. (D) 92 (Comm) the Court of Appeal distinguished between estoppel and acquiescence: see below, para.7–097. The right to avoid a contract for misrepresentation may be lost by acquiescence if the misrepresentee indicates that he will not avoid it and the other party acts on this to its detriment, at least if the representation was made after the misrepresentee knew of the facts giving him the right to avoid (at [22]).

[530] [2006] EWCA Civ 374. See also *Container Transport International Inc v Oceanus Mutual Underwriting Association (Bermuda) Ltd* [1984] 1 Lloyd's Rep. 476; *Motor Oil Hellas (Corinth Refineries SA v Shipping Corp of India (The Kanchenjunga)* [1990] 1 Lloyd's Rep. 391, 397–399.

[531] *Lindsay Petroleum Co v Hurd* (1874) L.R. 5 P.C. 221; *Erlanger v New Sombrero Phosphate Co* (1878) 3 App.Cas. 1218; *Clough v L. & N.W. Ry* (1871) L.R. 7 Ex. 26, 35; *Oelkers v Ellis* [1914] 2 K.B. 139; *Armstrong v Jackson* [1917] 2 K.B. 822; *Leaf v International Galleries* [1950] 2 K.B. 86.

[532] (1871) L.R. 7 Ex. 26, 34, 35.

[533] *Taite's Case* (1867) L.R. 3 Eq. 795; *Sharpley v Louth and East Coast Ry* (1876) 2 Ch D 663; *Re Scottish Petroleum Co* (1883) 23 Ch D 413; *Aaron's Reefs Ltd v Twiss* [1896] A.C. 273, 294; *Taylor v Oil and Ozokerite Co* (1913) 29 T.L.R. 515; *First National Reinsurance Co Ltd v Greenfield* [1921] 2 K.B. 260.

[534] *Oakes v Turquand* (1867) L.R. 2 H.L. 325.

[535] *Aaron's Reefs Ltd v Twiss* [1896] A.C. 273, 287; *Armstrong v Jackson* [1917] 2 K.B. 822; and see above, para.6–125.

[536] [1950] 2 K.B. 86. Denning L.J. and Lord Evershed M.R. said that the right to rescind for innocent misrepresentation must be barred if a right to reject for breach of condition would be barred by acceptance. It is not clear that a strictly analogous rule applies to rescission for innocent misrepresentation. It seemed doubtful when the courts held that the right to reject for breach of condition might be lost by acceptance after a matter of weeks: *Bernstein v Pamson Motors (Golders Green) Ltd* [1987] 2 All E.R. 220; but the decision of the Court of Appeal in *Clegg v Andersson* [2003] EWCA Civ 320, [2003] 2 Lloyd's Rep. 32 (below, para.43–315) seems much more generous and therefore an analogous approach might now be applied to loss of the right to rescind for misrepresentation.

goods.[536a] It seems doubtful whether mere lapse of time will bar rescission in other cases of completely innocent misrepresentation, and this will not be so in cases of fraud, nor where there has been breach of a fiduciary duty.[537]

Effect on representee. In considering whether the representee has lost his right to rescind by lapse of time, it may be important to inquire if the representee has been adversely affected by the delay.[538] Thus in *Morrison v Universal Marine Insurance Co*[539] it was said that rescission of a contract of marine insurance, the policy of which was voidable for non-disclosure of a material fact, would have been refused if there had been any evidence that the failure of the underwriters to avoid the contract after they had become aware of the defect had led the insured party to refrain from insuring elsewhere. But the fact that the representor has changed his position is not by itself a bar to rescission, so, e.g. a contract of guarantee can be rescinded by the guarantor notwithstanding that money has been lent by the representor in reliance on the guarantee.[540] But prompt action would doubtless be required once the representee knows the truth in a case of this nature. 6–128

Third-party rights. The intervention of a third party may prevent rescission. This is one of the risks run by the injured party if he delays in taking action, for if a third party acquires an interest in the subject-matter of the contract before the contract has been avoided a claim for rescission will not lie,[541] provided that the third party acted in good faith and gave consideration.[542] Thus, although there may be no duty to act within a prescribed time, it is in the representee's interest to act promptly, for the longer the delay, the greater the possibility of a third party acquiring rights in the subject-matter of the contract. This rule does not apply to void contracts, for in such cases the transferee has no title to pass to the third party[543]; it does apply to voidable contracts, for here the transferee has a good title until the contract is avoided.[544] Thus the rule may operate in all cases of misrepresentation (whether innocent, negligent or fraudulent) unless the effect of the misrepresentation is to make the contract void for mistake.[545] The effect on 6–129

536a See above, fn.525.

537 *Armstrong v Jackson* [1917] 2 K.B. 822.

538 See *Clough v L. & N.W. Ry* (1871) L.R. 7 Ex. 26, 34, 35; *Morrison v Universal Marine Insurance Co* (1873) L.R. 8 Ex. 197, 205; *Erlanger v New Sombrero Phosphate Co* (1878) 3 App. Cas. 1218, 1278. See also *Re Cape Breton Co* (1885) 29 Ch D 795 and *Ladywell Mining Co v Brookes* (1887) 35 Ch D 400.

539 (1873) L.R. 8 Ex. 197.

540 *Mackenzie v Royal Bank of Canada* [1934] A.C. 468.

541 *White v Garden* (1851) 10 C.B. 919; *Babcock v Lawson* (1880) 5 QBD 284; *Re L.G. Clarke* [1967] Ch. 1121.

542 *Scholefield v Templer* (1859) 4 De G. & J. 429, 433–434.

543 *Hardman v Booth* (1863) 1 H. & C. 803; *Cundy v Lindsay* (1878) 3 App. Cas. 459; *Ingram v Little* [1961] 1 Q.B. 31.

544 Sale of Goods Act 1979 s.23.

545 As, e.g. in *Cundy v Lindsay* (1877) L.R. 3 App. Cas. 459 and *Ingram v Little* (1892) L.R. 11 QBD 251; see above, paras 5–088 et seq. The rule that intervention of third party rights prevents rescission is normally invoked where a third party has acquired rights over the property transferred; but it can also apply where liability to third parties has been incurred before rescission is claimed and rescission would cause detriment to them: *Society of Lloyd's v Lyon* (unreported August 11, 1997).

third parties, in this case insured persons, may also prevent a name at Lloyd's from rescinding her agreement to become a name.[546]

6–130 **A "mere equity".** Until the contract is rescinded, the accepted view is that the misrepresentee has no proprietary right in the property transferred but only a "mere equity".[547]

6–131 **Assignments "subject to equities".** But this principle only applies to a transfer of goods and not to an assignment of contractual rights. If A is induced to sell goods to B by the fraud of B, and B resells the goods to C who takes in good faith and for value, C acquires a good title to the goods. But if A is induced to buy goods from B by the fraud of B, and B assigns the right to receive the purchase price to C, the rule that assignments are "subject to equities"[548] means that C gets no better right than B.

6–132 **Rescission by sub-buyer.** If a contract is induced by an innocent misrepresentation and that same innocent misrepresentation is passed on to a sub-buyer and in turn induces a subcontract, the sub-buyer may rescind the subcontract; if he does so, there is nothing to prevent the first representee from rescinding the original contract.[549]

6–133 **Executed contracts.** Until the passing of the Misrepresentation Act 1967 there was a further bar to rescission in certain cases of innocent misrepresentation, namely, the execution of the contract. This rule, often known as the rule in *Seddon v North Eastern Salt Co Ltd*[550] did not apply to cases of fraud, nor to cases of breach of fiduciary relationships,[551] and its application to particular types of contract was much disputed. The rule was, however, completely abrogated by s.1(b) of the Misrepresentation Act which provides that the performance of the contract shall be no bar to rescission for any misrepresentation where it would not have barred rescission for fraud. Although the Law Reform Committee (on whose Report the Act was based) had recommended that this rule should be retained for contracts for the sale of an interest in land, except for leases not exceeding three years,[552] the Act contains no special provision for such contracts. And despite the fact that the word "performed" is perhaps not wholly appropriate to contracts for the sale of an interest in land, it is thought that there can be no doubt that rescission of such contracts is now possible after execution of a conveyance or other grant in all cases of misrepresentation. Of course, the

---

[546] *Society of Lloyd's v Khan* [1998] 3 F.C.R. 93.

[547] *Clough v L. & N.W. Ry* (1871) L.R. 7 Ex. 26, 32, 34; *Bristol and West Building Society v Mothew* [1998] Ch. 1, 22; *Barclays Bank Plc v Boulter* [1999] 1 W.L.R. 1919, HL, at 1925; *Twinsectra Ltd v Yardley* [1999] Lloyd's Rep. Bank. 438 CA at [461]–[462]; *Shalson v Russo* [2003] EWHC 1637, *The Times*, September 3, 2003 Ch D (defendant did not hold property on constructive trust before rescission). For a full discussion see Cartwright, *Misrepresentation, Mistake and Non-disclosure* (2007), para.4.10 and Worthington [2002] R.L.R. 28.

[548] Below, para.19–070.

[549] *Abram S.S. Co v Westville Shipping Co* [1923] A.C. 773.

[550] [1905] 1 Ch. 326. See also *Senenayake v Cheng* [1966] A.C. 63, decided shortly before the 1967 Act was passed.

[551] *Armstrong v Jackson* [1917] 2 K.B. 822.

[552] Tenth Report, Cmnd.1782 (1962), paras 6 and 7.

execution of the contract may still be a bar to rescission on other grounds, for example, because it is evidence of affirmation,[553] or because restitutio in integrum is no longer possible.[554] Moreover, it is to be anticipated that a court might be more ready to exercise its discretion under s.2(2) of the Act of 1967 to award damages in lieu of rescission in cases where the contract has been executed.[555] But execution of the contract will no longer in itself be an absolute bar to rescission.

5. EXCLUSION OF LIABILITY FOR MISREPRESENTATION

Position at common law. At common law a person could not contract out of liability for fraud inducing the making of a contract with him, at least where the fraud was his own.[556] It is, however, possible that he could do so where the fraud was that of his employees[557] or agents[558] and there seems no doubt that it was possible, by a provision of the contract itself, to exclude or modify the normal consequences of innocent or negligent misrepresentation.[559] Such clauses were, however, subject to the normal principles of construction common to all exemption clauses.[560] 6–134

"No reliance" clauses. A clause that acknowledges that a party has not relied on a non-contractual representation may prevent that party showing that he was induced to enter the contract by a representation, as it may raise an "evidential estoppel". It will have that effect only if the party who made the representation entered the contract in the belief that the other had not relied on the representation: 6–135

---

553 Above, para.6–124.

554 Above, paras 6–115—6–122.

555 Above, para.6–102.

556 *S. Pearson & Son Ltd v Dublin Corp* [1907] A.C. 351; *HIH Casualty and General Insurance Ltd v Chase Manhattan Bank* [2003] UKHL 6, [2003] 2 Lloyd's Rep. 61 at [16], [76], [121]. This will include, in a case where there is a duty of disclosure (see below, para.6–142), fraudulent non-disclosure: *HIH Casualty and General Insurance Ltd v Chase Manhattan Bank* [2003] UKHL 6, at [21], [72].

557 See *John Carter (Fine Worsteds) Ltd v Hanson Haulage (Leeds) Ltd* [1965] 2 Q.B. 495.

558 This question was left open by the House of Lords in *HIH Casualty and General Insurance Ltd v Chase Manhattan Bank* [2003] UKHL 6, [2003] 2 Lloyd's Rep. 61, see at [16], [76]–[82]. In that case the clause was not in sufficiently clear and unmistakeable terms to exclude remedies for alleged fraud on the part of the agent.

559 *Boyd and Forrest v Glasgow Ry*, (1915) S.C. (HL) 20, 36. A properly worded clause which excludes a right of avoidance will be effective (assuming it is not affected by Misrepresentation Act 1967 s.3, see, para.6–136) notwithstanding a purported rescission of the contract as a whole by the misrepresentee: *Toomey v Eagle Star Insurance Co Ltd (No.2)* [1995] 2 Lloyd's Rep. 88.

560 Below, paras 14–005—14–019. Thus a clause stating that a contract of reinsurance was "neither cancellable nor voidable by either party" was held to apply only to cases of innocent misrepresentation or non-disclosure, and not to alleged negligence, nor to exclude the right to damages under Misrepresentation Act 1967 s.2(1): *Toomey v Eagle Star Insurance Co Ltd (No.2)* [1995] 2 Lloyd's Rep. 88. A disclaimer "without responsibility" does not prevent rescission on the ground of misrepresentation: *Crédit Lyonnais Bank Nederland v Export Credit Guarantee Department* [1996] 1 Lloyd's Rep. 1. However, a clause applying to "rights, obligations and liabilities arising . . . in connection with this contract" may apply to a claim for misrepresentation, *Strachan & Henshaw Ltd v Stein Industrie (UK) Ltd (No.2)* (1997) 87 B.L.R. 52.

> "... it may be impossible for a party who has made representations which he intended should be relied upon to satisfy the court that he entered into the contract in the belief that a statement by the other party that he had not relied upon those representations was true."[561]

However it has been pointed out that the clause may also be effective, even if it is known that the party did rely on a representation, if the parties have in fact agreed to conduct their affairs on the basis that there has been no reliance, so that an estoppel arises by convention.[562]

6–136 **Misrepresentation Act section 3.** Section 3 of the Act of 1967 limits the freedom of the parties to contract out of the effect of the Act in certain respects. The original s.3 was replaced by s.8 of the Unfair Contract Terms Act 1977, and s.3 is now as follows:

> "If a contract contains a term which would exclude or restrict—
>
> (*a*) any liability to which a party to a contract may be subject by reason of any misrepresentation made by him before the contract was made; or
>
> (*b*) any remedy available to another party to the contract by reason of such a misrepresentation,
>
> that term shall be of no effect except in so far as it satisfies the requirement of reasonableness as stated in section 11(1) of the Unfair Contract Terms Act 1977; and it is for those claiming that the term satisfies that requirement to show that it does."

The main change of substance between the current and the original s.3 is that under the original section it was *reliance* on the exempting provision which had to be shown to be reasonable; under the current s.3, it is the exempting term itself which has to be shown to be reasonable. Thus a very wide exempting term may be held unreasonable under the current s.3 while reliance on it might have been reasonable under the old s.3[563]; equally, a term may now be held reasonable where reliance on it in particular circumstances might formerly have been held unreasonable. A further change is that the current s.3 makes it clear that the onus is on a person claiming to rely upon an exempting term to show that it is reasonable under the relevant section of the Unfair Contract Terms Act. The

---

[561] Chadwick L.J. in *Watford Electronics Ltd v Sanderson CFL Ltd* [2001] EWCA Civ 317, [2001] Build. L.R. 143 at [40], referring to the requirements for evidential estoppel identified by the Court of Appeal in *Lowe v Lombank Ltd* [1960] 1 W.L.R. 196 and citing his own unreported decision in *E A Grimstead & Son Ltd v McGarrigan*, October 27, 1999. This dictum was applied in *Quest 4 Finance Ltd v Maxfield* [2007] EWHC 2313 (QB), [2007] 2 C.L.C. 706. Whether a non-reliance clause is caught by Misrepresentation Act s.3 is discussed below, para.6–138.

[562] *Peekay Intermark Ltd v Australia & New Zealand Banking Group Ltd* [2006] EWCA Civ 386, [2006] 2 Lloyd's Rep. 511 at [54]–[60], referring to *Colchester BC v Smith* [1991] Ch. 448, affirmed on appeal [1992] Ch. 421; *Donegal International Ltd v Zambia* [2007] EWHC 197 (Comm), [2007] 1 Lloyd's Rep. 397 at [465]. On estoppel by convention, see above, paras 3–107 et seq.

[563] In the *Howard Marine* case [1978] Q.B. 554 (above, para.6–068) Lord Denning M.R. was prepared to uphold reliance on an exempting clause under the old s.3 as reasonable; the majority of the court disagreed without giving reasons.

requirement of reasonableness is now stated in s.11(1) of the Unfair Contract Terms Act 1977 as a requirement that the term in question:

> " . . . shall have been a fair and reasonable one to be included having regard to the circumstances which were, or ought reasonably to have been, known to or in the contemplation of the parties when the contract was made."

Reasonableness under the Act is discussed below.[564]

Scope of section 3. The terms "any liability" and "any remedy" are presumably wide enough to cover provisions which would exclude or restrict a claim to damages, or the right to rescind, or the right to set up the misrepresentation by way of defence to an action.[565] The section applies not merely to provisions totally excluding the normal consequences of misrepresentation, but also to provisions which restrict any liability or remedy arising from a misrepresentation.[566] This means, for instance, that a provision barring rescission but allowing claims for damages would fall within the section, as also would a provision limiting the amount of damages or the time within which a claim may be made. What is more problematic is whether the section applies to a clause that is worded so as to exclude any liability for misrepresentation[567] from arising at all, by stating that one of the essential elements is missing.[568] Thus it has been held that the section does not prevent a principal from limiting the authority of his agent even though the effect is to exclude or restrict a liability to which the principal would otherwise be subject,[569] and it may not apply to a "no reliance" clause.[570] 6–137

Section 3 and no reliance clauses. Whether s.3 applies to clauses under which one party acknowledges that it has not relied on any statement made to 6–138

[564] See below, para.6–139.

[565] A right of set-off is a remedy for this purpose: *Skipskredittforeningen v Emperor Navigation* [1998] 1 Lloyd's Rep. 66, not following *Society of Lloyd's v Wilkinson (No.2)* [1997] 6 Re L.R. 214 on this point. See also *WRM Group Ltd v Wood* [1998] C.L.C. 189. But a term that purchasers of a lease would be permitted to enter into possession before completion "at their own risk" was held not to be within the section (though unreasonable if it was): *F. & H. Entertainments Ltd v Leisure Enterprises Ltd* (1976) 120 S.J. 331.

[566] It may not apply to clauses excluding liability for non-disclosure: *National Westminster Bank Plc v Utrecht-America Finance Co* [2001] EWCA Civ 658, [2001] 3 All E.R. 733 at [62] (point left open).

[567] Misrepresentation Act s.3 does not apply to clauses stating that the written document constitutes the entire contract and that particulars given do not constitute an offer or contract, but that is because such a clause does not purport to exclude liability for misrepresentation, but only to define what are the terms of the contract: *McGrath v Shah* (1989) 57 P. & C.R. 452.

[568] It has been pointed out that the problem is caused by the fact that s.3 has no equivalent to Unfair Contract Terms Act 1977 s.13, which defines "excluding or restricting liability" to include "excluding or restricting liability by reference to terms and notices which exclude or restrict the relevant obligation or duty": Peel (2001) 117 L.Q.R. 545, 548.

[569] *Overbrooke Estates Ltd v Glencombe Properties Ltd* [1974] 1 W.L.R. 1335, approved by the Court of Appeal in *Museprime Properties Ltd v Adhill Properties Ltd* [1990] 2 E.G.L.R. 196, 200.

[570] See next paragraph.

it[571] have been the subject of apparently conflicting views.[572] It is submitted that the question is whether a misrepresentation was made; the evidence as a whole, including the clause, might show that the representee did not rely on the misrepresentation. But if the contract was induced by misrepresentation, s.3 applies, and its effect cannot be excluded.[573] As it was put recently:

> "If a seller of a car said to a buyer 'I have serviced the car since it was new, it has had only one owner and the clock reading is accurate', those statements would be representations, and they would still have that character even if the seller added the words 'but those statements are not representations on which you can rely' . . . If, however, the seller of the car said 'The clock reading is 20,000 miles, but I have no knowledge whether the reading is true or false', the position would be different, because the qualifying words could not fairly be regarded as an attempt to exclude liability for a false representation arising from the first half of the sentence."[574]

6–139 **Reasonableness.** Reasonableness under the Act is discussed below (paras 14–089—14–099) and only selected points will be considered here.[575] It seems that the court must consider the reasonableness of the provision as a whole.[576] A clause may be invalid because, taken as a whole, it is too wide, even though it would not necessarily be unreasonable to exclude or restrict liability on the facts which have occurred. Thus a clause which purports to exclude liability for misrepresentation of any kind will be unreasonable, since it is not reasonable to exclude liability for fraud, and the clause as a whole will be invalid.[577] The court should not, however, hold a clause unreasonable because it might extend to some situation which is unlikely to occur.[578] But if the clause is too wide, the court cannot rewrite the clause in a reasonable fashion and, as the test under s.11(1) of

---

[571] See above, para.6–135.

[572] Compare *Cremdean v Nash* (1977) 241 E.G. 837 CA and *Watford Electronics Ltd v Sanderson CFL Ltd* [2001] EWCA Civ 317, [2001] Build. L.R. 142 at [40].

[573] *Cremdean v Nash* (1977) 241 E.G. 837 CA. See also *Thomas Witter Ltd v TBP Industries Ltd* [1992] All E.R. 573, 597–598; *Zanzibar v British Aerospace (Lancaster House) Ltd* [2000] 1 W.L.R. 2333, 2347.

[574] Toulson J. in *IFE Fund SA v Goldman Sachs International* [2006] EWHC 2887 (Comm), [2007] 1 Lloyd's Rep. 264 at [68]–[69]; affirmed without comment on this point [2007] EWCA Civ 811, [2007] 2 Lloyd's Rep. 449. The judge held that on the facts no representation had been made (see para.6–007, above). A "no reliance" clause was held to be ineffective under s.3 in *Leofelis SA v Lonsdale Sports Ltd* [2007] EWHC 451 (Ch).

[575] It has been held that condition 17 of the National Conditions of Sale (19th edn) was invalid as unreasonable under s.3 of the Misrepresentation Act: *Walker v Boyle* [1982] 1 W.L.R. 495. Condition 17 stated that replies to questions by the vendor or his agents do not obviate the need for the buyer to make his own inquiries and inspections, and are not to be treated as representations. See also *Southwestern General Property Co Ltd v Marton* (1982) 263 E.G. 1090; *White Cross Equipment Ltd v Farrell* (1982) 2 Tr.L.R. 21; *Cooper v Tamms* [1988] 1 E.G.L.R. 257; *Goff v Gauthier* [1991] 62 P. & C.R. 388.

[576] See below, para.14–100.

[577] *Thomas Witter Ltd v TBP Industries Ltd* [1992] All E.R. 573. cf. *Stewart Gill Ltd v Horatio Myer & Co Ltd* [1992] Q.B. 600; below, para.14–100. In *Skipskredittforeningen v Emperor Navigation* [1998] 1 Lloyd's Rep. 66 it was held not to be unreasonable to include in a loan agreement a no-set off clause which might apply even in cases of fraud.

[578] *Skipskredittforeningen v Emperor Navigation* [1998] 1 Lloyd's Rep. 66, 75–76.

the Unfair Contract Terms Act 1977 is whether the term was "a fair and reasonable one to be included", the court cannot allow the misrepresentor to rely on it so far as seems reasonable.[579] Thus it cannot uphold a provision in so far as it would bar rescission, but reject it in so far as it would bar a claim for damages. However, it is possible that a clause which is in distinct parts might be severed and the reasonable parts upheld. It has been said in the Court of Appeal that there are at least two good reasons why the courts should not refuse to give effect to an exclusion of remedies for misrepresentation in a commercial contract between experienced parties of equal bargaining power—a fortiori, where those parties have the benefit of professional advice. First, it is reasonable to assume that the parties desire commercial certainty; and secondly, it is reasonable to assume that the price to be paid reflects the commercial risk which each party—or, more usually, the purchaser—is willing to accept.[580]

Clauses covering breach. The section does not seem to apply to a provision which excludes or restricts liability arising solely from breach of a contractual term, whether the term is a promise or a representation of fact. But, read literally, the section would appear to apply to a provision which excludes or restricts liabilities or remedies arising both from misrepresentations as such, and from misrepresentations as contractual terms.[581] 6–140

Other statutory provisions affecting disclaimers. A clause aimed at preventing liability arising in tort under *Hedley Byrne & Co Ltd v Heller & Partners Ltd*[582] on the part of a business will be valid under the Unfair Contract Terms Act 1977 s.2(2) only if it satisfies the requirement of reasonableness under that Act.[583] The Unfair Terms in Consumer Contracts Regulations 1999[584] also affect clauses in consumer contracts which unfairly exclude or restrict the consumer's remedies for misrepresentation. For the most part it seems likely that the test of unfairness under the Regulations will produce substantially similar results to the reasonableness test of s.11 of the Unfair Contract Terms Act 1977. Any clause excluding or limiting liability for misrepresentation, however it is worded, will be within the Regulations provided that it is "in a contract concluded between a 6–141

[579] Compare the formulation used by the original version of s.3 before amendment by the 1977 Act: "[T]hat provision shall be of no effect except to the extent that . . . the court or arbitrator may allow reliance on it as being fair and reasonable in the circumstances of the case." But see the doubts expressed by Mance J. in *Skipskredittforeningen v Emperor Navigation* [1998] 1 Lloyd's Rep. 66, 75; and also *Bacardi-Martini Beverages Ltd v Thomas Hardy Packaging Ltd* [2002] EWCA Civ 549, [2002] 2 Lloyd's Rep. 379 at [26].

[580] See *National Westminster Bank Plc v Utrecht-America Finance Co* [2001] EWCA Civ 658, [2001] 3 All E.R. 733 at [60]–[61], citing an unreported judgment of Chadwick L.J. in *E A Grimstead & Son Ltd v McGarrigan* October 27, 1999; *Watford Electronics Ltd v Sanderson CFL Ltd* [2001] EWCA Civ 317, [2001] Build. L.R. 143 at [39].

[581] As already seen (above, para.6–105) s.1(a) of the 1967 Act provides that a misrepresentation continues to be effective as such even if it becomes a term of the contract. See also below, para.14–114.

[582] [1964] A.C. 465; above, para.6–081.

[583] *Smith v Eric S. Bush* [1990] 1 A.C. 831; see above, para.6–083 and below, para.14–092.

[584] SI 1999/2083; see below, Ch.15.

seller or supplier and a consumer" and "has not been individually negotiated".[585] Thus clauses limiting the authority of agents or defining the terms of the contract, which are not caught by s.3 of the Misrepresentation Act 1967,[586] will be covered.

6. CONTRACTS UBERRIMAE FIDEI

6–142 **Non-disclosure.** Mere non-disclosure of fact, material or not, does not ordinarily amount to misrepresentation, and the general rule is that in order to be actionable a representation must take an active form.[587] But in certain cases a stricter rule is enforced. The most important of these are the contracts uberrimae fidei[588] in which knowledge of the material facts generally lies with one party alone; that party is under a duty to make a full disclosure of these facts, and failure to do so makes the contract voidable. However, even if the non-disclosure is negligent, it does not give rise to liability in damages under Misrepresentation Act 1967 s.2(1) or, without more, at common law.[589] The duty varies in its extent from one type of contract to another. Contracts of insurance of every kind form the main group of contracts uberrimae fidei. Other examples generally included, though these are probably not all uberrimae fidei in the strict sense and do not involve such extensive duties of disclosure, are contracts to subscribe for shares in a company,[590] family settlements,[591] contracts for the sale of land,[592] contracts for suretyship,[593] and partnerships. To this list may be added general releases. Contracts of service are not uberrimae fidei[594] nor are contracts of sale of goods.[595]

6–143 **Rescission but not damages.** A breach of the duty to disclose will give rise to the right to rescind the contract but, it is submitted, not to a right to damages even if the other party kept quiet "fraudulently" in the sense of intended deliberately to mislead the claimant. In *Conlon v Simms* it was said that:

> ". . . where the breach of the duty of disclosure is fraudulent, a party to whom the duty is owed who suffers loss by reason of the breach may recover damages for that loss in

---

[585] Regulations 1999 reg.5(1).

[586] See above, para.6–137.

[587] See above, para.6–014.

[588] For the others, see above, paras 6–014—6–018. A party in whom trust and confidence is reposed may also have, in effect, a duty of disclosure: below, para.7–094.

[589] *Banque Keyser Ullman SA v Skandia (UK) Insurance Co Ltd* [1990] 1 Q.B. 665, 787–789, 790–805, affirmed on other grounds [1991] 2 A.C. 249. See above, para.1–134.

[590] Below, para.6–153.

[591] Below, para.6–155.

[592] Below, para.6–156.

[593] Below, para.6–158.

[594] *Bell v Lever Bros Ltd* [1932] A.C. 161, 227; *Nottingham University v Fishel* [2000] I.C.R. 1462.

[595] *Jewson & Sons Ltd v Arcos Ltd* (1932) 39 Com. Cas. 59.

the tort of deceit . . . Non-disclosure where there is a duty to disclose is tantamount to an implied representation that there is nothing relevant to disclose."[596]

This, with respect, is very doubtful, and cannot be supported on the ground given. It is well-established that breach of the duty of disclosure in insurance does not of itself give rise to an action for damages.[597] A negligent failure to speak may give rise to liability in damages but only if there is a "voluntary assumption of responsibility".[598] If silence when there is a duty to disclose amounted to an implied representation that there was nothing to disclose, that would make even a non-fraudulent non-disclosure into a positive misrepresentation for which damages could be recovered under Misrepresentation Act 1967 s.2(1), unless the non-disclosing party could show that he had reasonable grounds for believing that there was nothing to disclose. It is almost certain that without a voluntary assumption of responsibility there is no liability in damages for merely keeping silent, and it is submitted that this is so even if there was an intention to deceive.[599]

(a) *Insurance*

Contracts of insurance.[600] As a matter of law, all of these are uberrimae fidei, whatever their subject matter, that is whether they relate to marine, fire, life or burglary insurance, or to any other risk. Marine insurance is governed by the Marine Insurance Act 1906, which codified the existing law. Non-marine insurance is subject to the common law. It is thought to be contrary to good faith to withhold material facts from the insurer.[601] Such facts are generally known only 6–144

[596] [2006] EWCA Civ 1749 at [130]; see also at first instance [2006] EWHC 401 (Ch), [2006] 2 All E.R. 1024.

[597] See para.1–134 and para.6–142 at fn.589.

[598] *Banque Keyser Ullmann SA v Skandia (UK) Insurance Co Ltd* [1990] 1 Q.B. 665 at 794.

[599] Liability in damages for fraudulent non-disclosure had been mooted as a possibility by Rix L.J. in *HIH Casualty & General Insurance Ltd v Chase Manhattan Bank* [2001] EWCA Civ 1250, [2001] 2 Lloyd's Rep. 483 at [48], [164] and [168] but the point was neither argued nor decided. In the House of Lords, Lord Bingham did say that the deliberate withholding of information which the person knows or believes to be material, if done dishonestly or recklessly, may amount to a fraudulent misrepresentation: [2003] UKHL 6, [2003] 2 Lloyd's Rep. 61 at [21]. However this appears to refer to cases where in the circumstances a failure to disclose amounts to a positive misrepresentation, and it is not clear that Lord Bingham thought this included every case of a duty to disclose. Lord Hoffmann said that "nondisclosure (whether dishonest or otherwise) does not as such give rise to a claim in damages" (at [75]); he referred to the judgments in *Banque Keyser Ullmann SA v Skandia (UK) Insurance Co Ltd* [1990] 1 Q.B. 665, 777–781 and 788 ("without a misrepresentation there can be no fraud in the sense of giving rise to a claim for damages in tort") and [1991] 2 A.C. 249 at 280 (per Lord Templeman) and at 281 (per Lord Jauncey of Tullichettle). Moreover, in *Manifest Shipping Co v Uni-Polaris Insurance Co, The Star Sea* [2001] UKHL 1, [2003] 1 A.C. 469 at [46], Lord Hobhouse regarded the *Banque Keyser Ullman* case as deciding authoritatively that a breach of duty to disclose does not give rise to damages. Damages may be recovered in tort for deceit but even deliberate non-disclosure does not give rise to an action for deceit. See *Clerk & Lindsell on Torts*, 19th edn (2006), para.18–05; Cartwright, *Misrepresentation, Mistake and Non-disclosure*, 2nd edn (2007), para.17–36.

[600] See Hasson (1969) 32 M.L.R. 615 and Vol.II, paras 41–030 et seq. Proposals for reform of the law were made by the Law Commission, see Law Com. No.104, Cmnd.8064 (1980). They were not implemented and the Law Commission has now taken up the matter again, see below, fn.603.

[601] See *Carter v Boehm* (1766) 3 Burr. 1905, 1909; *London Assurance Co v Mansel* (1879) 11 Ch D 363, 367.

to the assured, and he is therefore under a duty to disclose them.[602] However, in practice the duty of disclosure has a very limited application to "retail" or "consumer" insurance because of the requirements of the Financial Services Authority and, even more pertinently, the decisions of the Financial Ombudsman Service as to when insurers are complying with a general requirement to treat customers fairly and reasonably.[603]

6–145 **Materiality.** A circumstance is material if it "would influence the judgment of a prudent insurer in fixing the premium, or determining whether he will take the risk." This is the definition given in the Marine Insurance Act 1906 s.18(2), and it was held in *Locker and Woolf Ltd v Western Australian Insurance Co Ltd*[604] that the definition applies to all forms of insurance. In *Pan Atlantic Insurance Co Ltd v Pine Top Insurance Co Ltd*[605] the House of Lords held that, for both marine insurance under Marine Insurance Act 1906 s.18(2) and non-marine insurance, the test of materiality is not whether the matter would have had a decisive effect on the prudent insurer's decision whether to accept the risk or at what premium, but whether it would have an effect on the mind of the prudent insurer in weighing up the risk.[606] In *St Paul Fire and Marine Insurance Co Ltd v McConnell Dowell Constructors Ltd*[607] it was held that a matter did not necessarily have to lead to an increase in the risk in order to be material; it was sufficient that the risk was different.[608] But in the *Pan Atlantic* case the House of Lords held that, in addition to being material, a misrepresentation or non-disclosure must have induced the making of the policy.[609] In this respect, the law on insurance contracts is parallel to the general law on positive misrepresentation.[610] Lord Mustill[611] refers to "a presumption in favour of causative effect", as there is in the case of a positive misrepresentation.[612]

6–146 **Duty on insurer also.** The obligation to disclose material facts is mutual and a duty also rests on the insurer to disclose all facts known to him which are

[602] A contract of marine insurance appears to be based on an implied condition that there is no misrepresentation or concealment: *Blackburn v Vigors* (1886) 17 QBD 552, 561, 562; *Pickersgill v London and Provincial Marine and General Insurance Co* [1912] 3 K.B. 614, 621. The duty of disclosure in non-marine insurance, on the other hand, is said to rest on a common law, and not on a contractual duty: *Joel v Law Union and Crown Insurance Co* [1908] 2 K.B. 863, 886; *Merchants and Manufacturers Insurance Co v Hunt and Thorne* [1941] 1 K.B. 295, 313. But see *Moens v Hayworth* (1842) 10 M. & W. 147, 157. It is otherwise of course if the common law obligation is superseded by a term in the contract itself.

[603] An account of the FSA Regulations and the FOS practice will be found in Law Commission, Joint Consultation Paper, *Insurance Contract Law: Misrepresentation, Non-disclosure and Breach of Warranty by the Insured* (LCCP 182, SLCDP 134, 2007) paras 3.5–3.54. The FOS applies the same approach in favour of some small business: para.5.165.

[604] [1936] 1 K.B. 408, 415. This was also the test applied in *Lambert v Co-operative Insurance Society Ltd* [1975] 2 Lloyd's Rep. 485.

[605] [1995] 1 A.C. 501.

[606] See further below, Vol.II, para.41–031.

[607] [1996] 1 All E.R. 96.

[608] [1996] 1 All E.R. 96, 107.

[609] [1995] 1 A.C. 501, 549–550.

[610] See above, paras 6–032—6–035.

[611] [1995] 1 A.C. 501, 542.

[612] See above, para.6–035, fn.178; and also *St Paul Fire and Marine Insurance Co Ltd v McConnell Dowell Constructors Ltd* [1996] 1 All E.R. 96, 112.

material either to the nature of the risk sought to be covered or to the recoverability of a claim under the policy.[613] In this case the test of materiality is whether the fact not disclosed would be taken into account by a prudent insured in deciding whether to place the risk with that insurer.[614]

The following have been held to be material facts and their non-disclosure made the contract in question voidable: that goods were insured upon a voyage for an amount in excess of their value[615]; that the vessel itself was over-insured[616]; that (in the particular circumstances of the case) the insured under a policy of burglary insurance was an alien[617]; that the insured had been convicted of robbery 12 years previously[618]; that in relation to an insurance comparable to that sought previous claims had been made.[619] On the other hand, certain details may on construction be held to be irrelevant,[620] such as the place where a lorry was to be garaged.[621] A circumstance that is material for one type of insurance is not necessarily material for another; for example, the fact that the risk has been refused by another company is material in life, fire, accident and burglary insurance, but not in marine insurance.[622] Whether a particular circumstance is material is a question of fact, and the opinion of the assured on its materiality is irrelevant.[623] **6–147**

In marine insurance the duty to disclose is defined as follows: **6–148**

> "Subject to the provisions of this section, the assured must disclose to the insurer, before the contract is concluded, every material circumstance which is known to the assured and the assured is deemed to know every circumstance which, in the ordinary course of business, ought to be known by him."[624]

---

613 *Carter v Boehm* (1766) 3 Burr. 1905; *Banque Keyser Ullman SA v Skandia (UK) Insurance Co Ltd* [1990] 1 Q.B. 665, 770–772, affirmed on other grounds but without disapproval of this statement of principle, [1991] 2 A.C. 249.

614 [1990] 1 Q.B. 665, 772.

615 *Ionides v Pender* (1874) L.R. 9 Q.B. 531; *Gooding v White* (1913) 29 T.L.R. 312.

616 *Thames and Mersey Marine Insurance Co v Gunford Ship Co Ltd* [1911] A.C. 529.

617 *Horne v Poland* [1922] 2 K.B. 364. But cf. *Associated Oil Carriers Ltd v Union Insurance Society* [1917] 2 K.B. 184.

618 *Woolcott v Sun Alliance & London Insurance Ltd* [1978] 1 W.L.R. 493; contrast *Reynolds and Anderson v Phoenix Assurance Co Ltd* [1978] 2 Lloyd's Rep. 440 (mere allegation of fraud need not be disclosed). Note the effect of the Rehabilitation of Offenders Act 1974 on cases of this kind, see s.4(2) and (3).

619 *Farra v Hetherington* (1931) 47 T.L.R. 465.

620 *Perrins v Marine Insurance Society* (1859) 2 E. & E. 317.

621 *Dawsons Ltd v Bonnin* [1922] 2 A.C. 413.

622 *London Assurance Co v Mansel* (1879) 11 Ch D 363; *Yager v Guardian Assurance Co* (1912) 29 T.L.R. 53; *Glicksman v Lancashire and General Assurance Co* [1927] A.C. 139; *Holts' Motors v South East Lancashire Insurance Co* (1930) 35 Com. Cas. 281; *Locker and Woolf Ltd v Western Australian Insurance Co* [1936] 1 K.B. 408.

623 *Lindenau v Desborough* (1828) 8 B. & C. 586, 592; *London Assurance Co v Mansel* (1879) 11 Ch D 363; *Joel v Law Union and Crown Insurance Co* [1908] 2 K.B. 863, 884; *Godfrey v Britannic Assurance Co Ltd* [1963] 2 Lloyd's Rep. 515; *Lambert v Co-operative Insurance Society Ltd* [1975] 2 Lloyd's Rep. 485.

624 Marine Insurance Act 1906 s.18(1). On the interpretation of this section see *PCW Syndicates v PCW Reinsurers* [1996] 1 W.L.R. 1136.

In non-marine insurance the duty may extend only to facts actually known to the assured.[625] If so, he is under no duty to disclose facts of which he is ignorant. A statement which is expressed to depend on the assured's state of mind will not be untrue simply because he was unaware of the true facts, provided that his statement of belief was genuine. For instance, a statement by the assured that he is in good health in relation to a proposed life policy will generally be construed to mean in good health to his own knowledge, and the contract cannot be rescinded on proof that at the time of the contract the assured's state of health was not what he believed it to be.[626] If, however, he is aware of a fact which a reasonable or prudent insurer might treat as material, he must disclose it; the test is not whether a reasonable man would think it material.[627]

6–149 **"Basis of the contract".** The duty to disclose may be enlarged by the terms of the contract, and insurers commonly provide that the declarations of the assured shall form the basis of the contract. In effect this means that the assured "warrants" that the information which he supplies is correct, the penalty for inaccuracy being the avoidance of the contract by the insurer. Thus the insurer may be discharged from liability[628] if the assured fails to disclose even a non-material fact,[629] or a fact never within his knowledge, or if he gives what has proved to be an inaccurate statement on a matter of opinion.[630] Where an attempt is made to enlarge the duty by the terms of the contract, the courts put a strict burden of proof upon the insurer.[631] But this has not prevented the courts from holding that even disclosure to a representative of the insurer is insufficient, if (as has in the past commonly been the case with some forms of insurance) the proposal form declares that any person filling in the form is deemed to be the agent of the insured, and not of the insurer.[632] More recently, however, it has been

---

625 *Blackburn, Low & Co v Vigors* (1887) 12 App. Cas. 531 (a marine insurance case before the Marine Insurance Act 1906); *Joel v Law Union and Crown Insurance Co* [1908] 2 K.B. 863, 884–885. In the *Economides v Commercial Union Assurance Co Plc* [1998] Q.B. 587 it was held that an insured who is not acting in the course of business has only to disclose material facts actually known to him; provided that he did not wilfully shut his eyes to the truth (so-called "Nelsonian blindness"), he is not under a duty to inquire further, for example by checking that his honest belief in the value of the property is in fact accurate. But see Vol.II, para.41–035.

626 *Wheelton v Hardisty* (1857) 8 E. & B. 232. But see *Macdonald v Law Union Insurance Co* (1874) L.R. 9 Q.B. 328.

627 *Lambert v Co-operative Insurance Society Ltd* [1975] 2 Lloyd's Rep. 485.

628 See *Bank of Nova Scotia v Hellenic Mutual War Risks (The Good Luck)* [1992] 1 AC 233, 263–4. The insurer may waive the breach and affirm the contract: Marine Insurance Act 1906 s.34(3).

629 *Anderson v Fitzgerald* (1853) 4 H.L.C. 484; *Condogianis v Guardian Assurance Co* [1921] 2 A.C. 125; *Dawsons Ltd v Bonnin* [1922] 2 A.C. 413. See Vol.II, para.41–041.

630 Again, the practical effect of such warranties is severely restricted in cases of consumer insurance by the FSA Regulations and the requirements of the Financial Ombudsman Service: see above, fn.603.

631 *Anderson v Fitzgerald* (1853) 4 H.L.C. 484; *Joel v Law Union and Crown Insurance Co* [1908] 2 K.B. 863; *Anstey v British National Premium Life Association Ltd* (1908) 99 L.T. 765.

632 *Newsholme Brothers v Road Transport and General Insurance Co Ltd* [1929] 2 K.B. 356; *Facer v Vehicle & General Insurance Co Ltd* [1965] 1 Lloyd's Rep. 113. Contra, *Bawden v London, Edinburgh and Glasgow Assurance Co Ltd* [1892] 2 Q.B. 534; this case was treated as virtually overruled by the *Newsholme Bros* case in the *Facer* case but now seems to have been rehabilitated by *Stone v Reliance Mutual Insurance Society Ltd* [1972] 1 Lloyd's Rep. 469. Such a clause might well be caught by Unfair Terms in Consumer Contracts Regulations 1999: see below, para.15–108.

held that if the representative is authorised by the insurer to fill in the forms and then secure the proposer's signature thereto, he may be held to be the agent of the insurer.[633]

Burden of proof. With regard to the burden of proof generally, the insurer must produce evidence to show non-disclosure, unless there is prima facie evidence of concealment. In that case the burden is on the assured to prove disclosure.[634] 6–150

Continuing duty. The duty to disclose continues until the contract is concluded. Thus if before the acceptance of the proposal a new material fact arises, or a fact thought to be non-material becomes material, this must be disclosed.[635] 6–151

Effect of Misrepresentation Act on insurance contracts. It has been seen above that the Act of 1967 has no application to cases of pure non-disclosure,[636] but most insurance contracts in effect convert what would be a non-disclosure into a positive misrepresentation constituting a term of the contract. It has also been seen above[637] that it is not clear whether s.2(2) of the Misrepresentation Act enables a court to refuse to allow rescission for misrepresentation where the statement in question was later incorporated as a term of the contract. If it did have this effect, the totally unexpected result might follow, that an insurer might no longer be able to repudiate liability for an immaterial misrepresentation, or even for a material misrepresentation which had no bearing on the risk which has occurred. But this is not generally thought to be the result of the 1967 Act[638]; and in any event it is very unlikely that the court would exercise its jurisdiction to prevent an insurer rescinding on the ground of misrepresentation by the insured.[639] 6–152

(b) *Contracts to take shares in companies*

Companies. Contracts to take shares in companies may be classified as uberrimae fidei because again the knowledge of the material facts lies with one party alone, namely, the promoters, directors and others responsible for the issue of the prospectus. It was long ago recognised that invitations to invest, made through a prospectus, could lead to much enrichment of individuals at the public expense, and at least from promoters the utmost good faith was required.[640] In time the legislature intervened to protect the public and to supplement the 6–153

---

633 *Stone v Reliance Mutual Insurance Society Ltd* [1972] 1 Lloyd's Rep. 469; see also *Maye v Colonial Mutual Life Assurance Society Ltd* (1924) 35 C.L.R. 14.

634 *Glicksman v Lancashire and General Assurance Co* [1925] 2 K.B. 593; [1927] A.C. 139.

635 *Allis Chalmers Co v Maryland Fidelity and Deposit Co* (1916) 114 L.T. 433; *Looker v Law Union and Rock Insurance Co* [1928] 1 K.B. 554; cf. *Blackley v National Mutual Life Association of Australasia Ltd* [1972] N.Z.L.R. 1038. See Vol.II, para.41–034.

636 Above, para.6–017.

637 Above, para.6–108.

638 See Hudson (1969) 85 L.Q.R. 524 and Vol.II, para.41–039 fn.283.

639 See above, para.6–102.

640 *Erlanger v New Sombrero Phosphate Co* (1878) 3 App. Cas. 1218.

common law. The present position is governed by Financial Services and Markets Act 2000 ss.80 and 81.[641] The legislation requires the disclosure of specified matters, and render those responsible liable in damages to anyone who has acquired securities to which the legislation applies,[642] and who has suffered loss as the result of the omission from the prospectus or, in the case listing particulars, the particulars, of any matter that should have been included.[643] However, mere disclosure does not of itself give a right to rescission.[644] It is this fact which provokes the doubt as to whether contracts to take shares in companies are properly classified as contracts uberrimae fidei. However, if failure to disclose makes the prospectus misleading by falsifying that which is stated, there is a remedy as for positive misrepresentation.[645] With regard to misrepresentations as distinct from non-disclosures, an untrue statement in the prospectus which has induced a person to subscribe for shares does of course give that person the right to rescind the contract, provided that he acts promptly and before winding-up proceedings have begun.[646]

6–154 The position of the promoters is also regulated by the common law. They have a fiduciary relationship with the company, and the rule is that they must not make a secret profit at its expense.[647] They are under a duty to disclose either to an independent board of directors, or to the intended shareholders, for instance by making a disclosure in the prospectus, any profit made by them on a sale of property to the company. A breach of this duty entitles the company to sue the promoters for damages, or to recover the profit,[648] or to rescind the contract.[649]

(c) *Family settlements*

6–155 **Family settlements.** In these and in negotiations for these there must not only be an absence of misrepresentation but a full communication of all material facts known to the parties. Any failure to disclose may be a ground for setting aside the settlement, and it is immaterial that information was withheld because of a

---

[641] See generally, Gower & Davies *Principles of Modern Company Law*, 7th edn (2003), pp.649–679.

[642] Thus investors who have bought on the market after dealing has commenced are now protected.

[643] Financial Services and Markets Act 2000 ss.86(1), 90(1) Note that the sections are without prejudice to any liability which may be incurred apart from the section or regulation: s.90(6). These provisions stem ultimately from the Directors Liability Act 1890, which was passed to reverse the effect of *Derry v Peek* (1889) 14 App.Cas. 337, so far as it applied to prospectuses.

[644] Gower & Davies, *Principles of Modern Company Law*, 7th edn (2003), p.675.

[645] See *Central Ry of Venezuela v Kisch* (1867) L.R. 2 H.L. 99.

[646] Further, a shareholder may rescind if misrepresentations are made in a document issued by the promoters before the company is formed: *Karberg's Case* [1892] 3 Ch. 1.

[647] *Erlanger v New Phosphate Co* (1878) 3 App. Cas. 1218; *Lagunas Nitrate Co v Lagunas Syndicate* [1899] 2 Ch. 392; *Re Leeds and Hanley Theatre of Varieties* [1902] 2 Ch. 809; see also below, para.9–054.

[648] *Gluckstein v Barnes* [1900] A.C. 240.

[649] *Erlanger v New Sombrero Phosphate Co* (1878) 3 App. Cas. 1218 (provided of course that restitutio in integrum is still possible).

mistaken opinion as to its accuracy or importance. In *Gordon v Gordon*[650] a division of property, based on the assumption that the eldest son was illegitimate, was set aside after 19 years on proof that the younger son had withheld knowledge of a marriage ceremony that had taken place between his parents before the birth of his brother. Lord Eldon said that "whether the omission of disclosure originated in design, or in honest opinion of the invalidity of the ceremony",[651] the agreement could not stand. On the other hand, in *Wales v Wadham*[652] it was held that a wife was under no duty to disclose to her husband, when they were negotiating for a financial settlement to be embodied in a consent order after divorce, that she intended to remarry. In the particular circumstances of the case, the parties had been negotiating a compromise on the basis that neither party was required to make a full disclosure. However, *Wales v Wadham* was overruled so far as it related to disclosure in proceedings for financial relief by the House of Lords in *Livesey v Jenkins*.[653] This held that the relevant statutory provisions required a court exercising jurisdiction to make financial provision or property adjustment between spouses to be placed in full possession of the facts, so that each side must make full disclosure.[654] These decisions leave it uncertain whether the common law today recognises family settlements as contracts uberrimae fidei.

(d) *Contracts for the sale of land*

Sales of land. Contracts for the sale of land are not uberrimae fidei in the sense that the vendor has to make to the purchaser a full disclosure of all material facts.[655] In the absence of actual misrepresentation[656] the general rule is caveat emptor. But certain qualifications must be made because the vendor is under a duty to disclose defects relating to title. Every material defect in the vendor's title must be disclosed, because if the title is in fact defective the vendor will be unable to perform his contract in the absence of a condition that the purchaser should accept a defective title. In consequence, if any such defect is not disclosed the purchaser may rescind the contract or resist a suit for specific performance. But it has been persuasively argued that there is in addition a duty on the vendor to disclose all latent defects in his title, since if an undisclosed latent defect appears the purchaser may apparently terminate the contract without waiting to see whether the vendor will be able to remove the defect before the date for 6–156

650 (1816–19) 3 Swans. 400; see also *Fane v Fane* (1875) L.R. 20 Eq. 698.

651 (1816–19) 3 Swans. 400, 477.

652 [1977] 1 W.L.R. 199.

653 [1985] A.C. 424. See above, para.6–019, fn.93.

654 Matrimonial Causes Act 1973 s.25, now replaced by Matrimonial and Family Proceedings Act 1984 s.3.

655 It had been intended that vendors (or their estate agents) of larger types of residential property would be required to provide on request a "Home Information Pack" including a "home condition report" prepared by a home inspector: see the Housing Act 2004, Pt 5 and the Home Information Pack Regulations 2006 (SI 2006/1503) reg.8. However, those Regulations were revoked before coming into force by SI 2007/1525 and a home condition report is now optional: see Home Information Pack (No.2) Regulations 2007 (SI 2007/1667) reg.9. See above, para.6–093.

656 See *Dyster v Randall* [1926] Ch. 932.

completion.[657] However, as it appears that all defects must be revealed whether known to the vendor or not, and that if a latent defect is not revealed the purchaser may recover damages for breach of contract, it seems that the duty must be based on an implied term of the contract.[658]

6–157 It seems that any fact which will prevent the purchaser from obtaining such a title as he was led to expect may constitute a defect in title.[659] So where the subject of the sale was a leasehold interest, and the lease contained onerous and unusual covenants which were not disclosed by the vendor, the purchaser was held to be entitled to rescind the contract.[660] It has also been suggested that a tenant who is selling his leasehold interest is bound to disclose receipt of notice from his landlord of an intention to proceed under a rent review clause.[661] A purchaser may, of course, contract to accept a defective title, but even an express agreement to this effect will not (it seems) save the vendor where he fails to disclose defects known to him.[662] A purchaser is not obliged to disclose any information he may have which may affect the value of the property; but it has been held that a purchaser who applies for planning permission in the name of the vendor prior to the exchange of contracts is acting as a self-appointed agent, and may thereby come under fiduciary duties to the vendor.[663]

(e) *Contracts of suretyship*

6–158 **Suretyship or insurance.**[664] It seems that contracts of suretyship are not contracts uberrimae fidei properly so-called, although they are sometimes said to bear certain characteristics of that class. One difficulty is that it may be a matter for doubt whether a given contract is one of suretyship or of insurance. In *Seaton v Heath*[665] Romer L.J. said that many contracts may with equal propriety be called contracts of insurance or contracts of suretyship, and that whether a contract requires uberrima fides or not depends not upon what it is called, but upon its substantial character and how it came to be effected. Commercial sureties, at least, are generally persons who know the risk they undertake without it being explained to them, and who if they do not know it, would make inquiry on the subject; in contracts of insurance, on the other hand, the person desiring to be insured has means of knowledge of the risk which the insurer does not possess, and he puts the risk before the insurer as a business proposition.

---

657 Harpum (1992) 108 L.Q.R. 208, relying on, inter alia, *Carlish v Salt* [1906] 1 Ch. 355 and *Reeve v Berridge* (1888) 20 QBD 423. The existence of such a duty was accepted by at least the majority of the Court of Appeal in *Peyman v Lanjani* [1985] Ch. 457, 482, 496–497.

658 Harpum (1992) 108 L.Q.R. 208, 332–333.

659 But see *Re Flynn and Newman's Contract* [1948] Ir.R. 104.

660 *Molyneux v Hawtrey* [1903] 2 K.B. 487.

661 *F. & H. Entertainments Ltd v Leisure Enterprises Ltd* (1976) 120 S.J. 331.

662 *Becker v Partridge* [1966] 2 Q.B. 155.

663 *English v Dedham Vale Properties Ltd* [1978] 1 W.L.R. 93; *Rignall Developments Ltd v Halil* [1988] Ch. 190.

664 See Vol.II, Ch.44.

665 [1899] 1 Q.B. 782, 792–793.

The position seems to be that while a contract of insurance requires a full disclosure of all material facts, a contract of suretyship does not.[666] Thus it has been held that a bank was under no duty to disclose to the guarantor of a customer's overdrawn account suspicions that the customer was defrauding him.[667] On the other hand, it seems that there is a limited duty of disclosure even in contracts of suretyship, though the nature and scope of this limited duty are hard to define. In *Levett v Barclays Bank Plc*[668] it was held that there is a duty to disclose to the surety any unusual feature of the contract between the principal debtor and the creditor which makes it materially different in a potentially disadvantageous respect from what the surety might naturally expect. In *Crédit Lyonnais Bank Nederland v Export Credit Guarantee Department*[669] it was held that any duty to disclose unusual features only applied to unusual features of the transaction itself, not to unusual features of the risk; and it did not extend to matters of which the bank had no knowledge, even if what it knew might have led it to make further enquiries. However, where a person guaranteed the honesty of a servant to an employer, who knew but did not disclose the fact that the servant had previously been dishonest while in his employment, the bond was held to be unenforceable when the servant subsequently committed a further act of dishonesty.[670] 6–159

Sureties given to banks on a non-commercial basis. It should be noted that the law which was developed to protect "surety wives" (principally wives who guarantee the debts of their husband's business), and which now apply to any guarantee to a bank given on a non-commercial basis[671] may have the practical effect of requiring the bank to disclose information to the surety. These rules are discussed in Ch.7.[672] 6–160

Binding authority to issue insurance. It has been suggested that an obligation to point out unusual facts, similar to that which appears to apply to suretyship,[673] may apply to a binding authority to issue insurance, so that unusual features of the coverholder to whom the authority is to be given should be pointed out.[674] 6–161

(f) *Partnership agreements*

Partnership. The fundamental duty of every partner is to show the utmost good faith in his dealings with the other partners. In *Conlon v Simms*, the Court of Appeal held that in negotiating a partnership agreement: 6–162

---

[666] *North British Insurance Co v Lloyd* (1854) 10 Ex. 523; *Lee v Jones* (1864) 17 C.B.(N.S.) 482; *Geest Plc v Fyffes Plc* [1999] 1 All E.R. (Comm) 672; below, paras 44–032 et seq.

[667] *National Provincial Bank v Glanusk* [1913] 3 K.B. 335; see also *Royal Bank of Scotland v Greenshields* (1914) S.C. 259; *Cooper v National Provincial Bank* [1946] K.B. 1.

[668] [1995] 1 W.L.R. 1260.

[669] [1996] 1 Lloyd's Rep. 200.

[670] *London General Omnibus Co v Holloway* [1912] 2 K.B. 72; see also *Phillips v Foxall* (1872) L.R. 7 Q.B. 666. For further discussion of these points see Vol.II, para.44–034.

[671] See below, para.7–111.

[672] See below, paras 7–059—7–096.

[673] See para.6–159.

[674] *Pryke v Gibbs Hartley Cooper Ltd* [1991] 1 Lloyd's Rep. 602, 616.

> "... a party owes a duty to the other negotiating parties to disclose all material facts of which he has knowledge and of which the other negotiating parties may not be aware".[675]

The duty of good faith applies during the continuance of the partnership, and during the winding up after dissolution. The duties of partners are regulated for the most part, in the absence of agreement to the contrary, by the Partnership Act 1890; and although the principle requiring the utmost good faith is not expressly enunciated by the Act, it is embodied in ss.28, 29 and 30. Thus a partner must account for any private profit made by him; so for instance, if a partner is buying from or selling to the firm, he cannot do either at a profit to himself.[676]

6–163 **Analogous agreements.** A duty of disclosure may arise as an implied term of an agreement which is not a partnership but which has "elements of joint enterprise or joint venture", but:

> "... wider duties will not lightly be implied, in particular in commercial contracts negotiated at arms' length between parties with comparable bargaining power, and all the more so where the contract in question sets out in detail the extent, for example, of a party's disclosure obligations".[677]

(g) *General releases*

6–164 **General releases.** In *Bank of Credit and Commerce International SA (In Liquidation) v Ali (No.1)*[678] Lord Nicholls said that where the party to whom a general release was given knew that the other party has or might have a claim and knew that the other party was ignorant of this, to take the release without disclosing the existence of the claim or possible claim could be unacceptable sharp practice. The law would be defective if it did not provide a remedy, and while the case did not raise the issue, he had no doubt that the law would provide a remedy.[679] Lord Hoffmann agreed:

> "There are different ways in which it can be put. One may say, for example, that inviting a person to enter into a release in general terms implies a representation that one is not aware of any specific claims which the other party may not know about. That would preserve the purity of the principle that there is no positive duty of disclosure. Or one could say, as the old Chancery judges did, that reliance upon such a release is against conscience when the beneficiary has been guilty of a suppressio veri or suggestio falsi.

---

[675] [2006] EWCA Civ 1749 at [127], relying on a dictum of Lord Atkin in *Bell v Lever Bros* [1932] A.C. 161 at 227 HL.

[676] *Bentley v Craven* (1853) 18 Beav. 75; *Dunne v English* (1874) L.R. 18 Eq. 524.

[677] *Ross River Ltd v Cambridge City Football Club Ltd* [2007] EWHC 2115 (Ch), [2008] 1 All E.R. 1004 at [197] (Briggs J.).

[678] [2001] UKHL 8, [2002] 1 A.C. 251, in which the House of Lords held that a general release was not effective to release a claim for "stigma" damages that neither party could have known about (see above, para.3–048).

[679] [2001] UKHL 8 at [32]–[33]. Lord Bingham preferred not to address this question (at [20]), and so it seems did Lord Clyde (at [87]).

> . . . a person cannot be allowed to rely upon a release in general terms if he knew that the other party had a claim and knew that the other party was not aware that he had a claim. I do not propose any wider principle: there is obviously room in the dealings of the market for legitimately taking advantage of the known ignorance of the other party. But, both on principle and authority, I think that a release of rights is a situation in which the court should not allow a party to do so. On the other hand, if the context shows that the parties intended a general release for good consideration of rights unknown to both of them, I can see nothing unfair in such a transaction."[680]

Whatever the basis on which this is to be explained, it would amount to creating a duty on a party negotiating for a general release to disclose a claim that he knows the other has or may have and which he knows the other is not aware of.

---

[680] [2001] UKHL 8 at [69]–[70].

Chapter 7

DURESS AND UNDUE INFLUENCE[1]

	PARA.
1. Introduction	7–001
2. Duress	7–003
(a) Introduction	7–003
(b) Nature of duress	7–004
(c) Types of illegitimate pressure	7–010
(i) Duress of the person	7–011
(ii) Duress of goods	7–012
(iii) Economic duress	7–014
(d) Causation	7–024
(e) Legitimacy of the demand	7–037
(f) Threats of actions not in themselves wrongful	7–045
(g) Parties to duress	7–051
(h) General effect of duress	7–053
3. Undue influence	7–056
(a) Introduction	7–056
(b) "Actual" undue influence	7–064
(c) Presumed undue influence	7–069
(i) Relationships giving rise to presumption of influence	7–071
(ii) Confidential relationship shown on facts in earlier decisions	7–079
(iii) A transaction not explicable by ordinary motives	7–086
(d) Rebutting the presumption	7–093
(e) Remedies for undue influence	7–097
(f) Undue influence by a third party	7–104
4. Unconscionable bargains and inequality of bargaining power	7–126

1. Introduction

Scope of chapter. This chapter deals with three further grounds on which a contract may be avoided: duress, undue influence and unconscionable dealing. In outline, a party may be able to avoid a contract for duress where he or she entered it because of a wrongful or illegitimate threat by the other party, normally because the threat left him or her with no practical alternative.[2] A contract may be voidable for undue influence where one party was subjected to pressure by the other or, more usually, where the other took advantage of the first party's trust and confidence.[3] Unconscionable dealing occurs where one party deliberately exploits the other's ignorance or weak position to obtain the other's agreement to 7–001

[1] See Cartwright, *Unequal Bargaining* (1991), Part III; N. Enonchong, *Duress, Undue Influence and Unconscionable Dealing* (2006).

[2] See below, paras 7–003—7–055.

[3] See below, paras 7–056—7–103.

a contract which is substantively unfair.[4] We will see that there may be some overlap between the three grounds. In particular, some cases that were decided on the basis of undue influence are now better regarded as examples of the more recently-developed "economic" duress,[5] while other cases may involve both undue influence and unconscionable dealing.[6]

7–002 **Unfair Commercial Practices.** The Unfair Commercial Practices Directive[7] requires Member States to prohibit, and to provide "adequate and effective" means to combat unfair commercial practices. These are defined so as to include conduct that falls within the scope of this chapter, such as "aggressive commercial practices"[8] and "harassment, coercion and undue influence".[9] However unfair commercial practices within the meaning of the Directive will not give rise to civil remedies for individual consumers, as the Directive is "without prejudice to contract law and, in particular, to the rules of validity, formation or effect of a contract".[10] Accordingly the Regulations passed to implement the Directive prohibit unfair commercial practices, but provide that an agreement shall not be void or unenforceable by reason only of a breach of the Regulations.[11]

2. DURESS[12]

(a) *Introduction*

7–003 **Introductory.** A contract which has been entered as the result of duress may be avoided by the party who was threatened. It has long been recognised that a threat to the victim's person may amount to duress[13]; it is now established that the same is true of wrongful threats to his property, including threats to seize his goods,[14] and of wrongful or illegitimate threats to his economic interests,[15] at least where the victim has no practical alternative but to submit.[16] In each case, the wrongful or illegitimate threat must have had some causal effect on his decision to enter the contract, but the causal requirements may differ between the various kinds of duress.[17]

---

[4] See below, paras 7–126—7–139.

[5] See below, para.7–048.

[6] See below, para.7–128.

[7] Directive 2005/28 on unfair commercial practices [2005] OJ L149/22. A useful summary of the Directive and its likely impact will be found in Twigg-Flesner (2005) 121 L.Q.R. 386.

[8] Directive 2005/29 art.8.

[9] Directive 2005/29 art.9.

[10] Directive 2005/29 art.3(1).

[11] Consumer Protection from Unfair Trading Regulations 2008 (SI 2008/1277) reg. 29; Business Protection from Misleading Marketing Regulations 2008 (SI 2008/1276) reg.29.

[12] Burrows, *Law of Restitution*, 2nd edn (2002), Ch.5; Goff and Jones, *Law of Restitution*, 7th edn (2007), Ch.10; Virgo, *Principles of the Law of Restitution*, 2nd edn (2006), pp.192–218.

[13] Below, para.7–011.

[14] Below, paras 7–012—7–013.

[15] Below, paras 7–014 et seq.

[16] Below, para.7–031.

[17] Below, paras 7–024—7–036.

(b) *Nature of Duress*

Basis of law relating to duress. It was at one time common to treat the legal rules relating to duress (and frequently also the equitable rules relating to undue influence) as resting on the absence of consent. A party who was subject to duress, or even undue influence, was often said to have had his will "overborne" so that he was incapable of making a free choice, or even of acting voluntarily. Most of the older cases cited in this chapter rest on this assumption; and even many modern decisions use the same kind of language.[18] But the basis of the law relating to these topics has been reconsidered in light of the speeches in the House of Lords in *Lynch v D.P.P. of Northern Ireland*.[19] This case was concerned with the defence of duress in the criminal law, and there are no doubt important differences between the civil and the criminal law on what can constitute duress; but the case contains by far the most extensive analysis of the juridical nature of duress in the law reports, and on this question, there appears to be no difference between the criminal and the civil law. Indeed, two of their Lordships in this case specifically relied upon the analogy of the law of contract.[20] All five members of the House of Lords in *Lynch*'s case rejected the notion that duress deprives a person of his free choice, or makes his acts non-voluntary.[21] Duress does not "overbear" the will, nor destroy it; it "deflects" it.[22] Duress does not literally deprive the person affected of all choice; it leaves him with a choice between evils.[23] A person acting under duress intends to do what he does; but does so unwillingly.[24] Lord Wilberforce specifically stated that: 7–004

> ". . . duress does not destroy the will, for example, to enter into a contract, but prevents the law from accepting what has happened as a contract valid in law."[25]

Similarly, Lord Simon of Glaisdale said that in the law of contract:

> "Duress again deflects without destroying, the will of one of the contracting parties. There is still an intention on his part to contract in the apparently consensual terms; but there is *coactus volui* on his side. The contrast is with *non est factum*. The contract procured by duress is therefore not void: it is voidable—at the discretion of the party subject to duress."[26]

---

[18] Even in *Barton v Armstrong* [1976] A.C. 104, 121, the dissenting speech of Lord Wilberforce and Lord Simon refers to the defence of duress as resting on the absence of true consent; and in several other modern cases courts have continued to use the same kind of language, see Atiyah (1982) 98 L.Q.R. 197.

[19] [1975] A.C. 653.

[20] The same analysis of the nature of duress is almost universally adhered to in America. For an early example, see Holmes J. in *Union Pacific Ry Co v Public Service Commission of Missouri* (1918) 248 U.S. 67, 70.

[21] *Lynch v D.P.P. of Northern Ireland* [1975] A.C. 653: Lord Morris of Borth-y-Gest at 670, 675; Lord Wilberforce at 680; Lord Simon of Glaisdale at 690–691, 695; Lord Kilbrandon at 703; and Lord Edmund-Davies at 709–711.

[22] Lord Simon, [1975] A.C. 653, 695.

[23] [1975] A.C. 653, 690–691.

[24] [1975] A.C. 653, 670, Lord Morris.

[25] [1975] A.C. 653, 680.

[26] [1975] A.C. 653, 695.

7–005 Notwithstanding these clear declarations of principle, in several important decisions relating to economic duress which post-date the *Lynch* decision the judges spoke of duress as negativing true consent and rendering the coerced party's actions non-voluntary.[27] For example, in *Pao On v Lau Yiu Long*[28] it was accepted by the Privy Council that economic duress might be recognised in principle by the law, but it was insisted that:

> "... the basis of such recognition is that it must amount to a coercion of will, which vitiates consent. It must be shown that the payment made or the contract entered into was not a voluntary act."[29]

However, in *Universe Tankships of Monrovia v I.T.W.F.*, Lord Diplock said that the rationale was that the party's consent was induced by pressure which the law does not regard as legitimate with the consequence that the consent is treated in law as revocable.[30] Similarly Lord Scarman, though dissenting in the result, agreed that the real issue is whether there has been illegitimate pressure, the practical effect of which is compulsion or absence of choice:

> "The classic case of duress is, however, not the lack of will to submit but the victim's intentional submission arising from the realisation that there is no practical choice open to him."[31]

Subsequent decisions have for the most part applied the test of whether the victim had a practical choice.[32]

7–006 **Importance of basis of duress.** No doubt in many circumstances the precise basis of duress will be immaterial; but in other circumstances it will be a matter of the greatest importance. For, so long as the doctrine of duress is treated as resting on an absence of consent, or of a voluntary act, it would seem immaterial what has caused the absence of consent, or the act to be involuntary. Duress would be a question of fact, and not of law. Further, absence of consent would logically render a contract void and not voidable. It is clear from *Lynch*'s case that all these propositions are inconsistent with the analysis of the nature of duress in the speeches in the House of Lords. Because duress does not destroy the will or the consent of the putative contracting parties, it is not possible to treat the issue as one of pure fact, nor is it immaterial what caused the will to be deflected, or the consent to be distorted. So, also, because duress does not truly deprive a

[27] See *Occidental Worldwide Investment Corp v Skibs A/S Avanti* [1976] 1 Lloyd's Rep. 293; *North Ocean Shipping Co Ltd v Hyundai Construction Co Ltd* [1979] Q.B. 705; *Pao On v Lau Yiu Long* [1980] A.C. 614; *Universe Tankships of Monrovia Inc v I.T.W.F.* [1983] 1 A.C. 366; see also *Syros Shipping Co v Elaghill Trading Co* [1981] 3 All E.R. 189.

[28] Above, and see below, para.7–016.

[29] *Pao On v Lau Yiu Long* [1980] A.C. 614, 636.

[30] [1983] 1 A.C. 366, 384.

[31] [1983] 1 A.C. 366, 400.

[32] e.g. *B. & S. Contracts & Design Ltd v Victor Green Publications Ltd* [1984] I.C.R. 419; *Vantage Navigation Corp v Suhail and Saud Bahwan Building Materials, The Alev* [1989] 1 Lloyd's Rep. 138. See Beatson, *The Use and Abuse of Unjust Enrichment* (1991), pp.109–117; and the remarks of Lord Goff in *Dimskal Shipping Co SA v ITWF* [1992] 2 A.C. 152, 166, agreeing with McHugh J.A. in *Crescendo Management Pty Ltd v Westpac Banking Corp* (1988) 19 N.S.W.L.R. 40, 45–46, that the "overbearing of the will" test is unhelpful.

party of all choice, but only presents him with a choice between evils, it is not possible to inquire simply whether the party relying on duress had "no choice"; the inquiry must necessarily be as to the nature of the choices he was presented with, and in what respect the choices differed from those ordinarily available in the market—where a person also has to choose, between paying the market price and going without. The question whether the doctrine rests on the absence of consent or on the use of illegitimate pressure may also affect questions of causation: on the latter approach, it may not be necessary to show that the threat was an overwhelming cause of the victim entering the contract.[33]

Analogy with fraud and mistake. Both in *Lynch*'s case and in *Barton v Armstrong*[34] the analogy with fraud and mistake has been relied upon by the courts. Thus (as shown by the quotation from Lord Simon's speech in *Lynch*'s case, above, para.7–004) duress renders a contract voidable rather than void; and in this respect it operates like fraud, and not like non est factum.[35] No doubt there will be extreme cases of duress, as there are extreme cases of fraud or mistake, in which non est factum is available as a plea and in which there is a total absence of consent; the gunman who actually helps himself to his victim's wallet is stealing it against his victim's consent, and in no sense obtaining it by means of a coerced contract. But (artificial though the distinction may seem in such a case) the gunman who *demands and is given* the wallet by the victim, is obtaining it by duress. As we will see, the analogy with fraud was also used in *Barton v Armstrong* to justify the view that, at least in a case of duress to the person, a contract entered into under duress may be avoided provided that the duress had some effect on the mind of the party threatened, even if he might have entered the contract anyway for other reasons. However, the contract will stand if it can be shown that the threat had no effect on his mind at all.[36] 7–007

Legitimacy of the pressure or threat. Once it is accepted that the basis of duress does not depend upon the absence of consent, but on the combination of pressure and absence of practical choice,[37] it follows that two questions become all-important.[38] The first is whether the pressure or the threat is legitimate; the second, its effect on the victim.[39] Clearly, not all pressure is illegitimate, nor even are all threats illegitimate. In ordinary commercial activity, pressure and even threats are both commonplace and often perfectly proper. Indeed, in one sense, all contracts are made under pressure: every offeror "threatens" that unless the offeree accepts the terms offered, he will not get the benefit of whatever goods or services are on offer. We shall see that the causal link between the pressure or 7–008

[33] See below, paras 7–024—7–036.

[34] [1976] A.C. 104.

[35] As to the defence non est factum, see above, paras 5–101—5–106. In *Barton v Armstrong* [1976] A.C. 104 Lord Cross, speaking for the majority, referred to the deeds as void (at 120), but he had previously referred to "setting aside a disposition for duress" (at 118). The dissenting minority seemed to consider that duress renders a contract voidable.

[36] Below, para.7–025. There may, of course, be some issues on which the analogy with fraud would be inappropriate and inapplicable, e.g. duress is not necessarily tortious: below, para.7–055.

[37] See further below, para.7–031.

[38] See *Universe Tankships of Monrovia Inc v I.T.W.F.* [1983] 1 A.C. 366, 384, 391, 400.

[39] See the next paragraph.

threat and the victim's action is also important,[40] but it cannot be said that the force or weight of the pressure or the threats is the decisive factor:

> "... for in life, including the life of commerce and finance, many acts are done under pressure, sometimes overwhelming pressure, so that one can say that the actor had no choice but to act."[41]

It therefore becomes essential to distinguish between legitimate and illegitimate forms of pressure. We shall see that whereas threats to the person and threats to commit a crime or tort are always treated as illegitimate, it is possible that in some circumstances a threat to break a contract if a demand is not met may not be regarded as illegitimate, depending on the nature of the demand.[42] Conversely, a threat to carry out an action which in itself is lawful but which is coupled with an illegitimate demand may constitute duress.[43]

7–009 **The effect of the threat.** For a contract made after there has been a wrongful or illegitimate threat, the threat must have had some causal effect on the victim's decision to enter the contract. However, the causal requirements differ between the various kinds of duress.[44] It is possible that in cases of "economic duress" there is a separate requirement that the victim had no reasonable alternative to agreeing to the contract, although an alternative interpretation is that the absence of a reasonable alternative is merely evidence that the threat had the necessary causal effect.[45]

(c) *Types of Illegitimate Pressure*

7–010 **Types of illegitimate pressure.** Violence to the person, and threats of such violence, have long been recognised as illegitimate forms of pressure. The law therefore allows a party to avoid any promise extorted from him by terror or violence, whether on the part of the person to whom the promise is made or that of his agent.[46] Contracts made under such circumstances are said to be made under duress,[47] a term derived from the common law, which took a narrow view as to the facts which would establish (as was then thought) the absence of free consent. At common law, duress consisted of actual or threatened violence or imprisonment.[48] Courts of equity, however, administered the wider doctrine of undue influence[49] which was applied chiefly to cases where some fiduciary

---

[40] See below, paras 7–024—7–036.

[41] *Barton v Armstrong* [1976] A.C. 104, 121, per Lord Wilberforce and Lord Simon dissenting, but not on this point.

[42] See below, paras 7–037—7–044.

[43] See below, paras 7–045—7–050.

[44] Below, paras 7–024—7–036.

[45] See below, para.7–036.

[46] For the parallel doctrine in cases concerning marriage, see *Scott v Sebright* (1886) 12 P.D. 21; *Griffith v Griffith* [1944] I.R. 35; *H. v H.* [1954] P. 258; *Szechter v Szechter* [1971] P. 286; *Singh v Singh* [1971] P. 226; Davies (1972) 88 L.Q.R. 549; Matrimonial Causes Act 1973 s.12. See also *Re Roberts (deceased)* [1978] 1 W.L.R. 653; *Hirani v Hirani* (1983) 4 F.L.R. 232.

[47] See generally, Beatson [1974] C.L.J. 97.

[48] 1 Roll.Abr. 687; Coke 2 Inst. 482.

[49] See below, paras 7–056 et seq.

relation existed between the parties, but was not in any way limited to them. Equity might therefore grant relief where the compulsion complained of was something less than that required by the common law. Since the Judicature Act 1873 it has been the duty of all courts to administer both doctrines concurrently and cases of coercion must be dealt with in the light of their combined effect. In recent years the courts have recognised that other forms of duress may be grounds for avoiding a contract: firstly, where there was a wrongful threat to seize the claimant's goods and secondly, where there was "economic duress". The latter blurs the traditional distinction between duress and undue influence.[50] In particular, there are cases in which equity will give relief against an agreement entered as the result of an improper threat to bring a prosecution against a member of the claimant's family. Traditionally, relief was given on the ground of actual undue influence, but it is strongly arguable that they are now to be regarded as falling within the doctrine of duress and they are so treated in this chapter.[51]

(i) *Duress of the Person*

Form of duress. Duress of the person may consist in violence to the person, or threats of violence, or in imprisonment whether actual or threatened.[52] The threat of violence need not be directed at the claimant[53]: a threat of violence against the claimant's spouse or near relation suffices[54] and a threat against the claimant's employees has been held to constitute duress.[55] It is suggested that a threat against even a stranger should be enough if the claimant genuinely believed that submission was the only way to prevent the stranger from being injured or worse.[56] 7–011

(ii) *Duress of Goods*

Duress of goods. It has been said that a threat to destroy or damage property may amount to duress.[57] It is now accepted that the same is true of a threat to seize or detain goods wrongfully, though for many years it was thought that such a threat could not amount to duress at common law. It used to be said that the distinction between duress of the person and duress of goods was that: 7–012

[50] See below, para.7–048.
[51] See below, para.7–048.
[52] For modern examples, see *Friedeberg-Seeley v Klass* (1957) 101 S.J. 275; *Barton v Armstrong* [1976] A.C. 104. But compare *R. v HM Att-Gen for England and Wales* [2003] UKPC 22 (threat to return member of armed forces to his unit lawful).
[53] See further below, para.7–051.
[54] *Kaufman v Gerson* [1904] 1 K.B. 591; cf. *Williams v Bayley* (1866) L.R. 1 H.L. 200 (threat to prosecute relation). See Goff & Jones, *Law of Restitution*, 7th edn (2007), para.10–004.
[55] *Royal Boskalis Westminster NV v Mountain* [1999] Q.B. 674 (threat to use employees as human shield); *Gulf Azov Shipping Co Ltd v Chief Idisi (No.2)* [2001] EWCA Civ 505, [2001] 1 Lloyd's Rep. 727 (detention of ship and crew).
[56] See further below, para.7–051.
[57] *Occidental Worldwide Investment Corp v Skibs A/S Avanti* [1976] 1 Lloyd's Rep. 293, 335.

> " . . . the former is a constraining force, which not only takes away the free agency, but may leave no room for appeal to the law for a remedy . . .; but the fear that goods may be taken or injured does not deprive anyone of his free agency who possesses that ordinary degree of firmness which the law requires all to exert."[58]

There is no evidence of any wider equitable rule concerning duress of goods, although it has for many years been well established that money paid in order to get possession of goods wrongfully detained, or to avoid their wrongful detention, may be recovered in an action for money had and received.[59] So in *Maskell v Horner*[60] tolls were levied on the plaintiff under a threat of seizure of goods. The tolls were in fact unlawfully demanded. Their payment was held to be recoverable as it had been made to avoid seizure of the goods and the plaintiff was entitled to recover the payments he had made under the illegal demand. Lord Reading C.J. said:

> "If a person pays money, which he is not bound to pay, under the compulsion of urgent and pressing necessity or of seizure, actual or threatened, of his goods, he can recover it as money had and received."[61]

It is nevertheless somewhat difficult to reconcile this rule with the traditional rule that duress of goods would not avoid a contract. A possible solution may be that money paid in this way can only be recovered if it has been paid under protest, without any binding agreement[62]; otherwise the absurd result must ensue that, although an agreement to pay money under duress of goods can be enforced, any money so paid will be recoverable by the person paying it as money had and received to his use. But there are cases inconsistent with the notion that duress can only be relied upon by someone who acted under protest[63]; and an alternative view is receiving increasing support. This is that the older cases denying relief are best explained as cases in which the claim was voluntarily compromised by the plaintiff.[64] The rule that duress of goods does not invalidate a contract only applies where the duress is in purported execution of legal process, such as distress or execution, brought in good faith.[65] Where this is the case, an agreement made to secure the release of the goods is a form of submission to legal process, and seizure of goods under legal process brought in good faith can scarcely be regarded as an illegitimate form of pressure.

---

[58] *Skeate v Beale* (1840) 11 A. & E. 983, 990; *The Unitas* [1948] P. 205, affirmed sub nom. *Lever Bros & Unilever N.V. v H.M. Procurator General* [1950] A.C. 536.

[59] *Astley v Reynolds* (1731) 2 Str. 915; *Atlee v Backhouse* (1838) 3 M. & W. 633; *Wakefield v Newbon* (1844) 6 Q.B. 276; *Oates v Hudson* (1851) 6 Exch. 346. Money paid to recover goods in the custody of the law is not paid under duress and cannot be recovered: *Liverpool Marine Credit Co v Hunter* (1868) L.R. 3 Ch. App. 479. See generally below, paras 29–090 et seq.

[60] [1915] 3 K.B. 106; below, para.29–090.

[61] [1915] 3 K.B. 106, 118.

[62] *Atlee v Backhouse* (1838) 3 M.& W. 633, 650; *Parker v Bristol & Exeter Ry* (1851) 6 Exch. 702, 705.

[63] See, e.g. *Spanish Government v North of England S.S. Ltd* (1938) 54 T.L.R. 852; *T.A. Sundell & Sons Pty Ltd v Emm Yannoulatos (Overseas) Pty Ltd* (1956) 56 S.R. (N.S.W.) 323; *Universe Tankships of Monrovia Inc v I.T.W.F.* [1983] 1 A.C. 366, 400.

[64] See Beatson, *The Use and Abuse of Unjust Enrichment* (1991), pp.105–106; *North Ocean Shipping* [1979] Q.B. 705, 719. On voluntary settlements see further below, para.7–028.

[65] See below, para.7–050; Goff & Jones, *Law of Restitution*, 7th edn (2007), para.10–005.

Recognition of duress of goods. This argument thus opened the door to a broad concept of duress of goods as a ground of relief in contract law, and the courts have now endorsed duress of goods.[66] As we shall see, they have also embraced a broader concept of "economic duress". At least one case that involved duress of goods was decided on this broader ground.[67] 7–013

(iii) *Economic Duress*

Recognition of economic duress. Three English cases, and one important Privy Council appeal, first recognised the possibility of the concept of economic duress. In substance this amounts to recognising that certain threats or forms of pressure, not associated with threats to the person, nor limited to the seizure or withholding of goods, may give grounds for relief to a party who enters into a contract as a result of the threats or the pressure. In *Occidental Worldwide Investment Corp v Skibs A/S Avanti*,[68] the charterers of two ships secured a renegotiation of the rate of hire, after a slump in market rates, by threatening the owners that they (the charterers) had no substantial assets, and that they would go bankrupt if the rates were not lowered. This threat was strongly coercive because, given the slump in the market, the owners would have had to lay up the tankers if the charterers had returned them, and would then have been unable to pay mortgage charges on the ships—all these facts being well known to the charterers. In fact the charterers' allegations, or threats, that they had no substantial assets and would go bankrupt if the rate of hire were not lowered, were false and fraudulent, and Kerr J. held that the owners were therefore entitled to avoid the renegotiated terms, and withdraw the ships, on the ground of fraud; but he recognised that the economic pressure of the threats might also have given rise to relief on the ground of duress, at least in principle. In the event, however, he denied relief on this ground because the owners' consent or will was not vitiated by the pressures, which were only normal commercial pressures. In light of the discussion of *Lynch*'s case, above, para.7–004, this ground of decision seems dubious; the question which the learned judge ought to have asked himself was not whether the owners' consent was negatived by the pressure, but whether the pressure was permissible pressure to exert.[69] Given his finding that the pressure was based on fraud, it would seem that duress should have been a further ground for relief, although in the circumstances it would have been immaterial, given that relief was available for fraud anyhow. 7–014

In *North Ocean Shipping Co Ltd v Hyundai Construction Co Ltd*[70] shipbuilders who were building a ship under a contract for the plaintiffs, threatened, 7–015

---

[66] *Occidental Worldwide Investment Corp v Skibs A/S Avanti* [1976] 1 Lloyd's Rep. 293; *North Ocean Shipping Co Ltd v Hyundai Construction Co Ltd* [1979] Q.B. 705; *Dimskal Shipping Co Ltd v I.T.W.F.* [1992] 2 A.C. 152, 165 (limitation to duress of the person now discarded). See further Goff & Jones, *Law of Restitution*, 7th edn (2007), paras 10–011—10–015.

[67] *The Alev* [1989] 1 Lloyd's Rep. 138; see Burrows, *Law of Restitution*, 2nd edn (2002), p.222.

[68] [1976] 1 Lloyd's Rep. 293, noted (1976) 92 L.Q.R. 496.

[69] It might, however, be said that his finding that consent was not negatived was tantamount to finding that the pressure was not of sufficient *weight* to constitute duress, see below, para.7–030.

[70] [1979] Q.B. 705.

without any legal justification, to terminate the contract unless the plaintiffs agreed (within a few days) to increase the price by 10 per cent. The owners had chartered the vessel to Shell at very favourable rates and feared that they would lose the charter if the vessel were delivered late, so they reluctantly acquiesced in this demand, but under protest, and without prejudice to their rights. Mocatta J. held[71] that this amounted to a case of economic duress, and that the plaintiffs would have been entitled, on that ground, to have refused payment of the additional 10 per cent. But he went on to hold that the owners had, by implication, affirmed the contract, or waived their right to avoid it for duress, even though they had not intended to do so; the basis for this part of his decision was that the owners had failed to raise the matter at any further stage, paying the extra instalments, and taking delivery of the ship in due course, and so giving the builders grounds for belief that the owners had affirmed the variation in price.

7–016 The Privy Council case is *Pao On v Lau Yiu Long*[72] in which again the allegation was made that a party had secured an amendment to a prior commercial transaction of some complexity, as a result of a threat to break his contract. Here also the Privy Council conceded that economic duress could be recognised in principle, but held that the plea was not made out on the facts. The speech of Lord Scarman emphasised that the defendant in this case had carefully considered his position when faced with the threatened breach of contract, and had concluded that it was in his interests to grant the concession demanded rather than to sue on the original contract. In determining the validity of the plea of duress in such circumstances, Lord Scarman said that:

> "... it is material to inquire whether the person alleged to have been coerced did or did not protest; whether, at the time he was allegedly coerced into making the contract, he did or did not have an alternative course open to him such as an adequate legal remedy; whether he was independently advised; and whether after entering the contract he took steps to avoid it."[73]

Lord Scarman did, however, draw attention to American case law which stressed the effectiveness of alternative remedies available to the party allegedly coerced; and it seems clear that it would no longer be regarded as an adequate answer to a plea of duress that the party coerced had a legal remedy which he could in due course have pursued in the courts. The all-important question in practice is whether, having regard to all the circumstances, that remedy is a practical and effective one. If it would have been, the complainant may have difficulty in persuading the court to grant relief.[74] If it would not, a case of duress may be made out.

---

[71] Relying, inter alia, on *Parker v G.W.R.* (1844) 7 M. & G. 253; *G.W.R. v Sutton* (1869) L.R. 4 H.L. 226; *Close v Phipps* (1844) 7 M. & G. 586; *Fernley v Branson* (1851) 20 L.J.Q.B. 178; *Nixon v Furphy* (1925) 25 S.R. (N.S.W.) 151; *Smith v William Charlick* (1924) 34 C.L.R. 38, 56; and *D & C Builders Ltd v Rees* [1966] 2 Q.B. 617, as to which see below, para.7–019.

[72] [1980] A.C. 614.

[73] [1980] A.C. 614, 635.

[74] See below, para.7–031, where the question whether absence of a reasonable alternative is a separate requirement is discussed.

The fourth case is *Universe Tankships of Monrovia v International Transport Workers Federation*[75] in which the defendant trade union had "blacked" the plaintiffs' ship in port, and refused to release her except on payment of a large sum of money; most of the money was claimed as back pay on behalf of seamen on the ship, but a part of it was a payment for the union's welfare fund. The Court of Appeal, affirming Parker J., held that the union's actions constituted duress which would prima facie have justified the shipowners in recovering the money, because the coercive nature of the threat was so powerful, and at common law involved unlawful pressure on various third parties to break their contracts. But the Court of Appeal went on to hold that the union's conduct was protected by the statutory immunities in the Trade Union and Labour Relations Act 1974, because it was in the course of, or in furtherance of, a trade dispute under that Act. The "trade dispute" defence was disallowed in the House of Lords where the finding of economic duress was not challenged. The decision involves rejection of the defendants' argument that a plea of duress requires the party guilty of the duress to appreciate that the other party is acting under duress. In effect, this was an attempt to revive, in a slightly different form, the argument that payments made under duress are only recoverable if they are paid under protest; as already seen (above, para.7–012) this view has been rejected in a number of previous cases. 7–017

The doctrine of economic duress is therefore now clearly established and its existence was accepted by the House of Lords in *Dimskal Shipping Co Ltd v I.T.W.F.*[76] It has been applied in a number of other cases.[77] For example, in *B. & S. Contracts & Design Ltd v Victor Green Publications Ltd*[78] the plaintiffs had contracted to erect an exhibition stand for the defendants at Olympia, but their workmen went on strike. To get the work done the defendants agreed to contribute £4,500 to pay off the workmen's claims. It was held by the Court of Appeal that this promise was made under duress as the defendants had no realistic alternative[79] but to promise to pay, given the serious threat to their economic interests. 7–018

Relationship between doctrine of consideration and economic duress. In the first three cases cited in paras 7–014—7–016, the parties were already in a contractual relationship; in these circumstances, a variation of the contract 7–019

---

[75] [1981] I.C.R. 129, reversed [1983] A.C. 366.

[76] [1992] 2 A.C. 152, 159, 160, 162, 165, 170.

[77] *B. & S. Contracts & Design Ltd v Victor Green Publications Ltd* [1984] I.C.R. 419; *Atlas Express Ltd v Kafco (Importers and Distributors) Ltd* [1989] Q.B. 833 (carrier refused to perform without extra payment after miscalculating number of cartons it could carry per load); *The Alev* [1989] 1 Lloyd's Rep. 138 (owner demanded "financial assistance" from consignee before it would deliver goods under freight pre-paid bills when charterer had failed to pay hire); *Carillion Construction Ltd v Felix (UK) Ltd* [2001] B.L.R. 1 (sub-contractor threatened to withhold performance if main contractor did not settle contested account); *Cantor Index Ltd v Shortall* [2002] All E.R. (D) (Nov) (payment made under threat to close customer's bets.) See also *Alec Lobb Ltd v Total Oil G.B. Ltd* [1983] 1 W.L.R. 87 (varied on other points, [1985] 1 W.L.R. 173); *Dimskal Shipping Co Ltd v I.T.W.F.* [1992] 2 A.C. 152; *CTN Cash and Carry Ltd v Gallaher Ltd* [1994] 4 All E.R. 714 (below, para.7–046); *Finance Ltd v Bank of New Zealand* (1993) 32 N.S.W.L.R. 50 (CA, N.S.W.).

[78] [1984] I.C.R. 419.

[79] On the question of absence of choice see below, para.7–031.

secured by one party as a result of threats to break the contract might until recently have been viewed as invalid on the ground of lack of consideration, irrespective of any issue of economic duress. Thus, in *D & C Builders Ltd v Rees*[80] the defendants, who owed the plaintiffs some £482, refused to pay anything unless the plaintiffs would accept £300 in full satisfaction of the claim; the plaintiffs (as the defendants knew) were in desperate financial straits, so that recourse to law was not a practicable remedy, and they accepted the £300, giving a receipt in full satisfaction. It was held that this was not a valid surrender of their claim to the balance because of the absence of consideration.[81] The case could, it is submitted, now be supported on the ground of economic duress. In contrast, in cases in which a promise is made to pay an additional sum to the promisee if the latter will perform its existing contractual duty, but where there is no duress, the law has recently undergone a marked change. In *Williams v Roffey Bros & Nicholls (Contractors) Ltd*[82] a carpentry subcontractor which had underpriced work on a number of flats was having difficulty in completing it on time. The contractor promised an additional payment for each flat finished. It was held that this promise was enforceable although the subcontractor was only performing its existing obligation; in the absence of duress the "practical benefit" to the contractor, that if the work was finished on time it would avoid liability for liquidated damages under the main contract, constituted consideration. Although in this case the subcontractor made no threat,[83] the decision suggests that not every case in which a party agrees to make an extra payment in order to obtain the performance originally promised is one of duress, nor perhaps will every agreement secured by a threat to break a contract be voidable. As will be seen later, a "threat" to break a contract which is in fact no more than a statement of the inevitable that will happen unless an extra payment is made may not amount to duress[84]; and even when a breach is not inevitable in that sense, a threat coupled with a demand for extra payment may sometimes be seen as legitimate.[85] Nor does the fact that there was some consideration rule out any question of duress. Where the consideration is only trifling, it is suggested that its inadequacy may be relevant in establishing that the variation of the contract has been secured by improper pressure.

7–020 **Non-contractual payments.** So far as the law of duress is concerned, there appears to be no difference between a payment made in pursuance of a contract or a variation of a contract procured under duress, and one made on a non-contractual basis in response to an illegitimate threat. Although in the first situation it is technically the case that the contract or contractual variation must

[80] [1966] 2 Q.B. 716; see also *T.A. Sundell & Sons Pty Ltd v Emm Yannoulatos (Overseas) Ltd* (1956) 56 S.R. (N.S.W.) 323.

[81] See above, para.3–116.

[82] [1991] 1 Q.B. 1. See above, para.3–068.

[83] See further below, para.7–031. Compare *South Caribbean Trading Ltd v Trafigura Beheever BV* [2004] EWHC 2676 (Comm), [2005] 1 Lloyd's Rep 128 at [107]–[109] (*Williams* doubted but not applicable because economic duress).

[84] See below, para.7–040.

[85] See below, paras. 7–037—7–044.

first be set aside, it seems that the definition of duress that applies in the two situations is the same.[86]

Different approaches to economic duress. Although the doctrine of economic duress is now firmly established, there remains considerable doubt and some disagreement over the circumstances in which relief will be granted, and how the decisions are best explained. It is evident from the dicta in *Occidental Worldwide Investment Corp v Skibs A/S Avanti*[87] and the decision in the *Pao On* case[88] that a party who has agreed to a contractual variation cannot always avoid the variation simply because the other party had threatened to break the contract if it was not varied and this threat had some influence on the party seeking relief. Something more must be shown. Those cases referred to the party's consent being vitiated. Now that the vitiation of consent approach has been discarded,[89] what additional elements have to be shown? 7–021

Special causal requirements? Earlier it was suggested that the critical questions are, first, the nature of the pressure or the threats and, secondly, their effect on the victim. One possible interpretation of the economic duress cases is that, compared to other cases of duress, there are additional requirements that go to the second element, causation. Possibly the claimant needs to show more than that his decision to enter the contract was affected by the illegitimate threat. He might, for instance, have to show that the threat was the overwhelming reason for the variation, or that in an objective sense he had no reasonable alternative—in other words, that any reasonable person in the same predicament would have acted in the same way. These arguments will be rejected. It will be submitted that the necessary causation is established if the claimant shows that, but for the threat, he would not have entered the contract, and that lack of a reasonable alternative should be treated as a matter of evidence rather than as an independent requirement. On the other hand, it would appear that, in contrast to physical duress, it is not sufficient that the economic duress was merely a reason for the victim entering the contract even though he might have concluded the contract for other reasons: the "but for" test must be satisfied. 7–022

Legitimacy of the demand. Another possible interpretation looks to the nature of the pressure or threat. It is arguable that for a contract to be voidable for economic duress, the threat must not only have been wrongful but illegitimate in the sense of being without any commercial or similar justification. It will be suggested that not every threat to break a contract is illegitimate in this sense, and that where the threat is one to breach a contract it will suffice only if it is made in support of a demand that is illegitimate. In the sections that follow we will consider first causation and lack of a reasonable alternative, and then the legitimacy of the demand. 7–023

---

[86] *CTN Cash and Carry Ltd v Gallaher Ltd* [1994] 4 All E.R. 714, 717.
[87] *Pao On v Lau Yiu Long* [1979] Q.B. 705; above, para.7–014.
[88] [1980] A.C. 614; above, para.7–016.
[89] See above, paras 7–004—7–009.

(d) *Causation*

7–024 **Causation in general.** In all cases of duress it is necessary that the victim's agreement was caused by the duress.[90] However, it appears that the nature of the causation required differs according to the nature of the duress.

7–025 **Causation in duress to the person.** In *Barton v Armstrong*[91] the Privy Council, relying on the analogy of fraud,[92] held that it was sufficient that the threat was a reason for the victim entering the contract: not only it did not have to be the predominant reason, but the victim was entitled to relief even if he had not shown that he would not have entered the contract without the threat. It would be up to the party who made the threat to show that it had not influenced the victim in any way.[93]

7–026 **Causation in duress to goods.** In cases of duress to goods, it seems that the threatened seizure must have been a significant cause[94] of the victim's agreeing to the contract or payment. Thus the victim will not be entitled to avoid the contract if he had an effective alternative remedy, for example to obtain an injunction to prevent the seizure, though it is recognised that a legal remedy may be of no avail if the victim has an urgent need for the goods.[95] The victim will also be unable to avoid the contract if it was a "voluntary settlement" of the other party's claim. The meaning of this is not wholly clear[96] but it appears that relief will be denied if the threat was not the reason for the victim agreeing to the other party's demand. Nor is it clear exactly what is meant by "significant cause". Relief will be denied if the threat did not influence the victim at all, so that it was not even "one of the reasons" for the victim agreeing to the other party's demand.[97] On the other hand, it seems unlikely that the courts will apply the analogy of fraud as they do in cases of duress to the person.[98] Thus the victim will not have the benefit of the reversed burden of proof in the same way as the victim of duress to the person[99] nor that it will suffice that the threat was merely "one reason" for his actions or "present to his mind".[100] It seems likely that the victim must show that, "but for" the threat, he would not have entered the contract. We will see that it has been said that this is the appropriate test of causation in economic duress[101] and, given the similarity of duress of goods and economic duress, the same test of causation seems appropriate.

---

[90] See the speech of Lord Goff in *Dimskal Shipping Co SA v I.T.W.F.* [1992] 2 A.C. 152, 165.
[91] [1976] A.C. 104.
[92] cf. above, para.6–035.
[93] [1976] A.C. 104, 120, 121.
[94] See the speech of Lord Goff in *Dimskal Shipping Co SA v I.T.W.F.* [1992] 2 A.C. 152, 165.
[95] *Astley v Reynolds* (1731) 2 Stra. 915, 916.
[96] See Burrows, *Law of Restitution*, 2nd edn (2002), p.212.
[97] cf. *Barton v Armstrong* [1976] A.C. 104, above, para.7–025.
[98] See para.7–025.
[99] cf. *Barton v Armstrong* [1976] A.C. 104.
[100] cf. above, para.6–035.
[101] See next paragraph.

Causation in economic duress: "but for". In *Dimskal Shipping Co SA v I.T.W.F.*[102] Lord Goff said that there may be duress where "the economic pressure may be characterised as illegitimate and has constituted a significant cause inducing the plaintiff to enter the relevant contract". This dictum indicates that, as cases of duress of goods,[103] the victim will not have the benefit of the reversed burden of proof in the same way as the victim of duress to the person,[104] nor will it suffice that the threat was merely "one reason" for his actions or "present to his mind". As Mance J. said in *Huyton v Cremer*,[105] by "significant cause" Lord Goff meant that what the judge termed the "relaxed view" of causation in the special context of duress to the person does not apply to economic duress.[106] Mance J. said: 7–027

> "... the minimum basic test of subjective causation in economic duress ought ... to be a 'but for' test. The illegitimate pressure must have been such as actually caused the making of the agreement, in the sense that it would not otherwise have been made either at all or, at least, in the terms in which it was made. In that sense, the pressure must have been decisive or clinching. There may of course be causes where a common sense relaxation ... is necessary, for example in the event of an agreement induced by two concurrent causes, each otherwise sufficient to ground a claim of relief, in circumstances where each alone would have induced the agreement."[107]

Adopting a "but for" test would place cases of economic duress on a par with cases of negligent or non-negligent misrepresentation.[108] This seems appropriate. Only in the special circumstances of duress to the person, as with cases of fraudulent misrepresentation, should relief be given merely because the threat or fraud had some influence on the mind of the victim.

Voluntary submission. Confirmation of the need for "but for" causation comes from indications that relief will be denied if the principal reason for the victim's agreement was that he was prepared to pay it anyway. This may have been relevant in the *Pao On* case,[109] where the actual decision seems to have rested on the fact that the defendants thought that they would lose very little by granting the amendment sought.[110] 7–028

Additional causal elements? After the passage quoted in para.7–027 above, Mance J. continued: 7–029

---

[102] [1992] 2 A.C. 152, 165.
[103] See previous paragraph.
[104] But note the contrary authority of *Crescendo Management Pty Ltd v Westpac Banking Corp* (1988) 19 N.S.W.L.R. 40
[105] *Huyton SA v Peter Cremer GmbH* [1999] 1 Lloyd's Rep. 620, 636.
[106] See also Goff & Jones, *Law of Restitution*, 7th edn (2007), paras 10–030—10–031.
[107] [1999] 1 Lloyd's Rep. 620, 636.
[108] See above, para.6–035.
[109] *Pao On v Lau Liu Long* [1980] A.C. 614, above, para.7–013. Birks, *Introduction to the Law of Restitution* (1985), p.183; compare Burrows, *Law of Restitution*, 2nd edn (2002) p.227.
[110] [1980] A.C. 614, 635.

"On the other hand it also seems clear that the application of a simple 'but for' test of subjective causation in conjunction with an actual or threatened breach of duty could lead too readily to relief being granted."

Thus it is seems that Mance J. considered that there may be other elements to economic duress.[111] Whether these relate to causation or to the nature of the threat remains to be discussed.

7–030 **"Predominant cause" not required.** As mentioned earlier,[112] some cases of economic duress applied the test of whether the victim's will was overborne so that he did not consent to the contract. This suggested that relief was only possible if the threat was the overwhelming reason for the victim's decision. However, the "overborne will" test has now been abandoned.[113] This, together with Lord Goff's dictum quoted above, suggests that the combination of threat and other pressures need not be overwhelming, "the only reason" the victim entered the contract.

7–031 **Reasonable alternative.** It is certainly relevant whether or not the victim had a reasonable alternative. The victim's lack of choice was emphasised by Lord Scarman in the *Pao On*[114] and *Universe Sentinel*[115] cases and has clearly been an important factor in those cases in which relief has been given.[116] It is not clear whether this is a prerequisite or merely evidential[117]; but it seems that if the victim had a reasonable alternative to submitting to the other party's demand, he will seldom obtain relief.[118] This is sometimes explicable on causal grounds. Thus a refusal, in breach of contract, to supply goods unless some extra consideration is supplied by the buyer, may lack genuine coercive force where alternative supplies are available in the market. Similarly, where the party claiming relief had adequate time to claim redress at law, and there is no reason to think that this would not protect or compensate him, submission to the threat may simply reflect that party's belief that his best interests would be served by such submission rather than by resort to the courts. The existence of a reasonable

---

[111] *Huyton SA v Peter Cremer GmbH & Co* [1999] 1 Lloyd's Rep. 620, 637. See also *Occidental Worldwide Investment Corp v Skibs A/S Avanti* [1976] 1 Lloyd's Rep. 293; above, para.7–014 where the plea of duress was rejected on the basis that the owners were subjected only to "normal commercial pressures".

[112] Above, para.7–005.

[113] Above, para.7–005.

[114] *Pao On v Lau Liu Long* [1980] A.C. 614, 635. See also Halson (1991) 107 L.Q.R. 649.

[115] "The classic case of duress is, however, not the lack of will to submit but the victim's intentional submission arising from the realisation that there is no practical choice open to him": [1983] 1 A.C. 366, 400.

[116] e.g. *North Ocean Shipping Co Ltd v Hyundai Construction Co Ltd* [1979] Q.B. 705; *B. & S. Contracts & Design Ltd v Victor Green Publications Ltd* [1984] I.C.R. 419; *The Alev* [1989] 1 Lloyd's Rep. 138. Cf. *Adam Opel GmbH v Mitras Automotive UK Ltd* [2007] EWHC 3252 (QB), [2007] All ER (D) 272 (Dec) (in circumstances, injunction not a adequate alternative to nullify pressure caused by threat to refuse to deliver supplies: at [33]).

[117] See Beatson *The Use and Abuse of Unjust Enrichment* (1991), pp.122–126.

[118] *Huyton SA v Peter Cremer GmbH* [1999] 1 Lloyd's Rep. 620, 638.

alternative may have been relevant in the *Pao On*[119] decision itself: Lord Scarman referred in general terms to American case law stressing the importance of examining the alternatives available to the party claiming relief.[120] But it is possible to argue that the existence of a reasonable alternative is not be just a matter of proving causation. It has been said that "economic duress can only provide a basis for avoiding a contract if there was no real alternative".[121] This suggests that a plea of duress would fail if a reasonable person would have thought that an alternative was practical, even if the actual victim did not and it is shown that he would not have entered the contract but for the threat.

Reasonable alternative: a matter of evidence. Mance J. has said that even though it is clear that the innocent party would never have acted as he did but for the threat, relief may be denied if he had "an alternative remedy which any and possibly some other reasonable persons would have pursued", so that he could have resisted the pressure.[122] He said where the threatened party had such an alternative, relief will seldom be appropriate. However, the judge also remarked that absence of a reasonable alternative was not "an inflexible third ingredient" (in addition to illegitimate pressure and causation).[123] It is submitted that absence of a reasonable alternative is not an absolute requirement but rather very strong evidence of whether the victim was in fact influenced by the threat. 7–032

Gravity of threat. For similar reasons it is likely that the threat must normally be one of some gravity. This is to some extent implicit in the factors to which attention must be had, as specified by Lord Scarman in the *Pao On* case.[124] For if attention must be paid to the alternative remedies available to the threatened party (and their effectiveness), it is evident that minor threats, even if unlawful or improper, can normally give no redress in contract law: the party threatened ought to pursue his other remedies. How serious the threats must be in order to constitute duress may depend on the physical and mental condition of the person threatened. Weakness of intellect or fear, whether reasonably entertained or not, may be relevant factors which should be taken into account.[125] However, it is submitted that the seriousness of the threat is also a matter of evidence as to whether the victim was coerced by the it (or possibly of whether he had a 7–033

---

[119] [1980] A.C. 614.

[120] For examples, see *Tristate Roofing Co of Uniontown v Simon* (1958) A.2d. 333, 335; *Gallagher Switchboard Corp v Heckler Electric Co* (1962) 229 N.Y.S. 2d. 623, 630.

[121] Sir John Donaldson M.R. in *Hennessy v Craigmyle & Co Ltd* [1986] I.C.R. 461, 468.

[122] *Huyton SA v Peter Cremer GmbH & Co* [1999] 1 Lloyd's Rep. 620, 638. The objective approach to whether there was a reasonable alternative is criticised in Goff & Jones, para.10–034; and the authors point out that in fact the courts seem quite ready to accept that the victim had no real alternative: *ibid*., pp.324–325.

[123] *Huyton SA v Peter Cremer GmbH & Co* [1999] 1 Lloyd's Rep. 620, 638. In *DSND Subsea Ltd v Petroleum Geo-services ASA* [2000] B.L.R. 530, para. 638, Dyson J. said "compulsion on, or lack of practical choice for, the victim" was one of "the ingredients of actionable duress"; but it is suggested that he did not mean lack of practical alternative to be an absolute requirement, since (also at [31]) he listed "whether the victim had any realistic practical alternative but to submit to the pressure" as one a range of factors to be taken into account: see below, para.7–044.

[124] Above, fn.119.

[125] *Scott v Sebright* (1866) 12 P.D. 21.

reasonable alternative, if, contrary to what was submitted above, that is required), rather than independent requirements.

7–034 **Protest.** In the *Pao On* case[126] it was said that it was relevant whether or not the victim protested. This again seems to be a question of evidence as whether or not the threat had a coercive effect. It has been accepted for many years that when a payment is made in order to avoid the wrongful seizure of goods, protest "affords some evidence . . . that the payment was not voluntarily made",[127] but that the fact that the payment was made without protest does not necessarily mean that the payment was voluntary.[128]

7–035 **Independent advice.** Likewise in the *Pao On* case[129] it was said that it is relevant whether or not the victim had independent advice. The relevance of this is perhaps less obvious: access to legal advice, for example, will not increase the range of options available to the victim, and lack of advice therefore cannot be an absolute requirement. However, whether or not the victim appreciated that he had an alternative remedy and what the practical implications of following it would be are relevant to the question of causation.[130]

7–036 **Conclusion on causation in economic duress.** It is submitted that for a contract to be voidable on the grounds of economic duress, the usual rule of causation should apply: the victim must show that "but for" the threat he would not have entered the contract.[131] It is not necessary that the victim shows that the threat was the predominant reason for him entering the contract or that it was particularly coercive. On the other hand, it is insufficient that the economic pressure was merely "a reason" for the victim entering the contract. The question of reasonable alternative is more difficult. The combination of a wrongful threat without which the innocent party would not have agreed to the contract and the absence of any reasonable alternative are clearly very important factors and some writers have argued that they are the ingredients of economic duress.[132] Others however have argued that other factors not related to causation are more relevant. These will explored in the next section and, as we shall see, there is some judicial support for this view. As to causation, it is submitted that while the victim will seldom obtain relief unless the threats were of some gravity or if he had a reasonable alternative, this is because without these factors he will fail to convince the court that he would not have entered the contract but for the threat, rather than absence of a reasonable alternative being an independent requirement of economic duress.[133]

---

[126] *Pao On v Lau Yiu Long* [1980] A.C. 614.

[127] *Maskell v Horner* [1915] 3 K.B. 106, 120.

[128] See below, para.29–111.

[129] Above, fn.126.

[130] *Hennessy v Craigmyle & Co Ltd* [1986] I.C.R. 461; N. Enonchong, *Duress, Undue Influence and Unconscionable Dealing* (2006), para.4–026.

[131] Contrast N. Enonchong, *Duress, Undue Influence and Unconscionable Dealing* (2006), paras 4–011—4–16, who favours applying the *Barton* test (see above, para.7–025).

[132] Virgo, *Principles of the Law of Restitution* 2nd edn (2005) p.215.

[133] See also N. Enonchong, *Duress, Undue Influence and Unconscionable Dealing* (2006), paras 4–020 and 4–024—4–025.

(e) *Legitimacy of the Demand*[134]

Threat to commit an unlawful act. As already indicated, it is clear that not all threats can be regarded as improper or illegitimate, and it is necessary in the law of duress to distinguish between legitimate and other forms of pressure or threats. Prima facie it is thought to be clear that a threat to commit an unlawful act will constitute an improper threat for the purposes of the law of duress.[135] Certainly a threat to commit a crime or a tort as a means of inducing the coerced party to enter into some contract must prima facie be improper.[136] However, this may not be true of every threatened wrong, particularly a threat to break a contract. 7–037

Threat to break a contract. When the threatened wrong is a breach of contract it seems that the victim will not necessarily be entitled to relief even if he would not have agreed "but for" the threat and had no reasonable alternative. As was suggested earlier, the decisions in *Occidental Worldwide Investment Corp v Skibs A/S Avanti*[137] and *Pao On v Lau Liu Long*[138] suggest that something more than this is required. It is possible that in cases where the threat is one of breach of contract, some additional factor is required. As we saw earlier, one possible "additional factor" is that the combination of the threat and commercial pressures were overwhelming, but that "causal" approach was rejected.[139] An alternative possibility is that the additional factor that may be required is that the threatened breach of contract must be regarded as "illegitimate pressure", and that in some circumstances a threat of a breach of contract may be regarded as not illegitimate. 7–038

Can a threatened breach be "legitimate"? This possibility is suggested by American cases. Where unexpected difficulties arise in the performance of a contract (even if they do not amount to frustrating circumstances) it is often commercially reasonable for one party to claim extra remuneration, or some other extra-contractual concession, as the price of his continuing with performance. In these circumstances, a threat to break the contract unless the extra consideration is forthcoming may well be regarded as a legitimate form of 7–039

[134] See Beatson, *The Use and Abuse of Unjust Enrichment* (1991), pp.117–129; Burrows, *Law of Restitution*, 2nd edn (2002) especially pp.225–234.

[135] In *Dimskal Shipping Co SA v ITWF, The Evia Luck* [1992] 2 A.C. 152 the House of Lords held that the question of whether economic pressure amounted to duress was *prima facie* a matter for the proper law of the contract, so that whether the conduct was lawful or not fell to be determined by the proper law of the contract rather than by that of the place where the threat was made. In *Royal Boskalis Westminster Nv v Mountain* [1999] Q.B. 674, 689, 730 it was said that, nonetheless, counsel had been correct to concede, in the light of *Kaufman v Gerson* [1904] 1 K.B. 591, that some forms of duress are so shocking that English law would not enforce a contract made under such duress irrespective of whether the threat would be acceptable, and the contract valid, under the governing law. See below, para.30–183.

[136] See the American *Restatement of Contract*, para.176(1).

[137] [1976] 1 Lloyd's Rep. 293; above, para.7–014.

[138] [1980] A.C. 614; above, para.7–016.

[139] See above, para.7–030.

commercial pressure[140] where the unanticipated difficulty means that he is genuinely unable to perform without an extra payment,[141] and possibly also if the threatening party acts in the bona fide belief that he is entitled to some extra payment or if the demand is in some sense "fair". We will consider these three possibilities in turn.

7–040 **Statement of the inevitable is not a threat.** A genuine inability to perform without the promised payment might have been significant in *Williams v Roffey Bros & Nicholls (Contractors) Ltd*[142] had the subcontractor demanded extra payment. On the facts there was no duress because no threat was made: the initiative for the extra payment came from the contractors.[143] If, however, the subcontractors had said that without extra payment, they would be unable to perform, and the main contractors had then promised the extra payment, it seems unlikely that the main contractors could have avoided the promise to pay extra on the ground of duress. There are a number of ways in which this result could be explained. One is that a party who truthfully states that, without the extra payment or concession demanded, he will be unable to perform is not making a threat; he is simply stating a fact.[144] This is not a matter of the words used; the courts have recognised that a threat may be implicit.[145] Thus where an agreement is entered into not because of a threatened breach of contract but through fear of prosecution, it was said that:

> "... not only is no direct threat necessary, but no promise need be given to abstain from a prosecution. It is enough if the undertaking were given to prevent a prosecution and that desire were known to those to whom the undertaking was given."[146]

A "veiled threat" has been held to constitute duress.[147] But if it is genuinely the case that the party will be forced to default if he is not paid extra, for instance

[140] See, e.g. *Goebel v Linn* (1882) 11 N.W. 284; *Linz v Schuck* (1907) 67 A. 286. There is a sense in which the *Pao On* case [1980] A.C. 614 also resembles these cases inasmuch as the variation obtained by the alleged duress was needed to put right what was an obvious commercial omission or mistake in the original contract.

[141] Posner (1977) 6 J.L.S. 411 makes the telling point that if a party will become bankrupt unless he is promised extra, it is very much in the promisor's interest to be able to make a binding promise to pay the extra amount in order to get the work finished, even though the promisor has no practical choice.

[142] [1991] 1 Q.B. 1; above, para.7–019.

[143] But see further below, para.7–042.

[144] Birks, *An Introduction to the Law of Restitution* (1985), p.183. Cf. *Biffin v Bignell* (1862) 7 H. & N. 877 , where it was held to be no duress to warn the promisor that the probable consequence of her failure to agree would be her continued detention in a lunatic asylum.

[145] See Birks [1990] L.M.C.L.Q. 342, 346.

[146] *Mutual Finance Co Ltd v John Wetton & Sons Ltd* [1937] 2 K.B. 389, 395. Thus in *Williams v Bayley* (1866) L.R. 1 H.L. 200 a father executed a mortgage to a banker, who insisted on this course as he had it in his power to prosecute the father's son for forgery. There was no direct threat of a prosecution, but the mortgage was executed in return for the delivery up of the documents forged. It was held that the mortgage was unenforceable in equity as the father was not a free and voluntary agent since he knew that unless he undertook the liability his son would be prosecuted.

[147] *B. & S. Contracts & Design Ltd v Victor Green Publications Ltd* [1984] I.C.R. 419.

because he will inevitably become bankrupt, he cannot be regarded as making a threat because he is powerless to prevent his default. It would seem appropriate to uphold any variation that the other party agrees or extra payment that he makes in such circumstances.[148] However, this is quite a narrow exception. It may be the case that it is not impossible for the party to perform without the extra payment but doing so will cause him very severe hardship.

Bad faith. Another approach is to say that a demand made in bad faith is illegitimate and may amount to duress.[149] There is some judicial support for the good or bad faith of the party exerting the pressure being relevant.[150] One difficulty, however, is to know what is meant by good faith or bad faith. It seems correct to say that a party who exploits the other's position to demand a payment that is unrelated to the contract, and to which he knows he has no legal or moral right, is guilty of economic duress.[151] However, a demand may constitute economic duress even though the demand is related to the contract, and it is not necessary that the threatening party was deliberately exploiting the victim's position.[152] One interpretation is that a party is in bad faith unless he honestly believes that his demand is legally justified,[153] but should every claim which is known not to have a legal basis be treated as one in bad faith? If a party makes a claim that it knows to be bad, any compromise that results may lack consideration,[154] so that the compromise is unenforceable on that ground. Provided however that there is other consideration, in some situations—for example, when a claim is made by a party who has been confronted with unexpected difficulty or expense not amounting to frustration[155]—it might be argued that the claim should not be regarded as illegitimate for the purposes of duress even though the party knows that there is no legal basis for it. But on existing authorities it seems that good faith in this sense does not preclude a finding of economic duress.[156] Similar circumstances may have obtained in the *North Ocean Shipping* case,[157] yet it was held that there was economic duress. Thus the role of good faith or bad faith in economic duress is uncertain. While one judge has expressed the view 7–041

[148] Halson (1991) 110 L.Q.R. 649.

[149] Birks at p.183; also [1990] L.M.C.L.Q. 342, 347.

[150] e.g. *DSND Subsea Ltd v Petroleum Geo-services ASA* [2000] B.L.R. 530 at [131]; *Adam Opel GmbH v Mitras Automotive UK Ltd* [2007] EWHC 3252 (QB), [2007] All ER (D) 272 (Dec) (no good faith belief that entitled to compensation demanded).

[151] Compare *B. & S. Contracts and Design Ltd v Victor Green Publications Ltd* [1984] I.C.R. 419, where the difficulty faced by the threatening party (a strike by its workers) was not related to the contract and may have been one it should have dealt with. See also *Adam Opel GmbH v Mitras Automotive UK Ltd* [2007] EWHC 3252 (QB), [2007] All ER (D) 272 (Dec) (claim so unreasonable that genuine belief would count for little: at [34]).

[152] *North Ocean Shipping Co Ltd v Hyundai Construction Co Ltd* [1979] Q.B. 705.

[153] But compare Goff & Jones, *Law of Restitution*, 7th edn (2007), para.10–051.

[154] Mance J. in *Huyton v Cremer* [1999] 1 Lloyd's Rep. 620, 637. This follows from cases such as *Wade v Simeon* (1846) 2 C.B. 528; 135 E.R. 1061: above, para.3–050.

[155] cf. below, Ch.23.

[156] See Birks and Chin in Beatson & Friedmann (eds), *Good Faith and Fault in Contract Law* (1995), pp.57–97, 62. See also *Huyten SA v Peter Cremer GmbH & Co* [1999] 1 Lloyd's Rep. 620, 637.

[157] [1979] Q.B. 705; above, para.7–015.

that good or bad faith is irrelevant,[158] other judges have said that the good or bad faith of the party making the threat may be a relevant factor.[159]

7–042 **Fairness of the demand.** In the cases, some of the demands appear to have been made in order to rectify an apparent imbalance in the existing contract; others appear to have been unrelated to any such factor. Where the demand is recognised by the "victim" as fair, that may lead to the conclusion that he was not really influenced by the threat so much as by a desire to help out the other party, and thus the necessary causal link will be missing.[160] But if it is clear that the threat did have a significant influence, it does not seem that the fact that the demand might rectify an imbalance in the contract will make the demand legitimate. In *Atlas Express Ltd v Kafco (Importers and Distributors) Ltd*[161] the plaintiffs miscalculated the number of cartons of the defendants' goods that they could carry on a trailer load for delivery to a retail chain and, when they discovered the truth, stated that they would not carry any more cartons without an extra payment. The defendants were heavily reliant on the contract with the retail chain and were unable to find an alternative carrier, so they agreed; but later they refused to pay the extra charges. Tucker J. held that their consent had been vitiated by duress.[162] Although the mistake was the plaintiffs' and unknown to the defendant, it seems likely that the latter did get the benefit of cheaper rates than normal for the goods to be carried. Nor would an evaluation of the "fairness" of the changed contract be consistent with the courts' normal approach.[163]

7–043 **Conclusion on legitimacy of threat to break contract.** It is thus difficult to state with confidence whether a threat of a breach of contract will ever be regarded as legitimate and, if so, in what circumstances. It is submitted that deliberate exploitation of the victim's position with a view to gaining some advantage, particularly one unrelated to the contract and to which the threatening party knows he is not entitled, is clearly illegitimate. At the other end of the scale, an apparent threat should not be treated as illegitimate if it was really no more than a true statement that, unless the demand is met, the party making it will be unable to perform. The difficult case is that of the party who has a genuine belief

[158] Kerr J. in *Occidental Worldwide Investment Corp v Skibs A/S Avanti* [1976] 1 Lloyd's Rep. 293, 335.

[159] *Huyton SA v Peter Cremer GmbH & Co* [1999] 1 Lloyd's Rep. 620, 637, though Mance J. described the argument that a threatened breach of contract may not represent illegitimate pressure if there was a reasonable commercial basis for the threat as "by no means uncontentious"; *DSND Subsea Ltd v Petroleum Geo-services ASA* [2000] B.L.R. 530 at [131], where Dyson J. said: "In determining whether there has been illegitimate pressure, the courts take into account a range of factors. These include whether there has been an actual or threatened breach of contract; whether the person allegedly exerting the pressure has acted in good or bad faith . . . " The relevant passage is quoted in full below, para.7–044.

[160] The attitude of the main contractors in *Williams v Roffey* [1991] 1 Q.B. 1 may be explained by the fact that the subcontractors appear to have under-priced the job.

[161] [1989] Q.B. 833.

[162] He also held that there was no consideration for the payment; but after the decision in *Williams v Roffey & Nicholls (Contractors) Ltd* [1991] 1 Q.B. 1, the presence or absence of consideration may depend on whether or not there was duress: see above, para.7–019.

[163] For a helpful discussion of "fairness" in this context, see Burrows, *Law of Restitution*, 2nd edn (2002) pp.232–233.

that he is legally entitled to the amount demanded. It is suggested that a demand made in good faith, in the sense that the party demanding has a genuine belief in the moral strength of his claim—for example, because he has encountered serious and unexpected difficulties in performing and will suffer considerable hardship if his demand is not met; or to correct an acknowledged imbalance in the existing contract—may in some circumstances also be treated as legitimate. Here the behaviour of the victim, for example whether he protests, will be relevant. First, as argued earlier,[164] it will go to causation: if the victim pays without protest, that may be evidence that he was not influenced by the threat. But secondly, payment without protest may leave the demanding party believing that the justice of his demand is admitted, whereas it will be harder for him to prove that he was acting in good faith if he ignores the victim's protests.

A range of factors. However, it is doubtful whether either the good faith of the party making the threat or the apparent fairness of his demand provides a touchstone by which to determine whether a threatened breach of contract which influenced the victim and which left him no reasonable alternative amounts to economic duress. In analogous doctrines, such as undue influence, the courts have refused to lay down precise limits to the doctrine.[165] This is with good reason: the facts with which they are presented can vary widely. We can expect the courts to maintain the same fluid approach to economic duress. It is clear that the threat must be made, as opposed to a warning being given.[166] The threat must influence the victim, at least to the extent that he would not have entered the contract from which he seeks relief "but for" the threat.[167] He will seldom have a remedy if he had a reasonable alternative.[168] The threat must normally be "illegitimate", and this normally[169] requires that the threat is of a breach of contract or other civil wrong.[170] But threat of a breach of contract which caused him to enter the contract or variation agreement may not suffice: he may have to show more than these facts, and what the additional facts will be is not rigidly defined. The degree of commercial pressure that combined with the threat to influence him, the good faith or bad faith of the party making the threat and possibly even the fairness of the latter's demand may all be taken into account.[171] In other words, the courts take into account a range of factors. As Dyson J. has said: 7–044

> "In determining whether there has been illegitimate pressure, the courts take into account a range of factors. These include whether there has been an actual or threatened breach of contract; whether the person allegedly exerting the pressure has acted in good or bad faith; whether the victim had any realistic practical alternative but to submit to the pressure; whether the victim protested at the time; and whether he affirmed and

[164] See above, para.7–034.
[165] See below, para.7–056.
[166] See above, para.7–040.
[167] See above, para.7–027.
[168] See above, para.7–032.
[169] For possible exceptions see below, para.7–045.
[170] See above, para.7–010.
[171] cf. Goff & Jones, *Law of Restitution*, 7th edn (2007), para.10–026, at fn.71. And note *R. v HM Att-Gen for England and Wales* [2003] UKPC 22 (threat to return member of armed forces to his unit lawful, but also demand that he sign a confidentiality agreement not unreasonable).

sought to rely on the contract. These are all relevant factors. Illegitimate pressure must be distinguished from the rough and tumble of the pressure of normal commercial bargaining."[172]

(f) *Threats of Actions not in Themselves Wrongful*

7–045 **Threat to commit otherwise lawful act.** Threatening to carry out something perfectly within one's rights will not normally amount to duress; for instance, a party who relies on his existing contractual rights to drive a hard bargain is not, on that ground alone, guilty of economic duress.[173] There can be no doubt that even a threat to commit what would otherwise be a perfectly lawful act may be improper if the threat is coupled with a demand which goes substantially beyond what is normal or legitimate in commercial arrangements. It was at one time suggested that it could not be unlawful to threaten to exercise one's legal rights, no matter what the motive.[174] But such a principle is too widely stated. There are, for example, many cases where a man who has a "right," in the sense of a liberty or capacity of doing an act which is not unlawful, but which is calculated seriously to injure another, will be liable to a charge of blackmail if he demands money from that other as the price of abstaining, e.g. from disclosing discreditable incidents in the victim's life.[175] Although it is, in general, true to say that a contract is not rendered voidable by reason of the fact that pressure has been lawfully applied so as to compel the promisor to accept its terms,[176] it is unlikely that a court would refuse to entertain an action at the suit of one who had paid money under a threat amounting to blackmail, or to set aside any agreement entered into as the result of such a threat.[177] In American law there are many illustrations of other threats to commit acts lawful in themselves which have been held to amount to duress when coupled with unreasonable demands.[178] For instance, a threat (lawfully) to dismiss an injured employee unless he accepted a manifestly low settlement for his injuries has been held to be unlawful duress.[179] It seems probable that a similar decision would be reached on such facts by an English court. On the other hand, care must be taken in treating threats lawful in themselves as amounting to duress, for otherwise threats commonly used in

---

[172] *DSND Subsea Ltd v Petroleum Geo-services ASA* [2000] B.L.R. 530 at [131]. Dyson J.'s statement was accepted as correct by both sides in the later case of *Carillion Construction Ltd v Felix (UK) Ltd* [2001] B.L.R. 1, also before Dyson J.

[173] *Alec Lobb Ltd v Total Oil G.B. Ltd* [1983] 1 W.L.R. 87 (varied on other points, [1985] 1 W.L.R. 173).

[174] *Allen v Flood* [1898] A.C. 1; *Ware and De Freville v Motor Trade Association* [1921] 3 K.B. 40; *Hardie and Lane Ltd v Chilton* [1928] 2 K.B. 306; *Chapman v Honig* [1963] 2 Q.B. 502; cf. *Quinn v Leathem* [1901] A.C. 495.

[175] *Thorne v Motor Trade Association* [1937] A.C. 797, 822; *Universe Tankships of Monrovia Inc v I.T.W.F.* [1983] 1 A.C. 366, 401.

[176] *Hardie and Lane Ltd v Chilton* [1928] 2 K.B. 306; *Eric Gnapp Ltd v Petroleum Board* [1949] 1 All E.R. 980.

[177] *Norreys v Zeffert* [1939] 2 All E.R. 187; *United Australia Ltd v Barclays Bank Ltd* [1941] A.C. 1, 29; *Universe Tankships of Monrovia Inc v I.T.W.F.* [1983] A.C. 366, 401.

[178] And see *Restatement of Contracts*, para.176(2).

[179] *Mitchell v C.C. Sanitation Co* (1968) 430 S.W. 2d. 933; cf. the somewhat similar facts in *Arrale v Costain Engineering Ltd* [1976] 2 Lloyd's Rep. 98, though there was no real duress in this case.

business (e.g. of lawful strikes[180]) would fall into the category of economic duress.

7–046 In *CTN Cash and Carry Ltd v Gallaher Ltd*[181] the plaintiffs had ordered goods from the defendants, who delivered them by mistake to the wrong warehouse, from which they were stolen. The defendants, honestly but wrongly believing that the goods were at the plaintiffs' risk, invoiced them. The plaintiffs refused to pay until the defendants threatened to withdraw the plaintiffs' credit facilities, which, it was said, would seriously jeopardise the plaintiffs' business. The defendants had the right to withdraw credit facilities at any time. The plaintiffs later sought repayment. The Court of Appeal upheld the trial judge's decision that no case of economic duress had been made out. Steyn L.J., with whom the other members of the Court agreed, said that the combination of the facts that: (i) the defendants were entitled to refuse to enter into any future contracts with the plaintiffs for any reason; and (ii), critically, that the defendants bona fide thought that the plaintiffs owed the sum in question, was sufficient to distinguish cases in which a plea of economic duress had succeeded. The fact that the defendants were in a sense in a monopoly position was irrelevant, the control of monopolies being as matter for Parliament. Although there are cases in which the courts have accepted that a threat of a lawful action coupled with a demand for payment may be illegitimate,[182] it would be a relatively rare case in which "lawful act duress" could be established in a commercial context.[183]

7–047 **Threat not to contract.** It is not clear whether a threat not to enter into a contract unless the threatener's terms are met could ever amount to improper pressure, for example where the threatener's terms are extortionate. There are a number of salvage cases in which extortionate demands have been made to rescue a vessel (or those on board) and the contracts so entered into have been set aside, or refused enforcement.[184] But these cases may rest upon the principle

---

[180] Threats of unlawful strikes are usually protected by the statutory immunities governing acts done in the course of furtherance of a trade dispute: see Trade Union and Labour Relations Consolidation Act 1992. But coercive threats falling outside these immunities will often constitute unlawful duress, see, e.g. *Universe Tankships of Monrovia Inc v I.T.W.F.* [1983] A.C. 366, above, para.7–017.

[181] [1994] 4 All E.R. 715.

[182] e.g. *Thorne v Motor Trade Association* [1937] A.C. 797.

[183] The threat, if not wrongful, must at least be immoral or unconscionable. There is nothing unconscionable in the owner of goods let on hire purchase threatening to repossess them when the hirer is in default and has not applied for relief against forfeiture: *Alf Vaughan & Co Ltd v Royscot Trust Ltd* [1999] 1 All E.R. 856. Nor is a threat to return a soldier to his unit unlawful: *R. v Att-Gen for England and Wales* [2003] UKPC 22.

[184] See *Akerblom v Price* (1881) 7 QBD 129; *The Rialto* [1891] P.175; *The Port Caledonia and the Anna* [1903] P.184; *The Crusader* [1907] P.196. See now Merchant Shipping Act 1995 s.224, which provides for the Salvage Convention 1989 (contained in Sch.11 to the Act) to have the force of law. The Convention provides in art.7:

"*Annulment and modification of contracts*

A contract or any terms thereof may be annulled or modified if—

(a) the contract has been entered into under undue influence or the influence of danger and its terms are inequitable; or

(b) the payment under the contract is in an excessive degree too large or too small for the services actually rendered."

Article 13 sets out criteria for fixing the proper reward.

of maritime law that a duty to rescue human life is imposed on putative rescuers, so that the threat not to rescue may be unlawful. Other cases can be put in which a threat not to act, or not to contract, may be lawful in itself, and yet may be strongly coercive, for example where the threatener is in a monopoly position. However, there are Commonwealth authorities which hold that a person who is under no duty to enter into a contract with another is entitled to set his own terms, even though these may seem extortionate and the other party may have little choice but to comply.[185]

7–048 **Threat to prosecute.** A threat to prosecute may itself be an unlawful threat if the charge is known to be false and the threat is made for malice or other improper motive. Such a threat would amount to a threat to commit the tort of malicious prosecution.[186] Consequently, a contract made as a result of such a threat would, it seems, be a clear case of a contract entered into as a result of duress, and if the other conditions are satisfied, would be voidable for that reason. Even at common law such action could constitute duress as to the person because the result of the prosecution could be the imprisonment of the threatened party, and this was sufficient to constitute duress as to the person[187]; in equity, an even broader view was taken, though most of the equitable cases were dealt with as instances of undue influence.[188] Thus in *Williams v Bayley*,[189] a father executed a mortgage to a banker, who insisted on this course as he had it in his power to prosecute the father's son for forgery. There was no direct threat of a prosecution, but the mortgage was executed in return for the delivery up of the documents forged. It was held that the mortgage was unenforceable in equity as the father was not a free and voluntary agent since he knew that unless he undertook the liability his son would be prosecuted. A threat to prosecute, even when perfectly proper in itself, in the sense that a prosecution would be justified, may amount to an improper threat for the purposes of the law, if it is coupled with a demand for restitution or for a promise of restitution or other contractual undertaking.[190] In *Mutual Finance Co Ltd v John Wetton & Sons Ltd*[191] a guarantee was obtained from a family company under an implied threat to prosecute a member of the family for the alleged forgery of a previous guarantee. The persons seeking to enforce the guarantee knew that at the time it was given the father of the alleged forger was so ill that the shock of the prosecution of his son was likely to endanger his life. The guarantee was held to be invalid on the basis of actual undue influence. It is submitted that today the wider equitable rule will prevail, so that a contract will be voidable if obtained by a threat of criminal prosecution or other lawful imprisonment, if the threat amounts to the use of illegitimate pressure.

---

[185] See, e.g. *Smith v William Charlick Ltd* (1924) 34 C.L.R. 38; *Morton Construction v City of Hamilton* (1961) 31 D.L.R. (2d) 323. See Goff & Jones at para.10–049.

[186] *Duke Cadaval v Collins* (1836) 4 A. & E. 858; *Flower v Sadler* (1882) 10 QBD 572.

[187] *Smith v Monteith* (1844) 13 M. & W. 427; *Mutual Finance Co Ltd v John Wetton & Sons Ltd* [1937] 2 K.B. 389, 395.

[188] See *Williams v Bayley* (1866) L.R. 1 H.L. 200.

[189] (1866) L.R. 1 H.L. 200.

[190] *Kaufman v Gerson* [1904] 1 K.B. 591.

[191] [1937] 2 K.B. 389.

Stifling a prosecution. An agreement obtained by threats to prosecute for a criminal offence may also be invalid on the ground that it involves the stifling of a prosecution for the offence.[192] In such a case, it is not sufficient for the party seeking to avoid the contract to show that his promise induced the other party to abstain from criminal proceedings.[193] He must go further and show that it was an express or implied term of the contract that there should be no prosecution.[194] An agreement of this nature is not only voidable on the ground of duress, but may be void as being contrary to public policy.[195] Money paid in pursuance of an illegal agreement is ordinarily irrecoverable; but the presence of duress may enable the party threatened to plead that he was not *in pari delicto*, and so he may recover his money by an action for money had and received.[196] The law will permit the compromise of a claim for damages, though made the subject of a criminal prosecution, in certain limited circumstances.[197] It is, however, submitted that a plea of duress might still be admitted to an action on a compromise of this nature if it were shown that it was arrived at by an illegitimate threat of a criminal prosecution. The modern trend seems to be to discourage the making of such contracts whenever serious crime is involved. If a contract is made without the matter being reported to the police there is a strong probability that the transaction will be held to amount to the stifling of a prosecution. And if the contract is made after the matter is reported to the police then there is a danger that it will amount to a conspiracy to pervert the course of justice.[198] To make a valid contract in such circumstances, it should be made absolutely clear that the innocent party is only compromising his *civil* claim for damages, and is neither threatening to report the matter to the police, nor to prosecute, nor offering not to do so. 7–049

Threat to institute civil proceedings. Since recourse to law is the remedy for redress provided by the law itself, it is obvious that prima facie a threat to enforce one's legal rights by instituting civil proceedings cannot be an unlawful or wrongful threat. Consequently a contract which is obtained by means of such a threat must prima facie be valid, and cannot be impeached on grounds of duress.[199] So an ordinary bona fide compromise is clearly a valid contract even though exacted under threats to bring (or defend) legal proceedings, or to appeal from a judgment already given. Even a threat to bring proceedings where there 7–050

---

[192] *Williams v Bayley* (1866) L.R. 1 H.L. 200; *Windhill Local Board v Vint* (1890) 45 Ch D 351; *Jones v Merionethshire Permanent Benefit Building Society* [1892] 1 Ch. 173; see also Criminal Law Act 1967 s.5(1), (5) and below, paras 16–035—16–037.

[193] *Flower v Sadler* (1882) 10 QBD 572; *Barnes v Richards* (1902) 71 L.J.K.B. 341.

[194] *Jones v Merionethshire Permanent Benefit Building Society* [1892] 1 Ch. 173 but the modern trend seems somewhat against this restricted view: see *R. v Panayiotou* [1973] 1 W.L.R. 1032.

[195] See below, para.16–037; *Keir v Leeman* (1846) 9 Q.B. 371.

[196] *Smith v Cuff* (1817) 6 M. & S. 160; *Davies v London and Provincial Marine Insurance Co* (1878) 8 Ch D 469. The same is generally true of fraud: *Atkinson v Denby* (1862) 7 H. & N. 934; *Shelley v Puddock* [1980] Q.B. 348.

[197] *Keir v Leeman* (1846) 9 Q.B. 371, 395; *Fisher & Co v Apollinaris Co* (1875) L.R. 10 Ch. App. 297; see also Criminal Law Act 1967 s.5(1), (5), and below, paras 16–035—16–037. See also Hudson (1980) 43 M.L.R. 532.

[198] See *R. v Panayiotou* [1973] 1 W.L.R. 1032.

[199] *Powell v Hoyland* (1851) 6 Exch. 67; *Ex p. Hall* (1882) 19 Ch D 580.

is no ground of action in law is prima facie not an unlawful threat, at least where the threat is made bona fide, and is not manifestly frivolous or vexatious.[200] On the other hand, the malicious institution of some forms of legal process or other civil proceedings is, at least in limited circumstances, a tort,[201] and a threat to institute proceedings which would constitute a tort will therefore prima facie constitute a threat to do something unlawful; consequently a contract entered into as a result of such a threat may be voidable on grounds of duress. It is not clear whether a threat to institute civil proceedings which is not unlawful in itself could ever constitute duress for present purposes, if it is coupled (for instance) with a wholly unjustified demand, or if it is made in special circumstances (for instance) in which the defendant has a particular fear of the publicity which may follow from a claim. In principle there seems no reason why such a threat should not amount to duress in appropriate circumstances, but for obvious reasons these are likely to be rare.[202]

(g) *Parties to Duress*

7–051 **By whom suffered.** As we saw earlier, there may be duress to the person when the threat is not to injure the party who makes the promise but a third person.[203] It was at one time said that the duress must be suffered by the party who enters into the contract, so that duress against a principal debtor would be no defence to an action on a bond against a surety.[204] But there is no modern authority to this effect, and it does not seem likely that a surety who gave an indemnity as the result of threats of violence to the principal debtor would be liable.[205] Similarly, if an agent enters into a contract for his principal, from the same fear of the inconvenience which may arise to the principal from the latter being kept in confinement as would affect the mind of the principal himself, such a contract will be voidable on the ground of duress.[206] So, too, duress to a wife will avoid a contract given under its influence by her husband,[207] duress to a child will avoid a contract obtained by means thereof from a parent,[208] and even duress to a more remote relative will suffice if a contract is entered into under its

[200] Decisions upholding the validity of compromises in such cases usually turn on the existence of consideration and have been dealt with above (paras 3–046 et seq.); although the presence of consideration is not conclusive that there is no duress (see above, para.7–019) it seems clear that a bona fide compromise could not be attacked on grounds of duress any more than on grounds of want of consideration.

[201] See, e.g. *Roy v Prior* [1971] A.C. 470.

[202] An example of a threat to take legal proceedings which in the circumstances amounted to improper pressure, and thus actual undue influence, is *Drew v Daniel* [2005] EWCA Civ 507, [2005] 2 F.C.R. 365.

[203] Above, para.7–011.

[204] Roll.Abr. 687, pl. 7; Bacon Abr. *Duress* (B); *Huscombe v Standing* (1607) Cro.Jac. 187. And see Vol.II, para.44–028.

[205] cf. above, para.7–011.

[206] *Cumming v Ince* (1847) 11 Q.B. 112.

[207] *Kaufman v Gerson* [1904] 1 K.B. 591.

[208] *Williams v Bayley* (1866) L.R. 1 H.L. 200.

influence.[209] Threats against the claimant's employees have been held to constitute duress.[210] Duress to a stranger was formerly thought to be ineffective,[211] and would no doubt be exceedingly rare. But if A takes B as a hostage and threatens to shoot him unless C signs a written agreement placed in front of him by A, it does not seem likely that the agreement would be held binding merely because B is a stranger to C. There are old cases holding that a contract made by a person in consideration of the discharge of a third party from illegal arrest is unenforceable as a mere *nudum pactum*.[212] In modern times it is, perhaps, more likely that a court would find consideration in such circumstances (for the promisor would not have made the promise unless he regarded the release of the third party as a benefit to him) but would hold the promise voidable for duress.

Duress exercised by third party. Where it is sought to avoid a contract on the ground of duress exercised, not by the party seeking to enforce the agreement, but by some third person, the party seeking to avoid the contract must prove that the other party knew of the duress,[213] or had constructive notice of it or had procured the making of the contract through the agency of the party who exercised the duress.[214] 7–052

(h) *General Effect of Duress*

Contract under duress is voidable.[215] Despite earlier doubts,[216] it now seems clearly established that a contract entered into under duress is voidable and not void[217]; consequently a person who has entered into a contract under duress may either affirm or avoid such contract after the duress has ceased[218]; and if he 7–053

[209] *Seear v Cohen* (1881) 45 L.T. 589; *Jones v Merionethshire Permanent Benefit Building Society* [1892] 1 Ch. 173.

[210] *Royal Boskalis Westminster NV v Mountain* [1999] Q.B. 674 (threat to use employees as human shield); *Gulf Azov Shipping Co Ltd v Chief Idisi (No.2)* [2001] EWCA Civ 505, [2001] 1 Lloyd's Rep. 727 (detention of ship and crew).

[211] 1 Roll.Abr. 687, pl. 6.

[212] *Smith v Monteith* (1844) 13 M. & W. 427; *Pole v Harrobin* (1782) 9 East. 416n.

[213] *Kesarmal s/o Letchman Das v Valliappa Chettiar (N.K.V.) s/o Nagappa Chettiar* [1954] 1 W.L.R. 380. In the case of a bill of exchange, the onus of proof is shifted by s.30(2) of the Bills of Exchange Act 1882, but this has been held not to apply where the holder seeking to enforce the instrument is the person to whom it was originally delivered and in whose possession it remains: *Talbot v Von Boris* [1911] 1 K.B. 854; *Hasan v Willson* [1977] 1 Lloyd's Rep. 431 (fraud). See also below, para.7–090.

[214] These propositions are based on the cases of misrepresentation and undue influence, see above, paras 6–021 et seq. and below, paras 7–104 et seq.

[215] This paragraph was accepted as stating the law correctly in *Capital Structures Plc v Time & Tide Construction Ltd* [2006] EWHC 591, [2006] B.L.R. 226 at [18]. Acquiescence is presumably also a bar, as it is in cases of misrepresentation and undue influence: see below, para.7–097.

[216] Lanham (1966) 29 M.L.R. 615. In *Barton v Armstrong* [1976] A.C. 104, 120, the majority of the Privy Council spoke of the contract as being void "so far as concerns" the plaintiff, but they were not adverting to this point. Indeed, the analogy with fraud which was relied upon by the majority supports the view stated in the text. See above, para.7–007, fn.35.

[217] See *Lynch v D.P.P. of Northern Ireland* [1975] A.C. 653, 695; *North Ocean Shipping Co Ltd v Hyundai Construction Co Ltd* [1979] Q.B. 705.

[218] *North Ocean Shipping Co Ltd v Hyundai Construction Co Ltd* [1979] Q.B. 705. See also *Pao On v Lau Yiu Long* [1980] A.C. 614.

has voluntarily acted under it with a full knowledge of all the circumstances he may be held bound on the ground of ratification,[219] or if, after escaping from the duress, he takes no steps to set aside the transaction, he may be found to have affirmed it.[220]

7–054 **Counter-restitution of benefits.** In some circumstances a person may not be able to avoid a contract he has entered into under duress unless he is able to restore the benefits he has received under the contract, at least in substantially the same form, or make an adequate monetary allowance. The position is the same as in cases of misrepresentation or undue influence[221]; there are not separate rules for duress at common law and other grounds on which a contract may be avoided in equity.[222] The court will:

> ". . . give . . . relief whenever, by the exercise of its powers, it can do what is practically just, though it cannot restore the parties precisely to the state there were in before the contract."[223]

However, the prime concern is to prevent unjust enrichment of the party who made the threat; that he should not be prejudiced is a secondary consideration and whether counter-restitution in any form will be required will depend on the circumstances of the case.[224] Thus where the agreement was a compromise under which all documents relating to the agreement were to be and had been destroyed, which (if the agreement were avoided) would benefit the party seeking to avoid and prejudice the other parties, it would not necessarily be impossible to avoid the contract for alleged duress even though pecuniary relief could not adequately restore the other parties' position.[225] It is submitted that counter-restitution or at least pecuniary compensation will normally be required where the transaction to be set aside involved an exchange from which the victim obtained some benefit.[226] In contrast, where the promise that it is sought to avoid

---

[219] *Ormes v Beadel* (1860) 2 De G.F. & J. 333.

[220] As in *North Ocean Shipping Co Ltd v Hyundai Construction Ltd* [1979] Q.B. 705, in which this passage was cited. See further below, para.7–097. In *Royal Boskalis Westminster NV v Mountain* [1999] Q.B. 674, 730, Phillips L.J. expressed some difficulty in saying that a contract has been avoided on the grounds of duress if it is governed by a foreign law which would afford no right of avoidance but where the duress was so unconscionable that English law would override the proper law of the contract (see above, para.7–037, fn.135). However, he considered that English law would not recognise the effects of the contract (at 731).

[221] See above, paras 6–115—6–120 and below, paras 7–098—7–103.

[222] *Halpern v Halpern (No.2)* [2007] EWCA Civ 291, [2008] Q.B. 195 at [70]–[73].

[223] *Erlanger v New Sombrero Phosphate Co* (1878) 3 App Cas 1218 at 1279.

[224] *Halpern v Halpern* (No.2) [2007] EWCA Civ 291 at [75]–[76]. For a case of fraudulent misrepresentation in which the judge seems to have taken the view that rescission was no longer possible because it was not possible to return the parties to their original position, see *Crystal Palace FC (2000) Ltd v Dowie* [2007] All E.R. (D) 135 (Jun) at [210]–[218].

[225] *Halpern v Halpern (No.2)* [2007] EWCA Civ 291, [2008] Q.B. 195; reversing [2006] EWHC 1728 (Comm), [2006] 3 All E.R. 1139.

[226] Compare Carnwath L.J.'s example of work being done that was not needed: [2007] EWCA Civ 291 at [74]. It may be that counter-restitution is not required if criminal fraud is used merely as a defence: see above, para.6–109, fn.459. It is possible that the same approach, which seems to be based on the *ex turpi causa* rule (see below, paras 16–164 and 16–168), would be applied in cases of duress were the duress to amount to a crime.

was merely one to pay an additional sum for a benefit already due under an existing contract,[227] there should be no requirement of counter-restitution.[228]

Damages for duress. As previously stated,[229] modern authorities have relied upon the analogy of fraud in adumbrating the law relating to duress. In particular, it now seems clear that a person may affirm a contract which would have been voidable for duress. In these circumstances it may be a matter of some importance to consider whether duress may constitute a tort, like fraud, so that damages may be obtained, either in addition to, or in lieu of, rescission of a contract entered into as a result of the duress. The leading authority on the tort of intimidation (or duress) is *Rookes v Barnard*[230] where the defendants conspired together to threaten to break their contracts of employment with the plaintiff's employer if he did not terminate the plaintiff's contract of employment. They were held liable to the plaintiff on the ground that a threat to break a contract was a sufficient unlawful act for the purpose of the tort of intimidation, at least where the intimidation is of a third party. Since it now appears clear that a threat to break a contract may, in appropriate circumstances, constitute unlawful duress in the law of contract, so that a variation of the contract thereby obtained may be voidable as a matter of contract law, it would seem that the doctrines of duress and intimidation are based on similar principles.[231] (It is, of course, also clear that a threat to commit a crime or a tort may equally constitute both duress in contract law, and intimidation in tort law.) If this is correct, it may be that, even where a person has affirmed a contract which is voidable for duress, damages could still be recovered in tort. In *Universe Tankships of Monrovia v I.T.W.F.*[232] Lords Diplock and Scarman expressed differing views on the point. The question was not considered in *North Ocean Shipping Co Ltd v Hyundai Construction Co Ltd*,[233] even though this case is a firm authority for holding that duress renders a contract voidable and not void. Yet it is arguable that this conclusion makes it all the more necessary to recognise that damages may be recovered for duress; for otherwise (as indeed was held in this case) the plaintiff who has lost his right to avoid will be left without any remedy for a wrongful act. 7–055

---

227 As in, e.g. *North Ocean Shipping Co Ltd v Hyundai Construction Co Ltd* [1979] Q.B. 705, see above para.7–015.

228 See Burrows at p.218.

229 Above, para.7–007.

230 [1964] A.C. 1129.

231 See *Universe Tankships of Monrovia Inc v I.T.W.F.* [1983] 1 A.C. 366, 385, 400. But cf. Lord Reid in *J. T. Stratford & Son Ltd v Lindley* [1965] A.C. 269, 325, where some doubt is thrown on the possible assimilation of two-party duress cases (where A coerces B) with three-party cases (where A coerces B who acts so as to cause loss to C). The reason for Lord Reid's doubts is that in the two-party case, unlike the three-party case, the plaintiff has a choice not to submit to the coercion, but to pursue his legal remedies. But this doubt seems to be disposed of by Lord Scarman's judgment in *Pao On v Lau Yin Long* [1980] A.C. 614 (above, para.7–016), where it is stressed that the question turns on the effectiveness of the remedy which the coerced party has.

232 [1983] A.C. 366, 385, 400. See Carty and Evans [1983] J.B.L. 218, 223–225. In *Dimskal Shipping Co SA v I.T.W.F.* [1992] 2 A.C. 152, Lord Goff followed Lord Diplock's analysis that economic duress is not a tort per se.

233 [1979] Q.B. 705, above, para.7–015.

3. UNDUE INFLUENCE[234]

(a) *Introduction*

7–056 **Equitable doctrine of undue influence.** The equitable doctrine of undue influence is a comprehensive phrase covering cases in which a transaction between two parties who are in a relationship of trust and confidence may be set aside if the transaction is the result of an abuse of the relationship. The transaction may be set aside if the claimant shows that the other party obtained it by abusing the relationship; this, as we shall see, is often termed "actual undue influence", but it is probably better to refer to such cases as ones in which undue influence is actually proved.[235] A transaction may also be set aside in the absence of direct proof if claimant shows the existence of a relationship of trust and confidence with the other party, and that the transaction is one that "calls for explanation".[236] Then it will be presumed that the transaction was the result of undue influence unless the presumption is rebutted. The doctrine extends to cases of coercion, domination, or pressure outside those special relations. As was said by Lord Chelmsford L.C.: "[t]he courts have always been careful not to fetter this useful jurisdiction by defining the exact limits of its exercise".[237] Although most of the cases in which undue influence has been successfully pleaded relate to gifts and guarantees,[238] the same principles apply to purchases at an undervalue or sales at an excessive price.[239] The difference between a gift and a contract that "calls for explanation" is for this purpose only a matter of degree.[240] The rules may also apply to contracts which are not obviously disadvantageous to the complainant at least where undue influence actually is shown.[241]

7–057 **Basis of doctrine.** At common law, the presence of duress was (as has been seen) traditionally justified on the ground that the duress prevented the party constrained from forming a full and independent resolution to contract. In equity, however, the application of the doctrine of undue influence was intended rather to ensure that no person should be allowed to retain the benefit of his own fraud or wrongful act. Cases treated as falling within the doctrine of undue influence included cases of coercion that are now seen as ones of duress, and were treated in the previous section,[242] but the doctrine was much wider than this. The equity view was well expressed in *Allcard v Skinner*[243]:

---

[234] See N. Enonchong, *Duress, Undue Influence and Unconscionable Dealing* (2006), Part II; Chen-Wishart (2006) 59 C.L.P. 231.

[235] See below, para.7–059.

[236] *Royal Bank of Scotland v Etridge (No.2)* [2001] UKHL 44, [2002] 2 A.C. 773 at [10]: see below, para.7–086.

[237] *Tate v Williamson* (1866) L.R. 2 Ch.App. 55, 61. See also Winder (1940) 3 M.L.R. 97; and see *Royal Bank of Scotland v Etridge (No.2)* [2001] UKHL 44, [2002] 2 A.C. 773 at [6].

[238] See below, para.7–105.

[239] *Tufton v Sperni* [1952] 2 T.L.R. 516, 526.

[240] *Wright v Carter* [1903] 1 Ch. 27, 52.

[241] Below, para.7–060.

[242] *Royal Bank of Scotland v Etridge (No.2)* [2001] UKHL 44, [2002] 2 A.C. 773 at [8]; see above, para.7–048.

[243] (1887) 35 Ch D 145, 190.

> "This is not a limitation placed on the action of the donor; it is a fetter placed upon the conscience of the recipient of the gift, and one which arises out of public policy and fair play."

Equity therefore acts on the conscience of the donee, not primarily on want of a true consent on the part of the donor. As a result, the equitable doctrine extends not only to cases of coercion, but to all cases "where influence is acquired and abused, where confidence is reposed and betrayed",[244] and to cases in which there is a danger that there may have been influence but proof of it is likely to be difficult[245]; in the latter type of case undue influence is presumed but the presumption may be rebutted on the facts.[246] But:

> " . . . the question is not whether [the party influenced] knew what she was doing, had done or was proposing to do, but how the intention was produced".[247]

Unconscionable conduct. As we have seen, traditional explanations of undue influence refer to the "conscience of the recipient", and modern cases often use similar phrases. Thus it has been said that "[t]he court of equity . . . sets aside transactions obtained by the exercise of undue influence because such conduct is unconscionable".[248] In a recent House of Lords case, actual undue influence was described as "a species of fraud" and from this was drawn the conclusion that the complainant need not show that she was "manifestly disadvantaged" by the transaction concerned.[249] And in the latest decision of the House of Lords, Lord Nicholls (whose opinion was supported by all their Lordships) referred variously to "the taking of unfair advantage",[250] "misuse" of influence,[251] "abuse of trust and confidence"[252] and a "connotation of impropriety".[253] However, it should be stressed that if there is a requirement that the defendant behaved unconscionably, this may on occasion be satisfied by behaviour that seems relatively innocuous.[254] Actual undue influence may occur not only if the defendant put pressure 7–058

---

[244] *Smith v Kay* (1859) 7 H.L.C. 750, 779.

[245] Lindley L.J. in *Allcard v Skinner* (1887) 35 Ch D 145, 183.

[246] See below, para.7–093.

[247] Lord Eldon L.C. in *Huguenin v Baseley* (1807) 14 Ves. 273, 300.

[248] *Dunbar Bank Plc v Nadeem* [1998] 3 All E.R. 876, 883–884, per Millett L.J. The other members of the court did not consider the question.

[249] Lord Browne-Wilkinson in *CIBC Mortgages Ltd v Pitt* [1994] 1 A.C. 200, 209. See further below, para.7–061. The analogy with fraud may also be relevant to causal issues: see below, para.7–068.

[250] *Royal Bank of Scotland v Etridge (No.2)* [2001] UKHL 44; [2002] 2 A.C. 773 at [8].

[251] [2001] UKHL 44 at [9].

[252] [2001] UKHL 44 at [10].

[253] [2001] UKHL 44 at [32].

[254] This has led for a call for undue influence cases to be re-classified as "plaintiff-sided", the core of the doctrine being that the complainant's dependency led to the impairment of her decision, rather than that the defendant took advantage. See Birks and Chin in Beatson and Friedmann (eds), *Good Faith and Fault in Contract Law* (1995), pp.57–97, who at p.59 cite dicta by the Australian High Court in *Commercial Bank of Australia Ltd v Amadio* (1983) 151 C.L.R. 447, 461, 474 to similar effect. Contrast N. Enonchong, *Duress, Undue Influence and Unconscionable Dealing* (2006), para.7–006; Chen-Wishart (2006) 59 C.L.P. 231.

on the claimant or subjected the claimant to excessive persuasion, but also it seems if the defendant abused the claimant's trust by making a decision for her rather than allowing her to make her own decision.[255] Nor in cases of actual undue influence need the transaction have been obviously disadvantageous to the claimant.[256] In cases of presumed undue influence it has long been accepted that the transaction may be set aside even though it is accepted that the defendant acted with propriety.[257] If there is unconscionability in such a case it must consist either in the defendant seeking to retain the benefit received now that it appears that the claimant did not enter the transaction freely, or perhaps in failing to point out to the claimant that the transaction was not to her advantage and ensuring that she took proper independent advice.[258] In either type of case it is immaterial that the person to whom the gift or promise is made derives no personal benefit from it.[259]

7–059 **Classes of undue influence.** In *Allcard v Skinner* Cotton L.J. classified the cases into two:

> "First, where the court has been satisfied that the gift was the result of influence expressly used by the donee for the purpose; second, where the relations between the donor and donee have at or shortly before the execution of the gift been such as to raise a presumption that the donee had influence over the donor. In such a case the court sets aside the voluntary gift, unless it is proved that in fact the gift was the spontaneous act of the donor acting under circumstances which enabled him to exercise an independent will and which justify the court in holding that the gift was the result of a free exercise of the donor's will. The first class of cases may be considered as depending on the principle that no one shall be allowed to retain any benefit arising from his own fraud or wrongful act. In the second class of cases the court interferes, not on the ground that any wrongful act has in fact been committed by the donee, but on the ground of public policy, and to prevent the relations which existed between the parties and the influence arising therefrom being abused."[260]

---

[255] See below, para.7–065.

[256] See below, para.7–060.

[257] e.g. *Cheese v Thomas* [1994] 1 W.L.R. 173; Chen-Wishart (1994) 110 L.Q.R. 173, 175; *Hammond v Osborn* [2002] EWCA Civ 885; *The Times*, July 18, 2002; Scott [2003] L.M.C.L.Q. 145.

[258] Compare *Hammond v Osborn* [2002] EWCA Civ 885, *The Times*, July 18, 2002, a case of gift in which it was held that the donor had not made an informed judgement. It was accepted that the recipient was not guilty of any reprehensible conduct. It appears that the exercise of undue influence consisted of failing to draw the donor's attention to the size of the gift he was making and to ensure that he obtained independent advice. It has been argued that the approach of the court in this case was inconsistent with the *Etridge* case: Scott [2003] L.M.C.L.Q. 145; but the explanation given in the text above is preferred. See also *Pesticcio v Huet* [2004] EWCA Civ 372, [2004] All E.R. (D) 36 (Apr), also a case of a gift; *Macklin v Dowsett* [2004] EWCA Civ 904, [2004] All E.R. (D) 95 (Jun) at [10]; *Turkey v Awadh* [2005] EWCA Civ 382, [2005] 2 F.C.R. 7 at [11] ("no need to show . . . either misconduct or that the deal was disadvantageous").

[259] *Ellis v Barker* (1871) L.R. 7 Ch. App. 104; *Allcard v Skinner* (1887) 35 Ch D 145; *Bullock v Lloyds Bank Ltd* [1955] Ch. 317. The doctrine is not limited to transactions which are in favour of, or which have been instigated by, the individual on whom reliance has been placed: *Naidoo v Naidu*, *The Times*, November 1, 2000.

[260] (1887) 36 Ch D 145, 171.

In *Barclay's Bank Plc v O'Brien*[261] Lord Browne-Wilkinson adopted a classification previously set out by the Court of Appeal,[262] labelling cases of actual undue influence as Class 1 and of presumed undue influence as Class 2. Class 2 was subdivided into cases in which there is a relationship between the parties such that it is presumed as a matter of law that undue influence had been used (Class 2A) and those in which for the presumption to arise it must be proved on the facts the existence of a relationship under which the complainant generally reposed trust and confidence in the defendant (Class 2B). However, in the subsequent House of Lords case of *Royal Bank of Scotland v Etridge (No.2)*[263] both these classifications and the statements about when a presumption of undue influence will arise were criticised. In particular, it was pointed out that no presumption of undue influence will arise unless the transaction between the parties is one that is not readily explicable by ordinary motives.[264] Further, Lord Hobhouse and Lord Scott criticised the "so-called Class 2B presumption" in particular.[265] And Lord Nicholls, whose opinion was supported by all their Lordships, remarked that the custom of distinguishing between cases of actual undue influence and presumed undue influence "can be confusing".[266] The question is more one of proof. The claimant may prove undue influence directly. Even if he does not do this, if nonetheless he shows that he placed trust and confidence in the other party in relation to the management of his affairs, and that the transaction in question is one that calls for explanation, that "will normally be sufficient, failing satisfactory evidence to the contrary, to discharge the burden of proof" and the transaction will be liable to be set aside.[267] The "presumption" "is descriptive of a shift in the evidential onus on a question of fact".[268]

Manifest disadvantage not essential. In *National Westminster Bank Plc v Morgan* Lord Scarman, giving the only full speech in the House of Lords, stated that relief for undue influence rests "not on some vague 'public policy' but specifically the victimisation of one party by the other".[269] The House, reversing the Court of Appeal,[270] held that the presumption that undue influence was used only arises if the transaction is "manifestly disadvantageous" to the person influenced.[271] Although most of the transactions which have been set aside were 7–060

---

[261] [1994] 1 A.C. 180, 189–190.

[262] In *Bank of Credit and Commerce International SA v Aboody* [1990] 1 Q.B. 923, 953.

[263] [2001] UKHL 44, [2002] 2 A.C. 773.

[264] [2001] UKHL 44 at [22]–[23]; below, para.7–086.

[265] See below, paras 7–079—7–085.

[266] [2001] UKHL 44 at [17].

[267] [2001] UKHL 44 at [14].

[268] [2001] UKHL 44 at [16]. See also the speeches of Lord Clyde (at [92]) and Lord Hobhouse (at [98]).

[269] [1985] A.C. 686, 705.

[270] [1983] 3 All E.R. 85.

[271] [1985] A.C. 686, 704, relying on a Privy Council decision on the Indian Contracts Act, *Poosathurai v Kannappa Chettiar* (1919) L.R. 47 Ind.App. 1. As Nourse L.J. put it in *Goldsworthy v Brickell* [1987] Ch. 378, 401: "... the presumption is not perfected and remains inoperative until the party who has ceded the trust and confidence makes a gift so large, or enters a transaction so improvident, as not to be reasonably accounted for on the ground of friendship, relationship, charity or other ordinary motives on which men act. Although influence might have been presumed beforehand, it is only then that it is presumed to have been undue."

obviously one-sided,[272] this decision seemed to represent a narrowing of the doctrine. For instance, in the Court of Appeal in *National Westminster Bank Ltd v Morgan* there had been some discussion of the position of the client who is induced by his solicitor to sell his house to the solicitor at a fair price but who regrets the sale for other reasons.[273] But as will be explained in the following three paragraphs, subsequent cases show that manifest disadvantage is not a necessary ingredient of any case of undue influence. In cases where undue influence has actually been shown, it has been rejected.[274] In cases in which there is not just a relationship of trust and confidence but a fiduciary relationship, it is not needed.[275] In cases in which the claimant cannot prove undue influence directly, the House of Lords have held that the test of manifest disadvantage should not be applied. Rather, the presumption will only arise if there is the necessary relationship of trust and confidence and " a transaction that cannot be explained by ordinary motives".[276]

7–061 **Undue influence actually proved.** In cases where undue influence has actually been shown,the party influenced is entitled to a remedy without more, unless the right to rescind has been lost[277]; it is not necessary to show that the transaction was manifestly disadvantageous to him or her.[278]

7–062 **Cases of abuse of confidence.** In a case in the Court of Appeal after *Morgan* it was pointed out that even if undue influence would not be a ground for upsetting a transaction that was not manifestly disadvantageous to the claimant, if the parties were in a fiduciary relationship the client might be able to obtain relief on the more limited ground of abuse of confidence.[279] This applies only between solicitor and client, principal and agent, trustee and beneficiary and persons in similar positions.[280] In these cases it is not necessary for the party seeking relief to show that the transaction is manifestly disadvantageous to him.[281] They are:

> " . . . founded on considerations of general public policy, *viz.* that in order to protect those to whom fiduciaries owe duties *as a class* from exploitation by fiduciaries *as a*

[272] As Lord Nicholls put it in *Royal Bank of Scotland v Etridge (No.2)* [2001] UKHL 44, [2002] 2 A.C. 77 at [12]: "[I]n the nature of things, questions of undue influence will not usually arise, and the exercise of undue influence is unlikely to occur, where the transaction is innocuous."

[273] [1983] 3 All E.R. 85, 90.

[274] See next paragraph.

[275] See below, para.7–062.

[276] See below, paras 7–063—7–086 et seq.

[277] See below, para.7–097 et seq.

[278] *CIBC Mortgages Ltd v Pitt* [1994] 1 A.C. 200, overuling *Bank of Credit and Commerce International SA v Aboody* [1990] 1 Q.B. 923 on this point; *Royal Bank of Scotland v Etridge (No.2)* [2001] UKHL 44, [2002] 2 A.C. 773, at [12], [156].

[279] *Bank of Credit & Commerce International SA v Aboody* [1990] 1 Q.B. 923, 943. See *Snell's Principles of Equity*, 31st edn (2005), para.38–26.

[280] [1990] 1 Q.B. 923, 943.

[281] In a leading case Lord Parmoor, delivering the judgment of the Privy Council, said that relief will be given "unless the person claiming to enforce the contract can prove, affirmatively, that the person standing in such a confidential position has disclosed, without reservation, all the information in his possession and can further show that the transaction was, in itself, a fair one": *Demara Bauxite Co Ltd v Hubbard* [1923] A.C. 673, 681–682.

class, the law imposes a heavy duty on fiduciaries to show the righteousness of the transactions."[282]

Abuse of confidence is outside the scope of this chapter.[283]

Cases in which the claimant relies on the presumption. The existence of the cases referred to in the last paragraph, and the fact that the House of Lords in *Morgan* was apparently not referred to them, seems to have led to that decision being the subject of some doubt in the later case of *CIBC Mortgages Plc v Pitt*.[284] (The actual decision in that case was that manifest disadvantage need not be shown in cases of actual undue influence.[285]) Lord Browne-Wilkinson, in a judgment with which the other members of the House agreed, pointed out the difficulty of reconciling *Morgan* with the abuse of confidence cases. He stated that "the exact limits of *Morgan* may have to be examined in the future".[286] But in the *Etridge* case the House of Lords held that the presumption of undue influence does not arise until it has been shown, first, that the complainant reposed trust and confidence in the other party, or the other party acquired ascendancy over the complainant; and secondly, that the transaction is not readily explicable by the relationship of the parties. The House held that the phrase "manifest disadvantage" should be abandoned because it had been misunderstood. Lord Nicholls said that in cases in which a wife had given a guarantee of the debts of her husband's business, in particular, it had sometimes led to the conclusion that such a guarantee was always manifestly disadvantageous because the wife undertakes a serious financial obligation and in return she personally receives nothing. This view was too narrow, and the better test to apply is that stated by Lindley L.J. in *Allcard v Skinner*.[287] Thus for a presumption to arise that undue influence has been exercised, it is not sufficient for the complaining party to show the existence of a confidential relationship. It must also be shown that the transaction cannot, in Lindley L.J.'s words, "reasonably [be] accounted for on the grounds of friendship, relationship, charity or other ordinary motives on which ordinary men act".[288] 7–063

(b) *"Actual" Undue Influence*

Express influence. If there is no special relationship, of the kind to be mentioned below, between the parties, the onus is upon the person seeking to 7–064

---

[282] Lord Browne-Wilkinson in *CIBC Mortgages Plc v Pitt* [1994] 1 A.C. 200, 209.

[283] See N. Enonchong, *Duress, Undue Influence and Unconscionable Dealing* (2006), Ch. 14.

[284] [1994] 1 A.C. 200. See below, para.7–113.

[285] Above, para.7–061.

[286] [1994] 1 A.C. 200. For criticism of the requirement see Capper (1998) 114 L.Q.R. 479, 487 and numerous further comments cited, at fn.44. In *Barclays Bank v Coleman* [2000] 1 All E.R. 385, 400, Nourse L.J., delivering the only full judgment, said that Slade L.J. in the Court of Appeal in *National Westminster Bank Ltd v Morgan* [2000] 1 All E.R. 385, had stated the law as it stood at the time accurately; and that not every transaction in which an unfair advantage is obtained is necessarily manifestly disadvantageous. While in that case the House of Lords had held that manifest disadvantage is required in Classes 2A and 2B, this "may not remain essential indefinitely". For the time being at least this prediction seems to have been inaccurate.

[287] *Royal Bank of Scotland v Etridge (No.2)* [2001] UKHL 44, [2002] 2 A.C. 773, per Lord Nicholls at [21]–[29]. See also the speech of Lord Scott at [156]–[158].

[288] *Allcard v Skinner* (1887) 36 Ch D 145, 185.

avoid the transaction to establish that undue influence was used.[289] This may be done by showing that there was coercion by the donee; these cases are probably now better viewed as cases of illegitimate pressure[290] and, accordingly, they were treated in the previous section. Undue influence may also be shown by proving that the stronger party exercised such a degree of domination or control over the mind of the weaker party that the latter's independence of decision was substantially undermined.[291] In *Bank of Credit and Commerce International SA v Aboody* Slade L.J., delivering the judgment of the Court of Appeal, said:

> "... we think that a person relying on a plea of actual undue influence must show that (a) the other party to the transaction ... had the capacity to influence the complainant; (b) the influence was exercised; (c) its exercise was undue; (d) that its exercise brought about the transaction."[292]

Many of the cases on this point have concerned spiritual "advisers", who have used their expert knowledge of the next world to obtain advantages in this.[293] In *Morley v Loughnan*[294] executors recovered from the defendant large sums of money obtained by him from their testator during the last seven years of his life, on the ground that they had been obtained by undue influence in the guise of religion, it being held unnecessary to decide whether there was a fiduciary or confidential relationship between the defendant and the testator.[295] There have also been cases where an employee obtained complete control over an employer of weak understanding,[296] and where an older man acquired a strong influence over a younger one, inducing him to execute securities for debts contracted by them in their career of mutual dissipation.[297] The transactions were set aside.

7–065 **Independent and informed judgment.** However, "importunity and pressure ... [are] neither always necessary nor sufficient".[298] The critical question is whether the complainant was allowed to exercise an independent and informed judgment. In *Bank of Montreal v Stuart* the wife succeeded in establishing undue influence even though the husband had put no pressure on her because none was

---

289 *Allcard v Skinner* (1887) 36 Ch D 145, 181.

290 Birks and Chin in *Good Faith and Fault in Contract Law*, pp.63–65; Capper (1998) 114 L.Q.R. 479, 484, 493. An example of actual undue influence that seems to have amounted to illegitimate pressure is *Drew v Daniel* [2005] EWCA Civ 507, [2005] 2 F.C.R. 365. Ward L.J. pointed out that in all cases of undue influence, "the critical question is whether or not the influence has invaded the free volition of the donor to accept or reject the persuasion or withstand the influence" (at [36]).

291 *Smith v Kay* (1859) 7 H.L.C. 750; *Bank of Montreal v Stuart* [1911] A.C. 120. See also *Coldunell Ltd v Gallon* [1985] Q.B. 429.

292 [1990] 1 Q.B. 923, 967.

293 *Norton v Relly* (1764) 2 Eden 286; *Nottidge v Prince* (1860) 2 Giff. 246; *Lyon v Home* (1868) L.R. 6 Eq. 655.

294 [1893] 1 Ch. 736.

295 It is such cases that Lord Nicholls may have had in mind when he said that undue influence includes "cases where a vulnerable person has been exploited": *Royal Bank of Scotland v Etridge (No.2)* [2001] UKHL 44, [2002] 2 A.C. 773 at [11].

296 *Bridgeman v Green* (1755) 2 Ves.Sen. 627; *Re Craig* [1971] Ch. 95. Whether there was actual influence depends on the individual involved, not on whether a normal person would be influenced: *Re Brocklehurst's Estate* [1978] Ch. 14, 40.

297 *Smith v Kay* (1859) 7 H.L.C. 750.

298 *Royal Bank of Scotland v Etridge (No.2)* [1998] 4 All E.R. 705, 712. See also *Dunbar Bank Plc v Nadeem* [1998] 3 All E.R. 876, 883.

needed as "she had no will of her own . . . she was ready to sign and do anything he told her to do".[299] In *Bank of Credit and Commerce International SA v Aboody*,[300] the wife trusted her husband in business matters and signed documents he put before her without question. Although there was also evidence that he bullied her and that she signed because she wanted peace, the Court of Appeal did not rely on these; it considered that if the husband had intentionally exploited her trust to get the wife to sign manifestly disadvantageous documents without explaining them to her, that would constitute undue influence.[301] As now in cases where undue influence is actually proved it is not necessary to prove that the transaction was manifestly disadvantageous in order to obtain relief,[302] it seems that a party who is shown to have exploited another's trust to get them to enter transactions without proper consideration or explanation will be held to be exercising undue influence, without more; the influenced party's mind is still "a mere channel through which the will of [the influencing party] operates".[303] As Lord Nicholls put it:

> "In cases of this . . . nature the influence one person has over another provides scope for misuse without any specific acts of persuasion. The relationship between two individuals may be such that, without more, one of them is disposed to agree to a course of action proposed by the other. Typically this occurs when one person places trust in another to look after his affairs and interests, and the latter betrays this trust by preferring his own interests."[304]

There is a close parallel between these cases of "actual" undue influence and cases in which undue influence may be presumed. In each case the capacity to influence the complainant exists because of the trust and confidence that the complainant had in the other party, at least in relation to the transaction in question. The fact that the confidence has been abused may be *presumed* from the fact that the complainant has entered a transaction that is not readily explicable by the relationship of the parties[305]; but if it is shown that the particular transaction was the result of the complainant simply following the other party's suggestions, and the latter did not allow the complainant to exercise his or her

---

[299] [1911] A.C. 120, 136–137. In *Royal Bank of Scotland v Etridge (No.2)* [1998] 4 All E.R. 705, 712, Stuart-Smith L.J. said that this would today be more readily classed as a Class 2B case. If there is a sufficient relationship for Class 2B (below, para.7–079) and also a transaction calling for explanation, it will be in the weaker party's interest to plead the case as Class 2B as it then is up to the other party to rebut the presumption of undue influence; but actual undue influence remains an attractive alternative if there is doubt about the nature of the relationship or the need for an explanation of the transaction.

[300] [1990] 1 Q.B. 923, 967.

[301] The court held that manifest disadvantage was essential to a plea of actual undue influence. As on the facts it did not consider the transactions to be manifestly disadvantageous, it refused relief.

[302] *CIBC Mortgages Plc v Pitt* [1994] 1 A.C. 200, overruling *Bank of Credit & Commerce International SA v Aboody* [1990] 1 Q.B. 923.

[303] *Bank of Credit and Commerce International SA v Aboody* [1990] 1 Q.B. 923, 969, referring to the observations of Jenkins and Morris L.JJ. in *Tufton v Sperni* [1952] 2 T.L.R. 516, 530, 532.

[304] *Royal Bank of Scotland v Etridge (No.2)* [2001] UKHL 44, [2002] 2 A.C. 773 at [9]. See the discussion in *McGregor v Michael Taylor & Co* [2002] 2 Lloyd's Rep. 468, where at [24]–[27] these are described as "trust me" cases.

[305] *McGregor v Michael Taylor & Co* [2002] 2 Lloyd's Rep. 468, at [21]; see further below, para.7–086.

own free and informed judgement, that will amount[306] to actual undue influence.[307] Manifest disadvantage is merely powerful evidence that undue influence has been exercised.[308] It is presumably this similarity which caused Lord Clyde in the *Etridge* case to doubt the utility of distinguishing between actual and presumed undue influence.[309]

7–066 In one sense, "actual" undue influence may be shown more readily when the complainant really did not exercise any choice than when she did so but under pressure:

> "Statements or conduct by a husband which do not pass beyond the bounds of what may be expected of a reasonable husband in the circumstances should not, without more, be castigated as undue influence."[310]

But:

> "... inaccurate explanations of a proposed transaction are a different matter. So are cases where a husband, in whom a wife has reposed trust and confidence for the management of their financial affairs, prefers his interests to hers and makes a choice for them both on that footing. Such a husband abuses the confidence he has. He fails to discharge the obligation of candour and fairness he owes a wife who is looking to him to make the major financial decisions."[311]

7–067 **Disregard of the victim's interests.** The House of Lords has held that in order to show actual undue influence, or rather if undue influence is actually shown to have been exercised,[312] it is not necessary to show that the transaction was "manifestly disadvantageous" or "one that called for an explanation".[313] However, the complainant may have to show that the other party at least "preferred his own interests". This phrase several times formed part of Lord Nicholls' description of 'actual undue influence' in the *Etridge* case.[314] In a case in which the wife simply signed whatever her husband put in front of her, it was said that the husband's influence was not "undue" because the transaction appeared at the time to be to her advantage: the husband was seeking to obtain for her an interest in a property which at the time was worth more than the amount charged, as he "was getting on":

> "The court of equity is a court of conscience. It sets aside transactions obtained by the exercise of undue influence because such conduct is unconscionable."[315]

---

306 Subject perhaps to the point to be discussed in para.7–067.

307 *Royal Bank of Scotland v Etridge (No.2)* [2001] UKHL 44, [2002] 2 A.C. 773 at [17]: "such a plaintiff may succeed even where this presumption was not available to him; for instance where the impugned transaction was not one which called for an explanation."

308 *Royal Bank of Scotland v Etridge (No.2)* [1998] 4 All E.R. 705, 713; cf. [2001] UKHL 44, [2002] 2 A.C. at [104].

309 [2001] UKHL 44 at [92]; and see further below, para.7–080.

310 *Royal Bank of Scotland v Etridge (No.2)* [2001] UKHL 44, [2002] 2 A.C. 773 at [32].

311 [2001] UKHL 44 at [33].

312 See above, para.7–059.

313 *CIBC Mortgages Plc v Pitt* [1994] 1 A.C. 200; *Royal Bank of Scotland v Etridge (No.2)* [2001] UKHL 44, [2002] 2 A.C. 773 at [12], [156].

314 See [2001] UKHL 44, [2002] 2 A.C. 773 at [9] (quoted above, text at fn.304) and [32].

315 *Dunbar Bank Plc v Nadeem* [1998] 3 All E.R. 876, 883–884, per Millett L.J. The other members of the court did not consider the question.

With respect, this interpretation is doubtful. In *CIBC Mortgages Plc v Pitt*[316] Lord Browne-Wilkinson said that actual undue influence was a species of fraud, and the victim is entitled to have the transaction set aside as of right. He continued:

> "No case decided before [*National Westminster Bank Plc v Morgan*][317] was cited (nor am I aware of any) in which a transaction proved to have been obtained by actual undue influence has been upheld nor is there any case in which a court has even considered whether the transaction was, or was not, advantageous."

It is submitted that in the context of parties who trust the other to the extent that they sign without question, the fact that they are deprived of the opportunity to make an independent and informed judgment in itself makes the influence undue. It may be true that the other party was not dishonest in the sense of intending to harm the complainant's interests; but in fraud cases it is no defence that there was no intent to injure; it suffices that the statement was known to be untrue or was made recklessly.[318] A parallel rule appears to apply in cases in which the complainant was deprived of the opportunity to make up his or her own mind as to the risk and benefits involved. The critical case would be one in which the stronger party made the decision without reference to the complainant's wishes, or without giving him full information, when at the time the transaction appeared to be one that was for the complainant's benefit but subsequently it turned out badly for the complainant and he now wishes to set it aside. It is submitted that denying the complainant the chance to decide for himself might amount to actual undue influence.[319]

Causation. As in cases of fraud, the fraud must have induced the contract, so actual undue influence must have influenced the contract.[320] However, the analogies with fraud and duress suggest that the undue influence need only be "a significant reason" for the complainant entering the contract,[321] rather than, for instance, the principal reason. What was less clear until recently was whether, as has been held in some fraud cases,[322] provided that the undue influence had some effect, it does not matter that the complainant would have entered the contract in any event. In *Bank of Credit and Commerce International SA v Aboody*[323] it was said that it would not be appropriate for the court to exercise its jurisdiction to set aside the contract "where the evidence establishes that on the balance of probabilities the complainant would have entered the contract in any event". But in 7–068

[316] [1994] 1 A.C. 200, 209.
[317] [1985] A.C. 686; above, para.7–052.
[318] Above, para.6–046.
[319] Not all commentators share this view. Compare N. Enonchong, *Duress, Undue Influence and Unconscionable Dealing* (2006), paras 9–004—9–007 (wrong-doing required, though not proof of any specific act); Chen-Wishart (2006) 59 C.L.P. 231, 265 ("an improvident outcome is practically indispensible even in class I coercion cases"; "substantive unfairness is of the essence of undue influence").
[320] See above, para.6–032.
[321] See above, paras 6–034 and 7–025.
[322] See above, paras 6–035 and 7–025.
[323] [1990] 1 Q.B. 923, 971.

UCB Corporate Services Ltd v Williams[324] the Court of Appeal held that, as undue influence is a species of fraud, it is no answer that the person influenced would have entered the transaction anyway: it is the fact that she has been deprived of the opportunity to make a free choice that founds her equity to set aside the transaction. The proposition in *Aboody's* case was said to be:

> "... flatly inconsistent with Lord Browne-Wilkinson's statement of principle[325] ... that a victim of undue influence is entitled to have the transaction set aside 'as of right'. The words 'as of right' seem ... to admit of only one meaning; *viz.*, regardless of other considerations."[326]

Presumably it would follow also that the same presumption applies as in fraud, so that it will be for the stronger party to show that the undue influence had no impact at all on the complainant's decision.[327]

(c) *Presumed Undue Influence*

7–069 **Presumption of influence from certain relationships.** If the parties were at the time of the transaction in one of certain types of relationship with each other, it is presumed that one party had influence over the other; and if it is shown that a transaction between them was one "not readily explicable by the relationship" between them, it will be presumed (or inferred)[328] that the transaction was the result of an abuse of the influence, unless the presumption is rebutted.[329] It is not necessary for the complainant to "prove that he actually reposed trust and confidence in the other party",[330] or that the other party dominated the relationship. These are the cases that Lord Browne-Wilkinson in *Barclays Bank Plc v O'Brien*[331] referred to as "Class 2A cases".[332] Once the transaction has been shown to be one requiring explanation, the onus is on the party taking the benefit to justify that it was free from undue influence.

7–070 **Relationship of influence shown on facts.** Outside the recognised relationships, if the plaintiff proves that at the time of the transaction "requiring explanation", a confidential relationship in fact existed between the parties, the presumption of undue influence will arise.[333] That at least has been the traditional view. These are the cases labelled by Lord Browne-Wilkinson as "Class 2B".[334]

---

[324] [2002] EWCA Civ 555 at [86].

[325] *CIBC Mortgages Plc v Pitt* [1994] 1 A.C. 200, 209.

[326] [2002] EWCA Civ 555 at [91].

[327] This is the rule suggested by the statement in *Bank of Credit and Commerce International SA v Aboody* [1990] 1 Q.B. 923, 971, see this paragraph, fn.323. For the rule in fraud cases see above, para.6–035.

[328] See below, para.7–072.

[329] *Allcard v Skinner* (1887) 36 Ch D 145, 181; *Royal Bank of Scotland v Etridge (No.2)* [2001] UKHL 44, [2002] 2 A.C. 773 at [18].

[330] *Royal Bank of Scotland v Etridge (No.2)* [2001] UKHL 44, [2002] 2 A.C. 773 at [18].

[331] [1994] 1 A.C. 180.

[332] See above, para.7–059.

[333] *Tufton v Sperni* [1952] 2 T.L.R. 516, 522; *Lloyds Bank Ltd v Bundy* [1975] Q.B. 326.

[334] In *Barclays Bank Plc v O'Brien* [1994] 1 A.C. 180: see above, para.7–059.

But the decision of the House of Lords in *Etridge*[335] has cast light on the existence of this class as a separate category. This is explored below.[336]

(i) *Relationships Giving Rise to Presumption of Influence*

Presumption of influence. Certain types of relationship give rise to a presumption that one party had influence over the other. This does not by itself give rise to a presumption that undue influence has been used by the stronger party, but if there is a transaction between the parties that cannot, in the words of Lindley L.J. in *Allcard v Skinner*,[337] "reasonably [be] accounted for on the grounds of friendship, relationship, charity or other ordinary motives on which ordinary men act,"[338] then a presumption does arise. Unless the stronger party raises sufficient doubt to rebut the presumption, the transaction will be set aside. 7–071

Nature of presumptions. It will be seen that in this class of case there may be two separate presumptions. The first arises from the nature of the relationship. It is simply a presumption that one party had influence over the other, and it is said to be "irrebuttable".[339] It is not, however, a presumption that undue influence has been exercised and it is not sufficient for the transaction to be set aside, even if the stronger party offers no evidence. A presumption or inference that there was undue influence arises, as we have just seen, only when there is a transaction that "calls for explanation".[340] This second presumption is not only rebuttable but was said in *Etridge*'s case to be merely an "evidential presumption".[341] This appears to mean that if the stronger party gives evidence that, on the balance of probabilities, means that there is doubt whether the transaction did result from undue influence, the weaker party will succeed only if he or she can show, again on the balance of probabilities, that it was: the overall burden remains on the party seeking to set aside the transaction.[342] 7–072

Dominating influence unnecessary. Despite the fact that in *Morgan* Lord Scarman had referred to a "dominating influence",[343] in cases of presumed undue influence it is immaterial whether one party has acquired a dominating influence over the mind of the other party[344]: 7–073

[335] *Royal Bank of Scotland v Etridge (No.2)* [2001] UKHL 44, [2002] 2 A.C. 773.

[336] See below, para.7–080.

[337] (1887) 36 Ch D 145, 185.

[338] This test is to be used instead of asking whether the transaction was "manifestly disadvantageous" to the weaker party: above, para.7–060.

[339] per Lord Nicholls in *Royal Bank of Scotland v Etridge (No.2)* [2001] UKHL 44, [2002] 2 A.C. 773 at [18]; but see Lord Clyde at [93].

[340] [2001] UKHL 44, [2002] 2 A.C. 773 at [14]; above, para.7–060.

[341] [2001] UKHL 44, [2002] 2 A.C. 773 at [16], [93] (semble), [104] and [153].

[342] Compare a legal presumption under which the burden of proof would shift to the stronger party to prove on the balance of probabilities that there was no undue influence. Before *Etridge* [2001] UKHL 44 there seems to have been little discussion of the exact nature of the presumption in undue influence cases. See further below, para.7–086.

[343] *National Westminster Bank Ltd v Morgan* [1985] A.C. 686, 707.

[344] *Lloyds Bank Ltd v Bundy* [1975] Q.B. 326.

"It is enough to show that the party in whom the trust and confidence is reposed is in a position to exert influence over him who reposes it."[345]

These cases depend:

". . . on the concept that once the special relationship has been shown to exist, no benefit can be retained from the transaction unless it has been positively established that the duty of fiduciary care has been entirely fulfilled."[346]

7–074 **Parent and child.** In the earliest cases in which benefits conferred by children upon their parents were set aside, the relief seems to have been extended on the ground of actual fraud.[347] Now, however, it is well established that the child reposes trust and confidence in the parent,[348] even though the child may have attained his majority not long before.[349] If a gift is made to a parent shortly after the child reaches the age of majority, the parent will be required to show that the child was acting independently of his influence.[350] This presumption can continue even after marriage,[351] although the duration of the presumption is a question of fact and degree in the circumstances of each particular case. Family arrangements, however, are treated more leniently:

"Transactions between parent and child may proceed upon arrangements between them for the settlement of property, and of their rights in property in which they are interested. In such cases the court regards the transactions with favour."[352]

But even so, if the parent gets a disproportionate advantage, the arrangement is likely to be set aside.[353] As between an adult child and elderly or senile parents, no presumption arises, but it may be possible to establish a case of undue influence on the facts.[354]

7–075 **Guardian and ward.** The presumption also applies to dealings between guardian and ward,[355] and the fact that the guardianship has legally terminated will not necessarily mean that the influence ceases, provided that there is still some control over the ward's property or actions.[356] Persons *in loco parentis* are

---

[345] *Goldsworthy v Brickell* [1987] Ch. 378, 404.

[346] *Lloyds Bank Ltd v Bundy* [1975] Q.B. 326 per Sir Eric Sachs at 346.

[347] *Glissen v Ogden* (1731) 2 Atk. 258; *Young v Peachy* (1741) 2 Atk. 254; *Cocking v Pratt* (1749) 1 Ves. Sen. 400.

[348] *Wright v Vanderplank* (1855) 2 K. & J. 1.

[349] *Archer v Hudson* (1844) 7 Beav. 551; *Berdoe v Dawson* (1865) 34 Beav. 603; *Powell v Powell* [1900] 1 Ch. 243; *London and Westminster Loan & Discount Ltd v Bilton* (1911) 27 T.L.R. 184.

[350] *Bainbrigge v Browne* (1881) 18 Ch D 188; *Bullock v Lloyds Bank Ltd* [1955] Ch. 317; *Re Pauling's Settlement Trusts* [1964] Ch. 303, 336.

[351] *Lancashire Loans Ltd v Black* [1934] 1 K.B. 380.

[352] *Baker v Bradley* (1855) 7 De G.M. & G. 597, 620; *Hartopp v Hartopp* (1855) 21 Beav. 259; *Jenner v Jenner* (1860) 2 De G.F. & J. 359; *Hoblyn v Hoblyn* (1889) 41 Ch D 200. cf. *Bullock v Lloyds Bank Ltd* [1955] Ch. 317.

[353] *Hoghton v Hoghton* (1852) 15 Beav. 278; *Turner v Collins* (1871) L.R. 7 Ch. App. 329.

[354] *Avon Finance Co Ltd v Bridger* [1985] 2 All E.R. 281. A very full survey of the doctrine of undue influence as applied to the elderly will be found in Burns (2003) 23 Legal Studies 251.

[355] *Hylton v Hylton* (1754) 2 Ves.Sen. 547; *Taylor v Johnston* (1882) 19 Ch D 603.

[356] *Hatch v Hatch* (1804) 9 Ves. 292.

also subject to the same surveillance by the court, such as uncle and niece,[357] stepfather and stepdaughter,[358] stepmother and stepdaughter,[359] elder and younger brother,[360] and even an executor and beneficiary,[361] where the relationship confers a power analogous to that of parental control.

Solicitor and client. Any gift or sale by a client to his solicitor will be regarded with considerable suspicion by the court.[362] The relationship between solicitor and client is not only sufficient to raise a presumption of undue influence should the client enter a manifestly disadvantageous transaction with the solicitor; as mentioned earlier, the solicitor is subject to the stricter regime of abuse of confidence.[363] The solicitor must show the utmost good faith in his dealings with his client,[364] and must not make any benefit for himself at his client's expense.[365] Even if the benefit is an indirect one, as where a gift is made to the solicitor's wife[366] or son,[367] and even if the relationship of solicitor and client has technically ceased,[368] the presumption will apply where the influence still continues between them.[369] 7–076

Other instances possibly within Class 2(A). The presumption applies to certain transactions between fiancé and fiancée.[370] It also applies to the relationship of medical man and patient,[371] trustee and cestui que trust,[372] and to a religious adviser and a person to whom he gives advice.[373] 7–077

---

[357] *Archer v Hudson* (1844) 7 Beav. 551.

[358] *Kempson v Ashbee* (1874) L.R. 10 Ch. App. 15.

[359] *Powell v Powell* [1900] 1 Ch. 243.

[360] *Sercombe v Sanders* (1865) 34 Beav. 382; cf. *Glover v Glover* [1951] 1 D.L.R. 657.

[361] *Grosvenor v Sherratt* (1860) 28 Beav. 659.

[362] For the analogous principles governing testamentary dispositions to solicitors, see *Wintle v Nye* [1959] 1 W.L.R. 284.

[363] Above, para.7–062.

[364] See above, paras 6–079—6–080; *Moody v Cox and Hatt* [1917] 2 Ch. 71.

[365] *Turrell v Bank of London* (1862) 10 H.L.C. 26; *Wright v Carter* [1903] 1 Ch. 27.

[366] *Liles v Terry* [1895] 2 Q.B. 679.

[367] *Barron v Willis* [1902] A.C. 271.

[368] *Demerara Bauxite Co Ltd v Hubbard* [1923] A.C. 673; *McMaster v Byrne* [1952] 1 All E.R. 1362.

[369] In *Markham v Karsten* [2007] EWHC 1509 (Ch), [2007] All E.R. (D) 377 it was said that the relationship of solicitor and client between two parties to a transaction should not be irrelevant merely because they were also in another well-recognised relationship in which influence, or the reposing of trust and confidence, might arise. On the contrary, the influence which was presumed to exist between solicitor and client might be strengthened if they were also in a marriage or domestic partner relationship. Nor was it correct to confine the presumption of influence, as between solicitor and client, to transactions of a legal rather than domestic nature. See at [35]–[36].

[370] *Cobbett v Brock* (1855) 20 Beav. 524; *Lovesy v Smith* (1880) 15 Ch D 655; *Re Lloyds Bank Ltd* [1931] 1 Ch. 289. Contrast *Zamet v Hyman* [1961] 1 W.L.R. 1442. Gifts between engaged couples may now also be set aside, if the marriage does not take place, under the Law Reform (Miscellaneous Provisions) Act 1970.

[371] *Mitchell v Homfray* (1881) 8 QBD 587; *Radcliffe v Price* (1902) 18 T.L.R. 466.

[372] *Ellis v Barker* (1871) L.R. 7 Ch. App. 104; *Beningfield v Baxter* (1866) 12 App. Cas. 167.

[373] *Huguenin v Baseley* (1807) 14 Ves. 273; *Lyon v Home* (1868) L.R. 6 Eq. 655; *Allcard v Skinner* (1887) 36 Ch D 145. It has been rightly pointed out that it is dangerous to assume that every relationship of this type, or of the other types just listed, will give rise to the presumption, as the relationship between the parties may not be confidential: Cartwright, *Unequal Bargaining* (1991), p.178.

7–078 **Value of the presumption.** In *Etridge*, Lord Nicholls stated that, in the relationships listed above, "the law presumes, irrebuttably, that one party had influence over the other".[374] Of course it does not follow that any transaction between parties in such a relationship will be set aside, even if it is not "readily explicable by the relationship between the parties".[375] The ascendant party may be able to rebut the presumption that he or she used undue influence.[376] But further, it is clear from the preceding paragraphs that it is not always possible to state with certainty when there will be a presumption of influence. Lord Clyde disputed "the utility of the further sophistication of sub-dividing 'presumed undue influence' into further categories".[377] Lord Nicholls further endorsed Treitel's view that the question is whether one party has reposed sufficient trust and confidence in the other, rather than whether the relationship between the parties belongs to a particular type, without apparently noting that Treitel was referring only to what used to be called "Class 2B" cases.[378] These statements might be taken as hints that in future the courts will abandon altogether the separate category of "presumed influence" and simply ask in each case whether the relationship was one of trust and confidence or of domination.

(ii) *Confidential Relationship shown on Facts in earlier Decisions*

7–079 **Confidential relationship shown on facts.** As stated earlier, an inference of undue influence may also arise if on the facts it is shown that the parties were in a confidential relationship although one would not be presumed to exist as a matter of law, and that the parties have entered a transaction that is "not otherwise readily explicable".[379] The cases in this section treated this as a separate category of presumed undue influence. In the light of the opinions expressed by the House of Lords in the *Etridge* case[380] this analysis may no longer be correct. It seems that these cases must now be viewed simply as instances of the kind of evidence that, combined with a transaction "not readily explicable by the relationship of the parties", may be sufficient to raise an inference that the transaction was procured by undue influence and, unless the other party displaces this inference, should be set aside.

7–080 **Confidential relationship shown on facts: a separate class?** In *Barclays Bank Plc v O'Brien*[381] Lord Browne-Wilkinson had said that in this type of case:

> " . . . if the complainant proves the de facto existence of a relationship under which the complainant generally reposed trust and confidence in the wrongdoer, the existence of such relationship raises the presumption of undue influence. In a Class 2(B) case therefore, in the absence of evidence disproving due influence, the complainant will

[374] *Royal Bank of Scotland v Etridge (No.2)* [2001] UKHL 44, [2002] 2 A.C. 773 at [18].
[375] [2001] UKHL 44 at [21].
[376] See above, para.7–059 and below, para.7–093.
[377] *Royal Bank of Scotland v Etridge (No.2)* [2001] UKHL 44, [2002] 2 A.C. 773 at [92].
[378] [2001] UKHL 44 at [10], referring to Treitel, *The Law of Contract*, 10th edn (1999), pp.380–381.
[379] The cases at one time referred to as falling within Class 2(B): see above, para.7–059.
[380] See above, para.7–059.
[381] [1994] 1 A.C. 180, at 189–190.

succeed in setting aside the impugned transaction merely by proof that the complainant reposed trust and confidence in the wrongdoer without having to prove that the wrongdoer exerted actual undue influence or otherwise abused such trust and confidence in relation to the particular transaction impugned."

In *Etridge* Lord Hobhouse said that it was difficult to apply this statement literally. First, it would seem to treat the husband as a " 'wrongdoer' without saying why when it is expressly postulated that no wrongdoing may have occurred".[382] This seems to refer to the point that the presumption of undue influence (which now requires a transaction not explicable by ordinary motives) is no more than a way of proving that undue influence did occur.[383] Secondly, Lord Hobhouse remarked that Lord Browne-Wilkinson referred to the complainant reposing trust and confidence *generally*, whereas a wife:

" . . . may be happy to trust her husband to make the right decision in relation to some matters but not others; she may leave a particular decision to him but not other decisions."[384]

He considered, and understood the other members of the court to agree, that "the so-called Class 2B presumption should not be adopted". The wife must prove her case by showing that she was the victim of an equitable wrong. This wrong may be an overt wrong, such as oppression; or it may be the failure to perform an equitable duty, such as a failure by one in whom trust and confidence is reposed not to abuse that trust by failing to deal fairly with her and have proper regard to her interests. She may discharge the burden of proof that rests on her by establishing a sufficient prima facie case to justify a decision in her favour on the balance of probabilities, the court drawing appropriate inferences from the primary facts proved.[385] Lord Scott spoke in rather similar terms[386]; and what Lord Hobhouse said was consistent with the remarks of Lord Clyde.[387] It does not seem inconsistent with what was said by Lord Nicholls,[388] who endorsed Treitel's view that the question is whether one party has reposed sufficient trust and confidence in the other, rather than whether the relationship between the parties belongs to a particular type.[389]

Thus it seems that cases in which a presumption of undue influence may arise because of the combination of a confidential relationship shown on the facts and a transaction not explicable otherwise should no longer be regarded as a separate category. Those facts are merely ways of proving that undue influence was used. Thus for a wife to able to have a transaction between her and her husband set aside, she will have to show, for example, that her husband took "unfair 7–081

[382] *Royal Bank of Scotland v Etridge (No.2)* [2001] UKHL 44, [2002] 2 A.C. 773 at [105].
[383] See above, para.7–069.
[384] [2001] UKHL 44, [2002] 2 A.C. 773 at [105].
[385] [2001] UKHL 44 at [107].
[386] [2001] UKHL 44 at [158]–[162].
[387] [2001] UKHL 44 at [92].
[388] In particular, [2001] UKHL 44 at [19].
[389] [2001] UKHL 44 at [10], referring to Treitel, *The Law of Contract*, 10th edn (1999) pp.380–381.

advantage of his influence . . . or her confidence in him".[390] This is not quite the same as what is required for a case of "actual" undue influence: that would need direct proof that he exerted undue pressure or took advantage of her confidence. But the dividing line is thin. If, for example, a wife shows that in respect a class of transactions including the particular transaction in question, she did not question her husband's decision in any way and simply signed what he put in front of her, she has established a case of actual undue influence, at least if she also shows that he preferred his own interests to hers.[391] She need not show "manifest disadvantage" or, in the phrase now preferred, that the transaction was not readily explicable by their relationship.[392] In such a case, what is the relevance of the transaction being disadvantageous to her? It seems that showing that the transaction was one that "calls for an explanation"[393] is no more than a piece of evidence that may be used to show that her husband did indeed abuse her trust when the evidence would otherwise fall short. The cases in what was formerly termed Class 2B must now be taken merely as examples of the kind of circumstances in which a combination of the nature of the relationship and the resulting transaction may provide sufficient evidence of undue influence for the complainant to succeed unless the other party can somehow rebut the evidential inference. It may be that in practice, however, any change as the result of the dicta in *Etridge*'s case is more formal than real. If the party shows that she placed trust and confidence in the other in relation to the relevant transaction, and that the transaction was obviously not in her interest, it seems that she will succeed unless the other can rebut the inference of undue influence, in much the same way as previously she would have benefited from a presumption that the other would have to rebut.

7–082 **Relationships that may be confidential.** The relevant type of confidential relationship may arise in "all the variety of relations, in which dominion is exercised by one person over another",[394] or where the complaint proves that he or she reposed trust and confidence in the wrongdoer. The classic statement is that of Lord Chelmsford in *Tate v Williamson*[395]:

> "Wherever two persons stand in such a relation that, while it continues, confidence is necessarily reposed by one, and the influence which naturally grows out of that confidence is possessed by the other, and this confidence is abused, or the influence is exerted to obtain an advantage at the expense of the confiding party, the person so availing himself of his position will not be permitted to retain the advantage, although the transaction could not have been impeached if no such confidential relationship existed."

Nevertheless, the "presumption" of undue influence does not arise merely because the relationship between the parties can be described as fiduciary (as, for

---

[390] [2001] UKHL 44 at [19].
[391] See above, para.7–067.
[392] See above, para.7–060.
[393] *Etridge's* case [2001] UKHL 44, Lord Nicholls at [17].
[394] *Huguenin v Baseley* (1807) 14 Ves. 273, 286, per Sir S. Romilly *arguendo*; *Smith v Kay* (1859) 7 H.L.C. 750, 779; *Lloyds Bank Ltd v Bundy* [1975] Q.B. 326.
[395] (1866) L.R. 2 Ch. App. 55, 61.

instance, that of principal and agent). It arises only where the fiduciary relationship is of a particular kind which, in the opinion of equity judges, is such as to raise the presumption.[396] For example, the relationship of bank manager and customer is not normally a confidential one in the relevant sense[397]; but when an elderly farmer, without consulting his solicitor, charged his property to his bank by way of guarantee of the debts of his son's company, and it was obvious that he was relying upon the bank manager for advice, a confidential relationship arose. As the manager neither explained the company's position fully nor suggested that the farmer get independent advice, the charge was set aside.[398]

Relationship may arise from transaction. It has been held that a confidential relationship may arise from the circumstances of the very transaction in question, e.g. if the defendant has advised and assisted the claimant over it and the claimant has relied on the defendant for that.[399] 7–083

Examples. The existence of a relationship of trust and confidence may be inferred from the fact that one party has entered an excessively onerous transaction at the request of the other (in the case in question, a junior employee with no stake in the business had at her employer's request given a second charge over her flat and an unlimited all monies guarantee of the employer's business debts).[400] But in such an extreme case the plaintiff may be able to set aside the transaction on the basis of unconscionability.[401] So, too, where a young man in financial difficulties sought the advice of a more experienced relative, who himself purchased the young man's property at a third of its proper price,[402] where a young woman granted a mining lease to her uncle and to the son of her father's executor, being advised to do so by the executor in whom she placed "the greatest confidence",[403] and where a member of a committee set up to establish a Moslem cultural centre in London was induced by a fellow member to buy the latter's house from him for the purpose at a price which greatly exceeded its market value,[404] the transactions were set aside on the ground that the defendants had failed to rebut the presumption of undue influence. 7–084

---

[396] *Smith v Kay* (1859) 7 H.L.C. 750, 771; *Re Coomber* [1911] Ch. 723.

[397] *National Westminster Bank Plc v Morgan* [1985] A.C. 686. If a bank takes it upon itself to explain the nature or effect of a guarantee to a customer, it will be liable for negligently misstating that nature or effect; and it was suggested that in some circumstances a bank might be under a duty to explain the nature of a guarantee to a guarantor before it is executed: *Cornish v Midland Bank Plc* [1985] 3 All E.R. 513.

[398] *Lloyds Bank Ltd v Bundy* [1975] Q.B. 326. See also *Re Craig* [1971] Ch. 95; *Horry v Tate & Lyle* [1982] 2 Lloyds Rep. 416.

[399] *Turkey v Awadh* [2005] EWCA Civ 382, [2005] 2 F.C.R. 7, referring to *Macklin v Dowsett* [2004] EWCA Civ 904, [2004] All E.R. (D) 95 (Jun). In that case the defendant, who was impecunious, had made an arrangement to give up his rights to land for a small sum unless he completed building a bungalow on the land within three years, which he was very unlikely to be able to do.

[400] *Crédit Lyonnais Bank Nederland NV v Burch* [1997] 1 All E.R. 144, especially at 154 and 158. See Chen-Wishart [1997] C.L.J. 60, 65–66.

[401] See below, para.7–128.

[402] *Tate v Williamson* (1866) L.R. 2 Ch. App. 55.

[403] *Grosvenor v Sherratt* (1860) 28 Beav. 659.

[404] *Tufton v Sperni* [1952] 2 T.L.R. 516.

7–085 **Husband and wife.** The presumption of influence does not apply between husband and wife.[405] In *Barclays Bank Plc v O'Brien*[406] the House of Lords recognised "a special tenderness of treatment afforded to wives" because in many cases:

> "... the wife demonstrates that she placed trust and confidence in her husband in relation to her financial affairs[407] and therefore raises a presumption of undue influence"

and because "sexual and emotional ties . . . provide a ready weapon for undue influence".[408] In contrast, in *Etridge*'s case the Members of the House were at some pains to emphasise that the courts should not be too ready to find undue influence as between husband and wife. Lord Nicholls said that:

> ". . . statements or conduct by a husband which do not pass beyond the bounds of what may be expected of a reasonable husband in the circumstances should not, without more, be castigated as undue influence."[409]

Lord Scott said that in the surety wife cases, that while there are cases in which the husband abused his wife's confidence in him, for example by over-estimating his prospects, misrepresenting his intentions or subjecting her to excessive pressure, "it should . . . be recognised that undue influence, though a possible explanation for the wife's agreement to become a surety, is a relatively unlikely one".[410]

(iii) *A Transaction not Explicable by Ordinary Motives*

7–086 **Transaction not explicable by ordinary motives.** As explained earlier, it is not sufficient in order to raise or inference that undue influence has been used that the parties were in the type of relationship in which influence of one over the other is presumed. It must also be shown that the transaction in question was, in the words of Lindley L.J. in *Allcard v Skinner*:

> "... not reasonably to be accounted for on the grounds of friendship, relationship, charity or other ordinary motives on which ordinary men act."[411]

This need not be shown if undue influence may be proved in other ways,[412] but in all cases in which there is no direct proof, the combination of a relationship in

[405] *Hoes v Bishop* [1909] 2 K.B. 390. See also *Grigby v Cox* (1750) 1 Ves.Sen. 517; *Nedby v Nedby* (1852) 5 De G. & Sm. 377; *Barron v Willis* [1899] 2 Ch. 578, 585; *Mackenzie v Royal Bank of Canada* [1934] A.C. 468; *Midland Bank Plc v Shephard* [1988] 3 All E.R. 17. But cf. *Cresswell v Potter* [1978] 1 W.L.R. 255n. and *Backhouse v Backhouse* [1978] 1 W.L.R. 243, below, para.7–128.

[406] [1994] 1 A.C. 180.

[407] Compare *Society of Lloyd's v Khan* [1998] 3 F.C.R. 93.

[408] *Barclays Bank Plc v O'Brien* [1994] 1 A.C. 180, 190. In *Barclays Bank Plc v Rivett* (1997) 29 H.L.R. 893 it was the wife who had influence over the husband.

[409] [2001] UKHL 44 at [32].

[410] [2001] UKHL 44 at [160]–[162].

[411] (1887) 36 Ch D 145, 185.

[412] *Etridge's* case [2001] UKHL 44, Lord Nicholls at [17]; above, para.7–059.

which influence exists and a transaction that "that cannot be explained by ordinary motives"[413] seems now to be taken as evidence that undue influence was used, and it will be sufficient to move the evidential burden of disproving undue influence to the other party.

Manifest disadvantage not the test. In *Etridge*[414] the House of Lords said that the "manifest disadvantage" test should be abandoned in favour of the test stated in the previous paragraph. The point seems to be that a transaction that is clearly disadvantageous to the complainant may not "call for an explanation". Thus even if the parties are in a confidential relationship, the fact that the weaker party has made a gift of moderate size to the other will not raise any presumption that undue influence was used.[415] More importantly, as between husband and wife, even a transaction that is in a narrow sense disadvantageous to the wife, such as a guarantee of her husband's business debts, will not necessarily raise the presumption: it may be explicable in terms of their relationship. In other words the question is not simply, was the transaction disadvantageous to the complainant but was it one that, given their relationship, "calls for explanation".[416] Moreover: 7–087

> ". . . the weight of the presumption will vary from case to case and will depend both on the nature of the relationship and on the particular nature of the impugned transaction."[417]

"Only explicable on the basis that undue influence has been used"? In *Mortgage Agency Services Number Two Ltd v Chater* the court said: 7–088

> "In our judgment the correct legal test is that set out by Lord Nicholls at paragraph [14] in *Etridge* . . . . In so far as the passage cited from Lord Scarman's speech in *Morgan* suggests a higher test, we prefer the reformulated test given by Lord Nicholls. We detect a possible distinction between a transaction explicable *only* on the basis that undue influence had been exercised to procure it (Lord Scarman) and one which called for an explanation, which if not given would enable the court to infer that it could only have been procured by undue influence (Lord Nicholls)."[418]

However in *Turkey v Awadh*,[419] in which *Mortgage Agency Services Number Two Ltd v Chater* does not appear to have been cited, the Court of Appeal held that a presumption of undue influence does not arise merely because the transaction called for an explanation. It must be one that cannot be explained by ordinary motives (as had been said by Lord Scott in *Etridge*'s case[420]); or, as the trial judge (Judge Cooke Q.C.) had put it:

---

[413] See below, para.7–088.
[414] [2001] UKHL 44, [2002] 2 A.C. 773 at [29], [156].
[415] See *Etridge's* case [2001] UKHL 44, [2002] 2 A.C. 773 at [24], [104], [156].
[416] [2001] UKHL 44 at [30], [158]. See further below, para.7–089.
[417] [2001] UKHL 44 per Lord Scott at [153]. On what is required to rebut the presumption see further below, para.7–093. A confidentiality clause signed by a soldier does not call for explanation: *R. v Att-Gen for England and Wales* [2003] UKPC 22.
[418] [2003] EWCA Civ 490 at [30].
[419] [2005] EWCA Civ 382, [2005] 2 F.C.R. 7.
[420] [2001] UKHL 44 at [220].

> " . . . whether, given the circumstances and the nature of the transaction, it says to the unbiased observer that absent explanation it must represent the beneficiary taking advantage of his position."[421]

The transaction must be looked at in its context and to see what its general nature was and what it was trying to achieve for the parties.[422] The judge's decision that, although neither party had given thought to the value of the property, the transaction was otherwise explicable by the circumstances (the transaction had family elements) was upheld. The difference between the two approaches seems to be that, according to the first case, providing the explanation for the transaction is part of the process by which the presumption is rebutted; whereas following the approach in *Turkey v Awadh*, if there is an explanation, no presumption arises in the first place. This would mean that the complainant, in order to show that there is a "transaction not explicable by ordinary motives" would have to show that it was not so explicable even in the circumstances of the case, for example, even though the complainant might be expected to want to provide for his family. This appears to be what Lord Nicholls intended, for in discussing the position as between husband and wife[423] he says that a guarantee of the husband's business debts is not:

> " . . . in the ordinary course . . . to be regarded as a transaction which, failing proof to the contrary, is explicable only on the basis that it has been procured by the exercise of undue influence by the husband."[424]

7–089 **What may be expected as between husband and wife.** As between husband and wife, it seems that with the change from requiring "manifest disadvantage" to that treating a transaction that is "not readily explicable by their relationship" as evidence that, combined with other evidence of undue influence, may suffice to raise an evidentiary presumption, may have been accompanied by a change of attitude towards what will satisfy this criterion. Earlier cases had suggested that a charge executed by a wife to secure her husband's business debts would be manifestly disadvantageous, even though she would benefit if the business were to thrive.[425] In *Etridge*'s case Lord Nicholls discussed at some length the "husband and wife" cases.[426] He said that it is not correct to take the narrow approach of saying that every guarantee of a husband's bank overdraft by the wife is manifestly disadvantageous to her:

---

[421] [2005] EWCA Civ 382 at [20]–[22].

[422] [2005] EWCA Civ 382 at [32].

[423] See next paragraph.

[424] *Etridge's* case [2001] UKHL 44 at [30].

[425] *Turner v Barclays Bank Plc* [1997] 2 F.C.R. 151, 165. In *Barclays Bank Plc v O'Brien* [1994] 1 A.C. 180, 199 Lord Browne-Wilkinson said quite simply that the charge to secure the husband's business debts was on the face of it "not to her financial advantage" because she had no direct pecuniary interest in the business, but there the question was whether the creditor was put on constructive notice of possible misrepresentation or undue influence and it seems that, as between the stronger and weaker party, more must be shown in order to raise the presumption of undue influence. See above, para.7–087 and compare below, para.7–113.

[426] [2001] UKHL 44 at [28]–[31].

"Ordinarily, the fortunes of husband and wife are bound up together. If the husband's business is the source of the family income, the wife has a lively interest in doing what she can to support the business."[427]

In Lord Nicholl's view, *in the ordinary course* [emphasis in the original], a guarantee of this kind is not to be regarded as explicable only on the basis of undue influence by the husband and thus prima facie evidence of undue influence. However, that applies only "in the ordinary course":

"There will be cases where a wife's signature of a guarantee or charge of her share in the matrimonial home does call for explanation."[428]

On one view of the previous law, wives who have signed guarantees of their spouses' business debts, and others in a similar position, will in future find it less easy to rely on the presumption of undue influence. However, it must be remembered that Lord Nicholls was discussing the facts necessary to give rise to an evidential presumption of undue influence. If the wife proves that the husband used undue influence (for example by showing that she left all such decisions to him and signed whatever he put in front of her), she does not need to rely on the presumption. Even though in practice questions are unlikely to arise if the transaction is innocuous, she may avoid the transaction without having to show that it was disadvantageous "either in financial terms or in any other way".[429] 7–090

Surety cases that call for explanation. In *Bank of Credit and Commerce International SA v Aboody* the Court of Appeal held that the question whether there was what was then termed manifest disadvantage: 7–091

"... must depend on two factors, namely (a) the seriousness of the risk of enforcement to the giver, in practical terms, and (b) the benefits gained by the giver in accepting the risk."[430]

The Court of Appeal refused to interfere with the trial judge's findings that, as the wife would receive substantial benefits if the business survived, and at the relevant times it had "more than an equal chance" or "at least a reasonably good chance of surviving", the transactions were not manifestly disadvantageous to the wife. Conversely, if the chances of the business surviving are not good or if the marriage is already in difficulties and were it to founder the wife would be left without her only substantial asset, the transaction may be manifestly disadvantageous.[431] But the disadvantage must:

---

427 [2001] UKHL 44 at [28].

428 [2001] UKHL 44 at [30]–[31].

429 [2001] UKHL 44 at [12]. See above, para.7–060. It should also be noted that Lord Nicholls, at [44], pointed out that a much lower threshold is required in order to put a third party, such as a bank, to whom the wife has given a guarantee or charge, "on inquiry": see below, para.7–111.

430 [1990] 1 Q.B. 923, 965. In *National Westminster Bank Plc v Morgan* [1985] A.C. 686 the charge was not manifestly disadvantageous as it was the only way to save the matrimonial home from repossession by another creditor.

431 See the CA decision in *Etridge's* case [1998] 4 All E.R. 705 at 716.

"... be obvious as such to any independent and reasonable persons who considered the transactions at the time with knowledge of all the relevant facts."[432]

This approach seems compatible with that of the House of Lords in *Etridge*'s case. If a wife gives a guarantee for a business that seems to be thriving, the transaction will be explicable by ordinary motives.[433] But a presumption will arise if the complainant who was induced to guarantee or execute a charge to secure the other party's business debts is merely an employee with no stake in the business[434]; indeed some such transactions have been so one-sided that they "shock the conscience of the court" and may be set aside as unconscionable bargains.[435]

7–092 **Examples from other contracts.** In the context of contracts generally, as opposed to guarantees, it is not easy to say what will be treated as "not reasonably to be accounted for on . . . ordinary motives" for the purposes of establishing an inference that undue influence has been used . Certainly, a sale at undervalue will suffice[436]; and so will a transaction which brings the weaker party significant benefits if the benefit is obviously outweighed by the risks involved.[437]

(d) *Rebutting the Presumption*

7–093 **Rebutting the presumption.** In order to rebut the presumption of undue influence, evidence must be adduced to satisfy the court "that the donor was acting independently of any influence from the donee and with the full appreciation of what he was doing".[438] The most usual, though not the only, way of rebutting the presumption is to prove that the claimant had competent and independent advice,[439] and the position of the defendant is stronger if the claimant's action was taken in accordance with, than if it was taken in spite of, such advice. Sometimes to show that the complainant had independent advice will be the only way of rebutting the inference of undue influence,[440] but circumstances may establish the fact that the claimant's will was freely exercised although no independent advice was given or although such advice was disregarded.[441] Conversely, proof of outside advice does not necessarily show that

[432] *Bank of Credit and Commerce International SA v Aboody* [1990] 1 Q.B. 923, 965.

[433] See above, para.7–089.

[434] *Steeples v Lea* [1998] 1 F.L.R. 138.

[435] *Crédit Lyonnais Bank Nederland NV v Burch* [1997] 1 All E.R. 144, 152. See further, below, para.7–128.

[436] *Mahoney v Purnell* [1996] 3 All E.R. 61.

[437] *Cheese v Thomas* [1994] 1 W.L.R. 129. It has been argued that a transaction under which the complainant parted with property at full market value may still be manifestly disadvantageous if it was not one that a party in similar situation would ordinarily be expected to have made, such as to sell the family land: Birks and Chin in Beatson and Friedmann (eds), *Good Faith and Fault in Contract Law* (1995), pp.57–97, at 83; but cf. para.7–060 above.

[438] *Inche Noriah v Shaik Allie Bin Omar* [1929] A.C. 127, 135.

[439] *Morley v Loughnan* [1893] 1 Ch. 736, 752; *Re Coomber* [1911] 1 Ch. 723; *Inche Noriah v Shaik Allie Bin Omar* [1929] A.C. 127.

[440] *Inche Noriah v Shaik Allie Bin Omar* [1929] A.C. 127 PC.

[441] [1929] A.C. 127, 135; *Re Estate of Brocklehurst* [1978] Ch. 141.

there was no undue influence: it is a question of fact to be decided on the evidence.[442]

Duty of confidence. In cases falling within the second of the two categories referred to in *Allcard v Skinner*[443] it is not to the point to attempt to "rebut the presumption" of undue influence by evidence that the donor's will was exercised free of domination. In cases of this kind what needs to be established is that the duty of confidence has been fulfilled. What constitutes fulfilment of that duty depends on the facts of the particular case, but in general the duty requires that the person liable to be influenced should be enabled to form an independent and informed judgment.[444] Where the case involves the giving of advice by a legal or other confidential adviser this no doubt means that the advice must be fairly and disinterestedly offered, and must also be reasonable and adequate advice in the circumstances. In other cases the question may not be so much as to any advice given by the defendant, but as to the availability of advice from other sources.[445] In some cases, such a duty may be held to require disclosure of material facts, and no real question arises of undue influence in the literal sense.[446] 7–094

Independent advice. On the subject of independent advice there have been varying statements of judicial opinion. In *Re Coomber*,[447] it was said that it is sufficient if an independent adviser sees that the donor understands what he is doing and intends to do it; he need not advise him to do it or not to do it. On the other hand, in *Powell v Powell*,[448] it was said: 7–095

> "The solicitor does not discharge his duty by satisfying himself simply that the donor understands and wishes to carry out the particular transaction. He must also satisfy himself that the gift is one which it is right and proper for the donor to make under all the circumstances, and if he is not so satisfied, his duty is to advise his client not to go on with the transaction, and to refuse to act further for him if he persists."

In *Royal Bank of Scotland v Etridge (No.2)* the Court of Appeal took a similar view,[449] but in the House of Lords, Lord Nicholls expressly disagreed.[450] It is not

---

[442] *Royal Bank of Scotland v Etridge (No.2)* [2001] UKHL 44, [2002] 2 A.C. 773 at [20].

[443] See above, para.7–050.

[444] *Lloyds Bank Ltd v Bundy* [1975] Q.B. 326, 342.

[445] cf. *Hammond v Osborn* [2002] EWCA Civ 885, *The Times*, July 18, 2002, a case of gift in which it was held that the donor had not made an informed judgement. It was accepted that the recipient was not guilty of any reprehensible conduct. It appears that the exercise of undue influence consisted of failing to draw the donor's attention to the size of the gift he was making and to ensure that he obtained independent advice.

[446] *English v Dedham Vale Properties Ltd* [1978] 1 W.L.R. 93.

[447] [1911] 1 Ch. 723.

[448] [1900] 1 Ch. 243, 247. See also *Barron v Willis* [1902] A.C. 271; *Wright v Carter* [1903] 1 Ch. 27.

[449] *Royal Bank of Scotland v Etridge (No.2)* [1998] 4 All E.R. 705, 715.

[450] [2001] UKHL 44, [2002] 2 A.C. 773 at [59]–[63]. Lord Nicholls said that *Powell v Powell* [1900] 1 Ch. 243 was an extreme case and Farwell J.'s statement "cannot be regarded as of general application".

for the solicitor to veto the transaction.[451] The decision whether to proceed is the decision of the client, not the solicitor. Only in exceptional cases where it is glaringly obvious that the complainant is being grievously wronged is the solicitor to be expected to decline to act further.

7–096 **Adequacy of advice.** It has been said that the independent adviser should ensure that the party entering the transaction understands it even where there has been no misrepresentation by the other party. It appears that if the solicitor does not have the relevant information or ask the relevant questions, the advice may be treated as inadequate and the presumption will not be rebutted. The Judicial Committee of the Privy Council considered this question in *Inche Noriah v Shaik Allie Bin Omar*,[452] where there was a gift of almost the whole of her property by an aged Malay widow to her nephew. The Board was of the opinion that independent advice might be effective even though it was not shown that the advice was taken; but then it must be given:

> " . . . with a knowledge of all relevant circumstances and must be such as a competent and honest adviser would give if acting solely in the interests of the donor."[453]

In the instant case, the gift was set aside, for although the widow had received independent advice from a solicitor, he did not know at the time that the gift comprised almost all of her property, nor did he advise her that she could equally well have benefited her nephew by will.[454]

(e) *Remedies for Undue Influence*

7–097 **Affirmation.**[455] A transaction entered into as the result of undue influence is voidable and not void. The right to rescind on the ground of undue influence may be lost either by express affirmation of the transaction by the victim,[456] by estoppel or by delay amounting to proof of acquiescence.[457] Although there can normally be no affirmation until the party knows he has the right to rescind, it has

---

[451] Or, in a case where the client is offering a guarantee to a third party bank (see below, para.7–105) by declining to confirm to the bank that he has explained the documents to the wife and the risks that she is taking upon herself. Lord Nicholls did not accept the view of the Court of Appeal that the availability of legal advice is insufficient to prevent the bank being fixed with constructive notice if the transaction is "one into which no competent solicitor could properly advise the wife to enter". *Etridge* was of course a "three-party" case but in this context, Lord Nicholls did not draw a distinction between two and three-party cases.

[452] [1929] A.C. 127.

[453] [1929] A.C. 127, 136.

[454] cf. below, para.7–116.

[455] This paragraph was cited with approval in *DSND Subsea Ltd v Petroleum Geo-services ASA* [2000] B.L.R. 530 at [146].

[456] *Mitchell v Homfray* (1881) 8 QBD 587; *Morse v Royal* (1806) 12 Ves. 355.

[457] *Allcard v Skinner* (1887) 36 Ch D 145; *Turner v Collins* (1871) L.R. 7 Ch. App. 329. See below, paras 28–136—28–142.

been doubted whether this is a hard and fast rule: "the whole of the circumstances must be looked at to see whether it is just that the complaining beneficiary should succeed".[458] Estoppel requires a clear and unequivocal representation that the claimant would not seek to set the agreement aside, intended to be acted on and in fact acted on by the other party to his detriment or in such a way that it would be inequitable to allow the claimant to go back on his representation.[459] In either case, to be of any value, the affirmation must take place after the influence has ceased:

> "The right to property acquired by such means cannot be confirmed in this court unless there be full knowledge of all the facts, full knowledge of the equitable rights arising out of those facts, and an absolute release from the undue influence by means of which the frauds were practised."[460]

Lapse of time in itself does not seem to constitute a bar to relief,[461] but it will provide evidence of acquiescence if the victim fails to take any steps to set aside the transaction within a reasonable time after he is freed from the undue influence.[462] And where he has himself failed to commence proceedings in this way during his lifetime, his personal representatives cannot do so after his death.[463]

Restitution. A complainant who has received no benefit under the contract may simply have it set aside.[464] If the complainant has received a benefit[465] and 7–098

[458] *Goldsworthy v Brickell* [1987] Ch. 378, 412 (Nourse L.J.) and 416 (Parker L.J.). Nourse L.J. considered that the defence might have succeeded on the basis that by the time of the alleged act of affirmation, the complainant had consulted solicitors. cf. *Lloyds Bank Plc v Lucken*, heard with the *Etridge* case, [1998] 4 All E.R. 705, 738, 751.

[459] *Goldsworthy v Brickell* [1987] Ch. 378, 410–411. In *Habib Bank Ltd v Tufail* [2006] EWCA Civ 374, [2006] All E.R. (D) 92 (Apr) Lloyd L.J. drew a distinction between affirmation, which requires knowledge of the right to rescind (at [19]) and acquiescence. Acquiescence can operate rather like promissory estoppel, though in *Goldsworthy v Brickell* [1987] Ch. 378 at 409, Nourse L.J. had pointed out that promissory estoppel is normally concerned with the giving up of rights under a contract whose validity is not in dispute, and its requirements are more formalised than those of acquiescence. Thus if before she seeks to avoid the contract the victim of undue influence or misrepresentation indicates that she will perform it, and the other party acts on that representation to its detriment, the victim will lose the right to avoid the contract, at least if the representation was made after she knew of the facts giving her the right to avoid (at [22]; Lloyd L.J. doubted whether the supposed further requirement that her representation be intended to be acted on added anything). If, as on the facts of the case, the other party cannot show that the representation, that solicitors had been instructed to sell the mortgaged property, led it to act differently, it cannot rely on acquiescence (at [25]) and the victim may still be entitled to avoid the contract. The case was one in which a mortgage to a bank had been entered into as the result of misrepresentation by a third party of which the bank had constructive notice (see below, paras 7–104 et seq.) but the same principle applies in a two-party case like *Goldsworthy v Brickell*.

[460] *Moxon v Payne* (1873) L.R. 8 Ch. App. 881, 885.

[461] *Hatch v Hatch* (1804) 9 Ves. 292; *Re Pauling's Settlement Trusts* [1964] Ch. 303.

[462] *Allcard v Skinner* (1887) 36 Ch D 145; cf. *Bullock v Lloyds Bank Ltd* [1955] Ch. 317.

[463] *Wright v Vanderplank* (1855) 2 K. & J. 1; *Mitchell v Homfray* (1881) 8 QBD 587.

[464] cf. *TSB Bank Plc v Camfield* [1995] 1 W.L.R. 430 (misrepresentation), above, para.6–118.

[465] It seems likely that in this context "benefit" refers to something received directly under the contract to be set aside or one inextricably linked with it (as in the case cited in the next note) rather than to, e.g. a benefit received by a wife through the successful operation of her husband's business for a period before the creditor sought to enforce the charge in question given by the wife.

rescinds, she must make restitution[466] and it has been said that her right to rescission is "conditional on her making counter-restitution".[467]

7–099 **Impossibility of restitution not necessarily a bar.** It is thought that, as between the parties, the fact that property transferred can no longer be returned as such to the complainant (for example, because an innocent third party has acquired rights over it) is not necessarily a bar to rescission on the grounds of undue influence. Instead, the defendant may be required to make counter-restitution by a monetary equivalent.[468] This is suggested by the cases discussed in the next two paragraphs.

7–100 **Account of profits with allowance.** Thus, a transaction entered into as a result of undue influence can be rescinded even though it has been fully executed, and even though restitutio in integrum is no longer fully possible, so long as the court can do substantial justice by ordering an account of profits with, if necessary, an allowance for work done by the defendant. Where a series of contracts between a young singer and his manager and agent was set aside after the singer had achieved world-wide success, it was held that the defendant could be made liable to account for all the profit made from the contracts, but subject to a reasonable allowance for his work under the transactions in question. This allowance could include a reasonable element of profit, but not so much as might have been obtained by the defendant if the plaintiff had been properly advised by independent advisers at the outset.[469]

7–101 **Equitable compensation.** It has been held that if restitutio in integrum is no longer possible, and the defendant does not retain any profits for which he may be made to account, the claimant may still be given "compensation in equity". In *Mahoney v Purnell*[470] May J. held that equitable compensation under *Nocton v Lord Ashburton*[471] is also available in such circumstances and the plaintiff could recover the value of what he had transferred, giving credit for what he had received. The judge described this as the practical equivalent of awarding damages, though it should be noted that equitable compensation will not include compensation for consequential losses.[472] Doubt has been expressed whether equitable compensation is available in every case of undue influence, or only those in which there is a fiduciary relationship of a narrower sort, such as between solicitor and client or beneficiary and trustee.[473] In *Bank of Credit and Commerce International SA v Aboody*[474] Slade L.J. treated such cases as different to normal cases of undue influence[475] and said that cases such as *Tate v*

[466] *Dunbar Bank Plc v Nadeem* [1998] 3 All E.R. 876; see also *Midland Bank Plc v Greene* [1994] 2 F.L.R. 827.

[467] *Dunbar Bank Plc v Nadeem* [1998] 3 All E.R. 876, 884.

[468] Burrows, *Law of Restitution*, 2nd edn (2002), p.246.

[469] *O'Sullivan v Management Agency Ltd* [1985] Q.B. 428, following the authorities relating to setting aside contracts for misrepresentation, above, paras 6–115 et seq.

[470] [1996] 3 All E.R. 61.

[471] [1914] A.C. 932 (a case of a mortgagee suing his solicitor, see para.6–078).

[472] See para.6–080, fn.339.

[473] See Heydon (1997) 113 L.Q.R. 8, 9 and para.6–080.

[474] [1990] 1 Q.B. 923, 943.

[475] See para.7–062.

Williamson[476] did not draw a sufficiently clear distinction between the two types of case; but there is no sign that May J. saw the case before him to be anything other than one of presumed undue influence. However, it has been argued persuasively that "equitable compensation" in this context should be understood as referring to pecuniary restitution of any unjust enrichment, which is appropriate in cases of undue influence. The case shows not that equitable compensation may be given when restitution is impossible, so much as that rescission need not be prevented by the fact that property cannot be returned *in specie*; as between the parties it may be effected in money.[477]

Sharing of loss. Conversely, where as the result of undue influence the claimant has contributed to the purchase of property which as a result of the transaction being set aside has to be sold, and the property does not fetch the price paid for it, the claimant is not entitled to the return of the full contribution he made. The principle is to prevent unjust enrichment of the other party and the sum obtained on sale of the property should be shared in the same proportions as the parties' original contributions to the purchase.[478] 7–102

Change of position. It has been noted that the decision described in the last paragraph might be viewed as a form of change of position defence to even monetary restitution; and that in *Allcard v Skinner*[479] the possibility of such a defence was recognised by all three Lords Justice, in that they considered that the complainant would have been able, had she taken steps in time, to recover from the religious order to which she had made her gifts only such sums as remained unspent in its hands.[480] 7–103

(f) *Undue Influence by a Third Party*

Undue influence by a third person. Where one party seeks to avoid a contract on the ground of undue influence by a third person, it must appear either that the third person was acting as the other party's agent, or that the other party had actual or constructive notice of the undue influence.[481] 7–104

Undue influence over a surety. In a number of cases a recurring situation has arisen.[482] In the typical case, a husband has wanted to borrow money from a creditor that has refused to proceed without having a guarantee secured by a charge over the matrimonial home, or similarly a charge without a personal 7–105

---

476 (1866) L.R. 2 Ch. App. 55.

477 Birks [1997] R.L.R. 72. But cf. Goff & Jones, *Law of Restitution*, 7th edn (2007), paras 11–012—11–013. See also above, para.6–120.

478 *Cheese v Thomas* [1994] 1 W.L.R. 129.

479 (1887) 36 Ch D 145.

480 Chen-Wishart (1994) 110 L.Q.R. 173, 177–178; *Allcard v Skinner* (1887) 36 Ch D 145, 164, 171, 186.

481 See *Bank of Credit and Commerce International SA v Aboody* [1990] 1 Q.B. 923, 973; *Barclays Bank Plc v O'Brien* [1994] 1 A.C. 180, discussed in the paragraphs that follow.

482 For a wide ranging study of the problem, see Fehlberg, *Sexually Transmitted Debt* (1997).

guarantee, from the wife. The wife's consent has been secured by undue influence[483] or misrepresentation[484] by the husband. Can the creditor enforce the guarantee? In some cases it was held that if the creditor had "left it to the husband" to get the wife's signature, the husband was acting as agent for the creditor[485] and it was therefore responsible for his misconduct.

7–106 **Constructive notice: *Barclays Bank v O'Brien*.** In *Barclays Bank Plc v O'Brien*, a case where the husband had secured his wife's signature by misrepresentation, the Court of Appeal[486] expressed the view that this "agency" approach was often artificial on the facts. It held that it was not just in cases in which the debtor was acting as the agent of the creditor in the true sense that the creditor would be unable to enforce the guarantee if the debtor had procured the surety's signature by misrepresentation. If the relationship between the debtor and a surety who charged property to secure the debt was one in which influence by the debtor over the surety and reliance on the debtor by the surety were natural and probable features, as in the case of husband and wife, and this was known to the creditor, a special rule applied. If the debtor procured the surety's consent by misrepresentation or undue influence, or the surety lacked an adequate understanding of the nature and effect of the transaction, and the creditor, whether by leaving it to the debtor to deal with the surety or otherwise, failed to take reasonable steps to try to ensure that the surety entered the transaction with adequate understanding and that the consent was a true and informed one, the creditor may not enforce the security given by the surety.[487]

7–107 In the House of Lords[488] this approach was rejected: there is no special theory in equity to protect wives.[489] The surety cannot set aside the transaction simply on the ground that she did not fully understand it.[490] However the appeal of the Bank was dismissed on the ground that it had constructive notice of the husband's misrepresentation. Lord Browne-Wilkinson, delivering the only full speech in the House of Lords, pointed out that there is a substantial risk that the wife may act as surety when the transaction is not to her advantage because of some legal or equitable wrong by the husband. Where the creditor is aware that the debtor and the surety are husband and wife, and the transaction is on its face not to the financial advantage of the surety as well as of the debtor, the creditor will be fixed with constructive notice of any undue influence, misrepresentation or other legal wrong by the debtor unless it has taken reasonable steps to satisfy itself that the surety has entered into the obligation freely and with knowledge of

483 e.g. *CIBC Mortgages Plc v Pitt* [1994] 1 A.C. 200.

484 *Kings North Trust Ltd v Bell* [1961] 1 W.L.R. 119; *Barclays Bank Plc v O'Brien* [1994] 1 A.C. 180.

485 See *Coldunell Ltd v Gallon* [1986] Q.B. 1184.

486 [1993] Q.B. 109.

487 Considerable reliance was placed on *Turnbull & Co v Duval* [1902] A.C. 429 PC.

488 [1994] 1 A.C. 180. In Scotland a similar result has been reached but via the different route of recognising a duty of good faith by the creditor towards the cautioner: *Smith v Bank of Scotland* 1997 S.L.T. 1061. In Australia, the problem has been approached through the doctrine of unconscionability (below, para.7–121): see Tjio (1997) 113 L.Q.R. 13. The *O'Brien* case has not been followed: *Garcia v National Australia Bank Ltd* [1998] 155 A.L.R. 614 High Ct.

489 *Turnbull & Co v Duvall* [1902] A.C. 429 PC was doubted.

490 *Barclays Bank Plc v O'Brien* [1994] 1 A.C. 180, 195.

the true facts.[491] It is the combination of the fact that the parties are husband and wife and that the transaction is on its face not to the wife's advantage that should put the creditor on notice.[492]

Lord Browne-Wilkinson said that where the creditor is aware that the debtor and the surety are husband and wife, and the transaction is on its face not one which is to the financial advantage of the surety as well as of the debtor, the creditor will be fixed with constructive notice of any undue influence, misrepresentation or other legal wrong by the debtor unless it has taken reasonable steps to satisfy itself that the surety has entered into the obligation freely and with knowledge of the true facts.[493] The creditor should explain to the surety the amount of her potential liability and of the risks involved, and advise her to seek independent legal advice before entering the guarantee[494]; and this should be done in a personal interview, as written warnings are often not read and are sometimes intercepted by the debtor.[495] The interview should not be attended by the husband. As in *O'Brien*'s case the bank's clerk, in disregard of her instructions, had not warned the wife of the risks involved nor recommended her to take legal advice before getting her to sign the documents charging the matrimonial home, the bank could not enforce the charge. If the bank has notice of facts rendering misrepresentation or undue influence not just possible but probable, it must insist that the wife actually is separately advised.[496] **7–108**

***Etridge*'s case.** The decision in *Barclays Bank v O'Brien*, and the many other decisions that followed it,[497] must be read in the light of the subsequent decision of the House of Lords in *Royal Bank of Scotland v Etridge (No.2)*,[498] and in particular the speech of Lord Nicholls, which gained the support of all their Lordships.[499] Reference to this case has already been made in relation to what amounts to undue influence.[500] The decision on constructive notice, and what steps the lender should take to avoid being fixed with constructive notice, is of equal or greater importance. **7–109**

Basis of the constructive notice rule. Lord Nicholls said that the decision in *Barclays Bank Plc v O'Brien*: **7–110**

"... is not a conventional use of the equitable doctrine of constructive notice . . .[501] The law imposes no obligation on one party to check whether the other party's

---

[491] [1994] 1 A.C. 180, 196.

[492] Compare *CIBC Mortgages Plc v Pitt* [1994] 1 A.C. 200, heard at the same time as *O'Brien* [1994] 1 A.C. 180: see below, para.7–113.

[493] *Barclays Bank Plc v O'Brien* [1994] 1 A.C. 180, 196.

[494] This much is required by the Banking Code of March 2008 para.13.4. This code was first adopted by banks and building societies (as the Code of Banking Practice) in March 1992. The code also provides that unlimited guarantees or security will not be taken.

[495] [1994] 1 A.C. 180, 198.

[496] [1994] 1 A.C. 180, 197.

[497] For a survey of many of the post-*O'Brien* cases see Fehlberg (1996) 59 M.L.R. 675.

[498] [2001] UKHL 44, [2002] 2 A.C. 773. This case and seven other appeals were heard together.

[499] See [2001] UKHL 44 at [3], [91], [100] and [192].

[500] See above, paras 7–059 et seq.

[501] [2001] UKHL 44 at [39].

concurrence was obtained by undue influence. Rather, *O'Brien* envisages that the steps taken by the bank will reduce, or even eliminate, the risk of the wife entering into the transaction under any misapprehension or as a result of undue influence by her husband. The steps are not concerned to discover whether the wife has been wronged by her husband in this way.[502] The steps are concerned to minimise the risk that such a wrong may be committed."[503]

O'Brien concerned suretyship transactions, which (outside commercial suretyship) is a one-sided transaction, so that the decision is aimed "at a class of contracts which has special features of its own".[504]

7–111 **When the bank is put on inquiry.** The bank is put on inquiry (strictly speaking not an accurate description of what the bank is required to do but now the accepted terminology[505]) by a combination of two things: a non-commercial relationship between the surety and the lender (see below, para.7–098) and a transaction which on its face is to the disadvantage of the surety (see below, para.7–099). The threshold that must be crossed before the bank is put "on inquiry" is deliberately set at a low level:

"... much lower than is required to satisfy a court that, failing contrary evidence, the court may infer that the transaction was procured by undue influence."[506]

The test stated by Lord Browne-Wilkinson[507] is to be taken to mean simply that a bank is put on inquiry whenever a wife offers to stand surety for her husband's debts.[508]

7–112 **Relationships giving rise to notice.** The same rule applies whether a husband stands surety for his wife's debts or one of an unmarried couple for the other's debts, provided the bank is aware of the relationship. Cohabitation is not essential.[509] It also applies where the bank knows that the parties are parent and child; knowledge of the relationship means that the bank must take reasonable steps to

[502] Thus the solicitor is not expected to satisfy himself that the wife is free from undue influence: see the criticism of statements made in *Etridge* in the Court of Appeal and applied in the conjoined case of *Kenyon-Brown v Desmond Banks & Co* ([2001] UKHL 44 at [181]–[182], per Lord Scott) and the decision of the House in the latter case (see at [90] and [374].)

[503] [2001] UKHL 44 at [41]. Compare the speech of Lord Scott, who though he said (at [192]) that he agreed fully with Lord Nicholls, said that the bank is to take steps to ensure that the wife understands the nature and effect of the transaction: see at [147], [164]–[165] and [191]. In contrast, Lord Hobhouse said that while comprehension was essential, the purpose was also to protect the wife's vulnerability to undue influence. He disagreed with Lord Scott if he meant that a belief by the bank that the wife understood the nature and effect of the transaction was sufficient. That was not the effect of Lord Nicholls' scheme (see at [111]).

[504] [2001] UKHL 44 at [43].

[505] *Etridge's* case [2001] UKHL 44 per Lord Nicholls at [44].

[506] [2001] UKHL 44 at [44]. For what will raise an inference that undue influence has been used, see above, paras 7–086—7–092.

[507] See above, para.7–108.

[508] [2001] UKHL 44 at [44].

[509] *Etridge's* case [2001] UKHL 44 at [47]. Lord Browne-Wilkinson had said that the rule applied to cohabitees: [1994] 1 A.C. 180, 198.

ensure that the child "knows what she is letting herself into".[510] And, as the principle should apply to any other relationship where trust and confidence are likely to exist,[511] and there is no rational cut-off point:

> ". . . the only practical way forward is to regard banks as 'put on inquiry' in every case where the relationship between the surety and the debtor is non-commercial."[512]

Transaction not on its face to the advantage of the surety. The bank is put on inquiry whenever a wife offers to stand surety for her husband's debts.[513] The bank is not put on inquiry if the money is advanced jointly to the couple, unless the bank is aware that the loan is being made for the husband's purposes.[514] Thus in *CIBC Mortgages Plc v Pitt*,[515] which was heard with *O'Brien*'s case, the loan appeared on its face to be a normal one for the joint benefit of husband and wife and therefore the creditor was not fixed with constructive notice of the undue influence used by the husband to secure the wife's agreement.[516] But if one party becomes surety for a company whose shares are held by both, the bank is put on inquiry, even if they have equal shareholdings or if the surety is also a director or secretary of the company.[517] 7–113

Reasonable steps. As to the steps that the lender should take to avoid being fixed with constructive notice of any undue influence that has occurred, Lord Nicholls stated in *Etridge* that for past transactions, the bank should have taken steps: 7–114

> ". . . to bring home to the wife the risk she is running by standing as surety and to advise her to take independent advice."[518]

For the future, however, Lord Nicholls said in *Etridge* that a bank will satisfy the requirements if it insists that the wife attend a private meeting with a representative of the bank at which she is told of the extent of her liability as surety, is warned of the risk she is running and is urged to take independent legal advice.[519] In exceptional cases the bank should insist that she be separately advised.[520]

Advice from a solicitor. In several of the cases subsequent to *O'Brien* (the facts of many of which occurred before the House of Lords' decision in that 7–115

[510] *Etridge's* case [2001] UKHL 44 at [84]. See also *Barclays Bank Plc v O'Brien* [1994] 1 A.C. 180, at 198; *Avon Finance Co Ltd v Bridger* (1979) [1985] 2 All E.R. 281 (vulnerable elderly parents providing security for the debts of their adult son.)

[511] [2001] UKHL 44 at [82].

[512] [2001] UKHL 44 at [87].

[513] [2001] UKHL 44 at [44].

[514] [2001] UKHL 44 at [48]; cf. *Allied Irish Bank Plc v Byrne* [1995] 2 F.L.R. 325.

[515] [1994] 1 A.C. 200.

[516] And see *Society of Lloyds v Khan* [1998] 3 F.C.R. 93 (Lloyds not put on notice when wife agreed to be a Name, which enabled her to undertake a risk in return for reward); *Mortgage Agency Services Number Two Ltd v Chater* [2003] EWCA Civ 490, [2004] 1 P. & C.R. 4 (joint loan to mother and son).

[517] *Etridge's* case [2001] UKHL 44 at [49].

[518] [2001] UKHL 44 at [50], referring to the steps described by Lord Browne-Wilkinson in *O'Brien*'s case [1994] 1 A.C. 180, 196–197 and referred to above, para.7–108.

[519] [2001] UKHL 44 at [50].

[520] [2001] UKHL 44 at [50].

case), the creditor had not itself advised the wife[521] but had relied on a certificate from a third party, typically a solicitor employed by the husband or by the creditor itself, that the wife had been given an explanation. If the wife has actually received such an explanation, this would go beyond what *O'Brien*'s case required in the normal case in that the wife actually receives advice.[522] In *Etridge*, Lord Nicholls said that if the bank (or other lender) prefers that the task be undertaken by an independent legal advisor, it will normally be enough to rely on a confirmation from a solicitor,[523] acting for the wife,[524] that he has advised the wife appropriately.[525] However, if the bank knows that the solicitor has not duly advised the wife, or knows facts from which it ought to have realised the wife has not received appropriate advice, the position will be different.[526]

7–116 **Steps the solicitor should take.** Lord Nicholls then set out in some detail the steps the solicitor should take:

> "[64] . . . As a first step the solicitor will need to explain to the wife the purpose for which he has become involved at all. He should explain that, should it ever become necessary, the bank will rely upon his involvement to counter any suggestion that the wife was overborne by her husband or that she did not properly understand the implications of the transaction. The solicitor will need to obtain confirmation from the wife that she wishes him to act for her in the matter and to advise her on the legal and practical implications of the proposed transaction.
>
> [65] When an instruction to this effect is forthcoming, the content of the advice require a solicitor before giving the confirmation sought by the bank will, inevitably, depend upon the circumstances of the case. Typically, the advice a solicitor can be expected to give should cover the following matters as the core minimum. (1) He will need to explain the nature of the documents and the practical consequences these will have for the wife if she signs them. She could lose her home if her husband's business does not prosper. Her home may be her only substantial asset, as well as the family's home. She could be made bankrupt. (2) He will need to point out the seriousness of the

[521] In *Royal Bank of Scotland v Etridge (No.2)* [1998] 4 All E.R. 705, 720, Stuart-Smith L.J. doubted if banks would be willing to do this even after *O'Brien*'s case, as it "is likely to expose the bank to greater risks than those from which it wishes to be protected".

[522] *Royal Bank of Scotland v Etridge (No.2)* [1998] 4 All E.R. 705, 720, Stuart-Smith L.J.

[523] In *Barclays Bank Plc v Coleman*, one of the cases heard with *Etridge*, the Court of Appeal had held that the bank was justified in relying on a certificate given by a legal executive to the effect that the wife had received advice, provided that the advice was independent and was given with the authority of the legal executive's principal ([2001] Q.B. 20 at [78]). The House of Lords dismissed the appeal, Lord Scott saying that the bank were entitled to believe that the solicitors would not entrust such a task to a legal executive with insufficient experience to carry out the task properly ([2001] UKHL 44 at [292].)

[524] Thus the bank cannot rely on a confirmation from a solicitor who was not acting for the wife: *National Westminster Bank Plc v Amin* [2002] UKHL 9, [2002] 1 F.L.R. 735.

[525] As Lord Hobhouse put it at [120]: "[T]he central feature is that the wife will be put into a proper relationship with a solicitor who is acting for her and accepts appropriate duties towards her." Lord Scott said that the bank could not assume that because a solicitor was acting for the wife, the solicitor's instructions extend to advising her on the transaction: see at [168] and the decision in the conjoined case of *UCB Home Loans Corp v Moore* at [90], [127] and [307]. If a solicitor is acting for the wife, the bank does not have to give express instructions on the steps to be taken or that legal advice must be provided to the wife independently, provided the solicitor confirms that she has received independent advice: *Bank of Scotland v Hill* [2002] EWCA Civ 1081, [2002] E.G.C.S. 152.

[526] *Royal Bank of Scotland v Etridge (No.2)* [2001] UKHL 44 at [51]–[57].

risks involved. The wife should be told the purpose of the proposed new facility, the amount and principal terms of the new facility, and that the bank might increase the amount of the facility, or change its terms, or grant a new facility, without reference to her. She should be told the amount other liability under her guarantee. The solicitor should discuss the wife's financial means, including her understanding of the value of the property being charged. The solicitor should discuss whether the wife or her husband has any other assets out of which repayment could be made if the husband's business should fail. These matters are relevant to the seriousness of the risks involved. (3) The solicitor will need to state clearly that the wife has a choice. The decision is hers and hers alone. Explanation of the choice facing the wife will call for some discussion of the present financial position, including the amount of the husband's present indebtedness, and the amount of his current overdraft facility. (4) The solicitor should check whether the wife wishes to proceed. She should be asked whether she is content that the solicitor should write to the bank confirming he has explained to her the nature of the documents and the practical implications they may have for her, or whether, for instance, she, would prefer him to negotiate with the bank on the terms of the transaction. Matters for negotiation could include the sequence in which the various securities will be called upon or a specific or lower limit to her liabilities. The solicitor should not give any confirmation to the bank without the wife's authority.

[66] The solicitor's discussion with the wife should take place at a face-to-face meeting, in the absence of the husband. It goes without saying that the solicitor's explanations should be couched in suitably non-technical language. It also goes without saying that the solicitor's task is an important one. It is not a formality.

[67] The solicitor should obtain from the bank any information he needs. If, the bank fails for any reason to provide information requested by the solicitor, the solicitor should decline to provide the confirmation sought by the bank."

Conflicts of interest. The solicitor may also act for the husband or the bank but, in advising the wife, he is acting for her alone (and therefore his knowledge is not imputed to the bank[527]). He must consider whether there is any conflict of interest and whether it would be in the best interests of the wife for him to accept instructions from her. If at any stage there is a real risk that other interests or duties may inhibit his advice to the wife he must cease to act for her.[528] 7–117

The bank and the solicitor. The bank should check directly with the wife the name of the solicitor she wishes to act for her, telling her that it will require written confirmation from the solicitor that he has explained to her fully the nature of the documents and their practical implications, so that she is not able later to dispute that he is bound by the documents she has signed. It must also send to the solicitor the necessary financial information.[529] If the solicitor is already acting for the husband and wife the wife should be asked if she would 7–118

[527] *Etridge's* case [2001] UKHL 44 at [77]. See also *Midland Bank Plc v Serter* [1995] 3 F.C.R. 711; *Halifax Mortgage Services Ltd v Stepsky* [1995] 3 W.L.R. 701; *Barclays Bank Plc v Thomson* [1997] 4 All E.R. 816.

[528] [2001] UKHL 44 at [74]. Lord Hobhouse, at [100], said that the guidance given by Lord Nicholls should be applied to past as well as future transactions, because it represented a reasonable response to being put on inquiry.

[529] *Etridge's* case [2001] UKHL 44 at [79]. Lord Hobhouse (at [114]) pointed out that this may require the husband's consent, and if he will not give it, this would be a clear indication to the bank and the solicitor that something may be amiss and that it ought not to rely on the wife being bound.

prefer a different solicitor to advise her.[530] If in exceptional circumstances the bank suspects that the wife is being misled by her husband or is not entering the transaction of her own free will, it must inform the solicitor of the facts giving rise to the suspicion.

7–119 **Procedure.** It will be for the wife or other surety to show that the bank had notice of the non-commercial relationship between her and the debtor, and that the transaction was, on its face, not to her advantage. The burden will then be on the bank or other lender to show that it has taken sufficient steps to prevent it being fixed with constructive notice.[531]

7–120 **Need the party guilty of undue influence be a party to the transaction?** In at least one case the bank was treated as having constructive notice of the wife's right to set aside the charge *as against the husband*.[532] It is clear, however, that it makes no difference that the husband is not a party to the charge:

> "The transferor wife is seeking to resile from the very transaction she entered into with the bank, on the ground that her apparent consent was procured by the undue influence or other misconduct, such as misrepresentation, of a third party (her husband)."[533]

7–121 **Replacement mortgages.** Where a mortgage granted by a wife to a bank was voidable against the bank because the bank had constructive notice of undue influence by the husband, a replacement of the mortgage may also be voidable against the bank even if at the time the replacement mortgage was given there was no undue influence, at least where the replacement mortgage is taken as a condition of discharging the original mortgage.[534] It does not matter that the new agreement is a fresh contract rather than a variation of the old one, provided that the replacement mortgage is between the same parties.[535] However, it seems that the replacement mortgage must be inseparable from the original mortgage, in the sense that the replacement mortgage was granted before the grantor became aware that she had a right to avoid the original one, and was granted in order to discharge it.[536]

---

[530] [2001] UKHL 44 at [79].

[531] *Barclays Bank Plc v Boulter* [1999] 1 W.L.R. 1919. Lord Hoffmann, delivering the only full judgment, said that enough facts must be pleaded to give rise to the presumption of constructive notice; but it would not be adequate to rely on inferences derived from statements tucked away in documents that were pleaded. However the Court of Appeal should be slow to intervene in the decision that an arguable defence had been raised: *National Westminster Bank Plc v Kostopoulos*, *The Times*, March 2, 2000.

[532] *TSB Bank Plc v Camfield* [1995] 1 W.L.R. 430 (a case of misrepresentation).

[533] *Royal Bank of Scotland v Etridge (No.2)* [2001] UKHL 44, [2001] 3 W.L.R. 1021, per Lord Nicholls at [39]. See also the speech of Lord Scott at [144]–[146]; *Banco Exterior Internacional SA v Thomas* [1997] 1 W.L.R. 221, 229, per Sir Richard Scott V.C.; Proksch [1997] 1 R.L.R. 71.

[534] *Yorkshire Bank Plc v Tinsley* [2004] EWCA Civ 816, [2004] 1 W.L.R. 2380 at [19].

[535] [2004] EWCA Civ 816 at [19]–[20].

[536] [2004] EWCA Civ 816 at [24], [32] and [39]. Compare *Wadlow v Samuel* [2007] EWCA Civ 155, [2007] All E.R. (D.) 370, where the relationship of trust and confidence had ceased by the time of the second agreement and the claimant had been advised on it.

7–122 **Loss of right to avoid by inconsistent action.**[537] Like the right to avoid a contract for undue influence by the other party, the surety's right against the lender may be lost. One way in which this may occur is by the surety acting inconsistently with her right to avoid the charge. In *First National Bank Plc v Walker*[538] the husband and wife had charged their jointly owned home to the bank as security for a loan to the husband's business. Subsequently they divorced and the wife applied for ancillary relief. A property adjustment order was made in her favour, ordering the husband to convey his interest in the property to the wife. Clause 4 stated that nothing in the conveyance should prejudice the charge to the bank. Shortly afterwards the wife served a defence to possession proceedings by the bank, alleging that the charge was voidable by reason of the bank's actual or constructive notice of undue influence by the husband. The Court of Appeal held that the wife, by taking the transfer of her husband's interest, had lost her right to pursue the defence to the property proceedings, as this would be inconsistent with her having taken the conveyance. To pursue it would be an abuse of process or (per Morritt V.C.[539]) estoppel, approbation and reprobation, affirmation or release might apply. The reasoning employed in the Court of Appeal, that the wife's claim to set aside the charge because of the undue influence of the other joint and several debtor is secondary to and parasitic on the existence of such a claim against the other debtor, and that she lost her right by acting as against him in a way that was inconsistent with avoidance, may not have survived the decision in *Etridge*'s case that the wife's right to avoid the charge is because of the bank's constructive notice by a third party. But it seems that the right to avoid may be lost by acting in such a way as against the surety itself.[540]

7–123 **Jointly-owned homes.** It is only the surety against whom the charge may not be enforceable. If the property charged is owned jointly by husband and wife, then even though the charge may not be enforceable against the wife, it may be against the husband; and the result may be that the court will still order the property to be sold[541] in order to realise the husband's share.[542]

7–124 **Other cases.** This doctrine of constructive notice should avoid the need for the somewhat strained approach used in a number of earlier cases to the effect that the creditor, by "leaving it to the debtor" to get the surety's signature, was appointing the debtor as its agent and was therefore in no better position than the

---

537 The right may also be lost by acquiescence, which is a form of inconsistent action: see above, para.7–097.

538 [2001] 1 F.C.R. 21.

539 [2001] 1 F.C.R. 21 at [55].

540 See *Walker* [2001] 1 F.C.R. 21 at [35], per Morritt V.C. The Vice Chancellor said that the wife's right to claim ancillary relief on the footing that the mortgage was valid, which would have the effect that each party shares the liability equally and the equity of redemption is reduced by the amount of the liability, was inconsistent with her right to avoid the charge, since that would throw the entire liability to the bank onto the husband and increase the value of the equity of redemption by a sum equal to the wife's share of the liability.

541 Under Trusts of Land and Appointment of Trustees Act 1996 s.14.

542 See *First National Bank Plc v Achampong* [2003] EWCA Civ 487, [2004] 1 F.C.R. 18, noted by Thompson [2003] Conv. 314.

debtor would have been.[543] There may still be cases in which the creditor is responsible for the husband's actions because it can be said, "without artificiality", that the husband was acting as agent of the creditor, but "such cases will be of very rare occurrence".[544] The agency argument may still apply also in cases not involving sureties. In *O'Sullivan v Management Agency Ltd*[545] it was held that where a person in a fiduciary relationship procures by undue influence contracts to be entered into with companies under his control and direction, the companies will be affected by the doctrine of undue influence even though they themselves were not in fiduciary relationships. In such a case it is immaterial that the undue influence is exercised in order to obtain a benefit for third parties rather than for the person himself exercising the undue influence.

7–125 **Volunteers.** Alternatively, it may suffice to set aside the contract if the person against whom relief is sought gave no consideration, i.e. he was merely a volunteer.[546] It is not possible to avoid the contract as against a bona fide purchaser for value without notice.[547] It is clear that a gift made to a person who has exercised no influence will not be set aside because there is in the same instrument a gift to a person within the suspect relationships, unless the instrument as a whole can be said to have been executed as a result of undue influence.[548]

4. UNCONSCIONABLE BARGAINS AND INEQUALITY OF BARGAINING POWER

7–126 **Equitable relief against unconscionable bargains.** There are a number of well-established areas of the law where equitable relief is available against harsh or unconscionable bargains, such as in the law relating to penalties,[549] forfeitures[550] and mortgages; there are also many legislative interferences with freedom of contract designed to protect those who enter into harsh or unconscionable bargains.[551] But it remains doubtful in modern law to what extent there is any general equitable principle entitling the courts to interfere with freedom of contract on the ground that the contract (or a part of it) is, in all the circumstances

---

[543] See above, para.7–106.

[544] *Barclays Bank Plc v O'Brien* [1994] 1 A.C. 180, 195.

[545] [1985] Q.B. 428.

[546] *Bridgeman v Green* (1755) Wilm. 58, 65; *Huguenin v Baseley* (1807) 14 Ves. 273.

[547] *Cobbett v Brock* (1855) 20 Beav. 524, 528; *O'Sullivan v Management Agency Ltd* [1985] Q.B. 428.

[548] *Wright v Carter* [1903] 1 Ch. 27.

[549] See below, paras 26–125 et seq.

[550] See below, paras 26–147—26–156.

[551] See in particular the Unfair Contract Terms Act 1977, below, paras 14–059 et seq. Unfair Terms in Consumer Contracts Regulations 1999, below Ch.15 and Consumer Credit Act 1974 ss.140A–140D (inserted by ss.19–22 of the Consumer Credit Act 2006; the provisions on extortionate credit bargains, former ss.137–140, have been repealed by s.70 and Sch.4 of the 2006 Act): see below, para.38–213.

of the case, a harsh and unconscionable bargain.[552] Until recent years, the legacy of nineteenth-century ideology in favour of freedom of contract has restricted the development of possible residuary principles of unconscionability, but there were for a time some signs of a possible resurgence of a broader equitable approach to unconscionable bargains.[553] Subsequently, the courts have shown a determination to adhere firmly to principles of freedom of contract, particularly in commercial contracts between businessmen.[554] However, it is clear that relief is possible in certain cases of unconscionable advantage taking and the real question is the scope of the principles involved, particularly that of relief against unconscionable bargains with persons suffering from some form of bargaining disadvantage.[555]

Salvage cases. Reference has been made above (para.7–047) to the power of the court to set aside unconscionable contracts for salvage services rendered to a vessel in distress. When these cases were first decided they may have been based upon some broader principle permitting the overriding of unconscionable contracts, but now they are more usually treated as an exceptional category. 7–127

Unconscionable bargains with poor and ignorant persons.[556] Another principle of equity which can be traced back to the old equitable rules permitting intervention for the protection of expectant heirs[557] has been used in modern times to justify a substantial broadening of this jurisdiction. The old equitable principle was reviewed and restated in *Fry v Lane*[558] where it was held that the court could set aside a purchase at a considerable undervalue from "a poor and ignorant man" who had received no independent advice. Here the property being sold consisted of reversionary rights, so the case fell squarely within the old principles about expectant heirs, but little stress was laid upon the nature of the property in the judgment in this case; indeed it was expressly said that the principle extended to a sale of property in possession. In two more modern 7–128

552 See Waddams (1976) 39 M.L.R. 369; Reiter (1981) 1 O.J.L.S. 347.

553 See, e.g. dicta of Lord Simon of Glaisdale in *Shiloh Spinners Ltd v Harding* [1973] A.C. 691, 726; Lord Diplock in *A. Schroeder Music Publishing Co v Macaulay* [1974] 1 W.L.R. 1308, 1315; *Burmah Oil Co v Bank of England*, *The Times*, July 4, 1981 (no relief for mere unfair bargain—there must be an unconscionable bargain—a bargain whose very terms reveal conduct which shocks the conscience of the court); and *Alec Lobb (Garages) Ltd v Total Oil (Great Britain) Ltd* [1985] 1 W.L.R. 173, in which the Court of Appeal did not rule out a broad doctrine of unconscionability, though it held that no unconscientious conduct had occurred. See also cases cited below, para.7–128.

554 See, e.g. *Photo Productions Ltd v Securicor Transport Ltd* [1980] A.C. 827; *The Chikuma* [1981] 1 W.L.R. 314; *Multiservice Bookbinding Ltd v Marden* [1979] Ch. 84; for a slightly earlier dictum to the same effect, see Lord Radcliffe in *Bridge v Campbell Discount Co Ltd* [1962] A.C. 600, 626; and, in the particular context of unconscionability, below, para.7–124.

555 See below, paras 7–129 et seq.

556 Bamforth [1995] L.M.C.L.Q. 538.

557 e.g. *Aylesford v Morris* (1873) L.R. 3 Ch. App. 484. See Treitel, *Law of Contract*, 12th edn (by Peel), para.10–040.

558 (1888) 40 Ch D 312. See also *Wood v Abrey* (1818) 3 Madd. 417; *Longmate v Ledger* (1860) 2 Giff. 157; *Clark v Malpas* (1862) 4 De G.F. & J. 401; *Baker v Monk* (1864) 4 De G.J. & S. 388; *Prees v Coke* (1870) L.R. 6 Ch. App. 645; *James v Kerr* (1888) 40 Ch D 449; *Rees v De Bernardy* (1896) 2 Ch. 437; cf. *Harrison v Guest* (1860) 8 H.L.C. 481.

decisions, on somewhat similar facts, it was held that the court could set aside a contract by a separated wife by which she gave up her rights in the matrimonial home in consideration of an indemnity against liability on the mortgage. In the first of these cases[559] Megarry J. held that the requirements of "poverty" and "ignorance" referred to in *Fry v Lane* were satisfied because the wife was a "member of the lower income group" and "less highly educated" (than whom, does not appear). In the second,[560] Balcombe J. was willing to follow Megarry J.'s decision, though the question did not strictly arise, where the wife "was certainly not wealthy", and was also not "ignorant", but in fact "an intelligent woman". These generous interpretations of the meaning of vague words like "poverty" and "ignorance" appear, on their face, to open the door to the possibility of relief in a substantial number of contracts where the terms are exorbitant or unconscionable, and the party aggrieved did not have independent advice, and since there have been a number of cases in which relief on the ground of unconscionability has been considered[561] and some in which it has been granted. Thus the Privy Council has set aside the renewal of a lease, on very unfavourable terms, granted by a plaintiff who was "somewhat slow" and who was put under pressure by the lessee while the plaintiff's usual advisor was away.[562] In *Crédit Lyonnais Bank Nederland NV v Burch*[563] the defendant had given a guarantee and charged her flat to secure the borrowings of her employer's company, in circumstances in which the transaction was manifestly disadvantageous to her. The case was decided on the ground that the bank had constructive notice of undue influence by the employer, but both Nourse and Millett L.JJ. suggested that it might have been argued that she had a direct right, as against the bank, to set aside the transaction on the grounds of unconscionability. The bank had only explained the nature of the transaction without giving the defendant adequate information as to the risks and should have known she had not taken independent advice.[564]

7–129 **Scope of the doctrine.** The doctrine of unconscionable bargains seems to be limited in three ways. The first is that the bargain must be oppressive to the complainant in overall terms; the second that it may only apply when the complainant was suffering from certain types of bargaining weakness; and the third that the other party must have acted unconscionably in the sense of

[559] *Cresswell v Potter* [1978] 1 W.L.R. 255n. (decided in 1968).

[560] *Backhouse v Backhouse* [1978] 1 W.L.R. 243.

[561] See *Multiservice Bookbinding Ltd v Marden* [1979] Ch. 84; *Alec Lobb (Garages) Ltd v Total Oil (Great Britain) Ltd* [1983] 1 W.L.R. 87; *Hart v O'Connor* [1985] A.C. 1000. Unconscionability was not found on the facts in *Pye v Ambrose* [1994] N.P.C. 53. The *Multiservice* and *Alec Lobb* cases draw on a line of authority relating to mortgages: see Bamforth [1995] L.M.C.L.Q. 538, 546. A plea of unconscionability was rejected on the facts in *Jones v Morgan* [2001] EWCA Civ 995, *The Times*, July 24, 2001.

[562] *Boustany v Piggott* (1995) 69 P. & C.R. 298; see also *Watkin v Watson-Smith*, *The Times*, July 3, 1986.

[563] [1997] 1 All E.R. 144, noted Chen-Wishart [1997] C.L.J. 60; Hooley and O'Sullivan [1997] L.M.C.L.Q. 17; Tijo (1997) 113 L.Q.R. 10.

[564] [1997] 1 All E.R. 144, 151, 152–153.

having knowingly taken advantage of the complainant. These points will be discussed in turn.[565]

An oppressive bargain. The modern cases in which relief has been granted or said to be available have all involved transactions which were substantively unfair in that the complainant was parting with property for much less than it was worth,[566] or getting nothing out of the transaction.[567] "The resulting transaction has been, not merely hard or improvident, but overreaching and oppressive" so that its terms, together with the conduct of the stronger party, "shock the conscience of the court".[568] In *Boustany v Piggott*[569] the original lease had reserved a rent of $833 per month and imposed an obligation of repair on the lessee; the new lease which was set aside at the instance of the lessor imposed no such obligation, while the rent was fixed at $1,000 per month for a 10-year period and the lease was renewable for a further 10 years at the same rent. Thus it is doubtful whether English courts would follow dicta in Australia[570] to the effect that inadequacy of consideration is not essential.[571] It is equally doubtful whether the doctrine would be applied as it has been in the United States[572] to a single harsh term such as a limitation of liability clause, unless the contract was oppressive overall.[573] 7–130

[565] In *Irvani v Irvani* [2000] 1 Lloyd's Rep. 412, 424, Buxton L.J., delivering the only full judgment in the Court of Appeal, said that this paragraph (in the 28th edn of this work) accurately sets out the limitations on the doctrine of unconscionability. The doctrine is quite distinct from that of undue influence, which: "[I]s concerned with the prior relationship between the contracting parties, and whether that was the motivation or reason for which the bargain was entered into." (In Australia it seems that the courts may be abandoning this distinction: see *Bridgewater v Leahy* [1998] HCA 66, [1998] 158 A.L.R 66 High Ct.) In *Bank of Credit and Commerce International SA v Ali (No.1)* [2000] I.R.L.R. 398 the Court of Appeal (Buxton L.J. dubitante) held that equity can give relief against a release of a claim on the ground of unconscionability where the release was procured by the other party's deliberate concealment of facts, if that party knew or believed that the party giving the release could not discover the facts and the releasing party had not in fact known of them. In the House of Lords ([2001] UKHL 8, [2002] 1 A.C. 251), the case was decided upon other grounds, but there is a suggestion by Lord Nicholls (at [32]–[33]) that in extreme cases, unconscionability might have a part to play. See above, para.5–013.

[566] *Cresswell v Potter* [1978] 1 W.L.R. 255n.; *Backhouse v Backhouse* [1978] 1 W.L.R. 243; *Watkin v Watson-Smith, The Times*, July 3, 1986; *Boustany v Piggott* (1995) 69 P. & C.R. 298.

[567] *Crédit Lyonnais Bank Nederland NV v Burch* [1997] 1 All E.R. 144.

[568] *Alec Lobb Ltd v Total Oil (Great Britain) Ltd* [1983] 1 W.L.R. 87, 94–95, per Peter Millett Q.C. sitting as a Deputy High Court Judge (reversed in part [1985] 1 W.L.R. 173); see also *Crédit Lyonnais Bank Nederland NV v Burch* [1997] 1 All E.R. 144, 152–153.

[569] (1995) 69 P. & C.R. 298.

[570] *Blomley v Ryan* (1956) 99 C.L.R. 362, 405; *Commonwealth Bank of Australia v Amadio* (1983) 151 C.L.R. 447, 475. But in the latter case (which was one of a guarantee, so that the complainant would not expect to receive anything) Deane J. said that the transaction might be unfair, unreasonable and unjust although there was no inadequacy of consideration.

[571] cf. the suggestion in *Langton v Langton* [1995] 2 F.L.R. 890 that the jurisdiction to set aside contracts on the ground of unconscionability does not extend to gifts, as this would mean that in the case of all gifts by poor and ignorant persons without independent advice, an onus would be placed on the recipient to show that the gift was fair, just and reasonable. Note that Capper (1998) 114 L.Q.R. 479 argues that "transactional imbalance" is not a precondition of relief but only evidential (at 491). He thus argues that unconscionability and undue influence can be assimilated.

[572] See below, para.7–136.

[573] cf. *Multiservice Bookbinding Ltd v Marden* [1979] Ch. 84.

7–131 **The complainant's circumstances.** As noted earlier,[574] the traditional requirement that the complainant be "poor and ignorant"[575] received a broad interpretation in some of the modern cases; and in a recent case[576] the majority of the Court of Appeal were prepared to say that relief could have been given to a young employee who had charged her flat to secure her employer's debts without discussing the requirement.[577] Commonwealth cases have allowed relief in a broad variety of "disabling" circumstances. In *Blomley v Ryan*[578] Fullagar J. listed as examples:

> "... poverty or need of any kind, sickness, age, sex, infirmity of body or mind, drunkenness, illiteracy or lack of education, lack of assistance or explanation where assistance or explanation is necessary."

And in *Commercial Bank of Australia v Amadio*[579] Deane J. said that the jurisdiction is established:

> "... as extending generally to circumstances in which ... a party to a transaction was under a special disability in dealing with the other party with the consequences that there was an absence of any reasonable degree of equality between them."

It is submitted that English law can give relief in an equally wide range of circumstances, provided that:

> "... one party has been at a serious disadvantage to the other, whether through poverty, or ignorance, or lack of advice, *or otherwise*, so that circumstances existed of which unfair advantage could be taken."[580]

7–132 **Unconscionable conduct.** A contract will not be set aside merely because the aggrieved party did not have independent advice and the consideration was inadequate. It must also be shown that the other party engaged in unconscionable conduct or an unconscientious use of power.[581] He must have behaved:

> "... in a morally reprehensible manner ... which affects his conscience ... The classic example of an unconscionable bargain is where advantage has been taken of a young, inexperienced or ignorant person to introduce a term which no sensible, well-advised ... person would have accepted."[582]

---

[574] Above, para.7–128.

[575] e.g. *Fry v Lane* (1888) 40 Ch D 312.

[576] *Crédit Lyonnais Bank Nederland NV v Burch* [1997] 1 All E.R. 144.

[577] See Hooley and O'Sullivan [1997] L.M.C.L.Q. 17, 23.

[578] (1956) 99 C.L.R. 362, 405.

[579] (1983) 151 C.L.R. 447, 474. In that case the complainants were elderly immigrants with limited knowledge of written English.

[580] *Alec Lobb Ltd v Total Oil (Great Britain) Ltd* [1983] 1 W.L.R. 87, 94–95, per Peter Millett Q.C. sitting as a Deputy High Court Judge (reversed in part [1985] 1 W.L.R. 173) (emphasis supplied). In *Barclays Bank Plc v Schwartz, The Times*, August 2, 1995 Millett L.J. observed that a person whose illiteracy or inability to speak English is taken advantage of may, in an appropriate case, be able to have the contract set aside on the grounds of unconscionability. See below, para.7–117.

[581] *Alec Lobb (Garages) Ltd v Total Oil (Great Britain) Ltd* [1985] 1 W.L.R. 173, 182.

[582] *Multiservice Bookbinding Ltd v Marden* [1979] Ch. 84, 110.

If there has been no equitable fraud, victimisation, taking advantage, overreaching or other unconscionable conduct, relief will not be granted.[583] Thus in *Hart v O'Connor*[584] the vendor was of unsound mind, but this was not apparent to the purchaser and the vendor appeared to be advised by a solicitor who had proposed the terms of the bargain. The Privy Council held that the contract could not be set aside on the grounds of insanity unless the vendor's incapacity was known to the purchaser,[585] nor as unconscionable because the purchaser had acted with complete innocence. In the words of Lord Brightman, there must be "procedural unfairness" as well as "contractual imbalance," though:

> "... contractual imbalance may be so extreme as to raise a presumption of procedural unfairness, such as undue influence or some other form of victimisation."[586]

In *Boustany v Piggott*[587] Lord Templeman, delivering the judgment of the Privy Council, agreed in general terms with the submissions of counsel for the appellant:

(1) there must be unconscionability in the sense that objectionable terms have been imposed on the weaker party in a reprehensible manner;

(2) "unconscionability" refers not only to the unreasonable terms but to the behaviour of the stronger party, which must be morally culpable or reprehensible;

(3) unequal bargaining power or objectively unreasonable terms are no basis for interference in equity in the absence of unconscionable or extortionate abuse where, exceptionally and as a matter of common fairness, "it is unfair that the strong should be allowed to push the weak to the wall";

(4) a contract will not be set aside as unconscionable in the absence of actual or constructive fraud or other unconscionable conduct; and

(5) the weaker party must show unconscionable conduct, in that the stronger party took unconscientious advantage of the weaker party's disabling condition or circumstances.[588]

---

583 *Hart v O'Connor* [1985] A.C. 1000; *Boustany v Pigott* [1993] N.P.C. 75 PC; *Westpac Banking Corp v Paterson* [2001] FCA 1630, [2001] 187 A.L.R. 168 (Federal Ct of Australia); *Portman Building Society v Dusaugh* [2000] 2 All E.R. (Comm) 221.

584 [1985] A.C. 1000.

585 Overruling *Archer v Cutler* [1980] 1 N.Z.L.R. 386; below, para.8–068. But the New Zealand court has rejected this approach to unconscionability: *Nichols v Jessup (No.2)* [1986] 1 N.Z.L.R. 237; see Bamforth [1995] L.M.C.L.Q. 538, 550.

586 *Hart v O'Connor* [1985] A.C. 1000, 1018. Lord Brightman's language seems to reflect American terminology, below, para.7–121. It is interesting to contrast the justification offered in *Redgrave v Hurd* (1881) 20 Ch D 1, 13, for rescission for innocent misrepresentation; it is moral fraud to insist on keeping the contract now you know the representation is false. cf. *Rooney v Conway* [1982] 5 N.I.J.B.

587 (1995) 69 P. & C.R. 298, 303.

588 Lord Templeman's statement of the law was adopted by Buxton L.J. in *Irvani v Irvani* [2000] 1 Lloyd's Rep. 412, 424, delivering the only full judgment in the Court of Appeal.

7–133 **Unconscionable conduct may be inferred.** In *Crédit Lyonnais Bank Nederland NV v Burch*[589] Millett L.J. pointed out that it would be necessary to show that the bank had imposed the objectionable terms in a morally objectionable manner, but said that impropriety might be inferred from the terms of the transaction itself in the absence of an innocent explanation.[590]

7–134 **Absence of independent advice.** The traditional statements of the rule on unconscionable bargains also state that the complainant must have acted without independent advice. However, it is submitted that the absence of such advice is not essential. In *Crédit Lyonnais Bank Nederland NV v Burch*[591] Millett L.J. said that the fact that the complainant had been offered independent advice would not necessarily save a transaction which was so harsh that no competent advisor could have recommended it. In *Boustany v Piggott*[592] a lawyer called on to prepare the documents had pointed out that their terms were disadvantageous but did not refuse to proceed with execution of the document; the Privy Council refused to interfere with the trial judge's finding that the transaction was unconscionable. It may be suggested that an oppressive transaction will only be saved by independent advice if the advisor explains fully to the complainant why the transaction is so disadvantageous and that she is under no obligation to agree to it, or to agree to the terms offered; and (in an extreme case) refuses to act on her behalf if she persists in going ahead.[593]

7–135 **Burden of showing fair, just and reasonable.** Once the conditions for relief are met, the burden shifts to the stronger party to show that the transactions are fair, just and reasonable.[594] In practice, this will mean showing either that, in the particular circumstances, the transaction was not in fact oppressive; or that the complainant was fully aware of what she was doing. This will normally come back to the question of whether she had received proper independent advice.

7–136 **Commonwealth and American developments.** It has already been stated that Commonwealth courts appear to be more in favour of a possible general doctrine of unconscionability.[595] There is a good deal of Canadian authority,[596] and in Australia the courts seem prepared to give relief in a wide range of circumstances provided that advantage has been taken,[597] and to apply the

---

589 [1997] 1 All E.R. 144.

590 [1997] 1 All E.R. 144, 153, referring to *Multiservice Bookbinding Ltd v Marden* [1979] Ch. 84, 110 and *Alec Lobb (Garages) Ltd v Total Oil (Great Britain) Ltd* [1983] 1 W.L.R. 87, 95.

591 [1997] 1 All E.R. 144.

592 (1995) 69 P. & C.R. 298.

593 cf. above, para.7–095.

594 *Aylesford v Morris* (1873) 8 Ch. App. 484, 490–491.

595 See generally Bamforth [1995] L.M.C.L.Q. 538, passim. In *Irvani v Irvani* [2000] 1 Lloyd's Rep. 412, 425, Buxton L.J., delivering the only full judgment in the Court of Appeal, said that he agreed with this paragraph in saying that the Commonwealth cases "do or may go beyond the limits of present English authority".

596 See, e.g. *Black v Wilcox* (1976) 30 D.L.R. (3d) 192; *Paris v Machnik* (1972) 30 D.L.R. (3d) 723; *Morrison v Coast Finance* (1965) 55 D.L.R. (2d) 710; and other cases cited in Waddams, *Law of Contracts*, 3rd edn, para.511 and Enman (1987) 16 Anglo-Am.L.R. 191.

597 *Blomley v Ryan* (1956) 99 C.L.R. 362.

criteria liberally.[598] In America an even broader doctrine of unconscionability is now a well-established principle of the law entitling courts to refuse to enforce contracts, or contractual clauses, which are harsh, exorbitant or unconscionable. The principle is partly statutory, deriving from s.2–302 of the Uniform Commercial Code, but is widely applied by American courts as a matter of common law where the Code is inapplicable. A distinction is generally drawn in American law between "procedural unconscionability" and "substantive unconscionability".[599] The former can be invoked where some element of oppression or wrongdoing (in a broad sense) has occurred in the process of making the contract: this enables courts to use doctrines like duress and undue influence as merely illustrative of a broader principle requiring that undue advantage or surprise should not be taken of a party; so matters like illiteracy, lack of knowledge of the English language, general inability to comprehend a complicated document, etc. may be treated as matters of procedural unconscionability. Substantive unconscionability, by contrast, goes to the actual substance of the contract and its terms. In practice substantive unconscionability covers excessively wide exclusion clauses on the one side, and grossly exorbitant or excessive prices, on the other. The leading commentary on the Uniform Commercial Code states that:

> "Most parties who assert 2–302 [sic. the Code section dealing with unconscionability] and most of those who have used it successfully in reported cases have been consumers. Most of these successful consumer litigants have been poor or otherwise disadvantaged. . . . The courts have not generally been receptive to pleas of unconscionability by one merchant against another."[600]

Unfair terms in consumer contracts. With the implementation of Council Directive 93/13 on Unfair Terms in Consumer Contracts,[601] English law may move slightly closer to the concept of "substantive unconscionability" since art.3 of the Directive defines a contractual term which has not been individually negotiated as unfair (and therefore not binding on the consumer): 7–137

> ". . . if, contrary to the requirements of good faith, it causes a significant imbalance in the parties' rights and obligations arising under the contract, to the detriment of the consumer."

Thus the Regulations[602] implementing the Directive apply to harsh clauses in standard form consumer contracts.[603] But it will not cover the cases of sales at undervalue which have formed the core of unconscionable bargain cases in

---

[598] *Commonwealth Bank of Australia v Amadio* (1983) 57 A.L.J.R. 358; Hardingham (1984) 4 O.J.L.S. 275; *Bridgewater v Leahy* [1998] H.C.A 66, [1998] 158 A.L.R. 66 High Ct; but see *Westpac Banking Corp v Paterson* [2001] F.C.A. 1630, [2001] 187 A.L.R. 168 Federal Ct (complainant's disadvantage must be sufficiently evident to other party to make it unconscionable for it to accept complainant's apparent assent). The decision in *Barclays Bank Plc v O'Brien* [1994] 1 A.C. 180 has not been followed: *Garcia v National Australia Bank Ltd* [1998] 155 A.L.R. 614 High Ct.

[599] Leff (1967) 115 Un. Pennsylvania L.R. 485.

[600] White & Summers, *Uniform Commercial Code*, 5th edn (2000), para.4–2, though see also para.4–9.

[601] See below, Ch.15.

[602] Unfair Terms in Consumer Contracts Regulations 1999 (SI 1999/2083).

[603] e.g. the "add-on" clause in *Williams v Walker Thomas Furniture* Co (1965) 121 U.S. App.D.C. 315, 350 F.2d 445.

England since under the Directive and the Regulations the adequacy of the price cannot be reviewed.[604]

7–138 **Statutory provisions.** Under the Consumer Credit Act 1974, a credit agreement which is the result of an unfair relationship may be reopened.[605] When the Act still provided for relief against extortionate credit bargains,[606] there was some disagreement as to whether the principles of unconscionability apply to this jurisdiction,[607] and the same uncertainty seems to arise with the new jurisdiction.

7–139 **Inequality of bargaining power.** A possible principle which is closely related to the broad idea of unconscionability, but slightly narrower in scope, is that of inequality of bargaining power. In *Lloyds Bank Ltd v Bundy*,[608] Lord Denning M.R. stated the single general principle, which, in his view, underlay many of the cases discussed in this chapter. He considered that the thread running through the cases was the concept of "inequality of bargaining power":

> "By virtue of it, the English law gives relief to one who, without independent advice, enters into a contract upon terms which are very unfair or transfers property for a consideration which is grossly inadequate, when his bargaining power is grievously impaired by reason of his own needs or desires, or by his own ignorance or infirmity, coupled with undue influences or pressures brought to bear on him by or for the benefit of the other."[609]

In *National Westminster Bank Plc v Morgan* Lord Scarman questioned (the other Law Lords all concurring) whether there was any need in the modern law to erect a general principle of relief against equality of bargaining power.[610] It is certainly unlikely that mere inequality of bargaining power, even when this leads to the exertion of considerable pressure, will be recognised as a ground for setting aside a contract. Even Lord Denning would not have given relief when the pressure was "the result of the ordinary interplay of forces".[611] And unless and until a general doctrine along the lines suggested by Lord Denning is recognised, it seems that a contract will only be set aside if it falls within one of the recognised categories of "victimisation" such as duress, undue influence or unconscionable advantage taking.

---

[604] 1999 Regulations art.4(2) and reg.6(2), below, paras 15–049—15–062.

[605] Consumer Credit Act 1974 ss.140A–140D, inserted by ss.19–22 of the Consumer Credit Act 2006; see below, para.38–213.

[606] The provisions on extortionate credit bargains, former ss.137–140 of the 1974 Act, have been repealed by s.70 and Sch.4 of the 2006 Act.

[607] cf. *Davies v Directloans Ltd* [1986] 1 W.L.R. 823, 831 and *Shahabina v Gyachi* Unreported 1989, cited in Bamforth [1995] L.M.C.L.Q. 538, 559.

[608] [1975] Q.B. 326; see too *Arrale v Costain Engineering Ltd* [1976] 2 Lloyd's Rep. 98; *Levison v Patent Steam Carpet Cleaning Co Ltd* [1978] Q.B. 69, 78–79; *Langdale v Danby*, *The Times*, November 24, 1981.

[609] *Langdale v Danby*, *The Times*, November 24, 1981. See also *A. Schroeder Music Publishing Co v Macaulay* [1974] 1 W.L.R. 1308, 1315.

[610] [1985] A.C. 686, 708. With respect, the question is not so much whether there is any need for a principle of this character as whether there may not be a need for a residuary principle to catch cases which may otherwise slip through the various statutory protections.

[611] *Lloyd's Bank v Bundy* [1975] Q.B. 326, 336.

Part Three
CAPACITY OF PARTIES

CHAPTER 8

PERSONAL INCAPACITY

		PARA.
1.	In general	8–001
2.	Minors	8–002
	(a) Generally	8–002
	(b) Contracts binding on a minor	8–007
	(i) Liability for necessaries	8–007
	(ii) Apprenticeship, service and other beneficial contracts	8–021
	(c) Contracts binding on a minor unless repudiated	8–030
	(d) Contracts unenforceable against a minor unless ratified	8–042
	(e) Third parties and incapacity	8–045
	(f) Liability of minor in tort and contract	8–046
	(g) Liability of minor to make restitution	8–048
	(h) Agency and membership of societies	8–058
	(i) Liability of parent or guardian	8–061
	(j) Procedure in actions	8–062
	(k) Disposition of property by minors	8–065
3.	Persons lacking mental capacity	8–068
4.	Drunken persons	8–080

1. IN GENERAL

Contractual incapacity. The incapacity of one or more of the contracting parties may defeat an otherwise valid contract. Prima facie, however, the law presumes that everyone has a capacity to contract; so that, where exemption from liability to fulfil an obligation is claimed by reason of want of capacity, this fact must be strictly established on the part of the person who claims the exemption. In English law, three classes of individuals are subject to some degree of personal contractual incapacity.[1] These are minors,[2] persons lacking the requisite mental **8–001**

[1] At common law, a married woman could not in general enter into a contract on her own account either with her husband or with a third party, but successive statutes from 1857 to 1949 progressively removed this incapacity (although an agreement between spouses may be held not to be a contract on the ground of a lack of intention to create legal relations: above, paras 2–168—2–169). However, some uncertainty remains as to the liability of a wife in respect of a contract concluded with her husband before marriage, this turning on whether or not the Law Reform (Married Women and Tortfeasors) Act 1935 s.1(c) reversed the effect of the decision in *Butler v Butler* (1885) 14 QBD 831 (affirmed on a different point (1885) 16 QBD 374). It is submitted that the broader reading of the 1935 Act so as to remove from the law this last vestige of the peculiar treatment of married women's contracting is the more likely given "society's recognition of the equality of the sexes": *Barclays Bank Plc v O'Brien* [1994] 1 A.C. 180, 188, per Lord Browne-Wilkinson (though this observation was made in another context).

[2] See below, paras 8–002 et seq.

capacity,[3] and drunken persons.[4] Abnormal weakness of mind short of such mental incapacity as prevents a person understanding the nature of the transaction, or immaturity of reason in one who has attained full age, or the mere absence of skill upon the subject of the particular contract, affords in itself no ground for relief at law or in equity,[5] although in certain cases, undue influence[6] or unconscionable dealing by the other party[7] or (perhaps) inequality of bargaining power may permit the transaction to be set aside as inequitable.[8] Moreover, illiteracy and unfamiliarity with the English language are not to be equated with disabilities like mental incapacity or drunkenness. According to Millett L.J. in *Barclays Bank Plc v Schwartz*,[9] although all four conditions are disabilities which may prevent the sufferer from possessing a full understanding of a transaction into which he enters:

> "... mental incapacity and drunkenness [may] not only deprive the sufferer of understanding the transaction, but also deprive him of the awareness that he [does] not understand it",

which is not the case as regards an illiterate or a person unfamiliar with English. Again, however, such a person may in an appropriate case claim that the transaction be set aside as a harsh and unconscionable bargain.[10] Moreover, if a person acting in the course of a business takes advantage of the lack of full understanding of the terms of a contract which he concludes with a consumer, this circumstance would be relevant to the issue of the unfairness of these terms under the Unfair Terms in Consumer Contracts Regulations 1999.[11]

2. MINORS[12]

(a) *Generally*

8–002 **Definition of minors.** The age of capacity, for the purposes of the law of contract (as for most other legal purposes) which was 21 at common law, was reduced to 18 by s.1 of the Family Law Reform Act 1969. Section 9 of the same

[3] See below, paras 8–068 et seq.

[4] See below, paras 8–080—8–081.

[5] *Osmond v Fitzroy* (1731) 3 P.Wms. 129; *Lewis v Pead* (1789) 1 Ves. Jun. 19 and see Barton (1987) 103 L.Q.R. 118.

[6] See above, paras 7–056 et seq.

[7] See above, paras 7–126 et seq.

[8] See above, para.7–139.

[9] *The Times*, August 2, 1995; *Hambros Bank Ltd v British Historic Buildings Trust* [1995] N.P.C. 179.

[10] Above, para.7–126.

[11] SI 1999/2083 and see below, para.15–087.

[12] The Report of the Committee on the Age of Majority (1967) Cmnd.3342 contained proposals for fundamental changes in the law relating to minors' contracts but the only recommendation which was implemented was the reduction of the age of majority to 18. Many other proposals for reform are canvassed in the Law Commission Working Paper No.81 on *Minors' Contracts* (1982), including a possible further reduction in the age of contractual capacity to 16. The Law Commission's *Report on Minors' Contracts* (1984) Law Com. No.134 led to the Minors' Contracts Act 1987, on which see below, paras 8–005, 8–045, 8–054—8–057.

Act also abolished the common law rule under which a person attained his majority on the day preceding the relevant anniversary of the birth.[13] Under this section a person is deemed to attain the age of 18 at the commencement of the eighteenth anniversary of his birthday. The Act also declares that a person who is not of full age may be described as a "minor" instead of an "infant".

Very young children. The cases at common law concerning the capacity of a minor to make contracts generally concern older children.[14] However, it has been doubted whether a very young child has the mental capacity to enter a contract, even where the contract is of a type which would normally be held valid, though voidable at common law. In *R. v Oldham Metropolitan BC Ex p. Garlick*,[15] Scott L.J. observed that: **8–003**

> "If a minor is to enter into a contract with the limited efficacy that the law allows, the minor must at least be old enough to understand the nature of the transaction and, if the transaction involves obligations on the minor of a continuing nature, the nature of those obligations."[16]

Thus, while he considered that a child well under the age of ten years could purchase sweets, a four-year-old could not contract for the occupation of residential premises.[17] This approach to the position of very young children can be related to that taken by the common law and by the Mental Capacity Act 2005[18] to mental incapacity in adults.[19]

Contracts binding on a minor. The only contracts which are binding on a minor are contracts for necessaries. There is, however, in the cases, a diversity of meanings given to the word "necessaries". In one sense, the term is confined to necessary goods and services supplied to the minor.[20] In another, it extends to contracts for the minor's benefit and in particular to contracts of apprenticeship, education and service.[21] It has long been customary for a distinction to be drawn between these two classes of contract and it remains convenient for the purposes of exposition, but it is doubtful whether any practical importance still attaches to it. **8–004**

Voidable contracts. Apart from contracts for necessaries and contracts of apprenticeship, education and service, the general rule at common law is that a **8–005**

---

[13] *Re Shurey, Savory v Shurey* [1918] 1 Ch. 263.

[14] At common law the age of majority was 21 years: see above, para.8–002.

[15] [1993] 1 F.L.R. 645. The decision of the Court of Appeal was affirmed by the House of Lords: [1993] A.C. 509.

[16] [1993] 1 F.L.R. 645, 662.

[17] [1993] 1 F.L.R. 645. The context of these observations was the challenge by two four-year-old boys of a local authority's refusal to accept their application for accommodation under the Housing Act 1985 s.62.

[18] ss.2 and 7.

[19] See below, paras 8–068—8–079.

[20] *Wharton v Mackenzie* (1844) 5 Q.B. 606; *Peters v Fleming* (1840) 6 M. & W. 42, 46; *Cowern v Nield* [1912] 2 K.B. 419, 422.

[21] *Walter v Everard* [1891] 2 Q.B. 369; *Roberts v Gray* [1913] 1 K.B. 520, 525, 528, 529; *Shears v Mendeloff* (1914) 30 T.L.R. 342.

minor's contracts are voidable at his option, i.e. not binding on the minor but binding on the other party.[22] Of these voidable contracts there are two classes:

(a) contracts which are binding on the minor unless he repudiates them during minority, or within a reasonable time of attaining his majority[23];

(b) contracts which are not binding on him unless and until he ratifies them after attaining his majority.[24]

Prior to the passing of the Minors' Contracts Act 1987, the second of these classes was partially governed by the Infants Relief Act 1874, which also introduced a fourth category of minors' contracts, namely those declared by s.1 to be "absolutely void". By s.1 of the 1987 Act, however, both these changes were abolished and the position returned to the common law.[25]

8–006 **Deeds.** In general a minor is bound by a deed to the same extent that he would be bound if the promise contained in the deed were parol. He is, therefore, liable on a deed which contains a promise to pay for necessaries.[26]

(b) *Contracts Binding on a Minor*

(i) *Liability for Necessaries*

8–007 **Liability for necessaries.** Executed contracts for "necessary" goods and services were binding on a minor at common law,[27] though this does not mean that the minor will be liable for the price of the goods or services as stipulated.[28] The common law was partially codified in relation to the sale and delivery of necessary goods by the Sale of Goods Act 1893.[29] Less clear is the position of executory contracts for necessaries.[30] The meaning of "necessaries" is an extended one for this purpose, by no means being confined to "necessities" in the ordinary sense.

8–008 **Meaning of necessaries.** Such things as relate immediately to the person of the minor, as his necessary food, drink, clothing, lodging and medicine, are

[22] This passage was relied on as an accurate statement of the law in *Proform Sports Management Ltd v Proactive Sports Management Ltd* [2006] EWHC 2903 (Ch); [2007] Bus. L.R. 93 at [34]. In many old cases certain types of minors' contracts were often said to be "void" but normally where the word "void" was used "voidable" was intended: *Williams v Moor* (1843) 11 M. & W. 256, 263–264.

[23] See below, paras 8–030 et seq.

[24] See below, paras 8–042 et seq.

[25] For the position obtaining under the Infants Relief Act 1874 governing contracts made before June 9, 1987 see the 25th edn of the present work, Vol.I, paras 569–574.

[26] *Walter v Everard* [1891] 2 Q.B. 369. As to the effect of a disposition of property by deed, see below, paras 8–065—8–067.

[27] *Peter v Fleming* (1840) 6 M. & W. 42; *Ryder v Wombwell* (1868) L.R. 4 Ex. 32. See below, para.8–011 as to the position of executory contracts for necessaries.

[28] Below, para.8–010.

[29] s.2 (now Sale of Goods Act 1979 s.3). Cf. Mental Capacity Act 2005 s.7, below, paras 8–074—8–075.

[30] See below, para.8–011.

clearly necessaries for which he is liable. But the term is not confined to such matters only as are positively essential to the minor's personal subsistence or support; it is also employed to denote articles purchased for real use, so long as they are not merely ornamental, or are used as matters of comfort or convenience only, and it is a relative term to be construed with reference to the minor's age and station in life.[31] The burden of showing that the goods supplied are necessaries is always on the supplier:

> "Having shewn that the goods were suitable to the condition in life of the infant, he [the tradesman] must then go on to show that they were suitable to his actual requirements at the time of the sale and delivery."[32]

Thus the fact that the minor was already sufficiently supplied with the goods in question will defeat any claim against him[33] even though this fact was unknown to the supplier.[34]

Contracts for necessaries must be beneficial. It has been held that even a contract for necessaries will not be binding on the minor if it contains harsh and oppressive terms so that the contract, taken as a whole, cannot be said to be for the minor's benefit.[35] So, for instance, in *Flower v London & North Western Ry Co*[36] it was held that a contract of carriage (though clearly a necessary in the circumstances) was void as against the minor because it contained a clause exempting the defendants from liability for injury to the minor even if caused by negligence. However, it is submitted that any judgment of the overall beneficial (or conversely prejudicial) effect of a minor's contract for necessaries should be viewed after the application of any relevant legislation governing the fairness of terms. So, for example, since 1977 a contract term purporting to exclude a business liability for personal injuries and death caused by negligence is ineffective in law[37]; and many types of terms in consumer contracts may be held 'not binding' on a minor/consumer as unfair.[38] 8–009

Liability for goods "sold and delivered". Section 3 of the Sale of Goods Act 1979 (replacing s.2 of the 1893 Act) provides that where necessaries are sold and delivered to a minor he must pay a reasonable price for them. "Necessaries" are defined by s.3(3) as goods suitable to the condition in life of the minor and to his actual requirements at the time of the sale and delivery. There are two 8–010

---

[31] *Peters v Flemming* (1840) 6 M. & W. 42; *Ryder v Wombwell* (1869) L.R. 4 Ex. 32; *Nash v Inman* [1908] 2 K.B. 1.

[32] *Nash v Inman* [1908] 2 K.B. 1, 5, per Cozens-Hardy M.R., *Maddox v Miller* (1813) 1 M. & S. 738; *Harrison v Fane* (1840) 1 M. & G. 550; *Brooker v Scott* (1843) 11 M. & W. 67; *Ryder v Wombwell* (1869) L.R. 4 Ex. 32.

[33] *Barnes & Co v Toye* (1884) 13 QBD 410; *Johnstone v Marks* (1887) 19 QBD 509; *Nash v Inman* [1908] 2 K.B. 1.

[34] *Barnes & Co v Toye* (1884) 13 QBD 410; *Johnstone v Marks* (1887) 19 QBD 509. See also *Bainbridge v Pickering* (1780) 2 W.Bl. 1325; *Brayshaw v Eaton* (1839) 7 Scott 183; *Foster v Redgrave* (1867) L.R. 4 Ex. 35n.

[35] *Fawcett v Smethurst* (1914) 84 L.J.K.B. 473.

[36] [1894] 2 Q.B. 65. See also *Buckpitt v Oates* [1968] 1 All E.R. 1145, 1147–1148.

[37] Unfair Contract Terms Ac 1977 s.2(1).

[38] Unfair Terms in Consumer Contracts Regulations 1999 (SI 1999/2083) and see below, paras 15–004 et seq.

difficult points arising out of the impact of this section on the common law which have not yet been resolved. First, it is uncertain whether a minor can be held liable on an executory contract for the purchase of necessaries; and, secondly, where such a contract is executed by the delivery of the goods to the minor, it is uncertain whether the goods must be necessary for the minor at the time of sale as well as at the time of delivery.

8–011 **Executory contracts for necessary goods.** Section 3 of the Sale of Goods Act 1979 deals only with the case of necessary goods *sold and delivered*; it does not in terms deal with the case of necessaries sold but not delivered to a minor, and such a case may, therefore, still be governed by the common law. But even at common law it is uncertain whether a minor could be liable on an executory contract for the purchase of necessary goods.[39] Whether a minor is so liable may depend on the view taken of the basis of the minor's liability, though this seems to restate the problem rather than to solve it. On the one hand it is argued that the minor is liable on such a contract quite apart from the Act, for a contract for necessaries is one which, despite his lack of age, a minor may make.[40] This may be supported by more recent authority which has recognised that a minor may give a valid consent, notably, to medical treatment,[41] and by analogy with decisions which have held a minor liable on an executory contract for education and training[42]: the reason why an older minor's contracts are not binding on him is a matter of legal policy rather than because he cannot consent.[43] On the other hand it is said that a minor's obligation to pay for goods supplied to him is not contractual at all but is restitutionary, arising *quasi ex contractu*.[44] Delivery would, therefore, be necessary, for without it the minor could not be said to be unjustly enriched at the seller's expense. The supporters of this view buttress their argument by pointing to the fact that the minor is bound to pay only a reasonable price for the goods, rather than the contractual price.[45] This, they say, does not suggest a consensual liability.[46] Moreover, if s.3 of the Sale of Goods Act 1979 were treated as superseding the common law, this would suggest that a minor would not be liable except where the goods were "sold and delivered".[47]

8–012 **Goods necessary when delivered, but not when sold, and vice versa.** The second problem is, to some extent, tied up with the first. At common law there seems to be no doubt that the crucial question was always whether the goods

---

[39] Miles (1927) 43 L.Q.R. 389.
[40] *Nash v Inman* [1908] 2 K.B. 1, 12.
[41] *Gillick v West Norfolk Area Health Authority* [1986] A.C. 112, 169. cf. *R. v D.* [1984] A.C. 778, 806 (consent to kidnapping).
[42] *Roberts v Gray* [1913] 1 K.B. 520; *Hamilton v Bennett* (1930) 94 J.P.N. 136; *Doyle v White City Stadium Ltd* [1935] 1 K.B. 110. See below, para.8–027.
[43] Treitel, *The Law of Contract*, 12th edn (2007 by Peel), para.12–008.
[44] *Nash v Inman* [1908] 2 K.B. 1, 8; *Elkington & Co Ltd v Amery* [1936] 2 All E.R. 86, 88; Birks, *An Introduction to the Law of Restitution* (1985), p.436. cf. *Re Rhodes* (1890) 44 Ch D 94, 105 and *Re J.* [1909] 1 Ch. 574, 577, and below, para.8–074 (mental incapacity).
[45] Sale of Goods Act 1979 s.3(2) and see Birks at p.436.
[46] *Pontypridd Union v Drew* [1927] 1 K.B. 214, 220.
[47] See below, para.8–012.

were necessary when delivered[48] and it was immaterial whether or not they were necessary when the contract was made. This again would seem to support the theory that the minor's liability is restitutionary rather than contractual, for if it were contractual it would be hard to see why a change of circumstances between the time of sale and the time of delivery should affect the liability of the minor. But whatever the position may have been at common law it is possible that s.3 of the Sale of Goods Act has resolved both questions. In *Nash v Inman*[49] the Court of Appeal appears to have treated this section as completely superseding the common law on the liability of a minor for necessary goods, and the wording of the section appears to support the view that the goods must be necessary both when sold and when delivered. If this is indeed the effect of the section it can hardly be supposed that a minor could today be held liable on a purely executory contract.[50]

Necessary services. Services as well as goods may be necessaries. So, for example, a contract for legal[51] or medical services[52] may be a contract for necessaries.[53] It has also been held that a contract by a widow (who was a minor) to pay for her husband's funeral was binding as for a necessary.[54] Unlike the uncertain position in respect of contracts to supply necessary goods, it is clear that executory contracts for necessary services may be enforced against a minor, at least in the context of apprenticeship or contracts for education. Thus, a minor's promise to pay part of the premium for his apprenticeship on gaining his majority has been enforced[55] and his (reasonable) restrictive covenant against competing with his master after service is concluded has been enforced by injunction after gaining his majority.[56] In *Roberts v Gray*, the Court of Appeal held a minor who had entered a contract to go on a tour with a professional billiard player liable in damages for failing to proceed with the tour.[57] The court considered that once it had been decided that a contract is one for necessaries not qualified by unreasonable terms, then it was binding on the minor, so as to allow the other contracting party all such remedies as were appropriate on breach.[58] The reasoning of these decisions runs counter to that which argues for a non-contractual basis of an infant's liability for necessaries.[59] The question whether 8–013

[48] Winfield (1942) 58 L.Q.R. 82.

[49] [1908] 2 K.B. 1, 7, 9.

[50] It is, however, arguable that the words of s.3 of the Sale of Goods Act "at the time of the sale and delivery" appear to contemplate one time only. See also Treitel, *The Law of Contract*, 12th edn (2007 by Peel), para.12–008. If a minor is liable on an executory contract it would have to be decided whether the goods must be necessary when sold, or at the time when they ought to have been delivered, or perhaps even when the minor refuses to take delivery.

[51] *Helps v Clayton* (1864) 17 C.B.(N.S.) 553; *De Stacpoole v De Stacpoole* (1887) 37 Ch D 139; *Re Jones (An Infant)* (1883) 48 L.T. 188.

[52] *Huggins v Wiseman* (1690) Carth. 110. But quaere whether this is still so having regard to the National Health Service.

[53] cf. the position as regards a person lacking mental capacity for necessary goods and services under the Mental Capacity Act 2005 s.7, below, para.8–075.

[54] *Chapple v Cooper* (1844) 13 M. & W. 252.

[55] *Walter v Everard* [1891] 2 Q.B. 369.

[56] *Gadd v Thompson* [1911] 1 K.B. 304.

[57] [1913] 1 K.B. 520. cf. Mathews (1982) 33 N.Ir.L.Q. 150, 154–155.

[58] [1913] 1 K.B. 520, 530.

[59] cf. above, para.8–011.

the services must be necessary only when rendered or whether they must also be necessary when ordered seems never to have been considered.

8–014 **Fact and law.** Whether the particular goods or services are necessaries has for many years been treated as a question of fact in each case, subject to there being some evidence on which they might properly be so found.[60] Today, however, it would seem that, while it is still a pure question of fact whether the minor is already well supplied with the goods or services in question, it is really a question of mixed fact and law or a matter of evaluating the facts whether the goods or services can be treated as necessaries in themselves.[61]

8–015 **Contracts for both necessaries and non-necessaries.** If a minor buys a quantity of goods, some of which may be necessaries, but a substantial number of which cannot be necessaries, it has been said that the minor will not be liable at all if the contract is one entire contract.[62] On the other hand the courts have sometimes allowed a claimant to recover for necessaries while disallowing a claim for non-necessaries without adverting to the question whether the contract was an entire contract.[63] Since the minor is not bound to pay the contract price but only a reasonable price, there seems no reason why this course should not always be followed.[64]

8–016 **Examples.** The following have been held to be necessaries (although it must be remembered that the usages of society change and articles which once were necessaries may no longer be held to be so and vice versa): engagement and wedding rings,[65] regimental uniform (for an enlisted soldier),[66] presents for a fiancée,[67] a racing bicycle for a youth earning (in 1898) 21s. a week,[68] the hire of horses[69] and for work done for them,[70] and the hire of a car to fetch luggage from a station six miles away.[71] On the other hand, the following have been held not to be necessaries: 11 fancy waistcoats for a Cambridge undergraduate already sufficiently supplied with clothing,[72] expensive dinners with fruit and confectionery for another undergraduate,[73] jewelled solitaire sleeve-links for the son of a deceased baronet,[74] a large quantity of tobacco for an army officer,[75] lessons

---

[60] *Ryder v Wombwell* (1868) L.R. 3 Ex. 90.

[61] cf. *Benmax v Austin Motor Co Ltd* [1955] A.C. 370.

[62] *Stocks v Wilson* [1913] 2 K.B. 235, 241–242. As to entire contracts, see below, para.24–043.

[63] See, e.g. *Ryder v Wombwell* (1868) L.R. 3 Ex. 90.

[64] Certainly this would be the right course if the minor's liability is restitutionary; see above, para.8–011.

[65] *Elkington & Co Ltd v Amery* [1936] 2 All E.R. 86.

[66] *Coates v Wilson* (1804) 5 Esp. 152.

[67] *Jenner v Walker* (1868) 19 L.T. 398; cf. *Hewlings v Graham* (1901) 70 L.J. Ch. 568; *Elkington & Co Ltd v Amery* [1936] 2 All E.R. 86.

[68] *Clyde Cycle Co v Hargreaves* (1898) 78 L.T. 296.

[69] *Hart v Prater* (1837) 1 Jur. 623; cf. *Harrison v Fane* (1840) 1 M. & G. 550.

[70] *Clowes v Brook* (1739) 2 Str. 1101.

[71] *Fawcett v Smethurst* (1914) 84 L.J.K.B. 473.

[72] *Nash v Inman* [1908] 2 K.B. 1.

[73] *Wharton v Mackenzie* (1844) 5 Q.B. 606.

[74] *Ryder v Wombwell* (1869) L.R. 4 Ex. 32.

[75] *Bryant v Richardson* (1866) L.R. 3 Ex. 93.

in flying for a law student,[76] a vanity-bag worth (in 1936) £20, 10s. bought by the son of an ex-cabinet minister for his fiancée,[77] a hunter for an impecunious cavalry officer,[78] a collection of snuff-boxes and curios[79] and a second-hand sports car.[80]

Trading contracts. A minor's trading contracts are not contracts for necessaries.[81] While there is no precise definition of a trading contract for this purpose, it has been held that a minor will not be liable in contract upon an agreement for services performed for him to enable him to carry on his trade,[82] or for goods supplied to him for the purposes of his trade,[83] or where he fails to deliver goods to a purchaser who has paid for them.[84] However, if the contract can be considered to be one by which the minor gains proficiency in a certain trade (as in a contract of service or apprenticeship) it will be binding on him if, viewed as a whole, it is for his benefit.[85] 8–017

Where a minor's contract is a "trading contract" the minor cannot be adjudicated bankrupt on this basis for he is not a debtor at law,[86] though he may be liable for (and be made bankrupt on account of) a tax debt.[87] It has even been held that a minor is not liable in restitution for the recovery of the price of goods sold by him but not delivered,[88] but the authority of this decision is open to doubt since it dates from a time when a restitutionary claim was thought to be founded on an "implied contract", and it has been persuasively argued that it "allows an antiquated and now discredited pleading fiction to influence substantive rights".[89] Moreover, the court now possesses a discretion to order the minor to transfer money, or property representing it, to the other contracting party under s.3(1) of the Minors' Contracts Act 1987.[90] 8–018

Necessaries for wife or children. There have been some extensions of the doctrine of minors' necessaries. Necessaries for a minor's wife are necessaries for him,[91] though he is not liable on contracts made by his wife unless he has 8–019

---

[76] *Hamilton v Bennett* (1930) 94 J.P.N. 136.
[77] *Elkington & Co Ltd v Amery* [1936] 2 All E.R. 86.
[78] *Re Mead* [1916] 2 I.R. 285.
[79] *Stocks v Wilson* [1913] 2 K.B. 235.
[80] *Coull v Kolbuc* (1969) 68 W.W.R. 76 (Alberta District Ct).
[81] *Lowe v Griffith* (1835) 1 Scott 458.
[82] *Re Jones, Ex p. Jones* (1881) 18 Ch D 109.
[83] *Mercantile Union Guarantee Corp Ltd v Ball* [1937] 2 K.B. 498. But where a minor used goods (supplied to him in his trade) for household purposes he was held liable: *Turberville v Whitehouse* (1823) 1 C. & P. 94.
[84] *Cowern v Nield* [1912] 2 K.B. 419.
[85] *Roberts v Gray* [1913] 1 K.B. 520; *Doyle v White City Stadium Ltd* [1935] 1 K.B. 110. cf. *Shears v Mendeloff* (1914) 30 T.L.R. 342; below, paras 8–021—8–029.
[86] *Re Jones, Ex p. Jones* (1881) 18 Ch D 109, 120; *Re Davenport* [1963] 1 W.L.R. 817.
[87] *Re A Debtor (No.564 of 1949)* [1950] Ch. 282.
[88] *Cowern v Nield* [1912] 2 K.B. 419.
[89] Goff & Jones, *Law of Restitution*, 7th edn (2002), p.643 and see below, para.29–009.
[90] See below, paras 8–054—8–057.
[91] *Rainsford v Fenwick* (1671) Carter 215; *Turner v Trisby* (1719) 1 Stra. 168.

authorised them.[92] Either spouse is bound by a contract to pay for the funeral of the other where he or she dies leaving no sufficient estate.[93]

8–020 **Loans for necessaries.** A minor cannot be made liable on a loan advanced to enable him to purchase necessaries.[94] If, however, the loan is actually expended on necessaries, the lender can recover the amount spent thereon under the equitable principle of subrogation laid down in *Marlow v Pitfield*.[95] A person who purchased necessaries for a minor at his request was held at common law to be entitled to sue the minor for money paid to his use.[96] It would seem that today such an action could be maintained either by treating the purchaser as a lender and entitled to invoke the principle of subrogation, or by treating the purchaser as the minor's agent.[97] Any security given in respect of a loan is unenforceable even though the money was required for necessaries[98] and an account stated is voidable despite the fact that some of the items in the account consist of necessaries.[99] A bill of exchange or promissory note is void both as against the minor and any third person although given in payment of necessaries.[100] But the person who supplied the necessaries can, of course, disregard the account stated or the security and sue for a reasonable price.[101]

(ii) *Apprenticeship, Service and other Beneficial Contracts*

8–021 **Beneficial contracts.** Since it is of obvious advantage to a minor that he should be able to fit himself for his future trade or profession and to obtain a livelihood, he may enter into contracts of apprenticeship, service, education and instruction, provided that these are beneficial to him. As was said by Kay L.J. in *Clements v London & North Western Ry Co*[102]:

> "It has been clearly held that contracts of apprenticeship and with regard to labour are not contracts to an action on which the plea of infancy is a complete defence, and the question has always been, both at law and in equity, whether the contract, when

---

[92] The wife's "agency of necessity" was abolished by s.41 of the Matrimonial Proceedings and Property Act 1970: see Vol.II, para.31–049.

[93] *Chapple v Cooper* (1844) 13 M. & W. 252. It was doubted whether a minor would be bound by a contract to pay for the funeral of a parent or other relative: 260. The common law rule that a husband is always bound to pay for his wife's funeral no longer obtains: *Rees v Hughes* [1946] K.B. 517.

[94] *Darby v Boucher* (1694) 1 Salk. 279.

[95] (1719) 1 P.Wms. 558; *Re National Permanent Benefit Building Society* (1869) L.R. 5 Ch. App. 309, 313; *Martin v Gale* (1876) 4 Ch D 428; *Lewis v Alleyne* (1888) 4 T.L.R. 560; *Orakpo v Manson Investments Ltd* [1978] A.C. 95; Birks, *An Introduction to the Law of Restitution* (1985), p.398. For a similar principle in a different context, see *The Mogileff* (1921) 6 Ll.L. Rep. 528; *The Fairport (No.5)* [1967] 2 Lloyd's Rep. 162.

[96] *Ellis* v *Ellis* (1689) Comb. 482; *Earle v Peale* (1712) 10 Mod. 67.

[97] See below, para.8–058.

[98] *Martin v Gale* (1876) 4 Ch D 428.

[99] *Williams v Moor* (1843) 11 M. & W. 256. At common law, an account stated may be ratified by the minor on reaching majority: 266. The Infants Relief Act 1874 s.1, which made void all accounts stated with infants, was repealed by the Minors' Contracts Act 1987 s.1.

[100] *Re Soltykoff, Ex p. Margrett* [1891] 1 Q.B. 413; cf. Bills of Exchange Act 1882 s.22(2).

[101] [1891] 1 Q.B. 413; *Walter v Everard* [1891] 2 Q.B. 369.

[102] [1894] 2 Q.B. 482, 491.

carefully examined in all its terms, is for the benefit of the infant. If it is so, the court before which the question comes will not allow the infant to repudiate it."

Apprenticeship. A minor may bind himself apprentice to an employer, and after the employer's death to his executors provided that they carry on the same trade in the same place.[103] The validity of such a contract depends on whether the contract is as a whole, beneficial to the minor at the time when it is entered into.[104] If the contract of apprenticeship imposes onerous terms[105] such as a penalty clause,[106] or a provision that his wages are to depend on the will of his employer,[107] or if it places the minor virtually in a position of entire subservience to his employer,[108] it will be unenforceable. The question of fairness will depend upon whether the clause was common to employment contracts at the time, or accorded with the current conditions of trade, so that the employer was reasonably justified in imposing it in protection to himself.[109] 8–022

A contract of apprenticeship must be made in writing[110] and it is usually made by deed under which the minor promises faithfully to serve his employer and the employer to provide proper instruction for the minor and to pay him wages. Although a minor may by contract bind himself apprentice, during the period of apprenticeship no action is maintainable against him on his covenant to serve in such a contract,[111] nor can an injunction be obtained to enforce a negative covenant in the contract.[112] Accordingly, at one time it was customary for the minor's father or mother to execute the contract so as to covenant for his due performance of the agreement.[113] After his apprenticeship has ceased, however, a restrictive covenant in such a contract may be enforced provided that the contract as a whole is for the minor's benefit.[114] 8–023

Rescission of contracts of apprenticeship. It has been held that a minor cannot validly agree to rescind a binding contract of apprenticeship unless its 8–024

---

[103] *Cooper v Simmons* (1862) 7 H. & N. 707.

[104] *De Francesco v Barnum* (1890) 45 Ch D 430; *Dillingham v Harrison* [1917] W.N. 305; *Mackinlay v Bathurst* (1919) 36 T.L.R. 31; *Chaplin v Leslie Frewin (Publishers) Ltd* [1966] Ch. 71; *Aylesbury Football Club (1997) Ltd v Watford Association Football Club Ltd* Unreported 2000 HC.

[105] *Meakin v Morris* (1884) 12 QBD 352; *De Francesco v Barnum* (1890) 45 Ch D 430.

[106] *De Francesco v Barnum* (1890) 45 Ch D 430, 439.

[107] *R. v Lord* (1850) 12 Q.B. 757; *Corn v Matthews* [1893] 1 Q.B. 310; *Meakin v Morris* (1884) 12 QBD 352; cf. *Green v Thompson* [1899] 2 Q.B. 1.

[108] *De Francesco v Barnum* (1890) 45 Ch D 430.

[109] *Leslie v Fitzpatrick* (1877) 3 QBD 229, 232.

[110] *Kirkby v Taylor* [1910] 1 K.B. 529; *MacDonald v John Twiname Ltd* [1953] 2 Q.B. 304; Apprentices Act 1814 s.2.

[111] *De Francesco v Barnum* (1889) 43 Ch D 165, 171, where it was noted that the master might correct him in service or complain to a justice of the peace to have the apprentice punished under the statute 5 Eliz. c.4. This power was abolished by the Family Law Reform Act 1969 s.11.

[112] (1889) 43 Ch D 165.

[113] Where a child is being "looked after" by a local authority within the meaning of the Children Act 1989 s.22 or is a person qualifying for advice and assistance within the meaning of s.24(2), the authority may undertake any obligation by way of guarantee under any deed of apprenticeship or articles of clerkship which he enters into: s.23(9) Sch.2 para.18(1).

[114] *Cornwall v Hawkins* (1872) 41 L.J.Ch. 435; *Fellows v Wood* (1888) 59 L.T. 513; *Evans v Ware* [1892] 3 Ch. 502; *Gadd v Thompson* [1911] 1 K.B. 304; cf. *Brown v Harper* (1893) 68 L.T. 488.

rescission would be beneficial and this will not normally be so, since if the contract is beneficial to him its dissolution cannot normally be beneficial.[115] In a later case this rule was held to mean that a master cannot terminate a contract of apprenticeship made with a minor on the ground of the latter's breach of his covenants to serve, etc. since the minor cannot by breaking his covenants do indirectly what he may not do directly.[116] However, in the same case it was noted that earlier authorities on the relationship of master and apprentice dated from a time when the master possessed real and considerable powers of domestic chastisement,[117] and that (in 1922) these powers no longer existed and that this social change justified an exception to be made to the master's inability to terminate for breach where:

> "[T]here is habitual and systematic conduct, arising out of the character of the apprentice, which renders it impossible that the work of service and of teaching should continue."[118]

8–025 **Contracts of employment.** A contract of employment entered into by a minor is dealt with by the law in the same manner as a contract of apprenticeship. A contract of employment may be binding even if the minor gives up certain rights available under the general law, at least if he gets something equally advantageous in return,[119] and an agreement to submit disputes to arbitration may also be binding if it forms part of a binding contract of employment.[120] But a contract containing a term by which his work and wages depend on the will of his employer[121] or by which, in consideration of special terms, he contracts to waive all claims for compensation for accident[122] is not binding on him. There are many statutory restrictions on the employment of minors under which it is in general unlawful to employ a person under the age of 13, and the employment of persons between 13 and 16 is subject to many restrictions.[123] An agreement in breach of these provisions would presumably be unenforceable against the minor.

8–026 **Covenants in restraint of trade.** If a minor enters into a contract of employment or apprenticeship containing a covenant restraining his freedom to compete after the termination of the contract, it must first be decided whether this provision would have been valid against an adult.[124] But a covenant of this kind

---

[115] *R. v Great Wigston (Inhabitants)* (1824) 3 B. & C. 484.

[116] *Waterman v Fryer* [1922] 1 K.B. 499.

[117] [1922] 1 K.B. 499, 506.

[118] [1922] 1 K.B. 499, 507, per Shearman J. citing *Learoyd v Brook* [1891] 1 Q.B. 431 as an example. cf. *Mcdonald v John Twiname Ltd* [1953] 2 Q.B. 304, 311 (conduct of apprentice falling short of these "extreme examples").

[119] *Clements v L. & N.W. Ry* [1894] 2 Q.B. 482.

[120] *Slade v Metrodent Ltd* [1953] 2 Q.B. 112.

[121] *R. v Lord* (1848) 12 Q.B. 757.

[122] *Flower v London & N.W. Ry Co* [1894] 2 Q.B. 65; *Butterfield v Sibbitt* [1950] 4 D.L.R. 302; *Buckpitt v Oates* [1968] 1 All E.R. 1145. Such a term would since 1977 not be effective: Unfair Contract Terms Act 1977 s.2(1).

[123] See Children and Young Persons Act 1933 s.18(1), as substituted by Children Act 1972 ss.1(2), 18(3), as amended by Employment of Children Act 1973 s.1(3) and Children (Protection at Work) (No.2) Regulations (SI 2000/2548) reg.2(1).

[124] See below, paras 16–104—16–115.

may not bind a minor even where it would have bound an adult.[125] Whether, if the covenant is void, it invalidates the whole contract of employment or apprenticeship may be a difficult question. It seems that in deciding this question regard must be had to the covenant only in so far as it would have been valid against an adult. If, therefore, the covenant is severable according to the ordinary principles governing severence,[126] the question is whether the enforceable part of the covenant (and not the whole covenant) is so unfair or oppressive as to render the whole contract not beneficial.[127] It seems to follow that if the whole covenant is void quite apart from the defence of minority it should be disregarded altogether in deciding whether the remainder of the contract is beneficial to the minor. Where, on the other hand, the covenant is itself valid and does not render the whole contract void, it may be enforced against the minor by injunction in the usual way.[128]

Education. At common law a minor could bind himself by a contract for instruction and education, on the same ground as other contracts for necessaries. Having regard to modern statutory provisions for compulsory and free schooling it is doubtful if it could still be regarded as necessary for a minor to contract for ordinary schooling below the school-leaving age except perhaps in very special circumstances.[129] But a minor can doubtless still bind himself with regard to other forms of education or instruction, and a minor has been held liable under a contract for singing lessons to be paid for by commission on his earnings as a singer.[130] That the contract is executory appears to be immaterial.[131] On the other hand, not every form of instruction or education is appropriate to the status and position of a particular minor, and a contract for unnecessary education is no more binding than a contract for unnecessary goods.[132] 8–027

Other beneficial contracts. The principle that contracts beneficial to a minor are binding on him is not confined to contracts for necessaries and contracts of employment, apprenticeship or education in a strict sense.[133] It extends also to other contracts which in a broad sense may be treated as analogous to contracts of service, apprenticeship or education.[134] So, for instance, a contract by a minor (who was a professional boxer) with the British Boxing Board of Control whereby he agreed to adhere to the rules of the Board was held binding on him because he could not have earned his living as a boxer without entering into the 8–028

---

[125] *Sir W.C. Leng & Co Ltd v Andrews* [1909] 1 Ch. 763; *Gadd v Thompson* [1911] 1 K.B. 304; *Express Dairy Co v Jackson* (1930) 99 L.J.K.B. 181, 183.

[126] See below, paras 16–194 et seq.

[127] *Bromley v Smith* [1909] 2 K.B. 235.

[128] See cases cited above fn.125.

[129] cf. *Practice Direction (Minor: School Fees)* [1980] 1 W.L.R. 1441; *Practice Direction (Minor: Payment of School Fees)* [1983] 1 W.L.R. 800; *Sherdley v Sherdley* [1988] A.C. 213, 225.

[130] *Mackinlay v Bathurst* (1919) 36 T.L.R. 31.

[131] cf. above, para.8–011.

[132] *Hamilton v Bennett* (1930) 94 J.P.N. 136.

[133] This paragraph in the previous edition was quoted as an accurate statement of the law in *Proform Sports Management Ltd v Proactive Sports Management Ltd* [2006] EWHC 2903 (Ch); [2007] Bus. L.R. 93 at [35].

[134] *Roberts v Gray* [1913] 1 K.B. 525.

agreement.[135] Similarly, it has been held that an agreement between a minor and a publisher for the publication of the minor's biography which was to be written by a "ghost writer" was binding on the minor.[136] So also, a contract between a group of under-age musicians (known as "The Kinks") whereby they appointed a company as their manager and agent was held binding as analogous to a contract of employment.[137] On the other hand, it has been held that a contract by which a footballer aged 15 engaged a person to act as his executive agent and representative in all matters relating to his work as a professional footballer was not analogous to contracts of employment, apprenticeship or education as the agent did not provide any training (which was provided by the professional club where he played) nor did it undertake any matters essential to his livelihood.[138] And there is no general principle to the effect that *any* contract beneficial to a minor is binding on him.[139] So a minor's trading contracts are not binding on him, even if beneficial.[140]

8–029 **Benefit.** Where the contract contains terms, some of which are beneficial to the minor and others not, the question is whether, taken as a whole, it is to his advantage. If it is, he is bound.[141] One stipulation may be so unfair to the minor that it affects the validity of the whole contract[142]; but if the agreement as a whole is for his benefit, in principle he cannot pick and choose and adopt those terms while rejecting those terms which are not beneficial or not clearly beneficial.[143] However, as in the case of contracts for necessaries, the question of the beneficial (or prejudicial) effect of a contract of employment should be judged after the application of any legal control on the effectiveness on any apparently prejudicial terms.[144]

(c) *Contracts Binding on a Minor unless Repudiated*

8–030 **Contracts for an interest of a permanent nature.** Where a minor enters into a contract which involves the acquisition of an interest in property of a permanent nature, with continuing obligations attached to it, he may avoid it at his option

---

135 *Doyle v White City Stadium Ltd* [1935] 1 K.B. 110.

136 *Chaplin v Leslie Frewin (Publishers) Ltd* [1966] Ch. 71.

137 *Denmark Productions Ltd v Boscobel Productions Ltd* (1967) 111 S.J. 715 reversed on other grounds [1969] 1 Q.B. 699; cf. *Shears v Mendeloff* (1914) 30 T.L.R. 342 where the contract contained oppressive terms and was void.

138 *Proform Sports Management Ltd v Proactive Sports Management Ltd* [2006] EWHC 2903 (Ch), [2007] Bus. L.R. 93 at [35]–[41].

139 *Martin v Gale* (1876) 4 Ch D 428, 431; *Mercantile Union Guarantee Corp Ltd v Ball* [1937] 2 K.B. 498; *Bojczuk v Gregorcewicz* [1961] S.A.S.R. 128; *Sellin v Scott* (1901) 1 S.R.(N.S.W.) Eq. 64; but cf. *Slade v Metrodent Ltd* [1953] 2 Q.B. 112, 115.

140 *Cowern v Nield* [1912] 2 K.B. 419, above, para.8–017.

141 *De Francesco v Barnum* (1890) 45 Ch D 430, 439; *Clements v London & N.W. Ry* [1894] 2 Q.B. 482; *Roberts v Gray* [1913] 1 K.B. 520; *Doyle v White City Stadium Ltd* [1935] 1 K.B. 110; *IRC v Mills* [1975] A.C. 38, 53.

142 *R. v Lord* (1848) 12 Q.B. 757; *Meakin v Morris* (1884) 12 QBD 352; *Corn v Matthews* [1893] 1 Q.B. 310; *Flower v London & N.W. Ry Co* [1894] 2 Q.B. 65; *Stephens v Dudbridge Ironworks Co* [1904] 2 K.B. 225; *Express Dairy Co v Jackson* (1930) 99 L.J.K.B. 181.

143 *Slade v Metrodent Ltd* [1935] 2 Q.B. 112.

144 Above, para.8–009.

either before, or within a reasonable time after, attaining his majority.[145] But until he does so avoid it, he is bound to carry out the obligations as they become due; and if he waits until attaining his majority before avoiding the contract, he must then act promptly and clearly, or he will be bound by the contract for its full term. The reason for this was explained by Parke B. in *North Western Ry Co v M'Michael*,[146] a case where a minor was sued for a call on railway shares. The learned Baron, after referring to various cases[147] in which it had been held that minor shareholders in railway companies were liable for calls on their shares whilst they were minors, continued:

> "They have been treated, therefore, as persons in a different situation from mere contractors, for then they would have been exempt; but in truth they are purchasers who have acquired an interest, not in a mere chattel, but in a subject of a permanent nature . . . and with certain obligations attached to it, which they were bound to discharge, and having been thereby placed in a situation analogous to an infant purchaser of real estate, who has taken possession, and thereby becomes liable to all the obligations attached to the estate, or instance, to pay rent in the case of a lease rendering rent . . . unless they have elected to waive or disagree to the purchase altogether, either during infancy or after full age, at either of which times it is competent for an infant to do so."[148]

Despite this explanation there does not seem to be any general principle to the effect that *any* contract conferring an interest in a subject matter of a permanent nature is valid until repudiated. There appear to be four types of case which fall within this category though it is not clear whether these are exhaustive. These are contracts to lease or purchase land, marriage settlements, contracts to subscribe for or to purchase shares, and partnerships. On the other hand, a contract of hire or of hire-purchase entered into by a minor as hirer is either valid (if for necessaries) or unenforceable against the minor without a need for repudiation.[149] **8–031**

Benefit. There is old authority for the view that the underlying principle is one of benefit to the minor—that is, if the contract were beneficial to the minor, he could not avoid it at all,[150] whereas if it were not beneficial, he was not bound at all.[151] But since the mid-nineteenth century it has been established that even if the contract is not beneficial, the minor is bound if he takes possession of the property, but only until he disclaims within the time stated.[152] **8–032**

Contracts to lease or purchase land. At common law a lease to a minor was voidable only,[153] but even during his minority he was liable for accrued rent, if **8–033**

---

[145] Presumably the minor could not affirm and then repudiate the transaction, even if he acted within a reasonable time. cf. the principle stated in para.8–033, below.

[146] (1850) 5 Exch. 114, 123, 124, 127, 128.

[147] *Cork and Bandon Ry v Cazenove* (1847) 10 Q.B. 935; *Leeds & Thirsk Ry Co v Fearnley* (1849) 4 Exch. 26.

[148] (1850) 5 Exch. 114, 123–124.

[149] See *Mercantile Union Guarantee Corp v Ball* [1937] 2 K.B. 498. For criticism see Treitel, *The Law of Contract*, 12th edn (2007 by Peel) paras 12–025—12–026.

[150] *Maddon v White* (1787) 2 Term R. 159.

[151] *Ketsey's Case* (1614) Cro. Jac. 320; Brownlow 120 (*Kirton v Elliott*, 2 Bulst. 69).

[152] *North Western Ry Co v M'Michael* (1850) 5 Exch. 114, 128.

[153] *Davies v Beynon-Harris* (1931) 47 T.L.R. 424.

he had gone into occupation.[154] If he continued in occupation after attaining his majority he was liable for rent which had accrued prior to that date.[155] He was entitled to repudiate the lease either during his minority or within a reasonable time of attaining full age.[156] It seems that a contract by a minor to purchase freehold land is also in this category, i.e. the contract is binding unless and until repudiated by the minor,[157] at all events where there are outstanding obligations on the minor after completion. If there are no such obligations outstanding the question is really academic for even if the minor can repudiate the contract after completion he cannot recover the purchase price.[158]

8–034 **Conveyances to minors.** Since 1926, a minor has not been able to acquire or hold any legal estate,[159] nor has a minor been able to be a tenant for life or exercise the powers of a tenant for life.[160] A conveyance or lease to a minor has taken effect only as an agreement for valuable consideration to execute a settlement in his favour, and in the meantime to hold the land in trust for him.[161] The 1925 property legislation did not, however, affect a minor's beneficial interest, or prevent his holding an equitable interest in settled land.[162] However, this position was altered by the Trusts of Land and Appointment of Trustees Act 1996 as the latter repealed the provisions of the earlier legislation regarding the effect of conveyance or lease to a minor,[163] and instead provided that after its commencement a conveyance of a legal estate to a minor will take effect as a declaration of trust and that, where immediately before its commencement a conveyance is operating as an agreement to execute a settlement in favour of a minor, the agreement ceases to have effect and subsequently operates instead as a declaration that the land is held in trust for the minor.[164] In effect, therefore, the common law rule with regard to leases to minors is preserved. Equity will not allow a minor who has had the benefit of the statutory trusts to affirm them upon his majority and afterwards to say that he is not liable upon their obligations.[165]

8–035 **Minors as successors to secured or statutory tenants.** In *Kingston upon Thames BC v Prince*[166] the question arose whether a minor who was otherwise qualified to succeed to a periodic tenancy under the provisions of the Housing

---

[154] *Blake v Concannon* (1870) 4 Ir. Rep. C.L. 323; *Kelly v Coote* (1856) 5 Ir. C.L.R. 469.

[155] *Blake v Concannon* (1870) 4 Ir. Rep. C.L.

[156] *Holmes v Blogg* (1818) 8 Taunt. 508.

[157] *Thurston v Nottingham Permanent Benefit Building Society* [1902] 1 Ch. 1, 9, affirmed [1903] A.C. 6; *Whittingham v Murdy* (1889) 60 L.T. 956.

[158] *Steinberg v Scala (Leeds) Ltd* [1923] 2 Ch. 452, a case dealing with the purchase of shares.

[159] Law of Property Act 1925 s.1(6).

[160] Settled Land Act 1925 ss.19, 20.

[161] Law of Property Act 1925 s.19; Settled Land Act 1925 s.27(1); *Kingston upon Thames BC v Prince* [1999] 1 F.L.R. 593.

[162] Law of Property Act 1925 s.19; Settled Land Act 1925 ss.26, 27.

[163] s.25(2) Sch.4 repealing Law of Property Act 1925 s.19; Settled Land Act 1925 s.27.

[164] Trusts of Land and Appointment of Trustees Act 1996 s.2 Sch.1 s.1(1), (3). The Act came into force on January 1, 1997: Trusts of Land and Appointment of Trustees Act 1996 (Commencement) Order 1996 (SI 1996/2974).

[165] *Davies v Beynon-Harris* (1931) 47 T.R.R. 424.

[166] [1999] 1 F.L.R. 593.

Act 1985 could do so despite her minority. The Court of Appeal held that such a minor could so succeed.[167] According to Hale J.:

> "... a minor is quite capable of becoming a tenant, albeit in equity. ... If there is nothing to stop a local authority granting a tenancy effective in equity to a minor in appropriate circumstances there can be no insuperable technical objection to Parliament rendering that equitable tenancy secure. If Parliament had wanted to limit these provisions to adults it could easily have done so: but it did not."[168]

The Court of Appeal therefore ordered that the minor be declared to be the secure tenant of the property in question until she reached the age of majority and the legal estate in relation to the said equitable tenancy be held on trust by the minor's mother until that time. Hale J. further observed that where a tenancy was for a term certain, an otherwise qualified minor could succeed the deceased tenant as a secured tenant under the 1985 Act: here:

> "... the deceased's estate will continue to hold the legal estate on trust for the minor until she reaches the age of 18 when she can call for a conveyance of the legal estate."[169]

Hale J. also noted with approval that "it has been established for some time, apparently uncontroversially, that a minor can succeed to a statutory tenancy under the Rent Acts".[170]

Marriage settlements. Further instances of contracts which are binding on a minor unless repudiated are to be found in marriage settlements and agreements for marriage settlements. They can be avoided by the minor within a reasonable time of coming of age.[171] But he must accept or reject them in their entirety. He cannot take the benefit and refuse to accept a burden.[172] If he elects to avoid the settlement, any interest taken by the minor in property brought into the settlement by the other party may be taken away to make up to the beneficiaries the loss which they have sustained because of the avoidance.[173] 8–036

Shareholder under age. A minor may be a shareholder in a company regulated by the Companies Clauses Consolidation Act 1845,[174] or by the Companies Act 1985, or in any corporation formed under a statute which authorises, either expressly or by implication, the membership of minors, or which by its nature 8–037

[167] [1999] 1 F.L.R. 593, 600 so interpreting Housing Act 1995 s.89.

[168] [1999] 1 F.L.R. 593, 601.

[169] [1999] 1 F.L.R. 593, 600, so interpreting Housing Act, 1995 s.90.

[170] [1999] 1 F.L.R. 593, 596, citing *Portman Registrars v Mohammed Latif* [1987] 6 C.L. 217 (Willesden County Court).

[171] *Burnaby v Equitable Revisionary Interest Society* (1885) 28 Ch D 416; *Cooper v Cooper* (1888) 13 App.Cas. 88; *Duncan v Dixon* (1890) 44 Ch D 211; *Edwards v Carter* [1893] A.C. 360. *Kingsman v Kingsman* (1880) 6 QBD 122, which appears to suggest that such a contract is void rather than voidable, can no longer be relied on.

[172] *Codrington v Codrington* (1875) L.R. 7 H.L. 854; *Hamilton v Hamilton* [1892] 1 Ch. 396. cf. *Re Vardon's Trusts* (1885) 31 Ch D 275 as to which see *Re Hargrove* [1915] 1 Ch. 398.

[173] *Hamilton v Hamilton* [1892] 1 Ch. 396; *Carter v Silber* [1891] 3 Ch. 553.

[174] s.79.

does not prohibit their membership.[175] A contract by a minor to subscribe for shares in the company may be repudiated either while he is under age or within a reasonable time of attaining full age,[176] but until he does so he is liable for calls made even while he is under age.[177] If he wishes to avoid the contract after coming of age he must do so promptly or he will be bound by acquiescence.[178]

8–038 **Purchase of shares.** If a minor purchases shares in the market and thereafter becomes registered as a shareholder there are two contracts whose validity may come into question, viz that between the minor and the company, and that between the minor and the vendor. In the nineteenth century there were a number of decisions concerning the validity of a transfer of partly paid-up shares to a minor, and the liability of the transferor to pay calls or to contribute in a winding up.[179] In these cases it was held that the transferor generally remained liable for calls notwithstanding that the minor had been registered as a shareholder. But although it was said in these cases that a transfer of shares to a minor was voidable none of them actually raised any question as to the validity of the contracts made between the minor on the one hand and the vendor or the company on the other. So far as the contract with the company is concerned the question is largely academic for the only liability likely to be enforceable against the shareholders is the obligation to pay calls, and partly paid-up shares are rarely met with today. But if the question were raised it would seem that the position must be the same as in the case of shares applied for by the minor and allotted to him by the company itself, i.e. the contract would be binding unless and until repudiated.[180] As to the contract between the minor and the vendor of the shares it is uncertain whether the contract is unenforceable against the minor, or whether it is voidable in the sense that it is binding until repudiated. It is submitted that such a contract would be unenforceable against the minor, but any price paid by him would be irrecoverable unless there was a total failure of consideration.[181]

---

175 *Seymour v Royal Naval School* [1910] 1 Ch. 806.

176 *Newry and Enniskillen Ry Co v Coombe* (1849) 3 Exch. 565; *North Western Ry Co v M'Michael* (1850) 5 Exch. 114; *Hamilton v Vaughan-Sherrin Electrical Engineering Co* [1894] 3 Ch. 589; *Re Alexandra Park Co* (1868) L.R. 6 Eq. 512.

177 *Leeds & Thirsk Ry v Fearnley* (1849) 4 Exch. 26; *Birkenhead, etc., Ry v Pilcher* (1850) 5 Exch. 121; *North Western Ry Co v M'Michael* (1850) 5 Exch. 114; *Dublin and Wicklow Ry v Black* (1852) 8 Exch. 181. Unless perhaps he has derived no advantage from the shares and is still a minor: *Newry and Enniskillen Ry v Coombe* (1849) 3 Exch. 565.

178 *Cork and Bandon Ry Co v Cazenove* (1847) 10 Q.B. 935; *Dublin and Wicklow Ry Co v Black* (1852) 8 Exch. 181.

179 *Gooch's Case* (1872) L.R. 8 Ch. App. 266; *Capper's Case* (1868) L.R. 3 Ch. App. 458; *Merry v Nickalls* (1872) L.R. 7 Ch. App. 733; *Lumsden's Case* (1868) L.R. 4 Ch. App. 31; *Curtis's Case* (1868) L.R. 6 Eq. 455; *Re Crenver and Wheal Abraham United Mining Co* (1872) L.R. 8 Ch. App. 45.

180 *Steinberg v Scala (Leeds) Ltd* [1923] 2 Ch. 452, a case of allotment and not purchase in the market; and see *Capper's Case* (1868) L.R. 3 Ch. App. 458, 461.

181 *Steinberg v Scala (Leeds) Ltd* [1923] 2 Ch. 452, 458. cf. *Hamilton v Vaughan-Sherrin Electrical Engineering Co* [1894] 3 Ch. 589. cf. below, paras 29–041 et seq. on recovery of money paid under a mistake of law.

Partnerships. A minor who becomes a member of a partnership is, as between himself and his partners, bound by the contract unless and until he repudiates it.[182] He does not become liable to partnership creditors for debts or liabilities incurred while he is a minor,[183] but if he repudiates the partnership agreement while still a minor or within a reasonable time of coming of age, his co-partners may insist on all partnership debts being paid and liabilities being met before the minor can draw any profits or capital from the firm.[184] It seems that the creditors may also avail themselves of this right of the minor's partners in appropriate proceedings.[185] Furthermore, even if the minor repudiates before attaining his majority he may still become liable for partnership debts subsequently incurred on the holding-out principle, by which a person who holds himself out as being a partner is bound to those who deal with the firm upon the faith of that supposed partnership.[186] 8–039

Effect of avoidance. In all contracts of this class, namely, contracts involving the acquisition of an interest in property of a permanent nature with continuing obligations attached to it, the effect of avoidance by the minor is that he escapes from liability to perform obligations which have not accrued at the time of avoidance. He has, however, to meet obligations which have already accrued[187]; moreover, he can recover nothing which he has paid under the contract unless there has been a total failure of consideration. So, where a minor paid a premium to the defendant on taking a lease from him, and entered upon and used and enjoyed the premises for a short period before he came of age, he could not recover the premium.[188] And where a minor applied for and was allotted shares in a company and paid the amounts due on allotment and on the first call, it was held that upon subsequently repudiating while still under age she could not recover back what she had paid, for although she had received no dividends she had received "the very consideration for which she bargained".[189] 8–040

Time of avoidance. What is a reasonable time after attaining majority will depend upon the circumstances of each particular case.[190] A minor cannot plead ignorance of his right to repudiate as an excuse for his failure to exercise that right within a reasonable time[191] nor even that the property had not yet come into possession, so that there was nothing certain on which the repudiation could operate.[192] 8–041

---

[182] *Goode v Harrison* (1821) 5 B. Ald. 147.

[183] *Lovell & Christmas v Beauchamp* [1894] A.C. 607.

[184] [1894] A.C. 607.

[185] [1894] A.C. 607, 611.

[186] *Goode v Harrison* (1821) 5 B. Ald. 147, 157; see Vol.II, paras 31–056 et seq.

[187] *Cork & Bandon Ry Co v Cazenove* (1847) 10 Q.B. 935. cf. *North Western Ry Co v M'Michael* (1850) 5 Exch. 114, 125; *Newry and Enniskillen Ry Co v Coombe* (1849) 3 Exch. 565.

[188] *Holmes v Blogg* (1818) 8 Taunt. 508; cf. *Re Burrows* (1856) 8 De G.M. & G. 254.

[189] *Steinberg v Scala (Leeds) Ltd* [1923] 2 Ch. 452. Insofar as *Hamilton v Vaughan-Sherrin Engineering Co* [1894] 3 Ch. 589 decides to the contrary, it must be taken to have been overruled. cf. below, paras 29–041 et seq. on recovery of payments made under a mistake of law.

[190] See *Carter v Silber* [1892] 2 Ch. 278, affirmed sub nom. *Edwards v Carter* [1893] A.C. 360; *Carnell v Harrison* [1916] 1 Ch. 328 (disapproving *Re Jones* [1893] 2 Ch. 461).

[191] *Carnell v Harrison* [1916] 1 Ch. 328.

[192] *Edwards v Carter* [1893] A.C. 360.

(d) *Contracts Unenforceable against a Minor unless Ratified*

8–042 **Contracts not binding until ratified.** The largest class of minor's contracts are enforceable by the minor,[193] but are not binding upon him unless he expressly ratifies them upon coming of age. For this purpose:

> "... in order to be a ratification there must be a recognition, by the debtor after he attained his majority, of the debt as a debt binding upon him".[194]

It is in this sense that general propositions as to minors' incapacity should be understood. Indeed, were it otherwise, the minor's incapacity, instead of being an advantage to him might in many cases turn greatly to his disadvantage.[195] The class includes all contracts other than those for necessaries, beneficial contracts of employment and contracts for the acquisition of a permanent interest in property which are valid unless expressly avoided.[196] Thus, a minor may sue but may not be sued upon an account stated[197] or upon a contract for the sale of goods (other than necessaries) or any other simple contract. It was also held, for example, (before the abolition of actions for breach of promise of marriage) that a minor could sue an adult for breach of promise of marriage,[198] although the adult could not sue the minor on such a promise.[199] And a minor can maintain an action for money had and received against an attorney for damages recovered by his next friend in an action brought on his behalf.[200] A minor cannot, however, obtain specific performance of a contract because the remedy would not be mutual,[201] at any rate not unless he has himself performed his side of the agreement.[202]

8–043 **Examples.** The general rule that a minor's contracts are not binding on him unless ratified on attaining his majority has the consequence that a minor is not, at common law, liable on a warranty of goods or chattels sold by him[203] even where the warranty is fraudulent.[204] Nor is he liable on the custom of the realm as an innkeeper.[205] He is not bound by an agreement to refer a dispute to

---

[193] See below, para.8–045.

[194] *Rowe v Hopwood* (1868–1869) L.R. 4 Q.B. 1, 3, per Cockburn C.J. (decided under the Statute of Frauds (Amendment) Act 1828 s.5).

[195] *Warwick v Bruce* (1813) 2 M. & S. 205; *Shannon v Bradstreet* (1803) 1 Sch. & Lef. 52, 58; *Re Smith's Trusts* (1890) 25 L.R. Ir. 439, 443.

[196] See above, paras 8–007, 8–030.

[197] *Williams v Moor* (1843) 11 M. & W. 256.

[198] *Holt v Ward* (1732) 2 Str. 937, 939.

[199] *Hale v Ruthven* (1869) 20 L.T. 404.

[200] *Collins v Brook* (1860) 5 H. & N. 700.

[201] *Flight v Bolland* (1828) 4 Russ. 298. By the same token, specific performance cannot be obtained against an adult who is co-defendant with a minor: *Lumley v Ravenscroft* [1895] 1 Q.B. 683, commented on in *Basma v Weekes* [1950] A.C. 441, 456.

[202] See below, para.27–046.

[203] *Howlett v Haswell* (1814) 4 Camp. 118.

[204] *Green v Greenbank* (1816) 2 Marsh. 485.

[205] *Williams v Harrison* (1691) Carth. 160; 1 Roll.Abr. *Action sur Case*, D (3).

arbitration[206]; nor by the recitals in a deed made during infancy[207]; nor by a release of a legal claim[208]; nor by a contract of guarantee.[209]

Ratification after full age. At common law, the general rule in this class of contract is that if, on attaining his majority, a minor ratifies a contract made by him during his minority, it will bind him although there may be no consideration for the new promise.[210] Formerly, this rule was replaced by s.2 of the Infants Relief Act 1874 which provided that debts contracted during infancy were made incapable of becoming binding by ratification by the minor on majority, unless new consideration for such ratification was provided.[211] This provision itself has been repealed,[212] returning the law relating to ratification to the position at common law. Ratification after reaching majority may be express or implied from the former minor's conduct.[213] 8–044

(e) *Third Parties and Incapacity*

Third parties. In general, lack of capacity of a minor is a personal privilege and does not prevent the other party being bound. However, there are circumstances where a third party has taken advantage of the invalidity of a minor's contract. Thus, for example, in one case an impresario employed an infant who had entered an unreasonable deed of apprenticeship with the plaintiff. The latter's action against the impresario for enticement was rejected by the court as the contract of apprenticeship was invalid as between its parties.[214] Similarly, where a minor has entered a contract which is not binding on him then a third party who induces him to enter another contract in circumstances which (putting aside the issue of minority) would constitute breach of contract is not liable in the tort of inducing breach of contract.[215] Another example used to be found in the liability of the guarantor of an infant's debts. By s.1 of the Infants Relief Act 1874, a loan to an infant was made absolutely void and there was authority that this meant that any guarantors of the loan were not bound by their guarantee.[216] However, s.2 of the Minors' Contracts Act 1987 expressly[217] provides that where a guarantee is 8–045

[206] Unless it forms one term of an otherwise beneficial contract of service, etc.: *Slade v Metrodent Ltd* [1953] 2 Q.B. 112.

[207] *Milner v Lord Harewood* (1810) 18 Ves. 259, 274; *Field v Moore* (1854) 7 De G.M. & G. 691.

[208] *Overton v Bannister* (1844) 3 Ha. 503; *Mattei v Vautro* (1898) 78 L.T. 682. But see now CPR 1998 r.21.10(2), which enables the court to sanction a compromise by a minor even where no proceedings are otherwise contemplated.

[209] *Re Davenport* [1963] 1 W.L.R. 817.

[210] *Southerton v Whitlock* (1726) 2 Str. 690; *Williams v Moor* (1843) 11 M. & W. 256, 298.

[211] See for its effect the 25th edn of the present work, paras 569–570.

[212] Minors' Contracts Act 1987 s.1.

[213] cf. *Brown v Harper* (1893) 68 L.T. 488.

[214] *De Francesco v Barnum* (1890) 45 Ch D 430, 438 and 443.

[215] *Proform Sports Management Ltd v Proactive Sports Management Ltd* [2006] EWHC 2903 (Ch), [2007] Bus. L.R. 93 at [33].

[216] *Coutts & Co v Browne-Lecky* [1947] K.B. 104.

[217] As s.1 of the Minors' Contracts Act 1987 repeals s.1 of the 1874 Act, it would otherwise have been arguable that a guarantor of an unenforceable (as opposed to a void) loan should be liable.

given in respect of an obligation of a party to a contract made after its commencement and that obligation is unenforceable against him (or he repudiates the contract) on the grounds of minority, then the guarantee is not unenforceable for that reason alone.[218] The extent to which a minor may give title to property, which may have consequences for third parties, is discussed below.[219]

(f) *Liability of Minor in Tort and Contract*

8–046 **Liability for tort.** In principle, minors are liable for the torts which they commit,[220] though the incidence of liability in tort may be affected by their age.[221] However, if the claim in tort arises out of a contract upon which the minor is not liable, the claimant may not treat the breach of that contract as a tort and sue accordingly:

> "If one delivers goods to an infant on a contract, knowing him to be a minor, he shall not be charged for them in trover or conversion."[222]

Therefore, where a minor, having hired a horse, injured it by riding it too hard, it was held that he was not liable in an action for the tort,[223] and where a minor obtained a loan by falsely misrepresenting his age he could not be made liable in damages for deceit.[224] In *Fawcett v Smethurst*[225] a minor hired a car to fetch his bag from the station six miles away. He met a friend with whom he drove on further. The car caught fire and was damaged on the extra journey without the negligence of the minor. It was held that he was not liable in tort, as the extra journey did not take his actions outside the scope of the contract, nor in contract, as the hiring did not render him liable for loss arising without fault on his part. Although the hiring itself might have been necessary, the contract would not have been binding on him had its effect been to render him liable without fault.

8–047 **Torts independent of the contract.** On the other hand, if the tort may properly be considered as arising independently of the contract or outside its ambit altogether, the minor can be made liable. So a minor who hired a mare "merely for a ride" and was warned at the hiring that she was unfit for jumping, having lent her to a friend who killed her by that act, was held to be guilty of a bare trespass, not within the object of the hiring, and to be consequently liable.[226] A minor who embezzled money belonging to his employer was held liable in an

---

[218] See also s.113(7) of the Consumer Credit Act 1974, as amended by the Minors' Contracts Act 1987 s.4.

[219] See below, paras 8–065—8–067.

[220] *Bristow v Eastman* (1794) 1 Esp. 172; *Defries v Davis* (1835) 1 Scott 594. cf. above, para.1–162.

[221] e.g. in the tort of negligence the standard of care varies according to the age of a child defendant: *McHale v Watson* [1966] A.L.R. 513 and cf. *Gough v Thorne* [1966] 3 All E.R. 398 (defence of contributory negligence).

[222] *Manby v Scott* (1659) 1 Sid. 109, 129; cf. *R. v McDonald* (1885) 15 QBD 323, 327.

[223] *Jennings v Rundall* (1799) 8 Term R. 335.

[224] *Johnson v Pye* (1665) 1 Sid. 258; *Stikeman v Dawson* (1847) 1 De G. & Sm. 90; *R. Leslie Ltd v Sheill* [1914] 3 K.B. 607, 612.

[225] (1915) 84 L.J.K.B. 473.

[226] *Burnard v Haggis* (1863) 14 C.B.(N.S.) 45. See also *Walley v Holt* (1876) 35 L.T. 631.

action for money had and received because he would have been liable in trover[227]; and one who hired a microphone and improperly parted with it to a friend was held liable in an action of detinue.[228] It is generally assumed that a minor who buys non-necessary goods cannot be sued in conversion even where he fails to pay the price and keeps the goods.[229] But it has been held that a bailee under age who refuses to return goods delivered to him by the bailor may be sued in detinue,[230] and that non-necessary goods sold to a minor can be recovered, when he refuses to pay for them, though the minor is not liable to damages for conversion.[231] It is more likely, however, that a court will exercise its discretion under s.3 of the Minors' Contracts Act 1987 to require a minor to transfer to the claimant any property acquired by the defendant under the contract, or any property representing it.[232]

(g) *Liability of Minor to make Restitution*[233]

Generally. In general a minor cannot be sued on his contracts, but this rule leaves open the question whether he may be made to make restitution to the other party for benefits conferred on him under the contract. Such benefits may consist of the receipt of money, goods, interests in land or services. Common law, equity and statute have different answers to this question of a minor's liability in restitution. **8–048**

At common law. The common law rule is that a minor is not liable to restore benefits conferred on him under a contract which is unenforceable against him, even if the contract results from his fraudulent misrepresentation of majority.[234] Despite this rule, however, three possible routes may exist to recovery. The first route is for the other contracting party to rely on an independent tort which the minor has committed, for example, conversion or deceit, damages for which may compensate him for the loss which he has suffered by the minor's retention of the benefit, even though this may not always be the same as the minor's gain.[235] The second route is for the other contracting party to find such an independent tort, "waive" it and sue for any money had and received in respect of property **8–049**

---

[227] *Bristow v Eastman* (1794) 1 Esp. 172; *Re Seager* (1889) 60 L.T. 665. cf. *Cowern v Nield* [1912] 2 K.B. 419.

[228] *Ballett v Mingay* [1943] K.B. 281.

[229] Atiyah (1959) 22 M.L.R. 273, 281. The view that the minor is not liable is supported by the generally accepted opinion that property in non-necessary goods may pass to the minor: *Stocks v Wilson* [1913] 2 K.B. 235, 246 and see Treitel, *The Law of Contract*, 12th edn (2007 by Peel), para.12–031. cf. Minors' Contracts Act 1987 s.3(1) which refers to "property acquired" by the minor and to the power of the court to order him to "transfer" such property.

[230] *Mills v Graham* (1804) 1 B. & P.N.R. 140 (minor refusing to return skins delivered for finishing). Detinue was abolished by s.2(1) of the Torts (Interference with Goods) Act 1977, and replaced by liability in conversion. See also *R. v McDonald* (1885) 15 QBD 323; *Robinson's Motor Vehicles Ltd v Graham* [1956] N.Z.L.R. 545.

[231] *Re Henderson* (1916) 12 Tas.L.R. 40; cf. *Hall v Wells* [1962] Tas.S.R. 122, 128–129.

[232] See below, paras 8–054 et seq.

[233] Goff and Jones, *The Law of Restitution*, 7th edn (2007), pp.642 et seq.

[234] *Johnson v Pye* (1665) 1 Sid. 258; *Liverpool Adelphi Loan Association v Fairhurst* (1854) 9 Exch. 422.

[235] See above, paras 8–047—8–048.

conferred on the minor.[236] The third possible route to recovery at common law would be to claim restitution of money paid under an unenforceable contract to a minor based on a total failure of consideration, but this route has been rejected by the courts.[237] It has, however, been convincingly argued that a distinction should be drawn for this purpose between the situation where the restitutionary claim in effect enforces the contract, as, for example, with a loan to a minor,[238] and where it does not do so, but merely restores the parties to the status quo ante.[239] In the latter situation, a restitutionary claim ought to be available. Similar considerations apply to the denial of quasi-contractual claims for the value of non-necessary goods and services supplied to a minor who has failed to pay the contractual price; for holding a minor even to a reasonable price would undermine his protection.[240] Thus in *Lemprière v Lange*, for example, a lease which a minor had taken was set aside and possession by him given up, but the court refused to award a sum to the lessor as damages for use and occupation of the land on the ground that the two remedies were incompatible.[241]

8–050 **In equity.** It is no answer at law to a plea of incapacity based on lack of age that the defendant at the time of entering into the contract fraudulently represented himself to be of full age, and that the other party believing this representation and on the faith of it contracted with him[242] nor did these facts before the Judicature Act form the subject of a good replication on equitable grounds to a plea of infancy.[243] But in certain cases equity will grant relief against the minor, not on the ground of enforcing the contract, or recovering the debt, but of an equitable liability resulting from the fraud. He will be compelled to restore his ill-gotten gains, or to release the party deceived from obligations or acts in law induced by the fraud.[244] This obligation is, however, strictly limited in extent.

8–051 **Restoration of gains.**[245] If a minor has obtained property by fraudulently misrepresenting his age,[246] he can be compelled to restore it; if he has obtained money, he can be compelled to refund it.[247] This remedy is an equitable one and arises quite independently of the contract.[248] It lasts, however, only so long as the

[236] *Bristow v Eastman* (1794) 1 Esp. 172 and see Goff and Jones at pp.634–636.

[237] *Cowern v Nield* [1912] 2 K.B. 491; *R. Leslie Ltd v Sheill* [1914] 3 K.B. 607. cf. *Thavorn v Bank of Credit & Commerce International SA* [1985] 1 Lloyd's Rep. 259 (where it was held that a minor was not liable to make restitution for monies received under a mistake of fact).

[238] *R. Leslie Ltd v Sheill* [1914] 3 K.B. 607.

[239] Goff and Jones at pp.643–644.

[240] Goff and Jones at p.635.

[241] (1879) 12 Ch D 675 and see below, para.8–053.

[242] *Johnson v Pye* (1665) 1 Sid. 258; *Liverpool Adelphi Loan Association v Fairhurst* (1854) 9 Exch. 422, 430; *Inman v Inman* (1873) L.R. 15 Eq. 260; *Levene v Brougham* (1909) 25 T.L.R. 265 (no estoppel).

[243] *Bartlett v Wells* (1862) 1 B. & S. 836; *De Roo v Foster* (1862) 12 C.B.(N.S.) 272.

[244] See Atiyah (1959) 22 M.L.R. 273.

[245] See generally Goff and Jones at pp.644 et seq. and below, Ch.29.

[246] The representation must be explicit and not inferential: *Stikeman v Dawson* (1847) 1 De G. & Sm. 90; *Maclean v Dummett* (1869) 22 L.T. 710; *Re Jones, Ex p. Jones* (1881) 18 Ch D 109, 120–121. See also *Nelson v Stocker* (1859) 4 De G. & J. 458.

[247] *Stocks v Wilson* [1913] 2 K.B. 235.

[248] *Re King, Ex p. Unity Joint Stock Mutual Banking Association* (1858) 3 De G. & J. 63; *Re Jones, Ex p. Jones* (1881) 18 Ch D 109; *Stocks v Wilson* [1913] 2 K.B. 235.

minor retains the property or money or, perhaps, the proceeds of the property or money. If he has sold the goods or spent the money, he cannot be compelled through a personal judgment to pay an equivalent sum out of his present or future resources, for this would be nothing but enforcing an unenforceable contract[249]; "[r]estitution stopped where repayment began".[250] In *Stocks v Wilson*,[251] however, a minor who had obtained non-necessary goods by fraudulently misrepresenting his age was held bound to account for the proceeds of their sale. This decision was criticised, although not expressly overruled by the Court of Appeal in *R. Leslie Ltd v Sheill*.[252] Sir Frederick Pollock[253] considered the decision to be correct on the principle of following the property (i.e. as represented by the money) and not otherwise. His view is supported by other textbook writers[254] and it is suggested that a fraudulent misrepresentation of full age by a minor will allow the person deceived to trace his property in equity by an action in rem similar to that possessed by a beneficiary in respect of trust property.[255]

"Bankruptcy Debt". Under the Insolvency Act 1986 s.382, a "bankruptcy debt" means any debt or liability to which a bankrupt is subject either at the commencement of the bankruptcy or to which he may become subject after the bankruptcy by reason of any obligation incurred before the commencement of the bankruptcy and for this purpose "liability" includes "a liability to pay money, . . . any liability in contract . . . and any liability arising out of an obligation to make restitution".[256] Thus, while a person who has loaned money to a minor may not prove this as a debt in the latter's bankruptcy, there being no enforceable liability against the minor,[257] if that person was induced to make the loan by the minor's fraudulent misrepresentation of age, then any equitable liability in the minor arising from the fraud may be proved as a "bankruptcy debt".[258] **8–052**

Release from obligations. A party who has been induced to enter into an obligation or to perform some act in law by the fraudulent misrepresentation of a minor that he is of full age will be released from that obligation and restored, where possible, to his former position. In *Clarke v Cobley*[259] the defendant, a minor, by such a misrepresentation, induced the plaintiff to accept a bond for the amount of two promissory notes drawn by the defendant's wife before her **8–053**

249 *R. Leslie Ltd v Sheill* [1914] 3 K.B. 607, 618.

250 [1914] 3 K.B. 607.

251 [1913] 2 K.B. 235, 247.

252 [1914] 3 K.B. 607.

253 Pollock, *Principles of Contract*, 13th edn (1950), p.64.

254 *Anson's Law of Contract*, 28th edn (Beatson, 2007), pp.226–228. Treitel, *The Law of Contract*, 12th edn (2007 by Peel), para.12–046. cf. Furmston, *Cheshire, Fifoot and Furmston's Law of Contract*, 15th edn (2007), pp.563–565.

255 cf. Goff and Jones at p.648; Atiyah (1959) 22 M.L.R. 273. See below, paras 29–162 et seq.

256 Insolvency Act 1986 s.382(4).

257 *Re Jones, Ex p. Jones* (1881) 18 Ch D 109 (decided under the old law). For the position as to loans for necessaries, see above, para.8–020.

258 *Re King, Ex p. Unity Joint-Stock Mutual Banking Association* (1858) 3 De G. & J. 63; *Stocks v Wilson* [1913] 2 K.B. 235, 246 and see above, paras 8–050—8–051.

259 (1789) 2 Cox. 173 (fraud must be presumed though not appearing specifically in the report).

marriage. The plaintiff accordingly gave up the notes. When the plaintiff discovered the fact of the defendant's incapacity he filed a bill after the defendant had attained majority, praying that the defendant might be ordered to execute a fresh bond, or to pay the money secured, or deliver back the notes to him. The court ordered this last and also that the defendant should not plead limitation to any action brought upon them or set up any other plea open to him when the bond was executed, but refused to decree payment of the money, holding that the court could do no more than see that the parties were restored to the same situation in which they were at the date of the bond. And where a minor obtained a lease by fraudulently misrepresenting that he was of full age, the court set it aside and ordered him to give up possession and to pay his costs.[260]

8–054 **Minors' Contracts Act 1987 section 3.** The most important means by which a minor may be ordered to make restitution of benefits obtained under a contract unenforceable against him is found in s.3 of the Minors' Contracts Act 1987, which provides that:

> "... the court may, if it is just and equitable to do so, require the defendant [minor] to transfer to the plaintiff [other contracting party] any property acquired by the defendant under the contract, or any property representing it."

This provision gives a considerable discretion to the court to order restitution of property acquired by a minor under a contract, unless it is one for necessaries and therefore binding on him.[261] It is wider than the equitable remedy already described which is only available where fraud on the part of the minor is established.[262]

8–055 **"Property".** Only property acquired by a minor under the contract is included: thus any property acquired by way of inducement to enter the contract falls outside the section. "Property" itself is not defined by the Act. Clearly, it includes chattels and it is submitted that it should be taken to include interests in land to the extent that a minor is permitted by law to hold them.[263] More difficult is the question whether "property" includes money. Although there is some authority in the context of the equitable relief against fraud for recovery of money representing the proceeds of sale of goods transferred,[264] this was subject to criticism.[265] The better view, it is submitted, is that money should be included within the statutory definition of property.[266] The concern to prevent indirect enforcement of a minor's contract which led to the refusal of recovery of monies in equity as at common law may be fully taken into account as a factor in the discretion which s.3 confers.

---

[260] *Lemprière v Lange* (1879) 12 Ch D 675. A claim by the lessor for damages for use and occupation was held inconsistent with this relief and dismissed. See also *Cory v Gertcken* (1816) 2 Madd. 40; *Overton v Banister* (1844) 3 Ha. 503; *Woolf v Woolf* [1899] 1 Ch. 343.

[261] See above, para.8–007.

[262] See above, para.8–050.

[263] See above, para.8–034.

[264] *Stocks v Wilson* [1913] 2 K.B. 235.

[265] *R. Leslie Ltd v Sheill* [1914] 3 K.B. 607.

[266] Treitel, *The Law of Contract*, 12th edn (2007 by Peel), para.12–041.

"Any property representing it". This phrase gives the court power to order the transfer, not only of property acquired by a minor, but also the product of its exchange, and, assuming money is included within the provision,[267] its proceeds on sale. This will give rise to a process of statutory tracing, for which cases at common law and in equity may, though in different contexts, serve as illustrations.[268] However, it has been suggested that certain difficulties encountered in these cases, for example the identification of the exchange product of proceeds in a mixed fund, may go to the discretion of the court to make an award under s.3.[269] For example, if a minor has sold non-necessary goods acquired under a contract of sale and placed the money in a bank account together with other monies, the court should hesitate to apply the rules as to tracing of money through accounts in equity which were constructed for and are appropriate to the context of trustees or fiduciaries.[270] In the minor's context, the effect of the award should not be, or even, perhaps, risk being, the payment out of his present or future resources of a sum equivalent to that owed under a contractual obligation. 8–056

Discretion. It is submitted that a court should look in deciding whether to make an order under s.3 at the general fairness of the contract which the minor has made. In particular, if the other contracting party took advantage of the minor's inexperience or tricked him, then the latter should not be held liable to restore property acquired. Clearly, the question whether a minor appears or does not appear to be of full capacity, even in the absence of misrepresentation as to full age, will be relevant to the exercise of the discretion. The most important issue in this exercise will be the balance between the need to preserve the minor's protection which is the basis of his contractual incapacity and the interests of the other contracting party in recovery of benefits conferred by him on the minor. 8–057

(h) *Agency and Membership of Societies*

Minor as principal. A minor cannot execute a valid power of attorney,[271] but he is bound by a contract made by his agent with his authority, where the circumstances are such that he would have been bound if he had himself made the contract.[272] A minor may validly appoint an agent where he earns his living in a manner which necessitates this.[273] And it seems that if a minor authorises an agent to purchase necessaries for him, and the agent pays for them, the minor can be compelled to reimburse the agent.[274] 8–058

---

[267] See above, para.8–055.

[268] See Goff and Jones, *The Law of Restitution*, Ch.2.

[269] Treitel at para.12–042.

[270] Goff and Jones at pp.88 et seq.

[271] *Zouch v Parsons* (1765) 3 Burr. 1794; *Olliver v Woodroffe* (1839) 4 M. & W. 650; *Doe d. Thomas v Roberts* (1847) 16 M. & W. 778, 780. An act done by an agent under a void power of attorney is itself void.

[272] See Vol.II, para.31–037; Megarry (1953) 69 L.Q.R. 446; Webb (1955) 18 M.L.R. 461. cf. *Shepherd v Cartwright* [1953] Ch. 728, 755, and see *G.(A.) v G.(T.)* [1970] 3 All E.R. 546, 549.

[273] *Denmark Productions Ltd v Boscobel Productions Ltd* (1967) 111 S.J. 715.

[274] See above, para.8–020.

8–059 **Minor as agent.** A minor can act as agent or as the donee of a power of attorney[275] but is not personally liable on the contracts entered into on behalf of his principal.[276]

8–060 **Membership of societies.** Subject to certain conditions, a minor may become an associate of a friendly society,[277] an industrial and provident society,[278] a trade union,[279] or a building society.[280]

(i) *Liability of Parent or Guardian*

8–061 **Parent not liable for minor's debts.** A parent may be ordered to provide financial relief for the benefit of his or her child,[281] but apart from agency[282] or personal contract, he is no more liable to pay a debt contracted by the child with a third party (even for necessaries) than a mere stranger would be.[283] The same principles apply in the case of a guardian and ward.

(j) *Procedure in Actions*

8–062 **Procedure.** Formerly, under the Rules of the Supreme Court and the County Court Rules, a minor sued by his next friend and defended by his guardian ad litem.[284] However, since the coming into effect of the Civil Procedure Rules 1998, proceedings involving minors (termed by these rules, "children") are governed by a uniform set of rules[285] under which "a child must have a litigation friend to conduct proceedings on his behalf" unless the court otherwise orders, and the former distinction between next friends and guardians ad litem is

---

[275] *Watkins v Vince* (1818) 2 Stark 368; *Re D'Angibau* (1880) 15 Ch D 228, 246.

[276] *Smally v Smally* (1700) 1 Eq. Cas. Abr. 283.

[277] Friendly Societies Act 1992 s.119A(1)(a).

[278] Industrial and Provident Societies Act 1965 s.20 (as amended).

[279] Explicit provision to this effect was formerly found in the Trade Union Act Amendment Act 1876 s.9 but this Act was repealed by the Industrial Relations Act 1971 and the right of a minor to be a member of a trade union seems now to depend on inference. cf. Trade Union and Labour Relations (Consolidation) Act 1992 s.174.

[280] Building Societies Act 1986 Sch.2 para.5(3), as amended by the Building Societies Act 1997 s.2(2)(b).

[281] Children Act 1989 s.15(1) Sch.1 para.1. See also Social Security Administration Act 1992 ss.105–108.

[282] e.g. where a parent expressly or impliedly authorises the minor to contract on his behalf or where his wife or some other person, such as his servant, has authority to pledge his credit: *Cooper v Phillips* (1831) 4 C. & P. 581; *Bazeley v Forder* (1868) L.R. 3 Q.B. 559; *Collins v Cory* (1901) 17 T.L.R. 242. cf. *Fluck v Tollemache* (1823) 1 C. & P. 5; *Urmston v Newcomen* (1836) 4 A. & E. 899; *Ruttinger v Temple* (1863) 4 B. & S. 491.

[283] *Fluck v Tollemache* (1823) 1 C. & P. 5.; *Shelton v Springett* (1851) 11 C.B. 452; *Mortimore v Wright* (1840) 6 M. & W. 482. cf. *Hesketh v Gowing* (1804) 5 Esp. 131; *Gore v Hawsey* (1862) 3 F. & F. 509 (illegitimate children recognised by father); *Greenspan v Slate* (1953) 97 A. 2d. 390 (parent liable for cost of emergency medical treatment to child though he had refused to authorise it); and see Goff and Jones, *The Law of Restitution*, para.17–023.

[284] RSC O.80 rr.1 & 2; CCR O.10, r.1.

[285] CPR Pt 21 (which also governs litigation involving mental patients). These rules came into force on April 26, 1999.

therefore no longer drawn.[286] Under these rules, special provision is made for the assessment of costs of proceedings where the claimant is a child and where money is ordered to be paid to him or for his benefit or where money is ordered to be paid by him or on his behalf.[287] No settlement, compromise or payment and no acceptance of money paid into court shall be valid, so far as it relates to the claim by a child without the approval of the court.[288] As regards the exercise of this power of approval, it has been held (under the former procedural rules which made similar provision[289]) that the court has no power to compel a compromise against the opinion of the minor's advisers[290] and that a compromise will not be sanctioned, although made in good faith, if not for the minor's benefit.[291]

Joint obligations. Where one of two joint contracting parties is a minor whose promise is voidable or unenforceable against him, there is no need to join him as a party to the action and the action may be maintained against the adult only; but if both are sued and the minor relies on his lack of capacity, a claimant may still recover against the adult defendant.[292] Moreover, in contrast with the position at common law,[293] since 1987 where a contract is entered by a minor and the latter's obligations are guaranteed by an adult, the unenforceability of those obligations against the minor shall not alone render the guarantee unenforceable.[294] 8–063

Defence of minority. Under the Civil Procedure Rules 1998, where a defendant denies an allegation in the claimant's particulars of claim, he must state his reasons for doing so[295] and so a child who intends to rely on a defence of minority to a claim for the enforcement of a contract should make this clear in the defence which he files. 8–064

(k) *Disposition of Property by Minors*

Disposition of property by delivery. A minor can clearly dispose of property under a contract which is binding on him, but there are also cases in which a minor can effectively dispose of property belonging to him under a contract which is not binding on him. So, for instance, it has been held that a gift of a 8–065

286 CPR r.21.1(2).
287 CPR r.48.5.
288 CPR r.21.10.
289 RSC Or.80, rr.10, 11; CCR Or.10 r.10.
290 *Re Birchall* (1880) 16 Ch D 41; *Norman v Strains* (1880) 6 P.D. 219. See also *Re Taylor's Application* [1972] 2 Q.B. 369.
291 *Rhodes v Swithenbank* (1889) 22 QBD 577; *Mattei v Vautro* (1898) 78 L.T. 682.
292 See, e.g. *Burgess v Merrill* (1812) 4 Taunt. 468; *Gillow v Lillie* (1835) 1 Scott 597; *Lovell & Christmas v Beauchamp* [1894] A.C. 607; *Wauthier v Wilson* (1912) 28 T.L.R. 239. See below, para.17–005.
293 *Coutts v Browne-Lecky* [1947] K.B. 104.
294 Minors' Contract Act 1987 s.2(1) and see Vol.II, para.44–036.
295 CPR r.16.5.

chattel by a minor is irrevocable after delivery.[296] And money paid by a minor under a contract which is voidable or unenforceable against him cannot be recovered by him unless there is a total failure of consideration,[297] although if the minor paid it under a mistake as to the voidable nature or unenforceability of the contract, he may be able to recover it on the basis of this mistake of law.[298]

8–066 **Disposition of property by grant.** A disposition of property not accompanied by delivery is, in general, ineffective against a minor.[299] So, for instance, an assignment of an interest in a trust fund by way of security (at least if it is intended to secure an unenforceable obligation) is, it seems, ineffective to pass any interest as against a grantor who is a minor.[300] And a mortgage granted by a minor to secure an unenforceable loan is itself unenforceable.[301] On the other hand, in *Chaplin v Leslie Frewin (Publishers) Ltd*,[302] it was held that a contract whereby a minor assigned the copyright in a written work to a publisher was effective to pass the copyright and that even if the contract was voidable the minor could not revoke the contract so as to restore the copyright to himself.

8–067 **Dispositions relating to land.** A minor cannot grant a legal estate in land. But a minor may convey an equitable interest in land, whether by way of outright sale or by way of lease only. So long as the transfer is executory only it seems that the minor would not be bound by it,[303] but the position may be different after the grantee has gone into possession.

3. PERSONS LACKING MENTAL CAPACITY

8–068 **General.** In the case of contracts other than for necessaries, the general rule is that a person who is mentally disordered or otherwise lacking in mental capacity is bound by his contract unless he can show both that this lack of capacity meant that he did not understand what he was doing and that the other

---

[296] *Taylor v Johnston* (1882) 19 Ch D 603, 608 and see *Pearce v Brain* [1929] 2 K.B. 310 (where it was held that a minor who delivers a chattel belonging to him under a contract "absolutely void" under s.1 of the Infants' Relief Act 1874 cannot recover it unless there has been a total failure of consideration). cf. Halsbury, *Laws of England*, 4th edn, Vol.20, para.10 and see *G.(A.) v G.(T.)* [1970] 3 All E.R. 546, 549.

[297] *Wilson v Kearse* (1800) Peake Add.Cas. 196; *Corpe v Overton* (1833) 10 Bing. 252, 259; *Re Burrows* (1856) 8 De G.M. & G. 254, 256; *Valentini v Canali* (1889) 24 QBD 166; *Steinberg v Scala (Leeds) Ltd* [1923] 2 Ch. 452.

[298] cf. *Kleinwort Benson v Lincoln City Council* [1998] 3 W.L.R. 1095, on which see below, para.29–041 et seq.

[299] *Zouch v Parsons* (1765) 3 Burr. 1794, 1807, 1808.

[300] *Inman v Inman* (1873) 15 Eq. 260. See also *Martin v Gale* (1876) 4 Ch D 428.

[301] *Nottingham Permanent Benefit Building Society v Thurston* [1903] A.C. 6, which was decided under the Infants' Relief Act 1874 and held that a mortgage to secure a void loan was itself void.

[302] [1966] Ch. 71. There are dicta in this case (at 94) which appear to suggest that a minor can never, by repudiating a voidable contract, recover property which has passed to the other party. This may be true (at least if there is no total failure of consideration) where the contract is voidable in the normal sense of the word, but it is doubtful if this is correct where the contract is void as against the minor, rather than voidable. cf. at 96.

[303] *Zouch v Parsons* (1765) 3 Burr. 1794.

party was aware of this incapacity.[304] On the other hand, where these two conditions are satisfied, the contract is voidable at his option.[305] This rule was laid down in *Imperial Loan Co Ltd v Stone*[306] where Lord Esher M.R. said:

> "When a person enters into a contract, and afterwards alleges that he was so insane at the time that he did not know what he was doing, and proves the allegation, the contract is as binding on him in every respect, whether it is executory or executed, as if he had been sane when he made it, unless he can prove further that the person with whom he contracted knew him to be so insane as not to be capable of understanding what he was about."

This means that in general:

> "... the validity of a contract entered into by a lunatic who is ostensibly sane is to be judged by the same standards as a contract by a person of sound mind, and is not voidable by the lunatic or his representatives by reason of 'unfairness' unless such unfairness amounts to equitable fraud which would have enabled the complaining party to avoid the contract even if he had been sane."[307]

The doctrines referred to here as "equitable fraud" (notably, relief under the doctrine of unconscionability) are discussed earlier in this work.[308]

Nature of understanding required. At common law, the understanding and 8–069
competence required to uphold the validity of a transaction depend on the nature of the transaction.[309] There is no fixed standard of mental capacity which is requisite for all transactions.[310] What is required in relation to each particular matter or piece of business transacted, is that the party in question should have an understanding of the general nature of what he is doing.[311]

Evidence of lack of capacity. At common law, the burden of proof as to a 8–070
lack of mental capacity to make a contract lies on the person alleging it.[312] If the party possessed the requisite mental capacity when the contract was made, evidence of previous or subsequent mental incapacity is not material,[313] but in a

---

[304] *Brown v Jodrell* (1827) M. & M. 105; *Niell v Morley* (1804) 9 Ves. 478; *Molton v Camroux* (1849) 4 Exch. 17; *Beavan v M'Donnell* (1854) 9 Exch. 309; *Jacobs v Richards* (1854) 18 Beav. 300; *York Glass Co v Jubb* (1925) 42 T.L.R. 1; *Hart v O'Connor* [1985] A.C. 1000, disapproving *Archer v Cutler* [1980] 1 N.Z.L.R. 386, noted Beatson (1981) 1 O.J.L.S 426. See Goudy (1901) 17 L.Q.R. 147; Wilson (1902) 18 L.Q.R. 21; Hudson (1984) 48 Conv. 32; (1986) 50 Conv. 178; *Irvani v Irvani* [2000] 1 Lloyd's Rep. 412, 425. cf. *Re F.* [1990] 2 A.C. 1 (medical treatment where inability to consent).

[305] *Manches v Trimborn* (1946) 115 L.J.K.B. 305; *Gibbons v Wright* (1954) 91 C.L.R. 423.

[306] [1892] 1 Q.B. 599, 601.

[307] *Hart v O'Connor* [1985] A.C. 1000, 1027, per Lord Brightman (PC).

[308] Above, paras 7–126 et seq.

[309] *Manches v Trimborn* (1946) 115 L.J.K.B. 305; cf. *In the Estate of Park* [1954] P. 112 and see Fridman (1963) 79 L.Q.R. 502, 518–519; *Re Beaney* [1978] 1 W.L.R. 770.

[310] *Gibbons v Wright* (1954) 91 C.L.R. 423.

[311] *In the Estate of Park* [1954] P. 112; *Bennett v Bennett* [1969] 1 W.L.R. 430; *Re Roberts* [1978] 1 W.L.R. 653 (capacity to marry); *Mason v Mason* [1972] Fam. 302 (consent to decree of divorce). cf. *Clarke v Prus* [1995] N.P.C. 41 in relation to gifts.

[312] *Imperial Loan Co Ltd v Stone* [1892] 1 Q.B. 599, 601.

[313] *Hall v Warren* (1804) 9 Ves. Jun. 605.

doubtful case it might create a suspicion that he was mentally incapable at the time of making the contract.[314] The mere existence of a delusion in the mind of a person making a contract is not conclusive of his inability to understand it, even though the delusion is connected with the subject-matter of the contract.[315] And evidence that he is well known in the neighbourhood to be mentally disordered is not admissible to prove that the other party knew of his lack of capacity.[316]

8–071 **Deeds.** A deed executed by a person who lacks mental capacity for some purposes may still be valid if he is capable of understanding the effect of the deed at the time of its execution.[317] Thus deeds executed during a lucid interval are valid.[318] However, as with contracts in general, a deed made with such a person may be set aside on equitable grounds, such as relief against unconscionability.[319]

8–072 **Ratification.** It would appear that a person who lacked mental capacity at the time of making a contract (so as to render it voidable in principle) may nevertheless be bound by it if he ratifies it subsequently after recovery or during an interval where he possesses the capacity to do so.[320]

8–073 **Decisions as to a person's mental capacity under the Mental Capacity Act 2005.** The new Court of Protection set up under the Mental Capacity Act 2005 with a comprehensive jurisdiction over the health, welfare and financial affairs of people who lack capacity[321] has the power to make declarations as to a person's capacity in relation to specified decisions or matters and on the lawfulness of any act done or to be done in relation to such a person[322] and it may either itself make decisions on behalf of a person lacking capacity in relation to a matter concerning that person's personal welfare or his property and affairs[323] or appoint another person (a "deputy") to make decisions on that person's behalf in relation to such a matter.[324] For this purpose, it is provided that a person:

> ". . . lacks capacity in relation to a matter if at the material time he is unable to make a decision for himself in relation to the matter because of an impairment of, or a disturbance in the functioning of, the mind or brain"[325]

and that:

---

[314] *M'Adam v Walker* (1813) 1 Dow. 148, 177, HL.

[315] *Jenkins v Morris* (1880) 14 Ch D 674.

[316] *Greenslade v Dare* (1855) 20 Beav. 284, 290.

[317] *Elliott v Ince* (1857) 7 De G.M. & G. 475; *Re Beaney* [1978] 1 W.L.R. 770. But see below, para.8–078.

[318] *Hall v Warren* (1804) 9 Ves. 605; *Selby v Jackson* (1844) 6 Beav. 192; *Birkin v Wing* (1890) 63 L.T. 80; *Re Beaney* [1978] 1 W.L.R. 770. cf. *Daily Telegraph Newspaper Co Ltd v McLaughlin* [1904] A.C. 776.

[319] See above, paras 7–056 et seq., paras 7–126 et seq.

[320] *Matthews v Baxter* (1873) L.R. 8 Ex. 132 (drunken person).

[321] Mental Capacity Act 2005 ss.15–19; Pt 2 in force on October 1, 2007 (Mental Capacity Act (Commencement No.2) Order 2007 (SI 2007/1897) art.2(1)(a) and (b)).

[322] Mental Capacity Act 2005 s.15.

[323] 2005 Act ss.16(1) and (2)(a), 17 and 18.

[324] 2005 Act s.16(2)(b). On "deputies" see further ss.16–21.

[325] 2005 Act s.2(1).

"... a person is unable to make a decision for himself if he is unable (a) to understand the information relevant to the decision, (b) to retain that information, (c) to use or weigh that information as part of the process of making the decision, or (d) to communicate his decision (whether by talking, using sign language or any other means."[325a]

In coming to their decisions, both the Court of Protection and any deputee which it appoints must follow new statutory principles and give effect to the best interests of the person affected by the lack of capacity.[326]

Liability for necessaries: the old law. At common law, a lunatic was held liable for necessaries on the basis of an "implied contract" with their supplier although it was realised that this was a "most unfortunate expression, because there cannot be a contract by a lunatic".[327] The liability was restricted to the situation where the person who supplies the necessaries acted with the intention of claiming payment rather than by way of gift[328] and is explained in the modern law by the need to reverse the incapable person's unjustified enrichment rather than by implied contract,[329] being an example of liability based on necessitous intervention.[330] This position at common law was amended by s.2 of the Sale of Goods Act 1893[331] (subsequently s.3 of the Sale of Goods Act 1979) which provided that: 8–074

"... where necessaries are sold and delivered to a minor or to a person who by reason of mental incapacity or drunkenness is incompetent to contract, he must pay a reasonable price for them.[332]

And further that:

" '... necessaries' meant goods suitable to the condition in life of such a person, and to his actual requirements at the time of the sale and delivery."

While s.3 of the 1979 Act (unlike the common law governing necessitous intervention) does not in terms subject the liability of a mentally incapable person for necessary goods to a condition that they were supplied with the intention of claiming payment rather than by way of gift, this restriction can be seen implicitly in its requirement that the goods be "sold". In common with the liability of minors for necessaries,[333] it is unclear whether this provision *defines* the liability of mentally incapable persons for necessary goods or whether it leaves open the possibility of liability arising at common law beyond its terms:

[325a] Mental Capacity Act s.3(1).

[326] ss.1, 4, 16(3) and 20(6).

[327] *Re Rhodes* (1890) 44 Ch D 94, 105 Cotton L.J.

[328] (1890) 44 Ch D 94, 107.

[329] *Re Rhodes* (1890) 44 Ch D 94; *Re J.* [1909] Ch. 574 (expressed in terms of "implied contract"). See above, para.8–011. The estate of a husband who is mentally disordered is also liable at common law for necessaries supplied to his wife: *Read v Legard* (1851) 6 Exch. 636. See Vol.II, para.31–049.

[330] Goff and Jones at para.17–020.

[331] s.2.

[332] Sale of Goods Act 1979 s.3(2) (as enacted).

[333] Above, paras 8–008—8–012.

it certainly leaves aside their liability for necessary *services* which remained governed by the common law. If s.3 were to define liability in respect of necessary goods, then liability would arise only when goods actually sold and delivered were necessary at the time of sale and delivery and not therefore to executory contracts for necessaries (as the goods would not be "sold and delivered") nor to contracts for goods necessary when sold but not necessary when delivered.[334] On the other hand, it has been said that s.3 does not preclude liability of a mentally incapable person arising for necessary goods under a contract which would be valid under the general common law rules on the ground that his mentally incapacity was unknown to the other contracting party.[335] And this must be right as otherwise where the other party does not know of his incapacity the mentally incapable person could be liable to the contract price for non-necessary goods but only a reasonable sum for necessary ones. Moreover, in some cases, a person's mental incapacity may be so severe that it cannot be said that "necessaries are sold and delivered" to him and yet in these circumstances it has been argued that the common law rules governing necessitous intervention should still apply.[336] Finally, it is submitted that, unlike the more arguable position as regards the liability of minors for necessaries,[337] the liability for necessaries under s.3 of a person who lacks the mental capacity to make a contract for necessary goods should not be seen as arising from contract but rather on the basis of the principle of unjustified enrichment.

8–075 **Liability for necessaries: the new law.** However, as from October 1, 2007, s.7 of the Mental Capacity Act 2005 removed the reference to mentally incapable persons from s.3 of the Sale of Goods Act and itself instead provided that:

> "If necessary goods or services are supplied to a person who lacks capacity to contract for the supply, he must pay a reasonable price for them".[338]

And that for this purpose "necessary" means "suitable to a person's condition in life and to his actual requirements at the time when the goods or services are supplied".[339] As has been noted, the 2005 Act provides an explanation of "lack of capacity" for this purpose,[340] a test which can be seen to be broadly consistent with the test previously applied by the courts,[341] but the shift of statutory locus of the provisions regarding necessary goods (and its addition of necessary

---

[334] cf. above, paras 8–010—8–012 concerning minors' liability.

[335] Treitel, *The Law of Contract*, 11th edn (2003), p.558.

[336] Treitel at p.558 referring to *Re Rhodes* (1890) 44 Ch D 94.

[337] Above, para.8–011.

[338] Mental Capacity Act 2005 s.7(1) (which came into force on October 1, 2007 (Mental Capacity Act (Commencement No.2) Order 2007 (SI 2007/1897) art.2(1)(d))). It is to be noticed that s.7(1) did not retain the phrase "sold and delivered" from s.3 of the 1979 Act and this avoids the difficulty that they appear to assume that the person was capable of *some* element of consent in order to be liable for necessaries: cf. Mathews (1982) 33 N. Ir. L.Q. 148.

[339] Mental Capacity Act s.7(2). The Mental Capacity Act 2005 Code of Practice para.6.58 (made under s.42 of the 2005 Act and to be taken into account in deciding questions which arise under it) explains that: "The aim is to make sure that people can enjoy a similar standard of living and way of life to those they had before lacking capacity."

[340] Above, para.8–073.

[341] Treitel at para.12–053.

services) into the 2005 Act brings with it the application of important new general principles governing mental capacity.[342] It is clear that these changes do not alter the general common law position which remains that a person lacking the capacity to enter a contract is liable on the contract (including for necessaries) unless the other party knew of this incapacity.[343] But the reference to goods being "sold" found in the 1979 Act is not present in s.7 of the 2005 Act and this raises the question whether liability may arise even where a person supplying the goods or services intended to do so gratuitously: this appears justified on the wording of s.7, but it is submitted that it would be a perverse and unintended result of the legislative changes. Rather, the omission of the reference to goods "sold" is to be seen in the need to allow a person severely affected by mental incapacity (such as a person in an advanced stage of Alzheimer's disease) to be liable for necessary goods supplied to him even where it is difficult to say that they were "sold" to him.

Effect of principal's lack of capacity upon agency. It has been held that at common law the insanity of a principal terminates the authority of an agent to act on the ground that where the principal "can no longer act for himself, the agent whom he has appointed can no longer act for him".[344] It is submitted that (with the important exception of lasting powers of attorney[345]) where a principal develops a lack of capacity in respect of a particular translation which he has entrusted to an agent, then the agent's actual authority to make such a transaction is also terminated. However, the agent's apparent authority may continue beyond such a time, and the agent may himself be liable for breach of an implied warranty of authority.[346] 8–076

Property and affairs under the control of the court. Under the Lunacy and Mental Treatment Acts 1890 to 1930 a person might be found to be of unsound mind by inquisition, and if so found was held to be incapable of making a valid disposition of property by deed even during a lucid interval,[347] though whether the validity of ordinary contracts was similarly affected was not clear. The reason for this rule was that the statutory purpose of protecting and administering the property of a person of unsound mind would be frustrated if he remained capable of disposing of it by contract. The Lunacy and Mental Treatment Acts were repealed[348] and provision for the court to make decisions or appoint deputies to make decisions for a person lacking mental capacity is now found in the Mental 8–077

---

[342] s.1.

[343] This is apparent from the Parliamentary passage of the Mental Capacity Act 2005 where an amendment was proposed (and then withdrawn) which would have altered this position so as to render a contract unenforceable in certain circumstances where it was made with a person lacking capacity to do so even though the other party was unaware of this incapacity: *Hansard*, HL Vol.670, cols 1469–1472.

[344] *Drew v Nunn* (1879) 4 QBD 661, 666–667.

[345] Below, para.8–078.

[346] *Drew v Nunn* (1879) 4 QBD 661; *Yonge v Toynbee* [1910] 1 K.B. 215. For further details on this point, see Vol.II, para.31–056.

[347] *Re Walker* [1905] 1 Ch. 160; *Re Marshall* [1920] 1 Ch. 284. cf. *In the Estate of Walker* (1912) 28 T.L.R. 466 (disposition by will).

[348] Mental Health Act 1959 Sch.8.

Capacity Act 2005.[349] The question remains under this Act whether a patient who has been found by a judge to lack capacity in relation to his property or affairs and whose property is therefore the subject of its powers of management can execute a valid deed or enter into a valid contract. It would seem that he cannot,[350] but the point awaits authoritative decision.

8–078 **Lasting powers of attorney.** The Mental Capacity Act 2005 Act made new provision for "lasting powers of attorney" which replaced the "enduring powers of attorney" provided for by the Enduring Powers of Attorney Act 1985.[351] Under the new provisions, a "lasting power of attorney" can include a power of attorney under which the donor confers on the donee authority to make decisions about the donor's property and affairs or specified matters concerning his property or affairs "and which includes authority to make such decisions in circumstances where [the donor] no longer has capacity".[352] At the time of the execution of the instrument conferring the lasting power of attorney, the donor must be adult and have "the capacity to execute it".[353] On the other hand, the donor may revoke the power "at any time when he has capacity to do so".[354]

8–079 **Legal estate vested in person lacking capacity.** By s.22(1) of the Law of Property Act 1925 (as amended by the Mental Capacity Act 2005[355]), where a legal estate in land (whether settled or not) is vested in a person lacking capacity within the meaning of the 2005 Act to convey or create a legal estate, a deputy appointed for him by the Court of Protection or (if no deputy is appointed for him) any person authorised in that behalf shall, under an order of the Court of Protection, or of the court, or under any statutory power, make or concur in making all requisite dispositions for conveying or creating a legal estate in his name and on his behalf. And by s.22(2) of the 1925 Act, if land subject to a trust of land is vested in a person who lacks capacity within the meaning of the 2005 Act to exercise his functions as trustee, a new trustee shall be appointed in the place of that person, or he shall be otherwise discharged from the trust, before the legal estate is dealt with by the trustees.[356]

4. DRUNKEN PERSONS

8–080 **Effect of drunkenness.** In *Pitt v Smith*[357] in 1811, Lord Ellenborough held that a person in a state of complete intoxication has "no agreeing mind"; and later, in an action for work and labour, held that proof that the plaintiff was drunk

[349] Mental Capacity Act 2005 ss.15, 16 and 18; Sch.7 para.1.

[350] Treitel at paras 12–56—12–57 (at least as regards contracts which potentially may interfere with the court's control over the property).

[351] Mental Capacity Act 2005 ss.9–14 (in force on October 1, 2007: Mental Capacity Act (Commencement No.2) Order 2007 (SI 2007/1897) art.2(1)(a)).

[352] Mental Capacity Act 2005 s.9(1).

[353] s.9(2)(c).

[354] s.13(2).

[355] Sch.6 para.4(2)(c).

[356] Sch.6 para.4(2)(c).

[357] (1811) 3 Camp. 33.

when he signed what the defendant insisted was an agreement, dispensed with the necessity of producing it, the instrument being a nullity.[358] It would appear that the test of incapacity by reason of drunkenness is the same as that for persons lacking mental capacity, viz whether the person alleged to be incapable was so drunk as not to understand what he was doing, and whether the other party knew of his condition.[359] A contract made in such circumstances is said to be voidable at the drunken person's option, and can accordingly be ratified by him when sober.[360] But other authorities suggest that equity has a wider jurisdiction to set aside an unfair or unconscionable transaction entered into by a person affected by drink.[361] It would seem that a similar approach would be taken to a contract made under the influence of intoxicating substances other than alcohol, notably drugs.[362] In *Barclays Bank Plc v Schwartz*,[363] Millett L.J. accepted that the reason for drunkenness of a party to a contract affecting its validity is that like mental incapacity it deprives a person not only of a full understanding of a transaction, but also of the awareness that he does not understand it.

Liability for necessary goods. For necessaries sold and delivered, the liability of a drunken person is, by s.3 of the Sale of Goods Act 1979,[364] similar to that of a minor. 8–081

[358] *Fenton v Holloway* (1815) 1 Stark. 126.

[359] *Gore v Gibson* (1845) 13 M. & W. 623; *Molton v Camroux* (1849) 4 Exch. 17; *Imperial Loan Co v Stone* [1892] 1 Q.B. 599; *Hart v O'Connor* [1985] A.C. 1000; *Irvani v Irvani* [2000] 1 Lloyd's Rep. 412, 425.

[360] *Matthews v Baxter* (1873) L.R. 8 Ex. 132.

[361] *Cory v Cory* (1747) 1 Ves. Sen. 19; *Cooke v Clayworth* (1811) 18 Ves. 12; *Butler v Mulvihill* (1823) 1 Bligh 137; *Wiltshire v Marshall* (1866) 14 L.T.(N.S.) 396; *Blomley v Ryan* (1956) 99 C.L.R. 362. cf. *Irvani v Irvani* [2000] 1 Lloyd's Rep. 412, 425. This question is related to the wider question whether or not English law accepts a wide doctrine of "unconscionability", on which see, above, paras 7–126 et seq.

[362] *Irvani v Irvani* [2000] Lloyd's Rep. 412.

[363] *The Times*, August 2, 1995.

[364] See above, para.8–010.

Chapter 9

CORPORATIONS AND UNINCORPORATED ASSOCIATIONS

	PARA.
1. Corporations	9–001
(a) Kinds of corporations	9–001
(b) Corporations in general	9–004
(c) Attribution of acts to a company	9–007
(d) Registered companies	9–011
(i) Contracts between companies and third parties	9–012
(ii) Contracts between companies and promoters or directors	9–054
(iii) Contracts between companies and their members	9–060
(iv) Contracts between companies and their auditors	9–062
2. Unincorporated associations	9–064
(a) Generally	9–064
(b) Clubs	9–072
(i) Members' clubs	9–073
(ii) Proprietary clubs	9–080
(c) Trade unions	9–081

1. Corporations

(a) *Kinds of Corporations*

Kinds of corporations. Corporations, which are legal *personae* just as much as are individuals,[1] are either sole or aggregate. They may also be classified as ecclesiastical and lay, or as statutory and non-statutory. Lay corporations may be either trading or non-trading.[2] **9–001**

Corporations sole and aggregate. A corporation sole consists of a single person and his successors in office, such as the Crown, an archbishop, bishop or parson, the Treasury Solicitor,[3] or the Public Trustee.[4] It would seem that the benefit[5] and burden[6] of contracts made with a corporation sole pass, on the death of the holder of the office, to his successor in office; and contracts purportedly made with the corporation during a vacancy in the office take effect on the **9–002**

[1] *Re Sheffield, etc. Building Society* (1889) 22 QBD 470, 476.

[2] There is also the European Economic Interest Grouping (EEIG) which is an entity distinct from its members: see the European Economic Interest Grouping Regulations 1989 (SI 1989/638) [1985] O.J. L199/1.

[3] Treasury Solicitor Act 1876 s.1.

[4] Public Trustee Act 1906 s.1.

[5] Law of Property Act 1925 ss.180(1) and 205(1)(xx), reversing the common law rule in *Howley v Knight* (1849) 14 Q.B. 240, 255.

[6] See Co.Litt. 144b, n.2.

vacancy being filled, subject to a right of disclaimer by the successor in office.[7] A corporation aggregate is a legal person composed of individual members, but with a continuous identity distinct from that of the members composing it.[8] It follows that it can hold property in its own right, that its rights and liabilities are unaffected by changes in its membership and that, generally speaking, its property but not that of its members is available to satisfy its liabilities.

9–003 **Companies Act 2006.** The Companies Act 1985 has been replaced by the Companies Act 2006 the provisions of which are to be brought into effect in stages. Five commencement orders have been made.[9] The Act is being phased in over a period of three years; the final implementation being October 1, 2009.[10] Section 1297 of the 2006 Act is a continuity of law provision. This section provides that where the 2006 Act re-enacts a provision repealed (with or without modification) by the Act, the repeal and re-enactment does not affect the continuity of the law. Also, and very importantly, where there are references in articles of association, resolutions and contracts referring to a provision in the 1985 Act which is replicated in the 2006 Act, the provisions of the 2006 Act will be applicable (even if there have been verbal changes) unless it is intended that a change should be affected by the 2006 Act.

(b) *Corporations in General*

9–004 **Corporation created by charter.** A corporation created by charter can, unless prevented by some statute regulating its proceedings,[11] contract and deal with its property in the same way as an individual.[12] Contracts made by it outside the terms of its charter are valid, but by making them the corporation renders itself liable to the revocation of its charter.[13] But a member may obtain an injunction to restrain a chartered company from acting on regulations which would materially change the character of the company and which could not have

[7] Law of Property Act 1925 s.180(3).

[8] As to the juristic nature of corporations, see Wolff (1938) 54 L.Q.R. 494; Hart (1954) 70 L.Q.R. 37; Gower & Davies' *Principles of Modern Company Law*, 7th edn (2003), Chs 1 and 2; *Rayner (Mincing Lane) Ltd v DTI* [1990] 2 A.C. 418; *Adams v Cape Industries Plc* [1990] Ch. 433.

[9] Companies Act 2006 (Commencement No.1, Transitional Provisions and Savings) Order 2006 (SI 2006/3428 (c.132)); Companies Act 2006 (Commencement No.2, Consequential Amendments, Transitional Provisions and Savings) Order 2007 (SI 2007/1093 (c.49)); Companies Act 2006 (Commencement No.3, Consequential Amendments, Transitional Provisions and Savings) Order 2007 (SI 2007/2194 (c.84)); Companies Act 2006 (Commencement No.4 and Commencement No.3 (Amendment)) Order 2007 (SI 2007/2607 (c.101)); Companies Act 2006 (Commencement No.5, Transitional Provisions and Savings) Order 2007 (SI 2007/3495 (c.150)).

[10] For the implementation programme see *The Companies Act 2006 updating you; updating your clients* (BERR, 2008). The commentary is based on the assumption that the 2006 Act has been brought into effect.

[11] See *Att-Gen v Manchester Corp* [1906] 1 Ch. 643.

[12] *Sutton's Hospital Case* (1612) 10 Co.Rep. 23a; *Baroness Wenlock v River Dee Co* (1887) 36 Ch D 674, 685n.; *R. v Bonanza Creek Gold Mining Co Ltd* [1916] 1 A.C. 566, 583–584; *Institution of Mechanical Engineers v Cane* [1961] A.C. 696, 724–725; *Pharmaceutical Society of Great Britain v Dickson* [1970] A.C. 403. See the Companies Act 2006 s.1043 Pt 33 Chs 1 and 2.

[13] See fn.9, above; and see *British South Africa Co v De Beers Consolidated Mines Ltd* [1910] 1 Ch. 354, 374–376; reversed on other grounds [1912] A.C. 52. cf. *Att-Gen, New Brunswick v St John* [1948] 3 D.L.R. 693.

been contemplated at the date of its incorporation.[14] But he cannot restrain the corporation, acting on the wishes of a majority of its members, from applying to the Crown for an alteration of the charter.[15]

Corporation created by statute. The powers of a corporation, whether sole or aggregate, created by statute are confined to those given expressly or by reasonable inference by the statute concerned.[16] If the subject-matter of a contract made by such a corporation is outside the scope of its constitution as defined by the statute, the contract is ultra vires and void.[17] This principle applies to all statutory corporations and not only to companies incorporated under the Companies Act.[18] However, the ultra vires rule as far as it affects a company registered under the 2006 Act has been abrogated by s.39 of the Act,[19] the overall purpose of this provision being to guarantee security of transactions between companies and persons with whom they deal. Ultra vires will still have relevance as regards director's authority to bind the company.[20] 9–005

Corporations regulated by legislation. Certain corporations, although not created by statute, are regulated by legislation. Thus, the powers of ecclesiastical corporations, sole and aggregate, are limited by particular statutory provisions[21]; and most charitable corporations[22] are subject to the control of the Charity Commissioners under the Charities Act 1993. 9–006

(c) *Attribution of Acts to a Company*

It is a trite observation that a company can only act through the instrumentability of individuals to, for example, enter into contracts. The question arises as to which individuals will bind the company so that it is liable under a contract. The answer to this question is provided by the rules of attribution whereby the acts of certain individuals are attributed to the company. The principles of attribution were analysed by Lord Hoffmann in *Meridian Global Funds Management Ltd v Securities Commission*.[23] First, there are the company's primary rules of attribution which are to be found normally in the company's constitution (the articles and memorandum of association) and which will determine who or which 9–007

---

[14] *Jenkin v Pharmaceutical Society of Great Britain* [1921] 1 Ch. 392. A similar action lies if the alteration is in restraint of trade.

[15] *Gray v Trinity College, Dublin* [1910] 1 Ir. R. 370.

[16] For local authorities see *Hazell v Hammersmith and Fulham London BC* [1992] A.C. 1.

[17] *Ashbury Ry Carriage and Iron Co v Riche* (1875) L.R. 7 H.L. 653.

[18] *Baroness Wenlock v River Dee Co* (1885) 10 App. Cas. 354. The doctrine of ultra vires is discussed further at below, paras 9–020 et seq. As to the application of this principle to overseas companies, see *Dicey and Morris on the Conflict of Laws*, 13th edn (2000), pp.1109–1116; *Janred Properties Ltd v Ente National Per Il Turismo (No.2)* [1986] 1 F.T.L.R. 246.

[19] Below, paras 9–027 et seq.

[20] See para.9–031—9–033.

[21] Ecclesiastical Leasing Acts 1842 and 1858; Ecclesiastical Leases Acts 1861, 1862 and 1865.

[22] On the nature of charitable companies see *Liverpool and District Hospital for Diseases of the Heart v Att-Gen* [1981] Ch D 193.

[23] [1995] A.C. 500 PC. See also *Bank of India v Morris* [2005] EWCA Civ 693, [2005] 2 B.C.L.C. 328.

organ of the company can enter into transactions on behalf of the company.[24] The primary rules of attribution may also be provided by the rules of company law, for example, the principle that the unanimous decision of all the shareholders of a solvent company, even though given informally, constitutes a decision of the company.[25] Coupled with the company's primary rules of attribution are general rules of attribution, namely, the principles of agency and vicarious liability.[26] There will be situations, however, where the primary and secondary rules of attribution do not provide an answer and in these situations the court will have to determine who, if anyone, for the particular matter under consideration is intended to count as the person whose acts are attributed to the company.

9–008 **Company's name.** The Business Names Act 1985 was repealed by the Companies Act 2006[27] and replaced by Pt 41[28] of that Act. Part 41 applies to a "person" carrying on business in the United Kingdom.[29] Chapter 1 of Pt 41 contains prohibitions on the use of sensitive names, broadly names that suggest a connection with a government department or which are subject to statutory regulations. Individuals and partnerships are required to set out details as to their names where they are trading under a "business name".[30] Such disclosure is also required in "business documents".[31] Failure to make such disclosure can have criminal consequences[32] and can affect the company's right to enforce any contract.[33] There are no longer display rules of names by corporate bodies. The Secretary of State may make regulations requiring every company to display its name in a specified way, to include its name in specified documents, and to provide its name in the course of business.[34] Section 83 deals with the civil consequences of failure to comply with the name disclosure regulations. Failure to comply affects the right of the company to bring proceedings arising out of any contract with respect to which the company was in breach of the name regulations, there is, however, no personal liability imposed on the directors in this situation.[35]

9–009 **Abolition of old rule requiring seal: other formalities.** The contracts of a corporation sole were never required to be made under seal.[36] But the old common law rule was that a corporation aggregate could contract only under

---

[24] See, e.g. art.70 of Table A Companies (Tables A–F) Regulations 1985 (SI 1984/805).

[25] *Multinational Gas and Petrochemical Co v Multinational Gas and Petrochemical Services Ltd* [1983] Ch. 258.

[26] See *New Zealand Guardian Trust Co Ltd v Brooks* [1995] 1 W.L.R. 96.

[27] Sch.16.

[28] This is excluded from those parts of the Act deemed to constitute "the Companies Act" as it applies to business names in general: see Companies Act 2006 s.2.

[29] s.1192(1).

[30] s.1200.

[31] s.1202.

[32] s.1205.

[33] s.1206.

[34] s.82.

[35] 1985 Act s.349(4) has not been replicated.

[36] Bl. Comm. Vol.I, at 475.

seal.[37] The scope of this rule had been greatly restricted by numerous statutory, common law and equitable exceptions; it did not apply to companies incorporated under the Companies Act[38] and it was finally abolished altogether by the Corporate Bodies Contracts Act 1960.

Deeds. Section 1(2) of the Law of Property (Miscellaneous Provisions) Act 1989, which defines what constitutes a deed, applies to companies. How a deed is to be executed by a company is set out in ss.44–47 of the 2006 Act. Section 46 dispenses with the need for a company to have a common seal in order to execute an instrument as a deed.[39] 9–010

(d) *Registered Companies*[40]

Registered companies. This section is principally concerned with companies registered under the Companies Acts, but many of the principles herein discussed also apply to corporations created by particular private or public Acts. 9–011

(i) *Contracts between Companies and Third Parties*

Pre-incorporation contracts. Contracts entered into before a company is registered can, prima facie, bind or confer rights only on the actual makers of the contract and not the company,[41] the reason for this being that a company could not be bound by a contract entered into when it was non-existent.[42] At common law such contracts could even be completely null and void if the persons purporting to sign on behalf of the company were not the real principals.[43] However, the courts are strongly disposed to give effect to pre-incorporation contracts and, acting on the maxim *ut res magis valeat quam pereat*, the agent more likely than not will be personally bound on the contract particularly where both parties were aware at the time of contracting of the non-existence of the company.[44] It must be emphasised, however, that at common law there was no general rule that a person acting for a non-existent principal would be automatically bound by the contract; in the final analysis the agent's liability turns on the 9–012

---

[37] *Yarborough v Bank of England* (1812) 16 East 6; *Ludlow Corp v Charlton* (1840) 6 M. & W. 815; *A.R. Wright & Son Ltd v Romford BC* [1957] 1 Q.B. 431.

[38] See now s.43 of the 2006 Act.

[39] s.47 deals with the execution of deeds by an attorney and requires an attorney to be appointed by deed.

[40] This is not a summary of company law, but only of the law applicable to the contracts of companies.

[41] *Kelner v Baxter* (1866) L.R. 2 C.P. 174; *Scott v Lord Ebury* (1867) L.R. 2 C.P. 255; *Wilson & Co v Baker, Lees & Co* (1901) 17 T.L.R. 473; *King v David Allen & Sons Billposting Ltd* [1916] 2 A.C. 54; Gross (1971) 87 L.Q.R. 367.

[42] See Law Commission, *Privity of Contract: Contracts for the Benefit of Third Parties* (Report No.242), paras 8.9–8.16.

[43] *Newborne v Sensolid (Great Britain) Ltd* [1954] 1 Q.B. 45; *Black v Smallwood* (1965–66) 117 C.L.R. 52. See also Vol.II, para.31–028.

[44] *Kelner v Baxter* (1866) L.R. 2 C.P. 174.

intention of the parties.[45] The common law was significantly modified by the need to implement Art.7 of the First Directive on Company Law which deals with pre-incorporation contracts.[46] Article 7 was first implemented by s 9(2) of the European Communities Act 1972, was consolidated into s.36(4) of the Companies Act 1985 and became s.36C of the 1985 Act[47] and is now restated in s.51 of the 2006 Act. What is stated in the text with respect to ss.36(4) and 35C is equally applicable to s.51. Commenting on s.36(4), Oliver L.J. in *Phonogram Ltd v Lane*[48] stated that it swept away the "subtle distinctions" of the common law so that:

> "[W]here a person purports to contract on behalf of a company not yet formed, then however he expresses his signature he himself is personally liable on the contract."[49]

Phonogram Ltd v Lane was the first case[50] to interpret s.36(4), and the Court of Appeal rejected attempts to construe narrowly the effect of the section. In particular, it rejected the argument that the phrase "subject to any agreement to the contrary" should be interpreted to relieve a person of liability where he signs the contract as agent, in that this could be taken as evincing an agreement that the person acting for the company was not to be personally liable.[51] A person acting for an unformed company could only avoid liability under s.36C where there was an "express agreement"[52] that he was not to be liable. Section 36C creates a deemed contract which confers mutual obligations and rights, that is, it not only confers obligations on the agent who acted for the non-existent company but also confers a right of enforcement against the other party to the contract provided it is a situation where the ordinary principles of the common law of agency would entitle the agent to enforce the contract against the third party.[53] In determining who is the "agent" for the purpose of the section it is the person who purported to make the contract for the company and there is no need to establish from the totality of the negotiations that the purported agent was the moving mind and will of the whole transaction.[54] Where a person contracts on behalf of a company which has been struck off the register, and later forms a new company, the section

[45] *Hawkes Bay Milk Corp v Watson* [1974] 2 N.Z.L.R. 236. Note also the possible liability of the putative agent for breach of warranty of authority: see *Bowstead on Agency*, 17th edn (2001), Art.100.

[46] First Directive 68/151 art.7 provides that: "If, before a company being formed has acquired legal personality, action has been carried out in its name and the company does not assume the obligations arising from such action, the persons who acted shall, without limit, be jointly and severally liable therefore, unless otherwise agreed."

[47] This was inserted by s.130(4) of the 1989 Act.

[48] [1982] 1 Q.B. 938, 946.

[49] [1982] 1 Q.B. 938, 944, per Lord Denning M.R.

[50] For other cases dealing with s.36(4) of the 1985 Act see: *Rover International Ltd v Cannon Film Sales Ltd* [1987] B.C.L.C. 540 (the subsection, as would be the case with s.51, does not affect foreign companies); *Oshkosh B'Gosh Inc v Dan Marbel Ltd* [1989] B.C.L.C. 507; *Cotronic (UK) Ltd v Dezonie* [1991] B.C.L.C. 721; *Badgerhill Properties Ltd v Cottrell* [1991] B.C.L.C. 805.

[51] e.g. as in *Newborne v Sensolid (Great Britain) Ltd* [1954] 1 Q.B. 45. See generally Prentice (1973) 89 L.Q.R. 518, 530–533.

[52] *Phonogram Ltd v Lane* [1982] 1 Q.B. 938, 940.

[53] *Braymist Ltd v Wise Finance Co Ltd* [2002] EWCA Civ 127, [2002] Ch. 273.

[54] [2002] EWCA Civ 127.

does not apply as the new company was not in contemplation when the contract was entered into.[55]

Section 36C does not affect the company itself, and it remains the law that a company is not entitled to the benefits of, or bound by the liabilities in, a contract entered into before it was incorporated. But in some circumstances a company may acquire rights or incur liabilities at law or equity in respect of a transaction originally entered into before the incorporation of the company. Broadly speaking, for a company to be so liable it must enter into a new contract after it has been incorporated, but it is arguable (as will be seen later) that a company can be liable in other circumstances. 9–013

At law. A company cannot ratify or adopt a contract made ostensibly on its behalf before its incorporation, since a person cannot by a subsequent ratification make himself liable as a principal where he was not in existence at the time of the original contract.[56] Before a company is bound it must enter into a new contract. If promoters purport to enter into a contract on behalf of a company before its incorporation, the facts may show that a new contract is made with the company after its incorporation on the terms of the old. But the circumstances relied on for this purpose must be necessarily referable to, or must necessarily imply, a new contract between the company and the other contracting party.[57] This is a question of fact.[58] Where the company's conduct is attributable to its mistaken belief that it was bound by the original contract[59] or is attributable to the performance by the company of a contract between it and, for example the promoters,[60] it will be difficult, if not impossible, to show that the company's conduct is necessarily referable to a new contract with the other contracting party. In *Rover International Ltd v Cannon Film Sales Ltd*[61] Harman J. rejected the argument that the doctrine of estoppel by convention could operate to preclude the company from claiming that it was not bound by a pre-incorporation contract if both parties to the contract had, after the company's incorporation, acted as though it were bound.[62] He reasoned that where estoppel by convention operates it must relate to an "assumption of agreed facts . . . (existing) before the contract or dealing is made or agreed" and as the company did not exist at the time the contract was entered into there was accordingly no basis on which the estoppel could operate. Admittedly, in *Amalagamated Investment and Property Co Ltd v* 9–014

[55] *Cotronic (UK) Ltd v Dezonie* [1991] B.C.L.C. 721.

[56] *Kelner v Baxter* (1866) L.R. 2 C.P. 174; *Melhado v Porto Alegre Ry* (1874) L.R. 9 C.P. 503; *North Sydney Investment & Tramway Co v Higgins* [1899] A.C. 263; *Scott v Lord Ebury* (1867) L.R. 2 C.P. 255, 267.

[57] *Natal Land, etc., Co v Pauline Colliery Syndicate* [1904] A.C. 120.

[58] *Howard v Patent Ivory Manufacturing Co* (1888) 38 Ch D 156.

[59] *Re Northumberland Avenue Hotel Co* (1886) 33 Ch D 16; *Bagot Pneumatic Tyre Co v Clipper Pneumatic Tyre Co* [1901] 1 Ch. 196, 203.

[60] *Howard v Patent Ivory Manufacturing Co* (1888) 38 Ch D 156, 164–168.

[61] [1987] W.L.R. 1597 (Harman J.); [1989] 1 W.L.R. 912. For other proceedings involving the parties see *Films Rover International Ltd v Cannon Film Sales Ltd* [1987] 1 W.L.R. 670 where Hoffmann J. stated that it "would be a blot on English jurisprudence if this contract, acted on by both sides, had now to be held null and void" (679).

[62] This argument was advanced in the 25th edn of this text, p.334.

Texas Commerce International Bank Ltd[63] the facts on which the estoppel was based existed at the time the purported contract was entered into, but it is submitted that it is an unnecessarily narrow reading of the estoppel doctrine to confine it to facts that existed at the time the contract was entered into. There is, however, no reason in principle why the estoppel should not date from the time the company is incorporated. The estoppel point was not pursued on appeal in the *Rover International* case,[64] but the court allowed a quantum meruit claim with respect to services rendered by the company after it had been incorporated. Where the company, after its incorporation, has taken possession of property belonging to the other contracting party in pursuance to the agreement,[65] or has agreed to modify the terms of the original contract,[66] it will be easier to infer the making of a new contract.

9–015 **In equity.** Equity also will not assist (in the sense of enforcing a contract) a person who has entered into a contract for the benefit of a corporation which, at the time of the making of the contract, did not exist, and it will not, it would seem, enforce such contracts unless they are enforceable at law.[67] It is true that there are certain late nineteenth-century decisions in which courts of equity did enforce such contracts on the ground that the company had "adopted" the promoters' contract[68]; but the distinction between ratification and adoption was never clear[69] and they can no longer be relied upon.[70] Another attempt to enforce pre-incorporation contracts against companies sought to utilise the device of the trust; thus where a promoter had contracted with third parties that a company not yet in existence should pay the third parties £2,000 in consideration for certain services by the third parties, and the promoter was in a position to sue the company for that remuneration, the promoter was held to be a trustee for the third parties of his right of action, and the third parties, being cestuis que trustent,

---

[63] [1982] Q.B. 84.

[64] [1989] 1 W.L.R. 912; noted (1989) 105 L.Q.R. 179 (Beatson). For other aspects of this case see below, para.9–017.

[65] See fn.63.

[66] *Howard v Patent Ivory Manufacturing Co* (1888) 38 Ch D 156, 166.

[67] In some nineteenth-century cases there are dicta that persons who perform services for an unformed company will have a claim in equity for payment on the grounds that it is "inequitable for a man not to pay for services of which he has taken the benefit", per James L.J., *Re Empress Engineering Co* (1880) 16 Ch D 125, 130. See also *Hereford South Wales Waggon & Engineering Co* (1876) 2 Ch D 621. These dicta are of doubtful authority: no case actually turns on their application; they are often cited in the context of a company having purportedly "adopted" the contract, a phrase used with no great clarity; they are scarcely compatible with subsequent authority and were rejected in *Re English and Colonial Produce Co Ltd* [1906] 2 Ch. 435, 442.

[68] *Spiller v Paris Skating Rink Co* (1878) 7 Ch D 368. The question of "adoption" was often bound up with the problem of part performance in connection with the Statute of Frauds (see above, paras 4–041—4–046) and it was sometimes suggested that part performance was itself a ground of liability in equity even in the absence of a binding contract (see *Wilson v West Hartlepool Ry* (1865) 2 De G.J. & S. 475) but it is clear today that this is not so: *Hunt v Wimbledon Local Board* (1878) 4 C.P.D. 48, 61.

[69] *Falcke v Scottish Imperial Insurance Co* (1886) 34 Ch D 234, 249–250.

[70] *Re Empress Engineering Co* (1880) 16 Ch D 125, 130; *Natal Land, etc., Co v Pauline Colliery Syndicate* [1904] A.C. 120.

could sue the company.[71] But the courts are increasingly reluctant to imply a trust in such circumstances,[72] and, in any event, as later decisions show, the promoter will not have any right of action to hold in trust for the benefit of a third party unless the company, *after its incorporation*, makes a contract with him.[73]

Pre-incorporation benefits. A company is under no liability, either at law or in equity, to pay for benefits rendered to it prior to its incorporation.[74] So, for instance, a company is not bound to reimburse a promoter in respect of the expense of incorporation[75] unless after it has been formed it enters into a binding contract to do so. Similarly, a company is not bound by any agreement made by its promoters that it will, when formed, pay something to a third party who has agreed not to oppose the formation of the company in consideration of such a payment.[76] There are some nineteenth-century cases concerning the incorporation of railway companies by private Acts of Parliament which suggest that the court will not allow such a company to exercise its statutory powers without performing undertakings contained in a contract made by the promoters with a third party, in consideration of which that party agreed not to oppose the formation of the company.[77] But equity will not interfere even to this extent unless the original contract would have been intra vires of the company if originally made by the company.[78] 9–016

Post-incorporation benefits. It may be that a company will benefit in a tangible way from acts arising under a pre-incorporation contract which does not give rise to any contractual claim by the other party to the contract. With the recognition of unjust enrichment as a ground for granting restitutionary remedies,[79] there are now a range of doctrines that can be invoked by the party providing the tangible benefit to obtain restitution for the benefit conferred. Where property or money has been transferred to a company pursuant to a pre-incorporation contract, the property or money may be recovered on the basis that 9–017

[71] *Touche v Metropolitan Ry Warehousing Co* (1871) L.R. 6 Ch. App. 671 (it is important to note that the court found that there was a trust of the company's promise to the promoter, although how the trust was actually constituted is not clear from the facts).

[72] *Re Empress Engineering Co* (1880) 16 Ch D 125; and see below, paras 19–065—19–066.

[73] *Re National Motor Mail Coach Co, Clinton's Claim* [1908] 2 Ch. 515.

[74] *Re English & Colonial Produce Co Ltd* [1906] 2 Ch. 435, disapproving dicta in *Re Hereford & South Wales Waggon, etc., Co* (1876) 2 Ch D 621; see also fn.63.

[75] *Re Hereford & South Wales Waggon, etc., Co* (1876) 2 Ch D 621.

[76] *Earl of Lindsey v Great Northern Ry* (1853) 10 Hare 664; *Earl of Shrewsbury v North Staffordshire Ry* (1865) L.R. 1 Eq. 593.

[77] *Earl of Shrewsbury v North Staffordshire Ry* (1865) L.R. 1 Eq. 593. These cases, decided before the consequences of the entity doctrine were fully appreciated, were considered to have been seriously "shaken" by the development of this doctrine: see Hodges, *A Law of Railways*, 7th edn, pp.141–152. There is much substance to this view which is not significantly undermined by a more relaxed doctrine of privity, as to hold the company bound would for all intents and purposes sweep away the learning on pre-incorporation contracts, something which is scarcely likely to happen. The promoters who gave the assurance may, of course, be liable if there is deceit or, perhaps, for negligent misrepresentation or breach of warranty of authority.

[78] *Earl of Shrewsbury v North Staffordshire Ry* (1865) L.R. 1 Eq. 593. See *Westdeutsche Landesbank Girozentrale v Islington LBC* [1996] A.C. 669. The effect (if any) of s.51 of the Companies Act 2006 on this type of case is uncertain. For the categories of company covered by s.51; see s.1 and Pt 33 of the 2006 Act.

[79] See Ch.30.

the transfer or payment was made under a mistake of fact.[80] Alternatively, recovery may be available on the grounds of failure of consideration in the sense that the plaintiff has not received any part of the consideration bargained for under the purported contract.[81] In *Westdeutsche Landesbank Girozentrale v LBC of Islington*[82] it was held that there was a general principle that moneys, paid under an ultra vires contract that was void ab initio, were recoverable on the grounds of total failure of consideration, or on equitable principles entitling a transferor to recover property that in equity belonged to him. Since a pre-incorporation contract is, like an ultra vires contract, void, these principles could also be applied to moneys paid to a company pursuant to a pre-incorporation contract.[83] Where benefits are conferred on a company on the basis of a pre-incorporation contract, the party providing the benefit will be entitled to a quantum meruit.[84]

9–018 It is submitted that money in the hands of a company can be "traced" no less when it has come into the company's hands as the result of a pre-incorporation contract than when it has done so as the result of an ultra vires contract,[85] and that the ordinary rules of equity also apply where a company has stood by and allowed another to expend money on its property in the mistaken belief, based on a pre-incorporation contract and known to the company, that he has some interest in that property.[86]

9–019 **Public companies: trading certificate.** A company which is registered as a public company shall not do business or exercise its borrowing powers unless it obtains a certificate from the registrar of companies.[87] Broadly speaking, the registrar is obliged to issue such a certificate once he has been satisfied that the company possesses the necessary allotted minimum share capital.[88] Failure to obtain a certificate can give rise to criminal and civil consequences. In particular, if a public company trades without a certificate and fails to obtain one within 21 days from being called upon to do so, the directors of the company shall be jointly and severally liable to indemnify the other party to the transaction in

---

[80] *Rover International Ltd v Cannon Film Sales Ltd* [1989] 1 W.L.R. 912. See Burrows, *The Law of Restitution*, 2nd edn (2002), p.129; Goff and Jones, *The Law of Restitution*, 6th edn (2002), pp.649–651.

[81] *Rover International Ltd v Cannon Sales Ltd* [1989] 1 W.L.R. 912; Burrows, at pp.393–396.

[82] See above, fn.78; see also *Kleinwort Benson Ltd v The South Tyneside MBC* [1994] 4 All E.R. 972.

[83] Moneys paid on behalf of a company before it is has been formed could not be recoverable by the company, the company has lost nothing. See *Rover International Ltd v Cannon Film Sales Ltd* [1989] 1 W.L.R. 912.

[84] *Rover International Ltd v Cannon Film Sales Ltd* [1989] 1 W.L.R. 912; *Cotronic (UK) Ltd v Dezonie* [1991] B.C.L.C. 721. In the latter case, the court held that s.34 of the 1985 Act did not preclude recovery.

[85] See below, para.9–026.

[86] See *Hunt v Wimbledon Local Board* (1878) 4 C.P.D. 48, 61. The same rules will apply where it is the company has expended the money on another's property.

[87] Companies Act 2006 s.761.

[88] s.761(2).

respect of any loss or damage suffered by him by reason of the failure of the company to comply with those obligations.[89]

Ultra vires contracts.[90] A company which owes its corporate existence to statute has not the inherent common law powers of chartered corporations.[91] Indeed, it has only capacity to enter into contracts authorised by the objects clause in its memorandum of association, or, in the case of companies not registered under the Companies Act 1985, by the terms of its special Act. Thus, it was held in *Ashbury Ry Carriage & Iron Co v Riche*[92] that any contract outside the scope of the objects clause is ultra vires of the company and void, even if the whole body of shareholders in the company assent to it.[93] A member of a company[94] is entitled to an injunction to restrain the company and its directors[95] from entering into an ultra vires contract or otherwise acting outside the powers of the company, e.g. criminally.[96] Although ss.35–35C of the Companies Act 1985 (originally s.9(1) of the European Communities Act 1972) greatly reduced the importance of the ultra vires doctrine, the provisions did not completely abrogate the effect of the doctrine, and there were some situations (although these were rare) where the common law doctrine had relevance. More importantly, as stated earlier, some knowledge of the common law is needed in order to understand fully the statutory modifications of the ultra vires doctrine. Accordingly, the common law position is discussed in the next six paragraphs, and the Companies Act 2006 is then considered.[97] At this point it must be emphasised that the development of the ultra vires doctrine since the *Riche* decision also witnessed judicial attempts, on the whole successful, to attenuate the doctrine so 9–020

[89] s.767.

[90] The provisions dealt with in this paragraph, ss.35–36C of the 1985 Act, have been replaced by ss.39–40 of the 2006 Act. This is particularly relevant to paras 9–027—9–034. Also of relevance is, inter alia, s.31 of the 2006 Act which provides that a company's objects are unrestricted unless the company's articles specifically restrict the objects. Under the 2006 Act, a company's memorandum cannot contain a statement of its objects (s.8). If a company has objects they will have to be in its articles (s.31). See para.9–028 for a more extended treatment.

[91] See above, para.9–004.

[92] (1875) L.R. 7 H.L. 653; and see *Att-Gen v Great Eastern Ry* (1880) 5 App. Cas. 473; *Wenlock (Baroness) v River Dee Co* (1885) 10 App. Cas. 354; *L.C.C. v Att-Gen* [1902] A.C. 165; *Att-Gen v Mersey Ry* [1907] 1 Ch. 81; [1907] A.C. 415; *Re Jon Beauforte (London) Ltd* [1953] Ch. 131; *Parke v Daily News Ltd* [1962] Ch. 927.

[93] "An *ultra vires* agreement cannot become *intra vires* by means of estoppel, lapse of time, ratification, acquiescence, or delay": *York Corp v Henry Leetham & Sons Ltd* [1924] 1 Ch. 557, 573; see also para.9–024.

[94] But not, in general, a creditor: *Mills v Northern Ry of Buenos Aires Co* (1870) L.R. 5 Ch. App. 621; *Cross v Imperial Continental Gas Association* [1923] 2 Ch. 553; *Lawrence v W. Somerset Mineral Ry Co* [1918] 2 Ch. 250; contrast *Maunsell v Midland G.W. (Ireland) Ry* (1863) 1 Hem. & M. 130. See also *Charles Roberts & Co Ltd v British Railways Board* [1965] 1 W.L.R. 396 (action for declaration by business competitor of a nationalised industry); and as to relator actions, see *Att-Gen v Crayford U.D.C.* [1962] Ch. 575.

[95] *Hoole v G.W. Ry* (1867) L.R. 3 Ch. App. 262. The right to restrain prospective ultra vires acts is based on the contract constituted by s.33 of the Companies Act 2006. A shareholder's standing to complain of past ultra vires acts gives rise to more complex problems: see *Smith v Croft (No.2)* [1988] Ch. 114.

[96] See Buckley, *The Companies Acts*, 15th edn (2000), para.35–190.

[97] Proposals for the reform of the ultra vires doctrine were put forward in a DTI consultative document: *Reform of the Ultra Vires Rule: A Consultative Report* (1986). These were partly implemented by ss.108–109 of the Companies Act 1989.

that a person dealing with a company will not be prejudiced by the latter's lack of capacity except in exceptional circumstances.

9–021 **Scope of the rule.** The phrase ultra vires "should be restricted to those cases where the transaction is beyond the capacity of the company and therefore wholly void".[98] The question whether the making of a particular contract is or is not ultra vires of the company depends upon the terms of the company's memorandum of association, which must state the company's objects.[99] Explaining the rule Lord Wrenbury[100] said:

> "The purpose, I apprehend, is twofold. The first is that the intending corporator who contemplates the investment of his capital shall know within what field it is to be put at risk. The second is that anyone who shall deal with the company shall know without reasonable doubt whether the contractual relationship into which he contemplates entering with the company is one relating to a matter within its corporate objects."

As was stated by Browne-Wilkinson L.J. in *Rolled Steel Products (Holdings) Ltd v British Steel Corporation*[101]:

> "The question whether a transaction is outside the capacity of the company depends solely upon whether, on the true construction of its memorandum of association, the transaction is capable of falling within the objects of the company."

At common law the doctrine is not dependent on the person dealing with the company having notice of the company's lack of capacity; it operates regardless of the third party's state of knowledge as regards the contents of the company's objects clause.[102] In a number of cases it was held that where a company exercised a power which it undoubtedly possessed but for a *purpose* which was ultra vires, and this purpose was known to the party dealing with the company, the contract would be ultra vires in the sense of being outside the capacity of the company and hence void.[103] However, in the *Rolled Steel* decision the Court of Appeal considered that these cases should be treated as cases dealing with an abuse of the company's powers, not with corporate capacity, with the result that the transactions in these cases would be enforceable against the company unless the party dealing with it had notice (actual or constructive) that the transaction

---

[98] *Rolled Steel Products (Holdings) Ltd v British Steel Corp* [1986] 1 Ch. 246, 303, per Browne-Wilkinson L.J. (see also Slade L.J. 297). The phrase should not therefore be used to refer to situations where directors abuse or exceed their authority or where the transaction is illegal.

[99] Companies Act 1985 s.2(1)(c). It has been said that a wider construction ought to be given to the memorandum of association of a commercial company than to the statute creating a company with special powers: *Att-Gen v Mersey Ry* [1907] 1 Ch. 81, 106 (reversed [1907] A.C. 415), but see *Charles Roberts & Co Ltd v British Railways Board* [1965] 1 W.L.R. 396, at 400. See para.9–028 on the current position with respect to objects clauses.

[100] *Cotman v Brougham* [1918] A.C. 514, 522; *Hazell v Hammersmith and Fulham LBC* [1992] 2 A.C. 1, 36–37; *Westdeutsche* [1996] A.C. 669.

[101] [1986] Ch. 246, 306.

[102] [1986] Ch. 246, 304. See also *Freeman & Lockyer v Buckhurst Park Properties (Mangal) Ltd* [1964] 2 Q.B. 480, 504.

[103] See, e.g. *Re Lee, Behrens & Co* [1932] 2 Ch. 46; *Re Jon Beauforte (London) Ltd* [1953] Ch. 131. cf. Insolvency Act 1986 s.238(5); *Westdeutsche Landesbank Girozentrale v Islington LBC* [1996] A.C. 669.

was in excess of or an abuse of the company's powers.[104] Normally a transaction falling within a company's objects clause will be within the vires of a company. However, in certain situations a provision in the objects clause may not be capable as existing as an object and may be merely an ancillary power; for example, the power to borrow.[105] Formerly parties dealing with companies were deemed to have notice of companies' memoranda of association[106] but this rule has now been abrogated.[107]

What contracts are ultra vires. It has been repeatedly asserted that the ultra vires doctrine must be reasonably applied, and that any contract made by a company which may fairly be regarded as incidental to or consequential upon those things which are authorised by the memorandum is not, unless expressly prohibited, to be held ultra vires.[108] This depends on the circumstances of each case. Thus a trading corporation has implied power to borrow money either upon security or otherwise,[109] to sell its property,[110] to purchase the subject matter of its business,[111] or to compromise claims made by or against it.[112] Wide powers given by general words in the memorandum of association may be construed as only ancillary to the company's main objects[113]; but this rule of construction may be excluded by the wording of the memorandum.[114] Not all the activities stated in a company's objects clause are necessarily objects in the strict sense, and "some of them may only be capable of existing as, or on their true construction are, ancillary powers".[115] Thus, for example, (as was stated earlier) a provision in a company's objects clause relating to borrowing will normally be treated as a power and not an independent object.[116] The courts have strained to interpret 9–022

[104] Where the third party has knowledge the contract would appear to be void ([1986] 1 Ch. 246, 306–307); *Jyske Bank (Gibraltar) Ltd v Spgeldmaes* Unreported July 29, 1999 CA. Quaere if the contract is enforceable by the company and therefore only voidable.

[105] *Rolled Steel Products (Holdings) Ltd v British Steel Corp* [1986] Ch. 246, 305.

[106] [1986] Ch. 246; *Ernest v Nicholls* (1857) 6 H.L.Cas. 401. Copies of all a company's public documents are available for inspection: Companies Act 2006 s.1085.

[107] See below, para.9–035.

[108] *Att-Gen v Great Eastern Ry* (1880) 5 App. Cas. 473, 478; *Peel v L. & N.W. Ry* [1907] 1 Ch. 5; *S. Pearson & Sons Ltd v Dublin & S.E. Ry* [1909] A.C. 217, 220; *Dundee Harbour Trustees v Nicol* [1915] A.C. 550; *Municipal Mutual Insurance Ltd v Pontefract Corp* (1917) 116 L.T. 671; *Evans v Brunner, Mond & Co* [1921] 1 Ch. 359; *Deuchar v Gas Light & Coke Co* [1925] A.C. 691; *Wimbledon & Putney Commons Conservators v Tuely* [1931] 1 Ch. 190; *City of Winnipeg v C.P.R. Co* [1953] A.C. 618.

[109] *General Auction Estate & Monetary Co v Smith* [1891] 3 Ch. 432.

[110] *Re Kingsbury Collieries Ltd and Moore's Contract* [1907] 2 Ch. 259; *Re Thomas (William) & Co Ltd* [1915] 1 Ch. 325.

[111] *Leifchild's Case* (1865) L.R. 1 Eq. 231.

[112] *Dixon v Evans* (1872) L.R. 5 H.L. 606; *Bath's Case* (1878) 8 Ch D 334.

[113] *Re German Date Coffee Co* (1882) 20 Ch D 169, 188. This case dealt with a petition to wind up a company on the grounds that its substratum had disappeared, a doctrine which although having a strong resemblance to that of ultra vires is not the same: *Cotman v Brougham* [1918] A.C. 514; *Re Tivoli Freeholds* [1972] V.R. 445.

[114] *Cotman v Brougham* [1918] A.C. 514; *Anglo-Overseas Agencies Ltd v Green* [1961] 1 Q.B. 1.

[115] *Rolled Steel Products (Holdings) Ltd v British Steel Corp* [1986] Ch. 246, 305.

[116] [1986] Ch. 246. Normally it will not be possible to elevate this power into an object by a provision in a company's objects clause requiring all the objects to be interpreted independently of each other, although in other situations the courts have given full effect to such a clause: see *Cotman v Brougham* [1918] A.C. 514.

objects clauses liberally so as to validate transactions. In *Re New Finance & Mortgage Co Ltd*[117] the operation of a petrol station was held to fall within the terms of an objects clause authorising the company to carry on the business of "merchants generally". Goulding J., in the course of his judgment opined that the company's entire "objects clause is too loosely drawn to be of any real value to subscribers or persons dealing with the company".[118]

9–023 **Opinion of the directors.** Whether a contract is ultra vires or not depends in principle on whether the memorandum does in fact authorise the transaction in question, and not on whether the directors think that it does.[119] But where a memorandum states that the company can carry on any business which, in the opinion of the board of directors, can be advantageously carried on in connection with, or as ancillary to, its authorised business, the position is different. In such circumstances the bona fide opinion of the directors that a business can be advantageously carried on in connection with, or as ancillary to, the company's principal business will suffice to render the former business intra vires.[120] The memorandum of a company may contain a statement that the powers of the company, or a particular power, must be exercised for "purposes of the company". Normally the court will construe this as being a limitation on the powers of the directors and *not* as a "condition limiting the company's corporate capacity".[121]

9–024 **No ratification or estoppel.** An ultra vires contract is not capable of ratification by a company[122]; nor can the company be estopped by deed[123] or otherwise[124] from showing that they had no power to do that which they profess to have done.[125]

9–025 **Effect of ultra vires borrowing.** A loan contracted by persons on behalf of a company which has no power to borrow does not create an indebtedness on the part of the company either at law or in equity.[126] Securities deposited by the company to secure such a loan can be recovered by it from the lender.[127] The

[117] [1975] 1 Ch. 420. See also *Newstead v Frost* [1980] 1 W.L.R. 135.

[118] *Newstead v Frost* [1980] 1 W.L.R. 135 at 425.

[119] *Tinkler v Wandsworth D.B.W.* (1858) 2 De G. & J. 261, 274 (directors cannot confer power on a statutory company by asserting that something falls within the spirit of the Act).

[120] *Bell Houses Ltd v City Wall Properties Ltd* [1966] 2 Q.B. 656. Although the statement to this effect in *Bell* was technically obiter, the Court of Appeal found the contract to be intra vires, it is generally considered to be correct: see *American Home Assurance Co v Tjmond Properties Ltd* [1986] B.C.L.C. 181 NZCA.

[121] *Rolled Steel Products (Holdings) Ltd v British Steel Corp* [1986] Ch. 246, 295.

[122] *Ashbury Railway Carriage & Iron Co v Riche* (1875) L.R. 7 H.L. 653; see below, para.9–028.

[123] *Ex p. Watson* (1888) 21 QBD 301.

[124] *Great N.-W. Central Ry v Charlebois* [1899] A.C. 114; *York Corp v Henry Leetham & Sons Ltd* [1924] 1 Ch. 557; see also fn.201, below; cf. *Islington Vestry v Hornsey U.D.C.* [1900] 1 Ch. 695.

[125] For the present statutory provision see below, paras 9–027 et seq.

[126] *Baroness Wenlock v River Dee Co* (1885) 10 App. Cas. 354; see generally Vann (1978) 52 A.L.J. 490.

[127] *Cunliffe Brooks & Co v Blackburn Benefit Building Society* (1882) 22 Ch D 61; (1884) 9 App. Cas. 857.

money borrowed cannot be recovered from the company upon an implied promise to repay, as money had and received by the company to the use of the lender.[128] But if any part of the money which has been borrowed has been applied in discharging the company's debts, the lender is entitled to have that part of the loan treated as valid.[129] However, the lender is not subrogated to any securities or priorities enjoyed by the creditors who are paid by means of his money, the reason for this being that the ultra vires unsecured creditors should not be put in a better position than the company's unsecured creditors.[130] Money which is in the company's hands as the result of an ultra vires loan is treated as money belonging to the purported lender. So long therefore as that money is identifiable or traceable the lender is entitled to recover it or to a charge on the fund of which it forms part.[131]

Recovery of property of money under ultra vires transaction.[132] Where money or property is transferred under an ultra vires contract it can be recovered on the ground that since the contract was wholly void there was an inadequacy of consideration.[133] However, this right or recovery would not be available if the defendant could invoke the defence of change of position, that is, the recipient of the money had so changed his position that it would be inequitable to compel him to make restitution or to make restitution in full.[134] 9–026

Sections 39–42. Article 9 of the First Directive on Company Law[135] requires member states to introduce legislation abrogating the doctrine of ultra vires so as to ensure security of transactions between companies and those with whom they contract. This aspect of the Directive was first implemented by s.9(1) of the European Communities Act 1972[136] which became s.35 of the 1985 Act. Section 35 was amended by s.108 of the Companies Act 1989 which inserted ss.35–35B 9–027

---

128 *Sinclair v Brougham* [1914] A.C. 398. See below, para.9–026. For criticisms of *Sinclair v Brougham* see *Westdeutsche Landesbank Girozentrale v Islington LBC* [1996] A.C. 669, 709–714.

129 *Re Cork and Youghal Ry* (1869) L.R. 4 Ch. App. 748; *Cunliffe Brooks & Co v Blackburn Benefit Building Society* (1882) 22 Ch D 61; *B. Liggett (Liverpool) Ltd v Barclays Bank Ltd* [1928] 1 K.B. 48; *Re Airedale Co-operative Worsted Manufacturing Society Ltd* [1933] Ch. 639. The onus is on the person claiming the money to establish the necessary factual connection: see *Westdeutsche Landesbank Girozentrale v Islington LBC* [1996] A.C. 689.

130 *Re Wrexham Mold and Connah's Quay Ry* [1899] 1 Ch. 440; Goff and Jones, *The Law of Restitution*, 6th edn (2002), pp.127, 162–163. On the limits of subrogation where the contract is illegal see *Orakpo v Manson Investments Ltd* [1978] A.C. 95.

131 *Sinclair v Brougham* [1914] A.C. 398, where the principle of *Re Hallett's Estate* (1880) 13 Ch D 696 as to the tracing and identification of blended money was explained and the method adopted in *Re Guardian Permanent Benefit Building Society (Crace Calvert's Case)* (1882) 23 Ch D 440 was criticised. See also *Re Diplock* [1948] Ch. 465, 518–519 (affirmed sub nom. *Ministry of Health v Simpson* [1951] A.C. 251). For other consequences of an ultra vires transaction see Goff and Jones at pp.641–649.

132 See below, paras 29–051 et seq.

133 Title to money or property can be transferred under an ultra vires contract: see *Ayres v South Australian Banking Corp* (1871) L.R. 3 P.C. 548; *Westdeutsche Landesbank Girozentrale v Islington LBC* [1996] A.C. 669, 689–690.

134 *Lipkin Gorman v Karpnale* [1991] 2 A.C. 548; see also below, paras 29–179 et seq.

135 First Directive 68/151 on Company Law [1968] OJ. L65/7.

136 See Prentice (1973) 89 L.Q.R. 518; Collier and Sealy (1973) C.L.J. 1.

into the 1985 Act.[137] The relevant provisions of the Companies Act 2006 are ss.39–42. These provisions also dealt with the interrelationship of ultra vires and director's authority.[138]

9–028 **Objects**. Fundamental changes were introduced to the doctrine of ultra vires and the role of objects clauses in a company's constitution by the Companies Act 2006. Section 8 of the 2006 Act provides that a company's memorandum must merely state that the subscribers[139] to it wish to form a company under the Act, agree to become members, and in the case of a company with a share capital, to take at least one share each.[140] Thus the memorandum no longer contains an objects clause. A company's objects (if any) will be contained in a company's articles of association. Section 31(1) of the 2006 Act provides that "[u]nless a company's articles specifically restrict the objects of the company, its objects are unrestricted". Provisions in the memorandum of pre-2006 Act companies (which would include objects) are now treated as provisions in the company's articles other than provisions required to be in the memorandum by s.8 of the 2006 Act.[141] Where a company amends it articles to add, remove or alter its objects, notice must be given to the registrar and the amendment is not effective until it is registered by the registrar.[142] The company's constitution binds the company and its members "to the same extent as if there were covenants on the part of the company and of each member to observe" its provisions.[143] Section 171 of the 2006 Act imposes on the directors a statutory duty to act in accordance with the company's constitution[144] (which would cover any objects) and the shareholders have standing to enforce such a duty.[145]

9–029 **Corporate capacity.** In reforming the doctrine of ultra vires so as to ensure security of transactions between companies and those with whom they deal, it is necessary to ensure that the validity of the transaction cannot be called into question on the grounds of the company's want of capacity. This is clearly done by s.39 of the 2006 Act which provides that the "validity of an act done by a company" shall not be called into question by reason of anything in the company's constitution. Any contract can be enforced by or against the company even though it is not authorised by the company's constitution. Since a company's objects clause both confers capacity and restricts it, this means that the restriction, implicit by stating objects in the articles, does not affect the validity

[137] These provisions were brought into effect on February 4, 1991. These reforms were based in part on a consultative report, *Reform of the Ultra Vires Rule* (DTI, 1986); see also "Modern Company Law—The Strategic Framework", Company Law Review Steering Committee (February 1999), Ch.5.3.

[138] See, in particular, s.35A of the 1985 Act.

[139] These are persons who subscribe their name to the memorandum: s.7.

[140] s.8(1).

[141] s.28.

[142] s.31(2)(c). Charitable companies will still have to restrict their objects under charities legislation: s.31(4).

[143] s.33(1) which replaces s.14 of the 1985 Act. There is, of course, no reference in s.33 to articles or memorandum but rather to the company's constitution which is defined in s.17 of the 2006 Act. See below, para.9–065.

[144] This was also the position at common law: see below, para.9–030.

[145] Pt 10 (derivative claims).

of any act entered into by the company. It is important to note that the section refers to an "act" of the company, a word that is of the widest import. The common law rule that a company could not ratify an ultra vires transaction has been jettisoned as ratification of such a transaction is now a matter of internal management given that the objects (if any) are now contained in the articles. Where a contract can be avoided because of a conflict of interest of a director who is a party to the contract, the European Court of Justice has held that this does not constitute a breach of Art.9(1) of the First Directive.[146] This deals with "abuse" of authority rather than "want" of authority.[147]

Ultra vires and director's duties. It is a breach of duty for directors to enter into an ultra vires transaction since as fiduciaries they must keep within the limit of their powers arising from the limit on their principal's capacity.[148] The reform of ultra vires so as to ensure security of transactions, does not require that a director's duty to the company to act within its objects should in any way be modified. Section 171(a) provides that a director must act in accordance with the company's constitution. 9–030

An agent only has authority to act for the benefit of his principal unless the parties otherwise agree.[149] The same rule applies to directors. As was stated by Lord Nicholls in *Criterion Properties Plc v Stratford UK Properties Ltd*[150]: 9–031

> "If a company (A) enters into an agreement with B under which B acquires benefits from A, A's ability to recover these benefits from B depends essentially on whether the agreement is binding on A. If the directors of A were acting for an improper purpose when they entered into the agreement, A's ability to have the agreement set aside depends upon the application of familiar principles of agency and company law. If, applying these principles, the agreement is found to be valid and is therefore not set aside, questions of 'knowing receipt' by B do not arise. So far as B is concerned there can be no question of A's assets having been misapplied. B acquired the assets from A, the legal and beneficial owner of the assets, under a valid agreement made between him and A. If, however, the agreement is set aside, B will be accountable for any benefits he may have received from A under the agreement. A will have a proprietary claim, if B still has the assets. Additionally, and irrespective of whether B still has the same assets in question, A will have the personal claim against B for unjust enrichment, subject always to the defence of change of position. B's personal accountability will not be dependent upon proof of fault or 'unconscionable' conduct on his part. B's accountability, in this regard, will be 'strict'."

Ultra vires and director's authority. The authority of directors entering into contracts binding on a company is also constrained by the ultra vires doctrine since directors either individually or collectively could not possess any greater 9–032

[146] *Co-operative Rabobank Vecht en Plassgebied BA v Minderland* (C–104/96) [1998] 2 B.C.L.C. 507.

[147] See below, para.9–032.

[148] *Re Faure Electric Accumulator Co* (1889) 40 Ch D 141; *Ferguson v Wilson* (1866) L.R. 2 Ch. 77; *Northern Counties Securities Ltd v Jackson & Steeple Ltd* [1974] 1 W.L.R. 1133; *Bowstead and Reynolds on Agency*, 18th edn (2006), paras 8–033, 8–036, 8–038.

[149] *Bowstead and Reynolds on Agency*; art.23 cited with approval in *Hopkins v T L Dallas Group Ltd* [2004] EWHC 1379 (Ch), [2005] 1 B.C.L.C. 543.

[150] [2004] UKHL 28, [2004] 1 W.L.R. 1846 at [4].

authority than their principal. If the doctrine of ultra vires is to be successfully abrogated it is also necessary to deal with this aspect of the problem. Section 40(1) provides that in "favour of a person dealing with a company in good faith" the power of the board shall be deemed to be free of any limitation flowing from the company's constitution; the same applies to the power of the directors to authorise others to act on behalf of the company.[151] Section 40 restates ss.35A and 35B of the 1985 Act and decisions dealing with these sections are equally applicable to s.40. Critical to the operation of this provision are the concepts of "dealing with" and "good faith". Both are defined in s.40(2). Section 40(2)(a) provides that a person deals with a company if he is a party to any act or transaction to which the company is a party. This would cover not only commercial transactions but also transactions which are gratuitous.[152] In *Smith v Henniker-Major & Co*[153] a director, at an inquorate board meeting, purported to assign to himself an asset of the company (a cause of action against the company's solicitors). This raised two issues: (a) was the failure to hold a quorate meeting a "limitation under the company's constitution" within s.35A(1) (s.40(1)); and (b) was a director a "person" protected by s.35A (s.40). As regards issue (a), Robert Walker L.J. considered that the question was what was the "irreducible minimum, if s.35A (s.40) is to be engaged".[154] In determining whether or not s.35A(1) (s.40(1)) applied it was necessary to distinguish "between a nullity (or non-event) and a procedural regularity"[155] the section only applying to the latter situation. On the facts Robert Walker L.J. held that the defect in the case, namely the inquorate board meeting, was a procedural irregularity and therefore fell within s.35A (s.40) as being a limitation under the company's constitution. Carnwarth L.J. considered the distinction between nullity and procedural irregularity to be unhelpful. He considered that the proper approach would be to determine if the act in question was carried out by someone appearing to be acting on behalf of the company,[156] and in the case he held that this test had been satisfied. As regards issue (b), the majority (Schiemann and Carnwarth L.JJ.) held that, at least on the facts of the case where the director was acting for the company, a director could not benefit from s.35A (now s.40 of the 2006 Act). In *EIC Services Ltd v Phipps*[157] the Court of Appeal held that in the case of a bonus issue of shares, which is an internal corporate arrangement with no alteration in the assets of liabilities of the company, a shareholder could not be held as dealing with the company within the terms of s.35A (s.40).

9–033 The definition of "good faith" is more tortuous and indirect. Section 40(2)(b)(iii) provides that a person shall not be treated as acting in bad faith by

[151] Note that this covers all limitations flowing from the company's constitution. Limitations on the directors' powers flowing from a resolution of any meeting or a class meeting of shareholders or any agreement of the members are covered: see s.40(3). On this type of constitutional limitation see, e.g. *Cane v Jones* [1980] 1 W.L.R. 1451.

[152] As, e.g. in *Parke v Daily News Ltd* [1962] Ch. 927; *Simmonds v Heffer* [1983] B.C.L.C. 298.

[153] [2002] EWCA Civ 762, [2002] 2 B.C.L.C. 655. For the first instance judgment of Rimer J. see [2002] B.C.C. 544.

[154] [2002] EWCA Civ 762, at [41].

[155] [2002] EWCA Civ 762.

[156] [2002] EWCA Civ 762 at [108].

[157] [2004] EWCA Civ 1069, [2005] 1 All E.R. 325.

reason of his knowing that the act or transaction is "beyond the powers of the directors under the company's constitution". This is not a definition of "good faith" but rather the singling out of a particular act as not constituting "bad faith." The reason for this is to found in Art.9(2) of the First Directive. This provides that the:

> "... limits on the powers of the organs of the company, arising under the statutes or from a decision of the competent organs, may never be relied on as against third parties, even if they have been disclosed."

This Article only deals with restrictions on the scope of an agent's or organ's[158] authority and not with the abuse of authority. Although the provision does not contain any "good faith" limitation it is clear from the debates on the implementation of the Directive that it was not designed to protect persons who were acting in bad faith,[159] for example, entering into a transaction which they knew the directors were entering into not in the interests of the company but in their own interests.[160] This position has been implicitly adopted by the ECJ.[161] Thus (s.40(2)(b)(iii)) attempts to steer between actions which are in excess of authority as opposed to acts which constitute an abuse of authority—the dividing line between these situations will often be wafer thin in that a failure by directors to observe the limitations of a company's objects clause may often be indicative of a failure to act in the interests of the company. Good faith should not be interpreted as "reasonableness"[162] and failure to understand a company's objects should not be taken as evidence of bad faith,[163] but the more implausible the interpretation the easier it will be for the company to show an absence of good faith.[164] There is a presumption that a person has dealt with the company in good faith and the onus is on the company to prove the contrary.[165]

Limitations on director's authority and shareholder rights. As we have already seen when discussing corporate capacity,[166] a member of a company has the right to compel the company to observe the company's articles and memorandum of association. If this right were not curtailed then, similarly with the abrogation of the ultra vires doctrine, it would be possible for shareholders by asserting this right to enforce indirectly limitations on the powers of directors 9–034

[158] The concept of organ does not fit neatly into English company law but would at least include the board and the shareholders in general meeting, including it is submitted, a class meeting of shareholders.

[159] See Stein, *Harmonization of European Company Law* (1970), p.294.

[160] See, e.g. *Rolled Steel Products (Holdings) Ltd v British Steel Corp* [1986] Ch. 246.

[161] *Co-operative Rabobank Vecht en Plassengebied BA v Minderhoud* (C–104/96) [1998] 1 W.L.R. 1025.

[162] *Barclays Bank Ltd v TOSG Trustfund* [1984] B.C.L.C. 1, 18 ("reasonableness is not a necessary ingredient of good faith" per Nourse J. at first instance); cf. Bills of Exchange Act 1882 s.90; Paget, *The Law of Banking*, 12th edn (2002), pp.444–445. See also *International Sales and Agencies Ltd v Marcus* [1982] 3 All E.R. 551, 559.

[163] For example, if the person dealing with the company reads but misinterprets the articles: see *Re Introductions Ltd* [1970] Ch. 199.

[164] See, e.g. the bank in *Re Introductions Ltd* [1970] Ch. 199; *Wrexham Association Football Club Ltd v Curcialmove Ltd* [2006] EWCA (Civ) 237, [2008] 1 B.C.L.C. 508 at [47].

[165] s.40(2)(b)(ii).

[166] See para.9–024.

against third parties. To prevent this from happening, s.40(4) provides that no proceedings by a member shall lie to enjoin a company from entering into a transaction in fulfilment of a legal obligation arising out of a previous act of the company and this would cover legal obligations arising because of s.40[167]; a member still retains the right to bring proceedings to restrain an action which is beyond the powers of the directors.[168]

9–035 **Constructive notice.** As previously stated,[169] it was a principle of company law that a person dealing with a company was deemed to have constructive notice of the company's public documents and, while there was some uncertainty as to what exactly fell within the category of public document for this purpose, it undoubtedly covered the company's memorandum and articles of association.[170] It is obviously a necessary corollary to the abrogation of the doctrine of ultra vires that this doctrine be also substantially repealed. This has been achieved by s.40(2) which provides that a person dealing with a company is not bound to enquire as to any limitation on the powers of the directors to bind the company or authorise others to do so.

9–036 **Ultra vires contracts involving directors.** It is not felt proper that a director should benefit from s.40 in the case of contracts in which the director was personally involved. Where a director of the company or of it's holding company or any person connected with such a director is a party to a transaction which exceeds any limitation on the powers of the directors, such transaction is voidable.[171] Also, irrespective of whether it is avoided, the director will be obliged to account to the company for any profit or to indemnify it for any loss.[172] Where a person (not a person connected with a director) who is a party to a contract along with a director to whom this provision applies, such person may petition the court to have the contract affirmed, severed or set aside on such terms as the court thinks fit.[173]

9–037 **Charitable companies.** Sections 39 and 40[174] do not apply to the acts of a company which is a charity except in favour of a person: (i) who gives full consideration in money or money's worth; (ii) does not know that the act is not permitted by the company or that it is beyond the powers of the directors; or (iii) does not know that at the time the relevant act was done that the company was a charity.[175] In any proceedings the burden of proving that the person knew that

---

[167] It remains a breach of duty for directors to enter into a transaction which is not authorised by the company's constitution: see CA 2006 s.171.

[168] s.40(4).

[169] See para.9–021.

[170] *Irvine v. Union Bank of Australia* (1877) 2 App. Cas. 399 PC; *Re London and New York Investment Corp* [1895] 2 Ch. 860.

[171] s.41(1), (2). See also s.41(4) (bars to the avoidance of the contract). See also below, para.9–060.

[172] s.41(3). Quaere if the liability under this subsection can be waived by the company. Other parties to the transaction can also be liable in the same way as directors but they are provided with a defence in s.41(4).

[173] s.41(6). The company may also make an application.

[174] The Charities Act 1993 Sch.6 para.20 has been repealed: see Sch.16 to the 2006 Act.

[175] s.42.

the company was a charity or knew that the act was not permitted by the company's constitution or was beyond the powers of the directors lies on the person asserting that fact.[176] There is added protection for persons who acquire an interest in or over property acquired from a charitable company.[177]

9–038 **Other applications of ultra vires principle.** The ultra vires doctrine has sometimes been invoked to explain the invalidity of certain types of contracts entered into by companies, though in truth these appear to have little to do with the contractual capacity of companies. For example, prior to the Companies Act 1981, a contract by a company to purchase its own shares was void,[178] and a contract by a company to provide financial assistance in connection with the purchase of its own shares was illegal and unenforceable.[179] Again, a contract entered into by a company will not be binding on it if its directors have not been acting bona fide in the interests of the company in making the contract and this is known to the other party to the contract.[180] But cases of this kind do not appear to involve questions of capacity and are explicable on other grounds[181] (e.g. illegality or agency) which do not properly fall within the scope of this chapter.

9–039 **Ratification of unauthorised act of officer.** If a contract is beyond the powers of the officer of the company by whom it was effected, it may be ratified by the company so as to become binding upon it.[182] This also applies to a contract which is outside a company's objects as the objects are now in the articles and the shareholders would be ratifying a breach of the articles, something which is a matter of internal management.[183] In addition, there may by

---

[176] s.42(3). Any affirmation of a transaction with a charity to which s.41 applies requires the written consent of the Charity Commissioners (s.42(4)).

[177] s.42(2).

[178] This was the old rule in *Trevor v Whitworth* (1887) 12 App. Cas. 409. Companies may now purchase their own shares provided certain statutory pre-conditions are satisfied: see Pt 18, Chs 1 and 4 of the 2006 Act; see also *Precision Dippings Ltd v Precision Dippings Marketing Ltd* [1986] Ch. 447 (the transaction in that case would have been more appropriately classified as illegal rather than ultra vires).

[179] *Victor Battery Co v Curry's Ltd* [1946] Ch. 242; *South Western Mineral Water Co Ltd v Ashmore* [1967] 1 W.L.R. 1110; *Armour Hick Northern Ltd v Whitehouse* [1980] 1 W.L.R. 1520 interpreting the Companies Act 1948 s.54. On financial assistance by a company in the purchase of its own shares see now Pt 18 Ch.2 of the 2006 Act.

[180] For a recent example, see *Re R.W. Roith Ltd* [1967] 1 W.L.R. 432. An agent (and this includes a director) only has authority to act for the benefit of his principal unless the parties otherwise agree: see *Criterion Properties Plc v Stratford UK Properties Ltd* [2004] 1 W.L.R. 1846. Where the contract is with a third party who has no notice of the director's want of good faith, the contract will be enforceable: *Rolled Steel Products (Holdings) Ltd v British Steel Corp* [1986] Ch. 246 (see also para. 9–031).

[181] See Gower & Davies, *Principles of Modern Company Law*, 7th edn (2003), pp.132–134; see also *Charterbridge Corp Ltd v Lloyds Bank* [1970] Ch. 62; *Heald v O'Connor* [1971] 1 W.L.R. 497.

[182] *Reuter v Electric Telegraph Co* (1856) 6 E. & B. 341, 348; *Allard v Bourne* (1863) 15 C.B.(N.S.) 468; *Rolled Steel Products (Holdings) Ltd v British Steel Corp* [1986] Ch. 246 clearly distinguishes the issues of corporate capacity and director's duties. But an attempt to confer authority on directors with respect to future transactions would be treated as an attempt to alter the articles of association for which a special resolution would be necessary: *Grant v UK Switchbank Ry* (1888) 40 Ch D 135.

[183] s.39; see above, para.9–027.

acquiescence in the act of the directors (if any) so that the company is estopped from objecting to its validity.[184] The test of acquiescence in such cases is whether the shareholders had notice of the way in which the affairs of the company were being conducted and were content not to oppose those acts which they knew were being done.[185] So, where everything that is done by the directors is known to and acquiesced in by a sole beneficial shareholder,[186] or by all shareholders with a right to attend and vote at a general meeting,[187] the company will be bound by the directors' acts whatever the company's constitution may say unless those acts are illegal. Where a corporation actually takes the benefit of a contract made in an irregular manner, the adoption will amount to ratification.[188]

9–040 ***Royal British Bank v Turquand.*** Where a director enters into a contract on behalf of a company, the company may be bound either by the ordinary rules of agency or by virtue of the rule in *Royal British Bank v Turquand.*[189] The latter has been variously described as part of the law of agency,[190] and as distinct from it,[191] but more recently authority has strongly favoured the first line of reasoning.[192] But it is generally agreed that this branch of the law presents exceptional difficulties although many of these have been reduced by s.40 of the 2006 Act. The general rule is that a stranger is entitled to assume that matters of internal management have been regularly carried out and that the formalities (if any) necessary to enable the company's officers to exercise their powers have been duly performed. But one who has notice that an agent of a company is contracting in excess of his authority cannot enforce that contract against the company.[193] Formerly notice of the memorandum and articles of association was imputed to every person having dealings with the company,[194] but this rule is effectively abrogated by s.40(2) of the 2006 Act.[195] The result of this seems to be that, whatever its original significance, the rule in *Turquand*'s case now falls to be treated in most cases as part of the ordinary law of agency. The section has thus

184 *Re Magdalena Steam Navigation Co* (1860) Johns. 690.

185 *Evans v Smallcombe* (1868) L.R. 3 H.L. 249, 256; and see *Phosphate of Lime Co Ltd v Green* (1871) L.R. 7 C.P. 43; *London Financial Association v Kelk* (1884) 26 Ch D 107; *Re Bailey Hay & Co Ltd* [1971] 1 W.L.R. 1357.

186 *Personal Service Laundry Ltd v National Bank Ltd* [1964] I.R. 49; *Walton v Bank of Nova Scotia* (1965) 52 D.L.R. (2d) 506.

187 *Re Duomatic Ltd* [1969] 2 Ch. 365.

188 *Smith v Hull Glass Co* (1852) 11 C.B. 897; *Re Bonelli's Telegraph Co, Collie's Claim* (1871) L.R. 12 Eq. 246, 259.

189 (1856) 6 E. & B. 327. See generally, Campbell, (1959–60) 75 L.Q.R. 469, 76 L.Q.R. 115.

190 Gower & Davies at pp.132–134.

191 Pennington, *Company Law*, 8th edn (2001), p.131.

192 *Freeman & Lockyer v Buckhurst Park Properties Mangal Ltd* [1964] 2 Q.B. 480; Nock (1966) Conv.(N.S.) 123, 163. cf. *Northside Developments Pty Ltd v Registrar-General* (1990) 64 A.L.J.R. 427.

193 *Rolled Steel Products (Holdings) Ltd v British Steel Corp* [1986] Ch. 246, 283 (per Slade L.J.), 304 (per Browne-Wilkinson L.J.).

194 See *Fountaine v Carmarthen Ry* (1868) L.R. 5 Eq. 316; *Crampton v Varnay Ry* (1872) L.R. 7 Ch. App. 562, 568; *Mahony v East Holyford Mining Co* (1875) L.R. 7 H.L. 869, 893; *County of Gloucester Bank v Rudry Merthyr Steam & House Coal Colliery Co* [1895] 1 Ch. 629.

195 Replacing s.35B of the 1985 Act.

made no longer applicable cases holding (for example) that where directors have, by the articles, a power to borrow only up to a certain amount, any loan beyond that amount will be beyond the authority of the directors and therefore not binding on the company.[196]

The rule in *Turquand*'s case,[197] however, does not apply where the circumstances are such as to put the third party on inquiry, as for example, where a bank negligently paid the cheques of a company signed by only one director,[198] or where the company's cheques were paid into a director's private account[199]; these decisions appear to be unaffected by s.40 of the 2006 Act because they do not depend on any limitations on the powers of the directors to bind the company arising from the company's constitution.[200] Another restriction on the operation of the rule at common law was that it could not apply to protect a third party who contracted with the company if, in some different capacity, e.g. as a director, he also acted on behalf of the company in making the contract.[201] These cases would now need to be interpreted in the light of s.41 of the 2006 Act which applies to a contract where the parties include a "director" irrespective of the capacity in which he enters into it.[202] 9–041

The rule cannot itself confer apparent authority. The rule in *Turquand*'s case was often treated as an application of estoppel and it followed that an outsider who had not in fact examined the company's public documents could not assert the existence of an apparent authority merely because of some provision in those documents. This aspect of the rule is unaffected by ss.39–40 of the 2006 Act. On the other hand, this in no way prevents an outsider from setting up an apparent authority on ordinary principles of agency where the company holds a person out as having authority otherwise than by provisions in its articles. Thus if a company's constitution provides that the powers, or certain of the powers, of the board of directors may be delegated to a managing director, and one director acts as a managing director to the knowledge of the board, then even though he has never been formally appointed as such, an outsider is entitled to assume that the director has in fact the authority which a managing director would normally 9–042

---

[196] *Irvine v Union Bank of Australia* (1877) 2 App. Cas. 366. A case which arguably was decided on a wrong application of the *Turquand* rule. In that case, Sir Barnes Pollock considered that the resolution authorising the director to borrow above the stipulated limit would have had to be registered under the Companies Act 1862 s.53, so that a person dealing with the company would have had notice of it. This in fact was not so, and the ordinary resolution increasing the directors' borrowing powers did not have to be registered.

[197] (1856) 6 E. & B. 327.

[198] *B. Liggett (Liverpool) Ltd v Barclays Ltd* [1928] 1 K.B. 48; cf. *South London Greyhound Racecourses Ltd v Wake* [1931] 1 Ch. 496; *Houghton & Co v Nothard, Lowe & Wills* [1927] 1 K.B. 246, affirmed [1928] A.C. 1.

[199] *A.L. Underwood Ltd v Bank of Liverpool & Martins* [1924] 1 K.B. 775.

[200] *International Sales and Agencies Ltd v Marcus* [1982] 3 All E.R. 551.

[201] *Morris v Kanssen* [1946] A.C. 459; *Smith v Henniker Mayor & Co* [2002] EWCA Civ 762, [2002] 2 B.C.L.C. 655. cf. *Hely-Hutchinson v Brayhead Ltd* [1968] 1 Q.B. 549, affirmed on different grounds, 573; see also *John v Rees* [1970] Ch. 345.

[202] Above, para.9–035.

have.[203] Where, however, the director enters into some transaction which would not normally be within the powers of a managing director and there is no holding out so as to make s.40 of the 2006 Act applicable, it may be that an outsider cannot rely on any apparent authority unless he has examined the articles, and the articles themselves show that a properly appointed managing director would have such authority.[204]

9–043 In *Freeman and Lockyer v Buckhurst Park Properties (Mangal) Ltd*,[205] where the authorities on this difficult question were reviewed by the Court of Appeal, Diplock L.J. stated the following four conditions which must be satisfied to entitle a contractor to enforce a contract entered into on behalf of a company by an agent without actual authority.

> "It must be shown: (1) that a representation that the agent had authority to enter on behalf of the company into a contract of the kind sought to be enforced was made to the contractor; (2) that such representation was made by a person or persons who had 'actual' authority[206] to manage the business of the company either generally or in respect of those matters to which the contract relates; (3) that he (the contractor) was

---

[203] *Freeman and Lockyer v Buckhurst Park Properties (Mangal) Ltd* [1964] 2 Q.B. 480. All the earlier authorities must now be read in the light of this case, see, e.g. *Biggerstaff v Rowatt's Wharf Ltd* [1896] 2 Ch. 93; *Dey v Pullinger Engineering Co* [1921] 1 K.B. 77; *Houghton & Co v Nothard, Lowe & Wills Ltd* [1927] 1 K.B. 246; *Kreditbank Cassel GmbH v Schenkers Ltd* [1927] 1 K.B. 826; *British Thomson-Houston Co Ltd v Federated European Bank Ltd* [1932] 2 K.B. 176; *South London Greyhound Racecourses Ltd v Wake* [1931] 1 Ch. 496; *Rama Corp v Proved Tin & General Investments Ltd* [1952] 2 Q.B. 147; *British Bank of the Middle East v Sun Life Assurance Co of Canada (UK) Ltd* [1983] 2 Lloyd's Rep. 9; *Rhoddian River Shipping Co SA v Halla Maritime Corp* [1984] 1 Lloyd's Rep. 373. See also Vol.II, paras 31–057—31–061.

[204] In the *Freeman and Lockyer* [1964] 2 Q.B. 480 case this was held to be the correct explanation of the *Houghton* [1927] 1 K.B. 246 case, the *Schenkers* [1927] 1 K.B. 826 case, and the *Rama* [1952] 2 Q.B. 147 case. As a matter of principle it is difficult to see how mere knowledge of the articles could operate to confer an apparent authority on a director: see *Houghton & Co v Nothard Lowe & Wills Ltd* [1927] 1 K.B. 246, 266.

[205] [1964] 2 Q.B. 480. See also *Hely-Hutchinson v Brayhead Ltd* [1968] 1 Q.B. 549. As to the authority of: (1) a company's secretary, see *Panorama Develoments (Guildford) Ltd v Fidelis Furnishing Fabrics Ltd* [1971] 2 Q.B. 711; (2) the individual director, see Leigh, *The Criminal Liability of Companies in English Law* (1969), pp.94–95. There is controversy as to whether being chairman of the board confers authority on the holder of this position greater than that of the ordinary director. Although there is some authority that it does (*British Thomson-Houston Co Ltd v Federated European Bank* [1932] 2 K.B. 176; *Clay Hill Brick Co Ltd v Rawlings* [1938] 4 All E.R. 100), it is difficult to appreciate why being appointed chairman should confer this additional authority; see generally Gower & Davies *Principles of Modern Company Law*, 7th edn (2003) at pp.158–160.

[206] There was, however, a difference of opinion in the Court of Appeal on this point. Pearson L.J. took the view that a director acting as the *alter ego* of a company may hold *himself* out qua agent as having the necessary authority: [1964] 2 Q.B. 480, 499, citing Greer L.J. in the *British Thomson-Houston* case [1932] 2 K.B. 176, 182, although the judgment of Greer L.J. provides scant support for this proposition. The *British Thomson-Houston* case was cited with approval by Browne-Wilkinson L.J. in *Egyptian International Foreign Trading Co v Soplex Wholesale Supplies Ltd and P.S. Refson & Co Ltd* [1985] 2 Lloyd's Rep 36, 43, but Kerr L.J. in the latter case, "as at present advised", considered that an agent's assurance as to his authority could not vest him with wider authority than he already possessed (at 46). For dicta which on the whole support Kerr L.J. see *Armagas Ltd v Mundogas SA* [1985] 1 Lloyd's Rep. 1, 37 and 67–68, [1986] A.C. 717, 733–735, 749. See also Diplock L.J. in *Freeman*: a "contractor cannot rely on the agent's own representation as to his actual authority" (at 505). These somewhat conflicting dicta were reconciled in *First Energy (UK) Ltd v Hungarian International Bank Ltd* [1993] B.C.L.C. 1409 on the grounds that while an agent, without actual authority or apparent authority, cannot enlarge his appearance of authority by his own

induced by such representation to enter into the contract, that is, that he in fact relied on it; and (4) that under its memorandum or articles of association the company was not deprived of the capacity either to enter into a contract of the kind sought to be enforced or to delegate authority to enter into a contract of that kind to the agent."[207]

It is important to note how these principles have been affected by ss.39–40 of the 2006 Act. Principle (4) has been abrogated. More importantly, principle (2) has also been virtually abrogated by s.40 since where that section applies the company will be bound by a transaction outside the authority of the directors even though no holding out was made by a person with actual authority to make one.

Section 161 of the Companies Act.[208] In some circumstances s.161 of the 2006 Act may also apply. That section provides that the "acts of a person acting as a director are valid notwithstanding that it is afterwards discovered: (a) "that there was a defect in his appointment"; (b) "that he was disqualified from holding office"; (c) "that he had ceased to hold office"; and (d) "that he was not entitled to vote on the matter".[209] Thus this section would appear, for example, to cover under age directors.[210] As stated in Buckley[211]: 9–044

"Endangering accuracy for the sake of brevity, it may be said that the effect of this section is that, as between the company and persons having no notice to the contrary, directors, etc., *de facto* are as good as directors, etc., *de iure*."

In some ways the section is wider than the rule in *Turquand*'s case[212] in that it may be relied upon not only by outsiders, but also by directors of the company and by the company itself; on the other hand, unlike the rule in *Turquand*'s case, s.161 will not apply unless there has been an "appointment", albeit a defective appointment, but does not apply where there is no appointment.[213] Neither the rule nor the section can be called in aid by a third party who knew or should have known of the defect.[214]

Forgeries. It has been said that the rule in *Turquand*'s case[215] does not apply where the document upon which it is sought to make the company responsible is a forgery.[216] But the three cases in which this question has arisen can all be explained on the ground either that the forged document was not put forward as genuine by an official acting within his actual or apparent authority, or that the 9–045

representation, he may nevertheless have apparent authority to communicate decisions of the company, for example, that the board of directors have approved of a particular transaction.

207 [1964] 2 Q.B. 480, 504–505.

208 s.285 is replaced with modifications by s.161 of the 2006 Act.

209 s.161 overrides s.160 ("appointment of directors of public company to be voted on individually").

210 They would be disqualified (s.157 and s.161(1)(b)) or cease to act (s.159 and s.161(1)(c)).

211 Buckley, *On the Companies Acts*, para.285–4.

212 (1856) 6 E. & B. 327.

213 *Morris v Kanssen* [1946] A.C. 459, 471.

214 *Kanssen v Rialto (West End) Ltd* [1944] Ch. 346; affirmed sub nom. *Morris v Kanssen* [1946] A.C. 459.

215 See above, fn.212.

216 *Ruben v Great Fingall Consolidated Co* [1906] A.C. 439, 443; *Kreditbank Cassel GmbH v Schenkers Ltd* [1927] 1 K.B. 826, 844; *South London Greyhound Racecourses Ltd v Wake* [1931] 1 Ch. 496.

outsider was put on inquiry.[217] This was the view taken by the High Court of Australia in *Northside Developments Pty Ltd v Registrar-General*[218] where the court stated that a company would be bound by a "forgery" where it was "estopped from denying the authority of the persons affixing the genuine seal and writing the genuine signature to it".[219] It is submitted therefore that where a document is made by an officer of a company who has apparent authority to do so, the rule can be applied and the company may be bound by the document even though the officer forged it for some purpose of his own.

9–046 **Registration of charges.**[220] A contract entered into by a company which involves a charge on its assets may require registration with the registrar of companies under Pt 25 of the Companies Act 2006. The most important types of charge covered by this section are charges to secure an issue of debentures; charges created by an instrument which, if executed by an individual, would require registration as a bill of sale; charges on land or any interest therein; charges on book debts; and floating charges on the undertaking or property of the company.[221] Prescribed particulars of a charge covered by s.860 must be delivered to the Registrar within 21 days after its creation.[222] Failure to deliver particulars of a charge[223] renders the charge void against a liquidator, an administrator and any creditor of the company, and also renders any debt secured by the charge immediately repayable.[224] The court has power under s.873 of the 2006 Act to extend the time for registration in various circumstances.

9–047 **Effect of winding up on company's contracts.** A compulsory winding up automatically brings the powers of a director to an end[225] and publication of the winding up order discharges all persons employed by the company, giving them

[217] See Gower & Davies at pp.163–164. Campbell (1960) 76 L.Q.R. 115, 130 et seq.

[218] (1990) 64 A.L.J.R. 427.

[219] (1990) 64 A.L.J.R. 427, 443. See also *Lonsdale Nominee Pty Ltd v Southern Cross Airlines Ltd* (1993) 10 A.C.S.R. 739. Where there is a forgery in the strict sense of the word, i.e. the name of a person is falsely appended to a document, then this would obviously not be binding on the company.

[220] For details, see *Buckley on the Companies Acts*, Division H; Gough, *Company Charges*, 2nd edn (1998). As to the conclusiveness of the Registrar's certificate of registration, see Companies Act 2006 s.869(6)(b); *R. v Registrar of Companies Ex p. Esal Commodities Ltd* [1986] Q.B. 1114. Part 25 of the 2006 Act restates but does not make any substantive changes to Pt XII of the 1985 Act. Section 894 of the 2006 Act enables the Secretary of State to amend Pt 25 by regulations which are subject to the affirmative resolution procedure. See *Company Law Review: Proposals for Reform of Part XII of the Companies Act 1985* (DTI, A Consultative Document, November 1994); *Registration of Security Interest: Company Charges and Property other than Land* (Law Commission Consultation Paper No.164, 2002).

[221] s.861(7).

[222] s.870.

[223] It is important to note that it is delivery of the particulars of the charge rather than registration which saves it from invalidity; see *N.V. Slavenburg's Bank v Intercontinental Natural Resources Ltd* [1980] 1 W.L.R. 1076.

[224] s.874.

[225] *Re Oriental Inland Steam Co* (1874) 9 Ch. App. 557, 560; *Fowler v Broad's Patent Night Light Co* [1893] 1 Ch. 724; *Gosling v Gaskell* [1897] A.C. 575, 587; *Measures Brothers v Measures* [1910] 2 Ch. 248, 256. In the case of a voluntary winding up, see Insolvency Act 1986 ss.91(2), 103. On the effect of winding up on the powers and office of directors, see Keay and Walton, *Insolvency Law: Corporate and Personal*, 1st edn (2003), pp.243–245.

a right to damages for wrongful dismissal.[226] The liquidator may waive the dismissal brought about by publication of the winding up order, and where he does so the old contract of employment continues.[227] Where the winding up is voluntary the powers of the directors likewise cease, except that the company in general meeting or the liquidator may sanction their continuance[228]; the passing of a resolution for voluntary winding up may, but does not necessarily, terminate general contracts of employment with the company so as to give the company's employees a right to damages for wrongful dismissal.[229] It may do so where the circumstances are such that the employee knows that the company cannot continue to fulfil its obligations,[230] or where, on the facts, the company has ceased to carry on business and there is no implied term in the contract of employment that the contract is subject to the continuance of business by the company.[231] Where an order is made by the court under s.900 of the Companies Act 2006 for the amalgamation of two companies, a contract of employment between a worker and the transferor company does not automatically become a contract of employment between the worker and the transferee company.[232]

Winding-up not a repudiation. On the other hand, the winding-up of a company is not by itself a repudiation of the contractual obligations of the company unless the personality of the company goes to the root of the contract,[233] though there are statutory provisions for the disclaimer of leases or other onerous or unprofitable contracts.[234] The liquidator has certain statutory powers to deal with the company's property some of which can only be exercised with the sanction of the court, the liquidation committee, or, in the case of a members' voluntary winding up, the members.[235] Where a liquidator, appointed by the 9–048

---

[226] *Re General Rolling Stock Co, Chapman's Case* (1866) L.R. 1 Eq. 346; *Ex p. Maclure* (1870) L.R. 5 Ch. 737; *Re R.S. Newman Ltd* [1916] 2 Ch. 309; *Re Oriental Bank Corp, MacDowall's Case* (1886) 32 Ch D 366. An employee's right to damages is not affected by the fact that he may, as a shareholder, have supported the resolution for voluntary winding up: *Fowler v Commercial Timber Co* [1930] 2 K.B. 1. See Vol.II, paras 174–175.

[227] *Re English Joint Stock Bank, Ex p. Harding* (1867) 3 Eq. 341.

[228] Insolvency Act 1986 ss.91(2), 103.

[229] *Midland Counties District Bank Ltd v Attwood* [1905] 1 Ch. 357; *Fox Bros (Clothes) Ltd v Bryant* [1979] I.C.R. 64; see also Vol.II, para.39–173.

[230] *Reigate v Union Manufacturing Co (Ramsbottom) Ltd* [1918] 1 K.B. 592.

[231] [1918] 1 K.B. 592; *Fowler v Commercial Timber Co* [1930] 2 K.B. 1, 6.

[232] *Nokes v Doncaster Amalgamated Collieries Ltd* [1940] A.C. 1014 (this was decided under s.427 of the 1985 Act which s.900 restates). See now the Transfer of Undertakings (Protection of Employment) Regulations 1981 (SI 1981/1794) and cf. Employment Protection (Consolidation) Act 1978 Sch.13 para.17 which operates for purposes of that Act and the Redundancy Payments Act 1965.

[233] *British Waggon Co v Lea* (1880) 5 QBD 149; cf. *Tolhurst v Associated Portland Cement Manufacturers Ltd* [1903] A.C. 414, commented on in *Nokes v Doncaster Amalgamated Collieries Ltd* [1940] A.C. 1014, 1019–1020; and see paras 19–054—19–055.

[234] See Insolvency Act 1986 s.178. This is a change from the old law: see *Re Hans Place Ltd* [1993] B.C.L.C. 768; *Re Morrish* (1882) 22 Ch D 410; *Re A.B.C. Coupler and Engineering Co Ltd (No.3)* [1970] 1 W.L.R. 702; *Warnford Investments Ltd v Duckworth* [1979] Ch. 127; *Re A.E. Realisations (1986) Ltd* [1987] B.C.L.C. 486. Such disclaimer does not release a guarantor of the rents from his guarantee: *Hindcastle Ltd v Barbara Attenborough Associates Ltd* [1997] A.C. 70. See also *Re Park Air Services Plc* [2000] 2 A.C. 172.

[235] Insolvency Act 1986 ss.165–167; see *Bateman v Ball* (1887) 56 L.J.Q.B. 291; *Hire Purchase Furnishing Co v Richens* (1887) 20 QBD 387.

court, performs a contract of the company without disclaimer or where he purports to make a new contract on its behalf, he acts as agent for the company[236] and there is no presumption that he does so in a personal capacity.[237]

9–049 **Dispositions of property in winding-up.** In a winding-up by the court any disposition of the property of the company, including things in action, and any transfer of shares, or alteration in the status of members of the company, made after the commencement of the winding up, is, unless the court otherwise orders, void.[238] The court has a wide discretion in this respect which will be exercised having regard to what is fair and just in all the circumstances, particular attention being paid to the question of good faith and the principle that a company's free assets should be distributed pro rata among the company's unsecured creditors.[239] The court will readily validate transactions entered into bona fide in the course of trade and completed before the date of the winding-up order[240]; but the court will not validate the payment of a debt by the company to a debtor who has notice of the presentation of a winding-up petition[241] unless it is a "necessary part of a transaction which as a whole is beneficial to the general body of unsecured creditors".[242] The court will also normally validate the sale of an asset at its full market value as this does not dissipate the company's assets.[243] Further, the court can only validate a disposition of property; a contract for the sale of goods by a company is not a disposition of property which can be validated by the court unless the property in the goods has passed to the purchaser.[244]

9–050 **Appointment of a receiver or manager.**[245] An administrative receiver is a receiver appointed under a floating charge where the charge holder has a charge

---

[236] *Re Anglo-Moravian Co* (1875) 1 Ch D 130.

[237] *Stead Hazel & Co v Cooper* [1933] 1 K.B. 840. Representative language was not used in this case although it is always prudent for a liquidator to contract clearly in a representative capacity.

[238] Insolvency Act 1986 s.127; *Mond v Hammond Suddards* [1996] 2 B.C.L.C. 470; *Hollicourt (Contractors) Ltd v Bank of Ireland* [2001] Ch. 555; *Re Tain Construction Ltd* [2003] 2 B.C.L.C. 374.

[239] *Re Steane's (Bournemouth) Ltd* [1950] 1 All E.R. 21; *Re T.W. Construction Ltd* [1954] 1 W.L.R. 540; *Re Clifton Place Garage Ltd* [1970] Ch. 477; *Re Operator Control Cabs Ltd* [1970] 3 All E.R. 657n.; *Re Argentum Reductions (UK)* [1975] 1 W.L.R. 186; *Re Gray's Inn Construction Co Ltd* [1890] 1 W.L.R. 711; *Re Tramway Building and Construction Co Ltd* [1987] B.C.L.C. 632; *Re Webb Electric Ltd* [1988] B.C.L.C. 382; *Denney v John Hudson & Co Ltd* [1992] B.C.L.C. 901.

[240] *Re Wiltshire Iron Co* (1868) L.R. 3 Ch. App. 443; *Re Park Ward & Co* [1926] Ch. 828; *Re French's (Wine Bar) Ltd* [1987] B.C.L.C. 437.

[241] *Re Civil Service & General Store Ltd* (1887) 57 L.J. Ch. 119; cf. *Re T.W. Construction Ltd* [1954] 1 W.L.R. 540.

[242] *Re Gray's Inn Construction Co Ltd* [1980] 1 W.L.R. 711, 719. See also *Denney v John Hudson & Co Ltd* [1992] B.C.L.C. 901.

[243] [1992] B.C.L.C. 901. In the case of a solvent company, the court will validate a disposition under CA 2006 s.127 provided that an intelligent and honest board of directors could reasonably take the view that the arrangements were in the best interests of the company. Only where bad faith or other exceptional circumstances are proved will the court decline to act under s.127; *Re Burton and Deakin Ltd* [1977] 1 W.L.R. 390.

[244] *Re Oriental Bank Corp, Ex p. Guillemin* (1883) 28 Ch D 634; *Re Wiltshire Iron Co* (1868) L.R. 3 Ch. App. 443.

[245] For the definition of receiver see Insolvency Act 1986 s.29. In particular note the definition of administrative receiver a term first introduced by the Insolvency Act 1986: see also s.251 of the 1986 Act.

or charges over all or substantially all of a company's assets.[246] Under the Enterprise Act 2002 s.250 the holder of a floating charge created after a date appointed by the Secretary of State will no longer be able to appoint an administrative receiver.[247] Holders of a floating charge created before this date will be able to appoint an administration receiver provided of course they satisfy the terms of s.29(2).[248] The appointment of a receiver and manager by the court operates to discharge the company's employees.[249] But the appointment of a receiver and manager out of court by debenture holders, so that he becomes an agent of the company, does not normally operate to discharge the company's employees.[250] At common law such an appointment will, however, operate to discharge the company's employees if the appointment is accompanied by a sale of the company's business,[251] or if the appointment is accompanied by or followed by a new agreement with the company's employees,[252] and probably only if the new contract is inconsistent with the old,[253] or if the company's employees occupy positions which would be inconsistent with the position of the receiver.[254] Section 44(1)(a) of the Insolvency Act 1986 makes an administrative receiver of the assets of a company the company's agent unless and until the company goes into liquidation, a device that is primarily designed to avoid the security holder who appointed him from being treated as a mortgagee in possession. An administrative receiver is also made personally liable on any contract entered into by him.[255] Such liability can be excluded and almost invariably is. The 1986 Act also makes an administrative receiver personally liable "on any contract of employment adopted by him in carrying out" his functions, but that he is not to be "taken to have adopted a contract of employment by anything done or omitted to be done within 14 days after his appointment".[256] Initially, there was considerable uncertainty as to what this section means and, in particular, whether mere acquiescence in the continuation of contracts of employment can constitute an adoption.[257] However, in *Powdrill v Watson*[258] the House of

---

[246] Insolvency Act 1986 s.29(2).

[247] This introduces new ss.72A–72H into the Insolvency Act 1986. The prohibition affects floating charges created after September 15, 2003 (SI 2003/2093).

[248] There are also a number of exemptions to the prohibition on appointing an administrative receiver: see Insolvency Act 1986 ss.72C–72H.

[249] *Reid v Explosives Co* (1887) 19 QBD 264 (note, however, the reservations of Fry L.J.); *Re Mack Trucks (Britain) Ltd* [1967] 1 W.L.R. 780; *Griffiths v Secretary of State for Social Services* [1974] Q.B. 468. This principle has not been followed in Australia: see *Spidad Holding v Popovic* (1995) 19 A.C.S.R. 108.

[250] *Griffiths v Secretary of State for Social Services* [1974] Q.B. 468; *Deaway Trading Ltd v Calverley* [1973] I.C.R. 546; see Vol.II, paras 174–175.

[251] *Re Foster Clark Ltd's Indenture Trusts* [1946] 1 W.L.R. 125. The position has now been substantially modified by the Transfer of Undertakings (Protection of Employment) Regulations 1981 (SI 1981/1794). See Vol.II, paras 39–171 et seq.

[252] *Re Mack Trucks (Britain) Ltd* [1967] 1 W.L.R. 780.

[253] *Griffiths v Secretary of State for Social Services* [1974] Q.B. 468, 486.

[254] *Griffiths v Secretary of State for Social Services* [1974] Q.B. 468; see Freedland, *The Contract of Employment* (1975), p.339.

[255] s.44(1)(b). On the nature of the administrative receiver's liability see *Re Atlantic Computer Systems Plc (No.1)* [1992] Ch. 505, 526.

[256] s.44(1)(b), (2). This was designed to overcome the decision in *Nicoll v Cutts* [1985] B.C.L.C. 322.

[257] Stewart, *Administrative Receivers and Administrators*, pp.96–99.

[258] [1995] 2 A.C. 394.

Lords held that a receiver will be taken to have adopted a contract of employment where he treats the continued contract as giving rise to a separate liability in the receivership. The House also decided that the receiver could not reject some of the terms of the contract but accept others, but that his liability could be limited to liabilities arising during the period when he was in office.[259]

9–051 The appointment of a receiver does not amount to a repudiation of the trading contracts of the company, except in special circumstances.[260] It is often claimed that the receiver is in a better position than the company in that he need not observe existing contracts and, in addition, such contracts cannot be specifically enforced against him.[261] To permit contracts to be enforced against the company, or to require the receiver to comply with them would reverse the order of priorities in that it would oblige the receiver to prefer the interests of unsecured creditors over the interests of the security holder that appointed him. It is for this reason that the receiver is in a better position than the company as regards the obligation to observe existing contracts.[262] Where a receiver and manager, appointed by the court, orders goods for the purpose of the business of the company, the inference is that he pledges his personal credit for the goods, looking for indemnity to the assets of the company; he is therefore not necessarily the agent of the company[263] though he may be in particular circumstances.[264] The same is true of receivers appointed out of court where although an agent of the company he is personally liable in contracts he enters into unless the contract states otherwise.[265] The authority of a receiver is terminated by the winding up of the company whether it is voluntary[266] or by the court.[267] Although the authority of a receiver to act on behalf of the company is prima facie terminated by a winding-up order, this does not mean that a receiver appointed by debenture holders can no longer sell or convey property charged to the debenture holders, in respect of which a power of sale exists.[268] He can still

---

[259] In the lower courts it was held that the receiver who adopted the contract would be liable for all outstanding liabilities: see [1995] 2 A.C. 394 where the judgment of Lightman J. is reported. Because of the threat of liability this resulted in receivers, and more importantly administrators who are similarly liable under s.19 of the 1986 Act, in terminating contracts of employment, s.44 and s.19 of the Act have been modified by the Insolvency Act 1994 so that receivers and administrators will only be liable for services on a contract of employment rendered during the administration or receivership after the adoption of the contract of employment (referred to as "qualifying liabilities").

[260] *Airlines Airspaces Ltd v Handley Page Ltd* [1970] Ch. 193. cf. *Rother Iron Works Ltd v Canterbury Precision Engineers* [1974] Q.B. 1; *George Barker (Transport) Ltd v Eynon* [1974] 1 W.L.R. 462.

[261] See, however, *Ash & Newman Ltd v Creative Devices Research Ltd* [1991] B.C.L.C. 403 where an injunction was granted to protect a pre-emption right of the plaintiff but the facts were exceptional in that the injunction did not prejudice the interests of the security holder.

[262] *Hill (Edwin) & Partners v First National Finance Corp Plc* [1989] B.C.L.C. 89; *Astor Chemicals Ltd v Synthetic Technology Ltd* [1990] B.C.L.C. 1, 11.

[263] *Burt, Boulton & Hayward v Bull* [1895] 1 Q.B. 276, 279. On the right of a court appointed receiver to be remunerated see *Mellor v Mellor* [1993] B.C.L.C. 30.

[264] *Lawson v Hosemaster Co Ltd* [1966] 1 W.L.R. 1300.

[265] Insolvency Act 1986 s.44(1)(b).

[266] *Thomas v Todd* [1926] 2 K.B. 571.

[267] *Gosling v Gaskell* [1897] A.C. 575; *Re S. Brown & Co Ltd* [1940] Ch. 961; see also *Bacal Contracting Ltd v Modern Engineering (Bristol) Ltd* [1980] 2 All E.R. 655, 658.

[268] *Sowman v David Samuel Trust Ltd* [1978] 1 W.L.R. 22.

exercise the in rem rights that his appointor has against the company's property.

9–052 **Receivers and the tort of inducing a breach of contract.** The question has arisen in a number of cases as to whether a receiver who does not observe a contract which the company has entered into before his appointment can be liable for the tort of inducing a breach of contract.[269] It has been held (not without misgivings) that a receiver cannot be held so liable in that the receiver as agent of the company is the alter ego of the company, the other party to the contract, and accordingly no possible action could lie against a person for procuring himself to induce a breach of contract.[270]

9–053 **Administrators.** The Enterprise Act 2002[271] replaces the administration procedure set out in Pt II of the Insolvency Act 1986. This procedure like its predecessor imposes significant constraints on the right of a person to enforce a transaction against a company in administration.[272] Specialist texts should be consulted with respect to these provisions.

(ii) *Contracts between Companies and Promoters or Directors*

9–054 **Promoters.** Promoters are the persons who procure the formation of a company and its "flotation".[273] The term "promoter" is not a legal term but depends upon the function being carried out with respect to the formation of the company. A promoter stands in a fiduciary relationship to the company both before and after its formation.[274] While, therefore, a promoter may make a profit out of the sale of his property to the company,[275] that profit must be disclosed to an independent board of directors or to the shareholders[276]; he may not take a secret commission from a person selling to the company,[277] and if he does so, the company may rescind the contract[278] or claim to recover the secret profit from the promoter,[279] or (at any rate in some cases) sue him for damages.[280] Where promoters acquired property before they began to promote the company and thereafter sold it to the company without disclosing that they were the vendors,

[269] The authorities are collected in *Welsh Development Agency v Export Finance Co Ltd* [1992] B.C.L.C. 148. See also *OBG Ltd v Allan* [2007] UKHL 21, [2007] 4 All E.R. 545.

[270] [2007] UKHL 21 at 171–173.

[271] s.248 inserts a new Sch.B1 into the 1986 Act; see Sch.16.

[272] See, e.g., paras 42–45 of Sch.B1.

[273] Flotation in this sense does not require that the company's securities be offered to the public; *Gifford v Willoughby's Mashonaland Expedition Co* (1899) 16 T.L.R. 24; *Torva Exploring Syndicate v Kelly* [1900] A.C. 612.

[274] *Erlanger v New Sombrero Phosphate Co* (1878) 3 App. Cas. 1218; *Emma Silver Mining Co v Lewis* (1879) 4 C.P.D. 396; *Lagunas Nitrate Co v Lagunas Syndicate* [1899] 2 Ch. 392, 428; *Gluckstein v Barnes* [1900] A.C. 240.

[275] *Omnium Electric Palaces Ltd v Baines* [1914] 1 Ch. 332.

[276] *Gluckstein v Barnes* [1900] A.C. 240; *Re Leeds & Hanley Theatres of Varieties Ltd* [1902] 2 Ch. 809; *Jubilee Cotton Mills Ltd v Lewis* [1924] A.C. 958.

[277] *Lydney & Wigpool Iron Co v Bird* (1886) 33 Ch D 85.

[278] See above, fn.274.

[279] See above, fn.276.

[280] *Re Leeds & Hanley Theatres of Varieties Ltd* [1902] 2 Ch. 809; *Jacobus Marler Estates v Marler* (1913) L.J.P.C. 167n.

it was held that rescission was the only right open to the company, as the promoters were not at the time of their purchase in a fiduciary position to the company.[281] If disclosure is relied on, it must be a genuine disclosure, that is to say, either a disclosure to a board of directors independent of the promoters,[282] or a communication to all the shareholders,[283] or a plain indication in the prospectus that the board of directors are acting for the promoters.[284]

9–055 **Directors.** Directors owe fiduciary obligations to the company and may not make any secret profit by virtue of their office.[285] But directors are in a more responsible position than promoters and neither they nor companies in which they are interested[286] can make an enforceable contract with the company, unless so authorised by the articles of association.[287] Such authorisation is in practice almost universally included in the articles of association, but even where it is given the interested director has a statutory obligation to disclose his interest fully.[288] In the absence of the necessary authority in the articles, or in the event of a failure to disclose an interest where there is such authority, the contracts will be voidable by the company.[289] It may be affirmed by the shareholders in general meeting[290] or (probably) by an independent board of directors,[291] or alternatively the company may rescind the contract if restitutio in integrum is still possible. The company cannot, however, claim both to affirm the contract and an account of profits unless actual fraud or breach of trust can be proved, as, for example,

[281] *Ladywell Mining Co v Brookes* (1887) 35 Ch D 400; cf. *Burland v Earle* [1902] A.C. 83. For statutory liability with respect to a defective prospectus see Financial Services and Markets Act 2000 ss.84, 85 and 150.

[282] *Gluckstein v Barnes* [1900] A.C. 240; *Burland v Earle* [1902] A.C. 83, above.

[283] *Salomon v Salomon & Co* [1897] A.C. 22; *Att-Gen for Canada v Standard Trust Co of New York* [1911] A.C. 498.

[284] *Lagunas Nitrate Co v Lagunas Syndicate* [1899] 2 Ch. 392.

[285] *Imperial Mercantile Credit Association v Coleman* (1873) L.R. 6 H.L. 189; *Parker v McKenna* (1874) L.R. 10 Ch. App. 96; *Kaye v Croydon Tramways Co* [1898] 1 Ch. 358; *Tiessen v Henderson* [1899] 1 Ch. 861; *Clarkson v Davies* [1923] A.C. 100; *Regal (Hastings) Ltd v Gulliver* [1942] 1 All E.R. 378; [1967] 2 A.C. 134n; *Industrial Development Consultants Ltd v Cooley* [1972] 1 W.L.R. 443. See now Pt 10 of the 2006 Act which contains a codification of the major directors' duties.

[286] *Flanagan v Great Western Ry* (1868) L.R. 7 Eq. 116; *Transvaal Lands Co v New Belgium Land Co* [1914] 2 Ch. 488.

[287] *Costa Rica Railroad Co v Forwood* [1901] 1 Ch. 746; *Re Republic of Bolivia Exploration Syndicate Ltd* [1914] 1 Ch. 139; see now s.177 of the 2006 Act.

[288] s.182. This section replaces s.317 of the Companies Act 1985. Failure to comply with s.317 did not render the contract void or voidable: *Hely-Hutchinson v Brayhead Ltd* [1968] 1 Q.B. 549; *Guinness Plc v Saunders* [1990] 2 A.C. 663. It would also appear that breach of s.317 did not vest in the company any right of action for damages for breach of statutory duty: *Castlereagh Motels Ltd v Davies-Roe* (1966) 67 S.R. (N.S.W.) 279; see also *Lee Panavision Ltd v Lee Lighting Ltd* [1992] B.C.L.C. 575; *Runciman v Walter Runciman Plc* [1992] B.C.L.C. 1084. The same would apply to s.182.

[289] *Transvaal Lands Company v New Belgium (Transvaal) Land and Development Co* [1914] 2 Ch. 488.

[290] *North West Transportation Co v Beatty* (1887) 12 App. Cas. 589. However, *Beatty* has been substantially modified by s.239 of the 2006 Act so that a shareholders' vote affirming the transaction must be passed by an independent majority of shareholders thus disregarding the votes of the director or anyone connected with him. For connected persons see s.252 of the 2006 Act.

[291] *Queensland Mines Ltd v Hudson* (1978) 52 A.L.J.R. 399 PC; noted (1979) 42 M.L.R. 711. It is important to note that in this case the shareholders were all aware of the director's conduct: see *Cane v Jones* [1980] 1 W.L.R. 1451 and above, para.9–039.

where a director has sold to the company property which he already held as trustee (expressly or constructively) for the company.[292] Where the director is guilty merely of non-disclosure, having, for example, acquired his interest in the property which he sold to the company before he became a director, the company may either affirm the sale and pay the price agreed or rescind the transaction altogether, but, unless the transaction falls within s.190 of the Companies Act 2006,[293] it cannot claim to affirm and yet to recover the profit made by the director.[294]

Companies Acts and directors' contracts. The Companies Acts contain extensive provisions designed to regulate transactions between directors and their companies, the overall purpose of these provisions being to prevent overreaching by directors and to compel disclosure to the members of the details of the transactions. Some types of transaction must be disclosed and approved in advance (e.g. loans,[295] payments made in connection with the loss of office),[296] while others merely have to be disclosed (e.g. emoluments).[297] These provisions are much too technical and extensive to be dealt with here and specialist texts on Company Law should be referred to. Of greater significance with respect to contracts between directors and their companies is s.177 of the Companies Act 2006,[298] which requires a director who has a direct or indirect interest in a proposed contract or arrangement with his company to make disclosure of his interest in the way set out in the section. Directors are also obliged to disclose interests in an existing transaction or arrangement.[299] There are also special provisions dealing with contracts which include as one of the parties a director of the company and with respect to that contract the board exceeds limitations on its powers under the company's constitution.[300] Such contracts are (subject to limitations) made voidable at the option of the company.[301] 9–056

Managing directors. The appointment of a managing director does not necessarily constitute a contract between the holder of that office and the company and in the absence of a contract he is removable according to the regulations in the company's constitution.[302] Even where a person is appointed as a managing 9–057

[292] *Re Leeds and Hanley Theatres of Varieties Ltd* [1902] 2 Ch. 809.

[293] Where the transaction is a substantial property transaction as defined in s.190 of the Companies Act 2006, and that section is not complied with, the director must account for any gain and are liable to indemnify the company for all losses (s.195); see *Joint Receivers and Managers of Niltan Carson Ltd v Hawthorne* [1988] B.C.L.C. 298; *Duckwari Plc v Offerventure Ltd (No.2)* [1999] 2 Ch. 253.

[294] *Re Cape Breton Co* (1884) 26 Ch D 221; 29 Ch D 795; *Burland v Earle* [1902] A.C. 83.

[295] s.197. Loans may also be subsequently affirmed within a reasonable period of time: s.214. The long standing prohibition on company loans to directors was abrogated by the 2006 Act.

[296] ss.215–219. See *Company Directors: Regulating Conflicts of Interest and Formulating a Statement of Duties* (Law Commission, Consultation Paper No.153).

[297] s.318.

[298] See also fn.287.

[299] ss.182–186. This is extended to a shadow director: s.187.

[300] s.41. The purpose of this provision is to deny to directors the full protection of ss.39 and 40. See above, para.9–034.

[301] s.41.

[302] An appointment without remuneration will normally mean that there is no contract: *Foster v Foster* [1916] 1 Ch. 532.

director pursuant to a contract to that effect the company can lawfully terminate the appointment at any time in accordance with the company's constitution if the appointment is not made for a specific term, though reasonable notice may be required in this event. A person appointed managing director cannot, in the absence of an agreement to that effect, claim to be entitled to continue as such so long as he remains a director.[303]

9–058 **Contract for term of years.** A managing director may, however, be employed in that capacity by a company under a contract for a term of years,[304] and if so his appointment cannot be lawfully revoked by the company before the expiration of that time by removing him from his directorship in accordance with the articles of association or s.168 of the 2006 Act.[305] Although the company's power to remove a director under s.168 cannot be taken away by contract,[306] the exercise of the power may be a breach of contract because a managing director who is removed from his position as a director will necessarily lose his post as managing director,[307] and the company will then be in breach of any contract to employ him as such. Even if remuneration is attached to the office and there is a contract, the contract may exceptionally (particularly where it is an informal parol agreement) be treated as being subject to the provisions of the company's constitution. In this event removal of the managing director in accordance with the company's constitution will not be a breach of contract.[308]

9–059 **Improper appointment.** If a managing director is improperly appointed, fees received by him as such may be recovered from him by the company.[309]

(iii) *Contracts between Companies and their Members*

9–060 **Purchase and allotment.** The contract between a company and a shareholder may be made in a number of ways. By s.112 of the Companies Act 2006, the subscribers to the memorandum of association are deemed to have agreed to become members of the company.[310] The phrase "agrees to become a member"

---

[303] *Foster v Foster* [1916] 1 Ch. 532.

[304] Service contract is defined in s.227 of the 2006 Act and it must be open for inspection by members; ss.228–229. These provisions apply to shadow directors; s.230.

[305] *Southern Foundries Ltd v Shirlaw* [1940] A.C. 701; *Shindler v Northern Raincoat Co Ltd* [1960] 1 W.L.R. 1038; *Cumbrian Newspapers Group Ltd v Cumberland and Westmoreland Newspaper and Printing Co Ltd* [1987] Ch. 10.

[306] See, however, *Bushell v Faith* [1970] A.C. 1099.

[307] *Re Alexander's Timber Co* (1901) 70 L.J. Ch. 767; *Bluett v Stutchbury's Ltd* (1908) 24 T.L.R. 469.

[308] *Read v Astoria Garage (Streatham) Ltd* [1952] Ch. 637; contrast *Shindler v Northern Raincoat Co Ltd* [1960] 1 W.L.R. 1038. This gives rise to difficult conceptual problems: see Trebilcock (1967) 31 Conv.(N.S.) 95; *Carrier Australia Ltd v Hunt* (1935) 61 C.L.R. 534.

[309] *Brown & Green v Hays* (1920) 36 T.L.R. 330; *Kerr v Marine Products* (1928) 44 T.L.R. 292; cf. *Craven Ellis v Canons Ltd* [1936] 2 K.B. 403.

[310] Companies Act 2006 s.112 makes it clear that the subscribers to the memorandum become members on registration of the company even if the company fails to enter their names in the register of members.

in s.112 does not require a binding contract and this requirement is satisfied where the name of a person is entered in the register of members with his consent.[311] However, in most cases,[312] the contract between the shareholder and the company will either be preceded by a purchase of shares from a third party or will be made by application to the company followed by allotment. In the former case the contract is probably made by the application of the prospective shareholder to be entered in the register followed by his being so entered. In the latter case the contract is constituted by an application to take shares, accepted by the company by a notification that shares have been allotted.[313] Notice of allotment must be given within a reasonable time or the application lapses.[314] It was held in *Houldsworth v City of Glasgow Bank*[315] that a person who had applied for and been allotted shares in a company could not, while he remained a member of the company, sue the company for damages for breach of his contract of membership,[316] or for damages for fraudulently inducing him to enter into it.[317] The only remedy used to be that of rescission of the contract and rectification of the register of members. The position has now been altered by s.655 of the 2006 Act,[318] which provides that being a member does not preclude an action for damages. Rescission of a contract of subscription will normally be ordered if the claimant succeeds in showing that he has been induced to take the shares by a material misrepresentation of fact on the part of the company. A misrepresentation made by a person acting on behalf of the company within the scope of his authority[319] or contained in a document which is, to the knowledge of the company, the basis of the contract to take shares,[320] is a good ground for rescission.[321] In most cases the representations complained of are contained in a prospectus issued by the company, and inasmuch as the offer to take shares is an offer to take them on the terms of the prospectus, the materiality of the statements contained in the prospectus will in most cases be beyond dispute.[322] If the shareholder does not rescind the contract and take steps to have the register

[311] *Re Nuneaton Borough Association Football Club Ltd* [1989] B.C.L.C. 454. This was decided under s.22 of the 1985 Act which s.112 restates.

[312] cf. *Mackley's Case* (1875) 1 Ch D 247.

[313] For the statutory rules relating to allotment and the effects of irregular allotment, see Companies Act 1985 ss.82–86 repealed in part by Financial Services Act 1986 Sch.17, settling the law left uncertain in *Jubilee Cotton Mills Ltd v Lewis* [1924] A.C. 958; *Re James Burton & Son Ltd* [1927] 2 Ch. 132.

[314] *Ramsgate Victoria Hotel Co v Montefiore* (1866) L.R. 1 Ex. 109.

[315] (1880) 5 App. Cas. 317; *Soden v British and Commonwealth Holdings Plc* [1997] 2 B.C.L.C. 501.

[316] *Re Addlestone Linoleum Co* (1887) 37 Ch D 191.

[317] *Western Bank of Scotland v Addie* (1867) L.R. 1 Sc. & Div. 145; *Houldsworth v City of Glasgow Bank* (1880) 5 App. Cas. 317.

[318] This was first introduced as s.111A of the 1985 Act by s.131 of the Companies Act 1989.

[319] *Lydney v Anglo-Italian Hemp Spinning Co* [1896] 1 Ch. 178; cf. *Lagunas Nitrate Co v Lagunas Syndicate* [1899] 2 Ch. 392.

[320] *Karberg's Case* [1892] 3 Ch. 1; *Collins v Associated Greyhound Racecourses* [1930] 1 Ch. 1.

[321] See above, Ch.6.

[322] See *Karberg's Case* [1892] 3 Ch. 1; *Mair v Rio Grande Rubber Estates* [1913] A.C. 853; *Re Pacaya Rubber & Produce Co* [1914] 1 Ch. 542.

rectified within a reasonable time,[323] and in any event before the commencement of the winding up of the company,[324] he loses his right of rescission; but this rule does not apply to a shareholder whose shares have been forfeited by the company and who has done nothing to affirm the contract, for he has ceased to be a shareholder and has become a debtor to the company.[325]

9–061 **Effect of articles.** The terms of the contract of membership of a company are contained in the memorandum and articles of association. Where a company prior to the 2006 Act had to possess articles and a memorandum the articles were subordinate to the memorandum and, in the case of inconsistency between them, the memorandum prevails. Provisions in the memorandum of such companies are now treated as provisions in its articles.[326] No provision is made in the 2006 Act for dealing with the unlikely event that a conflict might arise but the courts would probably follow the old law, so that any provision in the articles derived from the memorandum would prevail.[327] The extent to which the articles of association form an enforceable contract between the company and its individual members is determined by s.33 of the Companies Act 2006 which provides that the:

> " . . . provisions of a company's constitution bind the company and its members to the same extent as if there were covenants on the part of the company and of each member to observe those provisions."[328]

In *Hickman v Kent or Romney Marsh Sheep-Breeders' Association*,[329] Astbury J. made an elaborate examination of the cases, some of which decided that the articles of association created no contract between the company and its members and others that a company was entitled as against its members to enforce and restrain breaches of its regulations; he concluded "[i]t is difficult to reconcile these two classes of decisions and the judicial opinions therein expressed", but he went on to formulate the following rules:

(1) No article can constitute a contract between the company and a third person.[330]

(2) No right purporting to be given by an article to a person, whether a member or not, in a capacity other than that of a member, as, for instance,

---

[323] *First National Reinsurance Co v Greenfield* [1921] 2 K.B. 260.

[324] *Oakes v Turquand* (1867) L.R. 2 H.L. 325; *Reese River Silver Mining Co v Smith* (1869) L.R. 4 H.L. 64.

[325] *Aaron's Reefs v Twiss* [1896] A.C. 273.

[326] s.28.

[327] *Ashbury v Watson* (1885) 30 Ch D 376; *Rayfield v Hands* [1960] Ch. 1.

[328] This replicates the effect s.14 of the 1985 Act, there have been inconsequential linguistic amendments.

[329] [1915] 1 Ch. 881, 900; approved *Beattie v Beattie Ltd* [1938] Ch. 708. See also *Mutual Life Insurance Co of New York v The Rank Organisation Ltd* [1985] B.C.L.C. 11 (the contract constituted by the articles does not import the requirement that there be parity of treatment of shareholders of the same class); *Bratton Seymour Service Co Ltd v Oxborough* [1992] B.C.L.C. 693.

[330] *Melhado v Porto Alegre Ry* (1874) L.R. 9 C.P. 503; *Re Greene* [1949] Ch. 333.

a solicitor,[331] promoter[332] or director,[333] can be enforced against the company.

(3) Articles regulating the rights and obligations of the members generally as such do create rights and obligations between them and the company respectively.

The articles also constitute a contract been the members inter se.[334]

(iv) *Contracts between Companies and their Auditors*

Appointment and removal of auditors. Public companies must appoint auditors.[335] If the directors reasonably resolve that no such appointment is needed on the ground that audited accounts are unlikely to be required then auditors need not be appointed.[336] The appointment of auditors is made by the members.[337] Although the first auditors may be appointed by the directors,[338] auditors are normally elected at the general meeting at which the company's accounts are considered[339] and the terms of the auditor's remuneration will normally be determined by the members of the company.[340] The auditor's term of office must run from the conclusion of that meeting to the conclusion of the next such meeting,[341] and although an auditor may resign he must follow certain stipulated procedures.[342] By virtue of the Companies Act 2006 s.510, a company may by ordinary resolution remove its auditor from office, before the expiration of his term of office, any such removal is without prejudice to any claim for damages for breach of contract.[343] 9–062

Rules of industrial societies. It would appear that the rules of a society registered under the Industrial and Provident Societies Act 1965 (or earlier Acts 9–063

[331] *Eley v Positive Life Assurance Co* (1876) 1 Ex.D. 88; cf. *Cumbrian Newspapers Group Ltd v Cumberland and Westmoreland Herald Newspaper & Printing Co Ltd* [1987] Ch. 1, 16.

[332] *Pritchard's Case* (1873) L.R. 8 Ch. 956.

[333] *Browne v La Trinidad* (1887) 37 Ch D 1; *Beattie v Beattie Ltd* [1938] Ch. 708; contrast *Rayfield v Hands* [1960] Ch. 1, on which see Gower (1958) 21 M.L.R. 401, 465.

[334] *Rayfields v Hands* [1960] Ch. 1. See also *Re Royal Institution of Chartered Surveyors' Application* [1985] I.C.R. 330, 345–347 (relationship between members of a body corporate incorporated by Royal Charter). It has been argued that a member also has the right to compel a company to observe all of the provisions in the company's articles of association, a proposition which if accurate would provide a means for enforcing indirectly outsider rights. Although some cases recognise such a right, it has not constituted the basis of any decision and its status remains very uncertain. See generally, Wedderburn [1957] C.L.J. 194; [1958] C.L.J. 93.

[335] s.489(1).

[336] s.489(1).

[337] s.489(1). In certain restricted circumstances, the directors can appoint auditors: see s.489(3).

[338] s.489(3).

[339] s.489(4).

[340] s.492.

[341] s.495.

[342] ss.516–618.

[343] The Act contains other procedural provisions relating to the removal of an auditor: see ss.510–513 of the Act.

replaced by that Act) bind the members of such a society to the same extent as the articles of association bind the shareholders.[344]

2. UNINCORPORATED ASSOCIATIONS

(a) *Generally*

9–064 **Liability of unincorporated associations.** An unincorporated association is not a legal person and therefore cannot sue or be sued[345] unless such a course is authorised by express or implied statutory provisions as in the case of a trade union[346] and a trustee savings bank.[347] Nor can a contract be made so as to bind all persons who from time to time become members of such an association.[348] But a contract purportedly made by or with an unincorporated association is not necessarily a nullity.[349] If the person or persons who actually made the contract had no authority to contract on behalf of the members they may be held to have contracted personally.[350] On the other hand, if they had the authority, express or implied, of all or some of the members of the association to contract on their behalf, the contract can be enforced by or against those members as co-principals to the contract by the ordinary rules of agency.[351]

9–065 **Representative action.** By the rules of agency, therefore, a large number of members of an association may find themselves parties to a contract. In practice it would be impossible in such a case to join all the members as plaintiffs or defendants, and therefore recourse must be had to the device of a representative action. Order 15 r.12, of the Rules of the Supreme Court (which is preserved by the Rules of the Supreme Court Sch.1) provides that where there are numerous persons having the same interest in any proceedings,[352] the proceedings may be begun and, unless the court otherwise orders, continued by or against any one or more of them as representing all or as representing all except one or more of them. The attitude of the courts is to interpret the open textured language of O.15 r.12, in a liberal manner. Its language, according to Megarry V.C., is wide and

[344] *Biddulph & District Agricultural Society v Agricultural Wholesale Society* [1925] Ch. 769, [1927] A.C. 76.

[345] *London Association for Protection of Trade v Greenlands Ltd* [1916] 2 A.C. 15, 20, 38; *Steele v Gourley* (1886) 3 T.L.R. 118, 119; affirmed (1887) 3 T.L.R. 772. See, generally, Ford, *Unincorporated Non-Profit Associations* (1959); Keeler (1971) 34 M.L.R. 615.

[346] Trade Union and Labour Relations (Consolidation) Act 1992 s.10; *British Association of Advisers and Lecturers in Physical Education v National Union of Teachers* [1986] I.R.L.R. 497 CA; *E.E.T.P.U. v Times Newspapers Ltd* [1980] Q.B. 585.

[347] *Knight and Searle v Dove* [1964] 2 Q.B. 631. See Wedderburn (1965) 28 M.L.R. 62.

[348] See *Walker v Sur* [1914] 2 K.B. 930; *Jarrott v Ackerley* (1915) 85 L.J.Ch. 135.

[349] The *Regulatory Reform (Removal of 20 Member Limit in Partnership*, etc.) Order 2002 (SI 2002/3203) removed the size limits on partnerships imposed by s.716 of the 1985 Act. No size limitation on partnerships has been imposed by the 2006 Act.

[350] *Bradley Egg Farm v Clifford* [1943] 2 All E.R. 378.

[351] See Vol.II, Ch.31.

[352] *Barker v Allanson* [1937] 1 K.B. 463; *London Association for Protection of Trade v Greenlands Ltd* [1916] 2 A.C. 15, 39; *Janson v Property Insurance Co* (1913) 30 T.L.R. 49.

permissive and the rule should be used as "a flexible tool of convenience in the administration of justice".[353]

Requirements for representative action. In *Prudential Assurance Co Ltd v Newman Industries Ltd*[354] Vinelott J. reviewed the authorities relating to representative actions and formulated the following principles with respect to the bringing of such actions. 9–066

Not if it would confer new right of action. First, a representative action may not be brought if the effect of so doing is: 9–067

> "... to confer a right of action on a member of the class represented who would not otherwise have been able to assert such a right in separate proceedings, or to bar a defence which might otherwise be available to the defendant, in such separate proceedings."[355]

From this Vinelott J. reasoned that the plaintiff in a representative action will normally be only entitled to declaratory relief, although he may join with the representative action a claim for personal damages. Although this is the normal rule, in exceptional circumstances the court may grant damages in favour of the plaintiff in an action commenced in representative form.[356] Also, it may be that the contractual arrangements between the parties make it appropriate that there be an action in representative form.[357] An action of libel cannot be instituted under the rule where some of the members of the association might not have authorised the publication of the alleged libel, or might be out of the country.[358] Similarly, it was refused where an order was sought against the members at the date of the proceedings and the members had changed since the cause of action had arisen,[359] and, in an action for breach of a contract for the carriage of goods by sea, where the shippers in a general ship held different bills of lading and different defences might have been raised against them.[360]

Not to enforce a personal liability. Nor can representative proceedings under this rule be used in an action in which a personal liability, such as a judgment for money due or for damages, is sought to be enforced against the individual 9–068

---

[353] *John v Rees* [1970] Ch. 345, 370.

[354] [1981] Ch. 229; *CBS/SONY Hong Kong Ltd v Television Broadcasts Ltd* [1987] F.S.R. 262.

[355] [1981] Ch. 229, 254.

[356] *E.M.I. Records Ltd v Riley* [1981] 1 W.L.R. 923.

[357] *Irish Shipping Ltd v Commercial Union Assurance Co Plc* [1991] 2 Q.B. 206 (action in representative form against the lead underwriter of an insurance contract).

[358] *Mercantile Marine Service Association v Toms* [1916] 2 K.B. 243; *E.E.T.P.U. v Times Newspapers Ltd* [1980] Q.B. 585.

[359] *Barker v Allanson* [1937] 1 K.B. 463; *Roche v Sherrington* [1982] 2 All E.R. 426; cf. *Campbell v Thompson* [1953] 1 Q.B. 445. There is no reason why a representative action should not be instituted against those persons who were members when the cause of action arose, but in this event no order could be made affecting the assets of the association.

[360] *Markt & Co v Knight S.S. Co* [1910] 2 K.B. 1021.

members of the association.[361] In *Lord Churchill v Whetnall*,[362] where three subscribers to a fund brought an action for misrepresentation in the circular inviting subscriptions to the fund on behalf of themselves and the other 200 subscribers, it was held that there could be no representative action to establish the right of numerous persons to recover damages, each in his own several right, where the only right claimed was the right to recover such damages: before a subscriber could recover he would have to show that he had been induced by the representation and this could only be done in separate proceedings.[363] But where the association is possessed of funds in the hands of trustees, a plaintiff may sue proper persons as representatives of the association for a declaration of his right against the property belonging to the association, and, by adding the trustees as defendants, may obtain an order charging the funds which are in their hands and of which they are the legal owners.[364]

9–069 **Common interest.** The *Prudential Assurance* case also required that there must be an "interest" shared by all members: "there must be a common ingredient in the cause of action of each member of the class".[365] This to a large extent is nothing more than a rephrasing of the first requirement.

9–070 **For benefit of class.** The third, and related requirement, is that it is for the benefit of the class that the representative action be brought.[366] This, among other things, will require that all evidence relating to the claim is adduced to avoid any unfairness to members of the class who will be bound by the outcome of the litigation.

9–071 **Relation of unincorporated association to its members.** Inasmuch as unincorporated associations are generally not legal persons, but mere collective names for all their members, a contract made by one member with some person or persons on behalf of the association is a contract by a man with himself and others; and as no man can be both covenantor and covenantee upon a contract, it must be construed as a contract between the member and the other members.[367] If that contract is broken the injured member can sue and recover damages from

---

[361] *Walker v Sur* [1914] 2 K.B. 930; *Hardie and Lane v Chiltern* [1928] 1 K.B. 663. See, however, *Morrison S.S. Co Ltd v Greystoke Castle (Cargo Owners)* [1947] A.C. 265. It may also be noted that the new O.15 r.12 is in wider terms than the old O.16 r.9, and it is perhaps arguable that the cases denying the use of this procedure in an action for damages should not now be followed. But see *Prudential Assurance* [1981] Ch. 229, 244; *Roche v Sherrington* [1982] 2 All E.R. 426.

[362] (1918) 87 L.J. Ch. 524; *Wing v Burn* (1928) 44 T.L.R. 258; *Markt & Co v Knight S.S. Co* [1910] 2 K.B. 1021, 1035.

[363] See *Prudential Assurance* [1981] Ch. 229, 251.

[364] *Wood v McCarthy* [1893] 1 Q.B. 775; *Taff Vale Ry v Amalgamated Society of Railway Servants* [1901] A.C. 426, 443; *Linaker v Pilcher* (1901) 17 T.L.R. 256; *Ideal Films v Richards* [1927] 1 K.B. 374, 381.

[365] *Prudential Assurance Co Ltd v Newman Industries Ltd* [1981] Ch. 229, 255. Vinelott J. cited *Markt & Co v Knight S.S. Co* [1910] 2 K.B. 1021 and *Lord Churchill v Whetmall* (1918) 87 L.J. Ch. 524 as two cases where this requirement was not satisfied.

[366] *Prudential Assurance Co Ltd v Newman Industries Ltd* [1981] Ch. 229, 255.

[367] Law of Property Act 1925 s.82. See also *John v Matthews* [1970] 2 Q.B. 443; *Reel v Holder* [1981] 1 W.L.R. 1226.

those who have broken it,[368] though he cannot sue the association except where statutory authorisation for such a course can be found. But he may be faced with the difficulty that the wrongful act was committed by an agent of the association on behalf of its members, including himself. In that case it is possible that he may be unable to recover from his fellow members, whose responsibility, in the circumstances, will be no greater than his own. But the other members, in order to rely on such a defence, must show that the agent was really acting on behalf of the injured member; and, at any rate where the injury is a wrongful expulsion in breach of the rules, that will not be so.[369]

(b) *Clubs*[370]

Kinds of clubs. The principal bodies with regard to which these questions arise are clubs and trade unions. Clubs are unincorporated associations and may be formed for any purpose for which associations may be lawfully constituted. There are two principal types of club: members' clubs and proprietary clubs.[371] 9–072

(i) *Members' Clubs*

Members' liability. The question whether contracts purporting to have been made on behalf of an association bind all the members or only some (e.g. the committee) is one which turns on the general law of agency.[372] Thus, no member of a members' club is liable for the debts of the club except to the extent that he has expressly or impliedly authorised some official of the club to pledge his personal credit.[373] Clubs are not partnerships[374] and the: 9–073

> "... law, which was at one time uncertain, is now settled, that no member of a club is liable to a creditor except, so far as he has assented to the contract in respect of which such liability has arisen."[375]

Unless the rules expressly so provide,[376] the committee of a club has no authority to pledge the credit of the members by borrowing on debentures,[377] or by

---

368 See *Abbott v Sullivan* [1952] 1 K.B. 189, 193, 219; *Lee v Showmen's Guild of Great Britain* [1952] 2 Q.B. 329, 341.

369 *Bonsor v Musicians' Union* [1956] A.C. 104, 148–149, 153.

370 See Josling and Alexander, *The Law of Clubs*, 6th edn (1987).

371 The Friendly Societies Act 1974 s.7(2)(d) recognised the "working men's clubs" but this definition is not repeated in the Friendly Societies Act 1992. However, the social and philanthropic purposes that could be carried out by working men's clubs as defined in 1974 Act could be carried out by a body registered as a Friendly Society under the 1992 Act: see Sch.2 Pt D as amplified by s.7(2)(b) and s.10 of the 1992 Act.

372 See Vol.II, Ch.31: *Lascelles v Rathbun* (1919) 35 T.L.R. 347; *Shore v Ministry of Works* [1950] 2 All E.R. 228; *Prole v Allen* [1950] 1 All E.R. 476; cf. *Moshenan v Segar* [1917] 2 K.B. 325 dealing with proprietary clubs.

373 *Steele v Gourley* (1887) 3 T.L.R. 772; *Wise v Perpetual Trustee Co* [1903] A.C. 139.

374 [1903] A.C. 139.

375 *Re St James' Club* (1852) 2 De G.M. & G. 383, 387.

376 *Cockerell v Aucompte* (1857) 2 C.B.(N.S.) 440.

377 *Re St James' Club* (1852) 2 De G.M. & G. 383.

ordering work to be done for or goods to be supplied to the club[378]; but a member may make himself liable by ratifying the order.[379] Members of the committee of a club are liable in respect of contracts made by them on behalf of the club,[380] but not in respect of contracts made by officials of the club which they have not themselves authorised.[381] Where one committee man has paid out money under a contract on which another committee man also could have been sued, the former has a right of contribution against the latter in respect of such payment,[382] but he has no right of indemnity against the members of the club.[383]

9–074 **Relation of club to its members.** The relations between the members of a club are governed by a contract between the members which may be express or implied and which is usually found in the rules of the club[384]; membership of a club may also confer proprietary rights on members which will be of significance where the club is being dissolved.[385] In *Lee v Showmen's Guild of Great Britain*[386] Denning L.J. said:

> "It was once said by Sir George Jessel M.R. that the courts only intervened in these cases to protect rights of property: see *Rigby v Connol*[387]; and other judges have often said the same thing: see, for instance, *Cookson v Harewood*.[388] But Fletcher Moulton L.J. denied that there was any such limitation on the power of the courts: see *Osborne v Amalgamated Society of Railway Servants*[389]; and it has now become clear that he was right: see the cornporters' case, *Abbott v Sullivan*.[390] That case shows that the power of this court to intervene is founded on its jurisdiction to protect rights of contract.[391] If a member is expelled by a committee in breach of contract, this court will grant a declaration that their action is *ultra vires*. It will also grant an injunction to prevent his expulsion, if that is necessary to protect a proprietary right of his; or to protect him in his right to earn his livelihood: see *Amalgamated Society of Carpenters, etc. v Braithwaite*[392]; but it will not grant an injunction to give a member the right to enter a

---

378 *Flemyng v Hector* (1836) 2 M. & W. 172; *Hawke v Cole* (1890) 62 L.T. 658; *Draper v Earl Manvers* (1892) 9 T.L.R. 73.

379 *Delauney v Strickland* (1818) 2 Stark. 416.

380 *Lee v Bissett* (1856) 4 W.R. 233; *Re London Marine Insurance Association* (1869) L.R. 8 Eq. 176; *Duke of Queensbury v Cullen* (1787) 1 Bro. P.C. 396.

381 *Todd v Emly* (1841) 7 M. & W. 427; 8 M. & W. 505.

382 *Earl of Mountcashell v Barber* (1853) 14 C.B. 53.

383 *Wise v Perpetual Trustee Co* [1903] A.C. 139.

384 *Harington v Sendall* [1903] 1 Ch. 921; *Lee v Showmen's Guild of Great Britain* [1952] 2 Q.B. 329. On the liability of a club or its officers to its members in tort: see *Robertson v Ridley* [1988] 2 All E.R. 474.

385 *Re Sick and Funeral Society of St John's Sunday School, Golcar* [1973] Ch. 51.

386 [1952] 2 Q.B. 329, 341–342.

387 (1880) 14 Ch D 482, 487.

388 [1932] 2 K.B. 478, 481, 488.

389 [1911] 1 Ch. 540, 562.

390 [1952] 1 K.B. 189.

391 See, however, *Nagle v Feilden* [1966] 2 Q.B. 633, which suggests that in the case of associations which control entry to a trade or profession (such as the Jockey Club, the Stock Exchange or the Inns of Court) the court's power to grant redress is not confined to cases of contract. See also *R. v Jockey Club Ex p. RAM Racecourses Ltd* [1993] 2 All E.R. 225, 247–248. Detailed consideration of this question falls outside the scope of this work, but see below, para.9–087 fn.435, as to trade unions and paras 16–075 et seq. as to the doctrine of restraint of trade. cf. *Goring v British Actors Equity Association* [1987] I.R.L.R. 122, 127–128.

392 [1922] 2 A.C. 440.

> social club, unless there are proprietary rights attached to it, because it is too personal to be specifically enforced: see *Baird v Wells*.[393] That is, I think, the only relevance of rights of property in this connection. It goes to the form of remedy, not to the right."

But the absence of property rights may, in certain circumstances, be some evidence that the members did not intend that their club membership should create legal relations between them.[394] As a result of the contractual nature of the rules the court will interfere to prevent them being altered,[395] unless they are altered in accordance with a procedure prescribed therein[396] or with the consent of every member.

Expulsion of members. The court will not restrain the exercise by a club of a power, contained in its rules, to expel members unless it is shown that what has been done is, in fact, contrary to the rules or has been done in bad faith[397] or, at least where some sort of inquiry is contemplated, where the rules of natural justice have been infringed.[398] It has been said that to give one reason for expelling a member and to act upon another is evidence of bad faith.[399] In a case of expulsion it was held that the issues were whether the rules of the club had been observed, whether the committee had given the member a fair hearing and whether it had acted in good faith.[400] Every member of the committee must be summoned to the meeting or the proceedings may be invalidated.[401] Notice must be given to the member of the charge made against him and he must have a proper opportunity of being heard in his own defence[402]; a rule purporting to deprive him of this right would probably be invalid as contrary to public policy.[403] If a decision of a committee, based on the opinion of the committee, is challenged, the court will only interfere if there was no evidence upon which to base the opinion, in which case it will declare the decision ultra vires. The club cannot oust the jurisdiction of the courts by making the committee the final 9–075

[393] (1890) 44 Ch D 661, 675–676. But a right to vote may be protected by injunction: *Woodford v Smith* [1970] 1 W.L.R. 806.

[394] See *Rigby v Connol* (1880) 14 Ch D 482, 487 (this was based on the discredited theory that court intervention in the affairs of an association was only justified to protect rights of property).

[395] *Harington v Sendall* [1903] 1 Ch. 921.

[396] *Thellusson v Viscount Valentia* [1907] 2 Ch. 1.

[397] *Hopkinson v Marquis of Exeter* (1867) L.R. 5 Eq. 63; *Richardson-Gardner v Fremantle* (1870) 24 L.T. 81; *Dawkins v Antrobus* (1879) 17 Ch D 615; *Lambert v Addison* (1882) 46 L.T. 20. See Lloyd (1952) 15 M.L.R. 413.

[398] *Russell v Duke of Norfolk* [1949] 1 All E.R. 109; *Lawlor v Union of Post Office Workers* [1965] Ch. 712. cf. *Gaiman v National Association of Mental Health* [1971] Ch. 317.

[399] *D'Arcy v Adamson* (1913) 29 T.L.R. 367.

[400] *Lamberton v Thorpe* (1929) 141 L.T. 638, following *Maclean v Workers' Union* [1929] 1 Ch. 602.

[401] *Young v Ladies' Imperial Club Ltd* [1920] 2 K.B. 523.

[402] *Labouchere v Earl Wharncliffe* (1879) 13 Ch D 346; *Fisher v Keane* (1878) 11 Ch D 353; *Gray v Allison* (1909) 25 T.L.R. 531.

[403] *Lee v Showmen's Guild of Great Britain* [1952] 2 Q.B. 329, 342; *Faramus v Film Artistes' Federation* [1964] A.C. 925, 941; *John v Rees* [1970] Ch. 345; *Enderby Town Football Club Ltd v Football Association Ltd* [1971] Ch. 591.

arbiter on questions of law; and the construction of the rules is always a question of law.[404]

9–076 **Election.** Generally speaking, a person who is refused membership of an unincorporated association has no ground for legal redress.[405] It has, however, been suggested that if the grounds for such refusal are unlawful as being in restraint of trade, redress may be available.[406] But refusal to admit a person to membership of a *social* club could hardly be in restraint of trade.[407] A refusal to admit a person to membership of a club on the grounds of colour, race or ethnic or national origins may constitute a breach of s.25 of the Race Relations Act 1976.[408]

9–077 **Re-election.** Where the rules of an unincorporated association provide for re-election at stated intervals by the committee, the committee (somewhat surprisingly in the light of the rules relating to expulsion) is not bound to give a member notice of any objection to his re-election,[409] and provided that they act neither arbitrarily nor capriciously but in the honest exercise of their discretion, which in the absence of evidence to the contrary will be presumed, their decision cannot be questioned.[410]

9–078 **Resignation.** A member of a club may unilaterally resign his membership even in the absence of any provision in the club's rules, and such resignation may be inferred from long-continued non-payment of dues.[411]

9–079 **Officers' mess.** For goods supplied to an officers' mess neither an individual member of the mess[412] nor the commanding officer[413] can be made liable without evidence that he authorised his credit to be pledged and that he was the person to whom the seller gave credit.

(ii) *Proprietary Clubs*

9–080 **Proprietary clubs.** In a proprietary club the property and funds of the club belong to the proprietor who regulates the use of the property by the members in return for their subscriptions. The management is generally in the hands of a committee of members. Although it was formerly thought that the only remedy of a member of a proprietary club which had itself no property was against the

---

[404] *Lee v Showmen's Guild of Great Britain* [1952] 2 Q.B. 329; followed in *Barker v Jones* [1954] 1 W.L.R. 1005.

[405] *Faramus v Film Artistes' Association* [1964] A.C. 925, 947.

[406] *Nagle v Feilden* [1966] 2 Q.B. 633; *Reg v Disciplinary Committee of The Jockey Club* [1993] 1 W.L.R. 909, 933; *Bunbury v Lautro Ltd* [1996] C.L.C. 1273.

[407] [1996] C.L.C. 1273, 644, 653.

[408] The law on this is complicated and it is necessary to refer to specialist texts: see Feldman, *Civil Liberties & Human Rights*, 2nd edn (2002).

[409] *Cassel v Inglis* [1916] 2 Ch. 211.

[410] *Weinberger v Inglis* [1919] A.C. 606; cf. *Nagle* v *Fielden* [1966] 2 Q.B. 633.

[411] *Re Sick and Funeral Society of St John's Sunday School, Golcar* [1973] Ch. 51.

[412] *Hawke v Cole* (1890) 62 L.T. 658.

[413] *Lascelles v Rathbun* (1919) 35 T.L.R. 347.

proprietor,[414] it is now clear that this is not so.[415] But since members have no right of property in the case of a proprietary club, one who has been expelled by the committee cannot obtain relief by way of injunction, even though the proceedings were irregular, but will be left to obtain it in damages.[416]

(c) *Trade Unions*

Contractual capacity of trade unions. The law relating to the contractual capacity of trade unions has undergone some remarkable vicissitudes since the beginning of this century. Under the nineteenth-century statutes governing trade unions there was no express provision for incorporation, but the *Taff Vale* case,[417] which held that registered unions could be sued in their own name, resulted in a limited contractual capacity being conferred upon them.[418] Legislation on trade unions in the twentieth century has tended to confer some type of "corporate" status on trade unions.[419] The present position is to be found in s.10 of the Trade Union and Labour Relations (Consolidation) Act 1992 which provides that a trade union is not nor is it to be treated as a "body corporate".[420] However, despite this statutory denial of corporate status a trade union, so far as the capacity to enter into contracts is concerned, is treated as if it were a body corporate since it is expressly provided that a trade union is capable of entering into contracts[421] and that it can sue or be sued in its own name.[422] Any judgment or order made against a trade union is enforceable against any property held in trust[423] for it is as though it were a body corporate.[424] The agreements of a trade union are not void or voidable because they may be in restraint of trade.[425] Thus for most practical purposes in connection with contracts with third parties the position of a trade union has been equated with that of a body corporate. 9–081

Contracts between trade unions and their members. The relationship between a member of a trade union and the union itself is contractual, and the terms of the contract are to be found in the rules of the union.[426] A member of a trade union has in general the right to take proceedings to enforce compliance with the union's own rules in relation to matters such as election of officers and 9–082

[414] *Lyttleton v Blackburne* (1875) 45 L.J. Ch. 219; *Baird v Wells* (1890) 44 Ch D 661.
[415] *Lee v Showmen's Guild of Great Britain* [1952] 2 Q.B. 329.
[416] *Baird v Wells* (1890) 44 Ch D 661. cf. *Millennium Productions Ltd v Winter Garden Theatre (London) Ltd* [1946] W.N. 151; reversed sub nom. *Winter Garden Theatre (London) Ltd v Millennium Productions Ltd* [1948] A.C. 173.
[417] [1901] A.C. 426.
[418] See the 23rd edn of this work, paras 520–524.
[419] See, for example, s.2 of the Trade Union and Labour Relations Act 1974 (now repealed).
[420] s.10(1) and (2).
[421] s.10(1)(a).
[422] s.10(1)(b).
[423] s.12(1) provides that all the property of a trade union must be vested in trustees to be held on trust for it.
[424] s.12(2).
[425] s.11.
[426] *Bonsor v Musicians' Union* [1956] A.C. 104.

other internal regulations.[427] In general the court has no power to declare provisions of a trade union's rules to be void as unreasonable any more than it has with the provisions of any other contract.[428] However, in *Edwards v SOGAT*[429] the Court of Appeal, prior to the 1974 Act, struck down a union rule permitting capricious and arbitrary expulsion of a member, apparently on the ground that such a rule is contrary to public policy in so far as it permits such expulsion.[430] Section 46 of the Trade Union and Labour Relations (Consolidation) Act 1992 imposes a statutory duty on a trade union to ensure that its officers[431] are elected by secret ballot.[432] Re-elections for such offices must take place at intervals of not more than five years.[433]

9–083 **Expulsion and exclusion from a trade union.** Prior to the Industrial Relations Act 1971 the courts had protected members of a union against unlawful expulsion where it could be shown that the union had violated the procedure laid down in its own rules, and was thus in breach of its contract with its member. It was originally thought that the only remedy was by injunction but it was eventually held by the House of Lords that damages could also be awarded against the union.[434] It was also well established that a union, like any other domestic tribunal, must in general observe the rules of natural justice,[435] and it also seemed that the rules of the union could not validly exclude the rules of natural justice.[436] Where the rules of natural justice applied, a trade union, like the committee of a club,[437] was required to give a man notice of the charge against him and a reasonable opportunity of meeting it.[438] A trade union could not in any case oust the jurisdiction of the court and could not be made the final arbiter on questions of law[439]; and if it acted without evidence, the courts would interfere.[440] But the courts did not claim to act as courts of appeal from domestic tribunals and would not disturb a decision which was on a matter of opinion only.[441]

[427] See *Taylor v N.U.M. (Derbyshire Area)* [1985] B.C.L.C. 237 (on right of members to sue with respect to ultra vires disbursements of union assets).

[428] *Faramus v Film Artistes' Federation* [1964] A.C. 925, 943.

[429] [1971] Ch. 354.

[430] See generally, Rideout, *Principles of Labour Law*, 5th edn (1989), pp.395–432.

[431] These are defined in s.4(2).

[432] The voting procedures are set out in ss.47–52.

[433] s.46(1)(b).

[434] *Bonsor v Musicians' Union* [1956] A.C. 104. On the availability of an interlocutory injunction, see *Porter v N.U.J.* [1980] 1 I.R.L.R. 404.

[435] *Lee v Showmen's Guild of Great Britain* [1952] 2 Q.B. 329; Kidner, *Trade Union Law*, 2nd edn, Ch.3.

[436] *Russell v Duke of Norfolk* [1949] 1 All E.R. 109; *Lawler v Union of Post Office Workers* [1965] Ch. 712; *Taylor v National Union of Seamen* [1967] 1 W.L.R. 532; *Lee v Showmen's Guild of Great Britain* [1952] 2 Q.B. 329: *Faramus v Film Artistes' Federation* [1964] A.C. 925.

[437] See below, para.9–079.

[438] *Annamunthodo v Oilfield Workers' Trade Union* [1961] A.C. 945; *Breen v Amalgamated Engineering Union* [1971] 2 Q.B. 175.

[439] *Luby v Warwickshire Miners' Association* [1912] 2 Ch. 371; *Burn v National Amalgamated Labourers' Union* [1920] 2 Ch. 364; *Leigh v National Union of Railwaymen* [1970] Ch. 326; and see *Australian Workers' Union v Brown* (1948) 77 C.L.R. 601; *White v Kuzych* [1951] A.C. 585.

[440] *Lee v Showmen's Guild of Great Britain* [1952] 2 Q.B. 329, 340.

[441] [1952] 2 Q.B. 329.

Refusal of membership. No attempt to protect a worker from arbitrary or unreasonable refusal of membership could (it is thought) have succeeded at common law since no contractual relation could, *ex hypothesi*, be established between a would-be member and the union.[442] 9–084

Statutory protection of member's rights. Of greater importance than the common law in protecting a trade union member's rights are the statutory protections accorded to trade union members to prevent them from being excluded, expelled or disciplined on grounds that the statute treats as being unjustifiable.[443] 9–085

[442] In *Nagle v Feilden* [1966] 2 Q.B. 633, it was suggested that in some circumstances the court's power to intervene might extend beyond cases of contract, but in so far as this decision was based on the invalidity of an unreasonable restraint of trade it could have no application anyhow to a trade union by reason of s.3 of the Trade Union Act 1871, now replaced by s.11 of the Trade Union and Labour Relations (Consolidation) Act 1992. Indeed the wording of s.11 is more clearly calculated to exclude the argument suggested in *Nagle v Feilden*. See *Greig v Insole* [1978] 1 W.L.R. 302, 363; *Goring v Bristol Actors' Equity Association* [1987] I.R.L.R. 122, 127–128.

[443] The major statutory protections are to be found in Ch.V of the Trade Union and Labour Relations (Consolidation) Act 1992 as amended by ss.15 and 16 of the Trade Union Reform and Employment Rights Act 1993; ss.174–177 of the 1992 Act were replaced by s.14 of the 1993 Act.

CHAPTER 10

THE CROWN, PUBLIC AUTHORITIES AND THE EUROPEAN COMMUNITY

	PARA.
1. Introduction	10–001
2. Crown contracts	10–004
(a) Parliamentary control over Crown contracts	10–005
(b) Fettering of discretion	10–007
(c) Agency	10–009
(d) Crown Proceedings Act 1947	10–015
3. Public authorities	10–020
(a) The scope of statutory powers	10–021
(i) Express powers	10–021
(ii) Implied powers	10–023
(b) Fettering of discretion	10–027
(c) Proper exercise of powers	10–032
(d) Ultra vires and human rights	10–033
(e) Statutory reform of ultra vires	10–034
4. Tender process contracts	10–035
(a) Conditions for the implication of a tender process contract	10–036
(b) Contents of a tender process contract	10–038
5. Estoppel	10–039
6. Public procurement	10–044
(a) European Community legislation	10–044
(b) International and domestic procurement regimes	10–047

1. INTRODUCTION

The influence of public law concepts. The position of government contracts in English law is somewhat ambiguous. In contrast to many Continental jurisdictions, government contracts in English law do not have their own special category as a part of public law.[1] But, although government contracts are dealt with under the general principles of private law, the private law principles are frequently supplemented, modified or disapplied in response to the peculiar circumstances of governmental transactions. Often these alterations to the private law principles are either inspired by, or involve the direct borrowing, of public and constitutional law concepts. The result is a body of law which, although part 10–001

[1] Street, *Governmental Liability* (1953), p.81; Kahn-Freund and Wedderburn, foreword to Turpin, *Government Contracts* (1972), p.9, attributing the lack of a separate category to the "quirks of our legal history"; Auby [2007] P.L. 40.

of private law, has been strongly influenced by ideas more familiar to public lawyers.

10–002 **The European Community.** An express power to enter contracts is conferred on the European Community by art.288(1) of the EC Treaty.[2] That article states that any dispute should be resolved according to "the applicable law", which is typically identified in contracts entered by the European Commission (as the Community's representative) using a choice of law clause.[3] The Community possesses "the most extensive capacity accorded to legal persons".[4]

10–003 **Alternative remedies.** Although contracts made by government do not engage a special contractual regime, the involvement of government gives the potential for other bases of liability not normally open to private contracting parties. The three most obvious possibilities are judicial review, breach of human rights[5] and breach of the procurement regulations.[6] The possibilities of contractual issues being subjected to judicial review and the impact of the Human Rights Act 1998 were discussed in Ch.1.[7] A detailed treatment of the procurement regulations is beyond the scope of this chapter but Pt 6[8] of the Chapter contains an outline of the requirements and a discussion of the effect of a breach of the public procurement regulations on any contract that may have been made. But it should be noted that each of these potential alternatives is independent of contractual liability, and does not require a contract to have been concluded. Thus, breach of human rights focuses on whether the claimant's protected right has been invaded unjustifiably. The public procurement regulations set out a highly detailed, prescriptive series of obligations relating to the entire contracting process, breach of which may incur liability to any potential contracting party. Judicial review focuses on the improper exercise of power by a public authority; where the authority has failed to make good a legitimate expectation it has created, the factual basis for judicial review may be very similar to the factual basis for a claim for breach of contract.[9] But the remedies available for a successful application for judicial review are very different to those available in a successful action for breach of contract. Furthermore, the availability of judicial review in relation to commercial contracts is controversial.[10]

---

2 EC Treaty [2002] O.J. C 325, 24/12/2002 p.294.

3 Craig and de Burca, *EU Law*, 4th edn (2008), 600–601. See further, paras 30–047—30–070 below.

4 EC Treaty art.282.

5 Human Rights Act 1998.

6 Public Contracts Regulations 2006 (SI 2006/5); Utilities Contracts Regulations 2006 (SI 2006/6).

7 See above, paras 1–193 et seq. and 1–035 et seq. See further on judicial review: Fordham, *The Judicial Review Handbook*, 4th edn (2004); on human rights: Lester and Pannick (eds), *Human Rights Law and Practice*, 2nd edn (2004); on public procurement: Arrowsmith, *The Law of Public and Utilities Procurement*, 2nd edn (2005).

8 See below, paras 10–044—10–048.

9 e.g. *R. v North and East Devon Health Authority Ex p Coughlan* [2001] Q.B. 213 (authority promising tetraplegic patient a home for life if she would move from existing hospital accommodation).

10 *Hampshire CC v Supportways Community Services Ltd* [2006] EWCA Civ 1035; Arrowsmith (1990) 106 L.Q.R. 277; Freedland [1994] P.L. 86, 95–102; Bailey [2007] P.L. 444.

2. CROWN CONTRACTS[11]

Capacity. The Crown has an inherent, common law capacity to make contracts.[12] No statutory authority is needed. Whilst this contracting power can be seen as part of the prerogatives of the Crown—largely because it requires no Parliamentary approval[13]—it is probably more accurate to see it as part of the Crown's capacity to do whatever is not prohibited by law.[14] It follows that statutory provisions conferring contracting powers on Ministers are not strictly necessary; those sections are best explained in terms of the constitutional convention that a programme of expenditure should have prior statutory authorisation.[15] 10–004

(a) *Parliamentary Control Over Crown Contracts*

Express limitations. Where Parliament has limited the Crown's right to contract, any purported contract made outside those limits is void.[16] For instance, a statute might require specific legislative approval for contracts over a certain duration,[17] or prescribe a method for disposal of government property.[18] Failure to obtain approval, or to follow the prescribed method will be fatal to the validity of the contract. 10–005

Implied limitation. Whilst the Crown has an inherent capacity to make contracts, it has been settled, since the Revolutionary Settlement of 1688, that the Crown does not have control over public money.[19] Expenditure is controlled by Parliament; and Parliament exercises that control through the Appropriation Acts, which set out the amounts and purposes for which expenditure is authorised.[20] This fundamental constitutional principle may affect a contracting party's ability to recover payment under a contract with the Crown: if no appropriation covers the payment, no money can be paid over to the claimant. Thus, in *R. v Churchward*,[21] where the relevant parliamentary appropriation expressly excluded any payment being made to the claimant,[22] no payment was recoverable. On the facts of the case payment had only been promised "out of moneys 10–006

[11] Wade and Forsyth, *Administrative Law*, 9th edn (2004), Ch.21; Street, *Governmental Liability* (1953), Ch.III.

[12] Turpin, *Government Contracts* (1972), p.19; Daintith (1979) 32 C.L.P. 41, 42; Freedland [1994] P.L. 86, 91–92; Harris (1992) 108 L.Q.R. 626, 627, (2007) 123 L.Q.R. 225; Davies (2006) 122 L.Q.R. 98, 102.

[13] Daintith (1979) 32 C.L.P. 41, 42; Freedland [1994] P.L. 86, 91–92.

[14] Harris (1992) 108 L.Q.R. 626, (2007) 123 L.Q.R. 225, 226; see also Freedland's later view that, at least in relation to the Private Finance Initiative, government does not see itself as exercising a prerogative power when making contracts: [1998] P.L. 288, 292–294.

[15] Turpin, *Government Contracts* (1972), p.19; Daintith (1979) 32 C.L.P. 41, 44–45.

[16] *New South Wales v Bardolph* (1934) 52 C.L.R. 455, 496, per Rich J.

[17] *Commercial Cable Co v Government of Newfoundland* [1916] 2 A.C. 610.

[18] *Cugden Rutile (No 2) Pty Ltd v Chalk* [1975] A.C. 520.

[19] Bill of Rights 1688 art.4.

[20] e.g. Appropriation Act 2007.

[21] (1865) L.R. 1 Q.B. 173.

[22] *R. v Churchward* (1865) L.R. 1 Q.B. 173, 183.

to be provided by parliament", but Shee J. went on to say that, if this condition had not been expressed, such a condition:

> "... must on account of the notorious inability of the crown to contract unconditionally for such money payments in consideration of such services, have been implied in favour of the crown."[23]

Two of the other three judges did not deal with the point, and Cockburn C.J. indicated that he would not have implied such a condition precedent to payment. *Churchward*'s case is, therefore, in itself, ambiguous in relation to the implied condition advanced by Shee J.[24] But, in a series of later judgments Viscount Haldane emphasised the importance of legislative control over expenditure,[25] culminating in his speech in the House of Lords in *Att-Gen v Great Southern and Western Railway Co of Ireland*.[26] There, in a speech with which Lords Dunedin and Carson agreed, he emphatically endorsed the analysis of Shee J. in *Churchward*'s case, saying that:

> "However clear it may be that before the Revolutionary Settlement the Crown could be taken to contract personally, it is equally clear that since that Settlement its ordinary contracts only mean that it will pay out of funds which Parliament may or may not supply."[27]

It is, therefore, clear, that whilst the absence of a Parliamentary appropriation will not make a contract void, such an appropriation is a condition precedent of liability to pay.[28] The appropriation need not refer specifically to the particular contract—general terms suffice.[29]

(b) *Fettering of Discretion*

10–007 **Construction of Crown's obligations so as to avoid fettering.** Virtually every contractual promise restricts a promisor's future freedom of action. Under ordinary circumstances there is no policy objection to this, but where the promisor is the Crown, such restrictions have the potential to inhibit the Crown in its performance of duties or exercise of powers in the public interest. In order to avert this undesirable consequence, the courts avoid interpreting the Crown's

---

[23] *R. v Churchward* (1865) L.R. 1 Q.B. 173, 209.

[24] Sawer (1946) 62 L.Q.R. 23, 24; Street (1948) 11 M.L.R. 129, 131; Williams, *Crown Proceedings* (1948), p.10; Street (1949–1950) 8 *University of Toronto Law Journal* 32, 33–34; Street, *Governmental Liability* (1953), pp.85–87.

[25] *Commercial Cable Co v Government of Newfoundland* [1916] 2 A.C. 610; *Mackay v Att-Gen for British Columbia* [1922] 1 A.C. 457; *Auckland Harbour Board v The King* [1924] A.C. 318.

[26] [1925] A.C. 754.

[27] *Att-Gen v Great Southern and Western Railway Co of Ireland* [1925] A.C. 754, 773.

[28] See also *New South Wales v Bardolph* (1934) 52 C.L.R. 455. The judgment of Dixon J. contains a particularly helpful exposition of Viscount Haldane's views (see especially at 514). McTiernan J. described Shee J. in *Churchward* as stating: "the effect on the contract of [the Crown's] incapacity ... the exigency of binding constitutional practice fashions the promise of the Crown into a promise to pay out of moneys lawfully available under parliamentary appropriation."

[29] *New South Wales v Bardolph* (1934) 52 C.L.R. 455, 467–474, per Evatt J.; Street, *Governmental Liability* (1953), p.90, commenting that the opposite rule would be "disastrous"; Harris (2007) 123 L.Q.R. 225, 229.

contractual promises in way that would constrain the performance of its functions. Thus, in *Commissioners of Crown Lands v Page*[30] a tenant of Crown premises sought to have a covenant for quiet enjoyment implied into the lease; this covenant was breached, the tenant alleged, when the premises were requisitioned by the Minister of Works, acting under statutory powers. The Court of Appeal unanimously held that any implied term would not extend "to prevent the future exercise by the Crown of powers and duties imposed upon it in its executive capacity by statute".[31] Devlin L.J. held that, even if the covenant for quiet enjoyment had been express, he would have read it as, by necessary implication, excluding "those measures affecting the nation as a whole which the Crown takes for the public good".[32] It should be emphasised, however, that *Page*'s case does not support the proposition that the Crown is free to disregard its own contractual obligations with impunity. On the contrary, it was crucial that, on the facts, the Crown was exercising statutory powers in pursuance of the public interest. The Crown is subject to the general rule that a contracting party should neither disable himself from performance, nor prevent the other party from performing the contractual obligations[33]; but where performance has been disrupted by the passage of legislation, or the performance of some executive function, the disruption is not regarded as being a case of self-disablement or prevention by the Crown. Instead, the contract is seen as frustrated[34]; the fact that the frustrating event emanated from the Crown is regarded as irrelevant.[35]

Express terms fettering the Crown's discretion. Where an express term, properly construed, commits the Crown to exercising its executive functions in a particular way, the position is more controversial. In *R. v Rederiaktiebolaget Amphitrite*[36] the claimant steamship company had sent its vessel, during the First World War, to a British port. It had done so only after being given a guarantee by the Crown that the vessel would not be detained. The vessel was detained by the Crown, and the claimants sought damages for breach of contract. Rowlatt J. held that no damages were recoverable. He held that whilst the Crown was bound by commercial contracts it made, the facts of the case did not show such a contract. Rather, it was "an arrangement whereby the Government purported to give an assurance as to what its executive action would be in the future".[37] This arrangement was not contractually enforceable because: 10–008

> " . . . it is not competent for the Government to fetter its future executive action, which must necessarily be determined by the needs of the community when the question arises. It cannot by contract hamper its freedom of action in matters which concern the welfare of the State."[38]

---

[30] [1960] 2 Q.B. 274.
[31] *Commissioners of Crown Lands v Page* [1960] 2 Q.B. 274, 287.
[32] *Commissioners of Crown Lands v Page* [1960] 2 Q.B. 274, 292.
[33] *Board of Trade v Temperley S.S. Co Ltd* (1926) 26 Ll.L. Rep. 76; (1927) 27 Ll.L. Rep. 230.
[34] *Reilly v The King* [1934] A.C. 176.
[35] *William Cory & Son Ltd v London Corp* [1951] 2 K.B. 476, 487, per Harman L.J.
[36] [1921] 3 K.B. 500.
[37] *R. v Rederiaktiebolaget Amphitrite* [1921] 3 K.B. 500, 503.
[38] *R. v Rederiaktiebolaget Amphitrite* [1921] 3 K.B. 500, 503.

A similar principle was invoked by the House of Lords in *Nixon v Att-Gen*, where it was held that the Treasury Commissioners could not validly bind themselves as to how they would exercise discretionary powers relating to Civil servants' future superannuation payments.[39] But, whilst the decision in *The Amphitrite* has never been overruled, it has been treated subsequently with caution: for instance, in *Commissioners of Crown Lands v Page*[40] the Court of Appeal refused the opportunity to endorse it.[41] In *Robertson v Minister of Pensions*[42] Denning J. suggested that the broad principle from the *Amphitrite* case was a dictum, the ratio of the decision being that the statement of the Crown was not binding, since there was no intention to create legal relations.[43] It is true that Rowlatt J. said that the Crown's guarantee was "merely an expression of intention",[44] but he continued, in the next sentence, to explain that his "main reason" for reaching that conclusion was that the government could not validly fetter its future executive action. It is therefore submitted that Denning J.'s reading of the *Amphitrite* case is unconvincing.[45] Denning J. also suggested that the defence of executive necessity was based on an implied term. But this is directly contrary to the facts of the *Amphitrite* case, where the defence succeeded despite an express undertaking to exercise powers in a particular way: no term relating to executive necessity could have been implied, since it would have contradicted the express terms. Commentators have drawn attention to the lack of authority cited in *The Amphitrite*, and argued that the case should not be followed.[46] However, it is submitted that whilst the language used in the *Amphitrite* case was perhaps too broad,[47] its main support, and the best guide to interpreting its scope, is the analogous rule that statutory bodies have no power to fetter their own discretion.[48] Of course, the Crown's source of power is non-statutory,[49] but such reasoning by analogy was expressly endorsed by Devlin L.J. in *Commissioners of Crown Lands v Page*,[50] and would allow the important policy justifications underlying the non-fettering rule to be applied to the Crown.[51]

---

[39] *Nixon v Att-Gen* [1931] A.C. 184, 193: "If you find that the statutes give the Lords of the Treasury a discretion, that is their power, and their only power, and they cannot possibly by contract take themselves out of it."

[40] [1960] 2 Q.B. 274.

[41] See especially *Commissioners of Crown Lands v Page* [1960] 2 Q.B. 274, 293, per Devlin L.J. (no need to consider whether the Crown could fetter its future executive action by express words, since it was "most unlikely" ever to attempt to do so).

[42] [1949] 1 K.B. 227.

[43] *Robertson v Minister of Pensions* [1949] 1 K.B. 227, 231.

[44] *Amphitrite* case [1921] 3 K.B. 500, 503.

[45] Turpin, *Government Contracts* (1972), pp.21–22.

[46] Holdsworth (1929) 45 L.Q.R. 162, 166; Street (1948) 11 M.L.R. 129, 131; Williams, *Crown Proceedings* (1948), pp.9–10.

[47] *A v Hayden (No.2)* (1984) 59 A.L.J.R. 6, 8: "The suggestion made by Rowlatt J. in [*The Amphitrite*] that the government cannot by contract fetter its executive action in matters which concern the welfare of the State is too wide" (per Gibbs C.J.).

[48] J. Mitchell, *The Contracts of Public Authorities* (1954), p.57; Street, *Governmental Liability* (1953), pp.98–99; Turpin, *Government Contracts* (1972), p.22. For detailed analysis of the rule in its application to statutory bodies, see below, paras 10–027—10–031.

[49] See above, para.10–004.

[50] [1960] 2 Q.B. 274, 292. See also Harris (1992) 108 L.Q.R. 626, 644 (commenting on the courts' playing down the importance of the source of authority in judicial review cases).

[51] Davies (2006) 122 L.Q.R. 98, especially 104–105.

(c) *Agency*

10–009 **Agency in general.** Contracts made by Crown servants in the course of their service, or by Crown agents within the scope of their authority bind the Crown. The right to contract on behalf of the Crown must be established by reference to statute or otherwise; merely being a Crown servant is not enough.[52]

10–010 **Whether servant or agent of the Crown.** Since Crown contracts are subject to certain special rules, both substantive[53] and procedural,[54] it may be crucial to determine whether the contracting party has entered the contract as a servant or agent of the Crown. The starting point is the list of "authorised departments" published under Crown Proceedings Act 1947 s.17. These departments may institute "civil proceedings by the Crown",[55] and may be sued in "civil proceedings against the Crown"[56]; it can therefore be assumed that they are Crown servants or agents.[57] However, the list is not exhaustive. For contracting parties not on the list a common law test must be applied which balances a range of factors. The main factor to consider is the degree of control which the Crown is entitled to exercise over the party who is alleged to have made the contract on its behalf.[58] If that party has wide powers which can be exercised independently of the Crown, that will strongly suggest that the contracting party is not a Crown servant.[59] Conversely, if the Crown has the right to exercise a close degree of control, that will suggest that the contracting party is a Crown servant or agent. It should emphasised that, in ascertaining the degree of control, the statutory provisions setting out the contracting party's rights and duties are "highly important"[60]; whether, as a matter of fact, the Crown exerted its right of control is irrelevant.[61] It also seems that the statutory definition of rights and duties prevails over other statutory indications. Thus, in *Hills (Patents) Ltd v University College Hospital Board of Governors*[62] the question was whether the defendants occupied hospital premises as agents for the Minister of Health. Despite the statement in the National Health Service Act 1946 s.13 that hospital boards managed hospitals "on behalf of" the Minister, it was held that the Board's statutory duties to manage, control and maintain the hospital, and appoint its staff, meant that the board occupied as a principal, not as the Minister's agent. A second factor to consider is whether the contracting party is performing a

---

52 *Att-Gen for Ceylon v Silva* [1953] A.C. 461.

53 See above, 10–005—10–008.

54 Particularly under the Crown Proceedings Act 1947. For further discussion see below, paras 10–015—10–019.

55 Crown Proceedings Act 1947 s.17(2).

56 Crown Proceedings Act 1947 s.17(3).

57 Griffith (1951–1952) 9 *University of Toronto Law Journal* 169, 169; Treitel [1957] P.L. 321, 328.

58 *Bank voor Handel en Scheepvaart NV v Administrator of Hungarian Property* [1954] A.C. 584; Treitel [1957] P.L. 321, 327 (describing this criterion as "entitled, if not to exclusive recognition, at any rate to pre-eminence").

59 *Metropolitan Meat Industry Board v Sheedy* [1927] A.C. 899.

60 *Bank voor Handel en Scheepvaart NV v Administrator of Hungarian Property* [1954] A.C. 584, 616, per Lord Reid.

61 [1954] A.C. 584, 617.

62 [1956] 1 Q.B. 90.

function linked to an existing Crown prerogative. Thus, for instance, in *Bank voor Handel en Scheepvaart NV v Administrator of Hungarian Property*[63] both Lord Tucker and Lord Asquith were influenced in their decision that the Custodian of Hungarian Property was a Crown servant by the fact that his functions were linked to the Crown prerogative to wage war.[64] Similarly, in *Gilbert v The Corp of Trinity House*[65] it was held that the defendants' remoteness from the scope of the Crown's prerogative powers indicated that they were not Crown servants. It is submitted that the relationship between the contracting party's functions and the Crown's prerogative powers deserves only little weight. As has been powerfully pointed out, to emphasise the importance of the prerogative powers is, in effect, to confine the sphere of potential Crown servants to activities which, historically, were seen as the Crown's responsibility: it freezes the law in a condition which will inevitably fail to reflect contemporary understandings of the Crown's role.[66] Other relevant factors suggesting that a party is not a Crown servant are financial independence,[67] liability of property to be levied,[68] and incorporation.[69]

10–011 **Unauthorised contracts.** Where a Crown servant or agent enters a contract outside the scope of his actual authority, it will not bind the Crown unless the agent's authority can be established on some other basis. Although Lord Denning put forward the view that all contracts should bind the Crown where government officers or departments took it upon themselves to assume authority,[70] that view was rejected by dicta in the House of Lords,[71] and criticised persuasively in the literature.[72] The better view, it is submitted, is that the general principles of the law of agency apply to the Crown—in particular, that a contract will bind the Crown if the agent had either ostensible or usual authority to make it. Although ostensible authority is a form of estoppel,[73] it is treated as an exception to the

---

[63] [1954] A.C. 584.

[64] *Bank voor Handel en Scheepvaart NV v Administrator of Hungarian Property* [1954] A.C. 584, 628, per Lord Tucker 632, per Lord Asquith. See also *BBC v Johns (Inspector of Taxes)* [1965] 1 Ch. 32 (broadcasting outside province of government).

[65] (1886) 17 QBD 795. The test of whether the body in question is an "emanation" of the Crown, used in this case, has subsequently been disapproved: *Tamlin v Hannaford* [1950] 1 K.B. 18; *BBC v Johns (Inspector of Taxes)* [1965] 1 Ch. 32.

[66] Friedmann (1948) 22 A.L.J. 7; Friedmann (1950) 24 A.L.J. 275; Griffith (1951–1952) 9 *University of Toronto Law Journal* 169.

[67] *Metropolitan Meat Industry Board v Sheedy* [1927] A.C. 899.

[68] *Tamlin v Hannaford* [1950] 1 K.B. 18. Crown property cannot be levied: Crown Proceedings Act 1947 s.25(4).

[69] *Tamlin v Hannaford* [1950] 1 K.B. 18; *Hills (Patents) Ltd v University College Hospital Board of Governors* [1956] 1 Q.B. 90; cf. *Metropolitan Meat Industry Board v Sheedy* [1927] A.C. 899, 905: "[t]hat they were not incorporated does not matter". For a powerful argument that incorporation should be decisive against being a Crown servant or agent see Friedmann (1948) 22 A.L.J. 7; (1950) 24 A.L.J. 275.

[70] *Robertson v Minister of Pensions* [1949] 1 K.B. 227; *Falmouth Boat Construction Co Ltd v Howell* [1950] 2 K.B. 16.

[71] *Howell v Falmouth Boat Construction Co Ltd* [1951] A.C. 837.

[72] Treitel [1957] P.L. 321, 335–337.

[73] *Marubeni Hong Kong and South China Ltd v Government of Mongolia* [2004] EWHC 472 (Comm), [2004] 2 Lloyd's Rep. 198 at [124].

general principle that estoppel cannot be relied upon to rehabilitate a transaction entered in excess of powers.[74]

Ostensible authority. In order to establish ostensible authority it must be shown that the principal held out the agent as having authority; a representation by the agent as to the extent of his own authority is insufficient. In *Att-Gen for Ceylon v Silva*[75] the Privy Council indicated that the requirement of a representation by the principal limited the potential application of ostensible authority to the Crown: 10–012

> "No public officer, unless he possesses some special power, can hold out on behalf of the Crown that he or some other public officer has the right to enter into a contract in respect of the Crown when in fact no such right exists."[76]

Such a special power will be rare, although not impossible to find.[77] Alternatively, it might be shown that the agent had usual authority. For usual authority, no representation by the principal is necessary,[78] although the status of usual authority as a separate category is not uncontroversial.[79] In any case, it is submitted that any recognition that contracts outside an agent's actual authority bind the Crown should be made selectively. In particular, where the agent's authority is defined by statute, there is much force in the Privy Council's comment that to hold the Crown bound would be undesirable, because it would, in effect, be:

> "... to hold that public officers had dispensing powers because they then could by unauthorized acts nullify or extend the provisions of the [statute]."[80]

Furthermore, where the agent's actual authority is set out in statute, it is open to the other contracting party to ascertain the scope of that authority for himself; in these circumstances it is, therefore, justifiable not to enforce a contract made in excess of authority.[81]

---

[74] For the general principle see below, para.10–040.

[75] [1953] A.C. 461.

[76] *Att-Gen for Ceylon v Silva* [1953] A.C. 461, 479.

[77] Treitel [1957] P.L. 321, 338 fn.4 suggests that it might exist where the holding out was done by the "directing mind" of the relevant government department. cf. Turpin, *Government Contracts* (1972), p.35, where it is suggested that the "special power" would exist wherever an officer had actual authority to do the act that he was holding out the agent as having authority to do. In *Marubeni Hong Kong and South China Ltd v Government of Mongolia* [2004] EWHC 472 (Comm), [2004] 2 Lloyd's Rep. 198 it was held that the Mongolian Ministry of Justice had such a power in respect of the Minister of Finance's authority to sign a guarantee. (This aspect of the decision was not challenged on appeal: [2005] EWCA Civ 395, [2005] 1 W.L.R. 2497 at [6]).

[78] *Watteau v Fenwick* [1893] 1 Q.B. 346; Treitel [1957] P.L. 321, 336.

[79] See below, para.31–065, describing the cases as "extremely doubtful".

[80] *Att-Gen for Ceylon v Silva* [1953] A.C. 461, 481. See also *Bowstead and Reynolds on Agency*, 18th edn (2006), para.8–044; the same paragraph from the previous edn was quoted with approval in *Marubeni Hong Kong and South China Ltd v Government of Mongolia* [2004] EWHC 472 (Comm), [2004] 2 Lloyd's Rep. 198 at [124].

[81] Turpin, *Government Contracts* (1972), p.35.

10–013 **Personal liability of agents.** Where a Crown servant or agent has entered a contract as agent, he cannot be held liable for a breach of that contract.[82] Nor will a declaration be issued against him.[83] Only if it is found that he contracted personally, on his own behalf, will he be made liable.[84] This rule accords with the general position in the law of agency,[85] but the courts have also consistently made it clear that they are very reluctant to conclude that an individual Crown agent has contracted personally. The concern is that exposure to personal liability:

> "... would, in all probability, prevent any proper and prudent person from accepting a public situation at the hazard of such peril to himself."[86]

Thus, for instance, in *Dunn v Macdonald*[87] Lopes L.J. contrasted the position of public and ordinary agents, saying that for the former to be personally liable, "something special which would be evidence of an intention to be personally liable"[88] was needed. Similarly, in *Graham v His Majesty's Commissioners of Public Works and Buildings*[89] Ridley J. stated that even where an agent had:

> "... put his own name in the contract without saying that he was agent for the Crown, yet, if you could gather from the surrounding circumstances of the case that he did in fact contract as agent for the Crown, and in that capacity only, he would not be liable upon the contract."[90]

There is no reported instance in the last two hundred years of an individual Crown agent being held personally liable.[91] Where the agent is incorporated, on the other hand, the concern about exposing individuals to personal liability has no application, and the courts have been willing to find that the agent in fact contracted on its own behalf.[92]

---

[82] *Macbeath v Haldimand* (1786) 1 T.R. 172; *Unwin v Wolseley* (1787) 1 T.R. 674; *Rice v Chute* (1801) 1 East 579; *Palmer v Hutchinson* (1881) 6 App. Cas. 619.

[83] *Hosier Brothers v Earl of Derby* [1918] 2 K.B. 671.

[84] *Macbeath v Haldimand* (1786) 1 T.R. 172; *Prosser v Allen* (1819) Gow. 117; *Gidley v Lord Palmerston* (1822) 3 B. & B. 275; *Dunn v Macdonald* [1897] 1 Q.B. 555; *Commercial Cable Co v Government of Newfoundland* [1916] 2 A.C. 610.

[85] See below, para.31–084.

[86] *Gidley v Lord Palmerston* (1822) 3 B. & B. 275, 286, per Dallas C.J. See also *Macbeath v Haldimand* (1786) 1 T.R. 172, 181–182, per Ashhurst J.; *Unwin v Wolseley* (1787) 1 T.R. 674, 678, per Ashhurst J.

[87] [1897] 1 Q.B. 555.

[88] *Dunn v Macdonald* [1897] 1 Q.B. 555, 557.

[89] [1901] 2 K.B. 781.

[90] *Graham v His Majesty's Commissoners of Public Works and Buildings* [1901] 2 K.B. 781, 788. cf. *Auty v Hutchinson* (1848) 6 C.B. 266.

[91] cf. *Rice v Everitt* (1801) 1 East 583n, which turned on its own unusual facts. In *Samuel Bros, Ltd v Whetherly* [1907] 1 K.B. 709, [1908] 1 K.B. 104 the personal liability of the commanding officer of a volunteer corps was imposed under statutory regulations (Regulations for the Volunteer Force 1901 reg.407).

[92] e.g. *Graham v His Majesty's Commissioners of Public Works and Buildings* [1901] 2 K.B. 781 (Ridley J.); *International Railway Co v Niagara Parks Commission* [1941] A.C. 328.

Warranty of authority. Individual Crown agents cannot be sued for a breach of warranty of authority.[93] This departure from the general rules of agency[94] is justified by the same concern about exposure to personal liability which informs the courts' approach to the personal liability of Crown agents on contracts.[95] It is submitted that, as with the approach to personal liability under the contract, the concern about exposure to personal liability can have no application to incorporated servants or agents; and that, therefore, a breach of warranty of authority by such an incorporated servant or agent should be actionable. 10–014

(d) *Crown Proceedings Act 1947*

Purpose of the Act. Before 1947 the Crown could not be sued on its contracts by bringing an ordinary action for breach of contract or debt. Litigants had to use the petition of right procedure, as amended by the Petitions of Right Act 1860. This procedure, even as amended, was "antiquated and cumbersome",[96] and it came to be seen as an anachronistic defect in the law. Section 1 of the Crown Proceedings Act 1947 abolished the need to bring a petition of right to enforce a contractual claim in most cases. It provided that: 10–015

> "Where any person has a claim against the Crown after the commencement of this Act, and, if this Act had not been passed, the claim might have been enforced, subject to the grant of His Majesty's fiat, by petition of right, or might have been enforced by a proceeding provided by any statutory provision repealed by this Act, then, subject to the provisions of this Act, the claim may be enforced as of right, and without the fiat of His Majesty, by proceedings taken against the Crown for that purpose in accordance with the provisions of this Act."

The Act also repealed the Petitions of Right Act 1860.[97] However, it did not entirely remove a role for the petition of right. The Act has no application to proceedings "by or against . . . his Majesty in His private capacity"[98]; nor does it apply to proceedings:

> " . . . against the Crown . . . in respect of any alleged liability of the Crown arising otherwise than in respect of his Majesty's Government in the United Kingdom."[99]

Contractual liability coming under either of these heads can only be enforced using the petition of right procedure. And, since the 1947 Act repealed the Petitions of Right Act 1860 for all purposes, the petition must be in its pre-1860

[93] *Dunn v Macdonald* [1897] 1 Q.B. 401, 555; *The Prometheus* (1949) 82 Ll.L. Rep. 859. For criticism of *Dunn v Macdonald*, and suggestions that the decision is best explained on other grounds see Williams, *Crown Proceedings* (1948), p.3; Street, *Governmental Liability* (1953), p.93.

[94] See below, para.31–101—31–108.

[95] See previous paragraph.

[96] *Davidson v Scottish Ministers* [2005] UKHL 74, 2006 S.C.(H.L.) 41 at [8].

[97] Crown Proceedings Act 1947 s.39 and Sch.2. Both s.39 and Sch.2 were themselves repealed by Statute Law Revision Act 1950 s.1, but that did not have the effect of reinstating the provisions that had been repealed by the 1947 Act (see proviso to Statute Law Revision Act 1950 s.1).

[98] Crown Proceedings Act 1947 s.40(1).

[99] Crown Proceedings Act 1947 s.40(2)(b). The certificate of a Secretary of State to this effect is conclusive: s.40(3); *Trawnik v Lennox* [1985] 1 W.L.R. 532.

form.[100] This "most peculiar thing",[101] as Glanville Williams described it, was, apparently, intended.[102]

10–016 **Remedies against the Crown.** The Crown Proceedings Act 1947 introduced new rules relating to the availability of remedies. Section 21(1) provided as follows:

> "In any civil proceedings by or against the Crown the court shall, subject to the provisions of this Act, have power to make all such orders as it has power to make in proceedings between subjects, and otherwise to give such appropriate relief as the case may require:
> Provided that—
>
> (a) where in any proceedings against the Crown any such relief is sought as might in proceedings between subjects be granted by way of injunction or specific performance, the court shall not grant an injunction or make an order for specific performance, but may in lieu thereof make an order declaratory of the rights of the parties; and
> (b) in any proceedings against the Crown for the recovery of land or other property the court shall not make an order for the recovery of the land or the delivery of the property, but may in lieu thereof make an order declaring that the plaintiff is entitled as against the Crown to the land or property or to the possession thereof."

By removing the possibility of an injunction or an order for specific performance the subsection reduced the rights enjoyed by claimants. Before 1947 various government departments had been subject to awards of specific performance or injunctions in relation to contractual performance,[103] with courts commenting that the defendant's status did not call for any special treatment.[104] The same approach could be seen where statutes expressly provided that, in relation to Crown contracts, certain ministers could "sue and be sued"[105]; and there was also support for the idea that the mere fact of incorporation indicated that a department could be sued in the ordinary way.[106] The 1947 Act repealed those statutory provisions stating that departments could sue and be sued, but that left

---

[100] *Franklin v Att-Gen* [1974] 1 Q.B. 185; Street (1948) 11 M.L.R. 129, 132–133.

[101] Williams, *Crown Proceedings* (1948), p.8.

[102] Williams, *Crown Proceedings* (1948), p.8, fn.24, states that the situation "was pointed out to those responsible for the measure when it was a Bill before Parliament". It was, in fact, Williams himself who had done so, writing a letter to Lord Chorley which Chorley forwarded to the Lord Chancellor (Jacob [1992] P.L. 452, 481–482).

[103] *Rankin v Huskisson* (1830) 4 Sim. 13 (injunction against Commissioners of Woods and Forests); *Thorn v Commissioners of Her Majesty's Works and Public Buildings* (1863) 32 Beav. 490; *Corbett v The Commissioners of Her Majesty's Works and Public Buildings* (1868) 18 L.T. 548.

[104] See, for instance, *Thorn v Commissioners of Her Majesty's Works and Public Buildings* (1863) 32 Beav. 490, 493: "a public Government board cannot be treated in any different manner from that in which a private individual would be dealt with".

[105] Williams, *Crown Proceedings* (1948) 4. e.g. *Minister of Supply v British Thomson-Houston Co Ltd* [1943] 1 K.B. 478.

[106] *Graham v His Majesty's Commissioners of Public Works and Buildings* [1901] 2 K.B. 781, per Phillimore J.; *Roper v The Commissioners of his Majesty's Public Works and Buildings* [1915] 1 K.B. 45.

open the question whether incorporated departments could still be sued in the ordinary way, thereby circumventing the limitation on remedies contained in s.21(1). Commentators disagreed,[107] and the point has never been settled.[108] It is submitted, however, that the repeal of the statutory provisions expressly authorising departments to be sued showed a legislative intention that s.21(1) should be definitive. Furthermore, it would be undesirable as a matter of policy to allow the statutory definition of the position in s.21(1) to be undermined where the government department happened to be incorporated: there is no convincing reason to make such departments subject to more extensive remedies than those which are not incorporated.

Interim remedies. Where parties have applied for interim relief against the Crown, the language of s.21(1) has proved difficult to apply. Although parts of the subsection seem to confer a broad discretion (for instance, "power . . . to give such appropriate relief as the case may require"), it has been held that since a declaration is, in its nature, final, no interim declaration can be made against the Crown.[109] Whatever the merits of that analysis,[110] it is submitted that it has now been superseded by the Civil Procedure Rules, which expressly provide for interim declarations to be granted.[111] Since interim declarations are now available in "proceedings between subjects" they must also be available in proceedings against the Crown. 10–017

Specific remedies against Crown servants. Where a contract has been made by a Crown servant in the course of service or by a Crown agent acting within his authority, the servant or agent is not personally liable on the contract.[112] Hence, the question of specific remedies against such a servant or agent shall not arise. However, a contracting party might seek to prevent a breach of contract by the Crown by bringing proceedings in tort against the servant or agent responsible for the contractual performance. For instance, it might be alleged that the servant or agent's threatened acts will amount to the tort of inducing breach of contract by the Crown.[113] In such a situation Crown Proceedings Act s.21(2) would become relevant. That subsection states that: 10–018

> "The court shall not in any civil proceedings grant any injunction or make any order against an officer of the Crown if the effect of granting the injunction or making the order would be to give any relief against the Crown which could not have been obtained in proceedings against the Crown."

[107] Street (1948) 11 M.L.R. 129, 132; Williams, *Crown Proceedings* (1948), p.6; Street, *Governmental Liability* (1953), p.94.

[108] Wade and Forsyth, *Administrative Law*, 9th edn (2004), p.827, fn.79 that "in practice the procedure of the Act of 1947 is always used".

[109] *Underhill v Ministry of Food* [1950] 1 All E.R. 591; *International General Electric Co of New York Ltd v Commissioners of Customs and Excise* [1962] 1 Ch. 784.

[110] For criticism see Wade (1991) 107 L.Q.R. 4, 8.

[111] CPR r.25.1.

[112] See above, para.10–013.

[113] See generally, Oliphant (ed.), *The Law of Tort*, 2nd edn (2007), Ch.29.

The subsection has been described as "somewhat obscure"[114] and "of Delphic opaqueness".[115] One obscurity concerns its scope. Its language refers only to proceedings against an "officer" of the Crown. The Crown Proceedings Act states that:

> "'Officer' in relation to the Crown, includes any servant of His Majesty, and accordingly (but without prejudice to the generality of the foregoing provision) includes a Minister of the Crown and a member of the Scottish Executive."[116]

The language of the statutory definition is inclusive, rather than limiting, but it was said in *British Medical Association v Greater Glasgow Health Board*[117] that a hospital board admitted to be exercising functions on behalf of the Minister of Health[118] could not have been argued to be an officer of the Crown for the purposes of s.21(2).[119] No reasons were given for this assertion, and it is respectfully submitted that it is difficult to support: a legal person is perfectly capable of being a servant or agent of the Crown,[120] and nothing in the Crown Proceedings Act definition of "officer" indicates that a narrow approach is needed. Furthermore, the effectiveness of s.21(2) would be seriously undermined if it only prevented the circumvention of s.21(1) in relation to actions against a limited class of representatives of the Crown. It is therefore submitted that the assertion was mistaken, and that the decision of the House of Lords can be supported only on the ground that the special legislation creating hospital boards expressly provided for those boards to be liable as principals.[121]

10–019 **Injunctions against Crown servants.** A second obscurity in s.21(2) relates to its effect. The immediate aim of the sub-section may simply have been to reverse two earlier authorities, which had been doubted by commentators.[122] But the more difficult question is whether it, in effect, prevents any injunction being granted against a Crown servant in respect of activities in the course of service. In *M v Home Office*[123] it was held that s.21(2) did not have that effect; rather, it only prevented injunctions from being granted against Crown servants in a representative capacity (such as being the superior of a Crown servant who had

[114] Williams, *Crown Proceedings* (1948), p.136.

[115] *Davidson v Scottish Ministers* [2005] UKHL 74, (2006) S.C.(H.L.) 41 at [8], per Lord Nicholls.

[116] Crown Proceedings Act 1947 s.38(2).

[117] [1989] 1 A.C. 1211.

[118] *British Medical Association v Greater Glasgow Health Board* [1989] 1 A.C. 1211 at 1225. Quaere whether the admission was correct: in *Hills (Patents) Ltd v University College Hospital Board of Governors* [1956] 1 Q.B. 90 it was held that, although the statute stated that the defendants carried out their functions "on behalf of" the Minister of Health, their independence from ministerial control showed that they actually occupied hospital premises as principals, not as agents of the Minister.

[119] *British Medical Association v Greater Glasgow Health Board* [1989] 1 A.C.1211, 1226.

[120] *BBC v Johns (Inspector of Taxes)* [1965] 1 Ch. 32 at 79, where Diplock L.J. comments that it "has been increasingly the tendency over the last hundred years" that Crown agents are "fictitious persons—corporations"; Williams, *Crown Proceedings* (1948), p.117.

[121] *British Medical Association v Greater Glasgow Health Board* [1989] 1 A.C. 1211, 1226–1227; National Health Service (Scotland) Act 1978 s.2(8).

[122] Street (1948) 11 M.L.R. 129, 138; Williams, *Crown Proceedings* (1948), p.136; both authors refer to *Rankin v Huskisson* (1830) 4 Sim. 13 and *Ellis v Earl Grey* (1833) 6 Sim. 214.

[123] [1994] 1 A.C. 377.

actually committed a tort). The House of Lords supported this narrow reading by reference to the position before the Crown Proceedings Act came into force: before 1947 specific remedies had been available against individual servants who had committed torts.[124] The subsection, in their view, was intended to apply only to situations where no cause of action had previously been available; as they put it:

> " . . . it is only in those situations where prior to the Act no injunctive relief could be obtained that section 21 prevents an injunction being granted."[125]

This interpretation of s.21(2), particularly the reliance on the position before 1947, has been questioned, however. In *Davidson v Scottish Ministers*,[126] without expressing a concluded view, Lord Rodger put forward the following analysis:

> "There are, however, no words in subsection (2) which refer to the position before the passing of the 1947 Act. If, as seems likely, Lord Woolf was thinking of the closing words of the subsection, I would respectfully prefer to interpret them as referring to the hypothetical situation where the claimant or pursuer has brought proceedings against the Crown rather than against an officer of the Crown. The purpose of the subsection seems to be to prevent the claimant or pursuer from circumventing the ban on an injunction, interdict or order for specific performance against the Crown in subsection (1)(a) by seeking a similar remedy against an officer of the Crown."[127]

Lord Mance shared Lord Rodger's doubts about whether s.21(2) referred to the position prior to the 1947 Act. "However", he continued:

> "even without that phrase, the purpose of subsection (2) can hardly have been to remove or preclude a right on the part of a claimant to injunctive relief against an officer of the Crown threatening to commit a tortious act against the claimant."[128]

The matter has not been settled.[129] It is submitted that, of the two competing interpretations, Lord Rodger's view is the more persuasive. It avoids a strained reading of the statutory language, and, perhaps more importantly, it recognises that the 1947 legislation responded to deep-rooted dissatisfaction with the complexity and anachronisms of the existing law by redefining the relationship between the Crown and litigants. Lord Mance's objection to Lord Rodger's interpretation is, it is submitted, not convincing. There is no inherent reason why the subsection should not have removed a right to an injunction which existed

---

[124] *Raleigh v Goschen* [1898] 1 Ch. 73; *Hutton v Secretary of State for War* (1926) 43 T.L.R. 106. Actions against such individual servants were not caught by the general pre-1947 rule that the Crown was not liable in tort, because it was said that since the Crown could do no wrong, it could never authorise the commission of a tort (see *M v Home Office* [1994] 1 A.C. 377, 410).

[125] *M v Home Office* [1994] 1 A.C. 377, 413.

[126] [2005] UKHL 74, 2006 S.C. (H.L.) 41.

[127] *Davidson v Scottish Ministers* (2006) S.C.(H.L.) 41 at [93]. See also *British Medical Association v Greater Glasgow Health Board* [1989] 1 A.C. 1211 at 1226.

[128] *Davidson v Scottish Ministers* (2006) S.C.(H.L.) 41 at [102].

[129] In *Davidson v Scottish Ministers* (2006) S.C.(H.L.) it was anticipated that the matter would be settled when their Lordships heard the then pending appeal in *Beggs v Scottish Ministers* (see e.g. per Lord Mance at [103]). However, when the appeal in *Beggs* was heard, the appellant abandoned the points he had raised in relation to s.21. See *Beggs v Scottish Ministers* [2007] UKHL 3, [2007] 1 W.L.R. 455 at [28], per Lord Rodger and [51], per Lord Mance.

prior to the Act; on the contrary, the statutory repeal of the "sue and be sued" provisions took away precisely such a right in respect of particular government departments.

3. PUBLIC AUTHORITIES

10–020 **The position in outline.** Public authorities, as the creations of statute, have the capacity to enter contracts only to the extent that their statutory powers permit. Any contract entered outside those powers (ultra vires) is void; similarly, a contractual promise outside the statutory powers is unenforceable.[130] To determine whether a contract or contractual obligation is intra vires the public authority, three tests must be satisfied. First, the contract or obligation must be within the scope of the authority's statutory powers. Second, it must not unduly fetter the authority's discretion. Third, the authority's entering into the contract or obligation must have been as a result of a proper exercise of its powers.

(a) *The Scope of Statutory Powers*

(i) *Express Powers*

10–021 **Construction of statutory language.** In ascertaining whether the contract or promise in question is within the scope of the authority's statutory powers, the statute must be construed. No special rules of construction apply[131]—the aim is to identify a "reasonable" interpretation of the words.[132] Broad powers, such as the conferment on the revenue authorities of "all necessary powers for carrying into execution every Act of Parliament relating to inland revenue"[133] may call for lengthy exposition and analysis.[134] Others, in narrower terms, will present less difficulty.[135]

10–022 **Local Government (Contracts) Act 1997 section 1(1).** One particularly important statutory power is that conferred by Local Government (Contracts) Act 1997 s.1(1), which states that:

> "Every statutory provision conferring or imposing a function on a local authority confers power on the local authority to enter into a contract with another person for the provision or making available of assets or services, or both, (whether or not together with goods) for the purposes of, or in connection with, the discharge of the function by the local authority."

---

[130] For discussion of whether the ultra vires term can be severed from the contract, leaving the remainder of the contractual terms enforceable see *Re Staines Urban DC's Agreement; Triggs v Staines Urban DC* [1969] 1 Ch. 10 and para.16–194.

[131] *Att-Gen v London CC* [1901] 1 Ch. 781, 788; *Att-Gen v Manchester Corp* [1906] 1 Ch. 643, 653.

[132] *Att-Gen v London CC* [1901] 1 Ch. 781, 788.

[133] Inland Revenue Regulation Act 1890 s.1(2).

[134] e.g. *Al Fayed v A.G. for Scotland* [2004] S.T.C. 1703; Eden [2005] B.T.R. 21. For a similarly wide power relating to local authorities see Local Government Act 2000 s.2.

[135] e.g. *Horsnell v Boston BC* [2005] EWHC 1311 QB.

It has been held that a contract of insurance would not come within the section.[135a] No definition of "function" is given in the Act. It almost certainly bears the same meaning as "function" in the Local Government Act 1972 s.111, namely, any one of the "multiplicity of specific statutory activities the [authority] is expressly or impliedly under a duty to perform or has power to perform".[136] The requirement that a contract be "for the purposes of, or in connection with the discharge" of a function is not elaborated on further in the Act, and it has not been considered in case law. However, it is submitted that the test authorises the same contracts as would be authorised under the test for implying a power to contract[137]—namely, whether such a power is reasonably incidental to the relevant statutory purpose: in both tests the focus is on the nexus between the statutory power and the contract. The "reasonably incidental" test has received extensive judicial consideration which, it is submitted, should be used to guide the application of the test set out in s.1(1) of the 1997 Act. It is also submitted that the very general terms of s.1(1) should not be taken to override specific statutory limitations on a local authority's power to contract.[138]

(ii) *Implied Powers*

General principle. The scope of statutory powers is not limited to the express language of the statute. As Lord Selborne L.C. explained in *Att-Gen v Great Eastern Railway Co*[139] the ultra vires doctrine: 10–023

> "... ought to be reasonably, and not unreasonably, understood and applied, and that whatever may fairly be regarded as incidental to, or consequential upon, those things which the Legislature has authorized, ought not (unless expressly prohibited) to be held, by judicial construction, to be *ultra vires*."[140]

Lord Blackburn, in the same case, added that:

> "... those things which are incident to, and may reasonably and properly be done under the main purpose, though they may not be literally within it, would not be prohibited."[141]

The emphasis on first identifying the main purpose, then deciding what is incidental to it, was echoed by Lord Selborne L.C. shortly afterwards[142] and remains good law. The principle of implied powers was subsequently recognised by statute[143] in the Local Government Act 1972 s.111(1):

135a *R. v Brent LBC Ex p. Risk Management Partners Ltd* [2008] EWHC 692 (Admin).

136 *Hazell v Hammersmith and Fulham LBC* [1990] 2 Q.B. 697, 722. This definition, given by the Divisional Court, was approved by the Court of Appeal ([1990] 2 Q.B. 697, 785) and the House of Lords ([1992] 2 A.C. 1, 29, per Lord Templeman, 45, per Lord Ackner).

137 See below, paras 10–023—10–026.

138 e.g. the limitations on borrowing imposed by Local Government Act 1972 Sch.13 Pt I (as interpreted in *Hazell v Hammersmith and Fulham LBC* [1992] 2 A.C. 1).

139 (1880) 5 App. Cas. 473.

140 *Att-Gen v Great Eastern Ry Co* (1880) 5 App. Cas. 473, 478.

141 *Att-Gen v Great Eastern Ry Co* (1880) 5 App. Cas. 473, 481.

142 *Small v Smith* (1884) 10 App. Cas. 119, 129.

143 *Hazell v Hammersmith and Fulham LBC* [1990] 2 Q.B. 697, 722 DC, 785 CA, [1992] 2 A.C. 1, 29; *Akumah v Hackney LBC* [2005] UKHL 17, [2005] 1 W.L.R. 985, [24].

"... subject to the provisions of this Act ... a local authority shall have power to do any thing (whether or not involving the expenditure, borrowing or lending of money or the acquisition or disposal of any property or rights) which is calculated to facilitate, or is conducive or incidental to, the discharge of any of their functions."

Where an authority claims an implied power to charge, the test is narrower: rather than a reasonable implication, the power must be shown to arise by necessary implication.[144]

10–024 **Consistency with other statutory provisions.** An incidental power will only be implied if it is consistent with the express statutory provisions. Thus, where a statutory borrowing power was limited to a set amount "but not further or otherwise", no additional borrowing power could be implied.[145] Similarly, if the statutory provisions were intended to provide an exhaustive enumeration of powers, there will be no room for a further, implied power. In *Hazell v Hammersmith and Fulham LBC*,[146] for instance, it was held that Local Government Act 1972 Sch.13 Pt 1 established "a comprehensive code which defines and limits the powers of a local authority with regard to its borrowing"[147]; it followed that no further power to borrow could be implied. The same analysis has been applied to both housing[148] and planning[149] legislation.

10–025 **Incidental or ancillary power.** Where there is room for a power to be implied, the power can only authorise activities that are incidental to, or ancillary to, the public authority's functions. It is not enough that the contract is, in itself, profitable, useful or desirable.[150] There must, in other words be "a sufficient nexus"[151] between the authority's functions and the activity sought to be carried on. Thus, for instance, it is incidental to a local authority's duty to manage its housing for it to introduce a parking scheme on one of its housing estates.[152] Similarly, printing and bookbinding work is incidental to a variety of local authority functions.[153] However, the necessary nexus would be broken if the authority undertook additional work, for a profit, beyond what was necessary for its own functions.[154] The activity would then no longer be truly subsidiary to the

---

[144] *Att-Gen v Wilts United Dairies Ltd* (1921) 37 T.L.R. 884, (1922) 38 T.L.R. 781; *McCarthy & Stone (Developments) Ltd v Richmond Upon Thames LBC* [1992] 2 A.C. 48. Quaere whether Local Government (Contracts) Act 1997 s.1(1) includes a power for authorities to charge others for the provision of services by the authority. The statutory language seems broad enough to do so.

[145] *Baroness Wenlock v River Dee Co* (1885) 10 App. Cas. 354.

[146] [1990] 2 Q.B. 697; [1992] 2 A.C. 1.

[147] *Hazell v Hammersmith and Fulham LBC* [1992] 2 A.C. 1, 33. cf. *Re Northern Ireland Human Rights Commission* [2002] UKHL 25, [2002] NI236.

[148] *Crédit Suisse v Waltham Forest LBC* [1997] Q.B. 362; *Sutton LBC v Morgan Grenfell & Co Ltd* (1996) 29 H.L.R. 608. *R. (Kilby) v Basildon DC* [2006] EWHC 1892 (Admin), [2006] H.L.R. 46 at [2]–[16]; [2007] EWCA Civ 479, [2007] H.L.R. 39, per Rix and Moses L.JJ.

[149] *Bielecki v Suffolk Coastal CC* [2004] EWHC 3142 (QB).

[150] *Att-Gen v London CC* [1901] 1 Ch. 781, 802, [1902] A.C. 165, 169; *Hazell v Hammersmith and Fulham LBC* [1992] 2 A.C. 1, 31.

[151] *Hazell v Hammersmith and Fulham LBC* [1990] 2 Q.B. 697, 723.

[152] *Akumah v Hackney LBC* [2005] UKHL 17, [2005] 1 W.L.R. 985.

[153] *Att-Gen v Smethwick Corp* [1932] Ch. 562.

[154] *Att-Gen v Smethwick Corp* [1932] Ch. 562 at 566, per Eve J., 572, per Hanworth M.R. See also *Att-Gen v Fulham Corp* [1921] 1 Ch. 440; *Deuchar v Gas Light and Coke Co* [1925] A.C. 691.

main statutory purpose; it would be a separate business.[155] Furthermore, where a statutory power permits a function to be carried on within a defined geographical area, an ancillary power to operate outside that area will be unlikely.[156] It is also unlikely that an activity will be regarded as ancillary to the statutory purpose if it is not (or cannot be) restricted to those individuals who participate in the expressly permitted activity. Thus, for instance, in *Att-Gen v London CC*[157] the authority had express statutory powers to operate three tramway services, and claimed that it had implied power to operate a bus service between the termini of the three tramway lines. However, it was held that no such implied power existed because as a matter of fact the bus service was used by the general public, and as a matter of law the bus service could not be confined to tramway passengers.[158]

Sufficient connection with statutory function. There must also be a sufficiently close connection between the express statutory function and the activity claimed to be incidental to it, such that the activity can be said directly to facilitate the performance of that function. It is not enough that the activity facilitates some intermediate function which, in turn, facilitates the statutory function.[159] For instance, in *McCarthy & Stone (Developments) Ltd v Richmond Upon Thames LBC*[160] it was held that a local authority had acted ultra vires by charging developers for consultations with its planning officers before a formal planning application was made. The authority's statutory function was solely to adjudicate on planning applications; consultations with planning officers before the submission of a formal application were incidental to the performance of that statutory function, but to charge for those consultations was incidental only to the consultations, not the adjudication. Charging was, therefore, merely "incidental to the incidental",[161] and, therefore, too far removed from the duty to determine planning applications to be implicitly authorised by it. 10–026

(b) *Fettering of Discretion*

General principle. A contract or contractual obligation which unduly fetters the public authority's performance of its statutory functions will be ultra vires. The doctrine first emerged, and has also received the most attention, in cases concerning grants of servitudes.[162] The leading case is *R. v The Inhabitants of* 10–027

[155] *Hazell v Hammersmith and Fulham LBC* [1990] 2 Q.B. 697, 723.

[156] *Att-Gen v Manchester Corp* [1906] 1 Ch. 643; *Trustees of the Harbour of Dundee v D. & J. Nicol* [1915] A.C. 550.

[157] [1901] 1 Ch. 781 [1902] A.C. 165.

[158] See, similarly *Att-Gen v Mersey Railway Co* [1907] A.C. 415, especially 418, per Lord James.

[159] *Att-Gen v Manchester Corp* [1906] 1 Ch. 643; *Hazell v Hammersmith and Fulham LBC* [1990] 2 Q.B. 697, 724.

[160] [1992] 2 A.C. 48.

[161] *McCarthy & Stone (Developments) Ltd v Richmond Upon Thames LBC* [1992] 2 A.C. 48, 75. See also *R. v Brent LBC Ex p. Risk Management Partners Ltd* [2008] EWHC 692 (Admin).

[162] *Southport District Electric Supply Co Ltd v Corp of Southport* [1926] A.C. 355, 368, per Lord Sumner.

Leake,[163] where the question was whether commissioners of drainage could have granted a public right of way over an earth bank adjacent to the drain. The Court of Exchequer held, by a majority, that the commissioners did have such power, since, on the evidence before them, the grant of a public right of way was not incompatible with the performance of their statutory duties. The compatibility test from the *Leake* case has been applied "again and again"[164] in later cases, but it should be noted that the Court of Exchequer did not consider whether, as a matter of statutory construction, the commissioners had the power, either express or implied, to grant a right of way.[165] The failure to consider that point is easily explicable: the decision in the *Leake* case predated by more than forty years the House of Lords' decisions in *Ashbury Railway Carriage and Iron Co v Riche*,[166] *Att-Gen v Great Eastern Railway Company*[167] and *Small v Smith*,[168] which were to emphasise the statutory limitations on public authorities' powers.[169] Those House of Lords cases represent the current general approach to ultra vires: it follows, therefore, that whilst the *Leake* case articulates an important general principle, it does not set out a complete test for ultra vires. However, it should be noted that even in cases decided after *Ashbury Railway Carriage and Iron Co v Riche*,[170] the courts continued to apply the principle from the *Leake* case as the exclusive test for ultra vires where the issue concerned a right of way.[171] There is some authority to support the use of the incompatibility test as the sole criterion of ultra vires in other situations,[172] but this has been doubted,[173] and it is submitted that the doubts are well-founded. A more generous approach than normal to the question of vires may be justified in the case of public rights of way by the combination of the resulting benefit to the public at large,[174] and the policy

[163] (1833) 5 B. & Ad. 469.

[164] *British Transport Commission v Westmorland CC* [1956] 2 Q.B. 214, 227. For the House of Lords consideration of this case see [1958] A.C. 126.

[165] The only observation on this question was made by Denman C.J., who commented that good roads were "extremely useful for the general purposes of the drainage, by facilitating the conveyance of persons and property" (*Leake* (1833) 5 B. & Ad. 469, 487). Quaere whether this would be sufficient to satisfy the current test to imply an ancillary power to grant a *public* right of way (see above, para.10–025).

[166] (1875) L.R. 7 H.L. 653.

[167] (1880) 5 App. Cas. 473.

[168] (1884) 10 App. Cas. 119.

[169] These three cases in particular were highlighted by Neill L.J. in *Crédit Suisse v Allerdale BC* [1997] Q.B. 306, 337. See also *Baroness Wenlock v River Dee Co* (1885) 10 App. Cas. 354.

[170] (1875) L.R. 7 H.L. 653.

[171] *Grand Junction Canal Co v Petty* (1888) 21 QBD 273 (public right of way); *An Arbitration between E. Gonty and the Manchester, Re Sheffield and Lincolnshire Ry Co* [1896] 2 Q.B. 439 (private right of way); *Great Western Ry Co v Solihull Rural DC* (1902) 86 L.T. 852 (public right of way); *South Eastern Ry Co v Cooper* [1924] 1 Ch. 211 (private right of way); *British Transport Commission v Westmorland CC* [1956] 2 Q.B. 214, [1958] A.C. 126 (public right of way). cf. *Mulliner v Midland Ry Co* (1879) 11 Ch D 611 where Jessel M.R. took a narrower approach to construing the relevant statute in relation to the creation of a private right of way.

[172] *Foster v London, Chatham and Dover Ry Co* [1894] 1 Q.B. 711.

[173] *Trustees of the Harbour of Dundee v D. & J. Nicol* [1915] A.C. 550, 570–571, where Lord Parmoor stated that *Foster* [1894] 1 Q.B. 711 should be explained in terms of an implication from the express statutory powers.

[174] *The Board of Works for the Greenwich District v Maudslay* (1870) L.R. 5 Q.B. 397, 401–402, per Cockburn C.J.

of maximising land use.[175] But, since such an approach has the potential to authorise acts which are beyond the authority's express or implied statutory powers, its use should remain exceptional.

Application of the compatibility test. The compatibility test focuses on how the contract or contractual obligation in question affects the authority's performance of its statutory functions. The impact is judged in the first instance by setting the statutory powers and duties affected alongside the contractual undertaking.[176] The contractual term may be so wide-ranging,[177] or the statutory functions affected so fundamental[178] that it is clear that the authority's discretion has been unduly fettered.[179] However, it may be (and, perhaps, is more likely to be) necessary to prove the incompatibility by evidence. Such evidence need not demonstrate an immediate conflict between contractual performance and statutory functions,[180] but, on the other hand, the mere possibility of future incompatibility is not enough. Rather, an assessment must be made of the likelihood of incompatibility and of its potential severity.[181] Thus, although the doctrine is not limited to cases of servitudes,[182] it is not surprising that servitudes have provided the context in which it has been most frequently applied: the grant of a servitude in perpetuity creates an obvious permanent restriction on the authority's freedom of action. It is not finally settled whether the assessment should be made using only knowledge available at the time the contract was made, or whether all information available at the time of trial can be used.[183] It is submitted that the use of all available knowledge is preferable: the assessment of incompatibility is not based on what the parties ought to have contemplated, but on the actual effect of the contractual obligation; a more accurate and informed assessment of that effect can be made with knowledge of events occurring after the contract was formed.[184] 10–028

Promises not to exercise powers. The more straightforward cases of incompatibility concern express undertakings not to exercise particular powers; in these cases the question is, simply, what impact that undertaking has. Thus, in *Ayr Harbour Trustees v Oswald*[185] the trustees acquired, by compulsory purchase, a 10–029

[175] *British Transport Commission v Westmorland CC* [1958] A.C. 126, 142, per Viscount Simonds.

[176] *Great Western Ry Co v Solihull Rural DC* (1902) 86 L.T. 852, 853, per Collins M.R.

[177] e.g. *Creyke v Corp of the Level of Hatfield Chase* (1896) 12 T.L.R. 383 (alleged unrestricted right to take water from a clough to warp adjoining land).

[178] e.g. *Ayr Harbour Trustees v Oswald* (1883) 8 App. Cas. 623 (authority created to develop harbour undertaking not to exercise any powers to build on certain land). See further, Lord Sumner's comments on the case in *Birkdale District Electric Supply Co Ltd v Corp of Southport* [1926] A.C. 355, 372.

[179] *British Transport Commission v Westmorland CC* [1958] A.C. 126, 155, per Lord Radcliffe.

[180] *Great Western Ry Co v Solihull Rural DC* (1902) 86 L.T. 852, 855, per Cozens-Hardy L.J.

[181] *British Transport Commission v Westmorland CC* [1958] A.C. 126, especially 144, per Viscount Simonds.

[182] *Birkdale District Electric Supply Co Ltd v Corp of Southport* [1926] A.C. 355, 372, per Lord Sumner.

[183] *British Transport Commission v Westmorland CC* [1958] A.C. 126, 145, per Viscount Simonds; cf. 152–153, per Lord Radcliffe and 160, per Lord Cohen, favouring all available knowledge.

[184] cf. Turpin, *Government Contracts* (1972), p.24.

[185] (1883) 8 App. Cas. 623.

part of the claimant's land fronting the harbour; they argued that an undertaking not to exercise any of their statutory powers to build on that land should be taken into account when assessing the compensation due to the claimant for damage to his remaining land. But the House of Lords held that the promise was ultra vires, since to enforce it would have effectively given the trustees power to repeal their own statute,[186] and prevent them or their successors from developing the harbour in future. Similarly, where a statute conferred a power on a railway company to acquire land for the building of "works . . . or other purposes", a covenant by the company not to construct works on land acquired under that power was held to be ultra vires.[187] In both of these cases, it could be said that the promise disowned core parts of the authority's powers: as was later said of the *Ayr Harbour* case, the trustees there were seeking to "renounce . . . a part of their statutory birth-right".[188] By contrast, there was held to be no fetter where an authority had acquired land for one particular statutory purpose and had covenanted not to use the land for any other purpose.[189] Furthermore, if the promise is merely in relation to the renunciation of an ancillary power, it will not be held to be incompatible with the authority's performance of its functions. Thus, in *Stourcliffe Estates Co Ltd v Corp of Bournemouth*[190] an authority acquiring land for use as a public park had undertaken not to exercise its power to construct public toilets on the land. This promise, relating only to an ancillary power, was enforceable.[191]

10–030 **Positive promises.** Where the contractual obligation in question consists of a positive promise to act, the position is more complex. Such a promise may, in effect, equate to a promise not to perform a statutory duty—as, for instance, where magistrates with a duty to preserve the St Andrews golf links purported to grant an unlimited right of way over a road alongside the golf course. The grant was held to be ultra vires, since it deprived the magistrates of their power to regulate traffic along the road.[192] Such cases can be dealt with on the same basis as express renunciations of statutory powers. Where the positive promise does not effectively renounce a power, however, but commits the authority to exercising a power in a particular way, analysis has proved more problematic. In *York Corp v Henry Leetham and Sons Ltd*[193] the authority had the power to levy tolls on river users; it agreed with the defendants that rather than charging them per use of the river, it would accept a fixed annual payment in lieu. The contract was held ultra vires. In *Birkdale District Electric Supply Co Ltd v Corp of Southport*,[194] by contrast, a promise by a statutory corporation not to charge more for electricity than was charged in the neighbouring borough for a period of five

---

[186] *Ayr Harbour Trustees v Oswald* (1883) 8 App. Cas. 623, 639–640, per Lord Watson.

[187] *Heywood's Conveyance; Re Cheshire Lines Committee v Liverpool Corp* [1938] 2 All E.R. 230. See also *Re Staines Urban DC's Agreement; Triggs v Staines Urban DC* [1969] 1 Ch. 10.

[188] *Birkdale District Electric Supply Co Ltd v Corp of Southport* [1926] A.C. 355, 372.

[189] *Earl of Leicester v Wells-next-the-Sea Urban DC* [1973] 1 Ch. 110.

[190] [1910] 2 Ch. 12.

[191] See also *Blake v Hendon Corp* [1962] 1 Q.B. 283, 303.

[192] *Paterson v Provost of St Andrews* (1881) 6 App. Cas. 833. See similarly *Att-Gen v Corp of Plymouth* (1845) 9 Beav. 67. cf. *South Eastern Railway Co v Cooper* [1924] 1 Ch. 211 (wide grant of right of way intra vires because expressly subject to grantor's by-laws).

[193] [1924] 1 Ch. 557.

[194] [1926] A.C. 355.

years was held to be intra vires. Both cases ostensibly involved a public body committing itself to a certain method of implementing its power to charge, and the differing results have proved difficult to reconcile. Suggested grounds of distinction have included that in the *York* case the authority was effectively renouncing its power to charge[195]; and that the authority in the *York* case was not profit-making. The latter point had potentially dual significance: first, there was an obligation to apply the tolls to the upkeep of the river, and the funds for that enterprise should be maximised[196]; second, the importance of commercial freedom was far less for a non-profit public body.[197] Whatever the merits of the distinction between the two cases,[198] which may be fact specific, the two decisions illustrate the difficulty of drawing a line between a valid exercise of a discretion and an invalid fettering of that discretion; they also show how policy reasons may inform where that line is ultimately drawn.

Prioritisation of powers. Where an authority's undertaking has the effect of prioritising one of its powers at the expense of another, it is not seen as automatically engaging the rule against fettering. In *R. v Hammersmith and Fulham LBC Ex p Beddowes*,[199] for instance, an authority decided to carry out its duty to manage its housing by selling off part of a large complex of flats to a developer on terms that prohibited the council from letting the remainder of the flats in the complex to short-term tenants. These terms effectively committed any future council to selling the rest of the complex to developers. The Court of Appeal held that the restrictive covenants relating to short-term tenants were intra vires since they were reasonably made in pursuit of the statutory object of managing housing. Similarly, the grant of a long-term licence under statutory powers was held not to be subject to an implied term that the licence could be terminated if the authority wanted to use the land for some other statutory purpose.[200] In both instances, the authority was seen as having made a valid choice as to which of its powers to prioritise. 10–031

(c) *Proper Exercise of Powers*

General principle. The authority's power to contract must have been exercised properly, in accordance with its public law obligations.[201] The same is true 10–032

[195] *Southport Corp v Birkdale District Electric Supply Co Ltd* [1925] Ch. 794, 820, per Warrington L.J. Such an analysis is echoed by the reasoning in *Al Fayed v A.G. for Scotland* [2004] S.T.C. 1703.

[196] *Southport Corp v Birkdale District Electric Supply Co Ltd* [1925] Ch. 794, 822–823, per Sargant L.J.; *Birkdale District Electric Supply Co Ltd v Corp of Southport* [1926] A.C. 355, 366, per Earl of Birkenhead.

[197] *William Cory & Son Ltd v London Corp* [1951] 2 K.B. 476, 485–486, per Lord Asquith.

[198] The trial judge in the *Southport* case held that the *York* case was indistinguishable: *Southport Corp v Birkdale District Electric Supply Co Ltd* [1925] Ch. 63.

[199] [1987] 1 Q.B. 1050; noted by Tromans [1987] C.L.J. 377.

[200] *Dowty Boulton Paul Ltd v Wolverhampton Corp* [1971] 1 W.L.R. 204; the authority subsequently achieved its aims by exercising its statutory planning powers: *Dowty Boulton Paul Ltd v Wolverhampton Corp (No.2)* [1976] 1 Ch. 13.

[201] *Hazell v Hammersmith and Fulham LBC* [1990] 2 Q.B. 697; *Crédit Suisse v Allerdale BC* [1995] 1 Lloyd's Rep. 315; [1997] Q.B. 306.

of any power to vary the contractual terms.[202] Thus, for instance, where an authority entered multiple complex financial transactions despite lacking officers with the training or experience to deal with such transactions, and without having taken any legal advice, it was held that the authority's actions had been irrational, and, therefore, ultra vires.[203] Similarly, where an authority guaranteed the overdraft of a company, the fact that the guarantee was given in order to evade borrowing restrictions imposed by central government was held to amount to the pursuit of an improper purpose. The guarantee was, therefore, ultra vires.[204]

(d) *Ultra Vires and Human Rights*

10–033 **Impact of human rights on ultra vires.** Where a public body makes an ultra vires agreement conferring a right to property, the intended recipient of that property right may have a remedy for breach of his human rights.[205] According to European human rights jurisprudence, an ultra vires transaction purporting to confer a property right gives rise to a legitimate expectation of receiving that right; the legitimate expectation is, in itself, a possession for the purposes of art.1 Protocol No.1.[206] The right expected to be conferred may be an interest in property,[207] or it may relate to a component of the property, such as the existence of planning permission,[208] or the absence of any public navigation right over a stretch of river.[209] What is recognised as a legitimate expectation for these purposes is not dependent on domestic law definitions or classifications.[210] Any interference with the right must be for a legitimate aim[211] and proportionate.[212] The mere fact that the public authority is reverting to its statutory mandate does

[202] *Wandsworth LBC v Winder* [1985] 1 A.C. 461.

[203] *Hazell v Hammersmith and Fulham LBC* [1990] 2 Q.B. 697, 729–730 (DC; the point was not dealt with by either the CA or the HL).

[204] *Crédit Suisse v Allerdale BC* [1995] 1 Lloyd's Rep. 315, 343–347; [1997] Q.B. 306, 333–334. See also the dissenting judgment of Kerr L.J. in *R. v Hammersmith and Fulham LBC Ex p Beddowes* [1987] 1 Q.B. 1050.

[205] art.1 Protocol No.1, European Convention for the Protection of Human Rights and Fundamental Freedoms; *Stretch v United Kingdom* (2004) 38 E.H.R.R. 12, (2003) 5 E.H.R.L.R. 554.

[206] *Pine Valley Developments Ltd v Ireland* (1991) 14 E.H.R.R. 319. cf. *Al Fayed v AG for Scotland* [2004] S.T.C. 1703 at [120], where it was conceded that a forward taxation agreement, under which the taxpayer paid a set sum per year, instead of being subject to assessment on actual transactions, created an expectation that engaged art.1. It is difficult to reconcile this concession with the requirement that there should be the expectation of a property right.

[207] *Stretch v United Kingdom* (2004) 38 E.H.R.R. 12, (2003) 5 E.H.R.L.R. 554.

[208] *Pine Valley Developments Ltd v Ireland* (1991) 14 E.H.R.R. 319.

[209] *Rowland v Environment Agency* [2003] EWCA 1885, [2004] 2 Lloyd's Rep 55.

[210] *Beyeler v Italy* (2001) 33 E.H.R.R. 1224 at [100]. cf. *Al Fayed v AG for Scotland* [2004] S.T.C. 1703 at [120], where counsel for the defender reserved the right to argue "if the case went further" that an expectation under an ultra vires agreement was a nullity and could not, therefore, give rise to a legitimate expectation. An appeal to the House of Lords was lodged on January 31, 2005, but was not pursued.

[211] e.g. *Al Fayed v AG for Scotland* [2004] S.T.C. 1703; Eden [2005] B.T.R. 21 (forward taxation agreement repudiated in order to apply the taxation system equally to all taxpayers). *Pine Valley Developments Ltd v Ireland* (1991) 14 E.H.R.R. 319 (annulment of outline planning permission in order to protect the environment). Quaere, whether the aim of ceasing to act outside statutory powers should not automatically be regarded as a legitimate aim.

[212] e.g. *Rowland v Environment Agency* [2003] EWCA 1885, [2004] 2 Lloyd's Rep 55 (reinstatement of public navigation right carried out so as to cause minimal interference to riparian owner).

not automatically satisfy the tests of justification and proportionality; some form of compensation may be required.[213] The remedy for infringement of the right to property cannot require the defendant to confer the property interest which the claimant expected.[214] If it takes the form of compensation, the European Court of Human Rights has held that the sum awarded should reflect the proportion of the initial consideration paid that can be attributed to the ultra vires element of the transaction.[215] Such an award has been said to be based on unjust enrichment[216]; as such, it transcends the usual requirement that restitution is only available for a total failure of consideration.[217]

(e) *Statutory Reform of Ultra Vires*

Local Government (Contracts) Act 1997. The Local Government (Contracts) Act 1997 introduces a new procedure of certification by local authorities.[218] If a contract is certified, it takes effect "as if the local authority had power to enter into it (and had exercised that power properly in entering into it)".[219] In other words, it will be no defence to an action on the certified contract that the authority lacked capacity to enter it. The certification requirements must be strictly observed,[220] including the time limits prescribed.[221] The Act sets out a list of matters that the certificate must contain.[222] Most importantly, the certificate must identify the power under which the local authority purports to act,[223] and it must state that the contract is within s.4(3) or s.4(4) of the Act.[224] Section 4(3) states that a contract falls within the subsection: 10–034

> "... if it is entered into with another person for the provision or making available of services (whether or not together with assets or goods) for the purposes of, or in connection with, the discharge by the local authority of any of its functions"[225]

and it operates, or is intended to operate for at least five years.[226] Contracts within s.4(4) essentially relate to the financing or insurance arrangements connected with contracts within s.4(3). It appears, therefore, that the certification process

---

[213] *Stretch v United Kingdom* (2004) 38 E.H.R.R. 12; cf. *Pine Valley Developments Ltd v Ireland* (1991) 14 E.H.R.R. 319 (inherently risky nature of property development justified awarding no compensation where claimant deprived of planning permission).

[214] *Rowland v Environment Agency* [2003] 1 Lloyd's Rep 427 at [80] (Lightman J.); expressly approved by the Court of Appeal [2003] EWCA 1885, [2004] 2 Lloyd's Rep 55 at 85 (Peter Gibson L.J.) and [140] (Mance L.J.).

[215] *Stretch v United Kingdom* (2004) 38 E.H.R.R. 12 at [47]–[50].

[216] *Rowland v Environment Agency* [2003] EWCA 1885, [2004] 2 Lloyd's Rep 55 at 88.

[217] See above, para.29–054.

[218] Defined in Local Government Contracts Act 1997 s.1(3). The new procedure also applies (with amendments) to contracts made by Welsh government authorities: The Government of Wales Act 2006 (Local Government (Contracts) Act 1997) (Modifications) Order 2007 (SI 2007/1182).

[219] Local Government (Contracts) Act s.2(1).

[220] Local Government (Contracts) Act s.2(2).

[221] Local Government (Contracts) Act s.2(3) and s.2(5).

[222] Local Government (Contracts) Act s.3.

[223] Local Government (Contracts) Act s.3(2)(d).

[224] Local Government (Contracts) Act s.3(2)(c).

[225] Local Government (Contracts) Act s.4(3)(a).

[226] Local Government (Contracts) Act s.4(3)(b).

applies only to contracts for the provision of services for five years or more, and contracts ancillary to those contracts, although once a certificate has been issued, it cannot be invalidated "by reason that anything in the certificate is inaccurate or untrue".[227] It should be noted, however, that certification has no effect on either judicial review or audit review[228]: a certified contract may still be held to be of no effect under either of these procedures.[229]

4. Tender Process Contracts

10–035 **The nature of tender process contracts.** Where a party initiates a process of competitive tendering and tenders are submitted, a contract may come into existence between the party and the tenderers that governs the manner in which the competition will be conducted. Thus, in *Blackpool and Fylde Aero Club Ltd v Blackpool BC*[230] the council formally invited six parties to tender for a concession to operate pleasure flights from the local airport. The invitation to tender specified, amongst other things, the deadline for receipt of tenders and also stated that no late tenders would be considered. The claimants submitted a tender before the deadline, but as a result of a careless failure by Council staff to empty the post box at the town hall, it was treated as late and excluded from consideration. The Court of Appeal held that a contract should be implied between the parties; one of the terms of that contract was that if a conforming tender was submitted before the deadline, it would be "opened and considered in conjunction with all other conforming tenders or at least . . . will be considered if others are".[231] While in principle there seems nothing to prevent the implication of a similar contract where the party inviting tenders is a private body or person,[232] similar implied contracts are particularly likely to arise when the invitation is made by a public authority.

(a) *Conditions for the Implication of a Tender Process Contract*

10–036 **Legal conditions.** A contract arising out of the tender process will only be implied where both the legal and the factual matrix permit. So far as the legal matrix is concerned, the implication of a tender process contract may be precluded by the existence of another legal mechanism regulating the relationship of the parties. Thus, for instance, in *St George Soccer Football Association Inc v*

---

[227] Local Government (Contracts) Act s.4(1).

[228] Local Government (Contracts) Act s.5.

[229] See Local Government (Contracts) Act ss.6 and 7 for the consequences of such a finding.

[230] [1990] 1 W.L.R. 1195; noted by Adams and Brownsword (1991) 54 M.L.R. 281, Davenport (1991) 107 L.Q.R. 201. See also Arrowsmith (2004) 5 P.P.L.R. NA125.

[231] *Blackpool and Fylde Aero Club Ltd v Blackpool BC* [1990] 1 W.L.R. 1195, 1202.

[232] Though the public character of the defendant was relied on by the plaintiff as support for the existence of the contract as it had as a matter of public law a duty to comply with its standing orders (to consider tenders) and a fiduciary duty to ratepayers to act with reasonable prudence in managing its financial affairs: *Blackpool and Fylde Aero Club Ltd v Blackpool BC* [1990] 1 W.L.R. 1195, 1201; and Bingham L.J. gave some weight to this: *Blackpool and Fylde Aero Club Ltd v Blackpool BC* [1990] 1 W.L.R. 1195, 1202. See further below, para.10–037.

Soccer NSW Ltd,[233] the Supreme Court of New South Wales held that the implication of a tender process contract was precluded by the fact that the relationship between the parties was already governed by the constitution of the defendant. It is submitted that this decision reflects English law. It may also be the case that the existence of comprehensive statutory regulations prevents a tender process contract from being implied. In *Harmon CFEM Facades (UK) Ltd v Corporate Officer of the House of Commons*[234] it was argued that the existence of comprehensive statutory procurement regulations precluded the implication of a tender process contract.[235] This argument was held to be "correct".[236] But the judge went on to hold that, on the facts, to which the procurement regulations applied, there was a tender process contract. This conclusion seems to have been based on the possibility that the claimant's claim under the Regulations might fail.[237] The decision therefore seems to establish that the common law implied contract is subsidiary to the Regulations, and that there cannot be concurrent liability under both the Regulations and a tender process contract.[238]

Factual conditions. Once any legal obstacles to the implication of a tender process contract have been dealt with, the factual matrix must be examined, in order to ascertain whether the implication of a contract is justified. The express dealings and discussions between the parties may exclude any such implication.[239] If a tender process contract has not been negatived, a variety of factors must be assessed. In *Blackpool & Fylde Aero Club Ltd v Blackpool BC*[240] it was particularly emphasised that tenders had been solicited by the invitor,[241] there was a small number of invitees,[242] who were known to the invitor,[243] and the invitation set out a "clear, orderly and familiar" procedure.[244] Some weight was also given to the fact that the defendant was a local authority.[245] It seems that there is no need to identify a particular offer or acceptance in the facts (the Court 10–037

233 [2005] NSWSC 1288.

234 (1999) 67 Con. L.R. 1.

235 *Harmon CFEM Facades (UK) Ltd v Corporate Officer of the House of Commons* (1999) 67 Con. L.R. 1 at [209].

236 *Harmon CFEM Facades (UK) Ltd v Corporate Officer of the House of Commons* (1999) 67 Con. L.R. 1 at [215].

237 (1999) 67 Con. L.R. at [216]: "If Harmon cannot complain of the result under the 1991 Regulations does this not mean that the 1991 Regulations are not as comprehensive as they might first appear . . . "

238 A similar relationship exists between the Regulations and judicial review: *R. v Ministry of Defence Ex p Cookson & Clegg Ltd* [2005] EWCA Civ 811, [2006] E.L.R. 1092.

239 *Greville v Venables* [2007] EWCA Civ 878 at [36]–[40], per Lloyd L.J.

240 [1990] 1 W.L.R. 1195.

241 *Blackpool and Fylde Aero Club Ltd v Blackpool BC* [1990] 1 W.L.R. 1195 at 1202, per Bingham L.J.

242 *Blackpool and Fylde Aero Club Ltd v Blackpool BC* [1990] 1 W.L.R. 1195 at 1203, per Stocker L.J.

243 *Blackpool and Fylde Aero Club Ltd v Blackpool BC* [1990] 1 W.L.R. 1195 at 1202, per Bingham L.J.

244 *Blackpool and Fylde Aero Club Ltd v Blackpool BC* [1990] 1 W.L.R. 1195 at 1202, per Bingham L.J.

245 *Blackpool and Fylde Aero Club Ltd v Blackpool BC* [1990] 1 W.L.R. 1195 at 1202, per Bingham L.J.

of Appeal in the *Blackpool* case did not do so)[246]; but it is necessary to show an intention to create legal relations.[247] Subsequent English authorities have held that tender process contracts have come into existence in similarly formal contexts[248]; and there is Australian authority to support the view that no contract can be inferred where the tender process is highly informal.[249] Whether such a contract can only be implied where the party inviting tenders is a public body, is more controversial. As mentioned above, some weight seemed to be given to the defendant's status as a public body in the *Blackpool* case, and a similar emphasis can be seen in some Commonwealth authorities.[250] However, in *J & A Developments Ltd v Edina Manufacturing Ltd*[251] the High Court of Northern Ireland held that the implication of tender process contracts was not limited to cases of public authorities.[252] It is submitted that this is the better view: the fundamental question is whether a tender process contract can be inferred from the parties' conduct and is consistent with the surrounding legal and factual matrix; such an inference is perfectly possible where the party inviting tenders is not a public body.

(b) *Contents of a Tender Process Contract*

10–038 **The terms of tender process contracts.** The terms of a tender process contract are collected from the language used by the parties and supplemented by implication. Thus, for instance, an express undertaking by the invitor as to the grounds on which a tender would be disqualified would be part of the contract.[253] Similarly, the tender documents might incorporate an otherwise voluntary code of practice; that code will then form part of the contractual terms.[254] Where it is sought to imply terms, the courts have been cautious, and have tended to focus on questions relating to the procedure to be followed in the tendering competition. In *Blackpool & Fylde Aero Club Ltd v Blackpool BC*,[255] for instance, it was held that whilst there was an obligation to *consider* a conforming tender, there

---

[246] See similarly the exposition by the Supreme Court of Western Australia in *Dockpride Pty Ltd v Subiaco Redevelopment Authority* [2005] WASC 211 at [121], which acknowledged that, in the tender process context, "a contract may be made without the formalities of offer and acceptance". cf. *Prime Commercial Ltd v Wool Board Disestablishment Co Ltd* [2006] NZCA 295 at[15], where the Court of Appeal of New Zealand asserted that offer and acceptance must be shown in order for a tender process contract to be created.

[247] *Blackpool & Fylde Aero Club Ltd v Blackpool BC* [1990] 1 W.L.R. 1195 at 1202, per Bingham L.J. and 1204, per Stocker L.J.

[248] *Fairclough Building Ltd v BC of Port Talbot* (1992) 62 B.L.R. 82; *Harmon CFEM Facades (UK) Ltd v Corporate Officer of the House of Commons* (1999) 67 Con. L.R. 1. See also *Prime Commercial Ltd v Wool Board Disestablishment Co Ltd* [2006] NZCA 295 at [16]: "the less formal the tender process, the less scope there is for implying any, or at least any onerous, obligations on the party calling for tenders".

[249] e.g. *Hickinbotham Developments Pty Ltd v Woods* [2005] SASC 215, (2005) 92 S.A.S.R. 52.

[250] *Hickinbotham Developments Pty Ltd v Woods* [2005] SASC 215, (2005) 92 S.A.S.R. 52 at 57. See also Samuel (2004) 24 O.J.L.S. 335, 356–357.

[251] [2006] NIQB 85.

[252] *J & A Developments Ltd v Edina Manufacturing Ltd* [2006] NIQB 85 at [49].

[253] *Fairclough Building Ltd v Borough Council of Port Talbot* (1992) 62 B.L.R. 82 at 94, per Nolan L.J.

[254] *J & A Developments Ltd v Edina Manufacturing Ltd* [2006] NIQB 85.

[255] [1990] 1 W.L.R. 1195.

was no implied obligation about which tender should be accepted.[256] Nor, it was said, could there be an implied term that the invitor must accept one of the tenders that it received. The Court of Appeal also suggested that, on the facts of that case, a term could be implied not to consider late applications,[257] and not to make a decision before the deadline for receipt of applications had expired. Similarly, in *Fairclough Building Ltd v BC of Port Talbot*[258] it was held that the party inviting tenders could only exclude a conforming tender from consideration on reasonable grounds, such as a concern about the appearance of bias. On the other hand, there is no implied term that the competitive process must be free from apparent bias.[259] However, where the party inviting tenders is a public authority, there is some support for the view that more extensive terms may be implied. In *Harmon CFEM Facades (UK) Ltd v Corporate Officer of the House of Commons*[260] it was said that:

> "... it is now clear in English law that in the public sector where competitive tenders are sought and responded to, a contract comes into existence whereby the prospective employer impliedly agrees to consider all tenderers fairly (see the *Blackpool* and *Fairclough* cases)."[261]

The judge indicated that such contractual obligations derived from the European-inspired statutory procurement Regulations. Those Regulations govern not merely the procedure for considering or excluding tenders, but also deal with the methods of evaluating bids and selecting a winner. It is submitted, however, that the decision in the *Harmon* case should not be seen as imposing implied terms as to methods of evaluation and selection; rather, it should be read in the light of its facts, which concerned procedural unfairness, and in the context of its approving reference to the *Blackpool* and *Fairclough* cases. It is submitted that what the decision in the *Harmon* case establishes is that the requirements to consider conforming tenders and not to exclude them without reasonable cause are illustrations of a wider procedural principle to give equal opportunity to all bidders to make their case. Such a broad general principle may indeed only be applicable to tender processes initiated by public authorities, on the basis that higher standards of impartiality and fairness can be expected from state contractors. But, if the law is to reflect the "confident assumptions of commercial

---

[256] *Blackpool & Fylde Aero Club Ltd v Blackpool BC* [1990] 1 W.L.R. 1195 at 1204, per Stocker L.J. In *Harmon CFEM Facades (UK) Ltd v Corporate Officer of the House of Commons* (1999) 67 Con. L.R. 1 at [210] Humphrey Lloyd Q.C. commented that the *Blackpool* case "is perhaps no more than authority for the proposition that a contracting authority undertakes to consider all tenders received".

[257] *Blackpool & Fylde Aero Club Ltd v Blackpool BC* [1990] 1 W.L.R. 1195, 1201, per Bingham L.J. For criticism see Arrowsmith (1994) 53 C.L.J. 104, 128, who argues that an authority should be free to accept late tenders "provided that all bidders are treated equally". However, if all bidders are treated equally, that seems to be not so much an acceptance after the deadline as a moving of the deadline. Bingham L.J. seemed to have in mind a situation where only one tender had been accepted late; that would be a clear case of inequality of treatment.

[258] (1992) 62 B.L.R. 82.

[259] *Pratt Contractors Ltd v Transit New Zealand* [2004] B.L.R. 143.

[260] (1999) 67 Con. L.R. 1.

[261] *Harmon CFEM Facades (UK) Ltd v Corporate Officer of the House of Commons* (1999) 67 Con. L.R. 1 at [216].

parties",[262] as Bingham L.J. suggested in the *Blackpool* case, there seems to be no good reason why such a general principle of procedural fairness should not apply to all parties.[263]

5. ESTOPPEL

10–039 **General principles.** Equitable estoppel may be successfully invoked against the Crown[264] and public authorities,[265] but not to the same extent that it is available against private parties. There are four restricting factors. First, estoppel cannot be used to uphold an ultra vires transaction. Second, it cannot be used to prevent the performance of a statutory duty. Third, estoppel must not prevent or hinder the exercise of statutory powers. Fourth, estoppel has no role in matters of public law; where the circumstances are such that they would give rise to an estoppel in private law, they must be dealt with in public law using the doctrine of legitimate expectation.

10–040 **Estoppel and ultra vires.** Estoppel cannot prevent an act from being challenged on the ground of ultra vires.[266] For example, in *Rhyl Urban DC v Rhyl Amusements Ltd*[267] the Council had granted a succession of leases over Council land to the defendants in circumstances which would otherwise have estopped the Council from denying that it had the capacity to do so. However, it was said that "a plea of estoppel cannot prevail as an answer to a claim that something done by a statutory body is ultra vires",[268] and the supposed leases were held invalid.

10–041 **Estoppel and statutory duty.** Estoppel cannot be used to prevent the performance of a statutory duty, provided that the duty is imposed by a statute "enacted for the benefit of a section of the public".[269] In *Maritime Electric Co Ltd v General Dairies Ltd*[270] an electricity supplier had undercharged one of its customers by mistake; the customer had relied on the supplier's statements as to the amounts due, and there was evidence that it had suffered detriment as a result

[262] *Blackpool & Fylde Aero Club Ltd v Blackpool BC* [1990] 1 W.L.R. 1195 at 1201.

[263] Arrowsmith (1994) 53 C.L.J. 104, 127 describes any bidder in a competitive tendering process as "generally expect[ing] only that they will be given a fair opportunity to obtain the contract by demonstrating that they are able to offer the best value".

[264] e.g. *Orient Steam Navigation Co Ltd v The Crown* (1925) 21 Ll.L. Rep. 301; Street, *Governmental Liability* (1953), pp.156–157.

[265] e.g. *Crabb v Arun DC* [1976] Ch. 179.

[266] *Fairtitle v Gilbert* (1787) 2 T.R. 169; *Minister of Agriculture and Fisheries v Hulkin* Unreported 1948 summarised in *Minister of Agriculture and Fisheries v Matthews* [1950] 1 K.B. 148, 153–154; *Minister of Agriculture and Fisheries v Matthews* [1950] 1 K.B. 148; *Rhyl Urban DC v Rhyl Amusements Ltd* [1959] 1 W.L.R. 465.

[267] [1959] 1 W.L.R. 465.

[268] *Rhyl Urban DC v Rhyl Amusements Ltd* [1959] 1 W.L.R. 465 at 474.

[269] *Maritime Electric Co Ltd v General Dairies Ltd* [1937] A.C. 610 at 620. See also *R. v Blenkinsop* [1892] 1 Q.B. 43, 46, per Mathew J.; but quaere whether, if the facts of that case arose today, the authority would not be regarded as having made a determination as to the rate, which it would be bound by (*Re 56 Denton Road, Twickenham* [1953] 1 Ch. 51).

[270] [1937] A.C. 610.

of that reliance. However, it was held that no estoppel could be relied upon, because the supplier, in seeking payment of the full amount, was fulfilling its mandatory, unconditional statutory duty not to charge "a greater or less compensation for any service" than that fixed by statute.[271] The Privy Council was careful to limit its reasoning to statutory duties "enacted for the benefit of a section of the public, that is, on grounds of public policy in a general sense".[272] It is difficult to see what kinds of statutory duties would fail to satisfy this test, but their Lordships perhaps had in mind duties imposed under a private Act of Parliament.

Estoppel and the exercise of statutory powers. Estoppel cannot be used to prevent or hinder the exercise of statutory powers.[273] Thus, for instance, in *The Mayor, Aldermen and Burgesses of the Borough of Sunderland v Priestman*[274] it was held that a local authority could not be prevented from exercising its powers in relation to the upkeep of roads by any prior acts done as private contractors.[275] So far as hindering the exercise of a power is concerned, it was held in *Southend-on-Sea Corp v Hodgson (Wickford) Ltd*[276] that an estoppel which prevented the planning authority from adducing evidence in a dispute over the previous use of premises was not permissible.[277] However, the Court of Appeal also stated that the principle governing the availability of estoppels against public bodies was analogous to the principle preventing an authority from fettering its discretion by contract.[278] This indicates that not all estoppels will be held to hinder the authority's exercise of its statutory powers; rather, as with the fettering principle, an assessment must be made of the likely effect of upholding the estoppel. One situation where it would seem that an estoppel would not hinder the exercise of statutory powers is where an authority treats an application as validly made, despite it having some purely formal defect.[279] 10–042

Estoppel and public law. Where the facts of a case concern a matter of public law, estoppel has no role[280]; it cannot be asserted either by or against the public authority concerned.[281] Any questions which would have related to estoppel, if the matter had been one of private law, must be dealt with in terms of legitimate 10–043

[271] *Maritime Electric Co Ltd v General Dairies Ltd* [1937] A.C. 610, 616. Breach of this duty was punishable by fine.

[272] *Maritime Electric Co Ltd v General Dairies Ltd* [1937] A.C. 610, 620.

[273] *Southend-on-Sea Corp v Hodgson (Wickford) Ltd* [1962] 1 Q.B. 416.

[274] [1927] 2 Ch. 107.

[275] *The Mayor, Aldermen and Burgesses of the Borough of Sunderland v Priestman* [1927] 2 Ch. 107, 116. See similarly *Stockwell v Southgate Corp* [1936] 2 All E.R. 1343.

[276] [1962] 1 Q.B. 416.

[277] Since the case related to planning matters, it would not be dealt with today in terms of estoppel; rather, as a public law matter, it would be dealt with in terms of legitimate expectation. See below, para.10–043.

[278] *Southend-on-Sea Corp v Hodgson (Wickford) Ltd* [1962] 1 Q.B. 416, 424. For the principle that a statutory body cannot fetter its discretion by contract see above paras 10–027—10–031.

[279] *Wells v Minister of Housing and Local Government* [1967] 1 W.L.R. 1000, 1007. Lord Denning M.R. may have been mistaken in his application of this proposition to the facts of the case: see *R. (Reprotech (Pebsham) Ltd) v East Sussex CC* [2003] 1 W.L.R. 348 at [30].

[280] *R. (Reprotech (Pebsham) Ltd) v East Sussex CC* [2003] 1 W.L.R. 348.

[281] *Stancliffe Stone Co Ltd v Peak District National Park Authority* [2004] EWHC 1475 (QB), [2005] Env. L.R. 4 at [35].

expectation. This is not a mere matter of labelling[282]; in particular, any remedies in public law take into account the interests of the general public, whereas in private law they do not. What marks out an activity as relating to public law is difficult to define precisely. But it has been said that public law activities engage the public interest, and have an effect on members of the public who are not parties to the process to an extent that distinguishes them from private law matters, in which "interests only of those directly involved must be considered".[283] The main instances of estoppels being denied on the basis that the matter relates to public law are in the area of planning control[284]; it has also been held that estoppel could not be relied upon in a dispute over the granting of moorings in a public harbour.[285] The question of a Minister's authority to issue a commercial guarantee has, by contrast, been held not to fall within public law; it is governed by the private law principles of agency.[286]

6. PUBLIC PROCUREMENT

(a) *European Community Legislation*

10–044 Contracts made by the Crown, by public bodies and by the European Community are subject to fundamental principles of EC law such as freedom of movement of goods, freedom of establishment and freedom to provide services. The European Community has also made special legislative provision to regulate the formation of such contracts in a series of Directives,[287] which have been implemented in the

---

[282] *R. (Reprotech (Pebsham) Ltd) v East Sussex CC* [2003] 1 W.L.R. 348 at [34]; *R. (on the application of Wandsworth LBC) v Secretary of State for Transport Local Government and the Regions* [2003] EWHC 622 (Admin), [2004] 1 P. & C.R. 32 at [22].

[283] *R. (Reprotech (Pebsham) Ltd) v East Sussex CC* [2003] 1 W.L.R. 348 at [6].

[284] *R. (Reprotech (Pebsham) Ltd) v East Sussex CC* [2003] 1 W.L.R. 348; *South Bucks DC v Flanagan* [2002] EWCA Civ 690, [2002] 1 W.L.R. 2601; *R. (on the application of Wandsworth LBC) v Secretary of State for Transport Local Government and the Regions* [2003] EWHC 622 (Admin), [2004] 1 P. & C.R. 32; *Stancliffe Stone Co Ltd v Peak District National Park Authority* [2004] EWHC 1475 (QB), [2005] Env. L.R. 4.

[285] *Yarmouth (Isle of Wight) Harbour Commissioners v Harold Hayes (Yarmouth Isle of Wight) Ltd* [2004] EWHC 3375 (Ch), [2004] All E.R. (D) 66 (Dec.).

[286] *Marubeni Hong Kong and South China Ltd v Government of Mongolia* [2004] EWHC 472 (Comm), [2004] 2 Lloyd's Rep. 198 especially at [97]–[102] (summarising counsel's submission that public law concepts should apply), and [123]–[127] (rejecting that submission). The question of authority was not challenged on appeal: *Marubeni Hong Kong and South China Ltd v Government of Mongolia* [2005] EWCA Civ 395, [2005] 1 W.L.R. 2497 at [6].

[287] The current Directives are Directive 2004/17 coordinating the procurement procedures of entities operating in the water, energy, transport and postal services sectors [2004] OJ L134/1; Directive 2004/18 on the coordination of procedures for the award of public works contracts, public supply contracts and public service contracts [2004] OJ L34/114; Directive 89/665 on the coordination of the laws, regulations and administrative provisions relating to the application of review procedures to the award of public supply and public works contracts [1989] OJ L395/33; Directive 92/13 coordinating the laws, regulations and administrative provisions relating to the application of Community rules on the procurement procedures of entities operating in the water, energy, transport and telecommunications sectors [1992] OJ L76/14; Directive 2007/66 amending Council Directives 89/665 and 92/13 with regard to improving the effectiveness of review procedures concerning the award of public contracts [2007] OJ L335/31.

United Kingdom by statutory instruments.[288] The Directives and their implementing regulations apply to public works contracts, public supply contracts, public service contracts and to contracts made by entities operating in the water, energy, transport and postal service sectors; only contracts above a specified threshold value are affected.[289] A detailed account of these provisions is beyond the scope of this work,[290] but the guiding principle is that contracting authorities "shall treat economic operators equally and non-discriminatorily and shall act in a transparent way".[291] Equal treatment in relation to public works, public supply and public service contracts is ensured by restricting a contracting authority's choice of contractual procedure under normal circumstances to one of two defined methods—the open or the restricted procedure.[292] For particularly complex or unusual contracts there are two other possibilities: competitive dialogue and the negotiated procedure.[293] For utilities contracts there is a free choice between the open, the closed or the negotiated procedures.[294] Whichever procedure is selected, the only two permissible criteria on which to award a contract are the most economically advantageous tender, or the lowest price.[295] Transparency of treatment is attained by the imposition of mandatory obligations on the contracting authority relating to matters such as advertising that a contract is to be awarded[296] and giving reasons for both the exclusion of any tenderer and for the rejection of any bid.[297]

Remedies. Where a contracting authority has breached its duty under the Regulations it may be made liable in damages to disappointed bidders.[298] The regulations also enable a disappointed bidder to obtain interim relief, so as to suspend the procedure leading to the award of the contract; for this purpose, the general prohibition of injunctions against the Crown under the Crown Proceedings Act 1947 is waived.[299] However, the Regulations expressly provide that: 10–045

> "... the Court does not have power to order any remedy other than an award of damages in respect of a breach of the duty owed ... if the contract in relation to which the breach occurred has been entered into."[300]

---

[288] The Public Contracts Regulations 2006 (SI 2006/5); The Utilities Contracts Regulations 2006 (SI 2006/6).

[289] Directive 2004/17 arts 16–17; Directive 2004/18 arts 7–9; Public Contracts Regulations 2006 reg.8; Utilities Contracts Regulations 2006 reg.11; Public Contracts and Utilities Contracts (Amendment) Regulations 2007 (SI 2007/3542).

[290] For a detailed treatment see Arrowsmith, *The Law of Public and Utilities Procurement*, 2nd edn (2005).

[291] Directive 2004/18 art.2. See similarly Directive 2004/17 art.10.

[292] Directive 2004/18 art.28. Public Contracts Regulations 2006 reg.12.

[293] Directive 2004/18 arts 29–30. Public Contracts Regulations 2006 reg.12.

[294] Directive 2004/17 art.40. Utilities Contracts Regulations 2006 reg.14.

[295] Directive 2004/17 art.55(1); Directive 2004/18 art.53; Public Contracts Regulations 2006 reg.30; Utilities Contracts Regulations 2006 reg.30.

[296] Directive 2004/17 arts 41–44; Directive 2004/18 arts 35–37; Public Contracts Regulations 2006 reg.15(2); Utilities Contracts Regulations 2006 reg.16.

[297] Directive 2004/17 art.49; Directive 2004/18 art.41; Public Contracts Regulations 2006 reg.32; Utilities Contracts Regulations 2006 reg.33.

[298] Public Contracts Regulations 2006 reg.47; Utilities Contracts Regulations 2006 reg.45.

[299] Public Contracts Regulations 2006 reg.47(10); Utilities Contracts Regulations 2006 reg. 45(10). On the nature of that prohibition see above, paras 10–016—10–019.

[300] Public Contracts Regulations 2006 reg.47(9); Utilities Contracts Regulations 2006 reg.45(9).

In other words, a contract cannot be held to be unenforceable as a result of a breach of the Regulations.

10–046 **Reform of remedial position.** The limited remedy provided by the 2006 Regulations in relation to contracts already entered into reflected the limited requirements imposed on Member States by the relevant Directives.[301] However, those Directives have now been amended,[302] and the amended position must be given effect to in national legislation by December 20, 2009.[303] There are two crucial innovations. The first is the introduction of a "standstill period" between the final decision about awarding a contract and entering into such contract.[304] The second is that, for certain breaches, such as an initial failure properly to advertise that a contract was to be awarded, or entering the contract before the expiry of the "standstill period", the contract must be held to be "ineffective".[305] Although it is stated that "[t]he consequences of a contract being considered ineffective shall be provided for by national law",[306] the Directive indicates in outline what will be required:

> "National law may provide for the retroactive cancellation of all contractual obligations or limit the scope of the cancellation to those obligations which have still to be performed. In the latter case, Member States shall provide for the application of other penalties within the meaning of Article 2e(2)."[307]

National law may also confer a discretion on the Courts not to set aside a contract if there are "overriding reasons relating to a general interest [that] require that the effects of the contract should be maintained".[308] Where such a discretion is exercised, Member States must "provide for alternative penalties".[309] It can, therefore, be seen that the current Regulations will require extensive amendment. If it is decided that the consequences of ineffectiveness should extend to retroactive cancellation of all contractual obligations, the effect of the specified breaches in the Regulations will be equivalent to the situation where a contract has been concluded ultra vires the powers of a statutory body. It might, therefore, appear to follow that the appropriate consequences of cancellation should be claims for unjust enrichment.[310] However, the Directive clearly contemplates that the remedy should be punitive (it refers to "other penalties" if retroactive cancellation is not imposed), and this is problematic under existing English law. Of course, if the contract was proving advantageous to the authority, its cancellation would indeed be a punishment. But cancellation will not necessarily be penal; it might even be welcome: in several cases local authorities have sought to rely on their own lack of capacity to contract in order to escape from what have

---

[301] Directive 89/665 art.2; Directive 92/13 art.2.
[302] Directive 2007/66.
[303] Directive 2007/66 art.3.
[304] Directive 2007/66 art.1, new art.2a in 89/665.
[305] Directive 2007/66 art.1, new art.2d in 89/665.
[306] Directive 2007/66 art.1, new art.2d(2) in 89/665.
[307] Directive 2007/66 art.1, new art.2d(2) in 89/665.
[308] Directive 2007/66 art.1, new art.2d(3) in 89/665.
[309] Directive 2007/66 art.1, new art.2d(3) in 89/665.
[310] See further below, paras 29–054 et seq.

turned out to be bad bargains.[311] It is difficult to see how relieving an authority from such a bad bargain could be seen as a "penalty". If, alternatively, it is decided that ineffectiveness should only extend to the cancellation of obligations not yet due, or it is decided to confer a discretion on the courts not to set aside contracts, the concept of "alternative penalties" will have to be given effect to. The Directive provides that:

> "Alternative penalties must be effective, proportionate and dissuasive. Alternative penalties shall be:
>
> —the imposition of fines on the contracting authority; or
> —the shortening of the duration of the contract.
>
> Member States may confer on the review body broad discretion to take into account all the relevant factors, including the seriousness of the infringement, the behaviour of the contracting authority and, . . . the extent to which the contract remains in force.
>
> The award of damages does not constitute an appropriate penalty for the purposes of this paragraph."[312]

Whilst the concept of cancelling only future obligations is not entirely foreign to English law,[313] the provisions of the Directive require the exercise of discretions relating to both the punitive element of the award and alteration of the terms of the contract which go far beyond the powers currently exercised by the courts.

(b) *International and Domestic Procurement Regimes*

International agreements. Various international agreements require the United Kingdom to open its markets to the industry of particular countries outside the European Union. Such agreements do not, typically, have direct effect in English law, and may be implemented by conferring on economic entities from those countries the same rights as would be available to them under the European procurement legislation. For example, the obligations of Member States under the World Trade Organization Agreement on Government Procurement will be satisfied by applying the Community Directives on procurement to economic operators from those countries.[314] 10–047

Domestic legislation. Whilst there is no comprehensive domestic legislation dealing with public procurement, there are certain broad statutory obligations, especially in relation to public authorities, which may affect which contracts are entered, and on what terms. For instance, the Local Government Act 1999 imposes a duty on local authorities to: 10–048

> " . . . make arrangements to secure continuous improvement in the way in which [their] functions are exercised, having regard to a combination of economy, efficiency and value"[315];

---

[311] e.g. *Guiness Mahon & Co Ltd v Kensington & Chelsea Royal BC* [1999] Q.B. 215.
[312] Directive 2007/66 art.1, new art.2e(2) in 89/665.
[313] Local Government (Contracts) Act 1997 s.7.
[314] Directive 2004/17 preamble para.(14); Directive 2004/18 preamble para.(7).
[315] Local Government Act 1999 s.3(1).

the Local Government Act 1988 requires local authorities to exercise procurement functions without regard to certain "non-commercial" matters.[316] This latter obligation will be particularly significant where the contract in question is not governed by the European public procurement regime because, for instance, its value falls below the specified threshold.

[316] Local Government Act 1988 s.17.

CHAPTER 11

POLITICAL IMMUNITY AND INCAPACITY

		PARA.
1.	Foreign states, sovereigns, ambassadors and international organisations	11–001
2.	Alien enemies	11–024

1. FOREIGN STATES, SOVEREIGNS, AMBASSADORS AND INTERNATIONAL ORGANISATIONS

Foreign states and sovereigns: the common law rule. The rule at common law was that no independent foreign state or foreign sovereign could be sued in an English court without consent.[1] This immunity was derived from rules of public international law which had become part of English law.[2] The immunity extended both to direct actions against the state or sovereign and to indirect actions against its property. Formerly, foreign states were afforded immunity not only with regard to governmental activities but also with regard to their purely commercial activities.[3] This absolute theory was abandoned by the courts in favour of the more restricted approach under which immunity did not apply either to an action, whether in rem[4] or in personam,[5] against a ship belonging to a sovereign state, or one of its organs, if the ship was being operated as an ordinary trading ship, nor indeed to actions in personam generally in relation to ordinary commercial activities[6]; but did extend to governmental acts, *acta iure imperii*, of the sovereign state.[7] **11–001**

---

[1] *Duke of Brunswick v King of Hanover* (1844) 6 Beav. 1, (1848) 2 H.L.C. 1.

[2] *The Christina* [1938] A.C. 485, 490; *Thai-Europe Tapioca Services Ltd v Government of Pakistan* [1975] 1 W.L.R. 1485.

[3] *The Porto Alexandre* [1920] P. 30; *The Christina* [1938] A.C. 485, 490; *Kahan v Pakistan Federation* [1951] 2 K.B. 1003; *Baccus S.R.L. v Servicio Nacional del Trigo* [1957] 1 Q.B. 438.

[4] *The Phillippine Admiral* [1977] A.C. 373.

[5] *I Congreso del Partido* [1983] 1 A.C. 244, 261.

[6] *Trendtex Trading Corp v Central Bank of Nigeria* [1977] Q.B. 529; *Hispano Americana Mercantil SA v Central Bank of Nigeria* [1979] 2 Lloyd's Rep. 277; *Planmount Ltd v Republic of Zaire* [1981] 1 All E.R. 1110; *I Congreso del Partido* [1983] 1 A.C. 244, 261–262; *Alcom Ltd v Republic of Columbia* [1984] A.C. 580, 598–599.

[7] *I Congreso del Partido* [1983] 1 A.C. 244, 262, 272, 276; *Sengupta v Republic of India* [1983] I.C.R. 221; *Littrell v Government of the United States (No.2)* [1995] 1 W.L.R. 82. For discussion of the changes, see *J.H. Rayner (Mincing Lane) Ltd v Dept of Trade and Industry* [1989] Ch. 72, affirmed without reference to these points, [1990] 2 A.C. 418.

11–002 **Common law and State Immunity Act 1978.** The law of sovereign immunity was largely placed on a statutory basis by the State Immunity Act 1978.[8] The 1978 Act is not, however, a complete code and matters which are excluded from its scope will be governed by the rules developed by the common law. Thus the 1978 Act excludes proceedings relating to anything done by or in relation to the armed forces of a state while in the United Kingdom.[9] Such cases are subject to immunity under the common law rules.[10]

11–003 **Sovereign immunity and human rights.** In *Holland v Lampen-Wolfe*[11] the House of Lords held that to accord sovereign immunity to the defendant did not deprive the claimant of a fundamental right of access to the English court under art.6 of the European Convention on Human Rights since the immunity of a state was an attribute of the state itself under international law which all other states are, by international law, obliged to accept. In a series of cases the European Court of Human Rights has also held that application of the principles of state immunity was compatible with art.6 of the Convention.[12] The court maintained that while a limitation on a right of access to a court must pursue a legitimate aim and must be proportionate, according immunity to a state in civil proceedings was designed to achieve the legitimate aim of complying with international law by promoting comity and good relations between states through mutual respect for the sovereignty of states. Immunity which reflected generally held rules of public international law did not amount to a disproportionate restriction on the right of access to a court since some such restrictions, including those generally accepted in international law, were inherent. In *Jones v Ministry of the Interior of the Kingdom of Saudi Arabia*[13] the House of Lords assumed that art.6 of the Convention was engaged, as decided by the European Court of Human Rights in the above cases, but held that according sovereign immunity to the state and its servants, agents, officials or functionaries in respect of civil claims arising out of alleged acts of torture committed in the state was not disproportionate as inconsistent with a peremptory norm of international law. Lord Bingham of Cornhill, however, had reservations as to whether art.6 was engaged at all, since the rule

---

[8] See below, para.11–004.

[9] State Immunity Act 1978 s.16(2).

[10] *Littrell v Government of the United States (No.2)* [1995] 1 W.L.R. 82; *Holland v Lampen-Wolfe* [2000] 1 W.L.R. 1573. Since the 1978 Act is not retrospective (s.22(3)) it will only apply to matters which occurred after it entered into force (November 1978) but it is now most unlikely that matters which occurred before that date, which would be governed by the common law, will arise in practice. cf. *Planmount Ltd v Republic of Zaire* [1981] 1 All E.R. 1110; *Sengupta v Republic of India* [1983] I.C.R. 221.

[11] [2000] 1 W.L.R. 1573. See also *Matthews v Ministry of Defence* [2003] UKHL 4, [2003] 1 A.C. 1163.

[12] *Fogarty v United Kingdom* (2002) 34 E.H.R.R. 302; *Al-Adsani v United Kingdom* (2002) 34 E.H.R.R. 273, arising out of *Al-Adsani v Government of Kuwait*, *The Times*, March 29, 1995, 107 Int. L.R. 536; *McElhinney v Ireland* (2002) 34 E.H.R.R. 322, arising out of *McElhinney v Williams* [1996] 1 I.L.R.M. 276. See Fox (2001) 117 L.Q.R. 10; Garnett (2002) 118 L.Q.R. 367; Voyiakis (2003) 52 I.C.L.Q. 297; Lloyd Jones (2003) 52 I.C.L.Q. 463; Yang (2003) 74 B.Y.I.L. 333; Garnett (2005) 54 I.C.L.Q. 705.

[13] [2006] UKHL 26, [2007] 1 A.C. 270. See Seymour [2006] C.L.J. 479.

of international law is not that a state should not exercise over another state a jurisdiction which it has, but that save in cases recognised by international law, of which this case was not an example, a state has no jurisdiction over another state: it was therefore difficult to accept that a state had denied access to its court if it had no access to give.[14]

State Immunity Act 1978. The Act[15] applies both to cases where the question of the immunity of a foreign state arises directly in the proceedings as where the state is named as a defendant, and also to the common case of "indirect impleading", as where an action between two other parties puts the title to the state's goods in issue.[16] The basic principle of the Act is that a foreign state is immune from the jurisdiction of the English courts[17] whether or not it appears in the proceedings,[18] and the issue of immunity must be decided as a preliminary 11–004

[14] [2006] UKHL at [14]. See, to the same effect, Lord Hoffmann at [64] and *Holland v Lampen-Wolfe* [2000] 1 W.L.R. 1573, 1588, per Lord Millett. See also *AIG Capital Partners Inc v Republic of Kazakhstan* [2005] EWHC 2239 (Comm), [2006] 1 W.L.R. 1420 (restriction on the right of a party to enforce a judgment against a central bank (see State Immunity Act 1978 s.14(4) is legitimate and proportionate)); *Grovit v Nederlandsche Bank* [2005] EWHC 2944 (QB), [2006] 1 W.L.R. 3323 (according immunity to employees of immune central bank is legitimate and proportionate; affirmed on other grounds, [2007] EWCA Civ 712, [2008] 1 W.L.R. 51). See also *Aziz v Aziz* [2007] EWCA Civ 712, [2008] 2 All E.R. 501. In *Lechouritou v Dimosio tis Omospondiakis Dimokratias tis Germanias* (C-282/05) [2007] I.L. Pr. 216 the European Court of Justice found it unnecessary to decide whether immunity was compatible with the Brussels Convention on Jurisdiction and the Enforcement of Judgments in Civil and Commercial Matters 1968. In *Grovit v Nederlandsche Bank* it was held at first instance that immunity was compatible, but the point was not decided by the Court of Appeal. See also *Entico Corp Ltd v UNESCO* [2008] EWHC 531 (Comm), [2008] 1 Lloyd's Rep. 673 (immunity of international organisation).

[15] Implementing the 1972 European Convention on State Immunity: Cmnd.5081, though the Act is more extensive in scope. For discussion and references to relevant literature (which is copious) see *Dicey, Morris and Collins on the Conflict of Laws*, 14th edn (2006), paras 10–002—10–058: Cheshire and North, *Private International Law*, 13th edn (1999), pp.388–395. See also United Nations Convention on Jurisdictional Immunities of States and their Property (December 2004, not yet in force). For the text of the Convention see (2005) 44 Int. Leg. Mat. 803. Although not in force the Convention has been regarded as a strong indicator of international thinking on questions of sovereign immunity: see *AIG Capital Partners Inc v Republic of Kazakhstan* [2005] EWHC 2239 (Comm), [2006] 1 W.L.R. 1420; *Jones v Ministry of the Interior of the Kingdom of Saudi Arabia* [2006] UKHL 26, [2007] 1 A.C. 270; *Koo Golden East Mongolia v Bank of Nova Scotia* [2007] EWCA Civ 1443, [2008] 2 W.L.R. 1160. For comment on the Convention, see Denza (2006) 55 I.C.L.Q. 395; Fox (2006) 55 I.C.L.Q. 399; Gardiner (2006) 55 I.C.L.Q. 407; Hall (2006) 55 I.C.L.Q. 411; Dickinson (2006) 55 I.C.L.Q. 427; McGregor (2006) 55 I.C.L.Q. 437.

[16] e.g. *The Parlement Belge* (1880) L.R. 5 P.D. 197; *United States of America and Republic of France v Dollfus Mieg et Cie SA and Bank of England* [1952] A.C. 582. On the scope of the Act in respect of immunity from taxation, see *R. v IRC Ex p Camacq Corp* [1990] 1 W.L.R. 191 and below, para.11–005.

[17] The principle of immunity also precludes registration in England of a foreign judgment against a foreign state under the Administration of Justice Act 1920: see *AIC Ltd v Federal Government of Nigeria* [2003] EWHC 1357 (QB). See also Civil Jurisdiction and Judgments Act 1982 s.31.

[18] 1978 Act s.1. See *United Arab Emirates v Abdelghafar* [1995] I.C.R. 65; *Malaysian Industrial Development Authority v Jeyasingham* [1998] I.C.R. 307; *Military Affairs Office of the Embassy of the State of Kuwait v Caramba-Coker* (E.A.T./1054/02/RN, April 10, 2003); *Koo Golden East Mongolia v Bank of Nova Scotia* [2007] EWCA Civ 1443, [2008] 2 W.L.R. 1160. The burden of proof is upon the party asserting that the state is subject to the jurisdiction of the English court: *Donegal International Ltd v Zambia* [2007] EWHC 197 (Comm), [2007] 1 Lloyd's Rep. 397.

issue before the substantive action can proceed.[19] This immunity applies to any foreign or Commonwealth state, other than the United Kingdom, to the sovereign or other head of state in his public capacity and to the government or any department of that state.[20] It also applies to a "separate entity", such as a state corporation, not being a department of the state, where proceedings relate to something done by the separate entity in the exercise of sovereign authority and the state itself would have been immune.[21] It will be for the courts to develop criteria for determining what constitutes a separate entity. It is suggested, however, that the notion of separate entity does not extend to any agent of a foreign state. Rather, it should be regarded as limited to an entity owned or controlled by the foreign state since it is only if such ownership or control exists that an entity can realistically be regarded as capable of doing something in the exercise of sovereign authority.[22]

11–005 To the general principle of immunity there are several important and wide-ranging exceptions. The most important is that there is no immunity for a state's commercial transactions,[23] thus confirming the judicial developments confining the common law rule to *acta iure imperii*, though it may still be difficult to determine in any particular case the dividing line between commercial and

---

[19] *J.H. Rayner (Mincing Lane) Ltd v Dept of Trade and Industry* [1989] Ch. 72, 194–195, 252, affirmed without reference to this point, [1990] 2 A.C. 418: *A Co Ltd v Republic of X* [1990] 2 Lloyd's Rep. 520, 525; *Aziz v Republic of Yemen* [2005] EWCA Civ 754, [2005] I.C.R. 1391. A claim to immunity should be heard in public: *Harb v King Fahd Bin Abdul Aziz* [2005] EWCA Civ 632, [2006] 1 W.L.R. 578. See also *Aziz v Aziz* [2007] EWCA Civ 712, [2008] 2 All E.R. 501.

[20] s.14. See *Propend Finance Pty Ltd v Sing*, *The Times*, May 2, 1997, 111 Int.L.R. 111; *Bank of Credit and Commerce International (Overseas) Ltd v Price Waterhouse* [1997] 4 All E.R. 108. The immunity extends to servants or agents, officials and functionaries of a foreign state in respect of acts done by them as such in the foreign state: *Jones v Ministry of the Interior of the Kingdom of Saudi Arabia* [2006] UKHL 26, [2007] 1 A.C. 270. See also *Grovit v Nederlandsche Bank* [2005] EWHC 2944 (QB), [2006] 1 W.L.R. 3323; affirmed on other grounds, [2007] EWCA Civ 953, [2008] 1 W.L.R. 51.

[21] s.14. See *Kuwait Airways Corp v Iraqi Airways Co* [1995] 1 W.L.R. 1147 (for further proceedings, see *Kuwait Airways Corp v Iraqi Airways Co (No.2)* [2001] 1 W.L.R. 430; *Kuwait Airways Corp v Iraqi Airways Co* [2003] EWHC 31 (Comm), [2003] 1 Lloyd's Rep. 448); *Propend Finance Pty Ltd v Sing*, *The Times*, May 2, 1997, 111 Int.L.R. 611; *Ministry of Trade of the Republic of Iraq v Tsavliris Salvage (International) Ltd* [2008] EWHC 612 (Comm); see also *Koo Golden East Mongolia v Bank of Nova Scotia* [2007] EWCA Civ 1443, [2008] 2 W.L.R. 1160. For the position of a state's central bank or other monetary authority, see State Immunity Act 1978 s.14(3), (4); *AIC Ltd v Federal Government of Nigeria* [2003] EWHC 1357 (QB); *AIG Capital Partners Inc v Republic of Kazakhstan* [2005] EWHC 2239 (Comm), [2006] 1 W.L.R. 1420.

[22] *Dicey, Morris and Collins on the Conflict of Laws*, 14th edn (2006), para.10–09. See also *Re Rafidain Bank* [1992] B.C.L.C. 301; *Kuwait Airways Corp v Iraqi Airways Co* [1995] 1 W.L.R. 1147, (for further proceedings, see *Kuwait Airways Corp v Iraqi Airways Co (No.2)* [2001] 1 W.L.R. 430; *Kuwait Airways Corp v Iraqi Airways Co* [2003] EWHC 31 (Comm), [2003] 1 Lloyd's Rep. 448); *Propend Finance Pty Ltd v Sing*, *The Times*, May 2, 1997; 111 Int.L.R. 611; *Ministry of Trade of the Republic of Iraq v Tsavliris Salvage (International) Ltd* [2008] EWHC 612.

[23] s.3(1)(a): see *AIC Ltd v Federal Government of Nigeria* [2003] EWHC 1357 (QB) (proceedings resulting from application to register a foreign judgment against a foreign state under Administration of Justice Act 1920 relate not to the commercial transaction underlying the judgment, but to the judgment itself and such proceedings attract immunity). See also *Re Rafidain Bank* [1992] B.C.L.C. 301. The same principle applies in respect of proceedings for permission to enforce a foreign arbitration award under the Arbitration Act 1996 s.101: *Svenska Petroleum Exploration AB v Government of the Republic of Lithuania (No.2)* [2005] EWHC 2437 (Comm), [2006] 1 Lloyd's Rep. 181; affirmed [2006] EWCA Civ 1529, [2007] Q.B. 886.

governmental activity.[24] The funds in the bank account of a state's London embassy have been considered not to be used for commercial purposes.[25] There is no immunity for contractual obligations (whether arising out of a commercial transaction or not) to be performed in the United Kingdom[26]; or in the case of contracts of employment made or to be performed in the United Kingdom[27]; or as to claims for personal injury or damage to property caused by misconduct in the United Kingdom[28]; or in proceedings relating to immovables in the United Kingdom[29] or to an interest in other property by way of succession, gift or bona vacantia[30]; or in the case of proceedings relating to various forms of intellectual property[31]; or the administration of estates or trusts, or insolvency, even though a state may claim an interest in the property[32]; or where a state is a member of a corporate or unincorporate body constituted under United Kingdom law or controlled from the United Kingdom[33]; or in relation to various tax claims[34]; or

---

[24] *I Congreso del Partido* [1983] 1 A.C. 244, where the House of Lords divided 3:2 on this issue. Section 3(3) of the 1978 Act defines a "commercial transaction" as any contract and any guarantee or indemnity in respect of such a transaction or other financial obligation, or any other transaction or activity into which a state enters (apart from a contract of employment between a state and an individual) otherwise than in the exercise of sovereign authority. On this provision, see *Alcom Ltd v Republic of Colombia* [1984] A.C. 580; *Amalgamated Metal Trading Ltd v Dept of Trade and Industry, The Times*, March 21, 1989; *Kuwait Airways Corp v Iraqi Airways Co* [1995] 1 W.L.R. 1147 (for further proceedings, see *Kuwait Airways Corp v Iraqi Airways Co (No.2)* [2001] 1 W.L.R. 430; *Kuwait Airways Corp v Iraqi Airways Co* [2003] EWHC 31 (Comm); [2003] 1 Lloyd's Rep. 448); *Central Bank of Yemen v Cardinal Finance Investment Corp* [2001] Lloyd's Rep. Bank. 1; *Svenska Petroleum Exploration AB v Government of the Republic of Lithuania (No.2)* [2005] EWHC 2437 (Comm); affirmed [2007] EWCA Civ 1529, [2007] Q.B. 886; *Koo Golden East Mongolia v Bank of Nova Scotia* [2007] EWCA Civ 1443, [2008] 2 W.L.R. 1160. Staker (1995) 66 B.Y.I.L. 496; Fox (1996) 112 L.Q.R. 186. See also *Littrell v Government of the United States (No.2)* [1995] 1 W.L.R. 82; *Holland v Lampen-Wolfe* [2001] 1 W.L.R. 1573.

[25] *Alcom Ltd v Republic of Columbia* [1984] A.C. 580. See also *AIC Ltd v Federal Government of Nigeria* [2003] EWHC 1357 (QB).

[26] 1978 Act s.3(1)(b), though note the limitation, s.3(2). See *J.H. Rayner (Mincing Lane) Ltd v Dept of Trade and Industry* [1989] Ch. 72, 194–195, 222, 252, affirmed without reference to the point, [1990] 2 A.C. 418.

[27] s.4. This section does not apply to proceedings concerning the employment of the members of a mission within the meaning of the Convention scheduled to the Diplomatic Privileges Act 1964 or of the members of a consular post within the meaning of the Convention scheduled to the Consular Relations Act 1968 s.16(1)(a). See *Sengupta v Republic of India* [1983] I.C.R. 221; *United Arab Emirates v Abdelghafar* [1995] I.C.R. 65; *Arab Republic of Egypt v Gamal-Eldin* [1996] I.C.R. 13; *Ahmed v Government of the Kingdom of Saudi Arabia* [1996] I.C.R. 25; *Malaysian Industrial Development Authority v Jeyasingham* [1998] I.C.R. 307; *Government of the Kingdom of Saudi Arabia v Nasser* Unreported November 14, 2000 CA; Garnett (1997) 46 I.C.L.Q. 81; Garnett (2005) 54 I.C.L.Q. 705. And see *Fogarty v United Kingdom* (2002) 34 E.H.R.R. 302; *Al-Kadhimi v Government of Saudi Arabia* [2003] EWCA Civ 1689; *Aziz v Republic of Yemen* [2005] EWCA Civ 754, [2005] I.C.R. 1391.

[28] s.5; cf. *Military Affairs Office of The Embassy of the State of Kuwait v Caramba-Coker* (E.A.T./1054/02/RN, April 10, 2003).

[29] As with proceedings for breach of covenants in a lease: *Intpro Properties (UK) Ltd v Sauvel* [1983] Q.B. 1019. cf. *Re B (A Child) (Care Proceedings: Diplomatic Immunity)* [2002] EWHC 1751 (Fam); [2003] Fam. 16.

[30] 1978 Act, s.6.

[31] s.7.

[32] s.6(3). See *Re Rafidain Bank* [1992] B.C.L.C. 301.

[33] s.8. See *Maclaine, Watson & Co Ltd v International Tin Council* [1989] Ch. 253, 282–283, affirmed on other grounds, [1990] 2 A.C. 418.

[34] s.11.

as to claims arising from use of ships for commercial purposes[35] (again confirming an important common law development); or, finally, where the state has submitted to the jurisdiction of our courts.[36]

11–006 The 1978 Act also deals with a variety of procedural matters, such as service of process on a foreign state.[37] Power is given to restrict or extend the Act's immunities and privileges by Order in Council in relation to individual foreign states[38]; and provision is also made for the recognition here of foreign judgments involving the United Kingdom as a foreign state.[39] A certificate from the Secretary of State is conclusive evidence on the question as to whether for the purposes of the Act any country is a state, is part of a federal state and as to the person or persons to be regarded as the head or government of a state.[40]

11–007 **Acts of sovereign states.** In addition to the law relating to the immunity of foreign states or sovereigns, there are other circumstances in which an English court will decline to entertain proceedings involving sovereign states.[41] Under the "act of state" doctrine, the courts have no jurisdiction to investigate the propriety of an act of the Crown[42] performed in the course of its relations with a foreign state[43] and the concept of "act of state" may extend to cover acts authorised or ratified by the Crown in the exercise of sovereign power.[44] Furthermore, English courts have no jurisdiction, it appears, to investigate the

[35] s.10. See *Ministry of Trade of the Republic of Iraq v Tsavliris Salvage (International) Ltd* [2008] EWHC 612 (Comm).

[36] s.2; see *A Co Ltd v Republic of X* [1990] 2 Lloyd's Rep. 520; *Kuwait Airways Corp v Iraqi Airways Co* [1995] 1 W.L.R. 1147 (for further proceedings, see *Kuwait Airways Corp v Iraqi Airways Co (No.2)* [2001] 1 W.L.R. 429; *Kuwait Airways Corp v Iraqi Airways Co* [2003] EWHC 31, (Comm); [2003] 1 Lloyd's Rep. 448); *Mills v Embassy of the United States of America* Unreported May 9, 2000 CA; *Sabah Shipyard (Pakistan) Ltd v The Islamic Republic of Pakistan* [2002] EWCA Civ 1643; [2003] 2 Lloyd's Rep. 571. On submission in arbitration proceedings, see s.9; *Svenska Petroleum Exploration AB v Government of the Republic of Lithuania* [2005] EWHC 9 (Comm), [2005] 1 Lloyd's Rep. 515; *Svenska Petroleum Exploration AB v Government of the Republic of Lithuania (No.2)* [2005] EWHC 2437 (Comm), [2006] 1 Lloyd's Rep. 181; affirmed [2006] EWCA Civ 1529, [2007] Q.B. 886; *Donegal International Ltd v Zambia* [2007] EWHC 197 (Comm), [2007] 1 Lloyd's Rep. 397; *Ministry of Trade of the Republic of Iraq v Tsavliris Salvage (International) Ltd* [2008] EWHC 612 (Comm).

[37] ss.12–14; see *Alcom Ltd v Republic of Colombia* [1984] A.C. 580; *Westminster City Council v Government of the Islamic Republic of Iran* [1986] 1 W.L.R. 979; *Kuwait Airways Corp v Iraqi Airways Co* [1995] 1 W.L.R. 1147 (for further proceedings, see *Kuwait Airways Corp v Iraqi Airways Co (No.2)* [2001] 1 W.L.R. 429; *Kuwait Airways Corp v Iraqi Airways Co* [2003] EWHC 31, (Comm); [2003] 1 Lloyd's Rep. 448; *Crescent Oil and Shipping Services Ltd v Importang UEE* [1997] 3 All E.R. 428; *ABCI v De Banque Franco Tunisienne* [2003] EWCA Civ 205, [2003] 2 Lloyd's Rep. 146. And see *Soleh Boneh International Ltd v Government of the Republic of Uganda* [1993] 2 Lloyd's Rep. 208, 213; *Norsk Hydro ASA v State Property Fund of Ukraine* [2002] EWHC 2120 (Comm).

[38] s.15.

[39] ss.18–19.

[40] s.21(a). On the importance of the certificate, see *R. (on the application of Alamieyeseigha v Crown Prosecution Service* [2005] EWHC 2704 (Admin).

[41] See *Dicey, Morris and Collins on the Conflict of Laws*, 14th edn (2006), paras 5–041—5–050.

[42] The position of the Crown generally is discussed in Ch.10.

[43] e.g. *Secretary of State in Council of India v Kamachee Boye Sahaba* (1859) 13 Moo. P.C. 22, 75; *Salaman v Secretary of State of India* [1906] 1 K.B. 613.

[44] e.g. *Buron v Denman* (1848) 2 Exch. 167; *Nissan v Att-Gen* [1970] A.C. 179.

propriety of the acts of a foreign sovereign state recognised by Her Majesty's Government, where the act is performed on the territory of that state.[45] Indeed, there is now established a general principle that "the courts will not adjudicate upon the transactions of foreign sovereign states"—a principle which calls in such cases for "judicial restraint or abstention".[46] This principle does not, however, preclude an English court from ever taking cognisance of international law or from ever considering whether a violation of international law has occurred.[47] Thus, in appropriate circumstances, it is legitimate for an English court to have regard to the content of international law in deciding whether to recognise a foreign law on the grounds of public policy.[48] Further, the principle does not mean that the court must shut its eyes to a breach of an established principle of international law committed by one state against another when the breach is plain, since in such cases the standards being applied to adjudicate on the issues are clear and manageable and do not call for the exercise of judicial self-restraint.[49]

Foreign heads of state, ambassadors and their staffs. The immunity from suit of foreign ambassadors and members of their staffs is conferred by the Diplomatic Privileges Act 1964,[50] which enacts as part of the law of the United Kingdom certain articles of the Vienna Convention on Diplomatic Relations 11–008

[45] *Duke of Brunswick v King of Hanover* (1844) 6 Beav. 1, 57–58, (1848) 2 H.L.C. 1, 21–22, 26–27; *Carr v Fracis Times* [1902] A.C. 179–180; *Johnstone v Pedlar* [1921] 2 A.C. 262, 291; *Empresa Exportadora de Acuzar v Industria Azacurera Nacional SA* [1983] 2 Lloyd's Rep. 171, 194.

[46] *Buttes Gas and Oil Co v Hammer (No.3)* [1982] A.C. 888, 931; and see *J.H. Rayner (Mincing Lane) Ltd v Dept of Trade and Industry* [1990] 2 A.C. 418; *Arab Monetary Fund v Hashim (No.3)* [1991] 2 A.C. 114; *Kuwait Airways Corp v Iraqi Airways Co* [1995] 1 W.L.R. 1147 (for further proceedings, see *Kuwait Airways Corp v Iraqi Airways Co (No.2)* [2001] 1 W.L.R. 430; *Kuwait Airways Corp v Iraqi Airways Co* [2003] EWHC 31, (Comm); [2003] 1 Lloyd's Rep. 448); *Arab Monetary Fund v Hashim* [1993] 1 Lloyd's Rep. 543, 572, affirmed on this point [1996] 1 Lloyd's Rep. 589; *Philipp Brothers v Republic of Sierra Leone* [1995] 1 Lloyd's Rep. 289; *Westland Helicopters Ltd v Arab Organisation for Industrialisation* [1995] Q.B. 282; *R. v Home Secretary, Ex p Launder (No.2)* [1998] Q.B. 994; *R. v Home Secretary, Ex p. Johnson* [1999] Q.B. 1174; *Azov Shipping Co v Baltic Shipping Co* [1999] 2 Lloyd's Rep. 159; *Skrine & Co v Euromoney Publications Plc* [2002] I.L. Pr. 281, affirmed on other grounds, [2001] EWCA Civ 1479, [2002] E.M.L.R. 278; *Kuwait Airways Corp v Iraqi Airways Co (Nos 4 and 5)* [2002] UKHL 19, [2002] 2 A.C. 883; *R. (on the application of Abassi) v Secretary of State for Foreign and Commonwealth Affairs* [2002] EWCA Civ 1598, [2003] U.K.H.R.R. 76; *Republic of Ecuador v Occidental Exploration and Production Co* [2005] EWCA Civ 116, [2006] Q.B. 70; *AY Bank Ltd v Bosnia and Herzegovina* [2006] EWHC 830 (Ch), [2006] 2 All E.R. (Comm) 463; *Tajik Aluminium Plant v Ermatov* [2006] EWHC 2374 (Comm). See also *R. v Christian* [2006] UKPC 47, [2007] 2 W.L.R. 120; *R. (on the application of Al Rawi) v Secretary of State for Foreign Affairs* [2006] EWHC 972 (Admin); *Mbasogo v Logo Ltd* [2006] EWCA Civ 1370, [2007] Q.B. 846; *Tasarruf Mevduati Sigorta Fonu v Demirel* [2006] EWHC 3354 (Ch), [2007] 1 Lloyd's Rep. 223; affirmed on other grounds [2007] EWCA Civ 799, [2007] 1 W.L.R. 2508; *Total E & P Soudan SA v Edmonds* [2007] EWCA Civ 50, [2007] C.P.Rep. 20.

[47] *Kuwait Airways Corp v Iraqi Airways Co (Nos 4 and 5)* [2002] UKHL 19, [2002] 2 A.C. 883; *Republic of Ecuador v Occidental Exploration and Production Co* [2005] EWCA Civ 116; *AY Bank v Bosnia and Herzegovinia* [2006] EWHC 830 (Comm). Collins (2002) 51 I.C.L.Q. 485.

[48] *Kuwait Airways Corp v Iraqi Airways Co (Nos 4 and 5)* [2002] UKHL 19. See also *Republic of Ecuador v Occidental Exploration and Production Co* [2005] EWCA Civ 116.

[49] [2002] UKHL 19.

[50] The 1964 Act has been amended, mainly in minor respects, by the Diplomatic and other Privileges Act 1971, the State Immunity Act 1978, the Diplomatic and Consular Premises Act 1987 and the Arms Control and Disarmament (Privileges and Immunities) Act 1988.

(1961). These articles are set out in Sch.1 to the Act. Where a foreign sovereign or other head of a recognised state acts in his public capacity, effectively as the embodiment of the state, he is entitled to all the immunities which the state has under the State Immunity Act 1978.[51] When acting in a private capacity, however, such a foreign sovereign or other head of a recognised state is entitled to the immunities, with certain appropriate modifications, which are conferred by the Diplomatic Privileges Act 1964, since the 1978 Act extends those immunities to such persons.[52]

11–009 The immunity from suit of the chief representatives in the United Kingdom of countries of the Commonwealth and of the Republic of Ireland, and of members of their staffs, formerly depended on s.1(1) of the Diplomatic Immunities (Commonwealth Countries and Republic of Ireland) Act 1952. But that subsection has been repealed[53] and such immunity now depends on the Diplomatic Privileges Act 1964, i.e. on the Vienna Convention.[54]

11–010 **Categories of persons entitled to diplomatic immunity.** The Convention divides persons entitled to diplomatic immunity into three categories[55]: (1) "diplomatic agents," namely, the head of the mission and members of his diplomatic staff; (2) "members of the administrative and technical staff", e.g. persons employed in secretarial, clerical, communications and public relations duties; and (3) "members of the service staff", namely, members of the staff of the mission in its domestic service.

11–011 **Diplomatic agents.** Diplomatic agents enjoy immunity from criminal, civil[56] and administrative jurisdiction and from execution, except in three cases: (a) a real action relating to private immovable property situated in the United Kingdom (unless the property is held for the purposes of the mission,[57] and this does not include a diplomatic agents private residence)[58]; (b) an action relating to succession in which the diplomatic agent is involved as executor, administrator or beneficiary as a private person; and (c) an action relating to any professional or commercial activity exercised by the diplomatic agent outside his official

---

[51] State Immunity Act 1978 s.14; *Bank of Credit and Commerce International (Overseas) Ltd v Price Waterhouse* [1997] 4 All E.R. 108. On the immunity of a former head of state in the context of criminal liability, see *R. v Bow Street Metropolitan Stipendiary Magistrate Ex p. Pinochet Ugarte (No.3)* [2000] 1 A.C. 147. On heads of state, see generally, *Aziz v Aziz* [2007] EWCA Civ 712, [2008] 2 All E.R. 501; Watts (1994) 224 *Recueil des Cours*, III, 9.

[52] State Immunity Act 1978 s.20; *Bank of Credit and Commerce International (Overseas) Ltd v Price Waterhouse* [1997] 4 All E.R. 108; *R. v Bow Street Metropolitan Stipendiary Magistrate Ex p. Pinochet Ugarte (No.3)* [2000] 1 A.C. 147. The immunities extend to members of the family of the foreign sovereign or other head of a recognised state who form part of his household and to his private servants: 1978 Act s.20(1).

[53] Diplomatic Privileges Act 1964 s.8(4) and Sch.2.

[54] *Empson v Smith* [1966] 1 Q.B. 426; *Omerri v Uganda High Commission* [1973] I.T.R. 14; cf. *Sengupta v Republic of India* [1983] I.C.R. 221, 226.

[55] Diplomatic Privileges Act 1964 Sch.1 art.1.

[56] Including a divorce petition: *Shaw v Shaw* [1979] Fam. 62. For the position in relation to proceedings under the Child Abduction and Custody Act 1985, see *P v P (Diplomatic Immunity: Jurisdiction)* [1998] 1 F.L.R. 1026.

[57] *Alcom Ltd v Republic of Colombia* [1984] A.C. 580.

[58] *Intpro Properties (UK) Ltd v Sauvel* [1983] Q.B. 1019, 1032–1033.

functions.[59] A like immunity is conferred on the members of the family of a diplomatic agent forming part of his household.[60]

11–012 **Diplomatic premises.** The actual premises of a diplomatic (or consular mission) are inviolable,[61] as is the private residence of a diplomatic agent,[62] despite the fact that a diplomatic agent may not enjoy immunity from suit in respect of it.[63] However, the inviolability of diplomatic premises only applies to ones which are currently so used[64]; and the Diplomatic and Consular Premises Act 1987 gives the Secretary of State power to determine whether land has diplomatic or consular status.

11–013 **Administrative, technical and service staff.** The members of the administrative and technical staff of the mission, together with their families forming part of their respective households, and the members of the service staff of the mission, enjoy a like immunity, but with the important qualification that the immunity does not extend to acts performed outside the course of their duties.[65]

11–014 **Period of immunity.** Every person entitled to immunity from jurisdiction enjoys it from the moment he enters the United Kingdom to take up his post or, if he is already there, from the moment when his appointment is notified to the department of the Secretary of State concerned.[66] In the former case it would not seem necessary, in addition, that his appointment be notified to, or accepted by, the department of the Secretary of State concerned.[67] He can claim the immunity even if he only became entitled to it after the issue of the claim form.[68] When his functions come to an end, his immunity normally ceases at the moment when he leaves the country, or on the expiry of a reasonable period in which to do so[69]; but it continues to subsist in the case of acts performed in the exercise of his

[59] Vienna Convention art.31.

[60] Vienna Convention art.37(1).

[61] Vienna Convention art.22.

[62] Vienna Convention art.30; cf. *Agbor v Metropolitan Police Commissioner* [1969] 1 W.L.R. 703.

[63] *Intpro Properties (UK) Ltd v Sauvel* [1983] Q.B. 1019, 1033–1034.

[64] *Westminster City Council v Government of the Islamic Republic of Iran* [1986] 1 W.L.R. 979, 984–985.

[65] Vienna Convention art.37(2), (3). See *Government of the Kingdom of Saudi Arabia v Nasser*, Unreported November 14, 2000 CA; *Re B (A Child) (Care Proceedings: Diplomatic Immunity)* [2002] EWHC 1751, (Fam); [2003] Fam. 16.

[66] Vienna Convention art.39(1) and s.2(2).

[67] *R. v Secretary of State for the Home Department Ex p. Bagga* [1991] 1 Q.B. 485 in which the Court of Appeal, albeit in an immigration context, doubted the correctness of *R. v Governor of Pentonville Prison Ex p. Teja* [1971] 2 Q.B. 274; *R. v Lambeth Justices Ex p. Yusufu* [1985] Crim. L.R. 510 and *R. v Governor of Pentonville Prison Ex p. Osman (No.2)* [1989] C.O.D. 446 which appear to suggest that such notification and acceptance is necessary. *Ex p. Bagga* was followed by the Court of Appeal in the context of the State Immunity Act 1978 s.16(1) in *Ahmed v Government of the Kingdom of Saudi Arabia* [1996] I.C.R. 25. See *Dicey, Morris and Collins on the Conflict of Laws*, 14th edn (2006), para.10–070; *Jimenez v Inland Revenue Commissioners* [2004] S.T.C. 371; cf. Cheshire and North, *Private International Law*, 13th edn (1999), p.396.

[68] *Ghosh v D'Rozario* [1963] 1 Q.B. 106.

[69] *Re Regina and Palacios* (1984) 45 O.R. (2d) 269.

functions.[70] If a claim form is issued before immunity has ceased, then provided it has not been struck out, the proceedings may continue once the immunity has come to an end.[71] If he dies, the members of his family continue to enjoy the immunity to which they were entitled until the expiry of a reasonable period in which to leave the country.[72] The running of the Statute of Limitations is suspended during such time as the defendant enjoys diplomatic immunity.[73]

11–015 **Certificate of entitlement.** If in any proceedings any question arises whether or not any person is entitled to diplomatic immunity, a certificate issued by or under the authority of the Secretary of State stating any fact relating to the question is conclusive evidence of that fact.[74]

11–016 **British citizens.** Diplomatic immunity is restricted if the person entitled to it is a British citizen, a British Dependent Territories citizen or a British Overseas citizen.[75] Diplomatic agents who are such citizens or are permanently resident in the United Kingdom only enjoy immunity from jurisdiction in respect of official acts performed in the exercise of their functions, except in so far as additional immunities may be granted by the receiving state.[76] Other members of the staff of the mission and private servants of members of the mission who are such citizens or are permanently resident in the United Kingdom enjoy immunities only to the extent admitted by the receiving state.[77] The "extent admitted by the receiving state" and the "additional immunities" here referred to mean such as may be specified by Order in Council.[78] Members of the family of diplomatic agents or of members of the administrative or technical staff, or members of the service staff of the mission, enjoy no immunity from jurisdiction if they are British, British Dependent Territories or British Overseas citizens or are permanently resident in the United Kingdom.[79]

11–017 **Consular immunity.** The regulation of consular immunity so far as foreign consuls and their staffs are concerned is governed by the Consular Relations Act 1968[80] giving effect to certain articles of the Vienna Convention on Consular Relations 1963. In the case of civil proceedings, consular officers, who are defined as "any person, including the head of a consular post, entrusted in that

[70] Vienna Convention art.39(2); *Propend Finance Pty Ltd v Sing, The Times,* May 2, 1997, 111 Int.L.R. 611. cf. *Musurus Bey v Gadban* [1894] 2 Q.B. 352; *Zoernsch v Waldock* [1964] 1 W.L.R. 675. See also *R. v Bow Street Magistrate Ex p. Pinochet Ugarte (No.3)* [2000] 1 A.C. 147, 255–257, 270.

[71] *Shaw v Shaw* [1979] Fam. 62.

[72] Vienna Convention art.39(3).

[73] *Musurus Bey v Gadban* [1894] 2 Q.B. 352.

[74] Diplomatic Privileges Act 1964 s.4; and see *Engelke v Musmann* [1928] A.C. 433; *R. v Governor of Pentonville Prison Ex p. Teja* [1971] 2 Q.B. 274. cf. *Re P (Children Act: Diplomatic Immunity)* [1998] 1 F.L.R. 625, 626.

[75] See British Nationality Act 1981 s.51(3).

[76] Vienna Convention art.38(1) and s.2(2) of the Act.

[77] Vienna Convention art.38(2) and s.2(2) of the Act.

[78] s.2(6).

[79] Vienna Convention art.37 and s.2(2).

[80] As amended by the Diplomatic and other Privileges Act 1971 and the Diplomatic and Consular Premises Act 1987.

capacity with the exercise of consular functions",[81] and consular employees, who are any persons "employed in the administrative or technical service of a consular post",[82] shall not be amenable to the jurisdiction of the courts of this country in respect of acts performed in the exercise of consular functions. This immunity shall not apply, in the case of a contractual action, where such officer or employee did not contract expressly or impliedly as an agent of his sending state or in the case of an action by a third party for damage arising from an accident in the United Kingdom caused by a vessel, vehicle or aircraft.[83] Special provision is made for the fact that immunity from civil jurisdiction shall not be accorded to consular employees who carry on private gainful occupation in the United Kingdom.[84] The position of officers from the Commonwealth and the Republic of Ireland who perform duties substantially similar to those performed by consular officers from foreign countries is governed by the Diplomatic Immunities (Commonwealth Countries and Republic of Ireland) Act 1952[85] until such time as the provisions of the Consular Relations Act 1968[86] are applied to them by Order in Council.

International organisations. The International Organisations Acts 1968[87] and 1981, which replaced the International Organisations (Immunities and Privileges) Act 1950, empower the Crown by Order in Council to confer complete immunity from suit and legal process[88] upon any international organisation of which the United Kingdom and any other Sovereign power are members,[89] and to confer the like immunity from suit and legal process as is accorded to the head of a diplomatic mission upon representatives of the organisation or representatives of a member of any organs or committees of the organisation, and upon specified high officers of the organisation and persons employed by or serving on 11–018

---

[81] Consular Relations Act 1968 Sch.I art.1.

[82] Sch.I art.1.

[83] Vienna Convention art.43.

[84] Vienna Convention art.57.

[85] s.1(2).

[86] s.12 as substituted by the Diplomatic and other Privileges Act 1971.

[87] As amended by the Diplomatic and other Privileges Act 1971 and International Organisations Act 2005.

[88] Including winding up: *Re International Tin Council* [1989] Ch. 309. For further litigation involving the Tin Council and its immunities under the 1968 Act, see *J.H. Rayner (Mincing Lane) Ltd v Dept of Trade and Industry* [1989] Ch. 72; affirmed [1990] 2 A.C. 418; *Standard Chartered Bank v International Tin Council* [1987] 1 W.L.R. 641; *Shearson Lehman Bros Inc v Maclaine, Watson & Co Ltd* [1988] 1 W.L.R. 16, HL; *Maclaine, Watson & Co Ltd v International Tin Council* [1989] Ch. 253; *Maclaine, Watson & Co Ltd v International Tin Council (No.2)* [1989] Ch. 286. In *Mukoro v European Bank for Reconstruction and Development* [1994] I.C.R. 897 it was held that immunity extended to proceedings in an industrial tribunal under the Race Relations Act 1976 by an individual whose application for a post with the organisation had been rejected. The making of an Order in Council in relation to an organisation may lead to the conclusion that that organisation is thereby clothed with such legal personality as to be capable of entering into valid contracts: *J.H. Rayner (Mincing Lane) Ltd v Dept of Trade and Industry* [1990] 2 A.C. 415.

[89] International Organisations Act 1981 s.1(1), (2)(b) and Sch.1 Pt I para.1. The immunities conferred by s.1 may be extended to include representatives at conferences of the organisation in the United Kingdom: s.5A. On the compatibility of this immunity with art.6 of the European Convention on Human Rights, see *Entico Corp Ltd v UNESCO* [2008] EWHC 531 (Comm), [2008] 1 Lloyd's Rep. 673; *Waite and Kennedy v Germany* (2000) 30 E.H.R.R. 261 (European Court of Human Rights).

the organisation as experts or as persons engaged on missions for the organisation.[90] Similar immunity extends to the members of the official staff of such representatives, provided they are recognised as holding a rank equivalent to that of diplomatic agent,[91] and to the members of the family forming part of the household of such representatives, high officers and members of their official staffs holding diplomatic rank.[92] A limited immunity from suit extending only to things done or omitted to be done in the course of the performance of official duties is conferred upon specified subordinate officers and servants of the organisation[93] and upon members of the administrative or technical service of the representative[94] and members of their families forming part of their households.[95] However, no such immunities may be conferred on any person as the representative of the United Kingdom or as a member of his staff.[96]

11–019 **Other persons entitled to immunity.** Special provision is made in the Acts of 1968 and 1981 for conferring immunity on officers of specialised agencies of the United Nations,[97] and on other organisations of which the United Kingdom is not a member,[98] including international commodity organisations.[99] The Acts further provide for the grant of immunity from suit to the judges and registrars of any international tribunal and to parties to any proceedings before any such tribunal and to their agents, advisers or advocates and to any witnesses in or assessors for the purposes of any proceedings before any international tribunal,[100] and for the grant of similar immunity to the representatives of foreign states and their official staffs attending conferences in the United Kingdom.[101] (The Diplomatic Immunities (Conferences with Commonwealth Countries and the Republic of Ireland) Act 1961[102] makes similar provision for representatives of the Commonwealth and of the Republic of Ireland and their official staff attending conferences in the United Kingdom.) Orders in Council have been

---

[90] s.1(2)(c), (3), and Sch.1 Pt II para.9.
[91] Is.1(4) and Sch.1 Pt IV para.20.
[92] s.1(4) and Sch.1 Pt IV para.23.
[93] s.1(2)(d) and Sch.1 Pt III para.14.
[94] s.1(4) and Sch.1 Pt IV para.21.
[95] s.1(4) and Sch.1 Pt IV para.23(4).
[96] s.1(6)(b). This is subject to s.4 of the International Organisations Act 1981.
[97] s.2(1).
[98] s.4. In *Arab Monetary Fund v Hashim (No.3)* [1991] 2 A.C. 114 (see F.A. Mann (1991) 107 L.Q.R. 357; Marston (1991) C.L.J. 218) it was held that an international organisation of which the United Kingdom was not a member and which had been given legal personality under the law of the United Arab Emirates, where its headquarters were situated, had capacity to sue in England even though no legal capacity had been conferred upon it by English law. Attribution of legal personality by the law of the Emirates created a corporation capable of being recognised in England. Although the organisation was not entitled to immunity under the English Acts, it has been held that it may be entitled to immunity, in respect of official acts, under customary international law, that such immunity may be recognised by the English courts and, further, that the immunity may extend to senior officials of the organisation: *Arab Monetary Fund v Hashim* [1993] 1 Lloyd's Rep. 543, 573–574. As to waiver of this immunity, see below, para.11–020.
[99] s.4A (added to the 1968 Act by s.2 of the International Organisations Act 1981) and representatives at conferences organised by them in the United Kingdom: s.5A.
[100] s.5.
[101] s.6.
[102] s.1, as amended by the Diplomatic Privileges Act 1964 s.8(4) and Sch.2.

made applying the Acts of 1950, 1968 and 1981 to a large number of organisations and (in most cases) to their representatives, officers, etc.[103] Any Order in Council made under the 1950 Act in force at the time of the passage of the 1968 Act shall continue to have effect, notwithstanding the repeal of the 1950 Act, until revoked or varied.[104] Special statutes or Orders in Council made thereunder confer immunity from suit on a number of international organisations and their representatives in the United Kingdom.[105] The immunities of major international organisations of which the United Kingdom is a member, such as the United Nations, the European Economic Community[106] and the Council of Europe, and of persons employed by or connected with such organisations, are provided for in a variety of separate international agreements.[107]

Waiver of immunity: common law. At common law, both sovereign[108] and diplomatic[109] immunity could be waived by or on behalf of the foreign state concerned. But the doctrine was confined within narrow limits. In the first place, there could be no waiver except with full knowledge of the right and with the authority of the foreign sovereign or ambassador.[110] Secondly, waiver had to take place at the time when the court was asked to exercise jurisdiction[111]: it could not be inferred from a prior contract to submit to the jurisdiction of the court,[112] nor from the agreement to submit to arbitration,[113] nor even from an application to the court to set aside an arbitration award,[114] nor (semble) could it take place after judgment had been pronounced.[115] **11–020**

---

[103] See Halsbury's *Laws of England*, 4th edn, Vol.18, para.1598. As to the Immunity of the International Maritime Organisation, see SI 2002/1826.

[104] 1968 Act s.12(5).

[105] See, e.g. Commonwealth Secretariat Act 1966 s.1(2) and Sch., as amended by International Organisations Act 2005, ss.1–3. Although immunity is conferred on the Commonwealth Secretariat (as to which, see *Jananyagam v Commonwealth Secretariat* [2007] WL 919439 (EAT)), that immunity does not extend to the Commonwealth Secretariat Arbitration Tribunal, decisions of which may be reviewed under the Arbitration Act 1996: see *Mohsin v Commonwealth Secretariat* [2002] EWHC 377 (Comm); Arbitration (International Investment Disputes) Act 1966 s.4 and Sch., International Monetary Fund Act 1979 s.5(1); Overseas Development and Co-operation Act 1980 s.9; Multilateral Investment Guarantee Agency Act 1988 s.3.

[106] The EEC cannot claim sovereign immunity: *JH Rayner (Mincing Lane) Ltd v Dept of Trade and Industry* [1989] Ch. 72, 196–203, 252–253 CA, affirmed on other grounds, [1990] 2 A.C. 418.

[107] For a list of such agreements, see Halsbury's *Laws of England*, Vol.18, paras 1595–1596. See also, *J.H. Rayner (Mincing Lane) Ltd v Dept of Trade and Industry* [1989] Ch. 72, 203–205.

[108] *Duke of Brunswick v King of Hanover* (1844) 6 Beav. 1, 37, 38; *Sultan of Johore v Bendahar* [1952] A.C. 318.

[109] *Taylor v Best* (1854) 14 C.B. 487; *Re Suarez* [1918] 1 Ch. 176; *Dickinson v Del Solar* [1930] 1 K.B. 376; *R. v A.B.* [1941] 1 K.B. 454.

[110] *Re Republic of Bolivia Exploration Syndicate Ltd* [1914] 1 Ch. 139; *Baccus S.R.L. v Servicio Nacional del Trigo* [1957] 1 Q.B. 438; *R. v Madan* [1961] 2 Q.B. 1.

[111] *Mighell v Sultan of Johore* [1894] 1 Q.B. 149, 159, 161, 162–164; *Duff Development Co v Government of Kelantan* [1924] A.C. 797; *Kahan v Pakistan Federation* [1951] 2 K.B. 1003; *The Philippine Admiral* [1974] 2 Lloyd's Rep. 568, 586–587, affirmed [1977] A.C. 373.

[112] *Kahan v Pakistan Federation* [1951] 2 K.B. 1003; *Baccus S.R.L. v Servicio Nacional del Trigo* [1957] 1 Q.B. 438.

[113] *Duff Development Co v Government of Kelantan* [1924] A.C. 797.

[114] [1924] A.C. 797. See above, fn.3.

[115] *R. v Madan* [1961] 2 Q.B. 1.

11–021 **Submission to jurisdiction.** The State Immunity Act 1978 now makes express provision for a state to submit to the jurisdiction of the court and thereby waive its state immunity, but such waiver does not exclude the assertion of absolute privilege[116] nor does submission to the adjudicative jurisdiction of the courts necessarily imply submission to the enforcement jurisdiction of the courts.[117] There are detailed rules as to what constitutes submission[118] but one of their main effects is to free the doctrine of waiver from its narrow common law limits. Submission may, under the Act, be by prior written agreement and is permitted after a dispute has arisen.[119] A state is also deemed to submit if it institutes the proceedings[120] or if it intervenes, or takes any step, in proceedings unless it does so in reasonable ignorance of facts entitling it to immunity and immunity is then claimed as soon as reasonably practicable.[121] However, intervention merely to claim immunity or to assert an interest in property in circumstances where the state would have been entitled to immunity in any proceedings brought against it does not constitute submission.[122] A contractual waiver of immunity, without any submission to the jurisdiction of the court, is not a submission for the purposes of the Act[123]; nor is submission to be deduced from a choice of law clause.[124] Submission extends to any appeal, but not to any counterclaim unless it arises out of the same legal relationship or facts as the

---

[116] *Fayed v Al Tajir* [1988] Q.B. 712.

[117] State Immunity Act 1978 s.13(2); *Alcom Ltd v Republic of Colombia* [1983] A.C. 580. Where a state has agreed in writing to submit a dispute which has arisen or which, may arise to arbitration, the state cannot then claim immunity as respects proceedings in the courts of the United Kingdom which relate to the arbitration, unless there is a contrary provision in the agreement or the arbitration agreement is between States: State Immunity Act 1978 s.9: see *Ministry of Trade of the Republic of Iraq v Tsavliris Salvage (International) Ltd* [2008] EWHC 612 (Comm). Section 9 extends to proceedings for permission to enforce an arbitration award under Arbitration Act 1996 s.101, but probably does not extend to enforcement of an award against property of a state: s.13(2)(b); *Svenska Petroleum Exploration AB v Government of the Republic of Lithuania (No.2)* [2005] EWHC 2437 (Comm), [2006] 1 Lloyd's Rep.181; affirmed [2006] EWCA Civ 1529, [2007] Q.B. 886. See *Dicey, Morris and Collins on the Conflict of Laws*, 14th edn (2006), para.10–051.

[118] s.2. Section 2 is a complete statement of the circumstances in which a state submits for the purposes of the Act: *Svenska Petroleum Exploration AB v Government of the Republic of Lithuania (No.2)* [2005] EWHC 2437 (Comm), [2006] 1 Lloyd's Rep. 181.

[119] s.2(2). See *A Co Ltd v Republic of X* [1990] 2 Lloyd's Rep. 520; *Ahmed v Government of the Kingdom of Saudi Arabia* [1996] I.C.R. 25 (meaning of "written agreement"); *Propend Finance Pty Ltd v Sing, The Times*, May 2, 1997; 111 Int. L.R. 611; *Mills v Embassy of the United States of America*, Unreported May 9, 2000 CA; *Sabah Shipyard (Pakistan) Ltd v The Islamic Republic of Pakistan* [2002] EWCA Civ 1643, [2003] 2 Lloyd's Rep. 571; *Donegal International Ltd v Zambia* [2007] EWHC 197 (Comm), [2007] 1 Lloyd's Rep. 397.

[120] s.2(3)(a).

[121] s.2(3)(b), (5). See *Kuwait Airways Corp v Iraqi Airways Co* [1995] 1 Lloyd's Rep. 25 CA, reversed, in part, on other grounds, [1995] 1 W.L.R. 1147 HL (for further proceedings, see *Kuwait Airways Corp v Iraqi Airways Co (No.2)* [2001] 1 W.L.R. 429; *Kuwait Airways Corp v Iraqi Airways Co* [2003] EWHC 31 (Comm), [2003] 1 Lloyd's Rep. 448; *London Branch of the Nigerian Universities Commission v Bastians* [1995] I.C.R. 358; *Arab Republic of Egypt v Gamal-Eldin* [1996] I.C.R. 13; *Malaysian Industrial Development Authority v Jeyasingham* [1998] I.C.R. 307; *Aziz v Republic of Yemen* [2005] EWCA Civ 745; [2005] I.C.R. 1391.

[122] s.2(3), (4).

[123] *Svenska Petroleum Exploration AB v Republic of Lithuania (No.2)* [2005] EWHC 2437 (Comm); [2006] 1 Lloyd's Rep. 181; affirmed [2006] EWCA Civ 1529, [2007] Q.B. 886.

[124] s.2(2).

claim.[125] The head of a state's diplomatic mission is deemed to have authority to submit on behalf of the state,[126] as is any person who entered into a contract on behalf of the state in respect of proceedings arising out of the contract.[127] Submission to the jurisdiction is not submission to execution, though such process may be issued with the written consent of the state.[128]

Waiver of diplomatic or consular immunity. The Diplomatic Privileges Act 1964[129] and the Consular Relations Act 1968[130] provide that diplomatic and consular immunity may be waived by the sending state; and both Acts provide that a waiver by the head or acting head of the mission is deemed to be a waiver by that state.[131] Waiver must always be express, except that the initiating of proceedings precludes the plaintiff from invoking immunity from jurisdiction in respect of any counterclaim directly connected with the principal claim. But though waiver must be express, there is no requirement under the Acts (as there was at common law[132]) that it must take place at the time when the court is asked to exercise jurisdiction. The better view, it is submitted, is that there is no such requirement since although waiver is not defined, the term in both Acts is derived from international conventions and should not, therefore, be given the narrow interpretation attributed to it at common law.[133] Unfortunately, however, it has been held that diplomatic immunity cannot be waived by contract inter partes but only by an undertaking or consent, given when the court is asked to exercise jurisdiction,[134] a regressive view which, it is submitted, should not be followed.[135] Waiver of immunity from jurisdiction in civil or administrative proceedings does not imply waiver of immunity in respect of the execution of the judgment, for which a separate waiver is required.[136] 11–022

[125] s.2(6). See *Propend Finance Pty Ltd v Sing*, *The Times*, May 2, 1997, 111 Int. L.R. 611; cf. *Sultan of Johore v Bendahar* [1952] A.C. 318 (appeal); *High Commissioner for India v Ghosh* [1960] 1 Q.B. 134 (counterclaim).

[126] s.2(7). See *Ahmed v Government of the Kingdom of Saudi Arabia* [1996] I.C.R. 25; *Arab Republic of Egypt v Gamal-Eldin* [1996] I.C.R. 13; *Propend Finance Pty Ltd v Sing*, *The Times*, May 2, 1997; 111 Int.L.R. 611; *Malaysian Industrial Development Authority v Jeyasingham* [1998] I.C.R. 307; cf. *Donegal International Ltd v Zambia* [2007] EWHC 197 (Comm), [2007] 1 Lloyd's Rep. 397 (authority of Minister). On the method of waiver or submission, see *Fayed v Al Tajir* [1988] Q.B. 712, 733, 736–737.

[127] s.2(7). See *Ahmed v Government of the Kingdom of Saudi Arabia* [1996] I.C.R. 25.

[128] s.13(3); cf. *Re Suarez* [1917] 2 Ch. 131; *Duff Development Co v Government of Kelantan* [1923] 1 Ch. 385, [1924] A.C. 797, 810, 821, 830. See also *Mitchell v Ibrahim Al-Dahli* [2005] EWCA Civ 720 (undertaking by foreign state not to appeal costs order made against it does not imply waiver of immunity should enforcement of the costs order be sought).

[129] Sch.1 art.32.

[130] Sch.1 art.45.

[131] s.2(3); see *Propend Finance Pty Ltd v Sing*, *The Times*, May 2, 1997, 111 Int. L.R. 611; 1968 Act s.1(5).

[132] *Mighell v Sultan of Johore* [1894] 1 Q.B. 149; *Duff Development Co v Government of Kelantan* [1924] A.C. 797; *Kahan v Pakistan Federation* [1951] 2 K.B. 1003.

[133] See *Dicey, Morris and Collins on the Conflict of Laws*, 14th edn (2006) para.10–074; Cohn (1958) 34 B.Y.I.L. 360; F.A. Mann (1991) 107 L.Q.R. 362.

[134] *A Co Ltd v Republic of X* [1990] 2 Lloyd's Rep. 520, cogently criticised by F.A. Mann (1991) 107 L.Q.R. 362.

[135] F.A. Mann (1991) 107 L.Q.R. 362.

[136] Which waiver must also be given by an undertaking or consent given to the court when it is asked to exercise jurisdiction: *A Co Ltd v Republic of X* [1990] 2 Lloyd's Rep. 520.

11–023 **Waiver of other statutory immunities.** The possibility of waiver of the immunity is specifically provided for in Orders in Council made under the International Organisations Act 1968,[137] and in the Commonwealth Secretariat Act 1966,[138] and the Arbitration (International Investments Disputes) Act 1966.[139]

2. ALIEN ENEMIES[140]

11–024 **Who is an alien enemy.** At common law, the term "alien enemy" means any person irrespective of nationality who voluntarily[141] resides or who carries on business in any enemy or enemy-occupied country during a war in which the United Kingdom is engaged.[142] As will be seen,[143] an enemy subject who resides or carries on business in the United Kingdom or in a neutral or allied country is nearly always treated as an alien friend. Hence the test of enemy character at common law is a territorial and not a national one. It is an objective test and depends on facts, not on the prejudices, passions or patriotism of the individual concerned.[144] So during the Second World War a company incorporated in

[137] See, e.g. *Standard Chartered Bank v International Tin Council* [1987] 1 W.L.R. 641. A senior official of an international organisation which is entitled to immunity under customary international law (see above, para.11–019 fn.96) may also be entitled to immunity, as a matter of customary international law, from legal process in respect of official acts, but since the immunity is granted to the official for the benefit of the organisation, rather than for the individual official, then the immunity may be waived by the organisation, and, if it is so waived, there is no further bar to proceedings against the official: *Arab Monetary Fund v Hashim* [1993] 1 Lloyd's Rep. 543, 574.

[138] s.1(2) and Sch. para.8.

[139] Sch.1 arts 20, 21.

[140] The leading authorities on the procedural incapacity of alien enemies are the judgment of the full Court of Appeal in *Porter v Freudenberg* [1915] 1 K.B. 857; the dissenting judgment of Lord Sumner in *Rodriguez v Speyer Brothers* [1919] A.C. 59; and the judgment of Lord Wright in *Sovfracht (V/O) v Van Udens Scheepvaart en Agentuur Maatschappij (N.V. Gebr)* [1943] A.C. 203. See also McNair, *Legal Effects of War*, 4th edn (1966), Ch.3. The principles discussed in this section only apply when a technical state of war exists. See *Amin v Brown* [2005] EWHC 1670 (Ch), [2006] I.L. Pr. 67 where it was held that the procedural incapacity of an alien enemy only came into existence if a technical state of war existed between the United Kingdom and the relevant country and that there was no warrant for extending the disability to modern armed conflict which did not involve war in this sense. Accordingly, an Iraqi citizen resident in Iraq was entitled to proceed in the English court as claimant since the court was satisfied, on the basis of Ministerial statements, that Her Majesty's government's position was that there was not, and had not been, a state of war between the United Kingdom and Iraq. See also *Janson v Driefontaine Consolidated Mines* [1902] A.C. 484. Although the existence of hostilities is not uncommon, it is rare for a technical state of war to exist today: see *Amin v Brown* [2005] EWHC 1670 at [28]; Greenwood in *The Handbook of Humanitarian Law in Armed Conflicts* (Fleck, ed.), pp.43–44.

[141] e.g. not as a prisoner of war: *Vandyke v Adams* [1942] Ch. 155, a case under the Trading with the Enemy Act 1939. Contrast *Scotland v South African Territories Ltd* (1917) 33 T.L.R. 255.

[142] *Porter v Freudenberg* [1915] 1 K.B. 857; *Sovfracht (V/O) v Van Udens* [1943] A.C. 203; cf. *The Hoop* (1799) 1 C.Rob. 196; *McConnell v Hector* (1802) 3 Bros & P. 113; *O'Mealey v Wilson* (1808) 1 Camp. 482; *Roberts v Hardy* (1815) 3 M. & S. 533; *Janson v Driefontein Consolidated Mines* [1902] A.C. 484, 505; *Amin v Brown* [2005] EWHC 1670 at [28].

[143] Below, para.11–027.

[144] *Sovfracht (V/O) v Van Udens* [1943] A.C. 203, 219.

Holland and having its principal place of business in Rotterdam was held to be an alien enemy after the German occupation of Holland.[145]

Companies. A company registered in an enemy or enemy-occupied country is an alien enemy,[146] unless the control of its affairs is shifted to a country not occupied by the enemy.[147] But a company registered in the United Kingdom and carrying on business here may acquire enemy character by reason of the hostile residence or activities of its agents or other persons in de facto control of its affairs.[148] Thus where all the shares except one in an English company were held by Germans resident in Germany, and all its directors were Germans so resident, the company was treated as an alien enemy.[149] In that case it was said that a company registered in the United Kingdom but carrying on business in an enemy country is to be regarded as an alien enemy.[150] But that proposition is too widely stated, for the contrary has since been held.[151] 11–025

Trading with the Enemy Act 1939. The Trading with the Enemy Act 1939[152] contains a statutory definition of an "enemy". But this definition is limited to the purposes of the Act and does not affect the common law rule with regard to the separate question of an alien enemy's capacity to sue,[153] with which alone this section is concerned. 11–026

Alien enemy as claimant. An alien enemy cannot sue in the Queen's courts or take up the position of an *actor* in British litigation[154] save under royal licence.[155] The fact that the action was commenced before the outbreak of war does not enable an alien enemy to continue his action during the war,[156] nor can he appeal against a judgment given against him before the war.[157] He cannot appear as claimant in an interpleader issue.[158] The royal licence necessary to cure 11–027

---

[145] *Sovfracht (V/O) v Van Udens* [1943] A.C. 203. Contrast *The Pamia* [1943] 1 All E.R. 269, where a Belgian company moved its head office from Antwerp to Pittsburgh shortly after the German occupation of Belgium and so was held not to be an alien enemy.

[146] *Janson v Driefontein Consolidated Mines* [1902] A.C. 484; *Sovfracht (V/O) v Van Udens* [1943] A.C. 203.

[147] *The Pamia* [1943] 1 All E.R. 269.

[148] *Daimler Co Ltd v Continental Tyre and Rubber Co Ltd* [1916] 2 A.C. 307, 344. But it does not cease to be an English company and is therefore not immune from the Trading with the Enemy Act 1939: *Kuenigl v Donnersmarck* [1955] 1 Q.B. 515.

[149] *Daimler Co Ltd v Continental Tyre and Rubber Co Ltd* [1916] 2 A.C. 307.

[150] *Daimler Co Ltd v Continental Tyre and Rubber Co Ltd* [1916] 2 A.C. 307, 346.

[151] *Re Hicks* [1917] 1 K.B. 48.

[152] s.2, as amended by the Emergency Laws (Miscellaneous Provisions) Act 1953 s.2 and Sch.II para.3.

[153] *Sovfracht (V/O) v Van Udens* [1943] A.C. 203, 219, approving the view of the Court of Appeal on this point.

[154] *Porter v Freudenberg* [1915] 1 K.B. 857; *Sovfracht (V/O) v Van Udens* [1943] A.C. 203, 209.

[155] *Wells v Wiliams* (1697) 1 Ld. Raym. 282; *The Hoop* (1799) 1 C.Rob. 196, 201.

[156] See McNair at pp.84–86; *Le Bret v Papillon* (1804) 4 East 502; *Alcenius v Nigren* (1854) 1 E. & B. 217. See also *Geiringer v Swiss Bank Corp* [1940] 1 All E.R. 406; *Eichengruen v Mond* [1940] Ch. 785.

[157] *Porter v Freudenberg* [1915] 1 K.B. 857, 884.

[158] *Geiringer v Swiss Bank Corp* [1940] 1 All E.R. 406.

the claimant's incapacity to sue may be either express,[159] or inferred from the fact of his presence here with the knowledge and tacit approval of the Crown, e.g. if he registered under the Aliens Restriction Act 1914 and orders made thereunder.[160] Such a licence can be revoked,[161] but it is not revoked merely by the internment of the alien,[162] at any rate if the internment was an act of general policy adopted for the safety of the realm and was not due to a hostile act or attitude on the alien's part. The effect of a licence is to place the alien enemy under the protection of the Crown, with the result that in all respects except perhaps one[163] he is treated as an alien friend for procedural purposes.

11–028 The rule which debars an alien enemy from suing is an ancient rule of the common law which is based on public policy.[164] It is immaterial that Emergency Regulations made under the Trading with the Enemy Act 1939 would prevent the claimant from transmitting abroad the sum recovered until the end of the war, because he might more easily raise a loan from neutral sources on the security of a judgment debt than he could on the security of a simple contract debt, and so help to furnish the enemy country with the sinews of war.[165]

11–029 **Exceptions.** There are two or possibly three exceptions to the rule:

(1) In *Rodriguez v Speyer Bros*[166] it was held by a bare majority of the House of Lords (against powerful dissent by Lords Atkinson and Sumner) that an alien enemy could be joined as co-plaintiff in an action by a firm of partners of which he was formerly a member to recover a pre-war debt due to the firm, on the somewhat specious grounds that the rule should not be applied if to do so would inflict hardship not on the enemy but on British or neutral partners.[167] Lord Wright has said that this decision must be limited to its special facts.[168]

[159] See, e.g. *Fibrosa v Fairbairn* [1943] A.C. 32, 35, 39–40, and comments thereon in *Sovfracht v Van Udens* [1943] A.C. 203, 208; *The Brighton* [1951] 2 Lloyd's Rep. 65.

[160] *Princess Thurn and Taxis v Moffitt* [1915] 1 Ch. 58, approved in *Porter v Freudenberg* [1915] 1 K.B. 857, 874; *Vokl v Rotuna Hospital* [1914] 2 I.R. 549; cf. *Re Mary, Duchess of Sutherland* (1915) 31 T.L.R. 248, 394 (enemy national resident in a neutral country may sue). The Aliens Restriction Act 1914 was repealed by the Immigration Act 1971 s.34(1) Sch.6.

[161] *Netz v Ede* [1946] Ch. 224.

[162] *Schaffenius v Goldberg* [1916] 1 K.B. 284; cf. *Sparenburgh v Bannatyne* (1797) 1 Bos. & P. 163, where an enemy prisoner of war was allowed to sue.

[163] He may be unable to apply for a writ of habeas corpus: *The Three Spanish Sailors* (1779) 2 W.Bl. 1324; *Ex p. Liebmann* [1916] 1 K.B. 268; *R. v Bottrill* [1947] K.B. 41; but see Sharpe, *The Law of Habeas Corpus* (1976), pp.112–114.

[164] *Porter v Freudenberg* [1915] 1 K.B. 857, 880; *Rodriguez v Speyer Bros* [1919] A.C. 59, 66, 124; *Sovfracht (V/O) v Van Udens* [1943] A.C. 203, 213; *Amin v Brown* [2005] EWHC 1670 (Ch), [2006] I.L. Pr. 67.

[165] *Rodriguez v Speyer Bros* [1919] A.C. 59, 114; *Sovfracht (V/O) v Van Udens* [1943] A.C. 203, 212, 236, 252; *Amin v Brown* [2005] EWHC 1670 (Ch.), [2006] I.L. Pr. 67.

[166] *Rodriguez v Speyer Bros* [1919] A.C. 59.

[167] [1919] A.C. 59, 71.

[168] *Sovfracht (V/O) v Van Udens* [1943] A.C. 203, 233; cf. McNair at p.83, fn.4: "The House of Lords have in the *Sovfracht* case substantially repaired the damage done by the majority speeches in *Rodriguez v Speyer Brothers*."

(2) An alien enemy can be heard without a licence in the Prize Court if his claim is based on an international treaty or convention, but not otherwise.[169]

(3) There is ancient authority for the proposition that an alien enemy can sue *en autre droit*, e.g. as executor or administrator of a deceased person.[170] It is, however, an open question whether this authority would be followed at the present day.[171]

Alien enemy as defendant. There is no rule of common law which prevents an alien enemy from being sued if service or substituted service can be effected.[172] There may be difficulties about service,[173] but in time of war it is usual for the rules as to substituted service to be relaxed under statutory authority.[174] If he is sued, an alien enemy can appear and be heard in his defence and may take all such steps as may be deemed necessary for the proper presentation of his defence, and may appeal against any judgment given against him, for to hold otherwise would be contrary to natural justice.[175] He may plead a set-off, but he may not counterclaim,[176] nor take third party proceedings,[177] nor execute a judgment for costs during the war,[178] because in doing any of these things he would become an *actor*. He may be made bankrupt[179] and may prove in the bankruptcy of another,[180] but if his proof is rejected he may not take proceedings or challenge the trustee's decision, for in doing so he would become an *actor*.[181] 11–030

Limitation of actions. The Limitation (Enemies and War Prisoners) Act 1945[182] suspended the running of any period of limitation for the bringing of any action in which any person who would have been a necessary party was an enemy or was detained in enemy territory until he ceased to be so and for 12 months thereafter. 11–031

Illegal contracts with alien enemies. The rule which has been considered in this section, that an alien enemy has no *persona standi in judicio*, must be 11–032

[169] *The Möwe* [1915] P. 1; *The Glenroy* [1943] P. 109.

[170] *Brocks v Phillips* (1599) Cro. Eliz. 683; *Richfield v Udell* (1667) Carter 191; *Villa v Dimock* (1694) Skin. 370.

[171] See *Rodriguez v Speyer Bros* [1919] A.C. 59, 70, 102, 118, 137; and see McNair at p.86.

[172] *Robinson & Co v Continental Insurance Co of Mannheim* [1915] 1 K.B. 155; *Porter v Freudenberg* [1915] 1 K.B. 857, 880 et seq.

[173] These were discussed in *Porter v Freudenberg* [1915] 1 K.B. 857, 886–890, and *Churchill & Co v Lonberg* [1914] 3 All E.R. 137.

[174] See, e.g. Legal Proceedings against Alien Enemies Act 1915 (repealed in 1927); RSC O.9 r.14(b) (added in 1941 and repealed in 1964).

[175] *Porter v Freudenberg* [1915] 1 K.B. 857, 883–884.

[176] *Re Stahlwerk Becker A/G's Patent* [1917] 2 Ch. 272, 276.

[177] *Halsey v Lowenfeld* [1916] 2 K.B. 707.

[178] *Robinson & Co v Continental Insurance Co of Mannheim* [1915] 1 K.B. 155, 162.

[179] *Re Hilckes* [1917] 1 K.B. 48.

[180] *Ex p. Boussmaker* (1806) 13 Ves. 71.

[181] *Re Wilson and Wilson Ex p. Marum* (1915) 84 L.J.K.B. 1893.

[182] As amended. See *The Atlantic Scout* [1950] P. 266; Franks, *Limitation of Actions* (1959), Appendix II. For limitation generally, see below, Ch.29.

carefully distinguished from the rule that contracts involving trading or other intercourse with the enemy are illegal at common law as well as by statute. The two rules are often confused, but they differ fundamentally in that the former merely creates a procedural incapacity which lasts only so long as the war lasts, while the latter destroys the cause of action once and for all.[183] The latter rule has nothing to do with capacity, and is therefore considered elsewhere in this work.[184]

[183] See *Schmitz v Van der Veen & Co* (1915) 84 L.J.K.B. 861, 864; *Rodriguez v Speyer Bros* [1919] A.C. 59, 122.

[184] See below, paras 16–26—16–34.

Part Four
THE TERMS OF CONTRACT

CHAPTER 12

EXPRESS TERMS

		PARA.
1.	Proof of terms	12–002
	(a) Contractual undertakings and representations	12–003
	(b) Standard form contracts	12–008
2.	Classification of terms	12–019
	(a) Conditions	12–025
	(b) Warranties	12–031
	(c) Intermediate terms	12–034
3.	Construction of terms	12–041
	(a) General principles of construction	12–041
	(b) Ordinary meaning to be adopted	12–050
	(c) Whole contract to be considered	12–063
	(d) Effecting the intention of the parties	12–072
	(e) Construction against grantor	12–083
	(f) Ejusdem generis principle	12–087
	(g) Restriction by express provisions	12–091
	(h) Stipulations as to time	12–093
4.	Admissibility of extrinsic evidence	12–095
	(a) The parol evidence rule	12–096
	(b) Evidence as to the validity or effectiveness of the written agreement	12–106
	(c) Evidence as to the true nature of the agreement	12–113
	(d) Evidence to interpret or explain the written agreement	12–117
	(e) Evidence of custom or mercantile usage	12–127

Generally. Assuming that a contract has been validly created, it is necessary to consider the extent of the obligations imposed on the parties by the contract. In order to do this, the exact terms of the contract must be determined[1] and their comparative importance evaluated.[2] There may be some doubt about the interpretation of the contract, and resort will then have to be made to the principles of construction which have been laid down by the courts,[3] and also to those which govern the admissibility of evidence extrinsic to a written agreement.[4] **12–001**

1. PROOF OF TERMS

Proof of terms. Where the agreement of the parties has been reduced to writing and the document containing the agreement has been signed by one or both of them, it is well established that the party signing will ordinarily be bound **12–002**

[1] See below, paras 12–002 et seq.

[2] See below, paras 12–019 et seq.

[3] See below, paras 12–041 et seq.

[4] See below, paras 12–095 et seq.

by the terms of the written agreement whether or not he has read them and whether or not he is ignorant of their precise legal effect.[5] But it by no means follows that the document will contain all the terms of the contract: it may be partly oral, and partly in writing.[6] Further, many contracts are made solely by word of mouth[7] or are contained in or evidenced by documents which have not been signed by the party affected. In such cases, it will be necessary to prove which statements, or stipulations, were intended to be incorporated as terms of the contract or to have contractual effect.

(a) *Contractual Undertakings and Representations*

12–003 **Terms and representations.** During the course of negotiations leading to the conclusion of a valid and binding contract, a number of statements may be made, some of which may, and others may not, be intended to have contractual force. Some statements may be considered to be mere representations, intended to induce the other party to enter into the contract, but not imposing liability for breach of contract.[8] Others may be considered to be contractual terms, for the breach of which an action for damages will lie.[9] The question whether any particular statement is a mere representation or a contractual term is frequently a difficult one for the court. In reaching a conclusion it will take into account the following considerations: the importance of the truth of the statement[10]; the time which elapsed between the making of the statement and the final manifestation of consensus[11]; whether the party making the statement was, vis-à-vis the other party, in a better position to ascertain the truth of the statement[12]; and whether the

[5] *Parker v South Eastern Ry* (1877) 2 C.P.D. 416, 421; *Howatson v Webb* [1908] 1 Ch. 1; *The Luna* [1920] P. 22; *L'Estrange v Graucob Ltd* [1934] 2 K.B. 394; *McCutcheon v David MacBrayne Ltd* [1964] 1 W.L.R. 125, 132–134; *Bahamas Oil Refining Co v Kristiansands Tank-rederie A/S* [1978] 1 Lloyd's Rep. 211; *Charlotte Thirty Ltd v Croker Ltd* (1990) 24 Const. L.R. 46; *Toll (FGCT) Pty Ltd v Alphapharm Pty Ltd* (2004) 211 A.L.R. 342; *Peekay Intermark Ltd v Australia and NZ Banking Group Ltd* [2006] EWCA Civ 386, [2006] 2 Lloyd's Rep. 511 at [43]. But see *Jaques v Lloyd D. George & Partners Ltd* [1968] 1 W.L.R. 625, 630; *Tilden Rent-a-Car Co v Clendenning* (1978) 83 D.L.R. (3d) 400; *Crocker v Sundance Northwest Resorts Ltd* (1988) 51 D.L.R. (4th) 321; *Ocean Chemical Transport Inc v Exnor Craggs Ltd* [2000] 1 Lloyd's Rep. 446, 454. See further Spencer [1978] C.L.J. 104; Macdonald [1999] C.L.J. 413, 420; Peden and Carter (2005) 21 J.C.L. 96 and above, paras 5–101—5–106; below, para.4–132 et seq.

[6] See below, paras 12–096—12–099.

[7] See above, para.4–001.

[8] *Hopkins v Tanqueray* (1854) 15 C.B. 130; *Heilbut, Symons & Co v Buckleton* [1913] A.C. 30; *Routledge v McKay* [1954] 1 W.L.R. 615; *Oscar Chess Ltd v Williams* [1957] 1 W.L.R. 370. See also above, para.6–004.

[9] *Bannerman v White* (1861) 10 C.B.(N.S.) 844; *De Lassalle v Guildford* [1901] 2 K.B. 215; *Schawel v Reade* [1913] 2 I.R. 64; *Dick Bentley Productions Ltd v Harold Smith (Motors) Ltd* [1965] 1 W.L.R. 623; and see the cases cited in fnn.23–25, below.

[10] *Bannerman v White*, above. cf. *Oscar Chess Ltd v Williams*, above.

[11] *Routledge v McKay* [1954] 1 W.L.R. 615. See also *Pasley v Freeman* (1789) 3 Term Rep. 51, 57; *Schawel v Read* [1913] 2 I.R. 64; *Mahon v Ainscough* [1952] 1 All E.R. 337; *Inntrepreneur Pub Co v East Crown Ltd* [2000] 2 Lloyd's Rep. 611 at [10].

[12] *Dick Bentley Productions Ltd v Harold Smith (Motors) Ltd* [1965] 1 W.L.R. 623; *Esso Petroleum Co Ltd v Mardon* [1976] Q.B. 801. Contrast *Heilbut, Symons & Co v Buckleton* [1913] A.C. 30; *Gilchester Properties Ltd v Gomm* [1948] 1 All E.R. 493.

statement was subsequently omitted when the agreement was embodied in a more formal contract in writing.[13] But none of these criteria is conclusive[14] and the true test would seem to be whether there is:

> "... evidence of an intention by one or both parties that there should be contractual liability in respect of the accuracy of the statement."[15]

Such intention is to be ascertained objectively.[16] In *Oscar Chess Ltd v Williams*[17] a statement made to a motor dealer by a private vendor of a motor-car, based on a previous alteration of the car log-book by an unknown person, that the car was "a 1948 model", whereas in fact it had been first registered in 1939, was held by the Court of Appeal to be a mere representation. But in *Dick Bentley Productions Ltd v Harold Smith (Motors) Ltd*[18] a statement made by a motor dealer to a private purchaser, based on a reading of the mileometer, that it had done only 20,000 miles, whereas in fact it had done approximately 100,000, was held to be a warranty. The *Oscar Chess* case was distinguished on the ground that the vendor "honestly believed and on reasonable grounds that [the statement] was true", whereas the motor dealer in the latter case "stated a fact that should be within his own knowledge. He had jumped to a conclusion and stated it as a fact".[19] Such cases show that, in this area of contract, the circumstances of each case must be individually considered to ascertain the intention of the parties and that the criteria stated above furnish no decisive tests in law:

> "The intention of the parties can only be deduced from the totality of the evidence, and no secondary principles of such a kind can be universally true."[20]

Collateral contracts.[21] It may be difficult to treat a statement made in the course of negotiations for a contract as a term of the contract itself, either because the statement was clearly prior to or outside the contract or because the existence of the parol evidence rule[22] prevents its inclusion. Nevertheless, the courts are prepared in some circumstances to treat a statement intended to have contractual 12–004

[13] *Heilbut, Symons & Co v Buckleton* [1913] A.C. 30, 50; *Gilchester Properties Ltd v Gomm* [1948] 1 All E.R. 493. cf. *Miller v Cannon Hill Estates Ltd* [1931] 2 K.B. 113; *Inntrepreneur Pub Co v East Crown Ltd* [2000] 2 Lloyd's Rep. 611 at [10].

[14] *Heilbut, Symons & Co v Buckleton* [1913] A.C. 30, 50.

[15] [1913] A.C. 30, 51 (and see 38, 42); *Pasley v Freeman* (1789) 3 T.R. 51, 57; *Oscar Chess Ltd v Williams* [1957] 1 W.L.R. 370, 374; *Dick Bentley Productions Ltd v Harold Smith (Motors) Ltd* [1965] 1 W.L.R. 623, 629; *Esso Petroleum Co Ltd v Mardon* [1976] Q.B. 801. See also *J.J. Savage & Sons Pty Ltd v Blackney* (1970) 119 C.L.R. 435.

[16] *Inntrepreneur Pub Co v East Crown Ltd* [2002] 2 Lloyd's Rep. 611 at [10].

[17] [1957] 1 W.L.R. 370. See also *Routledge v McKay* [1954] 1 W.L.R. 615; *Dawson v Yeoward* [1961] 1 Lloyd's Rep. 431. cf. *Turner v Anquetil* [1953] N.Z.L.R. 952; *Beale v Taylor* [1967] 1 W.L.R. 1193.

[18] [1965] 1 W.L.R. 623.

[19] [1965] 1 W.L.R. 623, 628, 629.

[20] *Heilbut, Symons & Co v Buckleton* [1913] 1 A.C. 30, 51.

[21] See Paterson, *Collateral Warranties Explained* (1991) and para.18–005, below.

[22] See below, paras 12–096—12–105.

effect as a separate contract or warranty, collateral to the main transaction.[23] In particular, they will do so where one party refuses to enter into the contract unless the other gives him an assurance on a certain point[24] or unless the other promises not to enforce a term of the written agreement.[25] Thus in *De Lassalle v Guildford*[26] the claimant and the defendant negotiated for the lease of a house. The terms of the lease were arranged, but the claimant (the prospective tenant) refused to hand over the counterpart of the lease which he had signed unless the defendant assured him that the drains were in good order. The defendant gave this assurance, and the counterpart lease was thereupon handed to him. The drains were not in fact, in good order, and the claimant sued the defendant on his assurance, no reference to drains having been made in the lease itself. The Court of Appeal held that the assurance constituted a contract collateral to the lease on which the defendant was liable. However, in *Heilbut Symons & Co v Buckleton*,[27] Lord Moulton said:

> "Such collateral contracts, the sole effect of which is to vary or add to the terms of the written contract, are therefore viewed with suspicion by the law . . . Not only the terms of such contracts but the existence of an *animus contrahendi* on the part of all the parties to them must be strictly shown."

But more recently Lord Denning M.R. has stated[28] that "much of what was said in that case is entirely out of date".

12–005 It is undoubtedly true that the courts are nowadays much more willing to accept that a pre-contractual assurance gives rise to a collateral contract,[29] so that such collateral contracts are no longer rare. Where the assurance consists of a statement of present or past fact, there may be less need to infer a collateral contract, since a remedy in damages may be available under the Misrepresentation Act 1967[30] for a representation of fact. But where the assurance is as to the

---

[23] *Lindley v Lacey* (1864) 17 C.B.(N.S.) 578; *Mann v Nunn* (1874) 30 L.T. 526; *Spicer v Martin* (1888) 14 App. Cas. 12; *Jacobs v Batavia & General Plantations Trust Ltd* [1924] 1 Ch. 287; *Jameson v Kinmell Bay Land Co Ltd* (1931) 47 T.L.R. 593; *Miller v Cannon Hill Estates Ltd* [1931] 2 K.B. 113; *Birch v Paramount Estates* (1956) 167 E.G. 396; *Frisby v BBC* [1967] Ch. 932; *Quickmaid Rental Services v Reece* (1970) 114 S.J. 372, CA; *J. Evans & Son (Portsmouth) Ltd v Andrea Merzario Ltd* [1976] 1 W.L.R. 1078; *Esso Petroleum Co Ltd v Mardon* [1976] Q.B. 801; *Record v Bell* [1991] 1 W.L.R. 853; *Wake v Renault (UK) Ltd* (1996) 15 Tr. L.R. 514; *Procter & Gamble (Health and Beauty Care) Ltd v Carrier Holdings Ltd* [2003] EWHC 83 (TCC), [2003] B.L.R. 255; Wedderburn [1959] C.L.J. 58; Greig (1971) 87 L.Q.R. 179.

[24] *Morgan v Griffith* (1871) L.R. 6 Ex. 70; *Erskine v Adeane* (1873) L.R. 8 Ch. App. 756; *Newman v Gatti* (1907) 24 T.L.R. 18, 20; *Heilbut, Symons & Co v Buckleton* [1913] 1 A.C. 30, 47.

[25] *Couchman v Hill* [1947] K.B. 554; *Webster v Higgin* [1948] 2 All E.R. 127; *Harling v Eddy* [1951] 2 K.B. 739; *City of Westminster Properties (1934) Ltd v Mudd* [1959] Ch. 129; *Brikom Investments Ltd v Carr* [1979] Q.B. 467; cf. *Business Environment Bow Lane Ltd v Deanwater Estates Ltd* [2007] EWCA Civ 622, (2007) 32 E.G. 90.

[26] [1901] 2 K.B. 215.

[27] [1913] A.C. 30, 47. See also *Business Environment Bow Lane Ltd v Deanwater Estates Ltd* [2007] EWCA Civ 622.

[28] *J. Evans & Son (Portsmouth) Ltd v Andrea Merzario Ltd* [1976] 1 W.L.R. 1078, 1081; *Howard Marine & Dredging Co Ltd v A. Ogden & Sons (Excavations) Ltd* [1978] Q.B. 574, 590. See also *Esso Petroleum Co Ltd v Mardon* [1978] Q.B. 801, 817.

[29] *Esso Petroleum Co Ltd v Mardon* [1976] Q.B. 801. But compare *Howard Marine & Dredging Co Ltd v A. Ogden & Sons (Excavations) Ltd* [1978] Q.B. 574.

[30] s.2(1); see above, para.6–068.

future, the Act does not apply[31] and in such a case the claimant must prove a collateral contract or fail completely. Lord Denning M.R. has said[32]:

> "When a person gives a promise or an assurance to another, intending that he should act on it by entering into a contract, and he does act on it by entering into the contract, we hold that it is binding."

Consideration for the collateral contract is normally provided by entering into the main contract,[33] but a collateral contract may also be actionable even if the main contract is unenforceable, e.g. for illegality.[34] Breach of the collateral contract will give rise to an action for damages for its breach, but not as a general rule to a right to treat the main contract as repudiated. However, the effect of a collateral contract may be to vary the terms of the main contract[35] or to estop a party from acting inconsistently with it if it would be inequitable for him to do so.[36] 12–006

Third parties. A collateral contract may also be found to exist where the main contract is not between the claimant and the defendant, but between the claimant and a third party. In *Shanklin Pier Ltd v Detel Products Ltd*,[37] the claimants, owners of Shanklin Pier, wished to have their pier painted with suitable paint. They asked the defendants, a firm of paint manufacturers, whether their paint was suitable for this purpose, and were assured that it was. The claimants therefore caused to be inserted in a contract made between them and the contractors who were to paint the pier a stipulation that the defendants' paint should be used. The paint was entirely unsuitable, and the claimants sued the defendants on their assurance. It was held that the assurance constituted a contract, collateral to the contract for painting the pier, the consideration for which was the claimants' entry into the contract containing the stipulation that the defendants' paint should be used. Similarly a collateral contract may exist where the main contract is between the defendant and a third party, as in *Charnock v Liverpool Corp*,[38] where the main contract to repair a car was 12–007

[31] See above, para.6–006.

[32] *J. Evans & Son (Portsmouth) Ltd v Andrea Merzario Ltd* [1976] 1 W.L.R. 1078, 1081. But see *Heilbut Symons & Co v Buckleton* [1913] A.C. 30, 38, 42, 47, 49–50; *Jonathan Wren & Co Ltd v Microdec Plc* (1999) 65 Const. L.R. 157; *Inntrepreneur Pub Co v East Crown Ltd* [2000] 2 Lloyd's Rep. 611 at [11].

[33] cf. *De Lassalle v Guildford* [1901] 2 K.B. 215; *Hill v Harris* [1965] Q.B. 601.

[34] See below, para.16–176.

[35] *Wake v Renault (UK) Ltd* (1996) 15 Tr. L.R. 514.

[36] *Brikom Investments Ltd v Carr* [1979] Q.B. 467; but see above, para.3–133.

[37] [1951] 2 K.B. 854. See *Brown v Sheen & Richmond Car Sales Ltd* [1950] 1 All E.R. 1102; *Andrews v Hopkinson* [1957] 1 Q.B. 229; *Smith v Spurling Motor Bodies Ltd* (1961) 105 S.J. 967; *Yeoman Credit Ltd v Odgers* [1962] 1 W.L.R. 215; *Wells (Merstham) Ltd v Buckland Sand & Silica Ltd* [1965] 2 Q.B. 170. cf. *Drury v Victor Buckland Ltd* [1941] 1 All E.R. 269; *Independent Broadcasting Authority v E.M.I. Electronics* (1980) 14 Build. L.R. 1; *Lambert v Lewis* [1982] A.C. 225; *Law Debenture Trust Corp v Ural Caspian Oil Corp Ltd* [1993] 1 W.L.R. 138 (reversed on other grounds, [1995] Ch. 132).

[38] [1968] 1 W.L.R. 1498. cf. *Brown and Davis Ltd v Galbraith* [1972] 1 W.L.R. 997. See below, para.18–008.

between the repairer and an insurance company, but there was also a collateral contract between the repairer and the owner of the car that the repairer should do the repairs within a reasonable time.

(b) *Standard Form Contracts*

12–008 **Contracts in standard form.** A different problem may arise in proving the terms of the agreement where it is sought to show that they are contained in a contract in standard form, i.e. in some ticket, receipt, or standard form document. If a party signs a contractual document,[39] he will normally be bound by its terms.[40] More often, however, the document is simply made available to him before or at the time of making the contract, and the question will then arise whether the printed conditions which it contains have become terms of the contract.[41] The party to whom the document is supplied will probably not trouble to read it, and may even be ignorant that it contains any conditions at all. Yet standard form contracts very frequently embody clauses which purport to impose obligations on him or to exclude or restrict the liability of the person supplying the document.[42] Thus it becomes important to determine whether these clauses should be given contractual effect.

12–009 **Contractual document.** The document must be of a class which either the party receiving it knows, or which a reasonable man would expect, to contain contractual conditions. Thus a cheque book,[43] a time sheet,[44] a ticket for a deck chair,[45] a ticket handed to a person at a public bath house[46] and a parking ticket issued by an automatic machine[47] have been held to be cases:

> "... where it would be quite reasonable that the party receiving it should assume that the writing contained no condition and should put it in his pocket unread."[48]

On the other hand, a railway[49] or ship[50] ticket or a receipt for goods deposited[51] has been held to be a contractual document.

---

[39] cf. *Grogan v Robin Meredith Plant Hire* (1996) 15 Tr. L.R. 371 (non-contractual document).
[40] See the cases cited in para.12–002, fn.5, above.
[41] See Sales (1953) 16 M.L.R. 318; Clarke [1976] C.L.J. 51.
[42] See below, Ch.14.
[43] *Burnett v Westminster Bank* [1966] 1 Q.B. 742.
[44] *Grogan v Robin Meredith Plant Hire* (1996) 15 Tr. L.R. 371.
[45] *Chapelton v Barry U.D.C.* [1940] 1 K.B. 532.
[46] *Taylor v Glasgow Corp* (1952) S.C. 440.
[47] *Thornton v Shoe Lane Parking Ltd* [1971] 2 Q.B. 163.
[48] *Parker v South Eastern Ry* (1877) 2 C.P.D. 416, 422.
[49] *Thompson v L.M. & S. Ry* [1930] 1 K.B. 41.
[50] *Hood v Anchor Line (Henderson Bros) Ltd* [1918] A.C. 837; *Cockerton v Naviera Aznar SA* [1960] 2 Lloyd's Rep. 451.
[51] *Parker v South Eastern Ry* (1877) 2 C.P.D. 416; *Alexander v Ry Executive* [1951] 2 K.B. 882.

Time of notice. The conditions must be brought to the notice[52] of the party to be bound before or at the time when the contract is made. If they are not communicated to him until after the contract is concluded, they will be of no effect. In *Olley v Marlborough Court Ltd*[53] certain property of the plaintiff was stolen from his hotel bedroom owing to the negligence of the hotel management. On arrival at the hotel he had signed the hotel register which contained no mention of any exemption clauses, but in the bedroom there was a notice disclaiming liability for articles lost or stolen. It was held that the notice was ineffective as he had not been made aware of it until after the contract was made. 12–010

Course of dealing. Conditions will not necessarily be incorporated into a contract by reason of the fact that the parties have, on previous occasions, dealt with each other subject to those conditions.[54] But they may be incorporated by a "course of dealing" between the parties where each party has led the other reasonably to believe that he intended that their rights and liabilities should be ascertained by reference to the terms of a document which had been consistently used by them in previous transactions.[55] It should, however, be noted that a more relaxed approach is adopted in Art.23 of Council Regulation 44/2001[56] to the degree of *consensus* required for the incorporation of an exclusive jurisdiction clause.[57] 12–011

Usual trade conditions. Conditions usual in a particular trade may likewise be incorporated where both parties are in the trade and are aware that conditions 12–012

[52] For the meaning of notice, see below, para.12–013.

[53] [1949] 1 K.B. 532. See also *Thornton v Shoe Lane Parking Ltd* [1971] 2 Q.B. 163 (ticket proffered by automatic machine); *Hollingworth v Southern Ferries Ltd* [1977] 2 Lloyd's Rep. 70; *Daly v General Steam Navigation Co Ltd* [1979] 1 Lloyd's Rep. 257; *Dillon v Baltic Shipping Co* [1991] 2 Lloyd's Rep. 155 (ship tickets); *Metaalhandel JA Magnus B.V. v Ardfields Transport Ltd* [1988] 1 Lloyd's Rep. 197, 204 (conditions in invoice). cf. *Cockerton v Naviera Aznar SA* [1960] 2 Lloyd's Rep. 451.

[54] *McCutcheon v David Macbrayne Ltd* [1964] 1 W.L.R. 125 HL (no consistent course of dealing); *Hollier v Rambler Motors (A.M.C.) Ltd* [1972] 2 Q.B. 71 (only three or four times in five years).

[55] *J. Spurling Ltd v Bradshaw* [1956] 1 W.L.R. 461, 467; *Cockerton v Naviera Aznar SA* [1960] 2 Lloyd's Rep. 451; *Henry Kendall & Sons v William Lillico & Sons Ltd* [1969] 2 A.C. 31, 90, 91, 104, 105, 130; *Transmotors Ltd v Robertson Buckley & Co Ltd* [1970] 1 Lloyd's Rep. 224; *Eastman Chemical International A.G. v N.M.T. Trading Ltd* [1972] 2 Lloyd's Rep. 25; *Gillespie Bros & Co Ltd v Roy Bowles Transport Ltd* [1973] Q.B. 400; *S.I.A.T. di del Ferro v Tradax Overseas SA* [1978] 2 Lloyd's Rep. 470 (affirmed [1980] 1 Lloyd's Rep. 53); *Lamport & Holt Lines Ltd v Coubro & Scrutton (M. & I.) Ltd* [1981] 2 Lloyd's Rep. 659 (affirmed [1982] 2 Lloyd's Rep. 42); *McCrone v Boots Farm Sales Ltd* 1981 S.L.T. 103; *George Mitchell (Chesterhall) Ltd v Finney Lock Seeds Ltd* [1983] Q.B. 284, 295 (affirmed [1983] 2 A.C. 803); *Johnson Matthey Bankers Ltd v State Trading Corp of India Ltd* [1984] 1 Lloyd's Rep. 427; *Circle Freight International Ltd v Medeast Gulf Exports Ltd* [1988] 2 Lloyd's Rep. 427; *Balmoral Group Ltd v Borealis UK Ltd* [2006] EWHC 1900 (Comm), [2006] 2 Lloyd's Rep. 629 at [362]–[366]; cf. *Banque Paribas v Cargill International SA* [1992] 1 Lloyd's Rep. 96, 98; see Hoggett (1970) 33 M.L.R. 518.

[56] Regulation 44/2001 [2001] OJ L12/1, replacing art.17 of the Brussels Convention on Jurisdiction and the Enforcement of Judgments in Civil and Commercial matters (as amended).

[57] See *The Tilly Russ (M.S.)* [1985] 1 Q.B. 931; *Mainschiffahrts-Genossenschaft eG v Les Gravières Rhénanes SARL* [1997] Q.B. 1; *SSQ Europe SA v Johann & Backes OHG* [2002] 1 Lloyd's Rep. 465.

are habitually imposed and of the substance of those conditions, even if they are not referred to at the time of contracting.[58]

12–013 **Meaning of notice.** It is not necessary that the conditions contained in the standard form document should have been read by the person receiving it, or that he should have been made subjectively aware of their import or effect. The rules which have been laid down by the courts[59] regarding notice in such circumstances are three in number:

(1) If the person receiving the document did not know that there was writing or printing on it, he is not bound.

(2) If he knew that the writing or printing contained or referred to conditions, he is bound.

(3) If the party tendering the document did what was reasonably sufficient to give the other party notice of the conditions, and if the other party knew that there was writing or printing on the document, but did not know it contained conditions, then the conditions will become the terms of the contract between them.

12–014 **Reasonable sufficiency of notice.** It is the third of these rules which has most often to be considered by the courts. The question whether the party tendering the document has done all that was reasonably sufficient to give the other notice of the conditions is a question of fact in each case, in answering which the tribunal must look at all the circumstances and the situation of the parties.[60] But it is for the court, as a matter of law, to decide whether there is evidence for holding that the notice is reasonably sufficient.[61] Cases in which the notice has been held to be insufficient have been those where the conditions were printed on the back of the document, without any reference, or any adequate reference, on its face, such as, "[f]or conditions, see back",[62] where, on documents sent by fax, reference was made to conditions stated on the back, but those conditions were not in fact stated on the back or otherwise communicated,[63] or where the conditions were

---

[58] *British Crane Hire Corp Ltd v Ipswich Plant Hire Ltd* [1975] Q.B. 303; *Chevron International Oil Co Ltd v A/S Sea Team* [1983] 2 Lloyd's Rep. 256; *Laceys Footwear (Wholesale) Ltd v Bowler International Freight Ltd* [1997] 2 Lloyd's Rep. 369, 378; *Balmoral Group Ltd v Borealis UK Ltd* [2006] EWHC 1900 (Comm), [2006] 2 Lloyd's Rep. 629 at [357]. cf. *Salsi v Jetspread Air Services Ltd* [1977] 2 Lloyd's Rep. 57; *Neptune Orient Lines Ltd v J.V.C. (UK) Ltd* [1983] 2 Lloyd's Rep. 438; *Shipbuilders Ltd v Benson* [1992] 3 N.Z.L.R. 349; *Grogan v Robin Meredith Plant Hire* (1996) 15 Tr. L.R. 371.

[59] *Parker v South Eastern Ry* (1877) 2 C.P.D. 416, 421, 423; *Richardson, Spence & Co v Rowntree* [1894] A.C. 217; *Hood v Anchor Line (Henderson Bros) Ltd* [1918] A.C. 837; *McCutcheon v David Macbrayne Ltd* [1964] 1 W.L.R. 125; *Burnett v Westminster Bank* [1966] 1 Q.B. 742; *Thornton v Shoe Lane Parking Ltd* [1971] 2 Q.B. 163; *Shepherd Homes Ltd v Encia Remediation Ltd* [2007] EWHC 70 (TCC), [2007] Build. L.R. 135. See Clarke [1976] C.L.J. 51.

[60] *Parker v South Eastern Ry* (1877) 2 C.P.D. 416; *Richardson, Spence & Co v Rowntree* [1894] A.C. 217; *Hood v Anchor Line (Henderson Bros) Ltd* [1918] A.C. 837, 844, 847.

[61] *Thompson v L.M. & S. Ry* [1930] 1 K.B. 41.

[62] *Henderson v Stevenson* (1875) L.R. 2 H.L.(Sc.) 470; *Sugar v L.M. & S. Ry* [1941] 1 All E.R. 172; *White v Blackmore* [1972] 2 Q.B. 651, 664. cf. *Rolls Royce Power Engineering Plc v Ricardo Consulting Engineers Ltd* [2003] EWHC 2871 (TCC), [2004] 2 All E.R. (Comm) 129.

[63] *Poseidon Freight Forwarding Co Ltd v Davies Turner Southern Ltd* [1996] 2 Lloyd's Rep. 388.

obliterated by a printed stamp.[64] In many situations, however, the tender of printed conditions will in itself be sufficient.[65] It is not necessary that the conditions themselves should be set out in the document tendered: they may be incorporated by reference, provided that reasonable notice of them has been given.[66]

Onerous or unusual terms. Although the party receiving the document knows it contains conditions, if the particular condition relied on is one which is a particularly onerous or unusual term, or is one which involves the abrogation of a right given by statute, the party tendering the document must show that it has been brought fairly and reasonably to the other's attention.[67] "Some clauses which I have seen", said Denning L.J.[68]: 12–015

> " . . . would need to be printed in red ink on the face of the document with a red hand pointing to it before the notice could be held to be sufficient."

Personal disability. It is immaterial that the party receiving the document is under some personal, but non-legal, disability, such as blindness, illiteracy, or an inability to read our language.[69] Provided the notice is reasonably sufficient for 12–016

---

[64] *Richardson, Spence & Co v Rowntree* [1894] A.C. 217. On small and illegible print, see *Paterson Zochonis & Co Ltd v Elder, Dempster & Co Ltd* [1923] 1 K.B. 420, 441. cf. *P.S. Chellaram & Co Ltd v China Ocean Shipping Co* [1991] 1 Lloyd's Rep. 493, 519.

[65] *Parker v South Eastern Ry* (1877) 2 C.P.D. 416; *Hood v Anchor Line (Henderson Bros) Ltd* [1918] A.C. 837; *Cockerton v Naviera Aznar SA* [1960] 2 Lloyd's Rep. 451; *Budd v P. & O. Steam Navigation Co* [1969] 2 Lloyd's Rep. 262; cf. *Union Steamships v Barnes* (1956) 5 D.L.R. (2d) 535.

[66] *Circle Freight International Ltd v Medeast Gulf Exports Ltd* [1988] 2 Lloyd's Rep. 427; *Shearson Lehman Hutton Inc v Maclaine Watson & Co Ltd* [1989] 2 Lloyd's Rep. 570, 613; *Crédit Suisse Financial Products v Société Generale d'Enterprises* (1996) 5 Bank. L.R. 220, *Ocean Chemical Transport Inc v Exnor Craggs Ltd* [2000] 1 Lloyd's Rep. 446; *O'Brien v MGN Ltd* [2001] EWCA Civ 1279, [2002] C.L.C. 33; *Sumukan Ltd v Commonwealth Secretariat* [2007] EWCA Civ 243, [2007] 2 Lloyd's Rep. 87.

[67] *Parker v South Eastern Ry* (1877) 2 C.P.D. 416, 428; *Thornton v Shoe Lane Parking Ltd* [1971] 2 Q.B. 163; *Hollingworth v Southern Ferries Ltd* [1977] 2 Lloyd's Rep. 70; *Interfoto Picture Library Ltd v Stiletto Visual Programmes Ltd* [1989] Q.B. 433; *Dillon v Baltic Shipping Co* [1991] 2 Lloyd's Rep. 155; *A.E.G. (UK) Ltd v Logic Resource Ltd* [1996] C.L.C. 265; *Laceys Footwear v Bowler International Freight (Wholesale) Ltd* [1997] 2 Lloyd's Rep. 369, 384–385; *Ocean Chemical Transport Inc v Exnor Craggs Ltd* [2000] 1 Lloyd's Rep. 446, 451, *Amiri Flight Authority v BAE Systems Plc* [2003] EWCA Civ 1447, [2003] 2 Lloyd's Rep. 767. For the suggested extension of this principle to signed documents, see *Jaques v Lloyd D George & Partners Ltd* [1968] 1 W.L.R. 625, 630; *Tilden Rent-a-Car Co v Clendenning* (1978) 83 D.L.R. (3d) 400; *Ocean Chemical Transport Inc v Exnor Craggs Ltd* [2000] 1 Lloyd's Rep. 446, 454; *Montgomery Litho Ltd v Maxwell* 2000 S.C. 56; *Amiri Flight Authority v BAE Systems Plc* [2003] EWCA Civ 1447 at [14]–[16]; Macdonald [1999] C.L.J. 413, 422; above, para.12–002 fn.5. Contrast *Shearson Lehman Hutton Inc v Maclaine Watson & Co Ltd* [1989] 2 Lloyd's Rep. 570, 612; *HIH Casualty and General Insurance Ltd v New Hampshire Insurance Co* [2001] EWCA Civ 735, [2001] 2 Lloyd's Rep. 161 at [209]. Cf. also *Sumukan Ltd v Commonwealth Secretariat* [2007] EWCA Civ 1148; *Shepherd Homes Ltd v Encia Remediation Ltd* [2007] EWHC 70 (TCC) [2007] Build. L.R. 135 (terms not onerous or unusual).

[68] *J. Spurling Ltd v Bradshaw* [1956] 1 W.L.R. 461, 466.

[69] *Thompson v L.M. & S. Ry* [1930] 1 K.B. 41; cf. *Firchuk and Firchuk v Waterfront Cartage Division, etc., Ltd* [1969] 2 Lloyd's Rep. 533, 534. Quaere if the disability is known to the other contracting party: see *Geier v Kujawa Weston and Warne Bros (Transport) Ltd* [1970] 1 Lloyd's Rep. 364.

the class of persons to which the party belongs (e.g. passengers on a ship or railway) he will be bound by the conditions.

12–017 **Printed notices.** Where printed notices are exhibited, it may be sufficient if the party to be bound has, before or at the time of making the contract, had his attention drawn to the notices,[70] or received a printed document which refers him to the notices,[71] in circumstances which make it clear to him that the contract is subject to the conditions contained in the notices.[72] The reference may be circuitous provided it is clear.[73] It has, however, been stated by Denning L.J. that:

> "The party who is liable at law cannot escape liability by simply putting up a printed notice, or issuing a printed catalogue, containing exempting conditions. He must go further and show affirmatively that it is a contractual document and accepted as such by the party affected."[74]

In many situations it will nevertheless be sufficient to display a prominent public notice which can be plainly seen at the time of making the contract.[75] But the issue of a catalogue or brochure which states that the contract to be concluded will be subject to exempting conditions may not be sufficient to make the conditions terms of the contract if further steps to incorporate the conditions are not taken at the time the contract is concluded.[76]

12–018 **Statute.** Certain additional requirements of form have been imposed by statute on some classes of contract; for example, by the Carriers Act 1830 s.4, common carriers cannot limit their liability by publication of notices alone, but only by special contract.[77]

2. Classification of Terms

12–019 **Conditions and warranties.** Once it has been established that a certain stipulation is indeed a term of the contract, the question arises as to its comparative importance and effect. Traditionally, in English law, the terms of a contract have been classified as being either *conditions* or *warranties*, the difference

---

[70] *Birch v Thomas* [1972] 1 W.L.R. 294.

[71] *Watkins v Rymill* (1883) 10 QBD 178.

[72] cf. *Hollingworth v Southern Ferries Ltd* [1977] 2 Lloyd's Rep. 70.

[73] *Wyndham Rather Ltd v Eagle Star and British Dominions Insurance Co Ltd* (1925) 21 Ll.L. Rep. 214; *Thompson v L.M. & S. Ry* [1930] 1 K.B. 41; *Goodyear Tyre & Rubber Co v Lancashire Batteries* [1958] 1 W.L.R. 857.

[74] *Harling v Eddy* [1951] 2 K.B. 739, 748. See also *Olley v Marlborough Court Ltd* [1949] 1 K.B. 532, 549; *Adams (Durham) Ltd v Trust Houses Ltd* [1960] 1 Lloyd's Rep. 380; *Mendelssohn v Normand Ltd* [1970] 1 Q.B. 177, 182.

[75] *Olley v Marlborough Court Ltd* [1949] 1 K.B. 532, 549; *Ashdown v Samuel Williams & Sons Ltd* [1957] 1 Q.B. 409; *Thornton v Shoe Lane Parking Ltd* [1970] 1 Q.B. 177; *White v Blackmore* [1972] 2 Q.B. 651. Contrast *McCutcheon v David Macbrayne Ltd* [1964] 1 W.L.R. 125 HL; *Smith v Taylor* [1966] 2 Lloyd's Rep. 231; *Burnett v British Waterways Board* [1973] 1 W.L.R. 700.

[76] *Hollingworth v Southern Ferries Ltd* [1977] 2 Lloyd's Rep. 70.

[77] See Vol.II, para.36–028. But the common carrier is now virtually extinct.

between them being that any breach of a condition entitles the innocent party, if he so chooses, to treat himself as discharged from further performance under the contract,[78] and in any event to claim damages for loss sustained by the breach. A breach of warranty, on the other hand, does not entitle him to treat himself as discharged, but to claim damages only.

Intermediate terms. The dichotomy between conditions and warranties is not, however, exhaustive. The "more modern doctrine"[79] is that there exists a third category of "intermediate" (or "innominate") terms, the failure to perform which may or may not entitle the innocent party to treat himself as discharged, depending on the nature and consequences of the breach.[80] **12–020**

Fundamental terms. There was at one time some support for the view that, in addition to conditions, warranties and intermediate terms, the law recognises yet a fourth category of term, the "fundamental term".[81] The fundamental term has been described as part of the "core" of the contract,[82] the non-performance of which destroys the very substance of the agreement. It has been distinguished by Devlin J.[83] as being "something narrower than a condition of the contract" and as: **12–021**

> "... something which underlies the whole contract so that, if it is not complied with, the performance becomes totally different from that which the contract contemplates."

Examples usually cited are those where a seller delivers goods wholly different from the agreed contract goods or delivers goods which are so seriously defective as to render them in substance not the goods contracted for: e.g. the delivery of beans instead of peas,[84] of pinewood logs instead of mahogany logs,[85] or of a vehicle which is incapable or barely capable of self-propulsion instead of a motor car.[86] In each case, so it is said, there is a breach of the fundamental term, that is to say, of the "core" obligation to deliver the essential goods which are the subject-matter of the contract of sale.

The concept of the fundamental term has most often been employed in relation to exemption clauses. At one time it was asserted that, even though liability for a breach of condition might be excluded by an appropriately drafted exemption clause, no such clause could exonerate a party from failure to perform the fundamental term of an agreement. The House of Lords, however, has since held **12–022**

---

[78] See below, para.24–040.

[79] *Reardon Smith Line Ltd v Yngvar Hansen-Tangen* [1976] 1 W.L.R. 989, 998.

[80] See below, para.12–024.

[81] See below, paras 14–020, 14–024. See also Guest (1961) 77 L.Q.R. 98, 327; Montrose [1964] C.L.J. 60, 254; Reynolds (1963) 79 L.Q.R. 534; Lord Devlin [1966] C.L.J. 192; Jenkins [1969] C.L.J. 251.

[82] *Alderslade v Hendon Laundry Ltd* [1945] K.B. 189, 192.

[83] *Smeaton Hanscomb & Co Ltd v Sassoon I. Setty Son & Co* [1953] 1 W.L.R. 1468, 1470.

[84] *Chanter v Hopkins* (1838) 4 M. & W. 399, 404.

[85] *Smeaton Hanscomb & Co Ltd v Sassoon I. Setty Son & Co* [1953] 1 W.L.R. 1468, 1470.

[86] *Karsales (Harrow) Ltd v Wallis* [1956] 1 W.L.R. 17; *Yeoman Credit Ltd v Apps* [1962] 2 Q.B. 508; *Farnworth Finance Facilities Ltd v Attryde* [1970] 1 W.L.R. 1053.

that there is no rule of law that an exemption clause is inapplicable in the case of a "fundamental" or "total" breach.[87] The question is now whether the clause, on its true construction, applies to the breach which has occurred. No doubt, as a matter of construction, a court will be reluctant to ascribe to an exemption clause so wide an ambit as in effect to deprive one party's stipulations of all contractual force.[88] But, for the purpose of ascertaining the intention of the parties in this respect, it seems unnecessary to predicate the existence of a fundamental term, i.e. in considering whether an exemption clause covers the delivery of beans instead of peas, to say that the contract contains a "fundamental term" to deliver peas. There may also be difficulties in identifying the "core" of the particular contract: Is it to supply "peas" or "leguminous vegetables" or "agricultural produce"?[89] The quest for the fundamental term may well deflect the court from its proper task of ascertaining the true construction of the exemption clause into a barren enquiry as to whether the essential object of the contract has not been fulfilled at all or whether it has been fulfilled, but not in a way that the contract requires.

12–023 Whether any further consequences follow from the categorisation of a particular contractual obligation as a fundamental term is even more doubtful. It is possible to contend that s.11(4) of the Sale of Goods Act 1979,[90] which in certain circumstances precludes a buyer who has accepted the goods from subsequently rejecting them and treating the contract as repudiated, does not apply to the breach of a fundamental term.[91] This seems to be only an ex-post facto rationalisation of an independent principle (if such exists) that, for the purposes of s.35 of the 1979 Act, a buyer will not be deemed to have accepted goods that are wholly different from those agreed to be sold. It is also possible to assert that the breach of a fundamental term gives rise, not merely to a claim for damages, but to recover all money paid as upon a consideration which has totally failed.[92] But it seems better to regard the question whether or not there has been a total failure of consideration as dependent upon the facts of the case, rather than upon the breach of a "fundamental term".

12–024 In conclusion it is submitted that it is neither necessary nor desirable to create yet a fourth category of contractual term—the "fundamental term"—in addition to conditions, warranties and intermediate terms. In *Suisse Atlantique Société*

---

[87] *Suisse Atlantique Société d'Armement Maritime SA v N.V. Rotterdamsche Kolen Centrale* [1967] 1 A.C. 361; *Photo Production Ltd v Securicor Transport Ltd* [1980] A.C. 827; *Ailsa Craig Fishing Co Ltd v Malvern Fishing Co Ltd* [1983] 1 W.L.R. 964, 971; *George Mitchell (Chesterhall) Ltd v Finney Lock Seeds Ltd* [1983] 2 A.C. 803; see below, para.14–020.

[88] *Suisse Atlantique Société d'Armement Maritime SA v N.V. Rotterdamsche Kolen Centrale* [1967] 1 A.C. 361, 432. See also *Tor Line A.B. v Alltrans Group of Canada Ltd* [1984] 1 W.L.R. 48, 58–59. See below, para.14–007.

[89] See, e.g. *George Mitchell (Chesterhall) Ltd v Finney Lock Seeds Ltd* [1983] 1 W.L.R. 964; Lord Devlin [1966] C.L.J. 192, 212.

[90] Formerly s.11(1)(c) of the Sale of Goods Act 1893.

[91] See Vol.II, para.43–055.

[92] *Rowland v Divall* [1923] 2 K.B. 500; *Karflex Ltd v Poole* [1933] 2 K.B. 251; *Warman v Southern Counties Car Finance Corp Ltd* [1949] 2 K.B. 576; *Butterworth v Kingsway Motors Ltd* [1954] 1 W.L.R. 1286; *Karsales (Harrow) Ltd v Wallis* [1956] 1 W.L.R. 936. See also *Hain S.S. Co v Tate & Lyle Ltd* (1936) 41 Com.Cas. 350, 368, 369, and Vol.II, paras 38–368, 43–068, 43–112.

d'Armement Maritime SA v N.V. Rotterdamsche Kolen Centrale,[93] Lord Upjohn defined the expression "fundamental term" in language which clearly indicated that he regarded it as an alternative way of referring to a condition, i.e. a term which went to the root of the contract so that any breach of it entitled the innocent party to be discharged. There is therefore strong ground for the view that English law does not recognise any category of "fundamental terms" distinct from conditions.

(a) *Conditions*

Differing terminology. The word "condition" is sometimes used, even in legal documents, to mean simply "a stipulation, a provision" and not to connote a condition in the technical sense of that word.[94] Even within the sphere of the technical meaning attached to the word "condition", the terminology employed is, unfortunately, not uniform.[95] There may, for example, be conditions, the failure of which gives no right of action, but which merely suspends the rights and obligations of the parties.[96] The most commonly used sense of the word "condition" is that of an essential stipulation of the contract which one party guarantees is true or promises will be fulfilled. Any breach of such a stipulation entitles the innocent party, if he so chooses, to treat himself as discharged from further performance of the contract, and notwithstanding that he has suffered no prejudice by the breach. He can also claim damages for any loss suffered. 12–025

Conditions and other contract terms. The use of the word "condition" in this sense appears to have originated in the seventeenth century[97]: a stipulation might be regarded as so vital to the contract that its complete and exact performance by one party was a condition precedent to the obligation of the other party to perform his part.[98] In the modern law, the reason why a breach of a condition entitles the innocent party to treat himself as discharged has been said to be that conditions: 12–026

> ". . . go so directly to the substance of the contract or, in other words, are so essential to its very nature that their non-performance may fairly be considered by the other party as a substantial failure to perform the contract at all."[99]

---

[93] [1967] 1 A.C. 361, 422; see below, para.14–021.

[94] *L.G. Schuler A.G. v Wickman Machine Tool Sales Ltd* [1974] A.C. 235; cf. *Skips A/S Nordheim v Syrian Petroleum Ltd* [1984] Q.B. 509.

[95] See Stoljar (1953) 69 L.Q.R. 485.

[96] See below, para.12–027.

[97] See *Pordage v Cole* (1669) 1 Wms. Saund. 319; *Kingston v Preston* (1773) 2 Doug. 689, 691; *Boone v Eyre* (1777) 1 H.Bl. 273n.; *Cutter v Powell* (1795) 6 Term.R. 320; *Hongkong Fir Shipping Co Ltd v Kawasaki Kisen Kaisha* [1962] 2 Q.B. 26, 65; *Cehave N.V. v Bremer Handelsgesellschaft mbH* [1976] Q.B. 44, 57, 72. See also Chalmers, *Sale of Goods*, 2nd edn, p.164; Dawson [1981] C.L.J. 83, 87; and below, para.24–039.

[98] See also (marine insurance) Marine Insurance Act 1906 ss.33–41; *Bank of Nova Scotia v Hellenic Mutual War Risks Association (Bermuda) Ltd* [1992] 1 A.C. 233.

[99] *Wallis, Son & Wells v Pratt & Haynes* [1910] 2 K.B. 1003, 1012, per Fletcher Moulton J. (dissenting): approved [1911] A.C. 394; *L.G. Schuler A.G. v Wickman Machine Tool Sales Ltd* [1974] A.C. 235, 264, 272; *State Trading Corp of India Ltd v M. Golodetz Ltd* [1989] 2 Lloyd's Rep. 277, 282.

And the reason why *any* breach of condition has this effect has been put on the ground that the parties are to be regarded as having agreed that any failure of performance, irrespective of the gravity of the event that has in fact resulted from the breach, should entitle the other party to elect to put an end to all primary obligations of both parties remaining unperformed.[100] The parties may, by express words[101] or by implication of law,[102] agree that a particular stipulation is to be a condition of their contract. But they may also be held to have done so by necessary implication arising from the nature, purpose and circumstances of the contract,[103] and in this respect:

> "There is no way of deciding that question except by looking at the contract in the light of the surrounding circumstances, and then making up one's mind whether the intention of the parties, as gathered from the instrument itself, will best be carried out by treating the promise as a warranty sounding only in damages, or as a condition precedent by the failure to perform which the other party is relieved of his liability."[104]

12–027 **Promissory and contingent conditions.** A condition in the sense mentioned above may conveniently be termed a "promissory" condition, being a promise or assurance for the non-performance of which a right of action accrues to the innocent party.[105] This sense must be carefully distinguished from that of a "contingent" condition, i.e. a provision that on the happening of some uncertain event an obligation shall come into force, or that an obligation shall not come into force until such an event happens.[106] In this latter case, the non-fulfilment of the condition gives no right of action for breach[107]; it simply suspends the

---

[100] *Photo Production Ltd v Securicor Transport Ltd* [1980] A.C. 827, 849. See also *Bunge Corp v Tradax Export SA* [1981] 1 W.L.R. 711; *State Trading Corp of India Ltd v M. Golodetz Ltd* [1989] 2 Lloyd's Rep. 277.

[101] *Dawsons Ltd v Bonnin* [1922] 2 A.C. 413; *Lombard North Central Plc v Butterworth* [1987] Q.B. 527. But the terminology used may not be decisive: Sale of Goods Act 1979 s.11(3).

[102] e.g. Sale of Goods Act 1979, ss.11(3), 12(5A), 13(1A), 14(6), 15(3).

[103] *Bunge Corp v Tradax Export SA* [1981] 1 W.L.R. 711. See also the cases cited in para.12–037 below (mercantile contracts).

[104] *Bentsen v Taylor, Sons & Co* [1893] 2 Q.B. 274, 281. See also *Glaholm v Hays* (1841) 2 M. & G. 257, 266; *Re Comptoir Commercial Anversois and Power, Son & Co* [1920] 1 K.B. 868, 899; *Hongkong Fir Shipping Co Ltd v Kawasaki Kisen Kaisha* [1962] 2 Q.B. 26, 60; *Astley Industrial Trust Ltd v Grimley* [1963] 1 W.L.R. 584, 590; *L.G. Schuler A.G. v Wickman Machine Tool Sales Ltd* [1974] A.C. 235; *Bunge Corp v Tradax Export SA* [1981] 1 W.L.R. 711, 719, 725; *State Trading Corp of India Ltd v M. Golodetz Ltd* [1989] 2 Lloyd's Rep. 277, 282; *Compagnie Commerciale Sucres et Denrees v Czarnikow Ltd* [1990] 1 W.L.R. 1337, 1347; *Torvald Klaveness A/S v Arni Maritime Corp* [1994] 1 W.L.R. 1465, 1475–1476; Sale of Goods Act 1979 ss.11(3), 61(1).

[105] Stoljar (1953) 69 L.Q.R. 485.

[106] *London Passenger Transport Board v Moscrop* [1942] A.C. 332, 341; *Panoutsos v Raymond Hadley Corp of New York* [1917] 2 K.B. 473; *Aberfoyle Plantations Ltd v Cheng* [1960] A.C. 115; *Banque Keyser Ullmann SA v Skandia (UK) Insurance Co Ltd* [1990] 1 Q.B. 665 (affirmed on other grounds [1991] 2 A.C. 249); *Total Gas Marketing Ltd v Arco British Ltd* [1998] 2 Lloyd's Rep. 209. In *Damon Compania Naviera SA v Hapag-Lloyd International SA* [1985] 1 W.L.R. 435, it was held that a provision for payment of a deposit on signing a memorandum of agreement was not a condition precedent (i.e. contingent condition) to the formation of the contract, but was a fundamental term (i.e. promissory condition) of a concluded contract. cf. *Haugland Tankers AS v RMK Marine Gemi Yapin Sanayii ve Dentz Tasimaciligi Isletmesi AS* [2005] EWHC 321 (Comm), [2005] 1 Lloyd's Rep. 573 (payment of commitment fee condition precedent to exercise of option).

[107] Unless one party himself deliberately procures the non-fulfilment of the condition in certain circumstances: see below, paras 12–082, 13–012.

obligations of one or both parties.[108] In *Trans Trust S.P.R.L. v Danubian Trading Co Ltd*,[109] Denning L.J. considered a condition in a contract for the sale of goods whereby the buyer was to open a confirmed credit in favour of the seller, and said:

> "What is the legal position of such a stipulation? Sometimes it is a condition precedent to the formation of a contract, that is, it is a condition which must be fulfilled before any contract is concluded at all. In those cases the stipulation 'subject to the opening of a credit' is rather like a stipulation 'subject to contract.' If no credit is provided, there is no contract between the parties.[110] In other cases, a contract is concluded and the stipulation for a credit is a condition which is an essential term of the contract. In those cases the provision of the credit is a condition precedent, not to the formation of the contract, but to the obligation of the seller to deliver the goods. If the buyer fails to provide the credit, the seller can treat himself as discharged from any further performance of the contract and can sue the buyer for damages for not providing the credit."

The first of these instances provided by Denning L.J. is that of a contingent, and the second of a promissory, condition.

Conditions precedent. The liability of one or both of the contracting parties may become effective only if certain facts are ascertained to exist or upon the occurrence or non-occurrence of some further event. In such a case the contract is said to be subject to a condition precedent.[111] The failure of a condition precedent may have one of a number of effects.[112] It may, in the first place, suspend the rights and obligations of both parties, as, for instance, where the parties enter into an agreement on the express understanding that it is not to become binding on either of them unless the condition is fulfilled.[113] Secondly, one party may assume an immediate unilateral binding obligation, subject to a condition. From this he cannot withdraw[114]; but no bilateral contract, binding on 12–028

[108] See below, para.12–028.

[109] [1952] 2 Q.B. 297, 304.

[110] The analogy is not, however, an exact one, for in the case of a stipulation "subject to contract" no contract will usually come into existence at all (see above, para.2–118) whereas in the case of a contingent condition relating to the opening of a credit a contract normally comes into existence, though certain rights and obligations of the parties are suspended until the condition is fulfilled (see below, para.12–028).

[111] For the other use of the term "condition precedent" to mean a promissory condition, see above, para.12–026, below, para.24–039.

[112] See the analyses, e.g. in *Property and Bloodstock Ltd v Emerton* [1967] 2 All E.R. 839, affirmed [1968] Ch. 94; *United Dominions Trust (Commercial) Ltd v Eagle Aircraft Services Ltd* [1968] 1 W.L.R. 74, 82; *Wood Preservation Ltd v Prior* [1969] 1 W.L.R. 1077; *L.G. Schuler A.G. v Wickman Machine Tool Sales Ltd* [1972] 1 W.L.R. 840, 850, 854, 859 CA; affirmed [1974] A.C. 235, 250–251, 256 HL; *North Sea Energy Holdings NV v Petroleum Authority of Thailand* [1997] 2 Lloyd's Rep. 418, 429.

[113] *Pym v Campbell* (1856) 6 E. & B. 370; *Aberfoyle Plantations Ltd v Cheng* [1960] A.C. 115; *William Cory & Son Ltd v IRC* [1965] A.C. 1088; *Haslemere Estates Ltd v Baker* [1982] 1 W.L.R. 1109.

[114] *Smith v Butler* [1900] 1 Q.B. 694.

both parties, comes into existence until the condition is fulfilled.[115] Thirdly, the parties may enter into an immediate binding contract, but subject to a condition, which suspends all or some of the obligations of one or both parties pending fulfilment of the condition.[116] These conditions precedent are, however, normally contingent and not promissory, and in such a case neither party will be liable to the other if the condition is not fulfilled.

12–029 **Concurrent conditions.** The word "condition" has also been employed in the case of "concurrent conditions". Where the promises made by each party are to be fulfilled at the same time, or, at any rate, where each party's obligation is to depend on the readiness and willingness of the other to perform at that time, the promises are termed concurrent conditions. For example, in a contract of sale of goods, delivery of the goods and payment of the price are in the absence of a contrary intention concurrent conditions, that is to say, the seller must be ready and willing to give possession of the goods to the buyer in exchange for the price and the buyer must be ready and willing to pay the price in exchange for possession of the goods.[117] Similarly, when freight is payable on delivery of cargo, payment of the freight and delivery of the cargo are normally concurrent conditions.[118]

12–030 **Conditions subsequent.** The obligation of one or both parties may be made subject to a condition that it is to be immediately binding, but if certain facts are ascertained to exist or upon the occurrence or non-occurrence of some further event, then either the contract is to cease to bind or one or both parties are to have the right to avoid the contract or bring it to an end.[119] In such a case the contract is said to be subject to a condition subsequent. An example is provided by the case of *Head v Tattersall*[120] where A bought a horse from B which B warranted to have been hunted with the Bicester hounds. If it did not answer its description, A was to have the right to return it by a certain day. The horse did not answer its description and A accordingly returned it before the day. In the meantime, however, the horse had been injured without A's fault. It was held that the injury

---

[115] *United Dominions Trust (Commercial) Ltd v Eagle Aircraft Services Ltd* [1968] 1 W.L.R. 74; *Wood Preservation Ltd v Prior* [1969] 1 W.L.R. 1077; cf. *Eastham v Leigh, London & Provincial Properties Ltd* [1971] Ch. 871.

[116] *Worsley v Wood* (1796) 6 Term Rep. 710; *Clarke v Watson* (1865) 18 C.B.(N.S.) 278; *Re Sandwell Park Colliery Co* [1929] 1 Ch. 277; *Parway Estates Ltd v IRC* (1958) 45 T.C. 135; *Smallman v Smallman* [1972] Fam. 25; *North Sea Energy Holdings NV v Petroleum Authority of Thailand* [1907] 2 Lloyd's Rep. 418. cf. *Total Gas Marketing Ltd v Arco British Ltd* [1998] 2 Lloyd's Rep. 209 (contract ceases to bind). See also (insurance contracts), Vol.II, para.41–060.

[117] Sale of Goods Act 1979 s.28. See Vol.II, para.43–267.

[118] *Paynter v James* (1867) L.R. 2 C.P. 348; *Duthie v Hilton* (1868) L.R. 4 C.P. 138; *Vogeman v Bisley* (1897) 13 T.L.R. 172.

[119] *Total Gas Marketing Ltd v Arco British Ltd* [1998] 2 Lloyd's Rep. 209. Examples can also be found in the "excepted risks" clauses of charterparties (*Atlantic Maritime Co Inc v Gibbon* [1954] 1 Q.B. 88), and the power given to a landlord to re-enter in cases of breach of covenant (*Bashir v Commissioner of Lands* [1960] A.C. 44). The former are contingent conditions; the latter, promissory.

[120] (1871) L.R. 7 Ex. 7.

did not cause A to lose his right to return the horse and he could recover the purchase price paid.[121]

(b) *Warranties*

Warranties. The word "warranty" has been described as "one of the most ill-used expressions in the legal dictionary".[122] In many older cases, it was used in the sense of "condition"[123] and today it is very frequently used simply in the sense of a contractual undertaking or promise. In its most technical sense, however, it is to be understood as meaning a term of the contract, the breach of which may give rise to a claim for damages but not to a right to treat the contract as repudiated.[124] The use of the word "warranty" in this sense is reserved for the less important terms of a contract, or those which are collateral to the main purpose of the contract,[125] the breach of which by one party does not entitle the other to treat his obligations as discharged. But the emergence of the new category of "intermediate" terms seems likely to have reduced the number of occasions when a term will be classified as a warranty in this sense almost to vanishing point,[126] save in the very exceptional circumstances where a term has been specifically so classified by statute.[127] 12–031

"Warranty" upon election. Upon the occurrence of a breach of condition, the injured party may elect to treat the breach of condition as a breach of warranty only and not as a ground for treating the contract as repudiated[128]; or he may be compelled to do so where he goes on with the contract and takes some benefit under it.[129] In such a case he is sometimes said to sue on a "warranty *ex post facto*", although this expression is somewhat misleading since the breach is still that of a condition of the contract.[130] 12–032

Collateral warranties. Undertakings may be given that are collateral to another contract.[131] They may be considered to be independent of that other 12–033

---

[121] But Cleasby J. held ((1871) L.R. 7 Ex. 7, 13, 14) that, since the property in the horse had reverted to B, B had to bear the risk of loss which had occurred without A's fault in the meantime.

[122] *Finnegan v Allen* [1943] 1 K.B. 425, 430.

[123] *Behn v Burness* (1863) 3 B. & S. 751. In marine insurance, a promissory "warranty" is used to signify a condition precedent, the breach of which discharges the insurer from liability as from the date of breach: Marine Insurance Act 1906 ss.33–41; *Thomson v Weems* (1884) 9 App.Cas. 671, 684; *Bank of Nova Scotia v Hellenic Mutual War Risks Association (Bermuda) Ltd* [1992] 1 A.C. 233.

[124] *Hongkong Fir Shipping Co Ltd v Kawasaki Kisen Kaisha Ltd* [1962] 2 Q.B. 26, 70; Sale of Goods Act 1979 ss.11(3), 61(1).

[125] Sale of Goods Act 1979, s.61(1).

[126] But see *Palmco Shipping Inc v Continental Ore Corp* [1970] 2 Lloyd's Rep. 21; *Anglia Commercial Properties v North East Essex Building Co* (1983) 266 E.G. 1096.

[127] Sale of Goods Act 1979 ss.11(3), 12(5A). See also Supply of Goods (Implied Terms) Act 1973 s.8(3).

[128] Sale of Goods Act 1979 s.11(2).

[129] Sale of Goods Act 1979 s.11(4).

[130] *Wallis, Son & Wells v Pratt & Haynes* [1911] A.C. 394.

[131] See above, para.12–004; Wedderburn [1959] Camb.L.J. 58.

contract either because they cannot fairly be regarded as having been incorporated therein,[132] or because rules of evidence hinder their incorporation,[133] or because the main contract is defective in some way[134] or is subject to certain requirements of form[135] or is made between parties other than those by or to whom the undertaking is given.[136] Such undertakings are often referred to as collateral contracts, or "collateral warranties."

(c) *Intermediate Terms*

12–034 **Intermediate terms.** The advantage that arises from the classification of a particular term as a condition is that of certainty[137]: the party affected by the breach of such a term knows at once where he stands, i.e. that he is immediately and unequivocally entitled to treat the contract as repudiated and, for example in a contract of sale of goods, to reject the goods.[138] On the other hand, since *any* breach of condition gives rise to this right, it may be exercised irrespective of the gravity of the breach or of the consequences resulting from the breach. The innocent party may have suffered no, or only trifling, loss or damage by reason of the breach, but is nevertheless entitled to refuse further performance of the contract. In recent years, the courts have therefore curtailed the right of discharge which follows from the classification of a term as a condition by the creation of a new category of terms, adopting a more flexible approach to the consequences of breach and tending to encourage, rather than discourage, performance of the contract.[139] In *Hongkong Fir Shipping Co Ltd v Kawasaki Kisen Kaisha Ltd*,[140] the Court of Appeal refused to ascribe to the shipowner's obligation to deliver a seaworthy vessel the character of a condition, and Diplock L.J. said[141]:

> "There are, however, many contractual undertakings of a more complex character which cannot be categorised as being 'conditions' or 'warranties' . . . Of such undertakings all that can be predicated is that some breaches will and others will not give rise to an event which will deprive the party not in default of substantially the whole benefit which it was intended he should obtain from the contract; and the legal consequences of a breach of such undertaking, unless provided for expressly[142] in the contract, depend upon the nature of the event to which the breach gives rise and do not follow

---

[132] *Esso Petroleum Ltd v Mardon* [1976] Q.B. 801.

[133] See below, para.12–095.

[134] e.g. for illegality: see below, para.16–176.

[135] *Record v Bell* [1991] 1 W.L.R. 853.

[136] See above, para.12–007.

[137] *A/S Awilco of Oslo v Fulvia Spa (The Chikuma)* [1981] 1 W.L.R. 314, 322; *Bunge Corp v Tradax Export SA* [1981] 1 W.L.R. 711, 715, 718, 720, 725; *Compagnie Commerciale Sucres et Denrees v Czarnikow Ltd* [1990] 1 W.L.R. 1337, 1348; *Richco International Ltd v Bunge & Co Ltd* [1991] 2 Lloyd's Rep. 93, 99.

[138] Sale of Goods Act 1979 ss.11(3), 12(5A), 13(1A), 14(6), 15(3). But see the modification of remedies for breach of condition in non-consumer sales contained in s.15A of the 1979 Act; Vol.II, para.43–057.

[139] *Cehave N.V. v Bremer Handelsgesellschaft mbH* [1976] Q.B. 44, 70; *Bunge Corp v Tradax Export SA* [1981] 1 W.L.R. 711, 715, 179.

[140] [1962] 2 Q.B. 26.

[141] [1962] 2 Q.B. 26 at 70.

[142] Or impliedly: see *Bunge Corp v Tradax Export SA* [1981] 1 W.L.R. 711 and below, para.12–040.

automatically from a prior classification of the undertaking, as a 'condition' or a 'warranty.' "

The description that has been applied to such terms is that of "intermediate" or "innominate" terms.[143] Breach of such a term entitles the party not in default to treat the contract as repudiated only if the other party has thereby renounced his obligations under the contract,[144] or rendered them impossible of performance,[145] in some essential respect or if the consequences of the breach are so serious as to deprive the innocent party of substantially the whole benefit which it was intended that he should obtain from the contract.[146]

Instances of classification. A term is most likely to be classified as intermediate if it is capable of being broken either in a manner that is trivial and capable of remedy by an award of damages or in a way that is so fundamental as to undermine the whole contract. Thus, for example, a shipowner's obligation in a charterparty to provide a seaworthy vessel,[147] to load containers without any stability problem[148] or to commence and carry out the voyage agreed on with reasonable despatch,[149] or a clause by which the master of the ship was to act under the charterer's orders,[150] have been classified as intermediate terms, the breach of which does not entitle discharge unless the consequences are such as to deprive the charterer of substantially the whole benefit of the contract or to frustrate the object of the charterer in chartering the ship.[151] 12–035

Classification of terms in sale of goods contracts. The Sale of Goods Act 1979 and the Supply of Goods (Implied Terms) Act 1973 expressly define certain implied terms in contracts of sale of goods or hire-purchase as being "conditions" or "warranties".[152] There can be no doubt that such classification is binding. But in *Cehave N.V. v Bremer Handelsgesellschaft mbH*[153] it was argued that s.11(1) of the Sale of Goods Act 1893 created a statutory dichotomy which divided all terms in contracts for the sale of goods into conditions and warranties. 12–036

---

143 *Cehave N.V. v Bremer Handelsgesellschaft mbH* [1976] Q.B. 44, 60; *Bremer Handelsgesellschaft mbH v Vanden Avenne-Izegem P.V.B.A.* [1978] 2 Lloyd's Rep. 109, 113; *Bunge Corp v Tradax Export SA* [1981] 1 W.L.R. 711, 714, 717, 719, 724; *Aktion Maritime Corp of Liberia v S. Kasmas & Brothers Ltd* [1987] 1 Lloyd's Rep. 283; *Phibro Energy A.G. v Nissho Iwai Corp* [1990] 1 Lloyd's Rep. 38, 58–59.

144 See below, para.24–018.

145 See below, para.24–028.

146 See below, para.24–034.

147 *Hongkong Fir Shipping Co Ltd v Kawasaki Kisen Kaisha Ltd* [1962] 2 Q.B. 26; *Nitrate Corp of Chile Ltd v Pansuiza Compania de Navegacion SA* [1980] 1 Lloyd's Rep. 638.

148 *Compagnie Generale Maritime v Diakan Spirit SA* [1982] 2 Lloyd's Rep. 574.

149 *Freeman v Taylor* (1831) 8 Bing. 124; *Clipsham v Vertue* (1843) 5 Q.B. 565; *MacAndrew v Chapple* (1866) L.R. 1 C.P. 643.

150 *Federal Commerce & Navigation Co Ltd v Molena Alpha Inc* [1979] A.C. 757.

151 *MacAndrew v Chapple* (1866) L.R. 1 C.P. 643, 648.

152 See Vol.II, paras 38–362, 43–044, 43–061—43–103.

153 [1976] Q.B. 44. See also *Tradax International SA v Goldschmidt* [1977] 2 Lloyd's Rep. 604 (provision as to impurities); *Aktion Maritime Corp of Liberia v S. Kasmas & Brothers Ltd* [1987] 1 Lloyd's Rep. 283 (condition of vessel on delivery); *Total International Ltd v Addax BV* [1996] 2 Lloyd's Rep. 333 (provision as to quality). Contrast *Tradax Export SA v European Grain & Shipping Co* [1983] 2 Lloyd's Rep. 100.

The Court of Appeal rejected that argument and held that an express term "shipment to be made in good condition" was an intermediate term the breach of which had to be so serious as to go to the root of the contract in order to entitle the buyer to reject the goods. In *Reardon Smith Line Ltd v Yngvar Hansen-Tangen*[154] two charterparties were entered into in similar terms for the charter of a ship "to be built by the Osaka Shipbuilding Co Ltd and known as Hull No. 354", Owing to her size, the ship was built at a new yard by Oshima Shipbuilding Co Ltd (a company in which Osaka had a 50 per cent interest) and bore the yard or hull number Oshima 004, although she was still referred to in external documents as "called Osaka 354". The charterers sought to reject the vessel on the ground that, by analogy with contracts of sale of goods, the description of the ship was a condition of the contract, any departure from which justified rejection. The House of Lords held that they were not entitled to do so. On the other hand, terms, for example, in contracts of sale of goods that the goods contracted to be sold are afloat or already shipped,[155] or on board a ship "now at Rangoon"[156] or on a ship that will sail direct to the port of destination,[157] or that they are "under deck",[158] or as to the date of shipment,[159] have been held to be part of the description of the goods, and conditions. Also, a stipulation as to the place of delivery in an f.o.b. contract[160] and a stipulation "linerterms Rotterdam" in a c.i.f. contract[161] have been held to be conditions.

12–037 **Classification of time stipulations.**[162] A number of cases have arisen relating to the question whether contractual stipulations as to the time of performance should be construed as making time of the essence of the contract (i.e. as conditions) or as intermediate terms. At common law, stipulations as to the time of performance were normally regarded as being of the essence of a contract.[163] But in equity they were not generally so regarded,[164] in particular in relation to contracts for the sale of land, and today the equitable rule prevails.[165] The relationship between the common law and equitable rules was considered by the House of Lords in *United Scientific Holdings Ltd v Burnley BC*,[166] where it was

---

[154] [1976] 1 W.L.R. 989. See also *Sanko Steamship Co Ltd v Kano Trading Ltd* [1978] 1 Lloyd's Rep. 156.

[155] *Benabu & Co v Produce Brokers Co Ltd* (1921) 37 T.L.R. 609, 851; *Macpherson Train & Co Ltd v Howard Ross & Co Ltd* [1955] 1 W.L.R. 640, 642.

[156] *Oppenheimer v Fraser* (1876) 34 L.T. 524.

[157] *Bergerco U.S.A. v Vegoil Ltd* [1984] 1 Lloyd's Rep. 440.

[158] *Montagu L. Meyer Ltd v Travaru A/B; H Cornelius of Gambleby* (1930) 46 T.L.R. 553; *Messers Ltd v Morrison's Export Co Ltd* [1939] 1 All E.R. 92.

[159] *Bowes v Shand* (1877) 2 App. Cas. 455.

[160] *Petrotrade Inc v Stinnes Handel GmbH* [1995] 1 Lloyd's Rep. 142.

[161] *Soon Hua Seng Co Ltd v Glencore Grain Co Ltd* [1996] 1 Lloyd's Rep. 398.

[162] This paragraph was approved by Langley J. in *Haugland Tankers AS v RMK Marine Gemi Yapin Sanayii ve Dentz Tasimaciligi Isletmesi AS* [2005] EWHC 321 (Comm), [2005] 1 Lloyd's Rep. 573 at [31]. See also *Dalkia Utilities Services Plc v Celtech International Ltd* [2006] EWHC 63 (Comm), [2006] 1 Lloyd's Rep. 599 at [130].

[163] See below, para.21–011.

[164] See below, para.21–011.

[165] Law of Property Act 1925 s.41; below, para.21–012.

[166] [1978] A.C. 904 (especially at 928); below, para.21–012.

held that the time-table specified in rent review clauses for the completion of the various steps for determining the rent payable in respect of the period following the review was not of the essence. It is, however, clear that, although stipulations as to time will not ordinarily be construed as being of the essence, they will be so construed if expressly stated to be such[167] or if the court infers from the nature of the subject-matter of the contract or the surrounding circumstances that the parties intended them to have that effect.[168] In mercantile contracts, where it is of importance that the parties should know precisely what their obligations are and be able to act with confidence in the legal results of their actions, the courts will readily construe a stipulation as to time as a condition of the contract.[169] Thus stipulations, for example, as to the time within which a ship must be nominated[170] or is expected ready to load under a charterparty,[171] goods must be delivered under a contract of sale,[172] the loading port must be nominated,[173] the vessel provided,[174] notice of readiness to load must be given[175] and the goods must be ready to be delivered[176] under an f.o.b. contract, goods must be shipped,[177] documents tendered[178] and notice of appropriation given[179] under a c.i.f. contract, a letter of credit must be opened,[180] or hire paid under a time charter[181] have been held to be conditions, entitling the innocent party in the event of default in punctual performance to treat himself as discharged. But there is no presumption of fact or rule of law that time is of the essence in mercantile

[167] *Steadman v Drunkle* [1916] 1 A.C. 275, 279; *Financings Ltd v Baldock* [1963] 2 Q.B. 104, 120; *Bunge Corp v Tradax Export SA* [1980] 1 Lloyd's Rep. 294, 305, 307, 309, 310 (affirmed [1981] 1 W.L.R. 711); *Lombard North Central Plc v Butterworth* [1987] Q.B. 527.

[168] [1978] A.C. 904, 937, 941, 944, 950, 958; *Bunge Corp v Tradax Export SA* [1981] 1 W.L.R. 711, 728–729; *Universal Bulk Carriers Ltd v André et Cie SA* [2000] 1 Lloyd's Rep. 459, 464; *B.S. & N. Ltd v Micado Shipping Ltd (The Seaflower)* [2001] 1 Lloyd's Rep. 348, 350, 354; *MSAS Global Logistics Ltd v Power Packaging Inc* [2003] EWHC 1393 (Ch).

[169] *Bunge Corp v Tradax Export SA* [1981] 1 W.L.R. 711, 716.

[170] *Greenwich Marine Inc v Federal Commerce and Navigation Co Inc* [1985] 1 Lloyd's Rep. 580.

[171] *The Mihalis Angelos* [1971] 1 Q.B. 164. See also *Behn v Burness* (1863) 3 B. & S. 751; *Compania de Naviera Nedelka SA v Tradax Internacional SA* [1974] Q.B. 264.

[172] *Hartley v Hymans* [1920] 3 K.B. 475, 484; *Scandinavian Trading Co A/B v Zodiac Petroleum SA* [1981] 1 Lloyd's Rep. 81.

[173] *Gill & Duffus SA v Société pour l'Exportation des Sucres* [1986] 1 Lloyd's Rep. 322.

[174] *Olearia Tirrena SpA v N.V. Algemeene Oliehandel* [1973] 2 Lloyd's Rep. 86.

[175] *Bunge Corp v Tradax Export SA* above.

[176] *Compagnie Commerciale Sucres et Denrees v Czarnikow Ltd* [1990] 1 W.L.R. 1337.

[177] *Bowes v Shand* (1877) 2 App. Cas. 455.

[178] *Toepfer v Lenersan-Poortman N.V.* [1980] 1 Lloyd's Rep. 143; *Cerealmangimi SpA v Toepfer* [1981] 1 Lloyd's Rep. 337.

[179] *Reuter v Sala* (1879) 4 C.P.D. 239; *Bunge GmbH v Landbouwbelang G.A.* [1980] 1 Lloyd's Rep. 458. See also *Société Italo-Belge pour le Commerce et L'Industrie SA v Palm and Vegetable Oils (Malaysia) Sdn. Bhd.* [1981] 2 Lloyd's Rep. 695 (notice of shipment).

[180] *Pavia & Co SpA v Thurmann-Nielsen* [1952] 1 Lloyd's Rep. 153; *Ian Stach Ltd v Baker Bosley Ltd* [1958] 2 Q.B. 130; *Nichimen Corp v Gatoil Overseas Inc* [1987] 2 Lloyd's Rep. 46; *Transpetrol Ltd v Transol Olieprodukten B.V.* [1989] 1 Lloyd's Rep. 309. See also *Warde v Feedex International Inc* [1985] 2 Lloyd's Rep. 289 (nomination of bank). Contrast *State Trading Corp of India Ltd v M. Golodetz Ltd* [1989] 2 Lloyd's Rep. 277 (opening of counter-trade guarantee).

[181] *Mardorf Peach & Co Ltd v Attica Sea Carriers Corp of Liberia* [1977] A.C. 850; *A/S Awilco of Oslo v Fulvia Spa (The Chikuma)* [1981] 1 W.L.R. 314.

contracts[182] and a stipulation as to time in such a contract, may on its true construction, be found to be merely an intermediate term.[183]

12–038 **Effect of failure to perform on time.** Where one party to a contract fails to perform an obligation by the date fixed by the contract, the other party may be entitled, in certain circumstances, immediately to serve notice that he will treat the contract as discharged if the obligation is not performed within a reasonable time as stipulated in the notice. This matter is discussed in Ch.21 (Performance) later in this work[184]; but it is to be noted that, as a general rule, where the original stipulation as to the time of performance was merely an intermediate term, failure to perform the obligation within the time limited by the notice does not, in itself, constitute a repudiation irrespective of the consequences of the breach.[185]

12–039 **Force majeure clauses.** A clause in a contract of sale excusing delivery, or permitting the seller to postpone or suspend delivery upon the happening of events beyond his control (a force majeure clause)[186] may require that certain procedures are to be followed or notices given to the buyer before the seller is entitled to rely on the clause. Such measures may be a condition precedent on which the availability of the protection provided by the clause depends, or merely an intermediate term, the non-compliance with which does not necessarily deprive the seller of his right to rely on the clause. The classification depends, as Lord Wilberforce said in *Bremer Handelsgesellschaft v Vanden Avenne-Izegem P.V.B.A.*[187] on "(i) the form of the clause itself, (ii) the relation of the clause to the contract as a whole, (iii) general considerations of law". In that case, the House of Lords had to consider two such provisions. The first was a prohibition of export clause which required the sellers to advise the buyers "without delay" of impossibility of shipment by reason of such prohibition.[188] This was held to be an intermediate term, since it did not establish any definite time limit within which the advice was to be given.[189] The second provision, which took effect

[182] *Bunge Corp v Tradax Export SA* [1981] 1 W.L.R. 711, 719; *State Trading Corp of India Ltd v M. Golodetz Ltd* [1989] 2 Lloyd's Rep. 277; *Compagnie Commerciale Sucres et Denrees v Czarnikow Ltd* [990] 1 W.L.R. 1337, 1347; *Phibro Energy A.G. v Nissho Iwai Corp* [1991] 1 Lloyd's Rep. 38, 45, 48.

[183] See, for example, *State Trading Corp of India Ltd v M. Golodetz Ltd* [1989] 2 Lloyd's Rep. 277 (opening of counter trade guarantee); *Re Olympia & York Canary Wharf Ltd (No.2)* [1993] B.C.C. 159 (indemnity clause); *Torvald Klaveness A/S v Arni Maritime Corp* [1994] 1 W.L.R. 1465 (charterer's re-delivery of ship); *Universal Bulk Carriers Ltd v André et Cie SA* [2000] 1 Lloyd's Rep. 459 (obligation to narrow laycan period prior to first lay day); *ERG Raffinerie Mediterranée SpA v Chevron USA Inc* [2007] EWCA Civ 494, [2007] 1 C.L.C. 807 (loading time in f.o.b. contract).

[184] Below, para.21–014.

[185] See *Eshun v Moorgate Mercantile Co Ltd* [1971] 1 W.L.R. 722, 726; *Behzadi v Shaftesbury Hotels Ltd* [1992] Chs 1, 12; *Re Olympia & York Canary Wharf Ltd (No.2)*, [1993] B.C.C. 159; *Dalkia Utilities Services Plc v Celtech International Ltd* [2006] EWHC 63 (Comm), [2006] 1 Lloyd's Rep. 599 at [131]; *Shawten Engineering Ltd v DGP International Ltd* [2005] EWCA Civ 1359, [2006] Build. L.R. 1. Contrast Stannard (2004) 120 L.Q.R. 137, 155. See below, para.21–017.

[186] See below, para.14–137.

[187] [1978] 2 Lloyd's Rep. 109, 113.

[188] The clause is not accurately set out in the headnote.

[189] But see *Mamidoil-Jetoil Greek Petroleum Co SA v Okta Crude Oil Refinery AD* [2002] EWHC 2210 (Comm), [2003] 1 Lloyd's Rep. 1 ("shall give prompt notice to the other party" held to be a condition) [2003] EWCA Civ 617, [2003] 2 Lloyd's Rep. 645 at [34].

upon a number of events of force majeure, established a time-table of fixed periods within which the occurrence was to be notified, an extension of the shipping period claimed, and the buyers were to have the option of cancelling the contract. The stipulation as to time for claiming an extension was held to be a condition, punctual compliance with which was required as part of a "complete regulatory code". It was further held that a requirement of this second provision that the sellers should notify the buyers of the port or ports of loading from which it was intended to ship in consequence of the event of force majeure had to be precisely complied with.[190]

Conclusion. The conclusion[191] to be drawn from these cases is that a term of a contract will be held to be a condition: 12–040

(i) if it is expressly so provided by statute;

(ii) if it has been so categorised as the result of previous judicial decision (although it has been said that some of the decisions on this matter are excessively technical and are open to re-examination by the House of Lords)[192];

(iii) if it is so designated in the contract[193] or if the consequences of its breach, that is, the right of the innocent party to treat himself as discharged, are provided for expressly in the contract[194]; or

(iv) if the nature of the contract or the subject-matter or the circumstances of the case lead to the conclusion that the parties must, by necessary implication, have intended that the innocent party would be discharged from further performance of his obligations in the event that the term was not fully and precisely complied with.[195]

---

[190] See also *Tradax Export SA v André & Cie SA* [1976] 1 Lloyd's Rep. 416; *Berg (V.) & Son Ltd v Vanden Avenne-Izegem P.V.B.A.* [1977] 1 Lloyd's Rep. 499; *Toepfer v Schwarze* [1980] 1 Lloyd's Rep. 385.

[191] The conclusion set out in this paragraph was approved by the Court of Appeal in *B.S. & N. Ltd v Micado Shipping Ltd (The Seaflower)* [2001] 1 Lloyd's Rep. 341, 348, 350, 353.

[192] *Reardon Smith Line Ltd v Yngvar Hansen-Tangen* [1976] 1 W.L.R. 989, 998.

[193] *Bettini v Gye* (1876) 1 QBD 183, 187; *Financings Ltd v Baldock* [1963] 2 Q.B. 104, 120; *Bunge Corp v Tradax Export SA* [1980] 1 Lloyd's Rep. 294, 305, 307, 309, 310 (affirmed [1981] 1 W.L.R. 711); *Lombard North Central Plc v Butterworth* [1987] Q.B. 527; cf. *L.G. Schuler A.G. v Wickman Machine Tool Sales Ltd* [1974] A.C. 235; *Antaios Compania Naviera SA v Salen Rederierna A.B.* [1985] A.C. 191.

[194] *Hongkong Fir Shipping Co Ltd v Kawasaki Kisen Kaisha Ltd* [1962] 2 Q.B. 26, 70; *United Scientific Holdings Ltd v Burnley BC* [1978] A.C. 904, 937, 941, 944, 950, 958; *Bremer Handelsgesellschaft mbH v Vanden Avenne-Izegem P.V.B.A.* [1978] 2 Lloyd's Rep. 109, 113; *Photo Production Ltd v Securicor Transport Ltd* [1980] A.C. 827, 849; *Bunge Corp v Tradax Export SA* [1981] 1 W.L.R. 711. But see *Rice v Great Yarmouth BC* [2001] 3 L.G.L.R. 4 (CA) (right to terminate for "any" breach of contract limited to repudiatory breaches).

[195] *United Scientific Holdings Ltd v Burnley BC* [1978] A.C. 904, 937, 941, 944, 950, 958; *Bremer Handelsgesellschaft mbH v Vanden Avenne-Izegem P.V.B.A.* [1978] 2 Lloyd's Rep. 109, 113, 116; *Bunge Corp v Tradax Export SA* [1981] 1 W.L.R. 711, 716, 717, 720, 729; *Greenwich Marine Inc v Federal Commerce and Navigation Co Inc* [1985] 1 Lloyd's Rep. 580, 584; *State Trading Corp of India Ltd v M. Golodetz Ltd* [1989] 2 Lloyd's Rep. 277, 283; *Barber v NWS Bank Plc* [1996] 1 W.L.R. 641; *B.S. & N. Ltd v Micado Shipping Ltd* [2001] 1 Lloyd's Rep. 341, 350, 353, 356.

Otherwise a term of a contract will be considered to be an intermediate term.[196] Failure to perform such a term will ordinarily entitle the party not in default to treat himself as discharged only if the effect of breach of the term deprives him of substantially the whole benefit which it was intended that he should obtain from the contract.[197]

3. CONSTRUCTION OF TERMS[198]

(a) *General Principles of Construction*

12–041 **Construction.** The word "construction" refers to the process by which a court determines the meaning and legal effect of a contract. As such, it will embrace oral contracts as well as those in writing and implied terms as well as those that are expressed. In this chapter, however, the principles of construction discussed in the following paragraphs have mainly been developed in relation to written documents, and in this context "construction" denotes the process (sometimes referred to as *interpretation*) by which a court arrives at the meaning to be given to the language used by the parties in the express terms of a written agreement.

12–042 **Object of construction.** The object of all construction of the terms of a written agreement is to discover therefrom the common intention of the parties to the agreement.[199] The principles which govern the construction of contracts are the same at law and in equity,[200] for simple contracts and for specialties.[201]

12–043 **Intention of the parties.** The task of ascertaining the common intention of the parties must be approached objectively[202]: the question is not what one or other of the parties meant or understood by the words used, but:

---

[196] *Hongkong Fir Shipping Co Ltd v Kawasaki Kisen Kaisha Ltd* [1962] 2 Q.B. 26; *Cehave M.V. v Bremer Handelsgesellschaft mbH* [1976] Q.B. 44; *United Scientific Holdings Ltd v Burnley* [1978] A.C. 904, 928; *Bremer Handelsgesellschaft mbH v Vanden Avenne-Izegem P.V.B.A.* [1978] 2 Lloyd's Rep. 109, 113, 121, 128, 130; *Bunge Corp v Tradax Export SA* [1981] 1 W.L.R. 711, 715–716, 717, 719, 724; *Phibro Energy A.G. v Nissho Iwai Corp* [1990] 1 Lloyd's Rep. 38, 45, 58–59.

[197] See below, para.24–040.

[198] See generally, *Odgers' Construction of Deeds and Statutes*, 5th edn; *Norton on Deeds*, 2nd edn; Lewison, *Interpretation of Contracts*, 3rd edn; McMeel, *Construction of Contracts* (2006); Mitchell, *Interpretation of Contracts* (2007).

[199] *Marquis of Cholmondeley v Clinton* (1820) 2 Jac.& W. 1, 91.

[200] *Hotham v East India Co* (1787) Doug. 272, 277; *Eaton v Lyon* (1798) 3 Ves. 690, 692; *Re Terry and White's Contract* (1886) 32 ChD 14, 21; *Bank of Credit and Commerce International SA v Ali* [2001] UKHL 8, [2002] 1 A.C. 251 at [25].

[201] *Seddon v Senate* (1810) 13 East. 63, 74; *Total Transport Corp v Arcadia Petroleum Ltd* [1998] 1 Lloyd's Rep. 351, 362.

[202] *Mannai Investment Co Ltd v Eagle Star Life Assurance Co Ltd* [1997] A.C. 749, 767, 775, 782; *Investors Compensation Scheme Ltd v West Bromwich Building Society* [1998] 1 W.L.R. 896, 912–913. See also *Guardian Ocean Cargoes Ltd v Banco do Brasil SA* [1994] 2 Lloyd's Rep. 152; *Deutsche Genossenschaftsbank v Burnhope* [1995] 1 W.L.R. 1580, 1587; *Inntrepreneur Pub Co v East Crown Ltd* [2000] 2 Lloyd's Rep. 611 at [10].

"... the meaning which the document would convey to a reasonable person having all the background knowledge which would reasonably have been available to the parties in the situation in which they were at the time of the contract".[203]

The cardinal presumption is that the parties have intended what they have in fact said, so that their words must be construed as they stand.[204] That is to say the meaning of the document or of a particular part of it is to be sought *in the document itself*: "[o]ne must consider the meaning of the words used, not what one may guess to be the intention of the parties".[205] However, this is not to say that the meaning of the words in a written document must be ascertained by reference to the words of the document alone. In the modern law, the courts will, in principle, look at all the circumstances surrounding the making of the contract which would assist in determining how the language of the document would have been understood by a reasonable man.[206]

Further it has long been accepted that the courts will not approach the task of construction with too nice a concentration upon individual words. 12–044

"The common and universal principle ought to be applied: namely, that [an agreement] ought to receive that construction which its language will admit, and which will best effectuate the intention of the parties, to be collected from the whole of the agreement, and that greater regard is to be had to the clear intention of the parties than to any particular words which they may have used in the expression of their intent."[207]

Principles of construction. Certain principles of construction have been formulated by the courts. Previously, these principles, referred to as "rules", were applied somewhat rigidly and adhered to tenaciously (even though the application of one rule in preference to another might lead to an opposite result). However, it has been pointed out[208] that the modern approach to construction is: 12–045

"... to assimilate the way in which [contractual] documents are interpreted by judges to the common-sense principles by which any serious utterance would be interpreted in ordinary life."

As a result, most principles of construction are nowadays better regarded merely as guidelines or assumptions as to what the court may regard as the normal use

[203] *Investors Compensation Scheme Ltd v West Bromwich Building Society* [1998] 1 W.L.R. 896, 912.

[204] *IRC v Raphael* [1935] A.C. 96, 142; *British Movietonews v London and District Cinemas* [1952] A.C. 166.

[205] *Smith v Lucas* (1881) 18 ChD 531, 542. See also *Prenn v Simmonds* [1971] 1 W.L.R. 1381, 1385 HL; *Hyundai Merchant Marine Co Ltd v Gesuri Chartering Co Ltd* [1991] 1 Lloyd's Rep. 100, 103.

[206] See below, para.12–118; McMeel [1999] L.M.C.L.Q. 382.

[207] *Ford v Beech* (1848) 11 Q.B. 852, 866. See also *Smith v Packhurst* (1742) 3 Atk. 135, 136; *Lloyd v Lloyd* (1837) 2 My. & Cr. 192, 202; *SA Maritime et Commerciale of Geneva v Anglo-Iranian Oil Co Ltd* [1953] 1 W.L.R. 1379; affirmed [1954] 1 W.L.R. 496.

[208] By Lord Hoffmann in *Investors Compensation Scheme Ltd v West Bromwich Building Society* [1998] 1 W.L.R. 896, 912. See also *Don King Productions Ltd v Warren* [1998] 2 Lloyd's Rep. 176, 188; [1999] 1 Lloyd's Rep. 588.

of language and which assist judges to arrive at a reasonable interpretation of the parties' intentions, though subject to examination of the relevant circumstances surrounding the transaction. Some principles, on the other hand, such as the contra proferentem principle,[209] are of a different nature in that they are less obviously designed to ascertain the intentions of the parties and are more closely assimilated to "rules" in the traditional sense.

12–046 **Law and fact.** The construction of written instruments is a question of mixed law and fact. The expression "construction" as applied to a document includes two things, first, the meaning of the words; and, secondly, their legal effect, or the effect which is to be given to them.[210] Construction becomes a question of law as soon as the true meaning of the words in which an instrument has been expressed and the surrounding circumstances, if any, have been ascertained as facts.[211] However, the meaning of an ordinary English word,[212] of technical or commercial terms[213] and of latent ambiguities,[214] and the discovery of the surrounding circumstances (when they are relevant) are questions of fact.[215]

12–047 **Construction of contract not wholly in writing.** Where the contract does not depend solely on written documents, the question as to the character of the contract is properly one of fact.[216] But if a document is lost, so that secondary evidence of its contents is admissible, the construction of its terms is still a question of law and not of fact.[217]

12–048 **Electronic "documents".** It is submitted that an agreement which is concluded by electronic means, the terms of which are recorded electronically in a computer or on disc and which are capable of being retrieved and converted into readable form, should be regarded as a written agreement for the purposes of the application of principles of construction and the admissibility of extrinsic evidence.[218]

12–049 **Human Rights Act 1998.** The question whether courts, as public authorities, ought to construe contracts so as to be compatible with "Convention rights" under the European Convention on Human Rights, or whether they should do so

---

[209] See below, para.12–083.

[210] *Chatenay v Brazilian Submarine Telegraph Co Ltd* [1891] 1 Q.B. 79, 85.

[211] *Bowes v Shand* (1877) 2 App. Cas. 455, 462. See also *Neilson v Harford* (1841) 8 M. & W. 806, 823; *R. v Stephens* (1978) 139 C.L.R. 315; *R. v Spens* [1991] 1 W.L.R. 624, 631; *Sun Life Assurance Co of Canada v Lincoln National Life Insurance Co* [2004] EWCA Civ 1660, [2005] 1 Lloyd's Rep. 606 at [15]; cf. *R. v Adams, The Times*, January 28, 1993.

[212] *Cozens v Brutus* [1973] A.C. 854, 861; *Belgravia Navigation Co SA v Cannor Shipping Ltd* [1988] 2 Lloyd's Rep. 423.

[213] *Hill v Evans* (1862) 4 De G.F. & J. 288, 295.

[214] *Robinson v Great Western Ry* (1865) 35 L.J.C.P. 123.

[215] *Simpson v Margitson* (1847) 11 Q.B. 23.

[216] *Moore v Garwood* (1849) 4 Exch. 681; *Brook v Hook* (1871) L.R. 6 Ex. 89; *Maskelyne v Stollery* (1899) 16 T.L.R. 97.

[217] *Berwick v Horsfall* (1858) 4 C.B.(N.S.) 450.

[218] *Derby & Co Ltd v Weldon (No. 9)* [1991] 1 W.L.R. 652. See also Electronic Communications Act 2000; EC Directive on electronic commerce 2000/31 [2000] OJ L178/1. But there are some obvious practical difficulties with respect to volume, dispersal, durability and susceptibility to alteration.

if one of the parties is a public authority, has been discussed in an earlier chapter of this book.[219]

(b) *Ordinary Meaning to be Adopted*

Meaning of words.[220] Judges differ widely in their belief in the reliability of language and in the inherent meaning of words. In 1997 in *Mannai Investment Co Ltd v Eagle Star Life Assurance Co Ltd*[221] Lord Hoffmann said[222]: 12–050

> "It is of course true that the law is not concerned with the speaker's subjective intentions. But the notion that the law's concern is therefore with the 'meaning of his words' conceals an important ambiguity. The ambiguity lies in a failure to distinguish between the meanings of words and the question of what would be understood as the meaning of a person who uses words. The meaning of words, as they would appear in a dictionary, and the effect of their syntactical arrangement, as it would appear in a grammar, is part of the material which we use to understand a speaker's utterance. But it is only a part; another part is our knowledge of the background against which the utterance was made. It is that background which enables us, not only to choose the intended meaning when a word has more than one dictionary meaning but also . . . to understand a speaker's meaning, often without ambiguity, when he has used the wrong words."

Again in 1998, in *Investors Compensation Scheme Ltd v West Bromwich Building Society*,[223] he said:

> "The meaning which a document (or any other utterance) would convey to a reasonable man is not the same thing as the meaning of its words. The meaning of words is a matter of dictionaries and grammars; the meaning of the document is what the parties using those words against the relevant background would reasonably have been understood to mean."[224]

Some eighty years earlier Holmes J. had similarly commented:

---

[219] See above, paras 1–057, 1–061.

[220] See Farnsworth (1967) 76 Yale L.J. 939.

[221] [1997] A.C. 749. *Rennie v Westbury Homes (Holdings) Ltd* [2007] EWHC 164; [2007] N.P.C. 16; *Savings Bank of the Russian Federation v Refco Securities LLC* [2006] EWHC 857 (Comm), [2006] 2 All E.R. (Comm) 722.

[222] [1997] A.C. 749, 775.

[223] [1998] 1 W.L.R. 896. The principles set out by Lord Hoffmann in this case at 912–913 have subsequently been adopted in numerous cases: *Static Control Components (Europe) Ltd v Egan* [2004] EWCA Civ 392, [2004] 2 Lloyd's Rep. 429 at [12]–[14]; *BP Exploration Operating Co Ltd v Kvaerner Oilfield Products Ltd* [2004] EWHC 999 (Comm), [2005] 1 Lloyd's Rep. 307 at [47]–[48]; *Sirius International Insurance (Publ) v FAI General Insurance Ltd* [2004] UKHL 54; [2004] 1 W.L.R. 3251 at [19]; *Dairy Containers Ltd v Tasman Orient Line CV* [2004] UKPC 22, [2005] 1 W.L.R. 215 at [12]; *NBTY Europe Ltd v Nutricia International BV* [2005] EWHC 734 (Comm), [2005] 2 Lloyd's Rep. 350 at [31]; *Canmer International Inc v UK Mutual Steamship Assurance Assn (Bermuda) Ltd* [2005] EWHC 1694 (Comm), [2005] 2 Lloyd's Rep. 479 at [22]; *Absalom v TCRU Ltd* [2005] EWHC 1090 (Comm), [2005] 2 Lloyd's Rep. 735 at [25]; *Gastronome (UK) Ltd v Anglo-Dutch Meats (UK) Ltd* [2006] EWCA Civ 1233, [2006] 2 Lloyds' Rep. 587 at [14]; *Kershaw Mechanical Services Ltd v Kendrick Construction Ltd* [2006] EWHC 727 (Comm), [2006] 2 All E.R. (Comm) 722; *Forrest v Glasser* [2006] EWCA Civ 1086, [2006] 2 Lloyd's Rep. 392 at [20].

[224] [1998] 1 W.L.R. 896, 913.

"A word is not a crystal, transparent and unchanged, it is the skin of a living thought and may vary greatly in colour and content according to the circumstances and the time in which it is used."[225]

It would be unduly pessimistic to accept that human language is such that no sensible meaning can ever be given to the words in a document without reference to the circumstances in which those words came to be used. But even the "plain" and "obvious" meaning may take on a different meaning in the light of the circumstances prevailing when the document was made.[226] On the other hand the actual language used by the parties undoubtedly does impose constraints on the court's willingness to depart from the plain and obvious meaning. If the meaning of the words is clear and unambiguous, why should the court not assume that it was what the parties intended?[227] Moreover, an examination of all the factual circumstances that might point to an interpretation which differs from the one which the words themselves convey may lead to an unnecessary protraction of the judicial process. A balance has therefore to be struck. As Corbin remarked[228]:

"The more bizarre and unusual an asserted interpretation is, the more convincing must be the testimony that supports it. At what point the court should cease listening to testimony that white is black and that a dollar is fifty cents is a matter for sound judicial discretion and common sense."

The current approach of the courts to the construction of contracts is "neither uncompromisingly literal nor unswervingly purposive".[229] The instrument must speak for itself, but the words used must, as stated by Lord Hoffmann,[230] be understood to bear the meaning which they would convey to a reasonable man against the relevant background of the transaction.

12–051 **Adoption of the ordinary meaning of words.** The starting point in construing a contract is that words are to be given their ordinary and natural meaning.

---

225 *Towne v Eisner* (1918) 245 U.S. 416, 425.

226 See below, para.12–118.

227 *Melanesian Mission Trust Board v Australian Mutual Provident Society* [1997] 1 N.Z.L.R. 391, 394 (Lord Hope). See also *Sinochem International Oil (London) Co Ltd v Mobil Sales and Supply Corp* [2000] 1 Lloyd's Rep. 339, 346 (Kennedy L.J., dissenting); *HSBC Bank Plc v Liberty Mutual Insurance Co (UK) Ltd, The Times,* June 11, 2001.

228 (1944) 53 Yale L.J. 603, 623.

229 *Arbuthnott v Fagan* [1995] C.L.C. 1396, 1400 (Bingham M.R.).

230 This approach has been followed in numerous cases, including *Zeus Tradition Marine Ltd v Bell* [1999] 1 Lloyd's Rep. 703, 706; *Boats Park Ltd v Hutchinson* [1999] 2 N.Z.L.R. 1129; *First Realty Plc v Norton Rose* [1999] 2 B.C.L.C. 428; *Harbinger UK Ltd v GE Information Services Ltd* [2000] 1 All E.R. (Comm) 166; *Sinochem International Oil (London) Co Ltd v Mobil Sales and Supply Corp* [2000] 1 Lloyd's Rep. 339, 344; *Eridania Spa v Rudolf A Oetker* [2000] 2 Lloyd's Rep. 191, 196; *Association of British Travel Agents Ltd v British Airways Plc* [2000] 2 Lloyd's Rep. 209, 216; *City of London v Reeve & Co Ltd* [2000] Build. L.R. 211, 216; *Bank of Credit and Commerce International v Ali (No.5)* [2001] UKHL 8, [2002] 1 A.C. 251 at [8], [39]; *Sirius International Insurance (Publ) v FAI General Insurance Ltd* [2004] UKHL 54 at [19]; *Westerngeco Ltd v ATP Oil & Gas (UK) Ltd* [2006] EWHC 1164 (Comm), [2006] 2 Lloyd's Rep. 535 at [10]; *Multiplex Construction (UK) Ltd v Cleveland Bridge UK Ltd (No.2)* [2007] EWHC 145 (TCC), (2007) 111 Const. L.R. 48 at [155–157].

This is not necessarily the dictionary meaning of the word, but that in which it is generally understood. The courts assume that the parties have used language in the way that reasonable persons ordinarily do. So terms are:

> "... to be understood in their plain, ordinary, and popular sense, unless they have generally in respect to the subject-matter, as by the known usage of trade, or the like, acquired a peculiar sense distinct from the popular sense of the same words; or unless the context evidently points out that they must in the particular instance, and in order to effectuate the immediate intention of the parties to that contract, be understood in some other special and peculiar sense."[231]

Technical words. Prima facie the assumption is that technical words should have their technical meaning given to them unless something can be found in the context to exclude it,[232] for if a word is of a technical or scientific character, then its primary meaning is its technical and scientific meaning.[233] But: 12–052

> "... when it is clear from the context of an instrument in what sense words are used in that instrument, the sound rule of construction is to attribute to them that meaning, even though the words be technical and have technically a different meaning; for it is only so that you can effectuate the intention."[234]

Also:

> "... where it can be ascertained that a particular vernacular meaning is attributed to words under circumstances similar to those in which the [scientific] expression to be construed is found, the vernacular meaning must prevail over the scientific."[235]

Thus "petroleum" in a reservation in a conveyance was construed according to the vernacular, and not the scientific, meaning, and so was held to include gas in

[231] *Robertson v French* (1803) 4 East 130, 135. See also *Shore v Wilson* (1842) 9 Cl. & Fin. 355, 527; *Mallan v May* (1844) 12 M. & W. 511, 517; *Tielens v Hooper* (1850) 5 Exch. 830; *Grey v Pearson* (1857) 6 H.L. Cas. 61, 78, 106; *Beard v Moira Colliery Co* [1915] 1 Ch. 257, 268; *Royal Greek Government v Minister of Transport* [1949] 1 K.B. 525, 528; *Melanesian Mission Trust Board v Australian Mutual Provident Society* [1997] 1 N.Z.L.R. 391, 394 PC; *Charter Reinsurance Co Ltd v Fagan* [1997] A.C. 313, 384; *BP Exploration Operating Co Ltd v Kvaerner Oilfield Products Ltd* [2004] EWHC 999 (Comm), [2005] 1 Lloyd's Rep. 307 at [93]; *Thames Valley Power Ltd v Total Gas & Power Ltd* [2003] EWHC 2208 (Comm), [2006] 1 Lloyd's Rep. 441 at [25]; *Forrest v Glasser* [2006] EWCA Civ 1086, [2006] 2 Lloyd's Rep. 392 at [21]. Contrast *Staffordshire A.H.A. v South Staffordshire Waterworks Co* [1978] 1 W.L.R. 1387, 1394; *Charter Reinsurance Co Ltd v Fagan* [1997] A.C. 313, 391.

[232] *Laird v Briggs* (1881) 19 ChD 22, 34; *Monypenny v Monypenny* (1858) 4 K. & J. 174, 182; *Roddy v Fitzgerald* (1858) 6 H.L.C. 823, 877.

[233] *Holt & Co v Collyer* (1881) 16 ChD 718, 720.

[234] *Graham v Ewart* (1856) 1 H. & N. 550, 562; *Musgrave v Forster* (1871) L.R. 6 Q.B. 590, 596; *Holt & Co v Collyer* (1881) 16 ChD 718. See also (insurance contracts) below, para.41–058.

[235] *Michael Borys v Canadian Pacific Ry* [1953] A.C. 217, 223; *Lord Provost and Magistrates of Glasgow v Farie* (1888) 13 App.Cas. 657, 669; *Luigi Monta of Genoa v Cechofracht Co Ltd* [1956] 2 Q.B. 552.

solution in the liquid as it existed in the earth.[236] Yet even this distinction is not a rigid one to be applied without regard to the circumstances of the case.[237]

12–053 **Established judicial construction.** Where the same words or contractual provisions have for many years received a judicial construction, the court will suppose that the parties have contracted upon the belief that their words will be understood in the accepted legal sense.[238]

12–054 **Community directives.** A contract of a public and regulatory nature which has been drafted with a view to implementing a Community Directive should be construed in a manner compatible with the Directive.[239]

12–055 **Absurdity, inconsistency, etc.** In *Investors Compensation Scheme Ltd v West Bromwich Building Society*[240] Lord Hoffmann said[241]:

> "The 'rule' that words should be given their 'natural and ordinary meaning' reflects the common sense proposition that we do not easily accept that people have made linguistic mistakes, particularly in formal documents. On the other hand, if one would nevertheless conclude from the background that something must have gone wrong with the language, the law does not require judges to attribute to the parties an intention which they plainly could not have had."

So, the principle that words must be construed in their ordinary sense is liable to be departed from where that meaning would involve an absurdity[242] or would create some inconsistency with the rest of the instrument.[243] It may also not be

---

[236] *Michael Borys v Canadian Pacific Ry* [1953] A.C. 217. See also *Lovell and Christmas Ltd v Wall* (1911) 103 L.T. 588; *Tester v Bisley* (1948) 64 T.L.R. 184; cf. *Earl of Lonsdale v Att-Gen* [1982] 1 W.L.R. 887.

[237] *Michael Borys v Canadian Pacific Ry* [1953] A.C. 217, 223.

[238] *Thames and Mersey Marine Insurance Co v Hamilton, Fraser & Co* (1887) 12 App. Cas. 484, 490; *Pioneer Shipping Ltd v BTP Tioxide Ltd* [1982] A.C. 724, 735; *Skips A/S Nordheim v Syrian Petroleum Co Ltd* [1983] 2 Lloyd's Rep. 592, 597; *Navrom v Callitsis Ship Management SA* [1987] 2 Lloyd's Rep. 276, 278 (affirmed [1988] 2 Lloyd's Rep. 416); *Marc Rich & Co Ltd v Tourloti Compania Naviera SA* [1988] 2 Lloyd's Rep. 101, 105; *Chiswell Shipping Ltd v National Iranian Tanker Co* [1991] 2 Lloyd's Rep. 251, 257; *I.D.C. Group Ltd v Clark* [1992] 2 E.G.L.R. 184, 186; *British Sugar Plc v NEI Power Projects Ltd* (1997) 87 Build. L.R. 42, 50; *Rose v Stavrou, The Times*, June 3, 1999, *Cero Navigation Corp v Jean Lion & Cie* [2000] 1 Lloyd's Rep. 292, 294; *Sunport Shipping Ltd v Tryg-Baltica International (UK) Ltd* [2003] EWCA Civ 12, [2003] 1 Lloyd's Rep. 138 at [25], [56]; *Henry Boot Construction Ltd v Alstom Combined Cycles Ltd* [2005] EWCA Civ 814, [2005] 1 W.L.R. 3850 at [29]. But contrast *Wickman Machine Tool Sales Ltd v L.G. Schuler A.G.* [1974] A.C. 235; *Macedonia Maritime Co v Austin & Pickersgill Ltd* [1989] 1 Lloyd's Rep. 73.

[239] *White v White* [2001] UKHL 9, [2001] 1 W.L.R. 481.

[240] [1998] 1 W.L.R. 896.

[241] [1998] 1 W.L.R. 896, 913 (applied in *Sinochem International Oil (London) Co Ltd v Mobil Sales and Supply Group Corp* [2000] 1 Lloyd's Rep. 339, 344, 345, 346). cf. *Nippon Yusen Kubishiki Kaisha v Golden Strait Corp* [2003] EWHC 16 (Comm); [2003] 2 Lloyd's Rep. 592 at [10], [14].

[242] *Grey v Pearson* (1857) 6 H.L.C. 61, 106; *Abbott v Middleton* (1858) 7 H.L.C. 68, 114; *Thelluson v Rendlesham* (1859) 7 H.L.C. 429, 519; *Caledonian Ry v North British Ry* (1881) 6 App.Cas. 114, 130; cf. *Charter Reinsurance Co Ltd v Fagan* [1997] A.C. 313, 387; *Zeus Tradition Marine Ltd v Bell* [1999] 1 Lloyd's Rep. 703, 707.

[243] Words prima facie synonymous should be construed in the same sense throughout the instrument; *Re Birks* [1900] 1 Ch 417, 418, but there is no principle of general application to compel this: *Watson v Haggitt* [1928] A.C. 127.

applied, as Lord Hoffmann indicates, where there has been an obvious linguistic mistake[244] or where, if the words were construed in their ordinary sense, they would lead to a very unreasonable result or impose upon the contractor a responsibility which it could not reasonably be supposed he meant to assume.[245] In *Wickman Machine Tools Sales Ltd v L.G. Schuler AG*[246] Lord Reid said:

> "The fact that a particular construction leads to a very unreasonable result must be a relevant consideration. The more unreasonable the result, the more unlikely it is that the parties can have intended it, and if they do intend it the more necessary it is that they shall make their intention abundantly clear."[247]

Badly drafted contracts. In *Mitsui Construction Co Ltd v Att-Gen of Hong Kong*[248] Lord Bridge said (of a building contract) that the fact that the contract was badly drafted: 12–056

> ". . . affords no reason to depart from the fundamental rule of construction of contractual documents that the intention of the parties must be ascertained from the language they have used interpreted in the light of the relevant factual situation in which the contract was made. But the poorer the quality of the drafting, the less willing any court should be to be driven by semantic niceties to attribute to the parties an improbable and unbusinesslike intention, if the language used, whatever it may lack in precision, is reasonably capable of an interpretation which attributes to the parties an intention to make provision for contingencies inherent in the work contracted for on a sensible and businesslike basis."

Mercantile contracts. Although it has been stated that there is not in law any difference of construction between mercantile contracts and other instruments,[249] 12–057

---

[244] *Static Control Components (Europe) Ltd v Egan* [2004] EWCA Civ 392, [2004] 2 Lloyd's Rep. 428; *BP Exploration Operation Co Ltd v Kvaerner Oilfield Products Ltd* [2004] EWHC 999 (Comm), [2005] 1 Lloyd's Rep. 307 at [95]. Cf. *Armitage v Staveley Industries Plc* [2004] EWHC 2320 (Comm), [2004] Pens. L.R. 385; *Canmer International Inc v UK Mutual Steamship Assurance Assn (Bermuda) Ltd* [2005] EWHC 1694 (Comm), [2005] 2 Lloyd's Rep. 479 at [24]–[29]; *Forrest v Glasser* [2006] EWCA Civ 1086, [2006] 2 Lloyd's Rep. 392 at [24]; see also below, para.12–075.

[245] *Re Levy Ex p. Walton* (1881) 17 Ch D 746, 751; *Baumwoll Manufactur von Scheibler v Furness* [1893] A.C. 8, 15; *Dodd v Churton* [1897] 1 Q.B. 562, 566; *Miramar Maritime Corp v Holborn Oil Trading Ltd* [1984] A.C. 676, 682; *Antaios Compania Naviera SA v Salen Rederierna A.B.* [1985] A.C. 191, 200–201; *Harbinger UK Ltd v GE Information Services Ltd* [2000] 1 All E.R. (Comm) 166; *Kazakstan Wool Processors (Europe) Ltd v Nederlandsche Credietverzekering Maatschappij NV* [2000] 1 All E.R. (Comm) 708. Contrast *Jones v St John's College, Oxford* (1870) L.R. 6 Q.B. 115; *The Raven* [1980] 2 Lloyd's Rep. 266, 269; *Lakeport Navigation Co Panama SA v Anonima Petroli Italiana* [1982] 2 Lloyd's Rep. 205; *Pera Shipping Corp v Petroship SA* [1985] 2 Lloyd's Rep. 103, 107; *Eurico SpA v Phillipp Bros* [1987] 2 Lloyd's Rep. 215; *Benjamin Developments Ltd v Robt. Jones (Pacific) Ltd* [1994] 3 N.Z.L.R. 189; *City Alliance Ltd v Oxford Forecasting Services Ltd* [2001] 1 All E.R. (Comm) 233.

[246] [1974] A.C. 235.

[247] [1974] A.C. 235, 251. This dictum was cited with approval in *Wace v Pan Atlantic Group Ltd* [1981] 2 Lloyd's Rep. 339, 343; *Forsikringsaktieselskapet Vesta v J.N.E. Butcher Bain Dawes Ltd* [1989] 1 Lloyd's Rep. 330, 346; *Macedonia Maritime Co v Austin & Pickersgill Ltd* [1989] 2 Lloyd's Rep. 73, 81; *Niobe Maritime Corp v Tradax Ocean Transportation SA* [1995] 1 Lloyd's Rep. 579; *International Fina Services AG v Katrina Shipping Ltd* [1995] 2 Lloyd's Rep. 344, 350; *Charter Reinsurance Co Ltd v Fagan* [1997] A.C. 313, 355.

[248] (1986) 33 Build.L.R. 1, 14, PC. See also *Sinochem International Oil (London) Ltd v Mobile Sales and Supply Corp* [2000] 1 Lloyd's Rep. 339, 344.

[249] *Southwell v Bowditch* (1876) 1 C.P.D. 374, 376.

commercial documents "must be construed in a business fashion"[250] and "there must be ascribed to the words a meaning that would make good commercial sense".[251] Indeed, in *The Antaios*[252] Lord Diplock said that:

> " . . . if detailed semantic and syntactical analysis of words in a commercial contract is going to lead to a conclusion that flouts business commonsense, it must yield to business commonsense."

Moreover, in mercantile contracts, the words employed may have acquired a special meaning,[253] and this may be a different meaning from their natural one.[254] Hence it is that mercantile contracts are to be construed according to the usage and custom of merchants,[255] provided that the custom is not inconsistent with the agreement.[256] When such contracts contain peculiar expressions which have in particular places or trades a known meaning attached to them, the meaning of these expressions is a question of fact, although the meaning of the contract still remains a question of law.[257] Also:

> " . . . the custom of trade, which is a matter of evidence, may be used to annex incidents to all written contracts, commercial or agricultural, and others, which do not by their terms exclude it, upon the presumption that the parties have contracted with reference to such usage, if it is applicable."[258]

---

[250] *Southland Frozen Meat and Produce Export Co Ltd v Nelson Brothers Ltd* [1898] A.C. 442, 444. See also *Glynn v Margetson & Co* [1893] A.C. 351, 359; *Menth & Co v Ropner & Co* [1913] 1 K.B. 27, 32; *Lake v Simmons* [1927] A.C. 487, 509; *Digby v General Accident Fire and Life Assurance Corp Ltd* [1949] 1 K.B. 226, 246; *Mannai Investment Co Ltd v Eagle Star Life Assurance Co Ltd* [1997] A.C. 749, 771 ("a commercially sensible construction"); *Homburg Houtimport BV v Agrosin Private Ltd* [2003] UKHL 12, [2004] 1 A.C. 715 at [10] ("a business sense"); *Sirius International Insurance (Publ) v FAI General Insurance Ltd* [2004] UKHL 54, [2004] 1 W.L.R. 3251 at [19] ("a . . . commercial approach").

[251] *Miramar Maritime Corp v Holborn Oil Trading Ltd* [1984] A.C. 676, 682; *International Fina Services AG v Katrina Shipping Ltd* [1995] 2 Lloyd's Rep. 344, 350; *Axa Reinsurance (UK) Plc v Field* [1996] 3 All E.R. 517, 526; *Society of Lloyd's v Robinson* [1999] 1 All E.R. (Comm) 545, 551.

[252] *Antaios Compania Naviera SA v Salen Rederierna A.B.* [1984] A.C. 191, 201. See also *Shipping Corp of India Ltd v NBB Niederelke Schiffartsgesellschaft mbH & Co* [1991] 1 Lloyd's Rep. 77, 80; *Bankers Trust Co v State Bank of India* [1991] 2 Lloyd's Rep. 443, 456; *International Fina Services AG v Katrina Shipping Ltd* [1995] 2 Lloyd's Rep. 344, 350; *Charter Reinsurance Co Ltd v Fagan* [1997] A.C. 313, 355; but cf. 387; *Sinochem International Oil (London) Ltd v Mobil Sales and Supply Corp* [2001] 1 Lloyd's Rep. 339, 344; *Sirius International Insurance (Publ) v FAI General Insurance Ltd* [2004] UKHL 54 at [19]; *Mora Shipping Inc v Axa Corproate Solutions Assurance SA* [2005] EWCA Civ 1069, [2005] 2 Lloyd's Rep. 769 at [32]; *Absalom v TCRU Ltd* [2005] EWHC 1090 (Comm), [2005] 2 Lloyd's Rep. 735 at [25].

[253] See, e.g. *Care Shipping Corp v Itex Itagrani Export SA* [1993] Q.B. 1 ("sub-freights").

[254] See e.g. *Seacrystal Shipping Ltd v Bulk Transport Group Shipping Co Ltd* [1989] 1 Lloyd's Rep. 1, 6 ("whether in berth or not").

[255] *Re Walkers, Winser & Hamm and Shaw, Son & Co* [1904] 2 K.B. 152; *Upjohn v Hitchens* [1918] 2 K.B. 48; see below, para.12–132.

[256] *Gibbon v Young* (1818) 8 Taunt. 254; *Hayton v Irwin* (1879) 5 C.P.D. 130; *The Alhambra* (1881) 6 P.D. 68; *Re L. Sutro & Co and Heilbut, Symons & Co* [1917] 2 K.B. 348; *Westacott v Hahn* [1918] 1 K.B. 495; *Palgrave, Brown & Sons v S.S. Turid* [1922] 1 A.C. 397; see below, para.12–128.

[257] *Hutchinson v Bowker* (1839) 5 M. & W. 535; *Hill v Evans* (1862) 4 De G.F. & J. 288; see above, para.12–046.

[258] *Gibson v Small* (1853) 4 H.L.C. 353, 397.

Custom of particular place. There are also cases in which regard must be had to the usage or custom of the place where the contract was made or to which it had reference, in order to discover the meaning and intention of the parties. Where, therefore, it appeared that, in the place where a contract concerning a sale of cider was made, the word meant the juice of apples as soon as the juice was expressed, it was held that the contract must be construed to have been for the sale of cider in that sense of the word.[259] And so where a lease was granted of a warren in Suffolk, and the landlord covenanted to pay £60 per thousand rabbits which the tenant was bound to leave on the premises, and it appeared by custom in Suffolk in such cases that 1,000 rabbits meant 1,200, it was held that the landlord was only bound to pay for rabbits reckoned at that rate.[260] 12–058

On the other hand, there are occasions when the courts have refused to modify the natural meaning of a word in the light of custom, e.g. to attribute to the word "alongside" in contracts of affreightment a peculiar meaning derived from the custom of a port so as to increase the shipowner's obligation.[261] Moreover it is a question of fact in each case whether or not a contract containing terms which have a peculiar meaning owing to some usage or custom was in fact made with reference to that usage or custom, and the mere fact that such a custom exists in the district covered by the contract does not raise a conclusion in law that the meaning of the contract is to be governed by the custom.[262] 12–059

Special meaning. Although a contract must normally be construed in accord with the ordinary meaning of the expressions contained in it, by considering the circumstances and situation of the parties at the time, and the subject-matter of the agreement, the court may be enabled to ascertain a special meaning placed upon the words[263] and such special meaning then takes the place of the ordinary meaning for the purpose of construing the contract. Also words in ancient documents are to be interpreted according to the meaning which they bore at the date of the document.[264] 12–060

Law of Property Act section 61. By s.61 of the Law of Property Act 1925, in all deeds, contracts, wills, orders, and other instruments executed, made, or coming into operation after December 31, 1925, unless the context otherwise requires: 12–061

---

259 *Studdy v Sanders* (1826) 5 B. & C. 628.

260 *Smith v Wilson* (1832) 3 B. & Ad. 728. See below, para.12–130.

261 *Palgrave, Brown & Sons v S.S. Turid* [1922] 1 A.C. 397; *Aktieselskabet Dampsskibsselskabet Primula v Horsley* (1923) 40 T.L.R. 11; *Hillas & Co v Rederiaktiebolaget Aeolus* (1926) 32 Com. Cas. 169; cf. *Aktieselskab Helios v Ekman* [1872] 2 QBD 83; *Smith, Hogg & Co v Louis Bamberger & Sons* [1929] 1 K.B. 150.

262 *Clayton v Gregson* (1836) 5 A. & E. 302.

263 *Shore v Wilson* (1842) 9 Cl. & F. 355, 555; *Smith v Doe* (1821) 2 B. & B. 473, 550, 602; *Payne v Haine* (1847) 16 M. & W. 541; *Myers v Sarl* (1860) 3 E. & E. 306; *Perrin v Morgan* [1943] A.C. 399, 421; *Levermore v Jobey* [1956] 1 W.L.R. 697; *Sydall v Castings Ltd* [1967] 1 Q.B. 302; cf. *Hospital for Sick Children v Walt Disney Productions Inc* [1968] Ch. 52; *Zeus Tradition Marine Ltd v Bell* [1999] 1 Lloyd's Rep. 703, 706.

264 *Shore v Wilson* (1842) 9 Cl. & F. 355, 566; *North British Ry Co v Budhill Coal and Sandstone Co* [1910] A.C. 116, 128; *Earl of Lonsdale v Att-Gen* [1982] 1 W.L.R. 887, 924–928. See below, para.12–121.

(a) "month" means calendar month[265];

(b) "person" includes a corporation[266];

(c) the singular includes the plural and vice versa[267];

(d) the masculine includes the feminine and vice versa.

12–062 **Construction of general words.** The approach adopted to the construction of general words is that they are to be restricted according to the nature of the circumstances or of the person.[268] Thus where a railway company agreed *efficiently* to work and repair the railway and works demised, it was held that the word "efficiently" had to be construed according to the resources and powers of the particular company.[269] The same would no doubt apply (subject to the terms of the contract as a whole) to an obligation to take "reasonable steps" or to use "reasonable endeavours".

(c) *Whole Contract to be Considered*[270]

12–063 **The whole contract is to be considered.** Every contract is to be construed with reference to its object and the whole of its terms,[271] and accordingly, the whole context must be considered in endeavouring to collect the intention of the parties, even though the immediate object of inquiry is the meaning of an isolated word or clause[272]:

---

[265] Prior to 1926, the general rule was that "month" meant lunar month, but the rule was fortunately almost destroyed by exceptions. The word always meant calendar month in ecclesiastical law, in mercantile transactions, mortgages and statutes (since 1850), or where the meaning required it from the context: see *Schiller v Petersen* [1924] 1 Ch. 394, 417; Sale of Goods Act 1979 s.10(3).

A calendar month ends on the day of the next following month having the same number as that on which computation began, e.g. March 30 to April 30; but if the next month has no day of the same number, the calendar month ends on the last day of the next month, e.g. January 30 to February 28 or 29 (in leap year): *Dodds v Walker* [1981] 1 W.L.R. 1027, see also below, para.21–026. See also the Interpretation Act 1978 s.5 and Sch.1; *Wilkie v IRC* [1952] 1 Ch. 153.

[266] cf. *Deutsche Genossenschaftsbank v Burnhope* [1995] 1 W.L.R. 1580 HL.

[267] cf. *Re A Solicitor's Arbitration* [1962] 1 W.L.R. 353.

[268] *Verba generalia restringuntur ad habilitatem rei vel aptitudinem personae* (Bac.Max. 10). See below, para.12–123.

[269] *West London Ry v London and N.W. Ry* (1853) 11 C.B. 327, 356. See also *Burges v Wickham* (1863) 3 B. & S. 669, 698; *Booth v Alcock* (1873) L.R. 8 Ch. App. 663, 667; *Thames and Mersey Marine Insurance Co v Hamilton, Fraser & Co* (1887) 12 App. Cas. 484, 490; *Shell Tankers (UK) Ltd v Astro Comino Armadora SA* [1981] 2 Lloyd's Rep. 40.

[270] *Ex antecedentibus et consequentibus fit optima interpretatio* (2 Co.Inst. 317).

[271] *Throcmerton v Tracey* (1585) 1 Plow. 145, 161; *Hume v Rundell* (1824) 2 S. & S. 174, 177; *Richards v Bluck* (1848) 6 C.B. 437, 441; *Reid v Fairbanks* (1853) 13 C.B. 692, 730; *Re Strand Music Hall Co Ltd* (1865) 35 Beav. 153, 159; *Miller v Borner* [1900] 1 Q.B. 691.

[272] *Smith v Packhurst* (1742) 3 Atk. 135, 136; *Browning v Wright* (1799) 2 B. & P. 13; *Stavers v Curling* (1836) 3 Scott 740; *Turner v Evans* (1853) 2 E. & B. 512; *Glynn v Margetson* [1893] A.C. 351; *Midland Ry of Western Australia v State of Western Australia* [1956] 1 W.L.R. 1037; *Nereide SpA di Navigazione v Bulk Oil International Ltd* [1982] 1 Lloyd's Rep. 1; *Abu Dhabi National Tanker Co v Product Star Shipping Ltd* [1991] 2 Lloyd's Rep. 468, 478, [1993] 1 Lloyd's Rep. 397; *Cementation Piling and Foundations Ltd v Aegon Insurance Co Ltd* [1995] 1 Lloyd's Rep. 97, 101; *International Fina Services AG v Katrina Shipping Ltd* [1995] 2 Lloyd's Rep. 344, 350.

"It is a true rule of construction that the sense and meaning of the parties in any particular part of an instrument may be collected *ex antecedentibus et consequentibus*; every part of it may be brought into action in order to collect from the whole one uniform and consistent sense, if that may be done."[273]

And so Lord Davey said in *N.E. Ry v Hastings*,[274] quoting Lord Watson[275]:

"The deed must be read as a whole in order to ascertain the true meaning of its several clauses, and the words of each clause should be interpreted as to bring them into harmony with the other provisions of the deed if that interpretation does no violence to the meaning of which they are naturally susceptible."

For example, in the case of a bond with a condition, the condition may be read in order to explain the obligatory part of the instrument, e.g. where no species of money was mentioned, but the debtor was bound for 7,700[276]; and in determining the meaning of words which are used for the purpose of designating periods of time, such as the words "from" and "until",[277] the whole contract is to be taken into consideration.[278] Also, when the meaning of a contract for services is ambiguous, the court will take into consideration even the price agreed to be paid for those services for the purpose of enabling them to determine the extent of the service to be rendered under the contract.[279] **12–064**

Nevertheless: **12–065**

"... it has long been recognised ... that to seek perfect consistency and economy of draftsmanship in a complex form of contract which has evolved over many years is to pursue a chimera."[280]

Although the court is bound to have regard to the whole of the contract and the words used, it may be necessary to adapt the language in order to effect the intentions of the parties.[281]

Control by recitals. When the words in the operative part of an instrument are ambiguous, the recitals and other parts of the instrument may be used to discover the intention of the parties and to fix the appropriate meaning of those **12–066**

---

[273] *Barton v Fitzgerald* (1812) 15 East 529, 541; *Coles v Hulme* (1828) 8 B. & C. 568. See also *Trenchard v Hoskins* (1625) Winch. 93.

[274] [1900] A.C. 260, 267.

[275] *Chamber Colliery Co v Twyerould* (1893) reported [1915] 1 Ch. 268n., 272. See also *Sir Lindsay Parkinson & Co v Commissioners of H.M. Works and Public Buildings* [1949] 2 K.B. 632, 662.

[276] *Coles v Hulme* (1828) 2 B. & C. 568.

[277] See below, para.21–024.

[278] *R. v Stevens* (1804) 5 East 244; *Wilkinson v Gaston* (1846) 9 Q.B. 137.

[279] *Allen v Cameron* (1833) 1 C. & M. 832, 840.

[280] *Homburg Houtimport PV v Agrosin Private Ltd* [2003] UKHL 12, [2004] 1 A.C. 715 at [12], per Lord Bingham, citing *Simond v Boydell* (1779) 1 Dougl. 268; *Nelson Line (Liverpool) Ltd v James Nelson & Sons Ltd* [1908] A.C. 16, 20–21; *Hillas & Co Ltd v Arcos Ltd* (1932) 43 Ll.L. Rep. 35; *Chandris v Isbrandtsen-Moller Inc* [1951] 1 K.B. 240, 245.

[281] See below, para.12–072.

words.[282] But clear words in the operative part of an instrument cannot be controlled by recitals.[283]

12–067 **Several instruments.** Several instruments made to effect one object may be construed as one instrument, and be read together, but so that each shall have its distinct effect in carrying out the main design.[284] Thus, a lease and counterpart are two documents relating to one transaction and a palpable mistake in the lease may be corrected by reference to the counterpart, just as it might be by reference to other parts of the lease itself[285]:

> "Where several deeds form part of one transaction and are contemporaneously executed they have the same effect for all purposes such as are relevant to the case as if they were one deed."[286]

Yet although the words "contemporaneously executed" have been used, there is no doubt that this is not essential, so long as the court, having regard to the circumstances, comes to the conclusion that the series of documents represents a single transaction between the same parties.[287] So the articles of association of a company may be read to explain the memorandum[288] and a prospectus which invited applications for deposit notes on certain terms could be read together with a deposit note from which one of those terms had been omitted.[289]

12–068 **Supplemental instruments.** Under s.58 of the Law of Property Act 1925, any instrument expressed to be supplemental to a previous instrument shall, as far as may be, be read and have effect as if the supplemental instrument contained a full recital of the previous instrument.

12–069 **Alterations and deletions.** Evidence of prior negotiations is normally not admissible to construe a written contract[290] and drafts will not be admitted either to alter the language of the contract or to help in its interpretation.[291] So, where an instrument appears to have been altered while the parties were negotiating, the

---

[282] *Hesse v Albert* (1828) 3 M. & Ry 406; *Walsh v Trevanion* (1850) 15 Q.B. 733, 751; *Re Mitchell's Trusts* (1878) 9 Ch D 5, 9; *Leggott v Barrett* (1880) 15 Ch D 306, 311; *Re Moon Ex p. Dawes* (1886) 17 QBD 275, 286; *Orr v Mitchell* [1893] A.C. 238, 253, 254; *Crouch v Crouch* [1912] 1 K.B. 378; *Rutter v Charles Sharpe & Co* [1979] 1 W.L.R. 1429, 1433 (factual matrix).

[283] *Leggott v Barrett* (1880) 15 Ch D 306, 311; *Re Moon Ex p. Dawes* (1886) 17 QBD 275, 286. See also *Young v Smith* (1865) L.R. 1 Eq. 180, 183; *Dawes v Tredwell* (1881) 18 ChD 354, 358; *Foakes v Beer* (1884) 9 App. Cas. 605; *Australian Joint Stock Bank v Bailey* [1899] A.C. 396; *Royal Insurance Co Ltd v G. & S. Assured Investments Co Ltd* [1972] 1 Lloyd's Rep. 267, 274; *Rutter v Charles Sharpe & Co* [1979] 1 W.L.R. 1428, 1433.

[284] *Duke of Bolton v Williams* (1793) 2 Ves. 138; *Harrison v Mexican Rail Co* (1875) L.R. 19 Eq. 358; *Stott v Shaw* [1928] 2 K.B. 26.

[285] *Burchell v Clark* (1876) 2 C.P.D. 88; *Matthews v Smallwood* [1910] 1 Ch. 777.

[286] *Manks v Whiteley* [1912] 1 Chs 735, 754 (reversed on other grounds sub nom. *Whiteley v Delaney* [1914] A.C. 132); *Fowler v Hunter* (1829) 3 Y. & J. 506.

[287] *Smith v Chadwick* (1882) 20 ChD 27, 63; *Ford v Stuart* (1852) 15 Beav. 493; *Whitbread v Smith* (1854) 3 De G.M. & G. 727.

[288] *Re Capital Fire Insurance Association* (1882) 21 ChD 209, 212.

[289] *Jacobs v Batavia and General Plantations Trusts Ltd* [1924] 2 Ch. 329; cf. *Smith v Chadwick* (1882) 20 Ch D 27.

[290] See below, para.12–119.

[291] See below, para.12–119.

court cannot look at it as it originally stood compared with the alterations which were made in it, to see whether those alterations will throw any light upon the question of intention.[292] However, when the parties use a printed form, and delete parts of it, there is some authority for the view that regard may be paid to what has been deleted as part of the surrounding circumstances in the light of which the meaning of the words which they chose to leave in is to be ascertained.[293] But there is weighty authority to the contrary.[294] In any event, it is doubtful whether the court can look at the words deleted except to resolve an ambiguity in the words retained.[295] The position may nevertheless be different where alterations are made to an already concluded agreement. In *Punjab National Bank v De Boinville*[296] Staughton L.J. said:

> " . . . if the parties to a concluded agreement subsequently agree in express terms that some words in it are to be replaced by others, one can have regard to all aspects of the subsequent agreement in construing the contract, including the deletions, even in a case which is not, or not wholly, concerned with a printed form."

Also where a one-off contract has been drafted by reference to a standard form contract which formed the basis for its drafting, the court can take into account the omission from the one-off contract of words that appear in the standard form contract in order to resolve an ambiguity in the former document.[297]

Printed and written clauses. Where the contract is contained in a printed form with writing superadded, the written words, if there should be any reasonable doubt about the sense and meaning of the whole, are to have greater effect 12–070

[292] *Inglis v Buttery* (1878) 3 App. Cas. 552, 558, 569, 576; *Channel Islands Ferries Ltd v Sealink UK Ltd* [1987] 1 Lloyd's Rep. 559, 577 (affirmed [1988] 1 Lloyd's Rep. 323).

[293] *Baumwoll Manufactur von Scheibler v Gilchrest & Co* [1892] 1 Q.B. 253, 256; cf. [1893] A.C. 8, 15; *Gray v Carr* (1871) L.R. 6 Q.B. 522, 524, 529; *Stanton v Richardson* (1874) L.R. 9 C.P. 390; *Glynn v Margetson* [1893] A.C. 351, 357; *Caffin v Aldridge* [1895] 2 Q.B. 648, 650; *Santay & Co v Cox, McEllen & Co* (1921) 10 Ll.L. Rep. 459, 460; *Bailey Sons & Co v Ross, Smythe & Co* [1940] 3 All E.R. 60; *Louis Dreyfus et Cie v Parnaso Compania Naviera SA* [1959] 2 Q.B. 498; *London & Overseas Freighters Ltd v Timber Shipping Co SA* [1972] A.C. 1, 15; *Mottram Consultants Ltd v Bernard Sunley Ltd* [1975] 2 Lloyd's Rep. 197, 209; *Punjab National Bank v De Boinville* [1992] 1 W.L.R. 1138, 1148.

[294] *Ambatielos v Jurgens* [1923] A.C. 175, 185; *Sassoon v International Banking Corp* [1927] A.C. 711, 721; *City & Westminster Properties (1934) Ltd v Mudd* [1959] Ch. 129; *Finzel, Berry & Co v Eastcheap Dried Fruit Co* [1962] 1 Lloyd's Rep. 370, affirmed [1962] 2 Lloyd's Rep. 11; *Compania Naviera Termar SA v Tradax Export SA* [1965] 1 Lloyd's Rep. 198, 204; *Borthwick (Thomas) (Glasgow) Ltd v Bunge & Co Ltd* [1969] 1 Lloyd's Rep. 17; *Tradax Export v Volkswagenwerk* [1969] 2 Q.B. 599, 607; *Ben Shipping Co (Pte) Ltd v An-Board Bainne* [1986] 2 Lloyd's Rep. 285, 291; *Wates Construction (London) Ltd v Franthom Property Ltd* (1991) 7 Const. L.J. 243.

[295] *Louis Dreyfus et Cie v Parnaso Cia. Naviera SA* [1959] 1 Q.B. 498, reversed on other grounds [1960] 2 Q.B. 49.

[296] [1992] 1 W.L.R. 1138, 1149. See also *Centrepoint Custodians Pty Ltd v Lidgerwood Investments Pty Ltd* [1990] V.R. 411; *Trasimex Holdings SA v Addax* BV [1997] 1 Lloyd's Rep. 610, 614; *HIH Casualty and General Insurance Ltd v New Hampshire Insurance Co* [2001] EWCA Civ 735, [2001] 2 Lloyd's Rep. 161 at [83], [84]; *KPMG v Network Rail Infrastructure Ltd* [2007] EWCA Civ 363.

[297] *Team Services v Kier Management and Design* (1994) 63 Build. L.R. 76.

attributed to them than the printed words, inasmuch as the written words are the immediate language and terms selected by the parties themselves for the expression of their meaning, and the printed words are a general formula adapted equally to their case and that of all other contracting parties upon similar occasions and subjects.[298] Nevertheless, it is open to the parties to stipulate in their printed conditions of contract that written provisions appended to the printed form are not to override, modify or affect in any way the application or interpretation of that which is contained in the printed conditions, and effect must then be given to such a stipulation even though this is contrary to the ordinary rule.[299]

12–071 **Discrepancy between words and figures.** In the event of a difference between words and figures, the written words normally prevail.[300]

(d) *Effecting the Intention of the Parties*

12–072 **Parties' intention.** It is not open to the court to revise the words used by the parties, or to put upon them a meaning other than that which they ordinarily bear, in order to bring them into line with what the court may think the parties ought to have agreed, or what the court may think would have been a reasonable contract for the parties to make.[301] But if, from the document itself and the admissible background,[302] the intention of the parties can reasonably be discerned, then the court will give effect to that intention even though this involves departing from or qualifying particular words used. So the court will be prepared to restrict, transpose, modify, supply or reject words or terms in the document, provided the intention of the parties is plain in spite of the words. The duty of the court in this respect was summed up by Kelly C.B. in *Gwyn v Neath Canal Co*[303]:

---

[298] *Robertson v French* (1803) 4 East 130, 136; *Glynn v Margetson & Co* [1893] A.C. 351, 358; *Re L. Sutro & Co and Heilbut, Symons & Co* [1917] 2 K.B. 348, 358, 361; *Hadjipateras v Weigall & Co* (1918) 34 T.L.R. 360; *Société d'Avances Commerciales (London) Ltd v A. Besse & Co Ltd* [1952] 1 T.L.R. 644; *The Brabant* [1967] 1 Q.B. 588; *Kum v Wah Tat Bank Ltd* [1971] 1 Lloyd's Rep. 439, 445; *Naviera Amazonica Peruana SA v Compania Internacional de Seguros del Peru* [1988] 1 Lloyd's Rep. 116, 121; cf. *T. W. Thomas & Co v Portsea Steamship Co Ltd* [1912] A.C. 1; *Evergos Naftiki Eteria v Cargill Plc* [1997] 1 Lloyd's Rep. 35, 38; *Homburg Houtimport BV v Agrosin Ltd* [2003] UKHL 12, [2004] 1 A.C. 715.

[299] *Gold v Patman & Fotheringham Ltd* [1958] 1 W.L.R. 697, 701; *North West Metropolitan Regional Hospital Board v T. A. Bickerton & Son Ltd* [1970] 1 W.L.R. 607, 617; *English Industrial Estates Corp v George Wimpey & Co Ltd* [1973] 1 Lloyd's Rep. 118. But the written provisions may be looked at "to follow exactly what was going on", [1973] 1 Lloyd's Rep. 118, at 126, 128.

[300] *Saunderson v Piper* (1839) 5 Bing.N.C. 425; Bills of Exchange Act 1882 s.9(2).

[301] *Sinochem International Oil (London) Co Ltd v Mobil Sales and Supply Corp* [2000] 1 Lloyd's Rep. 339 at [29]; Lord Goff [1984] L.M.C.L.Q. 382, 391.

[302] See below, para.12–118.

[303] (1865) L.R. 3 Ex. 209, 215, cited with approval by Lord Lowry in *Forsikringsaktieselskapet Vesta v J. N. E. Butcher, Bain Dawes Ltd* [1989] 1 Lloyd's Rep. 331, 345. See also *Indian Oil Corp v Vanol Inc* [1991] 2 Lloyd's Rep. 634, 636.

"The result of all the authorities is, that when a court of law can clearly collect from the language within the four corners of a deed, or instrument in writing, the real intentions of the parties, they are bound to give effect to it by supplying anything necessarily to be inferred from the terms used, and by rejecting as superfluous whatever is repugnant to the intention so discerned."

Some examples of these expedients are discussed in the paragraphs which follow.

Restricting. Where some of the words in a printed form of charterparty were left in by oversight, instead of being struck out, the House of Lords restricted the printed words to those applicable to the particular agreement.[304] Also in *Glynn v Margetson*[305] there was a wide deviation clause in a bill of lading for the carriage of oranges from Malaga to Liverpool. The ship left Malaga for a port not on the way to Liverpool, and the oranges were damaged by the delay. The House of Lords held that the deviation clause must be restricted to conform with the intention of a voyage from Malaga to Liverpool with a perishable cargo; to hold otherwise would defeat the object and intent of the contract. 12–073

Transposing. "Words shall be transposed to support the intent of the parties"[306]; "[t]he law is not nice in grants, and therefore it doth often transpose words contrary to their order to bring them to the intent of the parties".[307] In a marriage settlement the words "[s]uch younger child or children" were made to include both sons and daughters by transposing a clause creating a power to make provision "for such younger children" and that containing a limitation to daughters.[308] 12–074

Modifying. It has already been noted that the grammatical or ordinary sense of the words of a contract may be departed from if this would lead to some absurdity or inconsistency with the rest of the instrument or if there has been an obvious linguistic mistake.[309] It is also open to the court to correct a misnomer[310] or mistaken designation in a contract: *Falsa demonstratio non nocet cum de* 12–075

---

[304] *Baumwoll Manufactur von Scheibler v Gilchrest & Co* [1893] A.C. 8, 15. See also *Dudgeon v Pembroke* (1877) 2 App. Cas. 284.

[305] [1893] A.C. 351, 357. See also *Davy Offshore Ltd v Emerald Field Contracting Ltd* [1992] 2 Lloyd's Rep. 142, 155. cf. *G.H. Renton & Co Ltd v Palmyra Trading Corp of Panama* [1957] A.C. 149; *Sudatlantica Navegacion SA v Devamar Shipping Corp* [1985] 2 Lloyd's Rep. 271, 274. See below, para.14–029.

[306] Comyns' Digest, art. "Parols," A.21.

[307] *Parkhurst v Smith* (1742) Wiles 327, 332; cf. *Magrath v McGeany* [1938] Ir. R. 309.

[308] *Fenton v Fenton* (1837) 1 Dr. & W. 66.

[309] See above, para.12–055.

[310] The law relating to misnomer was explored by Rix L.J. in *Dumford Trading AG v DAO Atlantrybflot* [2005] EWCA Civ 24, [2005] 1 Lloyd's Rep. 289, where this paragraph was cited (at [27]); but see below, para.12–124. See also *The Tutova* [2006] EWHC 2223 (Comm), [2007] 1 Lloyd's Rep. 104 at [10]; *Front Carriers Ltd v Atlantic and Orient Shipping Corp* [2007] EWHC 421 (Comm), [2007] 2 Lloyd's Rep. 131 at [44].

corpore constat.[311] So where the parties to a charterparty attached thereto a typed paramount clause which stated that:

> "... this *bill of lading* shall have effect subject to the provisions of the Carriage by Sea Act of the United States ... which shall be deemed to be incorporated herein,"

it was held that the erroneous description of the charterparty as a bill of lading did not defeat the intention of the parties that the document should be subject to the Act.[312] However, the court will not be inclined to engage in a "verbal manipulation" of a designation in a contract if the actual words used make perfectly good sense without any modification.[313] An obvious mistake in a written instrument can be corrected as a matter of construction without obtaining a decree in an action for rectification,[314] but there must be a clear mistake on the face of the instrument and it must be clear what correction ought to be made in order to cure the mistake.[315]

12–076 **Supplying.** In principle, the court will not interpolate words into a written instrument, of whatever nature, unless it is clear both that words have been omitted and what those words were.[316] But, in simple situations, the word "pounds", for example, when omitted, has been supplied after or before a figure in a bill of sale[317] or a bill of exchange,[318] and in deeds the name of the grantor,[319] the obligor[320] and the grantee[321] have been supplied. In more complex cases

---

[311] *Llewellyn v Jersey* (1843) 11 M. & W. 183, 189; *Morrell v Fisher* (1849) 4 Exch. 591, 604; *Cowen v Truefitt Ltd* [1899] 2 Ch. 309; *Eastwood v Ashton* [1915] A.C. 900, 914; *Whittam v W.J. Daniel & Co Ltd* [1962] 1 Q.B. 271, 277; *F. Goldsmith (Sicklesmere) Ltd v Baxter* [1970] Ch. 85; *Modern Buildings Wales Ltd v Limmer and Trinidad Co Ltd* [1975] 1 W.L.R. 1281; *Nittan v Solent Steel Fabrication Ltd* [1981] 1 Lloyd's Rep. 633; *Lamport & Holt Lines Ltd v Coubro & Scrutton (M. & I.) Ltd* [1981] 2 Lloyd's Rep. 659 (affirmed [1982] 2 Lloyd's Rep. 42); *Mohammed bin Abdul Rahman Orri v Seawind Navigation Co SA* [1986] 1 Lloyd's Rep. 36; *Coral (UK) Ltd v Rechtman* [1996] 1 Lloyd's Rep. 235; *Gastronome (UK) Ltd v Anglo-Dutch Meats (UK) Ltd* [2006] EWCA Civ 1233, [2006] 2 Lloyd's Rep. 587. Contrast *Internaut Shipping GmbH v Fercometal SARL* [2003] EWCA Civ 812, [2003] 2 Lloyd's Rep. 430 (mistake beyond misnomer).

[312] *Adamastos Shipping Co Ltd v Anglo-Saxon Petroleum Co Ltd* [1959] A.C. 133. In the Court of Appeal, it had been held that the paramount clause was meaningless and to be rejected: [1957] 2 Q.B. 233.

[313] *Miramar Maritime Corp v Holborn Oil Trading Ltd* [1984] A.C. 676. But see *Mannai Investment Co Ltd v Eagle Star Life Assurance Ltd* [1997] A.C. 749.

[314] *East v Pantiles Plant Hire Ltd* [1982] 2 E.G.L.R. 111 at 112; *Holding & Barnes Plc v Hill House Hammond Ltd* [2001] EWCA Civ 1334 at [14]; *Lafarge (Aggregates) Ltd v London Borough of Newham* [2005] EWHC 1337 (Comm), [2005] 2 Lloyd's Rep. 577 at [25]; *Dalkia Utilities Services Plc v Celtech International Ltd* [2006] EWHC 63, (Comm); [2006] 1 Lloyd's Rep. 599 at [109]; *Littman v Aspen Oil Broking Ltd* [2005] EWCA Civ 1579, [2006] 2 P. & C.R. 2.

[315] *East v Pantiles Plant Hire Ltd* [1982] 2 E.G.L.R. 11 at 112; cf. *KPMG v Network Rail Infrastructure Ltd* [2007] EWCA Civ 363 at [64].

[316] *Homburg Houtimport BV v Agrosin Private Ltd* [2003] UKHL 12, [2004] 1 A.C. 715 at [23]; *Cambridge Display Technology Ltd v El Dupont de Nernouts* [2004] EWHC 1415 (Ch) [2005] F.S.R. 14.

[317] *Mourmand v Le Clair* [1903] 2 K.B. 216; *Coles v Hulme* (1828) 8 B. & C. 568.

[318] *Elliott's case* (1777) 2 East P.C. 951; 1 Leach 175.

[319] *Lord Say and Seal's Case* (1711) 10 Mod. 41, 45.

[320] *Dobson v Keys* (1610) Cro.Jac. 261.

[321] Co.Litt. 7a.

concerning commercial contracts the courts have gone further and supplied such words as were required to make commercial sense of the agreement.[322]

Rejecting. It might be thought to be a sensible principle of construction that an interpretation which leaves part of the language of a document useless or creates surplusage is to be avoided. But this presumption has often been said to be of little value in the construction of commercial documents.[323] If there is in a contract a word or phrase to which no sensible meaning can be given[324] or which is mere surplusage,[325] it may be rejected to carry out the intention of the parties. Inconsistent or repugnant words or expressions, if they cannot be harmonised, must similarly be rejected. 12–077

Inconsistent or repugnant clauses. Where the different parts of an instrument are inconsistent, effect must be given to that part which is calculated to carry into effect the real intention of the parties as gathered from the instrument as a whole, and that part which would defeat it must be rejected.[326] The old rule was, in such a case, that the earlier clause was to be received and the later rejected[327]; but this rule was a mere rule of thumb, totally unscientific, and out of keeping with the modern construction of documents. To be inconsistent a term must contradict another term or be in conflict with it, such that effect cannot fairly be given to both clauses.[328] A term may also be rejected if it is repugnant to the intention of the parties as it appears from the document.[329] However, an effort should be made to give effect to every clause in the agreement and not to reject a clause unless it is manifestly inconsistent with or repugnant to the rest of 12–078

[322] *Tropwood A.G. of Zug v Jade Enterprises Ltd* [1982] 1 Lloyd's Rep. 232; *Homburg Houtimport BV v Agrosin Private Ltd* [2003] UKHL 12; cf. *Petroleo Brasileiro SA v Elounda Shipping Co* [1985] 2 Lloyd's Rep. 154; *City Alliance Ltd v Oxford Forecasting Services Ltd* [2001] 1 All E.R. (Comm) 233.

[323] *Royal Greek Government v Minister of Transport* (1949) 83 Ll.L. Rep. 228, 235; *Chandris v Isbrandtsen-Moller Inc* [1951] 1 K.B. 385, 392; *Total Transport Corp v Arcadia Petroleum Ltd* [1998] 1 Lloyd's Rep. 351, 357.

[324] *Smith v Packhurst* (1742) 3 Atk. 135, 136; *Stone v Yeovil Corp* (1876) 1 C.P.D. 691, 701; *Nicolene v Simmonds* [1953] 1 Q.B. 543. Contrast *British Electrical and Associated Industries (Cardiff) Ltd v Patley Pressings Ltd* [1953] 1 W.L.R. 280; *Tropwood A.G. of Zug v Jade Enterprises Ltd* [1982] 1 Lloyd's Rep. 232; *Commercial Union Assurance Co v Sun Alliance Insurance Group Plc* [1992] 1 Lloyd's Rep. 475, 480.

[325] *Waugh v Bussell* (1814) 5 Taunt. 707, 711; *Gray v Carr* (1871) L.R. 6 Q.B. 522, 536, 550, 557; *Burrell & Sons v F. Green & Co* [1914] 1 K.B. 293, 303; *Chandris v Isbrandtsen-Moller Co Inc* [1951] 1 K.B. 240, 245; *Carga del Sur Compania Naviera SA v Ross T. Smyth & Co Ltd* [1962] 2 Lloyd's Rep. 147, 154; *The Merak* [1965] P. 223; *Pera Shipping Corp v Petroship SA* [1985] 2 Lloyd's Rep. 103, 106–107; *Mangistaumunaigaz Oil Production Association v United World Trade Inc* [1995] 1 Lloyd's Rep. 617; *Total Transport Corp v Arcadia Petroleum Ltd* [1998] 1 Lloyd's Rep. 351, 357–358.

[326] *Walker v Giles* (1848) 6 C.B. 662, 702; *Love v Rowtor Steamship Co Ltd* [1916] 2 A.C. 527, 535; *Sabah Flour and Feedmills Sdn. Bhd. v Comfez Ltd* [1988] 2 Lloyd's Rep. 18; cf. *Taylor v Rive Droite Music Ltd* [2005] EWCA Civ 1300, [2006] E.M.L.R. 4.

[327] Shep.Touch. 88; *Doe d. Leicester v Biggs* (1809) 2 Taunt. 109, 113; *Forbes v Git* [1922] 1 A.C. 256, 259.

[328] *Pagnan SpA v Tradax Ocean Transportation SA* [1987] 2 Lloyd's Rep. 342, 350.

[329] *Adamastos Shipping Co Ltd v Anglo-Saxon Petroleum Co Ltd* [1959] A.C. 133.

the agreement.[330] Thus, if there is a personal covenant and a proviso that the covenantor shall not be personally liable under the covenant, the proviso is inconsistent and void.[331] But if a clause merely limits or qualifies without destroying altogether the obligation created by another clause, the two are to be read together and effect is to be given to the intention of the parties as disclosed by the instrument as a whole.[332]

12–079 **Clauses incorporated by reference.** If clauses are incorporated by reference into a written agreement, and those clauses conflict with the clauses of the agreement, then, in the ordinary way,[333] the clauses of the written agreement will prevail.[334] Moreover, the incorporating provision may be so general or wide as to have the effect of incorporating more than can make any sense in the context of the agreement, in which case the surplus may be rejected as insensible or inconsistent, or disregarded as "mere surplusage".[335] A term in a proposal for insurance which conflicts with a term of the policy will be overridden by the term of the policy.[336]

12–080 **Grammatical errors.** Errors of syntax are a particularly frequent source of disputes in relation to written contracts. However plain the syntax of a sentence may be, if it is clear from the content of the instrument and the admissible background[337] that the apparent grammatical construction cannot be the true one, then that which upon the whole is the true meaning prevails, in spite of the syntax of such particular sentence. So, in *Ewing v Ewing*,[338] a deed of partnership provided that the capital of a deceased partner should be paid out as at the last

---

[330] *Barton v Fitzgerald* (1812) 15 East 529, 541; *Bush v Watkins* (1851) 14 Beav. 425, 432; *Société Co-operative Suisse des Céréales et Matières Fourrageres v La Plata Cereal Co SA* (1947) 80 Ll.L.Rep. 530, 537; *Bremer Handelsgesellschaft mbH v J.H. Rayner & Co Ltd* [1979] 2 Lloyd's Rep. 216; *Sudatlantica Navegacion SA v Devamar Shipping Corp* [1985] 2 Lloyd's Rep. 271; *Pagnan SpA v Tradax Ocean Transportation SA* [1987] 2 Lloyd's Rep. 342, 349; *STX Pan Ocean Co Ltd v Ugland Bulk Transport AS* [2007] EWHC 1317 (Comm), [2008] 1 Lloyd's Rep. 86 at [18].

[331] *Furnivall v Coombes* (1843) 5 M. & G. 736. See also *Watling v Lewis* [1911] 1 Ch. 414; *Re Tewkesbury Gas Co* [1911] 2 Ch. 279 (affirmed [1912] 1 Ch. 1).

[332] *Williams v Hathaway* (1877) 6 ChD 544; *Forbes v Git* [1922] 1 A.C. 256, 259; *Walton (Grain & Shipping) Ltd v British Italian Trading Co Ltd* [1959] 1 Lloyd's Rep. 223, 227; *Pagnan SpA v Tradax Ocean Transportation SA* [1987] 2 Lloyd's Rep. 342, 351.

[333] cf. *Sabah Flour and Feedmills Sdn. Bhd. v Comfez Ltd* [1988] 2 Lloyd's Rep. 18; *The Northgate* [2007] EWHC 2796 (Comm), [2008] 1 Lloyd's Rep. 511 at [39], [53].

[334] *Adamastos Shipping Co Ltd v Anglo-Saxon Petroleum Co Ltd* [1959] A.C. 133, 155, 178–179; *Modern Buildings Wales Ltd v Limmer and Trinidad Co Ltd* [1975] 1 W.L.R. 1281, 1289; *Sabah Flour and Feedmills Sdn. Bhd. v Comfez Ltd* [1988] 2 Lloyd's Rep. 18, 20; *Metalfer Corp v Pan Ocean Shipping Co Ltd* [1998] 2 Lloyd's Rep. 632, 637; *Finagra (UK) Ltd v O.T. Africa Line Ltd* [1998] 2 Lloyd's Rep. 622, 627; *BCT Software Solutions Ltd v Arnold Laver & Co Ltd* [2002] EWHC 1298 (Ch), [2002] 2 All E.R. (Comm) 85 at [42]; cf. *Bayoil SA v Seaworld Tankers Corp (The Leonidas)* [2001] 1 Lloyd's Rep. 533 (no conflict between clauses).

[335] *Skips A/S Nordheim v Syrian Petroleum Co Ltd* [1983] 2 Lloyd's Rep. 592, 594; cf. *Miramar Maritime Corp v Holborn Oil Trading Ltd* [1984] A.C. 676, 683; *Balli Trading Ltd v Afalona Shipping Co Ltd* [1993] 1 Lloyd's Rep. 1, 6.

[336] *Thor Navigation Inc v Ingosstrakh Insurance* [2005] EWHC 19, [2005] 1 Lloyd's Rep. 547 (applying *Izzard v Universal Insurance* [1937] A.C. 773, 780).

[337] See below, para.12–118.

[338] (1882) 8 App.Cas. 822. See also *Wills v Wright* (1677) 2 Mod. 285; *Waugh v Middleton* (1853) 8 Exch. 352, 356.

balance by certain regular instalments "with interest thereon from the date of the last balance". The word "thereon" was held to refer not to the last instalment but was intended to be payable on the balance of the capital remaining unpaid. In *Investors Compensation Scheme Ltd v West Bromwich Building Society*[339] a majority of the House of Lords held that an exception from an assignment of "[a]ny claim (whether sounding in rescission for undue influence or otherwise)" should be construed to read "[a]ny claim sounding in rescission (whether for undue influence or otherwise)", thus limiting the exception. The background circumstances and the terms of related non-contractual documents showed, it was said, that the apparent syntax did not convey the intended meaning.

Saving the document. If the words used in an agreement are susceptible of two meanings, one of which would validate the instrument or the particular clause in the instrument, and the other render it void, ineffective or meaningless, the former sense is to be adopted. This principle is often expressed in the phrase *ut res magis valeat cum pereat*.[340] Thus, if by a particular construction the agreement would be rendered ineffectual and the apparent object of the contract would be frustrated, but another construction, though in itself less appropriate looking to the words only, would produce a different effect, the latter interpretation is to be applied, if that is how the agreement would be understood by a reasonable man with a knowledge of the commercial purpose and background of the transaction.[341] So, where the words of a guarantee were capable of expressing either a past or a concurrent consideration, the court adopted the latter construction, because the former would render the instrument void.[342] If one construction makes the contract lawful and the other unlawful, the former is to be preferred. Thus a bond conditioned "to assign all offices" will be construed to apply to such offices as are by law assignable.[343] 12–081

Party cannot rely on his own breach. It has been said that, as a matter of construction, unless the contract clearly provides to the contrary[344] it will be presumed that it was not the intention of the parties that either should be entitled to rely on his own breach of duty to avoid the contract or bring it to an end or 12–082

---

339 [1998] 1 W.L.R. 896. See also *Static Control Components (Europe) Ltd v Egan* [2004] EWCA Civ 392; [2004] 2 Lloyd's Rep. 429; *BP Exploration Operating Co Ltd v Kvaerner Oilfield Products Ltd* [2004] EWHC 999 (Comm), [2005] 1 Lloyd's Rep. 307 at [95]; *Cereal Investments Co (CIC) SA v ED&F Man Sugar Ltd* [2007] EWHC 2843 (Comm), [2008] 1 Lloyd's Rep. 355 at [19]; cf. *Armitage Staveley Industries Plc* [2004] EWHC 2320 (Comm), [2004] Pens. L.R. 385.

340 *Verba ita sunt intelligenda ut res magis valeat cum pereat*: Bac. Max. 3; Noy. Max. 50.

341 *Solly v Forbes* (1820) 2 B. & B. 38, 48. See also Co.Litt. 42a; *Mills v Dunham* [1891] 1 Ch. 576, 590; *Multiplex Construction (UK) Ltd v Honeywell Control Systems Ltd* [2007] Build. L.R. 195 at [57]–[58]; *Beckett Investment Management Group Ltd v Hall* [2007] EWCA Civ 613.

342 *Haigh v Brooks* (1839) 10 A. & E. 309; *Goldshede v Swan* (1847) 1 Exch. 154; *Steele v Hoe* (1849) 14 Q.B. 431; *Broom v Batchelor* (1856) 1 H. & N. 255. See also *Rowell Leakey & Co v Scottish Provident Institution* [1927] 1 Ch. 55, 65 (insurance policy).

343 *Harrington v Kloprogge* (1785) 2 B. & B. 678, note (a). See also *Lewis v Davison* (1839) 4 M. & W. 654. The same principle applies to the performance of a contract: if a payment is made in performance of a contract partly legal and partly illegal it is presumed that it is made in performance of the legal part of the contract: *A. Smith & Son (Bognor Regis) Ltd v Walker* [1952] 2 Q.B. 319.

344 *Micklefield v S.A.C. Technology Ltd* [1990] 1 W.L.R. 1002. See also *Richco International Ltd v Alfred C. Toepfer International GmbH* [1991] 1 Lloyd's Rep. 136.

to obtain a benefit under it.[345] This presumption applies only to acts or omissions which constitute a breach by that party of an express or implied contractual obligation,[346] or (possibly) of a non-contractual duty,[347] owed by him to the other party. Breach of a duty, whether contractual or non-contractual, owed to a stranger to the contract will not suffice.[348] However, such a "principle of construction" appears to be somewhat different in nature from those discussed above. It may therefore be that it is better regarded as depending on an implied term of the contract in question[349] or as one illustration of a more general principle that "[a] man cannot be permitted to take advantage of his own wrong".[350]

(e) *Construction against Grantor*

12–083 **Construction against grantor.** Another principle of construction is that a deed or other instrument shall be construed more strongly against the grantor or maker thereof.[351] This rule is often misinterpreted. It is only to be applied to

[345] *Alghussein Establishment v Eton College* [1988] 1 W.L.R. 587, HL. See also *Doe d. Bryan v Bancks* (1821) 4 B. & Ald. 401, 406; *Malins v Freeman* (1838) 4 Bing. N.C. 395, 399; *New Zealand Shipping Co v Société des Ateliers et Chantiers de France* [1919] A.C. 1, 6, 8, 9, 15; *Quesnel Forks Gold Mining Co Ltd v Ward* [1920] A.C. 222, 227; *Amalgamated Building Contractors Ltd v Waltham Holy Cross U.D.C.* [1952] 2 All E.R. 452, 455; *Cheall v Association of Professional Executive and Computer Staff* [1983] 2 A.C. 180, 189; *Ackerman v Protim Services* [1988] 2 E.G.L.R. 259; *Gyllenhammar & Partners International Ltd v Saur Brodogradevna Industrija* [1989] 2 Lloyd's Rep. 403, 412; *Micklefield v S.A.C. Technology Ltd* [1990] 1 W.L.R. 1002, 1007; *Richco International Ltd v Alfred C. Toepfer International GmbH* [1991] 1 Lloyd's Rep. 136, 144; *Cerium Investments v Evans* [1991] C.L.Y 1870 CA; *WX Investments Ltd v Begg* [2002] EWHC 925 (Ch), [2002] 1 W.L.R. 2849 at [12]. The breach may be deliberate or inadvertent: *Cheall v Association of Professional Executive and Computer Staff* [1983] 2 A.C. 180.

[346] *Cheall v Association of Professional Executive and Computer Staff* [1983] 2 A.C. 180; *Alghussein Establishment v Eton College* [1988] 1 W.L.R. 587; *Gyllenhammar & Partners International Ltd v Saur Brodogradevna Industrija* [1989] 2 Lloyd's Rep. 403; *J. Lauritzen A.S. v Wijsmuller B.V.* [1990] 1 Lloyd's Rep. 1, 13; *Antclizo Shipping Corp v Food Corp of India (The Antclizo) (No.2)* [1992] 1 Lloyd's Rep. 558, 567–568.

[347] *Cheall v Association of Professional Executive and Computer Staff* [1983] 2 A.C. 180; *Ackerman v Protim Services* [1998] 2 E.G.L.R. 259; *J. Lauritzen A.S. v Wijsmuller B.V.* [1990] 1 Lloyd's Rep. 1, 13; *Antclizo Shipping Corp v Food Corp of India (The Antclizo) (No.2)* [1992] 1 Lloyd's Rep. 558, 568.

[348] *Cheall v Association of Professional Executive and Computer Staff* [1983] 2 A.C. 180.

[349] *Richco International Ltd v Alfred C. Toepfer International GmbH* [1991] 1 Lloyd's Rep. 136. See also *Bulk Shipping A.G. v Ipco Trading SA* [1992] 1 Lloyd's Rep. 39, 43, and below, para.13–012.

[350] See, e.g. *Rede v Farr* (1817) 6 M. & S. 121, 124; *Doe d. Bryan v Bancks* (1821) 4 B. & Ald. 401, 409; *Roberts v Bury Commissioners* (1870) L.R. 4 C.P. 755; *Alfred C. Toepfer v Peter Cremer* [1975] 2 Lloyd's Rep. 118, 124; *Total Transport Corp v Amoco Trading Co* [1985] 1 Lloyd's Rep. 423, 426. But that principle is not absolute: *Cheall v Association of Professional Executive and Computer Staff* [1983] 2 A.C. 180, 189; *Alghussein Establishment v Eton College* [1988] 1 W.L.R. 587, 595; *Micklefield v S.A.C. Technology Ltd* [1990] 1 W.L.R. 1002; *Richco International Ltd v Alfred C. Toepfer International GmbH* [1991] 1 Lloyd's Rep. 136; *Decoma UK Ltd v Haden Drysys International Ltd* [2005] EWHC 2948 (TCC), (2005) 103 Const. L.R. 1. See also below, para.13–012.

[351] *Verba cartarum fortius accipiuntur contra proferentem* (Bac. Max. 3).

remove (and not to create) a doubt or ambiguity[352] and where the issue cannot otherwise be resolved by the application of ordinary principles of construction.[353] Nevertheless, despite certain doubts which have been cast upon it from time to time,[354] the principle has been constantly cited as a rule of construction from Coke's time to the present day.[355] For instance, Coke says[356], "[i]t is a maxim in law that every man's grant shall be taken by construction of law most forcibly against himself"; and in 1949, Evershed M.R. said:

> "We are presented with two alternative readings of this document and the reading which one should adopt is to be determined, among other things, by a consideration of the fact that the defendants put forward the document. They have put forward a clause which is by no means free from obscurity and have contended . . . that it has a remarkably, if not an extravagantly, wide scope, and I think that the rule *contra proferentem* should be applied."[357]

The justification for the rule has been said to be that: 12–084

> " . . . a person who puts forward the wording of a proposed agreement may be assumed to have looked after his own interests so that if the words leave room for doubt about whether he is intended to have a particular benefit there is reason to suppose that he is not."[358]

So, in the case of a guarantee, if the party who drafts it uses ambiguous language, such ambiguity will be taken more strongly against himself.[359] If a carrier gives two notices, limiting his responsibility in cases of loss of goods, he is bound by that which is least beneficial to himself.[360] A notice under which a 12–085

[352] *Borradaile v Hunter* (1843) 5 M. & G. 639; *Birrell v Dryer* (1884) 9 App. Cas. 345, 350; *Cornish v Accident Insurance Co* (1889) 23 QBD 453, 456; *London & Lancashire Insurance v Bolands Ltd* [1924] A.C. 836, 848; *Houghton v Trafalgar Insurance Co* [1954] 1 Q.B. 247; *Lakeport Navigation Co Panama SA v Anonima Petroli Italiana* [1982] 2 Lloyd's Rep. 205, 208; *Aqua Design & Play International Ltd v Kier Regional Ltd* [2002] EWCA Civ 797, [2003] B.L.R. 111; *Tektrol Ltd v International Insurance Co of Hanover Ltd* [2005] EWCA Civ 845, [2005] 2 Lloyd's Rep. 701 at [8].

[353] *Lindus v Melrose* (1858) 3 H. & N. 177, 182; *Lakeport Navigation Company Panama S.A. v Anonima Petroli Italiana SpA* [1982] 2 Lloyd's Rep. 205, 208; *Sinochem International Oil (London) Co Ltd v Mobil Sales and Supply Corp* [2000] 1 Lloyd's Rep. 339 at [37]; *Direct Travel Insurance v McGeown* [2003] EWCA Civ 1606 at [13]; *Egan v Static Control Components (Europe) Ltd* [2004] EWCA Civ 392, [2004] 2 Lloyd's Rep. 429 at [37].

[354] *Taylor v St Helens Corp* (1877) 6 ChD 264, 270, per Jessel M.R., but the cases on which he relies turned upon the construction of wills.

[355] *Manchester College v Trafford* (1679) 2 Show. 31; *Johnson v Edgware, etc., Ry* (1866) 35 Beav. 480, 484; *Neill v Duke of Devonshire* (1882) 8 App. Cas. 135, 149; *Homburg Houtimport BV v Agrosin Private Ltd* [2003] UKHL 12, [2004] 1 A.C. 715 at [144]; *Dairy Containers Ltd v Tasman Orient Line* CV [2004] UKPC 22, [2005] 1 W.L.R. 215 at [12]. The principle is now mandatory in respect of certain consumer contracts by reg.7 of the Unfair Terms in Consumer Contracts Regulations 1999 (SI 1999/2083); see below, para.15–131.

[356] Co.Litt. 36a, 183a, 183b.

[357] *John Lee & Son (Grantham) Ltd v Railway Executive* [1949] 2 All E.R. 581, 583.

[358] *Tam Wing Chuen v Bank of Credit and Commerce Hong Kong Ltd* [1996] 2 B.C.L.C. 69, 77 (Lord Mustill), applied in *Lexi Holdings Plc v Stainforth* [2006] EWCA Civ 988.

[359] *Hargreave v Smee* (1829) 6 Bing. 244, 248; *Adams v Richardson & Starling Ltd* [1969] 1 W.L.R. 1645, 1653; *Tam Wing Chuen v Bank of Credit and Commerce Hong Kong Ltd* [1996] 2 B.C.L.C. 69; *Coutts & Co v Stock* [2000] 1 W.L.R. 906, 914.

[360] *Munn v Baker* (1817) 2 Stark. 255.

party claims a general lien is to be construed against him.[361] And if an instrument is made in terms so ambiguous as to make it doubtful whether it is a bill or note, the holder may, as against the maker of the instrument, treat it as either at his election.[362] Important applications of this principle arise in the case of conditions, warranties and exceptions in insurance policies[363] and in the case of time-bar[364] and exemption clauses,[365] for it is usually the party who has drafted the document who is seeking to rely on the protection of its provisions.[366]

12–086 **Crown contracts.**

> "The King's grant is taken most strongly against the grantee, and most favourably for the King, although the thing which he grants came to the King by purchase or descent."[367]

This ancient rule is still applicable to grants of land or of an interest in land,[368] but it no longer applies to commercial contracts with the Crown.[369] In any event, it does not in any way override other principles of construction.[370]

(f) *Ejusdem Generis Principle*

12–087 **Ejusdem generis principle.** The so-called "rule" which is laid down with reference to the construction of statutes, namely, that where several words preceding a general word point to a confined meaning the general word shall not extend in its effect beyond subjects ejusdem generis (of the same class),[371] applies in principle to the construction of contracts.[372] The principle depends on the assumed intention of the framer of the instrument, i.e. that the general words were only intended to guard against some accidental omission in the objects of the kind mentioned and were not intended to extend to objects of a wholly

---

361 *Crumpston v Haigh* (1836) 2 Scott 684.

362 *Edis v Bury* (1827) 6 B. & C. 433; *Lloyd v Oliver* (1852) 18 Q.B. 471.

363 *Blackett v Royal Exchange Assurance Co* (1832) 2 Cr. & J. 244; *Petros M. Nomikos Ltd v Robertson* (1939) 64 Ll.L.Rep. 45; *Tektrol Ltd v International Insurance Co of Hanover Ltd* [2005] EWCA Civ 845, [2005] 2 Lloyd's Rep. 701 at [8]; and see Vol.II, para.41–058.

364 *Board of Trade (Minister of Materials) v Steel Bus. & Co Ltd* [1952] 1 Lloyd's Rep. 87; *Pera Shipping Corp v Petroship SA* [1985] 2 Lloyd's Rep. 103.

365 See below, para.14–009.

366 It has, however, been pointed out by Staughton L.J. in *Pera Shipping Corp v Petroship SA* [1984] 2 Lloyd's Rep. 363, 365, and in *Youell v Bland Welch & Co Ltd* [1992] 2 Lloyd's Rep. 127, 134, in relation to the application of the maxim, that the *proferens* is sometimes regarded as the draftsman of the document and sometimes as the party who seeks to rely on the protection of its provisions. These may not coincide.

367 *Willion v Berkley* (1562) 1 Plow. 223, 243; *Att-Gen v Ewelme Hospital* (1853) 17 Beav. 366, 385; *Feather v the Queen* (1865) 6 B. & S. 257, 283, 284; *Viscountess Rhondda's Claim* [1922] A.C. 359, 353; *Earl of Lonsdale v Att-Gen* [1982] 1 W.L.R. 887, 901.

368 *Earl of Lonsdale v Att-Gen* [1982] 1 W.L.R. 887.

369 *Lonrho Exports Ltd v Export Credit Guarantee Department* [1999] Ch. 158.

370 *Att-Gen v Ewelme Hospital* (1853) 17 Beav. 366, 386.

371 *Sandiman v Breach* (1827) 7 B. & C. 96, 100; *R. v Nevill* (1846) 8 Q.B. 452; *Re Stockport Ragged Schools* [1898] 2 Ch. 687; *Att-Gen v Brown* [1920] 1 K.B. 773.

372 *Cullen v Butler* (1816) 5 M. & S. 461; *Harrison v Blackburn* (1864) 17 C.B.(N.S.) 678; *Sun Fire Office v Hart* (1889) 14 App. Cas. 98, 103.

different kind. Indeed, this principle follows as a corollary of the principle that the whole contract is to be considered,[373] being simply that every word shall be taken in conjunction with the words that accompany it.[374] Therefore the words "all the perils" in the ordinary form of marine insurance policy include only perils of the sea or perils ejusdem generis therewith, because their meaning is restricted by the subject-matter, i.e. marine risks, and by the genus of perils mentioned specifically in the policy.[375] General words such as "other accidents beyond the charterer's control" occurring at the end of a list of specific exceptions in a charterparty are construed to cover only accidents similar to those expressly mentioned.[376] Where a lease contained a proviso for an abatement of rent in case the demised premises should at any time during the term "be destroyed or damaged by fire, flood, storm, tempest, or other inevitable accident", it was held that the words "inevitable accident" must be construed by the principle of ejusdem generis, that is, they must be taken to mean accident of a similar kind to "fire, flood, storm, or tempest," and not to include accidents occasioned by the acts or defaults of the contracting parties.[377]

No common category. The ejusdem generis principle cannot, however, be applied unless there is a class to which the general words can be restricted. Therefore, where the matters specifically referred to are so various that they fall into no common category the meaning of subsequent general words is not limited by relation to them. For instance, liability was repudiated in the event of "deficiency of men or owner's stores, breakdown of machinery, or damage to hull *or other accident*". It was held that the matters specifically referred to made up no common category, so that the general words "or other accident" extended to delay caused by stranding.[378] The class need not be definable with logical or scientific exactitude, provided it is reasonably clear what it includes and what it excludes; for example, "war and disturbance" sufficiently indicate a class that excludes damage from ice.[379] It has been held that where only one matter is specifically referred to, the principle cannot be applied, because a single species cannot constitute a class[380]; but there is no reason why in such a case the general words should not be limited with respect to the subject matter in relation to which 12–088

[373] See above, paras 12–063—12–071.

[374] The maxim is *noscitur a sociis*: *Newby v Sharpe* (1878) 8 Ch D 39, 52.

[375] *Thames and Mersey Marine Insurance Co v Hamilton, Fraser & Co* (1887) 12 App. Cas. 494, 490; *Bolivia Republic v Indemnity Mutual Marine Assurance Co* [1909] 1 K.B. 785; *Stott (Baltic) Steamers v Marten* [1916] 1 A.C. 304; Marine Insurance Act 1906 Sch.I r.12.

[376] *Fenwick v Schmalz* (1868) L.R. 3 C.P. 313; *Re Richardsons and Samuel* [1898] 1 Q.B. 261; *Mudie v Strick* (1909) 100 L.T. 701; *Thorman v Dowgate Steamship Co* [1910] 1 K.B. 410; *Hadjipateras v S. Weigall & Co* (1918) 34 T.L.R. 360; *Aktieselskabet Frank v Namague Copper Co* (1920) 25 Com. Cas. 212; *Jones v Oceanic Steam Navigation Co* [1924] 2 K.B. 730 (passage ticket). But see the cases on force majeure clauses in commercial contracts cited below, para.12–089 fn.383.

[377] *Saner v Bilton* (1878) 7 ChD 815; *Manchester Bonded Warehouse Co v Carr* (1880) 5 C.P.D. 507; *Barking and Dagenham LBC v Stamford Asphalt Co Ltd*, *The Times*, April 10, 1997.

[378] *S.S. Magnhild v McIntyre Bros & Co* [1920] 3 K.B. 321; [1921] 2 K.B. 97; *Tillmanns v S.S. Knutsford* [1908] 2 K.B. 385, 395, 403, 409; affirmed [1908] A.C. 406.

[379] *Tillmanns v S.S. Knutsford* [1908] 2 K.B. 385; *Thorman v Dowgate S.S. Co* [1910] 1 K.B. 410; *Re Richardsons and Samuel* [1898] 1 Q.B. 261.

[380] *R. v Special Commissioners* [1923] 1 K.B. 393; *Re Ellwood* [1927] 1 Ch. 455.

they are used.[381] In a commercial contract, if a class cannot be found, that is one factor indicating that the parties did not intend to restrict the meaning of the words; but it is not universally true that, whenever a class cannot be found, the words must have been intended to have their literal meaning, whatever other indications there may be to the contrary.[382]

12–089 **Canon of construction.** The ejusdem generis principle is not a rigid technical rule, but a mere canon of construction. It has been held that, in a commercial contract, where general words follow an enumeration of particular things, those words are prima facie to be construed as having their natural and larger meaning, and are not to be restricted to things ejusdem generis with those previously enumerated, unless there is something in the instrument which shows an intention so to restrict them.[383] Also where a charterparty contained an exemption from liability arising from "frost, flood, strikes . . . and any other unavoidable accidents or hindrances of what kind soever beyond their control delaying the loading of the cargo", it was held that the parties, by inserting the words, "of what kind soever", intended to exclude the ejusdem generis principle, and that the contract was to be construed so as to exclude delays caused by a block of other shipping at the loading port.[384] On the other hand, the words "or otherwise" may be subject to the ejusdem generis principle.[385]

12–090 Where specific words follow general words instead of preceding them, the House of Lords has held that, as a general rule, the generality of the earlier should not be restricted by the insertion of the subsequent words, which may be regarded simply as examples of what was meant by the general words.[386] Similarly, even if the specific words precede the general words, they may be regarded as examples of what is comprehended in the general words.[387]

(g) *Restriction by Express Provisions*

12–091 **Expressio unius.** The express mention in an instrument of a particular person, power or thing may show an intention to exclude any other similar person, power or thing: *expressio unius est exclusio alterius*.[388] Thus, where a deed conveyed to

---

[381] See above, para.12–062; *Newby v Sharpe* (1878) 8 ChD 39, 52.

[382] *Chandris v Isbrandtsen-Moller Co Inc* [1951] 1 K.B. 240, 246.

[383] *Andersen v Andersen* [1895] 1 Q.B. 749; *Chandris v Isbrandtsen-Moller Co Inc* [1951] 1 K.B. 240; *P.J. Vander Zijden Wildhandel N.V. v Tucker & Cross Ltd* [1975] 2 Lloyd's Rep. 240. Contrast *Tillmanns Co v S.S. Knutsford* [1908] 2 K.B. 385; *Crompton v Jarratt* (1885) 30 ChD 298 where the contrary presumption is said to be correct.

[384] *Larsen v Sylvester & Co* [1908] A.C. 295; *Earl of Jersey v Neath Poor Law Union* (1889) 22 QBD 555; *Belcore Maritime Corp v Filli Moretti Cereali SpA* [1983] 2 Lloyd's Rep. 66, 68; *CA Venezolana de Navegacion v BankLine* [1987] 2 Lloyd's Rep. 498, 507; see also *Archbishop of Canterbury's Case* (1596) 2 Co.Rep. 46a (general words following particular words will not be taken to include anything of a superior class to that to which the particular words belong).

[385] *Re Kershaw, Whittaker v Kershaw* (1890) 45 ChD; cf. *Keeble v Keeble* [1956] 1 W.L.R. 94.

[386] *Ambatielos v Anton Jurgens Margarine Works* [1923] A.C. 175. cf. *Herman v Morris* (1919) 35 T.L.R. 328; affirmed (1919) 35 T.L.R. 574.

[387] *Stornvaart Maatschappij Sophie H. v Merchants' Marine Insurance Co Ltd* (1919) 89 L.J.K.B. 834 HL.

[388] Co.Litt. 210a; *Blackburn v Flavelle* (1881) 6 App. Cas. 628, 634.

a mortgagee an iron foundry and two dwelling-houses, and the appurtenances, together with the fixtures in and about the said houses, it was held that the specification of the fixtures in the dwelling-houses showed that those in the foundry were not intended to pass, although they would have passed had the other not been mentioned.[389] This maxim has, however, been said to be a valuable servant but a bad master in the construction of documents. Failure to complete the *expressio* may be accidental[390] and the maxim can only be applied if the instrument can be considered to contain all the terms agreed upon by the parties.[391] But, even with this qualification, arguments based on the maxim seem unlikely to carry much weight at the present day.[392]

Expressum facit cessare tacitum. It has also been said that, where there is an express covenant in an instrument on a particular matter, no implication of any other covenant on the same subject-matter can be raised[393]: 12–092

> "Where the parties have entered into written engagements with expressed stipulations, it is manifestly not desirable to extend them by any implications; the presumption is that, having expressed some, they have expressed all the conditions by which they intend to be bound under that instrument."[394]

But again it is doubtful whether this principle has any serious role to play in the modern law.

(h) *Stipulations as to Time*

Time in contracts. Generally, the words "till" and "until" are considered to be ambiguous and may be either exclusive or inclusive, according to the subject-matter and context[395]; "from" may be taken to be either inclusive or exclusive,[396] although the general assumption is that the day of the date, act or event is to be 12–093

[389] *Hare v Horton* (1833) 5 B. & Ad. 715. See also *Wood v Rowcliffe* (1851) 6 Exch. 407; *Miller v Emcer Products Ltd* [1956] Ch. 304.

[390] *Colquhoun v Brooks* (1887) 19 QBD 400, 406; affirmed (1889) 14 App.Cas. 493.

[391] *Devonald v Rosser & Sons* [1906] 2 K.B. 728, 745.

[392] *Beaufort Developments (NI) Ltd v Gilbert Ash NI Ltd* [1999] A.C. 266, 275; *National Grid Co Plc v Mayes* [2001] UKHL 20, [2001] 1 W.L.R. 864 at [55], [67].

[393] Co.Litt. 183, 210a; *Mathew v Blackmore* (1857) 1 H. & N. 762, 772.

[394] *Aspdin v Austin* (1844) 5 Q.B. 671, 684. See also *Broome v Pardess Co-operative Society Ltd* [1940] 1 All E.R. 603, 612 (no implied term).

[395] *R. v Stevens* (1804) 5 East 244; *Dakins v Wagner* (1835) 3 Dowl. 535, 536; *Kerr v Jeston* (1842) 1 Dowl.(N.S.) 538, 539; *Startup v Macdonald* (1843) 6 M. & G. 593; *Rogers v Davis* (1845) 8 Ir.L.R. 399, 400; *Bellhouse v Mellor, Proudman & Mellor* (1859) 4 H. & N. 116, 123; *Isaacs v Royal Insurance Co* (1870) L.R. 5 Ex. 296; *Heinrich Hirdes GmbH v Edmund* [1991] 2 Lloyd's Rep. 546.

[396] *Lester v Garland* (1808) 15 Ves. Jun. 248, 258; *Wilkinson v Gaston* (1846) 9 Q.B. 137, 145; *Re North* [1895] 2 Q.B. 264, 269; *Sheffield Corp v Sheffield Electric Light Co* [1898] 1 Ch. 203, 209; *Scottish Metropolitan Assurance Co v Stewart* (1923) 14 Ll.L.Rep. 55; *Carapanayoti & Co Ltd v Comptoir Commercial André & Cie SA* [1972] 1 Lloyd's Rep. 139.

excluded in the computation.[397] This principle, however, is not an absolute one, and the wording of the contract or the intention of the parties may indicate a contrary construction.[398]

12–094 "On" or "upon" may mean either before the act done to which it relates, or simultaneously with the act done, or after the act done, according as reason and good sense require the interpretation with reference to the context, and the subject-matter of the agreement.[399]

4. ADMISSIBILITY OF EXTRINSIC EVIDENCE

12–095 **Written documents.** Where the parties appear to have embodied their agreement in a written document,[400] the question arises whether extrinsic evidence, that is to say, evidence of matters outside the document, is admissible so as to affect its content. Two issues are involved: first, whether it is permissible to adduce extrinsic evidence of terms other than those included, expressly or by reference, in the document; secondly, whether extrinsic evidence may be admitted to explain or interpret the words used in the document.

(a) *The Parol Evidence Rule*

12–096 **Whether document conclusive.** It is often said to be a rule of law that:

> "If there be a contract which has been reduced to writing, verbal evidence is not allowed to be given . . . so as to add to or subtract from, or in any manner to vary or qualify the written contract."[401]

---

[397] *Lester v Garland* (1808) 15 Ves. Jun. 248; *Ackland v Lutley* (1839) 9 A. & E. 879, 894; *South Staffordshire Tramways Co v Sickness and Accident Association* [1891] 1 Q.B. 402; *Radcliffe v Bartholomew* [1892] 1 Q.B. 161; *Goldsmiths' Co v West Metropolitan Ry* [1904] 1 K.B. 1, 5; *Stewart v Chapman* [1951] 2 K.B. 792; *Cartwright v MacCormack* [1963] 1 W.L.R. 18; *Re Figgis* [1969] Ch. 123; *London and Overseas Freighters Ltd v Timber Shipping Co SA* [1972] A.C. 1; *Alma Shipping Corp of Monrovia v Mantovani* [1975] 1 Lloyd's Rep. 115; *Dodds v Walker* [1981] 1 W.L.R. 1027 HL; *Zoan v Rouamba* [2000] 1 W.L.R. 1509. See also the "clear day" principle: *Young v Higgon* (1840) 6 M. & W. 49; *Thompson v Stimpson* [1961] 1 Q.B. 195; *Carapanayoti & Co Ltd v Comptoir Commercial André & Cie SA* [1972] 1 Lloyd's Rep. 139. See also below, para.21–024.

[398] *Pugh v Duke of Leeds* (1777) 2 Cowp. 714; *Cornfoot v Royal Exchange Assurance Corp* [1904] 1 K.B. 40; *English v Cliff* [1914] 2 Ch. 376; *Hare v Gocher* [1962] 2 Q.B. 641; *Trow v Ind Coope (West Midlands) Ltd* [1967] 2 Q.B. 299; *Bevan Ashford v Malin* [1995] I.R.L.R. 360; *Zoan v Rouamba* [2000] 1 W.L.R. 1509 (statute).

[399] *R. v Humphery* (1839) 10 A. & E. 335, 370; *R. v Arkwright* (1848) 12 Q.B. 960, 970; *Paynter v James* (1867) L.R. 2 C.P. 348, 354; *Wm. Cory & Son Ltd v IRC* [1964] 1 W.L.R. 529 (affirmed [1965] A.C. 1088); *Kuratau Land Co Ltd v Kahu Te Kuru* [1966] N.Z.L.R. 544, 547; *Air New Zealand Ltd v Nippon Credit Bank Ltd* [1997] 1 N.Z.L.R. 218, 221–222.

[400] For computerised "documents", see above, para.12–048.

[401] *Goss v Lord Nugent* (1833) 5 B. & Ad. 58, 64. See also *Countess of Rutland's Case* (1602) 5 Co.Rep. 25b, 26a; *Meres v Ansell* (1771) 3 Wils. 275; *Smith v Doe d. Jersey* (1821) 2 Brod. & Bing. 473, 541; *Smith v Jeffryes* (1846) 15 M. & W. 561; *Hitchin v Groom* (1848) 5 C.B. 515; *Evans v Roe* (1872) L.R. 7 C.P. 138; *Mercantile Agency Co Ltd v Flitwick Chalybeate Co* (1897) 14 T.L.R. 90; *Newman v Gatti* (1907) 24 T.L.R. 18; *Reliance Marine Insurance v Duder* [1913] 1 K.B. 256, 273; *Hitchings & Coulthurst Co v Northern Leather Co of America and Doushkess* [1914] 3 K.B. 907; *Jacobs v Batavia and General Plantations Trust Ltd* [1924] 1 Ch. 287, 295; *Tsang Chuen v Li Po*

Indeed, in 1897, Lord Morris[402] accepted that:

> "... parol testimony cannot be received to contradict, vary, add to or subtract from the terms of a written contract, or the terms in which the parties have deliberately agreed to record any part of their contract."

This rule is usually known as the "parol evidence" rule. Its operation is not confined to oral evidence: it has been taken to exclude extrinsic matter in writing, such as drafts,[403] preliminary agreements,[404] and letters of negotiation.[405] The rule has been justified on the ground that it upholds the value of written proof,[406] effectuates the finality intended by the parties in recording their contract in written form,[407] and eliminates "great inconvenience and troublesome litigation in many instances".[408]

However, the parol evidence rule is and has long been subject to a number of exceptions.[409] In particular, since the nineteenth century, the courts have been prepared to admit extrinsic evidence of terms additional to those contained in the written document if it is shown that the document was not intended to express the entire agreement between the parties.[410] So, for example, if the parties intend their contract to be partly oral and partly in writing, extrinsic evidence is admissible to prove the oral part of the agreement.[411] In *Gillespie Bros & Co v Cheney, Eggar & Co*,[412] Lord Russell C.J. stated **12–097**

> "... although when the parties arrive at a definite written contract the implication or presumption is very strong that such contract is intended to contain all the terms of their bargain, it is a presumption only, and it is open to either of the parties to allege that there was, in addition to what appears in the written agreement, an antecedent express stipulation not intended by the parties to be excluded, but intended to continue in force with the express written agreement."

Kwai [1932] A.C. 713, 727; *O'Connor v Hume* [1954] 1 W.L.R. 824, 830; *Rabin v Gerson Berger Association Ltd* [1986] 1 W.L.R. 526, 530; *Edwards v O'Connor* [1991] 2 N.Z.L.R. 542.

402 *Bank of Australasia v Palmer* [1897] A.C. 540, 545 (cited in *National Westminster Bank Ltd v Halesowen Presswork & Assemblies Ltd* [1972] A.C. 785, 818–819).

403 *Miller v Travers* (1832) 8 Bing. 244; *Inglis v Buttery* (1878) 3 App. Cas. 552; *National Bank of Australasia v Falkingham & Sons* [1902] A.C. 585.

404 *Evans v Roe* (1871–72) L.R. 7 C.P. 138; *Leggott v Barrett* (1880) 15 ChD 306, 309, 311; *Henderson v Arthur* [1907] 1 K.B. 10; *Newman v Gatti* (1907) 24 T.L.R. 18; *Hitchings & Coulthurst Co v Northern Leather Co of America and Doushkess* [1914] 3 K.B. 907; *Hutton v Watling* [1948] Ch. 398; *Youell v Bland Welch & Co Ltd* [1992] 2 Lloyd's Rep. 127. But see *HIH Casualty and General Insurance Ltd v New Hampshire Insurance Co* [2001] EWCA Civ 735, [2001] 2 Lloyd's Rep. 161 at [83].

405 *Mercantile Bank of Sydney v Taylor* [1893] A.C. 317.

406 *Pickering v Dowson* (1813) 4 Taunt. 779, 784.

407 *Inglis v Buttery* (1877–78) L.R. 3 App. Cas. 552, 577.

408 *Mercantile Agency Co Ltd v Flitwick Chalybeate Co* (1897) 14 T.L.R. 90.

409 See below, paras 12–106 et seq.

410 *Mercantile Bank of Sydney v Taylor* [1893] A.C. 317, 321.

411 *Harris v Rickett* (1859) 4 H. & N. 1; *Malpas v L. & S.W. Ry* (1866) L.R. 1 C.P. 336; *Gillespie Bros v Cheney Eggar & Co* [1896] 2 Q.B. 59; *J. Evans & Son (Portsmouth) Ltd v Andrea Merzario Ltd* [1976] 1 W.L.R. 1078; *Yani Haryanto v E.D. & F. Man (Sugar) Ltd* [1986] 2 Lloyd's Rep. 44, 46–47.

412 [1896] 2 Q.B. 59, 62.

It cannot therefore be asserted that, in modern times, the mere production of a written agreement, however complete it may look, will as a matter of law render inadmissible evidence of other terms not included expressly or by reference in the document:

> "The court is entitled to look at and should look at all the evidence from start to finish in order to see what the bargain was that was struck between the parties."[413]

12–098 **Scope of the rule.** It follows that the scope of the parol evidence rule is much narrower than at first sight appears. It has no application until it is first determined that the terms of the parties' agreement are wholly contained in the written document. The rule:

> ". . . only applies where the parties to an agreement reduce it to writing, and agree or intend that the writing shall be their agreement."[414]

Whether the parties did so agree or intend is a matter to be decided by the court upon consideration of all the evidence relevant to this issue. It is therefore always open to a party to adduce extrinsic evidence to prove that the document is not a complete record of the contract. If, on that evidence, the court finds that terms additional to those in the document were agreed and intended by the parties to form part of the contract, then the court will have found that the contract consists partly of the terms contained in the document and partly of the terms agreed outside of it. The parol evidence rule will not apply. If, on the other hand, the court finds that the document is a complete record of the contract, then it will reject the evidence of additional terms. But it will do so, not because it is required to ignore the additional terms or the evidence said to prove them, but because such evidence is inconsistent with its finding that the document does contain the whole terms of the parties' agreement.[415] No doubt, in practice, where a document is produced which appears to be a complete contract, a party will experience considerable difficulty in proving, on the balance of probabilities, that further contractual terms were agreed outside the written terms of the document. But extrinsic evidence of such terms is not ipso facto excluded.

12–099 **Law Commission Report.** In 1986, the Law Commission considered[416] whether it should recommend that the parol evidence rule be abolished or amended by statute. For this purpose, it was necessary for the Commission to analyse the rule in detail as to its applicability, width and effect. The Commission expressed the opinion[417] that:

> ". . . although a proposition of law can be stated which can be described as the 'parol evidence' rule it is not a rule of law which, correctly applied, could lead to evidence being unjustly excluded. Rather, it is a proposition of law which is no more than a

---

413 *J. Evans & Son (Portsmouth) Ltd v Andrea Merzario Ltd* [1976] 1 W.L.R. 1078, 1083.

414 *Harris v Rickett* (1859) 4 H. & N. 1, 7; *Turner v Forwood* [1951] 1 All E.R. 746, 749; *Air Great Lakes Pty Ltd v K.S. Easter (Holdings) Pty Ltd* (1985) 2 N.S.W.L.R. 309, 337; *State Rail Authority of New South Wales v Heath Outdoor Pty Ltd* (1986) 7 N.S.W.L.R. 170, 191.

415 *Wild v Civil Aviation Authority* Unreported September 25, 1987 CA.

416 Law Com.154, 1986, Cmnd.9700. See Marston [1986] C.L.J. 192.

417 Law Com.154, Cmnd.9700, para.2.7.

circular statement: [W]hen it is proved or admitted that the parties to a contract intended that all the express terms of their agreement should be as recorded in a particular document or documents, evidence will be inadmissible (because irrelevant) if it is tendered only for the purpose of adding to, varying, subtracting from or contradicting the express terms of that contract."

The general conclusion[418] reached by the Commission was:

"... that there is no *rule of law* that evidence is rendered inadmissible or is to be ignored solely because a document exists which looks like a complete contract. Whether it is a complete contract depends upon the intention of the parties, objectively judged, and not on any rule of law."

It is submitted that this general conclusion is correct.[419]

Extrinsic evidence to contradict document. More justification[420] might, however, be found for the parol evidence rule if deployed to prevent extrinsic evidence being adduced to vary or contradict the terms of a written document. It could be said then to fulfil a useful purpose in that it would emphasise the primacy traditionally accorded to the written text of complete contractual documents, where these exist.[421] But, where it appears that the parties did not intend to record all the terms of their agreement in a particular document, then on the same analysis extrinsic evidence would be admissible to prove other terms even if they varied or contradicted those in the document.[422] Thus if the terms of a document stipulated that payment should be made on a certain day, evidence would be admissible of a contemporaneous agreement outside the document that payment was to be deferred until a later day.[423] Or if the terms of the document provided that one party was to have the unqualified right to terminate the contract upon one month's notice in writing, evidence would be admissible to prove a contractual agreement outside the document that the contract should only determine by effluxion of time.[424] If there is an inconsistency, that is, if effect cannot fairly be given to both terms, then the court might reject that term which defeats 12–100

[418] Law Com.154, Cmnd.9700, para.2.17.

[419] The Commission's Report was referred to with approval in *Wild v Civil Aviation Authority* Unreported September 25, 1987 CA and in *State Rail Authority of New South Wales v Heath Outdoor Pty Ltd* (1986) 7 N.S.W.L.R. 170, 192. See also *Yani Haryanto v E.D. & F. Man (Sugar) Ltd* [1986] 2 Lloyd's Rep. 44, 46; *Youell v Bland Welch & Co Ltd* [1992] 2 Lloyd's Rep. 127, 133, 140.

[420] For modern instances of support for the rule, see *AIB Group (UK) Ltd v Martin* [2001] UKHL 63, [2002] 1 W.L.R. 94 at [4]; *Shogun Finance Ltd v Hudson* [2003] UKHL 62, [2004] 1 A.C. 919 at [49].

[421] cf. *Gillespie Brothers & Co v Cheney, Eggar & Co* [1896] 2 Q.B. 59, 62; Wedderburn [1959] C.L.J. 58, 62 (presumption only).

[422] But see e.g. *Angell v Duke* (1875) 32 L.T. 320; *Henderson v Arthur* [1907] 1 K.B. 10.

[423] *Young v Austen* (1869) L.R. 4 C.P. 553; *Maillard v Page* (1870) L.R. 5 Ex. 312 (in these cases the extrinsic agreement was in writing, as the contract was required to be in writing: see below, para.12–101).

[424] cf. *State Rail Authority of New South Wales v Heath Outdoor Pty Ltd* (1986) 7 N.S.W.L.R. 170, 191–192.

the object and intent of the parties as expressed in the whole of their agreement.[425] Of such a situation the Law Commission said[426]:

> " . . . it is no different in principle from that in which the parties agree two inconsistent terms both of which are set out in the same document. The court will have to decide which of the inconsistent terms more nearly represents the intention of the parties."

However, the difficulty of proving that the written document did not express the true and complete agreement of the parties may lead the party who alleges a promise or assurance inconsistent with the document to seek to establish a collateral contract or warranty[427] or (in appropriate cases) to seek rectification of the document on the ground that it did not express the concurrent intentions of the parties at the time of its execution.[428]

12–101 **Contracts required to be in or evidenced by writing.** Certain contracts are required by law to be in writing.[429] The effect of this requirement will be to exclude *oral* evidence which is offered for no other purpose than to contradict, vary, add to or subtract from the contract as contained in writing. In particular, the contracts of the various parties to a bill of exchange or promissory note must be in writing.[430] It is well established that, even as between immediate parties to a bill or note, evidence will not be admitted to prove an oral agreement to qualify the absolute undertaking of a party on the instrument, for example, to show that his liability is to be enforceable against him only in certain contingencies or that it is to be postponed to a time later than that expressed on the face of the instrument.[431] But:

> " . . . a written agreement on a distinct paper, to renew, or in other respects to qualify, the liability of the maker or acceptor, is good as between the original parties."[432]

Indeed it would seem that, as between immediate parties, evidence may always be given of a contemporaneous *written* agreement to vary the effect of the

[425] See above, para.12–078.
[426] Law Com.154, 1986, Cmnd.9700, para.2.16.
[427] See below, para.12–103.
[428] See above, para.5–107.
[429] See above, para.4–001.
[430] Bills of Exchange Act 1882 s.3(1) (drawer), s.17(1) (acceptor), s.32(1) (indorser), s.83(1) (maker).
[431] *Hoare v Graham* (1811) 3 Camp. 57; *Free v Hawkins* (1817) 8 Taunt. 92; *Woodbridge v Spooner* (1819) 3 B. & Ald. 233; *Campbell v Hodgson* (1819) Gow 74; *Moseley v Hanford* (1830) 10 B. & C. 729; *Foster v Jolly* (1835) 1 C.M. & R. 703; *Adams v Wordley* (1836) 1 M. & W. 374; *Besant v Cross* (1851) 10 C.B. 895; *Drain v Harvey* (1855) 17 C.B. 257; *Abrey v Crux* (1869) L.R. 6 C.P. 37; *Young v Austen* (1869) L.R. 4 C.P. 553, 556; *Maillard v Page* (1870) L.R. 5 Exch. 312, 319; *Stott v Fairlamb* (1883) 52 L.J.Q.B. 420; *New London Credit Syndicate v Neale* [1898] 2 Q.B. 487; *Hitchings and Coulthurst Co v Northern Leather Co of America and Doushkess* [1914] 3 K.B. 907.
[432] *Byles on Bills of Exchange*, 26th edn, p.401.

instrument and regulate their rights between themselves.[433] However, in the case of a contract for the sale or other disposition of an interest in land which is required by the Law of Property (Miscellaneous Provisions) Act 1989[434] to be made in writing and signed by or on behalf of each party to the contract, all the terms which the parties have expressly agreed must be incorporated in one document (or, where contracts are exchanged, in each).[435] Terms may be incorporated in a document either by being set out in it or by reference to some other document.[436] But, in the absence of such a reference in the signed document, evidence will not be admissible to prove that other terms were agreed in writing in addition to those set out in the document,[437] except to show that the document does not satisfy the statutory requirements.[438]

Where the contract is one which by statute must be evidenced by a note or memorandum in writing signed by the party to be charged or his agent, as in the case of a contract of guarantee,[439] the memorandum must contain a statement of the material terms of the contract.[440] Extrinsic evidence is not admissible to prove that the parties orally agreed material terms which ought to have been, but were not, included in the memorandum, since the admission of such evidence would plainly not satisfy the statute.[441] Parol evidence is, however, admissible to connect two or more documents, provided that the document which is signed by the party to be charged expressly or by implication refers to the other document or documents,[442] but not otherwise.[443] 12–102

Collateral contracts. Even though the parties intended to express the whole of their agreement in a particular document, extrinsic evidence will nevertheless be admitted to prove a contract or warranty collateral to that agreement.[444] The reason is that, "the parol agreement neither alters nor adds to the written one, but is an independent agreement".[445] Such evidence is certainly admissible in respect of a matter on which the written contract is silent.[446] In a number of older cases 12–103

---

[433] *Bowerbank v Monteiro* (1813) 4 Taunt. 844; *Young v Austen* (1869) L.R. 4 C.P. 553; *Maillard v Page* (1870) L.R. 5 Exch. 312, 319. But the written agreement must be supported by valuable consideration (*Bowerbank v Monteiro*; *McManus v Bark* (1870) L.R. 5 Exch. 65) and be between the same parties (*Salmon v Webb* (1852) 3 H.L.C. 310).

[434] See above, para.4–052.

[435] s.2(1).

[436] s. 2(2).

[437] But such terms may have effect as a collateral contract or warranty: see below, para.12–103.

[438] But see s.2(4) (rectification); above para.4–070.

[439] Statute of Frauds 1677 s.4.

[440] *Holmes v Mitchell* (1859) 7 C.B. N.S. 361. But cf. Mercantile Law Amendment Act 1856 (consideration need not be stated).

[441] *Holmes v Mitchell* (1859) 7 C.B. N.S. 361; *Sheers v Thimbleby & Son* (1897) 76 L.T. 709, 711. But extrinsic evidence will be admitted to show that, by reason of the omission, the memorandum does *not* satisfy the statute: see, e.g. *Beckett v Nurse* [1948] 1 K.B. 535 (on Law of Property Act 1925 s.40).

[442] *Timmins v Moreland Street Property Co Ltd* [1958] Ch. 110; *Elias v George Sahely & Co (Barbados) Ltd* [1983] A.C. 646; see above, para.4–028.

[443] But cf. *Sheers v Thimbleby & Son* (1897) 76 L.T. 709.

[444] See above, paras 12–004—12–006, 12–033; Wedderburn [1959] C.L.J. 58, 71.

[445] *Mann v Nunn* (1874) 30 L.T. 526, 527.

[446] See, e.g. *De Lassalle v Guildford* [1901] 2 K.B. 515.

it was stated that evidence of such a contract or warranty must not contradict the express terms of the written contract.[447] However, more recently, the courts have admitted evidence to prove an overriding oral warranty[448] or to prove an oral promise that the written contract will not be enforced in accordance with its terms.[449] Thus in *City of Westminster Properties (1934) Ltd v Mudd*[450] the draft of a new lease presented to a tenant contained a covenant that he would use the premises for business purposes only and not as sleeping quarters. The tenant objected to this covenant, and the landlords gave him an oral assurance that, if he signed the lease, they would not enforce it against him. The tenant signed the lease, but later the landlords sought to forfeit the lease for breach of this covenant. Harman J. held that the oral assurance constituted a separate collateral contract from which the landlords would not be permitted to resile. The collateral contract or warranty may be oral or informal[451] even though the main contract is one which is required by law to be in or evidenced by writing.[452]

12–104 **"Entire agreement" clauses.** The practice has developed[453] of including in written agreements of a formal character an "entire agreement" clause, for example:

> "This Agreement contains the entire and only agreement between the parties and supersedes all previous agreements between the parties respecting the subject-matter hereof; each party acknowledges that in entering into this Agreement it has not relied on any representation or undertaking, whether oral or in writing, save such as are expressly incorporated herein."

The purpose of such a clause is to achieve, by a somewhat roundabout route, the exclusion of liability for statements other than those set out in the written

---

[447] *Lindley v Lacey* (1864) 17 C.B.(N.S.) 578, 586, 587; *Morgan v Griffith* (1871) L.R. 6 Ex. 70, 73; *Erskine v Adeane* (1873) L.R. 8 Ch. App. 756, 766; *Angell v Duke* (1875) 32 L.T. 320; *Leggott v Barrett* (1880) 15 ChD 306, 314; *Newman v Gatti* (1907) 24 T.L.R. 18; *Henderson v Arthur* [1907] 1 K.B. 10; *Goldfoot v Welch* [1914] 1 Ch. 213, 218. See also *Maybury v Atlantic Union Oil Co Ltd* (1953) 89 C.L.R. 507, 518; *Donovan v Northlea Farms Ltd* [1976] 1 N.Z.L.R. 180 (where the other view was adopted).

[448] *Couchman v Hill* [1947] K.B. 554; *Webster v Higgin* [1948] 2 All E.R. 127; *Harling v Eddy* [1951] 2 K.B. 739; *Mendelssohn v Normand Ltd* [1970] 1 Q.B. 177, 184; *J. Evans & Son (Portsmouth) Ltd v Andrea Merzario Ltd* [1976] 1 W.L.R. 1078.

[449] *City and Westminster Properties (1934) Ltd v Mudd* [1959] Ch. 129. See also *Brikom Investments Ltd v Carr* [1979] Q.B. 467.

[450] [1959] Ch. 129. This case was referred to with approval in *Frisby v BBC* [1967] Ch. 932, 945; *Lee-Parker v Izzett (No.2)* [1972] 1 W.L.R. 775, 779; *Atlantic Lines and Navigation Co Inc v Hallam Ltd* [1983] 1 Lloyd's Rep. 188, 197. It might be thought that the same result could be reached by application of the principle of promissory estoppel (see above, para.3–085), but it would appear that that principle may not extend to pre-contractual negotiations: see *Secretary of State for Employment v Globe Elastic Thread Co Ltd* [1980] A.C. 506. Contrast, however, *Bank Negara Indonesia v Philip Hoalim* [1973] 2 M.L.J. 3, PC; *Brikom Investments Ltd v Carr* [1979] Q.B. 467, 484–485; *State Rail Authority of New South Wales v Heath Outdoor Pty Ltd* (1986) 7 N.S.W.L.R. 171.

[451] Unless its subject-matter is such that it is itself required to be in or evidenced by writing: *Daulia Ltd v Four Millbank Nominees Ltd* [1978] Ch. 231.

[452] See, e.g. *Angell v Duke* (1875) L.R. 10 Q.B. 174 (but such evidence was later rejected: (1875) 32 L.T. 320); *Record v Bell* [1991] 1 W.L.R. 853.

[453] The practice probably originated in the United States: see Uniform Commercial Code para.2–202. See also Peden and Carter (2006) 22 J.C.L. 1; Mitchell (2006) 22 J.C.L. 222; McMeel, *Construction of Contracts* (2007), Ch.24.

contract. The effect of the clause will necessarily depend upon its precise wording. It has been stated[454] that an "entire agreement" clause operates "to denude what would otherwise constitute a collateral warranty of legal effect", although an alternative explanation could be that it renders inadmissible extrinsic evidence to prove terms other than those in the written contract, since the parties have by the clause expressed their intention that the document is to contain all the terms of their agreement.[455] However, the language of the clause may not be apt to exclude representations[456] even if it excludes claims arising out of a collateral contract or warranty.[457] It should also not prevent use of extrinsic evidence to ascertain the meaning of an express term in the contract.[458] An entire agreement clause may be waived by a party who might otherwise have relied on it.[459]

Extrinsic evidence admissible. There are, in any event, a number of situations in which the written instrument is not conclusive evidence of the contract alleged to be embodied in it. These situations may be regarded either as exceptions to the parol evidence rule or simply as cases falling outside the rule.[460] They will now be discussed. 12–105

(b) *Evidence as to the Validity or Effectiveness of the Written Agreement*

No contract. Extrinsic evidence is admissible to show that what appears to be a valid and binding contract is in fact no contract at all. Thus evidence may be admitted to show that one or both parties contracted under a mistake,[461] or that 12–106

[454] *Inntrepreneur Pub Co Ltd v East Crown Ltd* [2000] 2 Lloyd's Rep. 611, 614; *Ravennavi SpA v New Century Shipbuilding Co Ltd* [2006] EWHC 733 (Comm), [2006] 2 Lloyd's Rep. 280; [2007] EWCA Civ 58, [2007] 2 Lloyd's Rep. 24.

[455] See *McGrath v Shah* (1989) 57 P. & C.R. 452. Contrast the view expressed by the Law Commission, Law Com.154, 1986, Cmnd.9700, para.2.15: "It may have a strong persuasive effect but if it were proved that, notwithstanding the clause, the parties actually intended some additional term to be of contractual effect, the court would give effect to that term because such was the intention of the parties."

[456] *Alman and Benson v Associated Newspapers Group Ltd* Unreported June 20, 1980; *Thomas Witter Ltd v T.B.P. Industries Ltd* [1996] 2 All E.R. 573; *Deepak Fertilisers and Petrochemicals Corp v ICI* [1999] 1 Lloyd's Rep. 387, 395; *South West Water Services Ltd v International Computers Ltd* [1999] Build. L.R. 420, 424; *Government of Zanzibar v British Aerospace (Lancaster House) Ltd* [2000] 1 W.L.R. 2333, 2344; *Sabah Shipyard (Pakistan) Ltd v Govt of Pakistan* [2007] EWHC 2602 (Comm), [2008] 1 Lloyd's Rep. 240 at [130] (deceit). If the statement sought to be excluded is a misrepresentation, then the clause may in any event be ineffective under s.3 of the Misrepresentation Act 1967 (as amended by s.8 of the Unfair Contract Terms Act 1977); see above para.6–136. cf. *Watford Electronics Ltd v Sanderson* CFL Ltd [2001] EWCA Civ 317, [2001] Build.L.R. 143, 155. See also ss.11, 13 of the 1977 Act, and below, paras 14–063, n.331, 15–105.

[457] *Deepak Fertilisers and Petrochemicals Corp. v ICI*, above, at 395; *Inntrepreneur Pub Co Ltd v East Crown Ltd*, above. See also *Exxonmobil Sales and Supply Corp. v Texaco Ltd* [2003] EWHC 1964 (Comm); [2003] 2 Lloyd's Rep. 686 (exclusion of implied terms based on usage or custom). cf., *Milburn Services Ltd v United Trading Group* (1995) C.I.L.L. 1109 (terms implied by necessity).

[458] *Proforce Recruit Ltd v Rugby Group Ltd* [2006] EWCA Civ 69 at [41] [59] [61]. See also *Air New Zealand Ltd v Nippon Credit Bank Ltd* [1997] N.Z.L.R. 218, 224.

[459] *SAM Business Systems Ltd v Hedley & Co* [2002] EWHC (TCC) 2733; [2003] 1 All E.R. (Comm) 465.

[460] See the Report of the Law Commission, Law Com.154, 1986, Cmnd.9700, paras 2.30, 2.31.

[461] *Pym v Campbell* (1856) 6 E. & B. 370, 374; *Raffles v Wichelhaus* (1864) 2 H. & C. 906. See above, para.5–001.

a person who signed the document was under a misapprehension as to the real nature of the transaction into which he had entered so that it was "not his deed" in law.[462] Also it may be shown that the writing was not intended by the parties to give rise to contractual obligations[463] or that the contract is void for non-compliance with a statute.[464]

12–107 **Documents that are not contracts.** The parol evidence rule has in any event only been applied to an instrument which is intended itself to be the formal and conclusive expression by the parties of their agreement.[465] If the document in question is not such an instrument, then extrinsic evidence is admissible to ascertain or interpret the intentions of the parties. Thus if a document is intended to be merely an informal memorandum of an agreement previously concluded, extrinsic evidence may be admitted to show that this informal memorandum does not embody the terms contained in the previous agreement.[466] A receipt,[467] an invoice,[468] a payment instruction[469] and even bills of lading,[470] have been held to come within this exception.

12–108 **Consideration.** Consideration is a necessary requirement for the formation of all contracts which are not made by deed.[471] Extrinsic evidence may therefore be admitted to show want of or failure of the consideration stated to have been given in a written instrument.[472] Thus the words in a bill of exchange "for value received" do not preclude the court from finding that no consideration has in fact been given.[473] Extrinsic evidence is also admissible to prove the true consideration where no consideration, or a nominal consideration, has been stated,[474] where the expressed consideration is in general terms or ambiguously stated,[475]

---

[462] See, e.g. *Foster v Mackinnon* (1869) L.R. 4 C.P. 704; *Lewis v Clay* (1898) 67 L.J.Q.B. 224; *Roe v R.A. Naylor Ltd* (1918) 87 L.J.K.B. 958, 964. Direct evidence of intention is always admissible where the *factum* of the instrument is impugned. See above, para.5–101, and below, para.12–114, n.501.

[463] *Bowes v Foster* (1858) 2 H. & N. 779; *Rogers v Hadley* (1863) 2 H. & C. 227; *Pattle v Hornibrook* [1897] 1 Ch. 25; *Orion Insurance Co Plc v Sphere Drake Insurance Plc* [1992] 1 Lloyd's Rep. 239, 273, 301.

[464] *Lockett v Nicklin* (1848) 2 Exch. 93; *Campbell Discount Co Ltd v Gall* [1961] 1 Q.B. 431.

[465] Or, in the case of a unilateral instrument such as a deed, the formal and conclusive expression of the intentions of the maker: *Rabin v Gerson Berger Association Ltd* [1986] 1 W.L.R. 526.

[466] *Orion Insurance Co Plc v Sphere Drake Insurance Plc* [1992] 1 Lloyd's Rep. 239; cf. *Hutton v Watling* [1948] Ch. 398.

[467] *Graves v Key* (1832) 3 B. & Ad. 313; *Allen v Pink* (1838) 4 M. & W. 140; *Lee v L. & Y. Ry* (1871) L.R. 6 Ch. App. 527; *Beckett v Nurse* [1948] 1 K.B. 535.

[468] *Holding v Elliott* (1860) 5 H. & N. 117.

[469] *Guardian Ocean Cargoes Ltd v Banco do Brasil SA* [1991] 2 Lloyd's Rep. 68.

[470] *Crooks v Allan* (1879) 5 QBD 38; *Moss Steamship Co v Whinney* [1912] A.C. 254, 264; *The Ardennes* [1951] 1 K.B. 55.

[471] See above, Ch.3.

[472] *Abbott v Hendrix* (1840) 1 M. & G. 791, 794, 796; *Young v Austen* (1869) L.R. 4 C.P. 553, 556; *Abrey v Crux* (1869) L.R. 5 C.P. 37, 45; *Equitable Office v Ching* [1907] A.C. 96; Law of Property Act 1925 s.67. But cf. *Roberts v Security Co* [1897] 1 Q.B. 111; Law of Property Act 1925 s.68.

[473] *Solly v Hinde* (1834) 2 Cr. & M. 516; *Abbott v Hendrix* (1840) 1 M. & G. 791, 795.

[474] *Gale v Williamson* (1841) 8 M. & W. 405; *Clifford v Turrell* (1845) 1 Y. & C.C.C. 138; *Pott v Todhunter* (1845) 2 Coll. 76; *Re Holland* [1902] 2 Ch. 360, 388.

[475] *Goldshede v Swan* (1847) 1 Exch. 154; *Hoad v Grace* (1861) 7 H. & N. 494.

or where the consideration is inaccurately recorded.[476] Also an additional consideration may be proved, provided it does not contradict the stated consideration.[477]

> "The rule is that, where there is one consideration stated in a deed, you may prove any other consideration which existed, not in contradiction to the instrument; and it is not in contradiction to the instrument to prove a larger consideration than that which is stated."[478]

Conditional contracts. Extrinsic evidence is admissible to show that, at the time a document was signed by the parties, they were agreed that it was not to take effect as a contract except on the fulfilment of a certain condition,[479] e.g. in the case of deeds, evidence of an escrow.[480] 12–109

Evidence of date. Extrinsic evidence is admitted to prove the actual date of delivery of a deed,[481] or the date of execution of a written instrument,[482] in contradiction of the date stated therein; and also, where it has no date, to show from what time a written instrument was intended to operate.[483] It is also admitted to show that the parties intended that an instrument should operate retrospectively from a specified date, act or event prior to the date on which the instrument was executed.[484] 12–110

Subsequent variation or discharge. The rule regarding the admissibility of extrinsic evidence applies merely to the discovery of the original intention of the parties as expressed in the instrument, and has no application to the variation[485] or discharge[486] of the contract by a subsequent agreement. 12–111

---

476 *Booker v Seddon* (1858) 1 F. & F. 196. It is a moot point whether extrinsic evidence is admissible to prove a real (e.g. smaller) consideration inconsistent with that expressed in the instrument. See *Ridout v Bristow* (1830) 9 Exch. 48; *Abbott v Hendrix* (1840) 1 M. & G. 791, 796; *Turner v Forwood* [1951] 1 All E.R. 746. The views of Lord Hardwicke in *Peacock v Monk* (1748) 1 Ves. Sen. 127, 128 must now be read with caution. See also *Woods v Wise* [1955] 2 Q.B. 29; *Peffer v Rigg* [1977] 1 W.L.R. 285, 293.

477 *Leifchild's Case* (1865) L.R. 1 Eq. 231; *Townend v Toker* (1866) L.R. 1 Ch.App. 446, 459; *Frith v Frith* [1906] A.C. 254; *Turner v Forwood* [1951] 1 All E.R. 746; *Pao On v Lau Yiu Long* [1980] A.C. 614.

478 *Clifford v Turrell* (1845) 1 Y. & C.L.C. 138, 149.

479 *Pym v Campbell* (1856) 6 E. & B. 370; *Wallis v Littell* (1861) 11 C.B.(N.S.) 369; *Lindley v Lacey* (1864) 17 C.B.(N.S.) 578; *Pattle v Hornibrook* [1897] 1 Ch. 25; cf. *Smith v Mansi* [1963] 1 W.L.R. 26.

480 *London Freehold and Leasehold Property v Lord Suffield* [1897] 2 Ch. 608, 622. See above, para.1–105.

481 *Jayne v Hughes* (1854) 10 Exch. 430.

482 *Hall v Cazenove* (1804) 4 East 477; *Pasmore v North* (1811) 13 East 517; *Armfield v Allport* (1857) 27 L.J.Ex. 42; Bills of Exchange Act 1882 s.13(1).

483 *Davis v Jones* (1856) 17 C.B. 625; Bills of Exchange Act 1882 ss.12, 20.

484 *Northern & Shell Plc v John Laing Construction Ltd* [2002] EWHC 2258, (2002) 85 Const. L.R. 179.

485 *Goss v Lord Nugent* (1833) 5 B. & Ad. 58, 64. But a contract required by law to be in or evidenced by writing can in principle only be varied by writing: see below, para.22–033.

486 *Morris v Baron & Co Ltd* [1918] A.C. 1; below, para.22–029.

12–112 **Fraud, illegality, etc.** Extrinsic evidence will always be admitted to defeat a deed or written contract on the ground of fraud,[487] illegality,[488] misrepresentation,[489] mistake[490] or duress.[491] Also in the application of equitable remedies such as specific performance or the refusal thereof,[492] rectification,[493] or rescission,[494] extrinsic evidence will be admitted to prove the grounds upon which relief is sought.

(c) *Evidence as to the True Nature of the Agreement*

12–113 **True nature of the agreement.** Extrinsic evidence is admissible to prove the true nature of the agreement, or the legal relationship of the parties,[495] even though this may vary or add to the written instrument.[496] Thus a conveyance may be shown to be merely a mortgage,[497] a sale and hire-purchase agreement to be an unregistered bill of sale,[498] and a sale of property to be a loan on security.[499]

12–114 **Evidence of agency.** Extrinsic evidence may also be adduced to show that one or both of the contracting parties to an agreement were agents for other persons and acted as such in making the contract so as to give the benefit or the burden of the contract to their undisclosed principals.[500] Such evidence relates to the factum of the written instrument.[501] It is therefore a moot point whether

---

487 *Pickering v Dowson* (1813) 4 Taunt. 779; *Dobell v Stevens* (1825) 3 B. & C. 623.

488 *Collins v Blantern* (1767) 2 Wils. 347; *Doe d. Chandler v Ford* (1853) 3 A. & E. 649; *Reynell v Sprye* (1852) 1 De G.M. & G. 660, 672; *Madell v Thomas & Co* [1891] 1 Q.B. 230. See also *Woods v Wise* [1955] 2 Q.B. 29 (evidence to support legality).

489 *Pennsylvania Shipping Co v Compagnie Nationale de Navigation* [1936] 2 All E.R. 1167.

490 See above, para.5–001.

491 See above, para.7–001.

492 *Martin v Pycroft* (1852) D.M. & G. 785; *Webster v Cecil* (1861) 30 Beav. 62. See below, Ch.27.

493 *Druiff v Parker* (1868) L.R. 5 Eq. 131; *Olley v Fisher* (1887) 34 ChD 367; *Henderson v Arthur* [1907] 1 K.B. 10, 13; *Lovell and Christmas Ltd v Wall* (1911) 104 L.T. 85; *Craddock Bros v Hunt* [1923] 2 Ch. 136, 151; *Hamed El Chiaty & Co v Thomas Cook Group Ltd* [1992] 2 Lloyd's Rep. 399, 407, 408.

494 *Paget v Marshall* (1884) 28 ChD 255.

495 *Steele v M'Kinlay* (1880) 5 App. Cas. 754, 778–779; *Macdonald v Whitfield* (1883) 8 App. Cas. 733, 745; *National Sales Corp Ltd v Bernardi* [1931] 2 K.B. 188; *McCall Bros Ltd v Hargreaves* [1932] 2 K.B. 423; *Yeoman Credit Ltd v Gregory* [1963] 1 W.L.R. 343; and see below, para.12–116.

496 Including direct evidence of intention.

497 *Re Duke of Marlborough* [1894] 2 Ch. 133.

498 *Madell v Thomas & Co* [1891] 1 Q.B. 230; *Polsky v S. & A. Services* [1951] 1 All E.R. 1062.

499 *Maas v Pepper* [1905] A.C. 102.

500 *Bateman v Phillips* (1812) 15 East 272; *Wake v Harrop* (1861) 30 L.J.Ex. 273; *McCollin v Gilpin* (1881) 29 W.R. 408; *Fred Drughorn Ltd v Rederiaktiebolaget Transatlantic* [1919] A.C. 203; *Danziger v Thompson* [1944] K.B. 654; *Epps v Rothnie* [1945] K.B. 562; *Finzel, Berry & Co v Eastcheap Dried Fruit Co* [1962] 1 Lloyd's Rep. 370; affirmed [1962] 2 Lloyd's Rep. 11. See Vol.II, para.31–064.

501 *Young v Schuler* (1883) 11 QBD 651; *Homburg Houtimport BV v Agrosin Private Ltd* [2003] UKHL 12, [2004] 1 A.C. 715 at [175]. See also *Internaut Shipping v Fercometal SARL* [2003] EWCA Civ 812, [2003] 2 Lloyd's Rep. 430 (evidence of no agency).

evidence can be given which is inconsistent with the written agreement. There is authority for the view that, where an action is brought against a party who has contracted in terms indicating that he is the real and only principal, evidence cannot be given that he contracted merely as agent as this would contradict the written agreement.[502] Thus where a party was described as "owner" of a ship[503] or as "proprietor" of a building site,[504] he being, in fact, merely the agent of an undisclosed principal, it was held, in an action by the principal on the contract, that evidence could not be received to show the fact of the agency so as to give the principal a right to sue on the contract. On the other hand, these cases may be explained as cases in which the personality of the contracting party was of sufficient importance to have become a term of the contract[505] or simply that they were wrongly decided.[506] The issue is still an open one.[507]

Where a person describes himself in a contract as agent of an unnamed principal, either he or the other contracting party may bring evidence to show that, although described as agent, he is in fact the principal.[508] 12–115

Evidence of suretyship. Evidence is admissible to show that a person who signed a document did so as surety, even though it might appear that he entered into the agreement as principal debtor or on behalf of another or in some other capacity.[509] 12–116

---

502 *Magee v Atkinson* (1837) 2 M. & W. 440; *Higgins v Senior* (1841) 8 M. & W. 834; *Humble v Hunter* (1848) 12 Q.B. 310; *Formby Bros v Formby* (1910) 102 L.T. 116. See Vol.II, para.31–067.

503 *Humble v Hunter* (1848) 12 Q.B. 310.

504 *Formby Bros v Formby* (1910) 102 L.T. 116.

505 *Fred Drughorn Ltd v Rederiaktiebolaget Transatlantic* [1919] A.C. 203, 210; *Rederiaktiebolaget Argonaut v Hani* [1918] 2 K.B. 247; *Collins v Associated Greyhound Racecourses Ltd* [1930] 1 Ch. 1. See Vol.II, para.31–068.

506 *Killick & Co v Price & Co* (1896) 12 T.L.R. 263, 274; *Fred Drughorn Ltd v Rederiaktiebolaget Transatlantic* [1919] A.C. 203, at 209; *Epps v Rothnie* [1945] K.B. 562, 565 (cases where the description was equivocal).

507 *Siu Yin Kwan v Eastern Insurance Co Ltd* [1994] 2 A.C. 199. See also *Crescent Oil and Shipping Services Ltd v Importang UEE* [1998] 1 W.L.R. 919, 931; *Homburg Houtimport BV v Agrosin Private Ltd* [2003] UKHL 12 at [175]; *Rolls Royce Power Engineering Plc v Ricardo Consulting Engineers Ltd* [2004] EWHC 2871, [2004] 2 All E.R. (Comm) 129; *Talbot Underwriting Ltd v Nausch Hogan & Murray Inc (The Jascons)* [2006] EWCA Civ 889, [2006] 2 Lloyd's Rep. 195 at [55]–[68]; *Ferryways NV v Associated British Ports* [2008] EWHC 225 (Comm), [2008] 1 Lloyd's Rep. 638; see Vol.II, para.31–068.

508 *Schmaltz v Avery* (1851) 16 Q.B. 655; *Carr v Jackson* (1852) 7 Exch. 392; *Adams v Hall* (1877) 37 L.T. 70; *Harper v Vigers* [1909] 2 K.B. 549; *Electrosteel Castings Ltd v Scan-Trans Shipping and Chartering Sdn. Bhd.* [2002] EWHC 1993, (Comm); [2003] 1 Lloyd's Rep. 190 at [36]; cf. *Fairlie v Fenton* (1870) L.R. 5 Ex. 169; *Sharman v Brandt* (1871) L.R. 6 Q.B. 720. See Vol.II, paras 31–096, 31–097.

509 *Hill v Wilcox* (1831) 1 M. & Rob. 58; *Ewin v Lancaster* (1865) 6 B. & S. 571; *Overend Gurney & Co v Oriental Finance Co* (1874) L.R. 7 H.L. 348; *Macdonald v Whitfield* (1883) 8 App. Cas. 733; *Young v Schuler* (1883) 11 QBD 651; *Gerald McDonald & Co v Nash & Co* [1924] A.C. 625; *V.H.S. Ltd and B.K.S. Air Transport Ltd v Stephens* [1964] 1 Lloyd's Rep. 460; *Sun Alliance Pensions Life & Investments Services Ltd v Webster* [1991] 1 Lloyd's Rep. 410.

(d) *Evidence to Interpret or Explain the Written Agreement*

12–117 **Evidence in aid of interpretation.** Different considerations apply to the admissibility of extrinsic evidence to interpret or explain a written agreement.[510] Extrinsic evidence of this sort does not usurp the authority of the written document or contradict, vary, add to or subtract from its terms. It is the writing which operates. The extrinsic evidence does no more than assist in its operation by assigning a definite meaning to terms capable of such explanation or by pointing out and connecting them with the proper subject matter.[511] Accordingly, no "parol evidence rule" (in the sense referred to above) will apply to such a situation.[512] However, the nature of the evidence that may be adduced, and the purposes for which it may be used, are subject to certain restrictions imposed by the law.

12–118 **Evidence of surrounding circumstances.** The willingness of the courts to admit extrinsic evidence as an aid to the interpretation of a written contract was established as long ago as 1842 by Tindal C.J. in *Shore v Wilson*,[513] when he said:

> "The general rule I take to be, that where the words of any written instrument are free from ambiguity in themselves, and where external circumstances do not create any doubt or difficulty as to the proper application of those words to claimants under the instrument, or the subject-matter to which the instrument relates, such instrument is always to be construed according to the strict, plain, common meaning of the words themselves; and that in such case evidence *dehors* the instrument, for the purpose of explaining it according to the surmised or alleged intention of the parties to the instrument, is utterly inadmissible. . . . The true interpretation, however, of every instrument being manifestly that which will make the instrument speak the intention of the party at the time it was made, it has always been considered an exception, or perhaps, to speak more precisely, not so much an exception from, as a corollary to, the general rule above stated, that where any doubt arises upon the true sense and meaning of the words themselves, or any difficulty as to their application under the surrounding circumstances, the sense and meaning of the language may be investigated and ascertained by evidence *dehors* the instrument itself; for both reason and common sense agree that by no other means can the language of the instrument be made to speak the real mind of the party."

But under the older restrictive view expressed in this statement, and endorsed in a number of subsequent cases, extrinsic evidence is admissible only where the sense and meaning of the words of the written instrument is doubtful or difficulty arises when it is sought to apply the language of the instrument to the circumstances under consideration. If the words have a clear and fixed meaning, not capable of explanation, extrinsic evidence would not be admissible to show that

---

[510] See Law Com.No.154, 1986, Cmnd.9700, para.1.2; referred to with approval in *Youell v Bland Welch & Co Ltd* [1992] 2 Lloyd's Rep. 127, 140.

[511] *Thorpe v Brumfitt* (1873) L.R. 8 Ch. App. 650; *Johnstone v Holdway* [1963] 1 Q.B. 601; *The Shannon Ltd v Venner Ltd* [1965] Ch. 682; *Perrylease Ltd v Imecar A.G.* [1988] 1 W.L.R. 463.

[512] *Colpoys v Colpoys* (1822) Jac. 451.

[513] (1842) 9 Cl. & Fin. 355, 565.

the parties meant something different from what they have written.[514] The more modern view, however, is that the words do not have to be vague, ambiguous or otherwise uncertain before extrinsic evidence will be admitted. Since the purpose of the inquiry is to ascertain the meaning which the words would convey to a reasonable man against the background of the transaction in question, the court is free (subject to certain exceptions) to look to all the relevant circumstances surrounding the transaction, not merely in order to choose between the possible meanings of words which are ambiguous but even to conclude that the parties must, for whatever reason, have used the wrong words or syntax.[515] So the court is entitled (and, indeed, bound) to enquire beyond the language of the document and see what the circumstances were with reference to which words were used, and the object appearing from those circumstances which the person using them had in view.[516] The court must place itself in the same "factual matrix" as that

---

[514] *Bank of New Zealand v Simpson* [1900] A.C. 182, 188. See also *Blackett v Royal Exchange Co* (1832) 2 C. & J. 244; *Inglis v Buttery* (1878) 3 App.Cas. 552; *Edward Lloyd Ltd v Sturgeon Falls Pulp Co* (1901) 85 L.T. 162; *Lovell & Christmas Ltd v Wall* (1911) 104 L.T. 85; *Kinlen v Ennis* [1916] 2 Ir.R. 299; *G.W. Ry v Bristol Corp* (1918) 87 L.J.Ch. 414; *London CC v Henry Boot & Sons Ltd* [1959] 1 W.L.R. 133, 1069; *Codelfa Construction Pty Ltd v State Railway Authority of New South Wales* (1982) 149 C.L.R. 337, 352; *Shearson Lehman Hutton Inc v Maclaine Watson & Co Ltd* [1989] 2 Lloyd's Rep. 570, 591; *Hamed El Chiaty & Co v Thomas Cook Group Ltd* [1992] 2 Lloyd's Rep. 399, 407; *Adams v British Airways Plc* [1995] I.R.L.R. 577.

[515] *Mannai Investment Co Ltd v Eagle Star Life Assurance Ltd* [1997] A.C. 749, 774; *Investors Compensation Scheme Ltd v West Bromwich Building Society* [1998] 1 W.L.R. 896, 913; *Simon Container Machinery Ltd v Emba Machinery Ltd* [1998] 2 Lloyd's Rep. 429, 433; *R. (Westminster City Council) v National Asylum Support Service* [2002] UKHL 38, [2002] 1 W.L.R. 2956 at [5]; cf. *L.G. Schuler A.G. v Wickman Machine Tool Sales Ltd* [1974] A.C. 235, 261; *Zeus Tradition Marine Ltd v Bell* [1999] 1 Lloyd's Rep. 703, 706–707.

[516] *Smith v Thompson* (1849) 8 C.B. 44; *Burges v Wickham* (1863) B. & S. 669; *The Curfew* [1891] P. 131; *River Wear Commissioners v Adamson* (1877) 2 App. Cas. 743, 763; *Mackill v Wright* (1888) 14 App.Cas. 106, 114, 116, 120; *Bank of New Zealand v Simpson* [1900] A.C. 182; *Charrington & Co Ltd v Wooder* [1914] A.C. 71, 77, 80, 82; *A/S Tankexpress v Compagnie Financière Belge des Petroles SA* [1949] A.C. 76; *Prenn v Simmonds* [1971] 1 W.L.R. 1381, 1383; 1384; *Moschi v Lep Air Services Ltd* [1973] A.C. 351, 354; *Reardon Smith Line Ltd v Yngvar Hansen-Tangen* [1976] 1 W.L.R. 989, 995, 997; *Bunge v Kruse* [1977] 1 Lloyd's Rep. 492, 495, 497, 498; *Harmony Shipping Co SA v Saudi-Europe Line Ltd* [1981] 1 Lloyd's Rep. 377, 417; *Shell Tankers (UK) Ltd v Astro Comino Armadora SA* [1981] 2 Lloyd's Rep. 40, 44, 45; *Wace v Pan Atlantic Group Inc* [1981] 2 Lloyd's Rep. 339, 343; *Perrylease Ltd v Imecar A.G.* [1988] 1 W.L.R. 463, 470; *Vitol BV v Compagnie Europeenne des Petroles* [1988] 1 Lloyd's Rep. 574, 576; *Shearson Lehman Hutton Inc v Maclaine Watson & Co Ltd* [1989] 2 Lloyd's Rep. 570, 590; *Forsikringsaktieselskapet Vesta v J.N.E. Butcher, Bain Dawes Ltd* [1989] 1 Lloyd's Rep. 330, 345; *Anangel Atlas Compania Naviera SA v I.H.I. Co Ltd* [1990] 2 Lloyd's Rep. 526, 552; *Bankers Trust Co v State Bank of India* [1991] 2 Lloyd's Rep. 443, 456; *Levett v Barclays Bank* [1995] 1 W.L.R. 1260; *International Fina Services AG v Katrina Shipping Ltd* [1995] 2 Lloyd's Rep. 344, 350; *Cresspark Ltd v Wymering Mansions Ltd* [1996] E.G.C.S. 63; *Mannai Investment Co Ltd v Eagle Star Life Assurance Ltd* [1997] A.C. 749, 775; *Investors Compensation Scheme Ltd v West Bromwich Building Society* [1998] 1 W.L.R. 896, 912; *Don King Productions Ltd v Warren* [1998] 2 Lloyd's Rep. 176, 189; *Ringway Roadmarking v Adbruj* [1998] 2 B.C.L.C. 625, 643; *NLA Group Ltd v Bowers* [1999] 1 Lloyd's Rep. 109, 110; *C. Itoh & Co Ltd v Companhia de Navegacao Lloyd Brasileiro and Steamship Mutual Underwriting Association (Bermuda) Ltd* [1999] 1 Lloyd's Rep. 115, 118; *Eridania SpA v Rudolf A Oetker* [2000] 2 Lloyd's Rep. 209, 217; *Static Control Components (Europe) Ltd v Egan* [2004] EWCA 392, [2004] 2 Lloyd's Rep. 429; *UCB Corporate Services Ltd v Thomason* [2004] 2 All E.R. (Comm) 774; *Sirius International Insurance (Publ) v FAI General Insurance Ltd* [2004] UKHL 43, [2004] 1 W.L.R. 3251 at [20]; *Canmer International Inc v Mutual Steamship Assurance Association (Bermuda) Ltd* [2005] EWHC 1694, (Comm); [2005] 2 Lloyd's Rep. 49 at [22]; *Barclays Bank Plc v Kingston* [2006] EWHC 533 (QB), [2006] 2 Lloyd's Rep. 59 at [29]; *Gastronome (UK) Ltd v Anglo-Dutch Meats Ltd*

in which the parties were.[517] In *Reardon Smith Line Ltd v Yngvar Hansen-Tangen*,[518] Lord Wilberforce said:

> "No contracts are made in a vacuum; there is always a setting in which they have to be placed. The nature of what is legitimate to have regard to is usually described as 'the surrounding circumstances' but this phrase is imprecise: it can be illustrated but hardly defined. In a commercial contract it is certainly right that the court should know the commercial purpose of the contract and this in turn presupposes knowledge of the genesis of the transaction, the background, the context, the market in which the parties are operating."

He further stated[519] that, just as the intention of the parties is to be ascertained objectively, so also:

> "... when one is speaking of aim, or object, or commercial purpose, one is speaking objectively of what reasonable persons would have in mind in the situation of the parties."

12–119 On the other hand, although evidence of the facts about which the parties were negotiating is admissible to explain what meaning was intended, the court is not entitled to look at what the parties to the contract said or did whilst the matter was in negotiation[520] nor are drafts or preliminary documents admissible in aid of its

---

[2006] EWCA Civ 1233, [2006] 2 Lloyd's Rep. 587; *Bull v Nottinghamshire and City of Nottingham Fire and Rescue Authority* [2007] EWCA Civ 240, [2007] B.L.G.R. 439.

[517] *Reardon Smith Line Ltd v Yngvar Hansen-Tangen* [1976] 1 W.L.R. 989, 997; *Thoresen Car Ferries Ltd v Weymouth Portland BC* [1977] 2 Lloyd's Rep. 156; *Staffordshire A.H.A. v South Staffordshire Waterworks Co* [1978] 1 W.L.R. 1387, 1395; *Hyundai Shipbuilding & Heavy Industries Co Ltd v Pournaras* [1978] 2 Lloyd's Rep. 502, 506; *Earl of Lonsdale v Att-Gen* [1982] 1 W.L.R. 887, 900; *Gill & Duffus SA v Société pour l'Exportation des Sucres SA* [1986] 1 Lloyd's Rep. 322, 325; *Investors Compensation Scheme Ltd v West Bromwich Building Society* [1998] 1 W.L.R. 896, 912; *Galaxy Energy International Ltd v Assurance foreningen Skuld* [1999] 1 Lloyd's Rep. 249, 253; *Association of British Travel Agents Ltd v British Airways Plc* [2000] 2 Lloyd's Rep. 209, 217.

[518] [1976] 1 W.L.R. 989, 995–996.

[519] [1976] 1 W.L.R. 989, 996. See also *Hvalfangerselskapet Polaris Aktieselskap Ltd v Unilever Ltd* (1933) 39 Com.Cas. 1, 3, 19, 25; *Anangel Atlas Compania Naviera SA v I.H.I. Co Ltd* [1990] 2 Lloyd's Rep. 526, 553.

[520] *Inglis v Buttery* (1878) 3 App. Cas. 552, 558; *Leggott v Barrett* (1880) 15 ChD 306, 311; *Millbourn v Lyons* [1914] 2 Ch. 231, 240; *Davis Contractors Ltd v Fareham U.D.C.* [1956] A.C. 696; *Prenn v Simmonds* [1971] 1 W.L.R. 1381, 1385; *Moschi v Lep Air Services Ltd* [1973] A.C. 331, 354; *L.G. Schuler A.G. v Wickman Machine Tools Ltd* [1974] A.C. 235; *Arrale v Costain Civil Engineering Ltd* [1976] 1 Lloyd's Rep. 98, 101, 103, 105; *The Raven* [1980] 2 Lloyd's Rep. 266, 270; *Sudatlantica Navegacion SA v Devamar Shipping Corp* [1985] 2 Lloyd's Rep. 271, 274; *Investors Compensation Scheme Ltd v West Bromwich Building Society* [1998] 1 W.L.R. 896, 913; *Aqua Design & Play International Ltd v Kier Regional Ltd* [2002] EWCA Civ 797, [2003] B.L.R. 111; *P&S Platt Ltd v Crouch* [2003] EWCA Civ 1110, [2004] 1 P. & C.R. 18; *NBTY Europe Ltd v Nutricia International BV* [2005] EWHC 734 (Comm), [2005] 2 Lloyd's Rep. 350 at [29]–[32]; *Absalom v TCRU Ltd* [2005] EWHC 1090 (Comm), [2005] 2 Lloyd's Rep. 735 at [25]; *Beazer Homes Ltd v Stroude* [2005] EWCA Civ 265; *Dornoch Ltd v Mauritius Union Assurance Co Ltd* [2006] EWCA Civ 389, [2006] 2 Lloyd's Rep. 475 at [31]–[37]; *Chartbrook Ltd v Persimmon Homes Ltd* [2007] EWHC 409 (Ch), [2007] 1 All E.R. (Comm) 1083 (affirmed [2008] EWCA Civ 183); *Nearfield Ltd v Lincoln Nominees Ltd* [2006] EWHC 2421 (Ch), [2007] 1 All E.R. (Comm) 441. But see *Canterbury Golf International Ltd v Yoshimoto* [2001] N.Z.L.R. 523, [2002] UKPC 40 at [25]; and the observations of Lord Nicholls in *Bank of Credit and Commerce International v Ali* [2001] UKHL 8, [2002] 1 A.C. 251 at [25], and in (2005) 121 L.Q.R. 577 at 582–588; *Proforce Recruit Ltd v Rugby Group Ltd* [2006] EWCA Civ 69 at [33]–[35]; McMeel (2003) 119 L.Q.R. 272.

interpretation,[521] except where it is sought to rectify the instrument[522] or to show that the parties negotiated on an agreed basis that the words used bore a particular meaning.[523] Evidence will also not be admitted to show what were the parties' subjective intentions with respect to the words used[524]:

> "The general rule seems to be that all facts are admissible which tend to show the sense which the words bear with reference to the surrounding circumstances of and concerning which the words were used, but that such facts as only tend to show that the writer intended to use words bearing a particular sense are to be rejected."[525]

In *Prenn v Simmonds*,[526] Lord Wilberforce summed up the position as follows:

> "In my opinion, then, evidence of negotiations, or of the parties' intentions, and *a fortiori* of [the claimant's] intentions, ought not to be received, and evidence should be restricted to evidence of the factual background known to the parties at or before the date of the contract, including evidence of the 'genesis' and objectively the 'aim' of the transaction."

More difficulty may, however, be encountered in practice in determining the extent of the surrounding circumstances which may properly be admitted as an aid to interpretation. In *Investors Compensation Scheme Ltd v West Bromwich Building Society*[527] Lord Hoffmann, referring to the matrix of fact, said: 12–120

> "Subject to the requirement that it should have been reasonably available to the parties . . . it includes absolutely anything which would have affected the way in which the language of the document would have been understood by a reasonable man".[528]

---

521 *Inglis v Buttery* (1878) 3 App. Cas. 552; *National Bank of Australasia v Falkingham* [1902] A.C. 585, 591; *Youell v Bland Welch & Co Ltd* [1992] 2 Lloyd's Rep. 127. But an earlier contract may be looked at for the purpose of interpreting a later contract, although this may be of limited utility where the later contract is intended to supersede the earlier one: *HIH Casualty and General Insurance Ltd v New Hampshire Insurance Co* [2001] EWCA Civ 735, [2001] 2 Lloyd's Rep. 161 at [83]; *Electrosteel Castings Ltd v Scan-Trans Shipping* [2002] EWHC 1993 (Comm); [2003] 1 Lloyd's Rep. 190 at [198]; *Multiplex Constructions (UK) Ltd v Cleveland Bridge (UK) Ltd (No.2)* [2007] EWHC 145 (TCC), (2007) 111 Constr. L.R. 48 at [150]. Cf. *Nearfield Ltd v Lincoln Nominees Ltd* [2006] EWHC 2421 at [68]–[70].

522 See above, para.5–107.

523 *Partenreederei M.S. Karen Oltmann v Scarsdale Shipping Co Ltd* [1976] 2 Lloyd's Rep. 708, 712; *Proforce Recruit Ltd v Rugby Group Ltd* [2006] EWCA Civ 69.

524 *IRC v Raphael* [1935] A.C. 96, 142; *Prenn v Simmonds* [1971] 1 W.L.R. 1381, 1385; *Reardon Smith Line Ltd v Yngvar Hansen-Tangen* [1976] 1 W.L.R. 989, 996; *Harmony Shipping Co SA v Saudi-Europe Line Ltd* [1981] 1 Lloyd's Rep. 377, 416; *Nearfield Ltd v Lincoln Nominees Ltd* [2006] EWHC 2421 at [63]. In *Rabin v Gerson Berger Association Ltd* [1986] 1 W.L.R. 526, opinions of tax counsel given shortly before or at the time of execution of certain trust deeds were held inadmissible; cf. McMeel (2003) 119 L.Q.R. 272.

525 *Grant v Grant* (1870) L.R. 5 C.P. 727, 728; approved in *London CC v Henry Boot & Sons Ltd* [1959] 1 W.L.R. 133, 138, CA and [1959] 1 W.L.R. 1069, 1075.

526 [1971] 1 W.L.R. 1381.

527 [1998] 1 W.L.R. 896.

528 [1988] 1 W.L.R. 896, 912–913.

But, in *Scottish Power Plc v Britoil (Exploration) Ltd*[529] in the Court of Appeal, Staughton L.J. expressed doubts about this proposition and complained that often a great deal of evidence was produced under the heading of surrounding circumstances, background or factual matrix which contributed little or nothing to the understanding of the parties' contract and so increased the cost of litigation. In his view "surrounding circumstances" should be confined to what the parties had in mind, and what was going on around them at the time when they were making the contract. In a subsequent case,[530] therefore, Lord Hoffmann was at pains to point out that, in the *Investors Compensation Scheme case*:

> "I did not think it necessary to emphasise that I meant anything which a reasonable man would have regarded as *relevant*. I was merely saying that there is no conceptual limit to what can be regarded as background . . . I was certainly not encouraging a trawl through 'background' which could not have made a reasonable person think that the parties must have departed from conventional usage."

12–121 **Special meaning of words.** It has already been stated that words must be understood in their plain and ordinary sense.[531] In those cases where they are to be understood in a special sense[532] extrinsic evidence is admissible to prove that special sense. Thus evidence may be called to explain technical terms of science or art,[533] to explain contemporary meanings of the words of an ancient document[534] and to translate a document in a foreign language.[535] Extrinsic evidence is also admissible to show that words are understood by participants in a particular market to have a special meaning[536] or that they have by custom or usage a peculiar meaning.[537]

12–122 **Identity of parties.** The identity of parties may be established by extrinsic evidence where it is not clear from the written instrument to whom it refers.[538] So, where a landlord handed to his tenant a letter addressed "[d]ear Sir" in which he promised to renew a lease, extrinsic evidence was admitted to identify the

---

[529] *The Times*, December 2, 1997. See also *NLA Group Ltd v Bowers* [1999] 1 Lloyd's Rep. 109, 112.

[530] *Bank of Credit and Commerce International SA v Ali* [2001] UKHL 8, [2002] 1 A.C. 251 at [39]. See also Lord Steyn in *Mannai Investment Ltd v Eagle Star Life Assurance Co Ltd* [1997] A.C. 749, 768.

[531] See above, para.12–051.

[532] See above, paras 12–052, 12–060.

[533] *Shore v Wilson* (1842) 9 Cl. & Fin. 355, 511. See also *L.G. Schuler A.G. v Wickman Machine Tools Sales Ltd* [1974] A.C. 235, 261 ("technical expressions").

[534] *Shore v Wilson* (1842) 9 Cl. & Fin 355, 501, 527, 545, 555–556; *Earl of Lonsdale v Att-Gen* [1982] 1 W.L.R. 887.

[535] *Shore v Wilson* (1842) 9 Cl. & Fin 355, 555–556; *Di Sora v Phillips* (1863) 10 H.L.C. 624, 633, 638.

[536] *Zeus Tradition Marine Ltd v Bell* [1999] 1 Lloyd's Rep. 703, 706–707.

[537] See below, paras 12–127—12–133.

[538] *Rossiter v Miller* (1878) 3 App.Cas. 1124; *Chapman v Smith* [1907] 2 Ch. 97; *Stokes v Whicher* [1920] 1 Ch. 411. cf. *Jarrett v Hunter* (1887) 34 ChD 182; *OTV Burwelco Ltd v Technical and General Guarantee Co* [2002] EWHC 2240, (TCC); [2002] 4 All E.R. 668 at [12].

proposed lessee, even though no mention of his name appeared in the agreement.[539] Extrinsic evidence will also be admitted to show in what capacity the parties contracted, e.g. to show which party was the buyer and which the seller,[540] or to correct a misnomer.[541]

Subject matter. The subject matter of the contract may similarly be identified by extrinsic evidence.[542] Thus evidence was admitted as to the quality and quantity of wool described in the written contract as "your wool",[543] as to the identity of the property which was the subject matter of a contract of sale[544] and as to its exact area,[545] as to the items of furniture assigned by a deed to which no schedule was attached[546] and as to the liability comprehended by a guarantee.[547] Extrinsic evidence is also admissible where it is sought to restrict the generality of an obligation by reference to the circumstances or the person.[548] 12–123

Equivocations. An equivocation arises when the words of the written contract are intended to refer to one person or thing only, and in fact refer to more than one person. In such a case, if it cannot be ascertained from the document itself which was intended, extrinsic evidence is admissible to resolve the ambiguity. Direct evidence of the party's intention is this time admissible. Thus if a person buys goods "ex Peerless from Bombay", and it is shown that there are two vessels of that name sailing from the port of Bombay, the parties may give evidence to show which vessel they themselves intended.[549] Likewise in the case of a bill or note, where there are two payees of the same name, the drawer or maker may give evidence to identify the intended payee.[550] However, in *Dumford* 12–124

---

[539] *Carr v Lynch* [1900] 1 Ch. 613.

[540] *Newell v Radford* (1867) L.R. 3 C.P. 52. See also above, para.12–114 (agency).

[541] *Willis v Barrett* (1816) 2 Stark. 29; *Dermatine Co Ltd v Ashworth* (1905) 21 T.L.R. 510; *Bird & Co v Thomas Cook & Son* [1937] 2 All E.R. 227, 230–231. But contrast *Shogun Finance Ltd v Hudson* [2003] UKHL 62, [2004] 1 A.C. 919 at [49]; *Dumford Trading AG v OAO Atlantrybflot* [2005] EWCA Civ 24, [2005] 1 Lloyd's Rep. 289 at [32]. See also *Gastronome (UK) Ltd v Anglo-Dutch Meats Ltd* [2006] EWCA Civ 1233, [2006] 2 Lloyd's Rep. 587 at [16] and below, para.12–124; *Almatrans SA v Steamship Mutual Underwriting Association (Bermuda) Ltd* [2006] EWHC 2223 (Comm), [2007] 1 Lloyd's Rep. 104.

[542] *L.G. Schuler A.G. v Wickman Machine Tools Sales Ltd* [1974] A.C. 235, 261; cf. *Compagnie Noga d'Importation et d'Exportation SA v Abacha* [2003] EWCA Civ 1100, [2003] 2 All E.R. (Comm) 915.

[543] *Macdonald v Longbottom* (1860) 1 E. & E. 977, 987.

[544] *Ogilvie v Foljambe* (1817) 3 Mer. 53, 61; *Owen v Thomas* (1834) My. & K. 353; *Bleakley v Smith* (1840) 11 Sim. 150; *Cowley v Watts* (1853) 17 Jur. 172; *Wood v Scarth* (1855) 2 K. & J. 33; *Shardlow v Cotterell* (1881) 20 ChD 90; *Plant v Bourne* [1897] 2 Ch. 281; *Harewood v Retese* [1990] 1 W.L.R. 333; *Freeguard v Rogers* [1999] 1 W.L.R. 375. cf. *Doe d. Norton v Webster* (1840) 12 A. & E. 442.

[545] *Scarfe v Adams* [1981] 1 All E.R. 843.

[546] *England v Downs* (1840) 2 Beav. 522; *McCollin v Gilpin* (1881) 6 QBD 516. See also *Burges v Wickham* (1863) 3 B. & S. 669, 698; *Savory v World of Golf* [1914] 2 Ch. 566; *Auerbach v Nelson* [1919] 2 Ch. 383; *L.G. Schuler v Wickman Machine Tool Sales Ltd* [1974] A.C. 235, 261. cf. *Caddick v Skidmore* (1857) 2 De G. & J. 52.

[547] *Heffield v Meadows* (1869) L.R. 4 C.P. 595; *Perrylease Ltd v Imecar A.G.* [1988] 1 W.L.R. 463; cf. *Holmes v Mitchell* (1859) 7 C.B.N.S. 361.

[548] See above, para.12–062.

[549] *Raffles v Wichelhaus* (1864) 2 H. & C. 906.

[550] *Sweeting v Fowler* (1815) 1 Stark. 106; *Stebbing v Spicer* (1849) 8 C.B. 827.

Trading AG v OAO Atlantrybflot,[551] Rix L.J. explored the law relating to *misnomer* and suggested that where there are two possible entities intrinsic evidence would not be admissible to identify the entity referred to, but if there is only one possible entity then it would be possible to use extrinsic evidence to identify a misdescribed party.

12–125 **Patent ambiguity.** In the case of a patent ambiguity, that is to say, a defect or ambiguity appearing on the face of the document which renders the words used unintelligible or meaningless, a rule is said to exist that any reference to matter outside the document is forbidden.[552] It is doubtful, however, whether such a principle applies today in respect of written contracts, except possibly in the case of total blanks in a document,[553] although evidence will not be admitted to show what the author himself intended to say.[554] The view has been expressed that evidence is admissible to give sense to words that are meaningless, but only:

> "... within the range of meaning which the words are capable of bearing in their ordinary and natural sense having regard to the aim and purpose of the transaction."[555]

On the other hand the language employed may, of course, be so vague or contradictory as to be incurable.

12–126 **Subsequent acts.** The admissibility of evidence to show that the parties have acted upon an instrument in a particular sense is probably confined to ancient documents.[556] Evidence of user, and of acts done in pursuance of an instrument, has been admitted to explain old, or obsolete, or even imperfect expressions to be found in ancient documents.[557] Attempts were, however made to extend admissibility to cases where the document was modern and the ambiguity patent.[558] The acts and conduct of the parties under the agreement were admitted to show the sense in which the parties to it used the language they employed, and their intention in executing the instrument as revealed by their language interpreted in

---

551 [2005] EWCA Civ 24, [2005] 1 Lloyd's Rep. 289 at [32]; *Almatrans SA v Steamship Mutual Underwriting Association (Bermuda) Ltd* [2006] EWHC 2223 (Comm), [2007] 1 Lloyd's Rep. 104. Cf. *Gastronome (UK) Ltd v Anglo-Dutch Meats Ltd* [2006] EWCA Civ 1233, [2006] 2 Lloyd's Rep. 587 at [16].

552 Bacon's *Law Tracts*, p.99; *Colpoys v Colpoys* (1822) Jacob 451; *Great Western Ry v Bristol Corp* (1918) 87 L.J. Ch. 414, 429; cf. *Watcham v Att-Gen of East African Protectorate* [1919] A.C. 533 (but see below, para.12–126, fn.559).

553 *R. v Ryan* (1811) Russ. & Ry 195; *In the Goods of De Rosaz* (1877) 2 P.D. 66, 69; cf. Bills of Exchange Act 1882 s.20.

554 *Clayton v Lord Nugent* (1844) 13 M. & W. 200 (will).

555 *Zeus Tradition Marine Ltd v Bell* [1999] 1 Lloyd's Rep. 703, 707 (Colman J.).

556 *Att-Gen v Parker* (1747) 3 Atk. 576, 577; *Lord Waterpark v Fennell* (1859) 7 H.L.C. 650; *North Eastern Ry v Lord Hastings* [1900] A.C. 260, 269; *L.G. Schuler A.G. v Wickman Machine Tool Sales Ltd* [1974] A.C. 235, 261, 270 (but see at 252, 261, 269, 272, questions of title to land).

557 *Duke of Beaufort v Swansea Corp* (1849) 3 Exch. 413, 425; *Earl de la Warr v Miles* (1880) 17 ChD 535, 573; *Neill v Duke of Devonshire* (1882) 8 App.Cas. 135, 156.

558 *Doe d. Pearson v Ries* (1832) 8 Bing. 178, 184; *Chapman v Bluck* (1838) 4 Bing.N.C. 187; *Van Diemen's Land Co v Table Cape Marine Board* [1906] A.C. 92, 96, 98; *Watcham v Att-Gen of East African Protectorate* [1919] A.C. 533.

this sense.[559] The House of Lords has now decisively rejected this extension and has held that:

> "... it is not legitimate to use as an aid in the construction of the contract anything which the parties said or did after it was made."[560]

Subsequent actions are therefore inadmissible to interpret a written agreement, although there are certain exceptions to this rule: (i) where the contract is oral or partly oral[561]; (ii) where a conveyance is unclear or ambiguous with respect to the land conveyed by it[562]; (iii) to show that an agreement, or a term of an agreement, is a sham[563]; (iv) to show whether there was a contract and what the terms of the contract were[564]; (v) to show that the terms of a contract have been varied or enlarged[565]; and (vi) to found an estoppel.[566]

(e) *Evidence of Custom or Mercantile Usage*

Generally. Extrinsic evidence is also admissible to show the custom of a particular locality or the usage of a particular trade. Evidence may therefore be adduced: (1) to prove that the words of a contract are used in a peculiar sense and 12–127

---

[559] *Watcham v Att-Gen of East African Protectorate* [1919] A.C. 533, 538. The authority of this case is now extremely fragile: *Gaisberg v Storr* [1950] 1 K.B. 107, 114; *Sussex Caravan Parks Ltd v Richardson* [1961] 1 W.L.R. 561, 568; *L.G. Schuler A.G. v Wickman Machine Tool Sales Ltd* [1974] A.C. 235, 261, 272.

[560] *James Miller & Partners Ltd v Whitworth Street Estates (Manchester) Ltd* [1970] A.C. 572, 603. See also 606, 611, 614; *Prenn v Simmonds* [1971] 1 W.L.R. 1381; *English Industrial Estates Corp v George Wimpey & Co Ltd* [1973] 1 Lloyd's Rep. 118; *Trollope & Colls Ltd v N.W. Metropolitan Regional Hospital Board* [1973] 1 W.L.R. 601, 611; *L.G. Schuler A.G. v Wickman Machine Tool Sales Ltd* [1974] A.C. 235, 252, 260, 265–270, 272; *Bushwall Properties Ltd v Vortex Properties Ltd* [1976] 1 W.L.R. 591, 603; *Arrale v Costain Civil Engineering Ltd* [1976] 1 Lloyd's Rep. 98; *Harmony Shipping Co SA v Saudi-Europe Line Ltd* [1981] 1 Lloyd's Rep. 409, 416; *Haydon v Lo & Lo* [1997] 1 W.L.R. 198, 205; *Full Metal Jacket Ltd v Gowlain Building Group Ltd* [2005] EWCA Civ 1809 at [17]; *Council of the City of Sydney v Goldspar Australia Pty Ltd* [2006] FCA 472 (Australia). Contrast *Wholesale Distributors Ltd v Gibbons Holdings Ltd* [2007] N.Z. S.C. 37; *Port Sudan Cotton Co v Govindaswamy Chettiar & Sons* [1977] 2 Lloyd's Rep. 5, 11; cf. McMeel (2003) 119 L.Q.R. 272.

[561] *Carmichael v National Power Plc* [1999] 1 W.L.R. 2042, 2051; *Maggs v Marsh* [2006] EWCA Civ 1058, Build. L.R. 395.

[562] *Ali v Lane* [2007] EWCA Civ 1532, [2007] 1 P. & C.R. 26; *Haycocks v Neville* [2007] EWCA Civ 78, [2007] 12 E.G. 56.

[563] *Antoniades v Villiers* [1990] 1 A.C. 417, 475; *Bankway Properties Ltd v Pensfold-Dunsford* [2001] EWCA Civ 528, [2001] 1 W.L.R. 1369 at [44].

[564] *James Miller & Partners Ltd v Whitworth Street Estates (Manchester) Ltd* [1970] A.C. 572, 603, 615; *Schuler A.G. v Wickman Machine Tool Sales Ltd* [1974] A.C. 235, 261; *Ferguson v John Dawson & Partners (Contractors) Ltd* [1976] 1 W.L.R. 1213, 1221, 1229; *Liverpool City Council v Irwin* [1977] A.C. 239, 283; *Port Sudan Cotton Co v Govindaswamy Chettiar & Sons* [1977] 2 Lloyd's Rep. 5, 11; *Wilson v Maynard Shipbuilding Consultants AB* [1978] Q.B. 665, 675, 677; *Todd v British Midland Airways Ltd* [1978] I.C.R. 959, 964, 967; *Mears v Safecar Security Ltd* [1983] Q.B. 54, 77; *Great North Eastern Ry Ltd v Avon Insurance Plc* [2001] EWCA Civ 780, [2001] 2 Lloyd's Rep. 649 at [29].

[565] *Ferguson v John Dawson & Partners (Contractors) Ltd* [1976] 1 W.L.R. 1213; *Carmichael v National Power Plc* [1999] 1 W.L.R. 2042, 2051.

[566] *Amalgamated Investment & Property Co Ltd v Texas Commerce International Bank Ltd* [1982] 2 Q.B. 84, 119 (estoppel by convention); *Carmichael v National Power Plc* [1999] 1 W.L.R. 2042, 2051.

different from the sense which they ordinarily bear[567]; and (2) to annex incidents to the contract upon which the contract is silent.[568] The former is admitted on the ground that:

> "... the intention of the parties, though perfectly well known to themselves, would often be defeated if the language were construed according to its ordinary import in the world"[569];

the latter because the parties commonly reduce into writing the special particulars of their agreement, but omit to specify the custom or usage, which is included, however, as of course by mutual understanding: "[t]he contract in truth is partly express and in writing, partly implied or understood and unwritten".[570]

12–128 **Conflict with written instrument.** It has frequently been stated[571] that both of these principles are subject to the qualification that the peculiar sense or incident which it is proposed by the evidence to attach to the terms of the contract must not vary or contradict the terms of the written instrument. But the principle as to whether evidence is admitted to vary a written instrument is perhaps easier to state than to apply, because in a sense any such evidence varies the written agreement:

> "The contract construed without the custom will be different from what it is if construed with the custom, and in that sense every admission of custom varies the written contract."[572]

Yet in interpretation, the custom or usage is being used merely as "a dictionary to explain what words in the contract mean"[573]; in annexing incidents, it is being used to imply a term as to which the contract is silent. Perhaps the best test is still that suggested by Lord Campbell C.J.[574]:

> "To fall within the exception of repugnancy, the incident must be such as if expressed in the written contract would make it insensible or inconsistent."

Nevertheless the distinction is by no means always easy to draw in practice.[575]

---

[567] See above, paras 12–057—12–058.
[568] See below, paras 12–131, 12–133, 13–018.
[569] *Brown v Byrne* (1854) 3 E. & B. 703, 715.
[570] *Brown v Byrne* (1854) 3 E. & B. 703.
[571] See, e.g. *Yates v Pym* (1816) 6 Taunt. 446; *Roberts v Barker* (1833) 1 Cr. & M. 808; *Cockburn v Alexander* (1848) 6 C.B. 791; *Spartali v Benecke* (1850) 10 C.B. 212, 223; *Brown v Byrne* (1854) 3 E. & B. 703, 715; *Re L. Sutro & Co and Heilbut, Symons & Co* [1917] 2 K.B. 348; *Westcott v Hahn* [1918] 1 K.B. 495; *London Export Corp Ltd v Jubilee Coffee Roasting Co Ltd* [1958] 1 W.L.R. 661, 675; *Danowski v Henry Moore Foundation, The Times*, March 19, 1996. See below, para.13–023.
[572] *Produce Brokers Co Ltd v Olympia Oil and Cake Co Ltd* [1917] 1 K.B. 320, 330; *Humfrey v Dale* (1857) 7 E. & B. 266, 275.
[573] [1917] 1 K.B. 320, 330.
[574] *Humfrey v Dale* (1857) 7 E. & B. 266, 275.
[575] Contrast *Palgrave, Brown & Sons v S.S. Turid* [1922] 1 A.C. 397, with *Smith, Hogg & Co v Louis Bamberger & Sons* [1929] 1 K.B. 150.

Requirements. No custom or usage will be considered by the court on the construction of a contract, unless it is notorious, certain and reasonable[576] and does not offend against the intention of any legislative enactment.[577] The notoriety of a custom or usage is a matter to be proved in evidence; but there are certain usages, which are so well known that judicial notice will be taken of them.[578] Mere trade practice is insufficient.[579] 12–129

Custom to interpret instrument. Evidence of the custom prevailing in a particular place or locality has therefore been admitted to show that, in Suffolk, "one thousand" rabbits meant 1,200[580] and what was meant by "regular turns of loading" according to the usage of the ports of the Tyne.[581] Evidence was also held to be admissible for the purpose of proving at what time, according to the custom of the port of Liverpool, a ship chartered to that port with a cargo of timber, should be deemed to have arrived at her place of discharge within the meaning of the charterparty[582] and to show, for example, the meaning of "alongside" and "delivery",[583] "discharge"[584] or "working day"[585] at a particular port. 12–130

Custom to annex terms. Terms have also been annexed by custom,[586] one case being the "customs of the country" which relate to a tenant's rights at the end of his tenancy.[587] Evidence of these is admissible. 12–131

Usage to interpret instrument. The invariable, certain and general usage of a particular trade has frequently been admitted to interpret the terms of a written contract.[588] Thus, where a contract was in these words, "sold eighteen pockets Kent hops at 100s.", and it appeared that a pocket contained more than a hundred weight, evidence was admitted to show that by the usage of the trade a contract so worded was understood to mean £5 per cwt.[589] Where a theatrical manager contracted with an actress to engage her for "three years" at a certain salary, it was held that extrinsic evidence might be given to show that, according to the uniform usage of that profession, the claimant was to be paid only during the 12–132

---

576 *Devonald v Rosser & Sons* [1906] 2 K.B. 728, 743; *Three Rivers Trading Co v Gwinear and District Farmers* (1967) 111 S.J. 831. See also the cases cited in para.13–018, below.

577 *Daun v City of London Brewery Co* (1869) L.R. 8 Eq. 155, 161.

578 *George v Davies* [1911] 2 K.B. 445.

579 *Cunliffe-Owen v Teather and Greenwood* [1967] 1 W.L.R. 1421, 1438; *Vitol SA v Phibro Energy A.G.* [1990] 2 Lloyd's Rep. 84, 90; *Pryke v Gibbs Hartley Cooper Ltd* [1991] 1 Lloyd's Rep. 602, 615; *Sucre Exports SA v Northern Shipping Ltd* [1994] 2 Lloyd's Rep. 266.

580 *Smith v Wilson* (1832) 3 B. & Ad. 728. See above, para.12–058.

581 *Leidemann v Schultz* (1853) 14 C.B. 38.

582 *Norden S.S. Co v Dempsey* (1876) 1 C.P.D. 654.

583 *Aktieselskab Helios v Ekman* (1872) 2 QBD 83.

584 *Petersen v Freebody* [1895] 2 Q.B. 294.

585 *British and Mexican Shipping Co Ltd v Lockett Brothers & Co Ltd* [1911] 1 K.B. 264; *Reardon Smith Line Ltd v Ministry of Agriculture, Fisheries and Food* [1963] A.C. 691, 726.

586 See below, para.13–018.

587 *Hutton v Warren* (1836) 1 M. & W. 466; *Dashwood v Magniac* [1891] 3 Ch. 306.

588 See above, para.12–058.

589 *Spicer v Cooper* (1841) 1 Q.B. 424.

theatrical season of each of those years.[590] Evidence of usage has similarly been admitted to resolve ambiguities.[591]

12–133 **Usage to annex terms.** Usage has also been employed to annex terms to the contract.[592] So, where goods are sold by sample, evidence of a custom of the trade as to returning or making an allowance for such of the goods as do not answer the sample is admissible.[593] In particular, evidence may be adduced to show that where a broker sells or buys goods without disclosing his principals, he is, according to the usage of the trade, himself liable as vendor or purchaser.[594]

---

[590] *Grant v Maddox* (1846) 15 M. & W. 737. See also *Hutchinson v Bowker* (1839) 5 M. & W. 535; *Myers v Sarl* (1860) 3 E. & E. 306; *Davis v Temco* [1992] C.L.Y. 2064.

[591] *Bold v Rayner* (1836) 1 M. & W. 343.

[592] *R. v Inhabitants of Stoke-on-Trent* (1843) 8 Q.B. 303; *Syers v Jonas* (1848) 2 Exch. 111; *Re Walkers, Winser & Hamm and Shaw, Son & Co* [1904] 2 K.B. 152; *Produce Brokers Co Ltd v Olympic Oil & Cake Co Ltd* [1916] 1 A.C. 314. See below, para.13–018.

[593] *Cooke v Riddelien* (1844) 1 C. & K. 561.

[594] *Humfrey v Dale* (1858) E.B. & E. 1004; *Fleet v Murton* (1871) L.R. 7 Q.B. 126; *Hutchinson v Thatham* (1873) L.R. 8 C.P. 482; *Pike v Ongley* (1887) 18 QBD 708. Contrast *Trueman v Loder* (1840) 11 A. & E. 589; *Robinson v Mollett* (1875) L.R. 7 H.L. 802; *Miller, Gibb & Co v Smith & Tyrer* [1917] 2 K.B. 141.

Chapter 13

IMPLIED TERMS

Nature of implied terms. So far, only express terms have been discussed, that is to say, those terms which are actually recorded in a written contract or openly expressed at the time the contract is made. But there are cases in which the law implies a term in a contract although it is not expressly included therein by the parties. **13–001**

Implication of terms. The problem of the implication of terms is one which frequently arises in the law of contract. In certain instances, the parties to a contract may have been content to express only the most important terms of their agreement, leaving the remaining details to be understood. The court will then be asked to imply a term or terms to remedy the deficiency. More often, however, a subsequent disagreement reveals that there are contingencies for which the parties have not provided in their express contract. The question is then whether the court can imply a term to cover the contingency which has unexpectedly emerged. The principles that govern the implication of terms differ from those which apply to the construction of express terms.[1] Nevertheless there is a certain affinity between the two processes[2] in that, in both cases, the court is seeking to establish what the parties must be taken to have agreed having regard to the commercial purpose of the contract as a whole and the relevant background of the transaction. **13–002**

Terms implied by law. The implication of a term is a matter of law for the court,[3] and whether or not a term is implied is usually said to depend upon the intention of the parties as collected from the words of the agreement and the surrounding circumstances.[4] In many classes of contract, however, implied terms have become standardised, and it is somewhat artificial to attribute such terms to the unexpressed intention of the parties. The court is, in fact, laying down a general rule of law that in all contracts of a defined type—for example, sale of goods, landlord and tenant, employment, the carriage of goods by land or **13–003**

---

[1] See above, Ch.12.

[2] *Codelfa Construction Pty Ltd v State Railway Authority of New South Wales* (1982) 149 C.L.R. 337, 345; *South Australia Asset Management Corp v York Montague* [1997] A.C. 191, 212. cf. *Equitable Life Assurance Society v Hyman* [2002] 1 A.C. 408, 458–459. See Lord Hoffmann (1998) 56 S.A.L.J. 656, 662; Kramer [2004] Camb. L.J. 384; McMeel, *The Construction of Contracts* (2007), p.226.

[3] *Re Comptoir Commercial Anversois and Power, Son & Co* [1920] 1 K.B. 868, 899; *O'Brien v Associated Fire Alarms Ltd* [1968] 1 W.L.R. 1916, 1923, 1925.

[4] *Insurance Co of Africa v Scor (UK) Reinsurance Co Ltd* [1983] 1 Lloyd's Rep. 551, 558; *Equitable Life Assurance Socy. v Hyman* [2002] 1 A.C. 408.

sea—certain terms will be implied, unless the implication of such a term would be contrary to the express words of the agreement.[5] Such implications do not depend on the intentions of the parties, actual or presumed, but on more general considerations.[6]

13–004 **Intention of parties.** In many cases, however, one or other of the parties will seek to imply a term from the wording of a particular contract and the facts and circumstances surrounding it. The court will be prepared to imply a term if there arises from the language of the contract itself, and the circumstances under which it is entered into, an inference that the parties must have intended the stipulation in question.[7] An implication of this nature may be made in two situations: first, where it is necessary to give business efficacy to the contract, and, secondly, where the term implied represents the obvious, but unexpressed, intention of the parties. These two criteria often overlap[8] and, in many cases, have been applied cumulatively,[9] although it is submitted that they are, in fact, alternative grounds.[10] Both, however, depend on the presumed common intention of the parties. Such intention is, in general, to be ascertained objectively and is not dependent on proof of the actual intention of the parties at the time of contracting.

[5] cf. *Johnstone v Bloomsbury H.A.* [1992] Q.B. 333; *Yarm Road Ltd v Hewdon Tower Cranes Ltd* [2002] EWHC 2265, (2002) 85 Const. L.R. 142.

[6] *Lister v Romford Ice and Cold Storage Co Ltd* [1957] A.C. 555, 576, 579, 594; *Greaves & Co (Contractors) Ltd v Baynham Meikle and Partners* [1975] 1 W.L.R. 1095, 1099, 1100; *Shell UK Ltd v Lostock Garage Ltd* [1976] 1 W.L.R. 1187, 1196; *Liverpool City Council v Irwin* [1977] A.C. 239, 255, 258; *Scally v Southern Health and Social Services Board* [1992] 1 A.C. 294, 307; *Spring v Guardian Assurance Plc* [1995] 2 A.C. 296, 320, 340, 353; *Ali Shipping Corp v Shipyard Trogir* [1998] 1 Lloyd's Rep. 643, 651; *Mahmud v Bank of Credit and Commerce International SA* [1998] A.C. 20, 34, 45; *Equitable Life Assurance Socy. v Hyman* [2002] 1 A.C. 408, 458, 459. Contrast *National Bank of Greece SA v Pinios Shipping Co* [1990] 1 A.C. 637; *Reid v Rush & Tompkins Group Plc* [1990] 1 W.L.R. 212, 233; *Industrie Chimiche Italia Centrale and Cerealfin SA v Alexander G. Tsavliris & Sons Maritime Co* [1990] 1 Lloyd's Rep. 517, 526; *Ashmore v Corp of Lloyd's (No.2)* [1992] 2 Lloyd's Rep. 620, 631 (one-off or sui generis contracts).

[7] *Hamlyn & Co v Wood & Co* [1891] 2 Q.B. 488, 494.

[8] See, e.g. *Alpha Trading Ltd v Dunnshaw-Patten Ltd* [1981] 1 Lloyd's Rep. 122, 128, 131.

[9] e.g. by Scrutton L.J. in *Reigate v Union Manufacturing Co (Ramsbottom) Ltd* [1918] 1 K.B. 592, 598, by Lord Tucker in *Lister v Romford Ice and Cold Storage Co Ltd* [1957] A.C. 555, 594, and by Lord Cross in *Liverpool City Council v Irwin* [1977] A.C. 239, 258. See also *B.P. Refinery (Westenport) Pty Ltd v Shire of Hastings* (1977) 52 A.L.J.R. 20, 26, PC; *Codelfa Construction Pty Ltd v State Ry Authority of New South Wales* (1982) 149 C.L.R. 337, 347; *Byrne v Australian Airlines Ltd* (1995) 185 C.L.R. 410, 422, 441; *Phillips Electronique Grand Public SA v British Sky Broadcasting Ltd* [1995] EMLR 472, 480, 482; *Association of British Travel Agents Ltd v British Airways Plc* [2001] 1 Lloyd's Rep. 169, 175, [2000] 2 Lloyd's Rep. 209, 219.

[10] *Mosvolds Rederi A/S v Food Corp of India* [1986] 2 Lloyd's Rep. 68; *Associated Japanese Bank (International) Ltd v Crédit du Nord SA* [1989] 1 W.L.R. 255, 263; *Barclays Bank Plc v Taylor* [1989] 1 W.L.R. 1066, 1076; *Marcan Shipping (London) Ltd v Polish S.S. Co* [1989] 2 Lloyd's Rep. 138, 144; *Lauritzen (J.) A/S v Wijsmuller B.V* [1990] 1 Lloyd's Rep. 1, 6; *Industrie Chimiche Italia Centrale and Cerealfin SA v Alexander Tsavliris & Sons Maritime Co* (*The Choko Star*) [1990] 1 Lloyd's Rep. 517, 524, 526; *Ashmore v Corp of Lloyds (No.2)* [1992] 2 Lloyd's Rep. 620, 627; *C. Itoh & Co Ltd v Compania de Navegacao Lloyd Brasileiro and S.S. Mutual Underwriting Association (Bermuda) Ltd* [1999] 1 Lloyd's Rep. 115, 120–121; *Modahl v British Athletic Federation Ltd* [2001] EWCA Civ 1447, [2002] 1 W.L.R. 1192 at [119].

Efficacy to contract. A term will be implied if it is necessary, in the business sense, to give efficacy to the contract. The general principle of law was thus stated by Bowen L.J. in *The Moorcock*[11]: 13–005

> "Now, an implied warranty, or, as it is called, a covenant in law, as distinguished from an express contract or express warranty, really is in all cases founded upon the presumed intention of the parties, and upon reason. The implication which the law draws from what must obviously have been the intention of the parties, the law draws with the object of giving efficacy to the transaction and preventing such a failure of consideration as cannot have been within the contemplation of either side; and I believe if one were to take all the cases, and there are many, of implied warranties or covenants in law, it will be found that in all of them the law is raising an implication from the presumed intention of the parties with the object of giving to the transaction such efficacy as both parties must have intended that at all events it should have."

In this situation, although there is an apparently complete bargain, the courts are willing to add a term on the ground that without it the contract will not work.[12]

The principle laid down in *The Moorcock* has been approved and applied many times. For example, a term has been implied into a contract for the use of a wharf that it was safe for a ship to lie at the wharf[13]; into a contract for a Turkish bath that the couches for reclining on were free from vermin[14]; into a charterparty that the charterer would not order the ship to proceed to a port impossible of access[15] and would indemnify the shipowner against loss incurred in complying with the charterer's orders[16]; into a contract of bailment, the purpose of which was the use of the goods by the bailee, an authority to do in relation to the goods all things reasonably incidental to their reasonable use[17]; into a contract for the printing of banknotes that the plates should not be allowed to get into the hands of unauthorised persons[18]; into a father's contract to pay such school bills of his son as should be approved by him, that such consent should not be unreasonably withheld[19]; into a contract between a "pop group" and their personal manager, that the latter would not do anything which he could reasonably foresee would destroy the mutual confidence which was required to exist between them[20]; into a contract to provide a package holiday that reasonable care and skill would be used in rendering the services which the tour operator had contracted to provide, 13–006

---

[11] (1889) 14 P.D. 64, 68.

[12] *Liverpool City Council v Irwin* [1977] A.C. 239, 254, 262; *Tai Hing Cotton Mill Ltd v Liu Chong Hing Bank Ltd* [1986] A.C. 80, 106; *CEL Group Ltd v Nedlloyd Lines UK Ltd* [2003] EWCA Civ 1716, [2004] 1 Lloyd's Rep. 381 at [20]–[21]; *Concord Trust v Law Debenture Trust Corp Plc* [2005] UKHL 27, [2005] 1 W.L.R. 1591 at [37].

[13] *The Moorcock* (1889) 14 P.D. 64.

[14] *Silverman v Imperial London Hotels Ltd* (1927) 137 L.T. 57.

[15] *Aktieselskabet Olivebank v Dansk Svolsyre Fabrik* [1919] 2 K.B. 162. Contrast *Eurico Spa v Philipp Brothers* [1987] 2 Lloyd's Rep. 215.

[16] *Triad Shipping Co v Stellar Chartering & Brokerage Inc* [1994] 2 Lloyd's Rep. 227.

[17] *Tappenden v Artus* [1964] 2 Q.B. 185.

[18] *Banco de Portugal v Waterlow & Sons Ltd* [1932] A.C. 452.

[19] *Addison v Brown* [1954] 1 W.L.R. 779.

[20] *Page One Records Ltd v Britton* [1968] 1 W.L.R. 157; *Denmark Productions Ltd v Boscobel Productions Ltd* [1969] 1 Q.B. 699.

whether these were carried out by the tour organiser or others[21]; into a contract for driving lessons that the vehicle provided would be covered by insurance[22]; into a contract of agency that the principal would not deprive the agent of his commission by committing a breach of the contract between himself and a purchaser which released the purchaser from his obligation to pay the purchase price[23]; into insurance contracts between underwriters and insureds that documents previously shown to the underwriters by the insureds' brokers, and in the possession of the brokers, should be made available to the underwriters[24]; into a contract between architects and a construction company that the architects would carry out their design work in such time as would enable the company to complete its contract with its client[25]; into a towage contract that the tug would proceed with all reasonable despatch[26]; and into a contract of sale of goods, where defective goods had been returned to the seller for repair, that the seller would inform the buyer of the nature of the defect and what had been done to repair it.[27]

13–007 **Obvious inference from agreement.** A term which has not been expressed may also be implied if it was so obviously a stipulation in the agreement that the parties must have intended it to form part of their contract.[28]

> "Prima facie that which in any contract is left to be implied and need not be expressed is something so obvious that it goes without saying; so that, if while the parties were making their bargain, an officious bystander were to suggest some express provision for it in the agreement, they would testily suppress him with a common, 'oh, of course'."[29]

---

[21] *Wong Mee Wan v Kwan Kin Travel Services* [1996] 1 W.L.R. 38; see also below, para.13–034.

[22] *British School of Motoring Ltd v Simms* [1971] 1 All E.R. 317.

[23] *Alpha Trading Ltd v Dunnshaw-Patten Ltd* [1981] 1 Lloyd's Rep. 122. But see *Marcan Shipping (London) Ltd v Polish Steamship Co* [1989] 2 Lloyd's Rep. 138, and Vol.II, para.31–148.

[24] *Goshawk Dedicated Ltd v Tyser & Co Ltd* [2006] EWCA Civ 54, [2006] 1 Lloyd's Rep. 566.

[25] *CFW Architects v Cowlin Construction Ltd* [2006] EWHC 6 (TCC), (2006) 105 Const. L.R. 116.

[26] *Ease Faith Ltd v Leonis Marine Management Ltd* [2006] EWHC 232, [2006] 1 Lloyd's Rep. 673.

[27] *J C Ritchie Ltd v Lloyd Ltd* [2006] UKHL 9, [2007] 1 W.L.R. 670 at [37].

[28] *Reigate v Union Manufacturing Co (Ramsbottom) Ltd* [1918] 1 K.B. 592, 605; *Weg Motors Ltd v Hales* [1961] Ch. 176, 192; *Bronester Ltd v Priddle* [1961] 1 W.L.R. 1294, 1304; *Hongkong Fir Shipping Co Ltd v Kawasaki Kisen Kaisha Ltd* [1962] 2 Q.B. 26, 69; *Gardiner v Moore* [1969] 1 Q.B. 55, 61; *Alpha Trading Ltd v Dunnshaw-Patten Ltd* [1981] 1 Lloyd's Rep. 122, 128; *K/S Stamar v Seabow Shipping Ltd* [1994] 2 Lloyd's Rep. 183, 191; *Fletamentos Maritimos SA v Effjohn International BV* [1995] 1 Lloyd's Rep. 311, 345; *Cargill International SA v Bangladesh Sugar & Food Industries Corp.* [1996] 2 Lloyd's Rep. 524, 531 (affirmed [1998] 1 W.L.R. 461); *C. Itoh & Co Ltd v Companhia de Navegacao Lloyd Brasileiro and Steamship Mutual Underwriting Association (Bermuda) Ltd* [1999] 1 Lloyd's Rep. 115, 120; *Weldon v GRE Linked Life Assurance Ltd* [2002] 2 All E.R. (Comm) 914, 919; *Modahl v British Athletic Federation Ltd* [2001] EWCA Civ 1447, [2002] 1 W.L.R. 1192 at [119]; *Paragon Finance Plc v Nash* [2001] EWCA Civ 1466, [2002] 1 W.L.R. 685 at [36].

[29] *Shirlaw v Southern Foundries (1926) Ltd* [1939] 2 K.B. 206, 227 (affirmed [1940] A.C. 701). This test was criticised by Lord Hoffmann in (1998) 56 S.A.L.J. 656, 662. For a different test, see *William Morton & Co v Muir Bros & Co* (1907) S.C. 1211, 1224; *JH Ritchie Ltd v Lloyd Ltd* [2007] UKHL 9, [2007] 1 W.L.R. 670 at [14], [18].

A term will not, however, thus be implied unless the court is satisfied that *both* parties would, as reasonable men, have agreed to it had it been suggested to them.[30] The knowledge or ignorance of each party of the matter to be implied, or of the facts on which the implication is based, is therefore a relevant factor.[31] Further, since:

> "... the general presumption is that the parties have expressed every material term which they intended should govern their contract, whether oral or in writing,"[32]

the court will only imply a term if it is one which must necessarily have been intended by them,[33] and in particular will be reluctant to make any implication "where the parties have entered into a carefully drafted written contract containing detailed terms agreed between them".[34]

Incomplete contract. There is yet another situation where a term may be implied. This is where the court is simply concerned to establish what the contract is, the parties not having themselves fully stated the terms: "[i]n this sense the court is searching for what must be implied".[35] In *Liverpool City Council v Irwin*[36] the contract by which dwelling units in a Council block were let to tenants consisted of "conditions of tenancy" which imposed obligations upon the tenants, but which were silent as to the contractual obligations of the landlord. The House of Lords implied an obligation on the part of the landlord to take reasonable care to keep the essential means of access and other communal 13–008

[30] *Luxor (Eastbourne) Ltd v Cooper*; [1941] A.C. 108; *Attica Sea Carriers Corp v Ferrostaal Poseidon Bulk Rederei GmbH* [1976] 1 Lloyd's Rep. 250; *Liverpool City Council v Irwin* [1977] A.C. 239, 258, 266; *Federal Commerce and Navigation Co Ltd v Tradax Export SA* [1977] 1 Lloyd's Rep. 217, 229 (affirmed [1977] 2 Lloyd's Rep. 301, 309); *Frobisher (Second Investments) Ltd v Kiloran Trust Co Ltd* [1980] 1 W.L.R. 425. cf. the misgivings felt by May L.J. in *Marcan Shipping (London) Ltd v Polish S.S. Co* [1989] 2 Lloyd's Rep. 138, 142.

[31] *The Moorcock* (1889) 14 P.D. 64, 68; *Partabmull Rameshwar v K.C. Sethia (1944) Ltd* [1950] 1 All E.R. 55 (affirmed [1951] 2 All E.R. 352n); *Spring v National Amalgamated Stevedores and Dockers Socy.* [1956] 1 W.L.R. 585; *Compagnie Algerienne de Meunerie v Katana Societa di Navigatione Marittima SpA* [1960] 2 Q.B. 115; *Jamil Line for Trading and Shipping Ltd v Atlanta Handelsgesellschaft Harder & Co* [1982] 1 Lloyd's Rep. 481.

[32] *Luxor (Eastbourne) Ltd v Cooper* [1941] A.C. 108, 137; *Kelly v Battershell* [1949] 2 All E.R. 830.

[33] *L. French & Co v Leeston Shipping Co* [1922] 1 A.C. 451, 455; *Trollope & Colls Ltd v N.W. Metropolitan Regional Hospital Board* [1973] 1 W.L.R. 601, 609; *Liverpool City Council v Irwin* [1977] A.C. 239; *Federal Commerce and Navigation Co Ltd v Tradax Export SA* [1977] 1 Lloyd's Rep. 217, 228–229 (affirmed [1977] 2 Lloyd's Rep. 301, 309); *Equitable Life Assurance Socy. v Hyman* [2002] 1 A.C. 408; *Clarion Ltd v National Provident Institution* [2000] 2 All E.R. 265; *Ennstone Building Products Ltd v Stanger Ltd* [2002] EWCA Civ 916, [2002] 1 W.L.R. 3059 at [33].

[34] *Jones v St John's College, Oxford* (1970) L.R. 6 Q.B. 115, 126; *Lynch v Thorne* [1956] 1 W.L.R. 303; *Shell UK Ltd v Lostock Garage Ltd* [1976] 1 W.L.R. 1187, 1200; *Codelfa Construction Pty Ltd v State Railway Authority of New South Wales* (1982) 149 C.L.R. 337, 346; *J. Lauritzen A/S v Wijsmuller B.V* [1990] 1 Lloyd's Rep. 1, 6; *Flamar Interocean Ltd v Denmac Ltd* [1990] 1 Lloyd's Rep. 434, 437; *Bedfordshire CC v Fitzpatrick Contractors Ltd* (1998) 62 Const. L.R. 64, 71; *Times Newspapers Ltd v George Weidenfeld & Nicolson Ltd* [2002] F.S.R. 29.

[35] *Liverpool City Council v Irwin* [1977] A.C. 239, 254.

[36] [1977] A.C. 239.

facilities in reasonable repair. In *Sim v Rotherham Metropolitan BC*[37] the contracts under which secondary school teachers were employed were in general silent as to the extent of the teachers' obligations as teachers. The court implied an obligation on their part to cover for absent colleagues during non-teaching periods if requested to do so. And in *Scally v Southern Health and Social Services Board*[38] contracts of employment of public health service employees contained a term, derived from a collective agreement reached between representatives of the employers and of the employees, whereby a valuable pension benefit was conferred upon an employee contingent upon action being taken by him to avail himself of the benefit. An employee could not, in all the circumstances, reasonably be expected to be aware of the term unless it was drawn to his attention. The House of Lords implied an obligation on the employer to take reasonable steps to bring the term in question to the employee's attention so that he might be in a position to enjoy the benefit. In this type of case, the implication does not appear so much to depend on the intentions of the parties, but resembles more closely an implication of law,[39] since the term is implied as a "legal incident"[40] of a definable category of contract, though only where certain circumstances exist.

13–009 **Where term not implied.** A term ought not to be implied unless it is in all the circumstances equitable and reasonable.[41] But this does not mean that a term will be implied merely because in all the circumstances it would be reasonable to do so[42] or because it would improve the contract[43] or make its carrying out more convenient[44]: "[t]he touchstone is always *necessity* and not merely *reasonableness*".[45] The term to be implied must also be capable of being formulated with

---

[37] [1987] Ch. 216. cf. *Bull v Nottinghamshire and City of Nottingham Fire and Rescue Authority* [2007] EWCA Civ 240, [2007] B.L.G.R. 439 (firefighters' contracts).

[38] [1992] 1 A.C. 294. cf. *University of Nottingham v Evett* [1999] 1 W.L.R. 594; *Crossley v Faithful & Gould Holdings Ltd* [2004] EWHC Civ 293, [2004] I.R.L.R. 377; and see para.1–032, above; Vol. II, para.39–144.

[39] But it is still subject to the test of necessity; *Liverpool City Council v Irwin* [1977] A.C. 239, 254, 262, 266; *Scally v Southern Health and Social Services Board* [1992] 1 A.C. 294.

[40] *Liverpool City Council v Irwin* [1977] A.C. 239, 255, 270.

[41] *Young & Marten v McManus Childs Ltd* [1969] 1 A.C. 454, 465; *Liverpool City Council v Irwin* [1977] A.C. 239, 262; *BP Refinery (Westenport) Pty Ltd v Shire of Hastings* (1977) 52 A.L.J.R. 20, 26, PC. But the Unfair Terms in Consumer Contracts Regulations 1999 (see Ch.15) do not apply to implied terms: *Baybut v Eccle Riggs Country Park Ltd, The Times*, November 13, 2006.

[42] *Hamlyn & Co v Wood & Co* [1891] 2 Q.B. 488, 491; *Reigate v Union Manufacturing Co (Ramsbottom) Ltd* [1918] 1 K.B. 592, 598; *Re Comptoir Commercial Anversois v Power, Son and Co* [1920] 1 K.B. 868, 899; *George Trollope & Son v Martyn Bros* [1934] 2 K.B. 437, 443; *R. v Paddington and St Marylebone Rent Tribunal* [1947] K.B. 984, 990; *British Movietonews v London and District Cinemas Ltd* [1952] A.C. 166; *Bundar Property Holdings Ltd v J. S. Darwen (Successors) Ltd* [1968] 2 All E.R. 305; *Lupton v Potts* [1969] 1 W.L.R. 1749; *Trollope & Colls Ltd v N.W. Metropolitan Regional Hospital Board* [1973] 1 W.L.R. 601; *Liverpool City Council v Irwin* [1977] A.C. 239; *Duke of Westminster v Guild* [1985] Q.B. 688; *Holding and Management (Solitaire) Ltd v Ideal Homes Northwest Ltd* [2004] EWHC 2408, [2004] Const. L.R. 114.

[43] *Trollope & Colls Ltd v N.W. Metropolitan Regional Hospital Board* [1973] 1 W.L.R. 601, 609; *Express Newspapers v Silverstone Circuits, The Independent*, June 16, 1989 CA.

[44] *Russell v Duke of Norfolk* [1949] 1 All E.R. 109.

[45] *Liverpool City Council v Irwin* [1977] A.C. 239, 266; *BP Refinery (Westenport) Pty Ltd v Shire of Hastings* (1977) 52 A.L.J.R. 20, 26; *Harmony Shipping Co SA v Saudi Europe Line Ltd* [1980] 1 Lloyd's Rep. 44; *Tai Hing Cotton Mill Ltd v Liu Chong Hing Bank Ltd* [1986] A.C. 80, 104; *Scally v Southern Health and Social Services Board* [1992] 1 A.C. 294; *Bedfordshire CC v Fitzpatrick*

sufficient clarity and precision.[46] But it may be that lack of precision in the criterion to be embodied in the term is not fatal to any implication, since:

> "... it is no novelty in the common law to find that a criterion on which some important question of liability is to depend can only be defined in imprecise terms which leave a difficult question for decision as to how the criterion applies to the facts of a particular case."[47]

A term will not be implied if it would be inconsistent with the express wording of the contract.[48]

No term was implied into a contract of employment that the employee was to be paid overtime for excess hours worked[49] or that he was not to be paid during absence owing to illness[50]; into a contract for the hire of a private detective that employees of the detective agency would not divulge confidential information[51]; into a contract for the sale and purchase of all grains manufactured over a certain period that the seller would retain his business[52]; into a contract of employment that the employer would take reasonable care to ensure that his employee's effects were not stolen[53] or that he would insure the employee when abroad against accidental injury or advise the employee to obtain such insurance for himself[54]; or that he would take reasonable care of the employee's economic 13–010

Contractors Ltd (1998) 62 Const. L.R. 64, 71; *Mousaka Inc v Golden Seagull Maritime Inc* [2002] 1 Lloyd's Rep. 797, 802. But in *Crossley v Faithful & Gould Holdings Ltd* [2004] EWCA Civ 293, [2004] I.R.L.R. 377, Morritt V.C. expressed the view that, in the case of a contract of employment, it was better to focus on questions of reasonableness, fairness and the balance of competing policy considerations rather than on the elusive concept of "necessity".

46 *Shell UK Ltd v Lostock Garage Ltd* [1976] 1 W.L.R. 1187, 1197, 1201. See also *R. v Paddington and St Marylebone Rent Tribunal* [1947] K.B. 984, 990; *Lister v Romford Ice and Cold Storage Co Ltd* [1957] A.C. 555, 574; *Trollope & Colls Ltd v N.W. Metropolitan Regional Hospital Board* [1973] 1 W.L.R. 601, 610, 614; *BP Refinery (Westenport) Pty Ltd v Shire of Hastings* (1978) 52 A.J.L.R. 20, 26; *Terkol Rederierne v Petroleo Brasilero SA* [1985] 1 Lloyd's Rep. 395, 401; *Ashmore v Corporation of Lloyds (No.2)* [1992] 2 Lloyd's Rep. 620, 628; *WX Investments Ltd v Begg* [2002] EWHC (Ch), [2002] 1 W.L.R. 2849 at [29]; *Armitage v Staveley Industries Plc* [2004] EWHC 2320, [2004] Pens L.R. 385; *Socimer International Bank Ltd v Standard Bank London Ltd* [2008] EWCA Civ 116, [2008] 1 Lloyd's Rep. 558 at [105], [110].

47 *Shell UK Ltd v Lostock Garage Ltd* [1976] 1 W.L.R. 1187, 1204.

48 *BP Refinery (Westenport) Pty Ltd v Shire of Hastings* (1977) 52 A.J.L.R. 20, 26; *Duke of Westminster v Guild* [1985] Q.B. 688, 700; *Eurico Spa v Philipp Brothers* [1987] 2 Lloyd's Rep. 215, 219; *Gyllenhammar & Partners International Ltd v Sour Brodogradevna Industrija* [1989] 2 Lloyd's Rep. 403, 415; *Yorkshire Water Services Ltd v Sun Alliance & London Insurance Plc* [1997] 2 Lloyd's Rep. 21, 33; *Fast Ferries One SA v Ferries Australia Pty Ltd* [2000] 1 Lloyd's Rep. 534, 541; *Times Newspapers Ltd v George Weidenfeld & Nicolson Ltd* [2002] F.S.R. 29; *WX Investments Ltd v Begg* [2002] EWHC 925 at [28]. *Hadley Design Associates Ltd v Westminster City Council* [2003] EWHC 1617, [2004] T.C.L.R. 1; *Fairfax Gerrard Holdings Ltd v Capital Bank Plc* [2006] EWHC 3439 (Comm), [2007] 1 Lloyd's Rep. 171; *Wootton Trucks Ltd v Man ERF UK Ltd* [2006] EWCA Civ 1042, [2006] Eu. L.R. 1217.

49 *Ali v Christian Salvesen Food Services Ltd* [1997] 1 All E.R. 721.

50 *Orman v Saville Sportswear Ltd* [1960] 1 W.L.R. 1055.

51 *Easton v Hitchcock* [1912] 1 K.B. 535.

52 *Hamlyn & Co v Wood* [1891] 2 Q.B. 488. See also *Rhodes v Forwood* (1876) 1 App. Cas. 256; But see Vol.II, para.31–148.

53 *Deyong v Shenburn* [1946] K.B. 277; *Edwards v West Herts Group Hospital Committee* [1957] 1 W.L.R. 415.

54 *Reid v Rush & Tompkins Group Plc* [1990] 1 W.L.R. 212; cf. Employers' Liability (Compulsory Insurance) Act 1969; Vol.II, paras 39–101, 41–097.

well-being by advising him of the financial consequences under an insurance scheme of his early retirement[55]; into a contract for the sale of a patent to a company that the company would keep the patent alive[56]; into a contract for the exchange of two incomplete housing estates that the building work was of good quality[57]; into a contract for the building of a school that the builder should have uninterrupted possession of, and access to, the site[58]; into a lease that the lessor would keep a drain in repair[59]; into a contract for the services of a handwriting expert that he should not voluntarily give assistance to the other side[60]; into a voyage charterparty that the charterers would indemnify the shipowners against claims made by the cargo-owners[61]; into a contract for the carriage of goods by sea that the master was authorised to contract on behalf of the cargo-owners with third parties other than as agent of necessity[62]; into a contract between banker and customer that the customer would take reasonable precautions in his business to prevent forgeries by his employees[63] or that the banker would advise the customer of a new type of interest-bearing account[64]; into a debenture that the debenture holder could appoint a receiver if his security was in jeopardy[65]; into a contract of insurance that the insurers would indemnify the insured in respect of expenditure incurred by him in preventing or minimising a loss which might fall to them under the policy[66]; into a contract between insurers and the assignee of the policy to inform him that the insured was dishonestly jeopardising the cover provided by the insurers[67]; into a contract between insurers and a reinsurer that they could recover a pro rata share of their costs of investigating, settling or defending claims on the underlying policies[68]; into a non-proportional insurance contract that the reinsured would act "prudently" or "reasonable carefully"[69]; into an agreement to submit disputes to arbitration that the claimant would proceed with the arbitration without undue delay[70]; into a contract of employment of a schoolmaster that he was required to occupy a house for the better performance of his duties as such[71]; into a highway maintenance contract that the contractor would not conduct itself in a manner calculated or likely to destroy or seriously damage the relationship of confidence and trust that existed between

[55] *Crossley v Faithful & Gould Holdings Ltd* [2004] EWCA Civ 293, [2004] I.R.L.R. 377.
[56] *Re Railway and Electric Appliances Co* (1888) 38 Ch D 597.
[57] *Barratt Southampton Ltd v Fairclough Building Ltd* (1988) 27 Const.L.R. 623.
[58] *Porter v Tottenham U.D.C.* [1915] 1 K.B. 776.
[59] *Duke of Westminster v Guild* [1985] Q.B. 688.
[60] *Harmony Shipping Co SA v Saudi Europe Line Ltd* [1980] 1 Lloyd's Rep. 44.
[61] *Ben Shipping Co (Pte) Ltd v An-Board Bainne* [1986] 2 Lloyd's Rep. 285.
[62] *Industrie Chimiche Italia Centrale and Cerealfin SA v Alexander G. Tsavliris & Sons Maritime Co* [1990] 1 W.L.R. 576.
[63] *Tai Hing Cotton Mill Ltd v Liu Chong Hing Bank Ltd* [1986] A.C. 80.
[64] *Suriya & Douglas v Midland Bank Plc*, *The Times*, March 29, 1999.
[65] *Cryne v Barclays Bank* [1987] B.C.L.C. 548, CA.
[66] *Yorkshire Water Services Ltd v Sun Alliance and London Insurance Plc* [1997] 2 Lloyd's Rep. 21.
[67] *Bank of Nova Scotia v Hellenic Mutual War Risks Association (Bermuda) Ltd* [1990] 1 Q.B. 818 (reversed on other grounds [1992] 1 A.C. 283).
[68] *Baker v Black Sea & Baltic General Insurance Co Ltd* [1998] 1 W.L.R. 974.
[69] *Bonner v Cox* [2005] EWCA Civ 1512, [2006] 2 Lloyd's Rep. 152.
[70] *Bremer Vulkan Schiffbau und Maschinenfabrik v South India Shipping Corp Ltd* [1981] A.C. 909.
[71] *Hughes v Greenwich LBC* [1994] 1 A.C. 170.

itself and the employer[72]; into a contract which provided for the obtaining of counsel's opinion that the opinion would only be valid if given on the basis of true facts or proper instructions[73]; into an exclusive purchasing agreement that the seller would not act in a way that was prejudicial to the buyer by selling directly to customers[74]; into an option agreement that payment had to be made within the original option period[75]; into a construction sub-contract that the sub-contractor would execute the works with such diligence and expedition as was reasonably required to meet the dates of the programme[76]; and into an estate agent's contract a term that the agent was entitled to commission only if he was the effective cause of the sale.[77]

Co-operation. The court may be willing to imply a term that the parties shall co-operate to ensure the performance of their bargain.[78] Thus: 13–011

> "... where in a written contract it appears that both parties have agreed that something shall be done, which cannot effectively be done unless both concur in doing it, the construction of the contract is that each agrees to do all that is necessary to be done on his part for the carrying out of that thing, though there may be no express words to that effect."[79]

However, the conditions for the implication of a term mentioned above must be satisfied.[80] Also the duty to co-operate and the degree of co-operation required is to be determined, not by what is reasonable, but by the obligations imposed-

---

[72] *Bedfordshire CC v Fitzpatrick Contractors Ltd* (1998) 62 Const. L.R. 64, 72 (but see Vol.II, para.39–143, on contracts of employment).

[73] *Interleasing (UK) Ltd v Morris* [2002] EWHC 1086 (Ch).

[74] *Ultraframe (UK) Ltd v Tailored Roofing System Ltd* [2004] EWCA Civ 585, [2004] 2 All E.R. (Comm) 692.

[75] *Rennie v Westbury Homes (Holdings) Ltd* [2007] EWHC 164, [2007] N.P.C. 18.

[76] *Multiplex Constructions UC Ltd v Cleveland Bridge UK Ltd* [2006] EWHC 1341 (TCC), (2006) 107 Const. L.R.1.

[77] *Dashwood v Fleurets Ltd* [2007] EWHC 1610 (QB), [2007] 34 E.G. 84.

[78] See Bateson [1960] J.B.L. 187; Burrows (1968) 31 M.L.R. 390, 402; Peden (2000) 15 J.C.L. 56.

[79] *Mackay v Dick* (1881) 6 App. Cas. 251, 263. See also *Hunt v Bishop* (1853) 8 Exch. 675; *Roberts v Bury Commissioners* (1870) L.R. 5 C.P. 310, 325; *Nelson v Dahl* (1879) 12 Ch D 568, 592 (affirmed (1881) 6 App. Cas. 38); *Sprague v Booth* [1909] A.C. 576, 580; *Kleinert v Abosso Gold Mining Co* (1913) 58 S.J. (PC) 45; *Harrison v Walker* [1919] 2 K.B. 453; *Colley v Overseas Exporters* [1921] 3 K.B. 302, 309; *Panamena Europa Navegacion v Frederick Leyland & Co Ltd* [1947] A.C. 428, 436; *Luxor (Eastbourne) Ltd v Cooper* [1941] A.C. 108, 118; *A. V. Pound & Co Ltd v M. W. Hardy & Co Inc* [1956] A.C. 588, 608, 611; *Sociedad Financiera de Bienes Raices v Agrimpex* [1961] A.C. 135; *Sunbeam Shipping Co Ltd v President of India* [1973] 1 Lloyd's Rep. 482, 486; *Schindler v Pigault* [1975] 1 C.L. 401; *Metro Meat Ltd v Fares Rural Co Pty Ltd* [1985] 2 Lloyd's Rep. 13, 14; *Merton LBC v Hugh Leach Ltd* (1985) 32 Build. L.R. 51; *Kurt A. Becher GmbH & Co K.G. v Roplak Enterprises SA* [1991] 2 Lloyd's Rep. 23, 30, 34; *Davy Offshore Ltd v Emerald Field Contracting Ltd* (1991) 27 Const. L.R. 138; *Nissho Iwai Petroleum Inc v Cargill International SA* [1993] 1 Lloyd's Rep. 80, 84; *Scottish Power Plc v Kvaerner Construction (Regions) Ltd* (1999) S.L.T. 721; *Goodway v Zurich Insurance Co* [2004] EWHC 137, (2004) 96 Const. L.R. 49; *Kellang Shipping SA v Axa Assurances Senegal* [2006] EWHC 2825 (Comm), [2007] 1 Lloyd's Rep. 16 at [24], [36]. See also above, para.12–082, below, para.24–032, Vol.II, para.37–075.

[80] *Siporex Trade SA v Banque Indosuez* [1986] 2 Lloyd's Rep. 146, 161; *North Sea Energy Holdings NV v Petroleum Authority of Thailand* [1997] 2 Lloyd's Rep. 418 (affirmed [1999] 1 Lloyd's Rep. 482).

—whether expressly or impliedly—upon each party by the agreement itself, and the surrounding circumstances.[81]

13–012 **Prevention of performance.** By the same token:

> "... if a party enters into an arrangement which can only take effect by the continuance of a certain existing state of circumstances, there is an implied engagement on his part that he shall do nothing of his own motion to put an end to that state of circumstances under which alone the arrangement can become operative."[82]

Also where a binding contract is subject to a condition precedent,[83] a term may be implied that a party will not do an act which, if done, would prevent fulfilment of the condition.[84] But these implications are not inevitable: the alleged term may be unreasonably wide[85] or the nature of the contract may indicate otherwise.[86] A term may also be implied that a right, remedy or benefit expressly conferred upon one party to a contract or to which he may be entitled shall not be available if that party relies on his own breach of the contract, to establish his claim.[87]

---

[81] *Mackay v Dick* (1881) 6 App. Cas. 251, 263; *Mona Oil Equipment and Supply Co Ltd v Rhodesia Rys Ltd* [1949] 2 All E.R. 1014; *Hargreaves Transport Ltd v Lynch* [1969] 1 W.L.R. 215; *Liverpool City Council v Irwin* [1977] A.C. 239; *Kurt A. Becher GmbH & Co K.G. v Roplak Enterprises SA (The World Navigator)* [1991] 2 Lloyd's Rep. 23, 30, 31, 34; *North Sea Energy Holdings NV v Petroleum Authority of Thailand* [1999] 1 Lloyd's Rep. 482, 492; *Jolley v Carmel Ltd* [2000] 2 E.G.L.R. 154, 159.

[82] *Stirling v Maitland* (1864) 5 B. & S. 840, 852. See also *Rhodes v Forwood* (1876) 1 App. Cas. 256, 272, 274; *Turner v Goldsmith* [1891] 1 Q.B. 544; *Ogdens Ltd v Nelson* [1905] A.C. 109; *Warren v Agdeshman* (1922) 38 T.L.R. 588; *C. French & Co Ltd v Leeston Shipping Co Ltd* [1922] 1 A.C. 451; *Southern Foundries (1926) Ltd v Shirlaw* [1940] A.C. 701; *William Cory & Son Ltd v City of London Corp* [1951] 2 K.B. 476, 484; *A. Hamson & Son (London) Ltd v S. Martin Johnson & Co Ltd* [1953] 1 Lloyd's Rep. 553; *Shindler v Northern Raincoat Ltd* [1960] 1 W.L.R. 1038; *The Unique Mariner (No.2)* [1979] 1 Lloyd's Rep. 37; *Merton LBC v Hugh Leach Ltd* (1985) 32 Build. L.R. 51; *Martin-Smith v Williams* [1999] E.M.L.R. 571; *CEL Group Ltd v Nedloyd Lines UK Ltd* [2003] EWCA Civ 1716, [2004] 1 Lloyd's Rep. 381 at [11], [22] and [23]. See also Bateson [1960] J.B.L. 187; Burrows (1968) 31 M.L.R. 390; above, para.2–153; Vol.II, para.37–074.

[83] See above, para.12–028.

[84] *Holme v Guppy* (1838) 3 M. & W. 387, 389; *Inchbald v Western Neilgherry Coffee, etc., Co* (1864) 17 C.B.(N.S.) 733; *Roberts v Bury Improvements Commrs.* (1870) L.R. 5 C.P. 310, 316; *Mackay v Dick* (1881) 6 App. Cas. 251; *Dodd v Churton* [1897] 1 Q.B. 562, 566; *Barque Quilpué Ltd v Brown* [1904] 2 K.B. 264, 271; *Hickman & Co v Roberts* [1913] A.C. 229; *Trollope v Martyn* [1934] 2 K.B. 436; *Amalgamated Building Contractors Ltd v Waltham Holy Cross U.D.C.* [1952] 2 All E.R. 452, 455; *Jebco Properties v Mastforce* [1992] N.P.C. 42; *Nissho Iwai Petroleum Co Inc v Cargill International SA* [1993] 1 Lloyd's Rep. 80; *Taylor v Rive Droite Music Ltd* [2005] EWCA Civ 1300, [2006] E.M.L.R. 4. See also below, para.24–032.

[85] *Philips Electronique Grand Public SA v British Sky Broadcasting Ltd* [1995] E.M.L.R. 472; *Times Newspapers Ltd v George Weidenfeld & Nicolson Ltd* [2002] F.S.R. 29.

[86] *Aspdin v Austin* (1844) 5 Q.B. 671; *European, etc., Mail Co v Royal Mail Steam Packet Co* (1861) 30 L.J.C.P. 247; *Rhodes v Forwood* (1876) 1 App. Cas. 256; *Hamlyn v Wood* [1891] 2 Q.B. 488; *Luxor (Eastbourne) Ltd v Cooper* [1941] A.C. 108; *William Cory & Son Ltd v City of London Corp* [1951] 2 K.B. 476; *Farr v Admiralty* [1953] 1 W.L.R. 565; *Thompson v Asda-MFI Group Plc* [1988] Ch. 241; *Davy Offshore Ltd v Emerald Field Contracting Ltd* (1991) 27 Const.L.R. 138; *Philips Electronique Grand Public SA v British Sky Broadcasting Ltd* [1995] E.M.L.R. 477; *Multiplex Construction (UK) Ltd v Honeywell Control Systems Ltd* [2007] EWHC 447 (TCC), (2007) 111 Const. L.R. 78; see Vol.II, paras 31–139, 37–074.

[87] See above, para.12–082. cf. *Richco International Ltd v Alfred C. Toepfer International GmbH* [1991] 1 Lloyd's Rep. 136, 144; *Bulk Shipping A.G. v Ipco Trading SA* [1992] 1 Lloyd's Rep. 39, 43.

Export and import licences. In international trade, contracts of sale of goods are frequently the subject of governmental restrictions and a licence may have to be obtained for the import or export of goods from one country to another. The parties will normally provide expressly who is to assume this responsibility, but, in the absence of any express provision, it will be necessary to imply a term as to whether the duty to obtain a licence rests upon the buyer or the seller.[88] Once the incidence of this duty has been determined, the court will then have to consider whether the party placed under the duty impliedly undertook to use his best endeavours to obtain a licence[89] or whether he undertook absolutely that a licence would be obtained.[90] In any event, both parties are under an obligation to co-operate with each other to the extent that is necessary for the obtaining of a licence.[91] 13–013

Occupiers of premises. Where persons enter or use, or bring or send goods to, any premises in exercise of a right conferred by contract with a person occupying or having control of the premises, the duty he owes them in respect of dangers due to the state of the premises or to things done or omitted to be done on them in so far as the duty depends on a term to be implied in the contract by reason of its conferring that right, is the "common duty of care".[92] The common duty of care is a duty to take such care as in all the circumstances of the case is reasonable to see that the visitor will be reasonably safe in using the premises for the purposes for which he is invited or permitted by the occupier to be there,[93] except in so far as the occupier is free to[94] and does extend, restrict modify or exclude that duty by agreement or otherwise.[95] However, the duty cannot be restricted or excluded by the contract so as to diminish the rights of third parties 13–014

[88] *H.O. Brandt & Co v H.N. Morris & Co* [1917] 2 K.B. 784; *J.W. Taylor & Co v Landauer & Co* [1940] 4 All E.R. 335; *Mitchell Cotts & Co (Middle East) Ltd v Hairco Ltd* [1943] 2 All E.R. 552; *A.V Pound & Co Ltd v M.W. Hardy & Co Inc* [1956] A.C. 588; *Congimex Companhia Geral, etc., SARL v Tradax Export SA* [1983] 1 Lloyd's Rep. 250. See *Benjamin's Sale of Goods*, 7th edn (2006), paras 18–309—18–312.

[89] *Re Anglo-Russian Merchant Traders Ltd and John Batt & Co (London) Ltd* [1917] 2 K.B. 679; *Brauer & Co (G.B.) Ltd v James Clark (Brush Materials) Ltd* [1952] 2 All E.R. 497. See also *Windschuegl Ltd v Pickering & Co Ltd* (1950) 84 Lloyd's Rep. 89, 93; *Société D'Avances Commerciales (London) Ltd v A. Besse & Co (London) Ltd* [1952] 1 T.L.R. 644, 646; *Compagnie Algerienne de Meunerie v Katana Societa de Navigatione Marittima SpA* [1959] 1 Q.B. 527; *Provimi Hellas A.E. v Warinco A.G.* [1978] 1 Lloyd's Rep. 373; *Coloniale Import-Export v Loumidis Sons* [1978] 2 Lloyd's Rep. 560, 562; *Benjamin's Sale of Goods* at paras 18–313—18–315.

[90] *Mitchell Cotts & Co (Middle East) Ltd v Hairco Ltd* [1943] 2 All E.R. 552; *Partabmull Rameshwar v Sethia (K.C.) (1944) Ltd* [1950] 1 All E.R. 51 (affirmed [1951] 2 All E.R. 352n.); *Peter Cassidy Seed Co Ltd v Osuustukkukauppa I.L.* [1957] 1 W.L.R. 273; *Congimex Companhia Geral, etc., SARL v Tradax Export SA* [1983] 1 Lloyd's Rep. 250.

[91] *A.V. Pound & Co Ltd v M.W. Hardy & Co Inc* [1956] A.C. 588, 608, 611; *Kyprianou v Cyprus Textiles Ltd* [1958] 2 Lloyd's Rep. 60.

[92] Occupiers' Liability Act 1957 s.5(1), superseding the rule in *Francis v Cockrell* (1870) L.R. 5 Q.B. 501.

[93] s.2(2).

[94] See the Unfair Contract Terms Act 1977 ss.1, 2, 3 (below) and *Monarch Airlines Ltd v London Luton Airport Ltd* [1998] 1 Lloyd's Rep. 403.

[95] Occupiers' Liability Act 1957 s.2(1). See also *Ashdown v Samuel Williams & Sons Ltd* [1957] 1 Q.B. 409; *White v Blackmore* [1972] 2 Q.B. 651 (notices).

who are entitled to enter by virtue of its provisions.[96] The same duty applies in relation to fixed and movable structures as it does to premises[97] but does not extend to the obligations imposed by any contract for the hire of, or for the carriage for reward of persons or goods in, any means of transport, or by any contract of bailment.[98]

13–015 **Fitness for habitation: sale of land.** It is well established that prima facie upon a contract for sale of a piece of land with a house on it, there is no warranty as to the habitability of the house.[99] The same rule would apply in the case of an uncompleted house, which is the subject matter of a sale, where the structure stands at the time of the sale. But where the vendor sells a piece of land and covenants to build or complete a house on it, there is, at common law, an implied term: (i) that the work will be done in a good and workmanlike manner; (ii) that he will supply good and proper materials; and (iii) that the house will be reasonably fit for human habitation when built or completed.[100] This implication may, however, be rebutted where the purchaser has himself expressly prescribed the way in which the work is to be done, and the work has been completed in accordance with his instructions.[101] The Defective Premises Act 1972[102] in addition, imposes on every person who takes on work for or in connection with the provision of a dwelling a similar statutory duty[103] (which cannot be excluded or restricted by any term of an agreement), subject to certain exceptions provided for in the Act. This statutory duty is owed to any person to whose order the dwelling is provided and also to every person who acquires an interest (whether legal or equitable) in the dwelling.[104]

13–016 **Fitness for habitation: leases.** In general, a landlord gives no implied undertaking that leased premises are or will be fit for habitation or for any particular use,[105] or that the premises can lawfully be used for any particular purpose.[106] But where a house or flat is let furnished, there is an implied covenant or warranty that it is reasonably fit for human habitation when let,[107] although there

[96] s.3(1)–(4).

[97] s.5(2).

[98] s.5(3).

[99] *Hoskins v Woodham* [1938] 1 All E.R. 692; *Lynch v Thorne* [1956] 1 W.L.R. 303, 305.

[100] *Lawrence v Cassell* [1930] 2 K.B. 83; *Miller v Cannon Hill Estates Ltd* [1931] 2 K.B. 113; *Jennings v Taverner* [1955] 1 W.L.R. 932; *Hancock v B.W. Brazier (Anerley) Ltd* [1966] 1 W.L.R. 1317; *Billyack v Leyland Construction Co Ltd* [1968] 1 W.L.R. 471; *King v Victor Parsons & Co* [1972] 1 W.L.R. 801. See also below, para.13–032 and Vol.II, para.37–080.

[101] *Perry v Sharon Development Co Ltd* [1937] 4 All E.R. 390, 394; *Lynch v Thorne* [1956] 1 W.L.R. 303; cf. *King v Victor Parsons & Co* [1972] 1 W.L.R. 801.

[102] ss.1, 2, 6. See also s.3 and Vol.II, para.37–083.

[103] *Alexander v Mercouris* [1979] 1 W.L.R. 1270; *Andrews v Schooling* [1991] 1 W.L.R. 783.

[104] Defensive Premises Act 1972 s.1.

[105] *Hart v Windsor* (1843) 12 M. & W. 68; *Sutton v Temple* (1843) 12 M. & W. 52; *Robbins v Jones* (1863) 12 M. & W. 68, 87; *Manchester Bonded Warehouse Co Ltd v Carr* (1880) 5 C.P.D. 507; *Bottomley v Bannister* [1932] 1 K.B. 458, 468. Contrast *Western Electric Ltd v Welsh Development Agency* [1983] Q.B. 796 (licence).

[106] *Edler v Auerbach* [1950] 1 K.B. 359; *Hills v Harris* [1965] 2 Q.B. 601.

[107] *Smith v Marrable* (1843) 11 M. & W. 5; *Collins v Hopkins* [1923] 2 K.B. 617.

is no obligation at common law to keep furnished or unfurnished premises in that condition or to repair them during the tenancy.[108] However, covenants on the part of the landlord are implied in the cases of houses let at a low rent[109] or for a short term.[110]

Buildings in multiple occupation. Where an essential means of access to units in a building in multiple occupation is retained by the landlord, a covenant may be implied on his part to use reasonable care to keep the essential means of access in reasonable repair and fit for use.[111] 13–017

When implied from usage or custom. If there is an invariable, certain and general usage or custom of any particular trade or place, the law will imply on the part of one who contracts or employs another to contract for him upon a matter to which such usage or custom has reference a promise for the benefit of the other party in conformity with such usage or custom[112]; provided there is no inconsistency between the usage and the terms of the contract.[113] To be binding, however, the usage must be notorious, certain and reasonable, and not contrary to law[114]; and it must also be something more than a mere trade practice.[115] But when such usage is proved, it will form the basis of the contract between the parties, and: 13–018

---

[108] *Sarson v Roberts* [1895] 2 Q.B. 395; *Sleafer v Lambeth BC* [1960] 1 Q.B. 43, 56–57; *Duke of Westminster v Guild* [1985] Q.B. 688; *Adami v Lincoln Grange Management Ltd* [1998] I.C.L. 379. See also *Warren v Keen* [1954] 1 Q.B. 15. Contrast *Mint v Good* [1951] 1 K.B. 517, 522; *Edmonton Corp v Knowles & Son Ltd* (1961) 60 L.G.R. 124; Defective Premises Act 1972 s.4(4).

[109] Landlord and Tenant Act 1985 ss.8, 9, 10.

[110] ss.11–17 (term less than seven years) as amended by s.116 of the Housing Act 1988.

[111] *Miller v Hancock* [1893] 2 Q.B. 177; *Liverpool City Council v Irwin* [1977] A.C. 239. See also Occupiers' Liability Act 1957 s.3(4) and Landlord and Tenant Act 1987 Pt. IV

[112] *Hutton v Warren* (1836) 1 M. & W. 466; *Dale v Humfrey* (1858) E.B. & E. 1004; *Tucker v Linger* (1882) 21 ChD 18, 33, 34 (affirmed (1883) 8 App. Cas. 508); *Pike, Sons & Co v Ongley & Thornton* (1887) 18 QBD 708; *Fox-Bourne v Vernon & Co Ltd* (1894) 10 T.L.R. 647; *Lord Eldon v Hedley Bros* [1935] 2 K.B. 1; *E.E. & Brian Smith (1928) Ltd v Wheatsheaf Mills Ltd* [1939] 2 K.B. 302; *Mount v Oldham Corp* [1973] 1 Q.B. 309; *British Crane Hire Corp Ltd v Ipswich Plant Hire Ltd* [1975] Q.B. 303; *Novorossisk Shipping Co v Neopetro Co Ltd* [1990] 1 Lloyd's Rep. 425, 431; *Tony Cox (Dismantlers) Ltd v Jim 5 Ltd* (1997) 13 Const.L.J. 209. See above, paras 12–127—12–133.

[113] See above, para.12–128; below, para.13–023. An "entire agreement" clause (see above, para.12–104) may exclude any such implication: *Exxonmobil Sales and Supply Corp v Texaco Ltd* [2003] EWHC 1964, (Comm); [2003] 2 Lloyd's Rep. 686.

[114] *Yates v Pym* (1816) 6 Taunt. 446; *Daun v City of London Brewery Co* (1869) L.R. 8 Eq. 155, 161; *Nelson v Dahl* (1879) 12 Ch D 568, 575 (affirmed (1881) 6 App. Cas. 38); *Re Walkers, Winser & Hamm and Shaw, Son & Co* [1904] 2 K.B. 152; *Ropner v Stoate Hosegood & Co* (1905) 10 Com. Cas. 73; *Cunliffe-Owen v Teather and Greenwood* [1967] 1 W.L.R. 1421, 1438, 1439; *Constan Industries of Australia Pty Ltd v Norwich Winterthur Insurance (Aust.) Ltd* (1986) 160 C.L.R. 226; *Pryke v Gibbs Hartley Cooper Ltd* [1991] 1 Lloyd's Rep. 602, 615; *Danowski v Henry Moore Foundation, The Times*, March 19, 1996 CA; *Exxonmobil Sales and Supply Corp v Texaco Ltd* [2003] EWHC 1964 (Comm); [2003] 2 Lloyd's Rep. 686 at [21].

[115] *Cunliffe-Owen v Teather and Greenwood* [1967] 1 W.L.R. 1421, 1438; *General Reinsurance Corp v Forsakringsaktiebolaget* [1983] Q.B. 856, 874; *Pryke v Gibbs Hartley Cooper Ltd* [1991] 1 Lloyd's Rep. 602, 615; *Vitol SA v Phibro Energy A.G.* [1990] 2 Lloyd's Rep. 84, 90; *Sucre Export SA v Northern Shipping Ltd* [1994] 2 Lloyd's Rep. 266.

> "... their respective rights and liabilities are precisely the same as if without any usage they had entered into a special agreement to the like effect."[116]

These usages are incorporated on the presumption that:

> "... the parties did not mean to express in writing the whole of the contract by which they intended to be bound, but a contract with reference to those known usages"[117]

or on the ground that "the courts are spelling out what both parties know and would, if asked, unhesitatingly agree to be part of the bargain".[118] However, even in cases where the party alleged to be liable upon an implied promise, arising solely from the usage of a particular trade, is not shown to have been cognisant of the usage, he can still be held to be liable by virtue of it.[119]

13–019 **Incorporation of collective employment agreements.** In relation to contracts of employment, particular problems arise as to whether the terms of collective agreements between trade unions and employers concerning industrial conditions in a particular trade can be impliedly incorporated by usage into an individual worker's contract of employment[120] as they can be by express reference.[121]

13–020 **Human rights.** The question whether a term may be implied into a contract to secure compliance with the Human Rights Act 1998 has been discussed in Ch.1 of this work.[122]

13–021 **Usage employed by one of the parties.** Where the usage is one which merely applies to the mode of dealing of a particular firm, a party cannot be bound thereby, unless he is shown to have had actual notice of it. To establish a usage it must be proved that a course of dealing has acquired such a notoriety, has been so well established and has become so universal in the particular trade, that it must be taken to be incorporated into any contract that is entered into by the parties dealing in this particular business.[123]

13–022 **When implied from previous course of dealing.** It is, however, clear that a term may be implied in any given case from the circumstances of the parties having consistently on former and similar occasions adopted a particular course of dealing. Thus, a covenant to pay interest or to allow interest to be added to principal at stated periods and to pay interest on the whole, has been held to be

---

[116] *Raitt v Mitchell* (1815) 4 Camp. 146, 149; *Produce Brokers Co Ltd v Olympia Oil and Cake Co Ltd* [1916] 1 A.C. 314, 324.

[117] *Hutton v Warren* (1836) 1 M. & W. 466, 475; *Gibson v Small* (1853) 4 H.L.C. 353, 397.

[118] *Liverpool City Council v Irwin* [1977] A.C. 239, 253; *Baker v Black Sea & Baltic General Insurance Co Ltd* [1998] 1 W.L.R. 974, 979.

[119] *Sutton v Tatham* (1839) 10 A. & E. 27; *Bayliffe v Butterworth* (1847) 1 Exch. 425; *Reynolds v Smith* (1893) 9 T.L.R. 494; *Hunt v Chamberlain* (1896) 12 T.L.R. 186.

[120] See Vol. II, para.39–045.

[121] See Vol. II, para.39–045.

[122] Above, para.1–062.

[123] *Houlder v General Steam Navigation Co* (1862) 3 F. & F. 170; *Salsi v Jetspeed Air Services Ltd* [1977] 2 Lloyd's Rep. 57.

implied from the fact that on former occasions the accounts between the parties have been stated and settled on that footing.[124] And it has been held that an oral contract between the buyer and seller of goods incorporated by a long course of dealing conditions printed on the back of "sold notes" as conditions of sale, in so far as a condition was appropriate to the oral contract.[125]

Express terms prevail. A custom or usage can only be incorporated into a contract if there is nothing in the express or necessarily implied terms of the contract to prevent such inclusion, and it can only be incorporated if it is not inconsistent with the tenor of the contract as a whole.[126] Thus a custom that commission was only payable to the broker who had negotiated a charterparty when freight was actually earned was ousted by an express term that commission was to be paid on the signing of the charter.[127] And a contract to ship rubber from the East to New York "direct and/or indirect" was alleged to have been duly carried out by shipping goods to the American Pacific seaboard and across the American continent to New York by train. Evidence of such a practice, said to have been common in the First World War, was disallowed as being contrary to the contract.[128] 13–023

Implication from words of recital. Where words of recital or reference manifest a clear intention that the parties should do certain acts, the courts may from these infer a covenant to do such acts, just as if the instrument had contained an express agreement to that effect.[129] So a recital in a separation deed that a wife had agreed to live apart from her husband implied a covenant by the wife to live apart.[130] Also where by charterparty it was agreed that the ship C, "expected to be at A about December 15", should with all convenient speed sail and proceed to that port and there receive a cargo, it was held that the words 13–024

---

[124] *Calton v Bragg* (1812) 15 East 223, 228; *Bruce v Hunter* (1813) 3 Camp. 467; *Newal v Jones* (1830) 1 Moo. & M. 449; *Re Marquis of Anglesey* [1901] 2 Ch. 548; cf. *Re Lloyd Edwards* (1891) 65 L.T. 453. But see Vol. II, para.38–269.

[125] *Henry Kendall & Sons v William Lillico & Sons Ltd* [1969] 2 A.C. 31, 90, 91, 104, 105, 130. See also *J. Spurling Ltd v Bradshaw* [1956] 1 W.L.R. 461; *Cockerton v Naviera Aznar SA* [1960] 2 Lloyd's Rep. 451; *Transmotors Ltd v Robertson Buckley & Co Ltd* [1970] 1 Lloyd's Rep. 224; *Eastman Chemical International A.G. v N.M.T. Trading Ltd* [1972] 2 Lloyd's Rep. 25; *Roberts v Elwells Engineers Ltd* [1972] 2 Q.B. 586, 593; *Gillespie Bros & Co Ltd v Roy Bowles Transport Ltd* [1973] Q.B. 400; *S.I.A.T. di del Ferro v Tradax Overseas SA* [1980] 1 Lloyd's Rep. 53; *Lamport & Holt Lines Ltd v Coubro & M. & I. Scrutton Ltd* [1981] 2 Lloyd's Rep. 659 (affirmed [1982] 2 Lloyd's Rep. 42). cf. *McCutcheon v David MacBrayne Ltd* [1964] 1 W.L.R. 125, HL; *Hollier v Rambler Motors (A.M.C.) Ltd* [1972] 2 Q.B. 71. See Hoggett (1970) 33 M.L.R. 518 and above, para.12–011.

[126] *London Export Corp Ltd v Jubilee Coffee Roasting Co Ltd* [1958] 1 W.L.R. 661, 675; *Kum v Wah Tat Bank Ltd* [1971] 1 Lloyd's Rep. 439, 445.

[127] *Les Affréteurs Réunis Société Anonyme v Walford* [1919] A.C. 801. See generally on this point, above, paras 12–128, 13–022.

[128] *Re L. Sutro & Co v Heilbut, Symons & Co* [1927] 2 K.B. 348. See also *Humfrey v Dale* (1857) 7 E. & B. 266, 274; *Tucker v Linger* (1883) 8 App. Cas. 508, 511; *Westacott v Hahn* [1918] 1 K.B. 495; *Palgrave, Brown & Son Ltd v S.S. Turid* [1922] 1 A.C. 397.

[129] *Saltoun v Houston* (1824) 1 Bing. 433; *Easterby v Sampson* (1830) 6 Bing. 644; *Courtney v Taylor* (1843) 6 M. & G. 851; *Great Northern Ry v Harrison* (1852) 12 C.B.(N.S.) 576, 609; *Knight v Gravesend, etc., Waterworks Co* (1857) 2 H. & N. 6; *Farrall v Hilditch* (1859) 5 C.B.(N.S.) 840; *Jackson v North Eastern Ry* (1877) 7 ChD 573; *Mackenzie v Childers* (1889) 43 Ch D 265.

[130] *Re Weston* [1900] 2 Ch. 164.

"expected, etc", amounted to a warranty that the ship was then in such a position that she might reasonably be expected to arrive by the day named.[131]

13–025 In contrast, however, with the use of words of recital in order to ascertain the meaning of a written contract,[132] the courts are reluctant to imply such a covenant in the absence of a manifest intention:

> "It is one thing for the court to effectuate the intention of the parties to the extent to which they may have, even imperfectly, expressed themselves, and another to add to the instrument all such covenants as upon a full consideration the court may deem fitting for completing the intentions of the parties, but which they, either purposely or unintentionally, have omitted."[133]

So the recital of an agreement does not create a covenant where there is an express covenant to be found in the witnessing part relating to the same subject-matter.[134]

13–026 **Implied restriction on contractual discretion.** A discretion conferred by contract in seemingly absolute terms may be restricted by the implication of a term: that the discretion should not be exercised dishonestly, for an improper purpose, capriciously, arbitrarily, or in a way that no reasonable person, acting reasonably, would act.[135] Similarly a contract which provides that one party shall not enter into a transaction with a third person without the consent of the other may be subject to an implied term that the consent shall not be unreasonably withheld.[136]

13–027 **Implied term as to duration of contract.** A contract which contains no express provision for its determination may yet be determined by reasonable notice on the part of one or both of the parties. The question whether a contract can be determined in this way is often said to depend upon the implication of a term, although it is probably better to regard it as depending upon the true construction of the agreement.[137] Nevertheless, since ex hypothesi, the agreement contains no provisions expressly dealing with determination, the question is not one of construction in the narrow sense of putting a meaning on language which the parties have used, but in the wider sense of ascertaining, in the light of all the admissible evidence and in the light of what the parties have said or

---

[131] *Corkling v Massey* (1873) L.R. 8 C.P. 395.

[132] See above, para.12–066.

[133] *Aspdin v Austin* (1844) 5 Q.B. 671, 684.

[134] *Dawes v Tredwell* (1881) 18 ChD 354, 359.

[135] *Abu Dhabi National Tanker Co v Product Star Shipping Ltd* [1993] 1 Lloyd's Rep. 397, 404; *Paragon Finance Plc v Nash* [2001] EWCA Civ 1466, [2002] 1 W.L.R. 685 at [31]; *Socimer International Bank Ltd v Standard Bank London Ltd* [2008] EWCA Civ 116, [2008] 1 Lloyd's Rep. 538 at [60]–[69]; see above, para.1–033. cf. *Paragon Finance Plc v Pender* [2005] EWCA Civ 760, [2005] 1 W.L.R. 3412. See also Vol.II, para.38–273.

[136] *Societa Explosivi Industriale SpA v Ordnance Technologies (VIC) Ltd* [2004] EWHC 48 (Comm), [2004] 1 All E.R. (Comm) 619. See also *Addison v Brown* [1954] 1 W.L.R. 779; *Lymington Marina Ltd v MacNamara* [2007] EWCA Civ 151.

[137] *Winter Garden Theatre (London) Ltd v Millennium Productions Ltd* [1948] A.C. 173, 195, 203; *Martin-Baker Aircraft Co Ltd v Canadian Flight Equipment Ltd* [1955] 2 Q.B. 556, 578; *Staffordshire A.H.A. v South Staffordshire Waterworks Co* [1978] 1 W.L.R. 1387, 1399–1403, 1405.

omitted to say in the agreement, what the common intention of the parties was in the relevant respect when they entered into the agreement.[138] Thus a contract to supply gas to a public authority in such quantities as it should require has been held determinable by either party on reasonable notice,[139] and a licence to occupy a theatre and to produce there stage plays, which gave to the licensee an option to extend the licence at stated intervals, but which contained no provisions for determination by the licensor, was held to be determinable by the licensor upon giving reasonable notice.[140] Similar constructions have been adopted in the case of contracts between employer and employee,[141] between principal and agent,[142] and between solicitor and client in respect of an indefinite retainer.[143]

Contractual licences. A licence coupled with the grant of an interest in land cannot be revoked so as to defeat the grant to which it is appurtenant.[144] Since the Judicature Act 1873 such a licence may be made either by deed or by a specifically enforceable agreement in writing.[145] On the other hand a "bare licence" is revocable at any time upon the licensor giving clear[146] and adequate[147] notice to the licensee. The position of a contractual licensee is that, if a licence is given for consideration and coupled with an agreement, whether express or implied, that it will not be revoked until the effluxion of a specified period of time or the happening of a particular event, it is irrevocable until the expiration of the period or the happening of the event.[148] An injunction will be granted to restrain the licensor from revoking the licence, or from acting in 13–028

[138] *Re Spenborough U.D.C.'s Agreement* [1968] Ch. 139, 147. See also *Llanelly Rail and Dock Co v L. & N.W. Ry* (1873) L.R. 8 Ch. App. 942; (1875) L.R. 7 H.L. 550. cf. Carnegie (1969) 85 L.Q.R. 392.

[139] *Crediton Gas Co v Crediton Urban Council* [1928] Ch. 174, 447. See also *Beverley Corp v Richard Hodgson & Sons Ltd* (1972) 225 E.G. 799; *Staffordshire A.H.A. v South Staffordshire Waterworks Co* [1978] 1 W.L.R. 1387; *Tower Hamlets LBC v British Gas Corp, The Times*, March 23, 1982. Contrast *Kirklees Metropolitan BC v Yorkshire Woollen District Transport Co* (1978) 77 L.G.R. 448; *Power Co Ltd v Gore DC* [1997] N.Z.L.R. 537; *Harbinger UK Ltd v GE Information Services Ltd* [2000] 1 All E.R. (Comm) 166.

[140] *Winter Garden Theatre (London) Ltd v Millennium Productions Ltd* [1948] A.C. 173; cf. *Australian Blue Metal Ltd v Hughes* [1963] A.C. 74.

[141] See Vol. II, paras 39–150, 39–154. Contrast *McClelland v Northern Ireland General Health Services Board* [1957] 1 W.L.R. 594 where express terms prevented such implication.

[142] *Martin-Baker Aircraft Co Ltd v Canadian Flight Equipment Ltd* [1955] 2 Q.B. 566. See Vol. II, para.31–149.

[143] *Milner & Son v Percy Bilton Ltd* [1966] 1 W.L.R. 1582.

[144] *Thomas v Sorrell* (1673) Vaughan 330; *Jones v Earl of Tankerville* [1909] 2 Ch. 440.

[145] *Walsh v Lonsdale* (1882) 21 Ch D 9 (or sufficient act of part performance).

[146] *Mellor v Watkins* (1874) L.R. 9 Q.B. 400.

[147] *Minister of Health v Bellotti* [1944] 1 K.B. 298; *Tool Metal Manufacturing Co Ltd v Tungsten Electric Co Ltd* [1955] 1 W.L.R. 761; *Australian Blue Metal Ltd v Hughes* [1963] A.C. 74.

[148] *Winter Garden Theatre (London) Ltd v Millennium Productions Ltd* [1948] A.C. 173; *Bannister v Bannister* [1948] 2 All E.R. 133; *Errington v Errington* [1952] 1 K.B. 290; *Hounslow LBC v Twickenham Gardens Development Ltd* [1971] Ch. 233 (not followed in *Mayfield Holdings Ltd v Moana Reef Ltd* [1973] 1 N.Z.L.R. 309); *Tanner v Tanner* [1975] 1 W.L.R. 1346; *Verrall v Great Yarmouth BC* [1981] Q.B. 202. cf. *Chandler v Kerley* [1978] 1 W.L.R. 693 (contractual licence impliedly revocable on reasonable notice). A licence may also be created by estoppel, or its revocation restrained in equity: see *Inwards v Baker* [1965] 2 Q.B. 29; *E.R. Ives Investment Ltd v High* [1967] 2 Q.B. 379; *Binions v Evans* [1972] Ch. 359; *D.H.N. Food Distributors Ltd v Tower Hamlets LBC* [1976] 1 W.L.R. 852; *Hardwick v Johnson* [1978] 1 W.L.R. 683; *Pascoe v Turner* [1979] 1 W.L.R. 431; *Williams v Staite* [1979] Ch. 291; *Re Sharpe* [1980] 1 W.L.R. 219; *Greasley*

pursuance of the purported revocation,[149] and the licensee may also claim damages for breach of contract[150] and for assault should he be forcibly ejected by the licensor.[151]

13–029 **Sale of goods, hire-purchase and hire.** Undertakings as to title, quality, fitness for purpose and correspondence with description or sample are implied into contracts of sale of goods by ss.12 to 15 of the Sale of Goods Act 1979,[152] into contracts of hire-purchase by ss.8 to 11 of the Supply of Goods (Implied Terms) Act 1973,[153] and into contracts for the hire of goods by ss.7 to 10 of the Supply of Goods and Services Act 1982.[154] The rule that a term will not be implied which is inconsistent with an express term[155] does not apply in the case of a statutory implied term: any conflict must be resolved as a matter of construction.[156]

13–030 **Supply of goods.** Undertakings in respect of the goods similar to those implied in the case of sale, hire-purchase and hire are implied into contracts for the transfer of goods, e.g. for work and materials, by ss.2 to 5 of the Supply of Goods and Services Act 1982.[157] These replace and extend[158] the undertakings previously implied by the common law, for example, into a contract for the manufacture of a set of false teeth,[159] for the repair of a motor car,[160] for the dyeing of a woman's hair,[161] for the supply and installation of a burglar-proof

---

v Cooke [1980] 1 W.L.R. 1306; *Grant v Edwards* [1986] Ch. 638; *Lloyds Bank Plc v Rosset* [1991] 1 A.C. 107; *Hammond v Mitchell* [1991] 1 W.L.R. 1127; *Matharu v Matharu, The Times*, May 13, 1994, CA cf. *Coombes v Smith* [1986] 1 W.L.R. 808. See also Moriarty (1984) 100 L.Q.R. 346 and above, para.3–137.

[149] *Winter Garden Theatre (London) Ltd v Millennium Productions Ltd* [1948] A.C. 173; *Foster v Robinson* [1915] 1 K.B. 149, 156. See also *Verral v Great Yarmouth BC* [1981] Q.B. 202 (specific performance), and the cases in equity cited in fn.148, above.

[150] *Kerrison v Smith* [1897] 2 Q.B. 445.

[151] *Hurst v Picture Theatres Ltd* [1915] 1 K.B. 1. Contrast *Wood v Leadbitter* (1845) 13 M. & W. 838; *Thompson v Park* [1944] K.B. 408; *Cowell v Rosehill Racecourse Ltd* (1936) 56 C.L.R. 605, but these cases are of doubtful authority: see *Verrall v Great Yarmouth BC* [1981] Q.B. 202.

[152] See Vol.II, paras 43–061 et seq. See also (on exclusion or restriction of liability) below, para.14–079.

[153] See Vol.II, paras 38–296, 38–362 et seq. See also (on exclusion or restriction of liability) below, para.14–078.

[154] See Vol.II, para.33–070. See also (on exclusion or restriction of liability), below, para.14–079.

[155] See above, para.13–023.

[156] *Yarm Road Ltd v Hewden Tower Cranes Ltd* [2002] EWHC 2265, (2002) 85 Const. L.R. 142.

[157] As amended by Sch.2 para.6 to the Sale and Supply of Goods Act 1994. See *Charlotte Thirty Ltd v Croker Ltd* (1990) 24 Const. L.R. 46; *Jonathan Wren & Co Ltd v Microdec Ltd* (1999) 65 Const. L.R. 157. See also (on exclusion or restriction of liability), below, para.14–079.

[158] See *Young and Marten Ltd v McManus Childs Ltd* [1969] 1 A.C. 454; *Gloucestershire CC v Richardson* [1969] 1 A.C. 480; Vol.II, para.43–014.

[159] *Samuels v Davis* [1943] K.B. 526.

[160] *G.H. Myers & Co v Brent Cross Service Co* [1934] 1 K.B. 46; *Herschtal v Stewart and Ardern Ltd* [1940] 1 K.B. 155; *Stewart v Reavell's Garage* [1952] 2 Q.B. 545.

[161] *Ingham v Emes* [1955] 2 Q.B. 366.

door,[162] for the inoculation of cattle,[163] and for the roofing[164] and erection[165] of a building.

Disposition of property. The covenants for title that are implied on a disposition of property are those set out in Part I of the Law of Property (Miscellaneous Provisions) Act 1994. "Property" is defined[166] in the same terms as in the Law of Property Act 1925, i.e. to include "a thing in action, and any interest in real or personal property". 13–031

Supply of services. In the case of a contract under which a person agrees to carry out a service, other than a contract of service or apprenticeship[167] and certain other excepted contracts,[168] where the supplier is acting in the course of a business,[169] there is an implied term that the supplier will carry out the service with reasonable care and skill. This term is implied by s.13 of the Supply of Goods and Services Act 1982.[170] If the contract is one for the supply of professional services, the degree of care and skill required of a professional man is that which is to be expected of a member of his profession (in the appropriate speciality, if he be a specialist) of ordinary competence and experience.[171] If the service is to be carried out by an artisan, then the work should be done in a good and workmanlike manner.[172] However, the special circumstances of the case may show that the supplier impliedly warrants that his services will produce a specified result or that the product of his service will be reasonably fit for the purpose for which it is required.[173] 13–032

---

[162] *Reg. Glass Pty v Rivers Locking System Pty* (1968) 120 C.L.R. 516. cf. *Davis & Co (Wires) v Afa-Minerva (E.M.I.)* [1974] 2 Lloyd's Rep. 27.

[163] *Dodd and Dodd v Wilson and McWilliam* [1946] 2 All E.R. 691.

[164] *Young and Marten Ltd v McManus Childs Ltd* [1969] 1 A.C. 434.

[165] *Gloucestershire CC v Richardson* [1969] 1 A.C. 480.

[166] s.1(4).

[167] Supply of Goods and Services Act 1982 s.12(2).

[168] Supply of Goods and Services Act 1982 s.12(4). The following orders have been made: Supply of Services (Exclusion of Implied Terms) Order 1982 (SI 1982/1771); Supply of Services (Exclusion of Implied Terms) Order 1983 (SI 1983/902); Supply of Services (Exclusion of Implied Terms) Order 1985 (SI 1985/1).

[169] By Supply of Goods and Services Act 1982 s.18(1), "business" includes a profession and the activities of any government department or local or public authority.

[170] Unless excluded (Supply of Goods and Services Act 1982 s.16): *Eagle Star Life Assurance Co Ltd v Griggs* [1997] C.L.Y. 991. See also (on exclusion or restriction of liability), above, paras 14–072, 14–079; and see Vol.II, paras 33–089, 37–082.

[171] *Bolam v Friern Hospital Management Committee* [1957] 1 W.L.R. 582, 586; *Chin Keow v Government of Malaysia* [1967] 1 W.L.R. 813; *Greaves & Co (Contractors) Ltd v Baynham Meikle and Partners* [1975] 1 W.L.R. 1095, 1100, 1102; *Saif Ali v Sidney Mitchell & Co* [1980] A.C. 198, 218, 220; *Whitehouse v Jordan* [1981] 1 W.L.R. 246, 263; *Maynard v West Midlands Regional Health Authority* [1984] 1 W.L.R. 634, 639; *Thake v Maurice* [1986] Q.B. 644; *Wilson v Best Travel Ltd* [1993] 1 All E.R. 353; *Matrix-securities Ltd v Theodore Goddard* [1998] S.T.C. 1; *Bolitho v City and Hackney Health Authority* [1998] A.C. 232.

[172] *Kimber v W. Willett Ltd* [1947] K.B. 570. See also Vol.II, paras 37–076, 37–082.

[173] *Samuels v Davis* [1943] K.B. 526; *Greaves & Co (Contractors) Ltd v Baynham Meikle and Partners* [1975] 1 W.L.R. 1095; *St Alban's City and DC v International Computers Ltd* [1996] 4 All E.R. 481. Contrast *Lynch v Thorne* [1956] 1 W.L.R. 303; *Thake v Maurice* [1986] Q.B. 644. See Vol.II, para.37–079.

13–033 By ss.14 and 15 of the 1982 Act, where, under a contract for the supply of a service by a supplier acting in the course of a business,[174] the time for the service to be carried out, or the consideration for the service, is not fixed or determined by the contract, left to be fixed or determined in a manner agreed by the contract or determined by the course of dealing between the parties, there are respectively implied terms that the supplier will carry out the service within a reasonable time and that the party contracting with the supplier will pay a reasonable charge.[175]

13–034 **Package travel, etc.** By the Package Travel, Package Holiday and Package Tours Regulations 1992[176] a number of terms are implied in favour of the consumer in contracts for the sale of package travel, package holidays and package tours. These include implied terms: that the contract contains certain elements specified in the Regulations and that these are communicated in writing to the consumer before the contract is made and a copy of them is supplied to him[177]; that the consumer may transfer his booking where he is prevented from proceeding with the package[178]; that if the organiser is constrained before departure to alter significantly an essential term of the contract, such as the price, he will notify the consumer as soon as possible in order to enable the consumer to take appropriate action and in particular to withdraw from the contract without penalty[179]; that if for that reason the consumer withdraws from the contract or if the organiser cancels the package, the consumer will be entitled to take a substitute package or to have repaid to him all moneys paid by him under the contract[180]; and that if a significant proportion of the services contracted for is not provided, the organiser will make suitable alternative arrangements at no extra cost and compensate the consumer for the difference between the services provided and those contracted for.[181] The Regulations also impose (subject to certain exceptions) a strict liability on the other party to the contract for the proper performance of the obligations under the contract, irrespective of whether such obligations are to be performed by that party or by other suppliers of services.[182]

---

[174] See above, fn.169.

[175] *Jonathan Wren & Co Ltd v Microdec Ltd* (1999) 65 Const. L.R. 157.

[176] SI 1992/3288, implementing Council Directive 90/314 [1990] OJ L158/59, and amended by SI 1998/1208, SI 2003/1376, SI 2003/1400. For the relationship between the Regulations and the (Athens) International Convention on the Carriage of Passengers and their Luggage by Sea (above, para.14–117 and Vol.II, para.36–064) see *Lee v Airtours Holidays Ltd* [2004] 1 Lloyd's Rep. 683. See also Grant and Urbanowitz [2001] J.B.L. 253; Chapman [2004] I.T.L.J. (3) 129.

[177] 1999 Regulations reg.9.

[178] 1999 Regulations reg.10.

[179] 1999 Regulations reg.12.

[180] 1999 Regulations reg.13.

[181] 1999 Regulations reg.14; *Charlson v Warner* [2000] C.L.Y. 4043 Cty. Ct.

[182] 1999 Regulations reg.15; *Charlson v Warner* [2000] C.L.Y. 4043; cf. *Evans v Kasmar Villa Holidays Ltd* [2007] EWCA Civ 1003, [2008] 1 W.L.R. 297.

Interest on commercial debts. A term is implied into contracts for the supply of goods and services[183] by the Late Payment of Commercial Debts (Interest) Act 1998 whereby any qualifying debt[184] created by the contract is to carry statutory interest subject to and in accordance with the Act.[185] 13–035

[183] Other than excepted contracts: Late Payment of Commercial Debts (Interest) Act 1998 s.2(5).

[184] Defined in s.3.

[185] s.1(1). See below, para.26–172.

CHAPTER 14

EXEMPTION CLAUSES[1]

		PARA.
1.	In general	14–001
2.	Principles of construction	14–005
3.	Fundamental breach	14–020
4.	Application of principles of construction to particular contracts	14–025
5.	Exemption clauses and third parties	14–039
6.	Statutory control of exemption clauses	14–059
	(a) Unfair Contract Terms Act 1977	14–059
	(b) Misrepresentation Act 1967	14–114
	(c) Other statutes	14–115
7.	Common law qualifications	14–132
8.	Force majeure clauses	14–137

1. IN GENERAL

Generally. It is a common feature of written contracts at the present day (and 14–001
in particular of those in standard form) that the person tendering the document will seek to absolve himself either wholly or in part from liability under the contract or from liability for a tort connected with the contract. In a contract for the sale of goods, for instance, the seller may require the buyer to agree that all conditions and warranties, whether express or implied, statutory or otherwise, in respect of the goods sold are to be excluded.[2] In other contracts, such as a contract for the supply of services, the supplier may seek to protect himself, his employees and sub-contractors, against liability, for example, for negligence. It can reasonably be argued that, in many commercial contracts where both parties are of equal bargaining power, such exclusion or restriction of liability does no more than apportion the risk between the parties, in respect of which one party will be expected to insure. Very often, however, the party imposing the condition is in an economically superior position and can dictate his own terms to the other.[3] So, acting within the general limits prescribed by the doctrine of freedom of contract, the courts have attempted to correct the imbalance by adopting principles of construction which require the party seeking to exclude or restrict his liability to do so in clear and unequivocal terms. Inequality of bargaining power, however, in itself, is not a ground for invalidating such a clause at common law.[4]

---

[1] See Lawson, *Exclusion Clauses and Unfair Contract Terms*, 7th edn (2003); Yates, *Exclusion Clauses in Contracts*, 2nd edn; MacDonald, *Exemption Clauses and Unfair Terms*, 2nd edn.

[2] *L'Estrange v Graucob* [1934] 2 K.B. 394.

[3] See the discussion of this issue in the English and Scottish Law Commission's joint report (2005) Law Com. No.292, Scottish Law Com. No.199.

[4] See below, para.14–135.

14–002 **Incorporation of exemption clauses.** The question whether an exemption clause contained in a written document or notice has been incorporated as a term of the contract is dealt with in the chapter on Express Terms.[5] The normal rule (where the document is not signed) is that the party affected by the clause will be bound if the party tendering the document has done what may reasonably be considered sufficient to give notice of the clause to persons of the class to which he belongs.[6] But a clause may be incorporated by course of dealing between the parties or because both parties are aware that it is the practice of the particular trade to contract subject to exempting conditions.[7]

14–003 **Types of exemption clause.** Exemption clauses may broadly be divided into three categories.[8] First, there are clauses which purport to limit or reduce what would otherwise be the defendant's duty, i.e. the substantive obligations to which he would otherwise be subject under the contract, for example, by excluding express or implied terms, by limiting liability to cases of wilful neglect or default, or by binding a buyer of land or goods to accept the property sold subject to "faults," "defects" or "errors of description". Secondly, there are clauses which purport to exclude or restrict the liability which would otherwise attach to a breach of contract, such as the liability to be sued for breach or to be liable in damages, or which take away from the other party the right to treat as repudiated or rescind the agreement. Thirdly, there are clauses which purport to exclude or restrict the duty of the party in default fully to indemnify the other party, for example, by limiting the amount of damages recoverable against him, or by providing a time-limit within which claims must be made. Traditionally, the approach of English judges has in all cases been to ascertain the liability of the defendant apart from the exemption clause, and then to consider whether or not the clause is sufficient to constitute a defence to that liability.[9] It has, however, been argued[10] that such an approach tends to be misleading, at any rate if applied to exemption clauses which fall within the first two categories. These directly limit the substantive contractual content of the promise and circumscribe the liability of the party in default. The whole contract ought therefore initially to be construed together with the exemption clause. There is considerable logical force in this contention. More recent dicta have tended to support it.[11] The task of the courts has been said to be[12]:

---

[5] See above, paras 12–173 et seq.

[6] *Parker v South Eastern Ry* (1877) 2 C.P.D. 416; *Richardson, Spence & Co v Rowntree* [1894] A.C. 217; *Hood v Anchor Line (Henderson Bros) Ltd* [1918] A.C. 837; *McCutcheon v David Macbrayne Ltd* [1964] 1 W.L.R. 125, HL; *Thornton v Shoe Lane Parking Ltd* [1971] 2 Q.B. 163; *Shepherd Homes Ltd v Encia Remediation Ltd* [2007] EWHC 70 (TCC), [2007] Build. L.R. 135.

[7] See above, paras 12–011, 12–012.

[8] *Kenyon, Sons & Craven Ltd v Baxter Hoare & Co Ltd* [1971] 1 W.L.R. 519, 522; *Trade and Transport Inc v Iino Kaiun Kaisha Ltd* [1973] 1 W.L.R. 210, 230. See also Dawson (1975) 91 L.Q.R. 380.

[9] *Rutter v Palmer* [1922] 2 K.B. 87, 92.

[10] Coote, *Exception Clauses* (1964).

[11] *Suisse Atlantique Société d'Armement Maritime SA v N.V. Rotterdamsche Kolen Centrale* [1967] 1 A.C. 361, 431; *Photo Production Ltd v Securicor Transport Ltd* [1980] A.C. 827, 851.

[12] *Hardwick Game Farm v Suffolk Agricultural Poultry Producers' Association* [1966] 1 W.L.R. 287, 309, 333, 343 (affirmed sub nom. *Henry Kendall & Sons v William Lillico & Sons Ltd* [1969] 2 A.C. 31 HL).

> "... to look at the event [resulting from the breach], and to ascertain from the words and conduct of the parties which created the contract between them what their presumed intention was as to what should be their legal rights and liabilities either original or substituted upon the occurrence of an event of this kind."

The traditional approach has for the most part, however, been adopted in the Unfair Contract Terms Act 1977.[13]

Exemption clauses distinguished from other similar clauses. Agreed damages clauses, by which the parties liquidate the damages payable upon breach, are not to be classified as exemption clauses, at least where the liquidated damages provision is a genuine pre-estimate of the loss likely to be suffered in the event of breach.[14] It has also been said that force majeure clauses are not exemption clauses.[15] Likewise ordinary arbitration clauses are "in essence mere machinery"[16] and so distinct from exemption clauses, being governed by separate rules.[17] But it is possible that a clause which bars one party's claim unless arbitration is begun within a specified time may be treated as an exemption clause in so far as it may be construed not to extend to cover a fundamental breach of contract.[18] 14–004

2. PRINCIPLES OF CONSTRUCTION

General principles. Exemption clauses must be expressed clearly and without ambiguity or they will be ineffective.[19] The clause must clearly express what 14–005

---

[13] See *Phillips Products Ltd v Hyland* [1987] 1 W.L.R. 659, 664; *Smith v Eric S. Bush* and *Harris v Wyre Forest DC* [1990] 1 A.C. 831, 857, 873; Coote (1978) 41 M.L.R. 312; Palmer and Yates [1981] C.L.J. 108; below, para.14–063.

[14] *Suisse Atlantique Société d'Armement Maritime SA v N.V. Rotterdamsche Kolen Centrale* [1967] 1 A.C. 361, 395, 411, 420, 436. cf. 406. See also below, para.14–021.

[15] *Fairclough Dodd & Jones Ltd v J.H. Vantol Ltd* [1957] 1 W.L.R. 136, 143; cf. *Cero Navigation Corp v Jean Lion & Cie* [2000] 1 Lloyd's Rep. 292, 299. But in practice they may have the same effect and be as strictly construed: see also below, paras 14–137—14–153.

[16] *Woolf v Collis Removal Service* [1948] 1 K.B. 11. See also *Atlantic Shipping Co Ltd v Louis Dreyfus & Co* [1922] 2 A.C. 250, 258; *Heyman v Darwins Ltd* [1942] A.C. 356, 373–375, 400. See also Unfair Contract Terms Act 1977 s.13(2); below, para.14–062. But see the Unfair Terms in Consumer Contracts Regulations 1999 (SI 1999/2803) as amended by SI 2001/1186 and s.89 of the Arbitration Act 1996; Vol.II, para.32–013.

[17] See Vol.II, para.32–176.

[18] *Atlantic Shipping Co Ltd v Louis Dreyfus & Co* [1922] 2 A.C. 250, 258; *Ford & Co Ltd v Cie Furness* [1922] 2 K.B. 797; *Smeaton Hanscomb & Co Ltd v Sasson I. Setty Son & Co (No.1)* [1953] 1 W.L.R. 1468. Sed quaere?

[19] *Ailsa Craig Fishing Co Ltd v Malvern Fishing Co Ltd* [1983] 1 W.L.R. 964, 966, 970. See also *Gilbert-Ash (Northern) Ltd v Modern Engineering (Bristol) Ltd* [1974] A.C. 689, 717–718; *Photo Production Ltd v Securicor Transport Ltd* [1980] A.C. 827, 846, 850; *Bem Dis a Turk Ticaret S/A TR v International Agri Trade Co Ltd* [1999] 1 Lloyd's Rep. 729; *How Engineering Services Ltd v Lindner Ceilings Floors Partitions Plc* (1999) 64 Const. L.R. 67, 79; *Cero Navigation Corp v Jean Lion & Cie* [2000] 1 Lloyd's Rep. 292, 297; *Stent Foundations Ltd v MJ Gleeson Group Plc* [2001] Build. L.R. 134; *Amiri Flight Authority v BAE Systems Plc* [2003] EWCA Civ 1447, [2003] 2 Lloyd's Rep. 767 at [25]; *Homburg Houtimport BV v Agrosin Private Ltd (The Starsin)* [2003] UKHL 12, [2004] 1 A.C. 715 at [144]; *Dairy Containers Ltd v Tasman Orient Line CV* [2004] UKPC 22, [2005] 1 W.L.R. 215 at [12]. See also (consumer contracts), below, para.15–129.

its intention is. In *J. Gordon Alison & Co Ltd v Wallsend Shipway and Engineering Co Ltd*,[20] a cylinder was sold by the defendants to the claimants "subject to our usual guarantee clauses". The clause relied on by the defendants "guaranteed" the purchaser against defects of material or workmanship for six months, but excluded liability for consequential damage. The question arose whether the guarantee clause was applicable to this particular contract, and the Court of Appeal held that it was not: "if a person was under a legal liability and wished to get rid of it he could only do so by using clear words".[21] Exemption clauses will therefore be construed strictly, and the degree of strictness appropriate to their construction may properly depend upon the extent to which they involve departure from the implied obligations ordinarily accepted by the parties in entering into a contract of a particular kind[22] and whether the clause purports entirely to exclude an obligation or liability or merely to limit the compensation recoverable from the party in default.[23] However, the principles of construction applicable to written contracts[24] apply equally to exemption clauses to ascertain what meaning the words were intended to bear.[25] If the clause is expressed clearly and unambiguously, there is no justification for placing upon the language of the clause a strained and artificial meaning so as to avoid the exclusion or restriction of liability contained in it.[26]

14–006 **Clause must extend to event.** Each clause must be considered according to its actual wording, but it must clearly extend to the exact contingency or loss which has occurred if it is to protect the party relying on it. Thus in a contract for the sale of goods, a stipulation that the goods are bought "as seen"[27] or the exclusion of liability for "latent defects"[28] will not exclude terms as to quality and fitness for purpose implied by the Sale of Goods Act, the exclusion of warranties will not necessarily exclude conditions,[29] and the exclusion of implied terms will not exclude those which are actually expressed.[30] The exclusion of liability for "consequential loss or damage" will not cover loss which directly and naturally results in the ordinary course of events from the breach, but only

[20] (1927) 43 T.L.R. 323.

[21] (1927) 43 T.L.R. 323, 324.

[22] *Photo Production Ltd v Securicor Transport Ltd* [1980] A.C. 827, 850. See also *Suisse Atlantique Société d'Armement Maritime SA v N.V. Rotterdamsche Kolen Centrale* [1967] 1 A.C. 361, 482.

[23] *Ailsa Craig Fishing Co Ltd v Malvern Fishing Co Ltd* [1983] 1 W.L.R. 964, 966, 970; *George Mitchell (Chesterhall) Ltd v Finney Lock Seeds Ltd* [1983] 2 A.C. 803, 814. Contrast *Darlington Futures Ltd v Delco Australia Pty Ltd* (1987) 68 A.L.R. 385.

[24] See above, para.12–041.

[25] *Sydney City Council v West* (1965) 114 C.L.R. 481.

[26] *Photo Production Ltd v Securicor Transport Ltd* [1980] A.C. 827, 846, 851; *George Mitchell (Chesterhall) Ltd v Finney Lock Seeds Ltd* [1983] 2 A.C. 803; *Darlington Futures Ltd v Delco Australia Pty Ltd* (1987) 68 A.L.R. 385.

[27] *Cavendish-Woodhouse v Mancey* (1984) 82 L.G.R. 376.

[28] *Henry Kendall & Sons v William Lillico & Sons Ltd* [1969] 2 A.C. 31.

[29] *Baldry v Marshall* [1925] 1 K.B. 260; *Wallis, Son & Wells v Pratt & Haynes* [1911] A.C. 394.

[30] *Andrews Bros Ltd v Singer & Co Ltd* [1934] 1 K.B. 17. See *Benjamin's Sale of Goods*, 7th edn (2006), paras 13–026 et seq.

loss which is less direct or more remote.[31] And a clause which provided that "the goods delivered shall be deemed to be in all respects in accordance with the contract" unless the buyer gave notice to the contrary within 14 days of the arrival of the goods, was held not to apply to a claim for damages for short delivery, i.e. in respect of goods not delivered.[32] A clause in a contract of sale or hire-purchase which merely excludes all conditions and warranties, express or implied, will not necessarily extend to the delivery of goods wholly different from the agreed contract goods.[33] A clause may therefore be too narrow in its terms to cover the obligation or liability which it is sought to exclude or restrict.[34]

Inconsistency with main purpose of contract. Conversely, an exemption clause may be so broad and general in scope that to apply it literally would create an absurdity or defeat the main purpose of the contract which the parties had in mind.[35] It is the duty of the courts to give effect to the intentions of the parties as exhibited in their agreement.[36] If, therefore, looking at the whole of the contract, its main purpose and intent is clear, the court will be justified in attributing to the clause a construction which is not inconsistent with that main purpose and intent.[37] Thus a wide deviation clause in a bill of lading was restrictively construed so as not to cover a deviation by the carrier inconsistent with the contract voyage,[38] and a clause in a bill of lading which provided that "the responsibility of the carrier shall be deemed to cease absolutely after the goods are discharged from the ship" was held not to cover a release of the goods to the consignees without production of the bill, as the bill expressly required the goods to be delivered "unto order or assigns".[39] Likewise the court will be 14–007

[31] *Millar's Machinery Co Ltd v David Way & Son* (1935) 40 Com. Cas. 204; *Saint Line Ltd v Richardsons Westgarth Ltd* [1940] 2 K.B. 99; *Croudace Construction Ltd v Cawood's Concrete Products Ltd* [1978] 2 Lloyd's Rep. 55; *British Sugar Plc v NEI Power Projects Ltd* (1997) 87 Build. L.R. 42; *Deepak Fertilisers and Petrochemicals Corp v ICI* [1999] 1 Lloyd's Rep. 387, 402–403; *BHP Petroleum Ltd v British Steel Plc* [1999] 2 Lloyd's Rep. 583, 597–600, [2000] 2 Lloyd's Rep. 277; *Pegler Ltd v Wang (UK) Ltd* [2000] Build. L.R. 218, 227; *Hotel Services (UK) Ltd v Hilton International Hotels (UK) Ltd* [2000] 1 All E.R. (Comm) 750; *Watford Electronics Ltd v Sanderson CFL Ltd* [2001] EWCA Civ 317; [2001] B.L.R. 218; *Ease Faith Ltd v Leonis Marine Management Ltd* [2006] EWHC 232; *Ferryways NV v Associated Pontish Ports* [2008] EWHC 225 (Comm), [2008] 1 Lloyd's Rep. 639 at [84]–[85]. But the correctness of this conclusion was reserved by Lord Hoffmann in *Caledonia North Sea Ltd v Norton (No.2) Ltd* [2002] UKHL 4, [2002] 1 All E.R. (Comm) 321 at [100].

[32] *Beck & Co v Szymanowski & Co* [1924] A.C. 43.

[33] See below, paras 14–027—14–028. But contrast *George Mitchell (Chesterhall) Ltd v Finney Lock Seeds Ltd* [1983] A.C. 803; below, para.14–023.

[34] For further examples, see *Pegler Ltd v Wang (UK) Ltd* [2000] Build. L.R. 218; *Britvic Soft Drinks Ltd v Messer UK Ltd* [2002] 1 Lloyd's Rep. 20, 59, 60 (affirmed [2002] EWCA Civ 548, [2002] 2 Lloyd's Rep. 368).

[35] *Suisse Atlantique Société d'Armement Maritime SA v N.V. Rotterdamsche Kolen Centrale* [1967] 1 A.C. 361, 398.

[36] See above, para.12–072.

[37] *Glynn v Margetson & Co* [1893] A.C. 351, 357; *Mitsubishi Corp v Eastwind Transport Ltd* [2004] EWHC 2924 (Comm); [2005] 1 Lloyd's Rep. 382 at [29].

[38] *Leduc v Ward* (1888) 20 QBD 475; *Glynn v Margetson & Co* [1893] A.C. 351; *Connolly Shaw Ltd v A/S Det Nordenfjeldske D/S* (1934) 49 Ll.L.Rep. 183.

[39] *Sze Hai Tong Bank Ltd v Rambler Cycle Co Ltd* [1959] A.C. 576; *Motis Exports Ltd v Dampskibsselskabet AF 1912 Aktieselskab* [2000] 1 Lloyd's Rep. 213, 216, 217; *East West Corp v*

reluctant to ascribe to an exemption clause a meaning which effectively absolves one party from all duties and liabilities:

> "One may safely say that the parties cannot, in a contract, have contemplated that the clause should have so wide an ambit as in effect to deprive one party's stipulations of all contractual force: to do so would be to reduce the contract to a mere declaration of intent."[40]

In *Tor Line A.B. v Alltrans Group of Canada Ltd*,[41] in a contract of charterparty, shipowners expressly accepted responsibility for delay in delivery of the vessel or for delay during the currency of the charter and for loss or damage to goods on board, if these were caused by unseaworthiness or other personal act or omission or default of the owners or their manager, but stated that they were: "... not to be responsible in any other case nor for damage or delay whatsoever and howsoever caused even if caused by the neglect or default of their servants." In breach of an express warranty, the ship was not of the dimensions specified in the charter. On the charterers' claim for financial loss consequent upon the breach of this warranty, the shipowners relied upon the exemption clause. The House of Lords held that the loss was not covered by the clause. One of the reasons put forward by Lord Roskill[42] in his judgment was that, if the clause were to be construed so as to allow a breach of the warranty to be committed or a failure to deliver the vessel at all to take place without financial redress to the charterers:

> "... the charter virtually ceases to be a contract for the letting of the vessel and the performance of services by the owners ... and becomes no more than a statement of intent by the owners in return for which the charterers are obliged to pay large sums by way of hire, though if the owners fail to carry out their promises as to description or delivery, are entitled to nothing in lieu."

He found it difficult to believe that this conclusion would accord with the "true common intention" of the parties. Nevertheless the intent of the clause may be to qualify the main purpose of the contract, so that there is no inconsistency.[43] And if the clause does not entirely exclude the liability of one party, but merely limits or reduces his liability, it does not render his contractual promises illusory.[44] Further, if in the context of the contract as a whole and of the business relationship between the parties the words of the clause are clear and fairly susceptible of one meaning only, then effect must in any event be given to the clause.[45]

DKBS 1912 [2003] EWCA Civ 83, [2003] 1 Lloyd's Rep. 238 at [85]. Contrast *Glebe Island Terminals Pty Ltd v Continental Seagram Pty Ltd* [1994] 1 Lloyd's Rep. 213.

[40] *Suisse Atlantique Société d'Armement Maritime SA v N.V. Rotterdamsche Kolen Centrale* [1967] 1 A.C. 361, 482.

[41] [1984] 1 W.L.R. 48.

[42] [1984] 1 W.L.R. 48, 58–59 (with whom all other members of the House of Lords agreed).

[43] See, e.g. *G.H. Renton & Co Ltd v Palmyra Trading Corp of Panama* [1957] A.C. 149.

[44] See, e.g. *Ailsa Craig Fishing Co Ltd v Malvern Fishing Co Ltd* [1983] A.C. 964, 971; *Swiss Bank Corp v Brink's Mat Ltd* [1986] 2 Lloyd's Rep. 79, 92–93; *Mitsubishi Corp v Eastwind Transport Ltd* [2004] EWHC 2924.

[45] *Swiss Bank Corp v Brink's Mat Ltd* [1986] 2 Lloyd's Rep. 79, [93]; *Darlington Futures Ltd v Delco Australia Pty Ltd* (1987) 68 A.L.R. 385.

"Four corners" rule. There is some authority for the view that any damage or liability sought to be covered by an exemption clause must fall within the "four corners" of the contract and not outside of it.[46] This principle could be said to derive support from cases which have held an exemption clause to be inapplicable where a carrier deviated without justification from the agreed or usual route,[47] or carried goods above deck in breach of his obligation to carry them under deck,[48] where a bailee stored goods in a place other than that agreed,[49] and where a carrier or bailee in breach of contract parted with possession of the goods to an unauthorised sub-contractor.[50] Such cases, however, may be sui generis.[51] They are better explained as cases where the exemption clause in question was, on its true construction, not intended to cover the breach which occurred[52] and not as establishing any general principle that an exemption clause will be construed to extend only to acts of a party or his servants which fall within the four corners of the contract.[53] In any event, the clause itself may redefine a party's obligations with respect to performance[54] or in its terms be intended to cover even a radical departure from the performance contemplated by the contract.[55] 14–008

Construction contra proferentem. This principle of construction embraces two differing, but closely related, principles.[56] First, since the party seeking to rely upon an exemption clause bears the burden of proving that the case falls 14–009

[46] *Alderslade v Hendon Laundry Ltd* [1945] K.B. 189, 192; *J. Spurling Ltd v Bradshaw* [1956] 1 W.L.R. 461, 465, 469; *Thomas National Transport (Melbourne) Pty Ltd v May & Baker (Australia) Pty Ltd* (1966) 115 C.L.R. 353, 376; *Suisse Atlantique Société d'Armement Maritime SA v Rotterdamsche Kolen Centrale* [1967] 1 A.C. 361, 412, 424, 434; *Levison v Patent Steam Carpet Cleaning Co Ltd* [1978] Q.B. 69, 85.

[47] *London & North Western Ry v Neilson* [1922] 2 A.C. 263, 272; see also below, para.14–029.

[48] *Royal Exchange Shipping Co Ltd v Dixon* (1886) 12 App. Cas. 11, 16, 19; *J. Evans & Sons (Portsmouth) Ltd v Andrea Merzario Ltd* [1976] 1 W.L.R. 1078, 1082, 1084, 1085. But *Wibau Maschinenfabric Hartman SA v Mackinnon Mackenzie & Co* [1989] 2 Lloyd's Rep. 494 (Hague-Visby rules) was overruled in *Daewoo Heavy Industries Ltd v Klipriver Shipping Ltd* [2003] EWCA Civ 45, [2003] 2 Lloyd's Rep. 1.

[49] *Lilley v Doubleday* (1881) 7 QBD 510; *Gibaud v G.E. Ry* [1921] 2 K.B. 426, 435; *Woolf v Collis Removal Service* [1948] 1 K.B. 11; see below, para.14–035.

[50] *Davies v Collins* [1945] 1 All E.R. 247; *Garnham, Harris & Elton Ltd v Ellis (Transport) Ltd* [1967] 1 W.L.R. 940; see below, para.14–038.

[51] *Photo Production Ltd v Securicor Transport Ltd* [1980] A.C. 827, 845. See also *Kenya Railways v Antares Co Pte Ltd* [1987] 1 Lloyd's Rep. 424, 430; *Daewoo Heavy Industries Ltd v Klipriver Shipping Ltd* [2003] EWCA Civ 45 at [15]–[44]; and below, para.14–029.

[52] [1980] A.C. 827. See also *Compania Portorafti Commerciale SA v Ultramar Panama Inc* [1990] 1 Lloyd's Rep. 310; *Parsons Corp v CV Scheepvaartonderneming "Happy Ranger"* [2002] EWCA Civ 694; [2002] 2 Lloyd's Rep. 857 (Hague-Visby Rules).

[53] See *Raymond Burke Motors Ltd v Mersey Docks and Harbour Co* [1986] 1 Lloyd's Rep. 155, 162 ("collateral" negligence); *Darlington Futures Ltd v Delco Australia Pty Ltd* (1987) 68 A.L.R. 385.

[54] *Photo Production Ltd v Securicor Transport Ltd* [1980] A.C. 827, 851.

[55] *George Mitchell (Chesterhall) Ltd v Finney Lock Seeds Ltd* [1983] 2 A.C. 803 (below, para.14–023); *Glebe Island Terminals Pty Ltd v Continental Seagram Pty Ltd* [1994] 1 Lloyd's Rep. 213.

[56] *Pera Shipping Corp v Petroship SA* [1984] 2 Lloyd's Rep. 363, 365; *Youell v Bland Welch & Co Ltd* [1992] 2 Lloyd's Rep. 127, 134.

within its provisions,[57] any doubt or ambiguity will be resolved against him and in favour of the other party.[58] Secondly, as in the case of any other written document,[59] in situations of ambiguity the words of the document are to be construed more strongly against the party who made the document and who now seeks to rely on them. In *John Lee (Grantham) Ltd v Ry Executive*[60] a railway warehouse was leased by the defendants to the plaintiffs. A clause in the lease exempted the defendants from liability for: " . . . loss or damage (whether by act or neglect of the company or their servants or agents or not) which but for the tenancy hereby created would not have arisen." Owing to a fire caused by the negligence of the defendants in allowing a spark to escape from a railway engine, goods in the warehouse were damaged. It was held that the words "which but for the tenancy hereby created would not have arisen" confined the exemption to liabilities created by the relationship of landlord and tenant. Although the clause was capable of a wider construction, it was ambiguous and would be construed more strongly against the defendants, the makers of the document.

14–010 **Liability for negligence.** Liability for negligence may be excluded or restricted if words are used which sufficiently indicate that the parties intended, in the context of their agreement, that such should be the case. Where a clause purports merely to limit the compensation payable by one party for loss or damage caused by his negligence, it is enough that the wording of the clause, when read as a whole, clearly and unambiguously has that effect.[61] But since it is inherently improbable that one party to the contract would intend to absolve the other party entirely from the consequences of the latter's own negligence,[62] more exacting standards are applied to clauses which are alleged to exclude

---

[57] See below, para.14–018.

[58] This appears to be the sense in which the principle was referred to in *Photo Production Ltd v Securicor Transport Ltd* [1980] A.C. 827, 847; *Ailsa Craig Fishing Co Ltd v Malvern Fishing Co Ltd* [1983] 1 W.L.R. 964, 969, 970; *George Mitchell (Chesterhall) Ltd v Finney Lock Seeds Ltd* [1983] 2 A.C. 803, 814; *Homburg Houtimport BV v Agrosin Private Ltd* [2003] UKHL 12, [2004] 1 A.C. 71 at [144]; *Dairy Containers Ltd v Tasman Orient Line CV* [2004] UK PC 22, [2005] 1 W.L.R. 215 at [12].

[59] See above, para.12–083. See also (consumer contracts), below, para.15–131.

[60] [1949] 2 All E.R. 581. See also *Webster v Higgin* [1948] 2 All E.R. 127; *Houghton v Trafalgar Insurance Co Ltd* [1954] 1 Q.B. 247; *Billyack v Leyland Construction Co Ltd* [1968] 1 W.L.R. 471; *Adams v Richardson & Starling Ltd* [1969] 1 W.L.R. 1645, 1653; *Pera Shipping Corp v Petroship SA* [1985] 2 Lloyd's Rep. 103.

[61] *Ailsa Craig Fishing Co Ltd v Malvern Fishing Co Ltd* [1983] 1 W.L.R. 964, 966, 970; *George Mitchell (Chesterhall) Ltd v Finney Lock Seeds Ltd* [1983] 2 A.C. 803, 814. See also *Continental Illinois National Bank & Trust Co of Chicago v Papanicolau* [1986] 2 Lloyd's Rep. 441, 444, and *Skipskredittforeningen v Emperor Navigation* [1998] 1 Lloyd's Rep. 66, 76 ("no set-off" clause) and *Ocean Chemical Transport Inc v Exnor Craggs Ltd* [2000] 1 Lloyd's Rep. 446, 452; *BHP Petroleum Ltd v British Steel Plc* [2000] 2 Lloyd's Rep. 277, 285 (time-limit clause). But see *HIH Casualty and General Insurance Ltd v Chase Manhattan Bank* [2003] UKHL 6, [2003] 2 Lloyd's Rep. 61 at [63]; *Frans Maas (UK) Ltd v Samsung Electronics (UK) Ltd* [2004] EWHC 1502 (Comm), [2004] 2 Lloyd's Rep. 251.

[62] *Gillespie Bros Ltd v Roy Bowles Transport Ltd* [1973] Q.B. 400, 419; *Ailsa Craig Fishing Co Ltd v Malvern Fishing Co Ltd* [1983] 1 W.L.R. 964, 970; *Sonat Offshore SA v Amerada Hess Development Ltd* [1988] 1 Lloyd's Rep. 145, 157; *Stent Foundations Ltd v Ms Gleeson Group Plc* [2001] Build. L.R. 134.

altogether liability for negligence. The duty of a court in approaching the consideration of such clauses was summarised in the form of three propositions in the opinion of the Privy Council delivered by Lord Morton in *R. v Canada S.S. Lines Ltd.*[63] These tests, or guidelines,[64] have been subsequently approved and applied both by the Court of Appeal[65] and the House of Lords[66]:

> "(1) If the clause contains language which expressly exempts the person in whose favour it is made (hereafter called 'the proferens') from the consequences of the negligence of his own servants, effect must be given to that provision . . . (2) If there is no express reference to negligence, the court must consider whether the words used are wide enough, in their ordinary meaning, to cover negligence on the part of the servants of the proferens. If a doubt arises at this point, it must be resolved against the proferens . . . (3) If the words used are wide enough for the above purpose, the court must then consider whether 'the head of damage may be based on some ground other than that of negligence' . . . The 'other ground' must not be so fanciful or remote that the proferens cannot be supposed to have desired protection against it; but subject to this qualification . . . the existence of a possible head of damage other than that of negligence is fatal to the proferens even if the words used are prima facie wide enough to cover negligence on the part of his servants."

Words wide enough to cover negligence. To satisfy the first test, there must be a clear and unmistakable reference to negligence or to a synonym for it.[67] In the absence of any such express reference, it is necessary to proceed to the second test. Words such as "at sole risk",[68] "at customers' sole risk",[69] "at owner's risk"[70] and "at their own risk"[71] will normally cover negligence, as will 14–011

[63] [1952] A.C. 192, 208. For a criticism of these propositions, see Palmer [1983] L.M.C.L.Q. 557.

[64] *Smith v South Wales Switchgear Co Ltd* [1978] 1 W.L.R. 165, 168, 178; *Lamport & Holt Lines Ltd v Coubro & Scrutton (M. & I.) Ltd* [1982] 2 Lloyd's Rep. 42, 45, 48–49, 51; *HIH Casualty and General Insurance Ltd v Chase Manhattan Bank* [2003] UKHL 6, [2003] 2 Lloyd's Rep. 61 at [11], [63], [116].

[65] *Gillespie Bros Ltd v Roy Bowles Transport Ltd* [1973] Q.B. 400; *Lamport & Holt Lines Ltd v Coubro & Scrutton (M. & I.) Ltd* [1982] 2 Lloyd's Rep. 42.

[66] *Smith v South Wales Switchgear Co Ltd* [1978] 1 W.L.R. 165; *HIH Casualty and General Insurance Ltd v Chase Manhattan Bank* [2003] UKHL 6 at [11].

[67] *Clark v Sir William Arrol & Co Ltd* (1974) S.L.T. 90, 92; *Smith v South Wales Switchgear Co Ltd* [1978] 1 W.L.R. 165, 169, 173; *Lamport & Holt Lines Ltd v Coubro & Scrutton (M. & I.) Ltd* [1982] 2 Lloyd's Rep. 42, 45, 47, 51; *Spriggs v Sotheby Parke Bernet & Co* [1986] 1 Lloyd's Rep. 487; *Shell Chemicals Ltd v P.&O. Roadtanks Ltd* [1995] 1 Lloyd's Rep. 297.

[68] *Forbes, Abbott & Lennard Ltd v G.W. Ry* (1927) 44 T.L.R. 97; *The Jessmore* [1951] 2 Lloyd's Rep. 512; *James Archdale & Co Ltd v Comservices Ltd* [1954] 1 W.L.R. 459; *Scottish Special Housing Association v Wimpey Construction U.K. Ltd* [1986] 1 W.L.R. 995; *Norwich City Council v Harvey* [1989] 1 W.L.R. 828.

[69] *Rutter v Palmer* [1922] 2 K.B. 87.

[70] *Burton & Co v English & Co* (1883) 12 QBD 218, 223; *Levison v Patent Steam Carpet Cleaning Co Ltd* [1978] Q.B. 69; cf. *Allan Bros and Co v James Bros & Co* (1897) 3 Com.Cas. 10, 12; *Svenssons Travaruaktiebolag v Cliffe Steamship Co* [1932] 1 K.B. 490, 496; *Exercise Shipping Co Ltd v Bay Maritime Lines Ltd* [1991] 2 Lloyd's Rep. 391.

[71] *Reynolds v Boston Deep Sea Fishing & Ice Co Ltd* (1921) 38 T.L.R. 22, 429; *Pyman S.S. Co v Hull and Barnsley Ry* [1915] 2 K.B. 729. Contrast *Woolmer v Delmer Price Ltd* [1955] 1 Q.B. 291.

words which clearly indicate an intention to exclude all liability without exception, for example, "no liability whatever"[72] or "under no circumstances"[73] or "all liability",[74] or all liability save that specified in the clause.[75] If the defendant merely disclaims liability for "any loss", he may be directing attention to the kinds of losses, and not to their cause or origin; so liability for negligence will not necessarily be excluded.[76] But if he says "however arising" or "any cause whatever", these words can cover losses by negligence.[77] Thus the words "howsoever caused",[78] "from whatever other cause arising",[79] "howsoever arising",[80] "arising from any cause whatsoever",[81] "relieves from all responsibility for any injury, delay, loss or damage, however caused"[82] have been held to be effective. Likewise a clause which excluded liability for any damage "which may arise from or be in any way connected with any act or omission of any person . . . employed by [the defendant]" has been held to be wide enough to cover negligence on the part of the defendant's servants.[83] However, the intention of the parties must be collected from the entire wording of the clause, and in construing the clause other parts of the contract which throw light on the meaning to be given to it are not to be ignored.[84] So, for instance, even such comprehensive words as "any liability . . . whatsoever",[85] "howsoever caused",[86] "any

---

[72] *Reynolds v Boston Deep Sea Fishing & Ice Co Ltd* (1921) 38 T.L.R. 22; *Gibaud v G.E. Ry* [1921] 2 K.B. 426; *Swiss Bank Corp v Brink's Mat Ltd* [1986] 2 Lloyd's Rep. 79. See also *HIH Casualty and General Insurance Ltd v Chase Manhattan Bank* [2003] UKHL 6, [2003] 2 Lloyd's Rep. 61 ("no liability of any nature").

[73] *Haigh v Royal Mail Steam Packet Co* (1883) 52 L.J.Q.B. 640; *Akerib v Booth* [1960] 1 W.L.R. 454 (reversed on other grounds [1961] 1 W.L.R. 367); *Harris Ltd v Continental Express Ltd* [1961] 1 Lloyd's Rep. 251; *J. Carter (Fine Worsteds) Ltd v Hanson Haulage (Leeds) Ltd* [1965] 2 Q.B. 495; *Photo Production Ltd v Securicor Transport Ltd* [1980] A.C. 827, 846. cf. *Taubman v Pacific Steam Navigation Co* (1872) 26 L.T. 704.

[74] *BHP Petroleum Ltd v British Steel Plc* [2000] 2 Lloyd's Rep. 277.

[75] *George Mitchell (Chesterhall) Ltd v Finney Lock Seeds Ltd* [1983] 2 A.C. 803; *Swiss Bank Corp v Brink's Mat Ltd* [1986] 2 Lloyd's Rep. 79.

[76] *Price v Union Lighterage Co* [1904] 1 K.B. 412 ("any loss of or damage to goods which can be covered by insurance").

[77] *Joseph Travers & Sons Ltd v Cooper* [1915] 1 K.B. 73, 101; *Gibaud v G.E. Ry* [1921] 2 K.B. 426, 437; *Rutter v Palmer* [1922] 2 K.B. 87, 94.

[78] *Austin v Manchester, Sheffield & Lincs. Ry* (1852) 10 C.B. 454; *The Stella* [1900] P. 161; *Joseph Travers & Sons Ltd v Cooper* [1915] 1 K.B. 73; *Ashby v Tolhurst* [1937] 2 K.B. 242; *Harris Ltd v Continental Express Ltd*; *White v Blackmore* [1972] 2 Q.B. 651; *Stag Line Ltd v Tyne Shiprepair Group Ltd* [1984] 2 Lloyd's Rep. 211, 222; see also *Hunt & Winterbotham (West of England) Ltd v B.R.S. (Parcels) Ltd* [1962] 1 Q.B. 617 ("however sustained").

[79] *Ashenden v L.B. & S.C. Ry* (1880) 5 Ex.D. 190; *Manchester, Sheffield & Lincs. Ry v Brown* (1883) 8 App. Cas. 703.

[80] *Pyman S.S. Co v Hull & Barnsley Ry* [1915] 2 K.B. 729; *Swiss Bank Corp v Brink's Mat Ltd* [1986] 2 Lloyd's Rep. 79; *Frans Maas (UK) Ltd v Samsung Electronics (UK) Ltd* [2004] EWHC 1502 (Comm), [2004] 2 Lloyd's Rep. 251. cf. *Bishop v Bonham* [1988] 1 W.L.R. 742.

[81] *A.E. Farr Ltd v Admiralty* [1953] 1 W.L.R. 965.

[82] *The Stella* [1900] P. 161.

[83] *Lamport & Holt Lines Ltd v Coubro & Scrutton (M. & I.) Ltd* [1982] 2 Lloyd's Rep. 42. See also *Monarch Airlines Ltd v London Luton Airport Ltd* [1998] 1 Lloyd's Rep. 403 ("act, omission, neglect or default").

[84] *Smith v South Wales Switchgear Co Ltd* [1978] 1 W.L.R. 165, 168.

[85] *Smith v South Wales Switchgear Co Ltd* [1978] 1 W.L.R. 165.

[86] *Raymond Burke Motors Ltd v Mersey Docks and Harbour Co* [1986] 1 Lloyd's Rep. 155.

loss howsoever arising"[87] and "at charterers' risk"[88] may be limited by their context and thus not extend to the negligence of the defendant which it is sought to exclude. On the other hand, where a clause in a charterparty expressly accepted liability for negligence *only* in certain specified respects, it was held that it necessarily followed that it excluded negligence in all other respects.[89]

Liable only if negligent. There is no longer any rule of law that, if the only liability of the *proferens* is for negligence, the clause *must* be construed so as to cover negligence otherwise it would lack subject matter[90]: the duty of the court is always to construe the wording of the clause in question to see what it means.[91] 14–012

Words applicable only to another ground of liability. Lord Morton's third test is more problematical. It derives from a rule of construction enunciated by Lord Greene M.R. in *Alderslade v Hendon Laundry Ltd*[92] that: 14–013

> "Where . . . the head of damage [liability for which is sought to be excluded] may be based on some other ground than that of negligence, the general principle is that the clause must be confined in its application to loss, occurring through that other cause, to the exclusion of loss arising through negligence."

To this statement Lord Morton added the qualification that the "other ground" must not be so fanciful or remote that the *proferens* cannot be supposed to have desired protection against it. Even with this important qualification, however, the Court of Appeal has subsequently cautioned against a too literal or over-legalistic approach.[93] In *Lamport & Holt Lines Ltd v Coubro & Scrutton (M. & I.) Ltd*, May L.J. said[94]:

> "In seeking to apply Lord Morton's third test, we should not ask now whether there is or might be a technical alternative head of legal liability which the relevant exemption clause might cover and, if there is, immediately construe the clause as inapplicable to negligence. We should look at the facts and realities of the situation as they did or must be deemed to have presented themselves to the contracting parties at the time the

---

[87] *Bishop v Bonham* [1988] 1 W.L.R. 742. See also *Sonat Offshore SA v Amerada Hess Development Ltd* [1988] 2 Lloyd's Rep. 145 ("any damage whatsoever").

[88] *Svenssons Travaruaktiebolag v Cliffe S.S. Co* [1932] 1 K.B. 490, 496; *Exercise Shipping Co Ltd v Bay Maritime Lines Ltd* [1991] 2 Lloyd's Rep. 391.

[89] *Mineralimportexport v Eastern Mediterranean Maritime Ltd* [1980] 2 Lloyd's Rep. 572. But contrast *Tor Line A.B. v Alltrans Group of Canada Ltd* [1984] 1 W.L.R. 48; *Airline Engineering v Intercon Cattle Meat* Unreported, January 24, 1983 CA; *Caledonia Ltd v Orbit Value Co Europe* [1994] 1 W.L.R. 221, 229 (affirmed [1994] 1 W.L.R. 1515).

[90] *Alderslade v Hendon Laundry Ltd* [1945] 1 K.B. 189, 192. See also *Rutter v Palmer* [1922] 2 K.B. 87, 92; *Forbes Abbott & Lennard Ltd v G.W. Ry* (1927) 44 T.L.R. 97, 98.

[91] *Hollier v Rambler Motors (A.M.C.) Ltd* [1972] 2 Q.B. 71, 80 (disapproving *Turner v Civil Service Supply Association* [1926] 1 K.B. 50; *Fagan v Green & Edwards Ltd* [1926] 1 K.B. 102); *Gillespie Bros Ltd v Roy Bowles Transport Ltd* [1973] Q.B. 400, 414; *Smith v South Wales Switchgear Co Ltd* [1978] 1 W.L.R. 165, 108; *Lamport & Holt Lines Ltd v Coubro & Scrutton (M. & I.) Ltd* [1982] 2 Lloyd's Rep. 42, 49, 51.

[92] [1945] 1 K.B. 189, 192.

[93] *Lamport & Holt Lines Ltd v Coubro & Scrutton (M. & I.) Ltd* [1982] 2 Lloyd's Rep. 42, 45, 50, 51.

[94] [1982] 2 Lloyd's Rep. 42, 50.

contract was made, and ask to what potential liabilities the one to the other did the parties apply their minds, or must they be deemed to have done so."

A number of cases provide examples[95] of the application of this third test: for instance, it has been illustrated[96] by reference to a common carrier whose liability for loss of or damage to the goods carried may be based on a ground, i.e. strict liability, independent of negligence.[97] And, where there were mutual exceptions in a charterparty in certain specified events including "errors of navigation", one of the reasons advanced for holding that negligent errors of navigation were not covered was that the clause was based on the assumption that a shipowner would be liable without negligence.[98] Lord Morton's third test was also applied in somewhat different circumstances in *Dorset CC v Southern Felt Roofing Co*[99] where a term in a building contract provided that the employer should bear the risk of "loss or damage in respect of the works by fire, lightning, explosion, aircraft and other aerial devices dropped therefrom". The Court of Appeal held that the term did not apply to fire caused by the contractor's negligence since, by the inclusion of events other than fire which might occur without the fault of any human agent, there were risks not fanciful or remote to which the term could relate other than negligence.

14–014 **Non-contractual notices.** In the absence of a contract, the effect of a notice excluding liability may be to defeat a claimant's claim for damages for negligence on the basis of volenti non fit injuria.[100]

14–015 **Indemnity clauses.** It is not unusual to find clauses by which one party does not merely exclude his liability in negligence to the other party but further requires the other party to indemnify him against his liability in negligence to third parties. The law presumes that a party will not readily be granted an

[95] An example often cited is that of *White v John Warwick & Co Ltd* [1953] 1 W.L.R. 1285; but see *Lamport & Holt Lines Ltd v Coubro & Scrutton (M. & I.) Ltd* [1982] 2 Lloyd's Rep. 42, 46. See also *R. v Canada S.S. Lines Ltd* [1952] A.C. 192, 210; *Re Polemis, Furness, Withy & Co Ltd* [1912] 3 K.B. 560; *Olley v Marlborough Court Ltd* [1949] 1 K.B. 532; *A.M.F. International Ltd v Magnet Bowling Ltd* [1968] 1 W.L.R. 1028; *Smith v South Wales Switchgear Co Ltd* [1978] 1 W.L.R. 165, 169, 174, 179; *Caledonia Ltd v Orbit Valve Co Europe* [1994] 1 W.L.R. 221, 228 (affirmed [1994] 1 W.L.R. 1515); *Shell Chemicals Ltd v P.&O. Roadtanks Ltd* [1995] 1 Lloyd's Rep. 297, 301; *Toomey v Eagle Star Insurance Co Ltd (No.2)* [1995] 2 Lloyd's Rep. 88, 92; *Stent Foundations Ltd v M.J. Gleeson Group Plc* [2001] Build. L.R. 134; *Casson v Ostley P.J. Ltd* [2001] EWCA Civ 1013, (2002) 18 Const. L.J. 145. cf. *Try Build Ltd v Blue Star Garages Ltd* (1998) 66 Const. L.R. 90; *HIH Casualty and General Insurance Ltd v North Hampshire Insurance Co* [2001] EWCA Civ 735, [2001] 2 Lloyd's Rep. 161 at [131]–[140]; *HIH Casualty and General Insurance Ltd v Chase Manhattan Bank* [2003] UKHL 6, [2003] 2 Lloyd's Rep. 61.

[96] *Rutter v Palmer* [1922] 2 K.B. 87, 90.

[97] See Vol.II, para.36–014.

[98] *Seven Seas Transportation Ltd v Pacifico Union Marina Corp* [1982] 2 Lloyd's Rep. 465, 475 (affirmed [1948] 1 Lloyd's Rep. 488). cf. *Industrie Chimiche Italia Centrale SpA v Nea Ninemia Shipping Co SA* [1983] 1 Lloyd's Rep. 310, 314.

[99] (1990) 6 Const.L.J. 37. See also *Sonat Offshore SA v Amerada Hess Development Ltd* [1988] 1 Lloyd's Rep. 145.

[100] *McCawley Ry v Furness* (1872) L.R. 8 Q.B. 57; *Buckpitt v Oates* [1968] 1 All E.R. 1145; *Bennett v Tugwell* [1971] 2 Q.B. 267; *Birch v Thomas* [1972] 1 W.L.R. 294. But contrast *Burnett v British Waterways Board Ltd* [1973] 1 W.L.R. 700 (employee acting under orders of his employer), s.149(3) of the Road Traffic Act 1988 and s.2(3) of the Unfair Contract Terms Act 1977. See also below, paras 14–051, 14–083.

indemnity against a loss caused by his own negligence.[101] Nevertheless there is no doubt that a party is entitled to an indemnity against even the consequences of his own negligence if the clause so provides either expressly or by necessary implication.[102] The three tests laid down by Lord Morton in *R. v Canada S.S. Co Ltd*[103] normally apply to indemnity clauses as well as exemption clauses.[104] If there is no express reference to negligence, the question is whether the words used are wide enough in their ordinary meaning to cover negligence on the part of the person seeking to be indemnified or his servants.[105] Even if the words used are wide enough for this purpose, the court must consider whether liability for the loss or damage mentioned in the clause may arise on some ground other than such negligence, which ground is not so fanciful or remote that the parties cannot be supposed to have intended the indemnity to apply to it.[106] The scope of the indemnity will therefore depend upon the wording of the particular clause and the intentions of the parties regarding it to be collected from the whole of their agreement.[107]

---

[101] *Walters v Whessoe* [1968] 1 W.L.R. 1056, 1057; *Smith v South Wales Switchgear Co Ltd* [1978] 1 W.L.R. 165, 168.

[102] But see Unfair Contract Terms Act 1977 s.2 (exclusion or restriction of liabililty for negligence), s.4 (unreasonable consumer indemnities); below, paras 14–071, 14–075; Unfair Terms in Consumer Contracts Regulations 1999 (SI 1999/2083); below, Ch.15.

[103] [1952] A.C. 192, 208; see above, paras 14–010—14–013.

[104] *Smith v South Wales Switchgear Co Ltd* [1978] 1 W.L.R. 165, HL; *Shell Chemicals Ltd v P.&O. Roadtanks Ltd* [1995] 1 Lloyd's Rep. 297; *Deepak Fertilisers and Petrochemicals Corp v ICI* [1999] 1 Lloyd's Rep. 387, 396. See also *Sonat Offshore SA v Amerada Hess Development Ltd* [1988] 1 Lloyd's Rep. 145 (off-hire payment clause). But see *Morris v Breaveglen Ltd* [1997] C.L.Y. 937 (clear intention).

[105] *Smith v South Wales Switchgear Co Ltd* [1978] 1 W.L.R. 165; *Deepak Fertilisers and Petrochemicals Corp v I.C.I.* [1999] 1 Lloyd's Rep. 387.

[106] *Smith v South Wales Switchgear Co Ltd* [1978] 1 W.L.R. 165, 169, 174, 179; *Caledonia Ltd v Orbit Valve Co Europe* [1994] 1 W.L.R. 221, 228 (affirmed [1994] 1 W.L.R. 1515); *Shell Chemicals Ltd v P.&O. Roadtanks Ltd* [1995] 1 Lloyd's Rep. 297.

[107] See (effective indemnities): *A.E. Farr Ltd v Admiralty* [1953] 1 W.L.R. 965; *Swan Hunter and Wigham Richardson Ltd v France, Fenwick Tyne & Wear Co Ltd (The Albion)* [1953] 1 W.L.R. 1026; *James Archdale & Co Ltd v Comservices Ltd* [1954] 1 W.L.R. 459; *Harris Ltd v Continental Express Ltd* [1961] 1 Lloyd's Rep. 251; *Westcott v J.H. Jenner Plasterers and Bovis* [1962] 1 Lloyd's Rep. 309; *Spalding v Tarmac Civil Engineering Ltd* [1967] 1 W.L.R. 1508; *Gillespie Bros & Co Ltd v Roy Bowles Transport Ltd* [1973] 1 Q.B. 400; *Blake v Richards & Wallington Industries* (1974) 16 K.I.R. 151; *Comyn Ching & Co (London) v Oriental Tube Co* [1981] Com.L.R. 67; *Scottish Special Housing Association v Wimpey Construction UK Ltd* [1986] 1 W.L.R. 995; *Thompson v T. Lohan (Plant Hire) Ltd* [1987] 1 W.L.R. 649; *Hancock Shipping Co Ltd v Deacon & Trysail (Private) Ltd* [1991] 2 Lloyd's Rep. 550; *Nelson v Atlantic Power and Gas* (1995) S.L.T. 46; *Morris v Breaveglen Ltd* [1997] C.L.Y. 937; *Smedvig Ltd v Elf Exploration UK Plc* [1998] 2 Lloyd's Rep. 659; *Deepak Fertilisers and Petrochemicals Corp v ICI* [1999] 1 Lloyd's Rep. 387. Contrast (ineffective indemnities) *A.M.F. International Ltd v Magnet Bowling Ltd* [1968] 1 W.L.R. 1028; *Walters v Whessoe Ltd* [1968] 1 W.L.R. 1056; *British Crane Hire Corp Ltd v Ipswich Plant Hire Ltd* [1975] Q.B. 303; *C. Davis Metal Producers Ltd v Gilyott & Scott Ltd* [1975] 2 Lloyd's Rep. 422; *Smith v South Wales Switchgear Co Ltd* [1978] 1 W.L.R. 165; *Actis Co Ltd v Sankis S.S. Co Ltd* [1982] 1 Lloyd's Rep. 7; *Sonat Offshore SA v Amerada Hess Development Ltd* [1988] 1 Lloyd's Rep. 145; *Dorset CC v Southern Felt Roofing Co* (1990) 6 Const.L.J. 37; *Caledonia Ltd v Orbit Valve Co Europe* [1994] 1 W.L.R. 1515; *Glebe Island Terminals Pty Ltd v Continental Seagram Pty Ltd* [1994] 1 Lloyd's Rep. 213; *Shell Chemicals Ltd v P.&O. Roadtanks Ltd* [1995] 1 Lloyd's Rep. 297; *Stirling v Norwest* (1997) S.L.T. 974; *Hawkins v Northern Marine Management Ltd* 1998 S.L.T. 1107; *Stent Foundations Ltd v M.J. Gleeson Group Plc* [2001] Build. L.R. 134.

14–016 **Deliberate breaches.** It has from time to time been suggested that, if the breach by one party evinces "a deliberate disregard of his bounden obligations",[108] it will not be covered by an exemption clause.[109] But there is no rule of law to prevent the exclusion or restriction of liability arising from even a deliberate act or omission by one party or his servants if the parties so intend.[110] In the *Suisse Atlantique* case,[111] Lord Wilberforce said[112]:

> "Some deliberate breaches . . . may be, on construction, within an exceptions clause (for example, a deliberate delay for one day in loading.) This is not to say that 'deliberateness' may not be a relevant factor: depending on what the party in breach 'deliberately' intended to do, it may be possible to say that the parties never contemplated that such a breach would be excused or limited."

It may therefore be relevant to consider whether an exemption clause was intended by the parties to cover deliberate misconduct[113] or a deliberate non-performance of the contract,[114] but "to create a special rule for deliberate acts is unnecessary and may lead astray".[115]

14–017 Some clauses, however, while disclaiming liability for loss or damage caused by negligence, accept liability for loss or damage due to "wilful neglect or default",[116] "wilful misconduct"[117] or "gross negligence".[118]

---

[108] *Sze Hai Tong Bank Co Ltd v Rambler Cycle Co Ltd* [1959] A.C. 576, 588.

[109] *Alexander v Ry Executive* [1951] 2 K.B. 882; *Swan Hunter and Wigham Richardson Ltd v France Tyne & Wear Co Ltd (The Albion)* [1953] 1 W.L.R. 1026, 1030; *Sze Hai Tong Bank Co Ltd v Rambler Cycle Co Ltd* [1959] A.C. 576; *Colverd & Co Ltd v Anglo-Overseas Transport Co Ltd* [1961] 2 Lloyd's Rep. 352, 363. For a time it was considered that a "deliberate" breach had to be one which could be attributed to the contracting party personally, and not one imputed vicariously through his employees or agents: *Chartered Bank of India v British India Steam Navigation Ltd* [1909] A.C. 369, as explained in *Sze Hai Tong Bank Co Ltd v Rambler Cycle Co Ltd* [1959] A.C. 576, 588; *John Carter (Fine Worsteds) Ltd v Harrison Haulage (Leeds) Ltd* [1965] 2 Q.B. 495, but it submitted that this view would no longer be followed. See Guest (1961) 77 L.Q.R. 98, 116.

[110] *Photo Production Ltd v Securicor Transport Ltd* [1980] A.C. 827; below, para.14–022; *Frans Maas (UK) Ltd v Samsung Electronics (UK) Ltd* [2004] EWHC 1052 (Comm), [2004] 2 Lloyd's Rep. 251 at [141]–[152].

[111] [1967] 1 A.C. 361; below, para.14–021.

[112] [1967] 1 A.C. 361, 435. See also at 394, 414, 415, 429.

[113] *Alexander v Ry Executive* [1951] 2 K.B. 882 (but see below, para.14–036, fn.209); *Sze Hai Tong Bank Ltd v Rambler Cycle Co Ltd* [1959] A.C. 576, 587; *Levison v Patent Steam Carpet Cleaning Co Ltd* [1978] Q.B. 69.

[114] *The Cap Palos* [1921] P. 458, 471, 472. Contrast *Compania Portorafti Commerciale SA v Ultramar Panama Inc* [1990] 1 Lloyd's Rep. 310 (Hague-Visby Rules).

[115] *Suisse Atlantique* case [1967] 1 A.C. 361, 435.

[116] On the meaning of this phrase, see *Re City Equitable Fire Insurance Co Ltd* [1925] 1 Ch. 407; *Circle Freight International Ltd v Medeast Gulf Exports Ltd* [1988] 2 Lloyd's Rep. 427; *Bovis International Ltd v Circle Line Partnerships* [1995] N.P.C. 128.

[117] On the meaning of this phrase, see *Hoare v G.W. Ry* (1877) 37 L.T. 186; *Lewis v G.W. Ry* (1877) 3 QBD 195, 206; *Graham v Belfast & Northern Counties Ry Co* [1901] 2 I.R. 13; *Forder v G.W. Ry* [1905] 2 K.B. 532; *Horabin v B.O.A.C.* [1952] 2 Lloyd's Rep 450; *Rustenberg Platinum Mines Ltd v SAA* [1977] 1 Lloyd's Rep. 564, 569; *National Semiconductors (UK) Ltd v UPS Ltd* [1996] 2 Lloyd's Rep. 212, 214; *Lacey's Footwear v Bowler International Freight (Wholesale) Ltd* [1997] 2 Lloyd's Rep. 369; *Thomas Cook Group Ltd v Air Malta Co Ltd* [1997] 2 Lloyd's Rep. 399; *Rolls Royce Plc v Heavylift-Volga DNEPR Ltd* [2000] 1 Lloyd's Rep. 653; *Patrick v Royal London Mutual Insurance Socy Ltd* [2006] EWCA Civ 421, [2006] 2 All E.R. (Comm) 344; *Denfleet International Ltd v TNT Global SPA* [2007] EWCA Civ 405, [2007] 2 Lloyd's Rep. 504. See also Vol.II, paras 35–036—35–040, 36–130.

14–018 **Burden of proof.** It is for the party seeking to rely on the exemption clause to show that the clause, on its true construction, covers the obligation or liability which it purports to restrict or exclude. It would also seem that, in general, it is for that party to prove that the claimant's case is within the clause.[119] If the promise is qualified by an exemption which covers the whole scope of the promise,[120] the claimant must bring himself within the promise as qualified.[121] Further, if there is an exception to the exemption, for example, in the event of wilful neglect or default,[122] then the burden rests upon the claimant to prove that his case falls within the exception.[123] The form is not, however, conclusive, and the matter is in every case a question of construction of the instrument as a whole.[124] In *Firestone Tyre & Rubber Co Ltd v Vokins & Co Ltd*,[125] where a lighterage clause provided that goods were carried only at owner's risk, excepting loss arising from pilferage and theft whilst in the course of transit, Devlin J. held that the onus was still on the lightermen to prove that the loss did not occur by theft or pilferage.

14–019 If the party seeking to rely on the clause makes out a prima facie case that the facts are such as to bring the case within the clause, then it appears that the claimant must disprove it by showing that the loss or damage was occasioned by an act or omission falling outside the clause.[126] However, in *Levison v Patent Steam Carpet Cleaning Co Ltd*,[127] where a clause in a contract of bailment was sufficient to exclude liability for negligence on the part of the bailee but not a "fundamental breach" of the contract, the Court of Appeal held that the onus was on the bailee to show that he was not guilty of a fundamental breach, although the same court had previously decided[128] to the contrary in a case involving a contract of carriage. With the final demise of the doctrine of "fundamental breach",[129] it is suggested that *Levison's* case

---

[118] On the meaning of this phrase, see *Red Sea Tankers Ltd v Papachristidis* [1997] 2 Lloyd's Rep. 547, 586.

[119] *The Glendarroch* [1894] P. 226, 231; *Munro Brice & Co v War Risks Association* [1918] 2 K.B. 78 (reversed on other grounds [1920] 3 K.B. 94). Contrast *Hurst v Evans* [1917] 1 K.B. 352.

[120] See, e.g. *Photo Production Ltd v Securicor Transport Ltd* [1980] A.C. 827; below, para.14–022.

[121] *Munro Brice & Co v War Risks Association* [1918] 2 K.B. 78 at 88.

[122] See above, para.14–017.

[123] *H.C. Smith Ltd v G.W. Ry* [1922] 1 A.C. 178; *Kenyon Son & Craven Ltd v Baxter Hoare Ltd* [1971] 1 W.L.R. 232; *Johnson Matthey & Co Ltd v Constantine Terminals Ltd* [1976] 2 Lloyd's Rep. 215; *Sig Bergesen DY. and Co v Mobil Shipping and Transportation Co* [1993] 2 Lloyd's Rep. 453, 462. cf. *Port Swettenham Port Authority v T.W. Wu & Co* [1979] A.C. 580, and fn.131, below, (bailment).

[124] *Munro Brice & Co v War Risks Association* [1918] 2 K.B. 78 at 89.

[125] [1951] 1 Lloyd's Rep. 32, followed in *Euro Cellular (Distribution) Plc v Danzas Ltd* [2003] EWHC 3161 (Comm), [2004] 1 Lloyd's Rep. 521 at [55].

[126] *The Glendarroch* [1894] P. 226, 231; *Shipping Corp of India Ltd v Gamlen Chemical Co (Australasia) Pty Ltd* (1980) 147 C.L.R. 142, 168.

[127] [1978] Q.B. 69. See also *Woolmer v Delmer Price Ltd* [1955] 1 Q.B. 291; *Euro Cellular (Distribution) Plc v Danzas Ltd* [2003] EWHC 3161 at [64].

[128] *Hunt & Winterbotham (West of England) Ltd v B.R.S. (Parcels) Ltd* [1962] 1 Q.B. 617.

[129] See below, para.14–024. *Levison's* case [1978] Q.B. 69 was decided before *Photo Production Ltd v Securicor Transport Ltd* [1980] A.C. 827 (below, para.14–022) but was not doubted in that case.

deserves reconsideration.[130] A bailor may nevertheless be assisted by the rule that it is for a bailee who is sued in respect of the loss of the goods bailed to prove that the loss occurred without his negligence.[131]

3. FUNDAMENTAL BREACH

14–020 **Supposed rule of law.** It was at one time supposed that a party to a contract would be precluded from relying upon an exemption clause contained in it where he had been guilty of a fundamental breach of contract or the breach of a fundamental term. Statements in certain cases[132] tended to encourage the view that there existed a rule of substantive law preventing a party from relying on an exemption clause in situations of fundamental breach or the breach of a fundamental term, regardless of the wording of the clause. It was predicated that there were certain breaches of contract ("fundamental breaches") which were so totally destructive of the obligations of the party in default that liability for such a breach could in no circumstances be excluded or restricted by means of an exemption clause. Similarly there existed a category of terms ("fundamental terms") which were narrower than a condition of the contract. A fundamental term, so it was said:

> "... underlies the whole contract so that, if it is not complied with, the performance becomes totally different from that which the contract contemplates."[133]

It was part of the "core" of the contract,[134] and "however extensive the exception clause may be, it has no application if there has been a breach of a fundamental term".[135] The two expressions "fundamental breach" and "breach of a fundamental term" were used to some extent interchangeably,[136] but formulated in this way they embodied a rule of law to be applied notwithstanding the agreement of the parties as expressed in the exemption clause.

---

[130] See *Glebe Island Terminals Pty Ltd v Continental Seagram Pty Ltd* [1994] 1 Lloyd's Rep. 213, 238; contrast *Euro Cellular (Distribution) Plc v Danzas Ltd* [2003] EWHC 3161.

[131] *Joseph Travers & Sons Ltd v Cooper* [1915] 1 K.B. 73; *Woolmer v Delmer Price Ltd* [1955] 1 Q.B. 291; *J. Spurling Ltd v Bradshaw* [1956] 1 W.L.R. 461, 466; *Houghland v R.B. Low (Luxury Coaches) Ltd* [1962] 1 Q.B. 694; *Levison v Patent Steam Carpet Cleaning Co Ltd* [1978] Q.B. 69, 82; *Port Swettenham Port Authority v T.W. Wu & Co* [1979] A.C. 580; *Victoria Fur Traders Ltd v Roadline (UK) Ltd* [1981] 1 Lloyd's Rep. 570; see Vol.II, paras 33–012, 33–049.

[132] *J. Spurling Ltd v Bradshaw* [1956] 1 W.L.R. 461, 465; *Karsales (Harrow) Ltd v Wallis* [1956] 1 W.L.R. 936, 940, 943; *Sze Hai Tong Bank Ltd v Rambler Cycle Co Ltd* [1959] A.C. 576, 587, 588, 589; *Yeoman Credit Ltd v Apps* [1962] 2 Q.B. 508, 520; *Charterhouse Credit Co Ltd v Tolly* [1963] 2 Q.B. 683, 710; *Astley Industrial Trust v Grimley* [1963] 1 W.L.R. 1468, 1470; see also above, para.12–021.

[133] *Smeaton Hanscomb & Co Ltd v Sassoon I. Setty, Son & Co* [1953] 1 W.L.R. 1468, 1470; see above, para.12–021.

[134] See Melville (1956) 19 M.L.R. 26.

[135] *Karsales (Harrow) Ltd v Wallis* [1956] 1 W.L.R. 936, 943.

[136] cf. *Suisse Atlantique Société d'Armement Maritime SA v N.V. Rotterdamsche Kolen Centrale* [1967] 1 A.C. 361, 393, 421; *Wathes (Western) Ltd v Austins (Menswear) Ltd* [1976] 1 Lloyd's Rep. 14, 19.

Suisse Atlantique case. The view that the principle of fundamental breach constituted a rule of law was, however, rejected by Pearson L.J. in *U.G.S. Finance Ltd v National Mortgage Bank of Greece*, where he said[137]: 14–021

> "As to the question of 'fundamental breach,' I think there is a rule of construction that normally an exception or exclusion clause or similar provision in a contract should be construed as not applying to a situation created by a fundamental breach of the contract. This is not an independent rule of law imposed by the court on the parties willy-nilly in disregard of their contractual intention. On the contrary it is a rule of construction based on the presumed intention of the contracting parties. . . . This rule of construction is not new in principle but it has become prominent in recent years in consequence of the tendency to have standard forms of contract containing exceptions clauses drawn in extravagantly wide terms, which would produce absurd results if applied literally."

This statement was unanimously approved by the House of Lords in *Suisse Atlantique Société d'Armement Maritime SA v N.V. Rotterdamsche Kolen Centrale*.[138] In that case, shipowners sued the charterers of a ship for damages for delays in loading and unloading the chartered vessel. The charterers relied on the usual demurrage clause in the charterparty as establishing the full measure of their liability; but the shipowners contended that this clause did not protect the charterers since the breaches of contract which caused the delays amounted to a fundamental breach of contract. They claimed damages at large. The House of Lords rejected this claim. Their Lordships held:

(i) that the demurrage clause was not an exemption clause but an agreed damages provision[139];

(ii) that, in any event, since the shipowners had not treated the charter as repudiated, they were still bound by its provisions[140]; and

(iii) that, even if the clause were an exemption clause, it plainly covered the breach alleged, whether or not this was "fundamental" in the sense that it would have entitled the shipowners to be discharged.[141]

Their Lordships were clearly of the opinion that any statement of the principle of fundamental breach as a rule of law could not be supported in principle or in the light of previous authority.[142] So far as the use of the expression "fundamental breach" was concerned, Lord Wilberforce pointed out[143] that it had been used in the cases to denote two quite different things, namely:

---

[137] [1964] 1 Lloyd's Rep. 446, 450. See also *Gibaud v G.E. Ry* [1921] 2 K.B. 426, 435; *The Cap Palos* [1921] P. 458, 470, 472; *L. & N.W. Ry v Neilson* [1922] 2 A.C. 263, 272; *Cunard S.S. Co v Buerger* [1927] A.C. 1, 13; *Frenkel v MacAndrews & Co Ltd* [1929] A.C. 545, 562; *Calico Printers' Association v Barclays Bank* (1931) 36 Com.Cas. 197, 203; *Connolly Shaw v Nordenfieldske S.S. Co* (1934) 50 T.L.R. 418.

[138] [1967] 1 A.C. 361; see Treitel (1966) 29 M.L.R. 546.

[139] See above, para.14–004.

[140] [1967] 1 A.C. 361, 395, 407, 413, 426, 437.

[141] [1967] 1 A.C. 361, 395, 407, 415, 426, 437.

[142] [1967] 1 A.C. 361, 392, 399, 405, 410, 425, 431–432.

[143] [1967] 1 A.C. 361, 431.

(i) a performance totally different from that which the contract contemplated;

(ii) a breach of contract more serious than one which would entitle the other party merely to damages and which (at least) would entitle him to refuse further performance of the contract.

There was no necessary coincidence between these two kinds of (so-called) fundamental breach. After giving a series of examples[144] of how the courts had approached the problem of a fundamental breach in the former sense, he concluded[145]:

> "The conception, therefore, of 'fundamental breach' as one which, through ascertainment of the parties' contractual intentions, falls outside an exceptions clause is well recognised and comprehensible."

On the other hand, Lord Reid said[146]:

> "General use of the term 'fundamental breach' is of recent origin, and I can find nothing to indicate that it means either more or less than the well known type of breach which entitles the innocent party to treat it as repudiatory and to rescind the contract."

While, therefore, their Lordships were agreed that the application of an exemption clause to a breach of contract was a matter of construction of the contract, the question whether and to what extent any special rules were applicable to cases of "fundamental breach" (in the sense of "total" as opposed to repudiatory breach), was to some extent left open.

14–022 **Securicor case.** Certain statements in the *Suisse Atlantique* case further suggested (perhaps by way of illustration only) that in particular instances of fundamental breach an exemption clause would or would be presumed to be inapplicable.[147] Moreover, in his speech Lord Reid said[148]:

> "I do not think that there is generally much difficulty where the innocent party has elected to treat the breach as a repudiation, bring the contract to an end and sue for damages. Then the whole contract has ceased to exist, including the exclusion clause, and I do not see how that clause can then be used to exclude an action for loss which will be suffered by the innocent party after it has ceased to exist."

Lord Reid's statement was taken up and extended by the Court of Appeal in subsequent cases[149] which held that the protection of an exemption clause ceased

[144] [1967] 1 A.C. 361, 432–435.

[145] [1967] 1 A.C. 361, 434. See also Lord Dilhorne, 393.

[146] [1967] 1 A.C. 361, 397. See also Lord Hodson, 410; Lord Upjohn, 422.

[147] See Lord Denning M.R. in *Levison v Patent Steam Carpet Cleaning Co Ltd* [1978] Q.B. 69; *Photo Production Ltd v Securicor Transport Ltd* [1978] 1 W.L.R. 856, 863.

[148] [1967] 1 A.C. 361, 398. See also Lord Upjohn, 425.

[149] *Harbutt's "Plasticine" Ltd v Wayne Tank and Pump Co Ltd* [1970] 1 Q.B. 447. See also *Farnworth Finance Facilities Ltd v Attryde* [1970] 1 W.L.R. 1053; *Eastman Chemical International A.G. v N.M.T. Trading Ltd* [1972] 2 Lloyd's Rep. 25; *Wathes (Western) Ltd v Austins (Menswear) Ltd* [1976] 1 Lloyd's Rep. 14 (where contract affirmed).

to be available to a party guilty of a repudiatory breach if the other party accepted the breach as terminating the contract or if the breach was of such a nature as to render the contract impossible of further performance. This departure was, however, condemned by the House of Lords in *Photo Production Ltd v Securicor Transport Ltd*.[150] In that case, the defendants agreed to provide a visiting patrol service to the claimants' factory at a charge of £8. 15s. a week. The contract contained an exemption clause, the most relevant part of which stated:

> "Under no circumstances shall the company [the defendants] be responsible for any injurious act or default by any employee of the company unless such act or default could have been foreseen and avoided by the exercise of due diligence on the part of the company as his employer."

An employee of the defendants deliberately lit a fire in the factory, and a large part of the premises was burned down. The Court of Appeal held[151] that the defendants, having been employed to safeguard the factory, had committed a fundamental breach of their contract with the claimants and that the exemption clause could not be construed to cover the act of their employee in setting the premises on fire. It was further held that the destruction of the factory brought the contract to an end by rendering further performance impossible so that the defendants could not rely on the exemption clause to protect them from the consequences of the breach. The House of Lords reversed the Court of Appeal's decision. Their Lordships unanimously rejected the view that a breach of contract by one party, accepted by the other as discharging him from further performance of his obligations under the contract, brought the contract to an end, and, together with it, any exemption clause.[152] The House further reaffirmed[153] the principle that the question whether an exemption clause protected one party to a contract in the event of breach, or in the event of what would (but for the presence of the exemption clause) have been a breach, depended upon the proper construction of the contract. They held that, as a matter of construction, the exemption clause in question clearly relieved the defendants from liability. The defendants had effectively modified their obligation to one of exercising due diligence in their capacity as employers. The clause apportioned the risk between the parties: the risk of arson not being accepted by the defendants having regard to the nature and cost of the services provided and falling on the claimants who could more economically insure against it.

George Mitchell case. A third leading case is that of *George Mitchell (Chesterhall) Ltd v Finney Lock Seeds Ltd*,[154] where the respondents ordered from the appellants, who were seed merchants, a quantity of Dutch winter white cabbage seeds. The seeds supplied were invoiced as "Finney's Late Dutch Special". Owing to errors by the appellants' suppliers and employees, the seeds were in 14–023

[150] [1980] A.C. 827. See also *Ailsa Craig Fishing Co Ltd v Malvern Fishing Co Ltd* [1983] 1 W.L.R. 964; *Lifesavers (Australasia) Ltd v Frigmobile Pty Ltd* (1983) 1 N.S.W.R. 431.

[151] [1978] 1 W.L.R. 856.

[152] [1980] A.C. 827, 844–845, 847–850, 853. See also s.9(1) of the Unfair Contract Terms Act 1977. An exception may exist in "deviation" cases; see below, para.14–029.

[153] [1980] A.C. 827, 845, 850–851, 853.

[154] [1983] 2 A.C. 803.

fact not of this variety but were autumn cabbage seeds. The resulting crop proved to be worthless and had to be ploughed in. In an action by the respondents for wasted expenditure and loss of anticipated profits, the appellants relied on their standard conditions of sale. These provided: first, that in the event of any seeds sold or agreed to be sold not complying with the express terms of the contract of sale, the limit of the appellants' obligation was to replace the seeds or refund the purchase price; secondly, that the appellants excluded:

> " . . . all liability for any loss or damage arising from use of any seeds . . . supplied by us and for any consequential loss or damage arising out of such use or any failure in the performance of or any defect in any seeds . . . supplied by us or for any other loss or damage whatsoever save for, at our option, liability for any such replacement or refund as aforesaid";

thirdly, that express or implied conditions and warranties not stated in the conditions were excluded. A majority of the Court of Appeal[155] held that, at common law, this wording was insufficient to limit the appellants' liability. Oliver L.J.[156] considered that the first condition applied only to seeds "sold or agreed to be sold" and so could only relate to goods which were actually the subject matter of the contract between the parties, i.e. winter white cabbage seeds. The second condition was merely a supplement to the first and did not cover a case where what had been supplied was wholly different from what had been ordered. The House of Lords, however, unanimously held that, at common law, the limitation was effective.[157] The second condition, read as a whole, unambiguously limited the appellants' liability to replacement of the seeds or a refund of the price. The defective seeds were seeds sold and delivered, just as clearly as they were seeds supplied, by the appellants to the respondents. The judgment of Oliver L.J. came, it was said[158]:

> " . . . dangerously near to reintroducing by the back door the doctrine of 'fundamental breach' which this House in *Securicor* . . . had so forcibly evicted from the front."

14–024 **Conclusion.** It is clear that there is now no rule of law by which exemption clauses are rendered ineffective in the face of a "fundamental breach" or the breach of a "fundamental term". In the *Photo Production* case, Lord Diplock stated[159] that, if the expression "fundamental breach" is to be retained, it should, in the interests of clarity, be confined to the ordinary case of a breach of which the consequences are such as to entitle the innocent party to elect to put an end to all primary obligations of both parties remaining unperformed. No express reference was made by him to the expression "fundamental term", but the inference is that there exists no category of terms which can be said to be in any

---

155 [1983] Q.B. 284 (Oliver and Kerr L.JJ., Lord Denning M.R. dissenting).

156 Kerr L.J. (with whom Oliver L.J. agreed) also based his decision on the ground that the clause was not sufficiently unambiguous to exclude liability for negligence: see above, para.14–010.

157 But the clause was, however, held unreasonable under the modified s.55 of the Sale of Goods Act 1979, as set out in para.11 of Sch.1 to that Act. See now the Unfair Contract Terms Act 1977; below, para.14–091.

158 [1983] 2 A.C. at 813.

159 [1980] A.C. 827, 849. See also the *Suisse Atlantique* case [1967] 1 A.C. 361, 397, 410, 422.

sense "fundamental" other than conditions.[160] On this basis, it is submitted that there is no presumption that, in inserting a clause of limitation or exclusion into their contract, the parties are not contemplating its application to a fundamental breach or the breach of a fundamental term.[161] The question is in all cases whether the clause, on its true construction, extends to cover the obligation or liability which it is sought to exclude or restrict.

4. APPLICATION OF PRINCIPLES OF CONSTRUCTION TO PARTICULAR CONTRACTS

Generally. The principles of construction mentioned in the second section of this chapter may now be illustrated in their application to particular contracts. Certain of the cases cited were, however, decided at a time when the principle of "fundamental breach" was to a greater or less extent recognised by the courts. Such cases should probably now be regarded as instances where an exemption clause was, as a matter of construction, held to be inapplicable. 14–025

Contracts of sale of goods: terms about title. Section 6(1) of the Unfair Contract Terms Act 1977[162] invalidates (except in the case of international sales)[163] any term exempting from the terms about title implied by s.12 of the Sale of Goods Act 1979. Even at common law, however, it is probable that the courts would be reluctant to hold that an exemption clause, framed in general terms, was intended by the parties completely to exclude liability for breach of the implied term on the part of the seller that he has a right to sell the goods, since "the whole object of a sale is to transfer property from one person to another."[164] They would have to be satisfied that the parties intended the transaction to be merely the sale and purchase of a chance (*emptio spei*) that the seller might or might not have a good title to the goods sold.[165] 14–026

Sale of goods: terms as to quality, etc. Section 6(2) of the 1977 Act[166] further invalidates the exclusion of the terms as to quality, fitness for purpose, and correspondence with description and sample, implied by ss.13 to 15 of the Sale of Goods Act 1979, if the buyer "deals as consumer".[167] In any other case, an exemption clause is enforceable only in so far as it satisfies the requirement of reasonableness.[168] But, at common law, if there is a gross disparity between the goods as described in the contract of sale and as delivered, a number of cases 14–027

---

[160] [1980] A.C. 827, 849. See also the *Suisse Atlantique* case [1967] 1 A.C. 361, 422; and above, para.14–021.

[161] But see Lord Upjohn in the *Suisse Atlantique* case [1967] 1 A.C. 361, 427 and Thomas J. in *China Shipbuilding Corp v Nippon Yusen Kabukishi Kaisha* [2000] 1 Lloyd's Rep. 367, 376.

[162] See below, para.14–078; Vol.II, para.43–072.

[163] See s.26 of the 1977 Act; below, para.14–110; Vol.II, para.43–110.

[164] *Rowland v Divall* [1923] 2 K.B. 500, 507. See also Guest (1961) 77 L.Q.R. 98, 100. Contrast Hudson (1957) 20 M.L.R. 236; (1961) 24 M.L.R. 690; and see Coote, *Exception Clauses* (1964), p.61.

[165] *Chapman v Speller* (1850) 14 Q.B. 621; *Eichholz v Bannister* (1864) 17 C.B.(N.S.) 708; *Bagueley v Hawley* (1867) L.R. 2 C.P. 625; *Warmings Used Cars v Tucker* [1956] S.A.S.R. 249. See also s.12(3) of the Sale of Goods Act 1979: Vol.II, para.43–072.

[166] See below, para.14–078; Vol.II, para.43–104; But see 1977 Act s.26 (international sales).

[167] Defined in s.12 of the 1977 Act; below, para.14–066; Vol.II, para.43–106.

[168] s.6(3). See below, para.14–084; Vol.II, para.43–108.

have held that an exemption clause, for example, which purports to require the buyer to take the goods "with all faults and imperfections", or to exclude the seller's liability for errors of description, or to take away the buyer's right to reject the goods, may be held not to apply to a failure to supply the contract goods.[169] Even a clause in the familiar form which excludes all conditions and warranties, express or implied by common law, statute or otherwise, may possibly not be construed to cover the delivery of goods which are wholly different from those contracted for.[170] However, there is no rule of law to prevent a seller, who—to use a familiar example—has contracted to deliver peas, from excluding or restricting his liability in the event that he delivers beans,[171] or permits him to substitute beans in their place,[172] provided that the clause is sufficiently unambiguous in its terms to admit of this construction.

14–028 **Hire purchase.** Section 6 of the Unfair Contract Terms Act 1977[173] contains provisions prohibiting, either absolutely or subject to certain qualifications, exclusion of the terms as to title, quality, fitness for purpose, and correspondence with description or sample implied by ss.8 to 11 of the Supply of Goods (Implied Terms) Act 1973.[174] At common law, principles have been applied to hire-purchase transactions which are similar to those applied to contracts of sale. It has been held, for example, that a clause in such terms as:

> ". . . no condition or warranty as to the condition or fitness for any purpose of the goods is given by the owner or implied herein"

will not be construed to extend to the supply of goods which are so defective that what is delivered is totally different from that promised.[175] It is also probable that

---

[169] *Shepherd v Kain* (1821) 5 B. & Ald. 240; *Nichol v Godts* (1854) 10 Exch. 191; *Wieler v Schilizzi* (1856) 17 C.B. 619; *Josling v Kingsford* (1863) 13 C.B.(N.S.) 447; *Azémar v Casella* (1867) L.R. 2 C.P. 677; *Bowes v Shand* (1877) 2 App. Cas. 455, 480; *Gorton v Macintosh* [1883] W.N. 103; *Wallis, Son and Wells v Pratt and Haynes* [1911] A.C. 394; *Wimble v Lillico* (1922) 38 T.L.R. 296; *Munro & Co Ltd v Meyer* [1930] 2 K.B. 312; *Green v Arcos Ltd* (1931) 47 T.L.R. 336; *Wilensko v Fenwick* [1938] 3 All E.R. 429; *Champanhac & Co Ltd v Waller & Co Ltd* [1948] 2 All E.R. 724; *Smeaton Hanscomb & Co Ltd v Sassoon I. Setty, Son & Co (No.1)* [1953] 1 W.L.R. 1468, 1470; *Boshali v Allied Commercial Exporters Ltd* (1961) 105 S.J. 987; *Suisse Atlantique Société d'Armement Maritime SA v N.V. Rotterdamsche Kolen Centrale* [1967] 1 A.C. 361, 404, 410, 427, 433; *Benjamin's Sale of Goods*, 7th edn (2006), paras 13–028, 13–029, 13–031, 13–032; Vol.II, para.43–112.

[170] *Pinnock Bros v Lewis and Peat* [1923] 1 K.B. 690; *Andrews Bros (Bournemouth) Ltd v Singer & Co Ltd* [1934] 1 K.B. 17, 23; *Suisse Atlantique Société d'Armement Maritime v N.V. Rotterdamsche Kolen Centrale* [1967] 1 A.C. 361, 404, 413, 432, 433. Contrast *L'Estrange v Graucob Ltd* [1934] 2 K.B. 394. See also *Beck & Co v Szymanowski & Co* [1924] A.C. 43, 48; *Pollock & Co v Macrae* (1922) S.C.(HL) 192; and below, para.14–028 fn.175 (hire purchase).

[171] *George Mitchell (Chesterhall) Ltd v Finney Lock Seeds Ltd* [1983] 2 A.C. 803 (although, at 813, Lord Bridge said "[i]n my opinion, this is not a 'peas and beans' case at all".).

[172] See Lord Devlin [1966] C.L.J. at 212.

[173] See below, para.14–078; Vol.II, para.38–370.

[174] See Vol.II, paras 38–296, 38–362.

[175] *Karsales (Harrow) Ltd v Wallis* [1956] 1 W.L.R. 936; *Yeoman Credit Ltd v Apps* [1962] 2 Q.B. 508; *Charterhouse Credit Ltd v Tolly* [1963] 2 Q.B. 683 (which was overruled in *Photo Production Ltd v Securicor Transport Ltd* [1980] A.C. 827); *Unity Finance Ltd v Hammond* (1962) 106 S.J. 327; *Suisse Atlantique* [1967] 1 A.C. 361, 402, 404, 425, 433; *Farnworth Finance Facilities Ltd v Attryde* [1970] 1 W.L.R. 1053; *Guarantee Trust of Jersey v Gardner* (1973) 117 S.J. 564 CA. Contrast *Handley v Marston* (1962) 106 S.J. 327; *Astley Industrial Trust Ltd v Grimley* [1963] 1 W.L.R. 584.

the courts would not construe a general exemption clause to have so wide an ambit as to negative the implied undertaking on the part of the owner that he has a good title to the goods let on hire, particularly in view of the fact that such terms as "owner" and "option to purchase" appear in the agreement.[176]

Carriage of goods: deviation. Contracts for the carriage of goods are controlled only to a limited extent by the Unfair Contract Terms Act 1977.[177] At common law, in a contract for the carriage of goods, any unnecessary deviation from the agreed or customary route constitutes a breach of the contract of affreightment.[178] Such a breach entitles the owner to treat himself as discharged, and, unless, with knowledge of the facts, he elects to affirm the transaction, the special terms of the contract (including any exemption clause) which are designed to apply to the contract journey are held to have no application to the deviating journey.[179] So strict is this rule that although the deviation has not been the cause of any loss to the owner's goods and is a mere incident in the voyage, nevertheless, once it has taken place the carrier is no longer entitled to rely on clauses of exemption contained in the contract, unless it can be shown that the loss would have happened in any event.[180] But even if the contract is treated as continuing, exemption clauses will be strictly construed, so that, for example, a disclaimer of liability for loss of or damage to goods "in transit" will not extend to cover a deviation.[181] Deviation cases are, however, sui generis and not to be extended.[182] Moreover, clauses which confer upon the carrier a liberty to deviate 14–029

[176] See Vol.II, para.38–296. For the implied undertakings of title at common law, see *Karflex Ltd v Poole* [1933] 2 K.B. 251; *Mercantile Union Guarantee Corp v Wheatley* [1938] 1 K.B. 490; *Warman v Southern Counties Car Finance Corp Ltd* [1949] 2 K.B. 576.

[177] See ss.2, 3 and Sch.1 paras 2, 3. See below, paras 14–071, 14–072, 14–106, 14–107. cf. para.14–111.

[178] *L. & N.W. Ry v Neilson* [1922] 2 A.C. 363 (carriage by land); *Hain S.S. Co Ltd v Tate & Lyle Ltd* (1936) 41 Com.Cas. 350 (carriage by sea). See also *Rotterdamsche Bank N.V. v B.O.A.C.* [1953] 1 W.L.R. 493, 502–503 (carriage by air); *Suisse Atlantique Société d'Armement Maritime SA v N.V. Rotterdamsche Kolen Centrale* [1967] 1 A.C. 361, 390, 399, 411, 422, 433; Coote, *Exception Clauses* (1964), p.80. See Vol.II, para.36–036.

[179] See *Davis v Garrett* (1830) 6 Bing. 716; *Leduc v Ward* (1888) 20 QBD 475; *The Dunbeth* [1897] P. 133; *Mallett v G.E. Ry* [1899] 1 Q.B. 309; *J. Thorley Ltd v Orchis S.S. Ltd* [1907] 1 K.B. 660; *Internationale Guano, etc. v Macandreir & Co* [1909] 2 K.B. 360; *Gunyon v S.E. & Chatham Ry Companies' Managing Committee* [1915] 2 K.B. 370; *J. Morrison & Co Ltd v Shaw, Savill & Albion Co Ltd* [1916] 2 K.B. 783; *London & N.W. Ry v Neilson* [1922] 2 A.C. 263; *U.S. Shipping Board v Bunge y Born* (1925) 31 Com. Cas. 118; *Cunard S.S. Co Ltd v Buerger* [1927] A.C. 1; *Stag Line Ltd v Foscolo, Mango & Co Ltd* [1932] A.C. 328; *Hain S.S. Co Ltd v Tate & Lyle Ltd* (1936) 41 Com. Cas. 350.

[180] *Suisse Atlantique* [1967] 1 A.C. 361, 442. cf. *Drew Brown v The Orient Trader* [1973] 2 Lloyd's Rep. 174.

[181] *L. & N.W. Ry v Neilson* [1922] 2 A.C. 263, 278.

[182] *Photo Production Ltd v Securicor Transport Ltd* [1980] A.C. 827, 845. In *Kenya Railways v Antares Pte Ltd* [1987] 1 Lloyd's Rep. 424, 430 and *State Trading Corp of India v M. Golodetz Ltd* [1989] 2 Lloyd's Rep. 277, 289, Lloyd L.J. stated that "they should now be assimilated into the ordinary law of contract", but this would be difficult to achieve while it remains the case that the protection of the clause goes in the absence of affirmation. See Baughen [1991] L.M.C.L.Q. 70. cf. *Daewoo Heavy Industries Ltd v Klipriver Shipping Ltd* [2003] EWCA Civ 451, [2003] 2 Lloyd's Rep. 1.

will, if clearly expressed, be upheld[183] although they will be so construed as not substantially to defeat the main purpose of the contract voyage.[184]

14–030 **Carriage of goods: delay.** It is also the duty of the carrier to carry the goods with all reasonable dispatch to their destination. An unreasonable and protracted delay may entitle the charterer or consignor to treat the contract as repudiated.[185] Delay will not necessarily lie outside the scope of an exemption clause,[186] but it will do so where the parties cannot be taken to have intended that the clause should extend to the period of the delay[187] or to a risk consequent upon the delay which is wholly at variance with the contract of carriage.[188]

14–031 **Carriage on deck.** Where a carrier of goods by sea undertakes to carry the goods under deck, an exemption clause which excludes or restricts his liability for loss or damage to the goods carried may be held to be inapplicable if the goods are carried on deck.[189] The same might apply if goods carried by land are similarly conveyed in an unauthorised manner.

14–032 **Road and seaworthiness.** A carrier of goods by land probably does not give any implied warranty, in the sense of an absolute undertaking, that he will provide a roadworthy vehicle or a competent and honest driver or crew.[190] At common law, however, a carrier of goods by sea, in the absence of an express stipulation to the contrary,[191] impliedly undertakes that his ship is seaworthy.[192] Although an undertaking of seaworthiness has been said "to underlie the whole contract of affreightment",[193] its breach will not entitle the shipper to be discharged unless the breach is such as to frustrate the commercial purpose of the

---

[183] *Mayfair Photographic Supplies (London) Ltd v Baxter Hoare & Co Ltd* [1972] 1 Lloyd's Rep. 410; *Trade and Transport Inc v Iino Kaiun Kaisha Ltd* [1973] 1 W.L.R. 210, 232.

[184] *Leduc v Ward* (1988) 20 QBD 475; *Glynn v Margetson* [1893] A.C. 351; *Potter v Burrell* [1897] 1 Q.B. 97, 104; *V.O.S. of Moscow v Temple S.S. Co Ltd* (1945) 173 L.T. 373, 376; *Suisse Atlantique* [1967] 1 A.C. 361, 393, 412, 427, 430.

[185] *Freeman v Taylor* (1831) 8 Bing. 124; *Scaramanga v Stamp* (1880) 5 C.P.D. 295; *Brandt v Liverpool, Brazil & River Plate Steam Navigation Co* [1924] 1 K.B. 575; *Cunard S.S. Co Ltd v Buerger* [1927] A.C. 1. See Vol.II, para.36–037.

[186] *Colverd & Co Ltd v Anglo-Overseas Transport Ltd* [1961] 2 Lloyd's Rep. 352. cf. *Marston Excelsior Ltd v Arbuckle Smith & Co Ltd* [1971] 1 Lloyd's Rep. 70.

[187] *The Cap Palos* [1921] P. 458 (towage); *Brandt v Liverpool, Brazil and River Plate S.N. Co* [1924] 1 K.B. 575, 597, 601; *Bontex Knitting Works Ltd v St John's Garage* [1943] 2 All E.R. 690; affirmed [1944] 1 All E.R. 381n. But see *Suisse Atlantique* [1967] 1 A.C. 361, 435.

[188] *Thomas National Transport (Melbourne) Pty Ltd v May & Baker (Australia) Pty Ltd* [1966] 2 Lloyd's Rep. 347.

[189] *Royal Exchange Shipping Co Ltd v Dixon* (1886) 12 App. Cas. 11, 16, 19; *J. Evans & Sons (Portsmouth) Ltd v Andrea Merzario Ltd* [1976] 1 W.L.R. 1078, 1082, 1084, 1085. Contrast *Kenya Railways v Antares Co Pte Ltd* [1987] 1 Lloyd's Rep. 424; *Daewoo Heavy Industries Ltd v Klipriver Shipping Ltd* [2003] EWCA Civ 451, [2003] 2 Lloyd's Rep. 1 (Hague-Visby or Hague rules).

[190] *Readhead v Midland Ry* (1869) L.R. 4 Q.B. 379; *J. Carter (Fine Worsteds) Ltd v Hanson Haulage (Leeds) Ltd* [1965] 2 Q.B. 495.

[191] Such a stipulation must be expressed in clear words and without ambiguity, or it will be insufficient: *Rathbone v McIver* [1903] 2 K.B. 378; *Elderslie v Borthwick* [1905] A.C. 93; *Nelson v Nelson* [1908] A.C. 16; *Chartered Bank v British India Steam Navigation Co* [1909] A.C. 369, 375; *The Rossetti* [1972] 2 Lloyd's Rep. 116.

[192] But under the Carriage of Goods by Sea Act 1971 Sch. art.III(1), the carrier is only bound to exercise due diligence to make the ship seaworthy. See also s.3 of the 1971 Act.

[193] *Atlantic Shipping and Trading Co Ltd v Louis Dreyfus & Co* [1922] 2 A.C. 250, 260.

contract.[194] Nevertheless, as a matter of construction, exceptions in the charter or bill of lading may not be read as applying to breaches of an obligation to provide a seaworthy ship[195] unless their meaning is clear and unambiguous.[196]

Misdelivery by carrier. Misdelivery of the goods does not, of itself, prevent the application of an exemption clause in a contract of carriage.[197] But where the main object and intent of the contract is that delivery should be made to a certain person or persons, the clause may be limited and modified to the extent necessary to give effect to that object and intent. In *Sze Hai Tong Bank Ltd v Rambler Cycle Co Ltd*[198] goods carried by sea were to be delivered "unto order or his assigns", but the contract provided that the responsibility of the carrier should be deemed to cease absolutely after the goods were discharged from the ship. After the goods were discharged from the ship, the carrier's agent released the goods to the consignees without production of the bill of lading. It was held that the exemption clause could not be construed to apply to a deliberate breach by the carrier of his primary obligation under the contract. 14–033

Bailment: acts inconsistent with bailment. Contracts of bailment for deposit may be controlled in certain situations by the Unfair Contract Terms Act 1977.[199] At common law, any act of a bailee which is basically inconsistent with the terms of the bailment, such as the sale,[200] pledge[201] or offering for sale[202] of the goods bailed, puts an end to the bailment and the immediate right to possession of the goods forthwith revests in the bailor.[203] It is probable that, in the absence of specific authority to do such acts, a court would hold that they were not within 14–034

---

194 *The Europa* [1908] P. 84; *Kish v Taylor* [1912] A.C. 604, 617; *Hongkong Fir Shipping Co v Kawasaki Kisen Kaisha* [1962] 2 Q.B. 26; see below, para.24–040.

195 *Tattersall v National S.S. Co Ltd* (1884) 12 QBD 297. See also *Steel v State Line S.S. Co* (1877) 3 App. Cas. 72.

196 *Kish v Taylor* [1912] A.C. 604; *Bank of Australasia v Clan Line* [1916] 1 K.B. 39; *Atlantic Shipping and Trading Co Ltd v Louis Dreyfus & Co* [1922] 2 A.C. 250, 257. *Petrofina SA of Brussels v Compagnie Italiana Transporto Olii Minerali of Genoa* (1937) 63 T.L.R. 650, 653. But see *Parsons Corp v CV Scheepvaartonderneming "Happy Ranger"* [2002] EWCA Civ 694, [2002] 2 Lloyd's Rep. 357 (Hague-Visby rules).

197 *Smackman v General Steam Navigation Co* (1908) 98 L.T. 396; *Chartered Bank v British India Steam Navigation Co* [1909] A.C. 369; *Pringle of Scotland v Continental Express* [1962] 2 Lloyd's Rep. 80; *Port Jackson Stevedoring Pty Ltd v Salmond and Spraggon (Australia) Pty Ltd* [1981] 1 W.L.R. 138; *Chellaram & Co Ltd v China Ocean Shipping Co* [1989] 1 Lloyd's Rep. 493. See also *Hollins v J. Davy Ltd* [1963] 1 Q.B. 844 (bailment), and Vol.II, paras 36–029, 36–040.

198 [1959] A.C. 576. See also *Alexander v Railway Executive* [1951] 2 K.B. 882 (bailment); *Sydney City Council v West* (1965) 114 C.L.R. 481; *Suisse Atlantique* case [1967] 1 A.C. 361, 411, 434; *Kanematsu (Hong Kong) Ltd v Eurasia Express Line* [1998] 1 C.L.Y. 4404; *Motis Exports Ltd v Dampskibsselskabet AF 1912 Aktieselskab* [2000] 1 Lloyd's Rep. 213, 216, 217; *East West Corp v DKBS 1912* [2003] EWCA Civ 83, [2003] Q.B. 1509 at [65]–[68], [85]. cf. *Port Jackson Stevedoring Pty Ltd v Salmond and Spraggon (Australia) Pty Ltd* [1981] 1 W.L.R. 138; *Nissho Iwai Australia Ltd v Malaysian International Shipping Corp Berhad* (1989) 86 A.L.R. 375; *Sucre Export SA v Northern Shipping Ltd* [1994] 2 Lloyd's Rep. 266; *Pyramid Sound NV v Briese Schiffahrts GmbH & Co* [1995] 2 Lloyd's Rep. 144.

199 ss.2, 3; see below, paras 14–071, 14–072.

200 *Fenn v Bittleston* (1851) 7 Exch. 152.

201 *Nyberg v Handelaar* [1892] 2 Q.B. 202.

202 *North Central Wagon and Finance Co v Graham* [1950] 2 K.B. 7.

203 See Vol.II, paras 33–014, 33–023, 33–034, 33–042, 33–051, 33–077.

the ambit of an exemption clause which simply limited or excluded the bailee's liability for loss of or damage to the goods bailed.[204]

14–035 **Storage in wrong place.** Likewise, under a contract of bailment:

> "If the bailee uses a place other than the agreed one for storing the goods, or otherwise exposes the goods to risks quite different from those contemplated by the contract, he cannot rely on clauses in the contract designed to protect him against liability within the four corners of the contract, and has only such protection as is afforded him by the common law."[205]

It should be emphasised, however, that this principle is again one of construction only: the terms of the contract may not require storage in a particular place, and may be otherwise sufficient to exclude liability for negligence, so that the bailee will not be liable.[206]

14–036 **Misdelivery by bailee.** Upon termination of the bailment, a bailee is normally under an obligation to return the goods to the bailor or his nominee. If he negligently delivers the goods to a person not entitled to receive them, this will not necessarily preclude him from relying on an exemption clause, which may well be construed to cover the misdelivery in question. In *Hollins v J. Davy Ltd*,[207] the claimant garaged his motorcar at the defendants' garage under a contract which excluded liability for misdelivery. An employee of the defendants honestly, but mistakenly, delivered the car to a person who fraudulently represented that he had the claimant's authority to collect it, and the car was lost. It was held that this act was covered by the exemption clause. On the other hand, in *Alexander v Ry Executive*,[208] where the officials in charge of a railway cloakroom permitted an unauthorised person to break open and remove the baggage of a depositor without the production of the cloakroom ticket, it was held that an exemption clause limiting liability for loss or misdelivery could not be relied upon to protect the railway executive. These cases are not easily distinguishable except on the ground that the former involved an honest, though

---

[204] *North Central Wagon and Finance Co v Graham* [1950] 2 K.B. 7, 15; *Alexander v Ry Executive* [1941] 2 K.B. 882, 889; *Garnham, Harris & Elton Ltd v Ellis (Transport) Ltd* [1967] 1 W.L.R. 940, 946.

[205] *Suisse Atlantique* case [1967] 1 A.C. 361, 412. See also at 392, 424, 434, and *Lilley v Doubleday* (1881) 7 QBD 510; *Gibaud v G.E. Ry* [1921] 2 K.B. 426, 435; *Alderslade v Hendon Laundry Ltd* [1945] K.B. 189, 192; *J. Spurling Ltd v Bradshaw* [1956] 1 W.L.R. 461, 465; *Mendelssohn v Normand Ltd* [1970] 1 Q.B. 177, 184; Coote, *Exception Clauses* (1964), p.99.

[206] *Harris v G.W. Ry* (1876) 1 QBD 515; *Gibaud v G.E. Ry* [1921] 2 K.B. 426; *Kenyon Son & Craven Ltd v Baxter Hoare & Co Ltd* [1971] 1 W.L.R. 519.

[207] [1963] 1 Q.B. 844. See also *Ashby v Tolhurst* [1937] 2 K.B. 242; *B.G. Transport Service Ltd v Marston Motor Co Ltd* [1970] 1 Lloyd's Rep. 371.

[208] [1951] 2 K.B. 882. See also *Tozer Kemsley & Millbourn (Australasia) Pty Ltd v Collier's Interstate Transport Service Ltd* (1956) 94 C.L.R. 384; *Sze Hai Tong Bank Ltd v Rambler Cycle Co Ltd* [1959] A.C. 576 (carriage); *Sydney City Council v West* (1965) 114 C.L.R. 481; *Levison v Patent Steam Carpet Cleaning Co Ltd* [1978] Q.B. 69.

negligent, error, whereas the latter was concerned with a misdelivery which was known to be unauthorised by the terms of the bailment.[209]

Theft or deliberate damage. A clause which is sufficient to exclude or restrict a bailee's liability for negligence may not in its terms be sufficient to exclude or restrict liability for theft by the bailee's servants, or damage by reckless or wilful misconduct.[210] 14–037

Sub-contracting. The terms of a contract of carriage or bailment may expressly or impliedly permit the carrier or bailee to sub-contract his obligations to a third party.[211] If the contract, on its true construction, does not authorise the carrier or bailee to sub-contract, or limits the persons who may properly be employed as sub-contractors, it would appear that the carrier or bailee will not be protected if he exceeds his authority by an exemption clause which is intended to apply only while the goods are in his possession or control.[212] 14–038

5. EXEMPTION CLAUSES AND THIRD PARTIES

Application to third parties. It not infrequently happens that one of the parties to a contract seeks to extend the burden of its exempting provisions to persons who are not in any direct contractual relationship with him, or endeavours to confer the benefit of those provisions on persons outside the contract, e.g. to his employees, agents or sub-contractors. At common law, the general rule is that the doctrine of privity of contract[213] prevents the application of an exemption clause to third parties, although this general rule is subject to a number of exceptions or qualifications.[214] The common law rule has, however, been fundamentally affected by the Contracts (Rights of Third Parties) Act 1999.[215] Exemption clauses are unequivocally brought within the purview of the Act.[216] In any case involving the application of an exemption clause to a third party it will therefore be necessary to consider whether and, if so, to what extent the common law rule has been altered by this statute. 14–039

The general common law rule: burden. At common law, two persons cannot by contract impose the burden of an exemption clause on one who is not 14–040

[209] In *Suisse Atlantique* case [1967] 1 A.C. 361, 435, Lord Wilberforce rejects the view that there is a separate category of "deliberate breaches" (see above, para.14–016) and explains *Alexander v Ry Executive* [1951] 2 K.B. 882 as a case of "total departure" from what was contractually contemplated. cf. *J. Carter (Fine Worsteds) Ltd v Hanson Haulage (Leeds) Ltd* [1965] 2 Q.B. 495.

[210] *Levison v Patent Steam Carpet Cleaning Co Ltd* [1978] Q.B. 69.

[211] See below, para.14–054, Vol.II, para.33–026.

[212] *Davies v Collins* [1945] 1 All E.R. 247; *Garnham, Harris & Elton Ltd v Ellis (Transport) Ltd* [1967] 1 W.L.R. 940; *The Berkshire* [1974] 1 Lloyd's Rep. 185.

[213] See above, para.3–036, below, Ch.18.

[214] See below, para.14–045.

[215] The Act applies to contracts made after May 11, 2000; s.10(2).

[216] s.1(b).

a party to that contract.[217] In *Haseldine v C.A. Daw & Son Ltd*,[218] the owners of a block of flats by contract employed the defendants to maintain a lift in the premises. This contract purported to exempt the defendants from liability for accidents due to their negligence.[219] A third party was injured owing to the negligent repair of the lift by the defendants. It was held that the defendants were not protected against an action in tort by the third party.

14–041 **Effect of the 1999 Act: burden.** The Contracts (Rights of Third Parties) Act 1999 does not alter the common law rule. But where, by virtue of the provisions of the Act, a contract confers upon a third party a "positive" right to enforce a contractual term, that right may be affected by an exemption clause in the contract which excludes or limits the liability of one of the parties for breach of that term.[220] Suppose that A (the promisor) enters into a contract with B (the promisee) which contains a term under which A is to render certain services to C (a third party), but the contract also contains an exemption clause which effectively excludes or limits the liability of A to B for breach of the term. If A fails to perform the services or fails to perform them satisfactorily, the exemption clause will be available as a defence to A in any proceedings brought by C under the Act to enforce his right to those services. The reason is that the Act provides that, where (in reliance on the Act)[221] proceedings for enforcement of a term are brought by a third party, the promisor is to have available to him by way of defence any matter that arises from or in connection with the contract and is relevant to the term, and would have been available to him by way of defence if the proceedings had been brought by the promisee.[222] The question, however, arises whether A can rely on the exemption clause as against C if, by statute, it would not have been available as a defence to A if the proceedings had been brought by B (for example, because it is caught by s.3 of the Unfair Contract Terms Act 1977[223] and is unreasonable). The position appears to be that, in general,[224] A can rely on the exemption clause where C is seeking to enforce against A a contractual liability arising under the contract between A and B notwithstanding the invalidity of the clause between A and B.[225]

14–042 **The general common law rule: benefit.** At common law, two persons cannot by contract confer the benefit of an exemption clause on one who is not a party

---

[217] *Leigh and Sillavan Ltd v Aliakmon Shipping Co Ltd* [1986] A.C. 785, 817. See also the cases cited in paras 14–056, 14–057, below (building contracts) and paras 14–055—14–056, below (carriage of goods and bailment). Contrast *Pyrene Co Ltd v Scindia Navigation Co Ltd* [1954] 2 Q.B. 402, which was said in *Scruttons Ltd v Midland Silicones Ltd* [1962] A.C. 446, 471 to be supportable only on the ground of an implied contract between the party seeking to rely on the exemption and the third party: see also *The Kapetan Markos (No.2)* [1987] 2 Lloyd's Rep. 321, 331.

[218] [1941] 2 K.B. 343. Contrast *Fosbroke-Hobbes v Airwork Ltd* [1937] 1 All E.R. 108, which is explicable (if at all) only on the ground that the contracting party contracted as agent for his guests; *Cockerton v Naviera Aznar SA* [1960] 2 Lloyd's Rep. 450, 461 (agency for wife).

[219] [1941] 2 K.B. 343, 379.

[220] See below, para.18–088.

[221] s.1; see below, para.14–043.

[222] s.3(2).

[223] Below, para.14–072.

[224] But see the position with respect to s.2(1) of the Unfair Contract Terms Act 1977, below, paras 14–071, 18–118. Contrast s.2(2) and s.7(2) below, paras 14–071, 14–079, 18–118.

[225] ss.1(4), 7(4); see below, para. 18–118. Law Com. No.242, 1996, 13, 10.

to that contract.[226] Thus it was held that an employee of the London Passenger Transport Board, who was sued by a passenger for damages in negligence, was not protected by the terms of a pass given to the passenger by the Board which expressly purported to exempt the employees of the Board from all liability[227]; that the master and boatswain of a ship, who were sued by a passenger alleged to have been injured by their negligence, were not protected by a clause inserted in the passenger's ticket by their employers[228]; that stevedores, who had negligently damaged a drum of chemicals while handling it, were not protected by a clause in the bill of lading which exempted the carriers of the goods from liability in excess of a certain pecuniary limit[229]; and that a licensor of technology and know-how was not protected by a clause in a contract between its licensee and the person to whom the technology and know-how was transferred.[230]

Effect of the 1999 Act: benefit. The Contracts (Rights of Third Parties) Act 1999 enables a third party, subject to certain conditions, to take advantage of an exemption clause inserted in a contract for his benefit. The provisions of the Act are dealt with more fully in Ch.18 of this work.[231] Section 1 of the Act sets out the circumstances in which a person who is not a party to a contract (a "third party") may in his own right enforce a term of a contract if the contract expressly provides that he may[232] or if the term purports to confer a benefit on him.[233] The Act makes it clear that it applies so as to enable a third party to avail himself of an exclusion or limitation clause as well as to enforce "positive" rights such as 14–043

---

[226] Contrast *London Drugs Ltd v Kuehne & Nagel International Ltd* (1992) 97 D.L.R. (4th) 261 (Supreme Court of Canada); noted (1993) 109 L.Q.R. 349; (1993) 56 M.L.R. 722.

[227] *Cosgrove v Horsfall* (1945) 62 T.L.R. 140. See also *Genys v Matthews* [1966] 1 W.L.R. 758, and below, para.14–052; cf. *Gore v Van der Lann* [1967] 2 Q.B. 31.

[228] *Adler v Dickson* [1955] 1 Q.B. 158.

[229] *Scruttons Ltd v Midland Silicones Ltd* [1962] A.C. 446. See also *Wilson v Darling Island Stevedoring and Lighterage Co Ltd* [1956] 1 Lloyd's Rep. 346; *Krawill Machinery Corp v Robert C. Head & Co Ltd* [1959] 1 Lloyd's Rep. 305; *Canadian General Electric Co Ltd v The "Lake Bosomtwe"* [1970] 2 Lloyd's Rep. 80; *Herrick v Leonard and Dingley Ltd* [1975] 2 N.Z.L.R. 566; *The Suleyman Stalskiy* [1976] 2 Lloyd's Rep. 609; *Lummus v East African Harbours Corp* [1978] 1 Lloyd's Rep. 317; *Circle Sales & Import Ltd v The Tarantel* [1978] 1 F.C. 269 (Canada); *Raymond Burke Motors Ltd v Mersey Docks and Harbour Co* [1986] 1 Lloyd's Rep. 155. Contrast *Cabot Corp v John W. McGrath Corp* [1971] 2 Lloyd's Rep. 351; *The Mormaclynx* [1971] 2 Lloyd's Rep. 476; *Cable & Montanari Inc v American Export Isbrandtsen Lines Ltd* [1968] 1 Lloyd's Rep. 260 (affirmed 386 F. 2d 839; (1967) cert. denied (1968) 390 U.S. 1013); *New Zealand Shipping Co Ltd v A.M. Satterthwaite & Co Ltd* (*The Eurymedon*) [1975] A.C. 154; *Tessler Bros (B.C.) Ltd v Italpacific Line and Matson Terminals Inc* [1975] 1 Lloyd's Rep. 210; *Eisen und Metall A.G. v Ceres Stevedoring Co Ltd* [1977] 1 Lloyd's Rep. 665; *Miles International Corp v Federal Commerce & Navigation Co* [1978] 1 Lloyd's Rep. 285; *Port Jackson Stevedoring Pty Ltd v Salmond and Spraggon (Australia) Pty Ltd* (*The New York Star*) [1981] 1 W.L.R. 138; *Godina v Patrick Operations Pty Ltd* [1984] 1 Lloyd's Rep. 333; *The Pioneer Container* [1994] 2 A.C. 324; *The Mahkutai* [1996] A.C. 650, 664–665; *Homburg Houtimport BV v Agrosin Private Ltd (The Starsin)* [2003] UKHL 12, [2004] 1 A.C. 715 (see also the principles relating to sub-bailments discussed below, para.14–054). See now Art.IV *bis* (2) of the Hague-Visby Rules contained in the Schedule to the Carriage of Goods by Sea Act 1971.

[230] *Deepak Fertilisers and Petrochemicals Corp v ICI* [1998] 2 Lloyd's Rep. 139, 163; [1999] 1 Lloyd's Rep. 387.

[231] Below, paras 18–088—18–120.

[232] s.1(1)(*a*).

[233] s.1(1)(b), subject to s.1(2) (contrary intention).

the right to payment of money or to the performance of some other obligation.[234] However, the third party must be expressly identified in the contract by name, as a member of a class or as answering a particular description but need not be in existence when the contract is entered into.[235] So, for example, if A (the promisor) enters into a contract with B (the promisee) by which A agrees that B's sub-contractors may avail themselves of a term of the contract which excludes or limits the liability of B to A, and A seeks to hold C, a sub-contractor of B, liable, C may rely on the term as a defence notwithstanding that there is no privity of contract between himself and A. In principle, it appears to be the intention of the Act that C is to enjoy no greater and no less a right to enforce the exemption clause by relying on it than if he had been a party to the contract.[236] Section 3(6) provides:

> "Where in any proceedings brought against him a third party seeks in reliance on section 1 to enforce a term of a contract (including, in particular, a term purporting to exclude or limit liability), he may not do so if he could not have done so (whether by reason of any particular circumstances relating to him or otherwise) had he been a party to the contract".

Thus if, in the above illustration, the term of the contract which excludes or restricts liability is ineffective because it is caught by s.3 of the Unfair Contract Terms 1977[237] and is unreasonable, C will not any more be entitled to rely on it against A than if he (C) had been a party to the contract.[238] The Act does not in so many words provide that the right of C, the third party, to rely on the term is commensurate with that of B, the promisee, but no doubt this will be the practical effect of the Act in most cases.

14–044 **Contracts excluded from the 1999 Act.** Certain types of contract are excluded (wholly or partly) from the application of the 1999 Act.[239] In particular these contracts include contracts for the carriage of goods by sea[240] and contracts for the carriage of goods by rail or road, or for the carriage of cargo by air, which are subject to the rules of the appropriate international transport convention.[241] However, it is expressly provided that a third party may in reliance on s.2 of the Act avail himself of an exclusion or limitation of liability in such a contract.[242]

14–045 **Common law exceptions preserved.** Section 7(1) of the 1999 Act specifically provides that the right conferred on a third party by s.1 "does not affect any right or remedy of a third party that exists or is available apart from this Act". The provisions of the Act supplement and are in addition to the exceptions to the privity of contract doctrine at common law. If, therefore, apart from the Act, a

---

[234] s.1(6).
[235] s.1(3), see below, para.18–094.
[236] s.1(4).
[237] Below, para.14–072.
[238] See below, para.14–072.
[239] s.6; see below, para.18–112.
[240] Defined in s.6(6)(7). See *Benjamin's Sale of Goods*, 7th edn (2006), Ch.18.
[241] Defined in s.6(8).
[242] s.6(5).

person could be bound by or take the benefit of an exemption clause in a contract to which he is not a party, then the situation remains unaffected by the Act. In most cases, where a third party claims to be entitled to the benefit of an exemption clause, he will rely on s.1 of the 1999 Act. But where the requirements of that section are not satisfied, for example, where the person claiming the benefit of the clause is not identified or not sufficiently identified in the contract, he can still fall back on a common law exception (if any is applicable) to the privity rule. Also, if it is sought to establish that a person is bound by an exemption clause in a contract to which he is not a party, this can only be done by reference to an exception to the privity rule at common law since the Act does not generally provide for the burden of an exemption clause to be imposed on third parties. It is therefore necessary to consider what exemptions exist to the doctrine of privity of contract apart from the Act.

Vicarious immunity. The proposition was at one time advanced that, at common law, where a contract contained an exemption clause, any employee or agent who acted under the contract could claim the same exemption as attached to the liability of his employer or principal.[243] This concept of "vicarious immunity" was, however, rejected by the House of Lords in *Scruttons Ltd v Midland Silicones Ltd*[244] where it was held that no such principle existed in English law so far as exemption clauses were concerned. 14–046

Agency. At common law a third party may be able to take the benefit of an exemption clause by showing that the party imposing the exemption clause was acting as agent in the transaction so as to bring the third party into a direct contractual relationship with the claimant.[245] This device was first employed in the nineteenth century in relation to railways. It frequently happened that passengers or goods might be transported over a network of independent railway companies before reaching their destination. The question arose whether the exemption clauses inserted in the contract of carriage with the contracting company could be made to extend to the others with whom there seemed to be no direct contractual relationship. The courts held that the contracting company should be treated either as agent for the passenger or consignor to contract with the other companies[246] or as their agent to contract with him.[247] In more modern times clauses are frequently encountered in standard form contracts whereby one contracting party, e.g. a carrier,[248] repairer[249] or building contractor[250] purports to contract on behalf of his employees, agents and the independent contractors employed by him, and to extend to such employees, agents and independent 14–047

---

243 *Elder Dempster & Co Ltd v Paterson, Zohonis & Co Ltd* [1924] A.C. 522, 534, 548, 565; *Mersey Shipping and Transport Co Ltd v Rea Ltd* (1925) 21 Ll.L.Rep. 375, 378; *Gilbert Stokes and Kerr Proprietary Ltd v Dalgety & Co Ltd* (1948) 81 Ll.L.Rep. 337; *Waters Trading Co Ltd v Dalgety & Co Ltd* [1951] 2 Lloyd's Rep. 385.

244 [1962] A.C. 446.

245 *Elder Dempster & Co Ltd v Paterson, Zohonis & Co Ltd* [1924] A.C. 522, 534; *Scruttons Ltd v Midland Silicones Ltd* [1962] A.C. 446, 474, 480.

246 *Hall v N.E. Ry* (1875) L.R. 10 Q.B. 437, 442.

247 *Hall v N.E. Ry* (1875) L.R. 10 Q.B. 437, 443; *Barrett v G.N. Ry* (1904) 20 T.L.R. 175.

248 See Vol.II, para.36–046.

249 *Stag Line Ltd v Tyne Ship Repair Group Ltd* [1984] 2 Lloyd's Rep. 211, 217.

250 *Southern Water Authority v Carey* [1985] 2 All E.R. 1077.

contractors protection from liability. Such clauses are—at least in the context of carriage of goods by sea—usually referred to as "Himalaya clauses".[251] In *Scruttons Ltd v Midland Silicones Ltd*[252] the House of Lords left open the question whether, at common law, stevedores could be protected by an exemption clause contained in a contract of carriage to which they were not a party if the carrier contracted as agent on their behalf. Lord Reid said[253]:

> "I can see a possibility of success of the agency argument if (first) the bill of lading makes it clear that the stevedore is intended to be protected by the provisions in it which limit liability, (secondly) the bill of lading makes it clear that the carrier, in addition to contracting for these provisions on his own behalf, is also contracting as agent for the stevedore that these provisions should apply to the stevedore, (thirdly) the carrier has authority from the stevedore to do that, or perhaps later ratification by the stevedore would suffice, and (fourthly) that any difficulties about consideration moving from the stevedore were overcome."

14–048 These four propositions were held to have been satisfied in *New Zealand Shipping Co Ltd v A.M. Satterthwaite & Co Ltd* (*The Eurymedon*).[254] In that case, the Judicial Committee, by a majority, held that a stevedore, who had negligently damaged goods in the course of unloading, was protected by a clause in a bill of lading which contained appropriate words exempting him from liability and which was stated to have been made by the carrier acting as agent on his behalf. An action against him by the shipper therefore failed. The Board considered that:

> " . . . the bill of lading brought into existence a bargain initially unilateral but capable of becoming mutual between the shipper and the [stevedore], made through the carrier as agent. This became a full contract when the [stevedore] performed services by discharging the goods. The performance of these services for the benefit of the shipper was the consideration for the agreement by the shipper that the [stevedore] should have the benefit of the exemptions and limitations contained in the bill of lading."[255]

This reasoning is, however, somewhat artificial, and the courts of certain Commonwealth jurisdictions initially showed a reluctance to follow the *Eurymedon* case or a readiness to find grounds for distinguishing it.[256] But it has subsequently been endorsed and justified on grounds of policy: that established commercial practice now requires the stevedore, in normal circumstances, to

---

[251] After the name of the cruise liner in *Adler v Dickson* [1955] 1 Q.B. 158.
[252] [1962] A.C. 446.
[253] [1962] A.C. 446, 474.
[254] [1975] A.C. 154 (noted (1974) 90 L.Q.R. 301).
[255] *The Eurymedon* [1975] A.C. 154, 167–168; cf. *Homburg Houtimport BV v Agrosin Private Ltd (The Starsin)* [2003] UKHL 12, [2004] 1 A.C. 715 at [163], [197].
[256] *Herrick v Leonard and Dingley Ltd* [1975] 2 N.Z.L.R. 566; *The Suleyman Stalskiy* [1976] 2 Lloyd's Rep. 609; *Lummus v East African Harbours Corp* [1978] 1 Lloyd's Rep. 317; *Circle Sales and Import Ltd v The Tarantel* [1978] 1 F.C. 269 (Canada). See Palmer and Rose (1976) 39 M.L.R. 466.

enjoy the benefit of contractual provisions in the bill of lading.[257] In *Port Jackson Stevedoring Pty Ltd v Salmond and Spraggon (Australia) Pty Ltd* (*The New York Star*),[258] after goods had been unloaded from a ship and placed in a shed on the wharf under the stevedore's control, a servant of the stevedore negligently delivered the goods to thieves without production of the bill of lading. The High Court of Australia held that the stevedore was not protected by a clause in substantially the same form as that considered in the *Eurymedon* case, since he was no longer acting on behalf of the carrier under the bill of lading. The carrier's responsibilities and immunities under the bill of lading had ceased when the goods were discharged from the ship. On appeal, the Judicial Committee again held that the stevedore was protected on the ground that, whereas the carrier's responsibility as a carrier terminated as soon as the goods left the ship's tackle, his responsibility as bailee under the bill of lading continued until the consignee took delivery of the goods. During this period, both the carrier and the stevedore were entitled to the protection conferred by the bill.

"Himalaya clauses" have therefore attained a degree of general acceptance.[259] **14–049** The technical nature of the *Eurymedon* principle is, however, "all too apparent".[260] In some cases, the courts have rejected its application on the ground that they were compelled to do so by established principles of the law of contract or of agency. Thus, the benefit of an exemption clause has been held not to extend to a third party because the contract did not make it clear that the third party was intended to be protected or that the contracting party contracted as agent for the third party as well as on his own behalf,[261] or because there was no act of the third party which could be identified as constituting acceptance of the offer made to him through the agent,[262] or because no agency could be established since the third party was at all relevant times unascertained,[263] or because the negligence of the third party in respect of which exemption was sought was collateral and not related to the performance of his duties under the contract.[264] Since the enactment of the Contracts (Rights of Third Parties) Act 1999 a third party is more likely now to rely simply and directly on the provisions of the Act than on the *Eurymedon* principle and so will be absolved from having to establish the

---

[257] *Port Jackson Stevedoring Pty Ltd v Salmond and Spraggon (Australia) Pty Ltd* [1981] 1 W.L.R. 138, 143. See also *The Mahkutai* [1996] A.C. 650, 664; *Homburg Houtimport BV v Agrosin Private Ltd (The Starsin)* [2003] UKHL 12, [2004] 1 A.C. 715 at [56].

[258] [1979] 1 Lloyd's Rep. 298, [1981] 1 W.L.R. 138. See also Reynolds (1979) 95 L.Q.R. 183; Reynolds (1980) 96 L.Q.R. 506; Coote [1981] C.L.J. 13; Clarke [1981] C.L.J. 17; Rose (1981) 44 M.L.R. 336, and the cases cited in the latter half of fn.229 para.14–042, above.

[259] *The Mahkutai* [1996] A.C. 650, 664–665; *Homburg Houtimport BV v Agrosin Private Ltd (The Starsin)* [2003] UKHL 12, [2004] 1 A.C. 715; *The Borgivigilant* [2003] EWCA Civ 935 at [34], [51], [93], [140]–[162], [192], [2003] 2 Lloyd's Rep. 520.

[260] *The Mahkutai* [1996] A.C. 650, 664.

[261] *Stone Vickers Ltd v Appledore Ferguson Shipbuilders Ltd* [1992] 2 Lloyd's Rep. 578, 585; *Homburg Houtimport BV v Agrosin Private Ltd (The Starsin)* [2003] UKHL 12; cf. *The Borgivigilant* [2003] EWCA Civ 935 at [17], [18], [33].

[262] *Raymond Burke Motors Ltd v Mersey Docks and Harbour Co* [1986] 1 Lloyd's Rep. 154.

[263] *Southern Water Authority v Carey* [1985] 2 All E.R. 1077. See also *The Suleyman Stalskiy* [1976] 2 Lloyd's Rep. 609.

[264] *Raymond Burke Motors Ltd v Mersey Docks and Harbour Co* [1986] 1 Lloyd's Rep. 154. cf. *Lotus Cars Ltd v Southampton Cargo Handling Plc* [2000] 2 Lloyd's Rep. 532, 543.

more esoteric requirements, e.g. authority and consideration,[265] of that principle.

14–050 **Trust.** Exemption clauses are sometimes found which provide that a party contracts, for the purpose of the clause, as trustee on behalf of third parties, e.g. associated companies, or his employees or sub-contractors. It has been doubted whether a trust of the benefit of an exemption clause would be effective,[266] but it is possible that such a trust would be upheld at common law (the contracting party acting as a bare trustee) provided that the identity of the beneficiaries of the trust was sufficiently certain.

14–051 **Agreement not to sue, etc.** An exemption clause which purports to negative the liability of a third party to a contract cannot be construed as a promise not to sue that third party.[267] However, the contract may contain an express or implied provision whereby one party promises the other that he will not institute legal proceedings against a third party, e.g. any employee or sub-contractor of the promisee.[268] In such a situation, the third party cannot, at common law, rely on the promise as a defence to an action brought against him. But the promisee could, if he has a sufficient interest in the enforcement of the promise, apply for an order or claim a declaration that the action be stayed or dismissed.[269]

14–052 **No voluntary assumption of risk.** An exemption clause which purports to protect a third party cannot ordinarily be construed as a voluntary assumption of risk by the promisor.[270]

14–053 **Occupier's liability.** The Occupiers' Liability Act 1957[271] provides that where an occupier of premises is bound by contract to permit persons who are strangers to the contract to enter or use the premises, the duty of care which he owes to them as his visitors cannot be restricted or excluded by that contract, but (subject to any provisions of the contract to the contrary) shall include the duty to perform his obligations under the contract, whether undertaken for their

[265] See *Homburg Houtimport BV v Agrosin Private Ltd (The Starsin)* [2003] UKHL 12 at [149], [163], [197].

[266] *Southern Water Authority v Carey*, above. See also *New Zealand Shipping Co Ltd v A.M. Satterthwaite & Co Ltd* [1971] 2 Lloyd's Rep. 389, 408 (at first instance); *Deepak Fertilisers and Petrochemicals Corp v ICI* [1998] 2 Lloyd's Rep. 139, 163; [1999] 1 Lloyd's Rep. 387, and below, para.18–086.

[267] *Gore v Van der Lann* [1967] 2 Q.B. 31; *Homburg Houtimport BV v Agrosin Private Ltd (The Starsin)* [2003] UKHL 12 at [24], [55], [100], [145], [195].

[268] Such a clause is not subject to ss.2 or 10 of the Unfair Contract Terms Act 1977 (below, paras 14–071, 14–081): *Neptune Orient Lines Ltd v J.V.C. (UK) Ltd* [1983] 2 Lloyd's Rep. 438.

[269] *Snelling v John G. Snelling Ltd* [1973] Q.B. 87; *Nippon Yusen Kaisha v International Import and Export Co Ltd* [1978] 1 Lloyd's Rep. 206; *European Asian Bank A.G. v Punjab & Sind Bank* [1982] 2 Lloyd's Rep. 356, 359; *Deepak Fertilisers and Petrochemicals Corp v ICI* [1999] 1 Lloyd's Rep. 387, 400–402. cf. *Gore v Van der Lann* [1967] 2 Q.B. 31; *Neptune Orient Lines Ltd v J.V.C. (UK) Ltd* [1983] 2 Lloyd's Rep. 438. See below, para.18–070.

[270] *Cosgrove v Horsfall* (1945) 62 T.L.R. 140; *Scruttons Ltd v Midland Silicones Ltd* [1962] A.C. 446; *New Zealand Shipping Co Ltd v A.M. Satterthwaite & Co Ltd* [1975] A.C. 154, 168, 173, 182; Unfair Contract Terms Act 1977 s.2(3). But see above, para.14–014; below, para.14–083. Compare also *Norwich City Council v Harvey* [1989] 1 W.L.R. 828, see below, paras 14–056 and 14–057.

[271] s.3(1).

protection or not, in so far as those obligations go beyond the obligations otherwise involved in that duty. This rule applies to regulate the obligations (qua occupier) of a person occupying or having control over any fixed or movable structure, including any vessel, vehicle or aircraft; and to the obligations of a person occupying or having control over any premises or structure in respect of damage to property, including the property of persons who are not themselves his visitors.[272]

Bailment.[273] A carrier, warehouseman or other bailee of goods may sub-contract to another performance of the contract between himself and the bailor and for that purpose deliver possession of the goods to the sub-contractor as sub-bailee. If the sub-bailee has sufficient notice that the original bailor is interested in the goods, then he is under a duty to the original bailor, as well as to the bailee, to use reasonable care to safeguard the goods while in his possession and he will be liable to the original bailor if the goods are lost or damaged[274] through his negligence notwithstanding the absence of any contract between them.[275] Since the sub-bailee is not a party to the contract between the bailee and the original bailor, he cannot rely upon an exemption clause contained in that contract,[276] unless the bailee contracted as agent on his behalf.[277] Nor, in principle, will the original bailor be bound by an exemption clause contained in the sub-contract between the bailee and sub-bailee to which the original bailor is not a party,[278] 14–054

[272] s.1(3).

[273] See Vol.II, paras 32–026—32–031 (bailment); para.36–046 (carriage). Palmer, *Bailment*, 2nd edn (1991), pp.1295, 1631; Palmer and Murdoch (1983) 46 M.L.R. 73; Palmer [1989] L.M.C.L.Q. 466; Adams and Brownsword (1990) 10 L.S. 12; Swadling [1993] L.M.C.L.Q. 9; Reynolds (1995) 111 L.Q.R., 8; Palmer & McKendrick (eds), *Interests in Goods*, 2nd edn (1998).

[274] Contrast *Bart v British West Indian Airways Ltd* [1967] 1 Lloyd's Rep. 239; *Mayfair Photographic Supplies (London) Ltd v Baxter Hoare & Co Ltd* [1972] 1 Lloyd's Rep. 410, 416; *Mitsui & Co Ltd v Novorossiysk Shipping Co (The Gudermes)* [1993] 1 Lloyd's Rep. 311.

[275] *Meux v G.E. Ry* [1895] 2 Q.B. 387; *Harris Ltd v Continental Express Ltd* [1961] 1 Lloyd's Rep. 251; *Morris v C.W. Martin & Sons Ltd* [1966] 1 Q.B. 716; *Learoyd Bros & Co v Pope and Sons (Dock Carriers) Ltd* [1966] 2 Lloyd's Rep. 142; *Lee Cooper Ltd v C.H. Jeakins & Sons Ltd* [1967] 2 Q.B. 1; *Moukataff v B.O.A.C.* [1967] 1 Lloyd's Rep. 396; *Gilchrist Watt & Sanderson Pty Ltd v York Products Pty Ltd* [1970] 1 W.L.R. 1262; *James Buchanan & Co Ltd v Hay's Transport Services Ltd* [1972] 2 Lloyd's Rep. 535; *Gillespie Bros & Co Ltd v Roy Bowles Transport Ltd* [1973] Q.B. 406; *C. Davis Metal Brokers Ltd v Gilyott & Scott Ltd* [1975] 2 Lloyd's Rep. 422; *Johnson Matthey & Co Ltd v Constantine Terminals Ltd* [1976] 2 Lloyd's Rep. 215, 220; *Victoria Fur Traders Ltd v Roadline (UK) Ltd* [1981] 1 Lloyd's Rep. 570; *China Pacific SA v Food Corp of India* [1982] A.C. 939, 957; *Hispanica de Petroleos SA v Vencedora Oceanica Navegacion SA (The Kapetan Markos N.L.) (No.2)* [1987] 2 Lloyd's Rep. 321, 332, 340; *The Pioneer Container* [1994] 2 A.C. 324, 341; *Spectra International Plc v Hayesoak Ltd* [1997] 1 Lloyd's Rep. 153, [1998] 1 Lloyd's Rep. 162; *Lotus Cars v Southampton Cargo Handling Plc* [2000] 2 Lloyd's Rep. 532; *East Westcorp v DKBS 1912* [2003] EWCA Civ 83, [2003] Q.B. 1509 at [25]; *Homburg Houtimport BV v Agrosin Private Ltd (The Starsin)* [2003] UKHL 12, [2004] 1 A.C. 715 at [132]–[138]; cf. *Targe Towing Ltd v Marine Blast Ltd* [2004] EWCA Civ 346, [2004] 1 Lloyd's Rep. 721 at [28].

[276] *Lee Cooper Ltd v C.H. Jeakins & Sons Ltd* [1967] 2 Q.B. 1; *Moukataff v B.O.A.C.* [1967] 1 Lloyd's Rep. 396.

[277] *The Mahkutai* [1996] A.C. 650, 667–668. See above, para.14–047.

[278] *Harris Ltd v Continental Express Ltd* [1961] 1 Lloyd's Rep. 251; *Learoyd Bros & Co v Pope and Sons (Dock Carriers) Ltd* [1966] 2 Lloyd's Rep. 142; *Lee Cooper Ltd v C.H. Jeakins & Sons Ltd* [1967] 2 Q.B. 1; *Moukataff v B.O.A.C.* [1967] 1 Lloyd's Rep. 396; *C. Davis Metal Brokers Ltd v Gilyott & Scott Ltd* [1975] 2 Lloyd's Rep. 422.

unless the bailee entered into the sub-contract as his agent.[279] However, it has been held that the original bailor is bound by the terms of the sub-bailment if he has expressly or impliedly consented to the bailee making a sub-bailment containing those terms: the original bailor cannot, despite the lack of any contractual relationship, disregard those terms against the sub-bailee.[280] Thus an exemption clause contained in the sub-contract which excludes or restricts the liability of the sub-bailee may protect the sub-bailee in an action against him by the original bailor. This principle was taken one step further, by Donaldson J. in *Johnson Matthey & Co Ltd v Constantine Terminals Ltd*,[281] who stated that the original bailor might be bound by an exemption clause in the sub-contract irrespective of whether the bailee was authorised to sub-bail the goods on terms to the sub-bailee. But the Judicial Committee of the Privy Council has subsequently held[282] that the sub-bailee can invoke the terms of a sub-bailment under which he receives the goods from the bailee as qualifying or otherwise affecting his responsibility to the original bailor only if the original bailor consented to them.

14–055 On the other hand, the courts have been reluctant to extend these principles to cases where the relationship between the claimant and the defendant who seeks to rely on the exemption clause is not one of bailor and bailee or sub-bailee.[283] So, for example, if it is agreed between the buyer and seller of goods that the seller will enter into a contract for the carriage of the goods to the buyer and for that purpose will bail the goods to a carrier on terms, then, if the goods are lost or damaged by the negligence of the carrier, the buyer will not be bound by an exemption clause contained in the contract of carriage to which he is not a

[279] *Morris v C.W. Martin & Sons Ltd* [1966] 1 Q.B. 716, 731, 741; and see above, para.14–048 fn.247. cf. *Victoria Fur Traders Ltd v Roadline (UK) Ltd* [1981] 1 Lloyd's Rep. 570.

[280] *Elder, Dempster & Co Ltd v Paterson, Zochonis & Co Ltd* [1924] A.C. 522, 564; *The Kite* (1933) 46 Ll.L.Rep. 83; *Morris v C.W. Martin & Sons Ltd* [1966] 1 Q.B. 716, 729–730, 741; *Johnson Matthey & Co Ltd v Constantine Terminals Ltd* [1976] 2 Lloyd's Rep. 215, 220; *Hispanica de Petroleos SA v Vencedora Oceanica Navegacion SA* (*The Kapetan Markos N.L.*) (*No.2*) [1987] 2 Lloyd's Rep. 321, 332, 340; *Singer Co (UK) Ltd v Tees and Hartlepool Port Authority* [1988] 2 Lloyd's Rep. 164; *Compania Portorafti Commerciale SA v Ultramar Panama Inc.* (*The Captain Gregos*) [1990] 2 Lloyd's Rep. 395, 405; *Dresser (UK) Ltd v Falcongate Freight Management Ltd* [1992] Q.B. 502, 511; *The Pioneer Container* [1994] 2 A.C. 324; *Spectra International Plc v Hayesoak Ltd* [1997] 1 Lloyd's Rep. 153; [1998] 1 Lloyd's Rep. 162; *Sonicare International Ltd v East Anglia Freight Terminal Ltd* [1997] 2 Lloyd's Rep. 48; *Homburg Houtimport BV v Agrosin Private Ltd (The Starsin)* [2003] UKHL 12, [2004] 1 A.C. 715 at [132]–[138]; *Sandeman Coprimar S.A. v Transitos y Transportes Integrales SL* [2003] EWCA Civ 113, [2003] 2 Lloyd's Rep. 172 at [53]–[66]; *East West Corp v DKBS 1912* [2003] EWCA Civ 83, [2003] Q.B. 1509 at [30].

[281] [1976] 2 Lloyd's Rep. 215. See also *Singer Co (UK) Ltd v Tees and Hartlepool Port Authority* [1988] 2 Lloyd's Rep. 164, 168; *Compania Portorafti Commerciale SA v Ultramar Panama Inc* (*The Captain Gregos*) [1990] 2 Lloyd's Rep. 395, 406; *Mitsui & Co Ltd v Novorossiysk Shipping Co* (*The Gudermes*) [1993] 1 Lloyd's Rep. 311, 327. Donaldson J. (at 222) left open the question whether a sub-bailee who himself damages the goods would also be able to rely upon the terms of the sub-contract.

[282] *The Pioneer Container* [1994] 2 A.C. 324.

[283] *Scruttons Ltd v Midland Silicones Ltd* [1962] A.C. 446; *Swiss Bank Corp v Brink's Mat Ltd* [1986] 2 Lloyd's Rep. 79, 98; *Leigh and Sillavan Ltd v Aliakmon Shipping Co Ltd (The Aliakmon)* [1986] A.C. 785, 818; *Compania Portorafti Commerciale SA v Ultramar Panama Inc (The Captain Gregos)* [1990] 2 Lloyd's Rep. 395, at 404, 405; *The Mahkutai* [1996] A.C. 650.

party[284] unless, in view of the nature and terms of the sales contract, the seller is taken to have bailed the goods to the carrier on behalf of the buyer so that the carrier is in possession of the goods as his bailee or sub-bailee.[285] In the absence of any such relationship between them, the carrier will have to establish an implied or collateral contract between himself and the buyer[286] or that the seller's rights of suit under the contract of carriage have been transferred to and vested in the buyer[287] or that he has attorned to the buyer by acknowledging that he holds the goods as bailee for the buyer on the terms of the contract of carriage.[288]

Building and construction contracts. Where a contractor is employed to carry out building or construction works or works of repair, it may be agreed or understood that the contractor ("the main contractor") will engage a sub-contractor or sub-contractors to execute part of the works. Since there is normally no privity of contract between the employer and the sub-contractors, any action brought by the employer against a sub-contractor in respect of loss or damage caused to him by the sub-contractor must be brought in tort for negligence. As a general rule, no such action will lie in respect of defects in the works which the sub-contractor is engaged to carry out.[289] But the employer is entitled to claim against a sub-contractor damages in tort for negligence if the sub-contractor negligently causes physical damage to the existing structure or to property other than the thing supplied by him.[290] The question, however, arises whether, in such an action, the sub-contractor can rely on an exemption clause contained in: (a) 14–056

[284] *Leigh and Sillavan Ltd v Aliakmon Shipping Co Ltd (The Aliakmon)* [1986] A.C. 785, 818; *Compania Portorafti Commerciale SA v Ultramar Panama Inc (The Captain Gregos)* [1990] 2 Lloyd's Rep. 395, 405.

[285] *Hispanica de Petroleos SA v Vencedora Oceanica Navegacion SA (The Kapetan Markos N.L.) (No.2)* [1987] 2 Lloyd's Rep. 321; *Homburg Houtimport BV v Agrosin Private Ltd (The Starsin)* [2003] UKHL 12, [2004] 1 A.C. 715 at [36]–[41], [64], [89], [92], [139]; *Scottish and Newcastle International Ltd v Othon Ghalanos Ltd* [2008] UKHL 11, [2008] 1 Lloyd's Rep. 462 at [47]; *Benjamin's Sale of Goods*, 7th edn (2006), paras 18–065, 18–148—18–149.

[286] *Compania Portorafti Commerciale SA v Ultramar Panama Inc (The Captain Gregos)* [1990] 2 Lloyd's Rep. 395 (BP claim). See also the "*Brandt v Liverpool*" contract (*Brandt v Liverpool etc. Steam Navigation Co* [1924] 1 K.B. 575) and *Benjamin's Sale of Goods* at paras 18–138—18–147. cf. *Borealis AB v Stargas Ltd (The Berge Sisar)* [2002] 2 A.C. 205.

[287] By statute under the Bills of Lading Act 1855 or (now) under the Carriage of Goods by Sea Act 1992 (see *Benjamin's Sale of Goods* at paras 18–102—18–122).

[288] *Cremer v General Carriers SA* [1974] 1 W.L.R. 341; and see Vol.II, para.33–030. Contrast *Mitsui & Co Ltd v Novorossiysk Shipping Co (The Gudermes)* [1993] 1 Lloyd's Rep. 311; *Sonicare International Ltd v East Anglia Freight Terminal Ltd* [1997] 2 Lloyd's Rep. 48. See *Benjamin's Sale of Goods* at para.18–066.

[289] *Simaan General Contracting Co v Pilkington Glass Ltd (No.2)* [1988] Q.B. 758; *D. & F. Estates Ltd v Church Commissioners for England* [1989] A.C. 177; *Greater Nottingham Co-operative Society Ltd v Cementation Piling and Foundations Ltd* [1989] Q.B. 71; *Murphy v Brentwood DC* [1991] 1 A.C. 398; *Department of the Environment v Thomas Bates and Son Ltd* [1991] 1 A.C. 499; *Warner v Basildon Development Corp* (1991) 7 Const. L.J. 146; *Nitrigin Eireann Teoranta v Inco Alloys Ltd* [1992] 1 W.L.R. 598. Contrast *Junior Books Ltd v Veitchi Co Ltd* [1983] 1 A.C. 520 (which must now be regarded as an exceptional case) and Vol.II, paras 37–092, 37–175.

[290] *Norwich City Council v Harvey* [1989] 1 W.L.R. 828; *Nitrigin Eireann Teoranta v Inco Alloys Ltd* [1992] 1 W.L.R. 598. For the problem of "complex structures", see *D. & F. Estates Ltd v Church Commissioners for England* [1989] A.C. 177, and *Murphy v Brentwood DC* [1991] 1 A.C. 398.

the main contract between the employer and the main contractor; or (b) his own sub-contract with the main contractor. The initial contractual arrangements between the employer, the main contractor and the sub-contractor may be such as to give rise to a contract between the employer and the sub-contractor.[291] But, even if no such direct contractual relationship exists between them, the sub-contractor may nevertheless be entitled to rely upon an exemption clause contained in the main contract between the employer and the main contractor. This may be justified either on the ground that the duty in tort owed by the sub-contractor to the employer is negatived or qualified by the clause,[292] or on the ground that, if the clause places a risk in whole or in part on the employer, the circumstances show that the sub-contractor contracted with the main contractor on a like basis.[293]

14–057 Whether the sub-contractor is also entitled to rely upon an exemption clause in his sub-contract with the main contractor is more problematical. Prima facie the employer would not be bound by a clause in a contract to which he was not a party.[294] But, again, the contractual arrangements between the employer, main contractor and sub-contractor may be such as to show that the employer knew of and consented to the clause as, for example, where the sub-contractor is a nominated sub-contractor and the employer is aware of and accepts the terms on which the sub-contractor agrees to carry out the works. In such a case it is submitted that the employer could be held to be bound by the exemption clause.[295]

14–058 **Effect of the 1999 Act.** The common law exceptions referred to above in relation to bailment and building and construction contracts operate independently of and are not affected by the limitations contained in the Contracts (Rights of Third Parties) Act 1999.[296] In particular, for example, where a sub-bailee or sub-contractor seeks the protection of an exemption clause in a contract to which he is not a party, he does not have to show that he is identified in the contract as the beneficiary of the clause by name, class, or description as he would in a case where he relies on s.1 of the 1999 Act.

---

[291] *Welsh Health Technical Services Organisation v Haden Young* (1987) 37 Build. L.R. 130.

[292] *Junior Books Ltd v Veitchi Co Ltd* [1983] 1 A.C. 520, 546; *Southern Water Authority v Duvivier* [1984] C.I.L.L. 90; *Southern Water Authority v Carey* [1985] 2 All E.R. 1077; *Welsh Health Technical Services Organisation v Haden Young* (1987) 37 Build. L.R. 130; *Norwich City Council v Harvey* [1989] 1 W.L.R. 828; *Pacific Associates Inc v Baxter* [1990] 1 Q.B. 993, 1022, 1033, 1038. Contrast *National Trust v Haden Young Ltd* (1995) 72 Build. L.R. 1.

[293] *Norwich City Council v Harvey* [1989] 1 W.L.R. 828. cf. *National Trust v Haden Young Ltd* (1995) 72 Build. L.R. 1.

[294] *Rumbelows Ltd v AMK* [1980] 19 Build. L.R. 33; *Twins Transport Ltd v Patrick and Brocklehurst* (1983) 25 Build. L.R. 65. See also *Leigh and Sillavan Ltd v Aliakmon Shipping Co Ltd (The Aliakmon)* [1986] A.C. 785, 817; *Simaan General Contracting Co v Pilkington Glass Ltd (No.2)* [1988] Q.B. 758, 782, 785.

[295] *Morris v C.W. Martin & Sons Ltd* [1966] 1 Q.B. 716, 729; *Rumbelows Ltd v AMK* [1980] 19 Build. L.R. 33, 49. See also *Junior Books Ltd v Veitchi Co Ltd* [1983] 1 A.C. 520, 534; *Muirhead v Industrial Tank Specialities Ltd* [1986] Q.B. 507, 525.

[296] s.1; see above, para.14–043.

6. STATUTORY CONTROL OF EXEMPTION CLAUSES

(a) *Unfair Contract Terms Act 1977*[297]

Unfair Contract Terms Act 1977. This Act derives substantially from recommendations made by the Law Commission and the Scottish Law Commission in their Second Report on Exemption Clauses.[298] The title of the Act is, however, somewhat misleading. In the first place, the control imposed by the Act is not limited to contract terms, but extends to non-contractual notices which exclude or restrict liability in tort.[299] Secondly, the Act does not seek to control unfair contract terms generally. It applies, for the most part,[300] only to terms that purport to exclude or restrict liability, that is to say, to exemption clauses. The Act does not, in general, affect the basis of liability,[301] so that the first inquiry must normally be whether or not the person seeking to rely on the terms is in fact under any obligation or liability, for example, for breach of contract or negligence, apart from the term.[302] Further, the Act does not affect the preliminary issues as to whether the alleged term is in fact a term of the contract,[303] and, if it is, whether on its true construction it applies to the obligation or liability which it purports to exclude or restrict.[304] 14–059

Pattern of control. The control exercised by the Act over exemption clauses in contracts is complex in nature and by no means comprehensive. There are three broad divisions of control. First, control over contract terms which exclude or restrict liability for "negligence",[305] which is defined[306] to mean the breach: 14–060

(a) of any obligation, arising from the express or implied terms of a contract, to take reasonable care or exercise reasonable skill in the performance of a contract;

(b) of any common law duty to take reasonable care or exercise reasonable skill (but not any stricter duty); and

---

[297] See Thompson, *Unfair Contract Terms Act 1977*; Rogers and Clarke, *The Unfair Contract Terms Act 1977*; Lawson, *Exclusion Clauses and Unfair Contract Terms*, 7th edn (2003); Coote (1978) 41 M.L.R. 312; Adams (1978) 41 M.L.R. 703; Sealy [1978] C.L.J. 15; Reynolds [1978] L.M.C.L.Q. 201; Palmer and Yates [1981] C.L.J. 108; Adams and Brownsword (1988) 104 L.Q.R. 94; Peel (1993) 56 M.L.R. 98; Brown and Chandler (1993) 109 L.Q.R. 41; Adams (1994) 57 M.L.R. 960.

[298] Law Com. No.69, Scot. Law Com. No.39 (1975). Pt I of the Act applies only to England and Wales and Northern Ireland; Pt II applies only to Scotland; and Pt III applies to the whole of the United Kingdom.

[299] Such notices are not dealt with in this chapter.

[300] But see ss.3(2)(b), 4.

[301] But see ss.3(2)(b), 4.

[302] See above, para.14–003; below, para.14–063.

[303] See s.11(2) and above, para.12–002.

[304] See s.11(2) and above, paras 14–005 et seq.

[305] ss.2, 5; below, paras 14–071—14–077. See also s.4; below, para.14–075.

[306] s.1(1).

(c) of the common duty of care imposed by the Occupier's Liability Act 1957.[307]

Secondly, control over contract terms[308] which exclude or restrict liability for breach of certain terms implied by statute or common law in contracts of sale of goods,[309] hire purchase[310] and in other contracts for the supply of goods.[311] Thirdly, a more general control in limited circumstances over contract terms which exclude or restrict liability for breach of contract[312] or which purport to entitle one of the parties to render a contractual performance substantially different from that reasonably expected of him or to render no performance at all.[313] However, the provisions of the Act may overlap, so that, in any given situation, it may be necessary to consider whether more than one section is relevant. Further, certain very important contracts are excepted, either wholly or subject to qualifications, from the operation of the Act.[314]

14–061 If the contract term is subject to the control of the Act, that control may assume one of two forms: the exclusion or restriction of liability may be rendered absolutely ineffective,[315] or it may be effective only in so far as the term satisfies the requirement of reasonableness.[316]

14–062 **Varieties of exemption clause.** Subject to certain exceptions,[317] the Act only applies to contract terms which "exclude or restrict" liability. In considering whether a contract term has this effect, the court is concerned with the substance and not the form of the provision.[318] Moreover, by s.13(1), the meaning of these words is extended so as also to prevent:

(a) "making the liability or its enforcement subject to restrictive or onerous conditions" (as, for example, in the case of terms which require a party to make a claim within a certain time-limit or to commence proceedings within a shorter time-limit than the normal limitation period)[319];

(b) "excluding or restricting any right or remedy in respect of the liability, or subjecting a person to any prejudice in consequence of his pursuing any

---

[307] See *Monarch Airlines Ltd v London Luton Airports Ltd* [1998] 1 Lloyd's Rep. 403.

[308] Whether in the same or in another contract between the same parties. cf. s.10; below para.14–081.

[309] s.6; see below, para.14–078; Vol.II, paras 43–072, 43–104.

[310] s.6; see below, para.14–078; Vol.II, para.38–370.

[311] s.7; see below, para.14–079.

[312] s.3(1)(2)(a). See also s.4; below, para.14–075.

[313] s.3(1), (2)(b).

[314] See below, paras 14–104—14–112.

[315] ss.2(1), 5, 6(1), (2), 7(2), (3A).

[316] See below, para.14–084.

[317] ss.3(2)(b), 4, 10.

[318] *Cremdean Properties Ltd v Nash* (1977) 244 E.G. 547, 551; *Phillips Products Ltd v Hyland* [1987] 1 W.L.R. 659, 666; *Johnstone v Bloomsbury H.A.* [1992] Q.B. 333, 346; *IFE Fund SA v Goldman Sachs International* [2006] EWHC 2887 (Comm), [2007] 1 Lloyd's Rep. 264 at [68].

[319] *BHP Petroleum Ltd v British Steel Plc* [1999] 2 Lloyd's Rep. 586, 592 (affirmed [2002] 2 Lloyd's Rep. 277); *Granville Oil and Chemicals Ltd v Davis Turner & Co Ltd* [2003] EWCA Civ 570, [2003] 2 Lloyd's Rep. 356.

such right or remedy" (as, for example, in the case of terms which preclude a party from relying on or enforcing a right of set-off[320] or which take away or limit his right to reject defective goods, or require him to pay the expenses of redelivery on rejection);

(c) "excluding or restricting rules of evidence or procedure" (as, for example, terms which state that acceptance of goods or services shall be conclusive evidence that they are in conformity with the contract).[321]

It would seem probable, however, that a genuine liquidated damages clause would not be subject to the Act,[322] and it is specifically provided that an agreement in writing to submit present or future differences to arbitration is not to be treated under Part I of the Act as excluding or restricting any liability.[323]

Certain sections[324] further prevent "excluding or restricting liability by reference to terms which exclude or restrict the relevant obligation or duty".[325] The purpose of this provision appears to be[326] to bring within the control of the Act terms, for example, which state that the seller gives no undertaking with respect to the quality or fitness for purpose of the goods sold or which state that a surveyor accepts no responsibility with respect to the accuracy of a valuation report supplied by him.[327] Exemption clauses of this nature do not purport to exclude to restrict *liability* for breach of an obligation or duty, but purport to exclude the relevant obligation (e.g. the conditions implied by s.14 of the Sale of Goods Act 1979) or duty (e.g. to use reasonable care and skill in carrying out the valuation). It may be difficult, however, to differentiate between contractual provisions which exclude or restrict the relevant obligation or duty, and those which define the scope of the obligation or which specify the duties of the parties. For example, a seller of kitchen utensils may expressly state that they are suitable to be used only on electric cookers and not with gas,[328] or a surveyor may stipulate that he undertakes to carry out a valuation of the property and not a full structural survey.[329] Further, there may be difficulty in distinguishing between 14–063

[320] *Stewart Gill Ltd v Horatio Myer & Co Ltd* [1992] Q.B. 600; *Fastframe Ltd v Lochinski* Unreported, March 3, 1993 CA (noted (1994) 57 M.L.R. 960); *Esso Petroleum Co Ltd v Milton* [1997] 1 W.L.R. 938; *Surzur Overseas Ltd v Ocean Reliance Shipping Co Ltd* [1997] C.L.Y. 906; *Skipskredittforeningen v Emperor Navigation* [1998] 1 Lloyd's Rep. 66; *Schenkers Ltd v Overland Shoes Ltd* [1998] 1 Lloyd's Rep. 498; *WRM Group Ltd v Wood* [1998] C.L.C. 189.

[321] See *Howard Marine and Dredging Co Ltd v A. Ogden & Sons (Excavations) Ltd* [1978] Q.B. 574; see below, para.14–090.

[322] See above, para.14–004 fn.14. But see Law Com. No.69, Scot. Law Com. No.39, 1975, para.166.

[323] s.13(2). But see Arbitration Act 1996, ss.89–92; Vol.II, para.32–013.

[324] ss.2 and 5–7 only.

[325] s.13(1). The contention has been put forward that clauses which "exclude" the relevant obligation or duty ipso facto limit the obligation or duty, or prevent its accrual: see Coote, *Exception Clauses* (1964); Coote [1970] C.L.J. 221; Coote (1977) 40 M.L.R. 31; Coote (1978) 41 M.L.R. 312; Palmer and Yates [1981] C.L.J. 108; and above, para.14–003.

[326] For a different view as to its purpose, see *Stewart Gill Ltd v Horatio Myer & Co Ltd* [1992] Q.B. 600, 605.

[327] *Smith v Eric S. Bush* and *Harris v Wyre Forest DC* [1990] 1 A.C. 831.

[328] See Macleod (1981) 97 L.Q.R. 550.

[329] *Gibbs v Arnold Son & Hockley* (1989) 45 E.G. 156. cf. *Roberts v J. Hampson & Co* [1990] 1 W.L.R. 94.

provisions which exclude or restrict the relevant obligation or duty, and those which prevent it from arising, such as a clause limiting the ostensible authority of an agent to give undertakings[330] or an "entire agreement" clause.[331] In *Smith v Eric S. Bush*,[332] a case concerning the common law duty to take reasonable care and a non-contractual notice disclaiming liability, Lord Griffiths read the relevant provisions of the Act as introducing a "but for" test, that is to say, whether the duty would exist "but for" the notice excluding liability. But it is submitted that this test could not always be satisfactorily applied to contract terms which, in effect, limit the extent of the obligation or duty which one party owes to the other or which even prevent the accrual of the obligation or duty in particular situations.[333]

14–064 It has, however, been stated that the Act:

> "... is normally regarded as being aimed at exemption clauses in the strict sense, that is to say, clauses in a contract which aim to cut down prospective liability arising in the course of performance of the contract in which the exemption clause is contained,"[334]

and not to liability already accrued.[335]

14–065 **Business liability.** The Act is concerned, for the most part,[336] with terms that exclude or restrict "business liability." This is defined as liability for breach of obligations or duties arising:

(a) from things done or to be done in the course of a business (whether his own business or another's); or

(b) from the occupation of premises used for business purposes of the occupier.[337]

"Business" is not defined by the Act, except to the extent that it is stated to include a profession and the activities of any government department or local or

---

[330] See *Overbrooke Estates Ltd v Glencombe Properties Ltd* [1974] 1 W.L.R. 1335; *Collins v Howell-Jones* (1981) 259 E.G. 331; *Museprime Properties Ltd v Adhill Properties Ltd* [1990] 2 E.G.L.R. 196, 200 (misrepresentation); above, para.6–137.

[331] *McGrath v Shah* (1989) 57 P. & C.R. 452; *Thomas Witter Ltd v TBP Industries Ltd* [1996] 2 All E.R. 573; *E.A. Grimstead & Son Ltd v McGarrigan* Unreported October 27, 1999 CA; *South West Water Services Ltd v International Computers Ltd* [1999] Build. L.R. 420, 424; *Inntrepreneur Pub Co v East Crown Ltd* [2000] 2 Lloyd's Rep. 611, 614; *Watford Electronics Ltd v Sanderson CFL Ltd* [2001] EWCA Civ 317, [2001] Build. L.R. 143, 155; *SAM Systems Ltd v Hedley & Co* [2002] EWHC (TCC) 2733; [2003] 1 All E.R. (Comm) 465; above, para.12–104. But see below, para.15–105.

[332] [1990] 1 A.C. 831, 857. See also *Phillips Products Ltd v Hyland* [1987] 1 W.L.R. 659.

[333] *Hurley v Dyke* [1979] R.T.R. 265 HL (tort) (but see 281, 282); *IFE Fund SA v Goldman Sachs International* [2006] EWHC 2887 (Comm), [2007] 1 Lloyd's Rep. 264 at [67]–[70]. Contrast *Harris v Wyre Forest DC* [1990] 1 A.C. 831 (reversing the decision of the Court of Appeal [1988] Q.B. 835) (tort); *Cremdean Properties Ltd v Nash* (1977) 244 E.G. 547 (misrepresentation); above, para.6–138; *Hughes v Hall* [1981] R.T.R. 430; Macdonald (1992) 12 L.S. 277.

[334] *Tudor Grange Holdings Ltd v Citibank N.A.* [1992] Ch. 53, 65.

[335] See also s.10; below, para.14–081.

[336] Except s.6 (implied terms in contracts of sale of goods and hire-purchase).

[337] s.1(3) (as amended by the Occupiers Liability Act 1984 s.2).

Thank you for purchasing Chitty on Contracts

☑ Don't miss important updates

So that you have all the latest information, Chitty on Contracts, 30th edition is supplemented annually. Sign up today for a Standing Order to ensure you receive the updating supplements as soon as they publish. Setting up a Standing Order with Sweet & Maxwell is hassle-free, simply tick, complete and return this FREEPOST card and we'll do the rest.

You may cancel your Standing Order at any time by writing to us at Sweet & Maxwell, PO Box 2000, Andover, SP10 9AH stating the Standing Order you wish to cancel.

Alternatively, if you have purchased your copy of **Chitty on Contracts** from a bookshop or other trade supplier, please ask your supplier to ensure that you are registered to receive the new supplements.

All goods are subject to our 30 day Satisfaction Guarantee (applicable to EU customers only).

Yes, please send me new supplements and /or new editions of Chitty on Contracts to be invoiced on publication, until I cancel the standing order in writing.

☐ All new supplements to the 30th edition

☐ All new editions and supplements

Title .... Name ....

Organisation ....

Job title ....

Address ....

Postcode ....

Telephone ....

Email ....

S&M account number (if known) ....

PO number ....

All orders are accepted subject to the terms of this order form and our Terms of Trading. (see www.sweetandmaxwell.co.uk). By submitting this order form I confirm that I accept these terms and I am authorised to sign on behalf of the customer.

Signed .... Job Title ....

Print Name .... Date ....

(LBU002) V6 10.2008 / CL / LV

Goods will normally be dispatched within 3-5 working days of availability. The price charged to customers, irrespective of any prices quoted, will be the price specified in our price list current at the time of dispatch of the goods, as published on our website, unless the order is subject to a specific offer or discount in which case special terms may apply. Delivery Charges are not made for titles supplied in the UK. For deliveries in Europe the following charges apply: £7/€10 for first item, £2.50/€4 for each additional item. For deliveries outside Europe please add £30/€42 for first item, £15/€21 for each additional item.

UK VAT is charged on all applicable sales at the prevailing rate (currently 17.5%) except in the case of sales to Ireland where Irish VAT will be charged at the prevailing rate. Customers outside the EU will not be charged UK VAT. UK VAT Number: GB 900 5487 43. Irish VAT Number: IE 9513874E. For customers in an EU member state (except UK & Ireland) please supply your VAT Number. VAT No ....

Thomson Reuters (Legal) Limited (Company No. 1679046. Registered in England & Wales. Registered Office and address for service: 100 Avenue Road, London NW3 3PF) trades using various trading names, of which a list is posted on its website at www.sweetandmaxwell.co.uk, and is part of Thomson Reuters.

SWEET & MAXWELL THOMSON REUTERS

NO STAMP
REQUIRED
WITHIN
U.K.

SWEET & MAXWELL
FREEPOST
PO BOX 2000
ANDOVER
SP10 9AH
UNITED KINGDOM

public authority.[338] The words "in the course of a business" appear to require that the thing done or to be done is an integral part of the business carried on or that there is a sufficient degree of regularity about the type of transaction in question.[339] The words "whether his own business or another's" presumably cover the activities of an agent in the course of his principal's business.

Dealing as consumer. A distinction is drawn in the Act between cases where a party to a contract "deals as consumer" in relation to another party, and cases where he does not so deal. In order that a party should have dealt as consumer, two conditions must be satisfied.[340] First, he must neither make the contract in the course of a business[341] nor hold himself out as doing so.[342] Secondly, the other party must make the contract in the course of a business.[343] In *R. & B. Customs Brokers Co Ltd v United Dominions Trust Ltd*,[344] it was held that a freight forwarding and shipping agency company had dealt as consumer when it entered into a conditional sale agreement with a finance company for the purchase of a motor car for personal and business use by one of its directors, on the ground that, to be in the course of a business, the transaction must be an integral part of the business carried on or, if only incidental thereto, be of a type regularly entered into. It was further stated[345] that the company had not "held itself out" as making the contract in the course of a business by submitting a finance application in the corporate name, giving the nature of the company's business, the number of years trading and the number of employees, and giving the names and addresses of the directors. **14–066**

In addition, in the case of a contract governed by the law of sale of goods or hire-purchase, or by s.7 of the Act (other contracts under which the ownership or possession of goods passes),[346] a third requirement must be satisfied[347]: the goods passing under or in pursuance of the contract must be of a type ordinarily supplied for private use or consumption.[348] This requirement does not, however, **14–067**

[338] s.14. A business need not necessarily be carried on with a view to profit: see *Roles v Miller* (1884) 27 Ch D 71, 88; *Town Investments Ltd v Department of Environment* [1978] A.C. 359. Contrast *Smith v Anderson* (1880) 15 Ch D 247, 258.

[339] *Havering LBC v Stevenson* [1970] 1 W.L.R. 1375; *Davies v Sumner* [1984] 1 W.L.R. 1301; *R. & B. Customs Brokers Co Ltd v United Dominions Trust Ltd* [1988] 1 W.L.R. 321.

[340] s.12(1)(a), (b).

[341] See above, para.14–065 fn.339.

[342] e.g., by producing a trade card or asking for a trade discount in appropriate circumstances. But cf., below, fn.345.

[343] See above, para.14–065, and *R. & B. Customs Brokers Co Ltd v United Dominions Trust Ltd* [1988] 1 W.L.R. 321, 336.

[344] [1988] 1 W.L.R. 321. See also *Rasbora Ltd v J.C.L. Marine Ltd* [1977] 1 Lloyd's Rep. 645 (private buyer of boat substitutes a company owned and controlled by him); *Peter Symmons & Co v Cook* (1981) 131 New L.J. 758 (partnership of surveyors purchase Rolls-Royce from car dealer); *Feldaroll Foundry Plc v Hermes Leasing (London) Ltd* [2004] EWCA Civ 747 (company purchases car for use of managing director). Contrast *St Alban's City and District Council v International Computers Ltd* [1996] 4 All E.R. 481, 490.

[345] [1988] 1 W.L.R. 321, 328–329.

[346] See below, para.14–079.

[347] s.12(1)(c).

[348] See Vol.II, para.43–106.

apply if the buyer or person to whom the goods are supplied is an individual.[349]

14–068 **Auction sales.** On a sale by auction or by competitive tender a buyer who is not an individual is not in any circumstances to be regarded as dealing as consumer. If the buyer is an individual, then he is not to be regarded as dealing as consumer where the goods are second hand goods sold at public auction at which individuals have the opportunity of attending the sale in person.[350]

14–069 **Agency.** The application of the concept of "dealing as consumer" is unclear where a private person (the principal) makes a contract through a commercial or professional agent. Under the ordinary principles of agency,[351] if the agency is disclosed,[352] then, whether or not the principal is named, it is the principal who is a party to and makes the contract, and not the agent. The private principal does not therefore "make the contract in the course of a business" even though the agent, when entering into the contract on his behalf, acts in the course of a business.[353] So, for example, if a private seller sells goods through a commercial agent to a private buyer, the buyer does not deal as consumer, because the seller does not make the contract in the course of a business. And if a private buyer buys goods through a commercial agent, he may still be held to have dealt as a consumer as he does not make the contract in the course of a business, unless it could be said that, by employing a commercial agent to act for him, he has "held himself out" as making the contract in the course of a business.

14–070 **Burden of proof as to dealing as consumer.** It is for those claiming that a party does not deal as consumer to show that he does not.[354]

14–071 **Negligence liability.** Restrictions are placed by s.2 of the Act on the power of a party to a contract to exempt himself from business liability[355] for negligence.[356] He cannot by reference to any contract term exclude or restrict his liability for death or personal injury[357] resulting from negligence.[358] Any such exclusion or restriction of liability is wholly ineffective. In the case of other loss or damage, he cannot so exclude or restrict his liability, except insofar as the term satisfies the requirement of reasonableness.[359] The words of s.2 are wide enough to include a term which purports to transfer from one contracting party to the other responsibility for injury or damage caused to the latter by negligence on the

[349] s.12(1A) (inserted by the Sale and Supply of Goods to Consumers Regulations 2002 (SI 2002/3045) reg.14(2)).

[350] s.12(2) (substituted by the Sale and Supply of Goods to Consumers Regulations 2002 (SI 2002/3045) reg.14(3)).

[351] See Vol.II, Ch.31.

[352] *Aliter* if the agency is not disclosed (the "undisclosed principal"): see Vol.II, para.31–064.

[353] Contrast Sale of Goods Act 1979 s.14(5).

[354] s.12(3).

[355] See above, para.14–065.

[356] See above, para.14–060.

[357] Defined in s.14.

[358] s.2(1). See also s.2(3) (voluntary acceptance of risk); *Johnstone v Bloomsbury H.A.* [1992] Q.B. 333, 343, 346.

[359] s.2(2). See also s.2(3) (voluntary acceptance of risk).

part of an employee of the former.[360] They do not extend to a term by which one party requires the other to indemnify him against injury or damage caused to third parties by his own negligence or that of his employees,[361] nor to a covenant not to sue a third party.[362]

Liability arising in contract. Section 3 of the Act applies generally to liability arising in contract and (unlike certain later sections) is not limited to contracts of a particular type. However, the section only applies as between contracting parties where one of them deals: 14–072

(i) as consumer[363]; or

(ii) on the other's written standard terms of business,

and in either case the liability which it is sought to exclude is a business liability.[364] The expression . . . "deals on the other's written standard terms of business" is not defined or explained by the Act,[365] but it would seem probable that "standard terms of business" would embrace the standard terms of a third party, e.g. a trade association, incorporated into the contract by reference or by course of dealing. Since, in any event, no two contracts are likely to be completely identical, but will at least differ as to subject matter and price, the question arises whether variations or omissions from or additions to standard terms thereby render them "non-standard" and, if they do not, whether all the terms then become standard terms. Where negotiations have taken place around standard terms before the contract is made, and amendments agreed, it is a question of fact whether one party can be said to have dealt on those standard terms.[366] If it is alleged that an ostensibly "one-off" contract is in fact the other's written standard terms of business, extensive disclosure may be involved to determine the terms on which contracts have been concluded with others. The burden of proving that he dealt on the others written standard terms of business appears to rest on the party who alleges that s.3 applies.[367]

[360] *Phillips Products Ltd v Hyland* [1987] 1 W.L.R. 659. See also *Flamar Interocean Ltd v Denmac Ltd* [1990] 1 Lloyd's Rep. 434.

[361] *Thompson v T. Lohan (Plant Hire) Ltd* [1987] 1 W.L.R. 649; *Hancock Shipping Co Ltd v Deacon & Trysail (Private) Ltd* [1991] 2 Lloyd's Rep. 550.

[362] *Neptune Orient Lines Ltd v J.V.C. (UK) Ltd* [1983] 2 Lloyd's Rep. 438; see above, para.14–051.

[363] See above, para.14–066.

[364] See above, para.14–065.

[365] But see *McCrone v Boots Farm Sales* 1981 S.L.T. 103 (on s.17 of the Act in Scotland) and *Flamar Interocean Ltd v Denmac Ltd* [1990] 1 Lloyd's Rep. 434, at 438.

[366] Compare *St Alban's City and District Council v International Computers Ltd* [1996] 4 All E.R. 481, 490–491, with *Salvage Assocation v Cap Financial Services* [1995] F.S.R. 654. See also *Chester Grosvenor Hotel Co Ltd v Alfred McAlpine Management Ltd* (1991) 56 Build. L.R. 115, 131; *South West Water Services Ltd v International Computers Ltd* [1999] Build. L.R. 420; *British Fermentation Products Ltd v Compare Reavell Ltd* (1999) 66 Const. L.R.1; *Pegler Ltd v Wang (UK) Ltd* [2000] Build. L.R. 218; *Hadley Design Associates Ltd v Westminster CC* [2003] EWHC 1617 (TCC), [2004] T.C.L.R. 1; *Ferryways NV v Associated British Ports* [2008] EWHC 225 (Comm), [2008] 1 Lloyd's Rep. 639 at [92]; Britton (2006) 22 Const. L.J. 23.

[367] *British Fermentation Products Ltd v Compare Reavell Ltd* (1999) 66 Const. L.R. 1.

14–073 In cases falling within s.3, as against the party dealing as consumer or on the other's written standard terms of business, the other party ("the *proferens*") cannot by reference to any contract term,[368] except in so far as the term satisfies the requirement of reasonableness, do either of two things:

(a) when himself in breach of contract, exclude or restrict any liability of his in respect of breach[369]; or
(b) claim to be entitled:
   (i) to render a contractual performance substantially different from that which was reasonably expected of him,[370]; or
   (ii) in respect of the whole or part of his contractual obligations to render no performance at all.[371]

It would appear to be the intention of (b) that it should apply where there is no breach of contract at all, but where the obligation as to performance has been limited or qualified.[372] An example might be, where one party deals as consumer, of a contract with a holiday tour operator who agrees to provide a holiday at a certain hotel at a certain resort, but who claims to be entitled, by reference to a term of the contract to that effect, in certain circumstances to accommodate the consumer at a different hotel, or to change the resort, or to cancel the holiday in whole or in part. An example in a commercial contract on written standard terms, might be that of a force majeure clause[373] by reference to which a seller of goods claims to be entitled to suspend or postpone delivery of the goods, or to deliver substitute goods, or to cancel the contract, upon the happening of events beyond his control. The argument could, however, be advanced[374] that the effect of clauses such as those mentioned is to define the scope of the obligation of the *proferens* with respect to performance: the contract must be read together with and subject to the clause.[375] The other party could not therefore reasonably expect that the *proferens* would render a contractual performance other than that as qualified by the clause, nor would there be any contractual obligation in respect of which the *proferens* would be claiming to render no performance at all. But it is submitted that a sensible meaning can in most cases only be given to paragraph (b) if one assumes that the contractual performance and contractual

[368] Whether in the same or in another contract between the same parties: cf. s.10; below, para.14–081.

[369] s.3(2)(a). See *Charlotte Thirty Ltd v Croker Ltd* (1990) 24 Const. L.R. 46; *St Alban's City and District Council v International Computers Ltd* [1996] 4 All E.R. 481.

[370] i.e. at the time the contract was made: *Shearson Lehman Hutton Inc v Maclaine Watson & Co Ltd* [1989] 2 Lloyd's Rep. 570, 612. See *Timeload Ltd v British Telecommunications Plc* [1995] E.M.L.R. 459.

[371] s.3(2)(b).

[372] *Shearson Lehman Hutton Inc v Maclaine Watson & Co Ltd* [1989] 2 Lloyd's Rep. 570, 611–612.

[373] See below, para.14–137.

[374] Treitel, *Frustration and Force Majeure* (1994), para.12–014.

[375] See above, para.14–003.

obligation referred to is the performance required and the obligation imposed by the contract apart from the contract term relied on.[376] The contractual performance reasonably expected of a party may, in appropriate cases be determined by the content of representations made by that party in pre-contract negotiations.[377]

Nevertheless it seems unlikely that a contract term entitling one party to terminate the contract in the event of a material breach by the other (e.g. failure to pay by the due date) would fall within paragraph (b), or, if it did so, would be adjudged not to satisfy the requirement of reasonableness.[378] Nor, it is submitted, would that provision extend to a contract term which entitled one party, not to alter the performance expected of himself, but to alter the performance required of the other party (e.g. a term by which a seller of goods is entitled to increase the price payable by the buyer to the price ruling at the date of delivery, or a term by which a person advancing a loan is entitled to vary the interest payable by the borrower on the loan).[379] A term of a contract of employment relating to the requirements for payment of a discretionary bonus has been held not to fall within s.3.[380] 14–074

Unreasonable indemnity clauses. A contract may stipulate that, if one party incurs liability (usually to third parties) as the result of the performance of the contract, he shall be entitled to be indemnified by the other party against the liability.[381] Section 4 of the Act provides that a person dealing as consumer[382] cannot by reference to any contract term be made to indemnify another person (whether a party to the contract or not) in respect of liability that may be incurred by the other for negligence[383] or breach of contract, except in so far as the contract term satisfies the requirement of reasonableness.[384] This provision applies whether the liability in question: 14–075

(a) is directly that of the person to be indemnified or is incurred by him vicariously; or

[376] *Zockoll Group Ltd v Mercury Communications Ltd (No.2)* [1998] I.T.C.L.R. 104. See above, para.14–003.

[377] *SAM Business Systems Ltd v Hedley & Co* [2002] EWHC 2733 (TCC); [2003] 1 All E.R. (Comm) 465.

[378] But see *Timeload Ltd v British Telecommunications Plc* [1995] E.M.L.R. 459 (termination not limited to cases where there was a good reason) and below, para.15–109. cf. *Hadley Design Associates Ltd v Westminster CC* [2003] EWHC 1617 (TCC), [2004] T.C.L.R. 1 (one month's termination clause in architects' contract not unreasonable).

[379] *Paragon Finance Plc v Nash* [2001] EWCA Civ 1466, [2002] 1 W.L.R. 685, at [76]–[77] (pet. dis. [2002] 1 W.L.R. 2303). But such a term in a consumer contract might be unfair and not binding on the consumer under the Unfair Terms in Consumer Contracts Regulations 1999, below, Ch.15.

[380] *Keen v Commerzbank AG* [2006] EWCA Civ 1536, [2007] I.R.L.R. 132.

[381] See above, para.14–015.

[382] See above, para.14–066.

[383] See above, para.14–060.

[384] s.4(1).

(b) is to the person dealing as consumer or someone else.[385]

The liability against which indemnity is sought must be a business liability.[386] An example would be a term in a contract for the hire of a motorcar which required the hirer to indemnify the car hire company against third-party claims arising out of the hirer's use of the car.

14–076 Indemnities given by persons who do not deal as consumer are not affected by s.4. Although s.2 of the Act inhibits the exclusion or restriction of liability for negligence,[387] nothing in that section will render ineffective a term of a contract by which one party requires the other (who does not deal as consumer) to indemnify him against his liability in negligence to third parties.[388]

14–077 **"Guarantee" of consumer goods.**[389] Section 5 of the Act renders absolutely ineffective the exclusion or restriction of business liability[390] for loss or damage resulting from the negligence[391] of a manufacturer or distributor of goods[392] by reference to any contract term or notice contained in or operating by reference to a guarantee of the goods[393] (such as is often provided by, for example, manufacturers of electrical equipment). But the goods must be of a type ordinarily supplied for private use or consumption,[394] and the loss or damage must arise from the goods proving defective while "in consumer use", that is, when a person is using them, or has them in possession for use, otherwise than exclusively for the purposes of business.[395] This section does not apply as between parties to a contract under or in pursuance of which possession or ownership of the goods passed.[396]

14–078 **Sale and hire purchase.** Section 6 of the Act[397] limits the ability of a seller of goods, or of the owner of goods let under a hire-purchase agreement, to exclude or restrict his liability in respect of breach of the terms implied by ss.12 to 15 of the Sale of Goods Act 1979[398] or ss.8 to 11 of the Supply of Goods (Implied Terms) Act 1973.[399] The content of s.6 is discussed in Volume II, Chs

---

[385] s.4(2).
[386] s.1(3); see above, para.14–065.
[387] See above, para.14–060.
[388] *Thompson v Lohan (Plant Hire) Ltd* [1987] 1 W.L.R. 649; *Hancock Shipping Co Ltd v Deacon & Trysail (Private) Ltd* [1991] 2 Lloyd's Rep. 550.
[389] See below, para.18–065. See also SI 2002/3045; SI 2008/1277; Vol.II, para.43–155.
[390] See above, para.14–065.
[391] See above, para.14–060.
[392] Defined in s.14.
[393] Defined in s.5(2)(b).
[394] See Vol.II, para.43–106.
[395] s.5(2)(a).
[396] s.5(2), e.g. as between buyer and seller.
[397] As amended by s.63 of and Sch.3 to the Sale of Goods Act 1979.
[398] See Vol.II, paras 43–072, 43–104 et seq.
[399] See Vol.II, paras 36–296, 38–362.

38 (Credit and Security)[400] and 43 (Sale of Goods),[401] of this work. The liabilities referred to in this section are not confined to business liabilities,[402] but they are confined to those which arise from breach of the statutory *implied* undertakings only.

Miscellaneous contracts under which goods pass. Section 7 of the Act is concerned with contract terms which exclude or restrict business liability for breach of an implied obligation in a contract "where the possession or ownership of the goods passes under or in pursuance of" the contract (other than a contract governed by the law of sale of goods or hire-purchase).[403] Examples of such contracts are contracts for the hire of goods or for work and materials. The obligation in the contract must be one which arises "by implication of law from the nature of the contract".[404] In most cases, the obligations to be implied in such contracts are those set out in ss.2 to 5 and 7 to 10 of the Supply of Goods and Services Act 1982.[405] In so far as any liability arises in respect of the goods' correspondence with description or sample, or their quality or fitness for any particular purpose, as against a person dealing as consumer the exclusion or restriction of that liability by reference to any contract term is absolutely ineffective.[406] As against a person dealing otherwise than as consumer, that liability can be excluded or restricted by reference to any contract term, but only in so far as the term satisfies the requirement of reasonableness.[407] Liability for breach of the obligations as to title, etc., arising under s.2 of the 1982 Act (e.g. in contracts for work and materials) cannot be excluded or restricted by reference to any contract term.[408] In the case of other contracts (e.g. contracts for the hire of goods,) terms excluding or restricting liability in respect of the right to transfer ownership of the goods or give possession, or the assurance of quiet possession to a person taking goods in pursuance of the contract, are subject to the test of reasonableness.[409] 14–079

Effect of breach. A term that is required to satisfy the test of reasonableness, and does so, may be given effect to notwithstanding that the contract has been terminated either by breach or by the innocent party electing to treat it as repudiated[410]; and the affirmation of the contract does not of itself exclude the requirement of reasonableness.[411] It would also seem that a term which is 14–080

---

[400] Vol.II, paras 38–298, 38–370.
[401] Vol.II, paras 43–072, 43–104.
[402] s.6(4). See above, para.14–065.
[403] Also excluded are goods passing on redemption of trading stamps: s.7(5).
[404] See above, paras 13–029, 13–030.
[405] ss.2–5 (work and materials); ss.7–10 (bailment for hire). See Vol.II, paras 33–070, 43–014.
[406] s.7(2). See Vol.II, para.33–075.
[407] s.7(3). See *Charlotte Thirty Ltd v Croker Ltd* (1990) 24 Const. L.R. 46; *Danka Rentals Ltd v XI Software Ltd* (1998) 17 Tr.L.R. 74.
[408] s.7(3A), inserted by s.17(2) of the Supply of Goods and Services Act 1982.
[409] s.7(4) (as amended).
[410] s.9(1). See also above, para.14–022.
[411] s.9(2).

rendered wholly ineffective in some respect by the Act is not rendered effective by the fact that the innocent party has affirmed the contract.

14–081 **Anti-avoidance provisions.** Certain anti-avoidance provisions are contained in the Act. Section 10 provides:

> "A person is not bound by any contract term prejudicing or taking away rights of his which arise under, or in connection with the performance of, another contract, so far as those rights extend to the enforcement of another's liability which this Part of this Act prevents that other from excluding or restricting."

The purpose of this provision has been said to be to prevent rights arising in favour of A under a contract between A and B from being affected by the terms of a secondary contract between A and C which take away or inhibit the exercise of those rights,[412] as, for example, where a term in a contract between a manufacturer of goods and the buyer purports to affect the rights of the buyer under the Sale of Goods Act against the retailer from whom he purchases the goods.[413] The scope of the section is, however, enigmatic. It employs the words "prejudicing or taking away rights" instead of the usual "excludes or restricts liability". The extended interpretation of the latter phrase[414] therefore does not apply. Also the reference to "the enforcement of another's *liability*" would preclude the application of s.10 to a case where the terms of the secondary contract purported to entitle a party to another contract to render a performance substantially different from that reasonably expected of him, or to render no performance at all.[415] It has been held that the section does not apply to the compromise or waiver of an existing contractual claim, e.g. to the release by a person of rights which have accrued to him as the result of the breach of another contract to which he is a party.[416]

14–082 Section 27(2) further prevents evasion of the Act by choice of a foreign law. This provision is considered in a later chapter (Conflict of Laws).[417]

14–083 **Assumption of risk.** Section 2(3) of the Act provides that, where a contract term (or notice)[418] purports to exclude or restrict liability for negligence a person's agreement to it or awareness of it is not of itself to be taken as indicating his voluntary acceptance of the risk.[419]

---

412 *Tudor Grange Holdings Ltd v Citibank N.A.* [1992] Ch. 53.

413 See s.55(3),(4) of the Sale of Goods Act 1893, inserted by s.4 of the Supply of Goods (Implied Terms) Act 1973, and repealed by the Unfair Contract Terms Act 1977 s.31(4) and Sch.4. But in *Neptune Orient Lines Ltd v J.V.C. (UK) Ltd* [1983] 2 Lloyd's Rep. 439, Parker J. held that s.10 had no application to a covenant not to sue a third party (see above, para.14–051) in tort.

414 s.13; see above, para.14–062.

415 s.3(2)(b); above, para.14–072 (there being no breach of contract).

416 *Tudor Grange Holdings Ltd v Citibank N.A.* [1992] Ch. 53 (noted (1992) 55 M.L.R. 866). See also Sch.1 para.5.

417 See below, paras 30–008, 30–068.

418 See above, para.14–059.

419 But see above, para.14–014.

Test of reasonableness. Except in those instances where the Act renders absolutely ineffective exclusion or restriction of liability, the contract terms controlled by the Act are subject to the requirement of reasonableness. In relation to a contract term, the requirement of reasonableness for the purposes of the Act (and of s.3 of the Misrepresentation Act 1967) is that: 14–084

> " . . . the term shall have been a fair and reasonable one to be included having regard to the circumstances which were or ought reasonably to have been, known to or in the contemplation of the parties when the contract was made."[420]

The time for determining the reasonableness of the term is the time at which the contract was made. That determination is therefore not affected by the nature or seriousness of the loss or damage caused, or the way in which the term is in fact operated or relied on,[421] except to the extent to which such events were or ought reasonably to have been in the contemplation of the parties at that time. Further, it would appear that circumstances known only to the party seeking to allege that the term is reasonable, for example, the experimental nature of the product or the fact that it had been purchased from a foreign supplier subject to an effective exclusion of liability of his part,[422] are irrelevant if they were not known, and could not reasonably have been known, to the other party at the time the contract was made.[423]

Guidelines. By s.11(2) of the Act, five guidelines are laid down in Sch.2[424] and regard is to be had to these in determining whether a contract term satisfies the requirement of reasonableness.[425] The guidelines are only made expressly applicable for the purposes of s.6 (sale of goods and hire-purchase) and s.7 (other contracts for the supply of goods), but they are frequently regarded as being of general application.[426] The guidelines are: 14–085

---

[420] s.11(1). Contrast s.11(3) (notices) and *First National Bank Plc v Loxley* [1996] E.G.C.S. 174.

[421] *Shearson Lehman Hutton Inc v Maclaine Watson & Co Ltd* [1989] 2 Lloyd's Rep. 570, 612. See also *Stewart Gill Ltd v Horatio Myer & Co Ltd* [1992] Q.B. 600; *Balmoral Group Ltd v Borealis UK Ltd* [2006] EWHC 1900 (Comm), [2006] 2 Lloyd's Rep. 629 at [420]–[421].

[422] See below, para.14–110.

[423] See also *Singer Co (UK) Ltd v Tees and Hartlepool Port Authority* [1988] 2 Lloyd's Rep. 164, 169; *Flamar Interocean Ltd v Denmac Ltd* [1990] 1 Lloyd's Rep. 434; *Overseas Medical Supplies Ltd v Orient Transport Services Ltd* [1999] 2 Lloyd's Rep. 273, 277; *Pegler Ltd v Wang (UK) Ltd* [2000] Build. L.R. 218 (availability of insurance may be relevant, but actual insurance position at time irrelevant).

[424] The guidelines are similar to those set out in s.55(5) of the Sale of Goods Act 1893 (inserted by s.4 of the Supply of Goods (Implied Terms) Act 1973, and now repealed).

[425] See Vol.II, para.43–107.

[426] *Flamar Interocean Ltd v Denmac Ltd* [1990] 1 Lloyd's Rep. 434, 438–439; *Stewart Gill Ltd v Horatio Myer & Co Ltd* [1992] Q.B. 600, 608. See also *Singer Co (UK) Ltd v Tees and Hartlepool Port Authority* [1988] 2 Lloyd's Rep. 164, 169; *St Alban's City and District Council v International Computers Ltd* [1995] F.S.R. 686 (affirmed [1996] 4 All E.R. 481); *Overseas Medical Supplies Ltd v Orient Transport Services Ltd* [1999] 2 Lloyd's Rep. 273, 277; *Pegler Ltd v Wang (UK) Ltd* [2000] Build. L.R. 218; *Granville Oil and Chemicals Ltd v Davis Turner & Co Ltd* [2003] EWCA Civ 570, [2003] 2 Lloyd's Rep. 356 at [15]; *SAM Business Systems Ltd v Hedley & Co* [2002] EWHC (TCC) 2733, [2003] 1 All E.R. (Comm) 465 at [67].

(a) the strength of the bargaining positions of the parties relative to each other, taking account (among other things) alternative means by which the customer's requirements could have been met[427];

(b) whether the customer received an inducement to agree to the term, or in accepting it had an opportunity of entering into a similar contract with other persons, but without having to accept a similar term[428];

(c) whether the customer knew or ought reasonably to have known of the existence and extent of the term (having regard, among other things, to any custom of the trade and any course of dealing between the parties)[429];

(d) where the term excludes or restricts any relevant liability if some condition is not complied with, whether it was reasonable at the time of the contract to expect that compliance with that condition would be practicable[430];

---

[427] See *R.W. Green Ltd v Cade Bros Farms* [1978] 1 Lloyd's Rep. 602; *George Mitchell (Chesterhall) Ltd v Finney Lock Seeds Ltd* [1983] 2 A.C. 803; *Singer Co (UK) Ltd v Tees and Hartlepool Port Authority* [1988] 2 Lloyd's Rep. 164; *St Alban's City and District Council v International Computers Ltd* [1995] F.S.R. 686; *Schenkers Ltd v Overland Shoes Ltd* [1998] 1 Lloyd's Rep. 498; *Thames Tideway Properties Ltd v Serfaty & Partners* [1999] 2 Lloyd's Rep. 110; *Overseas Medical Supplies Ltd v Orient Transport Services Ltd* [1999] 2 Lloyd's Rep. 273; *British Fermentation Products Ltd v Compair Reavell Ltd* (1999) 66 Const. L.R. 1.; *Watford Electronics Ltd v Sanderson CFL Ltd* [2001] EWCA Civ 317, [2001] Build. L.R. 143; *Granville Oil and Chemicals Ltd v Davis Turner & Co Ltd* [2003] EWCA Civ 57; *Frans Maas (UK) Ltd v Samsung Electronics (UK) Ltd* [2004] EWHC 1502 (Comm), [2004] 2 Lloyd's Rep. 251 at [159]; *Balmoral Group Ltd v Borealis UK Ltd* [2006] EWHC 1900 (Comm), [2006] 2 Lloyd's Rep. 629 at [407]–[409]; *Shepherd Homes Ltd v Encia Remediation Ltd* [2007] EWHC 70 (TCC), [2007] Build. L.R. 135. In *Denholm Fishselling Ltd v Anderson* (1991) S.L.T. (Sh. Ct.) 24, it was held that there was no preponderance of bargaining power where buyers might not be able to purchase except on similar standard conditions but nevertheless had a choice of suppliers.

[428] *R.W. Green Ltd v Cade Bros Farms* [1978] 1 Lloyd's Rep. 602; *George Mitchell (Chesterhall) Ltd v Finney Lock Seeds Ltd* [1983] 2 A.C. 803; *Singer Co (UK) Ltd v Tees and Hartlepool Port Authority* [1988] 2 Lloyd's Rep. 164; *Thames Tideway Properties Ltd v Serfaty & Partners* [1999] 2 Lloyd's Rep. 110; *Overseas Medical Supplies Ltd v Orient Transport Services Ltd* [1999] 2 Lloyd's Rep. 273; *Watford Electronics Ltd v Sanderson CFL Ltd* [2001] EWCA Civ 317; *Frans Maas (UK) Ltd v Samsung Electronics (UK) Ltd* [2004] EWHC 1502 at [410].

[429] See *George Mitchell (Chesterhall) Ltd v Finney Lock Seeds Ltd* [1983] 2 A.C. 803; *Charlotte Thirty Ltd v Croker Ltd* (1990) 24 Const. L.R. 46; *AEG (UK) Ltd v Logic Resource Ltd* [1996] C.L.C. 625; *Thames Tideway Properties Ltd v Serfaty & Partners* [1999] 2 Lloyd's Rep. 110; *Overseas Medical Supplies Ltd v Orient Transport Services Ltd* [1999] 2 Lloyd's Rep. 273; *British Fermentation Products Ltd v Compair Reavell Ltd* (1999) 66 Const. L.R. 1; *Watford Electronics Ltd v Sanderson CFL Ltd* [2001] EWCA Civ 317; *Britvic Soft Drinks Ltd v Messer UK Ltd* [2002] EWCA Civ 548, [2002] 2 Lloyd's Rep. 368; *Granville Oil and Chemicals Ltd v Davis Turner & Co Ltd* [2003] EWCA Civ 570; *Frans Maas (UK) Ltd v Samsung Electronics (UK) Ltd* [2004] EWHC 1502 at [411].

[430] See *R.W. Green Ltd v Cade Bros Farms* [1978] 1 Lloyd's Rep. 602; *Stag Line Ltd v Tyne Ship Repair Group Ltd* [1984] 2 Lloyd's Rep. 211; *Rees-Hough Ltd v Redland Reinforced Plastics Ltd* (1985) 2 Const. L.R. 109; *Sargant v CIT (England) (t/a Citalia)* [1994] C.L.Y. 566; *Knight Machinery (Holdings) v Rennie* 1995 S.L.T. 166; *Granville Oil and Chemicals Ltd v Davis Turner & Co Ltd* [2003] EWCA Civ 570.

(e) whether the goods were manufactured, processed or adapted to the special order of the customer.[431]

Further factors. The guidelines set out in Sch.2 to the Act are not, however, exhaustive and in *Overseas Medical Supplies Ltd v Orient Transport Services Ltd*[432] Potter L.J. identified no less than seven further factors going to the question of reasonableness which, in his view, had been regarded as relevant by the courts in previous cases. This list is obviously not a closed one. 14–086

Limits on amount. Exemption clauses in contracts frequently limit the liability in damages of one party to a fixed or determinable sum. Section 11(4) provides: 14–087

> "Where by reference to a contract term . . . a person seeks to restrict liability to a specified sum of money, and the question arises (under this or any other Act) whether the term or notice satisfies the requirement of reasonableness, regard shall be had in particular (but without prejudice to subsection (2) above[433] in the case of contract terms) to—(a) the resources which he could expect to be available to him for the purpose of meeting the liability should it arise; and (b) how far it was open to him to cover himself by insurance."

This provision was clearly designed to provide some alleviation to the small business, and to professional persons, who may not have the resources available to meet unlimited liability or who may not be able to obtain insurance or who may be exposed to claims in excess of the sums for which insurance cover can be obtained. But it might in some circumstances be construed to operate against those enterprises with such resources or which are able to insure.[434] It seems probable that the words "a specified sum of money" would embrace a determinable sum, e.g. the contract price. But it is more questionable whether (b) covers

[431] It is uncertain whether the existence of this factor would operate against or in favour of the customer, but it is submitted that it should operate against the customer and in favour of the supplier. But see *Edmund Murray Ltd v BSP International Foundations Ltd* (1992) 33 Const. L.R. 1. cf. *British Fermentation Products Ltd v Compair Reavell Ltd* (1999) 66 Const. L.R. 1; *Watford Electronics Ltd v Sanderson CFL Ltd* [2001] EWCA Civ 317.

[432] [1999] 2 Lloyd's Rep. 273, 276–277. See also *Balmoral Group Ltd v Borealis UK Ltd* [2006] EWHC 1900 (Comm), [2006] 2 Lloyd's Rep. 629 at [412]–[413].

[433] See above, para.14–085.

[434] The availability of insurance may be a relevant consideration in applying the test of reasonableness under s.11(1): see *George Mitchell (Chesterhall) Ltd v Finney Lock Seeds Ltd* [1983] 2 A.C. 803, 817 (below, para.14–091); *Rees-Hough Ltd v Redland Reinforced Plastics Ltd* (1985) 2 Const. L.R. 109; *Phillips Products Ltd v Hyland* [1987] 1 W.L.R. 659, 666–668; *Singer Co (UK) Ltd v Tees and Hartlepool Port Authority* [1988] 2 Lloyd's Rep. 164, 169; *Smith v Eric Bush* [1990] 1 A.C. 831, 858; *Overseas Medical Supplies Ltd v Orient Transport Services Ltd* [1990] 2 Lloyd's Rep. 273, 277; *Pegler Ltd v Wang* [2000] Build. L.R. 218; *Frans Maas (UK) Ltd v Samsung Electronics (UK) Ltd* [2004] EWHC 1502 (Comm), [2004] 2 Lloyd's Rep. 251 at [159]; *Balmoral Group Ltd v Borealis UK Ltd* [2006] EWHC 1900 (Comm) at [415]–[416]. But the actual insurance position of the parties at the time is normally irrelevant: *Flamar Interocean Ltd v Denmac Ltd* [1990] 1 Lloyd's Rep. 434; cf. *St Alban's City and District Council v International Computers Ltd* [1995] F.S.R. 686 (affirmed [1996] 4 All E.R. 481); *Salvage Association v Cap Financial Services* [1995] F.S.R. 654; *SAM Business Systems Ltd v Hedley & Co* [2002] EWHC (TCC) 2733, [2003] 1 All E.R. (Comm) 465.

the situation where insurance cover can be obtained, but only on terms which are uneconomic in relation to the margin of profit achieved.[435]

14–088 **Burden of proof.** The onus of proving that it was fair and reasonable to incorporate a term in a contract lies on the party so contending.[436] It is therefore unnecessary for a claimant to indicate in his statement of case that he intends to challenge the reasonableness of a term in a contract relied on by the defendant.[437]

14–089 **Judicial application of the reasonableness test.**[438] There is a growing body of reported cases which illustrate in general terms the way in which the courts may approach the test of reasonableness contained in the Act. However, they are of limited value as precedents since the position of the parties and the circumstances surrounding the transaction, and the precise wording of the clause in question, will necessarily differ in each particular situation.

14–090 **Decisions under earlier legislation.** A small number of decisions have been reported with respect to the reasonableness test contained in s.55 of the Sale of Goods Act 1893[439] (now repealed) or s.3 of the Misrepresentation Act 1967 (now amended in its wording by s.8 of the Unfair Contract Terms Act 1977), both of which sections however required the court to determine whether it would be fair and reasonable to allow *reliance* on the term, and not whether it was fair and reasonable to incorporate the term having regard to the circumstances at the time the contract was made.[440] In *Rasbora Ltd v J.C.L. Marine Ltd*[441] it was held (obiter)[442] that it was not fair and reasonable to allow a boatbuilder to rely on a term excluding all liability (other than a warranty to replace defective parts) when the boat was wholly destroyed by a fire, due to defective electrical installations, on the day following its acceptance by the buyer. In *R.W. Green Ltd v Cade Bros Farms*[443] a term in a contract for the bulk sale of seed potatoes providing a short time-limit for complaints in respect of latent defects could not be relied on by the seller when the potatoes were infected with a virus; but reliance on a term limiting the liability of the seller to the contract price was allowed, as the term had been in use for many years with the approval of negotiating committees acting on behalf of both buyers and sellers. And in *Howard Marine and Dredging Co Ltd v A. Ogden & Sons (Excavations) Ltd*[444] the Court of Appeal by a majority[445] held that it would not have been fair and

[435] cf., *Smith v Eric Bush* [1990] 1 A.C. 831, 858 (cost); *Shepherd Homes Ltd v Encia Remediation Ltd* [2007] EWHC 70 (TCC), [2007] Build. L.R. 135.

[436] s.11(5). See *AEG (UK) Ltd v Logic Resource Ltd* [1996] C.L.C. 265, 278.

[437] *Sheffield v Pickfords Ltd* [1997] C.L.C. 648.

[438] See Adams and Brownsword (1988) 104 L.Q.R. 94; Brown and Chandler (1993) 109 L.Q.R. 41; Adams (1994) 57 M.L.R. 960.

[439] Inserted by s.4 of the Supply of Goods (Implied Terms) Act 1973.

[440] But see *Howard Marine and Dredging Co Ltd v A. Ogden & Sons (Excavations) Ltd* [1978] Q.B. 574, 594.

[441] [1977] 1 Lloyd's Rep. 645.

[442] The sale was held to be a consumer sale: see above, para.14–066 fn.344.

[443] [1978] 1 Lloyd's Rep. 602.

[444] [1978] Q.B. 574; see above, para.6–068.

[445] Bridge and Shaw L.JJ. (but giving no reasons).

reasonable to allow reliance on a term in a contract for the hire of barges which provided that acceptance was to be conclusive evidence that the barges were fit for their intended use, even if the clause had been apt (which it was not) to cover a misrepresentation by the owners of the barges as to their deadweight capacity. Lord Denning M.R., however, considered that both the clause itself and reliance on it was fair and reasonable, since the parties were of equal bargaining power, the term was contained in negotiated drafts and it was a familiar term in charterparties and other commercial contracts, such as structural and engineering contracts.

In *George Mitchell (Chesterhall) Ltd v Finney Lock Seeds Ltd*[446] the appellant seed merchants, by their standard conditions of sale, limited their liability in respect of seeds that did not comply with the contract of sale to replacement of the seeds or refund of the price, but otherwise excluded all liability for loss or damage arising from the use of seeds supplied by them apart from such replacement or refund. The respondents, who were farmers, purchased from them for £201 a quantity of winter white cabbage seeds. The seeds in fact supplied were autumn cabbage seed; the crop failed; and the respondents claimed damages in excess of £60,000. The House of Lords held that it would not be fair or reasonable to allow the appellants to rely on the limitation of liability. Lord Bridge said that, in having regard to the various matters to which the relevant statutory provision directs attention[447]: 14–091

> "... the court must entertain a whole range of considerations, put them in the scales on one side or the other, and decide at the end of the day on which side the balance comes down."[448]

In the instant case, although a similar limitation of liability had for long been embodied without protest in the terms of the trade between seedsmen and farmers,[449] the practice was to negotiate settlements of farmers' claims for damages in excess of the price of the seeds if it was thought that the claims were genuine and justified. This indicated that reliance on the limitation would not be fair or reasonable. Two further facts weighted the scale in favour of the respondents: the error was due to the negligence of the appellants' organisation, and seedsmen could insure[450] against the risk of crop failure resulting from the supply of the wrong variety of seeds without materially increasing the price of seeds.

Reasonableness under Unfair Contract Terms Act 1977. So far as the 1977 Act is concerned, in *Walker v Boyle*,[451] where a vendor in response to preliminary inquiries represented that she was unaware of any boundary dispute connected with the property, although she ought to have known that there was such a dispute, it was held that condition 17 of the National Conditions of Sale, even 14–092

---

[446] [1983] 2 A.C. 803; see above, para.14–023.

[447] Sale of Goods Act 1979 s.55 (as amended) or s.11 of the Unfair Contract Terms Act 1977.

[448] [1983] 2 A.C. 803, 816.

[449] But never negotiated by representative bodies.

[450] See above, para.14–087 fn.434.

[451] [1982] 1 W.L.R. 495. See also *Southwestern General Property Co Ltd v Marton* (1982) 263 E.G. 1090 and above, para.6–139 fn.575.

with a statement that "accuracy is not guaranteed, and [the replies] do not obviate the need to make appropriate searches, inquiries and inspections", did not meet the test of reasonableness required by s.11 of the Act.[452] In *Stag Line Ltd v Tyne Shiprepair Group Ltd*[453] a term in a ship-repairing contract excluding liability on the part of the repairer for consequential economic loss was held to be reasonable, but not a condition that the shipowner should have no remedy unless he returned the vessel to the repairer's yard for repair, or to such other place as the repairer should direct. In *Phillips Products Ltd v Hyland*[454] the Court of Appeal held unreasonable in the circumstances[455] a term in a contract for the hire of an excavator and driver which provided that the driver was to be regarded as an employee of the hirer who alone was to be responsible for all claims arising in connection with the operation of the plant by the driver. In *Rees-Hough Ltd v Redland Reinforced Plastics Ltd*[456] a term in a contract for the supply of piping which excluded all liability of the seller unless notified of complaints within three months of delivery was held unreasonable. In *Smith v Eric Bush*[457] a non-contractual notice in a report by a building society surveyor disclaiming all liability for negligence in conducting the survey of a modest dwelling-house was held to be unreasonable in view of the fact that the report would be relied on by an intending purchaser of the property. In *Charlotte Thirty Ltd v Croker Ltd*[458] the court held unreasonable a term in a contract to design and build an industrial plant which exonerated the contractor from all liability except as provided in a six-month warranty to replace defective components if these were returned carriage paid to the contractor for adjudication. And in *Stewart Gill Ltd v Horatio Myer & Co Ltd*[459] a term in a contract for the supply and installation of a conveyor system, which provided that the purchaser was not to be entitled to withhold payment of any sum due to the supplier under the contract by reason of "any payment, credit, set-off . . . or for any other reason whatsoever", failed to satisfy the requirement of reasonableness.

14–093 In *St Alban's City and DC v International Computers Ltd*[460] a term in a computer software contract made with a local authority limited the liability of the supplier to £100,000, and in *Salvage Association v Cap Financial Services*[461] a term in a computer accounting contract limited the liability of the supplier to

---

[452] For the purposes of s.3 of the Misrepresentation Act 1967 (as amended).

[453] [1984] 2 Lloyd's Rep. 211.

[454] [1987] 1 W.L.R. 659. But contrast *Thompson v Lohan (Plant Hire) Ltd* [1987] 1 W.L.R. 649.

[455] The contract was on a "take it or leave it" basis, and the hirer had no control over the way the driver would do the work.

[456] (1985) 2 Const.L.R. 109. See also *Sterling Hydraulics Ltd v Dichtomatik Ltd* [2006] EWHC 2004 (QB), [2007] 1 Lloyd's Rep. 8 (defects to be reported within one week of delivery). Contrast *Expo Fabrics (UK) Ltd v Naughty Clothing* [2003] EWCA Civ 1165 (textiles: 20-day time limit held reasonable).

[457] [1990] 1 A.C. 831; see also *Harris v Wyre Forest DC* at [1990] 1 A.C. 831; *Davies v Idris Parry* (1988) 20 E.G. 92, 21 E.G. 74; *Beaton v Nationwide Anglia Building Society* (1991) 31 E.G. 218.

[458] (1990) 24 Const.L.R. 46. But see Vol.II, para.37–085 (construction contracts).

[459] [1992] Q.B. 600. See also *Fastframe Ltd v Lochinski* Unreported March 3, 1993 CA (noted (1994) 57 M.L.R. 960); *Esso Petroleum Co Ltd v Milton* [1997] 1 W.L.R. 938, 948, 954. But see the cases cited in para.14–095, fn.475, 476.

[460] [1995] F.S.R. 686 (affirmed [1996] 4 All E.R. 481).

[461] [1995] F.S.R. 654.

£25,000. Both were held to be unreasonable. In *Edmund Murray Ltd v BSP International Foundations Ltd*[462] the court held unreasonable a term in a contract for the sale of a drilling rig with detailed requirements for performance, which purported to exclude liability on the part of the seller for breach of both express and implied obligations, and in *AEG (UK) Ltd v Logic Resource Ltd*[463] a term in a contract for the sale of radar equipment which excluded all warranties and conditions implied by the Sale of Goods Act 1979 was held to be unreasonable despite the giving of an express warranty that the equipment was free of defects caused by faulty materials or bad workmanship. Also in *Timeload Ltd v British Telecommunications Plc*[464] the Court of Appeal held unreasonable a term in BT's standard terms and conditions which permitted BT to terminate the contract on one month's notice since the term was not limited to cases where there was a good reason for the termination.

In *Overseas Medical Supplies Ltd v Orient Transport Services Ltd*[465] the defendants undertook to carry medical equipment belonging to the claimants to be exhibited at an overseas exhibition and to ensure full insurance cover for the exhibits. The Court of Appeal refused to disturb the finding of the trial judge that a term which purported to limit the liability of the defendants to £600 in the event that occurred, namely a breach by the defendants of their contractual duty to insure the goods, was unreasonable. In *Pegler Ltd v Wang (UK) Ltd*,[466] terms in a contract for the supply of computer hardware and software excluding liability for indirect, special and consequential loss and imposing a two-year contractual limit for claims were held unreasonable because the supplier "had so misrepresented what [it] was selling that breaches of contract were not unlikely" and because the customer had no choice but to accept them. In *Britvic Soft Drinks Ltd v Messer UK Ltd*[467] the Court of Appeal held that clauses in a contract for the sale of bulk carbon dioxide to be used by the buyer for the carbonation of drinks, which purported to exclude the terms as to satisfactory quality and fitness for purpose implied by the Sale of Goods Act 1979, were unreasonable, and in *Bacardi-Martini Beverages Ltd v Thomas Hardy Packaging Ltd*[468] it held that a clause in a similar contract, which operated as a blanket exclusion of liability on the part of the seller for any loss or damage (with certain exceptions) sustained by the buyer, was likewise unreasonable. 14–094

On the other hand, in *R. & B. Customs Brokers Co Ltd v United Dominions Trust Ltd*,[469] where a finance company purchased a motorcar from a dealer and agreed to sell it under a conditional sale agreement to a commercial company, 14–095

[462] (1994) 33 Const. L.R. 1.
[463] [1996] C.L.C. 265.
[464] [1995] E.M.L.R. 459. Contrast *Zockoll Group Ltd v Mercury Communications Ltd* [1998] I.T.C.L.R. 104.
[465] [1999] 2 Lloyd's Rep. 273.
[466] [2000] Build. L.R. 248.
[467] [2002] EWCA Civ 548, [2002] 2 Lloyd's Rep. 368. See also *Balmoral Group Ltd v Borealis UK Ltd* [2006] EWHC 1900 (Comm), [2006] 2 Lloyd's Rep. 629 at [418].
[468] [2002] EWCA Civ 549, [2002] 2 Lloyd's Rep. 379.
[469] [1988] 1 W.L.R. 321. See also *W. Photoprint Ltd v Forward Trust Group Ltd* (1993) 12 Tr.L.R. 146, QBD.

Dillon L.J. expressed the opinion (obiter)[470] that a clause in the conditional sale agreement which excluded all conditions and warranties, express or implied, as to merchantability or fitness for purpose was in the circumstances reasonable, since the director who entered into the agreement on behalf of the buyer company was a man of commercial experience and the finance company never had possession of or inspected the car.[471] In *Singer Co (UK) Ltd v Tees and Hartlepool Port Authority*,[472] where a machine sub-bailed to a port authority was damaged in the course of loading, Steyn J. held reasonable a clause disclaiming responsibility for damage other than that arising from the proven negligence of the authority and a clause limiting the liability of the authority to a sum of £800 per tonne.[473] In *Sonicare International Ltd v East Anglia Freight Terminal Ltd*[474] a term in the National Association of Warehouse Keepers' conditions limiting liability to £100 per tonne was similarly held reasonable in the circumstances of that case. A "no set-off" clause in the standard conditions of the British International Freight Association (freight forwarders) was upheld as reasonable in *Schenkers Ltd v Overland Shoes Ltd*,[475] and "no set-off" clauses in loan and financial agreements have also been upheld.[476] A term in a freight forwarders' contract excluding liability for damage to goods unless suit was brought within nine months was likewise adjudged reasonable.[477]

14–096 Clauses limiting the amount of damages recoverable have been upheld as reasonable in *Moore v Yakeley Associates Ltd*,[478] where a term in the Royal Institute of British Architects' Standard Form limited the liability of an architect to £250,000, and in *Britvic Soft Drinks Ltd v Messer UK Ltd*[479] where there was a term in a contract for the sale of bulk carbon dioxide limiting the liability of the seller in respect of direct physical damage to property, and losses arising directly therefrom, whether through negligence or otherwise, to £500,000. In *Frans Maas (UK) Ltd v Samsung Electronics (UK) Ltd*[480] a clause in the BIFA (freight forwarders) contract limiting the damages recoverable in respect of loss by theft of mobile telephones (valued at £2m) to approximately £25,000 was upheld as

---

[470] [1988] 1 W.L.R. 321, 331–332. The company was held to be "dealing as consumer": see above, para.14–066.

[471] See also *Abbey National Business Equipment Leasing Ltd v Dora Ife* [2003] C.L.Y 723 (hire). But the fact that the finance company had not seen the goods was considered insufficient in *Sovereign Finance Ltd v Silver Crest Furniture* [1997] C.C.L.R. 76 (hire purchase) following *Purnell Secretarial Services v Lease Management Services* [1994] C.C.L.R. 127 (hire).

[472] [1988] 2 Lloyd's Rep. 164.

[473] This figure was below that of the Hague-Visby Rules (£1,210), the CMR convention (£5,195) and the Warsaw Convention (£10,050) at the relevant time.

[474] [1997] 2 Lloyd's Rep. 48.

[475] [1998] 1 Lloyd's Rep. 498.

[476] *Surzur Overseas Ltd v Ocean Reliance Shipping Co Ltd* [1997] C.L.Y. 906; *Skipskredittforeningen v Emperor Navigation* [1998] 1 Lloyd's Rep. 66; *WRM Group Ltd v Wood* [1998] C.L.C. 189.

[477] *Granville Oil Chemicals Ltd v Davis Turner & Co Ltd* [2003] EWCA Civ 570, [2003] 2 Lloyd's Rep. 450.

[478] (1999) 62 Const. L.R. 76 (affirmed [2000] C.L.Y. 810).

[479] [2002] 1 Lloyd's Rep. 20, see also *Bacardi-Martini Beverages Ltd v Thomas Hardy Packaging Ltd* [2002] 1 Lloyd's Rep. 62 (both decisions by Tomlinson J.). The point was not in issue in either case on appeal [2002] EWCA Civ 548; [2002] EWCA Civ 549; [2002] 2 Lloyd's Rep. 368; [2002] 2 Lloyd's Rep. 379.

[480] [2004] EWHC 1502 (Comm), [2004] 2 Lloyd's Rep. 251.

reasonable and in *Sterling Hydraulics Ltd v Dichtomatik Ltd*[481] a clause in a contract for trailer parts which restricted the seller's liability for defects to the value of the goods was likewise held to be reasonable.

14–097 In *Thames Tideway Properties Ltd v Serfaty & Partners*[482] terms in a contract for the handling of cargoes of waste paper which provided that goods handled would be at the sole risk of the customer and that the handling company should not be liable for any damage to the goods unless such damage was proved by the customer to have been caused by the neglect or default of the company or its employees were held to be reasonable. In *British Fermentation Products Ltd v Compair Reavell Ltd*[483] the court held reasonable a term in a contract for the supply of machinery which provided that the supplier undertook to repair or replace machinery which proved to be defective within 12 months of delivery if it was returned to him at his expense but stipulated that this was: "... in lieu of any warranty or condition implied by law as to the quality or fitness for any particular purpose of the goods."

14–098 A number of cases have emphasised the importance of upholding the agreed contract terms where experienced businessmen are involved and the parties are of equal bargaining power in terms of size and resources. In *Photo Productions Ltd v Securicor Transport Ltd*[484] (a case which did not involve consideration of any provision of the 1977 Act) Lord Wilberforce stated that, in commercial matters generally, when the parties were not of unequal bargaining power, and when risks were to be borne by insurance, Parliament's intention in the Act seemed to be one of "leaving the parties free to apportion the risks as they think fit ... and respecting their decisions".[485]

14–099 This was the approach adopted in *Monarch Airlines Ltd v London Luton Airport Ltd*[486] where a term in a contract between an airline and an airport operator excluded liability for damage to an aircraft caused by any act, omission, neglect or default on the part of the latter, except if done with intent to cause damage or recklessly with knowledge that damage would probably result. It was held that this term was reasonable on the ground that it was generally accepted in the market, its meaning was clear and both parties could make insurance arrangements on the basis of the term. It was also the approach adopted in *Watford Electronics Ltd v Sanderson CFL Ltd*[487] where the Court of Appeal,

[481] [2006] EWHC 2004 (QB), [2007] 1 Lloyd's Rep. 8 (but not a provision that defects were to be reported within one week of delivery).

[482] [1999] 2 Lloyd's Rep. 110.

[483] (1999) 66 Const. L.R. 1.

[484] [1980] A.C. 827.

[485] [1980] A.C. 827, 843 (applied in *IFE Fund SA v Goldman Sachs International* [2006] EWHC 2887 (Comm); [2007] 1 Lloyd's Rep. 264 at [52]–[54]).

[486] [1998] 1 Lloyd's Rep. 403.

[487] [2001] EWCA Civ 317, [2001] Build. L.R. 143 at [63]. See also *Salvage Association v CAP Financial Services* [1995] F.S.R. 654, 676; *Sam Business Systems Ltd v Hedley & Co* [2002] EWHC 2733, [2003] 1 All E.R. (Comm) 465 at [63]; *Granville Oil and Chemicals Ltd v Davis Turner & Co Ltd* [2003] EWCA Civ 570, [2003] 2 Lloyd's Rep. 356 at [31]; *Frans Maas (UK) Ltd v Samsung Electronics (UK) Ltd* [2004] EWHC 1502 (Comm), [2004] 2 Lloyd's Rep. 251 at [158]; cf. *Balmoral Group Ltd v Borealis UK Ltd* [2006] EWHC 1900 (Comm), [2006] 2 Lloyd's Rep. 629 at [404], [422]–[426].

reversing the decision of the trial judge, held reasonable a term in a contract for the supply of a bespoke integrated software system which excluded the liability of either party for indirect and consequential losses, whether arising from negligence or otherwise, and limited the liability of the supplier to the amount of the contract price. Chadwick L.J. said:

> "Where experienced businessmen representing substantial companies of equal bargaining power negotiated an agreement, they may be taken to have had regard to the matters known to them. They should, in my view, be taken to be the best judges of the commercial fairness of the agreement which they have made; including the fairness of each of the terms of that agreement."

14–100 **Powers of the court.** Although the Act uses the words "except in so far as the term satisfies the requirement of reasonableness",[488] it is the term as a whole that has to be reasonable and not merely some part of it.[489] Thus if the term as a whole is unreasonable, a party cannot be heard to say that the part of the term on which he relies is reasonable.[490] However, where a single provision in a contract consists of several sub-clauses or sentences, it may be difficult to identify what is "the term" for the purposes of the Act.

14–101 There is little doubt that the court's powers under the Act are limited to declaring the term either to be reasonable or unreasonable. The court could not rewrite the term by (say) increasing the amount specified in a limitation of liability clause to a sum which it considered to be fair and reasonable.[491] Nor (semble) could the court sever words which made the term unreasonable so as to render the term reasonable or limit the application of an unreasonable clause so as to produce a reasonable result.[492]

14–102 If a single term purports to exclude or restrict liability which by the Act cannot in any circumstances be excluded or restricted (for example, liability for death and personal injury resulting from negligence) and also liability which can be excluded or restricted subject to the test of reasonableness (for example, liability in negligence for other loss or damage), it would appear that the term, while being ineffective to exclude or restrict the former liability, could nevertheless be upheld as reasonable in respect of the restriction or exclusion of the latter liability.[493] But it could be argued that the term as a whole is rendered unreasonable by purporting to exclude or restrict the former liability as well as the latter.

---

[488] Or, in ss.6(3), 7(3), "only in so far as".

[489] *Stewart Gill Ltd v Horatio Myer & Co Ltd* [1992] Q.B. 600, 608. cf. *R.W. Green Ltd v Cade Bros Farms* [1978] 1 Lloyd's Rep. 602; above, para.14–090.

[490] *Stewart Gill Ltd v Horatio Myer & Co Ltd* [1992] Q.B. 600, 607. But see *Skipskredittforeningen v Emperor Navigation* [1998] 1 Lloyd's Rep. 66, 75; *Bacardi-Martini Beverages Ltd v Thomas Hardy Packaging Ltd* [2002] EWCA Civ 549, [2002] 2 Lloyd's Rep. 379 at [26].

[491] See *George Mitchell (Chesterhall) Ltd v Finney Lock Seeds Ltd* [1983] 2 A.C. 803, 816 (on the wording of s.55 of the Sale of Goods Act 1979 (as amended)).

[492] *Stewart Gill Ltd v Horatio Myer & Co Ltd* [1992] Q.B. 600.

[493] The point was left open by Parker J. in *George Mitchell (Chesterhall) Ltd v Finney Lock Seeds Ltd* [1981] 1 Lloyd's Rep. 476, 480.

Appeals. A decision by the judge of first instance as to whether the term was a fair and reasonable one to be included cannot accurately be described as an exercise of discretion. Nevertheless, since it involves the balancing of various considerations, Lord Bridge has said[494]: 14–103

> "... in my view... when asked to review such a decision on appeal, the appellate court should treat the original decision with the utmost respect and refrain from interference with it unless satisfied that it proceeded upon some erroneous principle or was plainly and obviously wrong."

Specific exceptions. Some or all of the provisions of the Act do not apply in the case of contracts of a type specified in the Act. 14–104

Schedule 1.[495] By para.1 of Sch.1 to the Act, ss.2 (negligence liability), 3 (liability arising in contract) and 4 (unreasonable indemnity clauses) do not extend to: 14–105

(a) any contract of insurance (including a contract to pay an annuity on human life)[496];

(b) any contract so far as it relates to the creation or transfer of an interest in land, or to the termination of such an interest, whether by extinction, merger, surrender, forfeiture or otherwise[497];

(c) any contract so far as it relates to the creation of a right or interest in any patent, trade mark, copyright, registered design, technical or commercial information or other intellectual property, or relates to the termination of any such right or interest[498];

(d) any contract so far as it relates:

(i) to the formation or dissolution of a company (which means any body corporate or unincorporated association and includes a partnership); or

494 *George Mitchell (Chesterhall) Ltd v Finney Lock Seeds Ltd* [1983] 2 A.C. 803, 810. See also *Edmund Murray Ltd v BSP International Foundations Ltd* (1994) 33 Const. L.R. 1; *St Alban's City and District Council v International Computers Ltd* [1996] 4 All E.R. 481, 491; *Overseas Medical Supplies Ltd v Orient Transport Services Ltd* [1999] 2 Lloyd's Rep. 273, 276; *Britvic Soft Drinks Ltd v Messer UK Ltd* [2002] EWCA Civ 548; [2002] 2 Lloyd's Rep. 368 at [19]; *Bacardi-Martini Beverages Ltd v Thomas Hardy Packaging Ltd* [2002] 2 Lloyd's Rep. 549, [2002] 2 Lloyd's Rep. 379 at [20]. cf. *Watford Electronics Ltd v Sanderson CFL Ltd* [2001] EWCA Civ 317, [2001] Build. L.R. 143; *Granville Oil and Chemicals Ltd v Davis Turner & Co Ltd* [2003] EWCA Civ 570, [2003] 2 Lloyd's Rep. 356 (first instance decision reversed).

495 See s.1(2).

496 But see below, para.15–055 (Unfair Terms in Consumer Contracts Regulations 1999).

497 *Electricity Supply Nominees Ltd v IAF Group Ltd* [1993] 1 W.L.R. 1059 (no-set-off clause in lease); *Cheltenham and Gloucester B.S. v Ebbage* [1994] C.L.Y. 3292 (mortgage); *Star Rider Ltd v Inntrepreneur Pub Co* [1998] 1 E.G.L.R. 53 (no-set-off clause in draft lease); *Unchained Growth III Plc v Granby Village (Manchester) Management Co Ltd* [2000] 1 W.L.R. 739 (no-set-off clause in lease). But see below, para.15–019 (Unfair Terms in Consumer Contracts Regulations 1999).

498 cf. *Salvage Association v Cap Financial Services* [1995] F.S.R. 654. Contrast Unfair Terms in Consumer Contracts Regulations 1999, below para.15–037.

(ii) to its constitution or the rights or obligations of its corporators or members;

(e) any contract so far as it relates to the creation or transfer of any right or interest in securities.[499]

14–106 Paragraph 2 of Sch.1 lists three contracts:

(a) any contract of marine salvage or towage;

(b) any charterparty of a ship or hovercraft; and

(c) any contract for the carriage of goods by ship[500] or hovercraft.[501]

These contracts are subject to s.2(1) (exclusion or restriction of liability for death or personal injury resulting from negligence), but otherwise ss.2 (negligence liability), 3 (liability arising in contract), 4 (unreasonable indemnity clauses) and 7 (miscellaneous contracts under which goods pass) do not extend to any such contract except in favour of a person dealing as consumer.

14–107 Paragraph 3 of Sch.1 deals with the situation where goods are carried by ship[502] or hovercraft[503] in pursuance of a contract which either:

(a) specifies that as the means of carriage over part of the journey to be covered; or

(b) makes provision as to the means of carriage and does not exclude that means.

In such a situation s.2(2) (exclusion or restriction of liability for loss or damage resulting from negligence other than death or personal injury), 3 (liability arising in contract) and 4 (unreasonable indemnity clauses) do not, except in favour of a person dealing as consumer, extend to the contract as it operates for and in relation to the carriage of goods by that means.

14–108 By para.4 of Sch.1 s.2(1) and (2) (negligence liability) do not extend to a contract of employment, except in favour of the employee.[504]

14–109 By para.5 of Sch.1 s.2(1) (exclusion or restriction of liability for death or personal injury resulting from negligence) does not affect the validity of any discharge and indemnity given by a person, on or in connection with an award to him of compensation for pneumoconiosis attributable to employment in the coal

---

[499] *Micklefield v S.A.C. Technology Ltd* [1990] 1 W.L.R. 1002.

[500] See Carriage of Goods by Sea Act 1971; Merchant Shipping Act 1981. But see also below, para.14–107.

[501] See Hovercraft (Civil Liability) Order 1971 (SI 1971/720) made under s.1 of the Hovercraft Act 1968. But see also below, para.14–107.

[502] See fn.500 (above).

[503] See fn.501 (above).

[504] See *Johnstone v Bloomsbury H.A.* [1992] Q.B. 333.

industry, in respect of any further claim arising from his contracting that disease.

International supply contracts. By s.26 of the Act, the limits imposed by the Act on the extent to which a person may exclude or restrict liability by reference to a contract term do not apply to liability arising under an international supply contract (as defined in subss.(3) and (4) of that section),[505] nor are the terms of such a contract subject to any requirement of reasonableness under s.3 (liability arising in contract) or s.4 (unreasonable indemnity clauses.) 14–110

Contractual provisions authorised or required by statute or international agreement. By s.29(1), nothing in the Act removes or restricts the effect of, or prevents reliance upon, any contractual provision which: 14–111

(a) is authorised or required by the express terms or necessary implication of an enactment[506]; or

(b) being made with a view to compliance with an international agreement to which the United Kingdom is a party, does not operate more restrictively than is contemplated by the agreement.

This subsection covers (inter alia), provisions in statutes and international conventions relating to the carriage of goods by sea[507] and of passengers, goods and luggage by land and air.[508] A specific temporary provision is made in the Act in respect of the Athens Convention 1974 on the carriage of passengers and their luggage by sea.[509]

Contractual provisions approved by a competent authority. By s.29(2) a contract term is to be taken for the purposes of the Act as satisfying the requirement of reasonableness if it is incorporated or approved by, or incorporated pursuant to a decision or ruling of, a competent authority[510] acting in the exercise of any statutory[511] jurisdiction or function and is not a term in a contract to which the competent authority is itself a party.[512] 14–112

Choice of English law clauses. Commercial contracts are frequently, by choice of the parties, made subject to English law, even though having no substantial connection with England. Section 27(1) of the Act[513] provides that, where the law applicable to a contract is the law of any part of the United 14–113

---

[505] See Vol.II, para.43–110.
[506] Defined in UCTA 1977 s.29(3).
[507] Carriage of Goods by Sea Act 1971; Merchant Shipping Act 1981.
[508] See below, para.14–117, and Vol.II, Chs 35 and 36.
[509] s.28. The Merchant Shipping Act 1995 Sch.6, now provides that the Athens Convention 1974, as amended by the 1976 protocol, is to have the force of law in the United Kingdom. See also SI 1998/2917.
[510] Defined in s.29(3).
[511] Defined in s.29(3).
[512] cf. *Timeload Ltd v British Telecommunications Plc* [1995] E.M.L.R. 459 ("approval" by Director General of Fair Trading not in exercise of statutory function).
[513] As amended by s.5 of and Sch.4 to the Contracts (Applicable Law) Act 1990.

Kingdom[514] only by choice of the parties (and apart from that choice would be the law of some country outside the United Kingdom) ss.2 to 7 of the Act do not operate as part of the law applicable to the contract.[515]

(b) *Misrepresentation Act 1967*

14–114 **Liability for misrepresentation.** Section 3 of the Misrepresentation Act 1967, as substituted by s.8 of the Unfair Contract Terms Act 1977, provides that, if a contract contains a term which would exclude or restrict:

(a) any liability to which a party to a contract may be subject by reason of any misrepresentation made by him before the contract was made; or

(b) any remedy available to another party to the contract by reason of such a misrepresentation;

that term shall be of no effect except in so far as it satisfies the requirement of reasonableness as stated in s.11(1) of the 1977 Act; and it is for those claiming that the term satisfies the requirement of reasonableness to show that it does. The implications of this section have been discussed in a previous chapter[516] and it is clear that it applies to a term which excludes or restricts any liability or remedy in respect of misrepresentations which have not become terms of the contract. It seems equally clear that it does not apply to a term which excludes or restricts any liability or remedy in respect of a breach of the terms of a contract, whether statements or promises, if those terms were never communicated as representations before the contract was made. It is, however, probable that s.3 will apply so as to inhibit the exclusion or restriction of the right to rescind a contract where a misrepresentation, first made independently, is subsequently incorporated as a contractual term.[517] But, in so far as a term excludes or restricts any liability or remedy based on an alleged breach of contract, its validity has to be tested by reference to the different scheme in the 1977 Act.[518]

(c) *Other Statutes*

14–115 **Further statutes.** In addition to the Unfair Contract Terms Act 1977 and the Misrepresentation Act 1967, certain other statutes and statutory instruments currently regulate the right to take advantage of exempting provisions.

---

[514] "United Kingdom" does not include the Channel Islands or the Isle of Man: Interpretation Act 1978 s.5 and Sch.1.

[515] See below, para.30–068, and *Surzur Overseas Ltd v Ocean Reliance Shipping Co Ltd* [1997] C.L.Y. 906. Cf. *Balmoral Group Ltd v Borealis UK Ltd* [2006] EWHC 1900 (Comm), [2006] 2 Lloyd's Rep. 629 at [435].

[516] See above, para.6–136, and see also Atiyah and Treitel (1967) 30 M.L.R. 369, 379–385 and above, para.14–090.

[517] See s.1(a) of the 1967 Act (and s.2(2)).

[518] *Skipskredittforeningen v Emperor Navigation* [1998] 1 Lloyd's Rep. 66, 75.

Carriage by road or rail.[519] The Public Passenger Vehicles Act 1981 invalidates a provision contained in a contract for the conveyance of a passenger in a public service vehicle which purports to restrict the liability of a person in respect of a claim which may be made against him in respect of the death of, or bodily injury to, the passenger while being carried in, entering or alighting from the vehicle, or purports to impose any conditions with respect to the enforcement of such liability.[520] The Carriage of Goods by Road Act 1965[521] regulates the international carriage of goods, by road. The International Transport Conventions Act 1983 gives the force of law to the Convention concerning International Carriage by Rail (COTIF),[522] as modified by the Vilnius protocol,[523] which regulates the international carriage of passengers and their luggage,[524] and the international carriage of goods,[525] by rail. Each of these "international" instruments contains provisions prohibiting contracting out. 14–116

Carriage by sea. The Carriage of Goods by Sea Act 1971,[526] which gives effect to the International Convention for the Unification of certain Rules of Law relating to Bills of Lading signed at Brussels in 1924 (the Hague Rules), as amended by the Protocol signed at Brussels in 1968 (the Hague-Visby Rules) imposes certain duties and obligations upon a carrier who enters into a contract for the carriage of goods by sea to which the Act applies, and invalidates any clause which relieves the carrier or the ship from liability for loss or damage to or in connection with goods arising from negligence, fault or failure in those duties or obligations, or which lessens such liability otherwise than as provided in the Act.[527] The Athens Convention of 1974, and the 1976 Protocol thereto, regulates the carriage of passengers and their luggage by sea[528] and in effect invalidates any contractual provision which seeks to reduce the liability of the carrier contrary to the terms of the Convention.[529] 14–117

Carriage by air.[530] The Warsaw Convention (as supplemented and amended) regulates the liability of a carrier by air in respect of the international carriage of goods, passengers and passengers' luggage. It is given statutory force by the 14–118

[519] See below, Vol.II, Ch.36.

[520] s.29. See also s.149 of the Road Traffic Act 1988 (agreements between driver and passenger) and Vol.II, para.36–062.

[521] Implementing the CMR (as amended by the Carriage by Air and Road Act 1979: see SI 1980/1966). See Vol.II, para.36–117.

[522] Cmnd. 8535. See Vol.II, para.36–078.

[523] Implemented by the Railways (Convention on International Carriage by Rail) Regulations 2005 (SI 2005/2092).

[524] Appendix A (CIV).

[525] Appendix B (CIM).

[526] See the Carriage of Goods by Sea Act 1971 (Commencement) Order 1977 (SI 1977/981).

[527] art.III r.8; *The Hollandia* [1983] 1 A.C. 565. See also Merchant Shipping Act 1981 ss.2–5. But see *Jindal Iron and Steel Co Ltd v Islamic Solidarity Shipping Co Jordan Inc* [2004] UKHL 49, [2005] 1 W.L.R. 1363 (transfer of responsibility).

[528] See Merchant Shipping Act 1995 s.183 and Sch.6; SI 1987/670, SI 1998/2917. See also *R. G. Mayor v P. & O. Ferries Ltd* [1990] 2 Lloyd's Rep. 144 and Vol.II, para.36–063.

[529] Athens Convention art.18.

[530] See below, Vol.II, Ch.35.

Carriage by Air Act 1961, which was amended by the Carriage by Air (Supplementary Provisions) Act 1962 and by the Carriage by Air and Road Act 1979,[531] and applies with modifications to non-international carriage by the Carriage by Air Acts (Application of Provisions) Order 2004.[532] The Convention imposes certain liabilities on the carrier which cannot be excluded or limited by special contract; but, under its provisions, the carrier is prima facie relieved from liability in excess of certain stated pecuniary limits.

14–119 **Insurance.** The Road Traffic Act 1988, s.148, invalidates certain limitations on cover and conditions precedent to liability in connection with claims in respect of third-party risks under a compulsory policy of insurance, although these do not affect the position between the insurance company and the insured himself.[533]

14–120 **Defective premises.** The Defective Premises Act 1972, s.6(3), provides that any term of an agreement which purports to exclude or restrict, or has the effect of excluding or restricting, the operation of any of the provisions of the Act,[534] or any liability arising by virtue of any such provision, is to be void.

14–121 **Employment and services.** The Law Reform (Personal Injuries) Act 1948 s.1(3), invalidates any provision contained in a contract of employment or apprenticeship, or in any agreement collateral thereto, in so far as it would have the effect of excluding or limiting any liability of the employer in respect of personal injuries caused to the person employed or apprenticed by the negligence of persons in common employment with him. Restrictions on contracting out are also found in the Employment Rights Act 1996.[535]

14–122 The Solicitors Act 1974 regulates the enforcement of agreements between solicitor and client as to remuneration for non-contentious[536] and contentious[537] business, and provides for the determination by the court of fairness and reasonableness of any such agreement.[538] A provision in an agreement with respect to contentious business that a solicitor shall not be liable for his negligence or that of any employee of his, is void if the client is a natural person who, in entering that agreement, is acting for purposes which are outside his trade, business or profession, and a provision in such an agreement that the solicitor shall be relieved from any responsibility to which he would otherwise be subject as a solicitor, is declared to be void by the Act.[539]

---

[531] See also SI 1998/1751, SI 1999/1312, SI 2002/263, SI 2004/1418, SI 2004/1899; European Parliament and Council Regulations 889/2002, 875/2004; Vol.II, paras 35–001—35–022.

[532] SI 2004/1899. See also EC Regulation 889/2002. See Vol.II, para.35–070.

[533] See Vol.II, para.41–100.

[534] See above, para.13–015.

[535] s.203. See Vol.II, Ch.39. See also Sex Discrimination Act 1975 s.77; Race Relations Act 1976 s.72; Trade Union and Labour Relations (Consolidation) Act 1992 s.288; Disability Discrimination Act 1995 s.9; National Minimum Wage Act 1998 s.49; Employment Relations Act 1999 s.14.

[536] s.140.

[537] s.59–66.

[538] ss.57(5), 61(2) (as amended).

[539] s.60(5), (6), inserted by the Legal Services Act 2007 Sch.16 para.56(c).

Unit trusts. Any provision of the trust deed of an authorised unit trust scheme is void in so far as it would have the effect of exempting the manager or trustee from liability for any failure to exercise due care and diligence in a discharge of his functions in respect of the scheme.[540] 14–123

Commodities. The warranty of fitness of animal feeding stuffs implied by the Agriculture Act 1970 has effect notwithstanding any contract or notice to the contrary.[541] Likewise the warranties arising from the statutory statements which are required to be given by that Act in relation to fertilisers and feeding stuffs,[542] and by regulations made under the Plant Varieties and Seeds Act 1964 in relation to seeds,[543] cannot be excluded. 14–124

Consumer protection. The Unfair Terms in Consumer Contracts Regulations 1999[544] are designed to protect the consumer against unfair contract terms. They implement Council Directive 1993/13 and apply in addition to and separately from the provisions of the Unfair Contract Terms Act 1977. A term which has not been individually negotiated and which is adjudged to be unfair under the Regulations is not binding on the consumer.[545] There are a number of important differences between the 1977 Act and the Regulations. For example, unlike the regime of the Act, no types of contract term are automatically rendered ineffective by the Regulations: all are subject to a test of "fairness". On the other hand, the Regulations do not apply to any business-to-business contracts but only to those with consumers. The list of exceptions contained in the Act is not reproduced in the Regulations so that such contracts will be subjected to the Regulations if made with consumers. But the major differentiating factor is that, although the Regulations may operate side by side with the 1977 Act to invalidate exemption clauses, i.e. terms which exclude or restrict liability, they are not so confined and apply to unfair contract terms generally. Accordingly, they have been dealt with in Ch.15 of this book.[546] The English and Scottish Law Commissions have proposed, in a joint report,[547] that the Act and the Regulations be replaced by a unified regime. The Regulations[548] also confer specific powers on the Office of Fair Trading, and on certain qualifying bodies,[549] to consider complaints that a contract term drawn up for general use is unfair and to apply for an injunction against any person appearing to them to be using, or recommending use of, an unfair term drawn up for general use in contracts concluded into consumers.[550] But similar powers have now been conferred by the Enterprise 14–125

540 Financial Services and Markets Act 2000 s.253. "Authorised unit trust scheme" is defined in s.237.
541 Agriculture Act 1970 s.72(3).
542 s.68(6).
543 Plant Varieties and Seeds Act 1964 ss.16, 17.
544 SI 1999/2083, as amended. See Ch.15.
545 reg.8.
546 Paras 15–001—15–139.
547 Law Com. No.292, Scot Law Com. 199 Feb.
548 regs 10–14. See also reg.15 (publication, information and advice).
549 Listed in Sch.1 Pt one of the Regulations.
550 Below, para.15–135.

Act 2002 with respect to infringements of the 1977 Act relating to consumers.[551]

14–126 The liability of a person by virtue of Pt I of the Consumer Protection Act 1987 to a person who has suffered damage caused wholly or partly by a defect in a product, or to a dependant or relative of such a person, cannot be limited by any contract term, by any notice or by any other provision.[552] A term contained in a regulated consumer credit or consumer hire agreement, or in an agreement related thereto, is void if, and to the extent that, it is inconsistent with a provision for the protection of the debtor or hirer or his relative or any surety contained in the Consumer Credit Act 1974 or in any regulation made under that Act.[553]

14–127 The terms implied by the Package Travel, Package Holidays and Package Tours Regulations 1992,[554] and the strict liability to the consumer imposed by reg.15 of those Regulations, are mandatory.[555]

14–128 Also mandatory are the rights of cancellation conferred by the Consumer Credit Act 1974,[556] by the Consumer Protection (Contracts concluded away from Business Premises) Regulations 1987[557] by the Consumer Protection (Distance Selling) Regulations 2000,[558] by the Financial Services (Distant Marketing) Regulations 2004,[559] and by the Timeshare Act 1992,[560] as are the restrictions on the efficacy of consumer arbitration clauses imposed by the Arbitration Act 1996.[561]

14–129 **Unfair Commercial Practices Directive.** This Directive (2005/29/EC)[562] has been implemented in the Consumer Protection from Unfair Trading Regulations 2008.[563] Breach of the provisions of the Regulations may constitute a criminal offence but will not render any agreement void or voidable.

14–130 **Interest on commercial debts.** By s.8 of the Late Payment of Commercial Debts (Interest) Act 1998[564] any contract terms are void to the extent that they purport to exclude the right to statutory interest conferred by the Act in relation to a debt for goods or services supplied, unless there is a substantial contractual remedy for late payment of the debt.[565] The parties may not agree to vary the

---

551 See below, para.14–131.
552 Consumer Protection Act 1987 s.7.
553 Consumer Credit Act 1974 s.173(1). See *Wilson v Robertsons (London) Ltd* [2005] EWHC 1425 (Ch), [2006] 1 W.L.R. 1248.
554 SI 1992/3288; above, para.13–034.
555 1992 Regulations r.15(5).
556 ss.67, 173(1); see Vol.II, paras 38–091—38–111.
557 SI 1987/2117 (as amended); Vol.II, paras 38–112, 43–136.
558 SI 2000/2334, amended by SI 2004/2095, SI 2005/55, SI 2005/869, SI 2008/1277.
559 SI 2004/2095 amended by SI 2008/1277; Vol.II, para.38–116.
560 Amended by SI 2003/2579. See Vol.II, para.38–113.
561 ss.89–92. See Vol.II, para.32–013.
562 Directive 2005/29 on unfair commercial practices [2005] OJ L149/22.
563 SI 2008/1277. See also SI 2008/1276 and above, para.1–018.
564 See below, paras 26–172 et seq.
565 Commercial Debts Act 1998 s.8(1).

right to statutory interest in relation to the debt unless either the right to statutory interest as varied or the overall remedy for late payment of the debt is a substantial remedy.[566] Further, any contract terms are void to the extent that they purport to confer a contractual right to interest that is not a substantial remedy for late payment of the debt, or vary the right to statutory interest so as to provide for a right to statutory interest that is not a substantial remedy for late payment of the debt, unless the overall remedy for late payment of the debt is a substantial remedy.[567] The meaning of "substantial remedy" is set out in s.9 of the Act. It requires (inter alia) an assessment whether or not it would be fair and reasonable to allow the remedy to be relied on to oust (or as the case may be) to vary the right to statutory interest that would otherwise apply in relation to the debt.[568] An injunction may in certain circumstances be applied for to restrain the use of an offending term.[569]

Enterprise Act 2002. Part 8[570] of the Enterprise Act 2002 provides for the more effective enforcement of certain consumer protection legislation. It repeals, replaces and extends similar provisions which were contained in Pt 3 of the Fair Trading Act 1973[571] and in the Stop Now Orders (EC Directive) Regulations 2001.[572] The Act enables the High Court or a county court, on application, to make an order directing a person to refrain from continuing, repeating or engaging in any act or omission which harms the collective interests of consumers[573] and which is contrary to law.[574] Two categories of infringement may be the subject of an application for such an order. The first[575] is a "domestic infringement" which includes (inter alia): 14–131

> " . . . an act or omission by which a person supplying or seeking to supply goods or services purports or attempts to avoid (to any extent) liability relating to the supply in circumstances where such avoidance is restricted or prevented under or by virtue of any enactment."[576]

Exemption clauses in contracts with consumers that are invalidated; for example, by the Unfair Contract Terms Act 1977[577] could constitute such infringements. The second[578] category is a "Community infringement" which:

> " . . . contravenes a listed[579] Directive as given effect by the laws, regulations or administrative provisions of an EEA State, or contravenes such laws, regulations or administrative provisions which provide additional permitted protection."

---

[566] s.8(3).
[567] s.8(4).
[568] s.9(1)(b).
[569] Late Payment of Commercial Debts Regulations 2002 (SI 2002/1674).
[570] ss.210–236. See para.15–139 below, and Vol.II, para.43–159.
[571] ss.34–43.
[572] SI 2001/1422 (implementing the EC Injunctions Directive 98/27).
[573] "Consumer" is defined in s.210.
[574] s.217.
[575] s.211; SI 2003/1593; SI 2008/1277.
[576] s.211(2)(g).
[577] See above, paras 14–059—14–113.
[578] s.212; SI 2003/1374; SI 2003/1376; SI 2005/2759; SI 2006/3363; SI 2006/3372; SI 2008/1277.
[579] Defined in s.210(7) and Sch.13.

An exemption clause in a consumer contract which is unfair and so not binding on the consumer under the Unfair Terms in Consumer Contracts Regulations 1999 (implementing Directive 1993/13)[580] could constitute such a community infringement.[581] Although the bodies entitled and most likely to apply for an enforcement order under the Act are the Office of Fair Trading (OFT) and local weights and measures authorities,[582] any other person or body may be designated an "enforcer" by an order made by the Secretary of State if he considers that it has as one of its purposes the protection of the collective interests of consumers.[583] The Enterprise Act 2002[584] also repealed Pt 2 of the Fair Trading Act 1973[585] which set up a Consumer Protection Advisory Committee and empowered the Secretary of State to follow up the Committee's reports by making orders prohibiting trade practices that were so adverse to consumers as to be inequitable. Existing orders made under the 1973 Act[586] are, however, continued in force.

7. COMMON LAW QUALIFICATIONS

14–132 **Misrepresentations as to effect of exemption clause.** A party who misrepresents, whether fraudulently or otherwise, the terms or effect of an exemption clause inserted by him in a contract will not be permitted to rely on it in the face of his misrepresentation. In *Curtis v Chemical Cleaning and Dyeing Co*[587] the claimant took a dress to the defendants' shop to be cleaned. She was asked to sign a receipt which contained a clause exempting the defendants from all liability for damage to the articles cleaned. When the claimant asked why she was required to sign the receipt, the defendants' employee replied that it merely covered risks such as damage to the beads and sequins on the dress. The dress was returned to the claimant badly stained. It was held that the defendants were not protected since their employee had represented the effect of the exemption clause to be narrower than was, in fact, the case. If the misrepresentation gives rise to a fundamental mistake as to the character of the document, non est factum may also be pleaded.[588]

---

[580] See below, Ch.15.

[581] See below, para.15–139.

[582] s.213(1).

[583] s.213(1)–(13); and s.213(5A) (inserted by SI 2006/3363; see, for example, the Financial Services Authority (SI 2004/935) and the Consumers' Association (SI 2005/917).

[584] s.10.

[585] ss.13–33.

[586] Consumer Transactions (Restrictions on Statements) Order 1976 (SI 1976/1813) amended by the Consumer Transactions (Restrictions on Statements) Order 1978 (SI 1978/127); Business Advertisements (Disclosure) Order 1977 (SI 1977/1918). The Mail Order Transactions (Information) Order 1976 (SI 1976/1812) was repealed by the Consumer Protection (Distance Selling) Regulations 2000 (SI 2000/2334).

[587] [1951] 1 K.B. 805. See also *Jaques v Lloyd D. George & Partners Ltd* [1968] 1 W.L.R. 625; *Mendelssohn v Normand Ltd* [1970] 1 Q.B. 177, 183–184, 186; *Charlotte Thirty Ltd v Croker Ltd* (1990) 24 Const.L.R. 46; *Lloyds Bank Plc v Waterhouse* [1993] 2 F.L.R. 97; cf. *Cockerton v Naviera Aznar SA* [1960] 2 Lloyd's Rep. 450; *Peekay Intermark Ltd v ANZ Banking Group Ltd* [2006] EWCA Civ 386, [2006] 2 Lloyd's Rep. 511.

[588] See above, paras 5–101—5–106.

Acknowledgments. Clauses are often inserted in standard form agreements whereby one party "acknowledges and agrees" that he has "not been induced to enter into the contract by any representation of the other party", or that he has "examined the goods", or that he has "not made known to the other party expressly or by implication the purpose for which the goods are required". In *Lowe v Lombank Ltd*[589] the Court of Appeal held that such a clause can only give rise to an estoppel, preventing the party making the acknowledgment from asserting the contrary, and cannot operate as a positive contractual obligation: 14–133

> "To call it an agreement as well as an acknowledgment by the plaintiff cannot convert a statement as to past facts, known by both parties to be untrue, into a contractual obligation, which is essentially a promise by the promisor to the promisee that acts will be done in the future or that facts exist at the time of the promise or will exist in the future."[590]

In order for such an estoppel to be effective, it must further be shown:

(i) that the acknowledgment is clear and unambiguous;

(ii) that the party making it intended it to be acted upon by the other party, or at any rate so conducted himself that a reasonable man in the other party's position would take the acknowledgment to be true and believe that it was meant that he should act on it[591];

(iii) that the other party in fact believed it to be true and was induced by such belief to act on it.[592]

In the particular case, which concerned an acknowledgment by a hirer under a hire-purchase agreement,[593] the court found that none of these requirements was satisfied, and so no estoppel arose. It has, however, more recently been said[594] that:

> "... there is no reason in principle why parties should not agree that a certain state of affairs should form the basis for the transaction whether it be the case or not"

and that, in such an event:

[589] [1960] 1 W.L.R. 196. See also *China Shipbuilding Corp v Nippon Yusen Kaisha* [2000] 1 Lloyd's Rep. 367, 373; *Watford Electronics Ltd v Sanderson Ltd* [2001] EWCA Civ 317, [2001] Build. L.R. 143 at [40]; *EA Grimstead & Son Ltd v McGarrigan* [1998–1999] Info. T.L.R. 384 (CA).

[590] [1960] 1 W.L.R. 196, 204.

[591] *Citizens' Bank of Louisiana v First National Bank of New Orleans* (1873) L.R. 6 H.L. 352.

[592] *Lowe v Lombank Ltd* [1960] 1 W.L.R. 196, 205; *E.A. Grimstead & Son Ltd v McGorrigan* [1998–1999] Info. T.L.R. 384.

[593] See Vol.II, para.38–373.

[594] By Moore-Bick L.J. in *Peekay International Ltd v ANZ Banking Group Ltd* [2006] EWCA Civ 386, [2006] 2 Lloyd's Rep. 511 at [56].

"... neither can subsequently deny the existence of the facts and matters upon which they have agreed, at least so far as those aspects of the relationship to which their agreement was directed."

The contract itself then gives rise to an estoppel.[595]

14–134 **Collateral warranties and guarantees.** A party who would otherwise be entitled to rely on an exempting provision will not be permitted to do so if he gives an express oral warranty which runs counter to the tenor of the written exemption.[596] A warranty given before the agreement is entered into may also be enforced as a collateral contract the consideration of which is the entering into of the written agreement.[597] Thus in *Webster v Higgin*[598] an oral warranty as to the present condition of a car was enforced as a collateral contract in return for which a contract of hire-purchase, which contained exempting provisions, was signed. Where goods are sold or otherwise supplied to a consumer[599] which are offered with a consumer guarantee,[600] the guarantee takes effect as a contractual obligation owed by the guarantor[601] under the conditions set out in the guarantee statement and the associated advertising.[602] This obligation cannot be negatived by an exemption clause in the contract of sale or supply.

14–135 **Unreasonable provisions.** It has been stated on a number of occasions that a clause which excludes or restricts liability should not be given effect if it is unreasonable, or if it would be unreasonable to apply it in the circumstances of the case, at least in contracts in standard form where there is inequality of bargaining power.[603] But it would seem that, except in those situations expressly provided for in the Unfair Contract Terms Act 1977 or (in respect of consumer contracts) by the Unfair Terms in Consumer Contracts Regulations 1999,[604] it is not open to a court to strike down an exemption clause merely on the ground that it is in substance unreasonable or unfair.[605] However, a strong plea for a wider

---

[595] [2006] EWCA Civ 386 citing *Colchester BC v Smith* [1991] Ch. 448, affirmed [1992] Ch. 421.

[596] *Couchman v Hill* [1947] K.B. 554; *Harling v Eddy* [1951] 2 K.B. 739; *Mendelssohn v Normand Ltd* [1970] 1 Q.B. 177. See also *J. Evans & Sons (Portsmouth) Ltd v Andrea Merzario Ltd* [1976] 1 W.L.R. 1078.

[597] See above, paras 12–004, 12–033.

[598] [1948] 2 All E.R. 127.

[599] Defined in the Sale and Supply of Goods to Consumers Regulations 2002 (SI 2002/3045) reg.2.

[600] Defined SI 2002/3045 reg.2.

[601] Defined SI 2002/3045 reg.2.

[602] Sale and Supply of Goods to Consumer Regulations (SI 2002/3045) reg.15. See also SI 2008/1277, Sch.2, para.97.

[603] *Van Toll v S.E. Ry* (1862) 12 C.B.(N.S.) 75, 88; *Parker v S.E. Ry* (1877) 2 C.P.D. 416, 428; *Watkins v Rymill* (1883) 10 QBD 178, 179; *Thompson v L.M. & S. Ry* [1930] 1 K.B. 41, 56; *John Lee & Sons (Grantham) Ltd v Railway Executive* [1949] 2 All E.R. 581, 584; *Gillespie v Roy Bowles Transport Ltd* [1973] Q.B. 400, 416; *Levison v Patent Steam Carpet Cleaning Co Ltd* [1978] Q.B. 69, 79; *Photo Production Ltd v Securicor Transport Ltd* [1978] 1 W.L.R. 856, 865 (reversed [1980] A.C. 827).

[604] Below, Ch.15.

[605] *Grand Trunk Ry of Canada v Robinson* [1915] A.C. 740, 747; *Ludditt v Ginger Coote Airways Ltd* [1947] A.C. 233, 242; *Photo Production Ltd v Securicor Transport Ltd* [1980] A.C. 827, 848. But see above, para.12–015 (notice of particularly onerous or unusual terms). See generally Tiplady (1983) 46 M.L.R. 601.

approach, based on a principle of good faith in contracts[606] was made by Brooke L.J. in *Lacey's Footwear (Wholesale) Ltd v Bowler International Freight Ltd*[607] when he said that he preferred to ask whether it was in all the circumstances fair to hold a party bound by the condition in question rather than:

> " . . . to have resort to interpretative devices of almost Byzantine sophistication to arrive at a result that the words of a contract do not mean what, on the face of it, they clearly do mean."

Fraud. No exemption clause can protect a person from liability for his own fraud[608] or require the other party to assume what he knows to be false.[609] But it is uncertain whether, there is any rule of law, based on public policy, which would prevent the exclusion by a principal of liability for fraud on the part of his agent acting as such[610] It is, however, clear that any such exclusion would have to be expressed in clear and unmistakable terms on the face of the contract so as to leave the other party in no doubt that fraud was covered.[611] **14–136**

8. FORCE MAJEURE CLAUSES[612]

Force majeure clauses. The expression "force majeure clause" is normally used to describe a contractual term by which one (or both) of the parties is entitled to cancel the contract[613] or is excused from performance of the contract, in whole or in part, or is entitled to suspend performance or to claim an extension of time for performance, upon the happening of a specified event or events beyond his control. Such clauses may assume a variety of forms, and a term "the usual force majeure clauses to apply" has been held void for uncertainty.[614] Force majeure clauses have been said not to be exemption clauses,[615] although it is **14–137**

[606] See below, para.15–068.

[607] [1997] 2 Lloyd's Rep. 369, 385 (making reference to the judgment of Bingham L.J. in *Interfoto Picture Library Ltd v Stiletto Visual Programmes* [1989] 1 Q.B. 433, 439 (above, para.12–015).

[608] *S. Pearson & Son Ltd v Dublin Corp* [1907] A.C. 351. See also *Kollerich & Cie. SA v State Trading Corp of India* [1980] 2 Lloyd's Rep. 32 (false certificates). Contrast *Tullis v Jackson* [1892] 3 Ch. 441 (criticised in *Czarnikow v Roth, Schmidt & Co* [1922] 2 K.B. 478, 488); *Compania Portorafti Commerciale SA v Ultramar Panama Inc* [1990] 1 Lloyd's Rep. 310 (Hague-Visby Rules); *Armitage v Nurse* [1998] Ch. 241 (trustees).

[609] *Re Banister* (1879) 12 Ch D 131.

[610] *HIH Casualty and General Insurance Ltd v Chase Manhattan Bank* [2003] UKHL 6, [2003] 2 Lloyd's Rep. 61 at [14]–[17]–[76]–[82]–[118]–[126].

[611] [2003] UKHL 6.

[612] See Treitel, *Frustration and Force Majeure*, 2nd edn (2004); McKendrick (ed.), *Force Majeure and Frustration of Contract*, 2nd edn (1995).

[613] The contract may even be cancelled automatically: *Continental Grain Export Corp v S.T.M. Grain Ltd* [1979] 2 Lloyd's Rep. 460; *Bremer Handelsgesellschaft mbH v Finagrain SA* [1981] 2 Lloyd's Rep. 259; *Pagnan SpA v Tradax Ocean Transportation SA* [1987] 2 Lloyd's Rep. 342.

[614] *British Electrical and Associated Industries (Cardiff) Ltd v Patley Pressings Ltd* [1953] 1 W.L.R. 280. But such a term could refer to clauses usual in a particular trade.

[615] *Fairclough, Dodd & Jones Ltd v J.H. Vantol Ltd* [1957] 1 W.L.R. 136, 143. See also *Trade and Transport Inc v Iino Kaiun Kaisha Ltd* [1973] 1 W.L.R. 210, 230–231; *The Super Servant Two* [1990] 1 Lloyd's Rep. 1, 7, 12. cf. *Cero Navigation Corp v Jean Lion & Cie* [2000] 1 Lloyd's Rep. 292, 299.

difficult to draw any clear line of demarcation between the two types of clause,[616] since the effect of each may be to relieve a contracting party of an obligation or liability to which he would otherwise be subject, and force majeure clauses may nevertheless be affected by the Unfair Contract Terms Act 1977.[617]

14–138 Frequently a number of events are specified and then followed by the words "or any other causes beyond our control". Such general words in a commercial document are prima facie to be construed as having their natural and larger meaning and are not limited to events ejusdem generis with those previously enumerated.[618] Moreover, the words "beyond our control" will normally be construed to refer, not only to the unspecified cases, but also to the specific events.[619] Clauses which excuse performance in general terms may be construed as force majeure clauses. Thus a clause in a contract of sale which provides that the date of delivery is approximate only, and that the seller is not to be responsible for any delay or non-delivery, does not confer upon him an absolute discretion whether to deliver or not and so render the contract nugatory, but only to excuse him if non-delivery is due to a cause outside his control.[620] In the absence of a clear indication to the contrary,[621] a force majeure clause will not be construed to cover events brought about by a party's negligence or wilful default, even though a specified event would in other contexts not be limited to an event occurring without negligence.[622]

14–139 A force majeure clause which is prefaced by such words as "while every effort will be made to carry out this contract" will be rendered nugatory unless the party relying on it has in fact made reasonable efforts to ensure that the contract is performed.[623]

14–140 **Burden of proof.** It is for a party relying upon a force majeure clause to prove the facts bringing the case within the clause.[624] He must therefore prove the

---

[616] See Treitel, *Frustration and Force Majeure*, para.12–014; McMeel, *The Construction of Contracts* (2007), para.22.35.

[617] See below, para.14–152.

[618] *Chandris v Isbrandtsen-Moller Co Inc* [1951] 1 K.B. 240, 245–246; *P. J. Vander Zijden Wildhandel N.V. v Tucker & Cross Ltd* [1975] 2 Lloyd's Rep. 240; *Navrom v Callitsis Ship Management SA* [1987] 2 Lloyd's Rep. 276, 281 (affirmed [1988] 2 Lloyd's Rep. 416). See also *Anderson v Anderson* [1895] 1 Q.B. 749, 753; *Larsen v Sylvester* [1908] A.C. 295. Contrast *Thorman v Dowgate S.S. Co* [1910] 1 K.B. 410; *Jenkins v Watford* (1918) 87 L.J.K.B. 136; *Sonat Offshore SA v Amerada Development Ltd* [1988] 1 Lloyd's Rep. 145, 149, 158, 163.

[619] *Frontier International Shipping Corp v Swissmarine Corp Inc* [2004] EWHC 8 (Comm), [2005] 1 Lloyd's Rep. 390 at [11], [27]–[28].

[620] *Barnett v Ira L. and A.C. Berk Pty Ltd* (1952) 52 S.R. (N.S.W.) 268. See also *Hartwells of Oxford Ltd v B.M.T.A.* [1951] Ch. 50; *Monkland v Jack Barclay Ltd* [1951] 2 K.B. 252.

[621] *Gyllenhammar & Partners International Ltd v Sour Brodogradevna Industrija* [1989] 2 Lloyd's Rep. 403, 406.

[622] *Sonat Offshore SA v Amerada Hess Developments Ltd* [1988] 1 Lloyd's Rep. 145; *The Super Servant Two* [1990] 1 Lloyd's Rep. 1.

[623] *B. & S. Contracts and Design Ltd v Victor Green Publications Ltd* [1984] I.C.R. 419.

[624] *Channel Island Ferries Ltd v Sealink U.K. Ltd* [1988] 1 Lloyd's Rep. 323, 327; *Mamidoil-Jetoil Greek Petroleum Co SA v Okta Crude Oil Refinery AD* [2003] 1 Lloyd's Rep. 1 at [54].

Other expressions. Other, wider expressions may, however, be used, e.g. "rendered uneconomic". 14–145

Specified events. The following words and phrases have been the subject of consideration by the courts: Act of God,[651] storm tempest or flood,[652] fire,[653] perils and dangers or accidents of the sea,[654] war,[655] warlike operations,[656] civil war,[657] riot,[658] civil commotion,[659] strikes,[660] acts of the Queen's enemies,[661] and prohibition of export.[662] However, expressions used in the context of one type of contract, for example, a policy of insurance or a charterparty, may not necessarily be appropriate in the context of another, such as a contract of sale of goods. Moreover, even if the circumstances do not fall precisely within the meaning of a particular specified event, they may still be operative by virtue of the addition of more general words in the clause. 14–146

"Force majeure". Sometimes the actual expression "force majeure" is employed. Force majeure is not a term of art in English law,[663] although it is well 14–147

[651] *Nugent v Smith* (1876) 1 C.P.D. 423, 437, 438, 441, 444; *Nichols v Marsland* (1876) 2 Ex.D. 1; *Greenock Corp v Caledonian Ry* [1917] A.C. 556.

[652] *Oddy v Phoenix Assurance Co Ltd* [1966] 1 Lloyd's Rep. 134; *S. & M. Hotels Ltd v Legal & General Assurance Socy. Ltd* [1972] 1 Lloyd's Rep. 157; *Young v Sun Alliance Ltd* [1977] 1 W.L.R. 104.

[653] *Thames and Mersey Marine Insurance Co Ltd v Hamilton Fraser & Co* (1887) 12 App. Cas. 484; *The Diamond* [1906] P. 282; *Tempus Shipping v Louis Dreyfus* [1930] 1 K.B. 699.

[654] *Thames and Mersey Marine Insurance Co Ltd v Hamilton Fraser & Co* (1887) 12 App. Cas. 484; *The Xantho* (1886) L.R. 11 P.D. 170, 503; *Hamilton Fraser & Co v Pandorf & Co* (1887) 12 App. Cas. 518; *The Glendarroch* [1894] P. 226; *E.D. Sassoon & Co v Western Assurance Co* [1912] A.C. 561; *Grant Smith & Co and McDonnell Ltd v Seattle Construction and Dry Dock Co* [1920] A.C. 162; *P. Samuel & Co Ltd v Dumas* [1924] All E.R. Rep. 66; *Canada Rice Mills Ltd v Union Marine and General Insurance Co Ltd* [1941] A.C. 55; *Goodfellow Lumber Sales v Verrault* [1971] 1 Lloyd's Rep. 185; *The Super Servant Two* [1990] 1 Lloyd's Rep. 1; *Great China Metal Industries Co Ltd v Malaysian International Shipping Corp Bhd.* [1999] 1 Lloyd's Rep. 512.

[655] *Curtis v Mathews* [1919] 1 K.B. 425; *Pesquieras v Beer* (1949) 82 Ll.L.Rep. 501, 514; *Kawasaki Kisen Kabushiki Kaisha v Banham S.S. Co Ltd (No.2)* [1939] 2 K.B. 544. See McKendrick (ed.) at Ch.8.

[656] *Clan Line Steamers Ltd v Liverpool and London War Risks Insurance Association Ltd* [1943] K.B. 209, 221. cf. *Pan American World Airways Inc v Aetna Casualty and Surety Co* [1974] 1 Lloyd's Rep. 207 (affirmed [1975] 1 Lloyd's Rep. 77). See McKendrick at Ch.8.

[657] *Spinney's (1948) Ltd v Royal Insurance Co Ltd* [1980] 1 Lloyd's Rep. 406.

[658] *London and Lancashire Fire Insurance Ltd v Bolands Ltd* [1924] A.C. 836.

[659] *Langsdale v Mason* (1780) 2 Marshall, 2nd edn, 791, 794.

[660] *Re Richardsons & Samuel* [1898] 1 Q.B. 261, 267, 268; *Williams v Naamlooze* (1915) 21 Com.Cas. 253, 257; *Seeberg v Russian Wood Agency* (1934) 50 Ll.L.Rep. 146; *Reardon Smith Line Ltd v Ministry of Agriculture* [1960] 1 Q.B. 439 (affirmed [1962] 1 Q.B. 42. This point did not arise in the House of Lords [1963] A.C. 691); *J. Vermaazs Scheepvaartbedrif N.V. v Association Technique de l'Importation Charbonnière* [1966] 1 Lloyd's Rep. 582; *Tramp Shipping Corp v Greenwich Marine Inc* [1975] 1 W.L.R. 1042; *B. & S. Contracts and Design Ltd v Victor Green Publications Ltd* [1984] I.C.R. 419; *Channel Island Ferries Ltd v Sealink (UK) Ltd* [1987] 1 Lloyd's Rep. 559; [1988] 1 Lloyd's Rep. 323. See McKendrick at Ch.6.

[661] *Russell v Niemann* (1864) 17 C.B.N.S. 163. cf. *Spence v Chadwick* (1847) 10 Q.B. 5.

[662] The number of cases is voluminous. See *Benjamin's Sale of Goods* at paras 18–342 et seq.; McKendrick at Ch.12; Treitel at Ch.12.

[663] *Hackney BC v Doré* [1922] 1 K.B. 431, 437; *Re Podair Trading Ltd* [1949] 2 K.B. 277, 286; *Thomas Borthwick (Glasgow) Ltd v Faure Fairclough Ltd* [1968] 1 Lloyd's Rep. 16, 28; *Navrom v Callitsis Ship Management SA* [1987] 2 Lloyd's Rep. 276, 281, 282 (affirmed [1988] 2 Lloyd's Rep. 416).

known in continental legal systems, for example that of France.[664] The meaning of force majeure may nevertheless be ascertained by reference. Thus the incorporation into a contract of sale of the Force Majeure (Exemption) Clause of the International Chamber of Commerce[665] will mean that a party is not liable for failure to perform any of his obligations in so far as he proves:

(1) that the failure was due to an impediment beyond his control; and

(2) that he could not reasonably be expected to have taken the impediment and its effects upon his ability to perform the contract into account at the time of the conclusion of the contract; and

(3) that he could not reasonably have avoided or overcome it or at least its effects.

14–148 It has rightly been observed that the concept of force majeure in English law is wider than that of "Act of God" or *vis major*,[666] as these latter expressions appear to denote events due to natural causes, without any human intervention.[667] In *Lebeaupin v Crispin & Co*[668] McCardie J. reviewed the previous authorities on force majeure, and it now seems that war,[669] strikes,[670] legislative or administrative interference, for example, an embargo,[671] the refusal of a licence,[672] or seizure,[673] abnormal storm or tempest,[674] flooding which inhibits shipment from river ports,[675] interruption of the supply by rail of raw material,[676] and even the

[664] Cod.Civ., para.1148; Carbonnier, *Droit Civil*, 19th edn (1995), Vol.IV, p.1620; Marty and Raynaud, *Droit Civil* (1988), II, Vol.I, p.552; Mazeaud and Chabas, *Leçons de Droit Civil*, 8th edn, Vol.II, p.573. But see *Jacobs v Crédit Lyonnais* (1884) 12 QBD 589; *Navrom v Callitsis Ship Management SA* [1987] 2 Lloyd's Rep. 276, 281, 282, for differences between French and English law.

[665] I.C.C. Publication No.421. See also the (draft) *Principles, Definitions and Model Rules of European Private Law* (2008), Vol.III, para.304 in much the same terms.

[666] *Matsoukis v Priestman & Co* [1915] 1 K.B. 681, 686; *Lebeaupin v Crispin & Co* [1920] 2 K.B. 714, 719.

[667] *Nugent v Smith* (1876) 1 C.P.D. 423, 427, 431, 444.

[668] [1920] 2 K.B. 714.

[669] *Zinc Corp v Hirsch* [1916] 1 K.B. 541, 544. cf. at 549.

[670] *Matsoukis v Priestman & Co* [1915] 1 K.B. 681; *Torquay Hotel Co Ltd v Cousins* [1969] 2 Ch. 106; cf. *Hackney BC v Doré* [1922] 1 K.B. 431; *B. & S. Contracts and Design Ltd v Victor Green Publications Ltd* [1984] I.C.R. 419.

[671] *Lebeaupin v Crispin & Co* [1920] 2 K.B. 714, 270; *Tradax Export SA v André et Cie* [1976] 1 Lloyd's Rep. 109. cf. *Re Podair Trading Ltd* [1949] 2 K.B. 277.

[672] *Walton (Grain) Ltd v British Italian Trading Co* [1959] 1 Lloyd's Rep. 223; *Coloniale Import-Export v Loumidis Sons* [1978] 2 Lloyd's Rep. 560. But see *Brauer & Co (G.B.) Ltd v James Clark (Brush Materials) Ltd* [1952] 2 All E.R. 497, 501; *Pagnan SpA v Tradax Ocean Transportation SA* [1987] 3 All E.R. 565.

[673] *Yrazu v Astral Shipping Co* (1904) 20 T.L.R. 153, 154–155; *The Turul* [1919] A.C. 515.

[674] *Lebeaupin v Crispin & Co* [1920] 2 K.B. 714, 720.

[675] *Alfred C. Toepfer v Peter Cremer* [1975] 2 Lloyd's Rep. 118; *Tradax Export SA v André et Cie* [1976] 1 Lloyd's Rep. 109; *Bunge GmbH v Alfred C. Toepfer* [1978] 1 Lloyd's Rep. 506; *Avimex SA v Dewulf & Cie* [1979] 2 Lloyd's Rep. 57.

[676] cf. *Intertradax SA v Lesieur-Tourteaux S.A.R.L.* [1978] 2 Lloyd's Rep. 509.

accidental breakdown of machinery[677] can amount to force majeure,[678] but not "bad weather, football matches or a funeral",[679] a failure of performance due to the provision of insufficient financial resources[680] or to a miscalculation,[681] a rise in cost or expense,[682] the failure by a third party to fulfil his contract,[683] or any act, negligence, omission or default on the part of the party seeking to be excused.[684] The words "force majeure" are, however, rarely unqualified. The type of circumstance envisaged by the parties will often be set out, so that those circumstances may apply to limit, extend or explain the meaning of "force majeure".[685] Further the clause may refer to performance being "prevented," "hindered" or "delayed" by force majeure.[686] The expression must therefore be construed with regard to the words which precede and follow it and also with regard to the nature and general terms of the contract.[687]

If the reference to force majeure is indeed unqualified, e.g. "subject to force majeure" or "force majeure excepted," then it is submitted that, in English law, performance of the relevant obligation must have been prevented by an event of 14–149

---

677 *Matsoukis v Priestman & Co* [1915] 1 K.B. 681; *Thomas Borthwick (Glasgow) Ltd v Faure Fairclough Ltd* [1968] 1 Lloyd's Rep. 16, 28. Sed quaere cf. *Sonat Offshore SA* v *Amerada Hess Development Ltd* [1988] 1 Lloyd's Rep. 145, 158.

678 See also *Yrazu v Astral Shipping Co* (1904) 20 T.L.R. 153, 154–155 (casualty to ship or cargo).

679 *Matsoukis v Priestman & Co* [1915] 1 K.B. 681, 687.

680 *The Concadoro* [1916] 2 A.C. 199.

681 *Yrazu v Astral Shipping Co* (1904) 20 T.L.R. 153. See also *Atlantic Paper Stock Ltd v St Anne Nackawic Pulp and Paper Co Ltd* (1975) 56 D.L.R. (3d) 409 (lack of business sense).

682 *Brauer & Co (G.B.) Ltd v James Clark (Brush Materials) Ltd* [1952] 2 All E.R. 497.

683 *Lebeaupin v Crispin* [1920] 2 K.B. 714. See also *Thomas Borthwick (Glasgow) Ltd v Faure Fairclough Ltd* [1968] 1 Lloyd's Rep. 16 (failure of Conference to provide vessel). cf. *John Batt & Co (London) Ltd v Brooker, Dore & Co Ltd* (1942) 72 Ll.L.Rep. 149; *Coastal (Bermuda) Petroleum Co Ltd v VTT Vulcan Petroleum SA (No.2)* [1996] 2 Lloyd's Rep. 383.

684 *New Zealand Shipping Co v Société des Ateliers et Chantiers de France* [1919] A.C. 1, 6; *Hong Guan & Co Ltd v R. Jumabhoy & Sons Ltd* [1960] A.C. 684, 700; *Sonat Offshore SA v Amerada Hess Development Ltd* [1988] 1 Lloyd's Rep. 145; *The Super Servant Two* [1990] 1 Lloyd's Rep. 1, 5–8, 11–13.

685 *Sonat Offshore SA v Amerada Hess Development Ltd* [1988] 1 Lloyd's Rep. 145, 158.

686 See above, paras 14–141, 14–143, 14–144.

687 *Lebeaupin v Crispin & Co* [1920] 2 K.B. 174, 702; *Re Podair Trading Ltd* [1949] 2 K.B. 277, 286; see also *Matsoukis v Priestman & Co* [1915] 1 K.B. 681 (excepted only the cause of force majeure and/or strikes); *Dixon & Sons v Henderson Craig & Co* [1919] 2 K.B. 778 (hindered or prevented by force majeure); *Brauer & Co (G.B.) Ltd v James Clark (Brush Materials) Ltd* [1952] 2 All E.R. 497 (prevented by force majeure); *Fairclough Dodd & Jones Ltd v J.H. Vantol Ltd* [1957] 1 W.L.R. 136 (prohibition of export or any other cause comprehended by force majeure); *Hong Guan & Co Ltd v R. Jumabhoy & Sons Ltd* [1960] A.C. 684 (subject to force majeure and shipment); *Tsakiroglou & Co Ltd v Noblee Thorl GmbH* [1962] A.C. 93 (force majeure preventing shipment); *Alfred C. Toepfer v Peter Cremer* [1975] 2 Lloyd's Rep. 118 (delay in shipment occasioned by any cause comprehended in the term force majeure); similarly, *Tradax Export SA v André et Cie* [1976] 1 Lloyd's Rep. 109, *Bunge GmbH v Alfred C. Toepfer* [1978] 1 Lloyd's Rep. 506, *Bremer Handelsgesellschaft mbH v Vanden-Avenne Izegem P.V.B.A.* [1978] 2 Lloyd's Rep. 109, *Avimex SA v Dewulf & Cie* [1979] 2 Lloyd's Rep. 57; *Marifortuna Naviera SA v Govt. of Ceylon* [1970] 1 Lloyd's Rep. 247 ("force majeure excepted"); *Huilerie l'Abeille v Société des Huileries du Niger* [1978] 2 Lloyd's Rep. 203 ("strikes . . . or any other cause comprehended by the term force majeure"); *The Super Servant Two* [1990] 1 Lloyd's Rep. 1 ("force majeure, . . . perils or danger and accidents of the sea").

force majeure and not merely hindered or rendered more onerous.[688] However, there does not appear to be any requirement that the circumstances alleged to constitute force majeure should be unforeseeable,[689] although the party seeking to be excused still bears the burden of proving that his non-performance was due to circumstances beyond his control and that there were no reasonable steps that he could have taken to avoid or mitigate the event or its consequences.[690]

14–150 **Conditions precedent.** A clause excusing performance, or permitting one party to postpone or suspend performance, may provide that certain procedures are to be followed or notices given to the other party within a stipulated period of time before he is entitled to rely on the clause. Such measures may be a condition precedent on which the availability of the protection provided by the clause depends,[691] or merely an intermediate term,[692] the non-fulfilment of which does not necessarily deprive him of his right to rely on the clause.[693] The other party may also be held to have waived, or to be estopped from asserting, non-compliance with the measures set out in the clause.[694]

---

[688] But, in the context of EC Regulations, the European Court has sometimes held that the expression force majeure is not limited to cases where performance is impossible, but extends to unusual circumstances, outside the control of the person concerned, the consequences of which, in spite of the exercise of all due care, could not have been avoided except at the cost of excessive sacrifice: see *Internationale Handelsgesellschaft v Einfuhr-und-Vorratsstelle* [1970] E.C.R. 1125; *De Jong Verenigde v V.I.B.* [1985] E.C.R. 2061. Contrast *Schwarzwaldmilch v Einfuhr-und-Vorratsstelle für Fette* (4/68) [1968] E.C.R. 377; *Valsabbia v EC Commission* [1980] E.C.R. 907. These cases are discussed in McKendrick (ed.), *Force Majeure and Frustration of Contract*, Ch.13.

[689] *Navrom v Callitsis Ship Management SA* [1987] 2 Lloyd's Rep. 276, 281, 282, and see above, para.14–140. Contrast Council Directive 90/314 on package travel, package holidays and package tours [1993] O.J. L158/59, art.4(6), which defines force majeure as "unusual and *unforeseeable* circumstances beyond the control of the party by whom it is pleaded, the consequences of which could not have been avoided even if all due care had been exercised": see the Package Travel, Package Holidays and Package Tours Regulations 1992 (SI 1992/3288) regs 13(3)(b), 15(2)(c)(i); *Charlson v Warner* [2000] C.L.Y. 4043 (Cty. Ct.).

[690] See above, para.14–140.

[691] *Tradax Export SA v André et Cie* [1976] 1 Lloyd's Rep. 416; *Finagrain SA Geneva v P. Kruse Hamburg* [1976] 2 Lloyd's Rep. 508; *Berg & Son Ltd v Vanden Avenne-Izegem P.V.B.A.* [1977] 1 Lloyd's Rep. 499; *Toepfer v Schwarze* [1977] 2 Lloyd's Rep. 380 (affirmed [1980] 1 Lloyd's Rep. 385); *Bunge GmbH v CCV Landbouwbelang G.A.* [1978] 1 Lloyd's Rep. 217; *Bremer Handelsgesellschaft mbH v Vanden Avenne-Izegem P.V.B.A.* [1978] 2 Lloyd's Rep. 109; *Intertradax SA v Lesieur Tourteaux S.A.R.L.* [1978] 2 Lloyd's Rep. 509; *Bremer Handelsgesellschaft mbH v C. Mackprang Jr* [1979] 1 Lloyd's Rep. 221; *Bunge GmbH v Alfred C. Toepfer* [1979] 1 Lloyd's Rep. 554; *Johnson Matthey Bankers Ltd v State Trading Corp of India* [1984] 1 Lloyd's Rep. 427; *Bremer Handelsgesellschaft mbH v Westzucker GmbH (No.3)* [1989] 1 Lloyd's Rep. 582; *Mamidoil-Jetoil Greek Petroleum Co SA v Okta Crude Oil Refinery AD* [2003] 1 Lloyd's Rep. 1, [2003] EWCA Civ 1031, [2003] 2 Lloyd's Rep. 635 at [34]. cf. *Hoecheong Products Co Ltd v Cargill Hong Kong Ltd* [1995] 1 W.L.R. 404 (certificate required only to attest to occurrence of force majeure event).

[692] See above, para.12–034.

[693] *Bremer Handelsgesellschaft mbH v Vanden Avenne Izegem P.V.B.A.* [1978] 2 Lloyd's Rep. 109, 113. See also *Bunge SA v Kruse* [1979] 1 Lloyd's Rep. 279 (affirmed [1980] 2 Lloyd's Rep. 142); *SHV Gas Supply and Trading SAS v Naftomar Shipping and Trading Co Ltd Inc* [2005] EWHC 2528 (Comm), [2006] 1 Lloyd's Rep. 163 at [39]; cf. *Tradax Export SA v André et Cie* [1976] 1 Lloyd's Rep. 416. See *Benjamin's Sale of Goods* at para.18–356.

[694] *Bremer Handelsgesellschaft mbH v Vanden Avenne Izegem P.V.B.A.* [1978] 2 Lloyd's Rep. 109; *Bremer Handelsgesellschaft mbH v C. Mackprang Jnr* [1979] 1 Lloyd's Rep. 221 (waiver or estoppel). Contrast *Finagrain SA Geneva v P. Kruse Hamburg* [1976] 2 Lloyd's Rep. 508; *Berg & Son Ltd v Vanden Avenne-Izegem P.V.B.A.* [1977] 1 Lloyd's Rep. 499; *Toepfer v Schwarze* [1977] 2 Lloyd's Rep. 380 (affirmed [1980] 1 Lloyd's Rep. 385); *Avimex SA v Dewulf & Cie* [1979] 2 Lloyd's

Insufficiency of goods. A supplier of goods may as a result of an event of force majeure have insufficient goods of the contract description to meet all his existing contracts, but nevertheless have at his disposal enough goods to satisfy one or more of those contracts. In such a case he may be entitled to rely upon an appropriately worded force majeure clause as an excuse for non-performance of those contracts which are unfulfilled, even though the clause refers to his being "prevented" from delivering the goods and not merely to his being "hindered" from doing so.[695] If he has a number of existing contracts to fulfil, but cannot fulfil all of them, he can rely upon force majeure as to the others.[696] He may allocate the available goods in any way which the trade would consider proper and reasonable, whether this is pro rata,[697] or in chronological order, or on some other basis.[698] But he cannot make any allocation to those of his customers to whom he has a non-legal moral commitment[699]; nor would it be reasonable to allocate supplies to new contracts in order to take advantage of a resultant rise in price.[700] 14–151

Unfair Contract Terms Act 1977. Clauses of the types mentioned above may attract the application of s.3 of the Unfair Contract Terms Act 1977.[701] It seems unlikely that a clause which merely permits one party to suspend, postpone or cancel performance upon the happening of events beyond his control would, in 14–152

Rep. 57; *Bunge SA v Kruse* [1979] 1 Lloyd's Rep. 279; *Bremer Handelsgesellschaft mbH v C. Mackprang Jnr* [1981] 1 Lloyd's Rep. 292; *Raiffeisen Hauptgenossenschaft v Louis Dreyfus & Co Ltd* [1981] 1 Lloyd's Rep. 345; *Tradax Export SA v Cook Industries Inc.* [1981] 1 Lloyd's Rep. 236 (affirmed [1982] 1 Lloyd's Rep. 385); *Bremer Handelsgesellschaft mbH v Finagrain SA* [1981] 2 Lloyd's Rep. 259; *Bunge SA v Compagnie Européenne des Cereales* [1982] 1 Lloyd's Rep. 306; *Bremer Handelsgesellschaft mbH v Raiffeisen Hauptgenossenschaft E.G.* [1982] 1 Lloyd's Rep. 599; *Bremer Handelsgesellschaft mbH v Bunge Corp* [1983] 1 Lloyd's Rep. 476; *Bremer Handelsgesellschaft mbH v Deutsche-Conti Handelsgesellschaft mbH* [1983] 1 Lloyd's Rep. 689; (no waiver or estoppel). See also *Panchaud Frères SA v Etablissements General Grain Co* [1970] 1 Lloyd's Rep. 53, 57; *Bunge SA v Kruse* [1980] 2 Lloyd's Rep. 142; *André et Cie v Cook Industries Inc* [1987] 2 Lloyd's Rep. 463. See *Benjamin's Sale of Goods* at para.18–357.

[695] *Bremer Handelsgesellschaft mbH v Continental Grain Co* [1983] 1 Lloyd's Rep. 269, 280–281, 291–294. See also *Westfalische Central-Genossenschaft GmbH v Seabright Chemicals Ltd* Unreported 1979 (Robert Goff J.) cited [1983] 1 Lloyd's Rep. 269, 291–294.

[696] *Tennants (Lancashire) Ltd v C.S. Wilson & Co Ltd* [1917] A.C. 508, 511–512; *Pool Shipping v London Coal Co of Gibraltar* [1939] 2 All E.R. 432; *Tradax Export SA v André et Cie. SA* [1976] 1 Lloyd's Rep. 416, 423; *Kawasaki Steel Corp v Sardol SpA* [1977] 2 Lloyd's Rep. 552, 555; *Bremer Handelsgesellschaft mbH v Vanden Avenne-Izegem P.V.B.A.* [1978] 2 Lloyd's Rep. 109, 115; *Intertradex SA v Lesieur Tourteaux S.A.R.L.* [1978] 2 Lloyd's Rep. 509, 513; *Bremer Handelsgesellschaft mbH v C. Mackprang Jr* [1979] 2 Lloyd's Rep. 221, 224; *Bremer Handelsgesellschaft v Continental Grain Co* [1983] 1 Lloyd's Rep. 269.

[697] For "pro-rating," see American Uniform Commercial Code ss.2–615(b), (c); *Benjamin's Sale of Goods* at paras 6–053, 8–103, 18–353; Hudson (1968) 31 M.L.R. 535, (1978) 123 S.J. 137.

[698] *Intertradex SA v Lesieur Tourteaux SARL* [1978] 2 Lloyd's Rep. 509, 512; *Bremer Handelsgesellschaft mbH v C. Mackprang* [1979] 2 Lloyd's Rep. 221, 224; *Westfalische Central-Genossenschaft GmbH v Seabright Chemicals Ltd*, Unreported 1979 cited [1983] 1 Lloyd's Rep. 269 at [291]–[294].

[699] *Pancommerce SA v Veecheema B.V.* [1983] 2 Lloyd's Rep. 304, 307.

[700] *Westfalische Central-Genossenschaft GmbH v Seabright Chemicals Ltd* Unreported 1979, above at fn.698.

[701] s.3(2)(b); above, para.14–073. Contrast Treitel, *Frustration and Force Majeure*, 2nd edn (2004), Ch.12.

a commercial contract, be held to be unreasonable,[702] although there are possibly circumstances where such a clause would be so held, for example, in an exclusive dealing agreement, if the seller was entitled to suspend delivery in such events, but the buyer was nevertheless not entitled, during the suspension, to purchase supplies from elsewhere.

14–153 **Unfair Terms in Consumer Contracts Regulations 1999.** These regulations are discussed in Ch.15.[703] A force majeure clause in a consumer contract may not be binding on the consumer if, contrary to the requirement of good faith,[704] it causes a significant imbalance in the parties' rights and obligations arising under the contract, to the detriment of the consumer[705] or if it is not drafted in plain, intelligible language.[706] Examples of unfair terms might be force majeure clauses which require the consumer to accept a suspension of performance or delayed or substitute performance without giving him the opportunity to cancel the contract, or which deny him a full refund in the event of cancellation of the contract by the seller or supplier upon the occurrence an event of force majeure.[707]

14–154 **Distance Selling Regulations 2000.** Regulation 19(7) of the Consumer Protection (Distance Selling) Regulations 2000[708] provides that, in the case of a contract concerning goods which is concluded between a supplier and a consumer by means of distance communication[709] where the supplier is unable to supply the goods ordered by the consumer within the time limited by the contract or the Regulations,[710] he may provide substitute goods of equivalent quality and price. But this possibility must have been provided for in the contract and the supplier must, prior to the conclusion of the contract, have given the consumer the information required by reg.7[711] and in the manner there laid down.[712] Substitution is, however, only permitted if the supplier is *unable* to supply the goods and this inability must arise because the goods are "not available".[713]

[702] See *Shearson Lehman Hutton Inc v Maclaine Watson & Co Ltd* [1989] 2 Lloyd's Rep. 570, 612. But see above, para.14–074 fn.378.
[703] See also above, para.14–125.
[704] See below, para.15–008.
[705] 1999 Regulations reg.5; below, para.15–071.
[706] 1999 Regulations reg.7; below, para.15–129.
[707] See, in particular, 1999 Regulations Sch.2 para.1(f)(g)(h)(j)(k) of the Regulations.
[708] SI 2000/2334, amended by SI 2004/2095, SI 2005/55, SI 2005/869, SI 2008/1277; see Vol.II, paras 38–115, 43–137.
[709] For the scope of the regulations, see Vol.II, para.43–137.
[710] 2000 Regulations reg.19(1); see Vol.II, para.43–137.
[711] 2000 Regulations reg.7(1)(b) and (c); see Vol.II, para.43–137.
[712] 2000 Regulations reg.7(2).
[713] 2000 Regulations reg.19(2).

CHAPTER 15

UNFAIR TERMS IN CONSUMER CONTRACTS

	PARA.
1. Introduction	15–001
2. The EC Directive on Unfair Terms in Consumer Contracts and the UK Regulations	15–004
3. The temporal application of the Regulations	15–011
4. The types of contracts governed by the Regulations	15–016
5. Contract terms excluded from the Regulations	15–038
6. The requirement of fairness	15–044
(a) Contract terms excluded from the requirement of fairness	15–045
(i) The exclusion of terms which have been "individually negotiated"	15–046
(ii) The partial exclusion of "core terms"	15–049
(b) The composite test of unfairness	15–064
(i) The basic test	15–065
(ii) Particular elements within the test of unfairness	15–070
(iii) The "indicative list" of terms	15–091
(iv) The time-frame for assessment of the fairness of a term	15–110
(v) The relative roles of the European Court, national courts, and the parties	15–115
(vi) The effects of a finding that a term is unfair	15–123
7. The requirement of plain and intelligible language	15–128
(a) The test	15–128
(b) The effects of failure to comply with the requirement of plain and intelligible language	15–130
8. Choice of law clauses	15–131
9. The prevention of unfair terms	15–132

1. INTRODUCTION

The general position. English law has long taken the view that acceptance of the principles of freedom of contract and the binding force of contracts rules out review of the fairness of either the contract as a whole or of particular terms of the contract.[1] As regards the fairness of the contract itself, this general position is expressed in various ways depending on the aspect of contractual unfairness which is in issue. Thus it is said that while a promise is not enforceable without the furnishing of consideration, this "value in the eyes of the law" need not be adequate and may indeed be nominal[2]: substantive inequality of bargain is not a ground for vitiation of a contract. Furthermore, as has already been seen, "unconscionable conduct" or "bad faith" are not without more grounds of vitiation of a contract, whether this unfair behaviour on the part of a party to a **15–001**

[1] See above, paras 1–011 et seq.
[2] See above, para.3–014.

contract occurs in the course of its negotiation or the course of its performance or non-performance.[3] As regards the fairness of particular contract terms, this general attitude at common law can be seen most explicitly in its approach to the validity of exemption clauses: for once agreed by the parties to a contract, they are effective to exclude liability both in contract and in tort,[4] even extending to liability for causing death and personal injuries by negligence.[5] However, while these statements remain true as a general statement of the position at common law, they must be qualified to a very considerable extent both as a matter of the common law and as a result of legislative innovation. Of the latter, the Unfair Contract Terms in Consumer Contracts Regulations 1999[6] are the widest in scope and the most distinctive in their tests of control. Having noted some other qualifications on the general principle of the effectiveness of contract terms, this chapter will discuss the effect of this very important legislation.

15–002 **Qualifications at common law.** There are two ways in which the effectiveness of particular contract terms has been qualified at common law. First, exceptionally, the courts have held that certain types of contract term are invalid. The clearest example is the penalty clause, the line between this type of clause and its effective relation, the liquidated damages clause, being drawn taking into account a range of considerations.[7] However, the courts have also held other types of clause ineffective, for example, a clause in a mortgage which attempts to fetter a mortgagor's equity of redemption,[8] and they may give relief against the apparent effect of forfeiture clauses in contracts of lease.[9] Other types of term are held ineffective if they are unreasonable in the circumstances, as is the case with covenants in restraint of trade, though this has traditionally been discussed as a matter of illegality rather than "contractual unfairness".[10] Secondly, the courts have become very demanding in the requirement that a particular contract term be agreed by both the parties (the requirement of notice) and that the term be expressed in a way which effectively covers the facts in the way which the party relying on the term seeks to establish (the issue of construction). The demanding approach to the requirement of notice became particularly apparent as regards exemption clauses,[11] but has been applied to other types of particularly surprising or potentially oppressive terms, especially where these are found in the small print of a complex set of standard terms.[12] It has also been in the context of exemption clauses where the courts have been most strict in their attitude to

[3] See above, paras 1–022 and 1–023.

[4] *Nicholson v Willan* (1804) 5 East 507.

[5] This is clear a fortiori from the effectiveness of non-contractual notices to this effect: e.g. *White v Blackmore* [1972] 3 All E.R. 158.

[6] SI 1999/2083. These regulations revoked and replaced the Unfair Terms in Consumer Contracts Regulations 1994 (SI 1994/3159) and see below paras 15–004 et seq.

[7] See below, paras 26–124 et seq.

[8] Gray and Gray, *Elements of Land Law*, 4th edn (2005) para.8–240.

[9] Bright, *Landlord and Tenant Law in Context* (2007), pp.702 et seq.

[10] See below, paras 16–075 et seq.

[11] See above, paras 12–008 et seq.

[12] See *Interfoto Picture Library Ltd v Stiletto Visual Programmes Ltd* [1989] 1 Q.B. 433.

construction, though the orthodox position never went beyond interpretation *contra proferentem*.[13]

Legislative control of the fairness of contract terms. The impact of legislation on the fairness of contract terms has been very considerable and by no means restricted to consumer contracts. This has often been effected by the creation of rights or obligations on the parties to particular types of contracts which are not susceptible of contrary exclusion by agreement, notably as regards contracts of consumer credit,[14] tenancy,[15] and employment.[16] Other than this regulation of particular types of contract, the most important restriction on the effectiveness of contract terms before 1995 was the Unfair Contract Terms Act 1977, which subjected exemption and limitation clauses in both consumer contracts and commercial contracts to very considerable restrictions.[17] While this Act also imposed a requirement of reasonableness on the effectiveness of indemnity clauses in consumer contracts,[18] until the Unfair Contract Terms in Consumer Contracts Regulations 1994[19] there was no system of control on the basis of fairness general to all or most other types of contract term. According to a report of the Office of Fair Trading, which was given a policing role in respect of unfair terms by the Regulations,[20] its experience in its first months of operation led it to believe that "the use of unfair terms in consumer contracts is widespread and amounts to a serious problem in the United Kingdom".[21] 15–003

2. THE EC DIRECTIVE ON UNFAIR TERMS IN CONSUMER CONTRACTS AND THE UK REGULATIONS

Legislative history. On April 5, 1993 the EC Council enacted a directive on Unfair Terms in Consumer Contracts ("the Directive").[22] The Directive was implemented into English law first by the Unfair Terms in Consumer Contracts Regulations 1994 ("the 1994 Regulations"), but these were revoked and replaced 15–004

---

[13] See above, paras 14–005 et seq. (with the exceptions there noted).

[14] See Consumer Credit Act 1974, and Vol.II, paras 38–090—38–098.

[15] Bright and Gilbert at Ch.6.

[16] See Vol.II, paras 39–207 et seq.

[17] See above, paras 14–059 et seq.

[18] Unfair Contract Terms Act 1977 s.4 and see above, para.14–075.

[19] SI 1994/3159. The Regulations came into force on July 1, 1995 but were revoked and replaced by the Unfair Terms in Consumer Contracts Regulations 1999 (SI 1999/2083), on which see below paras 15–004 et seq.

[20] 1994 Regulations reg.8.

[21] Office of Fair Trading, *Unfair Contract Terms*, Bulletin No.2 (September 1996), p.5.

[22] Directive 93/13 on unfair terms in consumer contracts [1993] OJ L95/21. For discussion of the Directive or the Unfair Terms in Consumer Contracts Regulations, see Dean (1993) 56 M.L.R. 581; Collins (1994) 14 O.J.L.S. 229; Macdonald (1994) J.B.L. 441; Hondius (1994) 7 *Journal of Contract Law* 34; Willett (1994) Con. L.J. 114; Beale in Beatson and Friedmann (eds), *Good Faith and Fault in Contract Law* (1995), Ch.9; Bright and Bright (1995) 111 L.Q.R. 655; Weatherill (1995) 3 *European Review of Private Law* 307, especially 316 et seq. cf. Joerges at 175; Collins at 353; de Moor at 257; Weatherill, *E.C. Consumer Law and Policy* (2005), pp.115 et seq.; Howells and Wilhelmsson, *E.C. Consumer Law* (1997), p.88 et seq.; Beatson, *Anson's Law of Contract*, 28th edn (2002) pp.200–203, 300 et seq.; Macdonald [1999] C.L.J. 413; Whittaker (2000) 116 L.Q.R. 95; Bright (2000) 20 L.S. 331; Whittaker (2004) ZEuP 75.

Regulations. Moreover, in its first decision on the interpretation of the Regulations, the House of Lords followed the interpretative practice of the European Court of Justice and on occasion looked at the recitals to the Directive as an aid to the interpretation of its text.[37] Given the equally authoritative nature of the different language versions of the Directive,[38] recourse may need to be had at times to language versions of its text other than English.[39] In the following discussion, therefore, while reference will be made to the terms of the Regulations, it being generally assumed that these reflect the Directive, where necessary reference will be made to the Directive itself.

15–008 In interpreting the terms of the Directive, an important distinction is to be drawn according to whether the European Court of Justice is likely to treat a particular issue as one on which a European view should be taken (giving rise to an "autonomous" or "independent" interpretation) or as one which should be left to the national laws of the Member States. For those issues where a particular legal concept is itself defined (at least in part) by the Directive, it is clear that an "autonomous" interpretation is at least to this extent to be taken.[40] However, for other concepts this choice is much more difficult, this being particularly acute in relationship to the notion of "consumer contract" and even "contract" itself.[41]

15–009 **Summary of impact of the 1999 Regulations.** The 1999 Regulations subject a very wide range of types of terms in consumer contracts to two requirements: (i) that the terms should be "fair"; and (ii) that when in writing they should be written in "plain, intelligible language" (the latter being sometimes referred to as a requirement of "transparency"). There are two levels of effect in respect of any failure to fulfill these requirements. At the level of the relationship between the parties to a contract, a term which fails the requirement of fairness is not binding on the consumer, while a term which fails the requirement of transparency is to be interpreted *contra proferentem* and may be subjected to the test of fairness even if it relates to the contract's price or main subject matter.[42] At a more general level, the 1999 Regulations empower the Office of Fair Trading (until April 2003, the Director General of Fair Trading) and a number of other bodies to bring proceedings for an injunction to prevent a person using a term which they consider is unfair or unclear.[43] Rather than invoking this power to institute proceedings which he earlier possessed under the Regulations, the Director General of Fair Trading adopted an educative and negotiating strategy, though at times requiring a particular business whose terms offended under the Regulations to give an undertaking that they will not in future use offending terms. The Office

[37] *Director General of Fair Trading v First National Bank Plc* [2001] UKHL 52, [2002] 1 A.C. 481.

[38] *Kyocera Electronics Europe GmbH v Hauptzollamt Krefeld* (Case C–152/01) [2003] E.C.R. I–13821 at para.32–33.

[39] See below, para.15–019 (concerning the application of the 1993 Directive to land contracts) and cf. Lord Rodger of Earlsferry's discussion of the German and French texts of art.4(2) of the Directive in *Director General of Fair Trading v First National Bank Plc* [2001] UKHL 52 at [64].

[40] e.g. "consumer": EC Directive 1993 art.2(b).

[41] See below, paras 15–034 et seq.

[42] Below, para.15–049.

[43] 1994 Regulations reg.8; 1999 Regulations reg.12, and see below, paras 15–133 et seq.

of Fair Trading has also published a series of bulletins reporting on and explaining the work of the Unfair Contract Terms Unit, these providing invaluable guidance as to the *likely* application of the test of unfairness by the courts.[44] In *Director General of Fair Trading v First National Bank Plc*[45] the Director exercised his power to apply to the court for an injunction restraining the bank's use of a particular term in its common-form loan agreement.

Possible further legislative reform. Further legislative reform of the control on unfair terms in consumer contracts may come from one or both of two directions. First, at the European level, the EC Commission has presented a report to the European Parliament and to the Council concerning the application of the Directive which raised a number of questions as to its interpretation and also its possible amendment,[46] and this report has been followed by a much wider review of eight directives of the "consumer *acquis*" including the Directive on unfair terms in consumer contracts.[47] Secondly, at the national level, the English and Scottish Law Commissions have published a joint report on proposed reforms to the legislation on unfair terms in contracts.[48] The proposals include the creation of a unified regime for the control of unfair terms in consumer contracts, putting together the controls at present found in the Unfair Contract Terms Act 1977 and the Unfair Terms in Consumer Contracts Regulations 1999; preserving the protection given by the Unfair Contract Terms Act 1977 in business contracts; and extending existing protection against unfair contract terms for consumers to small businesses. 15–010

3. THE TEMPORAL APPLICATION OF THE REGULATIONS

General. The temporal application of the 1994 and 1999 Regulations is not entirely straightforward. As has been noted, the starting-point is that the 1994 Regulations came into force on July 1, 1995 and the 1999 Regulations revoked them and themselves came into force on October 1, 1999.[49] 15–011

The terms of the Regulations. Neither set of Regulations made express provision as to the temporal application of the requirement of fairness affecting the binding force of contract terms as between the parties to consumer contracts, but at first sight, the words used by both sets of the Regulations could be thought of as suggesting that they affect the validity of any contract terms *in force* 15–012

---

[44] These bulletins are entitled *Unfair Contract Terms* and are available together with an number of other guides to the OFT's view of the application of the Regulations at *http://www.oft.gov.uk/* [Accessed June 18, 2008].

[45] [2001] UKHL 52, [2002] 1 A.C. 481 and see below, paras 15–056, 15–082 and see also *OFT v Abbey National Plc* [2008] EWHC 875 (Comm), below, paras 15–051—15–052, 15–059.

[46] European Commission, *Report on the Implementation of Directive 93/13/EEC on unfair terms in consumer contracts* COM(2000) 248 final of April 27, 2000.

[47] See EC Commission, *Green Paper on the Review of the Consumer Acquis*, COM(2006) 744 (which refers to earlier documents).

[48] Law Commission, Scottish Law Commission, *Unfair Terms in Contracts* (Law Com. No.292, Scot Law Com. No.199, 2005). The Government has accepted the recommendations in principle.

[49] 1994 Regulations reg.1; 1999 Regulations regs 1 & 2.

between contracting parties at the time of the coming into force of the Regulations (whether or not the contract was made on or after this date) as they provide that "[a]n unfair term in a contract concluded with a consumer by a seller of supplier shall not be binding on the consumer".[50] By contrast, as regards the requirement of transparency, both sets of Regulations provide that "[a] seller or supplier shall ensure that any written term of a contract is expressed in plain, intelligible language" and that "[i]f there is any doubt about the meaning of a written term, the interpretation which is most favourable to the consumer shall prevail"[51]: this formulation suggests that the requirement affects only contracts made after the coming into force of the requirement (and therefore of the Regulations). And the formulation of the provisions in the Regulations which empowered first the Director General of Fair Trading (the 1994 Regulations) and then various other bodies (the 1999 Regulations) to take a range of "preventive measures" suggests that while these powers arise only from the date of the coming into force of the respective Regulations, they can affect contract terms "drawn up for general use" before their coming into force, although any injunction could be granted by a court only where a person is still "using or recommending use of, an unfair term drawn up for general use in contracts concluded with consumers".[52]

15–013 **The 1993 Directive.** However, it is submitted that the temporal effect of the provisions in the two sets of Regulations is to be found in the 1993 Directive and in EC legal principle rather than in the terms of the Regulations themselves. In this respect, art.10 of the Directive expressly states that "[t]hese provisions shall be applicable to all contracts concluded after 31 December 1994", which is the date not later than which Member States were required to bring into force the laws, regulations and administrative provisions necessary to comply with the Directive.[53] In this respect, no distinction is made by the Directive between the requirements of fairness and "plain, intelligible writing" as between parties to a contract or the preventive measures which it requires to be available to "persons or organizations having legitimate interest under national law in protecting consumers".[54] Since national courts have a duty to interpret the implementing legislation of EC directives under the *Marleasing* case law "as far as possible, in the light of the wording and the purpose of the directive",[55] clearly the provisions in the UK Regulations which affect the validity and the interpretation of the terms of consumer contracts as between their parties affect all contracts "concluded" after their coming into force.[56] In the case of the "preventive measures"

---

[50] 1994 Regulations reg.5(1); 1999 Regulations reg.8(1).

[51] 1994 Regulations reg.6; 1999 Regulations reg.7.

[52] 1999 Regulations reg.12(1) and see *Office of Fair Trading v MB Designs (Scotland) Ltd* [2005] S.L.T. 691 at [23] OH of the Ct of Session (power exercised under Pt 8 of the Enterprise Act 2002 in respect of 'Community infringement) and see below, para.15–138.

[53] 1993 Directive art.10(1).

[54] 1993 Directive art.7.

[55] *Marleasing SA v La Comercial Internacional de Alimentacion SA* (C–106/89) [1990] E.C.R. I-04135 at para.[8]

[56] This fundamental non-retroactivity of national laws implementing the 1993 Directive has been upheld by the Italian Corte suprema di Cassazione: Cass. Civ., Sez. III 21 giugio 2004, no.11487.

provided for by the two sets of Regulations, art.10's provision as to the Directive's temporal effect appears less appropriate as they are aimed not so much at the making of any particular contract "concluded" but rather at the present and future use of offending terms as at the time of intervention by the person designated by national law for this purpose.

However, in the UK context, there is a discrepancy between the date set by the Directive for the coming into force of its requirements (December 31, 1994[57]) and the date of coming into force of the 1994 Regulations (July 1, 1995[58]). In this respect, in principle the case-law of the European Court of Justice would require a UK court to apply the provisions of the Regulations which govern the validity or interpretation of contract terms retrospectively to cover this six month gap only if the relevant provisions of the Directive were to be interpreted as conferring rights on the individuals concerned to invoke its provisions before national implementation, i.e. able to establish their "direct effect".[59] And the European case-law sets stringent conditions (including that the provisions of the Directive are "unconditional and sufficiently precise"[60]) for the recognition of "vertical direct effect" (that is, where an individual claims to rely on a Directive as against a Member State) and denies altogether recognition of "horizontal direct effect" (that is, where an individual claims to rely on a Directive as against another individual).[61] This being the case, it is submitted that a UK court bears no obligation to give effect to the 1993 Directive in relation to a contract made by a "non-State business"[62] and a consumer between January 1, 1995 and June 30, 1995 and will bear such an obligation in relation to a contract made between a "State business" and a consumer only if the relevant provision of the 1993 Directive is held to pass the conditions for recognition of direct effect. 15–014

The timing of the "conclusion" of the contract. This discussion makes clear, however, that the timing of the "conclusion" of the contract as between the parties is crucial to the temporal application of the Regulations. For this purpose, the question arises whether an autonomous or partly autonomous interpretation would be given to this concept by the European Court or whether it would be left to the laws and/or courts of Member States (and therefore to English law as regards the Regulations). An autonomous interpretation could be seen as furthering the Directive's general policy of harmonisation especially given the central 15–015

[57] 1993 Directive art.10(1).

[58] 1994 Regulations reg.1.

[59] *Dik* (C–80/87) [1988] E.C.R. 1601 (in the context of Directive 79/7 concerning equal treatment of men and women in social security [1977] OJ L299/13). It is submitted that an English court could not interpret national law prior to the promulgation of the 1994 Regulations so as to give effect to the Directive under the *Marleasing* duty of harmonious interpretation given the absence of any regulation of terms in general in consumer contracts in English law at the time: see further Craig and de Búrca, *EU Law: Text, Cases, and Materials*, 4th edn (2008) pp.288–296.

[60] S. Prechal, *Directives in EC Law* (OUP, 2nd edn 2005) pp.243 et seq.

[61] *Marshall I* (152/84) [1986] E.C.R. 723; *Faccini Dori* (C–91/92) [1994] E.C.R. 1–3325.

[62] On the inclusion of public bodies acting in the course of a business within the 1993 Directive generally, see below, para.15–024. The ECJ has taken a broad view of the concept of the State for the purposes of the doctrine of vertical direct effect: see *Foster v British Gas Plc* (C–188/89) [1990] E.C.R. I-3313 and Craig and de Búrca, *EU Law: Text, Cases, and Materials*, 4th edn (2008), pp.284–87.

importance of determining the contracts to which it applies, but against this there is the practical difficulty of constructing a European view of when a contract is "concluded" in the absence of any definition in the Directive itself and of any European "general law of contract" such as may be provided in future by a "Common Frame of Reference" (though the Advocates general to the Court already refer to the draft of such a document).[63] In many types of case, the application of the normal rules of offer and acceptance (whether national or European (drawn from a Common Frame of Reference)) will be straightforward, but some types of cases may be more difficult, notably, where contractual relations were first entered into by the parties before the coming into effect of the Regulations but were altered after this date.[64] Here it is submitted that *English* law would draw a series of distinctions in this sort of context. First, where the parties to a contract agree mutually to change the terms on which they deal, this agreement (if supported by consideration) may either constitute a variation of the contract (where the Regulations would not apply) or a rescission of the earlier contract and the creation of a new substituted contract (where the Regulations would apply), this depending on the intention of the parties to be gathered from the terms of the subsequent agreement and all the surrounding circumstances.[65] Secondly, where a fixed-term contract made before the coming into force of the Regulations contains express provision for its renewal, it is submitted that it would be a matter of construction of the nature of the power to renew whether on renewal under this provision after the Regulations, the contract between the parties constituted the same contract as before (not caught by the Regulations as "concluded" before their coming into effect) or a new contract (caught by the Regulations as "concluded" after their coming into effect)[66]; and it is further submitted that the same approach should be taken where "renewal" is made under an implied term in the original contract. Thirdly, it is submitted that where a term or terms of a contract made *before* the coming into effect of the Regulations are varied *after* this time but under an express power of variation contained in the original contract, in principle these new terms would nevertheless be contained in a contract concluded earlier so as to escape the application of the Regulations. However, if the European Court were to hold that an autonomous European view should be taken as to the "conclusion" of the contract it could approach it in two ways. Either it could try to construct a European legal analysis for each of the different types of situation outlined above in relation to English law drawn (where possible) from a Common Frame of Reference or other pan-European instruments. Or it could hold that the relevant time of "conclusion of

[63] On the Draft Common Frame of Reference (DCFR) see above, para.1–010 fn.57. The provisions on agreement are found at paras II.–4:201—II.–4:211. cf. *Masdar (UK) Ltd v EC Commission* (T–333/03) [2007] 2 All E.R. 261 where the Court of First Instance accepted reference to the work of the *Study Group on a European Civil Code* in order to develop a EC law of restitution for unjustified enrichment under art.288 (formerly 215) EC; *Hamilton v Volksbank Filder eG* (412/06) A.G. Poires Maturo at [24] (referring to time limits for the exercise of a right as being a "principle common to the laws of the Member States" and citing the possible future DCFR).

[64] cf. *OFT v Abbey National Plc* (the *Bank Charges* Case) [2008] EWHC 875 (Comm) at [442] and see below, para.15–059.

[65] See below, paras 22–028—22–029, 22–034.

[66] cf. however the special position of the renewal of a lease by a tenant under an express term where the exercise of the option to renew is said to create a fresh lease: *Rider v Ford* [1923] 1 Ch. 541 at 547.

the contract" *for the purposes of the 1993 Directive* was the making of the *terms* which would then bind the consumer absent intervention by the protections for consumers which this Directive provided. If such a special and purposive view were taken by the Court, then "new" contract terms made from "old" contracts could be caught by the Regulations.[67]

4. THE TYPES OF CONTRACTS GOVERNED BY THE REGULATIONS

Introduction. It is unfortunate that the Regulations (following the Directive) do not state definitively which types of contract fall within their controls. However, on closer examination a fairly clear picture emerges of the general position, though certain points remain for judicial determination. 15–016

The 1994 and 1999 Regulations contrasted. The 1994 Regulations were expressed in such a way as to suggest that they applied only to contracts for the sale of goods or for the supply of goods or services to consumers,[68] but this was potentially misleading for three reasons: (i) the notion of a contract for the supply of services has to be interpreted very widely indeed for the purposes of the Regulations; (ii) the better view (accepted by the Court of Appeal[69]) is that the Directive (and therefore its implementing regulations) govern contracts for the sale of land as well as goods; and (iii) it is by no means clear that the consumer has to be the "recipient" of the property or services supplied. In this respect, the 1999 Regulations follow even more closely the wording of the Directive[70] and thereby avoid appearing to take a view as to the range of consumer contracts governed by their provisions. Thus, the 1999 Regulations define "seller or supplier" for this purpose as: 15–017

> " . . . any natural or legal person who, in contracts covered by these Regulations, is acting for purposes relating to his trade, business or profession, whether publicly owned or privately owned."[71]

This leaves, however, the question as to the true range of contracts governed by either set of Regulations.

All consumer contracts? The English text of the Directive supports the use by the 1994 Regulations of the terms "seller of goods" and "supplier of services",[72] and in recital 10 of its preamble states that: 15–018

> " . . . whereas more effective protection of the consumer can be achieved by adopting uniform rules of law in the matter of unfair terms; whereas those rules should apply to all contracts concluded between sellers or suppliers and consumers."[73]

---

[67] The Draft Common Frame of Reference (on which see Vol.1, para.1–010 fn.57) would not, apparently, help here as it contains no provisions relevant to this purpose.

[68] 1994 Regulations reg.2(1) (definitions of the persons party to the contracts in question).

[69] *R. (on application of Khatun) v Newham LBC* [2004] EWCA Civ 55, [2005] Q.B. 37.

[70] 1993 Directive art.2(c).

[71] 1999 Regulations reg.3(1), "seller or supplier".

[72] See Directive 1993 art.2's definitions and art.4(1)'s reference to "the nature of the *goods* or services" (emphasis added).

[73] 1993 Directive recital 10.

However, this terminology of sale and supply is not used at the same points in the Directive in a number of its other language versions. So, for example, the second clause of the French text of recital 10 states that "whereas those rules should apply to *all* contracts between a *professionnel* and a consumer",[74] and this terminology is followed through into the text of the Directive where the person whose standard terms are to be caught by the Directive is described simply as a "*professionnel*", this French term referring to someone in business or a profession.[75] This is not to say that other language versions of the Directive do not refer to "sellers of property" and "suppliers of services", but they generally do so in a way which suggests that these phrases are used as a convenient way of describing the contracts which consumers do enter. In all, therefore, even at this formal textual level, these other versions of the Directive suggest that it applies in principle to *all consumer contracts* (as defined) and this is the view taken by some commentators.[76] Certainly it is clear from the terms of the Directive that the notion of "contract for services" in particular has to be understood in a remarkably broad manner. For at other times in the Directive, the assumption is made that types of contracts are included within its ambit which are clearly not "contracts for services" (nor sale) in any traditional English legal sense (for example, as contrasted with contracts of service),[77] notably contracts of insurance and for the supply of financial services.[78]

15–019 **Contracts for the sale, etc. of an interest in land.** If the arguments in the previous paragraph hold good then this suggests that prima facie the Directive was intended to apply to (consumer) contracts for the sale or other disposition of an interest in land, as to any other consumer contract, but the 1994 Regulations defined "seller" as "seller of goods"[79] and this followed the wording of the English version of the text of and preamble to the Directive.[80] However, there are both textual and more general arguments in favour of the inclusion of contracts for the sale or other disposition (or creation) of an interest in land within in the ambit of the Directive.[81] First, not merely do a number of other language versions

[74] (Emphasis added): "*que ces règles doivent s'appliquer à tout contrat conclu entre un professionnel et un consommateur*". Similar formulations are found in the Italian, Spanish and German versions of the Directive.

[75] 1993 Directive art.2. Similarly drafting is found in the Italian, Spanish and German versions of the Directive.

[76] Tenreiro (1993) 7 *Contrats-Concurrence-Consommation* 1; Trochu (1993) *D.S. Chron* 315, 317; Weatherill, *EU Consumer Law and Policy* (2005) p.117; Calais-Auloy and Steinmetz, *Droit de la consommation*, 6th edn (2003), p.179.

[77] See Vol.II, para.39–003.

[78] See 1993 Directive recital 19 and Annex, para.2.

[79] 1994 Regulations reg.2.

[80] See in particular 1993 Directive art.4(1), which states that "the unfairness of a contractual term shall be assessed, taking into account the nature of the goods or services for which the contract was concluded and by referring". The phrases "sellers of goods" or "sale of goods" are used in recitals 2, 5, 7, 19. The German version of the Directive refers in the preamble to "*Waren*" and art.4(1) to "*Güter und Dienstleistungen*". However, recital 10 agrees with the French, Spanish and Italian versions that the Directive applies in principle to "all contracts between a trader and a consumer": see above, para.15–018.

[81] See generally Bright and Bright, (1995) 111 L.Q.R. 655, whose view was cited with approval in *Kindlance v Murphy* Unreported 1997 N.I. Ch D and see *R. (on the application of Khatun) v Newham LBC* [2004] EWCA Civ 55, [2005] Q.B. 37.

of the Directive use a general word for property at the key points at which the English version uses "goods",[82] but they use a different term for "goods" at the beginning of the preamble as regards the classic phrase which in English appears as "free movement of goods".[83] In these other versions of the Directive there is therefore a contrast between the "free movement of goods" and the Directive which applies to "sellers of property". Secondly, and more generally, the broad interpretation given to the phrase "free circulation of goods and services" and the significance of the Directive for the free movement of persons also suggest that the European Court of Justice is likely to include contracts of sale, etc. of land within the scope of the Directive.[84] In *London Borough of Newham v Khatun*[85] the question arose whether the 1993 Directive (and therefore the 1999 Regulations) applies to the terms on which accommodation is let by a local authority pursuant to its duty under the homeless persons legislation contained in Pt VII of the Housing Act 1996. Having looked at the *travaux préparatoires* of the Directive, the Court of Appeal considered that these differences of terminology used by some of its different language versions to describe its subject matter "effectively demolish" the textual argument that the English version's reference to "seller of goods" point to the exclusion of contracts relating to land.[86] The Court of Appeal therefore held that the 1999 Regulations apply equally to contracts relating to land. Moreover, a few weeks after this decision, the European Court of Justice in *Freiburger Kommunalbauten GMbH Baugesellschaft & Co KG v Hofstetter*[87] was apparently content to assume that a contract for the purchase of a building to be constructed falls within the ambit of the 1993 Directive, although the issue of the application of the 1993 Directive to contracts relating to land was not before the court.

Examples. If the Regulations do indeed cover "land contracts," then an important application would be as regards "consumer sales of land", i.e. those where the seller is acting in the course of a business in selling whereas the buyer is not. These would include contracts (including option contracts) made between builders or developers and "consumers". So, in *Zealander v Laing Homes Ltd*,[88] where the application of the Regulations was assumed, the Technology and Construction Court held that an arbitration clause in a contract for a newly built 15–020

[82] Bright and Bright, (1995) 111 L.Q.R. 655 p.664 who note the French use of "*vendeur de biens*". This is true also of the Italian and Spanish versions of the Directive, which use "*venditori de beni*" and "*vendedor de bens*" respectively.

[83] 1993 Directive recital 1. The French version uses "*marchandises*", the Italian "*merci*", and the Spanish "*marcadorias*."

[84] Bright and Bright, at p.669; cf. Kappus, *Neue Juristische Wochenschrift* (1994), p.1847 (cited with approval by the influential Heinrichs, *Neue Juristische Wochenschrift* (1996), p.2190) who argues that the Directive does not apply to contracts for the sale of land as these are not to be regarded as part of the common market since they do not involve trans-border transactions (The amendment of the B.G.B. paras 305–310 so as to apply the control of unfair contract terms in Germany generally to land contracts removes the significance of the interpretation of the 1993 Directive there. Cf. Basedow, *Münchener Kommentar zum BGB* vol.1, 4th edn (2001) on para.24a of former A.G.B.-Gesetz (fn.11) who argues that contracts concerning land are included. The author is grateful to Professor N. Jansen of the University of Munster for these points.

[85] [2004] EWCA Civ 55, [2005] Q.B. 37.

[86] [2005] Q.B. 37 at [78]–[83].

[87] C–237/02 [2004] 2 C.M.L.R. 13 and see below, para.15–115.

[88] (2000) 2 T.C.L.R. 724.

house under the National House Builders Council "Build Mark" Agreement was unfair in that its effect would have been that the consumer purchaser would have to take separate proceedings as between those matters covered by the Agreement and those falling outside it, which would put Z at a financial disadvantage. So, in the circumstances as a whole, including the disparities between the parties, the clause should be struck down. It has been assumed at first instance that the terms of a contract under which a consumer borrows money on the security of a mortgage executed over a property purchased from a third party are subject to the controls of the Regulations,[89] and this was indeed also the case as regards the term governing payment of interest on default in the contract of consumer credit secured by a mortgage in *Director General of Fair Trading v First National Bank*.[90]

15–021 **Other types of contract.** It has been argued earlier that the better view is that 1993 Directive applies to all types of "consumer contract" and that the use in its English version of the language of the supply of "goods" and "services" must be seen broadly in this.[91] In particular, and especially given the use of more general terms in other language versions referring to the supply of "property", there is no reason to consider that contracts for the supply of non-physical property are not included within the ambit of the Directive (and therefore the Regulations) and there are indeed examples in the Annex to the Directive (appearing in Sch.2 to the 1999 Regulations) which assume that it applies to non-physical property, including transactions in transferable securities, financial instruments and to purchase or sale of foreign currency, traveller's cheques or international money orders denominated in foreign currency.[92] If this is so, then contracts of assignment or of the licensing of contractual rights (for example, a right to use computer software) would also be included within the ambit of the Regulations.

15–022 **"Consumer contracts".** Clearly, the Regulations do not apply *beyond* "consumer contracts", the "consumer" aspect of this category being defined by them by defining the parties to such a contract.

15–023 **"Sellers or suppliers".** Regulation 3(1) of the 1999 Regulations provide that:

> "'... seller or supplier' means any natural or legal person who, in contracts covered by these Regulations, is acting for purposes relating to his trade, business or profession, whether publicly owned or privately owned."[93]

Restricting consumer protection to situations where the other party is acting "in the course of a business" is familiar to English lawyers from the Unfair Contract

---

[89] *Kindlance v McBride* Unreported 1997 N.I. Ch D (where on a summons for possession of mortgaged property it was held that the Regulations did apply to contracts of mortgage); *Falco Finance Ltd v Gough* (1999) 17 Tr. L. 526 Macclesfield Cty Ct.

[90] [2001] UKHL 52, [2002] 1 A.C. 481.

[91] See above, para.15–018.

[92] 1999 Regulations Sch.2 para.2(c). On the role of this Schedule more generally, see below, para.15–091.

[93] cf. 1994 Regulations reg.2 "sellers", "suppliers" and "business".

Terms Act 1977, many of whose controls are restricted to exemption clauses governing "business liability",[94] but the proper interpretation for the purposes of the Directive (and therefore the Regulations) may differ.

Public bodies. The Regulations state expressly that "seller or supplier" includes "legal persons" which are "publicly owned" as long as they are "acting for purposes relating to [their] trade, business or profession". It is submitted that an "autonomous" and broad understanding should and would be taken of "legal persons" which are "publicly owned" for this purpose as the concern of the Directive is to harmonise an aspect of the contractual behaviour of persons dealing with consumers in the market in the interests of fair competition and of the protection of consumers: the exact legal nature of the supplier of the goods or services under national law should not matter for these purposes.[95] If this approach were followed, then the Regulations would cover (in the English context) companies incorporated under the Companies Acts whose shares (or some of whose shares) were publicly owned, but it would also cover truly public bodies such as local authorities. On the other hand, in some cases the restriction to where a public person (in the above sense) acts "for purposes relating to [their] trade, business or profession" may sometimes be problematic. Clearly included would be the provision of services such as car-parking or use of a swimming pool by a local authority where the latter is acting in a way no differently than other "commercial" operators in the market, where payment is required from the consumer and where English law recognises the existence of a contractual relationship.[96] It is submitted that the contractual provision of education by a publicly owned institution of higher education would also fall within this test for this purpose.[97] And it has been held that the provision of accommodation by a local authority under a contract of tenancy, pursuant to its duty under the homeless persons legislation contained in Pt VII of the Housing Act 1996, falls within the scope of the 1993 Directive, as this activity comes within the words "trade, business or profession" under art.2(c) of the Directive, despite the statutory context of this provision.[98] While the European Court has not had occasion to explain the phrase 'acting for purposes relating to his trade, business or profession' in the 1993 Directive, in *Veedfald v Århus Amtskommune* it pronounced on a similar expression found in the EC Directive concerning 15–024

[94] Unfair Contract Terms Act 1977 ss.1(3) (as amended) and 14.

[95] cf. above, para.15–005. An analogy may be drawn with the ECJ's case law governing "direct effect" noted at para.15–014 above, but against this must be put the very different legal purposes of this caselaw from a consumer protection directive.

[96] Indeed, the Director General of Fair Trading acting under the Regulations has criticised a term on which a public authority provided a car park to the public: OFT, *Unfair Contract Terms*, Bulletin No.1 (May 1996), p.42.

[97] On the contractual nature of this relationship see *Herring v Templeman* [1973] 3 All E.R. 569; Garner (1974) 90 L.Q.R. 6; Wade (1974) 90 L.Q.R. 157 and Whittaker (2001) 21 O.J.L.S. 103. The OFT has intervened in relation to the contracts made between a University incorporated under the Education Reform Act 1988 and its student: *Unfair Contract Terms*, Bulletin no.21 (May, 2003), pp.48–50.

[98] *London Borough of Newham v Khatun* [2004] EWCA Civ 55, [2005] Q.B. 37, above, para.15–019.

liability for defective products of 1985 and this may provide some guidance.[99] There, the defendant public hospital argued that as it had produced and used the product in question in the course of providing publicly funded health care for which its patient did not pay, it therefore did not do so for an economic purpose or in the course of [its] business within the meaning of the defence to liability provided by art.7(c) of the 1985 Directive.[100] However, the European Court disagreed, holding that the fact that products are manufactured for a service for which the patient has not paid and which is financed from public funds:

> "... cannot detract from the economic and business character of that manufacture. The activity in question is not a charitable one which could therefore be covered by the exemption from liability provided for in Article 7(c) of the Directive. Besides, the [defendant hospital] itself admitted at the hearing that, in similar circumstances, a private hospital would undoubtedly be liable for the defectiveness of the product pursuant to the provisions of the Directive."[101]

15–025 This last point was clearly addressed to the argument put to the Court that the application of the 1985 Directive's scheme of liability to public hospitals would have harmful consequences for public health care and place them at a disadvantage in relation to private health schemes.[102] While this decision concerned a provision in a defence to liability and the European Court interprets such defences narrowly (especially where they reduce the protection of consumers[103]), it does suggest that the Court is likely to interpret "course of business" in the 1993 Directive so as to further its purposes of the facilitation of the internal market by reducing distortions of competition and the furtherance of the protection of consumers.[104] And it also suggests an expansive approach to the understanding of "acting for purposes relating to his trade, business, or profession" for the purposes of defining the ambit of the 1993 Directive. Moreover, as will be explained below, if an autonomous interpretation of "contract" were taken by the European Court, other examples of the provision of public services at present not treated as contractual by English law may well be included.[105]

15–026 **A regular part of his business?** While the person whose terms are caught by the Regulations must be acting for purposes relating to his business in making the contract and not merely "in business", it is not clear whether or not the contract made by a business needs to form a regular part of that business. In English law, the answer to this question in relation to the phrase "acting in the course of a business" in statute has differed according to the legal context in question, though these opposite responses have in common the expansion of protection for

---

[99] *Veedfald v Århus Amtskommune* (C–203/99) [2001] E.C.R. 1–3569 at [15]; EC Directive 1985/374 on liability for defective products.

[100] This gives the producer a defence where he proves that "the product was neither manufactured by him for sale or any form of distribution for economic purpose or distributed by him in the course of his business".

[101] [2001] E.C.R. 1–3569 at [21].

[102] [2001] E.C.R. 1–3569 at [20].

[103] [2001] E.C.R. 1–3569 at [15].

[104] 1993 Directive recitals 1–2.

[105] See below, paras 15–034—15–035. On the application of the 1993 Directive to the provision of public services see Whittaker (2000) 116 L.Q.R. 95.

consumers.[106] In French law, by contrast, a "professional seller" (*vendeur professionnel*) is generally understood to refer either to a seller whose business is to sell the general type of property sold in the relevant transaction or who otherwise possesses a special skill or expertise in relation to the type of property sold.[107] In the absence of any clear guidance from the text or recitals of the Directive, the European Court of Justice would resolve the question by reference to its purposes in the light of general Community principle. In this respect, as has been noted, the legislation is expressed as intended to create a minimum protection for consumers throughout the European Union and by this means increase consumer confidence and thus the facilitation of the establishment of the internal market.[108] Given that the Directive's controls apply only to terms which have not been "individually negotiated", i.e. typically the supplier's own standard terms[109] and that often a consumer will not be aware or not fully aware of the nature of the business of the supplier and, therefore, whether or not the contract which he intends to conclude does or does not form a regular part of its business, it is submitted that the consumer should not be deprived of the protections of the Directive merely because the contract in question is unusual for the supplier.

Dealing with a view to profit? It is also a question whether a "business" requires an element of dealing with a view to making a profit. Clearly, most businesses do so, but as has been seen in relation to the Unfair Contract Terms Act 1977,[110] English authority suggests that no such additional requirement should be made.[111] This may be supported in the context of the Regulations by reference to the inclusion of the contractual provision of public services, which are often run other than with a view to profit-making.[112] 15–027

"Consumer". Regulation 3(1) of the 1999 Regulations provides that: 15–028

> " ' . . . consumer' means any natural person who, in contracts covered by these Regulations, is acting for purposes which are outside his trade, business or profession."[113]

This definition of the other party to "consumer contracts" differs from the definition found in the Unfair Contract Terms Act 1977.[114] First, this definition restricts consumers to "natural persons" and therefore a company cannot rely on the provisions of the Regulations even if it acts "for purposes which are outside

---

[106] *R. & B. Customs Brokers Co Ltd v United Dominions Trust Ltd* [1988] 1 W.L.R. 321 (Unfair Contract Terms Act 1977, s.12); *Stevenson v Rogers* [1999] Q.B. 1028 (Sale of Goods Act 1979 s.14(1)).

[107] Com. December 12, 1984, Bull. civ.IV, no.349.

[108] 1993 Directive recitals 5, 6 & 10.

[109] This will not always be the case: see below, para.15–046—15–048. But note, there is no restriction to acting on "standard terms *of business*" as under the Unfair Contract Terms Act 1977 s.3, above, para.14–072.

[110] See above, para.14–065.

[111] *Roles v Miller* (1884) 27 Ch D 71, 88; *Town Investments Ltd v Department of Environment* [1978] A.C. 359.

[112] Above, para.15–024.

[113] cf. 1994 Regulations reg.2, "consumer".

[114] s.12.

[its] business".[115] Secondly, a buyer of goods is not to be regarded as "dealing as consumer" under the 1977 Act if he is an "individual" and the goods are second hand goods sold at public auction at which individuals have the opportunity of attending the sale in person, whereas this restriction does not apply to the Regulations.[116] Thirdly, purchase by a consumer at an auction sale or by competitive tender is covered by the Regulations, though it is not by the Unfair Contract Terms Act.[117]

15–029 **European jurisprudence.** While the European Court of Justice has not had occasion to explain the notion of "consumer" for the purposes of the 1993 Directive, it has made clear that it will take an "autonomous" interpretation to this concept.[118] In this respect it is likely to take a fairly restrictive view for these purposes,[119] particularly when contrasted with the expansive view taken by English law for the purposes of the Unfair Contract Terms Act, where it has been held that a business which makes a contract of a kind which does not form a regular part of its business may "deal as consumer".[120] Certainly, the European Court has taken a restrictive view of "consumer" for the purposes of other European provisions. So, in *Di Pinto*[121] the question arose whether a trader could ever be a "consumer" for the purposes of the "door-step selling" Directive, whose art.2 uses the same defining language for "consumer" as does the 1993 Directive.[122] The European Court held that:

> "... the criterion for the application of protection lies in the connection between the transactions which are the subject of the canvassing and the professional activity of the trader: the latter may claim that the directive is applicable only if the transaction in respect of which he is canvassed lies outside his trade or profession. Article 2, which is drafted in general terms, does not make it possible, with regard to acts performed in the context of such a trade or profession, to draw a distinction between normal acts and those which are exceptional in nature."[123]

The Court added that:

> "Acts which are preparatory to the sale of a business, such as the conclusion of a contract for the publication of an advertisement in a periodical, are connected with the

[115] *Cape Snc v Idealservice Srl* (C–541/99 & C–542/99) [2001] E.C.R. 1–09049. For English law, the 1999 Regulations are extended to consumer arbitration agreements including as "consumer" for this purpose legal as well as natural persons: Arbitration Act 1996 s.90; *Heifer International Inc v Christiansen* [2007] EWHC 3015 (TCC), [2008] All E.R. (D) 120 (Jan) and see below, para.15–094.

[116] Unfair Contract Terms Act 1977 s.12(2) as substituted by the Sale and Supply of Goods to Consumers Regulations 2002 (SI 2000/3045) reg.14(3), themselves implementing Directive 1999/44 on certain aspects of the sale of consumer goods and associated guarantees. This rule applies to goods bought under a contract of hire-purchase.

[117] And see s.12(2).

[118] *Cape Snc v Idealservice Srl* [2001] E.C.R. 1–09049.

[119] Reich (1995) 4 *European Review of Private Law* 285, 292–293.

[120] Unfair Contract Terms Act 1977 s.12; *R. & B. Customs Brokers Co Ltd v United Dominions Trust Ltd* [1988] 1 W.L.R. 321.

[121] *France v Di Pinto* (361/89) [1991] E.C.R. I–1189.

[122] Directive 85/577 to protect the consumer in respect of contracts negotiated away from business premises [1985] OJ L372/31 art.2.

[123] [1991] E.C.R. I–1189 at [15].

professional activity of the trader although such acts may bring the running of the business to an end, they are managerial acts performed for the purpose of satisfying requirements *other than the family or personal requirements of the trader.*"[124]

The last italicised phrase could be seen as suggesting that a person does not act as a consumer unless contracting for one's "family or personal needs". In *Benincasa v Dentalkit*[125] the European Court considered the concept of consumer for the purposes of art.13 of the Brussels Convention,[126] upholding its previous view that this referred to "private final consumer"[127]:

"Consequently, only contracts concluded for the purpose of satisfying an individual's own needs in terms of private consumption come under the provisions designed to protect the consumer as the party deemed to be the weaker party economically."[128]

Furthermore, in *Gruber v Bay Wa AG*[129] (again for the purposes of art.13 of the Brussels Convention) the European Court of Justice held that a person who concludes a contract for goods intended for purposes which are in part within and in part outside his trade or profession (in the case itself, a farmer who bought tiles to roof a building used both for agricultural and for domestic purposes) may not rely on the special rules in the Convention provided for consumer contracts:

"... unless the trade or professional purpose is so limited as to be negligible in the overall context of the supply, the fact that the private element is predominant being irrelevant in that respect."[130]

The Court further held that a national court must assess whether this is the case by reference to all the evidence, but it:

"... must not take account of facts or circumstances of which the other party to the contract [the business supplier] may have been aware when the contract was concluded, unless the person who claims the capacity of consumer behaved in such a way as to give the other party to the contract the legitimate impression that he was acting for the purposes of his business."[131]

While this observation was made in the context of a person (the alleged "consumer") acting partly for business and partly for non-business purposes, it suggests more generally that a person who in fact contracts as a consumer but gives the "seller or supplier" the impression that he acts in the course of a business cannot rely on his status as consumer. Finally, it is to be noted that the

---

124 [1991] E.C.R. 1–1189 at [16] (emphasis added).

125 C–269/95 [1997] E.C.R. 1-3767.

126 Brussels Convention on Jurisdiction and the Enforcement of Foreign Judgments in Civil and Commercial Matters of September 27, 1968 itself replaced as from March 1, 2002 by the Council Regulation 44/2001 of 2001 on jurisdiction and the recognition and enforcement of judgments in civil and commercial matters [2001] OJ L12/1.

127 [1997] E.C.R. 1–3767 at [15]; *Shearson Lehman Hutton* (C–89/91) [1993] E.C.R. I–139 at [20], [22].

128 [1997] E.C.R. 1–3767 at [17].

129 C–464/01 [2005] E.C.R. 1–439.

130 [2005] E.C.R. 1–439 at [54].

131 [2005] E.C.R. 1–439 at [54].

analogy between "consumer" for the purposes of art.13 of the Convention and for the 1993 Directive was expressly drawn by Advocate-General Mischo in proceedings in which the European Court confirmed that a body corporate could not be a consumer for the latter's purposes.[132]

15–030 **United Kingdom case law.** In *Standard Bank London Ltd v Apostolakis*[133] the proper understanding of "consumer" for the purposes of the 1993 Directive arose in unusual circumstances. The defendants were wealthy individuals (a civil engineer and a lawyer) who had used their personal funds for dealings in foreign exchange under an "umbrella contract" with a bank in Athens, where they resided. The question arose as to the validity of an exclusive jurisdiction clause of the English courts in this contract, either under art.13 of the Brussels Convention or the 1999 Regulations. It was held first that this was a "consumer contract" for the purposes of art.13[134]:

> "It is certainly not part of a person's trade as a civil engineer or a lawyer . . . to enter into foreign exchange contracts. They were using the money in a way which they hoped would be profitable but merely to use money in a way which they hoped would be profitable is not enough . . . to be engaging in trade."[135]

According to the court, even if the wording used by the European Court in *Benincasa* were applied literally, the foreign exchange contracts:

> " . . . were for the purpose of satisfying the needs of [the defendants], defined as an appropriate use of their income, and that that need was a need in terms of private consumption. Consumption cannot be taken as literally consumed so as to be destroyed but rather consumer in the sense that a consumer consumes, *viz.* he uses or enjoys the relevant product."[136]

It was later assumed that the defendants were also "consumers" for the purposes of the 1993 Directive and held that, apart from this decision under the Convention, the choice of jurisdiction clause was "unfair" within the meaning of the 1999 Regulations.[137] By contrast, in *Prostar Management Ltd v Twaddle*,[138] a professional footballer claimed that he acted as "consumer" in relation to his receipt of services under a management agreement for the promotion of his career, profile and sponsorship. The Glasgow and Strathkelvin Sheriff Court had regard to the decisions of the European Court in *Di Pinto*[139] and *Benincasa*[140] and rejected this claim, holding that being a footballer was the defender's "trade

---

[132] *Cape Snc v Idealservice Srl* (C–541/99 & C–542/99) [2001] E.C.R. I–9049. (The ECJ did not advert to this point). Applied in *Evans v Cherry Tree Finance Ltd* Unreported April 13, 2007 Ch D (loan taken out by individual secured on business premises was a consumer contract as it fell outside his trade, business or profession).

[133] *Standard Bank London Ltd v Apostolakis (No.1)* [2000] I.L. Pr. 766 (Longmore J.); *Standard Bank London Ltd v Apostolakis (No.2)* [2001] Lloyd's Rep. Bank. 240 (Steel J.).

[134] [2000] I.L. Pr. 766.

[135] [2000] I.L. Pr. 766, 771, per Longmore J.

[136] [2000] I.L. Pr. 766, 773.

[137] *Standard Bank London Ltd v Apostolakis (No.2)* [2001] Lloyd's Rep. Bank. 240.

[138] [2003] S.L.T. (Sh. Ct.) 11.

[139] *France v Di Pinto* [1991] E.C.R. 1–1189.

[140] [1997] E.C.R. 1–3767.

or profession" and that the contract in question could not be regarded as being outside it.[141] Finally, in *Heifer International Inc v Christiansen*[142] it was held that an offshore company set up to purchase a residential property for its beneficial owners acted "for purposes outside [its] trade, business, or profession" when it entered contracts for the purchase and renovation of the property in question.[143]

15–031 **The "average consumer".** Having decided that a person is indeed a "consumer" for the purposes of the Regulations, the question arises as to the *standard* by which the consumer (and particular the consumer's understanding) is to be assessed, this being relevant in particular for the purposes of the requirement of "plain, intelligible language"[144] and of the requirement of fairness.[145] Various standards can be seen as reflected in the consumer *acquis* more generally: "confident" or sophisticated consumers; "average" consumers; and "vulnerable" consumers.[146] Neither the 1993 Directive itself nor the jurisprudence of the European Court interpreting it take a overt position on this question, but the Court has adopted for the purpose of other legislation the standard of the "average consumer" who is "reasonably well informed and reasonably observant and circumspect".[147] This standard is not, however, a uniform one and for this purpose it is useful to see how the Unfair Commercial Practices Directive of 2005[148] has interpreted the concept of "average consumer". The 2005 Directive creates a "general framework" for preventive measures of consumer protection and it is expressly stated as being "without prejudice to contract law",[149] but its treatment of the standard of average consumer both reflects the Court's existing jurisprudence of this notion and may influence the shape of its future development.[150] For this purpose, the 2005 Directive distinguishes between: (i) the

[141] [2003] S.L.T. (Sh. Ct.) 11 at [12]–[14].

[142] [2007] EWHC 3015 (TCC), [2008] All E.R. (D) 120 (Jan) at [243]—[250].

[143] The extended definition of a "consumer" so as to include a company is provided by the Arbitration Act 1996 s.90.

[144] Below, para.15–130.

[145] Below, para.15–087. See also below, para.15–058 (reasonable expectation of average consumer relevant to identification of "core terms").

[146] See further Weatherill in Weatherill and Bernitz (eds), *The Regulation of Unfair Commercial Practices under EC Directive 2005/29* (2007), Ch.7.

[147] Directive 2005/29 recital 18. This standard was accepted as applicable in the context of the 1993 Directive by Andrew Smith J. in *OFT v Abbey National Plc* (the *Bank Charges* Case) [2008] EWHC 875 (Comm) at [89] treating it as "an appropriate yardstick guide to whether a term is in plain intelligible language". On this case more generally see below, para.15–059. The ECJ case law in question can be seen in *Pippig Augenoptik GmbH & Co KG v Hartlauer Handelsgesellschaft mbH* (C–44/01) [2003] E.C.R. I–3095 at [55]; *De Landtsheer Emmanuel SA v Comité Interprofessionnel du Vin du Champagne* (381/05) [2007] Bus. L.R. 1487; *Lidl Belgium GmbH & Co KG v Etablissementen Franz Colruyt NV* (356/04) [2007] Bus. L.R. 492 at [78] (misleading advertising); *Gut Springenheide GmbH and Rudolf Trusky v Oberkreisdrektor des Kreises Steinfurt-Amft fur Lebensmitteluberwachung* (C–210/90) [1998] E.C.R. I–4657 (marketing standards for eggs); *Estée Lauder Cosmetics GmbH & Co OHG v Lancaster Group GmbH* (C–220/98) E.C.R. [2000] I-0117 (marketing of cosmetics).

[148] Directive 2005/29 on unfair commercial practices. This directive is implemented in English law by the Consumer Protection from Unfair Trading Regulations 2008 (SI no.1277).

[149] Directive 2005/29 art.3(2).

[150] Whittaker in Weatherill and Bernitz at Ch.8.

average consumer; (ii) the average member of the group where a commercial practice is directed to a particular group of consumers; and (iii) the average member of a clearly identifiable group of consumers who are particularly vulnerable to the practice or the underlying product because of their mental or physical infirmity, age or credulity in a way which the trader could reasonably be expected to foresee.[151] Similar distinctions could helpfully be drawn in the context of the fairness or transparency of contract terms especially as regards the extent to which a consumer could be expected to read and understand the terms of the contract, for while a national court would generally be justified in assessing these questions bearing in mind an "average consumer" (neither very sophisticated and careful nor, conversely, of under average intelligence or careless), where the business has targeted its goods or services (and therefore its contract terms) towards a particular group of consumers, then this standard should be varied so as to take this into account. It is submitted, moreover, that in the context of contract terms, this standard could be varied in either direction. So, if a business targets particularly vulnerable consumers (for example, offering loans to low-income or poor-credit would-be borrowers), then the "average consumer" should be to an extent lowered; but if a business targets its sophisticated financial products towards high-income individuals (who may be independently advised), then the "average consumer" should be to this extent highered. In this way, the "average consumer" is generally an objective standard variable according to its context. On the other hand, where a business knows (or, possibly, can reasonably foresee) that a *particular* consumer with whom it deals has a lesser likely understanding of its contract terms, then this would certainly be relevant to the assessment of the fairness of the terms (notably, as a result of the requirement of good faith),[152] but in this situation the Court may prefer instead to apply a subjective test of the understanding of a consumer by way of exception to the general standard of "average consumer". The important difference between the two approaches would lie in the treatment of the issue of the "plainness and intelligibility of the terms", which are relevant to the test of unfairness but also important for the exclusion found in reg.6(2) of the 1999 Regulations.[153]

15–032 **"Consumers" as "suppliers"?** Does the "supplier of the service" (in the special extended sense) have to be the person in business, the consumer its "recipient" or can consumers also be the "supplier"?[154] In this respect, the English version of arts 1 and 2 of the Directive, which describes the business party to the contract as the "seller or supplier" may be thought to support an understanding of a consumer as "recipient". Perhaps more significantly, the concern of the Directive with enhancing the fairness of competition of the supply of property and services may be thought to make sense only where the latter are

---

[151] This distinction is drawn from 2005 Directive art.5(b) and 5(3).

[152] Below, para.15–087.

[153] Below, para.15–055.

[154] cf. the position under the Unfair Contract Terms Act 1977 in relation to which it has been stated that "a person can deal as consumer in disposing of goods, no less than in acquiring goods or services": Treitel, *Law of Contract*, 12th edn (by Peel, 2007), para.7–051.

indeed competing, i.e. where their *provision* is by "businesses".[155] And in general, as has been seen the European Court has taken a restrictive interpretation of the notion of "consumer" even in the context of consumer protection legislation.[156] A key example of a person who satisfies the Regulations' definition of a consumer (in terms of a natural person acting for purposes which are outside his trade, business or profession),[157] but who *provides* rather than *receives* a service would be a non-business surety guaranteeing the debts of her husband's company to a bank, thereby providing a "financial service".[158] And in this particular type of situation, the High Court has held that the Regulations do not apply to contracts of guarantee made by a company director (the supposed "consumer") with a bank, for while the bank supplied a service to the principal debtor, in the contract between the bank and the guarantor "the benefit of the contract flows one way: from guarantor to lender".[159] On the other hand, other language versions of arts 1 and 2 of the Directive do not assume a sale or supply *by the business,* instead using terms to describe the non-consumer party to the contract such as *professionnel* in the French and *Gewerbetreibenden* in the German.[160] And the view that the Directive does not apply to contracts by which a consumer sells or supplies is not shared by the European Commission, which has observed that:

> "Although contracts for the sale of products or the provision of services are those most frequently concluded between professionals and consumers, the Directive also covers other contracts such as contracts pertaining to guarantees for the benefit of a financial institution or even cases in which the consumers themselves are sellers (provided the buyer is acting in the course of business)."[161]

On balance, it is submitted that the European Court is likely to follow this broader interpretation, applying the Directive to cases where consumers "supply" as well as receive.

"Consumers" as agents for non-consumers. Where an individual (A) makes a contract outside his trade, business or profession with a person (B) for the supply of goods or services within the course of the latter's business but A does so as agent for a third person (C) who acts in the course of his business, then 15–033

[155] cf. also the definition of "consumer contract" for the purposes of art.5(1) of the Rome Convention of June 19, 1980 on the law applicable to contractual obligations as: "[A] contract the object of which is the supply of goods or services to a person ('the consumer') for a purpose which can be regarded as being outside his trade or profession, or a contract for the provision of credit for that object."

[156] See above, para.15–029.

[157] Above, para.15–028.

[158] See for a discussion of this point in the context of suretyship Vol.II paras 44–138—44–140.

[159] *The Governor and Co of the Bank of Scotland v Singh* Unreported QBD, Mercantile Ct, H.H. Judge Kershaw, at [85]–[90] especially at [86], followed by *Manches LLP v Freer* [2006] EWHC 991 (QB); *Williamson v Governor of the Bank of Scotland* [2006] EWHC 1289 (Ch) at [42]–[46] (guarantee made by a partner in respect of the partnership debts). For further critical assessment of this caselaw, see Vol. 2, paras 44–138—44–140.

[160] cf. above, para.15–018.

[161] European Commission, *Report on Directive 93/13/EEC on unfair terms in consumer contracts* COM(2000) final of April 27, 2000, p.8, no.19. See also Calais-Auloy and Steinmetz, *Droit de la consommation*, 6th edn (2003) p.14.

the contract thereby formed between B (the supplier) and C (the principal)[162] does not count as a consumer contract and so falls outside the controls of the Regulations. However, where in such circumstances A also undertakes personal liabilities under the contract which he makes on behalf of the principal,[163] then the contract may qualify as a consumer contract and so fall within the Regulations for this purpose. So, it has been held that where after a fire an owner of a house (A) entered a contract for its reinstatement with a builder (B) as agent for his insurer (C) (which had exercised its contractual right to repair the property rather than pay an indemnity) but under which he (A) also undertook personal liabilities in respect of payment for the building work, then the terms of the contract could be assessed for fairness under the Regulations.[164]

15–034 **An autonomous view of "contract"?** So far in this discussion it has been assumed that the transaction which is (arguably) within the ambit of the Regulations qualifies as a "contract" within the meaning of this notion in English law. However, the question arises whether the European Court would indeed rely on the classifications of the domestic laws of the Member States for this purpose, or would instead adopt an autonomous view of this concept.[165] The European Court would decide between these two positions on the basis of which of them is likely to be most effective in enabling the Directive to achieve its purposes[166] and on the difficulty of constructing a European conception of contract for the purposes of the Directive.[167] As regards the latter, it is to be noted that the Court has already embarked on such an undertaking for the purpose of the Brussels Convention.[168] As regards the purposes of the Directive, both reduction in distortions in competition and the protection of consumers would be enhanced by the Court's taking an autonomous view of "contract" for the purposes of the Directive, for such a view would clearly enhance the harmonising purpose of the Directive and thereby make more effective its policy of consumer protection within the European Union.

15–035 If the European Court were to take such an autonomous view of contract, it is likely that it would do so on the basis of an agreement between the parties.[169] Such a view would require an English court to classify as contractual for the

---

[162] See Vol.II, para.31–055.

[163] See Vol.II, para.31–085.

[164] *Domsalla v Dyason* [2007] EWHC 1174 (TCC) at [92] (H.H.J. Thornton Q.C.).

[165] For this issue and development of the consequences noted in the following discussion, see Whittaker (2000) 116 L.Q.R. 95.

[166] cf. the approach of Att-Gen Sir Gordon Slynn in *Arcado SPRL v Haviland SA* (9/87) [1988] E.C.R. 1539 at [1548].

[167] *Tessili v Dunlop* [1976] E.C.R. 1473.

[168] Brussels Convention art.5(1) and see *Martin Peters Bauunternehmung GmbH v Zuid Nederlandse Aannemers Vereniging* (34/82) [1983] E.C.R. 987 and *Jakob Handt & Co GmbH v Traitements Mécano-chimiques des Surfaces SA* (26/91) [1992] E.C.R. I–3967.

[169] cf. *Jakob Handt & Co GmbH v Traitements Mécano-chimiques des Surfaces SA* [1992] E.C.R. 1–3967 and see Whittaker (2000) 116 L.Q.R. 95. The ECJ may also rely for this purpose on the definition of contract found in DCFR para.II.–1:101 in terms of "an agreement which gives rise to, or is intended to give rise to, a binding legal relationship".

purposes of the Directive a transaction which in English law is considered non-contractual. Three examples may be given. First, the laws of most of the Member States contain no requirement conceptually equivalent to English law's doctrine of consideration.[170] This raises the possibility of including within the ambit of the Directive the terms on which professional services are provided gratuitously. Secondly, the relationship between the beneficiary of a trust and the trustee may sometimes be considered "contractual" for the purposes of the Directive (and therefore the Regulations), even though it is not in the general English law.[171] Thirdly, some provisions of public services, such as water and electricity, may be held to be "contractual" for the purposes of the Regulations even though they are non-contractual under general English law.[172] In this respect, the European Commission has drawn attention to its statement in the European Council's minutes in connection with the adoption of the common position concerning art.2 of the Directive on the notion of the contract which "points out that the notion of contract also includes transactions involving supplies of goods or services in a regulatory framework".[173]

Contracts specifically excluded from the ambit of the 1994 Regulations. The 1994 Regulations were expressed as not applying to contracts relating to employment, contracts relating to succession rights, any contract relating to rights under family law and any contract relating to the incorporation and organisation of companies or partnerships.[174] While no similar provision is found in the 1999 Regulations, it is submitted that no substantial change has occurred. The exclusion of these contracts in the 1994 Regulations may be traced to recital 10 of the Directive, according to which: 15–036

> "... those rules [as to the protection of consumers] should apply to all contracts concluded between sellers or suppliers and consumers; whereas *as a result inter alia* contracts relating to employment, . . . must be excluded from this Directive."[175]

It would appear, therefore, that these types of contracts are excluded on the ground that they are not "consumer contracts" within the meaning of the Directive, this being emphasised by the list being expressed as a non-exhaustive

---

170 There is no more than a superficial conceptual similarity between *la cause* in French law and the doctrine of consideration and there is no similarity in terms of their respective overall functions: see Whittaker, in Bell, Beyron and Whittaker, *Principles of French Law*, 2nd edn (2008), pp.321–322; H. Kötz and A. Flessner, *European Contract Law* (trans. Weir, 1997), Vol.I, pp.54 et seq.

171 cf. *Gray v Taylor* [1998] 1 W.L.R. 1093 in which the Court of Appeal held that a person occupying an almshouse under a charitable trust was not a tenant.

172 For the non-contractual nature of the supply of electricity and water to domestic consumers (even though they pay), see the Electricity Act 1989 ss.16, 22 and *Norweb v Dixon* [1995] 1 W.L.R. 636 and the Water Industry Act 1991 ss.53–56 and *Read v Croydon Corp* [1938] 4 All E.R. 631. cf. the position in relation to gas under the Gas Act 1995 ss.7 and 8 amending Gas Act 1986 ss.7 and 8.

173 European Commission, *Report on Directive 93/13/EEC on unfair terms in consumer contracts*, COM(2000) final, p.15.

174 1994 Regulations reg.3(1) and Sch.1 (a)–(d).

175 Emphasis added.

one.[176] So, while these types of contracts are indeed excluded from the ambit of the 1999 Regulations, this results simply from the latters' restriction to consumer contracts.

There is, though, a particular difficulty with this interpretation. Generally contracts of employment will not count as "consumer contracts" as this is generally understood by the Directive, the reason being that neither the "supplier of the service" (the employee) *nor* the would-be recipient of the service (the employer) act for purposes outside their "trade, business or profession". However, in some circumstances the employer may appear to count as a "consumer". For example, if a private individual employs a nanny for his children (perhaps using for this purpose the standard terms of the nanny's professional association), it could be argued that the individual does so as a consumer of the professional services of the nanny. For while the latter does act "for purposes relating to his trade, business or profession",[177] the private individual is a "natural person . . . acting for purposes which are outside his trade, business or profession" within the meaning of art.1 of the Directive: here, there appears to be both a "consumer contract" and a contract of employment.[178] On the other hand, both the definition of "consumer" and "seller or supplier" are qualified in art.1 by the phrase "in contracts covered by this Directive" and this could be seen as a legal basis in the *text* of the Directive itself for excluding contracts of employment and the other contracts referred to in recital 10, even if they otherwise would fall within its general definition of "consumer contract". This is significant, for while recitals to a Directive may be used in the interpretation of its articles, they should not be used to reduce their ambit since this would detract from the principle of legal certainty.[179]

15–037 **Differences from the ambit of the Unfair Contract Terms Act 1977.** It will be apparent that the types of contracts governed by the Regulations differ significantly from those governed by the various provisions of the Unfair Contract Terms Act 1977. First, while the ambit of the Regulations is restricted to consumer contracts, a significant number of provisions of the 1977 Act apply to non-consumer contracts, notably, as regards any exclusion of liability for negligence,[180] of contractual liability in general where it arises from breach of a written standard term[181] and as regards the implied terms as to title, quality, etc.

---

[176] The choice of contracts actually mentioned may be explained by the influence on the drafting of the Directive of the German Standard Contracts Act of 1976, a provision of which applied to standard terms in general and from which these very same contracts were excluded: see *Gesetz zur Regelung des Rechts der Allgemeinen Geschäftsbedingungen* para.23 (on which see Markesinis, *The German Law of Obligations*, Vol.I; Markesinis, Lorenz and Dannemann, *The Law of Contract and Restitution: A Comparative Introduction* (1997), pp.211 et seq). (The German Standard Contracts Act 1976 itself was abrogated and replaced by a revised BGB para.307(1).)

[177] cf. *Prostar Management Ltd v Twaddle* [2003] S.L.T. (Sh. Ct.) 11, above, para.15–030.

[178] cf. *Keen v Commerzbank AG* [2006] EWCA Civ 1536, [2007] I.C.R. 623 at [77]–[101] (whether *employee* can be "consumer" of services by employer for the purposes of the Unfair Contract Terms Act 1977 s.3).

[179] cf. *Denkavit International B.V. v Bundesamt für Finanzen* (C–283/94, C–291/94 & C–292/94) [1996] E.C.R. I–05063 at [24]–[29] (concerning the use of Council minutes).

[180] Unfair Contract Terms Act 1977 Act s.2.

[181] s.3, above, paras 14–072—14–074.

in sale of goods.[182] Secondly, on the other hand, as regards consumer contracts, the net of the Regulations is rather wider than the 1977 Act, notably in their inclusion of contracts of insurance,[183] sale at auction of second-hand goods,[184] and contracts which relate to the creation or transfer of a right or interest in intellectual property.[185] Furthermore, if contracts for the sale, etc. of land are indeed governed by the Regulations, this marks a significant difference from the 1977 Act.[186] Thirdly, it should be noted that the 1977 Act may apply to non-contractual notices,[187] whereas the Regulations apply only to contract terms, though it has been noted that "contract" may be given for this purpose a meaning different from its general significance in English law.[188]

5. CONTRACT TERMS EXCLUDED FROM THE REGULATIONS

General. Unlike the Unfair Contract Terms Act 1977 (whose controls principally affect exemption clauses)[189] the types of contract terms caught by the Regulations are very varied; indeed, the starting-point of the Regulations (following the Directive) is that their controls apply to *all* types of terms, the legislation referring simply to "unfair terms in contracts concluded between a seller or a supplier and a consumer".[190] From this starting-point, there are two sets of derogations. First, the Regulations exclude altogether from their controls contract terms which reflect "mandatory statutory or regulatory provisions" and those which reflect "the provisions of international conventions". These exclusions (and the question as to whether the Regulations apply to implied terms) will be considered in the following paragraphs. Secondly, the two requirements created by the Regulations differ somewhat in the range of terms which they govern. So, the requirement that terms be in "plain, intelligible language" applies to *any written term* of the contract,[191] whereas the requirement of fairness applies to any term (whether written or oral)[192] "which has not been individually negotiated" unless that term defines the subject matter of the contract or its price 15–038

[182] s.6, above, para.14–078.

[183] These are excluded from ss.2–4 of the 1977 Act by s.1(2) and Sch.1 para.1(a).

[184] This is by virtue of the more restricted definition of consumer in this respect in s.12 of the 1977 Act, above, para.14–068.

[185] This type of contract is excluded from ss.2–4 of the 1977 Act by s.1(2) Sch.1 para.1(c) and see above, para.15–021.

[186] These are excluded from ss.2–4 of the 1977 Act by s.1(2) Sch.1 para.1(b). cf. above, para.15–019.

[187] ss.2 and 14.

[188] See above, para.15–034.

[189] See above, paras 14–059 et seq.

[190] 1999 Regulations reg.4(1); 1993 Directive arts 2(a), 3(1).

[191] 1993 Directive recital 11; 1999 Regulations reg.7; 1994 Regulations reg.6.

[192] It is perhaps unusual for an oral term to be other than "not individually negotiated", but it is conceivable, particularly given the rule as to the burden of proof as to this issue (on which see below, para.15–047), for example, where a trader simply stipulates orally that a particular non-refundable deposit must be paid for goods or where a trader's standard terms are read by its agents to the consumer over the telephone.

in a "plain, intelligible" way.[193] These qualifications on the general starting-point will be considered with the treatment of the requirements themselves.[194]

15–039 **Terms which reflect "mandatory statutory or regulatory provisions" of English law.**[195] The 1999 Regulations are expressed as not applying to:

> ". . . contractual terms which reflect . . . mandatory statutory or regulatory provisions (including such provisions under the law of any Member State or in Community legislation having effect in the United Kingdom without further enactment)."[196]

Here, the text of the 1999 Regulations follows more closely the text of the Directive than did the corresponding provision in the 1994 Regulations, for the latter (unlike art.2(1) of the Directive) did not qualify the phrase "statutory or regulatory provisions" by the adjective "mandatory".[197] In interpreting this adjective, recourse must be had to the preamble to the Directive, recitals 13 and 14 of which explain that:

> "Whereas the statutory or regulatory provisions of the Member States which directly or indirectly determine the terms of consumer contracts are presumed not to contain unfair terms; whereas, therefore, it does not appear to be necessary to subject the terms which reflect mandatory statutory or regulatory provisions . . .; whereas in that respect the wording 'mandatory statutory or regulatory provisions' in Article 1(2) also covers rules which, according to the law, shall apply between the contracting parties provided that no other arrangements have been established;
>
> Whereas Member States must however ensure that unfair terms are not included, particularly because this Directive also applies to trades, businesses or professions of a public nature."

Recital 13 makes clear that the adjective "mandatory" does not intend to restrict the category of legal rules which impose terms on the parties to a contract to those whose effect is *not* excludable by agreement, rules which are, therefore, "mandatory" in a normal sense, i.e. belonging to *ius cogens*.[198] Instead, the term allows the inclusion of rules which simply apply in the absence of any express contractual provision, but which *may* be the subject of contrary contractual exclusion, i.e. rules belonging to *ius dispositivum*.[199] However, this leaves open the question as to whether the term "mandatory" adds anything to the phrase "statutory or regulatory provisions". If it does not,[200] as was apparently the view

---

193 1999 Regulations regs 5(1), 6(2); 1994 Regulations reg.3.

194 Below, paras 15–129—15–130; 15–045—15–063 respectively.

195 For fuller discussion of the questions raised in this paragraph, see Whittaker (2000) 116 L.Q.R. 95, 116–119.

196 1999 Regulations reg.4(2)(a).

197 1994 Regulations reg.3(1) Sch.1 para.(e)(i).

198 This also rules out any association with the meaning found in private international law: see, for example, the Rome Convention on the law applicable to contractual obligations of June 19, 1980 art.7(1).

199 This is made clear by French jurists for whom the distinction between *ius cogens* (*loi impérative*) and *ius dispositivum* (*loi supplétive*) is traditional: see notably Ghestin and Marchessaux-Van Melle J.C.P. 1995 I.3854 at No.6.

200 If it were thought necessary to rescue reference to "mandatory" from redundancy, it could be interpreted as referring to a term which applies whether or not the parties agree *that it should apply*.

of the drafters of the 1994 Regulations, then this is a very wide category of exclusion of terms from the ambit of the controls of the Regulations, and one of particular importance in the provision of public services, where some or even many of the terms are set by legislation. This is certainly the context of the application of the exclusion found in art.1(2) of the Directive in other European national laws where the practice is more widespread of the setting of standard terms for certain services by administrative decree.[201]

However, it has been suggested that use by the Directive of the term "mandatory" refers to the jurisprudence of the European Court on "mandatory provisions" restricting the ambit of freedom of movement of goods associated with the famous *Cassis de Dijon* decision.[202] According to this view, terms ought not to be considered "mandatory" unless they are imposed in the general interest of the market and of its users, and not merely in those of the suppliers of the service. The importance of such a view would lie particularly in the context of the provision of public services, where terms are sometimes imposed on consumers in the interests of the public supplier.[203] While this position is clearly attractive as a matter of consumer protection in that it narrows art.1(2), it is not without difficulty. The *Cassis de Dijon* jurisprudence provides a Member State with grounds of justification for allowing obstacles to the free movement of goods, further to those found in art.30 of the EC Treaty,[204] where these obstacles are necessary to satisfy: 15–040

> "... mandatory requirements relating in particular to the effectiveness of fiscal supervision, the protection of public health, the fairness of commercial transactions, and the defence of the consumer."[205]

This therefore allows a Member State to have legal rules which derogate from the principle of freedom of movement of goods if these rules are justified in the interest, for example, of consumer protection or public health. However, this jurisprudence does not altogether fit into the law on unfair contract terms, for the nature of the public interest considerations in the two contexts are very different: for example, in the context of the application of the Directive to the provision of public services, a particular term imposed by law in a contract may be justified as a matter of national law on the basis of the organisation of the public service in question or on an idea such as the importance of the continuity of the public

[201] e.g. the standard terms on which passengers travel by train on the French national carrier, *SNCF*, on which see Whittaker in Freedland and Auby (eds), *The Public Law/Private Law Divide* (2006), pp.243, 249 et seq.

[202] *Rewe-Zentrale AG v Bundesmonopolverwaltung für Branntwein* (120/78) [1979] E.C.R. 649. For this view, see Tenreiro (1993) 7 *Contrats-Concurrence-Consommation* 1, 2; cited with apparent approval by Trochu (1993) *D.S. Chron* 315, 317. See also the joint report of the National Consumer Council and the French *Institut National de la Consommation* in Hall and Tixador (eds), *Rapport sur l'application de la Directive 93/13/1993 du Conseil du 5 avril 1993 concernant les clauses abusives dans les contrats conclus avec les consommateurs aux prestations de service public* (published by the European Commission on the internet, 1997), pp.118–119.

[203] National Consumer Council and the French *Institut National de la Consommation, Rapport sur l'application de la Directive 93/13/1993*, pp.117–118.

[204] Formerly art.36 EEC.

[205] See Craig and De Burca, *EU Law*, 4th edn (2008), p.677 et seq.

service. It is difficult to see how either a national court or the European Court could weigh this sort of "public interest" with the competing interest of consumer protection as expressed by the Directive's requirements of fairness and transparency. But it is even more difficult to see how an ordinary business supplier of services would be in a position to justify in the *public* interest the terms on which it deals, these terms being imposed on it by a Member State for reasons which may be not at all obvious. In conclusion, it is considered that these difficulties are likely to lead the European Court to adopt the wider view of art.1(2) of the Directive, with the result that all terms required to be included in a consumer contract by law would be excluded from its scope.[206]

15–041 A second question of interpretation of art.1(2) concerns what is meant by the word "reflect" in the phrase "contractual terms which reflect mandatory statutory or regulatory provisions". A narrow interpretation would be that this refers only to those contract terms which are required by legislation or regulation to be inserted in the contract in question. However, recital 13 of the Directive's reference to "provisions . . . which directly or indirectly determine the terms of consumer contracts" suggests a broader interpretation. An important category of case which may arguably come within the category of a term which is *indirectly* determined by legislation would be one where the terms of supply of a public service are drawn up by the (commercial) supplier of that service, but then subjected either to a requirement of approval by an administrative body or to a structure of review by a "watchdog" institution. If this approval or review were undertaken under "legislative or regulatory provisions" the latter could be said to "determine indirectly" the content of the contracts. On the other hand, a court could instead distinguish between those provisions which *determine* and those which *provide for approval* of the terms on which services are provided, only the former being within the terms of art.1(2).

15–042 **Terms which reflect "the provisions of international conventions".** The Regulations also provide that their requirements do not apply to: "contractual terms which reflect . . . the provisions or principles of international conventions to which the Member States or the Community are party".[207] As the Directive makes clear, this exclusion is particularly concerned to exclude terms in conventions "in the transport area",[208] notably the Warsaw Convention on international carriage by air.[209] It should be noted that the exception applies to terms which reflect national legislation which uses the *principles* of international conventions to which the Member States or the Community are party, such as in the area of domestic carriage of goods.

15–043 **No application to implied terms.** The question has arisen as to whether an implied term falls within the controls provided by the Regulations. In *Baybut v Eccle Riggs Country Park Ltd* the High Court noted that the Regulations are not

[206] This is assumed by Joerges, (1995) 3 *European Review of Private Law* 175 p.176.
[207] 1999 Regulations reg.4(2)(b); 1994 Regs reg.3(1) Sch.1 para.(e)(ii).
[208] 1993 Directive art.1(2).
[209] See Vol.II, paras 35–002 et seq.

expressly limited to express contract terms,[210] but nevertheless considered that they did not apply to implied terms of any type: not to terms implied by statute, as these fall within the exclusion of terms which reflect "mandatory statutory or regulatory provisions" or the "provisions of international conventions"[211]; nor to terms implied at common law, whether in law or "to make contracts work by filling a technical lacuna in the contract" on the basis that it is difficult to see how these terms (which are implied only where they are reasonable[212]) could ever be found unfair within the meaning of the Regulations.[213] The court also noted that all the examples given in the "indicative list" of terms which may be regarded as unfair in the Schedule to the 1999 Regulations are express terms,[214] to which it may be added that the exclusion from the requirement of fairness of individually negotiated terms makes little sense except in the context of express terms.[215] Finally, while the English version of the 1993 Directive is no more explicit on the question of implied term than the UK Regulations, some of its other language versions use words which are more appropriate to describe what an English lawyer would see as an express term: so the French version of art.1(1) of the Directive refers to its application to "*clauses abusives*"; the German version to "*mißbräuchliche Klauseln*". Overall, the better view is indeed that the Regulations have no application to implied terms as understood by English law.[216]

6. THE REQUIREMENT OF FAIRNESS

Introduction. It has been noted that the Regulations make two requirements of contract terms, that they be fair and that they be expressed in plain, intelligible language and that the range of terms to which these two requirements apply differs to a degree.[217] In this section, the first of these requirements will be examined. 15–044

(a) *Contract Terms Excluded from the Requirement of Fairness*

In general. It has been noted above that in general the Regulations apply to all types of express contract terms, with the exceptions of terms required by legislation or international convention.[218] However, there are two further restrictions on the terms governed by the requirement of fairness. 15–045

---

[210] Unreported November 2, 2006 Ch D at [20], referring to 1999 Regulations regs 4, 5 and 6(2).
[211] Unreported November 2, 2006 Ch D at [22] and see above, para.15–038.
[212] See above, paras 13–007 (text at fn.30), 13–009.
[213] Unreported November 2, 2006 Ch D at [22].
[214] Unreported November 2, 2006 Ch D at [23] and see below paras 15–091—15–107.
[215] Unreported November 2, 2006 Ch D at [23].
[216] This view was endorsed by Andrew Smith J. in *OFT v Abbey National Plc* [2008] EWHC 875 (Comm) at [102].
[217] See above, para.15–038.
[218] Above, paras 15–039—15–042.

(i) *The Exclusion of Terms which have been "Individually Negotiated"*

15–046 **"Where the term has not been individually negotiated".** The requirement of fairness is restricted to terms of standard form contracts, this being expressed negatively by the exclusion of individually negotiated terms.[219] This exclusion reflects earlier pressure on the drafters of the Directive from those (and notably two German lawyers, Brandner and Ulmer) who considered that the inclusion within the scope of the proposed directive of "individually negotiated terms" represented "a drastic restriction of the autonomy of the individual".[220] Clearly, there is considerable practical similarity between this exclusion and the familiar restriction of the requirement of reasonableness to "written standard terms of business" found in s.3 of the Unfair Contract Terms Act 1977, but there are also some technical differences.[221] First, the test in the Regulations includes within the requirement of fairness a *non-standard* term as long as it was drafted in advance and presented or imposed on the consumer; secondly, unlike the restriction found in s.3 where the "written standard terms" must be "the other's" (i.e. those of the person acting in the course of a business and relying on a contract term falling within the section's controls), under the Regulations the exclusion of "individually negotiated terms" leaves within the control of fairness standard terms other than those belonging to the seller or supplier, for example, terms proposed or promoted by a trade association or third party intermediary. And, thirdly, there is no requirement equivalent to s.3's restriction to "terms *of business*", a restriction which has led the courts to exclude from the test of reasonableness under the 1977 Act a standard term of employment of a bank on the basis that its relevant business for this purpose was banking.[222]

15–047 **"Individual negotiation".** Moreover, the Regulations weight the issue of individual negotiation firmly in favour of the consumer, providing that:

> " . . . a term shall always be regarded as not having been individually negotiated where it has been drafted in advance and the consumer has therefore not been able to influence the substance of the term."[223]

The Regulations also place the burden of proof as to the issue of individual negotiation on the person who claims that a term has been so negotiated.[224] Finally, it is also provided that:

> "Notwithstanding that a specific term or certain aspects of it in a contract has been individually negotiated, these Regulations shall apply to the rest of a contract if an overall assessment of it indicates that it is a pre-formulated standard contract."[225]

Thus, the presence of an individually negotiated term in a consumer contract does not necessarily exclude the application of the Regulations to the rest of the

---

[219] 1999 Regulations reg.5(1); 1994 Regulations reg.3.

[220] Brandner and Ulmer (1991) 29 C.M.L.R. 647 at 652; Howells and Wilhelmsson, *EC Consumer Law* (1997), p.91.

[221] On which cf. above, para.14–072.

[222] *Keen v Commerzbank AG* [2006] EWCA Civ 1536, [2007] I.C.R. 623 at [103]–[104].

[223] 1999 Regulations reg.5(2) and see 1994 Regulations reg.3(3).

[224] 1999 Regulations reg.5(4); 1994 Regulations reg.3(5).

[225] 1999 Regulations reg.5(3) and see 1994 Regulations reg.3(4).

contract. This means that, for example, the general terms of a standard form contract of consumer sale whose delivery date for the goods, price or other particular aspect of the contract has been "individually negotiated" will not escape the requirement of fairness altogether.

Standard terms put forward by the consumer. In *Bryen & Langley Ltd v Boston* the question arose as to how, if at all, the 1999 Regulations affected standard terms (here, terms of one of the JCT standard building contracts) put forward by a consumer (or rather by his professional advisers) and incorporated into a consumer contract.[226] In the Court of Appeal Rimer J. noted that the consumer before him had had: 15–048

> "... the opportunity to influence the terms on which the contractors were being invited to tender, even though he may not have taken it up; and [that] there is therefore at least an argument"

that the terms were not therefore "not individually negotiated"; but he expressed no view on this point which had not been argued, it being held instead that in these circumstances any term of the standard contract would not fail the requirement of fairness as it would not cause a significant imbalance in the rights and obligations of the parties to the detriment of the consumer *contrary to the requirement of good faith*.[227] It is submitted with respect that the latter reflects the correct approach. There is nothing in the provisions of the 1999 Regulations or the 1993 Directive to support the proposition that standard terms put forward by a consumer fall for that reason within their exclusion of individually negotiated terms, particularly bearing in mind that this exclusion is to be interpreted strictly following the general approach of the European Court of Justice to exceptions to European legislative schemes of consumer protection.[228] For while a consumer who proposes a set of standard terms may sometimes have "been able to influence the substance of the term" (by amending or deleting the standard terms which he himself proposes), this will not always be the case. Moreover, the exclusion from the requirement of fairness affects contract terms which have been the object of "individual negotiation", whereas a term in a set of standard terms proposed by the consumer remains standard (and often unknown to, or not understood by, the consumer and possibly even his professional advisers) and not therefore (at least normally) "*individually* negotiated". For these reasons, the putting forward of standard terms by a consumer should be dealt with in terms of the requirement of good faith, rather than in terms of their "individual negotiation".[229]

[226] [2005] EWCA Civ 973, [2005] All E.R. (D) 507 (Jul) on appeal from [2004] EWHC 2450 (TCC), 98 Con. L.R. 82.

[227] [2005] EWCA Civ 973 at [46] and cf. [2004] EWHC 2450 (TCC) at [43] (Judge Richard Seymour Q.C.).

[228] 1993 Directive art.3(1) and (2); 1999 Regulations reg.5(1)–(4). On the strict interpretation of exceptions see *Veedfald* (C–203/99) [2001] E.C.R. 1–3569; *EasyCar (UK) Ltd v Office of Fair Trading* (C–336/05) [2005] ECR I–1947, at [54].

[229] See below, para.15–086.

(ii) *The Partial Exclusion of "Core Terms"*

15–049 **The exclusion in the 1999 Regulations.** Regulation 6(2) of the 1999 Regulations (reflecting very closely art.4(2) of the Directive) provides that:

> "In so far as it is in plain intelligible language, the assessment of fairness of a term shall not relate—
>
> (a) to the definition of the main subject matter of the contract, or
> (b) to the adequacy of the price or remuneration, as against the goods or services supplied in exchange."[230]

This is an important provision, reflecting the focus of concern of the Directive on unfair *terms*, rather than on unfair *contracts* and so ruling out (in principle) from its ambit any review of contracts on the basis that they represent a bad bargain, from the point of view of the consumer. In the English context, it has become usual to refer to the exclusion contained in reg.6(2) as relating to "core terms", but before discussing its content and significance, it is worth explaining the background to the Directive's provision as the manner of its drafting gives rise to some difficulty.

15–050 **The *travaux préparatoires*.** The original proposal for a Directive governing unfair contract terms from the EC Commission did not contain any exclusion equivalent to art.4(2) as promulgated,[231] but this proposal met with some powerful criticism, of which the most forceful and obviously most successful was by two German lawyers, Brandler and Ulmer, whose very widely-known article was translated into English.[232] In common with their concern with the proposal's inclusion under the test of unfairness of "individually negotiated terms",[233] Brandler and Ulmer asked:

> " . . . whether the control is to extend to the terms specifying the principal obligations entered into in a contract and, in particular, to the reasonableness of the price in relation to the value of the goods or services to be provided."[234]

In their view, if this were so, it was open to a serious objection, since "[i]n a free market economy parties to a contract are free to shape the principal obligations as they see fit" and any control of the relationship between the price and the goods or services is "anathema to the fundamental tenets of a free market economy".[235] Instead, they proposed that:

> " . . . if the harmonization of the national laws of the Member States relating to the protection of consumers against unfair contract terms is to contribute to the balance of

---

[230] And cf. 1994 Regulations reg.3(2).

[231] EC Commission, Proposal for a Council Directive on unfair terms in consumer contracts COM(90) 322 fin.

[232] Brandner and Ulmer, (1991) 28 C.M.L.R. 645. For a (somewhat controversialist) account of the political process of the enactment of the Directive see Niglia, *The Transformation of Contract in Europe* (2003) pp.119–145.

[233] Above, para.15–046.

[234] Brandner and Ulmer at 655.

[235] Brandner and Ulmer at 656.

the parties' rights and obligations, this should be achieved not by the wholly unsuitable means of controlling the terms of the contract, but rather by *improving the transparency* in this area. The requirement of transparency is directed against terms which may *conceal* the principal obligations or the price and thus make it difficult for the consumer to obtain an overview of the market and to make what would (relatively speaking) be the best choice in a given situation."[236]

In reading art.4(2) of the Directive as promulgated, it is very striking that both elements of this argument (the exclusion of terms determining the price and principal obligations but also the proviso relating to their "transparency") are reflected; indeed, even the language which Brandner and Ulmer use to describe the question is echoed in the wording of art.4(2) and recital 19.[237] This background to art.4(2) draws attention to the double purpose of the provision. First, it seeks to ensure that the Directive does not interfere with the free operation of the market—which indeed, it seeks to facilitate by establishing the internal market,[238] encouraging the confidence of consumers in making transactions (especially cross-border),[239] and removing distortions in competition between sellers and suppliers.[240] Moreover, secondly, it is concerned to ensure that a consumer's choice in relation to the price and main subject matter of the contract is a genuine one, by what Brandler and Ulmer term the principle of transparency. This is therefore the purpose of the proviso to the exclusion found at the end of art.4(2) to the effect that review is excluded only "in so far as these terms are in plain intelligible language". However, it is also clear that the definition of the main subject matter of the contract ("the nature of the goods or services for which the contract was concluded"[241]) and the level of the price[242] were not excluded altogether from the purview of the Directive as they remain relevant for the assessment of terms which do not themselves define these essential elements.[243]

"Core terms" or "core issues"? Regulation 6(2) of the 1999 Regulations follows closely the wording of art.4(2) of the Directive but while the overall purpose of these provisions is clear, it is less clear how this purpose is intended technically to be achieved. This degree of uncertainty was reflected in a subtle change in its treatment by the two sets of regulations: in the 1994 Regulations, the text implementing art.4(2) of the Directive was placed as an exception under the heading "Terms to which these Regulations apply"; in the 1999 Regulations, the text implementing art.4(2) was placed in a provision headed "assessment of unfair terms", following in this respect the framework of the Directive itself. The 15–051

[236] Bradner and Ulmer at 645 (original emphasis).

[237] cf. Joerges (1995) *European Review of Private Law* 175, 184–185 noting the "decisive criticism" from Germany of the proposal for a Directive of 1990.

[238] 1993 Directive recitals 1, 6.

[239] 1993 Directive recital 7.

[240] 1993 Directive recital 2.

[241] 1993 Directive art.4(1).

[242] 1993 Directive recital 16 ("consumer having inducement to agree to term relevant to good faith"); recital 19 ("the price/quality ratio may nevertheless be taken into account in assessing the fairness of other terms").

[243] EC Commission, Report on the implementation of Council Directive 93/13 on unfair terms in consumer contracts COM(2000) 248 final, at III.1(c).

question of substance behind this difference is whether art.4(2) (and therefore reg.6(2)) excludes a category of terms from the ambit of the requirement of fairness ("core terms" or "core provisions") or whether (where it applies) it instead excludes certain types of issue from being taken into account by the courts ("core issues") in coming to their overall assessment of the fairness of a term under reg.5(1).[244] The *position* of art.4(2) of the Directive suggests the latter, as does the first part of its text ("*assessment* of the unfair nature of the terms *shall relate neither* to the definition of the subject-matter"). Moreover, it may be thought unusual for a particular term itself to "relate . . . to the adequacy of the price or remuneration, *as against* the goods or services supplied in exchange". On the other hand, the last phrase of art.4(2) suggests the exclusion of a category of term ("in so far as *these terms* are in plain intelligible language"): indeed, it is difficult to understand how a failure in the requirement of transparency could relate other than to a term or terms, so as to attract review on the grounds of fairness where otherwise there would be none under art.4(2). Finally, recital 19 states that:

> "... assessment shall not be made of *terms which describe* the main subject matter of the contract nor the quality/price ratio of the goods or services supplied,"[245]

continuing that:

> "... the main subject matter of the contract and the price/quality ratio may nevertheless be taken into account in assessing the fairness of *other* terms."[246]

So, as earlier indicated, it is not that these factors cannot generally be taken into account in the application of the test of fairness; the fairness of the overall bargain may be relevant to the fairness of the contract's incidental terms; but these factors cannot generally be taken into account where they are the central concern of the contract term in question, since the relevant term itself cannot be assessed for fairness. The view that reg.6(2) excludes a category of term appears to be reflected in the language used by members of the House of Lords in *Director General of Fair Trading v First National Bank Plc* in their interpretation of this provision, recourse being made to recital 19 for this purpose,[247] though it is to be recalled that this decision actually concerned reg.3(2)(b) of the 1994 Regulations.

15–052 However, having reviewed the textual arguments for and against these two interpretations of reg.6(2) outlined in the previous paragraph (and set out in an earlier edition of the present work), in *OFT v Abbey National Plc*[248] Andrew

---

[244] Whittaker (2001) 117 L.Q.R. 215, 219; Law Commission, *Unfair Contract Terms* (2002), Law Com. Consultation Paper, No.166, paras 3.19 et seq.

[245] cf. Law Com., Consultation Paper, No.166, para.3.28 which suggests that recital 19 may be read as recognising a difference between the rule against assessment of "terms which describe the main subject matter" and assessment of "the quality/price" itself, but this approach does not accord with all other language versions of recital 19, e.g. the French version.

[246] Emphasis added.

[247] [2001] UKHL 52, [2002] 1 A.C. 481 at [12], [34], [42]–[43].

[248] [2008] EWHC 875 (Comm).

Smith J. expressed the view (though strictly speaking obiter[249]) that reg.6(2)(b) excludes an assessment relating to the adequacy of the price from a term to which it applies on the ground that it is:

> "... difficult to understand how, if an excluded term construction is preferred, any real force can be given to the reference to 'adequacy' or indeed how exempted assessments are limited to those which concern the price/quality ratio or the essential bargain between the parties."[250]

However, the learned judge had "much sympathy" with the view that the distinction between the two interpretations of reg.6(2)(b) was:

> "... an elusive one to apply, increasingly so the more tightly the ambit of Regulation 6(2)(b) is confined to terms that deal with the adequacy of the price, rather than terms concerned with the price or remuneration."[251]

A resolution of the difficulty? It is submitted that the view adopted by Andrew Smith J. can be interpreted as leading to an interpretation of reg.6(2) of the Regulations (art.4(2) of the Directive) which combines the ideas of an excluded category of terms and an excluded category of issues and may appear therefore to provide something of a third position between the two positions outlined above.[252] According to such an interpretation, where a contract term defines the main subject-matter of the contract or sets the *main* price or remuneration for the property or services supplied (as opposed to a term which varies the price or sets modalities for its payment or the consequences of its non-payment[253]) (a "core term"), then, provided that it does so in a "plain, intelligible" way, the definition of the main subject matter and the adequacy of the price in relation to the property or services are not to be challenged on the grounds of fairness, but the term may be assessed on *other* grounds of unfairness. On the other hand, where a core term (defined in the above way) is not "plain and intelligible" then its definition of the main subject matter or adequacy of the price in relation to the property or services are themselves open to challenge on the grounds of unfairness. However, the difficulty with this interpretation lies not merely in the elusive nature of its practical implications,[254] but in the impossibility of applying the basic test of unfairness provided by the Regulations (and the Directive) to a "core term" without taking into account "core issues". For, it is surely meaningless to subject a term whose purpose is the allocation of the parties' rights and obligations regarding the main subject matter of the contract or its price to a test of unfairness based on a "significant imbalance in the parties rights and obligations" without reference to the effect of the term on the parties' 15–053

[249] [2008] EWHC 875 at [422]–[436]. The decision was decided on the basis that contract terms in question did not "relate to the adequacy of the price or remuneration, as against the goods or services supplied in exchange" within the meaning of reg.6(2)(b) of the Regulations; below, para.15–059.

[250] [2008] EWHC 875 at [424].

[251] [2008] EWHC 875 at [423].

[252] Above, para.15–051.

[253] Terms relating to the price of these sorts are clearly included within the test of fairness, below, paras 15–054, 15–098, 15–103.

[254] Above, para.15–052.

relative rights and obligations! And it is submitted that the *other* elements provided by the Directive for the assessment of the unfairness of a term cannot not be "taken into account" under art.4(1)[255] where the basic test of unfairness in art.3(1) could not have any meaningful application. Clearly, though, if this line of argument holds good, then the "third position" outlined above can be seen to dissolve into the position earlier preferred as a matter of the drafting of the text of art.4(2) and recital 19 of the Directive and suggested by its *travaux préparatoires*, that is, that art.4(2) excludes from assessment on the ground of unfairness a category of terms provided that they are expressed in plain and intelligible language.

15–054 **The distinction between "core terms" and other terms.** With respect to the position adopted by the learned judge in the *Bank Charges* case,[256] the better view,[257] therefore, remains that reg.6(2) excludes from the requirement of fairness terms which define either the subject matter of the contract or the adequacy of the price, this trying to capture a distinction between the term or terms which express the substance of the bargain and "incidental" (if important) terms which surround them.[258] In many cases it will be clear that the term whose fairness is challenged does not relate to the core of the contract and in this respect the inclusion of a particular type of term in the "grey list" found in Sch.2 to the Regulations will be particularly helpful,[259] as it describes terms which are potentially unfair and thereby assumes that these terms are subject to the requirement of fairness.[260] In this respect, terms governing the price to be paid by a consumer do not necessarily fall outside the requirement of fairness, for Sch.2 gives as an example of a term which *may* be unfair one which allows the other party to determine the price at the time of delivery of any goods supplied or to increase the price without giving the consumer a right to cancel the contract.[261] Moreover, as has earlier been noted, according to recital 19 of the Directive:

[255] See especially 1993 Directive art.4(1), and see para.15–074 et seq.

[256] Above, para.15–053.

[257] This view finds support in the view taken by the EC Commission official responsible for the Directive: Tenreiro and Ferioli, *Examen comparatif des législations nationales transposant la directive 93/13* in section "The integration of Directive 93/13 into the national legal systems" contribution to conference *The "Unfair Terms Directive" of 1999*, proceedings available at *http://ec.europa.eu/consumers/rights/gen_rights_en.htm 5* [Accessed June 19, 2008] (referring (in French) to art.4(2): "[T]he third limitation on the scope of application of the directive, that is to say, the exclusion of contract terms which concern the definition of the price and the main subject matter of the contract as long as these are plain and intelligible"); and see also Cámara Lapuente, *El control de las cláusulas "abusivas" sobre elementos esenciales del contracto* (2006), pp.16–18, 109–114, 117–118.

[258] The last phrase in the text was quoted with apparent approval by Lord Bingham of Cornhill in *Director General of Fair Trading v First National Bank Plc* [2001] UKHL 52 at [12].

[259] 1999 Regulations Sch.2; 1994 Regulations Sch.3.

[260] See below, para.15–091 et seq. for the list.

[261] See 1999 Regulations reg.5(5) Sch.2 para.1(l); 1994 Regulations reg.4(4) Sch.3 para.(l). Cf. EC Commission, *Report on the Implementation of Directive 93/13/EEC on unfair terms in consumer contracts* COM(2000) 248 final, p.15 which contends that: "[T]erms concerning the price do indeed fall within the remit of the Directive, since the exclusion concerns the adequacy of the price and remuneration as against the services or goods supplied in exchange and nothing else. The terms laying down the manner of calculation and the procedures for altering the price remain entirely subject to the Directive."

"... the main subject matter of the contract and the price/quality ratio may ... be taken into account in assessing the fairness of other [i.e. non-core] terms."

While this idea is not explicitly reflected in the Regulations, it may be included under their injunction to take into account in assessing the fairness of a term "*all* the other terms of the contract".[262]

Insurance contracts. The Directive itself recognises the potential difficulty in applying the exclusion found in art.4(2) and attempts to explain the distinction drawn in the previous paragraph in the context of one particular example, contracts of insurance.[263] So recital 19 states that: 15–055

"... it follows [from the exclusion of core terms] *inter alia*, that in insurance contracts, the terms which clearly define or circumscribe the insured risk and the insurer's liability shall not be subject to such assessment since these restrictions are taken into account in calculating the premium paid by the consumer."

On the basis of this explanation, the Law Commission has taken the view that "an exception to the cover may be taken as defining the cover", but subject to two conditions: first, that the term in question is in "plain intelligible language" and, secondly, that it substantially conforms to the way in which consumers perceived the bargain.[264] This second condition (which is not expressly provided by recital 19 nor by art.4(2) of the Directive) is related to the more general position taken by the Office of Fair Trading and the Law Commission (and described below) according to which the identification of the "main subject matter of the contract" should be viewed from the point of view of the consumer.[265] On the other hand, it is submitted that the type of clause found in a consumer insurance contract which *would* normally be subject to the requirement of fairness would be one which imposes conditions as to the time or other circumstances in which a claim may be brought or one which purports to impose a duty of disclosure on a consumer more burdensome than the law of *uberrimae fides* as neither of these types of clause would define or circumscribe the risk.[266]

[262] 1999 Regulations reg.6(1); 1994 Regulations reg.4(2). Emphasis added.

[263] There is no equivalent explanatory provision in either the 1994 or the 1999 Regulations.

[264] Law Commission, *Insurance Contract Law: Misrepresentation, Non-disclosure and Breach of Warranty by the Insured* (Law Com. No. 182, 2007), paras 2.72–2.94, especially 2.82 and 2.87. The Law Commission also discusses the position as to warranties made by the consumer: paras 2.95–2.102.

[265] Below, para.15–058.

[266] For example, a clause which makes the accuracy of *all* statements made during the course of negotiations a condition precedent to liability, which on its terms would prevent a consumer from claiming that such a statement was immaterial to the risk: see Vol.II, para.41–031. cf. *Bankers Insurance Co Ltd v South* [2003] EWHC 380, [2003] P.I.Q.R. P28 at [21] (exclusion in travel insurance agreed as defining "main subject matter of the contract"). The French administrative body charged with advising on the fairness of terms under its legislation implementing the Directive (this legislation retaining the exclusion of "core terms": *loi* no.95–96 of February 1, 1995, art.1, new arts L.132–1 et seq. *Code de la consommation*) has advised that a clause in a contract of car insurance which makes the indemnity subject to having the damage actually repaired is unfair: *Rapport de la Commission des clauses abusives* (1996), pp.18–20.

15–056 **The *First National Bank Plc* decision.** In *Director General of Fair Trading v First National Bank Plc*[267] the House of Lords took a restrictive approach to the interpretation of the exclusion of "core terms" from the test of fairness now found in reg.6(2) of the 1999 Regulations. There, a contract of consumer credit contained a term by which:

> ". . . interest on the amount which becomes payable [on default] shall be charged in accordance [with rates stipulated by the contract] . . . until payment after as well as before any judgment (such obligation to be independent of and not to merge with the judgment)."

The effect of this agreement (if valid) would be that where the bank obtains judgment against a borrower, interest would be payable at the contractual rate on the outstanding principal plus accrued interest unpaid at the date of judgment until the judgment is discharged by payment. It would prevent the independent obligation to pay interest to merge in the judgment, the provision for interest at the contractual rate continuing to apply after judgment. The bank argued that this contract term did not fall to be assessed for fairness under the Regulations because it concerned the adequacy of the bank's remuneration as against the services supplied, namely the loan of money.[268] The House of Lords disagreed. In the view of Lord Bingham of Cornhill:

> "The object of the Regulations and the Directive is to protect consumers against the inclusion of unfair and prejudicial terms in standard-form contracts into which they enter, and that object would plainly be frustrated if reg.3(2)(b) were so broadly interpreted as to cover any terms other than those falling squarely within it. In my opinion the term, as part of a provision prescribing the consequences of default, plainly does not fall within it. It does not concern the adequacy of the interest earned by the bank as its remuneration but is designed to ensure that the bank's entitlement to interest does not come to an end on the entry of judgment."[269]

As Lord Steyn observed:

> ". . . regulation 3(2) must be given a restrictive interpretation. Unless that is done regulation 3(2)(a) will enable the main purpose of the scheme to be frustrated by endless formalistic arguments as to whether a provision is a definitional or an exclusionary provision."[270]

In this respect, the fact that the contract term before them was a "default provision" clearly weighed with the House.[271] Having said this, though, in applying the test of fairness to this contract term, for the House of Lords the fact that it related to the payment of interest which was part of the "essential bargain"

---

[267] [2001] UKHL 52, [2002] 1 A.C. 481 and see Whittaker (2004) ZEuP 75.

[268] [2001] UKHL 52 at [10].

[269] [2001] UKHL 52 at [12]. References to reg.3(2)(b) refer to the 1994 Regulations.

[270] [2001] UKHL 52 at [34]. This restrictive approach to the interpretation of an exception to the Directive's scheme of protection is fully supported by the case law of the ECJ in the consumer *acquis*: *Veedfald* (C–203/99) [2001] E.C.R. I–3569 at [15]; *EasyCar (UK) Ltd v Office of Fair Trading* (C–336/03) [2005] E.C.R. I–1947 at [54].

[271] [2001] UKHL 52 at [11]–[12], [34], [43].

between the parties argued in favour of its fairness.[272] In the result, the House of Lords held that the term in question did *not* fall within the exclusion found in art.4(2) of the Directive, but nevertheless "carries into effect what the parties themselves would regard as the essence of the transaction" and was held valid.[273]

The relevance of the construction of the contract. In *Bairstow Eves London Central Ltd v Smith*,[274] the House of Lords' approach in the *First National Bank Plc* case[275] to this exclusion from the requirement of fairness was applied to clauses setting the fee in an estate agency contract made with a consumer vendor. Under the estate agents' standard terms, the "standard commission" payable to them was set at 3 per cent of the sale price of the property, but "early payment" attracted a "discount rate" of 1.5 per cent of the sale price, early payment being defined as payment of the full sum payable within 10 working days of completion of the sale. It was further provided that if such a full sum was not paid within this time, the "standard commission" would become payable together with interest at 3 per cent above base rate. After completing a sale, the vendor's solicitors did not pay the agent the *full* sum of the "discount rate" within the 10 day period (falling short by a mere £387), and so the estate agent claimed the "standard rate" plus interest. On being sued for this, the vendor argued that the terms of the contract setting the 3 per cent commission rate were unfair within the meaning of the 1999 Regulations, to which the agents countered that these terms were excluded from the requirement of fairness as they related to the "adequacy of the price or remuneration, as against the goods or services supplied in exchange" by reg.6(2). Gross J. held that the applicability of this exclusion turned on an issue of construction of the contract, viz whether the agreement provided for a 3 per cent commission rate (or price) with the vendors having an option (but no obligation) to pay 1.5 per cent (in which case reg.6(2) *would* apply) or an obligation to pay a price of 1.5 per cent, with a "default" provision exercisable at the estate agents' option to insist on payment of 3 per cent (in which case reg.6(2) *would not* apply).[276] In his view, the prevailing market, the pre-contractual negotiations between the parties, and their expectation that the 1.5 per cent commission would be paid within 10 days all indicated that *both* the parties to the contract contemplated an agreed operative price of 1.5 per cent with a default provision of 3 per cent.[277] This view of the parties' intention was not precluded by the language used by the agreement as set in its contractual matrix, even though "at first blush" the reference to the higher price as the "standard commission rate" and the lower as the "early payment discounted rate" suggested the opposite conclusion[278]: the idea that there was merely an option in the consumer (rather than an obligation) to pay the lower rate was "simply fanciful".[279] As a result, reg.6(2) 15–057

[272] [2001] UKHL 52 at [20] and see below, para.15–082.

[273] [2001] UKHL 52 at [56] per Lord Millett and see below, para.15–082.

[274] [2004] EWHC 263, [2004] 2 E.G.L.R. 25.

[275] *Director General of Fair Trading v First National Bank Plc* [2001] UKHL 52, [2002] 1 A.C. 481, above, para.15–056.

[276] [2004] EWHC 263 at [26].

[277] [2004] EWHC 263 at [27]

[278] [2004] EWHC 263 at [29]

[279] [2004] EWHC 263 at [30].

did not exclude this "default provision" from the requirement of fairness. Given that the view of the judge below that the clauses in question were unfair had not been appealed, the estate agent's claim to the higher commission rate failed.

15–058 **Reasonable understanding of "average consumer".** However, with respect, it is submitted that treating the issue whether a particular term falls within reg.6(2) as turning on construction of the term in the ordinary common law sense (and therefore on the intention of the parties as seen in their factual matrix) as to whether the term set the price itself or merely set a "default sum" is not appropriate in the context. For, the exclusion of "core terms" by reg.6(2) is contained in an EC directive aimed (in part) at the protection of consumers and this purpose should be borne in mind in setting the perspective from which the proper qualification of a contract term as relating neither to the definition of the main subject matter of the contract nor to the adequacy of the price and remuneration, on the one hand, as against the services or goods should be seen.[280] In this respect, the Director General of Fair Trading earlier expressed the view that:

> "... it would be difficult to claim that any term was a core term unless it was central to *how consumers perceived* the bargain. A supplier would surely find it hard to sustain the argument that a contract's main subject matter was defined by a term which a consumer had been given no real chance to see and read before signing it—in other words if that term had not been properly drawn to the consumer's attention."[281]

Rather than relying on the construction of the contract in the traditional way (the intention of both the contracting parties as viewed objectively), this view proposes that a court should look at the reasonable expectation of the consumer in question.[282] And in *OFT v Abbey National Plc* this view was accepted by the High Court as appropriate given the significance of the notion of an 'average consumer' in the jurisprudence of the European Court of Justice.[283]

15–059 **The Bank Charges case.** In *OFT v Abbey National Plc*, the High Court considered whether a number of terms in contracts governing the current accounts between six major clearing banks and their consumer customers fell within the test of unfairness.[284] The terms in question (which were contained in contracts currently in effect[285]) had in common that they imposed charges made by banks to their customers who have current accounts with them when they are requested or instructed to make a payment for which they do not hold the necessary funds in the account and which is not covered by a facility arranged by

---

[280] 1993 Directive art.4(2).

[281] Office of Fair Trading, *Unfair Contract Terms*, Bulletin no.2 (September 1993), p.13, para.2.26 (emphasis added).

[282] See further Law Com. No.166, paras 4.55–4.59 where it is recommended that future unifying legislation on unfair contract terms should make explicit the reasonable expectations of the consumer for this purpose.

[283] [2008] EWHC 875 at [388]. On "average consumer" generally, see above, para.15–031.

[284] [2008] EWHC 875 (Comm).

[285] The proceedings before the court were not concerned with standard from terms used in the past ("historical terms"): [2008] EWHC 875 (Comm) at [9].

the customer.[286] The question arose, inter alia, whether reg.6(2)(b) of the 1999 Regulations applied so that no assessment of the terms in question should "relate . . . to the adequacy of the price or remuneration, as against the goods or services supplied in exchange" should be undertaken by the court. The banks argued that the charges in question were the price or remuneration either on the ground that they formed part of the total remuneration provided by the customer for their banking services (the "whole package" argument) or on the ground that the charges in question were the price or remuneration for the service or services supplied in connection with the borrowing requests made by the consumer where no facility had been arranged in advance (the "specific services" argument).[287] Andrew Smith J. accepted that he should take a restrictive approach to the interpretation of reg.6(2), relying on the approach advocated by their lordships in the *First National Bank* case[288] and rejecting the argument that it applied only to "default provisions".[289] He then analysed in turn the situations in which consumers requested or instructed a payment to be made for which they do not hold the necessary funds in the account and which is not covered by a facility arranged by the customer, noting that the terms of the standard contracts treated such an [illegible] request (or deemed request) by the customer for an overdraft. He held that where the banks [illegible] on such an instruction, they cannot properly be said to supply services: the "real and essential service supplied by the Banks under the contracts with customers is that of paying upon the customer's instruction".[290] He further held that even where the banks do pay on such an instruction, they do not supply a service within the meaning of reg.6(2): while:

> ". . . the provision of an unarranged overdraft is part of the essential services supplied by a bank operating current accounts. . . . [t]he characterisation of what the Bank provides as an 'arranged overdraft' seems . . . to define it with too great a degree of particularity for the purpose of deciding whether the Bank is supplying a service within the meaning of Regulation 6(2)."[291]

Moreover, in his view, reg.6(2) requires for its application that the "price or remuneration" (a "compendious expression"[292]) is given "in exchange" for the goods or services supplied. In this respect, he held first that the payments in question were not made in exchange for the whole package of services supplied by the bank when operating a current account, nor were they its "price or remuneration".[293] And he further held that where an instruction was not paid by 15–060

---

[286] [2008] EWHC 875 (Comm) at [1].

[287] [2008] EWHC 875 (Comm) at [333].

[288] [2008] EWHC 875 (Comm) at [345]–[358] and see above, para.15–056. Andrew Smith J. expressed the view that the burden of proof rested on the bank to establish the exclusion from the test of unfairness contained in reg.6(2)(b) though stating that his decision did not depend on this view: [2008] EWHC 875 (Comm) at [337].

[289] [2008] EWHC 875 (Comm) at [356].

[290] [2008] EWHC 875 (Comm) at [370].

[291] [2008] EWHC 875 (Comm) at [376].

[292] [2008] EWHC 875 (Comm) at [384].

[293] [2008] EWHC 875 (Comm) at [398].

the bank, any charge was not in exchange for any service[294]; nor was a charge imposed where an instruction was paid:

> "In reality they are not charges in exchange for services involved in making payments, but charges levied because the services are supplied in particular circumstances."[295]

On these grounds, the terms which imposed charges on the consumer customers were not exempt from assessment under the test of unfairness as not terms which "relate . . . to the adequacy of the price or remuneration, as against the goods or services supplied in exchange".[296] And, for the learned judge, this accorded with the "essential bargain" between the banks and their customers which was a "free-if-in-credit" account and:

> "On no view does an assessment of the [charges in question] impinge upon the adequacy of the totality of the benefits received by the Bank in exchange for the package of services"

under such an arrangement.[297]

15–061 **Further examples.** The Director Gen[illegible] relation to an agreement [illegible] provided for delivery of goods in instalments, that a clause which made each delivery a separate contract was potentially unfair because (when combined with another term of the contract) it allowed the seller to increase the price between deliveries[298]: therefore where the parties' dealings in reality form one unitary transaction, a clause which purports to redefine the parties' relations in terms of a series of contracts is to be treated not as going to the subject matter of the contract, but rather as an incidental clause. It has been suggested that (on the assumption that land contracts fall within the ambit of the Regulations), the terms which define the nature of the interest created, and the amount of rent or service charge would qualify as core terms, but forfeiture clauses and "upwards only" rent review clauses would not and would, therefore, be vulnerable.[299]

15–062 **Complicated or unintelligible "core terms" subject to review.** As has been noted, the exclusion of core terms from the fairness requirement of the Regulations is only partial, for it is subject to the proviso that they are expressed in plain and intelligible language: where they are not the terms are for this reason subject to the test of unfairness.[300] In this way, an unintelligible or complicated term

---

[294] [2008] EWHC 875 (Comm) at [403].

[295] [2008] EWHC 875 (Comm) at [406].

[296] [2008] EWHC 875 (Comm) at [420].

[297] [2008] EWHC 875 (Comm) at [421].

[298] Office of Fair Trading, *Unfair Contract Terms*, Bulletin No.2 (September 1996), p.28. cf. *Baybut v Eccle Riggs Country Park Ltd* Unreported November 2, 2006 at [24] where a term setting the duration of a licence for an owner of a caravan to use a commercially operated static caravan park was considered to be a "core term" as it defined the main subject matter of the contract within the meaning of the 1999 Regulations reg.6(2).

[299] Bright and Bright (1995) 111 L.Q.R. 655 pp.670–671.

[300] 1999 Regulations reg.6(2); 1994 Regulations reg.3(2); and see *Bankers Insurance Co Ltd v South* [2003] P.I.Q.R. P.28 at [24] (exclusion in travel insurance held "plain and intelligible").

which defines the subject matter of the contract or provides for the calculation of the price may be assessed as to its fairness.[301] Again, it is submitted that the question of the plainness or intelligibility of such a term should be assessed according to the variable standard of the "average consumer" as earlier explained.[302]

Examples. In *OFT v Abbey National Plc*, the court considered whether a considerable number of terms which imposed the payment of sums of money in certain circumstances (as explained above) were plain and intelligible in a number of ways, holding that many were, but that some were not.[303] A possible further context in which this proviso may apply may be found in conditional fee agreements made with consumers. In 1990 legislation made provision for the lawfulness of such an agreement (defined as "an agreement with a person providing advocacy or litigation services which provides for his fees and expenses . . . to be payable only in specific circumstances"[304]) subject to the fulfilment of certain conditions which it set[305] and which empowered the Lord Chancellor to make regulations setting further conditions.[306] Many of the terms of conditional fee agreements would be classed as relating to their "main subject matter" (as defining the costs, expenses etc. to be covered by the agreement) or the calculation of the price (notably, by providing for a particular percentage of "success fee") so as to fall within the definition of "core terms",[307] but if these terms are contained in a consumer contract and are not expressed in "plain intelligible language" from the point of view of the "average consumer" then they would on this ground fall within the test of unfairness provided by the 1999 Regulations.[308] 15–063

(b) *The composite test of unfairness*

The test in the Regulations. The definition of unfairness contains both familiar and unfamiliar elements for English contract lawyers. Regulation 5(1) of the 1999 Regulations provides that: 15–064

> "A contractual term which has not been individually negotiated shall be regarded as unfair if, contrary to the requirement of good faith, it causes a significant imbalance in

---

[301] On the effect of such a decision on the contract, see below, para.15–125.

[302] Above, para.15–031.

[303] [2008] EWHC 875 (Comm), conclusion at [393]–[394]. cf. above, paras 15–059—15–060.

[304] Courts and Legal Services Act 1990 s.58(2)(a).

[305] Courts and Legal Services Act 1990 s.58(1), (3) & (4).

[306] While regulations were made under this power (principally the Conditional Fee Agreements Regulations 2000 (SI 2000/692)), these were revoked prospectively by the Condition Fee Agreements (Revocation) Regulations 2005 (SI 2005/2305) and have not been replaced.

[307] cf. The Law Society's Model Conditional Fee Agreement November 2005 and its accompanying "What you need to know" leaflet in Law Society, *Payment by Results* (October 2007) appendices 4 and 5 available at *http://www.lawsociety.org.uk*. Use of this standard form is not compulsory for solicitors, but solicitors are subject to important duties of information and explanation about the costs of matters under the Solicitors' Code of Conduct 2007 para.2.03(2).

[308] A possible exception would be where such a term is "required by law" by any regulations made under s.58(3)(c) of the Courts and Legal Services Act 1990 so as to fall within the exception to the ambit of 1999 Regulations which reg.4(2)(a) provides: see above, para.15–039.

> the parties' rights and obligations arising under the contract, to the detriment of the consumer."[309]

Regulation 6(1) further provides that:

> "Without prejudice to regulation 12,[310] the unfairness of a contractual term shall be assessed, taking into account the nature of the goods[311] or services for which the contract was concluded and by referring, at the time of the contract, to all the circumstances attending the conclusion of the contract and to all the other terms of the contract or another contract on which it is dependent."[312]

These provisions provide the basic framework for a sophisticated and composite test of unfairness, its combination of different ideas and considerations being clearly aimed at reducing the degree of uncertainty and discretion which is given to a court in requiring it to judge the fairness of a term. This test can be broken down into two principal elements: (i) the test of unfairness itself (including the significance of the requirement of good faith and the range of considerations relevant to its application); and (ii) the significance and contents of the "indicative" or "grey list" of terms found in Sch.2 of the 1999 Regulations,[313] to which may be added other illustrations of potentially unfair terms.

(i) *The Basic Test*

15–065 **General.** The basic test of unfairness of a term is that:

> "... contrary to the requirement of good faith it causes a significant imbalance in the parties' rights and obligations under the contract, to the detriment of the consumer."

The significance of this test has given rise to considerable comment,[314] and for some its use of the notion of good faith introduced into English law a new and somewhat alien concept, whose significance is far from clear. In this respect, it is helpful to bear in mind the origins of the reference to good faith, this flowing from its use in the German statute which significantly influenced the Directive.[315] In turn, this German statute can be seen as the legislative recognition of existing judicial controls on unfair contract terms, this law-making being justified by the

---

[309] cf. 1994 Regulations reg.4(1).

[310] See below, paras 15–133 et seq.

[311] On the appropriateness of this limitation to goods, see above, paras 15–017—15–019.

[312] cf. 1994 Regulations reg.4(2).

[313] 1994 Regulations Sch.3 and see below, paras 15–091 et seq.

[314] Collins at 229; Beale, Ch.9 pp.242 et seq.; Weatherill (1995) 3 *European Review Private Law* 307; Howells and Willhemson at p.88, pp.96 et seq.; Beatson pp.200–203, 300 et seq., pp.291 et seq.; Bright in Burrows and Peel, *Contract Terms* (2007), ch. 9.

[315] i.e. *Gesetz zur Regelung des Rechts der Allgemeinen Geschäftsbedingungen* ("Standard Contract Terms Act") of 1976, translated in part by Dannemann in Markesinis, Lorenz and Dannemann, at pp.908 et seq. (The German Standard Contracts Act 1976 itself was abrogated and replaced by a revised BGB para.307(1).) The first draft of the Directive was much closer to the German legislation, applying to commercial as well as to consumer contracts. Apart from the German law, the laws of some other Member States law have used the notion of good faith in their control of unfair contract terms, for example, Spanish law: Paisant, Recueil Dalloz Sirey 1995 Chronique p.99, p.100.

Civil Code's general provision requiring good faith of parties to contracts[316]: "good faith" in this context can be seen as little more than a convenient legal pigeon-hole in which to have placed within the structure of the Civil Code judicial developments which took into account a range of considerations deemed appropriate to the control in hand.[317] For this reason, it could be thought that the reference to "good faith" in the Directive is no more than a bow in the direction of these origins. Indeed, such a very limited significance to the phrase "contrary to the requirement of good faith" is adopted by some French writers[318] and this is reflected in its omission from France's implementing legislation.[319] For a French lawyer it is unnecessary for two reasons: first, because the French Civil Code already makes a general requirement of the performance of contracts in good faith[320] (an argument of no significance for English law), but, secondly, because a business supplier could not be considered to remain in good faith if he were to seek to enjoy the disproportionate advantages set out in the contract concluded with the consumer.[321] From this perspective, the requirement that the term "causes a significant imbalance in the parties' rights and obligations under the contract to the detriment of the consumer" is sufficient in itself.

"Significant imbalance" and the role of good faith. However, this French view of good faith misunderstands the particular function of the requirement of good faith in the scheme of the Directive. According to this scheme, the first and basic element of the requirement of fairness is that the term "causes a significant imbalance in the parties' rights and obligations arising under the contract, to the detriment of the consumer". However, not all contract terms which cause such a significant imbalance are to be held unfair. Recital 16 of the Directive explains, therefore, the special role of the requirement of good faith. 15–066

> "Whereas the assessment, according to the general criteria chosen, of the unfair character of the terms, in particular in sale or supply activities of a public nature providing collective services which take account of solidarity among users, must be *supplemented by a means of making an overall evaluation of the different interests involved; whereas this constitutes the requirement of good faith*; whereas, in making an assessment of good faith, particular regard shall be had to the strength of the bargaining positions of the parties, whether the consumer had an inducement to agree to the term and whether the goods or services were sold or supplied to the special order of the consumer; whereas the requirement of good faith may be satisfied by the seller or

[316] BGB para.242 and see Zimmermann, *The New German Law of Obligations* (2005), pp.173–178.

[317] Zimmermann and Whittaker, *Good Faith in European Contract Law* (2000), Ch.1. It is noteworthy that the German Standard Terms Act of 1976 did not attempt to explain the requirement of good faith by reference to the already elaborate case law based on para.242 BGB, but instead listed the clauses which are either necessarily void or are void if they fail a test of "reasonableness": see Standard Contract Terms Act 1976 paras 9–11.

[318] See Larroumet, *Droit Civil*, *Les obligations Le contrat*, 5th edn (2003), Tome 3, p.422; Paisant, at p.100.

[319] *Loi* 95/96 of February 1, 1995 art.L.132–1 al. 1 *Code de la consommation*. Again, this reflects French legislative and judicial tradition which preferred to use the notion of the abuse of rights (hence, "*clauses abusives*") rather than the (admittedly closely related) notion of good faith.

[320] art.1134 al. 3 C.civ.

[321] Paisant at p.100.

supplier where he deals fairly and equitably with the other party whose legitimate interests he has to take into account."[322]

15–067 So, according to the recital, the role of the requirement as to good faith is to ensure that the test of "significant imbalance" ("the general criteria chosen") is not applied in any sense mechanically, but rather the court should in making its assessment of a contract term look to "an overall evaluation of the interests involved". It is interesting, for this purpose, that while some of the factors which the recital mentions as being significant to this evaluation are familiar to English lawyers from the assessment of "reasonableness" under the Unfair Contract Terms Act 1977[323] and may indeed be thought to represent an attempt to interpret good faith particularly for the benefit of common lawyers, the recital gives as a first and particular context for this supplementary requirement of good faith as "sale or supply activities of a public nature providing collective services which take account of solidarity among users". The particular significance of this reference will be discussed later,[324] but its inclusion is important more generally in showing that the function of the requirement of good faith is to ensure that *all* possible relevant considerations may be taken into account in making the overall assessment of the fairness of a term, even where these considerations relate to the public interest and therefore not necessarily to the position of either of the parties to the contract. Furthermore, two of the other circumstances mentioned by the recital as possible elements in this "overall evaluation" illustrate circumstances in which a "significant imbalance in the parties' rights and obligations arising under the contract to the detriment of the consumer" may be justified and therefore fair: where:

> "... the consumer had an inducement to agree to the term [or] ... the goods or services were sold or supplied to the special order of the consumer."

Another element draws attention to the significance of the relative bargaining power of the parties (which will normally rest with the seller or supplier but which may exceptionally rest with the consumer). The final circumstance re-emphasises the inclusive nature of the requirement of good faith, stating that this may be satisfied:

> "... by the seller or supplier where he deals fairly and equitably with the other party whose legitimate interests he has to take into account."

This is clearly related to the requirement in art.4(1) of the Directive that in assessing the fairness of a term, a court should consider "to all the circumstances attending the conclusion of the contract".

---

[322] Emphasis added.

[323] Unfair Contract Terms Act 1977 s.11(1) and Sch.2. The elements specified by recital 16 were included in Sch.2 of the 1994 Regulations, expressly to be taken account of in the assessment of good faith. However, their omission from the text of the 1999 Regulations makes no substantive change as their presence in the preamble to the Directive requires them to be taken into account in the interpretation of its text and, therefore, the text of the 1999 Regulations.

[324] See below, para.15–081.

An autonomous concept of good faith. What all this means, therefore, is that the Directive does require an autonomous interpretation of the concept of good faith, but not one drawn from the significances or uses to which the concept (or related concepts) have been put in the laws of the Member States generally. The concept of good faith is autonomous in the sense that it is specifically European (rather than to be left to the interpretation of national law or national courts), but it is also autonomous in the sense that it is particular to the context of the control of unfair contract terms. It is submitted, therefore, that there is no need or occasion for the European Court (or the court of any Member State) to seek to establish a general *meaning* of good faith in contracts in European contract law, drawn from the domestic laws of the Member States. This is as well given that: 15–068

> "The notion of good faith (or its equivalents in the various languages . . .) actually means different things both *within* a particular legal system and *between* the legal systems."[325]

Indeed, this richness and variety of use is well illustrated by the context of unfair contract terms, for while German law long relied on its general provision on good faith as the legislative foundation of such a control,[326] French law resorted to a number of other techniques, some with a certain kinship to good faith and some not related at all.[327] So, while a German lawyer and a French lawyer may agree with the sort of general statement that good faith requires "fair and open dealing", they may well differ as to the points in their legal regulation of contracts at which they consider it necessary to invoke good faith and, where it applies, what it requires.

Fairness and good faith in the *First National Bank Plc* case. In *Director General of Fair Trading v First National Bank Plc*[328] the House of Lords had occasion to discuss the requirement of good faith and the test of unfairness more generally for the purposes of the Directive. In this respect, Lord Bingham of Cornhill noted the harmonising purpose of the Directive, but also that "the member states have no common concept of fairness or good faith, and that the Directive does not purport to state the law of any single member state".[329] As to good faith, he observed: 15–069

> "The requirement of good faith in this context is one of fair and open dealing. Openness requires that the terms should be expressed fully, clearly and legibly, containing no

[325] Zimmermann and Whittaker, *Good Faith in European Contract Law* (2000), p.690 and see above, para.1–025.

[326] BGB para.242.

[327] Whittaker in Bell, Boyron and Whittaker, *Principles of French Law*, 2nd edn (2008) p.356. French lawyers have long found mechanisms for controlling exemption clauses (often tied to the notion of *ordre public*), but when a legislative framework for more general (if *administrative*) intervention in unfair terms in consumer contracts was introduced in 1978, the association was with *abus de droit* rather than with *mauvaise foi*, though these two notions are closely related: see *loi* 78–23 of January 10, 1978 arts 35–38.

[328] [2001] UKHL 52, [2002] 1 A.C. 481; Macdonald (2002) 65 M.L.R. 763; Dean, (2002) 65 M.L.R. 773; Whittaker (2004) ZEuP 75.

[329] [2001] UKHL 52 at [13].

> concealed pitfalls or traps. Appropriate prominence should be given to terms which might operate disadvantageously to the customer. Fair dealing requires that a supplier should not, whether deliberately or unconsciously, take advantage of the consumer's necessity, indigence, lack of experience, unfamiliarity with the subject matter of the contract, weak bargaining position or any other factor listed in or analogous to those listed in Schedule 2 to the [1994] Regulations. Good faith in this context is not an artificial or technical concept; nor, since Lord Mansfield[330] was its champion, is it a concept wholly unfamiliar to British lawyers. It looks to good standards of commercial morality and practice. Regulation 4(1) lays down a composite test, covering both the making and the substance of the contract, and must be applied bearing clearly in mind the objective which the Regulations are designed to promote."[331]

Clearly, then, good faith is an extremely inclusive concept, potentially comprising elements of both procedural and substantive fairness.[332] However, with the greatest respect, the idea of a business "taking advantage" of the consumer (even if unconsciously) is potentially restrictive, having overtones of bad faith which is clearly unnecessary.[333] As to the specificity of the role of good faith for the purposes of the Regulations, Lord Hope of Craighead is most clear. For having referred to the commentary to the *Principles of European Contract Law* which note the considerable differences between the legal systems of the Member States "as to how powerful the penetration has been of the principle of good faith and fair dealing",[334] he continued that:

> ". . . in the present context there is no need to explore this topic in any depth. The Directive provides all the guidance that is needed as to its application."[335]

The concept of good faith is indeed special to its context and moulded by its function.

(ii) *Particular Elements within the Test of Unfairness*

15–070 **A composite test of unfairness.** It has been seen that the basic test on which courts must review the terms of consumer contracts comprises a number of elements. The overall requirement is that a term is judged unfair and for this purpose the starting point is the criterion of "significant imbalance", this then being qualified by the need to ensure the evaluation of all interests involved (under the requirement of good faith). The Directive (and the Regulations) then go further and specify a number of factors to be taken into account in determining the issue of fairness (the nature of the goods or services, all the circumstances attending the conclusion of the contract and all the other terms of the contract or of another contract on which it is dependent) and finally providing a list of

[330] See *Carter v Boehm* (1766) 3 Burr. 1905, 1910, quoted above, para.1–022.

[331] [2001] UKHL 52 at [17]. See also at [36] (Lord Steyn).

[332] Beale in Beatson and Friedman (eds), *Good Faith and Fault in Contract Law* (1995), Ch.9, p.245.

[333] cf. Macdonald (2002) 65 M.L.R. 763 at p.769.

[334] Lando and Beale (eds), *Principles of European Contract Law, Pts I & II* (combined and revised, 2000), p.116.

[335] [2001] UKHL 52 at [45], referring to recital 16 of the Directive. The text of this paragraph to the end of fn.336 was quoted with approval in *Domsalla v Dyason* [2007] EWHC 1174 (TCC) at [78] (H.H.J. Thornton Q.C.).

illustrative terms which *may* be unfair.[336] The following paragraphs will look at these elements in turn.

"A significant imbalance in the parties' rights and obligations arising under the contract, to the detriment of the consumer". This phrase encapsulates the key idea of the notion of unfairness for the purposes of both sets of Regulations, requiring that the *term* creates an imbalance in the parties' legal rights and obligations and that this imbalance pass a threshold of significance. Two aspects of this definition have become clear as a result of the Office of Fair Trading's work in policing terms in consumer contracts.[337] 15–071

Potential for unfairness. First, a clause will be judged according to its *potential* unfairness: if a clause could give rise to a "significant imbalance in the parties' rights", etc. (given the particular and concrete factors to be outlined below), then it is no answer for a seller or supplier wishing to rely on it to say that on the facts it does not do so nor that it was never intended to be relied on so as to do so.[338] So, for example, if a price variation clause gives a supplier an unlimited discretion to vary the price (a term which can for this purpose be assumed to be potentially unfair given its lack of limitation or justification[339]), then it would not be binding on the consumer with the result that even a moderate variation of the price (itself not in the context apparently unfair) would not be effective against the consumer: the unfairness of the term makes it "not binding" on the consumer. This feature of the test of unfairness required a significant change in thinking behind the drafting of terms for the contracts to which the Regulations apply: no longer should a legal adviser acting for a seller or supplier draw a clause in as wide terms as possible so as to allow the seller or supplier as much room for manoeuvre even if he is unlikely to need it, as such a wide clause is more likely to be held altogether ineffective. Instead, such a legal adviser must in the interest of his own client take into account the legitimate interests of the client's consumer customers as these are reflected in the pattern of considerations gathered under the requirement of fairness (and indeed, of plainness and intelligibility). 15–072

The significance of imbalance. Secondly, the Office of Fair Trading has attached very considerable significance to the notion of balance, so that a term which may look, prima facie, severely prejudicial to the rights of a consumer may yet be considered fair if it is counterbalanced by a corresponding term which could act to the consumer's advantage. Various examples of this thinking are 15–073

---

[336] See below, paras 15–091 et seq.

[337] The OFT publishes this work in three-monthly bulletins entitled, *Unfair Contract Terms*. Its work was collected together in OFT, *Unfair Contract Terms Guidance* (February 2001). These bulletins now include the work of "qualifying bodies" (on which, see below, paras 15–133, 15–138). It is to be noted that the way in which the test of unfairness will apply in disputes between the parties to a contract will differ in certain respects from the way in which it is to be applied by the Director General of Fair Trading (on which, see below, para.15–136), but these are not significant for present purposes.

[338] OFT, *Unfair Contract Terms*, Bulletin No.1 (May 1996), paras 1.2, p.5; Bulletin No.3 (March 1997), p.7; cf. *Stewart Gill Ltd v Horatio Myer & Co Ltd* [1992] Q.B. 600 (in relation to the reasonableness test under the Unfair Contract Terms Act 1977 s.11).

[339] And see 1999 Regulations Sch.2 para.1(*l*), below, para.15–103.

given in the Office's reports, such as a seller's right to increase prices being coupled with a realistic right in the consumer to get out of the contract without penalty.[340] Conversely, the forfeiture of a consumer's deposit where a customer chooses not to go ahead with a contract to supply a fitted kitchen was criticised for the absence of a counterbalancing right in a consumer to receive compensation of an equivalent amount if the supplier decided to cancel the contract.[341] Again, a term in a contract of membership of a fitness club was considered unfair in that it allowed the business to assign the contract to another party without obtaining the consent of the consumers, while they were unable to transfer the benefit of the contract.[342]

15–074 **Factors in fairness.** While in principle the Regulations are concerned with the unfairness of contract terms, rather than with the fairness of the parties' behaviour more generally, certain aspects of their mutual behaviour may be relevant in the assessment of fairness. For, as has been seen,[343] the Regulations require that in assessing the fairness of a term account shall be taken of the nature of the goods or services, all the circumstances attending the conclusion of the contract and all other terms of the contract or of a contract on which it is dependent.[344] While formally this provision requires certain factors to be taken into account (raising the possibility of arguing that only these should be), it is submitted that, quite apart from the inherent openness of the concept of fairness itself, other considerations may be taken into account in assessing fairness by way of application of the requirement of good faith which forms an element within the assessment of fairness.[345]

15–075 **"The nature of the goods or services".** In certain types of case, the nature of the goods or services could argue for the fairness of a term which in other contexts would clearly be unfair. So, for example, in *Bryen & Langley Ltd v Boston*[346] it was considered material to the issue of fairness of a term that the transaction before the court was not of a "normal 'consumer' type, like buying a television set", but, for the individual or individuals concerned, a major project such as the costly construction of a building which would be undertaken only with the benefit of appropriate professional advice. A second example may be found in the context of clauses allowing the forfeiture of a purchaser's deposit in contracts of sale of land. Here, at first sight the loss of ten per cent of the purchase price if the purchaser withdraws from the contract suggests that such a clause is unfair, but it may not be given the need of the seller to cover transaction costs and also to be indemnified for likely loss of profit on the transaction. Indeed, it may be under this heading that a court could properly consider the impact of (good)

---

[340] OFT, *Unfair Contract Terms*, Bulletin No.1 (May, 1996), paras 1.5, p.6.

[341] OFT, *Unfair Contract Terms*, Bulletin No.1, p.45.

[342] OFT, *Unfair Contract Terms*, Bulletin No.4 (December 1997), p.40.

[343] See above, para.15–064.

[344] 1999 Regulations reg.6(1); 1994 Regulations reg.4(1). On the reference to "goods", see above, para.15–019.

[345] See above, para.15–066.

[346] [2004] EWHC 2450 (TCC), 98 Con L.R. 82 at [45]; [2005] EWCA Civ 973, [2005] All E.R. (D) 507 (Jul) (appeal allowed on other grounds).

industry practice in relation to the type of contract in question in assessing a term's fairness.

"All the circumstances attending the conclusion of the contract". This is clearly a very inclusive formulation. Here, two possible factors will be mentioned, both of which can be thought of as relating to circumstances relating to the conclusion of the contract. First, the fact that a seller or supplier has put pressure on a consumer to conclude the contract or to do so in haste and without time to think about its significance would point strongly against the fairness of any term which prejudices the consumer, even if this pressure did not amount to either duress or undue influence within the meaning of the general law.[347] Secondly, the degree of genuine opportunity for the consumer to read, understand, consider and decide upon the terms of a contract is also an important factor in their overall fairness. This may be supported by reference to the Schedules' inclusion in the grey list of a term which has the object or effect of "irrevocably binding the consumer to terms with which he had no real opportunity of becoming acquainted before the conclusion of the contract".[348] Now, a term which irrevocably binds a consumer to the contract is typically to be found in any contract which does not provide for a consumer to withdraw from the contract and so, absent such a provision, the terms of any contract which the consumer did not have a real opportunity of being acquainted are vulnerable to a charge of unfairness. Positively, therefore, a seller or supplier whose explanatory precontractual brochure[349] makes clear the otherwise surprising terms on which he deals or whose staff follow a practice of advising their customers of the terms in a clear and intelligible manner may be more likely to succeed in arguing that the terms in question are fair. This links in with the common law's traditional concern with notice of terms,[350] but it goes further in that a "real opportunity" is referred to and it may be thought that the more theoretical the opportunity, the more likely a term is to be held to be unfair.[351] This approach to fairness is related to the Regulations' requirement that the contract terms themselves be expressed in plain and intelligible language[352] and it is therefore submitted that a lack of plainness or intelligibility is *relevant* to the assessment of a term under the Regulations' requirement of fairness. 15–076

Lack of plainness or intelligibility sufficient? What is more open to contention is whether a lack of plainness or intelligibility can render a term unfair 15–077

[347] See above, Ch.7.

[348] 1999 Regulations Sch.2(1)(i); 1994 Regulations Sch.3 para.1(i).

[349] OFT, *Unfair Contract Terms*, Bulletin No.2 (September 1996), para.2.22, p.12 (though considering this to be particularly a matter for the good faith of the trader).

[350] See above, paras 12–010 et seq.

[351] The common law approach appears, by contrast, to distinguish between the general law of notice, where the unusual or onerous nature of a contract term is relevant to the degree of notice required (*Interfoto Picture Library Ltd v Stiletto Visual Programmes Ltd* [1989] Q.B. 433) and the rule governing signed documents, where it is not: *L'Estrange v Graucob* [1934] 2 K.B. 394. See Treitel, *The Law of Contract*, 12th edn (2007 by Peel), paras 7–007—7–009.

[352] See below, para.15–129.

within the meaning of the Regulations without more.[353] The key hurdle to allowing it to do so is the first element of the composite test of unfairness, viz that the term must cause "a significant imbalance in the parties' rights and obligations arising under the contract, to the detriment of the consumer".[354] Clearly, a case can be imagined where a term (while not plain and intelligible) does not attempt to create such an imbalance (notably, where any imbalance is to the *benefit* of the consumer) and so would not be rendered unfair by the Regulations; but in this situation it is difficult to see why the consumer would wish to argue that such a term was "not binding" on him (though a body entrusted with a policing role in relation to unfair contract terms may nevertheless wish to intervene).[355] However, where a contract term either seeks to bind a consumer to a particular duty or seeks to create rights which do not benefit him (notably, as compared to his existing rights or the rights of the seller or supplier under the contract more widely), a court could find that such an "imbalance" in the rights and obligations of the parties was "significant" merely on the ground that the consumer was not able to appreciate its extent: as the Director General of Fair Trading has observed:

> "... it would clearly be difficult to maintain that unintelligible or ambiguous terms were *not* unfair if they had some potential for detriment to the consumer."[356]

The final step in this direction (noted without comment by the EC Commission) is that courts in some Member States have held that a failure in the requirement of transparency itself constitutes "unfairness" within the meaning of the Directive.[357] However, this equating of the two requirements contained in the Directive does not accord with the way in which they are set out in the Directive as distinct both in their content and even more in their effects.[358] Indeed, if a mere failure in transparency would lead without more to a failure in fairness this would render the distinctive treatment of the requirement of transparency entirely otiose.

15–078 **"All the other terms of the contract".** The Regulations require courts to take into account the other terms of the contract before them in assessing the fairness of a term. It is to be noticed that *all* the terms should be looked at, this including as has been noted, the contract's "core terms" which relate to its subject matter or price/quality ratio.[359] In the view of the Director General of Fair Trading, an example of "another term" of a contract which may argue for the fairness of a term which by itself looks unfair may be found in a term which

---

[353] cf. Study Group on a European Civil Code and Research Group on EC Private Law (Acquis Group), *Principles, Definitions and Model Rules of European Private Law*, Interim Outline edn (Sellier, 2008), *Draft Common Frame of Reference*, II.-9:402(2) which provides that "[i]n a contract between a business and a consumer a term which has been supplied by the business in breach of the duty of transparency . . . may on that ground alone be considered unfair".

[354] Regulations reg.5(1), above, para.15–071 and see Bright in Burrows and Peel, *Contract Terms* (OUP, 2007), pp.172 at 184–86.

[355] On this see below, para.15–134.

[356] OFT, *Unfair Contract Terms*, Bulletin No.2 (September 1996), p.8.

[357] EC Commission, *Report on the Implementation of Directive 93/13/EEC on unfair terms in consumer contracts* COM(2000) 248 final, p.18.

[358] Below, paras 15–123—15–128, 15–131.

[359] See above, paras 15–050 et seq. and Preamble to the Directive recital 19.

provides the consumer with a cooling-off period during which he may decide to cancel the contract without penalty.[360]

"The . . . terms . . . of another contract on which it is dependent". It would seem from the general formulation of this phrase that there is no requirement that the other contract on which the consumer contract is dependent must itself be a consumer contract within the meaning of the Regulations (though in the vast majority of situations it will be)[361] nor even that the other contract be between the same parties as the one whose term is to be assessed.[362] A situation in the consumer context in which two contracts are related may be found in the context of the financing of a consumer sale. Here, it would seem that whatever controls already exist on the fairness of the terms of either the sale or the financing contract,[363] the terms of the one may go to the fairness of the terms of the other. For example, the fairness of the terms of purchase of a house could be assessed taking into account the terms of a mortgage contract taken out by a consumer mortgagor. However, this example shows the difficulties that would arise in this respect, where the mortgagee is not also the seller, for it may be thought unfair for a mortgagee to be prejudiced by the terms of the sale of which it may know nothing and have even less control. This may lead a court to imply into the phrase "another contract" a requirement that this contract be between the parties to the consumer contract whose terms are to be assessed. 15–079

Factors in good faith specified by the 1994 Regulations. Schedule 2 of the 1994 Regulations provided that: 15–080

"In making an assessment of good faith, regard shall be had in particular to—

(a) the strength of the bargaining positions of the parties;
(b) whether the consumer had an inducement to agree to the term;
(c) whether the goods or services were sold or supplied to the special order of the consumer, and
(d) the extent to which the seller or supplier has dealt fairly and equitably with the consumer."[364]

A first important point to notice about this formulation is that it expressly allowed the possibility of recourse to other considerations in making an assessment of good faith. All four of the elements expressly mentioned are found in the preamble to the Directive[365] and all but (d) are very similar indeed to the "guidelines" for the application of the reasonableness test provided by the Unfair Contract Terms Act 1977.[366] This being the case, it is likely that the courts will

[360] OFT, *Unfair Contract Terms*, Bulletin No.2 (September 1996), p.12.

[361] For example, even if contracts for the sale of land fall outside the ambit of the Regulations this might not prevent the terms of a purchase of a house being relevant to the fairness of the terms of a mortgage.

[362] *cf. Domsalla v Dyason* [2007] EWHC 1174 (TCC) at [77] (wide range of contracts related to the consumer contract in question considered as part of "all the circumstances").

[363] Notably, under the Consumer Credit Act 1974 on which see Vol.II, Ch.38.

[364] 1994 Regulations reg.3(3) and Sch.2.

[365] 1993 Directive recital 16 (quoted above, para.15–066).

[366] Unfair Contract Terms Act 1977 Sch.2 (a), (b) and (e) and see above, paras 14–085 et seq.

refer in giving them significance to the existing case law on the 1977 Act, though bearing in mind the differences between the types of term which are subject to control under that Act (exemption clauses and indemnity clauses) and the type of term to be tested before them for assessment under the 1994 Regulations. However, the fourth consideration which Sch.2 of the 1994 Regulations listed was new and, moreover, seemed to invite a very different approach from the one to be taken under the 1977 Act, for "the extent to which the seller or supplier *has* dealt fairly or equitably with the consumer" suggested that the seller's or the supplier's conduct *after* the conclusion of the contract may also form an element within the test of his good faith. It is clear, though, from the text of the Directive that the requirement of good faith is intended to qualify the fairness of the term, not the fairness of a party's *post*-contractual behaviour and this being the case, the fourth consideration appears somewhat redundant, given the general test's reference to "all circumstances attending the conclusion of the contract".[367]

Unlike the 1994 Regulations, the 1999 Regulations do not attempt to explain the requirement of good faith. However, this does not mean that the factors previously set out in Sch.2 of the 1994 Regulations as factors to which regard should be had in the assessment of good faith are irrelevant to the assessment of good faith for the purposes of the 1999 Regulations, for the presence of these factors in the preamble to the Directive make it legitimate to refer to them in the interpretation of art.3(1)'s use of the requirement of good faith and, therefore any national implementing legislation.[368]

15–081 **Good faith and the provision of public services.** As noted earlier recital 16 of the preamble to the Directive prefaces its explanation of the considerations to which regard shall be had in the assessment of good faith by stating that:

> "... the assessment ... of the unfair character of terms, in particular in sale or supply activities of a public nature providing collective services which take account of solidarity among users, must be supplemented by a means of making an overall evaluation of the different interests involved; whereas this constitutes the requirement of good faith."

This reference to taking account of "solidarity among users" does not have any resonance for English lawyers (which is no doubt why it was omitted from the 1994 Regulations), but it may allude to the idea to be found, for example, in French administrative law which requires that those who use a public service must have equal access to it and be equally treated by it.[369] One result of this is that the public service is not allowed to discriminate between different classes of user of the service (notably as regards any charges to be paid) where to do so is not justified in the public interest.[370] Perhaps, then, this part of recital 16 invites

---

[367] 1994 Regulations reg.4(2); cf. 1999 Regulations reg.6(1) and see above, para.15–076.

[368] 1993 Directive recital 16 (quoted above, para.15–066).

[369] Bell in Bell, Boyron and Whittaker, *Principles of French Law*, 2nd edn (2008) pp.170–171 and for details see Chapus, *Droit administratif général*, Tome 1, 15th edn (2001), pp.609 et seq.

[370] Chapus at p.581. Another significance of the term "solidarity" in EC law is to be found in relation to social security schemes "based on the principle of solidarity", i.e. where benefits are not based on contributions: see *Decker v Caisse de Maladie des Employés Privés* (120/95), [1998] 1 All E.R. (EC) 673.

a court to take into account in assessing the fairness of terms on which public services are provided a general principle of equality of treatment. This may even be the case in relation to differential tariffs, for while terms which concern "the adequacy of the price or remuneration, as against the goods or services sold or supplied" are excluded from the requirement of fairness,[371] a term which differentiates unfairly in the charges to be paid for a public service as between different categories of customer may be held not to concern the adequacy of the price *in relation to* the goods or services provided. However, whatever the particular example which the drafters of the Directive had in mind, the reference makes clear that in an appropriate case a court should take into account interests other than those of the parties to the contract, including the public interest generally. It has been suggested that this degree of inclusiveness in the evaluation of the fairness of contract terms would allow a court to take into account their effect on the "Convention rights" of third parties as well as of the parties themselves under the Human Rights Act.[372] This suggestion finds some support from the opinion of A.G. Tizziano in *Mostaza Claro v Centro Móvil Milenium SL*,[373] where he saw the effect of an arbitration clause in a consumer contract which severely limited the consumer's right to a fair hearing as a significant element in the national court's holding of its unfairness, given that this right is "one of the fundamental rights deriving from the constitutional traditions common to the Member States".[374]

The test of unfairness applied in the *First National Bank Plc* case. In *Director General of Fair Trading v First National Bank Plc*[375] the Director General of Fair Trading challenged the fairness of a term in a contract of consumer credit the effect of which (if valid) would be that where the bank obtains judgment against a borrower, interest would be payable at the contractual rate on the outstanding principal plus accrued interest unpaid at the date of judgment until the judgment is discharged by payment. The Court of Appeal held that the term was unfair as the borrower's attention is not specifically drawn to the point of payment of interest at the contractual rate beyond judgment in instalments by the bank at or before the conclusion of the contract—nor indeed at any later stage.[376] In its view, the existence of the court's powers by statute to order payment by instalments and to modify the contractual rate of interest as a result does not prevent the term from operating unfairly "in a majority of cases where instalment orders are made without the consideration by the courts of those provisions".[377] The bank has the stronger bargaining position and the clause comes as an "unfair surprise". However, the House of Lords unanimously reversed this decision and held that the term was fair within the meaning of the Regulations. So, for Lord Bingham of Cornhill: 15–082

---

371 See above, paras 15–049 et seq.

372 See above, para.1–063; Whittaker (2001) 21 OJLS 193, 213.

373 (C–168/05) [2007] 1 C.M.L.R. 22.

374 [2007] 1 C.M.L.R. 222 at [59] quoting *Krombach v Bamberski* (C–7198) [2000] E.C.R. I–01935.

375 [2001] UKHL 52; [2002] 1 A.C. 481; Whittaker (2004) ZEuP 75.

376 [2000] Q.B. 672, 688.

377 [2000] Q.B. 672 per Peter Gibson L.J. The powers are contained in Consumer Credit Act 1974 ss.129, 136.

> "The essential bargain is that the bank will make funds available to the borrower which the borrower will repay, over a period, with interest. Neither party could suppose that the bank would willingly forgo any part of its principal or interest. If the bank thought that outcome at all likely, it would not lend. If there were any room for doubt about the borrower's obligation to repay the principal in full with interest, that obligation is very clearly and unambiguously expressed in the conditions of contract. There is nothing unbalanced or detrimental to the consumer in that obligation; the absence of such a term would unbalance the contract to the detriment of the lender."[378]

The unfairness of the situation in which consumer borrowers relied on the terms of judgments made against them for payment of their debt to lenders and were later surprised by a demand for payment of *contractual* interest under a term such as the one in issue was caused by the absence of procedural safeguards provided for a consumer on default by the applicable primary and secondary legislation rather than by the contract term itself.[379]

15–083 **Other factors in the assessment of good faith or fairness.** Other factors have been suggested as relevant to determining whether the requirement of good faith is satisfied, though most could equally well be thought of simply as going to the issue of fairness in general.

15–084 **Price/quality ratio.** A notable example is found in the preamble to the Directive which allows the "price/quality" ratio of the contract to be taken into account in assessing a term *other than* one which itself describes the main subject matter of the contract or the quality/price ratio of the goods or services supplied.[380] The relevance of the price/quality ratio to the fairness of incidental terms may be seen to be reflected in recital 16's reference to the consumer's receipt of an inducement as an element within the application of the requirement of good faith.

15–085 **EC recommendations.** It has been suggested that EC recommendations in the field of consumer protection, for example, as regards payment systems,[381] may be referred to by a court in assessing the fairness of a term.[382]

15–086 **Terms put forward by the consumer or his professional agent.** Where a consumer's professional agent put forward a standard set of terms which were held to have been incorporated into the contract, and thereby "imposed these terms" on the supplier of a service, the Court of Appeal has regarded:

> "... the suggestion that there was any lack of good faith or fair dealing by [the supplier] with regard to the ultimate incorporation of these terms into the contract as repugnant to common sense ... It was not for [the suppliers] to take the matter up with [the consumer] and ensure that he know what he was doing: they knew that he had the

---

[378] [2001] UKHL 52 at [20]. Lords Steyn, Hope of Craighead, Millett and Rodger of Earlsferry agreed.

[379] [2001] UKHL 52 at [23], [61], [66].

[380] 1993 Directive recital 19.

[381] Recommendation 94/489.

[382] Howells and Wilhelmsson *E.C. Consumer Law* (1997) at p.103.

benefit of the services of a professional . . . to advise him on the effects of the terms."[383]

In this way, even if a particular term of the standard contract (here, an arbitration clause) were found to cause a "significant imbalance in the parties' rights and obligations under the contract, to the detriment of the consumer" as envisaged by reg.5(1) of the 1999 Regulations, this would not be "contrary to the requirement of good faith", with the result that the contract term would not be unfair within the meaning of the Regulations. On the other hand, if a business supplier were to agree to a set of standard terms (perhaps promulgated by a trade association) proposed by a consumer which the supplier knows to be very prejudicial to the consumer's interests in circumstances where he also knows that the consumer is ignorant of this effect (especially where the consumer is not professionally advised), then the mere fact that the terms were proposed by the consumer should not be allowed to rule out the unfairness of any of its terms: in these circumstances, the supplier may be acting "contrary to the requirement of good faith" and one or more of the terms may be "unfair" given their effect on the relative rights and obligations of the parties and taking into account the other circumstances specified by the 1999 Regulations for this purpose.[384]

Particularly vulnerable consumers. It has earlier been argued that the general standard of the "average consumer" appropriate to the Directive (and therefore the Regulations) varies according to the context in which the business concludes its contracts. So, for example, where the consumers with whom a business contracts are particularly vulnerable "because of their mental or physical infirmity, age or credulity in a way which the trader could reasonably be expected to foresee"[385] then the standard of understanding to be expected of the terms in question on the part of the consumers must be lowered. Moreover, if a business takes advantage of the vulnerability of a consumer understood in this sense, then this would clearly be relevant to the issue of the business's failing to have 'dealt fairly and equitably with the consumer' and therefore the requirement of good faith,[386] even though the consumer possessed the requisite legal capacity to conclude the contract in question under the law governing minors' contracts or the law governing lack of mental capacity.[387] 15–087

The language type of the contract. In general, a domestic consumer contract governed by English law is normally to be expressed in the English language and 15–088

---

383 *Bryen & Langley Ltd v Boston* [2005] EWCA Civ 973, [2005] All E.R. (D) 507 (Jul) at [46], per Rimer J. (with whom Clarke ([56]) and Pill L.JJ. [56] agreed). This decision has been treated as holding generally that the arbitration provisions in the JCT Minor Works Contract "even if proffered by the contractor in circumstances which would make it procedurally unfair for the contractor to rely on them vis-à-vis a consumer, do not cause a significant imbalance in the parties' rights and obligations": *Domsalla v Dyason* [2007] EWHC 1174 (TCC) at [92], per H.H.J. Thornton Q.C. On the issue whether terms in these circumstances remain not "individually negotiated" see above, para.15–048.

384 Above, para.15–070.

385 This formulation is taken from Directive 2005/29 on unfair commercial practices art.5(3) and see above, para.15–031.

386 Above, para.15–066.

387 See above, paras 8–002 and 8–068 respectively.

where reference is made to the "intelligibility" of the language used this normally refers to the style of language rather than to its type. However, it should not be universally assumed that English should be the only language in which such a contract should be expressed: for if a seller or supplier contracts with consumers whose first language is known or can be foreseen by it to be other than English, then it may be "contrary to the requirement of good faith" for the business to rely entirely on terms set out in English.[388] So, for example, where a contract for the provision of financial services was made with consumers who were Greek and non-resident in the UK the court considered that there the term under consideration "called for *translation* and careful explanation".[389] A similar approach could also be taken in the case of a cross-border contract concluded via the internet and on terms set out on the seller or supplier's web-site.[390]

15–089 **Terms deemed to be unfair within the meaning of the Regulations.** While generally the question whether a contract term is "unfair" within the meaning of the Regulations is a matter for the composite test described in the preceding paragraphs, on occasion legislation has deemed a particular type of term in consumer contracts to be unfair within the meaning of the Regulations. This is true of arbitration clauses where they relate to claims for a "modest amount"[391] and also of contract terms:

> ". . . providing that a consumer bears the burden of proof in respect of showing whether a distance supplier or an intermediary complied with any or all of the obligations placed upon him resulting from the Directive"

of 2002[392] concerning the distance marketing of consumer financial services.[393]

15–090 **"Fairness" under the Regulations and "reasonableness" under the Unfair Contract Terms Act 1977.** It has been noted that some of the considerations to be taken into account by a court in assessing the fairness of a term for the purposes of the Regulations (in particular in relation to the requirement of good faith) are the same or very similar to those to be taken into account in assessing the "reasonableness" of a term under the Unfair Contract Terms Act 1977.[394] Moreover, while the specific factors which are to be taken into account may differ somewhat, the "definitions" of the two concepts are both very inclusive, allowing a court to take into account whatever factors it thinks right in judging whether a term should be enforced, as long as these relate to the term (as

---

[388] See further Whittaker, *Cambridge Yearbook of European Studies* (2006), Vol.8, Ch.10.

[389] *Standard Bank London Ltd v Apostolakis (No.2)* [2001] Lloyd's Rep. Bank 240, 250 (emphasis added).

[390] On which see Whittaker, *Cambridge Yearbook of European Studies* (2006), Vol.8, Ch.10, passim.

[391] Arbitration Act 1996 ss.89, 90; Unfair Arbitration Agreements (Specified Amount) Order 1999 (SI 1999/2167) which came into force on January 1, 2000 and see below, para.15–094.

[392] Directive 2002/65 concerning distance marketing of consumer financial services [2002] OJ L271/16.

[393] The Financial Services (Distance Marketing) Regulations 2004 (SI 2095) reg.24, amending 1999 Regulations regs. 3(1) and (5).

[394] See above, paras 14–084 et seq.; para.15–067.

opposed to post-contractual dealings between the parties).[395] There is, therefore, a profound similarity in the two tests in that they both require a court to decide whether a particular contract term *should* be enforceable according to a range of considerations, some of which relate to the contract itself and some of which relate to the relative positions of the parties to the contract or the circumstances in which the contract was made. All this does not mean, however, that the two tests have the same significance, but their differences do not stem from use of the language, on the one hand, of "reasonableness" and, on the other, of "fairness" and "good faith". Instead, they flow from the differences in ambit of the two pieces of legislation, in particular as regards the types of term to be tested. For while the Unfair Contract Terms Act 1977 deals almost exclusively with exemption clauses, the requirement of fairness in the Regulations affects any type of contract term as long as it is "incidental"[396] and has not been "individually negotiated".[397] Clearly, the type of considerations which are appropriate in judging the "fairness" of terms other than exemption clauses are likely to differ considerably from those which are appropriate to that context. There are indeed existing parallels for this in wider English law: so, for example, the factors which are to be taken into account by a court in judging the "reasonableness" of a term of a contract which is in restraint of trade are not the same as those in judging the "reasonableness" of an exemption clause: the terminology of reasonableness is shared but the impact of this requirement differs according to the type of term in question, and the factors in determining reasonableness differ according to the reasons for which the term is viewed with suspicion (whether excluding a person's claim which would otherwise exist or unduly fettering a person's freedom).[398] In a similar way, the application of the requirement of fairness for the purposes of the Regulations differs according to its context. In the result, therefore, while the application of the test of "fairness" for the purposes of the Regulations to exemption clauses is unlikely to differ from the application of the test of "reasonableness" under the 1977 Act, its application to other clauses will differ appropriately to the context of both the type of term and the type of contract in question.[399]

(iii) *The "Indicative List" of Terms*

Introduction. Both the 1994 and the 1999 Regulations contain identical "indicative and non-exhaustive list[s] of the terms which may be regarded as unfair".[400] This list is sometimes termed a "grey list" for the terms which it contains are not necessarily to be held unfair (a "black list"), but they will give rise to a forensic presumption of unfairness (that is to say, in practice it will be very useful in forensic argument for a consumer to be able to point to a term in 15–091

[395] This is made clear by the phrase in 1999 Regulations reg.6(1) directing the court to refer "*at the time of the conclusion of the contract*, to all the circumstances attending the conclusion of the contract": and see above, para.15–064.

[396] i.e. not a "core term:" see above, para.15–054.

[397] See above, para.15–046.

[398] cf. above, para.14–085 and below, paras 16–092 et seq.

[399] cf. though, the differences in relation to the burden of proof discussed above, paras 15–019 et seq.

[400] 1994 Regulations reg.4(4) Sch.3 para.1; 1999 Regulations reg.5(5) Sch.2 para.1.

the list as similar to the one which he challenges).[401] Given its illustrative nature, it is odd that the second paragraphs of the Schedules purport to restrict the scope of particular examples of terms found in the first paragraphs, but this reinforces the importance which was attached by the drafters of the Directive to the illustrative list.[402] Even so, it needs to be emphasised that a type of term included on the list may be held by a court to be fair in the circumstances before it.

15–092 The list in para.1 of Sch.2 of the 1999 Regulations includes a wide variety of terms and these not merely illustrate the application of the requirement of fairness, but also the range of types of terms which are subject to the Regulations' controls (in particular in contrast to the limited ambit of the Unfair Contract Terms Act 1977). In the following paragraphs, these terms will be noted and very briefly discussed, the examples retaining the letter which they bear in the Schedule.

15–093 **Exclusion or limitation clauses.** Terms which have the object or effect of:

"(a) excluding or limiting the legal liability of a seller or supplier in the event of the death of a consumer or personal injury to the latter resulting from an act or omission of that seller or supplier;

(b) inappropriately excluding or limiting the legal rights of the consumer vis-à-vis the seller or supplier or another party in the event of total or partial non-performance or inadequate performance by the seller or supplier of any of the contractual obligations, including the option of offsetting a debt owed to the seller or supplier against any claim which the consumer may have against him;

. . .

(q) excluding or hindering the consumer's right to take legal action or exercise any other legal remedy, particularly by requiring the consumer to take disputes exclusively to arbitration not covered by legal provisions, unduly restricting the evidence available to him or imposing on him a burden of proof which, according to the applicable law, should lie with another party to the contract."

Many of the terms within these examples would be classed as exemption clauses within the meaning of the Unfair Contract Terms Act 1977,[403] or would come within the broader category of contract term falling within s.3(2) of that Act.[404] However, the Regulations are not restrained by any such limiting definitions as are found in the 1977 Act, and, as the Office of Fair Trading has put it:

---

[401] The DCFR para.II.-9:411 is expressed as creating a formal presumption of unfairness.

[402] The ECJ has held that national legislation implementing the 1993 Directive need not itself include the list in the Directive's Annex. However: "Inasmuch as [it] is of indicative and illustrative value, it constitutes a source of information both for the national authorities responsible for *applying* the implementing measures and for individuals affected by those measures," and so its "form and method of implementation [must] offer a sufficient guarantee that the public can obtain knowledge of it". The Court held that the European Commission had failed to show that this requirement was not satisfied where (in Sweden) the Annex had been included in the *travaux préparatoires* of the implementing legislation and where these constitute an important aid to legislative interpretation: *Commission v Sweden* (C–478/99) [2002] E.C.R. I–0414.

[403] s.13 and see above, para.14–062.

[404] See above, paras 14–073—14–074.

"If a term achieves the same *effect* as an unfair exemption clause, it will be unfair whatever its form or mechanism. This applies, for instance, to terms which 'deem' things to be the case, or get consumers to declare that they are—whether they really are or not—with the aim of ensuring no liability arises in the first place."[405]

An example of a term which requires a declaration may be found in the case of a contract for the provision of medical services under which the consumer/patient declares that he knows medical facts which could only be known with any certainty by experts.[406] The High Court has found (in circumstances described as unusual) a "withholding notice clause" in the JCT Minor Works standard contract by which the consumer/employer's right of set off can be exercised only if the appropriate notices has been served in time to the building contractor to be unfair within the meaning of the Regulations.[407] Moreover, the Office of Fair Trading has interpreted the impact of clauses which limit the consumer's right to offset a debt broadly. So, in its view:

"There is no objection to terms which state the consumer's normal legal obligation to pay promptly and in full what is properly owing—i.e. [the] full price, on satisfactory completion of the contract. But suspicion falls on terms which say, *or clearly imply*, that the consumer must in all cases complete his payment of the whole contract price, without any deduction, as soon as the supplier chooses to regard his side of the bargain as finished. They are likely to be seen as excluding the right of set-off even if they do not actually mention that right."[408]

Arbitration and adjudication clauses. Sub-paragraph (q) quoted above,[409] refers to a term which requires a "consumer to take disputes exclusively to arbitration not covered by legal provisions". This may refer to arbitration or adjudication clauses which give no option to the consumer. Here, it has been specifically provided that an arbitration clause in a "consumer contract"[410] is deemed necessarily unfair where it relates to a claim for a "modest amount" set at the time of writing at £5,000.[411] However, even where a claim for more than this amount is subject under a consumer contract to arbitration or adjudication the relevant term may be held unfair.[412] So, for example, in *Zealander v Laing Homes Ltd*[413] the claimant had contracted to buy a new house and certain other 15–094

[405] OFT, *Unfair Contract Terms Guidance* (February 2001), p.4 (original emphasis).

[406] OFT, *Unfair Contract Terms*, Bulletin No.22 (August, 2003), pp.126–127.

[407] *Domsalla v Dyason* [2007] EWHC 1174 (TCC), at [94]–[97].

[408] *Unfair Contract Terms Guidance*, Bulletin No.22, p.13 (original emphasis).

[409] See above, para.15–093.

[410] The definition of "consumer contract" is somewhat wider for this purpose than for the purposes of the Regulations in general as it is provided that the consumer may be a legal person as well as a natural one: Arbitration Act 1996 s.90.

[411] Arbitration Act 1996 ss.89, 90; Unfair Arbitration Agreements (Specified Amount) Order 1999 (SI 1999/2167) which came into force on January 1, 2000.

[412] cf. *Mostaza Claro v Centro Móvil Milenium SL* (C–168/05) [2007] 1 C.M.L.R. 22, where a Spanish court considered unfair an arbitration clause in a consumer mobile telephone contract which referred all disputes to arbitration and gave the consumer a period of 10 days in which to refuse arbitration or, if she did not, to file submissions and present evidence in her defence. While the ECJ reaffirmed that the question whether a term is unfair within the meaning of the Directive is for national courts (above, para.15–115), A.G. Tizziano noted (at paras [32]–[37] and [49] of his Opinion) that this clause "severely limited" the consumer's fundamental right to a fair hearing.

[413] (2003) 19 Const. L.J. 350.

items from the defendant, this house being covered in part by the National House Builders Council "Build Mark" Agreement, which contained a compulsory arbitration clause. The Technology and Construction Court refused to stay his claim for damages in respect of defects in the house, holding that the clause was unfair within the meaning of the Regulations in that it created a "significant imbalance" between the parties since the claimant, who had been in a position of disparity with the defendant builder, would have to take separate proceedings for the matters covered by the "Build Mark" Agreement and those falling outside it, which would put the claimant at a financial disadvantage. Similarly, in *Picardi v Cuniberti*,[414] the same court held unfair a clause in a contract between two consumers and their architect under which either party could refer any dispute or difference to adjudication, the adjudicator to be appointed by the parties or, absent their agreement, nominated by the architect's own professional body. Applying the approach of Lord Bingham of Cornhill in *Director General of Fair Trading v First National Bank Plc*,[415] the court held that:

> "... a procedure which the consumer is required to follow, and which will cause irrecoverable expenditure in either prosecuting or defending it, is something which may hinder the consumer's right to take legal action. The fact that the consumer was deliberately excluded by Parliament from the statutory regime of the [Housing Grants Construction Regeneration Act 1996] reinforces this view."[416]

On the other hand, in *Westminster Building Co Ltd v Beckingham*[417] a private individual (the "consumer") who had commissioned a firm of builders to renovate his property under a contract falling outside the Housing Grants, Regeneration and Construction Act 1996 was held bound by an adjudication clause which it contained since this clause was not unfair in the circumstances: its terms were couched in plain and intelligible language and had been decided upon by the consumer's professional agents, chartered surveyors, who could have given him competent and objective advice as to its existence and effect.

15–095 **Choice of jurisdiction clauses.** In *Océano Grupo Editorial SA v Murciano Quintero* the European Court of Justice held that a choice of local jurisdiction clause in a consumer contract which purported to give jurisdiction to the court where the business supplier was established even though the consumers were domiciled in another part of Spain was unfair within the meaning of art.3 of the Unfair Terms in Consumer Contracts Directive 1993, the European Court seeing

---

[414] [2002] EWHC 2923. This decision was strictly obiter given that the court held that the term was not incorporated into the contract at common law.

[415] [2001] UKHL 52, [2002] 1 A.C. 481, above, para.15–082.

[416] [2002] EWHC 2923 at [131]. The court also noted that the guidance of the R.I.B.A. whose standard form the architect had used, clearly required its members individually to negotiate such an adjudication clause.

[417] [2004] EWHC 138 (TCC) at [31]. See similarly *Lovell Projects Ltd v Legg* (TCC) [2003] B.L.R. 452. cf. *Bryen & Langley Ltd v Boston* [2005] EWCA Civ 973, [2005] All E.R. (D) 507 (Jul) (arbitration clause in JCT standard contract held binding where the *consumer* imposed it on the supplier); *Heifer International Inc v Christiansen* [2007] EWHC 3015 (TCC), [2008] All E.R. (D) 120 (Jan) (Danish arbitration clause fair as inserted by consumer's own lawyers: the Regulations were "not intended to protect clients from their own legal advisers": at [299], per H.H.J. Toulmin Q.C.); and see above, para.15–086.

this type of term as falling within the category set out in sub-para.(q) of para.1 of the Annex to that Directive.[418] While this aspect of the European Court's decision has no direct significance for English law, in *Standard Bank London Ltd v Apostolakis (No.2)* its impact was extended by analogy to a choice of *national* jurisdiction clause.[419] In that case, the defendants were two wealthy individuals resident in Greece who had entered foreign exchange contracts with a bank in Athens and who had commenced proceedings on the contracts in Athens. The claimant bank failed in its proceedings in England for an injunction to restrain the defendants from continuing their proceedings in Greece. Steel J. expressed the view that, whether or not the case fell within art.13 of the Brussels Convention so as to give the Greek courts exclusive jurisdiction,[420] the term which gave exclusive jurisdiction to the English courts was unfair within the meaning of the Regulations given the cost and inconvenience of requiring the defendants to defend an action in England, the contrast with this requirement and the claimant's reservation to itself of a right to sue the defendants in England or in any country where they had assets or were amenable to suit and the fact that the defendants had been faced with "potentially confusing sets of jurisdiction clauses calling for translation and careful explanation", neither of which had taken place.[421]

"Potestative conditions." Terms which have the object or effect of: 15–096

> "(c) ... making an agreement binding on the consumer whereas provision of services by the seller or supplier is subject to a condition whose realisation depends on his own will alone."

It may be thought that in English law such a term may render the contract as a whole void for uncertainty or lack of consideration, in that it appears to give the seller or supplier an effective choice whether or not to do anything under the contract,[422] a term which in the Romanist terminology is known as a "potestative condition".[423] This term's presence in the list may be explained by the fact that this result is not uniformly shared throughout the Member States.[424] However, the idea that a term should not enable the seller or supplier to determine in his discretion the rights of a consumer under a contract may be significant for English law. Thus, the Office of Fair Trading has expressed the view that a clause in a contract between a car manufacturer and the purchaser of one of its cars

[418] *Océano Grupo Editorial SA v Murciano Quintero* (C–240/98 to C–244/98) [2000] E.C.R. I–4941, especially at [22] and see below, paras 15–115, 15–117.

[419] [2001] Lloyd's Rep. Bank 240.

[420] This was the main ground of the decision: *Apostolakis (No.2)* [2001] Lloyd's Rep. Bank 240 at [40]. Art.13 of the Brussels Convention is replaced by Regulation 44/2001, above, fn.126, art.15.

[421] [2001] Lloyd's Rep. Bank 240, 250. It had previously been held that these contracts were "consumer contracts" for the purposes of the 1999 Regulations: *Standard Bank London Ltd v Apostolakis (No.1)* [2000] I.L. Pr. 766 and see para.15–030, above.

[422] de Moor, (1995) 3 *European Review of Private Law* 257, 269, at fn.62 and cf. below, para.15–099.

[423] Thomas, *Textbook of Roman Law* (1976), p.237.

[424] For example, while such a term may lead to the annulment of a contract in French law (being termed a *condition potestative*, see art.1174 C. civ. and Nicholas, *The French Law of Contract*, 2nd edn (1991), pp.159 et seq.), it would not necessarily do so in German law (cf. German Standard Contract Terms Act 1976 para.10.3), replaced from 2000 by BGB para.308(3).

which subjected a consumer's right to return a car to its manufacturer to a condition that the car had not suffered a particular degree of damage "in the opinion of the [manufacturer's] dealer" is unfair.[425]

15–097 **Unbalanced forfeiture clauses.** Terms which have the object or effect of:

> "(d) . . . permitting the seller or supplier to retain sums paid by the consumer where the latter decides not to conclude or perform the contract, without providing for the consumer to receive compensation of an equivalent amount from the seller or supplier where the latter is the party cancelling the contract."

The type of terms described in this subparagraph include terms under which either a part-payment or deposit paid by a consumer may be forfeited and have proved to be a significant object of the Office of Fair Trading's work. In this respect, important factors in the fairness of such a term are the proportion between the sum to be forfeited and any loss to be suffered by the seller or supplier by the consumer's cancellation[426] and, as subpara.(d) mentions, the existence of any counter-balancing provision in the contract for the benefit of the consumer.

15–098 **Penalty clauses.** Terms which have the object or effect of: "(e) requiring any consumer who fails to fulfil his obligation to pay a disproportionately high sum in compensation". The type of term described in this subparagraph bears a considerable similarity to the common law understanding of a "penalty clause", since the disproportionately high nature of a sum to be paid on breach is an element within the distinction between a penalty and a (valid) liquidated damages clause. Clearly, though, clauses which are penal in their potential effect may be subjected to the test of fairness under the Regulations, whether or not they count as penalties in the technical common law sense.[427] So, for example, it has been held that a clause which requires a consumer to pay interest at 8 per cent over the Bank of England current base rate on sums due to the business under the contract 30 days after the issue of an account is unfair within the meaning of the 1999 Regulations, even though it constituted a genuine pre-estimate of damage likely to be suffered by the claimant in the event of non-payment and therefore not a penalty clause at common law,[428] this decision on the unfairness of the term resting principally on the grounds that the term was unusual and not balanced by a similar term governing unpaid monies such as damages which may fall due *to* the consumer.[429] Moreover, if terms in contracts between banks and other lenders and their consumer customers which impose charges on the customer where the

---

[425] OFT, *Unfair Contract Terms*, Bulletin No.1 (May 1996), p.46.

[426] OFT, *Unfair Contract Terms*, Bulletin No.2 (September 1996), p.26.

[427] cf. below, paras 26–109 et seq. In *Kindlance v Murphy* Unreported 1997 N.I. Ch D an "interest acceleration clause" in a contract of mortgage was held unfair within the meaning of the 1994 Regulations. For an example of the upholding as fair of a clause requiring a consumer to pay a sum on his own termination of the contract, see *Gosling v Burrard-Lucas* [1999] 1 C.L. 197. For further decisions on allegedly penalty-like terms in financial services contracts see *Evans v Cherry Tree Finance Ltd* Unreported April 13, 2007 Ch D (early redemption clause with six-month deferment unfair in the circumstances).

[428] *Munkenbeck & Marshall v Harold* [2005] EWHC 356 (TCC), [2005] All E.R. (D) 227.

[429] [2005] EWHC 356 (TCC) at [12] and [15].

customer exceeds the credit in his account or his previously agreed overdraft limit were ultimately held to be subject to the requirement of fairness,[430] then para.(e) of Sch.2 will be relevant to any decision as to their fairness.[431]

Cancellation clauses. Terms which have the object or effect of: 15–099

> "(f) . . . authorising the seller or supplier to dissolve the contract on a discretionary basis where the same facility is not granted to the consumer, or permitting the seller or supplier to retain the sums paid for services not yet supplied by him where it is the seller or supplier himself who dissolves the contract."

It could be argued that an executory contract which contains a term permitting either party to "dissolve" it without any prejudicial consequence (such as the payment of expenses or the loss of a deposit) is itself void for lack of consideration, for consideration is illusory where it is alleged to consist of a promise the terms of which leave performance entirely to the discretion of the promisor (unless something else of value in the eyes of the law is required instead).[432] However, this is clearly not the assumption of the Regulations (nor indeed of the Unfair Contract Terms Act 1977[433]), which is that such clauses are, in principle, valid. Moreover, from the point of view of consumer protection, it does not help a consumer to say that a clause which allows a seller or supplier to cancel without prejudicial consequence renders the contract as a whole void, for this releases the seller or supplier just the same, whereas a holding that the clause is unfair means merely that the *clause* does not bind the consumer, thereby leaving the *contract* binding for both. Conversely, however, a term which allows a seller or supplier to retain a deposit when the consumer cancels the contract may well be held fair. So, for example, a clause requiring the parents of a pupil accepted at an independent school to give a term's written notice when cancelling their acceptance of a place, failing which a term's fees would be payable has been held fair within the meaning of the Regulations.[434]

Terms relating to notice in contracts of indeterminate duration. Terms which have the object or effect of: 15–100

> "(g) . . . enabling the seller or supplier to terminate a contract of indeterminate duration without reasonable notice except where there are serious grounds for doing so."

Terms in a contract of indefinite duration which allow one or other party to terminate it are, in principle, valid in English law, as may be seen from the law

[430] See para.15–059 discussing *OFT v Abbey National Plc* [2008] EWHC 875 (Comm).
[431] This situation may, however, fall within the exclusion found in Sch.2 para.2(b) of the 1999 Regulations.
[432] See above, para.15–096.
[433] s.3(2) (b)(ii).
[434] *Broadwater Manor School v Davis* [1999] C.L.Y. 1801 Worthing County Court.

governing contracts of employment and partnerships.[435] Subparagraph (g) describes a term which seeks to provide for the termination of a contract of indefinite duration without reasonable notice (a concept familiar to the common law) unless there are serious grounds for doing so. The Office of Fair Trading has applied this example to a contract for the provision of estate agency services which allowed the agency to cancel the contract at any time, preferring its replacement with a term which allowed termination only on 14 days' notice.[436] It is to be noted, though, that para.2 of Sch.2 of the 1999 Regulations excludes from the scope of subpara.(g) a range of terms in contracts for the supply of financial services, transactions in transferable securities, etc.[437]

15–101 **"Automatic extension clauses."** Terms which have the object or effect of:

"(h) . . . automatically extending a contract of fixed duration where the consumer does not indicate otherwise, when the deadline fixed for the consumer to express this desire not to extend the contract is unreasonably early."

Thus, for example, a term in a contract for the provision of a vehicle declamping service which stipulated that the annual contract was to be renewed unless the consumer gave notice not less than four weeks before its expiry was considered potentially unfair by the Office of Fair Trading (it being coupled with a clause requiring the payment of a very high percentage of the annual fee if the period for notice was not observed).[438]

15–102 **Binding terms and the relevance of notice.** Terms which have the object or effect of: "(i) irrevocably binding the consumer to terms with which he had no real opportunity of becoming acquainted before the conclusion of the contract". As has already been noted, this example of a possible unfair term has very important implications.[439] For the vast majority of consumer contracts made on written standard terms contain a term which binds the consumer irrevocably to the contract, although some rely simply on a requirement of a consumer's signature. Where a contract does contain such a term, then subpara.(i) suggests that *this term* may be unfair in the absence of a real opportunity of knowing about *other terms* of the contract and if it is, *this term* (and therefore the contract as a

[435] See Vol.II, paras 39–154 et seq. as regards employment and the Partnership Act 1890 s.26(1) as regards partnerships.

[436] OFT, *Unfair Contract Terms*, Bulletin No.3 (March 1997), p.26.

[437] 1999 Regulations Sch.2 para.2(a) states that: "Subparagraph 1(g) is without hindrance to terms by which a supplier of financial services reserves the right to terminate unilaterally a contract of indeterminate duration without notice where there is a valid reason, provided that the supplier is required to inform the other contracting party or parties thereof immediately". Para.2(b) provides that subparagraph 1(g) does not apply to: "[T]ransactions in transferable securities, financial instruments and other products or services where the price is linked to fluctuations in a stock exchange quotation or index or a financial market rate that the seller or supplier does not control; and contracts for the purchase or sale of foreign currency, traveller's cheques or international money orders denominated in foreign currency." Identical provision was contained in the 1994 Regulations Sch.3(2).

[438] OFT, *Unfair Contract Terms*, No.2 (September 1996), p.18.

[439] See above, para.15–076.

whole) will not be binding on the consumer.[440] In this way, the Regulations allow a court to make more onerous requirements of notice than has been the case at common law.[441]

Variation clauses. Terms which have the object or effect of: 15–103

> "(j) . . . enabling the seller or supplier to alter the terms of the contract unilaterally without a valid reason which is specified in the contract;
>
> (k) enabling the seller or supplier to alter unilaterally without a valid reason any characteristics of the product or service to be provided;
>
> (l) providing for the price of goods to be determined at the time of delivery or allowing a seller of goods or supplier of services to increase their price."

These three examples of possibly unfair terms are clearly related, each allowing a seller or supplier to vary an aspect of the contract (whether its terms, its subject matter or its price) to the possible prejudice of the consumer. First, para.2(b) of Sch.2 to the 1999 Regulations provides that subpara.(j) is:

> " . . . without hindrance to terms under which a seller or supplier reserves the right to alter unilaterally the conditions of a contract of indeterminate duration, provide that he is required to inform the consumer with reasonable notice and that the consumer is free to dissolve the contract."[442]

So, it would seem that a term which allows variations of contract terms under these conditions is likely to be considered to be fair. As to variations in the subject matter, the fact that a term clarifies that any change in, for example, goods to be supplied will be made only if it improves the specification of those goods and that the consumer will bear no extra cost for such improvements argue in favour of its fairness.[443] On the other hand, a term which allows the seller or supplier to pass on any increased costs of the service through price increases to the consumer is likely to be unfair, given that this places:

> ". . . the risk of the contract price proving to have been a bad bargain on the consumer, who would be less likely to be able to anticipate such changes than a business",[444]

though this is less likely if another term allows the consumer to cancel the contract if the price is in fact raised.[445] Finally, it is to be noted that subparas (j) and (l) are stated as being limited in their scope in various ways regarding certain

---

[440] See below, para.15–123.
[441] See above, paras 12–010 et seq.
[442] cf. 1994 Regulations Sch.3 para.2(b).
[443] OFT, *Unfair Contract Terms*, Bulletin No.1 (May 1996), p.36 and see other examples at pp.17 and 38.
[444] OFT, *Unfair Contract Terms*, Bulletin No.1 (May 1996), p.44.
[445] OFT, *Unfair Contract Terms*, Bulletin No.2 (September 1996), pp.21 and 33.

terms in contracts for the provision of financial services, transactions in transferable securities, etc.[446]

15–104 **"Supplier's discretion" clauses.** Terms which have the object or effect of:

> "(m) . . . giving the seller or supplier the right to determine whether the goods or services supplied are in conformity with the contract, or giving him the exclusive right to interpret any term of the contract."

For example, a term in a contract for the repair of computers has been viewed as potentially unfair by the Office of Fair Trading where it gave the repairer the exclusive right to determine whether the goods were faulty, this being exacerbated by the possibility of the repairer being able to impose a fee before the goods were returned.[447]

15–105 **"Entire agreement clauses".** Terms which have the object or effect of:

> "(n) . . . limiting the seller's or supplier's obligation to respect commitments undertaken by his agents or making his commitments subject to compliance with a particular formality."

The first part of this subparagraph describes an important group of contract terms, which have been the subject of special consideration by the Office of Fair Trading and termed "entire agreement clauses".[448] These clauses are those which are aimed at enabling a business to escape liability for promises that conflict with or add to the commitments in the standard written contract (for instance, an agreement to a deadline by which goods will be supplied), to which may be added by analogy those clauses which are aimed at enabling a business to escape liability for misrepresentations (for example, that an item has sold in large quantities and that this is the last one in stock).[449] The Office of Fair Trading gives as a typical example a clause of a mobile telephone airtime contract which provided that:

---

[446] 1999 Regulations Sch.2 para.2 and 1994 Regulations Sch.3 para.2 states that: "(b) Subparagraph 1(j) is without hindrance to terms under which a supplier of financial services reserves the right to alter the rate of interest payable by the consumer or due to the latter, or the amount of other charges for financial services without notice where there is a valid reason, provided that the supplier is required to inform the other contracting party or parties thereof at the earliest opportunity and that the latter are free to dissolve the contract immediately; . . . (c) Subparagraphs 1(g), (j) and (l) do not apply to: transactions in transferable securities, financial instruments and other products or services where the price is linked to fluctuations in a stock exchange quotation or index or a financial market rate that the seller or supplier does not control; contracts for the purchase or sale of foreign currency, traveller's cheques or international money orders denominated in foreign currency; (d) Subparagraph 1(l) is without hindrance to price indexation clauses, where lawful, provided that the method by which prices vary is explicitly described."

[447] OFT, *Unfair Contract Terms*, Bulletin No.2 (September 1996), p.23.

[448] OFT, *Unfair Contract Terms*, Bulletin No.1 (May 1996), pp.15 et seq. An "entire agreement clause" seeks to ensure that a court concludes that it was the intention of the parties that a written document should contain all the terms of the contract, for in the absence of such a finding a court will look at the oral as well as the written agreement of the parties: see above, para.12–104 in relation to the "parol evidence rule".

[449] OFT, *Unfair Contract Terms*, pp.15 et seq.

"You [the consumer] agree that this Agreement is the complete and exclusive statement between us which supersedes all understandings or prior agreements oral or written and all representations or other communications between us relating to the subject matter of the Agreement."[450]

Another variety of this type of term may be found in a clause which unreasonably restricts or purports to restrict the authority of an agent of the seller or supplier, for example, where the latter is a company by requiring that only representations made in writing and signed by a director of the company shall bind the company.[451] So, it has been held that where in the context of a particular type of contract (such as for the supply of replacement doors and windows) there is a very clear risk of statements being made by salesmen agents which do not conform to the contract's written terms, this risk is:

"... sufficiently great to make it unfair and contrary to the requirement of good faith for a supplier of such products to make use of a term which restricts liability for such statements",

e.g. by requiring any representation or promise made before or at the time of conclusion of the contract to be added to the contract and signed by both parties.[452] More generally, while the Office of Fair Trading concedes that these sorts of clause are not always intended to cheat consumers and that their potential effect is "not invariably unfair",[453] in its experience "virtually all entire agreement clauses" drawn to its attention were potentially unfair.[454]

"Unequal opt out clauses". Terms which have the object or effect of: 15–106

"(o) obliging the consumer to fulfil all his obligations where the seller or supplier does not perform his".

An example of such a term may be found in a contract for the provision of airtime by a mobile telephone service which allowed its provider "from time to time without notice to suspend the Network service", but further provided that:

"Notwithstanding any suspension of the Network service . . . the Customer shall remain liable for all charges due throughout the period of suspension unless [the supplier] at its sole discretion determines otherwise."[455]

---

450 OFT, *Unfair Contract Terms*, pp.15 et seq.

451 OFT, *Unfair Contract Terms*, Bulletin No.2 (September 1996), p.60. Such a clause attempts to denude the agents of their apparent or ostensible authority: cf. Vol.II, paras 31–057 et seq.

452 *Office of Fair Trading v MB Designs (Scotland) Ltd* [2005] S.L.T. 691 at [46], per Lord Drummond Young (OH of the Ct of Sess, in the context of granting an interim order under Pt 8 of the Enterprise Act 2002, on which see para.15–139).

453 OFT, *Unfair Contract Terms*, Bulletin No.1 (May 1996), p.16 (factors in favour of a clause's fairness are its narrow terms; any balancing equal and opposite burden on the business or grant of an unequal advantage to the consumer; or the fact that it was specifically drawn to the attention of and explained to consumer).

454 OFT, *Unfair Contract Terms*, Bulletin No.1, p.17.

455 OFT, *Unfair Contract Terms*, Bulletin No.3 (March 1997), p.77.

Not surprisingly, given its width, the Office of Fair Trading considered that this particular example of an "unequal opt out clause" was potentially unfair, and negotiated its replacement with a clause which advised the consumer to arrange insurance to cover any monthly charges and provided for a refund by the provider of the service if the consumer is unable to use the services in certain circumstances for a continuous period of three days.[456]

15–107 **Assignment clauses.** Terms which have the object or effect of:

> "(p) . . . giving the seller or supplier the possibility of transferring his rights and obligations under the contract, where this may serve to reduce the guarantees for the consumer, without the latter's agreement."

Such a term is particularly likely to be unfair if the contract prevents the consumer from transferring his own rights under the contract, given the reference in the general test of unfairness to the need for rights to be balanced.[457] Moreover, the Office of Fair Trading has intervened so as to prevent certain consumer contracts from preventing the assignment by the consumer of his rights under the contract more generally. In its view, in the case of guarantees of goods sold, a consumer should generally be entitled to assign the benefit of the guarantee as:

> ". . . they can add substantial value to the main subject matter of the contract. If consumers cannot sell something still under guarantee with the benefit of that guarantee, they are effectively deprived of part of what they have paid for."[458]

On the other hand, the Office of Fair Trading accepts that suppliers have a legitimate interest in ensuring that they are not subject to baseless claims under guarantees and so there is no objection to terms which require the purchaser (or "assignee") of goods, if he or she wishes to rely on the guarantee, to establish that it was properly assigned or that the transfer is subject to the reasonable consent of the supplier.[459] In a different context, "non-transferable ticketing" in air-travel contracts has been the subject of criticism by the Office of Fair Trading.[460]

15–108 **Other potentially unfair terms.** The bulletins of the Office of Fair Trading contain a number of types of terms found in consumer contracts which it considers are likely to be considered to be unfair within the meaning of the Regulations.[461] These include terms which put on the consumer the onus to judge technical matters in which the supplier is expert but in which the consumer is not (for example, placing on a consumer the determination whether a driveway was ready for resurfacing with tarmacadam)[462]; terms where the apparent supplier of

---

[456] OFT, *Unfair Contracts Terms*, Bulletin No.3, p.77.

[457] See above, para.15–071.

[458] *Unfair Contract Terms Guidance* (February 2001), p.46.

[459] *Unfair Contract Terms Guidance*, p.46.

[460] OFT, *Unfair Contract Terms Bulletin* (July 1999) para.1.8.

[461] See in particular, OFT, *Unfair Contract Terms Guidance* (February 2001); *Guidance on Unfair Terms in Tenancy Agreements* (November 2001).

[462] OFT, *Unfair Contract Terms*, Bulletin No.3 (March 1997), p.24.

the service states in small print that he acts only as agent for another person (for example, in the provision of a holiday cottage)[463]; and "unfair enforcement clauses", for example, a term which grants to a seller of goods a right to enter the consumer's home and repossess the goods in certain circumstances without recourse to the court.[464] In the view of the Director General of Fair Trading this last type of clause "could be used to pressure a consumer to give up a legitimate claim to retain part of the contract price, and are entirely inappropriate in consumer contracts".[465]

Apart from these examples, an important type of term which may be thought of as vulnerable under the Regulations is one which allows the seller or supplier to terminate the contract on a minor breach by the consumer, whether this stems from a very slight breach of a significant term or the breach of a very minor term of the contract (notably, where the contract classes the terms in question as "conditions" as opposed to warranties).[466] Other types of clauses which may be thought to be potentially unfair are those which restrict a consumer's legal or equitable rights, such as in relation to discharge of a guarantee on variation of the contract or negligence in relation to the security[467]; a term which permits the supplier to pass on information about the consumer more freely or widely than would otherwise be allowed under the Data Protection Act[468]; a term which imposes on a consumer a duty of disclosure of all material facts in a contract where such a duty is not required by law (such as a contract of mortgage), especially where it places the issue of materiality within the decision of the supplier of the service; or a term which imposes on a consumer party to a contract of insurance a duty of disclosure which is more onerous than the law itself requires.[469] Moreover, it has been held that a contract term which provides that the consumer must indemnify the business in respect of its legal or other costs in any action or proceedings and pay it a reasonable sum in respect of time spent in connection with such an action or proceedings was unfair within the meaning of the 1999 Regulations, even though the court saw the force of the argument that such a term could protect the business against unfair treatment of the business by the customer who could use the business's unrecoverable costs to negotiate a discount on the unpaid contract price: the term remained unbalanced by any similar provision for the benefit of the consumer.[470] 15–109

[463] OFT, *Unfair Contract Terms*, Bulletin No.3, p.28.

[464] e.g. OFT, *Unfair Contract Terms,* Bulletin No.3 (December 1996), pp.26, 29.

[465] OFT, *Unfair Contract Terms* Bulletin No.3, p.29.

[466] See above, paras 12–009 et seq. and see Whittaker in Burrows and Peel, *Contract Terms* (OUP, 2007), 255, 262–63.

[467] This example depends on the wider interpretation being given to "consumer contract" as explained above, para.15–032. (Such a term would not come within Sch.2 para.1(b) of the 1999 Regulations as it would not relate to a right in respect of the other party's inadequate *performance*.) Another example may be found in a term which attempts to negative an *insurer's* duty of disclosure to the assured (on this duty, see Vol.II, para.41–031).

[468] OFT, *Unfair Contract Terms Guidance* (February 2001), p.48.

[469] On this duty, see Vol.II, paras 41–030 et seq.

[470] *Munkenbeck & Marshall v Harold* [2005] EWHC 356 (TCC), [2005] All E.R. (D) 227 at [12]–[15].

(iv) *The Time-frame for Assessment of the Fairness of a Term*

15–110 **General.** While it was common ground in the *First National Bank* case that:

> " . . . fairness must be judged as at the date the contract is made, although account may properly be taken of the likely effect of any term that is then agreed and said to be unfair,"[471]

on examination the issue of the relevant time for the assessment of fairness is not without difficulty and a distinction needs to be drawn between the assessment of a term as between the parties to a consumer contract (termed an "assessment *in concreto*" by the European Court) and assessment of a term in the context of preventive measures (termed an "assessment *in abstracto*" by the European Court).[472]

15–111 **Assessment as between the parties: the time-frame.** As between the parties to a consumer contract, the court assesses the fairness of the terms included in the contract before it and, as earlier explained, the basic test of unfairness focuses on the (purported) effect of the term on the relative rights and obligations of the parties to the contract.[473] In doing so, the assessment is "concrete" in the sense that it can take into account the particular circumstances of the making of the individual contract: were any terms not easily comprehensible actually explained to the consumer? did the business bring any pressure to bear on the consumer? more broadly, did the business "deal fairly and equitably with the other party"?[474] The facts relevant to these questions would typically *precede* the point at which the contract itself is concluded. In this respect, it is perhaps surprising that reg.6(1) of the 1999 Regulations provides that:

> " . . . the unfairness of a contractual term shall be assessed taking into account the nature of the goods or services for which the contract was concluded and by referring, *at the time of conclusion of the contract*, to all the circumstances attending the conclusion of the contract,"

following here exactly the wording of the Directive.[475] It is submitted, however, that purpose of setting "the time of conclusion of the contract" as the relevant point of reference is not to exclude prior circumstances but rather to exclude circumstances which occur *after* the conclusion of the contract: in principle the Directive is concerned with the fairness of contract terms not with the fairness of the behaviour of business parties in the course of performance or non-performance of the contract. On the other hand, the test of fairness does have a forward-looking aspect, for, as earlier explained, a contract term must be assessed

[471] *Director General of Fair Trading Plc v First National Bank Plc* [2001] UKHL 52, [2002] 1 A.C. 481 at [13], per Lord Bingham, quoted by Andrew Smith J in *OFT v Abbey National Plc (Bank Charges)* [2008] EWHC 875 (Comm) at [442]. Lord Bingham's proviso accords with the relevance of a term's potential for unfair results in determining its unfair nature: above, para.15–072.

[472] *Commission v Spain* (C–70/03) [2004] E.C.R. I-0799 at [16].

[473] Above, para.15–065.

[474] Above, para.15–066.

[475] 1993 Directive art.4(1).

according to its potential for unfairness, that is, whether it permits the business party to the contract to act in a way which would be unfair to the consumer.[476]

Assessment as between the parties: "the conclusion of the contract". Given what has just been said, the question arises of when a contract is to be held concluded for this purpose. It is submitted that the European Court would wish to take an autonomous view of this issue and one which applied to this issue and also to the question of the temporal application of the implementing legislation of the Directive in Member States. The latter topic has already been discussed and suggestions made as to its possible treatment by the European Court.[477] As has been explained there (and has recently been noted by the High Court[478]) the meaning or application of the expression 'the conclusion of the contract' may give rise to difficulty where "new" terms are introduced into the relationship between parties to a contract concluded earlier. 15–112

Assessment in preventive proceedings: the time-frame. However, the time-frame for the assessment of terms in proceedings brought by the Office of Fair Trading or by "qualifying bodies" under the 1999 Regulations may well differ.[479] For the purpose of preventive measures taken under reg.12 of the 1999 Regulations, the 1993 Directive provides that: 15–113

> "Member States shall ensure that, in the interests of consumers and of competitors, adequate and effective means exist to prevent the continued use of unfair terms in contracts concluded with consumers by sellers or suppliers."[480]

It adds that this shall include action before courts or administrative bodies:

> ". . . for a decision as to whether contractual terms drawn up for general use are unfair so that they can apply appropriate and effective means to prevent the continue use of such terms"[481]

and it makes clear that action can be taken against trade associations to the same end. The European Court has described the assessment of contract terms in this way as "in abstracto"[482] and this refers to the characteristic of these proceedings that they do not concern the terms of an individual contract, but rather to the terms applicable to contracts of a particular type or types made by a particular business, several businesses or merely recommended for use by a trade association. This "abstract" character means that *particular* circumstances of the conclusion of a contract cannot be taken into account by a court in its assessment of

---

[476] Above, para.15–072.
[477] Above, para.15–015.
[478] *OFT v Abbey National Plc (Bank Charges)* [2008] EWHC 875 (Comm) at [442].
[479] 1999 Regulations regs 10—13, below, para.15–133. The time-frame in respect of the assessment of the fairness or the "plain, intelligible" character of terms in the context of proceedings by "enforcers" under the Enterprise Act 2002 appears to be clear as these proceedings are aimed at orders against persons to stop breaking legislation enacted for consumers where it harms their collective interest: see below, para.15–139.
[480] 1993 Directive art.7(1).
[481] 1993 Directive art.7(2).
[482] *Commission v Spain* (C–70/03) [2004] E.C.R. I–0799 at [16].

fairness as they will differ from case to case. On the other hand, a court should take into account the general and likely circumstances surrounding the making of contracts in the area concerned and this suggests that the time-frame for the assessment of the terms of contracts in preventive proceedings is a present and future one, the court looking at the fairness of the terms of the contract (under the basic test) as at the date of the proceedings taking into account the *likely future* circumstances of the actual conclusion of contracts under the terms in question.[483]

15–114 **"Continued use".** There is, however, a question as to what is meant by "continued use" for the purposes of the preventive measures under the Regulations: does it refer to the continued use of terms in contracts already concluded between consumers and businesses or only to the continued use of terms for the making of future contracts? It may be thought that the wording of art.7 of the Directive (on which these preventive measures rest) suggests the latter, as does the way in which the European Court has described these measures (although in a case not addressed to this issue).[484] However, against this it may be countered that the Directive's purpose of the protection of consumers requires the discontinuance of *reliance* on unfair terms by businesses as long as the terms would themselves fall under the test of unfairness as between the parties to contracts "concluded" after the coming into force of the national legislation implementing the Directive.[485] In this way, the "non-binding" nature of a term as between the parties could be reinforced by the exercise of preventive measures by public authorities or others entrusted with this policing role. It is submitted that this way of thinking finds support from the decisions of the European Court holding that national courts have a duty to consider the unfairness of terms as between the parties of their own initiative, doing so partly on the ground that this accords with the preventive measures foreseen by art.7 of the Directive.[486] This suggests a link between the two types of control ("concrete" and "abstract") required by the Directive, which would, therefore, argue that the preventive measures of art.7 should be able to come in aid of the individual measure (the non-binding nature of any unfair contract terms) of art.6. On the other hand, it may be countered that this would extend the intervention of the 1993 Directive too far towards the control of unfair contractual behaviour rather than merely unfair contract terms; to which can be added that on implementation of the Unfair Commercial Practices Directive of 2005,[487] the reliance by a business of a term "not binding" between the parties within the meaning of the 1993 Directive could constitute an

[483] And see below, para.15–136.

[484] *Commission v Spain* [2004] E.C.R. I–0799 at [16] (referring to the task of courts under art.7 "to assess *in abstracto* the unfair character of a term which may be incorporated into contracts which have not yet been concluded.")

[485] See above, para.15–011 et seq.

[486] *Océano Grupo Editorial SA v Murciano Quintero* (C–240/98 to C–244/98) [2000] E.C.R. 1–4941; *Cofidis SA v Fredout* (C–473/2000) [2002] E.C.R. 1–10875; *Mostaza Claro v Centro Móvil Milenium SL* (C–168/05) [2007] 1 C.M.L.R. 22 and see below, para.15–117.

[487] Directive 2005/29 concerning unfair business-to-consumer commercial practices in the internal market and amending Council Directive 84/450, Directives 97/7, 98/27 and 2002/65 and Regulation 2006/2004 of the European Parliament and of the Council ("Unfair Commercial Practices") [2005] OJ L149/22. The Directive is implemented in UK law by the Consumer Protection from Unfair Trading Regulations 2008 (SI/1277).

"unfair commercial practice" within the meaning of the 2005 Directive and so attract the policing measures which the latter provides.[488]

(v) *The Relative Roles of the European Court, National Courts and the Parties*

The relative roles of the European Court of Justice and national courts in relation to the issue of fairness. In *Océano Grupo Editorial SA v Murciano Quintero* the European Court had itself ruled that a domestic jurisdiction clause in consumer contract was unfair within the meaning of the 1993 Directive with the result that the Spanish court applying for a preliminary ruling and seized of a claim by the business against the consumer was entitled to deny jurisdiction on the ground of the unfairness of this term.[489] However, when in *Freiburger Kommunalbauten GmbH Baugesellschaft & Co KG v Hofstetter*[490] it was asked directly by a national court to decide whether a clause in the consumer contract before it was unfair within the meaning of the 1993 Directive, the European Court refused to do so, noting that: 15–115

> ". . . in referring to concepts of good faith and significant imbalance between the rights and obligations of the parties, Art.3 of the [1993] Directive merely defines in a general way the factors that render unfair a contractual term that has not been individually negotiated."[491]

Given the range of factors which the Directive requires to be taken into account in assessing the fairness of a contract term:

> ". . . the consequences of the term under the law applicable to the contract must also be taken into account. This requires that consideration be given to the national law."[492]

So, while the European Court:

> ". . . may interpret general criteria used by the Community legislation in order to define the concept of unfair terms . . . it should not rule on the application of these general criteria to a particular term, which must be considered in the light of the particular circumstances of the case in question."[493]

---

[488] The Unfair Commercial Practices Directive applies to "unfair business-to-consumer commercial practices . . . before, during and after a commercial transaction in relation to a product:" art.3(1). "Unfair commercial practices" are explained in arts 5–9. On this Directive, see further Weatherill and Bernitz, *The Regulation of Unfair Commercial Practices under the EC Directive 2005/29* (2007), passim.

[489] *Océano* [2000] E.C.R. 1–4941 and see below, para.15–117.

[490] (C–237/02) [2004] 2 C.M.L.R. 13.

[491] [2004] 2 C.M.L.R. 13 at [19]–[21].

[492] [2004] 2 C.M.L.R. 13 at [21]; e.g. *Director General of Fair Trading Plc v First National Bank Plc* [2001] UKHL 52, [2002] 1 A.C. 481, above, para.15–082.

[493] [2004] 2 C.M.L.R. 13 at [22] distinguishing (at [23]) its earlier decision in *Océano Grupo Editorial SA v Murciano Quintero* [2000] E.C.R. 1–4941 on the basis that the clause there satisfied all the criteria necessary for it to be judged unfair without consideration of all the circumstances in which the contract was concluded or the advantages and disadvantages which the term would have under the applicable national law.

As a result, it is generally for a national court to decide whether a contract term satisfies the requirements for it to be regarded as unfair within the meaning of art.3(1) of the Directive.[494]

15–116 **Judicial discretion and domestic appeals.** In the context of the Unfair Contract Terms Act 1977, it has been said that while a decision on the reasonableness of a contract term is not merely an exercise of judicial discretion (and so in practice all but immune to appeal)[495] there "will sometimes be room for a legitimate difference of judicial opinion",[496] this indicating a judicial desire to discourage appeals on the issue of reasonableness.[497] While the test of unfairness for the purposes of the Regulations has a number of features in common with the test of reasonableness under the 1977 Act,[498] the composite character of the former requires courts to take into account a number of elements, each of which may require "interpretation" and not merely application. And English appellate courts have not appeared unwilling to reverse first instances decisions on the fairness of a term where they disagreed with their application of the test.[499]

15–117 **The power and duty of national courts to intervene of their own initiative.** In *Océano Grupo Editorial SA v Murciano Quintero*,[500] which concerned proceedings brought by suppliers against consumers, the European Court held that, at least where a term in a consumer contract was clearly unfair within the meaning of the Directive, the national court is entitled to raise the issue of fairness of its own initiative, this being necessary to ensure that the consumer enjoys effective protection in view of the real risk that he is unaware of his rights or encounters difficulties in enforcing them.[501] In the particular circumstances of the case, the term in question was a choice of local jurisdiction within Spain which chose the court of the place of establishment of the seller or supplier: here, the Spanish court was entitled to refuse jurisdiction on the basis that the clause was unfair within the meaning of the Directive. In *Cofidis SA v Fredout*,[502] the European Court implicitly rejected the argument that its *Océano Grupo Editorial SA* decision was limited to the special context of jurisdiction clauses, holding that the effectiveness of the protection for consumers contained in the Directive requires a national court to be able to intervene without time-limit despite a national legislative provision which would otherwise have prevented a consumer from relying on the invalidity of an unfair term on the expiry of a time-limit.

---

[494] [2004] 2 C.M.L.R. 13 at [25]. See also *Mostaza Claro v Centro Móvil Milenium SL* (C–168/05) [2007] 1 C.M.L.R. 22 at [22]–[23].

[495] See, e.g. the approach of the courts to the exercise of judicial discretion in relation to the award of a "just sum" under the Law Reform (Frustrated Contracts) Act 1943 s.1(3), below, para.23–088.

[496] *George Mitchell (Chesterhall) Ltd v Finney Lock Seeds Ltd* [1983] 2 A.C. 803, 816, per Lord Bridge.

[497] Treitel, *The Law of Contract*, 12th edn (2007), para.7–080.

[498] Above, para.15–090.

[499] e.g. *Director General of Fair Trading v First National Bank Plc* [2001] UKHL 52, [2002] 1 A.C. 481 reversing the CA [2000] Q.B. 672 which itself had reversed the HC; *Bryen & Langley Ltd v Boston* [2005] EWCA Civ 973, [2005] All E.R. (D) 507 (Jul).

[500] Joined Cases C–240/98 to C–244/98 [2000] E.C.R. 1–4941.

[501] [2000] E.C.R. 1–4941 at [26].

[502] C–473/2000 [2002] E.C.R. 1–10875.

While in both these decisions the European Court was careful to express its view in terms of a *power* in national courts to intervene of their own initiative,[503] in *Mostaza Claro v Centro Móvil Milenium SL*[504] the European Court went further, holding that national courts have a duty to intervene of their own initiative in order to ensure that the protection promised by the Directive is effectively ensured for consumers. In that case, the European Court ruled that a national court faced with a claim by a consumer for annulment of an arbitral award against her must annul the award if it considers that the arbitration clause on the basis of which the arbitration took place was invalid as an unfair term in a consumer contract within the meaning of the Directive, even though the consumer had not raised the issue of invalidity in the course of the arbitral proceedings and would normally be prevented from raising the issue by a subsequent action for annulment of the award as a matter of national procedural law. According to the Court:

> "The nature and importance of the public interest underlying the protection which the Directive confers on consumers justify . . . the national court *being required to assess of its own motion* whether a contractual term is unfair, compensating in this way for the imbalance which exists between the consumer and the seller or supplier."[505]

While it could be argued that the circumstances in which this statement was made were special in that the arbitration clause in issue was seen as compromising the consumer's fundamental right to a fair hearing,[506] nevertheless it is expressed very generally and grounded principally on art.6 of the Directive itself and on the nature of the protection which it provides.[507] Behind this case law of the European Court is an implicit recognition of the principle that national courts "know the law" (this principle being known widely under the Latin tag "*iura novit curia*") and specifically that they therefore are on notice as to the ambit of the protection required by the Directive so as to enable them—and indeed to require them—to intervene of their own initiative.[508]

The burden of proof as to fairness. In English law, the decision of an issue such as the reasonableness of a contract term is a matter requiring the allocation 15–118

[503] Whittaker (2001) 117 L.Q.R. 215, 217–218 (but arguing for recognition of such a duty).

[504] C–168/05 [2007] 1 C.M.L.R. 22.

[505] [2007] 1 C.M.L.R. 22 at [38] (emphasis added).

[506] [2007] 1 C.M.L.R. 22, Opinion of A.G. Tizziano, at [57] and [59]. The ECJ also relied in part on the fact that in the case before it Spanish national procedural law allowed a court to annul an arbitral award on the basis of a failure to observe national rules of public policy and this meant that as a matter of EC law a Spanish court must be able to do so on the grounds of Community public policy (the principle of equivalence): *Claro* at [35] applying *Eco Swiss China Time Ltd v Benetton International NV* (C–126/97) [1999] E.C.R. I–3055 at [37].

[507] Moreover, joined Cases C–240/98 *Océano Grupo Editorial SA v Murciano Quintero* [2000] E.C.R. 1–4941; Case C–473/2000 *Codifis CA v Fredout* [2002] E.C.R. 1–10875; and Case C–168/05 *Mostaza Claro v Centro Móvil Milenium SL* [2007] 1 C.M.L.R. 22 have been treated by the ECJ as examples of where the effectiveness of an EC directive requires the recognition of a duty on courts to invoke its provisions of its own initiative: *Van der Weerd v Minister van Landbouw, Natuur En Voedselkwaliteit* (C–222/05) Opinion of Att-Gen Maduro at [31] and judgment of ECJ [2007] 3 C.M.L.R. 7 at [40]–[41] distinguishing these cases from the case before it where no such duty was required.

[508] Whittaker (2001) 117 L.Q.R. 215.

of a burden of proof.[509] So, s.11(5) of the Unfair Contract Terms Act 1977 provides that "[i]t is for those claiming that a contract term or notice satisfies the requirement of reasonableness to show that it does". This provision reverses the normal burden of proof in civil cases at common law according to which burdens of proof rest on a person claiming something to establish it.[510] By contrast with the 1977 Act, neither the Regulations nor the Directive provide a rule for the burden of proof as to the issue of the fairness of a term, in contrast to the position as to the "individual negotiation" of a term where the burden is placed on the seller or supplier to show that a term is individually negotiated.[511] In theory, there are three possible approaches which the European Court of Justice could take if the question as to the proper burden of proof as to the fairness of a term were to be submitted to its decision: (i) that the issue of burden of proof as to fairness is a matter for national law; (ii) that an autonomous European view must be take as to the issue of burden of proof; and (iii) that the assessment of the fairness of a contract term for the purposes of the 1993 Directive is not itself a matter for the imposition of *any* burden of proof.

15–119 **A national or an autonomous rule of burden of proof?** It is submitted that the case law of the European Court of Justice already noted which holds that it is the duty of national courts to address the question of the fairness of a term in a consumer contract of their own initiative[512] is incompatible with a simple imposition of the burden of proof on consumers as to the issue of fairness, since it assumes that there is no need for the consumer to allege let alone to establish its unfairness. Moreover, the European Court's view that the role of national courts in this respect is a matter for Community law (rather than for national law by way of the principle of subsidiarity or under the principle of the procedural autonomy of Member States) suggests that the Court would also see the issue of burden of proof as to unfairness as one on which an autonomous view should be taken. In this respect, the general rule in the national laws of Member States is that it is for a person to establish what he alleges,[513] but to this it could be countered that the effectiveness of the protection of consumers requires that the burden of proof should lie on the seller or supplier, as it does in the Unfair Contract Terms Act 1977[514] and as it does under the 1993 Directive as to the "individual negotiation" of terms.[515]

[509] At common law, the reasonableness of a covenant in restraint of trade is considered an issue attracting a burden of proof, it being for the person seeking to rely on it to show its reasonableness: above, para.16–095. Some of the laws of other Member States treat issues such as the fairness of a contract term as one for burden of proof. So, e.g. the French legislation implementing the 1993 Directive expressly places the burden of proof on the issue of fairness on the consumer: art.L.132–1, al. 3 *Code de la consommation*.

[510] *Cross and Tapper on Evidence*, 11th edn (2007), p.130.

[511] 1993 Directive, art.3(2) para.3 and see above, para.15–047.

[512] [2000] E.C.R. 1–4941; *Cofidis* [2002] E.C.R. 1–10875; *Claro* [2007] 1 C.M.L.R. 22 and see above, para.15–117.

[513] "*Actori incumbit probatio*". See, for example, French law: art.1315 C. civ. and Ghestin and Goubeaux, *Droit civil, Introduction générale*, 3rd edn (1990), p.536; and German law: Stadler in Ebke and Finkin (eds), *Introduction to German Law* (1996), Ch.13, pp.357, 367.

[514] s. 11(5).

[515] 1993 Directive art.3(2); 1999 Regulations reg.5(4), above, para.15–047.

"Neutral" assessment of fairness. However, it is submitted that the European Court is more likely to hold that the issue of the fairness of a contract term is not itself an issue proper for the imposition of a burden of proof on either party to the contract, but rather for a neutral judicial assessment.[516] This is the position of the European Commission, which has expressed the view that: 15–120

> ". . . strictly speaking there is no problem concerning the burden of proof, because the unfair nature of a clause is not a matter of facts to be substantiated by the parties concerned, but a matter of law which the court must independently decide upon according to the rules of law (*jura novit curia*).[517] Unfairness is therefore very much a matter of law, but potentially may depend on elements of fact which the court may not know and this becomes for burden of proof for one or the other side which may want the clause to be declared unfair or not unfair as the case may be."[518]

This position may be supported at a textual level by noting the contrast between the Directive's provision of a rule governing the burden of proof as to the "individual negotiation" of a term[519] (a predominantly factual issue) and the issue of unfairness (an issue for judicial assessment). If this way of thinking were followed by the European Court, then a national court would have to decide the issue of the fairness of a contract term (whether this issue were raised by the consumer or of its own initiative) on the basis of the facts brought to its attention by the parties. These facts themselves (for example, as to the circumstances in which the contract was concluded[520]) would remain subject to burdens of proof following the normal rules of the national laws of the Member States (and thereby preserving to this extent the general principle of the procedural autonomy of Member States).[521]

Finally, it is submitted that the view that the issue of the fairness of a contract term under the Regulations is in principle a matter for a neutral assessment by the court, rather than being itself the object of a burden of proof is equally suitable to proceedings brought by the Office of Fair Trading or by one of the "qualifying 15–121

[516] cf. the approach of English law to the issue of reasonableness in unfair dismissal. For while an employer bears the burden of proof of showing that dismissal took place for reasons which were "potentially fair", once this has been shown, the tribunal assesses whether or not the employer "acted reasonably or unreasonably" as a "neutral issue", although the parties may adduce facts or arguments in support of their positions: *Boys and Girls Welfare Society v McDonald* [1996] I.R.L.R. 129, 132.

[517] i.e. "The court knows the law" and sometimes found as *curia novit legem.* The simple idea behind this maxim is that while in civil cases it is for the parties to bring the facts to the court, it is for the courts to apply the law to those facts, even in the absence of any legal submissions by the parties.

[518] Proceedings of the Conference, *"The Unfair Terms Directive: 5 years On"*, (July 1999), *The Implementation of Directive 93/13 into the National Legal Systems*, Final Report to Workshop 3, "The definition of 'unfairness' ", pp.141–142, available at *http://europa.eu.int/* [Accessed June 19, 2008].

[519] 1993 Directive art.3(2), para.3.

[520] See above, para.15–076.

[521] This principle was expressly recognised by the ECJ in *Mostaza Claro v Centro Móvil Milenium SL* [2007] 1 C.M.L.R. 22 at [24], though subject to the provisos that national procedural rules designed to protect Community rights in individuals must satisfy the principle of the effectiveness of the rights in question and be no less favourable than those governing similar domestic situations following the principle of equivalence.

bodies" for an injunction in their preventive roles.[522] One practical difference between the two types of way in which the issue of unfairness arises is that as between contracting parties it is likely attract more discussion as to the facts surrounding the making of the contract (which remain subject to burden of proof), whereas proceedings brought to prevent the continued use or recommendation for use of unfair terms are relatively more "abstract"[523] and by their nature less likely to require the consideration of facts which need to be established.[524]

(vi) *The Effects of a Finding that a Term is Unfair*

15–122 **"Not binding on the consumer".** Article 6(1) of the Directive provides that:

> "Member States shall lay down that unfair terms used in a contract concluded with a consumer by a seller or supplier shall, as provided for under their national law, not be binding on the consumer and that the contract shall continue to bind the parties upon those terms if it is capable of continuing in existence without the unfair terms."

The wording of reg.8 of the 1999 Regulations follows this formulation closely, except that understandably it omits reference to national law. The idea of an unfair contract term "not binding" a consumer was deliberately adopted by the EC legislator as a "neutral" way of expressing the effect of a finding of "unfairness", making clear the practical effect which it sought to achieve without adopting any one of the various terminologies or techniques used by national laws in similar circumstances (such as holding the term invalid, a nullity, void or "deemed not to have been written").[525]

15–123 **Examples of the "non-bindingness" of unfair terms.** In the vast majority of cases which concern the unfairness of "incidental terms" the effect of a finding of unfairness is straightforward and unproblematic. So, for example, a consumer is not affected by any purported exercise of any power granted by the term (such as a variation of the price or subject matter of the contract by the seller or supplier); not prejudiced by any allocation of risk indicated by the term (such as contained in an exemption clause); nor is the consumer obliged to conform to a procedure stipulated by the term (such as in the case of an arbitration clause or choice of jurisdiction clause). By contrast, in principle, the seller or supplier remains bound by the term, even if it is unlikely that a consumer would wish to

---

[522] See below, paras 15–133 et seq.; cf. *Director General of Fair Trading v First National Bank Plc* [2000] 1 W.L.R. 98, 112 where it is noted that counsel for the D.G.F.T. conceded that it was for him to show that the term used by the defendant bank was unfair.

[523] In *Commission v Spain* (C–70/03) [2004] E.C.R. I-0799 at [16] the ECJ distinguished between proceedings between parties to a consumer contract ("assessment in concreto") and "actions for cessation which involve persons or organisations representative of the collective interest of consumers" (under art.7 of the 1993 Directive) ("assessment in abstracto").

[524] Even here, however, facts may be relevant: e.g. a particular contract term may be more intelligible (and therefore more likely to be fair) if the business which uses it explains its significance either by a brochure or the practice of its agents.

[525] Tenreiro (1995) *European Review of Private Law* 273, 280 et seq.

hold him to it (given that ex hypothesi the term purports to cause a significant imbalance in his rights or obligations to his detriment).

Wider effect of "core term" not being binding as between parties. On the other hand, the situation may well be more difficult in relation to a "core term" (that is, one which expresses the substance of the bargain either in terms of its subject-matter or its price) which is not "plain and intelligible"[526] and which has thereby become subjected to the test of unfairness.[527] If such a term were held to be unfair (and not binding on the consumer), it may well be that the contract would be held "incapable of continuing in existence without the unfair term". If this were the case, the Regulations appear to assume that the contract as a whole ceases to bind *both* the parties: this appears to be the force of the phrase "[t]he contract shall continue to bind the *parties* if" contained in reg.8. However, this interpretation of the Regulations has a potentially unattractive result: for if a core term were held not binding on the consumer (since it was both unclear and unfair), it would appear that the seller or supplier could claim that on this ground he was not bound by the contract as a whole. However, this is unlikely to prove a frequent problem as it is unlikely that a consumer would wish to keep the seller or supplier to such a contract. 15–124

Restitutionary consequences of term "not binding". Neither the Directive nor the Regulations make provision regarding any possible restitutionary consequences of a finding that a term is "not binding" on the ground of its unfairness. The first question which arises is whether the European Court would consider this an issue on which it should take an "autonomous" view.[528] In this respect, its starting-point is likely to be that art.6(1) of the Directive expressly refers to an unfair term not binding the consumer "as provided for under their national law" and this neutrality as between the conceptual mechanisms of "non-bindingness" suggests that other possible consequential effects of "non-bindingness" (notably, as to the availability of restitution and its incidents) are similarly to be allocated to national law. However, against this position, it is to be recalled that the European Court has made clear (in the context of the question whether a national court should address the issue of unfairness of a term of its own initiative) that art.6(1) reflects a policy of protection of consumers which must be supported if need be by reference to the principle of effectiveness.[529] Furthermore, in the context of another Directive within the consumer *acquis*, the Court has allocated a particular issue to national laws in principle, while at the same time qualifying this application by reference to the principle of effectiveness.[530] Drawing on this case law, the Court could hold that while in principle the mechanism and nature of "non-bindingness" of an unfair contract term is for national laws, their interpretation and application of this concept should not 15–125

[526] See below, para.15–129.

[527] See above, paras 15–049—15–063.

[528] See above, para.15–008.

[529] Joined Cases C–240/98 *Océano Grupo Editorial SA v Murciano Quintero* [2000] E.C.R. 1–4941; Case C–473/2000 *Codifis CA v Fredout* [2002] E.C.R. 1–10875; Case C–168/05 *Mostaza Claro v Centro Móvil Milenium SL* [2007] 1 C.M.L.R. 22; above, paras 15–117—15–118.

[530] Case C–203/99 *Veedfald v Århus Amtskommune* [2001] E.C.R. 1–3569 (in the context of Directive 1985/374 concerning liability for defective products art.9) at [27]–[28].

compromise the effectiveness of the consumer's protection envisaged by the Directive. In practice, this could mean that where, for example, a consumer had paid money under an unfair contract term (such as a penalty clause, an unfair variation of price clause or an unintelligible[531] and unfair price determination clause), then the consumer should be able to recover this amount from the seller or supplier, for otherwise the protection of the consumer against this sort of unfair contract term would be rendered ineffective. However, if this were the case, the exact nature of this recovery and its incidents (for example, as regards any defence of change of position by the seller or supplier or contributory fault in the consumer) would in principle remain for national law.[532] In this respect, a possible legal ground of restitution in English law would be recovery under a mistake of law, the consumer paying under a mistake as to the legal effectiveness of the term under which he pays owing on the mistaken view that it is binding.[533]

15–126 **Terms "not binding" on consumer and third parties.** Where a contract term does not bind a consumer by reason of the 1999 Regulations, this may in certain circumstances have legal consequences for third parties to the contract. For example, if a term in a consumer contract which stipulates that the rights under it may not be transferred (e.g. a non-transferable air ticket[534]) is found unfair within the meaning of the Regulations, then if these rights would otherwise be transferable[535] the consumer would be entitled to assign them to a third party and the third party would receive valid assigned rights under the contract; and if the third party had incited the consumer to assign his rights under the contract knowing of the non-assignment clause, then that third party would nonetheless not be guilty of the tort of inducing breach of contract as the contract would not have been broken.[536] In the very different context of contingency fee agreements, if a litigant (the consumer) were not bound by a term of a contingency fee agreement setting his advocate's success fee (on the basis that the term was both not "plain and intelligible" and unfair[537]), then no costs order could be made by a court against a losing defendant (third party to the agreement) in respect of this fee since the court's statutory power to do so is restricted to

---

[531] This further requirement stems from the partial exclusion of 'core terms' from the test of unfairness: above, para.15–062.

[532] The principle of effectiveness would still apply so as to ensure that any national rules did not render the consumer's protection ineffective. This may be relevant to the application of the rules of limitation of actions normally applicable to the restitutionary action in question: on this issue cf. [2002] E.C.R. 1–10875 (national limitation period held unable to prevent court intervening as regards the fairness of a contract term) and *Hamilton v Volksbank Filder eG* (412/06) especially A.G. Maduro's Opinion at [24] ("The existence of a general principle of limitation should therefore be recognised, while leaving the Member States the necessary discretion to implement it in their respective legal systems").

[533] On this ground of restitution see below.

[534] cf. above, para.15–107.

[535] So, for example, the rights in question are not too personal: see below, paras 19–054—19–057.

[536] On the need for breach of contract (and not mere interference with contract) for this tort see *OGB Ltd v Allan, Douglas v Hello! Ltd, Mainstream Properties Ltd v Young* [2007] UKHL 21, [2008] 1 A.C. 1 at [34] et seq. where the tort was described as being an "accessory" liability to breach of contract.

[537] See above, para.15–063.

"fees *payable* under a conditional fee agreement which provides for a success fee": if the term is not binding against the consumer, then the success fee would not by payable under the agreement.[538]

Other consequences. Apart from the above consequences as between the parties to a consumer contract, the unfairness of a term in a consumer contract may attract preventive measures being taken by the Office of Fair Trading and a number of other "qualifying bodies".[539] 15–127

7. THE REQUIREMENT OF PLAIN AND INTELLIGIBLE LANGUAGE

(a) *The Test*

Regulation 7 of the 1999 Regulations provides that: 15–128

> "(1) A seller or supplier shall ensure that any written term of a contract is expressed in plain, intelligible language.
>
> (2) If there is any doubt about the meaning of a written term, the interpretation which is most favourable to the consumer shall prevail except in proceedings brought under regulation 12."[540]

Unlike the 1994 Regulations' equivalent provision (which was entitled "Construction of written contracts"),[541] this provision is entitled simply "Written contracts" and this is preferable given that the importance of this requirement runs well beyond the traditional and narrow concern of construction. There are two aspects of this requirement: first, relating to its content and, secondly, relating to its effects.

The place of the requirement in the Regulations. It has earlier been argued that the requirement that the terms of consumer contracts (whether written or otherwise) be in plain, intelligible language can be relevant to their assessment under the test of unfairness, even though the more likely position is that a mere failure in "plainness" or "intelligibility" does not without more render a contract term unfair.[542] However, the requirement in reg.7 of the 1999 Regulations is clearly distinct from the wider test of unfairness in that it focuses on the form of drafting of the terms, rather than either their intended legal effect or their accessibility. It is to be noted, however, that the requirement has two limbs: terms must be both plain and intelligible. These are distinct as: 15–129

---

[538] Courts and Legal Services Act 1990 s.58A(6) (emphasis added) and see CPR Pt 44.3A, Practice Direction about Costs supplementing Pts 43–47 CPR para.9.1.

[539] See below, paras 15–133 et seq.

[540] 1994 Regulations reg.6. On proceedings brought under reg.12, see below, paras 15–133 et seq.

[541] 1994 Regulations reg.6.

[542] Above, paras 15–076—15–077.

> "A term might be obscure and difficult to understand at all, but bear only one meaning for anyone who manages to fathom it."[543]

Since the promulgation of the 1994 Regulations, the implications of this double requirement for the drafting of English consumer contracts have been considerable. The general style of traditional English contractual drafting echoes the general style of English legislative drafting: it is precise, detailed and elaborate, consisting of long clauses (sometimes without punctuation), providing many definitions of the terms or expressions which they use and attempting to leave as little as possible to chance. In its defence, it may be argued that these characteristics allow the avoidance of disputes and, therefore, of litigation, but this assumes a degree of understanding of the complexities of the terminology used and its attendant legal implications which is absent in all but the most sophisticated of commercial parties: to a consumer of average intelligence it is incomprehensible.

The work of the Office of Fair Trading indicates the virtues towards which the drafter of a consumer contract should strive and which its own work has been aimed at promoting.[544] Its starting-point has been that the contracts should normally be comprehensible by the consumer without recourse to legal advice.[545] As a result of this, the contract should avoid legal jargon (such as, for example, "representation", "warranty", "consequential damages", "force majeure"), express itself in direct and ordinary language, notably by using the first and second person rather than by naming and defining the parties to the contract and minimise the number of cross-references. Headings in the contract are helpful, and the size of the print should be large enough to be legible without difficulty.[546]

(b) *The Effects of Failure to Comply with the Requirement of Plain and Intelligible Language*

15–130 **Construction *contra proferentem*.** Regulation 7 of the 1999 Regulations refers only to one of the effects of a failure in a term to fulfill the requirement of use of plain and intelligible language: that where there is as a result doubt as to its meaning it shall be interpreted in a way most favourable to the consumer. This effect does not seem to add much to the existing position at common law, which has long recognised a rule of construction that an ambiguous written instrument shall be construed against the person who made it: construction is *contra proferentem*.[547] Apart from this effect, any failure to fulfil the requirement of plain and intelligible language will attract preventive measures under Pt 8 of the

---

[543] *OFT v Abbey National Plc (Bank Charges)* [2008] EWHC 875 (Comm) at [87], per Andrew Smith J.

[544] See especially the essay in OFT, *Unfair Contract Terms*, Bulletin No.2 (September 1996), pp.8 et seq.; OFT, *Unfair Contract Terms Guidance* (February 2001), pp.52 et seq.

[545] According to the OFT, the standard normally to be used is that of an average consumer (see above, para.15–031).

[546] It is submitted that the requirement of "plain, intelligible writing" does not affect the language type in which it is to be drawn up, but that this type may be relevant to the test of unfairness: see Whittaker, *Cambridge Yearbook of European Studies* (2006), Vol.8, Ch.10, above para.15–088.

[547] See above, paras 12–083 et seq.

Enterprise Act 2002 and may also attract preventive measures under the 1999 Regulations themselves.[548] Moreover, as has been noted, a failure of a "core term" to be expressed in plain, intelligible language removes its general immunity from assessment on the ground of unfairness.[549]

8. CHOICE OF LAW CLAUSES

Choice of law clauses ineffective. It is to be noted that, in keeping with the Unfair Contract Terms Act 1977 though subtly differently,[550] the Regulations contain a provision aimed at preventing the avoidance of their provisions by an express choice of law. Regulation 9 of the 1999 Regulations provides that: 15–131

> "These Regulations shall apply notwithstanding any contract term which applies or purports to apply the law of a non-Member State, if the contract has a close connection with the territory of the Member States."[551]

While this provision clearly disallows an express choice of law to avoid the application of the Regulations where the law chosen belongs to a non-Member State, it allows the choice of the law of a Member State, relying in this respect on the effect of the Directive to ensure a minimum protection for consumers throughout the European Union.[552] The European Court of Justice has noted that art.6(2) of Directive (implemented in English law by reg.9 of the 1999 Regulations) "merely states that the contract is to have a close connection with the territory of the Member States" in order to attract the application of the 1993 Directive's provisions.[553] This "deliberately vague", "general expression seeks to make it possible to take account of various ties depending on the circumstances of the case" and so while the legislature of a Member State may properly seek to give it concrete effect by the use of presumptions, it cannot circumscribe it by:

> " . . . a combination of predetermined criteria for ties such as the cumulative conditions as to residence and conclusion of the contract referred to in Article 5 of the Rome Convention."[554]

---

[548] Below, paras 15–134, 15–139.

[549] 1999 Regulations reg.6(2), above, para.15–000.

[550] s.27.

[551] 1994 Regulations reg.7.

[552] cf. the provisions governing express choice of law in consumer contracts in the Rome Convention art.5(2), below, paras 30–094 et seq.

[553] *Commission v Spain* (C–70/03) [2004] E.C.R. I–0799 at [32]. The Rome Convention is itself replaced by an EC Regulation No.593 on the law applicable to contractual obligations ("Rome I"), [2008] OJ L177/6 art.5 of which would introduce a new connecting factor of the direction by the business of its business or commercial activities to the country of the consumer's habitual residence. The UK has decided to opt into this new regime: see Ministry of Justice Consultation Paper 05/09, *Rome I—Should the UK opt in?* (2008) and below, para.30–131.

[554] [2004] E.C.R. 1–0799 at [32] and [33].

9. THE PREVENTION OF UNFAIR TERMS

15–132 **Introduction.** Article 7 of Directive of 1993 required Member States to:

> "... ensure that, in the interests of consumers and of competitors, adequate and effective means exist to prevent the continued use of unfair terms in contracts concluded with consumers by sellers or suppliers."

And it further provided that these:

> "... means ... shall include provisions whereby persons or organizations, having a legitimate interest under national law in protecting consumers, may take action according to the national law concerned before the courts or before the competent administrative bodies for a decision as to whether contractual terms drawn up for general use are unfair, so that they can apply appropriate and effective means to prevent the continued use of such terms."

These requirements were implemented (or purportedly implemented) into English law by the 1994 Regulations by imposing duties and granting powers in relation to the policing of unfair terms to the Director General of Fair Trading.[555] While the 1999 Regulations retained this role for the Director General of Fair Trading, they also created similar duties and powers in a number of other bodies ("qualifying bodies"), entrusted with "watch-dog" roles for particular commercial sectors, but one of which—the Consumers' Association—is a private body with a very general concern with the protection of the interests of consumers. Two further changes have taken place as a result of the Enterprise Act 2002. First, the office of the Director General of Fair Trading was abolished and replaced with a body corporate, the Office of Fair Trading, to which the functions of the Director were transferred.[556] Secondly, Pt 8 of the Enterprise Act 2002 put in place a further layer of support for the protection of consumers by giving a number of "enforcers" strengthened powers to obtain courts orders (known as "enforcement orders") against businesses which do not comply with their legal obligations to consumers and it included failures by businesses to fulfil the requirements of fairness and of transparency under Unfair Terms in Consumer Contracts Regulations for this purpose.[557] One effect of these changes has been to create the possibility of the cross-border policing of unfair contract terms, as "Community enforcers" recognised by other Member States and published at the European level are empowered to bring proceedings before UK courts.[558]

15–133 **Policing measures and written contract terms which fail the requirement of "plain and intelligible writing".** While both art.7 of the 1993 Directive and the 1999 Regulations themselves[559] on their terms restrict the availability of these policing measures to *unfair* contract terms, the Director General of Fair Trading

---

555 1994 Regulations reg.8.

556 Enterprise Act 2002 ss.1, 2. This change came into effect on April 1, 2003: Enterprise Act 2002 (Commencement No.2, Transitional and Transitory Provisions) Order 2003 (SI 2003/766) art.2.

557 See further below, para.15–139.

558 Below para.15–139.

559 1999 Regulations regs. 12–14.

interpreted the policing role imposed on him by the Regulations as including a concern with their formal as well as their substantive fairness.[560] Often, such a role can be justified on the basis that any failure in plainness or intelligibility of contract terms forms an element within their wider unfairness.[561] However, the Director General took the view that these policing measures extend to written contract terms which fail the requirement of "plain and intelligible writing" in and of itself. The main argument in favour of this position rests on the following reasoning. Art.5(2) of the Directive provides that:

> "... the rule on interpretation [*contra proferentem* which applies where a term fails as not plain and intelligible] shall not apply in the context of the procedures laid down in Article 7(2),"

and Art.7(2) imposes on Member States the duty to provide for action to be taken by "persons or organisations, having a legitimate interest under national law in protecting consumers" to prevent the continued use of "unfair terms"; so, although art.7 refers expressly only to "unfair terms", art.5(2)'s exclusion of one aspect of its application under art.7 assumes that it will otherwise figure in the role accorded to persons by Member States under art.7. The main difficulty with this line of argument is that it appears to run contrary to the approach of the European Court of Justice in *Commission v Spain,* where it held that the reason why the rule of interpretation *contra proferentem* of ambiguous terms found in art.5 should not apply in proceedings under art.7 lies in the need to enhance the effectiveness of preventive proceedings against *unfair* terms[562] since otherwise a potentially unfair term could be rescued by interpretation. This reasoning appears to assume, therefore, that proceedings under art.7 cannot be founded *merely* on a failure of term to be plain and intelligible and this has apparently been accepted at first instance.[563] Whatever the proper view as to the question of the availability of policing measures under art.7 of the 1993 Directive, the various "enforcers" acting under Pt 8 of the Enterprise Act 2002 enjoy certain powers to intervene under that Act on the basis of a failure to fulfil the requirement of plain and intelligible writing in the 1993 Directive since the Consumer Injunctions Directive[564] (which Pt 8 implements) requires the introduction of injunctions aimed at the protection of the collective interests of consumers where there is "any act contrary" to the directives listed in its annex, and this annex includes the 1993 Directive *in toto*.[565]

The role of the Office of Fair Trading. Under the 1999 Regulations the Office of Fair Trading ("OFT") has a duty to consider any complaint made to it that any contract term drawn up for general use is unfair, unless the complaint appears to it to be frivolous or vexatious or unless a "qualifying body" has notified it that it will consider the complaint.[566] The OFT may apply for an 15–134

---

560 OFT, *Unfair Contract Terms*, Bulletin No.2 (September, 1996), p.9.
561 Above, paras 15–056—15–057.
562 *Commission v Spain* (C–70/03) [2004] E.C.R. I–0799 at [16] and [17].
563 *OFT v Abbey National Plc* [2008] EWHC 875 (Comm) at [86].
564 Directive 98/27 on injunctions for the protection of consumers' interests [1998] OJ L166/51.
565 Directive 98/27 art.1(2); Annex, No.9.
566 1999 Regulations reg.10(1). On the work of the OFT, see Bright (2000) 20 L.S. 331. For "qualifying body" see below, para.15–138.

injunction against any person appearing to it to be using or recommending use of an unfair term drawn up for general use in contracts concluded with consumers,[567] the decision whether or not to do so being subject to a requirement of giving reasons where it has resulted from a complaint.[568] Furthermore, the 1999 Regulations permit the OFT to take into account in reaching its decision as to the appropriateness of bringing proceedings any undertaking given to it by or on behalf of any person as to the continued use of such a term in contracts concluded with consumers.[569] The 1999 Regulations empower a court to which the OFT has applied to grant an injunction on such terms as it thinks fit, and this may relate not only to use of a particular contract term drawn up for general use but to any similar term or term having like effect used or recommended for use by *any person*.[570] They also give to the OFT powers to obtain documents and information from any person in order to facilitate the consideration of a complaint submitted to him as to an unfair term or to ascertain whether a person has complied with an undertaking or court order as to the continued use of a term in contracts concluded with consumers.[571] Finally, the Regulations require the OFT to publish details of any undertakings made to it or to a court or made by a court and empowers it to arrange for the dissemination of information and advice concerning the operation of the Regulations.[572]

15–135 **Application of the fairness test by the OFT.** There are some differences in the way in which the OFT has undertaken the assessment of a term under the Regulations, these reflecting its somewhat more abstract nature than the assessment of a term between parties to a contract. First, as regards the requirement of fairness:

> "... the Director General applies the same test [as would a court in relation to a term to be enforced against a consumer], but looking forward rather than back—in other words, considering the circumstances that are generally likely to obtain, not those attending the conclusion of a particular contract."[573]

Secondly, in assessing the fairness of a term from the point of view of its clarity and intelligibility, the Director considers that:

> "... in order for [art.5 of] the Directive to have its intended effect we should have regard to a term's least favourable meaning, if it is likely to be so understood by the average consumer."[574]

---

567 1999 Regulations reg.12(1).
568 1999 Regulations reg.10(2).
569 1999 Regulations reg.10(3).
570 1999 Regulations reg.12(3) and (4).
571 1999 Regulations reg.13.
572 1999 Regulations reg.15(3).
573 Edwards in OFT, *Unfair Contract Terms*, Bulletin No.4 (December 1997), p.21. (The references to the "Director" must now be understood to refer to the Office of Fair Trading: see above, para.15–133). For the relevance of particular circumstances attending the conclusion of a contract, see above, para.15–076. For discussion of issues relating to the time-frame for assessment of the unfairness of terms for these purposes, see above, paras 15–113—15–114.
574 OFT, *Unfair Contract Terms*, Bulletin No.2 (September 1996), p.9. On the legal justification for the role of the Office of Fair Trading in respect of terms which fail the "plain, intelligible" requirement, see above, para.15–134.

These differences of approach are likely to be reflected in the judicial assessments of terms which are the subject of an application for an injunction under the 1999 Regulations.[575]

Burden of proof in proceedings. It has been argued that the better view is that, as between the parties to a consumer contract, there is no burden of proof as to the issue of the fairness of a contract term as normally understood, but rather that the court should make a neutral assessment of this issue on the basis of those facts adduced by the parties to the proceedings.[576] It is submitted that this should also be the case as regards an application brought by the Office of Fair Trading or one of the "qualifying bodies" for the grant of an injunction.[577] Indeed, this is a context where a neutral assessment is even more appropriate given that the assessment is made much more in the abstract (for the generality of circumstances in which the allegedly unfair term is used or recommended for use) than is the case as between the parties to the consumer contract, where the particular circumstances of the conclusion of the contract in question may be relevant. On the other hand, it is submitted that a court will not grant an injunction against a business on such an application unless it is satisfied that the term in question is unfair, whether or not this is expressed in terms of placing a burden of proof on the applicant body. 15–136

"Qualifying bodies." Unlike the 1994 Regulations, the 1999 Regulations extend the power to police unfair terms in consumer contracts to a range of bodies other than the Office of Fair Trading. Rather than providing a general definition or set of criteria by which a body may qualify for the purpose of bringing proceedings for an injunction under the 1999 Regulations, the latter simply list in Sch.1 those bodies or classes of body which in law do so.[578] Apart from the Consumers' Association, the list includes regulators of former public utilities, such as the Gas and Electrictity Markets Authority but also, at a local level, every weights and measures authority.[579] Where a qualifying body notifies the Office of Fair Trading that it agrees to consider a complaint that any contract term drawn up for general use is unfair, it thereby comes under a duty to consider that complaint.[580] A qualifying body is empowered to bring proceedings for an 15–137

---

[575] 1999 Regulations reg.12.

[576] See above, paras 15–119—15–122.

[577] cf. *Director General of Fair Trading v First National Bank Plc* [2001] 1 W.L.R. 98, 112 where counsel for the D.G.F.T. conceded that it was for him to show that the term used by the defendant bank was unfair.

[578] 1999 Regulations reg.1 "qualifying body".

[579] The full list is as follows: the Information Commissioner; the Gas and Electricity Markets Authority; the Director General of Electricity Supply for Northern Ireland; the Director General of Gas for Northern Ireland; the Office of Communications; the Water Services Regulation Authority; the Rail Regulator; every weights and measures authority in Great Britain; the Department of Enterprise, Trade and Investment in Northern Ireland; the Financial Services Authority (whose functions for this purpose are treated as functions of that Authority under the Financial Services and Markets Act 2000); the Consumers' Association: 1999 Regulations, as amended by Unfair Terms in Consumer Contracts (Amendment) Regulations 2001 (SI 2001/1186) reg.2; Financial Services and Markets Act (Consequential Amendments and Repeals) Order 2001 (SI 2001/3649) art.583.

[580] 1999 Regulations reg.11(1).

injunction against any person appearing to that body to be using, or recommending for use, an unfair term drawn up for general use in contracts with consumers, subject to a condition of prior notification of the OFT.[581] In deciding whether or not to apply for an injunction, a qualifying body may take into account any undertaking given to it as to the continued use of the term and bears a duty to give reasons for its decision.[582] Qualifying bodies enjoy the same powers to obtain documents and information as does the OFT[583] and the courts' power to grant injunctions is the same as for proceedings brought by the OFT.[584]

15–138 **"Enforcement orders" under the Enterprise Act 2002.** In addition to the powers provided by the 1999 Regulations, the Office of Fair Trading and other persons or bodies may enjoy powers of enforcement under the Enterprise Act 2002. Under Pt 8 of that Act a number of bodies, termed "enforcers", may apply to the court for an "enforcement order" against a person to stop breaking legislation enacted for the benefit of consumers.[585] The Act distinguishes for this purpose between the infringement of domestic legislation and of European Community legislation, including within the latter for this purpose the Unfair Terms in Consumer Contracts Directive 1993.[586] "Enforcers" are divided into "general enforcers", which include the Office of Fair Trading and local weights and measures authorities in Great Britain; "designated enforcers", which are any public or private body in the United Kingdom which the Secretary of State designates as a person or body one of whose purposes is the protection of the collective interests of consumers and which include the Civil Aviation Authority, the Information Commissioner and the Rail Regulator[587]; "Community enforcers", which are qualified entities listed for this purpose by the European Community, the list including a number of public and private bodies (notably, consumers' associations)[588]; and "CPC enforcers", which are bodies or persons designated by the Secretary of State under the EC Regulation on consumer protection co-operation,[589] these including the Office of Fair Trading, local

---

581 1999 Regulations reg.12(2).

582 1999 Regulations regs 10(2), (3) and 11(2).

583 1999 Regulations reg.13(5).

584 1999 Regulations reg.12(3).

585 2002 Act Pt 8 came into force on June 20, 2003: The Enterprise Act 2002 (Commencement No.3, Transitional and Transitory Provisions and Savings) Order 2003 (SI 2003/1397) art.2. It replaced the Fair Trading Act 1973 Pt III and the Stop Now Orders (EC Directive) Regulations 2001 (SI 2001/1422). Its provisions concerning "community infringements" implemented into UK law the Directive 98/27 on injunctions for the protection of consumers' interests, as amended. It has been held that the conduct of a person taking place *before* the coming into force of Pt 8 of the Enterprise Act 2002 can form the basis of granting an order under it: *Office of Fair Trading v MB Designs (Scotland) Ltd* [2005] S.L.T. 691 at [23] OH of the Ct of Sess, where Pt 8 is discussed more generally. The powers contained in the Enterprise Act 2002 were extended by the Enterprise Act 2002 (Amendment) Regulations 2006 (SI 2006/3363) implementing arts 4(6) and 13(4) of the Regulation 2006/2004 on co-operation between national authorities responsible for the enforcement of consumer protection laws (the Regulation on consumer protection co-operation), as amended by Directive 2005/29.

586 Enterprise Act 2002 s.212; Enterprise Act 2002 (Pt 8 Community Infringements Specified UK Laws) Order 2003 (SI 2003/1374) art.3.

587 The Enterprise Act 2002 (Pt 8 Designated Enforcers: Criteria for Designation, Designation of Public Bodies as Designated and Transitional Provisions) Order 2003 (SI 2003/1399) art.5 Sch.1.

588 Directive 98/27. For the full list of those "recognised entities" so-entitled, see Commission Communication [2006] OJ C39/2.

589 Regulation 2006/2004.

weights and measures authorities and certain other public bodies and persons.[590] The inclusion of "Community enforcers" within the class of those entitled to apply for enforcement orders reflects the policy of the European Community to promote cross-border policing under its own consumer protection legislation.[591] The designation of "CPC enforcers" seeks to give effect to a policy of encouraging and facilitating co-operation between European national authorities in the enforcement of consumer protection.[592] Where a domestic or a Community infringement harms the collective interest of consumers,[593] an "enforcer" can apply to the court for an enforcement order, but only after engaging in appropriate consultation with the person against whom the order would be made aimed at achieving the cessation of the infringement and ensuring that such an infringement will not occur in the future or where the matter is one of urgency.[594] Where a court finds that an infringement has been committed by the defendant to proceedings brought under these provisions, it may make an enforcement order.[595]

---

[590] Enterprise Act 2002 s.213(5A) as inserted by SI 2006/3363.

[591] Directive 98/27 art.4.

[592] Regulation 2006/2004.

[593] Enterprise Act 2002 ss.211(1)(c), 212(1). On the requirement of "harming the collective interest of consumers" see *Office of Fair Trading v MB Designs (Scotland) Ltd* [2005] S.L.T. 691 at [23], [1], [13]–[16].

[594] Enterprise Act 2002 s.214.

[595] s.217.

Part Five
ILLEGALITY AND PUBLIC POLICY

CHAPTER 16

ILLEGALITY AND PUBLIC POLICY

	PARA.
1. Introduction	16–001
2. The position at common law	16–003
(a) Generally	16–003
(b) Objects which are illegal by common law or by statute	16–014
(c) Objects injurious to good government	16–019
(i) Domestic affairs	16–019
(ii) Foreign affairs	16–026
(d) Objects injurious to the proper working of justice	16–035
(i) Agreements to conceal offences and compromises	16–035
(ii) Other contracts affecting the course of justice	16–039
(iii) Ouster of jurisdiction	16–044
(iv) Maintenance and champerty	16–048
(e) Objects injurious to morality and marriage	16–067
(i) Immorality	16–067
(ii) Interference with marriage	16–070
(f) Contracts in restraint of trade	16–075
(i) Scope of the doctrine	16–075
(ii) Employer and employee	16–104
(iii) Vendor and purchaser of business	16–116
(iv) Partners	16–119
(v) Supply and acquisition of goods: restraints in vertical agreements	16–121
(vi) Restraints on the use of land or chattels	16–128
(vii) Supply and acquisition of goods: restraints in horizontal agreements	16–132
(viii) Labour and services: restraints in horizontal agreements	16–136
(ix) Invalidating and regulatory statutory provisions	16–141
3. Contracts unenforceable by statute	16–142
(a) General principles	16–142
(b) Statutory regulation of trading with the enemy	16–162
4. Enforcement of collateral and proprietary rights	16–164
(a) The maxim *ex turpi causa non oritur actio* and related rules	16–164
(b) Collateral transactions	16–176
(c) Recovery of money paid or property transferred under illegal contracts	16–177
5. Severance	16–194
6. Pleading and practice	16–204

1. INTRODUCTION

Underlying principle. The enforcement of contractual claims is in certain circumstances against public policy. The effects of public policy differ considerably depending upon the circumstances; thus, in some instances, one or both parties are prevented from suing upon some particular undertaking contained in **16–001**

the contract (or even, where the doctrine of severance[1] can be applied, upon part of some particular undertaking), whereas in other cases one or both parties are prevented from suing upon the contract at all. The diversity of the fields with which public policy is concerned, and of the circumstances in which a contractual claim may be affected by it, combine to make this branch of the law of contract inevitably complex—a complexity which has been aggravated by lack of systemisation and by the confusing terminology which has often been adopted. Much difficulty would be avoided, if whenever a plea of illegality or public policy were raised as a defence to a contractual claim, the test were applied: does public policy require that this claimant, in the circumstances which have occurred, should be refused relief to which he would otherwise have been entitled with respect to all or part of his claim?[2] In addition, once the court finds that the contract is illegal and unenforceable, a second question should be posed which would also lead to greater clarity: do the facts justify the granting of some consequential relief (other than enforcement of the contract) to either of the parties to the contract.[3] As will be seen, the courts, although not posing this question directly, have been willing to grant consequential relief to the parties to illegal contracts.[4] Further, much confusion would be avoided if contracts were no longer themselves categorised as being void for illegality or on grounds of public policy in the same kind of way as contracts are categorised as being void on other grounds.

16–002 **Plan of chapter.** It is proposed in this chapter to deal first with the different kinds of situation in which one or both parties to a contract are prevented by reason of public policy from enforcing a contractual claim which they would otherwise have been entitled to enforce; the authorities make it necessary to treat the position at common law and by statute separately; the enforcement of collateral and proprietary rights is dealt with next; and thirdly the doctrine of severance, by which the court may reject the illegal part of an agreement and enforce what remains as unobjectionable, is considered.

2. THE POSITION AT COMMON LAW

(a) *Generally*

16–003 **Public policy.** The seriousness and turpitude of the illegality which renders a contract unenforceable varies considerably.[5] The illegality can arise either from

[1] See below, paras 16–194 et seq.

[2] cf. *Imperial Chemical Industries Ltd v Shatwell* [1965] A.C. 656, 675, 678, 683, 693. On the application of a "public conscience" test in determining whether or not contracts should be enforced, see *Tinsley v Milligan* [1994] 1 A.C. 340; below, para.16–181.

[3] See, for example, the sophisticated approach as to remedies in The Illegality Defence In Tort (Law Comm. Consultation Paper No.160, 2001); Enonchong, *Illegal Transactions* (1998); *Daido Asia Japan Ltd v Rothen* Unreported July 24, 2001, at [21]; *Hewison v Meridian Shipping PTE* [2002] EWCA 1821, [2002] All E.R. (D) 146.

[4] See below, paras 16–176 et seq.

[5] See generally "Illegal Transactions: The Effect of Illegality On Contracts And Torts" (Law Com. Consultation Paper No.154, 1999).

statute or the common law and, particularly where the latter is involved, the courts are faced squarely with the issue of whether public policy requires that a contract (otherwise valid and enforceable) should not be enforced because it is tainted with illegality. Obviously a doctrine of public policy is somewhat open-textured and flexible, and this flexibility has been the cause of judicial censure of the doctrine.[6] On occasions it has been seen by the courts as being vague and unsatisfactory, "a treacherous ground for legal decision", "a very unstable and dangerous foundation on which to build until made safe by decision".[7] It is in the context of this doctrine that the unruly horse metaphor rode into the litany of the English lawyer.[8] However, the doctrine has had its defenders. For Winfield, the "variability of public policy is a stone in the edifice of the doctrine, and not a missile to be flung at it".[9] Lord Denning M.R. also viewed the doctrine with favour[10]: "[w]ith a good man in the saddle, the unruly horse can be kept in control. It can jump over obstacles". In many respects the discussions on the nature of the doctrine of public policy is a matter of temperament, and it often appears to be nothing more than a verbal dispute. Although it is not something about which one can be dogmatic, the following seems reasonably clear. First, it is inevitable that some doctrine of public policy would evolve with respect to the validity of contracts. As was stated by Sir William Holdsworth[11]:

> "In fact, a body of law like the common law, which has grown up gradually with the growth of the nation, necessarily acquires some fixed principles, and if it is to maintain these principles it must be able, on the ground of public policy or some other like ground, to suppress practices which, under ever new disguises, seek to weaken or negative them."

Secondly, public policy is not immutable: 16–004

> "Rules which rest on the foundation of public policy, not being rules which belong to the fixed customary law, are capable, on proper occasion, of expansion or modification. Circumstances may change and make a commercial practice expedient which formerly was mischievous to commerce."[12]

And vice versa, a practice which was once permissible may be proscribed.[13] Thirdly, there is some doubt as to whether the courts can create new heads of public policy rather than merely apply existing doctrines to new situations. This

---

[6] See generally Bell, *Policy Arguments in Judicial Decisions* (Clarendon Press, 1983), particularly Ch.VI dealing with restraint of trade.

[7] *Janson v Driefontein Consolidated Mines Ltd* [1902] A.C. 484, 500, per Lord Davey; and see 507.

[8] "It is a very unruly horse, and when once you get astride it you never know where it will carry you": *Richardson v Mellish* (1824) 2 Bing. 229, 252, per Burrough J. See also *Money Markets International Stockbrokers Ltd v London Stock Exchange* [2002] 1 W.L.R. 1150 at [80].

[9] (1928–29) 42 Harv. L. Rev. 76, 94.

[10] *Enderby Town Football Club Ltd v The Football Association Ltd* [1971] Ch. 591, 606.

[11] *History of English Law*, Vol.III, p.55.

[12] *Maxim Nordenfelt Guns and Ammunition Co v Nordenfelt* [1893] 1 Ch. 630, 666. See also *Nagle v Feilden* [1966] 2 Q.B. 633, 650; *Shaw v Groom* [1970] 2 Q.B. 504, 523; *Multiservice Bookbinding Ltd v Mardon* [1979] Ch D 84 where the court had to determine whether an index-linked money obligation was contrary to public policy and decided it was not.

[13] *Esso Petroleum Co Ltd v Harper's Garage (Stourport) Ltd* [1968] A.C. 269, 322–324, 333.

is an area where the precedents hunt in packs of two. Broadly speaking, there are two conflicting positions, that have been referred to as the "narrow view" and "the broad view".[14] According to the former, the courts cannot create new heads of public policy,[15] whereas the latter countenances judicial law-making in this area.[16] To a large extent this debate is verbal. There is a general agreement that the courts may extend existing public policy to new situations[17] and the difference between extending an existing principle as opposed to creating a new one will often be wafer-thin. There will, however, be an understandable reluctance on the part of the courts to create completely new heads of public policy because of the existence of governmental bodies charged with the specific task of law reform and a more activist legislature. However, where Parliament has clearly articulated a principle of public policy then the courts may be willing to extend it by analogy into the field of contract.[18] Lastly, and most importantly, there is a public policy in favour of upholding contracts freely entered into, a policy which of course the doctrine of illegality completely undermines. The point was made forcefully by Jessel M.R. in *Printing and Numerical Registering Co v Sampson*.[19]

> "It must not be forgotten that you are not to extend arbitrarily those rules which say that a given contract is void as being against public policy, because if there is one thing which more than another public policy requires, it is that men of full age and competent understanding shall have the utmost liberty of contracting, and that their contracts when entered into freely and voluntarily shall be held sacred and shall be enforced by courts of justice. Therefore, you have this paramount public policy to consider—that you are not likely to interfere with freedom of contract."

16–005 **Scope of public policy.** Objects which on grounds of public policy invalidate contracts may, for convenience, be generally classified into five groups: first, objects which are illegal by common law or by legislation[20]; secondly, objects injurious to good government either in the field of domestic[21] or foreign affairs; thirdly, objects which interfere with the proper working of the machinery of justice; fourthly, objects injurious to marriage and morality; and, fifthly, objects economically against the public interest. This classification is adopted primarily

---

[14] Lloyd, *Public Policy* (1953), pp.112–117.

[15] *Egerton v Earl Brownlow* (1853) 4 H.L.C. 1, 106–107, 122–124; *Janson v Driefontein Consolidated Mines Ltd* [1902] A.C. 484, 491, 500, 507.

[16] *Egerton v Earl Brownlow* (1853) 4 H.L.C. 1, 149–151; *Wilson v Carnley* [1908] 1 K.B. 729, 737–738. See also *Initial Services Ltd v Putterill* [1968] 1 Q.B. 396; *McLoughlin v O'Brian* [1983] 1 A.C. 410, 426–428, 441–443.

[17] *Egerton v Earl Brownlow* (1853) 4 H.L.C. 1, 149; *Montefiore v Menday Motor Components Co* [1918] 2 K.B. 241, 246.

[18] See, e.g. *Nagle v Feilden* [1966] 2 Q.B. 633; cf. *Newland v Simons & Willer (Hairdressers) Ltd* [1981] I.C.R. 521.

[19] (1875) L.R. 19 Eq. 462, 465.

[20] Amongst statutory restrictions should now be included those articles of the Treaties of the European Community and those regulations and directives made thereunder which, either by virtue of the Treaties themselves or of the case law of the European Court, are directly applicable to the United Kingdom: European Communities Act 1972 ss.2 and 3. On the concept of direct applicability of Community law, see Hartley, *The Foundations of European Community Law*, 6th edn (2007), Ch.7.

[21] For an unusual example under this head, see *Amalgamated Society of Ry Servants v Osborne* [1910] A.C. 87.

for ease of exposition. Certain cases do not fit clearly into any of these five categories. For example, an agreement was held unenforceable by reason of the undertaking contained in it on the part of one of the parties, a newspaper, not to publish any comment on the activities of a company with which the other party was connected (although this was also held to be injurious to trade and commerce as in restraint of trade).[22] Any undertaking not to disclose matters of legitimate public interest may be insufficient consideration to support a contract,[23] and, if the matters are such that in the public interest they ought to be disclosed, an undertaking not to disclose them certainly will not be enforced.[24] Although a contract may be associated with a particular illegality, the public policy underlying the illegality may be such that it results in the contract being enforceable. In *Hill v Secretary of State for the Environment, Food and Rural Affairs*[25] the defendant argued that the contract that it had entered into with the claimant was illegal as the director, who had acted for the claimant, had been declared a bankrupt and had therefore committed an offence under s.11 of the Company Directors Disqualification Act 1986 which prohibits an undischarged bankrupt from taking part in the management of a company. As the court pointed out, this proscription had been introduced to protect persons dealing with companies and, were the argument of the defendant to prevail, it would have the effect of prejudicing creditors since it would prevent the company from enforcing the contract. Accordingly, public policy favoured the claimant's rights of enforcement and the defendant's defence of illegality failed.[26]

It is against public policy to enforce an agreement which would deprive a party to the contract of his sole means of support.[27] And an agreement by which a moneylender imposed restrictions on the liberty of a borrower, reducing him to a position little better than that of a slave, was held void as contrary to public policy.[28] But where a father and son entered into an agreement for the payment of an annuity to the son upon conditions fettering the son's liberty, the father's object being to save him from moral and financial ruin, the agreement was held good.[29] Again, a contract to use undue influence, e.g. to procure a legacy, will be set aside in equity as contrary to public policy[30]; but a contract between expectant legatees to divide benefits after the death of a testator and meanwhile to abstain from using influence is good.[31] 16–006

[22] *Neville v Dominion of Canada News Co* [1915] 3 K.B. 556.

[23] *Brown v Brine* (1875) 1 Ex.D. 5; such an undertaking would seem not to render unenforceable an otherwise good contract: see *Jennings v Brown* (1842) 9 M. & W. 496.

[24] *Initial Services Ltd v Putterill* [1968] 1 Q.B. 396.

[25] [2005] EWHC 696 (Ch), [2006] 1 B.C.L.C. 601.

[26] See also para.16–167. The company could probably have enforced the contract without relying on any illegality.

[27] *King v Michael Faraday & Partners* [1939] 2 K.B. 753.

[28] *Horwood v Millar's Timber and Trading Co Ltd* [1917] 1 K.B. 305; cf. *A. Schroeder Music Publishing Co Ltd v Macaulay* [1974] 1 W.L.R. 1308.

[29] *Denny's Trustee v Denny* [1916] 1 K.B. 583.

[30] *Debenham v Ox* (1749) 1 Ves.Sen. 276; *Higgins v Hill* (1887) 56 L.T. 426.

[31] *Higgins v Hill* (1887) 56 L.T. 426; and so is a contract to sell an expected devise: *Cook v Field* (1850) 15 Q.B. 460.

16–007 **How illegality may affect a contract.** Illegality may affect a contract in a number of ways[32] but it is traditional to distinguish between: (1) illegality as to formation; and (2) illegality as to performance. Broadly speaking the first refers to the situation where the contract itself is illegal at the time it is formed, whereas the latter involves a contract which on its face is legal but which is performed in a manner which is illegal. In this latter situation it is possible for either both or only one of the parties to intend illegal performance. Where a contract is illegal as formed, or it is intended that it should be performed in a legally prohibited manner, the courts will not enforce the contract, or provide any other remedies arising out of the contract. The benefit of the public, and not the advantage of the defendant, being the principle upon which a contract may be impeached on account of such illegality, the objection may be taken by either of the parties to the contract. "The principle of public policy", said Lord Mansfield:

> "... is this: *ex dolo malo non oritur actio*. No court will lend its aid to a man who founds his cause of action upon an immoral or illegal act. If, from the plaintiff's own stating or otherwise, the cause of action appears to arise *ex turpi causa*, or the transgression of a positive law of this country, there the court says he has no right to be assisted. It is upon that ground the court goes; not for the sake of the defendant, but because they will not lend their aid to such a plaintiff. So if the plaintiff and the defendant were to change sides, and the defendant were to bring his action against the plaintiff, the latter would then have the advantage of it; for where both are equally at fault, *potior est conditio defendentis*."[33]

The rules on illegality have been criticised as being unprincipled but a better way of viewing them, as the previous dictum from *Holmon v Johnson* illustrates, is as "being indiscriminate in their effect and are capable therefore of producing injustice".[34] The "effect of illegality is not substantive but procedural", it prevents the plaintiff from enforcing the illegal transaction.[35] The "*ex turpi causa* defence," as was stated by Kerr L.J. in *Euro-Diam Ltd v Bathurst*[36]:

> "... rests on a principle of public policy that the courts will not assist a plaintiff who has been guilty of illegal (or immoral) conduct of which the courts should take notice. It applies if in all the circumstances it would be an affront to public conscience to grant the plaintiff the relief which he seeks because the court would thereby appear to assist or encourage the plaintiff in his illegal conduct or to encourage others in similar acts."

---

[32] The principle that a man is not permitted, either directly or through his representatives, to found a contractual claim on the commission of a crime is discussed at paras 16–168—16–174, below.

[33] *Holman v Johnson* (1775) 1 Cowp. 341, 343. The maxim is further explained in *Bowmakers Ltd v Barnet Instruments Ltd* [1945] K.B. 65, 72; *Standard Chartered Bank v Pakistan National Shipping Corp (No.2)* [2000] 1 Lloyd's Rep. 218, 227–228, 231–232; *Vellino v Chief Constable of the Greater Manchester Police* [2001] EWCA Civ 1249, [2002] 1 W.L.R. 218.

[34] *Tinsley v Milligan* [1994] 1 A.C. 340, 362.

[35] *Tinsley v Milligan* [1994] 1 A.C. 340, 374.

[36] [1990] Q.B. 1 (although the manner in which the court applied the illegality doctrine in this case was disapproved of in *Tinsley v Milligan* [1994] 1 A.C. 340, 363, the dictum quoted in the text must remain true as a general principle).

As will be seen later, illegal contracts are not devoid of legal effect,[37] but the ex turpi causa maxim entails that no action on the contract can be maintained. The Law Commission has stated that:

> "Generally, it seems that the commission of a legal wrong, or acting otherwise contrary to public policy, in the course of performing a contract does not, at common law, affect enforcement."[38]

Illegality will only preclude the enforcement of the contract where it has been:

> " . . . entered into with the purpose of doing [an] . . . unlawful or immoral act or the contract itself (as opposed to the mode of . . . performance) is prohibited by law."[39]

Illegality as to formation. Contracts may be illegal when entered into because they cannot be performed in accordance with their terms without the commission of an illegal act. Thus the contract may involve a breach of the criminal law, statutory or otherwise, or alternatively it may be a statutory requirement that the parties to the transaction possess a licence and where they do not the contract will be illegal as formed. An example of a contract which was illegal as formed is provided by *Levy v Yates*,[40] a case concerned with the former statutory rule that no play could be lawfully acted within 20 miles of London without a royal licence, which might be given only in certain circumstances. In that case the contract, between a theatre-owner and an impresario, was itself for the performance of a theatrical production prohibited by the statute. The contract was unenforceable since[41] "the agreement could not be carried into effect without a contravention of the law": the parties had contracted to do the very thing forbidden by the statute and the contract was therefore unenforceable. 16–008

Illegality as to performance. The illegality may arise because both or one of the parties may intend to perform the contract in an illegal manner. The court will deny its assistance where both or one[42] of the parties intended to perform the contract in an illegal manner or to effect some illegal purpose. In this situation it is customary to distinguish between the situation where the legally objectionable features were known to both parties and the situation where they are known only to one. 16–009

Both parties aware of legally objectionable features. Neither party can sue upon a contract if: 16–010

---

[37] Below, paras 16–176 et seq.

[38] *Illegal Transactions: The Effect of Illegality on Contracts and Trusts* (LC CP No.154, para.2.29) cited with approval in *Colen v Cebrian (UK) Ltd* [2003] EWCA Civ 1676, [2004] I.R.L.R. 210 at [44].

[39] *Coral Leisure Group Ltd v Barnett* [1981] I.C.R. 503 at 509.

[40] (1838) 8 A. & E. 129; cf. *Dungate v Lee* [1959] 1 Ch. 545.

[41] (1838) 8 A. & E. 129, 134. See also *Ewing v Osbaldiston* (1836) 2 My. & Cr. 53. Occasionally it will be difficult to classify a contract as being illegal as to formation as opposed to being illegal as performed: see *J. M. Allan (Merchandising) Ltd v Cloke* [1963] 2 Q.B. 340.

[42] Where a party is not aware of the *facts* when the contract is made as a result of which the contract cannot be performed legally, see below, paras 16–011 and 16–176 et seq. for his remedies. Ignorance of the law is no excuse; see below, para.16–012.

(a) both knew that its performance necessarily involved the commission of an act which, to their knowledge,[43] is legally objectionable, that it is illegal or otherwise against public policy; or

(b) both knew that the contract is intended to be performed in a manner which, to their knowledge[44] is legally objectionable in that sense; or

(c) the purpose of the contract is legally objectionable and that purpose is shared by both parties[45]; or

(d) both participate in performing the contract in a manner which they know to be legally objectionable.[46]

Ashmore, Benson, Pease & Co Ltd v A.V. Dawson Ltd[47] provides a good example of a contract which was illegal as to performance so as to bar either party from maintaining an action with respect to it. The defendants agreed to transport two boilers belonging to the plaintiffs and did so by carrying the boilers on lorries which could not lawfully carry the loads in question. The goods were damaged in the course of transit but the claim of the owner for damages was rejected; the owner of the goods not only knew that the goods were being transported in an illegal manner but had actually "participated" in the illegality in the sense of assisting the defendant carrier to perform the contract in an illegal manner. However, that a party commits some illegality in the course of performance does not result in his being unable to enforce the contract.[48]

> "The fact that a party has in the course of performing a contract committed an unlawful or immoral act will not by itself prevent him from further enforcing that contract unless the contract was entered into with the purpose of doing that unlawful or immoral act or the contract itself (as opposed to the mode of . . . performance) is prohibited by law."

Thus in *St John Shipping Corp v Joseph Rank Ltd*[49] the carrier was able to enforce its claim for freight even though it had illegally overloaded its vessel. However, the plaintiff company would not have been entitled to recover freight had it intended from the beginning to perform the contract in an illegal manner.

16–011 **Legally objectionable features unknown to one party.** It follows from what has been said that, if the performance of a contract necessarily and to the

[43] Knowledge of illegality by an agent generally has no less effect than knowledge by the principal: *Apthorp v Neville* (1907) 23 T.L.R. 575; cf. *Stoneleigh Finance Ltd v Phillips* [1965] 2 Q.B. 537, 572, 580.

[44] *Apthorp v Neville* (1907) 23 T.L.R. 575; cf *Stoneleigh Finance Ltd v Phillips* [1965] 2 Q.B. 537, 572, 580.

[45] *Alexander v Rayson* [1936] 1 K.B. 169, 182; *Edler v Auerbach* [1950] 1 K.B. 359; *Bigos v Bousted* [1951] 1 All E.R. 92; *J.M. Allan (Merchandising) Ltd v Cloke* [1963] 2 Q.B. 340.

[46] *Ashmore, Benson, Pease & Co Ltd v A. v Dawson Ltd* [1973] 1 W.L.R. 828.

[47] [1973] 1 W.L.R. 828.

[48] *Coral Leisure Group Ltd v Barnett* [1981] I.C.R. 503, 509; see also *Newland v Simons & Willer (Hairdressers) Ltd* [1981] I.C.R. 521, 530; *Hall v Woolston Hall Leisure Ltd* [2001] 1 W.L.R. 225.

[49] [1957] 1 Q.B. 267; see also below, para.16–147.

knowledge[50] of the plaintiff involves or has as its object the commission by one or both parties of an act known to be legally objectionable, the plaintiff cannot sue on the contract[51] and this is so irrespective of the state of knowledge of the defendant. But when the contract does not necessarily involve the commission of a legally objectionable act and the legally objectionable intention or purpose of one party is unknown to the other, the latter is not precluded from enforcing the contract.[52] Thus in *Archbolds (Freightage) Ltd v S. Spanglett Ltd*,[53] the A Co agreed with the B Co to carry goods in a van which, unknown to the B Co, was not licensed for the purpose. The contract, which was not expressly or impliedly prohibited by statute, involved the commission of a criminal offence by the A Co in using the van for this purpose. But since the B Co was unaware of this fact, it was not prevented from suing the A Co for failure to deliver the goods. And in *Bank für Gemeinwirtschaft Aktiengesellschaft v City of London Garages Ltd*[54] the A Co had accepted a bill of exchange drawn upon itself by B Co who later discounted the bill to C Co, a company resident in Germany. When sued by C Co for dishonour of the bill, A Co contended that the discounting of the bill to C Co amounted to the export of a bill of exchange which was unlawful under Exchange Control regulations without the permission of the Treasury. The Court of Appeal held that, as C Co did not know of B Co's failure to obtain Treasury permission and was entitled to assume that B Co had complied with the requirement, it was not precluded from suing upon the bill.[55] The justification for this result is that it would be inequitable for a person who enters into an apparently unobjectionable contract to be deprived of his rights thereunder merely because the other party had an unlawful object in mind in entering into the contract. To deprive the innocent party of his rights would merely "injure the innocent, benefit the guilty and put a premium on deceit".[56] But upon learning of the illegal object of the other, the innocent party must refuse to assist him by carrying the contract into effect; the innocent party in such circumstances has a quantum meruit for what he has already lawfully done.[57] Similarly in a case where the contract appears legally unobjectionable but the other party later elects to perform the contract in an illegal manner: the innocent party is not thereby deprived of his rights but

---

[50] i.e. knowledge of fact, not of law; see below, para.16–012.

[51] *Edler v Auerbach* [1950] 1 K.B. 359; *Nash v Stevenson Transport Ltd* [1935] 2 K.B. 341; *Ashmore, Benson, Pease & Co Ltd v A.V. Dawson Ltd* [1973] 1 W.L.R. 828.

[52] *Mason v Clarke* [1955] A.C. 778, 793, 805; *Bank für Gemeinwirtschaft Aktiengesellschaft v City of London Garages Ltd* [1971] 1 W.L.R. 149.

[53] [1961] 1 Q.B. 374; *Davidson v Pillay* [1979] I.R.L.R. 275; *Corby v Morrison* [1980] I.C.R. 564 (the test of knowledge is a subjective one). Where the contract is *ex facie* illegal, no question of knowledge arises: *Newland v Simons & Willer (Hairdressers) Ltd* [1981] I.C.R. 521. In *Hall v Woolston Hall Leisure Ltd* [2001] 1 W.L.R. 225, 249, Mance L.J. cast doubt on the reasoning and outcome of the *Newland* case.

[54] [1971] 1 W.L.R. 149. See also *Credit Lyonnais v P.T. Barnard & Associates* [1976] 1 Lloyd's Rep. 557.

[55] Contrast the position where the contract infringes a *foreign* exchange control regulation imposed consistently with the IMF Agreement and will be, if it is an "exchange contract", unenforceable in the United Kingdom under the Bretton Woods Agreement Act 1945, irrespective of the British party's ignorance of the foreign illegality: *Wilson, Smithett & Cope Ltd v Terruzzi* [1976] Q.B. 683. See below, paras 16–031 fn.162. On the status of the Bretton Woods Agreement, see *Dicey, Morris and Collins, The Conflict of Laws*, 14th edn (2006), pp.2009–2015.

[56] *Archbolds (Freightage) Ltd v S. Spanglett Ltd* [1961] 1 Q.B. 374, 387.

[57] *Clay v Yates* (1856) 1 H. & N. 73.

where he learns of the illegal mode of performance he must not participate in it but should do all reasonably within his power to avoid or prevent such performance.[58] If he goes on with the contract with knowledge of what is objectionable he cannot recover, except where the illegality is merely the breach of a by-law which is subsequently waived by the authority which made it, so that the other party lawfully enjoys benefits under the contract, and can modify the work done so as to comply with the by-law.[59] However, where a party to a contract knows that the other party may have an illegal purpose in mind this does not preclude recovery provided there is no participation in carrying out the illegal purpose; there is a difference between:

> ". . . the supply of an ordinary vehicle by a motor dealer in the ordinary course of business to a customer known to be a drug dealer, and the supply of a vehicle with special compartments for the concealment of drugs."[60]

16–012 **Parties' ignorance of the law.**

> "Where a contract is to do a thing which cannot be performed without a violation of the law, it is void, whether the parties knew the law or not."[61]

Thus, in *Miller v Karlinski*,[62] an employee, whose mode of payment amounted to a fraud on the Revenue, was held unable to recover arrears of salary, whether or not the parties knew that what they were doing was illegal. Equally, where a statute makes the contract itself illegal, the parties' ignorance of the law does not make it the less so.[63] Even where the contract is capable of lawful performance, if the express purpose for which it was made was to do something unlawful, failure by the parties, through ignorance of the law, to appreciate that the purpose was unlawful is irrelevant.[64] But where the contract is not unlawful on its face and is capable of performance in a lawful way and the parties merely contemplate that it will be performed in a particular way which would be unlawful, the parties, through ignorance of the law, failing to appreciate that fact, the contract may be

---

[58] *Ashmore, Benson, Pease & Co Ltd v A.V. Dawson Ltd* [1973] 1 W.L.R. 828. A possible way of analysing this situation is that the contract has been varied by the parties and the new agreed contractual performance is illegal. See *Archbolds (Freightage) Ltd v S. Spanglett Ltd* [1961] 1 Q.B. 374, 393.

[59] *Townsend (Builders) Ltd v Cinema News & Property Management Ltd* [1959] 1 W.L.R. 119.

[60] *Ango-Petroleum Ltd v TFB (Mortgages) Ltd* [2007] EWCA Civ 456, [2007] All E.R. (D) 243 at [78].

[61] per Blackburn J. in *Waugh v Morris* (1873) L.R. 8 Q.B. 202, 208. And see *Re Trepca Mines Ltd (No.2)* [1963] Ch. 199, 221.

[62] (1945) 62 T.L.R. 85; *Napier v National Business Agency Ltd* [1951] 2 All E.R. 264; *Tomlinson v Dick Evans "U" Drive Ltd* [1978] I.C.R. 639 (rule about defrauding Revenue applies even in case of a junior employee who goes along with employer's tax fraud); *Newland v Simons & Willer (Hairdressers) Ltd* [1981] I.C.R. 521; *Hall v Woolston Hall Leisure Ltd* [2001] 1 W.L.R. 225, 249.

[63] *Kiriri Cotton Co Ltd v Dewani* [1960] A.C. 192: *Re Mahmoud and Ispahani* [1921] 2 K.B. 716. The court may of course decide that breach of the statute does not render the contract unenforceable: see *Shaw v Groom* [1970] 2 Q.B. 504 and below, para.16–147.

[64] *J.M. Allan (Merchandising) Ltd v Cloke* [1963] 2 Q.B. 340.

enforced[65] on the ground that there was never a "fixed intention" to do that which was later discovered to be lawful and that while the parties "contemplated" such unlawful act, they did not "intend" to do it.[66] In other words, knowledge of the law is of evidential significance with respect to the parties' intended mode of performance. It is important in this situation that at least the party seeking to enforce the contract can carry it out in a legal manner. Where the parties do not intend to enter into an illegal transaction but make a mistake as to the characterisation of the contract, for example treating a contract of service as a contract for services for tax purposes so that it is illegal, the contract has been held to be enforceable.[67]

Compromises of illegal contracts. There is a manifestly obvious public policy in favour of encouragement and enforcement of compromises of disputes which the parties themselves have agreed to. Compromises result in a saving of public resources and probably produce an optimum result from the disputants' point of view in that they have agreed to one, and that this has not been imposed by a third-party mediator. However, to enforce compromises of illegal contracts would have the effect of undermining the public policy underlying the illegality doctrine: it would be paradoxical, to say the least, to permit a party to enforce the compromise of an illegal contract but not the illegal contract itself. Whether the compromise of an illegal transaction is itself enforceable depends on the question of whether the courts must give effect to the broad social policy underlying the illegality despite any private arrangement between the parties.[68] Normally this will mean that the compromise, like the illegal contract, is not enforceable. An interesting problem on the compromise of an allegedly illegal contract arose in *Binder v Alachouzos*.[69] A lent a sum of money to B which B refused to repay on the grounds that the transaction was one of moneylending and A was not a registered moneylender. A sued B, and after taking legal advice B compromised the action on the terms that he would repay the loan and not contend that the contract was one of moneylending. B then repudiated the compromise arguing that it, like the illegal contract, was unenforceable. The Court of Appeal upheld the compromise, but it did so on the grounds that the compromise was of a dispute of fact whether the contract was in actual fact an illegal moneylending contract.[70] This was not a case where a clearly illegal contract was compromised, assuming *arguendo* that such a contract could be compromised.[71] 16–013

---

[65] *Waugh v Morris* (1873) L.R. 8 Q.B. 202. cf. *Nash v Stevenson Transport Ltd* [1936] 2 K.B. 128.

[66] See *Reynolds v Kinsey* [1959] (4) S.A. 50 where the authorities are reviewed. cf. *Best v Glenville* [1960] 1 W.L.R. 1198.

[67] *Enfield Technical Services Ltd v Payne* [2007] I.R.L.R. 840 (parties in good faith mistakenly treating a contract of service as a contract for services for tax purposes).

[68] *Kok Hoong v Leon Cheong Kweng Mines Ltd* [1964] A.C. 993, 1014–1019 (estoppel by way of judgment in default could not operate with respect to illegal moneylending agreement). cf. *A.R. Dennis & Co Ltd v Campbell* [1978] Q.B. 365.

[69] [1972] 2 Q.B. 151.

[70] "In my judgment, a bona fide agreement of compromise such as we have in the present case (which is a dispute as to whether the plaintiff is a moneylender or not) is binding": [1972] 2 Q.B. 151, 158, per Lord Denning M.R.

[71] On compromises see above, paras 3–050—3–056.

(b) *Objects which are Illegal by Common Law or by Statute*

16–014 **Examples of criminality.** Criminal objects which disentitle a party to contractual relief include doing something forbidden by statute,[72] or delegated legislation,[73] such as infringing food and drug legislation[74] or exchange control legislation,[75] and the commission of offences at common law such as publication of a criminal libel[76] and blasphemy.[77] A fortiori the courts will not enforce a contract the object of which is such as to render the contract a criminal conspiracy,[78] e.g. to corrupt public morals[79] or to rig the market for shares in a company.[80] Whether an agreement to fight is illegal depends upon whether the infliction of the injury is of such a nature, or is inflicted under such circumstances, that its infliction is injurious to the public, which is a question of fact.[81] Similarly, a contract, even if made abroad, is illegal if its purpose is the infringement of the laws of England.[82] But mere knowledge that goods sold abroad may possibly be smuggled into England will not disentitle the seller to sue for their price.[83]

16–015 **Evasion of statute.** It is now established that it is not a criminal offence for any person, whether or not acting in concert with others, to do acts which are neither prohibited by Act of Parliament nor at common law, and do not involve dishonesty or fraud or deception, even though an object which Parliament hoped to achieve by its legislation may be thereby thwarted[84]: nor is it an offence to commit a conspiracy to effect a public mischief.[85] Even though agreements which frustrate the policy of an Act of Parliament are not per se criminal conspiracies, it may be uncertain whether such agreements are civilly enforceable. If, e.g. to take the facts of *Bhagwan*,[86] the owner of the vessel from which B disembarked in order to avoid immigration control had sued for his fare, could B have contended that the agreement was unenforceable since its purpose was to frustrate the policy of the Immigration Acts? It is submitted that unless the policy

[72] e.g. see below, paras 16–168, 16–172 but cf. below, para.16–176.

[73] e.g. see *Palaniappa Chettiar v Arunasalam Chettiar* [1962] A.C. 294.

[74] e.g. see *Langton v Hughes* (1813) 1 M. & S. 593; and *Askey v Golden Wine Co* [1948] 2 All E.R. 35.

[75] *Bigos v Bousted* [1951] 1 All E.R. 92; *Shaw v Shaw* [1965] 1 W.L.R. 537; cf. *Wilson, Smithett & Cope Ltd v Terruzzi* [1976] Q.B. 783.

[76] *Fores v Johnes* (1802) 4 Esp. 97; as to civil libels, see below, para.16–018.

[77] *Cowan v Milbourn* (1867) L.R. 2 Ex. 230; but see now *Bowman v Secular Society* [1917] A.C. 406, as to what constitutes blasphemy.

[78] As to where one or both parties are prohibited by statute from making a contract such as that sued upon, see below, paras 16–141 et seq.

[79] *Poplett v Stockdale* (1825) Ry & Mood. 337; and see *Shaw v D.P.P.* [1962] A.C. 220.

[80] *Scott v Brown, Doering, McNab & Co* [1892] 2 Q.B. 724; cf. *Harry Parker Ltd v Mason* [1940] 2 K.B. 590.

[81] *Lane v Holloway* [1968] 1 Q.B. 379; thus an ordinary boxing match with gloves is not unlawful: *R. v Coney* (1882) 8 QBD 534, 539; see also Buller, *Nisi Prius*, 7th edn, p.16; and *Hunt v Bell* (1822) 1 Bing. 1.

[82] *Clugas v Penaluna* (1791) 4 Term Rep. 466; *Waymell v Reed* (1794) 5 Term Rep. 599.

[83] *Pellecat v Angell* (1835) 2 Cr.M. & R. 311; and see *Holman v Johnson* (1775) 1 Cowp. 341.

[84] *D.P.P. v Bhagwan* [1972] A.C. 60; cf. *Zamir v Secretary of State for the Home Department* [1980] A.C. 365.

[85] *D.P.P. v Withers* [1975] A.C. 842.

[86] See above, fn.84.

of the Act in question is one already recognised by the courts as protected under existing heads of public policy, or the means used by the parties are unlawful or dishonest, the agreement is fully enforceable.[87]

Waiver of statutory rights. Difficult questions can arise where a person attempts by contract to waive a right conferred on him by statute. Although there is a general principle that a person may waive any right conferred on him by statute (*quilibet potest renunciare juri pro se introducto*) difficulties arise in determining whether the right is exclusively personal or is designed to serve other more broad public purposes. In the latter situation, public policy would require that the right be treated as mandatory and not be waivable by the party for whose benefit it operates. Whether a statutory right is waivable depends on the overall purpose of the statute and whether this purpose would be frustrated by permitting waiver. Thus in *Johnson v Moreton*[88] the House of Lords held that a tenant could not contract out of the protection afforded by s.24 of the Agricultural Holdings Act 1948 as this would undermine the overall purpose of the Act in promoting efficient farming in the national interest. A contract between a landlord and a statutorily protected tenant whereby the tenant promises to give up possession in return for the landlord's promise of a sum of money is not illegal as an attempt to contract out of the Rent Acts; and although the landlord cannot obtain possession otherwise than under the Acts,[89] the tenant, if he performs his part, can recover the sum promised.[90] 16–016

Fraud. Where the object of a contract is the perpetration of a fraud,[91] e.g. upon prospective shareholders in a company[92] or upon the Government,[93] or a trader[94] the contract is illegal. Such frauds are usually criminal[95] but the rule appears to be general; thus a creditor cannot enforce an agreement with an insolvent debtor under which the latter is to pay him an amount in excess of his share under a composition agreement since the agreement to do so is a fraud upon the other parties to the composition agreement.[96] Likewise it is against public policy to enforce an agreement where the purpose of both parties was to defeat the proper claims of the Commissioners of Inland Revenue[97] or of a rating 16–017

---

[87] See above, para.16–003.

[88] [1980] A.C. 37. See generally, Bennion, *Statutory Interpretation*, 5th edn (2007), pp.41–44

[89] *Barton v Fincham* [1921] 2 K.B. 291; see Megarry, *The Rent Acts*, 11th edn, pp.26–27.

[90] *Rajbenback v Mamon* [1955] 1 Q.B. 283; see Megarry, pp.26–27.

[91] Deliberate deceit, even in the absence of moral turpitude, is sufficient: *Brown Jenkinson & Co Ltd v Percy Dalton (London) Ltd* [1957] 2 Q.B. 621. This should be distinguished from contracts induced by fraud which are not necessarily illegal: see Treitel in Tapper (ed.), *Crime, Proof and Punishment, Essays in Memory of Sir Rupert Cross* (1981), p.107.

[92] *Begbie v Phosphate Sewage Co Ltd* (1875) L.R. 10 Q.B. 491.

[93] *Willis v Baldwin* (1780) 2 Doug. K.B. 450.

[94] *Berg v Sadler and Moore* [1937] 2 K.B. 158.

[95] See *R. v Scott* [1975] A.C. 819; Treitel in Tapper, above, fn.91 p.87. cf. Fair Trading Act 1973 Pt XI, brought into operation by Fair Trading Act 1973 (Commencement No.1) Order 1973 (SI 1973/1545) which provides for the regulation of pyramid selling and similar trading schemes.

[96] *Cockshott v Bennett* (1788) 2 T.R. 763; *Mallalieu v Hodgson* (1851) 16 Q.B. 689; cf. above, para.3–125.

[97] *Miller v Karlinski* (1945) 62 T.L.R. 85; *Napier v National Business Agency* [1951] 2 All E.R. 264; *Beauvale Furnishings Ltd v Chapman* [2000] All E.R. (D) 2038.

authority.[98] However, where the contract in question is remote from the illegality, the court will enforce the contract.[99]

16–018 **Other civil wrongs.** If a contract has as its object[100] the deliberate commission of a tort,[101] it would seem that the contract is illegal, even though no criminality or fraud is involved.[102] Thus a printer cannot recover the cost of printing matter which he knew to be libellous[103] and the purchaser cannot recover a sum of money deposited with the printer on account of the cost to be incurred in printing it.[104]

(c) *Objects Injurious to Good Government*

(i) *Domestic Affairs*

16–019 **Sale of public offices and contracts.** Contracts for the sale or transfer of public appointments, though they may not be prohibited in particular cases by the statutes relative to the sale of public offices,[105] are nonetheless contrary to public policy.[106] So also is a secret agreement to assign to another, in circumstances amounting to a fraud on the Government, the profits of a public contract, such as for the conveyance of the mails.[107] And where a clerk of the peace, appointed by the corporation of a borough under the Municipal Corporations Act 1882 and having fees attached to his office, entered into an agreement with the corporation to receive a salary and account to them for the fees, it was held that the agreement was against public policy, as the acceptor of an office of trust can make no bargain in respect of it, and the presumption is that the fees are required to enable the holder to perform the duties of his office.[108]

16–020 **Contracts by employees and members of public authorities.** It is an offence at common law for a public officer to accept a bribe or show favour[109]

---

[98] *Alexander v Rayson* [1936] 1 K.B. 169; cf. *Saunders v Edwards* [1987] 1 W.L.R. 1116.

[99] *21st Century Logistic Solutions Ltd v Madysen Ltd* [2004] EWHC 231 (QB), [2004] 2 Lloyd's Rep 92. (In this case a company that intended to evade the payment of VAT could nevertheless enforce a contract for the supply of goods, the avoidance of VAT not being an integral part of the contract.)

[100] As to whether a man can found a contractual claim on his deliberate commission of a tort, see above, paras 16–017—16–018.

[101] As to where the object is the deliberate procurement of a breach of contract with a third party, see Lauterpacht (1936) 52 L.Q.R. 494.

[102] See Pearce L.J. in *Brown Jenkinson & Co Ltd v Percy Dalton (London) Ltd* [1957] 2 Q.B. 621, 638, though the case concerned fraud; *Allen v Rescous* (1676) 2 Lev. 179.

[103] *Apthorp v Nevill* (1907) 23 T.L.R. 575; see above, para.16–011 as to the printer's proper course if he first learns of the libellous nature of the material after commencing performance of the contract.

[104] *Apthorp v Nevill* (1907) 23 T.L.R. 575; as to agreements to indemnify against civil liability for libel, see below, para.16–175.

[105] For the definition of a public officer under s.47(3) of the Solicitors Act 1932 (re-enacted by s.22 of the Solicitors Act 1974 and amended by Administration of Justice Act 1985 s.6), see *Beeston & Stapleford U.D.C. v Smith* [1949] 1 K.B. 656.

[106] *Blachford v Preston* (1799) 8 T.R. 89, 94; *Parsons v Thompson* (1790) 1 H.Bl. 322.

[107] *Osborne v Williams* (1811) 18 Ves. 379.

[108] *Liverpool Corp v Wright* (1859) 28 L.J. Ch. 868; and see *McCreery v Bennett* [1904] 2 Ir.R. 69.

[109] *R. v Whitaker* [1914] 3 K.B. 1283.

and a contract with such an object is undoubtedly unenforceable. It is now provided by statute that any officer with a direct or indirect pecuniary interest in a contract to be entered into by a local authority is to give notice that he is so interested and no officer is to take a fee or reward beyond his ordinary remuneration.[110] Members of local authorities are under a similar duty to disclose their interest if they are present at a meeting of the authority at which the contract is the subject of consideration.[111]

Procurement of honours. Though not exactly the sale of an office, an agreement to pay money in return for the procurement of a knighthood for the payer is against public policy since it gives a third person an immediate interest in procuring the title by means which are likely to be improper.[112] Likewise a will limiting estates to persons who should acquire the title of marquis or duke has been held against public policy,[113] but not, perhaps surprisingly, on condition of acquiring a baronetcy, as that was held not to involve public duties.[114] **16–021**

Assignment of pay, pensions, etc.[115] An agreement to assign or mortgage the salary of a public officer, i.e. one paid from national funds,[116] is against public policy; and the same is true of the pension attached to such an office.[117] For instance, the pay of a naval surgeon on active service cannot be assigned[118] nor can half-pay of an army officer.[119] A clerk of petty sessions cannot assign his salary.[120] But it has been held that there may be a lawful partnership in the profits of an office.[121] **16–022**

Neglect of duty. An agreement, the natural effect of which is to induce a public officer to neglect his duty or which would influence him to perform it in a particular way, is against public policy. Thus an agreement between one who held the offices of town clerk and clerk of the peace of a borough and an attorney, that the former would, for reward to him, recommend the latter to parties who **16–023**

[110] Local Government Act 1972 s.117; cf. *Mellis v Shirley and Freemantle Local Board of Health* (1885) 16 QBD 446. See above, para.10–027.

[111] Local Government Act 1972 s.94 (as amended by the Local Government and Housing Act 1989 Sch.11; Police and Magistrates' Courts Act 1994 Sch.4); repealed by Local Government Act 2000 s.107 as from a day to be appointed.

[112] *Parkinson v College of Ambulance Ltd* [1925] 2 K.B. 1. Such an agreement would now constitute an offence under the Honours (Prevention of Abuses) Act 1925.

[113] *Egerton v Earl Brownlow* (1853) 4 H.L.C. 1.

[114] *Re Wallace* [1920] 2 Ch. 274.

[115] See below, para.19–047.

[116] *Re Mirams* [1891] 1 Q.B. 594 (involving the assignment of the salary of the chaplain to a workhouse which was held not to be against public policy).

[117] *Grenfell v The Dean and Canons of Windsor* (1840) 2 Beav. 544. Such assignments may also be avoided by statute: e.g. see the Army Act 1955 s.203 (on which see *Roberts v Roberts* [1986] 1 W.L.R. 437), and the Air Force Act 1955 s.203; see also the Sale of Offices Act 1551 as extended by the Sale of Offices Act 1809 and the cases thereon cited in the 22nd edn of this work, paras 856–860. cf. Logan (1945) 61 L.Q.R. 240.

[118] *Apthorpe v Apthorpe* (1887) 12 P.D. 192.

[119] *Flarty v Odlum* (1790) 3 T.R. 681.

[120] *McCreery v Bennett* [1904] 2 Ir.R. 69.

[121] *Sterry v Clifton* (1850) 9 C.B. 110; and see *Collins v Jackson* (1862) 31 Beav. 645.

might want an attorney to conduct prosecutions arising in the town clerk's office, was held illegal.[122]

16–024 **Procurement of public benefits.** An agreement to induce a person who has access to persons of influence to use his position to procure a benefit from the Government is contrary to public policy.[123] Similarly the sale of a recommendation to be given on an application for a beer-house licence is contrary to public policy. But a contract between the tenant of a beer-house and brewers, one of whom was a magistrate, that, in consideration of their paying the costs of his application to the magistrates for a licence, he would tie the premises to them, was held not to be void although it involved the brewers supporting the application, on the ground, inter alia, that the agreement was not void for champerty since an application for a licence is not litigation, licensing sessions not being a court.[124]

16–025 **Withdrawal of opposition to Bill.** At any rate in the absence of any intention to practise a fraud on some individual or on the legislature, bargains between the promoters of a private Parliamentary Bill and a third party under which the promoters agree to purchase property from the third party[125] partly as an inducement for him to withdraw opposition to the proposed Bill, or to amend the Bill and pay the third party a sum of money, appear not to be contrary to public policy.[126] Although the court has jurisdiction to enforce by injunction a contract entered into by a person or corporation that they will not apply to Parliament, or will not oppose an application to Parliament, no such injunction appears ever to have been granted and judges have frequently stated that it is difficult to conceive a case in which such jurisdiction should be exercised.[127]

(ii) *Foreign Affairs*

16–026 **Trading with the enemy.** All trading with the enemy,[128] except with royal licence, is against public policy.[129] On the same principle "it is not competent to any subject to enter into a contract to do any thing which may be detrimental to

---

[122] *Hughes v Statham* (1825) 4 B. & C. 187l; *Savill Bros v Langman* (1898) 79 L.T. 44.

[123] *Montefiore v Menday Motor Components Co* [1918] 2 K.B. 241.

[124] *Savill Bros v Langman* (1898) 79 L.T. 44; cf. *Hughes v Statham* (1825) 4 B. & C. 187 and Criminal Law Act 1967 ss.13, 14.

[125] *Taylor v Chichester & Midhurst Ry* (1870) L.R. 4 H.L. 628.

[126] *Simpson v Lord Howden* (1842) 9 Cl. & Fin. 61; and see *Shrewsbury and Birmingham Ry Co v London and N.W. Ry Co* (1851) 17 Q.B. 652; *Edwards v Grand Junction Ry Co* (1836) My. & Cr. 650. "A landowner cannot be restricted of his rights because he happens to be a Member of Parliament": *Earl of Shrewsbury v North Staffordshire Ry* (1865) L.R. 1 Eq. 593, 613. See also, *Standards in Public Life* (First Report of the Committee on Standards in Public Life, Cm.2850–1), Ch.2.

[127] *Bilston Corp v Wolverhampton Corp* [1942] Ch. 391; *Ware v Grand Junction Waterworks Co* (1831) 2 Russ. & My. 470, 483; *Heathcote v North Staffordshire Ry Co* (1850) 2 Mac. & G. 100, 109; *Re London, Chatham & Dover Ry Arrangement Act* (1869) L.R. 5 Ch. App. 671.

[128] As to who is an enemy, see above, paras 11–024 et seq., and below, para.16–162.

[129] *Ertel Bieber & Co v Rio Tinto Co* [1918] A.C. 260, 273, 289; and see *The Hoop* (1799) 1 C.Rob. 196; *Ogden v Peele* (1826) 8 Dow. & Ry 1; as to illegality by statute, see below, paras 16–141 et seq. See further McNair, *Legal Effects of War*, 4th edn; and see below, paras 16–162—16–163, as to the frustrating effect of war.

the interests of" this country in time of war[130] or involving intercourse with or benefit to the enemy,[131] however insignificant in quantum[132] and notwithstanding the benefit which may accrue to this country from such a contract.[133] Nor may the contract merely be suspended during hostilities.[134] Thus, a contract by a British subject to insure an enemy against loss through capture by British ships is unenforceable ab initio, even though it was entered into before the commencement of hostilities.[135] Similarly, a contract of insurance on goods shipped from an enemy's port on board a neutral ship, the goods having been purchased in the enemy's country by the agent of the assured after hostilities had commenced, has been held to be against public policy.[136] An English company found to have enemy character by reason of enemy control[137] does not cease, in the eye of English law, to be an English company subject to this rule.[138]

Illegality under applicable foreign law.[139] Where the contract is governed by a system of law other than English, i.e. under the principles of English private international law, as now laid down in the Rome Convention on the law applicable to contractual obligations,[140] the law governing the contract is foreign, and the contract is unenforceable for illegality under the relevant doctrine of the foreign system, the contract is also unenforceable in England,[141] unless the vitiating illegality under the governing law is one that the English court declines to recognise because, e.g. it imposes an unfair discrimination upon one or both of the contracting parties.[142] 16–027

Performance contrary to public policy in place for performance. Where a contract governed by English law is contrary to the public policy of the state where it is to be performed, this will not necessarily constitute a bar to the 16–028

[130] *Furtado v Rogers* (1802) 3 Bos. & Pul. 191, 198.

[131] *Kuenigl v Donnersmarck* [1955] 1 Q.B. 515, 536; *Ertel Bieber & Co v Rio Tinto Co* [1918] A.C. 260, 274.

[132] *Bevan v Bevan* [1955] 2 Q.B. 277, 240.

[133] *The Hoop* (1799) 1 C.Rob. 196, 199–200.

[134] *Ertel Bieber & Co v Rio Tinto Co* [1918] A.C. 260.

[135] *Furtado v Rogers* (1802) 3 Bos. & Pul. 191; *Ertel Bieber & Co v Rio Tinto Co* [1918] A.C. 260, 273, 289–290.

[136] *Potts v Bell* (1800) 8 T.R. 548. As to the validity of insurance against seizure immediately before the outbreak of hostilities, see *Janson v Driefontein Consolidated Mines Ltd* [1902] A.C. 484, 499.

[137] See below, para.16–162.

[138] *Kuenigl v Donnersmarck* [1955] 1 Q.B. 515; and see at 539: "Many of the old decisions dating from a more liberal age which suggest that British subjects in enemy territory enjoy a measure of freedom in their dealings with the enemy are of doubtful authority today."

[139] See below, paras 30–355 et seq.; *Dicey, Morris and Collins on the Conflict of Laws*, 14th edn (2006), Ch.32.

[140] Applicable by virtue of the Contracts (Applicable Law) Act 1990.

[141] Rome Convention arts 8, 10.

[142] Rome Convention art.16; *Heriz v Riera* (1840) 11 Sim. 318; *Kahler v Midland Bank Ltd* [1950] A.C. 24; *Zivnostenska Banka National Corp v Frankman* [1950] A.C. 57; *MacKender v Feldia A.G.* [1967] 2 Q.B. 590, 601; *Re Lord Cable* [1977] 1 W.L.R. 7. As to meaning of applicable law see below, para.30–130 et seq.

contract being enforceable in England.[143] However, in *Lemenda Trading Co Ltd v African Middle East Petroleum Co Ltd*[144] Phillips J. stated that[145]:

> "... the English courts should not enforce an English law contract which falls to be performed abroad where: (i) it relates to an adventure which is contrary to a head of English public policy which is founded on general principles of morality, and (ii) the same public policy applies to the country of performance so that the agreement would not be enforceable under the law of that country.
>
> In such a situation international comity combines with English domestic policy to militate against enforcement."

Presumably condition (i) would be sufficient to prevent the contract from being enforced irrespective of the governing law or where the place of performance of the contract may be.[146] However, not all principles of public policy are necessarily of universal application and where the policy is based on "considerations which are purely domestic"[147] then this would not constitute a bar to enforcement of a contract that has to be performed abroad.

16–029 **Contracts legal under applicable law but not under English law.** Where the contract is, however, valid by its foreign governing law, will it be unenforceable in England because it would be regarded as illegal or contrary to public policy under the rules governing domestic contracts? Article 16 of the Rome Convention provides that the:

> "... application of a rule of law of any country specified by this Convention may be refused only if such application is manifestly incompatible with the public policy ('ordre public') of the forum."[148]

Under the previous law it was clear that if the contract involved criminality either by statute or at common law, then it might be unenforceable in England despite its validity under the governing law and it may be that this is still so if the criminality is serious enough.[149] Where, however, the contract, though not involving criminality, is alleged to offend against one of the recognised heads of English public policy, great care should be exercised by the courts in determining whether the domestic policy demands the non-enforcement of a contract with substantial or even exclusive foreign elements which is valid under the system of law with which it has the closest connection. It cannot, however, be said that the courts have carefully considered this problem; instead they have usually applied the English heads of public policy and held such contracts unenforceable in England.[150] In *Lemenda Trading Co Ltd v African Middle East Petroleum Co*

---

[143] Collier (1988) C.L.J. 169, 170 and cases there cited.

[144] [1988] Q.B. 448; *Tekron Resources Ltd v Guinea Investment Co Ltd* [2004] 2 Lloyd's Rep. 26.

[145] [1988] Q.B. 448, 461.

[146] [1988] Q.B. 448, 459.

[147] [1988] Q.B. 448.

[148] See generally, *Dicey & Morris on the Conflict of Laws*, 14th edn (2008), r.210.

[149] *Boissevain v Weil* [1950] A.C. 327; *Dicey & Morris* at r.210.

[150] *Grell v Levy* (1864) 16 C.B.(N.S.) 73; *Kaufman v Gerson* [1904] 1 K.B. 591; contrast the narrower and, it is submitted, better approach in *Addison v Brown* [1954] 1 W.L.R. 779. See also *Att-Gen of New Zealand v Ortiz* [1984] A.C. 1.

Ltd[151] the court held that the approach adopted in this paragraph would also "seem apposite in the case of an English law contract to be performed abroad".

16–030 Where again the contract is valid by its foreign governing law, but fails to comply with an English regulatory statute rendering similar domestic contracts void or unenforceable but not illegal, the courts have sometimes enforced the agreement,[152] sometimes not.[153] It is thought that the proper principle is that such agreements should be enforced unless the social policy expressed in the English statute is of such paramount importance that it must be applied even to a transaction with foreign elements or unless the contract, or its breach, has a substantial contact with England. This seems to accord with art.16 cited above; and also art.7.2 which allows the application of:

> ". . . . the rules of the law of the forum in a situation where they are mandatory irrespective of the law otherwise applicable to the contract".

16–031 **Illegality under foreign law applicable to contract.** Is a contract unenforceable in England in a case where it is illegal by a foreign law other than the law applicable to the contract? The decisions on this question are somewhat confusing, but the following propositions appear to represent the law before the adoption of the Rome Convention. First, the English courts would not enforce any contract the recognition of which might constitute a hostile act against a foreign friendly government. Thus, in *De Wütz v Hendricks*[154] the plaintiff, in order to raise a loan in support of Greek rebels against their Turkish government, deposited with the defendant certain papers. The loan having fallen through, the purpose of the transaction which encompassed the overthrow of a friendly government prevented the plaintiff recovering the papers. Likewise in *Regazzoni v K.C. Sethia (1944) Ltd*[155] a contract to export a commodity from India to South Africa contrary to the law of the former country was held unenforceable. And although the English courts have refused to enforce a penal law at the suit of a foreign state,[156] nevertheless they will not enforce a contract which involves the breach of such a law,[157] or grant equitable relief[158] to one whose claim is based on such breach unless the law in question was "repugnant to English conceptions

---

151 [1988] Q.B. 448, 459.

152 *Quarrier v Colston* (1842) 1 Ph. 147; *Saxby v Fulton* [1909] 2 K.B. 208; *Sayers v International Drilling Co* [1971] 1 W.L.R. 1176.

153 *Leroux v Brown* (1852) 12 C.B. 801; cf. *English v Donnelly* (1958) S.C. 494 and *Brodin v A/R Seljan* (1973) S.L.T. 198.

154 (1824) 2 Bing. 314.

155 [1958] A.C. 301. Se also *Mahonia Ltd v J.P. Morgan Chase Bank* [2003] 2 Lloyd's Rep. 911; *Mahonia Ltd v West LB AG* [2004] EWHC 1938 (Comm); *JSC Zestafoni G Nikoladze Ferroalloy Plant v Ronly Holdings Ltd* [2004] EWHC 245 (Comm), [2004] 2 Lloyd's Rep. 335, [2004] All E.R. (D) 10.

156 *Government of India v Taylor* [1955] A.C. 491. On what constitutes a penal law see *Att-Gen of New Zealand v Ortiz* [1984] A.C. 1.

157 *Regazzoni v K.C. Sethia Ltd* [1958] A.C. 301; cf. *Pye v B.G. Transport Service* [1966] 2 Lloyd's Rep. 300; *Fielding & Platt Ltd v Najjar* [1969] 1 W.L.R. 357.

158 *Re Emery's Investment Trusts* [1959] Ch. 410.

of what may be regarded as within the ordinary field of legislation or administrative order even in this country" or such that its enforcement would be against "morals".[159] English courts have also refused to enforce a contract where the common intention of the parties was to violate the law of a foreign friendly state.[160] The above principle, however, has not been extended to cases where there was a mere sale in England in the knowledge that the goods were to be imported into a foreign country contrary to the revenue law of that country[161] or where there was the giving of an English cheque as part of an arrangement which, as the parties knew and intended, would involve the doing of acts in a foreign country which were criminal by the laws of that country.[162] Nor has the fact that strict compliance with the contract would cause a party to perform illegal acts contravening exchange control regulations in the country of his residence, or place of business, prevented the English court from upholding the contract and awarding damages in the event of its breach.[163] The explanation of these cases was that performance of the contracts did not "necessarily" involve the doing of an act which was unlawful by the law of the place where it had to be carried out.[164] Difficulties have been encountered in ascertaining whether performance of a contract involves such an illegal act. In making this assessment it was said to be:

> " . . . immaterial whether one party has to equip himself for performance by an illegal act in another country. What matters is whether performance itself necessarily involves such an act."[165]

But all these matters may now require reconsideration in the light of the Rome Convention.[166]

16–032 **Contract forbidden in place of performance.** Secondly, it is said that English courts will not enforce a contract where performance of that contract is

---

[159] *Regazzoni v K.C. Sethia Ltd* [1958] A.C. 301, 327, per Lord Keith; see also Lord Somerville, 330; *Brokaw v Seatrain UK Ltd* [1971] 2 Q.B. 476; *Att-Gen of New Zealand v Ortiz* [1984] A.C. 1.

[160] *Foster v Driscoll* [1929] 1 K.B. 470; *Toprak Mahsullri Ofisi v Finagrain Compagnie Commerciale Agricole et Financière SA* [1979] 2 Lloyd's Rep. 98, 106–107; *Ispahari v Bank Melli Iran* (1997) T.L.R. 701; *Soleimany v Soleimany* (1998) C.L.C. 779, 792: "Nor will it [i.e. English law] enforce a contract governed by the law of a foreign and friendly state, or which requires performance in such a country, if performance is illegal by the law of that country." Although the courts will not enforce a contract illegal by the law of the country of performance, where it has been performed the courts may recognise its effect: *Royal Boskalis Westminster NV v Mountain* [1997] C.L.C. 816, 866.

[161] *Foster v Driscoll* [1929] 1 K.B. 470, 518.

[162] *Sharif v Azad* [1967] 1 Q.B. 605; cf. *Mansouri v Singh* [1986] 1 W.L.R. 1393. The contract in this case involved exchange control legislation, on which see *Dicey & Morris* at r.241; *United City Merchants (Investments) Ltd v Royal Bank of Canada* [1983] 1 A.C. 168, 188–191.

[163] *Kleinwort Sons & Co v Ungarische Baumwolle Industrie Aktiengesellschaft* [1939] 2 K.B. 678; *Kahler v Midland Bank Ltd* [1950] A.C. 24, 48; *Rossano v Manufactures' Life Assurance Co* [1963] 2 Q.B. 352. See, however, *Dicey & Morris* at r.241.

[164] *Libyan Arab Foreign Bank v Bankers Trust Co* [1989] Q.B. 728, 743–746.

[165] [1989] Q.B. 728, 269.

[166] Below, paras 30–017 et seq. and paras 30–117—30–120.

forbidden by the law of the place where it must be performed.[167] This proposition, for which there is authority,[168] would clearly apply where the English law is the law governing the contract. However, beyond this the proposition has been doubted; the cases supporting it have been considered in the final analysis to turn on other propositions,[169] or to have reflected the application of standard principles of contract law or principles of English public policy.[170] There does not appear to be any overriding requirement of English public policy rendering such contracts unenforceable where they are governed by a foreign system of law and are not regarded as illegal under that system.

Foreign laws of extraterritorial application. Thirdly, certain foreign laws are of extraterritorial application and may purport to make contracts illegal although these contracts do not necessitate any illegal acts within the foreign jurisdiction and although the parties to them do not contemplate such acts.[171] In such circumstances there is no authority that the English courts would refuse to enforce the contract solely on account of the extraterritorial application of the foreign law, and there are indications to the contrary.[172] 16–033

Knowledge of foreign illegality. Where illegality by foreign law is pleaded, it may be that one of the parties is unaware of the illegality of the transaction, or of the illegal purpose intended by the other party. In such circumstances, the principles discussed above, paras 16–011, 16–012, have been applied, except that, foreign law being regarded by an English court as a matter of fact, ignorance as to the actual content of the foreign rule would appear to be equivalent to a mistake of fact, not of law. Thus in *Fielding & Platt Ltd v Najjar*[173] English machinery manufacturers contracted with a Lebanese company to make and deliver an aluminium press for £235,000, payment to be made by promissory notes given by N, the company's managing director, and payable at intervals during the progress of the work. The English manufacturers began the work, presented the first note for payment, but it was not honoured. In an action upon the note N pleaded that the whole transaction was illegal and unenforceable in that it was agreed that the manufacturers should render invoices which they knew to be false for the purpose of deceiving the Lebanese authorities into admitting 16–034

---

[167] *Ralli Bros v Compania Naviera Sota y Aznar* [1920] 2 K.B. 287.

[168] *Ralli Bros v Compania Naviera Sota y Aznar* [1920] 2 K.B. 287; *Toprak Mahsulleri Ofisi v Finagrain Cie Commerciale Agricole et Financière SA* [1979] 2 Lloyd's Rep. 98; *Libyan Arab Foreign Bank v Bankers Trust Co* [1989] Q.B. 728.

[169] Reynolds (1992) 109 L.Q.R. 553.

[170] Reynolds (1992) 109 L.Q.R. 553; Collier, *Conflict of Laws*, 3rd edn (2001), pp.210–212; *Dicey, Morris and Collins* at paras 32–144—32–151; (discussing, inter alia, whether *Ralli Bros* survives the Rome Convention).

[171] e.g. the United States Sherman Act 1890; see the *Report of the Attorney-General's Committee to Study the Antitrust Laws* (1955), pp.66–67; Brewster et al., *Waller's Antitrust and American Business Abroad*, 3rd edn (1997).

[172] *British Nylon Spinners Ltd v Imperial Chemical Industries Ltd* [1953] Ch. 19; *Sharif v Azad* [1967] 1 Q.B. 605, 617. See also Protection of Trading Interests Act 1980. Under art.7(1) effect may be given to the mandatory rules of another country but this, by art.7(2), is not to restrict effect being given to the law of the forum where it is mandatory, irrespective of the law otherwise applicable to the contract.

[173] [1969] 1 W.L.R. 257.

goods into Lebanon under import licences which did not in fact cover these goods. The Court of Appeal held that the English manufacturers were entitled to succeed since, even on the assumption that the foreign illegality was capable of vitiating an English contract, it was not a term that the false invoices be made, so that the contract could be performed lawfully; and even if there were such a term, there was not sufficient evidence to show that the manufacturers appreciated the illegality or intended to participate in it.

(d) *Objects Injurious to the Proper Working of Justice*

(i) *Agreements to Conceal Offences and Compromises*

16–035 **Concealment of crime generally.** A provision in any agreement not to disclose misconduct of such a nature that it ought, in the public interest, to be disclosed to others is against public policy.[174] There is no confidence as to the disclosure of iniquity.[175] But it may well be permissible for a person against whom frauds have been, and are intended to be, committed to give a binding promise of secrecy, in order to obtain information relating to those frauds, which will enable him, by taking steps himself, to prevent the commission of future frauds. However, such a promise will be against public policy where it extends to frauds committed and contemplated against others to whom the communication of the information obtained would be of use in preventing the commission of such frauds.[176]

16–036 **Criminality of agreements to conceal an arrestable offence.** In many cases where there is, in effect, an undertaking not to disclose a crime, the crime amounts also to a civil wrong against the promisor and the undertaking is given as part of an agreement to compromise or settle the civil wrong; the question then arises whether the inclusion of the undertaking not to disclose the information or to instigate a public prosecution renders unenforceable the compromise of the civil wrong. Section 5 of the Criminal Law Act 1967 provides that where an arrestable offence[177] has been committed, anyone who knows or believes:

(i) that an arrestable offence[178] has been committed; and

(ii) that he has information which might be of material assistance in securing the prosecution or conviction of any offender for it,

is guilty of an indictable offence[179] if he accepts, for not disclosing that information, any consideration other than:

---

[174] *Initial Services Ltd v Putterill* [1968] 1 Q.B. 396. cf. *Schering Chemicals Ltd v Falkman Ltd* [1982] Q.B. 1; *Hubbard v Vosper* [1972] 2 Q.B. 84; *A. v Hayden* (1985) 59 A.L.J.R. 6. See also *Lion Laboratories Ltd v Evans* [1985] Q.B. 526; *Att-Gen v Guardian Newspapers Ltd (No.2)* [1990] 1 A.C. 109, 268–269.

[175] *Gartside v Outram* (1857) 26 L.J. Ch. 113, 114.

[176] *Howard v Odhams Press* [1938] 1 K.B. 1, 41–42.

[177] As to what is an arrestable offence, see Police and Criminal Evidence Act 1984 s.24(1).

[178] Police and Criminal Evidence Act 1984 s.24(1).

[179] Not necessarily the offence which has in fact been committed.

(a) the making good of loss or injury occasioned by the offence; or

(b) the making of reasonable compensation for that loss or injury.[180]

Otherwise the compounding of an offence (other than treason) is no longer a criminal offence by English law.[181]

An agreement, express or implied,[182] which is criminal by virtue of the provisions of s.5 of the Criminal Law Act 1967, is undoubtedly unenforceable civilly.[183] But are compromises of offences[184] other than those which are unlawful under s.5 of the Criminal Law Act 1967 enforceable? Where the consideration or part of it takes the form of a promise not to report the matter to the police, or not to initiate a prosecution, the transaction runs the risk of being considered a stifling of a prosecution and may be considered contrary to public policy. It is in any case clear that where a person has already made a statement with a view to the provision of evidence in support of criminal proceedings, even if that person is the victim of the alleged crime, that person becomes a witness and the promise to him of an inducement,[185] even by way of compensation for the loss or injury, to alter or withdraw the statement, constitutes the crime at common law of attempting to pervert the course of justice,[186] and is therefore unenforceable. It is clear that an agreement that would not be offensive to public policy is where the innocent party is seen clearly to be compromising *only* his civil claim, and is not offering either not to report the matter, or not to initiate a prosecution, or to withdraw statements already made. Whether other agreements, for example, one involving a promise not to bring a criminal action, would not be enforceable is not clear. Prior to the 1967 Act, an undertaking not to take action with respect to misdemeanours was binding and enforceable; where the agreement pertained to a crime which was a felony or a misdemeanour of a public nature it was not enforceable. What is left of the old learning in the light of both the abolition of the distinction between misdemeanours and felonies and s.5 of the Criminal Law Act 1967 is not clear. The commentators do not speak with a single voice.[187] 16–037

[180] Such an offence can be prosecuted only by or with the consent of the Director of Public Prosecutions: Criminal Law Act 1967 s.5(3).

[181] Criminal Law Act 1967 s.5(1); cf. *Flower v Sadler* (1882) 10 QBD 572.

[182] As to the implication of an agreement in such circumstances, see *William v Bayley* (1886) L.R. 1 H.L. 200; *Brook v Hook* (1871) L.R. 6 Ex. 89; *Whitmore v Farley* (1881) 45 L.T. 99; *McClatchie v Haslam* (1891) 65 L.T. 691; *Jones v Merionethshire Building Society* [1892] 1 Ch. 173. cf. *Howard v Odhams Press* [1938] 1 K.B. 1; *Bhowampur Banking Corp Ltd v Sreemati Durgesh Nandini Dasi* (1941) 68 L.R.I.A. 144, per Lord Atkin at 148. As to the possibility of a plea of duress or undue influence in such cases, see above, paras 7–045—7–047.

[183] See above, para.16–014.

[184] Criminal Law Act 1967 s.1(1) abolished as from January 1, 1968, the distinction between felonies and misdemeanours, and s.1(2) provides that, subject to the provisions of that Act, on all matters on which a distinction was previously made between felonies and misdemeanours, the law and practice is to be the law and practice applicable at the commencement of the Act in relation to misdemeanours. The special rules relating to the stifling of a prosecution of a felony have thus been abrogated.

[185] If part of the consideration is also a promise not to commence a civil action for damages, see below, para.16–188 for the principles on the possibility of severing the tainted from the untainted promise.

[186] *R. v Panayiotou* [1973] 1 W.L.R. 1032.

[187] See Hudson (1980) 43 M.L.R. 532.

Given that the courts appear to have been given an opportunity to reconsider the matter, the preferable solution would be to jettison completely the old rule and only strike down those compromises which were manifestly contrary to the public interest.[188]

16–038 **Trustees in bankruptcy.** The trustee in bankruptcy of one who has paid money or given security in pursuance of an agreement which is rendered illegal by s.5 of the Criminal Law Act 1967 is probably in no better position than the bankrupt and is therefore unable to recover[189] unless perhaps the payment was an offence against the bankruptcy laws.[190]

(ii) *Other Contracts Affecting the Course of Justice*

16–039 **Interference with course of justice.** Any contract which tends to abuse, prevent or impede the due course of justice is against public policy. A bond upon consideration that criminal proceedings shall be so conducted that the name of a certain person shall not be mentioned, or shall be mentioned only in such a way as not to damage him, is against public policy,[191] as is an agreement not to appear and give evidence at a criminal trial.[192] Similarly agreements to institute a prosecution as a means of gaining publicity,[193] or to consent to a verdict of not guilty in respect of a public nuisance,[194] have been held to be contrary to public policy. And a contract with one who has stood bail to indemnify him amounts to an indictable offence[195] and is unenforceable.[196] However, there are many circumstances in which parties can agree as to the future course of legal proceedings. Thus, for example, in a commercial agreement relating to the sale of land, it has been held not to be against public policy for one of the parties to agree to support the other party's application for planning permission.[197]

16–040 **Procurement of pardon and withdrawal of election petition.** An agreement to pay money, in consideration of a party using his interest to procure the pardon of a convict, is against public policy.[198] And so is an agreement in consideration of a money payment to withdraw an election petition in which charges of bribery

[188] Hudson (1980) 43 M.L.R. 532.

[189] cf. *Re Mapleback* (1876) 4 Ch D 150 as to the position at common law before 1968 (the trustee takes the estate subject to its limitations in the hands of the bankrupt).

[190] cf. *Re Campbell* (1884) 14 QBD 32 as to the position at common law before 1968; and see below, paras 20–024—20–025.

[191] *Lound v Grimwade* (1888) 39 Ch D 605.

[192] *Collins v Blantern* (1767) 2 Wils. 341; 1 Sm.L.C., 13th edn, p.406; cf. *Fulham Football Club Ltd v Cabra Estates Plc* [1993] P.L.R. 29, [1994] 1 B.C.L.C. 363.

[193] *Dann v Curzon* (1910) 104 L.T. 66.

[194] *Windhill Local Board v Vint* (1890) 45 Ch D 351.

[195] *R. v Porter* [1910] 1 K.B. 369.

[196] *Hermann v Jeuchner* (1885) 15 QBD 561 (money actually deposited with a surety was held not to be recoverable); *Consolidated Exploration & Finance Co v Musgrave* [1900] 1 Ch. 37; *Re Gurwicz* [1919] 1 K.B. 675.

[197] *Fulham Football Club Ltd v Cabra Estates Plc* [1994] 1 B.C.L.C. 363. A term in a settlement not to repeat claims made in proceedings was not against public policy: *Australia and New Zealand Bank Group Ltd v Cie Woga D'Importation et D'Exportation SA* [2007] EWHC (Comm) 293, [2007] 1 Lloyd's Rep 487.

[198] *Norman v Cole* (1800) 3 Esp. 253; but see *Lampleigh v Brathwait* (1615) Hob. 105.

are made,[199] it being in the public interest that the investigation should be carried out.

Winding up. An agreement by a shareholder in a company which is being compulsorily wound up that, in consideration of a sum of money, he would endeavour to postpone the making of a call or would support the claim of a creditor is unenforceable as being contrary to the policy of the insolvency legislation and perhaps also an interference with the course of public justice.[200] 16–041

Bankruptcy. All "composition" agreements between a debtor and creditor of a preferential character are unenforceable.[201] In addition the essence of such agreements being equality between the creditors, a creditor who has executed a composition deed is entitled to repudiate it against the other creditors if he afterwards discovers that they have been induced to execute the deed by means of a secret bargain for a payment to them in excess of the composition, even if the bargain was made after his own execution of the deed.[202] Similarly, agreements for the withdrawal of opposition to the discharge of a bankrupt are unenforceable.[203] But a contract by an undischarged bankrupt in consideration of a small loan to pay in full a debt due from him at the commencement of and provable in his bankruptcy is not void as being contrary to public policy or the principles of the law of bankruptcy.[204] 16–042

Divorce: collusive agreements. A collusive agreement between the parties[205] to matrimonial proceedings is an agreement or bargain between the parties or their agents whereby the initiation of the suit is procured or its conduct provided for.[206] At one time these were held to be unenforceable. However, in *Sutton v Sutton*[207] the court held that public policy, particularly in the light of s.1(2)(d) of the Matrimonial Causes Act 1973 (permitting divorce by agreement after two years' separation), no longer rendered a contract unenforceable on the grounds of collusion. In that case the parties, who had lived apart for three years, agreed to an amicable divorce on the grounds of two years' separation and as part of the arrangement the husband agreed to transfer title to the matrimonial home to the wife. The wife sought specific performance of this promise and, although she was unsuccessful on the grounds that the agreement was unenforceable as an attempt to oust the jurisdiction of the court, the court held that the principle that collusive 16–043

---

[199] *Coppock v Bower* (1838) 4 M. & W. 361.

[200] *Elliott v Richardson* (1870) L.R. 5. C.P. 744.

[201] *Mallalieu v Hodgson* (1851) 16 Q.B. 689; and see *Staines v Wainwright* (1839) 6 Bing.N.C. 174. See below, paras 20–027 et seq.

[202] *Re Milner* (1885) 15 QBD 605. And see *Re Myers* [1908] 1 K.B. 941; *Farmers' Mart v Milne* [1915] A.C. 106; *Re Johns* [1928] Ch. 737; cf. above, para.16–017.

[203] See *McKewan v Sanderson* (1875) L.R. 20 Eq. 65; *Kearley v Thomson* (1890) 24 QBD 742.

[204] *Wild v Tucker* [1914] 3 K.B. 36; and see *Jakeman v Cook* (1878) 4 Ex.D. 26 where the promisor was a discharged bankrupt.

[205] cf. *Prevost v Wood* (1905) 21 T.L.R. 694 as to an agreement between a petitioner and a third party with whom sexual relations took place.

[206] *Gosling v Gosling* [1968] P. 1, 11–12.

[207] [1984] Ch. 184; see Cretney and Masson, *Principals of Family Law*, revised edn (2003), Ch.14.

agreements were void and unenforceable, was no longer the law. If of course the parties fabricate the grounds on which a divorce is sought then this would make any agreement to do this unenforceable as an attempt to pervert the course of justice.[208]

(iii) *Ouster of Jurisdiction*

16–044 **Maintenance agreements.** Any provision by which a wife binds herself not to apply to the divorce court for maintenance is void as an ouster of the jurisdiction of the courts[209]: but one which, by purporting to make maintenance a debt enforceable at law, is now by statute[210] binding on the parties and provides consideration for a counter-promise, although on application to the court it may be varied or revoked.[211] But an agreement is not, even at common law, void as contrary to public policy merely because it limits a husband's right to apply to the courts for a reduction in his liability for maintenance for his wife[212] or because it ousts the jurisdiction of a foreign court.[213]

16–045 **Arbitration.**[214] If the parties seek by agreement to take the law out of the hands of the courts and into the hands of a private tribunal, except as permitted by the Arbitration Act 1996, then the agreement, to the extent that it deprives recourse to the courts in case of errors of law, is contrary to public policy.[215] In *Leigh v National Union of Railwaymen*,[216] it was held that, since the court's jurisdiction could not be ousted, the court was not bound by an express provision in a trade union's rules that domestic remedies must be exhausted first, though a plaintiff would have to show cause why the court should intervene; in the absence of any such provision, though the court would more readily grant relief, it might first require the plaintiff to resort to the domestic remedies. An arbitration clause per se does not at common law oust the jurisdiction of the court[217] and it was held in *Scott v Avery*[218] that a provision making an arbitration award a condition precedent to the bringing of an action did not oust the jurisdiction of the court. And it is not against public policy to agree that all claims are to be taken to arbitration and that unless this is done within a certain period (however

[208] Although there is a provision enabling the parties to refer an agreement to the court for approval, this procedure is now obsolete: see Rayden and Jackson, *Divorce*, 16th edn, p.508.

[209] *Hyman v Hyman* [1929] A.C. 601; *Bennett v Bennett* [1952] 1 K.B. 249; *Sutton v Sutton* [1984] Ch. 184, 195–198; Matrimonial Causes Act 1973 s.34.

[210] Matrimonial Causes Act 1973 s.34. As to the previous position at common law, see *Bennett v Bennett* [1952] 1 K.B. 249, 262, see also para.16–043. The private ordering of the consequences of divorce raises difficult issues: see Cretney and Masson.

[211] Matrimonial Causes Act 1973 s.35 (as amended).

[212] *Russell v Russell* [1956] P. 283.

[213] *Addison v Brown* [1954] 1 W.L.R. 779.

[214] See Ch.32.

[215] *Lee v Showmen's Guild of Great Britain* [1952] 2 Q.B. 329.

[216] [1970] Ch. 326.

[217] *Scott v Avery* (1856) 5 H.L.C. 811; *Edwards v Aberayron Mutual Ship Insurance Society* (1876) 1 QBD 563; *Hallen v Spaeth* [1923] A.C. 684.

[218] (1856) 5 H.L.C. 811.

short) a claim is to be deemed as having been waived.[219] The court will set aside an arbitrator's award if it seeks to give effect to a contract which is illegal or contrary to public policy.[220]

16–046 The Arbitration Act 1996 enables parties to enter into binding arbitration agreements which enable the parties to determine "how their disputes are resolved"[221] and to curtail the jurisdiction of the court to interfere with the arbitral procedure which they have established.[222] In order to oust effectively the jurisdiction of the court and to have the rights of the parties determined by arbitration, the parties must have entered into an arbitration agreement. An arbitration agreement is defined as any agreement by the parties in writing[223] to submit their disputes to arbitration.[224] Where an arbitration agreement within the meaning of the 1996 Act is entered into, certain provisions of the Act, referred to as mandatory provisions, have effect irrespective of any agreement of the parties to the contrary.[225] The effect of these mandatory provisions is to ensure that the dispute is resolved by the terms of the agreement and not by recourse to courts.[226]

16–047 **Questions of fact and expert evaluation.** There is no objection to the parties making a private tribunal the final arbiter on questions of fact.[227] Thus, it often happens that by the rules of a game or a race or competition a stated person is to decide who is the winner and so on and that his decision shall be final. Those questions must be decided by the designated person or persons.[228] Where an agreement provides that in the case of a dispute the services of an expert should be used and that his decision "shall be conclusive and final and binding for all purposes", this will be binding on the parties unless there has been fraud or bias on the part of the expert or he has been guilty of "mistake".[229] Mistake in this context requires the expert to have "departed from his instructions in a material respect"[230] for example, an expert who has been employed to value shares values

---

[219] *Atlantic Shipping & Trading Co Ltd v Louis Dreyfus & Co* [1922] 2 A.C. 250. But under s.12 of the Arbitration Act 1996 the court has power to extend the time: Ch.32.

[220] *David Taylor & Son Ltd v Barnett Trading Co* [1953] 1 W.L.R. 562; cf. *Birtley & District Co-operative Society Ltd v Windy Nook & District Industrial Co-operative Society Ltd (No.2)* [1960] 2 Q.B. 1; but see *Bellshill & Mossend Co-operative Society Ltd v Dalziel Co-operative Society Ltd* [1960] A.C. 832.

[221] s.1(b).

[222] s.1(c).

[223] s.5, note in particular s.5(3) and (6).

[224] s.6 (the dispute does not have to be contractual).

[225] s.4 and Sch.1.

[226] in particular, ss.9–11.

[227] *Baker v Jones* [1954] 1 W.L.R. 1005, 1010; *West of England Shipowners Mutual Insurance Association v Cristal Ltd* [1996] 1 Lloyd's Rep. 370. Such a decision, however, is open to challenge on the grounds of fraud or perversity: *West of England Shipowners'* [1996] 1 Lloyd's Rep. 370, 377–379.

[228] *Brown v Overbury* (1856) 11 Exch. 715; *Sadler v Smith* (1869) L.R. 5 Q.B. 40; *Cipriani v Burnett* [1933] A.C. 83.

[229] *Jones v Sherwood Computer Service Plc* [1989] 1 W.L.R. 277 (noted (1993) 109 L.Q.R. 385).

[230] *Jones v Sherwood Computer Service Plc* [1989] 1 W.L.R. 277, 287.

the wrong number of shares or values shares in the wrong company.[231] Accordingly, the determination of the expert will be binding if "he has answered the question in the wrong way" but if "he has answered the wrong question, his decision will be a nullity".[232] However, an attempt to oust completely the jurisdiction of the court in the sense that the parties are precluded from seeking judicial redress even if there is fraud or bias by the expert would be ineffective.[233]

(iv) *Maintenance and Champerty*

16–048 **Maintenance and champerty formerly crimes.** For many centuries prior to 1968 maintenance and champerty were crimes both at common law[234] and by statute.[235] However the Criminal Law Act 1967 now provides[236] that, as from January 1, 1968, "any distinct offence under the common law in England and Wales of maintenance (including champerty)" should be abolished; and the Act repealed[237] various old statutes relating to the two crimes. The Act further abolished[238] tortious liability for maintenance and champerty. But s.14(2) of the Act provides that:

> "... the abolition of criminal and civil liability under the law of England and Wales for maintenance and champerty shall not affect any rule of that law as to the cases in which a contract is to be treated as contrary to public policy or otherwise illegal."

16–049 **Public policy today respecting maintenance and champerty.** It is thought that the provisions of s.14(2) of the Criminal Law Act 1967 must mean that at least prima facie contracts which under the law before 1968 would have been unenforceable for maintenance[239] or champerty[240] are still to be unenforceable therefor, even though the criminality attaching to such contracts has been removed. In *Trendtex Trading Corp v Credit Suisse*,[241] Lord Roskill considered it plain from s.14(2) that:

---

[231] *Jones v Sherwood Computer Service Plc* [1989] 1 W.L.R. 277.

[232] *Nikko Hotels (UK) Ltd v MEPC Plc* [1991] 2 E.G.L.R. 103, 108. For other relevant authorities see (1993) 109 L.Q.R. 385.

[233] (1993) 109 L.Q.R. 385 discussing *Re Davstone Estate's Ltd Leases* [1969] 2 Ch. 378.

[234] Maintenance: *Pechell v Watson* (1841) 8 M. & W. 691; *Neville v London Express Newspaper Ltd* [1919] A.C. 368, 383, 386, indicating need to prove want of reasonable or probably cause; champerty: *Re Trepca Mines Ltd (No.2)* [1963] Ch. 199, 224; *Master v Miller* (1791) 4 T.R. 320, 340.

[235] See Criminal Law Act 1967, Sch.4.

[236] s.13(1)(a).

[237] s.13(1)(b) and Sch.4.

[238] s.14(1).

[239] See below, paras 16–050—16–053.

[240] See below, paras 16–054—16–066.

[241] [1982] A.C. 679, 702. See also the views of Lord Denning M.R. in the Court of Appeal that by striking down both the tort and crime of maintenance the Criminal Law Act 1967 also "struck down our old cases as to what constitutes maintenance, including champerty in so far as they were based on an outdated policy": [1980] 1 Q.B. 629, 653. Lord Denning considered that modern public policy could be found in *British Cash and Parcel Conveyors Ltd v Lamson Store Service Co Ltd* [1908] 1 K.B. 1006; *Martell v Consett Iron Co Ltd* [1955] Ch. 363; and *Hill v Archbold* [1968] 1 Q.B. 686.

"Parliament intended to leave the law as to the effect of maintenance and champerty upon contracts unaffected by the abolition of them as crimes and torts."

This is an area where the courts clearly recognise that public policy is subject to change in the light of, for example, the need to ensure access to civil justice.[242] Thus the recent reforms on "no win no fee" arrangements obviously effect a significant change in public policy with respect to maintenance and champerty.[243] In *Kellar v Williams*[244] Lord Carswell stated obiter that the:

" . . . content of public policy can change over the years, and it may now be time to reconsider the accepted [common law] prohibition [on conditional fees] in the light of modern practising conditions."[245]

Maintenance. A person is guilty of maintenance if he supports litigation in which he has no legitimate concern without just cause or excuse.[246] The mischief directed against is wanton and officious intermeddling with the disputes of others in which the defendant has no interest whatever and where the assistance he renders to one or the other party is without justification or excuse.[247] The bounds of justification and excuse for supporting litigation by others have been greatly widened over the past 50 years.[248] In the strict sense of the term, the doctrine of maintenance applies only to litigation[249] actually pending[250]; but unjustified *instigation* of actions by others is treated as "savouring of maintenance".[251] It is not the less maintenance because the maintained action was successful.[252] 16–050

---

[242] See *Giles v Thompson* [1993] 3 All E.R. 321, 348 CA, per Bingham M.R.; "the law on maintenance and champerty has not stood still, but has accommodated itself to changing times", per Lord Mustill in the House of Lords at [1994] 1 A.C. 142, 164. See also *Thai Trading Co v Taylor* [1998] 3 All E.R. 65 (this case was disapproved of in *Awwad v Geraghty & Co (A Firm)* [2000] 1 All E.R. 608. See Walters (2000) 116 L.Q.R. 371); *Bevan Ashford v Geoff Yeandle (Contractors) Ltd* [1999] Ch. 239. This decision involved the use of conditional fee arrangements with respect to alternative dispute resolution procedures and in this context it is now expressly recognised by the new s.58A of the Courts and Legal Services Act 1990 (introduced by s.27 of the Access to Justice Act 1999) that conditional fee arrangements apply to "any sort of proceedings for resolving disputes" (s.58A(4)). *Camdex International Ltd v Bank of Zambia* [1996] C.L.C. 1477, 1481: "The modern approach is not to extend the types of involvement in litigation that are considered objectionable. There is a tendency to recognise less specific interests as justifying the support of the litigation of another."

[243] These reforms are set out in the judgment of Steyn L.J. in *Giles v Thompson* [1993] 3 All E.R. 321. See also below, para.16–056.

[244] [2004] UKPC 30, [2004] All E.R. (D) 286.

[245] [2004] UKPC 30 at [21].

[246] *Hill v Archbold* [1968] 1 Q.B. 686; *Trendtex Trading Corp v Credit Suisse* [1980] 1 Q.B. 629, 663. See Winfield (1919) 35 L.Q.R. 50 on the history of maintenance. See also Walters (1996) 112 L.Q.R. 560.

[247] *British Cash and Parcel Conveyors Ltd v Lamson Store Service Co Ltd* [1908] 1 K.B. 1006, 1012; *Hill v Archbold* [1968] 1 Q.B. 686, 697; *Giles v Thompson* [1994] 1 A.C. 142, 164.

[248] See below, para.16–051.

[249] See *Re Trepca Mines Ltd (No.2)* [1963] Ch. 199; cf. *Moore v Usher* (1835) 7 Sim. 383, 388; cf. *Pickering v Sogex Services (UK) Ltd* (1982) 262 E.G. 770.

[250] *Flight v Leman* (1843) 4 Q.B. 883.

[251] *Flight v Leman* (1843) 4 Q.B. 883; *Greig v National Amalgamated Union of Shop Assistants* (1906) 22 T.L.R. 274.

[252] *Neville v London Express Newspaper Ltd* [1919] A.C. 368.

16–051 **Justification.** The doctrine of maintenance, being founded on considerations of public policy, "cannot at any time become frozen into immutable respectability"[253] but must be "reappraised in light of current notions of public policy and of international trading practices".[254] As long ago as 1883 it was said that it was unhelpful to go back very far in the authorities relating to justification[255] and the grounds of justification have been further greatly widened over the past 50 years,[256] so that Danckwerts J.'s judgment in *Martell v Consett Iron Co Ltd*[257] can now be taken as the foundation of the modern law.[258] In that case an association for the protection of the rights of owners and occupiers of fisheries and for the prevention of pollution of rivers supported an action by one of its members in respect of alleged pollution of a river flowing through the member's land. Danckwerts J. rejected the defendant's contention that the association was unlawfully maintaining the action, holding that "support of legal proceedings based on a bona fide community of pecuniary interest or religion or principle or problems" did not constitute maintenance.[259] The Court of Appeal, in affirming the decision, held that the defendants had not shown that the association was not acting in defence of the collective interests of its members on the principle of mutual protection.[260]

16–052 **Examples of justification.** It has been said that most of the actions in our courts today:

> "... are supported by some association or other, or by the state itself. Comparatively few litigants bring suits, or defend them, at their own expense. Most claims by workmen against their employers are paid for by a trade union. Most defences of motorists are paid for by insurance companies."[261]

It is clear that ordinarily none of those cases today constitutes maintenance.[262] Similarly a body is not guilty of maintenance in supporting an action for defamation brought by one of its officers where, if the defamatory words complained of are true, the officer is unfit to continue in the body's employment.[263] It has always been a justification for the maintenance of an action that

[253] *Martell v Consett Iron Co Ltd* [1955] Ch. 363, 375; *Giles v Thompson* [1994] 1 A.C. 142, 164.

[254] *Trendtex Trading Corp v Credit Suisse* [1980] 1 Q.B. 629, 663; see also [1982] A.C. 679, 702.

[255] *Bradlaugh v Newdegate* (1883) 11 QBD 1, 7; and see *Ellis v Torrington* [1920] 1 K.B. 399, 412.

[256] *Hill v Archbold* [1968] 1 Q.B. 686, 694, 697; *Trendtex Trading Corp v Credit Suisse* [1982] A.C. 679, 702; see also the Law Commission, *Proposals for the Reform of the Law Relating to Maintenance and Champerty* (1966), pp.3–4; *Giles v Thompson* [1993] 3 All E.R. 321, 330 CA.

[257] [1955] Ch. 363.

[258] *Hill v Archbold* [1969] 1 Q.B. 686, 694, 700; *Trendtex Trading Corp v Credit Suisse* [1982] A.C. 679, 702.

[259] *Martell v Consett Iron Co Ltd* [1955] Ch. 363, 387.

[260] *Martell v Consett Iron Co Ltd* [1955] Ch. 363, 389, 420, 430.

[261] *Hill v Archbold* [1968] 1 Q.B. 686, 694–695.

[262] *Hill v Archbold* [1968] 1 Q.B. 686; *Bourne v Colodense Ltd* [1985] I.C.R. 291.

[263] *Scott v National Society for the Prevention of Cruelty to Children* (1909) 25 T.L.R. 789; *Hill v Archbold* [1968] 1 Q.B. 686, where the Court of Appeal stated that *Oram v Hutt* [1914] 1 Ch. 98 CA and *Baker v Jones* [1854] 1 W.L.R. 1005 (Lynskey J.) would not now be decided as they were; contrast *Martell v Consett Iron Co Ltd* [1955] Ch. 363, 389, 414–419, 425.

the maintainer acted solely with a charitable motive, and that is so even though there was no ground for the maintainer's action which he took without reasonable inquiry.[264] There may be evidence of maintenance in a solicitor taking up an action for a poor person[265] though it is probable that he may do so if he acts bona fide and has perhaps satisfied himself that there is a proper cause of action.[266] Blood relationship would seem to be a justification for maintenance.[267] The courts, particularly in commercial cases, have recognised that a sufficient interest does not have to be proprietary in character and in *Trendtex Trading Corp v Credit Suisse*[268] Oliver L.J. was willing to go so far as to hold that maintenance would be justified "wherever the maintainer has a genuine pre-existing financial interest in maintaining the solvency of the person whose action he maintains". The interest, however, must be distinct from any benefit which arises under the contract which is allegedly illegal as constituting maintenance.[269] It has been held that despite the judgment of the Court of Appeal in *Prudential Assurance Co Ltd v Newman Industries Ltd*[270] a majority shareholder in a company possesses a sufficient interest so that an assignment to him of the company's cause of action is not against public policy.[271]

Effect of maintenance. In principle a contract of maintenance should be held to be unenforceable between the parties to it.[272] But even when maintenance was a crime, the illegal maintenance of an action was not a defence to the action, nor did it afford a ground for stay of proceedings.[273] The remedy of the other party to the litigation was before 1968 an action in tort. It would still appear to be the position that the court will not stay proceedings which are being maintained provided the proceedings do not constitute an abuse of the process of the court, that is, an action commenced in bad faith with no genuine belief in its merits but commenced for an ulterior purpose.[274] Also, the court does not have inherent jurisdiction to dismiss a maintained action which is not an abuse of the process 16–053

[264] *Harris v Brisco* (1886) 17 QBD 504; *Holden v Thompson* [1907] 2 K.B. 489; cf. *Cole v Booker* (1913) 29 T.L.R. 295.

[265] *Wiggins v Lavy* (1928) 44 T.L.R. 721, but that was before legal aid. See also para.17–056.

[266] *Ladd v London Road Car Co, The Times*, March 14, 1900.

[267] *Rothewel v Pewer* (1431) Y.B. 9 Hen. 6, 64, pl.713; *Pomeroy v Abbot Buckfast* (1443) Y.B. 22 Hen. 6; (1442) Y.B. 21 Hen. 6, 15, pl.30; and see *Harris v Brisco* (1886) 17 QBD 504, 512–513; 1 Hawkins P.C., 8th edn, p.488; cf. *Hutley v Hutley* (1873) L.R. 8 Q.B. 112.

[268] [1980] 1 Q.B. 629, 668. This view was implicitly endorsed in the House of Lords. There Lord Roskill was willing to hold that a genuine commercial interest was sufficient to enable an assignee of a cause of action to enforce it and on this reasoning the views of Oliver L.J. on what constitutes a sufficient justification for maintaining an action were implictly adopted; see [1982] A.C. 679, 703; see also *Brownton Ltd v Edward Moore Inbucon Ltd* [1985] 3 All E.R. 499; below, para.19–048.

[269] *Giles v Thompson* [1994] 1 A.C. 142, 163 HL.

[270] [1982] Ch. 204 (sharesholder had no standing to bring action where wrong to the company allegedly reduced the value of his shares) (cf. *Fischer (Great Britain) Ltd v Multi Construction Ltd* [1995] 1 B.C.L.C. 260; *Johnson v Gore Wood* [2002] 2 A.C. 1).

[271] *Circuit Systems Ltd & Basten v Zucken Redac (UK) Ltd* (1995) 11 Const. L.J. 201, 209 (on appeal this point did not have to be decided: [1996] 3 All E.R. 748).

[272] *Cole v Booker* (1913) 29 T.L.R. 295, 297; Lord Coleridge C.J.'s obiter dictum to the contrary in *Bradlaugh v Newdegate* (1883) 11 QBD 1, 4 cannot be taken to represent the law.

[273] *Martell v Consett Iron Co Ltd* [1955] Ch. 363.

[274] *Abraham v Thompson* [1997] 4 All E.R. 362. It is considered that *Grovewood Holdings Plc v James Capel & Co Ltd* [1995] Ch. 80 (dealing with a champertous agreement) is no longer good law: see note (1998) 114 L.Q.R. 207.

of the court because the maintainer declines to give an undertaking as to costs, or to make such an order itself.[275]

16–054 **Champerty.** Champerty has been defined as "an aggravated form of maintenance"[276] and occurs when the person maintaining another stipulates for a share of the proceeds of the action or suit[277] or other contentious proceedings where property is in dispute.[278] For champerty there must not only be interference on the suit but there must be the added factor of a division of the spoils.[279] There is an obvious relationship between maintenance and champerty, you cannot have the latter without the former but "there can still be champerty even if the maintenance is not unlawful".[280] In *Giles v Thompson*,[281] Lord Mustill was of the opinion that champerty as it related to an agreement by a solicitor to accept payment of his fees measured as a proportion of the damages recovered by his client survived largely as a rule of professional conduct.[282] While there undoubtedly have been significant changes in the rules relating to fee arrangements between solicitors and their clients which now permit arrangements which previously would have been champertous,[283] it is suggested that it would be going too far to treat the rule as being merely one of professional conduct. It is no justification for a champertous agreement that the contracting parties are related by blood.[284] The question arises whether the court can enjoin proceedings that are champertous. The reasoning in *Abraham v Thompson*[285] would suggest not. Where the plaintiff relies on a champertous assignment to sue, the action would be enjoined not, however, because of the champerty as such but because it is not possible to assign a cause of action.

16–055 **Champertous agreements between solicitor and client.** An agreement by a solicitor to provide funds for litigation[286] or without charge to conduct litigation,[287] in this country, in consideration of a share of the proceeds is champer-

---

[275] *Abraham v Thompson* [1997] 4 All E.R. 362. See also *Murphy v Young & Co's Brewery Plc* [1997] 1 Lloyd's Rep. 236. It is submitted that *McFarlane v E.E. Caledonia Ltd (No.2)* [1995] 1 W.L.R. 366 is no longer good law. The proper way to proceed is to seek an order against the maintainer under s.51 of the Supreme Court Act 1981. The court could make an order under s.51 against a shareholder of a company as a shareholder who funded or controlled a company's litigation in order to protect his own financial interests: see *CIBC Mellon Trust Co v Stolzenberg* [2005] EWCA Civ 628, [2005] 2 B.C.L.C. 618.

[276] *Giles v Thompson* [1993] 3 All E.R. 321, 328, CA.

[277] *Trendtex Trading Corp v Credit Suisse* [1980] 1 Q.B. 629, 663; *Re Trepca Mines Ltd (No.2)* [1963] Ch. 199, 219; *Haseldine v Hosken* [1933] 1 K.B. 822, 831; and see *Anderson v Radcliffe* (1858) E.B. & E. 806, 819, 825. Champerty only relates to legal proceedings: *Pickering v Sogex Services (UK) Ltd* (1982) 262 E.G. 770.

[278] *Re Trepca Mines Ltd (No.2)* [1963] Ch. 199, 224; *Master v Miller* (1791) 4 T.R. 320, 340.

[279] *Giles v Thompson* [1994] 1 A.C. 142, 161.

[280] *Thai Trading Co v Taylor* [1998] 3 All E.R. 65, 69. This case was disapproved of in *Awwad v Geraghty & Co (A Firm)* [2000] 1 All E.R. 608 but this does not affect this aspect of the judgment.

[281] [1994] 1 A.C. 142.

[282] *Giles v Thompson* [1994] 1 A.C. 142, 153–154.

[283] See below, para.16–056.

[284] *Hutley v Hutley* (1873) L.R. 8 Q.B. 112; cf. above, para.16–052.

[285] See fn.268, above.

[286] See above, para.16–052 as to assignments of rights to solicitors, see below, para.16–064.

[287] See above, para.16–052.

tous,[288] and this is so even though the agreement was made abroad.[289] It was argued in *Wallersteiner v Moir (No.2)*[290] that considerations of policy demanded an exception to this rule, namely where a shareholder intended to bring an action on behalf of a company against those in control of the company who had allegedly committed wrongs against it, such an action being extremely costly to the individual and, in the event of success, bringing him probably small personal benefit. But a majority[291] of the Court of Appeal refused to create such an exception. In *Awwad v Geraghty & Co (A Firm)*[292] it was held that at common law an agreement whereby the client would pay a lower fee if he lost but a higher fee if he won was illegal and unenforceable.[293] The agreements in *Awwad* and *Thai Trading* would now be valid under s.27 of the Access to Justice Act 1999.[294] An agreement whereby a solicitor obtained more than his profit costs (unless it was a permitted conditional fee), or a contingent fee, would probably be unenforceable.[295] Where a solicitor enters into a champertous agreement, he cannot recover from his client his own costs[296] or even his out-of-pocket expenses.[297] But the solicitor does not act champertously unless he is a party to the agreement or participates in it by voluntarily doing a positive act to assist the parties in its execution, and the mere fact that the solicitor knows or gets to know of a champertous agreement relating to litigation in which he is engaged does not prevent him from suing on an otherwise lawful retainer.[298] If a lawful retainer is subsequently varied by a champertous agreement, the solicitor probably cannot disregard the agreement and rely on his ordinary rights under the retainer.[299]

Non-champertous agreements between solicitor and client. Section 58 of the Courts and Legal Services Act 1990, as amended by s.27 of the Access to Justice Act 1999,[300] is designed to enable a solicitor and client to enter into a conditional fee agreement. A conditional fee agreement is one whereby a person providing advocacy or litigation services is only to be paid his fees or expenses 16–056

---

[288] *Re Masters* (1835) 4 Dowl. 18; *Strange v Brennan* (1846) 15 Sim. 346; *Hilton v Woods* (1867) L.R. 4 Eq. 432; *Earle v Hopwood* (1861) 9 C.B. (N.S.) 566; *Hutley v Hutley* (1873) L.R. 8 Q.B. 112; *Re A Solicitor* [1912] 1 K.B. 302; *Re A Solicitor* (1913) 29 T.L.R. 354; *Wiggins v Lavy* (1928) 44 T.L.R. 721. And see Solicitors Act 1974 s.59 (amended by Courts and Legal Services Act 1990 s.98).

[289] *Grell v Levy* (1864) 16 C.B. (N.S.) 73.

[290] [1975] Q.B. 373.

[291] Lord Denning was prepared to allow a "contingency fee" in such circumstances. See also *Trendtex Trading Corp v Credit Suisse* [1980] 1 Q.B. 629, 654, 663.

[292] [2000] 2 All E.R. 608.

[293] The court declined to follow *Thai Trading Co (A Firm) v Taylor* [1998] Q.B. 781 where such an agreement was upheld.

[294] This amended s.58 of the Courts and Legal Services Act 1990. See Current Law Statutes where the Lord Chancellor is reported as stating: "Section 58 is intended to bring into effect the judgment of the Court of Appeal in *Thai Trading* into Statute Law" (*Hansard*, HL Vol.596, cols 956–965).

[295] Courts and Legal Services Act 1990 s.58. A fee splitting agreement may be in breach of the Law Society Rules and unenforceable because it is accordingly illegal: see *Mohamed v Alaga Co* [1998] 2 All E.R. 720.

[296] *Wild v Simpson* [1919] 2 K.B. 544.

[297] *Re Trepca Mines Ltd (No.2)* [1963] Ch. 199.

[298] *Re Trepca Mines Ltd (No.2)* [1963] Ch. 199, 220–221.

[299] *Wild v Simpson* [1919] 2 K.B. 544, 565, disapproving *Grell v Levy* (1864) 16 C.B.(N.S.) 73; and see *Re Trepca Mines Ltd (No.2)* [1963] Ch. 199, 222.

[300] Access to Justice Act 1999 s.27.

in specified circumstances,[301] or which provides for a success fee.[302] Such an agreement must be in writing, relate to proceedings which can be the subject of conditional fee arrangements, and comply with the requirements (if any) specified by the Lord Chancellor.[303] Where the conditional fee provides for a success fee, the percentage increase must comply with any order made by the Lord Chancellor regulating the permitted percentage of increase.[304] Section 58 provides that agreements "shall not be unenforceable by reason of being a conditional fee agreement" as permitted by s.58 but that other conditional fee agreements shall be unenforceable.[305] Certain proceedings cannot be the subject matter of any form of conditional fee; these are criminal and family proceedings as defined in s.58A of the Courts and Legal Services Act 1990. There are other forms of fee agreement between a solicitor and client which are not treated as being champertous. There is no objection to a solicitor agreeing to charge no costs against his client.[306] And a solicitor and client may agree for a fixed remuneration in lieu of costs,[307] such agreement must be in writing and is subject to the proviso that no validity is given to any purchase by a solicitor of his client's interests in any action, suit or other contentious proceedings, or to any success.[308] The mere fact that a solicitor had conducted proceedings on credit or that he was aware of his clients lack of means did not entail that he was unlawfully maintaining that action.[309] Section 58 of the 1990 Act (as amended) only applies to those who could be described as "litigators", that is, advocates and those conducting the litigation.[310] Thus it has been held that an agreement where by accountants were paid 8 per cent of damages recovered for professional services in preparing claimants' claim but which did not involve the issue of liability, was not champertous.[311] An agreement made in England which is champertous is lawful if it relates to litigation in a country where champerty is lawful.[312] A similar result was reached where a claims' recovery agent in respect

[301] Court and Legal Services Act 1990 s.58(2)(a). For techniques available to the court to regulate costs in an action involving a conditional fee agreement: see *King v Telegraph Group Ltd* [2004] EWCA Civ 613, [2005] 1 W.L.R. 2282.

[302] Court and Legal Services Act 1990 s.58(2)(b).

[303] s.58(3). Various statutory instruments have been made with respect to conditional fee orders: see *Sharratt v London Central Bus Co Ltd* [2003] EWCA Civ 718, [2003] 4 All E.R. 590 where the law is fully analysed.

[304] Court and Legal Services Act 1990 s.58(4)(c). The agreement must also state this amount: s.58(4)(b).

[305] s.58(1).

[306] *Jennings v Johnson* (1873) L.R. 8 C.P. 425. Such an agreement precludes the recovery of costs by the client from the other party to the litigation, as costs are given by way of indemnity: *Gundry v Sainsbury* [1910] 1 K.B. 645.

[307] Solicitors Act 1974 ss.59–63 (contentious business); cf. s.57 (non-contentious business) (certain aspects of ss.57, 59, 60 and 61 of the 1974 Act have been amended by s.98 of the Courts and Legal Services Act 1990). See also para.16–064; *Electrical Trades Union v Tarlo* [1964] Ch. 720.

[308] Solicitors Act 1974 s.59(1); and see *Electrical Trades Union v Tarlo* [1964] Ch. 720.

[309] *Burstein v Times Newspapers Ltd* [2002] EWCA Civ 1739, [2002] All E.R. (D) 442.

[310] *R. (on the application of Factortame and others) v Secretary of State for Transport, Environment and the Regions (No.2)* [2002] EWCA Civ 932, [2002] 3 W.L.R. 1104.

[311] *R. (on the application of Factortame and others) v Secretary of State for Transport, Environment and the Regions (No.2)* [2002] 3 W.L.R. 1104; *Mansell v Robinson* [2007] EWHC (QB) 101, [2007] All E.R. (D) 279 (Jan.).

[312] *Papera Traders Co Ltd v Hyundai Merchant Marine Co Ltd (No.2)* [2002] EWHC 2130, (Comm), [2002] Lloyd's L.R. 692.

of damages to sea cargo, acted on a "no cure no pay" basis but if the claim was successful 5 per cent of the recovery would be paid to the agent.[313] However, situation where an expert was to give evidence on a contingent fee basis was highly undesirable and the court would seldom consent to an expert being instructed on a contingent fee basis.[314]

Agreements savouring of champerty: assignments of the right to litigate. In *Trendtex Trading Corp v Credit Suisse*,[315] the Court of Appeal and House of Lords fundamentally re-examined the law of maintenance and champerty in so far as it applied to the assignment of the right to litigate. Much simplified, the facts in that case were as follows. The plaintiff (T) sold cement, payment to be made by confirmed letter of credit. The issuing bank (CBN) failed to honour the letter of credit and T sued for payment. T was successful in the Court of Appeal but leave was given to CBN to appeal to the House of Lords. At this juncture T assigned its right of action against CBN to the defendants, Credit Suisse, to whom T was heavily indebted for financial assistance provided in connection with the cement contract and the litigation arising out of the dishonouring of the letter of credit. The agreement whereby T assigned its right of action to Credit Suisse also provided that Credit Suisse could assign the right of action to a third party which Credit Suisse eventually did. T subsequently considered that it had been duped by the defendants into making the assignment for what turned out to be a gross undervaluation, and sought to have the assignment set aside on the ground that the whole transaction was champertous.[316] The Court of Appeal upheld the assignment. The defendants had a close commercial relationship with the defendants which would have justified them in maintaining an action by the plaintiff or in participating in any proceeds of action and, in the light of this, Oliver L.J., could not see why the actual "assignment of the cause of action itself" should not also be valid.[317] Lord Denning M.R. saw no reason why the benefit of the right to sue for damages for breach of contract should not be assignable given that the benefit of the contract before breach was assignable.[318] However, the right to litigate about purely personal claims is not 16–057

[313] *Papera Traders Co Ltd v Hyundai Merchant Marine Co Ltd (No.2)* [2002] Lloyd's L.R. 692.

[314] *Papera Traders Co Ltd v Hyundai Merchant Marine Co Ltd (No.2)* [2002] Lloyd's L.R. 692. See also *Dal-Sterling Group Plc v W.S.P. South & West Ltd* Unreported August 18, 2001.

[315] [1980] Q.B. 629 CA; [1982] A.C. 679; *Kaukomarkkinat O/Y v "Elbe" Transport-Union GmbH (The "Kelo")* [1985] 2 Lloyd's Rep. 85; *24 Seven Utility Services Ltd v Rosekey Ltd* [2003] EWHC 3415 (QB), [2004] All E.R. (D) 288 (Feb).

[316] The Criminal Law Act 1967 s.14(2), has a bearing on this issue. As s.14(2) only applies to "cases in which *a contract* is to be treated as contrary to public policy or otherwise illegal", it may therefore be argued that completed assignments, which operate as transfers of property and not as contracts, are no longer to be avoided on grounds of public policy. It is submitted that such an argument would fail. Even before the passing of the Criminal Law Act 1967 such assignments were neither crimes nor tort but, being analogised with maintenance and champerty, were on the grounds of public policy simply treated as ineffective. These grounds of public policy remain unaffected by the Criminal Law Act 1967. See above, para.16–049.

[317] [1980] Q.B. 629, 670.

[318] [1980] Q.B. 629, 656–657. See also Oliver L.J., at 674: "For my part, I would be prepared to hold that where a cause of action arises out of a right which was itself assignable, the cause of action equally remains assignable."

assignable[319] and where a solicitor is involved the courts would not adopt such a tolerant attitude to the validity of the assignment:

> "... because an English court will not permit one of its own officers to put himself in a position in which his interest and duty may conflict."[320]

16–058 Broadly speaking the House of Lords supported the reasoning of the Court of Appeal, although it differed on the application of that reasoning to the facts of the instant case. Lord Roskill considered that Oliver L.J., had not failed[321] to distinguish between the interest:

> "... necessary to support an assignment of a cause of action and the interest which would justify the maintenance of an action by a third party."

If the assignee has:

> "... a genuine commercial interest in taking the assignment and in enforcing it for his own benefit (there was) no reason why the assignment should be struck down as an assignment of a bare cause of action or as savouring of maintenance."[322]

Lord Roskill did, however, disapprove[323] of the view of Lord Denning M.R. in the Court of Appeal that "[t]he old saying that you cannot assign a 'bare right of litigate' is gone"; this still remained a fundamental principle of English law and the assignee needed to demonstrate a commercial interest in the enforcement of the claim for the assignment to be valid.[324] The House of Lords considered that the assignment in this case was void because it was the first step in a transaction whereby the cause of action was to be assigned to a third party who had no legitimate commercial interest in the transaction. If the assignment had merely been to Credit Suisse it would have been valid.[325]

16–059 That the vice in *Trendtex* was that the assignment contemplated the assignee selling the claim to a stranger for a higher price than it had paid for it is clear from *Brownton Ltd v Edward Moore Inbucon Ltd*.[326] In that case the plaintiffs sought advice from A on the installation of computer equipment and on the basis of that advice purchased equipment from B. The equipment never worked. The

---

[319] *Trendtex Trading Corp v Credit Suisse* [1980] Q.B. 629, 657 and 674 (referred to by Oliver L.J. as "personal and non-assignable" contracts). Lord Denning also considered that the right to sue with respect to certain torts to property would also be assignable, but not with respect to personal torts (656–657). See, e.g. *British Cash and Parcel Conveyors Ltd v Lamson Store Service Co Ltd* [1908] 1 K.B. 1006.

[320] *Trendtex Trading Corp v Credit Suisse* [1980] Q.B. 629, 675, per Oliver L.J., citing *Grell v Levy* (1864) 16 C.B.(N.S.) 73. See also below, para.19–048.

[321] *Trendtex Trading Corp v Credit Suisse* [1982] A.C. 679, 703.

[322] *Trendtex Trading Corp v Credit Suisse* [1982] A.C. 679.

[323] *Trendtex Trading Corp v Credit Suisse* [1982] A.C. 679.

[324] *Giles v Thompson* [1994] 1 A.C. 142, 153 (a bare right of action is not assignable).

[325] One of the features of the assignment was that the plaintiffs assigned all rights even if the assignee recovered more than the debt owing from the plaintiff to the defendant. Lord Roskill considered this to be an agreement to divide the "spoils" between the defendant and the third party: *Trendtex Trading Corp v Credit Suisse* [1982] A.C. 679, 779. *Quaere* what the position would have been if recovery beyond the debt was repayable to the plaintiff.

[326] [1985] 3 All E.R. 499.

plaintiffs sued A for damages who in turn alleged that the defective operation of the equipment was due to the fault of B, whereupon the plaintiffs joined B as second defendants. A paid a sum of money into court in settlement of its liability towards the plaintiffs and the plaintiffs were willing to accept this as full satisfaction of its claim against both A and B provided it could reach a satisfactory arrangement on the costs of the various parties. When B refused to agree to any arrangement, A assigned to the plaintiffs any cause of action it might have against B arising out of installation of the equipment. B's claim that this assignment was champertous failed. The court found that the plaintiffs had a sufficient commercial interest to justify the assignment and this distinguished the case from *Trendtex* where the:

> " . . . contemplated assignment to the anonymous third party was objectionable . . . because he had no genuine pre-existing commercial interest in the outcome of the cause of action."[327]

The court also held that for the assignment to be valid it was not necessary that the "assignee's interest applied to every facet of the cause of action",[328] all that was needed was that the assignee possess a genuine commercial interest which had to be determined on an examination of the transaction as a whole. In addition, it was not fatal to the validity of an assignment that the assignee might be better off as a result of the assignment, or that the assignee might make a profit out of it.[329] However, where the "figures . . . were massively disproportionate", the figures being what the assignee paid and what he was liable to gain, then the agreement would be champertous.[330]

All previous authorities must now be read in the light of *Trendtex's* greater liberality on assignments of the right to litigate and its rejection of any broad rule supposedly prohibiting the assignment of the right to litigate for damages. What appears in the following paragraphs are examples of recurrent situations involving the assignment of a right to litigate. Of course, where the court permitted assignment before *Trendtex* then obviously it will also be permitted after it. Thus assignments of debts are permissible[331] (even though the assignee's object in taking the assignment was to make the debtor bankrupt),[332] or assignments of the fruits of an action,[333] or assignments of property (even though the property is 16–060

[327] *Brownton Ltd v Edward Moore Inbucon Ltd* [1985] 3 All E.R. 499, 509, per Lloyd L.J.

[328] *Brownton Ltd v Edward Moore Inbucon Ltd* [1985] 3 All E.R. 499, 505, per Sir John Megaw.

[329] Lloyd L.J. left open the question as to whether any profit would be returnable by the assignee to the assignor ([1985] 3 All E.R. 499, 509). If the assignment is out and out and not by way of security it is difficult to see why this should be so.

[330] *Advanced Technology Structures Ltd v Cray Valley Products Ltd* [1993] B.C.L.C. 723, 733–734.

[331] *Ellis v Torrington* [1920] 1 K.B. 399; *Defries v Milne* [1913] 1 Ch. 98.

[332] *Fitzroy v Cave* [1905] 2 K.B. 364 (see the observations on this case in *Trendtex* [1980] Q.B. 673). Similarly a person may acquire shares in a company for the express purpose of challenging acts of the directors in litigation: *Bloxham v Metropolitan Ry* (1868) L.R. 3 Ch. App. 337, 353.

[333] *Glegg v Bromley* [1912] 3 K.B. 474. See also (fraudulent claims relating to part of a claim under insurance policy vitiating whole claim), *Galloway v Royal Exchange (UK) Ltd* [1999] L.R.L.R. 209.

incapable of being recovered without litigation),[334] or assignments designed "to support or enlarge" a property interest which the assignee already possesses.[335] It may also be that the old distinctions between maintenance, champerty and assignment are being dissolved. As was stated by Lloyd L.J. in *Brownton Ltd v Edward Moore Inbucon Ltd*[336] there is no difference between the interest "required to justify a share in the proceeds, or the interest required to support an out-and-out assignment". On this reasoning involvement in litigation will be justified if it can be shown that the party in question has sufficient interest in the litigation.

16–061 **Assignment incidental to transfer of property.** An assignment of a right to litigate is good if it is incidental and subsidiary to a transfer of property.[337] The question is whether the subject-matter of the assignment is property with an incidental remedy for its recovery, or a bare right of action.[338] Thus a conveyance of property by a vendor who has previously conveyed that property to another by a deed voidable in equity is good, as the vendor retained an interest which he could dispose of and which carried with it a right of action to have the earlier deed set aside.[339] In *Williams v Protheroe*[340] the vendor and purchaser of an estate agreed that the purchaser, bearing the expense of certain suits which had been commenced by the vendor against an occupier for bygone rent, should have any rent recovered and also any sum that might be recovered for dilapidations, and that the purchaser might at his own expense use the name of the vendor in any action he might think fit to commence against the occupier for arrears of rent or dilapidations. It was held that this agreement was not illegal as amounting to champerty. In *Ellis v Torrington*[341] the plaintiff took an assignment of the benefit of certain covenants to repair contained in an expired underlease, having already purchased the fee simple of the property from another person. This assignment was held free from objection on the ground of champerty, the right of action on the covenants being so connected with the enjoyment of property as to be more than a bare right to litigate. It was held to be immaterial that the assignment was made later than the purchase of the property, and by a person other than the vendor. Again, in *Performing Rights Society Ltd v Thompson*[342] the plaintiff society had been formed as a company to protect the copyright interests of its members, who assigned their copyrights to the society and by its rules shared in all damages recovered by the society. This was held to be a legitimate business arrangement and not champertous. In *Camdex International Ltd v Bank of Zambia*,[343] the court held that the assignment of a debt in accordance with s.136 of the Law of Property Act 1925, in circumstances where it was contemplated

[334] *Dawson v Great Northern & City Ry* [1905] 1 K.B. 260.
[335] *Compania Colombiana de Seguros v Pacific Steam Navigation Co* [1965] 1 Q.B. 101.
[336] [1985] 3 All E.R. 499, 509.
[337] *Williams v Protheroe* (1829) 3 Y. & J. 129.
[338] *Glegg v Bromley* [1912] 3 K.B. 474, 490; *Technotrade Ltd v Larkstore Ltd* [2007] 1 All E.R. (Comm) 104.
[339] *Dickinson v Burrell* (1866) L.R. 1 Eq. 337.
[340] (1829) 3 Y. J. 129.
[341] [1920] 1 K.B. 399; and see *County Hotel & Wine Co Ltd v London & N.W. Ry Co* [1918] 2 K.B. 251 (affirmed on other grounds [1921] 1 A.C. 85).
[342] (1918) 34 T.L.R. 351.
[343] [1998] Q.B. 22.

that an action would be necessary in order to obtain payment, did not constitute maintenance. Also, such an assignment would not be contrary to public policy even if the assignor maintained some interest in the debt.

Assignment to person beneficially entitled to right. Where before the Judicature Act 1873 equity would have compelled A to exercise his rights against a contract breaker or tortfeasor for the benefit of B, those rights can validly be assigned by A to B and, subject to due compliance with s.136 of the Law of Property Act 1925, can be enforced by B in his own name at law.[344] Therefore an underwriter, who has indemnified his insured under a policy of insurance and has in consequence been legally assigned the insured's rights of action against third parties, may sue those third parties in his own name to enforce those rights of action.[345] 16–062

Assignment by trustee in bankruptcy and liquidator. Rights of action which are the property of a bankrupt and pass to his trustee in bankruptcy may be assigned by the trustee, even though they may be only bare rights of action. These are treated as saleable as being part of the assets for the benefit of creditors.[346] And an agreement between some of the creditors of a bankrupt and the trustee that an action of the bankrupt should be carried on at their private expense, on the terms of receiving a larger share of the fruits of the action, was held not to offend against the law of champerty.[347] It has also been held that an assignment of a cause of action can be made by a liquidator.[348] It is not possible for a company to obtain legal aid.[349] The combined effect of these rules has serious consequences for a company that goes into liquidation since it will often find it difficult to fund litigation unless the creditors are willing to put it in funds. To circumvent these rules, the question arises as to whether it is possible for the liquidator to assign a cause of action of the company to an individual with an interest in the litigation, for example, a director or the majority shareholder. The reason for such assignment is that the individual, unlike the company, is entitled to legal aid and not subject to a security for costs order. *Norglen Ltd (In Liquidation) v Reeds Rains Prudential Ltd*[350] involved such an assignment which, inter alia, provided that the fruits of the action would be first used to pay the company's creditors and any balance divided equally between the company and the assignee. The assignment was made under the liquidator's powers to sell 16–063

[344] *Compania Colombiana de Seguros v Pacific Steam Navigation Co* [1965] 1 Q.B. 101, 121.

[345] *Compania Colombiana de Seguros v Pacific Steam Navigation Co* [1965] 1 Q.B. 101; and see Vol.II, para.41–091.

[346] *Seear v Lawson* (1880) 15 Ch D 426; Insolvency Act 1986 s.314(1); *Weddell v J. A. Pearce & Major* [1988] Ch. 26; *Farmer v Moseley (Holdings) Ltd* [2001] 2 B.C.L.C. 572. See further below, para.20–019.

[347] *Guy v Churchill* (1888) 40 Ch D 481.

[348] *Freightex Ltd v International Express Co Ltd* Unreported April 15, 1980 CA. The assignment in this case was made to the managing director of the company who arguably had an interest, but the court considered that the language of the legislation, s.242(2)(a) of the Companies Act 1948, absolved the actions of the liquidator from the taint of maintenance or champerty. See now, Insolvency Act 1986 ss.166, 167, 436 and Sch.4.

[349] Legal Aid Act 1988 s.2(11); *Wallersteiner v Moir (No.2)* [1975] Q.B. 373.

[350] [1997] 3 W.L.R. 1177.

the company's property which includes choses in action.[351] The court held that the assignment was valid and on established principles was not subject to the rules relating to maintenance and champerty. It has been held that the rules relating to maintenance and champerty apply to the assignment of the fruits of an action (but not the cause of action itself) where the assignee agrees to fund the action.[352] This decision, without expressing any definite view, has been doubted.[353] It is submitted that these doubts are justified. There are no compelling reasons for placing such a gloss on the power of the liquidator to assign a cause action vested in the company. If an assignment of the fruits of an action where the assignee does not undertake to provide funding for the action is valid,[354] it is difficult to see why an undertaking to provide such funding should make a difference; and similar principles apply to an assignment of a bankrupt's cause of action by the trustee in bankruptcy.[355]

16–064 **Assignments of rights to solicitors.** A solicitor cannot lawfully purchase anything in litigation of which he has had the management,[356] nor can he purchase fruits of such litigation before judgment[357]; but an assignment of an action to a solicitor preceding his employment as such is good unless it would have been unenforceable as between strangers.[358] A solicitor may lawfully take from his client a security upon property which is the subject-matter of an action for advances already incurred in the action,[359] and he may take security from his client for his costs to be ascertained by taxation or otherwise.[360]

16–065 **Other agreements "savouring of champerty".** An agreement merely to communicate information to a person in consideration of receiving a share of property to be recovered thereby is unobjectionable, provided there is no suit pending and no stipulation that one shall be commenced.[361] But if it is a term of the agreement that the person giving the information and who is to share in what

[351] In so far as the assignees were eligible for legal aid and the company was not, the House of Lords considered that this was a matter for the Legal Aid Board. Regulations have now been passed to deal with this: see *Norglen Ltd (In Liquidation) v Reeds Rains Prudential Ltd* [1997] 3 W.L.R. 1177, 1187.

[352] *Grovewood Holdings Plc v James Capel & Co Ltd* [1995] Ch. 80. This case was not followed in *Re Movitor Pty Ltd* (1996) 19 A.C.S.R. 440.

[353] *Re Oasis Merchandising Services Ltd* [1998] Ch. 170, 179–180. This case held that the liquidator could not assign a cause of action under s.214 of the Insolvency Act 1986 (wrongful trading) as such a cause of action was not property vested in the company. See also *Farmer v Morseley (Holdings) Ltd* [2001] 2 B.C.L.C. 572, [2001] B.P.I.R. 473.

[354] *Glegg v Bromley* [1912] 3 K.B. 474.

[355] *Stein v Blake* [1996] 1 A.C. 243.

[356] *Hall v Hallet* (1784) 1 Cox 134; *Simpson v Lamb* (1857) 7 E. & B. 84; cf. *Strachan v Brander* (1759) 1 Eden 303.

[357] *Wood v Downes* (1811) 18 Ves. 120; *Simpson v Lamb* (1857) 7 E. & B. 84; *Pittman v Prudential Deposit Bank Ltd* (1896) 13 T.L.R. 110. There is also a dictum to the effect that public policy in this area may be more strict where solicitors are involved: *Trendtex Trading Corp v Credit Suisse* [1980] Q.B. 629, 674–675; above, para.16–057; *Giles v Thompson* [1994] 1 A.C. 142.

[358] *Davis v Freethy* (1890) 24 QBD 519.

[359] *Anderson v Radcliffe* (1858) E.B. 806, 819. cf. Turner L.J. in *Knight v Bowyer* (1858) 2 De G. & J. 421, 445.

[360] Solicitors Act 1974 s.65(1) (contentious business); s.56(6) (non-contentious business), as amended by Legal Services Act 2007 s.177; see also SI 1994/2616.

[361] *Sprye v Porter* (1856) 7 E. & B. 58; *Rees v De Bernardy* [1896] 2 Ch. 437.

may be recovered shall himself recover the property or actively assist in its recovery by procuring evidence or otherwise, the agreement is unenforceable as "savouring of champerty",[362] and will be set aside in equity,[363] though it may be on terms.[364]

16–066 **Effect of champerty.** A champertous agreement is certainly unenforceable as between the parties,[365] though sums actually advanced to the champertor under the agreement have sometimes been held to be recoverable.[366] In respect of any loss sustained in connection with a champertous agreement, a solicitor cannot maintain a claim on a policy of indemnity.[367] The champertous support of the plaintiff in an action is probably not a defence to the action and probably affords no ground for a stay of proceedings.[368] Where a champertous agreement is entered into, a solicitor who provides services under it cannot recover on the grounds of quantum meruit or any other basis for the services that he has rendered. However, where payment has been made to a solicitor under a champertous agreement and he has not behaved unconscionably towards the payor or has not been unjustly enriched, the payor is not entitled to recover the price of those services while retaining the benefit of them: the champertous agreement in this situation is simply unenforceable.[369]

(e) *Objects Injurious to Morality and Marriage*

(i) *Immorality*

16–067 **Cohabitation.**[370] Agreements by unmarried persons to cohabit obviously raise important questions of public policy as these agreements could be treated as being *contra bonos mores*[371] and therefore unenforceable. In a number of earlier authorities the courts adopted this position. Agreements in consideration of future illicit cohabitation, even though made under seal, have been held to be unenforceable.[372] But a promise given in consideration of past illicit cohabitation

---

362 *Stanley v Jones* (1831) 7 Bing. 369, 377; *Rees v De Bernardy* [1896] 2 Ch. 437; *Wedgerfield v De Bernardy* (1908) 25 T.L.R. 21.

363 Above, para.16–057.

364 *Strachan v Brander* (1759) 1 Eden 303.

365 *Hutley v Hutley* (1873) L.R. 8 Q.B. 112.

366 *James v Kerr* (1888) 40 Ch D 449.

367 *Haseldine v Hosken* [1933] 1 K.B. 822.

368 cf. above, para.16–053.

369 *Aratra Potato Co Ltd v Taylor Joynson Garrett* [1995] 4 All E.R. 695. This case was disapproved of in *Thai Trading Co v Taylor* [1998] 3 All E.R. 65 but it is submitted that this aspect of the judgment remains good law. In *Farjab v Symth* Unreported CA, August 28, 1998 the court held that champerty did not itself constitute a ground for staying proceedings; *Stocznia Gdanska SA v Laftrers Inc* [2001] 2 B.C.L.C. 116 is to the same effect.

370 See Cretney and Masson, *Principles of Family Law*, 7th edn (2002) para.17–004, Ch.6 and Ch.7.

371 "In this branch of the law the word 'immoral' connotes only sexual immorality": *Coral Leisure Group Ltd v Barnett* [1981] I.C.R. 503, 506.

372 *Benyon v Nettlefold* (1850) 3 Mac. & G. 94; *Ayerst v Jenkins* (1873) L.R. 16 Eq. 275.

is good as a voluntary promise, and can be enforced if made under deed,[373] or supported by some other consideration, but not otherwise.[374] A bond given for such consideration is not invalidated by the mere fact that the illicit cohabitation continues after its execution[375]; nor that the parties contemplated its continuance, provided their intention forms no part of the consideration for the bond.[376] An agreement by a man to pay a woman with whom he was cohabiting a sum down and an annuity for life if they should separate and she should continue single and not cohabit with one D.G. or anyone else, has also been held good as being a gift on condition that she remained sole and chaste[377]; and so was an agreement by a reputed father of an illegitimate child to pay the mother an annuity if she would maintain the child and keep their connection secret, the maintenance of the child being a sufficient consideration for the contract.[378]

16–068 Extra-marital cohabitation is obviously an area where values change[379] and the older authorities clearly reflect a marriage morality which is out of tune with contemporary mores. Recently the courts have been obliged to deal with legal problems arising out of unmarried persons setting up relatively stable domestic arrangements and when these problems have arisen the issue of illegality does not appear to have been argued. For example, in *Tanner v Tanner*[380] a married man had twins by his mistress and he provided the mistress and the twins with a house. When the man subsequently attempted to evict the mistress, the court held that there was an implied contract between the parties that the mistress could live in the house, the consideration given by the mistress being her relinquishment of a rent-controlled flat. Although the contract undoubtedly involved sexual relations outside of marriage, no question of illegality was raised and there is little doubt that the court would have been unsympathetic to such a plea.[381] One way of reconciling *Tanner v Tanner* with previous authority is that "an agreement for an immoral consideration is to be treated as enforceable, if there be any other, lawful consideration to support it".[382] From this it would follow that contractual

---

[373] per Lord Selborne L.C. in *Ayerst v Jenkins* (1873) L.R. 16 Eq. 275, 282; and see *Annandale, Marchioness of v Harris* (1728) 1 Bro.P.C. 250; 2 P.Wms. 432; *Turner v Vaughan* (1767) 2 Wils.K.B. 339; *Gray v Mathias* (1800) 5 Ves. 286; *Nye v Moseley* (1826) 6 B. & C. 133.

[374] *Beaumont v Reeve* (1846) 8 Q.B. 483. There is no public policy against enforcing such promises as they do not promote immorality and all that is needed is consideration to make the contract binding.

[375] *Hall v Palmer* (1844) 3 Hare 532; *Re Vallance* (1884) 26 Ch D 353.

[376] *Re Wootton Isaacson* (1904) 21 T.L.R. 89; cf. *Friend v Harrison* (1827) 2 Car. & P. 584.

[377] *Gibson v Dickie* (1815) 3 M. & S. 463.

[378] *Jennings v Brown* (1842) 9 M. & W. 496; see also *Hicks v Gregory* (1849) 8 C.B. 378; *Smith v Roche* (1859) 6 C.B.(N.S.) 223; *Ward v Byham* [1956] 1 W.L.R. 496; *Horrocks v Foray* [1976] 1 W.L.R. 230, 299.

[379] See above, para.16–003.

[380] [1975] 1 W.L.R. 1346; see also *Chandler v Kerley* [1978] 1 W.L.R. 693; *Bernard v Josephs* [1982] Ch. 391. cf. *Horrocks v Foray* [1976] 1 W.L.R. 230 (the court found that there was no contract between a man and his mistress, but the issue of illegality was not raised). See also on changing values as regards sexual mores; *Barclays Bank Plc v O'Brien* [1994] 1 A.C. 180, 188; *Fitzpatrick v Sterling Housing Association Ltd* [1998] Ch. 304, 308; [2001] 1 A.C. 27; *Mendoza v Ghaidan* [2002] EWCA Civ 1533, [2003] 1 F.L.R. 468.

[381] See, e.g. *Cook v Head* [1972] 1 W.L.R. 518; *Eves v Eves* [1975] 1 W.L.R. 1338.

[382] Barton (1976) 92 L.Q.R. 168, 169. See also *Eves v Eves* [1975] 1 W.L.R. 1338 at 1345C; *Paul v Constance* [1977] 1 W.L.R. 527.

arrangements involving unmarried parties to a relatively stable domestic arrangement will be enforceable and the older authorities will only apply to relationships which are wholly related to the provision of sexual services.[383]

Prostitution. An action is not maintainable to recover the rent of lodgings knowingly let for the purpose of prostitution[384] or to a man's mistress for the purposes of the liaison.[385] And where the landlord, although not aware of the true facts at the time of the letting, permitted the tenant to remain after discovering that she was using the lodgings for prostitution, it was held that he could not recover from her the rent which accrued after this had come to his knowledge and he had failed to take steps to evict her.[386] All covenants in an assignment of a lease of premises which the assignor knows the assignee intends to use as a brothel are similarly unenforceable.[387] But although the tenant of an apartment may be a prostitute, and the landlord is aware of her character, he may recover his rent if she does not use his premises for immoral purposes[388]; and, in the absence of evidence specifically to connect the contract with the prostitution,[389] a contract to sell clothes to a prostitute,[390] or to wash for her,[391] is good. Where a contract of employment requires the employee to procure prostitutes, this would be a contract entered into for an immoral purpose and would be illegal and unenforceable.[392] 16–069

(ii) *Interference with Marriage*[393]

Promise of marriage by married person. A promise by a married man to marry one who knew him to be already married was unenforceable as against public policy and as tending to immorality.[394] No action lay for breach of such 16–070

---

[383] See, e.g. *Marvin v Marvin* (1976) 557 P.2d. 104; *Bernard v Josephs* [1982] Ch. 391; *Heglibiston Establishment v Heyman* (1977) 36 P. & C.R. 351, 360–362; *Barclays Bank Plc v O'Brien* [1994] 1 A.C. 180, 188 ("Now that unmarried cohabitation, whether heterosexual or homosexual, is widespread in our society, the law should recognise this.") See generally Cretney, *Family Law in the Twentieth Century: A History* (OUP, 2003), pp.516–527.

[384] *Girardy v Richardson* (1793) 1 Esp. 13. Similarly a seller cannot recover the price of clothes furnished specifically to enable the purchaser to carry on her trade as a prostitute, the seller expecting to be paid from the profits thereof: *Bowry v Bennet* (1808) 1 Camp. 348; and see *Pearce v Brooks* (1866) L.R. 1 Ex. 213, para.16–164, below. Contrast *Lloyd v Johnson* (1798) 1 B. & P. 340 (a contract for the cleaning of a prostitute's clothes, in which it was said that the use to be made of the clothes was irrelevant at least where the clothes were of such a nature that the prostitute would need them anyhow). Generally, cf. *Shaw v D.P.P.* [1962] A.C. 220.

[385] *Upfill v Wright* [1911] 1 K.B. 506 (in *Heglibiston Establishment v Heyman* (1977) 36 P. & C.R. 351, 360–362 it was doubted if this case would today be decided the same way on its facts). cf. Vol.II, para.31–049.

[386] *Jennings v Throgmorton* (1825) R. & M. 251.

[387] *Smith v White* (1866) L.R. 1 Eq. 626.

[388] *Appleton v Campbell* (1862) 2 C. & P. 347.

[389] See fn.378, above.

[390] *Bowry v Bennett* (1808) 1 Camp. 348.

[391] *Lloyd v Johnson* (1798) 1 B. & P. 340.

[392] *Coral Leisure Group Ltd v Barnet* [1981] I.C.R. 503.

[393] As to the invalidity of agreements between husband and wife providing for their future separation, see *Brodie v Brodie* [1917] P.271.

[394] *Wilson v Carnley* [1908] 1 K.B. 729; *Spiers v Hunt* [1908] 1 K.B. 720; *Siveyer v Allison* [1935] 2 K.B. 403.

a promise even after the death of the wife.[395] So also with a similar promise by a married woman to marry after the death of her husband[396] or divorce.[397] A promise of marriage made by a married man in the interval between decree nisi and decree absolute was actionable if broken—since after the decree nisi the normal obligations and conditions of marriage have disappeared and consortium has come to an end.[398] Actions for breach of promise of marriage were abolished by s.1 of the Law Reform (Miscellaneous Provisions) Act 1970, so that the cases just discussed are, strictly speaking, obsolete. However, s.2 of the Act provides that "where an agreement to marry is terminated" the formerly engaged couple are to be treated for the purpose of certain rights in and disputes about property as if they had been married; and these provisions can obviously give rise to difficulty where a man has both a wife and an ex-fiancée. It may be that the difficulty can be mitigated by holding that an "agreement" in s.2 must not be contrary to public policy in the sense of the old law. But the analogy is not perfect, and the courts may take the view that, so long as the interests of the wife (or former wife) are protected, an ex-fiancée may sometimes be allowed to take the benefit of s.2 even though she could not before the Act have claimed damages. However, the Act is of very limited effect because, apart from the right to claim a share or enlarged share in a partner's property by having spent money on improvements to that property,[399] property rights between spouses are determined in accordance with the principles of property and trusts law.[400]

16–071 **Marriage brokage contract.** A marriage brokage contract, that is, an undertaking for reward to produce a marriage between two parties, is against public policy.[401] It has, however, been observed that "it is hard to see what is wrong with these [contracts] in modern times"[402] as many are made by quite respectable marriage bureaux. It may be that this is an area where the public policy embodied in the old cases is in need of reappraisal.

16–072 **Contracts in restraint of marriage.** A contract, the object of which is to restrain or prevent a party from marrying[403] or which is a deterrent to marriage in so far as it makes any person uncertain whether he may marry or not,[404] is against public policy. There appears to be no authority on contracts in partial

[395] *Wilson v Carnley* [1908] 1 K.B. 729.
[396] *Spiers v Hunt* [1908] 1 K.B. 720.
[397] *Prevost v Wood* (1905) 21 T.L.R. 684.
[398] *Fender v Mildmay* [1938] A.C. 1; *Psaltis v Schultz* (1948) 76 C.L.R. 547.
[399] Matrimonial Proceedings and Property Act 1970 s.37.
[400] *Pettitt v Pettitt* [1970] A.C. 777; *Mossop v Mossop* [1989] Fam. 77.
[401] *Hermann v Charlesworth* [1905] 2 K.B. 123. See also para.16–182.
[402] Atiyah, *The Law of Contract*, 5th edn (1995), p.323 (this passage is not repeated in the 6th edn).
[403] *Lowe v Peers* (1768) 4 Burr. 2225; affirmed Wilmot 364; and see *Baker v White* (1690) 2 Vern. 215; *Cock v Richards* (1805) 10 Ves. 429, 437; *Hartley v Rice* (1808) 10 East 22.
[404] *Re Fentem* [1950] 2 All E.R. 1073. In *Cartwright v Cartwright* (1853) 3 De G.M. & G. 382 it was held that a condition in an ante-nuptial agreement that the wife would forfeit her interest if she and her husband separated was against public policy since it contemplated the separation of husband and wife.

restraint of marriage. Should such a contract come before the courts, the authorities concerning testamentary conditions in partial restraint of marriage would probably be applied.[405]

Contract not to revoke will. A man may validly bind himself or his estate to make certain dispositions by his will.[406] And a contract not to revoke a will or not to alter its contents is not necessarily against public policy. But probably no action could be brought upon its breach by reason of the covenantor's subsequent marriage, for the will is on that event revoked by operation of law[407] and to that extent the covenant is bad as being in restraint of marriage and against public policy; but it is divisible and will be construed as a covenant against revocation by any other mode of revocation.[408] **16–073**

Parental responsibility. The Children Act 1989 confers automatic parental responsibility on parents of a child who are married to each other and on a child's unmarried mother.[409] The Act stipulates that: **16–074**

> "... a person who has parental responsibility for a child shall not surrender or transfer any part of that responsibility to another but may arrange for some or all of it to be met by one or more persons acting on his behalf."[410]

An unmarried father may also acquire parental responsibility by agreement with the child's mother made in prescribed form and recorded in the Principal Registry of the Family Division.[411] Local authorities have a statutory duty to make written agreements with the parent of any child it is looking after.[412] But such agreements cannot transfer parental responsibility to the authority, and are not legally binding.[413] The inherent jurisdiction of the court to make appropriate orders concerning the upbringing of children cannot be ousted by agreement between the parties.[414] Surrogacy agreements have been expressly declared to be unenforceable.[415] Although the courts have power to treat a financial settlement agreed between divorcing couples as final, this does not apply with respect to agreements regarding the maintenance of children.[416] An "absent parent" may be

---

405 See *Theobald on Wills* (16th ed., 2001), pp.665 et seq.

406 *Dufour v Pereira* (1769) Dick. 419; *Hammersley v Baron De Biel* (1845) 12 Cl. & F. 45; *Re Brookman's Trusts* (1869) L.R. 5 Ch. App. 182.

407 Wills Act 1837 s.18 (as substituted by the Administration of Justice Act 1982 s.18); cf. *Re Marsland* [1939] Ch. 820. (In this case the covenant not to revoke was only held to apply to revocation under s.20 of the Wills Act 1837, and not to revocation by operation of s.18. Thus the issue of public policy was not directly faced and the court did not feel obliged to express any opinion on it.)

408 *Robinson v Ommanney* (1883) 23 Ch D 285; *Theobald on Wills* at pp.665 et seq. As to the effects of an actionable breach, see *Synge v Synge* [1894] 1 Q.B. 466; *Central Trusts & Safe Deposit Co v Snider* [1916] 1 A.C. 266.

409 Children Act 1989 s.2(1), (2).

410 s.2(9).

411 s.4(1)(b); Parental Responsibility Agreement Regulations 1991 (SI 1991/1478).

412 Arrangements for Placement of Children (General) Regulations 1991 (SI 1991/890).

413 Children Act 1989 s.20(8).

414 *A. v C.* [1985] F.L.R. 4451.

415 Human Fertilisation and Embryology Act 1990 s.36.

416 *Minton v Minton* [1979] A.C. 593, 609.

required to pay child support maintenance to a "qualifying child" under the Child Support Act 1991 irrespective of the terms of an existing agreement between the child's parents covering the matter.

(f) *Contracts in Restraint of Trade*[417]

(i) *Scope of the Doctrine*

16–075 **General rule.** All covenants[418] in restraint of trade[419] are prima facie unenforceable at common law[420] and are enforceable only if they are reasonable with reference to the interests of the parties concerned and of the public. Unless the unreasonable part can be severed[421] by the removal of either part or the whole of the covenant in question, its inclusion renders the covenant[422] or the entire contract[423] unenforceable. A covenant in restraint of trade (if unreasonable) is void in the sense that courts will not enforce it, but if the parties wish to implement it they would not be acting illegally and the courts would not intervene to prevent them from doing so.[424] It also follows from this that where A and B enter into a contract which contains an unreasonable restraint and they deposit money with T for the purposes of the contract then neither could prevent T from dealing with the money on the terms set out in the contract.[425] The doctrine of restraint of trade is probably one of the oldest applications of the doctrine of public policy; cases go back to the second half of the sixteenth century[426] and as early as 1711 it was laid down in *Mitchel v Reynolds*[427] that a bond to restrain oneself from trading in a particular place, if made upon a reasonable consideration, is good, though if it be upon no reasonable consideration or to restrain a man from trading at all, it is void.

---

[417] See Heydon, *The Restraint of Trade Doctrine* (1971); Kamerling and Osman, *Restrictive Covenants under Common and Competition Law*, 4th edn (2004).

[418] As to conditions, see above, para.16–012; and as to the rules of trade associations and kindred bodies, see below, paras 16–132—16–133; cf. paras 16–135—16–138.

[419] If the contract is to be performed in England, the fact that its proper law is foreign will not prevent the application of the English rules of public policy: *Rousillon v Rousillon* (1880) 14 Ch D 351. As to covenants against competition abroad, see para.16–089.

[420] An agreement in restraint of trade is generally not unlawful at common law if the parties choose to abide by it; it is only unenforceable if a party chooses not to abide by it: *Mogul S.S. Co Ltd v McGregor, Gow & Co* [1892] A.C. 25; *Esso Petroleum Co Ltd v Harper's Garage (Stourport) Ltd* [1968] A.C. 269, 297; *Brekkes Ltd v Cattel* [1972] Ch. 105; cf. *Cooke v Football Association* [1972] C.L.Y. 516; *Boddington v Lawton* [1994] I.C.R. 478. But a third party injured by the operation of an agreement in restraint of trade may, it appears, obtain a declaration (*Eastham v Newcastle United F.C. Ltd* [1964] Ch. 413; *Greig v Insole* [1978] 1 W.L.R. 302) or an injunction (*Nagle v Feilden* [1966] 2 Q.B. 633).

[421] See below, paras 16–194—16–198.

[422] e.g. see *Goldsoll v Goldman* [1914] 2 Ch. 603, [1915] 1 Ch. 292. See below, para.16–188.

[423] e.g. see the *Esso* case [1968] A.C. 769. See below, paras 16–194 et seq.

[424] *Boddington v Lawton* [1994] I.C.R. 478. Where the restraint has third party effects, the third party affected may be able to challenge its validity: see para.16–135.

[425] *Boddington v Lawton* [1994] I.C.R. 478.

[426] Holdsworth, *History of English Law*, Vol.III, pp.56, 57; Wilberforce, Campbell and Elles, *The Law of Restrictive Trade Practices and Monopolies*, 2nd edn, paras 130, 135, 141–144.

[427] (1711) 1 P.Wms. 181.

Competition law. This section concentrates on the common law. It should, however, be kept in mind that contracts in restraint of trade or otherwise having a restrictive impact on trade, particularly horizontal or vertical agreements relating to the supply or acquisition of goods, will often have anti-competitive effects and are therefore potentially subject to domestic and European legislation dealing with this topic.[428] For example, art.81(1) of the Treaty of Rome[429] may render invalid certain restraints between vendors and purchasers.[430] The potential relevance of domestic and European competition law must therefore always be considered in this context. 16–076

Definition of restraint of trade. The definition of a covenant in restraint of trade presents peculiar conceptual difficulty. The reason for this is that to some extent all contracts are in restraint of trade by at least preventing the parties to them from trading with others, but there has been no suggestion that all contracts are or should be subject to the doctrine.[431] In the leading House of Lords case, *Esso Petroleum Co Ltd v Harper's Garage (Stourport) Ltd*[432] Lord Reid stated[433] that he "would not attempt to define the dividing line between contracts which are and contracts which are not in restraint of trade"; and Lord Wilberforce said[434] that "no exhaustive test can be stated—probably no precise non-exhaustive test" but that that was not to be regretted since[435]: 16–077

> " . . . the common law has often (if sometimes unconsciously) thrived on ambiguity and it would be mistaken, even if it were possible, to try to crystallise the rules of this or any aspect of public policy into neat propositions. The doctrine of restraint of trade is one to be applied to factual situations with a broad and flexible rule of reason."

In the same case Lord Hodson adopted[436] the test shortly before advanced by Diplock L.J. in the Court of Appeal in *Petrofina (Great Britain) Ltd v Martin*[437] who stated[438]: 16–078

---

[428] See Whish, *Competition Law*, 5th edn (2003), Ch.1; see, for example, *Cutsforth v Mansfield Inns Ltd* [1986] 1 W.L.R. 558; below, para.16–120 and paras 16–131 et seq.

[429] See Bellamy & Child, *Common Market Law of Competition*, 5th edn (2001), Vol.II, Ch.40.

[430] Bellamy & Child, *Common Market Law of Competition*, para.6–088. Treaty of Rome art.81 could also have a bearing on non-competition clauses in mergers, exclusive distribution and purchasing agreements.

[431] See, e.g. *British Motor Trade Association v Gray* (1951) S.C. 586.

[432] [1968] A.C. 269.

[433] [1968] A.C. 269, 298.

[434] [1968] A.C. 269, 332.

[435] [1968] A.C. 269, 331.

[436] [1969] A.C. 269, 317.

[437] [1966] Ch. 146.

[438] [1966] Ch. 146, 180; Diplock L.J.'s test probably requires a distinction to be drawn between obligations on the part of the covenantor which are in substance "positive", e.g. to sell to A 100 tons of cast iron of the covenantor's manufacture, and obligations which are in substance "negative", e.g. not to sell his cast iron to anyone other than A or to sell to A some percentage of his production (which is an obligation not to sell to others more than the remaining percentage thereof). The difficulty arises that, if the covenantor's production is unlikely to exceed 100 tons, the positive obligation to sell to A 100 tons may be more restrictive of the covenantor's economic liberty to trade with others than would be a negative obligation to sell to A 50 per cent of his production.

"A contract in restraint of trade is one in which a party (the covenantor) agrees with any other party (the covenantee) to restrict his liberty in the future to carry on trade with other persons not parties to the contract in such manner as he chooses."

Lord Morris said[439] that that was a "helpful exposition", provided that it was used "rationally and not too literally" and that the same was true of the dicta of Lord Denning M.R. in the *Petrofina* case where he had said[440]:

"Every member of the community is entitled to carry on any trade or business he chooses and in such manner as he thinks most desirable in his own interests, so long as he does nothing unlawful: with the consequence that any contract which interferes with the free exercise of his trade or business, by restricting him in the work he may do for others, or the arrangements which he may make with others, is a contract in restraint of trade. It is invalid unless it is reasonable as between the parties and not injurious to the public interest."

Finally, in the *Esso* case, Lord Pearce, on the basis that[441]:

". . . somewhere there must be a line between those contracts which are in restraint of trade . . . and those contracts which merely regulate the normal commercial relations between the parties,"

and said[442] that the doctrine of restraint of trade:

". . . does not apply to ordinary commercial contracts for the regulation and promotion of trade during the existence of the contract, provided that any prevention of work outside the contract, viewed as a whole, is directed towards the absorption of the parties' services and not their sterilisation."

16–079 **Criteria for application of doctrine.** The following general principles have, with varying degrees of certainty, been laid down:

16–080 (1) It has now long been established that there is no distinction in principle between partial and total restraints.[443]

16–081 (2) The doctrine is not confined to a limited number of kinds of contracts[444]; but there are certain categories of covenants to which the doctrine traditionally applies, in particular those by which an employee undertakes not to compete with his employer after leaving the employer's service[445] and those by which a trader who has sold his business agrees not thereafter to compete with the purchaser of the business[446]; and those categories will always be subjected, under the doctrine, to the test of reasonableness.

[439] *Esso Petroleum Co Ltd v Harper's Garage (Stourport) Ltd* [1968] A.C. 269, 307.
[440] [1966] Ch. 146, 169.
[441] [1968] A.C. 269, 327.
[442] [1968] A.C. 269, 328.
[443] See above, para.16–075.
[444] *Esso* case [1968] A.C. 269, 295, 306, 337; *Bridge v Deacons* [1984] A.C. 705.
[445] See below, para.16–102.
[446] See below, para.16–115.

(3) The doctrine is capable of applying where the restraint relates to the use of a particular piece of property as well as where it relates to the activities of an individual.[447] Thus restraints in mortgages and leases are subject to the doctrine. The application of the doctrine to *Tulk v Moxhay*[448] covenants is not, however, without difficulties and this will be dealt with later. 16–082

(4) There is strong authority for the proposition that contracts of a kind which have gained general commercial acceptance and have not been traditionally subject to the doctrine will generally not be subjected to it so as to impose upon a plaintiff the burden of justifying as reasonable their terms, though special features may bring particular contracts of that kind within the ambit of the doctrine.[449] However, public policy is not immutable and no guarantee of absolute immunity for any restraint is possible. As was stated by Lord Wilberforce in *Esso*, "absolute exemption for any restriction or regulation is never obtained".[450] Thus, for example, contracts whereby an employee on the termination of his employment agrees not to recruit former fellow employees is now probably subject to the restraint of trade doctrine.[451] 16–083

(5) The doctrine applies to restraints which operate during the continuance of the contract. This is well illustrated by *A. Schroeder Music Publishing Co Ltd v Macaulay*.[452] There the plaintiff, a young songwriter, agreed to work as such exclusively for the defendants, who were music publishers, for five years. He assigned to them full copyright of his existing works and in future works composed during the five years. The five years was extended to 10 years if the plaintiff's royalties exceeded £5,000. The defendants could determine the agreement at any time on one month's notice and could assign the benefit of it. Although the plaintiff's royalties depended upon whether the defendants exploited his compositions, there was no obligation on the defendants to exploit any composition of the plaintiff, and if the defendants failed to do so, the plaintiff could not do so even after the determination of the contract. Lord Reid held that the contract was unduly restrictive, it was not a commercially acceptable one "made freely by parties bargaining on equal terms",[453] "or moulded under the pressures of negotiation, competition and public opinion".[454] Lord Diplock, 16–084

---

[447] *Esso Petroleum Co Ltd v Harper's Garage (Stourport) Ltd* [1968] A.C. 269 where the principle was established in the case of land; and it would seem that similar considerations apply to other kinds of property.

[448] (1848) 2 Ph. 774.

[449] *Esso Petroleum Co Ltd v Harper's Garage (Stourport) Ltd* [1968] A.C. 269 per Lord Wilberforce, at 332–333, to some extent supported by Lord Reid, at 295 and by Lord Pearce, at 328. There is some authority for the alternative approach under which contracts if they contain restrictive elements are always subject to the doctrine but some are "prima facie" reasonable. See per Diplock L.J. in *Petrofina (Great Britain) Ltd v Martin* [1966] Ch. 146, 185.

[450] [1968] A.C. 269, 333.

[451] *Office Angels Ltd v Rainer-Thomas and O'Connor* [1991] I.R.L.R. 214 (employment agency could protect pool of temporary secretaries); Sales (1988) 104 L.Q.R. 600.

[452] [1974] 1 W.L.R. 1308; see also *Clifford Davis Ltd v W.E.A. Records Ltd* [1975] 1 W.L.R. 61; Cartwright, *Unequal Bargaining* (1991), pp.205–206; *Watson v Prager* [1991] 1 W.L.R. 726 (restraint of trade doctrine applied to contract between a boxer and manager and held to be against public policy because of the unreasonable imbalance between the rights and duties of the parties).

[453] per Lord Pearce in the *Esso* case [1968] A.C. 269, 323.

[454] per Lord Wilberforce in the *Esso* case [1968] A.C. 269, 332–333.

however, asked simply what was the relative bargaining power between the songwriter and publisher at the time of contracting and whether the publisher had used his superior bargaining power to exact from the songwriter promises that were unfairly onerous to him, i.e. "was the bargain fair?" There might be a presumption of fairness in cases of conventional commercial contracts established by long usage between equal bargaining partners, but this was not such a case. Where the restraint operates to protect the legitimate interests of the employer and was not as one sided as that in the *Schroeder* decision, it will normally be upheld. However, the absence of reciprocal obligation may be a factor in determining whether a restraint is reasonable.[455]

16–085 (6) There is authority for the proposition that it is not possible to invoke the doctrine where the restraint relates to the use or disposition of property acquired by the covenantor under the very agreement under which he accepted the restraint. This proposition found favour with Lord Reid in the *Esso* case:

> "Restraint of trade appears to me to imply that a man contracts to give up some freedom which otherwise he would have had. A person buying or leasing land had no previous right to be there at all, let alone to trade there, and when he takes possession of that land subject to a negative restrictive covenant he gives up no right or freedom which he previously had."[456]

This test, however, is not free from difficulty and at least three principal objections can be levelled against it.[457] First, it can be easily evaded: for example, A could lease land to B which B could then lease back to A by means of a lease containing a covenant in restraint of trade. There is, however, authority for the proposition that if the transaction is a sham[458] the court will look at the reality of the transaction even though formally it appears that the covenantor is not curtailing an existing freedom. In *Amoco Australia Pty Ltd v Rocca Bros Motor Engineering Co Pty Ltd*[459] the Privy Council applied the restraint of trade doctrine to a transaction somewhat similar to the one previously outlined and treated the lease and underlease as part of a single transaction. A somewhat similar approach was adopted in *Alec Lobb (Garages) Ltd v Total Oil (Great Britain) Ltd*[460] where a lease by a company of its premises to its petrol suppliers who leased them back to the sole shareholders of the company, the lease-back

---

[455] *Societa Explosivi Industriali SpA v Ordnance Technologies (UK) Ltd* [2004] EWHC 48 (Ch), [2004] 1 All E.R. (Comm) 619.

[456] [1968] A.C. 269, 298. See also at 309 (Lord Morris) and at 325 (Lord Pearce) for somewhat similar views. This principle was adopted in *Cleveland Petroleum Co Ltd v Darstone* [1969] 1 W.L.R. 116; see also *Stephens v Gulf Oil Canada Ltd* (1976) 11 O.L.R. (2d) 229; *Re Ravenseft Properties Ltd's Application* [1978] Q.B. 52, 67. A similar type of reasoning has been applied to a contract settling a dispute for infringement of an intellectual property right. Before the restraint of trade doctrine can apply, the restrainee must show that the restraint overreaches the extent of the intellectual property right concerned: *World Wide Fund for Nature v World Wrestling Federation Entertainment Inc* [2002] EWCA Civ 196, [2002] F.S.R. 32.

[457] See Heydon, *The Restraint of Trade Doctrine* (1971), pp.55–59.

[458] On the nature of sham transactions, see *Chase Manhattan Equities Ltd v Goodman* [1991] B.C.L.C. 997; *Welsh Development Agency v Export Finance Co Ltd* [1992] B.C.L.C. 148, 185–188.

[459] [1975] A.C. 561, PC.

[460] [1985] 1 W.L.R. 173.

containing a solus agreement, was held to be subject to the restraint of trade doctrine. The second objection to Lord Reid's test that the doctrine only applies where a covenantor curtails an existing freedom is that it is a test based on form rather than substance, as was illustrated by counsel in the course of argument in the *Esso* case.[461] Undoubtedly one of the reasons for the adoption of this test (or something like it) was to insulate *Tulk v Moxhay*[462] type covenants against the application of the restraint of trade doctrine. In *Quadramain Pty Ltd v Sevastapol Investments Pty Ltd*[463] the Australian High Court adopted the reasoning of Lord Reid and thus avoided having to deal with the application of the restraint of trade doctrine to a restrictive covenant which impinged on the commercial use to which land could be put.[464] Thirdly, even where a covenantor purportedly gives up an existing freedom but is insolvent and the restraint is part of a package enabling him to remain in business it is far from evident how such a constraint curtails in any significant sense an existing freedom.[465] It is submitted that as the restraint of trade doctrine is one founded on public policy its application should not be artificially curtailed. No doubt where the court is dealing with the type of restraint which has obtained widespread acceptance then this will be strong evidence of its reasonableness, but all restraints should be subject to the doctrine.

(7) There is authority for the principle that the doctrine does not apply to "ordinary commercial contracts for the regulation and promotion of trade during the existence of the contract".[466] But this would appear to be founded on the theory that the doctrine does not apply during the contract, a theory which has been rejected by the House of Lords.[467] **16–086**

(8) Whether a particular provision operates in restraint of trade is to be determined not by the form the stipulation takes but by its effect in practice.[468] Thus a covenant to share profits, or a levy/remission scheme of the traditional cartel type, may in certain circumstances of the case constitute restraint. Likewise, a provision that a salesman who had left his employment would forfeit the commission due to him if he obtained employment with a competitor of his ex-employer was held to be a restraint.[469] In other words, what does or does not **16–087**

---

461 [1968] A.C. 269, 289–290.

462 (1848) 2 Ph. 774 (although many such covenants will not actually restrain trade).

463 (1976) 8 A.L.R. 555. See also *Aberdeen Varieties Ltd v James F. Donald (Aberdeen Cinemas) Ltd* (1940) S.L.T. 58.

464 See also *Irish Shell Ltd v Elm Motors Ltd* [1984] I.R. 200. As to whether a restrictive covenant affecting the commercial user of land touches and concerns it see *Newton Abbot Co-operative Society Ltd v Williamson & Treadgold Ltd* [1952] Ch. 286.

465 *Alec Lobb (Garages) Ltd v Total Oil (Great Britain) Ltd* [1983] 1 W.L.R. 87, 164F (at first instance).

466 *Esso Petroleum Co Ltd v Harper's Garage (Stourport) Ltd* [1968] A.C. 269, 328. Lord Pearce also opined that the doctrine only applies where a restraint is directed towards the "sterilisation" of the covenantor's services. On this see Heydon, *The Restraint of Trade Doctrine* (1971), pp.61–63; and cf. *Watson v Prager* [1991] 1 W.L.R. 726.

467 *A. Schroeder Music Publishing Co Ltd v Macaulay* [1974] 1 W.L.R. 1308.

468 *Stenhouse Australia Ltd v Phillips* [1974] A.C. 391; *McIntyre v Cleveland Petrol Co Ltd* (1967) S.L.T. 95, 100.

469 *Sadler v Imperial Life Insurance Co of Canada Ltd* [1988] I.R.L.R. 388.

operate as a restraint is a matter of substance. It is also important to note that it is *trade* which must be restrained. While the courts have not given an exhaustive definition of what constitutes a trade, it is clear that it extends to a man's profession or calling.[470]

16–088 **Time of application.** Most authorities favour as the time for testing the validity of a restriction the date when the restriction was imposed.[471] It has also been held that an enforceable restriction may become temporarily unenforceable where it operates unfairly in changed circumstances[472]; this is generally considered not to be correct.

16–089 **Covenants by deed.** A covenant in restraint of trade which is contained in a deed requires justification no less than such a covenant contained in a simple contract.[473]

16–090 **Adequacy of consideration.** Subject to the test of reasonableness of the restraint, the courts will not inquire into the adequacy of the consideration.[474]

16–091 **Covenants against competition abroad.** Doubts have been expressed whether the rule against covenants in restraint of trade applies to covenants against competition outside the United Kingdom.[475] But these doubts appear to be unfounded; the question was fully argued before the Court of Appeal in *Commercial Plastics Ltd v Vincent*[476] where a covenant was struck down inter alia on the ground that it was worldwide, whereas on the facts the plaintiffs did not require protection outside the United Kingdom. Although that decision

---

[470] *Hepworth Manufacturing Co Ltd v Ryott* [1920] Ch. 1, 29.

[471] *Gledhow Autoparts Ltd v Delaney* [1965] 1 W.L.R. 1366, 1377; *Home Counties Dairies Ltd v Skilton* [1970] 1 W.L.R. 526, 533, 536; *Commercial Plastics Ltd v Vincent* [1965] 1 Q.B. 623, 644; *A. Schroeder Music Publishing Co Ltd v Macaulay* [1974] 1 W.L.R. 1308, 1309; *Watson v Prager* [1991] 1 W.L.R. 726, 738 ("The question of whether the . . . agreement is unenforceable on restraint of trade grounds must be tested by reference to the state of affairs at the date of the agreement.").

[472] *Shell (UK) Ltd v Lostock Garage Ltd* [1976] 1 W.L.R. 1187, 1198 (this was a minority view of Lord Denning M.R.).

[473] *Mallan v May* (1843) 11 M. & W. 653, 655; cf. *Homer v Ashford* (1825) 3 Bing. 322.

[474] *Hitchcock v Coker* (1837) 6 A. & E. 438; *Gravely v Barnard* (1874) L.R. 18 Eq. 518; *Nordenfelt v The Maxim Nordenfelt Guns and Ammunition Co Ltd* [1894] A.C. 535, 565; *Alec Lobb (Garages) Ltd v Total Oil (Great Britain) Ltd* [1985] 1 W.L.R. 173, 179. cf. *A. Schroeder Music Publishing Co Ltd v Macaulay* [1974] 1 W.L.R. 1308.

[475] See *Leather Cloth Co v Lorsont* (1869) L.R. 9 Eq. 345, 351; *Maxim Nordenfelt Guns & Ammunition Co v Nordenfelt* [1893] 1 Ch. 639, 651, [1894] A.C. 535, 554, 574; contrast *Dowden and Pook Ltd v Pook* [1904] 1 K.B. 45; and see *Lamson Pneumatic Tube Co v Phillips* (1904) 91 L.T. 363 where the Court of Appeal's judgments suggested that the matter was still open; cf. *Goldsoll v Goldman* [1915] 1 Ch. 292 where the plaintiff was able to succeed without taking the point; and dicta in *Vancouver Malt & Sake Brewing Co Ltd v Vancouver Breweries Ltd* [1934] A.C. 181, 191, which were obiter since the covenant in question was, it would seem, unreasonable in so far as it related to the whole of Canada, where it had been made so that its world-wide application was irrelevant. See also *Cooke v Football Association* [1972] C.L.Y. 516.

[476] [1965] 1 Q.B. 623, 630–631, 645. See also the decision of the New Zealand Court of Appeal in *Blackler v New Zealand Rugby Football League (Incorporated)* [1968] N.Z.L.R. 547, 569, per McCarthy J. expressing the views of the majority: "My view of the law . . . is that any restraint on employment, wheresoever, whether it is intended to operate in New Zealand, or only overseas, or both, is *prima facie* void."

related to a restraint on an ex-employee taking employment abroad, it is submitted that the same principle applies to covenants between traders since the courts ought to have the power to strike down unreasonable restraints on the British export trade.[477]

The test of reasonableness. While all restraints of trade to which the doctrine applies are prima facie unenforceable,[478] all, whether partial or total,[479] are enforceable if reasonable. As was said by Lord Macnaghten in *Nordenfelt v Maxim Nordenfelt & Co*[480]: 16–092

> "It is a sufficient justification, and indeed it is the only justification, if the restriction is reasonable—reasonable, that is, in reference to the interests of the parties concerned and reasonable in reference to the interests of the public, so framed and so guarded as to afford adequate protection to the party in whose favour it is imposed, while at the same time it is in no way injurious to the public." In determining reasonableness the court "*is* entitled to consider whether or not a covenant of a narrower nature would have sufficed for the convenantee's protection."[481]

Even if the restraint is unlimited in time[482] or in space[483] it will be upheld if it is reasonable,[484] although the absence of such a limit "is a remarkable feature prima facie needing justification".[485] Worldwide restrictions have passed muster in the courts, but only where the restrictions to be reasonably effectual had to be worldwide.[486] In determining reasonableness the court does not apply any doctrine of "proportionality", that is, an assessment of whether there is a substantial equivalence between the scope of the restraint and what the covenantor received for entering into it.[487] To introduce such a doctrine would be to revive the now

---

477 cf. *Bull v Pitney-Bowes Ltd* [1967] 1 W.L.R. 273, 276–277. If it produces effects in other member states of the EC, then it may be subject to art.85 of the Treaty: see Vol.II, paras 42–004 et seq.

478 But see also above, para.16–077.

479 *Nordenfelt v The Maxim Nordenfelt Guns & Ammunition Co* [1894] A.C. 535, 565; *Mason v Provident Clothing & Supply Co* [1913] A.C. 724; these authorities abolished the old distinction between total and partial restraints to be found in, e.g. *Mills v Dunham* [1891] 1 Ch. 576, 586; *Haynes v Doman* [1899] 2 Ch. 13, 30.

480 [1894] A.C. 535, 565; and see *Esso* case [1968] A.C. 269, 299. Restraints normally operate as to time, area, and activity, and must be reasonable with respect to these factors.

481 *Office Angels Ltd v Rainer-Thomas and O'Connor* [1991] I.R.L.R. 214, 220 (emphasis in the original, a master and servant case).

482 *Hitchcock v Coker* (1837) 6 A. & E. 438; *Haynes v Doman* [1899] 2 Ch. 13; *Fitch v Dewes* [1921] 2 A.C. 158.

483 *Nordenfelt v The Maxim Nordenfelt Guns and Ammunition Co* [1894] A.C. 535; *Lamson Pneumatic Tube Co v Phillips* (1904) 91 L.T. 363; *Caribonum Co Ltd v Le Couch* (1913) 109 L.T. 385, 587.

484 *Peters American Delicacy Co Ltd v Patricia's Chocolates & Candies Pty Ltd* (1947) 77 C.L.R. 574.

485 *Commercial Plastics Ltd v Vincent* [1965] 1 Q.B. 623, 644. In *Bridge v Deacons* [1984] A.C. 705, 717E–F (dealing with a restraint of five years' duration which was upheld) the court stated that "there appears to be no reported case where a restriction which was otherwise reasonable has been held to be unreasonable solely because of its duration"; see, however, *Scully (UK) Ltd v Lee* [1998] I.R.L.R. 259 where the court held that a non-solicitation clause of two years in an employment contract was unreasonable because of excessive duration. cf. Heydon at pp.158–162.

486 *Vancouver Malt & Sake Brewing Co Ltd v Vancouver Breweries Ltd* [1934] A.C. 181, 191.

487 *Allied Dunbar (Frank Weisenger) Ltd v Weisinger* [1988] I.R.L.R. 60.

discredited doctrine that in assessing the reasonableness of the restraint the court should also consider the adequacy of the consideration.[488]

16–093 **Legitimate interests of the parties.** In the case of the traditional categories of covenant to which the doctrine relates, the expression "the interest of the covenantee" connotes the proprietary or quasi-proprietary interest of an employer in his trade secrets and trade connections and of a purchaser of a business in the goodwill of the enterprise he has acquired. It is the protection of such interests which furnishes the sole justification for a restraint[489] and the restraint must therefore be no *more* than is reasonably necessary for that protection. Similarly, where an otherwise unreasonable restraint is contained in a mortgage, it can be justified by reference to the mortgage only if reasonably necessary to protect the mortgagee's interest in his security.[490] But with the recognition that the doctrine of restraint of trade applies generally and not only to the traditional categories of covenant, it is clear that a proprietary or quasi-proprietary interest is not in every case necessary to support a covenant and the statement that the covenant must be reasonable in the interests of the parties must be taken to mean that the restraint must be reasonable from their point of view. Thus too, while the well-known phrase that a man is not entitled to protect himself against competition per se may be helpful in the context of the traditional categories of covenant, where the justification for the covenant is to be found, if at all, in the protection of the covenantee's "interest", the phrase cannot usefully be applied to other kinds of restrictive covenant.[491] For example, agreements to restrict the production or supply of goods or to fix prices can be justified if, by protecting themselves from competition, the parties are not only acting reasonably from their own point of view but are not injuring[492] or are even benefiting[493] the public, so that there is no ground of public policy for refusing to enforce the agreement.

16–094 Indeed, with the recognition that a "legitimate interest" in the sense of a proprietary or quasi-proprietary interest is not necessary in all cases, it could be argued that such an interest is not necessary even in the traditional categories of restraint; e.g. if a worker agreed for a million pounds not to work for the rest of his life it is difficult to see why such an agreement is not "reasonable" between the parties (as distinct from in the public interest) simply because the employer is protecting himself from competition simpliciter and not protecting some trade

---

[488] *Allied Dunbar (Frank Weisenger) Ltd v Weisinger* [1988] I.R.L.R. 60 "Proportionality," however, may be a factor in obtaining an *Anton Piller* order (see now CPR Pt 25 PD–007) against an ex-employee: see *Lock International Plc v Beswick* [1989] 1 W.L.R. 1268, 1281 ("there must be *proportionality* between the perceived threat to the plaintiff's rights and the remedy granted").

[489] See *British Concrete Co Ltd v Schelff* [1921] 2 Ch. 563, 574–575; *Countryside Assured Financial Services Ltd v Deanne Smart* [2004] EWHC 1214.

[490] See below, para.16–121.

[491] See *Esso Petroleum Co Ltd v Harper's Garage (Stourport) Ltd* [1968] A.C. 269, 301, 329; *McEllistrim v Ballymacelligott Co-operative Agriculture and Dairy Society Ltd* [1919] A.C. 548, 563–564; *Daunay Day & Co Ltd v D'Alfhen* [1997] T.L.R. 334.

[492] cf. *Att-Gen of Commonwealth of Australia v Adelaide Steamship Co* [1913] A.C. 781.

[493] cf. Vol.II, paras 42–081 et seq.

secret or customer connection.[494] Conversely, on present authority, once a "legitimate interest" is shown by the covenantee, the covenant is generally treated as reasonable; but the existence of such an interest need not be a sufficient condition for establishing reasonableness between the parties, since the covenant may in such a case be reasonable from the covenantee's point of view but impose undue hardship upon the covenantor. In recent cases the court has recognised the problem created by elaborate conceptualism in the past, and is tending to insist that the restraint be both reasonably necessary for protection of the legitimate interests of the promisee and also commensurate with the benefits secured to the promisor under the contract.[495] It has been held in an employment contract that, where the employer specifically states the interest to be protected, he is not entitled to "seek to justify the contract by reference to some separate and additional interest that has not been specified".[496] The justification for this is that the employee may have sought legal advice and his legal advisers would be entitled to give him that advice on the basis of the stated purpose of the covenant. This reasoning would apply equally to other types of contracts.

Public interest and burden of proof.[497] The onus of establishing that a covenant is no more than is reasonable in the interests of the parties is on the person who seeks to rely on it[498]; if he establishes that it is no more than reasonable in the interests of the parties, the onus of proving that it is contrary to the public interest lies on the party attacking it.[499] At least where the restraint relates to the traditional categories of employer-employee or vendor-purchaser restraints, this onus will not be a light one.[500] But once an agreement is before the court it is open to the scrutiny of the court in all its surrounding circumstances as a question of law[501] and a determination of the issue whether the covenant should be enforced requires, as a matter of public policy, that a balance should be struck between freedom of trade and freedom of contract.[502] For long, attention was concentrated predominantly on the question of reasonableness in the interests of the parties so that, for example, in 1913 the Privy Council stated that[503]: 16–095

> "... their Lordships are not aware of any case in which a restraint, though reasonable in the interests of the parties, has been held unenforceable because it involved some injury to the public."

---

494 cf. *Higgs v Olivier* [1952] Ch. 311; *Wyatt v Kreglinger and Fernau* [1933] 1 K.B. 793.

495 *A. Schroeder Music Publishing Co Ltd v Macaulay* [1974] 1 W.L.R. 1308.

496 *Office Angels Ltd v Rainer-Thomas and O'Connor* [1991] I.R.L.R. 214, 219 (where the contract does not state the interest to be protected, the employer is entitled to look to the contract and the surrounding circumstances for the purpose of ascertaining the purpose which is to be protected).

497 See above, para.16–075.

498 *Morris Ltd v Saxelby* [1916] 1 A.C. 688, 700, 706; *Attwood v Lamont* [1920] 3 K.B. 571, 587, 588; *Kores Manufacturing Co Ltd v Kolok Manufacturing Co Ltd* [1959] Ch. 108.

499 *Morris v Saxelby* [1916] 1 A.C. 688, 700, 707.

500 *Att-Gen of Commonwealth of Australia v Adelaide S.S. Co Ltd* [1913] A.C. 781, 797. See, however, *Sherk v Horwitz* [1972] 2 O.R. 451; affirmed [1973] 1 O.R. 160.

501 *Esso Petroleum Co Ltd v Harper's Garage (Stourport) Ltd* [1968] A.C. 269, 318 per Lord Hodson; see below, para.16–097.

502 *Morris v Saxelby* [1916] 1 A.C. 688, 716; *Esso Petroleum Co Ltd v Harper's Garage (Stourport) Ltd* [1968] A.C. 296, 304–305.

503 *Att-Gen of Commonwealth of Australia v Adelaide S.S. Co* [1913] A.C. 781, 785.

But especially in cases falling outside the traditional categories of covenant to which most of the earlier authorities relate, the emphasis may well now have shifted from the interests of the parties to those of the public on the basis[504] that the doctrine is part of the wider doctrine of public policy and that, at any rate where the contract was freely entered into between traders, they are usually the best judges of their own interest.[505] But what is meant in this context by the public interest?[506] It could be taken to mean "the public welfare" or "general utility" to the public, a meaning which, though compelling the court to secure a difficult balance between this objective of public benefit and the other one of fairness to the individual trader, would be the modern equivalent of the "pernicious monopoly" of ancient times and would harmonise well with modern statutory philosophy against monopolistic practices that are inconsistent with welfare objectives.[507]

16–096 There is, however, now considerable authority for an alternate theory. Thus according to Ungoed-Thomas J. in *Texaco Ltd v Mulberry Filling Station Ltd*,[508] reasonableness with reference to the interests of the public "is part of the doctrine of restraint of trade which is based on and directed to securing the liberty of the subject and not the utmost economic advantage" and the:

> ". . . question which such reasonableness raises would thus not be whether the restraint might be less in a different organisation of industry or society, or whether the abolition of the restraint might lead to a different organisation of industry or society and thus, on balance of many considerations, to the economic or social advantage of the country, but whether the restraint is, in our industry and society as at present organised and with reference to which our law operates, unreasonable in the public interest as recognised and formulated in such principle or proposition of law. For my part, I prefer to decide that the restraints relied on in our case are reasonable in the interests of the public, not on balance of existing or possible economic advantages and disadvantages to the public but because there is, in conditions as they are, no unreasonable limitation of liberty to trade."[509]

---

504 *Esso Petroleum Co Ltd v Harper's Garage (Stourport) Ltd* [1968] A.C. 269; *Bull v Pitney-Bowes Ltd* [1967] 1 W.L.R. 273.

505 *Esso Petroleum Co Ltd v Harper's Garage (Stourport) Ltd* [1968] A.C. 296; and see *North Western Salt Co v Electrolytic Alkali Co* [1914] A.C. 461, 471; *English Hop Growers v Dering* [1928] 2 K.B. 174, 180.

506 In *Alec Lobb Garages Ltd v Total Oil Great Britain Ltd* [1985] 1 W.L.R. 173, 191E Waller L.J. considered it to be in the public interest to save a firm from bankruptcy.

507 e.g. Competition Act 1998; arts 81 and 82 EC.

508 [1972] 1 W.L.R. 814, 827, 828.

509 cf. *Dickson v Pharmaceutical Society of Great Britain* [1970] A.C. 403, 441, per Lord Wilberforce: "I would . . . hold [that the restraints do not survive the test] on the simple ground, which I think is the relevant ground in this connection, that there is nothing here to displace the normal proposition that the public has in the absence of countervailing considerations an interest in men being able to trade freely in the goods which they judge the public wants and that these restraints clearly, severely and arbitrarily restrict this freedom. More special arguments to the effect that the restraints might cause a reduction in the number of pharmacies I would regard as less secure: before I could accept them I should require persuasion, first, that this type of consideration may properly be taken into account in relation to the common law doctrine of restraint of trade (as contrasted with proceedings in the Restrictive Practices Court)." See also *A. Schroeder Music Publishing Co Ltd v Macaulay* [1974] 1 W.L.R. 1308, 1315, per Lord Diplock.

The difficulty with this view is that the requirement of public interest adds nothing to the requirement that the restraint be reasonable in the interests of the parties. Thus, if it is reasonable in their interest, then there is no undue interference with individual liberty and the public interest is satisfied; if it is not reasonable it must be because the liberty of one of the parties is unduly restricted and the agreement is ipso facto contrary to the public interest.[510] The two limbs of the traditional formula for assessing restraints are then simply tautologous. There may, however, be arguments of policy in favour of this alternate view: the court is dependent on the parties and their advisers to present the economic evidence on the question of the impact of the restraint upon general welfare; it might be thought that such a wide-ranging inquiry of fact should be subject rather to presentation by a representative of the public or to investigation by a public administrative agency,[511] although the American practice of "Brandeis briefs", if accepted by the English courts in this context, might meet the objection. It can also be argued that a common law court is not an appropriate forum for assessing economic evidence, making predictions upon it and balancing the interest of conflicting groups in society.[512] There is also the time and expense of litigation which may make it an inappropriate method for providing an answer to economic issues which may have to be decided expeditiously. The optimal solution may be to assign to a government department, for example, the Office of Fair Trading, the primary responsibility for making economic decisions with a limited review being carried out by the courts.

Construction. In construing a covenant in restraint of trade, the same principles of construction apply as to the construction of other written term.[513] Covenants in restraint of trade must be clear and definite.[514] In construing a covenant in restraint of trade between partners it has been held that: **16–097**

> "(1) . . . the question of construction should be approached in the first instance without regard to the question of legality or illegality; (2) that the clause should be construed with reference to the object sought to be obtained; (3) that in a restraint of trade case the object is the protection of one of the partners against rivalry in trade; [and] (4) the clause should be construed in its context and in the light of the factual matrix when the agreement was made."[515]

---

510 It is not inconceivable that an extremely onerous restraint contractually imposed upon an individual might secure enormous utility to the public. But, on the above theory, the restraint must be contrary to the "public interest". Sed quaere?

511 cf. the Competition Commission and the Commission of the EEC under arts 81 and 82 EC. See *Texaco v Mulberry Filling Station Ltd* [1972] 1 W.L.R. 814, 826.

512 See Stevens and Yamey, *The Restrictive Practices Court* (1965), Ch.3 and *Texaco v Mulberry Filling Station Ltd* [1972] 1 W.L.R. 814, 827.

513 *Beckett Investment Management Group Ltd v Hall* [2007] EWCA Civ 613, [2007] I.R.L.R. 793 at [11].

514 *Davies v Davies* (1887) 36 Ch D 359, where a covenant to retire from business "so far as the law allows" was held to be too vague to be enforceable. cf. *Express Dairy Co v Jackson* (1930) 99 L.J.K.B. 181.

515 *Clarke v Newland* [1991] 1 All E.R. 397, 402. These principles were put forward in connection with a restraint in the contract of a salaried partner, a status that can often be equated with that of an employee: see *Lindley & Banks on Partnership*, 18th edn (2002), p.259, fn.41. However, in the light of the courts' disfavour of restraints in employment contracts, these principles will be applied in that context with greater rigour.

The courts will attempt to construe a covenant so as to achieve the parties' intention where there has been a "mere want of accuracy of expression" with the consequence that the covenant will be upheld as not being too wide.[516] However, for this principle to apply it must be clear from the contract and the surrounding circumstances what exactly are the terms of the more limited covenant.[517] Reasonableness is a question of law,[518] that is, a question of the application by the court of a legal standard to the facts of the particular case. Therefore, although evidence of surrounding circumstances at the time the contract was made, such as the character of the business to be protected by the covenant, is admissible in the consideration of the requirements of that business,[519] evidence of the views, about reasonableness, of persons in the particular trade is inadmissible.[520]

16–098 **Factors determining unreasonableness.** The considerations which arise in determining the reasonableness of a covenant in restraint of trade differ according to the nature of the contract in which the covenant occurs.[521] It is therefore convenient to consider separately the question of the validity of such covenants in a number of different situations, although since the doctrine is of general application[522] and the categories of restraint of trade are not closed,[523] such situations are not exhaustive.[524]

16–099 **Covenant assignable.** The benefit of a covenant in restraint of trade is assignable, unless it is clear from the terms of the covenant that it is intended to be personal to the covenantee.[525] Thus the purchaser of the goodwill of a business is entitled to enforce covenants entered into for the protection of that business.[526]

---

[516] The phrase is that of Lindley M.R. in *Haynes v Dorman* [1899] 2 Ch. 13, 26. For recent examples of this, see *Business Seating (Renovations) Ltd v Broad* [1989] I.C.R. 729; *Clarke v Newland* [1991] 1 All E.R. 397; *Hollis & Co v Stokes* [2000] I.R.L.R. 712.

[517] *Mont v Mills* [1993] I.R.L.R. 172. It has been suggested that there is a difference of approach by the Court of Appeal in this case to that of the Court of Appeal in *Littlewoods Organisation Ltd v Harris* [1978] 1 W.L.R. 1472: see *Hanover Insurance Brokers Ltd v Schapiro* [1994] I.R.L.R. 82; *Advantage Business Systems Ltd v Hopley* [2007] EWHC (QB) 1783, [2007] All E.R. (D) 339 (Jul).

[518] *Dowden & Pook Ltd v Pook* [1904] 1 K.B. 45; *Mason v Provident Clothing Co Ltd* [1913] A.C. 724, 732; *Stenhouse Australia Ltd v Phillips* [1974] A.C. 391, 402.

[519] *Routh v Jones* [1947] 1 All E.R. 758; *Jenkins v Reid* [1948] 1 All E.R. 471; *Lyne-Pirkis v Jones* [1969] 1 W.L.R. 1293; *Peyton v Mindham* [1972] 1 W.L.R. 8. cf. *Rogers v Maddocks* [1892] 3 Ch. 346.

[520] *Haynes v Dorman* [1899] 2 Ch. 13; *North Western Salt Co v Electrolytic Alkali Co* [1914] A.C. 461, 471; *Mason v Provident Clothing Co* [1913] A.C. 724, 732.

[521] *Jenkins v Reid* [1948] 1 All E.R. 471.

[522] See above, para.16–075.

[523] *Esso Petroleum Co Ltd v Harper's Garage (Stourport) Ltd* [1968] A.C. 269; *Petrofina (Great Britain) Ltd v Martin* [1966] Ch. 146, 169.

[524] e.g. see above, para.16–004, text to fn.14.

[525] As in *Davies v Davies* (1887) 36 Ch D 359; see also *Berlitz School of Languages Ltd v Duchêne* (1903) 6 F. 181.

[526] *Elves v Crofts* (1850) 10 C.B. 241; *Jacoby v Whitmore* (1883) 49 L.T. 335; *Townsend v Jarman* [1900] 2 Ch. 698; *Welstead v Hadley* (1904) 21 T.L.R. 165; *Automobile Carriage Builders Ltd v Sayers* (1909) 101 L.T. 419.

Repudiation of contract. If the party in whose favour a covenant in restraint of trade is entered into wrongly repudiates the agreement in which the covenant is contained, the covenantor is thereby discharged from his obligation. Wrongful dismissal, therefore, puts an end to any restrictive covenant in a contract of employment.[527] But payment of wages in lieu of notice is not a wrongful dismissal amounting to a repudiation of the contract which frees the employee from such a restraint, unless the contract of employment is one which obliges the employer to provide work for the employee.[528] It may also be possible to recover profits made by the covenantor from the breach.[529] **16–100**

Restraints after repudiation by employer. In a number of recent cases the courts have held that a restraint in an employment contract, which applied no matter how the contract was terminated, was unreasonable in that it could apply even where the employer unlawfully terminated the contract.[530] The Court of Appeal recently held that these cases were misconceived. In *Rock Refrigeration Ltd v Jones*[531] it held, applying the reasoning in *General Billposting Co Ltd v Atkinson*,[532] that the effect of the acceptance by an employee of the repudiatory breach by the employer was to terminate the contract and with it the restraint clause. There therefore could be no question of construing the restraint to determine its reasonableness since it ceased to be binding on the employee. Phillips L.J. doubted whether the *General Billposting* case, decided in 1909, now reflected the law on the effect of repudiatory breach in the light of developments since that date. It is now clear that some clauses can survive the acceptance of a repudiatory breach and regulate the rights of the parties and he considered that in certain circumstances there was no good reason why this could not apply to a restraint of trade clause. Whether this is indeed the case will need to be decided in the future. What is clear, however, contrary to what Phillips L.J. considered,[533] is that the survival of such restraints is not necessary to protect the proprietary interests of the employer as these will be protected by normal common law doctrines.[534] **16–101**

Injunctions. If a covenant in restraint of trade is valid, a breach of it may be restrained by injunction, even though the contract in which the covenant is contained provides an alternative remedy[535]; but the plaintiff must elect which of **16–102**

---

[527] *General Billposting Co Ltd v Atkinson* [1909] A.C. 118; *Measures Bros v Measures* [1910] 2 Ch. 248; *S. W. Strange Ltd v Mann* [1965] 1 W.L.R. 629, 637; *Briggs v Oates* [1991] 1 W.L.R. 407.

[528] *Konski v Peet* [1915] 1 Ch. 530, distinguishing *General Billposting Co Ltd v Atkinson* [1909] A.C. 118. See also para.16–101; *Rock Refrigeration Ltd v Jones* [1997] 1 All E.R. 1 (noted (1997) 113 L.Q.R. 377).

[529] See Birks [1987] L.M.C.L.Q. 421: cf. Gurry, *Breach of Confidence*, Ch.XXII. See *Experience Hendrix LLC v PPX Enterprises Inc* [2003] EWCA Civ 323, [2003] 1 All E.R. (Comm) 830 at [32].

[530] See, e.g. *D. v M.* [1996] I.R.L.R. 192.

[531] [1997] 1 All E.R. 1 (noted (1997) 113 L.Q.R. 377).

[532] [1909] A.C. 118.

[533] *Rock Refrigeration Ltd v Jones* [1997] 1 All E.R. 1, 20.

[534] *Rock Refrigeration Ltd v Jones* [1997] 1 All E.R. 1, 14, per Morritt L.J.

[535] *National Provincial Bank v Marshall* (1888) 40 Ch D 112; *Texaco Ltd v Mulberry Filling Station* [1972] 1 W.L.R. 814.

the two remedies he will enforce.[536] The court, however, will normally not grant an injunction which would have the effect of a decree of specific performance of a contract for personal service[537] although the court will enforce negative covenants, e.g. not to perform services elsewhere,[538] but not one which would deprive the defendant of his means of livelihood.[539] A restrictive covenant may be enforceable by injunction even though the covenantor is a minor[540] or the covenant is contained in a deed of apprenticeship.[541] No injunction will be granted to a plaintiff who is unable or unwilling to fulfil his obligations under the contract.[542]

16–103 **Interlocutory injunction.** There are no special rules relating to the granting of an interlocutory injunction in connection with covenants in restraint of trade.[543] This can give rise to problems particularly with respect to restraints in employment contracts. Since to be valid the restraint will inevitably be of limited duration, the granting of an interlocutory injunction may have the effect of disposing of the matter in that the delays associated with litigation will entail that a reasonable time will have expired by the time the matter comes on for trial on the merits. To deal with this, the courts have held that matters involving restraint of trade in employment contracts are "singularly appropriate for a speedy trial".[544] Where this is not possible, it is then proper for the judge to go on to consider the chances of the plaintiff succeeding in the action.[545] The court had jurisdiction to grant an injunction on limited terms, for example, that an

---

536 *General Accident Assurance Corp v Noel* [1902] 1 K.B. 377. This was a claim for both an injunction and liquidated damages. Where, however, the damages relate to past breaches there is no reason in principle why the plaintiff should not obtain both damages and an injunction as they clearly relate to different heads of loss.

537 See *Whitwood Chemical Co v Hardman* [1891] 2 Ch. 416; *Ehrman v Bartholomew* [1898] 1 Ch. 671; *Rely-a-Bell Burglar and Fire Alarm Co Ltd v Eisler* [1926] Ch. 609; cf. *Irani v Southampton and S.W. Hampshire Area Health Authority* [1985] I.C.R. 590; *Evening Standard Co Ltd v Henderson* [1987] I.C.R. 588 where injunctions were granted to prevent breach of employment contracts. See further below, paras 27–060 and 27–061. *Brazier v Bramwell Scaffolding Ltd* [2001] UKPC 59; *Beckett Financial Services v Atkinson* Unreported November 6, 2001 (court would not grant an injunction where credible undertaking to comply with a covenant in restraint of trade was given); *Ace London Services Ltd v Charman* Unreported October 1, 2001 (injunctions granted where no undertakings were given).

538 *Catt v Tourle* (1869) L.R. 4 Ch. App. 654; *Warner Bros v Nelson* [1937] 1 K.B. 209; *Rely-a-Bell Burglar and Fire Alarm Co v Eisler* [1926] Ch. 609. cf. *Lumley v Wagner* (1852) 1 De G.M. & G. 604, 619; *Page One Records Ltd v Britton* [1968] 1 W.L.R. 157; *Evening Standard Co Ltd v Henderson* [1987] I.C.R. 588; *Warren v Mendy* [1989] 1 W.L.R. 853.

539 *Palace Theatre Ltd v Clensy* (1909) 26 T.L.R. 28 (interim injunction).

540 *Bromley v Smith* [1909] 2 K.B. 235; *Trevor André v Bashford* [1965] C.L.Y. 1984; provided, of course, that the contract is beneficial to the minor; cf. *Corn v Matthews* [1893] 1 Q.B. 310, 314; see above, paras 8–021 et seq.

541 *Gadd v Thompson* [1911] 1 K.B. 304.

542 *Measures Bros Ltd v Measures* [1910] 2 Ch. 248.

543 *Lawrence David Ltd v Ashton* [1991] 1 All E.R. 385 (it appears that the profession did consider that the *American Cyanamid* principles did not apply to restraint of trade covenants in employment contracts: 392).

544 *Lawrence David Ltd v Ashton* [1991] 1 All E.R. 385, 395.

545 *Lawrence David Ltd v Ashton* [1991] 1 All E.R. 385, 396; *Lansing Linde Ltd v Kerr* [1991] 1 All E.R. 418; *Business Seating (Reservations) Ltd v Broad* [1987] I.C.R. 729 (in both cases merits were considered and an interlocutory injunction refused).

employee on "garden leave" may not accept employment with a named firm.[546]

(ii) *Employer and Employee*

16–104 **Employee's activities after determination of employment.** The doctrine of restraint of trade has always been applied to covenants contained in contracts of employment[547] which limit the freedom of the employee to work after the termination of the employment.[548] Post-termination restraints if reasonable are enforceable.[549] In some situations it will be difficult to categorise a restraint as relating to an employment contract as opposed to a contract between a vendor and purchaser of business, and what appears to be an employment contract may in substance be a vendor and purchaser contract. For example, where a company bought out its "sales associates" practices the court held that the covenant in the contract of sale was to be "tested by the principles applicable as between vendor and purchaser" since the covenant had been:

> ". . . taken for the protection of the goodwill of the business sold to the plaintiffs by the defendant, rather than for the protection of the plaintiffs' present and future business as employer."[550]

Covenants in employment contracts are viewed by the courts much more jealously than the other of the principal traditional categories of covenant to which the doctrine applies, namely, covenants between the vendor and purchaser of a business.[551] The courts, however, clearly accept the enforceability of such covenants provided they satisfy the test of reasonableness and more recent authorities indicate that they will not adopt extravagant interpretations to render them void:

> "If a clause is valid in all ordinary circumstances which can have been contemplated by the parties, it is equally valid notwithstanding that it might cover circumstances which are so 'extravagant,' 'fantastical,' 'unlikely or improbable' that they must have been entirely outside the contemplation of the parties."[552]

---

546 *Symbian Ltd v Christensen* [2001] I.R.L.R. 77.

547 As to contracts between employers as to whom they will employ and on what terms, see below, paras 16–135 et seq. Although agreements "in gross" cannot be justified as reasonable, the doctrine applies in the ordinary way to contracts made on the determination of the employee's employment if the contract was related to a subsisting contract of employment: *Stenhouse Australia Ltd v Phillips* [1974] A.C. 391.

548 As to contracts which tie the employee only during the continuance of his employment, see below, para.16–114.

549 *Leeds Rugby Ltd v Harris* [2005] EWHC 1591 (QB), [2005] All E.R. (D) 286 (Jul).

550 *Allied Dunbar (Frank Weisinger) Ltd v Weisinger* [1988] I.R.L.R. 60, 64. See also *Systems Reliability Holdings Plc v Smith* [1990] I.R.L.R. 377.

551 *Nordenfelt v Maxim Nordenfelt Guns & Ammunition Co* [1894] A.C. 535, 566; *Morris Ltd v Saxelby* [1916] 1 A.C. 688, 701; *Attwood v Lamont* [1920] 3 K.B. 571, 586, 587.

552 *Home Counties Dairies Ltd v Skilton* [1970] 1 W.L.R. 526, 536, per Salmon L.J. See also 537, per Cross L.J. "the validity of a covenant is not to be tried by the improbabilities that might fall within its wording": *Edwards v Worboys* [1984] A.C. 724, 727 H, per Dillon L.J.; *Scully (UK) Ltd v Lee* [1998] I.R.L.R. 259. See also below, para.16–114.

Thus in *Home Counties Dairies Ltd v Skilton*[553] the defendant employee, a milkman, entered into a covenant whereby he agreed that for a period of one year from the termination of his employment that he would not serve or sell "milk or dairy produce" to any customer of his ex-employer. It was argued that the restraint relating to dairy produce resulted in the covenant being too wide, as it would preclude the employee from working for a grocery shop selling butter and cheese where there was a likelihood that the shop might be patronised by his ex-employer's customers. The Court of Appeal, reversing the trial judge, rejected this interpretation as being commercially unreasonable. From the obvious intentions of the parties, it was clear that the restraint was[554] "intended to restrict the employee's activities only when engaged in the same type of business as the employer's". On this interpretation the clause was valid as being reasonable to protect the customer-connection of the employer. Whether a particular contractual provision operates in restraint of trade is "to be determined not by the form the stipulation wears but . . . by its effect in practice".[555] What is reasonable in one type of relationship may not be reasonable in another.[556] Thus a provision which provides that an employee will be deprived of a pension if, on the cessation of his employment, he competed with his ex-employer will not be viewed as merely setting out the terms of his entitlement to the pension but will be treated as a provision designed to restrict competition and therefore subject to the restraint of trade doctrine.[557] Also, it is on this basis that a covenant restraining an ex-employee from approaching other members of the employer's workforce would be subject to the restraint of trade doctrine.[558]

16–105 It is for the employer who seeks to enforce such a covenant against an employee to show that it is reasonable in the interests of the parties and in particular that it is designed for the protection of some proprietary interest owned by the employer for which the restraint is reasonably necessary.[559] It has been said that the restraint must be reasonable not only in the interests of the covenantee but in the interests of both the contracting parties.[560] But provided

---

[553] *Scully (UK) Ltd v Lee* [1998] I.R.L.R. 259; see also *Business Seating (Renovations) Ltd v Broad* [1989] I.R.L.R. 729.

[554] [1970] 1 W.L.R. 526, 535. In adopting this approach to the construction of the restraint the court followed Lord Lindley M.R. in *Haynes v Dorman* [1899] 2 Ch. 13, 24–25. See also *Littlewoods Organisation Ltd v Harris* [1977] 1 W.L.R. 1472 in which Lord Denning M.R. criticised the literalist approach of the court in *Commercial Plastics Ltd v Vincent* [1965] 1 Q.B. 623. For authorities which would probably not be adhered to in light of the *Skilton* and *Littlewood* cases see Heydon, *The Restraint of Trade Doctrine* (1971), pp.129–131.

[555] *Stenhouse Australia Ltd v Phillips* [1974] A.C. 391, 402.

[556] *Allan Janes LLP v Jahal* [2006] EWHC 286 (Ch), [2006] I.C.R. 742 (a covenant unreasonable for a milk roundsman may not be unreasonable for a solicitor).

[557] *Bull v Pitney-Bowes Ltd* [1967] 1 W.L.R. 273; *Sadler v Imperial Life Assurance Co of Canada Ltd* [1988] I.R.L.R. 388 (commission payable to an agent after the termination of his employment ceased to be payable if he competed with his ex-employer held to be an unlawful restraint of trade).

[558] See generally, Sales (1988) 104 L.Q.R. 600.

[559] *Attwood v Lamont* [1920] 3 K.B. 57; [1916] 1 A.C. 688, 710; *Jenkins v Reid* [1948] 1 All E.R. 471; *Eastham v Newcastle United F.C. Ltd* [1964] Ch. 413, 431; *Greig v Insole* [1978] 1 W.L.R. 302; *Gordian Knot Ltd v Kenneth Towers* Unreported December 6, 2001.

[560] *Attwood v Lamont* [1920] 3 K.B. 571, 589.

that the covenant affords adequate, and no more than adequate, protection to the covenantee,[561] it seems that the requirement that the restraint must be reasonable in the interests of the parties is satisfied, for the court will not now inquire into the adequacy of the consideration for the covenant.[562] Yet a restraint which is reasonably necessary for the protection of the employer may be oppressive and fatal to the chance of the employee earning his living in this country. Probably the true view is that such a restraint, whether or not it be reasonable in the interests of the parties, is unreasonable in the interests of the public, which require that a man shall not be prevented from supporting himself by disposing of his labour in this country[563] and that the national economy should not be deprived of the services of experienced men.[564] Thus, in *Wyatt v Kreglinger & Fernau*[565] a retired employee was granted a pension on condition that after retirement from the employment he should be at liberty to engage in any other trade than the wool trade, otherwise the pension would cease. There was no covenant by the employee not to engage in the wool trade nor any limit of time or space. The Court of Appeal rejected the former employee's claim for arrears of the pension, holding that, assuming a contractual relationship was established, the contract was in restraint of trade and therefore void. The decision has been criticised[566] and is explicable, if at all, only on the ground than an otherwise gratuitous promise is not made enforceable by adding to it a condition, the substance of which is such that, had the promisee covenanted to comply with it, the promisor could not, on the ground of the covenant's unreasonable restraint of trade, have held him to it. The courts will grant, as a matter of independent relief, a declaration that such a condition is void.[567] A restraint otherwise unreasonable does not become reasonable merely because provision is made that the consent of the employer shall not be unreasonably withheld.[568] The court will not imply a term in order to save a covenant restraining an employee's post-employment conduct.[569] Nor will the court re-write a covenant in restraint of trade where the contract provides that the covenant, if unenforceable, should be rewritten with such minimum amendment as renders it enforceable.[570] A provision that the

---

561 *Morris v Saxelby* [1916] 1 A.C. 688, 707.

562 *Morris v Saxelby* [1916] 1 A.C. 688.

563 per Neville J. in *Leetham & Sons Ltd v Johnstone-White* [1907] 1 Ch. 189, 194.

564 *Bull v Pitney-Bowes Ltd* [1967] 1 W.L.R. 273, 277; *Mont v Mills* [1993] I.R.L.R. 173, 177 ("public policy clearly has regard too to the public interest in competition and in the proper use of an employee's skills"). It is on this basis that so-called "garden leave" arrangements can be challenged. These are arrangements whereby an employee is given paid leave normally ending in the termination of the employment relationship and in this way the employer can protect his interests against the disclosure of confidential information, as during the period of paid leave the employee would be under a contractual duty not to disclose any confidential information relating to his employer's business.

565 [1933] 1 K.B. 793; applied in *Bull v Pitney-Bowes Ltd* [1967] 1 W.L.R. 273. See also *Howard F. Hudson Pty Ltd v Ronayne* (1971) 46 A.L.J.R. 173.

566 See (1933) 49 L.Q.R. 465.

567 *Bull v Pitney-Bowes Ltd* [1967] 1 W.L.R. 273. cf. *Howard F. Hudson Pty Ltd v Ronayne* (1971) 46 A.L.J.R. 173.

568 *Chafer Ltd v Lilley* [1947] L.J.R. 231.

569 *Townends Group Ltd v Cobb* [2004] All E.R. (D) 421 (Nov).

570 *Townends Group Ltd v Cobb* [2004] All E.R. (D) 421 (Nov).

restraint should apply "for as long as permitted by law" ws too uncertain to have effect.[571]

16–106 **Competition.** Whether the restraint sought to be enforced in a particular case affords more than adequate protection to the business of the employer depends to some extent upon the requirements of that business.[572] Certain principles of general application, however, may be laid down. An employer is not entitled to protect himself against mere competition on the part of a former employee.[573] In the course of his employment the employee may have acquired additional skill in and knowledge of the trade or profession in which he has been engaged, so as to be a more formidable competitor upon the termination of a service; but that additional skill and knowledge belong to him and their exercise cannot lawfully be restrained by the employer.[574] So, where a film actor in the course of his employment acquired a reputation under a pseudonym it was held that a term of his contract of service restraining him from using the pseudonym after the termination of his employment was invalid as a partial restraint of trade.[575] Similarly, an employer cannot enforce a covenant requiring an ex-employee to disclose and assign inventions discovered after he has ceased to be an employee.[576]

16–107 **Protection by general law and by covenant.** The general law relating to breach of confidence[577] prohibits ex-employees from using information which:

> "... can fairly be regarded as a separate part of the employee's stock of knowledge which a man of ordinary honesty and intelligence would recognise to be the property of his old employer and not his own to do as he likes with."[578]

It is also impermissible for any employee to copy customer lists or deliberately memorise such information even though it may be in the public domain as he would be saved the expense and effort of bringing the information together.[579] An employer can only protect by means of a covenant, information that constitutes a trade secret and cannot protect information that is merely confidential and which the employee would be precluded by his duty of fidelity from disclosing

---

[571] *Days Medical Aids Ltd v Pihsiang Machinery Manufacturing Co Ltd* [2004] EWHC 44 (Comm), [2004] 4 All E.R. (Comm) 95.

[572] See *Mason v Provident Clothing Co* [1913] A.C. 724, 732; *Wincanton Ltd v Grammy* [2000] I.R.L.R. 716; *Dranez Anstalt v Hayek* [2002] EWCA Civ 1729, [2003] 1 B.C.L.C. 278.

[573] *Bowler v Lovegrove* [1921] 1 Ch. 642; *Attwood v Lamont* [1920] 3 K.B. 571, 589.

[574] *Leng & Co v Andrews* [1909] 1 Ch. 763, 773; *Mason v Provident Clothing Co* [1913] A.C. 724; *Stevenson Jordan and Harrison Ltd v Macdonald and Evans* [1952] 1 T.L.R. 101; *Axiom Business Computers Ltd v Jeannie Frederick* Unreported, November 20, 2003, Ct of Session.

[575] *Hepworth Manufacturing Co v Ryott* [1920] 1 Ch. 1.

[576] *Electric Transmission Ltd v Dannenberg* (1949) 66 R.P.C. 183.

[577] North [1968] J.B.L. 32; Jones (1970) 86 L.Q.R. 463; Gurry, *Breach of Confidence* (1984).

[578] *Printers & Finishers Ltd v Holloway* [1965] 1 W.L.R. 1, 5; *Under Water Welders & Repairers Ltd v Street and Longthorne* [1968] R.P.C. 498, 507; *Roger Bullivant Ltd v Ellis* [1987] I.C.R. 464. cf. *Schering Chemicals Ltd v Falkman Ltd* [1982] 2 Q.B. 1; *Thomas Marshall (Exports) Ltd v Guinie* [1979] Ch. 227; *Brooks v Olyslager Oms (UK) Ltd* [1998] I.R.L.R. 590 (information in the public domain not confidential); *CWS Dolphin Ltd v Simonet* [2001] 2 B.C.L.C. 704.

[579] *Robb v Green* [1985] 2 Q.B. 1; *Crowson Fabrics Ltd v Rider* [2007] EWHC Ch 2942, [2008] I.R.L.R. 288.

during his employment.[580] Thus there is considerable overlap between the protection afforded by the general law and that which can be acquired by a restraint of trade covenant. However, there is no basis for holding that the duty of confidentiality should be "trumped" by the public policy which underlies the law relating to covenants in restraint of trade.[581] However, a covenant can afford wider protection than the general law in a number of respects. First, the use of a covenant is evidence of the attitude of the employer that the information is a trade secret. While an employer cannot turn confidential information into a protectable trade secret merely by characterising it as a trade secret, the attitude of an employer towards the information is a factor relevant to the court's determination of whether it is a trade secret.[582] Secondly, even where the employer's interest, for the protection of which a covenant is taken, is in trade secrets, a covenant relieves the employer of the need to prove that the employee subjectively appreciated the confidentiality of the information in question, or that the information was separable from the employee's general stock of trade knowledge or indeed that the employee has actually used the information, it being sufficient to frame the covenant to cover, to a reasonable degree, clearly defined activities in which the employee would be likely to use the information.[583] Thirdly, the courts may be reluctant to imply a term as the employee will have had no opportunity of rejecting it[584] and this may have the effect of making the protection afforded by the law slightly narrower than that which can be acquired by covenant. Fourthly, the protection provided by the law will normally be unlimited as to time whereas that under a covenant is more likely than not to be limited as to time.[585] Lastly, a carefully drafted covenant will make it easier for an employer to obtain injunctive relief since it will facilitate the framing of an order in "sufficient detail to enable the [employee] to know exactly what information he is not free to use on behalf of his new employer".[586] A covenant in a contract of service whereby an employee agreed that, on the termination of his service, he could not for a period of 12 months deal with a company with which his employer had negotiated was not void for uncertainty.[587] An employer can protect his interests by a non-solicitation clause but, in many situations, a non-competition clause provides a more secure protection for the employer, as has been accepted by the courts. A non-competition clause is easier to apply and it avoids difficulties of what constitutes confidential information as to who was the employer's client.[588] It

---

580 *Faccenda Chicken Ltd v Fowler* [1987] Ch. 117 (this case will be analysed in greater detail below, para.16–109). On when information ceases to be confidential by publication, see *Speed Seal Products Ltd v Paddington* [1985] 1 W.L.R. 1327; and on the measure of damages see *Dawson & Mason Ltd v Potter* [1986] 1 W.L.R. 1419.

581 *Shepherds Investments Ltd v Walters* [2006] EWHC Ch 866, [2007] 2 B.C.L.C. 202 at [107].

582 *Faccenda Chicken Ltd v Fowler* [1987] Ch. 117, 138.

583 cf. *Printers & Finishers Ltd v Holloway* [1965] 1 W.L.R. 1; *Littlewoods Organisation Ltd v Harris* [1977] 1 W.L.R. 1472.

584 *Balston Ltd v Headline Filters Ltd* (1987) F.S.R. 330, 352.

585 *Balston Ltd v Headline Filters Ltd* (1987) 13 F.S.R. 330, 347–348.

586 *Lock International Plc v Beswick* [1989] 1 W.L.R. 1268, 1274 (grounds on which an *Anton Piller* order was sought not sufficiently particularised).

587 *International Consulting Services (UK) Ltd v Hart* [2000] I.R.L.R. 277.

588 *Thomas v Farr Plc* [2007] EWCA Civ 18, [2007] I.R.L.R. 419; see also *Extec Screens & Crushers Ltd v Rice* [2007] EWHC 1043 (QB).

may be that a person possesses a particular status and this precludes competition by that person. For example, a director must act in the best interests of the company and must not enter into a transaction in which his interests conflict with those of the company. Where these duties are applicable, thus restricting the competitive activities of the director against the company, the rules of public policy as to restraint of trade do not "trump" these duties.[589]

16–108 **Trade secrets and connection with customers.** An employer can by covenant lawfully prohibit an employee from accepting, after determination of his employment, a position in which he would be likely to utilise information as to secret processes or other trade secrets which have been acquired in the course of his employment.[590] Depending on the nature of the employment[591] he may also be able by covenant lawfully to prohibit the employee: (i) from setting up on his own, or accepting a position with one of the employer's competitors,[592] so as to be likely to destroy the employer's trade connection by a misuse of his acquaintance with the employer's customers or clients[593]; or (ii) at least from soliciting the former employer's customers[594]:

> "In fact the reason, and the only reason, for upholding such a restraint on the part of an employee is that the employer has some proprietary right, whether in the nature of trade connection or in the nature of trade secrets, for the protection of which such a restraint is—having regard to the duties of the employee—reasonably necessary."[595]

In determining whether a particular item of information is capable of protection, the court will take into consideration such matters as the nature of the employment and the information and whether the "employer impressed on the employee the confidentiality of the information."[596] Another factor of importance is the

---

[589] *Shepherds Investments Ltd v Walters* [2006] EWHC Ch 836, [2006] All E.R. (D) 213 (Apr).

[590] *Haynes v Doman* [1899] 2 Ch. 13; *Caribonum Co v Le Couch* (1913) 109 L.T. 385; *Clark v Electronic Applications (Commercial) Ltd* [1963] R.P.C. 234; *Brunning Group v Bentley* [1966] C.L.Y. 4489; *Littlewoods Organisation Ltd v Harris* [1977] 1 W.L.R. 1472; *Voaden v Voaden* Unreported February 21, 1997, Lindsay J. (Unreported)); *Polymasc Pharmaceutical Plc v Stephen Alexander Charles* [1999] F.S.R. 711.

[591] See below, para.16–109 and see *S. W. Strange Ltd v Mann* [1965] 1 W.L.R. 629.

[592] *Commercial Plastics Ltd v Vincent* [1965] 1 Q.B. 623, 640. The presence of an enforceable non-solicitation clause diminishes the need for a wider clause against doing business or, at least, increases the burden of justifying the wider clause: *Stenhouse Australia Ltd v Phillips* [1974] A.C. 391. But if a non-solicitation clause would clearly suffice it may be as hard to justify a clause against doing business that stands alone as it would be to justify a clause against doing business that stands alongside a non-solicitation clause. See also *Office Angels Ltd v Rainer-Thomas and O'Connor* [1991] I.R.L.R. 214; *Brake Bros Ltd v Ungless* [2004] EWHC (QB) 2799, [2004] All E.R. (D) 686 (Jul).

[593] *Baines v Geary* (1887) 35 Ch D 154; *Ropeways v Hoyle* (1919) 88 L.J. Ch. 446; *Fitch v Dewes* [1921] 2 A.C. 158; *Marion White Ltd v Francis* [1972] 1 W.L.R. 1423. Contrast *Lucas & Co Ltd v Mitchell* [1974] Ch. 129 (anti-solicitation covenant was severable from a trading covenant and enforceable).

[594] *S.W. Strange Ltd v Mann* [1965] 1 W.L.R. 629; *Lucas & Co Ltd v Mitchell* [1974] Ch. 129. Contrast *Spafax (1965) Ltd v Dommett* (1972) 116 S.J. 711, (where the word "customers" was said to be impossibly vague); *S.B.J. Stephenson Ltd v Mandy* [2000] I.R.L.R. 233.

[595] *Morris v Saxelby* [1916] A.C. 688, 710; *Faccenda Chicken Ltd v Fowler* [1987] Ch. 117, 137; *Fibrenetix Storage Ltd v Davis* [2004] EWHC (QB) 1359, [2004] All E.R. (D) 99 (Jun) (protection of pricing policies).

[596] *Faccenda Chicken Ltd v Fowler* [1987] Ch. 117, 137–138.

"separability" of the information from other non-confidential information that the employee possesses, although this is not "conclusive".[597] Where there are difficulties in identifying what constitutes confidential information, "a non-competition clause may be the satisfactory form of restraint, provided it is reasonable in time and space".[598] It is important to re-emphasise that it is not all confidential information that an employer can protect but only that which amounts to a "trade secret" or which prevents "some personal influence over customers being abused in order to entice them away".[599] In *Faccenda Chicken Ltd v Fowler*[600] it was held that the duty of fidelity which an employee owes to an employer during the continuance of the employment obliges an employee to maintain confidential information which could not be made the subject of a valid restraint on the termination of the employment relationship.[601] At first glance this appears anomalous as the restraint of trade doctrine applies equally during the continuance of the contract as on its termination, and one would have expected that what was protectible during the contract would also be protectible on its termination. It may be that an employee's duty of fidelity is designed to produce a harmonious working relationship and this may be the justification for a wider restraint as long as the employee remains in employment.[602]

The limitations on the permissible scope of a post-employment restrictive covenant with respect to confidential information put forward in *Faccenda Chicken* were considered "improbable as being the law" by Harman J. in *Systems Reliability Holdings v Smith*.[603] Although *Faccenda Chicken* is a judgment of the Court of Appeal, there is much to commend the judgment of Harman J. As a matter of public policy it is difficult to see why an employer should not be free by agreement to restrain the disclosure of confidential information. The principle in *Faccenda Chicken* will have a very limited scope if the definition of "trade secret" is extended to include information which might in "common parlance" not be considered trade secrets. Thus if the names of customers and the goods that they buy or other nontechnical information are classified as trade secrets,[604] 16–109

[597] *Faccenda Chicken Ltd v Fowler* [1987] Ch. 117.

[598] *Thomas v Farr Plc* [2007] EWCA Civ 18, [2007] I.R.L.R. 419 at [42].

[599] *Faccenda Chicken Ltd v Fowler* [1987] Ch. 117, 137; *Poly Lina Ltd v Finch* [1996] F.L.R. 75; *A.T. Poeton (Gloucester) Plating Ltd v Horton* [2001] I.C.R. 1208; *Dranez Anstalt v Hayek* [2002] 1 B.C.L.C. 693.

[600] [1987] Ch. 117.

[601] *Faccenda Chicken Ltd v Fowler* [1987] Ch. 117.

[602] *Mont v Mills* [1993] I.R.L.R. 172, 177 ("[o]nce the employment relationship ceases, there is no continuing occasion for loyalty" per Simon Brown L.J.).

[603] [1990] I.R.L.R. 377, 384. Harman J. considered that the dictum was obiter in that in *Faccenda Chicken* [1987] Ch. 117 the court was dealing with implied covenants. His own observation was also strictly obiter since he found that the restraint before him related to the sale of a business. See also *Balston Ltd v Headline Filters Ltd* [1987] F.S.R. 330, 347–348 (Scott J. had reservations about the judgment of Neill L.J. in the *Faccenda Chicken* case). See also *Lock International Plc v Beswick* [1989] 1 W.L.R. 1268; *Dranez Anstalt v Hayek* [2002] 1 B.C.L.C. 693. *Faccenda Chicken* was followed in *Roger Bullivant Ltd v Ellis* [1987] I.C.R. 464 and *Mammet Holdings Plc v Austin* [1991] F.S.R. 538.

[604] As two judges were willing to do in *Lansing Linde Ltd v Kerr* [1991] 1 W.L.R. 251, 260 (Staughton L.J.), 270 (Butler-Sloss L.J.). See also *TSB Bank Plc v Connell* (1997) S.L.T. 1254, 1260; *FSS Travel and Leisure Systems Ltd v Johnson* [1998] I.R.L.R. 382.

post-employment restraints could validly embrace a wide category of confidential information. A matter on which the law is undecided is whether an employer is entitled to protection where an employee is not seeking to earn his living but is "selling to a third party information which he acquired in confidence in the course of his former employment".[605] Given that the principal justification for the restraint of trade doctrine as applied to employment contracts is to enable an employee to earn his livelihood, there is much to be said for not permitting an employee to sell confidential information unconnected with the need for him to earn a living.

16–110 **Nature of connection with customers.** The validity of restrictive covenants by employees frequently depends upon the question whether their employment is of a confidential nature, so that, for example, the necessity of protecting the employer's trade connection has caused restrictive covenants by canvassers and travellers generally to be upheld.[606] Each case must be decided upon its own facts.[607] The courts have considered the reasonableness of restraints relating to solicitors and legal executives,[608] medical and dental practitioners,[609] actors,[610] commercial managers and agents,[611] canvassers and travellers,[612] shop assistants and salesmen,[613] bookmaker's assistants,[614] estate agents,[615] designers[616] and technicians.[617]

---

[605] *Faccenda Chicken Ltd v Fowler* [1987] Ch. 117, 139.

[606] Absence of control, by professional rules, over an unqualified employee may go to support the maintenance of a restraint: *Scorer v Seymour Jones* [1966] 1 W.L.R. 1419.

[607] What is acceptable for a senior manager may be held to be unenforceable against a more junior employee: see *Ginsberg v Parker* [1988] I.R.L.R. 483.

[608] *Whittaker v Howe* (1841) 3 Beav. 383; sed quaere; contrast *S. Nevanas Ltd v Walker and Foreman* [1914] 1 Ch. 413, 425; below, para.16–111; *Dendy v Henderson* (1855) 11 Ech. 194; *May v O'Neill* (1875) 44 L.J. Ch. 660; but see the *Nordenfelt* case [1894] A.C. 535, 563–564, 572–573; *Fitch v Dewes* [1921] 2 A.C. 158, 167 and the comments thereon in *S.W. Strange Ltd v Mann* [1965] 1 W.L.R. 629, 640.

[609] *Horner v Graves* (1831) 7 Bing. 735; *Mallan v May* (1843) 11 M. & W. 653; *Ballachulish Slate Quarries Co Ltd v Grant* (1903) 5 F. 1105; *Eastes v Russ* [1914] 1 Ch. 468 (pathologist); *Whitehill v Bradford* [1952] Ch. 236; *Macfarlane v Kent* [1965] 1 W.L.R. 1019; *Lyne-Pirkis v Jones* [1969] 1 W.L.R. 1293; *Peyton v Mindham* [1972] 1 W.L.R. 8.

[610] *Tivoli (Manchester) Ltd v Colley* (1904) 20 T.L.R. 437.

[611] *Lamson Pneumatic Tube Co v Phillips* (1904) 91 L.T. 363; *Millers Ltd v Steadman* (1915) 84 L.J.K.B. 2057; *S. Nevanas Ltd v Walker and Foreman* [1914] 1 Ch. 413.

[612] *Rousillon v Rousillon* (1880) 14 Ch D 351 (champagne trade); *Rogers v Maddocks* [1892] 3 Ch. 346 (malt liquors and, if required by his employer, aerated waters); *Underwood & Son v Barker* [1899] 1 Ch. 300 (hay and straw merchants); *Haynes v Dorman* [1899] 2 Ch. 13; *Barr v Craven* (1904) 89 L.T. 574 (insurance agency); *Continental Tyre Co v Heath* (1913) 29 T.L.R. 308; *Mason v Provident Clothing Co Ltd* [1913] A.C. 724.

[613] *S. Nevanas Ltd v Walker and Foreman* [1914] 1 Ch. 413; *Pearks Ltd v Cullen* (1912) 28 T.L.R. 371; cf. *Perls v Saalfeld* [1892] 2 Ch. 149; *Great Western and Metropolitan Dairies Ltd v Gibbs* (1918) 34 T.L.R. 344; *Whitmore v King* (1918) 87 L.J. Ch. 647; *Vincents of Reading v Fogden* (1932) 48 T.L.R. 613; *Attwood v Lamont* [1920] 3 K.B. 571; *Putsman v Taylor* [1927] 1 K.B. 741; *Home Counties Dairies Ltd v Skilton* [1970] 1 W.L.R. 526; *Lucas & Co Ltd v Mitchell* [1974] Ch. 129; *Spafax (1965) Ltd v Dommett* (1972) 116 S.J. 711; *Dairy Crest Ltd v Pigott* [1989] I.C.R. 92.

[614] *S.W. Strange Ltd v Mann* [1965] 1 W.L.R. 629.

[615] *Scorer v Seymour Jones* [1966] 1 W.L.R. 1419.

[616] *John Michael Design Plc v Cooke* [1987] 2 All E.R. 332.

[617] *Commercial Plastics Ltd v Vincent* [1965] 1 Q.B. 623.

Limits on scope of restraint. A covenant not to solicit[618] customers is valid even if it extends to people who, although customers at the beginning of the employee's employment, ceased to be so before its determination,[619] though not if it extends to those who become customers after the determination of the employment.[620] It is no objection to a covenant restraining dealings with customers of the employer that the identity of all the employer's customers may not be known to the covenantor, for the court would not grant an injunction against him or commit him for contempt for the breach of any injunction already granted if he could show that what he had done he had done inadvertently and would not be repeated.[621] Similarly a covenant ought not to be held invalid because hypothetical cases can be suggested when it might be unreasonable to apply it, if those circumstances were outside the contemplation of the parties to such an extent that they are to be excluded from its operation.[622] It is no objection to the enforcement of a non-solicitation covenant with respect to a particular customer that that customer has no intention of doing any further business with the employer: this is: 16–111

> "... the very class of case against which the covenant is designed to give protection ... the plaintiff does not need protection against customers who are faithful to him."[623]

Type of business in which employee was engaged. The employer is not entitled to protect by a restrictive covenant of any description any business except the business in which he employed the covenantor[624] (though a covenant which might appear unduly wide with regard to the business to be protected may, on its proper construction, be subject to an implied limitation as a result of which it is valid[625]). Thus a covenant by a tailor's assistant not to carry on any business within certain limits of space and time is therefore invalid, even though it would be valid were it confined to the business of a tailor.[626] So, too, a covenant by an employee of a company intended to protect not merely the business of that 16–112

---

[618] As to the meaning of solicitation see *Cullard v Taylor* (1887) 3 T.L.R. 698; cf. *Horton v Mead* [1913] 1 K.B. 154 and cases there cited in argument.

[619] *Plowman & Son Ltd v Ash* [1964] 1 W.L.R. 568; *Home Counties Dairies Ltd v Skilton* [1970] 1 W.L.R. 526.

[620] *Konski v Peet* [1915] 1 Ch. 530; *Express Dairy Co v Jackson* (1930) 99 L.J.K.B. 181; *Rayner v Pegler* (1964) 189 E.G. 967; *Gledhow Autoparts Ltd v Delaney* [1965] 1 W.L.R. 1366; *Business Seating (Renovations) Ltd v Broad* [1989] I.C.R. 79; *Austin Knight (UK) v Heinz* [1994] F.S.R. 52; *Anamark Plc v Sommerville* (1995) S.L.T. 749.

[621] *Gilford Motor Co v Horne* [1933] Ch. 935, 964; *Plowman & Son Ltd v Ash* [1964] 1 W.L.R. 568.

[622] *Clark v Electronic Applications (Commercial) Ltd* [1963] R.P.C. 234, 237; *Commercial Plastics Ltd v Vincent* [1965] 1 Q.B. 623, 644; above, para.16–104.

[623] *John Michael Design Plc v Cooke* [1987] 2 All E.R. 332, 334 (the unwillingness of the customer to deal with the employer is something that goes to damages).

[624] *Bromley v Smith* [1909] 2 K.B. 235; *Vandervell Products Ltd v McLeod* [1957] R.P.C. 185; *Rayner v Pegler* (1964) 189 E.G. 967; *Commercial Plastics Ltd v Vincent* [1965] 1 Q.B. 623, 640. On *Commercial Plastics Ltd v Vincent* see *Littlewoods Organisation Ltd v Harris* [1977] 1 W.L.R. 1472, 1480–1482, 1488–1489; above, para.16–104 fn.554.

[625] *Plowman & Son Ltd v Ash* [1964] 1 W.L.R. 568; *Home Counties Dairies Ltd v Skilton* [1970] 1 W.L.R. 526. See above, para.16–103.

[626] *Baker v Hedgecock* (1888) 39 Ch D 520; *Perls v Saalfeld* [1892] 2 Ch. 149; *Ehrman v Bartholomew* [1898] 1 Ch. 671; cf. *Mills v Dunham* [1891] 1 Ch. 576.

company but also the business of associated or subsidiary companies in which he does not serve is an unreasonable restraint.[627]

16–113 **Limits of space and time.** In considering whether or not a restraint is reasonable, limitations of space or time imposed upon it are usually of the greatest relevance.[628] The longer the duration of restriction and the greater the area over which it operates, the more difficult it is to prove that the restriction is reasonable.[629] Area restraints "will always be approached with caution by the courts since such restraints amount to a covenant against competition".[630] It has been said that:

> ". . . to preclude a former servant from carrying on his natural business in any part whatever of the United Kingdom is a very strong step and requires exceptional justification"[631];

a fortiori where the restraint is worldwide.[632] It has been held reasonable to impose a worldwide restraint on disclosing confidential information on an employee employed in the United Kingdom, the reasoning of the court being that business has become global and that national boundaries did not constrain the dissemination of confidential information.[633] On the other hand, covenants against solicitation, especially if taken from canvassers and travellers, are generally not invalidated by reason of the absence of any limit of space[634] or even, it would seem, of any limit of space or time.[635] But where the employer's business is exclusively for credit, the customer not dealing directly with an employee, it will often be difficult to establish the reasonableness of any area restriction since a mere covenant not to deal with customers on the books of the employer is likely to be sufficient.[636] In considering whether a particular restraint is reasonable in point of time the limit of space imposed shall be considered, and vice versa.[637] In reckoning a spatial limitation the distance will be measured on

---

[627] *Leetham & Sons Ltd v Johnstone-White* [1907] 1 Ch. 322; *Business Seating (Renovations) Ltd v Broad* [1989] I.C.R. 729. Contrast *Stenhouse Australia Ltd v Phillips* [1974] A.C. 391 where the employer's business was to some extent transacted for it by its subsidiaries as its agencies or instrumentalities and a covenant which protected the business so transacted for it was held to be reasonable.

[628] See above, para.16–092.

[629] *Herbert Morris Ltd v Saxelby* [1916] 1 A.C. 688, 715; *M. & S. Drapers v Reynolds* [1957] 1 W.L.R. 9; *Lucas & Co Ltd v Mitchell* [1974] Ch. 129; *Financial Collection Agencies (UK) Ltd v Batey* (1973) 117 S.J. 416; *Luck v Davenport-Smith* (1977) 242 E.G. 455.

[630] *Office Angels Ltd v Rainer-Thomas and O'Connor* [1991] I.R.L.R. 214, 221.

[631] *S. Nevanas Ltd v Walker and Foreman* [1914] 1 Ch. 413, 425; *Spencer v Marchington* [1988] I.R.L.R. 372. cf. *George Silverman v Silverman Ltd* (1969) 113 S.J. 563.

[632] See above, para.16–092 fn.485.

[633] *Scully (UK) Ltd v Lee* [1998] I.R.L.R. 259.

[634] *Plowman & Son Ltd v Ash* [1964] 1 W.L.R. 568, 572; *Home Counties Dairies Ltd v Skilton* [1970] 1 W.L.R. 526: cf. *Marley Tiles Ltd v Johnson, The Times*, October 16, 1981 (area restraint held to be unreasonable).

[635] *Dubowski v Goldstein* [1896] 1 Q.B. 478; *Mason v Provident Clothing Co* [1913] A.C. 724, 734, 741.

[636] *S.W. Strange Ltd v Mann* [1965] 1 W.L.R. 629; cf. *Macfarlane v Kent* [1965] 1 W.L.R. 1019, 1024; *Scorer v Seymour Jones* [1966] 1 W.L.R. 1419; *Lucas & Co Ltd v Mitchell* [1974] Ch. 129.

[637] *Fitch v Dewes* [1921] 2 A.C. 158, 163, 168.

the map (as the crow flies)[638] unless the parties have adopted some other measurement. The courts have recognised that because of the difficulties of recognising what is and what is not confidential, or who may or may not have been a customer of the employer, an anti-competition covenant which is reasonable as to space and time may be the "most satisfactory form of restraint".[639]

Breach. In considering whether a particular act constitutes a breach of such a restrictive covenant, it is important to note the exact terms in which the covenant is framed, and this is a question of construction. Thus, a covenant not to practise as a solicitor in a defined area is not broken by writing letters to persons resident in that area,[640] though a covenant not to do acts usually done by a solicitor is.[641] A covenant by a doctor not to practise within an area is broken by attendance on patients in that area, even though he does not solicit such patients,[642] but he does not "set up in practice," though he does "practise", by attending a few patients within the prohibited area at their own request, he having no residence or premises within the area[643]; a similar covenant by a house agent is broken by letting houses in the area, though his office is outside.[644] Nor was a covenant not to carry on business as an auctioneer and estate agent broken by the employee, after the employment had terminated, setting up in business as an "Estate Agent, A.A.I." (Associate of the Auctioneers' Institute). He held himself out as an estate agent only and the addition of "A.A.I." did not mean that he held himself out as an auctioneer.[645] An employee has been held to be concerned in[646] and engaged in the business which he serves[647] but not to carry it on or be concerned in carrying it on.[648] The creditor of a business is not concerned or interested in it.[649] An "interest" in a business means a precuniary or proprietary interest. A covenant by a man not to carry on or be in anywise interested in a business does not prevent the business being carried on by his wife as a separate trader and in which he takes no part,[650] but he will not be allowed to evade his covenant by the device of carrying on business under a title,[651] or by means of the formation of a limited company,[652] which is a mere cloak for his own activities. A covenant not to practise as a solicitor is not broken by acting as managing clerk to a solicitor, the test being whether in the work he does the relationship of solicitor and client is constituted between himself and the person for whom he acts.[653] 16–114

[638] *Mouflet v Cole* (1872) L.R. 8 Ex. 32. See *Atkyns v Kinnier* (1850) 4 Ex. 776 for a case where the parties adopted their own unit of measurement.
[639] *Turner v Commonwealth & British Minerals Ltd* [2000] I.R.L.R. 14, 117.
[640] *Woodbridge & Sons v Bellamy* [1911] 1 Ch. 326; *Freeman v Fox* (1911) 55 S.J. 650.
[641] *Edmundson v Render* [1905] 2 Ch. 320.
[642] *Rogers v Drury* (1887) 57 L.J. Ch. 504.
[643] *Robertson v Buchanan* (1904) 73 L.J. Ch. 408.
[644] *Hadsley v Dayer-Smith* [1914] A.C. 979.
[645] *Bowler v Lovegrove* [1921] 1 Ch. 642.
[646] *Hill & Co v Hill* (1886) 55 L.T. 769.
[647] *Pearks Ltd v Cullen* (1912) 28 T.L.R. 371.
[648] *Ramoneur & Co Ltd v Brixey* (1911) 104 L.T. 809.
[649] *Cory & Son v Harrison* [1906] A.C. 274.
[650] *Smith v Hancock* [1894] 2 Ch. 377; cf. *Scheckter v Kolbe*, 1955 (3) S.A. 109.
[651] *Smith v Hancock* [1894] 2 Ch. 377, cf. *Scheckter v Kolbe*, 1955 (3) S.A. 109.
[652] *Gilford Motor Co Ltd v Horne* [1933] Ch. 935.
[653] *Way v Bishop* [1928] Ch. 647.

Generally, however, to act as assistant to a professional man such as a surgeon[654] or an architect[655] amounts to carrying on that profession. Covenants often preclude an employee from "soliciting" the customers of his ex-employer. This prohibition obviously covers direct approaches and probably also extends to advertisements by the employee designed to bring his availability for business to the notice of the customers of his ex-employer.[656] This would be so even where the customers are a sub-group of a larger group of potential customers to whom the advertisement is directed.[657] There is, however, a distinction between soliciting and doing business, and an anti-solicitation clause would not preclude the employee from doing business with customers of his ex-employer who unprompted seek out his services.

The position of a subordinate in a commercial house is very different; and it has therefore been held that a salaried manager to a rag merchant does not carry on that business[658] nor is a salaried assistant to a jeweller interested either directly or indirectly in the jewellery business.[659] A manufacturer of margarine, who sells the margarine which he manufactures, does not carry on the business of provision merchant.[660] A covenant not to solicit the customers of a particular shop does not extend to the customers of the same business at a different shop.[661]

16–115 **Restraints during currency of employment.** It now appears probable that even restraints which operate only during the currency of employment are subject to the doctrine of restraint of trade, at any rate if they have as their objects the sterilising rather than the absorption of a man's capacity for work,[662] or perhaps are such that one of the parties is so unilaterally fettered that the contract loses its character of a contract for the regulation and promotion of trade and acquires the predominant character of a contract in restraint of trade.[663] It is also clear that a restraint of trade which applies when an employee is on garden leave is subject to the public policy in connection with restraints applying on termination.[664] When a contract ties the parties only during the continuance of the contract and

---

654 *Palmer v Mallet* (1887) 36 Ch D 411.

655 *Robertson v Willmott* (1909) 25 T.L.R. 681.

656 *Sweeney v Astle* [1923] N.Z.L.R. 1198, 1204–1205.

657 *Sweeney v Astle* [1923] N.Z.L.R. 1198.

658 *Allen v Taylor* (1871) 39 L.J. Ch. 627.

659 *Gophir Diamond Co v Wood* [1902] 1 Ch. 950; cf. *Scheckter v Kolbe* (1955) 3 S.A. 109.

660 *Lovell and Christmas Ltd v Wall* (1911) 104 L.T. 85; cf. *Automobile Carriage Builders Ltd v Sayers* (1909) 101 L.T. 419.

661 *Marshall & Murray Ltd v Jones* (1913) 29 T.L.R. 351.

662 *Esso Petroleum Co Ltd v Harper's Garage (Stourport) Ltd* [1968] A.C. 269, 328, 336; *Young v Timmins* (1831) 1 Cr. & J. 331. See also *Lido-Savoy Pty Ltd v Paredes* [1972] V.R. 297, distinguishing *Warner Bros Pictures Inc v Nelson* [1937] 1 K.B. 209. See also above, para.16–079.

663 *Esso Petroleum Co Ltd v Harper's Garage (Stourport) Ltd* [1968] A.C. 269, 328; *A. Schroeder Music Publishing Co Ltd v Macaulay* [1974] 1 W.L.R. 1308 and *Clifford Davies Ltd v W.E.A. Records Ltd* [1975] 1 W.L.R. 61; *Greig v Insole* [1978] 1 W.L.R 302, 325–327. In the light of these cases it is submitted that *Warner Bros Pictures Inc v Nelson* [1937] 1 K.B. 209, where onerous restrictions upon a film actress were considered not to be within the doctrine since they related to her period of employment, can no longer be relied upon.

664 *Symbian v Christensen* [2001] I.R.L.R. 77; *TFS Derivatives Ltd v Morgan* [2004] EWHC 3181 (QB), [2005] I.R.L.R. 246.

the negative ties are only those which are incidental and normal to the positive commercial arrangements at which the contract aims even though those ties exclude all dealings with others, there is probably no restraint of trade within the meaning of the doctrine and no question of reasonableness arises[665]; indeed in appropriate circumstances the courts will even imply a restraint, for example that employees, engaged in skilled work and having knowledge of their employers' manufacturing data, shall not in their spare time carry out similar work for competitors.[666]

(iii) *Vendor and Purchaser of Business*

Vendor and purchaser.[667] Restrictive covenants between vendor and purchaser are looked on with less disfavour by the court. "I think it is now generally conceded," said Lord Watson in *Nordenfelt v Maxim Nordenfelt Guns and Ammunition Co Ltd*[668]: 16–116

> " . . . that it is to the advantage of the public to allow a trader who has established a lucrative business to dispose of it to a successor by whom it may be efficiently carried on. That object could not be accomplished if, upon the score of public policy, the law reserved to the seller an absolute and indefeasible right to start a rival concern the day after he sold. Accordingly it has been determined judicially, that in cases where the purchaser, for his own protection, obtains an obligation restraining the seller from competing with him, within bounds which having regard to the nature of the business are reasonable and are limited in respect of space, the obligation is not obnoxious to public policy, and is therefore capable of being enforced."

In the vendor and purchaser situation the covenant is as important for the *vendor* as it is for the purchaser: if the vendor could not enter into a valid covenant in restraint of trade then he could not sell his goodwill as the purchaser would have no assurance that the vendor would not compete against him at some time in the future. In other words, an enforceable covenant is necessary to create a property right (a "vendible asset") in the vendor which he can sell.[669] Also, there may be a disparity of bargaining power between employers and employees which is not present in vendor and purchaser situations, although the extent to which this is presently the case in light of contemporary industrial relations practices is open to question. Deciding whether a covenant is taken to protect goodwill attached to the sale of a business is a matter of substance and not form. Thus where an employer allowed its retiring sales staff to capitalise the value of the contacts they had built up with customers and to be paid a lump sum for it on the cessation

---

[665] *Esso Petroleum Co Ltd v Harper's Garage (Stourport) Ltd* [1968] A.C. 269, 307, 328, 336, contrast at 317.

[666] *Hivac Ltd v Park Royal Instruments Ltd* [1946] Ch. 169.

[667] Also of relevance are the provisions of art.81 EC (on which see below, Vol.II, Ch.42); as a general proposition, a restrictive covenant which is ancillary to a legitimate transaction such as the sale of business with its associated goodwill and which is appropriately limited in subject-matter, geographical scope and time, would not normally infringe EC or domestic competition law: see *Remia and Nutricia v Commission* [1985] E.C.R. 2545.

[668] [1894] A.C. 535, 552.

[669] Blake (1960) 73 *Harvard Law Review* 625, at 646–648; *Attwood v Lamont* [1920] 3 K.B. 571; *Ronbar Enterprises Ltd v Green* [1954] 1 W.L.R. 815, 820–821.

of their employment, this was held to be the sale of goodwill (despite appearances to the contrary) and the restraint had to be evaluated accordingly.[670] The court went on to hold that a two-year anti-competition covenant was enforceable even though such a covenant in the employee-employer context would not have been valid.

16–117 The more benign attitude of the courts towards restraints in vendor and purchaser contracts is illustrated by *Nordenfelt* itself: in that case the court held that a covenant by a patentee and manufacturer of guns and ammunition with the purchasers of the goodwill of his business not to engage in the business of a manufacturer of guns and ammunition for 25 years was not too wide to be a valid restraint. The covenant must, however, have been taken in connection with a genuine sale of a business.[671] A naked covenant in restraint of trade is void.[672] Where the business sold was that of dealing in imitation jewellery in London, it was held that an agreement covering real jewellery and extending to a number of European countries was too wide.[673] Where the lease and goodwill of a hairdresser and tobacconist were sold, the vendor covenanting not to carry on such a business in a particular town during his life, the covenant was held to be unreasonable and void.[674] Where the sale of a goodwill is concerned, if the restriction as to space is considered to be reasonable, it is seldom that the restriction can be held to be unreasonable because there is no limit as to time.[675] The business sold is the only legitimate subject of protection; the purchaser cannot take a covenant protecting other businesses controlled by him.[676] Thus where a vendor sold business A, a gentlemen's hairdresser, he could not enforce against the purchaser a non-competition covenant protecting business B, a ladies' hairdressing business.[677] On the sale of a business with a covenant that the vendor:

> "... would not within ten years ... directly or indirectly carry on or assist in carrying on or be engaged, concerned, interested or employed in the business of a quarry within seventy-five miles of"

the quarry sold, it was held to be a breach of this covenant that the vendor had advanced money to his sons to start a similar business within the prohibited area

[670] *Allied Dunbar (Frank Weisinger) Ltd v Frank Weisinger* [1988] I.R.L.R. 60.

[671] The vendor of shares in a business may, in certain circumstances, be in the same position as the vendor of the business itself: *Connors Bros Ltd v Connors* [1940] 4 All E.R. 179; *Greening Industries Ltd v Penny* (1965) 53 D.L.R. (2d) 643; *Systems Reliability Holdings Plc v Smith* [1990] I.R.L.R. 377; above, para.16–109.

[672] *Vancouver Malt and Sake Brewing Co Ltd v Vancouver Breweries Ltd* [1934] A.C. 181, below, para.16–132. cf. above, para.16–095. As to agreements between co-operative societies delimiting their trading areas, see *Bellshill and Mossend Co-operative Society Ltd v Dalziel Co-operative Society Ltd* [1960] A.C. 832, especially 842; cf. *Re Doncaster Co-operative Society Ltd's and Retford Co-operative Society Ltd's Agreement* [1960] 1 W.L.R. 1186.

[673] *Goldsoll v Goldman* [1915] 1 Ch. 292. A covenant limited to the sale of imitation jewellery in the United Kingdom and Isle of Man was held to be severable and valid. See above, para.16–095; below, paras 16–194 et seq.

[674] *Pellow v Ivy* (1933) 49 T.L.R. 422.

[675] *Connors Bros Ltd v Connors* [1940] 4 All E.R. 179, 195.

[676] *British Reinforced Concrete Engineering Co Ltd v Schelff* [1921] 2 Ch. 563; *Vancouver Malt and Sake Brewing Co Ltd v Vancouver Breweries Ltd* [1934] A.C. 181.

[677] *Giblin v Murdoch* (1979) S.L.T. 5.

and had given them advice as to how to manage the new business.[678] On the sale of a company, its directors may agree not to compete with the purchaser. Such an agreement may be subject to competition legislation: see Vol.II, Ch.42.

Sale of goodwill without express restraint. Where the goodwill of a business is sold, there being no express agreement as to the vendor's refraining from future competition, the vendor may set up a rival business, but he is not entitled to canvass the customers of the old firm, and may be restrained by injunction from soliciting any person who was a customer of the old firm prior to the sale to continue to deal with the vendor, or not to deal with the purchaser.[679] The ground of this may be either that a man may not derogate from his own grant, or that the vendor had impliedly contracted not to solicit his former customers, or that it would be fraudulent to do so. "It is not right", observed Lord Macnaghten: 16–118

> "... to profess to purport to sell that which you do not mean the purchaser to have; it is not an honest thing to pocket the price and then to recapture the subject of sale, to decoy it away or call it back before the purchaser has had time to attach it to himself and make it his very own."[680]

For the same reason the vendor of a business may not represent that he is carrying on business in continuance of, or in succession to, the business carried on by his former firm.[681] The principle of *Trego v Hunt*[682] extends to the executors of a vendor who are executing a contract for the sale of the goodwill. No such covenant can be implied, however, on the part of a bankrupt where the business is sold by the trustee in bankruptcy, because the alienation is compulsory[683]; this is the case even though the bankrupt agreed to aid in realising the business.[684] A purchaser of a business and goodwill of a bankrupt has therefore no right to restrain the bankrupt from setting up a fresh business or from soliciting customers of the old business, and this even though the bankrupt has joined in the conveyance to the purchaser. This rule applies also to the sale of a debtor's business by a trustee of a deed of arrangement for creditors. This is also regarded as a compulsory alienation.[685]

(iv) *Partners*

Covenants on dissolution of partnership. Upon similar principles, including that of *Trego v Hunt* just referred to, restrictive covenants which operate upon the 16–119

---

678 *Batts Combe Quarry Ltd v Ford* [1943] Ch. 51.

679 *Trego v Hunt* [1896] A.C. 7, approving *Labouchere v Dawson* (1872) L.R. 13 Eq. 322. See also *Jennings v Jennings* [1898] 1 Ch. 378. Even if goodwill is not expressly mentioned, its sale is implied on the sale of a business: *Shipwright v Clements* (1871) 19 W.R. 599.

680 *Trego v Hunt* [1896] A.C. 7, 25.

681 *Churton v Douglas* (1859) Johns. 174.

682 [1896] A.C. 7. See Muir Hunter, *Personal Insolvency*, para.3–116.

683 *Cruttwell v Lye* (1810) 17 Ves. 335; *Walker v Mottram* (1881) 19 Ch D 355. This is because, unlike the situation where there is a voluntary alienation, there is no personal covenant when the alienation is compulsory.

684 *Farey v Cooper* [1927] 2 K.B. 384.

685 *Green & Sons (Northampton) Ltd v Morris* [1914] 1 Ch. 562; followed in *Farey v Cooper* [1927] 2 K.B. 384, 398 per Atkin L.J.

dissolution of a partnership are valid,[686] if they impose no wider restraint than the circumstances reasonably require.[687] In *Bridge v Deacons*[688] it was considered inappropriate to attempt to categorise covenants in partnership agreements as either falling within the vendor-purchaser or employer-employee categories; the court in such cases simply had to determine whether the covenant was no more than was necessary to protect the interests of the covenantee. A fortiori, such restrictive covenants are generally valid during the continuance of the partnership[689]; thus, an agreement by one of the proprietors of a theatre not to write plays for any other theatre is good.[690] In the absence of any express covenant an ex-partner (who has been paid the value of his share including his interest in the goodwill) on dissolution of the partnership may carry on a similar and competing business in his own name and may deal with customers of his former firm and he may advertise himself as having been connected with the business sold.[691] He may not directly or indirectly canvass them or persuade them to deal with himself and not with the old firm,[692] nor may he carry on his business in the name of the old firm or represent his business as still being that of the old firm.[693]

16–120 **Analogous agreements.** It is well established that the categories involving the restraint of trade doctrine are neither rigid not exclusive.[694] The traditional categories for applying the restraint of trade principles are vendor and purchaser and employment contracts. This obviously is a small sub-set of commercial relationships. In *Kall-Kwik (UK) Ltd v Frank Clarence Rush*[695] the court had to deal with the application of the restraint of trade doctrine to a franchise agreement whereby on the termination of the franchise, the franchisee was restrained

---

[686] As to consideration, see *Leighton v Wales* (1838) 3 M. & W. 545. See generally *Lindley & Banks on Partnership*, 18th edn (2002), paras 10–177 et seq. Restrictive covenants in partnership agreements are also subject to art.81 of the EC Treaty: see *Lindley & Banks on Partners*, 18th edn (2002), paras 10–236 et seq.

[687] See *Whitehill v Bradford* [1952] Ch. 236; the National Health Service Act 1977 (as amended) has not altered the position with regard to medical partnerships; *Kerr v Morris* [1987] Ch. 90. See also *Macfarlane v Kent* [1965] 1 W.L.R. 1019; *Ronbar Enterprises v Green* [1954] 1 W.L.R. 815; *Lyne-Pirkis v Jones* [1969] 1 W.L.R. 1293; *Peyton v Mindham* [1972] 1 W.L.R. 8. See also *Nella v Nella, Independent*, November 1, 1999, as to the meaning of "carry on business" in a restraint of trade covenant in a partnership agreement which the court held required some form of continuous trading activity and not merely preparatory steps.

[688] [1984] A.C. 705 PC. The court also held that a covenant otherwise reasonable was not against public policy because it prohibited a solicitor from soliciting clients of the firm: see also *Oswald Hickson Collier & Co v Carter-Ruck* [1984] A.C. 720; *Edwards v Worboys* [1984] A.C. 724. cf. *Geraghty v Minter* (1979–80) 142 C.L.R. 177; *Thurston Hoskin & Partners v Jewell Hill & Bennett* [2002] EWCA Civ 249.

[689] See above, para.16–135.

[690] *Morris v Colman* (1812) 18 Ves. 437.

[691] *Lindley & Banks on Partnership*, 18th edn (2002), pp.323–336.

[692] *Churton v Douglas* (1859) Johns. 174; *Macfarlane v Kent* [1965] 1 W.L.R. 1019.

[693] *Labouchere v Dawson* (1872) L.R. 13 Eq. 322; *Trego v Hunt* [1896] A.C. 7; cf. *Curl Bros Ltd v Webster* [1904] 1 Ch. 685. The executors of a deceased partner will be restrained from soliciting the customers of the old firm: *Boorne v Wicker* [1927] 1 Ch. 667.

[694] *Dawnay Day & Co v D'Alphen* [1997] T.L.R. 334 (a joint venturer had a sufficient interest to enforce an anti-competition covenant).

[695] [1996] F.S.R. 114.

from competing with the franchisor. The court held that such a restraint was more akin to a restraint in a vendor and purchaser situation. The franchisee had an obligation to transfer the "goodwill" attached to the franchise at the end of the franchise period and this was analogous to the situation where the vendor of property enters into a restraint in order to protect any goodwill transferred to the purchaser. Where a majority shareholder sells his shares and enters into a contract of service with the company which contains a covenant in restraint of trade, this could also be categorised as a vendor and purchaser covenant and not one relating to employment.[696] In *Convenience Co Ltd v Roberts*[697] the court held that the principles applicable to a franchise agreement were not identical to those applied to employee and employer or vendor and purchaser and cited with approval the dictum of Neuberger J. in *Dymond Plc v Reeve*[698] that a franchise agreement is closer to the vendor and purchaser agreement. Such a covenant can be seen as being necessary to protect the goodwill of the business.[699] In *Buchanan v Alba Diagnostics Ltd*[700] Lord Hoffmann upheld as valid a perpetual restraint in the assignment of a patent entitling the assignee to the rights of any improvement in the patent. He considered that it was in the public interest for inventors to be able to borrow money on the security of future rights,[701] and a clear implication of his reasoning is that the agreement was treated as being analogous to the sale of the goodwill of a business.

(v) *Supply and Acquisition of Goods: Restraints in Vertical Agreements*

Application of doctrine. The treatment of restraints in vertical agreements dealt with in this part (i.e. paras 16–121—16–131) will concentrate on English common law. However, this is an area in which EC law and UK competition law are of equal if not greater importance and this body of law must also be considered when dealing with these types of restraint.[702] Agreements between a supplier of goods[703] and one to whom he supplies them may be described as "vertical" agreements. Such agreements can usefully be treated separately from agreements between suppliers inter se and acquirers inter se, which may be termed "horizontal" agreements. Although the doctrine of restraint of trade is capable of applying to vertical agreements, they are, for various reasons, less 16–121

---

[696] *Alliance Paper Group Plc v Prestwich* [1996] I.R.L.R. 25. A term in a shareholders' agreement that the parties to it will not disclose confidential information is enforceable: see *Giles v Rhind* Unreported February 9, 2000.

[697] [2001] F.S.R. 625.

[698] [1999] F.S.R. 148, 153.

[699] *TSC Europe Ltd v Massey* [1999] I.R.L.R. 22 (however, the restraint in this case, an anti-solicitation covenant, was held to be unreasonable in that it applied to all employees no matter how junior, and to employees who joined the company after the covenantor had ceased his employment).

[700] [2004] UKHL 5, (2004) S.C. (H.L.) 9.

[701] *Buchanan v Alba Diagnostics Ltd* (2004) S.C. (H.L.) 9 at [29].

[702] See Vol.II, para.42–077. The court held in *Days Medical Aids Ltd v Pihsiang Machinery Co Ltd* [2004] EWHC 44 (Comm) that an agreement not invalidated by art.81 of the EC Treaty could not be subject to the common law restraint of trade doctrine.

[703] As to certain special rules relating to patented articles, see below, para.16–130.

likely to be rendered unenforceable by the doctrine than are horizontal agreements. A further distinction[704] as perhaps to be drawn between:

(a) restrictions which relate exclusively to the goods supplied under vertical agreements, e.g. that the goods shall not be resold for more or less than a certain price or to certain persons or classes of person or outside a certain area, and

(b) restrictions which relate to goods other than those supplied under the agreement, e.g. absolutely or conditionally that the seller shall not supply similar goods to others or that the buyer shall not acquire similar goods from others.

Agreements which contain restrictions relating only to the goods supplied thereunder may well fall outside the scope of the common law doctrine of restraint of trade since before making the agreement the person acquiring the goods had no right to deal with them at all and in making the agreement he therefore gave up no right but, rather, acquired a limited right.[705] The doctrine is certainly capable of applying to agreements which contain restrictions relating to goods other than those supplied under the agreement,[706] though it would seem that unless the agreement contains special, oppressive features, the doctrine will not be applied where the inclusion of such a restriction in such a transaction has gained general commercial acceptance[707] as perhaps, for example, where a wholesaler agrees to purchase his requirements of a particular class of goods exclusively from a manufacturer.[708]

---

[704] EC Treaty art.81(1) prohibits anti-competitive agreements, including vertical agreements, unless they satisfy the criteria set out in art.81(3). Regulation 2790/99 on categories of vertical agreements OJ [1999] L 336/21 grants block exemption to vertical agreements provided that a market share cap of 30% is not exceeded and omits certain "hardcore" restrictions. The Commission has published Guidelines on its approach to vertical agreements and this Regulation (OJ [2000] C291/1). The Competition Act 1998 entered into force on March 1, 2000. It contains the Ch.I and II prohibitions which are closely modelled on arts 81 and 82 EC. Vertical agreements, except for those fixing resale prices, are currently excluded from the Ch.I, but not Ch.II, prohibition (SI 2000/310). The Government has proposed to repeal this exclusion (*A World Class Competition Regime*, COM(2001) 5233, paras 8.14–8.16). In any event, vertical agreements would benefit from a parallel exemption by virtue of s.10 of the Competition Act together with block exemption Regulation 2790/99. Many vertical agreements will have anti-competitive effect entered into by suppliers with power over the market may have appreciable anti-competitive effect and thus caught by art.81(1): see Vol.II, para.42–096.

[705] cf. *Esso Petroleum Co Ltd v Harper's Garage (Stourport) Ltd* [1968] A.C. 269 (below, para.16–129), where such reasoning is applied in the case of restrictions relating to the use of land; and see *Elliman, Sons & Co v Carrington & Son Ltd* [1901] 2 Ch. 275; but contrast *British Motor Trade Association v Gilbert* [1951] 2 All E.R. 641, where however the plaintiffs had not supplied the goods.

[706] See *Palmolive Co (of England) Ltd v Freedman* [1928] 2 Ch. 264.

[707] Above, para.16–079.

[708] *Esso Petroleum Co Ltd v Harper's Garage (Stourport) Ltd* [1968] A.C. 269, 328, 336, 963; cf. *Petrofina (Great Britain) Ltd v Martin* [1966] 1 Ch. 146, 184–185. See also *A. Schroeder Music Publishing Co Ltd v Macaulay* [1974] 1 W.L.R. 1308 and *Clifford Davis Ltd v W.E.A. Records Ltd* [1975] 1 W.L.R. 61.

Exclusive purchasing[709]: solus petrol agreements. An important application of the doctrine has been to solus petrol agreements, i.e. agreements between petrol companies and the operators of petrol filling stations under which the latter are bound to acquire all their requirements of petrol, whether for resale at a particular station[710] or generally, from the petrol company. So in *Esso Petroleum Co Ltd v Harper's Garage (Stourport) Ltd*[711] the defendants had undertaken to purchase from the plaintiffs for the following four years and five months the plaintiffs' petrol at wholesale schedule prices for all the requirements of a station which the defendants operated and, if they sold the station during that time, to procure the buyer to enter into a similar solus agreement with the plaintiffs; the defendants had further undertaken to keep the garage open at all reasonable hours. The evidence relating to the reasonableness or otherwise of the length of the tie was meagre but in the circumstances, and influenced perhaps by the report of the Monopolies Commission on the Supply of Petrol to Retailers in the UK,[712] the House of Lords held that the tie, being for less than five years, was reasonable and that the agreement should therefore be upheld. But in the same case the House of Lords held unenforceable restrictions of a similar nature contained in a mortgage relating to another station of the defendants, since the restrictions were for 21 years. This further illustrates that where a covenant in restraint of trade, which would be invalid if contained in a simple contract, is incorporated in a mortgage,[713] it does not thereby become enforceable, unless, as it was in the *Esso* case, the covenant is no more than reasonable to protect the mortgagee's interest in the value of the land as security for his loan.[714] 16–122

Reasonableness in circumstances. In determining whether a solus agreement is enforceable or not, no simple rule can be applied since the court will have regard to all the terms of the agreement and the surrounding circumstances.[715] 16–123

---

709 As to cases decided before 1967 relating to exclusive purchasing, see generally the cases referred to in *Esso Petroleum Co Ltd v Harper's Garage (Stourport) Ltd* [1968] A.C. 269. It is important to note that all exclusive purchasing agreements will be affected by the EC Treaty, in particular art.81. See also the block exemption regulation which deals with solus petrol agreements: Commission Regulation 1984/83. Those exclusive purchasing agreements which appreciably restrict competition and affect inter Member States trade may be subject to art.81(1) of the EC Treaty, though they may be eligible block exemption conferred by Regulation 2790/99. See Vol.II, paras 42–033—42–034.

710 As to where the station was owned by the petrol company when the agreement was made, see below, para.16–129. art.5(a) of the Regulation 2790/99 (block exemption) exempts non-compete obligations in agreements for the lease of a petrol station and the supply of petrol for the duration of the agreement (as opposed to the normal five-year rule, see Vol.II, para.42–046).

711 [1968] A.C. 269, and see (1966) 82 L.Q.R. 307: (1966) 29 M.L.R. 541; [1967] Camb.L.J. 104; *Texaco Ltd v Mulberry Filling Station Ltd* [1972] 1 W.L.R. 814; *Amoco Australia Pty Ltd v Rocca Bros Co Engineering Pty Ltd* [1975] A.C. 561; *Cleveland Petroleum Ltd v Darstone Ltd* [1969] 1 W.L.R. 116; *Esso Petroleum Ltd v Niad Ltd* [2001] All E.R. (D) 324, (the court granted recovery of profits rather than damages for breach by the promisor of a solus type agreement). See also *Experience Hendrix LLC v PPX Enterprises Inc* [2003] EWCA Civ 323, [2003] 1 All E.R. (Comm) 801, at [30]–[32].

712 House of Commons Paper 1965 No.264; see below, para.16–123.

713 Restraints contained in mortgages may also be enforceable after redemption as invalid clogs on the equity of redemption: see Megarry and Wade, *The Law of Real Property*, 7th edn (2007), p.17.

714 [1968] A.C. 269 and see [1967] 2 Q.B. 514, 555, 578.

715 cf. below, para.16–126, and above, para.16–095.

The importance of evaluating the restraint in the light of all the surrounding circumstances is illustrated by *Alec Lobb (Garages) Ltd v Total Oil (Great Britain) Ltd*[716] in which the Court of Appeal upheld as reasonable a tie for 21 years. Previous to this it had been thought that, as a result of the *Esso* decision, a tie for longer than five years would not be valid unless perhaps the petrol company produced evidence of economic necessity justifying a longer period, something which the petrol company failed to do in *Alec Lobb*. In that case the plaintiff garage company, which was in financial difficulties, renegotiated its solus agreement with the defendant, its petrol supplier. The outcome was a lease and lease-back arrangement whereby the plaintiff company for a premium of £35,000 leased its garage to the defendant for 51 years at a peppercorn rent and the defendant leased it back for 21 years to the principal shareholders in the plaintiff company. The plaintiff company sought to have the lease set aside on a number of grounds, one of which was that the tie constituted an unreasonable restraint of trade. Despite the fact that the defendant produced no evidence of economic necessity, the Court of Appeal upheld the validity of the restraint. Dillon L.J. found that the company had as a matter of substance received £35,000 for the tie, something which was undoubtedly beneficial. In addition there were a number of other factors which rendered the tie unobjectionable:

(a) for planning reasons the site could only be used as a garage and it made little difference to the public whether the petrol sold on it came from the defendant or some other company;

(b) the plaintiff company could terminate the tie after seven years under a break clause;

(c) the premises had been subject to a tie for four years before the 21-year tie had been entered into.

Dunn and Waller L.JJ. were also influenced by the fact that to uphold the validity of the tie would encourage the rescue of firms on the verge of bankruptcy. The implication of this is that the more perilous a firm's financial condition, the longer the tie that can be extracted as a price of rescue. Where a tie is unreasonable, the remainder of the agreement may also be unenforceable if the deletion of the tie would alter the nature of the agreement.[717]

16–124 **Solus petrol agreements.** Apart from the common law, all solus petrol agreements in the United Kingdom were substantially affected by the undertakings given by the petrol companies to the Secretary of State. However, the Secretary of State accepted the release of the undertakings in 2000.[718] There is the possibility of such agreements being subject to a market investigation reference by the Office of Fair Trading to the Competition Commission under Pt 4 of the Enterprise Act 2002, in particular, where competition is restricted due to a network of vertical agreements.[719] Exclusive purchasing and supply obligations

---

[716] [1985] 1 W.L.R. 173 (noted (1985) 101 L.Q.R. 306).
[717] *Crehan v Courage Ltd (No.1)* [1999] Eu. L.R. 834.
[718] DTI Press Release P/2000/864.
[719] Vol.II, paras 42–133—42–134.

may infringe art.81(1) where they appreciably restrict competition and have an appreciable impact on trade between Member States.[720] The undertakings relate not only to the enforcement and determination of existing solus ties and the inclusion of solus ties in new agreements, but also to other terms of agreements between petrol companies and operators of petrol filling stations, including ties relating to lubricants and other goods sold by such stations, the making of certain commission and other arrangements, options and rights of pre-emption over petrol filling stations and the terms of leases and licences of company-owned filling stations. An exclusive supply obligation will usually fall within the prohibition in art.81(1) EC but may benefit from the block exemption for such agreements set out in EC Regulation 1984/83.

Tied public-houses.[721] Another and much older class of exclusive purchasing agreements comprises agreements under which breweries lease or sell public-houses on the terms that the publican shall buy his beer exclusively from the brewery.[722] Such agreements have long been enforced at common law[723] and would seem still to lie outside the common law doctrine of restraint of trade, either because of the general commercial acceptance which they have long enjoyed[724] or because the publican accepts the restrictions under the very agreement by which he acquires his interest in the public-house.[725] 16–125

Implied obligations and limits to rights of supplier. In considering whether an exclusive purchasing agreement is of a class which has gained general commercial acceptance and therefore falls outside the common law doctrine of restraint of trade,[726] or whether the agreement, though within the doctrine, is reasonable, it is probably relevant to consider the implied obligations of the supplier. Thus a covenant by a lessee of a public-house to take beer only from a particular brewery is subject to an implied condition that good and wholesome beer shall be supplied.[727] It has been said that this rule applies even though there is no specific agreement by the brewer to supply the publican with beer, apparently on the ground that the existence of the tying covenant amounts to an 16–126

---

[720] Where these conditions are satisfied the agreements may benefit from block exemption under Regulation 2790/99.

[721] See Vol.II, paras 42–033 et seq.

[722] Monopolies Commission, *Report on the Supply of Beer*, 1989, Cm.651; Supply of Beer (Tied Estate) Order 1989 (SI 1989/2390); Supply of Beer (Loan Ties, Licensed Premises and Wholesale Prices) Order 1989 (SI 1989/2258); Supply of Beer (Tied Estate) (Amendment) Order 1997 (SI 1997/1740); these ties will be governed by EC law and subject to the block exemptions referred to fn.721, above. The EC Commission's proposals for reform of competition policy towards disribution agreements do not include the retention of sector-specific rules for the beer sector: see the EC Commission "Communication on the application of the EC competition rules to vertical restraints" of September 30, 1998, s.V(3).

[723] *Hartley v Pehall* (1827) 1 Peake 178; *Catt v Tourle* (1869) L.R. 4 Ch. App. 654; *Clegg v Hands* (1890) 44 Ch D 503; *Esso Petroleum Co Ltd v Harper's Garage (Stourport) Ltd* [1968] A.C. 269 especially 333, 334. See also *Cutsforth v Mansfield Inns Ltd* [1986] 1 W.L.R. 536. But see below, para.16–125.

[724] See above, para.16–083; and see *Esso Petroleum Co Ltd v Harper's Garage (Stourport) Ltd* [1968] A.C. 269.

[725] As to covenants contained in conveyances and leases generally, see below, para.16–129.

[726] *Thornton v Sherratt* (1818) 8 Taunt. 529.

[727] *Courage & Co v Carpenter* [1910] 1 Ch. 262.

implied guarantee by the covenantee that he will at times supply liquor of good quality at reasonable prices in requisite quantities. An injunction against the publican will be granted only for so long a time as the brewers are prepared to supply him with beers of a reasonable quality at a reasonable price.[728]

16–127 **Exclusive selling agreements and co-operative marketing schemes.**[729] Subject to the consideration that it may be more onerous to require a buyer to take his whole supply from one source than to require a seller to sell his whole output to one buyer,[730] exclusive selling agreements are, it would seem, to be treated in the same way as exclusive buying agreements.[731] Thus an obligation imposed on a farmer to sell all his milk to an agricultural co-operative, with no power on the part of the farmer to terminate his obligation, has been held in restraint of trade and unreasonable[732] because in the circumstances it was an unusual and excessive fetter on the farmer's personal liberty.[733] Where such an obligation was imposed under a marketing scheme which had been accepted by the great majority of producers and contained no unusual features it was, in the circumstances, held to be reasonable and enforceable.[734]

(vi) *Restraints on the Use of Land or Chattels*

16–128 **Restraint affecting commercial use of land.** Where a restraint affecting the commercial use of land is accepted by one who enjoyed his interest in the land before the making of the arrangement under which the restraint was imposed, it is clearly established that the doctrine of restraint of trade applies to the same extent as it otherwise would.[735]

16–129 **Restraint contained in conveyance or lease.** There is authority for the proposition that where a restraint on the use of a particular piece of land, e.g. that the land shall not be used for the purposes of trade generally or of particular trades or that all the goods of some kind sold from the land shall be bought from a specified source, is imposed in a conveyance or lease of the land in question, the common law doctrine of restraint of trade does not apply. The purchaser or lessee of the land, before he made the agreement, had no right to use the land at all and in making the agreement he therefore gave up no right but, rather,

---

[728] *Catt v Tourle* (1869) L.R. 4 Ch. App. 654.

[729] See Vol.II, para.42–039.

[730] *Esso Petroleum Co Ltd v Harper's Garage (Stourport) Ltd* [1968] A.C. 269, per Lord Reid at 298.

[731] See above, paras 16–122—16–125.

[732] *McEllistrim v Ballymacelligott Co-operative Society Ltd* [1919] A.C. 548; *Joseph Evans & Co Ltd v Heathcote* [1918] 1 K.B. 418, where, however, since the association was a "trade union", the agreement fell within the Trade Union Acts 1871 and 1876 and was therefore sufficient to support an account stated, on which the plaintiffs were able to recover.

[733] See *Esso Petroleum Co Ltd v Harper's Garage (Stourport) Ltd* [1968] A.C. 269.

[734] *English Hop Growers Ltd v Dering* [1928] 2 K.B. 174; *Esso Petroleum Co Ltd v Harper's Garage (Stourport) Ltd* [1968] A.C. 269.

[735] *Esso Petroleum Co Ltd v Harper's Garage (Stourport) Ltd* [1968] A.C. 269. Such agreements may also be subject to the Competition Act 1998 and art.81.

acquired a limited right.[736] This reasoning is not, however, free from difficulty, as has been pointed out in para.16–079 *et seq.*, above.

Restraint on use of chattels. On similar reasoning, restraints on the use of a chattel which are imposed upon a party by the contract under which he acquires the chattel may well fall outside the common law doctrine of restraint of trade.[737] Where the restraint relates to chattels not acquired under the contract which imposes the restraint, the doctrine ought in principle to apply. And while in *United Shoe Machinery Co of Canada v Bruner*[738] the Privy Council upheld a condition in a demise of machines that no other machines of a like kind should be used by the lessee during the continuance of the contract, the reasons given for the decision are unsatisfactory.[739] 16–130

Patented articles and patent licences. Section 44 of the Patents Act 1977 contained provisions designed to prevent the owner of a patent or an interest in a patent using his patent to extend his patent monopoly beyond the terms of the patent, e.g. by requiring purchasers of the patented goods to acquire only from him or his nominees other goods or by prohibiting licensees of the patent from using articles, whether patented or not, which are not supplied by him or his nominees. Section 44 was repealed by s.70 of the Competition Act 1998. The practices proscribed by s.44, and other terms in licences of intellectual property rights might be caught by art.81(1) of the EC Treaty or the Ch.I prohibition in the Competition Act.[740] However, many such licences enjoy block exemption by virtue of Regulation 240/96 and would benefit from a so-called "parallel exemption" under domestic law.[741] 16–131

(vii) *Supply and Acquisition of Goods: Restraints in Horizontal Agreements*

Horizontal agreements classified. The treatment of restraints in horizontal agreements dealt with in this part (i.e. paras 16–132—16–135) will concentrate on English common law. However, this is an area in which EC law and United Kingdom competition law are of equal if not greater importance and this body of law must also be considered when dealing with these types of restraint.[742] The two most common classes of restrictive agreements between producers or suppliers of goods inter se are those between vendor and purchaser of a business under which the vendor accepts restrictions for the protection of the goodwill sold and agreements whereby two or more producers or suppliers accept restrictions as to 16–132

[736] *Esso Petroleum Co Ltd v Harper's Garage (Stourport) Ltd* [1968] A.C. 269, 298, 308, 309, 325; cf. 316, 334–335. See also *Cleveland Petroleum Co Ltd v Dartstone Ltd* [1969] 1 W.L.R. 116; *Robinson v Golden Chips (Wholesale) Ltd* [1971] N.Z.L.R. 257; *Amoco Australia Pty Ltd v Rocca Bros Motor Engineering Pty Ltd* [1975] A.C. 561; *Stephens v Gulf Oil Canada Ltd* (1976) 110 D.L.R. (2d) 229.

[737] See above, para.16–121.

[738] [1909] A.C. 330. This type of arrangement would now be subject to arts 81 and 82 EC and in the light of the size of the fines exigible for breach of these articles, the common law has a very limited role to play in this area.

[739] *Esso Petroleum Co Ltd v Harper's Garage (Stourport) Ltd* [1968] A.C. 269, 297.

[740] See Vol.II, Ch.42.

[741] See Vol.II, para.42–117.

[742] See Vol.II, paras 42–016, 42–081 et seq.

the prices at which or terms on which they will sell, or as to the quantities or descriptions of goods they will produce or sell or as to the persons to whom or areas in which they will sell.[743] Agreements between vendors and purchasers have already been discussed[744]; where the restraint is reasonably required for the protection of the goodwill sold, the restrictive covenant is usually enforceable, otherwise not. Thus where, on "the sale of the goodwill of a licence" to make beer, which in fact the seller had never made, the seller undertook not to make beer for 15 years thereafter, the undertaking was held unenforceable as a bare covenant against competition.[745]

16–133 **Employer's Association.** Section 128 of the Trade Union and Labour Relations (Consolidation) Act 1992 provides that the purpose of an unincorporated employers' association and, in so far as they relate to the regulation of relations between employers and workers or trade unions, the purposes of an employers' association which is a body corporate, shall not, by reason only that they are in restraint of trade, be unlawful so as, inter alia, to make any agreement or trust void or voidable. This provision replaces earlier ones[746] and makes clear that such an association is not illegal as it might otherwise be at common law. The expression "employers' association" is defined by s.122 of the 1992 Act to include any organisation (whether permanent or temporary) which consists wholly or mainly of employers or individual proprietors of one or more descriptions and is an organisation whose principal purposes include the regulation of relations between employers of that description or those descriptions and workers or trade unions.[747] The principal purposes of such an organisation may also include cartel purposes but, if they do so, then, applying the reasoning adopted in *Faramus v Film Artistes Association*,[748] it would seem that s.128 of the 1992 Act legalises only such agreements as are relevant or directed to the purposes of the organisation by virtue of which the organisation is an employers' association and not agreements which are relevant or directed only to other of the organisation's purposes. The point, however, is academic since *cartel* agreements fixing prices and quantities are never illegal at common law and therefore do not require statutory legitimation. But where "legalised" either under s.128 of the 1992 Act or at common law, such agreements are not thereby rendered enforceable in the courts and are enforceable, if at all, only if they would be at common law. However, s.128 of the 1992 Act further provides that no rule of an unincorporated employers' association nor, in so far as it relates to the regulation of

[743] There are many horizontal agreements where the anti-competitive effect of the restrictions is outweighed by its beneficial effects on technical progress or improved distribution, for example, agreements providing for co-operation on research and development.

[744] Above, paras 16–115—16–117.

[745] *Vancouver Malt and Sake Brewing Co v Vancouver Breweries* [1934] A.C. 181. As to co-operative marketing schemes see above, para.16–127.

[746] See the Trade Union Acts 1871 to 1906, particularly ss.3 and 4 of the Trade Union Act 1871, repealed and replaced by the Industrial Relations Act 1971, particularly ss.35 and 61; Trade Union and Labour Relations Act 1974 s.3(5).

[747] See *Greig v Insole* [1978] 1 W.L.R. 302, 356–362.

[748] [1964] A.C. 925.

relations between employers and workers or trade unions, any rule of an employers' association which is a body corporate, shall be unlawful or *unenforceable* by reason only that it is in restraint of trade. It would seem therefore that *none* of the *rules* of an *unincorporated* cartel is affected by the doctrine of restraint of trade, provided that the principal purposes of the cartel include the regulation of labour relations.[749]

Price-fixing agreements. Agreements between suppliers of goods as to the price at which they will sell their goods are subject to the common law doctrine of restraint of trade. This matter would now in all likelihood be dealt with under the Competition Act 1998 or art.82; it is difficult to imagine parties wanting to litigate about the validity at common law of a price-fixing arrangement.[750] **16–134**

Auction rings. An agreement by which the parties agree not to bid against each other at an auction and to divide the goods purchased, i.e. to establish a ring, has been held valid at common law as neither fraudulent nor in restraint of trade[751] but if made by a dealer it is a criminal offence[752] and therefore unenforceable. **16–135**

(viii) *Labour and Services: Restraints in Horizontal Agreements*[753]

Labour. Section 11 of the Trade Union and Labour Relations (Consolidation) Act 1992 provides that the purposes of any trade union shall not, by reason only that they are in restraint of trade, be unlawful so as, inter alia, to make any agreement or trust void or voidable. This provision is intended to make clear that the purposes of such an association are not illegal (as they might be at common law), and it does not render agreements made by such an association enforceable[754]; whether the agreement is enforceable still depends on the application of the common law rules relating to restraint of trade discussed below. The expression "trade union" is defined by s.1 of the 1992 Act to include any organisation (whether permanent or temporary) which consists wholly or mainly of workers of one or more descriptions and is an organisation whose principal purposes include the regulation of relations between workers of the description or those descriptions and employers or employers' associations. The wording of s.11 of **16–136**

---

[749] The validity of such rules may be affected by the Competition Act 1998 or by the EC Treaty. See above, paras 16–122, 16–124; Vol.II, paras 42–035 et seq.

[750] For a common law example, see *Att-Gen of Commonwealth of Australia v Adelaide Steamship Co Ltd* [1913] A.C. 781; and see *Cade & Sons Ltd v Daly Co Ltd* [1910] 1 I.R. 306; contrast *Urmston v Whitelegg Bros* (1890) 63 L.T. 455 (10-year world-wide price-fixing cartel held unreasonable). See further above, paras 16–121 *et seq.*

[751] *Rawlings v General Trading Co* [1921] 1 K.B. 635; and see *Cohen v Roche* [1927] 1 K.B. 169.

[752] The Auctions (Bidding Agreements) Act 1927 s.1 as amended by the Auctions (Bidding Agreements) Act 1969 ss.1, 2 and the Criminal Law Act 1977 Sch.13; s.3 of the 1969 Act entitles the vendor to avoid the contract of sale or alternatively to recover damages.

[753] As to restrictions imposed by an employer on his employees, see above, paras 16–103 et seq.

[754] See above, para.16–133.

the Act makes it clear that *none* of the *rules* of trade unions is affected by the doctrine of restraint of trade.[755]

16–137 An agreement between traders to regulate the wages and hours of employment of their workers for one year in accordance with the decision of the majority has been held to be against public policy and unenforceable at common law.[756] Similarly a rule of a trade protection society that no member should employ an employee who had left the service of another member without the consent in writing of his previous employer till after the expiration of two years was held invalid at common law.[757] Also, an arrangement between the organisers of a professional sport which restricts the way in which the participants in that sport may earn their livelihood may be invalidated if it constitutes an unreasonable restraint.[758] Indeed the validity of a contract of that nature may have to be judged by the same strict standards as would an individual covenant by an employee with his employer directed to the same end[759]; moreover while there may be very good reasons for the agreement from the employer's point of view, it may be against the public interest to interfere in such a way with the freedom of employees.[760] An employee who is injured by the operation of such an agreement between employers or by rules to such an effect of an association of employers, whether or not the terms of that agreement or of those rules are incorporated into the employee's contract of employment, may be granted a declaration against the employers or their association that the agreement or rules, as the case may be, are in unreasonable restraint of trade and therefore unenforceable,[761] and perhaps an injunction restraining the parties enforcing or purporting to enforce them.[762]

16–138 **Supply of services: common law.** Restrictive agreements relating to the supply of services are at common law subject to the doctrine of restraint of trade[763] upon the same principles as are restrictive agreements relating to the supply of goods.[764] Thus where a group of master stevedores agreed to divide among themselves the work at a particular port, it was held that a provision that a member who on the request of a customer did work which was allotted to

---

[755] This was designed to nullify the effect of *Edwards v Society of Graphic and Allied Trades* [1971] Ch. 365. See also *Greig v Insole* [1978] 1 W.L.R. 302, 365; *Associated Newspaper Group Ltd v Wade* [1979] 1 W.L.R. 697, 710 (restraint of trade does not mean interference with business).

[756] *Hilton v Eckersley* (1856) 6 E. & B. 47; and see *Mogul Steamship Co v McGregor, Gow & Co* [1892] A.C. 25, 42; (1889) 23 QBD 598, 619.

[757] *Mineral Water Bottle, etc., Society v Booth* (1887) 36 Ch D 465 (the members of the association could protect any confidential information); *Davies v Thomas* [1920] 2 Ch. 189, 195.

[758] *Eastham v Newcastle United F.C. Ltd* [1964] Ch. 413; *Greig v Insole* [1978] 1 W.L.R. 302; *Buckley v Tuttey* (1971) 125 C.L.R. 353.

[759] *Kores Manufacturing Co Ltd v Kolok Manufacturing Co Ltd* [1959] Ch. 108. See also above, para.16–104.

[760] *Esso Petroleum Co Ltd v Harper's Garage (Stourport) Ltd* [1968] A.C. 269, 300, 301.

[761] *Eastham v Newcastle United F.C. Ltd* [1964] Ch. 413; *Cooke v Football Association* [1972] C.L.Y. 516; *Greig v Insole* [1978] 1 W.L.R. 302.

[762] See *Nagle v Feilden* [1966] 2 Q.B. 633. See also *Cooke v Football Association* [1972] C.L.Y. 516 where a claim for damages for loss of wages was rejected as having no ground in contract or tort.

[763] *Collins v Locke* (1879) 4 App. Cas. 674; *Budget Rent-a-Car International Inc v Mamos Slough Ltd* (1977) 121 S.J. 374.

[764] See above, para.16–134.

another member should pay that other member an equivalent was valid at common law, but not a provision which in certain circumstances prevented a particular job from being accepted by any member.[765] Such an agreement would also infringe art.81 EC.

Supply of professional services. The regulation of professional services is as much subject to the common law doctrine of restraint of trade[766] as the regulation of other services,[767] at any rate where the profession engages in trade.[768] Public policy may invalidate rules of a body such as the Stewards of the Jockey Club which prevent a class of people, such as women, from exercising a calling over which the body has control[769] or rules of professional conduct laid down for a profession whether or not those rules are intended to be binding.[770] 16–139

Supply of labour: common law. Agreements between workers binding them to regulate their work in accordance with the decision of some outside body or otherwise curtailing the free right to dispose of labour are at common law subject to the doctrine of restraint of trade[771] upon the same principles as agreements between employers to regulate the acquisition of labour.[772] Such contracts have generally been held to be in unreasonable restraint of trade and therefore unenforceable at common law.[773] Where a union's rules impose unjustifiable restraints on members, others of its rules, e.g. for the payment to members of superannuation benefits, have been held also to be unenforceable.[774] Where the rules of a union imposed no restrictive obligations on the members, a rule which provided for the payment of strike pay to those who took part in an authorised strike was held to be enforceable at common law as no more than an insurance of the members against the consequences of a strike.[775] 16–140

(ix) Invalidating and Regulatory Statutory Provisions

Restrictive trade practices, (goods and services) monopolies. Many practices which are in restraint of trade, or which are designed to stifle competition, are dealt with by specific statutes. The legislation cover, inter alia, restrictive trading agreements relating to goods and services, restrictive labour practices, 16–141

[765] *Collins v Locke* (1879) 4 App. Cas. 674.

[766] See below, para.16–141 for statutory provisions.

[767] *Dickson v Pharmaceutical Society of Great Britain* [1970] A.C. 403.

[768] *Dickson v Pharmaceutical Society of Great Britain* [1970] A.C. 403, 455 but it is to be noted that the traditional categories of covenant in restraint of trade include covenants by doctors, dentists, solicitors, etc., who probably do not engage in trade.

[769] *Nagle v Feilden* [1966] 2 Q.B. 633.

[770] *Dickson v Pharmaceutical Society of Great Britain* [1970] A.C. 403. The professional services sector is mainly controlled under the Fair Trading Act 1973.

[771] *Hornby v Close* (1867) L.R. 2 Q.B. 153; *Mogul Steamship Co Ltd v McGregor, Gow & Co* [1892] A.C. 25, 59, 60; *Cullen v Elwin* (1904) 90 L.T. 840; *Boddington v Lawton, The Times*, February 4, 1994.

[772] See above, para.16–136.

[773] *Russell v Amalgamated Society of Carpenters and Joiners* [1912] A.C. 421; and see Citrine's *Trade Union Law*, 3rd edn, pp.44–45; Grunfeld, *Modern Trade Union Law* (1966), pp.64–71; *Boddington v Lawton* [1994] I.C.R. 478.

[774] *Miller v Amalgamated Engineering Union* [1938] Ch. 669.

[775] *Gozney v Bristol Trade and Provident Society* [1909] 1 K.B. 901.

resale price maintenance and the anti-competitive impact of monopolies. These statutory controls are dealt with in Vol.II, Ch.42.

3. CONTRACTS UNENFORCEABLE BY STATUTE

(a) *General Principles*

16–142 **Unenforceability by statute and common law distinguished.** The illegality which renders a contract unenforceable at common law may arise by statute.[776] Unenforceability by statute, on the other hand, arises where a statute itself on its true construction deprives one or both of the parties of their civil remedies under the contract in addition to, or instead of, imposing a penalty upon them. If the statute does so, it is irrelevant whether the parties meant to break the law or not. A significant distinction between cases of contracts which are unenforceable at common law because they were entered into with the object of committing an act illegal by statute and of contracts which are rendered illegal by statute is that in the former case one has to look to see what acts the statute prohibits; it does not matter whether or not it prohibits a contract; if a contract is deliberately made to do a prohibited act that contract will be unenforceable. In the latter case one has to consider, not what acts the statute prohibits, but what contracts it prohibits; but one is not concerned at all with the intent of the parties[777]; if the parties enter into a prohibited contract that contract is unenforceable[778] and ignorance by the parties of the law does not make it the less so.[779]

16–143 **The distinction illustrated.** The distinction between contracts prohibited by statute and those prohibited at common law is well brought out in *Dungate v Lee*,[780] where the existence of a partnership of a betting office was called in issue. One of the parties denied the existence of the partnership, contending that the bookmaker's permit required by statute was held by him alone and that any partnership would have been contrary to the provisions of the Betting and Gaming Act 1960. It was held that even if, in the course of the partnership, the unlicensed partner committed offences against the Act, the Act did not render the partnership itself illegal as all it required was that one partner be suitably qualified. Nor was the partnership agreement illegal at common law since it did not, by its terms, require the unlicensed partner to act illegally as a bookmaker

---

[776] See above, para.16–005.

[777] But the parties' knowledge may not be entirely irrelevant, since only one party may be expressly penalised by the statute and therefore the statute will normally deprive only him of his civil rights under it (see below, para.16–158). But if the other has knowledge of the illegality he may become an aider and abettor and accordingly find himself penalised and disabled from suing on the contract: *Archbolds (Freightage) Ltd v S. Spanglett Ltd* [1961] 1 Q.B. 374, 385, 393; *Ashmore, Benson, Pease & Co Ltd v A. v Dawson Ltd* [1973] 1 W.L.R. 828.

[778] See *St John Shipping Corp v Joseph Rank Ltd* [1957] 1 Q.B. 267, 283. In any given situation it may not be easy to determine whether a statute prohibits acts as opposed to contracts.

[779] *Kiriri Cotton Co Ltd v Dewani* [1960] A.C. 192.

[780] [1969] 1 Ch. 545; cf. *Langton v Hughes* (1813) 1 M. & S. 593.

in the conduct of the business and it was not entered into with an intention on the part of the partners that the unlicensed partner should so act.

Express voidness by statute. Statutes often provide expressly for the civil consequences of breach of their provisions and this is by far the preferable solution.[781] A contract may, by statute, be void without being illegal, the only penalty being that a contract made in contravention of the statute is entirely ineffective to create rights, as in the case of a contract made in contravention of the Gaming Acts 1845 and 1892; or again a contract may be unenforceable without being either illegal or void, in which case it is effective to alter the rights of the parties, although the altered rights are not enforceable by them.[782] However, if a contract is illegal, the effect is "to avoid the contract *ab initio* . . . if the making of the contract is expressly or impliedly prohibited by statute".[783] 16–144

Statute expressly not affecting validity. A statutory prohibition to which a criminal sanction is attached may also provide that it does not render any contract entered into in breach of its terms void or unenforceable.[784] Whether such a provision has no effect whatsoever on the parties' contractual rights and obligations will depend upon the language used and the statutory purpose underlying the legislation. Thus, although the statute may provide that breach of its prohibition does not render a contract void or unenforceable, the court may nevertheless refuse to enforce the contract because this would be assisting in the furtherance of something that is illegal.[785] 16–145

Statute silent as to civil rights. But where the statute is silent as to the civil rights of the parties but penalises the making or performance of the contract, the courts consider whether the Act, on its true construction,[786] is intended to avoid contracts of the class to which the particular contract belongs or whether it merely prohibits the doing of some particular act.[787] In the following paragraphs certain tests which have been applied by the courts are considered. However, it is important to note that where a contract or its performance is implicated with breach of a statute this does not entail that the contract is avoided. Where the Act does not expressly deprive the plaintiff of his civil remedies under the contract the appropriate question to ask is whether, having regard to the Act and the evils against which it was intended to guard and the circumstances in which the 16–146

---

[781] See, e.g. Trade Descriptions Act 1968 s.35; Fair Trading Act 1973 s.26; Human Rights Act 1998 s.6 (it is unlawful for a public authority to act in a manner incompatible with convention rights), see above, para.16–142.

[782] *Eastern Distributors v Goldring* [1957] 2 Q.B. 600, 614.

[783] per Devlin J., *Archbolds (Freightage) Ltd v Spanglett Ltd* [1961] 1 QB 374, 388. See also *D.R. Insurance Co v Central National Insurance Co of Omaha* [1996] C.L.C. 64, 68; *Royal Boskalis Westminster NV v Mountain* [1997] C.L.C. 816.

[784] This was the language used in s.8(3) of the Companies Securities (Insider Dealing) Act 1985 which has now been repealed but it is repeated in the replacement legislation: see Criminal Justice Act 1993 s.63(2).

[785] *Chase Manhattan Equities Ltd v Goodman* [1991] B.C.L.C. 897, 931–934. See also *S.C.F. Finance Co Ltd v Masri (No.2)* [1987] Q.B. 1002, 1026.

[786] The natural meaning of a penal statute is not to be extended by reasoning based on the substance of the transaction under scrutiny: *Re H.P.C. Productions Ltd* [1962] Ch. 466.

[787] See *Archbolds (Freightage) Ltd v S. Spanglett Ltd* [1961] 1 Q.B. 374, 389–390.

contract was made and to be performed, it would in fact be against public policy to enforce it.[788]

16–147 **Aids to statutory interpretation.** (1) Where a statute imposes a penalty on one or both of the parties to a contract, as a result of their entering into the contract or of their manner of performing it, the court will consider whether on the construction and purpose of the statute the doing of the particular act is forbidden as illegal or whether there is merely a charge imposed upon it. If the latter, it is clear that the contract itself is not prohibited. Thus where a tobacco manufacturer sued for the price of tobacco he had sold to the defendant, the fact that he was not licensed to sell tobacco and that his name was not painted on his place of business as required by statute did not prevent him from recovering since there was nothing in the Act to prohibit every sale and its only effect was to impose a penalty for the purpose of the Revenue, on the carrying on of the trade without complying with its requirements.[789] If, on the true construction of the statute:

> "... *the contract* be rendered illegal, it can make no difference, in point of law, whether the statute which makes it so has in mind the protection of the revenue or any other object. The sole question is whether the statute *means to prohibit the contract.*"[790]

If, on the other hand, the object of the statute is the protection of the public from possible injury[791] or fraud, or is the promotion of some object of public policy, the inference is that contracts made in contravention of its provisions are prohibited.[792] Thus where by statute it was not lawful:

> "... to sell, or to supply ... a motor-vehicle ... for delivery in such a condition that the use thereof on a road in that condition would be unlawful",

such a sale was held illegal and a cheque given for the price could not be sued on.[793] Similarly, it was by statute illegal to contract as a moneylender without registration; accordingly a moneylender's failure to register invalidated contracts made and securities taken by him the course of his business, since the whole

[788] *Shaw v Groom* [1970] 2 Q.B. 504; *Ailion v Spiekermann* [1976] Ch. 158; *Geismar v Sun Alliance and London Insurance Ltd* [1978] Q.B. 383.

[789] *Smith v Mawhood* (1845) 14 M. & W. 452; *Johnson v Hudson* (1809) 11 East 180.

[790] *Cope v Rowlands* (1836) 2 M. & W. 149, 157; *Smith v Mawhood* (1845) 14 M. & W. 452, 463; and see *Vita Food Products Inc v Unus Shipping Co Ltd* [1939] A.C. 277, 293; *Yin v Sam* [1962] A.C. 304. See below, paras 16–149, 16–154, 16–159 as to the extent of the unenforceability of the contract.

[791] *Vinall v Howard* [1953] 1 W.L.R. 987. And see Road Traffic Act 1988 s.18(4) and Sch.1, which makes it an offence to sell motor-cyclists' protective helmets which do not comply with specifications. Such statutes sometimes create statutory duties enforceable at the suit of the injured party, e.g. see Consumer Protection Act 1987 and regulations made thereunder: Vol.II, paras 43–138 et seq.

[792] *Victorian Daylesford Syndicate Ltd v Dott* [1905] 2 Ch. 624; *Little v Poole* (1829) 9 B. & C. 192; *Cope v Rowlands* (1836) 2 M. & W. 149; *Taylor v Crowland Gas & Coke Co* (1854) 10 Exch. 293. See, however, *St John Shipping Corp v Joseph Rank Ltd* [1957] 1 Q.B. 267.

[793] *Vinall v Howard* [1953] 1 W.L.R. 987, applying Road Traffic Act 1934 s.8 (reversed on the facts [1954] 1 Q.B. 375); by s.75(7) of the Road Traffic Act 1988 it is now expressly provided that the statutory prohibition of the sale of unroadworthy vehicles contained in that section shall not affect the validity of contracts or rights arising under contracts.

purpose of the Act was the protection of the public.[794] It has also been suggested[795] that:

> "... not a bad test to apply is to see whether the penalty in the Act is imposed once for all, or whether it is a recurrent penalty imposed as often as the act is done. If it be the latter, then the act is a prohibited act."

(2) The courts have also been reluctant to find contracts unenforceable because the illegality doctrine operates in an all or nothing way and there is no proportionality between the loss ensuing from non-enforcement and the breach of statute. This is to be contrasted with fines for criminal acts where some proportionality does pertain. This aspect of the matter caused concern to Devlin J. in *St John Shipping Corp v Joseph Rank Ltd*.[796] In that case the illegality involved the plaintiff overloading its ship and the defendants wished to hold back merely that portion of the freight which was earned by the overloading. But as Devlin J. pointed out the principle of illegality: 16–148

> "... cares not at all for the element of deliberation, or for the gravity of the infraction, and *does not adjust the penalty to the profits unjustifiably earned*."[797]

Thus, were the doctrine to have applied in that case, it would have entitled the defendants to hold back the full freight which was 40 times the maximum fine for the offence of overloading.[798] Coupled with this, non-enforcement may have the effect of punishing the offender twice where the statute contains its own penalty for breach.

(3) The courts have also been sensitive to the fact that non-enforcement may also result in unjust enrichment to the party to the contract who has not performed his part of the bargain but who has benefited from the performance by the other party. As was stated by Devlin J., in the *St John Shipping* case, non-enforcement of the contract may result in the forfeiting of a sum which: 16–149

> "... will not go into the public purse but into the pockets of someone who is lucky enough to pick up the windfall or astute enough to have contrived to get it."[799]

(4) The courts have also appreciated that the growth in statutory law (including delegated legislation) can result in the unwitting and quite innocent breach of the 16–150

---

[794] *Victorian Daylesford Syndicate Ltd v Dott* [1905] 2 Ch. 624. See now the Consumer Credit Act 1974 ss.21, 40(1) and Pt III (as amended): *Menaka v Lum Kum Chum* [1977] 1 W.L.R. 267. It may be, however, that even though the statute is designed to protect the public, precluding a member of the public from being able to sue on it will cause him prejudice. This was the essence of the problem in the reinsurance cases: see *Bedford Insurance Co Ltd v Instituto de Resseguros do Brasil* [1985] Q.B. 966; *Stewart v Oriental Fire and Marine Ins. Co Ltd* [1985] 1 Q.B. 988; *Phoenix General Insurance Co of Greece SA v Administration Asigurarilor, etc.* [1988] Q.B. 216. It is submitted that the proper policy is to allow the contract to be enforced by the innocent party: see Financial Services and Markets Act 2000 s.27. See also *Estate of Anandh v Barnet Primary Health Care Trust* [2004] EWCA Civ 5, [2004] All E.R. (D) 242 (Jan).

[795] *Victorian Daylesford Syndicate Ltd v Dott* [1905] 2 Ch. 624, 630.

[796] [1957] 1 Q.B. 267.

[797] [1957] 1 Q.B. 267, 281 (emphasis added). cf. *Archer v Brown* [1985] Q.B. 401, 423F–H.

[798] Treitel, "Contract and Crime" in Tapper (ed.), *Crime, Proof and Punishment*, p.95.

[799] [1957] 1 Q.B. 267, 288.

statute. In *Shaw v Groom*[800] the court held that failure to comply with the provision of the Rent Act requiring a landlord to provide a tenant with a rent book did not result in the landlord being unable to obtain the payment of rental arrears. One of the factors obviously influencing the court in reaching this conclusion was the growth in the volume of legislation which could easily result in the innocent transgression of some statutory prohibition.[801]

16–151 (5) Although the courts have recognised "the desirability of (their) . . . assisting to enforce a statute",[802] the consequence of this in driving from the seat of judgment sometimes innocent supplicants has also to be weighed in the balance.[803]

16–152 None of the above factors constitutes a litmus test which produces fore-ordained results. Obviously it would be preferable if the legislature were specifically to provide for the consequences of breach of the statute. Experience indicates that such legislative foresight is not always displayed, and where it is not the court must answer the question: does the:

> ". . . ambit and intent of the particular statute in the light of any other legislation affecting the subject matter . . . preclude the plaintiff recovering on the contract if he had committed the offence?"[804]

16–153 **Illegality through manner of performance.** The question of statutory illegality in a contract generally arises in connection with its formation, but it may also arise in connection with its performance,[805] since the effect of the statute may be to deprive one or both parties of their rights unless the contract is performed in a particular manner, or, to put the matter another way, the manner in which a contract is performed may turn it into the sort of contract that is prohibited by statute.[806] Thus, the seller of agricultural fertiliser, who omitted to give to the purchaser an invoice showing the composition of the fertiliser, was held unable to recover its price since the seller had not performed the contract in the only way in which the statute allowed it to be performed.[807] In another case[808] statutory regulations required that the seller of utility goods should furnish to the

---

800 [1970] 2 Q.B. 504. cf. *Anderson Ltd v Daniel* [1924] 1 K.B. 138.

801 *Shaw v Groom* [1970] 2 Q.B. 504, 521–522.

802 *Shaw v Groom* [1970] 2 Q.B. 504, 521.

803 *St John Shipping Corp v Joseph Rank Ltd* [1957] 1 Q.B. 267, 288.

804 *Shaw v Groom* [1970] 2 Q.B. 504, 520, per Sachs L.J.; see also Harman L.J., at 516. See also *Yango Pastoral Co Ltd v First Chicago Australia Ltd* (1978) 139 C.L.R. 410; *Fire and All Risk Ins. v Powell* [1966] V.R. 513; *Pavey & Mathews Pty Ltd v Paul* (1986–87) 162 C.L.R. 221 (allowing a quantum meruit claim by a builder with respect to work performed under an oral contract which by statute was made unenforceable by the builder unless it was in writing). See the very helpful guidance for determining whether breach of the statute renders a contract illegal and unenforceable: *Nelson v Nelson* (1995) 132 A.L.R. 133, 192–193.

805 *Anderson Ltd v Daniel* [1924] 1 K.B. 138, 149; *Ashmore, Benson Pease & Co Ltd v A. v Dawson Ltd* [1973] 1 W.L.R. 828.

806 *St John Shipping Corp v Joseph Rank Ltd* [1957] 1 Q.B. 267, 284.

807 *Anderson Ltd v Daniel* [1924] 1 K.B. 138; overruled by the Fertilisers and Feeding Stuffs Act 1926 s.1(2); *Marles v Philip Trant & Sons Ltd* [1954] 1 Q.B. 29, but see now Agriculture (Miscellaneous Provisions) Act 1954 s.12(1).

808 *B. & B. Viennese Fashions v Losane* [1952] 1 All E.R. 909.

buyer an invoice containing certain particulars. The plaintiff made a contract of sale for non-utility goods, to which the regulations did not apply; but he purported to perform it by delivering to the buyer, without objection, utility garments to which the regulations did apply; and he did not furnish the invoice. The Court of Appeal held that this contract was no less unenforceable than would have been a contract the initial terms of which provided for the sale of utility garments, and which could only have been lawfully performed by the delivery of the requisite invoice.

Unlicensed transactions. Where a statute or statutory instrument prohibits the doing of work otherwise than under a licence,[809] a contract under which unlicensed work is carried out will generally be unenforceable.[810] If there is in existence some licence, the illegality only extends to the excess by which the work exceeds the amount of the licence, unless there is an unseverable agreement to exceed the amount licensed.[811] 16–154

Unlicensed consumer credit business. Contracts made in contravention of the licensing provisions of the Moneylenders Acts were illegal and would not be enforced.[812] The latter are now being replaced by the Consumer Credit Act 1974, under s.40(1) of which a regulated agreement with a person who carries on consumer credit business while unlicensed is not illegal but is unenforceable against the debtor unless the Director General of Fair Trading orders otherwise. 16–155

Omission to register according to statute. Where a statute imposes an obligation to register contracts of a particular kind and provides penalties for failure to register, the non-registration of such a contract has been held not to render the contract itself unenforceable.[813] Such contracts may be expressly avoided by the statute. Thus, the Companies Act 1985[814] expressly avoids as against the liquidator and any creditor of a limited company mortgages and charges created by the company which have not been registered in accordance with the provisions of the Act.[815] 16–156

Illegal performance of legal contracts. The cases cited above might appear to support the proposition that an initially legal contract will be unenforceable on the basis that an illegality was committed in its performance. There is authority that in fact they were decided: 16–157

---

[809] cf. *Re Mahmoud and Ispahani* [1921] 2 K.B. 716, see below, para.16–155 (licence necessary for formation of contract).

[810] *Bostel Bros Ltd v Hurlock* [1949] 1 K.B. 74; *Jackson Stansfield & Sons v Butterworth* [1948] 2 All E.R. 558; *Woolfe v Wexler* [1951] 2 K.B. 154; *Howell v Falmouth Boat Construction Co Ltd* [1951] A.C. 837; *Smith & Son (Bognor Regis) Ltd v Walker* [1952] 2 Q.B. 319; *Young v Buckles* [1952] 1 K.B. 220.

[811] *Dennis & Co Ltd v Munn* [1949] 2 K.B. 327; *Frank W. Clifford Ltd v Garth* [1956] 1 W.L.R. 570. See also below, para.16–195.

[812] See Vol.II, para.43–015.

[813] *Wright v Horton* (1887) 12 App. Cas. 371.

[814] Companies Act 1985 s.395(1). See above, para.9–046.

[815] As to the effects of failure to furnish particulars of agreements which are subject to registration under the Competition Act 1998, see paras 42–116, 42–126.

> "... on the narrower basis that the way in which the contract was performed turned it into the sort of contract that was prohibited by statute."[816]

This would also be in keeping with the general principle that the mere fact that there is an illegality associated with the performance of the contract[817] does not render it illegal and unenforceable. Thus in *St John Shipping Corp v Joseph Rank Ltd*[818] cargo owners resisted a claim for freight on the ground that the carriers had so overloaded their ship with the cargo in respect of which the freight was claimed as to submerge the ship below the load line. Devlin J. held that although this amounted to a statutory offence, the legality of the contract was unaffected, since the statute in question was to be construed as prohibiting merely the act and not the contract under which it was done.

16–158 **Statute: one party only affected.** Statutes which prohibit certain contracts often impliedly recognise, for example by punishing only one of the parties, that the parties are not equally at fault, and therefore on their true construction only one of the parties to the contract is prevented from suing upon it. Accordingly, when:

> "... the policy of the Act in question is to protect the general public or class of persons by requiring that a contract shall be accompanied by certain formalities or conditions, and a penalty is imposed on the person omitting those formalities or conditions, the contract and its performance without those formalities or conditions is illegal, and cannot be sued upon by the person liable to the penalties."[819]

The other party to the contract is not deprived of his civil remedies because of the criminal default of the guilty party.[820]

16–159 **Statute affecting both parties.** In certain cases a statute may be construed to prohibit both parties from suing on a contract of the sort in question, e.g. since it makes them both guilty of a criminal offence in entering into the contract. In such cases, no matter how much more culpable one party is than the other, both are equally unable to sue upon the contract; and this is so even though the party who seeks to sue on the contract was at the time it was made ignorant of the facts which brought the contract within the statutory prohibition.[821] Thus in *Re*

---

[816] *St John Shipping Corp v Joseph Rank Ltd* [1957] 1 Q.B. 267, 284.

[817] *Coral Leisure Group Ltd v Barnett* [1981] I.C.R. 503, 508; see also above, para.16–146.

[818] [1959] 1 Q.B. 267; and see *Dungate v Lee* [1969] 1 Ch. 545; *Shaw v Groom* [1970] 2 Q.B. 504.

[819] *Anderson v Daniel* [1924] 1 K.B. 138, 147; *Crehan v Inntrepreneur Pub Company CPC* [2004] EWCA Civ 637, [2004] E.C.C. 28, the claimant, as a matter of Community Law, could not claim damages from his co-contractor with respect to an agreement which breached art.81 of the EC Treaty. The claimant in *Crehan* was not significantly responsible for any distortion of competition.

[820] *Marles v Philip Trant & Sons Ltd* [1953] 1 All E.R. 645 (there was no appeal from this party of Lynskey J.'s judgment with which Denning L.J. expressed his agreement [1954] 1 Q.B. 29, 36); *Ailion v Spiekermann* [1976] Ch. 158; see also cases on reinsurance cited in fn.794 to para.16–147, above.

[821] *Re Mahmoud and Ispahani* [1921] 2 K.B. 716. See also *Wilson, Smithett & Cope Ltd v Terruzzi* [1976] Q.B. 683; *United City Merchants (Investments) Ltd v Royal Bank of Canada* [1983] A.C. 168, 188–190; above, para.16–031 fn.156 for the effect of the Bretton Woods Agreement Act 1945 upon "exchange contracts".

Mahmoud and Ispahani[822] the plaintiff agreed to sell and the defendant to buy 150 tons of linseed oil. By a statutory order then in force it was illegal "to buy or sell or otherwise deal in" linseed oil unless both parties had a licence. The defendant did not have a licence. Irrespective of the parties' state of knowledge about the existence of licences the contract was illegal and unenforceable by either, since both were prohibited from making it and the prohibition was for the benefit of the public.[823] Since in this case the plaintiff had a licence and had been told by the defendant, albeit falsely, that he also had one, the plaintiff's failure to recover on the contract may seem rather inequitable. Similarly in *Yin v Sam*,[824] Malayan Rubber Regulations provided that "no person shall purchase . . . rubber . . . unless he shall have been duly licensed". A sold rubber to B, who, unknown to A, did not hold a licence. The Privy Council, purporting to apply *Re Mahmoud and Ispahani*[825] held that A could not recover the price. But the decision is to be questioned since, whereas in *Re Mahmoud and Ispahani*[826] the regulations made it illegal "to buy or sell", in *Yin v Sam*[827] the regulations apparently made it an offence only "to buy"; A was therefore not the subject of a direct statutory prohibition[828] nor himself guilty of a criminal offence[829] and ought therefore not to have been held to be statutorily deprived of his rights; nor should he have been barred at common law since he had no knowledge that the performance of the contract would necessarily involve the commission of a criminal offence by B.[830] It is not possible, however, to go so far as to state that an innocent party to a contract rendered illegal by statute will invariably be entitled to enforce the contract.[831]

Alternative cause of action. Even where a statute deprives a party of a civil remedy under a contract, he may, if in fact innocent of turpitude, be able to sue upon a collateral warranty or implied term that the requirements of the law had been complied with, or for the deceit, or perhaps the negligence, of the other in misrepresenting that fact. This will be dealt with in para.16–176. 16–160

Alteration of law pending action. Where the law is altered by statute while an action is pending, the rights of the parties will be decided according to the law 16–161

[822] [1921] 2 K.B. 716.

[823] *Re Mahmoud and Ispahani* [1921] 2 K.B. 716, 729. At 730 Scrutton L.J. left open the question of whether the plaintiff would have had a remedy for deceit: on this, see below, para.16–176.

[824] [1962] A.C. 304.

[825] [1921] 2 K.B. 716.

[826] [1921] 2 K.B. 716.

[827] [1962] A.C. 304.

[828] cf. *Re Mahmoud and Ispahani* [1921] 2 K.B. 716, 731–732 where Atkin L.J. expressed the view that a direct statutory prohibition sufficed even if the party prohibited could not be prosecuted because he lacked mens rea.

[829] See *Sayce v Coupe* [1953] 1 Q.B. 1.

[830] See *Archbolds (Freightage) Ltd v S. Spanglett Ltd* [1961] 1 Q.B. 374 (above, para.16–146), which was not cited.

[831] *Phoenix General Insurance Co of Greece SA v Halvanon Insurance Co Ltd* [1988] Q.B. 216, "Illegal Transactions: The Effect of Illegality On Contracts And Torts" (Law Com., Consultation Paper No.154, 1999).

as it existed at the time the action was commenced, unless the statute shows a clear intention to vary such rights by making its action retrospective.[832]

(b) *Statutory Regulation of Trading with the Enemy*

16–162 **Trading with the Enemy Act 1939.** Trading with the enemy is regulated and prohibited by the Trading with the Enemy Act 1939. By s.1 of the Act,[833] a person trading with or attempting to trade with the enemy is liable to a fine or imprisonment. By s.1(2), a person shall be deemed to have traded with the enemy:

"(a) ... if he has had any commercial, financial or other intercourse with or of the benefit of an enemy, and, in particular, if he has

(i) supplied any goods to or for the benefit of an enemy, or obtained any goods from an enemy or traded in or caused any goods consigned to or from an enemy or destined for or coming from enemy territory, or

(ii) paid or transmitted any money, negotiable instrument or security for money to or for the benefit of an enemy or to a place in enemy territory, or

(iii) performed any obligation to or discharged any obligation of any enemy whether the obligation was undertaken before or after the commencement of the Act, or

(b) if he has done anything which, by virtue of the provisions of the Act, is to be treated as trading with the enemy."

Anything done under the authority of a Secretary of State, the Treasury or the Department of Trade does not fall within the Act; nor does the receipt of a payment from an enemy of a sum due in respect of a transaction under which all obligations on the part of the person receiving payment had already been performed when the payment was received and had been performed at a time when the person from whom payment was received was not an enemy.[834]

16–163 By s.2(1) of the Act[835] an enemy means:

"(a) ... any state, or sovereign of a state, at war with Her Majesty;

(b) any individual resident in enemy territory[836];

---

[832] *Hitchcock v Way* (1837) 6 A. & E. 943; *Lauri v Renard* [1892] 3 Ch. 402, 421; *Re Athlumney* [1898] 2 Q.B. 547, 551; *Beadling v Goll* (1922) 39 T.L.R. 128; *Ward v British Oak Insurance Co Ltd* [1932] 1 K.B. 392, 397; *Croxford v Universal Insurance Co Ltd* [1936] 2 K.B. 253; *Re Nautilus Shipping Co Ltd* [1936] Ch. 17, 28; *Craxfords (Ramsgate) Ltd v Williams and Steer Manufacturing Co Ltd* [1954] 1 W.L.R. 1130; and see *York Estates v Wareham* (1950) 1 S.A. 125.

[833] As amended by the Emergency Laws (Miscellaneous Provisions) Act 1953 s.2 and Sch.II para.2.

[834] See *R. & A. Kohnstamm Ltd v Ludwig Krumm (London) Ltd* [1940] 2 K.B. 359.

[835] As amended by the Emergency Laws (Miscellaneous Provisions) Act 1953 s.2 and Sch.II para.3. See also s.2(2) of the Act of 1939.

[836] Resident means *de facto* resident: *Re Hatch* [1948] Ch. 592, distinguishing *Vandyke v Adams* [1942] Ch. 155, where it was held that a British prisoner of war is not resident in enemy territory for the purposes of the Act; and see *The Atlantic Scout* [1950] P. 266; *Vamvakas v Custodian of Enemy Property* [1952] 2 Q.B. 183.

(c) any body of persons (whether corporate or unincorporate) carrying on business in any place, if and so long as the body is controlled by a person who, under section 2 of the Act, is an enemy;

(d) any body of persons constituted or incorporated in, or under the laws of, a state at war with Her Majesty; and

(e) as respects any business carried on in enemy territory, any individual or body of persons (whether corporate or unincorporate) carrying on that business; but the expression does not include any individual by reason only that he is an enemy subject."

By s.15(1) of the Act, enemy territory means any area which is under the sovereignty of, or in the occupation of, a Power with whom Her Majesty is at war, not being an area in the occupation of Her Majesty or of a Power allied with Her Majesty.[837]

4. ENFORCEMENT OF COLLATERAL AND PROPRIETARY RIGHTS[838]

(a) *The Maxim Ex Turpi Causa Non Oritur Actio and Related Rules*

Ex turpi causa non oritur actio. When a contractual right is said to be unenforceable on the ground that ex turpi causa non oritur actio, sometimes all that is meant is that the general principles discussed earlier in this chapter[839] apply to deprive the party of a contractual remedy which he would otherwise have, though the maxim is generally confined to cases involving criminality or immorality. On other occasions the maxim is used with specific reference to unenforceability at common law on the ground that an apparently innocent contract was entered into for an objectionable purpose. Thus in *Pearce v Brooks*[840] the plaintiff sued the defendant, a prostitute, for the hire of a brougham which he knew was to be used by her in her calling. It was held that he could not recover and Pollock C.B. said: 16–164

> "I have always considered it was settled law that any person who contributes to the performance of an illegal act by supplying a thing with the knowledge that it is going to be used for that purpose, cannot recover the price of the thing so supplied. . . . Nor can any distinction be made between an illegal and an immoral purpose; the rule which is applicable to the matter is *ex turpi causa non oritur actio*."

This is, in effect, merely an application of the general common law principle that one who knowingly enters into a contract with an improper object cannot enforce

---

[837] See also s.15(1A), added by the Emergency Laws (Miscellaneous Provisions) Act 1953 s.2 and Sch.II para.8.

[838] See Williams (1942) 8 Camb.L.J. 51; Coote (1972) 35 M.L.R. 38; Merkin (1981) 97 L.Q.R. 420.

[839] See above, paras 16–010, 16–011; *Euro-Diam Ltd v Bathurst* [1990] 1 Q.B. 1, 34–37.

[840] (1866) L.R. 1 Ex. 213, 217. See also *K. v P. and J.* [1993] Ch. 140 (defence of ex turpi causa does not preclude a claim for contribution under the Civil Liability (Contribution) Act 1978). For the application of the ex turpi causa principle in tort see *Hall v Herbert* [1993] 2 S.C.R. 159 (noted, (1994) 110 L.Q.R. 357).

his rights thereunder. Where the *ex turpi* maxim is applicable, it applies to assignees.[841] The ex turpi causa principle is applicable to a claim by a body corporate where the directing mind and will of the company was responsible for the company perpetrating the illegality.[842]

16–165 **Tainting.** The maxim ex turpi causa non oritur actio is also applied to the case of an apparently innocent contract which is nevertheless vitiated by the illegality of another contract to which it is merely collateral—the illegality of the latter tainting the former.[843] Thus in *Spector v Ageda*[844] the plaintiff loaned money to the defendant to repay a loan which had been made by a third party to the defendant and which was an illegal moneylending transaction. The plaintiff knew that her loan was to be used to pay off the illegal loan and the issue which squarely faced the court was, Megarry J. stated[845]:

> "... whether a loan knowingly[846] made in order to discharge an existing loan that was wholly or partially illegal was itself tainted with illegality."

He answered the question in the affirmative; the second transaction was tainted by the illegality of the first and was accordingly unenforceable.

16–166 Analogous to the principle of tainting is the situation where an illegal contract involves a statutory entitlement which would apply to the contract had it been legal. The following are examples of this: (a) the claimant, a foreign national, who is not entitled to work in the United Kingdom, uses forged documents to obtain employment and alleges racial discrimination against his employer[847]; (b) an employee employed under an illegal contract (no tax or NIC deducted) alleges

---

841 *D.R. Insurance Co v Central National Insurance Co of Omaha* [1996] C.L.C. 64, 73, [1996] 1 Lloyd's Rep. 74, 82.

842 *Stone & Rolls Ltd v Moore Stephens* [2007] EWHC (Comm) 1826.

843 *Fisher v Bridges* (1854) 3 E.B. 642; *Geere v Mare* (1863) 2 H. & C. 339; *Clay v Ray* (1864) 17 C.B.(N.S.) 188; *Taylor v Chester* (1869) L.R. 4 Q.B. 309; *Bigos v Bousted* [1951] 1 All E.R. 92; *Hall v Woolston Hall Leisure Ltd* [1998] I.C.R. 651. See also below, paras 16–194 et seq. on severance.

844 [1973] Ch. 30; see also *Heald v O'Connor* [1971] 1 W.L.R. 497 involving the Companies Act 1948 s.54 (now replaced by Companies Act 2006 Pt 18 Ch.2); *Swan v Bank of Scotland* (1836) 10 Bli. (N.S.) 627; *Pye Ltd v B. G. Transport Service Ltd* [1966] 2 Lloyd's Rep. 300; *Geismar v Sun Alliance and London Insurance Ltd* [1978] Q.B. 383; *Euro-Diam Ltd v Bathurst* [1990] 1 Q.B. 1; *Saunders v Edwards* [1987] 1 W.L.R. 1116; *Re Berkeley Applegate (Investment Consultants) Ltd* [1989] Ch. 32, 53.

845 *Re Berkeley Applegate (Investment Consultants) Ltd* [1989] Ch. 32, 44.

846 From Megarry J.'s judgment it would appear that the party to the second transaction must actually know of the illegality or deliberately shut their eyes, and the mere fact that they ought to have known is not enough *Spector v Ageda* [1973] Ch. 30.

847 *Vakante v Addey & Stanhope School* [2004] EWCA Civ 1065, [2004] 4 All E.R. 1056 where the Court of Appeal (Civil Division) upheld the decision of the Employment Appeal Tribunal that illegality precluded the claimant from pursuing his racial discrimination claim. See also *Wheeler v Quality Deep Ltd* [2004] EWCA Civ 1085 where the lack of English and limited knowledge of tax and national insurance provisions were considered relevant in determining the extent to which the employee participated in an illegality.

sexual discrimination[848]; and (c) the claimant hires a motorcycle for courier work by presenting false documentation and is injured because of the negligent failure to maintain the motorcycle in a roadworthy condition.[849] As a matter of principle, unless the concurrent action, e.g. the statutory claim or the claim in tort, directly relies upon and seeks to enforce the illegal contract, there is no reason why the claimant's rights should not be enforceable. Where the cause of action is not causally linked with the contract, the illegality of the contract will not constitute a bar to the transaction.[850]

Limits to the maxim. It is not sufficient, in order to bring the claimant within the maxim, that he should merely be obliged to give evidence of an illegal contract as part of his case, as for instance where the illegal purpose has not been carried out; for the rule normally applies only where the action is founded upon the illegal contract, and is brought to enforce it.[851] In *Euro-Diam Ltd v Bathurst*,[852] Kerr L.J. held that the *ex turpi causa* defence must be "approached pragmatically and with caution". He considered that the defence would not succeed where "some reprehensible conduct on [the claimant's] part is disclosed in the course of the proceedings" but the claimant does not have to found his claim on any illegal act.[853] Where property has passed to a party,[854] his proprietary rights therein will be recognised and enforced notwithstanding that his purpose in taking the transfer was objectionable,[855] or that the transfer was otherwise made in pursuance of a contract which on grounds of public policy could not have been enforced.[856] 16–167

[848] *Hall v Woolston Hall Leisure Ltd* [2001] W.L.R. 225 (claimant could pursue claim as she was protected by a statutory tort and did not have to rely on the contract); *Hunt v Power Resources Ltd* [2004] All E.R. (D) 23 (Apr).

[849] *Flavis v Pauley* [2002] All E.R. (D) 436 (Oct) (matter referred to trial to determine whether defence of illegality was available).

[850] *Hall v Woolston Hall Leisure Ltd* [2001] W.L.R. 225; *Leighton v Michael* [1996] 1 I.R.L.R. 67; *Sweetman v Nathan* [2003] EWCA Civ 1115; *Sutton v Hutchinson* [2005] EWCA Civ 1773.

[851] *Taylor v Bowers* (1876) 1 QBD 291, 295, 300; *Bowmakers Ltd v Barnet Instruments Ltd* [1945] K.B. 65; *Belvoir Finance Co Ltd v Stapleton* [1971] 1 Q.B. 210; *Euro-Diam Ltd v Bathurst* [1990] Q.B. 1. It may be, however, that the wrongful conduct is of such a nature (e.g. benefiting by means of a collateral transaction from a crime) that the court will refuse to enforce the tainted transaction: *Geismar v Sun Alliance and London Insurance Ltd* [1978] Q.B. 383; *Hall v Woolston Hall Leisure Ltd* [2001] 1 W.L.R. 225. This case dealt with the application of the maxim to a claimant seeking a remedy for the statutory tort under the Sex Discrimination Act 1975 but the contract cases are discussed. See also *The Illegality Defence In Tort* (Law Commission, Consultation Paper No.160); *Hewison v Meridian Shipping Pte* [2002] EWCA Civ 1821, [2002] All E.R. (D) 146.

[852] [1990] 1 Q.B. 1. Although the "affront to the public conscience" test adopted by Kerr L.J. in *Euro-Diam Ltd v Bathurst* for determining the effect of illegality was rejected by the House of Lords in *Tinsley v Milligan* [1994] 1 A.C. 340, it is submitted that this aspect of his judgment remains good law. See below, paras 16–170, 16–176.

[853] *Euro-Diam Ltd v Bathurst* [1990] 1 Q.B. 1, 35–36.

[854] See below, para.16–178.

[855] *Feret v Hill* (1854) 15 C.B. 207; *Ayerst v Jenkins* (1873) L.R. 16 Eq. 275, 283, 284; *Alexander v Rayson* [1936] 1 K.B. 169, 184; *Edler v Auerbach* [1950] 1 K.B. 359, 373; cf. *Greenwood v Bishop of London* (1814) 5 Taunt. 727, 746; *Mason v Clarke* [1954] 1 Q.B. 460 (reversed on the facts on this point [1955] A.C. 778).

[856] See below, para.16–178.

16–168 **Benefits resulting from crime.** Closely akin to the maxim ex turpi causa non oritur actio is the rule that neither a party nor his representative is permitted to found rights upon his deliberate commission of a crime:

> "It is clear . . . that no person can obtain, or enforce, any rights resulting to him from his own crime; neither can his representative, claiming under him, obtain or enforce any such rights. The human mind revolts at the very idea that any other doctrine could be possible in our system of jurisprudence."[857]

The rule only makes unenforceable rights to money or property to which, but for the crime, the plaintiff would have had no right or title[858]; it does not apply where the right on which the plaintiff relies would no less have come into existence when it did, even had the plaintiff committed no crime.[859] And it has been said that:

> ". . . in these days there are many statutory offences which are the subject of the criminal law, and in that sense are crimes, but which would, it seems, afford no moral justification to a court to apply the maxim"[860];

> ". . . in each case it is not the label which the law applies to the crime . . . but the nature of the crime itself which in the end will dictate whether public policy demands the court to drive the applicant from the seat of justice."[861]

16–169 **Rights resulting from victim's death.** Where a husband insured his life for the benefit of his wife, and his wife was convicted of murdering him, neither the wife nor her assigns could recover the insurance money. It was held, however, that there was a resulting trust in favour of the murdered husband's estate, inasmuch as between his representatives and the insurers no question of public policy arose, and their rights were unaffected by the wife's crime.[862] Similarly when a man insured the life of another for his own benefit and then murdered him for the sake of the insurance money, the murderer's representatives could not

---

[857] *In the Estate of Crippen* [1911] P. 108, 112; *Re Giles* [1972] Ch. 544; *Geismar v Sun Alliance and London Insurance Ltd* [1978] Q.B. 383. cf. *Gray v Barr* [1971] 2 Q.B. 554; *Pitts v Hunt* [1991] 1 Q.B. 24; *Charlton v Fisher* [2001] EWCA Civ 112, [2001] 1 All E.R. (Comm) 769; *Dubai Aluminium Co Ltd v Salaam* [2000] 3 W.L.R. 910.

[858] *St John Shipping Corp v Joseph Rank Ltd* [1957] 1 Q.B. 267, 292. It also applies where a person who is injured by his accomplice in crime sues the accomplice or his estate in tort: *Pitts v Hunt* [1991] 1 Q.B. 24. See also *Thorne v Silverleaf* [1994] 1 B.C.L.C. 637, 645.

[859] *Marles v Philip Trant & Sons Ltd* [1954] 1 Q.B. 29.

[860] per Lord Wright M.R. in *Beresford v Royal Insurance Co Ltd* [1937] 2 K.B. 197, 220 (affirmed [1938] A.C. 586); *Marles v Philip Trant Sons Ltd* [1954] 1 Q.B. 29, 37; cf. *St John Shipping Corp v Joseph Rank Ltd* [1957] 1 Q.B. 267, 292.

[861] *R. v Chief National Insurance Commissioner* [1981] Q.B. 758, 765. See also *Thorne v Silverleaf* [1994] 1 B.C.L.C. 637.

[862] *Cleaver v Mutual Reserve Fund Life Association* [1892] 1 Q.B. 147, per Fry L.J. at 159 (making it clear, however, that the murderer should never benefit). Where the deceased and the killer held property as joint tenants, the forfeiture rule in all probability operates to "sever the joint tenancy in the proceeds of sale and in the rent and profits until sale" a result which can be achieved by treating the "beneficial interests as vesting in the deceased and survivors as tenants in common": per Vinelott J. in *Re K. (Deceased)* [1985] Ch. 85, 100H (the judgment of Vinelott J. was upheld on appeal [1986] Ch. 180).

recover on the policy.[863] The rule would also apply to a conviction for manslaughter.[864] However, a special verdict that the accused is "not guilty by reason of insanity" is, for this purpose, equivalent to a simple acquittal.[865]

The Forfeiture Act 1982. The Forfeiture Act 1982,[866] which started life as a private member's Bill, is intended to modify the public policy in cases such as *R. v Chief National Insurance Commissioner*[867] where the court held that a wife who had killed her husband forfeited statutory entitlements accruing because of his death despite the fact that in the circumstances there was little moral blame attached to the wife's conduct. This Act vests in the court a discretion to modify the "forfeiture rule" which is defined in s.1(1) as: 16–170

> " . . . the rule of public policy which in certain circumstances precludes a person who has unlawfully killed another from acquiring a benefit in consequence of that killing."

Thus it only applies to benefits acquired by the person who does the killing and not to a situation where the estate of the deceased benefits.[868] The court can modify the forfeiture rule in whole or in part[869] but only where it is satisfied that:

> " . . . having regard to the conduct of the offender and of the deceased and to such other circumstances as appear to the court to be material, the justice of the case requires the effects of the rule to be so modified in that case."[870]

The power to modify the forfeiture rule does not however apply "in the case of a person who stands convicted of murder".[871] In circumstances where a person "stands convicted of an offence of which unlawful killing is an element" the Act contains its own limitation period and an order can only be made where proceedings are commenced within a period of three months commencing with the conviction. In the first reported case applying the Act[872] a widow who had for many years been subjected to violent and unprovoked attacks by her husband accidentally shot him with his shotgun in circumstances where she feared another attack. She was convicted of manslaughter and given a non-custodial sentence. In

---

863 *Prince of Wales, etc., Association Co v Palmer* (1858) 25 Beav. 605.

864 *In the Estate of Hall* [1914] P. 1; *Re Giles* [1972] Ch. 54 (manslaughter by reason of diminished responsibility); cf. above, para.16–168 fn.861; *R. v Chief National Insurance Commissioner* [1981] Q.B. 758 (wife convicted of manslaughter not entitled to widow's allowance under s.24(1) of the Social Security Act 1975).

865 *Re Houghton* [1915] 2 Ch. 173, relating to the old verdict of "guilty, but insane" under s.2 of the Trial of Lunatics Act 1883, which is now repealed by s.1(1) of the Criminal Procedure (Insanity) Act 1964.

866 See (1983) 46 M.L.R. 62; Cretney (1990) 10 O.J.L.S. 289.

867 [1981] Q.B. 758.

868 See, e.g. *Beresford v Royal Insurance Co Ltd* [1937] 2 K.B. 197, CA.

869 Forfeiture Act 1982 s.5.

870 s.2(2).

871 s.5.

872 *Re K* [1985] Ch. 85, [1986] Ch. 180, CA. See also *Re Royse* [1985] Ch. 22; *Re S. (Deceased)* [1996] 1 W.L.R. 235; *Dunbar v Plant* [1997] 4 All E.R. 289 (in this case Phillips L.J. disapproved of the approach of the judge in *Re S.* [1996] 1 W.L.R. 235, 387).

these circumstances, given the relative lack of moral culpability on the part of the widow, Vinelott J. held that the forfeiture rule should not operate and his decision was upheld on appeal. The Court of Appeal considered it appropriate for the court in exercising its discretion under s.2(2) to take into consideration the widow's loyalty as a wife, the widow's mental distress at the time the accident occurred, the deceased's behaviour, and the deceased's own assessment of how the wife should be treated on his death.[873] The Court of Appeal has also held that in exercising its discretion under s.2(2), it was wrong for the court to consider that it had to do justice as between the parties, rather it had to take into consideration all aspects of the case.[874]

16–171 **Life insurance and suicide.** Until 1961 one who committed suicide when sane was guilty of a crime, committing as it were murder on himself, and a claim by his personal representatives on a life policy effected by him could not be enforced since it was treated as equivalent to a claim by a murderer or his representative on a policy effected by the murderer on the life of the person murdered.[875] Even before 1961, public policy was no bar to a claim on such a policy,[876] by assignees for value, at any rate to the extent of their actual interest,[877] or by the representatives of the deceased if he was insane at the time of his suicide.[878] Section 1 of the Suicide Act 1961 abrogated the rule of law whereby it was a crime for a person to commit suicide and it is thought that public policy is no longer a bar to any claim resulting from the suicide of the assured. But there may still be a distinction between suicide when sane and when insane. In the case of insane suicide, in the absence of any special condition that the policy is to be avoided by suicide, the policy continues to be enforceable as under the old law.[879] In the case of sane suicide, in the absence of any special condition, express or implied, that the policy shall not be avoided by suicide, policy moneys may still be irrecoverable by reason of the presumption[880] that the promise to pay on the happening of a specified event does not apply where that event was deliberately caused by the assured.[881] Where, however, the policy

---

[873] The court's discretion was not to be limited by the principles of the Inheritance (Provision for Family and Dependants) Act 1975.

[874] *Dunbar v Plant* [1997] 4 All E.R. 289, 302–303, 312–313.

[875] *Horn v Anglo-Australian, etc., Life Assurance Co* (1861) 30 L.J. Ch. 511; *Beresford v Royal Insurance Co Ltd* [1937] 2 K.B. 197, [1938] A.C. 586.

[876] As to the possibility of a claim by the deceased's personal representatives for return of the premiums, see *St John Shipping Corp v Joseph Rank Ltd* [1957] 1 Q.B. 267, 293.

[877] *Beresford v Royal Insurance Co Ltd* [1938] A.C. 586, 600; *Moore v Woolsey* (1854) 4 E. & B. 243.

[878] See fn.875, above.

[879] See fn.875, above.

[880] See *MacGillivray on Insurance Law*, 9th edn (1997), para.14–66.

[881] Thus under the old law, though claims by assignees for value were not barred by public policy (see fn.877, above), enforcement of such claims depended upon the insurance policy containing a promise to pay, either generally, or to assignees for value (*White v British Empire Mutual Life Insurance Co of New York* (1868) L.R. 7 Eq. 394; *Rowett Leakey & Co v Scottish Provident Institution* [1927] 1 Ch. 55; *Royal London Mutual Insurance Society Ltd v Barrett* [1928] Ch. 411), in the event of sane suicide.

contains a promise, express or implied, to pay in the event of suicide, there is no room for that presumption to operate.

Assured suffering death at the hands of the law. In *Amicable Society v Bolland*[882] where the assured was hanged for forgery, it was held that his assignees could not recover the sum for which his life was insured. The essential feature of the decision was that the court would not allow a claim in contract to be based on the contracting party's crime as a necessary constituent of the cause of action, even though an interval of time and circumstance separated the crime from the resulting death.[883] 16–172

Indemnity against liability resulting from commission of crime. An indemnity[884] against civil[885] or criminal,[886] liability resulting from the deliberate commission of a crime by the person to be indemnified generally cannot be enforced by the criminal or his representatives, the reason being that, on grounds of public policy, either the indemnity is subject to an implied exclusion which operates against the criminal and his representatives or they are under a personal disability or ban which prevents their suing on it.[887] Thus, in *Askey v Golden Wine Co Ltd*[888] a wholesaler, through his own gross negligence, incurred a fine and costs as a result of breaches of the Food and Drugs Act and had to refund money to his retailers. Denning J. held that it would be against public policy to permit him to recover his loss, by way of damages for conspiracy, from those responsible for the management of the company which supplied him with the goods and it is clear from the judgment that the learned judge would have held a claim against the company for damages for breach of contract in respect of such loss to be equally unenforceable. But probably, as in the case of the closely related rule that a man may not benefit from his own crime, this rule does not apply to every breach of the criminal law[889]; indeed, it has been said that the courts' refusal to permit a person who has committed an anti-social act to assert a resultant right depends not only on the nature of the anti-social act but also on the nature of the right asserted.[890] Thus, for example, the rule does not apply to every breach of the criminal law. It does not apply, for example, to the innocent commission of an offence of strict liability.[891] It is also clear that policies of insurance relating to motor accidents are enforceable, so that a motorist who has to pay damages for negligence can recover an indemnity from his insurers; and 16–173

---

882 (1830) 2 Dow. & Cl. 1, where, however, the assignees were volunteers.

883 *Beresford v Royal Insurance Co* [1937] 2 K.B. 197, 213; affirmed [1938] A.C. 586.

884 As to the right of contribution as between joint tortfeasors, see Civil Liability Contribution Act 1978.

885 *Haseldine v Hosken* [1933] 1 K.B. 822 (indemnity against solicitor's civil liability for champerty held unenforceable): but see now below, para.16–175.

886 *Colburn v Patmore* (1834) 1 Cr.M. & R. 73; *Fitzgerald v Leonard* (1893) 32 L.R.Ir. 675. cf. *Geismar v Sun Alliance and London Insurance Ltd* [1978] Q.B. 838.

887 *Hardy v Motor Insurers' Bureau* [1964] 2 Q.B. 745, 760, 765; *Charlton v Fisher* [2001] EWCA Civ 112, [2001] 1 All E.R. (Comm) 769.

888 [1948] 2 All E.R. 35. See above, para.16–169, fn.862.

889 cf. *R. v Chief National Insurance Commissioner* [1981] Q.B. 758, 765, per Lord Lane C.J.

890 *Hardy v Motor Insurers' Bureau* [1964] 2 Q.B. 745, 767–768.

891 *Gregory v Ford* [1951] 1 All E.R. 121; *Osman v J. Ralph Moss Ltd* [1970] 1 Lloyd's Rep. 313.

this is so even though the negligence was so gross[892] as to amount to manslaughter.[893] Perhaps this is to be explained on the ground that here the act to be indemnified is one intended by the law that people should insure against,[894] or that the social harm which would be caused by not enforcing such insurance rights outweighs the gravity of the anti-social act committed and the extent to which such acts will be encouraged by the enforcement of such rights.[895] With these cases should be contrasted *Gray v Barr*[896]; a husband shot and killed his wife's lover; it was held by the Court of Appeal that the husband could not recover under an insurance policy (even if it covered the occurrence) the damages which he had had to pay to the lover's estate. The husband had caused the victim's death in the course of deliberately committing an unlawful and dangerous act (threatening the lover with a loaded shotgun) which in the opinion of the Court of Appeal amounted to the crime of manslaughter, and to allow persons to enforce indemnities against the consequences of their own acts of armed violence would clearly be contrary to public policy. There was no evidence in this case whether the husband could satisfy the judgment without obtaining payment from the insurance company. The failure of the court to advert to this would indicate that it was not a relevant factor although the effect of the judgment might be to deprive an innocent party of compensation.

16–174 In *Cooke v Routledge*[897] the Northern Ireland Court of Appeal held that a driver could recover under his insurance policy the cost of a replacement vehicle in circumstances where he had crashed his car while driving with an excess of alcohol in his blood for which he was not convicted. The insurance company argued that as a matter of public policy no such recovery should be permitted. The court rejected this argument on the grounds[898]:

---

[892] As to the distinction between negligence and intention in such cases, see *Hardy v Motor Insurers' Bureau* [1964] 2 Q.B. 745. The *Hardy* case was approved by the House of Lords in *Gardner v Moore* [1984] A.C. 548 where an uninsured driver had deliberately driven his car at the plaintiff for which he was convicted.

[893] *Tinline v White Cross Insurance Association Ltd* [1921] 3 K.B. 327; *James v British & General Insurance Co Ltd* [1972] 2 K.B. 311; compare *Crage v Fry* (1903) 67 J.P. 240; *Cointat v Mynham & Son* [1913] 2 K.B. 220; reversed on a different point (1914) 30 T.L.R. 282: *R. Leslie Ltd v Reliable Advertising, etc., Agency Ltd* [1915] 1 K.B. 652; *Simon v Pawsons & Leafs Ltd* (1932) 38 Com. Cas. 151, with *Fitzgerald v Leonard* (1893) 32 L.R.Ir. 675 and *Askey v Golden Wine Co Ltd* [1948] 2 All E.R. 35.

[894] per Greer L.J. in *Haseldine v Hosken* [1933] 1 K.B. 822, 838; and see the difference of opinion between Denning and Hodson L.JJ. in *Marles v Philip Trant & Sons Ltd* [1954] 1 Q.B. 29, 39–40 and 44.

[895] *Hardy v Motor Insurers' Bureau* [1964] 2 Q.B. 745, 768. In *Hardy v Motor Insurers' Bureau* [1964] 2 Q.B. 745, 769, Diplock L.J. considered that an assured who had discharged his liability to the victim would not be able to enforce his contractual right to indemnity against the insurance company where the damages were connected with an intentional criminal act; cf. the case of insurance by employers which covers liability for breach of the Factories Act, where under the law before the Employers' Liability (Compulsory Insurance) Act 1969 the explanation put forward in the text to fn.894 above, would not have applied but which had never been suggested to be unenforceable, however gross the employer's negligence.

[896] [1971] 2 Q.B. 554.

[897] [1998] N.I.L.R. 174.

[898] *Cooke v Routledge* [1998] N.I.L.R. 174, 185f–g, per Carswell L.C.J.

> "Insurance companies and insured persons need to be able to ascertain their respective rights with some degree of certainty. It would be impossible for either to know in what circumstances cover would be afforded under a motor policy. As [counsel for the appellant] asked rhetorically in his argument on behalf of the appellant, what level of consumption of alcohol would prevent recovery? What degree of reckless driving would lead to an exclusion of liability? If excessive speed were to disentitle an insured from enforcing the policy, what degree of excess over the permitted limit would do so? And what if the repair of the vehicle had been grossly neglected by the insured?"

The court considered it was of importance that cases, such as *Gray v Barr*,[899] where a criminal act by the insured had precluded recovery, "concerned branches of insurance other than motor insurance".[900]

Indemnity against liability resulting from commission of tort. Where the act to be indemnified is not only a tort but also a crime, the position is that set out in the preceding paragraph. Where the act is a mere tort, the enforceability of an agreement to indemnify against liability resulting from its commission depends upon the nature of the act and the circumstances of its commission.[901] Thus a contract to indemnify a person against liability for an act which constitutes the tort of deceit is unenforceable.[902] So also an agreement to indemnify a person against liability for the publication of what he knows to be a libel is unenforceable.[903] But an indemnity against innocent publication of a libel is enforceable by virtue of the provisions of s.11 of the Defamation Act 1952 which enacts that an agreement for indemnifying any person against civil liability for libel in respect of the publication of any matter shall not be unlawful unless at the time of publication that person knows that the matter is defamatory, and does not reasonably believe that there is a good defence to any action brought upon it. And at common law, where, as a natural consequence of a breach of contract by one party, the other incurs liability for defamation, there is no rule of public policy which prevents the recovery by way of damages of the loss suffered by the first party as a result of his tort, at any rate where the commission of the tort was not deliberate.[904] 16–175

(b) *Collateral Transactions*

Alternative cause of action. Although the ex turpi causa principle precludes a plaintiff from being able directly to enforce an illegal contract, it does not prevent him from enforcing causes of action which are collateral to the contract. By this means the courts have to some extent mitigated the severity of the 16–176

---

[899] [1971] 2 Q.B. 554.

[900] *Cooke v Routledge* [1998] N.I.L.R. 174, 186h–g.

[901] See the dicta in *Hardy v Motor Insurers' Bureau* [1964] 2 Q.B. 745, 767–770. cf. *Adamson v Jarvis* (1827) 4 Bing. 66; *Betts & Drewe v Gibbins* (1834) 2 A. & E. 57; *Lister v Romford Ice & Cold Storage Co Ltd* [1957] A.C. 555; in all of which indemnities have been enforced.

[902] *Brown Jenkinson & Co Ltd v Percy Dalton (London) Ltd* [1957] 2 Q.B. 621.

[903] *Smith v Clinton* (1908) 99 L.T. 840.

[904] *Bradstreets British Ltd v Mitchell and Carapanayoti & Co Ltd* [1933] Ch. 190; *Daily Mirror Newspapers Ltd v Exclusive News Agency* (1937) 81 S.J. 924; *K. v P.* [1993] Ch. 140 (in an action against the defendant for conspiracy to defraud, the ex turpi causa maxim did not preclude the defendant from serving a contribution notice on a third party).

illegality doctrine. In *Strongman Ltd v Sincock*[905] the plaintiff carried out building work for which it did not possess the appropriate licence and thus was unable to bring an action on the contract for the work done. However, the defendant (an architect) had assured the plaintiff that he would obtain the necessary licence and the court held that this gave rise to a collateral contract on which the plaintiff could maintain an action. An action may also lie in fraud as occurred in *Shelley v Paddock*[906] where the plaintiff was induced to enter into an illegal contract for the sale of a house in Spain by the fraud of the defendant. Also, where the circumstances are appropriate, there is no reason why a plaintiff should not recover damages for negligent misrepresentation. It was once thought that it was essential for the plaintiff to show that he was ignorant of the illegality.[907] This was a point emphasised in both *Strongman Ltd v Sincock*[908] and *Shelley* v *Paddock*.[909] However, in *Saunders v Edwards*[910] the court allowed a plaintiff, who was a knowing party to an illegal contract, to recover damages for the fraud of the defendant. The plaintiff had purchased a flat from the defendant. The purchase price contained an inflated figure for fixtures and fittings which reduced the stamp duty payable by the plaintiff. Despite the fact that the court found that the plaintiff's conduct was tainted by the illegality connected with the evasion of stamp duty, the court allowed the plaintiff to recover damages for the fraud of the defendant in misrepresenting the extent of the property being sold. The court held that the "relative moral culpability" of the parties could be taken into consideration in deciding whether the plaintiff should be given a remedy which did not involve the enforcement of the contract.[911] As the moral culpability of the defendant greatly outweighed that of the plaintiff in the *Saunders* case, the court allowed the plaintiff to recover. In the light of the House of Lords disapproval in *Tinsley v Milligan*[912] of the approach of the court in the *Saunders* case, it is no longer proper to carry out a balancing exercise as to the relative culpability of the parties. However, the decision in *Saunders v Edwards*[913] can possibly be explained on the grounds that the plaintiff had "an unassailable claim for

---

[905] [1955] 2 Q.B. 525.

[906] [1980] Q.B. 348 (Brandon L.J., had serious doubts but he reluctantly agreed with the majority). It is also important to note that in *Shelley v Paddock* the fraud did not relate to the legality of the transaction, that is, the sale of the house: see (1978) 94 L.Q.R. 484. See also *Burrows v Rhodes* [1899] 1 Q.B. 816; *Dott v Brickwell* (1906) 23 T.L.R. 61; *Archbolds (Freightage) Ltd v S. Spanglett Ltd* [1961] 1 Q.B. 374, 392–393; *Southern Industrial Trust Ltd v Brooke House Motors Ltd* (1968) 112 S.J. 798.

[907] It was considered that if the plaintiff had knowledge of the illegality he would be *in pari delicto* with the defendant and thus unable to obtain the assistance of the court.

[908] [1955] 2 Q.B. 525, 536–537. Denning L.J. in that case also thought it important that the plaintiff was not negligent with respect to determining the existence of the illegality. cf. the degree of knowledge required where a contract is allegedly tainted with the illegality of some other transaction: above, para.16–165 fn.846.

[909] [1980] Q.B. 348, 357.

[910] [1987] 1 W.L.R. 1116; see also *Mitsubishi Corp v Alafouzos* [1988] 1 F.T.L.R. 47; *Hughes v Clewley (The "Siben") (No.2)* [1996] 1 Lloyd's Rep. 35.

[911] It was on this basis that the court distinguished *Alexander v Rayson* [1936] 1 K.B. 169. The court left open the issue of what would have happened had the defendant refused to complete and the plaintiff had sued for specific performance or damages (at 1125C). The court also considered that the dictum of Lindley L.J. in *Scott v Brown, Doering, McNab & Co* [1892] 2 Q.B. 724, 729 could not be applied literally in every situation (at 1127).

[912] [1994] 1 A.C. 340; [1993] 3 W.L.R. 126.

[913] [1987] 1 W.L.R. 1116.

damages for fraud which did not involve any reliance on the contract of sale itself".[914] Also, where services are rendered under a contract which is intended to be performed in an illegal manner, or which is illegal at its inception, a quantum meruit claim will not lie.[915] Such a claim would circumvent the public policy underlying the making of a contract illegal.

(c) *Recovery of Money Paid or Property Transferred under Illegal Contracts*[916]

Non-recovery of consideration. While cases in which the plaintiff seeks the enforcement of an illegal contract are governed by the maxim ex turpi causa non oritur actio, those in which he seeks some release from its operation fall within the principle *in pari delicto potior est conditio defendentis*. The result of the application of this principle is that where both parties, contracting on an equal footing, are aware of the illegal nature of the contract, whether it be on its face illegal or whether the common intention be to carry out the contract in an illegal manner, neither party can recover anything paid or transferred thereunder. So, in a contract to secure a title for the plaintiff in return for payment, the plaintiff, when he failed to receive his title, could not recover back what he had paid, the contract being *turpis* and the parties *in pari delicto*.[917] A fortiori where the defendant had performed his part of the agreement the plaintiff cannot set up the illegal nature of the transaction in order to recover a deposit or part payment. Thus in *Taylor v Chester*[918] the plaintiff failed to recover the half of a £50 banknote deposited with the defendant to secure payment by the plaintiff of the price of wines and suppers supplied by the defendant in her brothel for the purposes of a debauch and of loans of money by the defendant to the plaintiff for expenditure in riot, debauchery and immoral conduct. The court held that the plaintiff failed, since he could not make out his case "otherwise than through the medium and by the aid of the illegal transaction to which he was himself a party".[919] 16–177

Transfer of property under illegal transactions.[920] When property has been delivered in pursuance of an illegal agreement[921] and there is subsequently a dispute about the property between the transferor and the transferee, the question 16–178

[914] *Tinsley v Milligan* [1994] 1 A.C. 340, 360. On this reasoning, the point left open by the judge (see fn.911 above) would be answered in the negative.

[915] *Taylor v Bhail* [1996] C.L.C. 377 (cost of repairs inflated to defraud insurers). In *AL Barnes Ltd v Time Talk (UK) Ltd* [2003] EWCA Civ 402, *The Times*, April 9, 2003 the reasoning in *Taylor v Bhail* was considered to apply to cases where the contract was illegal as formed but not to a case where there was illegality in the performance of the contract.

[916] The approach in this section follows that of Treitel, *The Law of Contract*, 12th edn (by Peel, 2007), pp.541–565. See also Goff and Jones, *The Law of Restitution*, 7th edn (2007), Ch.24; Burrows, *The Law of Restitution*, 2nd edn (2002), pp.323–336.

[917] *Parkinson v College of Ambulance Ltd* [1925] 2 K.B. 1; and see *Shaw v Shaw* [1965] 1 W.L.R. 537.

[918] (1869) L.R. 4 Q.B. 309. See also *Bigos v Bousted* [1951] 1 All E.R. 92.

[919] (1869) L.R. 4 Q.B. 309, 314.

[920] See Higgins (1962) 25 M.L.R. 149: Grodecki (1955) 71 L.Q.R. 254.

[921] cf. below, para.16–179.

often arises whether the court should give effect to the transferee's interest[922] or disregard it and enforce the transferor's original rights. The fact that by reason of illegality the transferee could not have enforced the agreement under which the transfer was made does not necessarily mean that delivery to him of property thereunder will not pass to him the property or the interest in question. Thus where goods are delivered in pursuance of an illegal contract of sale, the property in them passes to the purchaser who will be entitled to damages against anyone, including the vendor, who thereafter wrongfully deprives him of those goods.[923] Where a person takes a lease of property intending to use it for an immoral purpose, he acquires an interest under the executed lease despite the intention to use the property for an immoral purpose.[924] It is now clear that property may pass under an illegal sale, although the goods have not been delivered to the buyer,[925] so that the buyer may obtain rights against a *third* person. But it would not appear that a buyer to whom property in goods has passed under an illegal contract can claim them, or damages for their conversion, from a *seller* who has never delivered them at all. Such a claim would not differ in substance from a claim for the delivery, or for damages for the non-delivery, of the goods under the illegal contract and its success would defeat the policy of the rule against the enforcement of such a contract.[926] Statutes may avoid not only the agreement in pursuance of which a transfer is made[927] but also the transfer itself so that the transferor can rely on his original title and recover the property from the transferee to whom, because of the statute, no property passed and who therefore cannot set up any interest in the property by way of defence to the claim.[928]

16–179 **Determination of limited interests created by illegal transactions.** Where the interest created by an illegal transaction was by the provisions of the transaction limited for a term, after the expiry of that term the transferor can probably recover the property. Thus, the owner of a house let to a prostitute could no doubt recover possession by ejectment at the end of the term, though he would be precluded from recovering rent if he knew the purpose to which it was intended to put the premises.[929] Whether an owner could recover possession for non-payment of rent (assuming the lease provides for this) where, for example,

---

[922] The transferor cannot claim to have retained the beneficial interest where, in order to establish the trust in his favour, he must rely on the illegal purpose of the transfer: *Palaniappa Chettiar v Aranasalam Chettiar* [1962] A.C. 294.

[923] *Singh v Ali* [1960] A.C. 167. And see *Taylor v Chester* (1869) L.R. 4 Q.B. 309; *Tinsley v Milligan* [1994] 1 A.C. 340, 374, per Lord Browne-Wilkinson: "the effect of illegality is not to prevent a proprietary interest in equity from arising or to produce a forfeiture of such right: the effect is to render the equitable interest unenforceable in certain circumstances." The court will not enforce a claim by a person claiming funds held by a person in the position of trustee (in this case a solicitor) where the claimant has to rely on his fraud: see *Halley v Law Society* [2003] EWCA Civ 97.

[924] *Feret v Hill* (1854) 15 C.B. 207.

[925] *Belvoir Finance Co Ltd v Stapleton* [1971] 1 Q.B. 210; cf. *Kingsley v Sterling Industrial Securities* [1967] 2 Q.B. 747, 783.

[926] Treitel, *The Law of Contract*, 12th edn (by Peel, 2007), p.554.

[927] See above, para.16–159.

[928] *Amar Singh v Kulubya* [1964] A.C. 142.

[929] *Jajbhay v Cassim* (1939) A.D. 537, 557 (S. Africa); *Alexander v Rayson* [1936] 1 K.B. 169, 186–187.

he knowingly rents premises for the purposes of prostitution is more problematical. It is difficult to see how the owner could recover without relying on the lease and accordingly he would be denied the assistance of the court. It has been argued that as the lease is illegal neither party can rely on it so that the tenant is a tenant at will and the owner can thereupon take steps to terminate the lease.[930] Although creative as a solution to the problem, it ignores the fact that illegal contracts can operate to transfer title and presumably any other proprietary interest. Accordingly, the tenant would acquire a limited interest under the lease and it would appear that the owner would therefore be unable to recover possession until the limited property interest of the tenant comes to an end.[931] On the other hand, money or property may be paid or transferred by way of security for the performance of an illegal act which is not performed; in such cases it is thought that a claim to recover the money or property, on the ground of the non-performance of the act for which payment was made, would fail. For had the money or property been paid or transferred outright by way of payment a claim based on a total failure of consideration would have failed.[932] Great difficulties arise however in the case where the property has been bailed under a contract which is illegal by common law or statute.

In *Bowmakers Ltd v Barnet Instruments Ltd*[933] the Court of Appeal formulated the rule to be applied in cases of bailment of chattels thus: **16–180**

> "In our opinion a man's right to possess his own chattels will as a general rule be enforced as against one who, without any claim or right, is detaining them or has converted them to his own use, even though it may appear either from the pleadings, or in the course of the trial, that the chattels came into the defendant's possession by reason of an illegal contract between himself and the plaintiff, provided that the plaintiff does not seek and is not forced either to found his claim on the illegal contract or to plead its illegality in order to support his claim."

In that case, illegal bailments of machinery under hire-purchase agreements were assumed to have been terminated, in some cases by the sale of the machinery by the bailees, and, in one other case, by their refusal to deliver the machinery up to the plaintiffs on demand. The bailments having been terminated, the plaintiffs were held entitled to rely on their proprietary interests in the machinery, and accordingly recovered damages for conversion.[934] The principal difficulty in the case arises with regard to the implicit finding that the latter bailment was terminated by the defendant bailees' refusal to deliver up the machinery on demand. If it were always possible for a bailor to terminate an illegal bailment on breach of its terms by the bailee, merely by demanding the return of the

---

[930] *Munro v Morrison* [1980] V.R. 83.

[931] See *Jajbhay v Cassim* (1939) A.D. 537.

[932] Contrast *Milner v Staffordshire Congregational Union Inc* [1956] Ch. 275, where the contract was statutorily unlawful only in the sense of being void and a deposit was therefore recoverable. And see *South Western Mineral Water Co Ltd v Ashmore* [1967] 1 W.L.R. 1110; below, para.16–201.

[933] [1945] K.B. 65, 71; applied in *Singh v Ali* [1960] A.C. 167 and also in *Belvoir Finance Co Ltd v Harold G. Cole & Co Ltd* [1969] 1 W.L.R. 1877; *Tinsley v Milligan* [1993] 3 W.L.R. 126.

[934] But if the action for conversion is statute-barred and the only cause of action is under the illegal bailment, the action will fail: *Thomas Brown & Sons v Fazal Deen* (1962) 108 C.L.R. 391 (Australia).

property bailed, little would be left of the general rule of non-recovery so far as bailments are concerned.[935] It has been argued that the hire-purchase agreement in *Bowmakers Ltd v Barnet Instruments Ltd* probably contained a cesser clause making the agreement determine on the failure of the hirer to pay instalments and thus the owner was entitled to recover the machinery which was still in the possession of the defendants.[936] There may also be special cases where a person is not entitled to recover property although his title to it is clear. An example of this type of case was given by Du Parcq L.J., in *Bowmakers Ltd v Barnet Instruments Ltd*[937] as occurring where the owner of obscene books attempts to recover them, and a similar result has been suggested where the owner of a weapon to be used to commit a serious crime tries to recover it.[938]

16–181 The principle in *Bowmakers* also applies to equitable interests. In *Tinsley v Milligan*[939] the plaintiff and the defendant contributed to the purchase of a house which was placed in the sole name of the plaintiff for the purpose of enabling the defendant to make fraudulent claims on the Department of Social Security. The plaintiff and defendant quarrelled and the plaintiff, having moved out of the house, commenced proceedings asserting ownership of the whole of the house. The defendant successfully counterclaimed for, inter alia, an order that the plaintiff held the house on trust in equal shares for the defendant and plaintiff. The House of Lords reasoned that the fact that the arrangement involved an illegality did not prevent an equitable interest from arising[940] and, since the fusion of law and equity, the principle in *Bowmakers* extended to equitable interests. As all that the defendant was seeking was recovery of an equitable proprietary interest which arose under a resulting trust, she could recover it without having to rely on the illegality. The majority of the House in *Tinsley v Milligan*[941] also rejected the argument that the "clean hands" maxim in equity precluded the plaintiff from recovering on the grounds of title. Although collateral rights, as in *Tinsley v Milligan*,[942] may arise out of an illegal contract, a collateral right normally involves a proprietary right and does not include a right of action on the contract itself.[943]

[935] Contrast *Bigos v Bousted* [1951] 1 All E.R. 92; *Archbolds (Freightage) Ltd v S. Spanglett Ltd* [1961] 1 Q.B. 374, 384. And see Hamson (1949) 10 Camb.L.J. 249; Paton, *Bailment in the Common Law* (1972), pp.34–36; Coote (1972) 35 M.L.R. 38.

[936] See Treitel, *The Law of Contract*, pp.548–549.

[937] [1945] K.B. 65, 72.

[938] Treitel at pp.553–554. See, however, Lord Goff's terrorist example in *Tinsley v Milligan* [1994] 1 A.C. 340, 362. See also *Webb v Chief Constable of Merseyside Police* [2000] 1 All E.R. 209, 22 (person could not recover, on the basis of title, controlled drugs seized by the police); *Costello v Chief Constable of Derbyshire Constabulary* [2001] EWCA Civ 381, [2001] 3 All E.R. 150.

[939] [1994] 1 A.C. 340.

[940] *Tinsley v Milligan* [1994] 1 A.C. 340, 373–374.

[941] [1994] 1 A.C. 340 (Lord Keith and Lord Goff dissenting). All of the law lords disapproved of the approach of the courts in *Thackwell v Barclays Bank Plc* [1986] 1 All E.R. 676; *Saunders v Edwards* [1987] 1 W.L.R. 1116; and *Euro-Diam Ltd v Bathurst* [1990] Q.B. 1 which had been followed by the majority of the Court of Appeal in *Tinsley v Milligan*.

[942] [1994] 1 A.C. 340.

[943] *Mahonia Ltd v JP Morgan Chase Bank* [2003] 2 Lloyd's Rep 911, at [27]. See also *Mahonia Ltd v West LB AG* [2004] EWHC 1938 (Comm).

***Locus poenitentiae*: presumption of advancement.** In *Tinsley v Milligan*[944] the House of Lords considered that its reasoning would not apply to a situation where there was a presumption of advancement between the plaintiff and the defendant[945] (in that the presumption would negative the resulting trust). This was the issue that was before the court in *Tribe v Tribe*.[946] In that case, a father transferred to his son shares in a company in order to protect them against the possible claims of his creditors, the shares to be held by his son on trust for him until he had settled the claims. Eventually, he settled with his creditors and sought to recover the shares from his son who refused to re-transfer them. The court held that the father could recover his shares. The court reasoned that provided the "illegal purpose has not been carried into effect in any way",[947] the father could recover his shares on the grounds that he did not intend to confer the beneficial interest on the son and therefore the presumption of advancement would be successfully rebutted. On the facts of the case the court held that as the illegal purpose had not been carried into effect since no deception had been practised on the father's creditors, the father could recover the shares. This decision extends, in a way that is unacceptable, the principles on the right of withdrawal with respect to illegal contracts, in that it enables the tranferor of property to recover it where the illegal purpose for which it was transferred in the first place is no longer needed to protect the transferor's interests.[948] Millett L.J. considered that the policy underlying the *locus poenitentiae* was the discouragement of fraud and therefore it necessarily also encouraged "withdrawal from a proposed fraud before it is implemented".[949] However, Millett L.J. recognised that in *Tribe v Tribe* recovery by the father would not be necessary to encourage withdrawal since the reason for the withdrawal was not a change of mind but simply that it was no longer needed.[950] This, rather than discouraging illegal contracts, produces the opposite effect since the transferor of property has nothing to lose and everything to gain by entering into the illegal transaction. On these grounds, *Tribe v Tribe* should be viewed as an extreme, if not wrong, application of the *locus poenitentiae* rule. 16–182

The approach in *Tinsley v Milligan*, depending as it does on proprietary concepts, was not followed in the important decision of the High Court of Australia, *Nelson v Nelson*.[951] It is not possible to do justice to the subtlety and scholarship of this judgment. *Nelson v Nelson* involved a contract designed to acquire for the transferor of property under the contract a statutory benefit to which she would not have been entitled had the transfer not been effected. Thus it was a situation on all fours with *Tinsley v Milligan*. Rather than adopt the proprietary based reasoning of *Tinsley v Milligan*, the approach of the High Court was to determine whether the statutory rule which rendered the contract illegal 16–183

---

[944] [1994] 1 A.C. 340. See Enonchony (1994) 14 O.J.L.S. 295.

[945] [1994] 1 A.C. 340, 372.

[946] [1996] Ch. 107; *Collier v Collier* [2002] EWCA Civ 1095, [2002] B.P.I.R. 1057. See Enonchong [1996] R.L.R. 78.

[947] *Tribe v Tribe* [1996] Ch. 107, 121, per Nourse L.J.; see also 135, per Millett L.J.

[948] See Rose (1996) 112 L.Q.R. 386.

[949] *Tribe v Tribe* [1996] Ch. 107, 134.

[950] [1996] Ch. 107, 135.

[951] (1995) 132 A.L.R. 133.

precluded relief and the court held that it did not. The court cited with approval the views of an American author to the effect:

> "... if illegality consists of the violation of a statute, courts will give or refuse relief depending upon the fundamental purpose of the statute."[952]

The majority also held that in granting relief the court could do it on terms; such a power enables the harshness of the illegality doctrine to be tempered in appropriate circumstances.

16–184 The *Bowmakers* principle can, as with the illegality doctrine in general, operate in a capricious way. The capriciousness of its operation was trenchantly criticised in the Australian Higher Court decision, *Nelson v Nelson*[953]:

> "The *Bowmakers* rule has no regard to the legal and equitable rights of the parties, the merits of the case, the effect of the transaction in undermining the policy of the relevant legislation or the question whether the sanctions imposed by the legislation sufficiently protect the purpose of the legislation. Regard is had only to the procedural issue; and it is that issue and not the policy of the legislation or the merits of the parties which determines the outcome. Basing the grant of legal remedies on an essentially procedural criterion which has nothing to do with the equitable positions of the parties or the policy of the legislation is unsatisfactory, particularly when implementing a doctrine that is founded on public policy."

16–185 **Class-protecting statutes.** The action for money had and received will also lie where it is clear from the statute which prohibits the making of the contract or the doing of the act in question that the parties are not to be treated as *in pari delicto*. Thus, as Lord Mansfield said in *Browning v Morris*[954]:

> "But where contracts or transactions are prohibited by positive statutes, for the sake of protecting one set of men from another set of men, the one, from their situation and condition, being liable to be oppressed or imposed upon by the other, there the parties are not *in pari delicto*; and in furtherance of these statutes, the person injured, after the transaction is finished and completed, many bring his action and defeat the contract."

The court will normally grant him relief without putting him on terms, as to impose terms as a condition precedent to the granting of relief would be virtually tantamount to enforcing the illegal contract.[955] For example, the Rent Act 1977 contains provisions[956] entitling a tenant to recover money which he could not

---

[952] *Nelson v Nelson* (1995) 132 A.L.R. 133, 149.

[953] (1995) 132 A.L.R. 133, 190.

[954] (1778) 2 Cowp. 790; *Barclay v Pearson* [1893] 2 Ch. 154; *Bonnard v Dott* [1906] 1 Ch. 740. In *Lodge v National Union Investment Co* [1907] 1 Ch. 300 it was held that the borrower could not recover his securities unless he repaid the money lent to him; but this decision has been distinguished out of existence: *Chapman v Michaelson* [1908] 2 Ch. 612; [1909] 1 Ch. 238; *Cohen v J. Lester Ltd* [1939] 1 K.B. 504; *Kasumu v Baba-Egbe* [1956] A.C. 539; cf. *Barclay v Prospect Mortgages Ltd* [1974] 1 W.L.R. 837. See also now Consumer Credit Act 1974 s.40(1) as amended by the Enterprise Act 2002 s.278.

[955] *Kasumu v Baba-Egbe* [1956] A.C. 539.

[956] e.g. Rent Act 1977 ss.119–125; see, e.g. *Steele v McMahon* [1990] 44 E.G. 65; *Saleh v Robinson* [1988] 36 E.G. 180. See also Housing Act 1980 s.79; *Ailion v Spiekermann* [1976] Ch. 158 (illegal premium on assignment); *Farrell v Alexander* [1977] A.C. 59.

lawfully have been required to pay; and in a case decided under an earlier Act it was held that he could recover an illegal premium even though he was a willing party to a fraudulent scheme to evade the Act.[957] It used to be thought that the prevalence of such provisions had made the old class-protecting rules obsolete,[958] until their reaffirmation by the Privy Council in *Kiriri Cotton Co Ltd v Dewani*[959]: a tenant paid his landlord a premium for a flat; by accepting the premium, the landlord committed an offence under a Rent Restriction Ordinance which did not expressly say that such premiums could be recovered. Nonetheless the tenant was allowed to recover the premium under the old rules relating to class-protecting statutes.

Oppression and fraud. A person can recover money paid or property transferred under an illegal contract if he was forced by the other party to enter into the illegal contract. "Oppression" is here used in a somewhat broad sense. Thus in *Atkinson v Denby*[960] the plaintiff was insolvent and offered to pay his creditors a dividend of 5s. in the pound. All the creditors were willing to accept the dividend in full settlement of their claims, except the defendants, who said he would only accept it if the plaintiff first paid him £50. The plaintiff did so, but was later allowed to recover the £50 on the ground that he had been forced to agree to defraud the other creditors.[961] Similarly, recovery is possible if the party entered into the contract as a result of the other party's fraudulent misrepresentation that the contract was lawful. Thus in *Hughes v Liverpool Victoria Legal Friendly Society*[962] the plaintiff effected a policy of insurance with the defendants on the life of a person in which he had no insurable interest. The contract was illegal,[963] but the plaintiff was able to recover the premiums he had paid as he had been induced to make the contract by the fraudulent representation of the defendants' agent that the policy was valid. The decisive factor in these cases is the fraud of the defendant and not the innocence of the plaintiff, although if the plaintiff is not innocent there can be no recovery.[964] The plaintiff would have failed if the representation that the policy was valid had been innocently made[965]; if, however, the misrepresentation is one of *fact* rather than law, and no bar to rescission has arisen, then the person who has been induced to enter the contract after the misrepresentation has been made, even *innocently*, would seem to have the right to rescind it and so recover his money or property.[966] 16–186

957 *Gray v Southouse* [1949] 2 All E.R. 1019.

958 See *Green v Portsmouth Stadium* [1953] 2 Q.B. 190; where the ratio now appears to be that the statute in question was passed, not to protect bookmakers, but to regulate racecourses.

959 [1960] A.C. 192.

960 (1862) 7 H. & N. 934; cf. *Smith v Cuff* (1817) 6 M. & S. 169; *Davies v London & Provincial Marine Insurance Co* (1878) 8 Ch D 469; *Erwin v Snelgrove* [1927] 4 D.L.R. 1028.

961 For a case where the "oppression" was caused by factors other than the other party's conduct see *Kiriri Cotton Co Ltd v Dewani* [1960] A.C. 190, 205, per Lord Denning; contrast *Bigos v Bousted* [1951] 1 All E.R. 92 (illness of daughter not sufficient to excuse party in making unlawful foreign exchange transaction).

962 [1916] 2 K.B. 482; *Reynell v Sprye* (1852) 1 De G.M. & G. 660.

963 Life Assurance Act 1774 s.1.

964 *Parkinson v College of Ambulance Ltd* [1925] 2 K.B. 1.

965 *Harse v Pearl Life Assurance Co* [1904] 1 K.B. 558.

966 This was assumed in *Edler v Auerbach* [1950] 1 K.B. 359 where, however, a bar to rescission had arisen. See Treitel, *The Law of Contract*, 12th edn (Peel, 2007), p.544.

16–187 **Mistake.**[967] There is some authority for the view that money can be recovered if it was paid under an excusable mistake of *fact* affecting the legality of the contract. In *Oom v Bruce*[968] the plaintiff as agent for the Russian owner of goods in Russia took out a policy of insurance with the defendant. Neither party knew (or could have known) that Russia had declared war on this country before the contract was made. It was held that the plaintiff could recover his premium as he was not guilty of any fault or blame in entering the illegal contract.

16–188 ***Locus poenitentiae*: general.**[969] Another exception to the general rule of non-recovery of money paid or property transferred under an illegal contract arises out of the parties' right to resile from such a contract while it is still executory and to recover anything already paid or transferred under the contract.[970] But:

(1) if the illegal purpose has been wholly or substantially effected; or

(2) if the parties have merely been frustrated in their illegal purpose,

the law allows no *locus poenitentiae*. It would also appear that where the contract involves gross moral turpitude or criminality then this doctrine will not apply.[971]

16–189 ***Locus poenitentiae*: performance.** The first requirement for the operation of the *locus poenitentiae* rule is that the illegal contract must not have been substantially performed. In *Taylor v Bowers*[972] A delivered his goods to B to put them out of reach of his creditors. B, by a fictitious bill of sale, without A's assent assigned them to a third party, who was aware of A's illegal purpose. A sought to repudiate the transaction and recover the goods from the third party. It was held he could do so, as the fraudulent purpose had not been carried out, and therefore A was not driven to rely on the illegal transaction between himself and B. C had no better title than B, as he knew how B had come to be possessed of the goods. The court will not allow a party to repudiate a contract merely because his illegal purpose has not yet been wholly performed; substantial performance will preclude his recovering. Thus in *Kearley v Thomson*[973] it was agreed that a solicitor's costs would be paid if he consented not to appear at a public examination of a bankrupt and not to oppose his discharge. The solicitor did not appear at his examination, and before any application for discharge was made, the plaintiff brought his action to recover back the money he had paid as costs. The contract was illegal and its substantial performance prevented recovery. *Taylor v Bowers*[974] and *Kearley v Thomson*[975] are difficult to reconcile. Perhaps *Taylor v*

---

[967] Treitel at p.544. On mistake of law see below, paras 29–041 et seq.

[968] (1810) 12 East 225.

[969] See Beatson (1975) 91 L.Q.R. 313; Merkin (1981) 97 L.Q.R. 420.

[970] *Bone v Ekless* (1860) 29 L.J.Ex. 438, 440; *Palaniappa Chettiar v Arunasalam Chettiar* [1962] A.C. 294, 302–303.

[971] See *Tappenden v Randall* (1801) 2 B. & P. 467.

[972] (1876) 1 QBD 291; *Symes v Hughes* (1870) L.R. 9 Eq. 475; *Tribe v Tribe* [1996] Ch. 107.

[973] (1890) 24 QBD 742; *Re National Benefit Assurance Co Ltd* [1931] 1 Ch. 46; *Parker (Harry) Ltd v Mason* [1940] 2 K.B. 590.

[974] (1876) 1 QBD 291.

[975] (1890) 24 QBD 742.

Bowers is to be explained as a case of bailment in which the plaintiff could disregard the illegal contract and rely on his continuing proprietary interest.[976] Or it may merely be that both are borderline cases, but that, on the view of the facts taken by the courts, whereas in *Taylor v Bowers* nothing irrevocable had yet been done in the performance of the illegal contract, in *Kearley v Thomson* a substantial part of it had clearly been performed. It has been argued that the "limit of the *locus poenitentiae* may well be at the point whereby recovery will not increase the chances of thwarting the illegal purpose"[977]: thus recovery was needed in *Taylor v Bowers*[978] to protect the interests of the plaintiff's creditors but no such recovery was required in *Kearley v Thomson*. Although, if this is adopted as the guiding principle, then arguably the courts should allow recovery up to the point where the contract has been performed.[979] This will provide the parties with the maximum opportunity to resile and thus defeat the carrying out of the illegal purpose, and will also not provide any incentive for the parties to perform in part as a ploy for preventing the operation of the *locus poenitentiae* principle.[980]

***Locus poenitentiae*: frustration.** The second requirement with respect to the *locus poenitentiae* principle is that the reason for the plaintiff's repudiation must be voluntary; the plaintiff must genuinely repent and not merely seek recovery because the illegal purpose of the contract has been frustrated. *Bigos v Bousted*[981] illustrates the operation of this requirement. There one party agreed to supply another party with lira. The agreement was illegal as it violated the prevailing exchange control legislation. The party who agreed to supply the lira failed to do so, and the other party brought an action to recover securities deposited in connection with the illegal agreement. His action was unsuccessful, the court reasoning that he had not repented but rather his reason for repudiating the agreement was merely that the other party had failed to carry it out.[982] 16–190

Marriage brokage contracts. For historical reasons the general rule of non-recovery after substantial performance does not apply to marriage brokage contracts. In such cases, equity had always allowed relief to the party dealing with the marriage broker owing to the jealousy with which contracts relating to marriage were regarded; and the common law courts adopted this equitable exception. In *Hermann v Charlesworth*,[983] therefore, although the defendant had 16–191

---

[976] See above, paras 16–177, 16–178.

[977] Beatson (1975) 91 L.Q.R. 313, 316; Treitel, "Contract and Crime" in Tapper (ed.), *Crime, Proof and Punishment*, pp.103–104.

[978] (1876) 1 QBD 291, 300, per Mellish L.J.: "To hold that the plaintiff is enabled to recover does not carry out the illegal transaction, but the effect is to put everybody in the same situation as they were before the illegal transaction was determined upon, and before the parties took steps to carry it out."

[979] See Burrows, *The Law of Restitution*, 2nd edn (2002), pp.429–430.

[980] See, e.g. *Harry Parker Ltd v Mason* [1940] 2 K.B. 590; Palmer, *Law of Restitution* (1978), Vol.II, p.216 dealing with *Hastelow v Jackson* (1828) 2 B. & C. 221.

[981] [1951] 1 All E.R. 92; *Tribe v Tribe* [1996] Ch. 107 above. See also Merkin (1981) 97 L.Q.R. 420, 428–431.

[982] It is unclear how far normal bars to rescission apply to withdrawal during the *locus poenitentiae*: see Burrows at pp.429–430.

[983] [1905] 2 K.B. 123; and see *Roberts v Roberts* (1730) 3 P.Wms. 66, 75, 76; *Cole v Gibson* (1750) 1 Ves.Sen. 503. See also para.16–071.

taken steps and incurred expense towards carrying out his part of a marriage brokage contract, the plaintiff was allowed to recover back money she had paid thereunder.

16–192 **Principal and agent.** A principal can recover from his agent money which he has paid to the agent, albeit for a legally objectionable purpose, provided that he instructs the agent to return it to him before the agent has paid it over under the contract,[984] at any rate if the purpose was not grossly criminal or turpitudinous or if the principal still enjoyed a *locus poenitentiae*.[985] Where money is received by an agent for his principal from a third party under an illegal contract it would seem that the principal may recover the money from the agent in an action for money had and received.[986] Where the receipt of the money is itself illegal and part of an illegal transaction in which both the principal and the agent are concerned,[987] or the agency itself is otherwise illegal,[988] the principal cannot recover the money from the agent; similarly in such a case in the absence of a *locus poenitentiae*,[989] the principal cannot recover from the agent money which he has paid to the agent for the purposes of the contract and which the agent has wrongfully appropriated to his own use.[990] Nor can a principal sue his agent for failure to perform a transaction which is, by common law or statute, void or otherwise unenforceable at the principal's suit.[991]

16–193 **Trustees and other fiduciaries.** A trustee who misapplies trust funds for an illegal purpose would, on the principles stated above, be unable to recover the funds thus advanced. The cestuis que trust, however, where they do not know of, or acquiesce in, the illegal transaction effected by their trustee, appear to be in a better position than he is to recover the trust property which has been illegally advanced and is traceable in the hands of third parties who would, in the absence of illegality, be bound to restore such property. It is submitted that there is no reason of policy why the beneficiary, if innocent of any illegal purpose, should be precluded from recovering in a proprietary action, provided, of course, a proprietary base to the claim can be shown. In any case it is clear that an innocent beneficiary may bring an action in personam against the trustee claiming damages for breach of trust, notwithstanding the latter's unlawful purpose. Thus in

---

[984] *Hampden v Walsh* (1876) 1 QBD 189; *Hastelow v Jackson* (1828) 8 B. & C. 221, 226; *Burge v Ashley & Smith Ltd* [1900] 1 Q.B. 744.

[985] *Bone v Eckles* (1860) 5 H. & N. 925; *Tennant v Elliott* (1791) 1 B. & P. 3; *Farmer v Russell* (1798) 1 B. & P. 296. As to *locus poenitentiae,* see above, paras 16–187 et seq.

[986] See *Sykes v Beadon* (1879) 11 Ch D 170, 194–195; and see *Bridger v Savage* (1885) 15 QBD 363; *De Mattos v Benjamin* (1894) 63 L.J.Q.B. 248; cf. *Rawlings v General Trading Corp* [1921] 1 K.B. 635, 642; *Hill v William Hill (Park Lane) Ltd* [1949] A.C. 530.

[987] *Nicholson v Gooch* (1856) 5 E. & B. 999, 1016; cf. *Jubilee Cotton Mills Ltd v Lewis* [1924] A.C. 958, 978.

[988] See *Harry Parker Ltd v Mason* [1940] 2 K.B. 590; *Kabel v Ronald Lyon Espanola S.A.* (1968) 208 E.G. 269. For criticisms of this requirement, see Merkin (1981) 97 L.Q.R. 420, 437–439.

[989] See above, fn.973.

[990] Above paras 16–180, 16–181.

[991] *Cohen v Kittell* (1889) 22 QBD 680.

Selangor United Rubber Estates Ltd v Cradock (No.3)[992] the plaintiff company, through its directors, lent money to various persons for the purpose of purchasing shares in itself, contrary to s.54 of the Companies Act 1948.[993] It was held that the company could claim damages[994] against its directors for breach of their fiduciary duty to the company to apply its funds for authorised purposes only, and against its bankers both for breach of their duty as constructive trustees of the company's accounts and also in contract for negligence in the running of its financial affairs.

5. SEVERANCE

Introductory. Where all the terms of a contract are illegal or against public policy or where the whole contract is prohibited by statute, clearly no action can be brought by the guilty party on the contract; but sometimes, although parts of a contract[995] are unenforceable for such reasons, other parts, were they to stand alone, would be unobjectionable. The question then arises whether the unobjectionable may be enforced and the objectionable disregarded or "severed".[996] The same question arises in relation to bonds where the condition is partly against the law.[997] 16–194

992 [1968] 1 W.L.R. 1555, 1652–1659.

993 The Companies Act 1948 s.54, has been repealed by the Companies Act 1981 Sch.4. On the provision of financial assistance by a company for the purchase or subscription of its shares see Companies Act 2006 Pt 18 Ch.2. Subsequent to *Selangor United Rubber Estates Ltd v Cradock (No.3)* [1968] 1 W.L.R. 1555 the courts interpreted the Companies Act 1948 s.54, as being for the protection of the company, despite the fact that criminal sanctions can be imposed on the company for breach of the section (s.54(2)), and thus the company could bring an action to recover any money or property transferred under the section. See above, para.9–038; *Belmont Finance Ltd v Williams Furniture Ltd (No.2)* [1980] 1 All E.R. 393; *Armour Hick Northern Ltd v Whitehouse* [1980] 1 W.L.R. 1520. See also *International Sales and Agencies Ltd v Marcus* [1982] 2 C.M.L.R. 46, 55.

994 Breach of s.54 (see now Companies Act 2006 Pt 18 Ch.2) would give rise to an action for breach of trust against the directors and any person who assisted in that breach: *Selangor United Rubber Estates Ltd v Cradock (No.3)* [1968] 1 W.L.R. 1555; *Belmont Finance Corp Ltd v Williams Furniture Ltd (No.2)* [1980] 1 All E.R. 393.

995 Where one contract is collateral to another and illegal contract, the former may be "tainted" by the illegality of the latter (see the authorities cited in para.16–165); the courts thus look at the substance of the matter and treat the two transactions as forming a single and unseverable arrangement. In *Spector v Ageda* [1973] Ch. 30, Megarry J. expressed the view *obiter* that where the original transaction is only partially illegal, e.g. by statute, then unless that partial illegality is shown to relate solely to some defined portion of the subsequent transaction, so that only that defined portion is affected, the *whole* of the subsequent transaction will be affected by the illegality. This means that the party to the subsequent transaction is put in a worse position than the party to the original illegal transaction, a view admitted by the judge to be "draconian", but consistent with the court's policy against devising means of preventing those who are implicated from burning their fingers more than to a limited extent. Similarly, individual covenants in a contract may be so closely connected that they stand or fall together, although the remainder of the contract may be severable: *Esso Petroleum Co Ltd v Harper's Garage (Stourport) Ltd* [1968] A.C. 269, 314, 321.

996 See Marsh (1948) 64 L.Q.R. 230, 347.

997 See *Baker v Hedgecock* (1889) 39 Ch D 520; *Kearney v Whitehaven Colliery Co Ltd* [1893] 1 Q.B. 700; *S. Nevanas & Co v Walker and Foreman* [1914] 1 Ch. 413, 423; *British Reinforced Concrete Engineering Co Ltd v Schelff* [1921] 2 Ch. 563.

16–195 **Partial statutory invalidity.** It was laid down in some of the older cases that there is a distinction between a deed or condition which is void in part by statute and one which is void in part at common law.[998] This distinction must now be understood to apply only to cases where the statute enacts that an agreement or deed made in violation of its provisions shall be wholly void.[999] Unless that is so, then provided the good part is separable from and not dependent on the bad, that part only will be void which contravenes the provisions of the statute. The general rule is that:

> "... where you cannot sever the illegal from the legal part of a covenant, the contract is altogether void; but, where you can sever them, whether the illegality be created by statute or by the common law, you may reject the bad part and retain the good."[1000]

Thus, a covenant in a lease that the tenant should pay "all parliamentary taxes", only included such as he might lawfully pay, and a separate covenant to pay the landlord's property tax, which it was illegal for a tenant to contract to pay, although void, did not affect the validity of the instrument.[1001] In some situations where there is a statutory requirement to obtain a licence for work above a stipulated financial limit but up to that limit no licence is required, the courts will enforce a contract up to that limit.[1002] There is some doubt whether this applies to a lump sum contract "for a single and indivisible work".[1003] Even in this situation if the cost element can be divided into its legal and illegal components, the courts will enforce the former but not the latter.[1004]

16–196 **General principles.** Although a number of authorities on the application of the doctrine of severance cannot easily be reconciled, it is submitted that two underlying principles have throughout guided the courts. First, the courts will not make a new contract for the parties, whether by rewriting the existing contract, or by basically altering its nature[1005]; secondly, the courts will not sever the

[998] *Maleverer v Redshaw* (1670) 1 Mod. 35; repudiated in *Collins v Blantern* (1767) 2 Wils.K.B. 341, 347, 351.

[999] *Doe d. Thompson v Pitcher* (1815) 6 Taunt. 359, 369.

[1000] *Pickering v Ilfracombe Ry* (1868) L.R. 3 C.P. 235, 250; *Payne v Brecon Corp* (1858) 3 H. & N. 572; *Pallister v Gravesend Corp* (1850) 9 C.B. 774; *Royal Exchange Assurance Corp v Sjorforsakrings Aktiebolaget Vega* [1901] 2 K.B. 567, 573; *Chemidus Wavin Ltd v Société Pour La Transformation Et L'Exploitation Des Resines Industrielles SA* [1978] 3 C.M.L.R. 514. cf. *Electrical Trades Union v Tarlo* [1984] Ch. 720, 731.

[1001] *Gaskell v King* (1809) 11 East 165; and see *Wigg v Shuttleworth* (1810) 13 East 87; *Howe v Synge* (1812) 15 East 440; *Greenwood v Bishop of London* (1814) 5 Taunt. 727; as to personal covenants in deeds where the real security is by statute void see *Mouys v Leake* (1799) 8 T.R. 411; *Gibbons v Hooper* (1831) 2 B. & Ad. 734.

[1002] *Frank W. Clifford Ltd v Garth* [1956] 1 W.L.R. 570.

[1003] *Frank W. Clifford Ltd v Garth* [1956] 1 W.L.R. 570, 572.

[1004] *United City Merchants (Investments) Ltd v Royal Bank of Canada* [1982] Q.B. 208, on appeal [1983] 1 A.C. 168. See also above, para.16–149.

[1005] Where a contract contains an ancillary provision which is illegal and which is for the benefit of the plaintiff, the court will normally be disposed to allow the plaintiff to waive it and enforce the contract: *Carney v Herbert* [1985] A.C. 301, 317A–B, PC.

unenforceable parts of a contract unless it accords with public policy to do so.[1006]

Contracts cannot be rewritten. The first limitation on the courts' power to sever the bad from the good is that they cannot make a new contract for the parties. Examples of one aspect of this limitation are provided by the courts' refusal to rewrite contracts which contain provisions in restraint of trade. The severance of the unreasonable part of the covenants in these cases is effected only where it is possible to do so by merely running a blue pencil through the offending part. For the blue pencil test to apply, it is essential that "the severed parts are independent of one another and can be severed without the severance affecting the meaning of the part remaining".[1007] Thus, in *Goldsoll v Goldman*,[1008] the defendant, who was a London dealer in imitation jewellery, on selling his business to the plaintiff, covenanted not to compete with the plaintiff as "a dealer in real or imitation jewellery in . . . any part of the United Kingdom, . . . the United States of America, Russia or Spain". The covenant was unreasonable in so far as it extended to real jewellery and to competition outside the United Kingdom, but was otherwise reasonable. It was held that the words "real or" and the listed places outside the United Kingdom could be severed leaving only a reasonable covenant which could be enforced. 16–197

Scope of agreement to be left unchanged. Although the courts will never effect a severance unless the illegal part can be "blue pencilled", it does not follow that they will always effect a severance when that is so.[1009] The court will not strike out words of a contract if to do so would "alter entirely the scope and intention of the agreement",[1010] there being "in truth but one covenant" and not two.[1011] The question of what is a single covenant and of what is the scope of an agreement is in each case one as to the proper construction of that particular covenant or agreement.[1012] Thus, where the business intended to be protected by a restrictive covenant contained several departments, it was held that a covenant 16–198

1006 For observations on the statement of principle in para.16–196, see *United City Merchants, etc.* [1982] Q.B. 208, 229–230, per Stephenson L.J.; *Sadler v Imperial Life Assurance Co of Canada Ltd* [1988] I.R.L.R. 388 at 393, cited with approval in *Beckett Investment Management Ltd v Hall* [2007] EWCA Civ 613, [2007] I.R.L. 793 at [35]–[36]. In *Sadler* (involving restraint of trade) the court held that severance required that: (i) "the unenforceable provision is capable of being removed without the necessity of adding to or modifying the wording that remains"; (ii) "the remaining terms are supported by consideration" and (iii) the removal of the unenforceable provisions does not alter the character of the contract" ([1988] I.R.L.R. 388, 393).

1007 *Business Seating (Renovations) Ltd v Broad* [1989] I.C.R. 729, 734. Where the covenant contains a number of separate and distinct prohibitions, severance will be more easy to effect: see *Ginsberg v Parker* [1988] I.R.L.R. 483.

1008 [1914] 2 Ch. 603, [1915] 1 Ch. 192; followed in *Ronbar Enterprises Ltd v Green* [1954] 1 W.L.R. 815; and see *Scorer v Seymour Jones* [1966] 1 W.L.R. 1419; *Francis Delzenne Ltd v Klee* (1968) 112 S.J. 583.

1009 *Attwood v Lamont* [1920] 3 K.B. 571, 578, 593.

1010 *Attwood v Lamont* [1920] 3 K.B. 571, 580; and see below, para.16–201.

1011 *Attwood v Lamont* [1920] 3 K.B. 571, 593; and see *Baker v Hedgecock* (1888) 39 Ch D 520; *Kenyon v Darwen Cotton Manufacturing Co Ltd* [1936] 2 K.B. 193; *James E McCabe Ltd v Scottish Courage Ltd* [2006] EWHC 538 (Comm).

1012 *Miles v Durham* [1891] 1 Ch. 576.

which restricted the covenantor from carrying on any of the sorts of business carried on by those departments, was a single covenant and was not severable in respect of the different sorts of business.[1013] Again, a covenant not to engage in a business in any one of several capacities was held to be a single covenant.[1014] *Goldsoll v Goldman*,[1015] on the other hand, provides an illustration where certain areas[1016] and types of business[1017] which a covenant in restraint of trade unreasonably covered were held to be severable. So too, a covenant not to disclose trade secrets may be severable from a covenant not to engage in a business.[1018] Where an employee's covenant not to interfere with customers of the employer[1019] is so construed that "customers" includes those persons who first become customers after the termination of the service, it will in ordinary circumstances be regarded as a single covenant and will not be severed so as to allow of its enforcement in respect of those who were customers during the service.[1020]

16–199 **Severance of a condition.** Many covenants in restraint of trade will be in conditional form and provide that X will receive £Y on condition that he refrains from doing a particular act. Assuming that the condition is in restraint of trade, the question arises as to whether the severance of the condition is at all possible in that it will transform a conditional obligation on the part of the covenantor into an absolute one; that is, payment of the £Y will be due even though X does not perform part of the bargain. This was the issue in *Marshall v N.M. Financial Management Ltd*.[1021] The case involved a provision in a contract for the payment of commission to a self-employed sales agent after the contract's termination. Payment of the commision was conditional on the ex-agent not competing with the defendant for a period of one year. The court held that the anti-competition covenant was in restraint of trade. The question before the court was whether the plaintiff as the party "who has been freed from an invalid restraint of trade can enforce the remainder of the contract without it".[1022] The court held that he could

[1013] *Attwood v Lamont* [1920] 3 K.B. 571; *British Reinforced Concrete Engineering Co Ltd v Schelff* [1921] 2 Ch. 563.

[1014] *British Reinforced Concrete Engineering Co Ltd v Schelff* [1921] 2 Ch. 563.

[1015] [1914] 2 Ch. 603, [1915] 1 Ch. 292.

[1016] And see *Mallan v May* (1843) 11 M. & W. 653; *Underwood & Son Ltd v Barker* [1899] 1 Ch. 300; *Hooper & Ashby v Willis* (1905) 94 L.T. 624; *Bromley v Smith* [1909] 2 K.B. 235; *Nevanas & Co v Walker and Foreman* [1914] 1 Ch. 413; *Putsman v Taylor* [1927] 1 K.B. 637, 741.

[1017] And see *Hooper v Willis* (1905) 94 L.T. 624; *Bromley v Smith* [1909] 2 K.B. 235.

[1018] *Caribonum Co Ltd v Le Couch* (1913) 109 L.T. 385, 587.

[1019] A covenant by a managing director against soliciting customers while so employed or afterwards has been upheld as not wider than necessary for the protection of the covenantee's trade: *Gilford Motor Co Ltd v Horne* [1933] Ch. 935.

[1020] *Konski v Peet* [1915] 1 Ch. 530; *East Essex Farmers Ltd v Holder* [1926] W.N. 230; *Express Dairy Co v Jackson* (1930) 99 L.J.K.B. 181; in *Baines v Geary* (1887) 35 Ch D 154 and *Dubowski & Sons v Goldstein* [1896] 1 Q.B. 478, the covenants were held to be severable; but unless distinguishable on the terms of the covenants, these two authorities probably cannot now be relied on: see *Continental Tyre Co v Heath* (1913) 29 T.L.R. 308. See also *S. Ivestone Records Ltd v Mountfield* [1993] E.M.L.R. 152.

[1021] [1997] 1 W.L.R. 1527.

[1022] *Marshall v N.M. Financial Management Ltd* [1997] 1 W.L.R. 1527, 1531.

since the "whole or substantially the whole [of the] consideration[1023] was not the restraint but the provision of the services that earned the commission.

Where a mortgage imposed upon the mortgagor an obligation, which was in unreasonable restraint of trade, to buy certain kinds of goods only from the mortgagee for 21 years, the unenforceability of the tie was so closely linked with the provision in the mortgage that it should be irredeemable for the same period, that this provision too was held to be unenforceable, though in other respects the enforceability of the mortgage itself was unaffected.[1024]

Rules of association in part objectionable. If the fundamental object of any association, whether it be a combination to fix prices or a trade union, is obnoxious to the law because it is an unreasonable restraint of trade, at common law the association is illegal and the agreement upon which it is founded is wholly unenforceable.[1025] So, for instance, where a society with the militant objects of a trade union combined with these the provident purposes of a friendly society and by its rules members might be expelled and their benefits forfeited for non-compliance with the decisions of committees directing the militant operations, it was held that the main object was illegal as being in restraint of trade and that as the provident rules were inseparably connected with that object, they were affected by its illegality and were therefore unenforceable.[1026] If the fundamental object of the association is not unlawful, the fact that certain of its rules are in unreasonable restraint of trade does not make the association unlawful though of course those particular rules cannot be enforced.[1027] 16–200

Illegality of part of the consideration. Many of the older authorities laid down that if a contract was made on several considerations, one of which was illegal, the whole contract was unenforceable and severance was impossible.[1028] Such a test is unworkable[1029] and, as has been recognised in more modern decisions, the partial illegality, and hence unenforceability, is only relevant in one of two ways. First, the severance of the offending clause may so alter the scope of the whole contract as to make it a new contract. The true test under this head is therefore whether the illegal promise is substantially the whole or main consideration for the promise now sought to be enforced. If it is, then the court will not sever it, leaving only a small part of the consideration to support the 16–201

1023 Citing Denning L.J., *Bennett v Bennett* [1952] 1 K.B. 249, 261.

1024 *Esso Petroleum Co Ltd v Harper's Garage (Stourport) Ltd* [1968] A.C. 269, 314, 321. cf. *Petrofina (Gt. Britain) Ltd v Martin* [1966] Ch. 146 where there was no mortgage and the unreasonable restraints were so pervasive as to vitiate the entire contract.

1025 *Hilton v Eckersley* (1856) 6 E. & B. 47. See above, paras 16–133—16–136 as to statutory position of such associations.

1026 *Russell v Amalgamated Society of Carpenters* [1912] A.C. 421; cf. *Swaine v Wilson* (1889) 24 QBD 252; *Finch v Oake* [1896] 1 Ch. 409.

1027 *Collins v Locke* (1879) 4 App. Cas. 674; *Osborne v Amalgamated Society of Ry Servants* [1911] 1 Ch. 540, 553.

1028 *Shackell v Rosier* (1836) 3 Scott 59; *Lound v Grimwade* (1888) 39 Ch D 605; *Jones v Merionethshire Permanent Benefit Building Society* [1891] 2 Ch. 587; [1892] 1 Ch. 173.

1029 Williston, *Contracts*, 9th edn, s.7–79; Marsh (1948) 64 L.Q.R. 230, 242.

promise of the defendant[1030]; otherwise it may. Thus, in *Goodinson v Goodinson*,[1031] a husband promised to make regular payments to his wife if she would forbear to bring any matrimonial proceedings against him, would indemnify him against her debts and would not pledge his credit for necessaries. The agreement not to commence matrimonial proceedings was against public policy as an attempt to oust the jurisdiction of the court; but as it did not form the main part of the consideration for the promise to make the payments, the court severed that part of the agreement and enforced the rest in favour of the wife.[1032] Similarly an employee can sue for his whole wages notwithstanding that his contract of employment imposes upon him a severable covenant in restraint of trade. An alternative approach is to be found in *South Western Mineral Water Co Ltd v Ashmore*[1033]; the illegal term of a contract was there severed, but the contract was thereby so altered in scope that it was held to be unenforceable; restitutio in integrum was therefore ordered and an order was made for the return of money paid under the contract. Such an order could not have been made but for the severance of the illegal term.[1034]

16–202 **Severance and public policy.** The second way in which the partial illegality of the consideration is relevant relates to the second of the two general principles mentioned above.[1035] This second limitation on the courts' power to sever the bad from the good is that they will not do so unless this accords with public policy. For example, part of the consideration for the promise of either party may be such as so gravely to taint the whole contract that there is no ground of public policy requiring the courts to assist either party by severing the offending parts[1036]: "[i]n all the cases a distinction is taken between a merely void and an illegal consideration".[1037] In this context illegal means that which amounts to a criminal offence or is *contra bonos mores*,[1038] where, on grounds of public policy, the illegality may, though does not invariably, preclude severance. Agreements the object of which is to defraud the Revenue,[1039] or which involve trading with the enemy,[1040] have been held to be incapable of severance.[1041] On the other

---

[1030] *Bennett v Bennett* [1952] 1 K.B. 249; see also *Putsman v Taylor* [1927] 1 K.B. 637, 639, affirmed [1927] 1 K.B. 741; *Chemidus Wavin Ltd v Société Pour La Transformation Et L'Exploitation Des Resines Industrielle SA* [1978] 3 C.M.L.R. 514 CA.

[1031] [1954] 2 Q.B. 118; see now Matrimonial Causes Act 1973 s.34.

[1032] And see *Kearney v Whitehaven Colliery Co* [1893] 1 Q.B. 700; *Furlong v Burns & Co* (1964) 43 D.L.R. (2d) 689; *Ailion v Spiekermann* [1976] Ch. 158.

[1033] [1967] 1 W.L.R. 1110. This case involved the application of Companies Act 1948 s.54, on which see above, para.16–193 fn.993.

[1034] See above, paras 16–177, 16–179 et seq.

[1035] Above, para.16–196.

[1036] *Kuenigl v Donnersmarck* [1955] 1 Q.B. 515, 537 (in this case the conditions for severance were not satisfied).

[1037] *Shackell v Rosier* (1836) 3 Scott 59, 74.

[1038] *Bennett v Bennett* [1952] 1 K.B. 249, 253–254; *Goodinson v Goodinson* [1954] 2 Q.B. 118, 120.

[1039] *Miller v Karlinski* (1945) 62 T.L.R. 85; *Napier v National Business Agency Ltd* [1951] 2 All E.R. 264.

[1040] *Kuenigl v Donnersmarck* [1955] 1 Q.B. 515.

[1041] This passage was cited with approval in *Hyland v J. H. Barker (North West) Ltd* [1985] I.C.R. 861, 863–864 where the court held that in determining the continuity of an employee's contract of employment the period during which he was paid an illegal tax-free allowance could not be taken into consideration.

hand, examples of mere voidness on grounds of public policy are agreements to oust the jurisdiction of the court[1042] and agreements which are merely in restraint of trade.[1043]

Employer and employee covenants in restraint of trade. There is authority for saying that, on grounds of public policy, the courts should be reluctant to sever in favour of an employer[1044] the unreasonable clauses in a covenant in restraint of trade made between employer and employee. Thus Lord Moulton in *Mason v Provident Clothing Co Ltd*[1045] expressed the view that parts of such a covenant should only be severed: 16–203

> "... in cases where the part so enforceable is clearly severable, and even so only in cases where the excess is of trivial importance, or merely technical, and not a part of the main purport and substance of the clause";

on the ground that it would:

> "... be *pessimi exempli* if, when an employer had exacted a covenant deliberately framed in unreasonably wide terms, the courts were to come to his assistance and, by employing their ingenuity and knowledge of the law, carve out of this void covenant the maximum of what he might validly have required."

"To hold otherwise," it has been said,[1046] is:

> "... to expose the covenantor to the almost inevitable risk of litigation which in nine cases out of ten he is very ill able to afford, should he venture to act upon his own opinion as to how far the restraint upon him would be held by the court to be reasonable, while it may give the covenantee the full benefit of unreasonable provisions if the covenantor is unable to face litigation."

However, more modern authorities[1047] appear to be in favour of applying to covenants in restraint of trade between employer and employee the same rule as to other covenants, that is to say, the rule that where the parts of a covenant really amount to separate and independent covenants they may be severed from one another, but not otherwise.[1048]

1042 *Czarnikow v Roth, Schmidt & Co* [1922] 2 K.B. 478; *Goodinson v Goodinson* [1954] 2 Q.B. 118.

1043 e.g. *Ronbar Enterprises Ltd v Green* [1954] 1 W.L.R. 815; and see *Mogul S.S. Co Ltd v McGregor, Gow & Co* [1892] A.C. 25, 46–47; *R. v Stainer* (1870) L.R. 1 C.C.R. 230.

1044 But the employee can sever on the ordinary principles so as, e.g. to sue for his whole wages during the continuance of his employment despite the fact that he is subject to an unreasonable restraint: see above, paras 16–194 et seq.; and cf. above, 16–115.

1045 [1913] A.C. 724, 745.

1046 *Goldsoll v Goldman* [1914] 2 Ch. 603, 613; affirmed [1915] 1 Ch. 292 cited with approval in *Attwood v Lamont* [1920] 3 K.B. 571, 595.

1047 *Francis Delzene v Klee* (1968) S.J. 583; *Lucas & Co Ltd v Mitchell* [1974] Ch. 129; *Stenhouse Australia Co Ltd v Phillips* [1974] A.C. 391. cf. *Ronbar Enterprises v Green* [1954] 1 W.L.R. 815, 820.

1048 *S. Nevanas & Co v Walker and Foreman* [1914] 1 Ch. 413, 423 (where it was said that the remarks of Lord Moulton cited above were not intended to apply where parts of a covenant are clearly severed by the parties themselves so as to amount to separate covenants); *Putsman v Taylor* [1927] 1 K.B. 637, 641; *Spink (Bournemouth) Ltd v Spink* [1936] Ch. 544.

6. PLEADING AND PRACTICE

16–204 **Presumption of legality.** The party alleging the illegality of the contract bears the legal burden of proving this fact[1049]; therefore if the contract be reasonably susceptible of two meanings or two modes of performance, one legal and the other not the legal burden of proving its illegality is undischarged and that interpretation is to be put upon the contract which will support it and give it operation.[1050] If the contract on the face of it shows an illegal intention, an evidential burden lies upon the party supporting the contract to bring evidence reasonably capable of showing the legality of the intention.[1051]

16–205 **Pleading of illegality.** Where a contract is ex facie illegal, the court will not enforce it, whether the illegality is pleaded or not; secondly, where the contract is not ex facie illegal, evidence of extraneous circumstances tending to show that it has an illegal object should not be admitted unless the circumstances relied on are pleaded; thirdly, where unpleaded facts, which, taken by themselves, show an illegal object, have been put in evidence (because, perhaps, no objection was raised or because they were adduced for some other purpose), the court should not act on them unless it is satisfied that the whole of the relevant circumstances are before it; but fourthly, where the court[1052] is satisfied that all the relevant facts are before it and it can clearly see from them that the contract had an illegal object, it may not enforce the contract, whether the facts were pleaded or not.[1053] It has been said that counsel is not acting improperly in inviting the court to consider the possible, though unpleaded, illegality of a transaction but that on the contrary counsel's duty is to prevent the court from enforcing illegal transactions.[1054]

16–206 **Costs.** Where a defendant successfully raises a plea of illegality, the ordinary rules as to costs apply.[1055]

[1049] *Hire-Purchase Furnishing Co v Richens* (1887) 20 QBD 387, 389.

[1050] *R. v Inhabitants of Haslingfield* (1814) 2 M. & S. 558; *Bennett v Clough* (1818) 1 B. & Ald. 461; *Lewis v Davison* (1839) 4 M. & W. 654, 657: *Mittelholzer v Fullarton* (1842) 6 Q.B. 989; *Edler v Auerbach* [1950] 1 K.B. 359, 368; *Archbolds (Freightage) Ltd v S. Spanglett Ltd* [1961] 1 Q.B. 374, 391–392. See also above, paras 16–005—16–011.

[1051] *Holland v Hall* (1817) 1 B. & Ald. 53.

[1052] The rule applies to appellate courts as well as to courts of first instance: *Snell v Unity Finance Ltd* [1964] 2 Q.B. 203.

[1053] *Edler v Auerbach* [1950] 1 K.B. 359, 371. See *Holman v Johnson* (1775) 1 Cowp. 341; *Evans v Richardson* (1817) 3 Mer. 469; *Scott v Brown, Doering, McNab & Co* [1892] 2 Q.B. 724; *Gedge v Royal Exchange Assurance Corp* [1900] 2 Q.B. 214; *North Western Salt Co v Electrolytic Alkali Co Ltd* [1913] 3 K.B. 422, 424; [1914] A.C. 461, 476, 477; *Montefiore v Menday Motor Components Co Ltd* [1918] 2 K.B. 241; *Alexander v Rayson* [1936] 1 K.B. 169, 190; *Commercial Air Hire Ltd v Wrightways Ltd* [1938] 1 All E.R. 89; *Palaniappa Chettiar v Arunasalam Chettiar* [1962] A.C. 294; *Snell v Unity Finance Co Ltd* [1964] 2 Q.B. 203; *Mercantile Credit Co Ltd v Hamblin* [1965] 2 Q.B. 242, 261–262, 276; *Crouch and Lees v Haridas* [1972] 1 Q.B. 158; *U.C.M. v Royal Bank of Canada* [1983] 1 A.C. 168, 169; the law is summarised in *Bank of India v Trans Continental Commodity Merchants Ltd* [1982] 1 Lloyd's Rep. 427, 429; *Birkett v Acorn Mechanics Ltd* [1999] 2 All E.R. (Comm) 429; *Pickering v JA McConville* [2003] EWCA Civ 554; *Bim Kemi AB v Blackburn Chemicals Ltd* [2004] EWHC 166 (Comm), [2004] EWCA Civ 1490 (court could take notice that agreement was illegal under art.81 of the EC Treaty); *Western Power Investment Ltd v Teeside Power Ltd* Unreported February 18, 2005.

[1054] *Mercantile Credit Co Ltd v Hamblin* [1964] 1 W.L.R. 423; affirmed on other grounds [1965] 2 Q.B. 242.

[1055] *Sphinx Export Co v Specialist Shippers* [1954] C.L.Y. 1440.

Part Six

JOINT OBLIGATIONS, THIRD PARTIES AND ASSIGNMENT

CHAPTER 17

JOINT OBLIGATIONS[1]

Introductory: definitions. Several liability arises when two or more persons make separate promises to another, whether by the same instrument or by different instruments. Thus if A and B covenant with C that they will each pay him £100, each is liable to pay £100[2]; their promises are cumulative and payment by one does not discharge the other.[3] 17–001

Joint liability arises when two or more persons jointly promise to do the same thing. There is only one obligation,[4] and consequently, performance by one discharges the others. Joint liability is subject to a number of strict and technical rules of law which are discussed in the paragraphs that follow. 17–002

Joint and several liability arises when two or more persons in the same instrument jointly promise to do the same thing and also severally make separate promises to do the same thing. Joint and several liability gives rise to one joint obligation and to as many several obligations as there are joint and several promisors. It is like joint liability in that the co-promisors are not cumulatively liable, so that performance by one discharges all; but it is free from most of the technical rules governing joint liability. 17–003

It should be emphasised that the above definitions—and the treatment in this chapter—focus on the standard *contractual* situations where the issues of several, joint, or joint and several liability arise. Particularly in mind is where the contractual liability is to pay an agreed sum (that is, a debt). Cutting across those definitions is joint and several liability in its traditional "tort" sense[5] of wrong-doers acting independently to cause the same damage to the same claimant: and 17–004

[1] See, generally, Williams, *Joint Obligations* (1949); Mitchell, *The Law of Contribution and Reimbursement* (2003).

[2] e.g. *Mikeover Ltd v Brady* [1989] 3 All E.R. 618.

[3] An exception is an original lessee's and a subsequent assignee's covenants to the lessor to pay rent. These are regarded as creating several but non-cumulative liability. Payment by one does discharge the other; and the rules of release for joint and several liability apply so that contractual release of one promisor releases the other. See Williams, *Joint Obligations* (1949), para.5; *Deanplan Ltd v Mahmoud* [1993] Ch. 151. For leases granted after 1995 the original tenant will generally be released from covenants in the lease once the lease has been assigned: see Landlord and Tenant (Covenants) Act 1995 ss.3 and 5. But under s.16 a tenant may enter into an "authorised guarantee agreement" to guarantee compliance with the covenants by the assignee.

[4] *King v Hoare* (1844) 13 M. & W. 494; *Kendall v Hamilton* (1879) 4 App. Cas. 504; *Re Hodgson* (1885) 31 Ch D 177, 188.

[5] For the tort definitions of several, joint, and joint and several liability, and the rules applying to them, see *Clerk & Lindsell on Torts*, 19th edn (2006), Ch.4. See also Williams, *Joint Torts and Contributory Negligence* (1951). The tort rules (e.g. on release) applicable to joint and several wrongdoers (e.g. release of one does not release the others; see *Clerk & Lindsell on Torts*, para.4–09)

a wrongdoer for these purposes can include a contract-breaker as well as a tortfeasor.[6] So if the same loss is caused to C by D1's breach of contract and D2's tort, D1 and D2 are jointly and severally liable to C.[7] This will mean that D1 and D2 are each liable for the whole of C's loss albeit that, if one defendant pays a disproportionate sum to the other, contribution can be recovered from the other defendant under the Civil Liability (Contribution) Act 1978.

17–005 **Creation of joint liability.** The presumption is that a promise made by two or more persons is joint so that express words are necessary to make it joint and several.[8] There are one or two special cases in which equity treats as joint and several an obligation which at law is joint, but they do not cover much ground and are of slight importance in the law of contract.[9] The liability of partners for partnership debts is a good example of joint liability, but it differs from the ordinary case of joint liability in that the estate of a deceased partner is liable for partnership debts (after satisfaction of personal debts) if the firm is unable to satisfy them itself.[10] So also the liability of two or more acceptors, drawers or indorsers of a bill of exchange to the holder thereof is joint.[11] In the case of promissory notes the liability is joint, or joint and several, according to the "tenor" of the note[12]; but if the note runs "I promise to pay" and is signed by two or more persons the liability is joint and several.[13] In the absence of words of severance, the liability of principal debtor and surety on a single promise is joint, but if there is not one single promise the general rule is that the liability is

---

appear to differ from the contractual rules applicable to joint and several promisors (e.g. release of one releases the others: see below, para.17–017).

[6] In the 1990s there was considerable debate over whether joint and several liability, in its tort sense, should be replaced by proportionate liability. The case for that reform was particularly urged by auditors in respect of contractual or tortious liability for negligence. For a rejection of that reform, see *Feasibility Investigation of Joint and Several Liability, by the Common Law Team of the Law Commission* (DTI Consultation Paper, 1996). See generally, R. Wright, "The Logic and Fairness of Joint and Several Liability" (1992) 23 Memphis State L.R. 45; M. Simpson, "Apportionment or Compensation? Joint and Several Liability Reconsidered" [1995] N.Z.L.J. 407; J. Payne, "Limiting the Liability of Professional Partnerships: In Search of this Holy Grail" (1997) 18 Company Lawyer 81; J. Freedman and V. Finch, "Limited Liability Partnerships: Have Accountants Sewn Up the 'Deep Pockets' Debate?" [1997] J.B.L. 387.

[7] This is so even though in relation to other promisors D1 might conceivably have been severally, jointly, or jointly and severally liable, in the standard contractual sense, to C.

[8] *White v Tyndall* (1888) 13 App. Cas. 263; *The Argo Hellas* [1984] 1 Lloyd's Rep. 296, 300. An example of joint and several liability being created by express words is provided by *AIB Group (UK) Ltd v Martin* [2001] UKHL 63, [2002] 1 W.L.R. 94. M and G, who had borrowed money both individually and jointly from a bank, covenanted under a mortgage to pay their debts to the bank and that their liability should be "joint and several". The difficult question of construction was therefore not whether G had joint and several liability with M but whether that joint and several liability of G extended to loans made to M alone rather than to M and G jointly. The House of Lords held that G's joint and several liability did extend to repaying loans made to M alone.

[9] Williams at para.12.

[10] Partnership Act 1890 s.9. But by reason of s.12 of the 1890 Act, a partner is jointly and severally liable with his co-partners for wrongs committed in the ordinary course of business of the firm.

[11] *Other v Iveson* (1855) 3 Drew. 177; *Re Barnard* (1886) 32 Ch D 447.

[12] Bills of Exchange Act 1882 s.85(1).

[13] s.85(2).

several.[14] Consequently the liability of a principal debtor and surety is prima facie joint and several.[15]

Words of severance. As to what constitute words of severance, the cases run to fine distinctions. Thus if A and B promise for themselves or either of them that they will pay £100, the promise is joint and several. But if they promise for themselves that they or either of them will pay £100 the promise is merely joint.[16] This is so even if they promise for themselves their executors and administrators[17]: for the reference to personal representatives is taken to mean the representatives of the survivor. 17–006

Contract by person with himself. At common law a joint contract between A and B on the one hand and B (or B and C) on the other was void, because a man cannot contract with himself.[18] This rule was altered (with retrospective effect) by s.82 of the Law of Property Act 1925, which provides that any agreement entered into by a person with himself and one or more other persons shall be construed and be capable of being enforced as if it had been made with the other person or persons alone. 17–007

Minors. A joint promise by an adult and a minor is binding on the adult though it may be unenforceable against or voidable by the minor.[19] A guarantee given by an adult of an obligation undertaken by a minor is not unenforceable against the adult merely because the principal obligation is unenforceable against or is repudiated by the minor.[20] 17–008

Joinder of parties. Since a joint promise creates only one obligation, the common law rule was that all the promisors who were still alive had to be joined as defendants to the action.[21] There were a number of exceptions to this rule which are detailed below; and since 1959 it has not applied to actions in the county court.[22] The rule does not appear to have been affected by the Civil Liability (Contribution) Act 1978, although that Act (as noted below, para. 17–015) has abolished the related common law rule that an action against a joint contractor served to bar any other proceedings against another joint contractor. But the Civil Procedure Rules have been amended since the commencement of 17–009

[14] *Lep Air Services Ltd v Rolloswin Investments Ltd* [1971] 1 W.L.R. 934, affirmed on other grounds sub nom. *Moschi v Lep Air Services Ltd* [1973] A.C. 331. As to the liability of an agent in cases where he is liable together with his principal, see Vol.II, para.31–085.

[15] *Re E.W.A.* [1901] 2 K.B. 642.

[16] *Wilmer v Currey* (1848) 2 De G. & Sm. 347; *Levy v Sale* (1877) 37 L.T. 709; *White v Tyndall* (1888) 13 App. Cas. 263.

[17] (1848) 2 De G. & Sm. 347. But cf. *Tippins v Coates* (1853) 18 Beav. 401.

[18] *Mainwaring v Newman* (1800) 2 Bos. & P. 120; *Neale v Turton* (1827) 4 Bing. 149; *Faulkner v Lowe* (1848) 2 Exch. 595; *Boyce v Edbrooke* [1903] 1 Ch. 836; *Ellis v Kerr* [1910] 1 Ch. 529; *Napier v Williams* [1911] 1 Ch. 361.

[19] *Gibbs v Merrill* (1810) 3 Taunt. 307; *Burgess v Merrill* (1812) 4 Taunt. 468; *Lovell and Christmas v Beauchamp* [1894] A.C. 607.

[20] Minors Contracts Act 1987 s.2, which reverses *Coutts and Co v Browne-Lecky* [1947] K.B. 104. See also s.4, which amends Consumer Credit Act 1974 s.113(7).

[21] Williams, *Joint Obligations*, para.15; *Cabell v Vaughan* (1669) 1 Wms. Saund. 290a; *Kendall v Hamilton* (1879) 4 App. Cas. 504, 542–544.

[22] County Courts Act 1984 s.48(1).

the 1978 Act. By Civil Procedure Rules 1998 r.2.2, the court may, on its own initiative, or on the application of an existing party or a person who wishes to become a party, order a person to be added as a new party if:

> "(a) . . . it is desirable to add the new party so that the court can resolve all the matters in dispute in the proceedings: or (b) there is an issue involving the new party and an existing party which is connected to the matters in dispute in the proceedings, and it is desirable to add the new party so that the court can resolve that issue."

17–010 Under the modern law, therefore, failure to join a party in the first instance can no longer be visited by any sanctions, except as to costs[23]; all that can happen is that the court may direct that he be joined. As stated above, the common law rule was that all joint contractors had to be joined as defendants but there were exceptions to this rule. There was no need to join one who was a discharged bankrupt,[24] or a person outside the jurisdiction,[25] or a minor as regards whom the contract was void or voidable,[26] or a person protected by the Limitation Act[27] (now the Act of 1980), or a member of a firm of common carriers,[28] or an undisclosed sleeping partner,[29] or an active partner where the defendant represented himself as being the sole contracting party.[30]

17–011 **Joinder of joint and several promisors.** If the obligation is joint and several the claimant has always been able to sue all the promisors together or such one of them separately as he thinks fit.[31] But the court's control over procedural matters now means that even in these cases joinder of another co-defendant may be directed where desirable.[32]

17–012 **Death of a joint contractor.** If one joint contractor dies, his obligation ceases and the whole obligation passes to the survivors or survivor and not to his personal representatives.[33] When the last surviving joint contractor dies, the obligation passes to his personal representatives because once there is only a

---

[23] See especially s.4 of the 1978 Act.

[24] Insolvency Act 1986 s.345(4).

[25] Civil Procedure Act 1833 s.8. This section was repealed by the Statute Law Revision and Civil Procedure Act 1883 s.4, but its principle is still applied by the courts although, under the Civil Procedure Rules 1998 r.6.20 permission to serve a claim form out of the jurisdiction may be granted where any person is a necessary or proper party to an action properly brought against some other person within the jurisdiction. See *Wilson Sons & Co v Balcarres Brook S.S. Co* [1893] 1 Q.B. 422.

[26] *Gibbs v Merrill* (1810) 3 Taunt. 307; *Burgess v Merrill* (1812) 4 Taunt. 468.

[27] Jacobs and Goldrein, *Pleadings: Principles and Practice* (1990), pp.200–201. One joint debtor may be protected by the Limitation Act and the other not where, e.g. the other has acknowledged the debt: Limitation Act 1980 s.31(6), below, para.17–026.

[28] Carriers Act 1830 s.5.

[29] *Ex p. Hodgkinson* (1815) 19 Ves. 291, 294; *Ex p. Norfolk* (1815) 19 Ves. 455, 458; *Mullett v Hook* (1827) M. & M. 89; *De Mautort v Saunders* (1830) 1 B. & Ad. 399; *Kendall v Hamilton* (1879) 4 App. Cas. 504, 513–514, 541.

[30] *Baldney v Ritchie* (1816) 1 Stark. 338; *Stansfeld v Levy* (1820) 3 Stark. 8.

[31] *Cabell v Vaughan* (1669) 1 Wms. Saund. 291, fn.4; Williams, *Joint Obligations* (1949), para.20; *Treitel on the Law of Contract*, 12th edn (Peel, 2007), para.13–006.

[32] CPR 1998 r.2.2.

[33] *White v Tyndall* (1888) 13 App. Cas. 263. Quaere whether this rule has been abolished by s.1(1) of the Law Reform (Miscellaneous Provisions) Act 1934: see Williams at para.25; Treitel at para.13–010.

single debtor, the obligation necessarily becomes several.[34] There is one exception to the rule that the personal representatives of one of a number of joint contractors are not liable: though partners are jointly liable for partnership debts, the estate of a deceased partner is also severally liable, subject however to the prior payment of his separate debts.[35]

Death of joint and several contractor. If one joint and several contractor dies, his several liability passes to his personal representatives.[36] 17–013

Discharge by performance. Payment of the debt by any one of a number of joint or joint and several debtors operates as a discharge of all, for in neither case is the obligation cumulative.[37] 17–014

Judgment against one joint debtor. At common law, the general rule was that a judgment against one joint debtor operated to bar an action against the others, even though the judgment was not satisfied.[38] This was explained on the ground that the debt was merged in the judgment, and also on the ground that joint debtors had a right to be sued together: but neither ground was satisfactory, and the rule was capable of working hardship. The rule applied to a judgment obtained by consent,[39] even if the defendant subsequently consented to the claimant's application to set aside the judgment in order that the claimant could sue another joint contractor.[40] The rule has now been abrogated by section 3 of the Civil Liability (Contribution) Act 1978.[41] This section applies to joint contractors generally, and is not confined to joint debtors.[42] 17–015

---

[34] *Calder v Rutherford* (1882) 3 Brod. & Bing. 302.

[35] Partnership Act 1890 s.9; cf. *Kendall v Hamilton* (1879) 4 App. Cas. 504, 538–539; *Re Hodgson* (1885) 31 Ch D 177.

[36] *Read v Price* [1909] 1 K.B. 577; Williams at para.30.

[37] Williams at para.42; *Banco Santander SA v Bayfern Ltd* [2000] 1 All E.R. (Comm) 776, 780.

[38] *King v Hoare* (1844) 13 M. & W. 494; *Kendall v Hamilton* (1879) 4 App. Cas. 504. There were exceptions to the general rule. For example, if the judgment was a foreign one (*Bank of Australasia v Nias* (1851) 16 Q.B. 717); or if the defendant in the second action agreed that his own liability should survive the judgment in the first action (*Duffner v Bowyer* (1924) 40 T.L.R. 700); or if the judgment was on an independent cause of action, such as a negotiable instrument given by one joint debtor (*Drake v Mitchell* (1803) 3 East 251; *Wegg Prosser v Evans* [1895] 1 Q.B. 108; *Badeley v Consolidated Bank* (1886) 34 Ch D 536, 556; affirmed (1888) 36 Ch D 238; *Goldrei, Foucard & Son v Sinclair* [1918] 1 K.B. 180); or, in relation to liquidated demands, where a judgment was signed against one or more joint debtors in default of notice of intention to defend or in default of defence (see CPR 1998 r.12.8 and Pt 24).

[39] *McLeod v Power* [1898] 2 Ch. 295.

[40] *Hammond v Schofield* [1891] 1 Q.B. 453. See Vol.II, para.31–071.

[41] But in *Morris v Wentworth-Stanley* [1999] 2 W.L.R. 470, it was held by the Court of Appeal that s.3 of the Civil Liability (Contribution) Act 1978 did not apply to a judgment obtained by consent: that judgment embodied an accord and satisfaction and the applicable rule was that an accord and satisfaction with one joint debtor released other joint debtors.

[42] It has been said that s.3 applies only to judicial determinations and not to arbitral awards: *The Argo Hellas* [1984] 1 Lloyd's Rep. 296, 304. Section 3 of the 1978 Act replaced s.6 of the Law Reform (Married Women and Tortfeasors) Act 1935, which abolished the "merger" doctrine in respect of joint tortfeasors only. By s.4 of the 1978 Act, if more than one action is brought in respect of the same damage, the claimant is to be deprived of his costs unless the court is of the opinion that there was reasonable ground for bringing the action.

17–016 **Judgment against one joint and several debtor.** When the liability is joint and several, a judgment against one debtor did not, even at common law, bar a several action against another.[43] But satisfaction of the judgment did so, for the obligation was not cumulative; hence payment by one, whether before or after judgment, discharged the others. At common law, it seems that a joint judgment against all the joint and several debtors, if unsatisfied, did not bar a several action against one of them[44]; nor did an unsatisfied several judgment against one bar a joint action against the others.[45] But these rules are of little importance now, having regard to the general words of s.3 of the Act of 1978.

17–017 **Release, accord and satisfaction and covenant not to sue.** The discharge of one joint debtor by a release in a deed[46] or by accord and satisfaction[47] discharges all, in accordance with the general principle that joint liability creates only one obligation[48]; and the same is true, illogical though it may seem, if one joint and several debtor is so discharged.[49] On the other hand, a covenant not to sue one joint or joint and several debtor does not discharge the others,[50] though it may leave the covenantee liable to pay contribution to the other debtors,[51] and thus deprive the covenant of some of its apparent effect.[52]

---

[43] *Lechmere v Fletcher* (1833) 1 C. & M. 623; *King v Hoare* (1844) 13 M. & W. 494, 505; *Blyth v Fladgate* [1891] 1 Ch. 337, 353.

[44] *Re Davison Ex p. Chandler* (1884) 13 QBD 50.

[45] (1884) 13 QBD 50, 53.

[46] Williams, *Joint Obligations* (1949), para.50.

[47] *Nicholson v Revill* (1836) 4 A. & E. 675; *Re E.W.A.* [1901] 2 K.B. 642; *Morris v Wentworth-Stanley* [1999] 2 W.L.R. 470; cf. *Cutler v McPhail* [1962] 2 Q.B. 292 (joint tortfeasors); contra, Williams at para.55, citing earlier authorities to the contrary, some of which, however, may be explained on the principle stated below at fn.54.

[48] In *North v Wakefield* (1849) 13 Q.B. 536, 541, the reason given was that otherwise the debtor released would be liable for contribution to the debtors not released and so the intention of the parties would be frustrated. But this reasoning seems dubious for it assumes what requires to be proved, viz. that the creditor intends to protect the debtor released against claims from his co-debtors. See *Ex p. Good, Re Armitage* (1877) 5 Ch D 46, 57 where Jessel M.R. said: "It is very dangerous for modern judges to endeavour to find modern reasons for these old rules". See also Williams at pp.111–112. Similar difficulty attends the rules relating to the discharge of a surety as a result of an agreement to discharge a principal debtor, see Vol.II, paras 44–078—44–084.

[49] *Nicholson v Revill* (1836) 4 A. & E. 675; *Re E.W.A.* [1901] 2 K.B. 642; *Deanplan Ltd v Mahmoud* [1993] Ch. 151; Williams at para.63. cf. *Jameson v Central Electricity Generating Board* [1999] 2 W.L.R. 141; a settlement, satisfying a claim against one joint and several tortfeasor, on its true interpretation extinguished the cause of action against the other joint and several tortfeasor. But *Jameson* did not lay down any rule of law that settlement with one joint and several tortfeasor inevitably precludes the claimant from bringing an action against another: *Heaton v Axa Equity and Law Life Assurance Society Plc* [2002] UKHL 15, [2002] 2 W.L.R. 1081. This case concerned two successive breaches of contract by different parties. The claimants settled with one contract-breaker, and then claimed against the other in respect of damages which had formed part of the settled claim. It was held that the sum accepted was not, on construction of the settlement, to be taken as fixing the full measure of the claimants' loss; they could therefore recover substantial damages from the defendants, giving credit for sums paid by the first contract-breakers in respect of matters covered in the instant claims.

[50] *Lucy Clayton v Kynaston* (1699) 12 Mod. 221, 415, 548; *Dean v Newhall* (1799) 8 T.R. 168; *Hutton v Eyre* (1815) 6 Taunt. 289 (joint tortfeasors).

[51] *Mallet v Thompson* (1804) 5 Esp. 178; *Hutton v Eyre* (1815) 6 Taunt. 289; Williams at para.52.

[52] As to the effect of a covenant, or agreement, not to sue a principal debtor on the liability of a surety, see Vol.II, paras 44–078—44–084.

The courts generally construe a release as a covenant not to sue if it contains an indication of intention that the other debtors are not to be discharged.[53] Moreover, even an accord and satisfaction with one joint or joint and several debtor will not discharge the others if the agreement, expressly or impliedly, provides that the creditor's rights against them shall be preserved.[54] 17–018

The distinction between a release and a covenant not to sue rests on the intention of the parties. A release involves total destruction of the debt or claim; a covenant not to sue implies that the creditor undertakes not to take proceedings against the debtor in question (the covenantee) while not necessarily abandoning his rights against any other party liable. In this context the term "covenant" does not bear its traditional meaning of a promise in a deed, but extends to any promise. 17–019

In practice the difficulty normally arises from the fact that, in making the agreement, the parties have overlooked the position of co-debtors, and it is not clear whether the creditor intends to reserve his rights against them or not.[55] If the agreement appears from its words to be a release and there are no words reserving rights against the other debtors, nor anything in the circumstances to rebut the prima facie meaning of words used, the agreement will release all the debtors[56]; but it would seem that the courts lean in favour of other debtors not being discharged by construing the agreement as a covenant not to sue or as a release but subject to an implied reservation of rights against other debtors.[57] 17–020

Sureties. Some special rules apply to joint or joint and several debtors who are sureties. For instance, an agreement to give time to a principal debtor without the consent of a surety discharges the surety unless there is an express reservation 17–021

---

[53] *Solly v Forbes* (1820) 2 Brod. & Bing. 38; *North v Wakefield* (1849) 13 Q.B. 536; *Thompson v Lack* (1846) 3 C.B. 540; *Price v Barker* (1855) 4 E. & B. 760; *Willis v De Castro* (1858) 4 C.B.(N.S.) 216; *Bateson v Gosling* (1871) L.R. 7 C.P. 9; cf. *Duck v Mayeu* [1892] 2 Q.B. 511 (joint tortfeasors); *Apley Estates Co v De Bernales* [1947] Ch. 217 (joint tortfeasors); *Gardiner v Moore* [1969] 1 Q.B. 55 (joint tortfeasors); *Bryanston Finance v de Vries* [1975] 1 Q.B. 703 (joint tortfeasors); *Watts v Adlington, The Times*, December 16, 1993 (joint tortfeasors).

[54] *Watters v Smith* (1831) 2 B. & Ad. 889; *Ex p. Good, Re Armitage* (1877) 5 Ch D 46; *Re Wolmershausen* (1890) 62 L.T. 541; *Re E.W.A.* [1901] 2 K.B. 642, 648–649; *Johnson v Davies* [1998] 3 W.L.R. 1299; *Sun Life Assurance Society Plc v Tantofex (Engineers) Ltd* [1999] 2 E.G.L.R. 135; cf. *Watts v Adlington, The Times*, December 16, 1993 (joint tortfeasors). See also *Heaton v Axa Equity and Law Life Assurance Society Plc* [2002] UKHL 15, [2002] 2 W.L.R. 1081 (a separate contract-breaker, albeit liable for the same damage to the claimant, was held not to be discharged by the claimant's settlement with another contract-breaker).

[55] *Re E.W.A.* [1901] 2 K.B. 642, 649.

[56] *Deanplan Ltd v Mahmoud* [1993] Ch. 151; *Morris v Wentworth-Stanley* [1999] 2 W.L.R. 470.

[57] *Watts v Adlington, The Times*, December 16, 1993 (which concerned joint tortfeasors). This case was followed in *Finlay v Connell Associates, The Times*, June 23, 1999 in deciding that a reservation of rights against a surety could be implied in an agreement not to sue a principal debtor. See also *Sun Life Assurance Society Plc v Tantofex (Engineers) Ltd* [1999] 2 E.G.L.R. 135, in which *Deanplan Ltd v Mahmoud* [1993] Ch. 151 was distinguished. The High Court of Australia in *Thompson v Australian Capital Television Pty Ltd* (1996) 186 C.L.R. 574 has removed the release rule altogether in respect of joint tortfeasors. See A. D. M. Hewitt, "Compromising With One Joint Tortfeasor" (1998) 72 A.L.J. 73.

of rights against the surety[58]; but an agreement to give time to one co-debtor without the consent of the other does not discharge them[59] unless they are sureties. These special rules as to sureties are fully discussed elsewhere in this work.[60]

17–022 **Material alteration.** As will be seen,[61] if a material alteration is made in a specialty or any other contractual document without the consent of the promisor, whether by the promisee or (possibly) by a stranger, when the document is in the custody of the promisee or his agent, such alteration discharges the promisor from all liability thereon.[62] The same rule applies to a contract entered into by joint or joint and several contractors.[63] There is no authority on the question whether a material alteration which discharges one operates also to discharge them all.

17–023 **Debtor becoming executor or administrator.** Where a debtor becomes executor or administrator of the estate of his creditor, the debt is extinguished, but the debtor may be accountable for the amount of the debt,[64] unless the creditor intended by appointing him as executor, to discharge the debt.[65] Although this rule is now statutory, previous authorities holding that co-debtors were necessarily discharged in these circumstances seem unaffected.[66] This result, however, does not prevent the executor or administrator from recovering contribution under the principle stated in para.17–027.[67] In the converse case where the creditor becomes executor to his debtor, the debt is not discharged unless the executor proves the will and has assets out of which he can pay the debt by means of his right of retainer.[68]

17–024 **Bankruptcy.** The discharge in bankruptcy of one joint or joint and several debtor does not discharge the others.[69]

17–025 **Voluntary arrangements with creditors.** Whether a voluntary arrangement with creditors entered into by an insolvent co-debtor, pursuant to the Insolvency Act 1986, does or does not discharge other co-debtors, who are not parties to the

[58] See Vol.II, para.44–094.

[59] *Swire v Redman* (1876) 1 QBD 536.

[60] See Vol.II, paras 44–091—44–101.

[61] Below, paras 25–020—25–023.

[62] *Pigot's Case* (1614) 11 Co.Rep. 26b; *Master v Miller* (1791) 4 T.R. 320, (1793) 5 T.R. 367.

[63] *Perring v Hone* (1826) 4 Bing. 29; *Gardner v Walsh* (1855) 5 E. & B. 83.

[64] See s.21A of the Administration of Estates Act 1925 (inserted by s.10 of the Limitation Amendment Act 1980).

[65] *Strong* v *Bird* (1874) L.R. 18 Eq. 315; *Re Applebee* [1891] 3 Ch. 422; *Re Bourne* [1906] 1 Ch. 697. The effect of these decisions is preserved by the wording of s.21A(1)(b) of the Administration of Estates Act 1925, but is now extended also to the case of the debtor who is appointed as administrator.

[66] *Cheetham v Ward* (1797) 1 Bos. & P. 630; *Jenkins v Jenkins* [1928] 2 K.B. 503.

[67] See *Jenkins v Jenkins* [1928] 2 K.B. 503, 506.

[68] *Lowe v Peskett* (1856) 16 C.B. 500; *Re Rhoades* [1899] 2 Q.B. 347.

[69] Insolvency Act 1986 s.281(7).

voluntary arrangement, will depend on the term of the voluntary arrangement.[70]

Limitation Act 1980. An acknowledgment or part payment of a debt or other liquidated pecuniary claim made by one joint debtor does not take a case out of the Limitation Act 1980 as regards the others,[71] unless: (1) it is made with their authority as agent for them[72]; or (2) a part payment (not an acknowledgment) is made before the expiration of the limitation period.[73] The reason for the second exception is that a part payment made before the expiration of the period enures for the advantage of all the joint debtors, hence it is thought fair that they should share the disadvantage too.[74] The rules appear to be the same for joint and several debtors as they are for joint debtors. **17–026**

Contribution between joint debtors. Joint and joint and several debtors have a restitutionary right of contribution among themselves: that is to say, if one has paid more than his share of the debt, he can recover the excess from the others in equal shares, subject to any agreement to the contrary.[75] In the absence of agreement to the contrary each co-debtor is liable for an equal share of the debt or obligation.[76] This right is statutory in cases where a county court judgment against one joint debtor has been satisfied.[77] The right of contribution is independent of any present right of the principal creditor. Thus one co-debtor can recover contribution from another although the principal creditor's right to recover from that other debtor has become statute-barred.[78] Again, the right to contribution may be enforced against the personal representatives of a deceased joint debtor,[79] even though (as we have seen)[80] they would not be liable to the creditor. (There is an exception to this rule in the case of lessees who are joint tenants: if one dies, the survivor cannot claim contribution in respect of rent from the personal representatives of the deceased lessee.[81]) If one joint or joint and **17–027**

---

[70] *Johnson v Davies* [1998] 3 W.L.R. 1299 (on the construction of its terms, the voluntary arrangement was held not to discharge co-debtors).

[71] Limitation Act 1980 s.31(6). See below, para.28–103.

[72] s.30(2).

[73] s.31(7).

[74] But the Law Commission has recommended that acknowledgments and part payments by one co-debtor should only affect the limitation period running against that debtor and not other co-debtors: see *Limitation of Actions* (Law Com No.270, 2001), paras 3.151, 3.155.

[75] *Deering v Earl of Winchelsea* (1787) 1 Cox 318; 2 Bos. & P. 270; *Hutton v Eyre* (1815) 6 Taunt. 289; *Coope v Twynam* (1823) Turn & R 426; *Pendelbury v Walker* (1841) 4 Y & C Ex 424; *Boulter v Peplow* (1850) 9 C.B. 493; *Batard v Hawes* (1853) 2 E. & B. 287; see Williams, *Joint Obligations* (1949), Ch.9; Goff and Jones, *The Law of Restitution*, 6th edn (2002), Ch.14.

[76] For an example of proportionate, rather than equal, contribution, see *Commercial Union Assurance Co Ltd v Hayden* [1977] Q.B. 804. A surety has a right of indemnity, not merely contribution: see Vol.II, paras 44–111 et seq.

[77] County Courts Act 1984 s.48(2); see above, para.17–009 fn.22.

[78] *Wolmershausen v Gullick* [1893] 2 Ch. 514; *Gardner v Brooke* [1897] 2 Ir.R. 6. Time begins to run, in respect of the right to contribution, only when that right crystallises by actual payment. See also Vol.II, paras 44–115 et seq.

[79] *Ashby v Ashby* (1827) 7 B. & C. 444, 449, 451–452; *Prior v Hembrow* (1841) 8 M. & W. 873; *Batard v Hawes* (1853) 2 E. & B. 287, 298.

[80] Above, para.17–012.

[81] *Cunningham-Reid v Public Trustee* [1944] K.B. 602.

several debtor is insolvent, the loss resulting from his insolvency is spread equally among the solvent debtors.[82]

17–028 It is a condition precedent to the right to recover contribution that the claimant should have been liable to pay the whole debt[83] and should have paid more than his share of it.[84] If he merely pays his share and no more, he has no present right to contribution: but he will acquire such right as soon as anything happens in the future which discharges the debt and thus brings it about that he has paid more than his share, for instance if the debt should become statute-barred.[85] Moreover, a surety against whom the principal creditor has obtained judgment for the full amount of the debt, but who has paid nothing in respect of that judgment, can obtain a prospective order directing a co-surety, on payment by the surety of his own share of the debt, to indemnify him against further liability, or (if the principal creditor is a party to the action) an order directing the co-surety to pay his proportion to the principal creditor.[86] A surety suing his co-sureties for contribution must join as defendants all those who are liable to make contribution, unless one of them is insolvent or there is some other good reason why he should not be joined.[87]

17–029 **Contribution between persons liable in respect of the same damage.** The rules stated in paras 17–027—17–028, above, only apply to co-debtors, i.e. persons liable in respect of the same *debt*.[88] Where two or more persons are liable in respect of the same *damage*, the position is now regulated by s.1 of the Civil Liability (Contribution) Act 1978.[89] Section 1(1) of this Act provides that:

> "... any person liable in respect of any damage suffered by another person may recover contribution from any other person liable in respect of the same damage (whether jointly with him or otherwise)."

This provision, as is made clear by the words in brackets, applies even where the liability arises out of two separate contracts, for example, where an architect and a builder, each employed under a separate contract, are both guilty of breaches of contract causing damage to the owner of the building.[90] The section would also

---

[82] *Peter v Rich* (1630) 1 Ch.Rep. 34; *Hitchman v Stewart* (1855) 3 Drew. 271; *Lowe v Dixon* (1885) 16 QBD 455. Before the Judicature Act 1873, the rule at law was otherwise. Since that Act, the rule in equity prevails.

[83] A debtor who was liable only for 50 per cent. of the debt but who has paid in full cannot recover contribution: *Legal & General Assurance Society Ltd v Drake Insurance Co Ltd* [1992] 1 Q.B. 887.

[84] *Davies v Humphreys* (1840) 6 M. & W. 153, 168–169; *Re Snowdon* (1881) 17 Ch D 44; *Stirling v Burdett* [1911] 2 Ch. 418.

[85] *Davies v Humphreys* (1840) 6 M. & W. 153, 169.

[86] *Wolmershausen v Gullick* [1893] 2 Ch. 514.

[87] *Hay v Carter* [1935] Ch. 397.

[88] As the Civil Liability (Contribution) Act 1978 does not apply to a claim for contribution from a co-debtor, the limitation period applicable to the 1978 Act, as laid down in s.10 of the Limitation Act 1980, does not apply to such a claim for contribution: *Hampton v Minns* [2002] 1 W.L.R. 1.

[89] The Act was based on the *Report on Contribution* of the Law Commission (Law Com. No.79, 1977); see generally Dugdale (1979) 42 M.L.R. 182; *Clerk & Lindsell on Torts*, 19th edn (2006), paras 4–12—4–25.

[90] Here the defendants would, in the contractual sense of the term, be severally liable but in the tort sense they would be jointly and severally liable; see above, para.17–004.

apply if one person were liable in contract and another in tort.[91] By ss.1(2) and (3) it is immaterial that the original liability of the claimant or the party from whom contribution is sought, has become statute-barred. But subject to s.1(3), "liability in respect of the same damage" refers to liability to the injured party at the time when contribution is being sought.[92]

"The same damage". In *Royal Brompton Hospital NHS Trust v Hammond*,[93] architects could not recover contribution from builders because the damage in respect of which the claims were brought by the owners against the architects and builders was not the same so as to fall within s.1(1) of the Civil Liability (Contribution) Act 1978. The damage caused by the builders' breach of contract was the failure to provide the building on time; whereas the damage caused by the architects, through negligently certifying an extension of time, was the impairment of the owners' ability to obtain full compensation in a settlement from the builders. It was emphasised by their Lordships that the statutory words "the same damage" must be applied without any glosses, extensive or restrictive. The wider interpretations of "the same damage" in some earlier cases[94] were expressly disapproved. On the other hand, *Eastgate Group Ltd v Lindsey Morden Group Inc*[95] was referred to without disapproval and the decision appears to be consistent with the reasoning of the House of Lords. In that case, the question was whether, on the sale of a company (LMG) to E, a liability of LMG to E for breach of warranties as to the value of the company was a liability for "the same damage" as a liability of LMG's accountants to E for negligent accounting. It was held by the Court of Appeal that the liability was for the same damage, namely that E had bought a company worth less than E reasonably expected it to be worth. The fact that the measure of damages might differ (as between contract 17–030

---

[91] *Royal Brompton Hospital NHS Trust v Hammond* [2002] UKHL 14, [2002] 1 W.L.R. 1397; *Eastgate Group Ltd v Lindsey Morden Group Inc* [2001] EWCA Civ 1446, [2001] 2 All E.R. (Comm) 1050.

[92] In *Co-operative Retail Services Ltd v Taylor Young Partnership Ltd* [2002] UKHL 17, [2002] 1 W.L.R. 1419 the House of Lords decided that those from whom contribution was sought were not "liable in respect of the . . . damage". Building works had been damaged by a fire, which on the assumed facts was due to the negligence (in breach of contract) of the main contractors, the electrical subcontractors, the engineer and the architect. By reason of a contractual arrangement, the main contractors and subcontractors were not liable to the building owners in respect of the fire damage (*i.e.* they had excluded their liability to pay compensation). No contribution could therefore be claimed from them by the engineer and architect.

[93] [2002] UKHL 14, [2002] 1 W.L.R. 1397.

[94] *Friends Provident Life Office v Hillier Parker May & Rowden* [1997] Q.B. 85 (restitution of money and compensation); *Hurstwood Developments Ltd v Motor & General & Andersley & Co Insurance Services* [2001] EWCA Civ 1785, [2002] Lloyd's Rep I.R. 185, (builder's defective work and insurance broker's failure to insure); *Bovis Lend Lease Ltd v Saillard Fuller & Partners* (2001) 77 Con.L.R. 134, 181–182 (builder's defective work and insurer's liability under policy of insurance). In *Charter Plc v City Index Ltd* [2007] EWCA Civ 1382 equitable liability for "knowing receipt" was treated as a wrong-based liability for compensation (rather than as being a liability to make restitution of an unjust enrichment). It therefore fell within the scope of the 1978 Act and the "knowing recipient" was held entitled to claim contribution from tortfeasors liable in respect of the same loss. The criticism of *Friends Provident* by the House of Lords in the *Royal Brompton* case was thought to be irrelevant to "knowing receipt".

[95] [2001] EWCA Civ 1446, [2001] 2 All E.R. (Comm) 1050.

and tort) did not contradict the view that the damage was the same. The 1978 Act therefore applied.

17–031 **Amount of contribution.** Section 2(1) of the 1978 Act provides that the amount of the contribution shall be:

> "... such as may be found by the court to be just and equitable having regard to the extent of that person's responsibility for the damage in question."

In this respect the Act makes a major change to the common law rules which still apply to cases of co-debtors; for under the rule stated in para.17–027, the debt can only be divided equally between the co-debtors. Under the Act, the liability can be apportioned unequally; in both cases, however, a complete indemnity can be awarded where appropriate.

17–032 **Effect of judgment or compromise.** Any judgment of a court is conclusive against the party from whom contribution is sought that the party claiming contribution was in fact liable for the damage in question.[96] A bona fide compromise is likewise conclusive, but in this case only assuming that the factual basis of the claim can be established.[97] The Act does not affect any contractual provision excluding or regulating a right to contribution, nor does it apply where a surety has a right to an indemnity as distinguished from a right to contribution.

17–033 **Contribution from party against whom limitation has run.** The Act, in replacing (as well as extending) the provisions of s.6 of the Law Reform (Married Women and Tortfeasors) Act 1935, has avoided some of the difficulties which arose under that Act where contribution was sought against a party who had been found (or was) not liable under a limitation statute.[98] Under the 1978 Act, it is expressly provided by s.1(3) that contribution can be sought from someone who has "ceased to be liable", and it seems clear that this remains the

---

[96] Civil Liability Act 1978 s.1(5).

[97] Civil Liability Act 1978 s.1(4). Where the facts are undisputed, and the compromise has been arrived at because of doubts about the law, the position seems to be that s.1(4) is irrelevant, and that contribution can only be claimed if both parties were "liable," which is explained by s.1(6) to mean: "... any such liability which has been or could be established in an action brought against him in England and Wales by or on behalf of the person suffering the damage." See, generally, *J. Sainsbury Plc v Broadway Malyan* [1999] P.N.L.R. 286. An assignor of a cause of action is not someone "by or on behalf of" whom an action could have been brought (by the assignee): *Bovis Lend Lease Ltd v Saillard Fuller & Partners* [2001] 77 Con.L.R. 134. But it was also held in that case that an insurer, assigned a cause of action to reinforce its existing right of subrogation, was to be treated as standing in the shoes of the assignor (the insured) at all times and therefore was to be taken to be "a person who suffered the damage". In *Baker & Davies Plc v Leslie Wilks Associates* [2005] EWHC 1179 (TCC), [2005] 3 All E.R. 603, it was held that the 1978 Act does apply—so that contribution can be claimed—even where a settlement requires a party to carry out work for, rather than to make a payment to, the person who has suffered the damage: that is, the word "payment" in s.1(4) includes a payment in kind.

[98] *Wimpey & Co Ltd v B.O.A.C.* [1955] A.C. 169; *Hart v Hall and Pickles Ltd* [1969] 1 Q.B. 405.

case even if he has actually been sued and successfully pleaded the Limitation Act.[99]

Assessment of contribution. The method of assessing the contribution under the 1978 Act follows the precedents previously set in s.6 of the 1935 Act and also the Law Reform (Contributory Negligence) Act 1945. In both these Acts the courts were given broad powers of apportioning liability (or responsibility) for damage in accordance with the "just and equitable" formula. In general it is well established that the courts must have regard to considerations of relative causative potency as well as to comparative blameworthiness under these provisions.[100] It is not wholly clear how easily these concepts are transferable from the tort context, where liability is usually based on negligence, to the contractual context where liability is usually strict, and does not involve "blameworthiness" except in the sense that any breach of contract may be said to be blameworthy. In a case of vicarious liability, comparative blameworthiness requires one to look at the blameworthiness of the person for whom the vicariously liable person was responsible: the vicariously liable person (e.g. the employer) stands in the shoes of the wrongdoer (e.g. the employee) and it is irrelevant that the vicariously liable person was non-blameworthy.[101] 17–034

Limits on right to contribution. It may also be worth noting that although the Act is designed to enable contribution to be obtained from any person liable in respect of the same damage, even though the liability of the parties arises from different legal sources (e.g. contract and tort), there will still be circumstances in which contribution will be unobtainable. For instance, a purchaser of defective goods who is held liable in negligence to a third party for damage caused by use of the goods, cannot claim contribution from the person who sold those goods to him if that person was not also liable to the third party; if the seller was guilty of a breach of the terms of the contract of sale, the purchaser may be able to recover a complete indemnity from the seller, depending on whether his own conduct has broken the causal link between the seller's breach and the third party's injury, but there can be no claim under the 1978 Act.[102] 17–035

---

[99] Or if he has settled: *Logan v Uttlesford DC* (1984) (C.A.T. No.263). Compare, as to the position before the coming into force of the 1978 Act, *Harper v Gray & Walker* [1985] 2 All E.R. 507.

[100] See, e.g. *Davies v Swan Motor Co* [1949] 2 K.B. 291 (contributory negligence); *Downs v Chappell* [1997] 1 W.L.R. 426 (contribution). In *Abbey National Plc v Matthews & Son* [2003] EWHC 925, [2003] 1 W.L.R. 2042, a claim for contribution was struck out where the terms of a compromise between C and D1 made it impossible to decide what amount of contribution was "just and equitable": the compromise precluded execution of C's judgment against D1 for any sum beyond the contribution that C (as assignee of D1's contribution claim) might be held entitled to from D2.

[101] *Dubai Aluminium Co Ltd v Salaam* [2002] UKHL 48, [2002] 3 W.L.R. 1913.

[102] See Hervey (1981) 44 M.L.R. 575, 576. In *Birse Construction Ltd v Haiste Ltd* [1996] 1 W.L.R. 675 a reservoir was defectively constructed: although D1 was liable to P (who was itself liable to X) and D2 was liable to X, D1 and D2 were not liable for the same damage to the same person and hence contribution could not be recovered by D1 and D2.

Chapter 18

THIRD PARTIES[1]

	PARA.
1. Introduction	18–001
2. The common law doctrine	18–003
(a) Parties to the agreement	18–004
(b) Party to the consideration	18–016
(c) Development of the common law doctrine	18–019
3. Scope	18–021
(a) Liability in negligence to third parties	18–022
(b) Liability to third parties for intimidation	18–040
(c) Liability to third parties in restitution?	18–042
4. Contracts for the benefit of third parties	18–043
(a) Effects of a contract for the benefit of a third party	18–043
(i) Promisee's remedies	18–044
(ii) Position between promisee and third party	18–072
(b) Exceptions to the doctrine	18–077
(i) Equitable exceptions	18–078
(ii) Contracts (Rights of Third Parties) Act 1999	18–088
(iii) Other statutory exceptions	18–121
5. Enforcement against third parties	18–133

1. Introduction

Preliminary. Our concern in this Chapter is with the extent to which persons can either take the benefit of, or be bound by, contracts to which they are not parties. Under the common law doctrine of privity of contract, the general rule is that contracts cannot be enforced either by or against third parties. The second limb of this rule (under which a contract cannot impose liabilities on anyone except a party to it) is generally regarded as just and sensible.[2] But its first limb (under which a contract cannot confer rights on anyone except a party to it) has been the subject of much criticism, culminating in a Report, issued by the Law Commission in 1996, on *Privity of Contract: Contracts for the Benefit of Third Parties*.[3] The recommendations of this Report have (where legislation for this **18–001**

[1] Finlay, *Contracts for the Benefit of Third Persons* (1939); Dold, *Stipulations for a Third Party* (1948); Furmston, *Third Party Rights* (2005); Corbin (1930) 47 L.Q.R. 12; Dowrick (1956) 19 M.L.R. 374; Furmston (1960) 23 M.L.R. 373; Wilson, 11 Sydney L.Rev. 230 (1987). Flannigan (1989) 105 L.Q.R. 564; Kincaid [1989] C.L.J. 454; Andrews (1988) L.S. 14.

[2] See below, para.18–133. The rule that a contract cannot in other respects bind a third party can be inconvenient in cases involving exemption clauses (and is therefore modified in a number of ways discussed in section 5 of Ch.14). It is further qualified in a number of ways to be discussed in section 5 of the present Chapter.

[3] Law Com. No.242 (hereafter "Report"). For an earlier proposal, see Law Revision Committee, 6th Interim Report (Cmnd. 5449) Section D.

purpose was necessary[4]) been implemented by the Contracts (Rights of Third Parties) Act 1999.The Act does not precisely follow the wording of the Draft Bill attached to the Law Commission's Report, but the changes in the wording do not, in general,[5] reflect any major departures from the policy of the recommendations in that Report: their object has rather been to secure the clearer and more effective implementation of that policy. For this reason, it is submitted that reference can appropriately be made to the Report in discussing the provisions of the 1999 Act; and such references will be made in this Chapter.

18–002 **Present structure of the subject.** It is important at the outset to make a point about the nature of the changes made by the 1999 Act, since this determines the present structure of the subject. A crucial passage in the Law Commission's Report states that "it is important to emphasise that, while our proposed reform will give some third parties the right to enforce contracts, there will remain many contracts where a third party stands to benefit and yet will not have a right of enforceability. Our proposed statute carves out a general and wide-ranging exception to the third party rule, but it leaves that rule intact for cases not covered by the statute."[6] The rights conferred on third parties by the 1999 Act therefore have the character of a new statutory exception[7] to the common law doctrine of privity; and the 1999 Act will be treated as such an exception in the present Chapter, though because of its importance a separate section will be devoted to it.[8] The new exception is, however, limited in two ways. First, a number of situations which have in the past been perceived as giving rise to problems resulting from the doctrine of privity are simply outside the scope of the new statutory exception and so are not affected by the provisions of the 1999 Act at all: this is, for example, true of many of the cases in which third parties who have suffered loss in consequence of the breach of a contract between others have sought a remedy in tort against the party in breach.[9] Secondly, the exception created by the 1999 Act is, in turn, under that Act, subject to exceptions[10] to

---

[4] For a situation in which this was *not* necessary, see Report, para.6.8 n.8, below, para.18–097.

[5] The exception is s.8 of the Act, subjecting the third party's rights to arbitration agreements, contrary to the views expressed in paras 14.14 to 14.19 of the Report: see para.18–095 below, and Vol.II, para.32–035.

[6] Report para.5.16; the importance of the point appears from the fact that it is repeated in almost identical terms in para.13.2 of the Report.

[7] See Lord Bingham's reference in *Heaton v Axa Equity & Law Life Assurance plc* [2002] UKHL 15; [2002] 2 A.C. 392 at [9] to "the limited class of contracts which either at common law or by virtue of the Contracts (Rights of Third Parties) Act 1999 was enforceable by . . . a third party." *cf. Alfred McAlpine Construction Ltd v Panatown Ltd* [2001] 1 A.C. 518 at 535 *per* Lord Clyde, saying that the 1999 Act had "made some inroads on the principle of privity" and Lord Browne-Wilkinson, *ibid.* at p.575, saying that the Act had "fundamentally affected" the law on this topic. It is respectfully submitted that these are more accurate statements than Lord Goff's reference *ibid* at p.544 to the "abolition" by the Act of the doctrine of privity, and his similar statement *in Johnson v Gore Wood & Co* [2002] 2 A.C. 1 at 40 ("recently abolished by statute"). See also *Ramco (UK) Ltd v International Insurance Co of Hanover* [2004] EWCA Civ 675, [2004] 2 All E.R. (Comm) 866 at [32], treating the third party's right of enforcement under the 1999 Act as an exception to the common law doctrine of privity.

[8] Below, paras 18–088 *et seq.*

[9] For further discussion of this point, see below, paras 18–022 *et seq.*

[10] See s.6 of the Act, discussed in paras 18–111—18–113, below.

which the third party's new statutory rights do not extend; and the effect of this is that in some[11] of these cases the common law doctrine of privity continues to apply. The 1999 Act also does not affect any rights which the third party has apart from its provisions[12]: thus it does not deprive the third party of rights which he has because the case falls either outside the scope of the common law doctrine or within one of the exceptions to it recognised either at common law, or in equity or under other legislation.[13] The scope of the common law doctrine and these other exceptions therefore continue to call for discussion, particularly because the content of rights available apart from the 1999 Act in some ways differs from that of the rights available under it.[14] The 1999 Act also (in accordance with the Law Commission's recommendations[15]) does not affect the common law rule that a contract cannot impose liabilities on a third party or (in general) otherwise bind him, so that this aspect of the common law doctrine, too, continues to call for discussion. Nor does the Act affect any rights of the promisee to enforce any term of the contract[16]: such questions as whether the promisee can recover damages in respect of the third party's loss will therefore continue to be governed by the rules which have been (and no doubt will further be) developed as a matter of common law. There is finally the point that the 1999 Act also does not apply to contracts made before the end of the period of six months beginning on the day on which it was it passed and came into force,[17] except where a contract[18] made within that period expressly provides that the Act is to apply to it.[19] The rules of law which were established before the 1999 Act therefore continue to apply to contracts made before the date specified in the Act or in any such contract. They also continue to apply in a significant number of other situations, described above,[20] to which the Act does not apply. These rules therefore still require discussion, even though a considerable number of the cases on which they are based would, if their facts occurred now, be decided differently (where they had denied the third party the right to enforce a term of the contract) or be decided on different grounds (where they had given the third party such a right). The result of all these points is that the 1999 Act may have improved, but that it has scarcely simplified the law on this topic.

---

[11] *e.g.* ss.6(2) and 6(3); under some of the other exceptions, the third party will be able to get rights by another legal route: *e.g.* under those stated in ss.6(1) and (5): see para.18–112, below.

[12] Section 7(1), below para.18–114; Report, para.12.12.

[13] Below, paras 18–078—18–087; 18–121—18–132. For an illustration of a situation in which the third party had rights both under the 1999 Act and under one of the judge-made exceptions to the doctrine of privity, see *Nisshin Shipping Co Ltd v Cleaves & Co Ltd* [2003] EWHC 2602; [2004] 1 All E.R. (Comm) 481.

[14] *e.g.*, ss.2 and 3 of the 1999 Act will not apply where the third party has rights apart from the Act; see further para.18–116, below.

[15] Report, paras 10.32, 7.6.

[16] 1999 Act, s.4.

[17] On November 11, 1999, when the Act received the Royal Assent: see s.10(2). Hence, subject to the exception mentioned at n.19 below, the Act does not apply to a contract made before May 11, 1999: see *Mulchrone v Swiss Life (UK) plc* [2005] EWHC 1808, [2006] Lloyd's Rep. I.R. 339 where the contract was made before the latter date, so that the Act did not apply.

[18] See s.10(3).

[19] *ibid.*

[20] At nn.9, 11.

2. THE COMMON LAW DOCTRINE

18–003 **Statement.** The common law doctrine of privity of contract means that a contract cannot (as a general rule) confer rights or impose obligations arising under it on any person except the parties to it. Two questions arise from this statement: who are the parties to the agreement? and has the claimant provided consideration for the promise which he is seeking to enforce?

(a) *Parties to the Agreement*

18–004 **Who are the parties?** Normally, the answer to this question is obvious enough: the parties to the agreement are the persons from whose communications with each other the agreement has resulted. There may, indeed, be factual difficulties in identifying these persons[21]; but such difficulties do not generally[22] raise any questions of legal principle. Problems as to the legal analysis of established or admitted facts can, however, arise in situations in which there is clearly an agreement, while it is doubtful exactly who the parties to it are; and difficulty in deciding who the parties to a particular contract are may also arise when there are several contracts which affect the same subject-matter and involve more than two parties. The rights of all the parties to such contracts arise independently of the Contracts (Rights of Third Parties) Act 1999 and are not limited by its provisions.[23] Situations in which such contracts may arise are discussed in the following paragraphs.

18–005 **Collateral contracts.**[24] A contract between two persons may be accompanied by a collateral contract between one of them and a third person relating to the same subject-matter. In *Shanklin Pier v Detel Products Ltd*[25] the claimants had employed contractors to paint a pier and instructed them for this purpose to buy

[21] *e.g. Stag Line Ltd v Tyne Ship Repair Group (The Zinnia)* [1984] 2 Lloyd's Rep. 211; *Empresa Lineas Maritimas Argentinas v The Oceanus Mutual Underwriting Association (Bermuda) Ltd* [1984] 2 Lloyd's Rep. 517; *Uddin v Ahmed* [2001] EWCA Civ 240; [2001] 3 F.C.R. 300; *Grecoair Inc v Tilling* [2004] EWHC 2851, [2005] Lloyd's Rep. I.R. 151; *Percy v Board of National Mission of the Church of Scotland* [2005] UKHL 73, [2006] 2 A.C. 28; *West Bromwich Albion Football Club v El Safty* [2006] EWCA Civ 1299, (2006) 92 B.M.L.R. 179; *cf. Independiente Ltd v Music Trading On-Line (HK) Ltd* [2007] EWCA Civ 111, [2007] 4 All E.R. 736, where the question was one of construction or implication; *Grosvenor Casinos Ltd v National Bank of Abu Dhabi* [2008] EWHC 511 (Comm), [2008] 2 Lloyd's Rep. 1.

[22] A highly specialised group of cases (beyond the scope of this book) concerns bills of lading issued in respect of goods shipped on a chartered ship: see *Carver on Bills of Lading*, 2nd ed., para.4–028 to para.4–056; *Homburg Houtimport BV v Agrosin Private Ltd (The Starsin)* [2003] UKHL 12; [2004] 1 A.C. 715.

[23] Contracts (Rights of Third Parties) Act 1999, s.7(1).

[24] Wedderburn [1959] C.L.J. 58; above, § 12–004.

[25] [1951] 2 K.B. 854; followed in *Wells (Merstham) Ltd v Buckland Sand & Silica Co Ltd* [1965] 2 Q.B. 170, even though in that case no specific main contract was contemplated when the collateral undertaking was given. As to sales by auction, see *Chelmsford Auctions Ltd v Poole* [1973] Q.B. 542, 550; *Morin v Bonhams & Brooks Ltd* [2003] EWHC 467 (Comm); [2003] 2 All E.R. (Comm) 36 at 28, 51; affirmed on other grounds [2003] EWCA Civ 1802, [2004] 1 All E.R. (Comm) 880; below, Vol. II, paras 31–011, 43–482; for similar reasoning, leading to the making of a contract "in the context of an associated and simultaneous set of transactions", see *Moody v Condor Insurance Ltd* [2006] EWHC 100 (Ch), [2006] 1 W.L.R. 1847 at [39].

paint made by the defendants. This instruction was given in reliance on a statement made by the defendants to the claimants that the paint would last for seven years. In fact it lasted for only three months. Although the main contract for the sale of paint was between the contractors and the defendants, it was held that there was also a collateral contract between the claimants and the defendants that the paint would last for seven years. The same reasoning may apply where a person buys goods from a dealer and is given a "guarantee" in the name of the manufacturer. Here the main contract of sale is between the customer and the dealer, but it seems that the "guarantee" could also be regarded as a collateral contract between the manufacturer and the customer.[26] Special legislation applies to certain guarantees given to consumers in respect of goods sold or supplied to them. Where the requirements specified in this legislation are satisfied, such guarantees take effect as contractual obligations[27] whether or not the requirements of a collateral contract[28] are satisfied; but these requirements continue to apply to manufacturers' guarantees not covered by this legislation, *e.g.* where the person to whom the guarantee is given is not a "consumer."[29] Again, a contract for the execution of building work between A and B may be performed, wholly or in part, through the instrumentality of a sub-contractor C, nominated by A but engaged by B. Such an arrangement usually gives rise to a contract between A and B and to one between B and C, but not to one between A and C[30]; but it is possible for a collateral contract to arise between these last two parties,[31] making C contractually liable to A. Similarly, where goods are bailed by A to B and A authorises B to sub-bail them to C, and B does so, then a collateral contract may arise between A and C, incorporating "via the agency of the bailee" (B) the terms of the sub-bailment from B to C.[32] Yet a further illustration of the possibility that a tripartite relationship may give rise to a collateral contract between parties who have not entered into any express contract with each other is provided by the situation in which an employment agency (A) enters into a contract with a worker (B) whom it supplies to an end user (C). In such cases, there may, in additions to the express contracts between A and B and between A and C,[33] be an implied (collateral) contract between B and C.[34] But the latter possibility is restricted by the usual requirements for such an implication. In particular, an implied contract between B and C will arise only if the implication is "necessary . . . to give

---

[26] For legislative control of exemption clauses in such guarantees, see above, Ch.14.

[27] Sale and Supply of Goods to Consumers Regulations 2002, (SI 2002/3045) reg.15(1), implementing Directive 1999/44/EC, Arts 2(e) and 6(1); for the meaning of "consumer" in this context, see reg.2.

[28] *i.e.*, those of consideration and contractual intention (below, paras 18–008 and 18–009).

[29] *e.g.*, on facts such as those of the *Shanklin Pier* case, above, n.25.

[30] *e.g. Simaan General Contracting Co v Pilkington Glass Ltd (No.2)* [1988] Q.B. 758; *National Trust v Haden & Young* (1994) 72 B.L.R. 1.

[31] *Holland Hannen & Cubitts (Northern) v Welsh Health Technical Services Ltd* (1987) 7 Con.L.R. 14; *cf. Welsh Health Technical Service Organisation v Haden Young* (1987) 37 Build.L.R. 130; *Greater Nottingham Co-operative Soc. Ltd v Cementation Ltd* [1989] Ch. 497; contrast *National Trust v Haden & Young*, above, where there was no such collateral contract; for C's possible liability to A in tort, see below paras 18–022—18–039.

[32] *Sandeman Coprimar SA v Transitos y Transportes Integrales SL* [2003] EWCA Civ 113; [2003] Q.B. 1270, at [63–65]

[33] For the nature of this relationship, see *Kalwak v Consistent Group Ltd* [2007] I.R.L.R. 560.

[34] For recognition of this possibility, see *Dacas v Brook Street Bureau*[2004] EWCA Civ 217, [2004] I.C.R. 1437; *Cable & Wireless plc v Muscat* [2006] EWCA Civ 220, [2006] I.C.R. 975.

business reality to the relationship between the parties",[35] i.e., between B and C.[36] Facts relevant to this issue would include the terms of the two express contracts referred to above and the conduct of B and C in the course of the relationship between them while B is rendering the services to C.

18–006 **Hire-purchase.** The collateral contract device can also be used where a dealer makes a representation to a customer in order to induce him to enter into a hire-purchase contract. The main contract of hire-purchase is usually between the customer and the finance company. Accordingly, a representation by the dealer as to the quality of the goods did not formerly impose any liability on the finance company[37]; but the dealer could be liable on the representation as a collateral contract.[38] If the transaction is a regulated agreement within the Consumer Credit Act 1974[39] a dealer who conducts antecedent negotiations is in certain circumstances deemed to do so as agent of the creditor as well as in his actual capacity.[40] The representation can therefore make the finance company liable under the main contract, while the dealer may still be liable on the representation as a collateral contract.[41]

18–007 **Payment by cheque or credit card.** A further situation in which a transaction involves several contracts is that in which a supply of goods or services is paid for by the use of a cheque card or credit card. Such a transaction involves three contracts: one between the supplier and the customer, a second between the customer and the issuer of the card, and a third between the issuer and the supplier of the goods.[42] The supplier therefore has a common law right of action against the issuer on this third contract.

18–008 **Consideration in collateral contracts.** To be enforceable as a collateral contract, a promise must be supported by consideration,[43] and in the cases considered in paragraphs 18–005 to 18–007 above there is no difficulty in explaining how this requirement was satisfied. In the *Shanklin Pier* case, the

---

[35] *James v Greenwich LBC* [2008] EWCA Civ 35 at [23], citing *The Aramis* [1989] 1 Lloyd's Rep. 213 at 224, and applying the general principle stated in para.2–160 above.

[36] Cases in which this requirement was not satisfied include the *James* case, above; *Cairns v Visteon UK Ltd* [2007] I.R.L.R. 175 and *Croke v Hydro Aluminium Worcester Ltd* [2007] I.C.R. 1303. For further discussion of this line of cases, see Vol.II, para.39–027.

[37] *Campbell Discount Co Ltd v Gall* [1961] 1 Q.B. 431; reversed on other points in *Branwhite v Worcester Works Finance Ltd* [1969] 1 A.C. 552 and *United Dominions Trust Ltd v Western* [1976] Q.B. 513.

[38] *Brown v Sheen & Richmond Car Sales Ltd* [1950] 1 All E.R. 1102; *Andrews v Hopkinson* [1957] 1 Q.B. 229; Diamond (1957) 21 M.L.R. 177; *cf. Astley, Industrial Trust Ltd v Grimley* [1963] 1 W.L.R. 584. As to damages, see *Yeoman Credit Ltd v Odgers* [1962] 1 W.L.R. 215.

[39] See Consumer Credit Act 2006, s.2; Vol.II, paras 38–002, 38–018.

[40] s.56(2); *cf.* also s.75.

[41] This follows from s.56(2), above, n.40.

[42] *Re Charge Card Services* [1987] Ch. 150; affirmed [1989] Ch. 497; *cf. Customs and Excise Commissioners v Diners Club Ltd* [1989] 1 W.L.R. 1196; *First Sport Ltd v Barclays Bank plc* [1993] 1 W.L.R. 1229 (where the card had been stolen and been presented by the thief to the retailer). A different analysis probably applies where the card is issued by the suppliers, as is the practice of some department stores: *Richardson v Worrall* [1985] S.T.C. 693, 720.

[43] *cf. Brikom Investments Ltd v Carr* [1979] Q.B 467, above, para.3–080, where no third party problem arose.

consideration was the instruction given by the claimants to their contractors[44]; in the building sub-contractor case, it is similarly the client's nomination of the sub-contractor; in the guarantee case it is the purchase by the customer of the goods from the dealer[45]; in the hire-purchase case it is the entering by the customer into a hire-purchase agreement with the finance company; in the cheque card or credit card case, it is the supply of the goods by the supplier to the customer, and the discount allowed by the supplier to the issuer of the credit card.[46] A case in which the problem of consideration gives rise to more difficulty is *Charnock v Liverpool Corp*.[47] A car had been damaged and was later repaired under a contract between the owner's insurance company and a garage. It was held that there was also a collateral contract between the owner and the garage (to do the repairs within a reasonable time), even though the owner did not pay or promise to pay the garage anything.[48] The consideration for the garage's promise was found in the owner's "leaving his car with the garage for repair."[49] This might not be a detriment to the owner, at least in the factual sense.[50] But it was a benefit to the garage in giving it the opportunity of making a contract for the repair of the car with the insurance company; and this benefit constituted the consideration for the garage's promise to the owner.

Contractual intention in collateral contracts. A promise will not amount to a collateral contract if it was made without contractual intention.[51] The need to satisfy this requirement is illustrated by *Alicia Hosiery Ltd v Brown Shipley Ltd*,[52] where the owner of goods in a warehouse pledged them to a bank and later sold them. The bank gave the buyer a delivery order addressed to the warehouseman but the latter refused to deliver the goods to the buyer who claimed damages from the bank. It was held that there was a contract between the buyer and the seller, and one between the seller and the bank, but none between the buyer and the bank as no intention to enter into such a contract had been shown.[53] Similarly, in *Independent Broadcasting Authority v E.M.I. Electronics*,[54] A had contracted with B for the erection of a television mast, on the terms that the actual work was 18–009

[44] In the *Shanklin Pier* case McNair J. said at 856: "I see no reason why there may not be an enforceable warranty between A [the defendant] and B [the plaintiff] supported by the consideration that B should cause C [the contractors employed by the plaintiffs] to enter into a contract with A [*viz.* to buy the paint from A]."

[45] *cf.*, in another context, *Penn v Bristol & West Building Society* [1997] 1 W.L.R. 1356, 1363 ("entering into some transaction with a third party").

[46] *Customs and Excise Commissioners v Diners Club Ltd* [1989] 1 W.L.R. 1196.

[47] [1968] 1 W.L.R. at 1498.

[48] *cf. Godfrey Davies Ltd v Culling and Hecht* [1962] 2 Lloyd's Rep. 349; *Cooter & Green Ltd v Tyrell* [1962] 2 Lloyd's Rep. 377; *Brown & Davies v Galbraith* [1972] 1 W.L.R. 997.

[49] [1968] 1 W.L.R. at 1505; *cf. West Bromwich Albion Football Club v El Safty* [2006] EWCA Civ 1299, [2006] B.M.L.R. 179.

[50] Above, para.3–006; the transfer of possession might subject the repairer to the obligations of a bailee, but these would not include an obligation to carry out the repairs. For reasoning similar to that in the *Charnock* case (above, n.47), see *International Petroleum Refining & Supply Ltd v Caleb Brett & Son Ltd* [1980] 1 Lloyd's Rep. 569, 594.

[51] *Heilbut, Symons & Co v Buckleton* [1913] A.C. 30, 47; above, para.2–166.

[52] [1970] 1 Q.B. 95.

[53] *cf.* also *Hannam v Bradford C.C.* [1970] 1 W.L.R. 937; *Construction Industry Training Board v Labour Force Ltd* [1970] 3 All E.R. 220.

[54] (1980) 14 Build.L.R. 1; *cf. Lambert v Lewis* [1982] A.C. 225; above, para.2–165.

to be done by C, a sub-contractor. C, who was not a party to the contract between A and B, wrote to A saying: "We are well satisfied that the structure will not oscillate dangerously." The mast having later collapsed, it was held that C's letter did not have contractual force as there was no *animus contrahendi* (though C was held liable in negligence). There will, *a fortiori*, be no collateral contract between A and C where these parties have deliberately chosen not to enter into a direct contract with each other.[55] And where A acquired shares from B which had previously been bought by B from C on the terms that certain payments were to be made to C in events which later happened, it was held that there was no collateral contract between A and C, obliging A to make the payments.[56] No intention on A's part to enter into such a contract could be inferred, while C did not know of A at the time of the alleged collateral contract and so equally lacked any intention to contract with A.

18–010 **Multilateral contracts.** When a person joins a club or other unincorporated association, he may contract with all the other members although he may be quite unaware of their identity and although he may be in direct communication only with the secretary.[57] Similarly, where an insurance policy was expressed to be between the assured and a syndicate of underwriters at Lloyd's, it was held nevertheless to constitute a number of separate contracts between the assured and each of the participating syndicates.[58] In the case of a company incorporated under the Companies Acts, s.33(1) of the Companies Act 2006 provides that "The provisions of a company's constitution bind the company and its members to the same extent as if there were covenants on the part of the company and of each member to observe those provisions." It seems appropriate to continue to refer to the effect of this subsection as giving rise to a "statutory contract"[59]; and so far as this contract takes effect between the members, it continues so to take effect between them in their capacity as such. In the case of a limited liability partnership incorporated[60] under the Limited Liability Partnerships Act 2000, the mutual rights and liabilities of the members *inter se* and between the members

---

[55] *Fuji Seal Europe v Catalytic Combustion Corp* [2005] EWHC 1649, 102 Con L.R. 47 (where, as in the *I.B.A.* case, above, n.54, C was held liable in tort).

[56] *Law Debenture Trust Corp. v Ural Caspian Oil Corp. Ltd* [1993] 1 W.L.R. 138, 142; reversed on another point [1995] Ch. 152.

[57] *Hybart v Packer* (1858) 4 C.B.(N.S.) 209; *Gray v Pearson* (1870) L.R. 5 C.P. 568; *Evans v Hooper* (1875) 1 Q.B.D. 45; *Lee v Showmen's Guild* [1952] 2 Q.B. 329 at 341; *Nutting v Baldwin* [1995] 1 W.L.R. 201. But in *Anderton v Rowland, The Times*, November 5, 1999, it was held that breach of the rules by one member did not, as a matter of construction, give another member a right of action in damages against the member guilty of the breach. And where a club was *owned by a company* of which the club's members were shareholders, the rules of the club were held to constitute contracts between each member and the company, and not between the members *inter se: Peskin v Anderson* [2000] 2 B.C.L.C. 1.

[58] *Touche Ross & Co v Colin Baker* [1992] 2 Lloyd's Rep. 207.

[59] *Soden v British Commonwealth Holdings* [1998] A.C. 298 at 323, stating the effect of the former s.14 of the Companies Act 1985, which is repealed by s.1295 and Sch.16 of Companies Act 2006 and replaced with modifications by s.33(1) of the 2006 Act. For a full discussion, see above para.9–061; for the position under the Contracts (Rights of Third Parties) Act 1999, see below, para.18–113.

[60] For the status of such a partnership as a body corporate, see Limited Liability Partnerships Act 2000, s.1(2)

and the partnership are governed by agreement between the members or between them and the partnership,[61] or, in the absence of such agreement, by regulations made under the Act governing such partnerships.[62]

Sporting competitions. Where a number of persons agree to enter into a competition subject to certain rules, it is often doubtful exactly who the parties to the resulting contract are. In one case it was held that the competitors in a regatta contracted not only with the committee of the organising club, but also with each other.[63] But in another case it was held that persons who had entered horses for races organised by the Jockey Club had contracted only with the Club and not with each other.[64] 18–011

Agency. Where a person negotiates a contract as agent between his principal and a third party, the contract will generally be between the principal and the third party. But it is sometimes doubtful whether a person acted as agent or on his own behalf.[65] In one case, a husband booked tickets on a cross-Channel ferry for himself and his wife and children. It was said that there was a "contract of carriage between the [wife] and the [carriers],"[66] presumably made by the husband as his wife's agent. Where a husband and wife lunched together at a restaurant, it was again held that there was a contract between the wife and the proprietor, though on the different ground that the husband and wife had each made a separate contract with the proprietor.[67] But if there were no such separate contracts and the host on such an occasion did not act as agent, it has been said that there would be a contract only between him and the restaurant proprietor.[68] 18–012

Sub-Agency. Similar problems arise where an agent employs a sub-agent.[69] 18–013
In some such cases there is privity of contract between principal and sub-agent, while in others the sub-agent is in a contractual relationship only with the agent

[61] Limited Liability Partnerships Act 2000, s.5(1)(a)

[62] *ibid.*, s.5(1)(c).

[63] *The Satanita* [1895] P. 248; affirmed sub nom. *Clarke v Dunraven* [1897] A.C. 59, where only Lord Herschell dealt with the point here discussed; *cf. Meggeson v Burns* [1972] 1 Lloyd's Rep. 223; *White v Blackmore* [1972] 2 Q.B. 651 (where there was no contractual intention).

[64] *Ellesmere v Wallace* [1929] 2 Ch. 1.

[65] See the authorities cited in nn.66–69, below.

[66] *Daly v General Steam Navigation Co Ltd (The Dragon)* [1979] 1 Lloyd's Rep. 257, 262; affirmed [1980] 2 Lloyd's Rep. 415; *cf. Wilson v Best Travel Ltd* [1993] 1 All E.R. 353, 355; *Bowerman v Association of British Travel Agents* [1995] N.L.J. 815 (holiday booked for pupil by her teacher); *Vitesse Yacht Charterers SL v Spiers (The Deverne II)* (contract to charter a yacht for a holiday taken by two persons together held to have been made by one of them on behalf of both).

[67] *Lockett v A.M. Charles* [1938] 4 All E.R. 170. *cf. Richards v Hughes* [2004] EWCA Civ 266, [2004] P.N.L.R. 35 (arguable that accountant advising parent about setting up a trust fund for the education of children owed a contractual duty, not only to the parents, but also to the children).

[68] *Jackson v Horizon Holidays Ltd* [1975] 1 W.L.R. 1468, 1473 (where *Lockett v A. M. Charles Ltd*, above was not cited).

[69] Such problems can arise in relation to "forwarding agents" see, *e.g. Jones v European General Express* (1920) 25 Com.Cas. 296; *Elektronska, etc. v Transped, etc.* [1986] 1 Lloyd's Rep. 49.

who employed him. In border-line cases of this kind, it is again clear that there is a contract, but doubtful who the parties to the contract are.[70]

18–014 **Mortgage valuations.** Problems as to parties can also arise where a house is valued at the instigation of a building society after a prospective purchaser has applied to it for a loan which is to be secured by a mortgage on the house. Where the valuation is carried out by a full-time employee of the building society, there will usually be a contract between the society and its employee, and one between the society and the borrower (under which the society will be vicariously liable for the valuer's negligence) but none between the valuer and the borrower.[71] Where, on the other hand, the valuation is carried out by an independent valuer, there may be a contract between him and the borrower[72] but this is not necessarily the case. If, for example, the independent valuer were appointed and paid by the society and reported directly to it, there is unlikely to be any contractual relationship between borrower and valuer, though the valuer will be liable to the borrower in tort if as a result of his negligence his report is inaccurate or incomplete and the borrower suffers loss.[73]

18–015 The reason why in the first of the above situations there is no separate contract between the valuer and the borrower is presumably that the valuer has no intention to contract with the borrower since he believes that he is merely carrying out his duties under his contract with the society.[74] The further suggestion that, in this situation, there is "seemingly no consideration for a contract by the valuer as principal"[75] is, with respect, harder to follow. It cannot mean that there is no consideration because the valuer is doing no more than performing his contract of employment, for it is now settled that the performance of a contractual duty owed to a third party can constitute consideration,[76] and in any event the question is whether there is consideration for the valuer's promise, and this consideration must move, not from him, but from the purchaser. Prima facie, such consideration is provided by the payment of the survey fee by the purchaser to the society, or by his entering into the mortgage transaction; and it is immaterial that this consideration does not move (at least directly) to the valuer; for so long as consideration moves from the promisee it need not move to the promisor.[77] Nor would such consideration be past, even if the fee had been paid before the valuer had been engaged; for the test for deciding whether consideration is past is a functional (rather than a strictly chronological) one, which is satisfied in the situation here under discussion since the consideration and the

---

[70] *Henderson v Merrett Syndicates Ltd* [1995] 2 A.C. 145; *Grosvenor Casinos Ltd v National Bank of Abu Dhabi* [2008] EWHC 511 (Comm), [2008] 2 Lloyd's Rep. 1 at [147]–[149]; see generally, Vol.II, Ch.31.

[71] *Halifax Building Society v Edell* [1992] Ch. 436. Nor could the borrower enforce a term of the valuer's employment contract by virtue of the Contracts (Rights of Third Parties) Act 1999: see s.6(3), below para.18–113.

[72] *Halifax Building Society v Edell*, above, at 454.

[73] See *Smith v Eric S. Bush* [1990] 1 A.C. 831.

[74] *cf.* above, para.2–180.

[75] *Halifax Building Society v Edell* [1992] Ch. 436, 454.

[76] Above, para.3–073.

[77] Above, para.3–039.

promise given in return are substantially one transaction.[78] Indeed, the assumption that it is so satisfied is supported by the view that there can be a contract between an independent valuer and the purchaser,[79] since the consideration which moves from the purchaser is exactly the same whether the valuer is an employee of the building society or an independent person.

(b) *Party to the Consideration*

18–016 **Relation to the rule that consideration must move from the promisee.**[80] It is disputed whether the rule that consideration must move from the promisee is the same as or different from the common law rule that only a party to the agreement can enforce it.[81] In the English cases the two rules have always led to the same result, which the judges have sometimes based on the first rule[82] and sometimes on the second.[83] To be entitled to enforce a promise, a person must (at common law) generally show (1) that it was made to him *and* (2) that consideration for it moved from him. The statement that consideration must move *from the promisee* simply assumes that the first requirement has been satisfied. If the rule were stated to be that consideration must move *from the party seeking to enforce the promise* it would be clearly distinct from the rule that only a party to the agreement can sue. A man might, for example, promise his daughter to pay £1,000 to any man who married her. A person who married the daughter with knowledge of and in reliance on such a promise might provide consideration for it, but would not be entitled to enforce it, as it was not addressed to him.[84]

18–017 In *Kepong Prospecting Ltd v Schmidt*[85] a third party made a claim to enforce a contract under the law of Malaysia, by which consideration need not move from the promisee. In rejecting the claim, the Privy Council said "It is true that s.2(*d*) of the Contracts Ordinance gives a wider definition of 'consideration' than that which applies in England, particularly in that it enables consideration to move from another person than the promisee, but the appellant was unable to show how this affected the law as to enforcement of contracts by third parties."[86] This decision seems therefore to support the view that the doctrine of privity is distinct from the rule that consideration must move from the promisee.

18–018 **Promises made to more than one person.** The doctrine of privity does not affect the enforceability by any promisee of promises made to a number of persons, whether jointly or severally or jointly and severally. The question whether one of the promisees can enforce such a promise if he has not provided any part of the consideration for it has been discussed in Chapter 3.[87]

---

[78] Above, para.3–026.
[79] Above, at n.72.
[80] Above, para.3–036.
[81] Furmston (1960) 23 M.L.R. at 383–384.
[82] See *Tweddle v Atkinson* (1861) 1 B. & S. 393.
[83] See *Price v Easton* (1833) 4 B. & Ad. 433 *per* Littledale and Patterson JJ.
[84] *cf. Uddin v Ahmed* [2001] EWCA Civ 204; [2001] 3 F.C.R. 300 at [20].
[85] [1968] A.C. 810.
[86] *ibid.* at 826.
[87] Above paras 3–041—3–044.

(c) *Development of the Common Law Doctrine*

18–019 **The doctrine established.** In the early authorities, there was support both for the view that a person could not,[88] and for the view that he could,[89] enforce a contract to which he was not a party. The point appeared to have been settled in 1861 by *Tweddle v Atkinson*,[90] where A promised B to pay a sum of money to B's son, C, on C's marriage to A's daughter. It was held that C could not enforce against A the promise that A hade made to B. This case was usually considered to have established the common law doctrine of privity,[91] which was approved by the House of Lords in 1915, when the principle that "only a person who is a party to the contract can sue on it" was said to be a "fundamental"[92] one in English law. This view was, indeed, judicially doubted in a number of cases[93]; but these doubts appeared to have been set at rest in 1961, when the House of Lords again affirmed the existence of the doctrine of privity of contract in holding that a person could not take the benefit of a limitation of liability clause contained in a contract to which he was not a party.[94] The view that a person could not enforce a contract to which he was not a party is also accepted in many later cases.[95] It

---

[88] *Bourne v Mason* (1668) 1 Ventris 6; *cf. Crow v Rogers* (1726) 1 Stra. 592; *Price v Easton* (1833) 4 B. & Ad. 433. For the history, see Holdsworth, *History of English Law*, VIII, pp.11–13, 40; E.J.P. (1954) 70 L.Q.R. 467; Scamell (1955) 8 C.L.P. 131; Palmer, 33 Am.Jl. of Legal History 3 (1989); Ibbetson in Barton (ed.), *Towards a History of the Law of Contract*, pp.67, 96–99; Palmer, *The Paths to Privity: The History of Third Party Beneficiary Contracts in English Law* (1992); Andrews, 69 Tulane L.Rev. 69 (1995).

[89] *Dutton v Poole* (1677) 2 Lev. 210; affirmed T.Raym. 302. *cf. Thomas v* —— (1655) Sty. 461; *Martyn v Hind* (1776) 2 Cowp. 437, 443; *Marchington v Vernon* (1787) 1 B. & P. 101, note (c).

[90] (1861) 1 B. & S. 393.

[91] *Gandy v Gandy* (1884) 30 Ch.D. 57, 69.

[92] *Dunlop Pneumatic Tyre Co Ltd v Selfridge & Co Ltd* [1915] A.C. 847, 853; for a similar, earlier, statement see *Keighley Maxsted & Co v Durant* [1901] A.C. 240, 246.

[93] *Smith and Snipes Hall Farm Ltd v River Douglas Catchment Board* [1949] 2 K.B. 500, 514–516; *Drive Yourself Hire Co (London) Ltd v Strutt* [1954] 1 Q.B. 250, 272–275. *Pyrene Co Ltd v Scindia Steam Navigation Co Ltd* [1954] 2 Q.B. 402, esp. at 426 (explained on other grounds in *Scruttons Ltd v Midland Silicones Ltd* [1962] A.C. 446, 471); *Rayfield v Hands* [1960] Ch. 1; Dowrick (1956) 19 M.L.R. 375. *cf.* Flannigan (1987) 103 L.Q.R. 564; Andrews (1988) 8 L.S. 14.

[94] In *Scruttons Ltd v Midland Silicones Ltd* [1962] A.C. 446; above, para.14–047. The Court of Appeal had taken a similar view of the continued existence of the doctrine in *Green v Russell* [1959] 2 Q.B. 226.

[95] *Rookes v Barnard* [1964] A.C. 1129; *Hepburn v A. Tomlinson (Hauliers) Ltd* [1966] A.C. 451; *New Zealand Shipping Co Ltd v A.M. Satterthwaite Ltd (The Eurymedon)* [1975] A.C. 154; *Port Jackson Stevedoring Pty Ltd v Salmond & Spraggon (Australia) Pty Ltd (The New York Star)* [1980] 1 W.L.R. 138; *Woodar Investment Development Ltd v Wimpey Construction UK Ltd* [1980] 1 W.L.R. 277; *Balsamo v Medici* [1984] 1 W.L.R. 951, 959–960; *Southern Water Authority v Carey* [1985] 2 All E.R. 1077, 1083; *The Forum Craftsman* [1985] 1 Lloyd's Rep. 291, 295; *Swiss Bank Corp. v Brink's-Mat Ltd* [1986] 2 Lloyd's Rep. 79; *Singer (UK) Ltd v Tees & Hartlepool Port Authority* [1988] 2 Lloyd's Rep. 164, 167; *J.H. Rayner (Mincing Lane) Ltd v D.T.I.* [1990] A.C. 643, 662; *Cia. Portorafti Commerciale SA v Panama Inc. (The Captain Gregos)* [1990] 1 Lloyd's Rep. 310, 318; *Law Debenture Trust Corp. v Ural Caspian Oil Corp. Ltd* [1993] 2 All E.R. 355, 365; (reversed on another point), [1995] Ch. 152; *Siu Yin Kwan v Eastern Insurance* [1994] 2 A.C. 199, 207; *Rhone v Stephens* [1994] 2 A.C. 310, 321; *K.H. Enterprise v Pioneer Container (The Pioneer Container)* [1994] 2 A.C. 324, 355; *White v Jones* [1995] 2 A.C. 207, 252, 266; *The Mahkutai* [1996] A.C. 650, 658; *Amsprop Trading Ltd v Harris Distribution Ltd* [1997] 1 W.L.R. 1025, 1028; *The Giannis NK* [1998] A.C. 605, 616; *Homburg Houtimport BV v Agrosin Private Ltd (The Starsin)* [2003] UKHL 12; [2004] 1 A.C. 715, esp. at [34], [146]. The point is perhaps left open in *Esso Petroleum Ltd v Hall Russell & Co* [1989] A.C. 643, 662.

also underlies the proposals for legislative reform to which reference has already been made.[96] and, indeed, the way in which these were implemented by the Contracts (Rights of Third Parties) Act 1999.

Beswick v Beswick. The leading modern authority is *Beswick v Beswick*.[97] A coal merchant transferred his business to his nephew who promised him (*inter alia*) that he would, after the uncle's death, pay an annuity to the uncle's widow. After the uncle's death, the widow became his administratrix. She brought an action to enforce the nephew's promise, suing both in her own right and as administratrix. In the Court of Appeal it was held, (1) by Lord Denning M.R., that the widow could sue in her own right at common law, notwithstanding the doctrine of privity: this doctrine was "at bottom . . . only a rule of procedure"[98] and could be overcome by simply joining the promisee as a party to the action[99]; (2) by Lord Denning M.R. and by Danckwerts L.J., that the widow could sue in her own right by virtue of s.56(1) of the Law of Property Act 1925[100]; and (3) by Lord Denning M.R. and by Danckwerts and Salmon L.JJ., that the widow could sue in her capacity as administratrix of the promisee and could in that capacity obtain an order of specific performance against the nephew, obliging him to pay the annuity to her for her own personal benefit. The House of Lords affirmed the decision on the third ground,[101] rejected the second[102] and found it unnecessary to express a concluded view on the first. But the speeches all assume the correctness of the generally accepted view that at common law a contract can be enforced only by the parties to it,[103] though the House of Lords has on a number of occasions indicated its willingness to reconsider this position.[104] Such a reconsideration has indeed been undertaken by a majority of the High Court of Australia, but in a decision in which so many divergent views were expressed that it provides no firm guidance for the development of the law.[105] The difficulties of reaching satisfactory results in this area through purely judicial reconsideration are formidable; they arise, in particular, in defining exactly what classes of 18–020

---

[96] See, above, para.18–001.

[97] [1968] A.C. 58; affirming [1966] Ch. 538; reversing [1965] 2 All E.R. 858.

[98] [1966] Ch. at 557.

[99] For criticism of this view, see para.18–075, below.

[100] Below, paras 18–122—18–125.

[101] [1968] A.C. 58; Goodhart (1967) 83 L.Q.R. 465; Fairest [1967] C.L.J. 149; Treitel (1967) 30 M.L.R. 687.

[102] See below, paras 18–124—18–125.

[103] [1968] A.C. 58, 72D, 81G, 92–93, 95G.

[104] *ibid.* at 72; *Woodar Investment Development Ltd v Wimpey Construction UK Ltd* [1980] 1 W.L.R. 277, 291, 297–298, 300; *Swain v Law Society* [1983] 1 A.C. 598, 611; *cf. Williams v Natural Life Health Foods Ltd* [1998] 1 W.L.R. 830, 837.

[105] *Trident Insurance Co Ltd v McNiece Bros Pty Ltd* (1988) 165 C.L.R. 107, where a claim under a liability insurance policy by a person who was not a party to it was upheld by a majority of five to two. But one member of the majority (Deane J.) was prepared to allow the third party's claim only under the well established trust exception to the doctrine of privity (below, para.18–078—18–086); while another (Gaudron J.) based her decision in favour of the third party, not on contract but on unjust enrichment, and said that this was "not an abrogation of the doctrine of privity of contract" (at 177, and see below, para.18–042). Only three of the seven members of the court can be said to have countenanced such an abrogation, and even their view may be restricted to the special insurance context with which the case was concerned. See also Edgell [1989] L.M.C.L.Q. 139; Kincaid (1989) 2 J.C.L. 160. For a different judicial approach in Canada, proceeding by means of developing an exception to the doctrine in the context of exemption clauses, see *London Drugs Ltd v Kuehne &*

third parties can acquire rights under the contract, and how these rights might be affected by attempts by the contracting parties to rescind the contract or to vary it, and by defences available between the contracting parties.[106] A satisfactory solution of such difficulties is more likely to be achieved by legislative reform,[107] such as that contained in the Contracts (Rights of Third Parties) Act 1999.[108] In a significant number of situations, however, third parties will not acquire rights by virtue of this Act[109]; and in many such situations the common law doctrine of privity will continue (at least for the time being)[110] to apply.

3. Scope

18–021 **General.** The common law doctrine of privity means, and means only, that a person cannot acquire rights, or be subjected to liabilities, *arising under* a contract to which he is not a party. For example, it means that, if A promises B to pay a sum of money to C, then C cannot sue A for that sum.[111] Similarly, if a contract between A and B contains a term purporting to exempt C from tortious liability to A, the doctrine of privity may prevent C from relying on that term in an action in tort brought against him by A.[112] But it does not follow that a contract between A and B cannot affect the legal rights of C indirectly. For example, in the situation just described, a clause in the contract between A and B can form the basis on which a separate collateral contract comes into existence between A and C, containing a promise by A to make the relevant terms of the contract between A and B available for the benefit of C[113]; such an agreement

Nagel International Ltd [1992] 3 S.C.R. 299; Waddams (1993) 109 L.Q.R. 349. *cf. Fraser River and Pile Dredge Ltd v Can-Drive Services Ltd* [2000] 1 Lloyds Rep. 199, where the Supreme Court of Canada, while refusing to engage in "wholesale abolition" of the doctrine of privity, continued to make "incremental changes" by holding that a third party could take the benefit of a "waiver of subrogation" clause in an insurance policy.

[106] See the discussion of these problems in American law (which in principle recognises the rights of third-party beneficiaries) in *Corbin on Contracts*, Chs 41–44.

[107] See Treitel (1966) 29 M.L.R. 657, 665; Reynolds (1989) 105 L.Q.R. 1, 3; above, para.18–001. Judicial reform is favoured by Steyn L.J. in *Darlington B.C. v Wiltshire Northern Ltd* [1995] 1 W.L.R. 68, 76, discussed in para.18–056 below. See also Beale (1995) J.C.L. 103.

[108] Below, para.18–088 *et seq. cf.*, in New Zealand, the Contract (Privity) Act 1982.

[109] Above, para.18–002.

[110] The passing of the 1999 Act has probably reduced the pressure for judicial reform.

[111] *Tweddle v Atkinson* (1861) 1 B. & S. 393; above, para.18–019.

[112] *Scruttons Ltd v Midland Silicones Ltd* [1962] A.C. 446; paras 14–047, 18–019 above; but there may be a contract between A and C, as in *New Zealand Shipping Co Ltd v A.M. Satterthwaite & Co Ltd (The Eurymedon)* [1975] A.C. 154; *Port Jackson Stevedoring Pty Ltd v Salmond & Spraggon (Australia) Pty Ltd (The New York Star)* [1980] 1 W.L.R. 138; above, para.14–048. Contrast, in Canada, *London Drugs Ltd v Kuehne & Nagel International Ltd* [1992] 3 S.C.R. 299. And see *The Mahkutai* [1996] A.C. 650, where the actual decision is based, not on the doctrine of privity, but on the fact that an exclusive jurisidiction clause was not, as a matter of construction, one of the "exceptions, limitations, provisions, conditions and liberties" of the contract on which the third party sought to rely. Hence it was not necessary to decide whether the English courts should, in cases of this kind, adopt the Canadian view taken in the *London Drugs* case [1992] 3 S.C.R. 299, but Lord Goff at 665 in *The Mahkutai* left the point open.

[113] This is often the effect of so-called Himalaya Clause in bills of lading: see *The Eurymedon*, above, n.112; *The New York Star*, above, n.112; contrast *The Mahkutai*, above, n.112 where such a clause failed to protect C for the reason given in that note; and *Homburg Houtimport BV v Agrosin Private Ltd (The Starsin)* [2003] UKHL 12; [2004] 1 A.C. 715, at [34], [93], [147], [196] where the

may also give rise to a bailment or sub-bailment between A and C by virtue of which C may be entitled to the benefit of, or be bound by, limitation or exemption clauses in the contract between A and B, even though the relationship between A and C is not contractual[114]; an agreement between A and B under which A accepts from B part payment of a debt owed by C to A in full settlement of that debt can benefit C by precluding A from suing C for the balance of the debt[115]; and *a fortiori* full performance by B of C's obligation to A can discharge that obligation. Conversely, a building contract between A and B may benefit C by defining his rights: *e.g.* by specifying the time at which payment becomes due to C under a subcontract between B and C for the execution of part of the work.[116] It is also possible for a contract between A and B to affect C adversely,[117] as in the bailment situation described above[118]; other ways in which a contract between A and B may so affect C are more fully discussed later in this Chapter.[119] At this stage, our concern is with a number of further situations in which a contract between A and B can operate to the advantage of C: in particular, with situations in which C may have a right of action against A in tort.

(a) *Liability in Negligence to Third Parties*

Duty of care may be owed to third party. While the primary effect of a contract between A and B is to oblige the parties to perform their promises to each other, the contract may also impose on A a duty of care to C, the breach of which will enable C to sue A in tort for negligence. The contract may, for example, have this effect because it gives rise between A and C to the relationship of passenger (or cargo-owner) and carrier,[120] bailor and sub-bailee,[121] or of 18–022

relevant term was invalid; and see generally the discussion of Himalaya Clauses in paras 14–048 to 14–049 above.

[114] *e.g. Elder Dempster & Co v Paterson Zochonis & Co* [1924] A.C. 522; *Morris v C.W. Martin & Co* [1966] 1 Q.B. 716, 729; above, para.14–054; Vol.II, paras 33–026, 33–027; *Carver on Bills of Lading*, 2nd ed. (2005) paras 7–027 to 7–045; 7–092 to 7–109.

[115] *Hirachand Punamchand v Temple* [1911] 2 K.B. 330; above, para.3–126 (where the effect on such facts of the Contracts (Rights of Third Parties) Act 1999 is also discussed); *cf. Johnson v Davies* [1999] Ch. 117 at 130. It is assumed that the payment was made with the debtor's authority and with the intention of discharging the debt: see *Crantrave Ltd v Lloyd's Bank plc* [2000] Q.B. 917, where the first of these requirements was not satisfied.

[116] *Co-operative Wholesale Society Ltd v Birse Construction Ltd* (1997) 84 B.L.R. 58.

[117] *e.g. West of England Shipowners Mutual Insurance Association (Luxembourg) v Cristal Ltd (The Glacier Bay)* [1996] 1 Lloyd's Rep. 370; *Banque Financière de la Cité v Parc (Battersea) Ltd* [1999] 1 A.C. 221.

[118] See above at n.114.

[119] Below paras 18–134—18–147.

[120] *Austin v G.W. Ry* (1867) L.R. 2 Q.B. 442; *Sammick Lines Co v Owners of the Antonis P. Lemos (The Antonis P. Lemos)* [1985] A.C. 771.

[121] *Moukataff v B.O.A.C.* [1967] 1 Lloyd's Rep. 396; *Bart v B.W.I.A.* [1967] 1 Lloyd's Rep. 239 (where the claim failed as the sub-bailee's duty was limited to one to keep safely, and did not extend to transmission of the package); *Hispanica de Petroles SA v Vencedora Oceanica Navegacion SA (The Kapetan Markos NL) (No.2)* [1987] 2 Lloyd's Rep. 321. Such a sub-bailment may also operate to the disadvantage of C (the head bailor) in that he may be bound by an exemption or lien clause in the contract between A (the head bailee) and B (the sub-bailee): see *Morris v C.W. Martin Ltd* [1966] 1 Q.B. 716, 719; *K.H. Enterprise v Pioneer Container (The Pioneer Container)* [1994] 2 A.C. 324; *Spectra International plc v Hayesoak Ltd* [1997] 1 Lloyd's Rep. 153; reversed on another ground [1998] 1 Lloyd's Rep. 162; *Sonicare International Ltd v EAFT Ltd* [1997] 2 Lloyd's Rep. 48;

building owner and subcontractor.[122] In a number of cases persons providing professional services, such as solicitors,[123] insurance brokers,[124] safety consultants[125] valuers and surveyors[126] have been held liable in tort to persons other than their immediate clients[127] for negligence in the performance of their contracts with these clients. Sometimes the provider of the services is liable in tort because his negligence in performing the contract with his client of itself causes loss to a third party: *e.g.* where a solicitor's negligence in failing duly to carry out his client's testamentary instructions causes an intended gift to a prospective beneficiary to fail.[128] Sometimes the defendant's negligence results in his making a

---

T. Comedy (UK) Ltd v Easy Managed Transport Ltd [2007] EWHC 611, [2007] 2 Lloyd's Rep. 397 at [64]. This application of the principle of sub-bailment results in the head bailor's being *bound* by terms in the contract between the head bailee and the sub-bailee. It must be distinguished from the situation in which the sub-bailee claims the *benefit* of a term in the contract between the head bailor and the head bailee, as in the *Elder Dempster* case, above n.114: see *The Mahkutai* [1996] A.C. 650, 667–668, *Carver, op. cit.* (above n.114), paras 7–098, 7–099. No sub-bailment arises merely because a sub-agent has received the proceeds of the sale of the principal's property from the buyer: *Balsamo v Medici* [1984] 1 W.L.R. 951.

[122] *British Telecommunications plc v James Thomson & Sons (Engineers) Ltd* [1999] 1 W.L.R. 9 where the loss caused by the subcontractor's negligence was physical damage to property of the owner *other* than the very thing supplied by the sub-contractor, so that the various difficulties discussed in relation to the *Junior Books* case [1983] 1 A.C. 520 (below, paras 18–023 to 18–027 and 18–036) did not arise.

[123] See the authorities cited in n.128 below.

[124] *Punjab National Bank v de Boinville* [1992] 1 W.L.R. 1138, 1152; *cf. Henderson v Merrett Syndicates Ltd* [1995] 2 A.C. 145; *Aiken v Stewart Wrightson Members Agency Ltd* [1995] 1 W.L.R. 1281; *BP plc v Aon Ltd* [2006] EWHC 424, [2006] 1 All E.R. (Comm) 789; Cane in (ed. Rose) *Consensus ad Idem, Essays in the Law of Contract in Honour of Guenter Treitel*, 96.

[125] *Driver v William Willett (Contractors) Ltd* [1969] 1 All E.R. 665; *cf. Dove v Banham's Patent Lock Ltd* [1983] 1 W.L.R. 1436; *Bailey v HSS Alarms Ltd, The Times*, June 20, 2000; contrast *Marc Rich & Co AG v Bishop Rock Marine Co Ltd (The Nicholas H)* [1996] A.C. 211.

[126] *Yianni v Edwin Evans & Sons* [1982] QB 438; *cf. Bourne v McEvoy Timber Preservation* (1975) 237 E.G. 496; *Davies v Pally* [1988] 20 E.G. 74; *Roberts v J. Hampson & Co* [1990] 1 W.L.R. 94; *Smith v Eric S. Bush* [1990] 1 A.C. 831 (where *Yianni's* case is cited with approval at 852–853, 864, 875); *Merrett v Babb* [2001] EWCA Civ, 214; [2001] Q.B. 1174; *Niru Battery Manufacturing Co v Milestone Training Ltd* [2002] EWHC 1425 (Comm); [2002] 2 All E.R. (Comm.) 705, at [60]; affirmed [2003] EWCA Civ 1466, [2004] 1 All E.R. (Comm) 193; *J. Jarvis v Sons Ltd v Castle Wharf Developments* [2001] EWCA Civ, 19; [2001] Lloyd's Rep. P.N. 208 (quantity surveyor employed by developer held to owe a duty to contractor working on the project, but claim failed for want of reliance); *Bellefield Computer Services Ltd v E Turner & Sons Ltd* [2003] EWCA Civ 1283; [2003] Lloyd's Rep. P.N. 53 (architects held to owe duty of care to subsequent occupiers but not to be in breach of it by reason of the limited nature of the services to be provided by them under the contract with their client); *cf. Halifax Building Society v Edell* [1992] Ch. 436, 454; contrast *Beaumont v Humberts* [1989] 29 E.G. 104.

[127] See also *Knight v Lawrence* [1991] 1 E.G.L.R. 143; *Barings plc v Coopers & Lybrand* [1997] 1 B.C.L.C. 498; *Medforth v Blake* [1999] N.L.J. 929.

[128] Below para.18–025; *Ross v Caunters* [1980] Ch. 287; *White v Jones* [1995] 2 A.C. 207; *cf. Smith v Clarement Haynes, The Times*, September 3, 1991; *Al Kandari v J.R. Brown & Co* [1988] Q.B. 665; *Rind v Theodore Goddard* [2008] EWHC 459 (Ch), [2008] P.N.L.R. 24. Contrast *Clarke v Bruce Lance & Co.* [1988] 1 W.L.R. 881 (solicitor acting for testator in a different transaction held to owe no duty to beneficiary); *Worby v Rosser* [2000] P.N.L.R. 140 (solicitor engaged by testator to draw up a new will held to owe no duty to beneficiary under an earlier will). For earlier discussion of *Ross v Caunters*, above, see *Banque Keyser Ullman SA v Skandia (UK) Insurance Co Ltd* [1990] Q.B. 659, 794–795; affirmed on other grounds [1990] 2 All E.R. 947; *Van Oppen v Clerk of the Bedford Charity Trustees* [1989] 1 All E.R. 273, 289; affirmed [1990] 1 W.L.R. 235; *Caparo Industries plc v Dickman* [1990] 2 A.C. 605, 635; *Murphy v Brentwood DC* [1991] 1 A.C. 398, 486.

misrepresentation to the third party and the loss is suffered by the latter in consequence of his acting in reliance on that representation: *e.g.* where a valuer employed by A negligently makes a report on the structure of a house and the report is communicated to B and induces him to buy the house for more than its true value[129]; or where an accountant employed by X negligently makes a report on the affairs of a company and the report induces Y to invest money in the company and to suffer loss by reason of the falsity of the report.[130] The types of relationships out of which such liability in tort for misrepresentation can arise are more fully discussed in Chapter 6.[131] The only point to be made here is that such liability can be incurred to the claimant even though the misrepresentation giving rise to it is made in the performance of a contract to which he is not a party.

The *Junior Books* case. A controversial extension of tort liability to a third party was made in *Junior Books Ltd v Veitchi Co Ltd*,[132] where B had undertaken to build a factory for C by a contract which entitled C to nominate sub-contractors. C nominated A as flooring sub-contractor; A in consequence entered into a contract with B; but no contract came into existence between A and C.[133] The floor later cracked and, on the assumption that this was due to A's negligence in doing the work, it was held that A was liable to C for the loss suffered by C in consequence of the fact that the work had to be done again. At first sight, this represented a considerable encroachment on the common law doctrine of 18–023

[129] See the authorities cited in n.126, above; contrast *Gran Gelato Ltd v Richcliff Group Ltd* [1992] Ch. 560 (vendor's solicitor not liable to purchaser for negligently representing his client's state of mind).

[130] See the overruling of *Candler v Crane Christmas & Co* [1951] 2 K.B. 164 in *Hedley Byrne v Heller & Partners Ltd* [1964] A.C. 465; *cf. Caparo Industries plc v Dickman* [1990] 2 A.C. 605, 625; *Morgan Crucible Co plc v Hill Samuel Bank plc* [1991] Ch. 295; *Killick v Pricewaterhouse Coopers* [2001] 1 B.C.L.C. 65; *Law Society v KPMG Peat Marwick* [2000] 1 W.L.R. 1921 (accountants employed by solicitors held to owe a duty of care to Law Society as trustee of its compensation fund); contrast *James McNaughton Paper Group v Hicks Anderson & Co* [1991] 2 Q.B. 113, where the circumstances in which the report was prepared negatived the duty.

[131] Above, paras 6–078 to 6–086.

[132] [1983] 1 A.C. 520; Jaffey [1983] C.L.J. 37; Palmer and Murdoch (1983) 46 M.L.R. 213; Jaffey (1985) 5 L.S. 77; Reynolds (1985) 11 N.Z.U.L.R. 215; Stapleton (1988) 104 L.Q.R. 213, 389; Huxley (1990) 53 M.L.R. 361; Beyleveld and Brownsword (1991) 54 M.L.R. 48. The Contracts (Rights of Third Parties) Act 1999 would probably not apply on such facts: below para.18–093.

[133] In *Greater Nottingham Co-operative Society Ltd v Cementation Piling & Foundations Ltd* [1989] Q.B. 71 there was such a contract between A and C, and it was held that A's duty to C was governed by that contract alone, and not by the general law relating to the tort of negligence; *cf. Welsh Health Technical Services v Haden Young* (1987) 37 Build.L.R. 130; *Sonat Offshore SA v Amerada Hess Development Co* [1988] 1 Lloyd's Rep. 145, 159; *Red Sea Tankers Ltd v Papachristidis (The Hellespont Ardent)* [1997] 2 Lloyd's Rep. 547, 593. But it has been recognised that breaches of duty arising out of certain contractual relationships may be actionable in tort as well as in contract; see *e.g. Forsikringsaktieselskapet Vesta v Butcher* [1989] A.C. 852, 860, affirmed, without reference to this point, *ibid* 880; *cf. Nitrigin Eirann Teoranta v Inco Alloys Ltd* [1992] 1 All E.R. 854, 856–857; *Saipem SpA v Dredging VO2 BV (The Volvox Hollandia) (No.2)* [1993] 2 Lloyd's Rep. 315, 322; *Henderson v Merrett Syndicates Ltd* [1995] 2 A.C. 145; *Holt v Payne Skillington* [1996] P.N.L.R. 179; *Sumitomo Bank Ltd v Banque Bruxelles Lambert SA* [1997] 1 Lloyd's Rep. 487, 512–514; *Weldon v GRE Linked Life Insurance Ltd* [2002] 2 All E.R. (Comm) 914 at 926–927; the same is true in the relationships described at nn.120 and 121 above. In *Sunny Metal and Engineering Pte Ltd v Ng Khim Ming Eric* (2006) 110 Con. L.R. 115 a sub-contractor who had entered into a contract not only with the main contractor but also with the owner was said to owe a duty of care to the latter in both contract and tort (High Court of Singapore).

privity; but the following discussion will show that later decisions have taken a highly restrictive view of the scope of the *Junior Books* case.

18–024 **Tort and contract of liability distinguished.** In the situations described in paragraphs 18–022 and 18–023 above, A's liability to C is in tort and not on the contract between A and B as such: both the basis and the standard of liability may differ according to whether A is being sued on the contract by B or in tort by C. Thus in the *Junior Books* case it does not seem that C could have sued A if A had wrongfully repudiated his contract with B and done no work under it at all, with the result that completion of the building was delayed and C suffered loss.[134]

18–025 **Omissions.** In one group of cases, A has indeed been held liable in tort to C for simple failure to take steps in the performance of his contract with B. These are cases, such as *White v Jones*,[135] which hold that where a solicitor (A) negligently fails to carry out his client's (B's) instructions to make a will in favour of C, then A can, after B's death, be held liable in tort to C for the value of the benefit lost by C as a result of A's failure to act. But one reason for this conclusion was that A's omission made him liable in tort, as well as for breach of contract, *even to his own client* B.[136] This would not have been the position if, in the *Junior Books* case,[137] A had wrongfully repudiated his contract with B or had simply failed to do any work under it: such a repudiation or omission would have made A liable to B only for breach of contract (and not in tort). The "disappointed beneficiary" cases are also distinguishable from the building contract cases for other reasons to be discussed in para.18–037 below; and they therefore do not support any general proposition that A's omission to perform his contract with B can give a cause of action in tort to C merely because, as a result of the omission, C suffers loss. Indeed, in *White v Jones* itself Lord Goff[138] recognised the general principle that in tort there was no liability for pure omissions; but he subjected[139] it to an exception where, as in that case, there had been an "assumption of responsibility"[140] by A towards C. The basis of that assumption seems to have been that A undertook a duty of care in relation to the provision of professional services, making him liable even to B in tort (as well as for breach of contract) for failure to act with due diligence and care. This reasoning would not apply to cases of A's simple failure to take any steps in the performance of his building contract with B, causing loss to C.

---

[134] In *G.A.F.L.A.C. v Tanter (The Zephyr)* [1984] 1 Lloyd's Rep. 58, 85, it was said at first instance that even the law of torts can sometimes impose "positive duties . . . recognised . . . only because a party has voluntarily undertaken them." This suggestion was disapproved on appeal; [1985] 2 Lloyd's Rep. 529: *cf. White v Jones* [1995] 2 A.C. 207, 261. No issue of privity arose in *The Zephyr*; the dispute was as to contractual intention (above, paras 2–159, 3–180).

[135] [1995] 2 A.C. 207 (below, para.18–037). *cf. Hooper v Fynmores* [2001] W.T.L.R. 1019.

[136] See n.133, above.

[137] [1983] 1 A.C. 520.

[138] at 258.

[139] *ibid.* at 268.

[140] *cf.* the discussion in para.3–180 above of A's possible liability to B for omissions where the relationship between A and B is not contractual because no consideration moved from B. In the cases with which the discussion in the present chapter is concerned, there is no doubt as to the existence of a contract with B, while the cases discussed in para.3–180 do not raise any third party problems.

18–026 **Further differences between tort and contract liability.** Further differences between contract and tort liability in cases involving three parties are that the contract between A and B might have made A strictly liable to B,[141] without proof of negligence, while negligence was an essential element of C's cause of action in tort against A; that in contract, B would have a cause of action against A as soon as the defective work was done, while in tort C's cause of action would only accrue when the resulting loss was suffered[142]; and that in B's action on the contract it is only necessary to show that the contract has been made and broken, while in C's action in tort, C must establish that there was a relationship between himself and A by virtue of which A owed him a duty of care and that C has suffered loss as a result of A's breach of that duty.[143]

18–027 **Restrictions on scope of the duty of care.** A relationship giving rise to a duty of care[144] is not established merely by showing that C has suffered foreseeable loss as a result of A's defective performance of his contract with B. In the *Junior Books* case, there were many special factors giving rise to such a relationship: A were nominated as sub-contractors by C; A were specialists in flooring and knew of C's requirements; C relied on A's special skills in laying floors; and A must have known that defects in the work could necessitate repairs and lead to C's suffering economic loss.[145] These factors (and in particular the extent of C's reliance on A's special skills) may have given rise to a "special relationship" and hence to a duty of care.[146] But such factors are unlikely to arise in the ordinary case where C suffers loss as a result of the defective performance by A of his contract with B. Accordingly, later authorities[147] have emphasised the exceptional nature of the circumstances in the *Junior Books* case. It has been said that those circumstances were "unique"[148]; that the case "cannot now be regarded as a useful pointer to the development of the law"[149]; or as "laying down any

---

[141] *e.g.* on facts such as those of *Donoghue v Stevenson* [1932] A.C. 562 liability for breach of contract in respect of defects in the goods sold would be strict (*Frost v Aylesbury Dairy Co Ltd* [1905] 1 K.B. 608), while the tort liability of, or to, a third party would have depended on negligence. This difference between contract and tort liability in such cases is reduced in importance by Pt I of the Consumer Protection Act 1987, introducing strict "product liability" to the ultimate consumer. But such liability is subject to important qualifications, so that it does not extend to many of the situations with which the discussion in this chapter is concerned.

[142] *Dove v Banham's Safety Locks Ltd* [1983] 1 W.L.R. 1463; *cf. Bell v Peter Browne & Co* [1990] 2 Q.B. 495.

[143] *Rothwell v Chemical & Insulating Co Ltd* [2007] UKHL 39, [2008] 1 A.C. 281. The question whether the claimants in that case had a claim against the defendants in contract (where proof of loss is not a requirement of a cause of action) was left open by Lords Hope (at [59]), Scott (at [74]) and Mance (at [105]). But that question could arise only where there was a contractual relationship between claimant and defendant; and the discussion in the text above is of situations in which there is *no* such relationship.

[144] Above, para.18–022.

[145] [1983] 1 A.C. 520, 546.

[146] *Murphy v Brentwood DC* [1991] 1 A.C. 398, 466, 481.

[147] Below, para.18–036, nn.205 and 206.

[148] *D. & F. Estates Ltd v Church Commissioners for England* [1989] A.C. 177, 202; *cf. Van Oppen v Clerk to the Bedford Charity Trustees* [1989] 1 All E.R. 273, 289; affirmed [1990] 1 W.L.R. 235; *Duncan Stevenson MacMillan v A.W. Knott Becker Scott Ltd* [1990] 1 Lloyd's Rep. 98; *Nitrigin Eirann Teoranta v Inco Alloys Ltd* [1992] 1 W.L.R. 498, 504.

[149] *Simaan General Contracting Co v Pilkington Glass Ltd (No.2)* [1988] Q.B. 758, 784.

principle of general application in the law of tort"[150]; that "it is really of no use as an authority on the general duty of care"[151]; and that the statement of principle in Lord Brandon's dissenting speech is to be preferred to the views of the majority.[152] The authority of the case is further undermined by the fact that the reasoning of the majority is to a considerable extent based on earlier decisions[153] which (so far as they hold defendants liable for economic loss)[154] have since been overruled by the House of Lords.[155] In consequence of these developments, the decision in the *Junior Books* case has been described as "discredited"[156] and "virtually extinguished."[157]

18–028 The duty owed by A to C in tort may also be less extensive than that owed by A to the other contracting party. This was, for example, the position where A was employed as solicitor by B who was guarantor of C's mortgage. It was held[158] that, although A might owe a duty of care to C, this duty did not extend to requiring A to explain the implications of the mortgage to C, since the imposition of such an extensive duty might give rise to a conflict between A's duty to his own client (B) and the alleged duty to C.

18–029 **Persons to whom duty is owed.** The law finally restricts the range of persons to whom the duty may be owed. Where, for example, a valuer was requested by a borrower to address a valuation of the property on which the loan was to be secured to "the prospective lender," it was held that the valuer owed no duty to that lender's assignee.[159] Similarly, counsel who had given advice to his client in litigation has been held to owe no duty of care in respect of that advice to the other party to the litigation[160]; and a solicitor engaged by one party to a transaction will not normally owe a duty of care to the other party, since the imposition of such a duty could give rise to a conflict of interest.[161] Such a duty

[150] *D. & F. Estates Ltd v Church Commissioners for England* [1989] A.C. 177, 202.

[151] *ibid.* at 215.

[152] *ibid.* at 202, 215; *Department of the Environment v Thomas Bates & Son Ltd* [1989] 1 All E.R. 1075, 1084; affirmed [1991] 1 A.C. 499; *Islander Trucking Ltd v Hogg Robinson & Gardner Mountain (Marine) Ltd* [1990] 1 All E.R. 826, 829; *cf. Murphy v Brentwood DC* [1991] 1 A.C. 398, 466, 469; and, in Scotland, *Strathford East Kilbride Ltd v Film Design Ltd*, 1997 S.C.L.R. 877.

[153] *i.e. Anns v Merton LBC* [1978] A.C. 728; *Dutton v Bognor Regis B. Co Ltd* [1972] 1 Q.B. 373.

[154] *Stovin v Wise* [1996] A.C. 923, 949.

[155] *Murphy v Brentwood DC* [1991] 1 A.C. 398. Contrast in Australia *Bryan v Maloney* (1995) 182 C.L.R. 609; in New Zealand (as accepted by the Privy Council) *Invercargill City Council v Hamlin* [1996] A.C. 624; in Canada *Winnipeg Condominium Corp. v Bird Construction Co Ltd* (1995) 121 D.L.R. (4th) 193 (where the defect made the building dangerous); and in Singapore *RSP Architects Planners & Engineers v Ocean Front Ltd* (1998) 14 Const.L.J. 139.

[156] *Societe Commerciale de Reassurance v ERAS International Ltd* [1992] 1 Lloyd's Rep. 570, 599.

[157] *Saipem SpA v Dredging VO2 BV (The Volvox Hollandia) (No.2)* [1993] 2 Lloyd's Rep. 315, 322; *Losinjska Plovidba v Transco Overseas Ltd (The Orjula)* [1995] 2 Lloyd's Rep. 395, 401.

[158] *Woodward v Wolfertrans*, *The Times*, April 8, 1997.

[159] *Barex Brothers Ltd v Morris Dean & Co* [1999] P.N.L.R. 344.

[160] *Connolly-Martin v Davis*, [1999] Lloyd's Rep. P.N. 790.

[161] *Dean v Allin & Watts* [2001] EWCA Civ 758; [2001] 2 Lloyd's Rep. 249, at [33].

may, however, arise in exceptional circumstances, *e.g.* where, in relation to a loan to be secured on a leasehold flat, the borrower engaged defendants as his solicitors and they knew that the lender had not engaged and did not intend to engage his own solicitor. The defendants were held liable in tort to the lender for failing effectively to secure the loan on the flat.[162] The existence of a duty of care to a person with whom the defendant was not in any contractual relationship may also be negatived by the fact that that person has an adequate remedy in respect of the loss in question against another potential defendant.[163]

Duty restricted by terms of contracts. The scope of any duty owed by A to C may, finally, be restricted by the terms of the contracts between A and B and between B and C. These contracts may be relevant for this purpose either in specifying exactly what it is that A is required to do, or in showing that C has assented to an exclusion or restriction of A's liability for defective performance.[164] 18–030

Economic loss and physical harm. Except where there is a special relationship between the parties, as in the misrepresentation cases discussed in Chapter 6, and in those in which the third party's claim is based on the defendant's breach of a contract, such as one to perform professional services, which involves, in addition to his obligations under that contract to the other party to it, an assumption of responsibility to a third party,[165] a claimant cannot rely on the breach of a contract to which he was not a party as giving him a cause of action in tort merely because, as a result of the breach, he has suffered economic loss, that is loss not taking the form either of personal injury or of physical damage to his property.[166] The importance of this point is illustrated by *Simaan General* 18–031

---

[162] This was the actual result in *Dean v Allin & Watts*, above.

[163] *Briscoe v Lubrizol Ltd* [2000] I.C.R. 694.

[164] *Junior Books* case [1983] 1 A.C. 520, 546, applied in *Southern Water Authority v Carey* [1985] 2 All E.R. 1077; doubted (though in another context) in *Leigh & Sillavan Ltd v Aliakmon Shipping Co Ltd (The Aliakmon)* [1986] A.C. 785, 817 (below para.18–034); see also *Pacific Associates Inc. v Baxter* [1990] 1 Q.B. 993; *cf. Norwich C.C. v Harvey* [1989] 1 All E.R. 1180, 1187; *John F. Hunt Demolition Ltd v ASME Engineering Ltd* [2007] EWHC 1507 (TCC), [2207] TCLR 6. And see above para.14–054.

[165] As, for example, in *Henderson v Merrett Syndicates* Ltd [1995] A.C. 145, *White v Jones* [1995] A.C. 207 and *BP plc v Aon Ltd* [2006] EWHC 424, [2006] 1 All E.R. (Comm) 789; and see the other authorities cited in para.18–022 above, nn.123–127; *cf. Parkinson v St James & Seacroft University NHS Trust* [2001] EWCA Civ, 530; [2002] Q.B. 266; *Rees v Darlington Memorial Hospital NHS Trust* [2003] UKHL 52; [2004] 1 A.C. 309, esp. at [131]. For a possible extension of the scope of such an "assumption" beyond contracts for professional services, see n.166, below.

[166] *Tate & Lyle Industries Ltd v G.L.C.* [1983] 2 A.C. 509, 530–531; *cf. London Congregational Union Inc. v Harriss* [1988] 1 All E.R. 15, 25; *Simaan General Contracting Co Ltd v Pilkington Glass Ltd (No.2)* [1988] 1 Q.B. 758, 781; *Greater Nottingham Co-operative Society Ltd v Cementation Piling & Foundation Ltd* [1989] Q.B. 71, 94; *Verderame v Commercial Union Assurance Co plc., The Times*, April 2, 1992; *Preston v Torfaen B.C.* [1993] E.G.C.S. 137; *Abou-Rahmah v Abacha* [2005] EWHC 2662 (QB), [2006] 1 All E.R. (Comm) 268 at [67]; affirmed [2006] EWCA Civ 1492, [2007] 1 All E.R. (Comm) 827 on other grounds, there being no appeal against the dismissal of the negligence claim: see at [7]. *cf.*, as to the restricted scope of such a duty, *Hill Samuel Bank v Frederick Brand Partnership* (1994) 10 Const.L.J. 72. See also *West Bromwich Football Club v El Safty* [2006] EWCA Civ 1299, (2006) B.M.L.R. 179 at [58]–[63], [80]–[84]; *OBG Ltd v Allan; Douglas v Hello! Ltd; Mainstream Properties Ltd v Young* [2007] U.K.H.L. 21, [2008] 1 A.C. 1 at [99] ("Even liability for causing economic loss by negligence is very limited"). For discussion of the tests which determine whether a defendant owes a duty of care in tort not to cause economic loss to the claimant,

Contracting Co v Pilkington Glass Ltd (No.2),[167] where the defendants had been nominated as suppliers of glass for incorporation in a building which was being erected by the claimants as main contractors for a client in Abu Dhabi. The glass had been sold by the defendants to a sub-contractor engaged by the claimants, so that there was no contract between claimants and defendants; the glass was perfectly sound but not of the colour specified in the contract of sale or in the main building contract. In consequence of this shortcoming, the claimants were not paid by their client and so suffered financial loss; but it was held that the defendants' breach of their contract with the sub-contractors did not give the claimants any right of action in tort against the defendants merely because that breach had caused the claimants to suffer financial loss. Similarly, it was held in *Balsamo v Medici*[168] that a sub-agent who negligently paid over the proceeds of the sale of the principal's property to a fraudulent impostor was not liable in tort to the principal for such negligence in handling the money; nor was he liable to the principal in contract as there was no privity of contract between the sub-agent and the principal. To uphold a tort claim in such a situation would, it was said, "come perilously close to abrogating the doctrine of privity altogether."[169] A doctor employed by a company to assess replies of job applicants to medical questionnaires has likewise been held to owe no duty in tort to those applicants[170]; while conversely a consultant surgeon who had given negligent advice in breach of his contract with a professional football player has been held not

---

see *Customs and Excise Commissioners v Barclays Bank plc* [2006] U.K.H.L. 28, [2007] 1 A.C. 181 where the claimant suffered such loss because the defendant bank failed to comply with an injunction which the claimant had obtained to freeze an account held by one of the bank's customers; and it was held that the bank owed no such duty to the claimant. The case does not directly affect the discussion in this Chapter since the claimant's loss did not result from any breach of the contract between the bank and its customer. In *European Gas Turbines Ltd v MSAS Cargo International Ltd* [2001] C.L.C. 880 a cargo-owner (C) recovered damages from a sub-contracting carrier (A) for purely economic loss resulting from breach of A's subcontract with the contracting carrier (B) as to the mode of carriage. There was no contract between A and C so that this conclusion is at first sight hard to reconcile with the other authorities cited in this note. The case may be explicable on the ground that C's agent had notified A of the importance to C of carriage by the stipulated mode and that A had accepted this position so as to give rise to an "assumption of responsibility" (*cf.* above, at n.165) to C to observe that stipulation.

[167] Above, n.166.

[168] [1984] 1 W.L.R. 951; Whittaker (1985) 48 M.L.R. 86 it seems that on facts such as those of *Balsamov Medici* the requirements of s.1(1), (2) and (3) of the Contracts (Rights of Third Parties) Act 1999 (below, paras 18–089, 18–091, 18–093) would not now be satisfied. *cf.* also *Michael Salliss & Co v E.C.A. Call* (1984) 4 Const. L.J. 125.

[169] [1984] 1 W.L.R. 951, 959–960. The soundness of the decisions discussed in this paragraph is not questioned in *Henderson v Merrett Syndicates Ltd* [1995] 2 A.C. 145, where the liability in tort of a subagent to a principal with whom he was in no contractual relationship was said at 195 to be based on the "most unusual" situation in that case. *cf. Hamble Fisheries Ltd v L. Gardner & Sons Ltd (The Rebecca Elaine)* [1999] 2 Lloyd's Rep. 1 at 8: "the dubious and lethal colonisation by the tort of negligence of the conceptual territory of contract" (engine manufacturer held not liable in negligence for purely economic loss, caused by failure of the engine, to owner of fishing boat with whom he was not in any contractual relationship); *Amiri Flight Authority v BAE Systems Ltd* [2003] 1 Lloyd's Rep. 50 at [35], varied, without reference to this point, [2003] EWCA Civ 1447; [2003] 2 Lloyd's Rep. 767.

[170] *Kapfunde v Abbey National plc*, [1998] I.R.L.R. 583 disapproving *Baker v Kaye* [1997] I.R.L.R. 219 so far as it holds that a duty was owed by the doctor to the applicant.

liable for financial loss suffered by the club which had employed the player but with which the surgeon was not in any contractual relationship.[171]

Requirement of "proximity". The point that is emphasised in cases such as the *Simaan* and *Balsamo* cases is that the claimants in them suffered no physical harm as a result of the defendants' acts or omissions. It does not follow that the mere fact of the claimant's having suffered foreseeable harm in this way is a sufficient condition of the defendant's liability in tort. The claimant must, in addition, show that there was a relationship of "proximity" between him and the defendant, and that it is fair, just and reasonable to impose a duty of care on the defendant.[172] The last of these requirements was held not to have been satisfied in *The Nicholas H*,[173] where a ship classification society had, in breach of its contract with shipowners, advised them that their ship could proceed on her current voyage until the cargo which she was then carrying had been discharged. In the course of that voyage the ship sank, and it was held that the owners of the cargo had no cause of action in tort against the society in respect of the loss of their cargo. The main reason given by the House of Lords for this conclusion was that the shipowners were, in turn, in breach of their contract of carriage with the cargo-owners; and that it was not fair, just or reasonable to impose on the classification society a liability to the cargo-owners in tort[174] since this would not be subject to the limitations of liability available to the shipowners under international Conventions[175] which have the force of law. The effect of holding 18–032

[171] *West Bromwich Albion Football Club v El Safty* [2006] EWCA Civ 1299, (2006) 92 B.M.L.R. 179.

[172] For these requirements, see, *inter alia, Caparo Industries plc v Dickman* [1990] 2 A.C. 605, 617–618 (where it is also said at 632 that "these requirements are, at least in most cases, merely facets of the same thing"); *Murphy v Brentwood DC* [1991] 1 A.C. 398, 480, 486; *X (Minors) v Bedfordshire C.C.* [1995] 2 A.C. 633, 739.

[173] *Marc Rich & Co AG v Bishop Rock Marine Co Ltd (The Nicholas H.)*, [1996] A.C. 211; see also the *X (Minors)* case, above, n.172 at 749; *Reeman v Department of Transport* [1997] 2 Lloyd's Rep. 648; *Architype Projects Ltd v Dewhurst McFarlane & Partners* [2003] EWHC 3341, [2004] P.N.L.R. 38; *R.M. Turton & Co Ltd v Kerslake & Partners* [2000] Lloyd's Rep. P.N. 967 (New Zealand CA).

[174] Nor had there been an "assumption of responsibility" (above, para.18–031) since the cargo-owners were "not even aware of [the classification society's] examination of the ship:" [1996] A.C. 211, 242.

[175] The Convention in question related to tonnage limitations; effect was given to this Convention by Merchant Shipping Act 1979 s.17 and Sch.4, now superseded by Merchant Shipping Act 1995, s.185 and Sch.7, Part I. The reasoning of the House of Lords is equally applicable to the contractual limitations and exceptions which protect the carrier by virtue of Carriage of Goods by Sea Act 1971 s.1(2) and Sch.: see *Marc Rich & Co v Bishop Rock Marine (The Nicholas H)* [1996] A.C. 211, 238. No similar policy reasons for protecting an aircraft inspection authority from liability for *personal* injury to a passenger were said to exist in *Perrett v Collins* [1998] 2 Lloyd's Rep. 225; *cf. Watson v British Boxing Board of Control Ltd* [2001] Q.B. 1134. Contrast *Sutradhar v Natural Environment Research Council* [2006] UKHL 33, [2006] 4 All E.R. 490 where a body which had carried out hydrogeological tests of artesian wells was held not liable to a consumer who had developed arsenical poisoning as a result of drinking water from the wells. *Perrett v Collins* (above) was distinguished at [37] on the ground that there, but not in the *Sutradhar* case, the defendants had a "measure of control" over the activity which caused the injury to persons with whom they had no contractual relationship.

classification societies liable in tort to cargo-owners would be to deprive shipowners of the benefits of these Conventions since the societies would pass this liability on to shipowners; and this would be an undesirable conclusion[176] particularly as loss suffered by cargo-owners in excess of the Convention limits was "readily insurable."[177]

18–033 **Defects in the very thing supplied insufficient.** Even where A's negligence in the performance of his contract with B has resulted in damage to "property," the scope of C's tort remedy is further restricted by the fact that "property" in this context normally refers to property belonging to C *other* than the very thing supplied by A under his contract with B. Thus where A sold goods to B who resold them to C, it was held that A would not be liable in tort to C merely because those goods disintegrated on account of a defect in them amounting to a breach of A's contract with B.[178] Nor, where goods are bought from a retailer, is the manufacturer liable to the buyer in tort[179] for negligence if the goods are defective and the defect is discovered before any injury, or harm to other property, has resulted. Even if the goods deteriorate by reason of the defect, the buyer's only loss is the financial or economic loss which he suffers because the defect has made them less valuable or because he discards them or incurs the cost of repairing them. Loss of this kind is not generally recoverable in tort,[180] though there may be an exception to this general rule where the defect is a source of danger in respect of which the claimant could become liable to third parties, so that money has to be spent in averting this danger.[181] The *Junior Books* case appears, indeed, to be inconsistent with the general rule; for the only "property" which could be said to have been damaged was the factory floor (which had cracked), and that damage was no more than a defect in the very thing supplied by A. The fact that A was nevertheless held liable in tort to C is now explicable (if at all) only by reference to the same special, or "unique," factors[182] which gave rise to the relationship of proximity in that case.

18–034 **Claimant having no title to thing damaged.** Even where A's breach of his contract with B does result in physical damage, the mere fact that the loss so

---

[176] *cf.* below para.18–034 at nn.190 and 191.

[177] *The Nicholas H* [1996] A.C. 211, 242.

[178] *Aswan Engineering Establishment Co v Lupdine Ltd* [1987] 1 W.L.R. 1; *cf. D. & F. Estates Ltd v Church Commissioners for England* [1989] A.C. 177, 202, 216; *Reid v Rush & Tompkins Group plc* [1990] 1 W.L.R. 212, 224; *Warner v Basildon Development Corp.* (1991) 7 Const.L.J. 146; *Holding & Management (Solitaire) Ltd v Ideal Homes Northwest Ltd* [2004] EWHC 2408, 96 Con. L.R. 114; affirmed [2005] EWCA Civ 59; *cf. Bacardi-Martini Beverages Ltd v Thomas Hardy Packaging Ltd* [2002] EWCA Civ 549; [2002] 2 All E.R. (Comm) 335 at [18] (contaminated ingredient used in manufacturing making finished product useless).

[179] For possible liability under a manufacturer's guarantee, see above, para.18–005.

[180] *Murphy v Brentwood DC* [1991] 1 A.C. 398, 469, 475; *cf. Nitrigin Eirann Teoranta v Inco Alloys Ltd* [1992] 1 W.L.R. 498.

[181] *Losinjska Plovida v Transco Overseas Ltd (The Orjula)* [1995] 2 Lloyd's Rep. 395, 402, where it was also arguable that the defective thing supplied by the defendant had caused physical harm to *other* property in which the claimant had a prior interest as lessee.

[182] Above, para.18–027 at n.148.

occasioned falls on C will not necessarily give C a right of action in tort against A in respect of that loss. In *The Aliakmon*[183] A, a carrier, had contracted with B for the carriage of a quantity of steel coils which B had sold to C. The goods were damaged, as a result of A's negligent breach of the contract of carriage, after the risk in them had passed to C under the contract of sale, but while B remained their owner. C had no claim under the contract of carriage as he was not a party to it[184]; and the House of Lords held that he also had no cause of action against A in tort in respect of the loss which he had suffered as a result of remaining liable for the full price of the goods in spite of the fact that they had been damaged in transit. This conclusion was based on a long line of authority[185] which had established "the principle of law that, in order to enable a person to claim in negligence for loss caused to him by reason of loss or damage to property, he must have had either the legal ownership of or a possessory title[186] to the property concerned at the time when the loss or damage occurred,"[187] or, where the loss is caused by continuing process, at the time when the cause of action in respect of it accrued.[188] It is not enough for him at the relevant time "to have only had contractual rights in relation to such property."[189] The House of Lords refused to create an exception to this principle where (as in *The Aliakmon*) the contractual right which C had under his contract of sale with B was one to have property and possession of the goods transferred to him at a later date. The main reason for this refusal was that the contract of carriage between A and B

---

[183] *Leigh & Sillavan Ltd v Aliakmon Shipping Co Ltd (The Aliakmon)* [1986] A.C. 785; Treitel [1986] L.M.C.L.Q. 294; Markesinis (1987) 103 L.Q.R. 354, 384–390; Tettenborn [1987] J.B.L. 12; *cf. Transcontainer Express Ltd v Custodian Security Ltd* [1988] 1 Lloyd's Rep. 128; *Mitsui & Co Ltd v Flota Mercante Grancolombiana SA (The Ciudad de Pasto)* [1988] 1 W.L.R. 1145; *Anonima Petroli Italiana S.p.A. v Marlucidez Armadora SA (The Filiatra Legacy)* [1991] 2 Lloyd's Rep. 337 at 339; *Mitsui & Co v. Novorossiysk Shipping Co (The Gudermes)* [1993] 1 Lloyd's Rep. 311 at 326; *The Hamburg Star* [1994] 1 Lloyd's Rep. 399 at 404–405; *The Seven Pioneer* [2001] 2 Lloyd's Rep. 57 (High Court of New Zealand). For a possible qualification, see *Virgo Steamship Co SA v Skaarup Shipping Corp. (The Kapetan Georgis)* [1988] 1 Lloyd's Rep. 352.

[184] The benefit of the contract of carriage had not been transferred to C under Bills of Lading Act 1855, s.1 as the property in the goods had not passed to him. On the facts of *The Aliakmon* rights under the contract of carriage would now be transferred to C by virtue of the Carriage of Goods by Sea Act 1992, s.2: see *White v Jones* [1995] 2 A.C. 207, 265. But cases can still be imagined where this would not be the case: see *Carver on Bills of Lading*, 2nd ed. (2005) para.5–108.

[185] Stretching from *Cattle v Stockton Waterworks Co* (1875) L.R. 10 Q.B. 453 to *Candlewood Navigation Corp. v Mitsui O.S.K. Lines (The Mineral Transporter)* [1986] A.C.1.

[186] A bailor of goods has been held to have a sufficient possessory title even after the transfer by him of his contractual rights under the contract giving rise to the bailment: *East West Corp. v DKBS 1912* [2003] EWCA Civ 83; [2003] 1 Lloyd's Rep 265 at [38]–[39], [49], [86]; *Scottish & Newcastle International Ltd v Othon Ghalanos Ltd* [2008] UKHL 11, [2008] 1 Lloyd's Rep. 462 at [46].

[187] [1986] A.C. 785 at 809.

[188] *Homburg Houtimport BV v Agrosin Private Ltd (The Starsin)* [2001] EWCA Civ 56; [2001] 1 Lloyd's Rep. 437, at [96] per Rix L.J., whose judgment was on this point affirmed on appeal: [2003] UKHL 12; [2004] 1 A.C. 715 at [40], [64], [90], [139].

[189] [1986] A.C. 785, 809. Griew, (1986) 136 N.L.J. 1201 suggests that the principle may have been qualified by Latent Damage Act 1986, s.3; but there is no hint in the legislative history of s.3 that such a qualification was intended. It can, in any event, only apply where the damage was still latent when the claimant became owner; and this was not the position in *The Aliakmon.* The point was left open in *The Starsin*, above, [2001] EWCA Civ, 56 at [119]–[128], [134], [202], [203], and not discussed in the House of Lords [2003] UKHL 12, above.

was expressed to be subject to an international Convention[190] which gave A (as carrier) the benefit of certain immunities from, and limitations of, liability; and to have held A liable in tort to C would have produced the undesirable result of depriving A of the protection of that contract,[191] since C (being a stranger to it) was no more bound by its terms than entitled to assert rights under it.

18–035 **Tort and contract damages contrasted.** Where a third party can recover damages in tort for the negligent performance of a contract between two others, the damages in such a tort action will not normally be assessed in the same way as they would be in a contractual action. In particular, certain kinds of loss are generally regarded as being recoverable only in a contractual action. This follows from the general principle that the object of awarding damages for breach of contract is to put the claimant into the same position as that in which he would have been if the contract had been performed, while in an action in tort that object is to put him back into the position in which he was before the tort was committed. The distinction is well illustrated by *Muirhead v Industrial Tank Specialities Ltd*[192] where the plaintiff, who owned a lobster farm, had entered into a contract for the installation of pumps, which later failed because of a defect in their electric motors. There was no contract between the plaintiff and the supplier of the motors but the plaintiff's claim against that supplier succeeded in tort in respect of the physical damage caused by that failure (*i.e.* the value of the lobsters which had died); and "any financial loss suffered by the plaintiff in consequence of that physical damage."[193] (*i.e.* the loss of profits on the sale of *those* lobsters). But a further claim "in respect of the whole economic loss suffered"[194] by the plaintiff (*i.e.* for loss of profits that he would have made from the installation, had it not been defective) was rejected: such damages might have been recoverable from the installer of the pumps in contract but they could not be claimed from the suppliers of the motors in tort.

---

[190] *i.e.* the Hague Rules set out in the Schedule to the Carriage of Goods by Sea Act 1924, now superseded in England by Carriage of Goods by Sea Act 1971.

[191] *cf. Simaan General Contracting Co v Pilkington Glass Ltd (No.2)* [1988] Q.B. 758, 782–783. For the suggestion that the position may be different where the potential tortfeasor has no such protection, see *Triangle Steel & Supply Co v Korean United Lines Inc.* (1985) 63 B.C.L.R. 66, 80 (the reasoning of which is in other respects inconsistent with that of *The Aliakmon*). See also *Sidhu v British Airways plc* [1997] A.C. 430, 450–451 stating that, in a case governed by the Conventions on international carriage by air, the only persons having the right to sue in respect of loss or damage to the goods were those specified in the Conventions for this purpose; in an action by such persons, the carrier would be entitled to the protection of the Conventions; see also *Re Deep Vein Thrombosis and Air Travel Group Litigation* [2006] UKHL 72, [2006] A.C. 495 at [3], [27], [29] and [62]. Under such Conventions, the carrier may be protected by their terms even against a person who is not a party to the contract but has a cause of action against the carrier by virtue of his title to the goods. It has been held that such an action can be brought only subject to the "scheme of liability" imposed by the Conventions: *Western Digital Corp. v British Airways plc* [2001] Q.B. 733 at 750, 754–755, 769. Where an original shipper transfers his contractual rights to a third party, he may retain rights against the carrier in bailment, but such rights will remain subject to the contractual terms on which the goods were originally bailed by him to the carrier: see *East West Corp. v DKBS 1912 A/S* [2003] EWCA Civ, 83; [2003] Q.B. 1509, especially at [50], [69].

[192] [1986] Q.B. 507; Whittaker (1986) 49 M.L.R. 469; Oughton [1987] J.B.L. 370.

[193] [1986] Q.B. at 533.

[194] *ibid.*

18–036 Considerable difficulty again arises in this connection from the *Junior Books*[195] case. The main question discussed in that case was whether any economic or financial loss could be recovered in a tort action in the absence of any allegation that the cracks in the floor were a source of danger to persons or to other property. In the exceptional circumstances of the case, this question was answered in the affirmative and on that basis most of the items of loss, in respect of which damages were said to be recoverable, can be explained in terms of the principles governing the assessment of damages in tort: this is, for example, true of the profits lost and of the wages and overheads wasted while the factory was closed for repairs to the floor. But it was also said that factory owners were entitled to the *cost of replacing the floor*[196]; and such an award would, by putting them into the position in which they would have been if the sub-contractor's promise had been performed, amount to an award of contract damages in spite of the fact that there was no contract between the factory owners and the sub-contractors.[197] On the normal basis of assessment in tort, the damages in respect of defects in the floor should not have included the cost of replacing the floor with a good one.[198] In the *Junior Books* case, Lord Keith explained this aspect of the case on the ground that, in replacing the floor, the factory owners had simply mitigated the loss of profit resulting from the defects in the floor originally provided[199]; and it is well established that expenses reasonably incurred in mitigation are recoverable.[200] But as this reasoning was not adopted by the other members of the House of Lords, an alternative explanation was given in the *Muirhead* case, namely that the same special (or unique) factors in the *Junior Books* case, which gave rise to the duty of care there,[201] also explain the assessment of damages.[202] This narrow view of the *Junior Books* case is supported by dicta in the *Junior Books* case itself[203]; by the fact that there is no subsequent similar[204] case in which a third party has recovered damages in tort to put him into the position in which he would have been if the contract between two others *had been performed* (as opposed to that in which he was *before it was*

[195] [1983] 1 A.C. 520; above, para.18–023 to 18–033; Grubb [1984] C.L.J. 111; Holyoak (1983) 99 L.Q.R. 591; Smith and Burns (1983) 46 M.L.R. 1 & 7.

[196] This was one of the items claimed; the question whether the claim was proved was not before the House of Lords, which decided only that there was a cause of action in respect of it if negligence were established.

[197] The case was governed by Scots law, which recognises a *jus quaesitum tertio*, but the conditions giving rise to such a right were not satisfied.

[198] *cf. Murphy v Brentwood DC* [1991] 2 A.C. 398, 469. Lord Roskill in the *Junior Books* case at 545 discusses (without reaching a definite conclusion) the question whether the pursuer in *Donoghue v Stevenson* [1932] A.C. 562 could have recovered damages "for the diminished value of the ginger beer"—not for the cost of replacing the contaminated with pure ginger beer. Even the former basis of assessment would seem to be ruled out by the authorities cited in para.18–033, n.178, above.

[199] [1983] 1 A.C. 520, 536.

[200] *cf.* below para.26–120.

[201] Above para.18–027.

[202] [1986] Q.B. 507, 523, 533–535.

[203] [1983] 1 A.C. 520, 533 (*per* Lord Fraser, who took the same narrow view of the *Junior Books* case in *The Mineral Transporter* [1986] A.C. 1, 24–25); and [1983] 1 A.C. 520, 546 (*per* Lord Roskill).

[204] For the different treatment of the "disappointed beneficiary" and analogous cases, see below, para.18–037—18–039.

broken); and by the fact that many later decisions[205] have made it highly unlikely that such damages will, in a future tort case of this kind be awarded to a third party. On the contrary, two House of Lords decisions have specifically rejected such claims.[206] In each case, a lessee claimed damages in tort for the cost of remedying defects alleged to be due to the negligence of a building contractor in the performance of a contract to which the lessee was not a party. In each case, the contractor was held not liable to the lessee in tort, even if he was negligent,[207] since the defects had been discovered before they had caused any personal injury, or damage to other property belonging to the lessees. To make the contractor liable for the purely economic loss suffered by the lessee in remedying the defect would "impose upon [the contractor] for the benefit of those with whom he had no contractual relationship the obligation of one who warranted the quality of"[208] his work. Such a result would have been inconsistent with the common law doctrine of privity; and these cases reinforce the view that tort liability in negligence to third parties has not wholly subverted (though it may have limited the scope of) that doctrine.

18–037 **Damages in "disappointed beneficiary" cases.** The general principle that a third party cannot recover damages in tort to put him into the position in which he would have been if a contract between two others had been performed is, at least at first sight, hard to reconcile with cases such as *White v Jones*,[209] where A had instructed his solicitor B to draw up a will containing bequests in favour of his daughters C and D, but B negligently and in breach of his contract with A had done nothing to carry out these instructions by the time of A's death. The House of Lords by a majority held that B was liable in tort to C and D, and that the damages to which they were entitled consisted of the amounts which they would have obtained under A's will, if B had duly carried out A's instructions. The case presented certain special features, namely that C had discussed A's testamentary intentions with B, and that the letter setting out A's wishes had been drafted by D's husband. The majority do not seem to restrict the principle of

---

[205] *i.e. Tate & Lyle Industries Ltd v G.L.C.* [1983] 2 A.C. 509; *Balsamo v Medici* [1984] 1 W.L.R. 951; *Candlewood Navigation Corp. v Mitsui O.S.K. Lines (The Mineral Transporter)* [1986] A.C. 1; *Muirhead v Industrial Tank Specialities Ltd* [1986] Q.B. 507; *Leigh & Sillavan Ltd v Aliakmon Shipping Co Ltd (The Aliakmon)* [1986] A.C. 785; *Aswan Engineering Establishment Co v Lupdine Ltd* [1987] 1 W.L.R. 1; *cf.* also *Smith v Littlewoods Organisation Ltd* [1987] A.C. 241, 280; *Yuen Kun Yeu v Att.-Gen. of Hong Kong* [1988] A.C. 175; *Simaan General Contracting Co v Pilkington Glass Ltd (No.2)* [1988] Q.B. 758; *Greater Nottingham Co-operative Society Ltd v Cementation Piling & Foundation Ltd* [1989] Q.B. 71, 84; *Davies v Radcliffe* [1990] 1 W.L.R. 821; *Parker-Tweedale v Dunbar Bank plc* [1991] Ch. 12, 24; *Deloitte Haskins & Sells v National Mutual Life Nominees* [1993] A.C. 774.

[206] *D. & F. Estates Ltd v Church Commissioners for England* [1989] A.C. 177; *Department of the Environment v Thomas Bates & Son Ltd* [1991] 1 A.C. 449.

[207] In the *D. & F. Estates* case, there was no such negligence as the builders had employed competent sub-contractors.

[208] [1989] A.C. 177, 207; *cf. ibid.* at 211–212.

[209] [1995] 2 A.C. 207 (Lords Keith and Mustill dissenting), approving the result (though not the reasoning) in *Ross v Caunters* [1980] Ch. 287, where B's negligence took the form, not of simply failing to carry out A's instructions, but of carrying them out ineffectively. *cf. Esterhuizen v Allied Dunbar Assurance plc*, [1988] 2 F.L.R. 668 (similar liability of company providing will making services) and (in Australia) *Hill v Van Erp* (1997) 142 A.L.R. 687, a case of actual misfeasance by the solicitor.

liability to such special circumstances[210] though they accept that there must be "boundaries to the availability of the remedy" which "will have to be worked out . . . as practical problems come before the courts."[211] It is, for example, an open question whether such a remedy would be available to a prospective beneficiary who had no previous connection with the testator or knowledge of his intentions; and it has been said that the solicitor would not be liable for the amount of the intended benefit where it would have been reasonable for the beneficiary to have taken proceedings against the estate for rectification of the will and so to have obtained that benefit.[212] But where the principle (whatever its precise scope may turn out to be) does apply, its effect is to put C into the position in which he would have been if the contract between A and B had been properly performed. Such cases are, however, distinguishable in several respects from those which hold that building contractors are not liable to third parties in respect of purely economic loss caused by defective work.[213] In the building cases, the third party's complaint is that he has not received the benefit of the contractor's performance. In the disappointed beneficiary cases, the benefit of which the third party is deprived is not that of the solicitor's work: the lost benefit was to be provided, not by the solicitor, but by the testator; it was not to be created by the solicitor's work, but existed independently of it. The third party is not entitled to the cost of curing the defects in the solicitor's work (*e.g.* to the cost of employing another solicitor to give effect to the testator's intention). On the contrary, it has been held that, if the defect is discovered when cure is still possible, the solicitor owes no duty to the beneficiary.[214] There are also the points that, if any duty is to be imposed on the solicitor to the disappointed beneficiary, the only realistic measure of damages is the value of the lost benefit; and that no more than nominal damages could be recovered from the solicitor by the client's estate, since it would have suffered no loss. The negligent solicitor would thus escape all substantial liability if he were not held liable to the disappointed beneficiary for the value of the lost benefit. In the building contract cases, on the other hand, the employer will usually have a substantial remedy against the defaulting builder for damages, amounting either to the cost of curing the defects in the work or to the difference between the value of the work which was done and that which should have been done; and such a remedy may be available to the employer, not only in respect of his own loss, but also (in appropriate circumstances) in respect of loss suffered by the third party.[215] For these reasons, it is

---

[210] [1995] 2 A.C. 207, 295.

[211] *ibid*, at 269. The alleged beneficiary's claim clearly cannot succeed without proof of the requisite testamentary intention in his favour: see *Gibbons v Nelsons* [2000] Lloyd's Rep. P.N. 603.

[212] On the question whether it would have been reasonable for the beneficiary to take rectification proceedings, contrast *Walker v Geo. H. Medlicott & Son* [1999] 1 All E.R. 685 with *Horsfall v Hayward* [1999] F.L.R. 1182.

[213] Above, para.18–036 at n.206. *cf.* also *Rees v Darlington Memorial Hospital NHS Trust* [2003] UKHL 52; [2004] 1 A.C. 309 at [131].

[214] *Hemmens v Wilson Browne* [1995] Ch. 223. But a claim by a person in a position analogous to that of a disappointed beneficiary may be available where the consequences of the adviser's negligence do not become apparent for many years after the transaction in question: *Richards v Hughes* [2004] EWCA Civ 266, [2004] P.N.L.R. 35.

[215] Below, paras 18–053 *et seq.*

submitted that the building contract cases can be distinguished from disappointed beneficiary cases such as *White v Jones*.

18–038 **Analogous situations.** The principle of the "disappointed beneficiary" cases has been extended to a number of closely analogous situations. One such extension was made in *Carr-Glynn v Frearsons*[216] where the solicitors' negligence took the form, not of failing to secure the proper execution of the will, but of failing to take steps to ensure that property specifically bequeathed to the beneficiary remained within the client's estate after her death.[217] Loss was thus suffered by the estate but the solicitors were nevertheless held liable to the intended legatee since the proceeds of any claim by the estate would have benefited, not that legatee, but the person entitled under the will to the residuary estate,[218] thus defeating the intention of the testatrix.[219] The decision can be explained on the ground that "the estate" is something of a legal abstraction, the loss being in fact suffered by the individual who under the will would, but for the solicitors' negligence, have received the property which was lost to "the estate"; and that the court looked behind that abstraction[220] so as to fashion a remedy for that individual. The alternative possibility that the estate might have had a claim against the solicitors in respect of the intended legatee's loss[221] was not considered, nor was any attempt made to reconcile the result with those building contract cases (discussed above[222]) in which a third party was held to have no remedy in tort against the contractor for pure economic loss. The principle of the "disappointed beneficiary" cases has also been extended to the situation in which the benefit of which the claimant was deprived as a result of the defendant's negligence was one which would have arisen on the death of the other contracting party, not under a will, but under a pension scheme. In *Gorham v British Telecommunications plc*[223] an insurance company sold a policy to a customer who had made it clear to the company that he was buying the policy to provide for his wife and dependant children in the event of his predeceasing them. The company negligently failed to advise the customer that these dependants would

---

[216] [1999] Ch. 326.

[217] The testatrix was joint owner of the property in question and the solicitors had negligently failed to advise her to sever the joint tenancy, so that on her death her share passed to the other co-owner by right of survivorship.

[218] For the right of an executrix to recover damages for the benefit of a residuary legatee in respect of loss to the estate caused by the negligence of a solicitor engaged by the executrix to administer the estate, see *Chappell v Somers & Blake* [2003] EWHC 1644 (Ch); [2004] Ch. 19, below, para.18–047 at n.264.

[219] *cf. Corbett v Bond Pearce* [2001] EWCA Civ 531; [2001] 3 All E.R. 769, where residuary gift in favour of a disappointed beneficiary was held invalid in legal proceedings the costs of which were paid out of the testatrix's estate. The solicitors whose negligence was the cause of the invalidity of that gift then settled the disappointed beneficiary's claim for the full value of the residuary estate, undiminished by those costs. It was held that the solicitors were not liable to the estate for such costs since to hold them so liable would (1) make them liable twice over the same loss; and (2) result in benefiting persons whom the testatrix (in accordance with her final testamentary intentions as expressed in the invalid will) no longer wished to benefit.

[220] In a way somewhat reminiscent of the process, well known in company law, of "lifting the corporate veil."

[221] See below, para.18–052, *et seq.* and n.218 above.

[222] Above, n.206.

[223] [2000] 1 W.L.R. 2129.

in that event have been better off if he had joined his employers' pension scheme; and it was held that the company was liable to the dependants for loss of benefits under the employers' scheme up to (but not beyond) the time when the company had corrected its original advice. The principle of *White v Jones*[224] applied because (as in that case) the customer had not himself suffered any loss, so that, if the dependants' claims had been rejected, then neither the persons who had suffered loss nor anyone else would have had any claim for established negligence; and because the advice had been given "in a context in which the interests of the dependants were fundamental to the transaction."[225] In both these respects, the case was closely analogous to that of a disappointed testamentary beneficiary.[226] The principle of those cases may also apply by analogy in favour of a claimant who has been deprived by the defendants breach of a contract to which the claimant was not a party of benefits which the claimant would, but for the breach, have obtained where those benefits would have arisen, not under a will, but under a trust.[227]

The "disappointed beneficiary" and analogous cases go further than any group of negligence cases in encroaching on the common law doctrine of privity of contract. Perhaps for this reason, they were described as "an unusual class of cases" in *Goodwill v Pregnancy Advisory Service*.[228] In that case, the defendant had arranged for one M to have a vasectomy and, after the operation had been carried out, told him that it had been successful and that he no longer needed to use any other method of contraception. Some three years later, M formed a sexual relationship with the claimant, to whom he communicated the information given to him by the defendant relating to the vasectomy; she ceased to use any method of contraception after having consulted her own general practitioner who told her that there was only a minute chance of her becoming pregnant. The vasectomy having undergone a spontaneous reversal, the claimant became pregnant by M and one reason for holding that the defendant was not liable to her in damages was that a doctor performing a vasectomy could not realistically be described as having been employed to confer a benefit on his patient's future sexual partners. The case was also said to be unlike the "disappointed beneficiary" cases in that dismissal of the claim would not produce the "rank injustice"[229] that would arise in those cases if in them the only person with a claim against the negligent solicitor were the testator's estate, which would have suffered no loss. In a sterilisation case, a substantial remedy for negligence (if established) would normally be available to the patient him (or her) self. Such damages may be 18–039

[224] [1995] 2 A.C. 207, above, para.18–037

[225] *Gorham's case*, above n.223, at 2142.

[226] *cf.* the reference in *Dean v Allin & Watts* [2001] EWCA Civ 758; [2001] 2 Lloyd's Rep. 249 (above, para.18–029) at [69] by Robert Walker L.J. to the "very special problems" which had arisen in *White v Jones* and *Gorham's* case, evidently not sharing the view of Lightman J. in *Dean v Allin & Watts*, above at [40] that the decision there represented a further extension of the principle in *White v Jones.*

[227] See *Richards v Hughes* [2004] EWCA Civ 266, [2004] P.N.L.R. 35.

[228] [1996] 1 W.L.R. 1397.

[229] [1996] 1 W.L.R. 1397, 1403; *cf.* above, n.226 and the description of *White v Jones* as having been "decided on special facts" in *Williams v Natural Life Health Foods* [1998] 1 W.L.R. 830 at 837.

recoverable[230] even though, because the operation is carried out under the National Health Service (NHS) there is no contract between the patient and either the doctor who performs the operation or the hospital in which it is performed. Such liability is generally thought to arise, independently of contract, under the normal principles which determine when the relationship between two persons is such as to impose on one of them a duty of care owed to the other, the breach of which is actionable in tort. In *Rees v Darlington Memorial Hospital NHS Trust*,[231] Lord Scott did indeed suggest that such liability could be explained on the ground that "The NHS patient is entitled to the benefit of the contractual duty owed by the doctor pursuant to his contract with his NHS employers (*cf. White v Jones*) . . . "[232] But no reference was made to this point by any of the other members of the House of Lords, a majority of whom awarded damages to the claimant on the basis that the hospital trust was liable on ordinary principles of tortious negligence, which Lord Scott was also prepared to apply as an alternative basis[233] for the award. It is not clear whether the "conventional"[234] sum awarded by the majority was intended to be compensatory[235] or to be based instead simply, as Lord Bingham said, on "some measure of recognition of the wrong done".[236] The case is therefore not direct authority on whether such an award is more closely analogous to damages for breach of contract[237] than to one for tort.[238]

(b) *Liability to Third Parties for Intimidation*

18–040 **Tort of intimidation.** The tort of intimidation is committed where A induces B to act to the detriment of C by threatening B with some unlawful course of conduct. In *Rookes v Barnard*[239] the House of Lords decided that a threat by A to break his contract with B is for this purpose a threat to do an unlawful act. Such a threat may therefore entitle C to sue A for intimidation; and in bringing such an action C will to some extent be relying on a contract to which he is not

---

[230] For limits on damages in such cases, see *McFarlane v Tayside Health Board* [2000] 2 A.C. 59; a full discussion of damages in "wrongful birth" cases is beyond the scope of this book.

[231] [2003] UKHL 52; [2004] 1 A.C. 309.

[232] *ibid.* at [131].

[233] *ibid.* at [132].

[234] *ibid.* at [8].

[235] *ibid.* at [123] *per* Lord Millett ("compensation by way of damages") and at [148] *per* Lord Scott ("a conventional sum to compensate the respondent").

[236] *ibid.* at [8]; in Lord Bingham's view, such an award "would not be, and would not be intended to be, compensatory". Lord Nicholls at [17] seems to take the same view.

[237] A view perhaps supported by Lord Scott at [148] ("to compensate the respondent for loss of the benefit that she was entitled to expect"); but see also at [131], regarding the distinction between contract and tort as irrelevant.

[238] A view perhaps supported by Lord Millett at [125], describing the purpose of the award as being "to compensate" for the . . . injury to the parents' autonomy."

[239] [1964] A.C. 1129. For restrictions on the scope of such liability where the unlawful conduct takes the form of acts done in the contemplation or furtherance of a trade dispute, see Trade Union and Labour Relation (Consolidation) Act 1992, s.219, as amended by Trade Union Reform and Employment Rights Act 1993, s.49(1) and Sch.8, para.72; for an extension of the principle in favour of an individual whose expected supply of goods or services is disrupted by unlawful acts inducing industrial action, see Trade Union and Labour Relations (Consolidation) Act 1992, s.235A, as inserted by Trade Union Reform and Employment Rights Act 1993, s.22.

a party. But the suggestion[240] that this position "outflanks" the common law doctrine of privity has been rejected by the House of Lords.[241] In the case put, C does not sue to enforce A's promise to B. "His cause of action is quite different."[242] C's complaint is not that A has broken his contract with B, but that A has coerced B into acting to C's detriment.

In *OBG Ltd v Allen; Douglas v Hello! Ltd; Mainstream Properties Ltd v Young*[243] Lord Hoffmann classified intimidation as "only one variant of the broader tort usually called 'causing loss by unlawful means'".[244] This classification does not affect the relationship between the doctrine of privity of contract and liability in tort for intimidation. 18–041

(c) *Liability to Third Parties in Restitution?*

Restitution. It has been suggested in Australia that the third party may have a claim in restitution where the promisor has received payment (or some other performance) from the promisee and has then failed or refused to perform the promise in favour of the third party; and that the measure of recovery on such a claim is the amount promised.[245] The suggestion was made where premiums under a policy of liability insurance for the benefit of a third party had been paid by the promisee to the promisor (the insurance company) which had then refused to pay the third party. The promisor's liability to the third party in restitution was said to be based on his unjust enrichment, and to arise in spite of the fact that there was no correlative impoverishment of the third party. But while it is true that liability in restitution is not based on loss to the claimant, it is (in the case put) based on gain to the defendant and it is hard to see what justification there can be for wholly disregarding this *basis* of restitutionary liability in determining its *measure*. And the argument that, to hold the promisor liable to the third party for the amount promised was "not an abrogation of the doctrine of privity of contract,"[246] merely because the liability was said to arise in restitution, is, it is submitted, inconsistent with the practical result of making the promisor so liable. We have seen that, in England, the promisor is not liable in tort where the practical effect of imposing such liability would be to abrogate the common law doctrine of privity[247]; and it is hard to see why the position should be different merely because the alleged basis of liability is restitution rather than tort. The suggestion that the promisor is liable in restitution to the third party for the amount promised, merely because the promisor has received performance from 18–042

[240] Wedderburn (1961) 24 M.L.R. 572, 577; accepted by Pearson L.J. in *Rookes v Barnard* [1963] 1 Q.B. 623, 695, but later rejected: below at n.241.

[241] *Rookes v Barnard* [1964] A.C. 1129, 1168, 1200, 1208, 1235; Hamson [1961] C.L.J. 189; [1964] C.L.J. 159; Hoffmann (1965) 81 L.Q.R. 116, 124–128.

[242] *Rookes v Barnard* [1964] A.C. 1129, 1208; if C were suing to enforce the contract, the damages might be quite different.

[243] [2007] UKHL 21, [2008] 1 A.C. 1.

[244] *ibid.*, at [7]; "broader" because causing loss by unlawful means "does not require threats": *ibid.*

[245] *Trident Insurance Co Ltd v McNiece Bros Pty Ltd* (1988) 165 C.L.R. 107, *per* Gaudron J.; this view does not seem to be shared by any other member of the Court; Soh (1989) 105 L.Q.R. 4.

[246] 165 C.L.R. at 177.

[247] Above, paras 18–031, 18–035.

the promisee is, moreover, inconsistent with the reasoning of *Beswick v Beswick*,[248] where it was assumed that the third party had no common law right to sue the promisor in her own name, in spite of the fact that the promisor had received performance in full from the promisee. The view that claims of the kind here discussed fall outside the scope of the doctrine of privity of contract must therefore be viewed with scepticism. The argument based on restitution would in any event be of no avail to the third party where the promisor was willing to pay and the issue was merely whether it should pay the third party or the promisee[249]: in such cases the promisor would not just be unjustly enriched so that there would be no basis for restitutionary liability.

The above discussion is based on the assumption that the promisor would be unjustly enriched if he were allowed to retain a payment received *from the promisee* in spite of his failure to perform his promise to pay the third party. There is the further possibility that the promisor may have received a benefit *from a third party*: for example, where A contracts to grant a development lease to B, a company controlled by C, and C incurs expense in improving A's land in anticipation of the development, which then fails to take place because of A's failure to perform his contract with B. In such a case, it is arguable that C may have a restitution claim against A.[250] To allow such a claim would not be inconsistent with the doctrine of privity since in such a case C's claim is not based on any promise made by A to B for the benefit of C; no such promise has been made. The basis and measure of any restitution claim which C may have against A is more closely analogous to cases in which restitution is granted in respect of benefits conferred under anticipated contracts which fail to come into existence.[251]

4. CONTRACTS FOR THE BENEFIT OF THIRD PARTIES

(a) *Effects of a Contract for the Benefit of a Third Party*

18–043 **General.** Although a contract for the benefit of a third party generally does not, at common law, entitle the third party to enforce rights arising under it, the contract remains nevertheless binding between promisor and promisee. The fact that the contract was made for the benefit of a third party does, however, give rise to special problems so far as the promisee's remedies against the promisor are concerned. Actual performance of the contract may also lead to disputes between promisee and third party.

(i) *Promisee's Remedies*

18–044 **Specific performance.** The promisee (or those acting for his estate) may seek specific performance of the contract. If, as in *Beswick v Beswick*,[252] such an order

---

[248] [1968] A.C. 58; above, para.18–020.

[249] See below, para.18–073; *cf.* such cases as *Re Schebsman* [1944] Ch. 83 and *Re Sinclair's Life Policy* [1938] Ch. 799 (below para.18–079).

[250] *Brennan v Brighton B.C., The Times*, May 15, 1997, where B was a company which had been wound up and so could no longer sue A for breach of the contract between them.

[251] Below, para.29–071.

[252] [1968] A.C. 58; above, para.18–020.

is obtained, the third party will in fact receive the benefit contracted for. But the scope of the remedy of specific performance is limited in various ways; these limitations, and their applicability to cases involving third parties, will be discussed in Chapter 27.[253] In the following paragraphs we shall therefore consider what other remedies may be available to the promisee if the contract is broken.

Restitution. The promisee might claim restitution of the consideration provided by him. But part performance of the promise in favour of the third party could defeat this remedy,[254] and it might also be unjust to restrict the promisee to it: for example, return of premiums could be a quite inadequate remedy where a policy of life insurance had been taken out for the benefit of a third party and had matured. 18–045

Claim for the agreed sum. The promisee might sue for payment to himself of the agreed sum. It may be objected that to allow such a claim would force the promisor to do something which he never contracted to do, *viz.* to pay the promisee when he contracted to pay the third party; and one view therefore is that the promisee cannot sue for the agreed sum,[255] save in the exceptional circumstances to be described later in this Chapter.[256] But the objection to allowing the promisee to claim payment to himself loses most of its force where the promisor would not in fact be prejudiced by having to pay the promisee rather than the third party (so long as such payment gave him a good discharge). In such a case, the contract may, on its true construction, be one to pay the third party or as the promisee shall direct,[257] so that it would not be inconsistent with its terms to allow the promisee to claim payment for himself. The promisee is a *fortiori* so entitled where the contract is one to pay him (the promisee) as nominee for the third party[258]: such a contract is not one for the benefit of a third party[259] in the sense of one purporting to give that party a right against the promisor. 18–046

Damages in respect of promisee's loss. The promisee might claim damages where he has suffered loss as a result of the promisor's failure to perform in favour of the third party. But in *Beswick v Beswick* the majority of the House of Lords[260] evidently thought that no such loss had been or would be suffered by the promisee, and that accordingly the damages recoverable by the uncle's (*i.e.*, the promisee's) estate for breach of the nephew's promise would be merely nominal. 18–047

---

253 Below, paras 27–049—27–053.

254 As there would be no "total failure of consideration"; and as "rescission" for breach could probably not be allowed unless the third party was willing to restore any performance received.

255 See *Coulls v Bagot's Executor and Trustee Co Ltd* [1967] A.L.R. 385 at 409–411; *cf. Beswick v Beswick* [1968] A.C. at 88, 101 (dealing with the remedy of damages: see below, para.18–047).

256 See *Cleaver v Mutual Reserve Fund Life Association* [1892] 1 Q.B. 147; *cf.* below, para.18–084.

257 *Tradigrain SA v King Diamond Shipping SA* (*The Spiros C*) [2000] 2 Lloyd's Rep. 319 at 331; below, para.18–073.

258 *The Turiddu* [1999] 2 Lloyd's Rep. 401 at 407.

259 *ibid.*

260 Lord Pearce thought that damages would be substantial: [1968] A.C. 58 at 88. It was not entirely clear whether he had in mind an action for *damages* or one for the *agreed sum*: see his reference at p.87 to "separate actions as each sum falls due".

Lord Upjohn explained that this would be the case because the promisee "died *without any assets* save and except the agreement which he hoped would keep him and then his widow for their lives."[261] It seems possible to deduce from this statement that damages might have been substantial if the promisee had had other assets—either because the widow might then have had a claim against those assets if the promise were not performed[262] or because the promisee or his estate would in fact, even if not legally obliged to do so, have made some other, wholly voluntary, provision for the widow. The loss suffered by the promisee would be the cost of making an alternative provision, and there is some authority for the view that damages for breach of contract may be recovered to compensate for such loss even though the provision is wholly voluntary.[263] *A fortiori* the promisee can recover substantial damages where he is under a legal obligation to make a payment to the third party and where this obligation would have been discharged if the promisor had paid the third party in accordance with the contract. Where loss is suffered by the promisee, substantial damages can, moreover, be recovered by the promisee even though the promisee is legally bound to pay those damages over to a third party. Thus where loss of income was suffered by the estate of a deceased person as a result of the negligence of solicitors retained by that person's executrix to administer the estate, the executrix recovered substantial damages in respect of that loss in her representative capacity as owner of the deceased's estate.[264] It made no difference that she was not entitled beneficially to the estate and was therefore obliged, as executrix, to hand over the damages to the residuary legatee under the deceased's will.

18–048 **Whose loss?** The question whether the loss had been suffered by the promisee or by a third party arose in *De Jongh Weill v Mean Fiddler Holdings*[265] where the claimant had been engaged by the defendant company as a financial consultant. He was to be remunerated partly by a specified fee but also on the terms that "warrants to purchase shares in the [defendant] company will be granted to a company representing my family interests."[266] It was clear from the antecedent negotiations that the grant of these warrants was to be the claimant's principal remuneration[267] and that "it was *he* who was to benefit in reality and the idea of

[261] [1968] A.C. 58 at 102 (italics supplied). See further para.18–062, below.

[262] *e.g.* under (at that time) the Inheritance (Family Provision) Act 1938, now Inheritance (Provision for Family and Dependants) Act 1975.

[263] *Admiralty Commissioners v SS. Amerika* [1917] A.C. 38, 61, where the actual decision was that payments voluntarily made to the victim of an alleged *tort* could not be recovered; on this point, see also *Esso Petroleum Co Ltd v Hall Russell & Co Ltd* [1989] A.C. 643 (where there was no causal link between the voluntary payment and the defendants' wrongdoing). For the possibility of recovering, as damages for breach of contract, voluntary payments to or benefits voluntarily conferred on, third parties see also *Banco de Portugal v Waterlow & Son Ltd* [1932] A.C. 452, where a bank recovered damages in respect of payments which it was not legally liable to make: below, para.26–104. And see the discussion in paras 18–053 and 18–058—18–066 below of *Linden Gardens Trust Ltd v Lenesta Sludge Disposals Ltd* [1994] A.C. 85 and of *Alfred McAlpine Construction Ltd v Panatown Ltd* [2001] 1 A.C. 518.

[264] *Chappell v Somers & Blake* [2003] EWHC 1644 (Ch), [2004] Ch. 19.

[265] [2005] All E.R. (D) 331 (Jul); Q.B.D., 22 July 2005; for earlier proceedings in this case, see [2003] EWCA Civ 1058.

[266] [2005] All E.R. (D) 331 (Jul), at [2], [25].

[267] *ibid.*, at [30].

a nominated company was just the way *he* was to be paid."[268] Judge Bruce Coles Q.C., after referring[269] to part of the discussion of the promisee's remedies in the previous edition of this book,[270] held that the loss resulting from the defendant's failure to issue the warrants to the nominated company had been suffered by the claimant himself and that damages in respect of it were therefore recoverable under the principle stated in paragraph 18–047 above.

Damages in respect of third party's loss: general rule. The starting point of the discussion in paragraphs 18–049 to 18–067 is the general rule that, in an action for damages, the claimant cannot recover more than the amount required to compensate him for his loss,[271] so that the a promisee cannot, in general, recover damages for breach of a contract made for the benefit of a third party[272] in respect of loss suffered, not by the promisee himself, but by that third party.[273] This general rule, was, indeed, denied by Lord Denning M.R. in *Jackson v Horizon Holidays Ltd*,[274] where the defendants had contracted with the claimant to provide holiday accommodation for the claimant, his wife and their two three-year-old children; and it was assumed that the wife and children were not parties to the contract.[275] The accommodation fell seriously short of the standard required by the contract, and the claimant recovered damages including £500 for "mental distress."[276] Lord Denning said that this sum would have been excessive compensation for the claimant's own distress.[277] He nevertheless upheld the award on the ground that the claimant had made a contract for the benefit both of himself and of his wife and children[278]; and that he could recover damages in respect of their loss as well as in respect of his own. But the authorities cited in 18–049

[268] *ibid.*

[269] *ibid.*, at [26].

[270] *i.e.*, 29th ed., paras 18–042 to 18–047.

[271] Below, para.26–020; *cf. White v Jones* [1995] 2 A.C. 207 (above, para.18–037), where the damages recoverable by the estate of the other contracting party would have been no more than nominal.

[272] *A fortiori*, a promisee cannot recover damages in respect of loss suffered by a third party *other* than one for whose benefit the contract was made. Thus if A agrees to buy goods from B which B intends to acquire from C, and A repudiates the contract so that B does not in turn buy the goods from C, then B cannot recover damages in respect of any loss suffered by C: *And so to Bed Ltd v Dixon*, Transcript November 21, 2000 at 46–49, 54 (Ch. D.). Similarly, it has been said that B could not recover damages in respect of loss suffered by B's intended supplier C in a case falling within an exception to the general rule stated in the present paragraph: *Smithkline Beecham plc v Apotex Ltd* [2006] EWCA Civ 658, [2007] Ch.71 at [94], where the main reason for actual decision was that there was no contract between A and B (at [86], [88]). Of course if B had *contracted* to acquire the goods from C and was in consequence of A's repudiation liable in damages to C, then B could recover the amount for which he was so liable from A as damages in respect of his (B's) *own* loss.

[273] *Albacruz (Cargo Owners) v Albazero (Owners) (The Albazero)* [1977] A.C. 774, 846; *Linden Gardens* case, above, n.263 at 114, and see below, para.18–058, at nn.335 and 336; Weir [1977] C.L.J. 24. See also *Ramco (UK) Ltd v International Insurance Co of Hanover* [2004] EWCA Civ 675, [2004] 2 All E.R. (Comm) 866 at [32]; the actual decision (that an insurance policy did not cover a third party's loss) turned on the wording of the policy.

[274] [1975] 1 W.L.R. 1468; Yates (1975) 39 M.L.R. 202.

[275] Contrast *Daly v General Steam Navigation Co Ltd (The Dragon)* [1979] 1 Lloyd's Rep. 257, 262; affirmed [1980] 2 Lloyd's Rep. 415, above, para.18–012.

[276] [1975] 1 W.L.R. 1468 at 1472.

[277] *ibid.*, at 1474.

[278] *ibid.*; *cf. McCall v Abelesz* [1976] Q.B. 585, 594.

support of this conclusion seem to contradict, rather than to favour, it.[279] Moreover, in *Beswick v Beswick*[280] a majority of the House of Lords said that the promisee's estate could have recovered no more than nominal damages as it had suffered no loss.[281] This is scarcely consistent with the view that the promisee under a contract for the benefit of a third party is, as a general rule, entitled to damages in respect of the third party's loss. James L.J. in *Jackson's* case seems to have regarded the £500 as compensation for the claimant's own distress.[282] No doubt this was increased by his witnessing the distress suffered by his wife and children; and if the promisee himself suffers loss he should not be prevented from recovering for it in full merely because the contract was in part one for the benefit of third parties, who also suffered loss.[283]

18–050 Lord Denning's approach to the question of damages in *Jackson's* case was disapproved by the House of Lords in *Woodar Investment Development Ltd v Wimpey Construction Co Ltd*[284]; though the actual decision in *Jackson's* case was supported on the ground that the damages there were awarded in respect of the claimant's own loss[285]; or alternatively on the ground that cases such as the booking of family holidays or ordering meals in restaurants[286] might "call for special treatment."[287] In the *Woodar* case itself, a contract for the sale of land provided that on completion the purchaser should pay £850,000 to the vendor and also £150,000 to a third party. The vendor claimed damages on the footing that the purchaser had wrongfully repudiated the contract and the actual decision was that there had been no such repudiation,[288] so that the issue of damages did not arise. But the question, what damages would have been recoverable in the *Woodar* case if there had been a wrongful repudiation, was described as "one of

---

279 Lord Denning M.R. relied on a dictum of Lush L.J. in *Lloyd's v Harper* (1880) 16 Ch.D. 290, 331, said to have been quoted by Lord Pearce in *Beswick v Beswick* "with considerable approval": [1975] 1 W.L.R. 1468 at 1473. In fact, Lord Pearce said that the dictum "cannot be accepted without qualification and regardless of the context": [1968] A.C. 58, 88; *cf. ibid.* at 101; he agreed with the view expressed in *Coulls v Bagot's Executor & Trustee Co Ltd* [1967] A.L.R. 385, 411, that Lush L.J.'s dictum must be confined to cases in which the contract creates a trust in favour of the third party: below, paras 18–078—18–086. *Lloyd's v Harper*, above, was treated as a case of trust by Fry J. at first instance, and by James and Cotton L.JJ in the Court of Appeal. Cases of trust fall within the exceptions stated in para.18–052, below to the general rule that in an action for damages the claimant can recover damages only in respect of his *own* loss.

280 [1968] A.C. 58.

281 Above, para.18–047.

282 [1975] 1 W.L.R. 1468 at 1474.

283 *cf. Radford v de Froberville* [1977] 1 W.L.R. 1262 (damages for failure to perform a contract to build a wall not reduced merely because the promisee had entered into the contract not only for his own benefit, but also for that of his tenants).

284 [1980] 1 W.L.R. 277.

285 *ibid.* at 283, 293, 297. Where a contract is made with a company and the breach causes loss to its subsidiary, damages can be recovered by the company since the value of its holding in the subsidiary will be reduced in consequence of the loss: *George Fischer (Great Britain) Ltd v Multi Construction Ltd* [1995] 1 B.C.L.C. 260.

286 *cf. Lockett v A.M. Charles Ltd* [1938] 4 All E.R. 170, where agency reasoning was used in such a situation.

287 [1980] 1 W.L.R. 277, 283. *cf. Calabar Properties Ltd v Stitcher* [1984] 1 W.L.R. 287, 290 where it was not disputed that a tenant's damages for her landlord's breach of his covenant to repair should include compensation for ill-health suffered by her husband.

288 Below, para.24–018.

great doubt and difficulty"[289]; presumably it would turn on such factors as whether the vendor was under a legal obligation to ensure that the third party received the payment, or whether, on the purchaser's failure to make the payment, the vendor had actually made it, or procured it to be made, from other resources available to him.

Criticism of the general rule. The assumption underlying *Woodar Investment Development Ltd v Wimpey Construction UK Ltd* thus seems to be that damages for breach of a contract for the benefit of a third party cannot, as a general rule, be recovered by the promisee in respect of a loss suffered only by the third party. At the same time, this position was described as "most unsatisfactory"[290] and said to be in need of reconsideration, either by the legislature or by the House of Lords in its judicial capacity.[291] It is unsatisfactory because it can give rise to what has been called a "legal black hole"[292] that is, to a situation in which the promisor has committed a plain breach which has caused loss to the third party whom the contracting parties intended to benefit[293] but none to the promisee, and in which no other remedy[294] (than damages in respect of the third party's loss) is available against the promisor. The general rule was again criticised in *Forster v Silvermere Golf and Equestrian Centre*,[295] where the claimant transferred land to the defendant who undertook to build a house on it and to allow the claimant and her children to live in it rent free for life. It was held that the claimant could recover damages in respect of her own loss but not in respect of any rights of occupation which her children might have enjoyed after her death. Dillon J. described this result as "a blot on our law and most unjust." It is submitted (on the basis of the explanation of *Beswick v Beswick*[296] given above)[297] that any expenses incurred by the claimant in making alternative provision for the accommodation of her children after her death could have been recovered as forming part of her own loss.[298] On the other hand, it is unlikely that the claimant could have secured the intended benefit for her children by seeking specific performance, for it does not seem that the defendant's obligation to build was defined with sufficient precision to enable the court to enforce it specifically.[299] 18–051

Damages in respect of third party's loss: exceptions in general. Judicial awareness of the unsatisfactory results which can flow from the general rule stated in para.18–051 above has led the courts to create a number of exceptions to that rule. For example substantial damages for breach of contract can be 18–052

[289] [1980] 1 W.L.R. 277 at 284.

[290] [1980] 1 W.L.R. 277 at 291; *cf.* 297–298; 300–301.

[291] *cf.* above, para.18–020 at nn.104–107.

[292] *Darlington B.C. Wiltshier (Northern) Ltd* [1995] 1 W.L.R. 68 at 79; for the origins of this metaphor, see *Alfred McAlpine Construction Ltd v Panatown Ltd* [2001] 1 A.C. 518 at 529

[293] See above, para.18–049 at n.272 for this requirement.

[294] *e.g.*, by way of specific performance, as in *Beswick v Beswick* [1968] A.C. 58

[295] (1981) 125 S.J. 397.

[296] [1968] A.C. 58.

[297] Above, para.18–047.

[298] Such a result could also, on the facts of the case, follow from the reasoning in para.18–054, below.

[299] Below, para.27–028.

recovered by a trustee even though the loss is suffered by his *cestui que trust*[300]; by an agent even though the loss is suffered by his undisclosed principal[301]; by a local authority even though the loss is suffered by its inhabitants[302]; and by a shipper of goods for breach of his contract of carriage with the shipowner in respect of the loss of the goods, even though that loss is suffered by a person to whom the shipper has sold the goods and to whom the risk and property in them has passed but who has not himself acquired any rights under the contract of carriage against the ship-owner[303]: it will be convenient to refer to this last rule as "the *Albazero* exception", after the leading modern case in which it is recognised.[304] In all these exceptional cases, a person recovers substantial damages for breach of contract, even though the breach caused no loss to him, but only to a third party. A similar possibility is recognised in the law of tort which, like the law of contract, starts with the principle that the claimant can recover "no more and no less than he has lost."[305] But where a third party voluntarily renders services in caring for a claimant who has suffered personal injury as a result of a tort, the claimant can recover damages from the wrongdoer in respect of the value of those services; and the "central objective" of such an award has been described as "compensating the voluntary carer,"[306] for whom such damages must be held on trust by the claimant.[307] In substance, though not in form, the claimant in such a case recovers damages in respect of the loss which has been

---

[300] See, for example, below para.18–083. *cf.*; *Pan Atlantic Insurance Co Ltd v Pine Top Insurance Co Ltd* [1988] 2 Lloyd's Rep. 505; below para.18–128. According to *Rolls Royce Power Engineering plc v Ricardo Consulting Engineers Ltd* [2003] EWHC 2871 (TCC), [2004] 2 All E.R. (Comm) 129 a contracting party cannot recover damages in respect of the third party's loss where the other contracting party did not, when the contract was made, know or have reason to know that the former party was contracting as trustee.

[301] See *Siu Yin Kwan v Eastern Insurance Co Ltd* [1994] 2 A.C. 199, 207.

[302] *St Albans C.C. v International Computers Ltd* [1996] 4 All E.R. 481.

[303] *Dunlop v Lambert* (1839) 2 Cl. & F. 626, 627 (as to which see *Alfred McAlpine Construction Ltd v Panatown Ltd* [2001] 1 A.C. 518 at 523 *et seq*). *cf. Obestain Inc. v National Mineral Development Corp. Ltd (The Sanix Ace)* [1987] 1 Lloyd's Rep. 465; *Wibau Maschinenfabric Hartman SA v Mackinnon Mackenzie & Co (The Chanda)* [1989] 2 Lloyd's Rep. 494 (overruled on another point in *Daewoo Heavy Industries Ltd v Klipriver Shipping Ltd (The Kapitan Petko Voivoda)* [2003] EWCA Civ 451; [2003] 1 All E.R. (Comm) 801). The rule was recognised by the House of Lords in *Albacruz (Cargo Owners) v Albazero (Owners) (The Albazero)* [1977] A.C. 774, but held inapplicable as the buyer had acquired his own contractual rights against the shipowner under Bills of Lading Act 1855, s.1 (now repealed and replaced by Carriage of Goods by Sea Act 1992); Weir [1977] C.L.J. 24. In the *Rolls Royce Power* case, above, n.300 the rule in *Dunlop v Lambert* (above) was said at [124] to apply only if, at the time of the contract, it was "in the actual contemplation of the parties that an identified third party or a third party who was a member of an identified class might suffer damage in the event of a breach of the contract." In the case of goods carried under a transferable bill of lading, this requirement will generally be satisfied since the transfer of such a bill must be within the carrier's contemplation. For discussion of another aspect of *Dunlop v Lambert*, above, see *Scottish & Newcastle International Ltd v Othon Ghalanos Ltd* [2008] UKHL 55, [2008] 1 Lloyd's Rep. 462 at [12], [39]–[40]. In the case of contracts to which the Carriage of Goods by Sea Act 1992 applies, a special statutory exception is created by s.2(4) of the Act to the general rule that a person can recover damages only in respect of his own loss; for a full discussion of this subsection, see *Carver on Bills of Lading*, 2nd ed., 2001, paras 5–075—5–082.

[304] *The Albazero*, above, n.303.

[305] *Hunt v Severs* [1994] 2 A.C. 350, 357.

[306] *ibid*. at 363.

[307] *Hughes v Lloyd* [2007] EWHC 3133 (Ch), [2008] W.T.L.R. 473; and see below, para.18–076. No such damages can be recovered where the voluntary carer is the tortfeasor: *Hunt v Severs* [1994] 2 A.C. 350; below para.18–076, n.434.

suffered by the third party in (for example) giving up his or her job so as to look after the injured claimant.

18–053 **Further exceptions: building contracts.** The list of exceptions stated in para.18–052 above should not be regarded as closed and the possibility of extending them or of creating further exceptions is illustrated by a line of building contract cases beginning with *Linden Gardens Trust v Lenesta Sludge Disposals Ltd*.[308] The speeches in that case raise the further question (also discussed in a number of later cases[309]) how far the process of extending the development there initiated can be taken in the direction of allowing the promisee to recover damages in respect of the third party's loss merely because the contract which has been broken was one for the benefit of a third party. In the *Linden Gardens* case, a building contract between parties described in it as employer and contractor provided for work to be done by the contractor by way of developing a site owned by the employer as shops, offices and flats. The site (but not the benefit of the contract) was later transferred by the employer to a third party, and it was assumed[310] for the purpose of the proceedings that the third party had suffered financial loss as a result of having to remedy breaches of the building contract committed after the transfer. In an action for breach of the building contract brought by the employer, the contractor argued that no loss had been suffered by the employer as he was no longer owner of the land when the alleged breaches occurred, and that the employer was therefore entitled to no more than nominal damages. In the House of Lords, this argument was rejected, and the employer's claim upheld,[311] on two distinct grounds.

18–054 **The "broader ground": promisee's expense of curing the breach.** Lord Griffiths upheld the employer's claim on what has become known as the "broader ground"[312] that the employer "ha[d] suffered financial loss because he ha[d] to spend money to give him the benefit of the bargain which the defendant had promised but failed to deliver."[313] He added that "the court will of course wish to be satisfied that the repairs have been or are likely to be carried out."[314]

---

[308] [1994] 1 A.C. 85.

[309] Below, paras 18–056 to 18–067.

[310] The case is reported on a preliminary issue of law, so that the alleged facts had not been proved.

[311] *cf. IMI Cornelius (UK) v Alan J. Bluor* (1993) 57 B.L.R. 108.

[312] *Linden Gardens* case [1994] A.C. 85 at 96–97; *Alfred McAlpine Construction Ltd v Panatown Ltd* [2001] 1 A.C. 518, *e.g.* at 532; all the other members of the House of Lords accepted and used this terminology.

[313] [1994] A.C. 85, 97. In fact the third party had reimbursed the employer in respect of this expenditure: see *ibid.* at 422; but this did not affect the question of liability.

[314] *ibid.* This requirement has been doubted on the ground that, in general, the court is "not concerned with what the plaintiff proposes to do with this damages:" *Darlington B.C. v Wiltshier Northern Ltd* [1995] 1 W.L.R. 68, 80. But it seems, with respect, that Lord Griffiths' requirement is concerned, not with the question what the plaintiff proposes to do with the damages, but with the question whether he has suffered any loss. In *Alfred McAlpine Construction Ltd v Panatown Ltd* [2001] 1 A.C. 518 at 592 Lord Millett (dissenting) rejects the above reasoning, apparently on the ground that the promisee is "bound to mitigate his loss" and "cannot increase it by entering into other arrangements." But, with respect, the mitigation rules only require the injured party to act reasonably (below, para.26–104) and in cases of the present kind this requirement would normally be satisfied where he made alternative provision to secure for the third party the benefit which the promisor has, in breach of the contract, failed to provide.

This approach is, it is submitted, consistent with the explanation given in *Beswick v Beswick*[315] of the fact that the damages there were regarded as no more than nominal: the court there could not be satisfied that the substitute provision for the widow was likely to be made, precisely because the promisee lacked the means to make it.[316] The essence of Lord Griffiths' reasoning is that the promisee recovers damages in respect of the loss which he himself suffers in ensuring that the third party receives the intended benefit. The "broader ground" therefore cannot apply where there is no practical possibility of curing the breach and so of securing the intended benefit to the third party. This was the position in the "family holiday" cases discussed in para.18–050 above.

18–055 **The "narrower ground": loss suffered by third party as transferee of the affected property.** Although Lord Keith had "much sympathy"[317] with, and Lord Bridge was "much attracted by,"[318] Lord Griffiths' reasoning, they (as well as Lord Ackner) preferred to base their decision on the "narrower ground"[319] stated by Lord Browne-Wilkinson. This treats the loss as having been suffered by the third party rather than by the employer, but concludes that the employer could nevertheless recover substantial damages as the case fell within the rationale of *Albazero* exception[320] to the general rule that a party can recover damages only in respect of his own loss. The rationale of this exception was that, in the carriage of goods cases to which it applies, the shipper and carrier must have contemplated that property in the goods might be transferred to third parties after the contract had been made, and that the shipper must therefore be treated in law as having made the contract of carriage for the benefit of all persons who might after the time of contracting acquire interests in the goods.[321] This rationale applied equally to the facts of the *Linden Gardens* case since the contractor could foresee that parts of the new development were going to be "occupied and possibly purchased by third parties" so that "it could be foreseen that damage caused by a breach would cause loss to a later owner."[322] The contractor could also foresee that a later owner would not have acquired rights under the building contract against the contractor since that contract expressly prohibited assignment by the employer without the contractor's written consent, which had not been sought. The effect of the *Linden Gardens* case was thus to extend the scope of the *Albazero* exception from contracts for the carriage of goods by sea to contracts generally, but it was consistent with two factors which had restricted the scope of that exception: namely that (a) the loss or damage was caused to property which had been transferred by one of the contracting parties to the third party; and (b) the third party had not acquired any rights under the building contract[323] and it

---

315 [1968] A.C. 58.

316 *ibid.* at 102; above para.18–047.

317 [1994] 1 A.C. 85, 95.

318 *ibid.* at 96.

319 *Alfred McAlpine Construction Ltd v Panatown Ltd* [2001] 1 A.C. 518, 575.

320 Above, para.18–052.

321 *The Albazero* [1977] A.C. 774 at 847; *HSBC Rail (UK) Ltd v Network Rail Infrastructure Ltd* [2005] EWCA Civ 1437, [2006] 1 W.L.R. 643 at [23].

322 [1994] 1 A.C. 85, 114.

323 *cf.* above, para.18–052 at n.303.

was foreseeable (by reason of the prohibition against assignment) that he would not do so. The significance of these factors is further considered in two later cases to be discussed in paras 18–056 and 18–058, below.

No transfer of affected property from promisee to third party. In *Darlington B.C. v Wiltshier Northern Ltd*[324] a local authority (the council) wished to develop land which it already owned. The building work was to be done by the defendant; finance was to be provided by a bank but this could not be done in the most obvious way, by a loan from the bank to the council, since such an arrangement would have violated government restrictions on local authority borrowing. The transaction was therefore cast in the form of two contracts: (1) a building contract in which the bank was the employer and the defendant the building contractor, and (2) a contract between the council and the bank, by which the bank undertook to procure the erection of the buildings on the site, to pay all sums due under the building contract and to assign to the council the benefit of any rights against the defendant to which the bank might be entitled at the time of the assignment. Clause 4(5) of this second contract provided that the bank was not to be liable to the council "for any incompleteness or defect in the building work," and it was this provision which was the principal source of the difficulties in the case. The bank duly assigned its rights against the defendant to the council which claimed damages as such assignee from the defendant in respect of defects in the work. Since an assignee cannot recover more than the assignor could have been done if there had been no assignment,[325] the question therefore arose what the bank could have recovered; and it was argued that it could have recovered no more than nominal damages since it had suffered no loss, having no interest in the land (or buildings) on which the work had been done and being protected by clause 4(5) from any liability to the council for defects in the work.[326] But the Court of Appeal rejected this argument and held that the bank could have recovered substantial damages from the defendant in respect of the council's loss and that it was this right which had been assigned to the council. This amounted to an extension[327] of the *Linden Gardens* case to a situation in which there was *no* transfer of the property affected by the breach from the promisee to the third party. This extension was later approved by the House of Lords,[328] so that, at least in the context of defective performance of 18–056

[324] [1995] 1 W.L.R. 68.

[325] See below, para.18–057.

[326] These difficulties are not, it is submitted, removed by Dillon L.J.'s alternative ground for decision, *viz.* that the bank was constructive trustee for the council of its contractual rights against the defendant: this reasoning merely pushes the enquiry back to the question what (if anything) the bank could have recovered from the defendant.

[327] [1995] 1 W.L.R. 68 at 79, *per* Steyn L.J. Dillon L.J. regarded the result in the *Darlington* case as a "direct application" of the *Linden Gardens* case: *ibid*, at p.75. Waite L.J. expressed his agreement with both the other judgments, though his reasoning seems to be closer to that of Dillon L.J. than to that of Steyn L.J. See also *John Harris Partnership v Groveworld Ltd* [1999] P.N.L.R. 697 (developer entitled to recover from architect retained by him loss suffered in part by a third party who had financed the building project).

[328] *Alfred McAlpine Construction Ltd v Panatown Ltd* [2001] A.C. 518 at 531, 566 *per* Lords Clyde and Jauncey; ibid, pp.545, 584, *per* Lords Goff and Millett (dissenting).

building contracts[329] such a transfer is no longer a necessary condition of the promisee's right to recover damages in respect of the third party's loss.

18–057 **Assignment of promisee's contractual right after transfer of affected property.** The effect of an assignment by the promisee (A) of his contractual rights against the promisor (B) to the third party (C) is further considered in *Offer-Hoare v Larkstore Ltd*.[330] In that case, a landowner (A) had commissioned B to report on the suitability of a site for development. The site was later sold by A to C who began work on it; during this work, there was a landslip which damaged adjoining properties, the owners of which made claims against C. A then assigned his rights under his contract with B to C who, as such assignee, claimed damages from B for breach of B's contract with A. B argued that C could recover no more than the loss that could have been recovered by A from B at the time of the assignment and that A at that time no longer had any claim for substantial damages against B since A had ceased to own the site before the assignment and before the landslip. The argument was rejected on the ground that A had acquired a cause of action for breach of contract against B when the report was produced and could have recovered substantial "damages for the landslip"[331] if A had remained owner of the land. The principle that an assignee cannot recover more than the assignee did not apply. The purpose of that principle was to protect the debtor from having to pay more to the assignee than he would have had to pay to the assignor "*had the assignment never taken place*. The principle is not intended to enable the contract breaker/debtor to escape all legal liability for breach of contract."[332] As B's exposure to the damages claimed was "the consequence of the landslip" and not "the consequence of the assignment,"[333] the principle did not protect B, so that C, standing in the shoes of A, recovered substantial damages from B.

18–058 **Third party having independent contractual rights against promisor.** In *Alfred McAlpine Construction Ltd v Panatown Ltd*[334] (the *Panatown* case), the facts resembled those of the *Darlington* case in that a building contract was again made, not between the building contractor and the company which owned the site (the owner), but between that contractor and another company (the employer) associated with the owner; the object of adopting this tripartite structure was to avoid VAT. On the day on which this contract was made, a separate contract (the "Duty of Care Deed") was made between the owner and the contractor. The obligations imposed on the contractor by this Deed were not precisely co-terminous with those imposed on him by the building contract; and the Deed did not, while the building contract did, contain an arbitration clause. The employer

[329] *Quaere* whether this extension will be applied in the carriage by sea context in which the exception originated: see *Carver on Bills of Lading*, 2nd ed (2005) para.5–062.

[330] [2006] EWCA Civ 1079, [2006] 1 W.L.R. 2926.

[331] *ibid.*, at [33].

[332] *ibid.*, at [43], *per* Mummery L.J., italics supplied; *cf. ibid.*, at 87, *per* Rix L.J.

[333] *ibid.*, at [43].

[334] [2001] 1 A.C. 518, discussed by Coote (2001) 117 l.Q.R. 81; reversing (1998) 58 Const.L.R. 58, discussed by Treitel (1998) L.Q.R. 527; for further proceedings, see [2001] EWCA Civ 284; (2001) 76 Con.L.R. 222.

alleged that the building work was seriously defective and in arbitration proceedings claimed damages from the contractor, who argued that the employer should recover no more than nominal damages since any loss resulting from the alleged defects in the work had been suffered, not by the employer (as the employer had never owned the property), but by the owner. The House of Lords, by a majority, upheld the contractor's argument and so rejected the employer's claim for substantial damages in respect of the owner's loss. It was accepted by the majority[335] and by one of the dissentients[336] that, as a general rule, a contracting party could not recover damages in respect of loss suffered, not by himself, but by a third party; and the question therefore arose whether the case could be brought within an exception to that general rule. This raised, in turn, the question whether either of the grounds for the decision in the *Linden Gardens* case[337] supported the employer's claim. It will be recalled that the "narrow" ground for that decision was derived from the "*Albazero* exception" under which a shipper of goods can sometimes recover damages in respect of a third party's loss.[338] That exception is, however, subject to the restriction that it does not apply where the third party had himself acquired contractual rights against the carrier,[339] usually by the transfer to the third party of a bill of lading.[340] In the *Panatown* case, the majority held (and the dissentients accepted) that the case fell within this restriction, so that the "*Albazero* exception" (and hence the "narrower ground" in the *Linden Gardens* case) did not apply because the Duty of Care Deed gave the owner an independent contractual right against the contractor. This point was, moreover, decisive even though that right did not arise under a *building* contract, so that in this respect the restriction was somewhat expanded: in the carriage by sea cases, the restriction normally[341] came into operation because the third party had acquired rights under a contract *of carriage*. Nevertheless, it is respectfully submitted that this aspect of the *Panatown* case is consistent with the rationale of the restriction. In the carriage by sea cases, this could and did apply even though the *content* of the third party's contractual right against the carrier was not the same as that of the shipper's right[342]; and it was based on the reasoning that, where the third party had its own contractual rights against the carrier, the exception did not apply "because it was not needed."[343] It was not needed because, where the third party had its own contractual rights against the party in breach, there was no risk of the "legal black hole" which had

---

[335] [2001] 1 A.C. 518, 522, 563, 575.

[336] Lord Millet, *ibid.*, 580–581; Lord Goff is more skeptical: see *ibid.*, at 538–539.

[337] [1994] 1 A.C. 85, above, para.18–053; referred to as the *St Martin* case throughout the speeches in the *Panatown* case.

[338] *The Albazero* [1977] A.C. 774; above, para.18–052.

[339] This was the position in *The Albazero*, above, itself, where the exception accordingly did not apply.

[340] Above, para.18–052, n.303.

[341] The restriction could also apply where the third party's contractual right against the carrier arose under an implied contract of the kind illustrated by *Brandt v Liverpool, etc., S.N. Co* [1924] 1 K.B. 575; see *The Albazero* [1977] A.C.A 774, 847.

[342] As in *The Albazero* [1977] A.C. 774.

[343] *Panatown* case [2001] 1 A.C. 518, 575; *The Albazero*, above, 846–848. The exception is similarly "not needed" where full effect can be given to the broken promise by an award of damages for the breach to the promisee: see *Smithkline Beecham plc v Apotex Europe Ltd* [2006] EWCA Civ 658, [2007] Ch.71, below, para.18–059 at n.348 and para.18–067.

driven judges to create exceptions to the general rule that a contracting party can recover damages only in respect of his own loss.[344]

18–059 The majority in the *Panatown* case further held that the existence of the third party's rights against the contractor under the Duty of Care Deed also precluded the employer from recovering damages under the "broader ground"[345] given by Lord Griffiths in the *Linden Gardens* case. In view of the existence of those rights, the employer had no pecuniary interest in curing the defects in the contractor's work.[346] Hence he neither had suffered nor would suffer any loss of his own, in consequence of the contractor's breach, and under the "broader ground" it is in respect of his *own* (not of the third party's) loss that the promisee recovers damages. This conclusion can, on the facts of the *Panatown* case, be supported for two further reasons. First, the creation or extension of exceptions to the general rule that a party can recover damages only in respect of his own loss is and should be driven and limited by necessity[347]: that is, by the need to guard against the risk of "legal black holes" of the kind described above; and in the *Panatown* case there was no such risk.[348] Secondly, the decision gives effect to the "contractual scheme"[349] created by the parties; and this point, so far from being undermined by the fact that the contractor's obligations to the owner under the Duty of Care Deed were not precisely co-terminous with his obligations to the employer under the building contract, is reinforced by this fact. As the parties had taken the "plain and deliberate course"[350] of giving the owner a "distinct entitlement"[351] against the contractor in respect of defects in the work, and as this entitlement was to be governed by the terms of one contract (the Duty of Care Deed), it followed that there was no good practical reason for holding the contractor liable in respect of the same defects on the terms of another contract (the building contract) for substantial damages to the employer, to whom these

[344] *Darlington B.C. v Wiltshier Northern Ltd* [1995] 1 W.L.R. 68, 79; above, para.18–051 at n.292. The reasoning of the *Panatown* case has likewise been said not to apply where the third party has its own independent right against the promisor, not in contract, but in tort, *Riyad Bank v Ahli United Bank* [2005] EWHC 279 (Comm), [2005] 2 Lloyd's Rep. 409 at [173] (affd without reference to this point [2006] EWCA Civ 780, [2006] 2 Lloyd's Rep. 292).

[345] Above, para.18–054; *Alfred McAlpine Construction Ltd v Panatown Ltd* [2001] 1 A.C. 518, 532.

[346] *ibid*, 574 and 577 (*per* Lords Jauncey and Browne-Wilkinson).

[347] See the references given in nn.343 and 344, above.

[348] *Panatown* case [2001] 1 A.C. 518, 574, *per* Lord Jauncey. There would likewise be no such "legal black hole" where A's only interest in the performance of the contract was to avoid the prejudice which failure in its performance might cause to himself and he had a remedy in damages in respect of that prejudice against B: see *Smithkline Beecham plc v Apotex Europe Ltd* [2006] EWCA Civ 658, [2007] Ch. 71 at [94], and below, para.18–067.

[349] *Panatown* case [2001] 1 A.C. at 577, *per* Lord Browne-Wilkinson; and see 76 Con. L.R 224 at 38 ("made their contractual bed") *cf. Henderson v Merrett Syndicates Ltd* [1992] 2 A.C. 145, 195, using the phrase "contractual structure" in the context of the faintly analogous question whether a contract between A and B can impose on a duty of care to C: see above, para.18–023 n.133; *cf. Greater Nottingham Co-operative Society Ltd v Cementation Piling & Foundation Ltd* [1989] Q.B. 71 (tort duty excluded by tripartite contractual structure); and *R.M. Turton & Co Ltd v Kerslake & Partners* [2000] Lloyd's Rep. P.N. 967 (New Zealand Court of Appeal). Contrast *Riyad Bank v Ahli United Bank (UK) plc* [2006] EWCA Civ 780, [2006] 2 Lloyd's Rep. 292 at [31], [32], [42] and [137], where the "contractual structure" did not exclude liability in tort to the third party.

[350] *Panatown* case [2001] 1 A.C. 519, 536, *per* Lord Clyde.

[351] *ibid.*

defects had caused no loss of his own. The fact that the "general rule" stated in para.18–049 above has been the subject of frequent judicial disapproval no doubt gives rise to the temptation to continue the process of eroding it by creating new or extending existing exceptions to it. But that criticism has occurred mainly in cases in which the third party problem was an inescapable consequence of normal commercial factors such as those which existed in the *Linden Gardens* case. The pressure for eroding the unpopular general rule is much less strong where the third party problem is, so to speak, manufactured by the parties for an ulterior motive, such as avoiding Government restrictions on borrowing, as in the *Darlington* case, or avoiding tax,[352] as in the *Panatown* case, where, in the view of the majority, any such pressure was eliminated for the further reason that the third party had his own contractual remedy against the party in breach under a separate contract between these parties.

Outstanding problems. The *Panatown* case is significant not only for the points it decides, but also for those which it leaves open. Some of these are discussed in paras 18–061 to 18–071 below. 18–060

Status of the "broader ground". The first such point relates to the effect of the case on the status of Lord Griffiths' "broader ground" in the *Linden Gardens* case. This ground forms the basis of the two dissenting speeches[353] in the *Panatown* case, and it is not the subject of any adverse comment from the majority,[354] whose speeches do not rule out the possibility of its being applied in the, perhaps more common, situation in which the third party has *no* contractual rights of his own against the promisor in respect of loss suffered by him in consequence of the defective services rendered under the contract between promisor and promisee. It seems that, even in such a situation, the majority would deny the employer's right to recover substantial damages under the "broader ground" unless *either* the condition stated by Lord Griffiths is satisfied, *i.e.* "the repairs have been or are likely to be carried out,"[355] *or* the employer has entered into a separate contract with the owner (the third party) undertaking liability in respect of defects in the contractor's work.[356] Where neither of these requirements is satisfied, the result of allowing the promisee (the employer) to recover the cost of repairs as damages for his own loss would be "unattractive" in that it would enable him to "put the money in his own pocket"[357] without carrying out or paying for the repairs: the technique of requiring him to hold the damages for the third party applies, on the authorities,[358] only where damages are recovered (under one of the exceptions to the general rule) in respect of the *third party's*, not in respect of the promisee's *own* loss. It follows that the requirements 18–061

[352] For the contrary view, see Lord Goff, dissenting, in *The Panatown* case, above, 556–557.
[353] Of Lords Goff and Millett.
[354] Lords Clyde, Jauncey and Browne-Wilkinson.
[355] *Linden Gardens* case [1994] 1 A.C. 85, 97; see further para.18–064 below at n.385.
[356] No such separate contract was established in *Panatown* case: see 76 Con.L.R. 224 at 35.
[357] *Panatown* case [2001] 1 A.C. 518, 571. This possible restriction on the scope of the broader ground is not considered in the discussion of that ground in the further proceedings in that case (76 Con.L.R. 224 at 20), being unnecessary to the decision at this stage.
[358] Below, para.18–076.

stated above[359] do not apply where the promisee's claim can succeed on the "narrow ground": in this respect, that ground is, paradoxically, broader than the "broader ground".

18–062 **Scope of the "broader ground".** If the "broader ground" is accepted for cases in which the third party has *no* contractual rights of his own against the promisor, then a further problem arises as to its scope. The example given by Lord Griffiths in support of the "broader ground" is one in which loss is caused by reason of the *defective* performance of a contract to render *services*.[360] The case put by him[361] is that of a husband who contracts with a builder to have his wife's house repaired; if the builder does the work defectively the husband is (so long as the other requirements of the "broader ground" are satisfied) entitled (in the example) to substantial damages, *i.e.*, to the cost of putting the defects right. Two questions then arise. The first is whether the rationale of the "broader ground" applies to cases in which the breach consists of a simple *failure* or *refusal* to perform (as opposed to cases of defective performance). And the second is whether it applies where the obligation which is not performed is one to do something other than to render services. The two questions come together in a case where, for a consideration provided or to be provided by A, a promise is made by B to A to pay a sum of money to C and B fails or refuses, wholly or in part, to perform that promise. Those were, in substance, the facts of *Beswick v Beswick*[362] where the majority of the House of Lords took the view that the damages recoverable by the estate would be no more than nominal. That may not, indeed, amount to a direct rejection of the "broader ground" in such cases. The reason given in *Beswick v Beswick* for the view that the promisee's damages would there have been merely nominal was that A's estate had no assets out of which it could make the payments to C which B had promised, but failed, to make.[363] But it is not clear whether in substance that reasoning is inconsistent with the "broader ground"; for, if the cost to A of securing the benefit intended for C is to be defrayed *out of the damages*, then it should not matter that A cannot provide that benefit out of his *other* assets, at least so long as A is solvent. The views expressed in *Beswick v Beswick* on the question of damages recoverable by the estate should, it is submitted, now be read subject to developments of the law as to damages in respect of a third party's loss in a number of later cases. The most directly relevant of these is the *Woodar* case[364] where it appears to be assumed that, as a general rule[365] A cannot recover substantial damages from B for B's failure to perform his promise to A to pay a sum of money to C. This

359 Above, at nn.355 and 356.

360 Lord Millett's dissent is restricted to this situation: [2001] 1 A.C. 518, 591; Lord Goff's dissent does not appear to be so restricted: see *ibid.* 545, 552–553.

361 *Linden Gardens* case [1994] 1 A.C. 85, 97. In *Rolls Royce Power Engineering plc v Ricardo Consulting Engineers Ltd* [2003] EWHC 2871 (TCC), [2004] 2 All E.R. (Comm) 129 at [128] it was said that the "broader ground" for the decision in the *Linden Gardens* case was not easy to apply "where the alleged damage is damage to, or failure to repair, property and there is no suggestion of consequential loss." It is, with respect, submitted that this restriction of the "broader ground" appears to be inconsistent with Lord Griffiths' example stated in the text above.

362 [1986] A.C. 58, above, para.18–020.

363 [1986] A.C. 58, 102; above, para.18–047.

364 [1980] 1 W.L.R. 277, above, para.18–050.

365 *i.e.* unless A can show that B's breach caused loss *to* A himself.

conclusion seems to be based on the assumptions that the loss is C's and that A cannot generally recover damages in respect of C's loss. It does not seem to preclude the possibility of A's recovering damages in respect of any loss which he himself might have suffered in consequence of B's breach: *e.g.* because A was under a contractual obligation to procure the payment to C or because A, acting reasonably, has made alternative provision for C.[366] Even in the absence of such factors, it is submitted that, in the light of the developments since the *Woodar* case,[367] the law should take account of the possibility that, unless B were held liable for substantial damages to A, then he might be under no substantial liability at all: in other words, that there would be a "legal black hole." In *Beswick v Beswick* and the *Panatown* case there were no such "black holes": in the former case, because of the availability of a satisfactory remedy for A against B by way of specific performance in favour of C,[368] in the latter because of the availability of a satisfactory remedy for C against B in damages under the separate contract between these parties.[369] If there is no such remedy and if the conditions in which A can (under the "broader ground") recover damages in respect of his *own* loss are not satisfied,[370] then the lack of any such remedy should, it is submitted be a ground for allowing A to claim damages in respect of C's loss. The need to avoid the legal "black hole" should generate this remedy; and this view is supported by *Offer-Hoar v Larkstore Ltd*[371] where, as noted in paragraph 18–057 above, C, suing as A's assignee, recovered substantial damages in respect loss suffered by C. Mummery L.J. justified this conclusion by saying[372] that, if B's contrary argument had succeeded, then B would have been liable to no-one for its breach, a conclusion which was evidently regarded as reducing that argument *ad absurdum*. Rix L.J. similarly said that the courts were willing to develop the law "to prevent the loss caused by the defendant's breach from disappearing into the proverbial black hole"[373] and that they were "anxious to see, if possible, that where a real loss has been suffered, then there should, if at all possible, be a real remedy which directs recovery from the defendant to the party which has suffered the loss."[374] That party, in the situation here under discussion, is C; and where A has suffered no loss himself, the result of allowing him to recover damages in respect of C's loss would also have the advantage of ensuring that these damages (as opposed to damages in respect of loss suffered by A) were to be held for C,[375] thus avoiding the "unattractive" result of allowing A to "put the money in his own pocket."[376]

It is submitted that the same approach is also appropriate to the case where the contract between A and B is one for services for the benefit of C which B simply **18–063**

---

[366] See above, paras 18–047, 18–050 and 18–051.
[367] *i.e.* in the *Linden Gardens* case [1994] A.C. 85, the *Darlington* case [1995] 1 W.L.R. 68 and the *Panatown* case [2001] 1 A.C. 518.
[368] Above, para.18–020.
[369] Above, para.18–057.
[370] See below, paras 18–064—18–067.
[371] [2006] EWCA Civ 1079, [2006] 1 W.L.R. 2926.
[372] At [44].
[373] At [84].
[374] At [85].
[375] Below, para.18–076.
[376] *Panatown* case [2001] 1 A.C. 518, 517.

fails or refuses to perform, instead performing them defectively, as in Lord Griffiths' example,[377] in which it seems to be assumed that A has paid for the work. Lord Griffiths does not discuss the case of total non-performance by B, presumably assuming that in such a case B would not have been paid.[378] If A then gets another builder to do the same work and that other builder charges no more than B would have charged, no loss will be suffered by A or by C; if the other builder charges more than B would have done, A will (subject to questions of mitigation[379] and remoteness) be able to recover the difference as damages for his *own* loss. The position will be substantially the same where A has paid B in advance and B has done no part of the work: in that case A will be entitled to claim restitution of his payment[380] together with damages for his own loss in respect of any extra cost of employing a substitute builder.[381] So in none of these cases of total non-performance is there any "legal black hole" and hence no need to generate a new remedy at the suit of A in respect of C's loss. The more difficult case is that of an advance payment by A followed by *part* performance by B in circumstances in which A himself has suffered no loss, *e.g.* because A was under no obligation to C to secure completion of the performance that B was to render and has neither himself taken any steps to secure that completion nor was likely to do so.[382] In such a case of partial performance there is considerable difficulty in holding B liable for partial restitution[383]; and if, in addition, the remedy of specific performance were not available (*e.g.* because the contract was one for personal services to be rendered by B[384]) then there would be at least a partial "legal black hole" and this fact should (it is again submitted) be a ground for allowing A to recover substantial damages from B in respect of C's loss.

18–064 **Use to which damages are put.** It will be recalled that, in his statement of the "broader ground" in the *Linden Gardens* case, Lord Griffiths said that the court would wish to be "satisfied that the repairs have been or are likely to be carried out."[385] In later cases, conflicting views have been expressed on the question whether this is an essential requirement for the operation of the "broader ground."

18–065 One view is that it is not, since (at least as a general rule[386]) a court in awarding damages is not concerned with the question what the claimant intends

[377] Above, para.18–062 at n.361.

[378] Performance of the work is in contracts of this kind *prima facie* a condition precedent of the right to be paid: *Morton v Lamb* (1797) 7 T.R. 125; *Miles v Wakefield MDC* [1987] A.C. 539, 561.

[379] *e.g.* damages on a "cost of cure" basis are not recoverable if the cost of cure is wholly disproportionate to the benefit to be derived from cure: below, para.26–017.

[380] There will be a "total failure of consideration:" below, para.29–055.

[381] See below, para.26–016.

[382] As in *Beswick v Beswick* [1968] A.C. 58, above, para.18–047.

[383] The "failure of consideration" would be only "partial:" see below, para.29–061.

[384] Below, para.27–021.

[385] [1994] 1 A.C. 85, 97; above, para.18–054; for further discussion, see below at paras 18–065—18–066.

[386] For a possible exception, see the discussion at para.26–016 below of the question whether cost of cure is recoverable where cure is not undertaken.

to do with these damages[387]: that question is said to be relevant only to the issue of the "reasonableness" of the claimant's conduct. This issue, however, arises, not for the purpose of determining the *existence* of a claim for substantial damages, but its *extent*: it may be relevant in determining whether damages in a two-party case are to be assessed on a difference in value or on a cost of cure basis,[388] or whether the claimant has failed to mitigate his loss[389]; but such questions arise only on the assumption that a claim for substantial damages does exist. A related argument in favour of the view that the claimant's intention with regard to the disposal of the damages is irrelevant is that he has been deprived by the defendant's breach of the benefit of his bargain, and this fact is, of itself, enough to support a claim for substantial damages.[390] This line of reasoning is, however, with respect, hard to reconcile with the principle that the victim of a breach has no claim to substantial damages if the breach has no adverse effect on him.[391] The assumption underlying this principle is that the mere failure to perform a contract does not suffice to sustain a claim for substantial damages: as Lord Clyde said in the *Panatown* case, "A breach of contract may cause a loss but is not in itself a loss in any meaningful sense."[392] In the cases here under consideration, the breach will have no adverse effect on *the claimant* (the promisee[393]) unless he has carried out, or intends to carry out, cure; and the argument that he has been deprived of his bargain cannot answer the question whether it must be shown that this deprivation has had an adverse effect on *him*: it merely pushes this question back one stage.

The alternative view is that damages in respect of the cost of curing the breach (and so of securing the intended benefit for the third party) can be recovered only if cure has been, or is likely to be, carried out. The main practical argument in favour of his view is that (as noted in para.18–061 above) it would be "unattractive" to allow the promisee to recover the cost of cure as damages in respect of his own loss and then to "put the money in his own pocket."[394] It is respectfully submitted that this is the preferable view. In a two-party case it is indeed generally[395] no concern of the court's what the claimant intends to do with the damages; but the rationale of this rule does not necessarily apply in a three-party case. That rationale in a two-party case is that the defendant has, by reason of the breach, inflicted injury, loss or damage on the person or property *of the claimant* (or has failed to improve, or to transfer, an asset belonging to, or to be **18–066**

---

[387] See the *Darlington* case [1995] 1 W.L.R. 68, 80; the *Panatown* case [2001] 1 A.C. 518, 556, 592 per Lords Goff and Millett, dissenting; *Ruxley Electronics and Construction Co v Forsyth* [1996] A.C. 344, 359 and 357; above, para.18–054, n.314.

[388] Below, para.26–016.

[389] Below, para.26–104.

[390] See the references to the *Darlington* and *Panatown* cases in n.387, above.

[391] *e.g.*, where a seller of goods in breach of contract fails to deliver and the goods are at the time of the failure worth less than the buyer had agreed to pay (but had not paid) for them.

[392] [2001] 1 A.C. 518, 534.

[393] Our concern here is with adverse *financial* effect on the claimant. A claim for damages for "loss of amenity" (below, para.26–084) will generally be one for loss suffered by the claimant, though in the family holiday cases (above, paras 18–049, 18–050) this loss may be increased by the claimant's witnessing the sufferings of his family in comfortless hotels. *Cf.* also below, para.26–082.

[394] *Panatown* case [2001] 1 A.C. 518, 571.

[395] See at n.386, above.

vested in, the claimant) who should therefore be able to deal in whatever way he pleases with the damages awarded to him in substitution of the interest of *his own* of which he has been deprived by the breach. For example, in the case of a contract to repair the claimant's own house, he could, but for the breach, have sold the house at a price reflecting the value of the repairs, had they been properly carried out, and then have disposed of the proceeds of the sale in any way he pleased; and so he should be able to dispose in the same way of the damages due to him for failure to carry out the repairs. Obviously, this reasoning cannot apply where the house is owned, not by the claimant, but by a third party. There is also the further point that, although in Lord Griffiths' example the claimant as a matter of legal principle recovers damages in respect of his *own* loss, as a practical matter the purpose of the award in such a case is to protect the interests of the third party. Where damages are awarded in respect of a third party's loss (under one of the exceptions to the general rule stated in paragraph 18–049 above) the court requires the promisee to hold these damages for the third party.[396] No such machinery is available where the damages are awarded in respect of the promisee's own loss; but a practical way of ensuring that the damages are in fact destined for the benefit of the third party is to require the promisee to show (as a condition of his entitlement to substantial damages) that they will be so used.

18–067 **No contract between claimant and defendant.** The principle established in the *Linden Gardens* case[397] assumes that there is a contract between A and B, the breach of which causes loss to C. The principle therefore did not apply in *Smithkline Beecham plc v Apotex Europe Ltd*[398] where, in legal proceedings between A and B, an interim injunction was granted to B to restrain A from dealing in England with a pharmaceutical product; and as a condition of the grant of the injunction, B was required to give an undertaking to the court to comply with any order which the court might, in later proceedings, make requiring B to compensate A for any loss which the injunction had caused to A. It was held that A could not invoke the *Linden Gardens* principle so as to recover damages in respect of loss suffered by A's supplier, C, in consequence of the injunction. One reason for this conclusion was that the cases in which that principle had been applied were "only about what damages [could] be recovered for a breach of contract"[399] and that the principle did not apply in the *Smithkline* case since in that case "there [was] in fact no contract between the parties [*i.e.* A and B]. The undertaking [was] given to the court."[400] This line of reasoning is, perhaps, not of itself conclusive since a principle akin to that of allowing a claimant to recover damages in respect of a third party's loss appears to be recognised in the law of tort.[401] The result in the *Smithkline* case was, however, also justified on the further ground that, even if there had been a contract between A and B on the terms of the undertaking, A's only interest in the performance of the hypothetical

[396] Below, para.18–076.
[397] [1994] 1 A.C. 85, above para.18–053.
[398] [2006] EWCA Civ 658, [2007] Ch. 71.
[399] *ibid.*, at [88].
[400] *ibid.*, at [86].
[401] See para.18–052 above.

contract was in A's not being restrained from dealing with the product, so that there was "no 'legal black hole' of the sort contemplated in *Linden Gardens*."[402] B would be liable to A for breach of B's hypothetical promise and full effect would be given to that promise by an award of damages to A in respect of the loss suffered by A as a result of the hypothetical breach.

Relation to third party's right. Even where, in one of the exceptional situations discussed above,[403] the promisee can recover damages in respect of the third party's loss, no right to enforce the contract is conferred directly on the third party, whose only claim will be to the fruits of any action which the promisee may decide to bring.[404] The third party will have a direct right against the promisor only under one of the exceptions to the doctrine of privity. On the facts of some[405] (though not of all)[406] of the cases discussed above, the third party would probably, if those facts recurred now, have such a right under the Contracts (Rights of Third Parties) Act 1999.[407] If the third party has such a right, then this very fact may restrict the number of situations in which the promisee can recover damages in respect of the third party's loss[408]; and it will probably reduce the pressure on the courts to extend the range of such situations.[409] But s.4 of the 1999 Act preserves the promisee's rights under the contract.[410] The question of his right to recover damages in respect of the third party's loss will therefore continue to arise and to be of practical importance: *e.g.* where the promisor has a defence against the third party which is not available against the promisee.[411] **18–068**

Negative promises. In paras 18–049 to 18–067 it has been assumed that the promise is positive in nature, *e.g.* to pay money, to deliver goods or to render some service. Where the promise is negative in nature, the promisee's most obvious remedy is an injunction to restrain the promisor's breach. This would, for example, be the position where A validly promised B not to compete with C. **18–069**

Promise not to sue a third party. A further type of negative promise which gives rise to special difficulty is a promise by A to B *not to sue* C. If, in breach **18–070**

[402] [2006] EWCA Civ 658 at [94].

[403] In paras 18–052 *et seq*.

[404] Below, para.18–076.

[405] *e.g.*, the *Woodar* case [1980] 1 W.L.R. 277 (above, 18–050). See Law Com. No.242, para.7–49; and probably the *Forster* case (1981) 125 S.J. 397 (above, para.18–051).

[406] *e.g.*, probably, the *Linden Gardens* case [1994] 1 A.C. 85 (above, para.18–053): see below, para.18–093.

[407] Below, paras 18–088 *et seq*. Section 1(1)(a) and (3) will make it possible to draw up contracts on facts similar to those of the *Linden Gardens* case, above, so as to confer a right of enforcement directly on the third party: see below, paras 18–089, 18–094.

[408] On the reasoning of *The Albazero* [1977] A.C. 774, and of *Alfred McAlpine Construction Ltd v Panatown Ltd* [2001] 1 A.C. 518, above, paras 18–052, 18–058, 18–059.

[409] The "legal black hole" referred to in the *Darlington* case [1995] 1 W.L.R. 68 at 79 would be much reduced in significance.

[410] See below, para.18–119.

[411] 1999 Act, s.3(4), below, para.18–109.

of such a promise, A nevertheless does sue C, it would not be appropriate for B to start a second action for an injunction to restrain A from proceeding with the first action; for such a step would lead to undesirable multiplicity of legal proceedings.[412] B's remedy is to ask the court to exercise its discretion[413] to stay A's action against C. In *Gore v Van der Lann*[414] the Court of Appeal held that B could obtain a stay of A's action against C only if two conditions were satisfied; there must be a definite promise by A to B not to sue C, and B must have a sufficient interest[415] in the enforcement of A's promise. This last requirement would not be satisfied unless, as a result of A's breach, B was exposed to the risk of incurring legal liability to C: for example where B had contracted with C to procure his release from a debt or liability to A, and would be put in breach of that contract by A's action against C.

18–071 *Snelling v John G. Snelling Ltd*[416] goes even further in giving effect to a promise of this kind. Three brothers had lent money to a family company of which they were directors. They agreed that if one of them resigned he should "forfeit" any money due to him from the company. One of them did resign and sued the company for the amounts due to him. By way of defence the company relied on the agreement between the brothers, and if matters had rested there the defence would have failed as the company was not a party to the agreement.[417] But the other two brothers applied to be joined as defendants to the action, adopted the company's defence and counterclaimed for a declaration that the third brother's loan was forfeited. It was held that they were entitled to such a declaration by virtue of the contract between them and the third brother.[418] Ormrod J. further held that they could obtain a stay of that brother's action against the company and that the most convenient way of disposing of the action against the company was to dismiss it. So far as the granting of the stay is concerned, the judgment is hard to reconcile with the requirement of a sufficient interest as explained in *Gore v Van der Lann*[419]; but it is submitted that Ormrod J.'s actual decision is consistent with the spirit of *Beswick v Beswick*.[420] If *the promisee* takes steps specifically to enforce the contract, the court should wherever possible grant such remedy as is most appropriate for that purpose. Normally this will be an order of specific performance or an injunction. The fact that the latter remedy is not appropriate to enforce a promise not to sue should not

---

[412] See Supreme Court Act 1981, s.49(2), replacing Supreme Court of Judicature (Consolidation) Act 1925, s.41.

[413] Under Supreme Court Act 1981, s.49(3).

[414] [1967] 2 Q.B. 31; Davies (1980) 1 L.S. 287; *cf. The Elbe Maru* [1978] 1 Lloyd's Rep. 206; *European Asian Bank AG v Punjab & Sind Bank* [1982] 2 Lloyd's Rep. 356; *Neptune Orient Lines Ltd v J.V.C. (UK) Ltd (The Chevalier Roze)* [1983] 2 Lloyd's Rep. 438.

[415] *e.g. Deepak Fertilisers & Chemical Corp. v ICI Chemicals & Polymers Ltd* [1999] 1 Lloyd's Rep. 387 at 401.

[416] [1973] 1 Q.B. 87; Wilkie (1973) 36 M.L.R. 214.

[417] [1973] 1 Q.B. at 95.

[418] *ibid.* at 96.

[419] [1967] 2 Q.B. 31, above, para.18–070.

[420] [1968] A.C. 58; above para.18–020.

deter the court from granting other remedies that serve substantially to enforce the promise. Such a remedy is, again, available only if it is sought *by the promisee.*[421] If, in the *Snelling* case, the two brothers had not applied to be joined to the action, the company could not have relied on the agreement between them and the third brother by way of defence.

(ii) *Position between Promisee and Third Party*

Introduction. The promisor may be willing to perform, or may actually perform, in favour of the third party, *e.g.* by paying him the agreed sum. These possibilities give rise to further problems between the third party and the promisee. In discussing these problems we shall in paras 18–073 to 18–076 assume that the case does not fall within any of the exceptions to the doctrine of privity which will be considered later in this Chapter.[422] 18–072

Promisor pays or is willing to pay. The promisor may actually pay or be willing to pay the third party in accordance with the contract, and the promisee may then claim that the third party is not entitled to keep the money for his own benefit but that he must hold it on behalf of the promisee. Such a claim is not likely to be made by the promisee himself, as he generally wants to benefit the third party. But it might be made by the promisee's trustee in bankruptcy, or by his personal representative on death. In *Beswick v Beswick* the House of Lords held that the third party was entitled to keep the money which the promisor was ordered to pay her, simply because it appeared from the true construction of the contract that this was the intention of the contracting parties.[423] It seems that this rule would apply equally to payments made willingly, *i.e.* without any order of the court.[424] Payments actually received by the third party can be claimed by the promisee only if, on the true construction of the contract, they were made to the third party as nominee for the promisee. Where the money has not yet been paid, the promisor and the promisee can agree to rescind or vary the contract[425]; and if they vary it so as to provide for payment to the promisee, the third party has no claim under the contract. But the question whether the promisee can unilaterally (*i.e.* without the consent of the promisor) demand that payment should be made to himself depends once again on the construction of the contract. If the contract can be construed as one to pay the third party "or as the promisee shall 18–073

---

[421] *cf. Heaton v Axa Equity and Law Life Assurance Society Ltd* [2002] UKHL 15; [2002] 2 A.C. 329, at [9] ("is enforceable by B", *i.e.* the promisee). No such promise had been made in that case.

[422] Below, paras 18–077—18–132.

[423] *Beswick v Beswick* [1968] A.C. 58, 71, 94, 96, on this point overruling *Re Engelbach's Estate* [1924] 2 Ch. 348 and doubting *Re Sinclair's Life Policy* [1938] Ch. 799. Earlier cases supporting the view stated in the text include *Ashby v Costin* (1888) 21 Q.B.D. 401; *Harris v United Kingdom, etc., Society* (1889) 87 L.T.J. 272; *Re Davies* [1892] 3 Ch. 63.

[424] This appears from the treatment in *Beswick v Beswick* of *Re Engelbach's Estate*, above, n.423, where the money had in fact been paid to the third party: see 93 L.J.Ch. 616, 617.

[425] The present discussion is (as stated in para.18–072 above) based on the assumption that the case does *not* fall within any of the exceptions (to be discussed in paras 18–077 *et seq.*) to the common law doctrine of privity of contract.

direct" then the promisee is entitled to demand payment to himself.[426] But the contract is not likely to be construed in this way where it is a matter of concern to the promisor that payment should be made to the third party, *e.g.* because the third party is a near relative of the promisor and it matters to the promisor that the third party should be provided for.[427]

18–074 **Revocable mandate.** The rules stated in para.18–073 above apply only if there is indeed a promise to pay the third party. In *Coulls v Bagot's Executor and Trustee Co Ltd*[428] an agreement between A and B provided for payment of royalties by B to A and concluded: "I [A] authorise . . . [B] to pay all money connected with this agreement to my wife . . . and myself . . . as joint tenants." The document was signed by A, B and A's wife. A majority of the High Court of Australia held that there was no *promise* by B to A to pay A's wife but only a *mandate* by A authorising B to pay A's wife (so that such payment would discharge B). This mandate was revocable and had been revoked by A's death. Consequently, the money (which B was willing to pay) belonged to A's estate and not to his wife. The third party would, *a fortiori*, not be entitled to the money if he were mentioned in the contract as a mere nominee in such a way as to indicate that no beneficial interest was intended to pass to him and that payment to him without the request of the promisee should not discharge the promisor.[429]

18–075 **Promisee refuses to sue.** A further problem arises where the promisee fails or refuses to take any action to enforce the promise. Lord Denning has suggested that, even at common law, the third party could in such a case circumvent the doctrine of privity by suing the promisor and joining the promisee as co-defendant.[430] But Diplock and Salmon L.JJ. have said that the action can (in cases not falling within any of the exceptions to the doctrine of privity) be brought only by the promisee[431]; and it is submitted that this is the correct view. Lord Denning's view is fundamentally inconsistent with the common law doctrine of privity, which was recognised in *Beswick v Beswick* and in many later cases.[432] It is also inconsistent with the reasoning of the cases on trusts of promises, to be discussed later in this Chapter[433]; for if the third party could always enforce the promise against the promisor by joining the promisee to the action, it would be pointless to insist that he must in addition show the existence of a trust.

---

[426] For an illustration of what is "probably" a contract to pay the third party or as the promisee shall direct, see *Tradigrain SA v King Diamond Shipping SA (The Spiros C)* [2002] 2 Lloyd's Rep. 319 at 331 (bill of lading making freight payable to a person other than contracting carrier; actual decision based on other grounds: *ibid.*, at 332). The same is true where a contract provides for some performance other than a payment of money to be rendered to a third party: *e.g. Mitchell v Ede* (1840) 11 Ad. & El. 888; *Elder Dempster Lines v Zaki Ishag (The Lycaon)* [1983] 2 Lloyd's Rep. 548.

[427] As in *Re Stapleton-Bretherton* [1941] Ch. 482.

[428] [1967] A.L.R. 385.

[429] *Thavorn v Bank of Credit & Commerce SA* [1985] 1 Lloyd's Rep. 259; *The Turridu* [1999] 2 Lloyd's Rep. 401.

[430] *Beswick v Beswick* [1966] Ch. at 557; *Gurtner v Circuit* [1968] 2 Q.B. 587, 596.

[431] *Gurtner v Circuit* [1968] 2 Q.B. at 599, 606.

[432] Above, para.18–020.

[433] Below, paras 18–078—18–086.

Promisee sues for damages or restitution. A final problem arises where the promisee sues but claims some form of relief other than specific performance in favour of the third party: *e.g.* where he claims damages, or recovery of the consideration provided by him. If such a claim succeeded, it would seem to lead to a judgment for payment to the promisee and not to the third party; and the question would arise whether the promisee could keep the payment for his own benefit or whether he would be bound to hold it for the third party. In tort, a person can sometimes recover damages for a loss suffered, not by himself, but by another; *e.g.* a husband may get damages for loss of earnings suffered by his wife in giving up her job to nurse him after an accident; and such damages must then be held on trust for the other person.[434] Similarly, where one person can recover damages for breach of contract in respect of loss suffered by another person in the exceptional cases mentioned in paras 18–052 to 18–056 above, those damages must be held for that other person.[435] This may also be the position in the cases "calling for special treatment,"[436] such as the booking of family holidays or ordering meals in restaurants. If, in such special cases, the promisee can recover damages in respect of the third party's loss, it may be that those damages, when recovered, would (as in the exceptional situations discussed in para.18–052 to 18–056) be held by the promisee as money had and received for the use of the third party.[437] But these exceptions apart, there does not appear (at least as a general rule) to be any similar possibility where the promisee claims damages for breach of a contract merely because the contract was made for the benefit of a third party. The general rule in such a case is that damages will be awarded only to compensate the promisee for his *own* loss,[438] and where the damages are awarded for such loss, it does not seem that the promisee can be under any obligation to pay over those damages (or any part of them) to the third party.[439] 18–076

[434] *Hunt v Severs* [1994] 2 A.C. 350, 363 following *Cunningham v Harrison* [1973] Q.B. 942, 952 and rejecting the contrary view in *Donelly v Joyce* [1974] Q.B. 454, 461–462. *cf. Allen v Waters* [1935] 1 K.B. 200 and *Dennis v L.P.T.B.* [1948] 1 All E.R. 779 as explained in (1956) 72 L.Q.R. 187; *Lowe v Guise* [2002] EWCA Civ 197; [2002] 3 All E.R. 454 at [38]; *Robertson v Wait* (1853) 8 Exch. 299. For further problems which may arise where the person who provides the nursing or other services in respect of which damages are claimed is also the tortfeasor (*e.g.* where tortfeasor and victim are members of the same family involved in the same motor accident) see *Hayden v Hayden* [1992] 1 W.L.R. 986 and *Hunt v Severs* [1994] 2 A.C. 350, holding that in such circumstances the claimant cannot recover damages in respect of the value of services voluntarily rendered by the tortfeasor himself.

[435] See, *e.g. Albacruz (Cargo Owners) v Albazero (Owners) (The Albazero)* [1977] A.C. 774, 842 and other authorities cited in para.18–052, above; and *cf. Conservative Central Office v Burrell* [1980] 3 All E.R. 43, 63; affirmed (without any reference to *Beswick v Beswick* [1986] A.C. 58) [1982] 1 W.L.R. 522; *O'Sulllivan v Williams* [1992] 3 All E.R. 385, 387, discussing *The Winkfield* [1902] P. 42; *Linden Gardens* case [1994] 1 A.C. 85, above, para.18–053); *John Harris Partnership v Groveworld Ltd* [1999] P.N.L.R. 697; Carriage of Goods by Sea Act 1992 s.2(4) ("for the benefit of the person who sustained the loss").

[436] *Woodar Investment Development Ltd v Wimpey Construction UK Ltd* [1980] 1 W.L.R. 277, 283.

[437] This was the view of Lord Denning M.R. in *Jackson v Horizon Holidays Ltd* [1975] 1 W.L.R. 1468, 1473. The strange result would be that the claimant was under some quasi-contractual or restitutionary liability to his two small children in respect of part of the £500 recovered as damages for distress.

[438] See above, paras 18–049—18–050, 18–054.

[439] *cf. Coulls v Bagot's Executor and Trustee Co Ltd* [1967] A.L.R. 385, 411.

(b) *Exceptions to the Doctrine*

18–077 **In general.** The doctrine of privity of contract is subject to many exceptions. Some of these, such as assignment and agency, are discussed in other parts of this work.[440] Others, such as covenants relating to land, are beyond its scope. In the following paragraphs of this Chapter, we shall discuss a further group of situations in which a third party can acquire rights under a contract by virtue of a number of equitable and statutory exceptions to the doctrine of privity. The most important of these is the "general and wide-ranging"[441] one which has been created by the Contracts (Rights of Third Parties) Act 1999. This Act preserves any right or remedy which the third party may have apart from its provisions.[442] The exceptions which were established before the Act came into force therefore still call for discussion, particularly because situations may arise in which it will be to the third parties' advantage to rely on one of these exceptions, rather than on the new one which has been created by the Act.[443]

(i) *Equitable Exceptions*

18–078 **Trusts of promises.**[444] Equity developed an exception to the doctrine of privity by making use of the concept of a trust of a chose in action. It accordingly held that where A made a promise to B for the benefit of C, the promise could be enforced by C against A if B had constituted himself trustee of A's promise for C.[445] This exception to the doctrine of privity was approved by the House of Lords in *Walford's* case[446] where C (a broker) negotiated a charterparty in which the shipowner (A) promised the charterer (B) to pay a commission to C. It was held that B was trustee of A's promise for C, who could accordingly enforce the promise against A.

---

[440] See Ch.19 and Vol.II, Ch.31. See also paras 14–039—14–058, above.

[441] Law Com No.242, para.5.16.

[442] s.7(1); this can apply not only to existing, but also to future, exceptions.

[443] See above, para.18–002, below, paras 18–114 to 18–116.

[444] Corbin, 46 L.Q.R. 12 (1930); *Contracts*, Ch.46; Jaconelli [1998] Conv. 88.

[445] *Tomlinson v Gill* (1756) Amb. 330; *cf. Gregory v Williams* (1817) Mer. 582; *Lloyd's v Harper* (1880) 16 Ch.D. 290; for recognition of the device at common law (allowing B to recover more than he had lost on the ground that he was bound to hold the surplus for C) see *Lamb v Vice* (1840) 6 M. & W. 467; *Robertson v Wait* (1853) 8 Ex. 299; *Prudential Staff Union v Hall* [1947] K.B. 685. For the effectiveness of a direction (not of a contractual nature) to executors in favour of a third party, see *Crowden v Aldridge* [1993] 1 W.L.R. 433. Our concern here is with the situation in which B constitutes himself as trustee *ab initio*, i.e. at the time of contracting. B may also constitute himself as trustee for C *after* that time. For the relationship between the latter possibility and an assignment to C by B of contractual rights against A, see *Barbados Trust Co Ltd v Bank of Zambia* [2007] EWCA Civ 148, [2007] 1 Lloyd's Rep. 723, below para.19–046.

[446] *Les Affréteurs Réunis SA v Leopold Walford (London) Ltd* [1919] A.C. 801; for the application on similar facts of s.1(2)(b) of the Contracts (Rights of Third Parties) Act 1999 (below, para.18–091) see *Nisshin Shipping Co Ltd v Cleaves & Co Ltd* [2003] EWHC 2602, [2004] 1 All E.R. (Comm) 481; *cf. Howard Houlder & Partners Ltd v Marine General Transporters (The Panaghia P)* [1983] 2 Lloyd's Rep. 653, 655; *Atlas Shipping Agency (UK) Ltd v Suisse Atlantique Société d'Armement Maritime SA* [1995] 2 Lloyd's Rep. 188. Contrast *Marcan Shipping (London) Ltd v Polish SS. Co (The Manifest Lipkowy)* [1989] 2 Lloyd's Rep. 138, where an agreement for the sale of a ship provided for deduction of the broker's commission from the price but seems to have contained no *promise* to pay the broker.

Intention to create a trust. A promisee will not be regarded as a trustee for the third party unless he has the intention to create a trust.[447] Such an intention can be made clear by using the word "trust" or "trustee,"[448] though even where this is done the further question[449] may arise whether the trust, which no doubt exists, is one in favour of the particular third party who seeks to enforce the promise which is the subject-matter of that trust.[450] A trust may, moreover, be created without using any particular form of words; and where the word "trust" or "trustee" has not been used, the question whether there is an intention to create a trust gives rise to very great difficulty. Thus in some cases[451] a promise to a person to provide for his dependants on his retirement or death has been held to create a trust in their favour, while in other cases[452] such a promise has been held not to have this effect.[453] Similarly, life insurance policies expressed to be for the benefit of third parties have in some cases been held to create trusts in their favour,[454] and in others to confer no enforceable rights on them.[455] And in some cases concerning other types of insurance[456] the courts have held that the third party could take advantage of the policy under the trust device,[457] while in others they have held that the third parties had no rights because of the doctrine of privity.[458] There is no point in trying to reconcile all these cases. They represent different stages in the development of the law. At one time, the courts were very ready to apply the trust device in order to protect the interests of the 18–079

---

[447] *Swain v Law Society* [1983] 1 A.C. 598, 620; Feltham (1982) 98 L.Q.R. 17.

[448] *Fletcher v Fletcher* (1844) 4 Hare 67; *Bowskill v Dawson* [1954] 1 Q.B. 288.

[449] For the purpose of the present discussion, it is assumed that formal requirements, such as that imposed by Law of Property Act 1925, s.53(1)(b), have been satisfied. As to the effect on the rights of third parties of failure to satisfy such requirements, see Feltham (1987) Conv. 246.

[450] See *Gandy v Gandy* (1844) 34 Ch.D. 57.

[451] *Re Flavell* (1883) 25 Ch.D. 89; *cf. Page v Cox* (1852) 10 Hare 163; *Re Gordon* [1940] Ch. 851; *Drimmie v Davies* [1899] 1 I.R. 176.

[452] *Re Schebsman* [1944] Ch. 83; *cf. Re Stapleton-Bretherton* [1941] Ch. 482. In *Re Miller's Agreement* [1947] Ch. 615 and *Beswick v Beswick* [1968] A.C. 58 it was conceded that there was no trust.

[453] In *Re Schebsman*, above, the argument that there was a trust was, paradoxically, advanced, not on behalf of the third parties, but on behalf of the promisee's trustee in bankruptcy. The point of the argument was to have the trust set aside under the Bankruptcy Act 1914, s.42 (now superseded by Insolvency Act 1986, s.339): see [1944] Ch. at 86. At 104 the argument is attributed to "Mr. Denning," who appeared for the third parties. But this must be a mistake; the corresponding passage in [1943] 2 All E.R. 768, 779 correctly attributes it to "counsel for the appellant," *i.e.* for the trustee in bankruptcy. As the company was willing to pay, the outcome of holding that there was *no* trust was that the third parties obtained the intended benefit (*cf.* above, para.18–073). In *Re Flavell*, above n.451, the same result followed from the decision that there *was* a trust.

[454] *Re Richardson* (1882) 47 L.T. 514; *Royal Exchange Assurance v Hope* [1928] Ch. 179; *Re Webb* [1941] Ch. 225; *Re Foster's Policy* [1966] 1 W.L.R. 222.

[455] *Re Burgess' Policy* (1915) 113 L.T. 443; *Re Clay's Policy of Assurance* [1937] 2 All E.R. 548; *Re Foster* [1938] 3 All E.R. 357; *cf. Re Engelbach's Estate* [1924] 2 Ch. 248 and *Re Sinclair's Life Policy* [1938] Ch. 799; these two cases were disapproved or doubted on another ground in *Beswick v Beswick* [1968] A.C. 58: see above, para.18–073, n.423.

[456] For statutory exceptions to the doctrine of privity in cases of insurance, see below, paras 18–126 to 18–131.

[457] *Waters v Monarch Fire and Life Assurance Co* (1856) 5 E. & B. 870; *Williams v Baltic Insurance Co* [1924] 2 K.B. 282; below, para.18–127; *Prudential Staff Union v Hall* [1947] K.B. 685; *cf.* Deane J. in *Trident General Ins. Co Ltd v McNiece Bros Pty Ltd* (1988) 165 C.L.R. 107 (above, para.18–020).

[458] *Vandepitte v Preferred Accident Insurance Corp.* [1933] A.C. 70; *Green v Russell* [1959] 2 Q.B. 226.

third party.[459] Later, they became more reluctant to apply the device because, once a contract was held to have created a trust in favour of the third party, the parties to that contract lost the right to vary it by mutual consent.[460] Although there are, therefore, no clear rules which determine the existence of a trust in cases of this kind, it is possible to extract from the cases a number of principles which will serve as some guide to the solution of future problems. These principles are discussed in paras 18–080 to 18–082 below.

18–080 **Intention to benefit third party necessary.** There must be an intention to benefit the third party.[461] If the promisee took the promise for his own benefit there will be no trust in favour of the third party.[462] The same may be true if it is as consistent with the facts that the promisee took the promise for his own benefit as for the benefit of the third party.[463] Conversely, the fact that the promisee had *not* intended to take the promise for his own benefit can be relied on to support the conclusion that there was a trust in favour of the third party.[464]

18–081 **Irrevocability of intention to benefit third party.** As a general rule,[465] the intention to benefit the third party must be irrevocable; so that a contract will not normally give rise to a trust in favour of the third party if, under the terms of the contract, the promisee is entitled to deprive the third party of the benefit by diverting it to himself or to other beneficiaries not mentioned in the contract.[466] On the other hand, the existence of such a power to divert the benefit will not negative the intention to create a trust where the power is expressed to be exercisable only for a limited period and is not in fact exercised within that period.[467] Nor will the existence of a trust necessarily be negatived where a contract names a group of beneficiaries, but reserves to the promisee a power to

---

[459] See *Hill v Gomme* (1839) 5 My. & Cr. 250; *Page v Cox* (1852) 10 Hare 163.

[460] *Re Schebsman* [1944] Ch. 83, 104; *Re Sinclair's Life Policy* [1938] Ch. 799.

[461] In *Talbot Underwriting Ltd v Naush Hogan & Murray Inc (The Jascon 5)* [2006] EWCA Civ 869, [2006] 2 Lloyd's Rep 195, it had been held that there could be no trust of a promise in favour of a third party if the contract did not contain any promise in favour of that party ([2005] EWHC 2395 at [70]–[71]). There is no reference to this unusually stringent requirement in the Court of Appeal.

[462] *West v Houghton* (1879) 4 C.P.D. 197; criticised in *Re Flavell* (1883) 25 Ch.D. 89, 98 and in *Lloyd's v Harper* (1880) 16 Ch.D. 290, 311.

[463] *e.g. Vandepitte v Preferred Accident Insurance Corp.* [1933] A.C. 70, where one relevant factor was that the insured was under the law governing the policy himself liable for the torts of the third party; contrast *Williams v Baltic Insurance* [1924] 2 K.B. 282. For the statutory position in such motor insurance cases, see below para.18–127.

[464] *Lyus v Prowsa Development Ltd* [1982] 1 W.L.R. 1044.

[465] For exceptions, see below at nn.467–469. For an earlier, contrary view, see below, n.466.

[466] *Re Sinclair's Life Policy* [1938] Ch. 799 (criticised on another ground in *Beswick v Beswick* [1968] A.C. 58, 96); and *cf. Re Schebsman* [1944] Ch. 83; some earlier authorities did not insist on this requirement: see *Hill v Gomme* (1839) 5 My. & Cr. 250; *Page v Cox* (1852) 10 Hare 163. A provision of the kind here under discussion would not fall within Contracts (Rights of Third Parties) Act 1999, s.2, since this applies only to rescission or variation *by agreement* between promisor and promisee: see below, paras 18–098, 18–099.

[467] *Re Foster's Policy* [1966] 1 W.L.R. 222.

redistribute the intended benefits among them in variation of the terms of the original contract.[468] And where a contract *by statute* creates a trust, a general provision purporting to entitle the promisee to divert the benefit to whom he pleases will not defeat the trust: on the contrary, such a power can be used only for the benefit of the objects of the trust.[469] The court may conclude that there was no intention irrevocably to benefit the third party even though the contract contains no express provision entitling the promisee to divert the benefit away from the third party. It may do so on the ground that the contract would, if it were held to give rise to a trust, unduly limit the freedom of action of the parties or of one of them: *e.g.* by restricting the promisee's freedom of movement[470] or by depriving the parties to the contract of their right to vary it by mutual consent.[471]

Intention to benefit third party not sufficient. The intention to benefit the third party is not, without more, sufficient, for an intention to make a gift must be distinguished from an intention to create a trust.[472] There are many cases in which the courts have refused to apply the trust device although the promisee clearly, irrevocably and without qualification intended to benefit the third party.[473] There must be an intention to create a trust; and it seems that such an intention will readily be found where the contract in favour of the third party is made in pursuance of some contractual[474] or fiduciary[475] obligation owed by the promisee to the third party. But the trust device has not been wholly confined to such cases—probably because the courts did not formerly insist very strictly on proof of intention to create a trust. The fact that they later came to do so accounts for the present more restricted scope of the trust device. 18–082

The intention to create a trust may, finally, be negatived on the ground that a trust is not necessary to give rights to the third party because he is entitled to

[468] *Re Webb* [1941] Ch. 225.

[469] *Re a Policy of the Equitable Life Assurance of the United States and Mitchell* (1911) 27 T.L.R. 213; *Re Fleetwood's Policy* [1926] 1 Ch. 48.

[470] *e.g. Re Burgess' Policy* (1915) 113 L.J. 43 (policy to become void if insured went "beyond the boundaries of Europe" without previously notifying insurers).

[471] *e.g. Re Schebsman* [1944] 83, 104 (parties "intended to keep alive their common law right consensually to vary the terms of the obligation"). The mere existence of such a right does not negative the statutory right of enforcement which third parties have under the Contracts (Rights of Third Parties) Act 1999: this is clear from s.2 of the Act (below, para.18–098).

[472] See *Richards v Delbridge* (1874) L.R. 18 Eq. 11; *Swain v Law Society* [1983] 1 A.C. 598, 620.

[473] *Re Clay's Policy of Assurance* [1937] 2 All E.R. 548; *Re Foster* [1938] 3 All E.R. 357; *Re Stapleton-Bretherton* [1941] Ch. 482; *Green v Russell* [1959] 1 Q.B. 28; *Re Cook's Settlement Trusts* [1965] Ch. 902. Under the Contracts (Rights of Third Parties) Act 1999, s.1(1)(b) and (2) it will suffice for the term to purport to confer a benefit on the third party, so long as it is not shown that the contracting parties did not intend the term to be enforceable by the third party. For the reasons given in para.18–002 above and para.18–116 below, however, it may be in the third party's interest to establish an intention to create a trust, so that he can rely on the trust exception rather than on the 1999 Act.

[474] See *Re Independent Air Travel Ltd, The Times*, May 20, 1961, where counsel, with the approval of the court, conceded this point.

[475] *Harmer v Armstrong* [1934] Ch. 65.

enforce the contract (even in the absence of a trust) under a statutory exception to the doctrine of privity.[476]

18–083 **Effects of the trust.** Two consequences generally flow from a finding that there is a trust in favour of a third party. First, the third party is entitled to sue the promisor for the money or property which the promisor had promised to pay or to transfer to him.[477] He must join the promisee as a party to the action[478] since if this were not done the promisor might be sued a second time by the promisee. As this rule as to joinder of parties exists for the benefit of the promisor, it can be waived by him.[479] Secondly, the third party is (as a general rule[480]) beneficially entitled to any money paid or payable under the contract; the promisee has no right to such money.[481] After *Beswick v Beswick*[482] the third party can generally keep money paid to him even if there is no trust.[483]

18–084 **Failure of the trust.** There are exceptional cases in which the promisee may be entitled to the money even though there was a trust. In *Cleaver v Mutual Reserve Fund Life Association*[484] a husband insured his life for the benefit of his wife by a policy which, by statute, created a trust in her favour.[485] The wife was convicted of murdering the husband and was therefore disqualified from enforcing the trust. It was held that the executors of the husband were entitled to the policy moneys. The decision can be criticised on the ground that the promisor should not have been held liable to pay the promisee when its promise was one to pay the third party.[486] But it seems that the destination of the payments was a matter of indifference to the insurance company and that there was nothing to show that the company would (even if there had been no conviction) have been in any way prejudiced by paying the husband's executors rather than the wife.[487] The actual decision may also turn on the interpretation of the statute creating the trust.[488]

---

476 *Swain v Law Society* [1983] 1 A.C. 598, esp. at 621.

477 But where a trustee engages a professional adviser for the purpose of administering the trust, a claim for negligence against that adviser cannot be brought by the beneficiary since such a claim is not part of the trust property (though any damages recovered by the trustee would be): *Bradstock Trustee Services Ltd v Nabarro Nathanson* [1995] 1 W.L.R. 1405.

478 *cf. Performing Right Society Ltd v London Theatre of Varieties* [1924] A.C. 1; *Howard Houlder & Partners v Marine General Transporters Co (The Panaghia P)* [1983] 2 Lloyd's Rep. 653, 655; *Atlas Shipping Agency (UK) Ltd v Suisse Atlantique Société d' Armement Maritime SA* [1995] 2 Lloyd's Rep. 188, 193; *Barbados Trust Co Ltd v Bank of Zambia* [2007] EWCA Civ 148, [2007] 1 Lloyd's Rep. 495 at [102].

479 As in *Les Affréteurs Réunis v Leopold Walford (London) Ltd* [1919] A.C. 801; *cf. William Brandt's Sons & Co v Dunlop Rubber Co* [1905] A.C. 454.

480 *i.e.* subject to the exceptions stated in para.18–084, below.

481 *Re Flavell* (1883) 25 Ch.D. 89; *Re Gordon* [1940] Ch. 851; *cf. Paul v Constance* [1977] 1 W.L.R. 527.

482 [1968] A.C. 58.

483 Above, para.18–073.

484 [1892] 1 Q.B. 147.

485 Married Women's Property Act 1882, s.11; below, para.18–126.

486 Ames, *Lectures*, 320; *Coulls v Bagot's Executor & Trustee Co Ltd* [1967] A.L.R. 385, 410–411, *per* Windeyer J. (dissenting); above para.18–046.

487 *cf.* above, para.18–073.

488 See [1892] 1 Q.B. 147, 157.

Kinds of promises which can be held on trust. The trust device has so far been applied only to promises to pay money or to transfer property. It is sometimes suggested that it might be applied to other kinds of promises, *e.g.* that an employer might hold the benefit of an exemption clause on trust for his employee.[489] But the present judicial tendency is to confine the trust device within narrow limits; and the suggestion has therefore been rejected on the ground that "the conception of a trust attaching to a benefit under an exclusion clause extends far beyond conventional limits."[490] A number of other techniques have, however, been developed for making the benefit of exemption clauses available to third parties.[491] 18–085

Relation of trust device to doctrine of privity. It has been argued[492] that, where the trust device applied and so conferred rights on a third party, there was before the Judicature Act 1873 a conflict between the rules of equity and those of common law; that, by virtue of that Act, the rules of equity now prevail[493]; and that a third party should now generally be entitled to enforce a contract made for his benefit. But this argument has not been accepted[494] and the trust device has been judicially described as "an *exception* to the rule of privity of contract."[495] The exception is of limited, if uncertain, scope and so does not give rise to a direct conflict between common law and equity. Even in equity, a third party could not enforce a contract merely because it was expressed to have been made for his benefit[496]: he had to show, in addition, that a trust had been created in his favour.[497] The argument that third parties were entitled to enforce contracts made for their benefit has been rejected in many cases since the 1873 Act; and although some of these decisions were based entirely on common law principles,[498] in others the equitable argument was considered and rejected.[499] 18–086

Covenants in marriage settlements. In equity a covenant to settle after-acquired property contained in a marriage settlement can be enforced by persons "within the marriage consideration," that is, by husband, wife and the issue of 18–087

[489] See the Himalaya clause in *New Zealand Shipping Co Ltd v A. M. Satterthwaite & Co Ltd (The Eurymedon)* [1975] A.C. 154; *Port Jackson Stevedoring Pty Ltd v Salmond & Spraggon (Australia) Pty Ltd (The New York Star)* [1980] 1 W.L.R. 138, above, para.14–048.

[490] *Southern Water Authority v Carey* [1985] 2 All E.R. 1077, 1083.

[491] Above, paras 14–039 to 14–049.

[492] *Drimmie v Davies* [1899] 1 I.R. 176, 182; Corbin (1930) 46 L.Q.R. 12, 36; *cf.* Langbein, 105 Yale L.J. 625, 646–647 (1997).

[493] Judicature Act 1873, s.25(11); now Supreme Court Act 1981, s.49(1).

[494] *Re Schebsman* [1943] 1 Ch. at 370; approved [1944] Ch. at 104.

[495] *Barbados Trust Ltd v Bank of Zambia* [2007] EWCA Civ 148, [2007] 1 Lloyd's Rep. 495 at [99], *per* Rix L.J. (italics supplied).

[496] Above, para.18–082.

[497] *Colyear v Mulgrave* (1836) 2 Keen 81. The actual decision has been criticised but without impairing the principle stated in the text: see *Page v Cox* (1852) 10 Hare 163; *Kekewich v Manning* (1851) 1 D.M. & G. 176.

[498] *e.g., Dunlop Pneumatic Tyre Co Ltd v Selfridge & Co Ltd* [1915] A.C. 847.

[499] *Re Burgess' Policy* (1915) 113 L.T. 443; *Re Clay's Policy of Assurance* [1937] 2 All E.R. 548; *Re Sinclair's Life Policy* [1938] Ch. 799; *Re Schebsman* [1944] Ch. 83; *Green v Russell* [1959] Q.B. 28.

the marriage. But the covenant confers no rights on mere volunteers such as the next-of-kin of the wife, or her children by a previous marriage.[500]

(ii) *Contracts (Rights of Third Parties) Act 1999*[501]

18–088 **Third party's right of enforcement.** "A general and wide-ranging exception to" the doctrine of privity is created by this Act, the central purpose of which[502] is to enable a third party to acquire rights under a contract if, and to the extent that, the parties to the contract so intend. Section 1(1) provides that a person who is not a party to the contract may in his own right enforce a term of the contract in the two situations to be described in paras 18–089 to 18–092 below. In discussing these situations and other provisions of the Act, it will be convenient to refer to the person who makes the promise which the third party is claiming to enforce (the promisor) as A, to the person to whom that promise is made (the promisee) as B[503] and to the third party as C.

18–089 **Express provision.** Under s.1(1)(a) of the 1999 Act, C can enforce a term of the contract if "the contract expressly provides that he may": *e.g.* where a contract contains a promise by A to B to pay £1,000 to C and goes on to provide that C is to be entitled to enforce the term which contains this promise. If the contract contains such a provision, there is no further requirement (as there is under s.1(1)(b), to be discussed in para.18–091 below) that the promise must have been made for C's own benefit: *e.g.* he can enforce the term even though the payment is to be made to him as trustee for D.[504] Express contractual provisions of the kind just described, to the effect that C is to be entitled to enforce the term containing the promise made by A to B, have hitherto been rare, presumably because under the doctrine of privity they would at common law have been ineffective. The 1999 Act provides a new drafting device to enable the contracting parties to give effect to their intention that C is to acquire an enforceable right against A. Apart from the Act, a similar result can be achieved by creating a trust of A's promise in favour of C[505] or by making him a co-promisee.[506] There is a procedural advantage in making use of the machinery of s.1(1)(a) in that, if C sues under this provision, he will not (it seems) need to join B as a party to the action[507]; though the court could order B to be so joined where claims against A

---

[500] *Hill v Gomme* (1839) 5 My. & Cr. 250, 254; *Re D'Angibau* (1880) 15 Ch.D. 228; *Green v Patterson* (1886) 32 Ch.D. 95, 107; *Re Plumptree's Marriage Settlement* [1910] 1 Ch. 609; *Re Cook's Settlement Trust* [1965] Ch. 902. These cases, apart from forming an exception to the doctrine of privity, are also hard to reconcile with the modern definition of consideration: *cf.* above, para.3–032; the statement in *Hill v Gomme*, above, that the children were "quasi-parties" is curiously reminiscent of the reasoning of *Dutton v Poole*, cited in para.18–019, above.

[501] See above, para.18–001; Stevens (2004) 120 L.Q.R. 292.

[502] Law Commission Report on *Privity of Contract: Contracts for the Benefit of Third Parties*, Law Com. No.242, (1996), hereafter "Report"; (ed.) Merkin & Faber, *Privity: the Impact of the Contracts (Rights of Third Parties) Act 1999*.

[503] *cf.* the definitions of "promisor" and "promisee" in s.1(7) of the 1999 Act.

[504] Report, para.7.5.

[505] Above, para.18–078.

[506] See *McEvoy v Belfast Banking Co* [1935] A.C. 24, above, para.3–044.

[507] This appears to follow from the words "in his own right" in s.1(1); *cf.* Report, para.14.3; *Mulchrone v Swiss Life (UK) Ltd plc* [2005] EWHC 1808, [2006] Lloyd's Rep. I.R. 339 at [14] ("exclusively in her [C's] own name").

were made by both B and C, or where A relied against C on a defence available to A against B,[508] since in such a case B's presence before the court is likely to be "desirable . . . so that the court can resolve all the matters in dispute in the proceedings."[509] If C does have a claim apart from the Act as the beneficiary of a trust of A's promise or as co-promisee, it may, in spite of the need to join B to the action, be in C's interest to pursue that claim since it would not be subject to other provisions of the Act which may restrict his rights under it: *e.g.* to those relating to the rescission or variation of the contract between A and B, or to defences available to A against B.[510]

Section 1(1)(a) is also likely to apply to terms such as Himalaya clauses,[511] contained in a contract between A and B by which A promises B that any exemptions from or limitations of liability available under that contract to B shall also be available for the benefit of C, who typically will be an employee, agent or subcontractor employed by B for the purpose of performing some or all of B's obligations under the contract. This follows from s.1(6) of the 1999 Act, by which references to C's "enforcing" a term which "excludes or limits liability"[512] are to be "construed as references to his availing himself of the exclusion or limitation." Words in the contract to the effect that C is to be protected by the exemption or limitation clause therefore amount in themselves to an express provision that C may enforce the clause[513]; no further words will be necessary. C's protection under the Act will, however, be based on a theory different from that which accounts for the effectiveness of Himalaya clauses at common law. The common law theory is that such clauses, and the conduct of the relevant parties, can give rise to a separate or collateral contract between A and C.[514] Under the Act, by contrast, C enforces a term of a contract to which he is *not* a party.[515] It follows that the agency requirements which exist at common law[516] are irrelevant for the purpose of the Act. On the other hand, under the Act C's right to "enforce" a Himalaya clause is subject to the provisions of the Act[517] while at common law the operation of such a clause is subject only to common law restrictions, and if C wishes to rely on his common law rights, in preference to those under the Act, it is open to him to do so.[518] For these (among other)[519] 18–090

---

[508] Under s.3 of the 1999 Act: see below, para.18–107.

[509] CPR, r.19.2(2)(a).

[510] See ss.2 and 3 (below, paras 18–098 to 18–106 to 18–108) and s.7(1) of the Act below, para.18–114).

[511] Above, para.14–049. For the effect of the 1999 Act on such clauses, see also *Carver on Bills of Lading*, 2nd ed. (2005), paras 7–074 to 7–079.

[512] This phrase would not include other terms in the contract on which C might wish to rely: *e.g.* not choice of forum clauses: see Report, para.14.9; *cf.*, at common law, *The Mahkutai* [1996] A.C. 650, where such a clause was held as a matter of construction not to have been covered by the Himalaya clause in that case. If, in a future case, a Himalaya clause were so drafted as to cover the choice of forum clause, the case would not fall within s.1(6) of the 1999 Act.

[513] Report, para.7.10.

[514] Above, para.14–047 to 14–049; *Homburg Houtimport BV v Agrosin Private Ltd (The Starsin)* [2003] UKHL 12; [2004] 1 A.C. 715 at [34], [93], [152], [153] and [196].

[515] s.1(1) ("a person who is not a party . . . ").

[516] Above, para.14–047.

[517] s.1(1); see especially ss.2 and 3, below paras 18–098—18–110.

[518] 1999 Act, s.7(1).

[519] See n.512, above; and see para.18–112 below.

reasons, what may be called the old law relating to Himalaya clauses retains a considerable degree of practical importance, so that it would not be safe to rely exclusively on the simpler forms of words that can protect third parties under the Act.

18–091 **Term purporting to confer benefit on third party.** Under subs.1(1)(b) of the 1999 Act, C may enforce a term of the contract if "the term purports to confer a benefit on him"; but his right to do so in such a case is subject to s.1(2), by which C has no such right "if on a proper construction of the contract it appears that [A and B] did not intend the term to be enforceable by" C.[520] These will probably be the most significant provisions of the 1999 Act and their interpretation is likely to give rise to a number of difficulties. It seems that a "benefit" within s.1(1)(b) can include any performance due under the contract between A and B: thus it can include a payment of money, a transfer of property, or the rendering of a service; it can also (by virtue of s.1(6)) include the benefit of an exemption or limitation clause. The requirement that the term must "purport" to confer a benefit on C has been held to mean that it must have "the effect of conferring a benefit"[521] on him. If that is the position, there is no further requirement that benefiting the third party must be "the predominant purpose or intent behind the term."[522] But it is submitted that it must be *a* purpose of the parties, so that it would not suffice for C to show merely that he would happen to benefit from the performance of the term where A and B had no intention at all to confer that benefit on him. The question whether A and B had any such intention would be one of construction.[523] If, for example, A were employed by B "to cut my hedge adjoining C's land", performance by A might benefit C, but the term would not "purport to confer a benefit" on C. The question of construction could be particularly hard to answer where A was a subcontractor employed by B to render services in relation to property owned by C.[524] Assuming that the *term* does purport to confer a benefit on C, it is then necessary to construe the *contract* as a whole to determine the nature and extent of C's right to enforce the term. This follows from s.1(4), under which "this section does not confer a right on [C] to enforce a term of a contract otherwise than subject to and in accordance

---

[520] For an apparent doubt whether this provision had been satisfied, see *Avraamides v Colwill* [2006] EWCA Civ 1553, *The Times* December 6, 2006 at [20]; the actual decision turned on s.1(3) of the 1999 Act (see below, para.18–094).

[521] *Prudential Assurance Co Ltd v Ayres* [2007] EWHC 775 (Ch), [2007] 3 All E.R. 946 at [28], reversed [2008] EWCA Civ 52 on the different ground that the contract, on its true construction, purported, not to *benefit* C, but to *restrict* C's rights.

[522] [2007] EWHC 775 at [28].

[523] *Nisshin Shipping Co Ltd v Cleaves & Co Ltd* [2003] EWHC 2602, [2004] 1 All E.R. (Comm) 481.

[524] An analogous problem arose, apparently under Brazilian law, in *Petromec Inc v Petroleo Brasileiro SA Petrobas* [2004] EWHC 1180 (Comm), [2005] 1 Lloyd's Rep. 219 where A, a sub-bareboat charterer of an oil production platform, took out a policy of insurance with B relating to the platform. It was held that no claim on the policy could be brought in his own right by C, a subcontractor engaged to do upgrading work on the platform, as A had not purported to insure for the benefit of C. In English law, similar reasoning could on such facts be applied to a claim brought under s.1(1)(b) of the 1999 Act. On appeal, the decision was affirmed without reference to the point of Brazilian law here discussed: [2005] EWCA Civ 891, [2006] 1 Lloyd's Rep. 121 (above, para.2–116 n.499).

with any other relevant terms of the contract." This provision would, for example, apply if the term which C was seeking to enforce provided for the payment to him of £1,000, but another term of the contract provided that claims under the former term must be made within one year. Yet a further and different question of construction arises (with regard to the intention of A and B) under s.1(2) (quoted above) and it appears from the wording of this subsection that the burden of proof under it rests on A,[525] or (in other words) that, if the term purports to confer a benefit on C, then there is a rebuttable presumption that the term is intended by A and B to be enforceable by C.[526] To rebut the presumption, A must (in the words of s.1(2)) show that "the parties" did not intend the term to be enforceable by C. Thus it is not enough for A to show that he did not so intend; he must show that neither he nor B had this intention. Nor is the presumption rebutted merely because in the contract A and B had reserved the right to rescind or vary the contract: this follows from the provisions with regard to such rescission or variation made in s.2 of the Act and discussed in paras 18–093 to 18–101 below. As the question of intention put in s.1(2) is there described as one of "construction", it seems that the evidence which A will be allowed to adduce for this purpose will, in general, be limited by the rules which restrict the types of evidence admissible on other questions of construction.[527] It follows from the structure of s.1 that the mere absence from the contract of any express statement that C is to have the right to enforce the term is not a bar to his entitlement under the section to do so[528]; but that effect will be given to an express contractual provision that C is not to have any such rights.

The operation of ss.1(1)(b) and (2) is illustrated by *The Laemthong Glory*[529] **18–092**
where, because of the bill the lading relating to goods which had been carried in a chartered ship had not reached the prospective receiver (A) by the time of the ship's arrival at the contractual destination, the goods were delivered to A against a letter of indemnity (LOI) issued by A to the charterer (B) and amounting to a contract between A and B. The LOI contained a promise to indemnify "you [B] your servants or agents" in respect of liability which might be incurred by reason of delivery of the goods at A's request without production of the bill of lading. It was held that this promise on its true construction purported to confer a benefit on the shipowner (C) within s.1(1)(b) of the 1999 Act as C had acted as one of B's "agents" within the meaning of the LOI in delivering the goods to A, and that the promise was enforceable by C against A. A had not discharged the burden imposed on him by s.1(2) of proving that the LOI was not intended by A and B to be enforceable by C.

Application to previous decisions? It is tempting to speculate how the **18–093**
provisions discussed in paras 18–089 to 18–092 above would apply to some of

[525] See *The Laemthong Glory*, below, para.18–092.

[526] Report, paras 7.5, 7.17.

[527] See above, para.12–096; but the rule that evidence is not admissible to ascertain the "parties' intention" (*Prenn v Simmonds* [1971] 1 W.L.R. 1381, 1385) can scarcely apply in the present context since the very purpose of the enquiry under s.1(2) is to determine what the parties intended.

[528] *Nisshin Shipping* case, above n.523.

[529] *Laemthong International Lines Co Ltd v Artis (The Laemthong Glory (No.2)* [2005] EWCA Civ 519, [2005] 1 Lloyd's Rep. 632.

the leading cases in which the doctrine of privity was applied before the 1999 Act. To some extent, indeed, such an exercise is likely to be fruitless since the courts have not in the past directed their attention to the issues which will arise under the Act. In *Beswick v Beswick*,[530] for example, the contract no doubt purported to confer a benefit on C; but no finding of fact was made (because such a finding would have been irrelevant) as to the intention of A and B on the issue of legal enforceability by C: it is conceivable that A could now succeed on this issue if, for example, he could show that A and B had, when the contract was made, instructed the solicitor who drafted it to do so in such a way as *not* to confer legally enforceable rights on C.[531] On the facts (if they now recurred), of a number of other cases, the position under the 1999 Act would, it is submitted be clearer. Thus in the "disappointed beneficiary" cases such as *White v Jones*[532] C would not get a right under the Act against A, the negligent solicitor, since the terms of the solicitor's retainer (even if they identified C[533]) would not purport to confer a benefit on C: the intended benefit was to come, not from A, but from B.[534] It is similarly unlikely that cases such as the *Junior Books* case,[535] in which A is a subcontractor employed by B to enable B to perform his contract with C, would be covered, even if the subcontract named C, since the purpose of such a subcontract would, *prima facie*, be to regulate the relations between A and B rather than to confer a benefit on C.[536] Cases such as the *Linden Garden* case[537] would likewise not be affected by section 1 since the mere possibility that land on which work is done by a building contractor (A) might be transferred to purchasers (C) from the owners (B) would not be sufficient to show that the term relating to the quality of the work purported to "confer a benefit" on such purchasers; nor would the contract, without more, adequately "identify"[538] such purchasers as third parties for the purpose of s.1(1). Nor, in circumstances such as those of the *Panatown* case,[539] would the mere fact that the building contractor (A) knew that the property on which he was working in pursuance of his contract with B belonged to someone other than B[540] suffice to show that the benefit was to be conferred on that other person (C): the answer to the question whether the work was being done for the benefit of C or B would depend on the contractual relations between B and C, of the details of which A might be wholly unaware. In the "family holiday" cases discussed in paras 18–049 to 18–050 above, the

[530] [1968] A.C. 58; above, para.18–020.

[531] It would have been easy, even before the 1999 Act, for the solicitor to have drafted the contract so as to make it enforceable by C, *e.g.* by expressly making B trustee for C (above, para.18–079) or by making C a joint promisee with B (see above, para.3–041). We do not know whether the solicitor explained these possibilities to A and B or whether he received any instructions from them on the point.

[532] [1995] 2 A.C. 207; above, para.18–037.

[533] Within s.1(3): see below, para.18–094.

[534] Report, para.7.25.

[535] *Junior Books Ltd v Veitchi Co Ltd* [1983] 1 A.C. 520; above, para.18–023.

[536] The case was a Scottish case and no claim was made in contract even though Scots law recognises a *jus quaesitum tertio* arising by way of contract.

[537] *Linden Gardens Trust Ltd v Lenesta Sludge Disposals Ltd* [1994] 1 A.C. 85; above, para.18–053.

[538] Within s.1(3), below para.18–094.

[539] *Alfred McAlpine Construction Ltd v Panatown Ltd* [2001] 1 A.C. 518, above, para.18–058.

[540] As appears to have been the position in *Darlington B.C. v Wiltshier Northern Ltd* [1995] 1 W.L.R. 68.

outcome under the Act would depend on the nature of the transaction. If the person making the booking supplied the names of other members of the family when the contract was made, those other members would probably acquire rights under s.1(1); but no such rights are likely to be acquired if a person simply rented a holiday cottage without giving the lessor any information as to the number or names of the persons with whom he proposed to share the accommodation. In many of the situations which have here been discussed, the question whether the contract purports to confer a benefit on C will be closely related to the question, to be discussed in para.18–094 below, whether C is adequately "identified" in the contract between A and B.

Identification of third party. Under s.1(3) of the 1999 Act, it is a requirement of C's right to enforce A's promise that C must have been "*expressly* identified in the contract [between A and B] by name, as a member of a class or as answering a particular description"[541]; and it follows from this requirement that C could not rely, for the purpose of s.1(1), on the argument that the contract referred to him by implication.[542] So long as C is identified in accordance with the requirements of s.1(3), there is no need for C to be in existence when the contract was made: for example a promise in favour of an unborn child, a future spouse or of an unformed company could be enforced by[543] such a third party when it came into existence. Although it is a *necessary* condition for the creation of C's rights under s.1(1) that he must be expressly identified in the contract between A and B, such identification is not a *sufficient* condition for this purpose, since a contract which identifies C does not necessarily purport to confer a benefit on him. If, for example, a portrait painter (A) were commissioned by a college (B) to paint a portrait of the head of the college (C) for display on its premises, the contract would not purport to confer a benefit on C, nor would A and B intend the contract to be enforceable by C. It would seem that C must be identified in such a way as to indicate that A and B intended to confer rights on C: thus the identification requirement would be satisfied where A promised B not to sue C for negligence but not where A promised B not to sue B for C's negligence.[544] The requirements of s.1(3) are, in other words, *additional* to those of s.1(2). Their operation may be illustrated by reference to the *Midland Silicones* case[545]: on the facts of that case, C would not be able to enforce the limitation clause since the contract between A and B contained no express reference to C (whether by name, 18–094

[541] Italics supplied.

[542] See *Avraamides v Colwill* [2006] EWCA Civ 1533, *The Times*, December 8, 2006 at [19], where on the transfer of B's business to A, A promised B to pay "any liabilities properly incurred by B." This was held not to amount to an express identification of one of B's former customers (even though A had also promised "to complete outstanding customer orders") since the "liabilities" to which it referred "would benefit third parties but of a large number of *unidentified* classes" (at [19], italics supplied). For similar reasons, facts such as those of *London Drugs Ltd v Kuehne & Nagel Ltd* [1992] 3 S.C.R. 299 would not, if they were governed by English law, appear to be governed by the Act.

[543] A company which did not at the time of the contract exist could, on coming into existence, by virtue of s.1(3) *enforce* a term made for its benefit (within s.1(1); but the rules relating to contracts made on behalf of such a company would continue to govern the extent to which such a company could be *bound* by a contract made on its behalf: Report paras 8.9 to 8.16; Companies Act 1985, s.36C (referred to in Report, para.8.9) has been replaced by Companies Act 2006, s.51.

[544] As, for example, in *Adler v Dickson* [1955] 1 QB 158.

[545] *Midland Silicones Ltd v Scruttons Ltd* [1962] A.C. 446; above, para.14–042.

by description or as a member of a class). In these circumstances, neither subsection would be satisfied: C would not be identified and this very fact would indicate that the contract did not purport to confer a benefit on him. Where a contract is (as it was in the *Midland Silicones* case) contained in or evidenced by a bill of lading, it is now likely to contain a Himalaya clause, which would be likely adequately to identify C within s.1(3) and also to satisfy the requirements of s.1(2), with the result that C would be entitled to "enforce"[546] the limitation clause. The question whether C is identified in such a way as to give him an enforceable right may itself raise a question of construction: *e.g.* where the words of the term are adequate to identify C but the term does not purport (or A and B do not intend) to confer a benefit on him.[547]

18–095 **Remedies.** Where C has a right to enforce a term of the contract by virtue of s.1(1) of the 1999 Act, he has this right in spite of the fact that he is not a party to the contract: the Act does not, in general, adopt the technique of transferring rights from B to C or of treating C as having acquired rights by means of the fiction that he has become a party to the contract.[548] It does, however, make use of such a fiction so far as C's remedies are concerned.[549] Section 1(5) provides that "For the purpose of exercising his right to enforce a term of the contract, there shall be available to the third party any remedy that would have been available to him in an action for breach of the contract if he had been a party to the contract (and the rules relating to damages, injunctions, specific performance and other relief shall apply accordingly)." It follows from this provision that C can invoke the same kinds of judicial remedies as would be available to B if no third party were involved, and that C can recover damages for loss of bargain (or "expectation" loss) even though the bargain was made, not with him, but with B. It also follows that the same principles which would limit B's remedies in a two-party case also apply to an action brought by C: for example, the principles of remoteness and mitigation and those which restrict the availability of specific relief.[550] The application of these principles may, however, lead to different practical results where the action is brought by C from those which would follow from them in an action brought by B. For example, in an action brought by C, the test of remoteness would be whether it was C's (not B's) loss which A ought reasonably have contemplated; the principles of mitigation would require the court to ask what steps C (not B) ought reasonably have taken to mitigate his loss; and the question whether specific relief should be refused on account of the

---

[546] See s.1(6), above, para.18–090.

[547] Such a question could arise on facts such as those in *Elder Dempster & Co Ltd v Paterson Zochonis & Co Ltd* [1924] A.C. 522, where the form of bill of lading used seems to have been based on the assumption that the goods would be carried by B but they were in fact carried by C and the words of the exemption clause in the bill happened to be apt to refer also to C. In the *Avraamides* case, above note 542, A's promise to B to "complete outstanding customer orders" seems to have been intended for the benefit of B rather than of any of B's customers.

[548] 1999 Act, s.7(4), below, para.18–117. This refers only to other legislation, but the principle that C is not to be treated as a party to the contract appears also to apply for the purpose of rules of common law: see below, para.18–097.

[549] Also for a number of other purposes relating to defences available to A against C: see s.3(4) and (6), below, para.18–109; and to arbitration provisions: see s.8, below, para.18–096.

[550] Report, paras 3.32, 3.33.

conduct of the claimant could receive one answer where the action was brought by C and another if it were brought by B.

Arbitration provisions. The contract containing the term which C seeks to enforce against A may also contain an arbitration clause amounting to a written arbitration agreement within the Arbitration Act 1996.[551] The 1999 Act provides that, if C seeks to enforce the former term against A, then C is to be treated as a party to the arbitration agreement.[552] It follows that, if C attempted to enforce that term *by action*, A could obtain a stay of that action under the 1996 Act and so secure compliance by C with the arbitration agreement.[553] A contract between A and B may also provide that C is to be entitled to submit to arbitration some dispute between himself and A *other* than one concerning the enforcement by C against A of one of the other terms of that contract. Such an arbitration provision cannot compel C to resort to arbitration of (for example) a tort claim between himself and A. But if the provision is a term which C is entitled to enforce under s.1 of the 1999 Act and is also a written arbitration agreement within the Arbitration Act 1996 and C chooses to submit the dispute with A to arbitration, then C is treated for the purpose of the 1996 Act as a party to the arbitration agreement so that the arbitration proceedings will be governed by the Act. 18–096

No requirement of consideration moving from third party. The 1999 Act does not impose any requirement that consideration for A's promise must move from C. It does not expressly provide that there is no such requirement[554]; the consequence follows from the fact that the Act gives C the right to enforce the term in question and is further supported by the general principle that C is not to be treated as a party to the contract between A and B.[555] Since the promise in contracts of the kind in question is made to B, the fact that C need not provide any consideration for it is not strictly an exception to the rule that consideration must move *from the promisee*, but it can be regarded as a quasi exception to that rule in the sense that C is a person in whose favour a promise is made and who can enforce it even though he may be no more than a gratuitous beneficiary. 18–097

Right to rescind or vary the contract by agreement. Under the judge-made rules relating to contracts for the benefit of third parties, one objection to the creation of such rights has been that it would deprive the contracting parties of their right to rescind or vary the contract by mutual consent.[556] The 1999 Act deals with this problem by means of a compromise: it specifies the circumstances in which A and B, *prima facie*, lose this right, while it at the same time enables them so to draw up their contract as to retain the right or to change the *prima facie* rules laid down in the Act which specify when it is lost. 18–098

---

551 Below, Vol.II, para.32–039.
552 1999 Act, s.8(1); *e.g. Nisshin Shipping Co Ltd v Cleaves & Co Ltd* [2003] EWHC 2602, [2004] 1 All E.R. (Comm) 481.
553 1999 Act, s.8(2).
554 Report, para.6.8 n.8.
555 See above, n.548.
556 This has been one reason for the restrictions on the scope of the equitable exception to the doctrine of privity by way of trusts of promises: above, para.18–079.

18–099 **General rule: C's consent required.** The general rule, stated in s.2(1) of the 1999 Act, is that, once C has acquired the right to enforce a term of the contract between A and B "under section 1", then, if one of the circumstances to be described in para.18–100 and 18–101 below has arisen, A and B may not, without C's consent, by agreement rescind or vary the contract so as to "extinguish or alter" C's entitlement. Rescission calls for no further comment here; but with regard to variation it should be noted that A and B are, under the general rule in s.2(1), precluded from varying the contract not only so as to extinguish but also so as to alter C's rights. An alteration may of course operate, not only to C's prejudice, but also to his advantage: *e.g.* where it purports to increase payments to be made to C under the term in question. Such a variation is unlikely to give rise to any problems between A and C, since C will presumably consent to it as soon as he hears of it. But the argument that C is entitled to enforce a term of a contract between A and B can also give rise to problems between one of these parties and outside interests: *e.g.* creditors of B in the event of B's insolvency.[557] Such persons may seek to invoke s.2(1) where the variation increases C's rights but where on the crucial date for the assertion of their rights C has either not yet acquired any knowledge of the variation or has not yet made any communication to A or done any other act from which his assent to the variation[558] can be inferred.

18–100 **Third party's assent to the term.** The first of the circumstances in which A and B may not, without C's consent, agree to rescind the contract, or to vary it in the ways described above[559] arises where C has communicated his assent to the term to A[560]; communication to B does not suffice for this purpose.[561] The assent may be by words or conduct[562]; and if it is "sent" to A by post or other means, it is not regarded as communicated to him "until received by him."[563] In other words, the "posting" rule, as developed in cases of contract formation[564] does not apply in the present context. "Sent" here seems to refer to some act done by C in order to communicate words of assent to A. The rule relating to an assent "sent" to A by post or other means is negative in nature: it states that the assent is not communicated to A until received by him. It thus leaves open the question whether an assent which has been so sent can take effect before it has actually come to A's notice: *e.g.* where it has been delivered to his address but not yet been read by him. If the overriding requirement is one of communication, it may not be satisfied in such a case. The expression "sent" also does not seem to be appropriate to refer to an assent by conduct; but it seems that such an assent must come to A's notice: this seems to follow from the general requirement that C's assent must be "communicated"[565] to A. No formality (such as writing) is

[557] As, for example, in *Re Schebsman* [1944] Ch. 83, above, para.18–079.
[558] See s.2(1)(a), below, para.18–100.
[559] Above, para.18–099.
[560] s.2(1)(a).
[561] This follows from the words "to the promisor" in s.2(1)(a).
[562] s.2(2)(a).
[563] s.2(2)(b).
[564] Above, para.2–048.
[565] s.2(1)(a).

required even for an assent in words,[566] so that an oral communication suffices.

Third party's reliance. The right to rescind or vary the contract is also barred where A is aware of C's having relied on the term,[567] or where A could reasonably have foreseen such reliance and it has actually taken place.[568] It would seem that, in such cases, C may be entitled, not merely to the promised performance, but also to damages in respect of his reliance loss: *e.g.* where he has travelled to the place specified in the contract for the receipt by him of the promised performance. This follows from the rule laid down by the 1999 Act with respect to C's remedies[569]; it also follows from this rule that C could not claim under both heads to the extent to which such a combination of claims would result in double recovery or in his being placed in a better position than that in which he would have been if A had performed his promise in accordance with its original terms.[570] 18–101

Consequences of attempted rescission or variation without C's consent. The general rule stated in s.2(1) is that A and B "may not" by agreement rescind the contract, or vary it in the ways described above, without C's consent. The most obvious consequence of this provision is that a purported rescission or variation without C's consent is simply *ineffective*, so that C can, in spite of it, enforce the term in question *against A*. But such enforcement may, because of the rescission, become a practical impossibility (*e.g.* because A has in consequence of the rescission put it out of his power to perform); and it is arguable that the purported rescission is also *wrongful*, so as to give C a remedy in damages *against B*, perhaps on the analogy of liability in tort for causing loss by unlawful means.[571] This possibility could have practical significance in the event of A's insolvency. 18–102

Contract conferring choices on promisee. Section 2(1) of the 1999 Act deals with the situation in which C has become entitled to enforce a term of the contract "under section 1" and A and B then attempt by agreement to rescind or vary the contract. This situation must be distinguished from that in which A promises B to perform in favour of C *or as B shall direct*. If, in such a case, B directs A to perform in favour of D (or of B himself) the contract is not varied. On the contrary, it is to be performed in accordance with its original terms, under which B has a choice as to the person to whom performance is to be rendered. The case therefore does not fall within s.2(1), so that the requirement of C's consent, as there stated, does not apply.[572] Another way of explaining this 18–103

---

566 Contrast the requirement of Law of Property Act, 1925, s.136(1), requiring written notice of an assignment.

567 s.2(1)(b).

568 s.2(1)(c).

569 s.1(5); above, para.18–095.

570 *e.g.* where it would have been necessary for C to incur the reliance expenditure in order to secure the benefit—perhaps by travelling to the place where it was to be conferred.

571 Below, para.18–135; the analogy is far from exact and its application would involve a significant extension of the tort.

572 *cf.* Report, para.10.3.

conclusion is to say that, in the case put, the mere making of the promise was not intended to confer an indefeasible right on C; for the fact that the contract gave B the power to divert the benefit away from C would indicate that A and B did not at this stage intend[573] the term to be enforceable by C if B exercised the power. A term of the present kind might, however, also *limit* B's power to divert the benefit away from C: *e.g.* by providing that the power was to be exercisable only for a specified period. After the end of that period, C could no longer be deprived of the benefit of A's promise by the unilateral act of B since the consent of A and B would then as a matter of common law be necessary to vary the contract; and any such variation would then be subject to the requirement of C's consent under s.2(1).

18–104 **Contrary provision in the contract.** The general requirement of C's consent to a rescission or variation of the contract,[574] contained in s.2(1) and stated in para.18–099 above, may be displaced by an express term of the contract. Section 2(3) envisages two possibilities. These are discussed in para.18–105.

18–105 *(1) Term dispensing with need for C's consent.* The first possibility, stated in s.2(3)(a), is for the express term to state that A and B may by agreement rescind or vary the contract, without the consent of C. Under such a term, it is open to A and B to rescind or vary the contract in spite of the fact that C has acquired a right by virtue of s.1(1) and in spite of the fact that the circumstances specified in s.2(1) have occurred: that is, even after communication of assent by C to A, or after reliance by C of which A is aware or which he could reasonably have been expected to foresee. It is not entirely clear whether it is enough for the express term to provide that A and B by agreement may rescind or vary the contract or whether it must go on to say in so many words that they may do so without the consent of C; but to be sure of achieving the desired result, A and B would be well advised to use the latter form of words.

(2) Term modifying requirement of C's consent. The second possibility, stated in s.2(3)(b), is for the express term to provide that the consent of C is required in circumstances other than those specified in s.2(1). For example, the term might provide that such consent was required only for a specified period or that it must be given in a specified form (*e.g.* by registered letter). Again, effect would be given to such provisions, so that in the first of the two examples just given, C's consent would no longer be needed (even after one of the circumstances described in s.2(1) had occurred) after the end of the period; while in the second it would be ineffective if not given in the specified form.

18–106 **Judicial discretion to dispense with consent.** Section 2(4) gives the court power, on the application of A and B, to dispense with the requirement of C's consent to a rescission or variation of the contract by agreement between A and B in two situations: (a) where C's consent cannot be obtained because "his whereabouts cannot reasonably be ascertained"; or (b) where he is mentally incapable of giving his consent. On a similar principle, the court has under s.2(5)

---

[573] Within s.1(2).

[574] Above, para.18–099.

the same power where it is alleged that C's consent is required because A could reasonably have foreseen that C would rely on the term[575] but it cannot reasonably be ascertained whether he has in fact relied on it. Where the court under these provisions dispenses with C's consent, it may order compensation to be paid to him[576]; such an order may presumably be made against either A or B or both of them.

Promisor's defences against third party. Section 3 of the 1999 Act contains an elaborate set of provisions which specify matters on which A can rely by way of defence, set-off or counterclaim against C in an action by C for the enforcement, "in reliance on section 1,"[577] of a term of the contract between A and B. 18–107

(1) General principle. The starting principle, stated in s.3(2), is that A can rely by way of defence, or set-off on any matter that "arises from or in connection with the contract [between A and B] and is relevant to the term" and would have been available to A if the proceedings (to enforce the term) had been brought by B. Under this principle, A could, for example, rely against C on a valid exemption clause in the contract between A and B[578]; and on the fact that the contract was void for mistake or voidable for misrepresentation,[579] or that it had been frustrated or that A was justified in refusing to perform it on account of B's repudiatory breach.

(2) Contrary provision. The general principle just stated can be excluded by a contrary provision in the contract: *i.e.* by a term in the contract between A and B that A is not to be entitled to rely on such matters against C[580]; though where the contract between A and B was wholly void such a term would appear to be of no more effect than the rest of the purported contract. The general principle can, conversely, be extended by an express term in the contract. Section 3(3) provides that A can (in addition to the matters referred to in s.3(2)) rely by way of defence or set-off against C on any matter if "an express term of the contract provides for it to be available to him [A] in proceedings brought by" C and it would have been so available to A in proceedings brought by B. Under this provision, A could rely against C on debts owed by B to A even though the debts arose out of other transactions, if the contract containing the term which C was seeking to enforce contained an express term that A was to be entitled to rely on those debts also against C. 18–108

(3) Defence against C only. There is a further possibility that A may have defences or counterclaims against C which he would not have against B: *e.g.* where A had been induced to enter into the contract with B by C's misrepresentation, or where C was indebted to A under another transaction. Section 3(4) 18–109

[575] See s.2(1)(c).
[576] s.2(6).
[577] s.3(1).
[578] *cf.* Report, para.10.31.
[579] See *Moody v Condor Insurance Ltd* [2006] EWHC 100 (Ch), [2006] 1 W.L.R. 1847 at [30].
[580] s.3(5).

enables A to rely on such matters against C if they could have been so relied on if C had been a party to the contract between A and B; though this rule, like the general principle stated in s.3(2), can be modified or excluded by an express term of that contract.[581]

18–110 *(4) Reliance on exemption clauses.* A rule analogous to the general principle of s.3(2) applies where the "enforcement" of the term by C takes the form of his availing himself of an exemption or limitation clause in his favour in the contract between A and B.[582] Section 3(6) provides that C cannot in this way "enforce" the term if he could not have done so, had he been a party to the contract. This restriction on C's right to enforce the term would, for example, apply if, by reason of the Unfair Contract Terms Act 1977[583] the clause had been invalid or if it had not satisfied the requirement of reasonableness as imposed by that Act; or if the clause was invalid under other legislation[584]; or C was guilty of a fraud on A and so could not have relied on the term (even though B might have been able to do so) by reason of the common law rule that an exemption clause does not protect a party from liability for his own fraud.[585]

18–111 **Exceptions to third party's entitlement.** A number of situations which *prima facie* fall within s.1 of the 1999 Act are excepted from the operation of that section by s.6. These exceptions fall into two groups. In cases which fall within the first group, C has, or can acquire, rights under the contract between A and B by virtue of some other rule of law; and the purpose of excepting these cases from the operation of s.1 is to preserve, not only C's rights, but also the conditions under which those rights arise under those other rules of law. In cases which fall within the second group, by contrast, C has, prima facie, no rights under other rules of law; and the purpose of excepting these cases from the operation of s.1 is to preserve in them the general rule of common law by which C acquires no rights under the contract between A and B. Such cases, in other words, continue to be governed by the common law doctrine of privity, subject to any limitations on its scope and to any exceptions to it that may exist at common law.

18–112 **The first group of exceptions.** The first of the above group of exceptions includes contracts on bills of exchange, promissory notes and other negotiable instruments[586]: third parties can acquire rights under such contracts under the rules relating to negotiability, discussed elsewhere in this book.[587]; and it is not the purpose of the Act to extend those rights.[588] It also includes contracts for the

---

[581] s.3(5) applies to s.3(4) as well as to s.3(2).

[582] See s.1(6), above para.18–090.

[583] Above, paras 14–059 *et seq.*

[584] See *Homburg Houtimport BV v Agrosin Private Ltd (The Starsin)* [2003] UKHL 12, [2004] 1 A.C. 715 where a Himalaya clause (above, para.14–048) was held not to protect a third party at common law by reason of its being void under Art.III. 8 of the Hague Rules. An attempt by the third party to "enforce" such a clause in reliance on s.1(6) of the 1999 Act would fail for the same reason by virtue of s.3(6) of that Act.

[585] Above, para.14–036.

[586] s.6(1).

[587] Below, Vol.II Ch.34.

[588] Report, para.12.6.

carriage of goods by sea which are governed by the Carriage of Goods by Sea Act 1992, and corresponding electronic transactions to which that Act may be applied by Order.[589] The carefully regulated scheme of the 1992 Act[590] for the acquisition of rights under such contracts by third parties (such as transferees of bills of lading) would be seriously disrupted if such third parties could acquire rights under the 1999 Act in circumstances in which no such rights would be acquired under the 1992 Act. The same is (*mutatis mutandis*) true of contracts for the international carriage of goods by rail, road and air, which are governed by international conventions having the force of law in the United Kingdom,[591] so that these contracts are likewise excepted from the operation of s.1 of the 1999 Act.[592] The present exception is, however, in turn, subject to an exception[593]: C is not precluded from taking the benefit of an exemption or limitation clause in a contract for the carriage of goods governed by the 1992 Act or by the international conventions referred to above merely because such legislation applies to the contract. Before the 1999 Act, C could in many cases, take the benefit of an exemption or limitation clause in the contract of carriage (*e.g.* where the contract contained a Himalaya clause). The legal reasoning on which this result was based was that a separate or collateral contract arose, by virtue of such a clause and the conduct of the parties, between A and C.[594] Since C *is a party* to this contract, his right to "enforce" it does not depend (in the words of the present exception) on any "reliance on . . . section" 1.[595] The effectiveness of Himalaya clauses would therefore not be directly affected by the present exception[596] to a *third party's* entitlement under s.1 to "enforce" an exemption or limitation clause. But one of the objects of the 1999 Act appears to have been to simplify the drafting of Himalaya clauses and to remove obstacles to their efficacy which might be encountered in establishing the separate contract between A and C,[597] and it is for this reason that the present exception to the operation of s.1 does not apply to exemption and limitation clauses in contracts of carriage which, for other purposes, fall within that exception.

The second group of exceptions. The second group of exceptions described in paragraph 18–111 above includes the contract which binds the company and its members by the terms of the company's constitution of virtue of s.33(1) of the 18–113

[589] s.6(5)(a); Carriage of Goods by Sea Act 1992, s.1(5), as amended by Communications Act 2003, s.406(1), Sch.17 para.17.

[590] For details of this scheme, see *Carver on Bills of Lading*, 2nd ed, (2005) paras 5–012—5–107, 8–002—8–016, 8–035—8–059; the 1992 Act (unlike the 1999 Act) provides not only for the acquisition of rights by, but also for the imposition of liabilities on, third parties.

[591] See below, Vol.II Chs 35 and 36.

[592] s.6(5)(b).

[593] s.6(5), "tailpiece".

[594] Above, paras 18–090, 14–047—14–048; *Homburg Houtimport BV v Agrosin Private Ltd (The Starsin)* [2003] UKHL 12, [2004] 1 A.C. 715 at [34], [93], [152], [153] and [196].

[595] s.1(1) confers a right of enforcement only on a "person who is *not* a party" to the contract.

[596] *i.e.*, that contained in s.6(5) of the 1999 Act.

[597] See Report, paras 2.35, 12.10; for the complexity of the drafting of Himalaya clauses and the difficulties which arise, or are thought to arise, in satisfying the common law requirement of a separate contract between A and C, see above, para.14–047—14–049.

Companies Act 2006.[598] The purpose of this exception is presumably to preserve the established limitations on the scope of this "statutory contract:"[599] *e.g.* the rule that this contract confers no rights on a director of the company as such.[600] The second group also includes contracts of employment and certain analogous contracts to the extent that such a contract will not give the employer's customer any right under s.1 of the 1999 Act to enforce any term of such a contract against the employee.[601]

18–114 **Third party's other rights unaffected.** Section 7(1) of the 1999 Act provides that "Section 1 does not affect any right or remedy of a third party that exists or is available apart from this Act." It follows that C continues, after the coming into force of the Act, to be able to enforce rights and to rely on defences arising under a contract between A and B, if before then he could have done so under exceptions to the doctrine of privity established at common law, in equity or under other legislation, or if he could have done so because the case fell outside the scope of the doctrine of privity of contract: these possibilities are discussed elsewhere in this Chapter.[602] C will, for example, continue to be able to enforce a promise made by A to B if there is a trust of the promise in his favour[603]; he will continue to be able to enforce collateral contracts between himself and A[604] and, in particular to be able to rely on Himalaya clauses by virtue of which an exemption or limitation clause in a contract between A and B becomes available to him.[605] Indeed, in some such cases the person seeking to enforce the term is not truly a "third party" within the 1999 Act.[606] The whole point of the collateral contract device is to establish a direct contractual relationship between the parties that have here been called A and C; and the legal basis for the efficacy of Himalaya clauses at common law is similarly that they make it possible for a contract of some kind to come into existence between A and C,[607] though this is not the same as "the contract" (*i.e.* that between A and B) containing the term on which C seeks to rely. Subsection 7(1) also preserves any rights which C may

---

[598] Replacing, with modifications, the effect of 14 of the Companies Act 1985, which is repealed by s.1295 and Sch.16 of Companies Act s.2006. S.33(1) of the latter Act is quoted in para.18–010 above.

[599] *Soden v British & Commonwealth Holdings plc (in Administration)* [1998] A.C. 298, 323.

[600] *Beattie v E. & F. Beattie Ltd* [1938] Ch. 708; *Rayfield v Hands* [1960] Ch. 1 is hard to reconcile with this principle: L.C.B.G., 21 M.L.R. 401. The limitations on the scope of the "statutory contract" referred to above seem not to be affected by the fact that this contract, which formerly arose by virtue of Companies Act 1985, s.14, now arises (after the repeal of that section by s.1295 and Sch.16 of Companies Act 2006) by virtue of 33(1) of the 2006 Act: see above, paras 18–010 and 18–113 note 598. Para. 108 of the Explanatory Notes to the 2006 Act states that "Like s.14(1) [of the Companies Act 1985] the provisions of this section [*i.e.*, s.33 of Companies Act 2006] are excepted from the general principle set out in s.1 of the Contracts (Rights of Third Parties) Act 1999 . . . " There is no express provision to this effect in the 2006 Act; but the effect of s.1297(5) of the 2006 Act appears to be that, once s.33(1) of the 2006 Act has come into force, the reference in s.6(2) of the 1999 Act to s.14 of the 1985 Act will have effect as being a reference to s.33 of the 2006 Act.

[601] ss.6(3), (4).

[602] Above, paras 18–005, 18–021, 18–077 *et seq*; below, paras 18–121 *et seq.*

[603] Above, paras 18–078 *et seq.*

[604] Above, paras 18–005 *et seq.*

[605] Above, paras 14–049, 14–050, 18–090, 18–112.

[606] s.1(1), ("not a party . . . ").

[607] See above, at n.604.

have to sue A in tort in respect of loss suffered by C in consequence of A's breach of his contract with B; we have seen that in such cases C will often have no rights under the 1999 Act.[608] C could also rely on the subsection to enforce rights arising under legislation coming into force after the 1999 Act or under new exceptions to the doctrine of privity of contract which might, after that Act, be developed by the courts.[609]

Although s.7(1) in terms states only that "Section 1" does not affect other rights and remedies available to C, it follows from the structure of the 1999 Act that many of its other provisions will likewise not apply where C's rights against A arise apart from the Act. Of particular significance are the points that the rules as to rescission and variation, contained in s.2, and the rules as to defences and related matters, contained in s.3, will not so apply, since s.2 applies only "where a third party has a right under section 1 to enforce a term of the contract"[610] and s.3 applies only "where, in reliance on section 1, proceedings for the enforcement of a term of a contract are brought by a third party."[611] **18–115**

The structure resulting from the distinctions drawn in paragraphs 18–115 to 18–107 is therefore a complex one. Four types of cases call for consideration. The first is that in which C has rights under the 1999 Act but none apart from it because the case falls within the scope of the doctrine of privity of contract but not within any of the judge-made or other legislative exceptions to it. Here C's rights and remedies are clearly subject to the provisions of the Act. The second is the case in which C has no rights under the Act (either because the requirements of its s.1 are not satisfied or because one of the exceptions listed in its s.6 applies) but in which he does have rights apart from the Act, because the case falls either outside the scope of the doctrine of privity of contract or within one of the judge-made or other legislative exceptions to it. Here the rights and remedies to which C is entitled are clearly not subject to the provisions of the Act.[612] The third is the case in which C has rights both under the Act and apart from it[613] (because the case falls outside the scope of the doctrine of privity of contract or within one of the judge-made or other legislative exceptions to it). It would seem that in such a case C can choose between making his claim under the Act (and so subject to its provisions) and apart from the Act (and so not subject to its provisions). If, for example, C has a cause of action against A in tort at common law, it may be to C's advantage to pursue that claim (rather than one which may also be, *prima facie*, available to him under s.1) since in making such a common law claim he would not, in general, be bound by an exemption clause in the contract between A and B, while he would be so bound if he made a claim under the Act.[614] The fourth is the case in which C has no rights under the Act and none under the existing rules of common law or under other legislative **18–116**

---

[608] Above, para.18–093.

[609] See below at n.615.

[610] s.2(1).

[611] s.3(1).

[612] *White v Jones* [1995] 2 A.C. 207 (above, paras 18–037, 18–093) illustrates this possibility.

[613] e.g. *Nisshin Shipping Co Ltd v Cleaves & Co Ltd* [2003] EWHC 2602, [2004] 1 All E.R. 481.

[614] s.3(2), above para.18–107.

exceptions to the doctrine of privity of contract. Here, C's only hope is to induce the court to create a new exception to the doctrine of privity[615] or (in the House of Lords) to reject that doctrine altogether. If C's claim were upheld on one of these grounds, it would plainly not be subject to the provisions of the 1999 Act.

18–117 **Nature of the third party's rights.** Although the 1999 Act for certain specified purposes[616] makes use of the fiction of treating C as if he were a party to the contract, it in general treats C's rights and defences as being *sui generis*.[617] It does not, in other words, except for those specified purposes, treat C as if he were deemed to be, or to have become, a party to the contract. In particular, the Act provides that C is not to be treated as a party to the contract between A and B for the purposes of other legislation.[618] For example, the references to a party or to the parties to a contract in the Law Reform (Frustrated Contracts) Act 1943 and in the Misrepresentation Act 1967 do not, under the 1999 Act include references to C. The same is true of the Unfair Contract Terms Act 1977. The point can be illustrated by supposing that a contract was made between A and B on A's standard terms of business, that a term of this contract conferred a benefit on C, that this term was enforceable by C by virtue of s.1 of the Act, and that the contract contained a term excluding or restricting A's liability for defects in the performance rendered to C. The requirement of reasonableness under s.3 of the 1977 Act[619] would not apply in favour of C since he was not one of the parties to the contract between A and B or a party who had dealt on A's standard terms: the requirement would apply only in favour of B.[620] The justification given by the Law Commission for this position is that to apply the 1977 Act in a three-party case would raise complex policy issues going beyond those involved in reforming the doctrine of privity.[621]

18–118 **Effect on Unfair Contract Terms Act 1977, section 2.** The relationship between the 1999 Act and the Unfair Contract Terms Act 1977 gives rise to the further difficulty that under s.2(1) of the 1977 Act[622] contract terms are void if they purport to exclude or restrict liability for death or personal injury resulting

---

[615] *e.g.* perhaps, to follow the Supreme Court of Canada's decision in *London Drugs Ltd v Kuehne & Nagel International Ltd* [1992] 3 S.C.R. 299 in recognising, at least to a limited extent, the principle of vicarious immunity: *cf.* above, para.18–021, n.112.

[616] See s.1(5), relating to C's remedies: above, para.18–095; s.3(4), relating to certain defences; s.3(6), relating to restrictions on the availability of exemption clauses: above, para.18–110; for a different technique, see s.7(3), relating to limitation of actions and s.8, relating to arbitration agreements (above, para.18–096; below Vol.II, para.32–039).

[617] A claim by C under the Contracts (Rights of Third Parties) Act 1999 is, however, a "matter relating to contract" within Art.5.1 of the Judgments Regulation (EC 44/2001; OJ 2001 L 12 p 1): *WPP Holdings Italy SRL v Benatti* [2007] EWCA Civ 263, [2007] 2 All E.R. (Comm) 525 at [53]–[55].

[618] 1999 Act, s.7(4). This provides that C is not to be so treated "by virtue of section 1(5) or 3(4) or 3(6)", above, n.616. No reference is made in s.7(4) to s.8, above, n.616, by virtue of which C *is* treated as a party to an arbitration agreement for the purpose of the Arbitration Act 1996.

[619] Above, para.14–072.

[620] Report, para.13.10; for B's right of enforcement, see below, para.18–119.

[621] Report, para.13.10 (vii) and (viii).

[622] Above, para.14–071.

from negligence and that under s.2(2)[623] contract terms are subject to the requirement of reasonableness if they purport to exclude or restrict liability for negligence in respect of other loss. Negligence here can include breach of a contractual duty of care,[624] so that a claim by C affected by s.2 of the 1977 Act could be brought either under the 1999 Act or in tort, apart from the latter Act. Where it is brought under the 1999 Act, a compromise solution[625] is adopted for cases of the kind here under discussion, *i.e.* for those in which C sues A for breach of a duty of care arising out of the contract between A and B, and A seeks to rely on a term of that contract excluding or restricting his liability for negligence. Where C in consequence of the breach suffers death or personal injury, the strong policy considerations against contract terms excluding or restricting A's liability for such harm prevail, so that nothing in the 1999 Act will affect C's right under s.2(1) of the 1977 Act to impugn the validity of a term excluding or restricting A's liability for such harm. But where C suffers other loss, the case is regarded as more closely analogous to the situation (described in para.18–117 above) that can arise under s.3 of the 1977 Act. Section 7(2) of the 1999 Act therefore provides that s.2(2) of the 1977 Act is not to apply where A's alleged negligence consists of the breach of an obligation arising from a term of a contract (between A and B) and the claim by C is brought under s.1 of the 1999 Act. In an action so brought by C, therefore, a term in that contract excluding or restricting A's liability for loss other than death or personal injury is not subject to the requirement of reasonableness under the 1977 Act.

Promisee's rights. At common law, the doctrine of privity of contract does **18–119** not preclude the promisee from enforcing the contract[626] and this position is preserved by s.4 of the 1999 Act, by which "Section 1 does not affect any right of the promisee to enforce any term of the contract." The contract between A and B can thus be enforced by B even where the 1999 Act also gives C the right to enforce one of its terms against A. On A's failure to perform that term in favour of C, B can therefore make any claims for the agreed sum, for other specific relief or for damages that would have been available to him at common law apart from the Act. There is also nothing in the Act that affects B's right to restitution[627] against A in the event of the latter's non-performance of the term in favour of C, even though B's right to restitution would not normally be a "right of [B] to enforce a term of the contract" within s.4. It would have this character only where the contract provided for the return by A of the consideration provided by B to A in the event of A's failure to perform in favour of C. The 1999 Act also contains nothing to affect the common law rules which govern the relative rights of B and C where A has performed, or is willing to perform, in favour of C.[628]

---

623 Above, para.14–071.

624 Unfair Contract Terms Act 1977, s.1(1)(a).

625 See Report, 13.12. The compromise is retained in Clauses 1(2) and 34(1) and Sch.5 para.40 of the Draft Unfair Contract Terms Act 2005 appended to the Law Commissions' Report on *Unfair Terms in Contracts*, Law Com. No. 292, Scottish Law Com. 199 (2005).

626 Above, para.18–043.

627 Above, para.18–045.

628 Above, para.18–073.

18–120 **Provision against double liability.** At common law, A's failure to perform in favour of C may, in circumstances discussed earlier in this Chapter,[629] give B a right to recover damages in respect of C's loss or in respect of expenses incurred by B in making good A's default: *e.g.* in completing A's unfinished, or in repairing A's defective, work. If, after B had recovered such damages, C were to make a claim against A under s.1 of the 1999 Act, there would be a risk of A's being made liable twice over for the same loss. Section 5 of the Act therefore directs the court in such circumstances "to reduce any award to [C] to such extent as it thinks appropriate to take account of the sum recovered by" B. Such a reduction would not prejudice C since, where damages had been recovered by B in respect of C's loss, these would have to be held by B for C[630]; and where B had incurred expense in curing A's breach, C's loss would be reduced in fact by his receipt of the intended benefit, though by a route other than that envisaged by the contract between A and B. Section 5 of the Act applies only where B has recovered "a sum" (*i.e.* of money) in respect of C's loss or B's expense in making good A's default. Thus it will normally apply where B has recovered damages, though the possibilities of its also applying where B has recovered the agreed sum or where he has made a successful claim for restitution do not appear to be excluded. It will not, however, apply where B has obtained an order for the specific performance of an obligation by A to render some performance to C other than the payment of money, or where B has obtained an injunction to enforce a negative promise made by A for the benefit of C. In such cases, C will obtain the performance due to him under the term made enforceable by him by virtue of s.1 and so will not have any right to damages for its non-performance. But C might, in addition to the receipt of the performance, claim damages from A, *e.g.* in respect of delay in rendering the performance. Such a claim is not, and should not be, affected by s.5 of the 1999 Act since its success would not make A liable twice over for the same loss.

(iii) *Other Statutory Exceptions*

18–121 A number of other exceptions to the doctrine of privity of contract were created by statute before the 1999 Act and continue to be available to the third party after the coming into force of that Act.[631] The most important of these exceptions are discussed in the paragraphs that follow.

18–122 **Law of Property Act, section 56(1).**[632] At common law a person could not take an immediate interest in property, or the benefit of any covenant, under an indenture purporting to be *inter partes*, unless he was named as a party to the

[629] Above, para.18–052—18–067.

[630] Above, para.18–076.

[631] See s.7(1) of the 1999 Act.

[632] Elliott (1956) 20 Conv. 43, 114; Andrews (1959) 23 Conv. 179; Wade [1964] C.L.J. 66; Furmston (1960) 23 M.L.R. 380–385; Ellinger (1963) 26 M.L.R. 396; all these comments on s.56(1) must now be read in the light of the decision of the House of Lords in *Beswick v Beswick* [1968] A.C. 58.

indenture.[633] The rule did not apply to deeds poll[634] or to indentures not *inter partes*.[635] In the case of such deeds, the grantee or covenantee never had to be named *as a party*, and it was eventually settled that he need not be named at all, so long as he was sufficiently designated.[636] Deeds no longer have to be indented for any purpose[637]; but the law still distinguishes between deeds *inter partes* and other deeds. That distinction has recently been restated as being one between a deed by which (i) "one or more of [the parties] makes a promise to the other" and (ii) one by which the parties executing it "seek to use the document as a means for each of them to make unilateral promises to a person not a party to it."[638] In the former case, the document is in the traditional terminology a deed *inter partes*, not enforceable at common law by a person who is not a party to it; in the latter case it is enforceable by such a person.[639] The old rule relating to indentures *inter partes*[640] still appears to apply to deeds *inter partes* which do not fall within the provisions (to be discussed below) of s.56(1) of the Law of Property Act 1925.

The common law rule with regard to indentures *inter partes* was modified by s.5 of the Real Property Act 1845,[641] which provided that "under an indenture executed after the first day of October 1845 an immediate estate or interest in any tenements or hereditaments and the benefit of a condition or covenant respecting any tenements or hereditaments may be taken although the taker thereof be not named a party to the said indenture." This enactment was limited to estates or interests in, and to conditions or covenants respecting, tenements or hereditaments, *i.e.* to real property.[642] It was later held that the enactment was further limited, in the case of covenants, to those which ran with the land.[643] **18–123**

Section 5 of the 1845 Act was replaced by s.56 of the Law of Property Act 1925, subs.(1) of which provides: "A person may take an immediate or other **18–124**

---

633 *Scudamore v Vanderstene* (1587) 2 CoInst. 673; *Storer v Gordon* (1814) 3 M. & S. 308; *Berkeley v Hardy* (1826) 5 B. & C. 355; *Southampton v Brown* (1827) 6 B. & C. 718; *Gardner v Lachlan* (1836) 8 Sim. 123. The rule was also applied to composition deeds; the cases on this subject are impossible to reconcile (see *Isaacs v Green* (1867) L.R. 2 Ex. 352, 355) but have become obsolete in view of the Deeds of Arrangement Act 1914, repealed in part by Insolvency Act 1985, s.235 and Sch.10, Pt III and amended by Insolvency Act 1986, s.439(2).

634 *cf.* above para.1–109.

635 *Cooker v Child* (1763) 2 Lev. 74; *Chelsea & Waldham Green Building Soc. v Armstrong* [1951] Ch. 853, discussed in *Moody v Condor Insurance Ltd* [2006] EWHC 100 (Ch), [2006] 1 W.L.R. 1847 at [24]–[27].

636 *Sunderland Marine Insurance Co v Kearney* (1851) 16 Q.B. 925, qualifying *Green v Horn* (1694) 1 Salk. 197.

637 Law of Property Act 1925, s.56(2).

638 *Moody v Condor Insurance Ltd* [2006] EWHC 100 (Ch), [2006] 1 W.L.R. 1847 at [16].

639 *ibid.*, at [18], where a deed of guarantee of instalments due under a contract for the sale of a company was held to fall into the second of the two categories distinguished in the text above.

640 *Beswick v Beswick* [1968] A.C. 58, 104B.

641 Replacing s.11 of the Transfer of Property Act 1844, which was not restricted to real property. For the history of this change see Davidson's *Concise Precedents in Conveyancing* (2nd ed., 1845), pp.10 *et seq. cf.* Treitel (1967) 30 M.L.R. 687, 688–689.

642 It is generally agreed that s.5 of the 1845 Act was confined to real property: see *Beswick v Beswick* [1968] A.C. 58, 87D, 104E.

643 *Forster v Elvett Colliery Co Ltd* [1908] 1 K.B. 629 (in the House of Lords, Lord Macnaghten reserved the point: *Dyson v Forster* [1909] A.C. 98, 102); *Grant v Edmonson* [1931] 1 Ch. 1.

interest in land or other property, or the benefit of any condition, right of entry, covenant or agreement over or respecting land or other property, although he may not be named as a party to the conveyance or other instrument." The 1925 Act further defines "property" to include "any thing in action."[644] In *Beswick v Beswick* Lord Denning M.R. and Danckwerts L.J. held that a promise in writing by A to B to pay a sum of money to C would, by virtue of this definition of "property," be within s.56(1) and so give C a right to enforce the promise against A.[645] But the House of Lords rejected this view, principally on the ground that the definition of "property" in the Act was stated to apply "unless the context otherwise requires." The context in s.56(1) did otherwise require, since s.56(1) was part of a consolidating Act and was designed to reproduce s.5 of the 1845 Act, which admittedly did not have the wide effect suggested for s.56(1).[646] There was, moreover, nothing in the legislative history of s.56(1) to support the view that the subsection was intended to abolish the doctrine of privity in relation to written contracts[647]; indeed, the legislative history gives some support to the view that no such change was intended.[648] The enacting words[649] of s.56(1) also give some support to this view. They refer to the case in which a person is not *named as* a party: not to the case in which he *is not* a party.[650]

18–125 Section 56(1) therefore does not apply to a bare promise in writing by A to B to pay a sum of money to C; and the correctness of a number of previous decisions to this effect[651] is reaffirmed by the House of Lords in *Beswick v Beswick*. But the question, to what other cases the subsection does apply, remains one of great difficulty. There is support in the speeches in *Beswick v Beswick* for the following limitations on the scope of s.56(1): namely, that it applies only (1) to real property[652] (2) to covenants running with the land[653]; (3) to cases where

[644] s.205(1)(xx).

[645] [1966] Ch. 538 (above, para.18–020), and see *Drive Yourself Hire Co (London) Ltd v Strutt* [1954] 1 Q.B. 250; criticised on this point by Wade [1954] C.L.J. 66.

[646] [1968] A.C. 58, 77C, 81C, 87C.

[647] [1968] A.C. 58, 73F, 84G, 104F; *cf.* Treitel (1966) 29 M.L.R. 657, 661.

[648] Before the passing of the 1925 Act, a number of reforming measures had been enacted. None of these contained any provisions from which the present s.56(1) is derived. In introducing one of the reforming Bills, which were consolidated, together with earlier Acts, in the 1925 property legislation, Lord Haldane L.C. said that no Parliamentary time would be needed for the consolidating bills "because they do not change what will then be the law": (1924) 59 H.L. Deb. 125. In view of his speech in *Dunlop Pneumatic Tyre Co Ltd v Selfridge & Co Ltd* [1915] A.C. 847, Lord Haldane could hardly have taken this view of the 1925 legislation if the effect of s.56(1) had been to reverse, for written contracts, the "fundamental principle" stated by him in that case at p.853, that "only a person who is a party to a contract can sue on it."

[649] But not the side-note, which reads in part "persons taking who are not parties . . . ".

[650] *cf.* below at nn.654 and 659.

[651] *Re Sinclair's Life Policy* [1938] Ch. 799; *Re Foster* [1938] 3 All E.R. 357; *Re Miller's Agreement* [1947] Ch. 615. A dictum in the last-mentioned case is doubted in *Beswick v Beswick* [1968] A.C. at 75F, but the actual decision is several times referred to with approval or at least without disapproval: at 76A, 80B, 86C, 106E.

[652] This view is stated by Lord Guest (at 87F) and perhaps shared by Lord Reid (at 76B) but doubted by Lord Upjohn (at 105F) with whom Lord Pearce agreed (at 94D). Lord Hodson says that "property" must be given "a limited meaning" (at 81C), but he does not say what that meaning is. *cf.* also *Southern Water Authority v Carey* [1985] 2 All E.R. 1077, 1083.

[653] This follows from Lord Guest's view in *Beswick v Beswick* [1968] A.C. 58 at 87A that s.56(1) has made no change at all in the law. Contrast Lord Reid's view that s.56(1) has not "substantially" (at 77C) altered the law; and *cf.* Lord Pearce's view of s.56(1) as an "enlargement" of its predecessor (at 93B) making no "substantial innovation"; and *cf.* Lord Upjohn at 105F.

the instrument is not merely for the benefit of the third party but purports to contain a grant to or covenant with him[654]; and (4) to deeds strictly *inter partes*.[655] But there is no clear majority in the speeches in favour of the imposition of all, some or even one of these restrictions, so that the precise scope of the subsection has not been clarified. There appear to be only three reported cases in which s.56(1) has actually been applied. The first case[656] is consistent with all four of the above limitations, the second[657] case is consistent only with the last two and it is not clear whether the third is consistent with any of them.[658] The third limitation was regarded as the operative one in the first two of the above three cases and in a number of other cases in which the courts have refused to apply the subsection[659]; and as it was, at any rate, not decisively rejected in *Beswick v Beswick*, it is probable that the subsection will be applied only where the requirements of this limitation are satisfied. There is also much to be said on historical grounds for the fourth limitation, which is consistent with all the cases, though it does not form a ground of decision in any of them. The scope of s.56(1) is further limited by a rule which it was not necessary to consider in *Beswick v Beswick*, namely, that a person cannot take the benefit of a covenant under the subsection unless he, or his predecessor in title, was in existence[660] and identifiable in accordance with the terms of the instrument at the time when it was made.[661]

Life insurance.[662] Section 11 of the Married Women's Property Act 1882 provides that where a man insures his life for the benefit of his wife or children, or where a woman insures her life for the benefit of her husband or children,[663] the policy "shall create a trust in favour of the objects therein named"; and this section also applies, by virtue of s.70 of the Civil Partnership Act 2004, to "a 18–126

[654] This view is regarded as a possible (though unsatisfactory) one by Lord Pearce (at 94D) and approved by Lord Upjohn (at 106D–F). It is rejected by Lord Guest (at 87B) and mentioned without comment by Lords Reid (at 74–75) and Hodson (at 81A).

[655] This view is stated by Lord Upjohn (at 107A), with whom Lord Pearce agreed (at 94D). It is also mentioned without comment by Lord Reid (at 76–77).

[656] *Re Ecclesiastical Commissioners' Conveyance* [1936] Ch. 430; *cf.* a dictum in *Re Windle* [1975] 1 W.L.R. 1628, 1631 (not affected on this point by the doubts expressed in *Re Kumar* [1993] 1 W.L.R. 224, 235).

[657] *Stromdale and Ball Ltd v Burden* [1952] Ch. 223.

[658] *OTV Birwelco Ltd v Technical & General Guarantee Co Ltd* [2002] EWHC 2240; [2002] 4 All E.R. 686, at [12]; the statement of the facts of the case leaves the point in doubt.

[659] See *White v Bijou Mansions* [1937] Ch. 610; affirmed [1938] Ch. 351; *Lyus v Prowsa Developments* [1982] 1 W.L.R. 1044, 1049; *Amsprop Trading Ltd v. Harris Distribution Ltd* [1997] 1 W.L.R. 1025. This is a more stringent requirement than those contained in s.1(1) and (2) of the Contracts (Rights of Third Parties) Act 1999.

[660] There is no such requirement under the Contracts (Rights of Third Parties) Act 1999: see s.1(3); above, para.18–094.

[661] *Kelsey v Dodd* (1883) 52 L.J.Ch. 34; *Westhoughton U.D.C. v Wigan Coal Co* [1919] 1 Ch. 159 (both these cases were decided under s.5 of the Real Property Act 1845, but the position under s.56(1) of the 1925 Act seems to be the same: *White v Bijou Mansions*, above n.659).

[662] For details of the exceptions discussed in this and the next five paragraphs, see Vol.II, Ch.41.

[663] Including illegitimate children: Family Law Reform Act 1969, s.19(1).

policy of assurance (a) effected by a civil partner on his own life, and (b) expressed to be for the benefit of his civil partner, or of his children, or of his civil partner and children, or any of them." Section 11 (as so extended) applies only where a person insures his or her own life and not where the policy is on the life of the beneficiary[664]; and it is restricted to policies for the benefit of spouses, civil partners and children and so does not apply in favour of other dependants.[665] These restrictions are not affected by the Contracts (Rights of Third Parties) Act, 1999[666]; but persons who have no rights under s.11 of the 1882 Act (as extended by s.70 of the 2004 Act) may, if the requirements of the 1999 Act are satisfied, acquire the more restricted[667] rights conferred on third parties by that Act. They may also have enforceable rights under the trust device discussed in para.18–078 above.[668]

18–127 **Motor insurance.** A person driving a motor vehicle with the consent of the owner can, by statute, take the benefit of a provision in his favour in the owner's insurance policy without having to prove that the owner intended to constitute himself trustee.[669]

18–128 **Insurance by persons with limited interests.** If a person insures for its full value property in which he has only a limited interest, he may be able to recover in full from the insurer but be liable to pay over to the other person interested any sum exceeding his own loss.[670] A number of real or supposed common law limitations on this principle have been removed by statute. Thus it has been

---

664 See *Re Engelbach's Estate* [1924] 2 Ch. 348 which is still good law on this point, although it has, on another point, been overruled (see above, para.18–073, n.423).

665 *Re Clay's Policy of Assurance* [1937] 2 All E.R. 548.

666 Law Com. No.242, para.12–27.

667 *e.g.* powers of cancellation or variation under s.2 of the 1999 Act do not apply where a trust has arisen under s.11 of the 1882 Act; *cf.* above, para.18–116.

668 *Re Foster's Policy* [1966] 1 W.L.R. 222.

669 Road Traffic Act 1988, s.148(7), replacing Road Traffic Act 1930, s.36(4); discussed in *Tattersall v Drysdale* [1935] 2 K.B. 174 and *Austin v Zurich, etc., Insurance* [1944] 2 All E.R. 243, 248. *cf.* also Transport Act 1980, s.61.

670 *Waters v Monarch Insurance Co* (1856) 5 E. & B. 870; *Hepburn v A. Tomlinson (Hauliers) Ltd* [1966] A.C. 451; *cf. Petrofina (UK) Ltd v Magnaload Ltd* [1984] Q.B. 127 (head contractor insuring for benefit of himself and sub-contractors); *Pan Atlantic Insurance Co Ltd v Pine Top Insurance Co Ltd* [1988] 2 Lloyd's Rep. 505 (same principle applied to reinsurance); *Sumitomo Bank Ltd v Banque Bruxelles Lambert SA* [1997] 1 Lloyd's Rep. 487, 495; *Glengate Properties Ltd v Norwich Union Fire Insurance Society* [1996] 2 All E.R. 487, 497. Contrast *Stone Vickers Ltd v Appledore Ferguson Shipbuilders Ltd* [1992] 2 Lloyd's Rep. 578, where the main contractors' insurance did not cover the subcontractors since the main contractors had no authority or intention to contract on behalf of the subcontractors; for similar reasoning, see *Colonia Versicherung AG v Amoco Oil Co* [1997] 1 Lloyd's Rep. 261, 270–272. The principle of *Waters v Monarch Insurance Co*, above, may also be displaced by the terms of the policy: see *Ramco (UK) Ltd v International Insurance Co of Hanover* [2004] EWCA Civ 675, [2004] 2 All E.R. (Comm) 866 at [32]. The loss of the insured may exceed the value of his interest, and even be suffered in spite of his having parted with that interest, by reason of his having undertaken a contractual obligation with respect to the property: *e.g.* an obligation to reinstate it in the event of damage by a peril covered by the insurance: *Lonsdale & Thompson Ltd v Black Arrow Group plc* [1993] Ch. 361. See also, *Simon Container Machinery v Emba Machinery* [1998] 2 Lloyd's Rep. 429 at 437.

provided that any person who has an interest in the subject-matter of a policy of marine insurance can insure "on behalf of and for the benefit of other persons interested as well as for his own benefit."[671] On a somewhat similar principle, where property is sold and suffers damage before the sale is completed, any insurance money to which the vendor is entitled in respect of the damage must be held by him for the purchaser, and be paid over to the purchaser on completion.[672]

Fire insurance. Where an insured house is destroyed by fire, "any person . . . interested" may require the insurance money to be laid out towards reinstating the house.[673] Thus a tenant may claim under his landlord's insurance; and vice versa.[674] **18–129**

Solicitors' indemnity insurance. Under s.37 of the Solicitors Act 1974, a scheme has been established by the Law Society for the compulsory insurance of solicitors against liability for professional negligence or breach of duty. The scheme takes the form of a contract between the Society and insurers, whereby the insurers undertake, on being paid the appropriate premiums, to provide indemnity insurance to solicitors. It has been held that the scheme gives rise to reciprocal rights and duties between the insurers and solicitors.[675] This result follows "by virtue of public law, not the ordinary English private law of contract"[676] for in operating the scheme the Society acts, not in its private capacity as a professional association, but in its public capacity, as a body one of whose functions is to protect members of the public against loss which they may suffer from dealings with solicitors. **18–130**

Third parties' rights against insurers. Our concern here is not with insurance contracts which purport to confer benefits on third parties, but with those which insure the promisee against liability to third parties. By statute, a third party may in certain circumstances enforce the rights of the insured under the policy[677] by proceeding against the insurance **18–131**

---

[671] Marine Insurance Act 1906, s.14(2).

[672] Law of Property Act 1925, s.47; for the definition of "property" see *ibid.* s.205(1)(xx). In contracts for the sale of land, s.47 is now commonly excluded: see Law Com. 191 (1990), para.3.2. *cf.* also Law of Property Act 1925, s.108 as to the application of insurance money where property is mortgaged.

[673] Fires Prevention (Metropolis) Act 1774, s.83.

[674] *Portavon Cinema Co v Price & Century Insurance Co* [1939] 4 All E.R. 601; *Mark Rowlands Ltd v Berni Inns Ltd* [1986] Q.B. 211; *Lonsdale & Thompson Ltd v Black Arrow Group plc* [1993] Ch. 361.

[675] *Swain v Law Society* [1983] 1 A.C. 598.

[676] *ibid.* at 611.

[677] Third Party (Rights against Insurers) Act 1930. See *Socony Mobil Oil Co Inc. v West of England Shipowners' Mutual Insurance Association (The Padre Island)* [1984] 2 Lloyd's Rep. 408; *Normid Housing Association Ltd v R. John Ralphs* [1989] 1 Lloyd's Rep. 265; *Bradley v Eagle Star Insurance Co Ltd* [1989] A.C. 957 (third party unable to sue insurer where insured had gone into liquidation before liability was established); *Duncan Stevenson MacMillan v A.W. Knott Becker Scott Ltd* [1990] 1 Lloyd's Rep. 98; *Lefevre v White* [1990] 1 Lloyd's Rep. 569, 577; *Firma C-Trade SA v Newcastle Protection and Indemnity Association (The Fanti and The Padre Island)* [1991] 2 A.C. 1; *Cox v Bankside* [1995] 2 Lloyd's Rep. 437, 457, 466–467; *Schiffahrtsgesellschaft Detlev von Appen v Voest Alpine Intertrading G.m.b.H.* [1997] 1 Lloyd's Rep. 179, 187; *Total Graphics Ltd v A.G.F. Insurance Ltd* [1997] 1 Lloyd's Rep. 599. *cf. Eagle Star Insurance Co Ltd v Provincial Insurance plc* [1994] A.C. 130, where the issue of contribution between insurers arose under legislation in force in the Bahamas giving third parties direct rights against insurers; *Charlton v Fisher* [2001] EWCA Civ 112;

company.[678] In the case of victims of motor accidents, these statutory rights are supplemented by an agreement originally made between the Motor Insurers' Bureau and the Minister of Transport.[679] This provides that the Bureau will pay any judgment (to the extent to which it remains unsatisfied) in respect of any liability which is required to be covered by a policy of insurance under the statutory scheme of compulsory motor insurance. At common law, a person who is injured in a road accident cannot technically sue on the agreement as he is not a party to it.[680] But the agreement may be specifically enforced by the appropriate Minister[681]; and although "the foundations in jurisprudence" of the agreement "are better not questioned,"[682] the Bureau's policy is not to rely on the doctrine of privity as a defence to claims by the injured parties themselves.[683] It is also now possible to draft the relevant agreements between the Bureau and the

---

[2002] Q.B. 578 at [96] (third party has no claim under the 1930 Act where the insured's claim against the insurer would fail on grounds of public policy since "as statutory assignee under the 1930 Act the third party simply stands in the shoes of the insured"); *Matadeen v Caribbean Insurance Co Ltd* [2002] UKPC 69, *The Times* January 20, 2003 (third party subject to same period of limitation as insured). For conflicting views on the question whether the third party had any right under s.1(3) before the insured's liability to the third party had been established, contrast *Nigel Upchurch Associates v Aldridge Estates Investment Co Ltd* [1993] 1 Lloyd's Rep. 533 (no such right) with *Centre Reinsurance International Co v Curzon International Ltd* [2004] EWHC 200 (Ch), [2004] 2 All E.R. (Comm) 28 (such a right can rise "notwithstanding that the insured's liability to the third party has yet to be established" (at [29]). The *Centre Reinsurance* case was varied on appeal, but not on the point here under discussion: [2005] EWCA Civ 115, [2005] 2 All E.R. (Comm) 28, where it was also held that s.1(3) was not intended to strike down provisions in the insurance contract itself which were designed to put the third party into a better position than that in which the insured would have been immediately before the statutory transfer of the insured's rights to the third party (at [83]). On further appeal, the decision of the Court of Appeal was reversed ([2006] UKHL 45, [2006] 1 W.L.R. 2863), but not on the points here under discussion. See also *Re T & N Ltd (No.3)* [2003] EWHC 1447 (Ch), [2007] 1 All E.R. (Comm) 851 at [30]–[33], distinguishing between (a) the rule that only those rights which the insured has against the insurer can be vested in the third party transferee and (b) the stage at which the transfer takes place, which may be "an earlier stage" than that at which the rights of the insured against the insurer are established. The present topic is not covered by the Contracts (Rights of Third Parties) Act 1999: see Law Com. No.242 para.12–21. For proposals for reform (relating largely to the procedure for enforcing such claims), see Law Com. No.272 (Cm. 5271).

[678] Third Parties (Rights against Insurers) Act 1930; *Bradley v Eagle Star Insurance Co Ltd* [1989] A.C. 957; Road Traffic Act 1988 ss.151–153 as amended by Road Traffic Act 1991 s.48 and Sch.4, para.66, s.83 and Sch.8; Michel [1987] L.M.C.L.Q. 228; and see Policyholders Protection Act 1975, s.7 for the rights of such persons where the company is in liquidation.

[679] See *Hardy v M.I.B.* [1964] 2 Q.B. 745, 770 and *White v London Transport Executive* [1971] 2 QB 721, 729; *White v White* [2001] UKHL 9; [2001] 1 W.L.R. 481 and see *ibid* at [7]; Vol.II, para.41–101.

[680] See *Gurtner v Circuit* [1968] 2 Q.B. 587.

[681] *ibid.*

[682] *Gardner v Moore* [1984] A.C. 548, 556.

[683] *Hardy v M.I.B.*, above, at 757; *Randall v M.I.B.* [1968] 1 W.L.R. 1900; *Persson v London County Buses* [1974] 1 W.L.R. 569; *Porter v Addo* [1975] R.T.R. 503. As the Bureau is interested in the outcome of the litigation between the injured party and the driver it may, at the court's discretion, be added as a party to such litigation: see *Gurtner v Circuit*, above, and contrast *White v London Transport Executive*, above n.684. Notice of proceedings against the driver must be served on the Bureau: *Cambridge v Callaghan*, *The Times*, March 21, 1997. For the enforceability of the agreement by third parties, see also *Charlton v Fisher* [2001] EWCA Civ 122; [2002] Q.B. 578, at [25], [82] and below at n.621a.

Secretary of State in such a way as to enable the victim to enforce them in his own right under s.1 of the Contracts (Rights of Third Parties) Act 1999.[684]

Defective premises. Under the Occupiers' Liability Act 1957, an occupier of premises who is bound by contract to permit persons who are strangers to the contract to enter or use the premises owes them (subject to any contrary provision in the contract) not only the common duty of care but also any stricter obligation he may undertake towards the other contracting party.[685] The Defective Premises Act 1972 imposes certain duties on a person who takes on work for or in connection with the provision of a dwelling. These duties are owed not only to the person to whose order[686] the dwelling is provided but also to any person who acquires an interest (whether legal or equitable) in the dwelling.[687] The Act also deals with the case where premises are let under a tenancy which puts on the landlord an obligation[688] to the tenant for the maintenance or repair of the premises. The landlord in such a case owes a duty to all persons, who might reasonably be expected to be affected by defects in the state of the premises, to take reasonable care to see that such persons are reasonably safe from personal injury or damage to their property caused by a relevant defect.[689] 18–132

5. ENFORCEMENT AGAINST THIRD PARTIES

General rule: third party not bound. The general rule is that a contract binds only the parties to it. This rule is regarded as an aspect of the doctrine of privity[690]; and in so far as A and B cannot by a contract between them impose an obligation to perform duties arising under that contract on C, the rule may seem to be so obvious that it scarcely needs to be stated: if a contract between A and B provided that C was to pay £100 to A, no-one would suppose that this contract could oblige C to make the payment. But the rule equally applies where the contract between A and B merely purports to deprive C of some right or to restrict his freedom of action, without imposing any obligation to perform on him: for example, a person is not bound by an exclusion clause contained in a contract to which he is not a party,[691] unless one of the exceptions to the doctrine of privity can be invoked against him[692] or unless he can be held to be so bound 18–133

[684] Above, para.18–089: see *Evans v Secretary of State for the Environment, Transport and the Regions* [2001] EWCA Civ 32, [2002] Lloyd's Rep. I.R. 1 at [4].

[685] Occupiers' Liability Act 1957, s.3(1).

[686] This will generally amount to a contract but the duty is imposed even where this is not the case.

[687] Defective Premises Act 1972, s.1.

[688] This will generally be contractual but might also be imposed (for example) by statute.

[689] Defective Premises Act 1972, s.4.

[690] This aspect of the doctrine is not affected by the Contracts (Rights of Third Parties) Act 1999: see above para.18–002. Hence where a contract between A and B was held, on its true construction, to purport, not to confer a *benefit* on C, but to *restrict* C's rights, it was said that "no question arises under the Contracts (Rights of Third Parties) Act 1999": *Prudential Assurance Co Lt v Ayres* [2008] EWCA Civ 52 at [42].

[691] *Leigh & Sullivan Ltd v Aliakmon Shipping Co Ltd (The Aliakmon)* [1986] A.C. 785.

[692] Above, para.14–040; *cf. Herd v Clyde Helicopters Ltd* [1997] A.C. 473, where legislation limiting the liability of a party to the contract was held to be effective as against a third party.

by virtue of some relationship (such as a bailment or sub-bailment on terms to which he had consented, incorporating the clause) between himself and the wrongdoer.[693]

18–134 **Exceptions to the doctrine of privity.** The discussion of the exceptions to the doctrine of privity in paras 18–077 to 18–132 above concerns situations in which a person can acquire *rights* under a contract to which he is not a party. It does not deal with the converse problem, whether *duties* can be imposed by such a contract on a third party. This possibility can, however, arise, under some of the exceptions to the doctrine which have been referred to in para.18–077, but which (for reasons there stated) are not discussed in this chapter; *e.g.* under the law of agency and under the law as to covenants relating to land.[694]

18–135 **Scope of the rule.** In cases governed by the general rule stated in para.18–133 above, a contract between A and B cannot impose a positive duty on C to render the performance specified in the contract; but the contract can impose legal restrictions on C's freedom of action in various other ways. For example, it may create a lien,[695] or a lease,[696] or an equitable interest, or give rise to a constructive trust affecting property,[697] and such interests can affect the rights of third parties who later acquire the property. Moreover, although a contract primarily creates rights and duties enforceable by the contracting parties against each other, it also incidentally imposes on third parties a duty not to induce one of the contracting parties to commit a breach of the contract. In the leading case of *Lumley v Gye*[698] it was held that a person who, knowing of a contract between two others,

[693] Above, para.14–054; *e.g. East West Corporation v DKBS 1912* [2003] EWCA Civ 83; [2003] Q.B. 1509, at [69] (where the exemption clauses were held on other grounds not to protect the defendants); *Scottish & Newcastle International Ltd v Othon Ghalanos Ltd* [2008] UKHL 11, [2008] 1 Lloyd's Rep. 462 at [46], [47].

[694] It can also arise under Carriage of Goods by Sea Act 1992, s.3, referred to in para.18–112 above.

[695] See *Faith v E.I.C.* (1821) 4 B. & Ald. 630; *Tappenden v Artus* [1964] 2 Q.B. 185; *Jare Trä AB v Convoys Ltd* [2003] EWHC 1488 (Comm); [2003] 2 Lloyd's Rep. 459. Contrast *Chellaram & Sons Ltd v Butler's Warehousing and Distributing Ltd* [1978] 2 Lloyd's Rep. 142 (third party not bound by agreement purporting to confer on sub-bailee a lien more extensive than that which would, but for such agreement, arise at common law). See also *T. Comedy (UK) Ltd v Easy Managed Transport Ltd* [2007] EWHC 611 (Comm), [2007] 2 All E.R. (Comm) 282 at [64] (third party bound by lien arising under contract of carriage by virtue of the doctrine of bailment on terms, referred to at n.693 above).

[696] As in *Ashburn Anstalt v Arnold* [1989] Ch. 1 (overruled on another ground in *Prudential Assurance Co Ltd v London Residuary Body* [1992] A.C. 386).

[697] See *Ashburn Anstalt v Arnold*, above, where the mere fact that C had notice of an earlier contract between A and B was said at 25–26 to be insufficient to give rise to a constructive trust on C's acquisition of the land affected by that contract; and where Fox L.J. (delivering the judgment of the court) at 17 disapproved dicta in *Errington* v *Errington* [1952] 1 K.B. 290, to the effect that a contractual licence to occupy land granted by A to B gave rise to an equitable interest binding third parties; Hill (1988) 51 M.L.R. 226; Oakley [1988] C.L.J. 353. *cf.* also *Binions v Evans* [1972] Ch. 359; Smith [1973] C.L.J. 81; *Re Sharpe* [1980] 1 W.L.R. 219; *Pritchard v Briggs* [1980] Ch. 338 (option to purchase); *Lyus v Prowsa Developments* [1982] 1 W.L.R. 1044; *Lloyd v Dugdale* [2001] EWCA Civ 1754; [2001] 48 E.G.C.S. 129.

[698] (1853) 2 E.&B. 216; for further proceedings, see 23 L.T. 66, 18 Jur. & 68 n., 23 L.J.Q.B. 116 n.; Waddams (2001) 117 L.Q.R. 431.

"maliciously", *i.e.* intentionally[699] induces one of them to commit a breach of it (*e.g.* by wrongfully refusing to perform it) is liable to the claimant for the tort of inducing a breach of the contract.[700] In some later cases, this tort was described as one of "interference" by C with contractual rights which A had under a contract between A and B. This terminology was based on authorities[701] which had supported the "unified theory"[702] that tort liability for inducing a breach of contract was "a species of a more general tort of actionable interference with contractual rights,"[703] But this "unified theory" was rejected[704] by the House of Lords in *OBG Ltd v Allan; Douglas v Hello Ltd; Mainstream Properties Ltd v Young*.[705] A sharp distinction was there drawn between two torts: that of inducing a breach of contract[706] and that of causing loss by unlawful means.[707] The details of this distinction are beyond the scope of a book on the law of contract. It suffices here to say that the former tort depends on C's having induced a breach by B, while the latter does not[708]; that the former tort does not, while the latter does, depend on C's having used means (to induce the breach) which are "independently unlawful"[709]; and that the mental elements of the two torts differ in that the former requires no more than an intention to induce the breach by B while the latter requires an intention to cause loss to A.[710] If, for example, A's claim is based on the allegation that C has *prevented* B from performing his

[699] "Maliciously" in *Lumley v Gye* (above, n.698) meant no more than that "the defendant intended to procure a breach of contract": *OBG Ltd v Allan; Douglas v Hello! Ltd*; *Mainstream Properties Ltd v Young* [2007] UKHL 21, [2008] 1 A.C. 1 at [8]; *cf.* at [189], [191]. It follows that C must have actual knowledge, not only of the existence of the contract between A and B, but also of the term in it alleged to have been broken by B: *ibid.*, at [39], [40]; though for this purpose C may be taken to have knowledge of a fact if he deliberately shuts his eyes to it: *ibid.*, at [41]. For the requirement of knowledge of the contract and intention to procure its breach, see also *Unique Pub Properties Ltd v Beer Barrels Mineral Waters Ltd* [2004] EWCA Civ 586, [2005] 1 All E.R. (Comm) 181. The relevant intention will be negatived where C honestly and genuinely believed that B's relevant conduct would not amount to a breach: *OBG* case, above, at [68]–[70], [200]–[202]; this is true even where C's belief is based on a mistake of law: *ibid*, at [202]; *Meretz Investments NV v ACP Ltd* [2007] EWCA Civ 1303 at [114], [119], [124], [180]. It follows from the requirement of an intention to induce a breach that C is not liable for the tort if he acts carelessly: "Negligent interference is not actionable": *OBG* case above at [191]; *Miller v Bassey* [2994] EMLR 44 is disapproved in the *OBG* case at [43], [166], [264]; and see *ibid* at [202], citing *British Industrial Plastics Ltd v Ferguson* [1940] 1 All E.R. 479 in favour of the view that the requisite intention may be negatived by C's honest, if eccentric, belief that the conduct induced was not a breach. C is also not liable for this tort if he believed that he was entitled to act in a way that would prevent B from performing B's contract with A: *Meretz* case, above, at [124], [179]. Where the intention to induce B to break his contract with A is established, there is no further requirement that C must intend to cause loss: see below, at n.710. To the extent that the contrary may be suggested in the *Meretz* case at [2], [127], the suggestions are, with respect, made *per incuriam*, and are inconsistent with *ibid.* at [124], [179].

[700] See below at n.706.

[701] *e.g., D.C. Thompson & Co v Deakin* [1952] Ch. 646: see *OBG Ltd v Allan; Douglas v Hello! Ltd; Mainstream Properties Ltd v Young* [2007] UKHL 21, [2008] 1 A.C. 1 at [26].

[702] *ibid.*, before [26], at [27], [28], [264]; *cf.* [306], [320].

[703] *ibid.*, at [27].

[704] See *ibid.*, at [32]; *cf.* at [172], [173], [264].

[705] Above, n.701.

[706] At [3]–[5], [39]–[44], [168]–[172].

[707] At [6]–[8], [45]–[60], [141]–[163].

[708] At [8].

[709] At [8]; *cf.* [32], [49], [51], [145], [148], [164].

[710] At [8], [47], [62], [141], [192]; for the mental element of the tort of inducing breach of contract, see further n.699 above.

contract with A, but without B's having committed any *breach* of it, then C's liability (if any) is for the "unlawful means" tort and will arise only if the requirements of *that* tort are satisfied.[711] Our concern in this Chapter is with the first of the two torts distinguished in the decision of the House of Lords referred to above,[712] *i.e.*, with that of inducing a breach of contract.

18–136 **Scope of the tort.** The effect of the tort of inducing a breach of contract may be, not only to restrict the activities of the person guilty of the wrongful interference, but also adversely to affect other third parties. For example, where a former employee disclosed the employer's trade secrets to a company which the employee controlled, and which used those trade secrets to secure an order from one of the employer's old customers, an injunction was granted not only to restrain the employee from using the trade secrets, but also to restrain the company from fulfilling its contract with the customer, whose remedy would have been in damages against the company.[713]

18–137 **Contracts affecting chattels.**[714] The rule in *Lumley v Gye*[715] may help to solve the problem which can arise where a person acquires a chattel which is the subject-matter of a contract previously made between two other persons. The problem is to what extent the acquirer may, although he is a stranger to that contract, be affected by it in his use of or dealing with the chattel. Such contracts may take a variety of forms. One possibility is that they may impose restrictions on the use or disposition of goods, *e.g.* by providing that the goods shall only be used along with others made by the same manufacturer, or that they shall only be sold in packets sealed by the manufacturer, or at fixed prices, or within specified limits of time or territory. Or they may require the use of some *particular* chattel for their performance, without creating any proprietary or possessory interest in the chattel: for example, in the case of a contract to carry cargo in a particular ship. Or they may provide for the hire of a chattel, or confer an option to purchase it, or do both these things, as in the case of hire-purchase agreements.

18–138 **Protection in special cases.** In a number of special cases the law protects such contractual rights against strangers who acquire the chattel in question with notice of the contractual rights. Thus where an option to purchase a chattel is *specifically* enforceable, it may be enforced against third parties who acquire the chattel with notice of the option.[716] The same would be true where a debtor gave an undertaking to his creditor that he would repay a loan of money out of specific property, and later created a charge over the property in favour of a third party.

---

[711] See the *OBG* case, above n.701 at [180], [189] ("there is no in-between hybrid tort of 'interfering with contractual relations'").

[712] At n.705. For the further distinction between the requirements of the tort of *causing loss* by unlawful means and that of *conspiracy* to cause loss by unlawful means, see the discussion of the *OBG* case in *Revenue and Customs Commissioners v Total Networks SL* [2008] UKHL 19, [2008] 2 All E.R. 143.

[713] *PSM International v Whitehouse* [1992] I.R.L.R. 279.

[714] Chafee (1928) 41 Harv.L.Rev. 945; Wade (1928) 44 L.Q.R. 51.

[715] (1853) 2 E. & B. 216; above, para.18–135.

[716] *Falcke v Gray* (1859) 4 Drew. 651, as explained in *Erskine Macdonald Ltd v Eyles* [1921] 1 Ch. 631, 641.

Since such an undertaking to repay is specifically enforceable, it would create a charge in equity over the property in favour of the creditor, and this would prevail against the third party unless he was a bona fide purchaser for value without notice.[717] This principle can, however, apply only where the contract is one which relates to specific property. It therefore did not apply where a property developer undertook in its contract with a builder to set up a retention fund and then charged its assets to a bank. Although the bank had express notice of the terms of the building contract, its charge was held not to be subject to the promise to create the retention fund since there was no specific property to which that promise could be said to relate.[718]

More general principle rejected. An attempt to establish a more general principle of protection of contractual rights affecting chattels against strangers acquiring them with notice of those rights was made in the charterparty case of *De Mattos v Gibson*, where Knight Bruce L.J. said: 18–139

> "Reason and justice seem to prescribe that, at least as a general rule, where a man, by gift or purchase, acquires property from another, with knowledge of a previous contract, lawfully and for valuable consideration made by him with a third person, to use and employ the property for a particular purpose in a specified manner, the acquirer shall not, to the material damage of the third person, in opposition to the contract and inconsistently with it, use and employ the property in a manner not allowable to the giver or seller."[719]

This principle came to be associated with the rule in *Tulk v Moxhay*,[720] relating to restrictive covenants affecting land. That rule was later confined to cases in which the claimant's interest in enforcing the covenant consisted in the ownership of land capable of being benefited.[721] This usually meant adjacent land, and since adjacency cannot be a satisfactory criterion of interest in the case of things that can be moved, the tendency of this development of the rule in *Tulk v Moxhay*, was to undermine the view that the general principle stated by Knight Bruce L.J. in *De Mattos v Gibson* could be applied to contracts affecting all kinds of property.[722] Nevertheless, in *Lord Strathcona SS. Co v Dominion Coal Co*[723] the Privy Council relied on that principle to hold that a time charterer of a ship had an interest[724] in the ship which he could enforce against a purchaser of the ship with notice of the charterparty: that purchaser was said to be "plainly in the position of a constructive trustee, with obligations which a court of equity will

---

[717] *Swiss Bank Corp. v Lloyd's Bank Ltd* [1982] A.C. 584, 598, 613, below, para.27–008; the actual decision was that the contract of loan did *not* create an obligation to repay out of specific property and hence was not specifically enforceable. *cf.* also *C.N. Marine Inc. v Stena Line A/B (The Stena Nautica) (No.2)* [1982] 2 Lloyd's Rep. 336 (where specific performance was denied). For the special position of mortgages of ships, see *The Shizelle* [1992] 2 Lloyd's Rep. 444.

[718] *MacJordan Construction Ltd v Brookmount Erostin Ltd* [1992] B.C.L.C. 350.

[719] (1858) 4 D. & J. 276, 282.

[720] (1848) 2 Ph. 774.

[721] *L.C.C. v Allen* [1914] 3 K.B. 642; the actual decision has been reversed by statute (see now Housing Act 1985, s.609) but the principle stated in the text remains unimpaired.

[722] See *Greenhalgh v Mallard* [1943] 2 All E.R. 234, 249.

[723] [1926] A.C. 108.

[724] *ibid.* at 123.

not allow him to violate."[725] The decision provoked adverse judicial criticism,[726] particularly because the land law analogies and the constructive trust reasoning on which it was based might lead to the third party's being made liable where he had only constructive notice of the earlier contract. Where that contract concerned the use or disposition of a chattel, such a conclusion was open to the objection that it might have the undesirable effect[727] of introducing the doctrine of constructive notice into commercial affairs. When a similar problem arose in *Port Line Ltd v Ben Line Steamers Ltd*,[728] Diplock J. therefore refused to follow the Privy Council's decision. Alternatively, he was prepared to distinguish that decision on the ground that the purchaser of the ship in the *Port Line* case merely knew the ship was subject to a time charter to the claimant, but did not have actual notice of the relevant terms of the charterparty specifying the precise extent of the claimants' rights under it.[729] Thus while the *Port Line* case rejects the general principle stated by Knight Bruce L.J. so far as it relates to contracts concerning chattels, it does not decide that a third party can always disregard such a contract when he acquires the chattel in question. Possible limitations on his freedom to do so are considered in the next eight paragraphs.

18–140 **Remedy.** Later authorities have restricted the principle stated in *De Mattos v Gibson*[730] by emphasising that the remedy there sought was simply an injunction to restrain the acquirer, C, from using the property inconsistently with the terms of the contract between A and B, known to C.[731] The principle therefore cannot impose any positive obligation on C to perform the terms of the contract between A and B. Thus where B acquired shares from A, promising to make payments to A on the occurrence of specified events, which later happened, it was held that that promise could not be enforced against C who later acquired the shares from B with knowledge of the contract between A and B, nor against D who acquired them from C with such knowledge.[732] An injunction on the principle of *De Mattos v Gibson* was not available against C or D as they were not proposing to act inconsistently with the contract between A and B: "they are merely proposing . . . to do nothing whatever."[733]

[725] *ibid.* at 125.

[726] *Clore v Theatrical Properties* [1936] 2 All E.R. 483, 490; *Greenhalgh v Mallard* [1943] 2 All E.R. 234; *cf.* the earlier criticisms of Knight Bruce L.J.'s principle in *Barker v Stickney* [1919] 1 K.B. 121, 132 (as to which see *Tito v Waddell (No.2)* [1977] Ch. 106, 300).

[727] See *Manchester Trust Ltd v Furness* [1895] 2 Q.B. 539, 545; *Westdeutsche Landesbank Girozentrale v Islington B.C.* [1996] A.C. 669, 704.

[728] [1958] Q.B. 146. The cases cited in para.18–135, n.697 all apply the constructive trust reasoning to contracts concerning land and do not, it is submitted, undermine the rejection of that reasoning in the *Port Line* case so far as contracts affecting the use or disposition of chattels are concerned.

[729] Hence the purchaser could not be held liable in tort: see above, para.18–135, below para.18–141, n.735.

[730] Above, para.18–139, n.719.

[731] *Swiss Bank Corp. v Lloyds Bank Ltd* [1979] Ch. 574, 581 (as to which see also below, n.663).

[732] *Law Debenture Trust Corp.* v *Ural Caspian Oil Corp. Ltd* [1993] 1 W.L.R. 138; reversed, on another point, [1995] Ch. 152.

[733] [1993] 1 W.L.R. 138, 146.

Third party's liability in tort.[734] Where a person acquires a chattel with actual knowledge[735] of the terms of a contract affecting it, he may, if his acquisition or use of the chattel is inconsistent with that contract, be liable in tort for inducing a breach of contract.[736] Thus in *British Motor Trade Association v Salvadori*[737] B bought a car and covenanted with A that he would not resell it for one year without first offering it to A. C bought the car from B within the year with notice of the covenant and was held liable to A for wrongfully inducing B to break his contract with A. It has been suggested that the decision of the Privy Council in the *Lord Strathcona* case[738] can be explained on the ground that the purchaser of the ship had committed this tort against the charterer.[739] The tort may be committed even though B was quite willing to break his contract with A. Thus in a case like *Salvadori's* it would be immaterial whether B or C began the negotiations for the sale of the car.[740] Indeed, C's tort liability may arise precisely where he and B collude in order to get rid (if they can) of a restriction imposed by the contract between B and A.[741] 18–141

Factors limiting tort liability. The merit of approaching the problem here under discussion through the law of tort is that it avoids the danger of importing the doctrine of constructive notice into this branch of the law. On the other hand, it is subject to two limitations: these are discussed in paras 18–143 and 18–144, below. 18–142

Lack of causal connection. First, the tort is not committed if the defendant's interference was not the cause of the claimant's loss. Thus in the *Lord Strathcona* case the shipowners, who were the defendants in the Privy Council proceedings,[742] had mortgaged the ship, after the conclusion of the charterparty. The mortgage gave the mortgagees a power to sell the ship, and it was held in other 18–143

---

[734] Wade (1926) 42 L.Q.R. 139.

[735] For the state of mind required to make a defendant liable for the tort of inducing a breach of contract, see *OBG Ltd v Allen; Douglas v Hello! Ltd; Mainstream Properties Ltd v Young* [2007] UKHL 21, [2008] 1 A.C. 1, above para.18–135 nn.699 and 710. Discussions of the requisite mental element of the tort in earlier cases must now be read subject to the *OBG* case, above. In the *Port Line* case (above, para.18–139) the third party assumed that the charterparty with which he was alleged to have interfered contained certain crucial terms to the same effect as those of another charterparty which he had made with one of the parties to the original contract. He therefore honestly and genuinely believed that his conduct would not induce a breach of the charterparty; and such a belief would exonerate him from liability for the tort: see the *OBG* case, above, at [68]–[70], [200]–[202] and the *Meretz* case, above para.18–125 n.699 at [124], [180].

[736] Above, para.18–135.

[737] [1949] Ch. 556; *semble*, that in such circumstances the agreement would now be likely to be exempted under Competition Act 1998, s.4 from potential invalidity under s.2 of that Act; *Rickless v United Artists Corp.* [1988] Q.B. 40, 58–59; *cf. Law Debenture Corp. v Ural Caspian Oil Corp. Ltd* [1993] 1 W.L.R. 138 (where the fifth defendant admitted liability on this ground); reversed on another point [1995] Ch. 152.

[738] [1926] A.C. 108, above, para.18–139.

[739] *Swiss Bank Corp. v Lloyds Bank Ltd* [1979] Ch. 581, 574; in the Court of Appeal it was conceded that there was "no substance" in the point: see [1982] A.C. 584, 598 and para.18–145, below, at n.755.

[740] *Sefton v Tophams* [1965] Ch. 1140, 1161, 1187; reversed without reference to this point [1967] A.C. 50.

[741] *Esso Petroleum Co Ltd v Kingswood Motors (Addlestone) Ltd* [1974] Q.B. 142.

[742] [1926] A.C. 108; above, para.18–139.

proceedings[743] that they were entitled to sell her free from the charterers' rights even though they knew of those rights.[744] The reason for this decision was that the shipowners could not have performed the charterparty, even if the ship had not been sold, because they were too poor to put her to sea. It was the poverty of the shipowners, and not the mortgagees' sale of the ship, which was the cause of the charterers' loss. Similarly, where breach of the contract has already been induced by C's acquisition of the property from B, there will be no tort liability for inducing breach of contract on D, who subsequently buys the property from C, even with knowledge of the contract between A and B, for D's conduct will not have played any part in inducing the original breach.[745] Nor will D in such a case be liable for interference with the remedies arising out of the broken contract[746] between A and B.

18–144 **Requirement of intentional wrongdoing.** Secondly, liability for interference with contractual rights is based on intentional wrongdoing.[747] It follows that, if a defendant negligently damaged a ship that was subject to a time charterparty, he would not commit this tort against the charterer; nor would he be liable to the charterer in negligence for purely economic loss, such as hire wasted or profits lost while the ship was, by reason of the damage, out of service.[748]

18–145 **Third party's knowledge: the time factor.** So far, in discussing the third party liability in tort for inducing a breach of contract, it has been assumed that C either knew or did not know of the contract between A and B. In the former situation, he could, but in the latter he could not, be liable for this tort.[749] There is also an intermediate situation, in which C at the time of his contract with B had no more than constructive notice of B's earlier contract with A, but then acquired actual knowledge of that contract before calling for (or receiving) performance of his own contract with B.[750] On such facts, the question arises whether C is liable to A for the tort of inducing a breach of the contract between A and B. That tort

---

[743] *The Lord Strathcona* [1925] P. 143; judgment in these proceedings was given four months earlier than that in the Privy Council proceedings. *cf.* also *De Mattos v Gibson* (1858) 4 D. & J. 276 where the charterer's claim eventually failed on a similar ground; and *The Myrto* [1977] 2 Lloyd's Rep. 243 (followed in *Anton Durbeck GmbH v Den Norske Bank ASA* [2005] EWHC 2497 (Comm), [2006] 1 Lloyd's Rep. 93 at [50]–[64], though in a part of the judgment said at [50] to be "*obiter*"); *Lyus v Prowsa Developments Ltd* [1982] 1 W.L.R. 1044, 1049 (as to which see also above para.18–080).

[744] *cf. Den Norske Bank ASA v Acemex Management Co* [2003] EWCA Civ 1559, [2004] 1 All E.R. (Comm) 904 (mortgagee of ship not obliged to defer the exercise of power of sale under the mortgage by reason of the fact that such exercise interferes with contracts for the carriage of goods in the ship made between the mortgagor and shippers of the goods).

[745] *Law Debenture Trust Corp. v Ural Caspian Oil Corp. Ltd* [1993] 1 W.L.R. 138, and see next note.

[746] *Law Debenture Trust Corp. v Ural Caspian Oil Corp.*, [1995] Ch. 152, reversing the decision at first instance (above, n.745) on this point.

[747] See above, para.18–135 n.699.

[748] *Candlewood Navigation Corp. v Mitsui O.S.K. Lines (The Mineral Transporter)* [1986] A.C. 1.

[749] Above, paras 18–135; 18–141.

[750] This was the position in *Swiss Bank Corp. v Lloyds Bank Ltd* [1982] A.C. 854; see [1979] Ch. 548, 568–596 and below, n.754.

is subject to the defence of "justification,"[751] which is certainly available to C where he had contracted with B *before* A had done so.[752] But the defence is a flexible one,[753] and the principle on which it is based appears to be equally applicable where C's contract with B was made *after* A's but in ignorance of it. The exercise by C of rights thus acquired in good faith against B should not, it is submitted, make C liable in tort to A.[754] Even in such a situation, however, C may be liable to A under the rules stated in para.18–138 above if the contract between A and B is specifically enforceable by A. Where the specific enforceability of this contract gives rise to an equitable interest, this can be asserted against C even though he had, when he contracted with B, only constructive notice of the contract. In such a case, the tort claim would be "of no value"[755] if, as has been submitted above, it arises only where C, when he contracted with B, had actual knowledge of A's rights; but it would equally be unnecessary,[756] since A could succeed against C on the different ground that the contract between A and B was specifically enforceable by A and therefore conferred an equitable interest on A.

Protection of "possessory rights." The further possibility here to be discussed relates to contracts under which possession of a chattel is, or is to be, transferred. The contracts in the *Strathcona* and *Port Line* cases were not of this kind: they were time charters, *i.e.* contracts under which a shipowner undertakes to render services by the use of a particular ship which remains in his possession.[757] Such charters must be contrasted with demise charters, which are contracts for the hire of a ship under which the shipowner does transfer, or undertake to transfer, possession of the ship to the charterer.[758] The nearest analogy in the 18–146

[751] See *OBG Ltd v Allan; Douglas v Hello! Ltd; Mainstream Properties Ltd v Young* [2007] UKHL 21, [2008] 1 A.C. 1 at [193].

[752] *Smithies v National Association of Operative Plasterers* [1909] 1 K.B. 310, 337; *Edwin Hill & Partners v First National Finance Corp. plc* [1989] 1 W.L.R. 225, 230; *Meretz Investments NV v ACP Ltd* [2007] EWCA Civ 1303 at [42], [142], [179]. For terms which may be imposed on C as a condition of obtaining relief against B, see *Guiness Peat Aviation (Belgium) N.V. v Hispania Lineas Aereas SA* [1992] 1 Lloyd's Rep. 190.

[753] *Glamorgan Coal Co v South Wales Miners' Federation* [1903] 2 K.B. 545, 574–575; *cf. Anton Durbeck GmbH v Den Norske Bank* [2005] EWHC 2497 (Comm), [2006] 1 Lloyd's Rep. 93, esp. at [68], [71] where A (a cargo-owner) contracted with B (a shipowner) for the carriage of goods which deteriorated and were lost when C (a bank) arrested and detained A's ship as security for a loan made by C to B before the contract of carriage between A and B, and it was held that C was not liable to A for the tort here under discussion.

[754] This was admitted in *Swiss Bank Corp. v Lloyds Bank Ltd*, above, n.672: see [1979] Ch. 548, 569–573.

[755] *Swiss Bank Corp. v Lloyds Bank Ltd* [1982] A.C. 584, 598, where it was held, on construction, that the contract did *not* impose an obligation to use the specific property for its performance and was *not* specifically enforceable: see below, para.27–008, n.31.

[756] [1982] A.C. 584, 598.

[757] *Ellerman Lines v Lancaster Maritime Co (The Lancaster)* [1980] 2 Lloyd's Rep. 497, 500; *Scandinavian Trading Co AB v Flota Petrolera Ecuatoriana (The Scaptrade)* [1983] A.C. 694, 702; *Hyundai Merchant Marine Co Ltd v Karander Maritime Co Ltd (The Niizura)* [1996] 2 Lloyd's Rep. 66, 72; *Homburg Houtimport BV v Agrosin Private Ltd (The Starsin)* [2003] UKHL 12, [2004] 1 A.C. 715 at [119].

[758] *Baumwoll Manufacturer v Furness* [1893] A.C. 8; *The Guiseppe di Vittorio* [1998] 1 Lloyd's Rep. 136, 156; *BP Operating Co Ltd v Chevron Transport (Scotland) Ltd* [2001] UKHL 50; [2003] 1 A.C. 197 at [78], [79].

land law to contracts for the hire of a chattel is a lease, and not a restrictive covenant. Hence the development of the doctrine of *Tulk v Moxhay*, discussed in para.18–139 above, need not affect cases concerning such contracts. One reason given by Diplock J. for his decision in the *Port Line* case was that a time charterer had "no proprietary *or possessory* rights in the ship."[759] It can be inferred that a "possessory right" might have been protected. Where the hirer of a chattel is in actual possession of it, he should certainly be protected against a third party who acquires the chattel with notice of the hirer's interest.

18–147 **Rights to future possession.** It is less clear whether, in this context, the words "possessory rights" refer only to the right *of* possession or extend also to a right *to* possession, *i.e.* whether a person who has a contractual right to the *future* possession of a chattel would similarly be protected against the third party. In *The Stena Nautica (No.2)*[760] B had demise-chartered his ship to A under a contract which also gave A an option to purchase her. Later, while B was in possession of the ship, he granted a second demise charter of her to C who had no knowledge of the earlier contract. A exercised his option to purchase and it was held that his only remedy was by way of damages against B: since A's option to purchase was not specifically enforceable,[761] A could not assert rights to the ship against C. The question whether A could assert his *right to possession as demise charterer* against C did not, strictly speaking, arise since A was suing, not to enforce that right, but rather his right as a person who had exercised an option to purchase. But it seems from the reasoning of the Court of Appeal that A's right to possession as demise charterer would have been protected only if the contract under which the right arose was one in respect of which the court was willing to make an order of specific performance.[762] The argument of commercial convenience which justified the decision in the *Port Line* case would seem to apply as much where a contract creates a right to the future possession of a chattel as where it creates the right to have some particular use made of the chattel. In each case the right is hard to discover and should not be enforced against a third party without actual knowledge of it; and adequate protection against a third party with such knowledge is provided by the rules relating to the tort of inducing a breach of contract.

[759] [1958] 2 Q.B. 146, 166 (italics supplied).

[760] *C.N. Marine Inc. v Stena Line A/B (The Stena Nautica) (No.2)* [1982] 2 Lloyd's Rep. 336.

[761] Below, para.27–014, n.56. A licence to occupy *land* can be enforced against a trespasser even by a licensee not yet in possession: *Dutton v Manchester Airport plc* [1999] 2 All E.R. 675.

[762] Above, para.18–138.

Chapter 19

ASSIGNMENT

		PARA.
1.	Assignment	19–001
	(a) Statutory assignments	19–006
	(b) Equitable assignments	19–020
	(c) Principles applicable to statutory and equitable assignments	19–042
	(i) What rights are assignable	19–042
	(ii) Validity of assignments against assignor's creditors and successors in title	19–058
	(iii) Priorities between successive assignees	19–068
	(iv) Assignments "subject to equities"	19–070
	(v) No assignment of liabilities	19–077
2.	Vicarious performance	19–081
3.	Assignment and negotiability	19–085
4.	Assignment, novation and acknowledgment	19–086

1. Assignment[1]

Assignment of choses in action: at common law. The term "things in action" or, as they are still called, choses in action, is used to describe "all personal rights of property which can only be claimed or enforced by action, and not by taking physical possession".[2] Contractual rights, being things in action as opposed to things in possession, were not assignable at common law without the consent of both contracting parties. This rule seems to have been based initially on the difficulty of conceiving of the transfer of an intangible, at any rate one of such a personal nature, and later on the desire to avoid maintenance, viz officious intermeddling in litigation. It was subject to two exceptions: (1) the benefit of a contract could be assigned to or by the Crown; (2) the holder of a bill of exchange could assign it by the law merchant.[3] Further, there were certain assignments by operation of law, e.g. on the death or bankruptcy of a contracting party.[4] Before 1875, the only methods of assigning contractual rights at law were by novation,[5] and by procuring the debtor's acknowledgment that he held for the assignee[6]: 19–001

[1] See Marshall, *The Assignment of Choses in Action* (1950); Biscoe, *Credit Factoring* (1975); Goode, *Legal Problems of Credit and Security*, 3rd edn (2003), Ch.5; Salinger, *Factoring Law and Practice*, 3rd edn (1999); Tolhurst, *The Assignment of Contractual Rights* (2006); M. Smith, *The Law of Assignment* (2007). See also Starke, *Assignments of Choses in Action in Australia* (1972). For conflict of laws in relation to assignment, see below, paras 30–123 to 30–125, 30–288 to 30–292.

[2] *Torkington v Magee* [1902] 2 K.B. 427, 430; reversed [1903] 1 K.B. 644.

[3] See Milnes Holden, *The History of Negotiable Instruments in English Law* (1955).

[4] See below, Ch.20.

[5] Below, para.19–086.

[6] Below, para.19–089.

both of these required the consent of the debtor. Powers of attorney could also be used to effect assignments, but these had considerable disadvantages, being normally revocable.[7]

19–002 **Assignment in equity.** The rule of equity, on the other hand, was to permit the assignment of contractual rights whether such rights were legal or equitable. If the rights were equitable (e.g. a legacy or a share in a trust fund), the assignee could sue in his own name, but it was necessary to make the assignor a party to the suit if he retained any interest in the subject-matter, for instance if the assignment was not absolute but conditional or by way of charge. If the right was a legal right, equity could compel the assignor to allow the assignee to use his name in a common law action.[8] The assignor had to be a party to such an action in order to bind him at law.

19–003 **Assignment under particular statutes.** The assignment of certain kinds of choses in action is now regulated by particular statutes. Examples are: bills of lading[9]; policies of life insurance[10]; policies of marine insurance[11]; shares in a company[12]; negotiable instruments[13]; patents[14]; and copyright.[15] Furthermore, to protect the creditors of insolvent assignors, provision has been made for the registration of certain assignments.[16]

19–004 **Statutory and equitable assignments.** General statutory provision for the assignment of choses in action was first made by s.25(6) of the Judicature Act 1873, which is now repealed and substantially re-enacted by s.136 of the Law of Property Act 1925. But an assignment which fails to comply with the statutory requirements is not necessarily invalid, for it may take effect as a perfectly good equitable assignment: "[t]he statute does not forbid or destroy equitable assignments or impair their efficacy in the slightest degree".[17] Indeed, it appears that for the purpose of the substantive law, there is often little (if any) advantage in a statutory assignment over an equitable assignment. To a considerable extent the rules governing them are identical, e.g. the rules relating to the question whether a particular right is assignable,[18] to priorities between successive assignees (at any rate in most cases)[19] and to the principle that assignments are "subject to equities".[20] Sometimes, as, e.g. with regard to consideration, the rules may be

---

[7] See Marshall at pp.67–69.
[8] *Hammond v Messenger* (1838) 9 Sim. 327.
[9] Carriage of Goods by Sea Act 1992.
[10] Policies of Assurance Act 1867 s.1.
[11] Marine Insurance Act 1906 s.50(2).
[12] Companies Act 2006 s.544, replacing Companies Act 1985 s.182(1); Stock Transfer Act 1963.
[13] Bills of Exchange Act 1882.
[14] Patents Act 1977 ss.30, 32.
[15] Copyright Designs and Patents Act 1988 ss.90, 94.
[16] Insolvency Act 1986 s.344; Companies Act 2006 ss.860–861, 863, 866–867, 874, replacing Companies Act 1985 ss.395–398; below, paras 19–060—19–066.
[17] *Brandt's Sons & Co v Dunlop Rubber Co* [1905] A.C. 454, 462.
[18] Below, para.19–042.
[19] Below, para.19–068.
[20] Below, para.19–070.

formulated differently, but appear to be substantially identical in result.[21] And even where the rules governing statutory and equitable assignments are different, e.g. with regard to the necessity for writing[22] and to assignments by way of charge,[23] the distinction is usually of little importance so far as the substantive law is concerned, because the rules of equity are often wider, but never narrower, than the rules governing statutory assignments.

Difference between statutory and equitable assignments. However, there is one very important procedural consequence which attaches to the distinction between statutory and equitable assignments. A statutory assignee can sue the debtor without joining the assignor as a party to the action,[24] whereas an equitable assignee often cannot do this.[25] Furthermore, it must be observed that whereas a statutory assignment passes a legal right to the assignee, an equitable assignment passes only an equitable right. In practice, as already observed, this usually makes little difference as a matter of substantive law to the efficacy of the assignment; but there are some situations where the distinction can prove of practical importance. For example, it has been held that an assignee of an option to renew a contract for services who had not given notice of his assignment to the other contracting party could not exercise the option: the reasoning is based on the fact that the assignment was equitable only.[26] 19–005

(a) *Statutory Assignments*

Law of Property Act 1925 section 136. This section provides as follows: 19–006

"(1) Any absolute assignment by writing under the hand of the assignor[27] (not purporting to be by way of charge only) of any debt or other legal thing in action, of which express notice in writing has been given to the debtor, trustee or other person from whom the assignor would have been entitled to claim such debt or thing in action, is effectual in law (subject to equities having priority over the right of the assignee) to pass and transfer from the date of such notice—

(*a*) the legal right to such debt or thing in action;

---

[21] Below, paras 19–019 and 19–027 et seq.

[22] Below, para.19–015.

[23] Below, para.19–012.

[24] Below, para.19–006.

[25] Below, paras 19–038—19–041.

[26] *Warner Bros Records Inc v Rollgreen Investments Ltd* [1976] Q.B. 430 (see Kloss (1975) 39 Conv.(N.S.) 261). But the authority of the case is somewhat distorted by the formulation of the question to which the Court of Appeal gave an answer, and some of the dicta may go further than was necessary for the decision of the case, which should perhaps be regarded as authority only upon the equitable assignment of options; quaere whether the result would have been the same had the assignment been oral, and so still equitable, but the assignee *had* given notice (even in the same letter). Note also that some aspects of the reasoning in this case were disapproved by a majority of the Court of Appeal (Peter Gibson L.J., with whom Waite L.J. agreed) in *Three Rivers D.C. v Bank of England* [1996] Q.B. 292.

[27] In view of the specific references to signature by an agent in ss.40 and 53 of the same Act, it would seem that signature by an agent is here insufficient, at any rate if he signs his own name: see *Wilson v Wallani* (1880) 5 Ex.D. 155; but cf. *Re Diptford Parish Lands* [1934] Ch. 151; Partnership Act 1890 s.6. See also *Bowstead & Reynolds on Agency*, 18th edn (2006), para.2–024.

(*b*) all legal and other remedies for the same; and

(*c*) the power to give a good discharge for the same without the concurrence of the assignor:

Provided that, if the debtor, trustee or other person liable in respect of such debt or thing in action has notice—

(*a*) that the assignment is disputed by the assignor or any person claiming under him; or

(*b*) of any other opposing or conflicting claims to such debt or thing in action;

he may, if he thinks fit, either call upon the persons making claim thereto to interplead concerning the same, or pay the debt or other thing in action into court under the provisions of the Trustee Act 1925.

(2) This section does not affect the provisions of the Policies of Assurance Act 1867."[28]

19–007 It will be seen that, in order that the section may apply, three conditions must be fulfilled:

(1) the assignment must be absolute and not purport to be by way of charge only;

(2) it must be in writing under the hand of the assignor;

(3) express notice in writing thereof must be given to the debtor or trustee.

The general effect of the section is to allow the assignee to sue the debtor in his own name instead of, as previously, having to sue in the name of the assignor and perhaps having to go to a court of equity to compel his joinder in the action. The section:

"... is merely machinery: ... it enables an action to be brought by the assignee in his own name in cases where previously he would have sued in the assignor's name, but only where he could so sue."[29]

19–008 **"Debt or other legal thing in action".** The phrase has been held to include the benefit of a contract for the sale of a reversionary interest,[30] and rights to claim indefinite sums of money, as for compensation under statute for the injurious affecting of land by a railway,[31] or for damages for loss in respect of which the assignee was the assignor's insurer.[32] A debt arising out of an existing contract, but payable at a future time, is capable of assignment under s.136.[33]

---

[28] This Act makes provision for the assignment of life insurance policies. See Vol.II, Ch.41.

[29] *Torkington v Magee* [1902] 2 K.B. 427, 435; reversed. [1903] 1 K.B. 644.

[30] *Torkington v Magee* [1902] 2 K.B. 427.

[31] *Dawson v G.N. & City Ry* [1905] 1 K.B. 260.

[32] *King v Victoria Insurance Co Ltd* [1896] A.C. 250; *Compania Colombiana de Seguros v Pacific S.N. Co* [1965] 1 Q.B. 101. See also *Re Battle's Feed Mill Ltd* (1975) 59 D.L.R. (3d) 488 (bankruptcy dividend).

[33] *Brice v Bannister* (1878) 3 QBD 569 (though the assignment in this case seems to have been treated as equitable); *Buck v Robson* (1878) 3 QBD 686; *Walker v Bradford Old Bank* (1884) 12 QBD 511; *Jones v Humphreys* [1902] 1 K.B. 10; *G. & T. Earle Ltd v Hemsworth R.D.C.* (1928) 44 T.L.R. 605, 758. Contrast *Law v Coburn* [1972] 1 W.L.R. 1238. See further, below, para.19–028.

Examples are future instalments of rent, future instalments of money due under an instalment contract, retention moneys under a building contract, future instalments of salary. A future chose in action in the strict sense is incapable of actual assignment, though it may be the subject of an agreement to assign, which will operate in equity in very much the same way as an actual assignment.[34]

In *Stein v Blake*[35] it was held by the House of Lords that, if A and B have mutual claims against each other and A becomes bankrupt, the effect of s.323 of the Insolvency Act 1986 is that the debt due to A ceases, on A's bankruptcy, to exist as a chose in action and is replaced by a new chose in action, namely the claim to the net balance owing.[36] Their Lordships went on to decide that, like any other chose in action, that right to the net balance (if any) can be assigned by the trustee in bankruptcy before it has been ascertained by the taking of an account between the trustee and B. **19–009**

In *Investors Compensation Scheme Ltd v West Bromwich Building Society*,[37] the House of Lords clarified that a right to rescind a mortgage is not a chose in action or part of a chose in action and an owner cannot therefore assign a right to rescission separately from his property. On the other hand, a right to damages is a chose in action which can be assigned. It followed that there was no objection to a clause in the Investors Compensation Scheme claim form by which investors assigned a right to damages against a building society to the Investors Compensation Scheme Ltd but which did not assign (because legally impossible) a right to rescission of the investors' mortgages with the building society. **19–010**

It might at first sight have been supposed that the expression "debt or other *legal* thing in action" was confined to legal choses in action; but the reference to a "trustee" militates against this and there is authority that the phrase includes equitable choses, or, as they are sometimes called, choses in equity.[38] The point seems, however, to be of no importance, for the principal effect of the section is to enable an assignee of a *legal* chose in action to sue alone in certain cases where he could not otherwise do so; the section seems to make no difference to the assignee of an equitable chose in action who can probably sue alone under the Act only in circumstances where he could do so in equity.[39] **19–011**

"Absolute . . . and not by way of charge". The assignment must be absolute and not purport to be by way of charge only. An assignment by way of mortgage may, however, be absolute within the meaning of the section, if there is an **19–012**

---

[34] Below, para.19–032.

[35] [1996] A.C. 243.

[36] The reasoning on this in *Farley v Housing and Commercial Developments Ltd* [1984] B.C.L.C. 442 was approved.

[37] [1998] 1 W.L.R. 896. A right to a vehicle registration mark is not a chose in action or, if it is, is not capable of being assigned: *Goel v Pick* [2006] EWHC 833 (Ch), [2007] 1 All E.R. 982.

[38] *Torkington v Magee* [1902] 2 K.B. 427, 430–431; reversed [1903] 1 K.B. 644; cf. *R. v Victoria Insurance Co* [1896] A.C. 250, 254; *Manchester Brewery v Coombs* [1901] 2 Ch. 608, 619; *Re Pain* [1919] 1 Ch. 38, 44–45.

[39] i.e. where the assignment is absolute: below, paras 19–040—19–041.

express[40] or implied[41] proviso for reassignment on repayment of the loan: for the reassignment would involve fresh notice to the debtor, who would thus be in no doubt as to whom he ought to pay the debt.[42] An assignment of all moneys due or to become due from the debtor, which was expressed to be by way of continuing security for all moneys due from the assignor to the assignee, has been held to be absolute.[43] On the other hand, where the assignor charged a sum which would become due to him from the debtor as security for advances made to him by the assignee, and assigned his interest in that sum until the advances were repaid to the assignee with interest, this was held to be by way of charge and not within the section.[44] The fact that the assignment is expressed to be by way of security for a loan does not by itself prevent it from being absolute,[45] though combined with other factors such expressions may have this effect.[46] Thus, a provision that the assignor was entitled to exercise all its rights over the property until in default under the loan agreement has prevented an assignment from being absolute.[47] The test seems to be, has the assignor unconditionally transferred to the assignee for the time being the sole right to the debt in question *as against the debtor*? If so, the assignment will be absolute; but if the debtor cannot tell whether to pay the assignor or the assignee without examining the state of accounts between them, it will be held to be by way of charge only. Much may depend on the language of the particular instrument; in construing it, the court will look at the whole of its language. The words italicised above are of crucial importance, for it is no concern of the debtor whether the assignor and assignee have some private arrangement for the disposal of the debt after it has been paid by the debtor. Thus the fact that the assignee is to hold the proceeds of the debt,[48] or the surplus proceeds beyond a stated amount,[49] on trust for the assignor does not prevent the assignment from being absolute.

19–013 **Absolute and conditional assignments.** Some cases distinguish between absolute and conditional assignments.[50] To conditional assignments similar criteria will be applied: if the assignor retains, by virtue of the condition, some interest in the debt, it is desirable that he be joined in proceedings regarding it, and the assignment is not absolute.

---

40 *Tancred v Delagoa Bay Co* (1889) 23 QBD 239.

41 *Durham Bros v Robertson* [1898] 1 Q.B. 765, 772.

42 [1898] 1 Q.B. 765.

43 *Hughes v Pump House Hotel Co* [1902] 2 K.B. 190.

44 *Durham Bros v Robertson* [1898] 1 Q.B. 765.

45 *Hughes v Pump House Hotel Co* [1902] 2 K.B. 190. See also *Care Shipping Corp v Latin American Shipping Corp* [1983] Q.B. 1005, 1016.

46 *Mercantile Bank of London Ltd v Evans* [1899] 2 Q.B. 613.

47 *The Halcyon the Great* [1984] 1 Lloyd's Rep. 283. See similarly *The Balder London* [1980] 2 Lloyd's Rep. 489.

48 *Comfort v Betts* [1891] 1 Q.B. 737; *Fitzroy v Cave* [1905] 2 K.B. 364.

49 *Burlinson v Hall* (1884) 12 QBD 347; *Bank of Liverpool and Martins Ltd v Holland* (1926) 43 T.L.R. 29.

50 e.g. *Durham Bros v Robertson* [1898] 1 Q.B. 765, 773; *Grey v Australian Motorists & General Insurance Co Pty Ltd* [1976] 1 N.S.W.L.R. 669; cf. *The Balder London* [1980] 2 Lloyd's Rep. 489, in which Mocatta J. spoke of the assignment being put "in suspense."

Part of a debt. An assignment of an unascertained part of a debt, e.g. of "so much of my salary" as amounts to a fixed sum and "any further sums in which I may hereafter become indebted to you", is not an absolute assignment.[51] And it is settled, though there were formerly doubts,[52] that an assignment of a definite part of a debt is not within the section.[53] This is because it would increase the burden on the debtor if the creditor were allowed to split up the debt into as many separate causes of action as he thought fit[54]; and also because conflicting decisions might result if the existence or amount of the debt was in dispute.[55] It will be seen that neither of these reasons holds good if the assignor and the assignees are all made parties to the action: and it must be remembered that an assignment which is not within the section because it is not absolute may nevertheless be a valid equitable assignment. The result is that if part of a debt is assigned, the assignee cannot sue for that part without joining the assignor, nor can the assignor sue for the balance without joining the assignee.[56] 19–014

Written assignment. The assignment must be in writing under the hand of the assignor. No particular form is however necessary: the writing can be quite informal.[57] A direction in writing by a creditor to his debtor to pay the assignee, handed to the assignee, may amount to an assignment,[58] but such a direction handed to the *debtor* will not by itself constitute an assignment unless there is evidence that the assignee has requested or consented to it[59]; and even if he has, the direction may constitute no more than authority to pay, and gives the assignee no rights. Thus the drawing of a cheque in favour of a third party does not constitute a statutory assignment of a bank balance or part of it.[60] 19–015

Written notice to the debtor. Under the statute notice in writing to the debtor is necessary. It is: 19–016

"... wrong to suppose that a separate document purposely prepared as a notice, and described as such, is necessary in order to satisfy the statute. The statute only requires

---

[51] *Jones v Humphreys* [1902] 1 K.B. 10.

[52] See *Brice v Bannister* (1878) 3 QBD 569; but the point was not argued, and in the Court of Appeal the assignment seems to have been treated as equitable. See also *Skipper v Holloway* [1910] 2 K.B. 630.

[53] *Forster v Baker* [1910] 2 K.B. 636; *Conlan v Carlow CC* [1912] 2 I.R. 535; *Re Steel Wing Co* [1921] 1 Ch. 349; *G. & T. Earle Ltd v Hemsworth R.D.C.* (1928) 44 T.L.R. 605, 758; *Williams v Atlantic Assurance Co* [1933] 1 K.B. 81, 100; *Walter and Sullivan Ltd v Murphy & Sons Ltd* [1955] 2 Q.B. 584; *Raiffeisen Zentralbank Österreich AG v Five Star General Trading LLC* [2001] EWCA Civ 68, [2001] 2 W.L.R. 1344 at [60], [75].

[54] *Durham Bros v Robertson* [1898] 1 Q.B. 765, 774.

[55] *Re Steel Wing Co* [1921] 1 Chs 349, 357.

[56] *Walter and Sullivan Ltd v Murphy & Sons Ltd* [1955] 2 Q.B. 584.

[57] *Re Westerton* [1919] 2 Ch. 104; *The Kelo* [1985] 2 Lloyd's Rep. 85, 89.

[58] *Brice v Bannister* (1878) 3 QBD 569; *Harding v Harding* (1886) 17 QBD 442; *Grey v Australian Motorists & General Insurance Co Pty Ltd* [1976] 1 N.S.W.L.R. 669.

[59] *Curran v Newpark Cinemas Ltd* [1951] 1 All E.R. 295. cf. below, para.19–022.

[60] *Schroeder v Central Bank of London Ltd* (1876) 34 L.T. 735, 736; Bills of Exchange Act 1882 s.53(1); cf. below, para.19–022. For the different position in Scotland see s.53(2); *Williams v Williams* (1980) S.L.T. 25.

> that information relative to the assignment shall be conveyed to the debtor, and that it shall be conveyed in writing."[61]

Thus a written demand for payment sent by the assignee to the debtor has been held sufficient.[62] Beyond this, however, the statute has been strictly construed, and it has been held that the notice must be unconditional,[63] and that written notice must be given, even though the debtor cannot read.[64] So also it is essential that the notice be given to the debtor himself: thus, where an insured assigned the proceeds of a policy and notice was given to the broker through whom the proceeds were collected, it was held that the notice was insufficient.[65] The notice is apparently invalid if it purports to identify the assignment by giving its date and that date is a wrong date[66]; though there is nothing in the section which requires the assignment to be dated at all, and it has been held that a notice is valid though it wrongly states that another notice has already been given.[67] On the other hand, the statute does not prescribe any limit of time within which notice must be given,[68] nor does it lay down that the notice must be given by any particular person.[69] It may consequently be given after the death of either the assignor or the assignee.[70] Notice must be given before the assignee starts his action,[71] though failure to do this will not prevent the assignee from proceeding

---

[61] *Van Lynn Developments Ltd v Pelias Construction Co Ltd* [1969] 1 Q.B. 607, 615. See also *Denney, Gasquet and Metcalfe v Conklin* [1913] 3 K.B. 177; cf. *James Talcott Ltd v John Lewis & Co Ltd* [1940] 3 All E.R. 592 (equitable assignment); see also *Herkules Piling Ltd v Tilbury Construction Ltd* (1992) 61 Build. L.R. 107 (the disclosure to the debtor of a document of assignment on discovery in an action by the assignor held to be insufficient notice for a legal or equitable assignment).

[62] *Van Lynn Developments Ltd v Pelias Construction Co Ltd* [1969] 1 Q.B. 607. But cf. *Warner Bros Records Inc v Rollgreen Investments Ltd* [1976] Q.B. 430 (exercise of option).

[63] *The Balder London* [1980] 2 Lloyd's Rep. 489, 495.

[64] *Hockley and Papworth v Goldstein* (1920) 90 L.J.K.B. 111.

[65] *Amalgamated General Finance Co Ltd v C.E. Golding & Co Ltd* [1964] 2 Lloyd's Rep. 163; *Magee v U.D.C. Finance Ltd* [1983] N.Z.L.R. 438. But cf. the position of an equitable assignment, below, para.19–020 fn.85.

[66] *Stanley v English Fibres Industries Ltd* (1899) 68 L.J.Q.B. 839; *W. F. Harrison & Co Ltd v Burke* [1956] 1 W.L.R. 419; criticised in (1956) 72 L.Q.R. 321 and explained in *Van Lynn Developments Ltd v Pelias Construction Co Ltd* [969] 1 Q.B. 607 at 612. The *Harrison* case [1956] 1 W.L.R. 418, 421 contains a suggestion that a misstatement of the amount of the debt might also vitiate the notice.

[67] *Van Lynn Developments Ltd v Pelias Construction Ltd* [1969] 1 Q.B. 607; *Grey v Australian Motorists & General Insurance Co Pty Ltd* [1976] 1 N.S.W.L.R. 669 (date referred to but no date inserted).

[68] There appears to be no authority on the question of whether notice can be given before the assignment takes place.

[69] *Bateman v Hunt* [1904] 2 K.B. 530, 538.

[70] *Walker v Bradford Old Bank* (1884) 12 QBD 511; *Bateman v Hunt* [1904] 2 K.B. 530; *Re Westerton* [1919] 2 Ch. 104.

[71] *Compania Colombiana de Seguros v Pacific Steam Navigation Co* [1965] 1 Q.B. 101, 128–129. It is arguable that this should no longer be the rule; and that instead a court could prevent any unfairness to defendants by exercising its discretion to disallow an application to amend the particulars of claim so as to add the assigned claim. Say, for example, a claimant is met by the defence that part (but not all) of what he is claiming is his company's, rather than his personal, claim. If he then takes a legal assignment from the company and gives written notice to the defendant, should he be able to apply for an amendment without bringing a fresh action? Or is the "rule" in the *Compania Colombiana* case a rigid one that would automatically mean that such an application would fail?

with his action on the footing that he is an equitable assignee.[72] In this event, however, the court may require the assignor to be made a party to the proceedings.[73]

"The date of such notice" in the section means the date when it is received by or on behalf of the debtor.[74] A debtor with notice of an absolute assignment is entitled, and indeed bound, to treat the debt as transferred to the assignee. Payment by the debtor to the assignor will therefore not give him a good discharge, and he will remain liable to pay the debt again to the assignee.[75] If notice is given late, equities which may come into existence prior thereto may be let in, e.g. the assignee must give credit for any payments made to the assignor by the debtor while the latter was in ignorance of the assignment. If there are more assignees than one, their priority is determined according to the dates on which they gave notice to the debtor.[76] It has been held that if the debtor pays his debt by cheque, he may disregard a subsequent notice that the debt has been assigned: he is under no duty to stop the cheque.[77] **19–017**

Since a creditor can assign by directing his debtor to pay the assignee it seems that a single written document could suffice to constitute both the assignment itself and the notice required by the section.[78] **19–018**

Consideration. Consideration is not required for a statutory assignment.[79] **19–019**

(b) *Equitable Assignments*

Notice. As has been seen above, an assignment cannot be effective under the statute unless written notice is given to the debtor, but an assignment may be perfectly valid in equity without any such notice.[80] Notice is, however, obviously desirable, since, as in the case of statutory assignments, until he receives it the debtor is entitled to treat the assignor as his creditor and to discharge his debt by **19–020**

---

[72] *Weddell v Pearce & Major* [1988] Ch. 26, 42, in which Scott J. rejected the obiter dicta in the *Compania Columbiana* case [1956] 1 Q.B. 101 to the extent that Roskill J. had there said that there was no valid equitable assignment.

[73] Below, paras 19–038—19–041.

[74] *Holt v Heatherfield Trust Ltd* [1942] 2 K.B. 1.

[75] *Jones v Farrell* (1857) 1 D & J 208; *Brice v Bannister* (1878) 3 QBD 569; Law of Property Act 1925 s.136; *The Halcyon the Great* [1984] 1 Lloyd's Rep. 283, 289. The debtor could prima facie recover the money paid to the assignor if paid under a mistake; below, paras 29–028—29–053.

[76] Below, paras 19–068—19–069.

[77] *Bence v Shearman* [1898] 2 Ch. 582.

[78] See *Curran v Newpark Cinemas Ltd* [1951] 1 All E.R. 295; *Cossill v Strangman* [1963] N.S.W.R. 1695.

[79] *Harding v Harding* (1886) 17 QBD 442; *Re Westerton* [1919] 2 Ch. 104; *Holt v Heatherfield Trust Ltd* [1942] 2 K.B. 1, 5.

[80] *Gorringe v Irwell India Rubber Works* (1886) 34 Ch D 128; *Re Patrick* [1891] 1 Ch. 82, 87; *Re Westerton* [1919] 2 Ch. 104; *Re City Life Assurance Co (Stephenson's Case)* [1926] Ch. 191; *Re Trytel* [1952] 2 T.L.R. 32; *Weddell v J. A. Pearce* [1988] Ch. 26. But as to options see *Warner Bros Records Inc v Rollgreen Investments Ltd* [1976] 2 Q.B. 430, above, para.19–005. On Australian and New Zealand cases see Chin-Aun (2002) 18 J.C.L. 107.

payment to him[81]; the giving of notice may prevent further equities attaching to the debt[82]; and may affect priorities.[83] From the debtor's perspective it seems that, if the debtor ignores a notice and pays the assignor, he is not discharged[84]: unless the debtor can secure the agreement of the assignor and assignee as to the amounts of their respective interests, it would certainly be unsafe for him to settle alone with either, the only safe course being to interplead. Where the assignment concerns a transaction in which an agent, such as a solicitor, was engaged on behalf of the debtor, notice to the agent will constitute notice to the debtor.[85]

19–021 **Means of assignment.** An assignor can assign a contractual right in equity in one of two main ways. He can inform the assignee that he transfers the chose to him[86]; or he can instruct the debtor to discharge the obligation by payment to, or performance for, the assignee.[87] Thus an agreement by merchants with a bank that payment for goods sold by the merchants should be remitted direct by the purchasers to the bank has been held to constitute a valid equitable assignment of the amounts to the bank.[88]

19–022 **Assignment or mandate.** On the other hand, a mere direction by a creditor to his debtor to pay money to a third person is not necessarily an assignment, for such a direction may be nothing more than a revocable mandate to the debtor.[89] So, where a person who was overdrawn at his bank directed his debtor to pay sums due to him directly to the credit of his account at the bank, this was held

---

[81] *Stocks v Dobson* (1853) 4 De G.M. & G. 11.

[82] Below, para.19–070.

[83] Below, paras 19–068—19–069.

[84] *Jones v Farrell* (1857) 1 D. & J. 208; *Brice v Bannister* (1878) 3 QBD 569; *Deposit Protection Board v Dalia* [1994] 2 A.C. 367 CA (Simon Brown L.J. dissented, reasoning, with respect incorrectly, that even after notice the debtor remains liable to the equitable assignor: the question did not arise in the House of Lords, [1994] 2 A.C. 391, which reversed the decision of the Court of Appeal in holding that, as a matter of statutory interpretation, only the original deposit maker, and not an assignee, was a "depositor" entitled to protection under s.58 of the Banking Act 1987); *Treitel on the Law of Contract*, 12th edn (Peel, 2007), para.15–022. See also above para.19–017 fn.75.

[85] *Magee v U.D.C. Finance Ltd* [1983] N.Z.L.R. 438.

[86] In *Kijowski v New Capital Properties Ltd* (1990) 15 Con. L.R. 1 this method of assignment was held not to be made out by an answer to enquiries before contract.

[87] These are the main ways of effecting a transfer. But provided there is the requisite intention, any other act by the transferor showing that he is transferring the chose in action appears to be sufficient: *Kijowski v New Capital Properties Ltd* (1990) 15 Con. L.R. 1; *Phelps v Spon-Smith & Co* [2001] B.P.I.R. 326; *Allied Carpets Group Plc v MacFarlane* [2002] EWHC 1155, [2002] P.N.L.R. 38. It is sometimes said that an assignment can also be effected by the assignor declaring himself trustee of the chose in action. It is not, however, clear that this should in all ways be equated with a transfer; and the effect of the rule in *Milroy v Lord* (1862) 4 De G.F. & J. 264, that equity will not perfect an imperfect gift, is that the implication of such a trust will be rare. See, however, *G.E. Crane Sales Pty Ltd v Commissioner of Taxation* (1971) 126 C.L.R. 177 (factoring arrangement); *Re Turcan* (1888) 40 Ch D 5.

[88] *Brandt's Sons & Co v Dunlop Rubber Co* [1905] A.C. 454. See further cases cited at para.19–025, below.

[89] *Percival v Dunn* (1885) 29 Ch D 128; *Re Gunsbourg* (1919) 88 L.J.K.B. 479; *Re Williams* [1917] 1 Ch. 1; *Rekstin v Severo, etc., and Bank for Russian Trade* [1933] 1 K.B. 47; *James Talcott Ltd v John Lewis & Co Ltd* [1940] 3 All E.R. 592; *Curran v Newpark Cinemas Ltd* [1951] 1 All E.R. 295; *Re Danish Bacon Co Ltd Staff Pension Fund Trusts* [1971] 1 W.L.R. 248.

not to be an assignment, but a mere revocable mandate.[90] Where similar instructions were given in another case, but were expressly declared to be irrevocable save with the consent of the bank, it was held that an assignment had been made,[91] but it has also been held in connection with statutory assignment that even an express provision of this nature did not make the instructions irrevocable unless the assignee had prior or subsequent knowledge of them.[92]

Known to assignee. Where an assignment is made by instructions to the debtor it is not clear whether it can have any effect at all before the assignee knows of the instructions and therefore has a chance to accept or decline the assignment. The cases cited above establish that the assignment is not effective as against the creditors of the assignor before the assignee knows of it, so that a creditor who serves a garnishee order on the assignor before the assignee gets to know of the purported assignment will have priority over the assignee.[93] It may be that such an assignment would be valid as against the assignor himself even before the assignee knows of the instructions to the debtor.[94] It has been held that an assignment made by letter is complete as soon as the letter is posted to the assignee,[95] but the proposition seems doubtful unless postal communication was in some way authorised or anticipated, as in the rules regarding the acceptance of contractual offers.[96] 19–023

Bill of exchange or cheque. As in the case of statutory assignments, a bill of exchange or cheque drawn on a banker or other fund holder is not an assignment of the amount for which the bill or cheque is drawn even if it is drawn for the precise amount of the debt due to the drawer.[97] 19–024

Formalities for equitable assignments. An equitable assignment of a legal chose in action need not be in writing, nor in any particular form.[98] On the other 19–025

[90] *Bell v London and North Western Ry* (1852) 15 Beav. 548; *Ex p. Hall* (1878) 10 Ch D 615.

[91] *Re Kent and Sussex Sawmills Ltd* [1947] Ch. 177. See also *British Eagle International Airlines Ltd v Cie Nationale Air France* [1973] 1 Lloyd's Rep. 414, 427; affirmed [1974] 1 Lloyd's Rep. 429.

[92] *Curran v Newpark Cinemas Ltd* [1951] 1 All E.R. 295. See also *Coulls v Bagot's Executor and Trustee Co Ltd* (1967) 119 C.L.R. 460, where some members of the High Court of Australia appear to have treated a direction as a revocable mandate even though it was intended to be irrevocable, and the payee knew of it.

[93] *Curran v Newpark Cinemas Ltd* [1951] 1 All E.R. 295; see also *Rekstin v Severo* [1933] 1 K.B. 47; *Re Hamilton* (1921) 124 L.T. 737.

[94] cf. *Standing v Bowring* (1885) 31 Ch D 282. An assignment made by declaration of trust probably requires no notice: see *Middleton v Pollock* (1876) 2 Ch D 104.

[95] *Alexander v Steinhardt, Walker & Co* [1903] 2 K.B. 208; sed quaere as the debt had arguably not yet arisen.

[96] *Timpson's Executors v Yerbury* [1936] 1 K.B. 645, 657.

[97] *Shand v Du Boisson* (1874) L.R. 18 Eq. 283; *Hopkinson v Forster* (1874) L.R. 19 Eq. 74; *Brown, Shipley & Co v Kough* (1885) 29 Ch D 848; Bills of Exchange Act 1882 s.53(1); cf. above, para.19–015.

[98] *Brandt's Sons & Co v Dunlop Rubber Co* [1905] A.C. 454, 462; *Re Wale* [1956] 1 W.L.R. 1346, 1350; *Kijowski v New Capital Properties Ltd* (1990) 15 Con.L.R. 1, 8; *Allied Carpets Group Plc v MacFarlane* [2002] EWHC 1155, [2002] P.N.L.R. 38 at [32]–[33]. See, e.g. *Re Westerton* [1919] 2 Ch. 104 (bank deposit receipt); *Cotton v Heyl* [1930] 1 Ch. 510 (proprietary interest in invention); *Re Wheeler* [1938] Ch. 725 (money due under building contract); *Thomas v Harris* [1947] 1 All E.R. 444 (insurance policy); *Re Tout & Finch Ltd* [1954] 1 W.L.R. 178 (retention money under building

hand, an equitable assignment of an equitable chose in action must be in writing[99] if it is caught by s.53(1)(c) of the Law of Property Act 1925, which provides:

> "A disposition of an equitable interest or trust subsisting at the time of the disposition must be in writing signed by the person disposing of the same, or by his agent thereunto lawfully authorised in writing or by will."[100]

It has been held that the word "disposition" in this paragraph must be given a wide meaning, and that it is apt to cover a direction by the holder of an equitable interest to the trustee to hold the property on trust for a third party, whether or not this is strictly an assignment of the equitable interest.[101] A fortiori a direct assignment should do the same. The paragraph does not prevent the holder of a beneficial interest in a trust fund from himself making an oral declaration of trust, and so constituting himself trustee of his own beneficial interest, for this is neither an assignment nor a "disposition" of his own interest.[102] Nor (it seems) does the provision apply where a person assigns the legal title to a chose in action together with an option to acquire the beneficial interest, and the transferee subsequently exercises this option orally. For in this case the beneficial interest

---

contract); *Letts v IRC* [1957] 1 W.L.R. 201 (shares); cf. *Re Williams* [1917] 1 Ch. 1 (insurance policy); *James Talcott Ltd v John Lewis & Co Ltd* [1940] 3 All E.R. 592 (invoice); *Spellman v Spellman* [1961] 1 W.L.R. 921 (hire-purchase agreement); *E. Pfeiffer Weinkellerei-Weineinkauf GmbH v Arbuthnot Factors Ltd* [1988] 1 W.L.R. 150 (reservation of title clause); *Colonial Mutual General Insurance Co Ltd v A.N.Z. Banking Group (New Zealand) Ltd* [1995] 1 W.L.R. 1140 PC (insurance policy). It was held in *Phelps v Spon-Smith & Co* [2001] B.P.I.R. 326 that, although no formalities are required for an equitable assignment, three necessary requirements on the particular facts were: first, the intention to assign; secondly, clear identification of the chose which was being assigned; and thirdly, some act by the assignor showing that he was passing the chose in action to the alleged assignee. None of these three was held to be satisfied. The third requirement (which Blackburne J., at [33], expressed as being "an outward expression by the assignor of his intention to make an immediate disposition of the subject matter of the assignment") was also held not to be made out in *Finlan v Eyton Morris Winfield* [2007] EWHC 914 (Ch), [2007] 4 All E.R. 143. Going the other way was *Coulter v Chief of Dorset Police* [2003] EWHC 3391 (Ch), [2004] 1 W.L.R. 1425 in which it was held that the benefit of a judgment (for costs) had been validly assigned in equity by a retiring chief constable to his successor. Patten J., at [16], said that there was: ". . . a sufficient outward manifestation of an intention that the successor office holder should obtain the benefits held on trust by a predecessor, for there to be an equitable assignment of the benefit of the judgment." On the question of whether the requirement of writing in the Copyright, Designs and Patents Act 1988 s.90(3) applies to an oral contract for the transmission of a legal interest in copyright, see *Western Front Ltd v Vestron Inc* [1987] F.S.R. 66, 76–78.

[99] Perhaps because of the difference in wording with Law of Property Act 1925 s.53(1)(b), which requires trusts of land to be *manifested and proved* by writing, it appears always to have been assumed that an oral disposition is void and not merely unenforceable.

[100] Quaere whether an equitable chose in action is necessarily an "equitable interest or trust". By s.53(2) it is expressly provided that the section does not affect the creation or operation of resulting, implied or constructive trusts, and in *Neville v Wilson* [1997] Ch. 144 the Court of Appeal held that an oral agreement to assign an equitable interest in shares constituted the promisor an implied or constructive trustee for the promisee, so that the requirement for writing contained in s.53(1)(c) was dispensed with by s.53(2). See further Hanbury and Martin, *Modern Equity*, 17th edn (2005), pp.79–94.

[101] *Grey v IRC* [1960] A.C. 1.

[102] *Grey v IRC* [1958] Ch. 690, 719; affirmed [1960] A.C. 1. Perhaps this should be regarded as a "sub-trust": see (1958) 74 L.Q.R. 180, 182. But see Pettit, *Equity and the Law of Trusts*, 10th edn (2006), p.89; [1960] A.C. at 16; above, para.19–021 fn.87.

passes not by virtue of any assignment or disposition to the transferor, but by virtue of the exercise of the option.[103]

Disposition of legal and equitable interests. Nor again does the paragraph apply where a person disposes of the entire interest, both legal and equitable, in a chose in action, for if it did, writing would be required in every case where a legal chose in action is assigned, unless the legal title were transferred without the beneficial interest.[104] So where the holder of the beneficial interest in some shares held on trust absolutely for him directed the trustees to transfer the legal title to the shares to a transferee with the intention that the transferee should also obtain the full beneficial interest, this was held not to be a disposition requiring writing under s.53(1)(c).[105] 19–026

Consideration needed for agreements to assign. The extent to which consideration is required for an equitable assignment is one of some difficulty.[106] It should first be observed that the question can only arise as between an assignor (or his successors in title) and assignee. So far as the debtor is concerned, the presence or absence of consideration appears to be immaterial. He cannot refuse to pay the assignee merely on the ground that there was no consideration for the assignment,[107] and, conversely, if he does pay the assignee after due notice has been given to him, it seems clear that the assignor cannot make him pay again. As between the assignor and the assignee the position broadly appears to be that consideration is required for an agreement to assign a chose in action, but is not required for an actual assignment of a chose in action.[108] Since a future chose in action is incapable of assignment in the strict sense, it follows that a purported assignment of a future chose can only operate as an agreement to assign, and as such requires consideration. There is no doubt however that dicta can be produced which suggest that consideration is always required.[109] 19–027

Distinction between existing and future choses in action. The distinction between an existing chose in action which is capable of immediate assignment, and a future chose in action which is only capable of being the subject of an agreement to assign, is one of difficulty. On the one hand, it is clear that a mere expectancy, not based on any existing legal right, can be nothing more than a 19–028

[103] This seems to follow from *William Cory & Son Ltd v IRC* [1965] A.C. 1088 though strictly speaking the decision is not inconsistent with the possibility that the exercise of the option to purchase in that case was invalidated by s.53(1)(c).

[104] *Vandervell v IRC* [1967] 2 A.C. 291. See also *Re Vandervell's Trusts (No.2)* [1974] Ch. 269; Harris (1974) 38 M.L.R. 557.

[105] *Vandervell v IRC* [1967] 2 A.C. 291. See also *Re Danish Bacon Co Ltd Staff Pension Fund Trusts* [1972] 1 W.L.R. 248.

[106] See Megarry (1943) 59 L.Q.R. 58; Hollond (1943) 59 L.Q.R. 129; Marshall, *The Assignment of Choses in Action* (1950), Ch.4; Sheridan (1955) 33 Can. Bar Rev. 284; Hall [1959] C.L.J. 99; Smith, *The Law of Assignment* (2007), paras 7.78—7.83.

[107] *Walker v Bradford Old Bank* (1884) 12 QBD 511; cf. *Harding v Harding* (1886) 17 QBD 442, but in this case the point was not taken, and in any event consideration was held to be unnecessary

[108] Below, paras 19–028—19–035.

[109] e.g. "For every equitable assignment . . . there must be consideration. If there be no consideration, there can be no equitable assignment": *Glegg v Bromley* [1912] 3 K.B. 474, 491.

future chose in action, and cannot, therefore, be transferred without consideration. Thus there cannot be an actual assignment of property which the assignor hopes to inherit from a person still alive at the date of the assignment[110] or of sums which the assignor hopes to receive under a contract not yet made.[111] On the other hand, sums which are certain to become payable in the future under an existing contract or other legal obligation are not treated for this purpose as future choses in action, but as existing choses in action. So, for instance, a loan repayable at a fixed future date, or rent payable in the future under an existing lease, is an existing chose in action, and is capable of actual assignment without consideration. So also the right to be paid sums in the future under an existing contract is an existing chose in action even though the precise amounts which will become payable are as yet unascertained, e.g. royalties payable under a patent licensing agreement already made.[112]

19–029 The most difficult cases concern those in which there is an existing legal obligation, by way of contract or otherwise, but it is uncertain whether anything will become due under it in the future, either because the obligation is conditional or because it may be terminated. On the one hand, it has been held that sums payable to a builder under an existing contract are an existing chose in action, even though the sums may never become payable if the builder fails to perform the contract.[113] It has even been held that an assignment by a person of sums which will be standing to his credit at his bank at his death is an assignment of an existing chose in action, and therefore needs no consideration, since it is a sum which will become payable under the existing contract between the assignor and his bank.[114] On the other hand, in *Norman v Federal Commissioner of Taxation*,[115] it was held by a majority of the Australian High Court that interest payable in the future on an existing loan was a mere expectancy, because the loan (not being made for a fixed period) might have been repaid before the interest became due.[116] It was also held (unanimously) in the same case that dividends which may become due in the future on shares already held in a company also constitute nothing more than an expectancy, and cannot therefore be assigned without consideration.

19–030 **Proceeds of existing obligation uncertain.** It is also to be noted that even where there is an existing chose in action which is capable of actual assignment,

[110] *Meek v Kettlewell* (1843) 1 Ph. 342; *Re Tilt* (1896) 74 L.T. 163; *Re Ellenborough* [1903] 1 Ch. 697; cf. *Kekewich v Manning* (1851) 1 De G.M. & G. 176; Hanbury and Martin, *Modern Equity*, 17th edn (2005), pp.139–141.

[111] *E. Pfeiffer Weinkellerei-Weineinkauf GmbH & Co v Arbuthnot Factors Ltd* [1988] 1 W.L.R. 150, 161.

[112] *Shepherd v Federal Commissioner of Taxation* (1965) 113 C.L.R. 385.

[113] *Hughes v Pump House Hotel Co Ltd* [1902] 2 K.B. 190.

[114] *Walker v Bradford Old Bank* (1884) 12 QBD 511.

[115] (1963) 109 C.L.R. 9. This case contains lengthy discussion of the principles relating to voluntary assignment of future property.

[116] This is the explanation of the case given by the High Court itself in *Shepherd v Federal Commissioner of Taxation* (1965) 113 C.L.R. 385.

the *proceeds* of that chose in action may constitute only an expectancy, assignment of which requires consideration. So in *Glegg v Bromley*,[117] where the proceeds of an action for defamation being brought by the assignor were "assigned" by her, it was assumed that this was a mere expectancy incapable of actual assignment. Again, in a New Zealand case[118] it was held that a purported assignment of "the first £500 of the net income which shall accrue to the assignor" from a certain trust fund in which he had a life interest was nothing more than an agreement to assign an expectancy and required consideration even though the assignment was under seal. Although the assignor's life interest was undoubtedly an existing chose in action and could have itself been assigned without consideration, the assignor had not in fact purported to assign the whole or even part of his actual life interest, but merely sums which he had expected to receive by virtue of that interest.

Agreement to assign existing chose in action in the future. It also seems that an agreement to assign an existing chose in action in the future (as distinguished from an actual assignment intended to operate forthwith) requires consideration. Thus, in *Re McArdle*,[119] five brothers and sisters were entitled to a testator's residuary estate subject to a life interest. The wife of one of the brothers executed and paid for certain improvements to a house which formed part of the estate. Subsequently the five brothers and sisters signed a document addressed to her which read: 19–031

> ". . . in consideration of your carrying out certain alterations and improvements to the property we agree that the executors shall repay to you from the estate when distributed £488 in settlement of the amount."

The Court of Appeal held that this document could not be construed as an equitable assignment[120] because it purported to be a contract to assign, and not an actual assignment. As such it required consideration, and the only consideration being past, it was not enforceable.

Agreement to assign expectancy supported by consideration. Although a mere expectancy is thus incapable of actual assignment, an agreement for valuable consideration to assign such an expectancy operates in equity to transfer the right to the chose in action as soon as it comes into existence provided only that it is sufficiently identifiable under the agreement.[121] No further action on the part of the assignor is necessary to convert an agreement to assign into an actual assignment. The effect of this equitable principle is that the assignee's interest is more than a mere matter of contract, even before the chose in action comes into 19–032

[117] [1912] 3 K.B. 474.

[118] *Williams v Commissioner of Inland Revenue* [1965] N.Z.L.R. 395.

[119] [1951] Ch. 669; criticised in (1951) 67 L.Q.R. 295.

[120] If it could, the fact that the consideration was past would not have made it invalid.

[121] *Tailby v Official Receiver* (1888) 13 App.Cas. 523; *Glegg v Bromley* [1912] 3 K.B. 474; *Cotton v Heyl* [1930] 1 Ch. 510; *Raiffeisen Zentralbank Osterreich AG v Five Star General Trading LLC* [2001] EWCA Civ 68, [2001] 2 W.L.R. 1344 at [80]–[81]. But, without consideration, the mere fact that the assignment is by deed is insufficient.

existence. So, for instance, in *Re Lind*,[122] a person agreed to assign, for valuable consideration, property which he expected to inherit on his mother's death, at that time his mother being still alive. The assignor became bankrupt, but secured his discharge before his mother's death. It was held that the assignees were entitled to the property inherited by the bankrupt from his mother since they had a valid equitable interest in it even before it became an existing chose in action. Had their interest been merely contractual the assignor's liability would have been discharged when he secured his discharge in bankruptcy.

19–033 **Consideration not needed for actual assignment of existing chose.** The better view seems to be that an actual assignment of an existing chose in action does not require consideration provided that the assignor has done everything which is necessary according to the nature of the property to transfer the title to it.[123] It is true that equity will not perfect an imperfect gift, and also that equity will not assist a volunteer; but it is also true that a person can make a gift of a chose in action no less than a chose in possession.[124] Failure to distinguish an actual transfer from the specifically enforceable contract to transfer referred to in the previous paragraph has however led to difficult and confusing dicta.[125] The better view is exemplified by *Holt v Heatherfield Trust Ltd*.[126] X, being indebted to the claimant, assigned to him a debt due from Y. The assignment was in writing and absolute, but before Y received notice of the assignment, the defendants served a garnishee order nisi on Y. The assignment was therefore not statutory but equitable. Atkinson J., having grave doubts whether the antecedent debt constituted sufficient consideration for the assignment in the absence of a forbearance to sue,[127] held that consideration was unnecessary.

19–034 **"Everything which is necessary".** The meaning of the requirement that the assignor must have done everything which is necessary according to the nature of the property to transfer the title to it to the assignee has been elucidated by certain cases on the assignment of shares in companies. If the assignor uses a

---

[122] [1915] 2 Ch. 345. See also *Joseph v Lyons* (1885) 15 QBD 280 (after-acquired stock-in-trade); *Re Gillott's Settlement* [1934] Ch. 97 (future trust income); *Re Trytel* (1952) 2 T.L.R. 32 (royalties); *Syrett v Egerton* [1957] 1 W.L.R. 1130 (future income); *Campbell, Connelly & Co Ltd v Noble* [1963] 1 W.L.R. 252 (copyright); *The Ugland Trailer* [1985] 2 Lloyd's Rep. 372, 374; *The Annangel Glory* [1988] 1 Lloyd's Rep. 45 (future sub-freights under a charter).

[123] See *Kekewich v Manning* (1851) 1 De G.M. & G. 176; *Harding v Harding* (1886) 17 QBD 442; *Re Griffin* [1899] 1 Ch. 408; *German v Yates* (1915) 32 T.L.R. 52; *Re Williams* [1917] 1 Ch. 1; *Holt v Heatherfield Trust Ltd* [1942] 2 K.B. 1; *Re Rose* [1949] Ch. 78; *Re McArdle* [1951] Ch. 669, 676–677; *Re Rose* [1952] Ch. 499; *Re Wale* [1956] 1 W.L.R. 1346; *Pulley v Public Trustee* [1956] N.Z.L.R. 771; *Letts v IRC* [1957] 1 W.L.R. 201; *Norman v Federal Commissioner of Taxation* (1963) 109 C.L.R. 9; *Shepherd v Federal Commissioner of Taxation* (1965) 113 C.L.R. 385. See also *Mascall v Mascall* (1984) 50 P. & C.R. 119 (voluntary conveyance of real property).

[124] Compare *Kekewich v Manning* (1851) 1 De G.M. & G. 176, with *Milroy v Lord* (1862) 4 De G.F. & J. 264. See also *Fortescue v Barnett* (1834) 3 My. & K. 36; *Voyle v Hughes* (1854) 2 Sm. & G. 18; *Re Patrick* [1891] 1 Ch. 82. But see *Olsson v Dyson* (1969) 120 C.L.R. 365, below, para.19–036, where a different view was taken by the High Court of Australia.

[125] See the dicta from *Glegg v Bromley* [1912] 3 K.B. 474, cited above, para.19–027 fn.109; see also *Re Westerton* [1919] 2 Ch. 104, 111.

[126] [1942] 2 K.B. 1.

[127] On this point see the judgment of Windeyer J. in *Norman v Federal Commissioner of Taxation* (1963) 109 C.L.R. 9 and (1943) 59 L.Q.R. 129, 208.

transfer which is not in the appropriate form,[128] or if Treasury consent to the transfer is required but the assignor dies before it is forthcoming,[129] he has not done everything which is necessary according to the nature of the property to transfer the title to the shares, and the assignment is inoperative unless made for value. On the other hand, if the assignor uses the right form of transfer but dies before the directors have registered the shares in the assignee's name, then the assignor has done everything in his power to transfer the title to the shares, and the assignment will operate in equity as from its date (and not from the date of registration), even if there is no consideration.[130] So if the assignor voluntarily assigns a debt to the assignee, but dies before notice is given to the debtor, it would seem that, as between the assignor's estate and the assignee, the assignment would take effect in equity as from its date: for notice to the debtor need not be, and is not usually, given by the assignor. If the assignment was in writing and absolute, it would be converted into a good statutory assignment if the assignee were to give written notice to the debtor after the death of the assignor.[131]

According to the Court of Appeal in *Pennington v Waine*,[132] an equitable assignment of shares may be valid even if the assignor has not done everything in his or her power to transfer the title to the shares. Rather it is sufficient that it would be unconscionable for the donor to change his or her mind; and that stage could be reached even before the share transfer form has been delivered to the donee or the company. Alternatively, it is sufficient that the donor and his or her agents have become agents for the donee for the purpose of submitting the share transfer to the company. Clarke L.J., going beyond Arden and Schiemann L.JJ., thought that, in any event and absent compelling reasons to the contrary, the execution of a stock transfer form should have effect as an equitable assignment without delivery of the form or share certificates to the donee or the company. 19–035

Defective statutory assignments. Difficult problems arise where a statutory assignment could have been used but the full requirements were not complied with. Where the defect is that no notice has been given to the debtor, it has been held that the assignment may be valid in equity without consideration, for the assignor has done all that he needed to do to transfer the chose, and notice can be given by the assignee.[133] Where the assignment was not made in writing, i.e. is oral, it will be void by statute if it ranks as a disposition of an equitable interest or trust.[134] If the subject-matter is a *legal* chose in action, it can still be argued that an assignor who has not made a statutory assignment has not done all that 19–036

[128] *Milroy v Lord* (1862) 4 De G.F. & J. 264.
[129] *Re Fry* [1946] Ch. 312.
[130] *Re Rose* [1949] Ch. 78; *Re Rose* [1952] Ch. 499; *Letts v IRC* [1957] 1 W.L.R. 201.
[131] As in *Re Westerton* [1919] 2 Ch. 104.
[132] [2002] 1 W.L.R. 2075.
[133] *Holt v Heatherfield Trust Ltd* [1942] 2 K.B. 1, above, para.19–033; *Magee v U.D.T. Finance Ltd* [1983] N.Z.L.R. 438. But as to options cf. *Warner Bros Records Inc v Rollgreen Ltd* [1976] Q.B. 30, above, para.19–005.
[134] Above, para.19–025.

he can to transfer the chose; hence the transaction can at best be regarded as an agreement to assign and requires consideration. This view has been adopted in the High Court of Australia.[135–136] A counter-argument is, however, that before 1875 an assignee of a legal chose in action could not sue in his own name and only had a right to compel the assignor in accordance with the agreement to allow his name to be used and that this agreement required consideration; but that since 1875 the assignee can sue in his own name, joining the assignor if necessary as co-defendant, so that consideration is no longer necessary for any assignment. This argument may go too far[137] and may be based on an imperfect understanding of the old cases.[138] Those cases do not in fact indicate a settled view, and it may be that the better approach is that the question whether an oral transaction is an assignment or an agreement to assign is to be collected from its terms and not prejudged by the application of supposed rules.[139]

19–037 Where the defect is that the assignment is non-absolute, it should be borne in mind that the distinction between absolute and non-absolute assignments is not the same as that between assignments and agreements to assign. The former distinction has the purpose of isolating those cases where, whether because the assignor may still have some interest in the debt assigned or because the debtor should not be subjected to successive actions on the same debt, it is desirable that all those involved be parties to litigation.[140] It would seem that whereas an assignment by way of charge shall normally be regarded as an agreement to assign, and so require consideration (which it would normally have in any case[141]) the assignment of part of a debt may rank as a completed assignment.[142] As before, the effect of a conditional assignment would depend on the interpretation of the condition.[143]

19–038 **Enforcement of legal chose in action equitably assigned.**[144] Before the Judicature Act 1873, an assignment of a legal chose in action could not usually have been enforced except in the name of the assignor because a legal chose in action had to be enforced in the common law courts, which would only recognise

---

[135–136] *Olsson v Dyson* (1969) 120 C.L.R. 365. See also *Anning v Anning* (1907) 4 C.L.R. 1049. Doubt was cast on some of the reasoning in *Olsson v Dyson* in *Corin v Patton* (1990) 169 C.L.R. 540 (High Court of Australia).

[137] *Treitel on the Law of Contract*, 12th edn (Peel, 2007), para.15–035.

[138] See *Re Westerton* [1919] 2 Ch. 104; *Treitel on the Law of Contract*, paras 15–027—15–036; below, paras 19–038—19–041.

[139] See *German v Yates* (1915) 32 T.L.R. 52 (discussed (1955) 33 Can. Bar Rev. 284, 294–296).

[140] Above, paras 19–012—19–014; below, paras 19–038—19–041.

[141] See *Matthews v Goodday* (1861) 31 L.J.Ch. 282; *Re Earl of Lucan* (1890) 45 Ch D 470.

[142] *Shepherd v Federal Commissioner of Taxation* (1965) 113 C.L.R. 385; see also *Re McArdle* [1951] Ch. 669, where the court appears to have been willing to construe a gift of part of a debt as an assignment had the circumstances been appropriate. Since part of a debt cannot be statutorily assigned, the reasoning in *Olsson v Dyson* (1969) 120 C.L.R. 365, is inapplicable: see *Re Smyth* [1970] Argus L.R. 919.

[143] Above, paras 19–012—19–013.

[144] See generally, Tolhurst (2002) 118 L.Q.R. 98.

the assignor as entitled to sue. After the passing of the Judicature Act, it has been held that, although assignments of legal choses not complying with the statute remain valid in equity,[145] and the assignee is entitled to sue in his own name, it also remains the position that, as a matter of practice, the assignee is normally required to join the assignor.[146] Where the assignment fails to be statutory because the assignor has not wholly disposed of his interest (e.g. where it is by way of charge only, or is of part of a debt only), or where there is a dispute as to whether the documents constitute an assignment,[147] joining the assignor serves a useful purpose. It ensures that all parties with an interest in the chose are brought before the court and that the debtor, if he is adjudged liable, obtains a complete discharge from his liability. But where the assignor retains no interest in the chose in action and the assignment only fails to be statutory, e.g. because it was not in writing or because no notice has been given, a requirement that the assignor be made a party to the proceedings would seem to serve no useful purpose and may be dispensed with.[148]

As the requirement that an equitable assignor be a party to a suit is procedural and not substantive, an action commenced by an equitable assignee is not a nullity and is effective to stop time running for the purposes of statutes of limitation[149] or a contractual limitation period.[150] The debtor may also waive the requirement that the assignor be joined.[151] In any event the Civil Procedure Rules 1998[152] provide that a court may order a person to be added as a new party either if this is desirable in order that the court can resolve all the matters in dispute in the proceedings; or if there is an issue involving the new party and an existing party, which is connected to the matters in dispute in the proceedings, and it is desirable to add the new party so that the court can resolve that issue. Where a claimant claims a remedy to which some other person is jointly entitled with him, all persons jointly entitled to the remedy must be parties unless the court orders otherwise; but if any such person does not agree to be a claimant, he must be made a defendant, unless the court orders otherwise. 19–039

145 *Brandt's Sons & Co v Dunlop Rubber Co* [1905] A.C. 454.

146 [1905] A.C. 454; and see also *Performing Right Society Ltd v London Theatre of Varieties Ltd* [1924] A.C. 1; *Williams v Atlantic Assurance Co* [1933] 1 K.B. 81; *Holt v Heatherfield Trust Ltd* [1942] 2 K.B. 1, 5; *The Aiolos* [1983] 2 Lloyd's Rep. 25; *Weddell v J.A. Pearce & Major* [1988] Ch. 26; *Three Rivers D.C. v Bank of England* [1996] Q.B. 292; *Hendry v Chartsearch Ltd, The Times*, September 16, 1998; *Raiffeisen Zentralbank Osterreich AG v Five Star General Trading LLC* [2001] EWCA Civ 68, [2001] 2 W.L.R. 1344 at [60]. In the rare converse case, an assignor wishing to recover for himself must join the assignee: *Walter and Sullivan Ltd v Murphy & Sons Ltd* [1955] 2 Q.B. 584; *Three Rivers D.C. v Bank of England* [1996] Q.B. 292.

147 *The Aiolos* [1983] 2 Lloyd's Rep. 25.

148 *The Aiolos* [1983] 2 Lloyd's Rep. 25, 33–34; *Weddell v J.A. Pearce & Major* [1988] Ch. 26, 40–41; *Raiffeisen Zentralbank Osterreich AG v Five Star General Trading LLC* [2001] EWCA Civ 68, [2001] 2 W.L.R. 1344 at [60].

149 *Weddell v J.A. Pearce & Major* [1988] Ch. 26; cf. *Compania Colombiana de Seguros v Pacific Steam Navigation Co* [1965] 1 Q.B. 101, 127–129.

150 *The Aiolos* [1983] 2 Lloyd's Rep. 25.

151 *Brandt's Sons & Co v Dunlop Rubber Co* [1905] A.C. 454.

152 CPR rr.19.2–3.

19–040 **Enforcement of equitable chose in action equitably assigned.** Even before the Judicature Act, an assignee of an equitable chose could sue alone to enforce his rights in the Court of Chancery if the assignment was absolute,[153] and this remains the position today, since there is nothing in the Judicature Act to impair this right.

19–041 Although there is no precise authority on the point, it seems that an equitable assignee of an equitable chose must join the assignor wherever the assignor retains an interest in the chose in question. It has already been seen that the reasoning underlying the decisions of the courts on the construction of s.136 of the Law of Property Act 1925 has been founded on the desirability of requiring all interested persons to be made parties to the proceedings; or, where part only of a debt has been assigned, of requiring the debt to be sued for in one action and not in several.[154] These considerations have prompted some of the decisions in which assignments have been held not to be statutory, since (as already seen) a statutory assignee can always sue alone. It would seem, therefore, that even an assignee of an equitable chose cannot sue alone without joining the assignor, wherever the assignor retains an interest in the chose; and, furthermore, that any other party (such as another assignee) who has an interest in it should also be joined.

(c) *Principles Applicable to Statutory and Equitable Assignments*

(i) *What Rights are Assignable*

19–042 **In general.** Despite the existence of the statutory form of assignment under s.136 of the Law of Property Act 1925, the assignability of a contractual right[155] in any given case is generally governed by the rules of equity existing before the Judicature Acts, and these rules now apply to statutory and equitable assignments alike.[156] There is also a number of particular statutory provisions prohibiting assignment in certain cases.[157]

19–043 **Rights declared by contract to be incapable of assignment.**[158] If rights arising under a contract are declared by the contract to be incapable of assignment, a purported assignment will be invalid as against the debtor. In the leading

---

[153] *Cator v Croydon Canal Co* (1841) 4 Y. & C.Ex. 405, 593; *Donaldson v Donaldson* (1854) Kay 711.

[154] Above, paras 19–012—19–004, 19–038.

[155] It seems that an irrevocable offer is assignable in the same way and subject to the same conditions as a contractual right: see *Whiteley v Hilt* [1918] 2 K.B. 808, 818; *R.A. Brierley Investments Ltd v Landmark Corp Ltd* (1966) 40 A.L.J.R. 425; *Warner Bros Records Inc v Rollgreen Investments Ltd* [1976] Q.B. 430. But this is an instance where an equitable assignment may be less effective than a legal assignment: above, para.19–005.

[156] *Tolhurst v Associated Portland Cement Manufacturers Ltd* [1902] 2 K.B. 660, 676; *Torkington v Magee* [1902] 2 K.B. 427, 430–431; reversed [1903] 1 K.B. 644.

[157] Below, para.19–047.

[158] See generally Allcock (1983) C.L.J. 328.

case of *Linden Gardens Trust Ltd v Lenesta Sludge Disposals Ltd*[159] the benefits of building contracts were purportedly assigned by lessees of the properties on which the building work was being carried out to assignees of the leases. Under the building contracts there was to be no assignment of the contract by either party without the other's consent. No such consent for the assignments was obtained.[160] It was held by the House of Lords that, on the true construction of the prohibition clause, the assignment of the benefit of the contract, rather than merely vicarious performance, was barred; and that no distinction was here being drawn by the parties between barring an assignment of the right to future performance, as opposed to the fruits, of the contract nor between barring an assignment of unaccrued, as opposed to accrued, causes of action.[161] Moreover there was no reason of public policy not to give effect to the prohibition clause, the legitimate commercial purpose of which was to ensure that the original parties to the contract were not brought into direct contractual relations with third parties.[162]

In *Hendry v Chartsearch Ltd*[163] the majority of the Court of Appeal (Millett and Henry L.JJ., Evans L.J. preferring to leave the point open) held that, where **19–044**

---

[159] [1994] 1 A.C. 85; Cartwright (1993) 9 Const.L.J. 281; Duncan Wallace (1994) 110 L.Q.R. 42; Tettenborn (1994) 53 C.L.J. 24. See also, following *Linden Gardens*, *Circuit Systems Ltd v Zuken-Redac (UK) Ltd* [1996] 3 All E.R. 748, CA; *Quadmost Ltd v Reprotech* [2001] B.P.I.R. 349; *British Energy Power & Energy Trading Ltd v Credit Suisse* [2007] EWHC 1428 (Comm), [2007] 2 Lloyd's Rep. 427. See also, prior to *Linden Gardens*, *Helstan Securities Ltd v Hertfordshire CC* [1978] 3 All E.R. 262; noted by Goode (1979) 42 M.L.R. 553. See further *United Dominions Trust Ltd v Parkway Motors* [1955] 1 W.L.R. 719 (benefits of hire-purchase agreement not assignable where agreement so states): the decision on the measure of damages in that case has been overruled by *Wickham Holdings Ltd v Brooke House Motors Ltd* [1967] 1 W.L.R. 295 but without affecting the assignment point (indeed the latter case proceeded on the assumption that either the benefit of the hire-purchase agreement was not assignable or that the prohibition against assignment was waived). A prohibition on assignment of a debt in a contract between a creditor and debtor does not operate to undermine the rights of a prior holder of a floating charge over that debt and it can therefore assign its rights, as chargee, over that debt: *Foamcrete (UK) Ltd v Thrust Engineering Ltd* [2002] B.C.C. 221. For a cogent criticism of this decision, see Tettenborn [2001] LMCLQ 472. *Linden Gardens* was applied in upholding a prohibition on an assignment of copyright in *New Zealand Payroll Software Systems Ltd v Advanced Management Systems Ltd* [2003] 3 N.Z.L.R. 1, noted by Thomas (2004) 120 L.Q.R. 218.

[160] In *Orion Finance Ltd v Crown Financial Management Ltd* [1994] 2 B.C.L.C. 607, although the defendant had not given its consent, the assignment was held valid because in the circumstances the defendant was estopped from denying that the assignment was valid.

[161] cf. *Flood v Shand Construction Ltd*, *The Times*, January 8, 1997, where a clause prohibiting assignment, without consent, of a building sub-contract but permitting the assignment of "any sum which is or may become due and payable under this sub-contract" was construed as permitting assignment of the right to recover sums already due, but not the right to claim damages or other sums that needed to be established as due and payable by litigation or arbitration or contractual machinery.

[162] See also *Oakdale (Richmond) Ltd v National Westminster Bank Plc* [1997] 1 B.C.L.C. 63, where a clause prohibiting a company from factoring, discounting, charging or assigning its book or other debts without the bank's consent was held to be necessary if banks were to lend on the security of book debts and, far from being anti-competitive under art.85 EC, it promoted competition because it enabled a company to obtain additional finance from its bank.

[163] *The Times*, September 16, 1998, CA.

there is a clause requiring consent, consent not to be unreasonably withheld,[164] it is fatal to the validity of the assignment that the debtor's consent was not sought; it is irrelevant that, on the facts, consent could not have been reasonably withheld.

19–045 However, it seems that a prohibited assignment can be effective as between assignor and assignee. It appears to have been in that context that Darling J. uttered his famous dictum that a prohibition "could no more operate to invalidate the assignment than it could interfere with the laws of gravitation".[165] In the *Linden Gardens* case Lord Browne-Wilkinson, giving the leading judgment, said:

> ". . . a prohibition on assignment normally only invalidates the assignment as against the other party to the contract so as to prevent a transfer of the chose in action: in the absence of the clearest words it cannot operate to invalidate the contract as between the assignor and assignee and even then it may be ineffective on the grounds of public policy."[166]

19–046 Moreover, it has been held that a covenant in a marriage settlement to settle after-acquired property could be enforced by the beneficiaries with respect to the proceeds of a life insurance policy that had been paid to the covenantor's executor, although the policy was expressed to be not assignable.[167] It has also been held that a purported assignment of a contract relating to the promotion and management of boxing that was ineffective at law, because the contract prohibited assignment and involved personal services, was effective in equity as a declaration of trust of the benefit of the contract.[168] On the facts, this ensured that the parties' commercial intentions were effected. The distinction between a prohibited and therefore invalid assignment and a valid declaration of trust of the benefit of a contract was further analysed in *Barbados Trust Co Ltd v Bank of Zambia*.[169] A clause in a loan facility prevented assignment by the lender other than to a bank or financial institution unless the borrower (the Bank of Zambia) gave its prior written consent. There was an assignment to a bank (the Bank of America). That bank, without the borrower's consent, declared itself a trustee of its rights under the loan for the claimant, which was neither a bank nor a financial

[164] See *British Gas Trading Ltd v Eastern Electricity Plc* Unreported, December 18, 1996 CA, where it was held, upholding Colman J., *The Times*, November 29, 1996, that Eastern had unreasonably withheld its consent to an assignment.

[165] *Tom Shaw & Co v Moss Empires Ltd* (1908) 25 T.L.R. 190, 191.

[166] [1994] 1 A.C. 85, 108. See also *Hendry v Chartsearch Ltd*, *The Times*, September 16, 1998.

[167] *Re Turcan* (1888) 40 Ch D 5. See also *Re Griffin* [1899] 1 Ch. 408 and *Re Westerton* [1919] 2 Ch. 104, where it was held that bank deposits had been validly assigned though the deposit receipts were expressed to be not transferable in both cases; and *Spellman v Spellman* [1961] 1 W.L.R. 921, 925, per Danckwerts L.J.

[168] *Don King Productions Inc v Warren* [2000] Ch. 291: (it was also held that the benefit of the contract could be partnership property even though non-assignable). For criticism of the decision in *Don King*, making the argument that one cannot have a trust of, or charge over, unassignable rights, see Turner, "Charges of Unassignable Rights" (2004) 20 J.C.L. 97.

[169] [2007] EWCA Civ 148, [2007] 1 Lloyd's Rep. 494.

institution. The Court of Appeal (Waller L.J. dissenting) held that there had been no initially valid assignment to the Bank of America and, without that initially valid assignment, there could be no subsequent valid declaration of trust. However, had there been an initially valid assignment, the majority (Waller and Rix L.JJ., Hooper L.J. dissenting) thought that the Bank of America's declaration of trust would have been effective. The prohibition on assignment to a non-bank did not also prohibit a declaration of trust because a declaration of trust and an assignment are different and, as a matter of construction, the prohibition here did not extend to a declaration of trust.[170]

Assignment prohibited by statute or public policy. Assignment of certain rights is prohibited by statute; for example, benefits under social security legislation are not assignable.[171] And in other cases an assignment may be void on grounds of public policy, e.g. an assignment of the salary of a public officer has been held to be void,[172] and the same may be true of an assignment by a wife of her right to maintenance.[173] 19–047

The assignment of a right of action by a party not entitled to legal aid (for example, because a corporate claimant) to a party so entitled (for example, the directors and shareholders of a company), where the object and effect of the assignment was to enable the assignee to obtain legal aid that would not have been available to the assignor, was not contrary to public policy or unlawful.[174] The same applied where the object, in effect, of the assignment was to enable the action to be brought by an assignee who, unlike the assignor, did not have to provide security for costs. 19–048

Assignments savouring of maintenance.[175] A chose in action is not assignable if the assignment savours of maintenance or champerty.[176] For this reason it has often been asserted that a bare right to litigate is not assignable.[177] The 19–049

[170] The majority (Hooper L.J. dissenting) was also of the view that, had there been a valid declaration of trust, the beneficiary under the trust could have itself enforced the contractual rights as it had invoked the procedure in *Vandepitte v Preferred Accident Insurance Corp of New York* [1933] A.C. 70 of joining the trustee as defendant.

[171] Social Security Administration Act 1992 s.187. See also, e.g. Superannuation Act 1972 s.5(1); Pensions Act 1995 s.91 (the right to a pension under an occupational pension scheme cannot be assigned other than in favour of one's widow, widower or dependant). The Unfair Terms in Consumer Contracts Regulations 1999 para.1(p) of Sch.2, list as a possible unfair term one which has the object or effect of: "... giving the seller or supplier the possibility of transferring his rights and obligations under the contract, where this may serve to reduce the guarantees for the consumer without the latter's agreement."

[172] See *Re Mirams* [1891] 1 Q.B. 594; above, para.16–022.

[173] *Re Robinson* (1884) 27 Ch D 160; *Watkins v Watkins* [1896] P. 222; *Clark v Clark* [1906] P. 331; *Pacquine v Snary* [1909] 1 K.B. 688.

[174] *Norglen Ltd v Reed Rains Provincial Ltd* [1999] 2 A.C. 1 HL (but in such circumstances the Legal Aid Board, in the exercise of its discretion, might refuse legal aid to the assignee); cf. *Sinclair v British Telecommunications Plc* [2000] 2 All E.R. 461 CA, below para.19–070 fn.254.

[175] This subject is dealt with in more detail above, paras 16–048 et seq.

[176] *Rees v De Bernardy* [1896] 2 Ch. 437; *Laurent v Sale & Co* [1963] 1 W.L.R. 829.

[177] *Prosser v Edmunds* (1835) 1 Y. & C. Ex. 481; *Dawson v Great Northern & City Ry* [1905] 1 K.B. 260, 271; *Glegg v Bromley* [1912] 3 K.B. 474, 489–490; *Defries v Milne* [1913] 1 Ch. 98; *Torkington v Magee* [1902] 2 K.B. 427, 433–434 (decision reversed [1903] 1 K.B. 644); *Trendtex Trading Corp v Credit Suisse* [1982] A.C. 679; *Giles v Thompson* [1994] 1 A.C. 142. Trustees in

principle has, however, been qualified in many important respects, and although in *Trendtex Trading Corp v Crédit Suisse*[178] it was said to remain a fundamental principle of our law, the House of Lords in that case recognised that it has limited scope in the modern law. Lord Roskill said:

> "If the assignment is of a property right or interest and the cause of action is ancillary to that right or interest, or if the assignee had a genuine commercial interest in taking the assignment and in enforcing it for his own benefit, I see no reason why the assignment should be struck down as an assignment of a bare cause of action or as savouring of maintenance."[179]

So it has been held that rights of action (even in tort) which are incidental and subsidiary to property may be validly assigned when the property is transferred.[180] Again, it has been held that an assignment of rights of action to an insurer who has paid a loss and would, apart from the assignment, have been able to sue the tortfeasor under the doctrine of subrogation in the name of the insured, may be effective to enable the insurer to sue in his own name.[181] It is also well established that a claim to a simple debt is assignable even if the debtor has refused to pay,[182] and even though this may be said in a sense to be an assignment of a "bare right to litigate".[183] The practice of assigning or "selling" debts to debt-collecting agencies and credit factors could hardly be carried on if the law were otherwise.[184]

---

bankruptcy and liquidators, however, are to some extent permitted by statute to make such assignments: Insolvency Act 1986 ss.167, 314, 436 Schs 4 and 5; *Guy v Churchill* (1888) 40 Ch D 481; *Re Park Gate Waggon Works* (1881) 17 Ch D 234; *Ogdens Ltd v Weinberg* (1906) 95 L.T. 567; *Ramsey v Hartley* [1977] 1 W.L.R. 686; *Freightex Ltd v International Express Co Ltd* Unreported April 15, 1980 CA; *Grovewood Holdings Plc v James Capel & Co Ltd* [1995] Ch. 80; *Re Oasis Merchandising Services Ltd* [1998] Ch. 170; *Norglen Ltd v Reed Rains Prudential Ltd* [1999] 2 A.C. 1, 11–12 HL.

[178] [1982] A.C. 679, discussed more fully, above, para.16–057.

[179] [1982] A.C. 679, 703. For a penetrating and persuasive criticism of the "genuine commercial interest" criterion in *Trendtex* and a call for a reconsideration of this area of the law so that assignments of rights to compensation are recognised as valid, subject to a few specific exceptions, see Tettenborn, "Assignment of Rights to Compensation" [2007] LMCLQ 392.

[180] *Dickinson v Burrell* (1866) L.R. 1 Eq. 337, 342 (right to rescind earlier conveyance); *Dawson v Great Northern & City Ry* [1905] 1 K.B. 260 (right to compensation for injurious affecting of land); *Ellis v Torrington* [1920] 1 K.B. 399 (breach of covenant relating to land); *G.U.S. Property Management Ltd v Littlewoods Mail Order Stores Ltd* (1982) S.L.T. 533 (delictual action for damage to building) noted by Street (1983) Conv. 404. But an order for possession is probably not assignable: *Chung Kwok Hotel Co v Field* [1960] 1 W.L.R. 1112. See generally above, para.16–061.

[181] *King v Victoria Insurance Co Ltd* [1896] A.C. 250; *Compania Colombiana de Seguros v Pacific Steam Navigation Co* [1965] 1 Q.B. 101; above, para.16–062. Even, probably, if the amount recoverable exceeds the loss suffered by the insurer: see *Compania Colombiana* [1965] 1 Q.B. 101, 121; *Trendtex Trading Corp v Credit Suisse* [1980] Q.B. 629, 656.

[182] *County Hotel and Wine Co Ltd v London & North Western Ry* [1918] 2 K.B. 251, 258–262; affirmed on other grounds [1919] 2 K.B. 29; [1921] 1 A.C. 85. See also *Ellis v Torrington* [1920] 1 K.B. 399.

[183] *Fitzroy v Cave* [1905] 2 K.B. 364.

[184] *Comfort v Betts* [1891] 1 Q.B. 737, 739; *Camdex International Ltd v Bank of Zambia* [1998] Q.B. 22. For an example of "factoring" see *G.E. Crane Sales Pty Ltd v Federal Commissioner of Taxation* (1971) 126 C.L.R. 177.

In the *Trendtex* case itself it was accepted that a creditor who has financed the transaction giving rise to the right of action will have a legitimate commercial interest in it and an assignment to him will be valid[185] unless it appears that the object of the assignment was not to protect that interest. On the facts the assignment was held void because it was a: 19–050

> "... step towards the sale of a bare cause of action to a third party who had no genuine commercial interest in the claim."[186]

However, the mere fact that the assignee seeks to enforce the assigned rights for another is not fatal where this is a legitimate part of its business activity.[187] So also the fact that the assignee might make a profit out of the assignment does not of itself render the agreement to assign champertous although the prospect of excessive profit can be taken into account in deciding whether the commercial interest is genuine.[188]

It appears, however, that a purported assignee has no legitimate commercial interest in a purely personal claim so that such a claim is non-assignable.[189] The most obvious example is the right to damages for a personal, as opposed to a proprietary, tort such as assault, defamation, or a tort causing personal injury. 19–051

It is also to be noted that even where a right of action is not assignable on the ground that it amounts to a "bare right to litigate" there is no objection to an agreement to assign the proceeds of an action.[190] In such a case no question of maintenance need arise, for the assignee is not himself given any right to sue the tortfeasor or debtor on the original cause of action. 19–052

The torts and crimes of maintenance and champerty were abolished by the Criminal Law Act 1967, but s.14(2) of that Act expressly provides that this is not to affect "any rule of law as to the cases in which a contract is to be treated as contrary to public policy or otherwise illegal". It is submitted that this phraseology should be interpreted to cover assignments as well as contracts to assign. In *Trendtex* Lord Roskill said that it: 19–053

---

[185] *Trendtex Trading Corp v Credit Suisse* [1980] Q.B. 629. Assignments have been held valid, applying the *Trendtex* test of a "genuine commercial interest" in, e.g. *The Kelo* [1985] 2 Lloyd's Rep. 85; *Bourne v Colodense Ltd* [1985] I.C.R. 291; *Brownton Ltd v Edward Moore Inbucon Ltd* [1985] 3 All E.R. 499; *South East Thames Regional H.A. v Lovell* (1985) 32 Build.L.R. 127; *24 Seven Utility Services Ltd v Rosekey Ltd* [2003] EWHC 3415 (QB); *Massai Aviation Services Ltd v Att-Gen for the Bahamas* [2007] UKPC 12. For the assignment of rights to solicitors, see above, para.16–064.

[186] [1980] Q.B. 629, 704.

[187] *The Kelo* [1985] 2 Lloyd's Rep. 85.

[188] *Brownton Ltd v Edward Moore Inbucon Ltd* [1985] 3 All E.R. 499. Quaere whether, if the assignee did make a profit, he is answerable to the assignor.

[189] *Trendtex Trading Corp v Credit Suisse* [1980] Q.B. 629, 656, per Lord Denning M.R., 671, 674, per Oliver L.J.; [1982] A.C. 679, 702.

[190] *Glegg v Bromley* [1912] 3 K.B. 474; *Gould v Skinner* [1983] Qd. 377.

"... seems plain that Parliament intended to leave the law as to the effect of maintenance and champerty upon contracts unaffected by the abolition of them as crimes and torts."[191]

19–054 **Personal contracts.** The benefit of a contract is only assignable in:

"... cases where it can make no difference to the person on whom the obligation lies to which of two persons he is to discharge it."[192]

It is to be noted that the question whether an assignment makes any difference to the debtor must be decided by the court on objective grounds, having regard to the nature of the contract and of the subject-matter of the rights assigned. It may in some circumstances make a great deal of difference to a debtor whether his creditor is of an indulgent character, or whether he is likely to enforce his legal rights ruthlessly, but considerations of this kind are ignored by the courts in determining whether a right is assignable or not.[193]

19–055 Prima facie contractual rights to, for example, the payment of money, and to the sale or occupation or use[194] of land, or to building work,[195] do not involve personal considerations and are capable of assignment. A right to be indemnified against a monetary liability may in some circumstances be assignable,[196] but the benefit of a motor vehicle insurance policy involves personal considerations and is not assignable.[197] Indeed, any contractual right involving personal skill on the part of the creditor, or other personal qualifications (such as his credit),[198] is incapable of assignment. Hence neither an author nor his publisher may assign the right to performance of the other's obligations under a publishing agreement, although an author's right to be paid royalties may be assigned[199]; and if the author has actually transferred the copyright in the work to the publisher, he can of course assign that as an item of property.[200] The right to employ a person under a contract of employment is clearly not assignable,[201] though wages or salary due to the employee are normally assignable by him.[202] The mere presence of an

---

[191] [1982] A.C. 679, 702.

[192] *Tolhurst v Associated Portland Cement Manufacturers Ltd* [1902] 2 K.B. 660, 668; affirmed [1903] A.C. 414.

[193] *Fitzroy v Cave* [1905] 2 K.B. 364 (where the purpose of the assignment was to procure the debtor's bankruptcy).

[194] *J. Miller Ltd v Laurence & Bardsley* [1966] 1 Lloyd's Rep. 90.

[195] *Charlotte Thirty Ltd and Bison Ltd v Croker Ltd* (1990) 24 Con. L.R. 46.

[196] *British Union and National Insurance Co v Rawson* [1916] 2 Ch. 476.

[197] *Peters v General Accident, etc., Ltd* [1938] 2 All E.R. 267.

[198] *Cooper v Micklefield Coal and Lime Co* (1912) 107 L.T. 457; *Cole v Wellington Dairy Farmers' Co-op Association* [1917] N.Z.U.L.R. 372.

[199] *Stevens v Benning* (1855) 6 De G.M. & G. 223; *Hole v Bradbury* (1879) 12 Ch D 886; *Griffiths v Tower Publishing Co* [1897] 1 Ch. 21; *Don King Productions Inc v Warren* [2000] Ch. 291, 319, per Lightman J.; decision affirmed [2000] Ch. 291 CA.

[200] Copyright, Designs and Patents Act 1988 s.90.

[201] *Nokes v Doncaster Amalgamated Collieries Ltd* [1940] A.C. 1014, 1026; *Denham v Midland Employers' Mutual Assurance Ltd* [1955] 2 Q.B. 437, 443; cf. *I.T. O'Brien v Benson's Hosiery (Holdings) Ltd* [1980] A.C. 562, 572. See also Transfer of Undertakings (Protection of Employment) Regulations 2006 (SI 2006/246).

[202] *Shaw v Moss' Empires and Boston* (1909) 25 T.L.R. 191; *Russell & Co v Austin Fryers* (1909) 25 T.L.R. 414. Subject to the rules as to public policy (above, para.16–003) and to statute (e.g. Merchant Shipping Act 1995 s.34(1)(c)).

arbitration clause in a contract does not as a general rule render the contract incapable of assignment.[203]

19–056 **Commercial contracts.** Rights arising under ordinary commercial contracts (e.g. for the sale of goods) are prima facie readily assignable, at least if there is no question of credit being granted to the assignee. But commercial contracts may sometimes be drafted so as to make the requirements of one of the parties a material consideration in determining the obligations of the other. In such circumstances there is often difficulty in deciding whether the benefit of the contract is assignable. In *Tolhurst v Associated Portland Cement Manufacturers Ltd*,[204] the defendant was the owner of certain land upon which there were chalk quarries. He sold part of this land to a company in order to enable the company to carry on there the business of manufacturing Portland Cement. He contracted to supply the company, which was in a small way of business, with 750 tons of chalk per week for 50 years "and so much more as the company shall require for the manufacture of Portland cement upon their said land". The company subsequently assigned the contract, sold its undertaking to the claimant company, which was in a large way of business, and went into voluntary liquidation. The House of Lords held that the new company was entitled to the benefit of the contract and could maintain an action against the defendant in its own name. There were two grounds for this decision: (1) The defendant's liability was measured by the capacity of the original company's land:

> ". . . the [original] company were not entitled to an unlimited supply of chalk, but only to so much as they might want for making cement on their own piece of land."[205]

Consequently the effect of the assignment was not to increase the burden on the defendant, for the original company might have increased its capital and worked its land more intensively; (2) By entering into a long-term contract the defendant must have contemplated that the benefit of it might be assigned.[206] The contract should therefore be construed as if it had been made between the defendant and his successors and assignees owners and occupiers of the quarries and the company, its successors and assignees owners and occupiers of the cement works.[207] On the other hand, in *Kemp v Baerselman*[208] the defendant contracted to supply X, a cake manufacturer, with all the eggs that he should require for manufacturing purposes for one year: and X undertook not to purchase eggs elsewhere. X transferred his business to a company, and it was held that the contract was not assignable, because the defendant's liability was not limited to the capacity of a particular piece of land, and because X's contract not to

---

203 *Shayler v Woolf* [1946] Ch. 320, explaining *Cottage Club Estates Ltd v Woodside Estates Co Ltd* [1928] 2 K.B. 463; *The Halcyon the Great* [1984] 1 Lloyd's Rep. 283, 289; *Montedipe SpA v JTP-Ro Jugotanker* [1990] 2 Lloyd's Rep. 11; *Baytur SA v Finagro Holding SA* [1992] 1 Q.B. 610.

204 [1902] 2 K.B. 660, [1903] A.C. 414.

205 [1903] A.C. 414, 423; in CA, 673.

206 [1903] A.C. 414, 419; in CA, 674–675.

207 [1903] A.C. 414, 420, 421, 423; *Nokes v Doncaster Amalgamated Collieries Ltd* [1940] A.C. 1014, 1020.

208 [1906] 2 K.B. 609.

purchase eggs elsewhere introduced a personal element inasmuch as this obligation would not have been binding on the assignee.[209]

19–057 **Contracts with companies.** It has been held that the fact that one of the parties to a contract is a limited company is no ground for assuming that the personality of that party is immaterial to the other party.[210] For example, the benefit of a publishing contract entered into by an author with a limited company is no more assignable by that company than is the benefit of such a contract with an individual publisher.[211] However, the personality of a company may change without any formal change in the legal identity of the company as, for example, where the ownership and management of the company pass into new hands,[212] or where direction passes into the hands of a receiver or liquidator.[213] Thus persons carrying on business in the form of a company may effectively (though not technically) assign all the company's contracts on a transfer of the business, provided that they transfer the company's shares, and not simply the company's assets, to the assignee. Had this course been adopted in, for example, *Tolhurst's* case[214] no difficulties would have arisen.

(ii) *Validity of Assignments against Assignor's Creditors and Successors in Title*

19–058 **General.** Even where an assignment is valid against the assignor, the position may be different between persons deriving title through the assignor on the one hand and the assignee on the other. Four different cases must be considered: the validity of an assignment against the assignor's personal representatives; the validity of an assignment against a trustee in bankruptcy of the assignor; the validity of an assignment against the liquidator or creditors of a company assignor; and the validity of an assignment against creditors generally. These four cases do not necessarily exhaust the cases in which some outside party may wish to dispute the validity of an assignment. For example, tax liability may in some cases turn on the validity of an assignment; in such circumstances it has been assumed that the question must be determined by inquiring whether the assignment is valid against the assignor.[215]

[209] Yet in *Tolhurst's* case [1903] A.C. 414 the assignor company was also bound to take all its chalk from Tolhurst, a point totally ignored in the House of Lords. The result of the decision seems to be that although the assignee was not bound by the duty to take chalk from the defendant, if it did take any, it was bound to take all its requirements of chalk for the manufacture of cement on that piece of land from him. See below, para.19–079. See also *National Carbonising Co Ltd v British Coal Distillation Ltd* (1936) 54 R.P.C. 41, 57.

[210] *Griffith v Tower Publishing Co* [1897] 1 Ch. 21; *Crane Co v Wittenberg A/S* Unreported December 21, 1999 CA.

[211] *Griffith v Tower Publishing Co* [1897] 1 Ch. 21.

[212] But in *Crane Co v Wittenberg A/S* Unreported December 21, 1999 CA, a manufacturing/distribution contract, which was expressly stated to be personal, was held not to be transferred when the company which was a party to the contract was taken over—i.e. merged—into another.

[213] See *Griffiths v Secretary of State for Social Services* [1974] Q.B. 468 (managing director's contract).

[214] [1974] Q.B. 468.

[215] See, e.g. *Vandervell v IRC* [1967] 2 A.C. 291 (surtax); *Re Rose* [1952] Ch. 499; *Letts v IRC* [1957] 1 W.L.R. 201; *Dalton v IRC* [1958] T.R. 45 (estate duty); and the cases cited above, which concerned stamp duty.

Personal representatives. It never seems to have been doubted that an assignor's personal representatives are bound by an assignment which was binding on the assignor,[216] even where the assignment was not intended to operate until the death of the assignor.[217] It has been suggested that an assignment not binding on the assignor may become binding on his death, inasmuch as an assignment without consideration may be revocable by the assignor but will not be revocable by his personal representatives.[218] This seems questionable, however, for if the "assignment" is truly revocable, then it seems that it cannot be an assignment in the strict sense at all[219]; and on the other hand, an actual assignment (as distinct from an agreement to assign) is not revocable merely because of want of consideration.[220] 19–059

Trustee in bankruptcy.[221] Prima facie the position of a trustee in bankruptcy is the same as that of the assignor himself, i.e. an assignment valid against the assignor will be equally valid against his trustee in bankruptcy. This could clearly cause grave injustice to creditors, especially in view of the effectiveness in equity of an agreement to assign future choses in action, and there are two important limitations on the principle that a trustee in bankruptcy is bound by assignments binding on the assignor. 19–060

First, an assignment of rights which cannot be *earned* by the assignor until after he has become bankrupt, in the sense that the consideration for the rights is not yet wholly executed by the assignor, is void as against the trustee in bankruptcy as from the commencement of the bankruptcy.[222] Thus, an assignment of sums already due to the assignor, or of sums which will become due to him without the need for any further action on his part, will be good against the trustee in bankruptcy; but an assignment of sums to be earned by the assignor in the future (that is, after the commencement of the bankruptcy) will be void as against the trustee from the commencement of the bankruptcy. 19–061

Secondly, s.344 of the Insolvency Act 1986 provides that a *general* assignment of existing or future book debts (or any class thereof) by a person engaged in trade or business is void against the assignor's trustee in bankruptcy as regards any debts not paid at the commencement of the bankruptcy unless the assignment has been registered as a bill of sale. This provision, however, does not apply to an assignment of debts due from specified creditors or under specified contracts, 19–062

---

216 *Re Westerton* [1919] 2 Ch. 104; *Re Rose* [1905] 1 Ch. 94. Moreover, notice after the death of the assignor is sufficient to comply with s.136 of the Law of Property Act 1925: see *Walker v Bradford Old Bank* (1884) 12 QBD 511; *Bateman v Hunt* [1904] 2 K.B. 530; *Re Westerton* [1919] 2 Ch. 104.

217 *Re Westerton* [1919] 2 Ch. 104.

218 *German v Yates* (1915) 32 T.L.R. 52; cf. *Errington v Errington* [1952] 1 K.B. 290, as explained in *National Provincial Bank Ltd v Hastings Car Mart Ltd* [1975] A.C. 1175, 1252.

219 See above, para.19–022.

220 Above, paras 19–019, 19–033.

221 See below, para.20–026.

222 *Ex p. Nichols* (1883) 22 Ch D 782; *Wilmot v Alton* [1897] 1 Q.B. 17; *Re Collins* [1925] Ch. 556; *Re Trytel* (1952) 2 T.L.R. 32; cf. *Drew & Co v Josolyne* (1887) 18 QBD 590.

nor to an assignment made on a bona fide transfer for value of the assignor's business, nor to an assignment made for the benefit of creditors generally.[223]

19–063 Apart from these particular cases, there are also other more general statutory provisions enabling an assignment to be set aside, by a trustee in bankruptcy, as a transaction at an undervalue, a preference, an extortionate credit transaction, or as a transaction defrauding creditors.[224]

19–064 An assignment made between the date of the petition and the making of the bankruptcy order will bind the trustee in bankruptcy against a bona fide purchaser for value without notice that the petition had been presented[225] but will otherwise be void unless the court has given its consent or has subsequently ratified the transaction.[226]

19–065 **Company liquidator or creditors.** The position of a liquidator of a company which, prior to the commencement of the winding up, has assigned any of its rights is basically the same as that of a trustee in bankruptcy; that is, apart from assignments of future earnings, and from particular statutory provisions, a liquidator is bound by an assignment which would be binding on the company itself. But the statutory provisions relating to companies differ markedly from those relating to individual bankrupts in this particular respect. Apart from the general provisions relating to preferences, extortionate credit transactions, and transactions at an undervalue,[227] which are similar to those applying to individual bankrupts, the requirements of the Companies Act only apply to assignments by way of charge, normally but not necessarily a floating charge. By ss.395–398 of the Companies Act 1985[228] a company is required to register, inter alia, a charge on book debts, and failure to comply with the Act renders the charge void against a liquidator[229] or any creditor.[230] On the other hand, these sections, unlike s.344 of the Insolvency Act 1986, apply to any charge over book debts, and not merely to a general charge or assignment. Further, failure to comply with the requirements of the Companies Act renders the charge void against any creditor of the company as well as against the liquidator.

19–066 An assignment which is absolute under s.136 of the Law of Property Act 1925 may sometimes nevertheless be an assignment by way of charge within the

---

[223] See Insolvency Act 1986 s.344(3)(b).

[224] Insolvency Act 1986 ss.339–349, 423–425. See below paras 20–027—20–031.

[225] Insolvency Act 1986 s.284(4).

[226] Insolvency Act 1986 s.284(1).

[227] Insolvency Act 1986 ss.238–246. The provisions governing transactions defrauding creditors (ss.423–425 of the 1986 Act) are the same as those for individual bankrupts.

[228] To be replaced by Companies Act 2006 ss.860–861, 863, 866–867, 874.

[229] See, e.g. *Orion Finance Ltd v Crown Financial Management Ltd* [1996] 2 B.C.L.C. 78 CA; *Orion Finance Ltd v Crown Financial Management Ltd (No.2)* [1996] 2 B.C.L.C. 382 CA. A liquidator includes, in certain circumstances, a person appointed in foreign proceedings in the nature of a winding-up: *N.V. Slavenburg's Bank v Intercontinental Natural Resources* [1980] 1 W.L.R. 1076, 1086–1087.

[230] On the meaning of creditor see Gough, *Company Charges*, 2nd edn (1998), pp.740–741; Goode, *Commercial Law*, 2nd edn (1995), pp.720–721; *Re Ehrmann Bros Ltd* [1906] 2 Ch. 697.

meaning of ss.395–398 of the Companies Act 1985.[231] Under s.136, as already seen,[232] the question is whether the assignor has unconditionally transferred to the assignee for the time being the sole right to the debt in question as against the debtor. But under the Companies Act, the question is whether the assignor retains any interest in the nature of an equity of redemption as against the assignee. Thus an assignment intended to operate by way of security, under which the right is vested in the assignee unless and until reassigned to the assignor, would be absolute under s.136 of the Law of Property Act,[233] but registrable as a charge under the Companies Act.[234] By s.409 of the Companies Act 1985 the registration requirements of ss.395–398 apply to charges made by a foreign company with a place of business in England.[235] This may be so even where the assignment is made abroad and the assignee is also a foreign company.[236]

Creditors. Except in the cases mentioned in the last two paragraphs, an assignment which is valid against an assignor will generally be valid against the assignor's creditors. Thus, except in those cases, a creditor cannot generally attach any debt already assigned by the assignor.[237] There is, however, one other possible case in which an assignment may be valid against an assignor but void against creditors. It has already been seen[238] that an assignment may be constituted by instructions given by the assignor to the debtor to pay the assignee. Where the assignee has no notice of the instructions, and has therefore had no chance to accept or decline the assignment, it has been held that the assignment is not binding on creditors of the assignor since it is incomplete.[239] It is thought that the assignment may be binding on the assignor himself in these circumstances.[240] **19–067**

(iii) *Priorities between Successive Assignees*

Priorities. As seen above, notice to the debtor is not necessary to perfect an equitable assignment as between assignor and assignee, but where there are **19–068**

---

[231] To be replaced by Companies Act 2006 ss.860–861, 863, 866–867, 874.

[232] Above, paras 19–012—19–014.

[233] Above, para.19–012.

[234] See *Re Kent and Sussex Sawmills Ltd* [1947] Ch. 177; *Re Miller, Gibb & Co* [1957] 1 W.L.R. 703; and *Paul and Frank Ltd v Discount (Overseas) Ltd* [1967] Ch. 348, in all of which assignments which were probably absolute under s.136 of the Law of Property Act were held to be registrable under the Companies Act. Certain reservations of title, commonly known as *Romalpa* clauses, may create a registrable charge (*Re Bond Worth Ltd* [1980] Ch. 228; *Borden (UK) Ltd v Scottish Timber Products Ltd* [1981] Ch. 25; *E. Pfeiffer Weinkellerei-Weinenkauf GmbH & Co v Arbuthnot Factors Ltd* [1988] 1 W.L.R. 150; *Tatung (UK) Ltd v Galex Telesure Ltd* (1989) 5 B.C.C. 325; *Re Weldtech Equipment Ltd* [1991] B.C.C. 16); Vol.II, paras 43-203—43-215. So also certain liens: *The Ugland Trailer* [1985] 2 Lloyd's Rep. 372; *The Annangel Glory* [1988] 1 Lloyd's Rep. 45. cf. a "block discount" agreement which constitutes an absolute assignment of debts and does not create a registrable charge: *Lloyds & Scottish Finance Ltd v Cyril Lord Carpets Sales Ltd* [1992] B.C.L.C. 609 HL.

[235] cf. Companies Act 2006 s.1052.

[236] *N.V. Slavenburg's Bank v Intercontinental Natural Resources Ltd* [1980] 1 W.L.R. 1076; *Re Oriel Ltd* [1984] B.C.L.C. 241.

[237] *Holt v Heatherfield Trust Ltd* [1942] 2 K.B. 1.

[238] Above, para.19–021—19–023.

[239] *Rekstin v Severo, etc., and Bank for Russian Trade* [1933] 1 K.B. 47.

[240] Above, para.19–023.

successive assignments (whether statutory or equitable), the rule in *Dearle v Hall*,[241] which originally related to equitable interests in pure personalty, regulates priorities. Under this rule the assignee who first gives notice to the debtor has the prior right, unless he knew of the earlier assignment when he took his assignment.[242] The fact that he knew of the earlier assignment when he gave notice is irrelevant.[243] Thus where a debt due to a firm was assigned by one partner to the defendants by writing and afterwards by the other partner to the claimant by deed, and the claimant gave notice to the debtor before the defendants, it was held that there was a valid equitable assignment to the claimant in priority to the defendants.[244] And a second statutory assignment will not prevail over an earlier equitable one merely because it confers a legal right upon the assignee[245]: in Phillips J.'s words in the *Pfeiffer* case:

> "... even if the [statutory] assignment is effected for value without notice of a prior equity, priorities fall to be determined as if the assignment had been effected in equity, not in law."[246]

The issue of priority must be distinguished from the rule that an assignee takes "subject to equities".[247] Such equities are independent of the assignments and prevail over all assignees.

19–069 **Nature of notice required.** In general, notice need not be formal for the purpose of conferring priority over a subsequent assignee: any kind of notice will suffice so long as the fact that assignment has taken place is brought to the notice of the debtor. A letter stating that the writers had authority to collect freight "against which we have made payments" was held a good notice.[248] And oral notice acquired in the ordinary course of business has been held sufficient, even

---

[241] (1823) 3 Russ. 1.

[242] *Dearle v Hall* (1823) 3 Russ. 1; see also *Lloyd v Banks* (1868) L.R. 3 Ch. App. 488; *Re Holmes* (1885) 29 Ch D 796; *Ward v Duncombe* [1893] A.C. 369; *Kelly v Selwyn* [1905] 2 Ch. 117; *Ellerman Lines Ltd v Lancaster Maritime Co Ltd* [1980] 2 Lloyd's Rep. 497; *The Attika Hope* [1988] 1 Lloyd's Rep. 439; *Compaq Computer Ltd v Abercorn Group Ltd* [1991] B.C.C. 484; *E. Pfeiffer Weinkellerei-Weinenkauf GmbH & Co v Arbuthnot Factors Ltd* [1988] 1 W.L.R. 150. The principle does not however apply in favour of a trustee in bankruptcy (*Re Anderson* [1911] 1 K.B. 896); a judgment creditor (*Scott v Lord Hastings* (1858) 4 K. & J. 633); nor a volunteer (*Justice v Wynne* (1861) 12 Ir.Ch.Rep. 289). For further discussion of this difficult topic see *Snell's Equity*, 31st edn (2005), pp.83–90; Smith, *The Law of Assignment* (2007), paras 15.65–15.122; Beale, Bridge, Gullifer, Lomicka, *The Law of Personal Property Security* (2007), paras 13.09–13.20. See also Goode (1976) 92 L.Q.R. 554–559; Donaldson (1977) 93 L.Q.R. 324; Goode (1977) 93 L.Q.R. 487; McLauchlan (1980) 96 L.Q.R. 90; Oditah (1989) 9 O.J.L.S. 513; De Lacy [1999] Conv. 311.

[243] *Mutual Life Assurance Society v Langley* (1886) 32 Ch D 460.

[244] *Marchant v Morton, Down & Co* [1901] 2 K.B. 829. *Joseph v Lyons* (1884) 15 QBD 280; *E. Pfeiffer Weinkellerei-Weinenkauf GmbH v Arbuthnot Factors Ltd* [1988] 1 W.L.R. 150.

[245] *E. Pfeiffer Weinkellerei-Weinenkauf GmbH v Arbuthnot Factors Ltd* [1988] 1 W.L.R. 150, 161–163. For a contrary approach, see Thomas (1951) 1 J.S.P.T.L. 480; Oditah (1989) 9 O.J.L.S. 513.

[246] [1988] 1 W.L.R. 150, 162. It was left open, 163, whether a statutory assignee, who has actually been paid the debt, can claim priority as a bona fide purchaser for value of the legal title to the payments received. This was conceded in favour of the assignee in *Compaq Computers Ltd v Abercorn Group Ltd* [1991] B.C.C. 484, 500. See also *Taylor v Blakelock* (1886) 32 Ch D 560.

[247] Below, paras 19–070—19–076.

[248] *Smith v S.S. Zigurds (Owners)* [1934] A.C. 209.

though no notice was given by the assignee.[249] But as regards the assignment of an equitable interest in real or personal property, s.137(3) of the Law of Property Act 1925 lays down that oral notice of the assignment to a trustee does not affect the priority of competing claims of purchasers in that equitable interest.

(iv) *Assignments "subject to equities"*

Assignments "subject to equities".[250] Assignments normally take effect "subject to equities". This was always so in equity,[251] and is also the position with a statutory assignment, for s.136 of the Law of Property Act 1925 lays down that an assignment takes effect "subject to equities having priority over the right of the assignee".[252] Thus, where a claim arises out of the contract under which the debt itself arises, and the claim affects the value or amount of the debt which one of the parties purported to assign for value, then if the assignee subsequently sues, the other party to the contract may set up that claim (including the right to set the contract aside[253]) by way of defence against the assignee as cancelling or diminishing the amount to which the assignee asserts his rights under the assignment.[254] Many of the cases have arisen in the context of receivership. The appointment of a receiver by a debenture-holder converts the incomplete assignment constituted by the debenture into a completed equitable assignment of the assets charged by it.[255] The authorities were reviewed in *Business Computers Ltd v Anglo-African Leasing Ltd*[256] and it was said that the result: 19–070

> "... is that a debt which accrues due before notice of an assignment is received, whether or not it is payable before that date,[257] or a debt which arises out of the same contract as that which gives rise to the assigned debt, or is closely connected with that contract,[258] may be set off against the assignee. A debt which is neither accrued nor

[249] *Re Worcester* (1868) L.R. 3 Ch.App. 555; *Lloyd v Banks* (1868) L.R. 3 Ch.App. 488; *Re Dallas* [1904] 2 Ch. 385, 399.

[250] See in general Derham, *Set-off*, 3rd edn (2003), Ch.13. See also Derham (1991) 107 L.Q.R. 126.

[251] *Mangles v Dixon* (1852) 3 H.L.C. 702, 731; *Phipps v Lovegrove* (1873) L.R. 16 Eq. 80, 88.

[252] Above, para.19–006.

[253] *Stoddart v Union-Trust* [1912] K.B. 181, 189.

[254] *Young v Kitchin* (1878) 3 Ex.D. 127; *Newfoundland Government v Newfoundland Ry* (1883) 13 App. Cas. 199; *Lawrence v Hayes* [1927] 2 K.B. 111; *Banco Santander SA v Bayfern Ltd* [2000] 1 All E.R. (Comm) 776 CA (assignee of the promise to pay under a letter of credit is subject to the "fraud exception" as the assignor would have been); *Sinclair v British Telecommunications Plc* [2000] 2 All E.R. 461 CA (where the assignor's action would have been stayed for failure to pay the costs of an earlier substantially similar action, the courts can grant a stay against the assignee to prevent it being in a better position than the assignor).

[255] *George Barker (Transport) Ltd v Eynon* [1974] 1 W.L.R. 462, 467. See also *Watson v Duff, Morgan & Vermont (Holdings) Ltd* [1974] 1 W.L.R. 450, 456.

[256] [1977] 1 W.L.R. 578.

[257] *Rother Iron Works Ltd v Canterbury Precision Engineers Ltd* [1974] Q.B. 1; *Biggerstaff v Rowatts Wharf Ltd* [1896] 2 Ch. 93.

[258] *Newfoundland Government v Newfoundland Ry* (1888) 13 App. Cas. 199, 213 (claims "flowing out of and inseparably connected with ... the transactions which also give use to the subject of the assignment"); *William Pickersgill & Sons Ltd v London & Provincial, etc., Ins. Co Ltd* [1912] 3 K.B. 614; *The Raven* [1980] 2 Lloyd's Rep. 266; cf. *Provident Finance Corp Pty Ltd v Hammond* [1978] V.R. 312; *The Evelpidis Era* [1981] 1 Lloyd's Rep. 54, 66; *The Dominique* [1989] A.C. 1056.

connected may not be set off even though it arises from a contract made before the assignment."[259]

The rationale for this is that, after notice of the assignment, the debtor cannot "do anything to take away or diminish the rights of the assignee as they stood at the time of the notice".[260] A direct claim by the debtor against the assignee may, however, be the subject of a set-off although it would not have been available against the assignor.[261]

19–071 **Claims for damages.** It is clear that provided a claim for unliquidated damages can be set off against the assignor,[262] it can also be set off against the assignee if it arises out of the transaction giving rise to the assigned debt, irrespective of whether the claim itself could have been assigned.[263] But in *Stoddart v Union Trust*[264] it was held that a claim for damages for fraudulently inducing the debtor to enter into the contract with the assignor could not be set up against the assignee unless the debtor rescinded the whole agreement. The decision appears to draw a distinction between a claim in tort for damages for fraud and a similar claim for breach of a term of the contract, and may turn on a procedural point.[265] In the somewhat analogous case where the fraudulent party becomes bankrupt (instead of assigning his rights) it has been held that the fraud may be set up as a defence against the trustee in bankruptcy.[266]

19–072 **Modification of "equities" rule.** Sometimes the rule that an assignee takes subject to equities is excluded or modified by statute,[267] or by the terms of the contract between the debtor and the assignor.[268]

---

259 [1977] 1 W.L.R. 578, 585 (Templeman J.). See also *Re Taunton, Delmard Lane & Co Ltd* [1893] 2 Ch. 175, 183; *Re Pinto Leite & Nephews* [1929] 1 Ch. 221; *Jeffryes v Agra & Mastermans Bank* (1866) L.R. 2 Eq. 674; *Watson v Mid-Wales Ry* (1867) L.R. 2 C.P. 593; *Re Pain* [1919] 1 Ch. 38; *The Khian Captain (No.2)* [1996] 1 Lloyd's Rep. 429; *Marathon Electrical Manufacturing Corp v Mashreqbank P.S.C.* [1997] 2 B.C.L.C. 460.

260 *Roxburghe v Cox* (1881) 17 Ch D 520, 526.

261 *The Raven* [1980] 2 Lloyd's Rep. 266.

262 *The Dominique* [1989] A.C. 1056.

263 *Young v Kitchin* (1878) 3 Ex. D. 127; *Newfoundland Government v Newfoundland Ry* (1883) 13 App. Cas. 199.

264 [1912] 1 K.B. 181. For criticism of this decision, see *Treitel on the Law of Contract*, 12th edn (Peel, 2007), para.15–041.

265 viz. that the debtor had "counterclaimed" for damages for the fraud against the assignee instead of merely setting the fraud up by way of defence; cf. above, para.6–106. See also *Lawrence v Hayes* [1927] 2 K.B. 111. The case was, however, followed in *Provident Finance Corp Pty Ltd v Hammond* [1978] V.R. 312.

266 *Jack v Kipping* (1882) 9 QBD 113; *Tilley v Bowman* [1910] 1 K.B. 745; cf. *Kitchen's Trustee v Madders* [1950] Ch. 134; see below, para.20–042. In none of these cases was there, or indeed could there have been, a counterclaim for damages for fraud, for this would have been a provable debt in the bankruptcy.

267 e.g. Marine Insurance Act 1906 s.50(2); Bills of Exchange Act 1882 s.38(2). On s.50, see *The Evelpidis Era* [1981] 1 Lloyd's Rep. 54.

268 *Re Agra and Masterman's Bank* (1867) L.R. 2 Ch.App. 391, 397; *Re Blakely Ordinance Co* (1867) 3 Ch. App. 154, 159–160. Such provisions are often inserted into debentures. See also *William Pickersgill & Sons Ltd v London & Provincial etc., Ins. Co Ltd* [1912] 3 K.B. 614. As to equities attaching to the debt in the hands of an intermediate assignor, see *Southern British National Trust Ltd v Pither* (1937) 57 C.L.R. 89. If the assignee in a notice of assignment to the debtor says "no set-off,"

Successive assignments. Where there have been several assignments, there is authority for the view that the rule that an assignee takes subject to equities does not include claims available against an intermediate assignee and that a claim or defence against the intermediate assignee could not be set-off in a claim by a subsequent assignee.[269] It has, however, been argued that where the claim or defence against the intermediate assignee arose after the first assignment it should be available in a claim by a subsequent assignee.[270] Moreover, where the assignment is statutory, as "the debt is transferred to the assignee and becomes as though it had been his from the beginning",[271] it is possible that the subsequent assignee would be required to sue in the name of the intermediate assignee and therefore be subject to such equities available against the intermediate assignee as arose before the subsequent assignee gave notice of the assignment to the debtor.[272] 19–073

Assignee cannot recover more than assignor. A further aspect of the idea that an assignee takes an assignment "subject to equities" is the principle that an assignee cannot recover more from the debtor than the assignor could have done had there been no assignment. For example, in *Dawson v Great Northern & City Ry Co*[273] the assignment of a statutory claim for compensation for damage to land did not entitle the assignee to recover extra loss suffered by reason of a trade carried on by him, but not the assignor, that the assignor would not have suffered. 19–074

The application of this principle has given rise to particular difficulty in relation to building contracts or tort claims for damage to buildings. Say, for example, a building is sold at full value along with an assignment to the purchaser of claims in contract or tort in relation to the building. The building turns out to need repairs as a result of a breach of the builder's contract with the assignor (whether that breach is prior, or subsequent, to the sale to the assignee) or of a tort (damaging the building prior to the sale). The assignee pays for the repairs. It might be argued that the assignor in that situation has suffered no loss so that, applying the governing principle that the assignee cannot recover more than the assignor, the assignee has no substantial claim. If correct, "the claim to damages would disappear . . . into some legal black hole, so that the wrongdoer escaped scot-free".[274] Acceptance of the argument would also nullify the purpose of the governing principle which is to avoid prejudice to the debtor and not to allow the debtor to escape liability. Perhaps not surprisingly, therefore, that 19–075

it is an interesting question, on which there appears to be no authority, whether the debtor is estopped from a set-off if, e.g. he continues to order goods from the assignor.

[269] *The Raven* [1980] 2 Lloyd's Rep. 266, 273; *Re Milan Railways Co* (1884) 25 Ch D 587, 593.

[270] *Treitel on the Law of Contract*, 12th edn (Peel, 2007), para.15–043.

[271] *Read v Brown* (1888) 22 QBD 128, 132.

[272] Derham, *Set-off*, 3rd edn (2003), para.17–48.

[273] [1905] 1 K.B. 260.

[274] *G.U.S. Property Management Ltd v Littlewoods Mail Order Stores Ltd* (1982) S.L.T. 533, 538, per Lord Keith.

argument was rejected in *Offer-Hoar v Larkstore Ltd.*[275] The Court of Appeal said that, in applying the principle that the assignee cannot recover more than the assignor, one should be asking what damages the assignor could itself have recovered had there been no assignment and *had there been no transfer of the land* to the assignee. Substantial damages were, therefore, recoverable where an assignor had sold its land to an assignee along with, or prior to, the assignment of the relevant cause of action relating to the land.

19–076 The problem has, in any event, normally been circumvented because of the courts' recognition that, where a third party is, or will become, owner of the defective or damaged property, there is an exception to the general rule that a contracting party can recover damages only for its own loss and not the loss of the third party.[276] Where the exception applies, the contracting party (the assignor) is entitled to substantial damages for the loss suffered by the third party (the assignee): by the same token, there is no question of an award of substantial damages to the assignee infringing the principle that the assignee cannot recover more than the assignor.

(v) *No Assignment of Liabilities*

19–077 **Consent of other party required for release of contracting party.** Everybody has a right to choose with whom he will contract and no-one is obliged without his consent to accept the liability of a person other than him with whom he made his contract. Consequently, the burden of a contract cannot in principle be transferred without the consent of the other party, so as to discharge the original contractor. As Sir R. Collins M.R. said in *Tolhurst* v *Associated Portland Cement Manufacturers Ltd*[277]:

> "Neither at law nor in equity could the burden of a contract be shifted off the shoulders of a contractor on to those of another without the consent of the contractee."

19–078 **Benefit and burden.** The principle that the burden of a contract cannot be transferred so as to discharge the original contractor without the consent of the other party means that, as a general rule, the assignee of the benefit of a contract involving mutual rights and obligations does not acquire the assignor's contractual obligations. Thus, where goods are purchased, and the seller assigns the right to the price to a credit factor, the factor is under no liability to the purchaser if the goods are defective although, in an action by the factor, the principle that assignments are subject to equities means that the purchaser will generally be

---

[275] [2006] EWCA Civ 1079, [2006] 1 W.L.R. 2926. See also *G.U.S. Property Management Ltd v Littlewoods Mail Order Stores Ltd* (1982) S.L.T. 533 (a Scottish delict case); *Linden Gardens Ltd v Lenesta Sludge Disposals Ltd* (1992) 57 B.L.R. 57, 80–81, per Staughton L.J.

[276] *Linden Gardens Trust Ltd v Lenesta Sludge Disposals Ltd* [1994] 1 A.C. 85; *Darlington BC v Wiltshier Northern Ltd* [1995] 1 W.L.R. 68; *Alfred McAlpine Construction Ltd v Panatown Ltd* [2001] 1 A.C. 518. The exception is based on *Dunlop v Lambert* (1839) 6 Cl. & F. 600 and *The Albazero* [1977] A.C. 774. For detailed discussion, see above, paras 18–050—18–063.

[277] [1902] 2 K.B. 660, 668 CA; *C.B. Peacock Land Co Ltd v Hamilton Milk Products Co Ltd* [1963] N.Z.L.R. 576; *Hirachand Punamchand v Temple* [1911] 2 K.B. 330, 80 L.J.K.B. 1155; *Linden Gardens Trust Ltd v Lenesta Sludge Disposals Ltd* [1994] 1 A.C. 85, 103. See also Birks and Beatson (1976) 92 L.Q.R. 188–202.

able to rely on any defence or claim which he could raise against the seller.[278] Similarly in *Pan Ocean Shipping Ltd v Creditcorp Ltd*[279] it was held by the House of Lords that an assignee of the payment of hire under a charterparty is not liable to the debtor (the charterer), whether in contract or restitution, to repay the hire paid for a period when the ship turned out to be off-hire: rather the liability to repay the unearned hire, which on the facts was contained in an express term of the charterparty, remained exclusively with the assignor. This was so irrespective of whether the debtor would have had a defence to an action for non-payment of hire by the assignee.

Conditional benefits. However, where contractual rights are assigned, the extent of those rights will be defined by the original contract. This means that (for example) an exemption clause in the original contract may be binding on the assignee.[280] Again, a patentee who assigned his patent by a contract which provided that certain payments were to be made to him was permitted to sue a company to which the assignees had later assigned their rights.[281] In *Tolhurst's* case,[282] the assignee acquired the benefit of a contract to supply chalk for the manufacture of Portland cement on a particular piece of land. The assignee was not bound by the duty to take chalk from Tolhurst,[283] but if it did take chalk, it was bound to obtain all its requirements for the manufacture of cement on that piece of land from him. Although these cases have sometimes been seen as applications of the principle that he who takes the benefit of a transaction must also bear the burden, it appears that they are examples of another principle; the conditional benefit principle.[284] The conditional benefit principle arises where the right assigned is only conditional or qualified, the condition being that certain restrictions shall be observed or certain burdens assumed. The restrictions or qualifications are an intrinsic part of the right which the assignee has to take as it stands.[285] The question whether a contract creates a conditional benefit is one of construction.[286] 19–079

"Pure" benefit and burden principle. In *Tito v Waddell (No.2)* Megarry V.C. distinguished the conditional benefit principle from what he termed the "pure principle of benefit and burden".[287] By a series of contracts, a mining 19–080

[278] Above, paras 20–068—20–069.
[279] [1994] 1 W.L.R. 161.
[280] See *Britain & Overseas Trading Ltd v Brooks Wharf Ltd* [1967] 2 Lloyd's Rep. 51; *National Carbonising Co Ltd v British Coal Distillation Ltd* (1936) 54 R.P.C. 41, 57 et seq. See also *Aspden v Seddon (No.2)* (1876) 1 Ex.D. 496, 509. In *Glencore International AG v Metro Trading International Inc* [1999] 2 All E.R. (Comm) 899, the assignee of the obligation to pay the price under a contract of sale was held "bound" by the exclusive jurisdiction clause in that contract (and such an assignment was held to fall within art.17 of the Brussels Convention, given effect to in the UK by the Civil Jurisdiction and Judgments Act 1982).
[281] *Werdman v Société Générale d'Electricité* (1881) 19 Ch D 246.
[282] [1903] A.C. 414; above, para.19–055.
[283] *National Carbonising Co Ltd v British Coal Distillation Ltd* (1936) 54 R.P.C. 41.
[284] See generally *Tito v Waddell (No.2)* [1977] Ch. 106, 290 et seq. See also *Pan Ocean Shipping Co Ltd v Creditcorp Ltd, The Trident Beauty* [1994] 1 W.L.R. 161, 171.
[285] [1977] Ch. 106, 290, 302.
[286] [1977] Ch. 106, 302.
[287] [1977] Ch. 106, 290, 302.

company acquired the right to extract phosphates on a Pacific island on the condition that it would "return all worked out lands to the original owners and . . . replant such lands". In 1920 the rights were transferred to government commissioners "subject to . . . the covenants and conditions therein contained". Megarry V.C. held that the right to extract phosphates given in the contracts between the owners and the company was not qualified by or conditional on the replanting obligations but that the "pure principle" of benefit and burden rendered the present commissioners liable to the owners for breach of the covenant to replant. But in *Rhone v Stephens*[288] the House of Lords cast doubt on Megarry V.C.'s views to the extent that he was recognising a "pure principle" that any party deriving any benefit from a conveyance must accept any burden in the same conveyance. Lord Templeman instead said that the condition must be relevant to the exercise of the right. On that basis, it was held that the fact that the roof of D's house was supported by C's cottage did not mean that C could enforce against D a covenant made by D's predecessor in title with C's to repair the roof.

2. VICARIOUS PERFORMANCE

19–081 **Vicarious performance.** A contracting party can in the case of many contracts enter into an arrangement by which some other person may perform for him, as far as he is concerned, the obligations of the contract, and the other contracting party will be obliged to accept that performance if it is performance in accordance with the terms of the contract. The contracting party will, however, be liable for any breach that may happen, and the other contracting party is not bound or, indeed, entitled to sue the substituted person for breach of contract,[289] although there may, of course, be a remedy in tort, e.g. where the substituted person negligently damages or causes the loss of goods entrusted to him. This is technically known as vicarious performance, and it is "quite a mistake to regard that as an assignment of the contract: it is not".[290]

19–082 It has been said that:

> "Whether or not in any given contract performance can properly be carried out by the employment of a subcontractor must depend on the proper inference to be drawn from the contract itself, the subject-matter of it, and other material surrounding circumstances."[291]

---

[288] [1994] 2 A.C. 310. See also *Thamesmead Town Ltd v Allotey* [1998] 37 E.G. 161.

[289] *Stewart v Reavell's Garage* [1952] 2 Q.B. 545. This is to be distinguished from where the debtor's promise is not one to render the performance but merely to arrange for the services to be performed by another person (as the debtor's agent). In respect of the latter type of promise, the debtor's only obligation at common law is to exercise reasonable care and skill in selecting a competent person to perform. For this distinction (albeit that the promise in question was held to be of the former type) see *Wong Mee Wan v Kwan Kin Travel Services Ltd* [1996] 1 W.L.R. 38. See also *Treitel on the Law of Contract*, 12th edn (Peel, 2007), para.17–011.

[290] *Davies v Collins* [1945] 1 All E.R. 247, 249; cf. *Nokes v Doncaster Amalgamated Collieries Ltd* [1940] A.C. 1014, 1019.

[291] *Davies v Collins* [1945] 1 All E.R. 247, 250; *Kollerich & Cie SA v The State Trading Corp of India* [1980] 2 Lloyd's Rep. 32.

Some contractual obligations are obviously too personal to admit to performance by anyone other than the original contracting parties: for example, a contract to paint a picture, or to write a play or a book.[292] A contractual obligation to store furniture[293] and to carry out building work,[294] has been held to be incapable of vicarious performance, because of the personal confidence reposed by the customer in the original contracting party. And in *Johnson v Raylton*[295] it was held that where a manufacturer of goods contracts to supply specific goods to a buyer, there is an implied term in the contract that the goods shall be those of the seller's own manufacture.[296] The case should, however, probably not be regarded as laying down a general rule still applicable in modern conditions, for clearly much must depend on the nature of the goods and the customs of the trade.[297] The terms of the contract may also throw light on the question whether it can be vicariously performed, the test being: Did the contracting party promise personal performance, or did he merely promise a result? In *Davies v Collins*,[298] the Court of Appeal hesitated to say that a contract to clean clothes was incapable of vicarious performance. They reached the conclusion that the particular contract in that case was not so capable because of the language of an exemption clause.

In *Robson and Sharpe v Drummond*,[299] the defendant hired a chariot from Sharpe for five years at a yearly rent, payable in advance each year, the chariot to be kept in repair and painted once a year by Sharpe. After three years Sharpe retired from business and purported to delegate performance of the contract to his partner Robson. It was held that the defendant was entitled to repudiate the contract and was not liable to pay the rent for the last two years. Lord Tenterden based his judgment on the ground that the defendant might have been induced to enter into the contract by reason of the personal confidence which he reposed in Sharpe, and therefore might have agreed to pay rent in advance. Littledale and Parke JJ. also said that the defendant had a right to the personal services of Sharpe, and to the benefit of his judgment and taste. On the other hand, in *British Waggon Co and Parkgate Waggon Co v Lea*,[300] the defendant hired 100 railway wagons from the Parkgate Waggon Company for seven years at a yearly rent payable quarterly, the wagons to be kept in repair by the company. After four years the Parkgate Company, which had gone into voluntary liquidation, assigned the benefit of the contract to the British Waggon Company and delegated performance of its obligations to the assignees. It was held that the defendant was 19–083

[292] *Tolhurst v Associated Portland Cement Manufacturers Ltd* [1902] 2 K.B. 660, 669, per Sir R. Collins M.R.; *Fratelli Sorrentino v Buerger* [1915] 1 K.B. 307, 313; *Southway Group Ltd v Wolff & Wolff* (1991) 57 B.L.R. 33, 52.

[293] *Edwards v Newland & Co* [1950] 2 K.B. 534.

[294] *Southway Group Ltd v Wolff & Wolff* (1991) 57 B.L.R. 33.

[295] (1881) 7 QBD 438.

[296] A clause to this effect was originally included in the Sale of Goods Bill 1889.

[297] The dissent of Bramwell L.J. puts strong arguments against the majority decision.

[298] [1945] 1 All E.R. 247.

[299] (1831) 2 B. & Ad. 303, a much criticised case. cf. *Boulton v Jones* (1857) 2 H. & N. 564; *Jaeger's Sanitary Woollen System Co v Walker & Sons* (1897) 77 L.T. 180.

[300] (1880) 5 QBD 149. See also *C.B. Peacocke Land Co Ltd v Hamilton Milk Producers Co Ltd* [1963] N.Z.L.R. 576.

not entitled to repudiate the contract. Cockburn C.J. laid down the general principle:

> "... that where a person contracts with another to do work or perform service, and it can be inferred that the person employed has been selected with reference to his individual skill, competency or other personal qualification, the inability or unwillingness of the party so employed to execute the work or perform the service is a sufficient answer to any demand by a stranger to the original contract for the performance of it by the other party, and entitles the latter to treat the contract as at an end, notwithstanding that the person tendered to take the place of the contracting party may be equally well qualified to do the service."[301]

He held that the principle did not apply to a contract for the repair of railway wagons—"a rough description of work which ordinary workmen conversant with the business would be perfectly able to execute"; and that the defendant could not have attached any importance to whether the repairs were done by the Parkgate Company or by a sub-contractor.

19–084 **Vicarious performance and agency.** As already seen, in a case of vicarious performance the original contracting party remains liable on the contract. There is nothing to prevent a person contracting on such terms that he is entitled either to perform the contract himself, or to secure performance by making a new contract with a third party as agent of the other contracting party. If such a new contract is in fact made the original contracting party may be subject to no further liability on the contract. Such an arrangement is not unusual in certain types of business,[302] though difficulty may sometimes arise in deciding whether the case is one of agency or of vicarious performance.[303] Whether it is the one or the other depends on the intention of the parties objectively ascertained.

3. ASSIGNMENT AND NEGOTIABILITY

19–085 **Assignment and negotiability.** Negotiable instruments, governed formerly by the law of merchants, differ in several ways from contracts which are assignable under the law as explained in the foregoing pages. In particular:

(a) They are transferable by delivery (or in some cases by delivery and indorsement) though it would be more accurate to say that the contract contained in them is transferred.

(b) No notice need be given to the debtor.

---

[301] (1880) 5 QBD at 153. cf. *Fratelli Sorrentino v Buerger* [1915] 3 K.B. 367, 370.

[302] Bills of lading, for example, may contain clauses permitting transhipment without further liability on the original contracting carrier: see *Scrutton on Charterparties*, 21st edn (2008), art.131. See also *Investors in Industry Commercial Property Ltd v Bedfordshire DC* [1986] 1 All E.R. 787, 807.

[303] e.g. if a person takes some article to a shop for repair and the shopkeeper sends it on to the manufacturer with the consent of the customer; cf. *Stewart v Reavell's Garage* [1952] 2 Q.B. 545; *Morris v C.W. Martin & Sons Ltd* [1966] 1 Q.B. 716; *The Pioneer Container* [1994] 2 A.C. 324.

(c) The right or contract embodied in them cannot be transferred without the instrument. Thus the rule in *Dearle* v *Hall*[304] as to priority of notice to the debtor has no application to negotiable instruments.[305]

(d) A bona fide transferee for value may obtain a good title even though the title of his transferor was defective. Thus the transferor of a negotiable instrument can give a better title than he himself has.[306]

4. ASSIGNMENT, NOVATION AND ACKNOWLEDGMENT

Novation. There is no doubt that with the consent of *both* contracting parties all contracts of any kind may be transferred, and the term "novation" has been introduced from Roman law to describe this species of transfer. Novation takes place where the two contracting parties agree that a third, who also agrees, shall stand in the relation of either of them to the other. There is a new contract and it is therefore essential that the consent of all parties shall be obtained[307]: in this necessity for consent lies the most important difference between novation and assignment. **19–086**

Most of the reported cases in English law have arisen either out of the amalgamation of companies, or of changes in partnership firms, the question being whether as a matter of fact the party contracting with the company or the firm accepted the new company or the new firm as his debtor in the place of the old company or the old firm.[308] That acceptance may be inferred from acts and conduct, but ordinarily it is not to be inferred from conduct without some distinct request.[309] Thus where a banking firm consisted of two partners and one died, the acceptance by a customer from the surviving partner of a fresh deposit note for a balance of a debt due was held sufficient evidence of novation to discharge the estate of the deceased partner, as the customer took the money out of a current account and placed it on deposit at the request of the surviving partner.[310] **19–087**

It should, however, be noted that the effect of a novation is not to assign or transfer a right or liability, but rather to extinguish the original contract and replace it by another. It is therefore necessary that consideration should be **19–088**

---

[304] (1823) 3 Russ. 1.

[305] See *Bence v Shearman* [1898] 2 Ch. 582.

[306] Bills of Exchange Act 1882 ss.29, 30, 38. But not if the bill is overdue: s.36(2). See also Consumer Credit Act 1974 s.125. See further Vol.II, Ch.34.

[307] e.g. *Rasbora Ltd v J.C.L. Marine Ltd* [1977] 1 Lloyd's Rep. 645; *The Blankenstein* [1985] 1 W.L.R. 435; *The Aktion* [1987] 1 Lloyd's Rep. 283, 310–311.

[308] *Wilson v Lloyd* (1873) L.R. 16 Eq. 60, 73; *Miller's Case* (1877) 3 Ch D 391; *Perry v National Provincial Bank* [1910] 1 Ch. 464; *Meek v Port of London Authority* [1918] 2 Ch. 96. For the use of novation or "quasi-novation" in analysing certain credit card transactions, see *Re Charge Card Services* [1989] Ch. 497, 513.

[309] *Re European Assurance Association Society Arbitration Acts, Conquest's Case* (1875) 1 Ch D 334; *Chatsworth Investments Ltd v Cussins (Contractors) Ltd* [1969] 1 W.L.R. 1. See also *Scarf v Jardine* (1882) 7 App. Cas. 345; *British Homes Assurance Corp v Paterson* [1902] 2 Ch. 404.

[310] *Re Head* [1894] 2 Ch. 236.

provided for the new contract.[311] If A owes B money and both parties agree with C that C, not A, is to pay the money to B, B provides consideration for C's promise to pay him by agreeing to release A; while A provides consideration for B's promise to release him by providing the new debtor, C.

19–089 **Acknowledgment.**[312] There is a distinct line of mainly nineteenth-century cases holding that where a person holds a fund for another and is directed by that other to pay it to a third party, and notifies the third party that he is willing to do so, the third party acquires a right of action for the money (even though the third party has provided no consideration). Such a transaction can obviously be said to be similar to an assignment. The proper assessment of these cases for the present day is however a matter of difficulty, for they antedate the formulation of the rules of privity of contract, trust, assignment and agency that are now accepted. The best explanation of the cases may rest on the idea of attornment of money. If this is so, it would seem essential that the doctrine is confined to funds and not extended to debts: yet in *Shamia v Joory*,[313] the only recent case in which the doctrine has been invoked, the full complexities were apparently not cited to Barry J. and he applied the doctrine to a mere debt. The extent to which this line of cases survives in view of the development of methods of assignment, and the significance to be attached to the individual cases, are highly doubtful.

[311] *Tatlock v Harris* (1789) 3 T.R. 174, 180. See also *Cuxon v Chadley* (1824) 3 B. & C. 591; *Wharton v Walker* (1825) 4 B. & C. 163. But there can be difficulty in seeing how consideration moves from the promisee: see *Olsson v Dyson* (1969) 120 C.L.R. 365, 390.

[312] Davies (1959) 75 L.Q.R. 220; Yates (1977) 41 Conv.(N.S.) 49; Goff and Jones, *The Law of Restitution*, 7th edn (2007), Ch.28; below, paras 29–194—29–196.

[313] [1958] 1 Q.B. 448; criticised by Goff and Jones at para.28–003.

Chapter 20

DEATH AND BANKRUPTCY

	PARA.
1. Death	20–001
2. Bankruptcy	20–015
(a) Contracts made prior to bankruptcy	20–018
(b) Vesting of property in trustee	20–024
(c) Trustee takes "subject to equities"	20–039
(d) Discharge of bankrupt	20–045
(e) Schemes of arrangement	20–050
(f) Contracts made after adjudication	20–053
(g) Second bankruptcies	20–057

1. Death

Introductory. The general rule at common law was that the maxim *actio personalis moritur cum persona* had no application to any breach of contract, except breach of a promise to marry.[1] Hence the personal representatives of a deceased contracting party could generally sue and be sued on contracts made by him in his lifetime. However, the operation of the maxim quoted above has been greatly circumscribed by the Law Reform (Miscellaneous Provisions) Act 1934 s.1(1) of which provides that on the death of any person after the commencement of the Act, all causes of action (with certain exceptions in tort) subsisting against or vested in him shall survive against or for the benefit of his estate. **20–001**

Actions by personal representatives. Wherever money due on a contract made with the deceased will, when recovered, be assets, the executor or administrator may sue for it in his representative capacity.[2] Therefore, when the defendant ordered a coat of one T, a tailor, but before the coat was finished T died, and the coat was afterwards finished and delivered by his administratrix, it was held that the value of the coat was recoverable in an action for goods sold and delivered by her as administratrix.[3] Again, where a person agreed to do certain work and died before it was begun and his executors did the work, using **20–002**

[1] *Pinchon's Case* (1611) 9 Co.Rep. 86b; *Hambly v Trott* (1775) 1 Cowp. 371, 375; *Raymond v Fitch* (1835) 2 Cr. M. & R. 588; *Phillips v Homfray* (1883) 24 Ch D 439, 456–457.

[2] *Marshall v Broadhurst* (1831) 1 Cr. & J. 403, 405; *Heath v Chilton* (1844) 12 M. & W. 632, 637; *Moseley v Rendell* (1871) L.R. 6 Q.B. 338; *Abbott v Parfitt* (1871) L.R. 6 Q.B. 346.

[3] *Werner v Humphreys* (1841) 2 M. & G. 853.

his materials, it was held that the executors might sue in that capacity for the value of the materials[4]; and in such a case they might also sue for work and labour as executors.[5] An executor may also sue in that capacity for goods sold by him in the course of carrying on and continuing as executor the testator's business, although the goods were acquired by the executor after the testator's death, provided they formed part of the assets.[6]

20–003 **Recovery of damages by personal representatives.** There is no rule of law which prevents a personal representative from recovering larger damages than the deceased could have recovered had he survived. Accordingly, where solicitors in breach of contract negligently advised a young man that he was tenant in fee simple of certain property and that he need take no steps to reduce it into possession, whereas in fact he was tenant in tail, and he died before barring the entail, his personal representatives recovered substantial damages, although if the deceased had lived he could only have recovered nominal damages, since the mistake could easily have been rectified.[7]

20–004 **When right of action arises.** An executor's title to the property of his testator is derived from the will and not from the grant of probate. He may therefore begin an action as executor before probate, but cannot complete his case without proving his title, and must accordingly obtain probate before the hearing.[8] An administrator's title is derived from the grant of administration, but upon the grant being made, his title relates back to the date of the intestate's death[9]; however, a subsequent grant of letters of administration cannot operate retrospectively to validate a writ which from the beginning was a nullity, e.g. as being issued in a representative capacity not possessed by the person issuing the writ.[10]

---

[4] *Marshall v Broadhurst* (1831) 1 Cr. J. 403.

[5] (1831) 1 Cr. J. 403; *Edwards v Grace* (1836) 2 M. & W. 190.

[6] *Aspinall v Wake* (1833) 10 Bing. 51; *Abbott v Parfitt* (1871) L.R. 6 Q.B. 346.

[7] *Otter v Church, Adams, Tatham & Co* [1953] Ch. 280. See also *Ross v Caunters* [1980] Ch. 297; *Clarke v Bruce Lance & Co (A Firm)* [1988] 1 W.L.R. 881; *White v Jones* [1995] 2 A.C. 207; *Hemmens v Wilson Browne* [1995] Ch. 223.

[8] *Thompson v Reynolds* (1872) 3 C. & P. 123; *Re Masonic, etc. Assurance Co* (1885) 32 Ch D 373. As to staying executor's action where the defendant admits the claim, but requires production of the probate, see *Webb v Adkins* (1854) 14 C.B. 401; *Tarn v Commercial Bank of Sydney* (1884) 12 QBD 294.

[9] *Wooley v Clarke* (1822) 5 B. & Ald. 744; *Foster v Bates* (1843) 12 M. & W. 226. Administrators now have the same rights and liabilities and are accountable in the same manner as executors: Administration of Estates Act 1925 s.21.

[10] *Ingall v Moran* [1944] K.B. 160; *Hilton v Sutton Steam Laundry* [1946] K.B. 65; *Burns v Campbell* [1952] 1 K.B. 15; *Finnegan v Cementation Co Ltd* [1953] 1 Q.B. 688. See also *Re Crowhurst Park* [1974] 1 W.L.R. 583. But cf. the different rule in actions for the recovery of land: Limitation Act 1980, s.26. The statement in the text appears to be unaffected by CPR r.17.4, which gives the court power in certain specified cases to allow amendments to the writ or pleadings, notwithstanding that the effect may be to deprive a party of a defence under the Limitation Act 1980: *Dawson (Bradford) v Dove* [1971] 1 Q.B. 330 (see fn.12). As to the effect of RSC O.20 r.5, the predecessor to CPR r.17.4, generally, see *Beck v Value Capital Ltd (No.2)* [1975] 1 W.L.R. 6; [1976] 1 W.L.R. 572; *Hancock Shipping Co Ltd v Kawasaki Heavy Industries Ltd* [1992] 1 W.L.R. 1025.

Actions against personal representatives. Similarly, in principle, the personal representatives of a contracting party are bound, so far as his assets will extend, to perform all his contracts although not named therein.[11] Special provision now exists enabling proceedings to be brought against a deceased person's estate prior to a grant of probate or administration.[12] 20–005

Personal contracts. The Law Reform (Miscellaneous Provisions) Act 1934 contains no exception for contracts involving personal skill, taste or confidence, such as a contract of service,[13] a contract to perform at a concert,[14] to paint a picture, to write a book, or to act as professional jockey to the owner of racehorses.[15] In such contracts, however, there is probably no cause of action to survive, as the contract is frustrated by the death of the party whose skill or other personal qualifications were relied upon.[16] The personal representatives are, however, entitled to sue for any money actually earned by the deceased under his contract, which has become due during his lifetime.[17] Further, where the contract is in such terms that the remuneration should continue after the service has ceased, the personal representatives may sue for remuneration accrued due after death.[18] And of course if a personal contract is broken by a contracting party during his lifetime, and one party subsequently dies, the cause of action survives the death and his personal representatives can sue or be sued for breach.[19] 20–006

It is thought that the question whether a contract is personal for this purpose is generally the same as whether the contract is personal for the purposes of the law relating to voluntary assignments and vicarious performance[20]; that is, the benefit of a contract which can be voluntarily assigned, and the burden of a contract which can be vicariously performed, will (subject to the terms of the contract itself) be transmissible to the personal representatives of the contracting parties.[21] It appears, however, that there are some cases in which the benefit of a contract will pass on the death of a party to his personal representatives, 20–007

---

[11] *Williams v Burrell* (1845) 1 C.B. 402; *Wills v Murray* (1850) 4 Exch. 843, 865; *Kennewell v Dye* [1949] Ch. 517, 521–522; *Youngmin v Heath* [1974] 1 W.L.R. 135. For the position of options see *Longbutt v Amoco Australia Pty Ltd* (1974) 4 A.L.R. 482.

[12] See RSC O.15 r.6A para.3, preserved by CPR Sch.1, which negatives *Dawson (Bradford) v Dove* [1971] 1 Q.B. 330. As regards bankruptcy see Insolvency Act 1986 s.421; Administration of Insolvent Estates Deceased Persons Order 1986 (SI 1986/1999).

[13] *Farrow v Wilson* (1869) L.R. 4 C.P. 744.

[14] cf. *Robinson v Davison* (1871) L.R. 6 Ex. 269.

[15] *Graves v Cohen* (1829) 46 T.L.R. 121. cf. *Phillips v Alhambra Palace Co* [1901] 1 Q.B. 59 (surviving partners who owned a music hall liable on contract with troupe of music hall performers); *Harvey v Tivoli (Manchester) Ltd* (1907) 23 T.L.R. 592 (surviving members of a troupe of music hall artistes cannot enforce contract against owner of music hall).

[16] *Stubbs v Holywell Ry* (1867) L.R. 2 Ex. 311, 314.

[17] *Stubbs v Holywell Ry* (1867) L.R. 2 Ex 311.

[18] *Wilson v Harper* [1908] 2 Ch. 370.

[19] *Shaw v Shaw* [1954] 2 Q.B. 429.

[20] As to personal contracts which cannot be voluntarily assigned or vicariously performed, see above, paras 19–042 et seq. As to personal contracts the benefit of which do not pass to a debtor's trustee in bankruptcy, see below, para.20–034.

[21] See, e.g. *Warner Engineering Co Ltd v Brennan* (1913) 30 T.L.R. 191; *Re Worthington* [1914] 2 K.B. 299; cf. *Collins v Associated Greyhound Racecourses* [1930] 1 Ch. 1.

although it may not be assignable inter vivos, e.g. in the case of third-party road traffic insurance policies.[22]

20–008 **Personal liability of personal representatives.** The general rule is that a personal representative is not personally liable on the contracts of the deceased: he is liable only to the extent of the assets of the estate. There is, however, a singular exception in the case of the covenants in a lease. Before entry and taking possession, the personal representatives of a tenant cannot be made personally liable as assignees of the term,[23] though they are liable to the extent of assets.[24] If they do enter, then they may be personally liable. Yet they may, by proper pleading, limit their liability for rent to the yearly value the premises might have yielded.[25] No such defence is, however, apparently allowed if the personal representative is sued after entry for a breach of the covenant to repair.[26]

20–009 **Confirmation of deceased's contract.** An administrator will generally be liable upon contracts which he confirms whether the contracts are made by the deceased or by an agent of the deceased: this is sometimes referred to as ratification, but does not seem to be a true application of agency principles.[27] However, confirmation of a contract made by an agent and a third party does not necessarily involve confirmation of a contract between the deceased and the agent of which the administrator may have been ignorant. Thus, where an agent, after the death of his principal, in pursuance of a contract made with him before the death sold the principal's goods, it was held that the principal's agreement to remunerate the agent was discharged by the death, and that confirmation of the sale by the administrator did not render him liable to remunerate the agent.[28]

20–010 **Executor carrying on business of testator.** Unless empowered to do so by the testator's will, an executor is not entitled to carry on the testator's business, except for the purpose of winding it up. If he does carry it on, whether with or without authority, he is personally liable upon the contracts he makes, and persons contracting with him have no remedy against the testator's assets.[29] The executor, if he has carried on the business in accordance with his duty, has a right to be indemnified out of the estate, and any profits made belong to the estate. He is not, however, entitled to be indemnified out of the estate in priority to the testator's creditors, even when empowered by the will to carry on the business,

[22] See *Peters v General Accident, etc., Ltd* [1938] 2 All E.R. 267 and *Kelly v Cornhill Insurance Co* [1964] 1 W.L.R. 158. It is implicit in this latter case that such a policy does not, in the absence of some express stipulation, come to an end on the death of the insured.

[23] *Wollaston v Hakewill* (1841) 3 M. & G. 297; *Rendall v Andreae* (1892) 61 L.J.Q.B. 630.

[24] *Youngmin v Heath* [1974] 1 W.L.R. 135.

[25] *Rendall v Andreae* (1892) 61 L.J.Q.B. 630; *Whitehead v Palmer* [1908] 1 K.B. 151.

[26] *Tremeere v Morrison* (1834) 1 Bing.N.C. 89; followed in *Sleap v Newman* (1862) 12 C.B.(N.S.) 116; *Rendall v Andreae* (1892) 61 L.J.Q.B. 630; *Woodfall's Law of Landlord and Tenant*, 28th edn (1978), Vol.I, para.17–168 and, more fully, para.1840.

[27] See *Foster v Bates* (1843) 12 M. & W. 226; Powell, *Law of Agency*, 2nd edn, p.388, n.7; cf. *Greenwood v Martins Bank Ltd* [1933] A.C. 51 (adoption of a forgery).

[28] *Campanari v Woodburn* (1854) 15 C.B. 400. A quantum meruit might have been available. As to this remedy, see below, paras 29–067—29–076. But cf. *Ex p. Phillips* (1887) 19 QBD 234.

[29] *Re Morgan* (1881) 18 Ch D 93; *Re Evans* (1887) 34 Ch D 597.

unless they consent to its being carried on.[30] The fact that the creditors stand by with knowledge that it is being carried on and without interference is not of itself sufficient to show consent.[31] Executors who carried on their testator's business under the powers of his will in the same firm name as before were held not to be partners, though no doubt joint debtors.[32] An administrator only has power to continue the intestate's business with a view to realising its assets. The statutory power[33] to postpone sale for such period as he may think proper may justify trading for purposes other than realisation especially in view of the duty of a personal representative to preserve the business as an asset.[34]

Liability on bills or notes. Where a person such as an executor is under an obligation to indorse a bill of exchange in a representative capacity, he may do so in such terms as to negative personal liability.[35] If he fails to do so he is personally liable.[36] 20–011

Executor de son tort. An executor *de son tort* is one who assumes the office of executor or interferes with the assets without having been appointed executor or having obtained a grant of administration.[37] He is liable in the same manner as a rightful executor[38]; and this rule includes the executor *de son tort* of an original rightful executor. But the executor of an executor *de son tort* is not liable for a breach of contract committed by the person with whose estate the executor *de son tort* has intermeddled, and similarly there is no such liability in the case of an executor of an administrator *de son tort*.[39] 20–012

Protection of representative on distribution of estate. A personal representative who has protected himself by advertisements[40] in accordance with s.27 of the Trustee Act 1925 may, at the expiration of the time fixed in the notice, distribute the property to which the notice relates, having regard only to the claims of which he has notice[41] and is not liable to any person of whose claim he has not had notice at the time of distribution. A creditor may, however, in spite of the distribution, follow the property or any property representing it into the hands of any person (other than a purchaser) who may have received it, in order 20–013

---

[30] *Dowse v Gorton* [1891] A.C. 190. Except where he has carried on only for such reasonable time as is necessary for selling the business as a going concern: 199.

[31] *Re Oxley* [1914] 1 Ch. 604; *Re East* (1914) 111 L.T. 101.

[32] *Re Fisher & Sons* [1912] 2 K.B. 491.

[33] Administration of Estates Act 1925 s.33(1).

[34] *Strickland v Symons* (1883) 22 Ch D 666, 671; (1884) 26 Ch D 245, see also *Garrett v Noble* (1834) 6 Sim. 504 (defence to action for breach of trust in continuing business).

[35] Bills of Exchange Act 1882 ss.31(5), 26(1).

[36] *King v Thom* (1789) 1 T.R. 487. cf. *Childs v Monins* (1821) 2 B. & B. 460; *Liverpool Borough Bank v Walker* (1859) 4 De G. & J. 24. See Vol.II, para.34–042.

[37] See, e.g. *Williams v Heales* (1874) L.R. 9 C.P. 177; *Stratford-upon-Avon Corp v Parker* [1914] 2 K.B. 562; Administration of Estates Act 1925 s.28.

[38] *Meyrick v Anderson* (1850) 14 Q.B. 719.

[39] *Wilson v Hodson* (1872) L.R. 7 Ex. 84.

[40] Or has been excused from the need to advertise by an order of the court: *Re Gess* [1942] Ch. 37. As to the form of such advertisements, see *Re Aldhous* [1955] 1 W.L.R. 459.

[41] *Guardian Trust and Executors Co Ltd v Public Trustee of New Zealand* [1942] A.C. 115.

to satisfy his claim,[42] and he need not join the representative in any such proceedings.[43]

20–014 **Payment and compounding of debts by executor.** By s.15 of the Trustee Act 1925, a personal representative may pay or allow any debt or claim[44] on any evidence that he thinks sufficient, and may accept any composition or any security for any debt and allow any time of payment of any debt, and may compromise, compound, abandon, submit to arbitration, or otherwise settle any debt, account, claim, or thing whatever relating to the testator's or intestate's estate. He is not bound to avail himself of the Limitation Act 1980 in an action brought against him by a creditor of his testator,[45] but he may not pay such a debt after it has been judicially declared by a court of competent jurisdiction to be statute-barred,[46] nor may he pay a debt which is unenforceable under the Statute of Frauds.[47]

2. BANKRUPTCY[48]

20–015 **Preliminary.** The bankruptcy of one or both parties to a contract may have a considerable effect upon their contractual obligations. Technically a debtor only becomes bankrupt on the making of a bankruptcy order,[49] which may take place some time after the commencement of bankruptcy proceedings, but the insolvency of a party to a contract prior to his bankruptcy may materially affect the obligations of the other party.

20–016 The property of a person adjudicated bankrupt vests in the trustee in bankruptcy and, for this purpose, the bankrupt's property includes choses in action. Thus the benefit of a contract made by a person later adjudicated bankrupt passes to his trustee.[50] Broadly speaking, the trustee in bankruptcy steps into the shoes of the bankrupt and, so far as the law of contract is concerned, the result of adjudication is to effect a form of assignment by operation of law. In addition, rights may sometimes pass to the trustee even though they did not belong to the

[42] Trustee Act 1925 s.27(2); Administration of Estates Act 1925 s.38.
[43] *Hunter v Young* (1879) 4 Ex.D. 256; *Re Frewen* (1889) 60 L.T. 953.
[44] Including a claim by a co-executor: *Re Houghton* [1904] 1 Ch. 622.
[45] *Stahlschmidt v Lett* (1853) 1 Sm. & G. 415; *Hill v Walker* (1854) 4 K. & J. 166; *Lowis v Rumney* (1867) L.R. 4 Eq. 451; *Midgley v Midgley* [1893] 3 Ch. 282, 297.
[46] *Midgley v Midgley* [1893] 3 Ch. 282.
[47] *Re Rownson* (1885) 29 Ch D 358.
[48] This section does not profess to be a summary of the whole of the law of bankruptcy, but only of the effect of bankruptcy on contracts. See generally *Muir Hunter on Personal Insolvency* (London: Sweet & Maxwell). (Bankruptcy is now dealt with in the Insolvency Act 1986. The second group of parts of the Act which deal with individual insolvency is entitled "Insolvency of Individuals; Bankruptcy".)
[49] Insolvency Act 1986 s.278(a).
[50] Below, para.20–019.

bankrupt.[51] Rights of a personal nature do not pass to the trustee,[52] and he may sometimes disclaim the burden of onerous contracts.[53] Where contracts vest in the trustee, he normally takes them "subject to equities" in the sense that the other contracting party may set up defences against him which would have been available against the bankrupt himself.[54] Purely personal defences cannot, however, be set up against the trustee,[55] and there are special statutory provisions relating to set-off.[56]

Once a bankruptcy order is made against a person, normal legal remedies cease to be available against him, so that he can no longer be sued for (inter alia) breach of contract. The remedy of the other contracting party is to prove for his loss or damage in the bankruptcy,[57] and once the bankrupt has been discharged all liabilities which could have been proved are finally discharged.[58] A bankrupt remains personally liable on contracts entered into by him *after* adjudication,[59] but since the bankrupt's property can on the application of his trustee in bankruptcy be made to vest in the trustee even where it is acquired after adjudication, the other contracting party may find that the bankrupt has no assets with which to meet any such liability.[60] In these circumstances it is possible to take new bankruptcy proceedings in which property acquired after the previous adjudication and still undistributed will pass to the second trustee.[61] 20–017

(a) *Contracts made Prior to Bankruptcy*

Grounds for creditor's bankruptcy petition. A creditor may present a bankruptcy petition against a debtor where the debtor owes him a debt for a liquidated sum which is unsecured[62] and which exceeds the "bankruptcy level"[63] and "the debtor either appears to be unable to pay or to have no reasonable prospect of being able to pay" the debt.[64] A creditor can satisfy the requirement of showing that the debtor is unable to pay his debt by serving a statutory demand 20–018

[51] Below, paras 20–024 et seq.
[52] Below, para.20–034.
[53] Below, para.20–035.
[54] Below, para.20–039.
[55] Below, paras 20–039 et seq.
[56] Below, para.20–039.
[57] Below, para.20–037.
[58] Below, para.20–046.
[59] Below, para.20–053.
[60] Insolvency Act 1986 s.305; paras 20–024 et seq. In special cases the other contracting party may be able to invoke the rule in *Ex p. James* (1874) L.R. 9 Ch. App. 609, below, para.20–022.
[61] Below, para.20–057.
[62] Where the debt is secured, the creditor may waive the security and present a bankruptcy petition: see s.269.
[63] The bankruptcy level is £750 and it can be altered by statutory instrument: Insolvency Act 1986 s.267. This must be owing at the time the petition is presented: see *Re Patel (A Debtor)* [1986] 1 W.L.R. 221; *Coulter v Chief Constable of Dorset Police* [2004] EWCA 1259, [2005] B.P.I.R. 62. See, however, *Lilley v American Express (Europe) Ltd* [2000] B.P.I.R. 70.
[64] s.267(2). The debtor may also present a petition: see s.272; *Re Coney* [1998] B.P.I.R. 333.

which the debtor fails to comply with within a three-week period or to have set aside.[65]

20–019 **Effect of presenting a bankruptcy petition.** The bankruptcy of an individual commences on the day on which a bankruptcy order is made.[66] The property comprised in the bankrupt's estate is defined by s.283 of the Insolvency Act 1986; broadly it is "all property belonging to or vested in the bankrupt at the commencement of the bankruptcy". The general principle of insolvency law is that the trustee in bankruptcy takes no better title to property than was possessed by the debtor and therefore excluded from the bankrupt's available property is any property held on trust by the bankrupt.[67] Property is given a very wide definition and includes "things in action" and "every description of property wherever situated".[68] In *Heath v Tang*[69] it was held that a bankrupt could not appeal against the judgment on which the bankruptcy order was based since this right of action was vested in the trustee.[70] Certain property is excluded from the estate of the bankrupt, the major categories being tools and equipment necessary to enable the bankrupt to carry on business and personal belongings.[71] Also certain actions which are personal to the bankrupt, for example, actions for damages for pain and suffering, do not vest in the trustee.[72] Where a person is adjudged bankrupt any disposition of property, if made between the day on which the petition is presented and the vesting of the estate in the trustee, is void except to the extent that it is made with the consent of the court or is ratified by it.[73] This section could obviously affect the validity of a contract involving a disposition or anything done under a contract entered into by the bankrupt after the presentation of a petition. It is important to note that it is only dispositions by the bankrupt that are affected and not dispositions made to him; it is thus possible for a person to make payment to the bankrupt and to obtain a good discharge until the estate is

[65] s.268(1). As regards inability to pay debts not yet due, see s.268(2). A document which purports to be a statutory demand is a statutory demand even though defective: *Re A Debtor (No.1 of 1987)* [1989] 1 W.L.R. 271; see also *Re A Debtor (No.1 of 1987)* [1989] 1 W.L.R. 461; *Practice Note (Bankruptcy: Service Abroad) (No.1 of 88)* [1988] 1 W.L.R. 461; *Practice Note (Bankruptcy: Prescribed Forms) (No.2 of 88)* [1988] 1 W.L.R. 557; *Re A Debtor (No.415–5D–1993), The Times*, December 8, 1993 (debtor faced with statutory demand not entitled to have it set aside because he offered security).

[66] Insolvency Act 1986 s.278(a); the bankruptcy continues until the debtor is discharged or the bankruptcy order is annulled: s.278(b). The 1986 Act does not make use of the doctrine of relation back formerly contained in s.37 of the Bankruptcy Act 1914.

[67] s.283(3)(a); see generally, Cork Report, Cmnd.8558 (1982), Ch.22.

[68] s.436. It also can include after acquired property: see para.20–017. On the effect of bankruptcy on joint tenancies: see *Re Dennis (A Bankrupt)* [1993] Ch. 72; *Re Palmer (Deceased) (A Debtor)* [1993] 4 All E.R. 812; *Re Pavlou (A Bankrupt)* [1993] 1 W.L.R. 1046, 1048.

[69] [1993] 1 W.L.R. 1421.

[70] A bankrupt who is dissatisfied with the conduct of the trustee can seek relief under s.303 of the 1986 Act.

[71] s.283(2); business is defined in s.436 to mean "trade or profession". Where the excluded property exceeds the cost of a reasonable replacement, it can be recovered from the bankrupt and a replacement provided: s.308. The matrimonial home will be dealt with in para.20–036.

[72] *Heath v Tang* [1993] 1 W.L.R. 1421, 1423.

[73] s.284(1). Section 284(2) extends the section to a "payment" whether in cash or otherwise. No indication is given as to how the court should exercise its discretion but presumably the court will follow the principles developed with respect to similar provision dealing with corporate insolvency: see s.127. Section 284(5) provides special rules with respect to banks.

vested in the trustee.[74] A person who deals with the bankrupt in good faith before the commencement of the bankruptcy,[75] who gives value and who has no notice of the presentation of the petition,[76] is protected.[77]

Proof of notice. It is probably for the person supporting the transaction to show that it was entered into without notice of the presentation of the bankruptcy petition.[78] He will probably have to establish that he had no knowledge or notice of any facts which would reasonably lead an ordinary man of business to conclude that a bankruptcy petition had been presented.[79] A statement by a creditor that he intends to present a bankruptcy petition would not be notice for the purpose of the section.[80] Notice to an agent is not necessarily notice to his principal, for example, notice to a sheriff's officer is not notice to the creditor,[81] but notice to a creditor's solicitor in the course of a particular matter in respect of which a solicitor has usual authority will be sufficient to fix the creditor with notice.[82] **20–020**

Assignments by bankrupt. Since s.284(4) has the effect of validating assignments of debts made by the bankrupt, it follows that payment by the debtor to the assignee is also validated. In such circumstances it is immaterial that the debtor had notice of an act of bankruptcy, provided only that the assignee had no such notice at the date of the assignment.[83] Moreover, even where there has been no assignment, a payment by a debtor to a third party at the request of the creditor (later made bankrupt) is within the protection of the section though in this case it is essential that the payer has no notice of an act of bankruptcy.[84] **20–021**

---

[74] s.306.

[75] Bankruptcy commences on the date on which the bankruptcy order is made: Insolvency Act 1986 s.278(a).

[76] It is important to note that it is notice of the petition and not the making of a statutory demand that is important. Notice of the making of a statutory demand may affect the question of good faith: *Muir Hunter on Personal Insolvency*, paras 3–153—3–154. On the meaning of good faith under s.46 of the Bankruptcy Act 1914, see *Re Simms* [1930] 2 Ch. 22; *Re Dalton* [1963] Ch. 336.

[77] s.284(4); enhanced protection is given to a bank where the bankrupt incurs a debt after the commencement of his bankruptcy: s.284(5); see generally *Muir Hunter on Personal Insolvency*, p.3079 (para.3–154). As regards actions against a debtor once bankruptcy proceedings have begun or an order made, see s.285; *Realisations Industrielles et Commerciales SA v Loescher* [1957] 1 W.L.R. 1026.

[78] *Re Dalton* [1963] Ch. 336, 351 (dealing with position under the Bankruptcy Act 1914).

[79] For the position under the Bankruptcy Act 1914, see *Smith v Osborn* (1858) 1 F. & F. 267; *Ex p. Snowball* (1872) L.R. 7 Ch. App. 534; *Ex p. Dawes* (1875) L.R. 19 Eq. 438; *Herbert's Trustee v Higgins* [1926] Ch. 794, 800.

[80] *Herbert's Trustee v Higgins* [1926] Ch. 794.

[81] *Ex p. Schulte* (1874) L.R. 9 Ch. App. 409. Strictly speaking a sheriff's officer is not the agent of the party on whose behalf he acts: *Hooper v Lane* (1857) 6 H.L.C. 443; *Barclays Bank v Roberts* [1954] 1 W.L.R. 1212.

[82] *Brewin v Briscoe* (1859) 28 L.J.Q.B. 329. See also *Re Dalton* [1963] Ch. 336 (notice to debtor's solicitor); see generally *Bowstead and Reynolds on the Law of Agency*, 18th edn (2006), paras 8–206—8–214.

[83] *Re Dalton* [1963] Ch. 336. It is also immaterial that the assignee does not actually claim payment from the debtor until after the receiving order, so long as he had no notice of an act of bankruptcy at the date of the assignment: *Re Seaman* [1896] 1 Q.B. 412.

[84] *Re Dalton* [1963] Ch. 336.

20–022 **The rule in *Ex p. James.*** The rule in *Ex p. James*,[85] governs situations in which, though in law the money or property belongs to the trustee for the creditors, the trustee is restrained from enforcing his claim to it or retaining it. The court will restrain the trustee whenever it would not be honourable or high minded for the trustee to assert his title.[86] The fact that the applicability of the rule depends upon a finding that the trustee has not met a high standard of moral, as distinct from legal, honesty has led to uncertainty and has been criticised.[87]

20–023 **Conditions of application of rule.** There are, however, other, more certain, prerequisites to the application of the rule. First, there must be some form of enrichment of the assets of the bankrupt by the person seeking to invoke the rule.[88] Secondly, the claimant must not normally be in a position to submit a proof of the claim in the bankruptcy: the rule should not give a creditor preference but should give relief where there would otherwise be none.[89] Finally, when the rule does apply, it applies only to the extent necessary to nullify the enrichment and not so as to restore the claimant to the status quo ante by compensating him for his full loss.[90] So, the court has allowed an execution creditor to recover money paid to the trustee under a mistake of law,[91] a wife to recover premiums paid (with the knowledge of the official receiver) in respect of her bankrupt husband's life policy,[92] a lender to recover a loan made to the bankrupt the day after the receiving order had been made,[93] agents to retain sums paid to them after the receiving order with the knowledge and approval of the official receiver,[94] a seller to retain the price of goods sold and delivered shortly after, but in ignorance of the making of a receiving order,[95] and executors to retain sums for funeral expenses and creditors for payment for necessaries

[85] [1874] L.R. 9 Ch. App. 609. See also *Re Byfield* [1982] Ch. 268; *Re Multi Guarantee Co Ltd* [1987] B.C.L.C. 257; *Commrs. of Customs & Excise v T.H. Knitwear Ltd* [1986] B.C.L.C. 195; *Hartgarten Ltd v Australian Gas Light Co Ltd* (1992) 8 A.C.S.R. 277; Goff and Jones, *The Law of Restitution*, 7th edn (2007), paras 5–012—5–016.

[86] *Re Wigzell* [1921] 2 K.B. 835, 850, 858; *Re Tyler* [1907] 1 K.B. 865; *Re Clark (A Bankrupt)* [1975] 1 W.L.R. 559, 564. A number of different phrases, all indicating moral opprobrium, have been used to describe the trustee's conduct.

[87] *Re Wigzell* [1921] 2 K.B. 835, 845, 850, 858; *Re Byfield* [1982] Ch. 268.

[88] *Government of India v Taylor* [1955] A.C. 491, 512–513; *Re Clark (A Bankrupt)* [1975] 1 W.L.R. 559, 563.

[89] *Re Clark (A Bankrupt)* [1975] 1 W.L.R. 559, 564, 566; *Re Gozzett* [1936] 1 All E.R. 79; *Re Multi Guarantee Co Ltd* [1987] B.C.L.C. 257, 270. This may explain the willingness of the court to intervene in *Re Thellusson* [1919] 2 K.B. 735. But cf. *Re Cushla Ltd* [1979] 3 All E.R. 415, 423.

[90] *Re Clark (A Bankrupt)* [1975] 1 W.L.R. 559, 564.

[91] *Ex p. James* [1874] L.R. 9 Ch. App. 609. Although a trustee who deals with a creditor will not be allowed to take advantage of a technical mistake bona fide committed by the creditor (*Re Tricks* (1885) 3 Morr. 15) the rule will probably not protect a creditor who makes such a mistake in his dealings with other creditors or the debtor: *Re Tyler* [1907] 1 K.B. 865; *Re Gozzett* [1936] 1 All E.R. 79. See also *Re Byfield* [1982] Ch. 268 (good faith payment by debtor's bank used to pay certain creditors not protected by the rule.)

[92] *Re Tyler* [1907] 1 K.B. 865.

[93] *Re Thellusson* [1919] 2 K.B. 735 (breadth of dicta questioned in *Re Wigzell* [1921] 2 K.B. 835, but see fn.89, above).

[94] *Re Wilson, Ex p. Salaman* [1926] Ch. 21.

[95] *Re Clark (A Bankrupt)* [1975] 1 W.L.R. 559.

supplied to the debtor out of money earned by him after the adjudication.[96] On the other hand, premiums paid in respect of life policies have in varying circumstances been held not to be protected,[97] builders who had erected buildings on the debtor's land immediately prior to bankruptcy could not recover because they had omitted to take a charge,[98] and counsel could not recover his fees where they had been paid to a deceased insolvent solicitor.[99]

(b) *Vesting of Property in Trustee*

Appointment of trustee. Between the making of a bankruptcy order and the vesting of the bankrupt's estate in the trustee, the official receiver is under a duty to act as the receiver and manager of the bankrupt's estate.[100] Once a bankruptcy order has been made it is normally the creditors in general meeting who will appoint the trustee of the bankrupt's estate.[101] No person can be appointed a trustee unless qualified to act as an insolvency practitioner in relation to the bankrupt.[102] The bankrupt's property vests immediately on the appointment of the trustee taking effect and there is no need for a conveyance, assignment or transfer.[103] 20–024

Vesting provisions mandatory. The vesting provisions of the Insolvency Act are, it would appear, mandatory, and contracting out is not permissible.[104] Thus a contract is invalid in so far as it provides that on the bankruptcy of one of the parties debts then due to him are not to pass to the trustee but are (for instance) to be offset or "cleared" against liabilities of the bankrupt to a third party.[105] 20–025

Choses in action. Prima facie all choses in action belonging to the bankrupt at the commencement of the bankruptcy pass to the trustee as part of the 20–026

[96] *Re Walter* [1929] 1 Ch. 647.

[97] *Tapster v Ward* (1909) 101 L.T. 503; *Re Phillips* [1914] 2 K.B. 689; *Re Stokes* [1919] 2 K.B. 256. The distinction between these cases and *Re Tyler* [1907] K.B. 865, may lie in the fact that in *Re Tyler* the trustee was aware of the existence of the policy and the payments.

[98] *Re Gozzett* [1936] 1 All E.R. 79.

[99] *Re Sandiford (No.2)* [1935] Ch. 681.

[100] s.287; an interim receiver can be appointed under s.286 and a special manager under s.370.

[101] ss.292–294.

[102] s.292(2). As to who is qualified to act as an insolvency practitioner, see s.388 and s.390.

[103] s.306; *Weddell v J.A. Pearce & Major* [1988] Ch. 26. For the definition of the bankrupt's estate see paras 20–015—20–016. On the vesting of after-acquired property, see s.307 and paras 20–026—20–027.

[104] This was the position under previous bankruptcy legislation: *Ex p. Mackay* (1873) L.R. 8 Ch. App. 643.

[105] *British Eagle International Airliner Ltd v Compagnie Nationale Air France* [1975] 1 W.L.R. 758; *Money Markets International Stockbrokers Ltd v London Stock Exchange Ltd* [2001] 2 B.C.L.C. 347; cf. *Horne v Chester and Fein Property Developments Pty Ltd* (1986) 11 A.C.L.R. 485. As regards companies, debt subordination agreements have been upheld: *Re British and Commonwealth Holdings Plc (No.3)* [1992] B.C.L.C. 322; *Re Maxwell Communications Corp Plc* [1993] 1 W.L.R. 1402.

bankrupt's property.[106] There is, however, nothing to prevent the trustee from reassigning a chose in action to the debtor.[107] Difficulties may arise where the bankrupt has purported to assign such a chose in action prior to the commencement of the bankruptcy. Generally such an assignment is valid and binding on the trustee as the successor in title of the assignor, but the trustee can upset such an assignment in two main cases.[108] First, an assignment of future choses in action which are not actually earned (in the sense that the whole consideration is not supplied) until after the commencement of the bankruptcy is void against the trustee.[109] Secondly, a general assignment of existing or future book debts (or any class thereof) by a trader is void against the trustee unless it has been registered as if it were a bill of sale.[110]

20–027 **Adjustment of prior transactions.** There are certain transactions entered into by a bankrupt prior to his bankruptcy which can be challenged by his trustee. If these transactions are successfully challenged they will be unenforceable against the estate of the bankrupt and the trustee may be able to recover with respect to them with the consequence that the bankrupt's estate will be increased for the benefit of his creditors. The transactions that may be challenged are: (i) transactions at an undervalue; (ii) preferences; (iii) extortionate credit transactions; and (iv) transactions defrauding creditors.

20–028 **Transactions at an undervalue.** A transaction at an undervalue is defined in section 339: it is a transaction in which a bankrupt makes a gift or otherwise receives no consideration, enters into a transaction in consideration of marriage, or enters into a transaction where the consideration provided by the other person to the contract is "significantly less, in money or money's worth", than the consideration provided by the bankrupt.[111] A transaction at an undervalue can only be challenged by the trustee if it is entered into at the "relevant time" which

[106] ss.283 and 436(4) ("property includes . . . things in action"). This includes most rights of action but not those arising from contracts for personal service to be performed, defamation, breach of confidence, or an action for damages for pain and suffering: *Bailey v Thurston & Co* [1903] 1 K.B. 137; *Wilson v United Counties Bank Ltd* [1920] A.C. 102; *Re Kavanagh* [1949] 2 All E.R. 264; [1950] 1 All E.R. 39n; *Heath v Tang* [1993] 1 W.L.R. 1421; *Re Landau (A Bankrupt)* [1998] Ch. 223. The bankrupt's home can in certain circumstances cease to form part of the estate: Insolvency Act 1986 s.283A (added by s.261(1) of the Enterprise Act 2002); *Re Byford* [2003] EWHC (Ch) 1267, [2003] B.P.L.R. 1089.

[107] *Ramsay v Hartley* [1977] 1 W.L.R. 686, 692–694; *Stein v Blake* [1996] A.C. 243. On the powers of a trustee in bankruptcy, see Insolvency Act 1986 s.314 and Sch.V.

[108] There are also provisions relating to transactions which can be set aside: see paras 20–023—20–024.

[109] *Wilmot v Alton* [1897] 1 Q.B. 17; *Re Collins* [1925] Ch. 556; *Re de Marney* [1943] Ch. 126 (the basis of the reasoning in these cases is that a bankrupt cannot create greater rights in an assignee than those which the bankrupt actually possesses); cf. *Re Davis & Co Ex p. Rawlings* (1888) 22 QBD 193; *Re Trytel* [1952] 2 T.L.R. 32.

[110] s.344, re-enacting the substance of s.43 of the Bankruptcy Act 1914. This prohibition does not apply to assignments from a specified debtor or under specified contracts, nor to assignments made on a bona fide transfer of an assignor's business, nor to an assignment made for the benefit of creditors generally: s.344(3)(b). As to the meaning of "book debts", see *Shipley v Marshall* (1863) 14 C.B.(N.S.) 566; *Paul & Frank Ltd v Discount Bank (Overseas) Ltd* [1967] Ch. 348; *Re Brightlife Ltd* [1987] Ch. 200, 208–209. See also *Hill v Alex Lawrie Factors* [2000] B.P.I.R. 1038, dealing with s.344(2).

[111] s.339(3): see *Re Kumar (A Bankrupt) Ex p. Lewis v Kumar* [1993] 1 W.L.R. 224.

is defined as a period of five years prior to the presentation of the bankruptcy petition and, provided the transaction was not entered into less than two years before the presentation of the bankruptcy petition, the bankrupt was insolvent or rendered insolvent[112] by the transaction.[113] The onus of showing insolvency is on the trustee but there is a presumption that the bankrupt was insolvent where the transaction is with an associate.[114] Where a transaction at an undervalue is shown to have taken place, the court can:

> "... make such order as it thinks fit for restoring the position to what it would have been if that individual had not entered into that transaction."[115]

No order can be made against a third party who is a bona fide purchaser for value unless he has notice of certain statutory prescribed circumstances which would allow the transaction to be set aside.[116]

Preferences. A preference occurs where a person does something which puts one of his creditors, or a surety or guarantor of his debts, in a better position than he would have been in the event of the person's bankruptcy had that thing not been done and the person providing the preference was influenced by a desire to put the other person in such a better position.[117] Such a transaction can only be challenged if the transaction was entered into within the six-month period before the presentation of the petition[118] and the individual is insolvent or rendered insolvent by the transaction.[119] As with transactions at an undervalue, the courts are given very wide remedial powers.[120] The relevant time for determining whether there is an intention to prefer is when the transaction is entered into and the fact that the debtor believes that he will be in a position to pay all his debts will not negative a preference.[121] 20–029

Extortionate credit transactions. The provision on extortionate credit transactions is modelled on ss.137 to 139 of the Consumer Credit Act 1974.[122] A transaction is an extortionate credit transaction if, having regard to the risk 20–030

---

[112] s.341(3) defines insolvency as an inability to pay debts as they fall due or the value of liabilities exceeds assets.

[113] s.341(1) and (2).

[114] s.341(2); associate is defined in s.435 and is qualified by s.341(2) to exclude a bankrupt's employee.

[115] s.339(2); the more specific powers of the court are spelled out in s.342.

[116] s.342(2)(b) and (4) as amended by the Insolvency (No.2) Act 1994.

[117] s.340(3). There is a rebuttable presumption that such was intended where the transaction was with an associate: see s.340(5). "Associate" is defined in s.435. Also the fact that something is done in pursuance to a court order does not prevent it from being a preference: see s.340(6).

[118] s.341(1)(c); where the transaction is entered into with an associate then it can be challenged within a two-year period: s.341(1)(b).

[119] For the definition of insolvency, see s.341(3).

[120] s.342.

[121] *Re F.P. & C.H. Mathews Ltd* [1982] Ch. 257 (dealing with a preference by a company under the previous insolvency legislation); *Re M.C. Bacon Ltd* [1990] B.C.L.C. 324 (dealing with preferences by a company under current legislation).

[122] See now Consumer Credit 2006 Act, Vol.II, para.39–198 et seq. The trustee in bankruptcy is precluded from making an application for relief under s.139(1)(a) of the Consumer Credit Act 1974 but must rely on his rights under the Insolvency Act: s.343(6).

accepted by the person providing the credit, it requires the debtor to make grossly exorbitant payment or otherwise grossly contravenes "ordinary principles of fair dealing".[123] A transaction can only be challenged if entered into within three years before the commencement of the bankruptcy.[124] Where the court finds that a bankrupt has entered into an extortionate credit transaction, it is given very wide remedial powers to deal with the issue.[125]

20–031 **Transactions defrauding creditors.** The definition of a transaction defrauding creditors in s.423[126] of the Insolvency Act 1986 (which applies to both individual bankruptcy and corporate insolvency[127]) is not unlike a transaction at an undervalue. Thus it applies to gifts, transactions in which a person receives no consideration, or where the consideration received is significantly less than the consideration provided.[128] For such a transaction to be caught, it must have been entered into for the purpose of putting the assets beyond the reach of those who would have a claim against the transferor, or otherwise prejudicing the interests of the transferor's creditors.[129] The advantage of this section over that relating to transactions at an undervalue is that no time limit for avoidance is fixed. In addition, the victim of the transaction may apply to have it set aside and not just the trustee in bankruptcy.[130]

20–032 **Contracts not terminated by bankruptcy.** A contract is not determined by the bankruptcy of one of the parties thereto.[131] Ordinarily the benefit of any contract made by the debtor passes to his trustee in bankruptcy as part of his property, subject to the trustee's right to disclaim unprofitable contracts,[132] and, if it is an executory contract, the trustee may complete it and receive the benefit for the estate[133]; he may give receipts[134] and, with the permission of the creditors' committee,[135] exercise various powers, e.g. he may sue on the contract, assign

[123] s.343(3). Where a trustee applies to have a transaction set aside under s.343 there is a presumption that it was extortionate: see s.343(3).

[124] s.343(2); on commencement of the bankruptcy, see s.278 and para.20–019.

[125] s.343(4).

[126] See *Arbuthnot Leasing International Ltd v Havelet Leasing Ltd (No.2)* [1990] B.C.C. 636; *Choan v Sagar* [1993] B.C.L.C. 661; *Re Ayala Holdings Ltd* [1993] B.C.L.C. 256; *Agricultural Mortgage Corp Plc v Woodward* [1995] 1 B.C.L.C. 1; *Barclays Bank Plc v Eustice* [1995] 2 B.C.L.C. 630; *IRC v Hashmi* [2002] 2 B.C.L.C. 489; *Gil v Baygreen Properties Ltd* [2004] EWHC 1732 (Ch), [2005] B.P.I.R. 95.

[127] *Re Shilena Hosiery Ltd* [1980] Ch. 219.

[128] s.423(1).

[129] s.423(3).

[130] s.424.

[131] *Ex p. Chalmers* (1873) L.R. 8 Ch. App. 289; *Morgan v Bain* (1874) L.R. 10 C.P. 15; *Re Sneezum* (1876) 3 Ch D 463; *Jennings' Trustees v King* [1952] Ch. 899. The case of the bankrupt's apprentices or articled clerks is dealt with by Insolvency Act 1986 s.348 (previously s.34 of the Bankruptcy Act 1914), which provides that if either party gives notice in writing to the trustee to that effect the agreement shall be discharged by the order and a part of any premium may be returned. Payment may also be made out of the Redundancy fund, see para.20–038.

[132] Below, para.20–049.

[133] *Ex p. Stapleton* (1879) 10 Ch D 586.

[134] s.314 Sch.V Pt II para.10.

[135] s.314.

the right of action to creditors[136] or even to the bankrupt,[137] sell the bankrupt's business (in a proper case even to a company promoted by himself and the creditors' committee[138]), or make any compromise of an action or claim.[139]

Effect on contractual rights. In some cases the rights of the trustee in respect of the bankrupt's contracts differ from the rights which the bankrupt would himself have had if he had remained solvent. Thus, in the case of the sale of goods, if a buyer becomes insolvent before the goods are delivered the seller may refuse to deliver them until paid in cash: 20–033

> "... when the insolvency of the purchaser had been declared the vendor [was] ... not bound to deliver any more goods until the price of the goods delivered ... as well as those which were to be delivered ... had been tendered to him."[140]

The vendor may also exercise the right of lien[141] even though he has agreed to give the buyer credit, and would not therefore have had any lien in the absence of insolvency of the buyer. So also, the seller's right of stoppage in transit only arises if the buyer is insolvent.[142] Where a person who has entered into a contract is subsequently adjudged bankrupt, the other party to the contract may apply to the court to be discharged. The court may discharge the contract on such terms as it thinks just and equitable and any damages payable by the bankrupt are provable as a bankruptcy debt.[143]

Contracts which do not pass. From the nature of certain contracts it follows that the benefit of them does not pass to the trustee. Contracts in which the personal skill of the bankrupt forms an essential part of the consideration are instances of these.[144] A right of action for the wrongful dismissal of the bankrupt 20–034

---

[136] s.314 Sch.V Pt I; *Guy v Churchill* (1888) 40 Ch D 481; *Seear v Lawson* (1880) 15 Ch D 426. These cases and those in the next three footnotes were decided under previous bankruptcy legislation but probably still reflect the law.

[137] *Seear v Lawson* (1880) 15 Ch D 426. *Ramsay v Hartley* [1977] 1 W.L.R. 686; *Stein v Blake* [1996] A.C. 243.

[138] *Stein v Blake* [1996] A.C. 243. *Re Spink* (1913) 108 L.T. 572.

[139] *Re Spink* (1913) 108 L.T. 572. *Re Ridgway* (1889) 6 Morr. 277; *Re A. & T. G. Ridgway* (1891) 8 Morr. 289; *Re Pilling* [1906] 2 K.B. 644.

[140] *Ex p. Chalmers* (1873) L.R. 8 Ch. App. 289, 293; this preceded what is now s.41(1)(c) of the Sale of Goods Act 1979. See *Benjamin's Sale of Goods*, 7th edn (2006), para.15–037; see also *Re Eastgate* [1905] 1 K.B. 465; *Tilley v Bowman Ltd* [1910] 1 K.B. 745 (right to repossess goods) but cf. *Re Wait* [1927] 1 Ch. 606 and Vol.II. para.43–471. There is no need to have recourse to Insolvency Act 1986 s.345 if the contract provides that bankruptcy is a terminating event: see *Cadogan Estates v McMahon* [2001] B.P.I.R.

[141] Sale of Goods Act 1979 s.41(1)(c).

[142] Sale of Goods Act 1979 ss.44–46; Vol.II, paras 43–346 et seq.

[143] s.345. Contracts will often provide that bankruptcy is a terminating event: see *Cadogan Estates v McMahon* [2001] B.P.I.R. 17.

[144] *Gibson v Carruthers* (1841) 8 M. & W. 321, 333; *Knight v Burgess* (1864) 33 L.J.Ch. 727; *Re Collins* [1925] Ch. 556. See also above, paras 19–054—19–055 (voluntary assignment of personal contracts) and para.20–006 (transmission of personal contracts on death); cf. *Re Worthington* [1914] 2 K.B. 299.

before his bankruptcy passes to his trustee.[145] Benefits payable under a permanent disability insurance policy constituted property of the bankrupt and passed to the trustee.[146] Rights of action in respect of injury to credit and reputation, or of personal injury, as opposed to injury to property, do not pass to the trustee in bankruptcy,[147] and in this type of case it seems that the trustee cannot even recover the fruits of the action received by the bankrupt[148]; unless perhaps the trustee obtains an order relating to the bankrupt's after-acquired property.[149] It is often difficult to determine if the proceeds of an action for breach of contract vest in the trustee for the benefit of the bankrupt's creditors. This difficulty is particularly acute in hybrid actions, that is, an action involving a claim:

> "... constituted by a single cause of action which is partly for personal injury or loss of reputation (to which the creditors are not entitled) and partly for financial loss (to which they normally are)."[150]

For example, in an action where there is a claim seeking the recovery of property (i.e. the loss of earnings), the cause of action vests in the trustee but if he recovers damages that are personal (i.e. damages for pain and nervous shock) he holds them on trust for the bankrupt.[151] The whole action, however, vests in the trustee,[152] who will hold any personal recoveries on trust for the bankrupt.[153] In *Grady v HM Prison Service*[154] the court held that a claim for unfair dismissal, for which the court could order reinstatement or re-engagement, was personal but that damages for wrongful dismissal constituted property of the bankrupt's estate. Sedley L.J. stated that the authorities tended:

> "... to place on the non-vesting side of the line a claim which is primarily directed at the restoration of a contractual relationship in which the claimant's skill and labour are the essential commodity."[155]

Difficult questions of characterisation arise with respect to claims that are connected with the fact that the bankrupt has gone into bankruptcy; obviously these claims are not pre-bankruptcy assets. In *Mulkerrins v Pricewaterhouse Coopers*[156] the House of Lords considered that a claim for damages against professional advisors who had given negligent advice resulting in the bankruptcy

---

[145] *Beckham v Drake* (1849) 2 H.L.C. 579, 596, 627; cf. *Wenlock v Moloney* (1967) 111 S.J. 437. As to the sale of such rights of action by the trustee, see above, para.16–063. For the position where the contract is unexecuted at the date of the bankruptcy and the breach occurs thereafter see: *Bailey v Thurston & Co Ltd* [1903] 1 K.B. 137; below, para.20–055.

[146] *Cork v Rawlins* [2001] EWCA Civ 202, [2001] 3 W.L.R. 300.

[147] *Wilson v United Counties Bank* [1920] A.C. 102, 120, 129–130; *Rose v Buckett* [1901] 2 K.B. 449; *Heath v Tang* [1993] 1 W.L.R. 1421.

[148] *Re Kavanagh* [1949] 2 All E.R. 264; [1950] 1 All E.R. 39n.

[149] See para.20–053.

[150] *Mulkerrins v Pricewaterhouse Coopers* [2003] UKHL 41, [2003] B.P.I.R. 1357 at [6].

[151] *Ord v Upton* [2000] Ch. 352; cf. *Cork v Rawlings* [2001] EWCA Civ 197, [2001] 3 W.L.R. 300.

[152] If the trustee decides not to pursue any action he can assign it to the bankrupt.

[153] *Ord v Upton* [2000] Ch. 352, 371.

[154] [2003] EWCA Civ 527, [2003] 3 All E.R. 745.

[155] [2003] EWCA Civ 527 at [24]. This was cited in *Mulkerrins v Pricewaterhouse Coopers* [2003] UKHL 41, [2003] 1 W.L.R. 1937 at [25] without comment.

[156] [2003] EWCA Civ 527.

did not vest in the trustee in bankruptcy in that the damages represented what the bankrupt had "lost by the making of the bankruptcy order".[157]

Disclaimer. Section 315 of the Insolvency Act 1986 enables the trustee to disclaim onerous property and for this purpose onerous property is "any unprofitable contract", property which is not saleable or readily saleable, or property that"may give rise to a liability to pay money or perform some other onerous act".[158] The disclaimer operates from the date on which the prescribed notice, which has to be filed in court, is indorsed by the court.[159] Any person who suffers loss or damage in consequence of the disclaimer may prove in the bankruptcy.[160] A notice of disclaimer with respect to property may not be given if the person interested in property had applied in writing to the trustee to decide whether to disclaim or not and 28 days have expired since that notice was given.[161] The trustee is deemed to have adopted any contract which he cannot disclaim by virtue of this section.[162] Disclaimer is the right to get rid of property or contracts which are onerous, any contract which is unprofitable, any property which is unsaleable or not readily saleable, or which gives rise to a liability to pay money or to perform any other contract.[163] Disclaimer is intended to affect the rights of third parties as little as possible; s.315(3) provides that disclaimer only operates to the extent that is necessary "for the purpose of releasing the bankrupt, the bankrupt's estate and the trustee from any liability".[164] 20–035

Matrimonial home. Special provision is made to protect the interests of the bankrupt and his spouse in the matrimonial home. Where a spouse has a charge[165] on the matrimonial home under Pt IV of the Family Law Act 1996 on the interest of the other spouse in the matrimonial home, the charge continues to subsist notwithstanding the bankruptcy of the other spouse.[166] On an application under s.33 of the 1996 Act[167] the court has to take into consideration the financial 20–036

---

[157] [2003] EWCA Civ 527 at [17].

[158] s.315. Special provision is made for the disclaimer of leases (s.317) and land subject to a rentcharge (s.318). Also leave of the court is required to disclaim property acquired under s.307 or s.308 (s.315(4)); *Re Hans Place Ltd* [1993] B.C.L.C. 768; *Hindcastle v Attenborough Associates Ltd* [1997] A.C. 70; *Re Park Air Services Plc* [2000] A.C. 172; *Re SSL Realisations (2002) Ltd* [2006] EWCA (Civ) 7, [2005] 1 B.C.L.C. 1 (dealing with the equivalent provision for companies).

[159] s.315(3)(a) and Winding Up Rules 1986 r.6.178(4).

[160] s.315(5).

[161] s.316. This time period can be extended: s.376; *Re Richardson* (1880) 16 Ch D 613.

[162] s.316.

[163] s.315(2). It is important to note that the lack of profitability of the contract does not have to flow from the onerous nature of the contract: cf. *Re Potters Oils Co Ltd* [1986] 1 W.L.R. 201. *Re Bastable Ltd* [1901] 2 K.B. 518 would probably be decided in the same way today but the reasoning would not be followed; there could be no disclaimer in that case because it would be depriving a purchaser of an interest and not merely relieving the bankrupt of an onerous obligation.

[164] *Stacey v Hill* (1900) 69 L.J.Q.B. 796, affirmed [1901] 1 K.B. 660. For disclaimer on the part of a company in liquidation see: *Re Potters Oils Ltd* [1986] 1 W.L.R. 201; *Re Distributors and Warehousing Ltd* [1986] B.C.L.C. 129; *Re A.E. (Realisations) Ltd* [1981] B.C.L.C. 486; *Re Hans Place Ltd* [1993] B.C.L.C. 768; *Hindcastle v Barbara Attenborough Associates Ltd* [1997] A.C. 70; *Re Park Air Services Plc* [2000] A.C. 172.

[165] A "matrimonial home right": see s.30 of the Family Law Act 1996.

[166] Family Law Act 1996 s.336(2).

[167] This section deals with the court's power to make occupation orders in favour of the person entitled to occupy a dwelling-house by virtue of the general law or s.30 of the 1996 Act.

resources of the spouse or former spouse[168] and the needs of any children[169] as well as the interests of the creditors.[170]

Also of relevance is the conduct of the spouse in contributing to the bankruptcy. The bankrupt is also given the right to occupy the dwelling-house provided he has a beneficial interest in it and there is someone under the age of 18 with whom the bankrupt shared the home at the time the bankruptcy petition was presented.[171] In this situation the bankrupt cannot be evicted except under a court order.[172] The right of occupation is treated as a charge under the Family Law Act 1996 and on an application to have the bankrupt evicted the court shall take into consideration not only the interests of the creditors but also the interests of the children but not "the needs of the bankrupt".[173] Where a bankrupt for whatever reason occupies the matrimonial home on condition that he makes payments to satisfy mortgage obligations or to satisfy other outgoings, he does not acquire any interest in the premises by reason of making the payments. If a dwelling-house forms part of the trustee's property and for any reason the trustee is unable to realise it, he may apply to the court for an order imposing a charge on the property for the benefit of the bankrupt's estate.[174]

20–037 **Remedies of contracting party against bankrupt.** A person who has entered into a contract with one who subsequently becomes bankrupt cannot generally sue either the bankrupt or the trustee; but an obligation under a contract is a "liability"[175] provable in the bankruptcy. All such debts and liabilities, except such wages or salary or other debts as are entitled to preferential payment,[176] are payable pari passu out of the estate.[177] The right of a creditor to prove in the debtor's bankruptcy is dealt with more fully in a subsequent part of this chapter.[178]

20–038 **Remedies of employee against bankrupt employer.** The Insolvency Act 1986 confers a limited preference on employees for unpaid wages and certain other entitlements.[179] To the extent that a claim falls outside the statutory limits it ranks as an ordinary debt. An employee has a statutory right to payment owed to him by his insolvent employer and this may often be a more valuable right than any personal claim he may have against his employer.[180] Where the Secretary of

[168] s.336(4)(c).

[169] s.336(4)(d).

[170] s.336(4)(a).

[171] s.337 (as amended by the Family Law Act 1996 s.66(1)).

[172] s.337(2)(a). Where the bankrupt is out of possession, then he can only regain it with a court order.

[173] s.337(5); where the application is made one year after the commencement of the bankruptcy it is presumed that the interests of the creditors prevail unless there are exceptional circumstances indicating otherwise: s.337(6).

[174] s.313 as qualified by s.313A for low value homes (added by s.283A(3) of the Enterprise Act 2002).

[175] ss.322 and 382(4).

[176] Below, para.20–038.

[177] s.328(3). Debts owed to a spouse are deferred to the claims of ordinary creditors: s.322.

[178] See below, para.20–049.

[179] ss.328, 386 and Sch.6.

[180] Employment Rights Act 1996 s.186; Vol.II, paras 39–191 et seq.

State makes a payment from the National Insurance Fund he is subrogated to the rights of the employee against the bankrupt employer, including any preferential claims.[181]

(c) *Trustee takes "Subject to Equities"*

General. Broadly speaking, a trustee in bankruptcy (like a voluntary assignee) acquires the property of the bankrupt "subject to equities". Thus a person who has been induced by fraud to sell property to a buyer who subsequently becomes bankrupt does not lose his right to rescind the contract and recover his property merely because it has passed to the trustee in bankruptcy.[182] So also where contractual rights have been validly assigned by the bankrupt before the commencement of the bankruptcy, the trustee takes the benefit of the contract subject to the rights of the assignee.[183] Exceptions to this principle have been discussed above.[184] On the other hand, the trustee in bankruptcy takes the property of the bankrupt free from purely personal claims binding on the bankrupt. 20–039

Set-off and mutual dealings. The right of set-off in bankruptcy does not rest on the same principle as the right of set-off between solvent parties (which is designed to prevent cross-actions) but is governed by s.323 of the Insolvency Act 1986. The section applies where before the commencement of the bankruptcy: 20–040

> " . . . there have been mutual credits, mutual debts or other mutual dealings between the bankrupt and any creditor of the bankrupt proving or claiming for a bankruptcy debt."[185]

Where such mutual dealings exist, an account is to be taken of what each party owes and the sums due from one party to the other with respect to mutual dealings between the parties shall be set off against each other.[186] Section 323(3) provides that sums due from the bankrupt shall not be included in any set-off if the other party "had notice at the time they became due" that a bankruptcy petition relating to the bankrupt was pending.[187] Were this provision to be applied literally, it would mean that a creditor could not set off sums due on a contract entered into before a bankruptcy petition was presented but which become due after the presentation of the petition. If such an interpretation were valid, this would severely curtail the right of set-off in a way that was probably not intended by the legislature. To deal with the alleged problem, a reform of s.323 was

---

[181] s.189.

[182] *Re Eastgate* [1905] 1 K.B. 465; *Tilley v Bowman* [1910] 1 K.B. 745; *A.W. Gamage Ltd v Charlesworth's Trustee* [1910] S.C. 257.

[183] *National Provincial Bank Ltd v Ainsworth* [1965] A.C. 1175, 1256–1258.

[184] Above, para.20–026.

[185] s.323(1); *Stein v Blake* [1996] A.C. 243.

[186] s.323(2).

[187] A petition would appear to be pending even though no order has been made on it: Derham, *Set-Off*, 3rd edn (2003), pp.456–457.

proposed in the Companies Bill 1989.[188] This was intended to make it clear that no debt or liability could be set-off which arose after the date on which the creditor had notice that a bankruptcy notice relating to the bankrupt was pending; thus debts incurred before but falling due after the debtor's bankruptcy could be set-off. However, it was decided that such a reform was not needed[189] and it was abandoned. Section 323(1) sets out the debts that are capable of being set-off and this refers to all "mutual credits, mutual debts and other mutual dealings". The requirement of being "due" is imposed by s.323(2), but this deals only with the time for the taking of an account and it is clear that unless a debt is due at the time of taking an account it cannot be the subject of set-off.[190]

20–041 The right of set-off under s.323 is mandatory and no contracting out of it is permissible.[191] The question whether there are sufficient mutual credits, debts or other dealings is determined at the date of the bankruptcy order.[192] As the object of the section is to do substantial justice between the parties[193] it has not been restrictively interpreted. Thus, it is not necessary that at the date of the order there should be mutual debts existing. If there are claims for the breach of contractual obligations[194] or other mutual demands which do not arise out of the contract[195] which will result in pecuniary liabilities they may be set off provided, in both cases, that the claims are provable in the bankruptcy. It has also been held that contingent debts and liabilities owed by the bankrupt may be set off in bankruptcy.[196] Whether the debt is a legal or an equitable debt is immaterial, for the bankruptcy jurisdiction proceeds upon equitable principles.[197] The claims on each side must be such as result in pecuniary liabilities. A debt cannot therefore be set off against a claim for the return of goods wrongfully detained, for the judgment in the latter case is for the return of the goods *in specie* and only in the

---

[188] Companies Bill cl.161.

[189] The reason for this is clear from *Stein v Blake* [1996] A.C. 243. See Goode, *Legal Problems of Credit and Security*, 3rd edn, pp.282–285.

[190] See Goode, at pp.282–285; Derham, *Set-Off*, pp.456–457. A debtor of a bankrupt cannot gain an advantage by acquiring the bankrupt's liabilities after the making of a bankruptcy order, but this in no way affects the interpretation being put forward in the text: see *Re Charge Card Services Ltd* [1987] Ch. 150, 190 (affirmed [1989] Ch. 497). cf. *Stein v Blake* [1996] A.C. 243.

[191] *National Westminster Bank Ltd v Halesowen Presswork & Assemblies Ltd* [1972] A.C. 785; *Re Cushla Ltd* [1979] 3 All E.R. 415. See also *Hong Kong and Shanghai Banking Corp v Kloeckner & Co AG* [1990] 2 Q.B. 514 (right of party to exclude contractual set-off).

[192] *Re Taylor* [1910] 1 K.B. 562; *Tilley v Bowman* [1910] 1 K.B. 745, 751; *Re A Debtor* [1927] 1 Ch. 410; *Re A Debtor* [1956] 1 W.L.R. 1226; cf. *Re Charge Card Services Ltd* [1987] 1 Ch. 150; [1989] Ch. 497.

[193] *Foster v Wilson* (1843) 12 M. & W. 191, 203–204; *Re Davies* (1867) L.R. 2 Ch. App. 808; *Re City Life Assurance Co Ltd* [1926] Ch. 191.

[194] *Re National Benefit Assurance Co* [1924] 2 Ch. 339; *Re City Life Assurance Co (Grandfield's Case)* [1926] Ch. 191.

[195] *Re D.H. Curtis (Builders) Ltd* [1978] Ch. 162; *Re Cushla Ltd* [1979] 3 All E.R. 415.

[196] *Re Charge Card Services Ltd* [1987] Ch. 150; [1989] Ch. 497; *Day & Dent Constructions Pty Ltd (In Liquidation) v North Australian Properties Pty Ltd (Provisional Liquidator Appointed)* (1982) 40 A.L.R. 399; Derham, *Set-Off*, pp.349–351. As regards contingent debts owed to the bankrupt see *Secretary of State for Trade and Industry v Frid* [2002] EWHC (Ch) 3192, [2004] 2 A.C. 506 (dealing with companies).

[197] *Bailey v Finch* (1871) L.R. 7 Q.B. 34; *Mathieson's Trustee v Burrup, Mathieson & Co* [1927] 1 Ch. 562.

alternative for their value.[198] On the other hand, where property is entrusted to a person for sale, this is a giving of credit.[199] So where a company employed a commission agent to sell its property, and the company owed the agent money by way of commission on earlier sales, it was held that, on the company going into liquidation, the agent was entitled to set off the sum due to him against the value of the property in his possession and still unsold.[200] There was, however, no set-off in respect of other property of the company in the agent's possession which had not been entrusted to him for sale.[201] A debt cannot be set off against a sum of money deposited for a specific purpose which failed owing to the bankruptcy,[202] at least where it would amount to a misappropriation for that money to be used for any other purpose.[203] The right of set-off may exist although one of the debts is secured[204]; to the extent that there is set-off the security is released.[205]

Set-off of unliquidated damages. A claim for unliquidated damages may be set off against a debt under the section.[206] Thus a claim for damages for fraudulent misrepresentation on the sale of a chattel was set off in an action by the bankrupt's trustee for the unpaid price, the fraudulent representation being not merely a personal tort but a breach of the obligation arising out of the contract of sale.[207] **20–042**

Debts must be mutual. In order that debts may be set off they must be mutual. For debts and credits to be mutual they must be between the same parties, in the same right and must be commensurable in the sense that at the relevant time both can be reduced to monetary terms.[208] This may be illustrated by *Re City Life Assurance Co Ltd (Stephenson's Case)*[209] where a policy holder mortgaged his policy to the company and the deed contained an absolute covenant to pay, but provided that so long as the premiums and interest and other obligations were paid the debt should not be called in. The company equitably assigned the mortgage to trustees for another class of policy holders, no notice of this being given to the mortgagor. The whole mortgage debt was outstanding at the time of the winding up of the company. The policy holder claimed to set off the amount due to him on his policy against his mortgage debt. It was held that as the **20–043**

---

[198] *Re Winter* (1878) 8 Ch D 225; *Eberle's Hotels & Restaurant Co v Jonas* (1887) 18 QBD 459; cf. *Re Thorne* [1914] 2 Ch. 438; *Ellis & Co's Trustee v Dixon-Johnson* [1925] A.C. 489; and contrast *Naoroji v Chartered Bank of India* (1868) L.R 3 C.P. 444; *Rolls Razor Ltd v Cox* [1967] 1 Q.B. 552.

[199] *Astley v Gurney* (1869) L.R. 4 C.P. 714; *Palmer v Day* [1895] 2 Q.B. 618.

[200] *Rolls Razor Ltd v Cox* [1967] 1 Q.B. 552. For criticisms of this case see Goode, *Principles of Corporate Insolvency*, 3rd edn (1997), pp.235–237.

[201] [1967] 1 Q.B. 552.

[202] *Re Pollitt* [1893] 1 Q.B. 455; *Re Mid-Kent Fruit Factory* [1896] 1 Ch. 567; *Re City Equitable Fire Insurance Co* [1930] 2 Ch. 293; Derham, *Set-Off*, pp.431–439.

[203] *National Westminster Bank Ltd v Halesowen Presswork & Assemblies Ltd* [1972] A.C. 785.

[204] *Ex p. Barnett* (1874) L.R. 9 Ch. App. 293; *Baker v Lloyds Bank Ltd* [1920] 2 K.B. 322.

[205] *M.S. Fashions Ltd v Bank of Credit and Commerce International SA (No.2)* [1993] Ch. 425.

[206] *Peat v Jones & Co* (1881) 8 QBD 147.

[207] *Jack v Kipping* (1882) 9 QBD 113; *Tilley v Bowman* [1910] 1 K.B. 745; cf. *Kitchen's Trustee v Madders* [1950] Ch. 134.

[208] *Re Cushla Ltd* [1979] 3 All E.R. 415, 420–421. See Derham, *Set-Off*, Ch.11.

[209] [1926] Ch. 191 (this dealt with s.31 of the Bankruptcy Act 1914).

equitable assignment was complete as between the company and their assignees without notice to the mortgagor, there was no mutual credit or mutual debt between the company and the policy holder within s.31, and the latter had no right of set-off in spite of the provisions of the mortgage deed. Warrington L.J.[210] observed that there was no mutuality because at the date of the winding up there was a debt due from the company to the policy holder, but no debt due from the policy holder to the company because the debt which had been so due had been effectively transferred to certain trustees. Therefore, at the date of the winding up there was no mutual credit or mutual debt which could come within the provisions of s.31 and be set off the one against the other.

20–044 A debt due to or from the trustee in bankruptcy as such cannot be set off against a debt due from or to the bankrupt. Therefore a person who has received money from the bankrupt under a transaction which is void as against the trustee (e.g. as a preference) cannot set off a debt due to him from the bankrupt against a claim by the trustee for that money.[211] Similarly a joint debt cannot be set off against a separate debt[212] nor can a debt due to an executor personally be set off against a debt due to him as personal representative of his testator.[213] Debts due in the same right in equity may be set off although they are not due in the same right at law,[214] and a debt due to an agent not known by the other party to have been acting as such may be set off against a debt due from him personally.[215]

(d) *Discharge of Bankrupt*

20–045 **Discharge.** Section 279 deals with the duration of bankruptcy.[216] A bankrupt is automatically discharged at the end of one year beginning on the date the bankruptcy commences.[217] This period can be shortened[218] or extended.[219] A new procedure called a bankruptcy restriction order has been introduced which is designed to enable the duration of bankruptcy to be extended where the bankrupt has been particularly culpable.[220]

20–046 **Effect of discharge.** Where a bankrupt is discharged, it releases him from all bankruptcy debts except:

---

[210] [1926] Ch. 191, 218.

[211] *Lister v Hooson* [1908] 1 K.B. 174.

[212] *Tyso v Petitt* (1879) 40 L.T. 132. cf. *Re Pennington and Owen Ltd* [1925] Ch. 825 (debt owed by a company could not be set off against debt owed to company by a firm of which the creditor was a member; also the principle in *Cherry v Boultbee* (1839) 4 My. & Cr. 442 did not apply in this situation).

[213] *Bishop v Church* (1748) 3 Atk. 691; *Nelson v Roberts* (1893) 69 L.T. 352.

[214] *Bailey v Finch* (1871) L.R. 7 Q.B. 34; for a criticism of this case see Derham at pp.647–648; *Re Willis, Percival & Co Ex p. Morier* (1879) 12 Ch D 491.

[215] *Lee v Bullen* (1858) 27 L.J.Q.B. 161 (note the brokers acted "and/or as agents").

[216] The current provision was inserted by s.256 of the Enterprise Act 2002.

[217] s.279(1).

[218] s.279(2).

[219] s.279(3)–(5).

[220] s.281A and Sch.4A (introduced by s.257 of the Enterprise Act 2002).

(a) from any bankruptcy debt which was incurred in connection with any fraud or fraudulent breach of trust[221];

(b) from any liability in respect of a fine[222];

(c) from any liability relating to damages for personal injuries[223];

(d) from any liability with respect to an order made in family or domestic proceedings[224];

(e) from any other bankruptcy debts as may be prescribed.[225]

It is important to note that discharge only releases a bankrupt from "bankruptcy debts" and therefore a debt which is not so classified is not released.[226]

An order of discharge does not release any person who at the date of the receiving order was a partner or co-trustee with the bankrupt, or was jointly bound or had made any joint contract with him, or any person who was surety or in the nature of surety for him.[227] It does, however, release the bankrupt from his liability, whether the debt was owed by him alone or jointly with others.[228] As an order of discharge releases the bankrupt from the debt, so it releases him from the operation of a collateral remedy for that debt, such as a licence to seize after-acquired goods.[229] It does not release him where the real effect of the transaction providing the collateral remedy is to assign after-acquired property. Such a transaction gives the assignee a right in rem against the property, which is not barred by the bankruptcy.[230] An order of discharge also releases the bankrupt from any liability for consequential damages which may result or arise from the non-payment of the debt.[231] 20–047

After the making of a bankruptcy order, no person who is a creditor of the bankrupt with respect to a provable debt can enforce any remedy with respect to that debt.[232] However, a promise to pay such a debt binds the bankrupt if made for a fresh consideration or otherwise by means binding in law,[233] and this will apply although the promise and consideration was made or given during the 20–048

---

[221] s.281(3).

[222] s.281(4); in the case of a fine in connection with an offence concerning the public revenue, the Treasury can consent to its discharge.

[223] s.281(5)(a); the court has a discretion to order that the bankrupt be discharged to whatever extent it considers appropriate from these debts.

[224] s.281(5)(b).

[225] s.281(6); see the Insolvency Rules 1986 r.6.223 (liability under s.1 of the Drug Trafficking Offences Act 1986 not discharged). For what constitutes a prescribed debt, see s.384(1).

[226] See s.382 on the definition of bankruptcy debt. See para.20–049.

[227] s.281(7).

[228] *Ex p. Hammond* (1873) L.R. 16 Eq. 614.

[229] *Thompson v Cohen* (1872) L.R. 7 Q.B. 527; *Cole v Kernot* (1872) L.R. 7 Q.B. 534n; *Collyer v Isaacs* (1881) 19 Ch D 342 (in these cases the court held that the committee merely had a personal right and not a proprietary interest).

[230] *Re Reis* [1904] 2 K.B. 769; (affirmed [1905] A.C. 442); *Re Lind* [1915] 2 Ch. 345. But if the agreement concerns chattels it may be void unless registered as a bill of sale.

[231] *Van Sandau v Corsbie* (1819) 3 B. & Ald. 13.

[232] s.285(3). A secured creditor can still enforce his security: s.284(5).

[233] *Jakeman v Cook* (1878) 4 Ex.D. 26; *Re Aylmer* (1894) 70 L.T. 244; *Re Bonacine* [1912] 2 Ch. 394. See also *Wild v Tucker* [1914] 3 K.B. 36. cf. *John v Mendoza* [1939] 1 K.B. 141.

bankruptcy.[234] It may be added that although a discharge releases the debtor from provable debts, it does not necessarily extinguish the obligation for all purposes.[235]

20–049 **Debts provable.** The debts provable in a bankruptcy are defined in the broadest possible terms in s.382 of the Insolvency Act 1986.[236] These include any debt or liability to which the bankrupt is subject at the commencement of the bankruptcy or to which he may be subject.[237] Liability means a liability to pay money or money's worth and it includes:

> "... any liability for breach of trust, any liability in contract, tort or bailment and any liability arising out of an obligation to make restitution."[238]

It is irrelevant that the debt or liability is present or future:

> "... whether it is certain or contingent or whether its amount is fixed or liquidated, or is capable of being ascertained by fixed rules or as matter of opinion."[239]

Where a bankruptcy debt bears interest, such interest is provable except in so far as it relates to interest accruing after the commencement of the bankruptcy.[240] Interest with respect to the period after the commencement of the bankruptcy is payable only if there is a surplus after the satisfaction of all of the bankruptcy debts.[241] Certain debts are not provable.[242] Thus a fine imposed for an offence and any obligation "arising under an order made in family or domestic proceedings"[243] are not provable. As well as these statutory exceptions, there are other debts which are not provable in the bankruptcy because they are such that the policy of the law will not allow the creditor to sue and consequently will not give the creditor a remedy in bankruptcy. Such debts are, for example, those given for an illegal or immoral consideration,[244] and in bankruptcy the existence of lawful consideration can be scrutinised even after judgment has been given against the bankrupt so that, as against him, the matter would be res judicata.[245] It is also

[234] *Wild v Tucker* [1914] 3 K.B. 36 (contract by undischarged bankrupt to pay in full a larger debt in consideration of smaller loan held a good contract).

[235] e.g. *Re Ainsworth* [1922] 1 Ch. 22 (gift by will to children equally, subject to proviso that one child must account for debt due to testator; bankrupt child must account for balance due after discharge). Also, of course, it does not release the bankrupt from debts which for whatever reason are not provable.

[236] See also the Insolvency Rules 1986 r.12.3.

[237] s.382(1)(a) and (b).

[238] s.382(4).

[239] s.382(3).

[240] s.322(2); for criticisms of the old law see Cork Report, 1982, Cmnd.8558, Ch.31.

[241] s.328(4); the rate of applicable interest is set out in s.328(5).

[242] See also para.20–046 on the effect of discharge.

[243] Insolvency Rules 1986 r.12.3(2); Insolvency Act 1986 s.281(5)(b). This probably effects a change in law by reversing the decision in *Curtis v Curtis* [1969] 1 W.L.R. 44; see *Muir Hunter on Personal Insolvency*, p.3222 (para.20–046).

[244] See above, Ch.16. Rule 12.3 of the Insolvency Rules 1986, which deals with provable debts, provides that: "Nothing in this Rule prejudices any enactment or rule of law under which a particular kind of debt is not provable, whether on the grounds of public policy or otherwise."

[245] *Ex p. Kibble* (1875) L.R. 10 Ch. App. 373; *Ex p. Banner* (1881) 17 Ch D 480; *Re Beauchamp* [1904] 1 K.B. 572; *Re Van Laun* [1907] 1 K.B. 155; [1907] 2 K.B. 23; *Re Mead* 2 Ir.R. 285; *Re A Debtor* [1927] 2 Ch. 367.

important to keep in mind that the definition of bankruptcy debt has important implications for discharge as it is with respect to these debts that the bankrupt is discharged so that he can have a fresh start.[246]

(e) *Schemes of Arrangement*

Voluntary arrangement. Part VIII of the Insolvency Act 1986 establishes a procedure for enabling a debtor to make what is referred to as a "voluntary arrangement"[247] with his creditors. A debtor intending to enter into a voluntary arrangement with his creditors can apply to the court for an interim order which precludes a bankruptcy petition from being presented against him and no other proceedings may be commenced against him.[248] The debtor's proposal must provide for a person—"the nominee"—to act in relation to the voluntary arrangement for the purpose of implementing its realisation. The court has a discretion as to whether to make an interim order.[249] If the court makes an interim order, the nominee has to report to the court as to whether a meeting of the debtor's creditors should be summoned to consider the debtor's proposal. If a creditors' meeting is called and it approves the voluntary arrangement (with or without modifications)[250] then broadly speaking it becomes binding on all persons who under the rules were entitled to notice of and to vote at the meeting of creditors held to approve the arrangement.[251] Provision is made for the implementation of the arrangement[252] and a creditor who is aggrieved by the arrangement can petition the court for relief.[253] 20–050

Deeds of arrangement.[254] Apart from proceedings in bankruptcy the creditors may agree to a voluntary deed of arrangement on the part of the debtor, though such a deed will not have the same effect in favour of a debtor as a 20–051

[246] The object (as was stated with respect to previous bankruptcy legislation) is that "the bankrupt is to be a freed man—freed not only from debts but from contracts, liabilities, engagements, and contingencies of every kind": *Ex p. Llynvi Coal and Iron Co* (1871) L.R. 7 Ch. App. 28, 32; and see *Ex p. Waters* (1873) L.R. 8 Ch. App. 562; *Flint v Barnard* (1888) 22 QBD 90.

[247] s.253(1). See also County Courts Act 1984 ss.112–117 (as amended by the Courts and Legal Services Act 1990 s.13); *Practice Direction (Bankruptcy: Voluntary Arrangements (No.1/91))* [1992] 1 W.L.R. 120, (making of an administration order.)

[248] s.252. As to who may make an application, see s.253.

[249] s.255. The grounds on which the court's jurisdiction is to be exercised are designed to prevent a debtor from misusing the procedure.

[250] No modification may affect the rights of a secured creditor without that creditor's consent: s.258(4). The proposal is treated as being made to creditors as a class and not to each creditor individually: *Re A Debtor (No.2389 of 1989)* [1991] 2 W.L.R. 578.

[251] s.260. The arrangement only affects creditors' rights as creditors and does not affect proprietory rights such as a landlord's right to forfeit a lease: *Re Mohammed Naeem (A Bankrupt) (No.18 of 1988)* [1990] 1 W.L.R. 48.

[252] s.263.

[253] s.262; *Re A Debtor (No.259 of 1990)* 1 W.L.R. 226 (the prejudice must be brought about by the unfairness stemming from the terms of the scheme).

[254] The Cork Committee recommended that the Deeds of Arrangement Act 1914 be repealed (paras 350–399), but this was not implemented. The relationship between the Insolvency Act 1986 and the Deeds of Arrangement Act 1914 is complex: see Muir Hunter at pp.2003–2005 (paras 20–001 et seq.).

discharge in bankruptcy. Section 2 of the Deeds of Arrangement Act 1914[255] provides that deeds of arrangement to which the Act applies[256] shall be void unless registered under the Act.

20–052 **Deed of arrangement and surety.** A deed of arrangement with creditors contained a proviso that the deed was not to affect the rights and remedies of the creditors against any surety. The executors of a surety for the debtor sued the latter to recover sums paid on her behalf under the deed. It was held that the covenant by creditors not to sue, as limited by the proviso, imported not only that the deed did not affect any creditors' rights against the surety but also that a surety's consequential rights against the debtor were not to be affected.[257]

(f) *Contracts made after Adjudication*

20–053 **Bankrupt's liability on contracts.** A bankrupt is clearly responsible upon any contract which he makes *after* he has been adjudicated bankrupt.

20–054 **After-acquired property.** As has been said above,[258] the effect of an adjudication in bankruptcy is to transfer to the trustee only such property as belongs to the bankrupt at the time of adjudication. A trustee can also obtain for the bankrupt's estate any "after-acquired" property, that is property which has devolved upon or which has been acquired by the bankrupt since the commencement of the bankruptcy.[259] Such property does not automatically vest in a trustee; before it does so the trustee must serve notice on the bankrupt and the trustee's title will be deemed to relate back to the time when the property was acquired by the bankrupt.[260] Certain types of after-acquired property are excluded.[261] Protection is provided for the bona fide purchaser for value who deals with the bankrupt without notice of the bankruptcy,[262] it is important to note that it is notice of the bankruptcy that is the determinative factor. The trustee's ability to obtain after-acquired property is subject to a time limit: by s.309 no notice (except with leave of the court) relating to after-acquired property may be served on the bankrupt after the end of a period of 42 days beginning with the day on which "it first

---

[255] See also Insolvency Act 1986 s.260(3) and s.388(2)(b).

[256] i.e. assignments of property, deeds or agreements for composition, deeds of inspectorship, letters of licence or other agreements for the purpose of carrying on or winding up a debtor's business; see s.1.

[257] *Cole v Lynn* [1942] 1 K.B. 142; following *Kearsley v Cole* (1846) 16 M. & W. 128, and *Close v Close* (1853) 4 De G.M. & G. 176. See further Vol.II, para.44–085, as to the effect of a scheme or deed of arrangement on the liability of a surety.

[258] Above, para.20–019.

[259] s.307.

[260] s.307(3). This involves a reversal of the decision in *Re Pascoe* [1944] Ch. 219 as was proposed by the Cork Report: see 1982, Cmnd.8558, Ch.26.

[261] This is property which does not form part of the bankrupt's estate: see Insolvency Act 1986 s.307(2).

[262] s.307(4). This protection applies whether or not a notice relating to after-acquired property has been served. For authorities dealing with the concept of value and bona fides in previous bankruptcy legislation: see *Re Bennett* [1907] 1 K.B. 149; *Hunt v Fripp* [1898] 1 Ch. 675; *Re Stokes* [1919] 2 K.B. 256; *Re Behrend's Trust* [1911] 1 Ch. 687 (marriage consideration); *Hosack v Robins (No.2)* [1918] 2 Ch. 339.

came to the knowledge of the trustee" that the property had vested in the bankrupt.[263] The trustee can also seek an order ("an income payments order") requiring the bankrupt to pay over to the trustee part of his income.[264] The court cannot make such an order where this would have the effect of reducing the income of the bankrupt below what is required to meet the reasonable domestic needs of the bankrupt and his family.[265]

Action by bankrupt. An undischarged bankrupt may sue on a contract made by him after his adjudication, unless his trustee intervenes.[266] Thus he may sue on a bill of exchange indorsed to him after adjudication,[267] or for rent in respect of premises let by him,[268] or for work and labour done,[269] or for goods sold,[270] or for specific performance of a contract for the sale of land.[271] And he may sue for wrongful dismissal, occurring after his adjudication, from employment under a contract made before it.[272] Once intervention is made by the trustee he cannot withdraw his intervention nor can the bankrupt deal in any way with the property.[273] **20–055**

Carrying on business of bankrupt. By s.314 of and Sch.5 to the 1986 Act, the trustee is given extensive powers to carry on the business of the bankrupt. Some of these powers can only be exercised with the consent of the creditors' committee, if there is one, and if one does not exist with the consent of the court. In certain circumstances a trustee in bankruptcy[274] can compel the suppliers of utilities[275] to continue to supply the business of a bankrupt. This power was introduced on the recommendations of the Cork Committee to deal with the practice of utilities insisting on the payment of old debts as a condition of future supply thus for all intents and purposes putting themselves in a preferential position.[276] If the trustee makes such a request to a utility covered by s.372, the utility may continue to supply the bankrupt but it cannot make it a condition of the continued supply that any outstanding charges owing by the bankrupt and arising before the bankruptcy order are paid.[277] However, as a condition of **20–056**

---

[263] s.309(1).

[264] s.310; see Cork Report, 1982, Cmnd.8558, paras 1158–1163.

[265] s.310(2).

[266] See above, para.20–054, dealing with after-acquired property.

[267] *Herbert v Sayer* (1844) 5 Q.B. 965: cf. *Drayton v Dale* (1823) 2 B. & C. 293; *Fyson v Chambers* (1842) 9 M. & W. 460.

[268] *Cook v Wellock* (1890) 24 QBD 658.

[269] *Jameson v Brick and Stone Co* (1878) 4 QBD 208; *Affleck v Hammond* [1912] 3 K.B. 162.

[270] *Cumming v Roebuck* (1816) Holt N.P.C. 172.

[271] *Dyster v Randall & Sons* [1926] Ch. 932.

[272] *Bailey v Thurston & Co Ltd* [1903] 1 K.B. 137. Where the wrongful dismissal occurred before the bankruptcy, the cause of the action passes to the trustee: *Beckham v Drake* (1849) 2 H.L.C. 579, 627. Above, paras 20–032—20–033.

[273] *Hill v Settle* [1917] 1 Ch. 319.

[274] Other office holders also have this right: see Insolvency Act 1986 s.372(1); for the equivalent in relation to companies see s.233.

[275] Gas, electricity and telecommunications: see Insolvency Act 1986 s.372(5).

[276] Cook Report, 1982, Cmnd.8558, Ch.33; on the legality of this practice see *Wellworth Cash & Carry (North Shields) Ltd v North Eastern Electricity Board* (1986) 2 B.C.C. 99, 265.

[277] s.372(2)(b).

continuing the supply the utility can make it a condition that the trustee guarantees the payment of any charges.[278]

(g) *Second Bankruptcies*

20–057 **Second bankruptcies.** Sections 334 and 335 deal with the special situation where a bankruptcy order is made against a person who is an undischarged bankrupt. These sections are designed to introduce the principle, indorsed by the Cork Committee, that:

> "... in most second and subsequent failures, the assets available are in the main the proceeds of the credit given to the bankrupt by his later creditors and that, in effect, goods supplied by them constitute the assets, and the proceeds thereof should not be shared by them with the creditors in some prior bankruptcy."[279]

In other words, assets acquired subsequent to an earlier bankruptcy should be used to meet the claims of creditors in a later bankruptcy. Where a bankruptcy petition is presented against a person already subject to a bankruptcy order which has not been discharged, a prescribed notice may be served on the trustee of the earlier bankruptcy which renders void the disposition of certain assets in the bankrupt's estate unless a court order validating the disposition is obtained.[280] Broadly speaking the assets covered are those assets acquired by the trustee of the first bankruptcy since the commencement of the first bankruptcy which are new assets. These are: (i) after-acquired property[281]; (ii) money derived from an order under s.310 (income payments)[282]; and (iii) property derived from either of the above.[283] These assets are also deemed to form part of the bankrupt's estate in the second bankruptcy.[284] The trustee of the first bankruptcy can prove in the second bankruptcy for any unsatisfied balance of debts provable in the first bankruptcy but is not entitled to any dividend on them until the creditors in the second bankruptcy have been satisfied in full.[285]

[278] s.372(2)(a).
[279] Cook Report, 1982, Cmnd.8558, para.1166.
[280] The court can also ratify such a disposition: see s.334(2).
[281] See above, para.20–054.
[282] See above, para.20–054.
[283] See s.334(3).
[284] s.335(1). They are however subject to a charge in favour of the trustee of the first bankruptcy for his bankruptcy expenses: see s.335(3).
[285] s.335(5) and (6).

Part Seven
PERFORMANCE AND DISCHARGE

CHAPTER 21

PERFORMANCE

		PARA.
1.	In general	21–001
2.	Time of performance	21–011
3.	Partial performance of an entire obligation	21–027
4.	Payment	21–039
	(a) In general	21–039
	(b) Appropriation of payments	21–059
	(c) Revalorisation: gold clauses and index-linking	21–068
	(d) Payment by negotiable instrument or documentary credit	21–073
	(e) Payment by credit or charge card	21–082
5.	Tender	21–083

1. IN GENERAL

Introduction. The general rule is that a party to a contract must perform exactly[1] what he undertook to do.[2] When an issue arises as to whether performance is sufficient, the court must first construe[3] the contract in order to ascertain the nature of the obligation (which is a question of law[4]); the next question is to see whether the actual performance measures up to that obligation (which is a question of "mixed fact and law" in that the court decides whether the facts of **21–001**

---

[1] On the doctrine of substantial performance, see below, para.21–032; on the doctrine of waiver, see below, paras 22–040 et seq.

[2] See below, paras 21–004, 21–032. cf. s.30 of the Sale of Goods Act 1979 (Vol.II, para.43–286). A party may be held to have failed to perform his contractual obligation, despite the existence of an exemption clause purporting to cover the matter, if as a matter of construction, the clause is held not to cover the loss which has been suffered: see above, paras 14–005 et seq. Under s.3(2)(b) of the Unfair Contract Terms Act 1977, two types of terms are ineffective unless they satisfy the test of reasonableness (as defined in s.11): they are terms under which a person acting in the course of a business and dealing either with a "consumer" (s.12) or on his "written standard terms of business" claims to be entitled either: "(i) [T]o render a contractual performance substantially different from that which was reasonably expected of him, or (ii) in respect of the whole or any part of his contractual obligation to render no performance at all." (See further above, paras 14–059 et seq.). A wide range of clauses may also be affected by the Unfair Terms in Consumer Contracts Regulations 1999 (see above, Ch.15).

[3] See also below, paras 21–027, 21–032, 21–037. On the construction of the terms of a contract, see above, paras 12–041 et seq.; on the question of the *order* in which the different promises of the parties have to be performed, see below, paras 21–027, 24–035—24–037.

[4] In addition to the cases cited in fnn.17 and 18, below see above, para.12–046, and *Dixon v Holdroyd* (1857) 7 E. & B. 903; *Parry v Great Ship Co Ltd* (1864) 4 B. & S. 556; *Edmundson v Longton Corp* (1902) 19 T.L.R. 15; *Vigers v Cook* [1919] 2 K.B. 475. cf. *Herbert Clayton and Jack Waller Ltd v Oliver* [1930] A.C. 209 (obligation to give actor "one of the three leading comedy parts in a musical play").

the actual performance satisfy the standard prescribed by the contractual provisions defining the obligation[5]). This means that although an appellate court, or a court reviewing the decision of an arbitrator, may not normally question a finding of pure fact by the lower court or arbitrator, it may review the construction of the contract and draw its own conclusion as to whether or not the facts amount to performance.[6]

21–002 The fact that a party to a contract has, in purported performance, acted in a way which may appear, in a commercial sense, to be just as valuable to the other party as the way specified in the contract does not amount to performance in law.[7] Thus, a contract to carry goods by sea from Singapore to New York with liberty to tranship at other ports was held not to be performed by their carriage partly by sea and partly by rail.[8]

21–003 **Promisor need not perform stipulation for his own benefit.** A party to a contract need not carry out a stipulation inserted solely for his own benefit.[9] Thus a covenant by a lessee to insure in the names of the lessors is not performed by insuring in their names and his own jointly[10]; nor a covenant by a lessee to insure in the joint names of the lessor and himself by the lessee insuring in his own name only[11]; but a covenant by a lessee to insure in the joint names of the lessor and himself is well performed by his insuring in the name of the lessor only.[12]

21–004 **Substituted or vicarious performance.** The promisor, in the absence of waiver[13] or subsequent variation by agreement,[14] cannot substitute for the agreed

---

[5] *Margaronis Navigation Agency Ltd v Henry W. Peabody & Co of London Ltd* [1965] 1 Q.B. 300, 318. Where A and B each enter into a contract with C and, subsequently, both A and B subcontract performance of their contractual obligations to the same sub-contractor, D, the question which contract (i.e. the contract between A and B or the contract between A and C) is being performed when D provides a service or delivers goods to C must be decided by reference to all the facts and circumstances of the case: *Albright & Wilson UK Ltd v Biachem Ltd* [2002] UKHL 37, [2002] 2 All E.R. (Comm) 753 (where, as a result of a mix-up, the sub-contractor delivered the goods which A had contracted to supply to C but the documents relating to the goods which B had contracted to supply—it was held that it was A that was in breach of contract, and not B, given that the documents were merely ancillary to the substance of what was taking place, namely the delivery of the goods).

[6] [1965] 1 Q.B. 300 cf. *Tsakiroglou & Co Ltd v Noblee Thorl GmbH* [1962] A.C. 93 (a frustration case: see below, para.23–015); *Pioneer Shipping Ltd v B.T.P. Tioxide Ltd* [1982] A.C. 724 (see below, para.23–096, fn.415).

[7] *Arcos Ltd v E.A. Ronaasen & Son* [1933] A.C. 470. The courts may, however, ignore a trivial failure to perform, under the de minimis principle: *Bremer Handelsgesellschaft mbH v Vanden Avenne-Izegem P.V.B.A.* [1978] 2 Lloyd's Rep. 109; *Margaronis Navigation Agency Ltd v Henry W. Peabody & Co of London Ltd* [1965] 1 Q.B. 300, 316; see also Vol.II, para.43–290.

[8] *Re L. Sutro & Co and Heilbut, Symons & Co* [1917] 2 K.B. 348. cf. *Tsakiroglou & Co Ltd v Noblee Thorl GmbH* [1962] A.C. 93, 113.

[9] *Beswick v Beswick* [1968] A.C. 58, 92.

[10] *Penniall v Harborne* (1848) 11 Q.B. 368.

[11] *Doe* d. *Muston v Gladwin* (1845) 6 Q.B. 953. As to severable contracts in such cases, see *Green v Low* (1856) 22 Beav. 625.

[12] *Havens v Middleton* (1853) 22 L.J. Ch. 746. (The lessor was in no way prejudiced by the departure from the contractual undertaking.)

[13] Below, paras 22–040 et seq.

[14] Below, paras 22–032 et seq.

performance anything different, even though the substituted performance might appear to be better than, or at least equivalent to, the agreed performance.[15] If no personal skill of or supervision by the promisor is envisaged by the contract, the promisor may arrange for performance by another person on his behalf[16]; but where the contract expressly or impliedly requires personal performance by the promisor, he may not delegate performance to any other person.[17]

Place of performance. If the contract does not specify where performance is to take place, the place of performance depends upon the implied intention of the parties, to be judged from the nature of the contract and all the surrounding circumstances.[18] If no place of performance is specified even by implication, but performance requires the concurrence of the promisee, the general rule is that the promisor must seek out the promisee and perform his promise wherever the promisee may be.[19] 21–005

Promises in the alternative. Where a contractual promise is in the alternative, in that the promisor agrees to do one of two or more things, the legal effect of the promise depends on the kind of alternative involved: there may be a promise to perform in one of two or more alternative ways, where the form of the promise *requires* an election to be made; or there may be a primary or basic obligation to perform in one way *unless* the party who holds the "option" chooses to substitute another way.[20] Under the first kind of alternative promise, there is no primary or basic obligation and there must be an election of an alternative by one of the parties. The contract may provide which party may choose the alternative to be performed[21]; in the absence of such a provision, the right to elect the alternative is impliedly vested in the promisor, the rule being that the party who is obliged to perform the first act may choose which alternative he wishes to perform.[22] If the promisee is entitled to elect between the alternatives, he must give notice of his election, and until such notice has been given 21–006

---

[15] *Legh v Lillie* (1860) 6 H. & N. 165; *Forman & Co Proprietary Ltd v The Liddesdale* [1900] A.C. 190; *Re L. Sutro & Co and Heilbut, Symons & Co* [1917] 2 K.B. 348 (see para.21–002); *Arcos Ltd v E.A. Ronaasen & Son* [1933] A.C. 470 (above, para.21–002).

[16] On such vicarious performance, see above, paras 19–081—19–084.

[17] *Davies v Collins* [1945] 1 All E.R. 247; *Martin v N. Negin Ltd* (1945) 172 L.T. 275; *Edwards v Newlands & Co* [1950] 2 K.B. 534.

[18] *Reynolds v Coleman* (1887) 36 Ch D 453; *Mutzenbecher v La Aseguradora Espanola* [1906] 1 K.B. 254. See also the cases on the place of payment, below, para.21–054. cf. *Comber v Leyland & Bullins* [1898] A.C. 524; *Re Parana Plantations Ltd* [1946] 2 All E.R. 214. On the place of delivery in a contract for the sale of goods, see s.29(1) and (2) of the Sale of Goods Act 1979; Vol.II, paras 43–273 et seq.

[19] This is the general rule in promises to pay money (see below, para.21–054), but it applies to other promises where the promisee must concur in performance: *Rippinghall v Lloyd* (1833) 5 B. & Ad. 742. cf. *Cranley v Hillary* (1813) 2 M. & S. 120.

[20] The second kind of alternative is discussed below, para.21–008.

[21] *Chippendale v Thurston* (1829) 4 C. & P. 98 (contract provided for notice to be given by one party). On the assessment of damages where the promisor could choose the method or extent of performance, see *Paula Lee Ltd v Robert Zehil & Co Ltd* [1983] 2 All E.R. 390 (below, para.26–048).

[22] *Layton v Pearce* (1778) 1 Dougl. 15; *Re Brookman's Trusts* (1869) L.R. 5 Ch. App. 182; *Reed v Kilburn Co-operative Society* (1875) L.R. 10 Q.B. 264; *Christie v Wilson* 1915 S.C. 645. However there is no rule of law to the effect that the right to elect the alternative is impliedly invested in the promisor. In all cases it is a question of construction of the contract: *Mora Shipping Inc v AXA*

the liability of the other party does not arise.[23] Once the person entitled to elect chooses the alternative to be performed,[24] he is absolutely bound by his choice[25] even though the chosen mode of performance afterwards becomes impossible to carry out.[26]

21–007 In the absence of any such election, if it becomes impossible to perform one alternative, it depends on the construction of the contract, in the particular circumstances, whether the promisor is still obliged to perform the remaining alternative, or whether he is discharged from his obligation[27]; normally, however, the promisor is still bound to perform another alternative[28]:

> "... if the court is satisfied that the clear intention of the parties was, that one of them should do a certain thing, but he is allowed at his option to do it in one or other of two modes, and one of the modes becomes impossible by the act of God, he is still bound to perform it in the other mode."[29]

In *Anderson v Commercial Union Assurance Co*[30] an insurance policy contained a condition giving the insurers the option "to reinstate or replace property damaged or destroyed instead of paying the amount of the loss or damage". The defendants argued that they would be discharged from performing either alternative if what had happened made it impossible for them to reinstate the property, but Bowen L.J. said:

> "It is clear law that if one of two things which have been contracted for subsequently becomes impossible, it becomes a question of construction whether, according to the true intention of the document, the obligor is bound to perform the alternative or is discharged altogether."[31]

Corporate Solutions Assurance SA [2005] EWCA Civ 1069, [2005] 2 Lloyd's Rep. 769 at [44], albeit that the natural meaning of a clause which imposes an obligation on a party to do A or B is likely to be that it is for the promisor to choose whether to do A or B

[23] *Vyse v Wakefield* (1840) 6 M. & W. 442; affirmed 7 M. & W. 126; *Thorn v City Rice Mills* (1889) 40 Ch D 357; *Narbeth v James* [1967] 1 Lloyd's Rep. 591, 598; affirmed on appeal [1968] 1 Lloyd's Rep. 168. See also *Rippinghall v Lloyd* (1833) 5 B. & Ad. 742; *Calaminus v Dowlais Iron Co Ltd* (1878) 47 L.J.Q.B. 575.

[24] On the time by which a selection must be made among "alternative cargoes," see *Brightman & Co v Bunge y Born Limitada Sociedad* [1924] 2 K.B. 619; affirmed on other grounds [1925] A.C. 799; *Reardon Smith Line Ltd v Ministry of Agriculture* [1963] A.C. 691, 717, 720.

[25] *Schneider v Foster* (1857) 2 H. & N. 4; *Rugg v Weir* (1864) 16 C.B.(N.S.) 471; *Gath v Lees* (1865) 3 H. & C. 558; cf. *Mallam v Arden* (1833) 10 Bing. 299. A tender of performance which is not up to the contractual requirements may, however, be withdrawn, and a proper tender substituted within the time fixed for performance (see below, para.21–090 fn.482).

[26] *Brown v Royal Insurance Society* (1859) 1 E. & E. 853.

[27] *Da Costa v Davis* (1798) 1 B. & P. 242; *Stevens v Webb* (1835) 7 C. & P. 60; *Marquis of Bute v Thompson* (1844) 13 M. & W. 487; *Barkworth v Young* (1856) 26 L.J. Ch. 153, 163; *Anderson v Commercial Union Assurance Co* (1885) 55 L.J.Q.B. 146, 150 (quoted below); *McIlquham v Taylor* [1895] 1 Ch. 53.

[28] *Barkworth v Young* (1856) 26 L.J. Ch. 153; *Brightman & Co v Bunge y Born Limitada Sociedad* [1924] 2 K.B. 619; *Reardon Smith Line Ltd v Ministry of Agriculture* [1963] A.C. 691, 717, 730. cf. below, para.21–008.

[29] *Barkworth v Young* (1856) 26 L.J. Ch. 153, 163.

[30] (1885) 55 L.J.Q.B. 146.

[31] (1885) 55 L.J.Q.B. 146, 150.

If, however, the promisor puts it out of his power to perform one alternative, he is bound to perform the other alternative.[32]

"Business" options. The second type of alternative promise is a "true" or "business" option, and it must be contrasted with a contractual obligation which may be performed in different ways (as discussed in the preceding paragraphs). In a "business" option, the contract specifies a single, primary or basic obligation to be performed in one way, unless the holder of the option chooses to substitute another way, and does so by the effective exercise of his option[33]; this power of choice is conferred by the contract on the option-holder "solely for his own advantage" and "in exercising the option . . . the holder is not bound to consider the convenience or the interest of the other party".[34] Hence, if performance of the primary obligation is impeded or frustrated, the option-holder is not obliged to exercise his choice so as to permit performance in the substituted way.[35] 21–008

When notice to perform is required. Some promises may be made conditional upon the happening of a particular event; the contract may stipulate that notice of the happening of the event must be given to the promisor by the other party, but in the absence of such a provision, the general rule is that where the matter does not lie more properly within the knowledge of the other party than of the promisor, such notice is not required.[36] So where houses were let on the understanding that the landlord was to repair a sea-wall necessary to preserve the houses, no notice to the landlord of want of repair was required.[37] Again, if A agrees to indemnify B against the acts of a third person, the liability attaches without B giving notice of such acts to A.[38] 21–009

In certain circumstances, however, notice requiring performance is necessary despite the absence of a clause in the contract requiring such notice:

---

[32] *McIlquham v Taylor* [1895] 1 Ch. 53 (following *Studholme v Mandell* (1698) 1 Ld.Raym. 279). cf. *Honck v Muller* (1881) 7 QBD 92. See also, in the context of "self-induced" frustration, the case of *J. Lauritzen AS v Wijsmuller BV (The Super Servant Two)* [1990] 1 Lloyd's Rep. 1 (below, paras 23–061—23–067).

[33] "There must, therefore, be some provision, express or implied, for its exercise within a reasonable time and for the communication of the election to the other party": *Reardon Smith Line Ltd v Ministry of Agriculture* [1963] A.C. 691, 731; *Libyan Arab Foreign Bank v Bankers Trust Co* [1989] Q.B. 728, 766.

[34] *Libyan Arab Foreign Bank v Bankers Trust Co* [1989] Q.B. 728, 766. Such a contractual provision will, however, in some circumstances fall within s.3 of the Unfair Contract Terms Act 1977: see above, para.21–001 fn.2; and paras 14–059 et seq.

[35] *Libyan Arab Foreign Bank v Bankers Trust Co* [1989] Q.B. 728, 766, 730. See also at 719–720.

[36] *Vyse v Wakefield* (1840) 6 M. & W. 442, especially 453–454; 7 M. & W. 126; *Dawson v Wrench* (1849) 3 Exch. 359, 362; *Murphy v Hurly* [1922] 1 A.C. 369 (distinguishing *Makin v Watkinson* (1870) L.R. 6 Ex. 25, below). As to the requirement of notice when one party has the right to choose the mode of performance in an alternative promise, see above, para.21–006; as to notice of dishonour of a bill, see the Bills of Exchange Act 1882 ss.48 and 49 (considered in Vol.II, para.34–110).

[37] *Murphy v Hurley* [1922] 1 A.C. 369 (The sea wall was not in the exclusive occupation of any tenant.)

[38] *Cutler v Southern* (1668) 1 Wms. Saund. 116; *Lilley v Hewitt* (1822) 11 Price 494. See Vol.II, para.44–068. But a demand is necessary where the surety promises "to pay on demand" if the principal debtor defaults: *Sicklemore v Thistleton* (1817) 6 M. & S. 9.

"The general rule is, that a party is not entitled to notice unless he has stipulated for it; but there are certain cases where, from the very nature of the transaction, the law requires notice to be given, though not expressly stipulated for."[39]

Thus, where only one party has knowledge of the relevant facts, notice is necessary[40]; so, if a landlord agrees to repair the inside of a house[41] or to keep drains in repair,[42] the tenant must give notice of the disrepair,[43] since:

"... the landlord is not the occupier of the premises and has no means of knowing what is the condition of the premises unless he is told."[44]

Notice to the landlord of the need for repair is also required where the covenant to repair is inserted by statute into the contract of letting[45]; this rule applies whether the defect is latent or patent.[46] But notice of disrepair is not necessary where the landlord retains in his own control that part of the premises whose defective condition causes the damage.[47]

21–010 **When request to perform is necessary.** Normally, no request or demand for performance is necessary[48] and the promisor is bound to perform his contractual obligation without being requested to do so; an illustration is the common case of a promise to pay a sum of money, either in general terms or on a specified day.[49] A request to perform is essential to complete the promisee's cause of action only if the contract expressly requires such a request,[50] or the nature of the contract shows that it is an implied condition precedent to the promisor's liability

---

[39] *Vyse v Wakefield* (1840) 6 M. & W. 442, 453. See also *Davies v McLean* (1873) 21 W.R. 264.

[40] *Makin v Watkinson* (1870) L.R. 6 Ex. 25; *London and South Western Ry v Flower* (1875) 1 C.P.D. 77, 85; *Manchester Bonded Warehouse Co v Carr* (1880) 5 C.P.D. 507.

[41] *Makin v Watkinson* (1870) L.R. 6 Ex 25; *Broggi v Robins* (1899) 15 T.L.R. 224; *Tredway v Machin* (1904) 91 L.T. 310. See also fn.45, below.

[42] *Hugall v M'Lean* (1885) 53 L.T. 94; *Torrens v Walker* [1906] 2 Ch. 166.

[43] Knowledge of the want of repair may come from a source other than the tenant: *Griffin v Pillet* [1926] 1 K.B. 17; *Uniproducts (Manchester) Ltd v Rose Furnishers Ltd* [1956] 1 W.L.R. 45; *O'Brien v Robinson* [1973] A.C. 912, 926.

[44] *Tredway v Makin* (1904) 41 L.T. 310, 311.

[45] *O'Brien v Robinson* [1973] A.C. 912 (Housing Act 1961 s.32; see now Landlord and Tenant Act 1985 s.11); *McCarrick v Liverpool Corp* [1947] A.C. 219. The landlord's right to enter and inspect the premises does not excuse the tenant from giving notice: [1947] A.C. 219.

[46] *O'Brien v Robinson* [1973] A.C. 912 (following *Morgan v Liverpool Corp* [1927] 2 K.B. 131).

[47] *Melles & Co v Holme* [1918] 2 K.B. 100; *Bishop v Consolidated London Properties Ltd* (1933) 102 L.J.K.B. 257; *British Telecommunications Plc v Sun Life Assurance Society Plc* [1996] Ch. 69 (although the court refrained from expressing a concluded view on the case where the defect is caused by an occurrence which is wholly outside the landlord's control). cf. also s.4(2) of the Defective Premises Act 1972.

[48] *Brown v Dean* (1833) 5 B. & Ad. 848; *Radford v Smith* (1838) 3 M. & W. 254, 258; *Hooper v Woolmer* (1850) 10 C.B. 370.

[49] *Gibbs v Southam* (1834) 5 B. & Ad. 911; *Walton v Mascall* (1844) 13 M. & W. 452; *Bell & Co v Antwerp, London & Brazil Line* [1891] 1 Q.B. 103, 107. On payment, see below, paras 21–039 et seq. It is a criminal offence for a creditor to "harass" his debtor with the object of coercing him to pay the debt: Administration of Justice Act 1970 s.40.

[50] e.g. *Rawson v Johnson* (1801) 1 East 203 (contract to deliver goods on request: if the buyer sues for non-delivery, he need only prove a request to deliver and his readiness to pay the price).

that a request for performance should be made. Thus, where the amount of a debt is uncertain and depends on facts known to the creditor, he must make a demand for a specific sum.[51] Similarly, no right of action against the drawer or indorser accrues on a bill of exchange or promissory note until a demand has been made[52]; a bank balance is not due until the depositor claims to withdraw it[53]; a bailor of chattels at will cannot sue for their return until there has been a demand and a refusal to return[54]; and where goods are consigned to an agent for sale on commission, an action will not lie against the agent for failure to account until such an account has been demanded from him.[55] Obviously, where a man has disabled himself from performing his contract, it is unnecessary to make any request or demand of performance.[56]

2. TIME OF PERFORMANCE[57]

Time "of the essence of the contract".[58] A number of difficulties surround the law relating to time stipulations in contracts. The first is that the phrase which is commonly employed, namely "time is of the essence of the contract", is potentially misleading in that the question in each case is whether time is of the essence of the particular term which has been broken, not whether time is of the essence of the contract as a whole.[59] The second is that, historically, common law and equity adopted a divergent approach to time stipulations in contracts. At common law a strict approach was taken so that, as was once stated by Sir John Romilly M.R.: 21–011

> " . . . at law time is always of the essence of the contract. When any time is fixed for the completion of it, the contract must be completed on the day specified, or an action will lie for breach of it."[60]

---

[51] *Brown v Great Eastern Ry* (1877) 2 QBD 406.

[52] Bills of Exchange Act 1882 s.45. (The acceptor is liable even where the bill has not been presented for payment: s.52(1).) cf. s.87. (See Vol.II, paras 34–106—34–107, 34–152, 34–192.)

[53] *Joachimson v Swiss Bank Corp* [1921] 3 K.B. 110; *Bagley v Winsome and National Provincial Bank Ltd* [1952] 2 Q.B. 236; *Arab Bank Ltd v Barclays Bank (Dominion, Colonial and Overseas)* [1954] A.C. 495; *Libyan Arab Foreign Bank v Bankers Trust Co* [1989] Q.B. 728, 748–749.

[54] *Cullen v Barclay* (1881) 10 L.R.Ir. 224; *Miller v Dell* [1891] 1 Q.B. 468. See Vol.II, para.33–010.

[55] *Topham v Braddick* (1809) 1 Taunt. 572.

[56] *Lovelock v Franklyn* (1846) 8 Q.B. 371; *Caines v Smith* (1846) 15 M. & W. 189, 190. An old illustration is *Short v Stone* (1846) 8 Q.B. 358, where A, who had promised to marry B, later married C instead. (Such promises no longer have legal effect: see below, para.26–019 fn.103.)

[57] Stoljar (1955) 71 L.Q.R. 527; Lindgren, *Time in the Performance of Contracts—Especially for the Sale of Land*, 2nd edn (Australia); Treitel, *The Law of Contract*, 12th edn (by Peel, 2007), paras 18–087—18–095; Carter, *Breach of Contract*, 2nd edn (1991), paras 538–568; J.E. Stannard, *Delay in the Performance of Contractual Obligations* (Oxford, 2007), especially Chs 1–3.

[58] J.E. Stannard, *Delay in the Performance of Contractual Obligations* (Oxford, 2007), Ch.2.

[59] *British and Commonwealth Holdings Plc v Quadrex Holdings Inc* [1989] Q.B. 842, 856–857.

[60] *Parkin v Thorold* (1852) 16 Beav. 59, 65.

However even at common law there were exceptional cases where time was held not to be of the essence of the contract.[61] But the thrust of the approach of the courts at common law was clear: stipulations as to time were generally of the essence of the contract, so that a party could treat the contract as repudiated if the other party's performance was not completed on the date stipulated by the contract. A different set of rules, however, evolved in equity where time was not of the essence of the contract, except in the three cases considered below:

> "The court of equity was accustomed to relieve against a failure to keep the date assigned . . . if it could do justice between the parties"[62]; "relief is given against mere lapse of time where lapse of time is not essential to the substance of the contract."[63]

21–012 **Law of Property Act 1925 section 41.** Section 41 of the Law of Property Act 1925,[64] provides that:

> "Stipulations in a contract, as to time or otherwise, which according to the rules of equity are not deemed to be or to have become of the essence of the contract, are also construed and have effect at law in accordance with the same rules."

Thus the rules at law are now the same as those in equity: the effect of s.41 is that:

> " . . . contractual stipulations as to time . . . shall not be construed as essential, except where equity would before 1875 have so construed them—i.e. only when the strict observance of the stipulated time for performance was a matter of express agreement or of necessary implication"[65];

or, in other words, s.41:

> " . . . does not negative the existence of a breach of contract where one has occurred,[66] but in certain circumstances it bars any assertion that the breach has amounted to a repudiation of the contract",[67]

---

[61] See, e.g. *Martindale v Smith* (1841) 1 Q.B. 389, 395 (although note the criticism levelled against the case by Lord Simon in *United Scientific Holdings Ltd v Burnley BC* [1978] A.C. 904, 941); Sale of Goods Act 1979 s.10(1); *Woolfe v Horne* (1877) 2 QBD 355; *Re Olympia & York Canary Wharf Ltd (No.2)* [1993] B.C.C. 159, 172.

[62] *Lock v Bell* [1931] 1 Ch. 35, 43. The equitable rule was developed in cases of the sale of land: see *Stickney v Keeble* [1915] A.C. 386, 415–416; *Williams v Greatrex* [1957] 1 W.L.R. 31. For the history of the law on stipulations as to time, see *United Scientific Holdings Ltd v Burnley BC* [1978] A.C. 904, 924–929, 940–945; *Raineri v Miles* [1981] A.C. 1050.

[63] *Lennon v Napper* (1802) 2 Sch. & Lef. 682, 684–685.

[64] Re-enacting s.25(7) of the Judicature Act 1873.

[65] *United Scientific Holdings Ltd v Burnley BC* [1978] A.C. 904, 943–944, per Lord Simon.

[66] This means that damages may be recovered for any loss caused by the breach: *Raineri v Miles* [1981] A.C. 1050 (below, para.21–018).

[67] *Raineri v Miles* [1981] A.C. 1050, 1059, per Buckley L.J., approved by the House of Lords in the same case: 1085.

which entitles the innocent party to treat the contract as terminated. Following the enactment of s.41, it is only in the three cases set out in the next two paragraphs that time is of the essence of a contract.[68]

Time made expressly or implicitly "of the essence". Time is of the essence: (1) Where the parties have expressly stipulated in their contract that the time fixed for performance must be exactly complied with,[69] or that time is to be "of the essence".[70] (2) Where the circumstances of the contract or the nature of the subject-matter indicate that the fixed date must be exactly complied with, e.g. the purchase of a leasehold house required for immediate occupation[71]; the sale of business land or premises,[72] such as a public-house as a going concern[73]; the sale of a reversionary interest[74]; the exercise of an option for the purchase or repurchase of property,[75] or for determining a lease under a "break" clause[76] or an option to acquire a leasehold interest *in futuro*[77] (since in these cases, "the parties on the exercise of the option, are brought into a new legal relationship"[78]); "mercantile contracts",[79] such as a contract for the sale of goods where a time is fixed for delivery,[80] or for the sale of shares liable to fluctuate in value (where the contract stipulated a time for payment),[81] or a charterparty under 21–013

[68] *United Scientific Holdings Ltd v Burnley BC* [1978] A.C. 904; *British and Commonwealth Holdings Plc v Quadrex Holdings Inc* [1989] Q.B. 842, 857; *Hammond v Allen* [1994] 1 All E.R. 307, 311.

[69] *Hudson v Temple* (1860) 29 Beav. 536; *Steedman v Drinkle* [1916] 1 A.C. 275; *Brickles v Snell* [1916] 2 A.C. 599; *Mussen v Van Diemen's Land Co* [1938] Ch. 253; *Harold Wood Brick Co Ltd v Ferris* [1935] 2 K.B. 198. The same result follows if the contract provides that the provision is to be a "condition" in this sense, or that any breach of the clause shall entitle the innocent party to "rescind" or terminate.

[70] *Lombard North Central Plc v Butterworth* [1987] Q.B. 527 (below, para.21–015).

[71] *Tilley v Thomas* (1867) L.R. 3 Ch. App. 61; *Hudson v Temple* (1860) 29 Beav. 536, 543.

[72] *Macbryde v Weekes* (1856) 22 Beav. 533; *Harold Wood Brick Co Ltd v Ferris* [1935] 2 K.B. 198.

[73] *Tadcaster Tower Brewery Co v Wilson* [1897] 1 Ch. 705, 711; *Lock v Bell* [1931] 1 Ch. 35.

[74] *Newman v Rogers* (1793) 4 Bro. C.C. 391.

[75] *Dibbins v Dibbins* [1896] 2 Ch. 348; *Hare v Nicoll* [1966] 2 Q.B. 130. cf. *Millichamp v Jones* [1982] 1 W.L.R. 1422.

[76] *United Scientific Holdings Ltd v Burnley BC* [1978] A.C. 904, 929; *Coventry City Council v J. Hepworth & Son Ltd* (1982) 46 P. & C.R. 170; *Metrolands Investments Ltd v J.H. Dewhurst Ltd* [1986] 3 All E.R. 659.

[77] Whether or not it is an option to renew an existing lease: *United Scientific Holdings Ltd v Burnley BC* [1978] A.C. 904, 929, 945, 961. An option to a tenant to determine his interest under a "break clause" must also be strictly complied with.

[78] [1978] A.C. 904, 945 (see also at 951, 961). cf. a rent review clause: below, para.21–018.

[79] *Reuter Hufeland & Co v Sala Co* (1879) 4 C.P.D. 239, 249; *Bunge Corp v Tradax Export SA* [1981] 1 W.L.R. 711, 716. See further above, paras 12–037 et seq.

[80] *Bowes v Shand* (1877) 2 App. Cas. 455, 463, 464; *Sharp v Christmas* (1892) 8 T.L.R. 687 (perishable goods); *Hartley v Hymans* [1920] 3 K.B. 475, 484. See below, Vol.II, para.43–275.

[81] *Hare v Nicoll* [1966] 2 Q.B. 130. See also *Re Schwabacher* (1908) 98 L.T. 127, 129; *Sprague v Booth* [1909] A.C. 576, 579–580; *British and Commonwealth Holdings Plc v Quadrex Holdings Inc* [1989] Q.B. 842, 857; *Grant v Cigman* [1996] 2 B.C.L.C. 24, 31 (although Judge Weeks Q.C. stated that the dicta in *Re Schwabacher* and *Hare v Nicoll* "may be too wide" and that: "[A] property company may be different from a trading company, and a company in one line of business may be different from a company trading in another less dynamic market." Ultimately, the question of is one of the interpretation of the particular contract: *Msas Global Logistics v Power Packaging Inc* [2003] EWHC 1393 (Ch), [2003] All E.R. (D) 211 (Jun.) at [43]–[47]. The implication that time is of the

which the owner is given the right to withdraw the vessel in default of "punctual payment" of hire.[82] However, the mere fact that the contract can be labelled "mercantile" or "commercial" does not determine the issue.[83] The question is whether the time specified in the particular clause was (expressly or by necessary implication) intended by the parties to be essential, e.g. because they needed to know precisely what were their respective obligations.[84] Thus, where the buyers were required to give 15 days' notice of readiness of the vessel so that the sellers could then nominate the port for loading, the House of Lords held time to be of the essence: performance by the buyer was a condition precedent to the seller's ability to perform his obligation.[85] (However, under the Sale of Goods Act 1979 s.10, unless a different intention appears from the terms of the contract, stipulations as to time of *payment* are not deemed to be of the essence of the contract of sale.[86])

---

essence may be made more readily where the subject-matter of the sale is not simply a parcel of shares in a private company, but the entirety of the shares: at [44]).

[82] *Mardorf Peach & Co Ltd v Attica Sea Carriers Corp of Liberia* [1977] A.C. 850 (approving *Tenax S.S. Co Ltd v Brimnes (Owners) (The Brimnes)* [1975] Q.B. 929). Time charters may now contain an "anti-technicality" clause requiring the owner to give notice before withdrawing the vessel: *Italmare Shipping Co v Ocean Tanker Co Inc (The Rio Sun) (No.2)* [1982] 3 All E.R. 273; *Afovos Shipping Co SA v Romano Pagnan and Pietro Pagnan* [1983] 1 W.L.R. 195. An anti-technicality clause must state that the hire has not been punctually paid and that charterers have a given period of time in which to pay up or risk losing the ship: *Schelde Delta Shipping BV v Astarte Shipping Ltd (The Pamela)* [1995] 2 Lloyd's Rep. 249.

[83] *Bunge Corp v Tradax Export SA* [1981] 1 W.L.R. 711, 729 (cf. at 716); *United Scientific Holdings Ltd v Burnley BC* [1978] A.C. 904, 924, 938, 950; *Torvald Klaveness A/S v Arni Maritime Corp* [1994] 1 W.L.R. 1465 (obligation to make timely redelivery in time charterparty held not to be a condition). *Re Simoco Digital UK Ltd: Thunderbird Industries LLC v Simoco Digital UK Ltd* [2004] EWHC 209 (Ch), [2004] 1 B.C.L.C. 541 at [14]; *Haugland Tankers AS v RMK Marine Gemi Yapim Sanayii ve Deniz Tasimaciliii Isletmesi AS* [2005] EWHC 321 (Comm), [2005] 1 Lloyd's Rep. 573; *Peregrine Systems Ltd v Steria Ltd* [2005] EWCA Civ 239, [2005] All E.R. (D) 215 (Mar) at [15].

[84] The *Bunge Corp* case [1981] 1 W.L.R. 711. See also *Scandinavian Trading Tanker Co A.B. v Flota Petrolera Ecuatoriana* [1983] 2 A.C. 694, 703–704; *Sport Internationaal Bussum BV v Inter-Footwear Ltd* [1984] 1 W.L.R. 776, 783, 793; *Hyundai Merchant Marine Co Ltd v Karander Maritime Inc (The Niizuru)* [1996] 2 Lloyd's Rep. 66, 71; *B.S. & N. Ltd (BVI) v Micado Shipping Ltd (Malta) (The "Seaflower")* [2001] 1 Lloyd's Rep. 341: *Tennara Ltd v Majorarch Ltd* [2003] EWHC 2601 (Ch) (on the facts it was held that time was not expressly or impliedly of the essence. Where time is not of the essence and there has been unreasonable delay in performance, a court may be able to infer that the delay nevertheless amounts to a repudiation of the contract where the consequences of the delay are sufficiently serious. When deciding whether or not the delay amounts to a repudiation of the contract, the court will have regard to all the facts and circumstances of the case.)

[85] The *Bunge Corp* case [1981] 1 W.L.R. 711. Other illustrations given in this case of time being of the essence in mercantile contracts include the date fixed for the sailing of a ship, for the opening of a banker's credit, or for payment against documents. See also *Toepfer v Lenersan-Poortmann N.V.* [1980] 1 Lloyd's Rep. 143 (seller's obligation to tender documents by a specified time); *Société Italo-Belge pour le Commerce et Industrie SA v Palm and Vegetable Oils (Malaysia) Sdn Bhd* [1982] 1 All E.R. 19 (seller's obligation to provide declaration of ship); *Gill & Duffus SA v Société pour l'Exportation des Sucres SA* [1985] 1 Lloyd's Rep. 621 ("at latest").

[86] See Vol.II, para.43–113. cf. s.48(3) of the Act (Vol.II, para.43–382). Similarly, the times of payment of bills of exchange regularly given under the terms of a long-term distributorship were not treated as of the essence: *Decro-Wall International SA v Practitioners in Marketing Ltd* [1971] 1 W.L.R. 361. cf. however, the time for payment of a deposit: *Portaria Shipping Co v Gulf Pacific Navigation Co Ltd* [1981] 2 Lloyd's Rep. 180.

Notice making time "of the essence".[87] (3) Where time was not originally of the essence of the contract, but one party has been guilty of undue delay, the other party may give notice[88] requiring the contract to be performed within a reasonable time.[89] Notice can be served at the moment of breach: it is not necessary to wait until there has been an unreasonable delay by the party in breach before serving the notice.[90] The period of notice given must, however, be reasonable and what is reasonable will depend upon all the facts and circumstances of the case.[91] Factors to which the courts will have regard in assessing the reasonableness of the period of notice include what remains to be done at the date of the notice; the fact that the party giving the notice has continually pressed for completion, or has before given similar notices which he has waived[92]; or that it is especially important for him to obtain early completion.[93] A party who elects to give notice immediately upon the breach of contract would be well advised to be "cautious" in his selection of the period to be included in the notice.[94] Notice making time of the essence of the contract can be given in relation to any term of the contract: entitlement to give notice is not confined to essential terms of the contract.[95] The party serving the notice must not himself be in default.[96] Once notice has been given, both parties are bound by it so that, if the party giving the notice is not ready to perform on the expiry of the notice, the other party may be 21–014

---

[87] J.E. Stannard, *Delay in the Performance of Contractual Obligations* (Oxford, 2007), Ch.8.

[88] No notice need be given if it is clear that the party in default does not intend to proceed: *Re Stone and Saville's Contract* [1963] 1 W.L.R. 163, 171. The inclusion in the contract of express provision for the service of a notice requiring performance within a specified time (where the recipient of the notice has failed to complete performance on the due date) does not exclude the rights and remedies at law or in equity which subsist apart from such notice: *Woods v Mackenzie Hill Ltd* [1975] 1 W.L.R. 613 (approved by the House of Lords in *Raineri v Miles* [1981] A.C. 1050, 1085–1086. Such a notice does not waive or expunge the previous breach of contract in failing to complete at the due date.)

[89] *Parkin v Thorold* (1852) 16 Beav. 59; *Green v Sevin* (1879) 13 Ch D 589; *Compton v Bagley* [1892] 1 Ch. 313; *Stickney v Keeble* [1915] A.C. 386; *Re Bagley and Shoesmith's Contract* (1918) 87 L.J. Ch. 626; *Hartley v Hymans* [1920] 3 K.B. 475; *Charles Rickards Ltd v Oppenhaim* [1950] 1 K.B. 616 (sale of goods); *United Scientific Holdings Ltd v Burnley BC* [1978] A.C. 904, 934, 946–947. cf. *Finkielkraut v Monohan* [1949] 2 All E.R. 234; *Thorpe v Fasey* [1949] Ch. 649; *Ajit v Sammy* [1967] 1 A.C. 255. cf. s.48(3) of the Sale of Goods Act 1979. The notice must make it sufficiently clear that time has been made of the essence: *Shawton Engineering Ltd v DGP International Ltd* [2006] 1 B.L.R. 1 at [44]

[90] *Behzadi v Shaftesbury Hotels Ltd* [1992] Ch. 1, in this respect overruling *Smith v Hamilton* [1951] Ch. 174 where Harman J. held that it was necessary to wait until there has been an unreasonable delay before serving the notice. Where the contract does not specify a date for completion it remains necessary to wait for a reasonable time before serving the notice but that is because it is only where there has been an unreasonable delay by the other party that there will be a breach of contract which justifies the serving of the notice: see *Mahase v Ramlal* [2003] UKPC 12 at [27].

[91] *Stickney v Keeble* [1915] A.C. 386; *Re Barr's Contract* [1956] Ch. 551; *Ajit v Sammy* [1967] 1 A.C. 255; *Behzadi v Shaftesbury Hotels Ltd* [1992] Ch. 1, 27; *Bidaisee v Sampath* (1995) 46 W.I.R. 461 PC; *Bedfordshire CC v Fitzpatrick Contractors Ltd* (1999) 62 Con. L.R. 64; *Barclays Bank Plc v Savile Estates Ltd* [2002] EWCA Civ 589.

[92] *Luck v White* (1973) 26 P. & C.R. 89 (the notice may be waived by the party who gave it re-opening negotiations, while failing to act upon the other party's neglect to comply with the notice). cf. *Buckland v Farmar & Moody* [1979] 1 W.L.R. 221.

[93] *Charles Richards Ltd v Oppenhaim* [1950] 1 K.B. 616.

[94] *Behzadi v Shaftesbury Hotels Ltd* [1992] Ch. 1, 24.

[95] *Re Olympia & York Canary Wharf Ltd (No.2)* [1993] B.C.C. 159, 171.

[96] *Mahase v Ramlal* [2003] UKPC 12 at [28].

entitled to terminate.[97] If, by notice, a party has made time of the essence, but later allows a further extension to another fixed date, time remains of the essence.[98] The notice procedure laid down in the contract may be held to be exhaustive of the rights of the parties so that it will not be open to them to serve a notice (for example, of shorter duration) under the general law rather than the contract.[99]

21–015 **Consequences of time being "of the essence".** In determining the consequences of a stipulation that time is to be "of the essence" of an obligation, it is vital to distinguish between the case where both parties agree that time is to be of the essence of the obligation and the case where, following a breach of a non-essential term of the contract, the innocent party serves a notice on the other stating that time is to be of the essence.[100] In the former case the effect of declaring time to be of the essence is to elevate the term to the status of a "condition"[101] with the consequences that a failure to perform by the stipulated time will entitle the innocent party to: (a) terminate performance of the contract and thereby put an end to all the primary obligations of both parties remaining unperformed[102]; and (b) claim damages from the contract-breaker on the basis that he has committed a fundamental breach of the contract ("a breach going to the root of the contract") depriving the innocent party of the benefit of the contract ("damages for loss of the whole transaction").[103]

21–016 **Loss of right to terminate: relief.** The right to terminate may, of course, be lost where the innocent party affirms the contract[104] or is held to have waived (or to be estopped from exercising) the right to terminate.[105] Additionally, equity may intervene to grant relief in cases of late payment of money due under a mortgage or rent due under a lease,[106] but equity will not intervene at the request of a purchaser who has failed to comply with an essential time stipulation in a contract for the sale of land.[107] The need for certainty in such cases is paramount and the very existence of a jurisdiction to grant relief in cases where it would be

[97] *Finkielkraut v Monohan* [1949] 2 All E.R. 234; *Quadrangle Development and Construction Co Ltd v Jenner* [1974] 1 W.L.R. 68; *Oakdown Ltd v Bernstein & Co* (1984) 49 P. & C.R. 282.

[98] *Buckland v Farmar & Moody* [1979] 1 W.L.R. 221, citing *Howe v Smith* (1884) 27 Ch D 89 and *Lock v Bell* [1931] 1 Ch. 35; *Etzin v Reece* [2002] All E.R. (D.) 405 (July).

[99] *Rightside Properties Ltd v Gray* [1975] Ch. 72; *Country and Metropolitan Homes Ltd v Topclaim Ltd* [1996] Ch. 307, 314–315. The position is, of course, otherwise where the parties expressly reserve "any other right or remedy" available: *Dimsdale Developments (South East) Ltd v De Haan* (1983) 47 P. & C.R. 1.

[100] *Ocular Sciences Ltd v Aspect Vision Care Ltd* [1997] R.P.C. 289, 432–433.

[101] In the sense examined above, paras 12–025 et seq.

[102] The first consequence was the only one mentioned by Lord Diplock in *Scandinavian Trading Tanker Co AB v Flota Petrolera Ecuatoriana* [1983] 2 A.C. 694, 703, when he referred to the effect of making time of the essence of an obligation. See also below, paras 24–047 et seq.

[103] *Lombard North Central Plc v Butterworth* [1987] Q.B. 527, 545, 546; *State Securities Plc v Initial Industry Ltd* [2004] All E.R. (D) 317 (Jan.).

[104] See below, paras 24–003—24–004.

[105] See below, paras 24–007—24–009.

[106] *G. and C. Kreglinger v New Patagonia Meat and Cold Storage Co Ltd* [1914] A.C. 25, 35; *Shiloh Spinners Ltd v Harding* [1973] A.C. 691, 722.

[107] *Union Eagle Ltd v Golden Achievement Ltd* [1997] A.C. 514; *Etzin v Reece* [2002] All E.R. (D) 405 (July) (*Union Eagle* applied to analogous case of an agreement to purchase freehold pursuant to the Leasehold Reform, Housing and Urban Development Act 1993).

unconscionable[108] for the vendor to exercise his right to terminate would detract from that need for a certain rule. The harshness of this general rule may, however, be tempered by the prospect of relief being granted in extreme cases. Where, for example, the vendor has been unjustly enriched by improvements made at the purchaser's expense, then the court may either relax the principle that specific performance will not be granted to a purchaser who has broken an essential condition as to time[109] or, preferably, recognise that the purchaser has a personal restitutionary claim against the vendor.[110]

Consequences of "time being made of essence". Where, however, notice is given by one party purporting to make "time of the essence" in respect of a breach of a non-essential term of the contract, the consequences are altogether different. Such a notice does not serve to make time of the essence so far as the obligations in the original contract are concerned, because one party cannot unilaterally vary the terms of a contract by turning what was previously a non-essential term of the contract into an essential term[111]: the notice "has in law no contractual import".[112] The effect of the notice is rather to bring to an end the interference of equity with the legal rights of the parties[113] so that the entitlement of the innocent party to terminate future performance of the contract is then governed solely by ordinary common law rules. Given that the notice cannot have the effect of turning the non-essential term of the contract into a condition, the party giving the notice can only terminate where the failure of the other party to comply with the terms of the notice goes to the root of the contract so as to deprive that party of a substantial part of the benefit to which he was entitled under the terms of the contract.[114] Failure to comply with the terms of the notice 21–017

[108] Such a jurisdiction has been developed in Australia: see, for example, *Legione v Hateley* (1983) 152 C.L.R. 406 and *Stern v McArthur* (1988) 165 C.L.R. 489. These developments generate too much uncertainty for English tastes.

[109] As has been done in Australia (see fn.108). The occasional English example can also be found (see *In Re Dagenham (Thames) Dock Co, Ex p. Hulse* (1873) L.R. 8 Ch. App. 1022) but the authorities are generally hostile to such an approach (see *Steedman v Drinkle* [1916] 1 A.C. 275). The English courts may "on some future occasion" have to consider whether to "relax" the principle in *Steedman v Drinkle* (see *Union Eagle Ltd v Golden Achievement Ltd* [1997] A.C. 514, 523B and see also *Bidaisee v Sampath* (1995) 46 W.I.R. 461, 466–467 where the point was left open by the Privy Council).

[110] It seems clear that Lord Hoffmann's preference in *Union Eagle Ltd v Golden Achievement Ltd* [1997] A.C. 514, 523 was for the development of an appropriate restitutionary remedy. There is much to be said for this view. It avoids the land being sterilised while the courts sort out whether or not the vendor is entitled to terminate, but at the same time it gives to the court a jurisdiction to remove any unjust enrichment which a vendor has obtained as a result of the termination. A further approach would be to develop the law of estoppel to deal with the case of the vendor who leads the purchaser to believe that the contractual time-scale will not be enforced.

[111] *Behzadi v Shaftesbury Hotels Ltd* [1992] Ch. 1, 12, 24; *Re Olympia & York Canary Wharf Ltd (No.2)* [1993] B.C.C. 159, 171–173; *Ocular Sciences Ltd v Aspect Vision Care Ltd* [1997] R.P.C. 289, 432–433; *Etzin v Reece* [2002] All E.R. (D) 405 (July).

[112] [1992] Ch. 1, 24.

[113] *Behzadi v Shaftesbury Hotels Ltd* [1992] Ch. 1, 12; *Re Olympia & York Canary Wharf Ltd (No.2)* [1993] B.C.C. 159, 173: *Dalkia Utilities Services Plc v Celtech International Ltd* [2006] EWHC 63 (Comm), [2006] 1 Lloyd's Rep. 599 at [131].

[114] *Behzadi v Shaftesbury Hotels Ltd* [1992] Ch. 1; *Ocular Sciences Ltd v Aspect Vision Care Ltd* [1997] R.P.C. 289, 432–433; *Dalkia Utilities Services Plc v Celtech International Ltd* [2006] EWHC 63 (Comm), [2006] 1 Lloyd's Rep. 599 at [131].

can therefore only be used as evidence of a repudiatory breach; it is not a repudiatory breach per se.[115]

21–018 **Where time is not of the essence.** Where none of the three exceptions mentioned in the preceding paragraphs applies, the effect of s.41 of the Law of Property Act 1925 (above) is that the breach of a stipulation as to time is not of itself a repudiatory breach[116] which entitles the innocent party to terminate further performance of the contract. Thus, in a contract for the sale and purchase of land, if the purchaser fails to complete on the date fixed for completion, the effect of s.41 is that the purchaser does not commit a repudiatory breach of contract (entitling the vendor to terminate the contract)[117] provided he either completes, or is ready to complete, within a reasonable time thereafter[118]: it is not essential for the purchaser to prove that he was ready and willing to complete on the date fixed for completion.[119] Even where time is not (or has not subsequently been made) of the essence in a contract for the sale and purchase of land, a failure to complete the contract on or before the date stipulated for completion is still a breach leading to liability to pay damages for any loss[120] caused by the delay in completion.[121] A further example comes from leases. The presumption is that time is not of the essence in the timetable specified in a rent review clause in a lease, under which various steps must be taken to determine the rent payable during the period following the review date[122]; strict adherence to the timetable will be necessary only if that is expressly stated, or if it is a "necessary implication" from the surrounding circumstances[123] (e.g. in the inter-relation between the rent review clause and other clauses).[124] The fact that the time specified in a rent review clause is held not to be of the essence does not itself

[115] *Behzadi v Shaftesbury Hotels Ltd* [1992] Ch. 1; *Astea (UK) Ltd v Time Group Ltd* [2003] EWHC 725 (TCC); [2003] All E.R. (D) 212 (Apr) at [147]–[148]. cf. *United Scientific Holdings Ltd v Burnley BC* [1978] A.C. 904, 946–947; *Louinder v Leis* (1982) 149 C.L.R. 509, 526.

[116] See below, paras 24–001 et seq. It would become such a breach only if it amounted to a substantial failure of performance.

[117] cf. the failure to pay the deposit: *Millichamp v Jones* [1982] 1 W.L.R. 1422; *John Willmott Homes Ltd v Read* (1985) 51 P. & C.R. 90.

[118] *Rightside Properties Ltd v Gray* [1975] Ch. 72, 83.

[119] *Rightside Properties Ltd v Gray* [1975] Ch. 72, 82 (following *Howe v Smith* (1884) L.R. 27 Ch D 89, 103, and *Stickney v Keeble* [1915] A.C. 386, 404).

[120] It should be noted in this context that the rule in *Bain v Fothergill* (1874) L.R. 7 H.L. 158 has been abolished by s.3 of the Law of Property (Miscellaneous Provisions) Act 1989 (below, para.26–091.)

[121] *Raineri v Miles* [1981] A.C. 1050 (following *Stickney v Keeble* [1915] A.C. 386, 415–416; *Phillips v Lamdin* [1949] 2 K.B. 33, 42). (Sometimes, however, the date for completion is "only a target": *Williams v Greatrex* [1957] 1 W.L.R. 31, 35.)

[122] *United Scientific Holdings Ltd v Burnley BC* [1978] A.C. 904; *Amherst v James Walker Goldsmith & Silversmith Ltd* [1983] Ch. 305 (mere delay, however lengthy, does not destroy the landlord's right to have the rent reviewed: the tenant can always serve notice on the landlord making time of the essence: above, para.21–014).

[123] The *United Scientific* case [1978] A.C. 904. (No question of damages was involved in this decision, but the failure to adhere to the timetable was clearly a breach of contract: *Raineri v Miles* [1981] A.C. 1050.)

[124] On the inter-relation between the timetable in a rent review clause and that in a "break" clause, see *Metrolands Investments Ltd v J.H. Dewhurst Ltd* [1986] 3 All E.R. 659.

mean that there is an implied term that the right to a review must be exercised within a reasonable time.[125]

21–019 **Other principles affecting the time fixed for performance.** Apart from the rules considered in the preceding paragraphs, the time fixed for performance may be postponed by waiver[126] or subsequent variation by agreement.[127] On the other hand, where, before the time fixed for performance, the party obliged to perform renounces his obligation, or puts it out of his power to perform, the other party may, at his option, treat this as an "anticipatory breach" without waiting for the time fixed for performance.[128]

21–020 **Where no precise time for performance is specified.**[129] Where a party to a contract undertakes to do an act, the performance of which depends entirely on himself, and the contract is silent as to the time of performance (or merely uses indefinite words such as "with all dispatch") the law implies an obligation to perform the act within a reasonable time having regard to all the circumstances of the case.[130] Thus, where, by the terms of a charterparty, the cargo was "to be discharged with all dispatch according to the custom of the port" of discharge, it was held by the House of Lords that this bound the charterer to discharge the cargo within a reasonable time, regard being had to every impediment arising out of the custom or practice of the particular port, which the charterer could not have overcome by the use of reasonable diligence.[131] Where the act to be done is one in which both parties to the contract are to concur, the implied engagement is not that the act shall be done within either a fixed or a reasonable time, or within the time usually taken, but that each shall use reasonable diligence in performing his part.[132] When deciding whether or not performance has taken place within a reasonable time, a court is not limited to what the parties contemplated or ought to have foreseen at the time of entry into the contract but can, with the benefit of hindsight, take account of a broad range of factors,

---

125 *Amherst v James Walker Goldsmith & Silversmith Ltd* [1983] Ch. 305.

126 Below, paras 22–040 et seq. But, in a contract requiring payment by instalments, time may continue to be of the essence despite a waiver of strict compliance with a fixed date for payment of earlier instalments: *Tropical Traders Ltd v Goonan* (1964) 111 C.L.R. 41, 52–55. See also *Bird v Hildage* [1948] 1 K.B. 91, 94–96; *Barclay v Messenger* (1874) 43 L.J. Ch. 449, 456.

127 Below, paras 22–032 et seq.

128 Below, paras 24–021, 24–030 et seq.

129 On the time for repayment of a loan, see Vol.II, Ch.38.

130 *Postlethwaite v Freeland* (1880) 5 App. Cas. 599; *Castlegate Shipping Co Ltd v Dempsey* [1892] 1 Q.B. 854; *Hick v Raymond* [1893] A.C. 22; *Carlton S.S. Co Ltd v Castle Mail Packet Co Ltd* [1898] A.C. 486; *Lyle Shipping Co Ltd v Cardiff Corp* [1900] 2 Q.B. 638; *Hulthen v Stewart & Co* [1903] A.C. 389; *Barque Quilpué Ltd v Brown* [1904] 2 K.B. 264; *Monkland v Jack Barclay Ltd* [1951] 2 K.B. 252; *Re Longlands Farm* [1968] 3 All E.R. 552; *Jolley v Carmel Ltd* [2000] 2 E.G.L.R. 153, 160; *National Car Parks Ltd v Baird (Valuation Officer)* [2004] EWCA Civ 967, [2005] 1 All E.R. 53 at [58] cf. *Hartwells of Oxford Ltd v British Motor Trade Association* [1951] Ch. 50. See also s.29(3) of the Sale of Goods Act 1979 (Vol.II, para.43–276); and *Charnock v Liverpool Corp* [1968] 1 W.L.R. 1498 ("reasonable time").

131 *Postlethwaite v Freeland* (1880) 5 App. Cas. 599. If performance is to be "in a customary manner," the manner is to be judged as at the time when performance is due: *Reardon Smith Line Ltd v Black Sea and Baltic General Insurance Co Ltd* [1939] A.C. 562; *Tsakiroglou & Co Ltd v Noblee Thorl GmbH* [1960] 2 Q.B. 318; affirmed [1962] A.C. 93, 113–114.

132 *Ford v Cotesworth* (1868) L.R. 4 Q.B. 127; (1870) L.R. 5 Q.B. 544.

including any estimate given by the performing party of the time which it would take for it to perform, whether the party for whose benefit the relevant obligation was to be performed needed to participate in the performance, whether it was necessary for a third party to collaborate with the performing party in order to enable it to perform, and the nature of the cause or causes of any delay in performance.[133]

21–021 **Meanings of general terms relating to time.** Where a contract is to be performed "directly", this does not mean "within a reasonable time", but "speedily", or "as soon as possible",[134] which is a more stringent obligation, like "immediately".[135] A contract by a manufacturer to supply certain specified goods "as soon as possible" means that he is to supply them, not within a time which he thinks reasonable, but within such a time as would be sufficient to enable a person, who had all the necessary appliances, to execute the contract, regard being had to the other contracts he may already have in hand.[136] Where under a policy of insurance notice of an accident was to be given "as soon as possible", it was held that all existing circumstances must be taken into account, including the available means of knowledge of the insured's personal representative of the existence of the policy.[137] The meaning of words referring to time may sometimes be explained by other terms of the contract. Thus, where the contract was to sell certain goods to the defendants:

> "... the said goods to be delivered forthwith, and the price to be paid by the defendants in cash in 14 days from the time of the making of the said contract,"

it was held that, by the use of the word "forthwith" in connection with the payment in 14 days, it was manifest that the parties intended the goods to be delivered at some time within 14 days.[138] Otherwise, "forthwith" means "without delay or loss of time".[139]

21–022 **Meaning of "day".**[140] The exact meaning of the word "day" in contracts, particularly in charterparties where the charterer is allowed so many days, has given rise to much litigation. Though every case must turn on the words of the particular contract, certain general rules of interpretation can be given. Usually, "days" include Sundays and holidays, unless there is a custom to the contrary, and this is the meaning of the words "running days"[141]; on the other hand, the

---

[133] *Peregrine Systems Ltd v Steria Ltd* [2005] EWCA Civ 239, [2005] All E.R. (D) 215 (Mar) at [15]; *Astea (UK) Ltd v Time Group Ltd* [2003] EWHC 725 (TCC), [2003] All E.R. (D) 212 (Apr) at [144].

[134] *Duncan v Topham* (1849) 8 C.B. 225.

[135] *Alexiadi v Robinson* (1861) 2 F. & F. 679.

[136] *Hydraulic Engineering Co Ltd v McHaffie* (1879) 4 QBD 670, 673; *Attwood v Emery* (1856) 1 C.B.(N.S.) 110, 115.

[137] *Verlest v Motor Union Insurance Co Ltd* [1925] 2 K.B. 137. As to these expressions of time, cf. Odgers, *Construction of Deeds and Statutes*, 5th edn, pp.126–140.

[138] *Staunton v Wood* (1851) 16 Q.B. 638; cf. *Hyde v Watts* (1843) 12 M. & W. 254.

[139] *Roberts v Brett* (1865) 11 H.L.C. 337, 355; *Hudson v Hill* (1874) 43 L.J.C.P. 273.

[140] See Odgers at pp.128–134.

[141] *Nielsen & Co v Wait, James & Co* (1885) 16 QBD 67, 71–73.

phrase "working days" excludes days when work is not ordinarily done,[142] and the terms of a contract may show that the word "day" has this meaning.[143] A day is a period of time as from midnight to midnight, and not a period of 24 consecutive hours,[144] unless it is clear that the latter was intended.[145] Where a person under an obligation to do an act has to do it on or before a specified day, he has the whole of that day to fulfil that obligation, viz until midnight.[146] It is a general rule that a day is indivisible; so in shipping contracts part of a day counts as a day,[147] but this is inapplicable where the day referred to is not a natural day, but an artificial period to be computed in accordance with the provisions of the contract.[148] The law will take account of parts of a day whenever that is intended by Parliament (or by the parties to a contract), as where the question concerns the sequence of events happening on the same day.[149] If a notice must be received by a specified person by a prescribed day, it must be received at a time when, as an ordinary matter of routine, it will convey the relevant information to that person or his agent, e.g. in the case of an office address, during normal business hours.[150]

Computation of time.[151] Expressions relating to time, in deeds and other instruments and documents, are (by the Interpretation Act 1978)[152] to be held to refer to Greenwich mean time, or, in the summer time period, to summer time.[153] **21–023**

---

[142] In *Lafarge (Aggregates) Ltd v London Borough of Newham* [2005] EWHC 1377 (Comm), [2005] 2 Lloyd's Rep. 577, Cooke J. stated that "in ordinary parlance in the UK, 'working days' are Mondays to Friday, excluding Christmas, Easter and Bank Holidays" (at [57]).

[143] *Commercial S.S. Co v Boulton* (1875) L.R. 10 QB 346; *Nielsen v Waite* (1885) 16 QBD 67; *Reardon Smith Line Ltd v Ministry of Agriculture* [1963] A.C. 691 ("weather working days" in a charterparty).

[144] *The Katy* [1895] P. 56; *Cartwright v MacCormack* [1963] 1 W.L.R. 18 (above, para.12–093). When payment has to be made on a specified day, it can (in the absence of any custom to the contrary) be made at any time up to midnight on that day: *Afovos Shipping Co SA v Romano Pagnan and Pietro Pagnan* [1983] 1 W.L.R. 195.

[145] *Cornfoot v Royal Exchange Assurance Corp* [1904] 1 K.B. 40; *Leonis S.S. Co v Rank (No.2)* (1908) 13 Com. Cas. 161, 295; *Momm v Barclays Bank International Ltd* [1977] Q.B. 790, 803 ("For banking purposes [a day] ends at the close of working hours . . . ").

[146] The *Afovos Shipping* case [1983] 1 W.L.R. 195, 201; *Schelde Delta Shipping BV v Astarte Shipping Ltd (The Pamela)* [1995] 2 Lloyd's Rep. 249.

[147] *Commercial S.S. Co v Boulton* (1875) L.R. 10 QB 346; *The Katy* [1895] P. 56; *Houlder v Weir* [1905] 2 K.B. 267; *L. & Y Ry v Swann* [1916] 1 K.B. 263.

[148] *Verren v Anglo-Dutch Brick Co (1927) Ltd* (1929) 45 T.L.R. 404, 556; *Carver's Carriage by Sea*, 13th edn (1982), Vols 1 and 2, paras 640, 1839–1859.

[149] *Eaglehill Ltd v J. Needham Builders Ltd* [1973] A.C. 992, 1006, 1010.

[150] *Rightside Properties Ltd v Gray* [1975] Ch. 72, 78–80; *The Brimnes (Tenax S.S. Co Ltd v The Brimnes (Owners))* [1975] Q.B. 929, 945–946, 967, 970. cf. *Eaglehill Ltd v J. Needham Builders Ltd* [1973] A.C. 992, 1011. cf. The *Afovos Shipping* case [1983] 1 W.L.R. 195.

[151] See above, para.12–093; below, para.21–026; on the computation of time for a period of limitation, see below, paras 28–062—28–063; and in a bill of exchange, see Vol.II, paras 34–014, 34–019.

[152] Interpretation Act 1978 ss.9, 23(3).

[153] Summer Time Act 1972. (By s.3(1), any reference to time in (inter alia) any "deed, notice or other document whatsoever" is to be taken as a reference to summer time during the period of summer time fixed by or under the Act.)

21–024 **Period from a date or event.** Where the time is to be computed *from* a certain date, or an act to be done on the happening of an event, the mode of calculating the time must depend on the circumstances of the particular contract.[154] The general rule is now well established that where a particular time is given from a certain date, within which an act is to be done, the day of the date is to be excluded,[155] but "there is no absolute rule with regard to the inclusion or exclusion of the day on which a particular event takes place", and the court has to decide the meaning of the particular contract.[156] The mode of calculation must therefore depend on the wording of the contract, and where the act done is one to which the party against whom time runs is privy the computation may be inclusive as he has had the benefit of some portion of the day included, but where this is not so and the event is foreign to the party against whom time runs, the general rule will be adopted. So it has been held that the words "not later than 21 days before" mean 21 full or clear days between, not counting the day from which the calculation is to be made.[157]

21–025 **Period within which to act.** Where a contract gives the first party a certain period of time in which to do some act, which period is between two other acts to be done by the second party, both the days for doing the second party's acts should be excluded from the computation of the period, so that the first party has the whole of the period of time in which to do his act.[158] But a notice to quit "within" a period of three months can mean "during" or "before or at the expiry of" the period, thus including the final moment of the period so as to amount to a full three months' notice.[159]

21–026 **Meaning and computation of "month".** By s.61 of the Law of Property Act 1925, in all deeds, contracts, wills, orders and other instruments executed, made or coming into operation after the commencement of the Act, unless the context otherwise requires, "month" means calendar month.[160] In the computation of a calendar "month," the House of Lords has upheld[161] the "corresponding date" rule, viz, that if a period of time in "months" is to be computed *from* or *after* a

---

[154] *Re North* [1895] 2 Q.B. 264, 269; *Lester v Garland* (1808) 15 Ves. 248. See above, para.12–093.

[155] *Goldsmiths' Co v West Metropolitan Ry* [1904] 1 K.B. 1, 5 (distinguished in *Hare v Gocher* [1962] 2 Q.B. 641 ("beginning with the commencement" of a statute); and in *Trow v Ind Coope (West Midlands) Ltd* [1967] 2 Q.B. 899 ("beginning with the date of . . . " in RSC Ord.6 r.8(1)); *Dodds v Walker* [1981] 1 W.L.R. 1027, above, para.12–093. See also *Radcliffe v Bartholomew* [1892] 1 Q.B. 161; *Stewart v Chapman* [1951] 2 K.B. 792; *Cartwright v MacCormack* [1963] 1 W.L.R. 18 ("15 days from the commencement date").

[156] *English v Cliff* [1914] 2 Ch. 376, 383. See above, para.12–093.

[157] *Carapanayoti & Co Ltd v Comptoir Commercial André & Cie SA* [1972] 1 Lloyd's Rep. 139. See also below, para.21–026.

[158] *Young v Higgon* (1840) 6 M. & W. 49, 54; *Re Railway Sleepers Supply Co* (1885) 29 Ch D 204; *Rightside Properties Ltd v Gray* [1975] Ch. 72, 80 (a period of "at least 21 days" between serving a notice and forfeiting a deposit).

[159] *Manorlike Ltd v Le Vitas Travel Agency, etc., Ltd* [1986] 1 All E.R. 573.

[160] See above, para.12–061. For similar provisions in other statutes, see s.10(3) of the Sale of Goods Act 1979; s.14(4) of the Bills of Exchange Act 1882; Interpretation Act 1978 Sch.1. (For the former rule, see *P. Phipps & Co Ltd v Rogers* [1925] 1 K.B. 14.)

[161] *Dodds v Walker* [1981] 1 W.L.R. 1027.

given date, that day is excluded from the computation,[162] and the period elapses at midnight on the corresponding day of the month of expiry.[163] Thus where under a statute, a tenant's application had to be made "not more than four months after the giving of the landlord's notice",[164] which was given on September 30, time began to run from midnight on that day (September 30/October 1) and ended at midnight on January 30/31.[165] No account is taken of the fact that some months have more days than others.[166] In the same enactment, the phrase permitting the application only if it was made "*not less* than . . . two months after" the landlord's notice has been interpreted to allow the application to be made on the corresponding date itself[167]: "[i]f the application is made on the corresponding date, it cannot be said to be either before or after the corresponding date".[168]

3. Partial Performance of an Entire Obligation[169]

Entire and divisible obligations. A contract is said to be "entire" when complete performance by one party is a condition precedent to the liability of the other[170]; in such a contract the consideration is usually a lump sum which is payable only upon complete performance by the other party (hence, the reference is sometimes to a "lump sum contract"). The opposite of an "entire contract" is a "divisible contract", which is separable into parts, so that different parts of the consideration may be assigned to severable parts of the performance, e.g. an agreement for payment pro rata.[171] 21–027

Yet the phrase "entire contract" is a misleading one in that the real issue in the cases is whether the "obligation" of the party in default is "entire", not whether the contract itself is entire. Of course, the contract may state that one party can only recover on the contract when he has completed his performance under the 21–028

---

162 See above, para.21–024.

163 *South Staffordshire Tramways Co Ltd v Sickness and Accident Assurance Association Ltd* [1891] 1 Q.B. 402. See also *Webb v Fairmaner* (1838) 3 M. & W. 473; *Freeman v Read* (1863) 4 B. & S. 174. cf. *Cartwright v MacCormack* [1963] 1 W.L.R. 18 ("15 days from. . .").

164 Under s.29(3) of the Landlord and Tenant Act 1954.

165 *Dodds v Walker* [1981] 1 W.L.R. 1027.

166 [1981] 1 W.L.R. 1027. If the relevant calendar month in which a period expires is too short to provide a corresponding date, the period expires on the last day of that month: *Migotti v Colvill* (1879) 4 C.P.D. 233.

167 *E.J. Riley Investments Ltd v Eurostile Holdings Ltd* [1985] 1 W.L.R. 1139 CA.

168 [1985] 1 W.L.R. 1139, 1141.

169 The law on "entire contracts" or, more accurately, entire obligations is reviewed in the Law Commission's Report (No.121 (1983)), paras 2.1–2.88 and Note of Dissent (pp.36–37). (This report is not to be implemented: see the 19th Annual Report of the Commission, para.2.11.) See also Treitel, *The Law of Contract*, 12th edn (by Peel, 2007), paras 17–030—17–047; Carter, *Breach of Contract*, 2nd edn (1991), paras 685–695; Williams (1941) 57 L.Q.R. 373, 490. (The enactment of the Law Reform (Frustrated Contracts) Act 1943 (below, para.23–074) has rendered obsolete some of the common law discussed in this article.)

170 *Hoenig v Isaacs* [1952] 2 All E.R. 176, 180–181. See also the authorities cited in fn.173, below.

171 See below, paras 21–037, 23–091. cf. ss.28 and 31 of the Sale of Goods Act 1979 (sale of goods to be delivered by instalments).

contract. In such a case it can be said that, from the perspective of such a party, there is no real point of distinction between an entire contract and an entire obligation because the contract may be said to be "entire" from his point of view. But in other cases the distinction may be clear. Where a contract makes provision for payment upon the completion of distinct stages of a construction contract, the completion of each stage being a condition precedent to the obligation to make a stage payment, the obligation to complete each stage may be said to be entire, even though the contract itself is clearly not entire. It is for this reason that the phrase "entire obligation" will be used in preference to "entire contract" in the following paragraphs.

21–029 **A matter of construction.** It is a question of construction whether the obligation is entire or divisible,[172] but in the reported cases the courts have tended to the view that in every lump-sum contract there is an implied term that no part of the price is to be recovered without complete performance.[173] In most modern contracts of any size, however, payments by instalments are specified, so that the law on entire obligations is not relevant to any obligation which has been completely performed.

21–030 **Partial performance of entire obligations.** Where a party has performed only part of an entire obligation[174] he can normally[175] recover nothing, neither the agreed price, since it is not due under the terms of the contract, nor any smaller sum for the value of his partial performance, since the court has no power to apportion the consideration.[176] The refusal of pro rata payment is based on the inability of the court, as a matter of construction, to add such a provision to the contract, and also upon the rule that the mere acceptance of acts of part performance under an express contract cannot, taken alone, justify the imposition of a restitutionary obligation to pay on a quantum meruit basis.[177] Thus where an employee is engaged for a fixed period for a lump sum, but fails to complete the

---

[172] *Appleby v Myers* (1867) L.R. 2 C.P. 651, 658; *Hoenig v Isaacs* [1952] 2 All E.R. 176, 178, 180; *Regent OHG Aisenstadt und Barig v Francesco of Jermyn Street Ltd* [1981] 3 All E.R. 327, 333–334. See below, para.21–037.

[173] *Appleby v Myers* (1867) L.R. 2 C.P. 651, 660–661 (where the court relied on *Cutter v Powell* (1795) 6 T.R. 320; *Jesse v Roy* (1834) 1 Cr. M. & R. 316; *Munroe v Butt* (1858) 8 E. & B. 738; *Sinclair v Bowles* (1829) 9 B. & C. 92, which were cases where particular terms in the contract supported such a conclusion: see the criticism in Williams (1941) 57 L.Q.R. 373, 389 et seq.); *The Madras* [1898] P. 90; *Sumpter v Hedges* [1898] 1 Q.B. 673; *Forman & Co Proprietary Ltd v Liddesdale* [1900] A.C. 190; *Small & Sons Ltd v Middlesex Real Estates Ltd* [1921] W.N. 245; *Heywood v Wellers* [1976] 1 Q.B. 446, 458.

[174] The failure to complete need not be a breach of contract: *Cutter v Powell* (1795) 6 T.R. 320. The contract in effect provides that the risk of non-completion is to be borne by the party undertaking the relevant obligation.

[175] For exceptions, see the doctrines of frustration (below, paras 23–085—23–087), acceptance of partial performance (below, para.21–035) and where the defendant prevents complete performance (below, para.21–036).

[176] *Cutter v Powell* (1795) 6 T.R. 320; *Bates v Hudson* (1825) 6 Dow. & Ry.K.B. 3; *Sinclair v Bowles* (1829) 9 B. & C. 92; *Adlard v Booth* (1835) 7 C. & P. 108; *Chanter v Leese* (1839) 5 M. & W. 698; *Appleby v Myers* (1867) L.R. 2 C.P. 651, 660; *The Madras* [1898] P. 90; *Sumpter v Hedges* [1898] 1 Q.B. 673; *Vigers v Cook* [1919] 2 K.B. 475; *Eshelby v Federated European Bank Ltd* [1932] 1 K.B. 423; *Bolton v Mahadeva* [1972] 1 W.L.R. 1009.

[177] See below, para.21–035.

term for a reason other than breach of contract by the employer, e.g. frustration,[178] the common law rule is that he can recover nothing.[179] In the famous case of *Cutter v Powell*[180] a seaman was to be paid a lump sum when he completed the voyage; he died before completion of the voyage and it was held that his executor could not recover pro tanto wages because it was an entire contract.[181] This was a case of non-feasance, but in a case of misfeasance, as where an employee completes a period of service but does bad work, the employee may recover his wages, subject to a deduction in respect of the bad work.[182] In contracts where wages or salaries are payable, however, the Apportionment Act 1870 has altered the common law rule, for by s.2:

> "... all rents, annuities, dividends, and other periodical payments in the nature of income ... shall ... be considered as accruing from day to day,[183] and shall be apportionable in respect of time accordingly."

By s.5, "annuities" include salaries and pensions, and it has been held that it also includes wages.[184]

Although nowadays building contracts of any size normally provide for payments by instalments, the common law rule on entire obligations was developed in cases concerning building contracts, or contracts for work and materials. Where the builder under a lump-sum contract fails to perform some of the agreed work, then, subject to the so-called doctrine of substantial performance,[185] he can 21–031

---

[178] See below, paras 23–037—23–039.

[179] *Spain v Arnott* (1817) 2 Stark. M.P.C. 256; *Huttman v Boulnois* (1826) 2 C. & P. 510; *Turner v Robinson* (1833) 5 B. & Ad. 789; *Lowndes v Stamford* (1852) 18 Q.B. 425; *Ridgway v Hungerford Market Co* (1853) 3 A. & E. 171; *Lilley v Elwin* (1848) 11 Q.B. 742; *Boston Deep Sea Fishing and Ice Co v Ansell* (1888) 39 Ch D 339, 360, 364–365.

[180] (1795) 6 T.R. 320. cf. Merchant Shipping Act 1995 s.38.

[181] On the facts, however, the decision could be based on a specific provision in the contract whereby complete performance was a condition precedent to recovery of any wages at all: similarly in *Appleby v Dods* (1807) 8 East 300 and *Jesse v Roy* (1834) 1 Cr. M. & R. 316. Particular terms of the contract affected the decisions in *Mapleson v Sears* (1911) 105 L.T. 639 and *Moriarty v Regent's Garage Co Ltd* [1921] 2 K.B. 766.

[182] *Sagar v H. Ridehalgh & Son Ltd* [1931] 1 Ch. 310, 324–326.

[183] A "day" means a calendar day and not a working day: *Re B.C.C.I. SA* [1994] I.R.L.R. 282 and *Thames Water Utilities v Reynolds* [1996] I.R.L.R. 186.

[184] *Moriarty v Regent's Garage Co Ltd* [1921] 1 K.B. 423 (held, Act applies to wages); reversed on another point: [1921] 2 K.B. 766; *Re William Porter & Co Ltd* [1937] 2 All E.R. 361, 363; Williams (1941) 57 L.Q.R. 373, 382–383; Matthews (1982) 2 L.S. 302. However, in *Item Software (UK) Ltd v Fassihi* [2003] EWHC 3116 (Ch), [2003] 2 B.C.L.C. 1 at [104] it was held, in this respect following *Boston Deep Sea Fishing and Ice Co v Ansell* (1888) 39 Ch D 339, that an employee was not entitled to recover a proportionate part of the unpaid salary where, on a proper construction of the contract, nothing was due until a date after the date of dismissal. The Court of Appeal in *Item Software (UK) Ltd v Fassihi* [2004] EWCA Civ 1244, [2004] I.R.L.R. 928 held that the effect of s.2 of the Act is that, unless the parties agree otherwise, the salary of an employee whose employment terminates part way through a pay period shall be apportioned and paid in respect of the period actually worked (with payment only becoming due and payable at the end of the relevant pay period). The decision of the Court of Appeal in *Boston Deep Sea Fishing and Ice Co Ltd v Ansell* (1888) 39 Ch D 339 was held not to stand in the way of this conclusion because the Act was not mentioned at any point in the case: it is therefore not an authority on the construction, scope or effect of the Apportionment Act.

[185] See below, para.21–032.

recover nothing for the work which was actually completed,[186] despite the fact that the other party may have received substantial benefit therefrom.[187] The building cases take the distinction between substantial non-feasance where recovery is denied, and misfeasance,[188] where recovery is permitted subject to a cross-action for damages.[189] If, however, under such a lump-sum contract the builder is guilty of a serious misfeasance, so that the work is substantially deficient, he can recover nothing.[190]

21–032 **Substantial performance.**[191] Considerable difficulty arises in the case where the part performer has substantially performed or substantially completed an entire obligation but has not completed full performance. In such a case there is some authority for the proposition that a doctrine of "substantial performance" can be applied so that the part performer is entitled to bring an action to recover the price, subject to a counterclaim for damages which will go in diminution of the price.[192] This "doctrine of substantial performance" has, however, been criticised on the ground that:

> " . . . it is based on the error that *contracts*, as opposed to particular *obligations*, can be entire. . . . To say that an obligation is entire *means* that it must be completely performed before payment becomes due. . . . In relation to 'entire' obligations, there is no scope for any doctrine of 'substantial performance.' "[193]

On the latter view a court is required to identify with some care the obligation which is alleged to be entire; for example, in *Hoenig v Isaac*[194] the obligation of the contractor to complete performance of the contract was entire, but the obligation to do so in a workmanlike manner was not, so that the presence of defects in his work did not act as a barrier to a claim under the contract. The obligation to do the work in a workmanlike manner not being entire, there was therefore no need to employ any doctrine of substantial performance. The same

---

[186] *Sumpter v Hedges* [1898] 1 Q.B. 673; *Forman & Co Proprietary v Liddesdale* [1900] A.C. 190; cf. *Sinclair v Bowles* (1829) 9 B. & C. 92; *Munro v Butt* (1858) 8 E. & B. 738; *Appleby v Myers* (1867) L.R. 2 C.P. 651 (the actual decision would probably be the same under the Law Reform (Frustrated Contracts) Act 1943: see below, para.23–086 fn.388); *Bolton v Mahadeva* [1972] 1 W.L.R. 1009.

[187] See the criticisms in Goff and Jones, *The Law of Restitution*, 7th edn (2007), paras 20–055—20–057.

[188] Some small non-feasance would also fall within the so-called doctrine of substantial performance (below, para.21–032): see *H. Dakin & Co Ltd v Lee* [1916] 1 K.B. 566, 578–579, 580.

[189] Below, para.21–033 fn.204.

[190] *Eshelby v Federated European Bank Ltd* [1932] 1 K.B. 423; *Bolton v Mahadeva* [1972] 1 W.L.R. 1009. See also the cases cited in fn.186, above. cf. *Vigers v Cook* [1919] 2 K.B. 475 (serious misfeasance by undertaker, who was held to be entitled to no remuneration at all under the contract).

[191] See generally Beck (1975) 38 M.L.R. 413.

[192] *Dakin v Oxley* (1864) 15 C.B.(N.S.) 646, 664–665; *Dakin v Lee* [1916] 1 K.B. 566; *Bolton v Mahadeva* [1972] 1 W.L.R. 1009; *Sim v Rotherham MBC* [1987] Ch. 216, 253; *Wiluszynski v Tower Hamlets LBC* [1989] I.C.R. 493, 499; *Williams v Roffey Bros & Nicholls (Contractors) Ltd* [1991] 1 Q.B. 1, 8–10, 17.

[193] Treitel *on The Law of Contract*, 12th edn (by Peel, 2007), para.17–039.

[194] *Hoenig v Isaacs* [1952] 2 All E.R. 176.

analysis can be applied to *Cutter v Powell*[195] because it has been pointed out that the court:

> "... did not decide that if [the seaman] had completed the main purpose of the contract, namely, serving as mate for the whole voyage, the defendant could have repudiated his liability by establishing that in the course of the voyage the sailor had, possibly through inadvertence, failed on some occasion in his duty as mate whereby some damage had been caused."[196]

Once again there is no need to resort to any notion of substantial performance because, only the obligation to complete performance being entire, the fact that a minor breach of contract had occurred would not have been sufficient to discharge the defendant from his obligation to pay.

On the other hand, it must be conceded that there is some authority which supports the existence of a doctrine of substantial performance in relation to entire contracts.[197] On this view, upon completion of substantial performance, the part performer will be entitled to claim the price, subject to a counterclaim for damages. This so-called doctrine of substantial performance may be excluded by an express provision of the contract[198]; "each case turns on the construction of the contract",[199] and "it is always open to the parties by express words to make entire performance a condition precedent" (to payment).[200] The onus of proof is upon the party claiming that it has substantially performed its obligations under the contract to prove that it has done so.[201] What is "substantial performance" will depend upon the nature of the contract and all the circumstances; if the contractor abandons performance, or does work entirely different in kind from that contracted for, it is clearly a case of substantial non-feasance and he may recover nothing.[202] Similarly, a builder who abandons work under a lump-sum contract can recover nothing[203]; but if the work is substantially completed, and it is only in some minor details that the workmanship falls below the contractual specifications, the builder may recover the agreed price, less a deduction based on the cost of making good the defects or omissions[204]: 21–033

[195] (1795) 6 T.R. 320 (see above, para.21–030).

[196] *Hoenig v Isaacs* [1952] 2 All E.R. 176, 178.

[197] See the authorities cited at fn.192, above.

[198] *Cutter v Powell* (1795) 6 T.R. 320; *Appleby v Myers* (1867) L.R. 2 C.P. 651, 660; *Hoenig v Isaacs* [1952] 2 All E.R. 176, 180–181.

[199] *Hoenig v Isaacs* [1952] 2 All E.R. 176, 178.

[200] [1952] 2 All E.R. 176, 181.

[201] *Close Invoice Finance Ltd v Belmont Bleaching and Dyeing Co Ltd* [2003] All E.R. (D) 304 (Apr).

[202] See the cases cited in fnn.186 and 198, above.

[203] *Sumpter v Hedges* [1898] 1 Q.B. 673. (Although the builder had in fact been paid part of the price, the Court of Appeal dealt with the case as a lump-sum contract.) See further McFarlane and Stevens (2002) 118 L.Q.R. 569.

[204] *H. Dakin & Co Ltd v Lee* [1916] 1 K.B. 566; *Hoenig v Isaacs* [1952] 2 All E.R. 176; *Kiely & Sons v Medcraft* (1965) 109 S.J. 829; *Bolton v Mahadeva* [1972] 1 W.L.R. 1009. See also *Boone v Eyre* (1779) 1 Hy. Bl. 273n; *Broom v Davis* (1794) 7 East 480n; *Basten v Butter* (1806) 7 East 479; *Mondel v Steel* (1841) 8 M. & W. 858, 870–871.

"In considering whether there was substantial performance . . . it is relevant to take into account both the nature of the defects and the proportion between the cost of rectifying them and the contract price."[205]

The rule applies to unimportant matters of non-feasance as well as to unimportant matters of misfeasance.[206] Notwithstanding these dicta it is suggested that there ought to be no room in English law for a doctrine of substantial performance: rather the court should inquire whether the particular obligation which is the subject matter of the litigation is entire. If it is not, non-performance of a part of that obligation should not, of itself, be a bar to an action to recover the price; but if it is, and the obligation has not been completely performed, it should not be possible for the part performer to bring an action on the contract to recover the price.

21–034 **Application to carriage of goods by sea.** A shipowner normally cannot recover freight unless the goods are carried to the agreed destination. If the goods are carried there, the fact that some breach of the shipowner's contract has caused damage to the goods in transit does not prevent recovery of the freight, subject to a cross-action for the damage.[207] In one case[208] a charterparty provided for payment of lump-sum freight; two-thirds of the cargo was delivered by the shipowner to its destination, despite the loss of the ship outside the port of discharge, and the House of Lords permitted recovery of the whole of the freight, on the ground (inter alia) that "a substantial part of the cargo"[209] had been delivered.[210]

21–035 **Acceptance of partial performance.** If the circumstances justify the inference that the parties have made a fresh contract, under which the original promisee agrees to accept and pay for partial performance of the original promise, or the requirements of a restitutionary claim have been made out, the recipient will be liable upon a quantum meruit[211] to pay a reasonable price for the work actually done, or the goods actually supplied.[212] The mere receipt of a benefit under the original contract is insufficient to justify the inference of such a promise or to establish a restitutionary claim, unless the party receiving the benefit had an opportunity to accept or reject it.[213] Sale of goods is an example where the buyer need not accept goods which are defective or insufficient in

---

[205] *Bolton v Mahadeva* [1972] 1 W.L.R. 1009, 1013.

[206] *Boone v Eyre* (1779) 1 Hy. Bl. 273n; *H. Dakin & Co Ltd v Lee* [1916] 1 K.B. 566.

[207] *Dakin v Oxley* (1864) 15 C.B.(N.S.) 646; *Henriksens Rederi A/S v T. H. Z. Rolimpex* [1974] Q.B. 233.

[208] *William Thomas & Sons v Harrowing S.S. Co* [1915] A.C. 58.

[209] [1915] A.C. 58, 66. cf. in the Court of Appeal [1913] 2 K.B. 171, 192; *Leiston Gas Co v Leiston U.C.* [1916] K.B. 428. See *Carver's Carriage by Sea*, 13th edn (1982), Vols 1 and 2, paras 1243, 1676.

[210] On the effect of an "expected peril" in the charterparty, which excused delivery of the balance of the cargo, see Williams (1941) 57 L.Q.R. 490, 500–501; Carver at paras 1667 et seq.

[211] On quantum meruit, see below, paras 29–066 et seq.

[212] *Christy v Row* (1808) 1 Taunt. 300; *Sumpter v Hedges* [1898] 1 Q.B. 673, 674. See also, in addition to the cases cited in fn.213, below, *Wheeler v Stratton* (1911) 105 L.T. 786; *Small & Sons Ltd v Middlesex Real Estates Ltd* [1921] W.N. 245.

[213] *Munro v Butt* (1858) 8 E. & B. 738; *Sumpter v Hedges* [1898] 1 Q.B. 673; *Forman & Co Proprietary Ltd v Liddesdale* [1900] A.C. 190; cf. *Shipton v Casson* (1826) 5 B. & C. 378.

quantity; if, however, the buyer does accept delivery, he must pay for them at the agreed rate.[214] Where a builder has abandoned a partially completed erection on the defendant's land, the mere fact that the defendant completes the building does not create a restitutionary obligation to pay for the value of the work already done by the builder under an "entire contract"[215]; the defendant is in possession of his own land, and he cannot be expected to abandon it or to keep the building unfinished.[216] Similarly, where repairs were agreed to be made to the defendant's chattel, the mere fact that he accepted the return of the chattel and used it does not of itself raise the implication that he agreed to pay for the actual repairs done to it despite the fact that the contractual obligation of the repairer had been only partially completed.[217] However, where a builder abandoned work under an "entire contract", but left materials on the site, it was held that he could recover a reasonable sum for the value of these materials when the owner used them to complete the building.[218] The owner had a choice whether or not to use the materials, which could have been returned to the builder.

Defendant preventing complete performance. If the other party to the contract wrongfully prevents the claimant from completing his performance, the claimant may either recover damages for breach of contract, or alternatively sue upon a quantum meruit to recover a reasonable remuneration for his partial performance.[219] **21–036**

Divisible (or severable) obligations. The question whether an obligation is entire or divisible depends on its construction in the light of all the circumstances.[220] In a divisible or severable obligation there is an express or implied agreement that payment will be made in proportion to the extent of performance. If the obligation is held to be divisible (as in the case of a contract to deliver goods by instalments at stated intervals, the price being fixed per item), the obligation to pay for a divisible part of the performance[221] is independent of the performance of other parts of the contract.[222] Blackburn J., speaking of a contract to work other materials into the defendant's property, said[223]: **21–037**

"Bricks built into a wall become part of the house; thread stitched into a coat which is under repair, or planks and nails and pitch worked into a ship under repair, become part of the coat or the ship; and therefore, generally and in the absence of something to show a contrary intention, the bricklayer, or tailor or shipwright is to be paid for the work and

---

214 s.30(1) of the Sale of Goods Act 1979 (see Vol.II, para.43–286). cf. *Hoenig v Isaacs* [1952] 2 All E.R. 176, 179–180, 181 (defendant used defective furniture made by plaintiff).

215 *Sumpter v Hedges* [1898] 1 Q.B. 673.

216 [1898] 1 Q.B. 673, 676.

217 *Forman & Co Proprietary Ltd v Liddesdale* [1900] A.C. 190.

218 *Sumpter v Hedges* [1898] 1 Q.B. 673.

219 *Planché v Colburn* (1831) 8 Bing. 14 (discussed below, para.29–066, where other authorities are cited).

220 See above, paras 21–001, 21–027; below, paras 23–091, 24–042—24–043.

221 The "entire obligation" rule applies to each part *viz.* the payment for each part is due only from completed performance of that part of the payee's obligations.

222 *Roberts v Havelock* (1832) 3 B. & Ad. 404; *Taylor v Laird* (1856) 1 H. & N. 266. cf. *Rosenthal & Sons Ltd v Esmail* [1965] 1 W.L.R. 1117; Vol.II, paras 43–293 et seq. See also Smith's *Leading Cases*, 13th edn, pp.1, 9 et seq.

223 *Appleby v Myers* (1867) L.R. 2 C.P. 651, 660–661.

materials he has done and provided, although the whole work is not complete. It is not material whether in such a case the non-completion is because the shipwright did not choose to go on with the work. . . ."[224]

21–038 **Independent promises.** Analogous to "divisible obligations" are the "independent promises" to be found mainly in the law of landlord and tenant, e.g. the rule that the tenant's promise to pay rent is independent of the landlord's promise to repair, so that at law the tenant cannot rely on the landlord's failure to repair as a justification for refusing to pay the rent.[225] However, under a bona fide cross-claim for damages against his landlord, the lessee may be entitled to an equitable set-off against his liability for the rent, provided the cross-claim has a sufficiently close connection with the claim for the rent.[226]

4. PAYMENT

(a) *In General*

21–039 **Payment.** All questions relating to payment of a sum of money in pursuance of a contract depend on the construction of the terms of the contract.[227] The creditor is entitled to require the payment to be made in legal currency.[228] The parties, however, may by subsequent variation,[229] waiver[230] or novation[231] substitute a different obligation from that originally undertaken, so that the original obligation of the debtor to make payment is varied or discharged. An illustration of such a discharge is a settlement of accounts, by which items on one side are agreed to be set off against items on the other side: if the two sides then balance, this is equivalent to payment on both sides[232]; if there is a balance on one side, which is paid in cash, this is likewise equivalent to payment of all sums on both sides.[233] Similarly, payment of a debt may be satisfied by the creditor agreeing to

---

[224] Citing *Roberts v Havelock* (1832) 3 B. & Ad. 404.

[225] *Taylor v Webb* [1937] 2 K.B. 283 (this decision was questioned, but on different grounds, by the House of Lords in *Regis Property Co Ltd v Dudley* [1959] A.C. 370). On the remedies of the tenant who has expended money on the repairs, see *Taylor v Beal* (1591) Cro. Eliz. 222; *Granada Theatres Ltd v Freehold Investment (Leytonstone) Ltd* [1959] Ch. 592; *Lee-Parker v Izzet* [1971] 1 W.L.R. 1688.

[226] *British Anzani (Felixstowe) Ltd v International Marine Management (UK) Ltd* [1980] Q.B. 137. See also *Melville v Grapelodge Developments Ltd* (1978) 39 P. & C.R. 179; *B.I.C.C. Plc v Burndy Corp* [1985] Ch. 232.

[227] *Re Charge Card Services Ltd* [1989] Ch. 497. See Goode, *Payment Obligations in Commercial and Financial Transactions* (1983). On questions of payment due in a foreign currency, see below, paras 30–331, 30–369—30–379.

[228] See below, para.21–086.

[229] See below, paras 22–032 et seq.

[230] See below, paras 22–040 et seq.

[231] See below, para.22–031.

[232] *Re Harmony and Montague Tin and Copper Mining Co* (1873) L.R. 8 Ch. App. 407, 414. See also *Livingstone v Whiting* (1850) 15 Q.B. 722.

[233] *Callander v Howard* (1850) 10 C.B. 290; *Re Harmony and Montague Tin and Copper Mining Co* (1873) L.R. 8 Ch. App. 407; *Larocque v Beauchemin* [1897] A.C. 358; *North Sydney Investment and Tramway Co Ltd v Higgins* [1899] A.C. 263. Where items are on one side only there is no such settlement of accounts: *Perry v Attwood* (1856) 6 E. & B. 691.

take goods in lieu of cash,[234] or to accept the method of charging the debt to a third party through the debtor's credit card,[235] or by both parties agreeing that a transfer in a banker's books from the debtor's account to the creditor's account shall amount to payment.[236] Payment of wages to a workman, however, must either be in current coin of the realm, or comply with statutory provisions.[237] An obligation to pay money can be frustrated.[238] Payment by negotiable instrument is examined below.[239]

Distinction between claims for payment of a debt and claims for damages.[240] There is an important distinction between a claim for payment of a debt and a claim for damages for breach of contract. A debt is a definite sum of money fixed by the agreement of the parties as payable by one party in return for the performance of a specified obligation by the other party or on the occurrence of some specified event or condition[241]; whereas, damages may be claimed from a party who has broken his primary contractual obligation in some way other than by failure to pay such a debt. (It is also possible that, in addition to a claim for a debt, there may be a claim for damages in respect of consequential loss caused by the failure to pay the debt at the due date.)[242] The relevance of this distinction is that rules on damages do not apply to a claim for a debt,[243] e.g. the claimant who claims payment of a debt need not prove anything more than his performance or the occurrence of the event or condition; there is no need for him to prove any actual loss suffered by him[244] as a result[245] of the defendant's failure to pay; the whole concept of the remoteness of damage[246] is therefore irrelevant; the law on penalties does not apply to the agreed sum[247]; and the claimant's duty to mitigate his loss does not generally apply.[248] 21–040

Payment by agent or third party. Where payment of a debt is made by a third person who is not jointly[249] liable (e.g. as co-contractor), the debt is not discharged unless the payment is made by the third person as agent for and on 21–041

[234] *Hands v Burton* (1808) 9 East 349; *Saxty v Wilkin* (1843) 11 M. & W. 622; *Smith v Battams* (1857) 26 L.J.Ex. 232.

[235] See below, para.21–082.

[236] *Bodenham v Purchas* (1818) 2 B. & Ald. 39. See the discussion, below, para.21–045.

[237] See Vol.II, paras 39–090—39–091.

[238] *Libyan Arab Foreign Bank v Bankers Trust Co* [1989] Q.B. 728, 749 but note the criticisms levelled against this proposition by Mann, *The Legal Aspect of Money*, 5th edn, pp.68 and 418. The current edition of Mann, 6th edn (2005), paras 3.04–3.05 does, however, recognise that frustration may have a limited role to play in such cases.

[239] See below, paras 21–073 et seq.

[240] See below, paras 26–009, 26–136; *Jervis v Harris* [1996] Ch. 195, 206–207. Payment in full of a debt extinguishes the creditor's cause of action: *Edmunds v Lloyd's Italic, etc. SpA* [1986] 1 W.L.R. 492, 495. (On interest, see below, paras 26–167—26–184.)

[241] See below, para.26–009 fn.55.

[242] See *Trans Trust SPRL v Danubian Trading Co Ltd* [1952] 2 Q.B. 297; *Wadsworth v Lydall* [1981] 1 W.L.R. 598; see generally, below, paras 26–098—26–099.

[243] See below, paras 26–009, 26–136, for a fuller discussion of these and other distinctions.

[244] See below, paras 26–001, 26–008.

[245] On causation, see below, paras 26–032 et seq.

[246] See below, paras 26–051 et seq.

[247] See below, para.26–125.

[248] See below, para.26–101.

[249] Or jointly and severally liable. On joint liability, see above, paras 17–001 et seq.

account of the debtor, and with his prior authority or subsequent ratification.[250] Even after the creditor has sued for the debt, the debtor can ratify such a payment by pleading payment.[251] Where payment is made by a third person on behalf of the debtor but without his authority, the creditor and the person who made the payment may together rescind the transaction at any time before the debtor has ratified the payment; the creditor may repay the money to the third person and thereupon the payment is at an end, so that the debtor cannot later purport to ratify the payment; the debtor therefore becomes again responsible.[252] The payment of a debt by one of a number of joint (or joint and several) debtors discharges all the debtors.[253]

21–042 **Payment to a third party.** If the creditor requests the debtor to pay the debt to a third party, such a payment is equivalent to payment direct to the creditor, and is a good discharge of the debt.[254]

21–043 **Payment to agent.** If payment is made to an agent of the creditor, this discharges the debt if it is made in the ordinary course of business, before the creditor demands payment to himself,[255] and while the agent has actual or ostensible authority from the creditor to receive the payment.[256] Payment to an ostensible agent, who is in fact without actual authority to receive the payment, is a valid discharge of the debt, e.g. where money is paid to a person apparently entrusted with the conduct of the creditor's business.[257] There is no general rule that an agent who is authorised to sell on behalf of his principal is also authorised to receive the purchase-money.[258] A solicitor has implied authority to receive payment of a debt for which he is instructed to sue[259]; he also has authority to

---

[250] *James v Isaacs* (1852) 12 C.B. 791; *Simpson v Eggington* (1855) 10 Exch. 845, 847; *Lucas v Wilkinson* (1856) 1 H. & N. 420; *Walter v James* (1871) L.R. 6 Ex. 124; *Purcell v Henderson* (1885) 16 L.R.Ir. 213, 223, 224; *Keighley, Maxsted & Co v Durant* [1901] A.C. 240; *Re Rowe* [1904] 2 K.B. 483; *Smith v Cox* [1940] 2 K.B. 558; *Owen v Tate* [1976] 1 Q.B. 402. *Pacific Associates Inc v Baxter* [1990] 1 Q.B. 993, 1033–1034; *Pacific and General Insurance Co Ltd v Hazell* [1997] L.R.L.R. 65, 79–80. See below, para.29–115, and Vol.II, paras 31–026—31–033, especially para.31–033; and Goff and Jones, *The Law of Restitution*, 7th edn (2007), para.1–018, fn.16; Birks and Beatson (1976) 92 L.Q.R. 188. cf. Burrows, *The Law of Restitution*, 2nd edn (2002), pp.293–302 and Friedmann (1983) 99 L.Q.R. 534. The authority of the debtor will often be presumed: see *Bennett v Griffin Finance* [1967] 2 QB 46 (Vol.II, para.38–309) and below, paras 29–113—29–119.

[251] *Belshaw v Bush* (1851) 11 C.B. 191.

[252] *Walter v James* (1871) L.R. 6 Ex. 124, 128.

[253] See above, para.17–014.

[254] *Roper v Bunford* (1810) 3 Taunt. 76; *Page v Meek* (1862) 32 L.J.Q.B. 4; cf. *Commercial Bank of Australia Ltd v Wilson & Co's Estate* [1893] A.C. 181. On payment into the creditor's bank account, see below, para.21–045; on payment by credit or charge card, see below, para.21–082.

[255] *Sanderson v Bell* (1834) 2 C. & M. 304.

[256] See Vol.II, paras 31–042—31–049.

[257] *Barrett v Deere* (1828) Moo. & M. 200; *Wilmott v Smith* (1828) Moo. & M. 238; *Bocking Garage v Mazurk* [1954] C.L.Y. 14. The claimant's wife may be so authorised: *Offley v Clay* (1840) 2 M. & G. 172. cf. *Galbraith and Grant Ltd v Block* [1922] 2 K.B. 155 (delivery of goods at buyer's premises to a person having ostensible authority to receive them).

[258] *Drakeford v Piercy* (1866) 7 B. & S. 515; *International Sponge Importers Ltd v Andrew Watt & Sons* [1911] A.C. 279; *Linck, Moeller & Co v Jameson & Co* (1885) 2 T.L.R. 206; *Butwick v Grant* [1924] 2 K.B. 483. Custom, however, may affect the agent's authority: *Catterall v Hindle* (1867) L.R. 2 C.P. 368 (broker).

[259] *Yates v Freckleton* (1781) 2 Dougl. 623; *Weary v Alderson* (1837) 2 M. & Rob. 127 (implied authority to receive payment extends to solicitor's London agent who issues the writ).

receive the consideration money for a deed when he produces it, if it contains a receipt for such money and is duly executed by the person entitled to give a receipt for the money.[260]

Payment to agent otherwise than in cash. The creditor's right to payment is not affected by a set-off which his debtor may have against the creditor's agent[261] unless this mode of dealing is sanctioned by a usage known to the creditor,[262] or the creditor allowed his agent to sell as apparent principal.[263] Nor can the debtor discharge his debt to the creditor by writing off a debt due to the debtor from the creditor's agent.[264] Prima facie, an agent who is authorised to receive payment (e.g. an auctioneer) has authority only to receive it in cash[265]; such an agent cannot bind his principal by accepting a bill of exchange without the express authority of the principal.[266] If such an agent in fact accepts a cheque and cashes it, or the proceeds are collected by his bank, that amounts to a payment in cash.[267] On the other hand, a principal who desires to authorise an agent to receive payment by cheque only and not in cash must plainly notify third parties dealing with his agent of the exact extent of the agent's authority; thus a notification that cheques drawn in payment must be drawn in a particular form does not exclude the presumption that payment may lawfully be made to the agent in cash and not by cheque at all.[268] 21–044

Payment or transfer into a bank account.[269] Where the creditor instructs the debtor to pay a sum due to him by making a payment to the credit of a specified bank account, the creditor has made the bank his agent to receive the payment, which is made as soon as the bank receives payment in cash, or by means of a banker's cheque,[270] draft, payment order or transfer which is treated 21–045

[260] Law of Property Act 1925 s.69; *King v Smith* [1900] 2 Ch. 425. See also Trustee Act 1925 s.23(3)(a).

[261] *Bartlett v Pentland* (1830) 10 B. & C. 760; *Barker v Greenwood* (1837) 2 Y. & C. Ex. 414; *Pearson v Scott* (1878) 9 Ch D 198; *Anderson v Sutherland* (1897) 2 Com. Cas. 65; *Matvieff v Crossfield* (1903) 8 Com. Cas. 120.

[262] *Scott v Irving* (1830) 1 B. & Ad. 605; *Stewart v Aberdein* (1838) 4 M. & W. 211; *Sweeting v Pearce* (1861) 9 C.B.(N.S.) 534; *Catterall v Hindle* (1867) L.R. 2 C.P. 368.

[263] *Cooke & Sons v Eshelby* (1887) 12 App. Cas. 271; *Ex p. Dixon* (1876) 4 Ch D 133 (factor selling in his own name); *Borries v Imperial Ottoman Bank* (1873) L.R. 9 C.P. 38; see Vol.II, para.31–070; cf. *Greer v Downs Supply Co* [1927] 2 K.B. 28.

[264] *Underwood v Nicholls* (1855) 17 C.B. 239; *Pearson v Scott* (1878) 9 Ch D 198.

[265] *Sweeting v Pearce* (1861) 9 C.B.(N.S.) 534, 540; *Blumberg v Life Interests and Reversionary Securities Corp* [1897] 1 Ch. 171; [1898] 1 Ch. 27. Such an agent has no authority to receive payment in other goods: *Howard v Chapman* (1831) 4 C. & P. 508; nor is a credit to the agent payment to his principal: *Crossley v Magnac* [1893] 1 Ch. 594. See also Vol.II, para.31–050.

[266] *Sykes v Giles* (1839) 5 M. & W. 645; *Williams v Evans* (1866) L.R. 1 Q.B. 352; *Hogarth v Wherley* (1875) L.R. 10 C.P. 630.

[267] *Bridges v Garrett* (1870) L.R. 5 C.P. 451; *Charles v Blackwell* (1877) 2 C.P.D. 151; *Walker v Barker* (1900) 16 T.L.R. 393; *Robinson v Marsh* [1921] 2 K.B. 640, 644; *Clay Hill Brick & Tile Co Ltd v Rawlings* [1938] 4 All E.R. 100; cf. *Pape v Westacott* [1894] 1 Q.B. 272 (cheque dishonoured).

[268] *International Sponge Importers Ltd v Watt & Sons* [1911] A.C. 279; cf. *Bradford & Sons v Price Bros* (1923) 92 L.J.K.B. 871.

[269] Goode, *Payment Obligations in Commercial and Financial Transactions* (1983), pp.90 et seq. See also King (1982) 45 M.L.R. 369; and below, Vol.II, paras 34–402 et seq.

[270] On receipt of the debtor's own cheque, or other negotiable instrument, as conditional payment, see below, para.21–074.

by banks as equivalent to cash.[271] When the contract requires "payment in cash" to be made into the payee's bank account, but the parties obviously do not expect the payment to be literally in cash (i.e. in pounds sterling, dollar bills or other legal tender), the payment or credit to the payee's account must be "the equivalent of cash, or as good as cash",[272] that is, by:

> "... any commercially recognised method of transferring funds the result of which is to give the transferee the [unfettered or unrestricted] right to the immediate use of the funds transferred."[273]

Thus, where a Telex credit transfer was made to the payee's bank account, and was treated as irrevocable under an Italian inter-bank scheme, but interest on the funds credited would not begin to run in favour of the payee until four days later, the House of Lords held[274] that "payment in cash" had not been made by the book entry of the receiving bank. "Payment in cash" meant that the payee whose account was credited must be able to use it immediately, e.g. by immediate transfer to a deposit account where it would earn interest; the fact that the receiving bank would allow the payee immediately to draw on the credit, but subject to his paying interest during the four days, did not make it equivalent to cash, since that arrangement was merely the equivalent of an overdraft facility.[275]

21–046 The point of time at which a transfer or credit payment into a bank account is "made" has been discussed, but not finally decided, in another House of Lords case,[276] where "payment in cash" was required by the contract. The payment was made by a payment order from another bank, under the provisions of an inter-bank settlement scheme, where the system of processing might have taken 24 hours before the payee's account was credited. Lord Salmon, without deciding the point:

> "... inclined to think that ... there is no real difference between a payment in dollar bills and a payment by payment orders which in the banking world are generally regarded and accepted as cash"[277]

(which view Lord Russell was also inclined to accept[278]); but Lord Fraser thought that the payment must be made "in sufficient time to allow for the period

---

[271] *A/S Awilco of Oslo v Fulvia SpA Di Navigazione of Cagliari (The Chikuma)* [1981] 1 W.L.R. 314 (see Vol.II, para.34–407); *The Brimnes (Tenax S.S. Co Ltd v The Brimnes (Owners))* [1975] Q.B. 929, 948, 964–965, 968–969.

[272] *The Chikuma* [1981] 1 W.L.R. 314, 320.

[273] *The Brimnes* [1973] 1 W.L.R. 386, 400 (approved by the House of Lords in *The Chikuma* [1981] 1 W.L.R. 314, 318–320, with the substitution of "unfettered or unrestricted" for "unconditional" as the adjective before "right"). The decision of the Court of Appeal in *The Brimnes* is reported at [1975] Q.B. 929.

[274] *The Chikuma* [1981] 1 WL.R. 314.

[275] [1981] 1 W.L.R. 314. (But see the criticism by Mann (1981) 97 L.Q.R. 379.)

[276–277] *Mardorf Peach & Co Ltd v Attica Sea Carriers Corp of Liberia* [1977] A.C. 850.

[278] [1977] A.C. 850, 889.

of processing normally required for the method of payment they had chosen".[279]

Payment by "in-house" transfer. In the case of "in-house" payments (viz, a transfer from one customer's account to another's within the same bank), the payment is made as soon as the bank accepts the payer's instructions and credits the payee's account; in other words, the payment is "made" as soon as the bank has set in motion the bank's internal process for crediting the payee's account (e.g. by preparing the instructions for the bank's computer) and before the payee receives any notice that this has been done.[280] Thus, where a bank received a Telex instruction (or "transfer order") from a customer to debit his account and to credit another customer's account, the payment was made when the staff of the bank accepted the instruction and marked the appropriate documents in the bank.[281] 21–047

Where payment must be to agent. There may be cases where payment must be made to the agent, and cannot validly be made to the principal, e.g. where an auctioneer has an unsatisfied lien on the proceeds of goods sold by him, it is no defence to an action by him for the price[282] that the buyer had paid the principal, unless the contract of sale permitted payment direct to the principal.[283] The same rule applies where the auctioneer has acted on the faith of an agreement between himself and the principal that the proceeds of the sale shall be disposed of in a particular way.[284] The buyer may rely upon any defence or set-off that he may have against the principal in respect of that part of the amount claimed by the auctioneer which, if recovered, he would be bound to hand over to the principal.[285] 21–048

Payment to joint creditors, partners, trustees, etc. The payment of a debt to one of a number of joint creditors discharges a debt owed to them jointly.[286] Similarly, as partnership is founded on agency, payment to one of a number of partners to whom a debt is jointly owed binds them all, even after a dissolution of the partnership: this position holds even where the debtor had notice before payment that the partners had appointed a third person to collect the debts due to 21–049

---

[279] [1977] A.C. 850, 885. (The other Lords did not deal with this point.) See also *Afovos Shipping Co SA v Romano Pagnan and Pietro Pagnan* [1983] 1 W.L.R. 195, 202, 204.

[280] *Momm v Barclays Bank International Ltd* [1977] Q.B. 790 (following *The Brimnes* [1973] 1 W.L.R. 386; and *Eyles v Ellis* (1827) 4 Bing. 112); *Royal Products Ltd v Midland Bank Ltd* [1981] 2 Lloyd's Rep. 194.

[281] *The Brimnes* [1975] Q.B. 929, 948–951, 963–966, 969. (The mere receipt of the Telex message does not constitute payment, since it is not a negotiable instrument: 949, 965, 969.)

[282] An auctioneer's special property in the goods entrusted to him entitles him to sue in his own name for the price of the goods: *Williams v Millington* (1788) 1 H.Bl. 81; *Benton v Campbell, Parker & Co Ltd* [1925] 2 K.B. 410, 416.

[283] *Robinson v Rutter* (1855) 4 E. & B. 954. See Macintyre, *The Law relating to Auctioneers and Estate Agents* (1957), pp.180–184; Harvey and Meisel, *Auctions Law and Practice*, 2nd edn (1995), pp.56–62.

[284] *Manley & Sons Ltd v Berkett* [1912] 2 K.B. 329.

[285] *Grice v Kenrick* (1870) L.R. 5 Q.B. 340; *Manley Sons Ltd v Berkett* [1912] 2 K.B. 329.

[286] *Wallace v Kelsall* (1840) 7 M. & W. 264; *Husband v Davis* (1851) 10 C.B. 645; *Powell v Brodhurst* [1901] 2 Ch. 160; *Barrett v Universal Island Records Ltd* [2006] EWHC 1009 (Ch), [2006] E.M.L.R. 21 at [214].

the firm, unless there is something in the notice which expressly takes away the right of the one partner to receive the money.[287] Payment of a debt to one of two trustees is a good discharge as to both.[288] But where bankers pay to one of several trustees money which should be held in their joint account, the bankers are not discharged as against the other trustees unless they authorised such payment[289]; for where money is paid into a bank on the joint account of persons who are not partners, the bankers are not discharged by payment to one of those persons without the authority of the others.[290] Payment of a debt to one of several executors or administrators is a good discharge[291]; and by the Administration of Estates Act 1925 s.27(2), where a representation[292] is revoked all payments and dispositions made in good faith to a personal representative[293] before the revocation are a valid discharge to the person making the same.[294]

21–050 **Bankruptcy.** Payments made to a bankrupt before the date of the bankruptcy order are considered in Ch.20.[295] The trustee in bankruptcy is empowered to give receipts for any money received by him, which receipts "effectually discharge the person paying the money from all responsibility in respect of its application".[296]

21–051 **Payment under a third party debt order.** Under CPR Pt 72, the court may, upon the application of any person who has obtained a judgment or order for the recovery or payment of money, order that all debts owing or accruing from some third person (known as a third party debt order[297]) to the judgment debtor shall be attached to answer the judgment or order. By CPR Pt 72.9, it is provided that payment made by or execution levied upon the garnishee under a final third party order[298] shall be a valid discharge to him as against the judgment debtor to the extent of the amount paid or levied, notwithstanding that the third party debt order is subsequently set aside or the judgment or order reversed. Moreover, this is not a mere rule of procedure. Payment under a third party debt order issued by

[287] *Porter & Bristow v Taylor* (1817) 6 M. & S. 156. But payment to the firm of a separate debt due to one partner is not payment of the debt unless the firm was authorised to receive it: *Powell v Brodhurst* [1901] 2 Ch. 160. See further *Lindley and Banks on Partnership*, 18th edn (2002), paras 12–58—12–59.

[288] *Husband v Davis* (1851) 10 C.B. 645.

[289] *Stone v Marsh* (1826) Ry. & M. 364, 369.

[290] *Innes v Stephenson* (1831) 1 Moo. & Rob. 145. cf. the similar rule in the case of Bank of England stock: *Welch v The Bank of England* [1955] Ch. 508.

[291] *Can v Read* (1749) 3 Atk. 695; *Jacomb v Harwood* (1751) 2 Ves. Sen. 265, 267; *Charlton v Durham* (1869) L.R. 4 Ch. App. 433.

[292] "Representation" and "personal representative" mean probate or administration and executor or administrator: Administration of Estates Act 1925 s.55(1)(xi) and (xx).

[293] s.55(1)(xi) and (xx).

[294] cf. cases before statutory provision: *Allen v Dundas* (1789) 3 T.R. 125; *Prosser v Wagner* (1856) 1 C.B.(N.S.) 289.

[295] Above, paras 21–018 et seq.

[296] Para.10 of Pt II of Sch.5 to the Insolvency Act 1986 (by virtue of s.314). Section 306 provides for the bankrupt's estate to vest in the trustee.

[297] Previously known as a garnishee order. See further N. Andrews, *English Civil Procedure* (2003), paras 39.26—39.38.

[298] cf. a payment made under a private arrangement: *Turner v Jones* (1857) 1 H. & N. 878; or a payment made on an order nisi: *Re Webster* [1907] 1 K.B. 623.

a competent court discharges the third party from any further liability anywhere,[299] provided that it is shown that payment was made under the compulsion of that order.[300] No third party debt order will be made where there is a substantial risk that the third party will be called on to pay the debt over again, e.g. by the court of a foreign country.[301]

Amount to be paid. Apart from subsequent variation by agreement,[302] accord and satisfaction[303] or the operation of promissory estoppel,[304] the payment of part of a liquidated sum of money due to the creditor is not a discharge of the whole debt,[305] even though the creditor purports to release the remaining obligation, since there is no consideration for the release.[306] If there is no liquidated sum due, and the amount is uncertain or disputed, payment of any sum subsequently agreed upon by the parties will constitute an accord and satisfaction.[307] 21–052

Time of payment. The time when payment is due to be made is a question of construction of the contractual terms.[308] Sometimes the time for payment must be implied from the circumstances of the contract: thus, where the claimant contracts to work upon the defendant's materials, and no time is fixed for payment of the agreed cost, the defendant must pay as soon as the claimant has completed the work and given the defendant a reasonable opportunity of seeing that the work has been properly done.[309] Money which is repayable on demand must be ready to be handed over to the creditor as soon as he demands it from the debtor: the only time which the creditor needs to give the debtor is time to get the money from some convenient place,[310] not time in which to negotiate a deal or a loan 21–053

---

[299] *Swiss Bank Corp v Boemische Industrial Bank* [1923] 1 K.B. 673 (distinguishing *Martin v Nadel* [1906] 2 K.B. 26). See also *Westoby v Day* (1853) 2 E. & B. 605; cf. *Turnbull v Robertson* (1878) 47 L.J.C.P. 294.

[300] *Gould v Webb* (1855) 4 E. & B. 933; *Turner v Jones* (1857) 1 H. & N. 878; *Wood v Dunn* (1866) L.R. 2 Q.B. 73.

[301] *Martin v Nadel* [1906] 2 K.B. 26; *Employers' Liability Assurance Corp Ltd v Sedgwick Collins & Co Ltd* [1927] A.C. 95; *Société Eram Shipping Co Ltd v Compagnie Internationale de Navigation* [2003] UKHL 30, [2004] 1 A.C. 260.

[302] Below, paras 22–032 et seq.

[303] Below, paras 22–012 et seq.

[304] Above, paras 3–085—3–102; cf. below, paras 22–040 et seq.

[305] Below, paras 22–016—22–018.

[306] Above, paras 3–115 et seq.

[307] Below, para.22–012; above, paras 3–046 et seq.

[308] See above, paras 12–041 et seq., 21–011 et seq.; below, para.21–089. In *Mardorf Peach & Co Ltd v Attica Sea Carriers Corp of Liberia* [1977] A.C. 850 it was assumed that payment due to be made into a banking account on a date which turned out to be a non-banking day must be made not later than the previous banking day. See also above, para.21–022 fn.144.

[309] *Hughes v Lenny* (1839) 5 M. & W. 183. In the case of a divisible obligation (above, para.21–037) where no time for payment has been fixed, the person performing the work may be entitled to claim payment for parts of the work already completed: *Roberts v Havelock* (1832) 3 B. & Ad. 404; *The Tergeste* [1903] P. 26.

[310] *Toms v Wilson* (1862) 4 B. & S. 442, 453 ("[H]e must have a reasonable time to get it from some convenient place. For instance, he might require time to get it from his desk, or to go across the street or to his bankers for it.") (approved in *Moore v Shelley* (1883) 8 App. Cas. 285, 293). The reasonableness of the opportunity given to a debtor (who is required to pay on demand) may depend on the debtor's knowledge (or means of knowledge) of the amount due, and on the information supplied by the creditor: *Bunbury Foods Pty Ltd v National Bank of Australia Ltd* (1984) 153 C.L.R. 491 High Ct of Aust.

which he hopes will produce the money.[311] The rules discussed above[312] as to exact compliance with the time fixed for performance of the contract apply to the time fixed for payment. It is therefore only in three cases recognised by equity[313] that a failure to make the payment on the fixed date amounts to a repudiatory breach of contract entitling the other party to terminate the contract. By s.10(1) of the Sale of Goods Act 1979, it is expressly enacted that unless a different intention appears from the terms of a contract for the sale of goods, stipulations as to time of payment are not of the essence of the contract.[314]

21–054 **Place of payment.** Where the place of payment is specified by the contract, the debtor must tender payment at that place in order to discharge his obligation.[315] Where no place of payment is expressly or impliedly specified by the contract, the general rule is that it is the debtor's duty to seek the creditor in order to pay him at his place of business or residence, if it is in England[316]; but the rule is not applicable to large employers of labour who maintain a regular pay-day and pay office.[317] Unless there is evidence of a contrary intention, the place for payment of a debt is the business place or residence of the creditor at the date when the debt was contracted.[318] If the contract specifies alternative places for payment, it is the duty of the party entitled to select the place to notify the other party; if it is for the creditor to select, there is no default in payment until he notifies the debtor which place of payment he selects.[319]

21–055 **Mode of payment.** Except where he has expressly or impliedly agreed to do so, the creditor is under no obligation to accept a negotiable instrument (such as a bill, note or cheque) in payment of the debt.[320] If the creditor does accept payment in this way, the effect upon the existence of the debt depends on the circumstances, and is discussed in detail in a separate section.[321]

---

[311] *R.A. Cripps & Son Ltd v Wickenden* [1973] 1 W.L.R. 944, 955. See also *Brighty v Norton* (1862) 3 B. & S. 305, 312; *Toms v Wilson* (1862) 4 B. & S. 442.

[312] Above, paras 21–011 et seq.

[313] Above, paras 21–011—21–017.

[314] Contrast stipulations as to the time of delivery, above, para.21–013 fn.80.

[315] Except where there is waiver or variation of the obligation to pay at the specified place: see below, paras 22–032—22–046; *Gyles v Hall* (1726) 2 P. Wms. 378 (debtor gave creditor notice of his intention to pay at a specified time and place; creditor made no objection, and therefore waived personal tender anywhere else).

[316] *Robey & Co v Snaefell Mining Co Ltd* (1887) 20 QBD 152; *The Eider* [1893] P. 119, 128; *Thompson v Palmer* [1893] 2 Q.B. 80; *Charles Duval & Co Ltd v Gans* [1904] 2 K.B. 685; *Fowler v Midland Electric Corp for Power Distribution Ltd* [1917] 1 Ch. 656. The general rule applies to a tenant: *Haldane v Johnson* (1853) 8 Exch. 689; also where the creditor was out of England when the contract was made, but not where the creditor left England after the date: *Fessard v Mugnier* (1865) 18 C.B.(N.S.) 286.

[317] *Riley v William Holland & Sons Ltd* [1911] 1 K.B. 1029, 1031.

[318] *Rein v Stein* [1892] 1 Q.B. 753, 758; *Charles Duval & Co Ltd v Gans* [1904] 2 K.B. 685; *Drexel v Drexel* [1916] 1 Ch. 251, 259, 260.

[319] *Thorn v City Rice Mills* (1889) 40 Ch D 357; cf. *Re Escalera Silver Lead Mining Co* (1908) 25 T.L.R. 87; *Re Harris Calculating Machine Co* [1914] 1 Ch. 920.

[320] See below, para.21–087. On payment by bankers' commercial credit, see Vol.II, paras 34–423 et seq., para.43–270. On payment into the creditor's bank account, see above, para.21–045.

[321] Below, paras 21–073—21–081.

Loss in post. Where a banknote, a cheque or other negotiable instrument is sent to the creditor by post, this does not normally amount to payment if it is lost in the post.[322] Where, however, a creditor expressly or impliedly authorises his debtor to transmit the amount of the debt by cheque through the post, the debtor is discharged if he complies with the authority by sending the cheque in a letter properly addressed to the creditor, even though it does not reach him.[323] The necessary authority is not to be implied from the mere fact that the previous course of dealing between the parties has been to send cheques by post,[324] though very little evidence of authority is required in addition to evidence of such a course of dealing. A request for a remittance by post amounts to an authority to send the sum in question by post in such a form as is appropriate to its amount. To send (in 1916) a sum as large as £48 in banknotes, even in a registered letter, was held to be unusual and inappropriate[325] and so was the sending by post of an uncrossed bearer cheque.[326] 21–056

Expressly or impliedly authorised mode. A particular mode of payment may be expressly or impliedly authorised by the contract[327]: thus where there is an automatic slot gas meter, payment is effectively made when coins are placed in the meter, as this is the mode of payment authorised by the supplier of the gas; if the money is subsequently stolen without the negligence of the payer, he is not liable.[328] Similarly, payment by credit or charge card may be a method of payment accepted by the creditor.[329] In a contract for the self-service supply of petrol, the garage undertakes to accept a particular charge card in payment if it displays a notice of its willingness to do so.[330] 21–057

Proof of payment: receipts. A payment may be proved by any evidence[331] but the usual method of proof is the production of a receipt[332] signed by the 21–058

---

[322] *Luttges v Sherwood* (1895) 11 T.L.R. 233; *Pennington v Crossley & Son* (1897) 77 L.T. 43; *Baker v Lipton Ltd* (1899) 15 T.L.R. 435; *Warnborough Ltd v Garmite Ltd* [2006] EWHC 10 (Ch) at [84], [93]. The fact that payment is usually made through the post is insufficient of itself to show that the creditor has assumed the risk of loss in the post.

[323] *Norman v Ricketts* (1886) 3 T.L.R. 182 (the cheque reached the hands of a third person who received payment); *Thairlwall v Great Northern Ry* [1910] 2 K.B. 509 (dividend warrant lost in the post; the stockholder would probably have been able to obtain another warrant under s.69 of the Bills of Exchange Act 1882 (see Vol.II, para.34–146) or to have brought an action on the warrant); but cf. *Tankexpress A/S v Compagnie Financière Belges des Petroles SA* [1949] A.C. 76 (letter delayed in the post); *Zim Israel Navigation Co Ltd v Effy Shipping Corp* [1972] 1 Lloyd's Rep 18 (affirmed [1972] 2 Lloyd's Rep. 91). cf. posting a letter giving notice of dishonour of a bill: *Walter v Haynes* (1824) Ry & M. 149; *Berridge v Fitzgerald* (1869) L.R. 4 Q.B. 639.

[324] *Pennington v Crossley & Son* (1897) 77 L.T. 43.

[325] *Mitchell-Henry v Norwich Union Life Insurance Society* [1918] 2 K.B. 67.

[326] *Robb v Gow* (1905) 8 F. 90 Court of Session.

[327] See above, para.21–045.

[328] *Edmundson v Longton Corp* (1902) 19 T.L.R. 15.

[329] See below, para.21–082.

[330] *Re Charge Card Services Ltd* [1989] Ch. 497.

[331] *Eyles v Ellis* (1827) 4 Bing. 112; *Mountford v Harper* (1847) 16 L.J.Ex. 184 (proceeds of cheque drawn by debtor received by creditor); *Gadderer v Dawes* (1847) 10 L.T.(O.S.) 109; *Douglas v Lloyds Bank Ltd* (1929) 34 Com. Cas. 263 (payment presumed from lapse of time where no explanation given for the delay: cf. *Cooper v Turner* (1819) 2 Stark. 497).

[332] The practice of giving receipts for ordinary debts paid by cheque has been largely discontinued since the enactment of s.3 of the Cheques Act 1957 which provides: "An unindorsed cheque which

creditor or his agent. A receipt is not conclusive but only prima facie evidence that the money has been paid.[333] Evidence may be given of the intention with which it was handed over[334] and of the circumstances generally[335]: thus a receipt given "in full discharge" does not exclude an implied agreement to pay interest not covered by the receipt.[336] Again, the effect of a receipt may be destroyed by proof that it was obtained by fraud or under a mistake of fact,[337] or that it formed part of a transaction which was merely colourable, because no money had in fact been paid.[338] Where, however, a document containing a receipt clause is relied on by third parties, different considerations prevail, and the person signing the document may be estopped, as against third parties, from denying receipt of the money.[339] A receipt may be in any form so long as the words are express.[340] A receipt for consideration money or securities in the body of a deed is a sufficient discharge for the same, without any further receipt being indorsed on the deed.[341] It is no longer necessary for a receipt to be stamped.[342]

(b) *Appropriation of Payments*

21–059 **Rights to appropriate payments.** Where several separate debts are due from the debtor to the creditor, the debtor may, when making a payment, appropriate the money paid to a particular debt or debts, and if the creditor accepts the payment so appropriated, he must apply it in the manner directed by the debtor[343]; if, however, the debtor makes no appropriation when making the payment, the creditor may do so.[344]

---

appears to have been paid by the banker on whom it is drawn is evidence of the receipt by the payee of the sum payable by the cheque."

[333] *Straton v Rastall* (1788) 2 T.R. 366; *Hawkins v Gardiner* (1854) 2 Sm. & G. 441; *Wilson v Keating* (1859) 27 Beav. 121.

[334] e.g. in full satisfaction of all claims: *Lee v Lancashire & Yorkshire Ry* (1871) L.R. 6 Ch. App. 527; *Ellen v G. N. Ry* (1901) 17 T.L.R. 453; cf. *Oliver v Nautilus Steam Shipping Co Ltd* [1903] 2 K.B. 639.

[335] e.g. *Graves v Key* (1832) 3 B. & Ad. 313.

[336] *Re W.W. Duncan & Co* [1905] 1 Ch. 307; cf. *Nathan v Ogdens Ltd* (1905) 94 L.T. 126.

[337] *Skaife v Jackson* (1824) 3 B. & C. 421; *Farrar v Hutchinson* (1839) 9 A. & E. 641; *Cesarini v Ronzani* (1858) 1 F. & F. 339; *Ward & Co v Wallis* [1900] 1 Q.B. 675.

[338] *Bowes v Foster* (1858) 2 H. & N. 779.

[339] *Rimmer v Webster* [1902] 2 Ch. 163; *Powell v Browne* [1907] W.N. 228; *Tsang Chuen v Li Po Kwai* [1932] A.C. 715.

[340] Sometimes the form is statutory as in the Bills of Sale Act (1878) Amendment Act 1882 s.9. See *Burchell v Thompson* [1920] 2 K.B. 80.

[341] Law of Property Act 1925 s.67.

[342] As from February 1, 1971, the former stamp duty of 2d. on a receipt for £2. or more was abolished by the Finance Act 1970 s.32 and Sch.7 para.2. (For the position when an unstamped receipt dated before that date is tendered in evidence, see s.14 of the Stamp Act 1891; *Sergeant and Sims on Stamp Duties*, para.1423).

[343] It is not open to a creditor to defeat a debtor's appropriation by challenging it, or disagreeing with it, before or after the payment is made, if he has not refused the payment or returned it within a reasonable time: *Thomas v Ken Thomas Ltd* [2006] EWCA Civ 1504 at [21], [22], [28].

[344] *Peters v Anderson* (1814) 5 Taunt. 596; *Simson v Ingham* (1823) 2 B. & C. 65; *Cory Bros & Co Ltd v Owners of Turkish S.S. "Mecca"* [1897] A.C. 286; *West Bromwich Building Society v Crammer* [2002] EWHC 2618 (Ch); *Thomas v Ken Thomas Ltd* [2006] EWCA Civ 1504 at [19]. On the appropriation of payments made under a regulated hire-purchase agreement or a conditional sale agreement, see Consumer Credit Act 1974 s.81 (see Vol.II, para.38–142).

Debtor's right to appropriate. It is essential that an appropriation by the debtor should take the form of a communication, express or implied, to the creditor of the debtor's intention to appropriate the payment to a specified debt (or debts), so that the creditor may know that his rights of appropriation as creditor cannot arise.[345] It is not essential that the debtor should expressly specify at the time of the payment, which debt or account he intended the payment to be applied to. His intention may be collected from other circumstances showing that he intended at the time of the payment to appropriate it to a specific debt or account.[346] Thus, where at the date of the payment some of his debts are statute-barred and others are not, it will be inferred (in the absence of evidence to the contrary) that the debtor appropriated the payment to the debts that were not so barred.[347] 21–060

Creditor's right to appropriate.[348] Where the debtor has not exercised his option, and the right to appropriate has therefore devolved upon the creditor,[349] he may exercise it at any time "up to the very last moment"[350] or until something happens which makes it inequitable for him to exercise it.[351] What is "the very last moment" depends on the circumstances of each case. In one instance the creditor was held entitled, in the witness-box during the course of his action, to exercise his right to appropriate a payment by his debtor, as nothing had previously happened to determine his right of election.[352] The creditor need not make his election in express terms. He may declare it by bringing an action or in any other way that makes his meaning and intention plain.[353] An entry in the creditor's books applying a payment to a particular debt does not constitute an election which will preclude the creditor from afterwards applying it to another debt, unless the entry has been communicated to the debtor.[354] Once, however, the election is made and communicated to the debtor, it is irrevocable.[355] 21–061

Creditor may not appropriate to an illegal or irrecoverable demand. The doctrine of appropriation does not entitle a creditor who receives money on 21–062

---

[345] *Leeson v Leeson* [1936] 2 K.B. 156, 161; *Stepney Corp v Osofsky* [1937] 3 All E.R. 289; *Thomas v Ken Thomas Ltd* [2006] EWCA Civ 1504 at [19].

[346] *Newmarch v Clay* (1811) 14 East 239, 244; *Shaw v Picton* (1825) 4 B. & C. 715; *Young v English* (1843) 7 Beav. 10; *Nash v Hodgson* (1855) 6 De G.M. & G. 474; *R. v Miskin Lower Justices* [1953] 1 Q.B. 533.

[347] *Nash v Hodgson* (1855) 6 De G.M. & G. 474; cf. a balance owing on a current account: *Re Footman Bower & Co Ltd* [1961] Ch. 443 (and see below, para.21–066).

[348] On the right of a secured creditor to appropriate the proceeds of sale of the security, see *Re William Hall (Contractors) Ltd* [1967] 1 W.L.R. 948.

[349] *Lowther v Heaver* (1889) 41 Ch D 248; *Potomek Construction Ltd v Zurich Securities Ltd* [2003] EWHC 2827 (Ch), [2004] 1 All E.R. (Comm) 672 at [69]. In the case of hire-purchase payments, see fn.344, above.

[350] *Cory Bros & Co v Owners of Turkish S.S. "Mecca"* [1897] A.C. 286, 294.

[351] *Thomas v Ken Thomas Ltd* [2006] EWCA Civ 1504 at [19].

[352] *Seymour v Pickett* [1905] 1 K.B. 715. See also *Smith v Betty* [1903] 2 K.B. 317.

[353] *Cory Bros & Co Ltd v Owners of Turkish S.S. "Mecca"* [1897] A.C. 286, 294.

[354] *Simson v Ingham* (1823) 2 B. & C. 65; cf. *Deeley v Lloyds Bank Ltd* [1912] A.C. 756, 783, 784.

[355] *Smith v Betty* [1903] 2 K.B. 317; *Seymour v Pickett* [1905] 1 K.B. 715; *Albermarle Supply Co Ltd v Hind & Co* [1928] 1 K.B. 307.

account from his debtor to apply it towards the satisfaction of a debt due under an illegal contract, or to a claim which does not constitute any legal or equitable demand against the debtor. Thus where the creditor makes two demands on his debtor, one arising out of a lawful contract, and the other out of an illegal contract, any payment by the debtor which is not specifically appropriated by the debtor must be applied to the lawful demand.[356]

21–063 **Appropriation to statute-barred debt.** A creditor may appropriate a payment to a debt barred by the Limitation Act 1980,[357] or to a debt which is unenforceable because of some formal defect in the contract.[358] But a creditor cannot appropriate a payment to a statute-barred debt after a judgment is given directing the ascertainment of the amount due from the debtor, excluding items which are statute-barred.[359]

21–064 **Guaranteed debt.** Where one of the debts is guaranteed by a surety, but the other is not, the ordinary rules as to appropriation apply; hence a payment by the debtor will not be appropriated to the guaranteed debt[360] unless there is evidence to show that the debtor (or failing him, the creditor) so appropriated it.[361] Thus a creditor receiving payments on account by the debtor is at liberty to appropriate them to a debt not covered by the guarantee; he is not bound by any implied contract with the surety to apply such payments in reduction of the guaranteed debt.[362]

21–065 **Instalments paid under a composition.** Where a debtor has made a composition with his creditors, and a creditor receives dividends upon a debt partly guaranteed by a third person, the dividends must not be appropriated to the excess of the debt above the sum guaranteed, but must be applied rateably to the whole debt, so that the surety is relieved from liability by the amount of the dividend on the part which is guaranteed.[363] Similarly, where the debtor has made

---

[356] *Wright v Laing* (1824) 3 B. & C. 165; *Keeping v Broom* (1895) 11 T.L.R. 595; *A. Smith & Son (Bognor Regis) Ltd v Walker* [1952] 2 Q.B. 319 (instalments paid to builder where part of the work was illegal because no licence had been granted); cf. *Lamprell v Billericay Union* (1849) 3 Exch. 283.

[357] *Mills v Fowkes* (1839) 5 Bing. N.C. 455; *Stepney Corp v Osofsky* [1937] 3 All E.R. 289. See below, para.28–128.

[358] *Cruikshanks v Rose* (1831) 1 Moo. & Rob. 100; *Philpott v Jones* (1834) 2 A. & E. 41; *Arnold v Poole Corp* (1842) 4 M. & G. 860; *Seymour v Pickett* [1905] 1 K.B. 715; *West Bromwich Building Society v Crammer* [2002] EWHC 2618 (Ch).

[359] *Smith v Betty* [1903] 2 K.B. 317.

[360] *Kirby v Duke of Marlborough* (1813) 2 M. & S. 18; *Plomer v Long* (1816) 1 Stark. 153; *Williams v Rawlinson* (1825) 3 Bing. 71; *Re Sherry* (1884) 25 Ch D 692.

[361] *Kinnaird v Webster* (1878) 10 Ch D 139; *Browning v Baldwin* (1879) 40 L.T. 248; cf. *Marryatts v White* (1817) 2 Stark. 101; *Pearl v Deacon* (1857) 1 De G. & J. 461.

[362] *Re Sherry* (1884) 25 Ch D 692.

[363] *Raikes v Todd* (1838) 8 A. & E. 846. See also *Bardwell v Lydall* (1831) 7 Bing. 489; cf. *Ellis v Emmanuel* (1876) 1 Ex. D. 157. cf. also the position in bankruptcy where the surety guarantees the whole debt, but the creditor received some payments: *Re Houlder* [1929] 1 Ch. 205 (following *Midland Banking Co v Chambers* (1869) L.R. 4 Ch. App. 398; *Re Sass* [1896] 2 Q.B. 12).

a composition with his creditors, under which instalments are payable in discharge of several debts, an instalment must be appropriated to all the debts rateably.[364] Where the creditor receives from the estate of the principal debtor a dividend on the whole of a debt payable by instalments, the surety is not entitled to have the whole of the dividend applied in discharge of any one instalment, but only rateably in part payment of each instalment as it becomes due.[365]

Current account: *Clayton's Case*. In the case of a current account, the normal presumption is that the creditor has not appropriated payments to particular items. In a current account there is "one blended fund"[366] into which all receipts and payments are carried in order of their respective dates: 21–066

> "In such a case, there is no room for any other appropriation than that which arises from the order in which the receipts and payments take place, and are carried into the account. Presumably, it is the sum first paid in, that is first drawn out. It is the first item on the debit side of the account, that is discharged, or reduced, by the first item on the credit side. The appropriation is made by the very act of setting the two items against each other."[367]

This presumption may be rebutted if a different intention can be inferred from the circumstances, e.g. by a particular mode of dealing, such as keeping separate accounts or the creation of a common fund, or by a stipulation between the parties.[368] It has also been stated that the rule is one of convenience rather than presumed intent so that it might not be applied when to do so would result in injustice or otherwise produce a solution which would be impracticable.[369]

Appropriation as between principal and interest. Where there is no appropriation by either debtor or creditor in the case of a debt bearing interest, the law will (unless a contrary intention appears) apply the payment to discharge any interest due before applying it to the earliest items of principal.[370] 21–067

---

[364] *Thompson v Hudson* (1871) L.R. 6 Ch. App. 320.

[365] *Martin v Brecknell* (1813) 2 M. & S. 39.

[366] *Clayton's Case* (1816) 1 Mer. 572, 608. See also *Bodenham v Purchas* (1818) 2 B. & Ald. 39; *Simson v Ingham* (1823) 2 B. & C. 65; *Field v Carr* (1828) 5 Bing. 13; *Hooper v Keay* (1875) 1 QBD 178; *London and County Banking Co Ltd v Ratcliffe* (1881) 6 App. Cas. 722; *Re Sherry* (1884) 25 Ch D 692, 702; *Egg v Craig* (1903) 89 L.T. 41; *Deeley v Lloyds Bank Ltd* [1912] A.C. 756; *Re Primrose (Builders) Ltd* [1950] Ch. 561; *Re Footman Bower & Co Ltd* [1961] Ch. 443; *Re Yeovil Glove Co Ltd* [1965] Ch. 148; *Re James R. Rutherford & Sons Ltd* [1964] 1 W.L.R. 1211.

[367] *Clayton's Case* (1816) 1 Mer. 572, 608.

[368] *Henniker v Wigg* (1843) 4 Q.B. 792; *City Discount Co v McLean* (1874) L.R. 9 C.P. 692; *Browning v Baldwin* (1879) 40 L.T. 248; *Cory Bros & Co Ltd v Owners of Turkish S.S. "Mecca"* [1897] A.C. 286; *Re British Red Cross Balkan Fund* [1914] 2 Ch. 419; *Bradford Old Bank v Sutcliffe* [1918] 2 K.B. 833 (current account and loan account kept separate); *Re Hodgson's Trusts* [1919] 2 Ch. 189; *Barlow Clowes International Ltd v Vaughan* [1992] 4 All E.R. 22.

[369] *Barlow Clowes International Ltd v Vaughan* [1992] 4 All E.R. 22, 42; *Commerzbank Aktiengesellschaft v IMB Morgan Plc* [2004] EWHC 2771 (Ch), [2005] 1 Lloyd's Rep. 298 at [42]–[48].

[370] *Income Tax Commissioner v Maharajadhiraja of Darbhanga* (1933) L.R. 60 I.A. 146, 157; cf. *Smith v Law Guarantee and Trust Society Ltd* [1904] 2 Ch. 569; *West Bromwich Building Society v Crammer* [2002] EWHC 2618 (Ch); *Potomek Construction Ltd v Zurich Securities Ltd* [2003] EWHC 2827 (Ch), [2004] 1 All E.R. (Comm) 672 at [69].

(c) *Revalorisation: Gold Clauses and Index-linking*[371]

21–068 **The nominalistic principle.** It has been a principle of English law since the seventeenth century that a debt payable at a future time involves an obligation to pay the nominal amount of the debt at the date of payment in whatever is legal tender for that currency at that date, irrespective of any fluctuations in the currency in which the debt is expressed between the date of the contract and the date of payment.[372] Thus, where English law is the law applicable to the contract,[373] a debt expressed in "pounds" may be discharged in whatever are "pounds" according to English law at the date fixed for payment,[374] and a debt expressed in a foreign currency, e.g. dollars, may be discharged by the same nominal amount of dollars at the date of payment, despite changes in the real value of the dollars.[375] The creditor runs the risk of depreciation of the currency, while the debtor runs the risk of its appreciation. If the law applicable to the contract is foreign, that law governs the obligations arising under the contract,[376] but such a foreign law will invariably adopt the nominalistic principle[377]; hence, it is for the law of the country in whose currency the debt is expressed to define what is legal tender for the purpose of discharging that debt.[378]

21–069 **Gold clauses.** In an attempt to avoid the operation of the nominalistic principle (above), creditors have adopted various clauses to protect themselves against the risk of depreciation of the currency.[379] The most popular device used by

---

[371] See, in general, Mann, *The Legal Aspect of Money*, 6th edn (2005), Chs 9–13; Downes (1985) 101 L.Q.R. 98; on American law, with discussion of English authorities, see Nussbaum, *Money in the Law, National and International* (1950).

[372] *Gilbert v Brett* (*le case de Mixt Moneys*) (1604) Davis 18; *British Bank for Foreign Trade v Russian Commercial and Industrial Bank (No.2)* (1921) 38 T.L.R. 65; *Ottoman Bank v Chakarian (No.2)* [1938] A.C. 260; *Sforza v Ottoman Bank of Nicosia* [1938] A.C. 282; *Pyrmont Ltd v Schott* [1939] A.C. 145; *Marrache v Ashton* [1943] A.C. 311; *Bonython v Commonwealth of Australia* [1951] A.C. 201; *Treseder-Griffin v Co-operative Insurance Ltd* [1956] 2 Q.B. 127. The rule is similar in all foreign systems of law: see *Dicey, Morris and Collins*, 14th edn (2006), paras 36–005 et seq.; Mann at paras 9–05 et seq.; Nussbaum at pp.171 et seq., 348 et seq.; Hauser (1959) 33 Tulane L. Rev. 307; Report on Foreign Money Liabilities, Law Commission Report No.124 (1983).

[373] On the law applicable to the contract, see below, paras 30–004, 30–047 et seq., 30–107 et seq., 30–170 et seq. and 30–186 et seq.

[374] *Treseder-Griffin v Co-operative Insurance Ltd* [1956] 2 Q.B. 127, 144. cf. *Bonython v Commonwealth of Australia* [1951] A.C. 201, 222. (On the problems which arise where the currency expression chosen may refer to two or more different currencies (e.g. "pound" or "dollar" or "franc") see *Dicey, Morris and Collins* at paras 36R–017 et seq.) See also paras 26–080—26–081, below.

[375] *Re Chesterman's Trusts* [1923] 2 Ch. 466; *Pyrmont Ltd v Schott* [1939] A.C. 145; cf. *Addison v Brown* [1954] 1 W.L.R. 779, 785. In an action in England, the court may give a judgment in a foreign currency: see below, para.30–376.

[376] See Ch.30, below.

[377] *Dicey, Morris and Collins* at paras 36–008 et seq. See also above, fn.372.

[378] See fn.372, above, and for illustrations, *R. v International Trustee* [1937] A.C. 500; *Pyrmont Ltd v Schott* [1939] A.C. 145; *Miliangos v George Frank (Textiles) Ltd* [1976] A.C. 443. The law applicable to the contract also determines whether the debtor is liable to make an additional payment by way of "revalorisation" where the currency has depreciated: *Dicey, Morris and Collins* at paras 36R–035 et seq. (English domestic law knows no such principle.)

[379] A "gold value" clause, below, will also protect a debtor against appreciation of the currency.

creditors today is a cost-of-living or other index.[380] But in the earlier part of the century and the post-war years the most usual type of protective clause was a so-called "gold clause"[381]; the validity, meaning, and effect of such a clause are determined by the law applicable to the contract.[382] In an ordinary domestic English case, or a conflicts case where English law is the law applicable to the contract, a clause referring to payment in gold of a specified standard of weight and fineness is presumed to be a gold value clause: it does not impose an obligation to pay gold or gold coins, but is used to ascertain or measure the amount of the debt, so that the debtor is obliged to pay in legal tender of the chosen currency the amount necessary at the date of payment to purchase gold or gold coins to the nominal amount of the debt.[383] This construction imports a special standard or measure of value which may be described sufficiently, though not with precise accuracy, as being the value which the specified unit of account would have if the currency were on a gold basis.[384]

The construction of a gold clause as a gold value clause is known as the *Feist* construction, following the decision of the House of Lords in *Feist v Société Intercommunale Belge d'Electricité*.[385] In this case a bond for £100 was issued in 1928 by the Belgian company bearing interest payable on March 1 and September 1 each year at 5212 per cent. and repayable in 1963 or earlier: 21–070

> "... in sterling in gold coin of the United Kingdom of or equal to the standard of weight and fineness existing on September 1, 1928."

The company claimed the right to pay the sum due on an interest coupon in whatever might be legal tender in England at the date of payment.[386] The House of Lords held that the proper law of the contract was that of England and that the holder was entitled to receive such a sum in sterling (i.e. English legal tender) as should represent the gold value of the nominal amount of each respective payment, such gold value to be ascertained in accordance with the standard of weight and fineness existing on September 1, 1928. Therefore, after the devaluation of the pound in 1931, the clause imposed an obligation to pay in depreciated pounds the amount necessary to purchase 100 gold pounds. Lord Russell of Killowen said[387]:

---

380 See below, para.21–072.

381 No legislation in the UK has invalidated such a clause (cf. the Joint Resolution of the United States Congress of June 5, 1933, and the Canadian Gold Clauses Act 1937, applied respectively in *R. v International Trustee* [1937] A.C. 500 and *New Brunswick Ry v British and French Corp Ltd* [1939] A.C. 1. Both provisions have now been repealed: *Dicey, Morris and Collins* at para.36–048).

382 *Dicey, Morris and Collins* at paras 36R–040 et seq.; arts 8(1), 10(1)(a) and (b) of the Rome Convention on the Law Applicable to Contractual Obligations (Contracts (Applicable Law) Act 1990 Sch.1); *R. v International Trustee* [1937] A.C. 500; below, paras 30–326—30–335.

383 *Dicey, Morris and Collins* at para.36R–040.; *Feist v Société Intercommunale Belge d'Electricité* [1934] A.C. 161.

384 *Syndic in Bankruptcy of Khoury v Khayat* [1943] A.C. 507, 511, 512; *Feist v Société Intercommunale Belge d'Electricité* [1934] A.C. 161, 172. Another formulation of the principle is that the debtor has to provide at the time of payment such an amount of currency as will buy the same amount of gold as could have been bought with the sum promised at the time of making the contract.

385 Above. See Mann at paras 11.19 et seq.

386 On legal tender, see below, para.21–086.

387 [1934] A.C. 161, 172 et seq.

> "The parties are referring to gold coin of the United Kingdom of a specific standard of weight and fineness not as the mode in which the company's indebtedness is to be discharged, but as being the means by which the amount of the indebtedness is to be measured and ascertained."

The *Feist* construction has been followed in conflict of laws cases where the applicable law was foreign[388] and when interpreting international conventions[389] but it has not yet been applied to any reported case dealing with a domestic English contract.[390] Although the statutes of many foreign countries have declared gold clauses to be illegal, some have now been repealed.[391]

21–071 **Other possible constructions of gold clauses.** Other constructions than the *Feist* construction are possible of particular gold clauses, since each clause depends on its own wording and context. First, the clause may show that the parties intended a sale of actual gold or bullion as a commodity, so that no monetary obligation was undertaken.[392] Secondly, the clause may refer to the actual medium in which the debt is to be discharged, e.g. a "gold coin" clause whereby the debtor agrees to pay actual gold coins. Thirdly, it may be a descriptive clause, which merely repeats the statutory definition of the legal unit of currency.[393] This third construction was adopted by a majority of the Court of Appeal in 1956[394] where the lessee under a domestic English lease covenanted to pay a rent of £1,900 "yearly during the said term either in gold sterling or in Bank of England notes to the equivalent value in gold sterling"; it was held that this clause merely imposed an obligation to pay £1,900 in current legal tender, i.e. pound notes, since a gold sovereign was worth no more than a pound note for the purposes of legal tender. It may be that this decision should have been based

---

[388] *New Brunswick Ry v British and French Trust Corp Ltd* [1939] A.C. 1; *Syndic in Bankruptcy of Khoury v Khayat* [1943] A.C. 507 (the law of Palestine was the same as English law on this point). cf. *R. v International Trustee* [1937] A.C. 500 (reversing the decision of the Court of Appeal [1936] 3 All E.R. 407, but approving the Court of Appeal's view that the clause was a gold value clause).

[389] *The Rosa S.* [1989] Q.B. 419; *Brown Boveri (Australia) Pty Ltd v Baltic Shipping Co (The Nadezhda Krupskaya)* [1989] 1 Lloyd's Rep. 518 New South Wales Court of Appeal; *The "Tasman Discoverer"* [2001] 2 Lloyd's Rep. 665 (New Zealand High Court, reversed on appeal on the ground that the issue before the court was one which related to the construction of a contract term and not an international convention or over-riding national legislation: [2002] 2 Lloyd's Rep. 528).

[390] In *New Brunswick Ry v British and French Trust Corp Ltd* [1939] A.C. 1, the law of New Brunswick was probably the applicable law, though the point was left open; in *Treseder-Griffin v Co-operative Insurance Society Ltd* [1956] 2 Q.B. 127 (discussed below, para.21–071) and in *Campos v Kentucky & Indiana Terminal Railroad Co* [1962] 2 Lloyd's Rep. 459 (decisions on domestic English law), the *Feist* case [1934] A.C. 161 was distinguished. See now below, para.21–072.

[391] *Dicey, Morris and Collins* at paras 36R–040—36–050; Nussbaum, *Money in the Law*, pp.280 et seq.

[392] *British and French Trust Corp v New Brunswick Ry* [1936] 1 All E.R. 13, 16. But the courts will lean against this construction unless this meaning is clearly expressed, since payment in gold, or export in gold, has been made subject to controls in many countries.

[393] e.g. *St Pierre v South American Stores (Gath and Chaves) Ltd* [1937] 3 All E.R. 349 (Chilean law); *Treseder-Griffin v Co-operative Insurance Ltd* [1956] 2 Q.B. 127 (discussed below); *Campos v Kentucky & Indiana Terminal Railroad Co* [1962] 2 Lloyd's Rep. 459 (see Mann (1963) 12 I.C.L.Q. 1005); cf. *Modiano Bros & Sons v Bailey & Sons* (1933) 47 Ll.L.Rep. 134, 141.

[394] *Treseder-Griffin v Co-operative Insurance Ltd* [1956] 2 Q.B. 127.

on the uncertainty of the intention of the parties, in that the words they used did not definitely indicate that the amount of indebtedness was to be fixed by the current value of gold.[395] The words were obviously chosen by the parties for some purpose, yet the majority of the Court of Appeal treated them as a surplusage; the decision can only be reconciled with that of the House of Lords in *Feist* if the absence of any reference to the weight and fineness of the gold in the former case is treated as crucial.[396]

Index-linking clauses in domestic contracts. In modern times, contracting parties (particularly lenders) have sought other methods to safeguard themselves against a decline in the purchasing power of the pound sterling.[397] In 1977, a court of first instance[398] upheld the validity of an English mortgage (made between businessmen who received separate legal advice) under which both the principal debt and interest were "index-related" to a foreign currency; although payments were due in pounds sterling, their amounts were to vary proportionately to the variation in the rate of exchange between the pound and the Swiss franc.[399] The lender had advanced £36,000 as the capital loan in 1966, and under "the Swiss franc uplift" he became entitled to capital repayments of £87,588 by 1976.[400] It has been pointed out,[401] however, that protection against decline in the domestic purchasing power of sterling would come from index-linking to a domestic index, such as the retail price index[402]; whereas the linking of a domestic debt to a foreign currency is less justifiable, since it could lead to drastic revalorisation as a result of international fluctuations which bear little relation to domestic events. **21–072**

---

[395] Nor did the clause fix any exact gold standard, such as the selling or buying price of gold coins, or of the content of gold coins, or of bullion. On this, see *Campos v Kentucky & Indiana Terminal Railroad Co* [1962] 2 Lloyd's Rep. 459, 469. See also *The Rosa S.* [1989] Q.B. 419, 426.

[396] See the criticisms of the decision in *Dicey and Morris on the Conflict of Laws*, 13th edn (2000), 36–025—36–027 (the relevant passages have been omitted from the 14th edn); Mann (1957) 73 L.Q.R. 181; Yale [1956] C.L.J. 169; Unger (1957) 20 M.L.R. 266. (Leave to appeal to the House of Lords was granted, but the appeal was compromised before hearing.)

[397] Rents under leases have, for centuries, been made dependent on the price of corn. See also Nussbaum, *Money in the Law* at pp.299 et seq.

[398] *Multiservice Bookbinding Ltd v Marden* [1979] Ch. 84. See Bishop and Hindley (1979) 42 M.L.R. 338. The High Court of Australia has upheld the index-linking of an obligation to a retail price index: *Stanwell Park Hotel Co Ltd v Leslie* (1952) 85 C.L.R. 189. The *Multiservice* decision has been followed in a case concerned with the interpretation of the Building Societies Act 1962: *Nationwide Building Society v Registry of Friendly Societies* [1983] 1 W.L.R. 1226. See also Downes (1985) 101 L.Q.R. 98.

[399] cf. *Howard Houlder and Partners Ltd v Union Marine Insurance Co* (1922) 10 Ll. L. Rep. 627.

[400] During the same period, however, the borrower's business in the new premises purchased with the loan had prospered considerably, and the value of the premises had also inflated substantially: [1979] Ch. 84, 102. The judge also held that the terms of the mortgage were not unfair, oppressive or morally reprehensible so as to entitle the court to relieve the borrower under equitable principles applicable to mortgages: 105–113.

[401] Bowles (1981) 131 New L.J. 4, 5.

[402] On "cost-of-living index" clauses, and other similar clauses, see Nussbaum, *Money in the Law* at pp.299 et seq. cf. Mann at paras 11.38–11.46. A cost-of-living index clause is of the same nature as a gold value clause, above, para.21–069.

(d) Payment by Negotiable Instrument or Documentary Credit

21–073 **Payment by negotiable instrument.**[403] Apart from express agreement,[404] a creditor is not bound to accept payment in any way except cash, i.e. legal tender.[405] If, however, he accepts a negotiable instrument,[406] such as a bill of exchange, promissory note or cheque, it is a question of fact[407] depending on the intention of the parties, whether it is taken in absolute satisfaction of the debt, or only in conditional satisfaction. In either event, the acceptance of the instrument gives the debtor a good defence to an action for the debt, at least until the instrument matures.[408]

21–074 **Conditional payment.** Normally where a creditor accepts a negotiable instrument for his debt it is presumed[409] to be taken by him as a qualified or conditional payment, and, accordingly, although the original debt is still due during the currency of the instrument, the creditor's remedy is suspended until it is due.[410] If it is then paid, this amounts to payment of the debt[411]; if it is dishonoured when it is presented for payment in the ordinary way,[412] the right to sue upon the

[403] The previous restrictions on payment of wages by cheque have been repealed: see Vol.II, para.39–091.

[404] On payment by bankers' commercial credit, see Vol.II, paras 34–423 et seq., 43–270. On payment by credit or charge card, see below, para.21–082.

[405] e.g. where the debtor, in answer to a demand for payment, sent to the creditor a post office order which was in fact defective, but could easily have been rendered effective by the creditor, it was held that this was no evidence of payment as the debtor had no right to put his creditor to the trouble of either correcting the mistake or of returning the defective post office order: *Gordon v Strange* (1847) 1 Exch. 477.

[406] cf. *Plimley v Westley* (1835) 2 Bing. N.C. 249 (note endorsed by debtor to creditor, but it was not negotiable).

[407] *Goldshede v Cottrell* (1836) 2 M. & W. 20; *Re Boys* (1870) L.R. 10 Eq. 467; *Re Romer and Haslam* [1893] 2 Q.B. 286; *Palmer v Bramley* [1895] 2 Q.B. 405. cf. *Re Charge Card Services Ltd* [1989] Ch. 497.

[408] The same result follows: (i) where the bill or note for the debt is given to the creditor by a third party: *Allen v Royal Bank of Canada* (1925) 95 L.J.P.C. 17 (see also *Belshaw v Bush* (1851) 11 C.B. 191, and cf. on the need for consideration in such circumstances: *Oliver v Davis* [1949] 2 K.B. 727); (ii) where the bill or note is, at the creditor's request, payable to a third person: *Price v Price* (1847) 16 M. & W. 232, 241; *National Savings Bank Association Ltd v Tranah* (1867) L.R. 2 C.P. 556.

[409] This presumption is not displaced merely because the cheque was handed over with a bank card: *Re Charge Card Services Ltd* [1987] Ch. 150, 166. The Court of Appeal reserved its view on this point: [1989] Ch. 497, 517.

[410] *Sayer v Wagstaff* (1844) 5 Beav. 415; *Belshaw v Bush* (1851) 11 C.B. 191; *Currie v Misa* (1875) L.R. 10 Ex. 153; affirmed (1876) 1 App. Cas. 554; *Ex p. Matthew* (1884) 12 QBD 506; *Re Romer & Haslam* [1893] 2 Q.B. 286, 296; *Felix Hadley & Co Ltd v Hadley* [1893] 2 Ch. 680; *Allen v Royal Bank of Canada* (1925) 95 L.J.P.C. 17; *Re Charge Card Services Ltd* [1987] Ch. 150, 511; *Fusion Interactive Communication Solutions Ltd v Venture Investment Placement Ltd* [2005] EWHC 736 (Ch), [2005] All E.R. (D) 111 (May) at [91]. See also *Griffiths v Owen* (1844) 13 M. & W. 58, 64.

[411] *Thorne v Smith* (1851) 10 C.B. 659; *Felix Hadley & Co Ltd v Hadley* [1893] 2 Ch. 680; *Re Home* [1951] Ch. 85, 89. Payment in part is pro tanto discharge: *Bottomley v Nuttall* (1858) 5 C.B.(N.S.) 122.

[412] *Re Raatz* [1897] 2 Q.B. 80 (debtor's commission of an available act of bankruptcy amounts to dishonour of negotiable instrument given to creditor).

original debt revives as if no negotiable instrument had been taken.[413] Hence, if interest was due on the debt, it continues to accrue after the date of acceptance of a cheque which is subsequently dishonoured.[414] It has been held that a claimant who accepts a cheque for part of the debt claimed by him cannot sign judgment in default of appearance for the full amount claimed unless the cheque is dishonoured.[415] Similarly, acceptance of an irrevocable documentary credit does not constitute absolute payment to the seller so as to release the buyer; if the credit is not honoured, the seller may sue the buyer.[416]

Bill or note from debtor's agent. A creditor does not lose his remedy against his debtor merely by taking for the debt a bill or note of the debtor's agent, even without the debtor's consent.[417] The debtor will be discharged if the creditor has the opportunity of receiving payment in cash from the debtor's agent, but, for his own convenience, elects to take the agent's (or a third party's) bill or note.[418] 21–075

Collateral security. A negotiable instrument may be given to the creditor as collateral security for the debt, so that the existing remedies for the debt are unaffected.[419] This was frequently held to be the intention of the parties when the debt was due under a deed, or another remedy (e.g. distress) was also available.[420] Thus, where a cheque was given for interest due on a debenture, there was not a conditional payment so as to release the security; where the cheque was not met and the company went into liquidation, the debenture-holder could still claim to be a secured creditor in respect of the interest.[421] Even where the debt is 21–076

[413] *Gunn v Bolckow, Vaughan & Co* (1875) L.R. 10 Ch. App. 491; *Cohen v Hale* (1878) 3 QBD 371; *Re Romer & Haslam* [1893] 2 Q.B. 286, 296; *D.P.P. v Turner* [1974] A.C. 357, 367–368, 369. Where the bill has been negotiated and is outstanding in the hands of a third party, the creditor's remedy is still suspended: *Davis v Reilly* [1898] 1 Q.B. 1; *Re A Debtor* [1908] 1 K.B. 344 (except where the third party is a trustee for the claimant: *National Savings Bank Association Ltd v Tranah* (1867) L.R. 2 C.P. 556; or agent for the claimant: *Hadwen v Mendisabal* (1825) 10 Moore C.P. 477). If, though the dishonoured bill has been negotiated, it has again been transferred to the creditor, the latter may sue on the original demand: *Tarleton v Allhusen* (1834) 2 A. & E. 32.

[414] *D.P.P. v Turner* [1974] A.C. 357, 368.

[415] *Bolt & Nut Co (Tipton) Ltd v Rowlands, Nicholls & Co Ltd* [1964] 2 Q.B. 10.

[416] *W.J. Alan & Co Ltd v El Nasr Export and Import Co* [1972] 2 Q.B. 189, 209–212, 221; *Maran Road Saw Mill v Austin Taylor & Co Ltd* [1975] 1 Lloyd's Rep. 156; *E.D. & F. Man Ltd v Nigerian Sweets and Confectionery Co Ltd* [1977] 2 Lloyd's Rep. 50; *Re Charge Card Services Ltd* [1989] Ch. 497, 511 (above, para.21–082). See Vol.II, paras 34–475—34–477.

[417] *Robinson v Read* (1829) 9 B. & C. 449.

[418] *Marsh v Pedder* (1815) 4 Camp. 257; *Smith v Ferrand* (1827) 7 B. & C. 19; *Strong v Hart* (1827) 6 B. & C. 160; *Robinson v Read* (1829) 9 B. & C. 449, 455; *Anderson v Hillies* (1852) 12 C.B. 499; *Litchfield Union v Greene* (1857) 1 H. & N. 884, 892. Other rules on agency may also apply to this situation: see Vol.II, paras 31–070—31–073. cf. *Everett v Collins* (1810) 2 Camp. 515 (cheque of debtor's "servants" rather than of his "agents").

[419] *Drake v Mitchell* (1803) 3 East 251; *Pring v Clarkson* (1822) 1 B. & C. 14; *Peacock v Pursell* (1863) 14 C.B.(N.S.) 728; *Re London, Birmingham and South Staffordshire Bank* (1865) 34 L.J. Ch. 418; *Modern Light Cars Ltd v Seals* [1934] 1 K.B. 32 (following *Re Rankin and Shiliday* [1927] N.I. 162).

[420] *Davis v Gyde* (1835) 2 A. & E. 623; *Worthington v Wigley* (1837) 3 Bing. N.C. 454; *Belshaw v Bush* (1851) 11 C.B. 191, 206; *Henderson v Arthur* [1907] 1 K.B. 10, 13–14; *Re J. Defries & Sons Ltd* [1909] 2 Ch. 423, 428 ("the mere giving of a cheque is not conditional payment of a secured debt so as to release the security"). cf. *Bolt & Nut Co (Tipton) Ltd v Rowlands Nicholls & Co Ltd* [1964] 2 Q.B. 10.

[421] *Re J. Defries & Sons Ltd* [1909] 2 Ch. 423.

secured, the acceptance of a negotiable instrument may, in the circumstances, be evidence of an agreement to suspend the remedy under the security.[422]

21–077 **Absolute payment.** If the creditor accepts a negotiable instrument in absolute satisfaction of the original debt, agreeing expressly or impliedly to take upon himself the risk of the instrument not being paid, the effect is to extinguish his right of action for the debt and to leave him without remedy except upon the instrument.[423] It is a question of fact in each case whether the instrument was accepted as absolute payment or not.[424]

21–078 **Invalid or forged instrument.** If the instrument given in payment is invalid[425] or forged,[426] the creditor may treat it as a nullity and sue to recover the debt immediately.[427]

21–079 **Duties of creditor holding a negotiable instrument.** Where a negotiable instrument, upon which the debtor is not primarily liable, is accepted by the creditor as conditional payment, he is bound to do all that a holder of such an instrument may do in order to get payment[428]; thus it is his duty to present a cheque within a reasonable time, and if he fails to do so, and the debtor is thereby prejudiced, the creditor is guilty of laches and makes the cheque his own, so that it amounts to payment of the debt.[429] Similarly, the creditor must give due notice of dishonour and take other necessary steps to preserve his remedy against the other parties secondarily liable.[430] It is necessary to give notice of dishonour to the debtor only where he is a party to the negotiable instrument to whom such notice is required to be given.[431] The creditor, however, is not under such strict duties if it is the debtor who is primarily liable on the negotiable instrument given

---

[422] *Baker v Walker* (1845) 14 M. & W. 465; *Palmer v Bramley* [1895] 2 Q.B. 405.

[423] *Smith v Ferrand* (1827) 7 B. & C. 19; *Sard v Rhodes* (1836) 1 M. & W. 153; *Sayer v Wagstaff* (1844) 5 Beav. 415; *Sibree v Tripp* (1846) 15 M. & W. 23 (distinguished on another point: *D. & C. Builders Ltd v Rees* [1966] 2 Q.B. 617 (above, para.3–116)); *Caine v Coulton* (1863) 1 H. & C. 764. It does not appear to be essential in such a case that the instrument should be negotiable: *Lewis v Lyster* (1835) 2 Cr. M. & R. 704, 706.

[424] cf. the position with payment by credit or charge card: below, para.21–082. cf. also where the creditor of a partnership, upon its dissolution, takes the bill or note of the continuing partners for the debt: *Thompson v Percival* (1834) 5 B. & Ad. 925; *Lyth v Ault* (1852) 7 Exch. 669.

[425] Older cases concern invalidity caused by an insufficient stamp: *Brown v Watts* (1808) 1 Taunt. 353; *Wilson v Vysar* (1812) 4 Taunt. 288; *Cundy v Marriott* (1831) 1 B. & Ad. 696. The stamp duty on bills of exchange and promissory notes was abolished as from February 1, 1971 (Finance Act 1970 s.32 and Sch.7 para.2).

[426] *Camidge v Allenby* (1827) 6 B. & C. 373, 385. As to the forged renewal of an existing bill, see *Bell v Buckley* (1856) 11 Exch. 631.

[427] Similarly where the debtor acted fraudulently: *Camidge v Allenby* (1827) 6 B. & C. 373, 382.

[428] *Bridges v Berry* (1810) 3 Taunt. 130; *Soward v Palmer* (1818) 8 Taunt. 277; *Peacock v Pursell* (1863) 14 C.B.(N.S.) 728.

[429] *Camidge v Allenby* (1827) 6 B. & C. 373; *Hopkins v Ware* (1869) L.R. 4 Ex. 268. cf. *Robson v Oliver* (1847) 10 Q.B. 704.

[430] *Holbrow v Wilkins* (1822) 1 B. & C. 10; *Bridges v Berry* (1810) 3 Taunt. 130; cf. *Goodwin v Coates* (1832) 1 M. & Rob. 221, 222, fn.(a).

[431] *Swinyard v Bowes* (1816) 5 M. & S. 62; cf. *Smith v Mercer* (1867) L.R. 3 Ex. 51 (notice of dishonour required to be given to the debtor in the particular circumstances).

as conditional payment; in this case the onus is on the debtor to show a sufficient reason for failing to pay when it fell due.[432]

Loss of instrument. If the creditor loses the bill or note, he may rely on s.70 of the Bills of Exchange Act 1882: in any action or proceeding upon a bill the court may order that the loss of the instrument shall not be set up, provided an indemnity be given against the claims of any other person upon the instrument in question.[433] 21–080

Alteration of instrument. If the creditor alters, in a material particular, a bill drawn upon a third party, he makes the bill his own, and although it may be dishonoured, it operates as payment by the debtor if the debtor's rights are affected by the alteration.[434] If the creditor alters a bill accepted by the debtor, he may, in the absence of fraud, still sue for the original debt where the debtor has not been prejudiced.[435] 21–081

(e) *Payment by Credit or Charge Card*

Credit or charge card schemes. A finance company issuing credit or charge cards to approved cardholders sets up a scheme under which it agrees with various retailers in the scheme that the cardholders may charge purchases to the company, which undertakes (in its contract with each retailer) to pay the retailer the total amounts so charged. When a retailer agrees that a cardholder may pay for a purchase by having the price charged in this way, he accepts payment by this method as an unconditional, absolute payment of the price under the contract of sale between himself and the cardholder (unless that contract provides otherwise).[436] The result is that if the finance company fails to pay the retailer the amount[437] so charged, the seller has no recourse against the cardholder for payment of the price in cash.[438] In its decision on this situation the Court of Appeal held that there is no general presumption that whenever payment is agreed to be made through a third party, by a method which involved the risk that the third party may not pay, the acceptance by the seller of that method of payment is conditional upon the third party actually making the payment to the creditor.[439] When a new form of payment is introduced, the question whether it 21–082

[432] *National Savings Bank Association Ltd v Tranah* (1867) L.R. 2 C.P. 556.

[433] *King v Zimmerman* (1871) L.R. 6 C.P. 466. For the previous position at common law, see *Crowe v Clay* (1854) 9 Exch. 604; cf. also s.69 of the Bills of Exchange Act 1882, as to the holder's rights to a duplicate of a lost bill.

[434] *Alderson v Langdale* (1832) 3 B. & Ad. 660 (the alteration deprived the debtor of his remedy on the bill against the third party); cf. Bills of Exchange Act 1882 s.64. See also below, paras 25–020, 25–024; *Byles on Bills of Exchange and Cheques*, 28th edn (2007), paras 20–01—20–28.

[435] *Atkinson v Hawdon* (1835) 2 A. & E. 628; and see *M'Dowall v Boyd* (1848) 12 Jur. 980.

[436] *Re Charge Card Services Ltd* [1989] Ch. 497.

[437] Less any discount agreed in the contract between the company and the retailer.

[438] *Re Charge Card Services Ltd* [1989] Ch. 497. (There are three contracts: one between the company and the cardholder (who undertakes to pay the company the amounts charged to his card); the second between the company and the retailer; and the third the contract of sale between the retailer and the cardholder.)

[439] [1989] Ch. 497, 511–512.

should be treated as absolute or conditional depends on its own circumstances.[440]

5. TENDER

21–083 **The principle of tender.** In many cases a party to a contract cannot complete his obligations without the concurrence of the other party, e.g. without his acceptance of goods when delivered, or his acceptance of money paid over. If the other party refuses to accept performance in such cases, he is preventing the promisor from fulfilling his contractual obligations, and the plea of tender is available to the promisor as a defence to a subsequent action against him for failure to perform. The plea is that the defendant has always been willing to complete his side of the contract, and has in fact done so as far as is possible without the concurrence of the other party. A plea of tender must be established by showing that the promisor made an unconditional offer to perform his promise in terms of the contract but that the promisee refused to accept performance.[441] The authorities deal mainly with tender of money due under a contract, but the principle may extend to other cases, such as delivery of goods under a contract of sale[442]: if the buyer refuses to accept the goods, but has had a reasonable opportunity to examine the goods to see that they comply with the contract, the seller is, by his tender, relieved of liability to deliver under the contract.[443]

21–084 **Tender of money.** Where a debtor is obliged to pay a specific sum of money to a creditor a successful plea of tender does not discharge the debt,[444] but if the creditor subsequently sues for the debt, the debtor may, by paying the money into court[445] and by proving the tender and his continued willingness to pay the debt since the tender,[446] bar any claim for interest[447] or damages after the tender[448]; the creditor will also be liable to pay the debtor his costs of the action, on the ground that the action should not have been brought.[449] A claim for unliquidated

---

[440] [1989] Ch. 497.

[441] *Dixon v Clark* (1848) 5 C.B. 365, 377 et seq.

[442] See Vol.II, paras 43–271 et seq., especially paras 43–306—43–323.

[443] *Startup v Macdonald* (1843) 6 M. & G. 593, 610; *Isherwood v Whitmore* (1843) 11 M. & W. 347. See Vol.II, paras 43–306, 43–323.

[444] *Canmer International Inc v UK Mutual S.S. Assurance Association (Bermuda) Ltd (The "Rays")* [2005] EWHC 1694 (Comm), [2005] 2 Lloyd's Rep. 479 at [53], citing R. Goode, *Payment Obligations in Commercial and Financial Transactions* (1983), pp.14–16.

[445] CPR Pt 36. (There are similar provisions in the County Court Rules.) Payment into court is essential for a successful defence of tender of money: CPR r.37.3; *Kinnaird v Trollope* (1889) 42 Ch D 610.

[446] *Dixon v Clark* (1848) 5 C.B. 365, 377.

[447] But where a *borrower* of money tenders the amount due for principal and interest, the tender does not stop interest running after the date of the tender unless there is evidence that the sum has been set aside and is available for payment at any time: *Barratt v Gough-Thomas* [1951] 2 All E.R. 48 (following *Edmondson v Copland* [1911] 2 Ch. 301).

[448] *Norton v Ellam* (1837) 2 M. & W. 461; *Graham v Seal* (1918) 88 L.J. Ch. 31. See also Vol.II, para.38–271.

[449] *Griffith v Ystradyfodwg School Board* (1890) 24 QBD 307. See also *Dixon v Clark* (1848) 5 C.B. 365, 377. cf. *Graham v Seal* (1918) 88 L.J. Ch. 31 (after valid tender by mortgagor the mortgagee will be liable to pay the costs of an action to redeem).

damages, not being a claim for a specific sum of money, cannot be met by a plea of tender.[450]

Amount to be tendered. The debtor must tender the full amount of the debt, since a creditor is not bound to accept less than the whole of his demand; hence, a tender of part of an entire demand is invalid.[451] If there are separate items in a claim, the debtor may make a valid tender in respect of particular items, if he appropriates his tender to such items.[452] A tender of more than is due is a valid tender of the amount due if the debtor does not require change[453]; but if the debtor does ask for change out of the larger sum, this is not a valid tender of the amount due, since a creditor is not obliged to give change.[454] If, however, the creditor does not object to the tender on this ground, but makes some other objection, or demands a larger sum,[455] the tender will be valid, because the creditor will be taken to have waived any objection as to change.[456] 21–085

Tender must be in legal currency. A payment or tender must be in legal currency[457]; what amounts to legal tender is specified by s.2 of the Coinage Act 1971 (as amended[458]). Coins made by the Mint are legal tender as follows: gold coins, for payment of any amount[459]; coins of cupro-nickel or silver of denominations of more than 10 pence, for payment of any amount not exceeding £10; coins of cupro-nickel or silver of denominations of not more than 10 pence, for payment of any amount not exceeding £5; coins of bronze, for payment of any amount not exceeding 20 pence. There is power by proclamation to "call in" coins[460] (which then cease to be legal tender) or to make other coins legal tender.[461] By s.1(2) and (6) of the Currency and Bank Notes Act 1954, a tender of a note or notes of the Bank of England expressed to be payable to bearer on 21–086

---

[450] *Greenwood v Sutcliffe* [1892] 1 Ch. 1, 10.

[451] *Dixon v Clark* (1848) 5 C.B. 365; *James v Vane* (1860) 29 L.J.Q.B. 169; *Read's Trustee in Bankruptcy v Smith* [1951] Ch. 439. A tender of part of a debt, after deduction of a set-off, is not strictly a legal tender: *Searles v Sadgrave* (1855) 5 E. & B. 639; *Phillpotts v Clifton* (1861) 10 W.R. 135; but such a tender may be relevant when the court exercises its discretion as to costs. A set-off accruing after the date of a tender of part does not validate the tender: *Cotton v Godwin* (1840) 7 M. & W. 147.

[452] *James v Vane* (1860) 29 L.J.Q.B. 169; cf. *Hardingham v Allen* (1848) 5 C.B. 793 (debtor failed to assign his tender of part to any particular item); *Strong v Harvey* (1825) 3 Bing. 304, 313. On appropriation, see above, paras 21–059 et seq.

[453] *Dean v James* (1833) 4 B. & Ad. 546. See also *Wade's Case* (1601) 5 Co.Rep. 114a; *Douglas v Patrick* (1790) 3 T.R. 683.

[454] *Betterbee v Davis* (1811) 3 Camp. 70; *Robinson v Cook* (1815) 6 Taunt. 336; cf. *Blow v Russell* (1824) 1 C. & P. 365.

[455] *Black v Smith* (1791) Peake 121.

[456] *Bevans v Rees* (1839) 5 M. & W. 306, 308. See also *Saunders v Graham* (1819) Gow 121; *Atkin v Acton* (1830) 4 C. & P. 208, 210.

[457] The common law requires that a tender shall be made in the current coin of the realm or in foreign money legally made current by proclamation. As to tender of foreign money in discharge of a debt due in that foreign currency, see *Société des Hôtels Le Touquet Paris-Plage v Cummings* [1922] 1 K.B. 451. See also below, paras 30–069—30–079).

[458] By s.1(3) of the Currency Act 1983.

[459] Provided their weight has not become less than that specified: Coinage Act 1971 s.2(1) (as amended).

[460] Coinage Act 1971 s.3(e).

[461] ss.2(1B), 3(EE) of the Coinage Act 1971 (as amended).

demand is legal tender for the payment of any amount. A tender of notes of a bank other than the Bank of England is not a legal tender,[462] but the creditor may waive his objection to the tender on that ground.[463]

21–087 **Tender by negotiable instrument.** A tender by negotiable instrument, such as a bill of exchange or cheque, is not a valid tender[464]; but the creditor may waive an objection to the form of the tender,[465] e.g. if he asks for payment by cheque[466] or objects to the tender only on another ground, such as the amount of the tender.[467] There is no custom obliging a vendor to accept a cheque for the payment of a deposit on a sale by auction.[468] Nor is a solicitor, who is authorised to accept a tender of money due on a mortgage, at liberty to accept a cheque: thus a tender of a cheque to him is insufficient.[469]

21–088 **Actual production of the money.** To constitute a valid tender there must either be an actual production of the money, or its production must be expressly or impliedly dispensed with by the creditor.[470] Issues as to what constitutes actual production of the money[471] and to whether the creditor dispensed with actual production of the money will depend on all the circumstances.[472] In one case,[473] where the debtor was obliged to make "payment in cash", the Court of Appeal held that such payment was not made until the creditor either received cash or what he was prepared to treat as the equivalent of cash, or had a credit available on which, in the normal course of business or banking practice, he could draw in the form of cash.[474]

21–089 **Time of tender.** Where by the terms of the contract the money is to be paid on a particular day, the tender to be valid must be made on that day.[475] Although

---

[462] Unless, of course, the contract provides that a sum of money expressed in a foreign currency is to be paid in England: see *Dicey, Morris and Collins on the Conflict of Laws*, 14th edn (2006), paras 36R–051—36–060.

[463] *Polglass v Oliver* (1831) 2 C. & J. 15.

[464] *Re Steam Stoker Co* (1875) L.R. 19 Eq. 416; *Blumberg v Life Interests and Reversionary Securities Corp* [1897] 1 Ch. 171; [1898] 1 Ch. 27; *Johnson v Boyes* [1899] 2 Ch. 73.

[465] See *Re Quebrada Co Ltd* (1873) 42 L.J. Ch. 277; *Cohen v Roche* [1927] 1 K.B. 169.

[466] *Cubitt v Gamble* (1919) 35 T.L.R. 223.

[467] *Jones v Arthur* (1840) 8 Dowl. 442; see also *Lockyer v Jones* (1796) Peake 239n.; *Cohen v Roche* [1927] 1 K.B. 169, 180.

[468] *Johnston v Boyes* [1899] 2 Ch. 73. See also *Pollway Ltd v Abdullah* [1974] 1 W.L.R. 493.

[469] *Blumberg v Life Interests and Reversionary Securities Corp* [1897] 1 Ch. 171.

[470] *Finch v Brook* (1834) 1 Bing. N.C. 253, 257; *The Norway (Owners of) v Ashburner* (1865) 3 Moo. P.C.(N.S.) 245; *Farquharson v Pearl Assurance Co Ltd* [1937] 3 All E.R. 124. See also *Dickinson v Shee* (1801) 4 Esp. 67; *Thomas v Evans* (1808) 10 East 101.

[471] e.g. *Alexander v Brown* (1824) 1 C. & P. 288; *Leatherdale v Sweepstone* (1828) 3 C. & P. 342; *Liddiard v Skelton* (1843) 1 L.T.(O.S.) 143; *Bishop v Smedley* (1846) 2 C.B. 90; *Humphrey v Chapman* (1846) 6 L.T.(O.S.) 413.

[472] *Douglas v Patrick* (1790) 3 T.R. 683; *Read v Goldring* (1813) 2 M. & S. 86; *Harding v Davis* (1825) 2 C. & P. 77; *Re Farley* (1852) 2 De G.M. & G. 936; cf. *Ryder v Townsend* (1825) 7 D. & Ry 119; *Empresa Cubana De Fletes v Lagonisi Shipping Co Ltd* [1971] 1 Q.B. 488, 505 (tender of a banker's payment slip may be "treated in commercial circles as cash"): the case has been overruled on another point: see the *Mardorf Peach* case [1977] A.C. 850, and below, para.21–089.

[473] *The Brimnes (Tenax S.S. Co Ltd v The Brimnes (Owners))* [1975] Q.B. 929.

[474] [1975] Q.B. 929, 963. See further the discussion in *Mardorf Peach & Co Ltd v Attica Sea Carriers Corp of Liberia* [1977] A.C. 850, 880, 885, 889 (referred to above, para.21–046).

[475] *Dixon v Clark* (1848) 5 C.B. 365, 378–379.

a tender cannot be effectually made after the actual commencement of an action for the recovery of the debt, that is, after the issue of the writ,[476] nevertheless, before the issue of a writ, a late tender of the amount due will normally have the same effect, in regard to interest and costs,[477] as would a valid tender on the due day.[478] Where a charterparty gave the owner an express power to withdraw the vessel on default in payment of hire, late payment made before the owner exercised his right to withdraw was held not to deprive the owner of that right.[479]

The acceptor of a bill payable at a future day cannot make a valid tender after the due day, although he pleads a tender of the amount of the bill with interest from the day it became due up to the day of the tender.[480] Where a bill or note is payable on demand, a valid tender may be made, at any time before an action has been brought, by tendering the amount due with interest up to the time of the tender.[481] In a contract for sale of goods an earlier invalid tender may be disregarded if the seller, within the time fixed for delivery, makes a subsequent valid tender.[482] 21–090

Tender must be unconditional. A tender, to be valid, must not be made upon any condition to which the creditor has a right to object.[483] The debtor cannot force the creditor to make an admission by accepting the money tendered on terms which the creditor is unwilling to accept. Thus, although a debtor tendering money may exclude any presumption against himself that the sum tendered is only in part payment of the debt, his tender will be invalid if it is made on condition that the creditor acknowledges that nothing more is due from the debtor.[484] So tenders of money "in full of the plaintiff's claims",[485] as "all that is due",[486] "as a settlement",[487] or "in payment of the half-year's rent due at Lady Day last",[488] have all been held invalid. 21–091

---

476 The defendant may of course pay the amount into court: CPR Pt 36.

477 See above, para.21–084.

478 *Briggs v Calverly* (1800) 8 T.R. 629; *Moffat v Parsons* (1814) 5 Taunt. 307 (tenders valid, though made after creditors had instructed their solicitors to act). See also *Johnson v Clay* (1817) 7 Taunt. 486, and the comment thereon in *Poole v Tumbridge* (1837) 2 M. & W. 223, 226; *Dixon v Clark* (1848) 5 C.B. 365, 378 (if creditor validly demands payment, and the debtor refuses, a subsequent tender is invalid); *Bennett v Parker* (1867) Ir. 2 C.L. 89, 95.

479 *Mardorf Peach & Co Ltd v Attica Sea Carriers Corp of Liberia* [1977] A.C. 850.

480 *Dobie v Larkam* (1855) 10 Exch. 776 (following *Poole v Tumbridge* (1837) 2 M. & W. 223; *Hume v Peploe* (1807) 8 East 168). See also *Dixon v Clark* (1848) 5 C.B. 365, 379.

481 *Norton v Ellam* (1837) 2 M. & W. 461, 463.

482 *Borrowman Phillips & Co v Free & Hollis* (1878) 4 QBD 500. See *Benjamin's Sale of Goods*, 7th edn (2006), para.12–031 and Apps [1994] L.M.C.L.Q. 525.

483 *Re Steam Stoker Co* (1875) L.R. 19 Eq. 416; *Bevans v Rees* (1839) 5 M. & W. 306, 309.

484 See the cases cited in fnn.485–488, below.

485 *Strong v Harvey* (1825) 3 Bing. 304, 313. cf. *Evans v Judkins* (1815) 4 Camp. 156; *Cheminant v Thornton* (1825) 2 C. & P. 50; *Gordon v Cox* (1835) 7 C. & P. 172.

486 *Sutton v Hawkins* (1838) 8 C. & P. 259; *Field v Newport, etc., Ry* (1858) 3 H. & N. 409.

487 *Mitchell v King* (1833) 6 C. & P. 237; cf. *Hough v May* (1836) 4 A. & E. 954 ("balance account").

488 *Marquis of Hastings v Thorley* (1838) 8 C. & P. 573. See also *Foord v Noll* (1842) 2 Dowl.(N.S.) 617; *Finch v Miller* (1848) 5 C.B. 428.

21–092 **Tender under protest, or subject to valid condition.** A tender of a sum of money "under protest",[489] or where the debtor states that he considers the amount tendered to be all that is due, or where the debtor reserves the right to dispute the amount due,[490] is not a conditional tender and is therefore valid; no condition has been imposed that the creditor must make an admission when accepting the money. Where a tender of a mortgage debt is made upon the condition that the mortgagee should immediately execute a re-conveyance (previously seen and approved) of the mortgaged premises, the tender is valid, since the mortgagor is merely insisting on his contractual rights[491]; the tender therefore stops interest running, and renders the mortgagee liable to pay the costs of an action to redeem.[492] The fact that the creditor disputes the amount due and refuses to receive the amount tendered by the debtor does not affect the validity of the tender or render it a conditional tender.[493]

21–093 **Request for receipt.** Since the stamp duty on receipts has been abolished,[494] it is no longer an offence to refuse to give a stamped receipt.[495] It is probably a conditional tender if the debtor demands a receipt as a condition of payment,[496] but not if he merely asks for a receipt without making it a condition of payment.[497]

21–094 **Tender to an agent.** A tender need not be made to the creditor personally, but may be made to an agent who has actual or ostensible authority from the creditor to receive the money.[498] Thus, where a landlord authorises his bailiff to distrain for rent, he gives him implied authority to receive a tender of rent and expenses.[499] After a solicitor has been instructed by the creditor to apply for payment of a debt and has written demanding payment to himself, a tender to the solicitor is valid.[500] So, where the solicitor demands payment at his office, a tender to any person who is in the office carrying on the business is sufficient.[501]

---

[489] *Manning v Lunn* (1845) 2 C. & K. 13; *Scott v Uxbridge and Rickmansworth Ry* (1866) L.R. 1 C.P. 596; *Greenwood v Sutcliffe* [1892] 1 Ch. 1.

[490] *Greenwood v Sutcliffe* [1892] 1 Ch. 1.

[491] *Graham v Seal* (1918) 88 L.J. Ch. 31.

[492] (1918) 88 L.J. Ch. 31.

[493] *Robinson v Ferreday* (1839) 8 C. & P. 752; *Henwood v Oliver* (1841) 1 Q.B. 409; *Bowen v Owen* (1847) 11 Q.B. 130.

[494] See above, para.21–058 fn.342.

[495] As was provided by s.103 of the Stamp Act 1891 for payment of a sum of £2 or more.

[496] *Laing v Meader* (1824) 1 C. & P. 257; cf. *Richardson v Jackson* (1841) 8 M. & W. 298. If the creditor refuses to accept the tender on some other ground, he cannot later maintain that a demand for a receipt invalidated the tender: *Jones v Arthur* (1840) 8 Dowl. 442; *Richardson v Jackson*.

[497] *Jones v Arthur* (1840) 8 Dowl. 442.

[498] *Kirton v Braithwaite* (1836) 1 M. & W. 310, 313; *Finch v Boning* (1879) 4 C.P.D. 143. See also the cases cited below, and compare the cases on payment to an agent, above, paras 21–043—21–048.

[499] *Hatch v Hale* (1850) 15 Q.B. 10. cf. *Boulton v Reynolds* (1859) 29 L.J.Q.B. 11 (a man left in charge of premises by the bailiff has no authority to receive rent). But where no place for payment of the rent is fixed, mere readiness to pay the money on the land is insufficient: *Haldane v Johnson* (1853) 8 Exch. 689.

[500] *Watson v Hetherington* (1843) 1 C. & K. 36. See also *Crozer v Pilling* (1825) 4 B. & C. 26 (valid tender of judgment debt and costs to plaintiff's solicitor on the record).

[501] *Watson v Hetherington* (1843) 1 C. & K. 36. See also *Wilmott v Smith* (1828) Moo. & M. 238; *Kirton v Braithwaite* (1836) 1 M. & W. 310.

The fact that the creditor has instructed his solicitor to commence proceedings to recover the debt does not affect the validity of a tender to the creditor's clerk, who was previously authorised to receive the money, and later told not to receive it because the matter was in the solicitor's hands.[502] If an apparent agent of the creditor, at the time of the tender, disclaimed authority to receive the money, the tender is invalid if in fact the apparent agent had no such authority.[503] If the money is due to a number of creditors jointly, a tender to any one of the joint creditors is valid, though the tender should be pleaded as a tender to the one on behalf of all the creditors.[504]

Tender by an agent. A tender need not be made by the debtor personally, but may be made on his behalf by his agent,[505] whether the agent is previously authorised by the debtor, or his unauthorised tender has been subsequently ratified by the debtor. So where an agent was authorised to tender part of a sum, but he tendered at his own risk the whole sum, the tender was held valid after it had been ratified by the debtor.[506] **21–095**

Failure to comply with valid demand. Since the principle of the defence of tender is that the defendant has always been ready to perform the contract,[507] if the claimant can show that performance of the contract was demanded[508] and refused at any time when by the terms of the contract he had a right to make such a demand, the plea of tender will fail, whether such demand and refusal took place before or after the tender.[509] An application to and refusal by one of two joint debtors is sufficient for this purpose.[510] **21–096**

---

502 *Moffat v Parsons* (1814) 5 Taunt. 307; *Caine v Coulton* (1863) 1 H. & C. 764; *Finch v Boning* (1879) 4 C.P. D 143, 146; cf. *Smith v Goodwin* (1833) 4 B. & Ad. 413 (a tender to the landlord is valid even after his broker has distrained for rent).

503 *Bingham v Allport* (1833) 1 Nev. & M. 398; *Finch v Boning* (1879) 4 C.P.D. 143.

504 *Douglas v Patrick* (1790) 3 T.R. 683. cf. payment to a joint creditor: above, para.21–049.

505 *Finch v Brook* (1834) 1 Bing. N.C. 253; *Farquharson v Pearl Assurance Co Ltd* [1937] 3 All E.R. 124 (mortgagee of insurance policy made valid tender of premium). See also *Cropp v Hambleton* (1586) Cro. Eliz. 48; and cf. payment by an agent: above, para.21–041.

506 *Read v Goldring* (1813) 2 M. & S. 86.

507 See above, para.21–083.

508 The demand may be made by an authorised agent, but an unauthorised demand cannot be subsequently ratified: *Coore v Calloway* (1794) 1 Esp. 115.

509 *Poole v Tumbridge* (1837) 2 M. & W. 223; *Cotton v Godwin* (1840) 7 M. & W. 147; *Brandon v Newington* (1842) 3 Q.B. 915; *Hesketh v Fawcett* (1843) 11 M. & W. 356; *Dixon v Clark* (1848) 5 C.B. 365, 378. Semble, that the effect of a tender cannot be defeated by the creditor showing a demand for payment by letter, since a personal demand should be made on the debtor so as to give him at the time of the demand an opportunity of paying the debt: *Edwards v Yeates* (1826) Ry & M. 360, 361.

510 *Peirse v Bowles and Spibey* (1816) 1 Stark. 323.

CHAPTER 22

DISCHARGE BY AGREEMENT

		PARA.
1.	In general	22–001
2.	Release	22–003
3.	Accord and satisfaction	22–012
4.	Rescission	22–025
5.	Variation	22–032
6.	Waiver	22–040
7.	Provision for discharge in the contract itself	22–048

1. IN GENERAL

Generally. The discharge of a contract by agreement is a subject of considerable artificiality and refinement. The niceties of legal reasoning which appear in this branch of the law are not easy to justify,[1] but are attributable in the main to two causes. In the first place, the doctrine of consideration, which plays so important a role in the formation of a binding contract, has also been applied to its discharge.[2] Thus a distinction has to be drawn between those contracts which have been wholly executed on one side (i.e. where one party has performed all his obligations under the agreement) and those which are executory on both sides (i.e. where both parties still have some obligations to perform). In the former case, the party seeking to be discharged must prove either a release by deed or some consideration agreed by the other party ("accord and satisfaction") in place of his existing obligation or in addition to it.[3] In the latter case, consideration can usually be found in the mutual release by each party of his rights under the contract.[4] Secondly, the evidentiary requirements of the Statute of Frauds 1677 which required certain important classes of contract to be evidenced by writing,[5] were capable of producing even more serious instances of injustice than those which the statute was designed to prevent. Within the limits available to them, the judges endeavoured to circumvent the statute in order that it should not be made a cloak for fraud. Thus, although the variation of the term of a contract required to be evidenced by writing has to be proved by writing,[6] the discharge of the entire agreement[7] and the waiver of contractual terms[8] can be effected by parol. These distinctions have declined greatly in importance since the almost total 22–001

[1] *Samuel v Wadlow* [2007] EWCA Civ 155 at [35].

[2] This was criticised by Sir Frederick Pollock, *Principles of Contract*, 13th edn (1950), p.150, as an unwarrantable extension.

[3] See below, paras 22–003, 22–012; see also "Waiver", below, paras 22–044 et seq.

[4] See below, paras 22–025 et seq.

[5] See above, paras 4–009 et seq.

[6] See below, para.22–033.

[7] See below, para.22–030.

[8] See below, para.22–041.

repeal of the Statute of Frauds by the Law Reform (Enforcement of Contracts) Act 1954[9] and a modern court may be unwilling to draw a distinction unless it is strictly necessary for it to do so.[10]

22–002 **Discharge of right of action arising from breach.** It will be convenient also to deal in this chapter with the discharge by agreement of a right of action arising from a breach of contract.

2. RELEASE

22–003 **Release by deed.** Where a contract has been executed by one party only, that is to say, where only one party has fully performed his obligations under the contract and the other party has some obligations still outstanding, the contract may be discharged at any time before breach by release by deed.[11] Also, where one party has committed a breach of the contract, it will be a defence for him to show that the other party has by deed released the cause of action accruing from such breach.[12] The employment of a deed dispenses with the necessity for consideration.[13]

22–004 **Parol release.** A mere parol release, whether oral or in writing, without valuable consideration amounts to *nudum pactum* and is normally insufficient to effect a discharge either at law[14] or in equity.[15] A parol release given in return for valuable consideration amounts to accord and satisfaction.[16]

22–005 **Construction of release.** No particular form of words is necessary to constitute a valid release, and any words which show an evident intention to renounce a claim or discharge the obligation are sufficient.[17] The normal rules relating to the construction of a written contract also apply to a release,[18] and so

---

[9] See above, para.4–009.

[10] *Samuel v Wadlow* [2007] EWCA Civ 155 at [34]–[46].

[11] *Foster v Dawber* (1851) 6 Exch. 839, 851. The need for a seal for the valid execution of an instrument as a deed by an individual was abolished when s.1 of the Law of Property (Miscellaneous Provisions) Act 1989 came into force.

[12] *Tetley v Wanless* (1867) L.R. 2 Ex. 275. See also *Barker v St Quintin* (1844) 12 M. & W. 441 (debt of record).

[13] *Preston v Christmas* (1759) 2 Wils.K.B. 86.

[14] *Pinnel's Case* (1602) 5 Co. Rep. 117a; *Fitch v Sutton* (1804) 5 East 230; *Harris v Goodwyn* (1841) 2 M. & G. 405; *Foster v Dawber* (1851) 6 Exch. 839, 851; *De Bussche v Alt* (1878) 8 Ch D 286; *Foakes v Beer* (1884) 9 App. Cas. 605 (see above, para.3–115). *Bank of Credit and Commerce International SA (In Liquidation) v Ali* [1999] I.C.R. 1068, 1078. If a receipt is given, expressing that money has been received in satisfaction of all demands, it is open to the parties to contradict such a receipt: *Foster v Dawber* (1851) 6 Exch. 839, 848. For exceptions to this rule, see above, paras 3–118—3–136; below, paras 22–016—22–018.

[15] *Byrn v Godfrey* (1798) 4 Ves. 6; *Tufnell v Constable* (1836) 8 Sim. 69; *Cross v Sprigg* (1849) 6 Hare 552 (reversed on other grounds: (1850) 2 Mac. & G. 113); *Jorden v Money* (1854) 5 H.L.C. 185; *Luxmore v Clifton* (1867) 17 L.T. 460. See also *Stackhouse v Barnston* (1805) 10 Ves. 453, 466. It is doubtful whether earlier cases in equity culminating in *Flower v Marten* (1837) 2 My. & Cr. 459, can now be considered good law. But see above, paras 3–085, 3–128 et seq.; below, paras 22–016—22–018, 22–044.

[16] See below, para.22–012.

[17] Co.Litt. 264; Com.Dig. *Release* (A.1); Bac.Abr. *Release* (A).

[18] See *Bank of Credit and Commerce International SA v Ali* [2001] UKHL 8, [2002] 1 A.C. 251 at [8], [26] and above, paras 12–041 et seq., para.12–095.

a release in general terms is to be construed according to the particular purpose for which it was made.[19] In order to ascertain the intention of the parties, the court will have regard to the terms of the contract as a whole:

> "... giving the words used their natural and ordinary meaning in the context of the agreement, the parties' relationship and all the relevant facts surrounding the transaction so far as known to the parties."[20]

The scope of a release drafted in general terms may be limited either by the existence of a dispute between the parties or by the parties' knowledge, at the time of entry into the release, of the existence of the claim. Where the parties have a particular dispute in mind when entering into the release, the scope of the dispute "provides a limiting background context to the document".[21] Even where the parties do not have a particular dispute in mind, the circumstances in which the release was given may suggest that the release should only apply to a particular subject matter.[22] The parties' knowledge of the existence of the claim at the time of entry into the release is more equivocal. The fact that the existence of the claim was unknown to both parties does not mean that such a claim falls outside the scope of the release. Parties who enter into a release frequently want to achieve finality and so the:

> "... wording of a general release and the context in which it was given commonly make plain that the parties intended that the release should not be confined to known claims."[23]

It would appear that a person will not be allowed to rely upon a release in general terms if he knew that the other party had a claim and also knew that the other

---

[19] *Bank of Credit and Commerce International SA v Ali* [2001] UKHL 8; [2002] 1 A.C. 251 at [8] and [26]. *L. & S.W. Ry v Blackmore* (1870) L.R. 4 H.L. 610, 623; *Solly v Forbes* (1820) 2 B. & B. 38, 47; *Morley v Frear* (1830) 6 Bing. 547, 555.

[20] *Bank of Credit and Commerce International SA v Ali* [2001] UKHL 8, [2002] 1 A.C. 251. In other words the courts will apply the general rules of interpretation as re-stated by Lord Hoffmann in *Investors Compensation Scheme Ltd v West Bromwich Building Society* [1998] 1 W.L.R. 896, 912–913 (on which see paras 12–043 et seq.), as qualified by Lord Hoffmann in *Bank of Credit and Commerce International SA v Ali* [2001] UKHL 8, [2002] 1 A.C. 251 at [39].

[21] *Bank of Credit and Commerce International SA v Ali* [2001] UKHL 8, [2002] 1 A.C. 251 at [41]. See also *Directors of the London and South Western Railway Co v Blackburn* (1870) L.R. 4 H.L. 610 and *Lyall v Edwards* (1861) 6 H. & N. 337.

[22] *Bank of Credit and Commerce International SA v Ali* [2001] UKHL 8, [2002] 1 A.C. 251 at [28]. On the facts of the case the release was held to be confined to matters relating to the termination of the employment relationship and so did not encompass a claim for stigma damages arising out of an alleged breach of an implied duty owed to the employees not to carry out a dishonest or corrupt business. A further factor influencing their Lordships was the fact that the existence of such a claim, as a matter of law, was unknown at the time of entry into the release (indeed, this factor was held to have been "crucial" by the Court of Appeal in *Mostcash Plc v Fluor Ltd* [2002] EWCA Civ 975, [2002] B.L.R. 411 at [59]). See also *Cole v Gibson* (1750) 1 Ves. Sen. 503, *Lindo v Lindo* (1839) 1 Beav 496 and *Grant v John Grant & Sons Pty Ltd* (1954) 91 C.L.R. 112.

[23] *Bank of Credit and Commerce International SA v Ali* [2001] UKHL 8, [2002] 1 A.C. 251 at [27]; *Mostcash Plc v Fluor Ltd* [2002] EWCA Civ 975, [2002] B.L.R. 411. A party who wishes to ensure that a claim, the existence of which is unknown at the time of entry into the release, is covered by the release should use clear words to this effect because the courts may be reluctant to conclude that such was the intention of the parties in the absence of clear words to that effect (*Bank of Credit and Commerce International SA v Ali* [2001] UKHL 8, [2002] 1 A.C. 251 at [10]).

party was not aware that he had a claim.[24] But the construction of any individual release will necessarily depend upon its particular wording and phraseology.[25]

22–006 **Covenants not to sue.** A covenant not to sue without any limitation as to time is equivalent to a release.[26] The reason for this rule appears to be a desire to avoid the circuity of action which would otherwise arise if the covenantee recovered precisely the same damage that he suffered by reason of the covenantor suing on the original agreement.[27] But, at common law, a covenant, or agreement for valuable consideration, not to sue for a limited time was not equivalent to a release and did not bar the action on the contract.[28] The covenant was construed as giving the covenantee merely a right of action for its breach if the covenantor sued before the expiry of the time so limited. It did not operate as a bar to the original action but gave an action for damages.[29] A court of equity, however, would grant an injunction to restrain the covenantor from suing within that time,[30] and the equitable rule now prevails so as to provide the covenantee with a complete defence in that event.[31]

22–007 **Joint contractors.** The distinction between a release and a covenant not to sue can, however, be of importance in relation to the liability of joint contractors. This topic has been dealt with in the chapter on joint obligations earlier in this book.[32]

22–008 **Conditional release.** A release will be good although made subject to avoidance by the happening of a condition subsequent, as, for example, by the non-fulfilment of a compromise.[33]

---

[24] The point did not arise for decision in the House of Lords in *Bank of Credit and Commerce International SA v Ali* [2001] UKHL 8, [2002] 1 A.C. 251 but Lord Nicholls (at [32]) and Lord Hoffmann (at [70]) were of the view that a person should not be allowed to rely upon a release in general terms if he knew that the other party had a claim and knew that the other party was not aware that he had a claim. Lord Bingham (at [20]) and Lord Clyde (at [87]) chose to express no view on the point. The majority of the Court of Appeal also concluded that courts have an equitable jurisdiction to grant relief to the releasor if it would be unconscionable for the releasee to rely on the words of a general release (*Bank of Credit and Commerce International SA v Ali* [2000] I.C.R. 1410).

[25] Co.Litt. 264B, 291b; *Tynan v Bridges* (1612) Cro. Jac. 301; *Cutler v Goodwin* (1721) 11 Mod. R. 344; *Tetley v Wanless* (1867) L.R. 2 Ex. 275.

[26] *Hodges v Smith* (1599) Cro. Eliz. 623; *Clayton v Kynaston* (1699) 12 Mod. R. 221, 222; *Smith v Mapleback* (1786) 1 T.R. 441, 446; *Ford v Beech* (1848) 11 Q.B. 852; *Keyes v Elkins* (1864) 5 B. & S. 240; *Boosey v Wood* (1865) 3 H. & C. 484.

[27] *Fowell v Forrest* (1670) 2 Wms. Saund. 47 fn.1; *Ford v Beech* (1848) 11 Q.B. 852, 871.

[28] It was a principle of law that a personal action, once suspended by the act of the parties, was for ever extinct. The courts would not therefore construe the covenant or agreement as a legal suspension of the claimant's right to sue since this would have the effect of precluding him from ever suing at all. See Williams, *Joint Obligations*, para.61; *Ford v Beech* (1848) 11 Q.B. 852, 867.

[29] *Deux v Jefferies* (1594) Cro. Eliz. 352; *Thimbleby v Barron* (1838) 3 M. & W. 210; *Ford v Beech* (1848) 1 Q.B. 852; *Webb v Spicer* (1849) 13 Q.B. 886, 898; *Ray v Jones* (1865) 19 C.B.(N.S.) 416. Contrast *Foley v Fletcher* (1858) 3 H. & N. 769; *Bailey v Bowen* (1868) L.R. 3 Q.B. 133.

[30] *Beech v Ford* (1848) 7 Hare 208.

[31] Supreme Court Act 1981 s.49.

[32] See above, paras 17–017—17–020.

[33] *Newington v Levy* (1870) L.R. 6 C.P. 180; *Hall v Levy* (1875) L.R. 10 C.P. 154. See also *Slater v Jones* (1873) L.R. 8 Ex. 186, 192.

Bills of exchange. The release of a bill of exchange or promissory note[34] need not be effected by deed nor is any consideration required for such discharge.[35] Section 62 of the Bills of Exchange Act 1882 provides that where the holder of a bill at or after its maturity absolutely and unconditionally renounces his rights against the acceptor the bill is discharged. The renunciation must be in writing, unless the bill is delivered up to the acceptor.[36] 22–009

Effect of misrepresentation. A release obtained by misrepresentation will be set aside.[37] 22–010

Pleading of release. A defence alleging a release must be specifically pleaded.[38] 22–011

3. ACCORD AND SATISFACTION

Definition. 22–012

> "Accord and satisfaction is the purchase of a release from an obligation whether arising under contract or tort by means of any valuable consideration, not being the actual performance of the obligation itself. The accord is the agreement by which the obligation is discharged. The satisfaction is the consideration which makes the agreement operative."[39]

Thus, although a release not in the form of a deed is normally ineffective to discharge a contract which is executory on one side only,[40] it will operate as a discharge if the other party agrees to accept some other or additional consideration in return for the right which he abandons.[41] Whether there is a release or a compromise depends upon the substance rather than the form of the transaction between the parties.[42]

Compromise. Where a claim is asserted by one party which is disputed by the other, they may agree to compromise their dispute on terms mutually agreed 22–013

---

[34] Bills of Exchange Act 1882 s.89.

[35] See *Chalmers and Guest on Bills of Exchange*, 16th edn (2005), 8–061.

[36] The rights of a holder in due course after such release are not affected if he takes without notice of the release: see s.62(2). See Vol.II, para.34–139.

[37] *Wild v Williams* (1840) 6 M. & W. 490; *Hirschfeld v L.B. & S.C. Ry* (1876) 2 QBD 1.

[38] Although the CPR no longer contain any express reference to a release, it is advisable to continue to plead the defence specifically. The new rules relating to the contents of the defence are set out in CPR Pt 16, 16.5.

[39] *British Russian Gazette and Trade Outlook Ltd v Associated Newspapers Ltd* [1933] 2 K.B. 616, 643; *Bank of Credit and Commerce International SA v Ali* [1999] I.C.R. 1068, 1078.

[40] See above, paras 3–078, 22–004.

[41] *Wilkinson v Byers* (1834) 1 A. & E. 106; *Steeds v Steeds* (1889) 22 QBD 537.

[42] *Bank of Credit and Commerce International SA v Ali* [1999] I.C.R. 1068, 1078, although it should be noted that, while Lightman J. regarded the agreement between the parties as a compromise, the Court of Appeal ([2000] I.C.R. 1410, 1431) held that its true purpose was "not to compromise identified claims but to release BCCI from unidentified claims". In the House of Lords it was accepted that the document was a release and not a compromise ([2001] UKHL 8, [2002] 1 A.C. 251 at [40]).

between them.[43] Once a valid compromise has been reached, it is not open to the party against whom the claim is made to avoid the compromise on the ground that the claim was in fact invalid, provided that the claim was made in good faith and was reasonably believed to be valid by the party asserting it.[44] Conversely, the claimant cannot avoid the compromise on the ground that there was in fact no defence to the claim, provided that the other party bona fide and reasonably believed that he had a good defence either as to liability or as to amount. In order to establish a valid compromise, it must be shown that there has been an agreement (accord) which is complete[45] and certain in its terms,[46] and that consideration (satisfaction) has been given or promised[47] in return for the promised or actual forbearance to pursue the claim. It is a good defence to an action for breach of contract to show that the cause of action has been validly compromised.[48]

22–014 **Form of accord.** At common law, accord and satisfaction was no answer to a claim on a specialty, but the rule was otherwise in equity and the latter now prevails.[49] The accord need not be in writing even if the contract which it is sought to discharge, or for the breach of which a claim is made, is required by law to be made or evidenced in writing.[50] An oral accord will suffice, unless the accord itself constitutes a contract or transaction which is required to be made[51] or evidenced[52] in writing.

22–015 **Executory satisfaction.** At one time, a number of cases appeared to establish the rule that satisfaction was of no effect unless it was executed. While the satisfaction remained executory, that is to say, so long as the agreement to give satisfaction remained unperformed, the original claim was not discharged, nor would any action lie for breach of the accord.[53] Even a tender of performance of the satisfaction agreed upon was adjudged insufficient.[54] Only executed satisfaction would suffice. This rule, however, was never completely accepted[55] and it is

[43] See Foskett, *The Law and Practice of Compromise*, 6th edn (2005).
[44] See above, para.3–052.
[45] See above, para.2–112.
[46] See above, para.2–139.
[47] See below, para.22–015.
[48] *British Russian Gazette and Trade Outlook Ltd v Associated Newspapers Ltd* [1933] 2 K.B. 616. See also *Knowles v Roberts* (1888) 38 Ch D 263, 272. Alternatively, the defendant may apply by summons for an order staying the proceedings and the court has jurisdiction to stay under the Supreme Court Act 1981 s.19.
[49] Supreme Court Act 1981 s.49; *Steeds v Steeds* (1889) 22 QBD 537.
[50] *Lavery v Turley* (1860) 6 H. & N. 239. See also below, para.22–030.
[51] e.g. a legal assignment: see above, para.19–006. See also Law of Property (Miscellaneous Provisions) Act 1989 s.2(1), above, paras 4–052—4–088.
[52] See above, para.4–009; Vol.II, Ch.44.
[53] *Peytoe's Case* (1612) 9 Co. Rep. 77b; *James v David* (1793) 5 T.R. 141; *Reeves v Hearne* (1836) 1 M. & W. 323; *Bayley v Homan* (1837) 3 Bing. N.C. 915; *Griffith v Owen* (1844) 13 M. & W. 58; *Gifford v Whittaker* (1844) 6 Q.B. 249; *Woods v Pickersgill* (1859) 1 F. & F. 710; *Edwards v Hancher* (1875) 1 C.P.D. 111.
[54] *Gabriel v Dresser* (1855) 15 C.B. 622.
[55] *Goring v Goring* (1602) Yelv. 11; *Good v Cheesman* (1831) 2 B. & Ad. 328; *Cartwright v Cooke* (1832) 3 B. & Ad. 701; *Ford v Beech* (1848) 11 Q.B. 852; *Crowther v Farrer* (1850) 15 Q.B. 677; *Henderson v Stobart* (1850) 5 Exch. 99; *Elton Crop Dyeing Co Ltd v Broadbent & Son Ltd* (1919) 89 L.J.K.B. 186; *Morris v Baron & Co* [1918] A.C. 1, 35.

now established that satisfaction may be executory.[56] The question is one of the construction of the accord: whether it was intended that the promise itself or the performance of the promise should discharge the original claim[57]:

> "The rational distinction seems to be, that if the promise be received in satisfaction, it is a good satisfaction; but if the performance, not the promise, is intended to operate in satisfaction, there will be no satisfaction without performance."[58]

In the modern law, therefore, a claimant may still insist upon the performance of some act by the other party in satisfaction of his claim. In that case, there is no satisfaction until performance, and the other party remains liable on the original claim until the satisfaction is executed.[59] More often, however, the claimant will agree to accept the other party's promise of performance in satisfaction of his claim. The original claim is then discharged from the date of the agreement[60] and cannot be revived. The claimant's sole remedy, in the event that the other party fails to perform, is by action for breach of the substituted agreement, and he has no right of resort to the original claim.[61] If he wishes to preserve his right to proceed with the original claim should the other party fail to perform, an express term should be incorporated in the agreement to that effect.[62]

Payment of part of a debt. Where there is a claim for a liquidated sum, the liability for which is not in dispute,[63] the acceptance of a smaller sum in satisfaction does not relieve the debtor for there is no consideration for the creditor's abandonment of the balance.[64] This rule, which is generally known as the rule in *Pinnel's Case*,[65] is nevertheless subject to a number of qualifications, the combined effect of which is substantially to undermine the rule. 22–016

Payment in different form, at earlier time, in different place. A debt may be discharged by the acceptance of something different in nature from part payment of the debt, for then there is accord and satisfaction.[66] Even if the satisfaction accepted is much less in value than the debt, it will constitute a good 22–017

---

[56] *British Russian Gazette and Trade Outlook Ltd v Associated Newspapers Ltd* [1933] 2 K.B. 616, 643–645; *Jameson v Central Electricity Generating Board* [1998] Q.B. 323, 335.

[57] [1933] 2 K.B. 616, 645, 655; *Green v Rozen* [1955] 1 W.L.R. 741.

[58] Smith, *Leading Cases*, 13th edn, p.385.

[59] *British Russian Gazette and Trade Outlook Ltd v Associated Newspapers Ltd* [1933] 2 K.B. 616, 652. But see the statements of Greer L.J.; 655 (counterclaim).

[60] [1933] 2 K.B. 616, 644; *Morris v Baron & Co* [1918] A.C. 1, 35.

[61] *British Russian Gazette and Trade Outlook Ltd v Associated Newspapers Ltd* [1933] 2 K.B. 616, 644, 654. See also the cases cited in fn.55, above, and *Green v Rozen* [1955] 1 W.L.R. 741.

[62] For the effect of such a provision, see *Smith v Shirley and Baylis* (1875) 32 L.T. 234.

[63] For the compromise of disputed claims, see above, para.3–046.

[64] *Richard and Bartlet's Case* (1584) 1 Leon. 19; *Pinnel's Case* (1602) 5 Co. Rep. 117a; *Cumber v Wane* (1721) 1 Str. 426; *Flitch v Sutton* (1804) 5 East 230; *Down v Hatcher* (1839) 10 A. & E. 121; *McManus v Bark* (1870) L.R. 5 Ex. 65; *Foakes v Beer* (1884) 9 App. Cas. 605; *Underwood v Underwood* [1894] P. 204; *Hookham v Mayle* (1906) 22 T.L.R. 241; *D. & C. Builders v Rees* [1966] 2 Q.B. 617; *Tiney Engineering v Amods Knitting Machinery* Unreported May 15, 1986 (C.A.T. No.440); *Re Selectmove* [1995] 1 W.L.R. 474; *Ferguson v Davies* [1997] 1 All E.R. 315, although Evans L.J. at (326) expressed no view on this issue. See above, para.3–115.

[65] (1602) 5 Co. Rep. 117a.

[66] See above, para.3–122.

discharge, since the courts will not inquire into the adequacy of consideration.[67] Also payment by a debtor at an earlier time or in a different place from that required by the original contract, if made at the request and for the benefit of the creditor,[68] will effect a discharge.[69]

22–018 **Exceptions.** Other important qualifications relate to part-payment by a third party,[70] compositions with creditors[71] and the *High Trees* principle.[72]

22–019 **Joint obligations.** The effect of accord and satisfaction on joint obligations has been dealt with in the chapter on joint obligations earlier in this book.[73]

22–020 **Bill of exchange.** No satisfaction is required for the discharge of a bill of exchange or promissory note.[74] The holder may renounce his rights in writing, or by delivery up of the bill to the acceptor.[75]

22–021 **Ineffective accord.** An accord may be vitiated by any circumstance that would render a contract void or voidable, for example, by misrepresentation,[76] mistake,[77] or duress.[78]

22–022 **Evidence of accord.** The question whether there has been an accord and satisfaction is a question of fact.[79] Thus, retention and use by a creditor of a cheque sent by a debtor in full and final satisfaction of a larger claim does not, as a matter of law, constitute an accord and satisfaction.[80] The intention of the

---

[67] See above, para.3–009.

[68] cf. *Vanbergen v St Edmund's Properties Ltd* [1933] 2 K.B. 223.

[69] *Pinnel's Case* (1602) 5 Co. Rep. 117a.

[70] See above, para.3–126.

[71] See above, para.3–125.

[72] See above, para.3–128.

[73] See above, para.17–017.

[74] See above, para.22–009.

[75] Bills of Exchange Act 1882 ss.62, 89; see Vol.II, para.34–139.

[76] e.g. *Hirschfield v L.B. & S.C. Ry* (1876) 2 QBD 1; *Gilbert v Endean* (1878) 9 Ch D 259; *Re Roberts* [1905] 1 Ch. 704; *Dietz v Lennig Chemicals Ltd* [1969] 1 A.C. 170; cf. *Wales v Wadham* [1977] 1 W.L.R. 199. See above, Ch.6.

[77] An example of a compromise being set aside on the ground of mistake is provided by the decision of the Court of Appeal in *Magee v Pennine Insurance Co Ltd* [1969] 2 Q.B. 507. However the Court of Appeal in *Great Peace Shipping Ltd v Tsavliris Salvage (International) Ltd* [2002] EWCA Civ 1407; [2003] Q.B. 679 (on which see above, para.5–060), held that *Magee* was no longer good law (see *Great Peace* at [136]–[140], [153] and [160]). A party seeking to set aside an agreement on the ground of common mistake must therefore satisfy the more stringent requirements laid down by the House of Lords in *Bell v Lever Bros Ltd* [1932] A.C. 161 (on which see para.5–028, above). This is likely to be an extremely difficult hurdle to overcome (see, for example, *Champion Investments Ltd v Ahmed* [2004] All E.R. (D) 28 (Aug)). In the exceptional case in which it is overcome, compromise may be vitiated by a mistake of law as well as a mistake of fact: *Brennan v Bolt Burden (A Firm)* [2004] EWCA Civ 1017; [2005] Q.B. 303 at [17]. See above, para.5–055.

[78] e.g. *D. & C. Builders v Rees* [1966] 2 Q.B. 617. See above, Ch.7.

[79] *Stour Valley Builders v Stuart, The Independent*, February 9, 1993 CA; cf. *Pereira v Inspirations East Ltd* (1992) C.A.T. 1048, discussed in more detail by Foskett, *The Law and Practice of Compromise*, 6th edn (2005), paras 3–33—3–44.

[80] *Day v McLea* (1889) 22 QBD 610; *Auriena Ltd v Haigh and Ringrose Ltd* (1988) Const. L.J. 200; *Stour Valley Builders v Stuart, The Independent*, February 9, 1993 CA; *Ferguson v Davies* [1997] 1 All E.R. 315; *Inland Revenue Commissioners v Fry* [2001] S.T.C. 1715; cf. *Hirachand Punamchand v Temple* [1911] 2 K.B. 330.

creditor in cashing the cheque must be objectively ascertained. Cashing a cheque or retention of a cheque without rejection is strong evidence of assent by the creditor[81] but it is not conclusive evidence so that a creditor who, at the moment of paying in the cheque or shortly thereafter makes clear that he is not assenting to the conditions imposed by the debtor will not be held to have entered into an accord and satisfaction.[82] The construction of any correspondence which, it is alleged, evidences the accord is, however, a question of law.[83]

Pleading. Both the accord and the satisfaction should be specifically pleaded.[84] 22–023

Judgment or order. A compromise may by consent be made the subject of a judgment or order of the court. A consent judgment will ordinarily extinguish by merger[85] the contract of compromise, but a consent order will not have this effect. It does not itself constitute a contract, but it is sufficient evidence of the contract of compromise on which it is based, and such contract is no less a contract and subject to the incidents of a contract because there is superadded the command of a judge.[86] Where an action has been commenced and a compromise has been reached on agreed terms, the usual form of order sought by consent is a *Tomlin* order,[87] which provides that all further proceedings in the action be stayed, except for the purpose of carrying such terms into effect, with liberty to apply[88] as to carrying such terms into effect. The court will, if necessary, in appropriate cases enforce the terms of a compromise contained in a *Tomlin* order by specific performance.[89] 22–024

4. RESCISSION

Rescission by agreement. Where a contract is executory on both sides, that is to say, where neither party has performed the whole of his obligations under 22–025

[81] *Stour Valley Builders v Stuart, The Independent*, February 9, 1993 CA; *Bracken v Billinghurst* [2003] EWHC 1333 (TCC), [2003] All E.R. (D) 488 (Jul).

[82] *Day v McLea* (1889) 22 QBD 610; *Stour Valley Builders v Stuart, The Independent*, February 9, 1993 CA; *Inland Revenue Commissioners v Fry* [2001] S.T.C. 1715; *Joinery Plus Ltd (In Administration) v Laing Ltd* [2003] EWHC 3513 (TCC), (2003) 87 Con.L.R. 87 at [91]–[96].

[83] *Bunge SA v Kruse* [1977] 1 Lloyd's Rep. 492; *Kitchen Design and Advice Ltd v Lea Valley Water Co* [1989] 2 Lloyd's Rep. 221; *Ferguson v Davies* [1997] 1 All E.R. 315.

[84] *Flockton v Hall* (1849) 14 Q.B. 380, 386. Although the CPR do not expressly require the defence to be specifically pleaded, it is advisable to continue to plead it specifically. The new rules relating to the contents of the defence are set out in CPR Pt 16 r.16.5.

[85] See below, para.25–007.

[86] *Wentworth v Bullen* (1829) 9 B. & C. 840, 850; *Lievesley v Gilmore* (1866) L.R. 1 C.P. 570.

[87] *Practice Note* [1927] W.N. 290. See *Chitty and Jacob's Queen's Bench Forms*, 21st edn (1996, now with 8th Cumulative Supplement), paras 1339, 1350; cf. *McCallum v Country Residences Ltd* [1965] 1 W.L.R. 657 (no consent).

[88] *Cristel v Cristel* [1951] 2 K.B. 725.

[89] *Anders Utkilens Rederi A/S v O/Y Lovisa Stevedoring Co A/B* [1985] 2 All E.R. 669.

it, it may be rescinded by mutual agreement, express or implied.[90] A partially executed contract can be rescinded by agreement provided that there are obligations on both sides which remain unperformed. Similarly, a contract which has been fully performed by one party can be rescinded provided that the other party returns the performance which he has received and in turn is released from his own obligation to perform under the contract. The consideration for the discharge in each case is found in the abandonment by each party of his right to performance or his right to damages, as the case may be.[91] A rescission of this nature must be distinguished from a repudiation by one party, which the other party may elect to treat as a discharge of the obligation,[92] and from the right to rescind which is given to one party in cases of fraud, misrepresentation, duress and undue influence, and in certain cases of mistake.[93] It depends upon the consent of both parties, to be gathered from their words or conduct and not upon the intimation by one of them that he does not intend to be bound by the agreement.[94]

22–026 **Effect of rescission.** A contract which is rescinded by agreement is completely discharged and cannot be revived.[95] The parties will frequently make express provision for the restoration of money paid or for payment for services performed or goods supplied under the contract prior to rescission. In the absence of such provision (express or implied) it may be possible to bring a restitutionary claim provided that the contract has been set aside.[96] Money paid may be recoverable where the consideration for the payment has wholly failed.[97] It is more doubtful whether a claim can be brought in the case where goods have been supplied or services provided prior to the rescission of the contract because, in the case where performance has not been completed, the party in receipt of the performance may be able to contend that it was not enriched by receipt of partial performance.[98]

22–027 **Abandonment.** It is open to the court to infer that the parties have mutually agreed to abandon their contract where the contract has been followed by a long period of delay or inactivity on both sides.[99] The party seeking to establish

---

[90] *Davis v Street* (1823) 1 C. & P. 18; *Foster v Dawber* (1851) 6 Exch. 839, 851; *Morris v Baron & Co* [1918] A.C. 1; *Rose & Frank Co v J.R. Crompton & Bros Ltd* [1925] A.C. 445.

[91] *Scarf v Jardine* (1882) 7 App. Cas. 345, 351; *Raggow v Scougall & Co* (1915) 31 T.L.R. 564.

[92] See below, para.24–047.

[93] See above, Chs 5, 6 and 7.

[94] *Ogilvy and Mather Ltd v Silverado Blue Ltd* [2007] EWHC 1285 (QB), [2007] All E.R. (D) 383 (May) at [21]; *Intense Investments Ltd v Development Ventures Ltd* [2006] EWHC 1628 (TCC), [2006] All E.R. (D) 346 (Jun) at [117].

[95] *R. v Inhabitants of Gresham* (1786) 1 Term Rep. 101. It is, of course, open to the parties to enter into a fresh agreement.

[96] *West v Downes* (1778) 1 Doug. K.B. 23; *Gompertz v Denton* (1832) 1 C. & M. 207.

[97] *Towers v Barratt* (1786) 1 Term Rep. 133; *Davis v Street* (1823) 1 C. & P. 18. See below, 29–054.

[98] *Lamburn v Cruden* (1841) 2 Man. & G 253.

[99] *André & Cie SA v Marine Transocean Ltd (The Splendid Sun)* [1981] Q.B. 64; *Tracomin SA v Anton C. Nielsen A/S* [1984] 2 Lloyd's Rep. 195; *Excomm Ltd v Guan Guan Shipping (Pte) Ltd* [1987] 1 Lloyd's Rep. 330 (above, paras 2–070, 2–076—2–077). See also *Tyers v Rosedale and Ferryhill Iron Co* (1875) L.R. 10 Ex. 195.

abandonment of a contract must show that the other party so conducted himself as to entitle him to assume, and that he did assume, that the contract was agreed to be abandoned *sub silentio.*[100]

22–028 **Substituted contract.** A rescission of the contract will also be implied where the parties have effected such an alteration of its terms as to substitute a new contract in its place.[101] The question whether a rescission has been effected is frequently one of considerable difficulty, for it is necessary to distinguish a rescission of the contract from a variation which merely qualifies the existing rights and obligations.[102] If a rescission is effected the contract is extinguished; if only a variation, it continues to exist in an altered form.[103] The decision on this point will depend on the intention of the parties to be gathered from an examination of the terms of the subsequent agreement and from all the surrounding circumstances.[104] Rescission will be presumed when the parties enter into a new agreement which is entirely inconsistent with the old, or, if not entirely inconsistent with it, inconsistent with it to an extent that goes to the very root of it.[105] The change must be fundamental[106] and:

> "... the question is whether the common intention of the parties was to 'abrogate', 'rescind,' 'supersede' or 'extinguish' the old contract by a 'substitution' of a 'completely new' or 'self-subsisting' agreement."[107]

It is not necessary to create a *scintilla temporis* between the old and the new agreement for there to be a rescission and replacement; it can be achieved concurrently in the same document.[108]

---

[100] *Paal Wilson & Co A/S v Partenreederei Hannah Blumenthal* [1983] 1 A.C. 854, 924; *Allied Marine Transport Ltd v Vale do Rio Doce Navegacao SA (The Leonidas D.)* [1985] 1 W.L.R. 925 (interpreting *Pearle Mill Co v Ivy Tannery Co Ltd* [1919] 1 K.B. 78); *Collin v Duke of Westminster* [1985] Q.B. 581; *MSC Mediterranean Shipping Co SA v B.R.E. Metro-Ltd* [1985] 2 Lloyd's Rep. 239; *Cie. Française d'Importation et Distribution v Deutsche Continental Handelsgesellschaft* [1985] 2 Lloyd's Rep. 592; *Gebr. van Weelde Scheepvaartkantor BV v Compania Naviera Sea Orient SA* [1987] 2 Lloyd's Rep. 223; *Food Corp of India v Antclizo Shipping Corp* [1988] 1 W.L.R. 603; *Tankrederei Ahrenkeil GmbH v Frahuil SA* [1988] 2 Lloyd's Rep. 486; *Thai-Europe Tapioca Service Ltd v Seine Navigation Co Inc* [1989] 2 Lloyd's Rep. 506.

[101] *Thornhill v Neats* (1860) 8 C.B.(N.S.) 831; *Hunt v S.E. Ry* (1875) 45 L.J.Q.B. 87; *Williams Bros v Agius Ltd* [1914] A.C. 510, 527; *Raggow v Scougall & Co* (1915) 31 T.L.R. 564; *Morris v Baron & Co* [1918] A.C. 1; *British & Beningtons Ltd v N.W. Cachar Tea Co Ltd* [1923] A.C. 48, 69; *Rose & Frank Co v J.R. Crompton & Bros Ltd* [1925] A.C. 445.

[102] *British & Beningtons Ltd v N.W. Cachar Tea Co Ltd* [1923] A.C. 48; *Royal Exchange Assurance v Hope* [1928] Ch. 179; and see the cases cited in para.22–033 fn.130, below.

[103] *Compagnie Noga D'Importation et D'Exportation SA v Abacha* [2003] EWCA Civ 1100; [2003] All E.R. (D) 400 (Jul) at [57].

[104] *United Dominions Trust (Jamaica) Ltd v Shoucair* [1969] 1 A.C. 340; *Compagnie Noga D'Importation et D'Exportation SA v Abacha* [2003] EWCA Civ 1100; [2003] All E.R. (D) 400 (Jul); *Sookraj v Samaroo* [2004] UKPC 50; *Samuel v Wadlow* [2007] EWCA Civ 155.

[105] *British & Beningtons Ltd v N.W. Cachar Tea Co Ltd* [1923] A.C. 48, 62.

[106] [1923] A.C. 48.

[107] [1923] A.C. 48, 67.

[108] *Compagnie Noga D'Importation et D'Exportation SA v Abacha* [2003] EWCA Civ 1100; [2003] All E.R. (D) 400 (Jul) at [57].

22–029 In *Morris v Baron & Co*[109] a written contract was entered into for the sale of some cloth. A dispute arose and legal proceedings were begun. The parties orally agreed that the action and counterclaim should be withdrawn, that an extension should be given to the buyer for payment of a sum owed by him under the contract and that he should have an option to purchase the goods remaining due to him instead of being bound to take delivery. The House of Lords held that the original contract of sale was discharged by the substituted agreement. Lord Dunedin commented:

> "The difference between variation and rescission is a real one, and is tested, to my thinking, by this: In the first case there are no such executory clauses in the second arrangement as would enable you to sue upon that alone if the first did not exist; in the second you could sue on the second arrangement alone, and the first contract is got rid of either by express words to that effect, or because, the second dealing with the same subject-matter as the first but in a different way, it is impossible that the two should be both performed."[110]

In order to extinguish the original contract, it is not necessary that the substituted agreement should have been performed; an executory contract is sufficient.[111] Nor is it necessary that it should amount to an enforceable agreement.[112]

22–030 **Form of rescission.** The old rule of the common law was that a contract under seal could only be rescinded by a contract under seal,[113] but in equity a rescission not under seal provided a good defence to an action on the deed. Since the Judicature Act 1873, the equitable rule prevails, so that now a deed can be rescinded by a written or oral agreement.[114] Even if the original contract is one which is required by law to be made in writing, as in the case of a contract for the sale or other disposition of an interest in land,[115] or to be evidenced by writing as in the case of those contracts within the Statute of Frauds 1677,[116] an oral agreement is sufficient to effect its discharge.[117] Nevertheless, the new agreement may itself be unenforceable unless so evidenced. Thus in *Morris v Baron & Co*[118] the original contract for the sale of cloth was one which was then required by s.4 of the Sale of Goods Act 1893[119] to be evidenced in writing. The subsequent oral agreement was sufficient to discharge the original contract, but

---

[109] [1918] A.C. 1.

[110] [1918] A.C. 1, 25–26.

[111] *Taylor v Hilary* (1835) 1 Cr. M. & R. 741.

[112] *Morris v Baron & Co* [1918] A.C. 1; *Rose & Frank Co v J.R. Crompton & Bros Ltd* [1925] A.C. 445; cf. *Firth v Midland Ry* (1875) L.R. 20 Eq. 100. See below, para.22–030.

[113] *Kaye v Waghorn* (1809) 1 Taunt. 428; *West v Blakeway* (1841) 2 M. & G. 729.

[114] *Berry v Berry* [1929] 2 K.B. 316; Supreme Court Act 1981 s.49.

[115] Law of Property (Miscellaneous Provisions) Act 1989 s.2(1). See above, para.4–052.

[116] ss.4 and 17, as amended by the Law Reform (Enforcement of Contracts) Act 1954. See above, para.4–009.

[117] Law of Property (Miscellaneous Provisions) Act 1989 s.2(1) requires that a contract falling within its scope be "*made* in writing" but does not regulate the discharge or unmaking of such a contract.

[118] [1918] A.C. 1.

[119] Re-enacting s.17 of the Statute of Frauds 1677; repealed by the Law Reform (Enforcement of Contracts) Act 1954. See above, para.4–009.

was itself unenforceable for want of writing. In the result, no action could be maintained on the original contract since this had been extinguished, nor on the subsequent agreement since this was unenforceable.[120]

Novation. Novation is a generic term which signifies: 22–031

> ". . . that there being a contract in existence, some new contract is substituted for it, either between the same parties (for that might be) or between different parties; the consideration mutually being the discharge of the old contract."[121]

In particular, however, it denotes the rescission of one contract and the substitution of another in which the same acts are to be performed by different parties.[122] A novation cannot be forced on a new party without his agreement. So, for example, if there is a contract for the sale and purchase of a ship under which it is agreed that the actual purchaser of the ship will be a company to be nominated by and substituted for the buyer by novation, such substitution must be accepted by the company, either by authorising the nomination or by ratifying it after it has been made.[123]

5. VARIATION[124]

Variation. The parties to a contract may effect a variation of the contract by modifying or altering its terms by mutual agreement.[125] In *Berry v Berry*[126] a husband and wife entered into a separation deed whereby the husband covenanted to pay to the wife a certain sum each year for her support. His earnings proved insufficient to meet this obligation, so they agreed in writing to vary the financial provisions. It was held that this variation was valid and enforceable, and that it could be set up by the husband as a defence to an action against him on 22–032

---

[120] See also *Williams v Moss Empires* [1915] 3 K.B. 242; *United Dominions Trust (Jamaica) Ltd v Shoucair* [1969] 1 A.C. 340.

[121] *Scarf v Jardine* (1882) 7 App. Cas. 345, 351; *The Tychy (No.2)* [2001] 1 Lloyd's Rep. 10, 24.

[122] Partnership Act 1890 s.7(3); *Miller's Case* (1877) 3 Ch D 391; *Scarf v Jardine* (1882) 7 App. Cas. 345 ; *Re Head* [1894] 2 Ch. 236; *Re United Railways of Havana and Regla Warehouses Ltd* [1960] Ch. 52, 84; *Chatsworth Investments Ltd v Cussins (Contractors) Ltd* [1969] 1 W.L.R. 1; cf. *Liversidge v Broadbent* (1859) 4 H. & N. 603; *Conquest's Case* (1875) 1 Ch D 334. See above, paras 19–086—19–088.

[123] *Damon Compania Naviera SA v Hapag-Lloyd International SA* [1985] 1 W.L.R. 435; cf. *Aktion Maritime Corp of Liberia v S. Kasmas & Bros Ltd* [1987] 1 Lloyd's Rep. 283, 311.

[124] See generally Wilken and Villiers, *The Law of Waiver, Variation and Estoppel*, 2nd edn (2002), Ch. 2.

[125] *Robinson v Page* (1826) 3 Russ. 114; *Goss v Lord Nugent* (1833) 5 B. & Ad. 58, 65; *Stead v Dawber* (1839) 10 A. & E. 57, 65; *Dodd v Churton* [1897] 1 Q.B. 562; *Fenner v Blake* [1900] 1 Q.B. 426; *Royal Exchange Assurance v Hope* [1928] Ch. 179. See Dugdale and Yates (1976) 39 M.L.R. 680.

[126] [1929] 2 K.B. 316.

the original deed. A mere unilateral notification by one party to the other, in the absence of any agreement, cannot constitute a variation of a contract.[127]

22–033 **Form of variation.** As in the case of a rescission of a contract, the terms of a deed or written instrument may be varied by a subsequent agreement, whether oral or written.[128] This may be reconciled with the rule that extrinsic evidence is not admissible to vary or qualify the terms of a written instrument, for that rule only relates to the ascertainment of the original intention of the parties, and not to a subsequent variation.[129] A contract required by law to be made in or evidenced by writing can only be varied by writing,[130] although, as we have seen, it can be rescinded by parol.[131] In *Goss v Lord Nugent*[132] the plaintiff agreed in writing to sell to the defendant certain plots of land. In an action by the plaintiff against the defendant for the purchase-money, the defendant pleaded that the title to one of the plots was defective. To this plea the plaintiff replied that the defendant had orally agreed to waive the defect and to accept the existing title. The court held that, since the contract was one which was required by law to be evidenced by writing,[133] the oral variation was not admissible and the defendant was entitled to succeed on the ground that a good title had not been made.

22–034 **Variation or recission?** Where the formal requirements apply to a variation but not to a rescission it is obviously important to determine whether there has been a mere variation of terms or a rescission, and this question may not be an easy one to answer.[134] The effect of a subsequent agreement—whether it constitutes a variation or a rescission—will depend upon the extent to which it alters the terms of the original contract. The test suggested by Lord Dunedin in *Morris v Baron & Co*[135] has already been referred to,[136] and in the same case Lord Haldane[137] said that, for a rescission:

[127] *Cowey v Liberian Operations Ltd* [1966] 2 Lloyd's Rep. 45; *T. Comedy (UK) Ltd v Easy Managed Transport Ltd* [2007] EWHC 611 (Comm), [2007] 2 Lloyd's Rep 397 at [29].

[128] *Berry v Berry* [1929] 2 K.B. 316. Statute may, of course, intervene to prescribe a particular form of variation (see, for example, s.82 of the Consumer Credit Act 1974 concerning an agreement to vary or supplement a consumer credit or consumer hire agreement: below, Vol.II, para.38–132).

[129] *Goss v Lord Nugent* (1833) 5 B. & Ad. 58, 64; see above, paras 12–095 et seq.

[130] *Robinson v Page* (1826) 3 Russ. 114; *Stead v Dawber* (1839) 10 A. & E. 57; *Marshall v Lynn* (1840) 6 M. & W. 109; *Noble v Ward* (1867) L.R. 2 Ex. 135; *Sanderson v Graves* (1875) L.R. 10 Ex. 234; *Plevins v Downing* (1876) 1 C.P.D. 220; *British and Beningtons Ltd v N.W. Cachar Tea Co Ltd* [1923] A.C. 48; *United Dominions Trust (Jamaica) Ltd v Shoucair* [1969] 1 A.C. 340; *Richards v Creighton-Griffiths (Investments) Ltd* (1972) 225 E.G. 2104; *New Hart Builders Ltd v Brindley* [1975] Ch. 342; *McCausland v Duncan Lawrie Ltd* [1997] 1 W.L.R. 38.

[131] See above, para.22–030.

[132] (1833) 5 B. & Ad. 58.

[133] Statute of Frauds 1677 s.4, re-enacted as s.40(1) of the Law of Property Act 1925, but subsequently repealed by s.2(8) of the Law of Property (Miscellaneous Provisions) Act 1989.

[134] In one modern case the distinction was stated to be "sterile", "artificial" and one "of legal theory which might have little commercial meaning for the parties": *Samuel v Wadlow* [2007] EWCA Civ 155 at [39], [40] and [45].

[135] [1918] A.C. 1, 5.

[136] See above, para.22–029.

[137] [1918] A.C. 1, 19.

"... there should have been made manifest the intention in any event of a complete extinction of the first and formal contract, and not merely the desire of an alteration, however sweeping, in terms which leave it still subsisting."

If the changes do not go "to the very root of the contract"[138] there is merely a variation.

Consideration. The agreement which varies the terms of an existing contract must be supported by consideration. In many cases, consideration can be found in the mutual abandonment of existing rights or the conferment of new benefits by each party on the other.[139] For example, an alteration of the money of account in a contract proposed or made by one party and accepted by the other is binding on both parties, since either may benefit from the variation.[140] Alternatively, consideration may be found in the assumption of additional obligations or the incurring of liability to an increased detriment.[141] The position is more difficult in the case of an agreement whereby one party undertakes an additional obligation, but the other party is merely bound to perform his existing obligations, or an agreement whereby one party undertakes an additional obligation, but for the benefit of that party alone. There is a line of authority of respectable antiquity which supports the view that in such a case the agreement will not be effective to vary the contract because no consideration is present.[142] But a more liberal approach has been adopted in some recent cases and the courts have been prepared to find consideration and enforce the agreement where it has conferred a practical benefit upon the promisor.[143] A mere forbearance or concession afforded by one party to the other for the latter's convenience and at his request does not constitute a variation, although it may be effective as a waiver or in equity.[144] Such a forbearance or concession need not be supported by consideration, and can be made orally even when the contract is one which is required to be made or evidenced in writing.[145] 22–035

Variation and collateral agreement. A variation of an existing agreement should be distinguished from a collateral agreement (or collateral warranty)[146] concluded before the main agreement is entered into under which one party agrees not to enforce a term of the main agreement[147] or assumes obligations in 22–036

[138] *British and Beningtons Ltd v N.W. Cachar Tea Co Ltd* [1923] A.C. 48, 62, 68.
[139] *Re William Porter & Co Ltd* [1937] 2 All E.R. 361.
[140] *Woodhouse A.C. Israel Cocoa Ltd SA v Nigerian Produce Marketing Co* [1972] A.C. 741, 757; *W.J. Alan & Co Ltd v El Nasr Export and Import Co* [1972] 2 Q.B. 189.
[141] *North Ocean Shipping Co Ltd v Hyundai Construction Co Ltd* [1979] Q.B. 705.
[142] *Stilk v Myrick* (1809) 2 Camp. 317; *Vanbergen v St Edmund's Properties Ltd* [1933] 2 K.B. 233; *Syros Shipping Co SA v Elaghill Trading Co* [1980] 2 Lloyd's Rep. 390; see above, paras 3–079—3–080. See also above, paras 3–115, 22–016—22–018 (payment of part of debt).
[143] *Williams v Roffey Bros & Nicholls (Contractors) Ltd* [1991] 1 Q.B. 1; *Anangel Atlas Compania Naviera SA v Ishikawajima-Harima Heavy Industries Co Ltd (No.2)* [1990] 2 Lloyd's Rep. 526; *Simon Container Machinery Ltd v Emba Machinery AB* [1998] 2 Lloyd's Rep. 429, 434–435.
[144] See above, para.3–085; below, para.22–040.
[145] See below, para.22–041.
[146] See above, paras 12–004, 12–103.
[147] *City and Westminster Properties (1934) Ltd v Mudd* [1959] Ch. 129.

addition to or at variance with those contained in the main agreement.[148] Such an agreement may not require to be evidenced by writing even though the main agreement requires to be made or evidenced in writing.[149] There seems to be no reason why such a collateral agreement should not be held to exist even if entered into after the conclusion of the main agreement, provided that there is present (and not merely past) consideration.[150]

22–037 **Variation and elucidation.** A variation should also be distinguished from the elucidation of a contract by the filling in of details which were agreed before the written contract was signed[151] or by the correction of mistakes which occurred when the contract was reduced to writing.[152]

22–038 **Effect of extra works.** Where, in a contract for the execution of specified works, it is provided that they shall be completed by a certain day, and that liquidated damages shall be payable by the contractor for non-completion to time, the general rule is that the employer will be unable to recover such liquidated damages if he orders extra work to be done which necessarily delays completion of the works.[153] However, the wording of the contract may be such that the original contract period continues to apply to the completion of the works even though additional work is ordered.[154] Alternatively, the contract may provide that the agreed date for completion shall be extended in the event that delay is caused by the additional work, in which case liquidated damages will be payable from that extended date if the works are not then completed.

22–039 **Unilateral power of variation.** At common law a contract may validly give to one contracting party the power unilaterally to vary the obligations of the parties to the contract. So, for example, in the case of a contract for the sale of goods, it is "a perfectly good contract to say that the price is to be settled by the buyer".[155] However, the power of one party unilaterally to vary the obligations of the parties may not be unlimited. The courts may imply into the contract a term the effect of which is to curtail that power.[156] In *Nash and Staunton v*

---

[148] *Erskine v Adeane* (1873) 8 Ch. App. 756; *De Lassalle v Guildford* [1901] 2 K.B. 215; *Brikom Investments Ltd v Carr* [1979] Q.B. 467; *Record v Bell* [1991] 1 W.L.R. 853; see above, paras 3–079, 12–103.

[149] *Record v Bell* [1991] 1 W.L.R. 853.

[150] See above, para.3–079.

[151] *Hudson v Revett* (1829) 5 Bing. 368; *Rudd v Bowles* [1912] 2 Ch. 60.

[152] *Bluck v Gompertz* (1852) 7 Exch. 362; see above, para.5–107.

[153] *Holme v Guppy* (1838) 3 M. & W. 387; *Russell v Sada Bandeira* (1862) 13 C.B.(N.S.) 149; *Dodd v Churton* [1897] 1 Q.B. 562; *Trollope & Colls Ltd v North West Metropolitan Regional Hospital Board* [1973] 1 W.L.R. 601, 607; *Astilleros Canarios SA v Cape Hatteras Shipping Co Inc* [1982] 1 Lloyd's Rep. 518. See generally *Keating on Construction Contracts*, 8th edn (2006), para.9–019 and also *Perini Pacific Ltd v Greater Vancouver Sewerage and Drainage District* (1966) 57 D.L.R. (2d) 307.

[154] *Macintosh v Midland Counties Ry* (1845) 14 M. & W. 548; *Legge v Horlock* (1848) 12 Q.B. 1015; *Jones v St John's College, Oxford* (1870) L.R. 6 Q.B. 115; *Tew v Newbold-on-Avon United District School Board* (1884) 1 Cab. & E. 260.

[155] *May and Butcher v R.* [1934] 2 K.B. 17, 21.

[156] See, for example, *Esso Petroleum v Addison* [2003] EWHC 1730 (Comm); *Mallone v BPB Industries Plc* [2002] EWCA Civ 126, [2002] I.C.R. 1045 and *Nash and Staunton v Paragon Finance Plc* [2001] EWCA Civ 1466, [2002] 1 W.L.R. 685.

Paragon Finance Plc[157] it was held that a lender's entitlement to vary interest rates was not completely unfettered. The court implied a term into the agreement to the effect that the rates of interest would not be set dishonestly, for an improper purpose, capriciously or arbitrarily, or in a way in which no reasonable mortgagee, acting reasonably, would do.[158] The legislature has also intervened to control clauses such as those which purport to entitle a lender unilaterally and in its absolute discretion to vary the rate of interest subject to notice to the debtor. Where such a provision is contained in a contract concluded between a seller or supplier and a consumer and that contract has not been individually negotiated, it may fall within the scope of the Unfair Terms in Consumer Contracts Regulations 1999.[159] Thus a contract term which enables the seller or supplier to alter the terms of the contract unilaterally without a valid reason which is specified in the contract,[160] or enables the seller or supplier to alter unilaterally without a valid reason any characteristics of the product or service to be provided,[161] or which provides for the price of the goods to be determined at the time of delivery, or allows a seller of goods or supplier of services to increase their price without in both cases giving the consumer the corresponding right to cancel the contract if the final price is too high in relation to the price agreed when the contract was concluded,[162] may constitute an unfair term which will not be binding upon the consumer.

6. WAIVER[163]

Waiver or forbearance. Where one party voluntarily accedes to a request by the other that he should forbear to insist on the mode of performance fixed by the contract, the court may hold that he has *waived* his right to require that the contract be performed in this respect according to its original tenor.[164] Waiver (in the sense of "waiver by estoppel" rather than "waiver by election"[165]) may also **22–040**

[157] [2001] EWCA Civ 1466, [2002] 1 W.L.R. 685. The Court of Appeal declined to follow dicta of Staughton L.J. in *Lombard Tricity Finance Ltd v Paton* [1989] 1 All E.R. 918, 923.

[158] On the facts of the case it was held that the borrowers had no real prospect of successfully establishing a breach of the implied term. The reason for the increase in interest rates was that the creditors were in financial difficulties and so had to increase their interest rates in order to protect their own financial position. It could not be said that they had acted dishonestly, capriciously, arbitrarily or wholly unreasonably in acting as they did. See also *Paragon Finance Plc v Pender* [2005] EWCA Civ 760, [2005] All E.R. (D) 307 (Jun).

[159] SI 1999/2083. See further above, Ch.15, where the scope of the Regulations and the definition of terms such as "seller or supplier", etc. is discussed in more detail.

[160] See Sch.2 to the 1999 Regulations para.1(j), (set out at para.15–103) although note the restricted applicability of this provision to the supply of financial services (para.2(b)).

[161] See Sch.2 to the 1999 Regulations para.1(k).

[162] See Sch.2 to the 1999 Regulations para.1(l), although note the restricted applicability of this provision to financial services (para.2(c)) and that it does not apply to "price-indexation clauses, where lawful, provided that the method by which prices vary is explicitly described" (para.2(d)).

[163] See generally Wilken and Villiers, *The Law of Waiver, Variation and Estoppel*, 2nd edn (2002), Chs 3–5.

[164] See above, para.3–081.

[165] The distinction between these two types of waiver is discussed, below para.24–007. See also *Motor Oil Hellas (Corinth) Refineries SA v Shipping Corp of India* [1990] 1 Lloyd's Rep. 391, 397–399.

be held to have occurred if, without any request, one party represents to the other that he will forbear to enforce or rely on a term of the contract to be performed or observed by the other party, and the other party acts in reliance on that representation.[166]

22–041 **Form of waiver.** A waiver may be oral or written or inferred from conduct[167] even though the provision waived is found in a contract required to be made in or evidenced by writing. It has been noted that any variation of a contract required to be made in or evidenced by writing must itself be made in or evidenced by writing.[168] If it is merely oral, it is of no effect. An oral forbearance or concession made by one party to the other does not require to be so evidenced, even if made at the latter's request.[169] Thus, what is ineffective as a variation may possibly have effect as a waiver. The formal requirements, in relation to such a contract, of rescission, variation and waiver were thus described by Goddard J. in *Besseler Waechter Glover & Co v South Derwent Coal Co*[170]:

> "If the parties agree to rescind their original contract and to substitute for it a new one, the latter must be evidenced by writing; so, too, if as a matter of contract the parties agree that the terms of the original agreement shall be varied, the variation must be in writing. But if what happens is a mere voluntary forbearance to insist on delivery or acceptance according to the strict terms of the written contract, the original contract remains unaffected, and the obligation to deliver and accept the full contract quantity still continues. . . . It does not appear to me to matter whether the request comes from one side or the other, or whether it is a matter which is convenient to one party or to both. What is of importance is whether it is a mere forbearance or a matter of contract."

The distinction between variation and waiver is, however, a difficult one to apply in practice,[171] particularly since a waiver may be consensual and be just as far reaching in its effect as a variation of the agreement. Fortunately, in respect of formal requirements,[172] it has become much less important since the almost total repeal of the Statute of Frauds by the Law Reform (Enforcement of Contracts) Act 1954.[173]

22–042 **Effect on party forbearing.** The party who forbears will be bound by the waiver and cannot set up the original terms of the agreement. If, by words or conduct, he has agreed or led the other party to believe that he will accept performance at a later date than or in a different manner from that provided in the

---

166 See above, 3–081, 3–085.

167 *Bruner v Moore* [1904] 1 Ch. 305; *Bremer Handelsgesellschaft mbH v Vanden Avenne-Izegem P.V.B.A.* [1978] 2 Lloyd's Rep. 109.

168 See above, para.22–033.

169 *Msas Global Logistics v Power Packaging Inc* [2003] EWHC 1393 (Ch), [2003] All E.R. (D) 211 (Jun).

170 [1938] 1 K.B. 408, 416, 417; *Msas Global Logistics v Power Packaging Inc* [2003] EWHC 1393 (Ch), [2003] All E.R. (D) 211 (Jun).

171 See *Besseler Waechter Glover & Co v South Derwent Coal Co* [1938] 1 K.B. 408; *Watson v Healy Lands* [1965] N.Z.L.R. 511; Dugdale and Yates (1976) 39 M.L.R. 680.

172 See Ch.4.

173 See above, para.4–009.

contract, he will not be able to refuse that performance when tendered.[174] However, in cases of postponement of performance, if the period of postponement is specified in the waiver, then, if time was originally of the essence, it will remain so in respect of the new date.[175] If the period of postponement is not specified in the waiver, the party forbearing is entitled, upon reasonable notice, to impose a new time-limit, which may then become of the essence of the contract.[176] Similarly, in other cases of forbearance, he may be entitled, upon reasonable notice, to require the other party to comply with the original mode of performance,[177] unless in the meantime circumstances have so changed as to render it impossible[178] or inequitable[179] so to do. He cannot treat the waiver as entirely without effect. If a seller of goods withholds delivery of the goods at the purchaser's request (i.e. if the seller waives the obligation of the purchaser to accept the goods within a certain time), he will still be under a duty to deliver within a reasonable time if so requested by the purchaser.[180]

Effect on party to whom forbearance is extended. Where one party has induced the other party to accede to his request, the party seeking the forbearance will not be permitted to repudiate the waiver and to rely on the letter of the agreement.[181] Thus in *Levey & Co v Goldberg*[182] the defendant agreed in writing to buy from the plaintiffs certain pieces of cloth over the value of £10[183] to be delivered within a certain period. At the oral request of the defendant, the plaintiffs voluntarily withheld delivery during that period. The defendant subsequently refused to accept delivery, and, when sued, contended that the plaintiffs themselves were in breach, as the oral agreement was insufficient to vary the terms of a contract which was required by law to be evidenced by writing. It was held that the forbearance by the plaintiffs at the request of the defendant did not constitute a variation but a waiver, and the plaintiffs were entitled to maintain their action. 22–043

[174] *Leather Cloth Co v Hieronimus* (1875) L.R. 10 Q.B. 140; *Bruner v Moore* [1904] 1 Ch. 305; *Panoutsos v Raymond Hadley Corp of New York* [1917] 2 K.B. 473; *Hartley v Hymans* [1920] 2 K.B. 475; *Besseler Waechter Glover & Co v South Derwent Coal Co* [1938] 1 K.B. 408; *Tankexpress A/S v Compagnie Financière Belge des Petroles SA* [1949] A.C. 76; *Plasticmoda Societa per Azioni v Davidsons (Manchester) Ltd* [1952] 1 Lloyd's Rep. 527; *Enrico Furst & Co v W.E. Fischer* [1960] 2 Lloyd's Rep. 340; *W.J. Alan & Co Ltd v El Nasr Export and Import Co* [1972] 2 Q.B. 189, 213.

[175] *Luck v White* (1973) 26 P. & C.R. 89; *Buckland v Farmar & Moody* [1979] 1 W.L.R. 221; *Nichimen Corp v Gatoil Overseas Inc* [1987] 2 Lloyd's Rep. 46.

[176] *Hartley v Hymans* [1920] 2 K.B. 475; *Charles Rickards Ltd v Oppenhaim* [1950] 1 K.B. 616; *Jacobson van der Berg & Co (UK) Ltd v Biba Ltd* (1977) 121 S.J. 333; *State Trading Corp of India Ltd v Compagnie Française d'Importation et de Distribution* [1983] 2 Lloyd's Rep. 679. See also *Ficom SA v Sociedad Cadex Ltda* [1980] 2 Lloyd's Rep. 118, 131.

[177] *Panoutsos v Raymond Hadley Corp of New York* [1917] 2 K.B. 473.

[178] *Leather Cloth Co v Hieronimus* (1875) L.R. 10 Q.B. 140.

[179] *Toepfer v Warinco A.G.* [1978] 2 Lloyd's Rep. 569, 576. See also above, para.3–083.

[180] *Tyers v Rosedale Ferryhill Iron Co* (1875) L.R. 10 Ex. 195.

[181] *Ogle v Earl Vane* (1868) L.R. 3 Q.B. 272; *Hickman v Haynes* (1875) L.R. 10 C.P. 598.

[182] [1922] 1 K.B. 688.

[183] Statute of Frauds 1677 s.17 (re-enacted as s.4 of the Sale of Goods Act 1893) required such a contract to be evidenced by writing. Both provisions have now been repealed by the Law Reform (Enforcement of Contracts) Act 1954.

22–044 **Consideration for waiver.** A waiver is also distinguishable from a variation of a contract in that there is no consideration for the forbearance moving from the party to whom it is given.[184] It may therefore be more satisfactory to regard this form of waiver, that is "waiver by estoppel", as analogous to, or even identical with, equitable forbearance or "promissory" estoppel.[185] Although consideration need not be proved, certain other requirements must be satisfied for such an estoppel to be effective: first, it must be clear and unequivocal; secondly, the other party must have altered his position in reliance on it, or at least acted on it.[186]

22–045 **Contracting out of waiver.** It would appear that there is no general principle of law that parties to a contract cannot restrict the operation of the doctrine of waiver by the terms of their contract.[187] In *State Securities Plc v Initial Industry Ltd*[188] Jonathan Gaunt Q.C., sitting as a Deputy Judge of the High Court, stated:

> "I can, however, see no reason in principle why the parties to an equipment lease . . . or other commercial contract, should not be free to stipulate that a particular act, such as payment of a rental instalment should not be taken to waive a right to terminate for an earlier breach. After all, such a provision may be very convenient and operate to the benefit of both parties. The finance company may want to encourage the lessee to correct the breach but not want him to fall behind with his payments while he does so. It may be in the interests of the lessee that the finance company should not have to take an early decision whether to terminate."[189]

However it cannot be assumed that the courts in all cases will give effect to a term of the contract which purports to exclude or limit the operation of the doctrine of waiver; in some circumstances the term of the contract may not

---

[184] *W.J. Alan & Co Ltd v El Nasr Export and Import Co* [1972] 2 Q.B. 189, 193. See also above, para.3–081.

[185] See above, para.3–085.

[186] *Woodhouse A.C. Israel Cocoa Ltd SA v Nigerian Produce Marketing Co Ltd* [1972] A.C. 741, 755, 758, 761, 762, 767–768, 781; *W.J. Alan & Co Ltd v El Nasr Export & Import Ltd* [1972] 2 Q.B. 189, 212–214, 215, 217; *Finagrain SA v P. Kruse* [1976] 2 Lloyd's Rep. 508, 534–535, 540, 546; *Bremer Handelsgesellschaft mbH v Vanden Avenne-Izegem P.V.B.A.* [1978] 2 Lloyd's Rep. 109, 127; *Bunge SA v Schleswig-Holsteinische Landwirtschaftliche Hauptgenossenschaft Eingetr GmbH* [1978] 1 Lloyd's Rep. 480, 490; *Bremer Handelsgesellschaft mbH v C. Mackprang* [1979] 1 Lloyd's Rep. 220, 225–226, 228, 230; *Avimex SA v Dewulf & Cie* [1979] 2 Lloyd's Rep. 57, 67–68; *Bremer Handelsgesellschaft mbH v Westzucker* [1981] 1 Lloyd's Rep. 207, 213; *Cremer v Granaria B.V.* [1981] 2 Lloyd's Rep. 583, 587; *Cerealmangimi SpA v Toepfer* [1981] 3 All E.R. 533; *Cook Industries Inc v Meunerie Liegeois SA* [1981] 1 Lloyd's Rep. 359, 368; *Société Italo-Belge pour le Commerce et l'Industrie v Palm and Vegetable Oils (Malaysia) Sdn Bhd* [1981] 2 Lloyd's Rep. 695, 700–702; *Bremer Handelsgesellschaft mbH v Finagrain Compagnie Commerciale, etc. SA* [1981] 2 Lloyd's Rep. 259, 263, 266; *Bremer Handelsgesellschaft mbH v Raiffeisen Hauptgenossenschaft E/G* [1982] 1 Lloyd's Rep. 599; *Bremer Handelsgesellschaft mbH v Deutsche Conti-Handelsgesellschaft mbH* [1983] 2 Lloyd's Rep. 45; *Allied Marine Transport Ltd v Vale do Rio Doce Navegacao SA* [1985] 1 W.L.R. 925; *Motor Oil Hellas (Corinth) Refineries SA v Shipping Corp of India* [1990] 1 Lloyd's Rep. 391. cf. *Scandinavian Trading Tanker Co AB v Flota Petrolera Ecuatoriana* [1983] 2 Q.B. 529, [1983] 2 A.C. 694. See above, para. 3–081; below, paras 24–007—24–009.

[187] *State Securities Plc v Initial Industry Ltd* [2004] All E.R. (D) 317 (Jan).

[188] [2004] All E.R. (D) 317 (Jan).

[189] [2004] All E.R. (D) 317 (Jan) at [57].

suffice to deny effect to a clear and unequivocal representation made by one party to the contract.[190]

Waiver of condition for benefit of one party. Where the terms of a contract include a provision which has been inserted solely for the benefit of one party, he may, without the assent of the other party, waive compliance with that provision and enforce the contract as if the provision had been omitted.[191] He will not be permitted to do so where the provision has been inserted for the benefit of both parties[192] or where there is in reality no concluded agreement.[193] 22–046

Waiver of breach. One party may waive his right to terminate a contract consequent upon a repudiation of the contract by the other party.[194] It is, however, important to distinguish between the case in which a party waives his right to treat the contract as repudiated but does not abandon his right to claim damages for the loss suffered as a result of the breach[195] and the case where the innocent party waives not only his right to terminate performance of the contract but also his claim for damages for the breach.[196] The former is an example of waiver by election,[197] whereas the latter is more properly classified as a species of waiver by estoppel.[198] 22–047

7. PROVISION FOR DISCHARGE IN THE CONTRACT ITSELF

Express provision. The parties may expressly provide in their contract that either or one of them is to have an option to terminate the contract.[199] This right 22–048

---

[190] *I-Way Ltd v World Online Telecom Ltd* [2002] EWCA Civ 413 (Court of Appeal refused to give summary judgment in a case in which the court was asked, in effect, to enforce a term of the contract which provided that "no addition, amendment or modification of this Agreement shall be effective unless it is in writing and signed by or on behalf of both parties").

[191] *Bennett v Fowler* (1840) 2 Beav. 302; *Hawksley v Outram* [1892] 3 Ch. 359; *Morrell v Studd and Millington* [1913] 2 Ch. 648; *F.E. Napier v Dexters Ltd* (1926) 26 Ll. L. R. 62, 63–64, 184, 187–188. See also *North v Loomes* [1919] 1 Ch. 378 and Sale of Goods Act 1979 s.11(2). Once he has waived the condition, either expressly or by conduct, he cannot then rely on it to deny his own liability: *Barrett Bros (Taxis) Ltd v Davies* [1966] 1 W.L.R. 1334.

[192] *Lloyd v Novell* [1895] 2 Ch. 744; *Burgess v Cox* [1951] Ch. 383; *Heron Garage Properties Ltd v Moss* [1974] 1 W.L.R. 148; *Gregory v Wallace* [1998] I.R.L.R. 387; *Wessex Reserve Forces and Cadets Association v White* [2005] EWHC 983 (QB), [2005] All E.R. (D) 310 (May).

[193] *Allsopp v Orchard* [1923] 1 Ch. 323.

[194] See below, para.24–007.

[195] *Motor Oil Hellas (Corinth) Refineries SA v Shipping Corp of India* [1990] 1 Lloyd's Rep. 391, 397–398.

[196] This is sometimes known as "total waiver"; see Sale of Goods Act 1979 s.11(2); *Benjamin's Sale of Goods*, 7th edn (2006), paras 12–034—12–036; Treitel, *The Law of Contract*, 12th edn by Peel, 2007), para.18–076 and below, para.24–007.

[197] See below, para.24–007.

[198] See below, para.24–007. There are important differences between the two types of waiver; see below, para.24–008 and Treitel at paras 18–074—18–080.

[199] In *Aktieselskabet Dampskibsselskabet Svendborg v Mobil North Sea Ltd* [2001] 2 Lloyd's Rep. 127, 130 David Steel J. said that he saw no reason to accord the word "terminated" in a termination clause anything other than "its ordinary meaning of coming, or being brought, to an end, however that result may have occurred". Thus he held that a repudiatory breach by either party accepted by the other constituted a "termination" within the meaning of the clause.

of termination may be exercisable upon a breach of contract by the other party (whether or not the breach would amount to a repudiation of the contract),[200] or upon the occurrence or non-occurrence of a specified event other than breach,[201] or simply at the will of the party upon whom the right is conferred. In principle, since the parties are free to incorporate whatever terms they wish for the termination of their agreement, no question arises at common law whether the provision is reasonable or whether it is reasonable for a party to enforce it,[202] unless the situation is one in which equity would grant relief against forfeiture.[203] However, certain statutes restrict the efficacy of such provisions,[204] and in certain circumstances a term of this nature would have to be shown to be fair and reasonable by virtue of the provisions of the Unfair Contract Terms Act 1977.[205] Where such a provision is contained in a contract concluded between a seller or supplier and a consumer and that contract has not been individually negotiated, it may also fall within the scope of the Unfair Terms in Consumer Contracts

---

[200] See below, para.24–001. A court may, however, interpret a clause entitling a party to terminate on the occurrence of any "breach of contract as applying only to a breach of contract which is repudiatory in nature": see *Rice (t/a Garden Guardian) v Great Yarmouth BC, The Times*, July 26, 2000. In *Rice* the local authority purported to terminate the contract under a term of the contract which stated that: "[I]f the contractor commits a breach of any of its obligations under the contract, the Council may, without prejudice to any accrued rights or remedies under the Contract, terminate the Contractor's employment under the Contract by notice in writing having immediate effect." The Court of Appeal concluded that the notion that this term entitled the council to terminate the contract at any time for any breach of any term flew in the face of commercial common sense (the contract was one which was designed to run for four years). The clause only gave the Council the right to terminate the contract on the occurrence of a repudiatory breach of contract and the Court of Appeal held that the trial judge had been entitled to conclude on the facts that there had not been a repudiatory breach of contract so that the Council was not entitled to terminate the contract. There is therefore a need for clearer drafting if one wishes to ensure a right to terminate in the event of a breach of a long-term contract. It may be possible to use the words "material breach" (see *National Power Plc v United Gas Co Ltd* Unreported July 3, 1998, Coleman J.; *Fortman Holdings Ltd v Modem Holdings Ltd* [2001] EWCA Civ 1235; *Dalkia Utilities Services Plc v Celtech International Ltd* [2006] EWHC 63 (Comm), [2006] 1 Lloyd's Rep. 599 at [90]–[102]) or "substantial breach" (see *Crane Co v Wittenborg A/S* Unreported, December 21, 1999 CA) but that simply opens the problem of establishing the meaning of "material" or "substantial" and the court may conclude that they are simply synonyms for a repudiatory breach. See further Thomas [2001] *International Company and Commercial Law Review* 26.

[201] See above, para.12–030 (conditions subsequent) and para.12–039 (force majeure clauses).

[202] *Financings Ltd v Baldock* [1963] 2 Q.B. 104, 115; *China National Foreign Trade Transportation Corp v Evlogia Shipping Co SA* [1979] 1 W.L.R. 1018.

[203] See, e.g. *Stockloser v Johnson* [1954] 1 Q.B. 476; *Barton Thompson & Co Ltd v Stapling Machines Co* [1966] Ch. 499; *Shiloh Spinners Ltd v Harding* [1973] A.C. 691; *Starside Properties Ltd v Mustapha* [1974] 1 W.L.R. 816; *B.I.C.C. Plc v Burndy Corp* [1985] Ch. 232; *Transag Haulage Ltd v Leyland DAF Finance Plc* [1994] B.C.C. 356; *On Demand Information Plc v Michael Gerson (Finance) Plc* [2001] 1 W.L.R. 155 and below, para.26–146 et seq. Contrast *Galbraith v Mitchenall Estates Ltd* [1965] 2 Q.B. 473; *Mardorf Peach & Co Ltd v Attica Sea Carriers Corp of Liberia* [1977] A.C. 850; *Afovos Shipping Co SA v R. Pagnan and Filli* [1983] 1 W.L.R. 195; *Scandinavian Trading Tanker Co AB v Flota Petrolera Ecuatoriana* [1983] 2 A.C. 694; *Sport Internationaal Bussum BV v Inter-Footwear Ltd* [1984] 1 W.L.R. 776; *Union Eagle Ltd v Golden Achievement Ltd* [1997] A.C. 514; *Etzin v Reece* [2002] All E.R. (D) 405 (July); *More OG Romsdal Fylkesbatar AS v The Demise Charterers of the Ship "Jotunheim"* [2004] EWHC 671 (Comm), [2005] 1 Lloyd's Rep. 181.

[204] e.g. Law of Property Act 1925 s.146; Consumer Credit Act 1974 ss.76, 86, 87, 98; Housing Act 1996 ss.81 and 82.

[205] s.3(2)(b)(ii); see above, para.14–073.

Regulations 1999.[206] Thus, a contract term which authorises a seller or supplier to dissolve a contract on a discretionary basis where the same facility is not granted to the consumer may constitute an unfair term which will not be binding upon the consumer.[207]

The fact that one party is contractually entitled to terminate the agreement in the event of a breach by the other party does not preclude that party from treating the agreement as discharged by reason of the other's repudiation or breach of condition,[208] unless the agreement itself expressly or impliedly provides that it can only be terminated by exercise of the contractual right.[209] Whether the procedure laid down for termination in the contract excludes, expressly or impliedly, the common law right to terminate further performance of the contract in respect of a breach which falls within the scope of the clause is a question of construction of the contract.[210] When interpreting a clause in a contract which lays down a procedure for termination of the contract, the court will have regard to the commercial purpose which is served by the termination clause and interpret it in the light of that purpose.[211] Strict or precise compliance with the termination clause may no longer be a necessary pre-requisite to a valid termination.[212] It can be a matter of some practical importance whether termination has taken place pursuant to a term of the contract or under the general law.[213] A contractual right to terminate can be exercised even if the breach is not repudiatory at common law.[214] On the other hand, a contractual right to terminate, of itself, says nothing about the remedial consequences of termination; that is to say, not every termination pursuant to an express term of the contract will entitle the party terminating the contract to loss of bargain damages. Thus, where a contracting party terminates further performance of the contract pursuant to a term of the contract, and the breach which has caused it to exercise that power is not a repudiatory breach, the party exercising the right to terminate may only be 22–049

[206] SI 1999/2083. See further above, Ch.15, where the scope of the Regulations and the definition of terms such as "seller or supplier", etc., is discussed in more detail.

[207] See Sch.2 to the 1999 Regulations para.1(f), set out at para.15–099.

[208] *Leslie Shipping Co v Welstead* [1921] 3 K.B. 420; *The Mihalis Angelos* [1971] 1 Q.B. 164; *Lombard North Central Plc v Butterworth* [1987] Q.B. 587.

[209] *Npower Direct Ltd v South of Scotland Power Ltd* [2005] EWHC 2123 (Comm) at [177].

[210] See, for example, *Lockland Builders Ltd v Rickwood* (1996) 77 Build. L.R. 38 where the contractually agreed procedure for dealing with the consequences of a particular breach was held impliedly to have excluded the common law right to terminate performance of the contract in respect of a breach which fell within the scope of the clause. However, the position would have been otherwise if the party in breach had evinced a clear intention not to be bound by the terms of the contract; in such a case the common law right to terminate and the right contained in the contract would have existed side by side (see Russell L.J. at 46 and Hirst L.J. at 50). A provision to the effect that the contractual right to terminate is "without prejudice to other rights and remedies" will generally suffice to persuade a court that the common law right to terminate has not been excluded.

[211] *Ellis Tylin Ltd v Co-operative Retail Services Ltd* [1999] B.L.R. 205, relying upon *Mannai Investment Co Ltd v Eagle Star Life Assurance Co Ltd* [1997] A.C. 749 and *Investors Compensation Scheme Ltd v West Bromwich Building Society* [1998] 1 W.L.R. 898.

[212] As was previously thought to be the case in cases such as *The Mihalis Angelos* [1971] 1 Q.B. 164; *Mardorf Peach & Co Ltd v Attica Sea Carriers Corp of Liberia* [1977] A.C. 850, 870; and *Afovos Shipping Co v Pagnan* [1983] 1 W.L.R. 195, 201.

[213] Although it can occasionally be difficult to tell whether a party has purported to terminate.

[214] See, for example, *Financings Ltd v Baldock* [1963] 2 Q.B. 104.

entitled to recover damages in respect of the loss which it has suffered at the date of termination and not for loss of bargain damages.[215] Where, however, the breach is also repudiatory[216] and that repudiatory breach has been accepted,[217] loss of bargain damages can be recovered[218] by relying on the contractual right to do so or by accepting the other party's repudiation of the contract. An example of a case in which the line between the two became distinctly blurred is provided by *Laing Management Ltd v Aegon Insurance Co (UK) Ltd*[219] where Judge Lloyd Q.C. concluded that reliance on a contractual right to terminate did not amount to an acceptance of a repudiatory breach and that therefore the contract remained alive for the benefit of both parties. The finding that the contract remained alive, notwithstanding the reliance on the express power to terminate, is a difficult one. A simpler analysis would have been to conclude that reliance on the express term in the contract did operate to discharge both parties from their obligation to perform under the contract but that the exercise of the right to terminate did not, of itself, entitle the plaintiff to recover loss of bargain damages.[220]

22–050 **Burden of proof.** It is for the party seeking to terminate the contract to prove the existence of the facts which justify the exercise of his contractual right to terminate.[221]

22–051 **Requirements as to notice.** Where the terms of the contract expressly or impliedly[222] provide that the right of termination is to be exercised only upon notice given to the other party, it is clear that notice must be given for the contract to be terminated pursuant to that provision.[223] Any notice must be sufficiently

---

[215] See, for example, *Financings Ltd v Baldock* [1963] 2 Q.B. 104; *Brady v St Margaret's Trust* [1963] 2 Q.B. 494; *Anglo-Auto Finance Ltd v James* [1963] 1 W.L.R. 1042; *United Dominions Trust (Commercial) Ltd v Ennis* [1968] 1 Q.B. 54. This separation of the right to terminate and the right to claim loss of bargain damages has been rejected by the Supreme Court of Canada in *Keneric Tractor Sales Ltd v Langille* (1987) 43 D.L.R. (4th) 171 and subjected to academic criticism, see Opeskin (1990) 106 L.Q.R. 293. An attempt to stipulate for a wider right of recovery in the contract in such a case may be invalid as a penalty clause: *Lombard North Central Plc v Butterworth* [1987] Q.B. 527.

[216] This is so whether it is repudiatory under the general law or by virtue of the decision of the parties to treat the term which has been broken as a condition of the contract: *Lombard North Central Plc v Butterworth* [1987] Q.B. 527. cf. Treitel [1987] L.M.C.L.Q. 143.

[217] A court may conclude that, having regard to the conduct of the parties, any repudiatory breach committed was not, in fact, accepted so that the contract must be regarded as continuing: see *United Dominions Trust (Commercial) Ltd v Ennis* [1968] 1 Q.B. 54 and *Laing Management Ltd v Aegon Insurance Co (UK) Ltd* (1998) 86 Build. L.R. 70.

[218] *Yeoman Credit Ltd v Waragowski* [1961] 1 W.L.R. 1124; *Overstone Ltd v Shipway* [1962] 1 W.L.R. 117; *Lombard North Central Plc v Butterworth* [1987] Q.B. 527.

[219] (1998) 86 Build. L.R. 70. For further discussion of the case, see *Dalkia Utilities Services Plc v Celtech International Ltd* [2006] EWHC 63 (Comm), [2006] 1 Lloyd's Rep. 599 at [139]–[142].

[220] See above, fn.215.

[221] See *Chandris v Isbrandtsen Moller Co Inc* [1951] 1 K.B. 240, 245–246; *P.J. Van der Zijden Wildhandel NV v Tucker & Cross Ltd* [1975] 2 Lloyd's Rep. 240 (force majeure clauses). See also above, para.14–137.

[222] See *Mardorf Peach & Co Ltd v Attica Sea Carriers Corp of Liberia* [1977] A.C. 850 (withdrawal of ship). See also *Abingdon Finance Co Ltd v Champion, Guardian*, November 6, 1961 (seizure of goods let on hire purchase).

[223] *Reliance Car Facilities Ltd v Roding Motors* [1952] 2 Q.B. 844. Contrast *Union Transport Finance Ltd v British Car Auctions* [1978] 2 All E.R. 385.

clear and unambiguous in its terms to constitute a valid notice[224]; but it is a question of construction in each case whether the notice must actually be communicated to the other party and whether it takes effect at the time of dispatch or of receipt.[225] The terms of the contract may further provide that notice can be given only after the occurrence of a specified event[226]; or that a specified period of notice be given; or that the notice is to be in a certain form (e.g. in writing); or that it should contain certain specified information; or that it should be given within a certain period of time. Prima facie the validity of the notice depends upon the precise observance of the specified conditions.[227] However, a consideration of the relationship of the notice requirements to the contract as a whole and regard to general considerations of law, may show that a stipulated requirement, for example, that notice be given "without delay",[228] was intended by the parties to be an intermediate term,[229] the non-observance of which would not invalidate the notice (unless the other party was seriously prejudiced thereby), but would give rise to a claim for damages only.[230]

Waiver of defects in notice. Where the requirements of notice have not been complied with, the party giving the notice may still be entitled to rely on it if the other party has expressly or by conduct waived the defect in the notice.[231] 22–052

[224] *Allam & Co Ltd v Europa Poster Services Ltd* [1968] 1 W.L.R. 638. See also *May v Borup* [1915] 1 K.B. 830; *Addis v Burrows* [1948] 1 K.B. 444; *Aegnoussiotis Shipping Corp of Monrovia v A/S Kristian Jebsens Rederi* [1977] 1 Lloyd's Rep. 268. cf. *P. Phipps & Co (Northampton and Towcester) Breweries Ltd v Rogers* [1925] 1 K.B. 14.

[225] *Scarf v Jardine* (1882) 7 App. Cas. 345, 348; *Re London and Northern Bank* [1900] 1 Ch. 220; *Tenax S.S. Co Ltd v The Brimnes* [1973] 1 W.L.R. 386; affirmed [1975] Q.B. 929; *Bremer Handelsgesellschaft mbH v Vanden Avenne-Izegem P.V.B.A.* [1978] 2 Lloyd's Rep. 109.

[226] *Afovos Shipping Co SA v Pagnan & Filli* [1983] 1 W.L.R. 195; *Telfair Shipping Corp v Athos Shipping Co SA* [1983] 1 Lloyd's Rep. 127.

[227] See *Afovos Shipping Co SA v Pagnan & Filli* [1983] 1 W.L.R. 195; *Tradax Exports SA v Dorada Compania Naviera SA* [1982] 2 Lloyd's Rep. 140; and the cases cited in fn.231, below. However the prima facie rule may have to give way on the facts of the case when regard is had to the underlying commercial purpose of the termination clause: *Ellis Tylin Ltd v Co-operative Retail Services Ltd* [1999] B.L.R. 205.

[228] *Bremer Handelsgesellschaft mbH v Vanden Avenne-Izegem P.V.B.A.* [1978] 2 Lloyd's Rep. 109.

[229] See above, para.12–034.

[230] *Bremer Handelsgesellschaft mbH v Vanden Avenne-Izegem P.V.B.A.* [1978] 2 Lloyd's Rep. 109, 113. See also *Bunge SA v Kruse* [1979] 1 Lloyd's Rep. 279; affirmed [1980] 2 Lloyd's Rep. 142.

[231] *Alfred C. Toepfer v P. Cremer* [1975] 2 Lloyd's Rep. 118; *Bremer Handelsgesellschaft mbH v Vanden Avenne-Izegem P.V.B.A.* [1978] 2 Lloyd's Rep. 109; *Bremer Handelsgesellschaft mbH v C. Mackprang* [1979] 1 Lloyd's Rep. 220; *Bunge GmbH v Alfred C. Toepfer* [1979] 1 Lloyd's Rep. 554. Contrast (no waiver) *V. Berg & Son Ltd v Vanden Avenne-Izegem P.V.B.A.* [1977] 1 Lloyd's Rep. 499; *Avimex SA v Dewulf Cie.* [1979] 2 Lloyd's Rep. 56; *Toepfer v Schwarze* [1980] 1 Lloyd's Rep. 385; *Bremer Handelsgesellschaft mbH v C. Mackprang* [1981] 1 Lloyd's Rep. 292; *Tradax Export SA v Cook Industries Inc* [1982] 1 Lloyd's Rep. 385; *Raiffeisen Hauptgenossenschaft v Louis Dreyfus & Co Ltd* [1981] 1 Lloyd's Rep. 345; *Bremer Handelsgesellschaft mbH v Westzucker* [1981] 1 Lloyd's Rep. 207; *Cook Industries Inc v Meunerie Liegeois SA* [1981] 1 Lloyd's Rep. 359; *Bremer Handelsgesellschaft mbH v Finagrain Compagnie Commerciale, etc., SA* [1981] 2 Lloyd's Rep. 259; *Bremer Handelsgesellschaft mbH v Westzucker (No.2)* [1981] 2 Lloyd's Rep. 130; *Bunge SA v Compagnie Européenne des Cereales* [1982] 1 Lloyd's Rep. 306; *Bremer Handelsgesellschaft mbH v Bunge Corp* [1983] 1 Lloyd's Rep. 476; *Bremer Handelsgesellschaft mbH v Deutsche-Conti Handelsgesellschaft mbH* [1983] 2 Lloyd's Rep. 45.

22–053 **Waiver of right to terminate.** Conversely, if one party is contractually entitled to terminate the agreement on breach by the other, he may be held to have waived his right to terminate.[232]

22–054 **Implied provision.** A contract which appears on its face to be perpetual and irrevocable may nevertheless be construed in the sense that it can be determined upon reasonable notice.[233] This topic has been dealt with in the chapter on Implied Terms earlier in this book.[234] An unlawful repudiation of the contract by one party cannot be relied on by him as a lawful determination upon reasonable notice under an implied term in the contract.[235]

22–055 **Determination of contract.** The parties may expressly provide that the contract shall ipso facto determine upon the happening of a certain event.[236] But such a provision is to be construed subject to the principle that no man can take advantage of his own wrong, so that one party may not be allowed to rely on such a provision where the occurrence of the event is attributable to his own act or default.[237]

---

[232] *Keith Prowse & Co v National Telephone Co* [1894] 2 Ch. 147; *Reynolds v General & Finance Facilities* (1963) 107 S.J. 889. Contrast (no waiver) *Mardorf Peach & Co Ltd v Attica Sea Carriers Corp of Liberia* [1977] A.C. 850; *China National Foreign Trade Transportation Corp v Evlogia Shipping Co SA of Panama* [1979] 1 W.L.R. 1018; *Bremer Handelsgesellschaft v Deutsche-Conti Handelsgesellschaft* [1983] 2 Lloyd's Rep. 45; *Scandinavian Trading Tanker Co A.B. v Flota Petrolera Ecuatoriana* [1983] 2 Q.B. 529; affirmed [1983] 2 A.C. 694; *Eximenco Handels A.G. v Partredereit Oro Chief* [1983] 2 Lloyd's Rep. 509.

[233] *Crediton Gas Co v Crediton U.D.C.* [1928] Ch. 174, 178; *Winter Garden Theatre (London) Ltd v Millenium Productions Ltd* [1948] A.C. 173; *Martin Baker Aircraft Co Ltd v Canadian Flight Equipment Ltd* [1955] 2 Q.B. 556; *Re Spenborough U.D.C.'s Agreement* [1968] Ch. 139; *Beverley Corp v Richard Hodgson & Sons Ltd* (1972) 225 E.G. 799; *Staffordshire AHA v South Staffordshire Waterworks Co* [1978] 1 W.L.R. 1387. Contrast *Kirklees Metropolitan BC v Yorkshire Woollen District Transport Co* (1978) 77 L.G.R. 448. See also Carnegie (1969) 85 L.Q.R. 392.

[234] See above, para.13–027.

[235] *Decro-Wall International SA v Practitioners in Marketing Ltd* [1971] 1 W.L.R. 361. See also *Bridge v Campbell Discount Co Ltd* [1962] A.C. 600.

[236] *Jay's Furnishing Co v Brand & Co* [1915] 1 K.B. 458; *Continental Grain Export Corp v S.T.M. Grain Ltd* [1979] 2 Lloyd's Rep. 460; *Bremer Handelsgesellschaft mbH v Finagrain SA* [1981] 2 Lloyd's Rep. 259. See also *British Leyland UK Ltd v Ashraf* [1978] I.C.R. 979 (employment), subsequently overruled in *Igbo v Johnson, Matthey Chemicals Ltd* [1986] I.C.R. 505.

[237] *Rede v Farr* (1817) 6 M. & S. 121, 124; *Doe d. Bryan v Bancks* (1821) 4 B. & Ald. 401, 406; *New Zealand Shipping Co v Société des Ateliers et Chantiers de France* [1919] A.C. 1, 6, 8, 9; *Quesnel Forks Gold Mining Co Ltd v Ward* [1920] A.C. 222; *Alghussein Establishment v Eton College* [1988] 1 W.L.R. 587. cf. *Cheall v Association of Professional Executive and Computer Staff* [1988] 2 A.C. 180; *Thompson v Asda M.F.I. Group Plc* [1988] Ch. 241; *Micklefield v S.A.C. Technology Ltd* [1990] 1 W.L.R. 1002; *Richco International Ltd v Alfred C. Toepfer International GmbH* [1991] 1 Lloyd's Rep. 136; see above, para.13–012.

CHAPTER 23

DISCHARGE BY FRUSTRATION[1]

		PARA.
1.	Introduction	23–001
2.	The test for frustration	23–007
3.	Illustrations of the doctrine	23–020
	(a) General	23–020
	(b) Common types of frustrating events	23–022
	(i) Subsequent legal changes and supervening illegality	23–022
	(ii) Cancellation of an expected event	23–033
	(iii) Delay	23–035
	(c) Application of the doctrine to common types of contracts	23–037
	(i) Personal contracts	23–037
	(ii) Charterparties	23–041
	(iii) Sale and carriage of goods	23–047
	(iv) Building contracts	23–049
	(v) Leases and tenancies	23–052
	(vi) Contracts for the sale of land	23–057
4.	The limits of frustration	23–058
5.	The legal consequences of frustration	23–070

1. INTRODUCTION

Introduction. A contract may be discharged on the ground of frustration when something occurs after the formation of the contract which renders it physically or commercially impossible to fulfil the contract or transforms the obligation to perform into a radically different obligation from that undertaken at the moment of entry into the contract. **23–001**

Frustration and mistake. Although the doctrine of frustration has some affinity with common mistake, in that both doctrines are essentially concerned with the allocation of risk of an unforeseen event which makes contractual performance more onerous or even impossible,[2] it is customary to treat the two doctrines separately on the ground that common mistake is concerned with a **23–002**

[1] Treitel, *Frustration and Force Majeure*, 2nd edn (2004); McKendrick (ed.), *Force Majeure and Frustration of Contract*, 2nd edn (1995). See also McElroy and Williams, *Impossibility of Performance* (1941); Gottschalk, *Impossibility of Performance in Contract* (1945); McNair and Watts, *The Legal Effects of War*, 4th edn, Ch.5; Webber, *Effect of War on Contracts*, 2nd edn, especially Parts III and IV. For an economic analysis of the doctrine of frustration, see Posner and Rosenfield (1977) 6 J. Leg. Stud. 83.

[2] See, e.g. *Amalgamated Investment & Property Co Ltd v John Walker & Sons Ltd* [1977] 1 W.L.R. 164; *Associated Japanese Bank (International) Ltd v Crédit du Nord* [1989] 1 W.L.R. 255, 264; *Jan Albert (HK) Ltd v Shu Kong Garment Factory Ltd* [1990] 1 H.K.L.R. 317; *Great Peace Shipping Ltd v Tsavliris Salvage (International) Ltd* [2002] EWCA Civ 1407; [2003] Q.B. 679 at [61]–[75].

common misapprehension which was present at the date of entry into the contract, whereas frustration is solely concerned with events which occur *after* the date of formation of the contract.[3]

23–003 **Narrow scope.** Although the doctrine of frustration is of respectable antiquity, having been established in its present form in 1863 in *Taylor v Caldwell*,[4] it currently operates within rather narrow confines. This is so for two principal reasons. The first is that the courts do not wish to allow a party to appeal to the doctrine of frustration in an effort to escape from what has proved to be a bad bargain: frustration is "not lightly to be invoked to relieve contracting parties of the normal consequences of imprudent commercial bargains".[5] The second is that parties to commercial contracts commonly make provision within their contract for the impact which various possible catastrophic events may have on their contractual obligations. Thus, force majeure clauses[6] and hardship and intervener clauses[7] are frequently inserted into commercial contracts. The effect of these clauses is to reduce the practical significance of the doctrine of frustration because, where express provision has been made in the contract itself for the event which has actually occurred, then the contract is not frustrated.[8] Therefore the wider the ambit of contractual clauses, the narrower is the practical scope of the doctrine of frustration.[9]

23–004 **Historical development.**[10] Prior to the watershed decision of the Court of Queen's Bench in *Taylor v Caldwell*[11] supervening events were not regarded as an excuse for non-performance because the parties could have provided for such eventualities in their contract.[12] Once a contracting party assumed an obligation

---

[3] It can sometimes be difficult to decide into which category a particular case falls; see, for example, *Amalgamated Investment & Property Co Ltd v John Walker & Sons Ltd* [1977] 1 W.L.R. 164 and *Gamerco SA v ICM/Fair Warning (Agency) Ltd* [1995] 1 W.L.R. 1226 (it has been argued that the latter case may have been too readily classified as an instance of frustration, see Carter and Tolhurst (1996) 10 J.C.L. 264, 265–266).

[4] (1863) 3 B. & S. 826.

[5] *Pioneer Shipping Ltd v B.T.P. Tioxide Ltd (The Nema)* [1982] A.C. 724, 752; *Edwinton Commercial Corp v Tsavliris Russ (Worldwide Salvage & Towage) Ltd (The Sea Angel)* [2007] EWCA Civ 547 at [111]. See also *Lee Chee Wei v Tan Hor Peow Victor* [2007] SGCA 22 at [48].

[6] See generally above, paras 14–137—14–154 and McKendrick (ed.), *Force Majeure and Frustration of Contract*, 2nd edn (1995), Ch.3.

[7] See generally Schmitthoff [1980] J.B.L. 82; Montague (1985) Int. Bus. Lawyer 135.

[8] *Joseph Constantine S.S. Line Ltd v Imperial Smelting Corp Ltd* [1942] A.C. 154, 163.

[9] In the case of an elaborately drafted contract a court may conclude, as a matter of interpretation, that the parties preferred the "certainty" of termination pursuant to one of the terms of the contract to the uncertainty of possible discharge under the doctrine of frustration: see *Total Gas Marketing Ltd v Arco British Ltd* [1998] 2 Lloyd's Rep. 209, especially 221–222.

[10] See generally Treitel, *Frustration and Force Majeure*, Ch.2 and Ibbetson in Rose (ed.), *Consensus Ad Idem* (1996), Ch.1.

[11] (1863) 3 B. & S. 826.

[12] *Paradine v Jane* (1646) Aleyn 26; *Atkinson v Ritchie* (1809) 10 East 530; *Barker v Hodgson* (1814) 3 M. & S. 267 (later held to be wrongly decided by Scrutton L.J. in *Ralli Bros v Compagnia Naviera Sota y. Aznar* [1920] 2 K.B. 287, 303); *Bute (Marquis of) v Thompson* (1844) 13 M. & W. 487; *Hills v Sughrue* (1846) 15 M. & W. 253; *Jervis v Tomkinson* (1856) 1 H. & N. 195; *Kirk v Gibbs* (1857) 1 H. & N. 810; *Brown v Royal Insurance Society* (1859) 1 E. & E. 853; *Re Arthur* (1880) 14 Ch D 603. The same rule was applied in equity: *Leeds v Cheetham* (1827) 1 Sim. 146, 150.

he was bound to fulfil it. The classic decision on this rule as to "absolute" contracts is *Paradine v Jane*,[13] where a lessee who was sued for arrears of rent pleaded that he had been evicted and kept out of possession by an alien enemy; such an event was beyond his control, and had deprived him of the profits of the land from which he expected to receive the money to pay the rent. He was nevertheless held liable on the ground that:

> ". . . where the law creates a duty or charge and the party is disabled to perform it and hath no remedy over, there the law will excuse him . . . but when the party of his own contract creates a duty or charge upon himself, he is bound to make it good, if he may, notwithstanding any accident by inevitable necessity, because he might have provided against it by his contract."[14]

Physical destruction of the subject matter. Although this rule was peculiar to English law, it continued to be enforced until 1863.[15] However, in 1863, in *Taylor v Caldwell*[16] the defendants had agreed to permit the plaintiffs to use a music-hall for concerts on four specified nights. After the contract was made, but before the first night arrived, the hall was destroyed by fire. Blackburn J., giving the judgment of the Court of Queen's Bench, held that the defendants were not liable in damages, since the doctrine of the sanctity of contracts applied only to a promise which was positive and absolute, and not subject to any condition express *or implied*. The court employed the concept of an implied condition to introduce the doctrine of frustration into English law, since it might appear from the nature of the contract that the parties must have known from the beginning that the fulfilment of the contract depended on the continuing existence of a particular person or thing. The court held that the particular contract in question was to be construed: 23–005

> ". . . as subject to an implied condition that the parties shall be excused in case, before breach, performance becomes impossible from the perishing of the thing, without default of the contractor . . . [17] The principle seems to us to be that, in contracts in which the performance depends on the continued existence of a given person or thing, a condition is implied that the impossibility of performance arising from the perishing of the person or thing shall excuse the performance. In none of these cases is the promise other than positive, nor is there any express stipulation that the destruction of the person or thing shall excuse the performance; but that excuse is by law implied, because from

---

[13] (1646) Aleyn 26. For fuller analysis of the case and its antecedents see Ibbetson in Rose (ed.), *Consensus Ad Idem* (1996), Ch.1.

[14] (1646) Aleyn 26, 27.

[15] There were some exceptions, e.g. no damages could be granted for breach of a promise to marry or of a contract for personal services if one party died (below, paras 23–037 et seq.), nor for the breach of a contractual promise when performance of that promise became illegal after the formation of the contract: *Atkinson v Ritchie* (1809) 10 East 530, 534–535. But the courts still refused to recognise any general principle that a party might be released from liability in the absence of an express condition which operated to release him in the particular events which occurred: *Hall v Wright* (1858) E.B. & E. 746, 789; *Kearon v Pearson* (1861) 2 H. & N. 386.

[16] (1863) 3 B. & S. 826.

[17] (1863) 3 B. & S. 826, 833–834.

the nature of the contract it is apparent that the parties contracted on the basis of the continued existence of the particular person or chattel."[18]

The principle of *Taylor v Caldwell* was soon applied in other cases[19] and was accepted by the legislature in relation to agreements for the sale of goods.[20]

23–006 **Frustration of the adventure.** Though the doctrine of frustration was first introduced into English law to cover situations where the physical subject-matter of the contract had perished (as in *Taylor v Caldwell*[21]), it was quickly extended to cases where, without any such physical destruction, the commercial adventure envisaged by the parties was frustrated. "Frustration of the common venture" first appeared in 1874 in *Jackson v Union Marine Insurance Co Ltd*[22] where a ship was required, under a charterparty, to proceed from Liverpool to Newport to load a cargo for San Francisco. On the first day out from Liverpool the ship ran aground, and it took six weeks to refloat her, and another six months to complete repairs. The jury was asked whether the time necessary for getting the ship off and repairing her so as to be a cargo-carrying ship was so long as to put an end in a commercial sense to the commercial speculation entered upon by the shipowner and the charterers. The jury answered in the affirmative, and the Court of Exchequer Chamber held that the charterparty ended upon the mishap. Bramwell B. said that the jury had found that "a voyage undertaken after the ship was sufficiently repaired would have been a different voyage . . . different as a different adventure".[23] With these decisions, the existence of the doctrine of frustration in English law was firmly established.

2. THE TEST FOR FRUSTRATION[24]

23–007 **Introduction.** Although the existence of the doctrine of frustration is now firmly established, its juristic basis remains rather uncertain. However in *J. Lauritzen AS v Wijsmuller BV (The Super Servant Two)*,[25] Bingham L.J. set out the following five propositions which describe the essence of the doctrine. These propositions, he stated, were "established by the highest authority" and were

[18] (1863) 3 B. & S. 826, 839.

[19] e.g. *Appleby v Myers* (1867) L.R. 2 C.P. 651.

[20] Sale of Goods Act 1893 s.7. See below, para.23–047. (But the legislature did not intend to disturb the rules as to risk: see Vol.II, para.43–036.)

[21] (1863) 3 B. & S. 826.

[22] (1874) L.R. 10 C.P. 125.

[23] (1874) L.R. 10 C.P. 125, 141.

[24] See Treitel, *Frustration and Force Majeure*, 2nd edn (2004), paras 16–006—16–016; Treitel, *The Law of Contract*, 12th edn (by Peel, 2007) paras 19–115—19–125; J. Beatson, *Anson's Law of Contract*, 28th edn (2002), pp.541–546; Cheshire, Fifoot and Furmston, *Law of Contract*, 15th edn (2007), pp.721–726; Webber, *Effect of War on Contracts*, 2nd edn, pp.404–478; McNair and Watts, *The Legal Effects of War*, 4th edn, pp.166 et seq., based on (1919) 35 L.Q.R. 84–100 and (1940) 56 L.Q.R. 173–207; Wade (1940) 56 L.Q.R. 519. For a comparison of the theories in different legal systems, see Smit (1958) 58 Col. L.R. 287; for an American assessment of the UK cases, see Schlegel (1969) 23 Rutgers L.Rev. 419.

[25] [1990] 1 Lloyd's Rep. 1.

"not open to question".[26] The first proposition was that the doctrine of frustration has evolved "to mitigate the rigour of the common law's insistence on literal performance of absolute promises"[27] and that its object was:

> "...to give effect to the demands of justice, to achieve a just and reasonable result, to do what is reasonable and fair, as an expedient to escape from injustice where such would result from enforcement of a contract in its literal terms after a significant change in circumstances."[28]

Secondly, frustration operates to "kill the contract and discharge the parties from further liability under it" and that therefore it cannot be "lightly invoked" but must be kept within "very narrow limits and ought not to be extended".[29] Thirdly, frustration brings a contract to an end "forthwith, without more and automatically".[30] Fourthly, "the essence of frustration is that it should not be due to the act or election of the party seeking to rely on it"[31] and it must be some "outside event or extraneous change of situation".[32] Finally, a frustrating event must take place "without blame or fault on the side of the party seeking to rely on it".[33]

No absolving power. While these propositions establish the essence of the doctrine of frustration and provide some guidance as to its limits, they do not explain precisely *why* it is that the courts intervene in these cases, except, at the broadest level, to give effect to the demands of justice. But this appeal to the demands of justice should not be taken to suggest that the court has a broad absolving power to set a contract aside whenever a change of circumstances causes hardship to one of the contracting parties. The proposition that the court has a power to impose a just and reasonable solution to the problem raised by the 23–008

[26] [1990] 1 Lloyd's Rep. 1, 8.

[27] Citing *Hirji Mulji v Cheong Yue S.S. Co Ltd* [1926] A.C. 497, 510; *Denny, Mott & Dickson Ltd v James B. Fraser & Co Ltd* [1944] A.C. 265, 275; *Joseph Constantine S.S. Line Ltd v Imperial Smelting Corp Ltd* [1942] A.C. 154, 171.

[28] Citing *Hirji Mulji v Cheong Yue S.S. Co Ltd* [1926] A.C. 497, 510; *Joseph Constantine S.S. Line Ltd v Imperial Smelting Corp Ltd* [1942] A.C. 154, 183, 193; *National Carriers Ltd v Panalpina (Northern) Ltd* [1981] A.C. 675, 701.

[29] Citing *Bank Line Ltd v Arthur Capel & Co* [1919] A.C. 435, 459; *Davis Contractors Ltd v Fareham U.D.C.* [1956] A.C. 696, 715, 727; *Pioneer Shipping Ltd v B.T.P. Tioxide Ltd* [1982] A.C. 724, 752. See also *Edwinton Commercial Corp v Tsavliris Russ (Worldwide Salvage & Towage) Ltd (The Sea Angel)* [2007] EWCA Civ 547 at [111].

[30] Citing *Hirji Mulji v Cheong Yue S.S. Co Ltd* [1926] A.C. 497, 505; *Maritime National Fish Ltd v Ocean Trawlers Ltd* [1935] A.C. 524, 527; *Joseph Constantine S.S. Line Ltd v Imperial Smelting Corp Ltd* [1942] A.C. 154, 163, 170, 171, 187, 200; *Denny Mott & Dickson Ltd v James B. Fraser & Co Ltd* [1944] A.C. 265, 274. See also *GF Sharp & Co Ltd v McMillan* [1998] I.R.L.R. 632.

[31] Citing *Hirji Mulji v Cheong Yue S.S. Co Ltd* [1926] A.C. 497, 510; *Maritime National Fish Ltd v Ocean Trawlers Ltd* [1935] A.C. 524, 530; *Denny, Mott & Dickson Ltd v James B. Fraser & Co Ltd* [1944] A.C. 265, 274; *Davis Contractors Ltd v Fareham U.D.C.* [1956] A.C. 696, 729.

[32] Citing *Paal Wilson & Co A/S v Partenreederi Hannah Blumenthal* [1983] 1 A.C. 854, 909.

[33] Citing *Bank Line Ltd v Arthur Capel & Co* [1919] A.C. 435, 452; *Joseph Constantine S.S. Line Ltd v Imperial Smelting Corp Ltd* [1942] A.C. 154, 171; *Davis Contractors Ltd v Fareham U.D.C.* [1956] A.C. 696, 729; *Paal Wilson & Co A/S v Partenreederei Hannah Blumenthal* [1983] 1 A.C. 854, 882, 909.

new circumstances[34] was rejected by the House of Lords in *British Movietonews Ltd v London and District Cinemas Ltd*.[35] Such a test is too wide, and gives too much discretion to the court; it ignores the limited data for the court's decision, and suggests that attention should be concentrated on the harshness of enforcing the contract in the new situation, without any inquiry whether the original obligation was radically different.[36]

23–009 **Basis of doctrine.** Although a number of judges have considered the basis of the doctrine of frustration, it is not clear that the issue gives rise to any practical consequences. The various theories "shade into one another" and a "choice between them is a choice of what is the most appropriate to the particular contract under consideration".[37] The principal theories which have been put forward are set out in the following paragraphs, before further consideration is given to the issue of whether or not any practical consequences flow from this debate.

23–010 **The implied term test.** The test which was originally adopted in *Taylor v Caldwell*[38] was the implied term test. The classic exposition of the test is to be found in the speech of Lord Loreburn in *F.A. Tamplin S.S. Co Ltd v Anglo-Mexican Petroleum Products Co Ltd*[39]:

> "A court can and ought to examine the contract and the circumstances in which it was made, not of course to vary but only to explain it, in order to see whether or not from the nature of it the parties must have made their bargain on the footing that a particular thing or state of things would continue to exist. And if they must have done so, then a term to that effect will be implied, though it be not expressed in the contract . . . . In most of the cases it is said that there was an implied condition in the contract which operated to release the parties from performing it, and in all of them I think that was at bottom the principle upon which the court proceeded. It is, in my opinion, the true principle, for no court has an absolving power, but it can infer from the nature of the contract and the surrounding circumstances that a condition which was not expressed was a foundation on which the parties contracted . . . . Were the altered conditions such that, had they thought of them, the parties would have taken their chance of them, or such that as sensible men they would have said, 'if that happens, of course, it is all over between us'?"

---

[34] *British Movietonews Ltd v London & District Cinemas Ltd* [1951] 1 K.B. 190, 202; cf. Cheshire, Fifoot & Furmston, *Law of Contract*, 15th edn (2007), pp.724–725 and Lord Denning's modified formulations in *Ocean Tramp Tankers v V/O Sovfracht (The Eugenia)* [1964] 2 Q.B. 226, 238 and in *Staffordshire A.H.A. v South Staffordshire Waterworks Co* [1978] 1 W.L.R. 1387, 1395; (pet. dis.) [1979] 1 W.L.R. 203 HL.

[35] [1952] A.C. 166.

[36] In *Notcutt v Universal Equipment Co (London) Ltd* [1986] 1 W.L.R. 641, 646–647 (below, para.23–038) the Court of Appeal rejected the suggestion that injustice was an *additional* factor to be considered after the factors which established a radical change in the obligation. In *Edwinton Commercial Corp v Tsavliris Russ (Worldwide Salvage & Towage) Ltd (The Sea Angel)* [2007] EWCA Civ 547 at [113], [132], the Court of Appeal affirmed that injustice is not an additional factor, but noted that "the dictates of justice" is a: "[R]elevant factor which underlies all and provides the ultimate rationale of the doctrine. If one uses this factor as a reality check, its answer should conform with a proper assessment of the issue of frustration."

[37] *National Carriers Ltd v Panalpina (Northern) Ltd* [1981] A.C. 675, 693, per Lord Wilberforce.

[38] (1863) 3 B. & S. 826.

[39] [1916] 2 A.C. 397, 403–404.

So it was by means of this test that the doctrine of frustration was first introduced into English law[40] and it was frequently accepted in later judgments.[41]

Objections to the implied term test. The implied term test has, however, been the subject of considerable criticism and it was finally laid to rest by the House of Lords in *National Carriers Ltd v Panalpina (Northern) Ltd*.[42] The following objections to it ought to be borne in mind when reading the older decisions. The first objection is that it is artificial and often fictitious in its operation, since there would seldom be a genuine common intention to terminate the contract upon the occurrence of the particular event in question.[43] The parties in the normal case have not foreseen the event, and even if they had, they would probably have "sought to introduce reservations, or qualifications or compensations".[44] Some judges, while paying lip-service to the test, have treated it as an objective one; for instance, in *Dahl v Nelson, Donkin & Co*,[45] Lord Watson said: 23–011

> "... the meaning of the contract must be taken to be, not what the parties did intend (for they had neither thought nor intention regarding it), but that which the parties, as fair and reasonable men, would presumably have agreed upon if, having such possibility in view, they had made express provision as to their several rights and liabilities in the event of its occurrence."

In *Davis Contractors v Fareham U.D.C.* Lord Radcliffe said that:

> "... the spokesman of the fair and reasonable man, who represents after all no more than the anthropomorphic conception of justice, is and must be the court itself."[46]

The implied term approach is also difficult to accept where the parties have actually foreseen the possibility of the event in question, or even inserted in their contract some express provision (short of termination of the contract) for the event which occurred, but the court nevertheless holds that the contract was frustrated by that event.[47]

Test of a radical change in the obligation. The test which found favour with the House of Lords in *Davis Contractors Ltd v Fareham U.D.C.*[48] and in later 23–012

---

[40] *Taylor v Caldwell* (1863) 3 B. & S. 826.

[41] e.g. *Bank Line Ltd v Arthur Capel & Co* [1919] A.C. 435, 455 (Lord Sumner); *Joseph Constantine S.S. Line Ltd v Imperial Smelting Corp Ltd* [1942] A.C. 154, 163 (Viscount Simon L.C.); *British Movietonews Ltd v London & District Cinemas Ltd* [1952] A.C. 166, 183 (Viscount Simon) and 187 (Lord Simonds); see also the references collected in McNair and Watts at pp.167–171.

[42] [1981] A.C. 675, 687, 702, 717 (cf. at 693, 694).

[43] *James Scott & Sons Ltd v Del Sel* (1922) S.C. 592, 597; *Davis Contractors Ltd v Fareham U.D.C.* [1956] A.C. 696, 728; *National Carriers Ltd v Panalpina (Northern) Ltd* [1981] A.C. 675, 687. See also *Horlock v Beal* [1916] 1 A.C. 486 (below, para.23–039).

[44] *Denny, Mott and Dickson Ltd v James B. Fraser & Co Ltd* [1944] A.C. 265, 275 (Lord Wright).

[45] (1881) 6 App. Cas. 38, 59.

[46] [1956] A.C. 696, 728.

[47] See below, para.23–059.

[48] [1956] A.C. 696 (for the facts, see below, para.23–050).

cases[49] may be formulated as follows: If the literal words of the contractual promise were to be enforced in the changed circumstances, would performance involve a fundamental or radical change from the obligation originally undertaken?[50] Thus, Lord Radcliffe said:

> "... frustration occurs whenever the law recognises that without default of either party a contractual obligation has become incapable of being performed because the circumstances in which performance is called for would render it a thing radically different from that which was undertaken by the contract. *Non haec in foedera veni.* It was not this that I promised to do .... There must be ... such a change in the significance of the obligation that the thing undertaken would, if performed, be a different thing from that contracted for."[51]

Lord Reid put the test for frustration in a similar way:

> "The question is whether the contract which they did make is, on its true construction, wide enough to apply to the new situation: if it is not, then it is at an end."[52]

Later in his speech,[53] he approved the words of Asquith L.J. that the question is whether the events alleged to frustrate the contract were:

> "... fundamental enough to transmute the job the contractor had undertaken into a job of a different kind, which the contract did not contemplate and to which it could not apply."[54]

It is submitted that the test put forward by Lord Reid is substantially the same as that of Lord Radcliffe.

---

[49] *National Carriers Ltd v Panalpina (Northern) Ltd* [1981] A.C. 675; *Pioneer Shipping Ltd v B.T.P. Tioxide Ltd* [1982] A.C. 724.

[50] This formulation does not cover the special case of supervening illegality (see below, para.23–023). With this formulation, compare that in *Williston on Contracts*, 3rd edn, Vol.18, para.1931, at 8: "The important question is whether an unanticipated circumstance has made performance of the promise vitally different from what should reasonably have been within the contemplation of both parties when they entered into the contract."

[51] [1956] A.C. 696, 729. This statement was explicitly approved by the House of Lords in *National Carriers Ltd v Panalpina (Northern) Ltd* [1981] A.C. 675, 688, 700, 702, 707, 717 and in *Pioneer Shipping Ltd v B.T.P. Tioxide Ltd (The Nema)* [1982] A.C. 724, 744, 751–752. Earlier approval was given in *Tsakiroglou & Co Ltd v Noblee Thorl GmbH* [1962] A.C. 93. It has also been cited with approval by the Court of Appeal in *William Sindall Plc v Cambridgeshire CC* [1994] 1 W.L.R. 1016, 1039 and in *Globe Master Management Ltd v Boulus-Gad Ltd* [2002] EWCA Civ 313.

[52] [1956] A.C. 696, 721. (Lord Somervell agreed with Lord Reid on this issue, 733.)

[53] [1956] A.C. 696, 723.

[54] *Sir Lindsay Parkinson & Co Ltd v Commissioners of Works* [1949] 2 K.B. 632, 667. See also the words of Lord Sumner in *Bank Line Ltd v Arthur Capel & Co* [1919] A.C. 435, 460: "I am of opinion that the requisitioning of the [ship] destroyed the identity of the chartered service and made the charter as a matter of business a *totally different thing*"; also the statement of Lord Simon in *British Movietonews Ltd v London & District Cinemas Ltd* [1952] A.C. 166, 185: "[I]f ... a consideration of the terms of the contract, in the light of the circumstances existing when it was made, shows that they never agreed to be bound *in a fundamentally different situation* which has now unexpectedly emerged, the contract ceases to bind at that point—not because the court in its discretion thinks it just and reasonable to qualify the terms of the contract, but *because on its true construction it does not apply in that situation*"; and that of Lord Dunedin in *Metropolitan Water Board v Dick, Kerr & Co Ltd* [1918] A.C. 119, 128: "An interruption may be so long as *to destroy the identity of the work* or service, when resumed, with the work or service interrupted." (Italics supplied.)

Confirmation of the test. In subsequent cases the House of Lords has expressly upheld the *Davis Contractors* formulation of the test for frustration.[55] In *National Carriers Ltd v Panalpina (Northern) Ltd*[56] Lord Simon restated the test as follows: 23–013

"Frustration of a contract takes place when there supervenes an event (without default of either party and for which the contract makes no sufficient provision) which so significantly changes the nature (not merely the expense or onerousness) of the outstanding contractual rights and/or obligations from what the parties could reasonably have contemplated at the time of its execution that it would be unjust to hold them to the literal sense of its stipulations in the new circumstances; in such case the law declares both parties to be discharged from further performance."[57]

Yet, at the same time it was said that the doctrine should be flexible and capable of new applications as new circumstances arise.[58]

Construction of the contract. Both Lords Reid and Radcliffe in *Davis Contractors* emphasised that the first step was to construe: 23–014

"... the terms which are in the contract read in the light of the nature of the contract, and of the relevant surrounding circumstances when the contract was made."[59]

From this construction the court should reach an impression of the scope of the original obligation, that is, the court should ascertain what the parties would be required to do in order to fulfil their literal promises in the original circumstances. This impression will depend on the court's estimate of what performance would have required in time, labour, money and materials, if there had been no change in the circumstances existing at the time the contract was made. The court should then examine the situation existing after the occurrence of the event alleged to have frustrated the contract, and ascertain what would be the obligation of the parties if the words of the contract were enforced in the new circumstances. Having discovered what was the original "obligation" and what would be the new "obligation" if the contract were still binding in the new circumstances, the last step in the process is for the court to compare the two obligations in order to decide whether the new obligation is a "radical" or "fundamental" change from the original obligation.[60] It is not simply a question

[55] *National Carriers Ltd v Panalpina (Northern) Ltd* [1981] A.C. 675; *Pioneer Shipping Ltd v B.T.P. Tioxide Ltd (The Nema)* [1982] A.C. 724 (three of their Lordships in the former case referred to it as "the construction test": 688, 702, 717); *Paal Wilson & Co A/S v Partenreederei Hannah Blumenthal* [1983] 1 A.C. 854, 909, 918–919.

[56] [1981] A.C. 675.

[57] [1981] A.C. 675, 700. (On the use of the word "unjust," see the use of "injustice," 701, and below, para.23–017.)

[58] [1981] A.C. 675, 692, 694, 701, 712.

[59] [1956] A.C. 696, 720–721, per Lord Reid; cf. 729, per Lord Radcliffe.

[60] "I turn then to consider the position after the Canal was closed, and to compare the rights and obligations of the parties thereafter, if the contract still bound them, with what their rights and obligations would have been if the Canal had remained open." Per Lord Reid, in *Tsakiroglou & Co Ltd v Noblee Thorl GmbH* [1962] A.C. 93, 118. "Whether a supervening event is a frustrating event or not, is, in a wide variety of cases, a question of degree ... ", per Lord Hailsham, in *National Carriers Ltd v Panalpina (Northern) Ltd* [1981] A.C. 675, 688.

whether there has been a radical change in the circumstances, but whether there has been a radical change in the "obligation" or the actual effect of the promises of the parties construed in the light of the new circumstances. Was "performance . . . fundamentally different in a commercial sense"?[61]

23–015 **Application of the test.** Their Lordships also agreed in *Davis Contractors* that it is a matter of law[62] for the court to construe the contract in the light of the facts existing at its formation and then "to determine whether the ultimate situation . . . is or is not within the scope of the contract so construed".[63] It has several times been emphasised in the House of Lords that "that conclusion is almost completely determined by what is ascertained as to mercantile usage and the understanding of mercantile men".[64] Hence, the court should seldom interfere with an arbitrator's application of the test to particular facts:

> " . . . when it is shown on the face of a reasoned award that the appointed tribunal has applied the right legal test, the court should in my view only interfere if on the facts found as applied to that right legal test, no reasonable person could have reached that conclusion. It ought not to interfere merely because the court thinks that upon those facts and applying that test, it would not or might not itself have reached the same conclusion, for to do that would be for the court to usurp what is the sole function of the tribunal of fact."[65]

23–016 **Objective test.** The House of Lords has accepted the view that the test for frustration is objective.[66] It is not a subjective inquiry into the actual or presumed intentions of the parties, as was suggested by the older criterion of the implied term, since the discharge of a contract on the ground of frustration occurs automatically upon the happening of the frustrating event, and does not depend upon any repudiation or other act of volition on the part of either party.[67] The fact that the parties, at the time of contracting, actually foresaw the possibility of the

[61] *Tsakiroglou & Co Ltd v Noblee Thorl GmbH* [1962] A.C. 93, 119. See to the same effect *Pioneer Shipping Ltd v B.T.P. Tioxide Ltd (The Nema)* [1982] A.C. 724, 752.

[62] [1956] A.C. 696, 723; cf. 729; *Tsakiroglou & Co Ltd v Noblee Thorl GmbH* [1962] A.C. 93.

[63] [1956] A.C. 696, 721.

[64] *Tsakiroglou & Co Ltd v Noblee Thorl GmbH* [1962] A.C. 93, 124, per Lord Radcliffe (cited with approval in *Pioneer Shipping Ltd v B.T.P. Tioxide Ltd (The Nema)* [1982] A.C. 724, 752; see also 738.)

[65] [1982] A.C. 724, 752–753, (per Lord Roskill, in a speech concurred in by all their Lordships). It is not "open to the court to impose its own view rather than adopt that of the arbitral tribunal" simply because "questions of frustration are ultimately questions of law" (at 753). cf. *International Sea Tankers Inc v Hemisphere Shipping Co Ltd (The Wenjiang)* [1982] 2 All E.R. 437; and below, para.23–035 fn.148; and para.23–097, especially fn.415.

[66] *Davis Contractors Ltd v Fareham U.D.C.* [1956] A.C. 696, 728 (per Lord Radcliffe: " . . . the true action of the court . . . consists in applying an objective rule of the law of contract").

[67] See the statement of Lord Sumner in *Hirji Mulji v Cheong Yue S.S. Co* [1926] A.C. 497, 510: "its legal effect [i.e. of frustration] does not depend on their intention, or their opinions or even knowledge as to the event which has brought this about . . . [Frustration] is irrespective of the individuals concerned, their temperaments and failings, their interests and circumstances." See also *Denny, Mott & Dickson Ltd v James B. Fraser & Co Ltd* [1944] A.C. 265, 274; *J. Lauritzen AS v Wijsmuller BV (The Super Servant Two)* [1990] 1 Lloyd's Rep. 1, 8. cf. the arguments of Goldberg (1972) 88 L.Q.R. 464. cf. also the principles on proving that a frustrating event was "self-induced": below, para.23–063; *F.C. Shepherd & Co Ltd v Jerrom* [1987] Q.B. 301, 321–323.

event or new circumstances in question does not necessarily prevent the doctrine of frustration from applying.[68]

Other tests. Various other theories have been put forward in an attempt to provide a coherent basis for the doctrine of frustration. As we have noted,[69] some judges have maintained that the doctrine seeks to give effect to the demands of justice, but these statements cannot be invoked to justify the conferral upon the courts of a wide-ranging discretion to re-write the parties' bargain in the name of "fairness and reasonableness". Another theory which has been invoked is that both parties have been discharged from further performance of their contractual obligations because of a total failure of consideration; but this rationalisation has been rejected by the House of Lords.[70] The final theory put forward by Lord Haldane in *Tamplin S.S. Co Ltd v Anglo-Mexican Petroleum Products Co Ltd*[71] and Goddard J. in *Tatem Ltd v Gamboa*[72] is that the doctrine is based on "the disappearance of the foundation of the contract." The difficulty with this theory lies in ascertaining the "foundation" of the contract[73]; the inquiry would appear to be one based on the construction of the contract and, if this is so, it is not easy to see how it differs from the construction theory. 23–017

Practical differences between the tests. It is therefore difficult to discern any practical consequence which flows from the different tests because, as Lord Wilberforce has stated, they appear to shade into each other.[74] The courts have regard to the construction of the contract, the effect of the changed circumstances on the parties' contractual obligations, the intentions of the parties (objectively construed) and the demands of justice in deciding whether or not a contract has been frustrated. No one factor is conclusive: the court will balance these different factors in determining whether a contract has been frustrated. On the other hand, it must be conceded that the basis of the doctrine is not unimportant in jurisprudential terms. A test based on a fictitious or artificial assumption (such as the implied term approach) may prevent a proper understanding of the function of the doctrine and of the role of the court in applying it. And the literal application of the one theory might lead to results which are incompatible with the rules which presently make up the doctrine of frustration. For example, the implied term theory, literally applied, may suggest that the question whether a contract is frustrated is one of fact, based on the intention of the parties, but it is clear law that the question whether a contract has been frustrated is one of law.[75] It is, however, unlikely that a modern court would apply a theory where it led to a result which was incompatible with the present rules and so it is submitted that 23–018

[68] See below, para.23–059.
[69] Above, para.23–007.
[70] *National Carriers Ltd v Panalpina (Northern) Ltd* [1981] A.C. 675, 687, 702.
[71] [1916] 2 A.C. 397, 406–407.
[72] [1939] 1 K.B. 132.
[73] *National Carriers Ltd v Panalpina (Northern) Ltd* [1981] A.C. 675, 687–688, 703.
[74] [1981] A.C. 675, 693.
[75] Above, para.23–015.

no practical consequences flow from the debate as to the correct conceptual basis of the doctrine of frustration.[76]

23–019 **A "multi-factorial" approach.** Rather than seek to identify a single, definitive test that can be applied in all cases, more recent authority supports a broader approach which seeks to take account of all of the facts and circumstances of the case when deciding whether or not a contract has been frustrated. This "multi-factorial"[77] approach has regard, among other factors, to the following:

> "... the terms of the contract itself, its matrix or context, the parties' knowledge, expectations, assumptions and contemplations, in particular as to risk, as at the time of contract, at any rate so far as these can be ascribed mutually and objectively, and then the nature of the supervening event, and the parties' reasonable and objectively ascertainable calculations as to the possibilities of future performance in the new circumstances."[78]

3. ILLUSTRATIONS OF THE DOCTRINE

(a) *General*

23–020 **Methods of classifying the cases on frustration.** Since the doctrine of frustration depends on the construction of the "obligation" created by the particular contract in the light of its own circumstances, reported decisions can be only a rough guide to the future application of the doctrine.[79] Nevertheless, the scope of the doctrine in practice must be gleaned from a study of the decisions in the law reports. The cases may be classified by reference either to the different types of frustrating events (such as a change in the law or subsequent illegality,[80] outbreak of war,[81] cancellation of an expected event[82] or delay[83]), or by reference to particular categories of contracts where frustration has been invoked (such as personal contracts,[84] charterparties,[85] sale and carriage of goods,[86] building contracts,[87] leases,[88] and contracts for the sale of land[89]). The doctrine of

[76] Treitel, *The Law of Contract*, 12th edn (by Peel, 2007), paras 19–115—19–125. Treitel, *Frustration and Force Majeure*, 2nd edn (2004), paras 16–013—16–016.

[77] *Edwinton Commercial Corp v Tsavliris Russ (Worldwide Salvage & Towage) Ltd (The Sea Angel)* [2007] EWCA Civ 547 at [111].

[78] [2007] EWCA Civ 547.

[79] See above, para.23–014 fn.60.

[80] Below, paras 23–022 et seq.

[81] Below, para.23–030.

[82] Below, paras 23–033—23–034.

[83] Below, para.23–035.

[84] Below, paras 23–037—23–040.

[85] Below, paras 23–041—23–046.

[86] Below, paras 23–047—23–048.

[87] Below, paras 23–049—23–051.

[88] Below, paras 23–052—23–056.

[89] Below, para.23–057.

executive necessity, according to which the Crown is unable to fetter by contractual undertakings the exercise in the future of its executive discretion, is discussed elsewhere in this Volume[90]; the discharge of contracts by the winding up of a company,[91] or by bankruptcy,[92] is also discussed elsewhere.

Illustrations of frustrating events. In addition to the frustrating events mentioned in the preceding paragraph, the following events may be taken as illustrations of the kind of events which have been held, in the circumstances of particular contracts, to bring the doctrine of frustration into operation: destruction by fire or other cause of the subject-matter of the contract,[93] an explosion or stranding disabling a ship,[94] requisitioning of the subject-matter of the contract by the government,[95] seizure of a ship[96] or expropriation of an oil concession[97] by a foreign government, incapacity or death of a person obliged to perform personal services,[98] and delay sufficiently long to frustrate the commercial adventure of the parties.[99] On the other hand, mere inconvenience, or hardship, or financial loss involved in performing the contract,[100] or delay which is within the commercial risk undertaken by the parties,[101] has been held insufficient to frustrate particular contracts. 23–021

[90] See above, paras 10–007—10–008.

[91] See above, paras 9–047—9–051.

[92] See above, paras 20–032 et seq.

[93] *Taylor v Caldwell* (1863) 3 B. & S. 826 (above, para.23–005) (distinguished in *New System Private Telephones (London) Ltd v Edward Hughes & Co* [1939] 2 All E.R. 844); *Appleby v Myers* (1867) L.R. 2 C.P. 651. cf. *Turner v Goldsmith* [1891] 1 Q.B. 544. cf. also *The Maira (No.2)* [1985] 1 Lloyd's Rep. 300 (contract for management of ship not frustrated by loss of the ship); affirmed on other grounds [1986] 2 Lloyd's Rep. 46.

[94] *Joseph Constantine S.S. Line Ltd v Imperial Smelting Corp Ltd* [1942] A.C. 154; *Jackson v Union Marine Insurance Co Ltd* (1874) L.R. 10 C.P. 125 (above, para.23–006).

[95] See the cases cited below, paras 23–024—23–026, 23–041—23–043, and below, para.23–047 fn.211.

[96] *Tatem v Gamboa* [1939] 1 K.B. 132 (below, para.23–044).

[97] *B.P. Exploration Co (Libya) Ltd v Hunt (No.2)* [1981] 1 W.L.R. 232 (appeal to HL dismissed [1983] 2 A.C. 352).

[98] See the cases cited below, paras 23–037—23–039.

[99] Below, para.23–035.

[100] *Davis Contractors Ltd v Fareham U.D.C.* [1956] A.C. 696, 729 (below, para.23–050); *National Carriers Ltd v Panalpina (Northern) Ltd* [1981] A.C. 675, 707; *Larrinaga & Co Ltd v Société Franco-Americaine des Phosphates de Médulla, Paris* (1923) 30 T.L.R. 316; *Hangkam Kwingtong Woo v Liu Lan Fong* [1951] A.C. 707; *Palmco Shipping Inc v Continental Ore Corp* [1970] 2 Lloyd's Rep. 21, 32 (a difference in expense between the expected and the actual performance is not sufficient to produce frustration); *United International Pictures v Cine Bes Filmcheck VE Yapimcilik AS* [2003] EWHC 798 (Comm), [2003] All E.R. (D) 278 (Apr) (abandonment of exchange rate mechanism held not to have frustrated a contract). See also the cases on Sale and Carriage of Goods cited below, paras 23–047—23–048. The proposition that an increase in expense is not, of itself, sufficient to produce frustration may not be absolute; see Beatson in Rose (ed.) *Consensus Ad Idem* (1996), Ch.6. On the question whether a term permitting determination upon notice may be implied into a long-term contract, see *Staffordshire A.H.A. v South Staffordshire Waterworks Co* [1978] 1 W.L.R. 1387; (pet. dis.) [1979] 1 W.L.R. 203 HL. cf. *Kirklees MBC v Yorks Woollen District Transport Co* [1978] L.G.R. 448; *Watford BC v Watford Rural Parish Council* (1988) 86 L.G.R. 524; *Islwyn BC v Newport BC* (1994) 6 Admin. L.R. 386. On the judicial response to problems caused by a fall in the value of money, see Downes (1985) 101 L.Q.R. 98; also above para.21–072; below paras 26–080—26–081.

[101] Below, para.23–035.

(b) *Common Types of Frustrating Events*

(i) *Subsequent Legal Changes and Supervening Illegality*

23–022 **Subsequent legal changes.** A subsequent change in the law or in the legal position affecting a contract is a well-recognised head of frustration; Parliament or another authority may intervene by legislative action, or the Government may exercise the royal prerogative or administrative powers so as to affect the legal situation of the contracting parties. In the leading case of *Baily v De Crespigny*[102] a lessor was held not liable for an alleged breach of his covenant that neither he nor his assigns would build on a piece of land adjoining the demised premises, when a railway company, under its powers derived from a subsequent statute, compulsorily acquired the land and erected a station on it. In delivering the judgment of the court, Hannen J. said:

> "The legislature by compelling him to part with his land to a railway company, whom he could not bind by any stipulation, as he could an assign chosen by himself, has created a new kind of assign, such as was not in the contemplation of the parties when the contract was entered into. To hold the defendant responsible for the acts of such an assignee is to make an entirely new contract for the parties."[103]

The court also held that it made no difference whether the company was only empowered or was obliged by the statute to build on the land.

23–023 **Changes affecting employment.** Contracts of service may also be frustrated by a subsequent change in the law. In *R. v Reilly*,[104] the appellant was appointed a member of a statutory board in Canada with a specified term of appointment and salary. During the tenure of the appointment the office was abolished by the repeal of the statute establishing the board. By petition of right the appellant claimed damages for breach of contract, but the Judicial Committee held that the contract was discharged, because further performance had become impossible by statute. Similarly, a solicitor's retainer agreement with a gas company was held to be frustrated by the nationalisation effected by the Gas Act 1948.[105]

23–024 **Supervening illegality.**[106] It is now customary to treat supervening illegality as an instance of frustration,[107] in that it is similar to frustration by a subsequent change in the law. Apart from the effect of an outbreak of war upon a contract, e.g. with a person who thereby becomes an alien enemy,[108] many wartime cases illustrate the power of the Government under statutory authority to forbid, whether temporarily or permanently, the performance of a contract, and so

---

[102] (1869) L.R. 4 Q.B. 180. See also *Islwyn BC v Newport BC* (1994) 6 Admin. L.R. 386.
[103] (1869) L.R. 4 Q.B. 180, 186–187.
[104] [1934] A.C. 176.
[105] *Studholme v South Western Gas Board* [1954] 1 W.L.R. 313. See also *Marshall v Glanvill* [1917] 2 K.B. 87.
[106] Treitel, *Frustration and Force Majeure*, 2nd edn (2004), Ch.8.
[107] McNair (1944) 60 L.Q.R. 160, 162–163. Supervening illegality is probably included in the term "frustration" in the Law Reform (Frustrated Contracts) Act 1943 (below, paras 23–074 et seq.).
[108] See below, para.23–030.

frustrate it. In *Metropolitan Water Board v Dick, Kerr & Co Ltd*,[109] under a contract made in July 1914, a reservoir was to be constructed and to be completed in six years from 1914, subject to a proviso that if the contractors should be impeded or obstructed by any cause the engineer should have power to grant an extension of time. Under the powers conferred by the Defence of the Realm Acts and Regulations, the contractors were obliged to cease work on the reservoir by order of the Ministry of Munitions in 1916. The House of Lords held that the contract was frustrated by supervening impossibility, and that the provision for extending the time did not apply to the prohibition by the Ministry. The interruption was of such a character, and likely to last so long, that if the work was to be resumed after the war, it would be a different undertaking altogether. Lord Finlay L.C. said that the interruption was:

> "... of such a character and duration that it vitally and fundamentally changed the conditions of the contract, and could not possibly have been in the contemplation of the parties to the contract when it was made."[110]

An express provision in the contract cannot exclude frustration by supervening illegality where this would be against public policy.[111]

Other war-time restrictions. In *Denny, Mott and Dickson Ltd v James B. Fraser & Co Ltd*[112] a contract for the sale and purchase of timber contained an option for the appellants to purchase a timber-yard (which was meanwhile let to them) if the contract was terminated on notice given by either party. By the Control of Timber (No.4) Order 1939 further trading transactions under the contract became illegal, but in 1941 the appellants gave notice to terminate the contract, and also to exercise their option to purchase the timber-yard. The House of Lords held that the option to purchase was dependent on the trading agreement, that the 1939 Order had operated to frustrate the contract, and that, consequently, the option to purchase lapsed upon the frustration since it arose only if the contract was terminated by notice. Temporary, war-time restrictions may not frustrate a long-term lease, which will continue in force for many years after the restrictions are lifted; so long as it exists, the restriction will, however, provide an excuse for not complying with a covenant in the lease.[113] 23–025

Exercise of statutory power. The same principle of supervening illegality operates where a statutory power in existence at the time of making the contract is subsequently exercised to render illegal the performance of the contract. Thus in *Re Shipton Anderson & Co and Harrison Bros & Co*[114] wheat was sold upon terms that payment in cash was to be made within seven days against a delivery 23–026

---

[109] [1918] A.C. 119. cf. *White & Carter Ltd v Carbis Bay Garage Ltd* [1941] 2 All E.R. 633.
[110] [1918] A.C. 119, 126.
[111] *Ertel Bieber & Co v Rio Tinto Co Ltd* [1918] A.C. 260 (below, para.23–030).
[112] [1944] A.C. 265.
[113] *Cricklewood Property and Investment Trust Ltd v Leightons Investment Trust Ltd* [1945] A.C. 221 (below, para.23–052). cf. *Eyre v Johnson* [1946] K.B. 481 (below, para.23–066 fn.319).
[114] [1915] 3 K.B. 676. Contrast *Walton Harvey Ltd v Walker and Homfrays Ltd* [1931] 1 Ch. 274.

order. But before delivery and before the property passed to the buyer the government requisitioned the wheat under an Act passed before the date of the contract; the contract was held to be frustrated so that the sellers were excused from performance.

23–027 **Supervening illegality under a foreign law.** Where a contract governed by English law as its applicable law is to be performed abroad, and that performance becomes illegal by the law of the place of performance (*lex loci solutionis*), the contract will not, according to common law rules, be enforced in England.[115] For the principle to apply, performance must include the doing in a foreign country of something which the laws of that country make it illegal to do; it is not enough that an act of performance is unlawful by the law of the country in which it happens to be done or that the contract is contrary to public policy according to the law of the place of performance.[116] The principle of frustration by supervening illegality operates where the change in the *lex loci solutionis* occurs after the formation of the contract but before its performance. Hence an English court will not enforce a contract governed by English law for the payment in Spain of freight under a charterparty exceeding the maximum amount fixed, after the making of the contract, by Spanish law.[117] A party relying on frustration by the *lex loci solutionis* must show that the illegality covered the whole of the period within which performance was due; thus where a foreign export control regulation prohibited performance of a contract during only part of the contract period, the exporters were held liable for failure to perform during the time no prohibition existed.[118]

23–028 **Limits to the rule.** A contract governed by English law is not frustrated where the *lex loci solutionis*, without making performance illegal, merely excuses a party from performance in full[119]; nor is an English contract frustrated because the party liable to perform would, by his performance, contravene the

---

[115] *Ralli Bros v Compania Naviera Sota y Aznar* [1920] 2 K.B. 287. For an illustration, see *The Nile Co for the Export of Agricultural Crops v H. & J.M. Bennett (Commodities) Ltd* [1986] 1 Lloyd's Rep. 555, 581–582. The same result would appear to be reached under art.8 of the Rome Convention on the Law Applicable to Contractual Obligations: Contracts (Applicable Law) Act 1990 Sch.1. See Cheshire and North, *Private International Law*, 13th edn, pp.601–602; below, para.30–168; *Dicey, Morris and Collins*, 14th edn (2006), paras 32–144—32–151. The latter point was referred to, but not resolved, by Cooke J. in *Tamil Nadu Electricity Board v ST-CMS Electric Co Private Ltd* [2007] EWHC 1713 (Comm), [2008] 1 Lloyd's Rep. 93 at [46].

[116] *Tamil Nadu Electricity Board v ST-CMS Electric Co Private Ltd* [2007] EWHC 1713 (Comm), [2008] 1 Lloyd's Rep. 93 at [47].

[117] *Ralli Bros v Compania Naviera Sota y Aznar* [1920] 2 K.B. 287; cf. *A.V. Pound & Co Ltd v M.W. Hardy & Co Inc* [1956] A.C. 588 (refusal by foreign authorities to grant export licence for performance of an English contract). On a partial prohibition by the *lex loci solutionis*, see *Benjamin's Sale of Goods*, 7th edn (2006), paras 18–348—18–355.

[118] *Ross T. Smyth & Co (Liverpool) Ltd v W.N. Lindsay (Leith) Ltd* [1953] 1 W.L.R. 1280. cf. *Walton (Grain and Shipping) Ltd v British Italian Trading Co Ltd* [1959] 1 Lloyd's Rep. 223.

[119] *Jacobs v Credit Lyonnais* (1884) 12 QBD 589 (the headnote of this case is misleading: see *Ralli Bros v Compania Naviera Sota y Aznar*, above, at 292, 297, 301); *Blackburn Bobbin Co Ltd v T.W. Allen & Sons Ltd* [1918] 2 K.B. 467.

law of the place of his residence, or of which he is a national (if that law is neither the applicable law nor the *lex loci solutionis*).[120]

Applicable law is a foreign law. It is uncertain whether illegality by the *lex loci solutionis* as such would have any effect in an English court if the law applicable to the contract was not English but a foreign law, and the place of performance was outside England.[121] In such cases, the effect of illegality by the *lex loci solutionis* would seem to be a matter for the applicable law, subject to the rules of English public policy.[122] The mere fact that performance has become illegal under the law of a foreign country does not of itself amount to frustration of the contract unless the contract expressly or impliedly requires performance in that country.[123] 23–029

Outbreak of war. The outbreak of war renders illegal all intercourse between British subjects (or other persons owing temporary allegiance to the Crown) and alien enemies.[124] Consequently, any contract which involves such intercourse is automatically dissolved by the outbreak of war, or by the party thereto becoming an alien enemy,[125] even though it contains a clause suspending its operation during the continuance of a state of war, for this would be void as against public policy.[126] Any contract which, though not actually made with a party who becomes an alien enemy, necessarily involves intercourse with or advantage to the enemy, is within the rule.[127] In other cases, where the outbreak of war does not itself render one party to the contract an alien enemy, the question whether 23–030

---

[120] *Dicey, Morris and Collins*, 14th edn (2006), para.32–145; *Kleinwort Sons & Co v Ungarische Baumwolle Industrie Aktien-Gesellschaft* [1939] 2 K.B. 678 (the principle of this case is clearly approved by three members of the House of Lords in *Kahler v Midland Bank* [1950] A.C. 24); *Fox v Henderson Investment Fund Ltd* [1999] 2 Lloyd's Rep. 303, 306.

[121] *Dicey, Morris and Collins* at paras 32–146—32–147.

[122] For a discussion of the common law rules, see Cheshire and North, *Private International Law*, 11th edn, pp.485–489; Mann (1937) 18 B.Y.B.I.L. 107. But see dicta to the contrary: *Zivnostenka Banka v Frankman* [1950] A.C. 57, 78; *Mackender v Feldia A.G.* [1967] 2 Q.B. 590, 601. The same doubt would appear to exist under the Rome Convention on the Law Applicable to Contractual Obligations. Article 7(1) of the Convention does not have the force of law in the United Kingdom (Contracts (Applicable Law) Act 1990 s.2(2)) and so cannot be invoked in the present context, although it is arguable that the contract could possibly be invalidated under arts 7(2), 10(2) or 16: see further below, para.30–355; Cheshire and North, *Private International Law*, 13th edn, pp.602–603; *Dicey, Morris and Collins*, 14th edn (2006), paras 32–148—32–151; Reynolds (1992) 108 L.Q.R. 553. For the position under the Rome I Regulation, see para.30–360.

[123] *Bangladesh Export Import Co Ltd v Sucden Kerry SA* [1995] 2 Lloyd's Rep. 1, 5–6.

[124] *Robson v Premier Oil and Pipe Line Co Ltd* [1915] 2 Ch. 124. See above, para.16–026; McNair and Watts, *Legal Effects of War*, 4th edn, especially Ch.3; Webber, *Effect of War on Contracts*, 2nd edn; Rogers, *Effect of War on Contracts* (1940); Trotter, *Law of Contract during and after War*, 4th edn. As to who is an alien enemy, see above, paras 11–024, 16–163; Trading with the Enemy Act 1939 s.2 (as amended); Howard, *Trading with the Enemy* (1943).

[125] *Esposito v Bowden* (1857) 7 E. & B. 763; *Ertel Bieber & Co v Rio Tinto Co Ltd* [1918] A.C. 260; *Naylor Benzon & Co Ltd v Krainische Industrie Gesellschaft* [1918] 2 K.B. 486. On the effect of war on a contract of agency, see Vol.II, para.31–164(iv).

[126] *Ertel Bieber & Co v Rio Tinto Co Ltd* [1918] A.C. 260.

[127] *Re Badische Co Ltd* [1921] 2 Ch. 331, 373–378. See also the *Fibrosa* case [1943] A.C. 32 (below, para.23–072).

the contract has been frustrated depends on the effect upon the contract of the acts done in furtherance of the war.[128]

23–031 **Accrued rights.** Accrued rights under a contract which has been frustrated (e.g. for a liquidated sum of money already due) are not destroyed,[129] though the right of suing in respect of such rights may be suspended for the duration of the war or so long as the claimant remains an alien enemy.[130] Thus, where a partnership agreement is dissolved by one partner becoming an alien enemy the enemy partner is nevertheless entitled to a share in the profits made thereafter by the English partner with the aid of the enemy partner's share of the capital.[131]

23–032 **Exceptions.** Some executory contracts, whose continuance in force is not against public policy, are not abrogated by one party becoming an alien enemy; for instance, a separation agreement by which a husband agrees to pay regular maintenance to his wife remains in force when she becomes an alien enemy, though during the war payments should be made to the Custodian of Enemy Property.[132]

(ii) *Cancellation of an Expected Event*

23–033 **The "coronation cases".** The cancellation of an expected event can, in exceptional circumstances, operate to frustrate a contract. That this is so can be demonstrated by reference to the "coronation cases", so-called because they arose out of actions brought in consequence of the postponement of the coronation processions in June 1902, owing to the illness of King Edward VII. These cases are important both because they show that the event which is alleged to have frustrated the contract need not result in the physical destruction of the subject-matter of the contract, but may frustrate the "commercial purpose" of the contract and because they also illustrate the narrow confines within which the doctrine of frustration currently operates. The most prominent of these cases is *Krell v Henry*,[133] where the defendant agreed in writing to hire rooms in the plaintiff's flat in Pall Mall on June 26 and 27 in order to see the coronation processions which had been announced for those days. The written contract made no express reference to the processions, but it was clear from the circumstances that both parties regarded the viewing of the processions as the sole purpose of the hiring. When the processions were postponed, the defendant declined to pay the balance of the agreed rent, and the Court of Appeal upheld his refusal, on the

[128] *Akties, Nord-Osterso Rederiet v E.A. Casper, Edgar & Co* (1923) 14 Ll. L. Rep. 203, 206; *Finelvet A.G. v Vinava Shipping Co Ltd* [1983] 1 W.L.R. 1469; *International Sea Tankers Inc v Hemisphere Shipping Co Ltd (The Wenjiang (No.2))* [1983] 1 Lloyd's Rep. 400, 405–406. On delay, see below, para.23–035.

[129] McNair and Watts at pp.135–144; *Schering Ltd v Stockholms Enskilda Bank Aktiebolag* [1946] A.C. 219; *Arab Bank Ltd v Barclays Bank* [1954] A.C. 495; *Re Claim by Helbert Wagg & Co Ltd* [1956] Ch. 323, 354.

[130] See above, paras 11–024—11–032.

[131] *Hugh Stevenson and Sons Ltd v Aktiengesellschaft für Cartonnagen-Industrie* [1918] A.C. 239.

[132] *Bevan v Bevan* [1955] 2 Q.B. 227.

[133] [1903] 2 K.B. 740. See Treitel, *Frustration and Force Majeure*, 2nd edn (2004), paras 7–006—7–014; McElroy & Williams (1941) 4 M.L.R. 241 and 5 M.L.R. 1.

ground that "the Coronation procession was the foundation of this contract and that the non-happening of it prevented the performance of the contract"[134] within the principle of *Taylor v Caldwell*.[135] The court also held that parol evidence was admissible to prove what was the subject-matter of the contract.[136] Similarly, in *Chandler v Webster*[137] another contract to let rooms "to view the first Coronation procession" was held to be frustrated by the postponement; the same result occurred with contracts to take seats on a stand built in order to view the procession.[138]

A different result was reached, however, in *Herne Bay Steamboat Co v Hutton*[139] where the plaintiffs' steamboat was engaged by the defendant to take passengers from Herne Bay on June 28 and 29, 1902, "for the purpose of viewing the Naval Review at Spithead and for a day's cruise round the fleet". The hire was £250, of which £50 was paid in advance, the balance to be paid before the vessel left Herne Bay. On June 25 the review was cancelled. The plaintiffs asked the defendant for instructions and for the balance of hire. As the defendant did not reply the plaintiffs used the vessel for their own purposes. In an action for the balance of the £250 the Court of Appeal held that it was payable, as: **23–034**

> "... the purpose of Mr. Hutton, whether of seeing the naval review or of going round the fleet with a party of paying guests, does not lay the foundation of the contract within the authorities,"[140]

such as *Taylor v Caldwell*. The case may also be explicable on another ground, namely, that as the fleet remained anchored in Spithead, it was still possible to use the vessel "for a day's cruise round the fleet", so that there had not been a complete failure of the fundamental purpose of the contract. *Krell v Henry* and *Herne Bay Steamboat Co v Hutton* are not entirely easy to reconcile.[141] But it is clear that it is *Krell* which is the exceptional case: it has been subject to much criticism[142] and as an authority it "is certainly not one to be extended".[143] The vital factor in *Krell* was probably that the flat was hired for the days but not the nights and so the only conceivable purpose of the contract was to view the coronation procession. Thus the case has been kept within very narrow confines

---

[134] [1903] 2 K.B. 740, 751.
[135] (1863) 3 B. & S. 826 (above, para.23–005).
[136] [1903] 2 K.B. 740, 754.
[137] [1904] 1 K.B. 493. (That part of the case dealing with the legal consequences of frustration is no longer good law: see below, paras 23–072 et seq.)
[138] *Blakeley v Muller* [1903] 2 K.B. 760n. cf. *Clark v Lindsay* (1903) 88 L.T. 198; *Griffith v Brymer* (1903) 19 T.L.R. 434 (although this is a case of common mistake because the "impossibility" was antecedent).
[139] [1903] 2 K.B. 683. See Gottschalk, *Impossibility of Performance in Contract* (1945), pp.16–18. cf. *Civil Service Co-operative Society v General Steam Navigation Co* [1903] 2 K.B. 756.
[140] [1903] 2 K.B. 683, 689.
[141] See the discussion of these cases in Treitel, *The Law of Contract*, 12th edn (by Peel, 2007), paras 19–041—19–043; Cheshire, Fifoot & Furmston, *Law of Contract*, 15th edn (2007), pp.727–728; McElroy & Williams (references in fn.133, above).
[142] See, for example, *Larrinaga & Co Ltd v Société Franco-Americaine des Phosphates de Médulla, Paris* (1923) 39 T.L.R. 316, 318.
[143] *Maritime National Fish Ltd v Ocean Trawlers Ltd* [1935] A.C. 524, 529 (Lord Wright).

so that it cannot be invoked by a party whose aim is simply to escape from what has proved to be a bad bargain.[144]

(iii) *Delay*

23–035 **Delay.**[145] It is often a difficult matter to decide whether a contract has been frustrated by an event or change in circumstances which causes unexpected delay in its performance. In *Pioneer Shipping Ltd v B.T.P. Tioxide Ltd (The Nema)*,[146] Lord Roskill, in a speech concurred in by all their Lordships, said:

> "... it is often necessary to wait upon events in order to see whether the delay already suffered and the prospects of further delay from that cause, will make any ultimate performance of the relevant contractual obligations 'radically different' ... from that which was undertaken by the contract. But, as has often been said, business men must not be required to await events too long. They are entitled to know where they stand. Whether or not the delay is such as to bring about frustration must be a question to be determined by an informed judgment based upon all the evidence of what has occurred and what is likely thereafter to occur.[147] Often it will be a question of degree whether the effect of delay suffered, and likely to be suffered, will be such as to bring about frustration of the particular adventure in question."[148]

For this purpose, causes of delay should not be divided into classes: a strike may cause frustration of a commercial adventure through delay as much as any other cause:

> "It is not the nature of the cause which matters so much as the effect of that cause upon the performance of the obligations which the parties have assumed one towards the other."[149]

To frustrate a contract, the delay must be abnormal, in its cause, its effects, or its expected duration, so that it falls outside what the parties could reasonably

144 *Amalgamated Investment & Property Co Ltd v John Walker & Son Ltd* [1977] 1 W.L.R. 164; *Pioneer Shipping Ltd v B.T.P. Tioxide Ltd (The Nema)* [1982] A.C. 724, 752. See also *Congimex Companhia Geral S.A.R.L. v Tradax Export SA* [1983] 1 Lloyd's Rep. 250, 253.

145 Treitel, *Frustration and Force Majeure*, 2nd edn (2004), paras 5–036—5–056; Howard in McKendrick (ed.), *Force Majeure and Frustration of Contract*, 2nd edn (1995) pp.122–131; Stannard (1983) 46 M.L.R. 738; J.E. Stannard, *Delay in the Performance of Contractual Obligations* (Oxford, 2007), paras 6.16–6.22 and Ch.12.

146 [1982] A.C. 724, 752.

147 "Commercial men must be entitled to act on reasonable commercial probabilities at the time they are called upon to make up their minds": per Lord Simon in *National Carriers Ltd v Panalpina (Northern) Ltd* [1981] A.C. 675, 706 (see also at 688) (following *Embiricos v Sydney Reid & Co* [1914] 3 K.B. 45, 54). As to the point of time when prospective delay must be judged, see *Watts, Watts & Co Ltd v Mitsui & Co Ltd* [1917] A.C. 227, 245–246; *Andrew Millar & Co Ltd v Taylor & Co Ltd* [1916] 1 K.B. 402; *Total Gas Marketing Ltd v Arco British Ltd* [1998] 2 Lloyd's Rep. 209, 222; *Edwinton Commercial Corp v Tsavliris Russ (Worldwide Salvage & Towage) Ltd (The Sea Angel)* [2007] EWCA Civ 547 at [89]; also below, para.23–043, and McNair (1940) 56 L.Q.R. 173, 201–205.

148 On such a question, an appellate court should be reluctant to interfere with the conclusion of the tribunal of fact: see above, para.23–015; below, para.23–097 fn.415. See *Kodros Shipping Corp v Empresa Cubana de Fletes (The Evia) (No.2)* [1983] 1 A.C. 736, 767–768; cf. *International Sea Tankers Inc v Hemisphere Shipping Co (The Wenjiang)* [1982] 2 All E.R. 437; *Adelfamar SA v Silos E. Mangimi Martini SpA* [1988] 2 Lloyd's Rep. 466, 471.

149 *Pioneer Shipping Ltd v B.T.P. Tioxide Ltd (The Nema)* [1982] A.C. 724, 754 (per Lord Roskill, citing *The Penelope* [1928] P. 180); *Eridania SpA v Rudolf A. Oetker (The Fjord Wind)* [1998] C.L.C. 1187.

contemplate at the time of contracting.[150] The fact that the delay was caused by "a new and unforeseeable factor or event" is a relevant matter.[151] The probable length of the delay must be assessed in relation to the nature of the contract, and to the expected duration of the contract after the delay is expected to end.[152] There can be no frustration if the delay in question was within the commercial risks undertaken by the parties.[153]

Illustrations. Many illustrations of the effect of delay on particular contracts will be found throughout this chapter: in relation to charterparties, delay caused by the stranding of the ship,[154] the requisitioning of the ship by the Government,[155] its seizure by insurgents,[156] the blocking of the Suez Canal,[157] or strikes[158]; in relation to building contracts, delay caused by war-time restrictions,[159] or by bad weather and unforeseen shortage of labour[160]; in relation to contracts of carriage, delay caused by the blocking of the usual route[161]; and in relation to leases, the prohibition of building,[162] or the closing of vehicular access to the property.[163] 23–036

(c) *Application of the Doctrine to Common Types of Contracts*

(i) *Personal Contracts*[164]

Death. The rule is stated by Pollock C.B. in *Hall v Wright*[165]: 23–037

> "All contracts for personal services which can be performed only during the lifetime of the party contracting are subject to the implied condition that he shall be alive to

---

[150] See the quotation, below, in para.23–030.

[151] See below, paras 23–050, 23–059.

[152] This is particularly important in leases (below, paras 23–052—23–056); charterparties (below, paras 23–041—23–046); and building contracts (below, paras 23–049—23–051).

[153] *Davis Contractors Ltd v Fareham U.D.C.* [1956] A.C. 696; *King v Parker* (1876) 34 L.T. 887 (delay in deliveries of coal due to strike held insufficient to frustrate contract of sale); *Trade and Transport Inc v Iino Kaiun Kaisha Ltd* [1973] 1 W.L.R. 210, 221–222; *Intertradex SA v Lesieur-Tourteaux S.A.R.L.* [1978] 2 Lloyd's Rep. 509, 514, 515–516; *Edwinton Commercial Corp v Tsavliris Russ (Worldwide Salvage & Towage) Ltd (The Sea Angel)* [2007] EWCA Civ 547 at [83]; approving [2006] EWHC 1713 (Comm) at [83]. (But see the comment of Lord Roskill on the court's imposing its own view on this issue, rather than adopting the view of the arbitral tribunal: *Pioneer Shipping Ltd v B.T.P. Tioxide Ltd* [1982] A.C. 724, 752–753; and fn.148, above.)

[154] Above, para.23–048.

[155] Below, paras 23–041—23–043.

[156] Below, para.23–044.

[157] Below, para.23–044.

[158] Below, para.23–045.

[159] Below, para.23–024.

[160] Below, paras 23–050—23–051.

[161] Below, para.23–048.

[162] Below, para.23–054.

[163] Below, para.23–055.

[164] See above, para.23–023; Vol.II, paras 39–168—39–170.

[165] (1858) E.B. & E. 746, 793. (The actual decision in this case, to the effect that supervening illness of the defendant did not frustrate a contract to marry, even though the defendant could not consummate the marriage without danger to his life, might not have been followed, quite apart from the change in the law which now prevents promises to marry from giving rise to legal rights: Law Reform (Miscellaneous Provisions) Act 1970 s.1. The case is discussed in more detail by Treitel, *Frustration and Force Majeure*, 2nd edn (2004), para.2–015. For a discussion of the previous law on frustration of a promise to marry, see Powell (1961) 14 C.L.P. 100, cf. *Stubbs v Holywell Ry* (1867) L.R. 2 Ex. 311.)

perform them; and, should he die, his executor is not liable to an action for the breach of contract occasioned by his death."

Thus, in *Graves v Cohen*[166] the court considered the effect upon a jockey's contract for personal services of the death of his employer, a racehorse owner. The court held that death frustrated his jockey's contract with him, since the contract created a relationship involving mutual confidence. However, in *Phillips v Alhambra Palace Co Ltd*[167] one partner in a firm of music-hall proprietors died after the firm had engaged a troupe of performers, but it was held that the contract was not frustrated, since it was not of such a personal character and so could be enforced against the surviving partners. Similarly, it has been held that a tenancy at a weekly rent is not determined by the death of the tenant.[168]

23–038 **Illness or incapacity.** The question whether a contract of employment has been frustrated[169] by the employee's illness or incapacity depends on whether it was of such a nature or likely to continue for such a period, that future performance of his contractual duties would be either impossible or radically different from that envisaged by the contract.[170] In applying this test, the court will treat as relevant factors the terms of the contract (including any sick pay provisions), the nature and expected duration of the employment, the period of past employment, and the prospects of recovery.[171] Thus, permanent illness may frustrate an apprenticeship,[172] while a short period of illness may frustrate a shorter-term contract.[173] A periodic contract of employment which is determinable by the employer by short notice may nevertheless be frustrated by illness or

---

166 (1930) 46 T.L.R. 121. See also *Morgan v Manser* [1948] 1 K.B. 184.

167 [1901] 1 Q.B. 59; for the converse case, cf. *Harvey v Tivoli (Manchester) Ltd* (1907) 23 T.L.R. 592.

168 *Youngmin v Heath* [1974] 1 All E.R. 461 (although the judgments do not discuss the case in terms of the doctrine of frustration).

169 Even where the contract of employment has not been frustrated, a dismissal of an employee on the grounds of ill-health may not be "unfair" within the relevant statutory provisions: see Vol.II, para.39–207. See Mogridge (1982) 132 New L.J. 795.

170 *Storey v Fulham Steel Works* (1907) 24 T.L.R. 89; *Condor v The Barron Knights Ltd* [1966] 1 W.L.R. 87; *Marshall v Harland & Wolff Ltd* [1972] 1 W.L.R. 899; *Hebden v Forsey & Son* [1973] I.C.R. 607; *Hart v A.R. Marshall & Sons (Bulwell) Ltd* [1977] 1 W.L.R. 1067; *Notcutt v Universal Equipment Co (London) Ltd* [1986] 1 W.L.R. 641; *GF Sharp & Co Ltd v McMillan* [1998] I.R.L.R. 632. See Howarth [1987] C.L.J. 47; *Harvey on Industrial Relations and Employment Law*, Vol.1, Div.A, paras 2077–2090 and Div.D, paras 359–368.

171 *Marshall v Harland & Wolff Ltd* [1972] 1 W.L.R. 899, 903–905. See Freedland, *The Contract of Employment* (1976), pp.301–311. cf. below, para.23–043. It may be that permanent incapacity alone will not suffice to frustrate a contract of employment, on the basis that the contract itself may, exceptionally, envisage the possibility that the employee will continue to be employed notwithstanding the fact that he or she is suffering a permanent incapacity: see *R. (Verner) v Derby City Council* [2003] EWHC 2708 (Admin), [2004] I.C.R. 535 at [66]. Lindsay J. concluded (at [68]) that in such a case the contract of employment continues to exist: "[I]n an entirely shadowy form in which, by reason of the employee's incapacity and retirement, the employer cannot require any performance and the employee cannot offer it."

172 *Boast v Firth* (1868) L.R. 4 C.P. 1. (Temporary illness, however, may give an employee a temporary excuse for failure to work: below, paras 23–066—23–072, and Vol.II, para.39–170.)

173 *Egg Stores (Stamford Hill) Ltd v Leibovici* [1977] I.C.R. 260 ("has the time arrived when the employer can no longer reasonably be expected to keep the absent employee's post open for him"?: 264).

injury which incapacitates the employee[174]: in *Notcutt v Universal Equipment Co (London) Ltd*, it was held that the contract was frustrated (by operation of law and thus without notice) as soon as it became clear that the employee's illness would prevent him from ever working again.[175] Illness may also provide an employee with a temporary excuse for non-performance of his contractual obligations without the contract being discharged by operation of the doctrine of frustration.[176]

Imprisonment or compulsory service. A sentence of imprisonment (or of Borstal training) upon an employee (except possibly in the case of a very short sentence) will frustrate his contract of employment or of apprenticeship as from the date of the sentence.[177] Detention during war-time may also frustrate a contract. In *Horlock v Beal*[178] a British ship was detained in a German port on the outbreak of the First World War and the crew imprisoned. The House of Lords held that the crew were not entitled to wages during their detention, which had rendered it impossible for them to fulfil their contract of employment. Other contracts of employment have been frustrated where a refugee, employed in England, was interned during the war,[179] and where a music-hall artiste was called up for service in the army.[180] **23–039**

Other events. If an arbitration is restricted to the submission of an identified, existing dispute to a named arbitrator, the agreement is frustrated if the arbitrator turns out not to be impartial.[181] But long delay in proceeding with an arbitration does not frustrate the agreement to submit the dispute to arbitration.[182] A **23–040**

---

[174] *Notcutt v Universal Equipment Co (London) Ltd* [1986] 1 W.L.R. 641.

[175] [1986] 1 W.L.R. 641.

[176] This, it is submitted, is the best explanation of the difficult case of *Poussard v Spiers and Pond* (1876) 1 QBD 410. The contract there was not automatically discharged as a result of the plaintiff's illness, rather, the defendants were given an option to terminate the contract and they chose to exercise that option. See further para.23–068 fn.325.

[177] *Hare v Murphy Bros Ltd* [1974] I.C.R. 603 (12 months' imprisonment); *F.C. Shepherd & Co Ltd v Jerrom* [1987] Q.B. 301 (Borstal training, which is for an indefinite period: the sentence would be "a substantial break in the period of training" under the apprenticeship agreement (at 320) which had not yet run for half the period). But see *Chakki v United Yeast Co Ltd* [1982] 2 All E.R. 446 (imprisonment may not frustrate the contract immediately upon sentence); *Harvey on Industrial Relations and Employment Law*, Vol.1, Div.D, paras 369–374.

[178] [1916] 1 A.C. 486 (distinguished in *Ottoman Bank v Chakarian* [1930] A.C. 277, where a temporary and limited disability did not frustrate a contract of service).

[179] *Unger v Preston Corp* [1942] 1 All E.R. 200. cf. *Nordman v Rayner & Sturges* (1916) 33 T.L.R. 87.

[180] *Morgan v Manser* [1948] 1 K.B. 184. See also *Marshall v Glanvill* [1917] 2 K.B. 87 (above, para.23–023). cf. *Hangkam Kwingtong Woo v Liu Lan Fong* [1951] A.C. 707 (agency not frustrated by agent being in enemy-occupied territory).

[181] *Bremer Vulkan Schiffbau und Maschinenfabrik v South India Shipping Corp Ltd* [1981] A.C. 909, 981.

[182] Delay was employed in an unsuccessful attempt to invoke the doctrine of frustration in a line of cases which arose out of agreements to arbitrate which had "gone to sleep" and then one party later attempted to revive the arbitration (the leading example is the decision of the House of Lords in *Paal Wilson & Co A/S v Partenreederei Hannah Blumenthal* [1983] 1 A.C. 854, discussed in the 27th edn of this work at para.23–025). The problem has now been resolved by statute giving to the arbitrator the power to dismiss any claim in a dispute referred to him if it appears to him that there has been an inordinate and inexcusable delay on the part of the claimant in pursuing the claim and that the delay either will give rise or is likely to give rise to a substantial risk that it is not possible to have a fair resolution of the issues or that it has caused, or is likely to have caused, serious prejudice to

separation agreement under which the husband covenants to pay maintenance to his wife is not frustrated by a subsequent decree of divorce obtained by the wife,[183] nor by a subsequent decree of nullity obtained by the husband on the ground of the wife's incapacity.[184] The doctrine of frustration has been held to be inapplicable to a consent order made in ancillary relief proceedings.[185] The Court of Appeal has left open the question whether the doctrine of frustration could ever apply to the status of marriage,[186] but it is submitted that it should not, because to frustrate a marriage under a doctrine of the common law would amount to adding to the grounds for divorce without legislation.

(ii) *Charterparties*[187]

23–041 **Requisitioning.** The doctrine of frustration has been frequently invoked in disputes concerning charterparties, and the application of the doctrine is well illustrated by such cases. A leading decision of the House of Lords is *Bank Line Ltd v Arthur Capel & Co*,[188] where a ship was let on a time charter of 12 months from the time she was delivered to the charterers. Before such delivery, however, the ship was requisitioned by the Government. The charterparty contained a special clause giving the charterers the option of cancelling the charter if the ship was not delivered by a fixed date or if she was commandeered by the Government during the currency of the charter, but the charterers did not exercise their option to cancel. Three months after the requisitioning the owners (who regarded the charterparty as frustrated) sold the ship to third parties subject to her release by the Government, and a month later she was released and the sale completed.

---

the respondent (Arbitration Act 1996 s.41(3)). Regard may be had to delay which occurred before arbitrators were given this statutory power (see *L'Office Cherifien des Phosphates v Yamashita-Shinnhon S.S. Co Ltd* [1994] 1 A.C. 486). The intervention of statute has removed the need to invoke the doctrine of frustration in this fact situation.

[183] *May v May* [1929] 2 K.B. 386. The result is the same if the divorce is obtained by the husband: *Charlesworth v Holt* (1873) L.R. 9 Ex. 38.

[184] *Adams v Adams* [1941] 1 K.B. 536. (In this case, as well as in *May v May*, above, it was open to either party to apply to the court for a variation of the agreement: see now s.35 of the Matrimonial Causes Act 1973; *Tomkins v Tomkins* [1948] P. 170.)

[185] *S v S (Ancillary Relief: Consent Order)* [2002] EWHC 223 (Fam); [2003] Fam. 1 at [30].

[186] *Kenward v Kenward* [1951] P. 124.

[187] *Scrutton on Charterparties*, 20th edn (1996), pp.23–31; Treitel, *Frustration and Force Majeure*, 2nd edn (2004), paras 5–052—5–054; see (in addition to the cases cited below) *Geipel v Smith* (1872) L.R. 7 Q.B. 404 (blockading of port); *Jackson v Union Marine Insurance Co Ltd* (1874) L.R. 10 C.P. 125 (stranding; above, para.23–006); *Dahl v Nelson, Donkin & Co* (1881) 6 App. Cas. 38 (dock authorities refused to admit ship because dock was full: held, charterer bound to permit unloading at alternative place mentioned in charterparty); *Lloyd Royal Belge SA v Stathatos* (1917) 34 T.L.R. 70 (ship detained by naval authorities for over two months); *Larrinaga & Co Ltd v Société Franco-Americaine des Phosphates de Médulla* (1923) 39 T.L.R. 316; *Hirji Mulji v Cheong Yue S.S. Co Ltd* [1926] A.C. 497 (requisitioning); *Court Line Ltd v Dant & Russell Inc* [1939] 3 All E.R. 314 (boom blocking river during war); *Joseph Constantine S.S. Line Ltd v Imperial Smelting Corp Ltd* [1942] A.C. 154 (explosion); *Blane S.S. Ltd v Minister of Transport* [1951] 2 K.B. 965 (stranding); *Atlantic Maritime Co Inc v Gibbon* [1954] 1 Q.B. 88 (marine insurance: restraint of princes clause); cf. *Hongkong Fir Shipping Co Ltd v Kawasaki Kisen Kaisha Ltd* [1962] 2 Q.B. 26 (delays caused by breakdowns and repairs where shipowners in breach); *Pioneer Shipping Ltd v B.T.P. Tioxide Ltd (The Nema)* [1982] A.C. 724 (long delay caused by strike at port of loading: see above, para.23–035); *Adelfamar SA v Silos E. Mangimi Martini SpA (The Adelfa)* [1988] 2 Lloyd's Rep. 466 (arrest of vessel by third party). See also the cases cited above, para.23–035 fn.148.

[188] [1919] A.C. 435.

The charterers brought an action for non-delivery of the ship, but the House of Lords held that the doctrine of frustration applied to time charters, and that the object of this charterparty had been frustrated by the requisitioning and detention of the ship, since the identity of the chartered service had been destroyed. The House also held that the doctrine of frustration had not been excluded by the special clauses of the charterparty. They merely gave the charterers an express option to cancel in the event of requisition, "without waiting to see or having to show that its object is thereby frustrated".[189] Their function was not to preclude resort to frustration.

The Tamplin case. Three years prior to *Bank Line* the House of Lords decided another case on frustration of a charterparty by requisitioning, namely, *F.A. Tamplin S.S. Co Ltd v Anglo-American Petroleum Products Co Ltd.*[190] In the latter case a ship was chartered under a time charter for five years to sail between any safe ports within certain limits as the charterers should direct. After the outbreak of the First World War, when the charter had nearly three years to run, the ship was requisitioned by the Admiralty and converted by structural alterations into a troopship. The owners contended that the charter had been determined by the requisitioning, but this was denied by the charterers, who were willing to continue to pay the agreed freight. The House decided by a majority that the interruption was not sufficient to frustrate the contract. Earl Loreburn said that both parties: 23–042

> "... would have been considerably surprised to be told that interruption for a few months was to release them both from a time charter that was to last five years ... I think that they took their chance of lesser interruptions and the condition I should imply goes no further than that they should be excused if substantially the whole contract became impossible of performance, or in other words, impracticable, by some cause for which neither was responsible."[191]

The fact that it was the shipowners rather than the charterers who were arguing that the contract was frustrated so that they could obtain the generous rates of compensation paid by the Government undoubtedly weighed with the majority.[192]

The impact of the interruption. The application of the doctrine of frustration will always depend on the particular facts of each case, but it is difficult to reconcile these two cases, except on the basis that in *Tamplin* the interruption was of a time charter for five years, while in *Bank Line* the interruption had a more serious effect, since the time charter was for the much shorter period of one year: 23–043

---

[189] [1919] A.C. 435, 456.

[190] [1916] 2 A.C. 397.

[191] [1916] 2 A.C. 397, 405–406.

[192] Lord Parker of Waddington thought that the doctrine of frustration could not apply to a time charter which "does not contemplate any definite adventure or object to be performed or carried out" ([1916] 2 A.C. 397, 425) but this opinion was later rejected by the House of Lords in *Bank Line Ltd v Arthur Capel & Co* [1919] A.C. 435, 443.

> "... the main thing to be considered is the probable length of the total deprivation of the use of the chartered ship compared with the unexpired duration of the charterparty .... The probabilities as to the length of the deprivation and not the certainty arrived at after the event are also material. The question must be considered at the trial as it had to be considered by the parties, when they came to know of the cause and the probabilities of the delay, and had to decide what to do."[193]

This approach to the problem of requisitioning is supported by the case of *Port Line Ltd v Ben Line Steamers Ltd*,[194] where Diplock J. held that a time charterparty for 30 months (of which 17 had expired) was not frustrated by a government requisitioning which was expected to last, and did in fact last, only about three months. At the time of derequisition of the vessel there was still 10 months of the charterparty to run and in these circumstances it could not be said that the contract was frustrated. The fact that the ship was requisitioned under the prerogative of the Crown, which meant that the Crown could retain the ship only for such period as was necessary for the defence of the realm was a relevant factor because it indicated that the requisition was "necessarily a temporary taking of possession".[195]

23–044 **Other frustrating events.** In *W.J. Tatem v Gamboa*[196] a ship was chartered by an agent of the Spanish Republican Government under a time charter for 30 days during the Spanish Civil War, in order to evacuate the civil population from north Spain. The hire of £250 a day (three times the normal rate) was payable until redelivery at a French port, and it was paid in advance for 30 days from July 1, when the charterers took over the ship. On July 14, she was seized by a Nationalist cruiser and detained until September 7. The risk of capture by the insurgents was known to the parties, but there was no provision for this event in the charterparty. The owners claimed hire at £250 a day from August 1 to September 11, the date of redelivery, but Goddard J. held that performance of the charterparty had been frustrated by the seizure.[197] In *The Eugenia*,[198] the Court of Appeal held that a time charterparty, starting at Genoa for a single "trip out to India via Black Sea" (for which the Suez Canal was the customary route) was not frustrated by the blocking of the canal in 1956. Although the voyage around the Cape of Good Hope was longer and more expensive, it was not a "fundamentally different" voyage, since the cargo of metal goods "would not be adversely

---

[193] *Bank Line Ltd v Arthur Capel & Co* [1919] A.C. 435, 454; *Court Line Ltd v Dant & Russell Inc* [1939] 3 All E.R. 314, 318. See above, para.23–041 fn.187; Howard in McKendrick (ed.), *Force Majeure and Frustration of Contract*, 2nd edn (1995), pp.129–138.

[194] [1958] 2 Q.B. 146, 161–163.

[195] [1958] 2 Q.B. 146, 161.

[196] [1939] 1 K.B. 132.

[197] In *Edwinton Commercial Corp v Tsavliris Russ (Worldwide Salvage & Towage) Ltd (The Sea Angel)* [2007] EWCA Civ 547 Rix L.J. explained this conclusion on the basis that "there was no question . . . of any possibility of recourse to a court to obtain a remedy against the unlawful seizure" (at [98]) with the consequence that the requisition "could not be rectified" (at [118]). On this basis *Tatem* is a case which is only applicable within narrow limits because in most cases, such as *The Sea Angel* [2007] EWCA Civ 547, it will be possible for the party affected to seek relief through the courts.

[198] *Ocean Tramp Tankers Corp v V/O Sovfracht (The Eugenia)* [1964] 2 Q.B. 226.

affected by the longer voyage and there was no special reason for early arrival".[199] On the other hand it was held that charterparties were frustrated when, following the outbreak of the war between Iran and Iraq, vessels were trapped for an indefinite period in the Shatt-al-Arab waterway.[200]

Examples not amounting to frustration. The reports contain other examples of cases in which an unexpected event has not released a party from his obligation under a charterparty. In *Thiis v Byers*[201] the master of a ship was obliged, at the place of discharge, to make the cargo of timber into rafts so that the charterer's agents could tow the rafts away. Rough weather prevented this method of unloading for four days, but it was held that when a given number of days is allowed to the charterer for unloading, he must "take the risk of any ordinary vicissitudes" which may delay the operation; hence he was liable for four days' demurrage. Similarly in *Budgett & Co v Binnington & Co*[202] a strike of dock labour did not release the consignees from their obligation to pay demurrage where the clause of the charterparty (incorporated in the bill of lading) fixed the number of lay-days and did not contain any exception for strikes.[203] *Budgett* may be contrasted with *The Penelope*,[204] where the general coal strike of 1926 frustrated a time charter under which the ship was to carry successive cargoes of coal from South Wales over a 12-month period; although the charterparty contained strike provisions, these were held to contemplate only an interruption due to a local withdrawal of labour, and not the total impossibility of any export of coal for more than eight months. 23–045

The Sea Angel. More recently, in *Edwinton Commercial Corp v Tsavliris Russ (Worldwide Salvage & Towage) Ltd (The Sea Angel)*,[205] a delay of just over three months towards the end of a 20-day charterparty, resulting from detention of the vessel by port authorities as security for the costs of pollution caused by another vessel, was held not to have frustrated the contract. That general risk was 23–046

[199] [1964] 2 Q.B. 226, 240. *The Eugenia* was followed (with reluctance) in *Palmco Shipping Inc v Continental Ore Corp* [1970] 2 Lloyd's Rep. 21. As a result of the 1956 closing of the canal, many later charterparties contained a "Suez Canal clause" which has been held to be intended to apply to a future closing of the canal: see *Achille Lauro Fu Gioacchino & Co v Total Societa Italiana Per Azioni* [1969] 2 Lloyd's Rep. 65.

[200] *Kissavos Shipping Co SA v Empresa Cubana de Fletes (The Agathon)* [1982] 2 Lloyd's Rep. 211; *Kodros Shipping Corp of Monrovia v Empresa Cubana de Fletes (The Evia) (No.2)* [1983] 1 A.C. 736; *International Sea Tankers Inc v Hemisphere Shipping Co Ltd (The Wenjiang) (No.2)* [1983] 1 Lloyd's Rep. 400; *Vinava Shipping Co Ltd v Fineluet A.G. (The Chrysalis)* [1983] 1 Lloyd's Rep. 503; Howard in McKendrick (ed.), *Force Majeure and Frustration of Contract*, 2nd edn (1995) pp.129–138. In *Edwinton Commercial Corp v Tsavliris Russ (Worldwide Salvage & Towage) Ltd (The Sea Angel)* [2007] EWCA Civ 547 Rix L.J. explained this conclusion on the basis that 'one cannot negotiate or litigate one's way out of such consequences of war' (at [98]). Thus the ability to negotiate or to litigate may deny to a party the ability to invoke the doctrine of frustration: see fn.197 above.

[201] (1876) 1 QBD 244.

[202] [1891] 1 Q.B. 35.

[203] Charterparties contain many express exceptions known as "excepted perils." See *Scrutton* at pp.204 et seq. For a case on the construction of an exceptions clause, see *Reardon Smith Line Ltd v Ministry of Agriculture* [1963] A.C. 691.

[204] [1928] P. 180.

[205] [2007] EWCA Civ 547.

foreseeable by the salvage industry, was provided for by the industry's terms, and formed part of the matrix of the charter. The Court of Appeal considered that the test of comparing the probable length of delay with the unexpired duration of the charter was only the starting point. Where the charterer assumes the general risk of delay, subject to express provision, it requires something special to frustrate the charter through mere delay.[206] This is particularly the case where the supervening event comes at the very end of a charter, and the effect on performance is purely a question of the financial consequences of the delay, rather than interrupting the heart of the adventure.[207]

(iii) *Sale and Carriage of Goods*

23–047 **Sale and carriage of goods.** Section 7 of the Sale of Goods Act 1979 provides a statutory rule for one instance of frustration:

> "Where there is an agreement to sell specific goods and subsequently the goods, without any fault on the part of the seller or buyer, perish before the risk passes to the buyer,[208] the agreement is avoided."[209]

Where only part of the goods have perished, the court may imply into the contract a term which deals with the resulting situation.[210] Apart from s.7, the normal principles of the common law apply where it is alleged that an agreement to sell goods has been frustrated.[211] Thus, an agreement to sell goods is not frustrated merely because performance of the contract would be commercially unprofitable,[212] at least where performance is still physically and legally possible. On this ground it was once doubted whether a contract for the sale of unascertained goods could ever be frustrated,[213] but it has been held that it can, at all

[206] [2007] EWCA Civ 547 at [131].

[207] [2007] EWCA Civ 547 at [118], [131].

[208] Once the risk has passed to the buyer, he must still pay the price, but the seller is discharged from his obligation to deliver: Vol.II, paras 43–218 et seq.

[209] See Vol.II, paras 43–035—43–038; *Benjamin's Sale of Goods*, 7th edn (2006), paras 6–035 et seq.; Atiyah, *The Sale of Goods*, 11th edn (2005), pp.355–360; McKendrick (ed.), *Sale of Goods* (2000), paras 4–003—4–015; Chalmers, *Sale of Goods*, 18th edn, pp.100–101; *Horn v Minister of Food* [1948] 2 All E.R. 1036. cf. *Elphick v Barnes* (1880) 5 C.P.D. 321; *Howell v Coupland* (1876) 1 QBD 258; *H.R. and S. Sainsbury Ltd v Street* [1972] 1 W.L.R. 834, 837 (below, para.23–068).

[210] See the discussion of *H.R. and S. Sainsbury Ltd v Street* [1972] 1 W.L.R. 834 below, in para.23–068.

[211] e.g. (in addition to the cases cited below) *Nickoll & Knight v Ashton, Edridge & Co* [1901] 2 K.B. 126 (agreement to sell goods to be shipped by specified ship which was stranded before shipment); *Re Shipton, Anderson & Co and Harrison Bros & Co* [1915] 3 K.B. 676 (above, para.23–026; requisition); *Dale S.S. Co Ltd v Northern S.S. Co Ltd* (1918) 34 T.L.R. 271 (requisition of ship while being built); *Fibrosa Spolka Akcyjna v Fairbairn Lawson Combe Barbour Ltd* [1943] A.C. 32 (below, para.23–072; place of delivery becoming enemy territory); *Denny, Mott & Dickson Ltd v James B. Fraser & Co Ltd* [1944] A.C. 265 (above, para.23–025; wartime prohibition). cf. *King v Parker* (1876) 34 L.T. 887; *Ross T. Smyth & Co (Liverpool) Ltd v W.N. Lindsay (Leith) Ltd* [1953] 1 W.L.R. 1280 (above, para.23–027).

[212] *Blackburn Bobbin Co v Allen & Sons* [1918] 2 K.B. 467; *Re Comptoir Commercial Anversois & Power, Son & Co* [1920] 1 K.B. 868; *Beves and Co Ltd v Farkas* [1953] 1 Lloyd's Rep. 103. See also *Davis Contractors Ltd v Fareham U.D.C.* [1956] A.C. 696, 729 (below, para.23–050); *Tsakiroglou & Co Ltd v Noblee Thorl GmbH* [1962] A.C. 93 (below, para.23–048).

[213] *Blackburn Bobbin Co v Allen & Sons* [1918] 1 K.B. 540, 550; *Re Thornett and Fehr and Yuills Ltd* [1921] 1 K.B. 219.

events where the importation of the goods from a particular country was the basis of the contract and where such importation has become impossible.[214] If a government does not place an absolute embargo on dealings in a certain commodity, but permits dealings subject to a licence being obtained, the seller cannot rely on frustration to excuse him from performance unless he actually applies for a licence and is refused.[215] Similarly, a seller of goods who makes an unqualified promise to sell goods bears the risk of a failure of the contemplated source of supply and so cannot invoke frustration where that source is not the specified source or the goods are not specific goods and it remains physically and legally possible for the supplier to make the delivery.[216]

Suez Canal cases. The closure of the Suez Canal in November 1956 led to a number of cases in which it was argued that CIF contracts for the sale of goods had been frustrated. In *Tsakiroglou & Co Ltd v Noblee Thorl GmbH*,[217] the House of Lords heard an appeal concerning a contract whereby the sellers agreed in October 1956 to sell Sudanese groundnuts for shipment during November–December 1956 from Port Sudan CIF Hamburg. On November 2 the Suez Canal was closed to navigation but the goods could have been shipped from Port Sudan round the Cape of Good Hope; this alternative route was three times longer than the route through the canal, and freightage was far more costly. The sellers claimed that the contract had been frustrated by the closure of the canal, but the House of Lords held that although the route via the Cape involved a change in the anticipated[218] method of performance of the contract, it was not such a fundamental change from the obligations undertaken in the contract as to frustrate it. It should be noted that a date had not been fixed for delivery in Europe, and that there was evidence that sufficient shipping was available to carry the 23–048

[214] *Re Badische Co Ltd* [1921] 2 Ch. 331, 381–383. (This case concerned frustration from supervening illegality—the outbreak of the war made it illegal to import the goods from Germany: see above, para.23–030.)

[215] *J.W. Taylor & Co v Landauer & Co* [1940] 4 All E.R. 335; see above, para.13–013; Vol.II, para.43–269 (export licences). cf. *Société Co-opérative Suisse des Cereales v La Plata Cereal Co SA* (1947) 80 Ll. L. Rep. 530 (an effective de facto prohibition against export frustrated the contract); *K.C. Sethia (1944) Ltd v Partabmull Rameshwar* [1950] 1 All E.R. 51, [1951] 2 All E.R. 352; *Pound & Co Ltd v Hardy & Co Inc* [1956] A.C. 588; *Dalmia Dairy Industries Ltd v National Bank of Pakistan* [1978] 2 Lloyd's Rep. 223, 253; affirmed on different grounds; *C. Czarnikow Ltd v Centrala Handlu Zagranicznego Rolimpex* [1979] A.C. 351. cf. *The Playa Larga* [1983] 2 Lloyd's Rep. 171 (complete breakdown of commercial relations between seller's and buyer's respective countries: contract held frustrated). See *Benjamin's Sale of Goods*, 7th edn (2006), paras 18–318—18–341 (where a distinction is drawn between cases of supervening imposition of licensing requirements, where the contract may be frustrated, and cases where the contract is stated to be "subject to licence" and one party fails to obtain a licence under a licensing system which was in existence at the moment of formation of the contract. The latter example, it is argued, is not a case of frustration but rather is a case in which a condition is "introduced" into the contract under which neither party is liable to perform unless a licence is obtained; Chalmers, *Sale of Goods*, 18th edn (1981), pp.39–42; Schmitthoff, *Export Trade*, 10th edn (2000), para.6–012.)

[216] *CTI Group Inc v Transclear SA (The Mary Nour)* [2007] EWHC 2070 (Comm), [2008] 1 Lloyd's Rep. 179 at [39].

[217] [1962] A.C. 93. cf. *Ocean Tramp Tankers Corp v V/O Sovfracht (The Eugenia)* [1964] 2 Q.B. 226 (above, para.23–044).

[218] The contract may not have been frustrated even if it had *specified* the Suez Canal route: *Tsakiroglou* [1962] A.C. 93, 112; see also *Palmco Shipping Co v Continental Ore Corp* [1970] 2 Lloyd's Rep. 21.

goods via the Cape. If the goods had been perishable, or if a definite date for delivery (rather than shipment) had been fixed, or if there had been a shortage of shipping to carry goods from Port Sudan to Europe via the longer route, the contract might well have been frustrated.[219]

(iv) *Building Contracts*

23–049 **Building contracts.**[220] If a builder contracts to do work on an existing building which is destroyed during the progress of the work the contract is frustrated. In *Appleby v Myers*,[221] the plaintiff contracted to erect certain machinery upon the defendant's premises for a fixed sum, but when the machinery was only partly erected an accidental fire destroyed the whole of the buildings and the machinery thereon. It was held that since the premises were entirely destroyed without the fault of either party, the contract was frustrated and both parties were excused. Again, government prohibition of, or restrictions on, building operations during wartime have often caused the frustration of building contracts.[222]

23–050 **The Davis Contractors case.** It is in building contracts that the best illustration may be found of the principle that "it is not hardship or inconvenience or material loss which calls the principle of frustration into play",[223] unless there is a radical change in the obligation. In *Davis Contractors Ltd v Fareham U.D.C.*[224] the plaintiffs agreed to build 78 houses for the defendants at a fixed price, the work to be completed in eight months. Due partly to bad weather, but also to an unforeseen shortage of labour caused by the unexpected lag in the demobilisation of troops after the war, the work took 22 months to complete, and cost the builders some £17,000 more than they anticipated. The builders claimed that the shortage of labour and the delay had frustrated the contract, so that they were entitled to sue for the £17,000 on a quantum meruit. The House of Lords unanimously held that the contract had not been frustrated. Viscount Simonds denied that:

> ". . . where, without the default of either party, there has been an unexpected turn of events, which renders the contract more onerous than the parties contemplated, that is by itself a ground for relieving a party of the obligation he has undertaken."[225]

Lord Reid said:

---

[219] *Ocean Tramp Tankers Corp v V/O Sovfracht (The Eugenia)* [1964] 2 Q.B. 226, 240, 243.

[220] *Hudson's Building and Engineering Contracts*, 11th edn (1995), paras 4–233—4–264; McInnis in McKendrick (ed.), *Force Majeure and Frustration of Contract*, 2nd edn (1995), Ch.10; *Keating on Construction Contracts*, 8th edn (2006), paras 6–030—6–046.

[221] (1867) L.R. 2 C.P. 651; in 16 L.T. 669 the contract is set out *in extenso*.

[222] *Metropolitan Water Board v Dick, Kerr & Co Ltd* [1918] A.C. 119 (above, para.23–024); *Federal Steam Navigation Co Ltd v Dixon & Co Ltd* (1919) 64 S.J. 67, HL; cf. *Innholders' Co v Wainwright* (1917) 33 T.L.R. 356 (suspension of contract).

[223] *Davis Contractors Ltd v Fareham U.D.C.* [1956] A.C. 696, 729.

[224] [1956] A.C. 696. See also *Wates Ltd v Greater London Council* (1983) 25 Build. L.R. 1; *Dryden Construction Co Ltd v Hydro-Electric Power Commission of Ontario* (1957) 10 D.L.R. (2d) 124.

[225] [1956] A.C. 696, 716.

"... the delay was greater in degree than was to be expected. It was not caused by any new and unforeseeable factor or event: the job proved to be more onerous but it never became a job of a different kind from that contemplated in the contract."[226]

A builder who undertook to perform such work for a definite lump sum undertook the commercial risk that delay would increase his costs.

Abnormal delay. In another case of delay in completing a building contract, Asquith L.J. laid down the following principles: 23–051

"A contract often provides that in the event of 'delay' through specified causes, the contract is not to be dissolved, but merely suspended, yet such a provision has been held not to apply where the delay was so abnormal, so pre-emptive, as to fall outside what the parties could possibly have contemplated in the suspension clause. In other words 'delay' though literally describing what has occurred, has been read as limited to normal, moderate delay, and as not extending to an interruption so differing in degree and magnitude from anything which could have been contemplated as to differ from it in kind."[227]

(v) *Leases and Tenancies*[228]

Leases and tenancies. For many years, there was uncertainty as to whether the doctrine of frustration could ever apply to a lease.[229] In 1945, in *Cricklewood Property and Investment Trust Ltd v Leightons Investment Trust Ltd*[230] the House of Lords decided unanimously that on the facts there had been no frustration of a long-term building lease by the imposition of building restrictions following the outbreak of war. On the question of principle, the House of Lords was evenly divided.[231] Viscount Simon[232] and Lord Wright[233] thought that on rare occasions a lease may be frustrated, as, for instance, if some vast convulsion of nature swallowed up the property altogether, or buried it in the depths of the sea. Lord Russell[234] and Lord Goddard,[235] however, thought that a lease is more than a contract in that it creates an estate in the land vested in the lessee, and that this estate in the land could never be frustrated, even though some contractual obligations under the lease might be suspended by wartime regulations. In 1980, 23–052

[226] [1956] A.C. 696, 724. See above, paras 23–012—23–016.

[227] *Sir Lindsay Parkinson & Co Ltd v Commissioners of Works* [1949] 2 K.B. 632, 665, citing *Metropolitan Water Board v Dick, Kerr & Co Ltd* [1918] A.C. 119 (above, para.23–024) as "a good illustration of this".

[228] Treitel, *Frustration and Force Majeure*, 2nd edn (2004), Ch.11.

[229] But a licence to occupy land could be frustrated: *Krell v Henry* [1903] 2 K.B. 740 (above, para.23–033); *Taylor v Caldwell* (1863) 3 B. & S. 826 (above, para.23–005); and a hire-purchase agreement (a lease of chattels) could be frustrated. cf. *British Berna Motor Lorries Ltd v Inter-Transport Co Ltd* (1915) 31 T.L.R. 200.

[230] [1945] A.C. 221; cf. Walford (1941) 57 L.Q.R. 339.

[231] The fifth member of the House expressed no opinion on the point.

[232] [1945] A.C. 221, 229.

[233] [1945] A.C. 221, 241.

[234] [1945] A.C. 221, 233–234.

[235] [1945] A.C. 221, 243–245.

in *National Carriers Ltd v Panalpina (Northern) Ltd*,[236] the majority in the House of Lords agreed with the reasoning of Viscount Simon and Lord Wright in the *Cricklewood* case, and thus held that the doctrine of frustration is, in principle, applicable to leases; but several of their Lordships considered that the doctrine would "hardly ever"[237] be applied to a lease.

23–053 **Illustrations of events frustrating leases.** Although there is no reported case in England in which a lease has been held to be frustrated, the reports do contain opinions on the types of situations in which the courts might so hold. The physical disappearance of the demised premises is the most obvious case: a convulsion of nature might "swallow up" the property, or bury it permanently under the sea[238]; or an upper floor flat might be totally destroyed by fire or earthquake.[239] Frustrating events not involving the physical disappearance of the land would include in the case of a building lease, subsequent legislation which permanently prohibited private building on the site[240]; or a fire which destroyed or seriously damaged the buildings on the demised premises.[241] More recently, in *Graves v Graves*,[242] although the Court of Appeal did not find it necessary to decide whether the agreement was frustrated, the same result was reached through the use of an implied term. A housing benefit office incorrectly told Mrs Graves that she could continue to receive housing benefit if she moved into a property owned by her ex-husband, despite the fact their daughter would be living with her. Receipt of this benefit was crucial to the agreement of both parties. The error was discovered several months after Mrs Graves had commenced a 12-month tenancy. It was held that, when it was clear that the housing benefit would not be received, the agreement was different in kind from that

---

[236] [1981] A.C. 675.

[237] [1981] A.C. 675, 692, 709. (The circumstances in which a lease might be frustrated would be "exceedingly rare": 692, 697, 715.) cf. Lord Wright in *Cricklewood Property and Investment Trusts Ltd v Leightons and Investment Trust Ltd* [1945] A.C. 221, 241.

[238] *Cricklewood Property and Investment Trusts Ltd v Leightons and Investment Trust Ltd* [1945] A.C. 221, 229; *National Carriers Ltd v Panalpina (Northern) Ltd* [1981] A.C. 675, 691, 700–701, 709. These examples were cited in *Holbeck Hall Hotel Ltd v Scarborough BC* (1998) 57 Con. L.R. 113, 152–153 where the judge was prepared to assume, without deciding the point, that an event of this nature would have operated to discharge the lease by frustration.

[239] *National Carriers Ltd v Panalpina (Northern) Ltd* [1981] A.C. 675, 690. See Megarry and Wade, *The Law of Real Property*, 6th edn (1999), para.14–189; *Woodfall's Law of Landlord and Tenant*, paras 11–041—11–042.

[240] *Cricklewood Property and Investment Trusts Ltd v Leightons and Investment Trust Ltd* [1945] A.C. 221, 229, 241. In *Rom Securities Ltd v Rogers (Holdings) Ltd* (1967) 205 E.G. 427, an agreement for a lease was frustrated by refusal of planning permission: see *National Carriers Ltd v Panalpina (Northern) Ltd* [1981] A.C. 675, 690, 694, 705 (where Lord Simon says that this was a case of frustration, although the judge dealt with it by implying a term), and 715. cf. the relevant American authorities: Corbin, *Contracts* (1962), Vol.6, paras 1356–1357; Williston, *Contracts*, 3rd edn (1978), Vol.18, para.1955. (In *Robertson v Wilson* (1958) 75 W.N. (N.S.W.) 503, a weekly tenancy was held to have been frustrated by the local authority's "closing order".)

[241] *National Carriers Ltd v Panalpina (Northern) Ltd* [1981] A.C. 675, 701, 713. (The consequences of fire would normally be covered by an express term in the lease.) On the earlier law dealing with the lessee's obligation to pay the rent even when the premises are destroyed, see McElroy and Williams (1941) 4 M.L.R. 241, 256–260. cf. *Taylor v Caldwell* (1863) 3 B. & S. 826 (a licence to use a hall: above para.23–005).

[242] [2007] EWCA Civ 660, [2007] All ER (D) 32 (Jul).

originally contemplated. A term was thus implied that, if housing benefit was not payable, the tenancy would come to an end.[243]

Prohibition on intended use. A clause in the lease restricting the use of the demised premises may be an important factor in deciding whether the lease has been frustrated by circumstances affecting that use. In the United States, leases which restricted the use of the premises to the conduct of a liquor saloon were held to have been frustrated by the enactment of provisions prohibiting that use.[244] The following passage in Corbin, *Contracts*[245] was cited with approval in the House of Lords in *National Carriers Ltd v Panalpina (Northern) Ltd*[246]: 23–054

"If there was one principal use contemplated by the lessee, known to the lessor, and one that played a large part in fixing rental value, a governmental prohibition or prevention of that use has been held to discharge the lessee from his duty to pay the rent. It is otherwise if other substantial uses, permitted by the lease and in the contemplation of the parties, remain possible to the lessee."

Events not frustrating leases. An event which causes an interruption in the expected use of the premises by the lessee will not frustrate the lease unless the interruption is expected to last for the unexpired term of the lease, or, at least, for a long period of that unexpired term. The lease at issue in *National Carriers Ltd v Panalpina (Northern) Ltd* was a 10-year lease of a warehouse. By a temporary order, the City Council closed the street which gave the only access to the warehouse. The House of Lords held that the lease was not frustrated since the closure was expected to last only for a year or a little longer, which would still allow the lease to run for three more years after the street re-opened. The length of the unexpired term was "a potent factor"[247]: 23–055

". . . the likely continuance of the term after the interruption makes it impossible for the lessee to contend that the lease has been brought to an end."[248]

In *Cricklewood*,[249] the lessee under a 99-year building lease claimed that wartime building restrictions had frustrated the lease. The House of Lords held that there had been no frustration, since the lease had over 90 years to run when the war broke out, and it was unlikely that the war would last for more than a small fraction of the whole term.[250] There are also a number of earlier decisions in which the courts, without basing their decisions solely on the then-current

---

243 [2007] EWCA Civ 660 at [40]–[42].

244 *Doherty v Monroe Eckstein Brewing Co* (1921) 191 N.Y.S. 59; *Industrial Development and Land Co v Goldschmidt* 206 P. 134 (1922). These cases are discussed by Treitel, *Frustration and Force Majeure*, 2nd edn (2004), paras 7–023—7–0024 and 11–022; Corbin, *Contracts* (1962), Vol.6, para.1356; Williston, *Contracts*, 3rd edn (1978), Vol.18, para.1955.

245 (1962), Vol.6, pp.475–476 (Lord Simon quoted the identical passage in (1951) Vol.6, p.391).

246 [1981] A.C. 675, 702, per Lord Simon. (Another similar passage from Corbin was also cited with approval by Lord Wilberforce, 695.)

247 [1981] A.C. 675, 706, per Lord Simon.

248 [1981] A.C. 675, 698, per Lord Wilberforce.

249 [1945] A.C. 221. (It was said in this case, however, that frustration might apply to a *covenant* in the lease: see below, para.23–066 fn.318.)

250 See also *Elizabeth Jones v Christos Emmanuel Cleanthi* [2006] EWCA Civ 171 at [84].

doctrine that a lease could never be frustrated, held that specific leases were not frustrated in the particular events which occurred.[251]

23–056 **The consequences of frustration of a lease.** In *National Carriers Ltd v Panalpina (Northern) Ltd*, it was said that a lease would be "automatically discharged on the happening of a frustrating event".[252] The legal operation of this automatic determination of the lease should be the same as where a lease is prematurely determined by other events, either as specified in the terms of the lease, or by operation of law (e.g. forfeiture by denial of title).[253] There is, however, little indication in the cases as to the consequential legal arrangements. If a lease were frustrated, the legal estate would presumably remain vested in the lessee (unless the land itself disappeared), but the lessee could be treated as a trustee for the lessor.[254] Difficulties may arise in relation to land registration. However, these difficulties may not be insuperable because a trust does not appear on the register and the court has power, in certain circumstances, to make an order for the alteration of the register, as does the registrar.[255] Thus it may be that the register could be altered in order to record the premature determination of a registered lease as a result of the frustration of that lease.[256] Some legal consequences may be governed by the Law Reform (Frustrated Contracts) Act 1943,[257] which will apply when a lease has been frustrated,[258] but it is clear that the draftsman did not specifically provide for the situation. There should be an

[251] *London and Northern Estates Co v Schlesinger* [1916] 1 K.B. 20 (the actual result in the case was approved by several of their Lordships in [1981] A.C. 675, 689, 694, 696, 715); *Whitehall Court Ltd v Ettlinger* [1920] 1 K.B. 680 (the actual result in this case was also approved by several of their Lordships in *National Carriers Ltd v Panalpina (Northern) Ltd)*; *Redmond v Dainton* [1920] 2 K.B. 256; *Matthey v Curling* [1922] 2 A.C. 180 (Lord Roskill has said that the result in this case depended on its particular facts: [1981] A.C. 675, 696, 715); *Swift v Macbean* [1942] 1 K.B. 375; *Eyre v Johnson* [1946] K.B. 481; *Simper v Coombs* [1948] 1 All E.R. 306; *Denman v Brise* [1949] 1 K.B. 22; *Yougmin v Heath* [1974] 1 W.L.R. 135.

[252] [1981] A.C. 675, 702.

[253] [1981] A.C. 675, 702.

[254] Interference with property rights has been accepted by the legislature in an analogous field, the rescission of a contract for innocent misrepresentation: the Misrepresentation Act 1967 permits such rescission after a contract has been performed (s.1), and as performance may involve a conveyance or lease of land, rescission of the contract would affect the property rights of the parties. (The Act does not exclude contracts for the sale or lease of an interest in land: above, para.6–133. But the court has a discretion under s.2(2) to award damages in lieu of rescission: above, para.6–096.)

[255] The power of the court and the registrar to make an order for the alteration of the register or to alter the register is set out in s.65 and Sch.4 to the Land Registration Act 2002. The power of the registrar to alter the register is slightly more extensive than the power of the court to make an order for alteration. There may be a difficulty in accommodating a power to alter the register to record the frustration of a registered lease with the express wording of Sch.4 but it may be that it will fall within the power to alter the register for the purpose of "bringing the register up to date" (Sch.4 paras 2(1)(a) and 5(1)(a)).

[256] The law relating to the registration of leases has undergone significant change as a result of the enactment of the Land Registration Act 2002: see generally Harpum and Bignell, *Registered Land: The New Law* (2002).

[257] See below, paras 23–074 et seq.

[258] This is recognised by Lord Wilberforce in *National Carriers Ltd v Panalpina (Northern) Ltd* [1981] A.C. 675, 697, and by Lord Simon, 707, who said: "The Act of 1943 seems unlikely to vouchsafe justice in all cases. As often as not there will be an all-or-nothing situation, the entire loss caused by the frustrating event falling exclusively on one party, whereas justice might require the burden to be shared."

obligation on the lessee to pay rent pro rata up to the date of the frustration, and for so long thereafter as he retains possession.[259]

(vi) *Contracts for the Sale of Land*

Contracts for the sale of land. The doctrine of frustration does not apply where a compulsory purchase order has been made relating to land which is the subject of a contract of sale but has not yet been formally conveyed to the purchaser.[260] Similarly, a contract for sale is not frustrated by the subsequent listing of the building as one of architectural or historical interest under planning legislation.[261] Upon the making of the contract, the purchaser is regarded in equity as the owner of the land (subject to payment of the purchase money); hence the purchaser is bound to complete, but will be entitled to the whole of the compensation money payable under the compulsory purchase order. It is doubtful whether the doctrine of frustration could ever apply to a contract for the sale of land,[262] though it has been suggested that it might if the frustrating event prevented the vendor from transferring any estate whatever to the purchaser.[263] 23–057

4. THE LIMITS OF FRUSTRATION

Express provision.[264] A clause in the contract which is intended to deal with the event which has occurred will normally preclude the application of the doctrine of frustration.[265] Frustration is concerned with unforeseen, supervening events, not events which have been anticipated and provided for in the contract itself.[266] Thus the effect of a force majeure clause or a hardship clause may be to 23–058

---

[259] For US cases on the point, see Williston, *Contracts*, 3rd edn (1978), Vol.18, para.1955.

[260] *Hillingdon Estates Co v Stonefield Estates Ltd* [1952] Ch. 627; *E. Johnson & Co (Barbados) Ltd v N.S.R. Ltd* [1997] A.C. 400, 406–407. cf. (on frustration of contracts for leases) *Lobb v Vasey Housing Auxiliary (War Widows Guild)* [1963] V.R. 239 and *Rom Securities Ltd v Rogers (Holdings) Ltd* (1967) 205 E.G. 427 (above, para.23–053 fn.240); *Denny, Mott and Dickson Ltd v James B. Fraser & Co Ltd* [1944] A.C. 265 (A trading contract held frustrated despite the fact that it contained ancillary provisions creating an option to purchase land and an agreement for a lease: see above, para.23–025 and *National Carriers Ltd v Panalpina (Northern) Ltd* [1981] A.C. 675, 704.)

[261] *Amalgamated Investment & Property Co v John Walker & Sons* [1977] 1 W.L.R. 164. (The listing greatly restricted the owner's freedom to develop the property.)

[262] cf. above, paras 23–052 et seq. (But *delay* in building a block of flats, caused by a landslip, may frustrate a contract for sale of a flat: *Wong Lai Ying v Chinachem Investment Co* (1979) 13 Build. L.R. 81.)

[263] The latter suggestion is probably an instance of supervening illegality: see above, para.23–024. If, however, the contract entitled the purchaser to vacant possession, the vendor cannot enforce the contract if he is prevented from giving possession (e.g. by requisitioning): *Cook v Taylor* [1942] Ch. 349 (see below, para.27–008 fn.29).

[264] Treitel, *Frustration and Force Majeure*, 2nd edn (2004), Ch.12.

[265] *Joseph Constantine S.S. Line Ltd v Imperial Smelting Corp Ltd* [1942] A.C. 154, 163; *Kuwait Supply Co v Oyster Marine Management (The Safeer)* [1994] 1 Lloyd's Rep. 637; *Bangladesh Export Import Co Ltd v Sucden Kerry SA* [1995] 2 Lloyd's Rep. 1: cf. *R. (Verner) v Derby City Council* [2003] EWHC 2708 (Admin), [2004] I.C.R. 535 at [66].

[266] The courts may, exceptionally, be able to imply that the contract has made provision for the alleged frustrating event where it is clear from the contract that one party was intended to assume the risk of the alleged frustrating event: *Larrinaga & Co Ltd v Société Franco-Americaine des Phosphates de Médulla, Paris* (1923) 39 T.L.R. 316.

shut out the doctrine of frustration because the contract, on its proper construction, will be held to have covered the event which has occurred.[267] Similarly, the presence of a price-escalation clause in a contract may make a court more reluctant to conclude that a sudden increase in prices has frustrated the contract.[268] But the courts are likely to construe such clauses narrowly and insist that the provision for the event be "full and complete"[269] before the conclusion is reached that frustration is excluded. The more catastrophic the event, the less likely it is that a clause will be held to cover the event which has occurred, unless particularly clear words are used.[270] Similarly, the fact that a force majeure clause makes provision for an extension of time on the occurrence of one of the stipulated events may indicate to the court that the clause was confined in its application to events which are capable of resolution within that particular timeframe: an event which renders further performance of the contract "unthinkable" may therefore not fall within the scope of the clause.[271] Further, the clause may not make complete provision for all the legal issues arising from the event.[272] For example, a clause may excuse *one* party from the consequences of delay, in the sense that it prevents the delay from constituting a breach of contract, but this does not necessarily exclude the operation of the doctrine of frustration so as to enable that party to hold the other party to the contract when delay occurs.[273] An express provision in the contract cannot, however, exclude frustration by supervening illegality where this would be against public policy.[274]

23–059 **Significance of a foreseen event.**[275] The parties to the contract may not have made express provision for the event which has occurred but they may have foreseen it happening. In such a case, the fact that the parties have foreseen the

---

[267] On force majeure clauses, see above, paras 14–137—14–154, *Benjamin's Sale of Goods*, 7th edn (2006), paras 8–095—8–097, 18–330—18–331, 19–124—19–126; *Schmitthoff's Export Trade: The Law and Practice of International Trade*, 10th edn (2000), 6–017—6–021; Cartoon [1978] J.B.L. 230. See also *RDC Concrete PTE Ltd v Sato Kogyo (S) PTE Ltd* [2007] SGCA 39, (2008) 115 Con. L.R. 154 at [53]–[65].

[268] *Wates Ltd v G.L.C.* (1983) 25 Build. L.R. 1.

[269] *Bank Line Ltd v Arthur Capel & Co* [1919] A.C. 435, 455; *Select Commodities Ltd v Valdo SA (The "Florida")* [2006] EWHC 1137 (Comm), [2007] 1 Lloyd's Rep. 1.

[270] *Metropolitan Water Board v Dick Kerr & Co Ltd* [1918] A.C. 119 (above, para.23–024). See also *Pacific Phosphate Co Ltd v Empire Transport Co Ltd* (1920) 36 T.L.R. 750; *The Penelope* [1928] P. 180 (above, para.23–045); *Fibrosa Spolka Akcyjna v Fairbairn Lawson Combe Barbour Ltd* [1943] A.C. 32; *Denny, Mott & Dickson Ltd v James B. Fraser & Co Ltd* [1944] A.C. 265, 284; *Kodros Shipping Corp of Monrovia v Empresa Cubana de Fletes (The Evia) (No.2)* [1983] 1 A.C. 736; *Edwinton Commercial Corp v Tsavliris Russ (Worldwide Salvage & Towage) Ltd (The Sea Angel)* [2007] EWCA Civ 547 at [83], approving [2006] EWHC 1713 (Comm) at [84]; also above, para.23–051.

[271] *Empresa Exportadora De Azucor v Industria Azucarera Nacional SA (The Playa Larga)* [1983] 2 Lloyd's Rep. 171, 189.

[272] *Bank Line Ltd v Arthur Capel & Co* [1919] A.C. 435, 455–456 (above, para.23–041).

[273] *Jackson v Union Marine Insurance Co Ltd* (1874) L.R. 10 C.P. 125, 144 (above, para.23–006).

[274] *Ertel Bieber & Co v Rio Tinto Co Ltd* [1918] A.C. 260 (above, para.23–024). In other cases of supervening illegality (such as export or import restrictions) express provision may exclude the operation of frustration: *Johnson Matthey Bankers Ltd v State Trading Corp of India* [1984] 1 Lloyd's Rep. 427.

[275] Treitel, *Frustration and Force Majeure*, 2nd edn (2004), Ch.13; Treitel, *The Law of Contract*, 12th edn (by Peel, 2007), paras 19–076—19–081; Hall (1984) 4 L.S. 300.

event but not made any provision for it in their contract will usually,[276] but not necessarily,[277] prevent the doctrine of frustration from applying when the event occurs. While an unforeseen event will not necessarily lead to the frustration of a contract,[278] a foreseen event will generally exclude the operation of the doctrine. The inference that a foreseen event is not a frustrating event is only a prima facie one and so can be excluded by evidence of contrary intention.[279] Thus, it is a question of construction of the contract whether the parties intended their silence to mean that the contract should continue to bind in that event,[280] or whether they intended the effect of the event, if it occurs, to be determined by any relevant legal rules.[281] If one party foresaw the risk, but the other did not, it will be difficult for the former to claim that the occurrence of the risk frustrates the contract.[282] On the other hand, a contract may be frustrated by supervening illegality, notwithstanding the fact that the war which has brought about the supervening illegality was foreseen.[283]

Event foreseeable but not foreseen. When the event was foreseeable but not actually foreseen by the parties, it is less likely that the doctrine of frustration will be held to be inapplicable.[284] Much turns on the extent to which the event was foreseeable.[285] The issue which the court must consider is whether or not one or 23–060

[276] *Tamplin S.S. Co Ltd v Anglo-Mexican Petroleum Co* [1916] 2 A.C. 397, 426; *Bank Line Ltd v Arthur Capel & Co* [1919] A.C. 435, 455, 462; *Gulnes (D/S A/S) v Imperial Chemical Industries Ltd* [1938] 1 All E.R. 24; *Davis Contractors Ltd v Fareham U.D.C.* [1956] A.C. 696, 731; *Paal Wilson & Co A/S v Partenreederei Hannah Blumenthal* [1983] 1 A.C. 854, 909; *McAlpine Humberoak Ltd v McDermott International Inc* (1992) 58 Build. L.R. 1, 18; Treitel, *The Law of Contract* 12th edn (by Peel, 2007), paras 19–076—19–081.

[277] *Maritime National Fish Ltd v Ocean Trawlers Ltd* [1935] A.C. 524, 529; *Tatem Ltd v Gamboa* [1939] 1 K.B. 132 (above, para.23–044); *Jennings and Chapman Ltd v Woodman, Matthews & Co* [1952] 2 T.L.R. 409, 412; *Ocean Tramp Tankers Corp v V/O Sovfracht (The Eugenia)* [1964] 2 Q.B. 226, 239; *Nile Co for the Export of Agricultural Crops v H. & J.M. Bennett (Commodities) Ltd* [1986] 1 Lloyd's Rep. 555, 582; *Adelfamar SA v Silos E. Mangimi Martini SpA (The Adelfa)* [1988] 2 Lloyd's Rep. 466, 471.

[278] *Davis Contractors Ltd v Fareham U.D.C.* [1956] A.C. 696; *British Movietonews Ltd v London and District Cinemas Ltd* [1952] A.C. 166.

[279] *Edwinton Commercial Corp v Tsavliris Russ (Worldwide Salvage & Towage) Ltd (The Sea Angel)* [2007] EWCA Civ 547 at [103] (but cf. [127])

[280] See, e.g. *Chandler Bros Ltd v Boswell* [1936] 3 All E.R. 179.

[281] For example, an intention that if the event were to happen, the parties would "leave the lawyers to sort it out": *Ocean Tramp Tankers Corp v V/O Sovfracht (The Eugenia)* [1964] 2 Q.B. 226, 239.

[282] *Walton Harvey Ltd v Walter and Homfrays Ltd* [1931] 1 Ch. 274; *Edwinton Commercial Corp v Tsavliris Russ (Worldwide Salvage & Towage) Ltd (The Sea Angel)* [2007] EWCA Civ 547 at [83], approving [2006] EWHC 1713 (Comm) at [84]; Treitel, *The Law of Contract*, 12th edn (by Peel, 2007), para.19–076.

[283] *Ertel Bieber & Co v Rio Tinto Co Ltd* [1918] A.C. 260 (above, para.23–024).

[284] *Edwinton Commercial Corp v Tsavliris Russ (Worldwide Salvage & Towage) Ltd (The Sea Angel)* [2007] EWCA Civ 547 at [104].

[285] The question is one of degree and so depends to a large extent on the facts and circumstances of the individual case. The courts have warned against the "over-refinement" of submissions on this issue and one can probably go no further than conclude that "the less that an event, in its type and its impact, is foreseeable, the more likely it is to be a factor which, depending on other factors in the case, may lead on to frustration": *Edwinton Commercial Corp v Tsavliris Russ (Worldwide Salvage & Towage) Ltd (The Sea Angel)* [2007] EWCA Civ 547 at [127].

other party has assumed the risk of the occurrence of the event.[286] The degree of foreseeability required to exclude the doctrine of frustration is, however, a high one:

> "'. . . foreseeability' will support the inference of risk-assumption only where the supervening event is one which any person of ordinary intelligence would regard as likely to occur, or . . . the contingency must be 'one which the parties could reasonably be thought to have foreseen as a real possibility.' "[287]

23–061 **Self-induced frustration.**[288]

> "The essence of frustration is that it should not be due to the act or election of the party seeking to rely on it."[289]

Thus, a contracting party cannot rely on "self-induced frustration, that is, on frustration due to his own conduct or to the conduct of those for whom he is responsible".[290] Although the concept of self-induced frustration is clearly established as a matter of general principle, the precise limits of the doctrine have not been clearly established. It is merely a "label" which has been used to describe:

> " . . . those situations where one party has been held by the Courts not to be entitled to treat himself as discharged from his contractual obligations."[291]

Thus frustration has been held to be "self-induced" where the alleged frustrating event was caused by a breach[292] or anticipatory breach of contract[293] by the party claiming that the contract has been frustrated, where an act of the party claiming that the contract has been frustrated broke the chain of causation between the

---

[286] *Edwinton Commercial Corp v Tsavliris Russ (Worldwide Salvage & Towage) Ltd (The Sea Angel)* [2007] EWCA Civ 547 at [104]. Many events are foreseeable but neither party assumes the risk of their occurrence. Death is the classic example. The death of an employee during the currency of his employment contract is a foreseeable event but it operates to discharge the contract of employment because neither party assumes the risk of its occurrence.

[287] Treitel, *Frustration and Force Majeure*, 2nd edn (2004), para.13–012. The quote at the end of the citation is taken from the case of *Mishara Construction Company Inc v Transit-Mixed Concrete Corp* 310 N.E. 2d 363, 367 (1974).

[288] Treitel, *Frustration and Force Majeure*, 2nd edn (2004), Ch.14. Swanton (1990) 2 J.C.L. 206.

[289] *J. Lauritzen AS v Wijsmuller B.V. (The Super Servant Two)* [1990] 1 Lloyd's Rep. 1, 8. See also *Bank Line Ltd v Arthur Capel & Co* [1919] A.C. 435, 452; *Maritime National Fish Ltd v Ocean Trawlers Ltd* [1935] A.C. 524, 530; *Joseph Constantine S.S. Line Ltd v Imperial Smelting Corp Ltd* [1942] A.C. 154, 170; *Ocean Tramp Tankers Corp v V/O Sovfracht (The Eugenia)* [1964] 2 Q.B. 226, 237; *Denmark Productions Ltd v Boscobel Productions Ltd* [1969] 1 Q.B. 699, 725, 736–737; *National Carriers Ltd v Panalpina (Northern) Ltd* [1981] A.C. 675, 700; *Edwinton Commercial Corp v Tsavliris Russ (Worldwide Salvage & Towage) Ltd (The Sea Angel)* [2007] EWCA Civ 547 at [83], approving [2006] EWHC 1713 (Comm) at [85].

[290] *Bank Line Ltd v Arthur Capel & Co* [1919] A.C. 435, 452.

[291] *J. Lauritzen A.S. v Wijsmuller BV (The Super Servant Two)* [1989] 1 Lloyd's Rep. 148, 154.

[292] *Ocean Tramp Tankers Corp v V/O Sovfracht (The Eugenia)* [1964] 2 Q.B. 226, 237; *Paal Wilson & Co A/S v Partenreederei Hannah Blumenthal* [1983] 1 A.C. 854; *Cheall v Assn. of Professional Executive and Computer Staff* [1983] 2 A.C. 180, 189.

[293] *New Zealand Shipping Co Ltd v Société des Ateliers et Chantiers de France* [1919] A.C. 1, 6.

alleged frustrating event and the event which made performance of the contract impossible,[294] and where the alleged frustrating event was not a supervening event or "something altogether outside the control of the parties".[295] A party who has been at fault or whose act was deliberate will generally be unable to invoke frustration because of the difficulty which such a party will inevitably face in showing the existence of a supervening event which is outside his control.[296]

Allocation of available supplies. Two leading cases which illustrate the scope of self-induced frustration are *Maritime National Fish Ltd v Ocean Trawlers Ltd*[297] and *J. Lauritzen AS v Wijsmuller BV (The Super Servant Two)*.[298] In the former case the appellants chartered a trawler, the *St Cuthbert*, from the respondents. It was fitted with an otter trawl, and both parties knew that under the Canadian Fisheries Act it was forbidden to use an otter trawl without a licence from the Minister of Fisheries. The appellants were operating four otter trawlers besides the *St Cuthbert*, but in reply to their application for five licences, the Minister stated that he would grant only three, leaving it to the appellant to choose three trawlers. They did not include the *St Cuthbert* in the three trawlers they named, but later claimed that the charterparty had been frustrated by the Minister's refusal of a licence. The Privy Council held that they could not rely on frustration, since they had by their own voluntary election prevented the *St Cuthbert* from being used as an otter trawl. The case is capable of two interpretations. The first is that the critical factor was not that the appellants had a choice as to the allocation of the licences, but that they chose to allocate the licences to their own vessels. The second is that the mere existence of a choice was sufficient to preclude the invocation of frustration. 23–062

In the second case, *J. Lauritzen AS v Wijsmuller BV (The Super Servant Two)*,[299] the defendants agreed to transport the plaintiffs' rig using one or other of two barges, *Super Servant One* or *Super Servant Two*. The defendants later made an internal decision to allocate the *Super Servant Two* to the performance of the contract with the plaintiffs but, before the time for performance of the contract, the *Super Servant Two* sank while transporting another rig in the Zaire River. The *Super Servant One* having been allocated to the performance of other concluded contracts, the defendants sought to argue that the sinking of the *Super Servant Two* had frustrated the contract between the parties. The Court of Appeal held that, whether or not the *Super Servant Two* sank as a result of negligence on the part of the defendants or their employees, the contract was not frustrated. If it sank as a result of negligence then, the court held, the contract was not 23–063

[294] *Maritime National Fish Ltd v Ocean Trawlers Ltd* [1935] A.C. 524 (where the fact that the party claiming frustration had a choice as to how to allocate the scarce resources (licences) was held to be sufficient to break the causal link between the alleged frustrating event and the event which made performance impossible, below, para.23–062).

[295] *Denmark Productions Ltd v Boscobel Productions Ltd* [1969] 1 Q.B. 699, 736.

[296] *J. Lauritzen AS v Wijsmuller BV (The Super Servant Two)* [1990] 1 Lloyd's Rep. 1, 10; cf. *Joseph Constantine S.S. Line Ltd v Imperial Smelting Corp Ltd* [1942] A.C. 154, 166–167.

[297] [1935] A.C. 524.

[298] [1990] 1 Lloyd's Rep. 1.

[299] [1990] 1 Lloyd's Rep. 1. See Treitel, *The Law of Contract*, paras 19–086—19–088; McKendrick [1990] L.M.C.L.Q. 153.

frustrated because negligence did not constitute a supervening event.[300] Although the House of Lords in *Joseph Constantine S.S. Co v Imperial Smelting Corp Ltd*[301] left open the question whether "mere negligence" would justify a finding that frustration was self-induced,[302] subsequent cases have concluded that negligence does exclude a finding of self-induced frustration by asserting that a frustrating event must arise "without blame or fault on the side of the party seeking to rely on it".[303] "Fault" in this context is not confined to a breach of a duty of care owed to the plaintiffs: such an interpretation would have confined the law within "a legalistic strait-jacket" and distracted attention from the real question, which is:

> "... whether the frustrating event relied upon is truly an outside event or extraneous change of situation or whether it is an event which the party seeking to rely on it had the means and opportunity to prevent but nevertheless caused or permitted to come about."[304]

23–064 If, on the other hand, the *Super Servant Two* sank without negligence on the part of the defendants, the contract was still not frustrated because, it was held, the cause of the non-performance of the contract was not the sinking of the *Super Servant Two* but the decision of the defendants not to use the *Super Servant One* in the performance of the contract with the plaintiffs. Yet to have allocated the *Super Servant One* to the contract with the plaintiffs would, doubtless, have exposed the defendants to liability to someone else to whom they had promised to supply either the *Super Servant One* or the *Super Servant Two*. On this analysis, it was the mere fact that the appellants in *Maritime National Fish*[305] had a choice which prevented them from invoking the doctrine of frustration. The effect of the decision of the Court of Appeal is to place a supplier whose source of supply partially fails in a very difficult position. There was some authority, prior to *Super Servant Two*, which appeared to suggest that a supplier in such a case could "prorate," that is to say the supplier would be discharged from further liability if he proportionately rationed the limited supply among his buyers and his regular customers.[306] But in *Super Servant Two* it was held that these cases turned upon the proper interpretation of a force majeure clause and were not illustrative of a general common law power to prorate.[307] In the light of the decision in *Super Servant Two*, a supplier would be well advised to include within his contract a force majeure clause which allows him to prorate in the event of a partial failure of supply. The contract in *Super Servant Two* did in fact

---

[300] [1990] 1 Lloyd's Rep. 1, 10.

[301] [1942] A.C. 154.

[302] [1942] A.C. 154, 166–167, 179, 195, 202.

[303] *J. Lauritzen AS v Wijsmuller BV (The Super Servant Two)* [1990] 1 Lloyd's Rep. 1, 8.

[304] [1990] 1 Lloyd's Rep. 1, 10.

[305] [1935] A.C. 524.

[306] *Tennants (Lancashire) Ltd v C.S. Wilson & Co Ltd* [1917] A.C. 495; *Intertradex SA v Lesieur Torteaux S.A.R.L.* [1978] 2 Lloyd's Rep. 509; *Bremer Handelsgesellschaft mbH v C. Mackprang Jr* [1979] 1 Lloyd's Rep. 221; *Continental Grain Export Corp v S.T.M. Grain Ltd* [1979] 2 Lloyd's Rep. 460, 473 and *Bremer Handelsgesellschaft mbH v Continental Grain Co* [1983] 1 Lloyd's Rep. 269. See generally on this line of cases, Hudson (1968) 31 M.L.R. 535 and (1979) 123 S.J. 137.

[307] *J. Lauritzen AS v Wijsmuller BV* [1990] 1 Lloyd's Rep. 1, 9; *Benjamin's Sale of Goods*, 7th edn (2006), paras 18–353—18–354.

contain a force majeure clause and this was held to be effective to excuse the defendants provided that the *Super Servant Two* sank without negligence on the part of themselves or their employees.[308]

23–065 **Onus of proof.** The House of Lords in *Joseph Constantine S.S. Line Ltd v Imperial Smelting Corp Ltd*[309] held that the onus of proving self-induced frustration lies on the party who asserts that this is the case. If A (the party relying on frustration) proves events which prima facie would frustrate the contract, the onus of proving that the frustration was self-induced is on the other party (B) who denies that the contract has been frustrated. B must then prove some default by A which caused the allegedly frustrating event. When A proves and relies on frustration, B cannot prevent its operation by proving that it had been induced by his own (B's) fault.[310] So the fact that it was an employee's (or apprentice's) criminal conduct which led to a sentence of imprisonment[311] or of Borstal training[312] being imposed on him does not amount to "self-induced" conduct so as to prevent frustration of his contract of employment (or apprenticeship) as alleged by his employer[313]:

> "What matters, however, in the case of self-induced frustration is that the party who is the 'self' cannot treat himself as being discharged."[314]

23–066 **Partial "frustration".** English law has great difficulty in dealing with the case where part of the contract has become impossible of performance. To use the expression partial "frustration" to encompass this situation is not strictly accurate because the effect of frustration is to "kill the contract and discharge the parties from further liability under it".[315] Yet in these cases it is clear that the contract as a whole is not discharged: the argument is the more limited one that the occurrence of some new circumstance may excuse (perhaps temporarily) the performance of a particular contractual obligation without frustrating the whole contract.[316] Thus temporary illness may excuse an employee for his failure to attend for work,[317] while building restrictions imposed during war-time or as a result of the listing of a building may temporarily excuse non-performance of a

308 [1990] 1 Lloyd's Rep. 1, 6–8; see above, para.23–063.

309 [1942] A.C. 154.

310 *F.C. Shepherd & Co Ltd v Jerrom* [1987] Q.B. 301; *Edwinton Commercial Corp v Tsavliris Russ (Worldwide Salvage & Towage) Ltd (The Sea Angel)* [2007] EWCA Civ 547 at [83], approving [2006] EWHC 1713 (Comm) at [85]. (It is submitted that the dictum at 319C-D is contrary to *Joseph Constantine S.S. Line Ltd v Imperial Smelting Corp Ltd* [1942] A.C. 154.)

311 *Hare v Murphy Bros Ltd* [1974] I.C.R. 603.

312 *F.C. Shepherd & Co Ltd v Jerrom* [1987] Q.B. 301.

313 See above, para.23–039.

314 *F.C. Shepherd & Co Ltd v Jerrom* [1987] Q.B. 301, 327. A similar statement is that "a party who has been in fault cannot rely on frustration due to his own wrongful act" (per Lord Porter in *Joseph Constantine S.S. Line Ltd v Imperial Smelting Corp Ltd* [1942] A.C. 154, 200).

315 *J. Lauritzen AS v Wijsmuller BV (The Super Servant Two)* [1990] 1 Lloyd's Rep. 1, 8.

316 cf. on the U.S. law, Williston, *Contracts*, 3rd edn (1978), Vol.18, paras 1956, 1957; Patterson (1961) 47 Virginia L. Rev. 798; and on South African law, Ramsden (1977) 94 S.A.L.J. 162.

317 See Vol.II, para.39–170.

covenant to build.[318] In some cases supervening illegality may excuse performance of a minor contractual obligation without the whole contract becoming frustrated.[319] These cases can be divided into two distinct categories.

23–067 **Force majeure clauses.** The first group concern the construction of clauses, such as force majeure clauses, which purport to relieve a party from the consequences of a failure to comply with a particular obligation. Thus in *Egham & Staines Electricity Co Ltd v Egham U.D.C.*[320] the council had made a contract with the electricity company for the supply of current for street lighting. If the supply failed due to "unavoidable cause over which the company had no control" payments for current were to abate in proportion. Public street lighting was forbidden by the Lighting (Restrictions) Order on the outbreak of war in 1939. The company sued to recover the full payments provided for by the contract, but it was held that the clause providing for abatement of payments had come into operation; the company was unable to fulfil its contract because it had become illegal to do so, and this illegality amounted to an "unavoidable cause" within the meaning of the clause. But this case tells us nothing about any common law doctrine of "partial frustration"; the court's task was simply to interpret the clause of the contract which was in issue.

23–068 **Partial excuse at common law.** The second group of cases do not turn on the construction of a clause in a contract but rather are based on a general common law doctrine. An example in this category is provided by the difficult case of *H.R. & S. Sainsbury Ltd v Street*.[321] The parties entered into a contract under which the defendant agreed to sell to the plaintiffs 275 tons of barley from a crop growing on a farm. Without any fault on the part of the defendant, the yield turned out to be only 140 tons. The defendant refused to supply the plaintiff with the 140 tons harvested and so the plaintiff buyers brought a claim for damages. The defendant claimed that, as a result of the partial failure of the harvest, he was excused from delivering any of the barley. This argument was rejected by the court. The plaintiffs did not claim damages for failure to deliver the other 135 tons, conceding that:

> " . . . it was an implied condition of the contract that if the defendant, through no fault of his, failed to produce the stipulated tonnage of his growing crop, he should not be required to pay damages."[322]

---

[318] *Cricklewood Property and Investment Trust Ltd v Leightons Investment Trust Ltd* [1945] A.C. 221, 233–234; *John Lewis Properties Plc v Viscount Chelsea* [1993] 2 E.G.L.R. 77, 82. See above, para.23–052.

[319] *Cricklewood Property and Investment Trust Ltd v Leightons Investment Trust Ltd* [1945] A.C. 221, 233–234 (see above, para.23–052). cf. *Matthey v Curling* [1922] 2 A.C. 180; *Eyre v Johnson* [1946] K.B. 481, 484; *Innholders Co v Wainwright* (1917) 33 T.L.R. 356.

[320] [1944] 1 All E.R. 107; cf. *Williams v Mercer* [1940] 3 All E.R. 292.

[321] [1972] 1 W.L.R. 834, noted (1972) 88 L.Q.R. 464.

[322] [1972] 1 W.L.R. 834, 835. The basis for this concession would appear to be *Howell v Coupland* (1874) L.R. 9 Q.B. 462; affirmed (1876) 1 QBD 258; *Barrow, Lane and Ballard Ltd v Phillip Phillips and Co Ltd* [1929] 1 K.B. 574.

But MacKenna J. held that the defendant remained bound to deliver the 140 tons of barley produced.[323] The case could be explained as one of "partial frustration": the obligation to deliver 135 tons of barley was frustrated by the failure of the crop, while the obligation to deliver the 140 tons remained valid and enforceable. But nowhere in the judgment of MacKenna J. is the word frustration used: the focus of his judgment is upon the implication of terms into a contract. This is not an altogether satisfactory basis for the decision because it does not explain *why* the court saw fit to refuse to imply a term into the contract relieving the defendant from his obligation to deliver the 140 tons. It is suggested that this case is not illustrative of a wider doctrine of "partial frustration" in English law[324] but rather it suggests that English law, in certain circumstances, recognises that a contracting party may have a partial excuse for non-performance of a contractual obligation.[325] It is on this ground that a seller is excused for his failure to deliver 135 tons of barley or an employee who is absent from work through temporary illness is excused for his failure to attend for work. There is no need to invoke "frustration" to explain this rule and it has not been so explained in a number of cases.[326] The use of the word "frustration" is positively misleading in so far as it suggests that the contract as a whole has been terminated when this is clearly not the case.

Limits of partial excuse. Once the basis of these decisions is recognised, the limits of this "partial excuse for non-performance" must be ascertained. In this respect *Sainsbury Ltd v Street*[327] presents an odd contrast with *Super Servant Two*.[328] In both cases there was a partial failure of supply: in the former the defendant was excused, in the latter, had it not been for the force majeure clause, the defendants would not have been excused. One point of distinction which does emerge is that in *Sainsbury* the defendant had entered into a contract with one buyer, while in *Super Servant Two* the defendants had entered into a number of 23–069

[323] Although the plaintiffs were not bound to accept delivery, given that the amount of barley produced was less than what was contracted for: Sale of Goods Act 1979 s.30(1). In the case of a non-consumer buyer, the buyer's right to reject is now limited by s.30(2A) of the Sale of Goods Act 1979.

[324] There are dicta which are hostile to the existence of "partial frustration": see *Kawasaki Steel Corp v Sardoil SpA (The Zuiho Maru)* [1977] 2 Lloyd's Rep. 552, 555; cf. *Schmitthoff's Export Trade: The Law and Practice of International Trade*, 10th edn (2000), para.6–013.

[325] See Treitel, *The Law of Contract*, 12th edn (by Peel, 2007), paras 17–059 and 19–049—19–050; *Benjamin's Sale of Goods*, 7th edn (2006), paras 18–353—18–354. See also *Poussard v Spiers and Pond* (1876) 1 QBD 410 where illness gave the plaintiff opera singer a temporary excuse for her non-performance of her contract with the defendants. The case has sometimes been viewed as an example of the operation of the doctrine of frustration but this explanation encounters the difficulty of explaining why the defendants had an option whether or not to rescind the contract. If the contract had indeed been frustrated it would have been discharged automatically, whereas, if the defendants had wished to hold the plaintiff to the terms of her contract, it seems clear that they could have done so: see further Treitel, *Frustration and Force Majeure*, 2nd edn (2004), para.5–060.

[326] See, e.g. *Sainsbury Ltd v Street* [1972] 1 W.L.R. 834; *Cricklewood Property and Development Trust Ltd v Leightons Investment Trust Ltd* [1945] A.C. 221, 233–234; *Libyan Arab Foreign Bank v Bankers Trust Co* [1989] Q.B. 728, 772; *John Lewis Properties Plc v Viscount Chelsea* [1993] 2 E.G.L.R. 77, 82. In *Cricklewood* Lord Russell clearly could not have been relying upon the doctrine of frustration because he had just strenuously denied that a lease could be frustrated (233); cf. *Sturke v S.W. Edwards Ltd* (1971) 23 P. & C.R. 185, 190.

[327] [1972] 1 W.L.R. 834.

[328] [1990] 1 Lloyd's Rep. 1.

different contracts with different parties. Yet it is difficult to see why this should be a relevant point of distinction. Rather, *Super Servant Two* illustrates a particularly robust approach on the part of the court, according to which a contracting party who has entered into more contracts than he has supplies, and who later wishes to be excused in the event of a partial failure of supply, "must bargain for the inclusion of a suitable *force majeure* clause in the contract".[329] But on this approach, *Sainsbury v Street* must be wrong because there the defendant could equally have protected himself by incorporating a carefully drafted force majeure clause into the contract. Such an approach would confine the doctrine of frustration within very narrow limits and, taken to its extreme, it could even be applied to cases of total failure of supply. This approach has the potential to "undermine the whole basis of the doctrine of frustration"[330] and it is suggested that, while there is much to be said for recognising that frustration operates within narrow confines,[331] this should not prevent the courts from recognising that a contracting party who, without fault on his part has been disabled from performing part of his contractual obligations, may be able to rely on the supervening event as an excuse for that non-performance.

5. THE LEGAL CONSEQUENCES OF FRUSTRATION[332]

23–070 **Common law.** Although the Law Reform (Frustrated Contracts) Act 1943 now provides for most of the legal consequences of frustration, it is still necessary to examine the common law on the subject, since some contracts fall outside the scope of the Act, and the interpretation of the Act itself demands a knowledge of the common law.

23–071 **Contract discharged automatically.** At common law frustration does not rescind the contract ab initio: it brings the contract to an end forthwith, without more and automatically,[333] in the sense that it releases both[334] parties from any

[329] [1989] 1 Lloyd's Rep. 148, 158. The Court of Appeal (above) did not dissent from the reasoning of Hobhouse J.

[330] Treitel, *The Law of Contract*, 12th edn (by Peel, 2007), para.19–088.

[331] Above, para.23–007.

[332] See Treitel, *Frustration and Force Majeure*, 2nd edn (2004), Ch.15; McKendrick (ed.), *Force Majeure and Frustration of Contract*, 2nd edn (1995), Ch.11; Burrows (ed.), *Essays on the Law of Restitution* (1991), Ch.6; Stewart and Carter [1992] C.L.J. 66; Burrows, *The Law of Restitution*, 2nd edn (2002), pp.359–372.

[333] *Hirji Mulji v Cheong Yue S.S. Co Ltd* [1926] A.C. 497, 505; *National Carriers Ltd v Panalpina (Northern) Ltd* [1981] A.C. 675, 712; *B.P. Exploration Co (Libya) Ltd v Hunt (No.2)* [1981] 1 W.L.R. 232, 241 (the House of Lords upheld the appeal, but without adverting to this point: [1983] 2 A.C. 352); *J. Lauritzen AS v Wijsmuller BV (The Super Servant Two)* [1990] 1 Lloyd's Rep. 1, 8.

[334] The theory that one party is discharged by frustration and the other party for failure of consideration resulting from that frustration (see Williams, *Law Reform (Frustrated Contracts) Act 1943*, pp.21–28; McElroy & Williams, *Impossibility of Performance*, pp.88–89, 99–100) is not accepted by the Act ("the *parties* thereto have *for that reason* been discharged": s.1(1) (italics supplied)) nor in various judicial statements (e.g. "[W]hen 'frustration' occurs . . . it does not merely provide one party with a defence in an action brought by the other. It kills the contract itself and discharges both parties automatically," per Viscount Simon in *Joseph Constantine S.S. Line Ltd v Imperial Smelting Corp Ltd* [1942] A.C. 154, 163; *National Carriers Ltd v Panalpina (Northern) Ltd* [1981] A.C. 675, 700.

further performance of the contract.[335] A court does not have the power at common law to allow the contract to continue and to adjust its terms to the new circumstances.

Recovery of money paid. Having set aside the contract, the initial response of the courts at common law was to let the loss lie where it fell. The origins of this rule can be found in the decision of the Court of Appeal in *Chandler v Webster*[336] where it was held that, while the effect of frustration was to release both parties from their obligations to perform in the future, frustration did not affect the obligations which had accrued prior to the date of frustration. Thus, on the facts of the case, not only was the plaintiff unable to recover the pre-payment which he had made before the frustrating event, but it was held that he remained liable to pay the balance of the sum which he had contracted to pay before that time. Although the Court of Appeal held that money paid was recoverable upon a total failure of consideration, it was held that such a total failure could only arise when the contract was set aside ab initio. The harshness of the rule laid down in *Chandler* was often acknowledged but it stood until 1943 when it was overruled by the House of Lords in the case of *Fibrosa Spolka Akcyjna v Fairbairn Lawson Combe Barbour Ltd*[337] in which English sellers agreed to sell certain machinery to Polish buyers, and to deliver it CIF Gdynia. The contract was made in July 1939, and in that month £1,000 was paid on account of the price. However before the sellers were able to complete the manufacture of the machines the contract was frustrated when Gdynia was occupied by the German army. The buyers sued to recover the £1,000 they had paid on the signing of the agreement. The House of Lords held that they were entitled to recover the money because there had been a total failure of consideration. They overruled *Chandler v Webster* and rejected the proposition that a total failure of consideration could arise only when a contract was set aside ab initio; it arose whenever money[338] was paid on a basis which wholly failed. 23–072

Defects in the common law. Although the result in *Fibrosa* represented an improvement upon the rule established in *Chandler*, the common law remained 23–073

[335] Some clauses in the contract may, however, be intended by the parties to survive frustration of the contract (e.g. an arbitration clause: see below, para.23–097: *B.P. Exploration Co (Libya) Ltd v Hunt (No.2)* [1983] 2 A.C. 352, 372 (see also the judgments below: [1981] 1 W.L.R. 232, 240–241; [1979] 1 W.L.R. 783, 829). And see s.2(3) of the 1943 Act (below, para.23–092).

[336] [1904] 1 K.B. 493; see also *Blakeley v Muller & Co* [1903] 2 K.B. 760n; *Civil Service Co-operative Society v General Steam Navigation Co* [1903] 2 K.B. 756 and *French Marine v Compagnie Napolitaine d'Eclairage et de Chauffage par le Gaz* [1921] 2 A.C. 494, 523.

[337] [1943] A.C. 32. Although it should be noted that the House of Lords expressly stated that their decision did not affect the law in relation to advance freight. Thus advance freight continues to be governed by a rule "analogous to what we all know as the rule in *Chandler v Webster*" (per Robert Goff J. in *The Lorna I* [1981] 2 Lloyd's Rep. 559, 560; affirmed [1983] 1 Lloyd's Rep. 373; and see also *The Karin Vatis* [1988] 2 Lloyd's Rep. 330). On advance freight see more generally Howard in McKendrick (ed.), *Force Majeure and Frustration of Contract*, 2nd edn (1995), pp.123–129.

[338] It should apply in the case of goods or services because total failure of consideration is logically applicable both to money claims and to non-money claims; see Birks, *An Introduction to the Law of Restitution* (1989), pp.230–231.

in a less than satisfactory state.[339] Three principal defects were apparent. The first was that the payer could only recover money paid upon a total failure of consideration; a partial failure of consideration did not give rise to a right of recovery.[340] The second was that the House of Lords was of the opinion that the payee could not set off against the money to be repaid any expenditure which had been incurred in the performance of the contract.[341] The third defect arose in relation to a claim by a provider of services. Where the frustrating event destroyed the work which had been done and payment was due only on the completion of the work, then the service provider was not entitled to bring a restitutionary claim to recover payment in respect of the work which he had done prior to the frustration of the contract.[342]

23–074 **Law Reform (Frustrated Contracts) Act 1943.**[343] These remaining defects in the common law compelled Parliament to intervene in the form of the enactment of the Law Reform (Frustrated Contracts) Act 1943. The Act applies only to a contract which is "governed by English law"[344]; that is to say, the crucial question is whether the law applicable to the contract is English law.[345] A further limiting factor is that the Act only applies to contracts which have become "impossible of performance or been otherwise frustrated". The Act does not specify when a contract is frustrated: it simply alters the legal consequences once the contract is held to have been frustrated under the rules of the common law. The generic expression "frustration" in s.1(1) probably includes cases where a contract is discharged by supervening illegality.[346] The Act does not apply to

---

339 For a fuller analysis of the decision of the House of Lords in *Fibrosa* [1943] A.C. 32 its implications for the common law rules and an assessment of the relevant common law principles, see Burrows (ed.), *Essays on the Law of Restitution* (1991), Ch.6.

340 *Whincup v Hughes* (1871) L.R. 6 C.P. 78.

341 Although it can be argued that the common law position was not as bleak as their Lordships in *Fibrosa* [1943] A.C. 32 made it appear; see Burrows at pp.154–165.

342 *Appleby v Myers* (1867) L.R. 2 C.P. 651. The same result is, however, likely to be reached under s.1(3) of the Law Reform (Frustrated Contracts) Act 1943 (below, para.23–084). The problem in a case such as *Appleby* lies in showing that the recipient of partial performance has been enriched. If the contract states that he is only required to pay on complete performance, why should the law say that he must pay on receipt of partial performance?

343 Based on the "Seventh Interim Report (Rule in *Chandler v Webster*)" of the Law Revision Committee, 1939, Cmnd.6009. Although the Act is based upon the recommendations of the Law Revision Committee, it is, in fact, wider in its scope than their recommendations and so in *B.P. Exploration Co (Libya) Ltd v Hunt (No.2)* [1979] 1 W.L.R. 783, 798, Robert Goff J. held that the Committee's report should not be used as an aid to the interpretation of the Act. See generally on the Act, Williams, *Law Reform (Frustrated Contracts) Act 1943*; Goff and Jones, *The Law of Restitution*, 7th edn (2007), paras 20–061 et seq.; McNair (1944) 60 L.Q.R. 160; Haycroft and Waksman [1984] J.B.L. 207; McKendrick (ed.), *Force Majeure and Frustration of Contract*, 2nd edn (1995), Ch.11; Treitel, *Frustration and Force Majeure*, 2nd edn (2004), paras 15–049—15–096.

344 Law Reform (Frustrated Contracts) Act 1943 s.1(1).

345 See below, Ch.30. See also *B.P. Exploration Co (Libya) Ltd v Hunt* [1976] 1 W.L.R. 788 where there was an argument before Kerr J. as to whether or not the proper law of the contract was English law. It does, however, seem rather strange that the draftsman has elected to use the proper law of the *contract* as the decisive factor when we are here concerned with an independent restitutionary claim which is, of course, distinct from an action on the contract.

346 Goff and Jones, *The Law of Restitution*, 7th edn (2007), para.20–061; McNair (1944) L.Q.R. 160, 162–163.

contracts which are discharged by subsequent agreement or breach.[347] Nor does it apply to contracts which are initially impossible of performance or to the discharge of a contract under an express provision of the contract, which provides for automatic cancellation of a contract on the occurrence of a specified event.[348]

Principle underlying Act. When seeking to interpret the Act it is important to have regard to the purpose which it seeks to achieve. In *B.P. Exploration Co (Libya) Ltd v Hunt (No.2)*[349] Robert Goff J. stated that the "fundamental principle underlying the Act itself is prevention of the unjust enrichment of either party to the contract at the other's expense"[350] and that its aim was not to "apportion the loss between the parties".[351] But the Court of Appeal dismissed this view, stating that the court got "no help from the use of words which are not in the statute".[352] The purpose behind the Act therefore remains a matter of some doubt, although it is suggested that the better view is that the Act does indeed seek to prevent unjust enrichment and can be analysed in restitutionary terms.[353] 23–075

Recovery of advance payments. Section 1(2) of the Act provides that: 23–076

> "All sums paid or payable to any party in pursuance of the contract before the time when the parties were so discharged (in this Act referred to as 'the time of discharge') shall, in the case of sums so paid, be recoverable from him as money received by him for the use of the party by whom the sums were paid, and, in the case of sums so payable, cease to be payable:
>
> Provided that, if the party to whom the sums were so paid or payable incurred expenses before the time of discharge in, or for the purpose of, the performance of the contract, the court may, if it considers it just to do so having regard to all the circumstances of the case, allow him to retain or, as the case may be, recover the whole or any part of the sums so paid or payable, not being an amount in excess of the expenses so incurred."

The principal effect of this subsection is to entitle a contracting party to recover money paid to the other contracting party prior to the frustrating event and it also relieves such a party of the obligation to pay any monies which were payable prior to the frustrating event but which had remained unpaid. The court has no

---

347 It would not therefore apply to the situation in *Sumpter v Hedges* [1898] 1 Q.B. 673, where the plaintiff, who abandoned his performance of a lump-sum contract, was unable to recover anything for his work up to that time. See above, para.21–033.

348 See McKendrick at pp.291–297.

349 [1979] 1 W.L.R. 783.

350 [1979] 1 W.L.R. 783, 799.

351 [1979] 1 W.L.R. 783. The basic structure of the Act is, first, to identify the benefit which has been obtained by the defendant at the expense of the plaintiff and then, broadly speaking to allow the plaintiff to recover so much (not exceeding the value of the benefit) as appears to the court to be just. Loss apportionment is not explicitly addressed within the Act except to the extent that the court has a discretion to allow the plaintiff to recover so much of the benefit as appears to the court to be "just". Contrast the view of Haycroft and Waksman [1984] J.B.L. 207, 225.

352 [1981] 1 W.L.R. 232, 243.

353 See generally Burrows at Ch.6.

discretion over the question whether a sum already paid is recoverable: the only discretion concerns the allowance for expenses.

23–077 **Changes from common law.** Section 1(2) goes beyond the common law rule laid down in *Fibrosa* in two respects. The first is that money paid is recoverable even upon a partial failure of consideration; the common law requirement that the failure be total has therefore been abolished in the case of frustration. One effect of this change may be to rescue a payer from his bad bargain because the prepayment is recoverable irrespective of the consideration which would have been received had the contract been performed.[354] The second respect in which s.1(2) goes beyond the rule in *Fibrosa* is that the payee may be entitled to set off against a claim by the payer "the amount of any expenses incurred before the time of discharge . . . in, or for the purpose of, the performance of the contract". The subsection gives rise to a number of interpretative difficulties.

23–078 **Paid or payable.** Subject to one exception, s.1(2) gives a cause of action to the payer and not to the payee. The one exception arises in the case where money payable by the "payer" to the payee before the time of discharge remains unpaid; in such a case the payee can rely upon s.1(2) to recover so much of his expenses, not exceeding the amount of the prepayment due, as is just.[355] Where no money is either paid[356] or is payable to the payee prior to the frustrating event but the payee nevertheless incurs expenditure in, or for the purpose of, the performance of the contract, the payee cannot recover under s.1(2).[357] Such sums are deemed by s.1(2) to be spent at the risk of the payee. No provision is made in the subsection for any increase in the sum recoverable by the claimant, or in the amount of the expenses to be allowed to the defendant, to take account of the time value of money,[358] although interest[359] may be awarded on a sum in respect of which judgment is given under the Act.[360]

23–079 **Breaches before discharge.** Nor does the subsection expressly release a promisor who has failed to perform his promise to do something (other than to pay money) before the time of discharge.[361] In such a case the promisor will be liable to pay damages for his breach of contract but he will not be able to bring the sum so paid into account under s.1(3) of the Act because it is not a benefit which was obtained "before the time of discharge". Where the claimant has, prior to the frustrating event, broken the contract between the parties, the defendant may have an accrued right to damages which may, in turn, be the

---

354 *B.P. Exploration Co (Libya) Ltd v Hunt (No.2)* [1979] 1 W.L.R. 793, 800.

355 This is because the proviso states that the payee may be able to "recover" in whole or in part any sums which were "payable" to him.

356 "Paid" would cover a sum actually paid, whether or not there was a contractual obligation to pay before the time of discharge.

357 Although a claim may be made under s.1(3) where the expenditure results in a valuable benefit being obtained by the other party. See below, para.23–084.

358 *B.P. Exploration Co (Libya) Ltd v Hunt (No.2)* [1979] 1 W.L.R. 783, 800: affirmed [1981] 1 W.L.R. 232, 244.

359 See below, para.23–087.

360 *B.P. Exploration Co (Libya) Ltd v Hunt (No.2)* [1979] 1 W.L.R. 783, 835–836; affirmed [1983] 2 A.C. 352, 373.

361 Treitel, *The Law of Contract*, 12th edn (by Peel, 2007), para.19–105.

subject of a set-off or counterclaim. But a prior breach by the claimant has no other impact upon the operation of either s.1(2) or s.1(3).[362]

The time of discharge. Since s.1(2) refers to money paid or payable before "the time of discharge" it may be important to fix the exact time of discharge. This will usually be the actual happening of the frustrating event but, if the frustration is caused by the non-occurrence of an expected event, the frustration may take effect when it first becomes generally known that the event will not happen. For instance, where a contract to hire rooms to view a procession is frustrated by the cancellation of the procession two days before it is due to take place, the time of discharge, according to *Krell v Henry*,[363] is the time of the official announcement of the cancellation.[364] Where money is paid after the time of discharge the recoverability of the payment will be governed by common law rules.[365] Thus where the payment was made after the time of discharge because the payor was unaware of the occurrence of the frustrating event, then the payment may be recoverable on the ground that it was made under a mistake of fact.[366] Where the payment was made because the payor, although aware of the occurrence of the event, was unaware that it amounted in law to a frustrating event, the payment may now be recoverable as a payment made under a mistake of law.[367] 23–080

The basis of the proviso. Although the payee may now be entitled to set off against a claim by the payer "the amount of any expenses incurred before the time of discharge . . . in, or for the purpose of the performance of the contract", it is difficult to establish the basis upon which the payee is entitled to seek to bring his expenditure into account. The consequence of this is that it is difficult, if not impossible, to ascertain with any confidence the amount which the payee will be entitled to retain. Various views have been put forward. First, it has been argued that the loss caused by the frustrating event should be divided equally between the parties on the ground that the: 23–081

> ". . . situation with which the Act is concerned is the familiar one in which one of two parties has to suffer loss for which neither is responsible",

and that in the "normal case" the just course "would be to order the retention or repayment of half the loss incurred".[368] Secondly, it has been argued that the

---

[362] *B.P. Exploration Co (Libya) Ltd v Hunt (No.2)* [1979] 1 W.L.R. 783, 808.

[363] [1903] 2 K.B. 740 (above, para.23–033).

[364] The court will not review the decision of an arbitrator who has, on reasonable grounds, found that the contract was frustrated on a particular date: see *Kodros Shipping Corp of Monrovia v Empresa Cubana de Fletes (The Evia) (No.2)* [1983] 1 A.C. 736, 767–768, followed in *Finelvet AG v Vinava Shipping Co Ltd* [1983] 1 W.L.R. 1469 (the arbitrator's choice of date must be within the permissible range of dates). On arbitration, see below, para.23–097.

[365] See McKendrick (ed.), *Force Majeure and Frustration of Contract*, 2nd edn (1995), p.230.

[366] Under the authority of *Barclays Bank Ltd v W.J. Simms Son & Cooke (Southern) Ltd* [1980] Q.B. 677, below paras 29–034 et seq.

[367] See generally *Kleinwort Benson Ltd v Lincoln City Council* [1999] 2 A.C. 349, below, paras 29–045 et seq.

[368] *The Law Reform (Frustrated Contracts) Act 1943*, pp.35–36. Such an approach has been expressly adopted in s.5(3) of the British Columbia Frustrated Contracts Act 1974.

payee should be entitled to retain the full amount of the expenditure incurred in the performance of the contract; a view supported by the English Law Revision Committee[369] and which also seems to receive some support from the judgment of Robert Goff J. in *B.P. Exploration Co (Libya) Ltd v Hunt (No.2)* who argued that the proviso constituted a "statutory recognition of the defence of change of position"[370] although this rationalisation is controversial.[371] The third view is that the court in deciding what is "just" is exercising a broad discretion, which discretion is not confined to the entitlement to bring expenditure into account but extends to the proportion of the repayment which the payee can retain or recover[372] and that therefore this discretion would be unduly circumscribed by the adoption of either of the other two views. These three views were considered by Garland J. in *Gamerco SA v I.C.M./Fair Warning (Agency) Ltd*[373] who concluded that he could see:

> "... no indication in the Act, the authorities or the relevant literature that the court is obliged to incline towards either total retention or equal division. Its task is to do justice in a situation which the parties had neither contemplated nor provided for, and to mitigate the possible harshness of allowing all loss to lie where it has fallen."[374]

The emphasis is thus placed on the "broad nature" of the discretion which the court enjoys and the imperative to do justice on the facts of the case.[375]

23–082 **Burden of proof.** The onus of proof is upon the payee to demonstrate that the requirements of the proviso have been satisfied.[376] An illustration of the importance of the location of the onus of proof is provided by *Lobb v Vasey Housing Auxiliary*,[377] a case decided under the Victorian Frustrated Contracts Act 1959.[378] The defendants were paid £1,250 by Mrs Smith for an exclusive licence to occupy a flat in a block of flats which they were building. Mrs Smith died before

---

[369] On the ground that it is "reasonable to assume that in stipulating for pre-payment the payee intended to protect himself against loss under the contract" (1939, Cmnd.6009, p.7). But it is doubtful whether the payee thinks of the possibility of frustration; he probably intends to protect himself against the possibility of the other party's insolvency or default in payment.

[370] [1979] 1 W.L.R. 783, 800.

[371] See further Burrows (ed.), *Essays on the Law of Restitution* (1991), pp.156–159. One version of the change of position defence requires that the defendant show that he "had materially changed [his] circumstances as a result of the receipt of the money" (*Storthoaks v Mobil Oil of Canada Ltd* (1975) 55 D.L.R. (3d) 1). But the provison does not require that the payee change his position "as a result of the receipt of the money". The expenditure can be incurred before the receipt of the payment and yet the payee remains entitled to invoke the proviso. The change of position rationalisation must be handled, if at all, with great care and must not be allowed to distort the meaning of the words actually used in the proviso. See further on change of position, *Lipkin Gorman v Karpnale* [1991] 2 A.C. 508 and below, paras 29–179—29–185.

[372] cf. *National Carriers Ltd v Panalpina (Northern) Ltd* [1981] A.C. 675, 707 where Lord Simon of Glaisdale did not think that the court was empowered by the Act to engage in loss apportionment and that, in consequence, there would often be an "all-or-nothing" situation.

[373] [1995] 1 W.L.R. 1226.

[374] [1995] 1 W.L.R. 1226, 1235.

[375] For an attempt to provide a structure for the exercise of this discretion see Burrows at Ch.6.

[376] *Gamerco SA v I.C.M./Fair Warning (Agency) Ltd* [1995] 1 W.L.R. 1226, 1235.

[377] [1963] V.R. 239.

[378] An Act which was modelled on the Law Reform (Frustrated Contracts) Act 1943.

her flat was completed. Her death was held to have frustrated the contract between the parties. Her executrix sued to recover the £1,250. The onus of proof was on the defendants to show that it was just in all the circumstances of the case for them to retain any part of the £1,250 and Hudson J. pointed out that, in the normal case they would sell the right to occupy the flat to someone else and so recover their expenses in that way. After an adjournment judgment was entered for the plaintiff for £1,175.[379] On this approach a payee whose expenditure results in a product which he can use in the performance of another contract may find it difficult to discharge the onus of proof.[380] A further consequence of the adoption of this approach may be that, where the payee fails to satisfy the onus, any loss lies on him but that, where he does satisfy the onus, he is entitled to retain or recover all the expenditure incurred in or for the purpose of the performance of the contract.

Allowance for expenses. In identifying the relevant "expenses" to be taken into account, it must be noted that expenses includes a reasonable sum for overhead expenses and for work or services personally performed.[381] These expenses must have been incurred "in, or for the purpose of, the performance of the contract". Pre-contract expenditure may not be recoverable on the ground that, at the time of the expenditure, there was no contract for the expenses to be incurred in "the performance of", although it can be argued that such expenditure was incurred "for the purpose of" the performance of the contract and so should be brought into account.[382] 23–083

Obligations other than to pay money. Section 1(3) states that: 23–084

> "Where any party to the contract has, by reason of anything done by any other party thereto in, or for the purpose of, the performance of the contract, obtained a valuable benefit (other than a payment of money to which the last foregoing subsection applies) before the time of discharge, there shall be recoverable from him by the said other party such sum (if any), not exceeding the value of the said benefit to the party obtaining it, as the court considers just, having regard to all the circumstances of the case and, in particular—
>
> (a) the amount of any expenses incurred before the time of discharge by the benefited party in, or for the purpose of, the performance of the contract, including any sums paid or payable by him to any other party in pursuance of the contract and retained or recoverable by that party under the last foregoing subsection, and

[379] The precise basis on which this sum was calculated does not emerge from the judgment.

[380] As was the case in *Davis and Primrose Ltd v Clyde Shipbuilding and Engineering Co Ltd* (1917) 1 S.L.T. 297. See also Treitel, *The Law of Contract*, 12th edn (by Peel, 2007), para.19–098 and for a slightly different argument to the same end see Williams at p.39 who argues that expenses in s.1(2) means "expenses after deduction of gains resulting from those expenses".

[381] Law Reform (Frustrated Contracts) Act 1943 s.1(4).

[382] It can also be argued that where the expenditure is incurred in the reasonable belief that a contract will be concluded it will be recoverable; see the examples given by Goff and Jones at para.20–064.

(b) the effect, in relation to the said benefit, of the circumstances giving rise to the frustration of the contract."

This is the most controversial and difficult provision in the Act, caused in large part by the failure of the draftsman to provide a definition of what constitutes a "benefit" and to identify with sufficient precision the time at which the benefit is to be valued. In *B.P. Exploration Co (Libya) Ltd v Hunt (No.2)*[383] Robert Goff J. held that the proper approach to the construction of the subsection is a three-stage one. At the first stage the valuable benefit must be identified; at the second stage the benefit must be valued; and at the third stage the court must consider the award of a just sum.

23–085 **(1) Identification of the benefit.** The "benefit," which must of course be non-monetary, could consist of either the "end product" of the services or the services themselves. Robert Goff J. concluded, as a matter of construction rather than one of principle,[384] that "in an appropriate case" it was the end product which was to be regarded as the benefit. It is not clear when it would not be "appropriate" to regard the end product as the benefit but there are a number of situations in which it has been argued that the benefit should be identified with the service itself. The general rule is therefore that regard must be had to the end product of the services when identifying the benefit. But there are at least two situations in which it is appropriate to have regard to the services themselves when identifying the benefit. The first case arises where the service, by its very nature, does not result in an end product, for example, "where the services consist of doing such work as surveying, or transporting goods".[385] Where there is no end product the court must simply ascertain the benefit which the defendant has obtained by virtue of the claimant's contractual performance, which benefit can only be measured by reference to the value of the services performed by the claimant under the contract.[386] The second case arises where the services performed result in an end product which has no objective value,[387] in which case the benefit must also be measured by reference to the value of the services provided under the contract.

23–086 There is a third situation in which it has been argued that a court should have regard to the value of the service performed, namely where the frustrating event results in the destruction of the end product itself. But in *B.P. Exploration Co (Libya) Ltd v Hunt (No.2)*, Robert Goff J. rejected this argument on two principal

---

[383] [1979] 1 W.L.R. 783.

[384] As a matter of principle he was of the view that the services themselves should be regarded as the benefit.

[385] [1979] 1 W.L.R. 783, 802.

[386] The conclusion that the existence of an end product was a necessary ingredient of a s.1(3) claim would arguably have led to ridiculous arguments as to what constitutes an "end product": see, for example, Birks, *An Introduction to the Law of Restitution* (1989), p.252.

[387] Robert Goff J. gave the example of a claimant who commences "the redecoration, to the defendant's execrable taste, of rooms which are in good decorative order": [1979] 1 W.L.R. 783, 803. In such a case, the work of the claimant may even reduce the value of the defendant's property but the services must nevertheless be regarded as a benefit because they were requested by their recipient.

grounds.[388] The first was that a distinction is drawn in s.1(3) between the claimant's performance and the defendant's benefit, thus indicating that the defendant's benefit cannot be regarded as the value of the claimant's performance. The second was that "benefit" in s.1(3)(b) clearly refers to the end product of the services rather than the services themselves.[389] This view has not, however, commanded universal assent, largely on the basis that s.1(3) applies where a valuable benefit has been obtained *before* the time of discharge and on the ground that the words immediately preceeding paras (a) and (b) ("having regard to all the circumstances of the case, and in particular") appear to be directed to the assessment of the just sum and not to the identification of the valuable benefit.[390]

(2) Valuing the benefit. Once the benefit has been identified, the court must then value it. The conclusion that it is the end product and not the services themselves which are to be regarded as the benefit gives rise to considerable difficulties in valuing the benefit because there is no necessary relationship between the services and the end product. A small service may result in an end product of great value, while a service of great value may result in an end product of no or minimal value. If the benefit is only partly attributable to the claimant's performance, the court should apportion the value of the benefit accordingly.[391] The wording of the subsection does not permit the court to take account of the time value of money so that the benefit is valued at the date of the frustrating event without regard to the money which the defendant may have obtained by selling the benefit before the date of the frustrating event,[392] although interest[393] may be awarded on a sum in respect of which judgment is given under the Act.[394] 23–087

Date of valuation. In *B.P. Exploration Co (Libya) Ltd v Hunt (No.2)* Robert Goff J. held that the benefit must be valued as at the date of the frustrating event. The difficulty with this proposition is that s.1(3) applies where "a valuable benefit has been obtained *before* the time of discharge". This suggests that the date of the valuation should be before the time of discharge and the point may yet be open for further argument. 23–088

Deduction of expenses. A further problem arises in relation to the role of s.1(3)(a), namely whether the expenses should be deducted from the benefit or from the just sum. Robert Goff J. held that the expenses were to be deducted from 23–089

[388] On this view the result of *Appleby v Myers* (1867) L.R. 2 C.P. 651 would be unaffected by s.1(3) of the Act.

[389] Further support for this view can be gleaned from the decision of the Newfoundland Supreme Court in *Parsons Bros Ltd v Shea* (1966) 53 D.L.R. (2d.) 86, a case decided under the similarly worded Newfoundland Frustrated Contracts Act 1956. See also McKendrick (ed.), *Force Majeure and Frustration of Contract*, 2nd edn (1995), pp.236–237.

[390] See, e.g. Treitel, *Law of Contract*, 12th edn (by Peel, 2007), para.19–103.

[391] *B.P. Exploration Co (Libya) Ltd v Hunt (No.2)* [1979] 1 W.L.R. 783, 802.

[392] [1979] 1 W.L.R. 783, 803–804.

[393] See below para.26–174 fn.911.

[394] [1979] 1 W.L.R. 783, 836; affirmed [1983] 2 A.C. 352, 373.

the value of the benefit and not from the just sum.[395] But, as we have already noted, the words immediately preceding para.(a) suggest that the expenses should be deducted from the just sum and not from the valuable benefit and, once again, the point may yet be open for further argument.[396]

23–090 **(3) The just sum.** The final step is for the court to assess the "just" sum to be awarded to the claimant. Robert Goff J. held that the aim of the court in assessing the just sum ought to be the "prevention of the unjust enrichment of the defendant at the plaintiff's expense"[397] but the Court of Appeal preferred a broader, discretionary approach, stating that "[w]hat is just is what the trial judge thinks is just" and that an appellate court is not entitled to interfere with the assessment of the just sum by the trial judge "unless it is so plainly wrong that it cannot be just".[398] This appears to leave the assessment of the just sum at the complete discretion of the trial judge. There are, however, certain factors which are clearly of relevance in the assessment of the just sum. The first is that the value of the benefit acts as a ceiling on the sum which the court can award so that the "just sum" cannot be greater than the value of the benefit obtained. The second is that the contractual allocation of risk is likely to be an important factor in the assessment of the just sum. It is "likely" that in most cases the claimant's claim will be limited to a rateable proportion of the contract price so that s.1(3) cannot be used to escape the consequences of a bad bargain.[399] The third point is that the process of assessing the just sum may bear some resemblance to the inquiry conducted by the court in an action for a quantum meruit or a quantum valebat.[400]

23–091 **Severability.** Section 2(4) of the Act provides:

> "Where it appears to the court that a part of any contract to which this Act applies can properly be severed from the remainder of the contract, being a part wholly performed before the time of discharge, or so performed except for the payment in respect of that part of the contract of sums which are or can be ascertained under the contract, the court shall treat that part of the contract as if it were a separate contract and had not been frustrated and shall treat the foregoing section of this Act as only applicable to the remainder of that contract."

Thus, where a contract can be divided into severable and distinct obligations (as opposed to being an "entire contract"[401]) the Act has no application to any obligation which has been completely performed. The Act does, however, apply to those several obligations which have not been completely performed, thus departing from the common law rule which was that no recovery was possible in

---

[395] [1979] 1 W.L.R. 783, 804.
[396] See Haycroft and Waksman [1984] J.B.L. 207, 220.
[397] [1979] 1 W.L.R. 783, 805.
[398] [1981] 1 W.L.R. 232, 238.
[399] [1979] 1 W.L.R. 783, 806.
[400] [1979] 1 W.L.R. 783, 805 and see also 825.
[401] See above, para.21–027.

respect of money paid or benefits conferred in the performance of a severable obligation which had not been completely performed.[402]

Contrary intention. Section 2(3) provides: 23–092

> "Where any contract to which this Act applies contains any provision which, upon the true construction of the contract, is intended to have effect in the event of circumstances arising which operate, or would but for the said provision operate, to frustrate the contract, or is intended to have effect whether such circumstances arise or not, the court, shall give effect to the said provision and shall only give effect to the foregoing section of this Act to such extent, if any, as appears to the court to be consistent with the said provision."[403]

Although it has been stated that, in deciding whether the parties have contracted out of the Act, a court will apply "ordinary principles of construction"[404] it has also been said that:

> "... where there is no clear indication that the parties did intend the clause to be applicable in the event of frustration, the court has to be very careful before it draws the inference that the clause was intended to be applicable in such radically changed circumstances."[405]

It is for the party who is seeking to rely upon s.2(3) to demonstrate that the clause was intended to operate in the circumstances which have actually happened; where the circumstances which have occurred are so devastating and unusual as to fall outside the ambit of the clause in question, then the Act may not have been excluded.

Implicit provision. A court will be particularly reluctant to imply a term that 23–093 the parties have made provision for the consequences of a frustrating event. But a clause which provides that one contracting party is under an obligation to maintain insurance against the consequences of the frustrating event would appear to be effective to exclude the operation of the Act so that the party upon whom the obligation to insure is imposed cannot bring a claim under the Act.[406] However the fact that a contract is entire and that the contract provides that payment is not due until the work is complete or until a date which is after the

---

[402] *Stubbs v Holywell Rly Co* (1867) L.R. 2 Ex. 311.

[403] It should be noted that we are here concerned with a clause which seeks to regulate the *consequences* of the frustration of a contract and not with a clause which seeks to make provision for an *event* which would otherwise frustrate the contract; where the parties make provision for what would otherwise be a frustrating event the effect of such a clause is to exclude the operation of the doctrine of frustration completely and the Act does not apply to a contract which has not been frustrated.

[404] [1979] 1 W.L.R. 783, 806.

[405] [1979] 1 W.L.R. 783, 829.

[406] [1979] 1 W.L.R. 783, 807A, although it should be noted that s.1(5) provides that: "[T]he court shall not take into account any sums which have, by reason of the circumstances giving rise to the frustration of the contract, become payable to that party under any contract of insurance unless there was an obligation to insure imposed by an express term of the frustrated contract or by or under any enactment."

date of the frustrating event does not "automatically preclude an award of damages under s.1(3)"[407] and it is only:

> "... if upon a true construction of the contract the plaintiff has contracted on the terms that he is to receive no payment in the event which has occurred, will the fact that the contract is 'entire' have the effect of precluding an award under the Act."[408]

23–094 **Effect of contracting out.** It is not, however, enough to contract out of the Act without making alternative provision for the consequences of frustration, because the effect of simply contracting out of the Act would appear to be to re-instate the common law as laid down in *Fibrosa Spolka Akcyjna v Fairbairn Lawson Combe Barbour Ltd.*[409] Contracting parties who wish to provide a different regime for the remedial consequences of frustration should make express provision to that effect in their contract.

23–095 **Supplementary provisions of the Act.** Section 1(6) of the Act states that the court may allow an action given by subs.(3) to be brought against one party to the contract, though the benefit was conferred on another party to it, or upon a stranger to the contract altogether. Section 2(2) of the Act provides that the Act binds the Crown.

23–096 **Contracts excluded from the Act.** Section 2(5) provides that the Act does not apply to four types of contract: (a) "any charterparty, except a time charterparty or a charterparty by way of demise"; (b) "any contract . . . for the carriage of goods by sea" (since commercial practice has developed well-known rules for insurance against the risks of these contracts[410]); (c) "any contract of insurance" (since there is a well-established principle that no part of a premium is legally recoverable where the subject-matter of the risk ceases to exist before the period of the insurance expires[411]); (d) any contract for the sale of specific goods which perish, whether or not the risk passed to the buyer before the date of perishing.[412] (Any other contract for the sale of goods will be governed by the Act,[413] as will

[407] [1979] 1 W.L.R. 783, 807.

[408] [1979] 1 W.L.R. 783.

[409] [1943] A.C. 32.

[410] Williams (1942) 6 M.L.R. 46, 54–55 and 72–74, 79. This exclusion from the Act preserves two common law rules: freight due in advance is still payable despite the fact that, after payment has fallen due, the voyage specified in the contract is frustrated; and a shipowner cannot recover part of the agreed freight *pro rata itineris peracti* when frustration occurs before completion of the voyage. See *Carver's Carriage by Sea*, 13th edn (1982), Vols 2 and 3, paras 779 et seq., 1691 et seq.

[411] *Tyrie v Fletcher* [1777] 2 Cowp. 666, and see below, Vol.II, para.41–057.

[412] This formulation of category (d) is an attempt to state the effect of a badly drafted provision of the Act, namely, s.2(5)(c) (as amended by the Sale of Goods Act 1979 s.63 and Sch.2 para.2). The provision appears to assume that the rules as to risk adequately cover the situation: see Vol.II, paras 43–218 et seq. Detailed arguments as to the effect of this involved provision may be found elsewhere, viz Williams (1942) 6 M.L.R. 46, 81–90; Goff & Jones at paras 20–079—20–081; Cheshire, Fifoot & Furmston, *Law of Contract*, 15th edn (2007), pp.746–748; Treitel, *Law of Contract*, 12th edn (by Peel, 2007), paras 19–111—19–114; Atiyah, *The Sale of Goods*, 11th edn (2005), pp.365–368. Section 7 is discussed in more detail in Vol.II, paras 43–035—43–038.

[413] Thus, the Act would apply where a contract for the sale of non-specific goods was frustrated, e.g. *Howell v Coupland* (1876) 1 QBD 258. cf. *H.R. and S. Sainsbury Ltd v Street* [1972] 1 W.L.R. 834 (above, para.23–068).

a contract for the sale of specific goods which is frustrated otherwise than by the "perishing" of the goods.)

Arbitration. The paucity of reported decisions on the operation of the Act is possibly due to the fact that the issues arising under the Act are particularly suitable for arbitration.[414] The questions whether a contract has been frustrated[415] and, if so, whether a claim under the Act arises[416] are within the scope of a wide arbitration clause in a contract, e.g. one providing for arbitration: 23–097

> "... if any dispute or difference shall arise or occur between the parties hereto in relation to any thing or matter arising out of or under this agreement"[417];

the arbitration clause survives the frustration for the purpose of the assessment of any consequential claim under the Act or for the purposes of an independent restitutionary claim.[418]

Services rendered or payments made after frustration. The Law Reform (Frustrated Contracts) Act 1943 has no application to benefits conferred after the date of the frustrating event. Where the parties enter into a fresh contract relating to the post-frustration performance, then that contract will obviously govern the relationship between the parties. Where no such contract is concluded the party who has conferred the benefit on the other party may be able to bring an independent restitutionary claim if he can show that the defendant has freely accepted the benefit of the post-frustration performance, in the sense that the recipient knew that the performance was being rendered non-gratuitously and elected to accept the performance, having had the opportunity to reject it.[419] In such a case the plaintiff may be able to recover the reasonable value of the services performed.[420] The only other ground upon which a restitutionary claim could be brought is mistake. Where the benefit has been conferred because the plaintiff was unaware of the occurrence of the frustrating event, then it may be 23–098

---

[414] *Pioneer Shipping Ltd v B.T.P. Tioxide Ltd* [1982] A.C. 724, 743–744; *Kodros Shipping Corp of Monrovia v Empresa Cubana de Fletes (The Evia) (No.2)* [1983] 1 A.C. 736. On arbitration clauses, see below, para.32–026.

[415] *Heyman v Darwins Ltd* [1942] A.C. 356, 366, 383, 400–401; *Kruse v Questier & Co Ltd* [1953] 1 Q.B. 669; *Government of Gibraltar v Kenney* [1956] 2 Q.B. 410; *Kodros Shipping* [1983] 1 A.C. 736 (the time of frustration). The House of Lords has held that the court should be reluctant to interfere with the conclusion of an arbitrator that a contract has been frustrated: it must be shown either that the arbitrator misdirected himself in law, or that the decision was such that no reasonable arbitrator could reach: *Pioneer Shipping* [1982] A.C. 724, 742–744, 752–754. (See above, para.23–015, especially fn.65; and para.23–035 fn.148.) To similar effect see *Kuwait Supply Co v Oyster Marine Management (The Safeer)* [1994] 1 Lloyd's Rep. 637.

[416] *Government of Gibraltar v Kenney* [1956] 2 Q.B. 410.

[417] [1956] 2 Q.B. 410.

[418] [1956] 2 Q.B. 410.

[419] See below, paras 29–054 et seq. and, more generally, Birks, *An Introduction to the Law of Restitution*, Ch.X.

[420] *Société Franco-Tunisienne d'Armement v Sidermar SpA* [1961] 2 Q.B. 278, 313 (overruled on another point: *Ocean Tramp Tankers Corp v V/O Sovfracht (The Eugenia)* [1964] 2 Q.B. 226); Furmston (1961) 24 M.L.R. 173; Giles (1964) 27 M.L.R. 351; *Codelfa Construction Pty Ltd v State Rail Authority of New South Wales* (1982) 149 C.L.R. 337.

possible to recover the value of the benefit conferred on the ground that it was given under a mistake of fact.[421] Where the benefit was conferred because the plaintiff was unaware that the event, as a matter of law, constituted a frustrating event, then the value of the benefit conferred may now be recovered on the ground that it was given under a mistake of law.[422]

[421] See below, paras 29–030—29–040 and, more generally, Goff and Jones at Ch.4.
[422] See below, paras 29–041—29–048 and *Kleinwort Benson Ltd v Lincoln City Council* [1999] 2 A.C. 349.

CHAPTER 24

DISCHARGE BY BREACH

		PARA.
1.	In general	24–001
2.	Renunciation	24–018
3.	Impossibility created by one party	24–028
4.	Failure of performance	24–034
5.	Consequences of discharge	24–047

1. IN GENERAL[1]

Discharge by breach. One party to a contract may, by reason of the other's breach, be entitled to treat himself as discharged from his liability further to perform his own unperformed obligations under the contract and from his obligation to accept performance by the other party if made or tendered.[2] The expression "discharge by breach" is commonly employed to describe the situation where he is entitled to, and does, exercise that right. Nevertheless, the expression is not wholly accurate, at least without further explanation. In the first place, not every breach of contract has this effect. Discharge from liability is not necessarily coincident with a right to sue for damages. The rule is usually stated as follows: "[a]ny breach of contract gives rise to a cause of action; not every breach gives a discharge from liability". Thus the main question discussed in this chapter is whether a party who admittedly has a claim for damages is also relieved from further performance by the other party's breach.[3] Secondly, although sometimes the innocent party is referred to as "rescinding" the contract **24–001**

[1] See Lord Devlin [1967] Camb. L.J. 192; Reynolds (1963) 79 L.Q.R. 534; Treitel (1967) 30 M.L.R. 139; Shea (1979) 42 M.L.R. 623; Beatson (1981) 97 L.Q.R. 389; Rose (1981) 34 C.L.P. 235; Carter, *Breach of Contract*, 2nd edn (1991).

[2] This principle would appear to apply to leases: see *Hussain v Mehlman* [1992] 2 E.G.L.R. 87; *Progressive House Pty Ltd v Tabali Pty Ltd* (1985) 157 C.L.R. 17; *Highway Properties Ltd v Kelly, Douglas & Co* (1971) 17 D.L.R. (3d) 710; cf. *Total Oil Great Britain Ltd v Thompson Garages (Biggin Hill) Ltd* [1972] 1 Q.B. 318. See further Pawlowski [1995] Conv. 379.

[3] While the general law entitles a party to refuse to continue with performance in circumstances to be discussed in this chapter, the terms of the contract between the parties may give to one or both of the parties a right to terminate the contract in the event of a breach of contract by the other party. The right so conferred may be broader than that which would otherwise exist under the general law; in other words, the clause may entitle a party to terminate in the event of a breach which would not otherwise be regarded by the law as a repudiatory breach. The scope of the termination clause is in all cases a question of interpretation of the particular clause, on which see further para.22–047 fn.200.

and the contract as being "terminated" by the breach, it is clear that the contract is not rescinded ab initio[4] nor is it extinguished by the breach.[5] The innocent party, or, in some cases, both parties, are excused from further performance of their primary obligations under the contract; but there is then substituted for the primary obligations of the party in default a secondary obligation to pay monetary compensation for his non-performance.[6] Thirdly, the innocent party is not ordinarily[7] bound to treat himself as discharged: if the contract is still executory, he may elect instead to treat it as continuing.[8] He may also waive his right of discharge, accept the defective performance of the other party, and content himself with damages, which are his remedy in any event.[9]

24–002 **A middle ground.** An innocent party, faced by a repudiatory breach, is therefore given a choice: he can either treat the contract as continuing ("affirmation" of the contract) or he can bring it to an end ("acceptance of the repudiation"). He must "elect" or choose between these options. Further, it is sometimes said that there is no other option open to the innocent party; that is to say, there is no "middle way" or "third choice".[10] This is true in the sense that there is no:

[4] *Heyman v Darwins Ltd* [1942] A.C. 356, 373, 399; *Johnson v Agnew* [1980] A.C. 367, 373; *Photo Production Ltd v Securicor Transport Ltd* [1980] A.C. 827, 844; *Bank of Boston Connecticut v European Grain and Shipping Ltd* [1989] A.C. 1056, 1098–1099; *State Trading Corp of India Ltd v M. Golodetz Ltd* [1989] 2 Lloyd's Rep. 277, 286. See below, para.24–047.

[5] *Photo Production Ltd v Securicor Transport Ltd* [1980] A.C. 827 (overruling *Harbutt's "Plasticine" Ltd v Wayne Tank and Pump Co Ltd* [1970] 1 Q.B. 447). See above, para.14–022; below, para.24–047.

[6] *R. V. Ward Ltd v Bignall* [1967] 1 Q.B. 534, 548; *Moschi v Lep Air Services Ltd* [1973] A.C. 331, 345, 350, 351; *Hyundai Ltd v Pournouras* [1978] 2 Lloyd's Rep. 502, 507; *Photo Production Ltd v Securicor Transport Ltd* [1980] A.C. 827, 848–851. See below, para.24–052.

[7] On the question of whether the wrongful dismissal of an employee from his contract of employment constitutes an exception to the rule, see Vol.II, para.39–185. See also *Thomas Marshall (Exports) Ltd v Guinle* [1979] Ch. 227 (repudiation by employee).

[8] *Avery v Bowden* (1855) 5 E. & B. 714; (1856) 6 E. & B. 953; *Frost v Knight* (1872) L.R. 7 Ex. 111, 112; *Johnstone v Milling* (1886) 16 QBD 460, 470; *Michael v Hart & Co* [1902] 1 K.B. 482, 492; *Tredegar Iron and Coal Co Ltd v Hawthorn Bros & Co* (1902) 18 T.L.R. 716; *Hain S.S. Co Ltd v Tate & Lyle Ltd* (1936) 41 Com. Cas. 350, 355, 363; *Heyman v Darwins Ltd* [1942] A.C. 356, 361; *Chandris v Isbrandtsen Moller Co Inc* [1951] 1 K.B. 240, 248; *Howard v Pickford Tool Co Inc* [1951] 1 K.B. 417, 421; *White & Carter (Councils) Ltd v McGregor* [1962] A.C. 413; *Cranleigh Precision Engineering Ltd v Bryant* [1965] 1 W.L.R. 1293; *Suisse Atlantique Société d'Armement Maritime SA v N.V. Rotterdamsche Kolen Centrale* [1967] 1 A.C. 361, 398, 418; *Decro-Wall International SA v Practitioners in Marketing Ltd* [1971] 1 W.L.R. 361, 368, 375, 381; *Mayfair Photographic Supplies Ltd v Baxter Hoare & Co Ltd* [1972] 1 Lloyd's Rep. 410, 417; *Lakshmijit v Sherani* [1974] A.C. 605; *Thomas Marshall (Exports) Ltd v Guinle* [1979] Ch. 227; *Tai Hing Cotton Mill Ltd v Kamsing Knitting Factory* [1979] A.C. 91; *Fercometal S.A.R.L. v Mediterranean Shipping Co SA* [1989] A.C. 788; *Vitol SA v Norelf* [1996] A.C. 800.

[9] *Bentsen v Taylor, Sons & Co* [1893] 2 Q.B. 274; *Wallis, Son and Wells v Pratt and Haynes* [1911] A.C. 394; *Hain S.S. Co Ltd v Tate & Lyle Ltd* (1936) 41 Com. Cas. 350; *Chandris v Isbrandtsen Moller Co Inc* [1951] 1 K.B. 240; *Suisse Atlantique Société d'Armement Maritime SA v N.V. Rotterdamsche Kolen Centrale* [1967] 1 A.C. 361; Sale of Goods Act 1979 s.11(2). See also below, para.24–003 (affirmation).

[10] *Bentsen v Taylor* [1893] 2 Q.B. 274, 279; *Fercometal S.A.R.L. v Mediterranean Shipping Co SA* [1989] A.C. 788, 799–801; *Motor Oil Hellas (Corinth) Refineries SA v Shipping Corp of India* [1990] 1 Lloyd's Rep. 391, 398–399.

"... third choice, as a sort of via media, to affirm the contract and yet be absolved from tendering further performance unless and until [the breaching party] gives reasonable notice that he is once again able and willing to perform."[11]

But the proposition that there is no middle way can be over-stated. There is a sense in which there is a middle way open to the innocent party in that he is given a period of time in which to make up his mind whether he is going to affirm the contract or terminate. This point was well-expressed by Rix L.J. in *Stocznia Gdanska SA v Latvian Shipping Co (No.2)*[12] when he stated:

"In my judgment, there is of course a middle ground between acceptance of repudiation and affirmation of the contract, and that is the period when the innocent party is making up his mind what to do. If he does nothing for too long, there may come a time when the law will treat him as having affirmed. If he maintains the contract in being for the moment, while reserving his right to treat it as repudiated if his contract partner persists in his repudiation, then he has not yet elected. As long as the contract remains alive, the innocent party runs the risk that a merely anticipatory repudiatory breach, a thing 'writ in water' until acceptance, can be overtaken by another event which prejudices the innocent party's rights under the contract—such as frustration or even his own breach. He also runs the risk, if that is the right word, that the party in repudiation will resume performance of the contract and thus end any continuing right in the innocent party to elect to accept the former repudiation as terminating the contract."[13]

The length of the period given to the innocent party in order to make up his mind will very much depend upon the facts of the case. The period may not be a long one because a party who does nothing for too long may be held to have affirmed the contract.[14] The length of time will also depend upon the time at which the innocent party's obligations fall due for performance. A contract remains in force until it has been terminated for breach so that a contracting party who has not elected to terminate the contract remains bound to perform his obligations unless the effect of the other party's breach is to prevent performance of the innocent party's obligation becoming due.[15]

Affirmation. Where the innocent party, being entitled to choose whether to treat the contract as continuing or to accept the repudiation and treat himself as discharged, elects to treat the contract as continuing, he is usually said to have "affirmed" the contract.[16] He will not be held to have elected to affirm the 24–003

[11] *Fercometal S.A.R.L. v Mediterranean Shipping Co SA* [1989] A.C. 788, 801.
[12] [2002] EWCA Civ 889, [2002] 2 Lloyd's Rep. 436; *Astea (UK) Ltd v Time Group Ltd* [2003] EWHC 725 (TCC), [2003] All E.R. (D) 212 (Apr).
[13] [2002] EWCA Civ 889 at [87].
[14] cf. *W.E. Cox Toner (International) Ltd v Crook* [1981] I.R.L.R. 443, 446 ("he is not bound to elect within a reasonable time or any other time"). See also the line of cases in which it has been held that mere delay by itself does not constitute affirmation (fn.23 below).
[15] See Treitel, *The Law of Contract*, 12th edn (by Peel, 2007), paras 18–001—18–022 and also paras 24–036 and 24–037.
[16] *Suisse Atlantique Société d'Armement Maritime SA v N.V. Rotterdamsche Kolen Centrale* [1967] 1 A.C. 361, 398; *Peyman v Lanjani* [1985] Ch. 457.

contract unless, first, he has knowledge of the facts giving rise to the breach,[17] and, secondly, he has knowledge of his legal right to choose between the alternatives open to him.[18] Affirmation may be express or implied. It will be implied if, with knowledge of the breach and of his right to choose, he does some unequivocal[19] act from which it may be inferred that he intends to go on with the contract regardless of the breach or from which it may be inferred that he will not exercise his right to treat the contract as repudiated.[20] Affirmation must be total: the innocent party cannot approbate and reprobate by affirming part of the contract and disaffirming the rest, for that would be to make a new contract.[21] Equally a party cannot affirm the contract for a limited period of time and then abrogate it on the expiry of that period of time.[22] Mere inactivity after breach does not of itself amount to affirmation,[23] nor (it seems) does the commencement of an action claiming damages for breach.[24] The mere fact that the innocent party

---

[17] *Matthews v Smallwood* [1910] 1 Ch. 777, 786; *U.G.S. Finance Ltd v National Mortgage Bank of Greece* [1964] 1 Lloyd's Rep. 446, 450; *Suisse Atlantique Société d'Armement Maritime SA v N.V. Rotterdamsche Kolen Centrale* [1967] 1 A.C. 361, 426; *Panchaud Frères SA v Etablissements General Grain Co* [1970] 1 Lloyd's Rep. 53, 57; *Kammins Ballrooms & Co Ltd v Zenith Investments (Torquay) Ltd* [1971] A.C. 850; *Peyman v Lanjani* [1985] Ch. 457; *Yukong Line Ltd of Korea v Rendsberg Investments Corp of Liberia* [1996] 2 Lloyd's Rep. 604, 607.

[18] *Kendall v Hamilton* (1879) 4 App. Cas. 504, 542; *Peyman v Lanjani* [1985] Ch. 457. cf. *Sea Calm Shipping Co SA v Chantiers Navals de L'Esterel* [1986] 2 Lloyd's Rep. 294; *Motor Oil Hellas (Corinth) Refineries SA v Shipping Corp of India* [1990] 1 Lloyd's Rep. 391, 398 where the issue was noted but not resolved; *Yukong Line Ltd of Korea v Rendsberg Investments Corp of Liberia* [1996] 2 Lloyd's Rep. 604, 607.

[19] *China National Foreign Trade Transportation Corp v Evolgia Shipping Co SA of Panama* [1979] 1 W.L.R. 1018; *Peyman v Lanjani* [1985] Ch. 457; *State Securities Plc v Initial Industry Ltd* [2004] All E.R. (D) 317 (Jan) (acceptance of rental payment held not to have amounted to an election to continue with the contract).

[20] *Pust v Dowie* (1863) 5 B. & S. 33; *Bentsen v Taylor, Sons & Co* [1893] 2 Q.B. 274; *Matthews v Smallwood* [1910] 1 Ch. 777; *Hain S.S. Co Ltd v Tate & Lyle Ltd* (1936) 41 Com. Cas. 350, 355, 363; *Temple S.S. Co v Sovfracht* (1945) 79 Ll. L. Rep. 1, 11; *Chandris v Isbrandtsen Moller Inc* [1951] 1 K.B. 240; *Denmark Productions Ltd v Boscobel Productions Ltd* [1969] 1 Q.B. 699, 731; *Suisse Atlantique Société d'Armement Maritime SA v N.V. Rotterdamsche Kolen Centrale* [1967] 1 A.C. 361; *Sea Calm Shipping Co SA v Chantiers Navals de L'Esterel* [1986] 2 Lloyd's Rep. 294; *Motor Oil Hellas (Corinth) Refineries SA v Shipping Corp of India* [1990] 1 Lloyd's Rep. 391, 398; *Laing Management Ltd v Aegon Insurance Co (UK) Ltd* (1998) 86 Build. L.R. 70, 108 (although the conclusion that the contract remained alive for the benefit of both parties does not sit easily with the fact that the plaintiffs had expressly relied upon an express power to terminate contained in the contract).

[21] *Suisse Atlantique Société d'Armement Maritime SA v N.V. Rotterdamsche Kolen Centrale* [1967] 1 A.C. 361, 398. See also *Johnstone v Milling* (1886) 13 QBD 460.

[22] *Norwest Holst Ltd v Harrison* [1985] I.C.R. 668, 683; *Walkinshaw v Diniz* [2001] 1 Lloyd's Rep. 632, 643.

[23] *Perry v Davis* (1858) 3 C.B.(N.S.) 769; *Cranleigh Precision Engineering Ltd v Bryant* [1965] 1 W.L.R. 1293; *Nichimen Corp v Gatoil Overseas Inc* [1987] 2 Lloyd's Rep. 46. See also *Clough v L.N.W. Ry* (1871) 7 Ex. 26; *Allen v Robles* [1969] 1 W.L.R. 193; *Cantor Fitzgerald International v Bird* [2002] I.R.L.R. 867. But see *Denmark Productions Ltd v Boscobel Productions Ltd* [1969] 1 Q.B. 699; *Scandinavian Trader Tanker Co AB v Flota Petrolea Ecuatoriana* [1981] 2 Lloyd's Rep. 425, 430; affirmed [1983] 2 A.C. 694.

[24] *General Billposting Co Ltd v Atkinson* [1909] A.C. 118; *Garnac Grain Co Ltd v H.M. Fauré & Fairclough Ltd* [1966] 1 Q.B. 650; affirmed [1968] A.C. 1130n. Equally, a decision not to pursue the remedy of specific performance does not commit the innocent party to accept a repudiatory or an anticipatory breach: *Bear Stearns Bank Plc v Forum Global Equity Ltd* [2007] EWHC 1576 (Comm) at [127].

has called on the party in breach to change his mind, accept his obligations and perform the contract will not generally, of itself, amount to an affirmation:

> "... the law does not require an injured party to snatch at a repudiation and he does not automatically lose his right to treat the contract as discharged merely by calling on the other to reconsider his position and recognize his obligation."[25]

But if the innocent party unreservedly[26] continues to press for performance or accepts performance by the other party after becoming aware of the breach and of his right to elect, he will be held to have affirmed the contract.

Affirmation irrevocable. Once the innocent party has elected to affirm the contract, and this has been communicated to the other party, then the choice becomes irrevocable.[27] There is no need to establish reliance or detriment by the party in default.[28] Thus the innocent party, having affirmed, cannot subsequently change his mind and rely on the breach to justify treating himself as discharged.[29] Nevertheless, in the case of a breach which is persisted in by the other party, the fact that the innocent party has continued to press for performance will not normally preclude him at a later stage from treating himself as discharged.[30] In such a case the innocent party is not terminating on account of the original 24–004

[25] *Yukong Line Ltd of Korea v Rendsberg Investments Corp of Liberia* [1996] 2 Lloyd's Rep. 604, 608. Moore-Bick J. added that, in his view, the courts should generally be "slow" to accept that the innocent party has committed itself irrevocably to going on with the contract and then leave it to "the doctrine of estoppel" (below, para.24–006) to remedy any potential injustice which may arise in the case where the party in breach has relied upon a representation by the innocent party which suggests that the contract has been affirmed. See also *Internet Trading Clubs Ltd v Freeserve (Investments) Ltd Plc* Unreported June 19, 2001 QBD.

[26] *Bremer Handelsgesellschaft mbH v Deutsche Conti Handelsgesellschaft mbH* [1983] 2 Lloyd's Rep. 45; *Cobec Brazilian Trading & Warehousing Corp v Alfred C. Toepfer* [1983] 2 Lloyd's Rep. 386 (waiver).

[27] *Hain S.S. Co Ltd v Tate & Lyle Ltd* (1936) 41 Com. Cas. 350, 355; *Peyman v Lanjani* [1985] Ch. 457; *Motor Oil Hellas (Corinth) Refineries SA v Shipping Corp of India* [1990] 1 Lloyd's Rep. 391; *Yukong Line Ltd of Korea v Rendsberg Investments Corp of Liberia* [1996] 2 Lloyd's Rep. 604, 607; *Laing Management Ltd v Aegon Insurance Co (UK) Ltd* (1998) 86 Build. L.R. 70, 108. However, affirmation may not be irrevocable in the case of an anticipatory breach of contract. In the case of an anticipatory breach, it has been argued that the innocent party ought to be entitled to go back upon his affirmation unless there has been some change of position by the party in breach in reliance upon the affirmation which would be prejudiced by the change of mind by the innocent party (see Treitel (1998) 114 L.Q.R. 22 and Treitel, *The Law of Contract*, 12th edn (by Peel, 2007), paras 17–089 et seq., a view which gains some support in principle from Thomas J. in *Stocznia Gdanska SA v Latvian Shipping Co* [2001] 1 Lloyd's Rep. 537, 566) and from Rix L.J. on appeal to the Court of Appeal, [2002] EWCA Civ 889, [2002] 2 Lloyd's Rep. 436 at [97]–[99].

[28] *Edm. J.M. Mertens & Co P.V.B.A. v Veevoeder Import Export Vimex BV* [1979] 2 Lloyd's Rep. 372, 384; *Telfair Shipping Corp v Athos Shipping Co SA* [1981] 2 Lloyd's Rep. 74, 87–88; affirmed [1983] 1 Lloyd's Rep. 127; *Peter Cremer v Granaria B.V.* [1981] 2 Lloyd's Rep. 583, 589; *Peyman v Lanjani* [1985] Ch. 457, 493, 500; *Sea Calm Shipping Co SA v Chantiers Navals de l'Esterel SA* [1986] 2 Lloyd's Rep. 294, 298; *Motor Oil Hellas (Corinth) Refineries SA v Shipping Corp of India* [1990] 1 Lloyd's Rep. 391, 398; *Yukong Line Ltd of Korea v Rendsberg Investments Corp of Liberia* [1996] 2 Lloyd's Rep. 604, 607.

[29] *Bentsen v Taylor Sons & Co* [1893] 2 Q.B. 274.

[30] *Tai Hing Cotton Mill Ltd v Kamsing Knitting Factory* [1979] A.C. 91; *Johnson v Agnew* [1980] A.C. 367; *Stocznia Gdanska SA v Latvian Shipping Co* [2002] EWCA Civ 889, [2002] 2 Lloyd's Rep. 436 at [94]–[100].

repudiation and going back on his election to affirm but rather is "treating the contract as being at an end on account of the continuing repudiation reflected in the other party's behaviour after the affirmation".[31] Nor, in the case of an ongoing contract, will affirmation in respect of one breach preclude the innocent party from treating himself as discharged by reason of further subsequent breaches.[32]

24–005 **Loss of right to terminate.** There are, however, circumstances where the innocent party may be deprived of his right to treat the contract as repudiated notwithstanding that he has no knowledge of the breach or of the right to choose which the law gives to him. For example, there will be circumstances where, even in the absence of an actual election, the innocent party will be regarded as having made its election, and decided not to terminate, when a reasonable time has passed and it has not sought to bring the contract to an end.[33] A statutory example is provided by s.11(4) of the Sale of Goods Act 1979 whereby a buyer may, in certain circumstances, be deprived of his right to reject the goods and to treat the contract as repudiated by his acceptance of the goods, regardless of his lack of knowledge of the breach.[34]

24–006 **"Inchoate doctrine" of consistency.** The example given in the last paragraph was relied on and extended by the Court of Appeal in *Panchaud Frères SA v Etablissements General Grain Co*,[35] a case which concerned a CIF contract for the sale of goods. Buyers of maize to be shipped in June/July 1965 accepted without objection shipping documents which included a bill of lading showing shipment on July 31 and also a certificate of quality which stated that the maize had been loaded in August. On arrival of the vessel the buyers rejected the maize on a ground subsequently found to be inadequate. Some three years later, at the hearing of an arbitration appeal, they became aware of late shipment, and then sought to justify their rejection on this ground. It was held that they were not

---

[31] *Safehaven Investments Inc v Springbok Ltd* (1996) 71 P. & C.R. 59, 68; *Stocznia Gdanska SA v Latvian Shipping Co* [2002] EWCA Civ 889, [2002] 2 Lloyd's Rep. 436 at [40] and [96].

[32] *Segal Securities Ltd v Thoseby* [1963] 1 Q.B. 887 (lease); *Yukong Line Ltd of Korea v Rendsberg Investments Corp of Liberia* [1996] 2 Lloyd's Rep. 604, 607.

[33] *Motor Oil Hellas (Corinth) Refineries SA v Shipping Corp of India* [1990] 1 Lloyd's Rep. 391, 398; *Kosmar Villa Holidays Inc v Trustees of Syndicate 1243* [2008] EWCA Civ 147, [2008] All E.R. (D) 448 (Feb) at [74].

[34] *Wallis Son & Wells v Pratt and Haynes* [1910] 2 K.B. 1003, 1015 (decision reversed [1911] A.C. 394); *Peyman v Lanjani* [1985] Ch. 457. See *Benjamin's Sale of Goods*, 7th edn (2006), para.12–038.

[35] [1970] 1 Lloyd's Rep. 53. See also *Woodhouse A.C. Israel Cocoa Ltd SA v Nigerian Produce Marketing Co Ltd* [1971] 2 Q.B. 23; affirmed [1972] A.C. 741; *Alma Shipping Corp v Union of India* [1971] 2 Lloyd's Rep. 494; *Alfred C. Toepfer v Cremer* [1975] 2 Lloyd's Rep. 118; *Waren Import Gesellschaft Krohn & Co v Alfred C. Toepfer* [1975] 1 Lloyd's Rep. 322; *Surrey Shipping Co Ltd v Cie Continentale (France) SA* [1978] 1 Lloyd's Rep. 191; *Bunge GmbH v Alfred C. Toepfer* [1978] 1 Lloyd's Rep. 506; *Avimex SA v Dewulf & Cie* [1979] 2 Lloyd's Rep. 57; *Procter & Gamble Philippine Manufacturing Corp v Peter Cremer GmbH & Co* [1988] 3 All E.R. 843, 848–852; *Glencore Grain Rotterdam BV v Lebanese Organisation for International Commerce* [1997] 4 All E.R. 514. cf. *V. Berg & Son Ltd v Vanden Avenne-Izegem P.V.B.A.* [1977] 1 Lloyd's Rep. 499.

entitled to do so. The case is best considered to have been decided on the relatively straightforward ground that a buyer under a CIF contract who accepts the documents will lose his right to reject the goods on the ground of their late shipment if he fails to notice the late shipment date when he takes up the documents.[36] Lord Denning M.R., however, stated[37] that the buyers were estopped by their conduct from setting up late shipment as a ground for rejection, in that they had led the sellers to believe that they were not relying on that ground and it would be unjust or unfair to allow them to do so when they had had full opportunity of finding out from the contract documents what the real date of shipment was, but did not trouble to do so. Winn L.J. agreed[38] that, having accepted the documents, the buyers could not properly thereafter turn round and say that the goods tendered were not contract goods. While doubting that there was anything which could be strictly described as an estoppel or quasi-estoppel, he considered that:

> "... there may be an inchoate doctrine stemming from the manifest convenience of consistency in pragmatic affairs, negativing any liberty to blow hot and cold in commercial conduct."[39]

The difficulty with the estoppel analysis is that there does not appear to have been any reliance by the sellers on any representation which was made by the buyers when they took up the documents. The "inchoate doctrine" referred to by Winn L.J. has received "no support"[40] in subsequent cases and has generally been invoked as an argument of "last resort".[41] In so far as the case can be analysed as an example of estoppel by conduct, it is now clear that there is no "separate doctrine"[42] which can be derived from *Panchaud Frères* alone and the conventional requirements of estoppel by conduct must be satisfied on the facts of any future case.[43]

Waiver and estoppel. Affirmation is sometimes regarded as a species of waiver, the innocent party "waiving" his right to treat the contract as repudiated.[44] But the word "waiver" is used in the law in a variety of different senses 24–007

[36] *B.P. Exploration Co (Libya) Ltd v Hunt* [1979] 1 W.L.R. 783, 810–811; *Glencore Grain Rotterdam BV v Lebanese Organisation for International Commerce* [1997] 4 All E.R. 514, 528, 530.

[37] [1970] 1 Lloyd's Rep. 53, 57–58. The estoppel explanation was preferred by Hirst J. in *Procter & Gamble Philippine Manufacturing Corp v Peter Cremer GmbH & Co* [1988] 3 All E.R. 843, 852.

[38] [1970] 1 Lloyd's Rep. 53, 60.

[39] [1970] 1 Lloyd's Rep. 53, 59.

[40] *Glencore Grain Rotterdam BV v Lebanese Organisation for International Commerce* [1997] 4 All E.R. 514, 529.

[41] *B.P. Exploration Co (Libya) Ltd v Hunt* [1979] 1 W.L.R. 783, 811.

[42] *Glencore Grain Rotterdam BV v Lebanese Organisation for International Commerce* [1997] 4 All E.R. 514, 530.

[43] *Glencore Grain Rotterdam BV v Lebanese Organisation for International Commerce* [1997] 4 All E.R. 514.

[44] See, e.g. Sale of Goods Act 1979 s.11(2).

and so bears "different meanings".[45] Two types of waiver are relevant here. The first type may be called "waiver by election" and waiver is here used to signify the "abandonment of a right which arises by virtue of a party making an election".[46] Thus it arises when a person is entitled to alternative rights inconsistent with one another and that person acts in a manner which is consistent only with his having chosen to rely on one of them.[47] Affirmation is an example of such a waiver, since the innocent party elects or chooses to exercise his right to treat the contract as continuing and thereby abandons his inconsistent right to treat the contract as repudiated.[48] It is important to appreciate that, in this context, the party who makes the election only abandons his right to treat the contract as repudiated; he does not abandon his right to claim damages for the loss suffered as a result of the breach.[49] A second type of waiver may be called "waiver by estoppel" and it arises when the innocent party agrees with the party in default that he will not exercise his right to treat the contract as repudiated[50] or so conducts himself as to lead the party in default to believe that he will not exercise that right.[51] This type of waiver does not exist as a separate principle[52] but is in fact an application of the principle of equitable estoppel deriving from the classic statement of Lord Cairns in *Hughes v Metropolitan Ry Co.*[53]

24–008 **Similarities and differences.** Both waiver by election and waiver by estoppel share some common elements. The principal similarity is that both would appear to require that the party seeking to rely on it (i.e. the party in default) must show a clear and unequivocal representation, by words or conduct, by the other party

---

[45] *Motor Oil Hellas (Corinth) Refineries SA v Shipping Corp of India* [1990] 1 Lloyd's Rep. 391, 397; *Kosmar Villa Holidays Inc v Trustees of Syndicate 1243* [2008] EWCA Civ 147, [2008] All E.R. (D) 448 (Feb) at [36]–[38]. See also Wilken and Villiers, *The Law of Waiver, Variation and Estoppel*, 2nd edn (2002), Ch.3 and above, paras 3–081, 22–040; below, para.24–009.

[46] *Motor Oil Hellas (Corinth) Refineries SA v Shipping Corp of India* [1990] 1 Lloyd's Rep. 391, 398.

[47] *Kammins Ballroom & Co Ltd v Zenith Investments (Torquay) Ltd* [1971] A.C. 850, 882–883; *China National Foreign Trade Transportation Corp v Evlogia Shipping Co SA of Panama* [1979] 1 W.L.R. 1018, 1024, 1034–1035; *Telfair Shipping Corp v Athos Shipping Co SA* [1981] 2 Lloyd's Rep. 74, 87; affirmed [1983] 1 Lloyd's Rep. 127; *Motor Oil Hellas (Corinth) Refineries SA v Shipping Corp of India* [1990] 1 Lloyd's Rep. 391, 398.

[48] *Peyman v Lanjani* [1985] Ch. 457; *Sea Calm Shipping Co SA v Chantiers Navals d'Esterel SA* [1986] 2 Lloyd's Rep. 294; *Motor Oil Hellas (Corinth) Refineries SA v Shipping Corp of India* [1990] 1 Lloyd's Rep. 391, 399; *Yukong Line Ltd of Korea v Rendsberg Investments Corp of Liberia* [1996] 2 Lloyd's Rep. 604, 607.

[49] The latter type of waiver, sometimes called "total waiver," is discussed, above, para.22–046; below para.24–009.

[50] See above, para.24–005.

[51] See the cases cited in fn.35, above.

[52] *Glencore Grain Rotterdam BV v Lebanese Organisation for International Commerce* [1997] 4 All E.R. 514, 530, where the Court of Appeal rejected the argument that any separate doctrine could be derived from the decision of the Court of Appeal in *Panchaud Frères SA v Etablissements General Grain Co* [1970] 1 Lloyd's Rep. 53, above, para.24–006.

[53] (1877) 2 App. Cas. 439, see above, para.3–085. There would also appear to be a common law species of waiver (sometimes referred to as "forbearance," see above, para.3–081) but the differences between the two appear to be very slight (see above, para.3–104). The equitable variety is most frequently relied upon in the courts.

that he will not exercise his strict legal rights to treat the contract as repudiated.[54] But there are also important differences between the two types of waiver. In the case of waiver by election the party who has to make the choice must either know[55] or have obvious means of knowledge[56] of the facts giving rise to the right, and possibly of the existence of the right.[57] But in the case of waiver by estoppel neither knowledge of the circumstances nor of the right is required on the part of the person estopped; the other party is entitled to rely on the apparent election conveyed by the representation.[58] Waiver by election is final and so has permanent effect,[59] whereas the effect of an estoppel may be suspensory only.[60] This difference may not be so marked in the context of waiver of breach because here the waiver may have permanent effect because, in some circumstances, it would be inequitable to allow the innocent party to retract his waiver. For example, in the case where a buyer assures a seller that the goods are in conformity with the contractual specifications, and the seller, in reliance upon these assurances, does not make a fresh conforming tender when he could have done, the buyer will be held to have waived any breach relating to the conformity of the goods and so the waiver will have permanent effect.[61] Finally, waiver by estoppel requires that the party to whom the representation is made rely on that representation so as to make it inequitable for the representor to go back upon his representation.[62] There is, however, no such requirement in the case of waiver by

---

[54] *Woodhouse A.C. Israel Cocoa Ltd SA v Nigerian Produce Marketing Co Ltd* [1972] A.C. 741, 758; *V. Berg & Son Ltd v Vanden Avenne-Izegem P.V.B.A.* [1977] 1 Lloyd's Rep. 499; *Finagrain SA v Kruse SA* [1976] 2 Lloyd's Rep. 508; *Bremer Handesgesellschaft mbH v C. Mackprang Jr* [1979] 1 Lloyd's Rep. 221, 228; *Avimex SA v Dewulf & Cie* [1979] 2 Lloyd's Rep. 57, 67; *Peter Cremer v Granaria BV* [1981] 2 Lloyd's Rep. 583; *Telfair Shipping Corp v Athos Shipping Co SA* [1981] 2 Lloyd's Rep. 74, 87; *Peyman v Lanjani* [1985] Ch. 457, 501; *Cobec Brazilian Trading and Warehousing Corp v Alfred C. Toepfer* [1983] 2 Lloyd's Rep. 386; *Bremer Handelsgesellschaft mbH v Deutsche Conti-Handelsgesellschaft mbH* [1983] 2 Lloyd's Rep. 45; *Nichimen Corp v Gatoil Overseas Inc* [1987] 2 Lloyd's Rep. 46; *Yukong Line Ltd of Korea v Rendsberg Investments Corp of Liberia* [1996] 2 Lloyd's Rep. 604, 607; *Tameside MBC v Barlow Securities Group Services Ltd* [2001] EWCA Civ 1, [2001] B.L.R. 113, 122. ("it is not the function of the court to resolve ambiguities and, unless it can find a reasonably clear and definite meaning, then it is not entitled to make the finding that the representation was indeed clear and unequivocal.") cf. *Bremer Handelsgesellschaft mbH v Vanden Avenne-Izegem P.V.B.A.* [1978] 2 Lloyd's Rep. 109, 126. See also above, paras 3–089—3–092.

[55] *U.G.S. Finance Ltd v National Mortgage Bank of Greece* [1964] 1 Lloyd's Rep. 446, 450; *Suisse Atlantique Société d'Armement Maritime SA v N.V. Rotterdamsche Kolen Centrale* [1967] 1 A.C. 361, 425; *Panchaud Frères SA v Etablissements General Grain Co* [1970] 1 Lloyd's Rep. 53, 57.

[56] *Bremer Handelsgesellschaft mbH v C. Mackprang Jr* [1979] 1 Lloyd's Rep. 221, 228; *Avimex SA v Dewulf & Cie* [1979] 2 Lloyd's Rep. 57, 67–68.

[57] *Peyman v Lanjani* [1985] Ch. 457 (affirmation).

[58] *Panchaud Frères SA v Etablissements General Grain Co* [1970] 1 Lloyd's Rep. 53, 57, 59 (see above, para.24–006); *Peyman v Lanjani* [1985] Ch. 457, 501; *Motor Oil Hellas (Corinth) Refineries SA v Shipping Corp of India* [1990] 1 Lloyd's Rep. 391, 399.

[59] *Motor Oil Hellas (Corinth) Refineries SA v Shipping Corp of India* [1990] 1 Lloyd's Rep. 391, 398. See also above, para.24–004.

[60] *Hughes v Metropolitan Ry Co* (1877) 2 App. Cas. 439, see above, para.3–096.

[61] *Toepfer v Warinco AG* [1978] 2 Lloyd's Rep. 569, 576. See above, paras 3–095, 3–097.

[62] *Finagrain SA v Kruse SA* [1976] 2 Lloyd's Rep. 508, 535; *Bremer Handelsgesellschaft mbH v Vanden Avenne-Izegem P.V.B.A.* [1978] 2 Lloyd's Rep. 109, 127; *Bunge SA v Schleswig-Holsteinische Landweretschaftliche Hauptgenossenschaft GmbH* [1978] 1 Lloyd's Rep. 480; *Société Italo-Belge pour le Commerce et l'Industrie SA v Palm and Vegetable Oils (Malaysia) Sdn Bhd* [1982] 1 All E.R. 19; *Peter Cremer v Granaria BV* [1981] 2 Lloyd's Rep. 583; cf. *Alfred C. Toepfer v P. Cremer* [1975] 2 Lloyd's Rep. 118, 123. See also above, paras 3–093—3–095.

election; once the election has been made it is final whether or not the party has acted in reliance upon the election having been made.[63] Waiver by estoppel is thus the "more flexible"[64] of the two doctrines.

24–009 **Other waivers.** Affirmation must be distinguished from a waiver by one party of a term of the contract inserted for his benefit,[65] or a "total" waiver by the innocent party of the breach itself by which he forgoes, not merely his right to treat himself as discharged by the breach, but also any claim for damages for the breach.[66]

24–010 **Effect of affirmation.** Where the innocent party, being entitled to treat himself as discharged by the other's breach, nevertheless elects to affirm the continued existence of the contract, he does not thereby necessarily relinquish his claim for damages for any loss sustained as a result of the breach.[67] Further, he may insist on holding the other party to the bargain and continue to tender due performance on his part.[68] In *White and Carter (Councils) Ltd v McGregor*,[69] the appellants, advertising contractors, agreed with the respondent, a garage proprietor, to display advertisements for his garage for three years. On the same day, the respondent repudiated the agreement and requested cancellation, but the appellants refused to cancel and performed their obligations under the contract. They then sued for the full contract price. The House of Lords, by a majority of three to two, upheld the claim. The appellants had elected to treat the contract as continuing and it remained in full effect. The decision in this case has not passed without criticism,[70] and one of the majority (Lord Reid) considered that the right to complete the contract and claim the price would not apply:

> "... if it can be shown that a person has no legitimate interest, financial or otherwise, in performing the contract rather than claiming damages."[71]

---

[63] *Motor Oil Hellas (Corinth) Refineries SA v Shipping Corp of India* [1990] 1 Lloyd's Rep. 391, 399; *Yukong Line Ltd of Korea v Rendsburg Investments Corp of Liberia* [1996] 2 Lloyd's Rep. 604, 607.

[64] *Kosmar Villa Holidays Inc v Trustees of Syndicate 1243* [2008] EWCA Civ 147, [2008] All E.R. (D) 448 (Feb) at [38].

[65] See above, para.22–045.

[66] Sale of Goods Act 1979 s.11(2); *Benjamin's Sale of Goods*, 7th edn (2006), paras 12–034—12–036. cf. *European Grain & Shipping Ltd v Peter Cremer* [1983] 1 Lloyd's Rep. 211.

[67] *Bentsen v Taylor, Sons & Co* [1893] 2 Q.B. 274; *Hain S.S. Co Ltd v Tate & Lyle Ltd* (1936) 41 Com. Cas. 350, 363; *Chandris v Isbrandtsen Moller Co Inc* [1951] 1 K.B. 240, 248; *Suisse Atlantique Société d'Armement Maritime SA v N.V. Rotterdamsche Kolen Centrale* [1967] 1 A.C. 361, 395.

[68] *Heyman v Darwins Ltd* [1942] A.C. 356, 361.

[69] [1962] A.C. 413. See also *Tredegar Iron and Coal Co Ltd v Hawthorn Bros & Co* (1902) 18 T.L.R. 716; *International Correspondence Schools v Ayres* (1912) 106 L.T. 845; *Anglo-African Shipping Co of New York Inc v Mortner* [1962] 1 Lloyd's Rep. 81, 94; *Decro-Wall International SA v Practitioners in Marketing Ltd* [1971] 1 W.L.R. 373; *Gator Shipping Corp v Trans-Asiatic Oil Ltd SA* [1978] 2 Lloyd's Rep. 357; *Asamera Oil Corp Ltd v Sea Oil and General Corp* (1979) 89 D.L.R. (3d) 1, 26.

[70] Goodhart (1962) 78 L.Q.R. 263; Furmston (1962) 25 M.L.R. 364; Scott [1962] Camb. L.J. 12. cf. Nienaber [1962] Camb. L.J. 213; Treitel, *The Law of Contract*, 12th edn (by Peel, 2007), paras 21–011—21–015.

[71] [1962] A.C. 413, 431. This dictum was applied or approved in *Attica Sea Carriers Corp v Ferrostaal Poseidon Bulk Reederei GmbH* [1976] 1 Lloyd's Rep. 250, 255; *Gator Shipping Corp v Trans-Asiatic Oil Ltd SA* [1978] 2 Lloyd's Rep. 357, 372–374; *Clea Shipping Corp v Bulk Oil International Ltd* [1983] 2 Lloyd's Rep. 645; *Stocznia Gdanska SA v Latvian Shipping Co* [1995] 2

Further, if the innocent party is unable to complete the contract without the co-operation of the other party, his only remedy is to sue for damages and not for the contract sum.[72] So an employee who is wrongfully dismissed can ordinarily only sue for damages[73] and not for his wages or salary.[74] But the fact that the remedies of the innocent party are restricted to damages does not mean that a discharge occurs at the moment of breach[75]; he may (in the case of an anticipatory repudiation) refuse to accept the repudiation and await the time fixed for performance, keeping the contract alive during the interval. In such a case, the innocent party is not required to mitigate his loss before the time for performance arrives.[76]

Effect if repudiation not accepted. If the innocent party elects to treat the contract as continuing, then it remains in existence for the benefit of the wrongdoer as well as of himself.[77] The wrongdoer is entitled to complete the contract and to take advantage of any supervening circumstance which would excuse[78] him from or diminish[79] his liability. The question, however, arises whether the wrongdoer may raise as a defence to liability the fact that the innocent party has failed to perform or is unable to perform his own obligations in some fundamental respect at the time appointed for performance. The answer to this question turns on the difficult case of *Braithwaite v Foreign Hardwood Co Ltd*.[80] In that 24–011

Lloyd's Rep. 592, 600–602 (Clarke J.); [1996] 2 Lloyd's Rep. 132, 138–139 CA. (It was unnecessary for the House of Lords in *Stocznia Gdanska* to consider this point on appeal ([1998] 1 W.L.R. 574, 581; *Ocean Marine Navigation Ltd v Koch Carbon Inc (The "Dynamic")* [2003] EWHC 1936 (Comm), [2003] 2 Lloyd's Rep. 693 at [23]; *Ministry of Sound (Ireland) Ltd v World Online Ltd* [2003] EWHC 2178 (Ch) at [64]–[66])). *Reichman v Beveridge* [2006] EWCA Civ 1659, [2007] Bus L.R. 412 at [17].

[72] [1962] A.C. 413, 430, 432, 439; *Finelli v Dee* (1968) 67 D.L.R. (2d) 293; *Denmark Productions Ltd v Boscobel Productions Ltd* [1969] 1 Q.B. 699; *Hounslow LBC v Twickenham Garden Developments Ltd* [1971] Ch. 233, 251–254; *Attica Sea Carriers Corp v Ferrostaal Poseidon Bulk Reederei GmbH* [1976] 1 Lloyd's Rep. 250, 256; *Telephone Rentals v Burgess Salmon* [1987] 5 C.L. 52; *Ministry of Sound (Ireland) Ltd v World Online Ltd* [2003] EWHC 2178 (Ch) at [49]–[61].

[73] In the absence of special circumstances the liability of an employer in damages for wrongful dismissal does not extend beyond the notice period which the employer could lawfully have given under the contract: *Boyo v Lambeth LBC* [1994] I.C.R. 727.

[74] *Denmark Productions Ltd v Boscobel Productions Ltd* [1969] 1 Q.B. 699; cf. *Boyo v Lambeth LBC* [1994] I.C.R. 727, 747 where Staughton L.J. inclined to the view that the wrongfully dismissed employee should be able to sue for his wages. See Vol.II, paras 39–193—39–195.

[75] See (contracts of employment): Vol.II, para.39–185. See also *Heymans v Darwins Ltd* [1942] A.C. 356, 371.

[76] *Shindler v Northern Raincoat Co Ltd* [1960] 1 W.L.R. 1038, 1048. When the time for performance arrives the doctrine of mitigation does come into play. The inapplicability of the doctrine of mitigation to cases of anticipatory breach has been criticised: see Burrows, *Remedies for Torts and Breach of Contract*, 3rd edn (2004) p.128.

[77] *Frost v Knight* (1872) L.R. 7 Exch. 111, 112; *Suisse Atlantique Société d'Armement Maritime SA v N.V. Rotterdamsche Kolen Centrale* [1967] 1 A.C. 361, 395, 419, 437–438; *Fercometal S.A.R.L. v Mediterranean Shipping Co SA* [1989] A.C. 788.

[78] *Frost v Knight* (1827) L.R. 7 Exch. 111, at 112; *Avery v Bowden* (1855) 5 E. & B. 714; (1856) 6 E. & B. 953 (below, para.24–024); *Heyman v Darwins Ltd* [1942] A.C. 356, 361; *Fercometal S.A.R.L. v Mediterranean Shipping Co SA* [1989] A.C. 788 (below, para.24–025).

[79] *Leigh v Paterson* (1818) 8 Taunt. 540; *Brown v Muller* (1872) L.R. 7 Ex. 319; *Tredegar Iron and Coal Co Ltd v Hawthorn Bros & Co* (1902) 18 T.L.R. 716; *Tai Hing Cotton Mill Ltd v Kamsing Knitting Factory* [1979] A.C. 91, 104.

[80] [1905] 2 K.B. 543. See Dawson (1980) 96 L.Q.R. 229; Carter [1989] L.M.C.L.Q. 81.

case, it was held that buyers of goods under a CIF[81] contract, who had wrongfully repudiated the contract, could not, in an action by the seller for damages for non-acceptance of a particular consignment of the goods, rely as a defence to liability upon the fact that part of the consignment covered by documents tendered to and refused by them did not answer to the quality specified by the contract. The case has been taken to establish the proposition that, if the innocent party elects to keep the contract alive notwithstanding a prior repudiation by the party in default, then so long as the repudiating party persists in his refusal to perform, he absolves the innocent party from his obligation to perform the contract in accordance with its terms.[82] Such a proposition may be defended on the ground that it would be an empty formality to require the innocent party to carry out his obligations under the contract in the face of a clear refusal by the other party to perform. But it is inconsistent with the principle that, if a repudiation is not accepted, the contract is kept alive for the benefit of *both* parties and the liabilities and obligations of the innocent party continue. In subsequent cases the facts of *Braithwaite* have been the subject of scrutiny,[83] and the opinion has been expressed that the documents covering the defective consignment were never tendered, but only offered to be tendered, and that at this stage the seller in fact accepted the buyers' repudiation and the contract was rescinded.[84] Alternatively, the House of Lords has stated[85] that the proposition sought to be derived from *Braithwaite* is wrong: there is no half-way house between affirmation (in which case the rights and obligations of both parties continue) and acceptance of the repudiation (in which case the rights and obligations of both parties which remain unperformed are discharged).[86]

24–012 Nevertheless, it may be that there are certain circumstances in which the innocent party may be released from performance of one or more of his obligations under the contract, notwithstanding the fact that he has not accepted the wrongdoer's repudiation. The first arises where the repudiating party has, by

[81] This appears from, e.g. the report in (1905) 74 L.J.K.B. 688. On the significance of this fact, see *Benjamin's Sale of Goods*, 7th edn (2006), paras 19–167—19–171, and see *Gill & Duffus SA v Berger & Co Inc* [1984] A.C. 382.

[82] [1905] 2 K.B. 543, 551. See *Brett v Schneideman Bros Ltd* [1923] N.Z.L.R. 938; *Peter Turnbull & Co Pty Ltd v Mundas Trading Co (Australia) Pty Ltd* (1954) 90 C.L.R. 235, 246; *Cerealmangimi SpA v Toepfer* [1981] 1 Lloyd's Rep. 337; *Bunge Corp v Vegetable Vitamin Foods (Private) Ltd* [1985] 1 Lloyd's Rep. 613.

[83] *Benjamin's Sale of Goods* at paras 9–011—9–016, 19–167—19–171.

[84] *Taylor v Oakes, Roncoroni & Co* (1922) 38 T.L.R. 349, 351, affirmed, 517; *Esmail v J. Rosenthal & Sons Ltd* [1964] 2 Lloyd's Rep. 447, 466 (this point was not discussed on appeal in *J. Rosenthal & Sons Ltd v Esmail* [1965] 1 W.L.R. 1117 HL); *Fercometal S.A.R.L. v Mediterranean Shipping Co SA* [1989] A.C. 788.

[85] *Fercometal S.A.R.L. v Mediterranean Shipping Co SA* [1989] A.C. 788. The correctness of *Braithwaite's Case* [1905] 2 K.B. 543 had been previously left open by the House of Lords in *J. Rosenthal & Sons Ltd v Esmail* [1965] 1 W.L.R. 1117 (Lord Pearson) and in *Gill & Duffus Ltd v Berger & Co Inc* [1984] A.C. 382, 395. See also *Cohen & Co v Ockerby & Co Ltd* (1917) 24 C.L.R. 288; *Taylor v Oakes, Roncoroni & Co* (1922) 38 T.L.R. 349, 517; *Bowes v Chaleyer* (1923) 32 C.L.R. 159, 169, 192, 197–199.

[86] But in *Segap Garages Ltd v Gulf Oil (Great Britain) Ltd, The Times*, October 24, 1988 (below, para.24–025); the Court of Appeal considered that a breach by the affirming party would be excused if he proved that it had been caused by or was due to the repudiatory breach. cf. *Foran v Wight* (1989) 168 C.L.R. 385, 409–410, 421–422, 447–449, 459. Equally, the fact that there is "no half-way house" does not deprive the innocent party of a period of time in which to decide whether or affirm or

words or conduct, represented to the innocent party that he will no longer require performance of a particular obligation under the contract, and the innocent party acts upon that representation. In such a case the repudiating party will be estopped from contending that the innocent party still remains bound by that obligation.[87] Secondly, where the repudiating party, by means of a breach of contract or other default, prevents the innocent party from performing his obligations under the contract he cannot rely upon that non-performance to reduce or eliminate his liability.[88] Finally, where the repudiating party stipulates for a mode of performance which is at variance with the terms of the contract and the innocent party attempts to comply with the new stipulation, the repudiating party cannot rely on a failure by the innocent party to perform his original obligations where that failure is attributable to his attempt to comply with the fresh stipulation.[89]

Acceptance of repudiation. Where there is an anticipatory breach, or the breach of an executory contract, and the innocent party wishes to treat himself as discharged, he must "accept the repudiation".[90] An act of acceptance of a repudiation requires no particular form.[91] It is usually done by communicating the decision to terminate to the party in default,[92] although it may be sufficient to lead evidence of an: 24–013

> "Unequivocal overt act which is inconsistent with the subsistence of the contract . . . without any concurrent manifestation of intent directed to the other party."[93]

---

terminate: *Stocznia Gdanska SA v Latvian Shipping Co* [2002] EWCA Civ 889, [2002] 2 Lloyd's Rep. 436 at [87] and see above, para.24–002.

[87] *Fercometal S.A.R.L. v Mediterranean Shipping Co SA* [1989] A.C. 788, 805–806. Estoppel could also arise if the repudiating party represents that he will not exercise a right conferred on him by the contract. A wider role for estoppel was acknowledged by Brennan J. in *Foran v Wight* (1989) 168 C.L.R. 385, 421–422.

[88] *Bulk Oil (Zug) AG v Sun International Ltd* [1984] 1 Lloyd's Rep. 531.

[89] *B.V. Oliehandel Jonglarid v Coastal International Ltd* [1983] 2 Lloyd's Rep. 463.

[90] *Heyman v Darwins Ltd* [1942] A.C. 356, 361. The appropriateness of the word "acceptance" has, however, been questioned: Smith, "Anticipatory Breach of Contract" in Lomnicka and Morse (eds), *Contemporary Issues in Commercial Law: Essays in Honour of A.G. Guest*, pp.175, 184–188.

[91] *Vitol SA v Norelf Ltd* [1996] A.C. 800, 810–811; *Stocznia Gdanska SA v Latvian Shipping Co* [2001] 1 Lloyd's Rep. 537, 563, 566. (Where the acceptance took the form of a notice to rescind which was in fact invalid. The important fact was held to be that the letter which constituted the acceptance unequivocally stated that the contractual obligations were at an end. The claimants had a right to terminate the contract and the fact that they did not set that ground out in the letter which constituted the acceptance was held to be irrelevant. The analysis of Thomas J. was upheld by the Court of Appeal but not without some hesitation: see [2002] EWCA Civ 889, [2002] 2 Lloyd's Rep. 436 at [88]–[92]. The safest course of action would have been for the innocent party expressly to have reserved its common law rights.)

[92] *Heyman v Darwins Ltd* [1942] A.C. 356, 361; *The Mihalis Angelos* [1971] 1 Q.B. 164, 204. The innocent party need not personally, or by an agent, notify the repudiating party of his election to treat the contract as at an end. It is sufficient that the fact of the election is brought to the attention of the repudiating party, for example, by notification by an unauthorised broker or by another intermediary may be sufficient: *Vitol SA v Norelf Ltd* [1996] A.C. 800, 811.

[93] *State Trading Corp of India Ltd v M. Golodetz Ltd* [1989] 2 Lloyd's Rep. 277, 286; *Holland v Wiltshire* (1954) 90 C.L.R. 409, 416. See also Dawson [1981] C.L.J. 83, 103. cf. *Vitol SA v Norelf Ltd (The Santa Clara)* [1993] 2 Lloyd's Rep. 301, 304 where Phillips J. preferred to leave open the question whether "an innocent party can accept an anticipatory repudiation by conduct which is not communicated to the party in anticipatory breach". When deciding whether or not inconsistent

In an appropriate case an acceptance of a repudiation may take the form of reliance on a contractual term which entitles the innocent party to terminate the contract. Where the conduct of the party in breach is such as to entitle the innocent party to terminate the contract either pursuant to a term of the contract or under the general law, the innocent party is not required to elect between its two rights to terminate and so can be treated as having terminated the contract both under the appropriate term of the contract and in accordance with its rights at common law.[94] Unless and until the repudiation is accepted the contract continues in existence for "an unaccepted repudiation is a thing writ in water".[95] Acceptance of a repudiation must be clear and unequivocal[96] and mere inactivity or acquiescence will generally not be regarded as acceptance for this purpose.[97] But there may be circumstances in which a continuing failure to perform will be sufficiently unequivocal to constitute acceptance of a repudiation. It all depends on "the particular contractual relationship and the particular circumstances of the case".[98] An example of a failure to perform which has been suggested as sufficient to constitute an acceptance is the following:

> "Postulate the case where an employer at the end of the day tells a contractor that he, the employer, is repudiating the contract and that the contractor need not return the next day. The contractor does not return the next day or at all. It seems to me that the contractor's failure to return may, in the absence of any other explanation, convey a decision to treat the contract as at an end."[99]

The requirement that the acceptance be communicated "clearly and unequivocally" is likely to mean that it is only where there has been a failure to carry out an act in relation to the party in breach that silence or inactivity will be sufficiently unequivocal for this purpose. Where the silence or inactivity relates to the performance of a contract to which the party in breach is not privy then it

---

actions amount to an acceptance of a repudiation, the courts apply an objective test: *Enfield London Borough Council v Sivanandan* [2004] EWHC 672 (QB), [2004] All E.R. (D) 73 (Apr) at [38]–[39].

94 *Dalkia Utilities Services Plc v Celtech International Ltd* [2006] EWHC 63 (Comm), [2006] 1 Lloyd's Rep. 599 at [135]–[144].

95 *Howard v Pickford Tool Co* [1951] 1 K.B. 417, 421. See also *Cranleigh Precision Engineering Ltd v Bryant* [1965] 1 W.L.R. 1293; *Thomas Marshall (Exports) Ltd v Guinle* [1979] Ch. 227; *Gunton v Richmond-on-Thames LBC* [1981] Ch. 448; *London Transport Executive v Clarke* [1981] I.C.R. 355; *State Trading Corp of India Ltd v M. Golodetz Ltd* [1989] 2 Lloyd's Rep. 277, 285; *Boyo v Lambeth LBC* [1994] I.C.R. 727 (although it should be noted that the court was rather reluctant to follow *Gunton*; see in particular the judgment of Staughton L.J. (747). cf. *Savage v Sainsbury Ltd* [1981] I.C.R. 1; and see Vol.II, para.39–185 (contracts of employment).

96 *Harrison v Northwest Holt Group Administration* [1985] I.C.R. 668; *Boyo v Lambeth LBC* [1994] I.C.R. 727; *Vitol SA v Norelf Ltd* [1996] A.C. 800; *Holland v Glendale Industries Ltd* [1998] I.C.R. 493; *Sookraj v Samaroo* [2004] UKPC 50 at [17]; *South Caribbean Trading Ltd v Trafigura Beheer BV* [2004] EWHC 2676 (Comm), [2005] 1 Lloyd's Rep. 128 at [129]–[130]; *Banham Marshall Services Unlimited v Lincolnshire CC* [2007] EWHC 402 (QB), [2007] All E.R. (D) 02 (Mar) at [52].

97 *Denmark Productions Ltd v Boscobel Productions Ltd* [1969] 1 Q.B. 699, 732; *State Trading Corp of India Ltd v M. Golodetz Ltd* [1989] 2 Lloyd's Rep. 277, 286; *Lefevre v White* [1990] 1 Lloyd's Rep. 569, 574, 576.

98 *Vitol SA v Norelf Ltd* [1996] A.C. 800, 811. In such a case the contractor may be absolved from his contractual obligation before he communicates his acceptance: *Potter v RJ Temple* [2003] All E.R. (D) 327 (Dec).

99 *Vitol SA v Norelf Ltd* [1996] A.C. 800, 811.

is unlikely that silence will be sufficiently unequivocal.[100] Once a repudiation has been accepted, the acceptance cannot be withdrawn.[101] If the parties thereafter resume performance of the contract, their rights are governed by a new contract, even if the terms remain the same.[102]

No reason or bad reason given. The general rule is well established that, if a party refuses to perform a contract, giving therefore a wrong or inadequate reason or no reason at all, he may yet justify his refusal if there were at the time facts in existence which would have provided a good reason, even if he did not know of them at the time of his refusal.[103] Thus when an employee brings an action against his employer, alleging that he has been wrongfully dismissed, the employer can rely on information acquired after the dismissal when seeking to justify the dismissal.[104] The general rule is the subject of a number of exceptions. First, a party cannot rely on a ground which he did not specify at the time of his refusal to perform "if the point which was not taken could have been put right".[105] Secondly, a party may be precluded by the operation of the doctrines of waiver or estoppel from relying on a ground which he did not specify at the time of his refusal to perform.[106] Thirdly, a party may be held to have accepted 24–014

[100] *Jaks (UK) Ltd v Cera Investment Bank SA* [1998] 2 Lloyd's Rep. 89, 96 (where the party alleged to be in breach was the bank under a letter of credit but the inactivity related to the non-performance of the contract of sale).

[101] *Scarf v Jardine* (1882) 7 App. Cas. 345, 361; *Motor Oil Hellas (Corinth) Refineries SA v Shipping Corp of India* [1990] 1 Lloyd's Rep. 391, 398. cf. Vold (1926) 5 Texas L. Rev. 9.

[102] *Aegnoussiotis Shipping Corp of Monrovia v A/S Kristian Jebsens Rederi of Bergen* [1977] 1 Lloyd's Rep. 268, 276.

[103] *Ridgway v Hungerford Market Co* (1835) 3 A. & E. 171, 177, 178, 180; *Baillie v Kell* (1838) 4 Bing N.C. 638; *Boston Deep Sea Fishing and Ice Co v Ansell* (1888) 39 Ch D 339, 352, 364; *Taylor v Oakes Roncoroni Co* (1922) 127 L.T. 267, 269; *British & Beningtons Ltd v N.W. Cachar Tea Co* [1923] A.C. 48, 71; *Etablissements Chainbaux S.A.R.L. v Harbormaster Ltd* [1955] 1 Lloyd's Rep. 303, 314; *Universal Cargo Carriers Corp v Citati* [1957] 2 Q.B. 401, 443–445; affirmed in part [1957] 1 W.L.R. 979, and reversed in part [1958] 2 Q.B. 254; *Denmark Productions Ltd v Boscobel Productions Ltd* [1969] 1 Q.B. 699, 722, 732; *The Mihalis Angelos* [1971] 1 Q.B. 164, 195, 200, 204; *Cyril Leonard & Co v Simo Securities Trust* [1972] 1 W.L.R. 80, 85, 87, 89; *Scandinavian Trading Co A/B v Zodiac Petroleum SA* [1981] 1 Lloyd's Rep. 81, 90; *State Trading Corp of India Ltd v M. Golodetz Ltd* [1988] 2 Lloyd's Rep. 182; *Sheffield v Conrad* (1988) 22 Con.L.R. 108; *South Caribbean Trading Ltd v Trafigura Beheer BV* [2004] EWHC 2676 (Comm), [2005] 1 Lloyd's Rep. 128 at [133]–[134]. The latter case demonstrates that there are limits to the willingness of the courts to speculate about the reaction of the innocent party to the breach of which he was unaware.

[104] *Ridgway v Hungerford Market Co* (1835) 3 A. & E. 171; *Baillie v Kell* (1838) 4 Bing N.C. 638; *Boston Deep Sea Fishing and Ice Co v Ansell* (1888) 39 Ch D 339; *Cyril Leonard & Co v Simo Securities Trust* [1972] 1 W.L.R. 80. The rule does not apply in cases of *unfair* dismissal: *Earl v Slater & Wheeler (Airline) Ltd* [1973] 1 W.L.R. 51; *W. Devis & Sons Ltd v Atkins* [1977] A.C. 931; cf. *Polkey v A.E. Dayton Services Ltd* [1988] A.C. 344; Vol.II, para.39–218.

[105] *Heisler v Anglo-Dal Ltd* [1954] 1 W.L.R. 1273, 1278; *Andre et Cie v Cook Industries Inc* [1987] 2 Lloyd's Rep. 463, 468–469; *Glencore Grain Rotterdam BV v Lebanese Organisation for International Commerce* [1997] 4 All E.R. 514, 526–527. But it would appear that the point must be one which could have been taken at the time.

[106] To invoke waiver or estoppel it is, however, necessary to show that there was an unequivocal representation made by one party, by conduct or otherwise, which was acted upon by the other. It may not be easy to establish the existence of such an unequivocal representation: *Glencore Grain Rotterdam BV v Lebanese Organisation for International Commerce* [1997] 4 All E.R. 514, 527, 530.

the goods so that he is no longer able to justify his refusal to perform.[107] However there does not appear to be any separate principle which would preclude a party from setting up a different ground simply because it would be unfair or unjust to allow him to do so.[108]

24–015 **Both parties in breach.** Where both parties are alleged to have committed a breach of contract, and it is asserted that each breach (taken independently) gives rise to a right to terminate further performance of the contract, regard must be had to the order in which the breaches occurred. Where one party (A) breaches the contract and that breach is followed by a breach by the other party (B) then, assuming that both breaches are repudiatory, the breach by party A will give party B the right to terminate future performance of the contract. If B exercises that right and accepts the repudiation his subsequent failure to perform his obligations under the contract will not constitute a breach of contract.[109] The position is rather more complex if B does not accept the breach and then himself commits a repudiatory breach of contract. In such a case can A accept the breach and terminate performance of the contract or does the fact that he has previously repudiated the contract prevent him from exercising his option to terminate? It is suggested that, in such a case, the effect of B electing to affirm the contract is to leave the primary obligations of both parties unchanged.[110] The contract therefore remains in existence for the benefit of A as well as for B so that A should be free to elect to terminate performance. Thus in *State Trading Corp of India v M. Golodetz Ltd*,[111] Kerr L.J. stated that:

> "If A is entitled to treat B as having wrongfully repudiated the contract between them and does so, then it does not avail B to point to A's past breaches of contract, whatever their nature. A breach by A would only assist B if it was still continuing when A purported to treat B as having repudiated the contract *and* if the effect of A's subsisting breach was such as to preclude A from claiming that B had committed a repudiatory breach. In other words, B would have to show that A, being in breach of an obligation in the nature of a condition precedent, was therefore not entitled to rely on B's breach as a repudiation."[112]

So unless the obligation of A to perform is a condition precedent to B's

---

[107] This has been held to be the true interpretation of the difficult case of *Panchaud Frères SA v Etablissements General Grain Co* [1970] 1 Lloyd's Rep. 53; see *B.P. Exploration Co (Libya) Ltd v Hunt* [1979] 1 W.L.R. 783, 811 and *Glencore Grain Rotterdam BV v Lebanese Organisation for International Commerce* [1997] 4 All E.R. 514, 528.

[108] Support for such a separate principle can be gleaned from dicta of the Court of Appeal in *Panchaud Frères SA v Établissements General Grain Co* [1970] 1 Lloyd's Rep. 53, 57, 59 but the proposition that some "separate doctrine" can be derived from *Panchaud Frères* alone has since been decisively rejected by the Court of Appeal: *Glencore Grain Rotterdam BV v Lebanese Organisation for International Commerce* [1997] 4 All E.R. 514, 528, 530.

[109] *Northern Foods Plc v Focal Foods Ltd* [2003] 2 Lloyd's Rep. 728, 748–750.

[110] *Heyman v Darwins Ltd* [1942] A.C. 356, 361; *Fercometal S.A.R.L. v Mediterranean Shipping Co SA* [1989] A.C. 788.

[111] [1989] 2 Lloyd's Rep. 277; See further Treitel (1990) 106 L.Q.R. 185, 188–190.

[112] [1989] 2 Lloyd's Rep. 277, 286.

obligation to perform, the fact that A is in breach of contract should not act as a barrier to A's ability to terminate on the ground of B's breach.[113]

Where both parties are simultaneously in breach of contract, there is authority for the proposition that neither party is entitled to terminate performance of the contract.[114] Thus, it has been held that where both parties agree to submit a dispute to arbitration, and there then follows a substantial period of delay during which neither party seeks to proceed with the reference to arbitration, each party is thereby guilty of a continuing breach of contract with the result that: 24–016

> "... neither [party] can rely on the other's breach as giving him a right to treat the primary obligations of each to continue with the reference as brought to an end."[115]

While a party who has committed a repudiatory breach of contract is not entitled to enforce the contract against a party who is ready and willing to perform his obligations under the contract, it is suggested that it does not follow that the fact that a party has committed a repudiatory breach should preclude him from accepting a repudiatory breach committed by the other party. As has already been stated, until the repudiatory breach has been accepted, the primary obligations of both parties remain unaffected and therefore it is suggested that the proposition that, in such a case, either party is entitled to accept the breach is more consistent with the underlying principles of English law.[116]

Circumstances of discharge. 24–017

> "The three sets of circumstances giving rise to a discharge of contract are tabulated by Anson as: (1) renunciation by a party of his liabilities under it; (2) impossibility created by his own act; and (3) total or partial failure of performance. In the case of the first two, the renunciation may occur or the impossibility be created either before or at the time for performance. In the case of the third it can occur only at the time or during the course of performance. Moreover, if the third be partial, the failure must occur in a matter which goes to the root of the contract. All these acts may be compendiously described as repudiation, though that expression is more particularly used of renunciation before the time for performance has arrived."[117]

---

[113] *DRC Distribution v Ulva Ltd* [2007] EWHC 1716 (QB), [2007] All E.R. (D) 357 (Jul) at [54].

[114] *Bremer Vulkan Schiffbau und Maschinenfabrik v South India Shipping Corp Ltd* [1981] A.C. 909; *Paal Wilson & Co A/S v Partenreederei Hannah Blumenthal* [1983] 1 A.C. 854.

[115] *Bremer Vulkan Schiffbau und Maschinenfabrik v South India Shipping Corp Ltd* [1981] A.C. 909, 987–988.

[116] See generally Treitel, *The Law of Contract*, 12th edn (by Peel, 2007), para.18–086.

[117] *Heyman v Darwins Ltd* [1942] A.C. 356, 397; *Universal Cargo Carriers Corp v Citati* [1957] 2 Q.B. 401, 436; affirmed in part [1957] 1 W.L.R. 979, and reversed in part [1958] 2 Q.B. 254. The question whether repudiation by "renunciation" of a contract differs in principle from what may be termed repudiation by non-performance was left open by Langley J. in *Amoco (UK) Exploration Co v British American Offshore Ltd* Unreported November 16, 2001 QBD, at [105]. It may be that it is easier to establish a repudiatory breach in the case of a renunciation than in the other categories. Thus in *Astea (UK) Ltd v Time Group Ltd* [2003] EWHC 725 (TCC), [2003] All E.R. (D) 212 (Apr) it was observed (at [151]) that "a flat refusal to continue performance will probably amount to a repudiation however much work has been done". Matters are likely to be more difficult in the case where the breach is alleged to take the form of defective work rather than an outright refusal to work.

2. RENUNCIATION

24–018 **Renunciation.** A renunciation of a contract occurs when one party by words or conduct evinces an intention not to perform, or expressly declares that he is or will be unable to perform, his obligations under the contract in some essential respect.[118] The renunciation may occur before or at the time fixed for performance.[119] An absolute refusal by one party to perform his side of the contract will entitle the other party to treat himself as discharged,[120] as will also a clear and unambiguous assertion by one party that he will be unable to perform when the time for performance should arrive.[121] Short of such an express refusal or declaration, however, the test is to ascertain whether the action or actions of the party in default are such as to lead a reasonable person to conclude that he no longer intends to be bound by its provisions.[122] The renunciation is then evidenced by conduct. Also the party in default:

> "... may intend in fact to fulfil (the contract) but may be determined to do so only in a manner substantially inconsistent with his obligations,"[123]

or may refuse to perform the contract unless the other party complies with certain conditions not required by its terms.[124] In such a case, there is little difficulty in holding that the contract has been renounced.[125] Nevertheless, not every intimation of an intention not to perform or of an inability to perform some part of a contract will amount to a renunciation. Even a deliberate breach, actual or threatened, will not necessarily entitle the innocent party to treat himself as discharged, since it may sometimes be that such a breach can appropriately be sanctioned in damages.[126] If the contract is entire and indivisible,[127] that is to say, if it is expressly or impliedly agreed that the obligation of one party is dependent or conditional upon complete performance by the other, then a refusal to perform

[118] See also *Martin v Stout* [1925] A.C. 359; *Brinkibon Ltd v Stahag Stahl und Stahlwarenhandelgesellschaft mbH* [1980] 2 Lloyd's Rep. 556; affirmed [1983] 2 A.C. 34 (place of renunciation).

[119] Where the renunciation takes place before the time fixed for performance, it is known as an anticipatory breach: below, para.24–021.

[120] *Freeth v Burr* (1874) L.R. 6 C.P. 208, 214; *Thompson v Corroon* (1992) 42 W.I.R. 157.

[121] *Anchor Line Ltd v Keith Rowell Ltd* [1980] 2 Lloyd's Rep. 351; *The Munster* [1982] 1 Lloyd's Rep. 370; *Texaco Ltd v Eurogulf Shipping Co Ltd* [1987] 2 Lloyd's Rep. 541.

[122] *Universal Cargo Carriers Corp v Citati* [1957] 2 Q.B. 401, 436; affirmed in part [1957] 1 W.L.R. 979 and reversed in part [1958] 2 Q.B. 254. See also *Morgan v Bain* (1874) L.R. 10 C.P. 15; *Bloomer v Bernstein* (1874) L.R. 9 C.P. 588; *Forslind v Becheley-Crundall* (1922) S.C. 173 HL; *Maple Flock Co v Universal Furniture Products (Wembley) Ltd* [1934] 1 K.B. 148, 157; *Laws v London Chronicle (Indicator Newspapers) Ltd* [1959] 1 W.L.R. 698; *Chilean Nitrate Sale & Corp v Marine Transportation Co Ltd* [1982] 1 Lloyd's Rep. 570, 580; *Re Olympia & York Canary Wharf Ltd (No.2)* [1993] B.C.C. 159, 168; *Nottingham Building Society v Eurodynamics Plc* [1995] F.S.R. 605, 611–612. cf. below, para.24–019.

[123] *Ross T. Smyth & Co v Bailey, Son & Co* [1940] 3 All E.R. 60, 72; *Federal Commerce & Navigation Co Ltd v Molena Alpha Inc* [1979] A.C. 757.

[124] *B.V. Oliehandel Jongkind v Coastal International Ltd* [1983] 2 Lloyd's Rep. 463.

[125] *Withers v Reynolds* (1831) 2 B. & Ad. 882; *Booth v Bowron* (1892) 8 T.L.R. 641.

[126] *Suisse Atlantique Société d'Armement Maritime SA v N.V. Rotterdamsche Kolen Centrale* [1967] 1 A.C. 261, 365. See below, para.24–041.

[127] See above, para.21–027; below, para.24–043.

or declaration of inability to perform any part of the agreement will normally entitle the party in default to treat himself as discharged from further liability.[128] But in any other case:

> "It is not a mere refusal or omission of one of the contracting parties to do something which he ought to do, that will justify the other in repudiating the contract; but there must be an absolute refusal to perform his side of the contract."[129]

If one party evinces an intention not to perform or declares his inability to perform some, but not all, of his obligations under the contract, then the right of the other party to treat himself as discharged depends on whether the non-performance of those obligations will amount to a breach of a condition of the contract[130] or deprive him of substantially the whole benefit which it was the intention of the parties that he should obtain from the obligations of the parties under the contract then remaining unperformed.[131] Words or conduct which do not amount to a renunciation will not justify a discharge.[132]

Unequivocal. The renunciation must be "made quite plain".[133] In particular, where there is a genuine dispute as to the construction of a contract, the courts may be unwilling to hold that an expression of an intention by one party to carry out the contract only in accordance with his own erroneous interpretation of it 24–019

[128] *Longbottom & Co Ltd v Bass Walker & Co Ltd* [1922] W.N. 245. See also *Ebbw Vale Steel Co v Blaina Iron Co* (1901) 6 Com. Cas. 33.

[129] *Freeth v Burr* (1878) L.R. 9 C.P. 208, 213, 214; *Chilean Nitrate Sales Corp v Marine Transportation Co Ltd* [1982] 1 Lloyd's Rep. 570, 572; *Aktion Maritime Corp of Liberia v S. Kasmas & Brothers Ltd* [1987] 1 Lloyd's Rep. 283, 306; *Torvald Klaveness A/S v Arni Maritime Corp* [1994] 1 W.L.R. 1465, 1476.

[130] See above, para.12–025; below, para.24–039.

[131] *Federal Commerce & Navigation Co Ltd v Molena Alpha Inc* [1979] A.C. 757; *Afovos Shipping Co SA v Pagnan & Filli* [1983] 1 W.L.R. 195, 203; *Weeks v Bradshaw* [1993] E.G.C.S. 65; *Amoco (UK) Exploration Co v British American Offshore Ltd* Unreported November 16, 2001 QBD at [105]; *Dalkia Utilities Services Plc v Celtech International Ltd* [2006] EWHC 63 (Comm), [2006] 1 Lloyd's Rep. 599 at [133]. When assessing the nature and effects of the breach the court is concerned to do so objectively: *Shyam Jewellers Ltd v Cheeseman* [2001] EWCA Civ 1818 at [58].

[132] *Franklin v Miller* (1836) 4 A. & E. 499; *Wilkinson v Clements* (1872) L.R. 8 Ch.App. 96; *Re Phoenix Bessemer Steel Co* (1876) 4 Ch D 108; *Cornwall v Henson* [1900] 2 Ch. 298; *Dominion Coal Co Ltd v Dominion Iron and Steel Co Ltd* [1909] A.C. 293; *Household Machines v Cosmos Exports* [1947] K.B. 217; *Thorpe v Fasey* [1949] Ch. 649; *Peter Dumenil & Co Ltd v James Ruddin Ltd* [1953] 1 W.L.R. 815.

[133] *Spettabile Consorzio Veneziana di Armamento di Navigazione v Northumberland Shipbuilding Co Ltd* (1919) 121 L.T. 628, 634, 635; *Woodar Investment Development Ltd v Wimpey Construction UK Ltd* [1980] 1 W.L.R. 277, 287, 288; *Anchor Line Ltd v Keith Rowell Ltd* [1980] 2 Lloyd's Rep. 351, 353; *Thompson v Corroon* (1993) 42 W.I.R. 157; *Nottingham Building Society v Eurodynamics Plc* [1995] F.S.R. 605; *Jaks (UK) Ltd v Cera Investment Bank SA* [1998] 2 Lloyd's Rep. 89, 92–93. This proposition applies to words and conduct said to demonstrate that a party is persisting in an earlier repudiation as well as to the earlier repudiation itself (*Safehaven Investments Inc v Springbok Ltd* (1996) 71 P. & C.R. 59, 69). See also *Warinco A.G. v Samor SpA* [1979] 1 Lloyd's Rep. 450; *Metro Meat Ltd v Fares Rural Co Pty Ltd* [1985] 2 Lloyd's Rep. 13; *Sanko S.S. Co Ltd v Eacom Timber Sales Ltd* [1987] 1 Lloyd's Rep. 487; *Alfred C. Toepfer International GmbH v Itex Itagram Export SA* [1993] 1 Lloyd's Rep. 360, 361; *Thompson v Corroon* (1993) 42 W.I.R. 157.

amounts to a repudiation[134]; and the same is true of a genuine mistake of fact[135] or law.[136] Even the giving of notice of rescission, or the commencement of proceedings by one party claiming rescission of the contract, does not necessarily entitle the other to treat the contract as repudiated, since such action may be taken in order to determine the respective rights of the parties, and so not evince an intention to abandon the contract.[137] On the other hand, it is, generally, no defence for a party who is alleged to have repudiated the contract to show that he acted in good faith.[138] The courts have struggled to reconcile the latter proposition with their reluctance to conclude that a party who has acted in good faith but was mistaken has thereby repudiated the contract. The result of this tension is that the cases in this area are not at all easy to reconcile.[139] The position would appear to be that it may not be a repudiation for one party to put forward his genuine but bona fide interpretation of what the contract requires of him[140] but that where that party performs in a manner which is not consistent with the terms of the contract, it is no defence for that party to show that he acted in good faith.[141]

24–020 **Employer and employee.** In respect of an action for wrongful dismissal at common law, or proceedings for unfair dismissal under statute, the question what acts or omissions amount to or justify such dismissal is dealt within the chapter on employment in Vol.II of this work.[142]

24–021 **Anticipatory breach.** If, before the time arrives at which a party is bound to perform a contract, he expresses an intention to break it, or acts in such a way as

---

[134] *James Shaffer Ltd v Findlay Durham & Brodie* [1953] 1 W.L.R. 106; *Sweet & Maxwell Ltd v Universal News Services Ltd* [1964] 2 Q.B. 699; *Woodar Investment Development Ltd v Wimpey Construction UK Ltd* [1980] 1 W.L.R. 277; *Telfair Shipping Corp v Athos Shipping Co SA* [1983] 1 Lloyd's Rep. 127; *The Design Company v Elizabeth King* Unreported July 7, 1992 CA; *Vaswani v Italian Motors (Sales and Services) Ltd* [1996] 1 W.L.R. 270; *Mitsubishi Heavy Industries Ltd v Gulf Bank K.S.C.* [1997] 1 Lloyd's Rep. 343, 354; *Orion Finance Ltd v Heritable Finance Ltd* Unreported March 10, 1997 CA.

[135] *Kent v Godts* (1855) 26 L.T.(o.s.) 88; *Peter Dumenil & Co Ltd v James Ruddin Ltd* [1953] 1 W.L.R. 815; *Alfred C. Toepfer v Peter Cremer* [1975] 2 Lloyd's Rep. 118.

[136] *Freeth v Burr* (1874) L.R. 9 C.P. 208, 214; *Mersey Steel & Iron Co v Naylor Benzon & Co* (1884) 9 App. Cas. 434. Contrast *Federal Commerce & Navigation Co Ltd v Molena Alpha Inc* [1979] A.C. 757.

[137] *Spettabile Consorzio Veneziano di Armamento di Navigazione v Northumberland Shipbuilding Co Ltd* (1919) 121 L.T. 628; *Woodar Investment Development Ltd v Wimpey Construction UK Ltd* [1980] 1 W.L.R. 277.

[138] *Federal Commerce & Navigation Co Ltd v Molena Alpha Inc* [1979] A.C. 757.

[139] In particular, the decisions of the House of Lords in *Woodar Investment Development Ltd v Wimpey Construction UK Ltd* [1980] 1 W.L.R. 277 and *Federal Commerce & Navigation Co Ltd v Molena Alpha Inc* [1979] A.C. 757 are not at all easy to reconcile. See also *Dalkia Utilities Services Plc v Celtech International Ltd* [2006] EWHC 63 (Comm), [2006] 1 Lloyd's Rep. 599 at [145]–[149]

[140] *Woodar Investment Development Ltd v Wimpey Construction UK Ltd* [1980] 1 W.L.R. 277; *James Shaffer Ltd v Findlay Durham and Brodie* [1953] 1 W.L.R. 106; *Sweet and Maxwell Ltd v Universal News Services Ltd* [1964] 2 Q.B. 699 and *Vaswani v Italian Motors (Sales) Ltd* [1996] 1 W.L.R. 270.

[141] *Federal Commerce & Navigation Co Ltd v Molena Alpha Inc* [1979] A.C. 757; *Farrant v The Woodroffe School* [1998] I.C.R. 184.

[142] Vol.II, paras 39–176—39–185 (wrongful dismissal); Vol.II, paras 39–207—39–242 (unfair dismissal).

to lead a reasonable person to the conclusion that he does not intend to fulfil his part,[143] this constitutes an "anticipatory breach"[144] of the contract and entitles the other party to take one of two courses. He may "accept"[145] the renunciation, treat it as discharging him from further performance, and sue for damages forthwith, or he may wait till the time for performance arrives and then sue.[146] On the other hand, where the anticipatory breach takes a continuing form,[147] the fact that the innocent party initially continued to press for performance does not normally preclude him from later electing to terminate the contract provided that the party in breach has persisted in his stance up to the moment of termination.[148]

Breach accepted. The first alternative was established by *Hochster v De la Tour*,[149] where a travelling courier sued his employer who wrote before the time for performance arrived that he would not require his services. The courier sued for damages at once and it was held that he was entitled to do so. In *Johnstone v Milling*[150] the effect of an anticipatory breach was thus stated by Lord Esher M.R.: 24–022

> "A renunciation of a contract, or, in other words, a total refusal to perform it by one party before the time for performance arrives, does not, by itself, amount to a breach of contract but may be so acted upon and adopted by the other party as a rescission of the contract as to give an immediate right of action. Where one party assumes to renounce the contract, that is, by anticipation refuses to perform it, he thereby, so far as he is concerned, declares his intention then and there to rescind the contract. . . . The other party may adopt such renunciation of the contract by so acting upon it as in effect to declare that he too treats the contract as at an end, except for the purpose of bringing

---

[143] *Forslind v Becheley-Crundall* (1922) S.C. 173 HL; *Universal Cargo Carriers Corp v Citati* [1957] 2 Q.B. 401; affirmed in part [1957] 1 W.L.R. 979 and reversed in part [1958] 2 Q.B. 254; *Greenaway Harrison Ltd v Wiles* [1994] I.R.L.R. 380 *Stocznia Gdanska SA v Latvian Shipping Co* [2001] 1 Lloyd's Rep. 537, 563; *Proctor & Gamble Ltd v Carrier Holdings Ltd* [2003] EWHC 83 (TCC), [2003] B.L.R. 255 at [35]; *Berkeley Community Villages Ltd v Pullen* [2007] EWHC 1330 (Ch), [2007] All E.R. (D) 36 (Jun) at [79].

[144] For a criticism of this expression, see *Bradley v H. Newsom Sons & Co* [1919] A.C. 16, 53; Dawson [1981] C.L.J. 83; Mustill, *Butterworth Lectures*, 1989–1990, p.1.

[145] See above, para.24–013.

[146] In *Berkeley Community Villages Ltd v Pullen* [2007] EWHC 1330 (Ch), [2007] All E.R. (D) 36 (Jun) at [83] Morgan J. left open the question whether, in the case where a claimant wishes not to bring the contract to an end, it is appropriate to grant an injunction to restrain a sale because it amounts to an anticipatory breach of a contingent future obligation.

[147] Not all anticipatory breaches are of a continuing nature: see, for example, *Howard v Pickford Tool Co Ltd* [1951] 1 K.B. 417.

[148] *Stocznia Gdanska SA v Latvian Shipping Co* [2002] EWCA Civ 889, [2002] 2 Lloyd's Rep. 436 at [94]–[100].

[149] (1853) 2 E. & B. 678; *Xenos v Danube, etc., Ry* (1863) 13 C.B.(N.S.) 825; *Frost v Knight* (1872) L.R. 7 Ex. 111; *Dominion Coal Co Ltd v Dominion Iron and Steel Co Ltd* (1909) 25 T.L.R. 309; *The Mihalis Angelos* [1971] 1 Q.B. 164.

[150] (1886) 16 QBD 460. For the measure of damages, see *Roper v Johnson* (1873) L.R. 8 C.P. 167; *Melachrino v Nickoll and Knight* [1920] 1 K.B. 693; *Millett v Van Heek & Co* [1921] 2 K.B. 369; *Wright v Dean* [1948] Ch. 686; *Sudan Import Co Ltd v Société Génerale de Compensation* [1958] 1 Lloyd's Rep. 310; *Garnac Grain Co Inc v H.M.F. Faure and Fairclough Ltd* [1966] 1 Q.B. 650 (on appeal [1968] A.C. 1130); *The Mihalis Angelos* [1971] 1 Q.B. 164; *Tai Hing Cotton Mill Ltd v Kamsing Knitting Factory* [1979] A.C. 91; *Chiemgauer Membran und Zeltbau GmbH v The New Millennium Experience Co Ltd*, *The Times*, January 16, 2001; and Vol.II, paras 43–412 et seq. and 43–425 et seq.

> an action upon it for the damages sustained by him in consequence of such renunciation."[151]

It is nevertheless clear that, in cases of anticipatory breach by renunciation of the contract, the cause of action is not the future breach; it is the renunciation itself.[152] The doctrine is not based on the fiction that the eventual cause of action may, in anticipation, be treated as a cause of action.[153] So, if the anticipatory breach is accepted as a discharge of the contract, it is not open to the party in breach subsequently to tender performance within the time originally fixed.[154] Further, the innocent party can claim damages at once even though his right to future performance of the contract is then only contingent.[155]

24–023 If the breach is accepted, the innocent party is relieved from further performance of his obligations under the contract. He is likewise relieved from proving, in any action against the party in default, that he was ready and willing at the date of the renunciation to perform the contract in accordance with its terms.[156] It follows that it is no defence to liability in such an action to show that, if the contract had not been renounced, the innocent party would not at the time fixed for performance have been able to perform it,[157] although proof of such inability to perform might possibly be material in the assessment of damages.[158]

---

[151] (1886) 16 QBD 460, 467. The proposition that a renunciation of the contract before the time for performance has arrived does not amount to a breach until it has been acted upon or adopted has been criticised on the ground that it is inconsistent with *Hochster v De la Tour* (1853) 2 E. & B. 678 and because whether or not there is a breach must depend on what the promisor does and not on what the promisee does thereafter: see Smith, "Anticipatory Breach of Contract" in Lomnicka and Morse (eds), *Contemporary Issues in Commercial Law: Essays in Honour of A.G. Guest*, pp.175, 178–182.

[152] *The Mihalis Angelos* [1971] 1 Q.B. 164; *Moschi v Lep Air Services Ltd* [1973] A.C. 331, 356.

[153] cf. *Frost v Knight* (1872) L.R. 7 Ex. 111, 114.

[154] *Xenos v Danube, etc., Ry* (1863) 13 C.B.(N.S.) 825.

[155] *Frost v Knight* (1872) L.R. 7 Ex. 111; *Synge v Synge* [1894] 1 Q.B. 466. Damages will generally, but not inevitably, be assessed at the date of the breach of contract. Exceptionally, damages may be reduced where subsequent events, known to the court at the time of the hearing, have reduced the value of the contractual rights in respect of which the claim has been brought: *Golden Strait Corp v Nippon Yusen Kubishika Kaisha (The Golden Victory)* [2007] UKHL 12, [2007] 2 W.L.R. 691. See further below, para.26–064.

[156] *Braithwaite v Foreign Hardwood Co Ltd* [1905] 2 K.B. 543, 551, 554; *Cooper, Ewing & Co Ltd v Hamel and Horley Ltd* (1922) 13 Ll. L. Rep. 466, 590, 593; *Taylor v Oakes Roncoroni & Co* (1922) 38 T.L.R. 349, 517; *British and Beningtons Ltd v North Western Cachar Tea Co Ltd* [1923] A.C. 48, 66; *Continental Contractors Ltd v Medway Oil and Storage Co Ltd* (1925) 23 Ll. L. Rep. 55, 124, 128, 132; *Rightside Property Ltd v Gray* [1975] Ch. 72, 82; *Gill & Duffus SA v Berger & Co Inc* [1984] A.C. 382, 395–396; *Chiemgauer Membran und Zeltbau GmbH v The New Millennium Experience Co Ltd, The Times*, January 16, 2001; *Marplace (Number 512) Ltd v Chaffe Street (A Firm)* [2006] EWHC 1919, [2006] All E.R. (D) 413 (Jul) at [321]. cf. Dawson (1980) 96 L.Q.R. 239. See also Lloyd (1974) 37 M.L.R. 121.

[157] *Aliter*, if at the time of the renunciation, there was already a breach of contract (albeit unknown) on the part of the innocent party: *Cooper, Ewing & Co Ltd v Hamel and Horley Ltd* (1922) 13 Ll. L. Rep. 466; *British and Beningtons Ltd v North Western Cachar Tea Co Ltd* [1923] A.C. 48, 72. cf. *Gill & Duffus SA v Berger & Co Inc* [1984] A.C. 382. See also above, para.24–014.

[158] *Braithwaite v Foreign Hardwood Co Ltd* [1905] 2 K.B. 543, 552; *Taylor v Oakes Roncoroni & Co* (1922) 38 T.L.R. 349; *British and Beningtons Ltd v North Western Cachar Tea Co Ltd* [1923] A.C. 48, 71, 72; *Continental Contractors Ltd v Medway Oil and Storage Co Ltd* (1925) 23 Ll. L. Rep. 55, 132, 133; *Esmail v Rosenthal & Sons Ltd* [1964] 2 Lloyd's Rep. 447, 466; [1965] 1 W.L.R. 1117; *The*

Breach not accepted. The second alternative[159] is illustrated by *Avery v Bowden*.[160] In that case there was a contract by charterparty that a ship should sail to Odessa and there take a cargo from the charterer's agent, the cargo to be loaded within a certain number of days. The ship arrived at Odessa and the master demanded a cargo, but the charterer's agent was unable to supply one. The master nevertheless continued to demand a cargo. Before the loading days had expired war broke out between England and Russia and performance became legally impossible. When the charterer was sued for breach of the charterparty, the defence was sustained that there had been no failure of performance before war broke out. Even, however, if the agent's conduct had amounted to an anticipatory renunciation of the contract, so that the shipowner would have been entitled to accept it and claim damages at once, he had lost the right to do so by electing to keep the contract alive, and it continued in force until it was discharged by frustration. In other words, if the second alternative is chosen, the contract subsists at the risk of both parties, and the anticipatory renunciation is ineffective. This is well expressed by Cotton L.J. in *Johnstone v Milling* where he says[161]: 24–024

> "The promisee, if he pleases, may treat the notice of intention as inoperative, and await the time when the contract is to be executed, and then hold the other party responsible for all the consequences of non-performance; but in that case he keeps the contract alive for the benefit of the other party as well as his own; he remains subject to all the obligations and liabilities under it, and enables the other party not only to complete the contract, if so advised, notwithstanding his previous repudiation of it, but also to take advantage of any supervening circumstances which would justify him in declining to complete it."

Thus in *Fercometal Sarl v Mediterranean Shipping Co SA*,[162] a voyage charterparty contained a clause entitling the charterers to cancel the charter should the vessel not be ready to load on or before July 9, 1982. Prior to that date the charterers prematurely purported to cancel it. This constituted an anticipatory breach and repudiation of the contract. The repudiation was not accepted by the shipowners. Nevertheless the nominated vessel was not ready to load by the due date and the charterers then sent a second notice cancelling the charter. The House of Lords held that the shipowners, by affirming the contract, had kept it alive for the benefit of both parties, so that the charterers were entitled, notwithstanding their previous repudiation, to cancel on the ground of the vessel's non-readiness to load in accordance with the terms of the charterparty. Also in *Segap* 24–025

Mihalis Angelos [1971] 1 Q.B. 164; *Gill & Duffus SA v Berger & Co Inc* [1984] A.C. 382, 392, 396, 397; *Chiemgauer Membran und Zeltbau GmbH v The New Millennium Experience Co Ltd*, *The Times*, January 16, 2001. In *Singh v Sardar Investments Ltd* [2002] EWHC 380 (Ch) Patten J. stated (at [60]) that it was not necessary for him to express any views about the correctness or otherwise of the decision in *Chiemgauer*.

[159] *Michael v Hart & Co* [1902] 1 K.B. 482; *Braithwaite v Foreign Hardwood Co Ltd* [1905] 2 K.B. 543; *Sinason-Teicher Inter-American Grain Corp v Oilcakes and Oilseeds Trading Co Ltd* [1954] 1 W.L.R. 935, 944; affirmed, 1394.

[160] (1855) 5 E. & B. 714; (1856) 6 E. & B. 953.

[161] (1886) 16 QBD 470.

[162] [1989] A.C. 788.

Garages Ltd v Gulf Oil (Great Britain) Ltd,[163] the defendants, in breach of contract, failed to supply motor fuel to the plaintiffs. This would have entitled the plaintiffs, had they chosen to do so, to treat the contract as repudiated, but they elected to treat it as still continuing. The plaintiffs nevertheless refused to pay for motor fuel already supplied. This refusal, under the terms of the contract, entitled the defendants to terminate the contract and they did so terminate it. The Court of Appeal held that the plaintiffs could recover damages in respect of non-delivery of motor fuel prior to the termination, but not in respect of the period following termination. By electing not to accept the defendants' repudiation, the plaintiffs had kept the contract alive for the benefit of both parties.

24–026 **Anticipatory breach and actual breach.** When establishing whether or not there has been a renunciation of the contract, there is no distinction between the tests for what is an anticipatory breach and what is a breach after the time for performance has arrived.[164] It follows, therefore, that where the conduct of the promisor is such as to lead a reasonable person to the conclusion that he does not intend to fulfil his obligations under the contract when the time for performance arrives, the promisee may treat this as a renunciation of the contract and sue for damages forthwith. The innocent party is not obliged to wait for the time for performance because the renunciation, coupled with the acceptance of that renunciation, renders the breach legally inevitable and the effect of the doctrine of anticipatory breach is precisely to enable the innocent party to anticipate an inevitable breach and to commence proceedings immediately.[165]

24–027 **Renunciation in the course of performance.** The law is similar where a party renounces a contract in the course of its performance, as, for instance, where the subject-matter is a sale of goods to be delivered by instalments. Thus, where the purchaser, after accepting some, refuses to take any more of the goods concerned, the vendor may sue him for damages at once without manufacturing and tendering the remainder.[166]

3. IMPOSSIBILITY CREATED BY ONE PARTY

24–028 **Impossibility.** Where one party has, by his own act or default,[167] disabled himself from performing his contractual obligations in some essential respect, the

[163] *The Times*, October 24, 1988 CA.

[164] *Thorpe v Fasey* [1949] Ch. 649, 661; *Universal Cargo Carriers Corp v Citati* [1957] 2 Q.B. 401, 438. The distinction between an anticipatory breach and an actual breach may have significant implications for limitation purposes: *Proctor & Gamble Ltd v Carrier Holdings Ltd* [2003] EWHC 83 (TCC), [2003] B.L.R. 255.

[165] *Universal Cargo Carriers Corp v Citati* [1957] 2 Q.B. 401, 438. The position is otherwise where the mode of anticipatory breach in issue is impossibility created by the act or default of one party. In such a case it is much more difficult to establish that the breach is inevitable, a point which was recognised by Devlin J. in *Citati* at 437. These difficulties are discussed below, para.24–029.

[166] *Withers v Reynolds* (1831) 2 B. & Ad. 882; *Cort v Ambergate, etc., Ry* (1851) 17 Q.B. 127.

[167] See also above, paras 23–059—23–062.

other party will be entitled to treat himself as discharged.[168] The inability to perform his contractual obligations must be established on the balance of probabilities and the fact that a party has:

> "... entered into inconsistent obligations does not in itself necessarily establish such inability, unless these obligations are of such a nature or have such an effect that it can truly be said that the party in question has put it out of his power to perform his obligations."[169]

The inability to perform need not be due to a deliberate act:

> "A party is deemed to have incapacitated himself from performing his side of the contract, not only when he deliberately puts it out of his power to perform the contract, but also when by his own act or default circumstances arise which render him unable to perform his side of the contract or some essential part thereof."[170]

So, where a person undertook to transfer certain furniture, but before he could do so a judgment creditor took the furniture in execution and sold it, his inability to perform, though not due to his own deliberate act, constituted a breach of the agreement.[171] However, where part only of one party's obligations are rendered impossible of performance, the other party will not be able to treat himself as discharged unless the resulting non-performance would amount to a breach of condition[172] or would deprive him of substantially the whole benefit of the contract.[173]

Impossibility and renunciation. In most cases where the impossibility created by one party has manifested itself by conduct, the innocent party will rely upon renunciation by conduct rather than impossibility, because renunciation is so much easier to establish.[174] Renunciation is to be preferred because the innocent party need only show that the conduct of the party in default was such as to lead a reasonable man to believe that he did not intend, or was not able, to perform his promise; whereas if the innocent party relies upon impossibility he must show that the contract was *in fact* impossible of performance due to the other party's default.[175] Nevertheless the innocent party would be well advised to 24–029

---

[168] *Sir Anthony Main's Case* (1596) 5 Co.Rep. 21a; *Bodwell v Parsons* (1808) 10 East 359; *Amory v Brodrick* (1822) 5 B. & A. 712; *Short v Stone* (1846) 8 Q.B. 358; *Caines v Smith* (1846) 15 M. & W. 189; *O'Neil v Armstrong* [1895] 2 Q.B. 418; *Ogdens Ltd v Nelson* [1905] A.C. 109; *Measures Bros Ltd v Measures* [1910] 2 Ch. 248; *British and Beningtons Ltd v North Western Cachar Tea Co Ltd* [1923] A.C. 48, 72. See also the cases cited in para.24–030 fn.178, below.

[169] *Alfred C. Toepfer International GmbH v Itex Itagrani Export SA* [1973] 1 Lloyd's Rep. 360, 362.

[170] Smith, *Leading Cases*, 13th edn (1929), Vol.II. p.40, cited by Devlin J. in *Universal Cargo Carriers Corp v Citati* [1957] 2 Q.B. 401, 441.

[171] *Keys v Harwood* (1846) 2 C.B. 905; *Powell v Marshall, Parkes & Co* [1899] 1 Q.B. 710 (bankruptcy); cf. *Re Agra Bank* (1867) L.R. 5 Eq. 160; *Jennings' Trustees v King* [1952] Ch. 899.

[172] See above, para.12–025; below, para.24–039.

[173] *Afovos Shipping Co SA v Pagnan & Filli* [1983] 1 W.L.R. 195, 203; see below, para.24–040.

[174] *Universal Cargo Carriers Corp v Citati* [1957] 2 Q.B. 401, 437; *Sanko S.S. Co Ltd v Eacom Timber Sales Ltd* [1987] 1 Lloyd's Rep. 487, 492.

[175] See below, para.24–030 fn.180.

rely on both grounds for treating the contract as at an end, because: (1) renunciation may not, for some reason,[176] be open to him; and (2) if he has misinterpreted the conduct of the other party and so rescinded for an inadequate reason he may still fall back on impossibility if it should subsequently appear that the other party was in fact incapable of performing his promise.[177]

24–030 **Anticipatory breach.** Anticipatory breach of contract may be constituted by impossibility as well as by renunciation, and similar principles apply to both. So where a shipowner agreed to charter a ship upon her release from government service, but before the release sold her to another person, it was held that he had put it out of his power to perform the agreement and the charterer was entitled to sue for damages forthwith. It was argued for the shipowner that he might have bought back the ship in time to fulfil the contract, but this was regarded as too speculative a possibility.[178] Also in *Universal Cargo Carriers Corp v Citati*,[179] where a charterer of a ship agreed to nominate a berth, to provide a cargo, and to finish loading, all before a certain day, and three days before this day had failed to do any of these things, it was held that the shipowner would be entitled to treat this default as an anticipatory breach of contract if it could prove that the charterer would not have been able to perform its obligations under the charter-party before the point in time at which the delay would have frustrated the commercial object of the venture. In this case it was held that it would not be sufficient for the innocent party to show that he had reasonable grounds for believing that the other party would be unable to perform at the appointed time; he would only be justified in treating himself as discharged if the other party was in fact unable to perform at that time: "[a]n anticipatory breach must be proved in fact and not in supposition".[180]

24–031 **No anticipation of express right to terminate.** Where it is alleged that one party has, by his own act or default, disabled himself from performing his contractual obligations at some future time and the contract also contains an express provision giving to the innocent party the right to terminate the contract in certain circumstances, care must be taken to establish the basis upon which the innocent party seeks to terminate the contract. Where the basis for the decision to terminate is the express right to determine the contract, the requirements of the

---

[176] *Universal Cargo Carriers Corp v Citati* [1957] 2 Q.B. 401, where Devlin J. held that the erroneous finding of the arbitrator created such a stituation (but see [1958] 2 Q.B. 254).

[177] *British & Beningtons Ltd v N.W. Cachar Tea Co* [1923] A.C. 48, 70; *Universal Cargo Carriers Corp v Citati* [1957] 2 Q.B. 401, 443.

[178] *Omnium D'Enterprises v Sutherland* [1919] 1 K.B. 618; *Lovelock v Franklyn* (1846) 8 Q.B. 371; *Synge v Synge* [1894] 1 Q.B. 466; *Guy-Pell v Foster* [1930] 2 Ch. 169; cf. *Alfred C. Toepfer International GmbH v Itex Itagrani Export SA* [1993] 1 Lloyd's Rep. 360, 362.

[179] [1957] 2 Q.B. 401; affirmed in part [1957] 1 W.L.R. 979 and reversed in part [1958] 2 Q.B. 254. cf. *Hongkong Fir Shipping Co Ltd v Kawasaki Kisen Kaisha Ltd* [1962] 2 Q.B. 26; *Trade and Transport Inc v Iino Kaiun Kaisha Ltd* [1973] 1 W.L.R. 210; *F. C. Shepherd & Co Ltd v Jerrom* [1987] Q.B. 301, 323, 327–328; Treitel, *Law of Contract*, 12th edn (by Peel, 2007), para.17–076.

[180] [1957] 2 Q.B. 401, 449–450; *Re Simoco Digital UK Ltd: Thunderbird Industries LLC v Simoco Digital UK Ltd* [2004] EWHC 209 (Ch), [2004] 1 B.C.L.C. 541 at [22]–[23]. But see *Embiricos v Sydney Reid & Co* [1914] 3 K.B. 45, 59 (frustration); *Hongkong Fir Shipping Co Ltd v Kawasaki Kisen Kaisha Ltd* [1962] 2 Q.B. 26, 57 (failure of performance); Treitel at paras 17–084—17–087; Carter (1984) 47 M.L.R. 422.

clause containing the right to terminate must be complied with. On the other hand, where reliance is placed on the inability of the party to perform his obligations under the contract at some future time, it must be demonstrated that the inability to perform relates to some essential aspect of the obligations of the party in breach. To be entitled to terminate, the innocent party must establish that he had a right to terminate on one or other ground. Where he can establish neither ground, he cannot justify his decision to terminate by combining the two grounds so as to apply the doctrine of anticipatory breach to the contractual right to terminate. It is not possible to anticipate a contractual right to terminate.[181] Either the conditions necessary to exercise the right have been satisfied or they have not.

Co-operation and prevention of performance. It has been noted that the court will readily imply a term that each will co-operate with the other to secure performance of the contract[182] and that neither party will, by his own act or default, prevent performance of the contract.[183] If one party is in breach of his duty to co-operate, so that performance of the contract cannot be effected, the other party will be entitled to treat himself as discharged.[184] It has also been said to be a general principle of law that, where performance of a condition precedent[185] is prevented by the act or default of one party, the contract is taken to have been duly performed by the other even though the condition has not been satisfied.[186] Thus, in *Mackay v Dick*[187] where a contract of sale of goods was subject to a condition precedent to be performed by the buyer, but which he neglected to perform, the seller was held entitled to sue for the price. This principle, however, is by no means always applicable,[188] and the party not in default may be compelled to treat the prevention of performance as a repudiation of the contract and to sue for damages for the breach. 24–032

Impossibility and frustration. Similar tests have been applied to determine whether or not a contract has become impossible of performance by reason of the 24–033

---

[181] *Afovos Shipping Co SA v Pagnan & Filli* [1983] 1 W.L.R. 195. This, it is suggested, is the correct interpretation of Lord Diplock's statement (at 203) that the doctrine of anticipatory breach by conduct which disables a party to a contract from performing one of his primary obligations under the contract has no application to a breach of punctual payment of hire clause in a time charterparty of a ship. In so far as Lord Diplock suggested that the doctrine of anticipatory breach applies only to fundamental breaches, his reasoning cannot be supported: see Treitel at para.17–083 and Carter, *Breach of Contract*, 2nd edn (1991), paras 744A and 744B.

[182] See above, para.13–011.

[183] See above, para.13–012.

[184] *Kyprianou v Cyprus Textiles Ltd* [1958] 2 Lloyd's Rep. 60; *Metro Meat Ltd v Fares Rural Co Pty Ltd* [1985] 2 Lloyd's Rep. 13. Contrast *Bremer Vulkan Schiffbau und Maschinenfabrik v South India Shipping Corp Ltd* [1981] A.C. 909 (both parties in breach of duty); *Dymocks Franchise Systems (N.S.W.) Pty Ltd v Todd* [2002] UKPC 50, [2002] 2 All E.R. (Comm) 849 at [62]–[63]. The inference that a refusal to co-operate is repudiatory will more readily be drawn in the case of a long-term contract which requires a greater degree of mutual co-operation between the parties.

[185] See above, para.12–028.

[186] *Hotham v East India Co* (1787) 1 Term Rep. 638, 645; *Smith v Wilson* (1807) 8 East 437, 443; *Thomas v Fredricks* (1847) 10 Q.B. 775; *Mackay v Dick* (1881) 6 App. Cas. 251; *Kleinert v Abosso Gold Mining Co Ltd* (1913) 58 S.J.(P.C.) 45.

[187] (1881) 6 App. Cas. 251.

[188] *Colley v Overseas Exporters* [1921] 3 K.B. 302; *Luxor (Eastbourne) Ltd v Cooper* [1941] A.C. 108. See also *Benjamin's Sale of Goods*, 7th edn (2006), para.16–023; Vol.II, para.31–148.

default of one party as have been applied to determine whether there has been a mutual discharge of the contract by reason of the doctrine of frustration.[189]

4. FAILURE OF PERFORMANCE

24–034 **Failure of performance.** Failure of performance, whether total or partial, may in certain circumstances entitle the other party to the contract to treat the contract as discharged. But this is not necessarily the case, and difficult questions of fact and law may arise.

24–035 **Relation of the promises.** In the first place, it is necessary to discover the relation to one another of the promises which form the contract. They may be either independent or dependent.[190] Promises are said to be independent when the obligation of one party is absolute and not conditional upon the performance by the other of his part of the bargain. They are said to be dependent when the obligation of one party depends upon the performance, or the readiness and willingness to perform, of the other[191]:

> "The question whether covenants are to be held dependent or independent of each other, is to be determined by the intention and meaning of the parties as it appears on the instrument, and by the application of common sense to each particular case; to which intention, when once discovered, all technical forms of expression must give way."[192]

24–036 **Independent mutual promises.** In the exceptional case of independent mutual promises, each party has his remedy on the promise made in his favour without performing his part of the contract[193] and conversely neither party can claim to be discharged from liability on the contract by reason of the failure of the other to perform his part. Thus in *Fearon v Earl of Aylesford*,[194] an action on a separation deed, it was said that a husband would be bound to perform a covenant to pay money to a trustee for his wife, even though the wife might have broken a covenant in the same deed not to molest her husband. But the tendency of the courts is against construing contracts as containing two independent promises. So, in *General Billposting Co Ltd v Atkinson*,[195] it was held that a man

---

[189] *Trade and Transport Inc v Iino Kaiun Kaisha Ltd* [1973] 1 W.L.R. 210, 221, citing *Davis Contractors Ltd v Fareham U.D.C.* [1956] A.C. 696 (above, para.23–050); *Tsakiroglou & Co Ltd v Noblee Thorl* [1962] A.C. 93 (above, para.23–048) and *The Eugenia* [1964] 2 Q.B. 226 (above, para.23–044). See also below, para.24–046.

[190] *Pordage v Cole* (1669) 1 Wms. Saund. 319; *Guy-Pell v Foster* [1930] 2 Ch. 169.

[191] Cited with approval in *Denmark Productions Ltd v Boscobel Productions Ltd* [1969] 1 Q.B. 699, 733.

[192] *Stavers v Curling* (1836) 3 Bing.N.C. 355, 368. cf. *Ritchie v Atkinson* (1808) 10 East 295, 306; *Huntoon Co v Kolynos* [1930] 1 Ch. 528, 558, 559 (where the test is stated in the same terms as the distinction between a condition and a warranty: see below, para.24–038).

[193] *Pordage v Cole* (1669) 1 Wms. Saund. 319, 320.

[194] (1884) 14 QBD 792, 800.

[195] [1909] A.C. 118. In *Rock Refrigeration Ltd v Jones* [1997] 1 All E.R. 1, 18–20 Phillips L.J. questioned the correctness of *General Billposting*, but the majority of the Court of Appeal were prepared to assume that it had been correctly decided. See further below, para.24–048 fn.262.

who had been wrongfully dismissed from his employment was no longer bound by a restrictive covenant contained in his contract of employment as his employers by their action had repudiated the contract. Similarly it has been held that mutual covenants as to draining land by adjoining owners were dependent on each other and not independent promises.[196] On the other hand, it has long been established that a tenant's covenant to pay rent is independent of the landlord's covenant to repair the premises; the tenant is not discharged from his obligation to pay rent merely because his landlord is unwilling to fulfil his obligation.[197] Also in contracts of apprenticeship the covenants of the master and apprentice are normally independent of each other.[198]

Dependent promises. Assuming that the promises are not independent, the question then arises whether it is any failure by one party to perform a dependent promise which entitles the other to treat himself as discharged from further performance. In historical terms, the right of discharge was said to turn upon the non-performance of a "condition precedent" in the contract.[199] Performance by one party of his promise or "covenant" was regarded as a condition precedent to the liability of the other. However, following the case of *Boone v Eyre*[200] in 1777, it was recognised that precise fulfilment of every promise was not necessarily a condition precedent, and Lord Mansfield said[201]: 24–037

> "Where mutual covenants go to the whole of the consideration on both sides, they are mutual conditions, the one precedent to the other. But where they go only to a part, where a breach may be paid for in damages, there the defendant has a remedy on his covenant, and shall not plead it as a condition precedent."

Thus, where one party failed to perform a promise which went to the whole of the consideration, the other party was released from performance as the former had not performed that which was a condition precedent to the latter's liability.[202] For example, in *Cutter v Powell*,[203] where a seaman undertook to serve as mate on a voyage for an enhanced sum to be paid in a single payment on completion of the voyage and died before that time, his wife was unable to recover quantum meruit for work done during that part of the voyage that he lived and served. The seaman's continuing to do his duty as mate during the whole voyage was a condition precedent to his recovering the stipulated sum. On the other hand, where the failure of performance went to part only of the consideration or, as it was later expressed,[204] did not go to the "root" or substantial consideration, the

[196] *Kidner v Stimpson* (1918) 35 T.L.R. 63.

[197] *Taylor v Webb* [1937] 2 K.B. 283 (but see *Regis Property Co Ltd v Dudley* [1959] A.C. 370).

[198] *Winstone v Linn* (1823) 1 B. & C. 460; cf. *Ellen v Topp* (1851) 6 Exch. 424.

[199] See *Pordage v Cole* (1669) 1 Wms. Saund. 319; *Kingston v Preston* (1773) 2 Doug. 689, 691; *Hongkong Fir Shipping Co Ltd v Kawasaki Kisen Kaisha* [1962] 2 Q.B. 26, 65; *Cehave N.V. v Bremer Handelsgesellschaft* [1976] Q.B. 44, 57, 72; *United Scientific Holdings Ltd v Burnley BC* [1978] A.C. 904, 927; *Hurst v Bryk* [2002] 1 A.C. 185, 193; Dawson [1981] C.L.J. 83, 87.

[200] (1777) 1 Hy. Bl. 273.

[201] (1777) 1 Hy. Bl. 273, 273n.

[202] e.g. *Smith v Wilson* (1807) 8 East. 437.

[203] (1795) 6 Term Rep. 320; see above, para.21–030; below, para.24–043.

[204] *Mersey Steel and Iron Co Ltd v Naylor, Benzon & Co* (1884) 9 App. Cas. 434, 444.

breach did not entitle the innocent party to be discharged from further liability, but to claim damages only. Further there were terms or "warranties", collateral to the main purpose of the contract, the breach of which did not relieve him from liability to perform.[205]

24–038 **Conditions and warranties.** By the end of the nineteenth century, there emerged a strong tendency to classify the terms of a contract as being either *conditions* (any breach of which entitled the innocent party to refuse further performance and treat himself as discharged) or *warranties* (which merely gave him a right to damages). In the Sale of Goods Act 1893, for example, certain implied stipulations were assigned to one or other category by statute.[206] Others were so assigned by virtue of judicial decisions.[207] Numerous cases turned on the question whether or not a particular statement or promise amounted to a condition. In one of these, *Bettini v Gye*,[208] Blackburn J. stated that, in the absence of an express declaration of intention by the parties, the test was:

> "... whether the particular stipulation goes to the root of the matter, so that failure to perform it would render the performance of the rest of the contract a thing different in substance from what the defendant had stipulated for."[209]

And in another case[210] Bowen L.J. remarked:

> "... it is often very difficult to decide ... whether a representation which contains a promise ... amounts to a condition precedent, or is only a warranty. There is no way of deciding this question except by looking at the contract in the light of the surrounding circumstances";

but he suggested that:

> "... in order to decide this question of construction, one of the first things you would look to is, to what extent the accuracy of the statement—the truth of what is promised—would be likely to affect the substance and foundation of the adventure which the contract is intended to carry out."

Such statements as these would suggest that, at that time, the basis for classifying a term as a condition depended on whether its breach would substantially defeat the purpose of the contract.

24–039 **Failure of performance: breach of condition.** The classification of contractual terms has been dealt with in an earlier chapter in this work.[211] It was there noted that, in the modern law, a term of a contract may be held to be a condition if it has been so categorised by statute or by judicial decision, or if the

[205] Sale of Goods Act 1979 ss.11(3), 61(1); Chalmers, *Sale of Goods*, 2nd edn (1981) p.164; 18th edn, p.373; above, para.12–031.
[206] Sale of Goods Act 1893 ss.12–15.
[207] See above, para.12–035.
[208] (1876) 1 QBD 183.
[209] (1876) 1 QBD 183, 188, citing Parke B. in *Graves v Legg* (1854) 9 Exch. 709, 716.
[210] *Bentsen v Taylor, Sons & Co* [1893] 2 Q.B. 274, 281.
[211] See above, para.12–019.

parties have so agreed in their contract, whether expressly or by necessary implication.[212] Any failure of performance which constitutes a breach of condition entitles the innocent party to treat himself as discharged from further liability under the contract.[213] The word condition has therefore broken free from its historical roots and can no longer be confined to an obligation which must be performed as a condition precedent to the liability of the other party.

Failure of performance: other situations. Where the failure of performance is not a breach of condition, but of an "intermediate" term,[214] it may still justify the innocent party in treating himself as discharged. But in such a case regard must be had to the nature and consequences of the breach in order to determine whether this right has arisen. A number of expressions have been used to describe the circumstances that warrant discharge, the most common being that the breach must "go to the root of the contract".[215] It has also been said that the breach must "affect the very substance of the contract",[216] or "frustrate the commercial purpose of the venture",[217] and, at the present day, a test which is frequently applied[218] is that stated by Diplock L.J. in *Hongkong Fir Shipping Co Ltd v Kawasaki Kisen Kaisha Ltd*[219]: 24–040

> "Does the occurrence of the event deprive the party who has further undertakings to perform of substantially the whole benefit which it was the intention of the parties as expressed in the contract that he should obtain as the consideration for performing those undertakings?"

---

[212] See above, para.12–040.

[213] See above, para.12–025.

[214] See above, para.12–034.

[215] *Davidson v Gwynne* (1810) 12 East 381, 389; *MacAndrew v Chapple* (1866) L.R. 1 C.P. 643, 648; *Poussard v Spiers* (1876) 1 QBD 410, 414; *Honck v Muller* (1881) 7 QBD 92, 100; *Mersey Steel and Iron Co v Naylor, Benzon & Co* (1884) 9 App. Cas. 434, 443; *Guy-Pell v Foster* [1930] 2 Ch. 169, 187; *Heyman v Darwins Ltd* [1942] A.C. 356, 397; *Suisse Atlantique Société d'Armement Maritime SA v N.V. Rotterdamsche Kolen Centrale* [1967] 1 A.C. 361, 442; *Decro-Wall International SA v Practitioners in Marketing Ltd* [1971] 1 W.L.R. 361, 374; *Cehave N.V. v Bremer Handelsgesellschaft mbH* [1976] Q.B. 44, 60, 73; *Federal Commerce & Navigation Co Ltd v Molena Alpha Inc* [1979] A.C. 757, 779.

[216] *Wallis, Son and Wells v Pratt and Haynes* [1910] 2 K.B. 1003, 1012.

[217] *Tarrabochcia v Hickie* (1856) 1 H. & N. 183; *MacAndrew v Chapple* (1866) L.R. 1 C.P. 643, 647, 648; *Stanton v Richardson* (1872) L.R. 7 C.P. 421, 433, 437; *Jackson v Union Marine Insurance Co* (1874) L.R. 10 C.P. 125, 145, 148; *Inverkip S.S. Co v Bunge* [1917] 2 K.B. 193, 201; *Astley Industrial Trust Ltd v Grimley* [1963] 1 W.L.R. 584, 599; *Trade and Transport Incorporated v Iino Kaiun Kaisha Ltd* [1973] 1 W.L.R. 210, 223.

[218] *Cehave N.V. v Bremer Handelsgesellschaft mbH* [1976] Q.B. 44, 82; *United Scientific Holdings Ltd v Burnley BC* [1978] A.C. 904, 928; *Photo Production Ltd v Securicor Transport Ltd* [1980] A.C. 827, 849; *Nitrate Corp of Chile Ltd v Pansuiza Compania de Navigacion* [1980] 1 Lloyd's Rep. 638 (affirmed [1982] 1 Lloyd's Rep. 570). See also *Freeman v Taylor* (1831) 8 Bing. 124, 138; *MacAndrew v Chapple* (1886) L.R. 1 C.P. 643, 648; *Decro-Wall International SA v Practitioners in Marketing Ltd* [1971] 1 W.L.R. 361, 380; *Federal Commerce & Navigation Co Ltd v Molena Alpha Inc* [1979] A.C. 757, 783; *Gunatunga v DeAlwis* (1996) 72 P. & C.R. 161, 171; *Alfred McAlpine Plc v BAI (Run-off) Ltd* [2000] 1 Lloyd's Rep. 437, 444; *Rubicon Computer Systems Ltd v United Paints Ltd* (2000) 2 T.C.L.R. 453; *Anglo Group Plc v Winther Brown & Co Ltd* (2000) 72 Con. L.R. 118, 160; *Astea (UK) Ltd v Time Group Ltd* [2003] EWHC 725 (TCC), [2003] All E.R. (D) 212 (Apr) [149]; *Northern Foods Plc v Focal Foods Ltd* [2003] 2 Lloyd's Rep. 728, 745.

[219] [1962] 2 Q.B. 26, 66.

In that case, the charterers of a ship sought to establish that they were discharged from further performance of the charterparty because of repeated break-downs of the ship due to the fact that it was unseaworthy. It was argued on their behalf that the obligation to provide a seaworthy vessel was a condition of the contract, any breach of which entitled them to treat the contract as repudiated. This argument was rejected by the Court of Appeal, which held that regard must be had to the consequences of the breach.[220] On the facts, the delays which had already occurred, and the delay which was likely to occur,[221] as a result of unseaworthiness, and the conduct of the shipowners in taking steps to remedy the same, were not, when taken together, such as to deprive the charterers of substantially the whole benefit which it was the intention of the parties they should obtain from further use of the ship under the charterparty. The charterers were therefore not entitled to treat themselves as discharged.

24–041 **Fundamental breach.** The principle of "fundamental breach" or the breach of a "fundamental term" was developed by the courts with a view to limiting the operation of exemption clauses, the rationale being that no party could exclude or restrict his liability for such a breach.[222] As so conceived, a fundamental breach was more far reaching in its effects (a "total breach")[223] than one which would justify discharge.[224] And a fundamental term was something narrower than a condition: it went to the "core" or substance of the contract.[225] However, in *Suisse Atlantique Société d'Armement Maritime SA v N.V. Rotterdamsche Kolen Centrale*,[226] the House of Lords expressed the view that the applicability of exemption clauses to particular breaches of a contract was in reality a rule of construction based on the presumed intention of the parties as expressed in the contract.[227] So far as the expression "fundamental breach" is concerned, Lord Reid said[228]:

> "General use of the term 'fundamental breach' is of recent origin and I can find nothing to indicate that it means more or less than the well-known type of breach which entitles the innocent party to treat it as repudiatory and to rescind the contract."

Accordingly, the expression would seem to be no more than a restatement, in differing terminology, of the principle that a particular breach or breaches may be such as to go to the root of the contract and entitle the other party to treat such

---

220 When considering the consequences of the breach the court may have regard to the cumulative effect of the breaches that have taken place: *Moschi v Lep Air Services Ltd* [1973] A.C. 331, 349; *Anglo Group Plc v Winther Brown & Co Ltd* (2000) 72 Con. L.R. 118, 160; *Rice (t/a Garden Guardian) v Great Yarmouth BC, The Times*, July 26, 2000.

221 Regard is to be had, not only to the actual consequences which have occurred, but also those which it can reasonably be foreseen will occur as a result of the breach: [1962] 2 Q.B. 26, 57, 63.

222 See above, para.14–020.

223 *Suisse Atlantique Société d'Armement Maritime SA v N.V. Rotterdamsche Kolen Centrale* [1967] 1 A.C. 361, 431.

224 See above, paras 14–020—14–021.

225 *Smeaton Hanscomb & Co Ltd v Sassoon I. Setty, Son & Co* [1953] 1 W.L.R. 1468, 1470; see above, para.12–021.

226 [1967] 1 A.C. 361; see above, para.14–021.

227 See above, para.14–021.

228 [1967] 1 A.C. 361, 397. See also 409–410, 421–422, 431.

breach or breaches as a repudiation of the whole contract.[229] Likewise, the expression "fundamental term" appears to mean no more than a condition, i.e. a stipulation which the parties have agreed (expressly or impliedly) to be, or which the general law regards as, a term which goes to the root of the contract so that any breach of that term may at once and without further reference to the facts and circumstances be regarded by the innocent party as justifying discharge.[230] This view that a fundamental breach was no more than a repudiatory breach was confirmed by Lord Diplock in *Photo Production Ltd v Securicor Transport Ltd*.[231] In that case, the House of Lords held that discharge consequent upon a fundamental, i.e. repudiatory, breach does not disentitle the guilty party from relying on an exemption clause in respect of that breach. It is therefore submitted that there is no separate category of "fundamental" breaches, or terms, producing different effects from those already discussed.[232]

Deliberate breach. The question whether or not a failure of performance is deliberate may be a relevant factor,[233] since it may indicate the attitude of the party in default towards future performance and so be evidence of an intent to renounce the contract.[234] But there is no separate category of "deliberate" breaches and Lord Wilberforce has said[235]: 24–042

> "Some deliberate breaches there may be of a minor character which can be appropriately sanctioned by damages. . . . To create a special rule for deliberate acts is unnecessary and may lead astray."

Entire obligations. The rule that the failure of performance must go to the root of the contract to justify discharge suffers an exception when the party in default has undertaken to complete performance of an obligation which is entire and indivisible, and has agreed that this shall be done before his claim to remuneration is due. In such a case, any failure of performance on his part will normally release the innocent party from liability.[236] The innocent party will not be bound to pay anything for the partial performance.[237] But even this exception may to some extent be mitigated by the so-called doctrine of "substantial performance", that is to say, if there is a trivial departure from the exact performance of an entire obligation, the innocent party will not be discharged 24–043

---

229 [1967] 1 A.C. 361, 422. See also *Thompson v Corroon* (1993) 42 W.I.R. 157.

230 [1967] 1 A.C. 361, 422.

231 [1980] A.C. 827, 849; above, para.14–022.

232 See above, paras 12–024, 14–024.

233 *Suisse Atlantique Société d'Armement Maritime SA v N.V. Rotterdamsche Kolen Centrale* [1967] 1 A.C. 361, 394, 414, 415, 429; *Rubicon Computer Systems Ltd v United Paints Ltd* (2000) 2 T.C.L.R. 453. The fact that the breach is "covert" may also be a relevant factor: *Northern Foods Plc v Focal Foods Ltd* [2003] 2 Lloyd's Rep. 728, 747.

234 For the coincidence between renunciation and failure of performance, see *Mersey Steel and Iron Co v Naylor, Benzon & Co* (1884) 9 App. Cas. 434, 441, 444.

235 [1967] 1 A.C. 361, 435.

236 *Ebbw Vale Steel, Iron and Coal Co v Blaina Iron and Tinplate Co* (1901) 6 Com. Cas. 35; *Eshelby v Federated European Bank Ltd* [1932] 1 K.B. 423; *Bolton v Mahadeva* [1972] 1 W.L.R. 1009.

237 See above, paras 21–027—21–038.

from liability under the agreement, although he will be entitled to a set-off or counterclaim for damages.[238]

24–044 **Divisible or severable obligations.** Contracts for the delivery of goods by instalments will more often be construed as containing divisible (or severable) obligations rather than one entire obligation.[239] A breach relating to one or more instalments must be considered in the light of its effect on the contract as a whole, so that the innocent party will not necessarily be entitled to treat the whole contract as repudiated by such a breach.[240] In the absence of an express renunciation of the contract, he will not be so entitled unless the other party's acts or conduct amount to "an intimation of an intention to abandon and altogether to refuse performance of the contract"[241] (that is to say, an implied renunciation)[242] or the failure of performance is such as to go to "the root or essence of the contract".[243] The most relevant factors have been said to be[244]:

> "First, the ratio quantitively which the breach bears to the contract as a whole, and secondly the degree of probability or improbability that such a breach will be repeated."

Thus the further the parties have proceeded with the performance of the contract, the less likely it is that one party will be entitled to claim that the contract has been discharged by a single breach.[245]

24–045 **Stipulations as to time.** The question whether a stipulation as to the time of performance is or is not "of the essence" and a condition of the contract has been considered in previous chapters.[246]

---

238 *H. Dakin & Co Ltd v Lee* [1916] 1 K.B. 566; *Hoenig v Isaacs* [1952] 2 All E.R. 176; *Williams v Roffey Bros & Nicholls (Contractors) Ltd* [1991] 1 Q.B. 1, 8–10. cf. *Vigers v Cook* [1919] 2 K.B. 475; *Eshelby v Federated European Bank Ltd* [1932] 1 K.B. 423; *Bolton v Mahadeva* [1972] 1 W.L.R. 1009. cf. Beck (1975) 38 M.L.R. 413. See also above, paras 21–032—21–033, where the existence of a doctrine of substantial performance is doubted.

239 See *Benjamin's Sale of Goods*, 7th edn (2006), paras 8–064 et seq.

240 Sale of Goods Act 1979 s.31(2); see Vol.II, para.43–293.

241 *Freeth v Burr* (1874) L.R. 9 C.P. 208, 213. See also *Bloomer v Bernstein* (1874) L.R. 9 C.P. 588; *Mersey Steel and Iron Co v Naylor Benzon & Co* (1884) 9 App. Cas. 434; *Dominion Coal Co Ltd v Dominion Iron and Steel Co Ltd* [1909] A.C. 293; *Household Machines v Cosmos Exports* [1947] K.B. 217; *Warinco AG v Samor SpA* [1979] 1 Lloyd's Rep. 450; *Bunge GmbH v C.C.V. Landbouwbelang G.A.* [1980] 1 Lloyd's Rep. 458.

242 See above, para.24–018.

243 *Mersey Steel and Iron Co v Naylor Benzon & Co* (1884) 9 App. Cas. 434, 443–444. See also *Hoare v Rennie* (1859) 5 H. & N. 19; *Jonassohn v Young* (1863) 4 B. & S. 296; *Clarke v Burn* (1866) 14 L.T. 439; *Coddington v Paleologo* (1867) L.R. 2 Ex. 193; *Simpson v Crippin* (1872) L.R. 8 Q.B. 14; *Honck v Muller* (1881) 7 QBD 92; *Millar's Karri and Jarrah Co v Weddel Turner & Co* (1908) 100 L.T. 128; *Taylor v Oakes, Roncoroni & Co* (1922) 127 L.T. 267; *Robert A. Munro Ltd v Meyer* [1930] 2 K.B. 312; *Maple Flock Co Ltd v Universal Furniture Products (Wembley) Ltd* [1934] 1 K.B. 148; *Ross T. Smyth & Co Ltd v T.D. Bailey, Son & Co* [1940] 3 All E.R. 60; *Amos & Wood Ltd v Kaprow* (1948) 64 T.L.R. 110; *Regent OHG Aisenstadt und Barig v Francesco of Jermyn Street* [1981] 3 All E.R. 327.

244 *Maple Flock Co Ltd v Universal Furniture Products (Wembley) Ltd* [1934] 1 K.B. 148, 157. See also *Millars Karri and Jarrah Co v Weddel Turner & Co* (1908) 100 L.T. 128, 129.

245 *Cornwall v Henson* [1900] 2 Ch. 298, 304.

246 See above, paras 12–037, 21–011.

"Frustration by breach" and frustration. Similar language has been used to describe the seriousness of the interference with performance of the contract that must be shown to have occurred to justify a discharge and to bring about a discharge of the contract by frustration.[247] Nevertheless, "frustration by breach" must be distinguished from the doctrine of frustration of a contract referred to in Ch.23.[248] Frustration by breach arises where the failure of performance is due to the act or default of one of the parties, but true frustration will only occur if the frustrating event was not caused by the fault of either party to the contract.[249] Further, where there has been frustration by breach, the innocent party may elect to affirm the contract; but where there is true frustration, the contract is determined automatically, and it cannot be continued by affirmation.[250] 24–046

5. CONSEQUENCES OF DISCHARGE[251]

Effect on contract. It has become usual to speak of the exercise by one party of his right to treat himself as discharged as a "rescission" of the contract. But, as Lord Porter pointed out in *Heymans v Darwins Ltd*[252]: 24–047

> "To say that the contract is rescinded or has come to an end or has ceased to exist may in individual cases convey the truth with sufficient accuracy, but the fuller expression that the injured party is thereby absolved from future performance of his obligations under the contract is a more exact description of the position. Strictly speaking, to say that on acceptance of the renunciation of a contract the contract is rescinded is incorrect."

This statement was unanimously approved by the House of Lords in *Johnson v Agnew*,[253] where Lord Wilberforce emphasised[254] that this so-called "rescission" is quite different from rescission ab initio, such as may arise for example, in cases of mistake, fraud or lack of consent. It has also become usual to speak of the contract as having been "terminated" or "discharged" by the breach. Again, however, these expressions may be somewhat misleading for they might suggest that the contract ceases for all purposes to exist in that event. Such an approach

247 *Jackson v Union Marine Insurance Co Ltd* (1874) L.R. 10 C.P. 125, 145, 147; *Trade and Transport Inc v Iino Kaiun Kaisha Ltd* [1973] 1 W.L.R. 210, 221; *Nitrate Corp of Chile Ltd v Pansuiza Compania de Navegacion SA* [1980] 1 Lloyd's Rep. 638, 648; affirmed sub nom. *Chilean Nitrate Sale & Corp v Marine Transportation Co Ltd* [1982] 1 Lloyd's Rep. 570.

248 See above, paras 23–001 et seq.

249 See above, paras 23–059—23–063. For consideration of "mixed causes", see *Nitrate Corp of Chile Ltd v Pansuiza Compania de Navegacion SA* [1980] 1 Lloyd's Rep. 638, 649.

250 *Hirji Mulji v Cheong Yue S.S. Co Ltd* [1926] A.C. 497, 509. cf. *B.P. Exploration Co (Libya) Ltd v Hunt (No.2)* [1979] 1 W.L.R. 783; affirmed [1983] 2 A.C. 352 (waiver).

251 See Shea (1979) 42 M.L.R. 623; Beatson (1981) 97 L.Q.R. 389; Rose (1981) 34 C.L.P. 235.

252 [1942] A.C. 356, 399.

253 [1980] A.C. 367. See also *Bank of Boston Connecticut v European Grain and Shipping Ltd* [1989] A.C. 1056, 1098–1099.

254 [1980] A.C. 367, 393.

was indeed adopted by the Court of Appeal in *Harbutt's "Plasticine" Ltd v Wayne Tank and Pump Co Ltd*[255] so as to prevent the party in default from relying on an exemption clause inserted in a contract which had been "terminated" by breach. But this case was overruled by the House of Lords in *Photo Production Ltd v Securicor Transport Ltd*.[256] The true position was there stated to be—where the innocent party elects to terminate the contract, i.e. to put an end to all primary obligations of both parties remaining unperformed—that:

> "(a) there is substituted by implication of law for the primary obligations of the party in default which remain unperformed a secondary obligation to pay money compensation to the other party for the loss sustained by him in consequence of their non-performance in the future and (b) the unperformed primary obligations of that other party are discharged."[257]

24–048 Of course, in assessing damages, the court must have regard to the terms of the contract in order to ascertain the performance promised in it,[258] including performance which would have fallen due after the date of discharge.[259] It must also give effect to terms of the contract which, for example, liquidate the damages recoverable[260] or exclude or restrict the remedies otherwise available for breach.[261] But, from the time of discharge, as a general rule both parties are excused from further performance of the primary obligations of the contract which each has still to perform. However, obligations for the resolution of disputes will remain in full force and effect,[262] "as may other clauses having a contractual function which is ancillary or collateral to the subject-matter of the

---

[255] [1970] 1 Q.B. 447.

[256] [1980] A.C. 827; see above, para.14–022.

[257] [1980] A.C. 827, 849, per Lord Diplock. See also *Moschi v Lep Air Services Ltd* [1973] A.C. 331, 345, 350, 351; *Thompson v Corroon* (1993) 42 W.I.R. 157, 172–173.

[258] *Heyman v Darwins Ltd* [1942] A.C. 356, 373; *F.J. Bloemen Pty Ltd v Council of the City of the Gold Coast* [1973] A.C. 115.

[259] *O'Neil v Armstrong, Mitchell & Co* [1895] 2 Q.B. 418; *Moschi v Lep Air Services Ltd* [1973] A.C. 331; *The Mihalis Angelos* [1971] 1 Q.B. 164. In particular, damages may be reduced where, subsequent events, known to the court at the time of the hearing, have reduced the value of the contractual rights in respect of which the claim has been brought: *Golden Strait Corp v Nippon Yusen Kubishika Kaisha (The Golden Victory)* [2007] UKHL 12, [2007] 2 W.L.R. 691. See above, para.22–022.

[260] See below, para.26–125.

[261] See above, para.14–022.

[262] *Port Jackson Stevedoring Pty Ltd v Salmond and Spraggon (Australia) Pty Ltd* [1981] 1 W.L.R. 138, 145. However, a restrictive covenant in a contract of employment will not generally survive where it is the employer who has repudiated the contract: *General Billposting Co Ltd v Atkinson* [1909] A.C. 118, above, para.16–101, although the correctness of this proposition has recently been questioned by Phillips L.J. in *Rock Refrigeration Ltd v Jones* [1997] 1 All E.R. 1, 18–20 on the basis that "the law in relation to the discharge of contractual obligations by acceptance of a repudiation has been developed and clarified" since *General Billposting* was decided. The employer may, however, be able to protect his property and trade secrets on the basis that his rights of property will survive the termination of the contract as a result of the employee's acceptance of his repudiatory breach (*Rock Refrigeration Ltd v Jones* [1997] 1 All E.R. 1, 14 and (on rather wider grounds) 20). The underlying uncertainty in this area relates to the scope of the decision of the House of Lords in *General Billposting,* on which see Freedland (2003) 32 I.L.J. 48.

contract".[263] Arbitration clauses which state without qualification that any difference or dispute which may arise under the contract shall be referred to arbitration will continue to apply notwithstanding the discharge.[264] Ultimately, it is a question of construction whether or not the parties intended the contractual obligation in question to survive the termination of the contract.[265] Moreover, in principle, only those primary obligations falling due after the date of discharge will come to an end; those which have accrued due at the time may still be enforceable as such.[266] Thus, while both parties are discharged from further performance of their primary obligations under the contract, "rights are not divested or discharged which have been unconditionally acquired".[267] The party in breach can therefore enforce against the innocent party such rights as it has "unconditionally acquired" by the date of termination.

Termination of partnership agreement. In *Hurst v Bryk*[268] the House of Lords was content to assume, without finally deciding,[269] that a partnership could 24–049

[263] *Yasuda Fire & Marine Insurance Co of Europe Ltd v Orion Marine Insurance Underwriting Agency Ltd* [1995] Q.B. 174 (principal's contractual right to inspect documents and computer databases relating to transactions entered into by agents held to have survived the termination of the agency agreement). The position is more difficult in relation to obligations of confidence. The Court of Appeal in *Campbell v Frisbee* [2002] EWCA Civ 1374, [2003] I.C.R. 141 held that the question whether an innocent party remains bound by an obligation of confidence following a wrongful repudiation of the contract by the other party was too uncertain to be resolved in summary proceedings. At first instance, [2000] EWHC 328 (Ch), Lightman J. held that the obligation of confidence of a service provider survived the acceptance by the service provider of the repudiation of her contract by the client. While the Court of Appeal concluded that the issue was not suitable for summary determination, they did acknowledge (at [22]) that they considered it unlikely that the innocent party in *Campbell* would be able to establish that Lightman J. had erred in his conclusions in a manner detrimental to her case. This suggests that obligations of confidence are likely to survive termination of the contract following a wrongful repudiation, whether the obligation of confidence survives as an express term of the contract or as a distinct equitable obligation (the latter view is preferred by Clarke (2003) 32 I.L.J. 43, 44–46, but questioned by Freedland (2003) 32 I.L.J. 48, 49). As has been noted (fn.256 above), the underlying problem is uncertainty as to the scope of the decision of the House of Lords in *General Billposting Co Ltd v Atkinson* [1909] A.C. 118.

[264] *Heyman v Darwins Ltd* [1942] A.C. 356; *F.J. Bloemen Pty Ltd v Council of the City of the Gold Coast* [1973] A.C. 115; *Moschi v Lep Air Services Ltd* [1973] A.C. 331, 351. Similarly, an adjudication provision in a contract will survive the discharge of the contract: *Connex South Eastern Ltd v MJ Building Services Group Plc* [2004] EWHC 1518 (TCC), [2004] B.L.R. 333 at [25].

[265] *Duffen v Frabo SpA* [2000] 1 Lloyd's Rep. 180, 194.

[266] *Bank of Boston Connecticut v European Grain and Shipping Ltd* [1989] A.C. 1056. See Beatson (1981) 97 L.Q.R. 389; and below, para.26–154.

[267] *McDonald v Dennys Lascelles Ltd* (1933) 48 C.L.R. 457, 476–477; *Bank of Boston Connecticut v European Grain and Shipping Ltd* [1989] A.C. 1056, 1098–1099; *Northern Developments (Cumbria) Ltd v J. & J. Nichol* [2000] B.L.R. 158, 165–166; *Hurst v Bryk* [2002] 1 A.C. 185, 199.

[268] [2002] 1 A.C. 185.

[269] In *Hurst v Bryk* [2002] 1 A.C. 185, both Lord Millett (at 196D–E) and Lord Nicholls (at 189D) expressly left open the question whether a partnership agreement can be automatically dissolved by an innocent partner or partners treating the other partner's or partners' breach as repudiatory. Lord Millett was of the view (at 196C) that it was arguable that, by entering into the relationship of partnership, the parties had submitted themselves to the jurisdiction of the court of equity and had thereby renounced their right by unilateral action to bring about the automatic dissolution of their relationship by acceptance of a repudiatory breach of the partnership contract. In other words, the issue was not whether acceptance of a repudiatory breach applied to the contract of partnership, but whether it operated to bring about the automatic dissolution of the partnership relationship (at 195A–B). cf. *Hitchman v Crouch Butler Savage Associates (A Firm)* (1982) 80 L.S. Gaz. 550.

be dissolved by one partner accepting his partner's or partners' repudiatory breach of the partnership agreement but held that, following termination, the innocent partner remains liable for the accrued and accruing liabilities of the partnership provided that these liabilities were incurred by the partnership when the innocent partner was a partner in the firm[270] and that the innocent partner also remains liable to his fellow partners to contribute to these liabilities.[271] However, in *Mullins v Laughton*[272] Neuberger J. subsequently held that the dissolution of a partnership by an accepted repudiation is not possible on the basis that the relationship between partners, while contractual, is also subject to equitable principles and to the principles to be found in the Partnership Act 1890.[273] On this basis, while an agreement to enter into a partnership agreement and an agreement whereby partners mutually undertake to observe certain obligations after the partnership has come to an end can be brought to an end by the acceptance of a repudiatory breach,[274] an acceptance of a repudiatory breach cannot be invoked in order to bring about the automatic dissolution of the partnership itself. The grounds on which a partnership can be dissolved are regulated principally by the provisions of the Partnership Act 1890 and these do not include the acceptance of a repudiatory breach.

24–050 **Position of innocent party.** Where the innocent party is entitled to, and does, treat himself as discharged by the other's breach, he is thereby released from future performance of his obligations under the contract.[275] Discharge also deprives him of any right as against the other party to continue to perform them.[276] After such discharge he is not bound to accept, or pay for, any further performance by the other party. If he has paid money under the contract to the party in default, he will be entitled to recover it by an action for money had and received,[277] but only if the consideration for the payment has totally failed.[278] A deposit paid by him to secure performance is, however, recoverable.[279]

---

[270] *Hurst v Bryk* [2002] 1 A.C. 185, 198.

[271] *Hurst v Bryk* [2002] 1 A.C. 185, 198–199. The innocent partner may have a claim for damages against his fellow partners in respect of the breach which brought about the dissolution of the partnership but these losses cannot be measured by reference to the contribution which he must make to the partnership's liabilities because his liability to contribute to them had accrued prior to the breach of the partnership agreement (199). He can recover damages only if he can show that the dissolution of the firm caused him loss which he would not otherwise have sustained.

[272] [2002] EWHC 2761 (Ch), [2003] Ch. 250.

[273] [2002] EWHC 2761 (Ch) at [87]–[93]. In this respect Neuberger J. followed the reasoning of Lord Millett in *Hurst v Bryk* [2002] 1 A.C. 185.

[274] *Hurst v Bryk* [2002] 1 A.C. 185, 193D.

[275] *Heyman v Darwins Ltd* [1942] A.C. 356, 399; *Moschi v Lep Air Services Ltd* [1973] A.C. 331, 345, 350, 351; *Photo Production Ltd v Securicor Transport Ltd* [1980] A.C. 827, 844, 848; *Thompson v Corroon* (1993) 42 W.I.R. 157, 173; cf. *Port Jackson Stevedoring Pty Ltd v Salmond and Spraggon (Australia) Pty Ltd* [1981] 1 W.L.R. 138.

[276] *Moschi v Lep Air Services Ltd* [1973] A.C. 331, 350, 351; *Photo Production Ltd v Securicor Transport Ltd* [1980] A.C. 827, 844.

[277] *Fibrosa Spolka Akcyjna v Fairbairn Lawson Combe Barbour Ltd* [1943] A.C. 32, 52, 65; *Kwei Tek Chao v British Traders and Shippers Ltd* [1954] 2 Q.B. 459, 475.

[278] See below, paras 29–054—29–057 and 29–063. The *total* failure requirement may not survive further judicial scrutiny, see *Goss v Chilcott* [1996] A.C. 788, 798. For academic criticism of the insistence upon a total failure see Burrows, *The Law of Restitution*, 2nd edn (2002), pp.333–336.

[279] See below, para.29–064.

Rights acquired before discharge. Although both parties are discharged from further performance of the contract, rights are not divested or discharged which have already been unconditionally acquired.[280] Rights and obligations which arise from the partial execution of the contract and causes of action which have accrued from its breach alike continue unaffected.[281] Where, at the time of discharge, money is due under the contract by the innocent party but that sum remains unpaid, the innocent party is not required to pay that sum if it would then be recoverable by him in a restitutionary claim (for example, on the ground that there had been a (total) failure of consideration). Otherwise, the innocent party can retain or recover sums paid or due before the time at which the repudiation is accepted by him[282] and may maintain an action for damages in respect of any cause of action vested in him at that time.[283] If the contract provides for payment of a deposit, which is forfeitable in the event of breach, the acceptance by the innocent party of the repudiation of the contract by the party in default does not preclude him from recovering and forfeiting the deposit if it is at that time due and unpaid.[284] Further in *Damon Compania Naviera SA v Hapag-Lloyd International SA*[285] the vendor and purchaser of three ships agreed that each would sign a memorandum of agreement within a reasonable time, whereupon the purchaser would be liable to pay a deposit of 10 per cent of the purchase price. The purchaser repudiated the contract by failing to sign the memorandum and this repudiation was accepted by the vendor. The Court of Appeal held that, even though the vendor had acquired no accrued right to the deposit at the time he accepted the repudiation, nevertheless at that time he had a vested right to sue the purchaser for damages for breach of his obligation to sign the memorandum, the measure of such damages being the amount of the deposit. However, in the case of contracts for the sale of land or goods, unless the contract otherwise provides, sums due as part payment of the purchase price from the party in default may be irrecoverable.[286] If the innocent party has expended labour or money under the 24–051

[280] *Collidge v Freeport Plc* [2007] EWHC 1216 (QB), [2007] All E.R. (D) 457 (May) at [9].

[281] *McDonald v Dennys Lascelles Ltd* (1933) 48 C.L.R. 457, 476–477; *Johnson v Agnew* [1980] A.C. 367, 396; *Damon Compania Naviera SA v Hapag-Lloyd International SA* [1985] 1 W.L.R. 435, 450; *Hurst v Bryk* [2002] 1 A.C. 185, 199; *SCI (Sales Curve Interactive) Ltd v Titus SARL* [2001] EWCA Civ 591, [2001] 2 All E.R. (Comm) 416 (albeit that, on the facts, it was held that the right invoked had not been unconditionally acquired prior to the termination of the contract). *Odfjfell Seachem A/S v Continental des Petroles et D'Investissements* [2004] EWHC 2929 (Comm), [2005] 1 Lloyd's Rep. 275 at [35].

[282] *Dewar v Mintoft* [1912] 2 K.B. 373, 387–388; *Damon Compania Naviera SA v Hapag-Lloyd International SA* [1985] 1 W.L.R. 435, 451. Contrast *Lowe v Hope* [1970] Ch. 94.

[283] *Damon Compania Naviera SA v Hapag-Lloyd International SA* [1985] 1 W.L.R. 435.

[284] *Brooks v Beirnstein* [1909] 1 K.B. 98; *Leslie Shipping Co v Welstead* [1921] 3 K.B. 420; *Chatterton v Maclean* [1951] 1 All E.R. 761; *Overstone Ltd v Shipway* [1962] 1 W.L.R. 117; *Galbraith v Mitchenall Estates Ltd* [1965] 2 Q.B. 473; *Hyundai Shipbuilding & Heavy Industries Co Ltd v Pournaras* [1978] 2 Lloyd's Rep. 502; *Hyundai Heavy Industries Co Ltd v Papadopoulos* [1980] 1 W.L.R. 1129; cf. *Wehner v Dene Steam Shipping Co* [1905] 2 K.B. 929; *China National Foreign Trade Transportation Corp v Evlogia Shipping Co SA of Panama* [1979] 1 W.L.R. 1018 HL (overpayment); *Thompson v Corroon* (1993) 42 W.I.R. 157, 173.

[285] [1985] 1 W.L.R. 435.

[286] *Palmer v Temple* (1839) 9 A. & E. 508; *Dies v British and International Mining and Finance Corp Ltd* [1939] 1 K.B. 724. See also *Mayson v Clouet* [1924] A. C. 980, 986; *McDonald v Dennys Lascelles Ltd* (1933) 48 C.L.R. 457, 477; *Hyundai Heavy Industries Co Ltd v Papadopoulos* [1980] 1 W.L.R. 1129, 1134, 1142, 1153; Beatson (1981) 97 L.Q.R. 389; and below, para.29–065. For the possibility of equitable relief, see below, para.26–148.

contract, or delivered goods to the party in default, but payment for these is not yet due, he will be entitled to sue for these on a quantum meruit or quantum valebat.[287] Otherwise, his remedy is to sue for damages for breach of contract.[288]

24–052 **Position of guilty party.** Upon discharge, the primary obligations of the party in default to perform any of the promises made by him and remaining unperformed come to an end, as does his right to perform them.[289] But for his primary obligations there is substituted by operation of law a secondary obligation to pay to the other party a sum of money to compensate him for the loss he has sustained as a result of the failure to perform the unperformed primary obligations.[290]

24–053 The party in default will not be entitled to recover any deposit paid by him as security for the performance of his obligations.[291] In principle, other sums paid by him under the contract before the time of discharge will likewise be irrecoverable.[292] But, unless the contract otherwise provides, he may be permitted to recover money paid as a part-payment of the purchase price where the contract is one for the sale of goods or land,[293] and it is possible that relief in equity may in certain circumstances be available.[294] Unpaid instalments which were due prior to the discharge of the contract remain payable by the party in default unless there has been a total failure of consideration in respect of these instalments, in which case they cease to be payable.[295]

24–054 Whether he has any claim to be recompensed for partial performance of the contract which he has broken will depend on whether the obligation is entire or divisible.[296] If it is entire, he will normally have no claim, unless there is evidence on which to ground the inference of a new contract or an independent restitutionary claim.[297] But if the obligation is not entire but divisible, he may be entitled to claim in respect of a divisible part of the performance completed[298] (subject to a counterclaim by the innocent party in respect of that part of the contract which remains unperformed). Where goods delivered under a contract of

[287] See below, para.29–066.

[288] But see the effect of a buyer's repudiation on the seller's rights in respect of goods: *Benjamin's Sale of Goods*, 7th edn (2006), para.15–107.

[289] *Hurst v Bryk* [1999] Ch. 1, 21–22.

[290] *Moschi v Lep Air Services Ltd* [1973] A.C. 331, 345, 350, 351; *Photo Production Ltd v Securicor Transport Ltd* [1980] A.C. 827, 848–851; *Port Jackson Stevedoring Pty Ltd v Salmond and Spraggon (Australia) Pty Ltd* [1981] 1 W.L.R. 138, 145.

[291] *Palmer v Temple* (1839) 9 A. & E. 508, 520; *Howe v Smith* (1884) 27 Ch D 87; *Linggi Plantations Ltd v Jagattheesan* [1972] 1 M.L.J. 89, 91 PC; *Thompson v Corroon* (1993) 42 W.I.R. 157, 173; and see below, para.29–064. But see Law of Property Act 1925 s.49(2).

[292] See above, para.24–051 fn.284, below, para.29–064.

[293] see above, para.24–051 fn.286, below, para.26–154.

[294] See below, para.26–147; Beatson (1981) 97 L.Q.R. 389.

[295] *Mirimskaya v Evans* [2007] EWHC 2073 (TCC), (2007) 114 Con. L.R. 131.

[296] See above, para.24–043; below, para.26–147.

[297] See above, paras 21–030—21–031.

[298] See above, paras 21–037, 24–044.

sale are not in conformity with the contract, and are rejected by the buyer, the property in the goods revests in the seller.[299]

Effect on guarantor. Where a creditor "accepts" his debtor's wrongful repudiation of the contract, and exercises his right to treat himself as discharged, this does not release a guarantor of the debtor from liability in respect of monies payable by the debtor after the date of discharge.[300] Nor is the guarantor released from liability in respect of sums due but unpaid at that time,[301] unless those sums could not have been recovered from the debtor himself[302] and the guarantee does not, on its true construction, require payment by the guarantor in the event of default in payment on the due date.[303] 24–055

[299] *Kwei Tek Chao v British Traders and Shippers Ltd* [1954] 2 Q.B. 459, 487; *Rosenthal & Sons Ltd v Esmail* [1965] 1 W.L.R. 1117, 1131.

[300] *Moschi v Lep Air Services Ltd* [1973] A.C. 331; see Vol.II, Ch.44.

[301] *Hyundai Shipbuilding and Heavy Industries Co Ltd v Pournaras* [1978] 2 Lloyd's Rep. 502; *Hyundai Heavy Industries Co Ltd v Papadopoulos* [1980] 1 W.L.R. 1129 HL; see below, para.29–065.

[302] See above, para.24–051 fn.286.

[303] *Hyundai Heavy Industries Co Ltd v Papadopoulos* [1980] 1 W.L.R. 1129 HL and see Vol.II, Ch.44.

Chapter 25

OTHER MODES OF DISCHARGE

		PARA.
1.	Merger	25–001
2.	Alteration or cancellation of a written instrument	25–020
3.	Miscellaneous modes of discharge	25–028

1. Merger

Merger by taking a higher security. In general, a debt or security by simple contract is extinguished by a specialty security being given for the same if the remedy on the latter is coextensive with that which the creditor had upon the former.[1] Thus, if a bond or covenant by the debtor is taken for or to secure a simple contract debt, the latter is merged in the former, because in contemplation of law the specialty is an instrument of a higher nature and gives the creditor a better remedy than he had for the original debt.[2] But in order for this principle to apply, two conditions must be fulfilled. First, the later security must be of a higher efficacy than that which it is sought to replace. Thus, if the securities are of equal degree, as in the case of an earlier and a later bond,[3] no merger will take place. A negotiable instrument is not a higher security for the purposes of this rule,[4] although the giving and taking of a bill or note may act as a discharge of a debt if the parties so intended.[5] Secondly, the remedy given by the higher security must be coextensive with the lower security, that is to say, it must secure the same obligation and be made between the same parties.[6] Thus, if one of two makers of a joint and several promissory note gives the holder a mortgage to secure the amount with a covenant to pay it, the other maker is not thereby discharged, for the remedy on the specialty is not coextensive with the remedy of the note.[7] And where a specialty is given for payments of amounts due or to 25–001

[1] *Acton v Symon* (1635) Cro. Car. 414; *Twopenny v Young* (1824) 3 B. & C. 208; *Price v Moulton* (1835) 10 C.B. 561; *Bristol and West Plc v Bartlett* [2002] EWCA Civ 1181, [2002] 4 All E.R. 544 at [22].

[2] *Price v Moulton* (1835) 10 C.B. 561.

[3] *Kidd v Boone* (1871) 40 L.J. Ch. 531. See also *Norwood v Grype* (1599) Cro. Eliz. 727; *Chetwynd v Allen* [1899] 1 Ch. 353.

[4] *Drake v Mitchell* (1803) 3 East 251.

[5] See above, paras 21–073—21–075.

[6] *Bell v Banks* (1841) 3 M. & G. 258; *Ansell v Baker* (1850) 15 Q.B. 20; *Mowatt v Lord Londesburgh* (1854) 3 E. & B. 307; *Chetwynd v Allen* [1899] 1 Ch. 353; *Lawrence v Cassel* [1930] W.N. 137; *Hissett v Reading Roofing Co Ltd* [1969] 1 W.L.R. 1757.

[7] *Ansell v Baker* (1850) 15 Q.B. 20. Where the remedy is not joint and several, but merely joint, it seems that merger will operate: *Owen v Homan* (1850) 3 Mc. & G. 378, 410; *Ex p. Flintoff* (1844) 3 M.D. & De G. 726; *Ex p. Hernaman* (1848) 12 Jur. 642. Contrast *Sharpe v Gibbs* (1864) 16 C.B.(N.S.) 527; *Holmes v Bell* (1841) 3 M. & G. 213; *Bell v Banks* (1841) 3 M. & G. 258. See Williams, *Joint Obligations*, para.49, and generally on joint obligations, above, Ch.17.

become due on a running account with a bank, the doctrine of merger, if it applies at all, could at most apply only to the indebtedness which existed at the date when the covenant was taken; for the specialty would otherwise be given in respect of a different future debt.[8]

25–002 **Collateral security.** If it appears on the face of the specialty or from the nature of the transaction that the specialty was intended only as an additional or collateral security, it will not operate as a merger.[9] So, where a banker took from A, his customer, and B, his surety, a bond conditioned for the payment of all sums already advanced or thereafter to be advanced to A, it was held that the bond was evidently intended only as a collateral security, that therefore there was no merger and that A might be sued for the balance of his account as on a simple contract debt.[10]

25–003 **Merger of contract in conveyance.**

> "It is well settled that, where parties enter into an executory agreement which is to be carried out by a deed afterwards to be executed, the real completed contract is to be found in the deed. The contract is merged in the deed. . . . The most common instance, perhaps, of this merger is a contract for the sale of land followed by conveyance on completion."[11]

Merger is not, however, inevitable, but depends upon the intention of the parties.[12] Merger may occur despite the fact that the terms of the conveyance differ from those in the contract; and, where a contract applies to many parcels of land, but the conveyance to only some of them, merger may operate distributively, i.e. *quoad* only the parcels conveyed.[13]

25–004 **Merger of rights and liabilities.** A contract may also be discharged where the rights and liabilities under it become vested, by assignment or otherwise, in the same person in the same right,[14] for a man cannot maintain an action against himself. This type of merger is more often encountered in the law of land,[15] e.g. where a tenant for a term of years retains the lease and acquires the reversion. An example in the law of contract is provided by s.61 of the Bills of Exchange Act

---

[8] *Barclays Bank Ltd v Beck* [1952] 2 Q.B. 47, 53.

[9] *Twopenny v Young* (1824) 3 B. & C. 208; *Ex p. Bate* (1838) 3 Deac. 358; *Yates v Aston* (1843) 4 Q.B. 182; *Norfolk Ry Co v M'Namara* (1849) 3 Exch. 628; *Ex p. Hughes* (1872) 4 Ch D 34; *Commissioner of Stamps v Hope* [1891] A.C. 476; *Barclays Bank Ltd v Beck* [1952] 2 Q.B. 47.

[10] *Holmes v Bell* (1841) 3 M & G. 213.

[11] *Knight Sugar Co Ltd v Alberta Ry & Irrigation Co* [1938] 1 All E.R. 266, 269.

[12] *Palmer v Johnson* (1884) 13 QBD 351, 357; *Clarke v Ramuz* [1891] 2 Q.B. 456, 461; *Lawrence v Cassel* [1930] 2 K.B. 83; *Barclays Bank Ltd v Beck* [1952] 2 Q.B. 47; *Hancock v B.W. Brazier (Anerley) Ltd* [1966] 1 W.L.R. 1317; *Hissett v Reading Roofing Co Ltd* [1969] 1 W.L.R. 1757; *Tito v Waddell (No.2)* [1977] Ch. 107, 284; *Gunatunga v De Alwis* (1996) 72 P. & C.R. 161, 180.

[13] *Tito v Waddell (No.2)* [1977] Ch. 107, 284–285.

[14] e.g. not as executor or administrator, to which special rules apply, below.

[15] See Megarry and Wade, *The Law of Real Property*, 6th edn (2000), paras 14–176—14–177. At common law merger was automatic; but by s.185 of the Law of Property Act 1925, the equitable rule now prevails; that merger depends upon the intention of the person who acquires the two estates. See *Capital and Counties Bank Ltd v Rhodes* [1903] 1 Ch. 631.

1882, which enacts that, when the acceptor of a bill is or becomes the holder of it at or after its maturity, in his own right, the bill is discharged.[16]

Debtor becomes creditor's personal representative. At common law, if a debtor became the personal representative of his creditor, the right of action for the debt was suspended, since he could not maintain an action against himself. But since the suspension of a personal action as the result of the voluntary act of a creditor prevented revival of the action, the result was that, if the creditor appointed the debtor his executor, the debt was extinguished when that appointment became effective on the creditor's death.[17] On the other hand, if the debtor became the administrator of the creditor's estate, this was not the voluntary act of the creditor, and the debt was therefore not extinguished, but was suspended for the duration of the administration.[18] In equity, however, a debtor who was appointed his creditor's executor was treated as having paid the debt to himself, and he was compelled to account for it as assets of the testator held by him[19] unless there was evidence of the testator's settled intention to release him from the debt.[20] But equity did not intervene in the case of a debtor who became administrator. This divergence between the rules applicable to executors and administrators has now been abolished, so that an administrator's debt is likewise extinguished (and not merely suspended), but he is likewise accountable for the amount of the debt as part of the creditor's estate.[21] 25–005

Creditor becomes debtor's personal representative. Where a creditor becomes the executor or administrator of his debtor's estate, the debt is not thereby extinguished or suspended.[22] However, he may retain[23] assets of the testator in payment of his debt in priority to other creditors of equal degree.[24] 25–006

Merger by judgment recovered. The mere pendency of an action for the recovery of a debt or damages is no bar to another action for the same breach of 25–007

---

[16] *Harmer v Steele* (1849) 4 Exch. 1; *Chalmers and Guest on Bills of Exchange*, 16th edn (2005), pp.519–521. See Vol.II, para.34–138.

[17] *Wankford v Wankford* (1704) 1 Salk. 299; *Cheetham v Ward* (1797) 1 B. & P. 630; *Freakley v Fox* (1829) 9 B. & C. 130; *Re Applebee* [1891] 3 Ch. 422. See also *Jenkins v Jenkins* [1928] 2 K.B. 501 and *Williams, Mortimer and Sunnucks on Executors, Administrators and Probate*, 18th edn (2000), para.51–17, and above, para.17–023.

[18] *Nedham's Case* (1610) 8 Co. Rep. 135a; *Seagram v Knight* (1867) L.R. 2 Ch.App. 620.

[19] *Selwin v Brown* (1735) 3 Brown P.C. 607; *Ingle v Richards* (1860) 28 Beav. 366; *Re Bourne* [1906] 1 Ch. 697.

[20] *Strong v Bird* (1874) L.R. 18 Eq. 316; *Re Pink* [1912] 2 Ch. 528; *Re James* [1935] Ch. 449. cf. *Re Freeland* [1952] Ch. 110.

[21] Administration of Estates Act 1925 s.21A (inserted by s.10 of the Limitation Amendment Act 1980).

[22] *Bowring-Hanbury's Trustee v Bowring-Hanbury* [1942] Ch. 276. See generally *Williams, Mortimer and Sunnucks on Executors, Administrators and Probate*, 18th edn (2000), para.51–20; (1943) 59 L.Q.R. 117; (1943) 6 M.L.R. 233.

[23] See below, para.28–131.

[24] Administration of Estates Act 1925 s.34(2). But the form of administration bond which a creditor is required to enter into in connection with an application for a grant of administration as creditor prohibits him from using his right of retainer to give himself an advantage over other creditors.

contract on which the claim to such a debt or damages is founded.[25] The defendant's remedy in such a case is either to consolidate the two actions[26] or to have the second action struck out on the basis that there are no reasonable grounds for bringing the claim.[27] But when a prior action has already been successfully brought by the claimant against the defendant in a court of record[28] for the identical demand,[29] and judgment has been recovered thereon, the cause of action is changed or merged into matter of record and the inferior remedy is merged in the higher.[30] In such a case, therefore, if the claimant sues upon the original promise or demand (even although it accrued upon a specialty), it will be a good defence that he has already recovered judgment against the defendant for the same cause of action.[31]

25–008 **Damages "once for all".** The general rule is that "damages resulting from one and the same cause of action must be assessed and recovered once for all".[32] So in one case[33] the claimant recovered from the defendant in one action as damages for the defendant's breach of contract the damages which a third party had recovered against the claimant. He then brought a second action to recover the costs incurred by him in defending the third party's action. It was held that recovery of judgment in the first action was a bar to the second. But where one contract contains separate promises, or there are separate breaches of the same promise, separate or successive actions may be brought for each breach, and judgment in one will be no bar to the other.[34] However, if a contract contains a single indivisible undertaking, different actions cannot be maintained for different breaches of it. Where, therefore, a builder who had agreed to build a bungalow in a good and workmanlike manner was sued in successive actions by the owner for breach of his contract, inefficiency of workmanship being alleged

[25] *Harley v Greenwood* (1821) 5 B. & Ald. 95, 101.

[26] CPR Part 3 r.3.1(2)(g).

[27] CPR Part 3 r.3.4(2)(a); County Courts Act 1984 s.35.

[28] See below, para.25–010.

[29] *Seddon v Tutop* (1796) 6 T.R. 607; *Hadley v Green* (1832) 2 Cr. & J. 374; *Wegg Prosser v Evans* [1895] 1 Q.B. 108; *Economic Life Assurance Society v Usborne* [1902] A.C. 147.

[30] *Greathead v Bromley* (1798) 7 T.R. 455; *King v Hoare* (1844) 13 M. & W. 495; *Stewart v Todd* (1846) 9 Q.B. 759; *Re European Central Ry* (1876) 4 Ch D 33; *Kendall v Hamilton* (1879) 4 App. Cas. 504; *Aman v Southern Ry* [1926] 1 K.B. 59. For the position in regard to judgment against one joint, or joint and several, debtor, see above, paras 17–015—17–016. For the effect of an arbitration award, see Vol.II, paras 32–128 et seq.

[31] But see *Buckland v Palmer* [1984] 1 W.L.R. 1109, 1115.

[32] *Brunsden v Humphrey* (1884) 14 QBD 141, 147; *Darley Main Colliery Co v Mitchell* (1886) 11 App. Cas. 127, 132; *Conquer v Boot* [1928] 2 K.B. 336, 343; *Clark v Urquhart* [1930] A.C. 28, 54. See also County Courts Act 1984 s.35. The general rule applies also to arbitrations: see Mustill and Boyd, *Commercial Arbitration*, 2nd edn (1989), p.411.

[33] *Furness, Withy & Co v Hall* (1909) 25 T.L.R. 233.

[34] *Bristowe v Fairclough* (1840) 1 M. & G. 143; *Brunsden v Humphrey* (1884) 14 QBD 141; *Ebbetts v Conquest* (1900) 82 L.T. 560; *Bake v French* [1907] 1 Ch. 428; *Brooks v Beirnstein* [1909] 1 K.B. 98; *Isaacs v Salbstein* [1916] 2 K.B. 139; *South Bedfordshire Electrical Finance Ltd v Bryant* [1938] 3 All E.R. 580; *National Coal Board v Galley* [1958] 1 W.L.R. 16; *Overstone Ltd v Shipway* [1962] 1 W.L.R. 117; *Telfair Shipping Corp v Inersea Carriers SA* [1983] 2 Lloyd's Rep. 351. See below, paras 26–013—26–015. But see also below, paras 25–011—25–014 (stay of proceedings where matters could and should have been raised).

in the first action and unsuitability of materials in the second, recovery of judgment in the first action was held to be a defence in the second.[35]

Interest. A judgment for interest only is no bar to a claim for the principal money.[36] But where there is a covenant to pay a principal sum, and judgment is obtained upon the covenant for that sum, any covenant to pay interest which is merely incidental to the covenant to pay the principal sum is merged in the judgment.[37] If, however, the covenant to pay interest is expressed in such a manner as to be independent of the covenant to pay the principal sum, it is not merged or extinguished in the judgment.[38] 25–009

County court judgments. A county court is a court of record.[39] Judgment recovered in a county court is therefore a good defence to an action in the High Court for the same cause,[40] provided that the county court was acting within its jurisdiction.[41] 25–010

Estoppel by judgment. Estoppel by judgment, or estoppel *per rem judicatam*, is a rule of evidence[42] whereby a party is debarred from relitigating a cause of action which has been conclusively determined by the judgment of a court of competent jurisdiction in previous proceedings between the same parties or their privies, or an issue raised and determined in such proceedings which it was necessary[43] to determine for the purpose of those proceedings.[44] Estoppel *per rem judicatam* has two principal branches: cause of action estoppel and issue estoppel. Cause of action estoppel arises: 25–011

> "[W]here the cause of action in the later proceedings is identical to that in the earlier proceedings, the latter having been between the same parties or their privies and having involved the same subject matter. In such a case the bar is absolute in relation to all

---

[35] *Conquer v Boot* [1928] 2 K.B. 336. But see (arbitrations) Vol.II, para.32–128.

[36] *Morgan v Rowlands* (1872) 41 L.J.Q.B. 187.

[37] *Ex p. Fewings* (1883) 25 Ch D 338. The judgment bears interest: see below, para.26–184.

[38] *Popple v Sylvester* (1882) 22 Ch D 98; *Economic Life Assurance Society v Usborne* [1902] A.C. 147.

[39] County Courts Act 1984 s.1(2).

[40] *Austin v Mills* (1853) 9 Exch. 288. See also *Vines v Arnold* (1849) 8 C.B. 632; *Webster v Armstrong* (1885) 54 L.J.Q.B. 236.

[41] *Briscoe v Stephens* (1842) 2 Bing. 213.

[42] *Vervaeke v Smith* [1983] 1 A.C. 145; *Republic of India v India Steamship Co Ltd* [1993] A.C. 410, 422.

[43] *Kok Hoong v Leong Cheong Kweng Mines Ltd* [1964] A.C. 993; *Penn Texas Corp v Murat Anstalt (No.2)* [1964] 2 Q.B. 647; *Fidelitas Shipping Co Ltd v V/O Exportchleb* [1966] 1 Q.B. 630, 640; *Mills v Cooper* [1967] 2 Q.B. 459, 468; *Carl Zeiss Stiftung v Rayner & Keeler Ltd (No.3)* [1970] Ch. 506; *Helmville Ltd v Astilleros Espanoles SA* [1984] 2 Lloyd's Rep. 569; *In Re State of Norway's Application (No.2)* [1990] 1 A.C. 723, 743, 752; *In Re B. (Minors) (Care Proceedings: Issue Estoppel)* [1997] Fam. 117, 121–122.

[44] The subject is one of considerable difficulty and refinement: see *Halsbury's Laws of England*, 4th edn (reissue), Vol.16(2) ("Estoppel"), paras 977 et seq.; *Cross and Tapper on Evidence*, 11th edn (2007) p.92 et seq. For estoppel by a default judgment, see *Howlett v Tarte* (1861) 10 C.B.N.S. 813; *New Brunswick Ry Co v British and French Trust Corp Ltd* [1939] A.C. 1; *Kok Hoong v Leong Cheong Kweng Mines Ltd* [1964] A.C. 993. Neither dismissal for want of prosecution (*Pople v Evans* [1969] 2 Ch. 255) nor the withdrawal of proceedings (*Owens v Minoprio* [1942] 1 K.B. 193) is a foundation for res judicata.

> points decided unless fraud or collusion is alleged such as to justify setting aside the earlier judgment."[45]

On the other hand, issue estoppel arises:

> "[W]here a particular issue forming a necessary ingredient in a cause of action has been litigated and decided and in subsequent proceedings between the same parties involving a different cause of action to which the same issue is relevant one of the parties seeks to re-open that issue."[46]

Both estoppels are founded "upon the public interest in finality of litigation rather than the achievement of justice as between the individual litigants".[47]

25–012 **Requirements.** Three requirements must be satisfied for a plea of estoppel *per rem judicatam* to succeed[48]: first, there must have been a final and conclusive judgment[49] on the merits[50] by a court of competent jurisdiction[51] in the earlier[52] proceedings; secondly, there must be identity of parties in the two sets of

---

[45] *Arnold v National Westminster Bank Plc* [1991] 2 A.C. 93, 104.

[46] [1991] 2 A.C. 93, 105.

[47] *Republic of India v India S.S. Co Ltd* [1993] A.C. 410, 415. See also *Duchess of Kingston's Case* (1776) 20 St. Tr. 573; *R. v Inhabitants of the Township of Hartington Middle Quarter* (1855) E. & B. 780; *Flittens v Allfrey* (1874) L.R. 10 C.P. 29; *Hoystead v Commissioner of Taxation* [1926] A.C. 155, 170; *Fidelitas Shipping Co Ltd v V/O Exportchleb* [1966] 1 Q.B. 630, 640; *Thoday v Thoday* [1964] P. 181, 197–198; *Mills v Cooper* [1967] 2 Q.B. 459, 468; *Carl Zeiss Stiftung v Rayner & Keeler Ltd (No.2)* [1967] 1 A.C. 853, 916, 917; *Vervaeke v Smith* [1983] 1 A.C. 145; *Thrasyvoulou v Secretary of State for the Environment* [1990] 2 A.C. 273, 289; *Johnson v Gore Wood & Co (A Firm)* [2002] 2 A.C. 1, 30–31 and 59; *Cross and Tapper on Evidence*, 11th edn (2007), pp.77–78.

[48] *Carl Zeiss Stiftung v Rayner & Keeler Ltd (No.2)* [1967] 1 A.C. 853, 909–910, 935, 943, 967–971; *D.S.V. Silo-und Verwaltungsgesellschaft mbH v Owners of the Sennar* [1985] 1 W.L.R. 490, 499.

[49] *Marchioness of Huntley v Gaskell* [1905] 2 Ch. 656; *Carl Zeiss Stiftung v Rayner & Keeler Ltd (No.3)* [1970] Ch. 506; *Midland Bank Trust Co Ltd v Green* [1980] Ch. 590; *Hines v Birkbeck College (No.2)* [1992] Ch. 33; *Buehler AG v Chronos Richardson Ltd* [1998] 2 All E.R. 960. See also the cases cited in para.25–017 fn.88, below.

[50] Where there has been a dismissal on the sole ground that the particular court has no jurisdiction, there has been no decision on the merits which would prevent the claimant from commencing proceedings before a court which did have jurisdiction: *Hines v Birkbeck College (No.2)* [1992] Ch. 33. Particular difficulties arise in the context of interlocutory rulings (*Carl Zeiss Stiftung v Rayner & Keeler Ltd (No.2)* [1967] 1 A.C. 853). A decision on an application to set aside a default judgment is unlikely to give rise to an estoppel in this context (*Mullen v Conoco Ltd* [1998] Q.B. 382). See below, para.25–017 fn.89.

[51] *The European Gateway* [1987] Q.B. 206; *Crown Estates Commissioners v Dorset CC* [1990] Ch. 297. In the case of adjudications subject to a comprehensive statutory code, there is a presumption that, where the statute has created a specific jurisdiction for the determination of any issue which establishes the existence of a legal right, res judicata applies unless an intention to exclude the principle can properly be inferred as a matter of construction of the relevant statutory provisions (*Thrasyvoulou v Secretary of State for the Environment* [1990] 2 A.C. 273, 289). Res judicata has been held to be applicable to arbitral tribunals (*Fidelitas Shipping Co Ltd v V/O Exportchleb* [1966] 1 Q.B. 630; *Dallal v Bank Mellat* [1986] Q.B. 441) and to industrial tribunals (*Munir v Jang Publications Ltd* [1989] I.C.R. 1). For the effect of findings of an industrial tribunal on subsequent common law actions, see *Turner v London Transport Executive* [1977] I.C.R. 952; *Green v Hampshire CC* [1979] I.C.R. 861. See also below, paras 25–016—25–019.

[52] But see below fn.58.

proceedings[53] or else the existence of privity between the respective claimants or defendants in the earlier proceedings and those in the later proceedings[54]; thirdly, there must be identity of subject matter in the two proceedings.[55]

25–013 **Issues not raised previously.** Both cause of action[56] and issue estoppel[57] may extend to issues which might have been put but were not raised and decided[58] in the earlier proceedings, although in special circumstances[59] the court may depart from this rule and permit the parties to raise such an issue. The court also has a power under rules of court and its inherent jurisdiction to stay or dismiss the action if a claimant seeks to raise in subsequent proceedings matters which were or should have been litigated in the earlier proceedings.[60] The courts will not, however, exercise their discretion in such a way as to deny to a claimant the right

---

[53] *Townsend v Bishop* [1939] 1 All E.R. 805; *Gleeson v J. Wippell & Co Ltd* [1977] 1 W.L.R. 510; *Hunter v Chief Constable of West Midlands* [1982] A.C. 529, 540–541; *C. (A Minor) v Hackney LBC* [1996] 1 W.L.R. 789; cf. *North West Water Ltd v Binnie & Partners* [1990] 3 All E.R. 547, where Drake J. rejected the argument that identity of parties was an essential ingredient of an issue estoppel. The parties must have litigated in the same capacity in both actions: *Marginson v Blackburn BC* [1939] 2 K.B. 426; cf. *House of Spring Gardens Ltd v Waite* [1991] 1 Q.B. 241, 252, where Stuart-Smith L.J. reserved his opinion as to whether the plaintiff's claim in *Marginson* should have been struck out as an abuse of process. See also his rationalisation of *Marginson* in *Talbot v Berkshire CC* [1994] Q.B. 290, 296–297.

[54] *Kinnersley v Orpe* (1780) 2 Dougl. K.B. 517; *Outram v Homewood* (1803) 3 East 346, 366; *Mercantile Investment and General Trust Co v River Plate Trust, Loan and Agency Co* [1894] 1 Ch. 578; *Carl Zeiss Stiftung v Rayner & Keeler Ltd (No.3)* [1970] Ch. 506; *Gleeson v J. Wippell & Co Ltd* [1977] 1 W.L.R. 510; *Hunter v Chief Constable of West Midlands* [1982] A.C. 259; *House of Spring Gardens Ltd v Waite* [1991] 1 Q.B. 241, 252–254.

[55] *Hoystead v Commissioner of Taxation* [1926] A.C. 155; *Marginson v Blackburn BC* [1939] 2 K.B. 426; *Bell v Holmes* [1956] 1 W.L.R. 1359; *Society of Medical Officers of Health v Hope* [1960] A.C. 551; *Randolph v Tuck* [1962] 1 Q.B. 175; *Wood v Luscombe* [1966] 1 Q.B. 69; *Re Mantey's Will Trusts (No.2)* [1976] 1 All E.R. 673. See also *Khan v Golechha International Ltd* [1980] 1 W.L.R. 1482; *Taylor v Vectapike Ltd* [1990] 2 E.G.L.R. 12; *Republic of India v India S.S. Co Ltd* [1993] A.C. 410; *Buehler AG v Chronos Richardson Ltd* [1998] 2 All E.R. 960 and *Cross and Tapper on Evidence*, 11th edn (2007), pp.103–105. In the case of issue estoppel, the decision on the issue must have been essential for the decision of the court and not merely collateral: see the cases cited in fn.43, above.

[56] *Arnold v National Westminster Bank Plc* [1991] 2 A.C. 93, 104, citing *Henderson v Henderson* (1843) 3 Hare 100, 114–115; *Hoystead v Commissioner of Taxation* [1926] A.C. 155, 170; *Yat Tung Investment Co Ltd v Dao Heng Bank Ltd* [1975] A.C. 581, 590.

[57] *Arnold v National Westminster Bank Plc* [1991] 2 A.C. 93, 106, citing *Fidelitas Shipping Co Ltd v V/O Exportchleb* [1966] 1 Q.B. 630, 642; *Brisbane City Council v Att-Gen for Queensland* [1979] A.C. 411, 425.

[58] The issue should have been decided as well as raised in the earlier proceedings: *Barrow v Bankside Agency Ltd* [1996] 1 W.L.R. 257 (plaintiff's claim not barred because it would not have been decided by the court in the earlier proceedings).

[59] *Henderson v Henderson* (1843) 3 Hare 100, 115; *Yat Tung Investment Co Ltd v Dao Heng Bank Ltd* [1975] A.C. 581, 590; *Talbot v Berkshire CC* [1994] Q.B. 290, 298–300; *Barrow v Bankside Agency Ltd* [1996] 1 W.L.R. 257; *Republic of India v India S.S. Co Ltd (No.2)* [1998] A.C. 878, 897–898; *Hodgkinson & Corby Ltd v Wards Mobility Services Ltd* [1998] F.S.R. 530.

[60] *Henderson v Henderson* (1843) 3 Hare 100, 115; *Greenhalgh v Mallard* [1947] 2 All E.R. 255; *Fidelitas Shipping Co Ltd v V/O Exportchleb* [1966] 1 Q.B. 630, 640; *Yat Tung Investment Co Ltd v Dao Heng Bank Ltd* [1975] A.C. 581, 590; *L.E. Walwin & Partners Ltd v West Sussex CC* [1975] 3 All E.R. 604; *Brisbane City Council v Att-Gen for Queensland* [1979] A.C. 411, 425; *Green v Hampshire CC* [1979] I.C.R. 861, 865–866; *Vervaeke v Smith* [1983] 1 A.C. 145; *Dallal v Bank Mellat* [1986] Q.B. 441, 452; *The European Gateway* [1987] Q.B. 206, 212, 221; *S.C.F. Finance Co Ltd v Masri (No.3)* [1987] Q.B. 1028, 1049; *Talbot v Berkshire CC* [1994] Q.B. 290, 296.

to bring "a genuine subject of litigation before the court".[61] The burden is therefore upon the defendant to establish that it is oppressive or an abuse of process for him to be subjected to the second action[62] and there will "rarely be a finding of abuse unless the latter proceeding involves what the court regards as unjust harassment of a party".[63] The question whether an action is an abuse of the court is "closely related"[64] to the question whether or not there is an estoppel *per rem judicatam* but it is not identical so that an action may be struck out on the ground that it is an abuse of the court where the plea of estoppel is not strictly made out.[65] Estoppel *per rem judicatam* may be raised as a defence,[66] but the more usual course is to apply to the court for an order that the statement of claim, or part thereof, be struck out and the action stayed or dismissed.[67]

25–014 **Issue estoppel: exceptional circumstances.** So far as cause of action estoppel is concerned, the rule appears to be absolute[68]: a party cannot relitigate the same cause of action even if new facts or law have subsequently come to light.[69] But there may be circumstances in issue estoppel where the justice of allowing the matter to be relitigated outweighs the hardship to the successful party in the first action in having to relitigate the point.[70] Thus a party may not be estopped if further material which is relevant to the correctness or incorrectness of the

---

[61] *Johnson v Gore Wood & Co (A Firm)* [2002] 2 A.C. 1, 22. The speech of Lord Bingham contains a particularly valuable review of the authorities.

[62] *Johnson v Gore Wood & Co (A Firm)* [2002] 2 A.C. 1, 59–60. Note also the impact of art.6 of the European Convention on Human Rights on the reasoning of Lord Millett (59).

[63] *Johnson v Gore Wood & Co (A Firm)* [2002] 2 A.C. 1, 31.

[64] *Dallal v Bank Mellat* [1988] Q.B. 441, 452. The closeness of the link can be seen in the fact that *Henderson v Henderson* (1843) 3 Hare 100 has been explained as an example of the extension of cause of action estoppel (*Arnold v National Westminster Bank Plc* [1991] 2 A.C. 93, 105) and of the exercise of the inherent jurisdiction of the court (*Yat Tung Investment Co Ltd v Dao Heng Bank Ltd* [1975] A.C. 581, 590). See to the same effect *Greenhalgh v Mallard* [1947] 2 All E.R. 255; *Hunter v Chief Constable of West Midlands* [1982] A.C. 529, 540; *The European Gateway* [1987] Q.B. 206, 212, 221; *S.C.F. Finance Co Ltd v Masri (No.3)* [1987] Q.B. 1028, 1049; and *Johnson v Gore Wood & Co (A Firm)* [2002] 2 A.C. 1, 31 ("separate and distinct" but having "much in common") and 59 (they are "all designed to serve the same purpose: to bring finality to litigation and avoid the oppression of subjecting a defendant unnecessarily to successive actions"); cf. *Barrow v Bankside Agency Ltd* [1996] 1 W.L.R. 257.

[65] *Yat Tung Investment Co Ltd v Dao Heng Bank Ltd* [1975] A.C. 581, 590; *Bragg v Oceanus Mutual Underwriting Association (Bermuda) Ltd* [1982] 2 Lloyd's Rep. 132, 137, 138–139; *J.H. Rayner (Mincing Lane) Ltd v Bank fur Gemeinwirtschaft AG* [1983] 1 Lloyd's Rep. 462, 469; *North West Water Ltd v Binnie & Partners* [1990] 3 All E.R. 547, 553; *House of Spring Gardens Ltd v Waite* [1991] 1 Q.B. 241, 254–255. The rule in *Henderson v Henderson* (1843) 3 Hare 100 has been held to apply where the first action concludes in a settlement, whereas the strict doctrine of *res judicata* would not apply in such a situation: *Johnson v Gore Wood & Co (A Firm)* [2002] 2 A.C. 1, 32–33 and 59.

[66] Although the CPR do not expressly require the defence to be specifically pleaded, it is advisable to continue to plead it specifically. The new rules relating to the contents of the defence are set out in CPR, Pt 16.5. See also *Morrison, Rose and Partners v Hillman* [1961] 2 Q.B. 266; *Lee v Citibank NA* [1981] H.K.L.R. 470 (irrelevancy of which proceedings were first commenced).

[67] *Carl Zeiss Stiftung v Rayner & Keeler Ltd (No.3)* [1970] Ch. 506.

[68] Subject to cases of covin, collusion and fraud and lack of jurisdiction; below, para.25–015.

[69] *Arnold v National Westminster Bank Plc* [1991] 2 A.C. 93, 104.

[70] *Carl Zeiss Stiftung v Rayner & Keeler Ltd (No.2)* [1967] 1 A.C. 853, 947; *Yat Tung Investment Co Ltd v Dao Heng Bank Ltd* [1975] A.C. 581, 590; *Arnold v National Westminster Bank Plc* [1991] 2 A.C. 93, 108–109. The better approach may, however, be to ask whether, in all the circumstances, a party's conduct is an abuse rather than to ask whether it amounts to an abuse and then, if it is, to

assertion and could not by reasonable diligence have been adduced by that party in the previous proceedings has since become available to him[71] or if there has been a change in the law subsequent to the previous proceedings.[72]

Ineffective judgments. A judgment obtained by covin, collusion or fraud is no bar to a subsequent action in respect of the same subject matter.[73] Similarly, a judgment obtained in a court which had no jurisdiction to pronounce it is without legal effect.[74] 25–015

Foreign judgments.[75] A judgment of a foreign court (including a court in another part of the United Kingdom) did not at common law operate in England as a merger of the original cause of action in respect of which the judgment was given.[76] However, by s.34 of the Civil Jurisdiction and Judgments Act 1982, no proceedings may be brought[77] by a person in England on a cause of action[78] in respect of which a judgment[79] has been given in his favour in proceedings 25–016

---

ask whether the abuse is excused or justified by special circumstances: *Johnson v Gore Wood & Co (A Firm)* [2002] 2 A.C. 1, 30–31.

[71] *Mills v Cooper* [1967] 2 Q.B. 459, 468. See also *Phosphate Sewage Co v Mollison* (1879) 4 App. Cas. 801; *Ladd v Marshall* [1954] 1 W.L.R. 1489, 1491; *McIlkenny v Chief Constable of West Midlands* [1980] Q.B. 283, 319–320; *Hunter v Chief Constable of West Midlands* [1982] A.C. 529, 541.

[72] *Arnold v National Westminster Bank Plc* [1991] 2 A.C. 93.

[73] *Duchess of Kingston's Case* (1776) 20 St.Tr. 573; *Girdlestone v Brighton Aquarium Co* (1879) 4 Ex.D. 107; *Abouloff v Oppenheimer & Co* (1882) 10 QBD 295; *Vadala v Lawes* (1890) 25 QBD 310; *Birch v Birch* [1902] P.130; *Nixon v Loundes* [1909] 2 Ir.Rep. 1; *Reg. v Humphreys* [1977] A.C. 1, 39. In the case of an English judgment, it is impeachable in an English court on the ground that it was obtained by fraud but only by the production and establishment of evidence newly discovered since the trial and not reasonably discoverable before the trial (*Boswell v Coaks (No.2)* (1894) 86 L.T. 365n). But in the case of a foreign judgment fresh evidence is not required before it can be attacked on the ground of fraud in an English court (*Abouloff v Oppenheimer & Co* (1882) 10 QBD 295). In *Owens Bank Ltd v Etoile Commerciale SA* [1995] 1 W.L.R. 44 the Privy Council noted this disparity of treatment in disapproving terms and, while they indicated a preference for the general application of the rule which presently governs English judgments, they stopped short of overruling *Abouloff*. However, the Privy Council went on to hold that the court does have an inherent power to prevent misuse of its process and that that power can be exercised to strike out a defence based on an allegation that a foreign judgment has been obtained by fraud where full particulars of the fraud have not been given. *Abouloff* has since been held to be inapplicable to the enforcement of a foreign arbitration award (*Westacre Investments Inc v Jugoimport-SPDR Holding Co Ltd* [1999] 3 Q.B. 740).

[74] *Rogers v Wood* (1831) 2 B. & Ad. 245.

[75] See Dicey, Morris and Collins, *The Conflict of Laws*, 14th edn (2006), Ch.14. See also Barnett, *Res Judicata, Estoppel and Foreign Judgments* (2001).

[76] *Smith v Nicolls* (1839) 5 Bing. N.C. 208; *Bank of Australasia v Harding* (1850) 9 C.B. 661; *Bank of Australasia v Nias* (1851) 16 Q.B. 717; *Carl Zeiss Stiftung v Rayner & Keeler Ltd* [1967] 1 A.C. 853, 917, 927, 938; *Re Flynn (No.2)* [1969] 2 Ch. 403, 412; *Republic of India v India S.S. Co Ltd* [1993] A.C. 410, 417, 423.

[77] Proceedings which are "continued" after judgment has been obtained in other proceedings involving the same parties or their privies fall within the scope of "brought" for this purpose: *Republic of India v India S.S. Co Ltd (No.2)* [1998] A.C. 878, 912.

[78] "Cause of action" is used in the technical sense of every fact which it would be necessary for the claimant to prove, if traversed, to obtain the relief which he claims: *Republic of India v India S.S. Co Ltd* [1993] A.C. 410, 419–421; *Black v Yates* [1992] Q.B. 526, 543–545.

[79] Defined in Civil Jurisdiction and Judgments Act 1982 s.50.

between the same parties, or their privies, in a court[80] in another part of the United Kingdom[81] or in a court of an overseas country,[82] unless that judgment is not enforceable or entitled to recognition in England. The effect of s.34 is to reverse the common law rule that a foreign judgment does not of itself extinguish the original cause of action in respect of which the judgment was given.[83] But it does not apply the doctrine of merger in judgment to foreign judgments.[84] So it does not exclude the jurisdiction of the court, but rather it provides a bar against proceedings by the claimant, which bar can be defeated by waiver or estoppel.[85] The claimant need not have been one of the original parties to the foreign proceedings, nor need the proceedings have been exclusively civil in character, provided that the judgment is enforceable or entitled to recognition in England.[86] In deciding whether or not the proceedings are between the same parties, or their privies, the court is likely to take a flexible approach and consider whether the reality is that the claim is between the same parties.[87]

25–017 **Foreign judgments in personam.** At common law, a foreign judgment in personam which is final and conclusive[88] on the merits[89] will be entitled to recognition in England,[90] provided that it is given by a court having jurisdiction

[80] s.50.

[81] s.50.

[82] s.50.

[83] *Republic of India v India S.S. Co Ltd* [1993] A.C. 410, 418; *Republic of India v India S.S. Co Ltd (No.2)* [1998] A.C. 878, 912; Davenport (1994) 110 L.Q.R. 25.

[84] [1993] A.C. 410, 423.

[85] [1993] A.C. 410, 423–424; *Showlag v Mansour* [1995] 1 A.C. 431, 441; *Republic of India v India S.S. Co Ltd (No.2)* [1998] A.C. 878.

[86] *Black v Yates* [1992] Q.B. 526, 546–549, distinguishing *Marginson v Blackburn BC* [1939] 2 K.B. 426 on the ground that it was a case of estoppel and not a case of merger (*quaere*, whether this argument can stand in the light of *Republic of India v India S.S. Co Ltd* [1993] A.C. 410) and on the broader ground that Parliament, when enacting s.34, could not have intended to limit the application of the section to previous proceedings in those countries which have an identical form of action to the English form of action brought by the claimant.

[87] *Republic of India v India S.S. Co Ltd (No.2)* [1998] A.C. 878, 896 CA.

[88] *Plummer v Woodburne* (1825) 4 B. & C. 625; *Scott v Pilkington* (1862) 2 B. & S. 11; *Nouvion v Freeman* (1889) 15 App. Cas. 1; *Beatty v Beatty* [1924] 1 K.B. 807; *Blohn v Desser* [1962] 2 Q.B. 116; *Colt Industries Inc v Sarlie (No.2)* [1966] 1 W.L.R. 1287; *Berliner Industriebank A.G. v Jost* [1971] 2 Q.B. 463; *Helmville Ltd v Astilleros Espanoles SA* [1984] 2 Lloyd's Rep. 569. cf. *Harrop v Harrop* [1920] 3 K.B. 386; *Re Macartney* [1921] 1 Ch. 522; *Westfal-Larson & Co A.S. v Ikerigi Compania Naviera SA* [1983] 1 Lloyd's Rep. 424. A foreign judgment may be final and conclusive even though it is subject to appeal or is under appeal; but cf. Administration of Justice Act 1920 s.9(2)(e); Foreign Judgments (Reciprocal Enforcement) Act 1933 ss.1(3), 5(1).

[89] *Carl-Zeiss Stiftung v Rayner & Keeler Ltd (No.2)* [1967] 1 A.C. 853, 917, 925, 967 (estoppel per rem judicatam). In the context of issue estoppel, a decision "on the merits" may be procedural in nature: *D.S.V. Silo-und Verwaltungsgesellschaft mbH v Owners of the Sennar* [1985] 1 W.L.R. 490. cf. *Charm Maritime Inc v Kyriakou* [1987] 1 F.T.L.R. 265 CA; *Harris v Quine* (1869) L.R. 4 Q.B. 653 (limitation); *Black-Clawson International Ltd v Papierworke-Aschaffenburg A.G.* [1975] A.C. 591 (limitation), but see now the Foreign Limitation Periods Act 1984 s.3.

[90] See Dicey, Morris and Collins at 14R–018. See also Administration of Justice Act 1920; Foreign Judgments (Reciprocal Enforcement) Act 1933; Dicey, Morris and Collins at 14R–161—14–184. Where there are two competing foreign judgments, each of which is pronounced by a court of competent jurisdiction and is final and not open to impeachment on any ground, then the general rule is that the earlier of them in time must be recognised and given effect to, to the exclusion of the latter, although there may be circumstances under which the party holding the earlier judgment may be estopped from relying on it: *Showlag v Mansour* [1995] 1 A.C. 431.

to give the judgment[91] and is not impeachable on grounds of fraud, public policy or breach of natural justice.[92] In the case of a judgment given by a court of a state party to the Brussels Convention on Jurisdiction and Enforcement of Judgments in Civil and Commercial Matters,[93] the Lugano Convention on Jurisdiction and Enforcement of Judgments in Civil and Commercial Matters[94] or the Council Regulation on Jurisdiction and the Recognition and Enforcement of Judgments in Civil and Commercial Matters[95] and which falls within the scope of either Convention or the Regulation, the judgment will (and must) be recognised in England.[96] Although certain exceptions are provided for in both Conventions and the Regulation,[97] these are very limited in nature and in particular an English court cannot ordinarily question the jurisdiction of the court by which the judgment was given.[98] Where the judgment is that of a court in another part of the United Kingdom, i.e. in Scotland or Northern Ireland, it would appear that such a judgment is entitled to recognition, and may be impeached, in accordance with the common law[99]; but the judgment cannot be refused recognition in England solely on the ground that, in relation to that judgment, the court which gave it was not a court of competent jurisdiction according to the rules of private international law in force in England.[100]

Estoppel by foreign judgment in personam. A foreign judgment which is entitled to recognition in England may also, if given in favour of the defendant, 25–018

[91] i.e. according to the rules of English private international law: see Dicey, Morris and Collins at 14R–048—14–098. See also Administration of Justice Act 1920 s.9(2)(a), (b); Foreign Judgments (Reciprocal Enforcement) Act 1933 ss.4(1)(a)(ii), 2(a); Civil Jurisdiction and Judgments Act 1982 s.33 (as amended by Sch.2 para.15 to Civil Jurisdiction and Judgments Act 1991).

[92] See Dicey, Morris and Collins at 14R–127—14–160. By statute, an overseas judgment may also be refused recognition if it is given in proceedings brought in breach of an agreement for settlement of a dispute: see Civil Jurisdiction and Judgments Act 1982 s.32 (as amended by Sch.2 para.14 to Civil Jurisdiction and Judgments Act 1991); *Tracomin SA v Sudan Oil Seeds Co Ltd (Nos 1 and 2)* [1983] 1 W.L.R. 1026, 1427; Dicey, Morris and Collins at 14R–090—14–093. See also Administration of Justice Act 1920 s.9(2)(c), (d), (f); Foreign Judgments (Reciprocal Enforcement) Act 1933 ss.4(1)(a)(iv), (v), 8(1), (2); *Owens Bank Ltd v Bracco* [1992] 2 A.C. 443; *House of Spring Gardens Ltd v Waite* [1991] 1 Q.B. 241; *Owens Bank Ltd v Etoile Commerciale SA* [1995] 1 W.L.R. 44.

[93] Brussels Convention (1968) together with the 1971 Protocol thereto, both as amended by the Convention on Accession (1978). See the Civil Jurisdiction and Judgments Act 1982 s.2(2) and Schs 1, 2, 3. See Dicey & Morris at 14R–183—14–229

[94] Lugano Convention (1988). See the Civil Jurisdiction and Judgments Act 1982 s.3A and Sch.3C.

[95] Regulation 44/2001 on jurisdiction and the recognition and enforcement of judgments in civil and commercial matters [2001] OJ L12/1. See the Civil Jurisdiction and Judgments Order 2001 (SI 2001/3929) art.3 and Schs 1, 2.

[96] Civil Jurisdiction and Judgments Act 1982 s.2(1) and Sch.1 paras 26, 29, 30 (Brussels Convention) and s.3(1) and Sch.3C paras 26, 29, 30 (Lugano Convention) and Civil Jurisdiction and Judgments Order art.3 and Sch.1 paras 33, 36, 37. The relationship between the two Conventions is regulated by art.54B of the Lugano Convention. The relationship between the Order and the two Conventions is regulated by arts 67 and 68 of the Order.

[97] Lugano and Brussels Conventions arts 27, 28 and Regulation 44/2001 arts 34, 35. An English court should not normally entertain a challenge to a Convention judgment in circumstances in which it would not permit a challenge to an English judgment: *Interdesco SA v Nullifire Ltd* [1992] 1 Lloyd's Rep. 180, 187–188.

[98] Lugano and Brussels Conventions art.28 and Regulation 44/2001 art.35.

[99] This would appear to be the effect of s.19 of the Civil Jurisdiction and Judgments Act 1982, since the section is negative in its wording. But see s.18 and Schs 6 and 7 (enforcement).

[100] s.19(1), (2) (subject to s.19(3)). For definitions, see s.50.

be relied upon to establish an estoppel *per rem judicatam*[101] and thus afford a good defence to an action in England between the same parties, or their privies, for the same matter.[102] Issue estoppel may arise in respect of an issue determined by previous proceedings in a foreign court.[103]

25–019 **Foreign judgment in rem.** A foreign judgment in rem, e.g. a judgment which determines the right to, or disposition of, some res[104] such as a ship or other chattel within the territorial jurisdiction of the foreign court,[105] probably acts as an assignment of the res.[106] The adjudication is recognised as binding upon the whole world.

2. ALTERATION OR CANCELLATION OF A WRITTEN INSTRUMENT

25–020 **Material alteration.** If a promisee, without the consent of the promisor, deliberately makes a material alteration in a specialty or other instrument containing words of contract, this will discharge the promisor from all liability thereon, even though the original words of the instrument are still legible.[107] The rationale for the rule is two-fold. First: "no man shall be permitted to take the chance of committing a fraud, without running any risk of losing by the event, when it is detected"[108] and, second, that the effect of the alteration renders the deed or instrument "no longer the deed or instrument of the party charged".[109] The rule consists of two principal elements. First, the alteration must have been made deliberately. The promisor is therefore not discharged if the alteration is made by accident[110] or by mistake.[111] Not every amendment or note will amount

[101] See above, paras 25–011—25–014.

[102] *Ricardo v Garcias* (1845) 12 Cl. & Fin. 368; *Société Generale de Paris v Dreyfus Bros* (1887) 37 Ch D 215; *Taylor v Holland* [1902] 1 K.B. 676, 681; *Jacobson v Frachon* (1927) 138 L.T. 386; *House of Spring Gardens Ltd v Waite* [1991] 1 Q.B. 241. See Dicey, Morris and Collins at 14–027—14–037, 14R–109—14–117.

[103] *Carl Zeiss Stiftung v Rayner & Keeler Ltd (No.2)* [1967] 1 A.C. 853, 918, 925–927, 966–967 (contrast at 937–938, 948–949); *Helmville Ltd v Astilleros Espanoles SA* [1984] 2 Lloyd's Rep. 569; *D.S.V. Silo-und Verwaltungsgesellschaft mbH v Owners of the Sennar* [1985] 1 W.L.R. 490, 499; *Black v Yates* [1992] Q.B. 526, 551–552; *Desert Sun Loan Corp v Hill* [1996] 2 All E.R. 847 (no issue estoppel arose because not sufficiently clear that the specific issue which arose before the court had been identified and decided against the defendant in the foreign court).

[104] *Fracis, Times & Co v Carr* (1900) 82 L.T. 698, 701.

[105] *The Henrich Björn* (1886) 11 App. Cas. 270, 276, 277; *Castrique v Imrie* (1870) L.R. 4 H.L. 414, 429; *Re Trufort* (1887) 36 Ch D 600.

[106] Dicey, Morris and Collins at 14R–099—14–108.

[107] *Pigot's Case* (1614) 11 Co. Rep. 26b (deed); *Master v Miller* (1791) 4 Term Rep. 320; *Croockewit v Fletcher* (1857) 1 H. & N. 893; *Sellin v Price* (1867) L.R. 2 Ex. 189, and cases cited in fn.130, below cf. *Hamelin v Bruck* (1846) 9 Q.B. 306; *Pattinson v Luckley* (1875) L.R. 10 Ex. 330. See generally *Norton on Deeds*, 2nd edn, p.34; Holmes (1897) 10 Harvard L.R. 457, 473; Williston (1904) 18 Harvard L.R. 105, 165. For the effect of alteration on joint obligations, see above, para.17–022; for negotiable instruments, see below 25–024 and Vol.II, para.34–141.

[108] *Master v Miller* (1791) 4 Term Rep. 320, 329; *Co-operative Bank Plc v Tipper* [1996] 4 All E.R. 366, 369–370, where the severity of the rule is noted by Roger Cooke J.

[109] *Raiffeisen Zentralbank Österreich AG v Crossseas Shipping Ltd* [2000] 1 W.L.R. 1135, 1143.

[110] *Hongkong and Shanghai Bank v Lo Lee Shi* [1928] A.C. 181.

[111] *Henfree v Bromley* (1805) 6 East 309; *Wilkinson v Johnson* (1824) 3 B. & C. 428.

to an "alteration".[112] Where, for example, the amendment is made in pencil, the court may infer that the amendment is not "an operative and final alteration"[113] but is merely an annotation or a suggestion.[114] Second, the alteration must have been material. The touchstone of materiality has been held to be whether or not:

> "... there has been some alteration in the legal effect of the contract or instrument concerned simply in the sense of some alteration in the rights and obligations of the parties."[115]

In order to show that the alteration is material the:

> "... would-be avoider should be able to demonstrate that the alteration is one which, assuming the parties act in accordance with the other terms of the contract, is one which is potentially prejudicial[116] to his legal rights or obligations under the instrument."[117]

Whether or not the would-be avoider:

> "... might or might not have assented to the alteration prior to affixing his signature, had he been requested to do so, is not a matter for investigation by the court when applying the rule."[118]

Material alteration by a stranger. More difficult to justify, however, is the supposed rule that a material alteration made by a stranger while the instrument is in the custody of the promisee discharges the promisor from his obligation.[119] The reason for this is said to be that the alteration of the instrument may raise a doubt as to its identity.[120] If this is so, the reason is both illogical and inadequate. 25–021

[112] It may be necessary in certain cases to distinguish between an "alteration" to a document and an "appendage" to the contract. Thus the addition of an incorrect date after the document has been signed may amount to an "appendage" rather than an alteration: *Moussavi-Azad v Sky Properties Ltd* [2003] EWHC 2669 (QB), [2003] All E.R. (D) 38 (Dec) at [49]. This may be thought to introduce an unnecessary element of sophistry into the rule and that the better view is that such an addition is an "alteration" and the vital question then becomes whether that alteration is "material".

[113] *Co-operative Bank Plc v Tipper* [1996] 4 All E.R. 366, 372.

[114] [1996] 4 All E.R. 366.

[115] *Raiffeisen Zentralbank Österreich AG v Crossseas Shipping Ltd* [2000] 1 W.L.R. 1135, 1146.

[116] It is not necessary to show that prejudice has in fact occurred. The rule is a salutary one which is aimed at the prevention of fraud and so it suffices to establish that the prejudice is potential: *Raiffeisen Zentralbank Österreich AG v Crossseas Shipping Ltd* [2000] 1 W.L.R. 1135, 1148. However there must be evidence from which a court can infer a potential prejudice: *Governor and Co of the Bank of Scotland v Henry Butcher & Co* [2003] EWCA Civ 67 at [73]–[74].

[117] *Raiffeisen Zentralbank Österreich AG v Crossseas Shipping Ltd* [2000] 1 W.L.R. 1135, 1148. The position may be otherwise where a bank note or negotiable instrument has been altered after its execution without the approval of the parties.

[118] *Raiffeisen Zentralbank Österreich AG v Crossseas Shipping Ltd* [2000] 1 W.L.R. 1135, 1150.

[119] *Pigot's Case* (1614) 11 Co. Rep. 26b; *Davidson v Cooper* (1844) 13 M. & W. 343; *Crookewit v Fletcher* (1857) 1 H. & N. 893, 912.

[120] *Sanderson v Symonds* (1819) 1 B. & B. 426, 430.

It is illogical, because the same doubt would be raised, whether or not the instrument was in the custody of the promisee, and it is inadequate, because extrinsic evidence would be admissible to prove the true words of the agreement.[121] On the other hand, if the reason for the rule is that an alteration made while the document is in the custody of the promisee raises a suspicion that it was made with his connivance or consent, the situation is already adequately covered, since it is incumbent on the party seeking to enforce an altered instrument to show that the alteration was made in such circumstances as not to invalidate it.[122] The acceptance of the rule would mean that an alteration by an officious burglar would discharge the contract.[123] Such a conclusion has rightly been doubted[124] and it is submitted that the rule should be discarded.

25–022 **Burden of proof.** The burden of proving that the promisee has, without the consent of the promisor, deliberately made a material alteration to a written instrument would appear to be on the promisor.[125] But, once it has been proved or it is apparent from the face of the instrument that it has been altered, the burden of proof switches to the promisee to show that the alteration was made in circumstances which were insufficient to discharge the promisee from all liability under the instrument (for example, by proving that the alteration was made before the promisor signed the document).[126] The question whether an alteration is material is a matter of law for the court.[127]

25–023 **Immaterial alteration.** An instrument is not discharged by an immaterial alteration, that is to say, one which does not alter the legal effect of the instrument or impose a greater liability on the promisor.[128] Cases in which the alteration has been held to be immaterial have been held to fall into two groups: (i) where it

---

[121] See above, para.12–105 et seq.

[122] *Johnson v Duke of Marlborough* (1818) 2 Stark. 313; *Bishop v Chambre* (1827) Moo. & M. 116.

[123] Williams, *Joint Obligations*, para.67.

[124] *Lowe v Fox* (1887) 12 App. Cas. 206, 217.

[125] There does not appear to be any authority in English law for this proposition but it flows from the general principle that he who alleges must prove. See generally on alterations *Phipson on Evidence*, 16th edn (2005), paras 40–27—40–30.

[126] *Johnson v Duke of Marlborough* (1818) 2 Stark. 313, 317; *Bishop v Chambre* (1827) M. & M. 116; *Henman v Dickinson* (1828) 5 Bing. 183; *Knight v Clements* (1838) 8 A. & E. 215, 220; *Cariss v Tatterswell* (1841) 2 M. & G. 890; *Clifford v Parker* (1841) 2 M. & G. 909, 911. See also *Halsbury's Laws of England*, 4th edn (2006 reissue), Vol.12(1), para.1056 and the notes to *Master v Miller* 1 Smith L.C., 13th edn, pp.807, 818. A different rule would appear to apply to deeds because, in the case of a deed, there is a presumption that the alteration was made before the deed was delivered, so that the promisor bears the burden of proving that the alteration was made after the deed was delivered: *Doe* d. *Tatum v Catomore* (1851) 16 Q.B. 745, 747; *Halsbury's Laws of England* at Vol.13, para.81.

[127] *Vance v Lowther* (1876) 1 Ex. D. 176, 178. The burden of proof would appear to be on the promisee to show that the alterations did not alter the liabilities of the parties on the instrument: *Koch v Dicks* [1933] 1 K.B. 307, 321.

[128] *Pigot's Case* (1614) 11 Co. Rep. 26b, as qualified in *Aldous v Cornwell* (1868) L.R. 3 Q.B. 573; *Bishop of Crediton v Bishop of Exeter* [1905] 2 Ch. 455 and *Moussavi-Azad v Sky Properties Ltd* [2003] EWHC 2669 (QB), [2003] All E.R. (D) 38 (Dec) at [48]–[51].

either was or could have been said that the alterations either rendered express, or had no effect upon (in the sense of adding nothing to), what the law would otherwise provide or imply[129]; and (ii) where the alteration corrects a mere "misdescription" which can be cured by parol evidence that a person or entity referred to has in fact been misdescribed and that the alteration merely corrects the error in description in accordance with the original intention.[130] Thus the addition, without the assent of the maker, of the words "on demand" to a promissory note did not vitiate the instrument, since the alteration only expressed the legal effect of the note as originally drawn.[131] The alteration in a charterparty of the time of sailing has been held to be material as it altered its legal effect.[132]

Negotiable instruments. By s.64(1) of the Bills of Exchange Act 1882, where a bill or acceptance is materially altered[133] without the assent of all parties liable on the bill, the bill is avoided, except as against a party who himself made, authorised or assented to the alteration, and subsequent indorsers[134]; provided that, where a bill has been materially altered, but the alteration is not apparent, and the bill is in the hands of a holder in due course, such holder may avail himself of the bill as if it had not been altered, and may enforce payment of it according to its original tenor.[135] 25–024

Bank of England notes. In the case of notes issued by the Bank of England, even an alteration which does not affect the contract may be sufficient to avoid the instrument. Thus where such notes had been fraudulently altered by erasing the numbers on them and substituting others with the object of preventing the notes from being traced, the Court of Appeal held that although the alteration did not vary the contract, it was material in the sense of altering the notes in an essential part and that the notes were therefore void.[136] 25–025

---

[129] See, e.g. *Aldous v Cornwell* (1868) L.R. 3 Q.B. 573; *Bishop of Crediton v Bishop of Exeter* [1905] 2 Ch. 455; *Caldwell v Parker* (1869) 3 I.R. Eq. 519.

[130] See, e.g. *Re Howgate and Osborn's Contract* [1902] 1 Ch. 451; *Lombard Finance Ltd v Brookplain Ltd* [1991] 1 W.L.R. 271, 274.

[131] *Aldous v Cornwell* (1868) L.R. 3 Q.B. 573. See also *Waugh v Bussell* (1814) 5 Taunt. 707; *Sanderson v Symonds* (1819) 1 B. & B. 426; *Wood v Slack* (1868) L.R. 3 Q.B. 379; *Decroix v Meyer* (1890) 25 QBD 343; *Re Howgate and Osborne's Contract* [1902] 1 Ch. 451; *Bishop of Crediton v Bishop of Exeter* [1905] 2 Ch. 455.

[132] *Croockewit v Fletcher* (1857) 1 H. & N. 893. See also *Davidson v Cooper* (1844) 13 M. & W. 343; *Re United Kingdom Shipowning Co Ltd* (1865) 2 De G.J. & Sm. 456; *Sellin v Price* (1867) L.R. 2 Ex. 189; *Suffell v Bank of England* (1881–82) L.R. 9 QBD 555; *Slingsby v District Bank* [1932] 1 K.B. 544; *Koch v Dicks* [1933] 1 K.B. 307.

[133] A material alteration is partly defined by s.64(2). See generally *Chalmers and Guest on Bills of Exchange*, 16th edn (2005), pp.532–534; *Byles on Bills of Exchange and Cheques*, 28th edn (2007), 20–15—20–18; and Vol.II, paras 34–141—34–142.

[134] *Master v Miller* (1791) 4 Term Rep. 320; *Burchfield v Moore* (1854) 23 L.J.Q.B. 261; *Woollatt v Stanley* (1928) 138 L.T. 620.

[135] *Scholfield v Londesborough* [1896] A.C. 514; *Imperial Bank of Canada v Bank of Hamilton* [1903] A.C. 49; *London Joint Stock Bank v Macmillan* [1918] A.C. 777.

[136] *Suffell v Bank of England* (1882) 9 QBD 555; *Slingsby v Westminster Bank* [1931] 1 K.B. 173; *Slingsby v District Bank* [1932] 1 K.B. 544; *Arab Bank v Ross* [1952] 2 Q.B. 216. cf. *Leeds Bank v Walker* (1883) 11 QBD 84; *Hongkong and Shanghai Bank v Lo Lee Shi* [1928] A.C. 181.

25–026 **Cancellation.** In early law, the accidental destruction or cancellation of a deed or of its seal prevented it being sued upon.[137] Now only the intentional cancellation by the promisee of a bond[138] or bill or promissory note[139] is sufficient.

25–027 **Loss.** The loss of a deed or written instrument does not destroy the obligation, but only affects the question of proving the instrument.[140] By s.69 of the Bills of Exchange Act 1882 the holder has the right to a duplicate of a lost bill.[141]

3. MISCELLANEOUS MODES OF DISCHARGE

25–028 **Death.** A personal contract is discharged by the death of either party.[142]

25–029 **Bankruptcy.** Proceedings in bankruptcy may act as a discharge of rights and liabilities under a contract.[143]

25–030 **Winding up.** The winding up of a company may result in a stay of proceedings in contract against the company and the discharge of the contract.[144]

25–031 **Set-off and counterclaim.** Where an action is brought for damages for breach of contract, the defendant may claim a set-off or counterclaim in the same action, and judgment may be given for the balance in favour of the claimant or the defendant.[145] This judgment operates to discharge the obligations involved in the claim and set-off or counterclaim. The position is otherwise where the defendant claims a set-off but does not make a counterclaim. In such a case the defendant can later issue fresh proceedings against the claimant even though the claimant has accepted a payment into court made by the defendant in settlement of the claimant's claim against the defendant and the allegations made by the defendant are essentially the same as those pleaded in his defence to the claimant's action.[146]

25–032 **Limitation.** A right of action arising out of a breach of contract may be barred or extinguished by the operation of the Limitation Act 1980 or other limitation enactment.[147]

---

[137] Shep.Touch. 69; *Nichols v Haywood* (1545) Dyer 59a (seal eaten by mice).

[138] *Bamberger v Commercial Credit Co* (1855) 15 C.B. 676, 693; *Perrott v Perrott* (1811) 14 East 423; *Carew v White* (1829) 2 Moo. & P. 558.

[139] Bills of Exchange Act 1882 s.63. See Vol.II, para.34–140.

[140] *Read v Price* [1909] 2 K.B. 724, 737.

[141] See also s.70 of the 1882 Act and Vol.II, paras 34–146, 34–147.

[142] See above, paras 20–006, 23–037; Vol.II, para.39–169.

[143] See above, paras 20–032—20–035, 20–037, 20–046—20–048.

[144] See above, paras 9–049—9–054.

[145] CPR rr.20.2, 16.6.

[146] *Hoppe v Titman* [1996] 1 W.L.R. 841. The Court of Appeal reached this conclusion with some reluctance but, on the facts, there was no suggestion from the plaintiffs, when the payment in was made, that it was intended to take into account and satisfy their own cause of action for breach of contract.

[147] See below, Ch.28.

Part Eight

REMEDIES FOR BREACH OF CONTRACT

CHAPTER 26

DAMAGES[1]

		PARA.
1.	Nature and kinds of damages	26–001
	(a) In general	26–001
	(b) Nominal damages	26–008
	(c) Claims for an agreed sum	26–009
	(d) Liquidated and unliquidated damages	26–010
	(e) Prospective loss and continuing breaches	26–013
	(f) Substitute performance (cost of completion or repairs)	26–016
	(g) Exemplary damages and depriving the defendant of his profit	26–019
	(h) Appeals against the assessment of damages	26–030
	(i) Third party beneficiaries	26–031
2.	Causation and contributory negligence	26–032
3.	Remoteness of damage	26–051
	(a) General rules	26–051
	(b) Timing of the assessment of damages	26–064
	(c) Loss of profits	26–066
	(d) Expenditure wasted or incurred as a result of the breach	26–072
	(e) Non-pecuniary losses	26–082
4.	Illustrations of the remoteness of damage and the assessment of damages	26–088
	(a) Sale of goods	26–088
	(b) Carriage of goods	26–089
	(c) Contracts concerning land	26–091
	(d) Contracts to pay or lend money	26–098
	(e) Sale of shares	26–100
5.	Assumption of responsibility	26–100A
6.	Mitigation of damage	26–101
7.	Penalty or liquidated damages	26–125
8.	The tax element in damages	26–157
9.	Interest and rate of exchange	26–167
	(a) Introduction	26–167
	(b) Damages for loss of interest at common law	26–168
	(c) Admiralty and equity	26–171
	(d) Statutory rights to interest	26–172
	(e) Statutory discretion to award interest	26–174
	(f) Interest of arbitration awards	26–183
	(g) Interest on judgment debts	26–184

[1] On the whole subject of damages, see *McGregor on Damages*, 17th edn (2003); Harris, Campbell and Halson, *Remedies in Contract and Tort*, 2nd edn (2002), Chs 1–17; Waddams, *The Law of Damages*, 3rd edn; Ogus, *The Law of Damages* (1973); Burrows, *Remedies for Torts and Breach of Contract*, 3rd edn (2004); Beale, *Remedies for Breach of Contract* (1980); Street, *Principles of the Law of Damages* (1962), especially Ch.10. For a comparison between common law and civil law, see Treitel, *Remedies for Breach of Contract* (1988), Chs IV to VII.

1. NATURE AND KINDS OF DAMAGES

(a) *In General*

26–001 **Introduction.** Subject to a few controls,[2] the parties to a contract may themselves specify in their contract the remedy available to the innocent party following the other's breach. In the absence of any such "tailor-made" clause on the remedy, the law on damages fills the gap with standard-form provisions on the assessment of money compensation which apply to all types of contract.[3] Until *Att-Gen v Blake*,[4] the traditional view was that damages for a breach of contract committed by the defendant are a compensation to the claimant for the damage, loss or injury he has suffered through that breach,[5] and this remains the normal rule.[6] The claimant is, as far as money can do it, to be placed in the same position as if the contract had been performed.[7] This implies a "net loss" approach in which the gains made by the claimant as the result of the breach (e.g. savings made because he is relieved from performing his side of a contract which has been terminated for breach; savings in taxation; benefits obtained from partial performance; or the salvage value of something left in his hands) must be set off against his losses arising from the breach (after he has taken reasonable steps to minimise those losses).[8] In assessing damages for breach of contract, the court can take account of only the defendant's[9] strict, legal obligations: it cannot take account of "the expectations, however reasonable, of one contractor that the other will do something that he has assumed no legal obligation to do".[10] Thus, if the contract-breaker had a choice of alternative methods of performance,

---

[2] e.g. the law on penalties below, paras 26–125 et seq.; and statutory controls such as the Unfair Contract Terms Act 1977 (above paras 14–057 et seq.), the Unfair Terms in Consumer Contracts Regulations 1999 (above, paras 15–001 et seq.) and the Consumer Credit Act 1974 (as amended by the Consumer Credit Act 2006) (below, Vol.II, paras 38–002 et seq.).

[3] Harris, Campbell and Halson, *Remedies in Contract and Tort*, 2nd edn (2002) pp.88–94.

[4] [2001] 1 A.C. 268 (see below, paras 26–022—26–026).

[5] *Robinson v Harman* (1848) 1 Ex. 850, 855; *Lock v Furze* (1866) L.R. 1 C.P. 441, 450–451, 453; *Livingstone v Rawyards Coal Co* (1880) 5 App. Cas. 25, 39; *Wertheim v Chicoutimi Pulp Co* [1911] A.C. 301, 307; *British Westinghouse Electric Co Ltd v Underground Electric Rys* [1912] A.C. 673, 689; *Watts & Co Ltd v Mitsui & Co Ltd* [1917] A.C. 227, 241; *Banco de Portugal v Waterlow & Sons Ltd* [1932] A.C. 452, 474; *Monarch S.S. Co Ltd v Karlshamns Oljefabriker (A/B)* [1949] A.C. 196, 220–221; *C. Czarnikow Ltd v Koufos* [1969] 1 A.C. 350, 414; *Johnson v Agnew* [1980] A.C. 367, 400; cf. below, paras 26–024—26–029.

[6] For exceptions see below, paras 26–019 et seq.

[7] For a recent use of this principle, see *Golden Strait Corp v Nippon Yusen Kubishika Kaisha* [2007] UKHL 12, [2007] 2 A.C. 353 at [9], [29], and [57] (see below, para.26–047).

[8] The language of "balancing" or "setting off" gains and losses is used by the House of Lords in the *British Westinghouse* case [1912] A.C. 673, 691, and in *Westwood v Secretary of State for Employment* [1985] A.C. 20, 44.

[9] It will on occasion take into account losses incurred by the claimant even though he was not legally obliged to incur them, e.g. payments made voluntarily to a third person injured as the result of the defendant's breach of contract. See below, para.26–078.

[10] *Lavarack v Woods of Colchester Ltd* [1967] 1 Q.B. 278, 294 (distinguished in a case of "unfair dismissal": *York Trailer Ltd v Sparkes* [1973] IRC 518; cf. *Janciuk v Winerite Ltd* [1998] I.R.L.R. 63, and in *Horkulak v Cantor Fitzgerald International* [2004] EWCA Civ 1287, [2005] I.C.R. 402, which involved a discretionary bonus clause). See also below, para.26–048.

damages will be assessed on the basis of his minimum legal obligation, viz on the alternative which would have been least onerous, or most beneficial to him.[11] If the claimant cannot establish an actual loss, he is entitled only to nominal damages.[12] Even where the claimant can prove his loss, damages are hardly ever a full recompense, since "it must be remembered that the rules as to damages can in the nature of things only be approximately just".[13]

Limitations on recovery. The law on damages places various conditions and restrictions on the principle that the claimant is generally entitled to recover all he has lost by the breach. Traditionally the principal general limitations on recovery have been (1) the "mitigation" rule, that a claimant cannot recover for losses which he could have avoided by taking reasonable steps[13a]; and (2) the "remoteness" rule, that the claimant will recover for losses only if they arose "in the usual course of things" or were losses that were contemplated by the parties at the time the contract was made.[13b] Following the very recent decision of the House of Lords in *Transfield Shipping Inc v Mercator Shipping Inc (The Achilleas)*[13c] it now seems that there is a third limitation of general application: (3) a claimant will not recover even losses that were not unlikely to occur in the usual course of things if the defendant cannot reasonably be regarded as assuming responsibility for losses of the particular kind suffered.[13d] Because the decision was handed down while this edition was in proof, it has not been possible to integrate the discussion of it fully into the text as a whole. It is dealt with principally in a separate new section.[13e] The remainder of the Chapter, and in particular the discussion of the remoteness rule, must be read in the light of this new section. The impact of this new limitation on recovery is far from clear. 26–001A

"Expectation" and "reliance" interests. A distinction has been drawn[14] between the "expectation interest" and the "reliance interest" of the claimant: the former relates to the gains or benefits[15] which he expected to receive from the completion of the promised performance of the other party's obligation but which were in the event prevented by the breach of contract committed by the latter[16]; the reliance interest relates to the expense or loss which the claimant has 26–002

---

[11] See below, para.26–048.

[12] See below, para.26–008.

[13] *Rodocanachi v Milburn* (1886) 18 0 67, 78. But see Street at Ch.5, and cf. the use of actuarial calculations approved by the House of Lords in *Wells v Wells* [1999] 1 A.C. 345.

[13a] See below, paras 26–101 et seq.

[13b] See below, paras 26–051 et seq.

[13c] [2008] UKHL 48, [2008] 3 W.L.R. 345.

[13d] See below, para.26–100C.

[13e] See below, paras 26–100A et seq.

[14] Street at pp.240–247; Fuller and Perdue (1937) 46 Yale L.J. 52, 373 (on this article, see Friedmann (1995) 111 L.Q.R. 628). (A third interest, the "restitution" interest, is protected by other rules: see below, paras 26–024, 29–054 et seq.) Another interest is the "performance interest"; see below, para.26–003.

[15] "Benefit" may include a personal or subjective, even idiosyncratic, benefit: see below, para.26–084.

[16] See, e.g. below, paras 26–066—26–071.

himself incurred in reliance on the promised performance[17] and which is wasted by the defendant's breach.[18] Both interests are protected by the law on damages, but it is not yet clear whether English law permits the claimant to recover both his expected profit on the contract and the consequential expense he has incurred in reliance on the defendant's promise.[19] In principle, he should be entitled to recover his expected *net* profit plus any of his incidental expenditure of a type reasonably contemplated by the parties at the time the contract was made, but not his *gross* profit (e.g. the full contract price) plus his disbursements which would have been incurred in earning that gross profit.[20]

26–003 **The "performance" interest.** Recent cases have recognised "that a party to a contract may have an interest in performance which is not readily measurable in terms of money".[21] This has occurred in two types of case. One is where the claimant has contracted for something which will benefit a third person. The damages available in this type of case were discussed in Ch.18.[22] It was in a case of this type that Lord Goff (dissenting) said that the courts may now be giving:

> "... fuller recognition of the importance of the protection of a contracting party's interest in the performance of his contract than has occurred in the past."[23]

The other is the exceptional class of cases like *Att-Gen v Blake*[24] in which the claimant has not suffered any loss but, because of the strong interest in performance, the courts have found it appropriate to order the defendant to account for his profits.[25] Academic writers have supported this approach, which they see as underlying restitutionary remedies for breach of contract.[26] Whenever the court makes an order for specific performance (or injunction) to force the promisor to fulfil exactly what he has undertaken to do (or refrain from doing) the remedy recognises the performance interest by giving the claimant exactly what was promised. But such a remedy has always been a discretionary one[27] and has not

---

[17] Costs incurred by the claimant in attempting to mitigate (see below, para.26–120) are incurred as a result of the defendant's breach and are therefore outside this definition.

[18] See, e.g. below, paras 26–063—26–068; Vol.II, paras 43–421—43–423. See also Owen (1984) 4 O.J.L.S. 393. The reliance interest includes the award of damages in some situations to restore the claimant to the position he would have been in if he had not entered a particular transaction: see below, para.26–070.

[19] Street at pp.243–245.

[20] Street at p.245; Morris L.J. (dissenting) in *Cullinane v British "Rema" Manufacturing Co* [1954] 1 Q.B. 292 (the majority of the Court of Appeal in this case held that the plaintiff must elect between claiming reliance expenditure and claiming loss of expected profits: see below, para.26–077 and Vol.II, paras 43–453—43–454).

[21] *Att-Gen v Blake* [2001] 1 A.C. 268, 282. On this case, see below, paras 26–024—26–029.

[22] See paras 18–046—18–071.

[23] *Alfred McAlpine Construction Ltd v Panatown Ltd* [2001] 1 A.C. 518, 551.

[24] [2001] 1 A.C. 268.

[25] See below, paras 26–019 et seq.

[26] Friedmann 111 (1995) L.Q.R. 628; Coote [1997] C.L.J. 537.

[27] Below, paras 27–003, 27–020.

been granted as a regular remedy for breach of contract, especially since it is not granted where damages would be "adequate".[28] But the new restitutionary remedies recognised in *Att-Gen v Blake*[29] go a considerable way to recognising that the claimant's interest in performance should be given legal protection.[30] But other academic writers[31] have warned that wider recognition of the performance interest could undermine some basic assumptions of the previous law. In particular, the rules on mitigation,[32] which are fundamental to the assessment of damages, often lead to the result that damages do not represent the full value of the defendant's promised performance because the damages have been assessed on the basis that the claimant should have taken reasonable steps after the breach of contract to avoid or minimise his loss caused by the breach. If the claimant can obtain adequate substitute performance from a third party, so as to give him the same benefit as he would have obtained from actual performance of the defendant's promise, his damages are prima facie only the difference in cost to him of obtaining that substitute performance, compared with what would have been the cost under the broken contract.[33]

Damages in lieu of specific performance or injunction. The court is empowered to award damages in addition to, or in substitution for an order for specific performance or an injunction: the assessment of damages under this power is examined in the next chapter.[34] 26–004

Concurrent liability. If the claimant is able to sue in tort (i.e. there is concurrent liability,[35] which has been considerably widened by *Henderson v Merrett*[36]) he will be able to take advantage of the more favourable rules on damages in tort, e.g. on remoteness of damage.[37] But concurrent liability in tort may benefit the defendant, e.g. in regard to contributory negligence.[38] 26–005

Kinds of damages: general and special damages. Various types of damages are distinguished for different purposes; the more important types are examined in the succeeding paragraphs. Thus, the distinction between general damages and special damages is mainly a matter of pleading and evidence. General damages are given in respect of such damage as the law presumes to result from the 26–006

---

[28] Below, para.27–005; cf. below, para.26–124.

[29] Above, fn.24.

[30] See also the new remedies (in Pt 5A of the Sale of Goods Act 1979) given to consumers in respect of the purchase of "non-conforming" goods, especially the use of specific performance to enforce the requirement to repair or replace non-conforming goods: see Vol.II, paras 43–114 et seq.

[31] Campbell and Harris 22 (2002) J. of L. Studies 208; Campbell [2003] J. Bus. L. 131, 141.

[32] Below, paras 26–101 et seq.

[33] Below, paras 26–016—26–018.

[34] Below, paras 27–077 et seq.

[35] See above, paras 1–117 et seq.

[36] [1995] 2 A.C. 145.

[37] Below, paras 26–051 et seq.

[38] Below, para.26–049.

infringement of a legal right or duty[39]: damage must be proved but the claimant cannot quantify exactly any particular items in it.[40] The main meaning[41] of special damages is that precise amount of pecuniary loss which the claimant can prove to have followed from the particular facts set out in his pleadings. Special damage must be specifically pleaded and evidence relevant to it cannot be adduced if only general damages have been pleaded,[42] since the purpose of pleading special damage is to prevent surprise at the trial by giving the defendant prior notice of any item in the claim for which a definite amount can be given in evidence, e.g. in a claim for wrongful dismissal, loss of salary during the period of notice required by the contract.[43] A claimant who bases his claim on precise calculations must give the defendant access to the facts on which they are based[44]: thus it was held that where loss of profits was not a necessary consequence of the alleged breach of contract the claim for such loss should be specifically pleaded, in order to give the defendant fair warning of the claim.[45]

26–007 **Difficulty of assessment.** The fact that damages are difficult to assess does not disentitle the claimant to compensation for loss resulting from the defendant's breach of contract.[46] Where it is clear that the claimant has suffered substantial loss, but the evidence does not enable it to be precisely quantified, the court will assess damages as best it can on the available evidence.[47] Similarly, the fact that the amount of that loss cannot be precisely ascertained, as, for example, where it depends on a contingency, does not deprive the claimant of a remedy. Where, if the defendant had fully performed his undertaking, there was only a chance that the claimant would acquire a benefit or make a profit, the court will discount the damages to reflect the likelihood that the benefit or profit would have been received.[48] The loss of profits suffered by a claimant as the result of the defendant's breach of contract frequently depends on many speculative factors, but the courts will always attempt to assess the amount of the loss.[49]

---

[39] Pollock, *Contracts*, 13th edn, p.536; cf. the cases on dishonouring a cheque, Vol.II, para.34–315.

[40] *Aerial Advertising Co v Batchelor's Peas Ltd* [1938] 2 All E.R. 788; and cf. *Sunley & Co Ltd v Cunard White Star Ltd* [1940] 1 K.B. 740. In *B.C. Sawmills v Nettleship* (1868) L.R. 3 C.P 499 it was presumed that delay in delivery had caused some loss and interest on the value of the goods was awarded by way of general damages.

[41] For other meanings, see Street at pp.18–22. One meaning which has been used is the reference to damages under the second rule in *Hadley v Baxendale* (1854) 9 Ex. 341 (below, paras 26–061 et seq.): see *President of India v La Pintada Compania Navegacion SA* [1985] A.C. 104, 125–127.

[42] *Hayward v Pullinger and Partners Ltd* [1950] 1 All E.R. 581; *Anglo-Cyprian Trade Agencies Ltd v Paphos Wine Industries Ltd* [1951] 1 All E.R. 873. See also *The Susquehanna* [1926] A.C. 655, 661; *National Broach and Machine Co v Churchill Gear Machines Ltd* [1965] 1 W.L.R. 1199 (this decision was accepted by the appellants in the House of Lords: [1967] 1 W.L.R. 384).

[43] *Hayward v Pullinger and Partners Ltd* [1950] 1 All E.R. 581. See Vol.II, para.39–194.

[44] *Perestrello e Companhia Limitada v United Paint Co Ltd* [1969] 1 W.L.R. 570.

[45] *Perestrello e Companhia Limitada v United Paint Co Ltd* [1969] 1 W.L.R. 570.

[46] *Chaplin v Hicks* [1911] 2 K.B. 786 (below, para.26–044); *Simpson v L.N.W. Ry* (1876) 1 QBD 274.

[47] *Tai Hing Cotton Mill Ltd v Kamsing Knitting Factory* [1979] A.C. 91, 106. cf. below, para.26–097.

[48] See below, paras 26–042—26–043.

[49] See below, paras 26–066—26–071.

(b) *Nominal Damages*

Nominal damages. Wherever the defendant is liable for a breach of contract, the claimant is in general entitled to nominal damages although no actual damage is proved[50]; the violation of a right at common law will usually entitle the claimant to nominal damages without proof of special damage.[51] Normally, this situation arises when the defendant's breach of contract has in fact caused no loss to the claimant, but it may also arise when the claimant, although he has suffered loss, fails to prove any loss flowing from the breach of contract,[52] or fails to prove the actual amount of his loss.[53] A regular use of nominal damages, however, is to establish the infringement of the claimant's legal right, and sometimes the award of nominal damages is "a mere peg on which to hang costs".[54] 26–008

(c) *Claims for an Agreed Sum*

Distinction between claims for payment of an agreed sum and claims for damages. There is an important distinction between a claim for payment of a debt and a claim for damages for breach of contract. A debt is a definite sum of money fixed by the agreement of the parties as payable by one party in return for the performance of a specified obligation by the other party or upon the occurrence of some specified event or condition[55]; damages may be claimed from a party who has broken his contractual obligation in some way other than failure to pay such a debt. (It is also possible that, in addition to a claim for a debt, there may be a claim for damages in respect of consequential loss caused by the failure to pay such a debt at the due date.[56]) The relevance of this distinction is that rules on damages do not apply to a claim for a debt, e.g. the claimant who claims 26–009

---

[50] *Marzetti v Williams* (1830) 1 B. & Ad. 415; *The Mediana* [1900] A.C. 113, 116; *Surrey CC v Bredero Homes Ltd* [1993] 1 W.L.R. 1361.

[51] *Ashby v White* (1704) 2 Ld. Raym. 938; *Constantine v Imperial Hotels Ltd* [1944] K.B. 693. On nominal damages when a bank wrongly dishonours a customer's cheque, see Vol.II, para.34–315.

[52] *Columbus & Co Ltd v Clowes* [1903] 1 K.B. 244; *Weld-Blundell v Stephens* [1920] A.C. 956; *Taylor & Sons Ltd v Bank of Athens* (1922) 91 L.J.K.B. 776; *James v Hutton and J. Cook & Sons Ltd* [1950] 1 K.B. 9; *Sykes v Midland Bank Executor and Trustee Co Ltd* [1971] 1 Q.B. 113. See below, paras 26–032 et seq.

[53] *Erie County Natural Gas and Fuel Co Ltd v Carroll* [1911] A.C. 105; cf. *Government of Ceylon v Chandris* [1965] 3 All E.R. 48; cf. *Tai Hing Cotton Mill Ltd v Kamsing Knitting Factory* [1979] A.C. 91, 106 (see above, para.26–007, text at fn.47); cf. also *Dean v Ainley* [1987] 1 W.L.R. 1729.

[54] *Beaumont v Greathead* (1846) 2 C.B. 494, 499. But costs are in the discretion of the court, and sometimes a claimant who recovers nominal damages will not receive costs: *Anglo-Cyprian Trade Agencies Ltd v Paphos Wine Industries Ltd* [1951] 1 All E.R. 873, 874.

[55] e.g. *Alder v Moore* [1961] 2 Q.B. 57 (below, para.26–145); *Hyundai Heavy Industries Co Ltd v Papadopoulos* [1980] 1 W.L.R. 1129, HL (guarantee: see Vol.II, Ch.44); *Damon Compania Naviera SA v Hapag-Lloyd International SA* [1985] 1 W.L.R. 435, 449 (suing in debt to recover an unpaid deposit); *Jervis v Harris* [1996] Ch. 195. See below, para.26–136; Vol.II, Ch.41 (contracts of insurance).

[56] See below, paras 26–098 et seq. Interest may also be payable on a debt: below, paras 26–167 et seq.

payment of a debt need not prove anything more than his performance[57] or the occurrence of the event or condition[58]; there is no need for him to prove any actual loss suffered by him[59] as a result[60] of the defendant's failure to pay; the whole concept of the remoteness of damage[61] is therefore irrelevant; the law on penalties does not apply to the agreed sum[62]; the claimant's duty to mitigate his loss does not generally apply[63]; and the claimant will usually be able to seek summary judgment.[64] The distinction may also be relevant where a contract provides for payment to be made by instalments; thus, under a hire-purchase agreement, a claim for arrears of instalments already due is a claim in debt quite distinct from a claim for damages for breach of the contract as a whole.[65] Under a contract for payment by instalments, no claim in respect of instalments due in the future may be brought as a claim for a debt, but if the party due to pay the instalments has committed a breach of his obligations which entitles the other party to terminate the contract, then, subject to the general rules on damages, an award of damages may be made in respect of the prospective loss of the future instalments, allowance being made for a discount on account of the earlier payment of a lump sum to be received under the judgment instead of the instalments spread over the future period.[66]

(d) *Liquidated and Unliquidated Damages*

26–010 **Liquidated and unliquidated damages.** The term liquidated damages is applied where the damages have been agreed and fixed by the parties (in respect of which the law has developed criteria for their validity[67]), or fixed by statute as in the case of damages against parties to a dishonoured bill of exchange.[68] Unliquidated damages is the term applied where the damages are at large and are to be assessed by the court; the rules as to remoteness of damage[69] are the main criteria for such damages.

---

[57] On the question when an action lies for the price under a contract for the sale of goods, see Vol.II, paras 43–390 et seq.

[58] See fn.55, above.

[59] See above, paras 26–001, 26–008.

[60] On causation, see below, paras 26–032 et seq.

[61] See below, paras 26–051 et seq.

[62] See below, para.26–136.

[63] *White and Carter (Councils) Ltd v McGregor* [1962] A.C. 413. (See below, para.26–122.)

[64] CPR Pt 24. A debt can be factored, viz sold to a financial institution.

[65] *Overstone Ltd v Shipway* [1962] 1 W.L.R. 117, 123, 129. (See Vol.II, para.38–325; cf. Vol.II, paras 38–188—38–191, 38–353.)

[66] *Interoffice Telephones Ltd v Robert Freeman Co Ltd* [1958] 1 Q.B. 190; *Robophone Facilities Ltd v Blank* [1966] 1 W.L.R. 1428; *Lombard North Central Plc v Butterworth* [1987] Q.B. 527 (below, para.26–141); *Stoeznia Gdanska SA v Latvian Shipping Co* [1998] 1 All E.R. 883 HL. On the question of the discount, see also *Overstone Ltd v Shipway* [1962] 1 W.L.R. 117 (approved by HL in *Christopher Moran Holdings Ltd v Bairstow* [2000] 2 A.C. 172, 180, 184, 188) and below, para.26–158, between fnn.823 and 824. On damages for prospective loss in general, see below, paras 26–013—26–015.

[67] Below, paras 26–109 et seq.

[68] Bills of Exchange Act 1882 s.57 (see Vol.II, para.34–120); *Re Rickett* [1949] 1 All E.R. 737.

[69] Below, paras 26–052 et seq.

Often the parties to a contract fix a sum as liquidated damages in the event of one specific breach, and leave the claimant to sue for unliquidated damages in the ordinary way if other types of breach occur.[70] Again, where there is provision for liquidated damages the claimant may, in appropriate cases, nevertheless elect to ask instead for an injunction to restrain a breach.[71] 26–011

Contract excluding or varying right to damages. At common law, the right of a contracting party to claim damages for a breach of the contract may be excluded by the express terms of the contract, provided that the language employed to do so is plain.[72] Subject to the law as to penalties[73] and to the general principles of the law of contract, such as illegality, the courts will enforce a contractual provision designed to operate in the event of a breach.[74] But the Unfair Contract Terms Act 1977 and the Unfair Terms in Consumer Contracts Regulations 1999 impose some statutory restrictions on attempts to exclude or limit liability for breach of contract.[75] 26–012

(e) *Prospective Loss and Continuing Breaches*

Prospective loss.[76] The general rule, in contract as well as in tort, is that damages for all prospective loss flowing from a single cause of action must be recovered once and for all in one action[77]: the claimant cannot recover damages for one part of his loss in one action, and then recover further damages for another part of his loss in a subsequent action.[78] Hence the claimant should claim at the same time damages for all his loss resulting or likely to result from the defendant's breach of contract, whether the loss is past or is reasonably anticipated in the future. Damages for prospective loss should take into account the contingencies of life and other uncertainties affecting the future.[79] The court may, 26–013

---

[70] e.g. *Aktieselskabet Reidar v Arcos Ltd* [1927] 1 K.B. 352. See below, para.26–125.

[71] But the claimant cannot have both an injunction and liquidated damages in respect of a single breach: *Sainter v Ferguson* (1849) 1 Mac. & G. 286; *Carnes v Nesbitt* (1862) 7 H. & N. 778; *General Accident Insurance Co v Noel* [1902] 1 K.B. 377. cf. the position if there are different breaches: *Imperial Tobacco Co v Parslay* [1936] 2 All E.R. 515; *Elsley v J. G. Collins Insurance Agencies Ltd* (1978) 83 D.L.R. (3d) 1 Sup.Ct. of Canada (injunction granted to restrain future breaches of employee's covenant not to compete, together with damages in respect of past breaches). See also *Upton v Henderson* (1912) 28 T.L.R. 398.

[72] On such exclusion or exemption clauses, see above, Ch.14.

[73] See below, paras 26–125 et seq.

[74] For illustrations, see below, paras 26–142—26–144.

[75] See above, paras 14–059 et seq., 15–004 et seq.

[76] On damages for sums of money payable in the future, see above, para.26–009.

[77] *Rowntree & Sons Ltd v Allen & Sons (Poplar) Ltd* (1936) 41 Com. Cas. 90. See above, para.26–007; s.35 of the County Courts Act 1984; cf. the same rule in tort: *Darley Main Colliery Co v Mitchell* (1886) 11 App. Cas. 127, 132. See also *Pegler v Ry Executive* [1948] A.C. 332.

[78] *Furness Withy & Co v Hall* (1909) 25 T.L.R. 233. See also *Conquer v Boot* [1928] 2 K.B. 336 (distinguished in *Purser and Co (Hillingdon) Ltd v Jackson* [1977] Q.B. 166 (successive arbitrations over different building defects)); *H.E. Daniels Ltd v Carmel Exporters and Importers Ltd* [1953] 2 Q.B. 242. Prospective loss falls within the rule: *Clarke v Yorke* (1882) 47 L.T. 381.

[79] e.g. *Johnston v G.W. Ry* [1904] 2 K.B. 250, 259–260. On discounting for contingencies in hypothetical situations, see below, paras 26–042 et seq.

however, defer the assessment of damages for future losses which are very uncertain.[80]

26–014 **Separate breaches.** There may be separate breaches of different promises in the same contract, giving rise to separate causes of action, as where there are successive breaches of an instalment contract[81]; in such a case, damages may be awarded for the separate breaches in separate actions.

26–015 **Continuing breaches of contract.** There is, however, a difference between a breach of contract which is a continuing one (giving rise to a continuing cause of action) and repeated breaches of recurring obligations.[82] With a continuing wrong, a fresh cause of action arises after recovery of damages in an earlier action, and the claimant may bring a second action to recover damages for loss arising after the earlier action. A former rule of court prescribed:

> "Where damages are to be assessed . . . in respect of any continuing cause of action, they shall be assessed down to the time of the assessment."[83]

An instance of a continuing breach of contract has been given by the Court of Appeal[84]:

> "For example, a contract of service for a specified term might contain a stipulation that the employee should not during the period of his service carry on or be concerned in any other business of the same kind as the employer's business. If the employee, in breach of such a stipulation, did proceed to carry out some other business of the kind in question, the breach would, we think, clearly be a continuing one, in that the employee would *de die in diem* be continuously in breach of the stipulation so long as the prohibited business was carried on."

(f) *Substitute Performance (Cost of Completion or Repairs)*

26–016 **Damages for the cost of completion, reinstatement or repairs.** In appropriate circumstances, damages may be assessed on the basis of what it will cost the claimant to obtain performance (or completion of performance) of the contractual undertaking by a third party.[85] Where the contract was one to transfer goods to the claimant, it is assumed that the claimant will obtain performance by

---

[80] *Deeny v Gooda Walker Ltd (No.3)* [1995] 4 All E.R. 289 (the plaintiff's future liabilities to policyholders could not be predicted with reasonable confidence; there was also the risk that, having received a substantial sum for future losses, the plaintiff might allow the damages to be dissipated before the policyholders' claims were made); cf. *Total Liban SA v Vitol Energy SA* [2001] Q.B. 643.

[81] *H.E. Daniels Ltd v Carmel Exporters and Importers Ltd* [1953] 2 Q.B. 242, 252; *National Coal Board v Galley* [1958] 1 W.L.R. 16, 26.

[82] *National Coal Board v Galley* [1958] 1 W.L.R. 16 (failure to work Saturday shifts at a colliery amounted to repeated breaches of a recurring obligation).

[83] RSC Ord.37 r.6. See *Hole v Chard Union* [1894] 1 Ch. 293; cf. the award of damages in lieu of an injunction: below, paras 27–077 et seq.

[84] *National Coal Board v Galley* [1958] 1 W.L.R. 16, 26.

[85] The advantages of this remedy are reviewed by Harris, Campbell and Halson, *Remedies in Contract and Tort*, 2nd edn (2002) pp.210–216.

purchasing goods which conform to the contractual requirements, and damages will be assessed as the difference between the cost (if reasonable) of the substitute purchase and the price fixed in the original contract (the rules of mitigation apply). In other situations, the damages are assessed as the difference between the market value of the defendant's performance in its defective or incomplete state, and the market value of the performance if it had been properly completed.[86] In a contract to perform services or for work and materials it will be assumed that the claimant will have the incomplete or defective performance completed or corrected and the damages will be assessed by the cost of getting this done; however, if the claimant will not have the work done or it would be unreasonable to do so, the damages will again be measured by the difference in value, which may be less than the cost of having the work done. The claimant is entitled to the reasonable cost of having the remedial work done if, in all the circumstances, it is (or was) reasonable for him to insist on having the work done.[87] Factors which are relevant to the issue of reasonableness include:

(i) the claimant has actually had the work done[88]; or

(ii) he undertakes to have it done[89] (but such an undertaking will not, on its own, make it reasonable for the claimant to have it done[90]); or

(iii) he shows a "sufficient intention" to have the work done if he receives damages on this basis[91]: the claimant's subjective intention is relevant.[92]

In *Ruxley Electronics and Construction Ltd v Forsyth*,[93] above, the House of Lords emphasised the role of reasonableness and held that where the cost of reinstatement was out of all proportion to the advantage to be gained by the 26–017

[86] *Tito v Waddell (No.2) (The Ocean Island case)* [1977] Ch. 106. In appropriate circumstances, damages may be awarded for loss of amenity, even the loss of a personal, subjective value in obtaining the benefit of performance: see below, para.26–084. Such a measure will fall between the cost of reinstatement and the diminution in market value.

[87] *Ruxley Electronics and Construction Ltd v Forsyth* [1996] A.C. 344 (see the comment by Poole (1996) 59 M.L.R. 272; and Coote [1997] C.L.J. 537); *Harbutt's "Plasticine" Ltd v Wayne Tank and Pump Co* [1970] 1 Q.B. 447, 473. On the question of the reasonableness of substitute performance in building contracts, see *East Ham Corp v Bernard Sunley & Sons Ltd* [1966] A.C. 406 (repairs carried out promptly when defect discovered); *Radford v De Froberville* [1971] 1 W.L.R. 1262 (commented on by Wallace in (1980) 96 L.Q.R. 101, 341); *Bevan Investments Ltd v Blackhall and Struthers (No.2)* [1973] 2 N.Z.L.R. 45; [1978] 2 N.Z.L.R. 97; *G.W. Atkins Ltd v Scott* (1980) 7 Construction L.J. 215, CA.

[88] *Jones v Herxheimer* [1950] 2 K.B. 106.

[89] The *Ocean Island* case [1977] Ch. 106, 333.

[90] *Ruxley Electronics and Construction Ltd v Forsyth* [1996] A.C. 344, 373.

[91] The *Ocean Island* case [1977] Ch. 106, 333; *Radford v De Froberville* [1971] 1 W.L.R. 1262, 1269–1270; cf. the tort case of *Dodd Properties Ltd v Canterbury City Council* [1980] 1 W.L.R. 433.

[92] The *Ruxley Electronics* case [1996] A.C. 344, 359, 372–373.

[93] [1996] A.C. 344. For an application of the case see *Sunrock Aircraft Corp Ltd v Scandinavian Airlines Sytem Denmark-Norway-Sweden* [2007] EWCA Civ 882, [2007] 2 Lloyd's Rep 612.

plaintiff from reinstatement,[94] it would be unreasonable for the plaintiff to insist on it. In this case, a swimming pool was not built to the depth specified in the contract but was sufficiently deep for diving according to normal standards so that the market value of the property was not reduced. It was held that it was unreasonable for the plaintiff to claim the cost of rebuilding the pool to the contractual specification. (However, the House of Lords did approve the award of £2,500 as damages for loss of amenity or loss of consumer surplus.)[95] But the courts have refused to assess damages at the cost of repairs where a surveyor negligently failed to report defects in a property purchased by the claimant in reliance on the report.[96]

26–018 The time at which the cost of repairs should be assessed is when it would have been reasonable for the claimant to begin repairs,[97] which may be as late as the date of the hearing if the claimant was acting reasonably in not mitigating earlier.[98]

(g) *Exemplary Damages and Depriving the Defendant of his Profit*

26–019 **Exemplary damages.**[99] Exemplary damages are damages awarded against the defendant as a punishment, so that the assessment goes beyond mere compensation of the claimant. Such "punitive" or "vindictive" damages were permitted in some cases of tort until 1964 when the House of Lords in *Rookes v Barnard*[100] severely restricted their use in such cases by specifying only two categories where they may be awarded at common law. The right to receive

---

94 On the question whether the "cost of cure" is disproportionate to the benefit, see *Channel Island Ferries Ltd v Cenargo Navigation Ltd (The Rozel)* [1994] 2 Lloyd's Rep. 161; cf. the use of reasonableness to decide whether the owner of a chattel damaged by negligence (tort) was entitled to the cost of replacing it rather than its market value: *Southampton Container Terminals Ltd v Hansa Schiffahrts GmbH (The Maersk Colombo)* [2001] EWCA Civ 717, [2001] 2 Lloyd's Rep. 275.

95 See below, para.26–084.

96 See below, para.26–093.

97 *Radford v De Froberville* [1971] 1 W.L.R. 1262; *London Congregational Union Inc v Harriss and Harriss* [1985] 1 All E.R. 335, 344 (the appeal did not deal with this point: [1988] 1 All E.R. 15); *Cormier Enterprises Ltd v Costello* (1980) 108 D.L.R. (3d) 472. See below, para.26–064; and, on the duty to mitigate in general, below, para.26–101; cf. the tort case of *Dodd Properties Ltd v Canterbury City Council* [1980] 1 W.L.R. 433.

98 *Radford v De Froberville* [1971] 1 W.L.R. 1262; *Dodd Properties Ltd v Canterbury City Council* [1980] 1 W.L.R. 433 (a tort case where a building was damaged by defendant's tort; plaintiff reasonably postponed repairs until defendant admitted liability); *Alcoa Minerals of Jamaica Inc v Broderick* [2002] 1 A.C. 371, PC (claimant entitled to wait until liability had been established for cost of repairs: a tort case); *Bevan Investments Ltd v Blackhall and Struthers (No.2)* [1973] 2 N.Z.L.R. 45 (commented on by Wallace (1980) 96 L.Q.R. 101, 115, and 341); *Perry v Sidney Phillips & Son* [1982] 1 W.L.R. 1297 (defendant denied liability).

99 See the Law Commission Report (Law Com. No.247, 1997), Pt III (paras 3.33–3.37, 3.45–3.47 refer to breach of contract cases); Smith (1997) 60 M.L.R. 360.

100 [1964] A.C. 1129, 1220–1231; the ruling was upheld by the House of Lords in *Cassell & Co Ltd v Broome* [1972] A.C. 1027 (libel), but it was not followed by the Privy Council in an appeal from Australia: *Australian Consolidated Press v Uren* [1969] 1 A.C. 590. The use of exemplary damages in tort was again examined by the House of Lords in *Kuddus v Chief Constable of Leicestershire* [2001] UKHL 29, [2002] 2 A.C. 122 and in *Borders (UK) Ltd v Metropolitan Police Commissioner* [2005] EWCA Civ 197 (see below, para.26–024 fn.137.

exemplary damages for breach of contract was, for many years before 1964,[101] confined to the single case of damages for breach of promise of marriage,[102] but this cause of action was abolished in 1970.[103] In 1909, the House of Lords in *Addis v Gramophone Co Ltd*[104] held that exemplary damages could not be awarded for wrongful dismissal: no compensation should be given for the plaintiff's injured feelings[105] even where the dismissal was carried out in a humiliating manner.[106] The principle of this decision is not confined to cases of wrongful dismissal, and it is submitted that it now prevents the recovery of exemplary[107] damages for any breach of contract.[108] However, in special circumstances, damages may be awarded for mental distress where the parties contemplated it as a not unlikely consequence of breach.[109]

Depriving the defendant of profit made through his breach. The tradi- 26–020
tional view was that when assessing damages for breach of contract, the court is "concerned with the [claimant's] loss and not with the [defendant's] profit, the latter being wholly irrelevant".[110] Until *Blake*'s case[111] in 2000, the only recognised exceptions to this principle were where the claimant had a remedy in restitution or could enforce a fiduciary obligation; or where he had a remedy in tort or had an interest in property used by the defendant without permission. In these latter two tupes of case, the claimant may be awarded damages on a broad

[101] In some cases last century, before *Addis v Gramophone Co Ltd* [1909] A.C. 488, exemplary damages for breach of contract were awarded, e.g. *Lord Sondes v Fletcher* (1822) 5 B. & Ald. 835; *Maw v Jones* (1890) 25 QBD 107.

[102] *Quirk v Thomas* [1916] 1 K.B. 516, 527, 531, 538.

[103] Law Reform (Miscellaneous Provisions) Act 1970 s.1 provides that an engagement to marry shall not have effect as a contract giving rise to legal rights. (See notes in (1971) 87 L.Q.R. 158, 314.)

[104] [1909] A.C. 488 (see further, below, para.26–083).

[105] Followed in *Bliss v S.E. Thames Regional H.A.* [1987] I.C.R. 700.

[106] Some of the general statements in the *Addis* case [1909] A.C. 488 have been qualified by the House of Lords in *Malik v Bank of Credit and Commerce International SA* [1998] A.C. 20 (see below, paras 26–083—26–087). In *Johnson v Gore Wood & Co* [2002] 2 A.C. 1 the House of Lords recognised that some "inroads" had been made into the general principle laid down by *Addis's* case, but refused to make further inroads. See below, para.26–083. cf. *Dunk v George Waller & Son Ltd* [1970] 2 Q.B. 163 (employer's breach of contract of apprenticeship: see Vol.II, para.39–196); *Edwards v Society of Graphical and Allied Trades* [1971] Ch. 354 (damages for wrongful expulsion from a trade union, leading to dismissal from employment, may include damages "for the difficulty the dismissal causes to a plaintiff in getting fresh employment": at 379).

[107] The decision in *Addis's* case [1909] A.C. 488 is wide enough to mean that aggravated damages (as sometimes available in tort) cannot be awarded in contract: see *Kralj v McGrath* [1986] 1 All E.R. 54, 61; and *Johnson v Gore Wood & Co* [2002] 2 A.C. 1 where a claim for aggravated damages was struck out.

[108] *Perera v Vandiyar* [1953] 1 W.L.R. 672; *Kenny v Preen* [1963] 1 Q.B. 499 (but both doubted in *McCall v Abelesz* [1976] Q.B. 585, 594). cf. *Lavender v Betts* [1942] 2 All E.R. 72 (action in tort in similar circumstances); cf. also *Drane v Evangelou* [1978] 1 W.L.R. 455 (exemplary damages awarded for trespass when landlord wrongfully evicted his tenant). The Supreme Court of Canada has allowed exemplary damages for breach of contract in exceptional circumstances: *Royal Bank of Canada v W. Gott & Associates Electric Ltd* (2000) 178 D.L.R. (4th) 385 (noted in 117 (2001) L.Q.R. 539); *Whiten v Pilot Insurance Co* (2002) 209 D.L.R. (4th) 257 (noted in 119 (2003) L.Q.R. 20).

[109] See below, para.26–083.

[110] *The Solholt* [1983] 1 Lloyd's Rep. 605, 608.

[111] *Att-Gen v Blake* [2001] 1 A.C. 268.

measure which is not necessarily related to a real loss he has suffered. These are briefly reviewed in turn.[112]

26–021 **Claim in restitution.** Restitutionary remedies may be used to deprive the defendant of a profit,[113] e.g. to deprive an agent of a bribe or secret profit[114] or an employee of profits arising from misuse of confidential information.[115] The equitable remedy of tracing property[116] and the wide use of the remedial device of a constructive trust,[117] have also been used to deprive a defendant of his profit. So the Privy Council held a defendant liable to account for the profits made through the wrongful use of a telegraph wire.[118] The House of Lords in *Blake*[119] reviewed and approved the earlier cases on interference with rights of property at common law and equity mentioned in both this and the next paragraph.

26–022 **Broad measures of damages in tort.** In tort, damages have often been awarded for unauthorised use of the claimant's land.[120] On a similar principle, damages for retaining goods or buildings beyond the period of a letting to the defendant are assessed at the ordinary letting value of their use[121]; the same approach has been used in assessing damages against a buyer who refused to remove the goods from the seller's premises.[122] It is not always the case that the claimant would have used the goods or land himself or have rented them to someone else.[123] A famous example was given by Lord Shaw: the owner of a horse which the defendant has ridden without permission may recover damages even though the horse may actually be the better for having been ridden.[124]

---

[112] In *Blake's* case [2001] 1 A.C. 268 the House of Lords upheld all the exceptions set out in this paragraph.

[113] Goff and Jones, *The Law of Restitution*, 7th edn (2007), para.20–024 et seq.; Dawson (1959) 20 Ohio State L.J. 175, 185–188. On restitutionary damages, see below, paras 26–024 et seq.

[114] Below, para.29–156.

[115] See Vol.II, paras 31–128—31–130, 39–061—39–063.

[116] Below, paras 29–164 et seq.

[117] Below, para.29–160. The US Supreme Court has used a remedial constructive trust to deprive a cynical contract-breaker of his profits: *Snepp v United States* 444 US 507 (1980), but the English Court of Appeal preferred not to use this concept: *Att-Gen v Blake* [1998] Ch. 439, 459. See below, paras 29–160 et seq. See also Deane J. (dissenting) in *Hospital Products Ltd v US Surgical Corp* (1984) 156 C.L.R. 41, High Ct of Australia.

[118] *Reid Newfoundland Co v Anglo-American Telegraph Co Ltd* [1912] A.C. 555 (a promise to account for the profits of breach). See also *Reading v Att-Gen* [1951] A.C. 507.

[119] [2001] 1 A.C. 268, 278–280.

[120] e.g. the wayleave cases, such as *Phillips v Homfray* (1871) L.R. 6 Ch. App. 770; or where the defendant had trespassed by tipping soil on the plaintiff's land: *Whitwham v Westminster Brymbo Coal and Coke Co* [1896] 2 Ch. 538; or where a landlord wrongfully ejected his tenant and the damages for trespass were assessed as a reasonable rent for the entire period of the trespass, whether or not the landlord had derived any benefit from using the property: *Inverugie Investments Ltd v Hackett* [1995] 1 W.L.R. 713 PC. See Cooke (1994) 110 L.Q.R. 420.

[121] *Strand Electric and Engineering Co Ltd v Brisford Entertainments Ltd* [1952] 2 Q.B. 246; *Swordheath Properties Ltd v Tabet* [1979] 1 W.L.R. 285.

[122] *Penarth Dock Engineering Co Ltd v Pounds* [1963] 1 Lloyd's Rep. 359 (the reasonable charge for storage facilities was allowed as damages).

[123] See *Experience Hendrix LLC v PPX Enterprises Inc and Edward Chaplin* [2003] EWCA Civ 323, [2003] 1 All ER (Comm) 830 at [25] (Mance L.J.).

[124] *Watson, Laidlaw & Co Ltd v Potts, Cassels and Williamson* (1914) 31 R.P.C. 104, 119.

Invasion of property interest. Where a breach of contract also amounts to the invasion of a property interest vested in the claimant, he may obtain a remedy which has the effect of depriving the contract-breaker of some of his profit.[125] So in the *Wrotham Park* case[126] where the defendant built on his land in defiance of a restrictive covenant in favour of the plaintiff, the damages (in lieu of an injunction[127]) were assessed at the price which the plaintiff could reasonably have expected to receive from a negotiated partial release from the covenant; this price could be a proportion of the profits expected to be made by the defendant. In *Blake*'s case[128] the House of Lords explicitly approved the basis of the award in *Wrotham Park*, preferring it to some inconsistent Court of Appeal authority.[129] It may be that in *Blake*'s case the compensation for loss of the opportunity to bargain was viewed as a form of restitutionary remedy rather than a form of damages, but subsequently the Court of Appeal has held it to be a form of compensatory damages, in contrast to the account of profits ordered in *Blake*'s case itself.[130] 26–023

The extension made by *Att-Gen v Blake*. In *Att-Gen v Blake*[131] the House of Lords, while upholding the exceptions set out in paras 26–020 and 26–023 above, extended the principles in two ways. First, the *Wrotham Park* basis was approved without it being restricted to the invasion of a property interest: 26–024

> "In a suitable case damages for breach of contract may be measured by the benefit gained by the wrong-doer from the breach. The defendant must make a reasonable payment in respect of the benefit he has gained."[132]

This basis is discussed further below under the heading of "partial disgorgement" of the defendant's profit.[133] Secondly, their Lordships held that *Blake*[134] was an "exceptional case" which entitled the court to go even further:

> "When exceptionally, a just response to a breach of contract so requires, the court should be able to grant the discretionary remedy of requiring the defendant to account to the plaintiff for the benefits he has received from his breach of contract . . . the

[125] e.g. *Lake v Bayliss* [1974] 1 W.L.R. 1073.

[126] *Wrotham Park Estate Co v Parkside Homes* [1974] 1 W.L.R. 798, approved by the House of Lords in *Blake's* case [2001] 1 A.C. 268; followed in *Bracewell v Appleby* [1975] Ch. 408.

[127] Supreme Court Act 1981 s.50 (formerly, Lord Cairns' Act).

[128] [2001] 1 A.C. 268.

[129] *Surrey CC v Bredero Homes Ltd* [1993] 1 W.L.R. 1361; *Jaggard v Sawyer* [1995] 1 W.L.R. 269. The cases subsequent to Wrotham Park are exhaustively analysed in *WWF-World Wide Fund for Nature v World Wrestling Federation Entertainment Inc* [2007] EWCA Civ 286, [2008] 1 W.L.R. 445.

[130] *WWF-World Wide Fund for Nature v World Wrestling Federation Entertainment Inc* [2007] EWCA Civ 286, [2008] 1 W.L.R. 445. It was necessary for the court to examine the *Wrotham Park* basis for assessing damages in order to reach its decision, which was based on the claimant's abuse of process in seeking such damages after inviting the judge below to decide whether to order an account of profits on the basis that there would be no claim for *Wrotham Park* damages: at [74].

[131] [2001] 1 A.C. 268. See below, paras 29–151 et seq.

[132] [2001] 1 A.C. 268, 283–284.

[133] See below, para.26–027.

[134] [2001] A.C. 268, 283–284.

> plaintiff's interest in performance may make it just and equitable that the defendant should retain no benefit from his breach of contract."[135]

> "A useful general guide, although not exhaustive is whether the plaintiff had a legitimate interest in preventing the defendant's profit-making activity and, hence, in depriving him of his profit."[136]

This principle is discussed below under the heading of "total disgorgement" (para.26–028). On the facts of *Blake* it was applied to entitle the Crown to all the royalties from a book which the traitor Blake had written and published in breach of the confidentiality agreement made by him when he entered the Secret Intelligence Service.

26–025 The decision in *Blake* opened the door to restitutionary damages in English law but it has left great uncertainty as to the circumstances in which such an award is justified.[137] The emphasis in *Blake* on the claimant's interest in "performance" is difficult to follow when his entitlement to specific performance is so limited and when the rules of mitigation so often require him to accept damages which are less than the value which performance by the defendant would have had for the claimant.[138] It must also be remembered that the defendant who avoids expense by breaching should in theory be treated as analogous to his making a profit through breach; but such an extension would fundamentally undermine commercial law.[139] It is submitted that an account of profits will be ordered only in the most exceptional cases. However, it does seem that damages on the more limited *Wrotham Park* basis may be awarded more readily than before *Blake*'s case. In the *Experience Hendrix* case,[140] the Court of Appeal followed *Blake* by awarding such damages on the *Wrotham Park* basis in a commercial case.[141]

26–026 **Disgorgement on a sliding scale.** The decision in *Experience Hendrix*, above, seems to recognise a sliding scale[142] of recovery, from partial disgorgement of wrongful profits (*Wrotham Park*) to total disgorgement (an account of

---

[135] [2001] A.C. 268, 284–285.

[136] [2001] A.C. 268, 285.

[137] Campbell and Harris 22 (2002) J. Leg. Studies 208; Campbell and Wylie [2003] C.L.J. 605; Campbell 65 (2002) M.L.R. 256; Goff and Jones, *The Law of Restitution*, 7th edn (2007) paras 20–024 et seq.; *McGregor on Damages*, 17th edn (2003) at Ch.12. *Blake* leaves future courts with the task "best hammered out on the anvil of concrete cases" of deciding how far the new remedies should go (per Lord Steyn [2001] A.C. 268, 291). In *Borders (UK) Ltd v Metropolitan Police Commissioner* [2005] EWCA Civ 197, *Blake* was used to justify the extension of exemplary damages to cover disgorgement of some of the profits made by D through tortious activity: see Campbell and Devenney [2006] C.L.J. 208.

[138] Above, para.26–003.

[139] See the articles cited above in fn.137. In *Blake* [2001] A.C. 268, 299, Lord Hobhouse (dissenting) feared "far reaching and disruptive" consequences for commercial law.

[140] *Experience Hendrix LLC v PPX Enterprises Inc and Edward Chaplin* [2003] EWCA Civ 323, [2003] 1 All ER (Comm) 830. (This case is extensively analysed by Campbell and Wylie [2003] C.L.J. 605.)

[141] In commercial cases an account of profits has been granted at first instance: *Esso Petroleum Co Ltd v Niad Ltd* [2001] All E.R. (D) 324; but refused in *WWF-WorldWide Fund for Nature v World Wrestling Federation* [2002] FSR 32 (affirmed without reference to this point [2002] EWCA Civ 196); and by a strong arbitral tribunal: *A. B. Corp v C. D. Co (The "Sine Nomine")* [2002] 1 Lloyd's Rep. 805 (ship wrongfully withdrawn from a charter) (noted by Beatson 118 [2002] L.Q.R. 377).

[142] Burrows, *The Law of Restitution*, 2nd edn (2002), pp.461–462.

profits) but gives very little indication of the factors which will guide a court to fix the level of damages in an individual case. In *Experience Hendrix*[143] the Court of Appeal used the factors relevant to the granting of an account of profits[144] as also relevant to their discretion to grant *Wrotham Park* damages. "Hypothetical release" damages as in *Wrotham Park* appear to be assessed on a discretionary basis and to be arbitrary in amount. The court may often have no information about the level of the defendant's profit from breach since the claimant may not be able to obtain such evidence. *Blake* and *Hendrix* give claimants an incentive to seek extensive disclosure from the defendant.[145]

Partial disgorgement on the *Wrotham Park* basis. On this basis, the claimant is awarded "hypothetical release" damages representing what the claimant could reasonably have charged for giving permission to the defendant to act contrary to his contractual undertaking. Such damages have been assessed at a modest level (5 per cent of the defendant's anticipated profit in *Wrotham Park*[146]; in *Experience Hendrix* "significantly in excess of 2%" as a royalty on retail sales (sums yet to be assessed).[147] Such partial disgorgement of the "wrongful" profits made through the breach was explained in *Experience Hendrix* on a restitutionary, not a compensatory, basis. In the later *WWF* case[148] it was held to be a form of compensatory damages. Whichever is correct, strict compensation for loss which the claimant can prove to have been caused by the breach is treated as irrelevant: the defendant is required to make a "reasonable" payment in respect of the benefit he has gained.[149] In another phrase, it is the "value of a bargaining opportunity",[150] but it does not matter that had the claimant's permission been sought it would never have given it.[151] At the very least it can be said that the same broad measure of damages previously applied in tort cases of deliberately wrongful interference may now be used in cases of breach of contract where the defendant acted in disregard of the claimant's rights,[152] but the latter cannot show that he suffered a loss. 26–027

Total disgorgement by an account of profits. In *Blake*[153] the House of Lords gave the claimant the "exceptional" remedy of an account of profits, which would amount to a total disgorgement of the profits made by the defendant as a 26–028

[143] [2003] EWCA Civ 323 at [44], [58].

[144] Below, para.26–028.

[145] Harris, Campbell and Halson, *Remedies in Contract and Tort*, 2nd edn (2002), pp.268–272, 491–494. See the comment of the arbitral tribunal in *A.B. Corp v C.D. Co (The "Sine Nomine")* [2002] 1 Lloyd's Rep. 805.

[146] *Wrotham Park Estate Co v Parkside Homes* [1974] 1 W.L.R. 798, 816.

[147] [2003] EWCA Civ 323 at [46].

[148] *WWF-World Wide Fund for Nature v World Wrestling Federation Entertainment Inc* [2007] EWCA Civ 286, [2008] 1 W.L.R. 445.

[149] *Experience Hendrix* case [2003] EWCA Civ 323 at [58]. Since *Att-Gen v Blake* there is no need for such damages to be available only where an injunction is not granted: *Experience Hendrix* at [34] and [56].

[150] *Experience Hendrix* case [2003] EWCA Civ 323 at [45]. See Sharpe and Waddams (1982) 2 Oxf. J. Leg.S. 290.

[151] See *Experience Hendrix LLC v PPX Enterprises Inc and Edward Chaplin* [2003] EWCA Civ 323, [2003] 1 All ER (Comm) 830 at [25] (Mance L.J.).

[152] See below, para.26–028.

[153] *Att-Gen v Blake* [2001] 1 A.C. 268, 285 G–H. See the quotation above, para.26–025.

result of the breach. In *Hendrix* an account of profits was not awarded on the particular facts[154] but it was recognised that such a remedy was possible in a commercial case[155] where the defendants made contracts with third parties to exploit music recordings. In *Blake* their Lordships avoided any definition of "exceptional" circumstances which would justify an account of profits as the remedy for breach of contract. It appears that no one factor is crucial. But judges have given some factors which may be relevant to their decision:

(a) The moral character of the defendant's conduct in breaching, e.g. was it "deliberate and cynical"; did it involve "doing exactly what one promised not to do"? In *Blake*, Lord Nicholls said that none of the following facts "would be, by itself, a good reason for ordering an account of profits", but by these words he implied that they might contribute to the cumulative weight in favour of that remedy:

> "... the fact that the breach was cynical and deliberate; the fact that the breach enabled the defendant to enter into a more profitable contract elsewhere; and the fact that by entering into a new and more profitable contract the defendant put it out of his power to perform his contract with the plaintiff."[156]

Other relevant factors in *Blake* were that the breach of contract involved committing a criminal offence[157]; and that he committed repeated breaches.[158] In *Experience Hendrix* in granting partial disgorgement the Court of Appeal took into account the fact that the defendant "did do the very thing it had contracted not to do"[159]; that the defendant "knew that it was doing something which it had contracted not to do"[160]; that it was a "deliberate breach",[161] a "flagrant contravention" of the defendant's obligation.[162] But prior to *Hendrix* courts did not treat moral considerations as relevant in commercial transactions.

(b) The question whether the claimant "had a legitimate interest in preventing the defendant's profit-making activity".[163] In *Blake*, the Crown's interest in protecting the Secret Service's information met this test but in *Experience Hendrix*, a case between commercial parties, such a legitimate interest was found because on orthodox rules the claimant would be confined to nominal damages—the claimant could not adequately prove any loss, or could prove only minor loss.[164] It is submitted that this

[154] The situation was not sufficiently exceptional for an account of all profits. See below, para.29–154.

[155] An account of profits in a commercial cases was granted at first instance in *Esso Petroleum Co Ltd v Niad Ltd* [2001] All E.R. (D) 324.

[156] [2001] 1 A.C. 268, 286 E–F.

[157] [2001] 1 A.C. 268, 286 G–H.

[158] [2001] 1 A.C. 268, 286 G. Repetition of breaches was an important factor in the *Niad* case [2001] All E.R. (D) 324.

[159] [2003] EWCA Civ 323 at [36].

[160] [2003] EWCA Civ 323 at [36].

[161] [2003] EWCA Civ 323 at [58].

[162] [2003] EWCA Civ 323 at [54].

[163] *Att-Gen v Blake* [2001] 1 A.C. 268, 285.

[164] *Experience Hendrix* [2003] EWCA Civ 323 at [58].

interpretation is too wide, because it could allow many claims to be based (at the claimant's choice) on either restitution or compensation for loss.

(c) The analogy with fiduciary obligations. Before the *Blake* decision it was clear that an account of profits could be awarded for breach of a fiduciary obligation: although Blake was not a fiduciary, their Lordships said that his obligation was "closely akin to a fiduciary obligation".[165] In effect, Blake extended the previous category of fiduciaries by creating a quasi-fiduciary out of a contractual obligation. In *Experience Hendrix* it was said that an account of profits was not justified on the facts because the defendant's situation was not analogous with a fiduciary's duty: "there is no direct analogy between [the defendant's] position and that of a fiduciary".[166] The concept that contractual obligations may give rise to remedies previously given only to genuine fiduciaries is unsatisfactory because it is uncertain and so unpredictable in its application.

Analogies with intellectual property rights. An account of profits has been a standard remedy for infringements of property rights such as passing off, infringement of trade marks, copyrights and breach of confidence.[167] So the House of Lords has treated the infringement of a patent as an injury to the claimant's property right so that damages were assessed as a royalty for every infringing article.[168] The facts in *Experience Hendrix* give a flavour of intellectual property rights,[169] but the remedy was not based on such rights. However, in one case at first instance the judge refused to treat a breach of restraint of trade (a contractual obligation) as sufficient to justify an account of profits, despite the facts giving the flavour of a trademark case. The judge said that the common law should not provide what statute provides for the infringement of an intellectual property right.[170] 26–029

(h) *Appeals Against the Assessment of Damages*

Power of appellate court to reassess damages. When the Court of Appeal hears an appeal[171] against the assessment of damages made by a judge sitting 26–030

[165] *Att-Gen v Blake* [2001] 1 A.C. 268, 287 F–G.

[166] *Experience Hendrix* [2003] EWCA Civ 323 at [37].

[167] *Att-Gen v Blake* [2001] 1 A.C. 268, 279.

[168] *Watson, Laidlaw & Co Ltd v Pott. Cassels and Williamson* (1914) 31 R.P.C. 104.

[169] Campbell and Wylie [2003] C.L.J. 605, 623–628.

[170] *World Wide Fund for Nature v World Wrestling Foundation Entertainment Inc* [2002] F.S.R. 32 at 63. (See above fn.141). See now the CA decision in the *World Wide Fund* case, above, para.26–027 fn.148.

[171] The appeal used to be by way of rehearing: CPR Sch.1: RSC Ord.59 r.3(1) which enabled the court to substitute its own view of the assessment of damages: *Flint v Lovell* [1935] 1 K.B. 354, 360; *Davies v Powell Duffryn Associated Collieries Ltd* [1942] A.C. 601, 616–617. Appeals are now normally limited reviews, CPR r.52.11, but CPR r.52.10 gives the Appeal Court all the powers of the lower court and power to alter its orders. The Court of Appeal is more willing to interfere with a judge's award than with a jury's award of damages: [1942] A.C. 601, 616; and if it reverses a decision for the defendant on the issue of liability, it will assess the damages itself: *Reaney v Co-operative Wholesale Society* [1932] W.N. 78; cf. the position in the Privy Council: *Ratnasingam v Kow Ah Dek* [1983] 1 W.L.R. 1235.

alone, without a jury, it applies similar principles to those followed previously in considering appeals against the award of damages by the verdict of a jury.[172] The court will interfere only if it is convinced that the trial judge acted upon some wrong principle of law,[173] or that the amount awarded was so extremely high or so very small as to make it, in the judgment of the Court of Appeal, an entirely erroneous estimate of the damages to which the claimant is entitled.[174] Great attention is paid to the opinion of the trial judge and the appellate court should be slow to reverse the judgment of the judge who saw and heard the witnesses.[175] In special situations, the appellate court may take account of circumstances affecting the assessment of damages which arise after the first instance trial,[176] e.g. if the fresh evidence showed that the "basic or fundamental assumption" underlying the judge's assessment had been "falsified by later events".[177]

(i) *Third Party Beneficiaries*

26–031 **Breach of promises intended to benefit third persons.** Chapter 18 of this work[178] includes a full discussion of the situations in which the promisee can recover either the agreed sum[179] due to be paid to a third person who is not a party to the contract[180] or substantial damages for breach of a promise intended to benefit such a person.[181]

---

172 The verdict of a jury awarding damages can be set aside only if the Court of Appeal upon consideration of all the circumstances comes to the conclusion that the damages awarded were so small or so large that 12 sensible jurors could not reasonably have awarded them: *Mills v Stanway Coaches Ltd* [1940] 2 K.B. 334, 340; *Phillips v London & S.W. Ry* (1879) 4 QBD 406; (1879) 5 QBD 78; or if the court is satisfied that the jury took into consideration matters which they ought not to have considered or had disregarded matters which they ought to have considered: *Smith v Schilling* [1928] 1 K.B. 429, 440. See also *Praed v Graham* (1889) 24 QBD 53; *Johnston v G.W. Ry* [1904] 2 K.B. 250; *Bocock v Enfield Rolling Mills Ltd* [1954] 1 W.L.R. 1303; *Nance v British Columbia Electric Ry* [1951] A.C. 601, 613; *Scott v Musial* [1959] 2 Q.B. 429; *Cavanagh v Ulster Weaving Co Ltd* [1960] A.C. 145; *Ward v James* [1966] 1 Q.B. 273.

173 e.g. *Benham v Gambling* [1941] A.C. 157; *Naylor v Yorkshire Electricity Board* [1968] A.C. 529; *Dingle v Associated Newspapers* [1964] A.C. 371; *Lai Wee Lian v Singapore Bus Service (1978) Ltd* [1984] A.C. 729 (all cases on torts).

174 *Flint v Lovell* [1935] 1 K.B. 354, 360 (approved in *Owen v Sykes* [1936] 1 K.B. 192). See also *Davies v Powell Duffryn Associated Collieries Ltd* [1942] A.C. 601, 616–617, 623–624; *Nance v British Columbia Electric Ry* [1951] A.C. 601, 613; *Warren v King* [1964] 1 W.L.R. 1, 9; *Morey v Woodfield (No.2)* [1964] 1 W.L.R. 16. cf. *Hinz v Berry* [1970] 2 Q.B. 40; *Bone v Seale* [1975] 1 W.L.R. 797 (nuisance case). For an appeal from a county court judge, see *Shave v J. W. Lees (Brewers) Ltd* [1954] 1 W.L.R. 1300.

175 *Powell v Streatham Manor Nursing Home* [1935] A.C. 243. See also *Smith v Schilling* [1928] 1 K.B. 429, 432–433 (similar remarks concerning the opinion of the trial judge who took the verdict of the jury).

176 *Edwards v Society of Graphical and Allied Trades* [1971] Ch. 354, 377, 384 (a contract case, following the tort case of *Murphy v Stone-Wallwork (Charlton) Ltd* [1969] 1 W.L.R. 1023); see also *Mulholland v Mitchell* [1971] A.C. 666.

177 *Hunt v Severs* [1993] Q.B. 815, 838 (a tort case: the House of Lords did not deal with this point: [1994] 2 A.C. 350).

178 See paras 18–043 et seq.

179 See above, para.26–009. (In many "third-party beneficiary" cases it is an agreed sum which is in question.)

180 On the common law doctrine of privity of contract, see above, paras 18–003 et seq.

181 The Contracts (Rights of Third Parties) Act 1999 does not affect the promisee's right to damages, s.4. See the Law Commission's Report: *Privity of Contract: Contracts for the Benefit of Third Parties* (Law Com. No.242, 1996) para.5.17; and above, paras 18–088 et seq.

2. Causation[182] and Contributory Negligence

Requirement of a causal connection. The important issue in remoteness of damage in the law of contract is whether a particular loss was within the reasonable contemplation of the parties,[183] but causation must first be proved: there must be a causal connection between the defendant's breach of contract[184] and the claimant's loss.[185] The claimant may recover damages for a loss only where the breach of contract was the "effective" or "dominant" cause of that loss.[186] The courts have avoided laying down any formal tests for causation: they have relied on common sense to guide decisions as to whether a breach of contract is a sufficiently substantial cause of the claimant's loss.[187] The answer to whether the breach was the cause of the loss or merely the occasion for the loss must "in the end" depend on "the court's commonsense" in interpreting the facts.[188] So where a company continued to trade after a negligent audit by the defendant failed to reveal the true financial position of the company, the Court of Appeal held that the auditor's breach of contract gave the company "the *opportunity* . . . to incur . . . trading losses: it did not *cause* those trading losses".[189] The trading losses flowed from trading, not auditing. 26–032

The problems of causation most likely to arise concern intervening acts of either a third party or of the claimant; but an issue of causation may also arise when the alleged loss is claimed on the basis of a hypothesis as to what the claimant or a third person would have done had the defendant not broken the contract.[190] 26–033

Intervening act of third party. Although the voluntary act of a third person intervening between the breach of contract by the defendant and the loss suffered by the claimant will normally "break the chain of causation", this will depend on the court's appraisal of the particular circumstances. Thus, where the negligence 26–034

---

[182] This topic has been developed mainly in the law of torts, but may arise in the law of contract (see Hart & Honoré, *Causation in the Law*, 2nd edn, Ch.11). No doubt the numerous decisions on causation in the law of torts may be used as analogies in the law of contract.

[183] See below, paras 26–052 et seq.

[184] The loss must have been caused by the breach itself, since "damages for breach of contract may . . . [not] be awarded . . . for loss caused by the manner of the breach": per Lord Steyn in *Malik v Bank of Credit and Commerce International SA* [1998] A.C. 20, 51 (citing *Addis v Gramophone Co* [1909] A.C. 488 (see below, para.26–083).

[185] *Monarch S.S. Co Ltd v Karlshamns Oljefabriker (A/B)* [1949] A.C. 196, 225; *Quinn v Burch Bros (Builders) Ltd* [1966] 2 Q.B. 370; *Sykes v Midland Bank Executor and Trustee Co Ltd* [1971] 1 Q.B. 113.

[186] *Galoo v Bright Grahame Murray* [1994] 1 W.L.R. 1360, 1374–1375. The breach of contract need not be the sole cause: below, para.26–038.

[187] This sentence was quoted with approval by the CA in *Galoo v Bright Grahame Murray* [1994] 1 W.L.R. 1360, 1374–1375.

[188] *Galoo v Bright Grahame Murray* [1994] 1 W.L.R. 1360; *Racing Drivers' Club Ltd v Hextall Erskine & Co* [1996] 3 All E.R. 667, 671–672, 681–682. See also *County Ltd v Girozentrale Securities* [1996] 3 All E.R. 834 CA (causation does not depend on the parties' contemplation).

[189] The *Galoo* case [1994] 1 W.L.R. 1360, 1375. The contrast between the "occasion" (or "opportunity") and the "cause" is also made in *Quinn v Burch Bros (Builders) Ltd* [1966] 2 Q.B. 370 (below, para.26–034).

[190] See below, paras 26–043—26–045.

of a solicitor (in breach of his contractual duty to his client) creates a risk for the client, an "error of judgment" made subsequently by counsel advising the client may not interrupt the chain of causation resulting from the solicitor's negligence.[191] Similarly, in a case where insurers were held liable to a bank, the mortgagee of a ship, for failing (in breach of contract) to notify the bank that the ship had been trading in a war zone prohibited by the terms of the insurance, the fact that the shipowners lied to the bank when seeking the re-financing of their loan, did not break the chain of causation between the breach of contract and the bank's loss as a result of the re-financing.[192]

26–035 If the defendant owes a contractual duty to the claimant to take care to ensure that an intervening and voluntary act of a third party is not permitted, then the defendant will be liable if he fails to take such care.[193] Thus a customer of a bank owes a duty to the bank to draw his cheques carefully so as not to facilitate fraud; where the customer drew a cheque in such a way that the amount could be readily altered, he was held liable to the bank for the increase forged by a third party, who obtained payment of the increased amount[194]:

> "The fact that a crime was necessary to bring about the loss does not prevent its being the natural consequence of the carelessness."[195]

26–036 There are, however, cases where although the intervening act of a third party was probably foreseeable, the defendant was held not liable for loss resulting from that act. In *Weld-Blundell v Stephens*,[196] the defendant, in breach of his contract, negligently left a libellous letter (written by the plaintiff) where it was read by a third party, who was likely to, and did, communicate its contents to the persons libelled; the latter recovered damages for libel from the plaintiff, who thereupon sued the defendant. The House of Lords, by a bare majority, held that the plaintiff could recover only nominal damages for the defendant's breach of contract, and not the damages and costs paid in the libel action, since the act of the third party was a "new and independent" cause.[197]

26–037 **Intervening act or omission of the claimant.** The doctrines of mitigation[198] and possibly of contributory negligence[199] may, in addition to causation, be relevant where the claimant, following the defendant's breach of contract, has

---

[191] *Cook v S.* [1966] 1 W.L.R. 635, 642 (the Court of Appeal did not discuss this aspect of the case: [1967] 1 W.L.R. 457; below, para.26–083). cf. *East Ham Corp v Bernard Sunley & Sons Ltd* [1966] A.C. 406 (failure of architect to notice defective work by builder).

[192] *Bank of Nova Scotia v Hellenic Mutual War Risks Association (Bermuda) Ltd* [1992] 1 A.C. 233, 266–268.

[193] *London Joint Stock Bank Ltd v Macmillan* [1918] A.C. 777. See also *De la Bere v Pearson* [1908] 1 K.B. 280; *Stansbie v Troman* [1948] 2 K.B. 48; *Marshall v Rubypoint Ltd* [1997] 25 E.G. 142; cf. *Cobb v G.W. Ry* [1894] A.C. 419.

[194] *London Joint Stock Bank Ltd v Macmillan* [1918] A.C. 777.

[195] [1918] A.C. 777, 794. See also the cases cited in fn.193, above.

[196] [1920] A.C. 956 (the intervening act was foreseeable: see at 974, 987, 991. But see Treitel, *The Law of Contract*, 12th edn (by Peel), para.20–096.

[197] *Weld-Blundell v Stephens* [1920] A.C. 956, 986.

[198] See below, para.26–101.

[199] See below, para.26–049. A similar problem arises when loss is caused by breaches of contract by both the claimant and the defendant: *Government of Ceylon v Chandris* [1965] 3 All E.R. 48.

suffered loss through his own voluntary act or omission. In *Quinn v Burch Bros (Builders) Ltd*[200] the defendants could have foreseen that their failure (in breach of contract) to supply the plaintiff, an independent contractor, with adequate equipment might result in an accident if he used unsuitable equipment. When this actually happened so that the plaintiff was injured, the Court of Appeal held that it was the voluntary choice of the plaintiff following the breach of contract which *caused* the accident; the breach of contract did not cause it but merely gave the plaintiff the opportunity to injure himself by his choice to use the unsuitable equipment, despite his appreciation of the risk involved.[201] Similarly, where a buyer engaged a third party to repair the defect in a machine supplied by the seller, but the buyer then failed to inspect the repairs before using the machine, the Court of Appeal held[202] that the cause[203] of the subsequent explosion was the negligence of the buyer in using the machine without inspecting it to see whether the defect had been adequately repaired.[204]

Other contract cases dealing with the causal effect of the claimant's intervening act mainly concern the actions of masters of ships in obeying instructions of the charterers. Thus where a charterer was obliged to nominate a safe port of loading, but nominated a port which in fact was unsafe, and the master of the ship acted reasonably in accepting the nomination, the owners of the ship were entitled to recover damages from the charterer for injury sustained by the ship[205]; the master of a ship cannot enter a port which is obviously unsafe and then charge the charterers with damage done, but normally "a man is entitled to act in the faith that the other party to a contract is carrying out his part of it properly".[206] If the claimant is put on the horns of a dilemma by the defendant's breach of **26–038**

[200] [1966] 2 Q.B. 370 (followed in *Sole v W. J. Hallt Ltd* [1973] Q.B. 574 (but it is submitted that this decision is unsatisfactory on this point); see also *O'Connor v B. D. Kirby & Co* [1972] 1 Q.B. 90.

[201] cf. *Galoo v Bright Grahame Murray* [1994] 1 W.L.R. 1360 (above, para.26–032). cf. also *Young v Purdy* [1997] P.N.L.R. 130. An analogous situation is dealt with in *Lambert v Lewis* [1982] A.C. 225 (below, para.26–109; Vol.II, para.43–443). This decision indicates that a buyer who negligently fails to discover a defect in the goods may not be able to recover from the seller for breach of his implied undertakings as to the quality of the goods: see Hervey (1981) 44 M.L.R. 575.

[202] *Beoco Ltd v Alfa Laval Co Ltd* [1995] Q.B. 137.

[203] It is submitted that mitigation (below, paras 26–101 et seq.) would be a more appropriate principle for the decision. The explosion was caused by the original defect (which had not been cured) but the buyer had failed, after discovery of the defect, to take reasonable steps to avoid further loss; instead of saying the buyer *caused* the further loss it would be better to say that he failed to avoid it when he unreasonably decided to use the machine without testing it after the repairs.

[204] Although the seller was liable for the cost of repairing the original defect, and for the loss of the buyer's profit while the original repairs were made, the seller was not liable for the cost of repairing the explosion damage, nor for the further loss of production after the explosion. The need for further repairs to remedy the original defect had been overtaken by the need for more extensive repairs due to the explosion, and the buyer could not recover damages for the loss of production during the notional period which would have been necessary for further repairs even if there had been no explosion.

[205] *Reardon Smith Line Ltd v Australian Wheat Board* [1956] A.C. 266, 282–283 (PC, approving the judgment of Devlin J. in *Compania Naviera Maropan SA v Bowaters Lloyd Pulp and Paper Mills Ltd* [1955] 2 Q.B. 68).

[206] *Compania Naviera Maropan SA v Bowaters Lloyd Pulp and Paper Mills Ltd* [1955] 2 Q.B. 68, 77.

contract, the defendant cannot escape liability if the claimant acts in a reasonable way.[207]

26–039 **Apportionment between claimant and defendant.** In one case, the Court of Appeal unusually allowed apportionment of causation between the claimant and the defendant.[208]

26–040 **Intervening events.** An intervening event which could reasonably be expected will not excuse the defendant for loss caused by the combined operation of the defendant's breach of contract[209] and the intervening event.[210] Thus in *Monarch S.S. Co Ltd v Karlshamns Oljefabriker (A/B)*[211] the defendants' ship was chartered to carry a cargo from Manchuria to Sweden. The ship should have reached Sweden in July 1939 but the defendants broke their contractual duty to provide a seaworthy ship and she was delayed till September. By this time war had broken out, and the vessel was ordered by the British Admiralty to unload at Glasgow. The plaintiffs (indorsees of the bills of lading) incurred expenses in forwarding the cargo to Sweden in neutral ships, and the House of Lords held that these could be recovered from the defendants. Reasonable business men, knowing of the possibility of war, would have foreseen that a delay might lead to the risk that the vessel would be diverted by the Admiralty. The House of Lords held that the cost of transhipment was due to, or caused by, the breach of contract, and was damage arising as a direct and natural consequence of the breach.[212]

26–041 **Two causes.** If a breach of contract is one of two causes, both co-operating and both of equal efficacy in causing loss to the claimant, the party responsible for the breach is liable to the claimant for that loss.[213] The contract-breaker is liable so long as his breach was "an" effective cause of his loss: the court need not choose which cause was the more effective.[214]

26–042 **The claimant's lost opportunities: hypothetical consequences.** The claimant may claim that, in the absence of the defendant's breach of contract, he might

[207] [1955] 2 Q.B. 68, 77, 88; cf. *Lambert v Lewis* [1982] A.C. 225.

[208] *Tennant Radiant Heat Ltd v Warrington Development Corp* [1988] 1 E.G.L.R. 41 (discussed below para.26–050, where later doubts in the Court of Appeal are noted).

[209] The defendant will not be liable if his breach did not contribute to the risk of the event occurring: see below, fn.212; cf. the cases dealing with a fall in the property market: below, para.26–094.

[210] *Monarch S.S. Co Ltd v Karlshamns Oljefabriker (A/B)* [1949] A.C. 196. See also *The Wilhem* (1866) 14 L.T. 636; cf. *Associated Portland Cement Manufacturers (1900) Ltd v Houlder Bros & Co Ltd* (1917) 86 L.J.K.B. 1495; *Diamond v Campbell-Jones* [1961] Ch. 22.

[211] [1949] A.C. 196.

[212] But if during the delayed voyage the ship ran into a typhoon and suffered damage, it could not be said that the delay caused the damage: [1949] A.C. 196, 215; cf. the explosion in *Beoco Ltd v Alfa Laval Co Ltd* [1995] Q.B. 137 (above, para.26–037) for which the plaintiff (the buyer) was held responsible, and which put an end to any continuing liability on the seller for the cost of further repairs even though the original defect was due to the seller's breach of contract.

[213] *Heskell v Continental Express Ltd* [1950] 1 All E.R. 1033, 1047–1048; *Banque Keyser Ullmann SA v Skandia (UK) Insurance Co Ltd* [1990] Q.B. 665, 813–814 (the decision of the HL did not deal with this point: [1991] 2 A.C. 249). The defendant may seek contribution from a third party who contributed to the causation of the loss and who would also have been liable to the claimant: s.1(1) of the Civil Liability (Contribution) Act 1978.

[214] *County Ltd v Girozentrale Securities* [1996] 3 All E.R. 834 CA.

have obtained a benefit or avoided a loss[215]: this consequence was not certain to follow proper performance of the contract but the breach deprived the claimant of the opportunity to benefit from it. The question usually arises when the defendant has failed to do something, but it could arise where his performance had been inadequate or deficient in some way. The law distinguishes threee situations: where the hypothetical consequence involves the hypothesis of the claimant's act, where it involves that of a third person and where it involves the occurrence of a contingency outside the control of either party to the contract. It seems, however, that the second and third cases are treated in the same way.

A hypothetical action of the claimant. This situation arises where a particular contingency depends on the hypothetical question whether the claimant himself would have acted in a certain way. It is illustrated by the case where a solicitor failed to give proper advice to his client and the issue is whether the client would have accepted the advice and acted on it in a particular way. The client must prove, on the balance of probabilities, that he would have done so: unless he can prove this, he fails to establish the causal link between the defendant's omission and the loss he would have avoided if he had accepted and acted on the hypothetical advice.[216] But if he can satisfy this burden of proof, it is not a case of loss of a chance, because the claimant has proved what he would have done and damages must be assessed on this basis.[217] 26–043

A hypothetical action of a third party. This situation arises where a particular contingency depends on whether a third party would have acted in a certain way.[218] Where the claimant claims that, in the absence of the breach of contract by the defendant, a third party would have acted in a particular way, so as to benefit the claimant, he need not prove that hypothetical action on the balance of probabilities. Provided that the claimant can prove[219] that in the absence of the breach there was a "real" or "substantial" (not a speculative) chance of the third party's action, the court must assess the chance of that action resulting (usually as a percentage) and then discount the claimant's damages for his loss by 26–044

[215] The question whether a past event occurred must be decided on the balance of probabilities —once the claimant proves that it was more likely than not to have occurred, the court treats it as a definite fact: *Davies v Taylor* [1974] A.C. 207, 213 (a tort case); it does "not raise any question of what might have been the situation in a hypothetical state of facts": *Hotson v East Berkshire A.H.A.* [1987] A.C. 750, 785; and so "chances" are not legally relevant. See Reece (1996) 59 M.L.R. 188.

[216] *Allied Maples Group Ltd v Simmons and Simmons* [1995] 1 W.L.R. 1602, CA; *Brown v K.M.R. Services Ltd* [1995] 4 All E.R. 598, 617, 638, CA. See also *Sykes v Midland Bank Executor and Trustee Co* [1971] 1 Q.B. 113.

[217] The case of *Otter v Church, Adams Tatham & Co* [1953] 1 Ch. 280, which decided the contrary, was criticised in the CA in both the *Allied Maples* case [1995] 1 W.L.R. 1602, 290; and *Sykes v Midland Bank Executor and Trustee Co* [1971] 1 Q.B. 113, 130.

[218] This issue could arise in a case where it was also relevant to decide how the claimant himself would have acted: the *Allied Maples* case [1995] 1 W.L.R. 1602. Loss of profits will always depend on many speculative factors, such as third parties continuing to deal with the claimant: this paragraph, however, deals with the loss of a specific opportunity.

[219] On the balance of probabilities: *North Sea Energy Holdings N.V. v Petroleum Authority of Thailand* [1999] 1 All E.R. (Comm) 173, 187, CA (no substantial chance shown).

reference to that percentage.[220] In the leading case of *Chaplin v Hicks*[221] the defendant, by a breach of contract in conducting a contest, deprived the plaintiff, one of 50 finalists, of the opportunity to compete for one of the 12 prizes. Although there could be no precision in calculating the value of her lost chance, she was entitled to substantial damages. Similarly, where the breach of contract caused the claimant to lose his chance of success in litigation, the question is what chance the claimant would have had of a favourable outcome. So where the client's claim became statute-barred because his solicitor failed to bring proceedings within time, the measure of the client's damages recovered from the solicitor was the expected proceeds of the original claim[222]: what he might have recovered in the original claim must be discounted by reference to his chances of success in recovering it.[223] However, "the more the contingencies, the lower the value of the chance or opportunity of which the plaintiff was deprived".[224] Where one contingency may depend on another, the chance should be evaluated as a percentage of a percentage.[225]

26–045 A similar approach to assessing damages is found in other "loss of a chance" cases not involving litigation: for instance, where through a solicitor's failure to give proper advice, the client lost the chance to negotiate better terms in a commercial transaction with a third party, who might have accepted such terms[226]; or where an author or actor lost the opportunity to enhance his reputation[227]; or where, but for the breach, there was a real or substantial chance that the claimant would have continued to make profits from "repeat orders" from customers.[228]

---

[220] The *Allied Maples* case [1995] 1 W.L.R. 1602. (CA: a claim in tort, but the facts also amounted to a breach of contract: the case was considered in *Bank of Credit and Commerce International SA v Ali (No.3)* [2002] EWCA 82, [2002] 3 All E.R. 750 (loss of the chance of employment)). See also *Maden v Clifford Coppock & Carter (A Firm)* [2004] EWCA Civ 1037, [2005] 2 All E.R. 43 (80 per cent chance of obtaining a particular level of damages in an out of court settlement). The chance of the third party's action can be considerably less than 50%. But no discount for contingency is appropriate if it is certain what the third party would have done: see *White v Jones* [1995] 2 A.C. 207, 228 CA; *Dickinson v Jones Alexander & Co* [1993] 2 F.L.R. 321.

[221] [1911] 2 K.B. 786 CA. (This case, and *Kitchen v Royal Air Force Association* [1958] 1 W.L.R. 563 were cited by the House of Lords in *Hotson v East Berkshire A.H.A.* [1987] A.C. 750, 782, 792–793 (a tort case).)

[222] *Kitchen v Royal Air Force Association* [1958] 1 W.L.R. 563, 575–576; *Cook v Swinfen* [1967] 1 W.L.R. 457; *Malyon v Lawrence, Messer & Co* [1968] 2 Lloyd's Rep. 539.

[223] cf. *Yeoman's Executrix v Ferries* (1967) S.L.T. 332 (the value of an "out-of-court" settlement of the plaintiff's claim).

[224] *Hall v Meyrick* [1957] 2 Q.B. 455, 471 (reversed by CA on other grounds).

[225] *Ministry of Defence v Wheeler* [1998] 1 All E.R. 790, CA. Where the claimant had different chances of success on different issues in litigation it is not appropriate to multiply the chances together; an overall view should be taken: *Hanif v Middleweeks* [2000] Lloyd's Rep. P.N. 920, CA.

[226] The *Allied Maples* case [1995] 1 W.L.R. 1602; *Stovold v Barlows* [1996] P.N.L.R. 91. cf. *First Interstate Bank of California v Cohen Arnold* [1996] P.N.L.R. 17 CA (negligence claim against accountants); *Davies v Taylor* [1974] A.C. 207 (loss of chance of widow's fatal accident claim); *Spring v Guardian Assurance* [1995] A.C. 296, 327 (tort claim for former employee's loss of reasonable chance of a particular employment).

[227] Below, para.26–087.

[228] *Jackson v Bank of Scotland* [2005] UKHL 3, [2005] 1 W.L.R. 377 (see below, para.26–071).

Other contingencies. The amount of the claimant's loss may depend on a contingency not involving hypothetical action by the claimant or a third person. If, at the time when damages are assessed, a relevant contingency has not yet occurred, the future risk that it might occur should be assessed as a percentage chance and damages adjusted accordingly: e.g. the risk that war might break out so as to entitle a party to cancel a long-term contract under a war clause. 26–046

Contingency has occurred by time of trial. If the contingency has actually occurred before the time of assessment, the damages should be assessed on the basis of the actual facts as then known, despite the fact that the contingency occurred only after the breach of contract. So where a charterparty to be performed over seven years contained a war clause, the House of Lords assessed damages for the charterer's repudiation on the basis that war had actually broken out before the time when damages were assessed so that the charterparty would have been brought to an end at that time.[229] The decision concerned only a contingency affecting the period of the charter: any loss arising from the reduction in the current rate of hire was determined as at the date of the breach. 26–047

The contract-breaker's opportunity to minimise the cost of performance.[230] A contingency may depend on whether the contract-breaker would have acted in a certain way. If the defendant fails to perform, when he had an option to perform the contract in one of several ways,[231] damages are assessed on the basis that he would have performed in the way which would have benefited him most,[232] e.g. at the least cost to himself.[233] So damages were assessed against charterers on the basis that they would have used their contractual entitlements to produce the least profitable result for the owners.[234] A similar situation arises where the contract-breaker had an option to terminate the contract: if the claimant accepts the anticipatory breach of the defendant as a ground for terminating the contract,[235] but the defendant could have exercised his option to terminate the contract so as to extinguish or reduce the loss caused by the anticipatory breach, the court will assess the damages for the breach on the assumption that the defendant would have exercised the option.[236] 26–048

---

[229] *Golden Strait Corp v Nippon Yusen Kubishika Kaisha* [2007] UKHL 12, [2007] 2 A.C. 353.

[230] cf. *Lavarack v Woods of Colchester Ltd* [1967] 1 Q.B. 278, 294 (above, para.26–001).

[231] See above, paras 21–006 et seq.

[232] But where the defendant had a choice of alternative methods of performance, the damages will be assessed on the basis of the method least onerous to him only where that method was reasonable in all the circumstances: *Paula Lee Ltd v Robert Zehil & Co Ltd* [1983] 2 All E.R. 390; cf. *Abrahams v Herbert Reiach Ltd* [1922] 1 K.B. 477.

[233] *Re Thornett, Fehr and Yuills* [1921] 1 K.B. 219; *Withers v General Theatre Corp* [1933] 2 K.B. 536; *Beach v Reed Corrugated Cases* [1956] 1 W.L.R. 807, 816–817; *Bunge Corp, New York v Tradax SA Panama* [1981] 1 W.L.R. 711, HL; *Johnson Matthey Banking v State Trading Corp of India* [1984] 1 Lloyd's Rep. 427 (sellers entitled to take advantage of 1.5% tolerance).

[234] *Spiliada Maritime Corp v Louis Dreyfus Corp* [1983] Com. L.R. 268. See also *Kaye Steam Navigating Co v Barnett* (1932) 48 T.L.R. 440; *Becher v Koplak Enterprises* [1991] 2 Lloyd's Rep. 23, CA.

[235] See above, paras 24–021—24–027, 24–030.

[236] *The Mihalis Angelos* [1971] 1 Q.B. 164 (see above, para.24–022); cf. the principles on which damages are assessed for wrongful dismissal: Vol. II, paras 39–193—39–196. cf. also the *Golden Strait* case [2007] UKHL 12, above, para.26–047.

26–049 **Contributory negligence.**[237] The Law Reform (Contributory Negligence) Act 1945 permits apportionment of loss by the reduction of the claimant's damages where he "suffers damage as the result partly of his own fault and partly of the fault of any other person".[238] Although the Act was obviously designed for claims in tort,[239] the definition of "fault" as (inter alia) "negligence" raises the question whether a defendant guilty of a breach of contract can take advantage of this provision if the claimant has himself contributed to causing his loss by some "fault" on his part. In *Vesta v Butcher*[240] the Court of Appeal accepted that three categories are relevant to this question: category 1, where the defendant is liable only in contract for breach of a strict duty (negligence being irrelevant); category 2, where the defendant is liable only in contract for breach of an obligation to take care (there being no corresponding duty of care in tort); and category 3, where the defendant's liability in contract is the same as his liability in negligence (the tortious duty of care arising independently of the contract). In *Vesta v Butcher*[241] the Court of Appeal held[242] that the Act of 1945 applied only to category 3 cases,[243] namely those where the breach of contract is co-extensive with the breach of the tortious duty.[244] In this situation it would be anomalous if the claimant could avoid the apportionment provisions of the Act by the simple device of suing only in

[237] Proposals to change the law were made in the Law Commission's Report No.219, *Contributory Negligence as a Defence in Contract* (1993). See the comment by Porat (1995) 111 L.Q.R. 228. The proposals were not accepted by the Government.

[238] s.1(1). At common law, the claimant's contributory negligence was a complete defence in an action in tort; the defence had never been applied (*eo nomine*) in an action in contract before 1945: see the discussion in Williams, *Joint Torts and Contributory Negligence* (1951), pp.214–222; and in the Law Commission's Report No.219 Pt II.

[239] Contributory negligence may be raised in a claim under s.2(1) of the Misrepresentation Act 1967: *Gran Gelato Ltd v Richcliff (Group) Ltd* [1992] Ch. 560, 572–575 (see above, para.6–074). But contributory negligence is no defence against a claim in deceit: *Standard Chartered Bank v Pakistan National Shipping Corp* [2002] UKHL 43, [2003] 1 A.C. 959 (above, para.6–064). (The case has an extensive discussion of the meaning of the word "fault" in the 1945 Act.)

[240] *Forsikrings Vesta v Butcher* [1989] A.C. 852, 860–867, 875, 879 (in the decision of the House of Lords, contributory negligence was not dealt with).

[241] [1989] A.C. 852.

[242] Following a New Zealand decision, *Rowe v Turner Hopkins and Partners* [1980] 2 N.Z.L.R. 550. The question had been examined by academic writers: Swanton (1981) 55 A.L.J. 278; Chandler (1989) 40 N.I.L.Q. 152; Anderson [1987] L.M.C.L.Q. 10.

[243] This decision has been followed (obiter) by the Court of Appeal in *Bank of Nova Scotia v Hellenic Mutual War Risks Association (Bermuda) Ltd* [1990] 1 Q.B. 818, 904. (The appeal was allowed by the House of Lords on another issue, with the result that contributory negligence was not considered: [1992] 1 A.C. 233, 266.) But the High Court of Australia has not followed the decision: *Astley v Austrust Ltd* [1999] Lloyd's Rep P.N. 758.

[244] In other words, the claim in contract is founded on an act or omission by the defendant which would also have given rise to liability in tort. Illustrations of category 3 are: *Sayers v Harlow U.D.C.* [1958] 1 W.L.R. 623 (see the comments on this case in *Vesta v Butcher* [1989] A.C. 852, 861, 866–867); *Vesta v Butcher* (insurers' claim against brokers for failing to inform reinsurers that the insured could not comply with a clause in the contract of reinsurance); *Platform Home Loans Ltd v Oyston Shipways Ltd* [2000] 2 A.C. 190 (lender suing valuer for negligent over-valuation of the security). The decision in *Vesta v Butcher* leaves open the question whether the Act of 1945 applies where the claimant's claim in tort is not co-extensive with his claim in contract: see the Law Commission's Report No.219 (1993), para.3.29.

contract.[245] The decision in *Vesta v Butcher* means that where the defendant's liability arises only in contract (categories 1[246]; and 2[247]) contributory negligence cannot be relied on to reduce the claimant's damages.

Recovery barred on other grounds. But even where the Act does not apply to claims founded only on contract, there are many situations where conduct of the claimant which would have constituted contributory negligence under the Act will bar his recovery on the ground of his failure to mitigate,[248] or his failure to prove causation—his own carelessness may be held to be the sole cause of the loss.[249] In one case, the Court of Appeal, after holding that contributory negligence did not apply to a Category 1 case, nevertheless reached a similar result by an unusual application of causation: a landlord's damages against his lessees for breach of a repairing covenant (a strict obligation) were reduced by 90 per cent because he (the landlord) had negligently failed to keep clear the drainage outlets of the roof.[250] The landlord's failure was held to be a concurrent cause of the collapse of the roof, to which 90 per cent of the total causation was assigned. 26–050

[245] Category 3 cases will be more frequent after the decision in *Henderson v Merrett* [1995] 2 A.C. 145 (see above, paras 1–158 et seq.) (especially where clients sue those providing professional services and advice). For an illustration see *U.C.B. Bank Plc v Hepferd Winstanley & Pugh* [1999] Lloyd's Rep. P.N. 963 CA.

[246] Illustrations of category 1 cases are: *Basildon DC v J.E. Lesser (Properties) Ltd* [1985] Q.B. 839 (claim for an indemnity under a deed); *Quinn v Burch Bros (Builders) Ltd* [1966] 2 Q.B. 370 (the Court of Appeal did not discuss contributory negligence: see above, para.26–037); *Tennant Radiant Heat Ltd v Warrington Development Corp* [1988] 1 E.G.L.R. 41 (but see below, fn.250); *Banque Keyser Ullmann SA v Skandia (UK) Insurance Co Ltd* [1990] Q.B. 665, 720–721 (neither the Court of Appeal, at 815–817, nor the House of Lords [1991] 2 A.C. 249 deal with this point); *Bank of Nova Scotia v Hellenic Mutual War Risks Association (Bermuda) Ltd* [1990] 1 Q.B. 818, 904; *Barclays Bank Plc v Fairclough Building Ltd* [1995] Q.B. 214 (strict undertakings by builder that roofing work should be done by specialists, and that the workmanship should be the best of its kind).

[247] Illustrations of category 2 cases are: *A.S. James Pty Ltd v Duncan* [1970] V.R. 705; *De Meza v Apple* [1974] 1 Lloyd's Rep. 508 (solicitor's claim for both negligence and breach of contract against auditors: the appeal did not deal with the point: [1975] 1 Lloyd's Rep. 498, 509; it is submitted that the decision at first instance is not consistent with *Vesta v Butcher* [1989] A.C. 852); *Marintrans (A.B.) v Comet Shipping Ltd* [1985] 1 W.L.R. 1270.

[248] Below, paras 26–101 et seq. For an illustration, see *Lambert v Lewis* [1982] A.C. 225 (below, para.26–109).

[249] Above, para.26–037.

[250] *Tennant Radiant Heat Ltd v Warrington Development Corp* [1988] 1 E.G.L.R. 41 (but the principle applied in this case was doubted by the Court of Appeal in *Bank of Nova Scotia v Hellenic Mutual War Risks Association (Bermuda) Ltd* [1990] 1 Q.B. 818, 904: the House of Lords did not deal with this point: [1992] 1 A.C. 233, 266). See also Bennett (1984–85) 4 *Litigation* 195, 197; the Law Commission's Report No.219 (fn.223, above), 3.13 to 3.15; and *Schering Agrochemicals Ltd v Resibel NVSA* Unreported; noted at (1993) 109 L.Q.R. 175.

3. REMOTENESS OF DAMAGE[251]

(a) *General Rules*

26–051 **Introduction.** The term "remoteness of damage" refers to the legal test used to decide which types of loss caused by the breach of contract may be compensated by an award of damages.[252] If there is no explicit clause in the contract dealing with the assessment of damages, the law supplies a standard test which specifies the extent of responsibility implicitly undertaken by the promisor. There is a reciprocal allocation of risks; the precise legal test is examined below, but it can be said in general terms that the promisor implicitly accepts responsibility for the usual consequences of a breach of the promise in question, while the promisee implicitly accepts the risk of any other consequences. (In other words, the promisee implicitly agrees not to hold the promisor responsible for unusual consequences.)[253] The test should ultimately depend on the express or implied intention of the parties, in the sense that a party who undertakes a contractual obligation when he knows that, if he breaks the contract, a particular kind of loss is likely to follow, is implicitly assuming responsibility unless he obtains the other party's agreement to an exclusion or restriction of liability clause in the contract. Hence, the promisor may be liable for an unusual type of loss where he is made aware of the risk and thus expressly or impliedly accepts responsibility for it.[254] However, following the very recent decision of the House of Lords in *Transfield Shipping Inc v Mercator Shipping Inc (The Achilleas)*[254a] it now seems that a defendant is not necessarily liable for losses, whether they were usual or unusual, merely because he knew or should have known that they were not unlikely to occur. There is an additional limitation, namely that a defendant will not be liable if he cannot reasonably be regarded as assuming responsibility for losses of the particular kind suffered. Thus the test of liability is no longer applied in a standardised fashion, depending on the principally factual questions of the likelihood or knowledge of the loss. There now appear to be two tests, the remoteness test and, in addition, whether in the particular circumstances it can be said that the defendant was implicitly undertaking responsibility. The second

[251] The term "remoteness of damage" has been distinguished from the term "measure of damages" (or "quantification"), the former referring to the rules as to which types of consequences or losses may be compensated, the latter to the method of assessing in money the compensation for a particular consequence or loss which has been held to be not too remote: Cheshire and North, *Private International Law*, 5th edn, pp.708–712 (approved in *D'Almeida Araujo v Becker* [1953] 2 Q.B. 329; see now 13th edn pp.86–88). This distinction, however, is not adopted in this chapter because it has not yet found favour with the courts in a domestic case: see *Handel (N.V.) My. J. Smits Import-Export v English Exporters Ltd* [1955] 2 Lloyd's Rep. 69, 72; affirmed at 317; *Boys v Chaplin* [1968] 2 Q.B. 1, 31; but the distinction has been accepted in a conflict of laws problem: *Boys v Chaplin* [1971] A.C. 356, 378–379, 382–383, 392–393, 394. cf. *Wroth v Tyler* [1974] Ch. 30, 60–62 (below, para.26–054).

[252] For a comparison between the rules on remoteness in tort and in contract, see Harris, Campbell and Halson, *Remedies in Contract and Tort*, 2nd edn (2002) pp.331–333; and Cartwright [1996] C.L.J. 488.

[253] In an exemption clause (see Ch.14, above), the promisee expressly accepts that the promisor is not to be liable for specified consequences.

[254] This is the second rule in *Hadley v Baxendale* (1854) 9 Ex. 341, below, para.26–061.

[254a] [2008] UKHL 48. See below, para.26–100C.

question appears to be one of law, not of fact.[254b] This new restriction on liability is discussed in a separate section of this Chapter,[254c] after the rules on remoteness have been described in this Section. Because the decision of the House of Lords appeared while this edition was already in proof, it has not been possible to integrate the discussion of it fully into the text as a whole. The remainder of this Section and Section 4 must be read in the light of Section 5 on assumption of responsibility.

Hadley v Baxendale. The classic statement of the rules regarding remoteness of damage in contract (which apply when the damages claimed are unliquidated) is to be found in the judgment of the Court of Exchequer in *Hadley v Baxendale*,[255] as interpreted in later cases.[256] In this case, the plaintiffs' mill was brought to a standstill by the breakage of their only crankshaft. The defendant carriers failed to deliver the broken shaft to the manufacturer at the time they had promised to do, and the plaintiffs sued to recover the profits they would have made had the mill been started again without the delay. The court rejected the claim on the ground that the facts known to the defendants were insufficient[257] to: 26–052

> ". . . show reasonably that the profits of the mill must be stopped by an unreasonable delay in the delivery of the broken shaft by the carriers to the third person."[258]

The judgment of the court was delivered by Alderson B., who said[259]: 26–053

> "Where two parties have made a contract which one of them has broken, the damages which the other party ought to receive in respect of such breach of contract should be such as may fairly and reasonably be considered either as arising naturally, *i.e.* according to the usual course of things, from such breach of contract itself, or such as may reasonably be supposed to have been in the contemplation of both parties, at the time they made the contract, as the probable result of the breach of it. Now, if the special circumstances under which the contract was actually made were communicated by the plaintiffs to the defendants, and thus known to both parties, the damages resulting from the breach of such a contract, which they would reasonably contemplate, would be the amount of injury which would ordinarily follow from a breach of contract under these special circumstances so known and communicated. On the other hand, if these special circumstances were wholly unknown to the party breaking the contract, he, at the most, could only be supposed to have had in his contemplation the amount of

[254b] See below, para.26–100D.
[254c] See below, paras 26–100A et seq.
[255] (1854) 9 Ex. 341. (See comments by Simpson (1975) 91 L.Q.R. 247, 273; Pugsley (1976) 126 New L.J. 420; Danzig (1975) 4 J. Leg. Stud. 249; Harris, Campbell and Halson at pp.92–93.)
[256] See below, para.26–054 et seq.
[257] *Victoria Laundry (Windsor) Ltd v Newman Industries Ltd* [1949] 2 K.B. 528, 537–538. (The headnote of *Hadley v Baxendale* (1854) 9 Ex. 341 is misleading.)
[258] *Hadley v Baxendale* (1854) 9 Ex. 341, 355. See also *Collins v Howard* [1949] 2 All E.R. 324.
[259] (1854) 9 Ex. 341, 354–355.

injury which would arise generally, and in the great multitude of cases not affected by any special circumstances, from such a breach of contract."

26–054 **Modern statement of the rule.** The principles laid down in *Hadley v Baxendale*, above, have been interpreted and restated by the Court of Appeal in 1949 in *Victoria Laundry (Windsor) Ltd v Newman Industries Ltd*[260] and by the House of Lords in 1967, in *Koufos v C. Czarnikow Ltd (The Heron II)*.[261] The combined effect of these cases may be summarised as follows: A type or kind of loss is not too remote a consequence of a breach of contract if, at the time of contracting (and on the assumption that the parties actually foresaw the breach in question), it was within their reasonable contemplation as a not unlikely result of that breach.[262] The following paragraphs expound the different aspects of this summary. It must be borne in mind that a loss may not be recoverable merely because it was not too remote, if in the circumstances it was not reasonable to assume that the defendant was accepting responsibility for it.[262a]

26–055 **Relevant date.** A preliminary point is that the question is what was contemplated by the parties at the time at which the contract was made, not what they may have contemplated at some later date such as the date of breach.[263]

26–056 **The *Victoria Laundry* case.** The three main propositions in the *Victoria Laundry* case were[264]:

"(2) In cases of breach of contract the aggrieved party is only entitled to recover such part of the loss actually resulting as was at the time of the contract reasonably foreseeable as liable to result from the breach. . . .

(3) What was at that time reasonably so foreseeable depends on the knowledge then possessed by the parties or, at all events, by the party who later commits the breach . . .

[260] [1949] 2 K.B. 528. (Some of the propositions in this case were cited with approval in *East Ham Corp v Bernard Sunley & Sons Ltd* [1966] A.C. 406, 440, 445, 450–451.) See below, para.26–066.

[261] [1969] 1 A.C. 350. The Court of Appeal has further considered these principles in *H. Parsons (Livestock) Ltd v Uttley Ingham & Co Ltd* [1978] Q.B. 791. (The two cases cited in the text at the beginning of para.26–054 are not limited in their application to loss of profits: [1978] Q.B. 791, 804–805, 805–806, 813. cf. at 802–804.)

[262] This sentence was quoted with approval by Stuart-Smith L.J. in *Brown v K.M.R. Services Ltd* [1995] 4 All E.R. 598, 621 (see also at 642–643). cf. the summary of Scarman L.J. in *H. Parsons (Livestock) Ltd v Uttley Ingham & Co Ltd* [1978] Q.B. 791, 807 ("The court's task . . . is to decide what loss to the plaintiff it is reasonable to suppose would have been in the contemplation of the parties as a serious possibility had they had in mind the breach when they made their contract."). The test is not one of "directness": *Ogilvie Builders Ltd v Glasgow City DC* (1995) S.L.T. 15. As to the judicial discretion involved in applying the test for remoteness, see Cooke [1978] C.L.J. 288. On the time when the test is applied, see *Jackson v Bank of Scotland* [2005] UKHL 3, [2005] 1 W.L.R. 377 at [35]–[36].

[262a] See below, paras 26–110A et seq.

[263] *Hadley v Baxendale* (1854) 9 Ex. 341, 354; *Victoria Laundry (Windsor) Ltd v Newman Industries Ltd* [1949] 2 K.B. 528, 539; *Jackson v Bank of Scotland* [2005] UKHL 3, [2005] 1 W.L.R. 377 at [35]–[36].

[264] [1949] 2 K.B. 528, 539–540 (propositions (1), (5) and (6) are omitted for reasons of space). For the facts in the case, see below, para.26–066.

(4) For this purpose, knowledge 'possessed' is of two kinds; one imputed, the other actual. Everyone, as a reasonable person, is taken to know the 'ordinary course of things' and consequently what loss is liable to result from a breach of contract in that ordinary course.... But to this knowledge, which a contract-breaker is assumed to possess whether he actually possesses it or not, there may have to be added in a particular case knowledge which he actually possesses, of special circumstances outside the 'ordinary course of things,' of such a kind that breach in those special circumstances would be liable to cause more loss."

The Heron II. In *The Heron II*[265] their Lordships did not agree upon a common formulation, but three of their Lordships[266] gave general approval to these and other[267] propositions in the *Victoria Laundry* case. Somewhat different formulations were adopted by Lords Reid and Upjohn: the former said that Alderson B. in *Hadley v Baxendale*, above: 26–057

"... clearly meant that a result which will happen in the great majority[268] of cases should fairly and reasonably be regarded as having been in the contemplation of the parties, but that a result which, though foreseeable as a substantial possibility, would only happen in a small minority of cases should not be regarded as having been in their contemplation."[269]

Lord Reid continued:

"The crucial question is whether, on the information available to the defendant when the contract was made, he should, or the reasonable man in his position would, have realised that such loss was sufficiently likely to result from the breach of contract to make it proper to hold that the loss flowed naturally from the breach or that loss of that kind should have been within his contemplation."[270]

Lord Upjohn stated:

"... the broad rule as follows: 'What was in the assumed contemplation of both parties acting as reasonable men in the light of the general or special facts (as the case may be) known to both parties in regard to damages as the result of a breach of contract.' "[271]

---

265 [1969] 1 A.C. 350. For the facts see below, para.26–089.

266 [1969] 1 A.C. 350, 399 (Lord Morris), 410–411 (Lord Hodson), 414–417 (Lord Pearce). (But Lord Reid, at 388–391, rejected parts of the *Victoria Laundry* [1949] 2 K.B. 528 propositions.)

267 See below, para.26–059.

268 Lord Hodson [1969] 1 A.C. 350, 411, also adopted the expression used in *Hadley v Baxendale* (1854) 9 Ex. 341: "in the great multitude of cases": (1854) 9 Ex. 341, 355, 356. On the degree of probability see below, para.26–059.

269 [1969] 1 A.C. 350, 384 (see also at 385). Both Lords Reid and Upjohn criticised the words "foreseeable" or "reasonably foreseeable" in the *Victoria Laundry* [1949] 2 K.B. 528 formulations: [1969] 1 A.C. 350, 389, 422–423; Lord Upjohn at 422–423, expressly preferred "contemplate" or "in contemplation" for cases in contract, and these are the words used by Lord Reid at 384–385.

270 [1969] 1 A.C. 350, 385.

271 [1969] 1 A.C. 350, 424.

There is no need for the breach itself to be within the contemplation of the parties: "It is clear that one starts from the assumption that the contract-breaker contemplates, at the date of the making of the contract, the occurrence of the particular breach which he, although at the time he may have no notion of it, is thereafter going to commit."[272]

26–058 **The type or kind of loss.**[273] The reference to "the loss" in the formulations of the test for remoteness of damage is to be interpreted as the type or kind of loss in question.[274] The:

> ". . . party who has suffered damage does not have to show that the contract-breaker ought to have contemplated, as being not unlikely, the precise detail of the damage or the precise manner of its happening. It is enough if he should have contemplated that damage *of that kind* is not unlikely."[275]

(There is a similar formulation in the test for remoteness of damage in tort: "the essential factor in determining liability is whether the damage is of such a kind as the reasonable man should have foreseen".[276]) If the parties ought to have contemplated a particular type of loss ("head of damage") they need not have contemplated the extent of that loss.[277] The application of the test for remoteness to a particular set of facts therefore depends largely on the judicial discretion[278]

---

[272] *Christopher Hill Ltd v Ashington Piggeries Ltd* [1969] 3 All E.R. 1496, 1523 (Court of Appeal: the House of Lords [1972] A.C. 441 reversed the decision on other grounds, without discussing *The Heron II* [1969] 1 A.C. 350); *H. Parsons (Livestock) Ltd v Uttley, Ingham & Co Ltd* [1978] Q.B. 791, 802, 807.

[273] This paragraph was quoted with approval by Stuart-Smith L.J. in *Brown v K.M.R. Services Ltd* [1995] 4 All E.R. 598, 621.

[274] In *The Heron II* [1969] 1 A.C. 350 Lord Reid spoke of "type of damage" (at 385–386), "loss of a kind which" (at 382, 383) and "type of loss" (at 385); while Lord Pearce spoke of "type of consequence" (at 417). See also *H. Parsons (Livestock) Ltd v Uttley, Ingham & Co Ltd* [1978] Q.B. 791, 801, 805, 806, 813.

[275] *Christopher Hill Ltd v Ashington Piggeries Ltd* [1969] 3 All E.R. 1496, 1524; *Brown v K.M.R. Services Ltd* [1995] 4 All E.R. 598, 621; *Kpohraror v Woolwich Building Society* [1996] 4 All E.R. 119, 126. See below, para.26–061 for the corresponding formulation in the second rule in *Hadley v Baxendale* (1854) 9 Ex. 341.

[276] *Overseas Tankship (UK) Ltd v Morts Dock & Engineering Co Ltd (The Wagon Mound)* [1961] A.C. 388, 426.

[277] *H. Parsons (Livestock) Ltd v Uttley, Ingham & Co Ltd* [1978] Q.B. 791, 804, 805, 813; *Brown v K.M.R. Services Ltd* [1995] 4 All E.R. 598, 621, 642–643; cf. *Wroth v Tyler* [1974] Ch. 30, 60–62 (dealing with the corresponding position under the second rule in *Hadley v Baxendale* (1854) 9 Ex. 341). But cf. the cases on loss of profits, below, para.26–066; Vol.II, paras 43–439—43–441, where the type of profits expected from the normal use of a profit-earning machine is used to place a cap on a claim for loss of a different type of profit caused by the breach of contract; *Vacwell Engineering Co Ltd v B.D.H. Chemicals Ltd* [1971] Q.B. 88; cf. also the limitation on the extent of a valuer's liability to a lender for a negligent over-valuation: *South Australia Asset Management Corp v York Montague Ltd* [1997] A.C. 191 (below, para.26–094).

[278] For recent illustrations, see *Balfour Beatty Construction (Scotland) Ltd v Scottish Power Plc* (1994) S.L.T. 807 (HL: not contemplated that interruption of electricity supply to a concrete batching plant would result in demolition and rebuilding of a partly-constructed aqueduct); *Kpohraror v Woolwich Building Society* [1996] 4 All E.R. 119 (CA: not contemplated that one day's delay by a bank in meeting a cheque might cause the plaintiff to lose the transaction in question or incur a trading loss in future).

to categorise losses into broad categories,[279] without requiring any contemplation of the precise manner in which the loss was caused, or of the precise details of the loss.[280] However, when a particular loss is likely to be extensive, it seems that the courts may be inclined to pay more attention to the likelihood of the precise combination of circumstances which caused it to occur.[280a] Moreover, when loss is extensive, it seems more likely that the court will find it unreasonable to assume that the defendant was accepting responsibility for it, whether or not it the defendant should have contemplated it as "not unlikely" to occur.[280b]

The degree of probability. What was in the contemplation of reasonable men obviously depends on the relevant degree of likelihood[281] that a particular kind of loss may occur, and this issue was extensively discussed in *The Heron II*.[282] Lord Reid used: 26–059

> " . . . the words 'not unlikely' as denoting a degree of probability considerably less than an even chance but nevertheless not very unusual and easily foreseeable."[283]

Although Lord Morris thought it unnecessary to choose any one phrase[284] he used "not unlikely to occur",[285] with "liable to result" as an alternative[286]; Lord Hodson accepted the latter phrase.[287] Both Lords Pearce[288] and Upjohn[289]

---

[279] As is illustrated by cases in later paragraphs of this chapter, e.g. loss of profits; physical damage to a chattel or building; illness or death of a person; illness or death of an animal; expenses incurred by the claimant in reliance on the contract; personal, subjective loss of amenity; damages and costs paid by the claimant to a third party as a result of the breach of contract leading to the claimant being held liable to the third party. cf. the similar broad interpretation of the "type" or "kind" of loss in the test for remoteness of damage in tort: *Overseas Tankship (UK) Ltd v Morts Dock & Engineering Co Ltd* [1961] A.C. 388; *Hughes v Lord Advocate* [1963] A.C. 837.

[280] *H. Parsons (Livestock) Ltd v Uttley, Ingham & Co Ltd* [1978] Q.B. 791, 811 ("contemplation that a hopper unfit for its purpose of storing food in a condition suitable for feeding pigs, might well lead to illness" of the pigs or their "physical injury" (at 805, 813), but not that it might lead to a specific type of serious illness (at 812, 813)). "Loss of profit" is obviously another "type" of loss: at 802–803, 813; see also below, paras 26–066 et seq. It seems that in contract cases involving loss of profit, a somewhat more precise test is applied than in tort cases. Thus in the *Victoria Laundries* case [1949] 2 K.B. 528, the court distinguished between profit from different activities. This may be explained by the same factors which seem to lead the courts to requiring a higher degree of probability than in contract cases: see below, para.26–059. In *Transfield Shipping Inc v Mercator Shipping Inc (The Achilleas)* [2008] UKHL 48 at [22]–[23], Lord Hoffmann pointed to the distinction drawn in *Victoria Laundry (Windsor) Ltd v Newman Industries Ltd* [1949] 2 K.B. 528 between loss of laundry profits and loss of profits from especially lucrative dyeing contracts as justifying the approach that the defendant could not be assumed to be taking responsibility for certain kinds of loss. See further below, paras 26–100A et seq.

[280a] See the speech of Lord Rodger in *Transfield Shipping Inc v Mercator Shipping Inc (The Achilleas)* [2008] 3 W.L.R. 345 discussed below at para.26–100C.

[280b] See below, paras 26–110A et seq.

[281] *Southern Portland Cement Ltd v Cooper* [1974] A.C. 623, 640.

[282] [1969] 1 A.C. 350. For the facts, see below, para.26–089.

[283] [1969] 1 A.C. 350, 383. (See also his statements at 388: "a very substantial degree of probability.")

[284] [1969] 1 A.C. 350, 397, 399.

[285] [1969] 1 A.C. 350, 406.

[286] [1969] 1 A.C. 350, 406. "Liable to result" was also one of the phrases accepted in the *Victoria Laundry Case* [1949] 2 K.B. 528, 540.

[287] [1969] 1 A.C. 350, 410–411. (Lord Reid, at 389, rejected this phrase.)

[288] [1969] 1 A.C. 350, 415.

[289] [1969] 1 A.C. 350, 425.

adopted the words "a real danger" or "a serious possibility"[290] which were the phrases used in the House of Lords in 1991.[291] (Four of their Lordships in *The Heron II* agreed that the colloquialism "on the cards" should not be used.[292]) It was also made clear that in contract cases it is not sufficient that the loss was "reasonably foreseeable", at least if this refers to the low probability that will satisfy the remoteness test in tort cases.[293] The contractual test requires a higher degree of probability than the test for remoteness in tort.[294] One reason for this may be that the remoteness rule in contract aims to encourage the parties to exchange information about unusual losses that might flow from breach. As Lord Reid said in *The Heron II*:

> "The modern rule in tort is quite different and it imposes a much wider liability. The defendant will be liable for any type of damage which is reasonably foreseeable as liable to happen even in the most unusual case, unless the risk is so small that a reasonable man would in the whole circumstances feel justified in neglecting it; and there is good reason for the difference. In contract, if one party wishes to protect himself against a risk which to the other party would appear unusual, he can direct the other party's attention to it before the contract is made, and I need not stop to consider in what circumstances the other party will then be held to have accepted responsibility in that event. In tort, however, there is no opportunity for the injured party to protect himself in that way, and the tortfeasor cannot reasonably complain if he has to pay for some very unusual but nevertheless foreseeable damage which results from his wrongdoing."

In tort cases, in contrast, the rule aims to protect the defendant from liability for events of very low probability.[295]

26–060 **Actual and imputed knowledge.** In general, it is necessary to consider the actual knowledge of the defendant (the promisor) only where he would not have been liable without that knowledge; normally the imputed knowledge of the defendant will be at least as great as (if not greater than) his actual knowledge.

[290] These words were rejected by Lord Reid (at 390), who also rejected "foreseeable as a real possibility" (at 385). *Victoria Laundry* [1949] 2 K.B. 528, 540, also accepted "a real danger" or "a serious possibility." (The latter phrase was used by the Court of Appeal in *H. Parsons (Livestock) Ltd v Uttley, Ingham & Co Ltd* [1978] Q.B. 791, 802, 805, 807.)

[291] *Bank of Nova Scotia v Hellenic Mutual War Risks Association (Bermuda) Ltd* [1992] 1 A.C. 233, 267.

[292] [1969] 1 A.C. 350, 390, 399, 415, 425. (It was yet another phrase used in *Victoria Laundry* [1949] 2 K.B. 528, 540.)

[293] [1969] 1 A.C. 350, 385, 411, 425.

[294] See Harris, Campbell and Halson, *Remedies in Contract and Tort*, 2nd edn (2002) at pp.331–333.

[295] See Bishop (1983) 12 JLS 241. The difference between the rules caused the Court some difficulty in *H. Parsons (Livestock) Ltd v Uttley, Ingham & Co Ltd* [1978] Q.B. 791, where there was liability in both trot and contract. Lord Denning M.R. said that in the test for remoteness of damage in contract there is a distinction between loss of profit (or only economic loss) cases, and physical damage (or expense) cases (at 802–803); but this distinction was not accepted by the other members of the Court of Appeal, and lacks supporting authority: see, per Orr L.J. at 804–805; and, per Scarman L.J. at 805–806. But no clear answer emerges from the other judgments. See Treitel, *Law of Contract*, 12th edn (by Peel, 2007), para.20–086, where the interesting suggestion is made that where a claimant in tort was in previous communication with the defendant, the contract rule should apply.

Actual knowledge may occasionally operate to the advantage of the defendant. For instance, Devlin J. has said:

> "If, however, a sub-sale is within the contemplation of the parties, I think that the damages must be assessed by reference to it, whether the plaintiff likes it or not. . . . If it is the plaintiff's liability to the ultimate user that is contemplated as the measure of damages and it is in fact used without injurious results so that no such liability arises, the plaintiff could not claim the difference in market value, and say that the sub-sale must be disregarded."[296]

The test for imputed knowledge has been said by Lord Wright[297] to be:

> " . . . what reasonable business men must be taken to have contemplated as the natural and probable result if the contract was broken. As reasonable business men, each must be taken to understand the ordinary practices and exigencies of the other's trade or business."[298]

The defendant's knowledge of the type of business conducted by the claimant may be a ground for imputing knowledge,[299] but the defendant cannot be expected to know the technical details of the claimant's activity where it involved complicated techniques.[300] Again, in contracts for the sale of goods, the defendant is normally taken to have known that the market price and the supply and demand of the market may change.[301] The kind of consequence which falls within the imputed knowledge of the defendant will be illustrated by cases throughout the rest of this section, and in particular, by cases on damages in contracts for the sale of goods.[302]

Actual knowledge of special circumstances. The so-called second rule in *Hadley v Baxendale*[303] applies when the loss (the "type or kind of loss"[304]) flowing from the breach of a particular contract is greater than, or different from what it would have been in normal circumstances. If actual knowledge of the 26–061

[296] *Biggin & Co Ltd v Permanite Ltd* [1951] 1 K.B. 422, 436. (The actual decision in this case was reversed on another ground: [1951] 2 K.B. 314 (see Vol.II, para.43–463).) See also *Bence Graphics International Ltd v Fasson UK Ltd* [1998] Q.B. 87 (below, paras 43–444, 43–446, where criticism by Treitel is noted); *The Heron II* [1969] 1 A.C. 350, 416; *Louis Dreyfus Trading Ltd v Reliance Trading Ltd* [2004] EWHC 525 (Comm), [2004] 2 Lloyd's Rep. 243 (see Vol.II, para.43–446 fn.2027). cf. *Trans Trust S.P.R.L. v Danubian Trading Co Ltd* [1952] 2 K.B. 297, 306.

[297] *Monarch S.S. Co Ltd v Karlshamns Oljefabriker (A/B)* [1949] A.C. 196, 224 (examined further in *Balfour Beatty Construction (Scotland) Ltd v Scottish Power Plc* (1994) S.L.T. 807, (1994) 71 B.L.R. 20 HL).

[298] See also *Bank of Nova Scotia v Hellenic Mutual War Risks Association (Bermuda) Ltd* [1992] 1 A.C. 233, 267.

[299] *Victoria Laundry (Windsor) Ltd v Newman Industries Ltd* [1949] 2 K.B. 528 (below, para.26–059); cf. *Diamond v Campbell-Jones* [1961] Ch. 22.

[300] *Balfour Beatty Construction (Scotland) Ltd v Scottish Power Plc* (1994) S.L.T. 807.

[301] *Interoffice Telephones Ltd v Robert Freeman Co Ltd* [1958] 1 Q.B. 190, 202 (below, para.26–069). The same holds for contracts for the carriage of goods: below, para.26–089.

[302] Below, paras 26–088, et seq.

[303] (1854) 9 Ex. 341 (above, para.26–052).

[304] *Wroth v Tyler* [1974] Ch. 30, 61.

defendant (the promisor) is relied upon to make him liable for exceptional losses resulting from breach of the contract in the special[305] circumstances, that knowledge must have existed at or before the making of the contract.[306] There is now authority in the House of Lords that the two rules in *Hadley v Baxendale* are not mutually exclusive; indeed, what kinds of loss are within the first rule and what kinds are only recoverable if within the second rule depends on how the relevant breach of contract is characterised and the degree of knowledge of the circumstances that the parties are assumed to have.[307] The second rule covers "heads of damage" not the quantum or extent of loss; thus, it is unnecessary for the parties to have contemplated the quantum of damages, or the extent of the loss, provided it falls within a contemplated type of loss.[308]

26–062 **Express or implied term as to liability not required.** An unsettled point is whether, when the loss is an unusual one, the remoteness rule will be satisfied if the defendant had bare knowledge of the special circumstances.[309] In 1868, Willes J. said[310]:

> "The mere fact of knowledge cannot increase the liability. The knowledge must be brought home to the party sought to be charged, under such circumstances that he must know that the person he contracts with reasonably believes that he accepts the contract with the special condition attached to it . . . knowledge on the part of the carrier is only important if it forms part of the contract. It may be that the knowledge is acquired

---

[305] The facts or circumstances do not have to be "unusual" before the second rule in *Hadley v Baxendale* (1854) 9 Ex. 341 may come into play: see *President of India v Lips Maritime Corp* [1988] A.C. 395, 411, 412.

[306] *Victoria Laundry (Windsor) Ltd v Newman Industries Ltd* [1949] 2 K.B. 528, 539 (Proposition 3, cited above, para.26–056); *Jackson v Bank of Scotland* [2005] UKHL 3, [2005] 1 W.L.R. 377 at [35]–[36]. See also *Hydraulic Engineering Co Ltd v McHaffie Goslett & Co* (1878) 4 QBD 670, 676; cf. *Kollman v Watts* [1963] V.L.R. 396 (knowledge acquired *after* the contract was made). The rules in *Hadley v Baxendale* encourage the efficient exchange of information. There is no need for the promisee to inform the promisor about the usual consequences of a breach of his promise, but if he intends the promisor to be responsible for an unusual type of risk he must inform the promisor of that risk, so that, by making the promise with that knowledge, the promisor is implicitly assuming responsibility for it. (The promisor can then increase the "price" he requires in exchange, or exclude liability.)

[307] *Jackson v Bank of Scotland* [2005] UKHL 3 at [46]–[49]. There is no need for a strict delineation between the two rules in *Hadley v Baxendale* (1854) 9 Ex. 341: *Transfield Shipping Inc v Mercator Shipping Inc (The "Achilleas")* [2006] EWHC 3030 (Comm), [2007] 1 Lloyd's Rep. 19 at [49]; affirmed [2007] EWCA Civ 901, [2007] 2 Lloyd's Rep. 555, on the same point see at [88] and [95]; reversed [2008] UKHL 48 but on a different ground, see below, para.26–100C.

[308] *Wroth v Tyler* [1974] Ch. 30, 60–62; cf. *Jackson v Bank of Scotland* [2005] UKHL 3 at [36]. cf. above, fn.251. cf., however, the cases on loss of profits, which show that a loss of profits from one use of a chattel may be treated as different from a loss of profits from another use: see below, para.26–066; Vol.II, paras 43–439, 43–441. cf. also *South Australia Asset Management Corp v York Montague Ltd* [1997] A.C. 191 (below, para.26–094).

[309] *Patrick v Russo-British Grain Export Co Ltd* [1927] 2 K.B. 535, 540.

[310] *British Columbia, etc., Saw Mill Co Ltd v Nettleship* (1868) L.R. 3 C.P. 499, 509. See also *Horne v Midland Ry* (1873) L.R. 8 C.P. 136, 139, 141, 145, 146–147 (*cf.* at first instance (1872) L.R. 7 C.P. 583, 591–592); *Elbinger Aktiengesellschaft v Armstrong* (1874) L.R. 9 Q.B. 473, 478; *Victoria Laundry (Windsor) Ltd v Newman Industries Ltd* [1949] 2 K.B. 528, 538; *Robophone Facilities Ltd v Blank* [1966] 1 W.L.R. 1428, 1448.

casually from a stranger, the person to whom the goods belong not knowing or caring whether he had such knowledge or not."

It is submitted, however, that it is unnecessary to hold that the defendant's acceptance of liability for unusual loss (in the special circumstances made known to him) can be enforced only where there is an express or implied term of the contract to that effect.[311] Nor does there have to be an "assumption of responsibility" in the sense required for liability for negligent misstatement.[312]

Casual knowledge of unusual risk will not suffice. The defendant will probably not be liable merely because he had gained knowledge of the unusual risk in a purely casual way. Although in *Hadley v Baxendale*[313] itself, "communication" was said to be the vital factor, it is submitted that a casual communication from a stranger is insufficient. It is essential that there should be communication of the special circumstances by or on behalf of the claimant to the defendant or his agent so as to show that the claimant thought it important that the defendant should know what other matters depended on his fulfilment of the contract; these facts may, in appropriate circumstances, lead to the inference that the defendant, as a reasonable man, was accepting the risk of special loss to the claimant.[314] 26–063

Assumption of responsibility? The remoteness rule is without doubt satisfied if, on the basis of his knowledge of the special circumstances, the reasonable man in the defendant's position at the time of contracting would have understood that, by making the promise in those circumstances, he was accepting responsibility for the risk of the type of loss in question. What was less clear is whether, once the defendant had the necessary knowledge, he might still be able to deny liability on the grounds that it was not reasonable to assume that he was accepting responsibility. Many dicta suggest that adequate knowledge suffices, so that the defendant will be liable unless he validly excludes his liability by a term of the contract. 26–063A

[311] See *Koufos v C. Czarnikow Ltd, The Heron II* [1969] 1 A.C. 350, 421–422 (*obiter*); *Satef-Huttenes Albertus SpA v Paloma Tercera Shipping Co SA* [1981] 1 Lloyd's Rep. 175, 183–184. Such a rule might create difficulties where the contract was required to be in writing, or evidenced by a memorandum in writing: see *Hydraulic Engineering Co Ltd v McHaffie Goslett Co* (1878) 4 QBD 670.

[312] *Transfield Shipping Inc v Mercator Shipping Inc (The"Achilleas")* [2007] EWCA Civ 901, [2007] 2 Lloyd's Rep. 555 at [115]. For "assumption of responsibility" in the context of negligent misrepresentation, see above, para.1–141. But see the decision of the House of Lords in *The Achilleas* [2008] UKHL 48, [2008] 3 W.L.R. 345, discussed below, paras 26–100A et seq.

[313] (1854) 9 Exch. 341, 354 (above, para.26–052).

[314] The cases on sub-sales, considered in Vol.II, paras 43–432—43–435, 43–446, 43–455, provide a good illustration of this principle. For other illustrations see *Panalpina International Transport Ltd v Densil Underwear Ltd* [1981] 1 Lloyd's Rep. 187, 191; the *Victoria Laundry* case [1949] 2 K.B. 528 (below, para.26–059); *Wadsworth v Lydall* [1981] 1 W.L.R. 598 (upheld by House of Lords in *President of India v La Pintada Compania Navegacion SA* [1985] A.C. 104, 125–127) (see below, para.26–145); *Kemp v Intasun Holidays Ltd* [1987] 2 F.T.L.R. 234 and below, paras 26–059, 26–062, 26–089.

> "Where knowledge of special circumstances is relied on, the assumption is that the defendant undertook to bear any special loss which was referable to those special circumstances".[315]

However, on occasions liability for losses of an unusual kind has been explained in terms of the defendant assuming responsibility for the loss in question:

> ". . . have the facts in question come to the defendant's knowledge in such circumstances that a reasonable person in the shoes of the defendant would, if he had considered the matter at the time of making the contract, have contemplated that, in the event of a breach by him, such facts were to be taken into account when considering his responsibility for loss suffered by the plaintiff as a result of such breach."[316]

This might be interpreted as meaning that the defendant would not be liable if, for some reason, it was reasonable for him to think that he was *not* undertaking responsibility. In previous editions of this work, it was suggested that in relation to liability for special circumstances, mere knowledge that an unusual loss might well follow a breach would not always suffice. There might not be liability if either it was clear from all the circumstances either that the defendant—to the knowledge of the plaintiff—did not wish to accept the risk of the unusual loss, or that a reasonable man in the place of the defendant would not, despite his knowledge of the special circumstances, have accepted the risk of the unusual loss.[317] These factors now seem to be relevant to the separate[318] question of whether the defendant can reasonably be assumed to have accepted responsibility.[318a] It is submitted that the remoteness rule is still satisfied if the loss in question is one that in the usual course of things was "not unlikely" to arise from the breach in question, or if, before the contract was made, the defendant was informed by the other party that a breach of contract might lead to an unusual kind of loss.

(b) *Timing of the Assessment of Damages*

26–064 **The relevant date for the assessment of damages.**[319] The general rule is that damages for breach of contract should be assessed as at the date when the cause of action arose, viz the date of the breach[320] (which rule usually applies where substitute performance is readily available in the market[321]):

---

[315] *Jackson v Bank of Scotland* [2005] UKHL 3, [2005] 1 W.L.R. 377, at [26]. Cf *Muhammad Issa el Sheikh Ahmad v Ali* [1947] A.C. 414, 427 (impecuniosity of one party in the contemplation of the parties: "damages which, on the facts found by the trial judge, might reasonably be expected to be in the contemplation of the parties").

[316] Robert Goff J. in the *Satef-Huttenes* case, above, at 183: (At 184, the learned judge spoke of "assuming responsibility for the risk of such loss in the event of" breach.) See also *Seven Seas Properties Ltd v Al-Essa (No.2)* [1993] 1 W.L.R. 1083, 1088.

[317] 29th edition, para.26—055. cf. *Robophone Facilities Ltd v Blank* [1966] 1 W.L.R. 1428, 1448.

[318] See below, para.26–100E.

[318a] See below, paras 26–100A et seq.

[319] Waddams (1981) 97 L.Q.R. 445. cf. below, paras 26–071, 26–072.

[320] *Miliangos v George Frank (Textiles) Ltd* [1976] A.C. 443, 468; *Johnson v Agnew* [1980] A.C. 367, 400 (see below, paras 26–091—26–092).

[321] See Vol.II, paras 43–400 et seq., paras 43–420 et seq.; and, on the doctrine of mitigation, below, paras 26–101 et seq.

"But this is not an absolute rule: if to follow it would give rise to injustice the court has power to fix such other date as may be appropriate in the circumstances."[322]

Thus, if, after a breach, the innocent party reasonably[323] continues to treat the contract as in force, damages may be assessed as at the later date "when (otherwise than by his default) the contract is lost",[324] viz when performance becomes impossible,[325] or when the innocent party terminates the contract.[326] (Any further delay in his receiving compensation should be met by the award of interest.[327]) If the claimant did not know of the breach of contract at the time it occurred, damages will usually be assessed as at the time when he should reasonably have discovered the breach, and was able to act on his knowledge,[328] e.g. by attempting to mitigate.[329] The assessment of damages at the cost of substitute performance[330] or at the cost of a reasonable attempt to mitigate[331] are other situations where the time for assessment may be postponed after the date of breach.

Inflation and interest rates. If the date for the assessment of damages is postponed so that the claimant is protected against inflation until that date, the full market rate of interest (which largely reflects current expectations of inflation) should not be awarded for any earlier period.[332] 26–065

[322] *Johnson v Agnew* [1980] A.C. 367, 401; *Kennedy v K. B. Van Emden & Co* (1997) 74 P. & C.R. 19; *Golden Strait Corp v Nippon Yusen Kubishika Kaisha* [2007] UKHL 12, [2007] 2 A.C. 353 at [79]–[80]. For the assessment of damages for anticipatory breach, see below, para.26–121; Vol.II, paras 43–412, 43–425. cf. below, para.26–122.

[323] In *Malhotra v Choudhury* [1980] A.C. 52, 77, 81, delay by the plaintiff led to the date for valuing a property being moved back one year from the date of judgment: see below, para.26–091.

[324] *Johnson v Agnew* [1980] A.C. 367, 401 (see below, para.26–091) citing *Ogle v Earl Vane* (1867) L.R. 2 Q.B. 275 (on appeal, L.R. 3 Q.B. 272) (see Vol.II, para.43–424); *Hickman v Haynes* (1875) L.R. 10 C.P. 598 (see Vol.II, para.43–408); and *Radford v De Froberville* [1977] 1 W.L.R. 1262. cf. below, para.26–109.

[325] *Johnson v Agnew* [1980] A.C. 367, 401. If the seller postponed delivery, but later repudiated, damages will be assessed at the date of the repudiation: *Barnett v Javeri & Co* [1916] 2 K.B. 390.

[326] For cases decided before *Johnson v Agnew* [1980] A.C. 367, where the damages were assessed at dates later than the original breach of contract, see below, para.26–091 fn.488.

[327] See below, paras 26–167 et seq.

[328] *East Ham Corp v Bernard Sunley & Sons Ltd* [1966] A.C. 406.

[329] *Van den Hurck v R. Martens & Co Ltd* [1920] 1 K.B. 850 (damages assessed as at the time when, after delivery of sealed packages, it was reasonable to expect them to be opened and the contents inspected: see Vol.II, para.43–444); *Cehave N.V. v Bremer Handelsgesellschaft mbH* [1976] 1 Q.B. 44 (damages assessed as at the date of arrival of the goods).

[330] See above, para.26–016. cf. the assessment of damages in tort for the cost of repairs to damaged property: *Dodd Properties Ltd v Canterbury City Council* [1980] 1 W.L.R. 433 (see above, para.26–018); *Alcoa Minerals of Jamaica Inc v Broderick* [2002] 1 A.C. 371, PC, and the comments of Waddams (1981) 97 L.Q.R. 445, 457–461 on the incentives to the claimant to maximise his damages which might arise from permitting postponement of the date for assessing damages.

[331] *County Personnel (Employment Agency) Ltd v Alan R. Pulver & Co* [1987] 1 W.L.R. 916, 925–926. See below, paras 26–079, 26–120.

[332] *Dodd Properties Ltd v Canterbury City Council* [1980] 1 W.L.R. 433. See Waddams (1981) 97 L.Q.R. 445, 454–455; and 1 O.J.L.S. 134 (1980); Swan (1980) 10 *Real Property Reports* (Canada) 267; Wallace (1980) 96 L.Q.R. 101, 115, 341 and (1982) 98 L.Q.R. 406.

(c) *Loss of Profits*

26–066 **Seller's liability for loss of profits.** The general principles of remoteness of damage in contract may be illustrated by cases where the claimant has claimed for loss of profits as a result[333] of the defendant's breach of contract.[334] A frequent instance is the delayed delivery of a profit-earning chattel.[335] In *Victoria Laundry (Windsor) Ltd v Newman Industries Ltd*[336] the plaintiffs agreed to buy a large boiler from the defendants, and a date was fixed for delivery. The plaintiffs sued for damages for delay in delivery, and claimed loss of profits in respect of:

(1) the large number of new customers they could have taken on had the boiler been installed; and
(2) the amount which they could have earned under special dyeing contracts with the Ministry of Supply.

The defendants knew that the plaintiffs were launderers and that they wanted the boiler for immediate use; the Court of Appeal held that with such knowledge the reasonable man could have foreseen that delay in delivery would lead to some loss of profits, though he would not have foreseen the loss of profits under the special contracts with the Ministry, since these were special circumstances not within the defendant's actual knowledge.[337] Hence the plaintiff could not recover all of the actual loss of profits which he had incurred under these contracts, but only the normal loss of business in respect of laundering and dyeing contracts to be reasonably expected.[338] Other cases support the principle that loss of profits may be awarded where there has been delayed delivery by a seller of a profit-earning chattel where it was within his reasonable contemplation that the buyer would use it to make profits[339]; or would have resold it at a profit[340]; or where the

[333] On the question of evaluating contingencies affecting the chance of making a profit, see above, paras 26–042—26–045.

[334] In *H. Parsons (Livestock) Ltd v Uttley, Ingham & Co Ltd* [1978] Q.B. 791, 802–803, Denning M.R. said that in the test for remoteness of damage in contract there is a distinction between loss of profit (or only economic loss) cases, and physical damage (or expense) cases; but this distinction was not accepted by the other members of the Court of Appeal, and lacks supporting authority: see, per Orr L.J. at 804–805; and, per Scarman L.J. at 805–806.

[335] *Hadley v Baxendale* (1854) 9 Ex. 341 (above, para.26–052); *Fletcher v Tayleur* (1855) 17 C.B. 21; *Wilson v General Iron Screw Colliery Co Ltd* (1877) 47 L.J.Q.B. 239; *Hydraulic Engineering Co Ltd v McHaffie Goslett & Co* (1878) 4 QBD 670; *Saint Lines Ltd v Richardsons Westgarth & Co* [1940] 2 K.B. 99; *Victoria Laundry (Windsor) Ltd v Newman Industries Ltd* [1949] 2 K.B. 528.

[336] Above. See Vol.II, para.43–439.

[337] See above, para.26–061. See *Brown v K.M.R. Services Ltd* [1995] 4 All E.R. 598, 621; *North Sea Energy Holdings N.V. v Petroleum Authority of Thailand* [1997] 2 Lloyd's Rep. 418, 438–439.

[338] If the defendant had been told of the special contracts, and should have realised, as a reasonable man, that he was undertaking responsibility for the loss of higher-than-usual profits in the case of breach, he would have been able to demand a higher price, or to cover himself with an exemption.

[339] *Cory v Thames Ironworks & Shipbuilding Co Ltd* (1868) L.R. 3 Q.B. 181. cf. *Re Trent and Humber Co* (1868) L.R. 4 Ch. App. 112 (delay by a repairer); *Steam Herring Fleet v Richards* (1901) 17 T.L.R. 731.

[340] See Vol.II, paras 43–432—43–435, 43–446, 43–455.

profit-earning chattel which was delivered was defective.[341] However, these cases must now be read in the light of the recent decision of the House of Lords in *Transfield Shipping Inc v Mercator Shipping Inc (The Achilleas)*[341a] that a claimant will not recover even losses that were not unlikely to occur in the usual course of things if the defendant cannot reasonably be regarded as assuming responsibility for losses of the particular kind suffered.[341b]

Contemplated loss may operate as a cap on recovery. In one case, where the defendant contracted to supply a profit-earning chattel, which the plaintiff intended to put to an exceptional use (outside the defendant's reasonable contemplation), the loss of profits expected under its normally contemplated use placed a ceiling on the damages recoverable by the plaintiff for the delay in delivery.[342] A loss of profits from normal use was contemplated as arising from the breach, and the plaintiff had in fact suffered such a loss to an amount beyond that ceiling.[343] Similarly, in the *Victoria Laundries* case[344] the buyer recovered the sum they would have earned from "normal" laundering and dyeing, though if the boiler had been delivered on time they would presumably have used it for the more profitable Government dyeing contracts. 26–067

Purchaser's intended use of land. In a contract to sell land or a leasehold interest in land, "special circumstances are necessary to justify imputing to [the] vendor a knowledge that the purchaser intends to use it in any particular manner" so as to entitle the purchaser to recover damages for loss of the profit he would have made from that use.[345] 26–068

Seller's claim for loss of profits. If the defendant, in breach of his contract, has refused to accept goods sold[346] or hired[347] to him by a dealer or goods manufactured for him,[348] but the claimant has found a third person who will take the goods by a similar contract (under which the claimant makes a similar profit), the claimant is entitled to recover his loss of profit on the defendant's contract 26–069

---

[341] *H. Parsons (Livestock) Ltd v Uttley, Ingham & Co* [1978] Q.B. 791, 810, 813; Vol.II, para.43–449. (Loss of "repeat orders" from the buyer's disappointed customers may also be recovered: see Vol.II, para.43–456.)

[341a] [2008] UKHL 48.

[341b] See below, paras 26–100A et seq.

[342] *Cory v Thames Ironworks and Shipbuilding Co Ltd* (1868) L.R. 3 Q.B. 181.

[343] This explanation is supported by the *Victoria Laundry* case [1949] 2 K.B. 528.

[344] See above, para.26–066.

[345] *Diamond v Campbell-Jones* [1961] Ch. 22; *Cottrill v Steyning and Littlehampton Building Society* [1966] 1 W.L.R. 753; *Malhotra v Choudhury* [1980] Ch. 52. See below, paras 26–091—26–092. cf. *Wright v Dean* [1948] Ch. 687; *G. & K. Ladenbau (UK) Ltd v Crawley & De Reya* [1978] 1 W.L.R. 266 (solicitors who were negligent in checking title, which delayed completion, held liable for interest for delayed receipt of profits on a resale within their reasonable contemplation).

[346] *W. L. Thompson Ltd v Robinson (Gunmakers) Ltd* [1955] Ch. 177.

[347] *Interoffice Telephones Ltd v Robert Freeman Co Ltd* [1958] 1 Q.B. 190; *Robophone Facilities Ltd v Blank* [1966] 1 W.L.R. 1428 (below, Vol.II, para.38–299). On damages for loss of profits under a hire-purchase agreement, see Vol.II, paras 38–326—38–328.

[348] *Re Vic Mill Ltd* [1913] 1 Ch. 465.

where the supply of such goods exceeds the demand; for in such a case the claimant has lost one profit he would otherwise have made.[349] If however, in similar circumstances, the demand for such goods exceeds the supply, the claimant will recover only nominal damages, since he has received the same profit through the substituted contract as he would have received if the defendant had performed his contract.[350] Other cases dealing with loss of profits in sub-contracts and "string" contracts are discussed in Vol.II.[351]

26–070 **Carrier's liability for loss of profits.** A carrier who fails to deliver goods within the agreed time may also cause loss of business profits to the consignee.[352] The normal measure of damages for delayed delivery is the difference between the market value of the goods on the due date of arrival and their market value on the actual date of delivery.[353] But:

> "... a carrier commonly knows less than a seller about the purposes for which the buyer or consignee needs the goods, or about other 'special circumstances' which may cause exceptional loss if due delivery is withheld."[354]

The amount of knowledge imputed to a carrier will therefore be limited in the usual case, and the consignee will be obliged to prove the carrier's actual knowledge of the special circumstances so as to show that the carrier must be taken as a reasonable man to have accepted the risk of unusual loss resulting from breach. In most reported cases, therefore, the carrier has escaped liability for the plaintiff's loss of profits because he lacked sufficient knowledge.[355] Exceptionally, however, the carrier may be liable where it is shown that, at the time of contracting, he knew of the facts which would lead to special loss if he failed to

---

[349] It is a "lost volume" case. This assumes that the claimant would have made both contracts. If his operation would have been operating at maximum efficiency in order to fulfil the first contract, he might not have taken on the second. See Beale, *Remedies for Breach of Contract* (1980), p.200.

[350] *Charter v Sullivan* [1957] 2 Q.B. 117. The claimant should also be entitled to recover any extra expenses incurred in making the substituted contract: see below, para.26–078. (To a certain extent, this decision and that in *W. L. Thompson Ltd v Robinson (Gunmakers) Ltd* [1955] Ch. 177, depend on the absence of an "available market" where the price fluctuates in accordance with supply and demand: see Vol.II, paras 43–400—43–410.)

[351] Vol.II, paras 43–432—43–435, 43–446, 43–455.

[352] On damages for delay in the carriage of passengers, see Vol.II, para.36–065.

[353] See below, para.26–089. On special conditions of carriage, see Vol.II, Ch.36.

[354] *Victoria Laundry (Windsor) Ltd v Newman Industries Ltd* [1949] 2 K.B. 528, 537. See also *Heskell v Continental Express Ltd* [1950] 1 All E.R. 1033, 1049, where Devlin J. expressed the view that knowledge of a sub-contract would be more easily imputed to a seller than to a carrier; *André et Cie SA v J. H. Vantol* [1952] 2 Lloyd's Rep. 282.

[355] *Hadley v Baxendale* (1854) 9 Ex. 341; *Gee v Lancs & Yorks Ry* (1860) 6 H. & N. 211; *British Columbia, etc., Saw Mill Co Ltd v Nettleship* (1868) L.R. 3 C.P. 499; *Horne v Midland Ry* (1873) L.R. 8 C.P. 131. But the fact that loss of profit under a special contract with a third party is not recoverable, does not prevent the carrier being liable for some damages for delay: *B. Sunley & Co Ltd v Cunard White Star Ltd* [1940] 1 K.B. 740 (interest awarded on the value of the goods for the period of the delay); *Koufos v C. Czarnikow Ltd, The Heron II* [1969] 1 A.C. 350 (damages for reduction in market value at date of late delivery: see below, para.26–089).

deliver or was late in delivering,[356] e.g. where the carrier knew that no substitutes would be available in the market at the place fixed for delivery, he may be liable for loss of "reasonable" resale profits suffered by the consignee.[357] However, liability in such cases may be limited by the recent decision of the House of Lords in *Transfield Shipping Inc v Mercator Shipping Inc (The Achilleas)*[357a] that a claimant will not recover even losses that were not unlikely to occur in the usual course of things if the defendant cannot reasonably be regarded as assuming responsibility for losses of the particular kind suffered.[357b]

Loss of future business. Subject to the rules on causation and remoteness, the contract-breaker may be liable for the claimant's loss of future profits from "repeat orders" from his previous customers which loss was caused by the particular breach of contract.[358] When loss of future profits is not too remote, the period of time for which the loss should be assessed is until the question whether any loss has been sustained has become "too speculative to permit the making of any award".[359] 26–071

(d) *Expenditure Wasted or Incurred as a Result of the Breach*[360]

Reliance expenditure arising from the claimant's performance. The claimant may claim damages for wasted expenditure which he incurred in reliance on the contract or as the result of the defendant's breach. The first category is where, before the breach, the claimant had incurred expenditure in reliance on his expectation that the defendant would perform his undertaking, but where the breach results in that expenditure being wasted, at least in part. The first type of this expenditure is that directly related to the claimant's own preparations for his performance, as where he has incurred the cost of labour and materials which will be wasted as a result of the breach.[361] This expenditure is part of the cost of the claimant's performance and if the defendant had fulfilled his side, the claimant would have received the benefit of the expenditure when he 26–072

---

[356] *Simpson v L.N.W. Ry* (1876) 1 QBD 274; *Jameson v Midland Ry* (1884) 50 L.T. 426; *Monte Video Gas and Dry Dock Co Ltd v Clan Line Steamers Ltd* (1921) 37 T.L.R. 866; *S.S. Ardennes (Cargo Owners) v S.S. Ardennes (Owners)* [1951] 1 K.B. 55 (loss of market); *Satef-Huttenes Albertus SpA v Paloma Tercera Shipping Co SA (The Pegase)* [1981] 1 Lloyd's Rep. 175. See also *Schulze & Co v G.E. Ry* (1887) 19 QBD 30; cf. *Ströms Bruks Aktiebolag v John & Peter Hutchison* [1905] A.C. 515.

[357] *Satef-Huttenes Albertus SpA v Paloma Tercera Shipping Co SA* [1981] 1 Lloyd's Rep. 175.

[357a] [2008] UKHL 48, [2008] 3 W.L.R. 345.

[357b] See below, paras 26–100A et seq.

[358] *Jackson v Bank of Scotland* [2005] UKHL 3, [2005] 1 W.L.R. 377 (breach of obligation to maintain confidence). See above, para.26–045; and Vol.II, paras 43–434, 43–456.

[359] *Jackson v Bank of Scotland* [2005] UKHL 3 at [37].

[360] See Owen (1984) 4 O.J.L.S. 393.

[361] The test of reasonableness in incurring the expenditure would not seem to be relevant (cf. the rule in mitigation for post-breach expenditure: below, para.26–078). But the expenditure must have been intended by the claimant to be part of his performance and must satisfy the remoteness rules.

received the benefit of the defendant's performance (e.g. the price). When the claimant terminates the contract on the ground of the breach, he may claim damages to cover his expenditure towards his own performance, but only to the extent that it has been wasted as a result of the breach.[362]

26–073 **The ceiling on recovery in an unprofitable contract.** If the claimant fully performed his side of the contract, he would not be entitled to recover from the defendant more than the value of the latter's performance viz the gross return (such as the price) to which the claimant was entitled under the contract. If the claimant is relegated to a claim to damages because he had only partly performed his side by the time the contract was terminated, the amount of the gross return to which he would be entitled upon full performance will be a ceiling on the recovery of damages for the expenditure incurred in his partial performance.[363] By suing for damages for his costs in performing in reliance on the contract, the claimant cannot recover more than he would have been entitled to if the defendant had not broken the contract.[364] The precise arithmetical method of implementing this principle has not yet been decided[365] but it is submitted that the claimant should be entitled to claim his performance expenditure actually incurred to the limit imposed by the gross return (or price) due for full performance.[366] The onus of proof is on the defendant to show (on the balance of probabilities) that the claimant would have made a loss on full performance of both sides of the contract and so would not have recouped all of his own costs in performing his side.[367] In the absence of such proof, the court will assume in the claimant's favour that he would have recouped all the costs incurred in his performance, and so will be willing to award damages to reimburse the claimant.[368] Usually the claimant will seek damages for this reliance expenditure rather than for his loss of expectations (his gross return, less future expenses avoided after the breach) only where he lacks adequate proof of his loss of expectations (e.g. profits),[369] or where he feared that it would have been a losing or unprofitable contract so that he would not be able to prove any net loss of

[362] If the claimant can salvage any items of value from his preparations for performance, the rules of mitigation require him to deduct from his claim the amount he obtained from selling the salvageable items to a third party (or the amount he ought reasonably to have obtained from doing so).

[363] This principle is inferred from two cases (*C. & P. Haulage v Middleton* [1983] 1 W.L.R. 1461; and *C.C.C. Films (London) Ltd v Impact Quadrant Films Ltd* [1985] Q.B. 16) although they were concerned not with the profitability of the individual contract which the defendant broke, but of the activity of which that contract was an essential part. On this see below, para.26–075.

[364] *C. & P. Haulage v Middleton* [1983] 1 W.L.R. 1461; *C.C.C. Films (London) Ltd v Impact Quadrant Films Ltd* [1985] Q.B. 16.

[365] Harris, Campbell and Halson, *Remedies in Contract and Tort*, 2nd edn (2002) at pp.124–127.

[366] This view is found (obiter) in the *C.C.C. Films* case [1985] Q.B. 16, 35. Harris, Campbell and Halson at pp.124–127, prefers this method to scaling down the claimant's damages by reference to the total of his costs incurred to date and the potential costs which (but for the breach) he would thereafter have incurred.

[367] *C.C.C. Films (London) Ltd v Impact Quadrant Films Ltd* [1985] Q.B. 16.

[368] [1985] Q.B. 16, 39–40.

[369] *Molling & Co v Dean & Son Ltd* (1902) 18 T.L.R. 216; *Anglia Television v Reed* [1972] 1 Q.B. 60.

expected profit.[370] The courts insist that the claimant has an unfettered choice as to which measure of damages to claim.[371]

Reliance expenditure not directed at performance. Before the breach the claimant may incur expenditure in reliance on the expected performance of the contract by the defendant where the expenditure was not incurred in or towards the performance of his own obligations; this is expenditure from which he expected to benefit, as part of the activity in which he was engaged, after he had received the benefit of the defendant's performance, but which the breach now renders futile. Subject to mitigation,[372] the claimant is entitled to damages to reimburse him for this expenditure, provided it was within the reasonable contemplation of the parties that it was not unlikely that the claimant would incur it in reliance on the contract, and that it would be wasted if the defendant committed the breach in question. (No test of reasonableness in incurring the expenditure has been imposed on the claimant, but if the expenditure was incurred unreasonably, it would not satisfy the remoteness test.) So where the buyer of goods had them repaired before he had to give them up to a third party (because it later emerged that the seller had no title to them), he recovered the cost of the repairs which was wasted from his point of view.[373] Other illustrations of the recovery of wasted expenditure are the cost of painting a machine before it was found to be defective[374]; the cost of transporting goods to a sub-buyer before they were examined and rejected[375]; and the cost of equipping a salvage expedition to a tanker which the buyer had been promised was on the "Journand Reef", when in fact neither the tanker nor the reef existed.[376] 26–074

Ceiling on recovery if claimant's activity would have been unprofitable. As with the case of performance expenditure discussed above,[377] the defendant may show[378] that the claimant entered into a contract as part of a 26–075

---

[370] This statement is probably restricted to a contract where the claimant intended to make a profit from his performance of the contract (viz it was not a consumer contract where the claimant intended to *use* the subject-matter of the contract).

[371] *Anglia Television v Reed* [1972] 1 Q.B. 60; *C.C.C. Films (London) Ltd v Impact Quadrant Films* [1985] Q.B. 16, 31–32. On the possibility of a "split" claim, see below, para.26–077.

[372] See below, para.26–101. The claimant's damages will be calculated on the basis that he took reasonable steps to realise the salvage value of anything left on his hands after the breach.

[373] *Mason v Burningham* [1949] 2 K.B. 545. See also *Steam Herring Fleet Ltd v V.S. Richards & Co Ltd* (1901) 17 T.L.R. 731 (expenses in preparing for a voyage; delay in delivering ship). See also *Saint Line Ltd v Richardsons, Westgarth & Co Ltd* [1940] 2 K.B. 99, 105.

[374] *Cullinane v British "Rema" Manufacturing Co Ltd* [1954] 1 Q.B. 292. See also *British Westinghouse Electric and Manufacturing Co Ltd v Underground Electric Rys Co of London Ltd* [1912] A.C. 673, 683 (cost of extra coal used by defective turbines); *Richard Holden Ltd v Bostock & Co Ltd* (1902) 18 T.L.R. 317 (beer wasted when ingredient found to be contaminated).

[375] *Molling & Co v Dean & Son Ltd* (1901) 18 T.L.R. 217.

[376] *McRae v Commonwealth Disposals Commission* (1950) 84 C.L.R. 377 (see above, para.5–033). The High Court of Australia dismissed a claim for loss of profit as speculative.

[377] Above, para.26–073. (The discussion in that paragraph applies to the present paragraph, subject to the proviso that the latter is not limited to the profitability of the contract in question, but applies to the profitability of the activity in question.)

[378] The onus of proof is on the defendant: *C.C.C. Films (London) Ltd v Impact Quadrant Films Ltd* [1985] Q.B. 16 (above, para.26–073).

commercial or profit-making activity and that he would have made an overall loss on that activity. The defendant must show that, from the gross return which the claimant expected to receive from exploiting or using the subject matter of his contract with the defendant,[379] he would not have recouped all of the expenditure incurred in reliance on the contract. Where the defendant can prove that, even if he had completely performed that contract, the claimant's gross return from his exploitation would not have covered that expenditure, the claimant's claim for wasted expenditure can succeed only to the extent that it would have been recouped.[380] (The same question as discussed above arises over the method of implementing this principle.[381])

26–076 **Expenditure incurred before making the contract.** The claimant may incur expense before entering the contract, but in the expectation that if such a contract is made, the expenditure will be needed to enable him to perform the contract (or to undertake the activity of which the expected contract will form part), and that he will be able to recoup the expenditure from the benefit of the defendant's performance of that contract (e.g. the price) or from the profits he expects to make from the activity in question. If, at the time of contracting, it was within the reasonable contemplation of the parties that the claimant would be able to recoup this expenditure in this way, he may recover damages for any wasted[382] part of the expenditure arising from the breach.[383] For instance, the overhead costs (premises, staff, etc.) will often be incurred by the claimant before he makes a particular contract: the defendant, when entering into the contract, can easily contemplate that the claimant will expect to recoup from it a contribution towards overheads.[384]

26–077 **Claiming for wasted expenditure in addition to net loss of expected profit.** In principle, the claimant should be entitled to claim damages both for his wasted expenditure incurred up to the date of his terminating the contract and also for the net loss of profit[385] which he would have made but for the breach. There can be no valid objection to this, provided the calculations show that there

---

[379] The relevant gross return is that expected from the claimant's whole undertaking, of which the contract with the defendant forms an essential part: *C & P Haulage v Middleton* [1983] 1 W.L.R. 1461. This point is implicitly recognised in *Cullinane v British "Rema" Manufacturing Co Ltd* [1954] 1 Q.B. 292.

[380] The *C.C.C. Films* case [1985] Q.B. 16; *C & P Haulage v Middleton* [1983] 1 W.L.R. 1461.

[381] See above, para.26–073.

[382] Under the rules of mitigation, a deduction must be made from the damages in respect of anything with a salvage value arising from the expenditure.

[383] *Anglia Television Ltd v Reed* [1972] 1 Q.B. 60 (the expenditure was part of the overall activity in which the plaintiff was engaged, the making of a film); *Lloyd v Stanbury* [1971] 1 W.L.R. 535, 546 (legal costs, and removal expenses: "the costs of performing an act required to be done by the contract"). See Ogus (1972) 35 M.L.R. 423. The question of a ceiling on recovery will be relevant: see above, paras 26–073, 26–075.

[384] The facts of the *C.C.C. Films* case [1985] Q.B. 16 show that the expenditure in question was incurred before the making of the subsidiary agreement broken by the defendant.

[385] The expected profit will either be from the particular contract (performance expenditure: above para.26–073) or from the profit-making activity of which it forms a part (above, para.26–075).

is no overlapping in the claimant's recovery, viz his net loss of profits is calculated by deducting from his expected gross return both the cost of his performance and reliance expenditure to the date of termination[386] and the cost of the further expenditure which he would have incurred after that date if he had completed his performance.[387] However, the Court of Appeal has ruled that the claimant must choose between claiming for his wasted reliance expenditure and claiming for his loss of expected profits, holding that he is not entitled to recover both.[388] This position is correct if it is interpreted to mean that the claimant should not recover both his *gross* return or profits expected under the contract (or from the activity in question)[389] and also the (now wasted) expenditure incurred in reliance on the contract which he had intended to meet from that gross return. But it is submitted that the ruling against a "split" claim cannot be justified if the claimant can show that there is no overlapping between the two claims.[390]

Expenditure incurred after, and as a result of the breach. Subject to the rules on causation and remoteness and to the test of acting reasonably,[391] the claimant may recover as damages the reasonable costs[392] incurred by him in mitigating the loss caused by the breach or in otherwise dealing with the consequences of breach.[393] So where the defendant delayed delivery of a crane sold to the plaintiff whom he knew to be an importer of timber, the plaintiff recovered the extra cost of man-handling timber at his wharf.[394] Other illustrations are the recovery of the cost of substitute performance by a third party[395]; the recovery of the amount of damages and costs paid by the claimant to a third party 26–078

[386] Allowance must be made for any salvage value.

[387] Macleod [1970] J.B.L. 19; Street, *Principles of the Law of Damages* (1962), pp.242–245; Beale, *Remedies for Breach of Contract* (1980), p.238.

[388] *Cullinane v British "Rema" Manufacturing Co Ltd* [1954] 1 Q.B. 292, 308. (This case is explored in more detail below, Vol.II, paras 43–453—43–454); *Anglia Television Ltd v Reed* [1972] 1 Q.B. 60, 63–64.

[389] In both the *Cullinane* [1954] 1 Q.B. 292 and *Anglia Television* [1972] 1 Q.B. 60 cases, above, the relevant profit-making related to the activity in which the plaintiff was engaged (processing clay for sale or making a proposed film) rather than to the individual contract.

[390] See *T.C Industrial Plant Pty Ltd v Robert's (Queensland) Pty Ltd* [1964] A.L.R. 1083; Stoljar [1975] 91 L.Q.R. 68. In *Hydraulic Engineering Co Ltd v McHaffie Goslett & Co* (1878) 4 QBD 670, both wasted expenses and profits were awarded, but it is not clear whether the latter were *net* profits. See also *Saint Line Ltd v Richardsons, Westgarth & Co Ltd* [1940] 2 K.B. 99 which accepted a claim involving both. The distinction between gross and net profits is recognised in *C.C.C. Films (London) Ltd v Impact Quadrant Films Ltd* [1985] Q.B. 16, 32.

[391] The cost of "reasonable" action may be recovered even if it later appears that some other action would have been better: *Gebruder Metelmann GmbH v NBR (London) Ltd* [1984] 1 Lloyd's Rep. 614, 634. cf. below, para.26–120.

[392] See below, para.26–120.

[393] *Richard Holden Ltd v Bostock & Co Ltd* (1902) 18 T.L.R. 317 (cost of sending notices to customers to minimise loss of business); *Heskell v Continental Express Ltd* [1950] 1 All E.R. 1033, 1046 (cost of trying to trace goods). On claims for interest charges incurred, see below, paras 26–167 et seq. On mitigation, see below, para.26–101.

[394] *John M. Henderson & Co Ltd v Montague L. Meyer Ltd* (1941) 46 Com. Cas. 209, 219–220. See also on the costs caused by delay, *Borries v Hutchinson* (1865) 19 C.B.(N.S.) 445 (extra freight and insurance); *Watson v Gray* (1900) 16 T.L.R. 308 (increased building costs).

[395] Above, para.26–016.

as a consequence of the defendant's breach of contract,[396] as where it was within reasonable contemplation of the parties that the buyer would probably resell the goods, and that the seller's breach in supplying defective goods was not unlikely to result in the buyer being liable to pay damages and costs to a sub-buyer for breach of the sub-contract[397]; the recovery of storage charges after the defendant refused to accept goods[398]; the recovery of the reasonable cost of rebuilding,[399] repairing or replacing[400] property of the claimant damaged or destroyed through the defendant's breach of contract; the recovery of medical or rehabilitation expenses when the breach causes physical injury to the claimant[401]; extra freight and insurance costs arising from late delivery of goods.[402] Unlike in the case of reliance expenditure, there is no question of this category being subject to a ceiling on recovery being fixed by the expected profitability of the contract or activity.[403]

26–079 **Damages assessed on a "no transaction" basis.** In a limited number of situations, where the claimant claims that he would not have entered into a particular transaction but for the defendant's negligent advice (or failure to advise), his damages have been assessed at the amount needed to restore him to the position he would have been in if he had never entered the transaction.[404] So in *Hayes v Dodd*[405] a solicitor negligently advised the plaintiff that he had a right of way to give access to the leasehold property he proposed to acquire as a site

---

[396] See Vol.II, para.43–436. The breach of contract may even result in a tortious claim by a third party against the claimant, the cost of which is within the remoteness test: *Mowbray v Merryweather* [1895] 2 Q.B. 640 (see Vol.II, para.43–461). The claimant's legal liability to a third person (even before it is discharged by payment) constitutes recoverable loss: *Total Liban SA v Vitol Energy SA* [2001] Q.B. 643.

[397] e.g. *Biggin v Permanite* [1951] 2 K.B. 314. See Vol.II, paras 43–463—43–446. If the claimant acts reasonably in reaching an out-of-court settlement with the third party, he may be entitled to recover the amount of the settlement: Vol.II, para.43–463. It is not necessary that he should have been under a legal obligation to pay the third party if it was reasonable to do so: *John F Hunt Demolition Ltd v ASME Engineering Ltd* [2007] EWHC 1507 (TCC), [2008] 1 All E.R. 180. On the recovery of a fine imposed on the claimant as the result of the defendant's breach of contract, see Vol.II, para.43–452.

[398] *Harlow & Jones Ltd v Panex (International) Ltd* [1967] 2 Lloyd's Rep. 509 (there was no available market). See also *S.S. Ardennes (Cargo Owners) v S.S. Ardennes (Owners)* [1951] 1 K.B. 55 (increased import duty payable).

[399] *Harbutt's "Plasticine" Ltd v Wayne Tank and Pump Co Ltd* [1970] 1 Q.B. 447. See also *Smith v Johnson* (1899) 15 T.L.R. 179 (mortar supplied by a builder was below standard; it was used for building a wall which the local authority later condemned as unsafe; the owner recovered from the builder the cost of pulling it down and of rebuilding). See also *Calabar Properties Ltd v Stitcher* [1984] 1 W.L.R. 287 (cost of alternative accommodation during repairs to flat occupied by tenant).

[400] *Bacon v Cooper (Metals) Ltd* [1982] 1 All E.R. 397.

[401] The decision in *Grant v Australian Knitting Mills Ltd* [1936] A.C. 85 supports the view that damages for personal injury caused by breach of contract should be assessed on a similar basis to that used in tort.

[402] *Borries v Hutchinson* (1865) 18 C.B.(N.S.) 445.

[403] See above, paras 26–073, 26–075.

[404] *Aneco Reinsurance Underwriting Ltd v Johnson & Higgins Ltd* [2001] UKHL 51, [2001] 2 All E.R. (Comm) 929 HL (advice to enter the transaction, as distinct from the provision of specific information).

[405] [1990] 2 All E.R. 815 CA.

for his business. There was no legally-enforceable vehicular right of way and the business failed through the lack of adequate access. Damages were assessed on the "no transaction" basis viz all the wasted expenditure incurred by the plaintiff (the initial cost of the lease and goodwill, rent, rates, insurance, bank interest and other expenses wasted until the time he reasonably gave up the business) *less* the amounts recovered by the plaintiff through selling the lease and his plant (the mitigation rules applied). An analogous case is where negligent advice from a solicitor led the client to take a disadvantageous underlease: the damages were the sum paid by the client over five years later to secure its surrender: *County Personnel (Employment Agency) Ltd v Alan R. Pulver and Co.*[406] In the *South Australia* case[407] the House of Lords said that the distinction between "no transaction" and "successful transaction" cases should be abandoned; but the House approved the two cases just mentioned on the basis of the mitigation or "extrication" principle ("a reasonable attempt to cope with the consequences of the defendant's breach of duty").[408] However, in *Hayes v Dodd* the damages went beyond "extrication" and covered *all* the plaintiff's wasted expenditure from the beginning of the transaction. It is clearly established that damages may be assessed on the "no transaction" basis when the defendant fraudulently induced the claimant to enter into the transaction,[409] and it is submitted that the same basis may be appropriate where the breach of contract destroys the whole purpose of the transaction into which the claimant entered in reliance on the defendant's advice.[410] So this basis applied where a lender claimed against a solicitor whose negligence did not concern the adequacy of the security[411] but was fundamental in the sense that in the absence of the negligence the lender would have refused to make any loan at all to the particular borrower.[412] Similarly, where a broker negligently advised the claimant to enter a transaction, he was held liable for all the losses suffered by the claimant from that entry.[413]

Loss in purchasing power of currency; and currency exchange loss. Debts or damages cannot be increased to take account of a fall in the domestic purchasing power of sterling between the time when the claimant's loss is 26–080

[406] [1987] 1 W.L.R. 916 CA.

[407] [1997] A.C. 191 (below, para.26–094) This case was followed in *Hok Sport Ltd v Aintree Racecourse Co Ltd* [2002] EWHC 3094, [2003] Lloyd's Rep. P.N. 148.

[408] [1997] A.C. 191, 218–219.

[409] *Smith New Court Securities Ltd v Scrimgeour Vickers Ltd* [1997] A.C. 254. The same result holds when the defendant negligently advised the claimant to enter the transaction: *Aneco Reinsurance Underwriting Ltd v Johnson & Higgins Ltd* [2001] UKHL 51; [2001] 2 All E.R. (Comm) 929.

[410] As in *Hayes v Dodd* [1990] 2 All E.R. 815 CA. The wasted expenditure must, of course, meet the remoteness test.

[411] The situation covered by analogy with the over-valuation formula in the *South Australia* case [1997] A.C. 191 (below, para.26–085).

[412] *Steggles Palmer* case (one of the cases brought by the *Bristol and West Building Society*, and reported in [1997] 4 All E.R. 582).

[413] *Aneco Reinsurance Underwriting Ltd v Johnson & Higgins Ltd* [2001] 2 All E.R. (Comm) 929 HL.

assessed and the date of judgment.[414] For domestic purposes,[415] sterling[416] is taken by English courts to be constant in value,[417] subject to the award of interest[418]; but this approach has led courts to find grounds for postponing the date when damages are assessed,[419] and to uphold various contractual clauses indexing debts to the value of gold, to a foreign currency, or to a price index.[420]

26–081 **Currency exchange loss.** Where a debt due in a foreign currency is not paid on time, and as a result the creditor suffers a currency loss which was within the reasonable contemplation of the parties, he may recover damages in respect of that loss.[421] The ordinary rules on remoteness of damage apply to a claim to recover a currency exchange loss caused by breach of contract.[422]

(e) *Non-pecuniary Losses*

26–082 **Physical loss, injury or inconvenience.** Normally, damages for breach of contract relate to financial loss (including loss of expected financial gains), but non-pecuniary losses may be recovered if they were within the contemplation of the parties as not unlikely to result from the breach. If the defendant's breach of contract caused physical injury to the claimant himself,[423] or to his property,[424] the claimant may recover damages for that injury, provided the test for remote-

---

414 *Philips v Ward* [1956] 1 W.L.R. 471 CA. See *Dicey, Morris and Collins on the Conflict of Laws*, 14th edn, Ch.36; Mann, *The Legal Aspect of Money*, 6th edn (2005), Chs 5, 7 and 10. See also above, paras 21–068 et seq. cf. a debt which is calculable in a foreign currency: see below, paras 30–357—30–378.

415 Sterling is treated as having a fluctuating exchange value in relation to any given foreign currency: *Miliangos v George Frank (Textiles) Ltd* [1976] A.C. 443 (see below, para.30–376).

416 For the award of debts and damages in a foreign currency, see below, para.30–376.

417 *Philips v Ward* [1956] 1 W.L.R. 471 CA 474 (citing *Di Ferdinando v Simon Smits & Co* [1920] 3 K.B. 409, 414; *S.S. Celia v S.S. Volturno* [1921] A.C. 544, 563; *Bishop v Cunard White Star Co* [1950] P. 240, 246). See also *Treseder-Griffin v Co-operative Insurance Society Ltd* [1956] 2 Q.B. 127, 144; *Tomkinson v First Pennsylvania Banking and Trust Co* [1961] A.C. 1007, 1069–1070; *The Teh Hu* [1970] P. 106.

418 Below, paras 26–167 et seq. If interest is awarded at full market rates, these may often largely compensate the claimant for inflation in the sense of loss of domestic purchasing power: see above, para.26–065, text at fn.332.

419 See above, para.26–064.

420 See above, paras 21–068—21–072. A long-term contract which in terms is binding indefinitely may nevertheless be interpreted as permitting determination by reasonable notice; the fact that the contract contains no provision for inflation is relevant: *Staffordshire Area Health Authority v South Staffordshire Waterworks Co* [1978] 1 W.L.R. 1387.

421 See below, paras 30–369 et seq. See *Aruna Mills Ltd v Dhanrajmal Gobindram* [1968] 1 Q.B. 655 (contemplated risk of devaluation) (which was approved by the House of Lords in *President of India v Lips Maritime Corp* [1988] A.C. 395, 425).

422 *President of India v Lips Maritime Corp* [1988] A.C. 395, 424.

423 *Wren v Holt* [1903] 1 K.B. 610 (defective food sold for human consumption); *Grant v Australian Knitting Mills Ltd* [1936] A.C. 85 (buyer of defective clothing contracted dermatitis); *Summers v Salford Corp* [1943] A.C. 283; *Godley v Perry* [1960] 1 W.L.R. 9.

424 *Henry Kendall & Sons v William Lillico & Sons Ltd* [1969] 2 A.C. 31; *Harbutt's "Plasticine" Ltd v Wayne Tank and Pump Co Ltd* [1970] 1 Q.B. 447 (the decision has been overruled on another point: *Photo Productions Ltd v Securicor Transport Ltd* [1980] A.C. 827); *H. Parsons (Livestock) Ltd v Uttley, Ingham & Co Ltd* [1978] Q.B. 791. See also the cases on repair and reinstatement, above, para.26–016.

ness is satisfied. Damages for personal injury caused by breach of contract may include compensation for pain and suffering and loss of amenity, as well as loss of earnings, which are normal heads of damages in the assessment of damages in tort for such injuries.[425] Similarly, where the breach of contract causes the claimant physical inconvenience or discomfort, he may recover damages,[426] as where the claimant suffered physical inconvenience and discomfort as the result of living in a defective house, or of vacating rooms while repairs were carried out.[427] But the quantum of such damages should be "modest".[428] If the remoteness test is satisfied, the claimant's damages for breach of contract may include compensation for loss incurred through the death of a human being, as, e.g. for loss of his wife's services, where the cause of action was independent of the death and the death was merely an item of damage.[429]

Mental distress and disappointment; nervous shock.[430] Normally, no damages in contract will be awarded for injury to the claimant's feelings, or for his mental distress, anguish, annoyance, loss of reputation[431] or social discredit caused by the breach of contract[432]; as where an employee is wrongfully dismissed in a humiliating manner.[433] Although in *Malik's* case[434] the House of 26–083

[425] Often there may be concurrent liability in tort for the personal injury or death, but there may be advantages in suing for breach of contract, e.g. in not having to prove the defendant's negligence.

[426] *Burton v Pinkerton* (1867) L.R. 2 Ex. 340, 349–351; *Hobbs v L.S.W. Ry* (1875) L.R. 10 Q.B. 111; *Bailey v Bullock* [1950] 2 All E.R. 1167; *Stedman v Swan's Tours* (1951) 95 S.J. 727; cf. below, para.26–083. cf. also *Farley v Skinner* [2001] UKHL 49, [2002] 2 A.C. 732 (a serious level of aircraft noise may cause physical inconvenience and discomfort: at [30]–[36], [57]–[60], [85]–[88], [108]. See below, para.26–084—26–085).

[427] *Perry v Sidney Phillips & Son* [1982] 1 W.L.R. 1297, CA; *Calabar Properties Ltd v Stitcher* [1984] 1 W.L.R. 287; *Watts v Morrow* [1991] 1 W.L.R. 1421, 1439–1443, 1445–1446, CA; damages may also cover the plaintiff's "mental suffering" directly related to the physical inconvenience: at 1445.

[428] *Watts v Morrow* [1991] 1 W.L.R. 1421 (the judge's award of £4,000 was reduced by the Court of Appeal to £750: at 1443, 1445). See also Franklin (1988) 4 Const. L.J. 264.

[429] *Jackson v Watson* [1909] 2 K.B. 193. See also *Priest v Last* [1903] 2 K.B. 148.

[430] Exemplary damages are not available for breach of contract: above, para.26–019.

[431] See below, para.26–086.

[432] *Addis v Gramophone Co Ltd* [1909] A.C. 488 (as interpreted by *Malik v Bank of Credit and Commerce International SA* [1998] A.C. 20). See also *Hamlin v G.N. Ry* [1856] 1 H. & N. 408; *Groom v Crocker* [1939] 1 K.B. 194; *Foaminol Laboratories Ltd v British Artid Plastics Ltd* [1941] 2 All E.R. 393 (loss of co-operation of advertisers); *Bailey v Bullock* [1950] 2 All E.R. 1167 (no damages for "annoyance or mental distress"); *Last-Harris v Thompson Bros* [1956] N.Z.L.R. 995; *Hayes v Dodd* [1990] 2 All E.R. 815, CA; *Watts v Morrow* [1991] 1 W.L.R. 1421, CA. Nor are damages recoverable for loss of the society of one's spouse or child; cf. *Jackson v Watson* [1909] 2 K.B. 193.

[433] *Addis v Gramophone Co Ltd* [1909] A.C. 488 (see above, para.26–019). The House of Lords later said that "damages for breach of contract may only be awarded for breach of contract, and not for loss caused by the manner of the breach": *Malik v Bank of Credit and Commerce International SA* [1998] A.C. 20, at 51 (per Lord Steyn, interpreting *Addis v Gramophone Co*). In *Eastwood v Magnox Electric Plc* [2004] UKHL 35, [2005] 1 A.C. 503, Lord Nicholls said (at [11]) that if the facts of *Addis* occurred today, the claimant would have a remedy at common law for breach of contract: see para.26–086, below. See also *Bliss v S.E. Thames Regional Health Authority* [1987] I.C.R. 700; *French v Barclays Bank Plc* [1998] I.R.L.R. 646 CA. But cf. the damages when a master wrongfully terminates a contract of apprenticeship: Vol.II, para.39–196. On damages for wrongful, or unfair dismissal, see below, paras 39–193 et seq., paras 39–232 et seq.

[434] [1998] A.C. 20.

Lords created a narrow exception to this principle,[435] it still holds as the general principle[436]: where a breach of an ordinary commercial contract may cause foreseeable anguish and vexation to the claimant, no damages are recoverable for that type of loss.[437] However, an exception applies in the enjoyment or "holiday" cases[438]: in the case of a failure, in breach of contract, to provide a holiday of the advertised standard or some other form of entertainment or enjoyment, damages may be awarded for the disappointment and mental distress caused by the breach of contract.[439] (The "loss of amenity" recognised by the House of Lords[440] could be viewed as an extension of the "loss of enjoyment" category.) A further exception arises where the purpose of the contract was to protect the claimant from annoyance or distress, e.g. where a woman employed solicitors to protect her from being molested by a former friend, who was causing her mental distress; the damages for the solicitors' failure to obtain protection for her included a sum for the foreseeable annoyance and mental distress which she continued to suffer as a result of their breach of contract.[441] Damages for breach of contract may be awarded to a mother for the mental distress caused by the loss of the company of her child.[442] Damages may also be awarded for nervous shock or an anxiety state (an actual breakdown in health) suffered by the claimant, if that was, at the time the contract was made,[443] within the contemplation of the parties as a not unlikely consequence of the breach of contract.[444]

26–084 **Loss of amenity.** In *Ruxley Electronics and Construction Ltd v Forsyth*[445] the House of Lords accepted that damages may be awarded for the "loss of amenity" suffered by the claimant where the purpose of the contract was to give him a subjective, even idiosyncratic pleasure or amenity. The defendant, in breach of

---

[435] See below, para.26–086.

[436] The House of Lords in *Johnson v Gore Wood & Co* [2002] 2 A.C. 1 maintained the *Addis* principle, while accepting the exceptions set out in para.26–083. The House held that the principle should not be restricted by further "inroads" (cf. at 50 where Lord Cooke of Thorndon doubts the permanence of *Addis* in English law). See also *Johnson v Unisys* [2001] UKHL 13, [2003] 1 A.C. 518 (in particular, per Lord Steyn, at 1082 et seq.); *Farley v Skinner* [2001] UKHL 49, [2002] 2 A.C. 732. On *Johnson v Unisys*, see para.26–086 below.

[437] *Hayes v Dodd* [1990] 2 All E.R. 815, CA.

[438] *Jarvis v Swans Tours Ltd* [1973] Q.B. 233; *Jackson v Horizon Holidays Ltd* [1975] 1 W.L.R. 1468; *Jackson v Chrysler Acceptances Ltd* [1978] R.T.R. 474; *Kemp v Intasun Holidays Ltd* [1987] 2 F.T.L.R. 234.

[439] cf. *Diesen v Samson* (1971) S.L.T. (Sh.Ct.) 49 (failure of photographer to attend a wedding). cf. also *Archer v Brown* [1985] Q.B. 401, 424–426 (deceit).

[440] *Ruxley Electronics and Construction Ltd v Forsyth* [1996] A.C. 344; *Farley v Skinner* [2001] UKHLR 49, [2002] 2 A.C. 732. See below, paras 26–084—26–085.

[441] *Heywood v Wellers* [1976] Q.B. 446. cf. damages for mental distress awarded against a solicitor whose negligence led to his client's wrongful conviction of a crime: *McLeish v Amoo-Gottfried & Co* (1994) 10 Prof. Negligence 102; *McLoughlin v Grovers* [2001] EWCA Civ 1743, [2002] P.I.Q.R. 20 222.

[442] *Hamilton-Jones v David & Snape (A Firm)* [2003] EWHC 3147 (Ch), [2004] 1 W.L.R. 924 (solicitor's failure allowed father to remove children from the UK).

[443] See above, para.26–054.

[444] *Cook v Swinfen* [1967] 1 W.L.R. 457. See also *Walker v Northumberland CC* [1995] 1 I.C.R. 702 (employee's nervous breakdown caused by excessive workload); *Barber v Somerset CC* [2004] UKHL 13, [2004] 1 W.L.R. 1089 (employee's psychiatric injury caused by work-related stress).

[445] [1996] A.C. 344 (see the comments by Poole (1996) 59 M.L.R. 272; and Coote [1997] C.L.J. 537).

contract, built a swimming pool whose depth was only six feet in the diving area, instead of the specified seven feet six inches. Despite evidence that a depth of six feet was perfectly safe for diving, and that the market value of the property was not adversely affected by the breach, the Court of Appeal[446] had allowed the full cost of re-building the pool. Their Lordships reversed this decision[447] and appeared to support the trial judge's award (not appealed) of £2,500 as substantial damages for "loss of amenity" because the purpose of the contract was "the provision of a pleasurable amenity". Two Lords agreed with Lord Mustill's speech: he upheld the award as representing the loss of the "consumer surplus", the personal, subjective gain which the claimant expected to receive from full performance—an advantage not measured by any increase in the market value of his property.[448]

The House of Lords again used the "loss of amenity" concept to award damages in *Farley v Skinner*[449] where the potential purchaser specifically asked his surveyor whether the property would be seriously affected by aircraft noise. A paragraph in the survey report said it was unlikely that the property would suffer greatly from such noise. In fact, it was close to a navigation beacon around which aircraft could be "stacked" on a spiral course at busy times at the nearby airport. The House of Lords held that it was sufficient for the award of damages that an important object of the contract was to give pleasure, relaxation or peace of mind—it need not be the sole or principal purpose of the contract to justify the award of damages for "loss of amenity" when the surveyor had failed to exercise reasonable care in making the report on noise. An award of £10,000 damages was upheld, even though the market value of the property, after taking account of the noise, was not less than the price paid by the purchaser.[450] It should be noted that the defendant make a specific statement about the amenity in response to a specific inquiry by the claimant.[451] 26–085

Loss of reputation. Damages for loss of reputation as such are not normally awarded for breach of contract, since protection of reputation is the role of the tort of defamation. However, where the breach of contract causes a loss of reputation which in turn causes foreseeable financial loss to the claimant, he may recover damages for that financial loss: in *Malik's* case,[452] the House of Lords 26–086

[446] [1994] 1 W.L.R. 650.

[447] Above, para.26–017.

[448] Lord Mustill cited the article by Harris, Ogus and Phillips (1979) 95 L.Q.R. 581 (which was also cited in *Farley v Skinner* [1994] 1 W.L.R. 650 at [21]). The *Ruxley Electronics* decision [1996] A.C. 344 decision is discussed in *Att-Gen v Blake* [2001] 1 A.C. 268, 298 (a dissenting speech). At 282, in Lord Nicholl's speech (approved by the majority) he said that: "The law recognises that a party to a contract may have an interest in performance which is not readily measurable in terms of money."

[449] [2001] UKHL 49, [2002] 2 A.C. 732.

[450] Awards should be "restrained and modest": [2001] UKHL 49 at [28].

[451] In earlier cases, in the absence of such specificity, damages have been refused for distress caused by reliance on a survey about the condition of a house: *Watts v Morrow* [1991] 1 W.L.R. 1421 CA; or for breach of a covenant for quiet enjoyment in a tenancy agreement: *Branchett v Beaney* [1992] 3 All E.R. 910 CA. However, damages may be awarded for "mental suffering" directly related to physical inconvenience and discomfort caused by breach of contract: *Watts v Morrow* [1991] 1 W.L.R. 1421, 1440–1445 (see above, para.26–082 fn.427).

[452] *Malik v Bank of Credit and Commerce International SA* [1998] A.C. 20. (See the article by Enonchong, which preceded this decision, (1996) 16 O.J.L.S. 617.)

held that where, by conducting a dishonest and corrupt business, the employer had broken his obligation to his employee (under the implied "trust and confidence" term[453]) the employee could recover damages for the financial loss suffered by him where his future employment prospects were prejudiced by the stigma of his former employment.[454] But in *Johnson v Unisys Ltd*[455] the House of Lords held that, in the light of the statutory scheme providing compensation for unfair dismissal, the common law should not construct a remedy of damages for the unfair manner of the dismissal. The claimant had recovered the maximum statutory compensation in the industrial tribunal, but later claimed, on the basis of the "trust and confidence" implied term, that the manner of his dismissal had caused his mental breakdown. This case has later been distinguished by the House of Lords, which held that an employee may have a common law claim for financial loss where his employer has acted unfairly towards him prior to, and independently of, his subsequent unfair dismissal.[456] However, it should be noted that in another case the House of Lords held that in his unfair dismissal claim an employee cannot recover compensation for non-economic or non-pecuniary loss, such as distress, humiliation or loss of reputation.[457]

26–087 Another line of authority covers cases where the contract gave an opportunity to the claimant to enhance his reputation as an author[458] or an actor[459]: damages may be awarded for loss flowing from a failure to provide promised publicity, which loss may include loss to existing reputation.[460] Subject to remoteness, damages are recoverable where the breach of contract causes loss of commercial reputation involving loss of trade.[461]

4. ILLUSTRATIONS OF THE REMOTENESS OF DAMAGE AND THE ASSESSMENT OF DAMAGES[462]

(a) *Sale of Goods*

26–088 **Sale of goods.** Many of the best illustrations of the rules for the remoteness of damage and for the assessment of damages will be found in cases on the sale

[453] See below, paras 39–143—39–144.

[454] *Malik's* case [1998] A.C. 20 was applied in *Bank of Credit and Commerce International SA v Ali (No.3)* [2002] EWCA 82, [2002] 3 All E.R. 750 (where it was held that the employees had failed to prove that the stigma had caused them actual financial loss).

[455] [2001] UKHL 13, [2003] 1 A.C. 518.

[456] *Eastwood v Magnox Electric Plc* [2004] UKHL 35, [2005] 1 A.C. 503.

[457] *Dunnachie v Kingston upon Hull City Council* [2004] UKHL 36, [2005] 1 A.C. 226 (interpreting s.123 of the Employment Rights Act 1996).

[458] *Tolnay v Criterion Film Productions Ltd* [1936] 2 All E.R. 1625; *Joseph v National Magazine Co Ltd* [1959] Ch. 14.

[459] *Clayton & Jack Waller Ltd v Oliver* [1930] A.C. 209; *Marbé v George Edwardes (Daly's Theatre) Ltd* [1928] 1 K.B. 269.

[460] *Malik's* case [1988] A.C. 20 above (overruling on this point *Withers v General Theatre Corp Ltd* [1933] 2 K.B. 536).

[461] *Malik's* case [1998] A.C. 20 at 115; *Cointax v Myham & Son* [1913] 2 K.B. 220 (below, para.43–456); *G.K.N. Centrax Gears Ltd v Matbro Ltd* [1976] 2 Lloyd's Rep. 555 (below, para.43–456); *Jackson v Bank of Scotland* [2005] UKHL 3, [2005] 1 W.L.R. 377 (see above, para.26–071).

[462] Further illustrations will be found in the various chapters of Vol.II of this work.

of goods, which are considered in some detail in Vol.II, Ch.43. Although these cases are often based on the provisions of the Sale of Goods Act 1893 (now consolidated in the 1979 Act), the relevant ss.50, 51, 53 and 54 incorporate former common law decisions on the sale of goods[463] so that cases decided on the Act may be useful analogies for determining the measure of damages for breaches of other types of contract which are still governed by common law rules. The cases discussed in Ch.43 of Vol.II illustrate the types of loss which have been found to be within the contemplation of the parties[464]; the duty to mitigate[465] (especially in cases of anticipatory breach[466]); and the assessment of damages for delay in delivery,[467] and for breaches of terms relating to the quality of the goods.[468] However, caution needs to be exercised in seeking to apply cases on sale of goods to other kinds of contract, simply because the factual circumstances and therefore what will normally be contemplated by the parties may well differ. For example, when a seller fails to deliver goods, the buyer's damages are usually assessed by the difference between the contract price and the market price at the date of delivery. The fact that the buyer has resold them at a higher price will normally be disregarded on the grounds that the buyer can buy replacement goods in the market to satisfy the sub-buyer. It is only when the parties contemplated that the buyer might re-sell the self-same goods, and thus would not be able to substitute other identical goods, that the buyer may recover loss of profit on the resale.[469] In contrast, it has been held that if a charterer re-delivers the vessel late, the owner may recover loss of profit on a new charter at above the market rate at the date of delivery. The parties will know that a following fixture is likely and that the owner will not be entitled to substitute another vessel.[470] However, the decision was reversed by the House of Lords[470a] on the apparently separate ground that a claimant will not recover even losses that were not unlikely to occur in the usual course of things if the defendant cannot reasonably be regarded as assuming responsibility for losses of the particular kind suffered.[470b]

(b) *Carriage of Goods*

Carriage of goods. If by default of the carrier the goods which he has contracted to deliver are lost or destroyed in transit the normal measure of damages is the market value of the original goods at the time when and place where they ought to have been delivered, less the freight payable under the 26–089

[463] *Barrow v Arnaud* (1846) 8 Q.B. 595, 609–610.

[464] e.g. loss of profits on sub-contracts: Vol.II, paras 43–446—43–455, 43–432, 43–435.

[465] Vol.II, para.43–400. See also below, paras 26–092 et seq.

[466] Vol.II, paras 43–412, 43–425.

[467] Vol.II, paras 43–437 et seq.

[468] Vol.II, paras 43–442 et seq.

[469] See below, para.43–441.

[470] *Transfield Shipping Inc v Mercator Shipping Inc (The Achilleas)* [2007] EWCA Civ 901, [2007] 2 Lloyd's Rep. 555.

[470a] *Transfield Shipping Inc v Mercator Shipping Inc (The Achilleas)* [2008] UKHL 48, [2008] 3 W.L.R. 345.

[470b] See below, paras 26–100A et seq.

contract upon safe delivery of the goods.[471] The price in a forward sale made by the consignee is usually irrelevant,[472] but it may be relevant if there is no market for such goods at the place of delivery.[473] Where the carrier delays in delivering the goods, the normal[474] measure of damages is the difference between the market value of the goods at their destination on the date they ought to have been delivered, and the market value at the actual date of delivery[475]; the same rule now applies to carriage of goods by sea.[476] The carrier's liability for loss of profits has already been discussed.[477] Occasionally the carrier may be liable for expenses incurred by the claimant in acquiring the nearest substitute when equivalent goods were not available in the market, and the claimant acted reasonably in incurring the expenses.[478]

26–090 If the defendant carries the goods to the wrong place, or completely fails to carry them at all, the claimant may either:

(a) engage substitute transport at the market rate and recover from the carrier the difference between that and the contractual rate, together with any difference between the market price of the goods at the actual time of delivery and the agreed time of delivery[479]; or

(b) purchase substitute goods at the agreed place of delivery, and recover from the carrier the difference between the cost of the substituted goods, and the total of the value of the original goods at the place of loading, freight and insurance (or at the wrong place of delivery, as the case may be).[480]

Where the owner of the goods fails to supply the goods for the agreed carriage, but the carrier ought reasonably to have obtained substitute cargo, the normal

---

[471] *Rodocanachi v Milburn* (1886) 18 QBD 67, 76. Even where the claimant has only a limited interest in the goods, he may recover their full value: *Crouch v L.N.W. Ry* (1849) 2 C. & K. 789. (See Vol.II, para.33–130.)

[472] *Rodocanachi v Milburn* (1886) 18 QBD 67. See also *Slater v Hoyle and Smith* [1920] 2 K.B. 11 (but on this case see now *Bence Graphics International Ltd v Fasson UK Ltd* [1998] Q.B. 87, which is discussed below, paras 43–444, 43–446); *The Arpad* [1934] P. 189.

[473] *O'Hanlan v G.W. Ry* (1865) 6 B. & S. 484; *The Arpad* [1934] P. 189.

[474] "Where there is a market it must be assumed to be in the contemplation of the parties as a grave danger that the goods may be sold on arrival so that if there is a delay one of the consequences may be loss of market": *Koufos v C. Czarnikow Ltd, The Heron II* [1969] 1 A.C. 350, 427.

[475] *Wilson v Lancs & Yorks Ry* (1861) 9 C.B.(N.S.) 632; *Collard v S.E. Ry* (1861) 7 H. & N. 79; *Schulze v G.E. Ry* (1887) 19 QBD 30; *Heskell v Continental Express Ltd* [1950] 1 All E.R. 1033, 1046.

[476] *Koufos v C. Czarnikow Ltd* [1969] 1 A.C. 350 HL, holding that the rule in *The Parana* (1877) 2 P.D. 118 was obsolete).

[477] See above, para.26–070.

[478] *Millen v Brash* (1882) 10 QBD 142; cf. *Romulus Films v William Dempster* [1952] 2 Lloyd's Rep. 535. Other expenses recoverable include the cost of searching for the missing goods: *Hales v L.N.W. Ry* (1863) 4 B. & S. 66; *Heskell v Continental Express Ltd* [1950] 1 All E.R. 1033, 1046.

[479] *Monarch S.S. Co v Karlshamns Oljefabriker (A/B)* [1949] A.C. 196. The claimant must act reasonably in his choice of one of the alternatives (a) or (b): at 217–218, 220; where neither alternative is possible, see *Watts, Watts & Co Ltd v Mitsui & Co Ltd* [1917] A.C. 227.

[480] *Ströms Bruk Aktiebolag v Hutchison* [1905] A.C. 515 (no substitute transport was available); *Nissho Co v Livanos* (1941) 57 T.L.R. 400. Consequential loss is also recoverable: *Heindal A/S v Questier* (1949) 82 Ll. L. Rep. 452 (perishable goods).

measure of damages is the difference between the agreed rate of freight, and the market rate (deducting in each case the cost of earning the freight).[481]

(c) *Contracts Concerning Land*[482]

Contracts for the sale or lease of land.[483] Full details of the damages recoverable for breaches of contracts relating to the sale or lease of land (including breaches of the covenants in a conveyance or lease) should be sought elsewhere.[484] In respect of contracts made after September 27, 1989 the restrictive rule in *Bain v Fothergill*[485] (which limited the vendor's liability) no longer applies.[486] Thus, a vendor who breaks his contract by failing to convey the land to the purchaser is liable to damages for the purchaser's loss of bargain and must pay damages calculated in accordance with the ordinary rules, viz the market value of the property at the fixed time for completion (or at a later time so long as it was reasonable[487] for the purchaser to continue to seek performance[488]), less the contract price.[489] The purchaser may claim the loss of profit he intended to make from a particular use of the land (e.g. by converting a building into flats and offices) only if the vendor had actual or imputed knowledge of special circumstances showing that the purchaser intended to use the land in that way.[490] 26–091

[481] *Smith v M'Guire* (1858) 3 H. & N. 554; *Aitken Lilburn v Ernsthausen* [1894] 1 Q.B. 773; *Wallems Rederij A/S v Muller* [1927] 2 K.B. 99, 105.

[482] On damages for defective building work, see above, para.26–016 fn.87.

[483] The usual remedy of a purchaser under such a contract is specific performance: see below, para.27–007.

[484] See *McGregor on Damages*, 17th edn (2003), Chs 22 and 23, and the standard textbooks on real property.

[485] (1874) L.R. 7 H.L. 158. The rule provided that where a vendor of land was unable to complete the contract through a defect in his title, no damages could be recovered (in the absence of fraud, misrepresentation, bad faith or default on the part of the vendor) for the loss of the purchaser's bargain. The exceptions to the rule were developed in a line of authorities, which are no longer cited in this work.

[486] Law of Property (Miscellaneous Provisions) Act 1989 s.3. (The Law Commission proposed the abolition of the rule: Report No.166.)

[487] *Malhotra v Choudhury* [1980] Ch. 52, 77, 81 (some unnecessary delay by the plaintiff led to the date for assessment being fixed one year before the hearing).

[488] cf. *Johnson v Agnew* [1980] A.C. 367, 401 (see below, paras 27–078—27–083: breach by purchaser). cf. *Suleman v Shahsavari* [1988] 1 W.L.R. 1181. In some cases decided before *Johnson v Agnew*, damages were assessed as at dates later than those originally fixed for completion (*Wroth v Tyler* [1974] Ch. 30 (as at the date of hearing); *Grant v Dawkins* [1973] 1 W.L.R. 1406; *Malhotra v Choudhury* [1980] Ch. 52), but the reasoning in these cases cannot now be supported, except to the extent that it is consistent with that in *Johnson v Agnew*.

[489] *Godwin v Francis* (1870) L.R. 2 C.P. 295; *Engel v Fitch* (1869) L.R. 4 Q.B. 659; *Re Daniel* [1917] 2 Ch. 405; *Diamond v Campbell-Jones* [1961] Ch. 22; *Chitholie v Nash & Co* (1973) 229 E.G. 786 (damages for breach of warranty of authority by vendor's agents). An express term in the contract of sale may regulate the rights of the parties in the event of the vendor's title proving to be defective: see the Law Society's General Conditions of Sale (condition 16(1)); and the National Conditions of Sale (condition 10(1)).

[490] *Diamond v Campbell-Jones* [1961] Ch. 22; *Cottrill v Steyning and Littlehampton Building Society* [1966] 1 W.L.R. 753; *Malhotra v Choudhury* [1980] Ch. 52, 80–81. A similar rule applies to claims by a purchaser for losses arising under a sub-contract: *Seven Seas Properties Ltd v Al-Essa (No.2)* [1993] 1 W.L.R. 1083; and to expenses incurred by the purchaser: *Lloyd v Stanbury* [1971] 1 W.L.R. 535, 546–547 (above, para.26–076).

26–092 If the vendor or lessor delays in completion, the normal measure of damages is the value of the use of the land for the period of delay, viz usually its rental value.[491] Where the purchaser of land fails to complete, the normal measure of damages is the contract price less the market price at the time fixed for completion,[492] plus any consequential expenses or loss.[493] Where the vendor reasonably tried to obtain performance by the purchaser, damages were assessed as at the later time when it was reasonable for him to give up seeking performance.[494]

26–093 **Valuer-surveyor's report to a purchaser.** Where, in breach of contract, the defendant surveyor negligently failed to report defects in the property purchased by the claimant in reliance on the report, the claimant's damages[495] should be assessed at the difference between the price paid by him and the market value of the property in its actual (defective) condition at the time of the purchase.[496] Since the surveyor did not contractually warrant that the property was in the condition which he reported, he is not liable to pay the difference between its hypothetical value in the reported condition and its market value in its actual condition.[497] The diminution in value measure does not depend on whether or not the claimant would have bought the property had the surveyor's report been carefully made.[498] But if, on learning of the defects which should have been

---

[491] *Royal Bristol Permanent Building Society v Bomash* (1887) 35 Ch D 390. See also *Jones v Gardiner* [1902] 1 Ch. 191; *Phillips v Lamdin* [1949] 2 K.B. 33. As to a lessor's delay, see *Jaques v Millar* (1877) 6 Ch D 153 (loss of profits allowed to lessee where lessor knew of his intended trade on the premises).

[492] *Laird v Pim* (1841) 7 M. & W. 474. A resale price may be evidence of the market price: *Noble v Edwards* (1877) 5 Ch D 378 (reversed on another point: 5 Ch D 392); *York Glass Co v Jubb* (1926) 134 L.T. 36.

[493] *York Glass Co v Jubb* (1926) 134 L.T. 36, 40. (The measure is similar where a lessee refuses to proceed with a contract to take a lease: *Marshall v Macintosh* (1898) 78 L.T. 750; cf. *Oldershaw v Holt* (1840) 12 A. & E. 590.)

[494] *Johnson v Agnew* [1980] A.C. 367, 401 (below, paras 27–078—27–083). See also *Suleman v Shahsavari* [1988] 1 W.L.R. 1181.

[495] In addition, the claimant may be able to recover damages for physical inconvenience: see above, para.26–082; or for "loss of amenity": see above, paras 26–084—26–085.

[496] *Watts v Morrow* [1991] 1 W.L.R. 1421, CA, following *Phillips v Ward* [1956] 1 W.L.R. 471, and *Perry v Sidney Phillips & Son* [1982] 1 W.L.R. 1297. See also *Gardner v Marsh & Parsons* [1997] 1 W.L.R. 489 (the fact that five years after the purchase the landlord, a third party, remedied the defect at his expense was held to be too remote to be taken into account in assessing the purchaser's damages against a surveyor). (In these cases the courts refused to assess damages at the cost of repairs; see above, paras 26–016 et seq.) In *Watts v Morrow*, the court left open the question as to *when* the market value should be ascertained: [1991] 1 W.L.R. 1421, 1437–1438. In *Dent v Davis Blank Furniss* [2001] Lloyd's Rep. P.N. 534 where a solicitor failed to advise the purchaser that part of the property was registered as common land, the judge applied the diminution in value test, not at the time of purchase but at the later date when the purchaser succeeded in partially mitigating his loss.

[497] *Watts v Morrow* [1991] 1 W.L.R. 1421, 1430, 1435. The relevant statement in the headnote is inaccurate; see also *Perry v Sidney Phillips & Son* [1982] 1 W.L.R. 1297, 1301–1302, 1304.

[498] *Watts v Morrow* [1991] 1 W.L.R. 1421, 1437–1438. The "excessive price" measure used in a purchaser's claim is not affected by the decision of the House of Lords in the *South Australia* case [1997] A.C. 191 (see below, para.26–094) where a lender's claim is based on a negligent overvaluation of the proposed security; *Patel v Hooper & Jackson* [1999] 1 W.L.R. 1792, 1801. The excessive price provides the measure of the purchaser's damages, whereas the initial deficiency in the value of the security provides only a limitation on the lender's damages. The excessive price measure has not been used when it would give the purchaser more than his actual loss: *Devine v Jefferys* [2001] P.N.L.R. 16.

reported, the claimant had immediately moved out and sold, he might have been able to recover (in addition to the diminution in value measure) his wasted costs.[499] However, the purchaser may be able to claim damages for "loss of amenity" from his surveyor if an important object of the contract was the enjoyment of that particular amenity, but which, as a result of the surveyor's breach of contract, was not obtained by the purchaser.[500]

Valuer-surveyor's report to a lender. In the *South Australia* case[501] the House of Lords imposed a limit[502] on the extent of damages payable by a valuer who negligently over-values the intended security and the security turns out to be inadequate through a combination of this and a fall in the value of the property. The lender's "ultimate loss" (viz the difference between: (i) the capital of the actual loan; and (ii) the net proceeds of realising the security, plus any repayments by the borrower) is caused by, and is not too remote a consequence of, the negligence[503] but the lender's damages for his capital loss may not exceed the extent of the initial deficiency in the supposed value of the security, viz the difference between the amount of the defendant's negligent over-valuation and what would have been a proper[504] valuation at the time of the loan.[505] Within this limit, however, the lender may recover his ultimate loss of capital even though it is due to a fall in the market value of the security since the loan was made. In addition to his claim for loss of capital, the lender may claim: (1) his reasonable expenses of realising the security; and (2) interest (see next paragraph). 26–094

The lender's claim for interest. In order to decide when interest on the damages should begin, the court must fix the date when the lender first suffers "loss". In a case in which a security has been overvalued, the lender's cause of action may not arise until the security is realised and the difference emerges between its value and the outstanding debt. However, it may be clear long before that date that the security has been overvalued and is inadequate; and if the 26–095

499 *Watts* [1991] 1 W.L.R. 1421, 1445. cf. the "no transaction" measure of damages used in *Hayes v Dodd* [1990] 2 All E.R. 815, CA (above, para.26–079).

500 *Farley v Skinner* [2001] UKHL 49, [2002] 2 A.C. 732 (see above, para.26–085).

501 *South Australia Asset Management Corp v York Montague Ltd* [1997] A.C. 191 (also known as the *B.B.L.* or *Banque Bruxelles* case). Lord Hoffmann, who gave the only speech, dealt almost exclusively with the scope of the valuer's limited duty of care under the tort of negligence, but he also said that the same result would follow from an implied term in the contract: at 211, 212. The High Court of Australia has not followed the *South Australia* case: *Kenny Good Pty Ltd v MGICA (1992) Ltd* [2000] Lloyd's Rep. P.N. 25.

502 cf. however, the "extrication" or "no transaction" cases recognised by the House of Lords in the *South Australia* case [1997] A.C. 191, 218–219 (see above, para.26–079).

503 *Nykredit Mortgage Bank Plc v Edward Erdman Group Ltd (No.2)* [1997] 1 W.L.R. 1627, HL, 1631, 1638. The *Nykredit* case and *Platform Home Loans Ltd v Oyston Shipways Ltd* [2000] 2 A.C. 190, explain the decision in the *South Australia* case [1997] A.C. 191.

504 See below, para.26–097.

505 The "amount of the loss . . . [is] limited to the extent of the overvaluation": the *Nykredit* case [1997] 1 W.L.R. 1627, 1632. The limitation on damages laid down in the *South Australia* case covers both categories previously recognised by *Swingcastle Ltd v Alastair Gibson* [1991] 2 A.C. 223, viz where, given a proper report, the lender: (1) would have lent nothing at all on the proposed security; and (2) would have lent a smaller sum. On the relevance of a mortgage indemnity guarantee policy for the benefit of the lender, see *Arab Bank Plc v John D. Wood Commercial Ltd* [2000] 1 W.L.R. 857, CA.

borrower ceases to pay interest on the loan, the lender is not obliged to wait to bring an action until the security has been realised. According to the *Nykredit* case,[506] the lender first suffers "loss" when the amount of the loan (plus interest) exceeds "the value of the rights acquired, namely the borrower's covenant and the true value of the over-valued property".[507] (This case creates the strange possibility of a fluctuating "loss" because it could be wiped out if the security later increased in value and reinstated if its value fell thereafter.[508]) The rate of interest should be fixed by the court[509] as compensation for the loss of the use of the capital lent to the borrower.[510]

26–096 **Analogous application of the *South Australia* case.** The formula placing a limit on the damages used in the *South Australia* case, above, has been applied by analogy where the negligence of a solicitor resulted in the lender believing it had more adequate security than it in fact had. The solicitor failed to tell the lender of facts which would have led it to doubt the valuation on which it was relying and so to obtain a second valuation: if this showed that the first was an overvaluation the solicitor would be liable only to the extent of the difference between the proper valuation and the overvaluation.[511]

26–097 **Assessing the "proper" valuation of property.** Where the court must fix the "proper" valuation of a property there is normally a range of valuations which might have been made by reasonably careful valuers; the court must choose the figure which it considers to be the most likely outcome of careful assessment: the defendant is not given the benefit of damages being assessed by reference to the highest figure which might have been given without negligence.[512]

(d) *Contracts to Pay or Lend Money*

26–098 **Contracts to pay money.** Most contracts contain a promise to pay money as part of the bargain between the parties. Although the agreed sum itself may be

---

506 [1997] 1 W.L.R. 1627.

507 [1997] 1 W.L.R. 1627, 1631. This "loss" could be suffered by the lender "from the inception of the loan transaction" (at 1632), or before the security is realised: "Realisation of the security does not create the lender's loss, nor does it convert a potential loss into an actual loss. Rather it crystallises the amount of a present loss . . . " (at 1633).

508 In the *Nykredit* case [1997] 1 W.L.R. 1627, 1631, Lord Nicholls spoke of the lender "currently" having no cause of action.

509 *Swingcastle Ltd v Alastair Gibson* [1991] 2 A.C. 223. (The House of Lords, however, envisaged the possibility that the lender could produce evidence as to how he would otherwise have used the money; at 239.)

510 The lender cannot recover the contractual (often penal) rate of interest undertaken by the borrower in the loan agreement, because to allow this would be to make the valuer a guarantor of the agreement between the lender and borrower: [1991] 2 A.C. 223.

511 *Colin Bishop*, one of the *Bristol and West Building Society* cases reported in [1997] 4 All E.R. 582. Similarly, if the lender obtains a valid title to only half the intended security, the damages should be limited to half of the initial value of the security: *Cooke and Borsay*, another of these cases.

512 The *South Australia* case [1997] A.C. 191 (following the Privy Council in *Lion Nathan Ltd v C-C. Bottlers Ltd* [1996] 1 W.L.R. 1438 (a contractual duty to take reasonable care in making a forecast of likely profits)).

recoverable as a debt,[513] it was for many years uncertain whether at common law the creditor could claim for any other loss resulting from the debtor's failure to pay the agreed sum at the fixed time.[514] Except in the few cases where interest was recoverable at common law,[515] the rule was believed to be that only nominal damages were recoverable for failure to pay money.[516] The House of Lords had confirmed that at common law interest cannot be awarded by way of *general* damages simply because payment of a debt had been delayed,[517] though it approved the decision of the Court of Appeal[518] that, if the test for remoteness based on knowledge of special circumstances is satisfied (the second rule in *Hadley v Baxendale*),[519] special damages may be awarded for interest paid and other expenses incurred by the claimant[520] in arranging alternative finance as the result of the defendant's breach of his obligation to pay a sum of money on a given date.[521] In earlier cases the defendant had been held liable for substantial damages where he undertook to maintain the claimant's financial credit.[522] In 2007, however, in *Sempra Metals Ltd v Commissioners of Inland Revenue*, the House of Lords severely restricted the rule that interest cannot be claimed by way of general damages.[523] It now applies only where the claimant has not pleaded or proved a loss resulting from the non-payment.[524] Further, the court is empowered by statute[525] in its discretion to award interest in an action, whether for debt or for damages.

In actions for the dishonour of bills of exchange and promissory notes, the measure of damages depends on statutory provisions.[526]

---

[513] See above, para.26–009; below, para.26–136.

[514] *London, Chatham and Dover Ry Co v South Eastern Ry Co* [1893] A.C. 429 (a claim for interest at common law). cf. *Trans Trust SPRL v Danubian Trading Co Ltd* [1952] 2 Q.B. 297; and see the criticism of the rule by Jessel M.R. in *Wallis v Smith* (1882) 21 Ch D 243, 257. On a contract to pay interest, see Vol.II, paras 38–265 et seq.

[515] e.g. dishonour of bills of exchange and promissory notes. See below, para.26–167; Vol.II, para.34–118.

[516] *London, Chatham and Dover Ry Co v South Eastern Ry Co* [1893] A.C. 429.

[517] *President of India v La Pintada Compania Navegacion SA* [1985] A.C. 104 (below, para. 26–144). The High Court of Australia has not followed this rule: *Hungerfords v Walker* (1989) 171 C.L.R. 125.

[518] *Wadsworth v Lydall* [1981] 1 W.L.R. 598. See the fuller discussion of this case, below, para.26–169.

[519] (1854) 9 Ex. 341. See above, paras 26–052 et seq.; The *President of India* case [1985] A.C. 104, 125–127.

[520] A currency loss arising from late payment has been held to fall within this principle: *President of India v Lips Maritime Corp* [1988] A.C. 395, 410–412, following *International Minerals and Chemical Corp v Karl O. Helm A.G.* [1986] 1 Lloyd's Rep. 81. See also below, paras 30–369 et seq.

[521] For other cases on recovery of interest, or interest charges paid, see below, paras 26–167 et seq. If the defendant's failure to pay on time entitles the claimant to terminate the contract, he may be entitled to recover general damages for the loss he suffers: *Yeoman Credit Ltd v Waragowski* [1961] 1 W.L.R. 1124; *Lombard North Central Plc v Butterworth* [1987] Q.B. 527 (below, para.26–141).

[522] *Rolin v Steward* (1854) 14 C.B. 595; *Wilson v United Counties Bank* [1920] A.C. 102; cf. *Larios v Bonany y Gurety* (1873) L.R. 5 P.C. 346; *Prehn v Royal Bank of Liverpool* (1870) L.R. 5 Ex. 92.

[523] [2007] UKHL 34, [2007] 3 W.L.R. 354.

[524] See below, para.26–170.

[525] See below, paras 26–174—26–182 and Vol.II, para.38–275.

[526] Bills of Exchange Act 1882 s.57 considered in Vol.II, para.34–118.

26–099 **Contracts to lend money.** In an action based on a lender's failure to provide the money promised, the normal measure of damages is the difference between the cost of a substitute loan in the market, and the cost of the contracted loan[527]: hence nominal damages will be usual, except where the claimant can obtain a loan elsewhere only "at a higher rate of interest, or for a shorter term of years, or upon other more onerous terms",[528] or where the claimant cannot raise another loan, and so fails to complete his purchase.[529]

(e) *Sale of Shares*

26–100 **Shares.** In an action for a seller's failure to transfer shares, the buyer may recover the market price of the shares on the day fixed for completion, less the contract price, since the principles of law governing damages in the sale of goods[530] are applied by analogy.[531] A buyer who obtains a decree of specific performance for the delivery of shares may also recover damages equal to the dividends declared by the company between the agreed date of delivery and the actual date (and interest thereon).[532] Where the buyer refuses to accept the shares, the seller may recover the difference between the contract price and the market price on the day fixed for completion.[533]

> "If the seller retains the shares after the breach, the speculation as to the way the market will subsequently go is the speculation of the seller, not of the buyer; the seller cannot recover from the buyer the loss below the market price at the date of the breach if the market falls, nor is he liable to the purchaser for the profit if the market rises."[534]

5. ASSUMPTION OF RESPONSIBILITY

26–100A **A new limitation.** In the light of the remoteness rules discussed in the previous sections of this Chapter, the traditional assumption of many contract lawyers[534a] has been that the victim of a breach of contract can recover for loss

---

[527] *South African Territories v Wallington* [1898] A.C. 309; *Astor Properties Ltd v Tunbridge Wells Equitable Friendly Society* [1936] 1 All E.R. 531; *Bahamas Sisal Plantation v Griffin* (1897) 14 T.L.R. 139. See Vol.II, para.38–234.

[528] *South African Territories v Wallington* [1897] 1 Q.B. 692, 696–697; affirmed [1898] A.C. 309.

[529] *Manchester and Oldham Bank v Cook* (1884) 49 L.T. 674, 678 (the lender knew the purpose for which the loan was required). See also *Astor Properties Ltd v Tunbridge Wells Equitable Friendly Society* [1936] 1 All E.R. 531.

[530] See Vol.II, paras 43–399 et seq., paras 43–419 et seq.

[531] *Shaw v Holland* (1846) 15 M. & W. 136. See also *Tempest v Kilner* (1845) 3 C.B. 249. cf. *Michael v Hart & Co* [1902] 1 K.B. 482.

[532] *Sri Lanka Omnibus Co v Perera* [1952] A.C. 76.

[533] *Jamal v Moolla Dawood & Co* [1916] 1 A.C. 175.

[534] [1916] 1 A.C. 175, 179.

[534a] "Where a loss is identified as occurring in the ordinary course of things, there is no basis, as far as remoteness is concerned, for imposing any further limit to its recovery": *Treitel, Law of Contract*, 12th edn by Peel (2007), para.20–087. See also Burrows, *Remedies for Torts and Breach of Contract*, 3rd edn (2004), 95–96.

which arose "in the usual course of things", or were "not unlikely",[534b] unless the loss was one that he should have avoided by taking reasonable steps.[534c] In relation to unusual kinds of loss, liability seemed to depend on whether the defendant had been told of the potential loss in sufficient detail and with sufficient force to bring it home to him that he should take it into account.[534d] Following the very recent decision of the House of Lords in *Transfield Shipping Inc v Mercator Shipping Inc (The Achilleas)*[534e] it now seems that a claimant will not recover, even for losses that were not unlikely to occur in the usual course of things, if the defendant cannot reasonably be regarded as having assumed responsibility for losses of the particular kind suffered. This seems not merely an aspect of the circumstances in which the parties will be held to have "had in contemplation" unusual kinds of loss, and so part of the remoteness rule, but an additional and probably separate requirement to the remoteness rule.[534f]

Previous authority on assumption of responsibility. Before the decision in *The Achilleas*,[524g] there had been a number of suggestions in the academic literature that the remoteness rule is best understood not as an external "default" standard to be applied when the parties have not agreed what losses they should nor should not be liable for, but as a reflection of their implied agreement as to the allocation of risks.[534h] Indeed in the previous edition of this work it was said that: 26–100B

> "... it can be said in general terms that the promisor implicitly accepts responsibility for the usual consequences of a breach of the promise in question, while the promisee implicitly accepts the risk of any other consequences."[534i]

Such an analysis might imply that the fact that a particular loss was not unlikely as the result of a breach might not suffice to make the contract-breaker liable were the circumstances such that it was not reasonable to suppose that the defendant was accepting responsibility for the kind of loss in question. This is particularly so when the loss was unusual. It was said above that it is not completely settled whether knowledge of special circumstances is enough to fix the defendant with liability for an unusual loss if he breaks the contract. It is argued that mere knowledge of the special circumstances is not enough for this purpose; but there need not be an express or implied term of the contract to the effect that the defendant accepted responsibility.[534j] It is sufficient if, on the basis

---

[534b] See above, para.26–054.

[534c] The "mitigation" rule: see below, paras 26–101 et seq.

[534d] See above, para.26–063.

[534e] [2008] UKHL 48, [2008] 3 W.L.R. 345.

[534f] Though Baroness Hale [(at [93]) describes the majority decision in *The Achilleas* as "adding a novel dimension to the way in which the question of remoteness in damage in contract is to be answered." See further below, para.26–100E.

[534g] *Transfield Shipping Inc v Mercator Shipping Inc (The Achilleas)* [2008] UKHL 48.

[534h] See e.g. Harris, Campbell and Halson, *Remedies in Contract and Tort*, 2nd edn (2002), 90; Kramer, "An agreement-centered approach to remoteness and contract damages" in McKendrick and Cohen (eds), *Comparative Remedies for Breach of Contract* (2005). The literature is helpfully surveyed in Robertson (2008) 28 Legal Studies 172.

[534i] Chitty on Contracts, 29th edn (2004), para.26–044.

[534j] See above, paras 26–062—26–063A.

of his knowledge of the special circumstances, the reasonable man in the defendant's position at the time of contracting would have understood that, by making the promise in those circumstances, he was assuming responsibility for the risk of the type of loss in question.[534k] But in previous editions of this work, it was suggested that in relation to liability for unusual circumstances, mere knowledge that an unusual loss might well follow a breach might not always suffice. There might not be liability if either it was clear from all the circumstances either that the defendant—to the knowledge of the plaintiff—did not wish to accept the risk of the unusual loss, or that a reasonable man in the place of the defendant would not, despite his knowledge of the special circumstances, have accepted the risk of the unusual loss.[534l] The courts, however, seem hitherto to have applied a test based on the defendant's knowledge.[534m] As a matter of general law,[534n] the only departure from this seems to be an unreported case in the Court of Appeal,[534o] which had held that mere knowledge that an unusual kind of loss might result from a breach is not enough if it would be unreasonable to impose liability for the loss or when the duty is limited. Waller L.J. held that to recover the unusual losses in issue in that case, the claimant would have to show not only that the special circumstances had been drawn to the defendant's attention but that the defendant accepted the risk.[534p] Sir Anthony Evans agreed, saying[534q]:

> "Even if the loss was reasonably foreseeable as a consequence of the breach of duty in question (or of contract, for the same principles apply), it may nevertheless be regarded as "too remote a consequence" or as not a consequence at all, and the damages claim is disallowed. In effect, the chain of consequences is cut off as a matter of law, either because it is regarded as unreasonable to impose liability for that consequence of the breach,[534r] or because the scope of the duty is limited so as to exclude it,[534s] or because as a matter of commonsense the breach cannot be said to have caused the loss, although it may have provided the opportunity for it to occur."[534t]

There do not appear to have been other English cases applying a general rule limiting liability to what is reasonable, even for unusual losses provided that they were contemplated by the parties.[534u] In relation to losses that might occur "in the usual course of things", in only two types of cases did there appear to be an additional limitation that the defendant must, as a matter of interpretation, be accepting responsibility for the loss. The first type of case is that of valuations provided to lenders, where in *South Australia Asset Management Corp v York Montague Ltd*[534v] it was held that a valuer who negligently undervalues the

[534k] See above, paras 26–063A.

[534l] 29th edition, para.26–055; see now above, para.26–063A. cf. *Robophone Facilities Ltd v Blank* [1966] 1 W.L.R. 1428, 1448.

[534m] See Robertson (2008) 28 Legal Studies 172, 183–188.

[534n] Compare the cases on negligent valuations for lenders, above, para.26–094.

[534o] *Mulvenna v Royal Bank of Scotland* [2003] EWCA Civ 1112.

[534p] At [26].

[534q] At [33] (footnotes as in the original).

[534r] *The Pegase* [1981] 1 Lloyds Reports 175 Robert Goff J.

[534s] *Banque Bruselles SA v Eagle Star* [the *South Australia* case] [1997] A.C. 191.

[534t] *Galoo Ltd v Bright Grahame Murray* [1994] 1 W.L.R. 1360.

[534u] See Robertson (2008) 28 Legal Studies 172, 183–188.

[534v] [1997] A.C. 191; see above, para.26–094.

property is not liable for the full amount of the lender's loss if there is a subsequent general fall in property prices. The second type of case is of damages for disappointment and the like, when the defendant is liable only if an important purpose of the contract was to provide enjoyment or to guard against the type of loss.[534w]

The Achilleas. In *Transfield Shipping Inc v Mercator Shipping Inc (The Achilleas)*[534x] the time-charterer of the ship was due to redeliver her by May 2, 2004 and had given notice that they would redeliver by then. The owners had then fixed the vessel for a new four to six-month hire to another charterer, under which the latest date for delivery to the new charterers was May 8. The first charterers sent the vessel on a last voyage which was expected to be completed in time but the vessel was delayed and was not redelivered until May 11. The new charterers agreed to accept her but, because freight rates had fallen, only at a reduced rate of hire. The owners claimed damages for the difference between the original rate and the reduced rate for the period of the new charter. The charterers argued that they were liable only for the difference between the market rate and the rate under the first charter for the nine days during which the owners were deprived of the use of their ship. Before the arbitrators it was conceded that it was not unlikely that late delivery would result in the loss of a following fixture. The arbitrators all accepted that the general understanding in the industry was that the charterer would be liable only for the lower amount, the difference between the original charter rate and the market rate for the period of the delay. There were a number of dicta which indicated that this would be the limit of liability, and the same thing was stated in various textbooks.[534y] One arbitrator concluded that therefore a reasonable person in the charterer's position would not understand that he was accepting liability for the loss of the following fixture, and that the charterers were therefore not liable for it; but the majority held that as that loss was not unlikely, it was recoverable. On appeal, both Christopher Clarke J.[534z] and the Court of Appeal[534aa] upheld the majority decision; but the House of Lords reversed the decision, though for differing reasons. Lord Rodger decided the case on the ground of remoteness: the loss in question was caused by a combination of the delay in redelivery and a sudden fall in market rates between the time the following fixture was made, and this combination was not sufficiently likely to bring the loss within the rule in *Hadley v Baxendale*.[534ab] Baroness Hale said that if it was correct to allow the appeal at all, as to which she continued to have doubts, it should be on this ground.[534ac] Lord Walker seems to have allowed the appeal on similar grounds,[534ad] but said[534ae] that he also agreed with the reasoning of Lords Hoffmann and Hope, which was very different. They held that it was not sufficient that a particular kind of loss was "not unlikely" if 26–100C

[534w] See above, paras 26–082 et seq.

[534x] [2008] UKHL 48, [2008] 3 W.L.R. 345.

[534y] Examples of the authorities are listed in the speech of Lord Hoffmann at [10].

[534z] [2006] EWHC 3030 (Comm), [2007] 1 Lloyd's Rep. 19.

[534aa] [2007] EWCA Civ 901, [2007] 2 Lloyd's Rep. 555.

[534ab] (1854) 9 Exch. 341 (above, para.26–052).

[534ac] At [93].

[534ad] At [83].

[534ae] At [87].

it was not reasonable to assume that the defendant had undertaken responsibility for it.[534af] In the circumstances it was not reasonable to assume that the charterers were accepting responsibility for the loss of the following fixture, and so the damages were limited to the difference between the market rate and the charter rate for the period of the delay in redelivery.

26–100D **A question of law, not of fact.** Application of the remoteness rule in *Hadley v Baxendale*[534ag] depends primarily on questions of fact: was the kind of loss in question one that was substantially likely or "not unlikely" to occur, or was the risk of an unusual loss brought home to the defendant at the time the contract was made in such a way that a reasonable person in his position would have taken it into account. In contrast, whether it was reasonable to assume that the defendant was assuming responsibility for the loss is a question of law.[534ah] Lord Hoffmann treated the question as closely analogous to the rule in the *South Australia* case[534ai] on negligent valuers, which is undoubtedly a rule of law. The question then is, in what circumstances will a defendant be held not to have assumed responsibility for a loss even if it was "not unusual", or if its likelihood had been drawn to his attention at the time the contract was made.

26–100E **Factors negating an assumption of responsibility.** It is clear that when Lords Hoffmann and Hope in *The Achilleas* held that a party will not be liable for losses that are "not unlikely" if it was not reasonable to assume that he was assuming responsibility for the loss, they considered that they were stating a rule of general application, not a special rule for charter-party contracts.[534aj] However, it is not easy to identify what facts will lead to the conclusion that there was no assumption of responsibility. Both their Lordships emphasised two general points. One was that the amount of loss, which would be determined by the terms and length of the following fixture, was something over which the charterers had no control; the other, that at the time the contract was made, the loss was completely unpredictable.[534ak] (The following fixture was made only shortly before the end of the charter.) Lord Hoffmann also emphasised more particular facts: that (as the arbitrators had found) the general understanding in the shipping market was that liability was restricted to the difference between the market rate and the charter rate for the overrun period,[534al] and that there had been a "uniform series of dicta" to the same effect.[534am] This might suggest that the effect of *The Achilleas* will be limited to cases in which there is a similar kind of understanding. He also pointed out that the owners might have avoided loss of the following fixture by refusing to undertake the last voyage.

[534af] Lord Hoffmann at [21]; Lord Hope at [30].

[534ag] (1854) 9 Exch. 341 (above, para.26–052).

[534ah] Lord Hoffmann in *The Achilleas* [2008] UKHL 48 at [25]; and see Baroness Hale at [93].

[534ai] *South Australia Asset Management Corp v York Montague Ltd* [1997] A.C. 191; see above, paras 26–094 and 26–100B.

[534aj] Lord Hope at [36].

[534ak] Lord Hoffmann at [24]; Lord Hope at [34].

[534al] At [6].

[534am] At [10].

"If it was clear to the owners that the last voyage was bound to overrun and put the following fixture at risk, it was open to them to refuse to undertake it."[534an]

Although Lord Hoffmann does not say so, the owners might also refuse the last voyage even if it were not illegitimate. This would of course render them liable in damages to the charterer for lost freight, or the cost of arranging another ship, but it would prevent risk to the following fixture. Lord Hope, in contrast, does not refer to these peculiar features of the case. Rather he seems to suggest that it may be unreasonable to assume that a party accepts responsibility for even a loss which is of a kind that is "not unlikely", if the fact that it is not quantifiable will make it hard for the party to price the risk adequately.[534ao] The case is thus open to the interpretation that it lays down a rule that may be applied in any case in which it will be difficult for a party to predict the amount of loss.

A separate rule? It is not wholly clear whether the limitation is an aspect of the remoteness rule or a separate rule. Baroness Hale refers to it as "adding a novel dimension to the way in which the question of remoteness in damage in contract is to be answered."[534ap] However Lord Hoffmann, after referring to the *South Australia* case[534aq] states that before considering the measure of damages: 26–100F

"... one must first decide whether the loss for which compensation is sought is of a "kind" or "type" for which the contract breaker ought fairly to be taken to have accepted responsibility."[534ar]

This seems to suggest a separate rule from remoteness. In most cases it will make little difference whether the "assumption of responsibility" is seen as part of the remoteness rule or as separate, but it may matter in cases of sales of goods. The Sale of Goods Act 1979 s.51(2) provides that for the buyer's damages:

"The measure of damages is the estimated loss directly and naturally resulting, in the ordinary course of events, from the seller's breach of contract."

If the restriction were part of the remoteness rule, it is submitted that this section would preclude its application in contracts for the sale of goods, at least where the loss is one that is "not unlikely" in the usual course of things. But it is submitted that the majority of the House of Lords see it as a separate rule which will therefore apply to contracts of sale of goods.

Evaluation. There may possibly be cases in which a simple application of the remoteness rule, so making the party in breach liable for any loss that was "not unlikely", will produce inappropriate results, for example by imposing a liability that is disproportionate to the value of the contract or, as in *The Achilleas*, that 26–100G

[534an] At [23].
[534ao] At [36].
[534ap] At [93].
[534aq] *South Australia Asset Management Corp v York Montague Ltd* [1997] A.C. 191, above, para.26–094.
[534ar] [2008] UKHL 48 at [15].

is simply hard to quantify.[534as] It is submitted, however, that this will rarely be the case. In *The Heron II*, Lord Reid explained that the rules of remoteness in tort and in contract are different because in contract cases the parties have the opportunity to direct the other party's attention to unusual risks.[534at] The implication is that if the party has been told of an unusual loss that might result were he to break the contract, he can safeguard his position. Either he can take extra precautions to avoid breach (and charge an appropriately increased price) or he can insist on a clause excluding or restricting his liability. In most cases, therefore, there is simply no need for the courts to provide additional protection by holding that it was not reasonable to think that the party was assuming responsibility. Contractual liability is of course based on express or implied agreement, and it is argued that the reason a party who has broken the contract should be held liable for losses that were not unusual, or which he had brought home to him might occur, is that (unless it is agreed otherwise) he can be taken to have agreed to compensate them. But it does not follow that liability for likely losses should be limited by a vague criterion such as "assumption of responsibility". Rather it is submitted that it is better to have a simple rule that the party in breach is be liable for all losses that are sufficiently likely to occur in the usual case, or whose likelihood has been brought home to him when the contract was made, unless he has validly excluded or restricted his liability. It has been cogently argued that there are limits to the extent that it is feasible to determine all issues by reference to an assumption of responsibility. In relation to the extent of liability for losses suffered by the innocent party as the result of a breach, there will seldom be any "factual foundation for making a determination as to whether the defendant implicitly assumed responsibility for the risk in question."[534au] It is thus to be hoped that the approach adopted by the majority in *The Achilleas* will be applied by the courts only in exceptional circumstances, such as those emphasised by Lord Hoffmann in that case.

6. MITIGATION OF DAMAGE

26–101 **Mitigation.** There are three rules often referred to under the comprehensive heading of "mitigation": they will be considered in turn. First, the claimant cannot recover damages for any part of his loss consequent upon the defendant's breach of contract which the claimant could have avoided by taking reasonable steps. Secondly, if the claimant in fact avoids or mitigates his loss consequent upon the defendant's breach, he cannot recover for such avoided loss, even though the steps he took were more than could be reasonably required of him under the first rule. Thirdly, where the claimant incurs loss or expense in the

---

[534as] Possible cases for such limitations are explored in Robertson (2008) Legal Studies 172, 191–195.

[534at] [1969] 1 A.C. 350, 386.

[534au] Robertson (2008) 28 Legal Studies 172, 196. The author suggests that if limits on liability are needed, other mechanisms might be used: at 191–193. For reasons given above, it is submitted that they will seldom if ever be needed.

course of taking reasonable steps to mitigate the loss resulting from the defendant's breach, the claimant may recover this further loss or expense from the defendant.

Purpose of mitigation role. The purpose of the rules on mitigation is to prevent the waste of resources in society, since they are obviously limited. Wherever the innocent party, following the defendant's breach, is able to find substitute performance from a third party, the mitigation rules give him a strong incentive to accept the substitute. The rules inevitably give some incentive to the defendant deliberately to break his contractual undertaking whenever he finds a better opportunity for the resources he intended to use in performing the contract: if he makes a higher profit on a new contract, he may be better off even after paying damages to compensate the original promisee (because these damages may be relatively low whenever substitute performance is readily available).[535] **26–102**

Avoidable loss. The first rule: **26–103**

> "... imposes on a plaintiff the duty of taking all reasonable steps to mitigate the loss consequent on the breach, and debars him from claiming any part of the damage which is due to his neglect to take such steps."[536]

It is not strictly a "duty" to mitigate, but rather a restriction on the damages recoverable, which will be calculated *as if* the claimant had acted reasonably to minimise his loss.[537] Only the claimant's *net* gain from his mitigating effort will be deducted—he may set off against his substitute profits or earnings the reasonable expenses incurred in obtaining them.[538] The position of the claimant under this rule is similar to that of a claimant in tort whose damages are reduced because of his contributory negligence.[539] The onus of proof is on the defendant, who must show that the claimant ought, as a reasonable man, to have taken certain steps to mitigate his loss,[540] and that the claimant could thereby have avoided some part of his loss.[541] Any loss which is directly caused by a failure

---

[535] This leads many writers on law-and-economics to argue that mitigation supports "efficient" breaches of contract (viz breaches which will leave society as a whole better off, while the original promisee is left no worse off). This "efficiency" argument is reviewed and criticised by Harris, Campbell and Halson, *Remedies in Contract and Tort*, 2nd edn (2002) at pp.11–21, 263–267, 279–280; see also Goetz and Scott (1983) 69 Virg.L.Rev. 967; and Macneil (1982) 68 Virg.L.Rev. 947; cf. above, para.26–055.

[536] *British Westinghouse Electric Co Ltd v Underground Electric Rys* [1912] A.C. 673, 689. See also *Le Blanche v L.N.W. Ry* (1876) 1 C.P.D. 286; *Tucker v Linger* (1882) 21 Ch D 18; *Macrae v H. G. Swindells (Trading as West View Garage Co)* [1954] 1 W.L.R. 597. The test for mitigation in a fraud case does not differ from that in any tortious or contractual claim: *Standard Chartered Bank v Pakistan National Shipping Corp* [1999] 1 All E.R. (Comm) 417 (upheld [2001] 1 All E.R. (Comm) 822 CA).

[537] *Darbishire v Warran* [1963] 1 W.L.R. 1067, 1075; *The Solholt* [1983] 1 Lloyd's Rep. 605, 608 CA.

[538] *Westwood v Secretary of State for Employment* [1985] A.C. 20, 44.

[539] See above, para.26–049.

[540] *Roper v Johnson* (1873) L.R. 8 C.P. 167; *Pilkington v Wood* [1953] Ch. 770; *Edwards v Society of Graphical and Allied Trades* [1971] Ch. 354; *Strutt v Whitnell* [1975] 1 W.L.R. 870.

[541] *Standard Chartered Bank v Pakistan National Shipping Corp* [2001] 1 All E.R. (Comm) 822, CA.

to meet this standard is not recoverable from the defendant. Thus an employee who has been wrongfully dismissed and unreasonably[542] refuses to accept another equally remunerative post to date from the dismissal is only entitled to nominal damages.[543]

26–104 **"Reasonable steps".** The claimant is not "under any obligation to do anything other than in the ordinary course of business"[544]; the standard is not a high one, since the defendant is a wrongdoer:

> "The law is satisfied if the party placed in a difficult situation by reason of the breach of a duty owed to him has acted reasonably in the adoption of remedial measures, and he will not be held disentitled to recover the cost of such measures merely because the party in breach can suggest that other measures less burdensome to him might have been taken."[545]

Questions about the reasonableness of the claimant's steps to mitigate his loss have arisen in cases (discussed elsewhere[546]) where the defendant has failed to complete the contractual work (e.g. building or repair work) and the claimant claims damages for the cost of substitute performance by a third party. But the claimant need not take risks with his money[547] in attempting to mitigate, nor need he take a step which might endanger his own commercial reputation, e.g. by enforcing sub-contracts.[548] The claimant is under no duty, even under an indemnity from the defendant, to embark on a complicated and difficult piece of litigation against a third party,[549] nor is the claimant required to sacrifice any of

[542] *Shindler v Northern Raincoat Co Ltd* [1960] 1 W.L.R. 1038; *Yetton v Eastwoods Froy Ltd* [1967] 1 W.L.R. 104. See Vol.II, para.39–193.

[543] *Brace v Calder* [1895] 2 Q.B. 253. See also *Beckham v Drake* (1849) 2 H.L.C. 579, 607–608; cf. *Harries v Edmunds* (1845) 1 Car. & Kir. 686; *British Ticket & Stamp Automatic Delivery Co v Haynes* [1921] 1 K.B. 377; *Houndsditch Warehouse Co v Waltex Ltd* [1944] K.B. 579. An employee dismissed without the minimum statutory notice must nevertheless seek alternative employment: *Westwood v Secretary of State for Employment* [1985] A.C. 20.

[544] *Dunkirk Colliery Co v Lever* (1878) 9 Ch D 20, 25 (approved by Lord Haldane in *British Westinghouse Electric Co Ltd v Underground Electric Rys* [1912] A.C. 673, 689).

[545] *Banco de Portugal v Waterlow* [1932] A.C. 452, 506. See also *Moore v DER Ltd* [1971] 1 W.L.R. 1476, 1479.

[546] See above, para.26–016 and the cases cited in fn.87 to that paragraph. See also *Farley v Skinner* [2001] UKHL 49, [2002] 2 A.C. 732 (above, para.26–085): it may be reasonable for a house purchaser not to sell and move out when he discovers a breach of contract affecting his use and enjoyment.

[547] *Jewelowski v Propp* [1944] K.B. 510; *Lesters Leather & Skin Co v Home and Overseas Brokers* (1948) 64 T.L.R. 569. The duty of the buyer to purchase substitute goods if the seller defaults (below, para.26–110, and Vol.II, para.43–420) will, of course, involve the buyer in expenditure, but the buyer will normally have available the money with which he intended to pay for the seller's goods. The impecuniosity of the claimant is discussed below, paras 26–105—26–108.

[548] *Finlay & Co v N. v Kwik Hoo Tong H.M.* [1929] 1 K.B. 400; *Banco de Portugal v Waterlow* [1932] A.C. 452 (which also, at 471, supports the proposition that the claimant need not act so as to injure innocent persons); *Anglo-African Shipping Co of New York Inc v J. Mortner Ltd* [1962] 1 Lloyd's Rep. 81, 94 (on appeal, [1962] 1 Lloyd's Rep. 610); *London and South of England Building Society v Stone* [1983] 1 W.L.R. 1242.

[549] *Pilkington v Wood* [1953] Ch. 770. cf. simple litigation: *Walker v Geo H. Medlicott & Son* [1999] 1 All E.R. 685 at 697 (a tort case).

his property or rights in order to mitigate the loss.[550] It has been suggested[551] that the claimant's duty to mitigate does not require him to guard against the effects of inflation per se, i.e. it does not apply to the risk of pure price increases which may lead to "inflationary increases in damages" after the date of the breach of contract.[552]

Impecuniosity of the claimant. A recent tort case in the House of Lords leads to the question whether the impecuniosity of the claimant could be relevant in a contractual claim. In *Lagden v O'Connor*[553] the House of Lords held that it would not follow the dicta in *The Liesbosch* case[554] to the effect that the plaintiff's impecuniosity was not relevant to the assessment of damages. *Lagden v O'Connor* was a claim in tort where the claimant's car had been damaged by the defendant's negligence. Since the claimant could not afford simply to hire a replacement car while his was being repaired (the car-hire firm would require him to make an up-front payment) he entered into a more expensive hire arrangement with an "accident hire" insurance company under which he need not pay anything in advance. The majority of their Lordships held that it was reasonably foreseeable that an impecunious claimant might reasonably incur the higher cost of credit hire because he had no other choice in obtaining a replacement car. Thus the claimant's foreseeable impecuniosity resulted in his entitlement to higher damages in tort than would have been awarded to others who could afford to pay for ordinary hire. This rule: 26–105

> "... requires the wrongdoer to bear the consequences if it was reasonably foreseeable that the injured party would have to borrow money or incur some other kind of expenditure to mitigate his damages."[555]

This language ("wrongdoer", "injured party") is not appropriate to a claim in contract where the main remoteness rule (the first rule in *Hadley v Baxendale*) is different from that in tort: the kind of loss within the reasonable contemplation of the parties at the time of making the contract.[556] But even in contract the claimant's impecuniosity might be relevant if it prevented him from choosing a cheaper form of mitigation. The rules on mitigation and those on remoteness are entwined in some cases, where what was "within reasonable contemplation" and what was "reasonable" mitigation are treated as inter-changeable concepts. In the *Monarch S.S.* case,[557] Lord Wright said (with reference to the decision of the House of Lords in *Muhammad Issa el Sheikh Ahmad v Ali*[558]) that:

---

[550] *Elliott Steam Tug Co v Shipping Controller* [1922] 1 K.B. 127, 140–141. cf. *Weir (Andrew) & Co v Dobell & Co* [1916] 1 K.B. 722.

[551] Libling and Feldman (1979) 95 L.Q.R. 270, 282. See also *Radford v De Froberville* [1977] 1 W.L.R. 1262, 1287; and Wallace (1980) 96 L.Q.R. 101, 341.

[552] See above, para.26–064 on the relevant date for the assessment of damages.

[553] [2003] UKHL 64, [2004] 1 A.C. 1067.

[554] [1933] A.C. 449, 460.

[555] [2003] UKHL 64, per Lord Hope at [61].

[556] See paras 26–051 et seq.

[557] *Monarch S.S. Co Ltd v Karlshamms Oljefabriker (A/B)* [1949] A.C. 196.

[558] [1947] A.C. 427.

> "... damages consequent on impecuniosity were held not too remote because ... the loss was such as might reasonably be expected to be in the contemplation of the parties as likely to flow from breach of the obligation undertaken."[559]

This means that the claimant's impecuniosity will be relevant in contract if it falls within the defendant's reasonable contemplation (as at the time of contracting) as not unlikely to affect the claimant's ability to mitigate after a breach of the particular undertaking, viz that the claimant would be likely to incur greater than usual expense (or higher than normal interest charges) in a reasonable attempt to mitigate. This test will not be easy for the claimant to satisfy if he cannot prove that the defendant actually knew of his impecuniosity (which is the situation examined in the next paragraph.) Thus, there is no reported case holding his impecuniosity to be relevant in relation to the market price rule in the sale of goods[560] or to the similar market price rule for breach of a contract of hire.[561]

26–106 **Actual knowledge of the claimant's impecuniosity.** The claimant's impecuniosity will be relevant in contract if the second rule in *Hadley v Baxendale* is satisfied viz if, at the time of contracting, the contract-breaker had actual knowledge of special circumstances under which a breach was likely to cause the claimant greater or different loss from that to be normally expected under normal circumstances.[562] The claimant's impecuniosity could be a "special circumstance" under this rule if, with his knowledge of it, the defendant could foresee that the claimant could mitigate his loss caused by the breach only by incurring greater expense than would be incurred by a financially secure person. The claimant must act "reasonably" in his mitigating actions but what is reasonable for a claimant known to be impecunious may be different from the case of a person with financial resources.[563] One of the mitigation rules is that the claimant is entitled to damages for any loss or expense incurred by him in reasonably attempting to mitigate his loss, even where this attempt was unsuccessful or led to greater loss.[564]

26–107 Several cases illustrate the position.[565] In *Wroth v Tyler*[566] the contract-breaker's knowledge of the plaintiffs' lack of resources was treated as relevant to their ability to mitigate.[567] Both the seller and the purchasers of a house contemplated at the date of the contract that there would be a rise in house prices after the contract; the seller knew that the purchasers:

> "... had no financial resources beyond [the price] that they could have put together for the purchase of [the seller's house] ... [The purchasers] were therefore to the [seller's] knowledge unable at the time of breach to raise a further £1500 to purchase an equivalent house forthwith, and so ... mitigate their loss."[568]

---

559 [1949] A.C. 196, 224.
560 See para.26–110 and Vol.II para.43–420.
561 See para.26–110 fn.582.
562 See paras 26–061—26–062.
563 On the question of actual knowledge, see para.26–061 fn.305.
564 See para.26–120.
565 See also para.26–110, below.
566 [1974] Ch. 30.
567 On the relevance of this knowledge, see para.26–106, above.
568 [1974] Ch. 30, 57.

In *Wadsworth v Lydall*,[569] on the dissolution of a farming partnership between the parties, the defendant was obliged to pay £10,000 to the plaintiff on a fixed date. The defendant knew that the plaintiff needed another farm and would be dependent on payment of that sum on that date to finance any purchase. When the defendant failed to pay, the Court of Appeal awarded the plaintiff as special damages the extra interest charges and legal costs incurred by him as a result of the breach.[570] In *Bacon v Cooper*[571] the rotor of the plaintiff's machine was damaged beyond repair as a result of the defendant's breach of contract. The only available replacement cost £41,500 which the plaintiff, a dealer in scrap metal, could not finance out of his own resources. It was held that the plaintiff had acted reasonably in obtaining it on hire purchase at a high rate of interest.[572] A further authority is *Trans Trust SPRL v Danubian Trading Co Ltd*.[573] The buyers undertook that a confirmed credit was to be opened forthwith in favour of the firm from which the sellers were obtaining the goods. The buyers knew that the sellers were not in a position themselves to open the necessary credit. The Court of Appeal held that the loss due to this impecuniosity of the sellers was not too remote because it was within the reasonable contemplation of the parties as likely to flow from the buyer's breach of contract in failing to obtain the credit.

Another case appears to accept the principle but it was found on the facts that the defendants did not know of the plaintiff's special financial arrangements. In *Compania Financiera "Soleada" SA v Hamoor Tanker Corp Inc*[574] the plaintiff's vessel was arrested in breach of contract: since it was reasonably foreseeable that the plaintiff would seek to obtain its release and for that purpose would obtain a guarantee for payment of the debt, the Court of Appeal held that the expense in doing so, if reasonable, would be recoverable either because it was within the remoteness rules, or as the expense of reasonable mitigation.[575] But because the particular financial arrangements between the plaintiffs and their bank were not known to the defendants, the high interest charges actually incurred by the plaintiffs were held to be "wholly unreasonable" and so not recoverable. **26–108**

The time for mitigating action. The time when the claimant should have mitigated may depend on when he discovered or ought to have discovered that the defendant had broken his contractual obligation.[576] So, as soon as the **26–109**

---

[569] [1981] 1 W.L.R. 598.

[570] See para.26–098.

[571] [1982] 1 All E.R. 397; see also para.26–169.

[572] The case was not explicitly put on the ground of the second rule in *Hadley v Baxendale* (1854) 9 Ex. 341 but on the reasonableness of mitigation, as was *Robbins of Putney Ltd v Meek* [1971] R.T.R. 345 (see para.26–110, below.)

[573] [1952] 2 Q.B. 297.

[574] [1981] 1 W.L.R. 274.

[575] Although Lord Denning preferred the former, his colleagues seemed to use the two concepts interchangeably.

[576] *East Ham Corp v Bernard Sunley & Sons Ltd* [1966] A.C. 406; *Van den Hurck v R. Martens & Co Ltd* [1920] 1 K.B. 850 (see Vol.II, para.43–444). One judge has held that the mitigation rules do not apply until the plaintiff knows of the breach: *Youell v Bland Welch & Co Ltd (The "Superhulls Cover" case)* [1990] 2 Lloyd's Rep. 431, 461–462; but another judge has applied the rules when the plaintiff should have known of the breach: *Toepfer v Warinco* [1978] 2 Lloyd's Rep. 569, 578. cf. Treitel at para.20–098.

claimant discovers that an item supplied to him by the defendant is unsafe because it is defective (in breach of the contract) he cannot continue to use it at the defendant's risk: he must either make it safe or replace it, since he cannot recover damages from the defendant for any loss which arose after he discovered[577] the defect but which he could reasonably have avoided by taking remedial steps.[578] After he knows (or ought to have known) of the breach, the claimant still has a reasonable time, depending on all the circumstances, before he must decide how to mitigate.[579] In the case of damages for the cost of repairs or reinstatement, it may be reasonable for the claimant to delay getting the repairs or remedial work done so long as there is a reasonable chance that the defendant will repair or cure the defect,[580] or until the time when the defendant has accepted liability or been held liable.[581]

26–110 **Sale of goods.** In contracts for the sale of goods, the normal rule for the measure of damages assumes that the innocent party should act immediately upon the breach, and buy or sell in the market, if there were an available market.[582] The relevance of the claimant's impecuniosity is discussed above.[583] The market price rule is fundamental to the sale of goods: if the seller fails to deliver, the buyer's damages are prima facie the difference between the contract price and the market price at the date of breach.[584] The rule assumes that the buyer should be able to finance the purchase of substitute goods at the time of the breach, even though he may not receive the damages until much later. The rule works reasonably well if he retains the balance of the price and there has not been a substantial rise in the market price. But the buyer's lack of financial resources could prevent his purchase of a substitute if he had paid the price (or a substantial deposit) in advance, or if the rise in price has been substantial. But to date none of these factors has prevented the application of the prima facie rule.[585] Actual knowledge of the buyer's lack of resources has been treated as relevant to the purchase of a house[586]; and the seller's decision to re-sell quickly because he was

---

[577] It has been argued that the same result should follow as soon as the claimant *ought* to have discovered the defect: *Benjamin on Sale of Goods*, 7th edn (2006), paras 17–059—17–060.

[578] *Lambert v Lewis* [1982] A.C. 225 (defective trailer coupling: see Vol.II, para.43–462).

[579] *C. Sharpe & Co Ltd v Nosawa* [1917] 2 K.B. 814, 821; *Asamera Oil Corp Ltd v Sea Oil & General Corp* (1978) 89 D.L.R. (3d) 1, Sup. Ct of Canada. If there is a rising market, the defendant may know that the claimant lacks the financial ability to buy a substitute, which may justify him in not attempting to do so: *Wroth v Tyler* [1974] Ch. 30. See also above, paras 26–064, 26–092; Vol.II, paras 43–422, 43–430.

[580] *Radford v De Froberville* [1977] 1 W.L.R. 1262.

[581] *Alcoa Minerals of Jamaica Inc v Broderick* [2002] 1 A.C. 371, PC (a tort case).

[582] See ss.50(3) and 51(3) of the Sale of Goods Act 1979; *Dunkirk Colliery Co v Lever* (1878) 9 Ch D 20, 25: see also *Alcoa Minerals of Jamaica Inc v Broderick* [2002] 1 A.C. 371. A similar rule applies in the case of contracts for the hire of goods (e.g. charterparties): where there is an available market in which to hire a substitute, the hirer's damages for breach by the owner in terminating the hire will normally be the difference between the contract rate and the market rate of hire for the remaining period of the contract: *Koch Marine Inc v D'Amica Societa di Navigazione A.R.L. (The "Elena D'Amico")* [1980] 1 Lloyd's Rep. 75, 87–90. cf. the position of the owner who retakes the goods after the hirer has broken his hire-purchase agreement: see Vol.II, paras 38–326—38–328.

[583] See above, paras 26–105—26–108.

[584] See Vol.II, para.43–419.

[585] See Benjamin's *Sale of Goods*, 7th edn (2006), para.17–008. On the prima facie nature of the rule, see Vol.II, para.43–420.

[586] *Wroth v Tyler* [1974] Ch. 30: see above, para.26–017.

short of liquid resources was held to be reasonable mitigation in *Robbins of Putney Ltd v Meek*.[587]

Another instance of mitigation arises where the defendant in breach of contract refuses to accept goods which he has agreed to buy,[588] but the claimant is able to sell the goods at the same price to a third person: if the state of the market is such that demand exceeds supply, so that the claimant could always find a purchaser for every article he could get from the manufacturer, he is entitled only to nominal damages from the defendant (and not his loss of profit on the repudiated sale) since he sold the same number of articles and made the same number of fixed profits as he would have done if the defendant had duly performed his contract.[589] If an exact substitute is not available to the buyer in the market, it is not clear whether he should be required to accept a "near equivalent,"[590] but if he does reasonably choose to do so, he can recover damages on the basis of the cost of the nearest available equivalent in quality and price.[591] 26–111

Mitigation and anticipatory breach in sale of goods. Where the claimant does not accept the defendant's anticipatory breach of contract,[592] there is generally no duty on the claimant to mitigate his loss before the actual breach on the due date for performance.[593] However, where the buyer repudiates the contract before delivery, the position may be different. If the goods have to be obtained or manufactured by the seller, and the property has not yet passed to the buyer,[594] then even if the seller is able to perform without the buyer's co-operation, his right to do so may be qualified as the result of *White and Carter (Councils) Ltd v McGregor*[595] unless the seller has a legitimate interest in continuing to perform.[596] 26–112

---

[587] [1971] R.T.R. 345 (sale of goods).

[588] If the property in the goods has passed to the buyer, the seller is entitled to the price, and no question of mitigation arises. See Vol.II, paras 43–390 et seq.

[589] *Charter v Sullivan* [1957] 2 Q.B. 117 (see s.50(3) of the Sale of Goods Act 1979). cf. the cases cited in Vol.II, paras 43–400—43–415.

[590] In cases of wrongful dismissal, any alternative employment can obviously be no more than a "near equivalent": see Vol.II, para.39–193.

[591] *Hinde v Liddell* (1875) L.R. 10 Q.B. 265; *Erie County National Gas and Fuel Co Ltd v Carroll* [1911] A.C. 105, 117. The nearest equivalent may be of superior quality and so higher in price: *Diamond Cutting Works v Treifus* [1956] 1 Lloyd's Rep. 216. The claimant may also recover any extra cost arising from his adapting the nearest substitute to suit his requirements, to the extent that goods of the contractual description would suit these requirements: *Blackburn Bobbin Co Ltd v T. W. Allen & Sons Ltd* [1918] 1 K.B. 540, 554 (appeal decided on another ground: [1918] 2 K.B. 467). Similarly, where a seller manufactured goods to the buyer's requirements, but he failed to accept them, the seller may recover as part of his damages the expense incurred in adapting the goods to suit another buyer: *Re Vic Mill Ltd* [1913] 1 Ch. 465, 473, 474.

[592] See above, para.24–024.

[593] *Brown v Muller* (1872) L.R. 7 Ex. 319; *Roper v Johnson* (1873) L.R. 8 C.P. 167; *Melachrino v Nickoll & Knight* [1920] 1 K.B. 693. See below, para.26–106; Vol.II, paras 43–412, 43–425. cf. *White and Carter (Councils) Ltd v McGregor* [1962] A.C. 413 (below, para.26–122).

[594] If the property in the goods has passed to the buyer, the seller is entitled to the price, and no question of mitigation arises. See Vol.II, paras 43–390 et seq.

[595] [1962] A.C. 413 (below, para.26–107).

[596] See below, para.26–124.

26–113 **Offer by defendant.** The opportunity to mitigate the loss may arise through an offer made by the party who committed the breach of contract: if the claimant unreasonably[597] refuses to accept the offer he is in breach of his duty to mitigate his loss.[598] Where a seller in breach of his contract declined to deliver goods on the agreed credit terms but offered to do so on terms of "cash on delivery", and the buyer refused and claimed as damages the difference between the contract price and the higher market price on the date for delivery, the refusal of the buyer to accept thee seller's offer, was held to be unreasonable, and resulted in a reduction in the damages.[599] Similarly, where the plaintiff bought a ship from the defendant, who could not deliver her on the agreed date, it was held that it would have been reasonable for the plaintiff to mitigate his loss by accepting her late delivery at the original price.[600] (The plaintiff was, of course, entitled to claim damages for any residual loss arising from the delay.) Where the vendor offered to repurchase a house which he sold with vacant possession but which was in fact occupied by a protected tenant, it was held that the buyer was not obliged by the doctrine of mitigation to accept the offer: his choice to retain the house and to sue for damages for the breach of contract was not to be subjected to the test of reasonableness.[601]

26–114 **Amount of damages or cost to the defendant?** It is not clear that *Payzu v Saunders*[602] was correctly decided. While the plaintiff's refusal of the defendant's offer to supply for cash at the original contract price increased the amount of damages claimed, it does not seem to have increased the overall cost to the defendant. The defendant would have been left with the original goods and could have sold them at the higher market price. It is submitted that the reasonableness of the claimant's actions should be judged by whether or not they increase the overall cost to the defendant rather than by whether they increase the amount of damages claimed.[603]

26–115 **Loss which is avoided cannot be recovered.** The second rule of mitigation concerns potential loss which is not actually suffered. If, by taking steps which could not reasonably have been required of him, the claimant has in fact avoided

---

[597] It is not reasonable for the offer to be on terms that the claimant should relinquish his claim against the defendant for damages: *Shindler v Northern Raincoat Co Ltd* [1960] 1 W.L.R. 1038.

[598] *Payzu v Saunders* [1919] 2 K.B. 581; *Houndsditch Warehouse Co v Waltex* [1944] K.B. 579; *Brace v Calder* [1895] 2 Q.B. 253 (contract of service). cf. *Edwards v Society of Graphical and Allied Trades* [1971] Ch. 354; *A.B.D. (Metals & Waste) Ltd v Anglo Chemical & Ore Co Ltd* [1955] 2 Lloyd's Rep. 456.

[599] *Payzu v Saunders* [1919] 2 K.B. 581. But a buyer who rejects goods on the ground of defective quality is not required to accept them if offered by the seller in mitigation since this would undermine the buyer's right to reject: *Heaven & Kesterton Ltd v Etablissements François Albiac & Cie* [1956] 2 Lloyd's Rep. 316.

[600] *The Solholt* [1983] 1 Lloyd's Rep. 605. (The Court of Appeal held that on the facts it would have been reasonable for the *buyer* to have taken the initiative in making the offer.)

[601] *Strutt v Whitnell* [1975] 1 W.L.R. 870; cf. *The Solholt* [1983] 1 Lloyd's Rep. 605; cf. also *Hussey v Eels* [1990] 2 Q.B. 227 (see below, fn.607). On the choice between remedies, see below, para.26–121.

[602] [1919] 2 K.B. 581.

[603] See the discussion in Bridge (1989) 105 L.Q.R. 398.

the potential loss resulting from the defendant's breach of contract, he cannot recover damages in respect of such potential loss[604]:

> "When in the course of his business [the claimant] has taken action arising out of the transaction, which action has diminished his loss, the effect in actual diminution of the loss he has suffered may be taken into account even though there was no duty on him to act."[605]

The claimant is entitled to damages only for his actual loss, which is assessed by taking account of all the items in his notional "profit and loss" calculation for the whole transaction.[606] The court is required to decide whether the claimant's actions arose *out of* his attempts to mitigate the potential loss resulting from the breach, or whether his actions were "independent" of his mitigating steps, so that any benefit to him should not be used to reduce the damages payable by the defendant.[607] So where a seller delivers defective goods, and the buyer acquires a substitute through which he gains a consequential benefit, e.g. a greater profit, this benefit must be set off against the cost of the substitute when the buyer sues the seller to recover such cost,[608] since the benefit arises directly from the act of mitigation.

Betterment as a result of mitigation. Damages will not be reduced where reasonable steps taken by by the claimant by way of mitigation result in a notional betterment of his position, unless the betterment will result in an immediate saving to the claimant or give him an advantage that is readily realisable. Thus, where a breach of contract caused the destruction of a building, and the owners acted reasonably both in deciding to rebuild and in choosing the plan for the new building, it was held that the defendants were not entitled to a reduction in damages (which consisted in the actual cost of rebuilding) on account of the "betterment" enjoyed by the claimants in having a new building in place of the old one—the claimants had no effective choice: but a reduction would be made for any extra accommodation or improvement going beyond 26–116

---

604 *British Westinghouse Electric Co Ltd v Underground Electric Rys* [1912] A.C. 673, 689, 690.

605 [1912] A.C. 673, 689. See also *R. Pagnan & Fratelli v Corbisa Industrial Agropacuaria Limitada* [1970] 1 W.L.R. 1306 (see Vol.II, para.43–428); and cf. *The World Beauty* [1969] P. 12; affirmed in part [1970] P. 144.

606 The amount of "avoided loss" to be deducted from his damages will be his *net* gain after deducting his reasonable expenses in earning the gross gain: *Westwood v Secretary of State for Employment* [1985] A.C. 20, 44.

607 *Hussey v Eels* [1990] 2 Q.B. 227, CA ((pet. dis.) [1990] 1 W.L.R. 414) (induced by defendant's misrepresentation, plaintiff bought and lived in a defective house for over two years, before reselling it at a profit to a developer: held, the resale profit arose from an independent transaction, and should not be taken into account in assessing the damages payable by defendant); *Needler Financial Services Ltd v Taber* [2002] 3 All E.R. 501.

608 *British Westinghouse* case [1912] A.C. 673 (and see Vol.II, para.43–445). (The principle was applied in the tort case of *Dimond v Lovell* [2002] 1 A.C. 384, 402–403.) See also *Erie County Natural Gas Co v Carroll* [1911] A.C. 105; *Hill v Showell* (1918) 87 L.J.K.B. 1106; *Nadreph Ltd v Willmett & Co* [1978] 1 W.L.R. 1537; *Levison v Farin* [1978] 2 All E.R. 1149 (the breach of contract resulted in a trading loss, which enabled the innocent party to claim a reduction in tax on subsequent profits: the tax benefit was deducted from the damages). cf. *Bellingham v Dhillon* [1973] Q.B. 304 (approved in *Dimond v Lovell* [2002] 1 A.C. 384, 402).

replacement.[609] Similarly, where, as a result of breach of contract, a partly-used working part of a machine had to be replaced with a new part which would last longer, the plaintiff was nevertheless entitled to the full cost of the replacement.[610] In contrast, in *British Westinghouse Electric Co Ltd v Underground Electric Rys*[611] the buyers replaced the defective turbines supplied with a newer design of much greater efficiency, and the saving to them was taken into account.

26–117 **Benefits independent of mitigation.** Where a seller of goods chooses not to resell upon the date of the buyer's breach (which is the normal date when his duty to mitigate must be tested[612]) but retains the goods for some time and resells at a gain when the market price later rises, the benefit to the claimant does not arise from any act of mitigation[613] and is irrelevant in assessing damages.[614] The seller could not have made the buyer liable for additional loss had the market price fallen after the date of the breach,[615] so he is entitled to the gain when the market price happens to rise after that date. The decision to retain the goods was an independent speculation by the seller. On a similar principle, advantages gained by the claimant from wholly independent transactions, especially those entered into before the defendant's breach of contract, as for example, a sum due under an insurance policy,[616] cannot be relied on in mitigation of loss arising from the defendant's breach.[617] So where the claimant, by another contract with a third

---

[609] *Harbutt's "Plasticine" Ltd v Wayne Tank and Pump Co Ltd* [1970] 1 Q.B. 447. (This case has been overruled by the House of Lords on another point: *Photo Production Ltd v Securicor Transport Ltd* [1980] A.C. 827 (above, para.14–022).)

[610] *Bacon v Cooper (Metals) Ltd* [1982] 1 All E.R. 397.

[611] [1912] A.C. 673. cf. *Re-Source America International Ltd v Platt Site Services Ltd* [2005] EWCA Civ 97, [2005] 2 Lloyd's Rep. 50 CA (the saved cost of refurbishment was deducted from the full cost of replacement).

[612] Sale of Goods Act 1979 s.50(3). See Vol.II, paras 43–399 et seq.

[613] *Jebsen v East and West India Dock Co* (1875) L.R. 10 C.P. 300.

[614] *Campbell Mostyn v Barnett* [1954] 1 Lloyd's Rep. 65 (distinguished in *R. Pagnan & Fratelli v Corbisa Industrial Agropacuaria Limitada* [1970] 1 W.L.R. 1306 where the claimant buyer finally accepted the *same* goods at a reduced price; but the *Pagnan Fratelli* case was itself distinguished in *Mobil North Sea Ltd v P.J. Pipe & Valve Co* [2001] EWCA Civ 741, [2001] 2 All E.R. (Comm) 289) (see Vol.II, para.43–428). See also *Jones v Just* (1868) L.R. 3 Q.B. 197 (breach by seller but loss avoided by buyer when market price later rose); *Jamal v Moolla Dawood* [1916] 1 A.C. 175; and *Hussey v Eels* [1990] 2 Q.B. 227, para.26–100 fn.607; *Gardner v Marsh & Parsons* [1997] 1 W.L.R. 489 (see para.26–093 fn.496).

[615] *Koch Marine Inc v D'Amico Società di Navigazione A.R.L. (The "Elena D'Amico")* [1980] 1 Lloyd's Rep. 75, 87–90.

[616] *Bradburn v G.W. Ry* (1874) L.R. 10 Ex. 1. Similarly, an employee's damages for wrongful dismissal should not be reduced by reference to a pension payable before his normal retirement age to the employee from his employer's pension scheme: *Hopkins v Norcross Plc* [1993] 1 All E. R. 565. (The pension entitlement was "earned" and thus "paid for" by the employee; and the pension scheme should be treated as a form of insurance.) See also Vol.II, para.39–193. The damages recoverable by a lender from a negligent valuer (see above, para.26–094) should not be reduced by the proceeds of a mortgage indemnity guarantee policy taken out with an insurer for the benefit of the lender: such a policy is for indemnity insurance, under which the insurer's rights of subrogation will prevent any question of double recovery by the lender: *Arab Bank Plc v John D. Wood Commercial Ltd* [2000] 1 W.L.R. 857 CA.

[617] *Lavarack v Woods of Colchester Ltd* [1967] 1 Q.B. 278. cf. *Brown v K.M.R. Services Ltd* [1995] 4 All E.R. 598, 640–641; *Mobil North Sea Ltd v P.J. Pipe & Valve Co* [2001] EWCA Civ 741, [2001] 2 All E.R. (Comm) 289.

party entered into before the defendant's breach of his contract with the claimant, has made an arrangement which should or does in fact prevent loss to the claimant from the defendant's breach, the defendant cannot rely on that other contract to reduce his damages[618]; it is *res inter alios acta*, or an extraneous circumstance. Even where a benefit to the claimant arises in the course of his mitigating action, there may not be a sufficient causal connection between the defendant's breach and that benefit to justify taking it into account in assessing the claimant's damages.[619]

Release of resources for other uses.[620] When the claimant terminates his contract with the defendant on the ground of the latter's breach of contract, the resources which the claimant would otherwise have devoted to his performance (whether capital, skill, labour, etc.) are always released for redeployment elsewhere. Even where there is no substitute or "near equivalent" use to which the claimant can be expected to devote his released resources (under the "avoidable loss" rule) he will always in practice devote them to some other use, which raises the application of the "avoided loss" rule. So an employee who was wrongfully dismissed will have his damages reduced *either* (under the "avoidable loss" rule) by the hypothetical earnings he should reasonably have earned for the relevant period in some similar employment *or* (whether or not the "avoidable loss" rule applied) by his *actual* earnings under another contract which he was able to undertake *only* as the result of the defendant's breach of contract.[621] If the claimant could not have undertaken the second contract but for the defendant's breach, and he deployed substantially the same skills, time and effort as he would have done in working for the defendant,[622] his earnings can legitimately be treated as substitute earnings even when the employment was different. If he is required to employ different skills in his new work, or to put in a greater effort, it is submitted that the courts should make allowance for this greater or different input from the claimant by deducting only a proportion of his substitute earnings.[623] 26–118

[618] *Haviland v Long* [1952] 2 Q.B. 80, especially at 84. See also *Joyner v Weeks* [1891] 2 Q.B. 31; *Slater v Hoyle and Smith* [1920] 2 K.B. 11 (buyer of defective goods able to avoid loss on sub-sale; but see *Bence Graphics International Ltd v Fassoun UK Ltd* [1998] Q.B. 87 (discussed below, paras 43–444, 43–446); the contrary decision of the Privy Council in *Wertheim v Chicoutimi Pulp Co* [1911] A.C. 301, may be wrong: see Vol.II, para.43–438 fn.1979).

[619] *Famosa Shipping Co Ltd v Armada Bulk Carriers Ltd (The "Fanis")* [1994] 1 Lloyd's Rep. 633.

[620] The arguments in this paragraph are developed more fully in Harris, Campbell and Halson *Remedies in Contract and Tort*, 2nd edn pp.115–120.

[621] *Jackson v Hayes Candy and Co Ltd* [1938] 4 All E.R. 587; *Collier v Sunday Referee Publishing Co* [1940] 2 K.B. 647, 653; *Lavarack v Woods of Colchester Ltd* [1967] 1 Q.B. 278.

[622] The causal test should be: (1) that the claimant used substantially the same resources as he would have done in the contractual activity; and (2) that the opportunity for the claimant to use them in the new activity would not have arisen *but for* the defendant's breach of contract, that is, it was the breach alone which released them for the alternative use. For instance, in *Hill v Showell* (1918) 87 L.J.K.B. 1106, 1108, the breach enabled the plaintiff to execute other profitable orders: it led to "the situation in which his machinery was rendered *free by reason of the breach*" (italics supplied).

[623] Some support for this is found in *Lavarack v Woods of Colchester Ltd* [1967] 1 Q.B. 278.

26–119 Except in the extremely rare situation where a resource cannot be redeployed to any other use at all, the release of resources always confers some benefit on the claimant, because he can find some use for them. But the courts have seldom taken this benefit into account where the alternative use chosen by the claimant was substantially different from his promised performance under the original contract. Where the alternative use has a similar goal (e.g. the earning of profits or wages), the courts have been more likely to take it into account in assessing damages. But, since there is nearly always some value to the claimant arising from the release of his resources, it is submitted that some assessment of that value should be made no matter where the redeployment is made.[624] However, it is submitted that the assessment should not deprive someone in the claimant's position of all incentive to redeploy: some incentive would remain if the court did not deduct the whole of the net benefit but left him to enjoy some of it as a reward for his initiative in seeking the alternative use.[625]

26–120 **Recovery of loss or expense suffered while attempting to mitigate.** The third rule of mitigation is that the claimant may recover damages for loss or expense incurred by him in reasonably[626] attempting to mitigate his loss following the defendant's breach, even when the mitigating steps were unsuccessful or in fact led to greater loss.[627] As most attempts are successful, it is in the interests of the defendant (as well as of the wider society) that the claimant, who is usually in the better position to minimise his loss, should be encouraged to try to do so: he may recover the cost of his reasonable attempt to "extricate" himself from the disadvantageous position in which he was placed by the breach.[628]

26–121 **Innocent party's choice between remedies.** The rules of mitigation do not apply to the innocent party's choice between different remedies open to him

---

624 For the causal test, see fn.622 above.

625 In *Lavarack v Woods of Colchester Ltd* [1987] 1 Q.B. 278, above (wrongful dismissal), the court took into account only *part* of the profit made by the plaintiff through his personal exertions in enhancing the value of his shares in the company where he took employment after his wrongful dismissal by the defendant. However, in *British Westinghouse Electric Co v Underground Electric Ry Co* [1912] A.C. 673 (see Vol.II, para.43–445) the House of Lords held that the *whole* of the benefit of the mitigating action of the plaintiff could be used to reduce the damages payable by the defendant, even though the plaintiff would not have been obliged under the "avoidable loss" rule to take that action: see Harris, Campbell and Halson, *Remedies in Contract and Tort*, 2nd edn (2002) at pp.119–120.

626 For an illustration of unreasonable expenses incurred by the claimant, see *Compania Financiera "Soleada" SA v Hamoor Tanker Corp Inc (The Borag)* [1981] 1 W.L.R. 274. cf. the tort case of *Dodd Properties Ltd v Canterbury City Council* [1980] 1 W.L.R. 433 (above, para.26–018 fn.98).

627 *Wilson v United Counties Bank* [1920] A.C. 102, 125; *Lloyds and Scottish Finance Ltd v Modern Cars and Caravans (Kingston) Ltd* [1966] 1 Q.B. 764, 782–783; *The World Beauty* [1970] P. 144, 156; *British Racing Drivers' Club Ltd v Hextall Erskine & Co* [1996] 3 All E.R. 667 (legal costs incurred by the plaintiff). See also *Erie County Natural Gas and Fuel Co Ltd v Carroll* [1911] A.C. 105, 119; cf. *Le Blanche v L.N.W. Ry* (1876) 1 C.P.D. 286; *Quinn v Burch Bros (Builders) Ltd* [1966] 2 Q.B. 370 (above, para.26–037); *Westwood v Secretary of State for Employment* [1985] A.C. 20, 44. cf. also the cases on reinstatement damages, above, para.26–016.

628 *County Personnel (Employment Agency) Ltd v Alan R. Pulver & Co* [1987] 1 W.L.R. 916, 926. This "extrication" principle was accepted by the House of Lords in *South Australia Asset Management Corp v York Montague Ltd* [1997] A.C. 191, 218–219 (see above, para.26–079).

following the other party's breach of contract: he is not bound to act "reasonably" in exercising his choice.[629] Thus, where the buyer commits an anticipatory breach by repudiating his obligation to take delivery of the goods before the date fixed for delivery, the seller has an option: he may either accept the repudiation and so treat it forthwith as a breach, or (subject to what was said earlier on the possible effect of the decision in *White and Carter (Councils) Ltd v McGregor*[630]) he may continue to treat the contract as binding and thus not accept the repudiation as a breach.[631] In exercising this choice between these alternative courses of action, the seller is not obliged to act "reasonably".[632] If the seller accepts the buyer's anticipatory repudiation, he is thereupon obliged to take reasonable steps to mitigate his loss[633]; but if the seller does not accept the anticipatory repudiation he does not have any duty to mitigate unless and until the buyer actually commits a breach of contract.[634] After the innocent party has terminated the contract, the rules on mitigation will apply to any claim for damages he makes; it may then be reasonable for him to act in a way which has the effect of nullifying the consequences of that decision, e.g. by entering into a new contract with the contract-breaker.[635]

Recovery of sum due on performance. By implication, the House of Lords has decided that the rules on mitigation do not apply to a claim for a debt due under a contract in return for the claimant's performance of his obligation[636]; such a claim is distinct from one for damages for breach of contract.[637] In *White and Carter (Councils) Ltd v McGregor*[638] the plaintiff refused to accept the defendant's anticipatory repudiation of the contract[639] and was able thereafter to complete the performance of his side of the contract without the co-operation of the defendant[640]; the majority of their Lordships held that the plaintiff could recover the full amount due for his performance: he was under no obligation to terminate the contract on the ground of the defendant's anticipatory breach and 26–122

629 *Strutt v Whitnell* [1975] 1 W.L.R. 870 (see above, para.26–113); *The Solholt* [1983] 1 Lloyd's Rep. 605, 608–609 CA; cf. *Lombard North Central Plc v Butterworth* [1987] Q.B. 527 (below, para.26–141).

630 [1962] A.C. 413; see above, para.26–112.

631 See above, paras 24–021 et seq.; and Vol.II, para.43–412. cf. Vol.II, paras 43–425—43–426.

632 *Tredegar Iron and Coal Co (Ltd) v Hawthorn Bros & Co* (1902) 18 T.L.R. 716, 716–717; *White and Carter (Councils) Ltd v McGregor* [1962] A.C. 413 (above, para.24–010; below, para.26–122); *Fercometal S.A.R.L. v Mediterranean Shipping Co SA* [1989] A.C. 788.

633 See Vol.II, para.43–412. cf. the situation when it is the seller's anticipatory repudiation: Vol.II, para.43–425.

634 See Vol.II, para.43–412; 43–425.

635 *The Solholt* [1983] 1 Lloyd's Rep. 605, 609. (See above, para.26–113.)

636 *White and Carter (Councils) Ltd v McGregor* [1962] A.C. 413 (a full statement of facts will be found above, para.24–010); followed in *Anglo-African Shipping Co of New York Inc v J. Mortner Ltd* [1962] 1 Lloyd's Rep. 81, 610; but distinguished in *Attica Sea Carriers Corp v Ferrostaal Poseidon Bulk Reederei GmbH (The Puerto Buitrago)* [1976] 1 Lloyd's Rep. 250, 254–256 and in *Clea Shipping Corp v Bulk Oil International Ltd (The Alaskan Trader)* [1984] 1 All E.R. 129.

637 See above, para.26–009.

638 [1962] A.C. 413.

639 On anticipatory breach, see above, paras 24–021 et seq.

640 *Hounslow LBC v Twickenham Gardens Developments Ltd* [1971] Ch. 233, 253–254 (plaintiff cannot insist on being given access to the defendant's land to enable him to complete work there). A wrongfully dismissed employee cannot sue for his wages as such, but is relegated to a claim for damages. See further next paragraph.

sue for damages. The two of their Lordships in the minority thought the plaintiff should have mitigated his loss by discontinuing his performance of the contract, but the majority held (by implication) that in the special circumstances of the casethere was no such duty on the plaintiff to act reasonably.[641]

26–123 **Price can be earned without defendant's co-operation.** The circumstances of the *White & Carter*[642] case were unusual, in that there was nothing which the defendant had to do or accept in order to enable the plaintiff to complete his performance. The claimant cannot ignore the defendant's repudiation, perform and claim the contract price if the price is not due at the time of the defendant's anticipatory repudiation, and the plaintiff can earn it only by performance which will require the defendant's co-operation.[643] Thus in two cases in which charterers of vessels have indicated that they have no further use for the vessel it has been held that the owners cannot simply keep the vessel idle and claim the hire; performance requires the charterers' co-operation.[644] Conversely, where according to the terms of the contract the price will become payable irrespective of the performance of the claimant's outstanding obligations, the claimant may recover it.[645]

26–124 **"Legitimate interest" in performing.** The difficulty of this situation is that the policy of the mitigation rules (viz to avoid the waste of resources and effort) seems to be contravened if the innocent party, following a repudiation, can elect (despite his knowledge that the expense of performance is now useless to the other party) to *continue* his performance of the contract so as to recover an agreed sum of money greater than the damages which the law would allow if the repudiation were treated at the time as a breach of contract.[646] Lord Reid, one of the majority in the *White and Carter* case, introduced a qualification, to the effect that the plaintiff could not insist on completing performance so as to be able to claim the agreed price as a debt, if he had "no legitimate interest, financial or otherwise, in performing the contract rather than claiming damages".[647] The Court of Appeal[648] has accepted this qualification, and a judge at first instance[649]

---

[641] As to whether the principle will extend to the sale of goods, see Lord Keith (dissenting) [1962] A.C. 413, 437; above, para.26–112; and *Benjamin's Sale of Goods*, 7th edn (2006), paras 16–022, 16–059.

[642] *White and Carter (Councils) Ltd v McGregor* [1962] A.C. 413.

[643] *Hounslow LBC v Twickenham Gardens Developments Ltd* [1971] Ch. 233, 253–254.

[644] *Attica Sea Carriers Corp v Ferrostaal, etc., GmbH (The Puerto Buitrago)* [1976] 1 Lloyd's Rep. 250; *Clea Shipping Corp v Bulk Oil International Ltd (The Alaskan Trader)* [1984] 1 All E.R. 129.

[645] *Ministry of Sound (Ireland) Ltd v World On-line Ltd* [2003] EWHC 2178 (Ch), [2003] 2 All E.R. (Comm) 823.

[646] See [1962] Camb.L.J. 12, 213; (1962) 78 L.Q.R. 263; (1962) 25 M.L.R. 364. cf. the American Law Institute's *Restatement of the Law of Contracts*, s.338, especially Comment (c). (See (1962) 78 L.Q.R. 263, 267.)

[647] [1962] A.C. 413, 431. This standard could be interpreted so as to bring it close to the reasonableness standard in the mitigation rules.

[648] *Attica Sea Carriers Corp v Ferrostaal, etc., GmbH (The Puerto Buitrago)* [1976] 1 Lloyd's Rep. 250, 254–256.

[649] *Clea Shipping Corp v Bulk Oil International Ltd (The Alaskan Trader)* [1984] 1 All E.R. 129. In *Ministry of Sound (Ireland) Ltd v World On-line Ltd* [2003] EWHC 2178 (Ch), [2003] 2 All E.R. (Comm) 823 the point was said not to arise.

has applied it to a shipping dispute, where for seven months the plaintiff shipowner kept a ship at anchor with a full crew ready to sail, despite the fact that the defendant treated the charterparty as ended.

7. PENALTY OR LIQUIDATED DAMAGES[650]

Damages fixed by the parties. Where the parties to a contract agree that, in the event of a breach, the contract-breaker shall pay to the other a specified sum of money, the sum fixed may be classified by the courts either as a penalty (which is irrecoverable) or as liquidated damages (which are recoverable).[651] The clause is enforceable if it does not exceed a genuine attempt to estimate in advance the loss which the claimant would be likely to suffer from a breach of the obligation in question[652]: it is enforceable irrespective of the loss actually suffered. The purpose[653] of the parties in fixing a sum is to facilitate recovery of damages without the difficulty and expense of proving actual damage[654]; or to avoid the risk of under-compensation, where the rules on remoteness of damage might not cover consequential, indirect or idiosyncratic loss[655]; or to give the promisee an assurance that he may safely rely on the fulfilment of the promise.[656] Often the parties to a contract fix a sum as liquidated damages in the event of one specific breach, and leave the claimant to sue for unliquidated damages in the ordinary way if other types of breach occur.[657] Where there is provision for liquidated 26–125

---

[650] The Law Commission, in its Working Paper No.61 (1975), made proposals for reform of the law on penalty clauses and on forfeiture of moneys paid. For a critique of the law, see Kaplan (1977) 50 S. Calif. L. Rev. 1055. For an empirical study of the use of liquidated damages in the travel industry, see Milner (1979) 42 M.L.R. 508. Some businessmen are reluctant to enforce agreed damages clauses for delay: Beale and Dugdale (1975) 2 Brit.J. Law and Soc. 45, 55.

[651] A valid agreed damages clause is probably not subject to the Unfair Contract Terms Act 1977 (above, paras 14–059 et seq.), even if it set at a figure below, the likely loss, since the sum will be payable in any event: see Treitel's *Law of Contract*, 12th edn (by Peel, 2007), paras 7–052 and 20–127. cf. however, the Unfair Terms in Consumer Contracts Regulations 1999 (above, paras 15–004 et seq., below, para.26–156).

[652] cf. a performance bond, which is *not* an estimate of the damage which might be caused by a breach of contract: *Cargill International SA v Bangladesh Sugar & Food Industries Corp* [1996] 4 All E.R. 563; *Comdel Commodities Ltd v Siporex Trade SA* [1997] 1 Lloyd's Rep. 424 CA.

[653] For an economic analysis of agreed damages clauses, see Goetz and Scott (1977) 77 Col.L.R. 554; Rea (1984) 13 J.Leg.Stud. 147. See also Harris, Campbell and Halson, *Remedies in Contract and Tort*, 2nd edn (2002) at Ch.9.

[654] *Clydebank Engineering and Shipbuilding Co Ltd v Don Jose Ramos Yzquierdo y Castaneda* [1905] A.C. 6, 11.

[655] *Robophone Facilities Ltd v Blank* [1966] 1 W.L.R. 1428, 1447–8. The agreed sum may take account of loss likely to be suffered which may not fall within the normal remoteness test: *Robert Stewart & Sons Ltd v Carapanayoti & Co Ltd* [1962] 1 W.L.R. 34, 39; *Philips Hong Kong Ltd v Att-Gen of Hong Kong* (1993) 61 Build. L.R. 49, 60–61 (the agreed sum may be justified by knowledge of "special circumstances").

[656] The clause may also operate as a limitation on liability: below, para.26–124. The present legal test, which is restricted to expected *loss*, does not permit the promisee to justify the sum fixed as a reasonable incentive to the promisor to perform his promise, nor as a disincentive to the promisor not to commit a *deliberate* breach: Harris, Campbell and Halson at pp.136–139.

[657] e.g. *Aktieselskabet Reidar v Arcos Ltd* [1927] 1 K.B. 352.

damages, the claimant may nevertheless, in appropriate cases, elect to ask for an injunction instead of enforcing the liquidated damages.[658]

26–126 **Reluctance to find clause penal.** The Privy Council[659] has cited with approval[660] the view of Dickson J. in the Supreme Court of Canada that:

> "... the power to strike down a penalty clause is a blatant interference with freedom of contract and is designed for the sole purpose of providing relief against oppression for the party having to pay the stipulated sum. It has no place where there is no oppression."[661]

Therefore, where there is no suggestion of oppression, "the court should not be astute to decry a 'penalty clause' ".[662] The:

> "... courts are predisposed ... to uphold [liquidated damages clauses]. This predisposition is even stronger in the case of commercial contracts freely entered into between parties of comparable bargaining power."[663]

However, the correct question is not whether one party secured the clause by the use of unequal bargaining power or oppression, but whether or not the clause is a genuine pre-estimate of the likely loss:

> "... whether a provision is to be treated as a penalty is a matter of construction to be resolved by asking whether at the time the contract was entered into the predominant contractual function of the provision was to deter a party from breaking the contract or to compensate the innocent party for breach. ... The question that has always had to be addressed is therefore whether the alleged penalty clause can pass muster as a genuine pre-estimate of loss."[664]

Courts of equity held that if the sum fixed was unenforceable as a penalty to ensure that the promise was not broken, the promisee should nevertheless receive by way of damages the sum which would compensate him for his actual loss.[665] The Court of Appeal has held that the strict legal position is that the innocent party can sue on the penal clause, but "it will not be enforced ... beyond the sum which represents [his] actual loss"[666]; and that the law on penalties also applies

---

[658] See the cases cited, above, para.26–011 fn.71. Agreed damages clauses do not bar the remedy of rejection of the goods: *Benjamin's Sale of Goods*, 7th edn (2006), para.13–036.

[659] *Philips Hong Kong Ltd v Att-Gen of Hong Kong* (1993) 61 Build. L.R. 49, 58.

[660] The view was also cited with approval in the High Court of Australia: *Esanda Finance Corp Ltd v Plessing* (1989) 166 C.L.R. 131, 140.

[661] *Elsey v J.G. Collins Insurance Agencies Ltd* (1978) 83 D.L.R. (3d.) 1, 15.

[662] *Robophone Facilities Ltd v Blank* [1966] 1 W.L.R. 1428, 1447.

[663] *Alfred McAlpine Capital Projects Ltd v Tilebox Ltd* [2005] Build. L. R. 271 (TCC) at [48].

[664] *Lordsvale Finance Plc v Bank of Zambia* [1996] Q.B. 752, 762–4, cited with approval in *Euro London Appointments Ltd v Claessens International Ltd* [2006] EWCA Civ 385, [2006] 2 Lloyd's Rep 436 at [30].

[665] Story, *Equitable Jurisprudence*, para.1316. The assessment of damages is according to common law; there is no equitable rule on damages where a clause has been held to be penal: *AMEV-UDC Finance Ltd v Austin* (1986) 60 A.L.J.R. 741.

[666] *Jobson v Johnson* [1989] 1 W.L.R. 1026, 1040 (see also at 1038, 1039–1042, 1049). (cf. however, the dictum in *Scandinavian Trading Tanker Co AB v Flota Petrolera Ecuatoriana (The Scaptrade)* [1983] 2 A.C. 694, 702. ("The classic form of relief against such a penalty clause has been to refuse to give effect to it, but to award the common law measure of damages for the breach of the primary obligation instead.")

to a clause which, upon breach, obliges the contract-breaker to transfer some property to the innocent party.[667] The Privy Council has treated the forfeiture of money held by the innocent party (for the breaching party) as subject to rules akin to (but not identical to) those on penalties,[668] but no English case has yet done so.[669]

Statement of penalty rules. The question whether a sum stipulated for in a contract is a penalty or liquidated damages is a question of law.[670] Lord Dunedin in delivering his opinion in *Dunlop Pneumatic Tyre Co Ltd v New Garage and Motor Co Ltd*[671] summed up the law in the following propositions: 26–127

> "(1) Though the parties to a contract who use the words 'penalty' or 'liquidated damages' may prima facie be supposed to mean what they say, yet the expression used is not conclusive. The court must find out whether the payment stipulated is in truth a penalty or liquidated damages. . . . [672]
>
> (2) The essence of a penalty is a payment of money stipulated as *in terrorem* of the offending party; the essence of liquidated damages is a genuine pre-estimate of damage.[673]
>
> (3) The question whether a sum stipulated is a penalty or liquidated damages is a question of construction to be decided upon the terms and inherent circumstances of each particular contract, judged of at the time of the making of the contract, not as at the time of the breach.[674]

---

[667] *Jobson v Johnson* [1989] 1 W.L.R. 1026, 1034–1036, 1042, 1049. Such a clause will be penal if the value of the property at the time of transfer exceeds the actual loss of the innocent party: at 1037, 1042, 1047–1048. (Sed quaere: if the *Dunlop* case [1915] A.C. 79 is followed, the test should be whether, at the time of contracting, the parties made a genuine pre-estimate both of the expected value of the property to be transferred and of the loss expected to be caused by breach, and then expected that the two would approximately match.) On the relief granted in *Jobson v Johnson*, see below, para.26–153.

[668] *Workers Trust & Merchant Bank Ltd v Dojap Investments Ltd* [1993] A.C. 573, 578 (a case on a deposit: see below, para.26–153).

[669] See below, para.26–151.

[670] *Sainter v Ferguson* (1849) 7 C.B. 716, 727.

[671] [1915] A.C. 79, 86–88. The law laid down in the *Dunlop* case has not been significantly altered by the *Philips Hong Kong* case (1993) 61 Build. L.R. 49: *Jeancharm Ltd v Barnet Football Club Ltd* [2003] EWCA Civ 58, [2003] 92 Con. L. R. 26.

[672] "But no case . . . decides that the term used by the parties themselves is to be altogether disregarded, and I should say that, where the parties themselves call the sum made payable a 'penalty,' the onus lies on those who seek to show that it is to be payable as liquidated damages": *Willson v Love* [1896] 1 Q.B. 626, 630. See *Alder v Moore* [1961] 2 Q.B. 57, 65; *Robert Stewart & Sons Ltd v Carapanayoti & Co Ltd* [1962] 1 W.L.R. 34. cf. the *Workers Trust* [1993] A.C. 573, 579.

[673] *Clydebank Engineering and Shipbuilding Co Ltd v Don Jose Ramos Yzquierdo y Castaneda* [1905] A.C. 6. See also *Bridge v Campbell Discount Co Ltd* [1962] A.C. 600, 622; *Photo Production Ltd v Securicor Transport Ltd* [1980] A.C. 827, 850; *Cameron-Head v Cameron & Co* (1919) S.C. 627; the *Workers Trust* case [1993] A.C. 573. It should be noted that by s.24 of the Agricultural Holdings Act 1986 "notwithstanding any provision in a contract of tenancy of an agricultural holding making the tenant liable to pay a higher rent or other liquidated damages" for breach of covenant, etc. the landlord may not recover for any such breach any sum "in excess of the damage actually suffered."

[674] *Public Works Commissioner v Hills* [1906] A.C. 368, 376; *Webster v Bosanquet* [1912] A.C. 394. cf. however, the Unfair Terms in Consumer Contracts Regulations 1999 (below, para.26–156).

(4) To assist this task of construction various tests have been suggested which, if applicable to the case under consideration, may prove helpful or even conclusive.[675] Such are:

(a) It will be held to be a penalty if the sum stipulated for is extravagant and unconscionable in amount in comparison with the greatest loss which could conceivably be proved to have followed from the breach.[676]

(b) It will be held to be a penalty if the breach consists only in not paying a sum of money, and the sum stipulated is a sum greater than the sum which ought to have been paid. . . .[677]

(c) There is a presumption (but no more) that it is a penalty when 'a single lump sum is made payable by way of compensation, on the occurrence of one or more or all of several events, some of which may occasion serious and others but trifling damage.'[678]

On the other hand:

(d) It is no obstacle to the sum stipulated being a genuine pre-estimate of damage, that the consequences of the breach are such as to make precise pre-estimation almost an impossibility. On the contrary, that is just the situation when it is probable that pre-estimated damage was the true bargain between the parties."[679]

26–128 **"Genuine" pre-estimate.** It has been held that:

" . . . the test does not turn upon the genuineness or honesty of the party or parties who made the pre-estimate. The test is primarily an objective one."

---

[675] *Pye v British Automobile Commercial Syndicate Ltd* [1906] 1 K.B. 425.

[676] *Clydebank Engineering and Shipbuilding Co Ltd v Don Jose Ramos Yzquierdo y Castaneda* [1905] A.C. 6, 17; *Webster v Bosanquet* [1912] A.C. 394; *Cooden Engineering Co Ltd v Stanford* [1953] 1 Q.B. 86; cf. *Bridge v Campbell Discount Co Ltd* [1962] A.C. 600 (below, para.26–136).

[677] *Kemble v Farren* (1829) 6 Bing. 141. See also *Astley v Weldon* (1801) 2 B. & P. 346; *Wallis v Smith* (1882) 21 Ch D 243, 256–257. The breach may involve more than a failure to pay: *Thos. P. Gonzales Corp v F. R. Waring (International) Pty Ltd* [1986] 2 Lloyd's Rep. 160, 163. A discount for prompt payment, however, does not make the undiscounted sum a penalty; nor is it a penalty where a loan agreement provides for a modest increase in the rate of interest, which operates only from the date of the borrower's default: *Lordsvale Finance Plc v Bank of Zambia* [1996] Q.B. 752 (a one per cent increase: if, however, the increase operated retrospectively, it might be a penalty); cf. *Jeancharm Ltd v Barnet Football Club Ltd* [2003] EWCA Civ 58, [2003] 92 Con. L. R. 26 (interest rate for late payment of five per cent per week held to be a penalty).

[678] *Lord Elphinstone v Monkland Iron & Coal Co Ltd* (1886) 11 App. Cas. 332, 342. See *Kemble v Farren* (1829) 6 Bing. 141, 148; *Magee v Lavell* (1874) L.R. 9 C.P. 107, 115; *Ford Motor Co v Armstrong* (1915) 31 T.L.R. 267 (see below, para.26–132); *Michel Habib Raji Ayoub v Sheikh Suleiman* [1941] 1 All E.R. 507, 510; *Cooden Engineering Co Ltd v Stanford* [1953] 1 Q.B. 86, 98; *Interoffice Telephones Ltd v Robert Freeman Co Ltd* [1958] 1 Q.B. 190, 194. The parties, in such a case, should fix separate sums for the various possible breaches: *Imperial Tobacco Co v Parslay* [1936] 2 All E.R. 515.

[679] See *Clydebank Engineering and Shipbuilding Co Ltd v Don Jose Ramos Yzquierdo y Castaneda* [1905] A.C. 6, 11; *Webster v Bosanquet* [1912] A.C. 394, 398; *English Hop Growers Ltd v Dering* [1928] 2 K.B. 174; *Imperial Tobacco Co v Parslay* [1936] 2 All E.R. 515, 519; *Philips Hong Kong Ltd v Att-Gen of Hong Kong* (1993) 61 Build. L.R. 49, 60 PC (the impact of delay by one contractor on other contracts).

In the same case the judge considered that one strand of the test in the reported cases was "whether the level of damages stipulated was reasonable".[680]

Pre-estimate of damage. The word "damage" must mean "net loss" after taking account of the claimant's expected ability to mitigate his loss.[681] The fact that the damage is difficult to assess with precision strengthens the presumption that a sum agreed between the parties represents a genuine attempt to estimate it and to overcome the difficulties of proof at the trial.[682] Even where the consequences of a breach are precisely ascertainable, a sum reserved by the contract may be intended by the parties as an agreed estimate of damage in order to avoid the expense and difficulty of assessment.[683] **26–129**

Fluctuating sums. Although a valid agreed damages clause may specify a graduated scale of sums payable according to the varying extent of the expected loss,[684] a sum which is liable to fluctuate according to extraneous circumstances will not be classified as liquidated damages.[685] In a railway construction contract it was provided that in the event of a breach by the contractor he should forfeit "as and for liquidated damages" certain percentages retained by the government of money payable for work done as a guarantee fund to answer for defective work, and also certain security money lodged with the government. The Judicial Committee held that this was a penalty, since it was not a definite sum, but was: **26–130**

> "... liable to great fluctuation in amount dependent on events not connected with the fulfilment of this contract. It is obvious that the amount of retained money ... depended entirely on the progress of those contracts, and that further, as those moneys are primarily liable to make good deficiencies in these contract works, the eventual sum available ... could not in any way be estimated as a fixed sum."[686]

Minimum payment clause. A "minimum payment" clause in a hire-purchase or hiring agreement that applies when the hirer is in breach of the contract by refusing to continue with it,[687] will usually be held to be a penalty if it provides for the same total sum to be payable by the hirer irrespective of how **26–131**

---

[680] *Alfred McAlpine Capital Projects Ltd v Tilebox Ltd* [2005] Build. L. R. 271 (TCC) at [48].

[681] The question whether the parties may give their own meaning to "loss" is mentioned below, para.26–141, text after fn.723.

[682] *Dunlop Pneumatic Tyre Co Ltd v New Garage Motor Co Ltd* [1915] A.C. 79; *English Hop Growers Ltd v Dering* [1928] 2 K.B. 174; *Imperial Tobacco Co v Parslay* [1936] 2 All E.R. 515; *Robophone Facilities Ltd v Blank* [1966] 1 W.L.R. 1428, 1447; *Philips Hong Kong Ltd v Att-Gen of Hong Kong* (1993) 61 Build. L.R. 49 (the loss to a governmental body caused by delay in construction was especially difficult to assess).

[683] *Diestal v Stevenson* [1906] 2 K.B. 345.

[684] See below, para.26–135, for graduated damages.

[685] *Public Works Commissioner v Hills* [1906] A.C. 368, 376. In a case concerning a deposit, which was held to be unreasonable in amount, the Privy Council followed this case: *Workers Trust & Merchant Bank Ltd v Dojap Investments Ltd* [1993] A.C. 573 (below, para.26–151).

[686] *Public Works Commissioner v Hills* [1906] A.C. 368, 376 (followed in *Jobson v Johnson* [1989] 1 W.L.R. 1026, 1036).

[687] Compare below, para.26–136.

long the agreement has been in force[688] or "regardless of the seriousness or triviality of the breach in question".[689] (But the position in regard to the assessment of damages at common law will be different if the parties made the term into a condition, any breach of which entitled the innocent party to terminate the contract.[690])

26–132 **Single sum payable upon different breaches.** The mere fact that the same amount is made payable upon the breach of several undertakings of varying importance is by no means conclusive.[691] It may be that the amount is not disproportionate to the least important of these undertakings, and therefore represents a genuine attempt at an agreed estimate of real damage.[692] In *Dunlop Pneumatic Tyre Co Ltd v New Garage and Motor Co Ltd*,[693] dealers in tyres agreed not to resell any tyres bought from the manufacturers to any private customers at less than the manufacturers' current list prices, not to supply them to persons whose supplies the manufacturers had decided to suspend, not to exhibit or export them without the manufacturers' consent, and to pay £5 by way of liquidated damages for every tyre sold or offered in breach of the agreement. It was held that the £5 was not a penalty and thus was recoverable as liquidated damages.[694]

26–133 In *Ford Motor Co v Armstrong*,[695] however, the retailer in a similar case agreed to pay £250 as "the agreed damage which the manufacturer will sustain" upon the breach of any one of several covenants (similar to those in the *Dunlop* case, above), and the Court of Appeal by a majority held that this (in 1915) was a penalty, since it was an arbitrary and substantial sum, and made payable for various breaches differing in kind, some of which might cause only trifling damage. The high amount of the agreed sum in this case showed that it could not be a genuine pre-estimate of loss, as in the *Dunlop* case.

26–134 However, the cases on covenants in restraint of trade[696] have generally treated the sum payable for a breach as a sum stipulated for the breach of a single obligation, although it "is capable of being broken more than once, or in more

---

[688] *Lamdon Trust Ltd v Hurrell* [1955] 1 W.L.R. 391. See also *Anglo-Auto Finance Co Ltd v James* [1963] 1 W.L.R. 1042; *United Dominions Trust (Commercial) Ltd v Ennis* [1968] 1 Q.B. 54.

[689] cf. *Lombard North Central Plc v Butterworth* [1987] Q.B. 527.

[690] Above, para.12–025, below, para.26–141.

[691] See r.4(c) in Lord Dunedin's proposition, above, para.26–127.

[692] *Wallis v Smith* (1882) 21 Ch D 243; *Pye v British Automobile Commercial Syndicate Ltd* [1906] 1 K.B. 425; *Dunlop Pneumatic Tyre Co Ltd v New Garage and Motor Co Ltd* [1915] A.C. 79; *Philips Hong Kong Ltd v Att-Gen of Hong Kong* (1993) 61 Build. L.R. 49, 62–63 (Privy Council refers to: ". . . the error of assuming that, because in some hypothetical situation the loss suffered will be less than the sum quantified in accordance with the liquidated damage provision, that provision must be a penalty.").

[693] [1915] A.C. 79.

[694] The House of Lords took the view that the £5 did not apply to the second and third obligations (not to sell to prohibited person, and not to exhibit without permission).

[695] (1915) 31 T.L.R. 267.

[696] *Crisdee v Bolton* (1827) 3 C. & P. 240; *Price v Green* (1847) 16 M. & W. 346, 354; *Reynolds v Bridge* (1856) 6 E. & B. 528, 541.

ways than one".[697] Again, if a sum is payable upon different breaches, it may nevertheless be recoverable as liquidated damages where:

> "... the damage caused by each and every one of those events, however varying in importance, may be of such an uncertain nature that it cannot be accurately ascertained"[698]

or where the stipulated sum is taken as an average or mean figure of the losses probably incurred in the different events.[699]

Graduated damages. In building contracts and other similar contracts the courts have upheld as liquidated damages a system of graduated sums which increase in proportion to the seriousness of the breach, e.g. so much per week for delay in performance,[700] or so much according to the number of items in question.[701] If in a building contract there is no such graduation the sum fixed is more likely to be held to be a penalty.[702] The sum must be graduated so that it changes in the right direction. Depreciation obviously increases over time, so a sum said to be compensation for depreciation is not a genuine pre-estimate of loss if it *decreases* over time as a hirer pays more instalments.[703] 26–135

The scope of the law on penalties. The law on penalties is not applicable to many sums of money payable under a contract.[704] Thus, it is not relevant where the claimant claims an agreed sum (a debt) which is due from the defendant in 26–136

[697] *Dunlop Pneumatic Tyre Co Ltd v New Garage and Motor Co Ltd* [1915] A.C. 79, 98 (see also at 92–93); *Law v Redditch Local Board* [1892] 1 Q.B. 127, 136.

[698] *Dunlop Pneumatic Tyre Co Ltd v New Garage and Motor Co Ltd* [1915] A.C. 79, 95–96. See also *Galsworthy v Strutt* (1848) 1 Ex. 659, 666–667.

[699] *Dunlop Pneumatic Tyre Co Ltd v New Garage and Motor Co Ltd* [1915] A.C. 79, 99; *English Hop Growers Ltd v Dering* [1928] 2 K.B. 174, 182.

[700] *Clydebank Engineering Co v Don Jose Ramos Yzquierdo y Castaneda* [1905] A.C. 6; *Philips Hong Kong Ltd v Att-Gen of Hong Kong* (1993) 61 Build. L.R. 49, 60, PC; *Alfred McAlpine Capital Projects Ltd v Tilebox Ltd* [2005] Build. L. R. 271, TCC. See also *Law v Redditch Local Board* [1892] 1 Q.B. 127; *Cellulose Acetate Silk Co Ltd v Widnes Foundry (1925) Ltd* [1933] A.C. 20 (below, para.26–142). The party entitled to the benefit of a liquidated damages clause in the event of failure to complete on time cannot take advantage of it if the delay is partly due to his own fault: *Peak Construction (Liverpool) Ltd v McKinney Foundations Ltd* (1971) 69 L.G.R. 1, 11, 16. Demurrage under a charterparty is a case of graduated liquidated damages: *President of India v Lips Maritime Corp* [1988] A.C. 395, 422–423.

[701] *Elphinstone v Monkland Iron and Coal Co* (1886) 11 App. Cas. 332; *Diestal* v *Stevenson* [1906] 2 K.B. 345.

[702] e.g. *Public Works Commissioner v Hills* [1906] A.C. 368 (above, para.26–130). See also *Re Newman* (1876) 4 Ch D 724.

[703] *Bridge v Campbell Discount Co Ltd* [1962] A.C. 600. ("It is a sliding scale of compensation, but a scale that slides in the wrong direction": at 623.) If it slides in the right direction, the clause is more likely to be held valid: *Phonographic Equipment (1958) Ltd v Muslu* [1961] 1 W.L.R. 1379. cf. *Lombank Ltd v Excell* [1964] 1 Q.B. 415.

[704] But Bingham L.J. has adverted to the possibility of "a disguised penalty clause": *Interfoto Picture Library Ltd v Stiletto Visual Programmes Ltd* [1988] 1 All E.R. 348, 358 (see above, para.1–022).

return for the claimant's performance of his obligations,[705] or which is due upon the occurrence of an event other than a breach of the defendant's contractual duty owed to the claimant.[706] In *Campbell Discount Co Ltd v Bridge*,[707] a hire-purchase agreement permitted the hirer at his option to terminate the hiring during the period of the agreement, and provided that the hirer should thereupon pay a sum by way of agreed compensation for the depreciation of the chattel; the Court of Appeal held that the owner could recover the agreed sum, since being payable upon an event not constituting a breach of the agreement, it fell outside the scope of the law as to penalties. In the House of Lords[708] the decision was based on a different view of the facts,[709] but four of their Lordships expressed obiter their views on the ruling of the Court of Appeal; two agreed that the law as to penalties was inapplicable, but two were prepared to hold that the hirer was entitled to some relief.

26–137 **Sum payable on event other than breach.** However, a later House of Lords case appears to support the restriction upon the scope of the law on penalties. In the *Export Credits Guarantee* case,[710] the House held that the law did not apply to a clause providing for the contract-breaker (the defendant) to pay a specified sum to the plaintiff upon the happening of a certain event which was *not* the breach of a contractual duty owed by the defendant to the plaintiff. So it could not be a penalty where the defendant had agreed to reimburse the plaintiff the amount paid by the plaintiff to third parties under a guarantee (even where the plaintiff's obligation to meet the guarantee arose on the occasion of the defendant's breach of his contractual duties owed to other parties).[711] Although the case concerned a guarantee in a complex commercial arrangement and the plaintiff was claiming only the sum it had actually lost, their Lordships' limitation on the scope of the law on penalties was expressed in such wide terms that it would prevent many other clauses from being subject to that law, for example a sum payable by one party should it exercise an option as to perform at a later

[705] *White and Carter (Councils) Ltd v McGregor* [1962] A.C. 413 (above, para.26–122). The contrast between a debt and liquidated damages is drawn by the House of Lords in *President of India v Lips Maritime Corp* [1988] A.C. 395, 422–423, 424.

[706] *Export Credits Guarantee Department v Universal Oil Products Co* [1983] 1 W.L.R. 399 (see below, para.26–137); *Euro London Appointments Ltd v Claessens International Ltd* [2006] EWCA Civ 385, [2006] 2 Lloyd's Rep 436 (a condition precedent imposing no obligation). See also *Jervis v Harris* [1996] Ch. 195, 206–207.

[707] [1961] 1 Q.B. 445 (following *Associated Distributors Ltd v Hall* [1938] 2 K.B. 83); see Vol.II, paras 38–313—38–314. The decision is based on the non-statutory law. For statutory regulation of hire-purchase agreements, see Vol.II, paras 38–321 et seq.

[708] [1962] A.C. 600.

[709] viz that the hirer had committed a breach. The law on penalties applies to a minimum payment clause if the agreement is in fact terminated on the ground of the hirer's breach: *Cooden Engineering Co Ltd v Stanford* [1953] 1 Q.B. 86; *Lamdon Trust Ltd v Hurrell* [1955] 1 W.L.R. 391. See Vol.II, paras 38–329—38–334.

[710] *Export Credits Guarantee Department v Universal Oil Products Co* [1983] 1 W.L.R. 399. It is unfortunate that the short speech in this case made no attempt to discuss the opinions expressed in the *Campbell Discount* case [1962] A.C. 600. See also *Euro London Appointments Ltd v Claessens International Ltd* [2006] EWCA Civ 385, [2006] 2 Lloyd's Rep 436 (a condition precedent imposing no obligation).

[711] *Export Credits Guarantee Department v Universal Oil Products Co* [1983] 1 W.L.R. 399.

date than anticipated (but not required).[712] Although statutory protection is available in some cases[713] the common law position is unsatisfactory; for instance, an honest hirer, who terminates his hire-purchase agreement when he finds that he cannot keep up the instalments, is in a worse position than the hirer who simply breaks his agreement by failing to pay the instalments.[714]

Other cases outside the law on penalties. It is uncertain how far the law applies to a clause which imposes on the contract-breaker adverse consequences other than the payment of money or forfeiture of money already paid, or of proprietary or possessory rights held by him.[715] The law does not apply where one party to the contract is given an option to choose a particular method of performance, subject to his making a stipulated payment to the other[716]; or where a member of a pooling agreement failed to pay his levy to finance litigation and was excluded from sharing in the proceeds of the litigation.[717] The law on penalties may apply to a clause which entitles the innocent party to withhold a payment (which would otherwise be due to the contract-breaker) on the ground that he has failed "to comply with any of the conditions" of the contract.[718] 26–138

Incentive payments. The reverse of an agreed damages clause is an incentive payment such as an extra payment for early completion. The law on penalties does not apply to a clause providing for an *increase* in the price if certain targets in the contract are bettered or if costs are reduced; similarly, the price for a specially-manufactured machine may be graduated according to its efficiency in operation. A Government report has recommended that in building contracts incentive payments should be preferred to agreed damages clauses.[719] 26–139

Acceleration clauses. An "acceleration" clause is often found in contracts providing for payment by instalments: on default in paying one instalment, all future instalments become immediately payable as one sum. Although the operation of these clauses produces results which may be "penal", the courts have 26–140

---

[712] In *M&J Polymers Ltd v Imerys Minerals Ltd* [2008] EWHC 344 (Comm), [2008] All ER (D) 445 (Feb) it was held that a "take or pay" clause is subject to the penalty rules (though it was held on the facts not to be a penalty). It is submitted that this will depend on the form of the clause. It will not be subject to the penalty rules if the buyer is simply obliged to pay for a minimum quantity with an option whether or not to take delivery of all the goods. On the facts of the case, however, it was held that the buyer was in breach of an obligation to order a certain quantity (at [41]). The death or bankruptcy of a party might be another event, not constituting a breach, upon which money is to be paid. cf. *Mount v Oldham Corp* [1973] Q.B. 309 (claim for a term's school fees in lieu of notice withdrawing a pupil).

[713] Below, paras 26–152 and 26–155—26–156.

[714] See the Law Commission's Working Paper No.61 (1975), paras 17–26.

[715] This was considered by the High Court of Australia in *Forestry Commission of N.S.W. v Stefanetto* (1976) 133 C.L.R. 507 (on the contractor's breach, the owner of the land was entitled to use the contractor's plant to complete the work). On clauses requiring the contract-breaker to transfer property to the innocent party, see above, para.26–126; below, para.26–153.

[716] *Fratelli Moretti SpA v Nidera Handelscompagnie B.V.* [1981] 2 Lloyd's Rep. 47, 53.

[717] *Nutting v Baldwin* [1995] 1 W.L.R. 201.

[718] *Gilbert Ash (Northern) Ltd v Modern Engineering (Bristol) Ltd* [1974] A.C. 689. cf. *The Vainqueur José* [1979] 1 Lloyd's Rep. 557, 577–578.

[719] Banwell Report (Report of the Committee on Placing and Management of Contracts for Building and Civil Engineering Work) (HMSO, 1964), para.9.22.

usually enforced them on the ground that they do not increase the contract-breaker's overall obligation.[720] The Court of Appeal has held that it is not a penalty for an acceleration clause in a contract of loan to provide that, upon failure to pay an agreed instalment, the whole capital of the loan becomes immediately due and repayable.[721] But it might be held to be a penalty if it provided that, upon such failure, future interest (viz payments not yet due) should be payable immediately.[722]

26–141 **Damages following termination by the innocent party under an express term.** Where the hirer has neither repudiated the hiring (or hire-purchase) agreement, nor committed a "fundamental breach" of it, but the owner terminates it in the exercise of an express power to do so conferred by the agreement, the owner's damages are limited to loss suffered through any breaches up to the date of the termination.[723] This is, in effect, the measure of loss defined by law and the parties are not free to define it otherwise. A clause that provides for a larger sum to be paid, such as a "minimum payment" clause or one providing for recovery of the amount of future payments, even with deductions for any savings made,[724] will be void as a penalty.[725] It should be noted, however, that this principle does not apply where the contract made the broken term into a condition, any breach of which entitled the innocent party to terminate (e.g. a clause making compliance with time "of the essence"[726]). In this case the innocent party may both terminate the contract and recover damages for the loss of the bargain (viz in respect of all the outstanding obligations of the other party).[727] A clause that makes the hirer liable for a genuine pre-estimate of the

---

[720] *Protector Endowment Loan Co v Grice* (1880) 5 QBD 592 (a loan case); *Wallingford v Mutual Society* (1880) 5 App. Cas. 685. See Goode [1982] J. Bus. L. 148; cf. *Wadham Stringer Finance Ltd v Meaney* [1981] 1 W.L.R. 39, 48 (see Vol.II, para.38–252). The High Court of Australia has sometimes upheld acceleration clauses (*I.A.C. (Leasing) Ltd v Humphrey* (1972) 126 C.L.R. 131 (see also Vol.II, para.38–333)) but sometimes not (holding them to be penalties): *O'Dea v Allstates Leasing Systems (W.A.) Pty Ltd* (1983) 152 C.L.R. 359; Muir (1985) 10 Sydney L.R. 503; *AMEV-UDC Finance Ltd v Austin* (1986) 162 C.L.R. 170; cf. *Esanda Finance Corp Ltd v Plessing* (1989) 166 C.L.R. 131.

[721] *The Angelic Star* [1988] 1 Lloyd's Rep. 122, 125, 127.

[722] *The Angelic Star* [1988] 1 Lloyd's Rep. 122. cf. *Lordsvale Finance Plc v Bank of Zambia* [1996] Q.B. 752 (see above, para.26–127 fn.677).

[723] *Financings Ltd v Baldock* [1963] 2 Q.B. 104. (A "minimum payment" clause specifying a larger sum will be held to be a penalty: see above, para.26–127.) The principle stated in the text has been regularly followed by the Court of Appeal: *Brady v St Margaret's Trust Ltd* [1963] 2 Q.B. 494; *Charterhouse Credit Co Ltd v Tolly* [1963] 2 Q.B. 683; *United Dominions Trust (Commercial) Ltd v Ennis* [1968] 1 Q.B. 54; *Capital Finance Co Ltd v Donati* (1977) 121 S.J. 270; *Lombard North Central Plc v Butterworth* [1987] Q.B. 527. See also the Australian cases cited, above, para.26–122 fn.650.

[724] In *Lombard North Central Plc v Butterworth* [1987] Q.B. 527 the contract contained a formula under which the owner was entitled to arrears, all future instalments that would have fallen due had and agreement not been terminated less a discount for accelerated payment. It omitted an allowance for the resale value of the repossessed goods. This would have prevented it being a genuine pre-estimate of the loss, but even had it provided for an allowance, the clause would have been a penalty for the reason stated in the text following.

[725] *Lombard North Central Plc v Butterworth* [1987] Q.B. 527.

[726] See above, paras 21–011 et seq.

[727] The *Lombard* case [1987] Q.B. 527. See Treitel [1987] L.M.C.L.Q. 143; Beale (1988) 104 L.Q.R. 355.

owners' full loss in such a case will be valid. The Court of Appeal decided that the clause making prompt payment "of the essence" when it would not be so otherwise[728] is not itself subject to the law on penalties.[729] The difference between the two types of clause (viz an express power to terminate, and a clause making time of the essence) is "one of drafting form and wholly without substance".[730] The result is that the position of the parties may be changed by a simple, small change in the terminology of the contract which makes every term a "condition" in the sense of a term any breach of which entitles the promisee to terminate.[731] This follows, however, not from the law on penalties but from the firmly established rule that the parties are free to agree that any term of the contract is a condition.[732]

"Underliquidated damages". The parties may agree that in the event of breach, the party in breach will pay a sum which is demonstrably less than a pre-estimate of the likely loss (sometimes called an "underliquidated damages clause"). This will not prevent it being a valid liquidated damages clause.[733] These clauses are often the basis of the insurance arrangements to be made by the parties. A clause of this type may operate as a limitation of the party's liability. For that reason it is likely to be construed in the same way as other clauses limiting liability.[734] It is probable that an underliquidated damages clause is not caught by the Unfair Contract Terms Act 1977[735] because it does not merely exclude or restrict one party's liability: the same amount is payable whether the actual loss is greater or less.[736] However, were such a clause to occur in a consumer contract, it would seem to fall within the Unfair Terms in Consumer Contract Regulations 1999 if the term had not been individually negotiated.[737] 26–142

Can damages exceed the sum fixed in penal clause? A clause which is not a genuine pre-estimate, e.g. because it stipulates for more than the likely loss, and 26–143

[728] In the *Lombard* case [1987] Q.B. 527, it was held that, according to common law principles, the hirer had not committed a repudiatory breach of the contract: at 543–545. The court nevertheless awarded as damages at common law almost the same sum which it had previously found not to be a genuine pre-estimate of loss (a penalty).

[729] The *Lombard* case [1987] Q.B. 527, 536–537. But cf. *Gilbert Ash (Northern) Ltd v Modern Engineering (Bristol) Ltd* [1974] A.C. 689 (above, para.26–138).

[730] The *Lombard* case [1987] Q.B. 527, 546.

[731] Would the law uphold a clause providing expressly that for any breach, however trivial, the damages shall be assessed on the basis that the whole benefit of the contract has been lost by the other party? cf. decisions on mitigation, such as *The Solholt* [1983] 1 Lloyd's Rep. 605 (above, para.26–113).

[732] See above, para.12–026.

[733] *Cellulose Acetate Silk Co Ltd v Widnes Foundry (1925) Ltd* [1933] A.C. 20. The Unfair Contract Terms Act 1977 may now apply to such a clause: *St Albans City Council v International Computers Ltd* [1996] 4 All E.R. 481; see above, paras 14–059 et seq.

[734] cf. the rule that the effect of an exemption clause depends on the construction of the contract: *Suisse Atlantique Societe d'Armement Maritime v N.V. Rotterdamsche Kolen Centrale* [1967] 1 A.C. 361; *Photo Production Ltd v Securicor Transport Ltd* [1980] A.C. 827 (see above, paras 14–022 et seq.).

[735] See above, paras 14–059 et seq., and in particular para.14–062.

[736] See Treitel's *Law of Contract*, 12th edn (by Peel, 2007), paras 7–052 and 20–127.

[737] See above, Ch.15.

which is therefore a penalty, may be ignored if it is for less than the actual damage suffered. Where a charterparty contained the following clause: "[p]enalty for non-performance of this agreement proved damages, not exceeding estimated amount of freight", it was held that the clause provided a penalty and not a limitation of liability, so that the party complaining of non-performance was entitled to recover damages for his actual loss although it exceeded the estimated amount of freight.[738] It is unsettled whether this principle applies to penalty clauses in other types of contract, so as to entitle the claimant to ignore the sum stipulated as a penalty (where it was clearly not intended to limit liability) and to sue for damages for a greater amount to compensate him for his actual loss.[739]

26–144 **"Invoicing back" clauses.** The express terms of the contract may not only exclude or limit the innocent party's right to claim damages for breach of contract,[740] but may also provide other provisions intended to apply in the event of a breach. Subject to the law as to penalties,[741] and to the effect of the Unfair Contract Terms Act 1977,[742] the courts will enforce these terms, despite the unexpected results which may occur. In one case,[743] a clause in a contract for the sale of goods provided that if the sellers made default in shipping, the contract should "be closed by invoicing back the goods" at the closing price fixed by the London Corn Trade Association. The sellers failed to ship, and the Association declared a closing price, which, because of a fall in market price, was lower than the contract price, so that a balance was due in favour of the sellers. Nevertheless, the Court of Appeal enforced the clause, despite the fact that the sellers were the party in default.[744] An "invoicing back" clause may not be interpreted as the exclusive remedy,[745] e.g. the clause may not prevent the buyer obtaining damages

---

[738] *Wall v Rederiaktiebolaget Luggude* [1915] 3 K.B. 66 (approved by the House of Lords in *Watts, Watts & Co Ltd v Mitsui & Co Ltd* [1917] A.C. 227). But this case may require reconsideration in the light of the *Suisse Atlantique* case [1967] 1 A.C. 361 (where a demurrage clause was held to be an agreed damages clause) and the *Photo Production* case [1980] A.C. 827.

[739] In *Cellulose Acetate Silk Co Ltd v Widnes Foundry (1925) Ltd* [1933] A.C. 20, 26, the House left: " . . . open the question whether, where a penalty is plainly less in amount than the prospective damages, there is any legal objection to suing on it or, in a suitable case, ignoring it and suing for damages." cf. dicta to the effect that the penalty fixes the maximum recoverable: *Wilbeam v Ashton* (1807) 1 Camp. 78; *Elphinstone v Monkland Iron & Coal Co* (1886) L.R. 11 App. Cas. 332, 346; *Elsley v J.G. Collins Insurance Agencies Ltd* (1978) 83 D.L.R. (3d) 1, 14–16; *W. & J. Investments Ltd v Bunting* [1984] 1 N.S.W.L.R. 331, 335–336. See also Hudson (1974) 90 L.Q.R. 31; Gordon (1974) 90 L.Q.R. 296; Hudson (1975) 91 L.Q.R. 25; Barton (1976) 92 L.Q.R. 20; Hudson (1985) 101 L.Q.R. 480; Treitel at para.20–128.

[740] On exemption clauses, see Ch.14, above.

[741] Above, paras 26–125 et seq.

[742] See above, paras 14–059 et seq.

[743] *Lancaster v J. F. Turner & Co Ltd* [1924] 2 K.B. 222 (Scrutton L.J. dissenting); followed in *J.F. Adair & Co Ltd v Birnbaum* [1939] 2 K.B. 149 (and the earlier case noted, 173); *Podar Trading Co Ltd v Tagher* [1949] 2 K.B. 277. cf. *Laing, Son & Co Ltd v Eastcheap Dried Fruit Co Ltd* [1961] 2 Lloyd's Rep. 277.

[744] Some clauses are drafted differently and avoid this difficulty, e.g. the clause may apply only to the defaulting buyer, and only if the market price has fallen: *Alexandria Cotton and Trading Co (Sudan) Ltd v Cotton Co of Ethiopia Ltd* [1963] 1 Lloyd's Rep. 576.

[745] *Roth, Schmidt & Co v D. Nagase & Co Ltd* (1920) 2 Ll. L. Rep. 36 (CA: the clause did not expressly exclude the right to reject the goods or to recover damages upon rejection).

for his loss of profits,[746] and judges have interpreted such clauses restrictively.[747] An "invoicing back" clause may also allow a percentage of the market price to be added to, or deducted from, the price, which if reasonable, will be upheld as liquidated damages covering items of loss not covered by the price alone.[748]

Reimbursement is not a penalty. If a contract provides that in a certain event a sum of money paid under the contract is to be repaid to the original payer, the reimbursement cannot be a penalty.[749] So where the defendant received an insurance payment on the basis of his permanent disablement the insurers were able to enforce his undertaking to pay them "a penalty" of the same amount if he took part in a specified sport in future.[750] 26–145

Deposits and forfeiture of sums paid.[751] This, and the following paragraph, deal with the law apart from the Law of Property Act 1925 s.49(2) and Consumer Credit Act 1974[752]; many situations, however, will be covered by the provisions of those statutes. A contract may, instead of fixing a sum to be paid upon breach, provide that a sum already paid shall be forfeited[753] upon breach by the party who paid it.[754] Alternatively, a sum may be paid as a deposit, in which case the sum is forfeited if the payer breaks the contract.[755] English courts have always treated such a forfeiture clause as different from a sum payable upon breach. It is true that though in *Workers Trust Merchant Bank Ltd v Dojap Investments Ltd* the Privy Council said, in general terms, that the law on penalties applies to: 26–146

> "... a contractual provision which requires one party in the event of his breach of the contract to pay or forfeit a sum of money to the other party."[756]

---

[746] *Re Bourgeois and Wilson Holgate & Co* (1920) 25 Com. Cas. 260 (the Court of Appeal decided in this case that the seller in these circumstances could not enforce the clause against the buyer).

[747] One judge has held that the interpretation of a clause which requires damages to be paid *to* the defaulting party is contrary to "natural justice": *Cassir, Moore & Co Ltd v Eastcheap Dried Fruit Co* [1962] 1 Lloyd's Rep. 400, 402. See also the qualifications suggested in *Lancaster v J. F. Turner & Co Ltd* [1924] 2 K.B. 222, 231; *J.F. Adair & Co Ltd v Birnbaum* [1939] 2 K.B. 149, 169.

[748] *Robert Stewart & Sons Ltd v Carapanayoti & Co Ltd* [1962] 1 W.L.R. 34.

[749] *Alder v Moore* [1961] 2 Q.B. 57 (approving *Re Apex Supply Co Ltd* [1942] Ch. 108).

[750] *Alder v Moore* [1961] 2 Q.B. 57.

[751] See Goff and Jones, *The Law of Restitution*, 7th edn (2007), paras 20–041—20–046; *McGregor on Damages*, 17th edn (2003), paras 13–075 et seq.; the Law Commission, Working Paper No.61 (1975) ("Penalty Clauses and Forfeiture of Moneys Paid"), paras 50, 65, 66; Smith [2001] C.L.J. 178; cf. *Commissioners of Public Works v Hills* [1906] A.C. 368 (recovery of amount deposited as "security" in a building contract; above, para.26–130).

[752] See below, paras 26–152 and 26–155.

[753] The payee "forfeits" the sum where he retains it for his own beneficial use, having freed himself of any further obligations under the contract by terminating the contract on account of the payer's breach. It is then up to the payer to challenge the forfeiture if he has any legal ground for doing so.

[754] If the sum is a deposit paid by the buyer (viz a sum intended to be received by the seller as a security for the completion of the purchase by the buyer) it will be assumed that it is intended to be forfeited to the seller if the buyer defaults: *Howe v Smith* (1884) 27 Ch D 89, 97–98 (below, para.29–064); *Stockloser v Johnson* [1954] 1 Q.B. 476, 490 ("or the money is expressly paid as a deposit (which is equivalent to a forfeiture clause)"). The court has power to order the return of a deposit paid under a contract for the sale of land: see below, para.26–152.

[755] *Howe v Smith* (1889) 27 Ch D 89.

[756] [1993] A.C. 573, 578. This was a case of a deposit of an amount held to be unreasonable and thus recoverable by the contract-breaker (subject to a cross-claim for any loss suffered by the innocent party).

However, the rules applied in that case differ from the penalty rules[757]; and modern English courts[758] do not appear to apply the penalty rules to deposits or clauses providing for the forfeiture of sums paid.

26–147 **Purchase by instalments and pre-payment of price.** Traditionally, the courts were willing to grant relief against "forfeiture" clauses in only two situations; and, as will be seen below,[759] the relief was of a limited form, which if the payee was entitled to terminate the contract, did not include ordering a return of the sums paid. The first type of case is of landlord and tenant. There has been a long history of equitable relief against forfeiture of leasehold interests viz where a clause in the lease entitled the landlord to repossess the premises if the tenant failed to pay an instalment of the rent.[760] The second situation was where the contract-breaker has been purchasing land by paying the price by instalments: it is clearly established that if, under a contract to purchase land by instalment payments, the purchaser defaults in payment of an instalment of the price, the court has jurisdiction in a proper case to relieve him against a clause providing for forfeiture of the instalments already paid, by granting him an extension of time within which he could pay the instalment now due.[761] It is implicit in these cases that payment within the extended period would preserve the purchaser's contractual rights in the same way as payment by the time originally agreed would have done.

26–148 It is only relatively recently that the courts have begun to grant a limited type of relief against forfeiture in a wider range of situations. A condition said to be necessary before equitable relief may be granted is that the forfeiture clause was inserted in order:

> "... to secure a stated result which can effectively be attained when the matter comes before the court, and where the forfeiture provision is added by way of security for the production of that result."[762]

The wider development began in 1954 with *Stockloser v Johnson*[763]: there was a provision, in a contract to purchase plant and machinery by instalment payments, that upon default by the buyer, the seller might terminate the contract and forfeit the instalments already paid. The majority of the Court of Appeal held that

[757] See below, para.26–151.

[758] This has occasionally been done in the past: see *Pye v British Automobile Commercial Syndicate* [1906] 1 K.B. 425 and *Public Works Commissioner v Hills* [1906] A.C. 368, P.C.

[759] Below, para.26–150.

[760] See also s.146 of the Law of Property Act 1925. See also fn.762, below.

[761] *Re Dagenham (Thames) Dock Co* (1972–73) L.R. 8 Ch. App. 1022; *John H. Kilmer v British Columbia Orchard Lands Ltd* [1913] A.C. 319; *Steedman v Drinkle* [1916] 1 A.C. 275; *Mussen v Van Diemen's Land Co* [1938] Ch. 253; *Starside Properties Ltd v Mustapha* [1974] 1 W.L.R. 816. (Time was not made "of the essence" in this contract: cf. above, para.26–141.) The Privy Council has refused to extend this principle: *Union Eagle Ltd v Golden Achievement Ltd* [1997] A.C. 514 (see the comments by Heydon (1997) 113 L.Q.R. 385); and Stevens (1998) 61 M.L.R. 255). See Lang (1984) 100 L.Q.R. 427; Harpum [1984] C.L.J. 134.

[762] *Shiloh Spinners Ltd v Harding* [1973] A.C. 691, 723. (The case concerned the right to forfeit (re-enter upon) leasehold property for failure to repair fences and to maintain works for the protection of adjoining property.)

[763] [1954] 1 Q.B. 476. (See also Vol.II, para.38–324.)

the court has an equitable jurisdiction to relieve against forfeiture of such instalments, even after termination of the contract, if in the actual circumstances of the case the clause was penal and it would be oppressive and unconscionable for the seller to retain all the instalments. In 1983, the House of Lords upheld the jurisdiction to relieve against forfeiture, but limited it to contracts concerning the transfer or creation of proprietary or possessory rights.[764] Thus it did not apply to the facts of the case before the House, where a shipowner withdrew his ship (chartered under a time charter[765]) on the ground of the charterer's failure to make punctual payment of an instalment of hire. Similarly, the House of Lords has refused relief against the forfeiture of "mere contractual licences" to use certain names and trade marks.[766] But Court of Appeal granted relief (in the form of an extension of time in which a payment could be made by the defendant) in a commercial contract which provided that his failure to pay a sum on time would entitle the plaintiff to claim an assignment of patent rights held by the defendant.[767] The House of Lords[768] has granted relief to the lessee of chattels from their forfeiture: the House held that the court's power to make an interim order for the sale of chattels (which formed the subject-matter of the proceedings) did not prejudice the lessee's right to seek relief from forfeiture. The proceeds of sale stood in the place of the chattels and relief could be given by an order deciding the proportions in which the parties were entitled to the money; it did not matter that the lessee could not be restored to possession.

Form of relief: additional time to pay. Under this equitable principle, the courts will seldom do more than give the contract-breaker more time in which to pay the sum he had failed to pay on time. This relief has the effect that the contract-breaker does not forfeit the rights which he had under the contract, provided he pays within the time fixed by the court. 26–149

Return of payments subject to forfeiture clause. If the contract-breaker is unable to pay, or if the contract has already been terminated, the position is less clear. Traditionally, the courts have been more reluctant[769] to allow recovery of money already paid by the contract-breaker (i.e. to grant affirmative relief)[770] 26–150

---

[764] *Scandinavian Trading Tanker Co AB v Flota Petrolera Ecuatoriana (The Scaptrade)* [1983] 2 A.C. 694 (followed in *Union Eagle Ltd v Golden Achievement Ltd* [1997] A.C. 514 (PC, failure by ten minutes to pay balance of purchase price on time, when time was "of the essence": see Heydon (1997) 113 L.Q.R. 385; Stevens (1998) 61 M.L.R. 255). See also *The Laconia* [1977] A.C. 850, 869–870, 873–874, 878, 887; cf. the High Court of Australia in *Legione v Hateley* (1983) 46 A.L.R. 1; *Ciavarella v Balmer* (1983) 153 C.L.R. 438; and in *Stern v McArthur* (1988) 165 C.L.R. 489.

[765] A charter by demise would have given the charterer a possessory interest in the ship.

[766] *Sport Internationaal Bussum B.V. v Inter-Footwear Ltd* [1984] 1 W.L.R. 776 (followed in *Crittall Windows Ltd v Stormseal (UPVC) Window Systems Ltd* [1991] R.P.C. 265). But it is not a purely contractual right where a hirer is entitled to indefinite possession of chattels so long as he makes hire payments: hence relief against forfeiture is available: *On Demand Information Plc v Michael Gerson (Finance) Plc* [2002] UKHL 13, [2003] 1 A.C. 368 at [29].

[767] *B.I.C.C. Plc v Burndy Corp* [1985] Ch. 232, 251–252. (The line drawn between this and the *Sport Internationaal* case [1984] 1 W.L.R. 776 is not justifiable in commercial terms.)

[768] *On Demand Information Plc v Michael Gerson (Finance) Plc* [2002] UKHL 13.

[769] *Dies v British and International Mining and Finance Corp Ltd* [1939] 1 K.B. 724 (sale of goods); *Stockloser v Johnson* [1954] 1 Q.B. 476, 483, 489–490; *Mayson v Clouet* [1924] A.C. 980 (sale of land); *Galbraith v Mitchenall Estates Ltd* [1965] 2 Q.B. 473.

[770] cf. below, para.26–151.

than to deny recovery of a sum (a penalty) agreed to be payable upon breach by the contract-breaker (i.e. to grant negative relief) or to give more time to him to make a payment. In one case, the House of Lords directed the relief at the proceeds of sale where the court had made an interim order for sale pending the outcome of the litigation.[771] On the facts of *Stockloser v Johnson*, above, although the majority of the court were prepared to order that money paid be returned if it would be unconscionable for the seller to keep it, they did not think that the seller's conduct in retaining £4,750 out of the £11,000 price in one contract, and £3,500 out of the £11,000 price on another, was unconscionable, because the buyer had already received substantial benefits in the form of royalties.[772] In any event, subsequent cases tended to follow the view of the third judge, Romer L.J., that there could be relief only if there had been fraud, sharp practice or unconscionable conduct on the part of the seller.[773] In a Privy Council case in 1906, the contract-breaker obtained an order that the deposit he had paid in advance to the innocent party should, despite a forfeiture clause, be repaid to him (subject to his paying damages for the actual loss caused to the innocent party by the breach of contract),[774] but this case has not to date been followed in England.[775]

26–151 **Return of deposit.** However, a more recent Privy Council case involving a contract for the sale of land requiring a 25 per cent deposit has come closer to applying the penalty rues to a deposit. In *Workers Trust Merchant Bank Ltd v Dojap Investments Ltd*[776] it was accepted that the 10 per cent deposit which is customary in contracts for the sale of land may be forfeited by the seller on the buyer's default, irrespective of the amount of the seller's loss. However, a larger deposit would be valid only if the seller could show that it was reasonable to demand one; and in the absence of that the whole deposit was invalid and must be repaid, subject to a cross-claim for any loss suffered by the seller. It remains to be seen whether English courts will follow the lead of the Privy Council in treating deposits in this way, though the question is unlikely to arise in relation to contracts for the sale of land because of the English courts have a statutory power to order the return of a deposit.[777] The approach of the Privy Council seems less than satisfactory, however. It is not a simple application of the penalty rules, since it seems that "customary" deposits cannot be challenged. It is not clear why a 10 per cent deposit does not require justification, since it does not appear to be a genuine pre-estimate of the seller's loss, nor whether similar deposits are permissible in other contexts, such as deposits given when goods are ordered.[778] It is possible that the Privy Council assumed that all deposits other

---

[771] *On Demand Information Plc v Michael Gerson (Finance) Plc* [2002] UKHL 13.

[772] [1954] 1 Q.B. 476, 484, 492.

[773] See *Galbraith v Mitchenall Estates Ltd* [1965] 2 Q.B. 473.

[774] *Public Works Commissioner v Hills* [1906] A.C. 368 (above, para.26–130).

[775] Though the penalty rules were assumed to apply to a sum paid by way of deposit in *Pye v British Automobile Commercial Syndicate Ltd* [1906] 1 K.B. 425 (held not penal).

[776] [1993] A.C. 573.

[777] See next paragraph.

[778] If the sale is to a consumer, the deposit might be challenged under the Unfair Terms in Consumer Contract Regulations 1999, see below, para.26–156.

than in sales of land cases have to be "reasonable" or genuine pre-estimates of the loss, but this was not stated.[779]

Law of Property Act 1925 section 49(2). This provides: 26–152

> "Where the court refuses to grant specific performance of a contract, or in any action for the return of a deposit, the court may, if it thinks fit, order the repayment of any deposit."

This provision is restricted to contracts for the sale or exchange of any interest in land.[780] Apart from this provision, the vendor would be obliged to return the deposit only where he was in breach of contract[781]; the statutory discretion conferred on the court by s.49(2) enables the court to make an order where the justice of the case requires it.[782] The scope of application of this section was for a time thought to be narrow. It was said that it:

> "... was passed to remove the former hardship which existed where a defendant had a good defence in equity to a claim for specific performance but no defence in law, and, therefore, the deposit was forfeited ... outside that ambit [the jurisdiction] should only be exercised, if at all, sparingly and with caution."[783]

It now seems to be accepted that "repayment must be ordered in any circumstances which make this the fairest course between the two parties".[784] But an order will not be made in every case in which the purchaser defaults, even if the vendor does not suffer any loss: rather, the case must be somehow exceptional for an order to be made for the return of a standard 10 per cent deposit.[785] The court's jurisdiction cannot be excluded by the parties.[786]

Other forms of forfeiture provision. In *Jobson v Johnson*[787] the contract-breaker was granted relief against a clause which required him, upon breach, to 26–153

---

[779] See Beale (1993) 109 L.Q.R. 524.

[780] Law of Property Act 1925 s.49(3).

[781] *Best v Hamand* (1879) 12 Ch D 1; *Re Scott and Alvarez's Contract* [1895] 2 Ch. 603; *Beyfus v Lodge* [1925] Ch. 350; *James Macara Ltd v Barclay* [1945] K.B. 148, 156.

[782] *Finkeilkraut v Monohan* [1949] 2 All E.R. 235, 237–238. (cf. *James Macara Ltd v Barclay* [1945] K.B. 148, 156).

[783] *Michael Richards Properties Ltd v Corp of Wardens of St Saviour's Parish, Southwark* [1975] 3 All E.R. 416, 424 (Goff J.).

[784] *Universal Corp v Five Ways Properties Ltd* [1979] 1 All E.R. 553, 555 (Buckley L.J.) See also *Schindler v Pigault* [1975] 30 P. C.R. 328; *County and Metropolitan Homes Survey Ltd v Topclaim Ltd* [1997] 1 All E.R. 254 (effect of exclusion of Law of Property Act 1925 s.49(2)); *Omar v El Wakil* [2001] EWCA Civ 1090.

[785] See *Omar v El Wakil* [2001] EWCA Civ 1090, [2002] 2 P. & C.R. 3 at [37], [49] and [55]; *Tennaro Ltd v Majorarch Ltd* [2003] EWHC 2601 (Ch), [2003] 47 E.G. 154 (C.S.) at [84]; *Aribisala v St James Homes (Grosvenor Dock) Ltd* [2008] EWHC 456 (Ch), [2008] All ER (D) 201 (Mar).

[786] *Aribisala v St James Homes (Grosvenor Dock) Ltd* [2007] EWHC 1694 (Ch), [2007] 37 E.G. 234, [2007] 2 P. & C.R. DG25.

[787] [1989] 1 W.L.R. 1026, 1037, 1045–1046.

re-transfer some property to the innocent party. The relief was given in the form of an option to the innocent party to accept a sale of the relevant property by the court, with his receiving out of the proceeds the amount of his actual loss, and the surplus going to the contract-breaker.[788]

26–154 **Recovery of other prepayments.** If in a contract of sale there is no express forfeiture clause of the type discussed in the preceding paragraphs, and the seller terminates the contract upon the buyer's default, the buyer may recover any prepayment or instalments paid in part payment of the price, subject to a cross-claim by the seller for damages for the breach of contract.[789] Thus, in *Dies v British and International Mining and Finance Corp Ltd*,[790] where a buyer repudiated his contract to purchase goods, he was nevertheless held to be entitled to recover a substantial prepayment (not in the nature of a deposit) made by him, subject to a deduction in respect of the actual damage suffered by the seller through the breach of contract: the court held that if it permitted the whole prepayment to be retained by the seller, it would be permitting the retention of a penalty, not liquidated damages.[791] This decision has been distinguished by two of their Lordships in the House of Lords[792] on the ground that it concerned a sale of existing goods where no expenditure was intended to be incurred by the seller in reliance on the advance payment. It has been persuasively argued[793] that the question should depend on the construction of the clause in the contract requiring the advance payment: was the right to retain the payment intended to be conditional upon performance by the payee of his obligations, or was it intended to be a security for performance of the payer's obligations?

26–155 **The Consumer Credit Act 1974.** Some of the problems created by contractual provisions requiring payments on the occurrence of specified events will be governed by the Consumer Credit Act 1974, which is discussed in Vol.II of

---

788 The other option offered to the innocent party was to accept an order for specific performance, (i.e. to compel re-transfer of the property) if a court-directed inquiry showed that the present value of the property did not exceed the innocent party's actual loss: [1989] 1 W.L.R. 1026, 1037, 1045–1046.

789 *Palmer v Temple* (1839) 9 A. & E. 508; *Mayson v Clouet* [1924] A.C. 980; *Dies v British and International Mining and Finance Corp Ltd* [1939] 1 K.B. 724; *Stockloser v Johnson* [1954] 1 Q.B. 476, 483, 489–490; Williams, *Vendor and Purchaser*, 4th edn, p.1006.

790 [1939] 1 K.B. 724 (followed in *Rover International Ltd v Cannon Film Sales Ltd* [1989] 1 W.L.R. 912).

791 See also *R. v Ward Ltd v Bignall* [1967] 1 Q.B. 534 (Vol.II, para.43–389).

792 *Hyundai Heavy Industries Co Ltd v Papadopoulos* [1980] 1 W.L.R. 1129, 1142–1143, 1147–1148. (The contract in this case was for work and material supplied in the course of building a ship, and so it was treated as analogous to a building contract: see Beatson (1981) 97 L.Q.R. 389, 401–404; *Stocznia Gdanska SA v Latvian Shipping Co* [1998] 1 W.L.R. 574 HL.) The *Dies* [1939] 1 K.B. 724 case was also distinguished in the *Hyundai* case 1134–1136, on the ground that there was a total failure of consideration in *Dies*: see below, para.29–054.

793 Beatson (1981) 97 L.Q.R. 389, 391–401. See also Dixon J. in *McDonald v Dennys Lascelles Ltd* (1933) 48 C.L.R. 457, 477 (following termination of the contract "rights are not divested or discharged which have already been *unconditionally* acquired" (italics supplied)); and the *Fibrosa* case [1943] A.C. 32, 65 ("[t]he condition of retaining it [the advance payment] is eventual performance"; cf. at 75).

this work.[794] For instance, s.100(1) provides that where a debtor under a regulated hire-purchase (or a regulated conditional sale) agreement[795] has prematurely terminated the agreement, he shall be liable to pay the difference between the sums already paid or payable by him and one-half of the total price; but by s.100(3) the court may order payment of a smaller sum if that would be equal to the loss sustained by the creditor.[796] The court is also empowered to intervene if it determines that the relationship between the creditor and the debtor is "unfair".[797] It may determine that the relationship is unfair because of one or more of the following:

(a) any of the terms of the agreement or of any related agreement;

(b) the way in which the creditor has exercised or enforced any of his rights under the agreement or any related agreement;

(c) any other thing done (or not done) by, or on behalf of, the creditor (either before or after the making of the agreement or any related agreement).[798]

The court may, for example, require the creditor, or any associate of his, to repay (in whole or in part) any sum paid by the debtor or by a surety, reduce or discharge any sum payable by the debtor or by a surety by virtue of the agreement, or alter the terms of the agreement or of any related agreement.[799] The Act will therefore cover many of the situations which arise in practice, and the common law and equitable rules will not need to be applied. Thus, it is uncertain how far the principle discussed in paras 26–147—26–149, above, applies to hire-purchase[800] or hiring[801] agreements so as to permit the court to grant relief to a hirer against a clause providing for the forfeiture of instalments already paid or for a "minimum payment" by the hirer upon his termination of the agreement.[802] When a hire-purchase agreement is terminated by the owner

---

794 paras 33–082 et seq. deal with hiring agreements, while paras 38–002 et seq. deal with the other agreements within the scope of the Act.

795 Definitions of these agreements are examined in Vol.II, paras 38–336 et seq.

796 See Vol.II, paras 38–348—38–349; cf. the similar power conferred on the court by s.132 in the case of a regulated consumer hire agreement.

797 Consumer Credit Act 1974 ss.140A–140D, inserted by Consumer Credit Act 2006 ss.19–22. These provisions replace ss.137–140 on "extortionate credit bargains", which are repealed by s.70 and Sch.4 of the 2006 Act. See further below, paras 38–198 et seq.

798 s.140A(1).

799 s.140(B)(1). These powers can be exercised in relation to any credit agreement where the debtor is an individual (as defined in s.189(1), as amended: see para.38–015, above) or any related agreement (as defined in s.140C(4)). The fact that the agreement is an exempt, and not a regulated, agreement is immaterial, except that no order can be made in connection with a credit agreement which is an exempt agreement by virtue of s.16(6C). The new provisions came into force on April 6, 2007 (SI 2007/123 (c.6)).

800 *Campbell Discount Co Ltd v Bridge* [1961] 1 Q.B. 445, CA (on appeal, the case was decided on another point: [1962] A.C. 600); see Vol.II, paras 38–331—38–334; Diamond (1956) 19 M.L.R. 498 and (1958) 21 M.L.R. 199; Prince (1957) 20 M.L.R. 620.

801 *Galbraith v Mitchenall Estates Ltd* [1965] 2 Q.B. 473; *Barton Thompson & Co Ltd v Stapling Machines Co* [1966] Ch. 499.

802 See the proposals for reform in the Law Commission's Working Paper No.61, *Penalty Clauses and Forfeiture of Moneys Paid* (1975).

upon the hirer's default, the common law as to penalties[803] and the provisions of the Act will often protect the hirer against clauses requiring further payments, e.g. for "depreciation"; the common law rules apply to similar clauses in hiring agreements.[804] The question whether a depreciation clause is a penalty or not depends on the construction of the clause in the light of all the circumstances surrounding the particular agreement.[805]

26–156 **The Unfair Terms in Consumer Contracts Regulations 1999.**[806] These Regulations provide that in a contract between a business and a consumer an "unfair term" will not be binding on the consumer.[807] The Regulations give illustrations of terms which will, prima facie, be regarded as unfair: relevant to clauses fixing damages is "(e) requiring any consumer who fails to fulfil his obligation to pay a disproportionately high sum in compensation". So a consumer will be able to appeal to this standard, as well as to the common law on penalties.

8. THE TAX ELEMENT IN DAMAGES

26–157 **The tax element in damages.**[808] In *British Transport Commission v Gourley*,[809] a decision on the assessment of damages for loss of earnings following personal injuries caused by negligence, the House of Lords held that income tax (including the higher rates) must be taken into account in assessing damages for either actual or prospective loss of earnings. The main principle to be applied is that damages are to compensate the claimant only in respect of what he has lost, and in view of the incidence of taxation, he has in such a case lost only his *net* earnings. The rule in *Gourley*'s case (above) will apply only where two conditions are satisfied[810]: (1) the money, for the loss of which damages are awarded, would have been subject to tax as income[811]; and (2) the damages awarded to the

[803] *Bridge v Campbell Discount Co Ltd* [1962] A.C. 600, upholding the decision of the Court of Appeal in *Cooden Engineering Co Ltd v Stanford* [1953] 1 Q.B. 86; *Anglo Auto Finance Co Ltd v James* [1963] 1 W.L.R. 1042, 1049.

[804] *Robophone Facilities Ltd v Blank* [1966] 1 W.L.R. 1428.

[805] *Lombank Ltd v Excell* [1964] 1 W.L.R. 415 (interpreting *Phonographic Equipment (1958) Ltd v Muslu* [1961] 1 W.L.R. 1379).

[806] SI 1999/2083.

[807] See above, paras 15–004 et seq.

[808] *Whiteman on Income Tax*, 3rd edn (1988), paras 25–01 et seq.; Simon's *Direct Tax Service* (looseleaf), paras E4.8321—E4.836. See the Seventh Report of the Law Reform Committee, *Effect of Tax Liability on Damages*, 1958, Cmnd.501; Stevenson and Orr [1956] B.T.R. 1; Dworkin [1967] B.T.R. 315, 373.

[809] [1956] A.C. 185.

[810] The defendant must show that the second condition is satisfied: *Stoke-on-Trent City Council v Wood Mitchell & Co Ltd* [1980] 1 W.L.R. 254. (This was not a contract case.) Then the onus of proof is on the claimant to prove his damage, and thus to show that the first condition is inapplicable: *Hall v Pearlberg* [1956] 1 W.L.R. 244.

[811] Thus where the claimant is deprived of a capital asset and his damages represent its capital value, no question of income tax arises unless he also claims for loss of profits: cf. *Hall v Pearlberg* [1956] 1 W.L.R. 244; *Sykes v Midland Bank Executor and Trustee Co Ltd* [1969] 2 Q.B. 518, 536–537 (reversed on a different ground: [1971] 1 Q.B. 113). See below, para.26–163.

claimant are not subject to tax[812] in his hands.[813] If these conditions are satisfied, the rule in *Gourley*'s case will apply to the assessment of damages in contract.[814]

26–158 **Taxation on damages for wrongful dismissal.**[815] By Income Tax (Earnings and Pensions) Act 2003 ss.401(1) and 403(1),[816] any payments made on a person's retirement or removal from any office or employment are taxable[817]; the terms of the Act are wide enough to cover damages awarded for loss of earnings in an action for wrongful dismissal, although it was no doubt primarily intended to apply to agreed compensation for loss of office.[818] Tax is not chargeable on the first £30,000 of any such payment[819]; and the excess over £30,000 is subject to income tax in the normal way.[820] It has not been held (as might have been expected) that since the taxation rules covered the situation, the rule in *Gourley*'s case was ousted: instead the Court of Appeal has held that the rule in *Gourley*'s case continues to apply to the assessment of damages for wrongful dismissal where the damages are under the exempted amount (at that time, £5,000).[821] Although the court discussed the position where both the lost earnings and the damages are taxable,[822] the position where damages for wrongful dismissal exceed the exempted amount was not finally decided. At first instance it was later held that in this event notional tax should be deducted as if the total award was only for the exempted amount[823]; on the facts of the particular case, the exempted amount of £5,000 represented future earnings of £5,850 over the remaining years of the contract of employment (discounted on the basis of the cost of an annuity) and the tax to be deducted was calculated on this gross sum, after the other income of the plaintiff was taken into account to calculate the rate of tax. A second solution adopted in Scotland[824] was to assess the damages as if the whole

---

812 On the position where the damages are subject to capital gains tax (below, para.26–166).

813 See below, para.26–163. By Income Tax (Trading and Other Income) Act 2005 s.751(1) (replacing s.329 of the Income and Corporation Taxes Act 1988), where the court awards a sum which includes interest on damages in respect of personal injuries or death, that interest is not regarded as income for any income tax purpose. See *Mason v Harman* [1972] R.T.R. 1.

814 But see the splitting of the award into taxable and non-taxable elements in cases of wrongful dismissal: *Phipps v Orthodox Unit Trusts Ltd* [1958] 1 Q.B. 314 (below, para.26–159); *Parsons v B.N.M. Laboratories Ltd* [1964] 1 Q.B. 95 (below, para.26–158). cf. below, para.26–165 fn.855.

815 See Powell (1981) 10 I.L.J. 239; *Whiteman on Income Tax*, 3rd edn, Ch.15.

816 Replacing ss.148 and 188 of (and Sch.11 to) the Income and Corporation Taxes Act 1988.

817 There are a number of exemptions: see e.g. s.309 of the 2003 Act. Where an ex-employee takes legal action to recover compensation for loss of employment there is an extra-statutory exemption granted by the Inland Revenue (dated September 2, 1993) exempting his legal costs from ss.401–406: see *Simon's Direct Tax Service*, para.E4.827 and Concession A81.

818 s.401(1) refers to any payment made "either directly or indirectly in consideration or in consequence of, or otherwise in connection with, the termination of a person's employment".

819 s.403(1).

820 On the question whether the first £30,000 might be subject to capital gains tax, see Whiteman at para.15–15.

821 *Parsons v B. N. M. Laboratories Ltd* [1964] 1 Q.B. 95 (on the provision now superseded by the 2003 Act).

822 See below, para.26–165.

823 *Bold v Brough, Nicholson & Hall Ltd* [1964] 1 W.L.R. 201 (followed in *Basnett v J. & A. Jackson Ltd* [1976] I.C.R. 63, 74).

824 *Stewart v Glentaggart Ltd* (1963) S.L.T. 119. See Simon's *Direct Tax Service* (looseleaf), para.E4.833; McGregor, *Damages*, 17th edn (2003), para.14–045 (which submits that the 1998 substitution of s.148 (see now ss.401–403 of the 2003 Act) avoided the problem).

award was subject to the *Gourley* principle, and then to add to that sum a further amount which would be sufficient to cover the tax payable by the plaintiff on the excess over the exempted amount (at that time, £5,000). This is the more precise method, since it will meet the claimant's exact loss[825]; but it suffers from the disadvantage that the addition to the award of the amount of tax may cause the amount of tax payable to be increased. The second method has been adopted at first instance in England,[826] and it is submitted that it is the better method.[827]

26–159 **Method of calculating tax.** Where the damages are calculated in respect of a number of years, the *Gourley* calculation will spread the payments and the relevant tax over the same number of years.[828] The House of Lords[829] has emphasised that the courts cannot make an elaborate assessment of the claimant's tax liability, but should act on broad lines. The rate of tax to be considered is the effective rate of tax applicable to the claimant's earnings, and not the standard rate of tax[830]; moreover, the relevant rates of tax are those in force at the time of the court's judgment.[831] If the claimant's rate of tax depends partly on unearned income, the court may pay comparatively little regard to the unearned income in fixing the deduction for tax on his prospective earned income from the defendants, since the claimant is able to dispose of his private capital at any time, e.g. by settlements, covenants or gifts.[832]

26–160 **Loss of part of earnings.** Where the claimant's claim for loss of earnings represents only part of his earnings for the relevant tax year, the lost earnings are treated as the top slice of the claimant's notional total income for that year. In *Lyndale Fashion Manufacturers v Rich*[833] the plaintiff was awarded a sum as damages for loss of commission following the wrongful termination of his appointment as a salesman. The Court of Appeal held that the amount of tax to be deducted under the *Gourley* principle was to be calculated by treating the gross sum for loss of commission as the top slice of the plaintiff's notional income for the relevant year. (The notional total comprised his actual receipts in that year and the gross amount of the damages.) This top slice would therefore attract to itself all the additional tax applicable to the notional total income for that year.[834] It was also held that any expenses which would have been incurred

---

825 It is possible under this method for the award to be higher than the claimant's gross loss: *Shove v Downs Surgical* [1984] 1 All E.R. 7.

826 *Shove v Downs Surgical* [1984] 1 All E.R. 7.

827 Whiteman at para.15–023 also submits that this method should be followed. (See above, fn.824).

828 *Re Houghton Main Colliery Co Ltd* [1956] 1 W.L.R. 1219.

829 *British Transport Commission v Gourley* [1956] A.C. 185, 203, 207, 215.

830 [1956] A.C. 185, 207.

831 [1956] A.C. 185, 209.

832 *Beach v Reed Corrugated Cases Ltd* [1956] 1 W.L.R. 807 (wrongful dismissal).

833 [1973] 1 W.L.R. 73. (McGregor at para.14–046, criticises the view taken in this case that the damages would not be taxable in the hands of the plaintiff. In para.14–047 he relies on the decision of the House of Lords in *Deeny v Gooda Walker (No.2)* [1996] 1 W.L.R. 426 (see below, para.26–163 fn.841).

834 The Court of Appeal did not accept the view taken in *Re Houghton Main Colliery Ltd* [1956] 1 W.L.R. 1219 that the partial loss was not to be treated as any particular part of the claimant's income, so as to attract a higher or lower rate of tax.

in earning the lost commission should be set against the assumed additional income. The defendant is entitled to reasonable particulars of the claimant's taxable income from other sources, and of his tax assessments and allowances, since these particulars are directly relevant to the assessment of the claimant's net loss of earnings[835]; elaborate particulars, however, might increase costs, and are unnecessary, since:

> " . . . particulars should be limited to what is really reasonably necessary to enable the party seeking them to know what case he has to meet."[836]

Foreign tax laws. Foreign tax laws are to be treated in the same way as United Kingdom tax laws in this connection: if the claimant in a claim for loss of earnings is subject to foreign fiscal laws under which no tax is payable on the damages it would seem that the rule in *Gourley*'s case (above) would apply.[837] 26–161

National insurance contributions; tax rebates. On the basis of the approach adopted in *Gourley*'s case, it has been held that in the assessment of damages for wrongful dismissal, a deduction should be made for the employee's national insurance contributions which the employer would have been obliged to deduct from the employee's wages[838]; an income tax rebate received in respect of a period of unemployment should also be taken into account to reduce damages for loss of earnings during that period.[839] 26–162

Instances where the Gourley principle is irrelevant. If a sum awarded as damages for loss of profit would be subject to tax in the hands of the claimant, the tax element should be ignored in assessing damages, even though the tax likely to be levied on the damages may be less than that which would have been levied on the income (if it had been received).[840] The general principle is that if the sum paid as damages would have been taxable as income if it had been paid by the defendant without dispute, then the damages themselves are subject to 26–163

---

[835] *Phipps v Orthodox Unit Trusts Ltd* [1958] 1 Q.B. 314 (following *Monk v Redwing Aircraft Co Ltd* [1942] 1 K.B. 182, where the claimant was compelled to give particulars of other employment he had undertaken since his wrongful dismissal).

[836] *Phipps v Orthodox Unit Trusts Ltd* [1958] 1 Q.B. 314, 321.

[837] *Julien Praet et Cie SA v H. G. Poland Ltd* [1962] 1 Lloyd's Rep. 566 (where damages for breach of contract are subject to foreign taxation, the rule in *Gourley*'s case does not apply). In *John v James* [1986] S.T.C. 352, a complicated situation created possible tax liabilities in seven foreign countries (as well as the UK) over many years, but the judge calculated damages without making any deductions on account of tax.

[838] *Cooper v Firth Brown Ltd* [1963] 1 W.L.R. 418 (Vol.II, para.39–198). In a personal injury tort case, a deduction has also been made from the claimant's lost wages in respect of the contributions he did not have to make to a pension scheme to which he was obliged to belong as one of the terms of his employment: *Dews v National Coal Board* [1988] A.C. 1. (Any diminution in his ultimate pension should be valued separately: at 14–15, 18.)

[839] *Hartley v Sandholme Iron Co Ltd* [1975] Q.B. 600 (a tort case). cf. also the question of deducting a redundancy payment from damages for wrongful dismissal: see Vol.II, para.39–199.

[840] *Parsons v B.N.M. Laboratories Ltd* [1964] 1 Q.B. 95; *Diamond v Campbell-Jones* [1961] Ch. 22, 37; *Julien Praet et Cie, SA v H. G. Poland Ltd* [1962] 1 Lloyd's Rep. 566. (See, however, the splitting of damages for wrongful dismissal into separate parts—taxable and non-taxable: above, para.26–158.) cf. *Burmah S.S. Co v IRC* (1931) 16 T.C. 67.

income tax.[841] Thus, in a claim against a vendor for breach of a contract to sell land, the purchaser, a dealer in real estate, was held entitled to a sum equal to the gross amount of his profit (namely, the difference between the purchase price and the market value of the land at the date of the breach) since any damages recovered by the claimant would attract tax as part of the profits of his business.[842] Damages in respect of goods which constitute the claimant's trading stock are treated as a taxable revenue receipt.[843] If the goods would have represented a capital asset in the claimant's hands, and the damages are in respect of their capital value, the first condition in *Gourley* is not satisfied; but where the claimant recovers damages for loss of use of such goods (or for interest on their value[844]) the damages will be treated as a trading receipt in the calculation of his trading profits.[845] Other awards held to be taxable in the hands of the recipient were for loss of rent from a tenant who failed to comply with a valid notice to quit[846]; and for damages received by a Lloyd's Name from his agent.[847]

26–164 **Salvage services.** There are conflicting decisions of two judges at first instance on the question whether liability to tax is a relevant factor in assessing an award for salvage services.[848] It is submitted that the better view is that[849] the rule in *Gourley*'s case (above) is only applicable to diminish an award for damages for loss of personal earnings where the damages are not subject to tax, and thus not applicable to increase the assessment of a salvage award merely because the profit of the salvor is taxable.[850]

26–165 **Where both the lost earnings (or profits) and the damages are taxable.** The Court of Appeal[851] has upheld the practice that in cases where both the lost earnings or profits and the damages to be awarded would be taxable, the

---

[841] *Whiteman on Income Tax*, 3rd edn, paras 25–01 et seq. See *Deeny v Gooda Walker (No.2)* [1996] 1 W.L.R. 426 (HL, "payments in compensation for what would have been revenue items in the trade": at 437).

[842] *Diamond v Campbell-Jones* [1961] Ch. 22. cf. *Lyndale Fashion Manufacturers v Rich* [1973] 1 W.L.R. 73 (where the *Gourley* principle was applied to damages for loss of a salesman's commission; but McGregor at para.14–046, argues that the damages should have been treated as taxable).

[843] *Sommerfelds v Freeman* [1967] 1 W.L.R. 489.

[844] *Riches v Westminster Bank* [1947] A.C. 390 (interest awarded as damages held to be taxable); *The Norseman* [1957] P. 224 (interest).

[845] *Burmah S.S. Co v Inland Revenue Commissioners* (1931) 16 T.C. 67 (a Scots case).

[846] *Raja's Commercial College v Gian Singh & Co Ltd* [1977] A.C. 312; cf. *Stoke-on-Trent City Council v Wood Mitchell & Co Ltd* [1980] 1 W.L.R. 254 (loss of profits as part of statutory compensation for compulsory acquisition); *London and Thames Haven Oil Wharves Ltd v Attwooll* [1967] Ch. 772 (loss of trading profits: the dictum of Diplock L.J. in this case was discussed by the HL in *Deeny v Gooda Walker Ltd (No.2)* [1996] 1 W.L.R. 426.)

[847] *Deeny v Gooda Walker Ltd (No.2)* [1996] 1 W.L.R. 426.

[848] *The Telemachus* [1957] P. 47; *The Makedonia* [1958] 1 Q.B. 365; cf. *The Frisia* [1960] 1 Lloyd's Rep. 90, 94, 95, 96. McGregor at para.14–013, fn.36, submits that the decision in *The Telemachus* was wrong. On salvage, see below, para.29–136.

[849] *The Makedonia* [1958] 1 Q.B. 365.

[850] Hall (1957) 73 L.Q.R. 212, 219–220; (1958) 74 L.Q.R. 168; (1958) 21 M.L.R. 301.

[851] *Parsons v B.N.M. Laboratories Ltd* [1964] 1 Q.B. 95 ("[I]t is impossible to maintain that there can be derived from *Gourley's* case any principle requiring taxation to be taken into account in assessing damages in a situation where both the lost earnings or profits and the damages are taxable": at 136). See also *Julien Praet et Cie SA v H. G. Poland Ltd* [1962] 1 Lloyd's Rep. 566.

incidence of taxation should be ignored. The tax on the damages is left to be set off against the tax on the lost earnings or profits; "rough justice is done and a great expenditure of time and costs is saved by ignoring the tax on both sides"[852] even though the actual amounts of tax, if calculated precisely, might differ widely.[853] However, one judge has considered the incidence of taxation on both sides, in a commercial case where failure to do so would have given the plaintiff substantially more than his actual loss.[854] In some instances the court has divided the award of damages into two separate elements, one being taxable while the other is not.[855]

Capital gains tax. Capital gains tax is charged upon gains accruing to a person on the disposal of assets.[856] The list of types of property subject to capital gains tax includes: "21(1)(*a*) options, debts and incorporeal property generally" (which is wide enough to cover rights of action[857]); and: 26–166

> "22(1)(*a*) [C]apital sums received by way of compensation for any kind of damage or injury to assets or for the loss, destruction or dissipation of assets or for any depreciation or risk of depreciation of an asset."

Many instances of the receipt of damages in contract will therefore be liable to capital gains tax[858] and so the *Gourley* principle will not apply.[859] There is a wider ground, for it seems that whenever the asset lost by the claimant would have been subject to capital gains tax, the damages recovered by him in respect of its value will also be subject to the tax.[860] However, the Act provides[861] that:

---

852 *Parsons v B.N.M. Laboratories Ltd* [1964] 1 Q.B. 95, 135. It was similarly assumed that the damages would be taxable in *Dickinson v Jones Alexander & Co* [1993] 2 F.L.R. 321.

853 Exceptional cases might justify separate assessments of tax: *Parsons v B.N.M. Laboratories Ltd* [1964] 1 Q.B. 95, 137.

854 *Amstrad Plc v Seagate Technology Inc* (1997) 86 Build. L.R. 34.

855 *O'Sullivan v Management Agency and Music Ltd* [1985] Q.B. 428 (CA: claim for accounting of profits, some of which would not be taxable in the plaintiff's hands, because of the time period in question). cf. the contrary opinion at first instance in *John v James* [1986] S.T.C. 352. See also above, para.26–158 (where awards of damages for wrongful dismissal are discussed: such awards have been split into taxable and non-taxable parts) and the opinion of Lord Hunter in *Stewart v Glentaggart Ltd* (1963) S.L.T. 119 (above, para.26–158).

856 Taxation of Chargeable Gains Act 1992 s.1(1). See Simon's *Direct Tax Service* (looseleaf), Cl. 319, Cl.325–Cl.328; Whiteman, *Capital Gains Tax*, 4th edn; Sumption, *Capital Gains Tax* (looseleaf); McGregor at paras 14–062 et seq.

857 cf. Taxation of Chargeable Gains Act 1992 s.51(2). See also *O'Brien v Benson's Hosiery* [1979] S.T.C. 735 (payment by employee for release from a contract of employment was an "asset" for the purposes of capital gains tax).

858 Since the deriving of a capital sum may be a disposal of assets, a seller's damages for the buyer's failure to accept the goods may be subject to capital gains tax.

859 McGregor, paras 14–063—14–065; Whiteman at paras 6–29 et seq., 7–73 to 7–74. If damages for breach of contract awarded to a buyer or seller amount to a trading receipt in the hands of the recipient and thus liable to income tax, they will not be liable to capital gains tax: s.37 of the 1992 Act; Sumption at para.A.18.03.

860 cf. *Zim Properties v Procter* [1985] S.T.C. 90 (criticised by McGregor at paras 14–063—14–065). See also the Extra-Statutory Concession dated December 19, 1988 (see Whiteman at 18th Cum. Supp., paras 6–29 to 6–36; Sumption at D.33).

861 s.51(2).

"... sums obtained by way of compensation or damages for any wrong or injury suffered by an individual in his person or in his profession or vocation are not chargeable gains",

for the purposes of the taxation of capital gains. This provision exempts many heads of damages in tort from the new tax but it is conceivable that the words "any wrong ... suffered by an individual ... in his profession or vocation" could apply to some damages in contract, unless it is held that no breach of contract is a "wrong" in this context.[862]

9. INTEREST[863] AND RATE OF EXCHANGE

(a) *Introduction*

26–167 **Introduction.** It has always been open to the parties to make express provision in their contract for the payment of interest, which the courts will enforce[864] (except in situations covered by specific statutory provision[865]). The courts were sometimes prepared to infer an agreement to pay interest where the inference could be based on the course of dealing between the parties[866] or on a relevant trade usage.[867] In the absence of such an express or implied provision for the payment of interest, however, interest was not payable. In 1893 in the *London Chatham* case[868] the House of Lords decided that the common law does not permit the award of interest by way of general damages for delay in payment of a debt beyond the date when it was contractually due. Various statutes gave an entitlement to interest, or empowered the courts to award interest, in certain types of case.[869] In 1934 the courts were given a general statutory discretion to award interest in proceedings for debt or damages, and this was subsequently extended.[870] In 1985 the House[871] refused to depart from its previous decision,

---

[862] Provision is made for the postponement of the capital gains charge in certain circumstances, e.g. if the recipient of damages uses them to repair damaged property: s.23 of the Act. (See also ss.152–154.)

[863] See also Vol.II, paras 38–254 et seq.; *McGregor on Damages*, Ch.15.

[864] See Vol.II, paras 38–265 et seq. But see below, para.26–156 fn.858.

[865] By ss.137–140 of the Consumer Credit Act 1974 the court was empowered to reopen certain transactions where the rate of interest is "grossly exorbitant". These sections have now been replaced by ss.140A–140D (inserted by Consumer Credit Act 2006 ss.19–22), which apply when there is an unfair relationship between creditor and debtor. See above, para.26–155 and below, Vol.II, paras 38–213 et seq.) cf. ss.244 and 343 of the Insolvency Act 1986. See also below, para.26–172.

[866] *Re Anglesey* [1901] 2 Ch. 548. See also *Great Western Insurance Co v Cunliffe* (1874) L.R. 9 Ch. 525; *Re Duncan & Co* [1905] 1 Ch. 307.

[867] *Ikin v Bradley* (1818) 8 Taunt. 250; *Page v Newman* (1829) 9 B. & C. 378, 381. cf. the implied term arising under the Late Payment of Commercial Debts (Interest) Act 1998 (below, para.26–172; Vol.II. paras 38–275 et seq.).

[868] *London, Chatham and Dover Railway Co v South Eastern Railway Co* [1893] A.C. 429.

[869] See below, paras 26–172 et seq. and 26–174.

[870] See below, para.26–174 et seq.

[871] *President of India v La Pintada Compania Navegacion SA* [1985] A.C. 104 (which was further considered by the House of Lords in *President of India v Lips Maritime Corp* [1988] A.C. 395). See Mann (1985) 101 L.Q.R. 30.

though it approved a Court of Appeal decision[872] that damages could be recovered in some circumstances. Recently, however, the House has said that damages for loss of interest should be recoverable whenever the loss has been pleaded and proved.[873]

(b) *Damages for Loss of Interest at Common Law*

The starting point: no recovery. The starting point for the discussion may be taken the decision of the House of Lords in the *London Chatham* case[874] in 1893. There it was treated as well settled that as a general rule, debts do not carry interest, nor are damages available for simple later payment, so that a debtor who pays late discharges his obligation by paying the sum originally due. The House viewed this rule without enthusiasm,[875] and it is perhaps not surprising that ultimately it first should be the subject of a major exception[876] and later reduced almost to vanishing point.[877] 26–168

Finance charges on particular transaction contemplated. In 1981 an exception to the common law rule was created by the Court of Appeal[878] (and was expressly approved by the House of Lords in 1985[879]). This was that [illegible] rule in *Hadley v Baxendale*[880] (the remoteness test where a promisor with [illegible] not normally within contemplation had assumed responsibility for a type of loss [illegible] awarded where, as the result of the defendant failing [illegible]tisfied, special damages could be [illegible] money when it was due, the claimant had actually incurred interest charges[882] in obtaining finance from another source. The defendant knew that the claimant needed the payment to finance a purchase, and that, if the defendant failed to make the payment, the claimant would need to borrow the amount elsewhere. An analogous situation arose where the plaintiff was buying a machine on hire-purchase. The defendant's breach of contract led to the need to replace an expensive part of it; since it was found that the plaintiff acted reasonably in buying the replacement on hire-purchase, the defendant was held liable to pay the finance charges.[883] 26–169

Loss of interest compensable if pleaded and proved. However, in the *Sempra Metals* case[884] the House of Lords went further than the Court of Appeal. 26–170

---

[872] *Wadsworth v Lydall* [1981] 1 W.L.R. 598. (See below, para.26–169.)

[873] *Sempra Metals Ltd v Commissioners of Inland Revenue* [2007] UKHL 34, [2007] 3 W.L.R. 354.

[874] *London, Chatham and Dover Ry Co v South Eastern Railway Co* [1893] A.C. 429.

[875] See e.g. [1893] A.C. 429, at 440, 441 and 443.

[876] See next paragraph.

[877] See para.26–170.

[878] *Wadsworth v Lydall* [1981] 1 W.L.R. 598. (See above, para.26–098.)

[879] *The President of India* case [1985] A.C. 104, at 125–127.

[880] (1854) 9 Ex. 341.

[881] Above, paras 26–061—26–063.

[882] *Compania Financiera "Soleada" SA v Hamoor Tanker Corp Inc (The Borag)* [1981] 1 W.L.R. 274 (interest charges held unreasonable).

[883] *Bacon v Cooper (Metals) Ltd* [1982] 1 All E.R. 397 (see above, para.26–116).

[884] *Sempra Metals Ltd v Commissioners of Inland Revenue* [2007] UKHL 34, [2007] 3 W.L.R. 354.

It severely restricted the rule in the *London Chatham* case of 1893. Although the actual decision in the *Sempra Metals* case was on the remedy in restitution, four of their Lordships took the opportunity to limit the effect of the *London Chatham* rule to cases where the claimant does not plead or prove any losses arising from late payment of the debt due to him: the rule still prevents the award of damages for "an unparticularised and unproved claim" for interest losses.[885] But their Lordships held that at common law it is always in principle open to a claimant to plead and prove his actual interest losses (including a loss of compound interest) caused by late payment of a debt.[886] (Such a claim is subject to all the ordinary rules on damages, such as those on remoteness and mitigation,[887] and presumably also the new requirement that it was reasonable to assume that the defendant was assuming responsibility for the loss.[887a]) The actual decision in the *Sempra Metals* case permitted a claim in restitution for compound interest where a payment had been made under a mistake of law (to which a more favourable limitation rule applied than in the case of a damages claim).

(c) *Admiralty and Equity*

26–171 **Admiralty—equity jurisdiction.** In some jurisdictions outside the common law, interest could be awarded by the court, e.g. in the Admiralty [illegible] salvage award,[888] or in the equitable jurisdiction of [illegible]

(d) *Statutory Rights to Interest*

26–172 **Interest on commercial debts.** Interest is payable on certain debts under a term implied into contracts by the Late Payment of Commercial Debts (Interest) Act 1998. The Act applies to "a contract for the supply of goods or services"[890] where both parties are acting in the course of a business.[891] It is an implied[892]

---

[885] [2007] UKHL 34 at [96].

[886] [2007] UKHL 34 at [16]–[17], [94]. [100], [132] and [154]. (Lord Mance rejected the invitation to revisit the common law rule.)

[887] On the relevance of the impecuniosity of the claimant, see above, paras 26–105—26–108.

[887a] *Transfield Shipping Inc v Mercator Shipping Inc (The Achilleas)* [2008] UKHL 48, [2008] 3 W.L.R. 345. See above, paras 26–100A et seq.

[888] *The Aldora* [1975] Q.B. 748; *The Rilland* [1979] 1 Lloyd's Rep. 455.

[889] *Wallersteiner v Moir (No.2)* [1975] Q.B. 373, 388, 406; *O'Sullivan v Management Agency and Music Ltd* [1985] Q.B. 428 (fiduciary relationship). The award of interest in equity was examined (especially in relation to compound interest) in *Westdeutsche Landesbank Girozentrale v Islington LBC* [1996] A.C. 669 (below, para.26–174 fn.192) and in the *Sempra Metals* case [2007] UKHL 34.

[890] Defined by s.2(2), (3) and (4). (Some other relevant definitions are found in s.16). Certain contracts are excepted by s.2(5) (as amended): consumer credit agreements; mortgages, pledges, charges or other securities. s.12 makes provision for the conflict of laws.

[891] s.2(1). The meaning of "business" includes a profession and the activities of any government department or local or public authority (s.2(7)). By the Late Payment of Commercial Debts (Interest) Act 1998 (Commencement No.5) Order 2002 (SI 2002/1673), the provisions of the Act apply to businesses of all sizes and to the public sector.

[892] In cases where the contract provides "a substantial remedy" (as defined in s.9) for late payment of the debt, s.1(3) and Pt II of the Act (ss.7–10) permit the parties to oust or vary the right to statutory interest conferred by s.1(1).

term in any such contract that any "qualifying debt"[893] created by the contract carries simple interest (called "statutory interest" in the Act).[894] The rate of statutory interest (or the formula for calculating it) is to be prescribed by order of the Secretary of State.[895] Once statutory interest begins to run on a qualifying debt, the supplier is entitled to a fixed sum of compensation in addition to the statutory interest.[896]

Period and rate of statutory interest. Where the parties agree a date for payment of the debt, statutory interest starts to run on the next day[897]; but when the debt relates to an obligation to make an advance payment,[898] the debt is treated as created on the day when the supplier's obligation is performed.[899] In other cases, statutory interest runs after the period of 30 days from the performance of the obligation to which the debt relates[900]; or from the day when the purchaser has notice of the amount of the debt.[901] Statutory interest ceases to run when the interest would cease to run if it were carried under an express contract term.[902] But statutory interest does not run for any period where "by reason of any conduct of the supplier",[903] "the interests of justice require".[904] 26–173

(e) *Statutory Discretion to Award Interest*

Statutory power to award interest. A statutory provision may empower the court to award interest in particular circumstances, e.g. where a bill of exchange 26–174

[893] As defined by s.3(1). s.3(2) and (3) exclude debts where any other enactment or any rule of law confers a right to interest or to charge interest. By s.13, the Act applies to a qualifying debt despite any assignment of the debt or the transfer of the duty to pay it, or any change in the identity of the parties, whether by assignment, operation of law or otherwise.

[894] s.1(1).

[895] s.6. Currently set at 8% over the official dealing rate of the Bank of England: SI 2002/1675. For the purposes of s.6 the official dealing rate in force on June 30 applies in respect of interest which starts to run during the following six-month period July 1 to December 31, and the rate in force on December 31 applies to interest starting during the six-month period January 1 to June 30.

[896] s.5A, inserted by Late Payment of Commercial Debts Regulations 2002 (SI 2002/1674). The amount of compensation is fixed on a scale under the regulations by reference to the size of the debt (see reg.2(4)): £40 for an unpaid debt up to £999; £70 from £1,000 to £9,999; and £100 for £10,000 and over. (The compensation is intended for recovery costs.)

[897] s.4(3). The agreed date "may depend on the happening of an event or the failure of an event to happen": s.4(3). s.14 extends the application of the Unfair Contract Terms Act 1977 to a contract term postponing the time when a qualifying debt would otherwise arise.

[898] ss.4(4) and 11.

[899] s.11(3). s.11(4) to (7) prescribe detailed rules on advance payments in respect of part performance or the hire of goods.

[900] s.4(5)(a). If the debt arises from a period of hire of goods, the 30 days runs from the last day of that period: s.4(6).

[901] If the amount is unascertained, the 30-day period runs from the day when the purchaser has notice of the sum claimed: s.4(5)(b).

[902] s.4(7).

[903] s.5(1). "Conduct" includes any act or omission (s.5(5)) and may be relevant whether it occurs before or after the time when the debt is created (s.5(4)).

[904] s.5(1) and (2). By s.5(3) a reduced rate of statutory interest may apply if "the interests of justice require". For possible analogies, see above paras 15–064 et seq. on "unfairness", and above, para.14–084 on "reasonableness".

has been dishonoured.[905] The first general discretionary power was enacted in 1934[906] and is now found in two separate statutes covering the main courts.[907] (It should be noted that those statutes do not confer on the creditor a right to interest[908]). The High Court[909] and the county court[910] are empowered, in proceedings for the recovery of a debt or damages,[911] to include "in any sum for which judgment is given" simple[912] interest[913]; subject to any rules of court,[914] the court is given a discretion to fix the rate of interest,[915] to decide whether the interest should be on "all or any part of" the debt or damages, and for "all or any part of the period between the date when the cause of action arose" and either the date of payment (of any sum paid before judgment) or the date of judgment.[916] The claimant[917] is also entitled (subject to a similar[918] judicial discretion as to the rate of interest, the period for which it is payable, and whether it should be on all

---

[905] Bills of Exchange Act 1882 s.57. In the enactment of general powers to award interest (discussed below), this provision has been preserved: s.3(1)(c) of the Law Reform (Miscellaneous Provisions) Act 1934; s.35A(8) of the Supreme Court Act 1981; and s.69(7) of the County Courts Act 1984. See also below Vol.II, para.38–275.

[906] The Law Reform (Miscellaneous Provisions) Act 1934 s.3(1).

[907] The new statutory provisions were the result of the Law Commission's *Report on Interest* No.88, 1978, Cmnd.722a. The Law Commission has since proposed further improvements, including that the court should have power to award compound interest. See *Pre-Judgment Interest on Debts and Damages* (Law Com. No.287, 2004).

[908] cf. above, para.26–172; below, para.26–182.

[909] By s.35A of the Supreme Court Act 1981 (which was inserted by s.15 of and Sch.1 to the Administration of Justice Act 1982). For the power given to arbitrators, see below, para.26–157.

[910] By s.69 of the County Courts Act 1984. Section 3 of the Law Reform (Miscellaneous Provisions) Act 1934 which is examined in the 25th edition of this work (Vol.I, paras 1745–1747) remains in force for courts of record other than the High Court and county court.

[911] The House of Lords held that the words "any debt or damages" in s.3(1) of the 1934 Act, above: ". . . are very wide, so that they cover any sum of money which is recoverable by one party from another, either at common law or in equity or under a statute of the kind here concerned." (viz the Law Reform (Frustrated Contracts) Act 1943.) *B.P. Exploration Co (Libya) Ltd v Hunt (No.2)* [1983] 2 A.C. 352, 373. This statement should also apply to ss.35A and 69 of the present Acts, above.

[912] *Wentworth v Wiltshire CC* [1993] 2 All E.R. 256, 269 (also at 263) (not a contract case). Section 3 of the 1934 Act explicitly excluded "the giving of interest upon interest": see *Bushwell Properties Ltd v Vortex Properties Ltd* [1975] 1 W.L.R. 1649 ("the court is not to award interest on such part of the sum claimed as represents contractual interest": at 1660). (The decision was reversed on another point: [1976] 1 W.L.R. 591.) The Law Commission has recommended that the courts be given power to award compound interest: see *Pre-Judgment Interest on Debts and Damages* (Law Com. No.287, 2004).) (Both the Canadian and Australian courts have allowed compound interest: see McInnes 118 (2002) L.Q.R. 516.) In equity, compound interest has been awarded for profits made through breach of a fiduciary duty: *Wallersteiner v Moir (No.2)* [1975] Q.B. 373. In *Westdeutsche Landesbank Girozentrale v Islington LBC* [1996] A.C. 699, the House of Lords held that in equity compound interest may be awarded only in cases of fraud or against a trustee (or other person in a fiduciary position) in respect of profits improperly made by him. See also *Mathew v T.M. Sutton Ltd* [1994] 1 W.L.R. 1455, 1463.

[913] For interest on arbitration awards and judgment debts, see below, paras 26–183, 26–184.

[914] See below, para.26–179.

[915] See below, paras 26–178—26–179.

[916] subs.(1) of ss.35A and 69 respectively. After the judgment, interest is payable under a different authority: see below, para.26–184. On the time of "entering up" a judgment, see *Parsons v Mather & Platt Ltd* [1977] 1 W.L.R. 855.

[917] In the Act, the "plaintiff" is defined as the person seeking the debt or damages: s.35A(7) and s.69(6) respectively.

[918] As in subs.(1) above.

or only part of the debt or damages) to the award of simple interest where the defendant pays the whole of a debt to the claimant after proceedings for its recovery were instituted but before any judgment.[919] Where an action has been brought for damages for breach of contract, payment of the amount claimed prior to the hearing does not extinguish the cause of action[920]: hence, when the payment does not include interest on the amount claimed, the court can still award the damages and interest under the statute.[921] It should be noted, however, that neither enactment[922] gives the court a discretionary power to award interest on any sum paid late before any proceedings for its recovery have been begun.[923] This applies to late payment of the whole or part of a debt and to a sum paid as damages before the commencement of proceedings.[924] But interest may arise as of *right* under other statutory provisions,[925] such as under the Late Payment of Commercial Debts (Interest) Act 1998.[926] Any claim for interest, whether under the statutory provisions or otherwise, must be specifically pleaded.[927] Special rules apply to the award of interest on damages in respect of death or personal injuries.[928]

Exercise of the discretion to award interest. The basic principle[929] is that the court should award interest wherever the defendant's breach of contract deprived the claimant of the opportunity to put the subject-matter of the claim to work to earn profits or income.[930] So where the buyer failed to pay the price of goods sold and delivered to him, interest has been awarded: 26–175

> "... on the simple commercial basis that if the money had been paid at the appropriate commercial time, the other side would have had the use of it."[931]

---

[919] Subs.(3) of ss.35A and 69 respectively. (This provision is wider than s.3 of the 1934 Act.)

[920] *Edmunds v Lloyd Italico, etc., SpA* [1986] 1 W.L.R. 492, 495. (The payment merely gives rise to an equitable set-off which could be used as a potential cross-claim.)

[921] *Edmunds v Lloyd Italico, etc., SpA* [1986] 1 W.L.R. 492. (The defendant could resist any attempt to levy execution on the judgment which failed to give credit for the amount already paid.)

[922] See fnn.909 and 910, above.

[923] *I.M. Properties Plc v Cape & Dalgleish (A Firm)* [1999] Q.B. 297 CA. In *President of India v La Pintada Compania Navigacion SA* [1985] A.C. 104, 129–131, the House of Lords considered this to be a gap in the law. cf. *Mathew v T.M. Sutton Ltd* [1994] 1 W.L.R. 1455.

[924] *I.M. Properties Plc v Cape & Dalgleish* [1999] Q.B. 297 CA. (The court also said that the court had no power to award interest on any sum paid by a third party in reduction of the plaintiff's claim against the defendant: at 306, but cf. 308).

[925] See below, para.26–182.

[926] Above, paras 26–172 et seq.

[927] CPR r.16.4(2): the claimant must give details of the legal basis of the claim and, where a specified amount of money is claimed, the percentage rate claimed, the date from which it is claimed, the total amount claimed up to the date of calculation, and the daily rate at which interest accrues after that date.

[928] 1981 Act s.35A; s.69(2) of the 1984 Act. (In particular the court is required, in the absence of special reasons, to award interest on such damages.) See *McGregor on Damages*, 17th edn (2003), paras 15–046 et seq. and standard textbooks on tort.

[929] cf. the statement in a personal injury (tort) case: *Jefford v Gee* [1970] 2 Q.B. 130, 146.

[930] Interest should be awarded only on money which has been wrongfully withheld: *Business Computers Ltd v Anglo-African Leasing Ltd* [1977] 1 W.L.R. 578, 587–8.

[931] *Kemp v Tolland* [1956] 2 Lloyd's Rep. 681, 691. cf. *Marsh v Jones* (1889) 40 Ch D 563.

Where the seller failed to deliver the goods, the buyer's damages should include interest on the normal measure of the damages, viz the difference between the contract price and the market price for substitute goods available at the date fixed for delivery.[932] Again, where the claimant has reasonably incurred expenditure as the result of the defendant's breach,[933] interest should be awarded as damages in respect of that expenditure.[934] The court should not award interest if that would give the claimant double recovery for the same loss: the use of property, or the receipt of the income arising from its use, is the equivalent of interest earned by a sum of money.[935] For instance, if the seller retains income-producing property, which would have been transferred to the buyer had he paid the price, the seller should not be given interest on the price if he is entitled to the income arising from the property during the delay until the price is paid.[936] Where the breach of contract deprives the claimant of the use of land or goods, and the court awards him damages for the loss of that use (e.g. loss of rents or profits), he should not also be awarded interest on the value (or price) of the land or goods.[937]

26–176 **Period of interest.** In principle, interest should run only from the date (after accrual of the cause of action) when the claimant incurred the loss in question.[938] The court has a discretion to fix a later date,[939] as where the claimant has unreasonably delayed bringing his action.[940] A question about the relevant dates from which interest should run arises when the claimant was insured against the particular loss. In one case,[941] the Court of Appeal was prepared to award interest on damages for the period after the plaintiffs were in fact indemnified by their insurers in respect of the loss. The court implied a term into the contract of insurance, to the effect that the plaintiffs could retain any interest awarded which accrued before the insurers paid the plaintiffs, but that any interest for a later period must go to the insurers.

---

932 *Panchaud Frères v Pagnan and Fratelli* [1974] 1 Lloyd's Rep. 394, 411, 414. See Vol.II, paras 43–420 et seq.

933 See above, paras 26–078, 26–120.

934 *Harbutt's "Plasticine" v Wayne Tank and Pump Co* [1970] 1 Q.B. 447. (Overruled on another point: see above, para.14–022.)

935 *Fletcher v Tayleur* (1855) 17 C.B. 21, 29 (delay in building a ship); *British Columbia Saw Mill Co Ltd v Nettleship* (1868) L.R. 3 C.P. 499, 507 (delay in obtaining replacement for goods lost by carrier); *Jaques v Millar* (1877) 6 Ch D 153 (lease); cf. *Bushwall Properties Ltd v Vortex Properties Ltd* [1975] 1 W.L.R. 1649 (reversed on another point: [1976] 1 W.L.R. 591).

936 cf. *Janred Properties Ltd v Ente Nazionale Italiano per il Turismo* [1989] 2 All E.R. 444, 456–457.

937 *Trafigura Beheer BV v Mediterranean Shipping Co SA* [2007] EWCA Civ 794, [2007] 2 Lloyd's Rep. 622 at [42] (conversion).

938 *Harbutt's "Plasticine" v Wayne Tank and Pump Co* [1970] 1 Q.B. 447; *Metal Box Co Ltd v Currys Ltd* [1988] 1 W.L.R. 175 (tort: damages for value of destroyed chattel). cf. above, para.26–078.

939 This is illustrated in cases not involving breach of contract: *General Tire and Rubber Co v Firestone Tyre and Rubber Co* [1975] 1 W.L.R. 819 (infringement of patent); *B.P. Exploration Co (Libya) v Hunt (No.2)* [1979] 1 W.L.R. 783 (upheld in [1983] A.C. 353) (restitution following frustration).

940 *Metal Box Co Ltd v Currys Ltd* [1988] 1 W.L.R. 175. Another illustration of a later date is the payment of demurrage: *President of India v Lips Maritime Corp* [1988] A.C. 395, 424–425.

941 *H. Cousins & Co v D. and C. Carriers Ltd* [1971] 2 Q.B. 230.

No power where interest already running. The relevant statutes provide that interest in respect of a debt must not be awarded "for a period during which, for whatever reason, interest on the debt already runs".[942] Hence, if the contract itself fixes interest, the court can only enforce that provision: its statutory power does not override the contractual provision, e.g. the court may not fix a different rate of interest. 26–177

Rates of interest. The court is empowered to award interest "at different rates in respect of different periods".[943] In business[944] contexts, the rate of interest should reflect the current commercial rate.[945] The approach of the Commercial Court is to award interest at a rate which broadly represents the rate at which the successful party would have had to borrow the amount recovered over the period in question.[946] The Court of Appeal has upheld the practice of the Commercial Court to award interest at a borrower's rate of 1 per cent above the base rate prevailing from time to time,[947] but this is only a presumption which can be displaced if its application would be unfair to either party.[948] The Court of Appeal has recognised that the borrowing costs of small businesses are often higher than for first class borrowers for whom one per cent above base rate is appropriate: interest on damages at three per cent above base rate was awarded.[949] 26–178

Rules of court may be made[950] fixing the rate of interest which the court may award by reference to the rate fixed from time to time for judgment debts under the Judgments Act 1838[951] or by reference to a rate for which any other enactment provides. The Civil Procedure Rules 1998 contain provisions about interest when the claimant seeks judgment by default, when the claimant makes an offer or when the defendant makes a payment into court. Where the claimant claims interest on a specified amount of money (under s.35A of the 1981 Act or 26–179

[942] s.35A(4) of the 1981 Act and s.69(4) of the 1984 Act respectively. See below, para.26–182.

[943] 1981 Act, s.35A(6); s.69(5) of the 1984 Act. Delay by the claimant in progressing his claim may be reflected in a reduced rate of interest for the overall period (instead of depriving him of all interest for the period of the delay): *Derby Resources A.G. v Blue Corinth Marine Co Ltd (No.2)* [1998] 2 Lloyd's Rep. 425.

[944] In cases where one party is a private person, the Court of Appeal is reluctant to interfere with the judge's discretion in fixing the rate of interest: *Watts v Morrow* [1991] 1 W.L.R. 1421, 1443–1444, 1446.

[945] cf. *The Mecca* [1968] P. 665, 672.

[946] *Cremer v General Carriers SA* [1974] 1 W.L.R. 341, 355–358.

[947] *Polish S.S. Co v Atlantic Maritime Co* [1985] Q.B. 41, 67 (followed in *Metal Box Co Ltd v Currys Ltd* [1988] 1 W.L.R. 175, 182–183 (insurers subrogated to a claim in tort for loss of chattels)). For a recent example *see National Westminster Bank Plc v Rabobank Nederland* [2007] EWHC 1742 (Comm), [2007] All E.R. (D) 477. (Base rate replaces the minimum lending rates and the London Interbank Offered Rate, previously used: see *Cia Banca de Panama SA v George Wimpey & Co Ltd* [1980] 1 Lloyd's Rep. 598, 615–617; *Shearson Lehman Hutton Inc v Maclaine Watson & Co Ltd* [1990] 3 All E.R. 723, 732–733.)

[948] The *Shearson Lehman* case [1990] 3 All E.R. 723, 733. Evidence is admissible as to the rate at which persons with the general attributes of the claimant could have borrowed the money: *Tate & Lyle Food and Distribution Ltd v G.L.C.* [1982] 1 W.L.R. 149, 154–155.

[949] *Jaura v Ahmed* [2002] EWCA Civ 210, [2002] 4 C.L. 130.

[950] Under s.35A(5) of the 1981 Act. See CPR r.12.6, below.

[951] Judgments Act 1838 s.17. See below, para.26–184.

s.69 of the 1984 Act) at a rate no higher than that payable on judgment debts[952] at the date when the claim form was issued, a default judgment may include the amount of interest to the date of judgment.[953] If the claim is for a different rate of interest, the default judgment must exclude interest but judgment may be entered for interest to be decided by the court.[954] A claimant's Pt 36 offer which offers to accept a sum of money, or a Part 36 payment notice (which accompanies a payment into court) will, unless it indicates to the contrary, be treated as inclusive of all interest until the last date on which it could be accepted without needing the court's permission.[955]

26–180 **Debt or damages in foreign currency.** When the debt or damages are calculated in a foreign currency, the rate of interest should be the commercial borrowing rate in that currency in the relevant country.[956]

26–181 **Rate of exchange.** The question of the appropriate rate of exchange when the debt or damages for breach of contract are calculable in a foreign currency is examined in Ch.30.[957]

26–182 **Interest due as of right.** The general statutory powers to award interest which have been examined in the preceding paragraphs do not apply where interest is payable under the terms of the contract itself[958] or under some other special provision.[959] Thus, the Late Payment of Commercial Debts (Interest) Act 1998 confers on the creditor a right under an implied term to "statutory interest" on "qualifying debts" where both parties are acting in the course of a business.[960] Similarly, where the contract itself[961] entitles the seller to claim interest on the price, the seller is not dependent on the exercise of the court's discretion and the court can award interest only at the rate specified in the contract.[962] A suitably

---

[952] See below, para.26–184.

[953] CPR r.12.6.

[954] CPR r.12.6(2). The procedure for deciding the amount of interest is set out in CPR r.12.7.

[955] CPR r.36.22. If the offer or notice is expressed not to include interest, it must state whether interest is offered, and, if so, the amount offered, the rate offered and the period for which it is offered: CPR r.36.22(2).

[956] *Miliangos v George Frank (Textiles) (No.2)* [1977] Q.B. 489, 497; *Helmsing Schiffahrts v Malta Drydocks Corp* [1977] 2 Lloyd's Rep. 444, 449. See further below, paras 30–369—30–378; and Bowles and Phillips (1976) 39 M.L.R. 196.

[957] Below, paras 30–369—30–378.

[958] For illustrations, see Vol.II, paras 38–265 et seq. In a contract of loan where the lender is given a discretion to vary the interest rate, there is an implied term to the effect that the rates of interest will not be set dishonestly, for an improper purpose, capriciously or arbitrarily: *Paragon Finance Plc v Staunton* [2001] EWCA Civ 1466, [2002] 1 W.L.R. 685.

[959] By s.35A(4) of the Supreme Court Act 1981 and s.69(4) of the County Courts Act 1984 the court must not award interest in respect of a debt "for a period during which, for whatever reason, interest on the debt already runs".

[960] Above, para.26–172; below, Vol.II, paras 38–275 et seq.

[961] A course of dealing between the parties, or the custom or usages of a particular trade, may lead to an implied term that interest may be charged: see above, para.26–167.

[962] Consumer Credit Act 1974 ss.140A–140D enable the court to re-open certain transactions: see above, para.26–155. (cf. ss.244 and 343 of the Insolvency Act 1986). See Vol.II, paras 38–213 et seq.

worded contractual clause may fix interest to run beyond judgment for the debt.[963]

(f) *Interest on Arbitration Awards*

Arbitration awards. At common law an arbitrator has no power to award general damages in respect of interest on debts paid late.[964] But s.49 of the Arbitration Act 1996[965] provides that (unless the parties agree otherwise) the arbitral tribunal may award simple or compound interest from such date at such rates and with such rests as it considers meets the justice of the case. Such interest may be awarded on the whole or any part of: (a) the amount awarded in respect of any period up to the award[966]; and (b) any amount which was claimed in the arbitration and outstanding at the commencement of the arbitral proceedings, but was paid before the award was made in respect of any period up to the date of payment.[967] This power is similar to that granted to courts[968] but wider in that compound interest may be awarded.[969] But the arbitral tribunal cannot award interest on a debt which was paid late but before the proceedings began.[970] 26–183

(g) *Interest on Judgment Debts*

Interest on judgment debts and arbitration awards. A special enactment prescribes the rate of interest on a High Court judgment debt from the time of entering up the judgment[971]: the current rate is fixed from time to time by 26–184

---

[963] *Economic Assurance Society v Usborne* [1902] A.C. 147. It is not an "unfair term" under the Unfair Terms in Consumer Contracts Regulations 1999 in a loan agreement that interest at the contractual rate would be charged until payment after (as well as before) any judgment: *Director General of Fair Trading v First National Bank Plc* [2001] UKHL 52, [2002] 1 A.C. 481. See above, para.15–069; below Vol.II, para.38–277.

[964] *President of India v La Pintada Compania Navegacion SA* [1985] A.C. 104. See above, para.26–147. (In the same case it was held that the Admiralty jurisdiction does not extend to the award of interest on debts already paid, nor to the award of compound interest.)

[965] Since an arbitration agreement impliedly empowers the arbitrator to decide the dispute according to the law existing at the date of his award, Arbitration Act 1996 s.49 applies to all arbitration agreements under the Act, whenever made: *Food Corp of India v Marastro Compania Naviera SA of Panama (The Trade Fortitude)* [1987] 1 W.L.R. 134 (decided on the previous Act).

[966] See below, para.26–184 for interest after the date of the award.

[967] s.49(3). By s.49(6) the provisions in s.49(3) do not affect any other power of the tribunal to award interest, e.g. above, para.26–182.

[968] See above, paras 26–174 et seq. The power of the arbitral tribunal applies whether the sum claimed is a debt or damages: *Edmunds v Lloyd Italico, etc. SpA* [1986] 1 W.L.R. 492, 495–496 (decided on the preceding Act).

[969] See above, para.26–174.

[970] See the *President of India* [1985] A.C. 104. (cf. above, para.26–174).

[971] Judgments Act 1838 s.17 (as amended by s.44(1) of the Administration of Justice Act 1970 which empowers the making of an order amending the rate of interest in s.17). The interest runs from the time of entering up a judgment, on which see *Parsons v Mather & Platt Ltd* [1977] 1 W.L.R. 855 (approved by the Court of Appeal in *Erven Warnink B.V. v J. Townend & Sons (Hull) Ltd* [1982] 3 All E.R. 312). An order for payment of costs ranks as a judgment; but interest on costs cannot be ordered from a date earlier than the date on which judgment was given: *Nykredit Mortgage Bank Plc v Edward Erdman Group Ltd* [1997] 1 W.L.R. 1627 HL (a decision on RSC Ord.42 r.1 that an order for costs cannot be backdated to the date on which judgment had been given in a lower court).

statutory instrument.[972] County Court judgments[973] for £5,000 or more also carry interest at the same rate.[974] The rate of interest is fixed at the rate in force at the time the judgment was entered up: it does not fluctuate in accordance with later statutory instruments made before the judgment or award is satisfied.[975] By statute,[976] an arbitrator has discretion to decide whether an award should or should not carry interest.[977] By the Arbitration Act 1996[978] an arbitral tribunal may award simple or compound interest from the date of the award (or any later date) until payment: it has discretion to fix the rates of interest and the rests (if any).

[972] For judgments entered up after April 1, 1993, the rate is 8%: see Judgment Debts (Rate of Interest) Order 1993 (SI 1993/564). On the time from which interest begins to run, see CPR r.40.8. However, a clause in the contract may explicitly fix a rate to run on a judgment for a debt: see above, para.26–182.

[973] By s.74 of the County Courts Act 1984 the Lord Chancellor is empowered to provide by order that county court judgments or orders shall carry interest.

[974] The County Courts (Interest on Judgment Debts) Order 1991 (SI 1991/1184). Some judgments are excluded from the provision. By SI 1998/2400 (L.9) county court judgments in respect of qualifying debts under the Late Payment of Commercial Debts (Interest) Act 1998 (see above, para.26–172) are included in the 1991 Order.

[975] *Rocco Giuseppe & Figli v Tradax Export SA* [1984] 1 W.L.R. 742; cf. the decision of the Privy Council on a New Zealand provision: *Rowling v Takaro Properties Ltd* [1988] 1 All E.R. 163.

[976] Arbitration Act 1996 s.49(4).

[977] Under the previous statutory power (s.20 of the Arbitration Act 1950) it was held that if the arbitration award was silent on the question, it automatically carried interest: *Continental Grain Co v Bremer Handelsgesellschaft mbH (No.2)* [1984] 1 Lloyd's Rep. 121.

[978] s.49(4).

CHAPTER 27

SPECIFIC PERFORMANCE AND INJUNCTION[1]

	PARA.
1. Introduction	27–001
2. The "adequacy" of damages	27–005
3. Contracts not specifically enforceable	27–020
4. Other grounds for refusing specific performance	27–030
5. Mutuality of remedy	27–046
6. Specific performance and third parties	27–049
(a) Claim by promisee	27–050
(b) Claim by third party	27–053
7. Specific performance with compensation	27–054
8. Injunction	27–060
9. Damages and specific performance or injunction	27–077

1. INTRODUCTION

Generally. The common law did not specifically enforce contractual obligations except those to pay money.[2] Specific enforcement of other contractual obligations was available only in equity. For the claimant, this was often a more advantageous remedy than the common law remedy of damages. With reference to this equitable remedy, Fry L.J. in his work on *Specific Performance* wrote: 27–001

> "If a contract be made and one party to it make default in performance, there appears to result to the other party a right at his election either to insist on the actual performance of the contract, or to obtain satisfaction for the non-performance of it. It may be suggested from this that it follows . . . that it ought to be assumed that every contract is specifically enforceable until the contrary be shown. But so broad a proposition has never, it is believed, been asserted by the judges of the Court of Chancery or their successors in the High Court of Justice, though if prophecy were the function of a law writer, it might be suggested that they will more and more approximate to such a rule."[3]

This prophecy has not been wholly fulfilled, for the scope of the remedy remains subject to many limitations.

Bases of limitations on the remedy. These limitations are based on a number of factors. The first is "the heavy-handed nature of the enforcement mechanism,"[4] by reason of which specific enforcement leads (more readily than an 27–002

---

[1] Fry, *Specific Performance* (6th ed.); Jones and Goodhart, *Specific Performance* (2nd ed., 1996); Sharpe, *Injunctions and Specific Performance* (2nd ed.); Spry, *Equitable Remedies* (5th ed.).

[2] See above, paras 26–009, 26–122; below, para.27–004.

[3] See now 6th ed., p.21; *cf.* Burrows (1984) 4 L.S. 102.

[4] *Co-operative Insurance Society Ltd v Argyll Stores (Holdings) Ltd* [1998] A.C. 1, 12.

award of damages) to attachment of the defendant's person.[5] But this is an important factor only where the contract calls for "personal" performance, by the defendant himself. Where the contract is not of this kind, it can be specifically enforced without personal constraint[6]: *e.g.* by sequestration, the appointment of a receiver[7] or by the execution of a formal document by an officer of the court.[8] The second is that the specific enforcement of certain contracts, especially of those for the sale of goods or shares for which there is a market, could, in effect, conflict with the requirement that the claimant must mitigate his loss by making a substitute contract where this was reasonably possible.[9] Although certain limitations on the scope of specific enforcement are thus justifiable, others are more open to debate: this is, in particular, true of the limitations which are based on the arguments that in certain situations specific relief is either unnecessary or impracticable.[10] In a number of later authorities, some of these reasons are no longer regarded as entirely convincing, so that these cases support some expansion in the scope of the remedy.[11] The most recent decision of the House of Lords[12] on the point may, however, foreshadow some degree of return to a more restrictive view, though with modern justifications.

27–003 **Scope of the remedy.** The jurisdiction to order specific performance is based on the existence of a valid, enforceable contract. The scope of the remedy is in one respect wider than that of an action for damages, since specific performance may be ordered before there has been any breach.[13] It will not be ordered if the contract suffers from some defect, such as failure to comply with formal requirements or mistake or illegality, which makes the contract invalid or unenforceable: these matters are discussed elsewhere in this book. But even if the contract is unimpeachable in these respects, specific performance will not necessarily be ordered; and the present chapter is mainly concerned with limitations on the availability of the remedy where the contract is not defective.

27–004 **Meaning of "specific performance".** The term "specific performance" will here be used in its traditional sense, to refer to the remedy available in equity to compel a person actually to perform a contractual obligation. Where a person has

[5] *cf. Enfield LBC v Mahoney* [1983] 1 W.L.R. 749, where even imprisonment failed to induce compliance with an order for specific restitution. "Lawful arrest or detention of a person for non-compliance with the lawful order of a court" is permitted by Human Rights Act 1998, Sch.1, Pt I, art.5(1)(b).

[6] *cf.* Corbin, *Contracts*, para.1138.

[7] *Miliangos v George Frank (Textiles) Ltd* [1976] A.C. 443, 494, 497.

[8] *Astro Exito Navegacion SA v Southland Enterprise Co Ltd (The Messiniaki Tolmi)* [1983] 2 A.C. 787.

[9] Above, para.26–103; *Buxton v Lister* (1746) 3 Atk. 383, 384; *Re Schwabacher* (1908) 98 L.T. 127; *cf. Colt v Nettervill* (1725) 2 P.Wms. 301 (defendant given option of transferring shares or paying the difference between contract and market price on date fixed for performance). See also *Whiteley Ltd v Hilt* [1918] 2 K.B. 808.

[10] *e.g.* below, paras 27–015, 27–026.

[11] *e.g.* below, paras 27–005, 27–017, 27–023.

[12] *Co-operative Insurance Society Ltd v Argyll Stores Ltd* [1998] A.C. 1.

[13] *Roy v Kloepfer Wholesale Hardware and Automotive Corp.* [1951] 3 D.L.R. 122; *Thomas Feather & Co v Keighley Corp.* (1953) 52 L.G.Rev. 30; *Hasham v Zenab* [1960] A.C. 316; (1960) 76 L.Q.R. 200. And see below, para.27–078, n.428.

under a contract become liable to pay a fixed sum of money, the actual performance of that obligation can be enforced by bringing an action for that sum, *e.g.* where a seller of goods sues for the price or where a person who has done work sues for the agreed remuneration. But such actions are not usually described in English law as actions for specific performance and are not subject to the limitations on the scope of that remedy which are considered in the following sections[14] of the present chapter.

2. THE "ADEQUACY" OF DAMAGES

Appropriateness of the remedy. The historical foundation of the equitable jurisdiction to order specific performance of a contract is that the claimant cannot obtain a sufficient remedy by the common law judgment for damages.[15] Hence the traditional view was that specific performance would not be ordered where damages were an "adequate" remedy.[16] Typically, this would be the case where the claimant could readily make a substitute contract for a performance equivalent to that promised by the defendant: the claimant would then be adequately compensated by damages based on the difference between the cost (or market price) of the substitute, and the contract price. Indeed, an award of specific performance in such a case could conflict with the mitigation requirement and be oppressive to the defendant.[17] Some of the early authorities[18] approach this problem by asking whether damages would *in fact* adequately compensate the claimant. At a later stage in the development of the subject, the courts tended rather to ask whether damages were *likely* to be an adequate remedy for breach of the *type* of contract before the court.[19] But more recently the courts have reverted to the earlier approach, by asking whether specific performance was the most *appropriate* remedy in the circumstances of each case.[20] The question is not whether damages are an "adequate" remedy, but whether specific performance will "do more perfect and complete justice than an award of damages."[21] The point was well put in a case in which an interim injunction was sought: "The standard question . . . , 'Are damages an adequate remedy?' might perhaps, in 27–005

[14] The mitigation rules may sometimes be relevant to the issue whether the action for the agreed sum is available: see above, para.26–108. For the relevance of these rules to claims for specific performance, see above, para.27–002 at n.9.

[15] *Harnett v Yielding* (1805) 2 Sch. & Lef. 549, 553.

[16] *Co-operative Insurance Society Ltd v Argyll Stores (Holdings) Ltd* [1998] A.C. 1, 11; *Bankers Trust Co v P.T. Jakarta International Hotels Development* [1999] 1 Lloyd's Rep. 910 at 911.

[17] See *Re Schwabacher* (1908) 98 L.T. 127 and other authorities cited in para.27–002 n.9. For oppression in cases of specific relief by way of injunction, see also below, para.27–063.

[18] *e.g. Adderley v Dixon* (1824) 1 S. & S. 607, 610.

[19] *e.g. Cohen v Roche* [1927] 1 K.B. 169.

[20] *Beswick v Beswick* [1968] A.C. 58, 88, 90–91, 102; *cf. Coulls v Bagot's Executor and Trustee Co* [1967] A.L.R. 385, 412.

[21] *Tito v Waddell (No.2)* [1977] Ch. 106, 322; *Rainbow Estates Ltd v Tokenhold Ltd* [1999] Ch. 64 at 72–73.

the light of the authorities in recent years, be rewritten: 'Is it just, in all the circumstances, that a plaintiff should be confined to his remedy in damages?' "[22]

27–006 **Where action for agreed sum available.** A similar approach has been adopted to the analogous question whether specific performance could be ordered where the common law action for the agreed sum is also available. At one time, a negative answer was given to this question, apparently because the common law remedy was regarded as an "adequate" one.[23] But the current view is that specific performance can be ordered in cases of this kind, if in all the circumstances it is the most appropriate remedy.[24]

27–007 **Land.** The law takes the view that the purchaser of a particular piece of land or of a particular house (however ordinary) cannot, on the vendor's breach, obtain a satisfactory substitute, so that specific performance is available to the purchaser.[25] It seems that this is so even though the purchaser has bought for resale. Even a contractual licence to occupy land, though creating no interest in the land[26] can be specifically enforced.[27] A vendor of land, too, can get specific performance[28]; for damages will not adequately compensate him if he cannot easily find another purchaser or if he is anxious to rid himself of burdens attached to the land. It seems to make no difference that the land is readily saleable to a third party; or even that after contract but before completion a compulsory

---

[22] *Evans Marshall & Co Ltd v Bertola SA* [1973] 1 W.L.R. 349, 379 (and see the subsequent proceedings: [1975] 2 Lloyd's Rep. 373); *cf.* in a different but analogous context *Miliangos v George Frank (Textiles) Ltd* [1976] A.C. 443.

[23] *e.g. Crampton v Varna Ry* (1872) L.R. 7 Ch.App. 562, 567 ("a money contract not enforceable in this court").

[24] *e.g. Beswick v Beswick* [1968] A.C. 58; the burden is on the claimant to show that the common law remedy is not adequate: *C.N. Maritime Inc v Stena Line A/B (The Stena Nautica) (No.2)* [1982] 2 Lloyd's Rep. 336, 348.

[25] Fry, *Specific Performance*, para.62; unless he elects to claim damages, as in *Meng Long Development Pte Ltd v Jip Hong Trading Co Pte Ltd* [1985] A.C. 511. Damages are, however, an adequate remedy for breach of a "lock-out" agreement relating to land (above, para.2–121) since such an agreement is intended merely to protect the prospective purchaser from wasting costs and does not give him any right to insist on conveyance of the land: *Tye v House* [1997] 2 E.G.L.R. 171.

[26] See *Ashburn Anstalt v Arnold* [1989] Ch. 1; overruled on another ground in *Prudential Assurance Co Ltd v London Residuary Body* [1992] A.C. 386.

[27] *Verrall v Great Yarmouth B.C.* [1981] Q.B. 202. *cf. Dutton v Manchester Airport plc* [1999] 2 All E.R. 657, where the claim by the licensee was not against the landlord but against a trespasser.

[28] *Lewis v Lechmere* (1722) 10 Mod. 503, 505; *Kenney v Wexham* (1822) 6 Madd. 355; *Adderley v Dixon* (1824) 1 S. & S. 607, 622; *Clifford v Turrell* (1841) 1 Y. & C.C.C. 138; *Walker v Eastern Counties Ry* (1848) 6 Hare 594; *Miliangos v George Frank (Textiles) Ltd* [1976] A.C. 443, 496; *cf. Amec Properties v Planning Research & Systems* [1992] 1 E.G.L.R.70 (specific performance against prospective lessee). Where the purchaser has been allowed to go into possession and has then failed to complete, and the vendor has not elected between rescission and specific performance, the court may (unless the contract otherwise provides) order the purchaser either to perform or to vacate the premises: see *Greenwood v Turner* [1891] 2 Ch. 144; *Maskell v Ivory* [1970] Ch. 502; *Attfield v D.J. Plant Hire & General Contractors* [1987] Ch. 141.

purchase order is made in respect of it.[29] Yet in such cases damages (based on the difference between the contract price and the resale price, or the compensation payable on the compulsory acquisition) would seem normally to be an adequate (in the sense of an entirely appropriate) remedy.

Difficulty of quantifying damages. In a number of other situations damages are considered to be an inadequate remedy because of the difficulty of quantifying them. For this reason specific performance may be ordered of a contract to execute a mortgage in consideration of money advanced at or before the time of the contract,[30] and of a term of a contract of loan giving the creditor the right to have the loan repaid out of specific property[31]: the value to the creditor of obtaining security for a debt cannot be precisely quantified. For the same reason, specific performance can be ordered of a contract to pay (or to sell) an annuity,[32] of a contract to indemnify,[33] of a sale of debts proved in bankruptcy[34] and of a promise in a letter of indemnity to secure the release of a ship in the event of her being arrested by reason of the shipowner's delivering the goods without production of the bill of lading.[35] Damages may also be an inadequate remedy because 27–008

[29] *Hillingdon Estates Co v Stonefield Estates Ltd* [1952] Ch. 627. (The actual decision may be explicable on the ground of the purchaser's delay.) But specific performance cannot be ordered where the land is sold with vacant possession and before the time for completion the land is requisitioned and possession of it is taken by the requisitioning authorities, for in that case the vendor will be unable to perform his contractual obligation to give possession: *Cook v Taylor* [1942] 1 Ch. 349; *cf. James Macara Ltd v Barclay* [1945] K.B. 148 (action for return of deposit); contrast *Re Winslow Hall Estates Co* [1941] Ch. 503 (possession not taken); the last two cases are not easy to reconcile on the issue of exactly when possession was taken by the acquiring authority. The contract is not frustrated by the mere making of the order (above, para.23–057) but after title to the land has vested in the acquiring authority by virtue of the compulsory purchase, the vendor's remedy is in damages and not by way of specific performance: *E. Johnson & Co (Barbados) v NSR Ltd* [1997] A.C. 400.

[30] *Ashton v Corrigan* (1871) L.R. 13 Eq. 76. *cf. Swiss Bank Corp. v Lloyds Bank Ltd* [1982] A.C. 584, 595; affirmed *ibid.* at 610; above, para.18–138; below, n.31.

[31] *Swiss Bank Corp. v Lloyd's Bank Ltd* [1979] Ch. 548; reversed [1982] A.C. 584 but on the ground that the contract did not, on its true construction, contain any such term. This was also the position in *Kingcroft Insurance Co Ltd v H.S. Weaver (Underwriting) Agencies Ltd* [1993] 1 Lloyd's Rep. 187, 193; *cf. Napier & Ettrick v Hunter* [1993] 1 A.C. 713 recognising that an insurer's right of subrogation gives him an equitable interest in the insured's rights of action.

[32] *Kenney v Wexham* (1822) 6 Madd. 355; *Swift v Swift* (1841) 31 I.R.Eq. 267; *Beswick v Beswick* [1968] A.C. 58, below, para.27–050.

[33] *Ranelaugh (Earl) v Hayes* (1683) 1 Vern. 189; *Sporle v Whayman* (1855) 20 Beav. 607; *Anglo-Australian Life Assurance Co v British Provident Life and Fire Society* (1862) 3 Giff. 521; *Ascherson v Tredegar Dry Dock & Wharf Co Ltd* [1909] 2 Ch. 401. The terms of the decree in *(Earl) Ranelaugh v Hayes*, above, were disapproved insofar as they related to future contingent liabilities in *Lloyd v Dimmack* (1877) 7 Ch.D. 398 and in *Hughes-Hallett v Indian Mammoth Gold Mines Co* (1882) 22 Ch.D. 561; and see Fry, *Specific Performance* (6th ed.), para.1612. But the court may (it seems) grant a declaration in such a case: *Household Machines Ltd v Cosmos Exporters Ltd* [1947] K.B. 217.

[34] *Adderley v Dixon* (1824) 1 S. & S. 607.

[35] *Laemthong International Lines Co Ltd v Artis (The Laemthong Glory)* [2004] EWHC 2738 (Comm), [2005] 1 Lloyd's Rep. 632 at [47], [49], [51]; affirmed [2005] EWCA Civ 519, [2005] 1 Lloyd's Rep. 688, where there was no reference to the issue of specific enforceability and the shipowner's claim is said at [19] to be one for a declaration that the promisors were obliged by the letter of indemnity to take specified steps to secure the release of the ship. For enforceability of the letter of indemnity by the shipowner as a third party (that letter having been addressed by the receiver of the goods to the charterer of the ship), see above, para.18–092.

the claimant's loss is difficult to prove[36] or because certain items of loss[37] are not or may not be, legally recoverable, because of the difficulty of enforcing a judgment for damages in a foreign country,[38] because of the delays which may occur (even in a domestic case) in securing the actual payment of damages,[39] or quite simply because the defendant may not be "good for the money."[40]

27–009 **Damages nominal.** In *Beswick v Beswick*[41] specific performance was ordered of a promise to pay an annuity to a third party. One reason[42] why this form of relief was granted was that damages were an inadequate remedy since (in the view of the majority of the House of Lords) they would be purely nominal, the promisee or his estate having suffered no loss.[43] The point here is not that the promisee would be inadequately compensated by damages. It is rather that the party in breach would be unjustly enriched (if damages were the sole remedy) by being allowed to retain the entire benefit of the promisee's performance, while rendering only a small part of his own.

27–010 **Other factors.** Specific performance may be ordered on grounds unconnected with the question whether the claimant has suffered or is likely to suffer material or financial loss for which he could be satisfactorily compensated by damages. Specific performance has, for example, been ordered of a contract to grant a licence to use a hall for a political meeting; and one reason for making the order was said to be that this form of relief would promote freedom of speech and assembly.[44]

---

[36] *Decro-Wall International SA v Practitioners in Marketing Ltd SA* [1971] 1 W.L.R. 361; *cf. The Laemthong Glory*, above n.35, [2004] EWHC 2738 (Comm) at [47] (damages for detention of a ship "never an entirely straightforward matter"); *Thames Valley Power Ltd v Total Gas & Power Ltd* [2005] EWHC 2208 (Comm), [2006] 1 Lloyd's Rep. 441 (below, para.27–017) at [64] ("the almost impossible task in calculating any damages"); but this factor is not decisive as "such difficulties frequently arise in litigation": *Société des Industries Metallurgiques SA v Bronx Engineering Co Ltd* [1975] 1 Lloyd's Rep. 465, 468; *Hollis v Stocks* [2000] UKCLR 685, below, para.27–060.

[37] See *Hill v C.A. Parsons Ltd* [1972] 1 Ch. 305; *Evans Marshall & Co Ltd v Bertola SA* [1973] 1 W.L.R. 349 (injury to employment prospects or reputation were formerly regarded as items of loss which could not be recovered by an employee: see now *Malik v B.C.C.I.* [1998] A.C. 20).

[38] *The Laemthong Glory*, above n.33a, [2004] EWHC 2738 (Comm) at [47] ("the enforcement of judgments in Yemen is a matter of some difficulty").

[39] *Thames Valley Power Ltd v Total Gas and Power Ltd* [2005] EWHC 2008 (Comm), [2006] 1 Lloyd's Rep. 441 at [64], below, para.27–017.

[40] *Evans Marshall & Co Ltd v Bertola SA*, above n.37, at 380. *cf. Associated Portland Cement Manufacturers Ltd v Teigland Shipping A/S (The Oakworth)* [1975] 1 Lloyd's Rep. 581, 583; *Eximenco Handels AG v Partrederiet Oro Chef (The Oro Chef)* [1983] 2 Lloyd's Rep. 509, 521; but not merely because the defendant has no assets in the jurisdiction: *Locobail International Finance Ltd v Agroexport (The Sea Hawk)* [1986] 1 W.L.R. 657, 665; *Lawrence David Ltd v Ashton* [1989] I.C.R. 123, 134. See also *Themehelp Ltd v West* [1996] Q.B. 84; *Kall-Kwik Printing (UK) v Bell* [1994] F.S.R. 674.

[41] [1968] A.C. 58; above, para.18–020; below, para.27–050. For the effect on such facts of the Contracts (Rights of Third Parties) Act 1999, see above para.18–093.

[42] For others, see above, para.27–008, at n.32; below, para.27–050.

[43] [1968] A.C. 58, 81, 102; *cf.* 73, 83; above, para.18–047. Lord Pearce thought that damages would be substantial: [1968] A.C. 58, 88 above, 18–047, n.260.

[44] *Verrall v Great Yarmouth B.C.* [1981] Q.B. 202. For the relevance of this factor, see also Human Rights Act 1998, s.12; *Imutran Ltd v Uncaged Campaigns Ltd* [2001] 2 All E.R. 385.

Availability of substitute. Damages are considered to be an adequate remedy where the claimant can readily get the equivalent of what he contracted for from another source. For this reason specific performance is not generally ordered of contracts for the sale of commodities,[45] or of government stock,[46] or of shares which are readily available in the market[47]: damages (based on the difference between the contract and the market price) are generally a satisfactory remedy in such cases. On the other hand, a contract to subscribe for shares in a company is specifically enforceable[48]; and so is a contract to buy shares which are not readily available in the market,[49] even (it seems) although the directors of the company have a discretion to refuse to register the transfer.[50] 27–011

Loans of money. A contract to lend money cannot, as a general rule, be specifically enforced at the suit of either party[51]: it is assumed that damages, based on current rates of interest, are an adequate remedy. However, s.740 of the Companies Act 2006 provides that a contract to take up and pay for debentures in a company may be specifically enforced.[52] 27–012

... of goods: non-delivery. Section 52 of the Sale of Goods Act 1979 gives 27–013
"for breach of a contract to ... specific performance where an action is brought
section deals only with cases in which this remedy ... ascertained goods." Although the
... ught by the buyer, the court also has power to order specific performance at the suit of the seller.[53]

---

[45] *Buxton v Lister* (1746) 3 Atk. 383, 384; above, para.27–002; *cf. Garden Cottage Foods Ltd v Milk Marketing Board* [1984] A.C. 130 (no injunction against refusal, in violation of Art.86 (now Art.82) of the European Community Treaty, to supply butter to a distributor, as his loss of profits could easily be assessed); and see below, para.27–017.

[46] *Cud v Rutter* (1719) 1 P.Wms. 570.

[47] *Re Schwabacher* (1908) 98 L.T. 127, 128; *Chinn v Hochstrasser* [1979] Ch. 447; reversed on other grounds [1981] A.C. 533.

[48] *Odessa Tramways Co v Mendel* (1878) 8 Ch.D. 235; *Sri Lanka Omnibus Co v Perera* [1952] A.C. 76.

[49] *Duncuft v Albrecht* (1841) 12 Sim. 189; *Cheale v Kenward* 1858) 3 De G. & J. 27; *Langen & Wind Ltd v Bell* [1972] Ch. 685; *Jobson v Johnson* [1989] 1 W.L.R. 1026; *cf. Pao On v Lau Yiu Long* [1980] A.C. 614, where this point was conceded; *Harvela Investments Ltd v Royal Trust Co of Canada (C.I.) Ltd* [1986] A.C. 207 (shares not available in the market and giving a controlling interest in the company); *Grant v Cigman* [1996] 2 B.C.L.C. 24; *Pena v Dale* [2003] EWHC 1065, [2004] B.C.L.C. 508 at [135] (option to purchase shares in a private company specifically enforced).

[50] *Hawkins v Maltby* (1867) L.R. 3 Ch.App. 188, 194; *Stray v Russell* (1859) 1 E. & E. 888 but see *Bermingham v Sheridan, Re Waterloo Life Assurance Co (No.4)* (1864) 33 Beav. 660; *Poole v Middleton* (1861) 29 Beav. 646. Specific performance of a contract to buy shares will not (save in exceptional circumstances) be ordered against a purchaser after an order has been made for the company to be wound up since the transfer of the shares would be void against the company: *Sullivan v Henderson* [1973] 1 W.L.R. 333.

[51] *Rogers v Challis* (1859) 27 Beav. 175; *Sichel v Mosenthal* (1862) 30 Beav. 371; *cf. Handley Page Ltd v Commissioners of Customs & Excise* [1970] 2 Lloyd's Rep. 459.

[52] Reversing *South African Territories v Wallington* [1898] A.C. 309.

[53] *Astro Exito Navegacion SA v Southland Enterprise Co Ltd (The Messiniaki Tolmi)* [1982] Q.B. 1248; affirmed without reference to this point [1983] 2 A.C. 787 (sale of ship.) For earlier authorities on the availability of the remedy to the seller, contrast *Shell-Mex Ltd v Elton Cop Dyeing Co* (1928) 34 Com.Cas. 39, 47 with *Elliott v Pierson* [1948] 1 All E.R. 939, 942. One practical effect of an order of specific performance at the suit of the seller would be to enable the seller to get the price in a case falling outside s.49 of the Sale of Goods Act 1979. Another practical effect of such an order would be to compel the buyer to perform his duty to take delivery: *cf. P & O Nedlloyd BV v Arab Metals*

27–014 The object of s.52[54] was to enlarge the scope of the remedy, which appeared to have been restricted to cases in which the claimant could not get a satisfactory substitute because the goods were "unique." For the purpose of specific relief, heirlooms, great works of art and rare antiques were regarded as "unique"[55]; and it seems that the courts went some way towards recognising a concept of commercial "uniqueness". Thus a contract to supply a ship, or machinery or other industrial plant which could not readily be obtained elsewhere might be specifically enforced.[56] Another special factor which may induce the court to order specific performance of a contract for the sale of goods is that the goods form the contents of a house which is being sold by the same seller to the same buyer, either by the same contract or by a separate contemporaneous one.[57] The court is particularly ready to order specific performance in such a case if removal of the goods would damage the land, but the remedy is not limited to such circumstances.[58] It has also been suggested that under s.52 the court could specifically enforce a contract for the sale of growing timber (so long as it was ascertained[59]) which was to be severed, whether by the vendor or by the purchaser.[60]

27–015 Under s.52, the discretion to order specific performan[illegible] nevertheless cases in which the goods are "[illegible] took the view that [illegible] discretion should be sparingly exercised. One reason for this view is that the specific enforceability of a contract for the sale of goods

Co [2006] EWCA Civ 1717, [2007] 2 All E.R. (Comm) 401 where it was assumed that the obligation to take delivery of goods imposed by a contract of carriage could be specifically enforced by the carrier at the end of the carriage operation.

[54] And of its precursor, s.2 of the Mercantile Law Amendment Act 1856, which gave effect to a recommendation in the 2nd Report of the Mercantile Law Commission (1855). See Vol.II, para.43–470.

[55] *Pusey v Pusey* (1684) 1 Vern. 273; *Somerset v Cookson* (1735) 3 P.Wms. 390; *Lowther v Lowther* (1806) 3 Ves. 95; a slightly wider view may be taken by *Falcke v Gray* (1859) 3 Drew. 651, 658.

[56] See *Nutbrown v Thornton* (1804) 10 Ves. 159; *North v G.N. Ry* (1860) 2 Giff. 64; *Behnke v Bede Shipping Co* [1927] 1 K.B. 649 the latter decision might have been, but was not, based on the fact that the subject matter was a ship: see *Bathynay v Bouch* (1881) 50 L.J.Q.B. 221 and *cf.* Lord Simon's statement in *Mardorf Peach & Co Ltd v Attica Sea Carriers Corp. of Liberia (The Laconia)* [1977] A.C. 850, 873–874 that "In some respects the law of contract already treats a ship as if she were a piece of realty." See also *Lingen v Simpson* (1824) 1 S. & S. 600 (pattern books); *cf. Land Rover Group Ltd v UPF (UK) Ltd* [2002] EWHC 3183; [2003] B.C.L.C. 222 at [52] (mandatory injunction to enforce obligation to supply chassis to car manufacturer); contrast *Soc. des Industries Metallurgiques SA v Bronx Engineering Co Ltd* [1975] 1 Lloyd's Rep. 465 (machinery available from another source). See also *C.N. Marine Inc. v Stena Line A/B (The Stena Nautica) (No.2)* [1982] 2 Lloyd's Rep. 336, where the Court of Appeal recognised that "specific performance can be made in the case of ship" (at 347) but refused to make such an order as the claimant had failed to show that he had a special need for the ship or that damages would not be an adequate remedy; *Eximento Handels AG v Partrederiet Oro Chef (The Oro Chef)* [1983] 2 Lloyd's Rep. 509, 520–521; *Allseas International Management Ltd v Panroy Bulk Transport Ltd (The Star Gazer)* [1985] 1 Lloyd's Rep. 370; *Gyllenhammer Partners International v Sour Brodogradevna* [1989] 2 Lloyd's Rep. 403, 422.

[57] *Record v Bell* [1991] 1 W.L.R. 853, 862.

[58] *ibid.*

[59] See below, para.27–016, n.66.

[60] *Jones v Tankerville* [1909] 2 Ch. 440, 445.

might give the buyer an equitable interest in the goods,[61] and this could adversely affect third parties who had only constructive (but no actual) notice of that interest: *e.g.* it could give the buyer priority over not only unsecured but also secured creditors where he had paid for the goods and the seller had then become insolvent.[62] But a restrictive view of the scope of specific performance in contracts for the sale of goods has been taken even where no such prejudice to third parties was likely to result. For example, in *Cohen v Roche*[63] the court refused specific performance to the buyer of a set of Hepplewhite chairs, saying that they were "ordinary articles of commerce and of no special value or interest."[64] This seems to amount to a refusal to exercise the discretion under s.52 on the ground that the goods were not "unique" in the sense of the old law.[65]

"Specific or ascertained" goods. Section 52 refers to goods which are "specific or ascertained."[66] The section therefore does not apply where the goods are unascertained because they are purely generic (*e.g.* where the sale is of "1,000 tons of wheat"). Where the goods are unascertained because they form an undifferentiated part of an identified bulk, a distinction must, as a result of amendments to the Sale of Goods Act made in 1995,[67] be drawn between two 27–016

[61] For the view that specific enforceability does not necessarily give rise to an equitable interest, see *Tailby v Official Receiver* (1888) 13 App.Cas 523, 548; *Re London Wine Co (Shippers)* [1986] P.C.C. 121, 149. *cf.* also *Leigh & Sillavan Ltd v Aliakmon Shipping Co (The Aliakmon)* [1986] A.C. 785, where it was said at 812–813 that equitable "ownership" or "title" did not pass under a contract for the sale of unascertained goods on "appropriation" of particular goods to the contract; but damages for breach of the contract would clearly have been an adequate remedy (above, para.27–011) so that the question whether an equitable interest in goods can pass under a specifically enforceable contract for the goods remains an open one.

[62] It was the fear of giving the buyer priority over secured creditors that was the main reason why specific performance was refused in *Re Wait* [1927] 1 Ch. 606: see esp. 640. The buyer's problems in that case arose from the general rule, laid down by Sale of Goods Act 1979 s.16, that property under a contract of sale cannot pass in goods which are unascertained: see *Re Goldcorp Exchange Ltd* [1995] 1 A.C. 74; contrast *Re Stapylton Fletcher* [1994] 1 W.L.R. 1181, where the goods were segregated from the seller's own stock after sale. The buyer's interests are now in turn protected by a statutory exception to the general rule in s.16: see s.20A, discussed after n.69, below. Insolvency of the defendant is not a ground for refusing specific performance where the remedy is normally available as a matter of course: *Amec Properties v Planning Research and Systems* [1992] 1 E.G.L.R. 70.

[63] [1927] 1 K.B. 169.

[64] At 181; contrast *Phillips v Lamdin* [1949] 2 K.B. 33 (Adam style door). And see *Rawlings v General Trading Co* [1921] 1 K.B. 635 where specific performance of an undertaking to deliver a quantity of shell cases was ordered without argument as to the remedy. The actual decision in that case has been reversed by the Auctions (Bidding Agreements) Act 1927 on a point unconnected with specific performance.

[65] *i.e.* before the enactment of its precursor in 1856: see above, n.52. For criticism see Treitel [1966] J.B.L. 211.

[66] "Specific" refers primarily to goods "identified and agreed on at the time a contract of sale is made:" Sale of Goods Act 1979 s.61(1); for an extension of the definition, see below at n.68. "Ascertained" is not defined in the Act but seems to mean "identified in accordance with the agreement after the time a contract of sale is made:" *Re Wait* [1927] 1 Ch.606, 630; or identified in any other way: *Thames Sack & Bag Co Ltd v Knowles* (1918) 88 L.J.K.B. 585, 588.

[67] By Sale of Goods (Amendment) Act 1995.

types of cases. The first consists of cases in which the part sold is expressed as a *fraction or percentage* of the bulk: *e.g.* half the cotton shipped on the *Peerless*. Such a contract is one for the sale of specific goods so long as the bulk was identified and agreed on when the contract was made,[68] and the court therefore has a discretion to order specific performance of it under s.52 of the 1979 Act. The second consists of cases in which the part sold is expressed as a *specified quantity* of unascertained goods to be taken from an identified bulk[69]: *e.g.* 5,000 bales out of the cargo of cotton shipped or to be shipped on the *Peerless*, on which 10,000 bales are shipped in bulk. In such a case[70] the buyer can become owner in common of the goods to the extent that he has paid for them[71] and so he would have less need[72] to seek specific performance of the seller's promise to deliver in order to to secure priority over other creditors in the event of the seller's insolvency. He would, however, acquire such ownership, not because the goods were specific or ascertained, but in spite of the fact they remained unascertained.[73] Cases of this kind are therefore not covered by the words of s.52, which refer to the court's discretion to order specific performance of a contract to deliver "specific or ascertained" goods. It is doubtful whether s.52 applies to a contract to deliver goods to be manufactured or produced by the seller, since such goods may not be "specific or ascertained."

27–017 **Specific enforcement of contracts not within section 52.** It is also an open question whether specific performance may be ordered in a case falling outside s.52. The section does not in terms say that specific performance is available to a buyer *only* where the contract is one to deliver goods which are "specific or ascertained"; and, where the goods are not of this kind, it is arguable that the remedy should be available on the general principle governing its scope. It should, in other words, be available where, in the particular case, the buyer cannot in fact obtain a substitute or be adequately compensated by damages. This might, for example, be the case where a person who had agreed to make and supply components for a manufacturer then repudiated his undertaking to do so. In such a case, damages for the manufacturer's loss of profits might not be adequate since they "would be a poor consolation if the failure of supplies forces a trader to lay off staff and disappoint his customers (whose affections may be transferred to others) and ultimately forces him towards insolvency . . . "[74] The

[68] Sale of Goods Act 1979, s.61(1), definition of "specific goods" as amended by s.2(a) of the 1995 Act; the bulk must (as in our example) be identified and agreed on when the contract was made.

[69] As in *Re Wait* [1927] 1 Ch. 606.

[70] Sale of Goods Act 1979 s.20A(1), as inserted by s.1(3) of the 1995 Act.

[71] *ibid.* s.20A(2).

[72] The buyer's property acquired by virtue of s.20A(2) would not necessarily prevail against a competing interest such as that of a bank to which documents of title representing the goods had been pledged, as in *Re Wait*, above; and where it did not so prevail the court would be unlikely to order specific performance to disturb this state of affairs: see *Benjamin's Sale of Goods* (7th ed.), paras 18–299, 19–204.

[73] Sale of Goods Act 1979, s.20A(1) refers to the goods (in a case of the present kind) as "a specified quantity of *unascertained* goods".

[74] *Howard E. Perry & Co v British Railways Board* [1980] 1 W.L.R. 1375, 1383.

view that specific performance could be ordered on such grounds[75] seemed at one stage to have been abandoned[76]; but some more recent cases give it fresh support. During a steel strike in 1980 a manufacturer of steel obtained an order for the specific delivery of a quantity of steel belonging to him against a rail carrier who (in fear of strike action[77]) had refused to allow it to be moved.[78] Specific delivery was ordered because during the strike "steel [was] available only with great difficulty, if at all."[79] It is submitted that in such circumstances specific enforcement of a seller's duty to deliver should similarly be available to a buyer. This view is supported by a case in which, during the "energy crisis" in 1973 an interim injunction was granted to stop an oil company from cutting off supplies of petrol to a garage, since alternative sources of supply were not available.[80] The goods in this case were purely generic and the case supports the view that an obligation to deliver goods may be specifically enforced in a case that is not covered by s.52 because the goods are not "specific or ascertained."[81]

This view is further supported by *Thames Valley Power Ltd v Total Gas and Power Ltd*[82] where A had in 1995 contracted with B for the supply of gas by B to A for 15 years at a price which was to vary after the first two years according to a formula depending on the movement of various indices; B knew[83] that A (a "single purpose company"[84]) needed the supply to perform a contract with C. In 2005, B purported to invoke a *force majeure* clause as justifying their refusal to continue to supply gas under the contract. Christopher Clarke J held that B's refusal was not so justified; and he further held (though it was "not strictly necessary to decide the point"[85]) that B's obligation to supply gas under the contract was specifically enforceable. One reason for this view was that the basis of the contract was to assure A "of a source of supply from a first-rate supplier 27–018

[75] Supported by some early cases: see *Taylor v Neville* (unrep.), cited with approval in *Buxton v Lister* (1746) 3 Atk. 386 and in *Adderley v Dixon* (1824) 1 S. & S. 607; but disapproved in *Pollard v Clayton* (1855) 1 K. & J. 462.

[76] See *Fothergill v Rowland* (1873) L.R. 17 Eq. 137; *Pollard v Clayton* (1855) 1 K. & J. 462; *Dominion Coal Co v Dominion Iron and Steel Co* [1909] A.C. 293. Contrast *Donnell v Bennett* (1883) 23 Ch.D. 835 taking a more liberal view.

[77] *cf.* below, para.27–031.

[78] *Howard E. Perry & Co v British Railways Board* [1980] 1 W.L.R. 1375.

[79] *ibid.* at 1383.

[80] *Sky Petroleum Ltd v V.S.P. Petroleum Ltd* [1974] 1 W.L.R. 576; *cf.* also *Total Oil Great Britain Ltd v Thompson Garages (Biggin Hill) Ltd* [1972] 1 Q.B. 318. *Wake v Renault*, *The Times*, August 1, 1996 could be explained on the same ground, though the case gives rise to difficulties discussed in para.27–071 at n.406, below.

[81] This possibility was doubted in *Re London Wine Co (Shippers)* [1986] P.C.C. 121, 149; but in that case it was not necessary to reach a conclusion on the specific enforceability of a contract for the delivery of goods which were not "specific or ascertained" since on the facts damages were clearly an adequate remedy: *cf.* above, para.27–011.

[82] [2005] EWHC 2208 (Comm), [2006] 1 Lloyd's Rep. 441.

[83] *ibid.*, at [49].

[84] *ibid.*

[85] *ibid.* at [63]. B had indicated that, if they were held not to be protected by the *force majeure* clause, then they would continue to supply gas to A under the terms of the contract between A and B: *ibid.*, at [58].

for a 15-year term", so that if they were confined to a claim for damages they would be deprived of "substantially the whole benefit that the contract was intended to give them."[86] This amounts to saying that damages were not an adequate remedy because no substitute was available.[87] Another reason for the availability of specific performance was that the task of assessing damages was "almost impossible"[88] in view of the uncertainty about the movement, over the unexpired term of the contract, of the indices that were to determine the price. And a third reason for the inadequacy of damages lay in the delay likely to be encountered in securing their actual payment, which might have led to A's insolvency before the end of the 15 year term.[89] No reference is made in the judgment to s.52; but where, for reasons such as those given above, damages are not a satisfactory remedy, then it is, with respect, consistent with the principles governing specific relief[90] to hold that such relief is available even in cases not falling squarely within the section.

27–019 **Defective delivery of goods supplied to consumers.** The concept of specific performance in s.52 is that of a remedy for *non-delivery* of goods; but there is the further possibility that specific relief may be sought in respect of *defective delivery, i.e.* delivery of goods which are not in conformity with the contract. This possibility is recognised by recent amendments[91] to the Sale of Goods Act 1979, by which a buyer who deals as consumer and to whom goods are sold by a commercial seller may, if the goods are not in conformity with the contract, require the seller to repair or replace them.[92] The remedy of specific performance is made available to enforce the seller's duty to comply with such a requirement,[93] and this extension of the remedy is, it is submitted, consistent with the principles governing specific relief in English law. Damages are unlikely to be the most appropriate remedy for a consumer who has bought (for example) an appliance which malfunctions; while hardship to the seller is avoided by a number of restrictions on the new remedies described above. Thus repair or replacement cannot be ordered if either remedy is impossible,[94] nor can one of these remedies be ordered if it is "disproportionate" to the other.[95] Specific performance can also be refused where another of the new remedies (such as

[86] *ibid.*, at [63].

[87] See para.27–011 above.

[88] *Thames Valley Power* case, above n.82, at [64]; *cf.* para.27–011 above.

[89] *Thames Valley Power* case, above n.82, at [64]; *cf.* para.27–008 at n.38.

[90] Especially with the principles stated in paras 27–008 and 27–011.

[91] Made by Sale and Supply of Goods to Consumers Regulations 2002, (SI 2002/3045), implementing Dir. 1999/44/EC, [1999] O.J. L171/12. The Regulations provide similar remedies where goods are supplied to a consumer under a contract other than one of sale: see the amendments made to the Supply of Goods and Services Act 1982 by reg.9 of the above Regulations. For the sake of brevity, the following discussion is confined to cases of sale. See also Harris, (2003) 119 L.Q.R. 541.

[92] Sale of Goods Act 1979, ss.48A(2) (a) and 48B, as inserted by reg.5 of the above Regulations; for dealing as consumer, see Sale of Goods Act 1979, s.61(5A).

[93] Sale of Goods Act 1979, s.48E(2), as inserted by reg.5 of the above Regulations.

[94] Sale of Goods Act 1979, s.48B(3)(a); *cf.* below, para.27–041.

[95] Sale of Goods Act 1979, s.48B(3)(b); *cf.* below, para.27–031.

price reduction) provided by the recent amendments[96] is "appropriate",[97] *i.e.* more appropriate than specific relief.[98]

3. CONTRACTS NOT SPECIFICALLY ENFORCEABLE

General. Specific performance of certain types of contracts may be refused, whether or not damages are an adequate remedy. In these cases the reason for refusing the remedy is not that it is unnecessary, but that it may be undesirable to grant it or impracticable to enforce it. **27–020**

Contracts involving personal service. It has long been settled that a contract of personal service (or employment) will not, as a general rule, be specifically enforced at the suit of either party.[99] The principle applies where a company director's service agreement is wrongfully determined by the company[100]; but the court may by injunction restrain one director from interfering with the exercise by another director of his powers as such.[101] **27–021**

Contracts of employment. The reason why specific enforcement is not available against an employee is that such an order is thought to interfere unduly with his personal liberty: it is this ground of policy which accounts for the rule, so that "questions of the adequacy of damages are irrelevant to this issue."[102] Legislative force is given to this principle by the Trade Union and Labour Relations (Consolidation) Act 1992, s.236 of which provides that no court shall compel an employee to do any work by ordering specific performance of a contract of employment or by restraining the breach of such a contract by injunction.[103] Conversely, an employer could not be forced to employ: it was thought to be difficult or undesirable to enforce the continuance of a "personal" relationship between unwilling parties. This principle is also reflected in the provisions of the Employment Rights Act 1996[104] as to the remedies for "unfair" **27–022**

---

[96] For price reduction, see the new s.48C, inserted by reg.5 of the Regulations referred to in n.91, above.

[97] Sale of Goods Act 1979, s.48E(3) and (4).

[98] Above, at para.27–005.

[99] *Johnson v Shrewsbury & Birmingham Ry* (1853) 3 D.M. & G. 914; *Brett v East India Shipping Co* (1864) 2 H. & C. 404; *Britain v Rossiter* (1879) 11 Q.B.D. 123, 127; *Rigby v Connol* (1880) 14 Ch.D. 482, 487; *cf. Whitwood Chemical Co v Hardman* [1891] 2 Ch. 416 (injunction); *Taylor v N.U.S.* [1967] 1 W.L.R. 532 (declaration); *Chappell v The Times Newspapers* [1975] 1 W.L.R. 482 (injunction); *Scandinavian Tanker Trading Co AB v Flota Petrolera Ecuatoriana (The Scaptrade)* [1983] 2 A.C. 694, 700–701; *cf. Wishart v National Association of Citizens' Advice Bureaux* [1990] I.C.R. 794 (where no employment relationship ever came into existence); *Wilson v St Helen's BC* [1999] 2 A.C. 52 at 77.

[100] *Bainbridge v Smith* (1889) 41 Ch.D. 462.

[101] *Pulbrook v Richmond Consolidated Mining Co* (1878) 9 Ch.D. 610; *Hayes v Bristol Plant Hire Ltd* [1957] 1 W.L.R. 49; *cf. British Murac Syndicate v Alperton Rubber Co* [1915] 2 Ch. 186.

[102] *Young v Robson Rhodes* [1999] 3 All E.R. 524 at 534.

[103] Injunctions in respect of industrial action may lie against the *organisers* of such action, *e.g.* under Trade Union and Labour Relations (Consolidation) Act 1992, ss.226 or 235A (inserted by Trade Union Reform and Employment Rights Act 1993, s.22) but not against *individual employees*.

[104] Pt X.

dismissal (which is not normally a breach of contract at all). Under the Act, a tribunal may order the reinstatement or re-engagement of the employee, but if such an order is not complied with, the employer can, in the last resort, only be ordered to pay compensation.[105] In practice, reinstatement is "effected in only a tiny proportion of . . . cases"[106] so that it is compensation which is the employee's "primary remedy."[107] Where an employee is dismissed in breach of contract, his normal remedy is a claim for damages or a declaration that the dismissal was *wrongful*: not specific enforcement, or a declaration that the dismissal was *invalid*.[108] The statutory right to return to work[109] after maternity, parental or paternity leave appears likewise not to be specifically enforceable.[110]

27–023 **Exceptions.** The arguments usually advanced in support, of the equitable principle stated in para.27–021 above are no longer wholly convincing[111] and the principle is subject to a growing list of exceptions. A person who is dismissed

---

[105] Employment Rights Act 1996, ss.113–117. Under ss.129(9) and 130 of the 1996 Act, orders may be made for the continuation of the contract, but these do not give rise to the remedy of specific performance; *cf.* also Sex Discrimination Act 1975, ss.65(1)(c), 65(3)(a), 71(1); Race Relations Act 1976, ss.56(1)(c), 56(4); Reserve Forces (Safeguard of Employment) Act 1985, ss.10, 17 and 18; Trade Union and Labour Relations (Consolidation) Act 1992, ss.152–167 (as amended by s.49 and Schs 7 and 8 of Trade Union Reform and Employment Rights Act 1993) (dismissal on grounds related to trade union membership or activities); Disability Discrimination Act 1995; s.8(5) and Sch.3, para.2(1).

[106] *Johnson v Unisys Ltd* [2001] UKHL 13; [2003] 1 A.C. 518 at [78] *per* Lord Millett; Lord Steyn at [23] states the proportion to be "only about three per cent." Contrast the view of Sedley L.J. in *Grady v Prison Service* [2003] EWCA Civ 527; [2003] I.C.R. 753 at [24], describing the remedy for unfair dismissal as being "primarily directed at the restoration of a contractual relationship."

[107] *Johnson v Unisys Ltd*, above n.106 at [23].

[108] *Francis v Kuala Lumpur Councillors* [1962] 1 W.L.R. 1411; *Vidyodaya University Council v Silva* [1965] 1 W.L.R. 77; *Gunton v London Borough of Richmond-upon-Thames* [1981] Ch. 448; *Marsh v National Autistic Society* [1993] I.C.R. 453; *cf. Mezey v South West London and St George's Mental Health N.H.S. Trust* [2007] EWCA Civ 106, [2007] I.R.L.R. 244 (injunction against invalid *suspension* of employee). A declaration may also be made that a *decision* by a disciplinary committee leading to dismissal was void for failure to comply with the rules of natural justice: *Stevenson v United Road Transport Union* [1977] I.C.R. 893; but this does not amount to a declaration that the *contract* remains in operation: *ibid.* at 906; *cf. R. v Berkshire H.A. Ex p. Walsh* [1985] Q.B. 152 (judicial review not available as remedy for allegedly wrongful dismissal of senior nursing officer by Health Authority since no "public law" issue was involved); *R. v Derbyshire C.C. Ex p. Noble* [1990] I.C.R. 808; *McLaren v Home Office* I.C.R. 824 (claim by prison officer raised no issue of public law); *Roy v Kensington, etc., Family Practitioner Committee* [1992] 1 A.C. 624 (private law remedy available to general practitioner in respect of practice allowance); contrast *R. v Secretary of State for the Home Department Ex p. Benwell* [1985] Q.B. 554 (judicial review available as a remedy for allegedly wrongful dimissal of prison officer; not followed on other grounds in *R. v Secretary of State for the Home Department Ex p. Broom* [1986] Q.B. 198); *R. v Civil Service Appeal Board Ex p. Bruce* [1989] I.C.R. 171 (judicial review refused to dismissed civil servant as other, preferable, remedies avaliable); *R. v Crown Prosecution Service Ex p. Hogg, The Times,* April 14, 1994 (no judicial review of dismissal of lawyer employed by Crown Prosecution Service). For exceptions to this aspect of the principle against specific enforceability, see below after n.116.

[109] Employment Rights Act 1996, Pt VIII, as substituted by Employment Relations Act 1999, ss.7, 8 and 9 and Sch.4 and amended by Employment Act 2002, s.1, and see *ibid*, s.17; Maternity and Parental Leave Regulations 1999, (SI 1999/3312), reg.18.

[110] The Regulations cited in n.109 above do not specify civil remedies for infringement of the right.

[111] See Clark (1969) 32 M.L.R. 532.

from a public office in breach of the terms of his appointment may be entitled to reinstatement[112]; and the Visitor of a University has power to order the reinstatement of a wrongfully dismissed lecturer (even where such a remedy would not be available in the ordinary courts),[113] such a dismissal being, if it amounts to a violation of the University's Statutes, not merely wrongful but also invalid.[114] The continuance or creation of a "personal" relationship may be enforced where an injunction is granted against expulsion from a social club,[115] or against the refusal of a professional association to admit a person to membership.[116] The right to exclude persons from membership of certain charitable associations is also restricted; for though such bodies have the right to exclude persons whom they in good faith regard as likely to damage their objectives, they must not adopt arbitrary procedures to that end: they may, for example, be required to invite persons who are about to be excluded to give reasons why they should be admitted.[117]

More generally, the modern relationship of employer and employee is often less personal than the old relationship of master and servant was believed to be; and there are signs that the courts are prepared to re-examine or qualify the traditional equitable principle in the light of this development.[118] Industrial conditions may in fact force an employer to retain an employee whom he would prefer to dismiss or to dismiss one whom he is perfectly willing to retain. For example, in *Hill v C.A. Parsons Ltd*[119] employers were forced by union pressure

---

[112] *Ridge v Baldwin* [1964] A.C. 40; Ganz (1967) 30 M.L.R. 288; *Malloch v Aberdeen Corp.* [1971] 1 W.L.R. 1578; *Chief Constable of the North Wales Police v Evans* [1982] 1 W.L.R. 1155; *R. v Secretary of State for the Home Department Ex p. Benwell* [1985] Q.B. 554 (above, n.108); *McLaughlin v H.E. the Governor of the Cayman Islands* [2007] UKPC 50, [2007] 1 W.L.R. 2839 (declaration that such a dismissal was ineffective in law to determine the officer's tenure of office and consequential financial relief). *cf. Jones v Lee* (1979) L.G.R. 213 (injunction against dismissal of teacher.) The line between "ordinary" and "public" employment is by no means clear cut: see *Barber v Manchester Regional Hospital Board* [1958] 1 W.L.R. 181; *Tucker v Trustees of the British Museum* [1967] C.L.Y. 1430; and criticisms of the *Vidyodaya University* case, above n.108, in *Malloch v Aberdeen Corp.*, above, at 1595.

[113] *Thomas v University of Bradford* [1987] A.C. 795, 824; for subsequent proceedings, see [1992] 1 All E.R. 964, where it was held by the Visitor that the lecturer's removal would have been invalid for procedural irregularities if these had not been waived by the lecturer.

[114] *Pearce v University of Aston (No.2)* [1991] 2 All E.R. 469. The Visitor's decision on the interpretation of the University's Statutes is not subject to judicial review: *R. v Hull University Visitor Ex p. Page* [1993] A.C. 682 (where the Visitor had held the dismissal to be in accordance with those Statutes).

[115] *Young v Ladies Imperial Club Ltd* [1920] 2 K.B. 522; below, para.27–072. See also Disability Discrimination Act 1995, s.21F(2)(b) (inserted by Disability Discrimination Act 2005, s.12) making it unlawful to discriminate against disabled persons by refusing them admission to private clubs. Enforcement of these provisions appears to be by criminal sanctions; there is no reference in the legislation to orders for specific relief.

[116] *cf. Nagle v Feilden* [1966] 2 Q.B. 633; below, para.27–075; doubted on the availability of specific relief in *R. v Disciplinary Committee of the Jockey Club Ex p. Aga Khan* [1993] 1 W.L.R. 909, 933.

[117] *Royal Society for the Prevention of Cruelty to Animals v Att.-Gen.* [2002] 1 W.L.R. 448.

[118] See *C.H. Giles & Co Ltd v Morris* [1972] 1 W.L.R. 307. *cf.* (in Scotland) *Peace v Edinburgh CC* [1999] I.R.L.R. 417.

[119] [1972] 1 Ch. 305; Hepple [1972] C.L.J. 47; *cf. Irani v Southampton, etc. H.A.* [1985] I.C.R. 590 (where the employers retained confidence in an employee but had dismissed him because of differences between him and another employee); *Powell v London Borough of Brent* [1988] I.C.R.

to dismiss an employee. The dismissal amounted to a breach of contract and the court issued an injunction to restrain the breach, thus in effect re-instating the employee. As the employers and the employee were perfectly willing to maintain their relationship, the decision does not seem to violate the spirit of the general equitable principle against the specific enforcement of employment contracts. An injunction to restrain dismissal can also be issued in respect of a period during which no services are to be rendered under the contract. Thus where an employee had been suspended on full pay while disciplinary proceedings against him were in progress, it was held that the employers could be restrained from dismissing him before the disciplinary proceedings had run their full course.[120]

27–024 **Other contracts involving "personal" service.** The equitable principle of refusing specific performance extends to contracts involving personal service even though they are not contracts *of* service. Thus it has been held that an agreement to allow an auctioneer to sell a collection of works of art cannot be specifically enforced by either party[121]; and that specific relief was not available to compel a fee-paying school to reinstate a pupil who had been excluded for alleged misconduct, since the "breakdown of trust" had made it undesirable to require the parties "to co-exist in a pastoral and educational relationship."[122] Similarly an agreement to enter into a partnership will not be specifically enforced[123] as "it is impossible to make persons who will not concur carry on a business jointly for their common advantage."[124] But a contract for the sale of a share in a partnership may be specifically enforced where it does not involve

176; *Hughes v Southwark L.B.C.* [1988] I.R.L.R. 55; for recognition of the approach adopted in these cases, see *Lauritzencool AB v Lady Navigation Inc* [2005] EWCA Civ 579, [2005] 1 W.L.R. 3686 at [11]. *Jones v Gwent C.C.* [1992] I.R.L.R. 521, 526 goes even further and is hard to reconcile with the authorities cited in n.108, above; and *Grady v Prison Service* [2003] EWCA Civ 527; [2003] 3 All E.R. 745 at [22] ("rare case").

[120] *Robb v Hammersmith and Fulham B.C.* [1991] I.R.L.R. 72. *Young v Robson Rhodes* [1999] 3 All E.R. 524; below, para.27–067; *Gryf-Lowczowski v Hitchinbroke Healthcare NHS Trust* [2005] EWHC 2407, [2006] I.R.L.R. 100.

[121] *Chinnock v Sainsbury* (1861) 30 L.J.Ch. 409; *cf. Mortimer v Beckett* [1920] 1 Ch. 571.

[122] *R. v Incorporated Froebel Educational Institute, Ex p. L* [1999] E.L.R. 488 at 493; *cf. R. v Fernhill Manor School* [1993] F.L.R. 620 (no judicial review of expulsion from private school). For statutory power to order reinstatement of state school pupils, see School Standards and Framework Act 1998, ss.66, 67, discussed in *R. (on the application of L) v Governors of J. School* [2003] UKHL 9; [2003] 1 All E.R. 1012. *cf. A v Lord Grey's School* [2004] EWCA Civ 382, [2004] Q.B. 1231 where *damages* were recovered by a pupil whose expulsion from a state school was found to amount to breach of the Human Rights Act 1998, Sch.1 Pt II, Art. 2 and whose request for *reinstatement* had been denied.

[123] *Scott v Rayment* (1868) L.R. 7 Eq. 112; *England v Curling* (1844) 8 Beav. 129, 137.

[124] *England v Curling*, above, at 137. On the same principle, specific performance has been refused of a house-sharing arrangement which had been made between members of a family who later quarrelled: *Burrows and Burrows v Sharp* (1991) 23 H.L.R. 82, where the basis of liability was not contract but proprietary estoppel; *cf. Internet Trading Clubs Ltd v Freeserve (Investments) Ltd*, Transcript June 19, 2001 at 30 (refusal specifically "to enforce an ongoing business relationship"); *Malcolm v Chancellor Masters and Scholars of the University of Oxford, The Times*, December 19, 1990 (specific performance of a contract to publish a book refused as the process of publication would have required continued co-operation between author and publishers; for further related proceedings, see [2002] EWHC 10; [2002] E.L.R. 277).

personal service or continuing personal relations between the contracting parties.[125] Even where personal service or a continuing personal relationship is involved, the court can order the execution of a formal partnership agreement and leave the parties to their legal remedies on the agreement.[126] Similarly, the court can order the execution of a service contract even though that contract, when made, may not be specifically enforceable.[127]

Services not of a "personal" nature. Specific performance is refused in the above cases because the courts are reluctant to force the parties to enter into, or to continue in, a personal relationship against the will of one of the parties. It follows that the refusal of specific performance on this ground is limited to cases in which the services are personal in nature. Specific enforcement of a contract for the supply of services which are not of this nature may, indeed, be refused on some other ground, e.g. because "mutual confidence [has] broken down" between the person to whom the services were to be provided and their provider.[128] But there is no general rule against the specific enforcement of a contract merely because one party has contracted to provide services.[129] Thus specific performance can be ordered of a contract to publish a piece of music,[130] and sometimes of contracts to build.[131] It has, indeed, been suggested that a time charterparty cannot be specifically enforced against the shipowner because it is a contract for services[132]; but the services that the shipowner undertakes to provide under such a contract will often be no more personal than those to be rendered by a builder under a building contract. Denial of specific performance in the case of time charters is best explained on other grounds.[133] 27–025

Constant supervision. The court will not specifically enforce a contract under which one party is bound by continuous duties, the due performance of 27–026

[125] See *Dodson v Downey* [1901] 2 Ch. 620. *cf. Pena v Dale* [2003] EWHC 1065, [2004] 2 B.C.L.C. 508, where specific performance was ordered of an agreement by which A, a shareholder in a private company, granted an option to B to acquire a minority shareholding in the company. Since exercise of the option would not give B any right to participate in the day to day management of the company, the existence of personal animosity between A and B was no bar to specific relief (at [136]).

[126] As in *England v Curling* (1844) 8 Beav. 129, where the object of obtaining such an order was to prevent one of the contracting parties from competing in business with the other and to procure a judicial determination of the exact terms that had been agreed.

[127] *C.H. Giles & Co Ltd v Morris* [1972] 1 W.L.R. 307; *cf. Posner v Scott-Lewis* [1987] Ch. 25.

[128] *Vertex Data Sciences Ltd v Powergen Retail* [2006] EWHC 1340 (Comm), [2006] 2 Lloyd's Rep. 591 at [42] (no injunction to restrain recipient of outsourcing services from terminating the contract).

[129] *e.g. Regent International Hotels v Pageguide, The Times,* May 13, 1985 (injunction against preventing claimant company from managing a hotel); *Posner v Scott-Lewis* [1987] Ch. 25 (below, para.27–026); *Lauritzencool AB v Lady Navigation Inc* [2005] EWCA Civ 579, [2005] 1 W.L.R. 3686, below, para.27–070.

[130] *Barrow v Chappel & Co* (unreported) cited in *Joseph v National Magazine Co* [1959] Ch. 14. It is assumed that it can be clearly shown exactly what is to be published: *cf.* below, para.27–042.

[131] Below, para.27–028.

[132] *Scandinavian Tanker Co AB v Flota Petrolera Ecuatoriana (The Scaptrade)* [1983] 2 A.C. 694, 700–701; *Lauritzencool AB v Lady Navigation Inc*, above n.129 at [9], where counsel reserved the right "to ask the House [of Lords] to review this proposition . . . "

[133] See below, para.27–026 at n.141.

which might require constant supervision by the court.[134] In *Ryan v Mutual Tontine Association*[135] the lease of a service flat gave the tenant the right to the services of a porter who was to be "constantly in attendance." Specific enforcement of this right was refused on the ground that it would have required "that constant superintendence by the court, which the court in such cases has always declined to give."[136] For the same reason the courts have refused specifically to enforce a tenant's undertaking to cultivate a farm in a particular manner[137]; the obligations of a railway company to operate signals and to provide engine power[138]; a contract to keep an airfield in operation[139]; a contract to keep a shop open[140]; the obligations of a shipowner under a voyage charterparty[141]; and a contract to deliver goods by instalments.[142] The difficulty of supervision is also one ground that has been given for the refusal of the courts in some cases specifically to enforce contracts to do building work[143] or to keep buildings in repair.[144] But in such cases specific performance is sometimes ordered and no practical difficulty seems to have arisen in enforcing such orders.[145] This suggests that the "difficulty" of supervision has been somewhat exaggerated; and various devices at the court's disposal can be used to overcome it. The court can,

[134] This principle plainly does not apply to continuous obligations to pay money, *e.g.* under an agreement to pay an annuity, for it is well settled that such an agreement can be specifically enforced: above, para.27–008.

[135] [1893] 1 Ch. 116.

[136] *ibid.* at 123. In *Vertex Data Science Ltd v Powergen Retail Ltd* [2006] EWHC 1340 (Comm), [2006] 2 Lloyd's Rep. 591 at [42] the principle was, unusually, applied because the services to be supplied *by the claimant* would require constant supervision. For this case, see also above, para.27–025.

[137] *Rayner v Stone* (1762) Eden 128; *Phipps v Jackson* (1887) 56 L.J.Ch. 550; *cf. Hill v Barclay* (1810) 16 Ves.Jun. 402 (tenant's covenant to repair); contrast *Jeune v Queens Cross Properties Ltd* [1974] Ch. 97 (landlord's covenant to repair); *Barrett v Lounava (1982) Ltd* [1990] 1 Q.B. 348 (landlord's implied covenant to repair).

[138] *Powell Duffryn Steam Coal Co v Taff Vale Ry* (1874) L.R. 9 Ch.App. 331; *Blackett v Bates* (1865) L.R. 1 Ch.App. 117.

[139] *Dowty Boulton Paul Ltd v Wolverhampton Corp.* [1971] 1 W.L.R. 204; for later proceedings in this case, see [1973] Ch. 94.

[140] *Braddon Towers Ltd v International Stores Ltd* [1987] E.G.L.R. 209 (decided in 1959); *Co-operative Insurance Society Ltd v Argyll Stores (Holdings) Ltd* [1998] A.C. 1, below, para.27–027.

[141] *De Mattos v Gibson* (1858) 4 D. & J. 276. The view expressed in *Scandinavian Tanker Co A.B. v Flota Petrolera Ecuatoriana (The Scaptrade)* [1983] 2 A.C. 694, 700–701, that a time charter cannot be specifically enforced against the shipowner, is best explained on the ground that such enforcement would require too much supervision.

[142] *Dominion Coal Co v Dominion Iron & Steel Co* [1909] A.C. 293. But see above, para.27–017, at n.80. In *Thames Valley Power Ltd v Total Gas and Power Ltd* [2005] EWHC 2208, [2006] 1 Lloyd's Rep. 441 (above, para.27–017) the court declared that a buyer was "entitled to damages and an order by way of specific performance" of the suppliers' obligation under a long term contract for the supply of gas. At the time of the order, the contract had nearly five years to run but no reference was made to any difficulty of supervision, perhaps because the suppliers had indicated their willingness to continue the supply if the decision on the issue of liability went against them (at [58]).

[143] Below, para.27–028.

[144] *Flint v Brandon* (1803) 8 Ves. 159; *Wheatley v Westminster Brymbo Coal Co* (1869) L.R. 9 Eq. 538; but see *Jeune v Queens Cross Properties Ltd*, above, n.137.

[145] See *Storer v G.W. Ry* (1842) 2 Y. & C.C.C. 48 (agreement to construct and "for ever thereafter to maintain one neat archway": specific performance decreed); *Kennard v Cory Bros* [1922] 2 Ch. 1 (mandatory injunction to keep a drain open); *Rainbow Estates Ltd v Tokenhold Ltd* [1999] Ch. 64.

for example, appoint a receiver to perform the acts specified in the order,[146] or appoint an expert to act as officer of the court for the purpose, or it can authorise the claimant to appoint a person to act as agent of the defendant for the purpose of performing those acts.[147] Where the acts to be done under the contract are not to be done by the defendant personally, the court can order him simply to enter into a contract to procure those acts to be done. From this point of view, *Ryan v Mutual Tontine Association*[148] may be contrasted with *Posner v Scott-Lewis*[149] where the lessor of a block of luxury flats covenanted, so far as lay in his power, to employ a resident porter to perform a number of specified tasks. It was held that the covenant was specifically enforceable in the sense that the lessor could be ordered to appoint a resident porter for the performance of those tasks.

Competing factors. This balancing of arguments for and against ordering specific performance in cases of the kind discussed in paragraph 27–026 above is well illustrated by *Co-operative Insurance Society Ltd v Argyll Stores (Holdings) Ltd*[150] where a 31-year lease of premises for use as a food supermarket in a shopping centre contained a covenant by the tenant to keep the premises "open for retail trade during the usual hours of business". Some six years after the commencement of the lease, the supermarket was running at a loss and the tenant ceased trading there. The main reason given by the House of Lords for refusing to order specific performance was the difficulty of supervising the enforcement of the order since the question whether it was being complied with might require frequent reference to the court. For this purpose, Lord Hoffmann distinguished between orders (such as that sought here) "to carry on an activity" and orders "to achieve a result." In the latter case, "the court . . . only has to examine the finished work"[151] so that compliance with the order could be judged *ex post facto*: it was on this ground that the cases in which building contracts had been specifically enforced[152] were to be explained. It should, however, be emphasised that difficulty of supervision was not the sole ground for refusing specific performance. Lord Hoffmann referred also to a number of other factors, such as the "heavy-handed nature of the enforcement mechanism"[153] by proceedings for contempt; the injustice of compelling the tenant to carry on business at a loss which might well exceed the loss which the landlord would be likely to suffer if the covenant were broken; and the fact that it was not "in the public interest for the courts to require someone to carry on business at a loss if there is any plausible alternative by which the other party can be given compensation,"[154] *i.e.* by way of damages. Reliance on such factors suggests that, if the court attaches sufficient importance to the claimant's interest in specific enforcement, it will not 27–027

[146] *cf. Gibbs v David* (1870) L.R. 20 Eq. 373 (receiver appointed in a rescission action to run a mine.)

[147] *cf.* Law of Property Act 1925, s.101; Insolvency Act 1986, s.44 (as amended by Insolvency Act 1994, s.2).

[148] Above at n.135.

[149] [1987] Ch. 25; Jones [1987] C.L.J. 21.

[150] [1998] A.C. 1.

[151] *ibid.* at 13; all the other members of the House of Lords agreed with Lord Hoffmann's speech.

[152] Below, para.27–028.

[153] [1988] A.C. 1, 12.

[154] *ibid.* at 15.

be deterred from granting such relief merely on the ground that such a course will require constant supervision. The outcome in each case will depend on the "cumulative effect"[155] of this factor together with any others which favour[156] or (as in the *Co-operative Insurance* case) militate against specific relief.[157]

27–028 **Building contracts: specific enforcement against builder.** The general rule is that a contract to erect a building cannot be specifically enforced against the builder. There seem to be three reasons for this rule. First, damages may be an adequate remedy if another builder can be engaged to do the work. Secondly, the contract may be too vague to be specifically enforced if it fails to describe the work to be done under it with sufficient certainty.[158] And thirdly, specific enforcement of the contract may require more supervision than the court is willing to provide.[159] But where the first two reasons do not apply, the third has not been allowed to prevail. Specific performance of a contract to erect or to repair buildings can therefore be ordered if (i) the work is precisely defined; (ii) damages will not adequately compensate the claimant; and (iii) the defendant is in possession of the land on which the work is to be done so that the claimant cannot get the work done by another builder.[160]

27–029 **Building contracts: specific enforcement against owner.** The converse question may also arise whether the builder can, in effect, compel the owner to allow him to complete the work. In *Hounslow (London Borough) v Twickenham Gardens Ltd*[161] a building contract gave a builder a contractual licence to enter the owner's land to execute the agreed work. The licence was held to be irrevocable till the work had been done, but the owner wrongfully purported to terminate it and sought an injunction to restrain the builder from entering the land, and damages for trespass. These claims failed as the purported termination

---

[155] *ibid.* at 16.

[156] See *Luganda v Service Hotels* [1969] 2 Ch. 206 (mandatory injunction ordering defendants to allow a protected tenant, who had been wrongfully locked out of a room in a residential hotel, to resume his residence in the hotel); *cf. Films Rover International Ltd v Cannon Film Sales Ltd* [1987] 1 W.L.R. 670, 682 (for further proceedings, see [1989] 1 W.L.R. 912); *Sutton Housing Trust v Lawrence* (1987) 19 H.L.R. 520.

[157] *cf. Shiloh Spinners Ltd v Harding* [1973] A.C. 691, 724 where difficulty of supervision is said to be no longer a bar to relief against forfeiture for breach of a covenant to repair (as it had been in *Hill v Barclay* (1810) 16 Ves.Jun. 402), but the possibility is recognised that such difficulty sometimes "explains why specific performance cannot be granted." *cf.* also the interpretation of these remarks in *Co-operative Insurance Society Ltd v Argyll Stores (Holdings) Ltd* [1998] A.C. 1, 14 as relating to relief against forfeiture rather than to the availability of specific performance and doubting their interpretation in *Tito v Waddell (No.2)* [1977] Ch. 106, 322.

[158] As in *Mosley* v. *Virgin* (1796) 3 Ves. 184; *cf.* below, para.27–042.

[159] Above, para.27–026.

[160] *Wolverhampton Corp. v Emmons* [1901] 1 Q.B. 515, as modified by *Carpenters Estates Ltd v Davies* [1940] Ch. 160; *Jeune v Queens Cross Properties Ltd* [1974] Ch. 97 (landlord ordered to restore collapsed balcony in performance of repairing covenant); *Price v Strange* [1978] Ch. 337, 357; *cf.* Landlord and Tenant Act 1985, s.17; *Gordon v Selico* (1986) 278 E.G. 53; *Barrett v Lounava* [1990] 1 Q.B. 348; *Tustian v Johnson* [1993] 2 All E.R. 675, 681; reversed in part on other grounds [1993] 3 All E.R. 534; *Rainbow Estates Ltd v Tokenhold Ltd* [1999] Ch. 64, 69, 75; and see *Channel Tunnel Group Ltd v Balfour Beatty Construction Ltd* [1993] A.C. 334, where the House of Lords took the view that it had jurisdiction to restrain a building contractor by injunction from stopping work, but refused such relief as a matter of discretion.

[161] [1971] Ch. 233; contrast *Mayfield Holdings v Moana Reef* [1973] 1 N.Z.L.R. 309.

was wrongful and ineffective. It seems, however, that if the licence had not been irrevocable, or if the owner's active co-operation had been required for the completion of the work, the builder's sole remedy would have been in damages.[162]

4. OTHER GROUNDS FOR REFUSING SPECIFIC PERFORMANCE

General. Specific performance is a discretionary remedy.[163] It may be refused although the contract is binding at law and cannot be impeached on some specific equitable ground (such as undue influence); although damages are not an adequate remedy[164]; and although the contract does not fall within the group of contracts, discussed above, which will not be specifically enforced. But the discretion to refuse specific performance is "not an arbitrary . . . discretion but one to be governed as far as possible by fixed rules and principles."[165] In particular, the court may refuse to order specific performance on the grounds to be discussed in the following paragraphs. Its discretion to refuse specific performance on such grounds cannot be excluded by the terms of the contract.[166] 27–030

Severe hardship to defendant. Specific performance may be refused on the ground that the order will cause severe hardship to the defendant. Thus in *Denne v Light*[167] the court refused specific performance, against the buyer, of a contract to purchase farming land wholly surrounded by land which belonged to others and over which the buyer would have no right of way. Specific performance may also be refused where the cost of performance to the defendant is wholly out of proportion to the benefit which performance will confer on the claimant[168]; and where the defendant can put himself into a position to perform only by taking legal proceedings against a third party (especially if the outcome of such proceedings is in doubt.)[169] Severe hardship may be a ground for refusing specific performance even though it results from circumstances which arise after the conclusion of the contract, which affect the person of the defendant rather than the subject matter of the contract, and for which the claimant is in no way responsible. For example, in *Patel v Ali*[170] a purchaser's claim for specific performance of a contract for the sale of a house was rejected after a four-year 27–031

---

[162] *cf. Finelli v Dee* (1968) 67 D.L.R. (2d) 393.

[163] *Scott v Alvarez* [1895] 2 Ch. 603, 612; *Stickney v Keeble* [1915] A.C. 386, 419.

[164] *Co-operative Insurance Society Ltd v Argyll Stores (Holdings) Ltd* [1998] A.C. 1, 12 ("even when damages are not an adequate remedy").

[165] *Lamare v Dixon* (1873) L.R. 6 H.L. 414, 423; *Holliday v Lockwood* [1917] 2 Ch. 56, 57; *Co-operative Insurance Society Ltd v Argyll Stores (Holdings) Ltd* [1998] A.C. 1, 16.

[166] *Quadrant Visual Communications Ltd v Hutchison Telephone (UK) Ltd* [1993] B.C.L.C. 442.

[167] (1857) 8 D.M. & G. 774; *cf. Wedgewood v Adams* (1843) 6 Beav. 600. See also *Sullivan v Henderson* [1973] 1 W.L.R. 333, above, para.27–011, n.50; *Jaggard v Sawyer* [1995] 1 W.L.R. 269 (injunction); *Insurance Co v Lloyd's Syndicate* [1995] 1 Lloyd's Rep. 273, 276 (injunction).

[168] *Tito v Waddell (No.2)* [1977] Ch. 106, 326; *Morris v Redland Bricks Ltd* [1970] A.C. 652.

[169] *Wroth v Tyler* [1974] Ch. 30 (where an additional ground for refusing specific performance was that the third party against whom the proceedings would have to be taken was the defendant's wife, so that the proceedings would tend to split up the family); *cf. Watts v Spence* [1976] Ch. 165, 173.

[170] [1984] Ch. 238.

delay (for which neither party was responsible), the vendor's circumstances having during this time changed disastrously as a result of her husband's bankruptcy and of an illness which had left her disabled. On the other hand, "mere pecuniary difficulties" would "afford no excuse."[171] Thus the purchaser of a house will not be denied specific performance merely because the vendor finds it difficult, on a rising market, to acquire alternative accommodation with the proceeds of the sale.[172] Nor will specific performance be refused merely because compliance with the order exposes the defendant to the risk of a strike by his employees.[173]

27–032 **Unfairness and surprise.** The court may refuse specific performance of a contract which has been obtained by means that are unfair, even though they do not amount to grounds on which the contract can be invalidated. In *Walters v Morgan*[174] the defendant agreed to grant to the claimant a mining lease over land which the defendant had only just bought. Specific performance was refused on the ground that the defendant was "surprised and was induced to sign the agreement in ignorance of the value of his property."[175] It seems that mere failure by the claimant to disclose factors which affect the value of the property, or the defendant's willingness to contract with him, would not be a ground for refusing specific performance. Something more must be shown: for example, that the claimant has taken unfair advantage of his superior knowledge. In *Walters v Morgan* the court relied on the fact that the claimant had hurried the defendant into the transaction before he could discover the true value of the property. On the same principle it seems that specific performance may be refused where the claimant has taken advantage of the defendant's drunkenness, though it was not so extreme as to invalidate the contract at law.[176] The claimant's failure to disclose his own breach of the contract, reducing the value of the subject matter,[177] has also been held to be a ground for refusing specific performance, even though the non-disclosure was not a ground for setting the contract aside at law.

27–033 **Inadequacy of consideration.** The authorities on inadequacy of consideration as a ground for refusing specific performance are not easy to reconcile. On the one hand it is settled that *mere* inadequacy of consideration is not a ground for refusing to grant the remedy.[178] On the other hand the statement that inadequacy of consideration is not a ground for refusing specific performance

---

[171] *ibid.* at 288; *cf. Francis v Cowcliffe* (1977) 33 P. & C.R. 386.

[172] *Mountford v Scott* [1975] Ch. 258; *cf. Easton v Brown* [1981] 3 All E.R. 278.

[173] *Howard E. Perry & Co v British Railways Board* [1980] 1 W.L.R. 1375.

[174] (1861) 3 D.F. & J. 718; *cf. Evans v Llewellin* (1781) 1 Cox C.C. 333; *Quadrant Visual Communications v Hutchison Telephone (UK) Ltd* [1993] B.C.L.C. 442; contrast *Mountford v Scott* [1975] Ch. 258.

[175] (1861) 3 D.F. & J. (1861) 718, 723.

[176] *Malins v Freeman* (1837) 2 Keen 25, 34. The same principle would probably apply where the defendant's judgment was impaired by drugs: see *Irani v Irani* [2000] 1 Lloyd's Rep. 412 at [425], where it was the *validity* of the contract, not any question of the *remedy* for its breach, that was in issue.

[177] *Quadrant Visual Communications v Hutchison Telephone (UK) Ltd*, above, n.161.

[178] *Collier v Brown* (1788) 1 Cox C.C. 428; *Western v Russell* (1814) 3 v & B. 187; *Haywood v Cope* (1858) 25 Beav. 140.

unless it is "such as shocks the conscience and amounts in itself to conclusive and decisive evidence of fraud"[179] is probably too narrow, even when allowance is made for the possibility that fraud may have had a wider meaning in equity than at law. The best view seems to be that specific performance may be refused where inadequacy of consideration is coupled with some other factor not necessarily amounting to fraud or other invalidating cause at law—for example, surprise[180] or unfair advantage taken by the claimant of his superior knowledge or bargaining position,[181] even though such other circumstances do not justify rescission of the contract.[182] Specific performance may also be refused on the ground of mistake, even though the mistake does not affect the validity of the contract at law.[183]

Lack of consideration. On the principle that equity will not aid a volunteer, specific performance will not be ordered of a gratuitous promise[184] even though it is binding at law because it is made by deed or supported by a nominal consideration[185] so that an action at law for the agreed sum or for damages can successfully be brought upon it. Where such a promise is made to a trustee for the benefit of a third party, it has been held that the trustee ought not to enforce the promise at law against the promisor[186] unless the promise can be considered to create a trust which is "already perfect."[187] Under the Contracts (Rights of Third Parties) Act 1999, promises for the benefit of a third party are (if the statutory requirements are satisfied) enforceable not only by the promisee, but also by the third party,[188] who has the right of enforcement even though he has not provided any consideration for the promise.[189] The third party has, moreover, available to him any remedy, including specific performance, that "would have been available to him in an action for breach of the contract if he had been a party to the contract".[190] Nothing in the Act, however, affects the principle that equity will not aid a volunteer. Hence it is clear that if, between promisor and promisee, the contract is binding at law only because it is contained in a deed or supported 27–034

[179] *Coles v Trecothick* (1804) 9 Ves. 234, 246.

[180] Above, para.27–032; *cf. Mortlock v Buller* (1804) 10 Ves. 292.

[181] *Falcke v Gray* (1859) 4 Drew. 651.

[182] See *Mortlock v Buller*, above.

[183] *e.g., Malins v Freeman* (1837) 2 Keen 25; after *Great Peace Shipping Ltd v Tsavliris Shipping International (The Great Peace)* [2002] EWCA Civ 1407, [2003] Q.B. 679 (above, paras 5–060, 5–061) a mistake which is not sufficiently "fundamental" to invalidate the contract at law is no longer a ground for rescission in equity, but it could be a ground for refusal of specific performance.

[184] *Jeffreys v Jeffreys* (1841) Cr. & Ph. 138.

[185] See *Re Parkin* [1892] 3 Ch. 510; *Cannon v Hartley* [1949] Ch. 213. Contrast *Gurtner v Circuit* [1968] 2 Q.B. 587 where the agreement between the Minister and the Motor Insurers' Bureau was said to be specifically enforceable by the Minister. The agreement was made by deed but no consideration seems to have moved from the Minister. *cf.* above, para.18–181.

[186] *Re Pryce* [1917] 1 Ch. 234; *Re Kay* [1939] Ch. 239; criticised by Elliott (1960) 76 L.Q.R. 100; Hornby (1962) 78 L.Q.R. 228; Matheson (1966) 29 M.L.R. 397; Barton (1975) 91 L.Q.R. 236; Meagher and Lehane (1976) 92 L.Q.R. 427. This rule does not apply where a promise in favour of a third party volunteer is made to a promisee who has provided consideration: *Beswick v Beswick* [1968] A.C. 58. above, para.18–020, below, paras 27–050, 27–051.

[187] *Fletcher v Fletcher* (1844) 4 Hare 67, 74.

[188] Above, paras 18–088 *et seq.*

[189] Above, para.18–097.

[190] s.1(5) of the 1999 Act.

by no more than nominal consideration (moving from the promisee), then equity will not order specific performance at the suit of the third party, any more than it will do so at the suit of the promisee. It is less clear what the position would be in the more usual case in which substantial consideration is provided by the promisee but none is provided by the third party. One possible view is that, since the third party is in such a case a volunteer, specific performance will not be ordered in his favour. But this would make the reference to specific performance in the Act, as one of the remedies available to the third party, largely nugatory. The courts may, therefore, prefer to take the view that the equitable principle applies only to gratuitous promises and that specific performance can be ordered at the suit of the third party, even though he has not provided any consideration for the promise, so long as substantial consideration for it has been provided by the promisee.

The principle that equity will not aid a volunteer does not, moreover, apply where an option to buy land is granted by an instrument for which no substantial consideration is given but which is binding because it is made by deed or supported by a nominal consideration. Such an option has some of the characteristics of an offer coupled with a legally binding promise not to revoke[191]; and it may therefore be exercised notwithstanding an attempted revocation. The resulting contract *of sale* can be specifically enforced[192] so long as that contract is supported by substantial consideration. The equitable principle likewise does not affect the validity of a *completed gift*: it is concerned with the enforceability of gratuitous *promises*.[193]

27–035 **Conduct of the claimant.** "The conduct of the party applying for [specific] relief is always an important element for consideration."[194] Thus specific performance may be refused if the claimant fails to perform a promise which he made in order to induce the defendant to enter into the contract, but which is neither binding contractually, nor (because it relates to the future) operative as a misrepresentation.[195] Specific performance may also be refused if the claimant's main object in seeking this form of relief is to avoid a set-off that could have been raised against a claim by him for damages.[196] A similar view may be taken where the claimant has made misrepresentation but the right to rescind for that misrepresentation has been lost. If the right has been lost by reason of the defendant's affirmation of the contract,[197] he will not be allowed to rely on the misrepresentation as a defence to specific performance since he in turn would be guilty of "unconscionable inconsistency in conduct"[198] in seeking, after affirmation, to invoke the misrepresentation for this purpose. But his conduct would not

---

[191] See above, para.3–172, n.943.

[192] *Mountford v Scott* [1975] Ch. 258.

[193] *T Choithram International SA v Pagarani* [2001] 1 W.L.R. 1; *Pennington v Waine* [2002] EWCA Civ 227; [2002] 1 W.L.R. 2075.

[194] *Lamare v Dixon* (1873) L.R. 6 H.L. 414, 413; *Chappell v Times Newspapers Ltd* [1975] 1 W.L.R. 482; *Wilton Group v Abrams* [1990] B.C.C. 310, 317 ("commercially disreputable" agreement).

[195] *Lamare v Dixon*, above.

[196] *Handley Page Ltd v Commissioners of Customs and Excise* [1970] 2 Lloyd's Rep. 459.

[197] Above, paras 6–124—6–128.

[198] *Geest plc v Fyffes plc* [1999] 1 All E.R. (Comm) 672, 694.

be open to such criticism where the right to rescind had been lost by *impossibility of restitution* arising otherwise than from the defendant's conduct.[199] Hence, in a case of this kind the misrepresentation, though no longer a ground for rescission, could be relied on as a defence to the equitable remedy of specific performance.[200]

For the purpose of the principle stated in para.27–035, it may suffice if the claimant has acted unfairly in performing the contract, even though he has not broken any promise. Specific enforcement of a solus petrol agreement[201] has accordingly been denied to an oil company on the ground that the company had given discounts to other garages and had thereby made it impossible for the defendant garage to trade on the terms of the agreement except at a loss.[202] On the other hand, a claimant would not be acting inequitably merely by denying benefits to a defendant if the claimant had done so in accordance with the scheme under which the benefits were to be provided and with the claimant's previously announced policy in operating the scheme.[202a] 27–036

An action could formerly be brought on a contract for the sale of land against a party who had provided written evidence of it by one who had not.[203] It had, however, been held that the principle stated in para.27–035 above was a ground for denying specific performance to a purchaser of land if he refused to perform a stipulation to which he had agreed, but which could not be enforced against him for want of written evidence.[204] A contract for the sale of land must now be made (and not merely evidenced) in writing signed by the parties and the writing must incorporate all the terms on which they have expressly agreed.[205] Hence if the stipulation in question was such a term, but was not contained in the documents, specific performance would now be refused on the different ground that no contract had come into existence. An alternative possibility is that the stipulation might have been intended to take effect as a collateral contract.[206] In that event, the main contract would be valid but the reasoning of the cases referred to above might still lead the court to refuse specific performance to the purchaser if it considered that the vendor would not be adequately protected, after being ordered to perform, by his claim for damages for breach of the collateral contract.[207] 27–037

Contracts expressed to be terminable. If a contract is expressed to be revocable by the party against whom an order of specific performance is sought, 27–038

[199] Above, paras 6–115 *et seq.*
[200] *Geest plc v Fyffes plc*, above, n.198, at p.694.
[201] Above, para.16–124.
[202] *Shell UK Ltd v Lostock Garages Ltd* [1977] 1 W.L.R. 1187.
[202a] *Ministry of Justice v Prison Officers Association* [2008] EWHC 239 (QB), [2008] I.R.L.R. 380.
[203] Law of Property Act 1925, s.40, replacing part of Statute of Frauds 1677, s.4, and now repealed by Law of Property (Miscellaneous Provisions) Act 1989, ss.1(8) and 4 and Sch.2; and see above, para.4–010.
[204] See *Martin v Pycroft* (1852) 2 D.M. & G. 785, 795; *Scott v Bradley* [1971] Ch. 850.
[205] Law of Property (Miscellaneous Provisions) Act 1989, s.2(1).
[206] Above, para.4–076.
[207] *i.e.* on the principle of "mutuality" as now understood: below, para.27–048.

the order will be refused as the defendant could render it nugatory by exercising his power to terminate.[208] On this ground a contract to enter into a partnership at will is not specifically enforceable.[209] The same is true of a contract for a lease which by virtue of the contract itself would contain a stipulation enabling the defendant to determine the lease as soon as it was executed[210]; but a tenancy from year to year, determinable by either party by half a year's notice to quit, is specifically enforceable.[211]

27–039 **Conditional contracts.** On a principle similar to that stated in para.27–038 above, an obligation which, under the contract alleged to give rise to it, is subject to a condition precedent not within the control of the party seeking the remedy will not be specifically enforced before the condition has occurred[212]; here too the making of the order could turn out to be nugatory if the condition were not satisfied. The occurrence of the condition will remove this obstacle to specific performance.[213]

27–040 **Inutility.** The courts will not ordinarily order specific performance of an agreement for a lease, where the term to be granted under the agreement will have expired by the time the order is made.[214] Similarly, specific performance will not be ordered of an agreement for a lease at the suit of a tenant who has so conducted himself that the landlord would have been justified in forfeiting the lease, had it been granted.[215] Specific performance of a promise to issue share warrants has likewise been refused where "the time for the exercise of the option which ought to have been issued" had "long since expired."[216]

27–041 **Impossibility.** Specific performance will not be ordered against a person who has agreed to sell land which he does not own and cannot compel the owner to convey to him,[217] "because the court does not compel a person to do what is impossible."[218] The position is the same where a person has agreed to assign a lease and the landlord withholds his consent, without which the assignment

---

[208] *Wheeler v Trotter* (1737) 3 Swan. 174n. *cf. R (Supportways Community Services Ltd) v Hampshire CC* [2006] EWCA Civ 1035, [2006] B.L.G.R. 836 (relief by way of the public law remedy of judicial review not available to compel (specific) performance of a contract after it had been terminated).

[209] *Hercy v Birch* (1804) 9 Ves. 357; *Sheffield Gas Co v Harrison* (1853) 17 Beav. 294; *cf. Wheeler v Trotter* (1737) Swan. 174n.; but contrast *Allhusen v Borrie* (1867) 15 W.R. 739.

[210] See *Lewis v Bond* (1853) 18 Beav. 85.

[211] *Lever v Koffler* [1901] 1 Ch. 543; but see *Clayton v Illingworth* (1853) 10 Hare 451, in which, however, the suit was dismissed merely "in the absence of any authority"; and *cf. Gray v Spyer* [1922] 2 Ch. 22 (tenancy for year.)

[212] *Chattey v Farndale Holdings Inc.* [1997] 1 E.G.L.R. 153.

[213] *cf. Wu Koon Tai v Wu Yau Loi* [1997] A.C. 179, 189.

[214] *Walters v Northern Coal Mining Co* (1855) 5 De G.M. & G. 629; *cf. Anon. v White* (1709) 3 Swan. 108n.; *Nesbitt v Meyer* (1818) 1 Swan. 223.

[215] *Gregory v Wilson* (1851) 9 Hare 683.

[216] *De Jongh Weill v Mean Fiddler Holdings* [2005] All E.R. (D) 331 (Jul) (Q.B.D., July 22, 2005) at [75]; for earlier proceedings in this case, see [2003] EWCA Civ 1058.

[217] See *Castle v Wilkinson* (1870) L.R. 5 Ch.App. 534; *Watts v Spence* [1976] Ch. 165; *cf. Elliott & Elliott (Builders) Ltd v Pierson* [1948] Ch. 453 (where the vendor sold land owned by a company that he controlled).

[218] *Forrer v Nash* (1865) 35 Beav. 167, 171.

cannot lawfully be effected.[219] Impossibility of enforcing an order of specific performance (*e.g.* because the defendant is not, and has no assets, within the jurisdiction) may also be a reason for refusing to make such an order.[220]

Vagueness. An agreement may be so vague that it cannot be enforced at all, even by an action for damages.[221] But although an agreement is definite enough to be enforced in some form of legal proceedings, it may still be too vague to be enforced specifically.[222] Thus specific performance has been refused of a contract to publish an article as to the exact text of which the parties disagreed.[223] The reason for refusing specific performance in these cases appears to be that the court would find it difficult or impossible to state in its order precisely what the defendant was bound to do in obedience to the order; and precision is essential since failure to comply with the court's order may lead to attachment for contempt.[224] An agreement is not, however, too vague to be specifically enforced merely because it is expressed to be subject to such amendments as may reasonably be required by one (or by either) party.[225] 27–042

Goodwill. The difficulty of precisely formulating the court's order was at one time thought to prevent the specific enforcement of contracts for the sale of goodwill alone, without business premises. Thus in one case involving such a contract Sir William Grant M.R. asked rhetorically: "In what way . . . is the court to decree the transfer of such a business? What is it that I am to direct [the vendor] to do?"[226] But in *Beswick v Beswick*[227] specific performance was ordered of a contract for the sale of goodwill without business premises at the suit of the personal representative of a vendor who had performed his part; and it was said by two members of the House of Lords that specific performance could have been ordered against the vendor, if he had not yet made the transfer.[228] The older, contrary, authorities[229] were not cited; but it seems that they have been made 27–043

---

[219] *Wilmott v Barber* (1880) 15 Ch.D. 96; *Warmington v Miller* [1973] Q.B. 877. And see *Sullivan v Henderson* [1973] 1 W.L.R. 333; above, para.27–011, n.50; contrast *Rose v Stavrou* [2000] L.&T.R. 133, where the remedy sought was not specific performance but a declaration.

[220] *Locobail International Finance Ltd v Agroexport (The Sea Hawk)* [1986] 1 W.L.R. 657, 665.

[221] Above, para.2–133, *Waring & Gillow v Thompson* (1912) 29 T.L.R. 154.

[222] *Collins v Plumb* (1810) 16 Ves. 454 as explained in *Catt v Tourle* (1869) L.R. 4 Ch.App. 654, 658; *Wilson v Northampton & Banbury Junction Railway Co* (1874) 9 Ch.App. 279, as explained in *Tito v Waddell (No.2)* [1977] Ch. 106, 322–323; *cf. Vertex Data Science Ltd v Powergen Retail Ltd* [2006] EWHC 1340 (Comm), [2006] 2 Lloyd's Rep. 591 (above, para.27–027) at [46].

[223] *Joseph v National Magazine Co* [1959] Ch. 14; *cf. Slater v Raw, The Times,* October 15, 1977.

[224] *cf. Lawrence David Ltd v Ashton* [1989] I.C.R. 123, 132; *Lock International plc v Beswick* [1989] 1 W.L.R. 1268.

[225] *Sweet & Maxwell Ltd v Universal News Services Ltd* [1964] 2 Q.B. 699; *Alpenstow Ltd v Regalian Properties plc* [1985] 1 W.L.R. 721.

[226] *Bozon v Farlow* (1816) 1 Mer. 459, 472.

[227] [1968] A.C. 58.

[228] *ibid.* at 89B, 97C.

[229] *Bozon v Farlow*, above; *Baxter v Connolly* (1820) 1 J. & W. 576; *Coslake v Till* (1826) 1 Russ. 376; *Thornbury v Bevill* (1842) 1 Y. & C.C.C. 554, 565; *Darbey v Whitaker* (1857) 3 Drew. 134, 139.

obsolete by the growing legal[230] and commercial precision of the concept of goodwill.

27–044 **Contract specifically enforceable in part only.** In *Ryan v Mutual Tontine Association*[231] the court refused specifically to enforce a landlord's undertaking to have a porter "constantly in attendance"; and it seems unlikely that the court would, even now, order the landlord to enter into a contract with a porter *on such terms*.[232] A claim that the landlord should be ordered simply to appoint a porter was also rejected on the ground that "when the court cannot grant specific performance of the contract as a whole, it will not interfere to compel specific performance of part of a contract."[233] This does not mean that the court cannot order specific performance of one individual obligation out of a number imposed by a contract[234]: it means only that it will not make such an order in relation to one such obligation if it cannot so enforce the rest of the contract.[235] Even in this restricted sense, the rule is by no means an absolute one. Thus where a monetary adjustment can be made in respect of the unperformable part the court may order specific performance with compensation.[236]

27–045 **Mistake, misrepresentation and delay.** Specific performance may be refused on the ground of mistake, misrepresentation and delay even where these factors do (or did) not justify rescission or bar a common law remedy such as damages or the action for the agreed sum. The effect of these factors on the availability of specific performance is discussed elsewhere in this book.[237]

5. MUTUALITY OF REMEDY

27–046 **Requirement of mutuality of remedy.** The court will sometimes refuse to order specific performance at the suit of one party if it cannot order it at the suit of the other. Thus where a party who undertakes to render personal services or to perform continuous duties cannot claim specific performance,[238] the remedy is, for that reason, not available against him[239]; and for the same reason a minor

---

[230] See *Trego v Hunt* [1896] A.C. 7.

[231] [1893] 1 Ch. 116; above para.27–026.

[232] An order requiring the landlord to enter into a contract with a porter could be made where the landlord's undertaking specified the tasks to be done by the porter, as in *Posner v Scott-Lewis* [1988] Ch. 25, above para.27–026.

[233] *Ryan v Mutual Tontine Association* [1893] 1 Ch. 116, 123.

[234] See *Odessa Tramways Co v Mendel* (1878) 8 Ch.D. 235, where such an order was made.

[235] *Rainbow Estates Ltd v Tokenhold Ltd* [1999] Ch. 64, 72–73; *Odessa Tramways Co v Mendel* (1878) 8 Ch.D. 235 (where contract is severable, specific performance of each part can be separately ordered); *Internet Trading Club Ltd v Freeserve Investments Ltd* [2001] E.B.L.R. 142, at [30], where specific performance of an unseverable part was refused.

[236] Below, paras 27–054 to 27–059.

[237] Above, paras 5–063, 6–103; below, paras 28–134 *et seq*.

[238] Above, paras 27–021, 27–022, 27–024, 27–026, 27–028.

[239] *Blackett v Bates* (1865) L.R. 1 Ch.App. 117; *cf. Page One Records Ltd v Britton* [1968] 1 W.L.R. 157 (injunction); a dictum in *Warren v Mendy* [1989] 1 W.L.R. 853, 866 rejects the requirement of mutuality even in this situation, but the ground for refusing specific relief is that stated in para.27–065 below.

cannot get specific performance.[240] Such cases were explained on the ground that the remedy of specific performance must be mutual; and it was said that this requirement had to be satisfied at the time when the contract was made.[241]

27–047 **Qualifications of the requirement.** There are, however, many cases in which specific performance can be ordered in favour of a party even though it could not at the time of contracting have been ordered against him.[242] If A promises to grant a lease of land to B who in return undertakes to build on the land, B's promise to build may not be specifically enforceable[243]; but if he actually does perform that promise he can get specific performance of A's promise to grant the lease.[244] Specific performance cannot be ordered against a person who sells land which he does not own and cannot force the owner to convey to him[245]; but if he becomes owner before the purchaser repudiates[246] he can get specific performance.[247] Conversely, a vendor with defective title may be compelled to convey at a reduced price although he could not himself have got specific performance.[248] It seems that a person of full age can get specific performance of a voidable contract made during minority even though he could have elected to repudiate the contract.[249] And a victim of fraud or innocent misrepresentation can get specific performance although he may be entitled to rescind the contract, so that it could not be enforced against him.[250]

27–048 **Time when requirement must be satisfied.** Cases of the kind described in para.27–047 above show that the requirement of mutuality does not have to be satisfied at the time of contracting: the crucial time is that of the hearing.[251] The requirement was reformulated by Buckley L.J. in *Price v Strange*: the court "will not compel a defendant to perform his obligations specifically if it cannot at the same time ensure that any unperformed obligations of the plaintiff will be specifically performed, unless, perhaps, damages would be an adequate remedy

---

[240] *Flight v Bolland* (1828) 4 Russ. 296; *Lumley v Ravenscroft* [1895] 1 Q.B. 683.

[241] Fry, *Specific Performance* (6th ed.), pp.219, 386. Here we are concerned with mutuality of remedy as a *necessary* requirement. It is also sometimes regarded as a *sufficient* condition when it is said that specific performance can be ordered against a contracting party *merely because* the remedy is available *to* him: this is one reason why specific performance is available *against* a purchaser of land, above, para.27–007. The phrase "lack of mutuality" is also sometimes used to refer to the situation in which a contract purports to be made by an exchange of promises one of which is not binding. In such a case there is no mutuality *of obligation* and accordingly there may be no contract at all; above, paras 3–165 to 3–169.

[242] This possibility was formerly illustrated by the rule that specific performance of a contract for the sale of land could be ordered against a party who had signed a note or memorandum of the contract by one who had not: see *Seton v Slade* (1802) 7 Ves. 265; *Martin v Pycroft* (1852) 2 D.M. & G. 785, 795. Now neither party would have a right of action since no contract would come into existence unless it was in writing signed by both: Law of Property (Miscellaneous Provisions) Act 1989, s.2(1).

[243] Above, para.27–028.

[244] *Wilkinson v Clements* (1872) L.R. 8 Ch.App. 96.

[245] Above, para.27–041.

[246] *Halkett v Dudley* [1970] 1 Ch. 590, 596; *cf. Cleadon Trust v Davies* [1940] 1 Ch. 940.

[247] *Hoggart v Scott* (1830) 1 Russ. & My. 293; *Wylson v Dunn* (1887) 34 Ch.D. 569.

[248] *Mortlock v Buller* (1804) 10 Ves. 292, 315; *Wilson v Williams* (1857) 3 Jur.(N.S.) 810.

[249] *Clayton v Ashdown* (1714) 9 Vin.Abr. 393 (G. 4) 1.

[250] Above, para.6–103.

[251] *cf. E. Johnson & Co (Barbados) Ltd v NSR Ltd* [1997] A.C. 400, 410–411.

for any default on the plaintiff's part."[252] The defendant in that case had promised to grant an underlease to the plaintiff who had in return undertaken to execute certain internal and external repairs. It was admitted that the plaintiff's undertakings were not specifically enforceable; and it seems that he could not have obtained specific performance of the promise to grant the underlease before any of the repairs had been done. For in that case the only remedy available to the defendant for default on the plaintiff's part might have been in damages, and this might have been inadequate,[253] especially if the plaintiff was of doubtful solvency. But in fact the plaintiff had done the internal repairs and had been wrongfully prevented from doing the external ones by the defendant, who later had these done at her own expense. As by the time of the hearing all the repairs had been completed, specific enforcement of the defendant's promise to grant the underlease would not expose her to the risk of having no remedy except damages in the event of the plaintiff's default; and specific performance was ordered on the terms that the plaintiff make an allowance in respect of the repairs done by the defendant. The principle that mutuality is judged by reference to the time of the hearing similarly accounts for the rule that a person who has been induced to enter into a contract by misrepresentation can specifically enforce the contract against the other; for by seeking this remedy he affirms the contract[254] and so gives the court power to hold him to it.[255] The court has no such power when specific performance is claimed on behalf of a minor: "the act of filing the bill by his next friend cannot bind him"[256] (*sc.* to perform his side of the bargain.) Similarly, it seems that lack of mutuality would still be good reason for refusing specific performance to A where A agreed to serve B in consideration of B's promise to convey a house to him and B repudiated before A had completed the agreed service.

6. SPECIFIC PERFORMANCE AND THIRD PARTIES

27–049 **Introduction.** Where A promises B to render some performance in favour of C, two problems can arise with regard to the specific enforceability of A's

[252] [1978] Ch. 337, 367–368; adopting Ames, 3 Col.L.Rev. 1; *Rainbow Estates Ltd v Tokenhold Ltd* [1999] Ch. 64, 69, 75. See also *Sutton v Sutton* [1984] Ch. 184 where the argument of lack of mutuality was rejected because one of the claimant's promises had been performed, even though another was not binding. Specific performance was refused on grounds of public policy, above, para.16–044.

[253] *cf. National Provincial Building Society v British Waterways Board* [1992] E.G.C.S. 149 where specific performance of a contract for the sale of land was claimed by an assignee of the purchaser's rights and it was held to be a defence that the purchaser's obligation to develop the land remained unperformed and no satisfactory remedy was available to the vendor as the purchaser had been compulsorily wound up without sufficient assets to meet the vendor's claim. If the claimant can be ordered to give additional, satisfactory security, he can obtain an order of specific performance even though he has not yet performed and is not ordered immediately to do so: *Langen & Wind Ltd v Bell* [1972] Ch. 685.

[254] Above, para.6–124.

[255] This reasoning still holds good in the situation described in the text above. It was formerly used to explain the now obsolete rule stated in n.242 above: see *Martin v Mitchell* (1820) 2 J. & W. 413, 427; *Flight v Bolland* (1828) 4 Russ. 298, 301.

[256] *Flight v Bolland*, above, at 301.

promise. The first is whether B can specifically enforce the promise against A; the second is whether C can do so.

(a) *Claim by Promisee*

Promisee seeking specific performance in favour of third party. In *Beswick v Beswick*[257] A promised B (in return for B's transfer of his business to A) to pay an annuity to B's widow, C, after B's death. The House of Lords held that this promise could be specifically enforced by B's personal representative (who happened to be C) against A.[258] Thus A was ordered to pay the annuity to C, who in this way obtained the benefit of a contract to which she was not a party even though the case did not fall within any exception to the common law doctrine of privity of contract.[259–260] Under the Contracts (Rights of Third Parties) Act 1999,[261] C will in many such cases be entitled in his or her own right to enforce against A the term in the contract containing the promise in favour of C; and where C takes this course, the need for B to seek specific performance in favour of C will be much reduced. But it will not be altogether eliminated since there may still be situations in which C will not have any such right against A because the requirements set out in the 1999 Act for the acquisition of such rights by C have not been satisfied.[262] The Act also expressly preserves B's right to enforce any term of the contract against A even where C has acquired a right of enforcement against A.[263] The scope of B's remedy by way of specific performance therefore continues to call for discussion. 27–050

In holding that this remedy was available to B, the House of Lords in *Beswick v Beswick* stressed three points: (1) (that B's remedy at law was inadequate as the damages, which he could recover would in the view of the majority of the House, be merely nominal[264]); (2) that the promisor (A) had received the entire consideration for his promise[265]; and (3) that the contract could have been specifically enforced *by* A, had B refused to perform his promise to transfer the business.[266] It is also relevant to the issue of specific enforceability that A's promise was one to pay an annuity and so would have been specifically enforceable if it had been made to B for his own benefit[267]; that, apart from his inadequate remedy by way of damages, B had no other, more satisfactory,

[257] [1968] A.C. 58; above, paras 18–020; Goodhart (1967) 83 L.Q.R. 465; Fairest [1967] C.L.J. 149; Treitel (1967) 30 M.L.R. 687.

[258] Similar orders had been made in *Keenan v Handley* (1864) 12 W.R. 930; affirmed (1864) 2 D.J. & S.; *Peel v Peel* (1869) 17 W.R. 586; *Drimmie v Davies* [1899] 1 I.R. 176 (but in this case there was probably a trust in favour of the third party); and in *Hohler v Aston* [1920] 2 Ch. 420.

[259–260] Above, Ch.18.

[261] Above, paras 18–088 *et seq.*

[262] *e.g.* because the requirements of ss.1(1) and (2) are not satisfied; see above para.18–093 for the question whether they would be satisfied on the facts of *Beswick v Beswick*, above.

[263] s.4 of the 1999 Act.

[264] *ibid.* at 81E, 102A; *cf.* at 73B, 83F. Lord Pearce, alone, thought that damages would be substantial, *ibid.* at 88F. *cf.* above, para.18–047.

[265] At 83A, 89B, 97C, 102C; *cf.* at 73C; and see *Hart v Hart* (1881) 18 Ch.D. 670, 685.

[266] At 89B, 97C; as to the specific enforceability of B's promise, see above, para.27–049.

[267] Above, para.27–008. The first three cases cited in n.258, above, were also annuity cases; the contract in the fourth case was a contract for the disposition of an interest in land and so specifically enforceable.

remedy at law[268]; and that, if the promise had been made to B for his own benefit, specific performance would not have been refused on any of the other grounds (than the availability of satisfactory remedy at law) which have been discussed in this Chapter.[269]

27–051 **Possible limitations on the remedy.** It therefore does not follow from *Beswick v Beswick* that the promisee can in all cases of contracts for the benefit of a third party obtain an order of specific performance in favour of the third party. In particular, the case is not direct authority for the availability of such a remedy in any of the following cases: (1) where the promisee has a remedy at law other than for nominal damages: *e.g.* for substantial damages,[270] for recovery of the consideration provided by him,[271] or for the agreed sum[272]; (2) where the promisor has not received the whole (or any part of) the consideration for his promise; (3) where the contract, if wholly executory, could not have been specifically enforced by the promisor[273]; and (4) where the promise sued upon would not have been specifically enforceable by the promisee, if it had been made to him for his own benefit. It is submitted that in such cases specific performance should neither be granted merely because the contract provides for performance in favour of a third party, nor refused merely because it would not have been available, had there been no third party in the case. As a general principle, it is submitted that the promisee should be able to obtain specific performance in favour of the third party whenever that is the most appropriate method of enforcing the contract which was actually made.[274] But it should be open to the defendant to resist specific enforcement by showing that this remedy would lead to one of the undesirable results against which the established limitations on the scope of the remedy[275] are meant to provide protection.

27–052 **Examples.** The scope of the promisee's remedy of specific performance in favour of third parties may be illustrated by a series of examples. In discussing these, an attempt will be made to apply the general statement made at the end of the preceding paragraph; but in the present state of the authorities some of the solutions which will be put forward can be no more than tentative.

(*a*) A promises[276] B to render personal services to C. B should not be able to obtain specific performance in favour of C, because the policy of the rule

[268] Possible remedies are referred to in para.27–052 (examples (e) and (f)).
[269] *i.e.* in paras 27–030—27–045 above.
[270] Above, para.18–047.
[271] Above, para.18–045. This remedy was probably not available in *Beswick v Beswick*. There was no "total failure of consideration," both by reason of the facts stated in n.279 below, and because A had made one payment to the widow.
[272] Above, para.18–046. The mere fact that the action for the agreed sum is available to the claimant is no bar to specific performance: see *Miliangos v George Frank (Textiles) Ltd* [1976] A.C. 443.
[273] The requirement of mutuality of remedy could give rise to difficulty in such a case: see below, para.27–052 at n.278.
[274] See especially [1968] A.C. 58, 88G, 102B and the citation with approval by Lord Pearce at 90–91 of a dictum of Windeyer J. in *Coulls v Bagot's Executor & Trustee Co Ltd* (1967) 40 A.L.J.R. 471, 488; and *cf.* above, para.27–005.
[275] See especially, paras 27–021—27–022, above.
[276] The "promises" in this and the following examples are assumed to be binding contractually.

against the specific enforcement of contracts to render personal services[277] applies no less where the services are to be rendered to a third party than where they are to be rendered to the promisee.

(*b*) A promises B to pay £1,000 to C immediately, in return for B's promise (as yet unperformed) to serve A for one year. B should not be able to obtain specific performance in favour of C, because the grant of this remedy would expose A to the hardship which the requirement of mutuality of remedy[278] is intended to prevent.

(*c*) The facts are as in (*b*), except that B has performed the service. Specific performance in favour of C should not be refused merely because A could not, when the contract was made, have obtained specific performance against B. Now that A has got the whole of what he bargained for, he cannot suffer the hardship which the requirement of mutuality is intended to prevent.[279]

(*d*) A promises B to pay £1,000 per annum to C for 10 years in return for B's promise (as yet unperformed) to transfer to A 100 shares in the X company; the shares are freely available in the market. Specific performance in favour of C should not be refused to B merely because specific performance could not have been ordered against him.[280] The hardship against which the mutuality rule is intended to protect A can here be prevented by making the order in favour of C conditional on B's making the agreed transfer. Specific performance in favour of C might, however, be properly refused if the factors mentioned in example (*g*) below operate so as to cause hardship to A.

(*e*) Examples (*b*) and (*d*) can be varied by supposing part performance by B. It is submitted that this should not generally affect the outcome; but that, by way of exception to this general principle, specific performance in favour of C should, perhaps, be ordered in a case like example (*b*) if B had substantially (though not completely) performed his promise so that the risk of hardship to A as a result of the order was minimal.[281]

(*f*) A (an insurance company) promises B to pay a sum of money to C in 20 years' time. The contract does not fall within any of the exceptions to the doctrine of privity of contract.[282] B has duly paid all the premiums. B should be able to obtain specific performance in favour of C though in a two-party case B's remedy would have been, not an order for specific performance, but an action for the agreed sum.[283] It should make no difference that B might, in the event of A's refusal or failure to pay C have

---

[277] Above, para.27–021.

[278] Above, para.27–046.

[279] Above, para.27–048. In *Beswick v Beswick* itself the contract provided that B should serve A as consultant for life in return for a payment of £6 10s. per week. This stipulation had been performed and was also held not to destroy "mutuality" because of its minimal importance (see [1968] A.C. at 97C).

[280] Above, para.27–011; damages would be an adequate remedy for A in a two-party case.

[281] *cf.* example (c) at n.279 above.

[282] Above, paras 18–077—18–132.

[283] Above, para.27–006. And see above, para.27–051, at n.270.

a substantial remedy at common law: *e.g.* for the recovery of the premiums as paid on a total failure of consideration,[284] or for the agreed sum (*e.g.* if he is named as an alternative payee),[285] or for substantial damages in respect of foreseeable loss arising from A's default.[286] In spite of the availability of such common law remedies, specific performance in favour of C is here the most appropriate[287] remedy for the enforcement of the contract; and to grant it would not conflict with any of the policies limiting the scope of the remedy in a two-party case.

(*g*) A promises B that, in return for an immediate payment of £100 by B he will supply 10 tons of coal to C in six months' time. A fails to deliver as agreed; and after breach the market price rises. If the promise had been made to B for his own benefit, B would have been bound to mitigate by taking reasonable steps to procure a substitute (*i.e.* by buying against A in the market where this was possible.) One reason for refusing B specific performance in such a case is that the grant of the remedy would in substance deprive A of the benefit of the mitigation rule.[288] It is not easy to see how this rule can be applied to contracts for the benefit of a third party; for if the promisee's damages are nominal[289] he can hardly mitigate, and it does not seem that there can (at common law[290]) be any requirement that the third party must take steps to mitigate loss. Yet specific performance in favour of C could cause considerable hardship to A in such a case and should probably be refused if such hardship is established.

(b) *Claim by Third Party*

27–053 **Effect of Contracts (Rights of Third Parties) Act 1999.** Under this Act, C is in many cases entitled in his own right to enforce against A the term in the contract between A and B containing A's promise in favour of C.[291] The Act expressly lists specific performance as one of the remedies available to C where it would have been available to him "if he had been a party to the contract;" and

---

[284] Above, para.18–044. To restrict B to such a remedy would be unjust if the policy had matured and its value at the maturity was worth substantially more than the premiums which had been paid.

[285] For the question whether, or when in the case of a contract to pay money to a third party an action for the agreed sum can be brought by the promisee, see above, para.18–046.

[286] *e.g.* if B had contracted with C to procure A's payments to C, or was otherwise under a legal obligation to ensure that they (or corresponding payments) were made, or (possibly) if it was foreseeable that B would make a substitute provision for C in the event of A's default, whether or not B was under a legal obligation to do so; above, para.18–054; Treitel (1967) 30 M.L.R. 687. For the question whether B could recover damages in respect of C's loss, see above paras 18–052 *et seq.*

[287] See, above, para.27–005 at n.22. *cf. Gurtner v Circuit* [1968] 2 Q.B. 587 as to which see above, para.27–034, n.185; *Sears v Tanenbaum* [1969] 9 D.L.R. (3d) 425.

[288] Above, para.27–002. This argument would apply even if the case fell within s.52 of the Sale of Goods Act 1979, *e.g.* because the goods were ascertained.

[289] *cf.* above, para.27–009.

[290] If C (not B) brings the action under s.1(1) of the Contracts (Rights of Third Parties) Act 1999, he would be required, by virtue of s.1(5) to comply with the mitigation rules.

[291] Above, paras 18–088 *et seq.*

it states that the rules relating to specific performance "shall apply accordingly."[292] Some such rules will apply to a claim by C in the same way as they apply to one by B: *e.g.*, if A's promise is one to render personal services to C, that promise will not be specifically enforceable at the suit of either B or C. Other rules will obviously apply with some modification; *e.g.*, if A promises B to pay a lump sum to C, then the most appropriate remedy for B might be specific performance in equity, while for C it would be a common law action for the agreed sum. Where C claims specific performance of A's promise under the 1999 Act, the application of the limitations on the scope of the remedy will need to be worked out on a case by case basis in the light of the policies which have given rise to these limitations in two-party cases.

7. SPECIFIC PERFORMANCE WITH COMPENSATION[293]

Misdescription. Apart from stipulations relating to errors or misdescription, a vendor of land could not at law sue on an executory contract if the land did not correspond with the contractual description. But in such cases equity could order specific performance with "compensation"—*i.e.* with adjustment of the purchase price. This jurisdiction may be exercised where the area of the land sold is less than that stated in the contract,[294] where there is a defect of title,[295] and where there is a physical defect.[296] 27–054

A vendor may obtain specific performance with compensation provided that the misdescription is not fraudulently or wilfully made,[297] that it does not affect the substance of the purchaser's bargain,[298] and that adequate compensation for the defect or deficiency can be made by a monetary adjustment.[299] A purchaser may succeed in a claim for specific performance with compensation even though the misdescription is of a degree of seriousness that would preclude the grant of the remedy to the vendor.[300] But the remedy will not be granted to a purchaser where it will prejudice third parties,[301] where it will inflict undue hardship on the vendor,[302] where the purchaser knows the true facts at the time of contracting,[303] 27–055

---

[292] s.1(5) of the 1999 Act.

[293] Harpum [1981] C.L.J. 108.

[294] *Aspinalls to Powell and Scholefield* (1889) 60 L.T. 595.

[295] *Burrow v Scammell* (1881) 19 Ch.D. 175.

[296] *Shepherd v Croft* [1911] 1 Ch. 521; *cf. Lyons v Thomas* [1986] I.R. 666 (where the defects arose after contract).

[297] *Price v Macaulay* (1852) 2 De G.M. & G. 339, 345; *Shepherd v Croft* [1911] 1 Ch. 521; *Re Belcham & Gawley's Contract* [1930] 1 Ch. 56 (where the vendor knew of the existence of the defect).

[298] *Re Fawcett & Holmes' Contract* (1889) 42 Ch.D. 150; *Jacobs v Revell* [1900] 2 Ch. 858; *Watson v Burton* [1957] 1 W.L.R. 19; *cf. Flight v Booth* (1834) 1 Bing.N.C. 370; *Re Puckett & Smith's Contract* [1902] 2 Ch. 258; *Ridley v Oster* [1939] 1 All E.R. 618; *Walker v Boyle* [1982] 1 W.L.R. 495.

[299] *Cato v Thompson* (1882) 9 Q.B.D. 616, 618.

[300] Williams, *Vendor and Purchaser* (4th ed.), p.725.

[301] *Willmot v Barber* (1880) 15 Ch.D. 96 (covenant not to assign lease without licence of lessor).

[302] *Durham v Legard* (1865) 34 Beav. 611; *Rudd v Lascelles* [1900] 1 Ch. 815.

[303] *Castle v Wilkinson* (1870) L.R. 5 Ch. 534.

or where compensation cannot readily be assessed in money.[304] In these cases the purchaser may be entitled to rescind; but if he seeks specific performance he can enforce the contract only without compensation.[305] This rule also applies where there is no misdescription in the contract but only a misrepresentation inducing it[306]; but under s.2(2) of the Misrepresentation Act 1967 the court has in such a case a discretion to declare the contract subsisting and to award "damages" in lieu of rescission.[307] The effect of the exercise of this discretion would probably be similar to that of specific performance with compensation. The main difference between the old equitable and the new statutory powers is that the former was exercisable only before,[308] while the latter can be invoked even after, completion.[309]

27–056 **Condition against error or misdescription.** A contract for the sale of land may provide that errors and misdescriptions shall not annul the sale but shall give rise to a claim for compensation; sometimes the provision may purport to exclude the purchaser's right to compensation for error or misdescription. The first question in such a case is as to the true construction of the provision. Generally it will not apply to defects of title[310]; but it is not invariably restricted to physical defects and may apply where the extent of a restrictive covenant is wrongly stated in the contract.[311]

27–057 A provision of the kind described in para.27–056 above will not help the vendor where the misdescription was wilful or fraudulent,[312] so that in such a case the purchaser can resist a claim for specific performance and rescind the contract. The position was held to be the same[313] where the defect was substantial[314] and where compensation could not readily be assessed in money.[315] These cases seem to be applications of what later became known as the doctrine of fundamental breach[316] and similar cases would now seem to turn on the

---

[304] *Rudd v Lascelles*, above, n.302.

[305] *Durham v Legard*, above, n.302.

[306] *Gilchester Properties Ltd v Gomm* [1948] 1 All E.R. 493; *cf. Clayton v Leech* (1889) 41 Ch.D. 103; *Rutherford v Acton-Adams* [1915] A.C. 866.

[307] Above, paras 6–096—6–102.

[308] *Joliffe v Baker* (1883) 11 Q.B.D. 255; *Clayton v Leech* (1889) 41 Ch.D. 103; the position is different where the contract expressly provides for compensation: below, para.27–058 at nn.330 and 331.

[309] Misrepresentation Act 1967, s.1(b) leads to this result.

[310] *Re Beyfus and Master's Contract* (1888) 39 Ch.D. 110; and see *Debenham v Sawbridge* [1901] 2 Ch. 98, 107, 108.

[311] *Re Courcier and Harrold's Contract* [1923] 1 Ch. 565.

[312] *Duke of Norfolk v Worthy* (1808) 1 Camp. 337; *Re Terry and White's Contract* (1886) 32 Ch.D. 14, 29; *Shepherd v Croft* [1911] 1 Ch. 521, 531; see above, paras 6–134, 14–136.

[313] *Flight v Booth* (1834) 1 Bing.N.C. 370; *Jacobs v Revell* [1900] 2 Ch. 858; *Re Puckett and Smith's Contract* [1902] 2 Ch. 258; *Lee v Rayson* [1971] 1 Ch. 613.

[314] See *Dimmock v Hallett* (1866) L.R. 2 Ch.App. 21; *Re Terry and White's Contract* (1886) 32 Ch.D. 14, 29; *Re Fawcett and Holmes' Contract* (1889) 42 Ch.D 150; *Re Puckett and Smith's Contract* [1902] 2 Ch. 258; *Lee v Rayson* [1917] 1 Ch. 613; contrast *Re Courcier and Harrold's Contract* [1923] 1 Ch. 565; *Beyfus v Lodge* [1925] Ch. 350; *Watson v Burton* [1957] 1 W.L.R. 19.

[315] *Brooke v Rounthwaite* (1846) 5 Hare 298; *Rudd v Lascelles* [1900] 1 Ch. 815; and see Williams, *Vendor and Purchaser* (4th ed.), pp.728–732.

[316] Above, para.14–020.

construction of the provision in question[317] rather than on any substantive rule making it impossible to exclude the court's power to order specific performance with compensation. Provisions of the present kind are not subject to the requirement of reasonableness under ss.2 to 4 of the Unfair Contract Terms Act 1977[318] since those sections do not apply to any contract so far as it relates to the creation or transfer of an interest in land.[319] The point may be important where a developer enters into a contract for the sale of a house on "written standard terms" which would otherwise be subject to the requirement of reasonableness under s.3 of the Act. It has been held that the Unfair Terms in Consumer Contracts Regulations 1999[320] apply to contracts for the sale of an interest in land by a commercial supplier to a consumer.[321] It follows that terms of the kind here under discussion in such a contract would not bind the consumer if they were "unfair" within the meaning given to that expression in the Regulations.[322]

Effects of misdescription as a misrepresentation. Further problems as to the effectiveness of a condition against error or misdescription can arise where the misdescription did not form part of the contract but was only a misrepresentation inducing it; or where it originated as such a misrepresentation and was later incorporated in the contract as one of its terms. In such cases, the representee can rescind the contract for misrepresentation,[323] and if the misrepresentation related to a matter that was substantial this right to rescind would not normally be affected by a condition of the kind here under discussion.[324] If, on the other hand, the matter misrepresented was *not* substantial, it is likely that the court would, even in the absence of such a condition, reject a claim to rescind for misrepresentation; more probably, it would declare the contract as subsisting and award damages in lieu of rescission.[325] The further question then arises, whether a condition against error or misdescription would, in such a situation, be ineffective under s.3 of the Misrepresentation Act 1967.[326] Under this section, a contract term which would exclude or restrict any remedy available to a contracting party by reason of a misrepresentation made before the contract was made is subject to the requirement of reasonableness. Before the Act, it was held that a condition which excluded the right to rescind *and* the right to compensation entitled the vendor to enforce the contract without compensation.[327] Now, such a condition might well be regarded as unreasonable in so far as it excluded the purchaser's right to compensation, or his right to rescind for a misrepresentation relating to a matter that was of substantial importance.[328] But if the matter misrepresented 27–058

---

317 *Photo Production Ltd v Securicor Transport Ltd* [1980] A.C. 827; *George Mitchell (Chesterhall) Ltd v Finney Lock Seeds Ltd* [1983] 2 A.C. 803; above, paras 14–022, 14–023.

318 Above, paras 14–059 *et seq*.

319 Unfair Contract Terms Act 1977, Sch.1, para.1(c).

320 SI 1999/2083.

321 *London Borough of Newham v Khatun* [2004] EWCA Civ 55, [2005] Q.B. 37.

322 See above, para.15–019.

323 Misrepresentation Act 1967, s.1(a); above, para.6–105.

324 Above, at n.314.

325 Misrepresentation Act 1967, s.2(2); above, para.6–097.

326 As amended by Unfair Contract Terms Act 1977, s.8; above, paras 6–136—6–140.

327 *Re Courcier and Harrold's Contract* [1923] 1 Ch. 565.

328 *Walker v Boyle* [1982] 1 W.L.R. 495; *cf. Cremdean Properties Ltd v Nash* (1877) 244 E.G. 547; *South Western General Property Co v Marton* (1982) 263 E.G. 263.

was of only minor importance, and the condition, while excluding the right to rescind, *provided* for compensation, it is submitted that the requirement of reasonableness would normally be satisfied. For such a condition would not prejudice the purchaser: it would only give contractual effect to the right that the vendor would have had, even in the absence of the condition, to specific performance with compensation, or to the result that the court would be likely to reach under s.2(2) of the Misrepresentation Act 1967.[329] Indeed, in one respect a condition in these terms might even benefit the purchaser; for the equitable rule that compensation could be claimed only *before* completion[330] does not apply where the contract contains such a provision.[331]

27–059 **Compensation to vendor.** A condition which provides for compensation may also entitle the vendor to compensation for errors to his disadvantage.[332]

8. INJUNCTION

27–060 **Negative contracts.** Where a contract is negative in nature, or contains an express negative stipulation, breach of it may be restrained by injunction.[333] In such cases an injunction is normally granted as a matter of course, though since it is an equitable, and thus in principle a discretionary, remedy, it may be refused on the ground that its award would cause such "particular hardship"[334] to the defendant as to be oppressive to him.[335] An injunction would not be "oppressive" merely because observance of the contract was burdensome to the defendant[336] or because its breach would cause little or no prejudice to the claimant,[337] for, in deciding whether to restrain breach of a negative stipulation, the court is not normally concerned with "'the balance of convenience or inconvenience.'"[338] This rule, however, applies only to a *prohibitory* injunction restraining a defendant from *future* breaches. If he has already broken his contract (*e.g.* by fencing land that he promised to leave open) he may be ordered by a *mandatory*

---

[329] Above, at n.325.

[330] Above, para.27–055, at n.308.

[331] *Bos v Helsham* (1866) L.R. 2 Ex. 72; *Re Turner and Skelton* (1879) 13 Ch.D. 130; *Palmer v Johnson* (1884) 13 Q.B.D. 351.

[332] *Leslie v Thompson* (1851) 9 Hare 268.

[333] *Martin v Nutkin* (1724) 2 P.Wms. 266. An injunction cannot be granted to restrain a party to a contract from doing acts which have, because the contract has been brought to an end, ceased to be breaches of the contract: see *Medina Housing Association v Case* [2002] EWCA Civ 2001; [2003] 1 All E.R. 1084. It is, of course, possible for a negative stipulation to continue to apply after positive obligations of performance have come to an end, whether by notice or by lapse of time, as in the restraint of trade cases discussed in para.27–068, below.

[334] *Insurance Co v Lloyd's Syndicate* [1985] 1 Lloyd's Rep. 273, 276 (where there was no such hardship). *cf.* above, para.27–031 (severe hardship).

[335] See below, para.27–063.

[336] *cf.* above, para.27–031.

[337] *Kemp v Sober* (1851) 1 Sim.(N.S.) 517; *Tipping v Eckersley* (1855) 2 K. & J. 264; *Marco Productions Ltd v Pagola* [1945] K.B. 111; *Hollis v Stocks* [2000] UKCLR 685.

[338] *Doherty v Allman* (1878) 3 App.Cas. 709, 720; *cf. Warner Bros Pictures Inc. v Nelson* [1937] 1 K.B. 209, 217; *Wakeham v Wood* (1982) 43 P. & C.R. 40; *Att.-Gen. v Barker* [1990] 3 All E.R. 257, 262.

injunction actually to undo the breach. Such an order *is* subject to a "balance of convenience" test, and may, accordingly, be refused if the prejudice suffered by the defendant in having to restore the original position heavily outweighs the advantage that will be derived from such restoration by the claimant.[339] On the other hand, the court will also, in applying the balance of convenience test, take account of the nature of the breach. Thus where the defendant had in breach of a restrictive covenant erected a building so as to block the claimant's sea view, a mandatory injunction was granted as the breach had been committed deliberately, with full knowledge of the claimant's rights, and as damages would not have been an adequate remedy.[340]

Interim injunctions. Applications for interim injunctions are likewise subject (*inter alia*) to the "balance of convenience" test[341]; except where there is "a plain and uncontested breach of a clear covenant not to do a particular thing."[342] One application of the balance of convenience test is to cases where the injunction is sought for such a period that to grant it would amount in substance to a final resolution of the dispute between the parties. The court will, in considering such a claim for interim relief, take into account the likelihood of the claimant's success at the eventual trial.[343] The court can also take into account the financial prejudice which is likely to be suffered either by the claimant if the injunction is refused,[344] or by the defendant if it is granted,[345] and if at the trial the dispute 27–061

339 *Sharp v Harrison* [1922] 1 Ch. 502; *Shepherd Homes Ltd v Sandham* [1971] Ch. 340; for subsequent proceedings, see [1971] 1 W.L.R. 1062; *Films Rover International Ltd v Cannon Film Sales* [1987] 1 W.L.R. 670 (for further proceedings, see [1989] 1 W.L.R. 912); *Sutton Housing Trust v Lawrence* (1987) 19 H.L.R. 520 (mandatory and prohibitory injunction); *Reed v Madon* [1989] Ch. 408; *Land Rover Group Ltd v UPF (UK) Ltd* [2002] EWHC 3183, [2003] B.C.L.C. 122 at [60], where the "balance of convenience" test was applicable also on the principle stated in para.27–061 below as the injunction was an interim one.

340 *Wakeham v Wood* (1982) 43 P. & C.R. 40; *cf. Mortimer v Bailey* [2004] EWCA Civ 1514, [2005] 2 P. & C.R. 9 (where the main issue was whether there had been undue delay in applying for a mandatory injunction to pull down an extension built in breach of covenant.

341 *Texaco Ltd v Mulberry Filling Station Ltd* [1972] 1 W.L.R. 814; *Evans Marshall & Co v Bertola* [1973] 1 W.L.R. 349; *Clifford Davis Management Ltd v W.E.A. Records Ltd* [1975] 1 W.L.R. 61; *Mike Trading & Transport Ltd v R. Pagnan & Fratelli* [1980] 2 Lloyd's Rep. 546; *Locobail International Finance v Agroexport (The Sea Hawk)* [1986] 1 W.L.R. 657; *Kerr v Morris* [1987] Ch. 90, 112; *Films Rover International v Cannon Film Sales Ltd* [1987] 1 W.L.R. 670, for further proceedings see [1989] 1 W.L.R. 912; *Evening Standard Co Ltd v Henderson* [1987] I.C.R. 588; *Provident Financial Group Ltd v Hayward* [1989] I.C.R. 160; *Lock International plc v Beswick* [1989] 1 W.L.R. 1268; *Channel Tunnel Group v Balfour Beatty Construction Ltd* [1993] A.C. 334; *GFI Group Inc. v Eaglestone*, [1994] I.R.L.R. 119; *Series 5 Software v Clarke* [1996] 1 All E.R. 853; *Tate & Lyle Industries v Cia. Usina Bulhoes* [1997] 1 Lloyd's Rep. 355; *Townsend Group Ltd v Cobb* [2004] EWHC 3432, *The Times*, December 1, 2004. For the principles governing such injunctions, see generally *American Cyanamid Co v Ethicon Ltd* [1975] A.C. 396; *Fellowes v Fisher* [1976] Q.B. 122 and *Lawrence David Ltd v Ashton* [1989] I.C.R. 123 (holding these principles to be applicable in restraint of trade cases).

342 *Hampstead and Suburban Properties Ltd v Diomedous* [1969] 1 Ch. 248, 259; *cf. Att.-Gen. v Barker* [1990] 3 All E.R. 257.

343 *Cambridge Nutrition Ltd v B.B.C.* [1990] 3 All E.R. 523; *Lansing Linde Ltd v Kerr* [1991] 1 W.L.R. 251, 258–259; *Imutran v Uncaged Campaigns Ltd* [2001] 2 All E.R. 385.

344 *Themehelp Ltd v West* [1996] Q.B. 84, doubted on another point in *Group Josi Re v Walbrook Ins. Co Ltd* [1996] 1 W.L.R. 1152, 1162.

345 *Cambridge Nutrition Ltd v B.B.C.* [1990] 3 All E.R. 523; *P. I. International Ltd v Llewellyn* [2005] EWHC 407, [2005] U.K.C.L.R. 530.

were to be resolved in that party's favour. An award of damages to that party might then be an "inadequate" remedy for reasons discussed earlier in this Chapter[346]: *e.g.* because there was an appreciable risk of the other party's not being able to pay the amount of the award.

27–062 **Exclusive alternative remedy.** An injunction will not be granted to restrain breach of a restrictive covenant affecting land against a body which has acquired the land under statutory powers where the legislation has provided an exclusive remedy by way of statutory compensation.[347]

27–063 **Oppression.** We shall see later in this Chapter[348] that the court has power by statute to award damages in lieu of specific performance or injunction. That power is likely to be exercised if the injury to the claimant is small, if it can readily be estimated in money, if compensation in money would adequately compensate the claimant and if the grant of an injunction would be oppressive to the defendant.[349] These conditions were satisfied, and an injunction was accordingly refused, in *Jaggard v Sawyer*,[350] where the defendants had built a house on land which could be reached only by committing a breach of covenant and a trespass against neighbouring house-owners, including the plaintiff. An injunction restraining such access would have rendered the new house "landlocked and incapable of beneficial ownership"[351]; and this would have been oppressive as the defendants had acted "openly and in good faith"[352] and not "in blatant disregard of the plaintiff's rights"[353] in building the house. The test is, again, one of *oppression*,[354] rather than one of *balance of convenience*: if the plaintiff had sought interlocutory relief *before* the house had been built, she "would almost certainly have obtained it"[355]

27–064 **Express negative promises.** Specific performance will not generally be ordered of contracts of personal service[356]; and the same principle generally

[346] Above, para.27–008 at n.40.
[347] *Brown v Heathlands Mental Health N.H. Trust* [1996] 1 All E.R. 133.
[348] See below, para.27–077.
[349] See the tort case of *Shelfer v City of London Electric Light Co* [1895] 1 Ch. 287, 322–333. The requirements stated in the text above do not apply where it is the *defendant* who claims that specific relief is the more appropriate remedy since in such a case the grant of the injunction cannot be oppressive to him: *Marcic v Thames Water Utilities (No.2)* [2001] 4 All E.R. 327 reversed on another ground [2003] UKHL 66; [2004] 1 All E.R. 135.
[350] [1995] 1 W.L.R. 269.
[351] *ibid.* at 288.
[352] *ibid.* at 289.
[353] *ibid.* at 283.
[354] *cf.* above at n.338.
[355] [1995] 1 W.L.R. at 289, *cf.* 283. See also the similar case of *Gafford v Graham*, (1998) 76 P. & C.R. D18; and the tort case of *Regan v Paul Properties Ltd* [2006] EWCA Civ 1391, [2007] Ch. 135 where the claimant had begun to protest five months before interference with his right to light by the defendant became imminent and was granted injunctive relief. Contrast the further tort case of *Watson v Croft Promosport Ltd* [2008] EWHC 759 (QB), [2008] 3 All E.R. 1171 at [85]–[87] where an injunction was refused and damages in lieu were awarded to the victims of the tort as there had been "considerable delay" in bringing the proceedings and the claimants had themselves shown their "willingness to accept compensation instead of an injunction" in respect of a noise nuisance.
[356] Above, para.27–021.

precludes the specific enforcement of such a contract by an injunction restraining the employee from committing a breach of his positive obligation to work or the employer from dismissing the employee in breach of contract.[357] But a contract to render personal services may contain an express negative promise which can be enforced by injunction without indirectly compelling the employee to work for the employer, or the employer to employ the employee. In *Lumley v Wagner*[358] the defendant had agreed with Mr Lumley to sing at the Drury Lane theatre on two nights a week for a period of three months, and not to use her talents at any other theatre during that period, without Mr Lumley's written consent. She then agreed for a larger payment to sing during the three months for Mr Gye at Covent Garden, and to abandon the agreement with Mr Lumley. Lord St. Leonards L.C. granted an injunction, restraining her from singing for Mr Gye. He said: "It is true that I have not the means of compelling her to sing, but she has no cause of complaint if I compel her to abstain from the commission of an act which she has bound herself not to do."[359] On the same principle, breach of negative stipulation against performing services as an actor for anyone except the employer may be restrained by injunction.[360] Such an injunction may provide an inducement to perform the positive obligation, but it falls short of indirectly compelling the employee to do the agreed work.

No indirect specific performance. Breach of a negative stipulation in a contract for personal services will not, however, be restrained by injunction where the effect of the court's order would be to leave the defendant with no alternatives except to perform the services or to remain idle. If, therefore, compliance with the negative promise which it is sought to enforce would preclude him from working for anyone else in any trade or profession whatsoever, an injunction will be refused.[361] Where the promise is merely one not to work in a *particular* capacity (*e.g.* as a singer or as an actress) for third parties, one view is that the promise may be enforced by injunction because the injunction would not prevent the employee from earning a living by doing other types of work.[362] But it might be quite unreasonable to expect an employee to do this; and more recent cases support the view that an injunction should not be granted except where it leaves the employee with some other *reasonable* means of earning a living.[363] They have arisen where professional entertainers or athletes 27–065

357 *Whitwood Chemical Co v Hardman* [1891] 2 Ch. 416, disapproving *Montagu v Flockton* (1873) L.R. 16 Eq. 189; *Mortimer v Beckett* [1920] Ch. 571; *Rely-a-Bell Co Ltd v Eisler* [1926] Ch. 609; *Chappell v The Times Newspapers Ltd* [1975] 1 W.L.R. 482; *cf.* Trade Union and Labour Relations (Consolidation) Act 1992, s.236; *Evans Marshall & Co v Bertola SA* [1973] 1 W.L.R. 349; *Scandinavian Tanker Trading Co AB v Florta Petrolera Ecuatoriana (The Scaptrade)* [1983] A.C. 694, 701; *City & Hackney H.A. v NUPE* [1985] I.R.L.R. 252; *Alexander v Standard Telephone and Cables Ltd* [1990] I.C.R. 291. For an exception to the general rule, see *Hill v C.A. Parsons & Co Ltd* [1972] 1 Ch. 305, above, para.27–023.

358 (1852) 1 De G.M. & G. 604.

359 At 619. See further n.368, below.

360 See, *e.g. Grimston v Cunningham* [1894] 1 Q.B. 125; *Robinson & Co Ltd v Heuer* [1898] 2 Ch. 451; *Tivoli (Manchester) v Colley* (1904) 20 T.L.R. 437; *Warner Bros v Nelson* [1937] 1 K.B. 209.

361 *Ehrman v Bartholomew* [1898] 1 Ch. 671.

362 *Warner Bros Pictures Inc. v Nelson* [1937] 1 K.B. 209; and see below, n.369.

363 Unless this was the position, the grant of an injunction might also be regarded as oppressive: *cf.* above, para.27–063.

have entered into long-term exclusive contracts with managers, in whom they then lost confidence. It has been held that the managers could not obtain injunctions either against their clients,[364] or against third parties with whom those clients had entered into substitute management contracts,[365] if the effect of the injunction would "as a practical matter"[366] force the clients to make use of the services of the original manager; and this would commonly be the case since such persons cannot successfully work without a manager.

27–066 **Injunction imposing undue pressure on employee.** An injunction, in cases of the kind discussed in para.27–065 above, will always put some pressure on the defendant to perform his positive obligation to render the agreed services; and the view that this factor is, of itself, a ground for refusing to grant the injunction[367] is, with respect, hard to reconcile with the reasoning of *Lumley v Wagner*.[368] The crucial question, in these cases, is whether the injunction would put *undue* pressure on an employee to perform his positive obligation to work; and this question can give rise to difficult issues of fact and degree. In one case[369] a newspaper reporter undertook during the term of his contract not to work for others; the contract provided for termination by 12 months' notice. The reporter gave only two months' notice of termination, and it was held that he could be restrained by injunction from breach of the negative stipulation. This was said not to subject him to undue pressure since the employers had undertaken to go on paying him, to allow him to go on working for them for the rest of the contract period, and not to claim damages if he should choose simply to draw his pay without doing such work. But the position might have been different if the employers had merely undertaken to go on paying him, without allowing him to work. In such cases, the court can balance the employee's interest in continuing to work (so as to maintain his skill and reputation) against any prejudice likely to be suffered by the employer if the employee works for a third party; and, where the remedy is discretionary,[370] the court may refuse to grant the injunction if it is satisfied that breach of the negative stipulation will not seriously prejudice

[364] *Page One Records Ltd v Britton* [1968] 1 W.L.R. 157.

[365] *Warren v Mendy* [1989] 1 W.L.R. 853, citing criticism of *Warner Bros. Inc. v Nelson* (above, n.362) in *Nichols Advance Vehicle Systems Inc. v De Angelis* (1979), unreported); McLean [1990] C.L.J. 15.

[366] *Page One Records Ltd v Britton* [1968] 1 W.L.R. 157, 166. *Lumley v Wagner* was distinguished at 165 on the ground that Mr. Lumley had undertaken no obligation except to pay money; but in fact he also made a promise which was negative in substance, *viz.* that certain parts were to "belong exclusively" to the defendant.

[367] *Young v Robson Rhodes* [1999] 3 All E.R. 524 at 534 ("to coerce the defendants . . . ").

[368] (1852) 1 D.M. & G. 694, above, para.27–064. *Lumley v Wagner* was cited by counsel, but not referred to it in the judgment, in *Young v Robson Rhodes*, above, n.367. It seems that the defendant in the former case was not in fact "coerced" into performing her positive obligation to sing at the claimant's theatre: see Waddams, 117 L.Q.R. 431 at 440. The two cases may be distinguishable on the ground that there was no *express* negative covenant in *Young v Robson Rhodes*, above.

[369] *Evening Standard Co Ltd v Henderson* [1987] I.C.R. 588.

[370] Above, paras 27–060—27–061 at nn.339–344; *cf. Delaney v Staples* [1992] A.C. 687, 692–693 and *William Hill Organisation Ltd v Tucker* [1998] I.R.L.R. 313, discussing so-called "garden leave."

the employer.[371] *A fortiori*, injunctive relief will be denied to the employer where his refusal to allow the employee to work amounts to a breach of the contract of employment on the employer's part.[372]

Services not of a personal nature. The discussion in paragraph 27–066 above is concerned with contracts of employment and reflects the reluctance of the courts to enforce negative stipulations in contracts of employment by injunction where the effect of so doing would be to put undue pressure on an employee to perform his positive obligation to serve. Where, however, the contract is one to render services which are not of a personal nature, an injunction in (substantially) negative terms may be available against a party who has promised to provide the services, even though the practical effect of such an injunction may be to compel performance of that party's positive obligation to render the services. A shipowner who has let his ship out under a time charter may, for example, be restrained by injunction from employing the ship inconsistently with the charterparty.[373] 27–067

Restraint of trade. Another type of contract containing a negative promise which is often enforced by injunction is that restraining an employee or the vendor of a business from competition with the employer or purchaser.[374] Such contracts are at common law invalid unless reasonable,[375] while the cases discussed in para.27–066 assume that the promise is valid and turn on the question whether an injunction would indirectly compel specific performance of the positive obligations of the contract. Yet it is arguable that the purpose of the negative stipulation in *Lumley v Wagner*[376] was to restrain competition, as it might have been physically possible for the defendant to sing at Drury Lane for two nights a week and to sing elsewhere on other nights. Yet the judgement does not discuss the question whether the contract was invalid for restraint of trade. It used to be thought that the two lines of cases could be distinguished on the ground that the former concerned the validity of covenants which took effect *after* employment; while the latter concerned the remedy for breaches of covenants operating *during* employment. There may be considerable force in this view where the term of the engagement is fairly short (as it was in *Lumley v Wagner*) since in such a case the negative stipulation is likely to be reasonable, and therefore valid under the rules relating to restraint of trade, by reason of its limited duration. But there are other situations in which the distinction between covenants operating after and those operating during employment may be hard to 27–068

[371] *Provident Financial Groups plc v Hayward* [1989] I.C.R. 160; contrast *Symbian Ltd v Christensen* [2001] I.R.L.R. 77, restraining the defendant from working for a specified competitor during the period of "garden leave."

[372] *William Hill Organisation Ltd v Tucker* [1998] I.R.L.R. 313.

[373] *Lauritzencool AB v Lady Navigation Inc* [2005] EWCA Civ 579, [2005] 1 W.L.R. 3686, below para.27–070.

[374] See above, paras 16–075 *et seq.*

[375] See above, para.16–092.

[376] (1852) 1 De G.M. & G. 604; above para.27–064.

draw or not obviously relevant in the present context, especially where a service contract is a long-term one or gives the employer a series of options to renew it,[377] or where long periods of notice have to be given to terminate the contract.[378] Stipulations which operate during employment (no less than those which operate thereafter) can therefore sometimes have their validity tested under the restraint of trade doctrine[379]; but even where their *validity* is not subject to these tests, the *remedy* of injunction is likely to be granted only where these tests are satisfied.[380] The employer will be allowed to enforce such a stipulation by injunction only if this remedy will not put the sort of pressure on the employee that was discussed in para.27–066 above.[381] It is further submitted that, even where a covenant in restraint of trade takes effect after the period of service, and is valid, it may be appropriate not to enforce it by *injunction* (but only by an action for damages) if the grant of an injunction would leave the employee with no other reasonable means of making a living than to comply with the covenant. In such a case, the grant of an injunction might well be regarded as oppressive and refused on that ground, and the employer be left to his remedy in damages.[382]

27–069 **Severance.** A negative stipulation which is too widely expressed to be enforced by injunction as it stands may be severed and enforced in part. Severance is not here governed by the rules relating to severance of promises in illegal contracts. The question is not whether severance alters the nature of the contract but simply whether an injunction to enforce such part of the negative stipulation as the claimant specifies amounts to indirect specific performance of a positive obligation which will not be specifically enforced. In *Warner Bros Pictures Inc v Nelson*[383] a film actress agreed to act for the claimants for a fixed period during which she undertook not only that she would not *act* for third parties, but also that she would not "*engage in any other occupation*" without the claimant's written consent. The claimants applied for an injunction to restrain her from acting for third parties. The court could clearly not restrain her from breach of all the negative undertakings, since that would force her to choose between idleness and performance of the obligation to serve. But this objection was "removed by the restricted form in which the injunction is sought."[384] The defendant was

---

[377] See the terms of the contracts in *Warner Bros v Nelson* [1937] 1 K.B. 209 and *cf. Eastham v Newcastle United Football Club Ltd* [1964] Ch. 413.

[378] *e.g.* in cases of "garden leave". See *Symbian Ltd v Christensen* [2001] I.R.L.R. 77, assuming that the restraint of trade doctrine can apply to such cases.

[379] *Young v Timmins* (1831) 1 Cr. & J. 331 as explained in *Esso Petroleum Co Ltd v Harper's Garage (Stourport) Ltd* [1968] A.C. 269, 328–329; *A. Schroeder Music Publishing Co Ltd v Macaulay* [1974] 1 W.L.R. 1308; *Clifford Davis Management Ltd v W.E.A. Record Ltd* [1975] 1 W.L.R. 61; above, para.16–115.

[380] *William Hill Organisation Ltd v Tucker* [1998] I.R.L.R. 313; *Symbian Ltd v Christensen*, above, n.378 at [52].

[381] See above para.27–066 at nn.369 and 370, and *Delaney v Staples* [1992] 1 A.C. 687, 692–693.

[382] *cf.* above, para.27–063.

[383] [1937] 1 K.B. 209.

[384] *ibid.* at 219; *cf. William Robinson & Co Ltd v Heuer* [1898] 2 Ch. 451; *Provident Financial Group plc v Hayward* [1989] I.C.R. 150, 160; *Symbian Ltd v Christensen*, above, n.378.

restrained simply from acting for third parties.[385] Of course, if the negative stipulation, though operating only during employment, had been as a whole invalid for restraint of trade, the question of severance would have been determined by the principles governing the severance of promises in illegal contracts.[386]

Implied negative promises. An injunction to restrain the breach by an employee of a stipulation in a contract of employment will be issued only if the contract contains an *express* negative promise.[387] The remedy has been restricted in this way because in employment cases an injunction may put so much economic pressure on the person who is to render the service that he will in fact be forced to perform the positive part of the contract, and compulsion of this kind is traditionally regarded as undesirable.[388] But where the defendant's obligation is not one to render personal services, there is less objection to an injunction which puts pressure on him to perform his positive undertaking, even though it may not be specifically enforceable; and in cases of this kind the courts have been willing to *imply* negative stipulations and to restrain their breach by injunction. Thus an injunction has been issued to prevent a shipowner from using a ship under charter inconsistently with the charterparty,[389] or fixing her with any third party during the period of the charterparty,[390] to restrain breach of a promise to give a "first refusal" to purchase of land,[391] to restrain breaches of various exclusive dealing agreements,[392] and of agreements to submit disputes to arbitration.[393] Similarly, a seller of uncut timber has been restrained from interfering with the right of the buyer to enter the land to cut down the timber and to take it away: this was "not specific performance in the sense of compelling the vendor 27–070

[385] See above, para.27–065 for the question whether the injunction, even in these limited terms, left the defendant with a *reasonable* alternative means of earning a living.

[386] Contrast the *Warner Bros* case, above, n.383, with *Gledhow Autoparts Ltd v Delaney* [1965] 1 W.L.R. 1366.

[387] *Mortimer v Beckett* [1920] 1 Ch. 571. An apparent exception is *Hivac v Park Royal Scientific Instruments* [1946] Ch. 169 but the injunction was there issued to restrain breach of a duty imposed by law rather than to restrain breach of an implied negative promise. *cf. Printers & Finishers Ltd v Holloway* [1965] 1 W.L.R. 1; *Cranleigh Precision Engineering Ltd v Bryant* [1965] 1 W.L.R. 1293.

[388] Above, para.27–065.

[389] *Sevin v Deslandes* (1860) 30 L.J. (Ch.) 457; *De Mattos v Gibson* (1859) 4 D. & J. 276; *Lord Strathcona Steamship Co v Dominion Coal Co* [1926] A.C. 108, as to which see above, para.18–139; *Associated Portland Cement Manufacturers Ltd v Teigland Shipping A/S (The Oakworth)* [1975] 1 Lloyd's Rep. 581; *Lauritzencool AB v Lady Navigation Inc* [2005] EWCA Civ, [2005] 1 W.L.R. 3686.

[390] *ibid.*

[391] *Manchester Ship Canal v Manchester Racecourse Co* [1901] 2 Ch. 37.

[392] *Donnell v Bennett* (1883) 22 Ch.D. 835; *Metropolitan Electric Supply Co v Ginder* [1901] 2 Ch. 799; *Decro-Wall International SA v Practitioners in Marketing Ltd* [1971] 1 W.L.R. 361; *Evans Marshall & Co v Bertola SA* [1973] 1 W.L.R. 349, and see above, paras 16–121—16–135. *Fothergill v Rowland* (1873) L.R. 17 Eq. 132 requires an express negative stipulation even in these cases but has not been followed on this point.

[393] *Bankers Trust Co v P.T. Jakarta International Development* [1999] 1 Lloyd's Rep. 910 at 911 (injunction against proceedings in *foreign* court; in respect of *English* court proceedings, the remedy would be by way of a stay of the proceedings: below Vol.II paras 32–045 *et seq.*).

to do anything. It merely prevents him from breaking his contract."[394] In such cases of commercial arrangements "involving the employment of no named individuals"[395] it is not an objection to the grant of an injunction that the "practical effect" of this form of relief would be to "compel performance"[396] in the sense that the "only realistic course" which the injunction left to the defendants was to perform the positive obligations imposed by the contract.[397]

27–071 In the above cases, a negative stipulation, though not express, can readily be implied, and its enforcement by injunction does not amount to indirect specific performance. The position would be different where the vagueness of the positive part of the contract made it impossible to say precisely what the defendant had undertaken *not* to do[398]; and also where the only negative stipulation which could be implied was one that would embrace the whole positive obligation. For example, if a seller had simply contracted to deliver a quantity of unascertained generic goods such as "100 tons of coal" an injunction "not to break the contract" or "not to withhold delivery" would be indistinguishable from an order of specific performance and would not normally[399] be granted.[400] And the implication of a narrower negative stipulation (*e.g.* not to sell to anyone else) would not fairly arise from the contract. Similarly, in a case[401] arising out of a number of time charterparties, it was held that the shipowners could not be restrained by injunction from "taking any step preventing the performance of" the contracts[402]; but injunctions were granted in the more restricted form of restraining them from employing the vessels in question inconsistently with the charterparties or fixing them with third parties during the period of the charterparties. A distinction was there drawn between an injunction giving rise to *practical* compulsion to perform (of the kind described in para.27–070 above) and one which was "*as a matter of law* pregnant with an affirmative obligation to perform",[403] such as one "not to break the contract" or "not to take steps to prevent its performance." An injunction of the latter kind was "tantamount to"[404] or "juristically indistinguishable from" an order of specific performance[405] and so not available in respect of contracts which were not specifically enforce-

---

[394] *Jones v Tankerville* [1909] 2 Ch. 440, 443; *cf. London Borough of Hounslow v Twickenham Gardens Ltd* [1971] Ch. 223; above, para.27–029; (1971) 87 L.Q.R. 309.

[395] *Lauritzgencool AB v Lady Navigation Inc* [2005] EWCA Civ 579; [2005] 1 W.L.R. 3686 at [35].

[396] *ibid.*, at [19], [20].

[397] *ibid.*, at [33].

[398] *Bower v Bantam Investments Ltd* [1972] 1 W.L.R. 1120.

[399] For exceptional cases in which such contracts could be specifically enforced, see above, para.27–017, at n.80.

[400] *cf.* Fry, *Specific Performance* (6th ed.), para.857; *Whitwood Chemical Co v Hardman* [1891] 2 Ch. 416, 426; *Scandinavian Trading Co AB v Flota Petrolera Ecuatoriana (The Scaptrade)* [1983] 2 A.C. 694, 701.

[401] *Lauritzencool AB v Lady Navigation Inc* [2005] EWCA Civ 579, [2005] 1 W.L.R. 3686.

[402] See the decision at first instance in the *Lauritzencool* case above, [2004] EWHC 2607 (Comm); [2005] 1 All E.R. (Comm), so far as it relates to para.12(a) of the relief claimed. There was no appeal against this aspect of the decision when it was affirmed and injunctions were granted in the more restricted form described in the text above, after n.402.

[403] *Lauritzencool* case, above n.380, [2005] EWCA Civ 579 at [6], italics supplied.

[404] *ibid.*

[405] *ibid.*, at [10], quoting from *The Scaptrade*, above n.400 at 700.

able.[406] An injunction which did not result in such *legal* compulsion to perform the contract was available to restrain breach of a contract, such as a charterparty, even though it resulted in *practical* compulsion of the kind referred to above. Such practical compulsion was a ground for refusing an injunction in personal service cases of the kind discussed in para.27–065 above but the same objection to this form of relief did not extend to cases in which the services to be rendered under the contract were not of the same personal nature.[407]

Expulsion from associations. The rules of a members' club or trade union may have contractual force; and wrongful expulsion from such an association in breach of its rules may be restrained by injunction.[408] Where the expulsion is wrongful because the proper procedure for expulsion has not been followed,[409] the court may nevertheless refuse an injunction on the ground that the procedural defect did not cause any prejudice to the claimant.[410] And where the statutory right of an individual not to be expelled from a trade union is infringed, the only remedies provided by the statute are by way of declaration and compensation.[411] **27–072**

Injunction against refusal to contract. Generally a person cannot be restrained by injunction from refusing to contract with another; but there are at least three possible exceptions to this rule. These are discussed in the three following paragraphs. **27–073**

Legislative provisions against refusal to contract. The first exception (or group of exceptions) arises under legislative provisions making it unlawful to refuse to enter into a contract with a person on certain specified grounds, such as that person's race, sex, religion or belief, sexual orientation,[412] age or the fact that **27–074**

---

[406] Above, at n.400. The apparently contrary decision in *Wake v Renault (UK) Ltd*, *The Times*, August 1, 1996 (injunction "not to terminate" a distributorship agreement which still had some years to run and was not specifically enforceable as it would require "constant supervision" (above, paras 27–026—27–027)) is, with respect, of doubtful authority. The case was not cited in the *Lauritzencool* decision and its authority is undermined to the extent that its reasoning was based on the reasoning of the decision of the Court of Appeal in *Co-operative Insurance Society Ltd v Argyll Stores Ltd* which was reversed on appeal: [1998] A.C.1, above para.27–027.

[407] Above, para.27–067.

[408] *e.g. Young v Ladies Imperial Club Ltd* [1920] 2 K.B. 523; *Lawlor v Union of Post Office Workers* [1965] Ch. 712; *R. v Disciplinary Committee of the Jockey Club Ex p. Aga Khan* [1993] 1 W.L.R. 909, 933; and see above, paras 9–072—9–080.

[409] See, for example, *Royal Society for the Prevention of Cruelty to Animals v Att.-Gen.* [2002] 1 W.L.R. 448, above, para.27–023.

[410] *Glynn v Keele University* [1971] 1 W.L.R. 487; Wade (1971) 87 L.Q.R. 320.

[411] Trade Union and Labour Relations (Consolidation) Act 1992, ss.174 to 177, as substituted by Trade Union Reform and Employment Rights Act 1993, s.14.

[412] Equality Act 2006, Parts 2 and 3. Part 2 contains detailed provisions specifying the situations in which discrimination on grounds of religion or belief is prohibited; refusal to contract could fall within these provisions: e.g. under s.46, relating to the provision of goods, facilitation and services; or s.47, relating to the disposal of premises or access to a benefit or facility provided by a manager of premises. Part 3 is an enabling provision under which regulations may be made "about discrimination or harassment on grounds of sexual orientation" (s.81(1)). Regulations made before the passing of the 2006 Act (and continued in force by it) which govern discrimination in employment on grounds of religion or belief or of sexual orientation, are cited below in n.418. For age discrimination in employment, see Employment Equality (Age) Regulations 2006, SI 2006/1031, and below, at n.418.

he suffers from a disability. Such refusal may in certain circumstances, and subject to the provisions of the relevant statutes, be restrained by injunction.[413] An injunction may similarly be granted (and damages awarded) against persons whose withholding of supplies from distributors amounts to an abuse of a dominant position contrary to European Community[414] or United Kingdom[415] competition law.[416] On the other hand, the only remedies provided by legislation for infringement of the statutory right not be excluded from a trade union are by way of declaration and compensation.[417] The same is true of the remedies provided by legislation for discrimination in employment on grounds of religion or belief, sexual orientation or age.[418] On the other hand, it seems that injunctive relief may be available in cases of unlawful discrimination on the ground of sexual orientation in fields other than employment, e.g. by suppliers of goods, facilities and services and by educational establishments.[419]

---

[413] Race Relations Act 1976, Pts II and III and ss.56, 57 and 72; Sex Discrimination Act 1975, Pts II and III and ss.65, 66; Disability Discrimination Act 1995, ss.4, 5, 12, 16F and 19 (for the meaning of "disability" in this context, see *Chacon Navas v Eurest Collectivadas* [2006] 3 CMLR 40, where the issue arose under EC Directive 2000/78, implemented by Disability Discrimination Act 1995 (Amendment) Regulations 2003, S.I. 2003/1673). The Equality Act 2006, s.24 empowers the Commission for Equality and Human Rights (created by s.1) to apply for an injunction against a person whom it "thinks . . . likely to commit an unlawful act" restraining that person from committing that act. For this purpose, an act is "unlawful" if it is "contrary to the provisions of the equality enactments" (s.34). These enactments are listed in s.33 (as amended by Employment Equality (Age) Regulations 2006, S.I. 2006/1031, Sch.8 para.40). The list includes legislation which makes discrimination unlawful on grounds of sex, race, disability, sexual orientation, religion or belief or age. Where the Commission has entered into an agreement with a person "not to commit an unlawful act of a specified kind" (s.23(1)(a)(i)), the Commission may apply to a county court for an order requiring that person "to comply with his undertaking" (s.24(3)(a)): such an order would amount to specific enforcement of the agreement. A claim that a person has done "anything that is unlawful" by virtue of Part 2 of the Act (which deals with discrimination on grounds of religion or belief) may be brought (apparently by a person claiming to have been prejudiced by such conduct) "by way of proceedings in tort" (s.66). It is envisaged that such proceedings will normally result in an award of damages but they could also result in a *quia timet* injunction against anticipated or threatened conduct which is "unlawful" within the 2006 Act (*cf.* the reference to s.34, above). See also s.21F of the 1995 Act (inserted by Disability Discrimination Act 2005, s.12) making it unlawful for private clubs to discriminate against disabled persons by refusing or deliberately omitting to accept their applications for membership. Enforcement appears to be by criminal prosecution rather than by injunction. The Human Rights Act 1998, s.1 and Sch.1, Pt.I, art.14 prohibits many forms of discrimination and s.6 of the Act makes it "unlawful" for a "public authority" to act inconsistently with this prohibition, which could be contravened by such an authority's unlawful refusal to enter into a contract: see above, para.1–043. At common law refusal to contract was sometimes punishable and actionable against persons exercising the "common callings": see *R. v Ivens* (1835) 7 C. & P. 213; *Constantine v Imperial Hotels Ltd* [1944] K.B. 593; but there seems to be no reported case in which such a refusal was restrained by injunction.

[414] European Community Treaty, Art.82 (formerly Art.86).

[415] Competition Act 1998, s.18.

[416] *Garden Cottage Foods Ltd v Milk Marketing Board* [1994] A.C. 130.

[417] The legislative provisions cited in n.411 above apply to exclusion, no less than to expulsion, from trade unions; *cf.*, also Disability Discrimination Act 1995, s.13.

[418] Employment Equality (Religion or Belief) Regulations 2003 (SI 2003/1660) Reg. 30; Employment Equality (Sexual Orientation) Regulations 2003 (SI 2003/1661) Reg. 30; these two SIs remain in force after the coming into force of the Equality Act 2006: see ss.33(1)(g) and 33(1)(h) of that Act; Employment Equality (Age) Regulations 2006 (SI 2006/1031), Reg. 38.

[419] Equality Act (Sexual Orientation) Regulations 2007 (SI 2007/1263), Reg.20(1)(a) provides for a civil remedy by way of proceedings in tort, in which the court may grant any remedy that the High Court could grant in proceedings for judicial review (Reg.22(1)(a)). It appears from the restrictions

Rules of associations restricting the right to work. The second exception to the general rule stated in paragraph 27–073 above arises where the refusal is based on the rules of an association and unreasonably deprives a person of the right to work in some trade or profession. In *Nagle v Feilden*[420] the claimant was refused a trainer's licence by the stewards of the Jockey Club on the sole ground that she was a woman. It was held that her claim for (*inter alia*) an injunction against the stewards ordering them to grant her a licence ought not to have been struck out as disclosing no cause of action; and it seems that the court was sympathetic to her claims on the merits. On the facts of *Nagle v Feilden* an injunction could now be issued on the ground that the refusal constituted unlawful sex discrimination[421]; but the common law principle recognised in the case could (if still valid[422]) also apply where such a refusal gave effect to a policy of discrimination that was not in terms made unlawful by legislation. This might be the position where a person was refused admission to an association, and so deprived of the opportunity of exercising a profession, on political grounds that had no bearing on his competence in that profession.[423] 27–075

Aiding and abetting breach of an injunction. The third exception to the general rule stated in para.27–073 above is illustrated by *Acrow Automation v Rex Chainbelt Inc.*[424] The defendant company refused to supply components to a manufacturer in obedience to instructions given by an associated company; these instructions had been given in breach of an injunction against the latter company not to interfere with the manufacturer's business. It was held that the defendant company (which knew of the injunction) could be restrained from obeying the associated company's instructions, and that it could be ordered to make reasonable efforts to supply the manufacturer, since its refusal to supply him amounted to aiding and abetting a breach of the injunction against the associated company. These orders against the defendant company were made even though there was no previous contract between the defendant company and the manufacturer for the supply of the goods in question. 27–076

9. DAMAGES AND SPECIFIC PERFORMANCE OR INJUNCTION

Statutory power to award damages in lieu of specific performance or injunction. Power to award damages in addition to or "in substitution for" specific performance or injunction was conferred on the Court of Chancery by s.2 of the Chancery Amendment Act 1858 (also known as Lord Cairns' Act). That 27–077

---

on the availability of injunctive relief in Reg.22(2)(a) that such relief may be available in cases not covered by this restriction (which precludes such relief in proceedings against public authorities where it might prejudice criminal proceedings or investigations).

420 [1966] 2 Q.B. 633.

421 Sex Discrimination Act 1975, s.13.

422 Its validity was doubted in *R. v Disciplinary Committee of the Jockey Club Ex p. Aga Khan* [1993] 1 W.L.R. 909, 993.

423 See the example given in *Nagle v Feilden* [1966] 2 Q.B. 633 at 655 ("the colour of his hair").

424 [1971] 1 W.L.R. 1676.

power is now vested in the High Court by s.50 of the Supreme Court Act 1981.[425] Since claims for specific performance (or injunction) can, by virtue of s.49 of that Act, be combined with claims for damages, it is normally unnecessary to resort to the special power to award damages in lieu of those remedies. But it may still sometimes be to the claimant's advantage to invoke that jurisdiction, and its exercise has also given rise to certain special problems with regard to the assessment of damages.

27–078 **No completed cause of action at law.** Damages may be awarded in lieu of specific performance or injunction even though there is no completed cause of action at law. Thus in *Leeds Industrial Co-operative Society Ltd v Slack*[426] the House of Lords held that damages could be awarded in lieu of a *quia timet* injunction in respect of a tort which had not yet been committed and which was, therefore, not yet actionable at law.[427] A similar possibility exists where one party to a contract has committed an anticipatory breach by repudiating the contract before performance was due, and the other, instead of "accepting" the repudiation, seeks to uphold the contract and sues for specific performance. In such case the court could make an order for specific performance at once[428] even though performance was not yet due at the time of the action; and it seems that the court can, in its discretion, award damages under the Act even though there was, when the proceedings were commenced, no right to damages at common law.[429] However, a party is not in anticipatory breach of contract merely because the other fears that he will commit a breach of it; and where there is neither a present breach nor a wrongful repudiation, an injunction is not available against the former party,[430] so that there can be no award of damages in lieu. On the principle of *Slack's* case it seems, moreover, that the power to award damages in lieu of an injunction could also be exercised where an injunction is available as a matter of judge-made law against refusal to contract[431]; and that such damages could be awarded even though the refusal gave rise to no claim for damages at common law. Where the refusal is wrongful under legislation of the kind described in paragraph 27–074 above, rights to a *quia timet* injunction and to

---

[425] See Jolowicz [1975] C.L.J. 224; Pettit [1977] C.L.J. 367; [1978] C.L.J. 51.

[426] [1924] A.C. 851. In this case it was the defendant who asked that damages (rather than an injunction) should be awarded.

[427] In *Meretz Investments NV v ACP* [2006] EWHC 74, [2007] Ch. 197 at [252] it was said at first instance that damages in lieu of a *quia timet* injunction would only exceptionally be awarded "before any damage at all had been suffered." On appeal, paragraph [252] of the decision at first instance was cited ([2007] EWCA Civ 1303 at [33],[62]) but not on the present point, and the actual decision was that the defendants were liable in damages for actual breach of contract: [2007] EWCA Civ 1303 at [2], [71], [161].

[428] *Hasham* v *Zenab* [1960] A.C. 316, above, para.27–003 (but the order will be for performance on the due day).

[429] *cf. Oakacre Ltd v Claire Cleaners (Holdings) Ltd* [1982] Ch. 197. For another former illustration of the power (now made obsolete by Law of Property (Miscellaneous Provisions) Act 1989, s.2), see *Price v Strange* [1978] Ch. 337, 358.

[430] *Veracruz Transportation Inc.* v *V.C. Shipping Inc. (The Veracruz I)* [1992] 1 Lloyd's Rep. 356; *The P.* [1992] 1 Lloyd's Rep. 470; *cf. Zucker v Tyndall Holdings plc* [1992] 1 W.L.R. 1127; *Mercantile Group (Europe) A.G. v Aiyela* [1994] Q.B. 366, 375.

[431] Above, paras 27–075—27–076.

damages in lieu are likely to be regulated by that legislation.[432] An injunction may also be available to a third party where a contract between two others is invalid for restraint of trade; and in such cases it is arguable that damages may be awarded in lieu even though the third party has no cause of action for breach of contract against the parties to the contract in question.[433]

Assessment of damages. There was formerly some support for the view that the assessment of damages might be more favourable to the claimant under Lord Cairns' Act than at common law where the value of the subject matter had risen between the time of breach and the time of judgment. This view rested on the assumption that common law damages for wrongful failure to deliver or to convey the subject-matter of the contract were necessarily based on the difference between the contract price and the market value of the subject matter *at the time of breach*. On this assumption, any subsequent increase in market value between breach and judgment was, at common law, liable to cause prejudice to the victim of the breach. In *Wroth v Tyler*,[434] for example, the defendant entered into a contract to sell a house to the claimants for £6,000. The sale was to be completed in October 1971, by which time the value of the house had risen to £7,500. Meanwhile (in July 1971) the defendant had repudiated the contract; but in January 1972 the claimants started proceedings for specific performance and damages. Judgment in the action was given in January 1973, by which time the house was worth £11,500. Megarry J. held that specific performance, though in principle available, should not be ordered[435] and that damages should be awarded in lieu. He assessed these by reference to the value of the house at the time, not of breach, but of judgment,[436] *i.e.* not at £1,500 but at £5,500. One reason for assessing the damages by reference to the latter time was that they were awarded, not at common law, but under the Act, "in substitution for . . . specific performance." Such damages must, it was said, "constitute a true substitute for specific performance,"[437] and "be a substitute giving as nearly as may be what specific performance would have given."[438] But even at common law the aim of damages is to put the claimant "in the same position . . . *as if* the contract had been 27–079

---

[432] *e.g.* Sex Discrimination Act 1975, s.65; Race Relations Act 1976, s.57, as amended by Race Relations (Remedies) Act 1994; Disability Discrimination Act 1995, ss.4, 5, 12 and 19; Competition Act 1998, ss.47A and 47B, as inserted by Enterprise Act 2002, ss.18 and 19; Equality Act 2006, ss.65, 66; above, para.27–074 n.412. See also *Garden Cottage Foods Ltd v Milk Marketing Board* [1984] A.C. 130 (above, para.27–074) where the right to damages was said at 141 to be based on breach of statutory duty.

[433] According to *Newport Association Football Club v Football Association of Wales Ltd* [1995] 2 All E.R. 87 the mere availability to the third party of a declaration that the contract is in restraint of trade is a cause of action; but this is hard to reconcile with the reasoning of *Eastham v Newcastle United Football Club Ltd* [1964] Ch. 413, according to which the court may grant a declaration to the third party even though that party has *no* "cause of action."

[434] [1974] Ch. 30.

[435] See above, para.27–031.

[436] *cf. Hulbert v Avens* [2003] EWHC 76 (Ch) (equitable compensation assessed as at time of judgment). For the possibility of assessment by reference to an even later time, see *Grant v Dawkins* [1973] 1 W.L.R. 1406.

[437] [1974] Ch. 30, 58.

[438] *ibid.* at 59. *cf. Biggin v Minton* [1977] 1 W.L.R. 701, 704.

performed"[439]; and there seems to be no difference in substance between the phrases "as if . . . performed" and "in substitution for . . . specific performance." Both state the same general objective; neither is followed through to its logical conclusion. The judgment in *Wroth v Tyler* itself appears to recognise the possibility that part of the claimants' loss could have been too remote,[440] and the mitigation rules[441] can also reduce the amount recoverable in lieu of specific performance.[442] In *Johnson v Agnew*[443] the House of Lords accordingly expressed the view that the assessment of damages was governed by the same principles whether the damages were awarded under the Act or at common law. Even at common law damages are not invariably assessed by reference to the date of breach. This method of assessment is adopted where it would have been reasonable for the claimant at that date to have mitigated his loss, *e.g.* by making a substitute contract; but if, for some reason, this is not the case, the damages will be assessed by reference to some other date.[444] In *Wroth v Tyler* the claimants had (as the defendant knew)[445] no financial resources beyond the £6,000 that they had raised for the purpose of completing their contract with the defendant. By the time of breach they therefore could not reasonably have been expected to avoid any part of their loss by making a substitute purchase, since similar houses were financially out of their reach. The decision must now be explained on this ground and not by reference to any supposed distinction between the assessment of damages at common law and under the Act.[446] Where the claimant cannot show that the breach has caused him any loss, the principles which determine whether he can nevertheless recover damages in respect of the defendant's gain, or whether the court will exercise its discretion to order an account of profits,[447] appear likewise to be the same whether the claim is made under the Act or at common law.[448] There seems similarly to be no difference between the assessment of damages in lieu of injunction under the Act and assessment apart from the Act where damages are based on the amount for which the claimant would

---

[439] *Robinson v Harman* (1848) 1 Exch. 850, 855; above, para.26–001.

[440] [1974] Ch. 30, 61; above, paras 26–051 *et seq.*

[441] Above, para.26–101.

[442] See *Radford v De Froberville* [1977] 1 W.L.R. 1262, 1286; *cf. Grant v Dawkins* [1973] 1 W.L.R. 1406.

[443] [1980] A.C. 367, 400. This decision also makes it hard to accept the suggestion that damages under the Act can, as a general rule, be based on the defendant's gain (rather than, as at common law, on the claimant's loss): see *Surrey C.C. v Bredero Homes Ltd* [1993] 1 W.L.R. 1361; *Jaggard v Sawyer* [1995] 1 W.L.R. 269. For *other* grounds for making a discretionary award based on the contract-breaker's gain, see *Att.-Gen. v Blake* [2001] 1 A.C. 268 (above, para.26–024) where conflicting views are expressed at 283, 291 and 298 as to the correctness of the decision in the *Bredero* case.

[444] [1980] A.C. 367, at 401; above, para.26–064; *cf. Suleman v Shahsavari* [1988] 1 W.L.R. 1181.

[445] *Wroth v Tyler* [1974] Ch. 30, 57; but for this fact the loss might well have been (at least in part) too remote: see above, para.26–060.

[446] *cf. Trafigura Beheer BV v Mediterranean Shipping Co SA* [2007] EWHC 944 (Comm), [2007] 2 All E.R. (Comm) 149 where specific restitution of goods could have been ordered (at [117]) but common law damages in tort were assessed by reference to the value of the goods at the time of judgment (at [131]–[133]) without any suggestion that the damages were awarded in lieu of specific restitution under Supreme Court Act 1981, s.50.

[447] Above, paras 26–024 *et. seq.*

[448] *cf.* the discussion of the Act in *Att.-Gen. v Blake* [2001] 1 A.C. 268, 281.

have been willing to negotiate the sale of the right infringed by the defendant's conduct.[449]

The general principle that there is no difference between the assessment of damages at common law and that of damages in lieu of specific performance or injunction is based on the assumption that the damages are claimed in respect of the same breach of contract or other cause of action. The principle obviously cannot apply where there is no cause of action at common law, *e.g.* where specific relief is sought in equity in respect of threatened or future breaches.[450] 27–080

Damages and specific performance. Damages may be awarded in addition to specific performance. For example, where a vendor's title is subject to an incumbrance and this amounts to a breach of contract, he can be ordered to convey what title he has and to pay damages based on the cost of discharging the incumbrance.[451] The court may also award damages as to part of a contract and specific performance or injunction as to the rest,[452] and damages for delay in completion in addition to specific performance.[453] Where the court grants an injunction to restrain future breaches of a contract, it can likewise award damages in respect of past breaches, *i.e.* in respect of those which had already taken place before the injunction was granted.[454] 27–081

Damages after specific performance. Where an order of specific performance has been made but not been complied with, one course of action open to the injured party is to apply to the court for enforcement of the order. There was formerly some support for the view that this was the only remedy available to him, and that he could not, after having first obtained an order of specific performance, then rescind the contract and claim damages.[455] But this view was rejected by the House of Lords in *Johnson v Agnew*.[456] In that case, vendors of land were (as the purchaser knew) relying on the proceeds of sale to pay off a mortgage on the land. The purchaser failed to pay, even after specific performance had been ordered against her, with the result that the land was sold by the mortgagee. It followed that the vendors could no longer convey the land in exchange for the price and that they were therefore not in a position to enforce the order of specific performance. The House of Lords held that the vendors were 27–082

---

449 *Lunn Poly Ltd v Liverpool and Lancashire Properties* [2006] EWCA Civ 430, [2006] 2 E.G.L.R. 29; for this basis of assessment, see above, paras 26–023, 26–024.

450 See *Jaggard v Sawyer* [1995] 1 W.L.R. 269, 291–292; *cf. Att.-Gen. v Blake* [2001] 1 A.C. 268, 281.

451 *Grant v Dawkins* [1973] 1 W.L.R. 1406.

452 *Soames v Edge* (1860) Johns. 669.

453 *Ford-Hunt v Raghbir Singh* [1973] 1 W.L.R. 738; *cf. Oakacre Ltd v Claire Cleaners (Holdings) Ltd* [1982] Ch. 197 (damages for delay in substitution for specific performance). For the availability of damages for delay, see *Raineri v Miles* [1981] A.C. 1050 (where no issue as to specific performance arose).

454 *Experience Hendrix LLC v PPX Enterprise Inc* [2003] EWCA Civ 323; [2003] 1 All E.R. (Comm) 830 at [34].

455 See *Capital & Suburban Properties Ltd v Swycher* [1976] Ch. 319 and the authorities there cited; and see below, n.456.

456 [1980] A.C. 367, disapproving *Capital & Suburban Properties Ltd v Swycher*, above, n.455.

entitled to damages, not only under the Act,[457] but also at common law. It would seem that the vendors could similarly have obtained damages if the order of specific performance had been obtained, and then not been complied with, by the purchaser.[458]

27–083 In *Johnson v Agnew*[459] the reason why the vendors could not enforce the order of specific performance was that they had been disabled, in consequence of the purchaser's default, from performing their side of the bargain. But the reasoning of the House of Lords is not restricted to this type of situation. It is based on the general rules applicable to cases of repudiatory breach and therefore applies even where no such disability results. The right to damages is subject only to the restriction that, where an order of specific performance has been made and not complied with, the party who had obtained the order must apply to the court for the dissolution of the order "and ask the court to put an end to the contract."[460] The choice between enforcement of the order of specific performance and damages thus seems to be a matter for the injured party; and the reasoning of *Johnson v Agnew* suggests that damages can be awarded, after failure to comply with an order of specific performance, whenever that party elects to claim damages.

27–084 **Limits of the court's power.** The power to award damages under s.50 of the Supreme Court Act 1981 exists only where the court has "jurisdiction to entertain an application for an injunction or specific performance."[461] If the court has such jurisdiction, the power to award damages in lieu can be exercised even though the court in its discretion refuses to order specific relief[462]; but it will not be exercised where no attempt is made to seek specific relief, where any chance of obtaining such relief has been lost (*e.g.* by lapse of time), and where the only claim made was one for damages at common law.[463] Under s.49 of the Act, common law damages can be awarded where specific performance or an injunction is claimed, even though the case is not one in which specific relief could have been ordered.[464]

---

457 Such damages had been awarded in *Biggin v Minton* [1977] 1 W.L.R. 701.

458 The contrary was decided in *Sing v Nazeer* [1979] Ch. 474. But as that case followed *Capital & Suburban Properties Ltd v Swycher* (above, n.455) which is now disapproved (above, n.456), the claim for damages should now be allowed.

459 Above, para.27–082.

460 *Johnson v Agnew* [1980] A.C. 367, 394; *G.K.N. Distributors v Tyne Tees Fabrication* (1985) 50 P. & C.R. 403.

461 *Hipgrave v Case* (1885) 28 Ch.D. 356; *Lavery v Pursell* (1888) 39 Ch.D. 508; *Price v Strange* [1978] Ch. 337, 359.

462 *e.g. Wroth v Tyler* [1974] Ch. 30 (where specific relief was refused for reasons stated in para.27–031, above); *Jaggard v Sawyer* [1995] 1 W.L.R. 269 (where specific relief was refused for the reasons stated in para.27–063, above).

463 *Surrey C.C. v Bredero Homes Ltd* [1993] 1 W.L.R. 1361. For conflicting views as to the correctness of this decision, see above, para.27–079, n.443.

464 As in *Dominion Coal Co Ltd v Dominion Iron & Steel Co* [1909] A.C. 293; *cf. Proctor v Bayley* (1889) 42 Ch.D. 390 (decided under earlier similar legislative provisions).

CHAPTER 28

LIMITATION OF ACTIONS[1]

		PARA.
1.	Periods of limitation	28–001
2.	Accrual of the cause of action	28–031
3.	Computation of the period	28–062
4.	The running of time	28–064
5.	Extension of the period	28–071
	(a) Disability	28–074
	(b) Fraud, concealment or mistake	28–081
	(c) Acknowledgment and part payment	28–092
	(d) Agreement of the parties	28–106
6.	Abridgement of the period	28–112
7.	Commencement of proceedings	28–116
8.	The statute bars the remedy, not the right	28–126
9.	Limitation in equity	28–134

1. PERIODS OF LIMITATION

Introductory. It is the policy of the law that there should be an end to litigation and that "stale demands"[2] should be suppressed. The reasons for this policy have been said to be[3]: first, that defendants should be protected against claims being made on them after a long period during which they may have lost the evidence available to them to rebut those claims; secondly, that claimants should be encouraged not to go to sleep on their rights, but to institute proceedings without unreasonable delay; thirdly, that defendants should be in a position to know that, after a given time, an incident which might have led to a claim against them is finally closed. The state also has an interest in ensuring that trials **28–001**

[1] See generally McGee, *Limitation of Actions*, 5th edn (2006); Prime and Scanlon, *The Modern Law of Limitation*, 2nd edn (2001); Merkin, Oughton and Lowry, *Limitation of Actions* (1998); Di Mambro, *Butterworth's Law of Limitation* (2000, looseleaf); Law Commission Report, *Limitation of Actions* (Law Com. No.270, 2001). For conflict of laws in relation to limitation of actions, see below, paras 30–347—30–348.

[2] *Cholmondeley v Clinton* (1820) 2 J. & W. 1; 4 Bli. 1; *A'Court v Cross* (1825) 3 Bing. 329, 333; *R.B. Policies at Lloyd's v Butler* [1950] 1 K.B. 76.

[3] *Report of the Committee on Limitation of Actions in Cases of Personal Injury*, 1962, Cmnd.1829, para.17; Law Reform Committee, *Twentieth Report*, 1974, Cmnd.5630; *Twenty-First Report*, 1977, Cmnd.6923, paras 1.7–1.14; *Twenty-Fourth Report*, 1984, Cmnd.9390; Law Commission Consultation Paper No.151, *Limitation of Actions* (1998), paras 1.22–1.38.

are heard at a time when there is sufficient reliable evidence and in promoting legal certainty for the benefit not only of potential defendants but also third parties. Accordingly, the legislature has laid down certain periods of limitation after the expiry of which no action can be maintained. The principal statute to which reference must be made for the law of limitation of actions is the Limitation Act 1980.[4] Subject to exceptions which do not affect the law of contract, the Act applies to proceedings by or against the Crown as it applies to proceedings between subjects[5]; but it does not apply to any action or arbitration for which a period of limitation is prescribed by or under any other enactment.[6] The main provisions of the Act so far as it affects the law of contract are discussed in the following pages.

28–002 **Simple contracts.** By s.5 of the 1980 Act, no action[7] founded on simple contract can be brought after the expiration of six years from the date on which the cause of action accrued. The section must also:

> "... be taken to cover actions for money had and received, formerly actions on the case ... though the words used cannot be regarded as felicitous."[8]

Restitutionary claims will, therefore, in general be barred after six years,[9] although they may be affected by the special provisions of the Act relating to fraud, concealment or mistake[10] or the fact that they are equitable claims.[11] An action for an account cannot be brought after the expiration of any time limit under the Act which is applicable to the claim which is the basis of the duty to account.[12]

28–003 **Specialties.** By s.8 of the 1980 Act, no action upon a specialty can be brought after the expiration of 12 years from the date when the cause of action accrued[13]: but this does not affect any action for which a shorter period of limitation is prescribed by any other provision of the Act.[14] The words "action upon a specialty" refer to any action to enforce an obligation created or secured by an

---

[4] The Act has been amended by the Latent Damage Act 1986 (below, paras 28–010—28–012), by the Consumer Protection Act 1987 (below, para.28–009), by the Defamation Act 1996 s.5 (defamation and malicious falsehood) and by the Arbitration Act 1996 (below, paras 28–115, 28–125).

[5] s.37(1).

[6] s.39.

[7] Defined in s.38(1).

[8] *Re Diplock* [1948] Ch. 465, 514, followed in *Kleinwort Benson Ltd v Sandwell BC* (1993) 91 L.G.R. 323, 382–384.

[9] *Kleinwort Benson Ltd v Lincoln CC* [1999] 2 A.C. 349. See Goff and Jones, *The Law of Restitution*, 7th edn (2007), Ch.43; McLean [1989] C.L.J. 472; Burrows, *The Law of Restitution*, 2nd edn (2002), pp.542–555.

[10] See below, para.28–021.

[11] See below, para.28–131.

[12] s.23. cf. *Tito v Waddell (No.2)* [1977] Ch. 106, 250–251; *Att-Gen v Cocke* [1988] Ch. 414; *Paragon Finance Plc v Thakerar & Co* [1991] 1 All E.R. 400, 415.

[13] s.8(1).

[14] s.8(2).

instrument which is executed as a deed.[15] They extend to an action for damages.[16] However, the period of limitation prescribed by the Act to recover arrears of rent[17] or arrears of interest on a mortgage[18] is six years even if the lease or mortgage is by deed.

The Companies Act 1985 provides that the memorandum and articles of association of a company shall, when registered, bind the company and the members thereof to the same extent as if they respectively had been signed and sealed by each member and contained covenants on the part of each member to observe all their provisions.[19] Further, all money payable by any member to the company under the memorandum or articles is a specialty debt due from him to the company.[20] The liability of contributories on a winding-up is also in the nature of a specialty debt.[21] There is little doubt that the obligations between a company incorporated under the Companies Acts and its members arising out of the memorandum and articles are contractual.[22] But judicial opinion is divided as 28–004

[15] Or under a statute (except where s.9 applies as in, e.g., *Re Farmizer (Products) Ltd* [1997] 1 B.C.L.C. 589): *Collin v Duke of Westminster* [1985] Q.B. 581; *Rahman v Sterling Credit Ltd* [2001] 1 W.L.R. 496. In *Hill v Spread Trustee Co Ltd* [2006] EWCA Civ 542, [2007] 1 W.L.R. 2404, it was held that a claim, under s.423 of the Insolvency Act 1986, by a trustee in bankruptcy for the avoidance of a transaction is subject to a six-year limitation period under s.9 (statute) or the 12-year limitation period under s.8 (specialty). On the facts, it did not matter which of these two was applied. The cause of action ran from the date when the bankruptcy order was made. In another case on s.423 brought by a creditor, s.8, and not s.9, was held to be applicable because the initial remedy sought was a challenge to the validity of a property transfer rather than to recover a sum of money; and the cause of action was held to accrue when the creditor became a victim which was when he became "capable of being prejudiced" by the transfer: *Giles v Rhind* [2007] EWHC 687 (Ch), affirmed [2008] EWCA Civ 118. For contracts under seal, see *Leivers v Barber, Walker & Co Ltd* [1943] 1 K.B. 385, 398; *Whittall Builders Co Ltd v Chester-le-Street D.C.* (1986) 11 Const. L.R. 40. But the requirement of a seal for a deed executed by an individual was abolished by the Law of Property (Miscellaneous Provisions) Act 1989, and see also (deeds executed by companies) ss.43–47 of the Companies Act 2006; above, paras 1–090, 1–091, 1–095 et seq. See, generally, *Matadeen v Caribbean Insurance Co Ltd* [2002] UKPC 69; [2003] 1 W.L.R. 670. The execution of a document under seal is itself not sufficient to make it "clear on its face" that it is intended to be a deed and therefore a specialty: see above, para.1–097. Also in *Re Compania de Electricidad de la Provincia de Buenos Aires Ltd* [1980] Ch. 146, it was held that an action to enforce an obligation which was merely acknowledged or evidenced by a sealed instrument was not an "action upon a specialty".

[16] *Aiken v Stewart Wrightson Members' Agency Ltd* [1995] 1 W.L.R. 1281.

[17] s.19. See also *Romain v Scuba TV Ltd* [1997] Q.B. 887 (action against guarantor of lessee).

[18] s.20(5). See also *Re Compania de Electricidad de la Provincia de Buenos Aires Ltd* [1980] Ch. 146 (arrears of interest on bond). But where the mortgagor is seeking to redeem or the mortgagee is accounting to the mortgagor for the surplus, more than six years' interest may be retained by the mortgagee: *Edmunds v Waugh* (1866) L.R. 1 Eq. 48; *Holmes v Cowcher* [1970] 1 W.L.R. 834; *Ezekiel v Orakpo* [1997] 1 W.L.R. 340. The limitation period for an action to recover a principal sum of money secured by a mortgage or the proceeds of the sale of land is 12 years from the date on which the right to receive the money accrued: s.20(1). See, generally on s.20, *Bristol & West Plc v Bartlett* [2002] EWCA Civ 1181, [2003] 1 W.L.R. 284; *Scottish Equitable Plc v Thompson* [2003] EWCA Civ 225; [2003] H.L.R. 48; *West Bromwich Building Society v Wilkinson* [2005] UKHL 44, [2005] 1 W.L.R. 2303; *Gotham v Doodes* [2006] EWCA Civ 1080, [2007] 1 W.L.R. 86.

[19] s.14(1).

[20] s.14(2).

[21] s.508. See also *Buck v Robson* (1870) L.R. 10 Eq. 629; *Re Muggeridge* (1870) L.R. 10 Eq. 443 (calls on shares).

[22] *Hickman v Kent or Romney Marsh Sheep Breeders' Association* [1915] 1 Ch. 881. cf. *Rayfield v Hands* [1960] Ch. 1.

to the appropriate period of limitation to be applied to an action by a member against the company to recover dividends or capital repayable on a reduction of capital. In *Re Artisans' Land and Mortgage Corp*,[23] Byrne J. applied the period of limitation then applicable to actions upon specialties. But in the later case of *Re Compania de Electricidad de la Provincia de Buenos Aires Ltd*[24] Slade J. held that the six-year period applied, on the ground that, while the Companies Act 1948[25] provided that the deemed contract constituted by the memorandum and articles was to be treated as if executed by the members under seal, and for money payable by members to the company to be specialty debts, it did not make the same provision with respect to the obligations of the company to members or money payable by the company to members under the deemed contract.

28–005 **Contracts (Rights of Third Parties) Act 1999.** This Act enables a person who is not a party to a contract (a "third party") in certain circumstances to enforce a term of the contract.[26] In ss.5 and 8 of the 1980 Act the references to an action founded on a simple contract and an action upon a specialty shall respectively include references to an action brought by the third party relating to a simple contract or to a specialty.[27]

28–006 **Personal injuries and death.** In the case of any action for breach of duty existing by virtue of a contract where the damages claimed by the claimant consist of or include damages for personal injuries to the claimant or any other person, neither the period applicable to simple contracts[28] nor that applicable to specialties[29] applies, but the limitation period is three years from: (a) the date on which the cause of action accrued; or (b) the date of the claimant's knowledge (if later) of certain facts relevant to his right of action against the defendant.[30] "Personal injuries" includes any disease and any impairment of a person's mental or physical condition.[31] But it has been held that an action against insurance brokers for damages for breach of duty (in failing to arrange insurance so that the claimant is unable to recover against his insurers for personal injury) is not within s.11 because the damages claimed do not include damages in respect of personal injuries.[32] And a claim under the Third Party (Rights Against Insurers) Act 1930 is not a claim for damages in respect of personal injuries

[23] [1904] 1 Ch. 796, following *Smith v Cork and Bandon Ry* (1870) I.R. 5 Eq. 65; *Re Drogheda Steam Packet Co* [1903] 1 Ir. R. 512. Byrne J. also considered whether an action for sums due for repayment of capital under a scheme of arrangement, sanctioned by the court in the exercise of its statutory jurisdiction, would be an action to recover sums "recoverable by virtue of any enactment", for which the period is six years under s.9 of the 1980 Act, but did not decide this point. cf. Preston and Newsom, *Limitation of Actions*, 3rd edn, p.58; Franks, *Limitation of Actions* (1959), p.84; *Cork and Bandon Ry v Goode* (1853) 13 C.B. 826.

[24] [1980] Ch. 146.

[25] s.20(1), now, with slightly different wording, s.33(1) of the Companies Act 2006.

[26] See above, para.18–088.

[27] Contracts (Rights of Third Parties) Act 1999 s.7(3).

[28] s.11(2).

[29] ss.8(2), 11(2).

[30] ss.11, 14. See *Clerk & Lindsell on Torts*, 19th edn (2006), paras 33–36—33–68.

[31] s.38(1).

[32] *Ackbar v C.F. Green & Co Ltd* [1975] Q.B. 582. cf. *Howe v David Brown Tractors (Retail) Ltd* [1991] 4 All E.R. 30 CA; *Bennett v Greenland Houchen & Co* [1998] P.N.L.R. 458 CA.

because it is a claim for an indemnity once a claim for damages has been quantified.[33]

28–007 An action under the Fatal Accidents Act 1976 cannot be brought after the expiration of three years from: (a) the date of death; or (b) the date of knowledge of the person for whose benefit the action is brought of certain facts relevant to his right of action against the defendant, whichever is the later.[34]

28–008 A discretion is, however, vested in the court to override the time limits mentioned above.[35]

28–009 **Product liability.** In the case of an action for damages by virtue of Pt I of the Consumer Protection Act 1987[36] in which the damages claimed by the claimant consist of or include damages for personal injuries to the claimant or any other person or loss of or damage to any property, the limitation period is three years from whichever is the later of: (a) the date on which the cause of action accrued; and (b) the date of knowledge of the injured person of certain facts relevant to his right of action against the defendant or, in the case of loss of or damage to property, the date of knowledge of the claimant or (if earlier) of any person in whom his cause of action was previously vested.[37] The normal three-year time limit in respect of Fatal Accident Act claims also applies.[38] The court has a discretion to override these time limits,[39] except where the damages claimed by the claimant are confined to damages for loss of or damage to any property.[40]

However, there is an overall long-stop period of 10 years after which any action for damages by virtue of Pt I of the 1987 Act is barred and extinguished.[41] This 10-year period usually begins to run from the time when the defendant[42] supplied the product to another.[43] A product is supplied, or in the words of Directive 85/374 "put into circulation", when it is taken out of the manufacturing process operated by the producer and enters a marketing process in the form in which it is offered to the public in order to be used or consumed.[44]

28–010 **Latent damage in actions for the tort of negligence.** Section 14A of the Limitation Act 1980[45] prescribes a special time limit for negligence actions

---

[33] *Burns v Shuttlehurst Ltd* [1999] 1 W.L.R. 1449.

[34] Limitation Act 1980 ss.12, 13, 14. See *Clerk & Lindsell on Torts* (19th edn (2006)), para.33–68.

[35] Limitation Act 1980 s.33. *Clerk & Lindsell on Torts* (19th edn, (2006)), paras 33–53—33–66.

[36] See Vol.II, para.43–138.

[37] Limitation Act 1980 s.11A (inserted by s.6 of and Sch.1 to the Consumer Protection Act 1987) and s.14 (as so amended). See *Clerk & Lindsell on Torts*, 19th edn (2006), para.33–81.

[38] Limitation Act 1980 ss.12, 13, 14 (as so amended); see above, para.28–007.

[39] Limitation Act 1980 s.33 (as so amended).

[40] Limitation Act 1980 s.33(1A).

[41] Limitation Act 1980 s.11A(3). This cannot be overridden: s.33(1A).

[42] Being a person to whom s.2(2) of the 1987 Act applies, i.e. the producer or ostensible producer or the importer of the product into a Member State of the EU.

[43] i.e. the "relevant time" within the meaning of s.4 of the 1987 Act. But see s.4(2)(b).

[44] *O'Byrne v Sanofi Pasteur MSD Ltd* [2006] 1 W.L.R. 1606, [2006] 2 C.M.L.R. 24 ECJ.

[45] Introduced by s.1 of the Latent Damage Act 1986.

(other than actions involving personal injuries)[46] where the facts relevant to the cause of action are not known at the date on which the cause of action accrues. It is important to appreciate that this section applies only to an action for damages for *negligence*.[47] Although it might be thought that the word "negligence" was intended to extend to breach of a contractual duty, for example, to use reasonable care and skill,[48] it has been held[49] that the section is restricted to actions in tort for negligence, on the ground (inter alia) that it provides[50] that the six-year period of limitation applicable to actions founded on tort[51] is not to apply to actions within its scope, but does not similarly disapply the six-year period applicable to actions founded on simple contract.[52] It follows that the section will only be of assistance to a contracting party who has a concurrent or independent cause of action in tort for negligence.[53] A contractual cause of action continues to accrue at the date of breach and the limitation period is not extended by reason of the fact that the damage caused by the breach is latent. A claimant who sues in contract cannot therefore rely on this section and will have to rely (if at all) on s.32(1)(b) of the Act, viz that a fact relevant to his right of action has been deliberately concealed from him by the defendant.[54]

28–011 In cases to which s.14A of the Act applies, the period of limitation is either: (a) six years from the date on which the cause of action accrued,[55] that is to say the date on which damage first occurred; or (b) three years from the earliest date (the "starting date") on which the claimant or any person in whom the cause of action was vested before him[56] first had both the knowledge required for bringing an action for damages in respect of the relevant damage[57], and a right to bring

[46] s.11; see above, para.28–006.

[47] s.14A(1). It therefore does not apply to an action for damages for breach of a strict duty imposed by statute, e.g. under the Defective Premises Act 1972. Nor does it apply to a claim for damages under s.2(1) of the Misrepresentation Act 1967 because under s.2(1) there is no onus on the claimant to prove negligence: *Laws v The Society of Lloyd's* [2003] EWCA Civ 1887, *The Times,* January 23, 2004 at [78]–[93].

[48] See below, para.28–033.

[49] *Iron Trades Mutual Insurance Co Ltd v Buckenham Ltd* [1989] 2 Lloyd's Rep. 85; *Société Commerciale de Reassurance v Eras International Ltd* [1992] 1 Lloyd's Rep. 570, 601–603; *West Bromwich Building Society v Mander Hadley & Co, The Times*, March 9, 1998.

[50] s.14(A)(2). See also s.32(5) (introduced by s.2(2) of the 1986 Act).

[51] s.2.

[52] s.5.

[53] See below, para.28–033.

[54] See below, para.28–084. For the relationship between ss.14A and 14B and s.32(1)(b), see s.32(5).

[55] s.14A(4)(a).

[56] s.14A(5). In *Graham v Entec Europe Ltd* [2003] EWCA Civ 1177, [2003] 4 All E.R. 1345, it was held that, where an insurer is bringing a subrogated action in the insured's name, the insurer's knowledge—including the knowledge of its loss adjuster—is relevant under s.14A.

[57] s.14A(6), (7), (8), (9). See *Iron Trades Mutual Insurance Co Ltd v Buckenham Ltd* [1989] 2 Lloyd's Rep. 85; *Horbury v Craig Hall & Rutley* [1991] E.G.C.S. 81; *Bradstock Trustee Services Ltd v Nabarro Nathanson* [1995] 1 W.L.R. 1405; *Hallam-Eames v Merrett Syndicates Ltd* [1996] 7 Med. L.R. 122; *Higgins v Hatch & Fielding* [1996] 1 E.G.L.R. 133; *Wilson v Le Fevre Wood & Royle* [1996] 1 P.N.L.R. 107; *Hamlin v Edwin Evans* [1996] P.N.L.R. 398; *Finance for Mortgages Ltd v Farley & Co* [1996] E.G.C.S. 35; *Henderson v Merrett Syndicates Ltd (No.3)* [1997] L.R.L.R. 247; *Perry v Moysey* [1998] P.N.L.R. 657; *Birmingham Midshires Building Society v Infields* [1999] Lloyd's Rep. P.N. 133; *Mortgage Corp Plc v Lambert & Co* [1999] Lloyd's Rep. P.N. 947; *Oakes v Hopcroft* (2000) 56 B.M.L.R. 136; *Fennon v Anthony Hodari & Co* [2001] Lloyd's Rep P.N. 183;

such an action, if that three-year period expires later than the six-year period.[58] For the purposes of the section, a person's knowledge includes knowledge which he might reasonably have been expected to acquire from facts observable or ascertainable by him or from facts ascertainable by him with the help of appropriate expert advice which it is reasonable for him to seek.[59] Thus if the damage inflicted is latent and is not discovered or discoverable until (say) five, or even seven, years after it first occurred, the claimant will have three years from the starting date in which to bring his action in respect of that damage. But if the damage is discovered or becomes discoverable one year after it first occurs, then the claimant's right of action will not become time-barred until six years from the date on which it first occurred. The burden of establishing that his case falls within the section rests upon the claimant.[60] This may be tried as a preliminary issue.[61]

In *Howard v Fawcetts*[62] s.14A was examined for the first time by the House of Lords. It was held that a claim against an accountant for negligent advice (or failure to advise), leading to loss-making investment in 1994 and 1995, was statute-barred. The claimant had had the relevant knowledge in December 1998, more than three years before commencing proceedings in December 2001. The case principally turned on the interpretation of s.14A(8)(a): "that the damage was attributable in whole or in part to the act or omission which is alleged to constitute negligence". Their Lordships adverted to the apparent tension between s.14A(8) and s.14A(9). According to the latter: "knowledge that any acts or omissions did or did not, as a matter of law, involve negligence is irrelevant". Their Lordships recognised that knowledge that the defendant had given "flawed" advice was necessary under s.14A(8)(a); and that the courts could safely look for knowledge that, factually, "something had gone wrong" without contravening s.14A(9). **28–012**

Actions to which s.14A applies cannot be brought after the expiration of 15 years from the date (or, if more than one, from the last of the dates) on which there occurred any act or omission: (a) which is alleged to constitute negligence; and (b) to which the damage in respect of which damages are claimed is alleged to be attributable (in whole or in part).[63] This 15-year long-stop is an absolute **28–013**

New Islington & Hackney Housing Association Ltd v Pollard, Thomas and Edwards Ltd [2001] Build. L.R. 74; *Lloyd's Bank Plc v Burd Pearse* [2001] Lloyd's Rep. P.N. 452; *Bowie v Southorns* [2003] P.N.L.R. 7; *McCarroll v Statham Gill Davies* [2003] EWCA Civ 425, [2003] P.N.L.R. 25.

[58] s.14A(4)(b).

[59] s.14A(10) (but see the qualification to this subsection where the person has taken all reasonable steps to obtain expert advice). Section 14A(10) therefore makes clear that constructive knowledge may be sufficient. For a consideration of s.14A(10), see *Gravgaard v Aldridge & Brownlee* [2004] EWCA Civ 1529, [2005] P.N.L.R. 19.

[60] *Iron Trades Mutual Insurance Co Ltd v Buckenham Ltd* [1989] 2 Lloyd's Rep. 85, 98: cf. *Nash v Eli Lilly and Co* [1993] 1 W.L.R. 782, 796. See also below, para.28–061.

[61] *Busby v Cooper, The Times*, April 2, 1996.

[62] [2006] UKHL 9, [2006] 1 W.L.R. 682. The approach to s.14A(8) in *Hallam-Eames v Merrett Syndicates Ltd* [1996] 7 Med. L.R. was approved, while that in *HF Pension Trustees Ltd v Ellison* [1999] P.N.L.R. 894 was disapproved.

[63] s.14B(1), inserted by s.1 of the Latent Damage Act 1986.

bar[64] to the remedy[65] and operates even though the cause of action has not yet accrued[66] and even though the starting date for the extension available in respect of latent damage has not yet occurred.[67]

28–014 **Loans.** The 1980 Act contains special provisions in respect of the time limit for actions in respect of certain loans.[68] It is not clear, however, whether these provisions apply if the contract of loan is executed as a deed. It is probable that the action is then upon a specialty and subject to the 12-year period.[69]

28–015 **Contribution.** Where under s.1 of the Civil Liability (Contribution) Act 1978 any person becomes entitled to a right to recover contribution in respect of any damage from any other person, no action to recover contribution by virtue of that right is to be brought after the expiration of two years from the date on which that right accrued.[70]

28–016 **Action on a judgment.** By s.24(1) of the 1980 Act, an action upon a judgment obtained in England or Wales is barred after the expiration of six years from the date on which the judgment became enforceable.[71] In *Lowsley v Forbes*[72] the House of Lords held that "an action upon a judgment" does not include proceedings to execute a judgment (such as proceedings for a charging order or a garnishee order). This was followed in *Ridgeway Motors (Isleworth) Ltd v ALTS Ltd*[73] in holding that a winding up or bankruptcy petition by a judgment creditor is not "an action upon a judgment" within s.24(1) of the 1980 Act. According to the Court of Appeal "an action upon a judgment" has the special meaning of a "fresh action" brought upon a judgment in order to obtain a second judgment, which can be executed. Insolvency proceedings, whether personal or corporate, do not fall within the scope of that special meaning. By s.24(2) no arrears of interest in respect of any judgment can be recovered after the expiration of six years from the date on which the interest became due.[74] A foreign judgment of a court of competent jurisdiction gives rise to an implied

---

[64] Subject to s.32(5); below, para.28–091, fn.353.

[65] But the long-stop does not extinguish the claimant's right of action: *Financial Services Compensation Scheme Ltd v Larnell (Insurances) Ltd* [2005] EWCA Civ 1408, [2006] 2 W.L.R. 751.

[66] s.14B(2)(a).

[67] s.14B(2)(b).

[68] s.6; see below, para.28–036.

[69] The action does not appear to be one "for which a shorter period of limitation is prescribed by any other provision of this Act" (s.8(2)) as under s.6(1) only s.5 of the Act is involved.

[70] s.10. See also below, para.28–051 (accrual of right). That the Civil Liability (Contribution) Act 1978 does not apply to a claim for contribution from a co-debtor means that the two-year limitation period applicable to the 1978 Act does not apply to such a claim for contribution: *Hampton v Minns* [2002] 1 W.L.R. 1.

[71] For the purposes of s.24, an order for costs becomes enforceable and time starts to run when the costs are quantified and certified by the process of taxation, and not before: *Chohan v Times Newspapers Ltd* [2001] 1 W.L.R. 1859.

[72] [1999] 1 A.C. 329.

[73] [2005] EWCA Civ 92, [2005] 1 W.L.R. 2871.

[74] This sub-section does apply to the recovery of interest by way of execution after six years: *Lowsley v Forbes* [1999] 1 A.C. 329.

contract to pay the amount of the judgment,[75] and the six-year period for actions founded on simple contract applies to an action upon such a judgment.[76]

Action on an award. An arbitrator's award is usually enforced by summary procedure under s.66 of the Arbitration Act 1996.[77] But it may also be enforced by bringing an action on the award, and this is the only method available in some situations, for example if the submission to arbitration was not in writing.[78] An action to enforce the award of an arbitrator, where the submission was not by deed, cannot be brought after the expiration of six years from the date on which the cause of action accrued.[79] 28–017

Equitable relief. The time limits prescribed by ss.5 and 8 of the Act[80] in respect of actions upon simple contracts and specialties do not apply to any claim for specific performance of a contract or for an injunction or for other equitable relief, except in so far as they may be applied by analogy.[81] Such claims may, however, be barred by laches or acquiescence, equitable doctrines which are discussed elsewhere in this chapter.[82] 28–018

Breach of trust or fiduciary duty. Actions for breach of trust and breach of fiduciary duty are distinct from actions for breach of contract; and commonly such actions are brought outside a contractual context. Nevertheless, where one contracting party owes fiduciary duties to the other, an action for breach of fiduciary duty may be brought. It may therefore be thought helpful here to refer, albeit very briefly, to the law on limitation of actions for these equitable causes of action. As regards breach of trust, the crucial section of the Limitation Act 1980 is the complex s.21. The basic regime of that section is that there is a six-year limitation period, running from the date when the right of action accrued, for a breach of trust[83] but that actions for fraudulent breach of trust or to recover trust property or its proceeds are excluded and have no statutory limitation period.[84] As regards a breach of fiduciary duty outside s.21, the courts tend to apply a six- 28–019

---

[75] *Grant v Easton* (1883) 13 QBD 302; *Re Flynn (No.2)* [1969] Ch. 403.

[76] This does not apply to the enforcement of a judgment registered under the Administration of Justice Act 1920, the Foreign Judgments (Reciprocal Enforcement) Act 1933 or Pts I and II of the Civil Jurisdiction and Judgments Act 1982. But certain time limits for registration are imposed by the 1920 and 1933 Acts.

[77] See below, para.32–168.

[78] See below, para.32–169.

[79] Limitation Act 1980 s.7; for accrual of the cause of action, see below, paras 28–059—28–060.

[80] s.7 (actions to enforce arbitral award); s.9 (statute) and s.24 (actions on judgments) are also inapplicable.

[81] s.36(1). As to the application of the statute by analogy, see below, para.28–135.

[82] s.36(2); below, paras 28–136—28–137.

[83] s.21(3).

[84] s.21(1). See *Tito v Waddell (No.2)* [1977] Ch. 106, 247–249; *Armitage v Nurse* [1998] Ch. 241; *Gwembe Valley Development Co Ltd v Koshy* [2003] EWCA Civ 1048; *Re Loftus* [2006] EWCA Civ 1124, [2007] 1 W.L.R. 1124. In the last case, it was further held that where the Limitation Act 1980 lays down that there is no limitation period prescribed by the Act (as, e.g. under s.21(1) for fraudulent breach of trust or to recover trust property), that does not preclude the operation of laches and acquiescence. See below, para.28–139.

year limitation period by analogy under s.36(1) of the Limitation Act 1980.[85] A six-year limitation period also applies to the equitable wrong of dishonest assistance in a breach of trust either because it falls within s.21(3) or by analogy to torts under s.36(1).[86]

28–020 **Special limitation periods.** Certain statutes provide periods of limitation which differ from those provided by the Limitation Act 1980.[87] These, so far as they affect the law of contract, are as follows:

28–021 **Salvage.** Article 23 of the International Convention on Salvage, contained in Sch.11 to the Merchant Shipping Act 1995, prescribes that any action relating to payment under the Convention is to be time-barred if judicial or arbitral proceedings are not instituted within a period of two years from the day on which the salvage operations are terminated (although the period may be extended by declaration to the claimant). Actions for an indemnity may be instituted within the time allowed by the *forum* where the proceedings are instituted.

28–022 **Carriage by sea.** Where the Hague-Visby Rules are incorporated in a contract of affreightment by the Carriage of Goods by Sea Act 1971,[88] the carrier[89] and the ship are discharged[90] from all liability whatsoever in respect of the goods, unless suit[91] is brought within one year of their delivery[92] or of the date when they should have been delivered.[93] This period may, however, be extended if the parties so agree after the cause of action has arisen.[94] An action for an indemnity against a third person may nevertheless be brought even after the expiration of the year if brought within the time allowed by the law of the court seised of the

---

[85] *Soar v Ashwell* [1893] 2 Q.B. 390, 393; *Taylor v Davies* [1920] A.C. 636, 652; *Paragon Finance Plc v Thakerar & Co* [1999] 1 All E.R. 400; *Coulthard v Disco Mix Club Ltd* [2000] 1 W.L.R. 707; *Cia de Seguros Imperio v Heath (REBX) Ltd* [2001] 1 W.L.R. 112; *Harrison (Properties) Ltd v Harrison* [2001] EWCA Civ 1467, [2002] 1 B.C.L.C. 162; *Gwembe Valley Development Co Ltd v Koshy* [2003] EWCA Civ 1048. cf. *James v Williams* [2000] Ch. 1. See below, para.28–135.

[86] *Cattley v Pollard* [2006] EWHC 3130 (Ch), [2007] Ch. 353.

[87] s.39.

[88] See ss.1, 2, 4, 5.

[89] cf. *Freedom General Shipping SA v Tokai Shipping Co Ltd* [1982] 1 Lloyd's Rep. 73.

[90] The cause of action is extinguished: see below, para.28–126; (Hague Rules) *Aries Tanker Corp v Total Transport Ltd* [1977] 1 W.L.R. 185; *Casillo Grani v Napier Shipping Co* [1984] 2 Lloyd's Rep. 481; *Payabi v Armstel Shipping Corp* [1992] Q.B. 907.

[91] "Suit" includes arbitration: *The Merak* [1965] P. 223; *Nea Agrex SA v Baltic Shipping Co Ltd* [1976] Q.B. 933; see also below, para.28–115. The suit may be in another competent jurisdiction: *The Nordglimt* [1988] Q.B. 183, distinguishing *Compania Columbiana de Seguros v Pacific Steam Navigation Co* [1965] 1 Q.B. 101. See also *Central Insurance Co Ltd v Seacalf Shipping Corp* [1983] 2 Lloyd's Rep. 25; *Hispanica de Petroleus SA v Vencedora Oceania Navegacion SA* [1986] 1 Lloyd's Rep. 211; *Government of Sierra Leone v Marmaro Shipping Co Ltd* [1989] 2 Lloyd's Rep. 130; *Transworld Oil (USA) Inc v Minos Naviera SA* [1992] 2 Lloyd's Rep. 48; *Mauritius Oil Refineries Ltd v Stolt-Nielsen Nederlands BV* [1997] 1 Lloyd's Rep. 273. Contrast *Thyssen Inc v Calypso Shipping Corp SA* [2000] 2 Lloyd's Rep. 243 (suit brought in incompetent jurisdiction).

[92] See *The Beltana* [1967] 1 Lloyd's Rep. 531.

[93] Sch. art.III r.6.

[94] See *The Clifford Maersk* [1982] 1 W.L.R. 1292; *Mitsubishi Corp v Castletown Navigation Ltd* [1989] 2 Lloyd's Rep. 383 (Hague Rules). cf. *Alma Shipping Corp v Union of India* [1971] 2 Lloyd's Rep. 494, 502 (after expiry of period new agreement required).

case,[95] i.e. in an English court, within the six-year period of limitation applicable to simple contracts.[96]

The Athens Convention of 1974 relating to the carriage of Passengers and their Luggage by Sea (as amended by the 1976 Protocol thereto) has the force of law in the United Kingdom.[97] It provides[98] for a two-year limitation period in respect of any action for damages arising out of the death of or personal injury to a passenger[99] or for the loss of or damage to luggage. The commencement of the period depends on the nature of the claim made, but in general is not earlier than the date of disembarkation or the date when disembarkation should have taken place. The period may be extended by written declaration of the carrier or by written agreement of the parties after the cause of action has arisen. 28–023

Carriage by air. The Carriage by Air Act 1961[100] applies to the international carriage by air of persons, baggage and cargo for reward or gratuitously by an air transport undertaking. The right to damages in respect of the carrier's liability is extinguished if an action[101] is not brought within two years,[102] reckoned from the date of arrival at the destination, or from the date on which the aircraft ought to have arrived, or from the date on which the carriage stopped.[103] Similar provisions are contained in the Carriage by Air Act (Application of Provisions) Order 2004[104] in cases to which the 1961 Act (or EC legislation) does not apply. 28–024

Carriage by rail. The Railways (Convention on International Carriage by Rail) Regulations[105] gives the force of law to the Convention (as modified by the Vilnius Protocol) concerning International Carriage by Rail (COTIF).[106] Under the Convention, the periods of limitation for actions for damages based on the liability of the railway in case of death of, or personal injury to, passengers are: (a) for the passenger, three years from the day after the accident; and (b) in a case where the claimant is not the passenger himself, three years from the day after the death of the passenger, subject to a maximum of five years from the day after the 28–025

---

95 Sch. art.III r.6 *bis*.

96 See *China Ocean Shipping Co v Andros* [1987] 1 W.L.R. 1213. cf. Limitation Act 1980 s.10 (claims to contribution), above, para.28–014.

97 Merchant Shipping Act 1995 Sch.6.

98 Athens Convention 1974 art.16.

99 The court's discretion to override the time-limit for such claims contained in s.33 of the 1980 Act (above, para.28–008) does not apply to this two-year period: *Higham v Stena Sealink Ltd* [1996] 1 W.L.R. 1107.

100 For the complex web of relevant statutory provisions and amendments, see below, Ch.35.

101 Or arbitration: Carriage by Air Act 1961 s.5(3).

102 That this two-year period is the relevant limitation period follows from s.39 of the Limitation Act 1980, which saves other limitation enactments. Moreover, s.33(2) of the 1980 Act uses the 1961 Act to illustrate the point that there is only a discretion to disapply s.12(1) (laying down the time limit for actions under the Fatal Accidents Act 1976) where the reason why the person injured could no longer maintain an action was because of the s.11 time limit and not some other time limit.

103 Sch.1 art.29 (see Vol.II, para.35–017). See also s.5 of the Act and s.3(2) of the Carriage by Air (Supplementary Provisions) Act 1962; s.4(4) of the Limitation Act 1963. For the time limits for complaints, see Sch.1 art.26 to the 1961 Act and Vol.II, paras 35–053, 35–064, 35–065.

104 SI 2004/1899; see Vol.II, para.35–070.

105 SI 2005/2092.

106 See Vol.II, para.36–078.

accident.[107] The Convention also contains limitation provisions with respect to other actions arising from a contract for the international carriage of passengers and luggage by rail[108] and for actions arising from a contract for the international carriage of goods by rail,[109] the period of limitation being in general one year with an extension to two years in certain cases. The starting point of the limitation period varies according to the nature of the claim,[110] but in the case of carriage of goods: (a) in actions for compensation for total loss, it runs from the thirtieth day after the expiry of the transit period; and (b) in actions for compensation for partial loss, for damage or for exceeding the transit period, it runs from the day when delivery took place.[111]

28–026 **Carriage by road.** Under the Carriage of Goods by Road Act 1965,[112] which gives effect to the Convention on the Contract for the International Carriage of Goods by Road (CMR), the period of limitation is one year, or, in the case of wilful misconduct or equivalent, three years.[113] The period of limitation begins to run: in the case of partial loss, damage or delay in delivery, from the date of delivery; in the case of total loss, from the thirtieth day after the expiry of the agreed time limit or where there is no agreed time limit from the 60th day from the date on which the goods were taken over by the carrier; and in all other cases, on the expiry of three months after the making of the contract of carriage.[114]

28–027 **Sale of goods.** By the Uniform Laws on International Sales Act 1967, where the Uniform Law of International Sales (ULIS) applies,[115] the buyer loses his right to rely on lack of conformity with the contract at the expiration of a period of one year after he has given notice as provided in art.39.[116] Such notice must be given promptly after he has discovered the lack of conformity or ought to have discovered it, and must in any event be given within a period of two years from the date on which the goods were handed over, unless the lack of conformity constituted a breach of a guarantee covering a longer period.[117]

28–028 **Employment.** Unless the employee has previously made a claim for a redundancy payment by notice in writing given to his employer and in certain other cases, a claim for such a payment cannot be entertained by an employment tribunal after the end of the period of six months beginning with the relevant date

---

[107] COTIF, Appendix A (CIV) art.60(1); Vol.II, para.36–116. For the time limits for complaints, see art.58; Vol.II, para.36–115.

[108] COTIF, Appendix A (CIV) art.60(2)(3); Vol.II, para.36–116. For the time limits for complaints, in respect of registered luggage, see art.59; Vol.II, para.36–115.

[109] COTIF, Appendix B (CIM) art.48; Vol.II, para.36–098. For the time limits for claims, see art.47; Vol.II, para.36–097.

[110] COTIF, Appendix A (CIV) art.60(3); Appendix B (CIM) art.48(2).

[111] COTIF, Appendix B (CIM) art.48(2)(a), (b).

[112] See Vol.II, para.36–117.

[113] Carriage of Goods by Road Act 1965 Sch. art.32(1) see below, Vol.II, para.36–143. For the time limits for complaints, see art.30 and Vol.II, para.36–142.

[114] See Vol.II, para.36–143.

[115] See Vol.II, para.43–003.

[116] Uniform Laws on International Sales Act 1967 Sch.1 art.49(1) (unless he has been prevented from exercising his right because of fraud on the part of the seller). But see art.49(2).

[117] art.39(1).

(usually the date of termination of his employment).[118] And an employment tribunal cannot consider a complaint of unfair dismissal unless it is presented to the tribunal before the end of the period of three months beginning with the effective date of termination or within such further period as the tribunal considers reasonable in a case where it is satisfied that it was not reasonably practicable for the complaint to be presented within the period of three months.[119] Short periods of limitation are further provided for proceedings where an employer has not provided an employee with a statement of terms of employment[120] and in respect of guarantee payments.[121]

Legal proceedings by the employer of a worker in retail employment for the recovery from the worker of any amount in respect of a cash shortage or stock deficiency cannot be instituted after the end of a period of 12 months beginning with the date when the employer established the existence of the deficiency or (if earlier) the date when he ought reasonably to have done so, unless he has within that period made a statutory demand for payment in respect of that amount.[122] An employment tribunal cannot entertain a complaint in respect of unauthorised deductions from the wages of a worker or an unlawful payment to an employer unless it is presented within the period of three months from the date of payment of the relevant wages or the date of the receipt of the payment by the employer or within such further period as the tribunal considers reasonable in a case where it is satisfied that it was not reasonably practicable for the complaint to be presented within the period of three months.[123] 28–029

The Equal Pay Act 1970,[124] the Sex Discrimination Act 1975,[125] the Race Relations Act 1976[126] and the Disability Discrimination Act 1995[127] also establish time limits within which proceedings must be brought. 28–030

2. ACCRUAL OF THE CAUSE OF ACTION

Meaning of cause of action. Section 5 of the Limitation Act 1980 provides that the action "shall not be brought after the expiration of six years from the date on which the cause of action accrued". The ascertainment of this date is often a question of some difficulty. There is no definition of the term "cause of action" 28–031

[118] Employment Rights Act 1996 s.164(1). But see s.164(2). See Vol.II, para.39–253.
[119] s.111(2). But see s.111(3)(4). See Vol.II, para.39–236.
[120] s.11(4) (three months); Vol.II, para.39–040.
[121] s.34(2) (three months); Vol.II, para.39–085.
[122] s.20(5); see Vol.II, para.39–093.
[123] s.23(2)–(4); see Vol.II, para.39–091.
[124] s.2(5) (as amended).
[125] s.76 (as amended).
[126] s.68 (as amended).
[127] Sch.3 Pt.I para.3.

in the Act, and therefore the old law is still applicable. In 1888 it was defined by Lord Esher as:

> "... every fact which it would be necessary for the plaintiff to prove, if traversed, in order to support his right to the judgment of the court."[128]

In 1891 Lindley L.J. said "it has always been held that the statute runs from the earliest time at which an action could be brought."[129] And in 1927 Lord Dunedin defined cause of action to mean "that which makes action possible".[130] There must also be in existence at this moment a competent claimant and a competent defendant.[131] There is no competent defendant if, e.g. he enjoys diplomatic privilege[132] or, being a corporation, it has been dissolved in the country of its incorporation.[133] On the other hand, the mere fact that the defendant cannot be traced, so that in practice the claimant cannot start proceedings, does not prevent the cause of action from accruing.[134] Where a claim arises at or after the death of an intestate and not before (e.g. for a debt payable after the death of the creditor or debtor) it appears to be the rule that there is no competent claimant or defendant, as the case may be, in the interval between the death and the grant of letters of administration so that the cause of action does not accrue until the grant of letters.[135] This is because the title of an administrator is derived from the grant and he cannot sue or be sued until a grant is made. There is also some authority for saying that if at the time when the cause of action would have accrued the potential claimant and defendant were one and the same person, so that the hand to pay and the hand to receive were the same, the cause of action does not accrue and time does not begin to run.[136] It should be noted that what is said above about

---

[128] *Read v Brown* (1888) 22 QBD 128, 131. See also *Cooke v Gill* (1873) L.R. 8 C.P. 107, 116; *Coburn v Colledge* [1897] 1 Q.B. 702, 706, 707; *Central Electricity Board v Halifax Corp* [1963] A.C. 785, 800, 806. *Letang v Cooper* [1964] 1 Q.B. 232, 242; *Paragon Finance v Thakerar & Co* [1999] 1 All E.R. 405.

[129] *Reeves v Butcher* [1891] 2 Q.B. 509, 511.

[130] *Board of Trade v Cayzer, Irvine & Co* [1927] A.C. 610, 617. See also *Letang v Cooper* [1965] 1 Q.B. 232, 242.

[131] *Thomson v Lord Clanmore* [1900] 1 Ch. 718, 728–729 (Vaughan Williams L.J.).

[132] *Musurus Bey v Gadban* [1894] 2 Q.B. 352.

[133] *Re Russo-Asiatic Bank* [1934] Ch. 720, 738.

[134] *R.B. Policies at Lloyd's v Butler* [1950] 1 K.B. 76; Goodman (1966) 29 M.L.R. 366. cf. *Clark v Forbes Stuart (Thames Steel) Ltd* [1964] 1 W.L.R. 836; Limitation Act 1980 ss.14(1)(c), 14(1A)(c), 14A(8)(c).

[135] *Jolliffe v Pitt* (1715) 2 Vern. 694; *Murray v East India Co* (1821) 5 B. & Ald. 204; *Douglas v Forrest* (1828) 4 Bing. 686, 704; *Pratt v Swaine* (1828) 8 B. & C. 285; *Burdick v Garrick* (1870) L.R. 5 Ch. App. 233, 241; *Chan Kit Sam v Ho Fung Ham* [1902] A.C. 257; *Meyappa Chetty v Supramanian Chetty* [1916] 1 A.C. 603, 610. But there is some doubt about whether this rule can stand subsequent to RSC Ord.15 r.6A—now CPR r.19.8—which was made by virtue of s.2 of the Proceedings against Estates Act 1970 (now repealed). There are also statutory limitation provisions for particular causes of action which presumably override any such rule, e.g. Limitation Act 1980, ss.11(5), 12(2). See also s.26 of the Limitation Act 1980 (recovery of land). For accrual after date of death where there is an executor, see *Webster v Webster* (1804) 10 Ves. Jun. 93; *Flood v Patterson* (1861) 29 Beav. 295; *Knox v Gye* (1871) L.R. 5 H.L. 656; *Lovett v Ambler* (1876) 3 Ch D 198; *Meyappa Chetty v Supramanian Chetty* [1916] 1 A.C. 603, 608.

[136] *Binns v Nichols* (1866) L.R. 2 Eq. 256; *Re Pardoe* [1906] 1 Ch. 265.

competent parties refers only to the accrual of the cause of action. It does not refer to the suspension of the statute once time has begun to run.[137]

General rule in contract. The general rule in contract is that the cause of action accrues, not when the damage is suffered, but when the breach takes place[138]: 28–032

> "In an action of assumpsit, the Statute of Limitations begins to run not from the time when the damage results from breach of the promise, but the time when the breach of promise takes place."[139]

The gist of an action for breach of contract is the breach, and not any resulting damage which may be occasioned thereby. Consequently, the Act runs from the time when the contract is broken, and not from the time at which any damage resulting therefrom is sustained by the claimant. Therefore, although such damage may occur within six years before the action is brought, the action will be barred if the contract was broken before that period. For example, in an action for breach of warranty or condition against a seller of goods, the cause of action accrues when the goods are delivered, and not when the defect is discovered.[140]

Concurrent liability in tort. It is, however, well established that in the tort of negligence the cause of action arises when the damage is suffered and not when the act or omission complained of occurs. If, therefore, a claimant has, independently of or in addition to any cause of action in contract, a cause of action in tort for negligence, time will not begin to run in respect of his claim in tort until the damage is sustained. In a number of cases it was held that an action for negligence against, for example, a solicitor[141] or architect[142] was contractual in nature, so that the cause of action accrued when his negligent act or omission took place.[143] But more recent cases have held that the existence of a contractual relationship between the parties does not necessarily exclude a concurrent or independent cause of action in tort.[144] So an action may be brought in tort for negligence in respect of professional services rendered, for example, by a 28–033

137 As to this, see below, paras 28–065—28–066.

138 *Gould v Johnson* (1702) 2 Salk. 422; *Battley v Faulkner* (1820) 3 B. & Ald. 288; *Short v M'Carthy* (1820) 3 B. & Ald. 626; *Howell v Young* (1826) 5 B. & C. 259; *Walker v Milner* (1866) 4 F. & F. 745; *Gibbs v Guild* (1881) 8 QBD 296, 302.

139 *Howell v Young* (1826) 5 B. & C. 259, 265.

140 *Battley v Faulkner* (1820) 3 B. & Ald. 288; *Lynn v Bamber* [1930] 2 K.B. 72, 74.

141 *Short v M'Carthy* (1820) 3 B. & Ald. 626; *Brown v Howard* (1820) 2 Brod. & B. 73; *Howell v Young* (1826) 5 B. & C. 529; *Bean v Wade* (1885) 2 T.L.R. 157; *Wood v Jones* (1889) 61 L.T. 551; *Groom v Crocker* [1939] 1 K.B. 194; *Somers v Erskine* [1944] Ir.R. 368; *Clark v Kirby-Smith* [1964] Ch. 506. See also *Cook v Swinfen* [1967] 1 W.L.R. 457; *Heywood v Wellers* [1976] Q.B. 446; *Rowe v Turner Hopkins & Partners* [1980] N.Z.L.R. 550.

142 *Bagot v Stevens Scanlon & Co Ltd* [1966] 1 Q.B. 197.

143 *Clark v Kirby-Smith* [1964] Ch. 506; *Bagot v Stevens Scanlan & Co Ltd* [1966] 1 Q.B. 197.

144 *Henderson v Merrett Syndicates Ltd* [1995] 2 A.C. 145. See above, paras 1–105—1–147, 28–010—28–012.

solicitor,[145] insurance broker,[146] architect[147] or engineer[148] within six years of the date when the claimant first sustains damage.[149]

28–034 Where the negligence has induced the claimant to enter into a contract (with the defendant or a third party), the cause of action in the tort of negligence (including liability under s.2(1) of the Misrepresentation Act 1967) will often accrue when that contract is entered into.[150] But it may accrue at a later date, e.g. when the claimant incurs expenditure or sustains other damage in consequence of having entered into the contract.[151] In *Law Society v Sephton & Co*[152] the House of Lords held that the Law Society's cause of action in the tort of negligence against an accountant only accrued when claims were made by former clients of a corrupt solicitor for compensation from the Solicitors Compensation Fund. Prior to then, the Law Society had only a contingent liability to pay out compensation. Such a pure contingent liability, which might or might not eventuate, did not count as damage so as to constitute the accrual of a cause of action. This situation was to be distinguished from that dealt with in almost all the prior English cases, which concerned entering into disadvantageous transactions or suffering a diminution in value of an asset.

28–035 **Successive and continuing breaches.** Where the innocent party elects to treat himself as discharged from further performance consequent upon a breach of the contract,[153] time begins to run immediately. For instance, if there is an anticipatory breach accepted by him as a repudiation of the contract, his cause of action

---

145 *Midland Bank Trust Co Ltd v Hett, Stubbs & Kemp* [1977] Ch. 384; *Forster v Outred & Co* [1982] 1 W.L.R. 86; *D.W. Moore & Co Ltd v Ferrier* [1988] 1 W.L.R. 267; *Bell v Peter Browne & Co* [1990] Q.B. 495; *Khan v Falvey & Co* [2002] EWCA Civ 400, [2002] P.N.L.R. 28; *McCarroll v Statham Gill Davies* [2002] EWCA Civ 425, [2003] P.N.L.R. 25.

146 *Iron Trades Mutual Insurance Co Ltd v Buckenham Ltd* [1989] 2 Lloyd's Rep. 85; *Islander Trucking Ltd v Hogg Robinson & Gardner Mountain (Marine) Ltd* [1990] 1 All E.R. 826; *Punjab National Bank v De Boinville* [1992] 1 W.L.R. 1138; *Knapp v Ecclesiastical Insurance Group Plc* [1998] P.N.L.R. 172. See also *Société Commerciale de Reassurance v Eras International Ltd* [1992] 1 Lloyd's Rep. 570 (insurance management agreement); *Henderson v Merrett Syndicates Ltd* [1995] 2 A.C. 145 (Lloyd's underwriting agents).

147 *Kensington and Chelsea and Westminster Area Health Authority v Wettern Composites Ltd* [1985] 1 All E.R. 346; *London Congregational Union Inc v Harriss & Harriss* [1988] 1 All E.R. 15; *Wessex Regional Health Authority v HLM Design* (1994) 10 Const. L.J. 165; *New Islington & Hackney Housing Association Ltd v Pollard, Thomas and Edwards Ltd* [2001] Build. L.R. 74.

148 *Pirelli General Cable Works Ltd v Oscar Faber and Partners* [1983] A.C. 1; *Wessex Regional Health Authority v HLM Design* (1994) 10 Const. L.J. 165.

149 For extension of the period in cases of latent damage in the tort of negligence, see above, paras 28–010—28–012.

150 See *Forster v Outred & Co* [1982] 1 W.L.R. 86; *D.W. Moore & Co Ltd v Ferrier* [1988] 1 W.L.R. 267; *Iron Trades Mutual Insurance Co Ltd v Buckenham Ltd* [1989] 2 Lloyd's Rep. 85; *Bell v Peter Browne & Co* [1990] 2 Q.B. 495; *Islander Trucking Ltd v Hogg Robinson & Gardner Mountain (Manne) Ltd* [1990] 1 All E.R. 826; *Knapp v Ecclesiastical Insurance Group Plc* [1998] P.N.L.R. 172; *Byrne v Hall Pain & Foster* [1999] 1 W.L.R. 1849; *McCarroll v Statham Gill Davies* [2002] EWCA Civ 425, [2003] P.N.L.R. 25.

151 *Toprak Enerji Sanayi A.S. v Sale Tilney Technology Plc* [1994] 1 W.L.R. 840; *Wardley Australia Ltd v State of Western Australia* (1992) 175 C.L.R. 514; *UBAF Ltd v European American Banking Corp* [1984] Q.B. 713, 726; *Nykredit Mortgage Bank Plc v Edward Erdman Group Ltd (No.2)* [1997] 1 W.L.R. 1627.

152 [2006] UKHL 22, [2006] 2 W.L.R. 1091.

153 For discharge by breach, see above, Ch.24.

accrues at once, and not from the failure of the party in default subsequently to perform at the time fixed for performance.[154] But if there are one or more breaches which do not give rise to a discharge either because they are not sufficiently fundamental or because the innocent party declines to accept them as having that effect, each will give rise to a separate cause of action.[155] There may also be a series of breaches of a single covenant. Examples are failure to pay instalments of interest[156] or rent.[157] Or the breach may be a continuing one, e.g. of a covenant to keep in repair.[158] In such a case the claimant will succeed in respect of so much of the series of breaches or the continuing breach as occurred within the six (or 12) years before action brought. If the breach consists in a failure to act, it may be held to continue *die in diem* until the obligation is performed or becomes impossible of performance or until the innocent party elects to treat the continued non-performance as a repudiation of the contract. Thus the failure of a solicitor to register an interest in land will ordinarily constitute a continuing breach of his retainer, and the client's cause of action will not become barred until six years after registration ceases to be possible.[159]

Money lent. At common law, where no time for repayment was specified in a contract of loan, or where the loan was expressed simply to be repayable "on demand", the lender's cause of action in general[160] accrued when the loan was made and time began to run from that moment.[161] As a result, once the loan was outstanding for more than six years (which not infrequently happens in the case of loans between friends or members of a family)[162] the lender's right to recover the money lent became barred notwithstanding that no demand for repayment had been made. But by s.6 of the Limitation Act 1980, if: (a) a contract of loan does not provide for repayment of the debt on or before a fixed or determinable date; and (b) does not effectively (whether or not it purports so to do) make the obligation to repay the debt conditional on demand for repayment made by or on behalf of the creditor or any other matter, then the right of action on the contract of loan is not barred after six years from the date of the loan.[163] Instead, the six-year period does not start to run unless and until a demand *in writing* for repayment of the debt is made by or on behalf of the creditor (or, where there are joint creditors, by or on behalf of any one of them).[164] However, the section establishes an exception in the case where, in connection with taking the loan, the debtor enters into any collateral obligation to pay the amount of the debt or any 28–036

[154] *Reeves v Butcher* [1891] 2 Q.B. 509.

[155] *Arnott v Holden* (1852) 18 Q.B. 593.

[156] *Bowyer v Woodman* (1867) L.R. 3 Eq. 313. See s.20(5)(6)(7). But cf. below, para.28–036.

[157] *Archbold v Scully* (1861) 9 H.L.C. 360. See s.19.

[158] *Spoor v Green* (1874) L.R. 9 Ex. 99, 111. There was held to be no continuing obligation to deliver goods of the correct quality, so that there was a simple breach at the time of delivery, in *VAI Industries (UK) Ltd v Bostock & Bramley* [2003] EWCA Civ 1069, [2003] B.L.R. 359.

[159] *Midland Bank Trust Co Ltd v Hett, Stubbs & Kemp* [1979] Ch. 384.

[160] For exceptions, see below, para.28–039 (banker and customer); para.28–046 (guarantees).

[161] *Rumball v Ball* (1712) 10 Mod. 39; *Garden v Bruce* (1868) L.R. 3 C.P. 300; *Re Brown's Estate* [1893] 2 Ch. 300, 305; *Bradford Old Bank v Sutcliffe* [1918] 2 K.B. 833, 840, 845–846, 848, 849; *Tate v Crowdson* [1938] Ch. 869, 881; *Lloyd's Bank v Margolis* [1954] 1 W.L.R. 644, 648.

[162] *Twenty-First Report of the Law Reform Committee*, 1977, Cmnd.6923, paras 3.19–3.26.

[163] For agreements made by deed, see above, para.28–003.

[164] See, generally, *Boot v Boot* [1996] 2 F.C.R. 713.

part of it (as, for example, by delivering a promissory note[165] as security for the debt) on terms which would exclude the application of the section to the contract of loan if they applied directly to repayment of the debt.[166]

28–037 Where the contract of loan does provide for repayment of the debt on or before a fixed or determinable date, or does effectively make the obligation to repay conditional upon a demand for repayment[167] or any other matter,[168] it is a question of construction when the lender's cause of action accrues. Thus where there was a loan for five years with interest, and the lender was entitled to call in the loan on any default in the payment of interest, it was held that the lender's cause of action accrued on the first such default taking place.[169]

28–038 Once the right to recover the principal sum is barred, arrears of interest falling due within six years before the action is brought are also irrecoverable, for the interest is accessory to the principal.[170]

28–039 **Banker and customer.** The relationship between banker and customer is the contractual one of debtor and creditor, not that of trustee and cestui que trust.[171] It is well settled that, unless the contrary is agreed, a demand by the customer is a condition precedent to repayment, whether the money is on current or deposit account.[172] Accordingly time runs from the date of the demand[173] and not from the date when the account was opened or the money paid in, so that banks may be faced with claims that have lain dormant for years. However, in one case, money on a deposit account was unclaimed for 60 years, there being no evidence of repayment or of a demand for repayment, and the court drew the inference from all the circumstances that the money had at some time been repaid.[174] Where sums are wrongly debited to the customer's account, time runs from the date on which the customer demands repayment of the credit balance remaining when those sums are left out of account.[175] If the relationship of banker and customer is terminated before a demand is made, e.g. by dissolution of the bank, the money thereupon becomes repayable.[176]

---

[165] Defined in s.6(4).

[166] s.6(2). See *Boot v Boot* [1996] 2 F.C.R. 713; *Von Goetz v Rogers* Unreported July 29, 1998 CA.

[167] *Lloyds Bank v Margolis* [1954] 1 W.L.R. 644 (legal charge with covenant to repay on demand given as collateral security); and see below, para.28–039 (customer's account with bank).

[168] *Re McHenry* [1894] 3 Ch. 240.

[169] *Reeves v Butcher* [1891] 2 Q.B. 509.

[170] *Hollis v Palmer* (1836) 2 Bing. N.C. 73; *Cheang Thye Phin v Lam Kin Sang* [1929] A.C. 670; *Elder v Northcott* [1930] 2 Ch. 422.

[171] *Foley v Hill* (1848) 2 H.L.C. 28.

[172] *Joachimson v Swiss Bank Corp* [1921] 3 K.B. 110; *Arab Bank v Barclays Bank* [1954] A.C. 495; *Hart v Sangster* [1957] Ch. 329. See also *Re Dillon* (1890) 44 Ch D 76, 81.

[173] But repeated demands do not start time running afresh: *Bank of Baroda v Mahomed* [1999] Lloyd's Rep. Bank 14.

[174] *Douglass v Lloyds Bank* (1929) 34 Com. Cas. 263.

[175] *National Bank of Commerce v National Westminster Bank* [1990] 2 Lloyd's Rep. 514. cf. 517 (account ultimately in debit).

[176] *Re Russian Commercial Bank* [1955] Ch. 148.

Overdrafts. An overdraft is a loan by the banker to the customer. At common law, in the case of an overdraft repayable on demand, a demand was in general not a condition precedent to bringing an action and time ran against the banker in respect of each advance from the time when it was made.[177] But now, by virtue of s.6 of the 1980 Act, time will not as a normal rule start to run against the banker until a demand in writing is made for repayment of the advance. 28–040

Negotiable instruments.[178] The liability to the holder of the acceptor of a bill or the maker of a note payable at a fixed or determinable future time arises upon the maturity of the instrument,[179] unless presentment for payment is necessary to charge the acceptor or maker, in which case the liability arises at the date of presentment.[180] Therefore, on a bill payable on a certain date, or at a certain period after date, the limitation period runs from the time it falls due.[181] In the case of a bill drawn payable after sight, presentment for acceptance is necessary in order to fix the maturity of the instrument.[182] If a bill is payable at a fixed period after sight, the liability of the acceptor arises at the end of the fixed period calculated from the date of acceptance.[183] 28–041

If a bill or note is payable at sight[184] or on demand, the liability of the acceptor or maker to the holder arises on the date of acceptance or, in the case of a note, on the date of the note (or of its issue if later), and no demand is necessary to establish liability.[185] Accordingly, the limitation period will run from that time. It would appear that the cause of action by the holder of a cheque against the drawer, being the party primarily liable on the instrument, likewise accrues on the date of the cheque (or of its issue if later).[186] 28–042

As regards the drawer of a bill and the indorser of a bill or note, time begins to run in his favour when he receives notice of dishonour, or, if notice of dishonour is excused, from the date of dishonour.[187] If a bill is dishonoured by non-acceptance, and afterwards by non-payment, no fresh cause of action accrues 28–043

---

177 *Parrs Banking Co v Yates* [1898] 2 Q.B. 460. Contrast *Lloyds Bank v Margolis* [1954] 1 W.L.R. 644 (legal charge with covenant to repay on demand given as collateral security).

178 See *Byles on Bills of Exchange*, 27th edn, pp.428–438; *Chalmers and Guest on Bills of Exchange*, 16th edn, paras 7–56—7–60.

179 Except where a bill is accepted after maturity, when time runs from the date of acceptance: Bills of Exchange Act 1882 s.10(2).

180 Bills of Exchange Act 1882 ss.19(2)(c), 52, 87.

181 *Montague v Perkins* (1853) 22 L.J.C.P. 187.

182 Bills of Exchange Act 1882 s.39(1).

183 Bills of Exchange Act 1882 ss.11(1), 14(2), (3); *Holmes v Kerrison* (1810) 2 Taunt. 323.

184 Bills of Exchange Act 1882 s.10(1)(a).

185 *Norton v Ellam* (1837) 2 M. & W. 461; *Re Brown's Estate* [1893] 2 Ch. 300, 304; *Re British Trade Corp* [1932] 2 Ch. 1. But see Bills of Exchange Act 1882 ss.19(2)(c), 52(2), 87(1) (presentment for payment). Contrast (instruments payable at a certain period *after* demand): *Thorpe v Booth* (1826) Ry. & M. 388; *Re Rutherford* (1880) 14 Ch D 687.

186 *Robinson v Hawksford* (1846) 9 Q.B. 52, 59; *Laws v Rand* (1857) 3 C.B. (N.S.) 442, 449; *Re Bethell* (1887) 34 Ch D 561.

187 Bills of Exchange Act 1882 ss.43, 47, 48, 50(2), 55, 87(2), (3); *Kennedy v Thomas* [1894] 2 Q.B. 759.

to the holder against the drawer by reason of the dishonour by non-payment.[188]

28–044 It would seem that the cause of action of a drawer of a bill, and of the indorser of a bill or note, who has been compelled to pay the instrument accrues against the acceptor or maker on the making of the payment.[189] Likewise, with respect to the claim of an indorser against the drawer of a bill or prior indorsers of a bill or note, it would seem that the cause of action arises when he is compelled to and does pay the instrument.[190]

28–045 **Securities.** In the case of registered securities, time begins to run in respect of payment of dividends from the date on which the dividend is declared or from the date provided by the declaration for its payment, whichever is the later,[191] and in respect of a scheme or reduction of capital involving an immediate repayment of capital on the date when the scheme or reduction becomes effective.[192] In the case of bearer securities, the question arises whether the document must be presented to the company before the liability of the company accrues, and this is to be determined by reference to the company's articles of association and the terms on which the securities were issued.[193]

28–046 **Principal and surety.** Unless otherwise agreed in the contract of guarantee, the liability of the surety to the creditor arises on the principal debtor's default, so that time begins to run in favour of both of them at that moment.[194] If the surety undertakes to pay on demand, a demand is a condition precedent to liability and the creditor's cause of action accrues only when a demand is made and not complied with.[195] Where it was agreed that the guarantee should be a continuing one and should apply to the balance that was then or might at any time thereafter be owing, it was held that this was a guarantee of each debit balance as it was constituted, so that the cause of action accrued not when each advance was made to the principal debtor, but when the debit balance in question was constituted.[196]

28–047 Unless otherwise agreed, the surety's implied right to an indemnity from the principal debtor accrues when the surety's liability to the creditor is ascertained,

---

[188] *Whitehead v Walker* (1842) 9 M. & W. 506; *Wilkinson v Verity* (1871) L.R. 6 C.P. 206, 209.

[189] Bills of Exchange Act 1882 ss.57, 59. But since the claim is analogous to that of a surety against the principal debtor (para.28–047, below), it is arguable that the cause of action arises when his liability to pay is ascertained, or even when he receives notice of dishonour.

[190] Bills of Exchange Act 1882 s.55(1)(2). But contrast *Webster v Kirk* (1852) 17 Q.B. 944 (date of receipt of notice of dishonour).

[191] *Bond v Barrow Haematite Steel* [1902] 1 Ch. 353; *Re Compania de Electricidad de la Provincia de Buenos Aires Ltd* [1980] Ch. 146.

[192] *Re Artisans' Land and Mortgage Corp* [1904] 1 Ch. 796; *Re Compania de Electricidad de la Provincia de Buenos Aires Ltd* [1980] Ch. 146.

[193] *Re Compania de Electricidad de la Provincia de Buenos Aires Ltd* [1980] Ch. 146.

[194] *Parrs Banking Co v Yates* [1898] 2 Q.B. 460.

[195] *Re Brown's Estate* [1893] 2 Ch. 300; *Bradford Old Bank v Sutcliffe* [1918] 2 K.B. 833; *Esso Petroleum Co Ltd v Alstonbridge Properties Ltd* [1975] 1 W.L.R. 1474; *Bank of Baroda v Patel* [1996] 1 Lloyd's Rep. 390.

[196] *Wright v New Zealand Farmers' Co-operative Association* [1939] A.C. 439. cf. *Hartland v Jukes* (1863) 1 H. & C. 667.

and time runs from that moment.[197] If a surety pays a statute-barred debt, he cannot recover the amount from the principal debtor.[198]

As between co-sureties, the right to contribution of one who has paid more than his share accrues at the time of such payment,[199] and of one who has been called upon to pay the whole of the debt at the time the claim of the creditor against him is established.[200] It is immaterial that, at the time of the action for contribution, time has run out between the creditor and the co-surety.[201] 28–048

Indemnity against liability. Where a contract of indemnity is to indemnify a person against liability to a third party (e.g. under a liability insurance policy), the general modern rule is that the limitation period starts to run when the indemnifying party's liability is established by judgment, arbitration or binding settlement.[202] However, that general rule is subject to the construction of the contract of indemnity.[203] This may mean that the indemnifying party is liable as soon as the indemnified party is liable (that is, even before any establishing of that liability by, for example, judgment).[204] At the other extreme, the contract may on its true construction provide that the indemnity is conditional on actual payment by the indemnified party in which case the cause of action will accrue only when such payment has been made.[205] 28–049

Non-liability insurance. Under a non-liability insurance policy, a cause of action would appear to accrue, in the case of insurance against loss, when the casualty causing the loss occurs[206]; and in the case of life or accident insurance, upon the occurrence of the event which gives rise to the claim.[207] But regard must be had to the terms of the policy; on its true construction it may be that the 28–050

[197] *Wolmershausen v Gullick* [1893] 2 Ch. 514; *Re Richardson* [1911] 2 K.B. 705, 709.

[198] *Coneys v Morris* [1922] 1 Ir.R. 81.

[199] *Davies v Humphreys* (1840) 6 M. & W. 153; *Re Snowdon* (1881) 17 Ch D 44.

[200] *Wolmershausen v Gullick* [1893] 2 Ch. 514; cf. *Robinson v Harkin* [1896] 2 Ch. 415 (contribution between co-trustees).

[201] *Wolmershausen v Gullick* [1893] 2 Ch. 514.

[202] *County & District Properties Ltd v C. Jenner & Son Ltd* [1976] 2 Lloyd's Rep. 728 (Swanwick J.); *R. H. Green & Silley Weir v British Rys Board* [1985] 1 W.L.R. 570 (Dillon J.); *Telfair Shipping Corp v Inersea Carriers SA* [1985] 1 W.L.R. 553 (Neill J., who distinguished an indemnity against liability from a general indemnity, express or implied); *Bradley v Eagle Star Insurance Co Ltd* [1989] A.C. 957; *North Atlantic Insurance Co Ltd v Bishopsgate Insurance Co Ltd* [1998] 1 Lloyd's Rep. 459; *City of London v Reeve & Co Ltd* [2000] Build. L.R. 211, 215.

[203] *Telfair Shipping Corp v Inersea Carriers SA* [1985] 1 W.L.R. 553, 566; *Firma C-Trade S.A. v Newcastle Protection and Indemnity Association* [1991] 2 A.C. 1; *Total Liban SA v Vitol Energy SA* [1999] 2 Lloyd's Rep. 700.

[204] *Bosma v Larsen* [1966] 1 Lloyd's Rep. 22.

[205] *Firma C-Trade SA v Newcastle Protection and Indemnity Association* [1991] 2 A.C. 1.

[206] *Chandris v Argo Insurance Co Ltd* [1963] 2 Lloyd's Rep. 65, approved in *Castle Insurance Co Ltd v Hong Kong Islands Shipping Co Ltd* [1984] A.C. 226. See also *Scott Lithgow v Secretary of State for Defence* (1989) 45 Build. L.R. 1 HL; *Firma C-Trade SA v Newcastle Protection and Indemnity Association* [1991] 2 A.C. 1, 35; *Bank of America National Trust and Savings Association v Chrismas* [1994] 1 All E.R. 401; *Callaghan v Dominion Insurance Co Ltd* [1997] 2 Lloyd's Rep. 541; *Universities Superannuation Scheme Ltd v Royal Insurance (UK) Ltd* [2000] 1 All E.R. (Comm) 266.

[207] *Re Haycock's Policy* (1876) 1 Ch D 611; *London & Midland Bank v Mitchell* [1899] 2 Ch. 161. See also *Virk v Gan Life Holdings Plc* (2000) 52 B.M.L.R. 207.

liability of the insurer will not arise unless and until a claim is made or certain other conditions are satisfied.[208]

28–051 **Civil Liability (Contribution) Act 1978.** In respect of the special two-year period of limitation[209] for claiming contribution under s.1 of the Civil Liability (Contribution) Act 1978, the right of action to recover contribution accrues on the date on which judgment is given or an arbitral award made.[210] Where there are separate judgments (or arbitration awards) in relation to liability and quantum, the two-year period runs from the judgment on quantum.[211] In the absence of any judgment or award, if the person entitled to recover contribution in respect of any damage makes or agrees to make any payment to one or more persons in respect of that damage (whether he admits any liability in respect of the damage or not), time begins to run from the earliest date on which the amount to be paid by him is agreed between him (or his representative) and the person (or each of the persons, as the case may be) to whom the payment is to be made.[212]

28–052 **Sale of goods.** In a contract of sale of goods, the property in which has passed to the buyer,[213] the seller's right of action for the price accrues at the time for payment specified in the contract or, if no time is specified, when the seller informs the buyer that he is ready and willing to deliver the goods.[214] If the sale is upon credit, the right of action accrues upon the expiry of the period allowed.[215] The buyer's right of action for breach of the implied term as to title accrues at the time of sale or (in the case of an agreement to sell) at the time when the property is to pass,[216] and in the case of a breach of the term as to quiet possession when the buyer's possession is disturbed.[217] Otherwise the buyer's right of action for breach of an express or implied warranty relating to goods accrues when the goods are delivered, and not when the defect is discovered or damage ensues.[218] Where there is a wrongful neglect or refusal to deliver or accept and pay for the goods, the Sale of Goods Act 1979[219] provides that an action may be maintained for damages for non-delivery or non-acceptance. Normally time would appear to run from the time or times when the goods ought to have been delivered or accepted as the case may be,[220] except in the case of an anticipatory breach accepted as a repudiation of the contract, when the limitation period runs from that time.[221] The buyer's right of action for damages

---

[208] *Virk v Gan Life Holdings Plc* (2000) 52 B.M.L.R. 207.

[209] Limitation Act 1980 s.10(1); above, para.28–014.

[210] s.10(2), (3).

[211] *Aer Lingus Plc v Gildercroft Ltd* [2006] EWCA Civ 4, [2006] 1 W.L.R. 1173.

[212] s.10(2), (4). In *Knight v Rochdale Healthcare NHS Trust* [2003] EWHC 1831 (QB), [2003] 4 All E.R. 417 it was held that time ran from the date of the agreement even though that agreement was later embodied in a consent order: that is, s.10(4) of the Limitation Act 1980 applied, not s.10(3).

[213] Sale of Goods Act 1979 s.49(1). But see s.49(2).

[214] s.28.

[215] *Helps v Winterbottom* (1831) 2 B. & Ad. 431.

[216] Sale of Goods Act 1979 s.12(1). But see s.32 of the Limitation Act 1980; below, paras 28–084—28–086.

[217] Sale of Goods Act 1979 s.12(2)(b).

[218] *Battley v Faulkner* (1820) 3 B. & Ald. 288; *Walker v Milner* (1866) 4 F. & F. 745.

[219] ss.50(1), 51(1).

[220] ss.50(3), 51(3).

[221] See above, para.28–035.

for delay in delivery of goods which are nevertheless accepted by him would appear to accrue at the time or times when the goods ought to have been delivered.

Work and services. Unless a time for payment is otherwise agreed, the right to claim payment upon an entire contract accrues when the work is completed.[222] This applies to work done by a solicitor, although by statute[223] he cannot bring an action to recover costs until one month after delivery of a proper bill. He is thus deprived of at least one month of the six-year limitation period.[224] The contractual cause of action for breach of duty in respect of defective work arises when the breach of duty occurs[225] and not when the defect is discovered or damage ensues.[226] Failure to carry out the work may nevertheless amount to a continuing breach of the contract.[227] However, there may be a separate action in tort for negligence, and the tortious cause of action will not accrue until the claimant first suffers damage.[228] 28–053

Building contracts. In building contracts, except in cases of fraud or concealment, any cause of action in contract in respect of defective work accrues when the contractor is in breach of his express or implied obligations under the contract (normally on practical or substantial completion), and not from the time when the defect is discovered or damage occurs. If the contractor delays in completing the works or fails to complete the works in whole or in part, the cause of action presumably accrues when the works ought to have been completed[229] or when the employer elects to treat the failure of performance as a repudiation of the contract.[230] 28–054

There may, however, be an alternative cause of action in the tort of negligence against the contractor where the works which he is employed to carry out are defective.[231] The cause of action arises when relevant injury or damage is sustained, even though this may be later than the completion of the works.[232] Moreover, special limitation provisions apply to latent damage (other than personal injury) in the tort of negligence.[233] 28–055

Defective Premises Act 1972. Under s.1 of the Defective Premises Act 1972, any cause of action in respect of duty imposed by the Act (the duty to build 28–056

[222] *Emery v Day* (1834) 1 Cr. M. & R. 245, 248.

[223] Solicitors Act 1974 s.69.

[224] *Coburn v Colledge* [1897] 1 Q.B. 702.

[225] *Bagot v Stevens Scanlan & Co Ltd* [1966] 1 Q.B. 197.

[226] *Bagot v Stevens Scanlan & Co* [1966] 1 Q.B. 197. See also the cases cited in para.28–032, above.

[227] See above, para.28–035.

[228] See above, para.28–033.

[229] *Kitney v Jones Lang Wootton* (1988) 20 E.G. 88.

[230] *Pegler Ltd v Wang (UK) Ltd* [2000] Build. L.R. 218.

[231] *Dove v Banhams Patent Locks Ltd* [1983] 1 W.L.R. 1436; *Murphy v Brentwood DC* [1991] 1 A.C. 398; *Department of the Environment v Thomas Bates and Son Ltd* [1991] 1 A.C. 499; *Nitrigen Eireann Teoranta v Inco Alloys Ltd* [1992] 1 W.L.R. 598.

[232] *Dove v Banhams Patent Locks Ltd* [1983] 1 W.L.R. 1436; *Nitrigen Eireann Teoranta v Inco Alloys Ltd* [1992] 1 W.L.R. 598.

[233] See above, paras 28–010—28–012.

dwellings properly) is deemed, for the purposes of limitation, to have accrued at the time the dwelling was completed; but if after that time a person who has done work for or in connection with the provision of a dwelling does further work to rectify the work he has already done, any such cause of action in respect of that further work is deemed for those purposes to have accrued at the time the further work was finished.[234]

28–057 **Breach of trust etc.** The right of action by a beneficiary to recover trust property or in respect of any breach of trust normally accrues upon the breach of trust being committed.[235] Time does not normally begin to run between partners in respect of any claim arising out of the partnership until it is dissolved[236] or until an act of ouster occurs.[237]

28–058 **Restitution.** The claimant's cause of action will normally accrue when he pays money to the defendant or to the defendant's use.[238] But the running of time may be postponed in the case of fraud, concealment or mistake,[239] or be affected by the fact that the relief claimed is equitable[240] or that the defendant is a constructive trustee.[241]

28–059 **Arbitration and award.** The parties can agree that the award of an arbitrator shall be a condition precedent to a right to bring an action on the contract.[242] This is known as a "*Scott v Avery*" clause.[243] Since the effect of such a term in an arbitration agreement is that no cause of action accrues in respect of any matter required by the agreement to be referred until an award is made under the agreement, it was formerly held that time ran from the date of the award and not from the date of the original cause of arbitration, and that no limitation period was applicable at all for arbitration proceedings.[244] But s.13(3) of the Arbitration Act 1996 now provides that, in determining for the purposes of the Limitation

---

[234] Defective Premises Act 1972 s.1(5). See *Alderson v Beetham Organisation* Ltd [2003] EWCA Civ 408, [2003] 1 W.L.R. 1686. Since the liability is strict, the extension in respect of latent damage in actions in tort for negligence under s.14A of the 1980 Act (above, paras 28–010—28–012) is not available.

[235] *Re Swain* [1891] 3 Ch. 233; *Re Somerset* [1894] 1 Ch. 231; *Thorne v. Heard* [1895] A.C. 495.

[236] *Knox v Gye* (1872) L.R. 5 H.L. 656; *Noyes v Crawley* (1878) 10 Ch D 31. cf. *Betjemann v Betjemann* [1895] 2 Ch. 474; *Gopala Chetty v Vijayaraghavachariar* [1922] 1 A.C. 488.

[237] *Barton v North Staffs Ry* (1888) 38 Ch D 458, 463.

[238] *Baker v Courage & Co* [1910] 1 K.B. 56; *Re Jones* [1914] 1 Ir.R. 188; *Anglo-Scottish Beet Sugar Corp Ltd v Spalding U.D.C.* [1937] 2 K.B. 607, 609, 627; *Re Diplock* [1948] Ch. 465, 513; *Maskell v Horner* [1915] 3 K.B. 106; *Re Mason* [1928] Ch. 385, 392; [1929] 1 Ch. 1; *Re Blake* [1932] 1 Ch. 54, 60; *Kleinwort Benson Ltd v Sandwell BC* (1993) 91 L.G.R. 323, 382–384; *Kleinwort Benson Ltd v South Tyneside Metropolitan BC* [1994] 4 All E.R. 972, 978; *Kleinwort Benson Ltd v Lincoln City Council* [1999] 2 A.C. 349, 409; *Fuller v Happy Shopper Ltd* [2001] 2 Lloyd's Rep. 49. See generally McLean [1989] C.L.J. 472; Goff and Jones, *The Law of Restitution*, 7th edn (2007), Ch.43; Burrows, *The Law of Restitution*, 2nd edn (2002), pp.542–555. See also above, para.28–002.

[239] See below, paras 28–081—28–091.

[240] See below, para.28–134, and *Tito v Waddell (No.2)* [1977] Ch. 106.

[241] See s.21 of the Act. But see above, para.28–018.

[242] See Vol.II, para.32–041.

[243] *Scott v Avery* (1856) 5 H.L.C. 811.

[244] *Board of Trade v Cayzer, Irvine & Co* [1927] A.C. 610.

Acts[245] when a cause of action accrued, any provision that an award is a condition precedent to the bringing of legal proceedings in respect of a matter to which an arbitration agreement applies is to be disregarded.

The limitation period for the enforcement of an arbitral award accrues when the claimant is entitled to enforce the award.[246] Alternatively, if the claim is for damages for breach of an implied promise to pay the award, then it accrues when a reasonable time to pay the award has elapsed.[247] 28–060

Burden of proof. In principle it might be expected that the defendant, having pleaded the statute,[248] would bear the burden of proving that the claimant's cause of action accrued outside the limitation period and was in consequence statute-barred.[249] However, there is weighty authority for the view that the burden of proof is on the claimant to show that his cause of action accrued within the statutory period.[250] In *Cartledge v E. Jopling and Sons Ltd*[251] the Court of Appeal so held. But in the House of Lords[252] Lord Pearce placed a gloss on this proposition when he stated that, although the initial onus was on the claimant, once he had satisfied that onus, the burden passed to the defendant to show that the apparent accrual of a cause of action was misleading and that in reality the cause of action accrued at an earlier date. Nevertheless it is not sufficient for the claimant to prove, for example, that a breach of contract occurred at some time during the limitation period. In *London Congregational Union Inc v Harriss & Harriss*[253] Ralph Gibson L.J. stated that the claimant must show, on the balance of probabilities, that the cause of action accrued, i.e. came into existence, on a day within the period of limitation. Only then would the onus shift to the defendant. The burden of proof may less often be of significance in contractual actions than actions in tort, but may still be of importance in certain cases.[254] 28–061

---

[245] Defined in s.13(4) of the 1996 Act.

[246] *International Bulk Shipping and Services Ltd v Minerals and Metals Trading Corp of India* [1996] 1 All E.R. 1017.

[247] *Agromet Motoimport v Maulden Engineering Co (Beds.) Ltd* [1985] 1 W.L.R. 762; *International Bulk Shipping Ltd v Minerals and Metals Trading Corp of India* [1996] 1 All E.R. 1017.

[248] See below, para.28–107.

[249] *Lochgelly Iron & Coal Co Ltd v McMullen* [1934] A.C. 1, 35.

[250] *Hurst v Parker* (1817) 1 B. & A. 92; *Beale v Nind* (1821) 4 B. & A. 566, 571; *Wilby v Henman* (1834) 2 C. & M. 658; *Darley Main Colliery Co v Mitchell* (1886) 111 App. Cas. 127, 135; *O'Connor v Isaacs* [1956] 2 Q.B. 288, 364; *Cartledge v E. Jopling and Sons Ltd* [1963] A.C. 758; *London Congregational Union Inc v Harriss and Harriss* [1988] 1 All E.R. 15; *Crocker v British Coal Corp* (1996) 29 B.M.L.R. 159; *Arab Monetary Fund v Hashim* [1996] 1 Lloyd's Rep. 589, 607–608. For an approach which puts the burden of proving limitation on the defendant, see the decision of the Victorian Supreme Court in *Pullen v Gutterridge, Haskins & Davey Pty Ltd* (1992) Aust. Torts. Rep. 81, noted by Mullany (1993) 109 L.Q.R. 215.

[251] [1962] 1 Q.B. 189, 202, 208.

[252] *Cartledge v E. Jopling and Sons Ltd* [1963] A.C. 758, 784 (with whom the other members of the House of Lords effectively agreed).

[253] [1988] 1 All E.R. 15, 30.

[254] *Chandris v Argo Insurance Co Ltd* [1963] 2 Lloyd's Rep. 65, 73; *N.V. Stoomv Maats "De Maas" v Nippon Yusen Kaisha* [1980] 2 Lloyd's Rep. 56 (overruled on other grounds in *Kodros Shipping Corp of Monrovia v Empresa Cubana de Fletes (No.2)* [1983] 1 A.C 736); *Arab Monetary Fund v Hashim* [1996] 1 Lloyd's Rep. 589.

3. COMPUTATION OF THE PERIOD

28–062 **Commencement of the period.** The computation of the period may require the court to determine the precise day on which the period starts running. In the preceding section of this chapter it was pointed out that in actions for breach of contract, the cause of action accrues when the breach takes place and not when the damage is suffered. But does the cause of action accrue on the day of the breach or on the following day? If the breach consists in failure to do something on a particular day, e.g. to pay money, and the person who has to do the act has the whole of that day in which to do it,[255] the cause of action is not complete until the commencement of the following day, and it would seem that time begins to run from and is inclusive of the day when the cause of action accrues.[256] On the other hand, if the breach consists in the doing of a positive act (e.g. the delivery of defective goods under a contract of sale), or of an event, no doubt the cause of action accrues on the day when the act is done or the event occurs. Nevertheless, it is now settled law that the day of the act or event is to be excluded from the computation of the period within which the action should be brought, and time begins to run from the following day.[257]

28–063 **End of the period.** If the period of limitation ends on a Sunday or some other day when the court offices are closed, and the necessary act (e.g. the issue of a claim form) is one which can only be done if the court office is open on the day when time expires, the period is extended until the next day on which the court office is open.[258]

4. THE RUNNING OF TIME

28–064 **Introductory.** The general principle is that once time has started to run it continues to do so until proceedings are commenced or the claim is barred.[259] The principle (if any is possible in so technical a matter) is that a claimant who is in a position to commence proceedings, and neglects to do so, accepts the risk that some unexpected subsequent event will prevent him from doing so within

[255] See *Afovos Shipping Co SA v R. Pagnan & Filli* [1983] 1 W.L.R. 195.

[256] *Gelmini v Moriggia* [1913] 2 K.B. 549 (failure to pay a promissory note) would appear still to be good law on this point. cf. Sale of Goods Act 1979 s.29(5); *Roper v Johnson* (1873) L.R. 8 C.P. 167, 179; *Bremer Handelsgesellschaft mbH v Vanden Avenne-Izegem P.V.B.A.* [1978] 2 Lloyd's Rep. 109.

[257] *Radcliffe v Bartholomew* [1892] 1 Q.B. 161; *Marren v Dawson Bentley & Co Ltd* [1961] 2 Q.B. 135; *Pritam Kaur v S. Russell & Sons Ltd* [1973] Q.B. 336.

[258] *Pritam Kaur v S. Russell & Sons Ltd* [1973] Q.B. 336, not following *Gelmini v Moriggia* [1913] 2 K.B. 549 and *Morris v Richards* (1881) 45 L.T. 210. See also *Hodgson v Armstrong* [1967] 2 Q.B. 299; CPR r.2.8(5); *The Clifford Maersk* [1982] 1 W.L.R. 1292.

[259] *Prideaux v Webber* (1661) 1 Lev. 31; *Rhodes v Smethurst* (1840) 6 M. & W. 351; *Homfray v Scroope* (1849) 13 Q.B. 509; *Fenny v Brice* (1865) 18 C.B.(N.S.) 393; *Boatwright v Boatwright* (1873) L.R. 17 Eq. 71; *Re Benzon* [1914] 2 Ch. 68; *Bowring-Hanbury's Trustee v Bowring-Hanbury* [1943] Ch. 104. But see below, para.28–082. For the principle of "suspension" in some civil law jurisdictions, see Law Commission Consultation Paper No.151, *Limitation of Actions* (1998), paras 10.137–10.140, 10.162–10.165.

the statutory period.[260] The principle is illustrated by a famous group of seventeenth-century cases deciding that the closing of the courts during the Civil War did not suspend the running of time.[261] Thus, if a cause of action has accrued in favour of or against a person who subsequently dies, the fact of his death will not suspend the running of the limitation period even though there may be an interval of time between his death and the grant of letters of administration.[262] However, in the case of a personal injuries action,[263] if the person injured dies before the expiration of the limitation period, the period as respects the cause of action surviving for the benefit of the estate of the deceased by virtue of s.1 of the Law Reform (Miscellaneous Provisions) Act 1934 is extended to three years from the date of death, or the date of the personal representative's knowledge of certain facts relevant to his right of action against the defendant, whichever is the later.[264]

Personal representatives. Before 1980, if a debtor became the administrator of his creditor, the running of time was suspended for the duration of his appointment, because during that time it was impossible for him to sue himself.[265] This rule did not apply when the creditor by will appointed the debtor his executor. In such a case, since the appointment was a voluntary act, the common law held that the appointment extinguished the debt,[266] although equity intervened by treating the debtor-executor as if he had paid the debt to himself, so that he became accountable for the amount of the debt as being an asset of the estate.[267] The two situations have now been assimilated by s.21A of the Administration of Estates Act 1925,[268] and the running of time is no longer suspended if the debtor becomes his creditor's administrator. Instead, if a debtor becomes his deceased creditor's executor (by representation) or administrator, his debt[269] is thereby extinguished, and he is accountable for the amount of the debt as part of the creditor's estate, as if he had been appointed as an executor by the creditor's will.[270] **28–065**

The running of time is not suspended or otherwise affected in the converse case where the creditor becomes executor or administrator of his debtor, since he can satisfy his debt by exercising his right of retainer.[271] **28–066**

---

260 *Re Benzon* [1914] 2 Ch. 68, 76.

261 e.g. *Prideaux v Webber* (1661) 1 Lev. 31.

262 *Rhodes v Smethurst* (1840) 6 M. & W. 351; *Fergusson v Fyffe* (1841) 8 Cl. & Fin. 121, 140; *Fenny v Brice* (1865) 18 C.B.(N.S.) 393; *Boatwright v Boatwright* (1873) L.R. 17 Eq. 71; *Bowring-Hanbury's Trustee v Bowring-Hanbury* [1943] Ch. 104. See also CPR r.19.8.

263 See above, paras 28–006—28–008.

264 Limitation Act 1980 ss.11(5), 11A(3), 14.

265 *Seagram v Knight* (1867) L.R. 2 Ch. App. 628, a complicated case which is discussed fully in *Bowring-Hanbury's Trustee v Bowring-Hanbury* [1943] Ch. 104.

266 *Nedham's Case* (1610) 8 Co. Rep. 135a.

267 *Re Greg* [1921] 2 Ch. 243.

268 Inserted by s.10 of the Limitation Amendment Act 1980 and amended by s.40(2) of and Sch.3 to the Limitation Act 1980. See the *Twenty-First Report of the Law Reform Committee*, 1977, Cmnd.6923, paras 3.85–3.93.

269 Or liability: s.21A(3) of the 1925 Act.

270 s.21A(1), subject to the exception in s.21A(2).

271 See below, para.28–131.

28–067 **Abrogation of arbitration award or agreement.** An exception to the rule that, once time has started to run, it runs continuously is provided by s.13(2) of the Arbitration Act 1996. Where the court orders that an arbitration award is to be set aside or to be of no effect (in whole or in part), the court may further order that the period between the commencement of the arbitration and the date of the order of the court shall be excluded in computing the time prescribed by the Limitation Acts[272] for the commencement of proceedings (including arbitral proceedings) with respect to the dispute which is the subject matter of the award.

28–068 **International carriage.** Further exceptions to the rule that time runs continuously are contained in certain international conventions relating to carriage by land. Under the Convention on the Contract for the International Carriage of Goods by Road (CMR)[273] and the Convention concerning International Carriage by Rail (COTIF),[274] a written claim, which has been duly made, suspends the period of limitation until the date on which the carrier rejects the claim by notification in writing and returns any documents accompanying the claim.[275] This principle is familiar in continental law; but in English law it is confined to claims arising under these conventions.

28–069 **Limitation (Enemies and War Prisoners) Act 1945.** The running of any limitation period may be suspended by virtue of this Act.[276]

28–070 **Bankruptcy and winding-up.** The presentation of a petition by a petitioning creditor is an action within the Limitation Act 1980 and so stops time from running against him.[277] Otherwise, the making of a bankruptcy order stops time running in respect of all claims against the bankrupt which are provable in the bankruptcy,[278] and the making of a winding-up order against a company has a similar effect.[279] However, the making of an administration order does not stop time running for limitation purposes.[280] Where a company has been dissolved, the court may make an order under s.651 of the Companies Act 1985 declaring the dissolution to have been void and, if it does so, it has a discretionary power to order that the period between the dissolution and the restoration of the company to the register should not count towards limitation.[281]

---

272 Defined in s.13(4) of the 1996 Act.

273 Carriage of Goods by Road Act 1965 Sch. art.32(2); see above, para.28–025; Vol.II, para.36–143.

274 Appendix A (CIV) art.60(4); Appendix B (CIM) art.48(3); see above, para.28–024; Vol.II, paras 36–098, 36–115.

275 *Microfine Minerals and Chemicals Ltd v Transferry Shipping Co Ltd* [1991] 2 Lloyd's Rep. 630.

276 See above, para.11–031.

277 Limitation Act 1980 s.38(1) "action"; *Re Karnos Property Co Ltd* [1989] B.C.L.C. 340; *Re Cases of Taffs Well Ltd* [1992] Ch. 179; *Re A Debtor (No.50A–SD–1995)* [1997] Ch. 310.

278 *Re General Rolling Stock Co* (1872) L.R. 7 Ch. App. 646, 649; *Re Cullwick* [1918] 1 K.B. 646, 653 (receiving orders). cf. *Re Benzon* [1914] 2 Ch. 68.

279 *Re General Rolling Stock Co* (1872) L.R. 7 Ch. App. 646; *Re Cases of Taffs Well Ltd* [1992] Ch. 179. See also *Re Art Reproduction Co Ltd* [1952] Ch. 89 (passing of resolution for voluntary winding up).

280 *Re Maxwell Fleet and Facilities Management Ltd* [2001] 1 W.L.R. 323.

281 cf. *Smith (deceased) v White Knight Laundry Ltd* [2001] 3 All E.R. 862.

5. EXTENSION OF THE PERIOD

Extensions. The Limitation Act 1980 contains a number of provisions, the effect of which will be to extend the time within which an action must be brought beyond that normally applicable. The Act affords such extensions in a number of differing ways. 28–071

It has already been pointed out that, in the case of actions for damages for personal injuries[282] and by virtue of Pt I of the Consumer Protection Act 1987,[283] the applicable three-year period of limitation runs from the date on which the cause of action accrued or the date of the claimant's knowledge (if later) of certain facts relevant to his cause of action against the defendant. This "date of knowledge" principle may also serve, in effect, to extend the limitation period where such a cause of action survives for the benefit of the injured person's estate by virtue of s.1 of the Law Reform (Miscellaneous Provisions) Act 1934[284] and where an action is brought under the Fatal Accidents Act 1976.[285] Again, by s.14A of the Limitation Act 1980, the limitation period for latent damage (other than personal injury) in the tort of negligence is extended to either six years from the date on which the cause of action accrued or three years from the date of the claimant's knowledge (if later).[286] 28–072

Provision is, however, made in the Act for more general extensions in certain contingencies. These statutory extensions are dealt with in the paragraphs which follow, together with the extension of the limitation period by agreement of the parties. 28–073

(a) *Disability*

Disability. The Act allows a claimant further time in which to bring proceedings if he was, at the commencement of the limitation period, under a disability, i.e. was a minor or a person of unsound mind.[287] 28–074

Limitation Act 1980 section 28. If on the date when any right of action accrued for which a period of limitation is prescribed by the Act,[288] the person to whom it accrued was under a disability, the action may be brought at any time before the expiration of six years from the date on which he ceased to be under a disability or died (whichever first occurred) notwithstanding that the period of limitation has expired.[289] This does not apply to actions for which a period of 28–075

[282] See above, para.28–006.
[283] See above, para.28–009.
[284] Limitation Act 1980 ss.11(5), 11A(3), 14.
[285] See above, para.28–007.
[286] See above, paras 28–010—28–012.
[287] s.38(2). For the definition of "a person of unsound mind", see s.38(3), (4). See also *Kirby v Leather* [1965] 2 Q.B. 367.
[288] But see below, para.28–080 for exceptions. s.28 also does not apply to any cause of action under s.3 of the Latent Damage Act 1986: see s.3(3) of the 1986 Act.
[289] s.28(1).

limitation is prescribed by or under any other enactment.[290] It will be observed that the period allowed after the cesser of disability or death is (subject to the exceptions discussed below)[291] six years, and this is so even though the action is on a specialty. The disability must exist when the cause of action accrued: subsequent disability is of no effect.[292] There is therefore, no extension of time under this section if the right of action first accrues to some person not under a disability, even if that person is one through whom the person under a disability claims.[293]

28–076 **Successive disabilities.** The wording of s.28 ("ceased to be under *a* disability") makes it clear that if the claimant is under successive disabilities with no interval of time between them, e.g. is a minor when the cause of action accrues and is of unsound mind at the time of attaining his majority, he will have until the expiration of six years from the cesser of the latter disability in which to bring his action.[294] On the other hand, if a person under a disability dies and is succeeded by a person also under a disability, no further extension of time is allowed by reason of the disability of the second person.[295]

28–077 **Joint claimants.** It was held under the Limitation Act 1623 that if there are a number of joint claimants or creditors, but not all of them under disability when the cause of action accrues, the running of time is not postponed.[296]

28–078 **Shorter extensions.** In the case of the special two-year time limit for claiming contribution under s.1 of the Civil Liability (Contribution) Act 1978,[297] only two years is allowed as an extension of time under s.28 of the 1980 Act[298]; and in the case of the three-year periods prescribed for actions in respect of personal injuries,[299] for actions under Pt I of the Consumer Protection Act 1987[300] and for actions under the Fatal Accidents Act 1976,[301] only a three-year extension is allowed.

28–079 **Limitation Act 1980 section 28A.** Similar provision to that contained in s.28 is made in s.28A of the 1980 Act for negligence actions in respect of latent damage where the claimant or other relevant person was under a disability on the

---

290 s.39.

291 Below, paras 28–078—28–079.

292 *Purnell v Roche* [1927] 2 Ch. 142.

293 s.28(2). See also s.38(5), (6).

294 cf. *Borrows v Ellison* (1871) L.R. 6 Ex. 128 (decided on s.16 of the Real Property Limitation Act 1833).

295 s.28(3).

296 *Perry v Jackson* (1792) 4 T.R. 416.

297 s.10; see above, para.28–014.

298 s.28(5).

299 ss.11, 28(6); see above, para.28–006. In *Byrne v Motor Insurers' Bureau* [2008] EWCA Civ 574 it was held that the Untraced Drivers' Agreement between the Motor Insurers' Bureau and the Secretary of State (by which the MIB agrees to compensate for an otherwise actionable death or personal injury caused by an untraced driver) infringes Directive 84/5 in imposing a three-year limitation period without any disability extension.

300 ss.11(A), 28(7)(b) (inserted by s.6 of and Sch.1 to the Consumer Protection Act 1987); see above, para.28–009.

301 ss.12(2), 28(6); see above, para.28–007.

"starting date" for reckoning the extended period of limitation prescribed by s.14A(4)(b) of the Act.[302] In this case, three years is allowed as an extension of time from the date when he ceased to be under a disability or died.[303]

Long-stop periods. Section 28 does not apply to the 10-year long-stop period for actions under Pt I of the Consumer Protection Act 1987,[304] and no action to recover land or money charged on land can be brought by virtue of the section after the expiration of 30 years from the date on which the right of action accrued to the claimant or to some person through whom he claims.[305] Section 28A of the Act does not enable an action to be brought after the end of the 15-year long-stop period for negligence actions not involving personal injuries.[306] **28–080**

(b) *Fraud, Concealment or Mistake*

Limitation Act 1980 section 32. Section 32 of the 1980 Act applies if the claimant's action is based on the fraud of the defendant or if a fact relevant to his right of action has been deliberately concealed from him by the defendant or if his action is for relief from the consequences of a mistake. The limitation period does not begin to run until the claimant discovers or with reasonable diligence could have discovered the fraud, concealment or mistake. The section does not, in its terms, extend the period of limitation, but postpones the commencement of the period, although its effect may be to enable an action to be brought more than six years after the date when the cause of action in fact accrued.[307] **28–081**

Where the claimant's action is based on the fraud of the defendant[308] or the action is for relief from the consequences of a mistake,[309] all the relevant circumstances must necessarily be in place when the cause of action accrues. It is therefore apt for s.32(1) to provide that the limitation period "shall not *begin* to run" until discovery or imputed discovery by the claimant of the fraud or mistake. The question, however, arises whether, once the limitation period has started to run, any deliberate *subsequent* concealment[310] will suspend or interrupt its running, or extend the period. In *Sheldon v R.H.M. Outhwaite (Underwriting Agencies) Ltd*[311] Saville J. held that a deliberate concealment[312] which occurred after the claimant's cause of action accrued nevertheless produced the effect that the period of limitation would not begin to run until the claimant discovered, or **28–082**

[302] See above, paras 28–010—28–012. The s.28A extension applies only where s.28 does not apply to the action.

[303] s.28A(1).

[304] ss.11A(3), 12(1), 28(7)(a) (inserted by s.6 of and Sch.1 to the Consumer Protection Act 1987); see above, para.28–009.

[305] s.28(4).

[306] ss.14B, 28A(2) (inserted by ss.1, 2 of the Latent Damage Act 1986); see above, para.28–012.

[307] *Eddis v Chichester Constable* [1969] 2 Ch. 345, 362.

[308] s.32(1)(a); below, para.28–083.

[309] s.32(1)(c); below, para.28–088.

[310] s.32(1)(b); below, paras 28–084—28–086.

[311] *The Times*, December 8, 1993.

[312] Under s.32(1)(b).

could with reasonable diligence have discovered, the concealment. The decision of Saville J. was reversed by the Court of Appeal but, on appeal to the House of Lords, his interpretation of s.32 was, by a majority, confirmed.[313] The consequence is that, in the case of a concealment taking place after the accrual of the cause of action, time will start running again and run for the full period from actual or imputed discovery of the concealment. Moreover, it seems that even concealment subsequent to the expiration of the original limitation period will produce this effect. The result seems to be an odd one which is unlikely to have been intended by the legislature.

28–083 **Fraud.** Section 32(1)(a) of the Limitation Act 1980 provides that where the action is based upon the fraud of the defendant, the period of limitation shall not begin to run until the claimant has discovered the fraud or could with reasonable diligence have discovered it. This provision is, however, of limited scope because it only covers cases where the cause of action requires the allegation and proof of fraud in the strict sense, e.g. as in actions for fraudulent misrepresentation or deceit.[314] It is submitted that an action under s.2(1) of the Misrepresentation Act 1967, though equated for some purposes to an action based on fraud,[315] would not fall within s.32(1)(a).

28–084 **Concealment.** Section 32(1)(b) of the Act provides that where any fact relevant to the claimant's right of action[316] has been deliberately concealed from him by the defendant, the period of limitation shall not begin to run until the claimant has discovered the concealment or could with reasonable diligence have discovered it. It is further provided that a deliberate commission of a breach of duty in circumstances in which it is unlikely to be discovered for some time amounts to deliberate concealment of the facts involved in that breach of duty.[317] The use of the word "deliberate" indicates that an unwitting (even if negligent) concealment of a relevant fact or commission of a breach of duty is not enough.[318] It also appears that no fraud or dishonesty on the part of the defendant need be proved. Where there is a deliberate commission of a breach of duty, e.g. a breach of contract, it is unnecessary to show that the defendant took active steps to conceal the breach: all that is required is that it is committed "in circumstances in which it is unlikely to be discovered for some time".

---

313 [1996] A.C. 102.

314 *Beaman v A.R.T.S Ltd* [1949] 1 K.B. 550, 558, 567; *Clef Aquitaine SARL v Laporte Materials (Barrow) Ltd* [2000] 3 All E.R. 493; *Barnstaple Boat Co Ltd v Jones* [2007] EWCA Civ 727, [2008] 1 All E.R. 1124.

315 *Royscot Trust Ltd v Rogerson* [1991] 2 Q.B. 297; see above, para.6–070.

316 Defined in s.38(9). The recovery of interest by way of execution on a judgment is not a "right of action" within s.32(1)(b): *Lowsley v Forbes* [1999] 1 A.C. 329. Nor (semble) is the defendant's concealment of himself or his assets a fact relevant to the claimant's action.

317 s.32(2). In *Giles v Rhind* [2008] EWCA Civ 118 it was held that a claim for the avoidance of a transaction under s.423 of the Insolvency Act 1986 involves an allegation of a "breach of duty" within s.32(2) of the 1980 Act; "breach of duty" in that subsection should not be narrowly construed as applying only to, for example, a tort, breach of contract, or breach of an equitable duty to the claimant.

318 *Re Coole* [1920] Ch. 536; *King v Victor Parsons & Co* [1973] 1 W.L.R. 29, 33, 36; *Kaliszewska v Clague* [1984] C.I.L.L. 131; *Cave v Robinson, Jarvis & Rolf* [2002] UKHL 18; [2003] 1 A.C. 384.

28–085 In *Brocklesby v Armitage and Guest*[319] the Court of Appeal held that, for the purposes of the concealment provisions, it did not matter that the defendant did not know that he was committing a breach of duty provided that he was acting intentionally in what he was doing. So, for example, a defendant who gave negligent legal advice could be said to have deliberately concealed a fact relevant to the claimant's right of action because the advice was given intentionally. But in *Cave v Robinson Jarvis & Rolf*[320] that interpretation of s.32 was rejected by the House of Lords. It was held that the concealment provisions are triggered only where the defendant knew that he had committed or was committing a breach of duty; inadvertant want of care was insufficient. In the words of Lord Millett:

> "... section 32 deprives a defendant of a limitation defence in two situations: (i) where he takes active steps to conceal his own breach of duty after he has become aware of it; and (ii) where he is guilty of deliberate wrongdoing and conceals or fails to disclose it in circumstances where it is unlikely to be discovered for some time. But it does not deprive a defendant of a limitation defence where he is charged with negligence if, being unaware of his error or that he has failed to take proper care, there has been nothing for him to disclose."[321]

28–086 The provisions on concealment were intended to give effect to a recommendation of the Law Reform Committee[322] that para.(b) of s.26 of the Limitation Act 1939 should be reformulated in a way "which reproduces in a more readily intelligible form the construction placed upon that paragraph by the courts".[323] It may therefore be that cases on the 1939 Act will be of some assistance in illustrating the operation of the 1980 Act provisions. Examples are: the furtive and surreptitious taking of coal under ground from the claimant's land where the trespass would not be found out "for many a long day"[324]; a husband's failure to disclose the true amount of his income, having contracted to pay a proportion of it to his wife under a maintenance agreement[325]; a married man's representing himself as single for the purposes of a subsequent ceremony of marriage with the claimant or a subsequent failure to reveal that the second ceremony was bigamous[326]; a reckless sale of bailed goods without communication with the bailor[327]; a solicitor's failure to inform his client that an ex gratia payment had been offered by an alleged tortfeasor, which would have revealed the possibility of a cause of action on the part of the client against the solicitor in negligence[328];

---

[319] [2002] 1 W.L.R. 598n. This was applied in *Liverpool Roman Catholic Trustees Inc v Goldberg* [2001] 1 All E.R. 182.

[320] [2002] UKHL 18; [2003] 1 A.C. 384.

[321] *Cave v Robinson, Jarvis & Rolf* [2002] UKHL 18 at [25].

[322] *Twenty-First Report*, 1977, Cmnd.6923, paras 2.22–2.25, 2.35. But s.32(1)(b) differs in wording from the reformulation of the Committee.

[323] *Twenty-First Report*, 1977, Cmnd.6923, para.2.22.

[324] *Bulli Coal Mining Co v Osborne* [1899] A.C. 351.

[325] *Legh v Legh* (1930) 143 L.T. 451.

[326] *Beyers v Green* [1936] 1 All E.R. 613; *Shaw v Shaw* [1954] 2 Q.B. 429. But see now the Law Reform (Miscellaneous Provisions) Act 1970 ss.1, 6, 7(2) (cause of action abolished).

[327] *Beaman v A.R.T.S. Ltd* [1949] 1 K.B. 550.

[328] *Kitchen v R.A.F. Association* [1958] 1 W.L.R. 563.

the failure of a builder to disclose the deliberate breach by him of a building contract by using defective bricks[329] or inadequate foundations[330]; and the failure to warn the purchaser of a house of a known risk of subsidence due to the fact that the house had been constructed on unsuitable ground.[331] Cases decided under s.32(1)(b) of the 1980 Act have mainly concerned bad work knowingly done by builders, which was subsequently covered up so that the defects were unlikely to be discovered for some time,[332] and allegations in respect of professional negligence by solicitors.[333] The burden of proof rests upon the claimant.[334]

28–087 **Fraud or concealment by agent.** The fraud or concealment may be that of an agent of the defendant or of any person through whom the defendant claims or his agent.[335] In the case of concealment, the word "agent" may include an independent contractor employed by the defendant.[336] The defendant is to be treated as claiming "through" another person if he became entitled by, through, under or by the act of that other person to the right claimed.[337] In the case of property, it has been held that a defendant claims property through another person if he derives his title to the property from that person.[338] And an innocent volunteer claims through a person who fraudulently directs another's money to him.[339]

28–088 **Mistake.** Section 32(1)(c) of the Act provides that where the action is for relief from the consequences of a mistake, the period of limitation shall not begin to run until the claimant has discovered the mistake or could with reasonable diligence have discovered it.[340] The corresponding paragraph in the Limitation Act 1939[341] received a somewhat narrow interpretation in *Phillips-Higgins v Harper*,[342] where it was said that:

---

[329] *Clark v Woor* [1965] 1 W.L.R. 650.

[330] *Applegate v Moss* [1971] 1 Q.B. 406.

[331] *King v Victor Parsons & Co* [1973] 1 W.L.R. 29.

[332] *Gray v T P Bennett & Son* (1987) 43 Build. L.R. 63; *Kijowski v New Capital Properties* (1990) 15 Con. L.R. 1.

[333] *Tunbridge v Buss Murton & Co, The Times*, April 8, 1997; *Markes v Coodes* [1997] P.N.L.R. 252; *Cave v Robinson Jarvis & Rolf* [2002] UKHL 18; [2003] 1 A.C. 384; *Williams v Fanshaw Porter & Hazelhurst* [2004] EWCA Civ 157, [2004] 1 W.L.R. 3185. The *Williams* and *Cave* decisions were applied in holding that there had been deliberate concealment of re-tests and their results in *AIC Ltd v ITS Testing Services (UK) Ltd, The Kriti Palm* [2006] EWCA Civ 1601, [2007] 1 Lloyd's Rep. 555 (in which one of the claims was for breach of contract).

[334] *Tunbridge v Buss Murton & Co, The Times*, April 8, 1997 (pleading).

[335] s.32(1).

[336] *Applegate v Moss* [1971] 1 Q.B. 406; *King v Victor Parsons & Co* [1973] 1 W.L.R. 29 (but both of these cases were decided on s.26(b) of the Limitation Act 1939); *Ryles v Chaudry* [1999] Lloyd's Rep. P.N. 454.

[337] s.38(5).

[338] *Eddis v Chichester Constable* [1969] 2 Ch. 345, 356–357, 362–363.

[339] *G.L. Baker Ltd v Medway Building and Supplies Ltd* [1958] 1 W.L.R. 1216.

[340] *Peco Arts Inc v Hazlitt Gallery Ltd* [1983] 1 W.L.R. 1315.

[341] s.26(c).

[342] [1954] 1 Q.B. 411; affirmed [1954] 2 All E.R. 51n.

"... it applies only where the mistake is an essential ingredient of the cause of action, so that the statement of claim sets out, or should set out, the mistake and its consequences and pray for relief from those consequences."[343]

In that case the defendant employer had underpaid the claimant, who had not realised what payments were due to her. Pearson J. held that only six years' arrears were recoverable: the claimant's action was to recover moneys due to her under a contract, and was not an action "for relief from the consequences of a mistake". The result seems somewhat anomalous because, if there is an overpayment by mistake, the person paying can claim the benefit of the provision. It is also to be noted that s.32(1)(c) does not require that the action be "based upon" a mistake[344]; nor does it require that the mistake should be that of the claimant. A mistake of law is sufficient.[345]

Reasonable diligence. In cases arising under s.32(1), time begins to run when the claimant discovers the fraud, concealment or mistake, or could with reasonable diligence have discovered it. What is "reasonable diligence" must vary with the particular context in which that expression is to be applied.[346] It does not require the claimant to use all means of discovery available to him, but only to do that which an ordinary prudent person, having regard to all the circumstances, would do.[347] The burden of proof rests upon the claimant.[348] **28–089**

Purchaser for valuable consideration. Section 32(3) of the Act protects innocent purchasers for valuable consideration by enacting that nothing in s.32 shall enable any action to recover, or recover the value of,[349] any property, or to enforce any charge against, or set aside any transaction affecting, any property, to be brought against the purchaser of the property or any person claiming through him[350] in any case where the property has been purchased for valuable consideration by an innocent third party since the fraud or concealment or (as the **28–090**

[343] [1954] 1 Q.B. 411, 419. cf. *Ministry of Health v Simpson* [1951] A.C. 251, 277; *Deutsche Morgan Grenfell Group Plc v Inland Revenue Commissioners* [2006] UKHL 49, [2006] 3 W.L.R. 781 at [146]–[147].

[344] As in s.32(1)(a) "based upon the fraud" of the defendant. See Franks, *Limitation of Actions* (1959), pp.206–207 and (in equity) Brunyate, *Limitation of Actions in Equity*, pp.254–257.

[345] *Kleinwort Benson Ltd v Lincoln CC* [1999] 2 A.C. 349; *Deutsche Morgan Grenfell Plc v Inland Revenue Commissioners* [2006] UKHL 49, [2006] 3 W.L.R. 781.

[346] *Peco Arts Inc v Hazlitt Gallery Ltd* [1983] 1 W.L.R. 1315, 1322–3.

[347] [1983] 1 W.L.R. 1315, 1323. See also *Ecclesiastical Commissioners for England v N.E. Ry* (1877) 4 Ch D 845, 861; *Rawlins v Wickham* (1858) 3 De G.L.J. 304; *Chetham v Hoare* (1870) L.R. 9 Eq. 571; *Vane v Vane* (1873) L.R. 8 Ch. App. 383, 390n; *Willis v Howe* [1893] 2 Ch. 545; *Betjemann v Betjemann* [1895] 2 Ch. 474, 480; *Paragon Finance Plc v Thakerar & Co* [1999] 1 All E.R. 400, 418; *UCB Home Loans Corp v Carr* [2000] Lloyd's Rep. P.N. 754; *Clef Aquitaine SARL v Laporte Materials (Barrow) Ltd* [2000] 3 All E.R. 493, 504–505; *Ezekiel v Lehrer* [2002] EWCA Civ 16, [2002] Lloyd's Rep. P.N. 260.

[348] *Peco Arts Inc v Hazlitt Gallery Ltd* [1983] 1 W.L.R. 1315; *Paragon Finance Plc v Thakerar & Co* [1999] 1 All E.R. 400.

[349] See *Eddis v Chichester Constable* [1969] 2 Ch. 345, 357 (extension to conversion).

[350] Defined in s.38(5); see para.28–087 fn.333, above.

case may be) the transaction in which the mistake took place. A purchaser is an innocent third party for the purposes of the section:

(a) in the case of fraud or concealment of any fact relevant to the claimant's right of action, if he was not a party to the fraud or concealment of that fact and did not at the time of the purchase know or have reason to believe that the fraud or concealment had taken place[351]; and

(b) in the case of mistake, if he did not at the time of the purchase know or have reason to believe that the mistake had been made.

28–091 **Application of section 32.** Fraud, concealment and mistake postpone the running of time only in the case of an action for which a period of limitation is prescribed by the Act[352] and do not apply (except to the extent expressly provided therein) to other limitation enactments.[353] The section also does not apply to an action under the Fatal Accidents Act 1976[354] or to the 10-year long-stop period for actions under Pt I of the Consumer Protection Act 1987.[355] On the other hand, in the case of an action to which s.32(1)(b) (concealment) applies, neither the three-year extension for negligence actions in respect of latent damage[356] nor the 15-year long-stop period for negligence actions not involving personal injuries[357] will come into operation.[358]

(c) *Acknowledgment and Part Payment*

28–092 **Origin of the doctrine.** The Jacobean statute of 1623 contained no provision that an acknowledgment of a debt or part payment thereof should extend the period of limitation. At least as early as 1699, however, the judges held that if the defendant made a fresh promise to pay the debt, time began to run anew from the date of the promise.[359] From this it followed that an acknowledgment or part payment had the same effect if, but only if, a fresh promise to pay could thereby be inferred.[360] This judicial process was described by Lord Sumner as "the task of decorously disregarding an Act of Parliament".[361] The judge-made doctrine was recognised by two statutes, one of which required that the acknowledgment should be in writing and signed by the person chargeable,[362] while the

[351] See *Eddis v Chichester Constable* [1969] 2 Ch. 345 (knowledge of agent attributed to principal).
[352] s.32(1).
[353] s.39.
[354] s.12(3).
[355] ss.11A(3), 32(4A), inserted by s.6 of and Sch.1 to the Consumer Protection Act 1987; see above, para.28–009.
[356] s.14A; see above, para.28–011.
[357] s.14B; see above, para.28–012.
[358] s.32(5), inserted by s.2(2) of the Latent Damage Act 1986.
[359] *Hyleing v Hastings* (1699) 1 Ld. Raym. 389.
[360] *Tanner v Smart* (1827) 6 B. & C. 603.
[361] *Spencer v Hemmerde* [1922] 2 A.C. 507, 519.
[362] Statute of Frauds Amendment Act 1828 (Lord Tenterden's Act) s.1.

other made the signature of his duly authorised agent sufficient.[363] For specialty debts the Civil Procedure Act 1833 abolished the requirement (productive of so much litigation) that there must be an implied promise to pay: but this requirement continued to exist for simple contract debts until 1940. All these statutes were repealed by the Limitation Act 1939.

Limitation Act 1980 section 29. The 1980 Act lays down a uniform rule for specialty and simple contract debts by providing that where any right of action has accrued to recover any debt or other liquidated pecuniary claim,[364] and the person liable therefor acknowledges the claim or makes any payment in respect of it, the right is to be treated as having accrued on and not before the date of the acknowledgment or payment.[365] A current period of limitation may be repeatedly extended under this rule by further acknowledgments or payments; but a right of action, once barred by the Act, cannot be revived by any subsequent acknowledgment or payment.[366] However, the Act goes on to provide that payment of a part of the rent or interest due at any time shall not extend the period for claiming the remainder then due, but any payment of interest shall be treated as a payment in respect of the principal debt.[367] The effect of this provision seems to be that part payment of an instalment of rent merely operates as an acknowledgment of the landlord's title, while part payment of an instalment of interest operates (for the purposes of limitation) as part payment of the principal sum.[368] 28–093

Form of the acknowledgment. The acknowledgment must be in writing and signed by the person making it.[369] But extrinsic evidence is admissible to identify the debt to which the acknowledgment refers,[370] to ascertain the amount of the debt,[371] to show the date of the acknowledgement,[372] or to link one document with another (so that when read together there is an acknowledgement).[373] Extrinsic evidence has also been admitted as secondary evidence of a lost written acknowledgment.[374] As to the requirement of writing, the following (inter alia) 28–094

---

[363] Mercantile Law Amendment Act 1856 s.13.

[364] *Amontilla Ltd v Telefusion Plc* (1987) 9 Con. L.R. 139 (quantum meruit held to be liquidated pecuniary claim). cf. McLean [1989] C.L.J. 472, 477–479.

[365] s.29(5).

[366] s.29(7). Contrast the position before the Limitation Amendment Act 1980, and see s.40(1) of and Sch.2 para.5 to the Limitation Act 1980.

[367] s.29(6).

[368] Franks, *Limitation of Actions* (1959), p.227.

[369] s.30(1). For the meaning of signature in this context, see *Good Challenger Navegante SA v Metalexportimport SA* [2003] EWHC 10, [2003] 1 Lloyd's Rep. 471, 487. In *Bradford and Bingley Plc v Rashid* [2006] UKHL 37, [2006] 1 W.L.R. 2066 letters were held to be admissible to prove an acknowledgement despite the "without prejudice" rule.

[370] *Read v Price* [1909] 2 K.B. 724, 737, 738; *Jones v Bellgrove Properties Ltd* [1949] 2 K.B. 700.

[371] *Bird v Gammon* (1837) 3 Bing. N.C. 883; *Cheslyn v Dalby* (1840) 4 Y. & C.Ex. 238, 241; *Jones v Bellgrove Properties Ltd* [1949] 2 K.B. 700; *Dungate v Dungate* [1965] 1 W.L.R. 1477; *Kamouh v Associated Electrical Industries International Ltd* [1980] Q.B. 199; *Re Overmark Smith Warden Ltd* [1982] 1 W.L.R. 1195, 1204.

[372] *Edmunds v Downes* (1834) 1 Cr. & M. 459, 463; *Jayne v Hughes* (1854) 10 Exch. 430.

[373] *McGuffe v Burleigh* (1898) 78 L.T. 264.

[374] *Haydon v Williams* (1830) 7 Bing. 163; *Read v Price* [1909] 2 K.B. 724.

will qualify: correspondence,[375] an account rendered,[376] a recital in a deed,[377] a company's balance sheet,[378] an affidavit,[379] and a pleading.[380]

28–095 **What constitutes acknowledgment.** What amounts to an acknowledgment is a question of construction and there is a high authority for saying that decided cases are of little value as precedents.[381] A decision on one debtor's words is not much help in construing another's. In reading cases decided under former Statutes of Limitation in regard to simple contracts, it must be remembered that the court was primarily concerned with the question whether a promise to pay could be implied, and not with the question whether there was an acknowledgment. Under the present law, all that is needed is an admission by the debtor that there is a debt or other liquidated pecuniary claim outstanding and of his legal liability to pay it. It is not necessary that the acknowledgment should specify the amount of the debt if it can be ascertained by other means.[382] But it must acknowledge a claim, not merely that there may be a claim,[383] and it must further acknowledge that the claim exists at the date of the acknowledgment or that it existed on a day which falls within the appropriate period of limitation next before action brought.[384] A mere acknowledgment of certain facts which, if taken in isolation, would give rise to liability, but which are alleged by the person who is said to have given an acknowledgment not to give rise to a liability by reason of other surrounding circumstances, is not sufficient.[385] Thus a "confession and avoidance" denying liability on the ground of an alleged set off or cross-claim does not constitute an acknowledgment.[386] Nor does a "without prejudice" worksheet sent or shown to the other party as part of the negotiation process.[387] The statement relied upon as an acknowledgment must be taken as a whole; the creditor is not entitled to pick out parts and ignore others.[388]

---

375 But not if written "without prejudice", *Re River Steamer Co* (1871) L.R. 6 Ch. App. 822, 831; *Cadle Co v Hearley* [2002] 1 Lloyd's Rep. 143.

376 *Hony v Hony* (1824) 1 Sim. & S. 568.

377 *Howcutt v Bonser* (1849) 3 Ex. 491.

378 *Re Gee & Co (Woolwich) Ltd* [1975] Ch. 52; see below, para.28–101.

379 *Tristram v Harte* (1841) 3 Ir. Eq. R. 386. cf. *Bowring-Hanbury's Trustee v Bowring-Hanbury* [1943] Ch. 104.

380 *Goode v Job* (1858) 1 E. & E. 6; *Grindell v Bass* [1920] 2 Ch. 487; *Wright v Pepin* [1954] 1 W.L.R. 635, 642. cf. *Re Flynn (No.2)* [1969] 2 Ch. 403.

381 *Spencer v Hemmerde* [1922] 2 A.C. 507, 519.

382 *Jones v Bellgrove Properties Ltd* [1949] 2 K.B. 700; *Dungate v Dungate* [1965] 1 W.L.R. 1477; *Bradford and Bingley Plc v Rashid* [2006] UKHL 37, [2006] 1 W.L.R. 2066; *Habib Bank Ltd v Central Bank of Sudan* [2006] EWHC 1767 (Comm), [2007] 1 All E.R. (Comm) 53.

383 *Good v Parry* [1963] 2 Q.B. 418; *Kamouh v Associated Electrical Industries International Ltd* [1980] Q.B. 199.

384 *Howcutt v Bonser* (1849) 3 Ex. 491; *Re Gee & Co (Woolwich) Ltd* [1975] Ch. 52; *Re Overmark Smith Warden Ltd* [1982] 1 W.L.R. 1195. Contrast *Consolidated Agencies Ltd v Bertram Ltd* [1965] A.C. 470 PC where it was held that an acknowledgment of past liability was ineffective.

385 *Re Flynn (No.2)* [1969] 2 Ch. 403, 412.

386 *Re Flynn (No.2)* [1969] 2 Ch. 403; *Surrendra Overseas Ltd v Sri Lanka Government* [1977] 1 W.L.R. 565. If the set off or cross-claim goes to only part of the debt, the statement may amount to an acknowledgment of indebtedness for the balance: at 575.

387 *Lia Oil SA v ERG Petroli SpA* [2007] EWHC 505 (Comm), [2007] 2 Lloyd's Rep. 509.

388 *Surrendra Overseas Ltd v Sri Lanka Government* [1977] 1 W.L.R. 565, 575; *National Westminster Bank Plc v Powney* [1991] Ch. 339.

If the creditor stands in a fiduciary relationship to the debtor, he may be unable to rely on an acknowledgment made without independent advice, since he cannot derive any benefit from his position.[389]

What constitutes part payment. Part payment is merely a species of acknowledgment. All that need (and must) be shown is that the part payment constitutes an admission that the balance of the debt remains due,[390] and not that an implied promise to pay the balance can be inferred. Many of the older cases are therefore no longer reliable guides. 28–096

Section 29(5) of the Limitation Act 1980 requires that the payment must be made "in respect of" the claim. A payment cannot acquire this character by any act of the creditor but only by the act of the debtor or his agent. Hence, if several distinct debts are due, and the debtor makes a part payment without appropriating it to any particular debt, an appropriation by the creditor towards satisfaction of one debt (whether it be statute-barred or not) cannot make the payment one "in respect of" the claim to that debt.[391] 28–097

The rule in *Clayton's Case*[392] applies to all current accounts, not merely to banking accounts. So if goods are supplied over a period of time and paid for by lump sums bearing no exact relationship to the amount of the buyer's indebtedness at any particular moment, each new credit must prima facie be treated as discharging the earliest outstanding debit. This may be important in ascertaining how far the balance in the account is contributed to by statute-barred items. But it does not affect the true nature of the debt itself, which is a single debt for the amount of the balance due for the time being. Hence a payment "generally on account" is a payment in respect of the whole balance due; it is not a payment in respect of particular items contributing to that balance.[393] 28–098

The payment need not necessarily be in money,[394] though this is usually the case. 28–099

Parties to the acknowledgment or part payment. The acknowledgment or payment may be made by the agent of the person liable and must be made to the person or to the agent of the person whose claim is being acknowledged, or in respect of whose claim the payment is being made.[395] An acknowledgment or part payment made by a stranger who is not an agent of the debtor is of no effect.[396] It is clear, however, that the agent need not be expressly authorised to 28–100

---

[389] *Lloyd v Coote and Ball* [1915] 1 K.B. 242.

[390] *Re Footman Bower & Co Ltd* [1961] Ch. 443; *Surrendra Overseas Ltd v Sri Lanka Government* [1977] 1 W.L.R. 565, 577; *Kleinwort Benson Ltd v South Tyneside Metropolitan BC* [1994] 4 All E.R. 972.

[391] *Re Footman Bower & Co Ltd* [1961] Ch. 443, 449. See also above, para.21–063.

[392] (1816) 1 Mer. 572. See above, para.21–066.

[393] *Re Footman Bower & Co Ltd* [1961] Ch. 443.

[394] *Hart v Nash* (1835) 2 Cr.M. & R. 337; *Hooper v Stephens* (1835) 4 A. & E. 71; *Bodger v Arch* (1854) 10 Ex. 333; *Re Wilson* [1937] Ch. 675.

[395] Limitation Act 1980 s.30(2).

[396] *Newbould v Smith* (1886) 33 Ch D 127; *Re Edwards* [1937] Ch. 553; *UCB Corporate Services Ltd v Kohli* [2004] EWHC 1126 (Ch), [2004] 2 All E.R. (Comm) 422.

make an acknowledgment: it is sufficient if the making of the acknowledgment is within his general authority.[397] An acknowledgment or part payment made to a stranger who is not an agent of the creditor is likewise ineffective.[398] It has also been said that an acknowledgment must be either delivered to the creditor or his agent by or with the authority of the debtor or his agent or expressly or implicitly addressed to and actually received by the creditor or his agent.[399] In any event, communication of the acknowledgment is required.[400]

28–101 A statement in an Inland Revenue affidavit sworn by an executor in order to obtain probate was held to be a mere statement of facts and not an acknowledgment of anything to anybody.[401] On the other hand, statements in the balance-sheet of a company (being implicitly addressed to those creditors whose debts are referred to in it) can amount to an acknowledgment if communicated to the creditor or his agent.[402] Thus, a balance-sheet presented to the shareholders at an annual general meeting, signed by chartered accountants as agents of the company and by two directors, was held to be an acknowledgment of a debt owed to a shareholder who was present at the meeting.[403] But a balance-sheet signed by directors showing debts in which they are beneficially interested, e.g. for directors' fees or loans to the company, is not a sufficient acknowledgment by the company[404] unless all the members of the company have agreed to the directors' acknowledgment of the debt.[405]

28–102 A minor can make an effective acknowledgment or part payment during minority in respect of a contract which is binding on him, e.g. for necessaries.[406]

28–103 **Effect of acknowledgment and part payment on other persons.** The Act draws an important distinction between acknowledgment and part payment as regards their effect on persons other than the maker or payer. An acknowledgment of a debt or other liquidated pecuniary claim binds the acknowledgor

---

[397] *Chinnery v Evans* (1864) 11 H.L.C. 115; *Wright v Pepin* [1954] 1 W.L.R. 635; distinguishing *Bowring-Hanbury's Trustee v Bowring-Hanbury* [1943] Ch. 104 (the solicitor's letter).

[398] *Batchelor v Middleton* (1848) 6 Hare 75, 83; *Stamford Banking Co v Smith* [1892] 1 Q.B. 765.

[399] *Re Compania de Electricidad de la Provincia de Buenos Aires Ltd* [1980] Ch. 146.

[400] [1980] Ch. 146; see also *Re Beavan* [1912] 1 Ch. 196; *Lloyd v Coote* [1915] 1 K.B. 242.

[401] *Bowring-Hanbury's Trustee v Bowring-Hanbury* [1943] Ch. 104, which, however, was decided under the old law under which an implied promise to pay was necessary.

[402] *Re Atlantic and Pacific Fibre Importing Co Ltd* [1928] Ch. 836; decided under the Civil Procedure Act 1833, under which such communication was unnecessary; *Jones v Bellgrove Properties Ltd* [1949] 2 K.B. 700; *Re Gee & Co (Woolwich) Ltd* [1975] Ch. 52, not following *Consolidated Agencies Ltd v Bertram Ltd* [1965] A.C. 470 (decided under s.19 of the Indian Limitation Act 1908); *Re Compania de Electricidad de la Provincia de Buenos Aires Ltd* [1980] Ch. 146; *Stage Club v Millers Hotels Pty* (1982) 150 C.L.R. 535. cf. *Re Overmark Smith Warden Ltd* [1982] 1 W.L.R. 1195 (statements of affairs made on appointment of receiver and on winding-up).

[403] *Jones v Bellgrove Properties Ltd* [1949] 2 K.B. 700.

[404] *Re Coliseum (Barrow) Ltd* [1930] 2 Ch. 44; *Re Transplanters (Holding Company) Ltd* [1958] 1 W.L.R. 822; contrast *Ledingham v Bermejo Estancia Co Ltd* [1947] 1 All E.R. 749.

[405] *Re Gee & Co (Woolwich) Ltd* [1975] Ch. 52.

[406] *Willins v Smith* (1854) 4 E. & B. 180.

and his successors, but does not bind any other person.[407] By successors are meant the personal representatives of the acknowledgor and any other person on whom the liability in respect of the debt or claim may devolve by reason of death or bankruptcy or otherwise.[408] But a part payment binds all persons liable in respect of the debt or claim (e.g. other joint debtors or sureties).[409] The distinction may be illustrated by the case of joint debtors. If A and B are jointly indebted to C, and A acknowledges the debt, the acknowledgment binds only A and his successors and not B. But if A makes a part payment, this binds B also. The reason for this distinction is that since a part payment operates for the advantage of all the joint debtors, it is only fair that they should share the disadvantage too.[410]

Exclusions. The rules as to acknowledgment and part payment do not apply to an action to recover contribution under s.1 of the Civil Liability (Contribution) Act 1978[411] nor to an action under the Fatal Accidents Act 1976[412]; nor do they apply to periods of limitation prescribed by or under any other enactment.[413] 28–104

Pleading. As a general rule, the acknowledgment or part payment should be pleaded in the particulars of claim and not in the reply.[414] 28–105

(d) *Agreement of the Parties*

Agreement of the parties. It appears that the parties may by contract postpone the commencement of the limitation period by agreeing that the cause of action shall not accrue until some act or event occurs, e.g. service of a written notice of claim. 28–106

Pleading the statute. A party is not bound to rely on limitation as a defence if he does not wish to do so. In general, the court will not raise the point *suo officio* even if it appears from the face of the pleading that the relevant period of limitation has expired.[415] A defendant who wishes to rely on limitation must, in his defence, give details of the expiry of any relevant limitation period relied on.[416] Even where the effect of the statute is to extinguish the claimant's title to land[417] or goods,[418] it would not be sufficient simply to deny that title[419] and the 28–107

---

407 s.31(6).

408 s.31(9).

409 s.31(7). *UCB Corporate Services Ltd v Kohli* [2004] EWHC 1126 (Ch), [2004] 2 All E.R. (Comm) 422 (part payment by a principal debtor bound the surety).

410 Law Revision Committee's Fifth Interim Report, p.28.

411 s.10(5); see above, para.28–014.

412 s.12(3).

413 s.39.

414 *Busch v Stevens* [1963] 1 Q.B. 1.

415 But the court will take the point on behalf of a person under a disability: *Re E.G.* [1914] 1 Ch. 927.

416 CPR 16 PD–13.

417 Limitation Act 1980 s.17.

418 s.3(2); see Vol.II, para.43–264.

419 See also CPR r.16.5.

statute should be specifically pleaded.[420] Where it is clear that there is a defence of limitation, the defendant can apply to strike out a statute-barred claim on the ground that the statement of case discloses no reasonable grounds for bringing the claim or that the statement of case is an abuse of the court's process.[421]

28–108 **Agreements not to plead the statute.** An express or implied agreement not to plead the statute, whether made before or after the limitation period has expired, is valid if supported by consideration (or made by deed) and will be given effect to by the court.[422] The effect of such an agreement is, however, by no means certain. On one view, the agreement will be enforced by preventing the defendant from relying on the statute.[423] But on another view, the agreement merely enables the claimant to have a separate action (or counterclaim) for damages for breach of the agreement.[424] It is submitted that the former view is preferable. In any event, to constitute an enforceable agreement, there must (in the absence of a deed) be consideration for the defendant's promise not to plead limitation as a defence, and this may be found, for example, in mutual promises by each party that accounts between them should be settled without reference to the length of time they have been running[425] or in an express or implied forbearance on the part of the claimant to sue.[426]

28–109 **Estoppel.** In certain cases it has been said that the defendant is estopped from pleading the statute.[427] If the circumstances render it impossible to imply any forbearance to sue on behalf of the claimant, and there is no other consideration for the defendant's promise, this may be the only course available to the claimant to prevent the defendant from raising the defence. It is doubtful, however, whether the ordinary principles of estoppel by representation are applicable, since there is often no representation of existing or past fact. But the claimant might, in appropriate cases, be entitled to rely on estoppel by acquiescence[428] or by convention[429] or upon the principle of equitable or promissory estoppel stated in *Hughes v Metropolitan Ry*[430] The question has been previously raised and

---

[420] Contrast Franks, *Limitation of Actions* (1959), p.265.

[421] CPR r.3.4. See *Ronex Properties Ltd v John Laing Construction Ltd* [1983] Q.B. 398, 405–406; *Leicester Wholesale Fruit Market Ltd v Grundy* [1990] 1 W.L.R. 107.

[422] *Lade v Trill* (1842) 11 L.J. Ch. 102; *Pearson v Dublin Corp* [1907] A.C. 351, 368; *Lubovsky v Snelling* [1944] K.B. 44.

[423] *Lade v Trill* (1842) 11 L.J. Ch. 102.

[424] *East India Co v Paul* (1850) 7 Moo.P.C. 85, 112.

[425] *Lade v Trill* (1842) 11 L.J. Ch. 102.

[426] *Lubovsky v Snelling* [1944] K.B. 44.

[427] *Wright v John Bagnell & Sons Ltd* [1900] 2 Q.B. 240; *Rendall v Hill's Dry Dock and Engineering Co Ltd* [1900] 2 Q.B. 245; *Kaliszewska v Clague* [1984] C.I.L.L. 131; *Commonwealth v Verwayen* (1990) 64 A.L.J.R. 540; *Cotterrell v Leeds Day* [2001] W.T.L.R. 435.

[428] cf. *K. Lokumal & Sons (London) Ltd v Lotte Shipping Co Pte Ltd* [1984] 1 Lloyd's Rep. 322, [1985] 2 Lloyd's Rep. 28.

[429] *K. Lokumal & Sons (London) Ltd v Lotte Shipping Co Pte Ltd* [1984] 1 Lloyd's Rep. 322. cf. *Hillingdon LBC v ARC Ltd (No.2)* [2000] 3 E.G.L.R.97; *Llanelec Precision Engineering Co Ltd v Neath Port Talbot CBC* [2000] 3 E.G.L.R. 158. See above, para.3–108.

[430] (1877) 2 App. Cas. 439; above, paras 3–085—3–107.

discussed[431] whether, under that principle, the promisee must have suffered some detriment in reliance on the promise or whether it is sufficient that he has in fact relied on it so that it would be inequitable for the promisor to go back on the promise. Where no express extension has been sought and obtained, a claimant may encounter difficulty in establishing that a sufficiently clear and unambiguous representation or promise has been made to him or that he has suffered a detriment or even acted in reliance on the representation or promise if made.[432]

Terms of agreement or promise. Further difficulties may arise in construing the terms of the agreement or promise, e.g. whether the defendant undertakes not to plead the statute or merely to suspend the running of time, whether the undertaking is conditional or unconditional and whether it is permanent in effect or merely temporary (the defendant being entitled on reasonable notice to resile from his undertaking or to start time running again), or is for a reasonable time only.[433] **28–110**

Negotiations. The fact that the parties have entered into negotiations for the settlement of their dispute will not, without more, suspend or otherwise affect the running of time or prevent the defendant from relying on the statute, even though the limitation period may expire before the negotiations are concluded.[434] But in *Wright v John Bagnall & Sons Ltd*,[435] and again in *Lubovsky v Snelling*,[436] the claimant had an action in tort against the defendant which was subject to a very short limitation period. Before the period had expired, negotiations took place between representatives of the parties in the course of which liability was admitted subject to the question of quantum. Soon after the period expired the claimant issued a writ and the defendant pleaded the statute. In both cases it was held that the action succeeded: in the former case because the defendant was estopped from pleading the statute, and in the latter case because there was an implied agreement not to plead the statute. Previously, the safest course for a claimant to pursue was to issue a writ within the period but not to serve it until the negotiations broke down. This practice may now be of limited utility, since **28–111**

---

[431] Above, paras 3–093—3–094.

[432] *Alma Shipping Corp v Union of India* [1971] 2 Lloyd's Rep. 494, 502; *K. Lokumal & Sons (London) Ltd v Lotte Shipping Co Pte Ltd* [1985] 2 Lloyd's Rep. 28; *Kenya Rys v Antares Co Pte Ltd* [1986] 2 Lloyd's Rep. 633; [1987] 1 Lloyd's Rep. 424; *P.S. Chellaram & Co Ltd v China Ocean Shipping Co* [1991] 1 Lloyd's Rep. 493; *Blaenau Gwent BC v Robinson Jones Design Partnership Ltd* (1997) 53 Const. L.R. 31; *Rowan Companies Inc v Lambert Eggink Offshore Consultants VOF* [1999] 2 Lloyd's Rep. 443, 448–449; *Tameside MBC v Barlow Securities Group Services Ltd* [2001] EWCA Civ 1, [2001] Build. L.R. 113; *Seechurn v Ace Insurance SA-NV* [2002] EWCA Civ 67, [2002] 2 Lloyd's Rep. 390; *Super Chem Products Ltd v American Life and General Insurance Co Ltd* [2004] UKPC 2, [2004] 2 All E.R. 358.

[433] *Waters v Earl of Thanet* (1842) 2 Q.B. 757.

[434] *Hewlett v L.C.C.* (1908) 72 J.P. 136.

[435] [1900] 2 Q.B. 240; distinguished in *Rendall v Hill's Dry Dock and Engineering Co Ltd* [1900] 2 Q.B. 245.

[436] [1944] K.B. 44; distinguished (admittedly on narrow grounds) in *The Sauria and The Trent* [1957] 1 Lloyd's Rep. 396.

a claim form must be served within four months, unless the court makes an order extending the period.[437] But a claimant may commence legal proceedings to protect its position and then apply for a stay of proceedings to allow for settlement of the case.[438]

6. ABRIDGEMENT OF THE PERIOD

28–112 **Agreement of the parties.** It is open to the parties to a contract to stipulate in the contract that legal or arbitral[439] proceedings shall be commenced within a shorter period of time than that provided in the Limitation Act 1980. Such stipulations are not uncommon in commercial agreements and their effect may be (depending on the precise wording of the stipulation) to bar or extinguish any right of action, or to deprive a party of his right to have recourse to particular proceedings, e.g. arbitration,[440] after the expiration of the agreed time limit. It is also open to the parties to agree that one party shall be released from liability or the other party's claim shall be extinguished or become barred unless a claim has been presented within a stipulated period of time.[441]

28–113 **Exemption and other restrictive clauses.** Clauses imposing a shorter time limit than that allowed by the 1980 Act may, even at common law, be regarded as exemption clauses,[442] so that, for example, they will be strictly construed[443] and be ineffective in the case of claims based on personal fraud.[444] In the case of contracts to which the Unfair Contract Terms Act 1977 applies,[445] to the extent that that Act prevents the exclusion or restriction of any liability, it also prevents: (i) making the enforcement of the liability subject to restrictive conditions[446]; and (ii) excluding or restricting any right or remedy in respect of the liability.[447] Contract terms which abridge the limitation period may therefore be subject to the control of the 1977 Act. Similar considerations probably apply in respect of remedies for misrepresentation under s.3 of the Misrepresentation Act 1967.[448]

---

[437] See below, para.28–116.

[438] See CPR rr.3.1(2)(f), 26.4.

[439] *Atlantic Shipping Co Ltd v Louis Dreyfus & Co* [1922] 2 A.C. 250; see below, para.28–115; below, para.32–058.

[440] See below, para.32–058.

[441] See, e.g. *Metalimex Foreign Trade Corp v Eugenie Maritime Co Ltd* [1962] 1 Lloyd's Rep. 378; *Babanaft International Co SA v Avant Petroleum Inc* [1982] 1 W.L.R. 871; *Indian Oil Corp v Vanol Inc* [1991] 2 Lloyd's Rep. 634; *Crown Estate Commissioners v John Mowlem & Co* [1994] 10 Const. L.J. 311; below, para.32–062.

[442] See above, Ch.14.

[443] *Bunge SA v Deutsche Conti-Handelsgesellschaft mbH (No.2)* [1981] 1 Lloyd's Rep. 352, 358. See above, para.14–005.

[444] See above, para.14–136.

[445] See above, paras 14–059—14–113.

[446] s.13(1)(a).

[447] s.13(1)(b).

[448] As amended by s.8 of the Unfair Contract Terms Act 1977; see above, para.14–114.

In addition to the statutes referred to above, a number of other statutes regulate exempting provisions[449] and their wording may likewise extend to prevent abridgement of the limitation period.

Special limitation periods. The special limitation periods established by enactments[450] other than the 1980 Act are, in general,[451] mandatory and cannot be shortened by agreement of the parties. 28–114

Arbitration. By s.12 of the Arbitration Act 1996, where an arbitration agreement to refer future disputes to arbitration provides that a claim shall be barred, or the claimant's right extinguished, unless the claimant takes within a time fixed by the agreement some step to begin proceedings, or to begin other dispute resolution procedures which must be exhausted before arbitral proceedings can be begun, the court may by order extend the time for taking the step. This section replaced s.27 of the Arbitration Act 1950, though the grounds on which the court may grant an extension of time are now more limited.[452] It is specifically provided that an order under s.12 "does not affect the operation of the Limitation Acts".[453] A similar provision in s.27 of the 1950 Act was interpreted to mean that, where the one-year time bar contained in art.III r.6, of the Hague Rules was imported by the parties into their contract, the court had power to grant an extension of time under s.27,[454] but not where the time bar in art.III r.6, of the Hague-Visby Rules was rendered applicable by the Carriage of Goods Act 1971.[455] It is probable that the same result would be reached under the 1996 Act since "the Limitation Acts" are defined to mean, in England and Wales, the Limitation Act 1980, the Foreign Limitation Periods Act 1984 and any other enactment (whenever passed) relating to the limitation of actions.[456] 28–115

7. COMMENCEMENT OF PROCEEDINGS

Legal proceedings. A cause of action will be barred unless legal proceedings[457] in respect of that cause of action are commenced by the claimant within the limitation period. Proceedings are started when the court issues a claim form at the claimant's request or on the day on which the form was received by the 28–116

[449] See above, para.14–115. In particular, the Unfair Terms in Consumer Contracts Regulations 1999 (SI 1999/2083); above, Ch.15.

[450] See above, para.28–019.

[451] But see, e.g. the Uniform Laws on International Sales Act 1967 Sch.1 art.3; and above, para.28–027.

[452] See below, para.32–059.

[453] Arbitration Act 1996 s.12(5).

[454] *The Merak* [1965] P. 223; *Nea Agrex SA v Baltic Shipping Co Ltd* [1976] Q.B. 933; *Consolidated Investment & Contracting Co v Saponaria Shipping Co Ltd* [1978] 1 W.L.R. 986.

[455] *Kenya Rys v Antares Co Pte Ltd* [1987] 1 Lloyd's Rep. 424; see below, para.32–062.

[456] s.13(4).

[457] By s.38(1) of the 1980 Act, "action" includes any proceedings in a court of law.

court office (if earlier).[458] The claim form must normally be served within four months[459] after the date of its issue.[460] But the claimant may apply within that period for an order extending the period within which the form must be served.[461] The court has a discretion whether or not to make the order. Under the old Rules of the Supreme Court, however, the court would not exercise its power to grant an extension if the relevant period of limitation had expired, unless good reason existed for doing so.[462] That approach can still be illuminating, albeit not binding, under the Civil Procedure Rules.[463] An application may even be made after the four month period has expired. But the court may then make an order only if the court has been unable to serve the claim form or the claimant has taken all reasonable steps to serve the form but has been unable to do so, and in either case the claimant has acted promptly in making the application.[464] If the claim form is served, but not within the four months or the extended period specified in the court order, the defendant should file an acknowledgment of service and make an application under Pt 11 of the Civil Procedure Rules. This must be done within the period for filing a defence.[465]

28–117 Proceedings must be commenced by a person properly entitled to bring them.[466] An equitable assignee may commence proceedings and so stop time from running even though the assignor has not been joined as a party to the action[467] and even though notice of the assignment has not been given to the defendant until after the claim form has been issued.[468] A claim form issued within the limitation period but without the authority of the nominal claimant is not a nullity. The nominal claimant could subsequently ratify and adopt the claim notwithstanding the expiration of the period.[469]

---

458 CPR 7PD, r.5.1; *Barnes v St Helens MBC* [2006] EWCA Civ 1372, [2007] 1 W.L.R. 879. For commencement of arbitration proceedings, see above, para.32–064.

459 Where the claim form has been issued for service outside the jurisdiction, the period is six months: CPR r.7.5(3). See also *Saris v Westminster Transport SA* [1994] 1 Lloyd's Rep. 115.

460 CPR r.7.5. Under the old rules, the date of issue of the writ was included in the computation of the four months: *Trow v Ind Coope (West Midlands) Ltd* [1967] 2 Q.B. 899. If there was more than one defendant, the writ had to be served on the particular defendant within the four months: *Jones v Jones* [1970] 2 Q.B. 576; *Payabi v Armstel Shipping Corp* [1992] Q.B. 907.

461 CPR r.7.6(1), (2).

462 *Battersby v Anglo-American Oil Co Ltd* [1945] K.B. 23; *Heaven v Road and Rail Wagons Ltd* [1965] 2 Q.B. 355; *Chappell v Cooper* [1980] 1 W.L.R. 958; *Wilkinson v Ancliff (B.L.T.) Ltd* [1986] 1 W.L.R. 1352; *Kleinwort Benson Ltd v Barbrak Ltd* [1987] A.C. 597; *Waddon v Whitecroft Scovell Ltd* [1988] 1 W.L.R. 309 HL; *Goldenglow Nut Food Co v Commodin (Produce) Ltd* [1987] 2 Lloyd's Rep. 569; *Doble v Haymills (Contractors), The Times*, July 5, 1988 CA; *Baly v Barrett, The Times*, May 19, 1989 HL; *The Vita* [1990] 1 Lloyd's Rep. 528; *De Pina v M.S. "Birka" Beutler Schiffahrts K.G.* [1996] 1 Lloyd's Rep. 31. The extension will be for no longer period than is shown to be justified: *Baly v Barrett*.

463 *Bua International Ltd v Hai Hing Shipping Co Ltd* [2000] 1 Lloyd's Rep. 300, especially 306.

464 CPR r.7.6(3).

465 CPR r.15.4.

466 But see below, para.28–118 (amendment).

467 See above, para.19–039.

468 *Weddell v J.A. Pearce & Major* [1988] Ch. 26. Contrast *Compania Columbiana de Seguros v Pacific Steam Navigation Co* [1965] 1 Q.B. 101, 127, 129.

469 *Presentaciones Musicales SA v Secunda* [1994] Ch. 271.

Amendments to statement of case after the end of the limitation period.[470] The Civil Procedure Rules[471] empower the court to allow a party to amend his statement of case in three specific cases where a period of limitation[472] has expired. These cases are as follows: 28–118

(1) An amendment to correct a mistake as to the name of a party, but only where the mistake was genuine and not one which would cause reasonable doubt as to the identity of the party in question.[473]

(2) An amendment to alter the capacity in which party claims if the new capacity is one which that party had when the proceedings started or has since acquired.[474]

(3) An amendment whose effect will be to add or substitute a new claim,[475] but only if the new claim arises out of the same facts or substantially the same facts as a claim in respect of which the party applying for permission to amend has already claimed a remedy in the proceedings.[476]

---

[470] See s.35 of the Act and *Twenty-First Report of the Law Reform Committee*, 1977, Cmnd.6923, paras 5.12–5.29.

[471] CPR r.17.4.

[472] Defined to mean a period of limitation under the Limitation Act 1980, the Foreign Limitation Periods Act 1984 s.190 of the Merchant Shipping Act 1995, or any other statutory provision. See also s.39 of the 1980 Act. Contrast (Hague Rules) *Casillo Grani v Napier Shipping Co* [1984] 2 Lloyd's Rep. 481, 487; *Payabi v Armstel Shipping Corp* [1982] Q.B. 907; *Transworld Oil (USA) Inc v Minos Compania Naviera SA* [1992] 2 Lloyd's Rep. 48; but see *Empresa Cubana Importadora de Alimentos v Octavia Shipping Co SA* [1986] 1 Lloyd's Rep. 273; *Katzenstein Adleu Industries (1975) Ltd v The Borchard Lines Ltd* [1988] 2 Lloyd's Rep. 274. The 10-year-long stop period under the Consumer Protection Act 1987 (see above, para.28–009) has been held to be a "period of limitation" for the purposes of the rules: *Horne-Roberts v SmithKline Beecham Plc* [2001] EWCA Civ 2006, [2002] 1 W.L.R. 1662. But in *O'Byrne v Aventis Pasteur MSD Ltd* [2008] UKHL 34 the House of Lords has referred to the ECJ the question of whether this approach is consistent with the product liability directive.

[473] CPR r.17.4.3, formerly RSC Ord.20 r.5(3). As to this, see *Rodriguez v Parker* [1967] 1 Q.B. 116; *Mitchell v Harris Engineering Co Ltd* [1967] 2 Q.B. 703; *Kamouh v A.E.I. International Ltd* [1980] Q.B. 199; *Evans Construction Co Ltd v Charrington & Co Ltd* [1983] Q.B. 810; *Birmingham City DC v C. Bryant & Son* (1987) 9 Con. L.R. 128; *Katzenstein Adler Industries (1975) Ltd v The Borchard Lines Ltd* [1988] 2 Lloyd's Rep. 274; *Thistle Hotels Ltd v Sir Robert McAlpine & Sons Ltd*, *The Times*, April 11, 1989; *The Sardinia Sulcis* [1991] 1 Lloyd's Rep. 201; *The Lu Shan* [1991] 2 Lloyd's Rep. 386; *Transworld Oil (USA) Inc v Minos Compania Naviera Inc* [1992] 2 Lloyd's Rep. 48; *International Bulk Shipping and Services Ltd v Minerals and Metals Trading Corp of India* [1996] 1 All E.R. 1017.

[474] CPR r.17.4.4, formerly RSC Ord.20 r.5(4). See also s.35(7), (8) of the Act. See *Haq v Singh* [2001] EWCA Civ 957, [2001] 1 W.L.R. 1594.

[475] cf. *The Jangmi* [1989] 2 Lloyd's Rep. 1 (change of date).

[476] CPR r.17.4.2, formerly RSC Ord.20 r.5(5). See also s.35(2)(a), (5)(a), (8) of the Act; *Chatsworth Investments Ltd v Cussins (Contractors) Ltd* [1969] 1 W.L.R. 1; *Brickfield Properties Ltd v Newton* [1971] 1 W.L.R. 862; *Beck v Value Capital Ltd* [1976] 1 W.L.R. 572; *Empresa Cubana Importadora de Alimentos v Octavia Shipping Co SA* [1986] 1 Lloyd's Rep. 273; *S.S. Mutual Underwriting Association Ltd v Trollope & Colls Ltd* (1986) 33 B.L.R. 77; *Fannon v Backhouse*, *The Times*, August 22, 1987 CA; *Birmingham City DC v C. Bryant & Son* (1987) 9 Con. L.R. 128; *Kakkar v Szelke* [1988] F.S.R. 97; *Hancock Shipping Co Ltd v Kawasaki Heavy Industries Ltd* [1992] 1 W.L.R. 1025; *Arab Monetary Fund v Hashim* [1993] 1 Lloyd's Rep. 543, 593; reversed on other grounds [1996] 1 Lloyd's Rep. 589; *Sion v Hampstead Health Authority*, *The Times*, June 10, 1994 CA; *Clarke (E.) & Sons (Coaches) v Axtell Yates Hallett* (1994) 30 Const. L.R. 123; *Paragon Finance Plc v Thakerer & Co* [1999] 1 All E.R. 400; *Lloyds Bank Plc v Rogers* [1999] 3 E.G.L.R. 83; *Stewart v Engel* [2000] 1 W.L.R. 2268; *Shade v Compton Partnership* [2000] P.N.L.R. 218; *Savings and*

28–119 In addition, the Civil Procedure Rules[477] provide for a change of parties after the end of a period of limitation.[478] The court may add or substitute a party only if the relevant limitation period was current when the proceedings were started, and the addition or substitution is necessary. The addition or substitution of a party is necessary only if the court is satisfied that the new party is to be substituted for a party who was named in the claim form in mistake for the new party, or the claim cannot properly be carried on by or against the original party unless the new party is added or substituted as claimant or defendant, or the original party has died or had a bankruptcy order made against him and his interest or liability has passed to the new party.[479]

28–120 However, in a claim for personal injuries, the court may in addition add or substitute a party where it directs that s.11 or s.12 of the 1980 Act[480] shall not apply to the claim by or against the new party or where it directs that the issue of whether those sections apply is to be determined.[481]

28–121 The court has not otherwise any power to allow a new claim to be made in the course of any action after the expiry of any time limit under the Act which would affect a new action to enforce that claim.[482]

Investment Bank Ltd v Fincken [2001] EWCA Civ 1639; *The Times*, November 15, 2002; *Goode v Martin* [2001] EWCA Civ 1899, [2002] 1 W.L.R. 1828; *Smith v Henniker-Major & Co* [2002] EWCA Civ 762, [2003] Ch. 182; *Laws v The Society of Lloyd's* [2003] EWCA Civ 1887, *The Times*, January 23, 2004; *Furini v Bajwa* [2004] EWCA Civ 412, [2004] 1 W.L.R. 1971; *Charles Church Developments Ltd v Stent Foundations Ltd* [2006] EWHC 3158 (TCC), [2007] 1 W.L.R. 1203; *Finlan v Eyton Morris Winfield* [2007] EWHC 914 (Ch), [2007] 4 All E.R. 143.

[477] CPR r.19.5. See also s.35(2)(b), (5)(b), (8) of the Act (cf. s.35(6)). In *Kenya Rys v Antares Co Pte Ltd* [1987] 1 Lloyd's Rep. 424, 432, 433, the Court of Appeal expressed the opinion that s.35 of the Act does not apply to arbitrations in respect of the addition or substitution of a new party.

[478] Defined in the same way as in fn.467, above.

[479] CPR r.19.5. See *International Distillers and Vinters Ltd v J.F. Hillebrande*, *The Times*, January 25, 2000; *Horne-Roberts v SmithKline Beecham Plc* [2001] EWCA Civ 2006, [2002] 1 W.L.R. 1662. See also the previous RSC Ord.15 r.6(6); *Liff v Peasley* [1980] 1 W.L.R. 781 (joinder of defendant after claim against him statute-barred disallowed) and *Mitchell v Harris Engineering Co Ltd* [1967] 2 Q.B. 703, 717, 721; *Branff v Holland & Hannen and Cubitts (Southern) Ltd* [1969] 1 W.L.R. 1533; *Lucy v W.T. Henleys Telegraph Works Co Ltd* [1970] 1 Q.B. 393; *Marubeni Corp v Pearlstone Shipping Corp* [1978] 1 Lloyd's Rep 38; *Gawthrop v Boulton* [1979] 1 W.L.R. 268; *Ketteman v Hansel Properties Ltd* [1987] A.C. 189; *Birmingham City DC v C. Bryant & Son* (1987) 9 Con. L.R. 128; *Hancock Shipping Co Ltd v Kawasaki Heavy Industries Ltd* [1992] 1 W.L.R. 1025; *Payabi v Armstel Shipping Corp* [1992] Q.B. 907; *Bank of America National Trust and Savings Association v Christmas* [1994] 1 All E.R. 401; *Bradstock Trustee Services Ltd v Nabarro Nathanson* [1995] 1 W.L.R. 1405; *Parsons v George* [2004] EWCA Civ 912, [2004] 1 W.L.R. 3264; *Adelson v Associated Newspapers Ltd* [2007] EWCA Civ 701, [2007] 4 All E.R. 330; *O'Byrne v Aventis Pasteur MSD Ltd* [2007] EWCA Civ 939, [2008] P.I.Q.R. P3.

[480] See above, paras 28–006—28–007.

[481] s.33; see above, para.28–008.

[482] *Kennett v Brown* [1988] 1 W.L.R. 582 was overruled in *Welsh Development Agency v Redpath Dorman Long Ltd* [1994] 1 W.L.R. 1409. But an order for the substitution of a party as claimant under the previous RSC Ord.15 r.7, did not involve the making of a "new claim": *Yorkshire Regional Health Authority v Fairclough* [1996] 1 W.L.R. 210; *Industrie Chimiche Italia Centrale v Alexander G. Tsavliris & Sons Maritime Co* [1996] 1 W.L.R. 774.

Defence, set-off and counterclaim. When a defendant is sued, he can raise any matter which is properly in the nature of a defence, without fear of being met by a plea of limitation.[483] But if he makes a cross-claim, either by way of set-off or counterclaim, he may be time-barred. Section 35 of the Limitation Act 1980 provides that, for the purposes of the Act,[484] any claim by way of set-off or counterclaim[485] is deemed to be a separate action and to have been commenced on the same date as the original action.[486] Thus a set-off or counterclaim can be made by an original defendant against an original claimant[487] notwithstanding the expiry of any time limit under the Act, provided that the time limit had not expired on the date of commencement of the original action. However, the court has a discretion to order that it be dealt with separately from the claim of the claimant against the defendant[488] and it may do so notwithstanding that any such action would be barred by limitation.[489] 28–122

A further difficulty which arises is that it is a matter of considerable refinement whether a particular cross-claim is to be treated as a defence or matter of set-off.[490] Section 53(1) of the Sale of Goods Act 1979, for example, provides that the buyer may set up against the seller a breach of warranty in diminution or extinction of the price,[491] and such a claim is therefore to be treated as a defence.[492] Lord Denning M.R. has further put forward the view, in respect of the comparable provision in the Limitation Act 1939,[493] that the word "set-off" meant only a set-off as permitted by the statutes of set-off, and did not apply to an "equitable set-off" pleaded in extinction or diminution of the claim.[494] On this view, if a cross-claim arises out of the same transaction as the claim, or out of a transaction that is closely related to the claim,[495] 28–123

[483] *Henriksens Rederi A/S v T.H.Z. Rolimpex* [1974] Q.B. 233.

[484] s.35 does not apply to any action or arbitration for which a period of limitation is prescribed by or under any other enactment: s.39. See (on the previous common law) *Walker v Clements* (1850) 15 Q.B. 1046 (set-off); *Lowe v Bentley* (1928) 44 T.L.R. 386 (counterclaim); and see s.40(1) Sch.2 paras 6, 8(2).

[485] s.35(2).

[486] s.35(1)(b).

[487] s.35(3) ("original set-off or counterclaim"); *JFS (UK) Ltd v DWR Cymru Cyf* [1999] 1 W.L.R. 231.

[488] CPR r.20.9(1).

[489] *Ernst & Young v Butte Mining Plc* [1997] 1 W.L.R. 1485.

[490] See *Mondel v Steel* (1841) 8 M. & W. 858; *Henriksens Rederi A/S v T.H.Z. Rolimpex* [1974] Q.B. 233; *Aries Tanker Corp v Total Transport Ltd* [1977] 1 W.L.R. 185; *Axel Johnson Petroleum v MG Mineral Group AG, The Jo Lind* [1992] 2 All E.R. 163.

[491] See Vol.II, para.43–442.

[492] s.28.

[493] *Henriksens Rederi A/S v T.H.Z. Rolimpex* [1974] Q.B. 233, 246. But see Cairns and Roskill L.JJ., 254, 264. Lord Denning's view was followed (obiter) by Hobhouse J. in *Kleinwort Benson Ltd v Sandwell B.C.* (1993) 91 L.G.R. 323, 386.

[494] See, e.g. *Morgan & Son v S. Martin Johnson & Co* [1949] 1 K.B. 107; *Hanak v Green* [1958] 2 Q.B. 9; *Federal Commerce & Navigation Co Ltd v Molena Alpha Inc* [1978] Q.B. 974; affirmed [1979] A.C. 757; *The Raven* [1980] 2 Lloyd's Rep. 266; *British Anzani (Felixstowe) Ltd v International Marine Management (UK) Ltd* [1980] Q.B. 137; *Fuller v Happy Shopper Markets Ltd* [2001] 2 Lloyd's Rep. 49; CPR r.16.6.

[495] See also *Mondel v Steel* (1841) 8 M. & W. 858.

it is to be treated as an equitable defence[496] and is time-barred only in equity.[497]

28–124 **Part 20 claims.** Section 35(1) of the Limitation Act 1980 provides that, for the purposes of the Act,[498] a new claim made in or by way of third-party proceedings is to be deemed to be a separate action and to have been commenced on the date on which those proceedings were commenced.[499] The result may be (assuming that the situation is not one to which s.1 of the Civil Liability (Contribution) Act 1978 applies)[500] that if a claimant starts proceedings against a defendant at a time when the defendant's cause of action against the third party is, or is on the point of becoming, time-barred, the defendant will have lost or may lose the opportunity of obtaining relief over against the third party. "Third-party proceedings" is defined to mean any proceedings brought in the course of any action against a person not previously a party to the action, other than proceedings brought by joining any such person as defendant to any claim already made in the original action by the party bringing the proceedings.[501] The rule set out above thus applies to a larger range of proceedings than would usually be considered as "third-party proceedings", and extends to other Pt 20 claims for example, a counterclaim by a defendant against an added party.

28–125 **Arbitral proceedings.** The Limitation Acts[502] apply to arbitral proceedings as they apply to legal proceedings,[503] and an arbitrator no less than a judge is bound to give effect to defences based thereon.[504] The arbitration must therefore be commenced before the expiration of the relevant limitation period. The parties are free to agree when arbitral proceedings are to be regarded commenced for the purposes of the Limitation Acts.[505] If there is no such agreement, the rules set out in s.14 of the Arbitration Act 1996 may apply. These are considered in the chapter on Arbitration Clauses later in this book.[506]

---

[496] Supreme Court of Judicature Act 1873 s.24; Supreme Court of Judicature (Consolidation) Act 1925 ss.38, 41; now see the Supreme Court Act 1981 s.49.

[497] s.36(2); *Filross Securities Ltd v Midgeley* (1998) 43 E.G. 134. Contrast *Aries Tanker Corp v Total Transport Ltd* [1977] 1 W.L.R. 185 (Hague Rules) and, e.g. Carriage of Goods by Road Act 1965 Sch. art.32(4); *Impex Transport Aktieselskabet v AG Thames Holdings Ltd* [1981] 1 W.L.R. 1547; *Casillo Grani v Napier Shipping Co* [1984] 2 Lloyd's Rep. 481.

[498] The subsection does not apply to any action or arbitration for which a period of limitation is prescribed by or under any other enactment (s.39) and enactments imposing special periods of limitation (see above, para.28–019) may grant an extension of time for third-party proceedings.

[499] s.35(1)(a).

[500] See above, para.28–014.

[501] s.35(2).

[502] Defined in s.13(4) of the Arbitration Act 1996.

[503] Arbitration Act 1996 s.13(1).

[504] *Board of Trade v Cayzer, Irvine & Co* [1927] A.C. 610, 614; *Naamlooze, etc. Vulcaan v A/S Ludwig Mowinckel Rederi* (1938) 43 Com. Cas. 252 HL; *Christian Salvesen (Properties) Ltd v Central Electricity Generating Board* (1984) 48 P. & C.R. 465; *Compagnie Europeenne de Cereals SA v Tradax Export SA* [1986] 2 Lloyd's Rep. 301.

[505] s.14(1). See *Transpetrol Ltd v Erkali Shipping Co Ltd* [1989] 1 Lloyd's Rep. 62.

[506] Vol.II, para.32–059. See also Carriage by Air Act 1961 s.5(3); Carriage of Goods by Road Act 1965 s.7(2)(a); Limitation Act 1980 s.40(2) and Sch.3 paras 5, 6.

8. The Statute Bars the Remedy, not the Right

General. Except for the provisions governing extinction of title in relation to land,[507] and goods,[508] and the 10-year long-stop period for actions under Pt I of the Consumer Protection Act 1987,[509] the effect of limitation under the Limitation Act 1980 is merely to bar the claimant's remedy and not to extinguish his right.[510] Limitation is a procedural matter, and not one of substance: the right continues to exist even though it cannot be enforced by action. In contrast, limitation provisions in certain other enactments, such as the Carriage by Air Act 1961[511] and the Carriage of Goods by Sea Act 1971,[512] extinguish the right. Where special statutory periods of limitation are applied, regard must be had to the particular language and intent of the statute in each case. A procedural bar does not go to the jurisdiction of the court or of an arbitral tribunal.[513] 28–126

Obtaining payment in other ways. In those cases where the remedy only is barred by the 1980 Act, if a debtor pays a statute-barred debt, he cannot subsequently recover the money on the ground that it was not due.[514] Further, though the creditor cannot recover a statute-barred debt by action, he can obtain satisfaction in a number of other ways. 28–127

Appropriation.[515] If a debtor makes a payment without appropriating it to any particular debt, the creditor may at any time before the commencement of proceedings appropriate it to a statute-barred debt.[516] If neither party makes an appropriation, the court will presume that the payment was made in respect of debts which were not statute-barred.[517] But if the debtor has no opportunity of exercising his right of appropriation, then the creditor cannot do so. Thus, he may not appropriate money of the debtor which happens to be in his hands to a statute-barred debt,[518] for that would be not appropriation but set-off. 28–128

---

507 s.17.

508 s.3(2); see Vol.II, para.43–264.

509 s.11A(3); above, para.28–009.

510 *Royal Norwegian Government v Constant & Constant and Calcutta Marine Engineering Co Ltd* [1960] 2 Lloyd's Rep. 431, 442.

511 Sch.1 art.29; see above, para.28–024; Vol.II, paras 35–017, 35–070.

512 Sch. art.3 r.6; *Kenya Rys v Antares Co Pte Ltd* [1987] 1 Lloyd's Rep. 424. See also (Hague Rules) *Goulandris Bros v Goldman* [1958] 1 Q.B. 74, 105, 106; *Aries Tanker Corp v Total Transport Ltd* [1977] 1 W.L.R. 185; *Casillo Grani v Napier Shipping Co* [1984] 2 Lloyd's Rep. 481, 487; *Payabi v Armstel Shipping Corp* [1992] Q.B. 907; *Bua International Ltd v Hai Hing Shipping Co Ltd* [2000] 1 Lloyd's Rep. 300, 310.

513 *Leif Hoegh & Co A/S v Petrolsea Inc* [1992] 1 Lloyd's Rep. 45, 49.

514 *Bize v Dickason* (1786) 1 T.R. 286, 287.

515 See above, para.21–059.

516 *Mills v Fowkes* (1839) 5 Bing. N.C. 455; *Nash v Hodgson* (1855) 6 De G.M. & G. 474, 480–481; *Friend v Young* [1897] 2 Ch. 421, 433, 437.

517 *Nash v Hodgson* (1855) 6 De G.M. & G. 474.

518 *Waller v Lacy* (1840) 1 M. & G. 54; *Coneys v Morris* [1922] 1 Ir.R. 81, 91–93; *Kleinwort Benson Ltd v Sandwell B.C.* [1994] 4 All E.R. 890, 943–945.

28–129 **Account stated.** The parties are at liberty to include a statute-barred debt in an account stated and thus render it enforceable by action.[519]

28–130 **Deduction from legacy, etc.** If a legatee owes money to his testator's estate, the personal representatives may deduct the debt from the legacy, even if the debt is statute-barred.[520] The same principle applies to a debt owed by a person entitled on intestacy.[521] But it does not apply to a debt owed by a specific legatee of chattels not represented by money in the hands of the personal representatives,[522] nor where the legatee was not himself the debtor but only the personal representative of a deceased debtor.[523]

28–131 **Executor's right of retainer.** A personal representative may choose to pay a statute-barred debt,[524] unless (perhaps) his fellow personal representative objects,[525] and may therefore exercise his right of retainer in respect of such a debt due to himself.[526] However, this is an anomalous principle which is not to be extended: it does not apply to a debt which has been judicially declared to be statute-barred, for in that case the executor would be failing to rely on the defence of res judicata as well as on that of limitation.[527] And the position is different if an order has been made in an administration action. Once such an order has been made, any beneficiary[528] or creditor[529] may insist on the statute being pleaded, except against a creditor who obtained the order and did not have the statute pleaded against him at that earlier stage.[530]

28–132 **Trustee's right to indemnity for expenses.** On similar principles, a trustee has been held entitled to recoup himself out of the trust estate in respect of costs and expenses which he had paid, although they were statute-barred.[531]

28–133 **Creditor's lien.** A creditor who has a lien on goods belonging to the debtor which are in his possession may exercise it in respect of statute-barred debts.[532]

---

519 *Ashby v James* (1843) 11 M. & W. 542.

520 *Courtenay v Williams* (1844) 3 Hare 539; affirmed 15 L.J. Ch. 204; *Coates v Coates* (1864) 33 Beav. 249; *Gee v Liddell (No.2)* (1866) 35 Beav. 629; *Poole v Poole* (1871) L.R. 7 Ch. App. 17; *Re Rownson* (1885) 29 Ch D 358; *Re Akerman* [1891] 3 Ch. 212; *Re Taylor* [1894] 1 Ch. 671.

521 *Re Cordwell's Estate* (1875) L.R. 20 Eq. 644.

522 *Re Savage* [1918] 2 Ch. 146.

523 *Re Bruce* [1908] 2 Ch. 682.

524 *Stahlschmidt v Lett* (1853) 1 Sm. & G. 415; *Hill v Walker* (1858) 4 K. & J. 166; *Lowis v Rumney* (1867) L.R. 4 Eq. 451.

525 See *Midgley v Midgley* [1893] 3 Ch. 282, 297; *Astbury v Astbury* [1898] 2 Ch. 111, 115. The point has never been decided.

526 *Stahlschmidt v Lett* (1853) 1 Sm. & G. 415; *Hill v Walker* (1858) K. & J. 166.

527 *Midgley v Midgley* [1893] 3 Ch. 282.

528 *Shewen v Vanderhorst* (1831) 1 R. & M. 347; *Moodie v Bannister* (1859) 4 Drew. 432; cf. *Re Wenham* [1892] 3 Ch. 59, applying the same principle to an originating summons taken out by the executors.

529 *Fuller v Redman (No.2)* (1859) 26 Beav. 614.

530 *Briggs v Wilson* (1854) 5 De G.M. & G. 12; *Fuller v Redman (No.2)* (1859) 26 Beav. 614.

531 *Budgett v Budgett* [1895] 1 Ch. 202.

532 *Spears v Hartly* (1800) 3 Esp. 81; *Higgins v Scott* (1831) 2 B. & Ad. 413; *Curwin v Milburn* (1889) 42 Ch D 424; *Re Brockman* [1909] 2 Ch. 170.

9. LIMITATION IN EQUITY[533]

Introductory. The earliest Statutes of Limitation applied only to common law actions. However, where an equitable remedy was sought in the protection or enforcement of a legal right, a court of equity would act "in obedience" to the statutes,[534] and if an equitable claim was closely analogous to a claim which was covered by the Statutes, the court would apply the same period of limitation "by analogy".[535] But, in cases not covered by any statutory period, equity developed its own doctrines of laches and acquiescence, under which the claimant was barred from equitable relief if he had not shown reasonable diligence in prosecuting his claim or appeared to have waived his rights.[536] "Nothing can call forth this court into activity", said Lord Camden in 1767[537]: 28–134

> "... but conscience, good faith and reasonable diligence. Where these are wanting, the court is passive and does nothing. Laches and neglect are always discountenanced and therefore, from the beginning of this jurisdiction, there was always a limitation to suits in this court."

These equitable doctrines rest on the same basis as the law of limitation, that stale demands should not be enforced: but with this difference, that while statute ordinarily prescribes a fixed time limit which applies in general irrespective of the conduct of the parties, the equitable doctrines look primarily at the conduct of the claimant and its effect on the defendant or on third parties, so that the length of time which will bar the claim varies greatly in accordance with the circumstances and the type of relief sought. The result is, as has been observed,[538] that a certain vagueness is apt to surround the equitable doctrines of delay. From 1833 onwards the Statutes of Limitation tended more and more to encroach on the field in which the equitable doctrines were applied. The Limitation Act 1980 provides expressly for the limitation of certain claims in equity.[539] Nevertheless, the existence of the equitable doctrines continues to be recognised by the Act, since nothing in the Act is to affect any equitable jurisdiction to refuse relief on the ground of acquiescence or otherwise.[540] Further, the Act provides

---

533 See Brunyate, *Limitation of Actions in Equity* (1932).

534 See *Beckford v Wade* (1805) 17 Ves. 87, 97; *Hovenden v Annesley* (1806) 2 Sch. & Lef. 607; *Cholmondeley v Clinton* (1821) 4 Bli. 1, 119; *Knox v Gye* (1872) L.R. 5 H.L. 656, 674; *Gibbs v Guild* (1882) 9 QBD 59, 74–75.

535 See, e.g. *Re Robinson* [1911] 1 Ch. 502; *Re Mason* [1928] Ch. 385, [1929] 1 Ch. 1; *Re Blake* [1932] 1 Ch. 54 (action to recover money paid wrongly by trustee to recipient analogous to common law action for money had and received). But see now *Re Diplock* [1948] Ch. 465, 498, 501, 502, 515, 516.

536 *Smith v Clay* (1767) 3 Bro. C.C. 639n.

537 *Smith v Clay* (1767) 3 Bro. C.C. 639n.

538 *Erlanger v New Sombrero Phosphate Co* (1878) 3 App. Cas. 1218, 1231.

539 e.g. s.16 (claims to redeem mortgaged land), s.20 (claims to recover money secured by a mortgage or the proceeds of sale), s.21 (claims in respect of trust property or for breach of trust), s.22 (claims in respect of personal estate of a deceased person).

540 s.36(2). But in *Re Pauling's Settlement Trusts* [1962] 1 W.L.R. 86, 115 Wilberforce J. said that laches, as distinct from acquiescence, cannot be invoked where there is a statutory limitation period; and this was approved by the Court of Appeal [1964] Ch. 303, 353. It was also approved in *Re Loftus* [2006] EWCA Civ 1124, [2007] 1 W.L.R. 1124 at [37]. See also *P & O Nedlloyd BV v Arab Metals Co, The UB Tiger* [2006] EWCA Civ 1717, [2007] W.L.R. 2288 (where the case was not one of laches by mere delay). See also below, para.28–139.

that neither the time limit under s.5 for actions founded on simple contract nor that under s.8 for actions on a specialty are to apply to any claim for specific performance of a contract or for an injunction or for other equitable relief, except in so far as any provision thereof may be applied by the court by analogy.[541] The effect of this "somewhat diffident" language is to limit the analogous application of ss.5 and 8 of the Act to claims of a kind for which no express provision is to be found elsewhere in the statute.[542]

28–135 **The statute applied by analogy.** The statute may be applied to an equitable claim by analogy.[543] One important example in the modern law is afforded by claims for a final injunction to protect a legal right. So long as the right itself is not barred (i.e. so long as the claimant could recover damages for its infringement), he retains his right to an injunction,[544] although delay or other circumstances may induce the court to withhold an injunction and award damages in lieu of an injunction.[545] (It is quite different if the claimant seeks an interim remedy. In that case the utmost promptitude is required and a delay of more than a month or two, unless explained, is usually fatal.[546]) There is also some authority for saying that the statute will be applied by analogy to claims for rescission[547] of a contract, with the result that the claimant's claim will be barred if his delay exceeds six years.[548] But, in such a case, even if the statute is applied by analogy, a claim for rescission may be barred, short of the statutory period, on account of acquiescence, laches or affirmation. In *P & O Nedlloyd BV v Arab Metals Co, The UB Tiger*[549] it was held, in a careful judgment by Moore-Bick L.J., that the usual contractual limitation period of six years does not apply by analogy under s.36(1) to a claim for specific performance.[550] This is because there is no directly equivalent remedy at common law to specific performance and because specific performance does not even require there to be an existing breach of contract.[551] Laches can, however, apply. The view was also expressed

[541] s.36(1). This also applies to s.7 (arbitration awards), s.9 (statutory claims) and s.24 (actions on judgments). In *P & O Nedlloyd BV v Arab Metals Co, The UB Tiger* [2005] EWHC 1276, [2005] 1 W.L.R. 3733, Colman J. held that a declaration was not "equitable relief" within s.36(1). Rather it was statutory so that normal time limits within the Limitation Act 1980 apply.

[542] *Re Diplock* [1948] Ch. 465, 515. cf. *Poole Corp v Moody* [1945] K.B. 350.

[543] s.36(1). As regards breach of fiduciary duty, see, e.g. *Knox v Gye* (1872) L.R. 5 H.L. 656; *Paragon Finance Plc v Thakerar & Co* [1999] 1 All E.R. 400; *Coulthard v Disco Mix Club Ltd* [2000] 1 W.L.R. 707; *Cia de Seguros Imperio v Heath (REBX) Ltd* [2001] 1 W.L.R. 112; *Gwembe Valley Development Co Ltd v Koshy* [2003] EWCA Civ 1048. See also above, para.28–018.

[544] *Imperial Gas Light and Coke Co v Broadbent* (1859) 7 H.L.C. 600; *Fullwood v Fullwood* (1878) 9 Ch D 176; *Jamieson v Jamieson* (1898) 15 R.P.C. 169, 179. See below, para.28–139.

[545] *Shaw v Applegate* [1977] 1 W.L.R. 97.

[546] *G.W. Ry v Oxford, etc. Ry* (1853) 3 De G.M. & G. 341.

[547] *Molloy v Mutual Reserve Life Insurance Co* (1906) 94 L.T. 756; *Oelkers v Ellis* [1914] 2 K.B. 139; *Armstrong v Jackson* [1917] 2 K.B. 822.

[548] In *Kleinwort Benson Ltd v Sandwell BC* [1994] 4 All E.R. 890, 943, Hobhouse J. noted that it was common ground between the parties that, in so far as s.5 of the 1980 Act applied to an action for money had and received, the same limitation period by reason of s.36 would apply to the equitable remedy (after tracing) sought by the bank.

[549] [2006] EWCA Civ 1717, [2007] 1 W.L.R. 2288.

[550] See also *Williams v Greatrex* [1957] 1 W.L.R. 31. cf. Beatson, "Limitation Periods and Specific Performance" in Lomnicka and Morse (eds), *Contemporary Issues in Commercial Law* (1997), pp.9–23.

[551] As shown in *Hasham v Zenab* [1960] A.C. 316.

that even if, contrary to the court's view, there were a statutory limitation period applicable to specific performance, laches comprising more than mere delay could still apply.[552]

Acquiescence.[553] 28–136

> "If a person having a right, and seeing another person about to commit, or in course of committing, an act infringing upon that right, stands by in such a manner as really to induce the person committing the act, and who might otherwise have abstained from it, to believe that he assents to its being committed, he cannot afterwards be heard to complain of the act."[554]

In this sense of the term (which has been described as the only proper one)[555] acquiescence by the claimant amounts to the waiver of his rights and raises a species of estoppel preventing him from subsequently enforcing them. The conduct of the claimant need not necessarily bear any relation to lapse of time, because it may take place before or at the time when his rights are violated. Mere delay by the claimant in seeking relief does not amount to acquiescence.[556] The essential ingredients of the defence are, however, by no means clear. In *Willmott v Barber*,[557] Fry J. laid down no less than five requirements, but it has been said[558] that more recent cases indicate:

> " . . . a very much broader approach which is directed rather at ascertaining whether, in particular individual circumstances, it would be unconscionable for a party to be permitted to deny that which, knowingly or unknowingly,[559] he has allowed or encouraged another to assume to his detriment than to inquiring whether the circumstances can be fitted within the confines of some preconceived formula serving as a universal yardstick for every form of unconscionable behaviour."

Laches. The term "laches" is sometimes used to denote acquiescence. But, in 28–137 a narrower sense, the essence of the doctrine of laches is that if the claimant has not been reasonably diligent in seeking relief, and in consequence the position of the defendant has been prejudiced or it would now be unjust or unreasonable to grant the relief, the claimant will be debarred from pursuing his remedy on the

---

552 See below, para.28–139.

553 See s.36(2).

554 *De Bussche v Alt* (1878) 8 Ch D 286, 314. See also *Archbold v Scully* (1861) 9 H.L.C. 360, 383; *Shaw v Applegate* [1977] 1 W.L.R. 970.

555 *Duke of Leeds v Earl of Amherst* (1846) 2 Ph. 117, 123. cf. *Life Association of Scotland v Siddall* (1861) 3 De G.F. & J. 58, 72.

556 *Jones v Stones* [1999] 1 W.L.R. 1739.

557 (1880) 15 Ch D 96, 105–106.

558 *Taylors Fashions Ltd v Liverpool Victoria Trustee Co Ltd* [1982] Q.B. 133n; *Amalgamated Investment & Property Co Ltd v Texas Commerce International Bank Ltd* [1982] Q.B. 84, 103; *Habib Bank Ltd v Habib Bank AG* [1981] 1 W.L.R. 1265, 1285; *Jones v Stones* [1999] 1 W.L.R. 1739. But contrast *The August P. Leonhardt* [1985] 2 Lloyd's Rep. 28; *Att-Gen of Hong Kong v Humphreys Estate (Queen's Gardens) Ltd* [1987] A.C. 114; *Matharu v Matharu, The Times*, May 13, 1994 CA; *Baird Textiles Holdings Ltd v Marks & Spencer Plc* [2002] 1 All E.R. (Comm) 737. See also above, para.3–138.

559 cf. *Pauling's Settlement Trusts* [1964] Ch. 303 (where it was held that a claimant cannot be held to have acquiesced unless he knew, or ought to have known, what his rights were). See also *Re Howlett* [1949] 1 Ch. 767, 775. As regards laches, see below, para.28–140.

ground of laches. What amounts to reasonable diligence and what circumstances will render it inequitable to grant the relief will vary with the type of relief sought and the facts of the particular case.

28–138 **Statements of the doctrine.** The most authoritative statement of the doctrine is that of Lord Selborne in *Lindsay Petroleum Co v Hurd*[560]:

> "Now the doctrine of laches in courts of equity is not an arbitrary or a technical doctrine. Where it would be practically unjust to give a remedy, either because the party has, by his conduct, done that which might be fairly regarded as equivalent to a waiver of it, or where by his conduct and neglect he has, though perhaps not waiving that remedy, yet put the other party in a situation in which it would not be reasonable to place him if the remedy were afterwards to be asserted, in either of these cases, lapse of time and delay are most material. But in every case, if an argument against relief which otherwise would be just, is founded on mere delay, that delay of course not amounting to a bar by any Statute of Limitations, the validity of that defence must be tried upon principles substantially equitable. Two circumstances always important in such cases, are, the length of the delay and the nature of the acts done during the interval, which might affect either party and cause a balance of justice or injustice in taking the one course or the other, so far as relates to the remedy."

In *Erlanger v New Sombrero Phosphate Co*[561] Lord Blackburn, after quoting this statement with approval, went on to say:

> "I have looked in vain for any authority which gives a more distinct and definite rule than this; and I think, from the nature of the inquiry, it must always be a question of more or less, depending on the degree of diligence which might reasonably be required, and the degree of change which has occurred, whether the balance of justice or injustice is in favour of granting the remedy or withholding it. The determination of such a question must largely depend on the turn of mind of those who have to decide, and must therefore be subject to uncertainty; but that, I think, is inherent in the nature of the inquiry."[562]

28–139 **Delay where statute applies.** Delay short of the statutory period is ordinarily no bar in cases where a statutory limitation provision is applicable either directly or by analogy.[563] In such cases the claimant is entitled to the full statutory period, though the court retains an equitable jurisdiction to refuse relief on the ground of

---

[560] (1874) L.R. 5 P.C. 221, 239 (wrongly attributed in the report to Sir Barnes Peacock).

[561] (1878) 3 App. Cas. 1218, 1279.

[562] These statements by Lord Selborne and Lord Blackburn have often been cited with approval: see, e.g. *Re Sharpe* [1892] 1 Ch. 154, 168; *Rochefoucald v Boustead* [1897] 1 Ch. 196, 210–211; *Weld v Petre* [1929] 1 Ch. 33, 51–52, 63; *Agbeyegbe v Ikomi* [1953] 1 W.L.R. 263, 266–267; *Nwakobi v Nzekwu* [1964] 1 W.L.R. 1019, 1025; *Nelson v Rye* [1996] 1 W.L.R. 1378, 1392; *Frawley v Neill, The Times*, April 5, 1999.

[563] *Archbold v Scully* (1861) 9 H.L.C. 360, 383; *Knox v Gye* (1872) L.R. 5 H.L. 656; *Fullwood v Fullwood* (1878) 8 Ch D 176; *Re Baker* (1881) 20 Ch D 230; *Re Maddever* (1884) 27 Ch D 523; *Re Pauling's Settlement Trusts* [1964] Ch. 303, 353; *Re Loftus* [2006] EWCA Civ 1124, [2007] 1 W.L.R. 1124 at [37]. See also *P & O Nedlloyd BV v Arab Metals Co, The UB Tiger* [2006] EWCA Civ 1717, [2007] 1 W.L.R. 2288 (where the case was not one of laches by mere delay). But if a limitation period applies by analogy to rescission, laches short of that may bar that remedy: see paras 28–135, 28–144.

acquiescence or otherwise.[564] In contrast, laches, as well as acquiescence, is not precluded by a section in the Limitation Act (for example, s.21(1)) which lays down that there is no limitation period prescribed by the Act.[565]

Awareness of facts. The claimant must be aware of the relevant facts[566] (though he need not know of the exact nature of his rights[567]) and therefore there is no question of laches while the claimant is under disability[568] or undue influence.[569] The principle that ignorance negatives laches may account for the fact that delay will not count against the claimant where the existence of the material cause of action has been concealed from him by fraud or unconscionable behaviour on the part of the defendant[570] or where he is under a mistake.[571] Alternatively it could be said that, in such circumstances, it would not be just or reasonable to deprive the claimant of the relief to which he would otherwise be entitled.[572] 28–140

Prejudice to defendant. It is a relevant subject for inquiry whether the claimant's delay has prejudiced the defendant, e.g. if he has lost the evidence necessary to rebut the claim or has been spending money on the property to the knowledge of the claimant.[573] If the defendant has not been so prejudiced, and no third parties are involved, the court may well treat the claimant's delay as immaterial.[574] In *Nelson v Rye*[575] Laddie J. left open the question whether a defendant must prove a causal link between the delay and prejudice of which he complains. 28–141

Mere delay. Statements may be found suggesting that mere delay will not bar the claimant's claim if there is no evidence of acquiescence on his part or of prejudice to the defendant. Thus, in *Life Association of Scotland v Siddal*[576] Turner L.J. said: 28–142

564 Limitation Act 1980 s.36(2).

565 *Re Loftus* [2006] EWCA Civ 1124, [2007] 1 W.L.R. 1124.

566 *Life Association of Scotland v Siddall* (1861) 3 De G.F. & J. 58, 74; *Lindsay Petroleum Co v Hurd* (1874) L.R. 5 P.C. 221, 241; *Allcard v Skinner* (1887) 36 Ch D 145, 188; *Re Howlett* [1949] Ch. 767, 775. cf. *Nelson v Rye* [1996] 1 W.L.R. 1378.

567 *Stafford v Stafford* (1857) 1 De G. & J. 193, 202; *Molloy v Mutual Reserve Life Insurance Co* (1906) 94 L.T. 756.

568 *Duke of Leeds v Earl of Amherst* (1846) 2 Ph. 117.

569 *Allcard v Skinner* (1887) 36 Ch D 145; *Bullock v Lloyds Bank Ltd* [1955] Ch. 317.

570 *Booth v Earl of Warrington* (1714) 4 Bro. P.C. 163; *Gibbs v Guild* (1882) 9 QBD 59; *Molloy v Mutual Reserve Life Insurance Co* (1906) 94 L.T. 756; *Oelkers v Ellis* [1914] 2 K.B. 139; *Armstrong v Jackson* [1917] 2 K.B. 822. See also above, para.28–084.

571 *Brooksbank v Smith* (1836) 2 Y. & C. Ex. 58; contrast *Denys v Shuckburgh* (1840) 4 Y. & C. Ex. 42, where the mistake could have been discovered with reasonable diligence. See also above, para.28–088.

572 *Turner v General Motors (Australia) Pty Ltd* (1929) 42 C.L.R. 352, 370.

573 *Turner v Collins* (1871) L.R. 7 Ch. 329; *Watts v Assets Co* [1905] A.C. 317, 333; cf. *Shaw v Applegate* [1977] 1 W.L.R. 970; *Nelson v Rye* [1996] 1 W.L.R. 1395, 1396.

574 *Gresley v Mousley* (1859) 4 De G. & J. 78, 95; *Beauchamp v Winn* (1873) L.R. 6 H.L. 232; *Re Garnett* (1885) 31 Ch D 1; *Blake v Gale* (1886) 32 Ch D 571, 578; *Re Sharpe* [1892] 1 Ch. 154, 168; *Re Lacey* [1907] 1 Ch. 330, 350; *Weld v Petre* [1929] 1 Ch. 33.

575 [1996] 1 W.L.R. 1378, 1396 (disapproved on other grounds in *Paragon Finance Plc v Thakerar & Co* [1999] 1 All E.R. 400, 415).

576 (1861) 3 De G.F. & J. 58, 72–73.

"Length of time where it does not operate as a statutory or positive bar operates, as I apprehend, simply as evidence of assent or acquiescence. The two propositions of a bar by length of time and by acquiescence are not, as I conceive, distinct propositions. They constitute but one proposition, and that proposition, when applied to a question of this description, is that the *cestui que trust* assented to the breach of trust."

But in the same case Lord Campbell, while expressing his concurrence with Turner L.J.'s statement, was careful to add that:

"... although the rule be that the onus lies on the party relying on acquiescence to prove the facts from which the consent of the cestui que trust is to be inferred, it is easy to conceive cases in which from great lapse of time, such facts might and ought to be presumed."[577]

It is submitted that the question always is whether, in the circumstances, it would be inequitable to grant relief by reason of the delay,[578] and it may be that if the claimant's delay is very great, his claim will be rejected as a stale demand without further inquiry.[579]

28–143 **Specific performance.** A person asking for specific performance of a contract seeks a discretionary remedy and has an option whether to pursue it or claim damages: he must therefore exercise his option promptly and show himself to be "ready, desirous, prompt and eager".[580] Unexplained delay of more than a few months is usually fatal: and this is especially true if the property is speculative or precarious or liable to fluctuate in value, e.g. a mine,[581] a public-house,[582] or a short leasehold interest.[583] However, it will be a sufficient explanation of the delay if the purchaser has been let into possession and requires merely to clothe his enjoyment of the property with the legal estate.[584] But this doctrine does not apply if the claimant was in possession under some other title than that of the contract which he seeks to enforce: for instance, if a tenant for years claims to exercise an option to purchase the freehold.[585]

28–144 **Rescission.** A person seeking to rescind a contract which is voidable for misrepresentation or otherwise has an election either to affirm or rescind the

[577] *Life Association of Scotland v Sidda* (1861) 3 De G.F. & J. 58, 77.

[578] *Parkin v Thorold* (1852) 16 Beav. 59, 73; *Clegg v Edmonson* (1857) 8 De G.M. & G. 787, 814; *Fitzgerald v Masters* (1956) 95 C.L.R. 420, 433; *Re Jarvis* [1958] 1 W.L.R. 815; *Lamshed v Lamshed* (1963) 109 C.L.R. 440, 453.

[579] Contrast *Brooks v Muckleston* [1909] 2 Ch. 519 (40 years' delay in foreclosing a mortgage of an advowson held to bar the claim) with *Weld v Petre* [1929] 1 Ch. 33 (18 years' delay in redeeming a mortgage of shares held not to bar the claim). In neither case was a statute of limitations applicable either expressly or by analogy. But see *Re Eustace* [1912] 1 Ch. 561.

[580] *Milward v Earl of Thanet* (1801) 5 Ves. 720n; *Eads v Williams* (1854) 4 D.M. & G. 674; *Oriental Inland Steam Co Ltd v Briggs* (1861) 4 De G.F. & J. 191, 194–195.

[581] *Eads v Williams* (1854) 4 D.M. & G. 674; cf. *Clegg v Edmondson* (1857) 8 De G.M. & G. 787.

[582] *Mills v Haywood* (1877) 6 Ch D 196.

[583] *Lehmann v McArthur* (1868) L.R. 3 Ch. App. 496.

[584] *Crofton v Ormsby* (1806) 2 Sch. & Lef. 583, 603; *Shepheard v Walker* (1875) L.R. 20 Eq. 659; *Williams v Greatrex* [1957] 1 W.L.R. 31 (where a delay of 10 years was held to be no bar).

[585] *Mills v Haywood* (1877) 6 Ch D 196.

contract. He must therefore act promptly if he wishes to rescind[586]: for it is inequitable that he should be allowed to wait and see whether it pays him to rescind or not, for that would be gambling on a certainty at the other party's expense. This is especially true of contracts for the sale or allotment of shares in companies, where the utmost promptness is required.[587] The allottee is not permitted to wait and see whether the company will prosper. Third persons may perhaps deal with the company on the faith of his being a member. Hence a delay of even a few weeks after discovery of the misrepresentation could be fatal. And it has been held that a buyer of goods could not rescind for innocent misrepresentation five years after the making of the contract, although he acted promptly as soon as he discovered the truth.[588]

Setting aside voluntary settlements. A person seeking to set aside a gift or voluntary settlement on the ground of undue influence is in a different position from one who seeks to rescind a commercial contract in that he takes no benefit from the transaction, and is therefore in a less equivocal position. Consequently, he is allowed a longer time in which to exercise his rights after the influence has ceased to operate and he becomes aware of the facts. But a delay of several years will raise an inference of acquiescence sufficient to defeat the claim.[589] Thus, in *Allcard v Skinner*[590] gifts made under religious influence by an inmate of a convent to the lady superior for the benefit of the sisterhood could not be recalled six years after she left the convent, changed her religion, and received independent advice: for there was not only inactivity but positive evidence of conduct amounting to confirmation of the gift. On the other hand, in *Bullock v Lloyds Bank*[591] a settlement made under the undue influence of her father by a young lady just of age was successfully impeached four years after the influence ceased and she became aware of her rights, during which time she unsuccessfully tried to persuade the trustee to exercise its power of revocation under the settlement. A longer time may be allowed for setting aside gifts made by mistake.[592] 28–145

Rectification. The rectification of deeds and contracts on the ground of mistake is subject to the doctrine of laches, but it seems that the claimant is allowed a longer time for claiming rectification than he is for setting aside a 28–146

---

586 *Lindsay Petroleum Co v Hurd* (1874) L.R. 5 P.C. 221; *Erlanger v New Sombrero Phosphate Co* (1878) 2 App. Cas. 1218; *Molloy v Mutual Reserve Life Insurance Co* (1906) 94 L.T. 756. See above, para.6–124. But see *Peyman v Lanjani* [1985] Ch. 457 (knowledge of right to rescind required).

587 *Taite's Case* (1867) L.R. 3 Eq. 795; *Sharpley v Louth and East Coast Ry* (1876) 2 Ch D 663; *Re Scottish Petroleum Co* (1883) 23 Ch D 413; *Aaron's Reefs Ltd v Twiss* [1896] A.C. 273, 294; *Taylor v Oil and Ozokerite Co* (1913) 29 T.L.R. 515; *First National Reinsurance Co Ltd v Greenfield* [1921] 2 K.B. 260; see above, para.6–127.

588 *Leaf v International Galleries* [1950] 2 K.B. 86; see above, para.6–127.

589 *Wright v Vanderplank* (1856) 8 De G.M. & G. 133 (10 years' delay a bar); *Turner v Collins* (1871) L.R. 7 Ch. App. 329 (nine years' delay a bar); *Allcard v Skinner* (1887) 36 Ch D 145 (six years' delay a bar); contrast *Bullock v Lloyds Bank Ltd* [1955] Ch. 317 (four years' delay not a bar).

590 (1887) 36 Ch D 145.

591 [1955] Ch. 317.

592 *Re Garnett* (1885) 31 Ch D 1 (20 years).

voluntary settlement or gift.[593] At any rate this is true if all parties have acted throughout on the claimant's version of what they really intended[594]: for in that case no one is prejudiced by the delay.

[593] *Wolterbeek v Barrow* (1857) 23 Beav. 423 (rectification allowed 34 years after date of deed and four years after discovery of mistake); *Turner v Collins* (1871) L.R. 7 Ch. App. 329 (rectification of voluntary settlement allowed though rescission barred).

[594] *M'Cormack v M'Cormack* (1877) 1 L.R. Ir. 119 (35 years' delay no bar); *Burroughes v Abbott* [1922] 1 Ch. 86 (12 years' delay no bar).

Part Nine
RESTITUTION

CHAPTER 29

RESTITUTION[1]

	PARA.
1. Introduction	29–001
(a) Nature of restitution	29–001
(b) Historical introduction	29–005
(c) The theoretical basis of restitution	29–009
2. Unjust enrichment	29–018
(a) The content of the unjust enrichment principle	29–018
(b) Enrichment	29–020
(c) At the expense of the claimant	29–025
(d) The grounds of restitution	29–028
(e) Mistake	29–029
(f) Failure of consideration	29–054
(g) Ultra vires receipts by the Revenue and public authorities	29–083
(h) Compulsion	29–087
(i) Necessity	29–130
(j) Exploitation	29–137
3. Restitution for wrongs	29–139
(a) General principles	29–139
(b) Tort	29–141
(c) Breach of contract	29–151
(d) Equitable wrongdoing	29–155
4. Proprietary restitutionary claims	29–158
(a) Establishing proprietary rights	29–158
(b) Following and tracing	29–162
(c) Proprietary restitutionary claims	29–170
5. Defences	29–176
(a) Estoppel	29–176
(b) Change of position	29–179
(c) Settlement of an honest claim	29–186
6. Miscellaneous restitutionary claims	29–191
(a) Account stated	29–191
(b) Account	29–193

[1] For a full treatment of the subject matter of this Chapter, see Birks, *An Introduction to the Law of Restitution* (1985); Virgo, *The Principles of the Law of Restitution*, 2nd edn (2006); Burrows, *The Law of Restitution*, 2nd edn (2002); Goff and Jones, *The Law of Restitution*, 7th edn (2007); Hedley and Halliwell (eds), *The Law of Restitution* (2002). See also Beatson, *The Use and Abuse of Unjust Enrichment* (1991); Burrows (ed.), *Essays on the Law of Restitution* (1991); Mitchell, "Unjust Enrichment" in Burrows (ed.), *English Private Law*, 2nd edn (2007); Maddaugh and McCamus, *The Law of Restitution*, 2nd edn (2004); Mason and Carter, *Restitution Law in Australia* (1995); Palmer, *The Law of Restitution* (1978) (four Vols); Stoljar, *The Law of Quasi-Contract*, 2nd edn (1989); *The American Law Institute's Restatement of the Law of Restitution, Quasi-Contracts and Constructive Trusts* (1937); Winfield, *The Law of Quasi-Contracts* (1952) (also his *Province of the Law of Tort* (1931), Ch.7).

1. INTRODUCTION

(a) *Nature of Restitution*[2]

29–001 **The essence of restitution.** The law of restitution is concerned with whether a claimant can claim a benefit from the defendant, rather than whether the claimant can be compensated for loss suffered. Restitutionary remedies are therefore distinct from those which are traditionally available in contract or in tort, as was recognised by Lord Wright[3]:

> "It is clear that any civilised system of law is bound to provide remedies for cases of what has been called unjust enrichment or unjust benefit, that is, to prevent a man from retaining the money of, or some benefit derived from, another which it is against conscience that he should keep. Such remedies in English law are generically different from remedies in contract or in tort, and are now recognised to fall within a third category of the common law which has been called quasi-contract or restitution."

The House of Lords has recognised that restitutionary remedies are available where the defendant has been unjustly enriched at the expense of the claimant.[4] It appears, however, that this is not the only principle which will trigger restitutionary remedies, since such remedies may also be awarded where the defendant has obtained a benefit by the commission of a wrong[5] or where the claimant can bring a claim to recover property held by the defendant in which the claimant has a proprietary interest.[6]

29–002 **Common law.** The obligation to make restitution can arise in a wide variety of situations, but their common framework is that they involve a special relationship between two persons where the law imposes a duty on one person to pay a sum of money or, exceptionally, to deliver specific property to another. This relationship is based either upon the involuntariness of the payment or transfer, its qualified nature, or the conduct of the transferee. A restitutionary claim resembles a contractual one in that liability is imposed upon one person to pay money or transfer property to another person, yet it differs radically in that restitutionary liability is imposed by the law irrespective of the agreement of the parties. Indeed, the law of restitution is subordinate to the law of contract in that, if a contractual relationship subsists between the parties, the contractual regime

---

[2] Burrows at pp.1–7; Goff and Jones at pp.3–12; Virgo at pp.1–18.

[3] *Fibrosa Spolka Akcyjna v Fairbairn Lawson Combe Barbour Ltd* [1943] A.C. 32, 61. See also Lord Wright of Durley, *Legal Essays and Addresses* (1939), p.6.

[4] *Lipkin Gorman (A Firm) Ltd v Karpnale* [1991] 2 A.C. 548. See also *Woolwich Equitable Building Society v IRC* [1993] A.C. 70; *Westdeutsche Landesbank Girozentrale v Islington LBC* [1996] A.C. 669; *Kleinwort Benson Ltd v Glasgow CC* [1999] 1 A.C. 153; *Banque Financière de la Cité v Parc Battersea Ltd* [1999] 1 A.C. 221; *Kleinwort Benson Ltd v Lincoln CC* [1999] 2 A.C. 349; *Foskett v McKeown* [2001] 1 A.C. 102; *Deutsche Morgan Grenfell Group Plc v IRC* [2006] UKHL 49, [2007] 1 A.C. 558.

[5] See below, paras 29–139 et seq.

[6] *Foskett v McKeown* [2001] 1 A.C. 102. See below, para.29–172.

will prevail.[7] Restitutionary liability, although like tortious liability in that it is imposed upon the defendant by operation of law, differs from such liability in that it need not be founded on the commission of any wrongdoing, although, as will be seen, such remedies are sometimes available where the defendant has profited from the commission of a tort.[8]

Equity. The common law has not been alone in providing restitutionary remedies. Equity independently developed some principles which are aimed at the same result of giving up to the claimant benefits obtained. In equity such restitutionary remedies may involve restoring value to the claimant or the return of property obtained or its traceable substitute. In equity restitutionary principles have been influential in a number of ways. First in the constructive trust, whereby a defendant is deemed to be a trustee of property for the claimant by operation of law, so that the claimant as beneficiary is able to recover what is due to him.[9] Secondly, the better developed rules of tracing in equity enable the claimant to recover property or its substitute from the defendant, despite being mixed with other property[10] Thirdly, there is the equitable remedy of an account of profits which involves the return of value to the claimant when the defendant has profited from the commission of an equitable wrong.[11] Fourthly, the equitable doctrine of acquiescence has enabled relief to be given to a person who has expended money on the property of another.[12] Fifthly, the equitable concept of unconscionability has proved important in the development of certain grounds of unjust enrichment, especially those relating to the exploitation of the claimant by the defendant.[13] In the United States these different principles of common law and equity have been amalgamated into a single topic in the law called "Restitution", as is evidenced by the volume published in 1937 entitled *The American Law Institute's Restatement of the Law of Restitution, Quasi-Contracts and Constructive Trusts*.[14] English lawyers are now aware of the interrelation of law and equity in the field of restitution,[15] and it has been said that, in the context 29–003

[7] *Guinness Plc v Saunders* [1990] 2 A.C. 663, 697–8 (Lord Goff); *Taylor v Motability Finance Ltd* [2004] EWHC 2619 (Comm) at [23] (Cooke J.); *Mowlem Plc v Stena Line Ports Ltd* [2004] EWHC 2206; *S and W Process Engineering Ltd v Cauldron Foods Ltd* [2005] EWHC 153 (TCC); *Lumbers v W Cook Builders Pty Ltd* [2008] HCA 27, para.46 (Gleeson C.J.). The contract itself may provide for a restitutionary (gain-based) remedy, but this is a contractual rather than a restitutionary remedy within the distinct law of restitution.

[8] See below, paras 29–141 et seq.

[9] See below, para.29–160.

[10] See below, para.29–164.

[11] See below, para.29–155.

[12] See below, para.29–161; *Ramsden v Dyson* (1866) L.R. 1 H.L. 83; *Plimmer v Wellington Corp* (1884) 9 App. Cas. 699, 710; *Blue Haven Enterprises Ltd v Tully* [2006] UKPC 17, see Watts (2006) 122 L.Q.R. 553. See also Birks at pp.277–279, 290–293. cf. Burrows (1988) 104 L.Q.R. 576, 583–586; and *The Law of Restitution*, p.123.

[13] See below, paras 29–137 et seq.

[14] Seavey and Scott (1938) 54 L.Q.R. 29; Winfield at p.529; Lord Wright, *Legal Essays and Addresses*, pp.34 et seq. For the history of the unjust enrichment principle in the United States see Kull [2005] O.J.L.S. 297.

[15] Winfield (1948) 64 L.Q.R. 46. See also Lord Wright (1936) 6 C.L.J. 305 (reprinted in his *Legal Essays and Addresses*, p.1); Holdsworth (1939) 55 L.Q.R. 37; *Nelson v Larholt* [1948] 1 K.B. 339, 343 (see also Denning (1949) 65 L.Q.R. 37); *Lipkin Gorman v Karpnale Ltd* [1991] 2 A.C. 548, 581; *Westdeutsche Landesbank Girozentrale v Islington LBC* [1994] 4 All E.R. 890 QB and CA, [1996] A.C. 669; *Tribe v Tribe* [1996] Ch. 107; Birks at pp.32–33, 71–72, 81–82, 154–156, 163–164, 277–279, 359–362, 420–423; Goff and Jones at p.11, Chs 3, 7, 11, 33 and 34; Virgo (ed. Getzler),

of restitution for unjust enrichment, there is no need to treat the action for money had and received and an action for an equitable remedy "as any longer depending upon different concepts of justice".[16] Accordingly, in this Chapter some indication will be given of the scope of equitable claims and restitutionary remedies.

29–004 **Classification.** There is no generally accepted method of classifying the instances of restitution. Writers[17] have suggested various methods of classification, in lieu of the old method of classifying by the form of action used, e.g. the action for money had and received, the action for money paid, quantum meruit (for the value of services provided) or quantum valebat (for the value of goods transferred). But these causes of action were abolished by the Common Procedure Act 1852 and, whilst they are useful to describe the nature of the benefit obtained by the defendant, they do not assist in the definition of the cause of action.[17a] Alternatively, a pragmatic classification can be adopted with reference to the route by which a particular type of benefit was received,[18] such as "restitution" where the defendant is obliged to restore or pay for a benefit received from the claimant, "reimbursement" where the defendant is obliged to repay the claimant in respect of money paid by the claimant to a third person, "liability to account to the claimant" for money received from a third party and "recompense", such as quantum meruit claims for services rendered. But with the recognition of the unjust enrichment principle by the House of Lords and, further, the apparent recognition that the law of restitution is founded on three distinct principles, this pragmatic classification will not be adopted here, especially because the nature of the claim is typically affected neither by the nature of the benefit nor the route by which it was received. Consequently, the classification adopted in this chapter will focus on the nature of the underlying claim. The final section of this chapter consists of a number of miscellanous claims which might once have been treated as restitutionary, but are better now treated as analytically distinct. These claims are included in this chapter for convenience only.

Rationalizing Property, Equity and Trusts: Essays in Honour of Edward Burn (2003), Ch.5; Mason [2007] R.L.R. 1.

[16] *Westdeutsche Landesbank Girozentrale v Islington LBC* [1994] 4 All E.R. 890, 914 (Hobhouse J.); see also [1996] A.C. 669.

[17] Goff and Jones at pp.81–83; Winfield, *Province of the Law of Tort* (1931), pp.148–149 (also *Quasi-Contracts* (1952), pp.26–27); Clarence Smith (1956) 19 M.L.R. 255; Munkman, *The Law of Quasi-contracts* at pp.19–20; Birks at pp.99–108; Burrows at pp.1–15; Virgo at pp.6–18.

[17a] In *Yeoman's Row Management Ltd v Cobbe* [2008] UKHL 55 the House of Lords recognised a distinct restitutionary claim in quantum meruit but without explaining what needed to be proved to establish such a claim or how it differed from a claim in unjust enrichment which was also recognised, as was a claim for a consideration which has wholly failed. The better view is that these all form the same cause of action which is properly characterised as one in unjust enrichment.

[18] As adopted in some of the earlier editions of this work.

(b) *Historical Introduction*[19]

Writs of assumpsit, debt and account. Although the origin of the action of assumpsit was some positive act of negligent misfeasance, it had become the regular remedy for breaches of contract at the beginning of the seventeenth century, and so was considered as the main remedy to enforce consensual obligations. The action of debt was an alternative remedy to enforce such obligations, but it was also used to remedy some claims which were not based on consent, such as claims for a liquidated sum of money due as a penalty under a statute, as a forfeiture under a by-law, as a customary fine or levy, or as a judgment debt. Debt also lay to recover money which had been paid to the defendant for a specific purpose (e.g. to pay to a third person) which the defendant had failed to carry out.[20] The old action of account also embraced some obligations which were not necessarily contractual: in general, it lay to enforce the duty of a guardian, bailiff or receiver to account to the plaintiff for moneys received on his behalf.[21] But by the development of the notion of a "constructive" receiver, account came to be used to recover money paid under a mistake, or money paid for a consideration which had wholly failed.[22] Thus account as well as debt covered some instances of liability to pay money imposed by operation of the law, and not voluntarily assumed under an agreement. 29–005

Development of *indebitatus assumpsit.* However, following *Slade's Case*,[23] *indebitatus assumpsit* became a complete alternative to the old writ of debt, and it inherited the wide scope of debt over not only consensual obligations but also some obligations classified in modern law as restitutionary. The rapid development of *indebitatus assumpsit* in the seventeenth century led to cases where the court permitted the newer and better remedy to replace debt and also account for non-contractual claims, e.g. to recover customary dues levied on foreign goods exposed for sale,[24] and to recover a customary fine due to the plaintiff as lord of the manor.[25] In some respects, *indebitatus assumpsit* extended the scope of restitutionary remedies: it was allowed upon a quantum meruit to claim a reasonable remuneration where the plaintiff had rendered services or supplied goods to the defendant at the latter's request, but the parties had not fixed the sum 29–006

---

[19] Goff and Jones at pp.3–11; Jackson, *History of Quasi-Contract* (1936); Winfield, *Quasi-Contracts* (1952), pp.1–25; Holdsworth, *History of English Law*, Vol.VIII, pp.88–98; Simpson, *A History of the Common Law of Contract* (1975), pp.489 et seq.; Baker, *An Introduction to English Legal History* (2002), 4th edn, Ch.21; Baker and Milsom, *Sources of English Legal History* (1986), pp.463–481; Birks and McLeod (1986) 6 O.J.L.S. 46; Ibbetson, *A Historical Introduction to the Law of Obligations* (1999), Part 4.

[20] Fifoot, *History and Sources of the Common Law: Tort and Contract* at pp.222–223; Baker at p.362; Ibbetson, *Law of Obligations*, pp.132–133. In modern law the term used would be "paid on a consideration which had wholly failed".

[21] Fifoot at pp.268 et seq. See Stoljar (1964) 80 L.Q.R. 203.

[22] Fifoot at pp.272–273; Baker at pp.363–365.

[23] (1602) 4 Co. Rep. 91a, 92b. See Simpson (1958) 74 L.Q.R. 381; Fifoot at pp.281 et seq., 489 et seq.; Baker [1971] C.L.J. 51, 213; Ibbetson (1984) 4 O.J.L.S. 295.

[24] *City of London v Goree* (1677) 2 Levinz 174, 3 Keble 677. (The phrase "*quasi ex contractu*" was used in the judgment.)

[25] *Shuttleworth v Garnett* (1688) 3 Mod. 240, 3 Lev. 261. See also *City of York v Toun* (1700) 5 Mod. 444, 2 Ld. Raym. 502.

to be paid, although it was obvious in the circumstances that neither party intended the services to be gratuitous, or the goods to be a gift.[26] *Indebitatus assumpsit* soon was employed to remedy many widely differing situations, often under the common formula that the sum of money claimed was "had and received to the use of the plaintiff". Thus it lay to recover money paid under a mistake,[27] or extorted from the plaintiff by duress of his goods,[28] or paid to the defendant on a consideration which totally failed,[29] or to recover profits received by the defendant while wrongfully usurping an office belonging to the plaintiff,[30] or as an alternative remedy to trover for the tort of conversion.[31]

29–007 **Implied promise.** It was only by historical accident that all these causes of action were based on the common remedy of *indebitatus assumpsit*, and the courts treated the alleged promise to pay as purely fictitious. The "promise" or obligation to pay was imposed by the law, and any genuine promise was plainly contrary to the facts, especially when the defendant was actually a tortfeasor. Lord Atkin, referring to such a case, said[32]:

> "... it was necessary to create a fictitious contract: for there was no action possible other than debt or assumpsit on the one side and action for damages for tort on the other... The law, in order to do justice, imputed to the wrongdoer a promise which alone as forms of action then existed could give the injured person a reasonable remedy... These fantastic resemblances of contracts invented in order to meet requirements of the law as to forms of action which have now disappeared should not in these days be allowed to affect actual rights."

But even though the allegation of a "promise" within the action of *indebitatus assumpsit* for money had and received to the use of the plaintiff was treated as ficititious by the courts, after the abolition of the forms of action by the Common Law Procedure Act 1852 some courts considered that the contractual framework of these actions was not merely a matter of procedure but was one of substantive law. The most important statement of this view was in *Sinclair v Brougham*[33] where Lord Sumner said:

> "All these causes of action are common species of the genus '*assumpsit.*' All now rest, and long have rested, upon a notional or imputed promise to pay."

In *Sinclair v Brougham* a building society carried on an ultra vires banking business. On the winding up of the society, the House of Lords held that the depositors could not sue in a common law action for money had and received,

---

[26] Fifoot at pp.360–363. Quantum meruit was introduced especially to cover services rendered by innkeepers, common carriers, and others exercising a "common calling". See *Warbrook v Griffin* (1609) 2 Brownlow 254; *Rogers v Head* (1610) Cro.Jac. 262.

[27] *Tomkyns v Barnet* (1693) Skin. 411.

[28] *Astley v Reynolds* (1731) 2 Strange 915.

[29] *Martin v Sitwell* (1690) 1 Show. 156.

[30] *Howard v Wood* (1680) 2 Levinz 245.

[31] *Lamine v Dorrell* (1705) 2 Ld. Raym. 1216.

[32] *United Australia Ltd v Barclays Bank Ltd* [1941] A.C. 1, 27–29.

[33] [1914] A.C. 398, 452.

since the law could not imply a promise to repay where an actual promise would have been ultra vires the society:

> "The law cannot *de jure* impute promises to repay, whether for money had and received or otherwise, which, if made *de facto*, it would inexorably avoid."[34]

But it is clear that the "notional or imputed promise" mentioned by Lord Sumner was:

> "... a legal fiction, intrinsically bound up with the defunct action of assumpsit and expressly abolished by s.49 of the Common Law Procedure Act 1852."[35]

Lord Wright said that Lord Sumner's observation "was not necessary for the decision of the case". He did not understand why or how Lord Sumner's statement "closed the door to any theory of unjust enrichment in English law":

> "It would indeed be a *reductio ad absurdum* of the doctrine of precedents. In fact, the common law still employs the action for money had and received as a practical and useful, if not complete or ideally perfect, instrument to prevent unjust enrichment, aided by the various methods of technical equity which are also available, as they were found to be in *Sinclair v Brougham*."[36]

The fate of the implied contract theory. The "implied contract" theory found other judicial and academic support since *Sinclair v Brougham*,[37] but has been severely criticised as artificial by many judges and writers.[38] The implied 29–008

[34] [1914] A.C. 398, 452 (see also at 415, 417). The House, however, was able to extend an equitable proprietary claim to the case, and to give "a sort of rough justice" by dividing the assets pari passu between the shareholders and the depositors in proportion to the sums which they had severally contributed. On this aspect of the case, see below, para.29–172, and see generally above, para.9–025.

[35] Munkman, *Quasi-Contracts*, p.8.

[36] *Fibrosa Spolka Akcyjna v Fairbairn Lawson Combe Barbour Ltd* [1943] A.C. 32, 64.

[37] See, for example, *Morgan v Ashcroft* [1938] 1 K.B. 49, 62–63 (Lord Greene M.R., contra Scott L.J. at 75–77); *Transvaal and Delagoa Bay Investment Co Ltd v Atkinson* [1944] 1 All E.R. 579; *Re Diplock* [1947] 1 Ch. 716, 724 (Wynn-Parry J.); [1948] Ch. 465, 480–481 CA; *Bossevain v Weil* [1950] A.C. 327, 341 (Lord Radcliffe); *Reading v Att-Gen* [1951] A.C. 507, 513 (Lord Porter); *Ministry of Health v Simpson* [1951] A.C. 251, 275 (Lord Simonds); *Orakpo v Manson Investments Ltd* [1978] A.C. 95, 104 (Lord Diplock); *Stoke on Trent CC v Wass* [1988] 1 W.L.R. 1406; *Guinness Plc v Saunders* [1990] 2 A.C. 663, 689 (Lord Templeman); *Taylor v Bhail* [1996] C.L.C. 377.

[38] *Brooks Wharf and Bull Wharf Ltd v Goodman Bros* [1937] 1 K.B. 534, 545; *United Australia Ltd v Barclays Bank Ltd* [1941] A.C. 1, 27–29 (Lord Atkin); *Fibrosa Spolka Akcyjna v Fairbairn Lawson Combe Barbour Ltd* [1943] A.C. 32, 61–64 (Lord Wright); *Nelson v Larholt* [1948] 1 K.B. 339, 343 (Denning J.); *Larner v LCC* [1949] 2 K.B. 683; *Kiriri Cotton Co Ltd v Dewani* [1960] A.C. 192, 204–205; Denning (1949) 65 L.Q.R. 37; *Hussey v Palmer* [1972] 1 W.L.R. 1286; *Att-Gen v Nissan* [1970] A.C. 179, 228 (Lord Pearce) (approving Winn L.J.'s dicta in [1968] 1 Q.B. 286, 352); *Lipkin Gorman v Karpnale Ltd* [1991] 2 A.C. 548, 559, 578 (Lord Goff); *Woolwich Equitable B.S. v IRC* [1993] A.C. 70, especially 196–197 (Lord Browne-Wilkinson); *Westdeutsche Landesbank Girozentrale v Islington LBC* [1996] A.C. 669, especially 710 (Lord Browne-Wilkinson) (see also at 688 (Lord Goff), 718 (Lord Slynn), 720 (Lord Woolf), 738 (Lord Lloyd)); *Kleinwort Benson Ltd v Lincoln CC* [1999] 2 A.C. 349. See also Lord Wright (1938) 6 Camb. L.J. 305 (reprinted in his *Legal Essays and Addresses*, pp.1–33).

contract theory does not elucidate the vital question, which is: "In what circumstances will the law impose restitutionary liability"? Furthermore, not all cases in which an action for money had and received or a quantum meruit has succeeded are consistent with the theory.[39] It was "unequivocally and finally" rejected by the House of Lords in *Westdeutsche Landsbank Girozentrale v Islington LBC*.[40]

(c) *The Theoretical Basis of Restitution*

29–009 **Introductory.** For many years the theoretical basis of restitutionary liability has been controversial. Although in most cases a claimant must bring his claim under a recognised head of liability and not rely on a sweeping generalisation, the underlying theory needs to be examined since it influences the development of the subject, especially when a court is asked to extend or restrict the scope of a specific rule in restitution. Thus, in one case, the fact that no general theory was accepted led the court to reject the relevance of arguments by analogy[41] whereas in another the acceptance of an underlying principle led to the recognition of a new defence.[42] The search is not to discover a precise rule on which liability in restitution can be tested, but to discover theoretical principles or common factors which underlie the categories of restitution which already exist.

29–010 **Two main theories.** The implied contract theory was once influential as providing a theoretical foundation for the subject, but it is now discredited as artificial, based on a fiction and misleading and has been rejected by the courts.[43] More recently the controversy about the proper theoretical basis for the law of restitution has focused on two alternative theories. The first is unjust enrichment, whereby the law of restitution is equated with the unjust enrichment principle, so that restitutionary remedies are only available where the defendant has been unjustly enriched at the expense of the claimant. The second is a composite theory whereby restitutionary remedies are available either where the defendant has been unjustly enriched, or where the defendant has profited from the commission of a relevant wrong or where the defendant has interfered with the claimant's proprietary rights. Although recent authority is consistent with the second theory,[44] the first theory still has strong proponents. There are also other theories

[39] *Craven Ellis v Cannons Ltd* [1936] 2 K.B. 403; *Brook's Wharf and Bull Wharf Ltd v Goodman Bros* [1937] 1 K.B. 534. See also *Re Rhodes* (1890) 44 Ch D 94, 105. But cf. *Guinness Plc v Saunders* [1990] 2 A.C. 663 (Lord Templeman) for apparent acceptance of implied contract as the basis of quantum meruit claims.

[40] [1996] A.C. 669, 710 (Lord Browne-Wilkinson). See also at 718, (Lord Slynn), 720 (Lord Woolf), 738 (Lord Lloyd). See also *Kleinwort Benson Ltd v Glasgow CC* [1999] 1 A.C. 153; *Roxborough v Rothmans of Pall Mall Australia Ltd* (2002) 76 A.L.J.R. 203, High Ct of Australia at [20], per Gleeson C.J., Gaudron and Hayne JJ.; at [63], per Gummow J.; and at [156]–[164], per Kirby J.

[41] *Orakpo v Manson Investments Ltd* [1978] A.C. 95. See below, paras 29–079, 29–173. For criticism of this see Davies (1978) 41 M.L.R. 330, 334. cf. *Spottiswood's* case (1855) 6 De G.M. & G. 345, 371–372, below, para.29–122; *Pavey and Matthews Pty Ltd v Paul* (1986–1987) 162 C.L.R. 221, 256–257 (Deane J.).

[42] *Lipkin Gorman v Karpnale Ltd* [1991] 2 A.C. 548. See below, paras 29–179—29–185.

[43] See above, para.29–008.

[44] See especially *Foskett v McKeown* [2001] A.C. 102.

relating to the subject, including some adherents to the implied contract theory and others who argue that the true basis of a number of situations in which restitution is granted is a principle by which the claimant's reasonable reliance on a defendant's words or conduct is protected.[45]

The principle of unjust enrichment. The American Law Institute's *Restatement of the Law of Restitution, Quasi-Contracts and Constructive Trusts* concisely states that "a person who has been unjustly enriched at the expense of another is required to make restitution to the other".[46] Although there is no general cause of action in English law for unjust enrichment, it has been explicitly recognised by the House of Lords in *Lipkin Gorman v Karpnale Ltd* that the concept of unjust enrichment lies at the heart of, and is the principle underlying, the individual instances in which the law does give a right of recovery in restitution.[47] However, despite the strong support of several judges including Lords Wright,[48] Atkin,[49] Denning,[50] Pearce[51] and Goff[52] and numerous academic writers,[53] the precise shape of English law has until recently been formed against a background of scepticism.[54] 29–011

---

[45] Fuller & Purdue (1936) 46 Yale L.J. 52; Atiyah, *The Rise and Fall of Freedom of Contract* (1979), pp.764 et seq.; Beatson, *The Use and Abuse of Restitution* (1991), Ch.2; Stoljar, *The Law of Quasi-Contract*, 2nd edn, pp.9–10. Goff and Jones recognise that not all the instances of restitution they deal with are based on benefit to or enrichment of the defendant; see at pp.22–24, 28 and Ch.26.

[46] (1937), para.1. See Kull [2005] O.J.L.S. 297.

[47] [1991] 2 A.C. 548, 559, 578. See also *Woolwich Equitable B.S. v IRC* [1993] A.C. 70, especially 196–197 (Lord Browne-Wilkinson); *Westdeutsche Landesbank Girozentrale v Islington LBC* [1996] A.C. 669, especially 710 (Lord Browne-Wilkinson) (see also at 688 (Lord Goff), 718 (Lord Browne-Wilkinson), 720 (Lord Woolf), 738 (Lord Lloyd)); *Kleinwort Benson Ltd v Lincoln CC* [1999] 2 A.C. 349. These built on *Fibrosa Spolka Akcyjna v Fairbairn Lawson Combe Barbour* [1943] A.C. 32, especially Lord Wright at 61 (quoted at para.29–001, above).

[48] *Brook's Wharf and Bull Wharf Ltd v Goodman Bros* [1937] 1 K.B. 534, 545; *Fibrosa Spolka Akcyjna v Fairbairn Lawson Combe Barbour Ltd* [1943] A.C. 32, 61–64; Lord Wright (1938) 6 Camb. L.J. 305 (reprinted in his *Legal Essays and Addresses*, pp.1–33).

[49] *United Australia Ltd v Barclays Bank Ltd* [1941] A.C. 1, 27–29.

[50] *Nelson v Larholt* [1948] 1 K.B. 339, 343; *Larner v LCC* [1949] 2 K.B. 683; *Kiriri Cotton Co Ltd v Dewani* [1960] A.C. 192, 204–205; (1949) 65 L.Q.R. 37; *Hussey v Palmer* [1972] 1 W.L.R. 1286.

[51] *Att-Gen v Nissan* [1970] A.C. 179, 228 (approving Winn L.J.'s dicta in [1968] 1 Q.B. 286, 352).

[52] As well as *Lipkin Gorman v Karpnale Ltd* [1991] 2 A.C. 548 and *Woolwich Equitable B.S. v IRC* [1993] A.C. 70, see *B.P. (Exploration) Co (Libya) Ltd v Hunt (No.2)* [1979] 1 W.L.R. 788, 799 (Robert Goff J.); affirmed [1981] 1 W.L.R. 232 CA; [1983] 2 A.C. 352 HL; *British Steel Corp v Cleveland Bridge and Engineering Co Ltd* [1984] 1 All E.R. 504, 511 (Robert Goff J.); *Whittaker v Campbell* [1984] Q.B. 318, 327 (Robert Goff L.J.); *R. v Tower Hamlets LBC Ex p. Chetnik Developments Ltd* [1988] A.C. 858, 882 (Lord Goff).

[53] e.g. Winfield, *Province of the Law of Tort* (1931), pp.119–141 (also his *Quasi-Contracts* (1952), pp.9–23; (1937) 53 L.Q.R. 447; (1939) 55 L.Q.R. 161; [1932] *Bell Yard* 32); Munkman, at pp.7–20; Friedmann (1937) 53 L.Q.R. 449; also (1938) 16 Can. Bar Rev. 247, 365; Birks at pp.34–39; Burrows at pp.5–7.

[54] *Orakpo v Manson Investments Ltd* [1978] A.C. 95, 104 (Lord Diplock). See also *Bossevain v Weil* [1950] A.C. 327, 341 (Lord Radcliffe); *Reading v Att-Gen* [1951] A.C. 507, 513 (Lord Porter); *Ministry of Health v Simpson* [1951] A.C. 251, 275 (Lord Simonds); *Stoke on Trent CC v Wass* [1988] 1 W.L.R. 1406; *Guinness Plc v Saunders* [1990] 2 A.C. 663, 689 (Lord Templeman), and the academic adherents of the implied contract theory; Holdsworth (1939) 55 L.Q.R. 37 (cf. Winfield at p.161); Landon (1937) 53 L.Q.R. 302; Landon [1931] *Bell Yard* 19; Gutteridge (1934) 5 Camb. L.J.

29–012 **The action for money had and received.** In 1760 Lord Mansfield sought to rationalise the action for money had and received to the use of the claimant in the following well-known passage[55]:

> "This kind of equitable action to recover back money which ought not in justice to be kept is very beneficial, and therefore much encouraged. It lies for money which, *ex aequo et bono*, the defendant ought to refund; it does not lie for money paid by the plaintiff, which is claimed of him as payable in point of honour and honesty, although it could not have been recovered from him by any course of law; as in payment of a debt barred by the Statute of Limitations, or contracted during his minority, or to the extent of principal and legal interest upon a usurious contract, or for money fairly lost at play: because in all these cases the defendant may retain it with a safe conscience, though by positive law he was debarred from recovering . . . [T]he gist of this kind of action is that the defendant, upon the circumstances of the case, is obliged by the ties of natural justice and equity to refund the money."

The equity (*aequum et bonum*) to which Lord Mansfield referred was not the technical system of equity of the Court of Chancery, but the *jus naturale* of the Roman law.[56] It was merely a synonym for "natural justice" and has for this reason often been criticised as vague and uncertain:

> "Whatever may have been the case 146 years ago, we are not now free in the twentieth century to administer that vague jurisprudence which is sometimes attractively styled 'justice as between man and man.' "[57]

29–013 **Judicial recognition.** The criticism that the principle of unjust enrichment is too vague to be of any practical use[58] overlooks the fact that there is a considerable body of case law dealing with the grounds of restitution, so that judges are not called upon to use their own sense of justice in order to apply or develop the law. The judges will follow the existing precedents, which cover most of the likely problems of restitution, and if an extension of the law is sought, the meaning to be attached to "unjust enrichment" will be gleaned from those precedents. Lord Mansfield's view of quasi-contractual obligation was accepted by many in the nineteenth century,[59] though it was attacked in the first half of the

---

204, 223–229; Radcliffe (1938) 54 L.Q.R. 24. See also Atiyah, *An Introduction to the Law of Contract*, 5th edn, pp.45–6; *Morris v Tarrant* [1971] 2 Q.B. 143, 160–162 (Lane J.). Allen (1938) 54 L.Q.R. 201 attempted to show that both unjust enrichment and constructive contract were essential to the law of quasi-contract.

[55] *Moses v Macferlan* (1760) 2 Burr. 1005, 1012. The actual decision in the case, which set aside the judgment of a competent court otherwise than by appeal, was not followed later: *Marriott v Hampton* (1797) 7 T.R. 269. See Winfield (1944) 60 L.Q.R. 341, 342–343. See also Lord Mansfield in *Towers v Barrett* (1786) 1 T.R. 133, 134; *Weston v Downes* (1778) 1 Dougl. (KB) 23, 24.

[56] *Baylis v Bishop of London* [1913] 1 Ch. 127, 137; *Sinclair v Brougham* [1914] A.C. 398, 417, 454–456 (Lord Sumner).

[57] *Baylis v Bishop of London* [1913] 1 Ch. 127, 140, per Hamilton L.J. See also *Holt v Markham* [1923] 1 K.B. 504, 513 (Scrutton L.J.).

[58] But the similar principles of the reasonable man and of public policy, which are frequently employed in the law of torts and contract (and are accepted by the legislature, e.g. s.2(2) of the Occupiers' Liability Act 1957) are not considered too vague. See Winfield (1928) 42 Harv. L.R. 97. See also the fundamental principle of proportionality within the law relating to human rights.

[59] e.g. *Kelly v Solari* (1841) 9 M. & W. 54; *Edwards v Bates* (1844) 7 Man. & G. 590; *Freeman v Jeffries* (1869) L.R. 4 Ex. 189, 199. See also Bullen & Leake, *Precedents of Pleadings*, 3rd edn (1868), p.44.

twentieth century by judicial[60] and academic[61] adherents of the "implied contract" theory. However, in recent years Lord Mansfield's approach has been strongly supported[62] and was relied on in the decisions of the House of Lords developing the law by recognising the defence of change of position, the liability to make restitution of ultra vires receipts of tax, and of money paid in pursuance of an ineffective contract.[63]

Statutory recognition. The unjust enrichment principle has also been recognised by statute. The Torts (Interference with Goods) Act 1977 s.7(4) imposes a liability to reimburse upon a person who, as a result of enforcement of a double liability in proceedings for wrongful interference with goods, is "unjustly enriched to any extent". Furthermore, the separation in the Insolvency Act 1986 s.382(4), of liabilities arising out of contract, tort, trust and bailment from those "arising out of an obligation to make restitution" may provide implicit support for the principle of unjust enrichment and the statutory power to refund overpayments of rates has been said to create "a statutory remedy of restitution ... to prevent the unjust enrichment of the rating authority at the expense of the ratepayer".[64] It has been recognised that the rationale of the Civil Liability (Contribution) Act 1978 is to ensure that a defendant is not unjustly enriched where the defendant's liability to a third party has been discharged by the claimant who is also liable to the third party.[65] Finally, statutory rights to recover overpaid tax are subject to the *defence* that repayment would unjustly enrich the claimant.[66] 29–014

The state of the unjust enrichment principle. In conclusion, it does not follow from the absence of a general cause of action in English law for unjust enrichment that the specific remedies provided are not justifiable by reference to the principle of unjust enrichment, even if they were originally framed without primary reference to it,[67] and the modern cases show an increasing tendency to cut through technicality to perceive and define the underlying principle.[68] In *Uren v First National Home Finance Ltd*[69] it was held that English law does not yet recognise a free-standing claim of unjust enrichment such that the claimant can simply plead an enrichment which is unjust. Rather, the claimant needs to 29–015

---

60 e.g. Lord Sumner in *Sinclair v Brougham* [1914] A.C. 398, 452–456; Greene M.R. in *Morgan v Ashcroft* [1938] 1 K.B. 49, 62–63 (contra Scott L.J. at 75–77); *Re Diplock* [1947] 1 Ch. 716, 724 (Wynn-Parry J.); [1948] Ch. 465, 480–481 CA.

61 Above, fn.54.

62 Above, para.29–011.

63 *Lipkin Gorman v Karpnale Ltd* [1991] 2 A.C. 548; *Woolwich Equitable B.S. v IRC* [1993] A.C. 70 and *Westdeutsche Landesbank Girozentrale v Islington LBC* [1996] A.C. 669 respectively.

64 *R. v Tower Hamlets LBC Ex p. Chetnik Developments Ltd* [1988] A.C. 858, 882 (Lord Goff). cf. *BP Exploration Co (Libya) Ltd v Hunt (No.2)* [1981] 1 W.L.R. 232, 243 (CA got "no help from the use of words which are not in the statute"—re the Law Reform (Frustrated Contracts) Act 1943 s.1(3)).

65 *Dubai Aluminium Co Ltd v Salaam* [2002] UKHL 48; [2003] 2 A.C. 366 at [76] (Lord Hobhouse).

66 Value Added Tax Act 1994 s.80(3) as amended. See *Marks and Spencer Plc v Commissioner of Customs and Excise* (C–309/09) (2008). See also below, para.29–086.

67 Dawson, *Unjust Enrichment* (1951), pp.116–117.

68 *Woolwich Equitable B.S. v IRC* [1993] A.C. 70, 166 (Lord Goff).

69 [2005] EWHC 2529 (Ch).

establish either that the claim falls within one of the recognised grounds of restitution or within a new ground which is a justifiable extension from the established grounds. English law has now joined US jurisdictions,[70] Australian law,[71] Canadian law,[72] Scots law,[73] French law[74] and Roman-Dutch law[75] in accepting the principle of unjust enrichment.

29–016 **Absence of basis.** The historical development of the subject has affected the way the principle manifests itself; thus English law has not recognised a general action for the recovery of money on the ground that it was not due, a *condictio indebiti*, but, as we shall see, has recognised specific grounds which a claimant seeking restitution must establish.[76] Professor Peter Birks in *Unjust Enrichment*, 2nd edn (2005) argued that there is a single reason for the reversal of unjust enrichment, namely the absence of legal justification for receipt of a benefit. In *Deutsche Morgan Grenfell Group Plc v IRC*[77] Lord Walker tentatively welcomed the absence of basis analysis of unjust enrichment, by virtue of which it is sufficient that the claimant can establish that there was no basis for the defendant's enrichment (such as a contract, gift or statutory obligation), although he did not adopt the absence of basis approach.[78] It follows that it remains necessary for the claimant to establish that the claim falls within one of the established grounds of restitution.[79]

29–017 **Different causes of action within restitution.** An alternative theory of restitution assumes that the award of restitutionary remedies is not confined to situations where the defendant has been unjustly enriched. Rather, restitutionary remedies are available by reference to three distinct principles. The first of these is the unjust enrichment principle itself. Secondly, such remedies may also be awarded where the defendant has benefited from the commission of some form

---

[70] e.g. *The American Law Institute's Restatement of the Law of Restitution, Quasi-Contracts and Constructive Trusts*, art.1 (and comment (c) thereon); J. P. Dawson, *Unjust Enrichment* (1951); Palmer, *The Law of Restitution* (1978) (four Vols). For earlier commentary, see *Woodward on Quasi-Contracts* (1913); *Keener on Quasi-Contracts* (1926).

[71] *Pavey and Matthews Pty Ltd v Paul* (1987) 69 A.L.R. 57. For an important attack on the validity of the principle in Australia, see Gummow J. in *Roxborough v Rothmans of Pall Mall Australia Ltd* (2002) 76 A.L.J.R. 203 High Ct of Australia, but cf. Beatson and Virgo (2002) 118 L.Q.R. 352. See also *Farah Constructions Pty Ltd v Say-Dee Pty Ltd* [2007] HCA 2 and *Matthew Lumbers v W. Cook Builders Pty Ltd* [2008] H.C.A. 27.

[72] *Deglman v Guaranty Trust Co of Canada* [1954] S.C.R. 725; *Pettkuss v Becker* [1980] 2 S.C.R. 834; *Rawluk v Rawluk* [1990] 1 S.C.R. 70; *Garland v Consumer's Gas Distributors Inc* [2004] 1 SCR 629; *Pacific National Investments Ltd v Corp of the City of Victoria* (2004) SCC 75.

[73] *Morgan Guaranty Trust Co of N.Y. v Lothian R.C.* (1995) S.C. 151, 229; *Shilliday v Smith* (1998) S.L.T. 976, 978.

[74] Gutteridge and David (1934) 5 Camb. L.J. 204.

[75] e.g. *Hussenabai Hassanally v Mohamed Muheeth Mohamed Cassim* [1960] A.C. 592; *Willis Faber Enthoven Ltd v Receiver of Revenue* (1992) (4) S.A. 202.

[76] See *NEC Semi-Conductors Ltd v IRC* [2006] EWCA Civ 25, [2006] S.T.C. 606 at [161] (Mummery L.J.); *Primlake Ltd (In Liquidation) v Matthews Associates* [2006] EWHC 1227 (Ch) at [335] (Lawrence Collins J.).

[77] [2006] UKHL 49, [2007]1 A.C. 558.

[78] See also Lord Hoffmann in *Deutsche Morgan Grenfell Group Plc* [2006] UKHL 49 at [21].

[79] See generally Burrows, "Absence of Basis: The New Birksian Scheme" in Burrows and Rodgers (eds), *Mapping the Law: Essays in Honour of Peter Birks* (2006), p.33; Baloch (2007) 123 L.Q.R. 636.

of wrongdoing, such as certain torts,[80] equitable wrongs[81] and, exceptionally, for breach of contract.[82] In such cases the cause of action is founded on the wrongdoing rather than unjust enrichment. Thirdly, restitution may also be awarded where the defendant has interfered with property in which the claimant has a legal or equitable proprietary interest. In such claims the underlying cause of action is the vindication of the claimant's property rights rather than unjust enrichment.[83] This latter principle remains controversial, with a number of jurists preferring to explain restitutionary claims to substitute property as founded on unjust enrichment.[84] How the claim is characterised matters as regards what needs to be proved to establish the claim and the application of defences.

2. UNJUST ENRICHMENT

(a) *The Content of the Unjust Enrichment Principle*

The elements of unjust enrichment. The principle of unjust enrichment requires: first, that the defendant has been enriched by the receipt of a benefit; secondly, that this enrichment is at the expense of the claimant; thirdly that the retention of the enrichment be unjust and finally that there is no defence or bar to the claim.[85] The development of the law of restitution in England has meant that the principle of unjust enrichment has not manifested itself in a general action for the recovery of money paid and other benefits conferred on the ground that they were not due,[86] but instead as a number of specific substantive grounds upon which restitution may be ordered. In *Moses v Macferlan* Lord Mansfield stated that the action for money had and received: 29–018

> " . . . lies for money paid by mistake; or upon a consideration which happens to fail; or for money got through imposition (express or implied); or extortion; or an undue advantage taken of the claimant's situation, contrary to the laws made for the protection of persons under those circumstances."[87]

Where a sum has been paid which is not due but the payer cannot establish a ground for recovery, it is not recoverable.[88] But the non-recognition of the

[80] See below, para.29–141.

[81] See below, para.29–155.

[82] See below, para.29–151. See Lord Millett, "*Jones v Jones* Property or Unjust Enrichment?" in Burrows and Rodgers (eds), *Mapping the Law* p.265.

[83] *Foskett v McKeown* [2001] 1 A.C. 102, 109 (Lord Browne-Wilkinson). See also 115 (Lord Hoffmann), 118 (Lord Hope) and 129 (Lord Millett). See below, para.29–172.

[84] See especially Birks [2001] C.L.P. 231; Burrows (2001) 117 L.Q.R. 412. cf. Lord Millett, *Mapping the Law: Essays in Honour of Peter Birks*, p.265.

[85] See *Banque Financière de la Cité v Parc (Battersea) Ltd* [1999] 1 A.C. 221, 234, per Lord Hoffmann, who added that a further question was whether there were any reasons of policy for denying a remedy. See also *Portman B.S. v Hamlyn Taylor Neck* [1998] 4 All E.R. 202, 206 (Millett L.J.); *Lloyds Bank Plc v Independent Insurance Co* [2000] Q.B. 110, 123 (Waller L.J.); *Rowe v Vale of White Horse D.C.* [2003] EWHC 388 (Admin), [2003] 1 Lloyd's Rep. 418; *McDonald v Coys of Kensington* [2004] EWCA Civ 47, [2004] 1 W.L.R. 2775.

[86] Birks [2001] C.L.P. 231; para.29–017, above.

[87] (1760) 2 Burr 1005, 1007.

[88] *Woolwich Equitable B.S. v IRC* [1993] A.C. 70, 165, 172 (Lord Goff); *Uren v First National Home Finance Ltd* [2005] EWHC 2529 (Ch) at [16], per Mann J. See above, para.29–016.

principle of unjust enrichment in the past has meant that the concepts of "benefit", "at the expense of the claimant" and "unjustness" of retention have tended to develop in a fragmented way within the substantive categories in which relief has been given[89] and sometimes, as in the former rules that only mistakes as to liability gave rise to restitution[90] and that in general a payment under a mistake of law was not recoverable,[91] in an unsatisfactory way.

29–019 **Defences and bars.** Where a ground of restitution is established, relief will nevertheless be denied if a recognised defence or bar is applicable.[92] Restitution will be denied where the defendant cannot be restored to his original position,[93] the claimant is estopped,[94] the defendant is a bona fide purchaser,[95] or where public policy precludes restitution.[96] It is also denied where the benefit was conferred:

(a) as a valid gift;

(b) pursuant to a valid common law, equitable or statutory obligation owed by the claimant to the defendant[97];

(c) by the claimant while performing an obligation owed to a third party[98];

(d) in submission to an honest claim, under process of law or a compromise of a disputed claim[99]; and

(e) by the claimant acting "voluntarily" or "officiously".[100]

In practice the most important of these are the requirements that the claimant is not a volunteer and that the defendant can be restored to his original position.

[89] For detailed discussion see the appropriate sections of this Chapter, below.

[90] See below, para.29–030.

[91] See below, para.29–041.

[92] See Goff and Jones at pp.53–81.

[93] This includes change of position by the defendant (below, para.29–179) and inability to make *restitution in integrum* of any benefit received by the claimant seeking restitution (above, paras 5–128, 6–115).

[94] See above, paras 3–085 et seq.; below, para.29–176.

[95] See below, para.29–175. On the relationship between bona fide purchase and change of position, see *Lipkin Gorman v Karpnale Ltd* [1991] 2 A.C. 548; Birks [1991] L.M.C.L.Q. 473; Millett (1991) 107 L.Q.R. 71, 82.

[96] See below, paras 29–039, 29–077. See also *R. Leslie Ltd v Sheill* [1914] 3 K.B. 607; *Boissevain v Weil* [1950] A.C. 327.

[97] *Brittain v Rossiter* (1879) 11 QBD 123, 127; *Gilbert & Partners v Knight* [1968] 2 All E.R. 248, 250 (Harman L.J.); *Pan Ocean Shipping Ltd v Creditcorp Ltd* [1994] 1 W.L.R. 161, 164, 165 (Lord Goff); *Portman B.S. v Hayman Taylor Neck* [1998] 4 All E.R. 202; Burrows [1994] Rest. L. Rev. 52; where the transaction is void see below, paras 29–074, 29–076.

[98] *Brown & Davies Ltd v Galbraith* [1972] 1 W.L.R. 997; *Pan Ocean Shipping Ltd v Creditcorp Ltd* [1994] 1 W.L.R. 161, 166, 170–171; *Esso Petroleum v Hall Russell & Co* [1989] A.C. 643; *Matthew Lumbers v W. Cook Builders Pty Ltd* [2008] H.C.A. 27.

[99] See above, para.7–028; below, paras 29–038, 29–186.

[100] Goff and Jones at pp.70–72. See *Falke v Scottish Imperial Insurance Co* (1886) 34 Ch D 234; *Ruabon S.S. Co v The London Assurance* [1990] A.C. 6, 10. See also *Owen v Tate* [1976] Q.B. 402; below, paras 29–109—29–112. cf. *G.N. Ry v Swaffield* (1874) L.R. 9 Ex. 132; *Matheson v Smiley* [1932] 2 D.L.R. 787.

(b) *Enrichment*

The nature of the enrichment.[101] This may take the form of a direct addition to the recipient's wealth, such as by the receipt of money,[102] or an indirect one, for instance where an inevitable expense has been saved. The most common example of the second type of benefit is the discharge of an obligation of the defendant, whether by paying his creditor[103] or abating a nuisance[104] or performing some other service[105] for which he is primarily responsible. 29–020

Non-monetary benefits. There have been difficulties in the development of restitutionary claims in respect of non-monetary benefits.[106] These are, in part, due to the fact that: 29–021

> " . . . by their very nature services cannot be restored: nor in many cases can goods be restored, for example where they have been consumed or transferred to another."[107]

Furthermore, even where the benefit takes the form of an increase in the value of the defendant's property, the increase can only be realised by forcing a sale.[108] In the case of the rendering of services as opposed to the payment of money, "the identity and value of the resulting benefit to the recipient may be debatable".[109] Services may take many forms and while some result in an indirect accretion to the defendant's wealth, for instance by improving his property, other "pure" services do not. The fact that services cannot be restored and the influence of the implied contract theory has meant that they were often not regarded as beneficial so as to give rise to a quantum meruit unless the defendant had requested the services or, knowing that they were to be paid for, had freely accepted[110] or

[101] Goff and Jones at pp.17–42; Birks at pp.114–132; Stevens, "Three Enrichment Issues" in *Mapping the Law*, p.65.

[102] *Kelly v Solari* (1841) 9 M. & W. 54 (below, para.29–030); *Brook's Wharf and Bull Wharf Ltd v Goodman Bros* [1937] 1 K.B. 534 (below, para.29–102).

[103] *Exall v Partridge* (1799) 8 T.R. 208 (below, para.29–103). See also *National Bank of Egypt International Ltd v Oman Housing Bank SAOC* [2002] EWHC 1760 (Comm), [2003] 1 All E.R. (Comm) 246.

[104] *Gebhardt v Saunders* [1892] 2 Q.B. 452 (below, para.29–107).

[105] Below, paras 29–121 et seq.

[106] Birks at pp.109–128; Jones (1977) 93 L.Q.R. 273

[107] *B.P. Exploration Co (Libya) Ltd v Hunt (No.2)* [1979] 1 W.L.R. 783, 799, affirmed by the House of Lords [1983] 2 A.C. 352.

[108] In *Greenwood v Bennett* [1973] 1 Q.B. 195 (below, para.29–053) a sale had, in fact, taken place. See also Goff and Jones at pp.244–247.

[109] *B.P. Exploration Co (Libya) Ltd v Hunt (No.2)* [1979] 1 W.L.R. 783, 799 (Robert Goff J.); affirmed by the Court of Appeal [1981] 1 W.L.R. 232 and by the House of Lords [1983] 2 A.C. 352 See also Birks at pp.109–128, 131–132; Burrows at pp.16–25; Virgo at pp.70–72; Jones (1977) 93 L.Q.R. 273; Goff and Jones at pp.20–28, 30–35; Barker (2001) 54 C.L.P. 255.

[110] But see now *Rowe v Vale of White Horse D.C.* [2003] EWHC 388 (Admin), [2003] 1 Lloyd's Rep. 418, 421 (Lightman J.) where free acceptance was recognised, obiter, as relevant to establish both an enrichment and a ground of restitution where home-owners had received sewerage services without charge. Free acceptance was not established on the facts because there had been no acquiescence by the defendant in the supply of services for a consideration. See also *McDonald v Coys of Kensington* [2004] EWCA Civ 47, [2004] 1 W.L.R. 2775 (free acceptance could be established on the facts) at [32] (Mance L.J.). See Goff and Jones at pp.20–24.

acquiesced in them.[111] Many, but not all, such cases are capable of analysis as a genuine implied contract.[112] These cases do not depend upon the service adding to the defendant's wealth; the service per se is treated as a benefit.[113] Thus, restitution has been given in respect of plans prepared in anticipation of the conclusion of a contract by a developer but rendered useless when the landowner decided not to proceed,[114] and in respect of work done by a person on his own property at the request of prospective tenants when negotiations for a lease broke down.[115] The better view is that that "if in fact the performance of services has conferred no benefit on the person requesting them, it is pure fiction to base restitution on a benefit conferred"[116] and it is more realistic to see the basis of liability as the protection of the claimant's reasonable reliance.[117] Restitution will not be given if the dealing between the parties shows that the risk is to be borne by the party rendering the services.[118]

29–022 **Service resulting in incontrovertible benefit.** There is also authority that treats a service as beneficial where it results in an "incontrovertible benefit" to the defendant.[119] With the possible exception of necessitous intervention to preserve life or health,[120] only services that result in an accretion to the defendant's wealth can constitute an incontrovertible benefit. Goff and Jones state that incontrovertible benefit is established:

---

[111] *Ellis v Hamlen* (1810) 3 Taunt 52, 53; *Nemes v Ata Chaglayan*, Unreported, October 11, 1982 CA; *Marston Construction Co Ltd v Kigass Ltd* [1989] 46 B.L.R. 109. cf. *Bookmakers Afternoon Greyhound Services Ltd v Wilfred Gilbert Staffordshire Ltd* [1994] F.S.R. 723, 742–744.

[112] Below, para.29–073. See *S and W Process Engineering Ltd v Cauldron Foods Ltd* [2005] EWHC 153 (TCC) at [51]–[55].

[113] *William Lacey (Hounslow) Ltd v Davis* [1957] 1 W.L.R. 932; *Brewer Street Investments Ltd v Barclay Woollen Co* [1954] 1 Q.B. 428, 433–434 (Somervell L.J.), 438 (Denning L.J.); *British Steel Corp v Cleveland Bridge and Engineering Co Ltd* [1984] 1 All E.R. 504. cf. *Sumpter v Hedges* [1898] 1 Q.B. 673; *Wiluszynski v Tower Hamlets LBC* [1989] I.C.R. 493. See also *Independent Grocers Co-operative Ltd v Noble Lowndes Superannuation Consultants Ltd* [1993] 60 S.A.S.R. 525. Below, paras 29–071, 29–073.

[114] *William Lacey (Hounslow) Ltd v Davis* [1957] 1 W.L.R. 932; *Sabemo v N. Sydney M.C.* [1977] 2 N.S.W.L.R. 880; *Marston Construction Co Ltd v Kigass Ltd* [1989] 46 B.L.R. 109; *Countrywide Communiations Ltd v ICL Pathway Ltd* [2000] C.L.C. 324; *Bridgewater v Griffiths* [2000] 1 W.L.R. 524; *Yeoman's Row Management Ltd v Cobbe* [2008] UKHL 55 (services in obtaining grant of planning permission).

[115] *Brewer St Investments Ltd v Barclays Woollen Co Ltd* [1954] 1 Q.B. 428.

[116] *Coleman Engineering v North American Aviation* (1967) 420 P2d 713, 729 (Traynor C.J.). See also Beatson, *Unjust Enrichment*, pp.21–44; Jones (1980) 18 U.W.Ont.L.R. 447. cf. Birks at pp.44–46, 271, 275.

[117] Above, para.29–010 fn.45.

[118] *Regalian Properties Plc v London Dockland Development Corp* [1995] 1 W.L.R. 212. See also *Bookmakers Afternoon Greyhound Services Ltd v Wilfred Gilbert Staffordshire Ltd* [1994] F.S.R. 723; *Matthew Lumbers v W. Cook Builders Pty Ltd* [2008] H.C.A. 27.

[119] *Craven-Ellis v Canons Ltd* [1936] 2 K.B. 403 (below, para.29–076); *Greenwood v Bennett* [1973] 1 Q.B. 195, 202 (Lord Denning), below, para.29–053; *Procter & Gamble Corp v Peter Cremer GmbH & Co* [1988] 3 All E.R. 843, 855–856 (Hirst J.); *Re Berkeley Applegate Ltd* [1989] Ch. 32, 50–51; *Rowe v Vale of White Horse DC* [2003] EWHC 388 (Admin), [2003] 1 Lloyd's Rep. 418, 421 (Lightman J.); *McDonald v Coys of Kensington* [2004] EWCA Civ 47, [2004] 1 W.L.R. 2775.

[120] *Matheson v Smiley* [1932] 2 D.L.R. 787; *G.N. Ry v Swaffield* (1874) L.R. 9 Ex. 132; below, paras 29–132 et seq.

"... if a reasonable person would conclude that he has been saved an expense which he otherwise would necessarily have incurred or where he has made, in consequence of the plaintiff's acts, a realisable financial gain."[121]

Receipt of goods. The receipt of goods may also constitute a benefit and, although where title has not passed to the recipient the proper claim will be in tort for wrongful interference to goods,[122] where title has passed it would seem that the principles governing services will apply by analogy and in an appropriate case result in the court awarding a *quantum valebat*.[123] 29–023

Interest. In *Sempra Metals (formerly Metallgesellschaft Ltd) Ltd v IRC*[124] the House of Lords held that a taxpayer which had paid tax too early in breach of EC law could establish that the Revenue had been unjustly enriched, with the enrichment consisting of the Revenue's use of the money until the tax was properly due. This enrichment was valued with reference to compound interest which the defendant would have had to pay to borrow an equivalent amount of money to that which had been received from the taxpayer and which, for the Revenue, was a rate which was lower than the commercial rate. This claim for the use value of money will be available for all unjust enrichment claims where money has been paid which was not due to the defendant. So, for example, any claimant who pays money by mistake has two restitutionary claims at common law, one for the amount paid and one for the defendant's use value of that money. Whilst not formally overruling *Westdeutsche Landesbank Girozentrale v Islington LBC*,[125] which had held that compound interest could only be awarded in respect of equitable claims, the House of Lords in *Sempra Metals* held, in *obiter dicta*, that compound interest should be generally available as of right for unjust enrichment claims at common law. 29–024

(c) *At the expense of the claimant*

Enrichment at the claimant's expense.[126] In many cases the increase in the defendant's wealth is the direct result of, and is matched by, a corresponding diminution in the claimant's wealth.[127] Sometimes this direct correspondence does not exist but restitution is still awarded. This will usually be by virtue of a principle other than unjust enrichment, such as the commission of a wrong where the defendant has profited from a third party in breach of a duty owed to the 29–025

---

[121] Goff and Jones at p.24. cf. Birks at pp.121–124 (only realised benefits suffice) and see Burrows at pp.18–20 and Virgo at pp.74–81. Now see *McDonald v Coys of Kensington* [2004] EWCA Civ 47, [2004] 1 W.L.R. 2775 (incontrovertible benefit where the benefit is readily returnable): at [37] (Mance L.J.).

[122] Torts (Interference with Goods) Act 1977. But see below, paras 29–141 et seq. (waiver of tort). See also proprietary restitutionary claims, below, paras 29–158 et seq.

[123] See Goff and Jones at p.28.

[124] [2007] UKHL 34, [2008] 1 A.C. 561.

[125] [1996] A.C. 669.

[126] *Halifax B.S. v Thomas* [1996] Ch. 217, 227 (Peter Gibson L.J.). Goff and Jones at pp.42–46; Burrows at pp.25–41; Virgo at Ch.5

[127] This is so in all cases of money paid; e.g. *Kelly v Solari* (1841) 9 M. & W. 54 (below, para.29–030); *Brook's Wharf and Bull Wharf Ltd* [1937] 1 K.B. 534 (below, para.29–102); *Uren v First National Home Finance Ltd* [2005] EWHC 2529 (Ch) at [22] (Mann J.).

claimant, or where the defendant has indirectly obtained property in which the claimant has a proprietary interest.

29–026 **The suggested need for "privity" between the parties.** One consequence of the implied contract theory was the view that the money sought to be recovered by an action for money had and received should have been received by the defendant under such circumstances as to create a privity between him and the claimant. It is difficult to say what this "privity" meant. It appears that an analogy was sought from the ordinary rules of contract. But the "implied contract" theory is based upon historical fictions which are no longer relevant, and has been rejected. Accordingly, this notion of "privity" is unnecessary in restitution. As Lord Wright said in one case[128]:

> "The obligation [to repay] is imposed by the court simply under the circumstances of the case and on what the court decides is just and reasonable having regard to the relationship of the parties. It is a debt or obligation constituted by the act of the law, apart from any consent or intention of the parties or privity of contract."

Winfield concluded[129] that most of the cases cited in support of the privity concept turn upon agency. They in fact lay down the rule of the law of agency that where the principal entrusts his agent with money to be paid to a third party, the latter cannot recover the money from the agent unless, on the facts, the agent has become also the agent of the third party.[130] Thus any mention of the absence of "privity" was unnecessary in these cases, most of which date from a period before the modern development of restitution.[131] The reference to "privity" may mean that a benefit received by the defendant is, as a general rule, not regarded as "at the claimant's expense" where conferred by a third party, so that restitution must be founded on the vindication of property rights instead.[132] In all other cases, however, the need for "privity" in this context should now be taken to mean simply that on the facts the claimant and defendant must have come into the factual relationship recognised by the appropriate rule of restitution, so that a direct obligation lies upon the defendant to make restitution to the claimant.[133] So, for example, where the defendant has intercepted an enrichment which would otherwise have been transferred to the claimant by a third party, this will be

---

[128] *Brook's Wharf and Bull Wharf Ltd v Goodman Bros* [1937] 1 K.B. 534, 545.

[129] *Quasi-Contracts* (1952), pp.14–17 (also his *Province of the Law of Tort* (1931), pp.134–138). See also Jackson, *History of Quasi-Contract* (1936) passim, especially pp.121–122.

[130] e.g. *Stephens v Badcock* (1832) 3 B. & Ad. 354; *Howell v Batt* (1833) 2 Nev. & M. (K.B.) 381; *Cobb v Beake* (1845) 6 Q.B. 930 (see also the other cases cited by Winfield, *Quasi-Contracts*, p.15). The agent may, on the facts, have appropriated the money to the third party: *Williams v Everett* (1811) 14 East. 582; *Moore v Bushell* (1827) 27 L.J. Ex. 3 (on this principle, see below, paras 29–194, 29–195).

[131] e.g. *Jones v Carter* (1845) 8 Q.B. 134 (a decision before the Gaming Act 1845 in which a stakeholder was held not liable to return a stake).

[132] See below, paras 29–158, 29–170.

[133] The New Zealand Court of Appeal has denied the need for any special "privity": *Thomas v Houston Corbett & Co* [1969] N.Z.L.R. 151.

treated as an enrichment at the expense of the claimant.[134] There must be some causal connection between the claimant and the defendant's enrichment.[135]

Rejection of "passing on" defence. In some cases the claimant is able to obtain restitution even though he has been able to pass on the loss, in the form of increased charges, to his customers.[136] In such cases a defence of "passing on" is not recognised, because the law is concerned with the enrichment of the defendant at the expense of the claimant and not with what happened to the claimant following the defendant's enrichment.[137] However, in *Marks and Spencer Plc v Commissioners of Customs and Excise*[138] Lord Walker of Westingthorpe recognised that passing on is recognised as a possible defence to any restitutionary claim. His Lordship cited *Roxborough v Rothmans of Pall Mall Australia Ltd*[139] in support of this conclusion, but that decision expressly rejected the passing on defence in Australia. 29–027

(d) *The grounds of restitution*[140]

The rationales of the grounds of restitution. There are a number of different grounds of restitution which operate to determine whether the defendant's receipt of an enichment can be considered to be unjust. These grounds of restitution have a number of different rationales. Some operate on the basis that the claimant's intention to benefit the defendant can be treated as absent, vitiated or qualified in some way. Others operate by virtue of the defendant's unconscionable conduct.[141] Still others exist by virtue of policy justifications.[142] The grounds of restitution are not closed.[143] The burden is placed on the claimant to establish the factor which renders it unjust for the defendant to retain an enrichment, rather than a burden being placed on the defendant to establish that it was unjust for a liability to be imposed on him.[144] 29–028

---

[134] See *Official Custodian for Charities v Mackey (No.2)* [1985] 1 W.L.R. 1308. See Birks at p.134; Virgo at pp.108–112. cf. Burrows at pp.35–38; Smith (1991) O.J.L.S. 481.

[135] *Uren v First National Home Finance Ltd* [2005] EWHC 2529 (Ch) at [23] (Mann J.).

[136] *Kleinwort Benson v Birmingham CC* [1997] Q.B. 380 See Burrows at pp.591–596; Virgo at Ch.25. See also *Mason v New South Wales* (1959) 102 C.L.R. 108, 146; *Roxborough v Rothmans of Pall Mall Australia Ltd* (2002) 76 A.L.J.R. 203 High Ct of Australia; *Kingstreet Investments Ltd v New Brunswick (Finance)* [2007] 1 S.C.R. 3 Supreme Ct of Canada; McInnes (2007) 123 L.Q.R. 365; Williams [2007] R.L.R. 130. See also Rush, *The Defence of Passing On* (2006).

[137] cf. the defence of change of position which is concerned with changes in the defendant's position following receipt of the enrichment. See below, para.29–179.

[138] [2005] UKHL 53, [2005] C.M.L.R. 3 at [25].

[139] *Marks and Spencer Plc v Commissioners of Custom and Excise* [2005] C.M.L.R. 3 at [25].

[140] Goff and Jones at pp.46–52; Burrows at pp.41–51; Virgo at Ch.6.

[141] See, for example, *Rowe v Vale of White Horse DC* [2003] EWHC 388 (Admin); [2003] 1 Lloyd's L.R. 418 where free acceptance was recognised as a ground of restitution, albeit not established on the facts, where services were provided in circumstances where the defendant had not rejected them when there was an opportunity to do so and the defendant, as a reasonable person, should have known that the claimant expected to be paid for the services.

[142] Restitution from public authorities on the ground of ultra vires receipt has been rationalised in this way. See below, para.29–083.

[143] *CTN Cash and Carry Ltd v Gallaher* [1994] 4 All E.R. 714, 720 (Sir Donald Nicholls V.C.).

[144] *Rowe v Vale of White Horse DC* [2003] 1 Lloyd's L.R. 418, 422 (Lightman J.). See also *Kleinwort Benson Ltd v Lincoln CC* [1999] 2 A.C. 349, 408 (Lord Hope); Chen-Wishart in Johnston and Zimmermann (eds), *Unjustified Enrichment* (2002) pp.159–193.

(e) *Mistake*[145]

29–029 **Enrichment.** Although most of the cases involving restitution for mistake concern money payments, there may be restitution of other benefits conferred as the result of a mistake, such as a transfer of property made under a mistake,[146] services rendered under a mistake,[147] such as improvements to land and chattels made as a result of a mistake[148] and where credit has been given in an account as a result of a mistake as to a material fact.[149]

29–030 **Mistake of fact: "supposed liability" rule.** It has long been clear that money paid under a mistake of the payer as to a material fact is, in certain circumstances, recoverable. Mistake in this context means lack of knowledge of the absence of liability,[150] but it is notoriously difficult to make an authoritative statement of the principles upon which recovery is based.[151] Broadly speaking, there are two approaches: one based on the nature of the mistake, permitting recovery only for certain types of mistake; the other, which now prevails, based on the effect of the mistake, prima facie permitting recovery whenever the mistake causes the payment. Much of the difficulty seems to be due to the application of dicta, made in the context of particular facts, to quite different facts, as if they established principles of general application.[152] Thus, while the decision of the Court of Exchequer in *Kelly v Solari*[153] can be seen as the basis of the modern law, the statement of Parke B. can lead to distortion if accepted as a definition of the boundaries of recovery. He said that:

> "... where money is paid to another under the influence of a mistake, that is upon the supposition that a specific fact is true, which would entitle the other to the money, but which fact is untrue, and the money would not have been paid if it had been known to the payer that the fact was untrue, an action will lie to recover it back."[154]

In that case a payment was made to the executrix of the assured by an insurance company which had forgotten that the policy had lapsed owing to the non-

---

[145] Goff and Jones at pp.187–303; Birks at pp.146–173; Burrows at Ch.3; Virgo at Ch. 8; Sheehan (2000) L.S. 538.

[146] *Gibbon v Mitchell* [1990] 1 W.L.R. 1304; *Lady Hood of Avalon v Mackinnon* [1909] 1 Ch. 476; *Re Butlin's S.T.* [1976] 1 Ch. 251

[147] See below, para.29–051.

[148] See below, paras 29–051, 29–161.

[149] *Skyring v Greenwood* (1825) 4 B. & C. 281; *Ward & Co v Wallis* [1900] 1 Q.B. 675, 679; *Branwhite v Worcester Works Finance Ltd* [1969] 1 A.C. 552. Contrast *British and North European Bank Ltd v Zalzstein* [1927] 2 K.B. 92.

[150] *Kleinwort Benson Ltd v Lincoln CC* [1999] 2 A.C. 349, 408–411 (Lord Hope). See also at 401 (Lord Hoffmann). See also *David Securities Pty Ltd v Commonwealth Bank of Australia* (1991–1992) 175 C.L.R. 353, 374 (Mason C.J.); below, para.29–034. See Sheehan (2000) L.S. 538 who argues that a mistake involves an actual belief (rather than ignorance or forgetfulness) in something which can be proved not to be the case at the time it is acted upon. But see below, para.29–033.

[151] *Weld-Blundell v Synott* [1940] 2 K.B. 107, 112 (Asquith J.); *Commercial Bank of Australia v Younis* [1979] 1 N.S.W.L.R. 444, 447 (Hope J.A.).

[152] *Commercial Bank of Australia v Younis* [1979] 1 N.S.W.L.R. 444; *Morgan v Ashcroft* [1938] 1 K.B. 49, 72 (Scott L.J.).

[153] (1841) 9 M. & W. 54; 11 L.J. Ex. 10. See also *Milnes v Duncan* (1827) 6 B. & C. 671.

[154] *Kelly v Solari* (1841) 9 M. & W. 54, 58. The report in the *Law Journal* is materially different in omitting any reference to entitlement; 11 L.J. Ex. 10, 13.

payment of the premium. Recovery was allowed and, in the context, the reference to "entitlement" is perfectly acceptable. However, together with a dictum of Bramwell B. in *Aiken v Short*, at one time it was taken to restrict recovery to cases in which the mistake was as to:

"... a fact which, if true, would make the person liable to pay the money; not where, if true, it would merely make it desirable that he should pay the money."[155]

Unsatisfactoriness of "supposed liability" rule. In fact the "supposed liability" rule itself could not explain all the decisions and it could have no application to cases of mistaken gifts of money. The true position would appear to be that "liability" mistakes are merely the commonest instance of what suffices to ground recovery, especially where the payment is associated with the performance of contractual obligations.[156] Thus, in *Kerrison v Glynn Mills, Currie & Co*[157] the House of Lords permitted recovery of money mistakenly paid in anticipation of a future liability. Again, in *Sybron Corp v Rochem Ltd*[158] a payment of accrued benefits under a pension scheme, which provided that in cases of early retirement such benefits were to be dealt with at the discretion of the trustees, was made in ignorance of the payee's breach of duty to disclose the fraud of his subordinates with whom he acted. The accrued benefits had been paid under a mistake of fact induced by the payee's breach of duty and the Court of Appeal allowed the payer to recover. Moreover, an agent who pays money to a third party mistakenly believing that he has his principal's authority to make the payment may recover it even where the principal is in fact liable to the third party payee.[159] A payment made by an agent acting under a mistake of fact is recoverable although the principal himself, or another agent, knows the true facts.[160] 29–031

Rejection of "supposed liability" rule. Bramwell B.'s dictum in *Aiken v Short*[161] has been rejected as an exhaustive statement of the law on two occasions 29–032

[155] (1856) 1 H. & N. 210, 215; 25 L.J. Ex. 321; below, para.29–038; *Deutsche Bank v Beriro & Co Ltd* (1895) 1 Com. Cas. 255, 259; *Re Bodega Co Ltd* [1904] 1 Ch. 276, 286; *Steam Saw Mills Co Ltd v Baring Bros & Co Ltd* [1922] 1 Ch. 244, 250 (Lord Sterndale M.R.). See also the formulation of the rule in *National Westminster Bank Ltd v Barclays Bank International Ltd* [1975] Q.B. 654, 675 (Kerr J.). The most restrictive interpretation of these dicta required the mistake to be "between" payer and payee: *Chambers v Miller* (1862) 13 C.B.(N.S.) 125, 133; but this has since been rejected (*Colonial Bank v Exchange Bank of Yarmouth, Nova Scotia* (1885) 11 App. Cas. 84; *Imperial Bank of Canada v Bank of Hamilton* [1903] A.C. 49; *Barclays Bank Ltd v W.J. Simms, Son and Cooke (Southern) Ltd* [1980] Q.B. 677).

[156] *Morgan v Ashcroft* [1938] 1 K.B. 49, 64, 71 (Scott L.J.).

[157] (1911) 81 L.J.K.B. 465.

[158] [1984] Ch. 112. cf. *Horcal Ltd v Gatland* [1984] I.R.L.R. 288 (no breach of duty at relevant date).

[159] *Colonial Bank v Exchange Bank of Yarmouth, Nova Scotia* (1885) 11 App. Cas. 84; *Anglo-Scottish Beet Sugar Corp Ltd v Spalding U.D.C.* [1937] 2 K.B. 607; *Turvey v Dentons (1923) Ltd* [1953] 1 Q.B. 218. Money mistakenly paid by a third party to an agent for transmission to the principal is also recoverable before the agent has paid the money to the principal: *Buller v Harrison* (1777) 2 Cowp. 565; *British American Continental Bank v British Bank for Foreign Trade* [1926] 1 K.B. 328.

[160] *Anglo-Scottish Beet Sugar Corp Ltd v Spalding U.D.C.* [1937] 2 K.B. 607; *Turvey v Dentons (1923) Ltd* [1953] 1 Q.B. 218. See also Birks at pp.159–164.

[161] (1856) 1 Hurl. & N. 210.

by the Court of Appeal. In *Morgan v Ashcroft* Sir Wilfrid Greene M.R. sought to confine it to "cases where the only mistake is as to the nature of the transaction" which should not, for instance, prevent recovery where a payment is made under a mistake as to the identity of the payee.[162] Scott L.J. went further and was not prepared to accept the dictum as authoritative.[163] Secondly, in *Larner v L.C.C.*[164] payments made by a local authority in the mistaken belief that it was under a moral obligation to pay were recovered. The authority had voluntarily promised, "until further order", to pay all their employees on war service the difference between their service pay and civilian pay. Larner was overpaid because he failed to inform the authority of increases in his service pay, but he defended the action by alleging that the payments were voluntary and were not made in discharge of any legal liability. The Court of Appeal rejected this, saying that, although under no legal obligation to pay, the authority:

> ". . . for good reasons of national policy, made a promise to the men which they were in honour bound to fulfil. The payments . . . were not mere gratuities. They were made as a matter of duty."[165]

These decisions show that it is not necessary for the mistake to induce belief in a legal liability to pay.[166] Although it may be possible to accommodate some of them within Bramwell B.'s dictum by adopting a very broad concept of liability, in such a diluted form it is inadequate as a general principle and attempts have been made to formulate an alternative test.

29–033 **Fundamental mistake.** In *Norwich Union Fire Insurance Society Ltd v W.H. Price Ltd* Lord Wright stated that it is:

> " . . . essential that the mistake relied on should be of such a nature that it can properly be described as a mistake in respect of the underlying assumption of the contract or transaction or as being fundamental or basic."[167]

The use of the term "fundamental" may be misleading because of the danger of confusing the basis upon which mistaken payments are recovered with that upon which a contract is avoided for mistake.[168] It has been said that recovery of mistaken payments can legitimately be granted on a generous basis where there is no contract that would need to be avoided because the policy favouring finality

---

[162] [1938] 1 K.B. 49, 66.

[163] *Morgan v Ashcroft* [1938] 1 K.B. 49, 71.

[164] [1949] 2 K.B. 683. cf. *Lowe v Wells Fargo & Co Express* (1908) 96 P. 74; *Lady Hood of Avalon v Mackinnon* [1909] 1 Ch. 476; *Re Butlin's S.T.* [1976] 1 Ch. 251; *Barder v Caluori* [1988] A.C. 20. See Seah [2007] R.L.R. 93.

[165] [1949] 2 K.B. 683, 688.

[166] See also *Rover International Sales Ltd v Cannon Film Sales Ltd (No.3)* [1989] 1 W.L.R. 912, 933 (Dillon L.J.); *Australian and New Zealand Banking Group Ltd v Westpac Banking Corp* (1988) 78 A.L.R. 157, 161 High Ct of Australia; *Nurdin and Peacock Plc v DB Ramsden and Co Ltd* [1999] 1 W.L.R. 1249.

[167] [1934] A.C. 455, 463. See also *Morgan v Ashcroft* [1938] 1 K.B. 49, 64–67, 77 (Scott L.J.); *Jones v Waring & Gillow Ltd* [1926] A.C. 670, 696 (Lord Sumner); *Bank of New South Wales v Murphett* [1983] V.R. 489; *Australia and New Zealand Banking Group Ltd v Westpac Banking Corp* (1988) 78 A.L.R. 157, 160–161.

[168] See above, paras 5–017, 5–030; below, para.29–159.

of contract does not apply if there is no transaction to rescind except the payment itself.[169] However, although the policy favouring finality of contract may be stronger than that favouring finality in other transactions, there is no *a priori* reason for this to be the case. In any event, whatever the reason for the difference, it would seem that the test of mistake in restitution is broader than that in contract.[170] Thus, mistakes as to creditworthiness and arithmetical mistakes have sufficed to allow the recovery of payments[171] and the mistake need not be shared by the payee, nor need he know of it.[172] Furthermore, the word "mistake" in this context not only signifies a positive belief in the existence of something which in reality does not exist, but it may also include forgetfulness and sheer ignorance of something relevant to the transaction.[173] On the other hand, a misprediction as to the nature of a future transaction does not provide the basis for a claim to recover money as having been paid under a mistake, because the payer is a risk-taker.[174] It is possible that the requirement that the mistake be fundamental in fact involves no more than that, without the mistake, the payment would not have been made.[175] If, however, the payment is due under a contract between the payer and the payee, the payment cannot be recovered unless the contract itself is held void or is discharged.[176]

Causative mistake. The recognition of the principle of unjust enrichment puts into question tests based on the nature of the mistake.[177] In *Barclays Bank Ltd v W.J. Simms, Son and Cooke (Southern) Ltd* it was stated that: 29–034

---

[169] Goff and Jones at p.193; Palmer at paras 11.2, 14.1; Palmer, *Mistake and Unjust Enrichment* (1962), pp.8, 25.

[170] e.g. *Midland Bank Plc v Brown Shipley & Co Ltd* [1991] 2 All E.R. at 690, 700–701 (Waller J.).

[171] *Kerrison v Glyn, Mills, Currie & Co* (1911) 81 L.J.K.B. 465; *Weld-Blundell v Synott* [1940] 2 K.B. 107. See also *Re Butlin's S.T.* [1976] 1 Ch. 251 (voluntary settlement).

[172] The mistake may be fraudulently induced by a third person; *R. E. Jones Ltd v Waring & Gillow Ltd* [1926] A.C. 670.

[173] See, e.g. *Lucas v Worswick* (1833) 1 M. & R. 293; *Kelly v Solari* (1841) M. & W. 54; *Lady Hood of Avalon v Mackinnon* [1909] 1 Ch. 476; *Home and Colonial Insurance Co Ltd v London Guarantee Accident Co* (1928) 45 T.L.R. 134; *Saronic Shipping Co Ltd v Huron Liberian Co Ltd* [1979] 1 Lloyd's Rep. 341; affirmed [1980] 2 Lloyd's Rep. 26; *David Securities Pty Ltd v Commonwealth Bank of Australia* (1992) 66 A.L.J.R. 768, 776; *Kleinwort Benson Ltd v Lincoln CC* [1999] 2 A.C. 349, 409. See Sheehan fn.150, above. On the position where the payer is negligent, see below, para.29–036.

[174] *Dextra Bank & Trust Co Ltd v Bank of Jamaica* [2002] 1 All E.R. (Comm) 193 PC.

[175] *David Securities Pty Ltd v Commonwealth Bank of Australia* (1992) 66 A.L.J.R. 768, 777; *Bank of New South Wales v Murphett* [1983] 1 V.R. 489; *Australia and New Zealand Banking Group Ltd v Westpac Banking Corp* (1988) 78 A.L.R. 157, 161. cf. Birks at pp.156–159. On the causation test, see below, para.29–033.

[176] *Norwich Union v W.H. Price Ltd* [1934] A.C. 455; *Barclays Bank Ltd v W.J. Simms, Son and Cooke (Southern) Ltd* [1980] Q.B. 677, 695 (Robert Goff J.).

[177] *Air Canada v British Columbia* [1989] S.C.R. 1161, 1200 (La Forest J.); *David Securities v Commonwealth Bank of Australia* (1992) 66 A.L.J.R. 768, 776, 787; *Woolwich Equitable Building Society v IRC* [1993] 1 A.C. 70, 192 (Lord Jauncey); *Kleinwort Benson Ltd v Lincoln CC* [1999] 2 A.C. 349, 373 (Lord Goff). On whether it is necessary for the payee to be "unjustly enriched" by the mistaken payment, see *Portman B.S. v Hamlyn Tyler Neck* [1998] 4 All E.R. 202; *Norwich City Council v Stringer* (2001) 33 H.L.R. 15 CA; *Roxborough v Rothmans of Pall Mall Australia Ltd* (2002) 76 A.L.J.R. 203 High Ct of Australia.

> "... if a person pays money to another under a mistake of fact which causes him to make the payment, he is *prima facie* entitled to recover it."[178]

Support for this causation test, which has since been recognised by the High Court of Australia,[179] is found in speeches in several decisions of the House of Lords,[180] including in *Kleinwort Benson Ltd v Lincoln CC* where it was stated that the payer "must prove that he would not have made the payment had he known of his mistake at the time when it was made" and that the function of mistake is to show that the benefit which had been received was an unintended benefit.[181]

29–035 **Burden of proof.** It appears that the burden of proving the causative effect of the mistake will not be heavy, at any rate if the mistake is serious, and it has been said that it is an "irresistible inference" that a payer who is mistaken about or ignorant of a material fact would not have made the payment had he known the true position.[182] Where, however, the payer would not have appreciated the significance of a fact, recovery may be refused on the ground that the payment was made in settlement of a claim.[183] The mistake must be the effective cause of the payment. The position is similar where the payer is aware that there is an issue of law which is relevant but, being in doubt as to what the law is, pays without waiting to resolve that doubt. A person who pays when in doubt takes the risk that he may be wrong.[184] In *Deutsche Morgan Grenfell Group Plc v IRC*[185] it was recognised that a claimant who suspects that there is no liability to pay the defendant but does so, may not be able to recover the payment, although their Lordships gave a variety of reasons for this conclusion. Lord Brown considered that suspicion negated the mistake,[186] whereas Lord Hoffmann considered that

---

[178] [1980] Q.B. 677, 695 (Robert Goff J.). See also *Lloyds Bank Plc v Independent Insurance Co Ltd* [2000] Q.B. 110. See further Vol.II, para.34–129.

[179] *David Securities Pty Ltd v Commonwealth Bank of Australia* (1992) 66 A.L.J.R. 768, 777.

[180] *Kleinwort, Sons and Co v Dunlop Rubber Co* (1907) 97 L.T. 263, 264 (Lord Loreburn); *Kerrison v Glyn, Mills, Currie and Co* (1912) 81 L.J.K.B. 465, 470 (Lord Atkinson), 471 (Lord Shaw), 472 (Lord Mersey); *R.E. Jones Ltd v Waring & Gillow Ltd* [1926] A.C. 670, 679–680 (Viscount Cave L.C.), 686 (Lord Shaw), 691, 692 (Lord Sumner). See also *Banque Financière de la Cité v Parc Battersea Ltd* [1999] 1 A.C. 221 and *Deutsche Morgan Grenfell Group Plc v IRC* [2006] UKHL 49, [2007] 1 A.C. 558.

[181] [1999] 2 A.C. 349, 408 (Lord Hope). See also at 373 (Lord Goff). See also *Nurdin and Peacock Plc v DB Ramsden and Co Ltd* [1999] 1 W.L.R. 1249 (payment prima facie recoverable where there was a mistake and it related directly and closely to the payment and to the relationship between the payer and payee, particularly where there would have been no payment if the mistake had not been made); *Dextra Bank & Trust Co Ltd v Bank of Jamaica* [2002] 1 All. E.R. (Comm) 193 PC, at [28]–[30]; *Maersk Air Ltd v Expeditors International (UK) Ltd* [2003] 1 Lloyd's Rep. 491; *Papamichael v National Westminster Bank Plc* [2003] 1 Lloyd's Rep. 34.

[182] *Saronic Shipping Co Ltd v Huron Liberian Co Ltd* [1979] 1 Lloyd's Rep. 341, 362–366 (affirmed [1980] 2 Lloyd's Rep. 26).

[183] *Home and Colonial Insurance Co Ltd v London Guarantee Accident Co* (1928) 45 T.L.R. 134. See below, para.29–186.

[184] *Kleinwort Benson Ltd v Lincoln CC* [1999] 2 A.C. 349, 410 (Lord Hope); *Cobbold v Bakewell Management Ltd* [2003] EWHC 2289 (Ch) at [19] (Rimer J.). See below, para.29–187.

[185] [2006] UKHL 49, [2007] 1 A.C. 558.

[186] [2006] UKHL 49 at [162].

the suspicious claimant might be considered to be a risk-taker.[187] The preferable view is that of Lord Hope,[188] namely that the claimant's suspicions will mean that the payment will not have been caused by the mistake but because the claimant has taken a calculated risk about the existence of the liability to pay.

Negligence: payer with means of knowledge. The fact that the payer was in a position to discover all the relevant circumstances concerning the payment, may possibly, as a matter of evidence, support the inference that he had actual knowledge of those circumstances or that he has represented that reasonable care was used in making and checking the payment. There is, however, no conclusive rule of law that, because a person has the means of knowledge, he must be taken to have actual knowledge.[189] Thus, a person paying money under a mistake of fact is not prevented from recovering it merely because he was negligent in failing to discover the true facts.[190] Parke B., in *Kelly v Solari*, said that recovery was possible, "however careless the party paying may have been in omitting to use due diligence to inquire into the fact".[191] So money paid to a defendant under a mistake of fact can be recovered even though the claimant had forgotten the facts which disentitled the defendant from receiving it,[192] or the money was paid in ignorance of a fact which the claimant could have discovered at the time of payment if he had availed himself of his means of knowledge.[193] In *Dextra Bank & Trust Co Ltd v Bank of Jamaica*[194] the Privy Council rejected the concept of "relative fault" or any suggestion to "balance the equities" between payer and recipient for the purposes of the defence of change of position, provided the recipient acted in good faith. Of course, if the claimant pays the money intentionally, waiving any inquiry into the facts, e.g. a payment made in submission to an honest claim, it is irrecoverable.[195] Again, if the payer was aware that there was 29–036

[187] [2006] UKHL 49 at [27].

[188] [2006] UKHL 49 at [65]

[189] *Bell v Gardiner* (1842) 4 M. & G. 11, 24; *Brownlie v Campbell* (1880) 5 App. Cas. 925.

[190] *Weld-Blundell v Synott* [1940] 2 K.B. 107; *Turvey v Dentons (1923) Ltd* [1953] 1 Q.B. 218, 224 (Pilcher J.); *Chase Manhattan Bank N.A. v Israel-British Bank (London) Ltd* [1981] Ch. 105. cf. s.4(3) of the Cheques Act 1957 (see Vol.II, para.34–358).

[191] (1841) 9 M. & W. 54, 59. The position in Scotland differs since the mistake must be "excusable" and this will be difficult to show where there is negligence: *Taylor v Wilsons Trustees* (1975) S.C. 146, 148, 156, 159.

[192] *Kelly v Solari* (1841) 9 M. & W. 54 (approved by PC in *Imperial Bank of Canada v Bank of Hamilton* [1903] A.C. 49 and by the House Lords in *R.E. Jones Ltd v Waring & Gillow Ltd* [1926] A.C. 670). See also *Lucas v Worswick* (1833) 1 Moo. & R. 293; *Commonwealth of Australia v McCormack* (1982) 69 F.L.R. 9; *R.B.C. Dominion Securities Inc v Dawson* (1994) 111 D.L.R. (4th) 230.

[193] *Townsend v Crowdy* (1860) 8 C.B.(N.S.) 477; *Durrant v Ecclesiastical Commissioners* (1880) 6 QBD 234; *Stanley Bros Ltd v Nuneaton Corp* (1913) 108 L.T. 986; *Avon CC v Howlett* [1983] 1 W.L.R. 605, 617–619 (Slade L.J.); *R.B.C. Dominion Securities Inc v Dawson* (1994) 111 D.L.R. (4th) 230; *Scottish Equitable Plc v Derby* [2001] 3 All E.R. 818.

[194] [2002] 1 All E.R. (Comm) 193.

[195] *Beevor v Marler* (1898) 14 T.L.R. 289. See also *Kelly v Solari* (1841) 9 M. & W. 54, 58, 59; *Woolwich Equitable B.S. v IRC* [1993] A.C. 70, 98 (Glidewell L.J.), 165, 174 (Lord Goff), 200–201 (Lord Slynn); *David Securities Pty Ltd v Commonwealth Bank of Australia* (1992) 66 A.L.J.R. 768, 774–776, 788; *Westdeutsche Landesbank Girozentrale v Islington LBC* [1994] 4 All E.R. 890 (affirmed [1996] A.C. 669). See below, para.29–039.

doubt as to whether the payment was due but paid without waiting to resolve that doubt, it will not be recoverable: "a state of doubt is different from that of mistake".[196]

29–037 **Qualification to causation principle.** This broad principle of recovery is attractive where the payee still has the money, for there is then a true superfluity in his assets. But unless the payee has a wide range of defences available, for instance to protect changes of position and security of transactions, it can operate unfairly. This was recognised in *Barclays Bank Ltd v W.J. Simms, Son and Cooke (Southern) Ltd* by Robert Goff J. who qualified the principle of recovery by stating[197] that a claim may fail if:

> "(a) . . . the payer intends that the payee shall have the money at all events, whether the fact be true or false, or is deemed in law so to intend; or (b) the payment is made for good consideration,[198] in particular if the money is paid to discharge and does discharge, a debt owed to the payee (or a principal on whose behalf he is authorised to receive the payment) by the payer or by a third party by whom he is authorised to discharge the debt; or (c) the payee has changed his position in good faith, or is deemed in law to have done so."

The first two did not apply in that case and it was held there was no evidence of any change of position so the judge did not have to consider these questions.[199]

29–038 **Payments made for good consideration.** Money paid in discharge of a genuine legal obligation cannot be recovered merely because the payer was induced to fulfil his legal obligation by a mistake. As Lord Hope stated, "The payee cannot be said to have been unjustly enriched if he was entitled to receive the sum paid to him".[200] For example,[201] where the claimant paid money due under a contract to agents of a foreign government in ignorance of the fact that a revolution had broken out which subsequently led to the downfall of the government, it was not recoverable even though the claimant would not have made the payment had he known what was happening[202].

---

[196] *Kleinwort Benson Ltd v Lincoln CC* [1999] 2 A.C. 349, 410 (Lord Hope). See also above, para.29–035.

[197] [1980] Q.B. 677, 695. See also *Lloyds Bank Plc v Independent Insurance Co Ltd* [2000] Q.B. 110.

[198] cf. *Commonwealth of Australia v McCormack* (1982) 69 F.L.R. 9. See below, para.29–038.

[199] For the view that there was in fact a change of position, see Goode (1981) 97 L.Q.R. 254, 259.

[200] *Kleinwort Benson Ltd v Lincoln CC* [1999] 2 A.C. 349, 408. See also *Lloyds Bank Plc v Independent Insurance Co Ltd* [2000] Q.B. 110.

[201] *Kerrison v Glyn, Mills, Currie & Co* (1910) 15 Com. Cas. 241, 247–248; reversed on the facts (1911) 81 L.J.K.B. 465; 17 Com. Cas. 41; *Steam Saw Mills Co Ltd v Baring Bros & Co Ltd* [1922] 1 Ch. 244, 251, 254; *British American Continental Bank v British Bank for Foreign Trade* [1926] 1 K.B. 328, 336–337, 341, 344.

[202] *Steam Saw Mills Co Ltd v Baring Bros & Co Ltd* [1922] Ch. 244.

"... the money was paid, not under a mistake of fact as to the existence of an obligation; it was paid in pursuance of an obligation which in fact existed"[203]

and was effective to discharge that obligation. Where, however, the claimant paid money under a contract to agents of the other party in ignorance of the fact that the contract had already been repudiated by the other party, it was held that the payment was recoverable because it did not discharge any legal obligation.[204] *Aiken v Short*,[205] which was the basis for the view that only "liability" mistakes sufficed to permit repayment, is in fact an example of failure to recover a payment which was effective to discharge a debt. The plaintiff bankers paid a sum of money to the defendant in discharge of a debt owed by one Carter to the defendant which was secured by a mortgage on property which supposedly belonged to Carter. The plaintiffs purchased the property from Carter subject to the defendant's interest on the understanding that they would pay off Carter's debt to the defendant. The plaintiffs paid the defendant because they believed that they were getting rid of the encumbrance on their title and, when it transpired that Carter did not in fact own the property, they claimed to recover the sum as having been paid under a mistake of fact. The Court of Exchequer held that the money was irrecoverable. The payment was authorised by Carter[206] and was effective to discharge the debt; the defendant therefore gave consideration for the payment.[207] The operation of this rule is also illustrated by cases in which a bank mistakenly pays a third party who presents a cheque drawn upon it by a customer. The question whether the bank may recover the payment depends on whether the payment was with or without mandate.[208] Thus, where the bank pays, having overlooked notice of the customer's death or his instructions countermanding the cheque, the bank will be able to recover the payment.[209] Because it has paid without mandate the bank cannot debit the customer's account and the payment does not discharge the customer's debt to the payee. Where, however, the bank mistakenly thinks the customer has sufficient funds or overdraft facilities to meet the cheque, the payment will be irrecoverable.[210] The payment is within the bank's mandate, the bank is therefore entitled to have recourse to the customer and the payment does discharge the customer's debt to the payee.

---

[203] [1922] Ch. 244, 254.

[204] *British American Continental Bank v British Bank for Foreign Trade* [1926] 1 K.B. 328; *Commonwealth of Australia v McCormack* (1982) 69 F.L.R. 9 (overpayment of sum due under lease paid having forgotten about previous part payment, recovered).

[205] (1856) 1 H. & N. 210; above, para.29–030.

[206] (1856) 1 H. & N. 210, 214, 215. This was said to be a "crucial" fact in the case: *Barclays Bank Ltd v W.J. Simms, Son and Cooke (Southern) Ltd* [1980] Q.B. 677, 687 (Robert Goff J.).

[207] cf. *Customs and Excise Commissioners v National Westminster Bank Plc* [2002] EWHC 2204 (Ch), [2003] 1 All E.R. (Comm) 327: unsolicited payment to a creditor's bank account would not discharge a debt unless it was accepted as doing such.

[208] *Barclays Bank Ltd v W.J. Simms, Son and Cooke (Southern) Ltd* [1980] Q.B. 677, 699–700 (Robert Goff J.).

[209] [1980] Q.B. 677. This would appear to be the case whether or not the customer's account was adequate to meet the cheque; Vol.II, para.34–131.

[210] *Pollard v Bank of England* (1871) L.R. 6 Q.B. 623; *Barclays Bank Ltd v W.J. Simms, Son and Cooke (Southern) Ltd* [1980] Q.B. 677, 699–700; *Lloyds Bank Plc v Independent Insurance Co Ltd* [2000] Q.B. 110.

29–039 **Other bars to recovery.** Payments made in submission to a claim and under compromises are normally irrecoverable.[211] If parties agree in good faith to compromise a disputed claim, the compromise is binding, even though the claim might in fact be without proper foundation.[212] Furthermore, a mistaken payment which is prima facie recoverable might not be recovered on grounds of public policy where granting a remedy would indirectly frustrate the policy of a statutory or common law rule.[213] Thus, in *Morgan v Ashcroft*[214] a bookmaker, by a clerical mistake, overpaid the defendant on a betting account, and sued to recover the excess. The Court of Appeal rejected his claim, primarily because the court could not examine the state of the account between the parties since that would be to recognise wagering transactions as producing legal obligations (contrary to the Gaming Act 1845). As Scott L.J. said, the:

> "... statutory veto upon the reception of evidence about gaming transactions ... creates a special impediment, and in effect constitutes a special defence to the action for money had and received",

by which "the law prevents the plaintiff from saying that he intended anything but a present".[215]

29–040 **Previous notice and demand.** It has been said that in order to entitle a party to bring an action to recover money on the ground that it was paid by mistake, notice of the mistake must have been given to the defendant and a demand made for the return of the money.[216] But it has been held that a right of restitution arises immediately following overpayment[217] and it is submitted that failure to give notice of the claim before action should be relevant only to the court's discretion in awarding costs.[218] It may be, however, that the giving of notice is a condition

---

[211] See generally, above, paras 3–050—3–054, 7–028, 29–019 and, in the context of mistake; *Kelly v Solari* (1841) 9 M. & W. 54, 59; above, para.29–029; *Grains & Fourrages SA v Huyton* [1997] 1 Lloyd's Rep. 628 (limits of contractual compromise); Andrews [1989] L.M.C.L.Q. 431; Arrowsmith in Burrows (ed.), *Essays on the Law of Restitution* (1991), Ch.2; Goff and Jones at pp.59–62, 209–212.

[212] See above, para.3–050 and, on the question whether the compromise may be invalidated by common mistake, paras 5–050 and 29–047; *Holmes v Payne* [1930] 2 K.B. 301. cf. *Huddersfield Banking Co Ltd v Henry Lister & Son Ltd* [1895] 2 Ch. 273.

[213] Goff and Jones at pp.74–81.

[214] [1938] 1 K.B. 49. See also *Thavorn v Bank of Credit & Commerce SA* [1985] 1 Lloyd's Rep. 259.

[215] [1938] 1 K.B. 49, 71, 77. cf. *Lipkin Gorman v Karpnale Ltd* [1989] 1 W.L.R. 1340, 1366 (Parker L.J.), 1384 (Nicholls L.J.); [1991] 2 A.C. 548, 577 (Lord Goff). The Gaming Act 1845 was repealed by the Gambling Act 2005; see Vol.II, para.40–001.

[216] *Kelly v Solari* [1841] 9 M. & W. 54, 58; *Freeman v Jeffries* (1869) L.R. 4 Ex. 189, 199, 200. In cases of mistaken payment of a forged negotiable instrument notice must be given on the day of the payment: *Cocks v Masterman* (1829) 9 B. & C. 902; *National Westminster Bank Ltd v Barclays Bank International Ltd* [1975] 1 Q.B. 654; *Barclays Bank Ltd v W.J. Simms, Son and Cooke (Southern) Ltd* [1980] Q.B. 677, 701–703 (Robert Goff J). See Vol.II, paras 34–126—34–131. This may be an example of estoppel: Goff and Jones at pp.880–884.

[217] *Fuller v Happy Shopper Markets Ltd* [2001] 2 Lloyd's Rep. 49.

[218] In *Colonial Bank v Exchange Bank of Yarmouth, Nova Scotia* (1885) 11 App. Cas. 84, 90 the Privy Council said that the recipient, when first informed of the mistake in making the payment, would have been justified in not repaying until he had checked the facts.

precedent to the right to bring an action, but not to the liability to repay. In another case, where the payer and payee were acting under the same mistake, this rule requiring a previous demand was not applied and the period of limitation was held to run from the date of payment.[219]

Mistake of law: formerly not a ground for restitution. Despite a dubious legal foundation[220] and the difficulty of drawing any clear dividing line between "law" and "fact"[221] for many years, as a general rule money paid under a mistake as to the general law, or as to the legal effect of the circumstances under which it is paid, but with full knowledge of the facts, was irrecoverable.[222] The rule reflected concern to protect security of receipts,[223] especially in the absence of a defence of change of position.[224] **29–041**

Examples of payments made under a mistake of law. A mistake as to the existence or construction of a statute is clearly one of law,[225] as is a mistaken view of regulations issued under statutory authority.[226] Mistakes as to the effect of general rules of common law or of equity also constitute mistakes of law. Thus, where a tenant paid rent to an equitable mortgagee with notice that the mortgagee claimed it in that capacity, the payments were made under a mistake of law.[227] Mistakes in construing a will,[228] such as a mistake as to the technical requisites for the creation of a valid charitable trust,[229] are also mistakes of law. **29–042**

---

219 *Baker v Courage & Co* [1910] K.B. 56. See also *Anglo-Scottish Beet Sugar Corp v Spalding U.D.C.* [1937] 2 K.B. 607, 609. On the limitation period in such cases, see above, para.28–088.

220 See Palmer at para.14.27; Evans, *An Essay on the Action of Money Had & Received* (1802) reprinted [1998] R.L. Rev. 1, 5–8; *Kleinwort Benson Ltd v Lincoln CC* [1999] 2 A.C. 349. See on the whole topic, Winfield (1943) 59 L.Q.R. 327 (summarised in Winfield, *Quasi-Contracts* (1952), pp.38–51); Law Commission Consultation Paper No.120 (1991), Pt II.

221 Winfield (1943) 59 L.Q.R. 327. cf. Wilson (1963) 26 M.L.R. 609. See also *Eaglesfield v Marquis of Londonderry* (1875) 4 Ch D 693, 703; *West London Commercial Bank v Kitson* (1884) 13 QBD 360, 363 (the same problem arises in connection with the rule that, to have legal effect, a representation must be one of fact, not of law: see above, para.6–013).

222 See *Bilbie v Lumley* (1802) 2 East 469; *Brisbane v Dacres* (1813) 5 Taunt. 143; *East India Co v Tritton* (1854) 3 B. & C. 280, 290; *Platt v Bromage* (1854) 24 L.J. Ex. 63; *R. v William Whiteley Ltd* (1910) 101 L.T. 741, 745; *Sawyer & Vincent v Window Brace Ltd* [1943] K.B. 32, 34; *Westdeutsche Landesbank Girozentrale v Islington LBC* [1994] 4 All E.R. 890, 933 (Hobhouse J.); affirmed [1996] A.C. 669.

223 See *Mistakes of Law and Ultra Vires Public Authority Receipt and Payments* (Law Com. C.P. No.120, 1991), paras 2.28–2.35; (Law Com. No.227, Cm. 2731), paras 2.25–2.38, 5.18.

224 See below, para.29–179.

225 *Sharp Bros and Knight v Chant* [1917] 1 K.B. 771; *R. v National Pari-Mutuel Association Ltd* (1930) 47 T.L.R. 110; *Sawyer & Vincent v Window Brace Ltd* [1943] K.B. 32. See now Rent Act 1977 s.57. See also *Orphanos v Queen Mary College* [1985] A.C. 761 (mistake of law where contractual meaning given to phrase in mistaken belief that this is its statutory meaning).

226 *Holt v Markham* [1923] 1 K.B. 504.

227 *Finck v Tranter* [1905] 1 K.B. 427. But cf. *Newsome v Graham* (1829) 10 B. & C. 234; *Cripps v Reade* (1796) 6 T.R. 606; *Barber v Brown* (1856) 1 C.B.(N.S.) 121.

228 *Rogers v Ingham* (1876) 3 Ch D 351.

229 cf. *Ministry of Health v Simpson* [1951] A.C. 251 (in the CA, *Re Diplock* [1948] Ch. 465, 480 the mistake was also regarded as one of law, so that the common law remedy for money received was excluded).

29–043 **Exceptions to the mistake of law bar.** There were, however, exceptional cases in which payments made under a mistake of law were recoverable. Some of these were in fact cases in which the payer could establish an alternative ground for restitution.[230] Thus, where an illegal payment was made under a contract, but the parties were not *in pari delicto*,[231] the payment could be recovered although it was made under a mistake of law in that neither party knew that the contract was illegal.[232] Similarly, recovery has always been permitted where the mistake of law which led to the payment was caused by an ultra vires demand by the revenue or possibly any public authority,[233] by fraud, undue influence or breach of a fiduciary obligation on the part of the recipient[234] or where it was caused by oppression[235] and, possibly, compulsion.[236] Other exceptions to the rule occured where the payment was made by the court or an officer of the court,[237] and where public funds were disbursed without legal authority.[238] The House of Lords in *Cooper v Phibbs*[239] held that ignorance of the existence of a private right of property was a mistake of fact, although this ignorance was based on a mistaken interpretation of the law. Equity has, in certain cases, given relief when a payment has, at least in part, depended on a mistake of law; thus a trustee or personal representative who has overpaid a beneficiary through a mistake of law may deduct the overpayment from future payments due to the beneficiary.[240] Furthermore, the court will not allow one of its officers, such as a

---

230 *Westdeutsche Landesbank Girozentrale v Islington LBC* [1994] 4 All E.R. 890, 933 (Hobhouse J.) affirmed [1996] A.C. 669.

231 See above, para.16–177.

232 *Kiriri Cotton Co Ltd v Dewani* [1960] A.C. 192; see above, para.16–185. cf. *Harse v Pearl Life Assurance Co* [1904] 1 K.B. 558.

233 *Woolwich Equitable Building Society v IRC* [1993] A.C. 70; *Deutsche Morgan Grenfell Group Plc v IRC* [2006] UKHL 49, [2007] 1 A.C. 558; see below, para.29–084.

234 *West London Commercial Bank Ltd v Kitson* (1884) 13 QBD 360, 363; *Ward & Co v Wallis* [1900] 1 Q.B. 675, 678; *Shelley v Paddock* [1980] Q.B. 348; *Rogers v Ingram* (1876) 3 Ch D 351, 355–356.

235 *Smith v Bromley* (1760) 2 Doug. 696n, 697 (Lord Mansfield).

236 Below, para.29–087. The commonest instances of such compulsion were payments to public bodies: *Steele v Williams* (1853) 8 Ex. 625; *Hooper v Exeter Corp* (1887) 56 L.J.Q.B. 457; *Eadie v Township of Brantford* [1967] S.C.R. 573; 63 D.L.R. (2d) 561; below, para.29–094.

237 *Re Birkbeck Permanent Benefit Building Society* [1915] 1 Ch. 91.

238 *R. v Auckland Harbour Board* [1924] A.C. 318, 326–327.

239 (1867) L.R. 2 H.L. 149. The distinction is criticised by Palmer at para.16.4(*c*). The decision was applied in *Anglo-Scottish Beet Sugar Corp Ltd v Spalding U.D.C.* [1937] 2 K.B. 607, 615–617 (Atkinson J.); *Meadows v Grand Junction Waterworks Co* (1905) 69 J.P. 255; *Stanley Bros Ltd v Corp of Nuneaton* (1912) 107 L.T. 760. See also *Norwich Union Fire Insurance Society Ltd v W. H. Price Ltd* [1934] A.C. 455, 462–463 (Lord Wright found nothing in *Bell v Lever Bros Ltd* [1932] A.C. 161 to overrule Lord Westbury's dicta in *Cooper v Phibbs*); *Sybron Corp v Rochem Ltd* [1984] Ch. 112.

240 *Dibbs v Goren* (1849) 11 Beav. 439; *Re Musgrave* [1916] 2 Ch. 417; *Gibbon v Mitchell* [1990] 1 W.L.R. 1304, 1309 (Turner L.J.); *Ogden v Trustees of the RHS Griffiths 2008 Settlement* [2008] EWHC 118 (Ch). cf. *Re Horne* [1905] 1 Ch. 76. See further *Stone v Godfrey* (1854) 5 De G.M. & G. 76, 90; *Allcard v Walker* [1896] 2 Ch. 369, 381; Winfield (1943) 59 L.Q.R. 327, 328–333. It is possible to trace in equity despite a mistake of law: *Sinclair v Brougham* [1914] A.C. 398, 452 (Lord Sumner) (below, para.29–164). See also the discussion in *Minister of Health v Simpson* [1951] A.C. 251, 269–275 (Lord Simonds). cf. *Re Diplock* [1948] Ch. 465, 479–480. In other contexts deductions have been said to be anomalous and have not been permitted: *R. v Tower Hamlets LBC Ex p. Chetnik Developments Ltd* [1988] A.C. 858, 876–877 (Lord Bridge); *Sharp Bros & Knight v Chant* [1917] 1 K.B. 771 CA.

trustee in bankruptcy or official receiver, to retain money paid to him under a mistake of law where it would be contrary to fair dealing to do so.[241] The principle in these cases, known as the rule in *Ex p. James*,[242] is not restricted to payments under mistake of law and appears to be based on the need to prevent unjust enrichment.[243]

Criticism of the bar to restitution. The main criticisms of the bar were as follows.[244] First, it allowed a payee to retain a payment which would not have been made but for the payer's mistake, "whereas justice appears to demand that money so paid should be repaid unless there are special circumstances justifying its retention".[245] Secondly, the distinction between mistakes of fact which could ground liability and mistakes of law which could not produced results which appeared to be capricious. So a payment by an insurer would be irrecoverable where, as in *Bilbie v Lumlie*,[246] the underwriter had failed to appreciate that he could repudiate the policy for non-disclosure, but not where, as in *Kelly v Solari*,[247] he forgot that the premium had not been paid. Thirdly, the rule became uncertain and unpredictable in its application because of the difficulty of drawing the distinction between mistakes of fact and law and because of the many exceptions and qualifications to the rule. In practice the scope of the rule was narrowed by the rather artificial distinction made between mistakes of general law and mistakes as to private rights, since the latter grounded recovery.[248] Many of the cases in which the rule was applied can in fact be explained as examples of the irrecoverability of payments made in settlement of an honest claim.[249] 29–044

Rejection of the bar to restitution. The rule has been held not to be part of the law of Scotland.[250] It has also been rejected by the Supreme Court of Canada, the High Court of Australia and the Appellate Division of the Supreme Court of 29–045

241 *Ex p. James* (1874) L.R. 9 Ch. App. 609; *Ex p. Simmonds* (1885) 6 QBD 308; *Re Opera Ltd* [1891] 2 Ch. 154 reversed on other grounds: [1891] 3 Ch. 260; *Re Tyler* [1907] 1 K.B. 865; *Re Thellusson* [1919] 2 K.B. 735; *Re Wigzell* [1921] 2 K.B. 835, 851 (Lord Sterndale M.R.); *Re Wyvern Developments Ltd* [1974] 1 W.L.R. 1097, 1105 (Templeman J.); *Re Sandiford (No.2)* [1935] Ch. 681; *Taylor v Wilson's Trustees* (1975) S.C. 146; *Re Multi Guarantee Co Ltd* [1987] B.C.L.C. 257; *Re T.H. Knitwear (Wholesale) Ltd* [1988] Ch. 275.

242 (1874) L.R. 9 Ch. App. 609; see above, para.20–022 for a fuller discussion.

243 *Government of India v Taylor* [1955] A.C. 491, 513 (Lord Keith); cf. *Re Clark (A Bankrupt)* [1975] 1 W.L.R. 559; *Re Byfield* [1982] Ch. 267; *Re Multi Guarantee Co Ltd* [1987] B.C.L.C. 257.

244 They are summarised by Lord Goff in *Kleinwort Benson Ltd v Lincoln City Council* [1999] 2 A.C. 349, 370–372. For a fuller account see Law Com. C.P. No.120 (1991), paras 2.24–2.26 and Law Com. No.227 (1994), paras 2.5–2.15.

245 [1999] 2 A.C. 349.

246 (1802) 2 East 469.

247 (1841) 9 M. & W. 54, above, para.29–030.

248 *Cooper v Phibbs* (1867) L.R. 2 H.L. 149, 170 (Lord Westbury).

249 e.g. *Bilbie v Lumlie* (1802) 2 East 469; *Home & Colonial Insurance Co Ltd v London Guarantee Accident Co* (1928) T.L.R. 135. See further below, para.29–186.

250 *Morgan Guaranty Trust Co of New York v Lothian R.C.* (1995) S.C. 151.

South Africa.[251] In England the acceptance in 1991[252] of the principle of unjust enrichment made it difficult to continue to defend a distinction between mistakes of fact and law, and the recognition of a defence of change of position[253] at the same time has dealt with some of the legitimate concerns about the security of receipts. By 1994, when the Law Commission recommended the abolition of the rule,[254] it was clearly "on the turn",[255] and, in 1998 the House of Lords, in *Kleinwort Benson Ltd v Lincoln City Council*,[256] held that it was not part of English law. In *Kleinwort Benson Ltd v Lincoln City Council*[257] the claimant bank sought to recover payments made to the defendants under interest rate swaps contracts believed to be binding but subsequently held ultra vires.[258] Over half of the payments had been made more than six years before the claim was brought, but less than six years after the House of Lords held that the contracts were ultra vires. The claim was statute barred unless it was for relief from the consequences of a mistake, in which case s.32(1) of the Limitation Act 1980 provided that the period of limitation only began to run when the bank either discovered the mistake or could with reasonable diligence have discovered it. The bank could not have discovered the true position until it was held that the contracts were ultra vires. It was held that the rule barring restitutionary claims to money paid under a mistake of law should no longer be maintained as part of English law. There is therefore a general right to recover money paid under a mistake, whether of fact or law, subject to the defences available in the law of restitution. Although there was unanimity as to the desirability in principle of abrogating the rule, their Lordships were divided as to whether this should be done judicially. This was due to a difference of opinion as to the position where, after a payment has been made, the law changed by judicial decision. The majority held that a payment made under a settled understanding of the law which is subsequently departed from by judicial decision was recoverable in restitution on the ground of mistake of law. The judges in the minority considered that such a payment was not made under a mistake of law, and were not prepared to abolish the rule barring restitution in respect of payments made under a mistake of law if that meant that such a payment would be recoverable. This aspect of the decision is considered further below.[259]

---

[251] *Air Canada v British Columbia* [1989] S.C.R. 1161; *David Securities Pty v Commonwealth Bank of Australia* (1992) 66 A.L.J.R. 768; *Willis Faber Enthoven (Pty) Ltd v Receiver of Revenue* (1992) (4) S.A. 202(A). It has been legislatively modified in New Zealand (Judicature Amendment Act 1958 s.94A) and Western Australia L.R. (Property, Perpetuities and Succession) Act 1962 ss.23, 24.

[252] In *Lipkin Gorman (A Firm) Ltd v Karpnale* [1991] 2 A.C. 548.

[253] Below, para.29–179.

[254] *Restitution: Mistakes of Law and Ultra Vires Public Authority Receipts and Payments* (Law Com. No.227, 1994).

[255] *Friends' Provident Life Office v Hillier Parker* [1997] Q.B. 85, 97 (Auld L.J.).

[256] [1999] 2 A.C. 349; on appeal from [1997] Q.B. 380.

[257] [1999] 2 A.C. 349. See also *Deutsche Morgan Grenfell v IRC* [2006] UKHL 49, [2007] 1 A.C. 558.

[258] In *Hazell v Hammersmith & Fulham LBC* [1992] 2 A.C. 1, above, para.10–024.

[259] Below, para.29–047.

Mistake of law: principles governing recovery. It was held in *Kleinwort Benson Ltd v Lincoln City Council*[260] that the questions raised in a claim for restitution of money paid under a mistake of law are the same as those raised in a claim for restitution of money paid under a mistake of fact: was there a mistake, did the mistake cause the payment, and did the payee have a right to receive the sum which was paid to him? Retention of the money is prima facie unjust if the payer paid because he thought he was obliged to do so and it subsequently turns out that he was not. Lord Hope stated that, although it may be more difficult to establish that there has been a mistake of law than a mistake of fact, there is no essential difference in principle with regard to the payer's state of mind or with regard to the state of facts or the law, which must be determined at the time of payment.[261] But his Lordship considered that there was no reason in principle for the mistake to be one that is capable of being discovered at the same time as when the payment was made.[262] The prima facie right to recover a mistaken payment is subject to the ordinary defences to restitutionary claims which are concerned to protect the stability of closed transactions, i.e. change of position, compromise[263] and settlement of an honest claim, the last of which is likely to assume an increased importance despite its current somewhat uncertain scope, since many of the cases in which recovery was barred by the mistake of law rule can be explained as examples of such settlements.[264] The House considered, but rejected, a number of other limits to recovery. Thus, the suggestion that restitution is barred where the payee honestly believes that he was entitled to the money, which would exclude recovery in a very large proportion of cases, was rejected.[265] It was also held that restitution is not barred where the transaction under which the money was paid has been fully performed (although this would bar a restitutionary claim based on failure of consideration).[266] Moreover, a bare majority held that a payment made under a settled understanding of the law which is subsequently departed from by judicial decision is made under a mistake of law and is therefore recoverable.[267] Nevertheless Lord Goff left open the possibility that other defences might be developed from judicial decisions in the future.[268] 29–046

[260] [1999] 2 A.C. 349.

[261] [1999] 2 A.C. 349, 409 (Lord Hope). See above, para.29–034—29–035. Also *Nurdin and Peacock Plc v D.B. Ramsden and Co Ltd* [1999] 1 W.L.R. 1249.

[262] [1999] 2 A.C. 349, 409 (Lord Hope).

[263] See *Brennan v Bolt Burdon* [2004] EWCA Civ 1017, [2005] Q.B. 303; above, para.5–055.

[264] Above, para.29–044.

[265] [1999] 2 A.C. 349, 384–385 (Lord Goff), 413 (Lord Hope). This had been suggested by Brennan J. in *David Securities Pty Ltd v Commonwealth Bank of Australia* (1991–92) 175 C.L.R. 353, 398–399.

[266] [1999] 2 A.C. 349, 385–387 (Lord Goff), 413 (Lord Hope); cf. Birks (1993) 23 U.W. Aus. L.R. 195.

[267] Below, para.29–047. In *Brennan v Bolt Burdon* [2004] EWCA Civ 1017, [2005] Q.B. 303 Maurice Kay L.J. stated that he was: ". . . reluctant to countenance as a mistake of law a situation in which it is generally known or ought to be known that the law in question is about to be reconsidered on appeal." See above, para.5–055.

[268] *Kleinwort Benson Ltd v Lincoln City Council* [1999] 2 A.C. 349, 382.

29–047 **Changes in the law.**[269] Where the law is changed by *legislation* a payment made or service rendered in accordance with the previous law cannot be recovered since there was clearly no mistake when it was made.[270] Where the law is changed by a *judicial decision*, however, the position differs. Such a change may occur either by the overruling of an earlier decision, or by changing what had previously been generally regarded as the law. The traditional working assumption upon which the common law proceeds is that judges declare law but do not make it. Thus, where the common law changes, a legal fiction (known as the declaratory theory) means that the law is regarded as having always been what the judicial decision has stated it to be. By a bare majority, the House of Lords held in *Kleinwort Benson Ltd v Lincoln City Council*[271] that the logical consequence of the declaratory theory is that the pre-decision payment must be regarded as mistaken and is therefore recoverable: "common sense does not easily accommodate the concept of retrospectivity".[272] This is so both where the law was established by a judicial decision which is subsequently overruled and where, as in *Kleinwort Benson Ltd* itself, the law was arguably "settled" as a matter of practice but without a decision in point.[273] The position may well differ, however, where the payment was made pursuant to a judgment of the court and that judgment is afterwards overruled by a higher court in a different case: "the obligation to pay is to be found in the order which has been made by the court".[274] Lord Browne-Wilkinson and Lord Lloyd took a different view of the general effect of a change in the law or a settled understanding of the law by judicial decision. They considered that such a payment was not made under a mistake because where a decision of a court has in fact changed the law, "retrospectivity cannot falsify history."[275] If at the date of the payment it was the law that the payer was liable, the payer was not labouring under a mistake at that

[269] See generally *Restitution: Mistakes of Law and Ultra Vires Public Authority Receipts and Payments* (Law Com. No.227, 1994), paras 5.1–5.13.

[270] *Kleinwort Benson Ltd v Lincoln City Council* [1999] 2 A.C. 349, 381 (Lord Goff). But the position may be different where the legislation is retrospective; at 400 (Lord Hoffmann).

[271] [1999] 2 A.C. 349, 381.

[272] [1999] 2 A.C. 349, 399 (Lord Hoffmann). See also at 379 (Lord Goff), 410 (Lord Hope). In *Deutsche Morgan Grenfell Group Plc v IRC* [2006] UKHL 49, [2007] 1 A.C. 558 at [23] Lord Hoffmann accepted that a mistake of law could be considered to be a "deemed" mistake. Following the decision of the House of Lords in *Spectrum Plus Ltd* [2005] UKHL 41, [2005] A.C. 680, the courts may exceptionally make a decision which is prospective in effect only. If a judgment only operates prospectively it will not be possible to construct a retrospective mistake.

[273] Payments made under public law transactions, such as taxes and similar charges, might, because of the large numbers of payments and considerations of the public interest, be treated differently from those under private law transactions: *Kleinwort Benson Ltd v Lincoln City Council* [1999] 2 A.C. 349, 381 (Lord Goff).

[274] [1999] 2 A.C. 349, 410 (Lord Hope). For Lord Browne-Wilkinson and Lord Lloyd this case is a fortiori their view of the general effect of a change in the law or a settled understanding of the law by judicial decision. But cf. Lord Goff and Lord Hoffmann, at 381–383, 399.

[275] [1999] 2 A.C. 349, 358 (Lord Browne-Wilkinson), 393 (Lord Lloyd). For support see *Henderson v Folkestone Waterworks Co* (1885) 1 T.L.R. 329 and, although less clearly, *Derrick v Williams* [1939] 2 All E.R. 559, 565 (Sir Wilfrid Greene M.R.). See also *Brennan v Bolt Burdon* [2004] EWCA Civ 1017, [2005] Q.B. 303 especially at [50] (Bodey J.). But see also *Mercury Machine Importing Corp v City of New York* (1957) 144 N.E. 2d 400 (New York); *Julian v Mayor of Auckland* [1927] N.Z.L.R. 453 (New Zealand); *Torrens Aloha Pty Co v Citybank NA* [1997] 72 F.C.R. 581 (Australian).

date: the subsequent change in the law could not create a cause of action which, *ex hypothesi*, did not exist at the relevant time.

Advantages of mistake of law as a ground of restitution. A mistake as to a liability to pay tax to the Inland Revenue also constitutes a mistake of law.[276] In such circumstances the taxpayer can choose to bring a claim founded on mistake of law or on the ultra vires nature of the receipt.[277] The advantage of founding the claim on mistake of law is that it will enable the claimant to gain the benefit of an extended limitation period under s.32(1)(c) of the Limitation Act 1980, which applies to claims involving a mistake and for which time does not begin to run until the mistake could reasonably have been discovered.[278] 29–048

Personal and proprietary remedies. The normal remedy for the recovery of money paid under mistake is the action for money had and received, a personal remedy. However, the effect of the claimant's mistake may sometimes operate so that the claimant retains or is given a new proprietary interest in the property which was received by the defendant. Where the claimant retains or is given an equitable proprietary interest equitable proprietary remedies may be available.[279] 29–049

Equitable remedies. The equitable remedy of rescission of a contract on the ground of misrepresentation[280] may also be viewed as an instance of restitution, since the consequences of rescission include the restitution of benefits transferred by the representee in pursuance of the contract and an indemnity against liabilities necessarily incurred by the representee as a result of the contract.[281] Similarly, rectification[282] of a written document which by a mistake fails to give effect to a prior oral agreement may also lead to restitutionary relief. Full discussion of these remedies will be found in previous Chapters.[283] 29–050

Mistaken repairs or improvements to another's goods. The position of a person who has mistakenly expended money or effort in repairing or improving goods belonging to another person depends on whether a claim is made against him by the owner of the goods for wrongful interference with them, or whether 29–051

[276] *Deutsche Morgan Grenfell Group Plc v IRC* [2006] UKHL 49, [2007] 1 A.C. 558; Goymour [2007] C.L.J. 24; Häcker (2007) 123 L.Q.R. 177; Mitchell [2007] R.L.R. 123.

[277] *Woolwich Equitable Building Society v IRC* [1993] A.C. 70, below, para.29–083.

[278] See above, para.28–088.

[279] See below, para.29–172. *Westdeutsche Landesbank Girozentrale v Islington LBC* [1996] A.C. 669, 714–715 (Lord Browne-Wilkinson) doubting *Chase Manhattan Bank NA v Israel-British Bank (London) Ltd* [1981] Ch. 105 but cf. *Banque Financière de la Cité v Parc (Battersea) Ltd* [1999] 1 A.C. 221; *Thavron v Bank of Credit & Commerce International SA* [1985] 1 Lloyd's Rep. 259; *Re Goldcorp Exchange Ltd (In Receivership)* [1995] 1 A.C. 74, 103 and *Friends' Provident Life Office v Hillier Parker May & Rowden (A Firm)* [1997] Q.B. 85, 105–106 (Auld L.J.); *A.G.I.P. (Africa) Ltd v Jackson* [1990] Ch. 265; affirmed [1991] Ch. 547; Goff and Jones at pp.214–218; Virgo at pp.608–612; cf. Stoljar at pp.131–132, 138.

[280] See above, paras 6–103 et seq.

[281] See above, paras 6–115 et seq.

[282] See above, paras 5–107 et seq.

[283] See above, paras 5–107 et seq., 6–103 et seq.

the claim is brought against the owner by the repairer or improver for the value of the repairs or improvement.

29–052 **Claims by owner: statutory allowance.** Where the owner brings a claim for wrongful interference under the Torts (Interference with Goods) Act 1977 against a person who has improved[284] the goods in the honest but mistaken belief that he had title to them, s.6(1) of the Act provides that an allowance shall be made in respect of the improvement to the extent to which the value of the goods is attributable to it.[285] Section 6(2) provides for an equivalent allowance where the action is brought against a bona fide transferee from the improver whether or not the improver was in good faith; but s.6(3) provides that where a transferee who is a purchaser has received this allowance, then, in proceedings by him against the seller for recovery of the price on the ground of total failure of consideration,[286] a bona fide seller (who may be the improver) shall be entitled to the allowance. Where the owner seeks an order for delivery to him of the goods under s.3(2) of the Act in circumstances in which an allowance under s.6 would have been made, the court is given discretion to require, as a condition for delivery of the goods, that the allowance be made to the defendant. The Act, however, only applies where the improver acts in the honest belief that he had good title[287] to the goods and it has no application where the owner has reacquired the goods without the aid of the court.[288] It would appear that the Act is, in some respects, narrower than the common law which indirectly permitted an allowance in respect of improvements by fixing the damages in actions for conversion as the value of the goods in their unimproved state even where there was no mistake as to title.[289]

29–053 **Claims by the improver.** The position is less easy to state in view of the paucity of authority. Where the owner of the goods has requested, freely accepted or acquiesced in the improvement, the improver should, by analogy to the cases

---

284 This would appear to include all acts of the defendant which increase the value of the goods, although cf. *Palmer on Bailment*, 2nd edn, p.257. See also Law Reform Committee, Cmnd.4774, para.89.

285 This would appear to enact the pre-existing common law: *Greenwood v Bennett* [1973] 1 Q.B. 195 (following *Peruvian Guano Ltd v Drefus Bros & Co* [1892] A.C. 166, 175–176; and *Livingstone v Raywards Coal Co* (1880) 5 App. Cas. 25). See (1973) C.L.J. 23 and (1973) 36 M.L.R. 89; Birks (1974) 27 C.L.P. 13, 19 et seq.; Matthews (1981) C.L.J. 340; Sutton in Finn (ed.), *Essays on Restitution*, Ch.7.

286 See below, para.29–054. Section 6(2) refers to the recovery of damages by the transferee but this would seem to be a reference to the action for the price mentioned in s.6(3).

287 This would not include an improvement done with knowledge that title was disputed. cf. at common law, *Reid v Fairbanks* (1853) 13 C.B. 692.

288 Quaere whether the owner of the goods that have been improved is liable for conversion of the "improvement" unless it has become part of the goods by accession. Accession will occur where the improver has acted wrongfully: *Spence v Union Marine Insurance Co* (1868) L.R. 3 C.P. 427, 437–438; *Indian Oil Corp v Greenstone Shipping SA (Panama)* [1988] Q.B. 345; Goff and Jones at pp.101–102.

289 *Munro v Willmott* [1949] 1 K.B. 295 (a claim in detinue). cf. *Sachs v Miklos* [1948] 2 K.B. 23 (value of the goods bailed appreciated over time). Although the Torts (Interference with Goods) Act 1977 s.12 would give a bailee who has taken reasonable steps to communicate with the bailor the right to sell the bailed goods, he is obliged to account to the bailor for the proceeds of sale less any costs of sale, but not apparently for the value attributable to an improvement unless it can be said to be a cost incurred in the adoption of the best method of sale reasonably available; s.12(5)(a).

on improvements to land, be entitled to claim.[290] The nature of the relief will depend on the circumstances of the case but, in principle, the improver should be entitled to the reasonable value of his services even if this is not reflected in the value of the goods. Apart from cases of acquiescence, the present state of the authorities[291] would seem to preclude the improver having any claim, even one limited to any increase in the value of the goods attributable to the improvement. In *Greenwood v Bennett*[292] Cairns L.J. doubted that such a claim could be made.[293] However, Lord Denning M.R. was prepared to allow a person, who had improved a car honestly believing himself to be its owner, a direct claim against the owner[294]:

> "The court will order the plaintiffs, if they recover the car, or its improved value, to recompense the innocent purchaser for the work he has done on it. No matter whether the plaintiffs recover it with the aid of the court, or without it, the innocent purchaser will recover the value of the improvements he has done to it."[295]

In the context of that case, in which the true owner had realised the increased value by selling the car, this may be unexceptionable but it should be noted that where an increase in value has not been realised it is only possible to regard it as a benefit for the purpose of a restitutionary claim if one is willing to force a sale upon the owner.[296]

(f) *Failure of Consideration*[297]

General principles. Where money has been paid under a transaction that is or becomes ineffective the payer may recover the value of the money provided that the consideration for the payment has totally failed. Although the principle is not confined to contracts[298] most of the cases are concerned with failed contracts. In that context failure of consideration occurs where there has been a complete 29–054

[290] Below, para.29–161; Goff and Jones at pp.244–247.

[291] In particular the cases on "voluntariness", below, para.29–109, especially *Falke v Scottish Imperial Insurance Co* (1886) 34 Ch D 234; (below, para.29–115). See also *Forman & Co Proprietary Ltd v Ship "Liddelsdale"* [1900] A.C. 190; *Sumpter v Hedges* [1898] 1 Q.B. 673.

[292] [1973] 1 Q.B. 195, 203 (Cairns L.J.). See also Matthews (1981) C.L.J. 340, 351–358.

[293] [1973] 1 Q.B. 195.

[294] The third member of the court, Phillimore L.J., did not advert to this point.

[295] [1973] 1 Q.B. 195, 202.

[296] Birks at pp.121–124. See also *B.P. Exploration Co (Libya) Ltd v Hunt (No.2)* [1979] 1 W.L.R. 783, 799, 803 (Robert Goff J.); Beatson (1981) 97 L.Q.R. 389, 410–411; Matthews (1981) C.L.J. 340, 366 for the difficulty in treating this as a benefit.

[297] Burrows at Ch.10; Goff and Jones at Ch. 20; Virgo at Ch.12; Virgo in Johnston and Zimmermann (eds), *Unjustified Enrichment: Key Issues in Comparative Perspective* (2002), Ch.4; Stoljar (1959) 75 L.Q.R. 53; "Pecuniary Restitution on Breach of Contract" (Law Com. No.121, 1983), paras 1.6–1.8, 3.1–3.11.

[298] *Martin v Andrews* (1856) 7 E. & B. 1 (recovery of conduct money paid to subpoenaed witness when action settled before trial); *Chillingworth v Esche* [1924] 1 Ch. 97 (recovery of deposit paid under transaction expressed to be "subject to contract" when no contract concluded through actions of payer). See also below, para.29–074 (void contracts).

failure of the performance for which the payer had bargained.[299] Thus, the failure is judged from the payer's point of view and:

> "... when one is considering the law of failure of consideration and of the quasi-contractual right to recover money on that ground, it is generally speaking, not the promise which is referred to as the consideration, but the performance of the promise."[300]

The failure has to be total because the consideration is "whole and indivisible", and the courts will not divide or apportion it unless the parties have done so.[301] This is partly because one cannot assume that all parts of the payee's performance are equally valuable and that the contract price is earned incrementally,[302] but historically it was also because of the non-recognition in English law of the principle of unjust enrichment.[303] Thus, any performance of the actual thing promised, *as determined by the contract*, is fatal to recovery under this heading. As Lord Goff said in *Stocznia Gdanska SA v Latvian S.S. Co*[304]:

> "... the test is not whether the promisee has received a specific benefit, but rather whether the promisor has performed any part of the contractual duties in respect of which the payment is due."

29–055 **Total failure of consideration and detrimental reliance.** At common law a total failure of consideration may occur even though the payee has incurred expense in partly performing his side of the contract, though this will turn on whether that performance can be considered to have been "bargained-for".[305] The line between irrelevant detrimental reliance and benefit may be very fine, and sometimes can appear to turn solely upon the formal classification of the contract in question. Thus, where a contract for the sale of textile machines was later discharged for frustration, the fact that the seller had done a considerable

---

[299] *Fibrosa Spolka Akcyjna v Fairbairn Lawson Combe Barbour Ltd* [1943] A.C. 32 (above, para.23–072); *Comptoir d'Achat et de Vente du Boerenbond Belge SA v Luis de Ridder Limitada* [1949] A.C. 293 (below, para.29–056); *Branwhite v Worcester Works Finance Ltd* [1969] 1 A.C. 552; *Rover International Ltd v Cannon Film Sales Ltd (No.3)* [1989] 1 W.L.R. 912, noted (1989) 105 L.Q.R. 179; *Stocznia Gdanska SA v Latvian S.S. Co, Latreefers Inc* [1998] 1 W.L.R. 574; *Roxborough v Rothmans of Pall Mall Australia Ltd* (2002) 76 A.L.J.R. 203 (High Court of Australia), paras 16, 101–109, 164–173 and cases cited in following footnotes. cf. *Taylor v Motability Finance Ltd* [2004] EWHC 2619 (Comm) at [25] (Cooke J.), where the judge appears to suggest that the test of whether the consideration has failed totally depends on substantial performance by the claimant, whereas the true position is that it typically depends on whether there has been performance by the other party to the contract.

[300] *Fibrosa Spolka Akcyjna v Fairbairn Lawson Combe Barbour Ltd* [1943] A.C. 32, 48, per Viscount Simon. Where, as in certain insurance contracts, the payer bargains for the promise the general rule will not apply: *Tyrie v Fletcher* (1777) 2 Cowp. 666. See below, para.29–082. For reconsideration of the requirement of totality, see *Goss v Chilcott* [1996] A.C. 788 and see below, para.29–063.

[301] As where there is a sale at a unit price; *Biggerstaff v Rowatt's Wharf* [1896] 2 Ch. 93, 100; *Ebrahim Dawood Ltd v Heath Ltd* [1961] 2 Lloyd's Rep. 512; on which see further below, para.29–062.

[302] *Whincup v Hughes* (1871) L.R. 6 C.P. 78, 81.

[303] (1871) L.R. 6 C.P. 78, 82, 84. On this see above, para.29–011.

[304] [1998] 1 W.L.R. 574, 588.

[305] [1998] 1 W.L.R. 574, 588.

amount of work in manufacturing them did not prevent the buyer recovering a prepayment as having been paid on a total failure of consideration.[306] On the other hand, in a shipbuilding contract for work and materials, it has been said that work done by the builders in drawing up plans and starting the construction amounted to a contractual benefit which prevented there from being a total failure of consideration.[307] What is relevant is the bargained-for performance and not the formal classification of the contract as one for sale or sale and services. The classification merely reflects the fact that in contracts for work and materials the purchaser is paying for the work as well as for the end-product while in contracts of sale he is only paying for the end-product.[308] In the former cases the reliance on the form of services rendered by the payee is to be regarded as the bargained-for performance, in other cases it is not. Thus, where a prepayment was made under a distributorship agreement, it was recoverable despite the fact that, after entering the agreement, the licensor-payee had paid a substantial sum to a third party to buy back rights to films subject to the agreement.[309] The bargained-for performance was the opportunity for the licensee to earn a share of gross receipts under the distributorship and thus the consideration had wholly failed as a result of the invalidity of the agreement.

Illustrations of total failure of consideration. Where money was paid to brokers to purchase goods in accordance with instructions, but the brokers did not make the contract authorised by their principals, it was held that the money could be recovered by the principals on the basis of a total failure of consideration.[310] Similarly, bondholders who had subscribed money for a purpose which failed were entitled to recover their money from the bank which held the subscriptions.[311] In another case sellers were bound to deliver at Antwerp a quantity of rye then in a ship en route to Antwerp, and the buyers paid the price against a delivery order directed to the sellers' agents at Antwerp; but the Germans occupied the town and the cargo was sold by the sellers in Lisbon where the ship discharged. The House of Lords held that the consideration had wholly failed so that the buyers were entitled to recover the price.[312] Again, 29–056

[306] *Fibrosa Spolka Akcyjna v Fairbairn Lawson Combe Barbour Ltd* [1943] A.C. 32, and see [1942] 1 K.B. 12, 14.

[307] *Hyundai Heavy Industries Ltd v Papadopoulos* [1980] 1 W.L.R. 1129, 1134, 1148 (Viscount Dilhorne and Lord Fraser); *Stocznia Gdanska SA v Latvian Shipping Co, Latreefers Inc* [1998] 1 W.L.R. 574; *Salvage Association v C.A.P. Financial Services Ltd* [1995] F.S.R. 654. See also *Maersk Air Ltd v Expeditors International (UK) Ltd* [2003] 1 Lloyd's Rep. 491, 497.

[308] Beatson (1981) 97 L.Q.R. 398, 402–403, 407–408, 412–413; Palmer, *The Law of Restitution* (1978), para.4.2.

[309] *Rover International Ltd v Cannon Film Sales Ltd (No.3)* [1989] 1 W.L.R. 912, 932, 936–937 (Dillon L.J.)

[310] *Bostock v Jardine* (1865) 3 H. & C. 700.

[311] *R. v Royal Bank of Canada* [1913] A.C. 283. See also *National Bolivian Navigation Co v Wilson* (1880) 5 App. Cas. 176.

[312] *Comptoir d'Achat et de Vente du Boerenbond Belge SA v Luis de Ridder Limitada* [1949] A.C. 293. (This was really a case of frustration (at 313) but since the facts occurred before 1943, the House of Lords did not refer to the Law Reform (Frustrated Contracts) Act 1943, but followed the common law principles laid down in *Fibrosa Spolka Akcyjna v Fairbairn Lawson Combe Barbour Ltd* [1943] A.C. 32 (above, para.23–072). Had it been a normal CIF contract the case would have been decided differently: cf. the view of the facts taken by the Court of Appeal [1947] 2 All E.R. 443.)

where the names of the drawer and the acceptor were forged to a bill of exchange, and the bill was discounted by the plaintiffs for the defendants (who had indorsed it), it was held that, since the genuineness of the acceptance was of the essence of the description of a bill, there was a total failure of consideration entitling the plaintiffs to recover from the defendants the amount paid to them.[313] In general, where an ultra vires issue of shares is made, the subscribers are entitled to recover their money; but if a subscriber to an ultra vires issue of shares has sold his shares, he cannot allege that as far as he is concerned there has been a total failure of consideration.[314]

29–057 **Artificiality of distinctions.** The role of the contractual specification means that it is not true to say that there can be a total failure of consideration only where the payer received no benefit at all in return for the payment.[315] The concept of total failure of consideration can ignore real benefits received by the payer if they are not the benefits bargained for and despite significant detrimental reliance by the payee. Thus, in cases of the sale of a car by a non-owner, the price paid has been recovered despite substantial intermediate enjoyment of the car by the purchaser[316] even where the vendor is subsequently able to perfect his title[317] and where the value of the car has depreciated considerably.[318] This is because the benefit for which the payer had bargained, namely title to the car, had not been obtained. Similarly, if the purchaser of an estate pays the purchase money and enters into possession of the land but, before the conveyance is executed, he is evicted in consequence of a defect in the vendor's title, he can recover the purchase-money.[319] Again, an instalment paid under a film distributorship agreement was said to be recoverable despite the receipt of films because the relevant

---

[313] *Gurney v Womersley* (1854) 4 E. & B. 133.

[314] *Linz v Electric Wire Co of Palestine Ltd* [1948] A.C. 371 (quaere, if the subscriber retains the shares but has received a dividend: at 377). This decision of the Privy Council is criticised in Goff and Jones at p.493, fn.28 and may be difficult to reconcile with *Westdeutsche Landesbank Girozentrale v Islington LBC* [1994] 4 All E.R. 890, 929 (Hobhouse J.); *Guiness Mahon & Co Ltd v Kensington & Chelsea RLBC* [1998] 2 All E.R. 272 in relation to closed swap transactions. cf. *Wilkinson v Lloyd* (1845) 7 Q.B. 27 (recovery of purchase price of shares when directors refused to register the transfer).

[315] Carter and Tolhurst (2001) 9(1) A.P.L.R. 1.

[316] *Rowland v Divall* [1923] 2 K.B. 500; 129 L.T. 755. See further *Barber v N.W.S. Bank* [1996] 1 W.L.R. 641. This rule does not apply where the payer parts with the property for value: *Linz v Electric Wire Co of Palestine Ltd* [1948] A.C. 371.

[317] *Butterworth v Kingsway Motors Ltd* [1954] 1 W.L.R. 1286.

[318] [1954] 1 W.L.R. 1286. The car was bought for £1,275 and used for nearly a year. When it was returned it was worth about £800. For criticisms of this and other similar cases, and proposals for reform, see Law Com. Working Paper No.65 (1975), Pt IV. The same principles apply to hire purchase: *Karflex Ltd v Poole* [1933] 2 K.B. 251; *Warman v Southern Counties Finance Corp Ltd* [1949] 2 K.B. 576; Vol.II, para.38–296. cf. *Yeoman Credit Ltd v Apps* [1962] 2 Q.B. 508, 521, 525; *Kelly v Lombard Banking Co Ltd* [1959] 1 W.L.R. 41, below, para.29–061.

[319] *Johnson v Johnson* (1802) 3 B. & P. 162. See also *Wright v Colls* (1849) 8 C.B. 150. *Aliter* if the purchaser negligently fails to discover an error in the title until after completion (*Allen v Richardson* (1879) 13 Ch D 524), or if after the conveyance has been executed the purchaser is evicted by a title to which the covenants in the conveyance do not extend (*Clare v Lamb* (1875) L.R. 10 C.P. 334, 338; *Clayton v Leech* (1889) 41 Ch D 103; *Debenham v Sawbridge* [1901] 2 Ch. 98). cf. also *Hunt v Silk* (1804) 5 East. 449.

bargain was the opportunity to earn a share of gross receipts with the certainty of recouping the advance and no receipts had been earned.[320]

Contract discharged or ineffective. Money will only be recoverable on this ground where the contract is discharged.[321] This requirement has practical importance where, as in the case of breach of contract, discharge operates at the election of the innocent party.[322] A contract-breaker will therefore only be able to recover money where the other party has elected to accept the breach as discharging the contract.[323] The requirement is irrelevant where the contract is ineffective ab initio[324] (e.g. for informality or incapacity) or where, as in the case of frustration, it is discharged automatically.[325] Where the payer has received a benefit from the payee it must, as a general rule, be restored before he can recover his money.[326] Further, at least in some cases of breach of contract and frustration, recovery is only possible where there is no express or implied term in the contract making the payment irrecoverable.[327] 29–058

Comparison with damages.[328] Where the payee is in breach of contract the unjust enrichment claim is an alternative to an action for damages for breach of contract.[329] This will be an attractive option in cases in which the payer has made a bad bargain[330] or where his damages will be limited or irrecoverable. This may 29–059

[320] *Rover International Ltd v Cannon Film Sales Ltd (No.3)* [1989] 1 W.L.R. 912, 924–925, per Kerr L.J. See also *Westdeutsche Landesbank Girozentrale v Islington LBC* [1994] 4 All E.R. 890, 929 (Hobhouse J.); affirmed [1996] A.C. 669.

[321] *Kwei Tek Chao v British Traders and Shippers Ltd* [1954] 2 Q.B. 459, 475 (Devlin J.); *Weston v Downes* (1778) 1 Doug. 23; *Goodman v Pocock* (1850) 15 Q.B. 576.

[322] Above, para.24–001.

[323] *Dies v British and International Mining and Finance Corp Ltd* [1939] 1 K.B. 724, discussed below, para.29–065. But cf. *Roxborough v Rothmans of Pall Mall Australia Ltd* (2002) 76 A.L.J.R. 203 High Ct of Australia.

[324] *Rover International Ltd v Cannon Film Sales Ltd (No.3)* [1989] 1 W.L.R. 912; *Westdeutsche Landesbank Girozentrale v Islington LBC* [1994] 4 All E.R. 890, 929 (Hobhouse J.), [1996] A.C. 669; *Eastbourne BC v Foster* [2001] EWCA Civ 1091 (employee bound to return monies received under void employment arrangement but at the same time entitled to a defence of change of position).

[325] Above, para.23–071.

[326] *Towers v Barratt* (1786) 1 T.R. 133; *Baldry v Marshall* [1925] 1 Q.B. 260. In certain circumstances, as in the cases of sale by a non-owner, above, para.29–057, where the goods have been repossessed by the true owner, the payer is relieved from the duty to restore. N.B. that certain benefits, such as use of chattels (but cf. *Rowland v Divall* [1923] 2 K.B. 500, above, para.29–057), occupation of land or receipt of services, are non-returnable and in such cases the money will be irrecoverable: *Hunt v Silk* (1804) 5 East. 449; *Harrison v James* (1862) 7 H. & N. 804. Although, if the benefit received can be valued, quaere whether money paid can be recovered if the claimant transfers the value of the benefit received to the defendant.

[327] *Fibrosa Spolka Akcyjna v Fairbairn Lawson Combe Barbour Ltd* [1943] A.C. 32, 67 (Lord Wright). See also the Law Reform (Frustrated Contracts) Act 1943 s.2(3) and the power to contract out of other rights to restitution; Goff and Jones at pp.56–58; Virgo at pp.40–42.

[328] Dawson (1959) 20 Ohio St.L.J. 175; Treitel, *The Law of Contract*, 10th edn (2003), pp.1056–1057; Palmer, *The Law of Restitution* (1978), paras 4.1 et seq.; Birks [1987] L.M.C.L.Q. 421; Goodhart [1995] Rest. L. Rev. 3; Beale (1996) 112 L.Q.R. 205, 208. For comparison of damages and quantum meruit, see below, para.29–066 and on availability of restitutionary damages for breach of contract see below, para.29–151.

[329] See above, Ch.24.

[330] *Bush v Canfield* (1818) 2 Conn. 485; *B.P. Exploration Co (Libya) Ltd v Hunt (No.2)* [1979] 1 W.L.R. 783, 800 (Robert Goff J.); affirmed [1981] 1 W.L.R. 232 CA; [1983] 2 A.C. 352 HL. Although the latter case concerned claims under the Law Reform (Frustrated Contracts) Act 1943

be the result of requirements such as remoteness, the duty to mitigate and restrictions as to the kind of loss that is recoverable. Restitution, therefore, has a clear advantage over a claim for compensation for reliance losses since such a claim will not succeed if the defendant shows the reliance loss is greater than the expected profit.[331] Apart from this, the unjust enrichment claim has procedural and evidential advantages in that it is a liquidated claim.[332] It will also be attractive in those exceptional cases in which a total failure of consideration is established despite the receipt of a benefit by the payee. This is because an action for damages, but not an action for money had and received, would take account of such benefits.[333] However, the unjust enrichment claim does have disadvantages. The most obvious is that the claimant's loss of profits are only recoverable as damages and not by an action for money had and received, but there are others. Thus, in cases of sale, where a buyer has paid in advance for goods that he is entitled to reject, in principle he can return the goods and recover the money.[334] But if he has spent money on the goods while they are in his possession, this will be recoverable in an action for damages[335] but not in an action for restitution of the price.[336] The ground of total failure of consideration may also trigger a proprietary restitutionary claim, at least where the defendant knew of the total failure when money was received from the claimant.[337]

29–060 **Partial failure of consideration: statute.** Under the provisions of the Law Reform (Frustrated Contracts) Act 1943,[338] where a contract is frustrated, money paid under the contract may be recovered (subject to a claim or set-off for expenses incurred by the recipient of the payment) even though there has been only a partial failure of consideration.[339] The Act would now apply to a case like *Ferns v Carr*,[340] where a solicitor had received a premium from an articled clerk, who was to be in his office for five years, but the solicitor died before the five

---

s.1(2) the principle would appear to be the same. The objection that this reverses the contractual allocation of risks has not apparently been accepted, possibly because the law favours liquidated claims, because the stringency of the requirements needed to establish a total failure of consideration mean that the issue will rarely arise and because, on facts such as those in *Bush v Canfield*, the payee-seller would otherwise get something for nothing. See also Palmer, *The Law of Restitution* (1978), Vol.1, pp.382–383, 392–393.

[331] *C.C.C. Films (London) Ltd v Impact Quadrant Films Ltd* [1985] Q.B. 16; above, paras 26–073, 26–075.

[332] *Biggerstaff v Rowatt's Wharf* [1896] 2 Ch. 93, 105.

[333] *Rowland v Divall* [1923] 2 K.B. 500; above, para.29–057; but compare *Warman v Southern Counties Car Finance Corp Ltd* [1959] 2 K.B. 576, 582–583 (any enrichment at expense of owner not seller). On damages, see *Harling v Eddy* [1951] 2 K.B. 739.

[334] e.g. *Baldry v Marshall* [1925] 1 Q.B. 260, above, para.29–058.

[335] *Mason v Burningham* [1949] 2 K.B. 545.

[336] See above, para.29–052 for the provisions of s.6(3) of the Torts (Interference with Goods) Act 1977 in relation to actions for the return of the price on the ground of total failure of consideration.

[337] *Re Farepak Food and Gifts Ltd* [2006] EWHC 3272, [2006] All E.R. (D) 265. See also *Nesté Oy v Lloyd's Bank Plc* [1983] 2 Lloyd's Rep. 658. See below, para.29–160.

[338] The Act is fully discussed above in paras 23–074 et seq.

[339] *B.P. Exploration Co (Libya) Ltd v Hunt (No.2)* [1979] 1 W.L.R. 783, 800 (Robert Goff J.); affirmed [1981] 1 W.L.R. 232, CA; [1983] 2 A.C. 352 HL. The common law rule was limited to total failure of consideration; *Fibrosa Spolka Akcyjna v Fairbairn Lawson Combe Barbour Ltd* [1943] A.C. 32, above, para.23–072.

[340] (1885) 28 Ch D 409; and see *Whincup v Hughes* (1871) L.R. 6 C.P. 78.

years were completed; under the common law it was held that the clerk could not recover any part of the premium from the solicitor's estate. The court is empowered by the Law Reform (Frustrated Contracts) Act 1943 s.1(3) to order a party to a contract which is subsequently frustrated to pay for a "valuable benefit" obtained by him under the contract.[341] It has been said that:

> "... the fundamental principle underlying the Act itself, is prevention of the unjust enrichment of either party to the contract at the other's expense."[342]

Where a partnership is prematurely determined, the court has statutory power to order the return of all or part of a premium paid by a partner for admission to the firm.[343]

Partial failure of consideration: common law. Apart from these cases and unless the contract is divisible,[344] an unjust enrichment claim to recover money paid does not lie if the claimant has derived some of the benefit for which he bargained.[345] So, where a vendor sold a patent right and the purchaser paid the price, used the patent right and enjoyed a benefit from it, but it afterwards appeared that the patent was invalid, it was held that the purchaser could not claim restitution of the purchase-money.[346] Again, a passenger on a cruise ship which sank on the 10th day of a 14-day cruise could not claim restitution of the cruise fare.[347] In another case[348] a hirer paid an initial sum of £186 to a finance company under a hire-purchase agreement "in consideration of the option to purchase" a car. He used the car for over 12 months, paying the monthly instalments under the agreement, but then the finance company validly terminated the agreement because the hirer allowed a judgment creditor to levy execution against him. The hirer claimed recovery of his initial payment on the ground that there had been a total failure of consideration in that he never obtained the option, but the Court of Appeal rejected this contention, holding that the option was an existing right from the moment of signing the contract, notwithstanding that it could not be exercised until certain conditions had been fulfilled. The question whether the retention of all the money received by the 29–061

---

[341] For full details, see above, paras 23–084 et seq.

[342] *B.P. Exploration Co (Libya) Ltd v Hunt (No.2)* [1979] 1 W.L.R. 783, 799 (Robert Goff J.); affirmed [1981] 1 W.L.R. 232 CA; [1982] 2 A.C. 352 HL. In contrast, the Court of Appeal got "no help from the use of words which are not in the statute" [1981] 1 W.L.R. 232, 243.

[343] Partnership Act 1890 s.40.

[344] Below, para.29–062. On partial performance of an "entire" contract, see above, paras 21–027—21–037.

[345] *Hunt v Silk* (1804) 5 East 449. cf. *Steinberg v Scala (Leeds) Ltd* [1923] 2 Ch. 452 (above, para.8–040); *Linz v Electric Wire Co of Palestine Ltd* [1948] A.C. 371; *Michalinos & Co Ltd v Scourfield* (1950) 83 Ll. L. Rep. 494.

[346] *Taylor v Hare* (1805) 1 B. & P.N.R. 260; and see *Lawes v Purser* (1856) 6 E. & B. 930; *The Salvage Association v C.A.P. Financial Services Ltd* [1995] F.S.R. 654.

[347] *Baltic S.S. Co v Dillon* (1993) 67 A.L.J.R. 228 High Ct of Australia.

[348] *Kelly v Lombard Banking Co Ltd* [1959] 1 W.L.R. 41. See also *Yeoman Credit Ltd v Apps* [1962] 2 Q.B. 508, 521, 525. cf. *Warman v Southern Counties Car Finance Corp Ltd* [1949] 2 K.B. 576 (above, para.29–057: intermediate enjoyment of a car is not a "benefit" where vendor has no title).

finance company amounted to the retention of a penalty and not liquidated damages was apparently not raised in this case.[349]

29–062 **Partial failure of consideration in a divisible contract.** A claim in restitution to recover part of the money already paid to the defendant will sometimes lie where the contract can be regarded as divisible, and some part of the consideration relating to a divisible part of the contract has wholly failed. Lord Porter has said[350]:

> "If a divisible part of the contract has wholly failed, and part of the consideration can be attributed to that part, that portion of the money so paid can be recovered."

Thus, where the plaintiff ordered and paid for a specified tonnage of goods at a price of "18s. per cwt.", but, on delivery of the goods, it was discovered that less than the specified tonnage had been shipped, it was held that the plaintiff might recover the sum overpaid.[351] The question of divisibility may also arise in contracts where delivery is to be made in instalments.[352] Whether a contract is divisible and whether apportionment can take place has traditionally been an issue of construction based on the presumed intention of the parties. However, in *Goss v Chilcott* the Privy Council suggested that apportionment is not limited to the intention of the parties and may also occur as a matter of law in those cases in which it can be carried out without difficulty, for instance, where the benefit received by the payer was, as in that case, a monetary one.[353] In that case it was acknowledged that a loan could be apportioned between principal and interest. This is not controversial, but Lord Goff delivering the judgment of the Board suggested that, if required, he would also apportion the principal so that any repayments made of the principal would not prevent there being a restitutionary claim based on failure of consideration but would merely reduce the restitutionary claim to the balance of the loan.

29–063 **Reconsideration of the total failure requirement.** The recognition of the principle of unjust enrichment in English law may lead to reconsideration of the requirement that the failure of consideration be total. Although the Law Commission has recommended that it be maintained[354] this has been criticised[355] as leading to asymmetry between the position of claims for the recovery of money and claims for recompense for services where quantum meruit will lie even

---

[349] See *Stockloser v Johnson* [1954] 1 Q.B. 476 (above, para.26–148); *Dies v British and International Mining and Finance Corp Ltd* [1939] 1 K.B. 724; *Mayson v Clouet* [1924] A.C. 980 (below, para.29–065). cf. *Galbraith v Mitchenall Estates Ltd* [1965] 2 Q.B. 473 (Vol.II, para.38–324); *Sport International Poussum B.V. v Inter-Footwear Ltd* [1984] 1 W.L.R. 776.

[350] *Fibrosa Spolka Akcyjna v Fairbairn Lawson Combe Barbour Ltd* [1943] A.C. 32, 77.

[351] *Deveaux v Conolly* (1849) 8 C.B. 640. See also *Biggerstaff v Rowatt's Wharf Ltd* [1896] 2 Ch. 93; *Behrend & Co Ltd v Produce Brokers Co Ltd* [1920] 3 K.B. 530; *Ebrahim Dawood Ltd v Heath Ltd* [1961] 2 Lloyd's Rep. 512.

[352] See above, paras 23–091, 24–044.

[353] [1996] A.C. 788, 798.

[354] "Pecuniary Restitution on Breach of Contract" (Law Com. No.121, 1983).

[355] Birks at pp.259–264; Burrows (1984) 47 M.L.R. 762 at pp.333–336; Goff and Jones at pp.552–555; Virgo at pp.323–326.

where some counter-performance has been rendered.[356] It is also inconsistent with the approach of equity to rescission. In neither situation have the courts regarded the difficulty of placing a value upon the contractual performance rendered as insurmountable. The fine and sometimes artificial distinctions produced by the concept of total failure of consideration has already been noted[357] as has the distinction between entire and divisible contracts.[358] It is also the case that courts are willing to avoid the total failure of consideration rule by dividing the contract, sometimes artificially, and holding that there has been a total failure in relation to the parts not performed.[359] In the High Court of Australia it has been said that "if counter-restitution is relatively simple . . . , insistance on total failure of consideration can be misleading or confusing"[360] and that:

> " . . . where both parties have impliedly acknowledged that the consideration can be 'broken up' or apportioned . . . , any rationale for adhering to the traditional rule requiring *total* failure of consideration disappears."[361]

The Privy Council has shown support for one of these methods of relaxing the requirement for total failure of consideration, namely apportionment.[362] Moreover, in *Westdeutsche Landesbank Girozentrale v Islington LBC*,[363] Lord Goff expressed support for the reformulation of the total failure of consideration rule. However, he subsequently affirmed the total failure requirement in *Stocznia Gdanska SA v Latvian S.S. Co, Latreefers Inc.*[364]

Recovery of deposits.[365] Where a sum of money is paid under a contract and the contract is not completed, the right of the payer to claim the return of the money depends on the construction of the particular terms of the contract.[366] If it is called a "deposit" then, if nothing is said expressly about the conditions governing it, it will be taken to be required as a security for the completion of the contract by the payer and will be forfeited to the other party if the payer fails to 29–064

---

356 Below, paras 29–066—29–069.

357 Above, paras 29–057, 29–061.

358 Above para.21–027.

359 Above, para.29–062.

360 *David Securities Pty Ltd v Commonwealth Bank of Australia* (1992) 66 A.L.J.R. 768, 779. See also *Roxborough v Rothmans of Pall Mall Australia Ltd* (2002) 76 A.L.J.R. 203 High Ct of Australia (tax included in cost of goods but held to be a distinct part of the consideration paid by buyers).

361 (1992) 66 A.L.J.R. 768, 780. Note also *Westdeutsche Landesbank Girozentrale v Islington LBC* [1996] A.C. 669, 682–683 (Lord Goff); *D.O. Ferguson & Associates v Sohl* (1992) 62 Build. L.R. 92; *White Arrow Express Ltd v Lamey's Distribution Ltd* (1995) 15 Tr. L.R. 69, CA, noted Beale (1996) 112 L.Q.R. 205. But cf. *Pan Ocean Shipping Co Ltd v Creditcorp Ltd* [1994] 1 W.L.R. 161, 164–166 (Lord Goff).

362 *Goss v Chilcott* [1996] A.C. 788, above, para.29–062.

363 [1996] A.C. 669, 682–683. But cf. *Stocznia Gdanska SA v Latvian S.S.* [1998] 1 W.L.R. 574, 590 (Lord Goff).

364 [1998] 1 W.L.R. 574.

365 On recovery of a deposit paid to the other party's agent, see Vol.II, para.31–110.

366 *Howe v Smith* (1884) 27 Ch D 89, 97–98; *Harrison v Holland* [1922] 1 K.B. 211. See also *Smith v Butler* [1900] 1 Q.B. 694; *Shuttleworth v Clews* [1910] 1 Ch. 176. cf. *R. V. Ward Ltd v Bignall* [1967] 1 Q.B. 534; *Workers' Trust and Merchant Bank Ltd v Dojap Investments Ltd* [1993] A.C. 573. In the sale of land, the conditions of sale will usually contain express provisions relating to the deposit. See also below, paras 29–197—29–198.

perform his side of the contract.[367] If only part of the agreed deposit has actually been paid, the better view is that, provided the obligation to make the payment has accrued, the innocent party can sue to recover the balance of the deposit.[368] A deposit may be recovered in the case of purchase on a condition which is not performed.[369] It is also prima facie recoverable where it is paid during the negotiations for a contract and no binding contract is concluded.[370] As regards contracts for the sale or exchange of any interest in land, the court has a discretion to order repayment of any deposit where the justice of the case requries it.[371] It may also be possible to seek equitable relief from forfeiture in respect of deposits and other payments required as security for performance where the forfeiture provision is penal[372] and it would be unconscionable for the payee to retain the payment. This jurisdiction, based on *Stockloser v Johnson*,[373] is fully discussed in Ch.26.[374]

29–065 **Part payments not intended to be deposits.**[375] Different principles apply if there is a substantial prepayment of the purchase price which is not intended to be in the nature of a deposit or earnest. In this situation the payer may still have a claim for recovery, despite the fact that the non-performance of the contract was due to his own fault. Thus, where a buyer repudiated his contract to purchase goods, he was nevertheless held to be entitled to recover a substantial prepayment made by him, subject to a deduction in respect of the actual damage suffered by the seller through the breach of contract.[376] This was because the

[367] *Howe v Smith* (1884) 27 Ch D 89, 97–98. But see the proposals of the Law Commission's Working Paper No.61 (1975), paras 49–67.

[368] *Hinton v Sparkes* (1868) L.R. 3 C.P. 161, 166; *The Blankenstein* [1985] 1 W.L.R. 435. cf. *Lowe v Hope* [1970] 1 Ch. 94; *Johnson v Jones* [1972] N.Z.L.R. 313, 318. But *Hinton v Sparkes* was not cited to Pennycuick J. in *Lowe v Hope* and *Johnson v Jones* concerned an express forfeiture clause which only applied to "moneys paid". These cases appear inconsistent with the principle that discharge of contract only operates prospectively; applied to moneys due as instalments in *Hyundai Heavy Industries Co Ltd v Papadopoulos* [1980] 1 W.L.R. 1129; *Stocznia Gdanska SA v Latvian S.S.* [1998] 1 W.L.R. 574, below, para.29–065. See also Law Com. Working Paper No. 61, para.59; Carter and Tolhurst (2001) 9(1) A.P.L.R. 1.

[369] *Wright v Newton* (1835) 2 C.M. & R. 124.

[370] *Chillingworth v Esche* [1924] 1 Ch. 97.

[371] Law of Property Act 1925 s.49(2). See above, para.26–152.

[372] Despite their similar functions, clauses requiring payment as security for performance are distinguished from penalty clauses (above, para.26–125) which provide for payment *after* breach. Although *Public Works Commissioners v Hills* [1906] A.C. 368 supports the application of the rules governing penalty clauses and liquidated damages clauses to stipulations for security for due performance, in the present state of the law, this is doubtful; *Linggi Plantations Ltd v Jagatheesan* (1972) 1 M.L.J. 89, 91, per Lord Hailsham L.C. cf. *Workers Trust & Merchant Bank Ltd v Dojap Investments Ltd* [1995] A.C. 573. See Law Commission Working Paper No.61 (1975), paras 57–67.

[373] [1954] 1 Q.B. 476.

[374] See above, paras 26–148, 26–150. See also Goff and Jones at pp.540–546.

[375] Beatson (1981) 97 L.Q.R. 389; *The Use and Abuse of Unjust Enrichment* (1991) Ch.3; above, para.26–131.

[376] *Dies v British and International Mining and Finance Corp Ltd* [1939] 1 K.B. 724. See above, para.26–154 (distinguished in *Elson v Prices Tailors Ltd* [1963] 1 W.L.R. 287). For the same principle in other types of contract, see *Mayson v Clouet* [1924] A.C. 980; *McDonald v Dennys Lascelles Ltd* (1933) 48 C.L.R. 457 (contracts for the sale of land); *Rover International Ltd v Cannon Film Sales Ltd (No.3)* [1989] 1 W.L.R. 912, 932 (Kerr L.J.), 936 (Dillon L.J.) (film distribution contract).

right to the payment was conditional upon the subsequent completion of the contract.[377] However, where, as in a contract for work and materials, the contractual obligations of the party to whom a part payment or an instalment is made mean that he is bound to incur expenses before completing performance, the right to the payment will be unconditional and the payment will be irrecoverable although it is not required as security for due performance.[378]

Quantum meruit for work done where the contract is terminated by breach. According to Winfield[379] there is only one instance of quantum meruit which is properly regarded as restitutionary. Alderson B. put it as follows: 29–066

> "Where one party has absolutely refused to perform, or has rendered himself incapable of performing, his part of the contract, he puts it in the power of the other party either to sue for a breach of it, or to rescind the contract and sue on a quantum meruit for the work actually done."[380]

Although the matter is not free from doubt the better view is that such a quantum meruit claim is grounded on the failure of consideration.[381] In a leading case, *Planché v Colburn*,[382] the defendants engaged Planché to write a volume for publication in the defendant's proposed series of "The Juvenile Library". After Planché had written some of his work, the defendants abandoned the whole publication, and it was held that Planché might, without tendering his completed work, sue to recover reasonable remuneration for his work already done.[383] In *Prickett v Badger*[384] an agent was employed to sell land at a certain price, but

---

[377] *Palmer v Temple* (1839) 9 A. & E. 508, 521; *McDonald v Dennys Lascelles Ltd* (1933) 48 C.L.R. 457, 477; *Fibrosa Spolka Akcyjna v Fairbairn Lawson Combe Barbour Ltd* [1943] A.C. 32, 65 (Lord Wright); *Guardian Ocean Cargos Ltd v Banco de Brasil SA (Nos 1 & 3)* [1994] 2 Lloyd's Rep. 152.

[378] *Hyundai Heavy Industries Co Ltd v Papadopoulos* [1980] 1 W.L.R. 1129. Although that case does not make it entirely clear whether the distinction from *Dies v British International Mining and Finance Corp Ltd* [1939] 1 K.B. 724 is based on the fact that in *Dies* the consideration for the payment had totally failed or on the need, on facts such as those in *Hyundai* [1980] 1 W.L.R. 1129 (above, para.29–055), to protect the reliance of the performer (on which, see Beatson at pp.401–405; *The Use and Abuse of Unjust Enrichment* (1991), pp.56–61), in *Rover International Ltd v Cannon Film Sales Ltd* [1989] 1 W.L.R. 912, it was said to be based on total failure of consideration. See also *Stocznia Gdanska SA v Latvian S.S. Co* [1998] 1 W.L.R. 574.

[379] *Province of the Law of Tort* (1931), pp.157–160; *Quasi-Contracts* (1952), pp.51–60. See also Winfield (1947) 63 L.Q.R. 35; Birks at pp.226–234, 239–242; Goff and Jones at pp.515–518.

[380] *De Bernardy v Harding* (1853) 8 Ex. 822, 824. See to the same effect *Luxor (Eastbourne) Ltd v Cooper* [1941] A.C. 108, 140–141 (Lord Wright). See also Birks at pp.268–279.

[381] Burrows at pp.343–344; Virgo at p.308. Although in *Yeoman's Row Management Ltd v Cobbe* [2008] UKHL 55 the House of Lords recognised a claim for quantum meruit, in respect of work done in anticipation of a contract being made, which was distinct from a separate claim apparently founded on total failure of consideration which was itself apparently distinct from a claim in unjust enrichment, although it is unclear what the difference between the three claims is.

[382] (1831) 8 Bing. 14, 16, Tindal C.J. said: "I agree that when a special contract is in existence and open, the plaintiff cannot sue on a *quantum meruit*", also reported in 5 Car. & P. 58 and 1 M. & S. 51. See, on this point, *Weston v Downes* (1778) 1 Doug. 23.

[383] It is, however, unclear how the defendant can be considered to have been enriched since no benefit had been received by the defendant. See Burrows at p.17; Virgo at p.66. cf. Birks at pp.126–127, 129.

[384] (1856) 1 C.B.(N.S.) 296. The position of such an agent employed to effect a sale was fully considered by the House of Lords in *Luxor (Eastbourne) Ltd v Cooper* [1941] A.C 108. See Vol.II, paras 31–138 et seq.

although he found a purchaser, the owner refused to sell and wrongfully revoked the agent's authority. The agent successfully sued for reasonable remuneration for his work and labour up to that date.

29–067 **Quantum meruit and contractual remedies.** In *Taylor v Motability Finance Ltd*[385] a distinction was drawn between claims involving goods and services and claims involving money, with the assumption being that the ground of total failure of consideration only applied to the latter claim. In this case the defendant terminated an employment contract with the claimant. The claimant argued that this constituted a repudiatory breach so that a restitutionary remedy could be awarded outside of the contract for the work done grounded on total failure of consideration. This argument was rejected because the claimant had fully performed the contract by providing services to the defendant and so, although the primary obligation to perform had been revoked, the contractual regime subsisted in terms of the secondary obligation to pay damages for breach. It appears from this decision that where a claimant has paid money to the defendant and has received nothing in return, the contractual regime no longer applies once the contract has been discharged, so that a restitutionary claim will lie.[386] Where, however, goods or services are provided by the claimant who has substantially performed the contract, the contractual regime still governs the award of remedies despite the repudiation of the contract.[387] The creation of such a distinction dependent on the nature of the enrichment received by the defendant is difficult to defend.

29–068 **Bad bargains.** Where the innocent party has made a bad bargain the damages for breach may well be less than the reasonable value of the work he has done. In such circumstances the claimant would wish to obtain a restitutionary remedy rather than damages which would be affected by the contractual limit. It has been unclear whether a restitutionary remedy is available to the innocent party in such circumstances or whether any claim for reasonable remuneration will be limited to a rateable proportion of the contract price. The weight of United States authority favours the view that the quantum meruit should not be limited in this way,[388] the Privy Council has held that the measure of relief in a quantum meruit is the actual value of the work and that the profitability of the contract is irrelevant[389] and the Law Commission has recommended that a quantum meruit granted to an innocent party should not be based on the contract price.[390] Until

[385] [2004] EWHC 2619 (Comm).

[386] [2004] EWHC 2619 (Comm) at [25] (Cooke J).

[387] [2004] EWHC 2619 (Comm).

[388] The most notable instance is *Boomer v Muir* (1933) 24 P. 2d 570, in which $258,000 was awarded as the value of the work done over and above the price paid, although only $20,000 was still due under the contract. See also the authorities cited by Palmer, *The Law of Restitution* (1978), Vol.I, pp.389–390.

[389] *Slowey v Lodder* [1904] A.C. 442; affirming (1900) N.Z.L.R. 321; *Reynard Construction (ME) Pty Ltd v Minister of Public Works* (1992) 26 N.S.W.L.R. 234; *Newton Woodhouse v Trevor Toys Ltd* Unreported December 20, 1991 CA; *Rover International Ltd v Cannon Film Sales Ltd (No.3)* [1989] 1 W.L.R. 912 (below, para.29–076; see also above, para.29–055) supports this approach although the contract in that case was void.

[390] Law Comm. No.121, para.2.52 on which see Birks at pp.262–263. See in general, Birks [1987] L.M.C.L.Q. 421.

recently the matter does not appear to have been considered explicitly in England.[391] However, in *Taylor v Motability Finance Ltd*[392] Cooke J. stated that there is no justification for the award of a restitutionary remedy which is in excess of the contractual limit since the award of such a remedy would put the claimant in a better position than he would have been in had the contract been fulfilled, which would be unjust. He emphasised that, when determining the quantum meruit, regard should be had to the contract both as a guide to the value which the parties put on the service and to ensure justice between the parties.

Relevance of the contract price. Although it might be thought wrong to allow the innocent party to "reverse" the contractual allocation of risks[393] and difficult to value the benefit without regard to the contract price,[394] it has also been argued that the contract price was agreed in the context of a contemplated complete performance and that this would not necessarily have been agreed for part performance.[395] The presence of economies of scale may mean that it does not follow that a person who agrees to pave 10 miles of road for a specified price would have agreed to pave 10 yards at a prorated price.[396] Furthermore, to allow a party in breach to reduce the award by reference to the contract price in effect awards him "a portion of his anticipated profit on the contract despite the fact that he was the contract breaker".[397] Finally, the contrast with claims for the recovery of money paid under contracts on the ground that there has been a total failure of consideration should be noted. In those cases the objection that recovery might reverse the contractual allocation of risks does not appear to have been taken.[398] An alternative to prorating the contract price is to limit the quantum meruit to the total contract price. This has been justified on the ground that it fully protects the claimant's expectations but avoids giving him a "windfall".[399] However, it does so by awarding the person who has committed a 29–069

[391] *Inchbold v Western Neilgherry Coffee, etc.* (1864) 17 C.B.(N.S.) 733 may suggest the use of the contract price as a ceiling but the judgments make no clear distinction between damages and a quantum meruit. See also *Burchall v Gowrie & Blockhouse Collieries* [1910] A.C. 614 (contract price used to value services). cf. *De Bernardy v Harding* (1853) 8 Ex. 822; *Prickett v Badger* (1856) 1 C.B.(N.S.) 296.

[392] [2004] EWHC 2619 (Comm) at [26].

[393] Burrows at p.346 would restrict the quantum meruit to a proration of the contract price unless there is incontrovertible benefit.

[394] *Burchall v Gowrie & Blockhouse Collieries* [1910] A.C. 614; *B.P. Exploration Co (Libya) Ltd v Hunt (No.2)* [1979] 1 W.L.R. 783, 822, 825 (Robert Goff J.). See also Law Com. Working Paper No.65 (1975), paras 26–32 for other difficulties of valuation. See further Law Com. No.121, paras 2.50–2.57. In *ERDC Group Ltd v Brunel University* [2006] EWHC 687 (TCC) quantum meruit was assessed with reference to the contract price where the claim for quantum meruit arose for work done after the expiry of a letter of appointment which had provided a contractual basis for the previous work.

[395] Palmer (1959) 20 Ohio State L.J. 264; *The Law of Restitution* (1978), Vol.I, pp.404–406.

[396] *The Law of Restitution* (1978), Vol.I, pp.404–406. This example is taken from the facts of *Kehoe v Rutherford* (1893) 27 A. 912 in which only a proportionate part of the price was recovered.

[397] Palmer at p.401. See also *Prickett v Badger* (1856) 1 C.B.(N.S.) 296, 306.

[398] Above, para.29–059.

[399] Goff and Jones at pp.516–518. Of the various solutions in the US cases, they prefer that in *Wuchter v Fitzgerald* (1917) 163 P. 819.

repudiatory breach which has led to the contract being discharged[400] a portion of his contractual expectations and has the consequence of producing disequilibrium between the position of a claimant who has done a small proportion of the work, where the contract price limit would in fact rarely apply, and the position of one who has done the bulk of the work, where the limit would be more likely to apply.[401]

29–070 **Claim of the party in breach.** Normally, the party in breach cannot recover for goods supplied or services rendered, even if the innocent party terminates further performance of the contract[402]; he may, however, be able to claim payment for the performance of a divisible part of a contract which is not an "entire" contract,[403] or in certain special situations.[404]

29–071 **Quantum valebat and quantum meruit to fix a price or remuneration.** If no price for goods sold has been fixed in the contract of sale, the law will imply that a reasonable price is to be paid, and, in an action for *quantum valebant*, the court will, as "a question of fact dependent on the circumstances of each particular case", decide what is a reasonable price.[405] Similarly, in a contract for work to be done, if no scale of remuneration is fixed, the law imposes an obligation to pay a reasonable sum (quantum meruit).[406] The circumstances must clearly show that the work is not to be done gratuitously before the court will, in the absence of an express contract, infer that there was a valid contract with an

---

400 On discharge, see above, Chs 22–24.

401 Beatson at pp.14–15. In the road example, if the contract price was £1 million, and the market price was £2 million, the limit would only affect a claimant who had completed more than half the work.

402 See in general, *Pecuniary Restitution on Breach of Contract* (Law Com. No.121, 1983), Pt II.

403 See by analogy, *Roberts v Havelock* (1832) 3 B. & Ad. 404; *Taylor v Laird* (1856) 25 L.J. Ex. 328. See also *Miles v Wakefield MBC* [1987] A.C. 539 but cf. *Wiluszynski v Tower Hamlets LBC* [1989] I.C.R. 493.

404 Above, paras 21–032—21–038. Note especially the doctrine of substantial performance, above, para.21–032, acceptance of short delivery under an entire contract for the sale of goods, Sale of Goods Act 1979 s.30(1); Vol.II, paras 43–317 et seq., and the position of freight after a deviation, *Hain S.S. Co Ltd v Tate & Lyle Ltd* (1934) 39 Com. Cas. 259, 271–272; (1936) 41 Com. Cas. 350, 358, 367–368, 373; Goff and Jones at pp.549–555, but cf. Beatson (1981) 97 L.Q.R. 389, 413–414, *Restitution*, pp.66–69. See also *Miles v Wakefield MBC* [1987] A.C. 539, but cf. *Wiluszynski v Tower Hamlets LBC* [1989] I.C.R. 493. See also *Item Software v Fassihi* [2004] EWCA Civ 1244, [2005] I.C.R. 450, where the Apportionment Act 1870 was applied to enable an employee who had been dismissed to recover a proportionate part of his monthly salary for the period he had actually worked, despite his breach of the contract of employment.

405 Sale of Goods Act 1979 s.8(2); *Foley v Classique Coaches Ltd* [1934] 2 K.B. 1. (cf. above, paras 2–128 et seq.).

406 e.g. *Way v Latilla* [1937] 3 All E.R. 759 HL; *William Lacey (Hounslow) Ltd v Davis* [1957] 1 W.L.R. 932; *British Steel Corp v Cleveland Bridge & Engineering Co Ltd* [1984] 1 All E.R. 504. See Ball (1983) 99 L.Q.R. 572; Beatson at pp.5–8; McKendrick (1988) 8 O.J.L.S. 197. See also *Lagos v Grunwaldt* [1910] 1 K.B. 41, 48; *Robins v Power* (1858) 4 C.B.(N.S.) 778. cf. *Re Richmond Gate Property Co Ltd* [1965] 1 W.L.R. 335. If the person at whose request the work is done subsequently promises a definite sum as remuneration, the so-called rule in *Lampleigh v Braithwaite* (1615) Hob. 105 may apply: see above, para.3–029.

implied term that a reasonable remuneration would be paid[407]; this principle may extend to services performed in anticipation that negotiations will lead to the conclusion of a contract, provided that the services were requested or acquiesced in by the recipient.[408] In this context, it has been said that quantum meruit is not truly restitutionary, since it is only "an incident in assessing the amount due under an ordinary contract where the amount is blank".[409] It is, however, difficult to accept this in the case of services rendered in anticipation that a contract would be entered into later[410] and, in such a case, a quantum meruit is not subject to contractual defences such as a claim for late delivery.[411] It has been said that these may be examples of:

> "... cases not founded on contract, nor in tort, nor upon the application of any equitable doctrine or principle, where there may be recovery."[412]

In *British Steel Corp v Cleveland Bridge & Engineering Co Ltd*[413] Robert Goff J. said that the obligation imposed in such cases sounds in restitution and not in contract.[414] This approach was endorsed by the House of Lords in *Yeoman's Row Management Ltd v Cobbe*.[414a]

Additional remuneration. An action for quantum meruit may allow recovery of a reasonable sum as additional remuneration for extra work by a building contractor, where, although the contract permitted the owner to order extra work, the amount of extra work actually ordered was so great as to go beyond the scope of the contract and entitle the builder to claim that he should not be limited to the maximum profit fixed by the contract.[415] The same principle has been applied to a contract of employment, where, in lieu of an increase of salary, the employer promised to pay a bonus on the net trading profits of the business but the method of assessing the bonus was never agreed.[416] 29–072

---

407 *Lampleigh v Braithwaite* (1615) Hob. 105.

408 *William Lacey (Hounslow) Ltd v Davis* [1957] 1 W.L.R. 932; *Peter Lind & Co Ltd v Mersey Docks and Harbour Board* [1972] 2 Lloyd's Rep. 234; *Sabemo v N. Sydney Municipal Council* [1977] 2 N.S.W.L.R. 880; *Marston Construction Co Ltd v Kigass Ltd* [1989] 46 B.L.R. 109; *Regalian Properties Plc v London Dockland Development Corp* [1995] 1 W.L.R. 212; *Countrywide Communications Ltd v ICL Pathway Ltd* [2000] C.L.C. 324; *Yeoman's Row Management Ltd v Cobbe* [2008] UKHL 55. cf. *Brewer Street Investments Ltd v Barclays Woollen Co Ltd* [1954] 1 Q.B. 428.

409 Winfield, *Quasi-Contracts* (1952), p.53.

410 *William Lacey (Hounslow) Ltd v Davis* [1957] 1 W.L.R. 932, 939; *Brewer Street Investments Ltd v Barclays Woollen Co Ltd* [1954] 1 Q.B. 428, 435–436. See also Goff and Jones at Ch.26.

411 *British Steel Corp v Cleveland Bridge & Engineering Co Ltd* [1984] 1 All E.R. 504.

412 *Sabemo v N. Sydney Municipal Council* [1977] 2 N.S.W.L.R. 880, 897, noted Davies (1981) 1 O.J.L.S. 300.

413 [1984] 1 All E.R. 504, 511; *Countrywide Communications Ltd v ICL Pathway Ltd* [2000] C.L.C. 324.

414 See above, paras 29–021—29–023 for doubts as to whether this is always based on unjust enrichment.

414a [2008] UKHL 55.

415 *Parkinson (Sir Lindsay) & Co Ltd v Commissioners of Works* [1949] 2 K.B. 632. cf. *Gilbert & Partners v Knight* [1968] 2 All E.R. 248.

416 *Powell v Braun* [1954] 1 W.L.R. 401. But cf. above, paras 3–065 et seq.; Vol.II, para.39–074.

29–073 **Implied and substituted contract for services.** The court may infer from the facts a contract to pay for services to be rendered, although this entails disregarding the actual intention of the parties at the time; as, for instance, where both parties, under a mistake of fact, assumed that the defendant was entitled to claim, without charge, the services of the particular fire brigade he had summoned.[417] But no obligation arises unless there is an express or implied request from the defendant to the claimant for the work to be done or the services to be rendered. Any claim would be founded on the contract rather than by reference to the unjust enrichment principle. Apart from the exceptional cases of salvage,[418] agency of necessity,[419] and services or benefits provided in an emergency,[420] or of limited cases where the claimant innocently repairs or improves the defendant's chattels,[421] English law at present appears hostile to claims for services rendered or work done in the absence of a contract (express or implied) between the parties.[422] The mere receipt of a benefit, when the defendant had no real option to accept or reject it, does not justify a claim for quantum meruit.[423] The term quantum meruit is also used where the parties have not performed the terms of their contract, but it can be inferred from their conduct that they have tacitly agreed to substitute another contract for the first one. Here any relief is granted under the contract rather than through the operation of the law of restitution. In *Steven v Bromley & Son*[424] Bankes L.J. summarised the facts by saying:

> "When the charterers tendered a cargo which was outside the charterparty, and for which no rate of freight had been agreed, the inference is justified that they made an offer to the owners to pay a reasonable freight if the cargo were accepted for carriage."

In the same case Atkin L.J. gave an illustration from the law as to the sale of goods[425]:

> "If I order from a wine merchant twelve bottles of whisky at so much a bottle and he sends me ten bottles of whisky and two of brandy and I accept them, I must pay a reasonable price for the brandy."

---

[417] *Upton-on-Severn R.D.C. v Powell* [1942] 1 All E.R. 220.

[418] Below, para.29–136. On improvements to land carried out by a limited owner or tenant see Munkman, *The Law of Quasi-Contracts* at p.95, and cf. below, para.29–161.

[419] Below, para.29–130; Vol.II, para.31–034.

[420] Below, para.29–131.

[421] Above, para.29–051.

[422] *Falcke v Scottish Imperial Insurance Co* (1887) 34 Ch D 234, 248–249. See Goff and Jones at pp.20–28, 53–54.

[423] *Forman & Co Proprietary Ltd v Ship "Liddesdale"* [1900] A.C. 190. See also *Taylor v Laird* (1856) 1 H. & N. 266; *Sumpter v Hedges* [1898] 1 Q.B. 673 (see below, para.29–080); *Bookmakers Afternoon Greyhound Services Ltd v Wilfred Gilbert Staffordshire Ltd* [1994] F.S.R. 723. cf. *Owen v Tate* [1976] Q.B. 402 (see below, paras 29–109—29–112).

[424] [1919] 2 K.B. 722, 726; *The Batis* [1990] 1 Lloyd's Rep. 345, 352–353 (Hobhouse J.).

[425] [1919] 2 K.B. 722, 728. cf. *Chandris v Isbrandtsen-Moller Co Inc* [1951] 1 K.B. 240, 248 et seq., (Devlin J.) where this principle is discussed in a charterparty case; *Sumpter v Hedges* [1898] 1 Q.B. 673, where the principle was recognised, although the plaintiff failed on the facts. See also above, para.21–035.

The obligation in such a case is genuinely contractual rather than restitutionary.

Payments made under a void contract. Many instances of restitution on the ground of total failure of consideration may arise where payments have been made under a void contract. If a contract is void ab initio for mistake[426] any payment or credit received[427] made under the apparent contract is recoverable.[428] Thus, where the plaintiff paid the purchase-money for an annuity on the life of A, but both parties were ignorant of the fact that A had died some days previously, he was entitled to recover the whole of the money since the contract lacked subject-matter and was therefore void: the consideration had totally failed.[429] Again, where a company paid instalments under a distributorship agreement which had in fact been made before its incorporation, it was entitled to recover such instalments as were paid after its incorporation; the agreement was void and the consideration for the instalments had totally failed.[430] Similarly, where money was lent to a bank in circumstances where the bank lacked the capacity to borrow the money, the loan could be recovered by the lender.[431] 29–074

Absence of consideration. Recovery in cases of payments under a void contract has been put on a basis wider than that of total failure of consideration. It has been held that money paid under void interest rate swap agreements can be recovered because it has been paid for "no consideration" or in the "absence of consideration", even if benefits have been received by the payer and the contract has been fully performed.[432] Where payments have been made both ways restitution is only available to a party on the basis that he gives credit for what he has received[433] and if it is possible to return the parties to their original positions.[434] Where a contract is rendered void by statute, it is a matter of statutory interpretation to discover whether money paid under such an apparent 29–075

[426] See above, para.5–009.

[427] A credit received, albeit only in account, is equivalent to payments for this purpose: *Branwhite v Worcester Works Finance Ltd* [1969] 1 A.C. 552.

[428] *Branwhite v Worcester Works Finance Ltd* [1969] 1 A.C. 552. See the discussion of *Bell v Lever Brothers* [1932] A.C. 161 (above, para.5–028) between Landon and Tylor: (1935) 51 L.Q.R. 650; (1936) 52 L.Q.R. 27, 478; (1937) 53 L.Q.R. 118.

[429] *Strickland v Turner* (1852) 7 Ex. 208; *Kennedy v Thomassen* [1929] 1 Ch. 426. For a review of the authorities, see *Westdeutsche Landesbank Girozentrale v Islington LBC* [1994] 4 All E.R. 890, 921–924 (Hobhouse J.).

[430] *Rover International Ltd v Cannon Film Sales Ltd* [1989] 1 W.L.R. 912.

[431] *National Bank of Egypt International Ltd v Oman Housing Bank SAOC* [2002] EWHC 1760 (Comm); [2003] 1 All E.R. (Comm) 246.

[432] *Westdeutsche Landesbank Girozentrale v Islington LBC* [1994] 4 All E.R. 890; affirmed [1996] 2 A.C. 669; *Guinness Mahon & Co Ltd v Kensington & Chelsea RLBC* [1998] 2 All E.R. 272. See also *Woolwich Equitable B.S. v IRC* [1993] A.C. 70, 197 (Lord Browne-Wilkinson). On "no consideration" see also *Friends' Provident Life Office v Hillier Parker May & Rowden (A Firm)* [1997] Q.B. 85, 98; *Primlake Ltd (In Liquidation) v Matthews Associates* [2006] EWHC 1227 (Ch) at [335] (Lawrence Collins J.). cf. *Commissioner of State Revenue (Vic) v Royal Insurance Australia Ltd* (1994) 182 C.L.R. 51, 67. See Birks, *Unjust Enrichment*, 2nd edn (2005), Chs 5 and 6.

[433] *Guiness Mahon & Co Ltd v Kensington & Chelsea RLBC* [1998] 2 All E.R. 272. Where the payer has received a non-monetary benefit, he will probably be liable to a quantum meruit or a *quantum valebat*, below, para.29–076.

[434] *Kleinwort Benson Ltd v S. Tyneside MBC* [1994] 4 All E.R. 972, 987–990 (Hobhouse J.); *Eastbourne BC v Foster* [2002] I.C.R. 234.

contract is recoverable.[435] For example, where a wagering contract was void under the Gaming Act 1845, money paid to the winner of the wager could not be recovered by the loser[436]; but money advanced on a bill of sale which is void for want of form or for non-registration may be recovered, with reasonable interest.[437]

29–076 **Services rendered or goods supplied under a void contract.** In *Craven-Ellis v Canons Ltd.*[438] Craven-Ellis was appointed managing director of a company by an agreement under the company's seal, and his remuneration was fixed. But this contract was void, since neither Craven-Ellis nor the directors who purported to execute the contract had obtained their qualification shares within two months after appointment (as required by the articles of association). The "directors" could therefore not bind the company, but the Court of Appeal held that the fact that Craven-Ellis had done work under a contract which was void did not disentitle him from recovering on a quantum meruit, since the company (either through qualified directors or through its shareholders) had accepted the benefit of his services,[439] knowing that the services were not intended to be gratuitous. Greer L.J. said[440]:

> "The obligation to pay reasonable remuneration for the work done when there is no binding contract between the parties is imposed by a rule of law, and not by an inference of fact from the acceptance of services or goods."

The Lord Justice thus appears to adopt the view that in these circumstances the obligation is purely restitutionary. There are, however, difficulties with the court's view that liability was imposed on the basis of free acceptance[441] because, at the material time, there was no one with authority to act, acquire knowledge, make a request or enter an agreement for the company.[442] The case

[435] On restitution of money transferred under an ultra vires contract, see *Westdeutsche Landesbank Girozentrale v Islington LBC* [1996] A.C. 669, above, paras 9–017, 29–058.

[436] *Morgan v Ashcroft* [1938] 1 K.B. 49, above, para.29–039. The Gaming Act 1845 was repealed by the Gambling Act 2005: see Vol.II, Ch.40. cf. *Lipkin Gorman v Karpnale Ltd* [1991] 2 A.C. 548 (where owner of stolen money recovered it from casino). See Vol.II, para.40–028.

[437] *Davies v Rees* (1886) 17 QBD 408; *North Central Wagon Finance Co Ltd v Brailsford* [1962] 1 W.L.R. 1288.

[438] [1936] 2 K.B. 403 (distinguished in *Re Richmond Gate Property Co Ltd* [1965] 1 W.L.R. 335). See Lord Denning (1939) 55 L.Q.R. 54; Evans (1966) 29 M.L.R. 608; Birks at pp.118–119, 229; [1971] C.L.P. 110, 119–122. See now *Westdeutsche Landesbank Girozentrale v Islington LBC* [1996] A.C. 669, above, para.29–075. cf. *Guinness Plc v Saunders* [1990] 2 A.C. 663; *Lawford v Billericay R.D.C.* [1903] 1 K.B. 772; *Société Franco Tunisienne D'Armement v Sidermar SpA* [1961] 2 Q.B. 278, 313 (Pearson J.) (above, para.23–098: the continued performance of a contract following frustration); the decision was overruled by the Court of Appeal on the issue of frustration: *Ocean Tramp Tankers Corp v V/O Sovfracht (The Eugenia)* [1964] 2 Q.B. 226 (above, para.23–059); (1964) 27 M.L.R. 351; (1961) 24 M.L.R. 173.

[439] It was assumed that the directors had had the opportunity either to accept or reject the plaintiff's services. cf. *Boulton v Jones* (1857) 27 L.J. Ex. 117 (above, para.5–090) and the cases cited above, para.29–073.

[440] *Craven-Ellis v Canons Ltd* [1936] 2 K.B. 403, 412.

[441] See above, para.29–021.

[442] [1936] 2 All E.R. 1066, 1069, per Croom Johnson K.C. *arguendo*.

is better seen as an early example of liability imposed because of incontrovertible benefit.[443] Greer L.J. pointed out that if the services "had not been performed by the plaintiff, [the company] would have had to get some other agent to carry [them] out".[444] The Court of Appeal in *Rover International Ltd v Cannon Film Sales (No.3)*[445] appears to support this view of *Craven-Ellis* in so far as it did not consider whether anything in the nature of an express or implied request was necessary to found a claim for a quantum meruit by a company for services rendered after its incorporation but under a pre-incorporation contract. Kerr L.J. said that the task of the court was to carry out a process of equitable restitution. The Court also held that the quantum meruit was not to be limited by reference to the claimant's entitlement under the purported contract, primarily because that was irrelevant to a remedy which only arose due to the invalidity of the contract. An action for wrongful interference with property may be brought in respect of goods delivered under the apparent contract.[446]

Illegal contracts. If money is paid under a contract which is illegal, and not merely void, the general rule is that it cannot be recovered: *in pari delicto potior est conditio defendentis*.[447] Both the general rule and the exceptions are fully discussed in the chapter on Illegality.[448] 29–077

Services provided under illegal contracts. When an innocent party learns that the other party to the contract has an illegal object in mind, the innocent party, although he must refuse to continue with the performance of the contract, may sue on a quantum meruit for the lawful work he has already done.[449] 29–078

Money paid under unenforceable contract. The mere fact that one party has paid money to another under a contract which he cannot enforce against the latter because of non-compliance with a statute requiring written evidence or on grounds of public policy will not entitle the payer to recover the money automatically, for such a contract is not void, but merely unenforceable.[450] A total failure of consideration must be proved before restitution can be claimed in these 29–079

[443] See above, para.29–022. Birks [1971] 24 C.L.P. 110, 120 et seq. argues convincingly for this explanation. See also Birks at pp.118–119, 229; Goff and Jones at pp.586–590. cf. Lord Denning (1939) 55 L.Q.R. 54 (acceptance by whole body of shareholders); Lord Templeman in *Guinness Plc v Saunders* [1990] 2 A.C. 663.

[444] [1936] 2 K.B. 403, 412.

[445] [1989] 1 W.L.R. 912; (1989) 105 L.Q.R. 179. See also *Cotronic (UK) Ltd v Dezonie* [1991] B.C.L.C. 721.

[446] *Cundy v Lindsay* (1878) 3 App. Cas. 459 (above, paras 5–088, 5–094); Torts (Interference with Goods) Act 1977.

[447] e.g. *Parkinson v College of Ambulance Ltd* [1925] 2 K.B. 1.

[448] See above, Ch.16.

[449] *Clay v Yates* (1856) 1 H. & N. 73 (above, para.16–011). See also *Mohamed v Alaga & Co* [1999] 3 All E.R. 699.

[450] On requirements of writing, see *Sweet v Lee* (1841) 3 Man. & G. 452, 467–468. See also *Shaw v Woodcock* (1827) 7 B. & C. 73, 84; *Thomas v Brown* (1876) 1 QBD 714, 723, and see Ch.4, above. On public policy, see *Aratra Potato Co Ltd v Taylor Joynson Garrett (A Firm)* [1995] 4 All E.R. 695; Ch.16, above.

circumstances and restitution will not, in any event, be given if it would run counter to the policy of the statute in question.[451]

29–080 **Work done under an unenforceable contract.** A person who renders services under a contract that is unenforceable will be entitled to a quantum meruit if the other party has failed to carry out his part, provided the restitutionary claim does not undermine the policy of the statute (or common law rule) rendering the contract unenforceable.[452] Although there is English authority to this effect which shows that the basis of the claim is restitution rather than implied contract,[453] the clearest examples are provided by the decisions of the Supreme Court of Canada and the High Court of Australia. Thus, in *Deglman v Guaranty Trust Co of Canada and Constantineau*,[454] a nephew, who rendered services to his aunt under an oral agreement by which she had agreed to bequeath a house to him, was entitled to reasonable remuneration for the services on her failure to do so since she had received the benefits of full performance of the contract. Again, in *Pavey & Matthews Pty Ltd v Paul*,[455] a quantum meruit was granted to a licensed builder who had renovated a cottage under an unenforceable oral contract. It was held that the claim was an independent restitutionary claim arising from the acceptance of the benefits accruing to the defendant from the plaintiff's execution of the work for which the ineffective contract provided. In these cases it was accepted that the contract had been fully performed by the claimant.[456] Where it is not, or where performance is alleged to be defective, if the basis of the claim is the acceptance of performance, the defendant who has not in fact received the bargained-for performance might not be deemed to have accepted non-conforming performance and might not therefore be liable.[457] Alternatively, in the case of a contract unenforceable for lack of writing, where there is an allegation of non-conformity with the promised performance, then, if the purpose of the statutory requirement is to avoid disputes as to what was agreed, this might be undermined by a restitutionary quantum meruit.

---

[451] *Orakpo v Manson Investments Ltd* [1978] A.C. 95. See also *Dimond v Lovell* [2002] 1 A.C. 384, H.L.

[452] *Pavey & Matthews Pty Ltd v Paul* (1987) 69 A.L.R. 577, 584–585, on which see Beatson (1988) 104 L.Q.R. 13; Ibbetson (1988) 8 O.J.L.S. 312.

[453] *Scarisbrick v Parkinson* (1869) 20 L.T. 175; *Pulbrook v Lawes* (1876) 1 QBD 284; *Scott v Pattison* [1923] 2 K.B. 723 (and see, on the relevance of the local custom, the fuller reports in: 39 T.L.R. 557; 129 L.T. 830; 92 L.J.K.B. 886); *James v Thomas H. Kent & Co Ltd* [1951] 1 K.B. 551, 555–556 (Somervell L.J.); *Vedatech Corp v Crystal Decisions (UK) Ltd* [2002] EWHC 818 (Ch) (a claim for quantum meruit and unjust enrichment in the alternative in respect of provision of services in return for software revenue under alleged oral agreement). See further Goff and Jones at Ch.21; Denning (1925) 41 L.Q.R. 79. These cases concern lack of writing, on which see, above, paras 4–003, 4–041 et seq., 4–075 et seq.

[454] [1954] 3 D.L.R. 785.

[455] (1987) 69 A.L.R. 577.

[456] In *Pavey's* (1987) 69 A.L.R. 577 case the owner of the cottage denied the reasonableness of the charges claimed by the builder.

[457] *Sumpter v Hedges* [1898] 1 Q.B. 673. See also *Wiluszynski v Tower Hamlets LBC* [1989] I.C.R. 493. But cf., albeit in another context, *British Steel Corp v Cleveland Bridge & Engineering Ltd* [1984] 1 All E.R. 504 (above, para.29–071) where allegedly non-conforming performance gave rise to a quantum meruit.

Minors' contracts. Money paid by a minor under a contract which is unenforceable against him,[458] will be recoverable provided there has been a total failure of consideration.[459] Where money is paid to a minor, at common law[460] the adult will not be permitted to recover in restitution on the ground of a total failure of consideration if that would "in a roundabout way" contravene the policy of the law and indirectly enforce the unenforceable contract.[461] By s.3(1) of the Minors' Contracts Act 1987 the court is given discretion to require the minor to transfer to the other party "any property" acquired under the contract "or property representing it" if it is just and equitable to do so. Although the matter is not entirely free from doubt, it is possible that "property" will be held to include money, since otherwise there would be no power to order the transfer of the proceeds if the minor has resold the goods he bought under the unenforceable contract.[462] 29–081

Recovery of premiums where a policy of insurance is avoided. The premium paid under a policy of insurance may be recovered if the risk insured against does not exist, and this fact was not known to the parties[463]: the consideration has totally failed. Where a policy of marine insurance is avoided by the insurer on the ground of the misrepresentation or concealment by the assured of a material fact, the assured, if not guilty of fraud, may recover all premiums which he has paid under the policy.[464] 29–082

(g) *Ultra vires Receipts by the Revenue and Public Authorities*[465]

Ultra vires demands. In *Woolwich Equitable Building Society v I.R.C.*[466] it was held that a payment made pursuant to a demand for tax that was ultra vires because of the invalidity of the relevant subordinate legislation was recoverable. Lord Goff stated that: 29–083

---

458 On the Minors' Contracts Act 1987, see above, Ch.8.

459 *Steinberg v Scala (Leeds) Ltd* [1923] 2 Ch. 452; *Pearce v Brain* [1929] 2 K.B. 310. cf. *Valentini v Canali* (1889) 24 QBD 166 (claim may lie where restitutio in integrum is possible). But note that the first case concerned a voidable contract and the other two contracts were "absolutely void" under the Infants Relief Act 1874, which was repealed by the Minors' Contracts Act 1987. See further above, para.8–005; Goff and Jones at pp.639–641.

460 Common law restitutionary remedies are preserved by the Minors' Contracts Act 1987 s.3(2).

461 *R. Leslie Ltd v Shiell* [1914] 3 K.B. 607, 613 (Lord Sumner); *Thavorn v Bank of Credit & Commerce SA* [1985] 1 Lloyd's Rep. 259. cf. *Cowern v Neild* [1912] 2 K.B. 419.

462 "Law of Contract Minors' Contracts" (Law Com. No.134, 1984), para.4.21; above, para.8–055.

463 *Pritchard v The Merchant's and Tradesman's Mutual Life Assurance Society* (1858) 3 C.B.(N.S.) 622; *Tyrie v Fletcher* (1777) 2 Cowp. 666, 668 (Lord Mansfield); *Re Cavalier Insurance Co Ltd* [1989] 2 Lloyd's Rep. 430.

464 *Anderson v Thornton* (1835) 8 Ex. 425, 428; and see Marine Insurance Act 1906 s.84(1). cf. *St John Shipping Corp v Joseph Rank Ltd* [1957] 1 Q.B. 267, 293 (Devlin J.).

465 Burrows at Ch.13; Goff and Jones at Ch.27; Virgo at Ch.14.

466 [1993] 1 A.C. 70. See also Beatson (1993) 109 L.Q.R. 401; Birks [1992] P.L. 580; Alder (2002) 22(2) L.S. 165.

"... money paid by a citizen to a public authority in the form of taxes or other levies paid pursuant to an ultra vires demand by the authority is *prima facie* recoverable by the citizen as of right."[467]

In holding this the House consciously reformulated the law which hitherto precluded recovery unless the payment was made under mistake or compulsion.[468] The reasons given for enunciating a new restitutionary right lay in constitutional law and, in particular, art.4 of the Bill of Rights 1688,[469] the existence of a right to repayment of sums levied by a public body contrary to rules of EU law,[470] the unattractive contrast with the position of money paid by the Crown which, if paid without authority, is recoverable,[471] and the fact that demands by the Revenue and other governmental bodies are implicitly backed by the coercive powers of the state and may well entail unpleasant economic and social consequences.

29–084 **Scope of right.** The *Woolwich* principle is applicable when money has been paid to a public authority as a result of a mistake of law.[472] In *Deutsche Morgan Grenfell Group Plc v IRC*[473] the House of Lords recognised that, if statutory provisions for recovery of taxes are not available,[474] claims for restitution of tax paid by mistake can be founded at common law either on the *Woolwich* principle or on the ground of mistake of law and the claimant can choose the preferable ground. The practical consequence of this decision is that the claimant can choose to rely on the extended limitation period under s.32(1)(c) of the Limitation Act 1980 which applies to claims involving mistake and for which time does not begin to run until the mistake could reasonably have been discovered.[475] It is submitted that the *Woolwich* principle should extend to cases in which the public authority has made no demand for payment, for example where an ultra vires tax is paid in reasonable anticipation of a demand.[476] Although Lord Goff and Lord Slynn expressly reserved the question of whether the principle extends to cases in which the tax or other levy has been wrongfully exacted for reasons other than

---

467 [1993] 1 A.C. 70, 177. See also 196 (Lord Jauncey), 198 (Lord Browne-Wilkinson); *British Steel Plc v Customs and Excise Commissioners* [1997] 2 All E.R. 366 CA.

468 [1993] 1 A.C. 70, 168 (Lord Goff), 171 (Lord Goff), 196 (Lord Jauncey), 204 (Lord Slynn). See also *Att-Gen v Wilts United Dairies Ltd* (1921) 37 T.L.R. 884 CA; (1922) 127 L.T. 822 HL; *R. v Brocklebank Ltd* [1925] 1 K.B. 52 (although recovery there was barred by the Indemnity Act 1920); *Congreve v Home Office* [1976] Q.B. 629, 652 (Lord Denning M.R.); Birks in Finn (ed.), *Essays in Restitution*, pp.164 et seq.; Cornish (1987) 14 Jo. Mal. and Comp. 41. See also *R. v Tower Hamlets LBC Ex p. Chetnik Developments Ltd* [1988] A.C. 858 (judicial review of refusal to exercise express discretion to repay overpayment of rates).

469 [1993] 1 A.C. 70, 172 (Lord Goff).

470 [1993] 1 A.C. 177 (Lord Goff). See *Administrazione delle Finanze dello Stato v SpA San Giorgio* (199/82) [1983] E.C.R. 3595; *Metallgesellschaft Ltd v IRC* (C-397/98) [2001] Ch. 620, noted Virgo (2002) 1 B.T.R. 4.

471 [1993] 1 A.C. 70; *R. v Auckland Harbour Board* [1924] A.C. 318.

472 [1993] A.C. 70, 177, 205.

473 [2006] UKHL 49, [2007] 1 A.C. 558. See Virgo [2007] B.T.R. 27.

474 See below, para.29–085.

475 See above, para.28–088.

476 Beatson (1993) 109 L.Q.R. 401, 405; Burrows at p.448; Law Commission Consultation Paper No.120, para.3.90.

that the demand was ultra vires, for example because the authority has misconstrued the relevant statute or regulation,[477] such misconstruction is an error of law and likely in virtually all cases to be ultra vires.[478] The *Woolwich* principle has been held not to apply where a landlord, who had received overpayments of housing benefits, repaid them to the local authority, although a defect in the notice meant that the council could not in fact have enforced the recovery of the money.[479] Although the council's demand was defective, it was not backed by coercive powers and it would have been open to the council to go though the process correctly and make a second regular and valid demand. It is not entirely clear whether the *Woolwich* principle extends beyond taxation to licence fees or unauthorised charges for the provison of services by statutory utilities, hitherto dealt with under the *colore officii* principle.[480] While explicit guidance was not given on the range of bodies subject to the principle, it is submitted that it should apply to public bodies whose authority to charge is subject to and limited by public law principles, and to other bodies whose authority to charge is solely the product of statute, and thus limited.[481]

Statutory provisions. The restitutionary right is, in the context of taxation, limited by statutory provisions for the recovery of overpayments. The broadest is the right to recover any payment of VAT that is not due[482]; the narrowest is the more discretionary remedy in s.33 of the Taxes Management Act 1970 for the recovery of overpaid income tax,[483] corporation tax,[484] capital gains tax, or petroleum revenue tax by reason of an error or mistake in a tax return as is "reasonable and just".[485] There is no right of recovery where the error reflected "the practice generally prevailing" when the return was made. Where, moreover, a statutory appeal mechanism is applicable to the facts, it appears that the payee will be required to seek its remedy through the statutory framework.[486] Further, although the claim is based on the ultra vires nature of the receipt, it appears that it is not a precondition to recovery that this be established in judicial review 29–085

[477] [1993] A.C. 70, 177 (Lord Goff), 205 (Lord Slynn).

[478] *Re Racal Communications Ltd* [1981] A.C. 374. It will anyway constitute a mistake of law.

[479] *Norwich City Council v Stringer* (2001) 33 H.L.R. 15.

[480] *Steele v Williams* (1853) 8 Ex Ch. 625; *Hooper v Exeter Corp* (1887) 56 L.J.Q.B. 457; *Queens of the River S.S. Co Ltd v Conservators of the River Thames* (1899) 15 T.L.R. 474 (harbour dues and pier charges); *South of Scotland Electricity Board v British Oxygen Co Ltd* [1959] 1 W.L.R. 587 (electricity charges). See below, paras 29–094—29–097; *Att-Gen v Wilts United Dairies Ltd* (1921) 37 T.L.R. 884; *R. v Brocklebank Ltd* [1925] 1 K.B. 52; *Mason v New South Wales* (1959) 102 C.L.R. 108.

[481] [1993] A.C. 70, 79, 138 (Glidewell and Butler-Sloss L.JJ.); *AEM (Avon) Ltd v Bristol City Council* [1999] L.G.R. 93. See Beatson (1993) 109 L.Q.R. 401, 406–418. cf. *Green v Portsmouth Stadium Ltd* [1953] 2 Q.B. 190 (where the principle would not apply because, but for the statute, there would have been no limit on the amount the defendant would have been able to charge). See *Waikato Regional Airport Ltd v The Att-Gen (on behalf of the Director General of Agriculture and Forestry)* [2003] UKPC 50, [2004] 3 N.Z.L.R. 1, where the *Woolwich* principle was extended to the recovery of governmental levies.

[482] Value Added Tax Act 1994 s.80 as amended. See Virgo [1998] B.T.R. 582.

[483] Claims for recovery which fall under this provision canot be brought at common law: *Monro v H.M. Revenue and Customs* [2008] EWCA Civ 306.

[484] See now Finance Act 1998 Sch.18 para.51.

[485] See also Inheritance Tax Act 1984 s.241; Council Tax (Administration and Enforcement) Regulations 1992 (SI 1992/613).

[486] *Woolwich Equitable Building Society v IRC* [1993] A.C. 70, 168–170 (Lord Goff).

proceedings.[487] The right of recovery is a private law right, albeit one arising from the background of public law.[488]

29–086 **Defences.** Restitution will not be awarded where the payment was made to close the transaction.[489] Further, the recognition of the defence of change of position means that in principle where a public authority can show that it has so changed its position that it would be inequitable to allow the claim it should have a defence.[490] Although Lord Goff doubted the advisability of imposing special limits upon recovery in the case of ultra vires levies to deal with the problem that a right of recovery might lead to serious disruption of public finances,[491] the question of whether a payer who has "passed on" to others, for instance by price increases, the higher cost he has borne because of the overpayment should be precluded from recovery, was left open.[492] This defence is permitted by EU law[493] provided it is shown that the charge has been borne entirely by a party

---

487 [1993] A.C. 70, 200 (Lord Slynn) and see Lord Goff's suggestion (at 174) that the right of recovery might need to be limited by strict time limits which implies that the three-month time limit for judicial review proceedings does not apply. In *Woolwich* there had been judicial review proceedings: *R. v IRC Ex p. Woolwich Equitable Building Society* [1990] 1 W.L.R. 1400, and see [1993] A.C. 70, 169 (Lord Goff).

488 See *Lonrho Plc v Tebbit* [1992] 4 All E.R. 280, 288; *Roy v Kensington and Chelsea and Westminster F.P.C.* [1992] 1 A.C. 624. It is now possible to obtain a restitutionary remedy in an application for judicial review: CPR r.54.3(2). Such proceedings are subject to a three-month limitation period. It is possible to seek restitution without prior judicial review proceedings and so avoid this shorter limitation period (*British Steel v Customs and Excise Commissioners* [1997] 2 All E.R. 366) although this has been criticised as an abuse of process: *NEC Semi-Conductors v IRC* [2006] EWCA Civ 25, [2006] S.T.C. 606 at [97] (Sedley L.J.). The validity of the non-judicial review route to obtain restitution from a public authority remains unclear after the recent decisions of the House of Lords in *Deutsche Morgan Grenfell Group Plc v IRC* [2006] UKHL 49, [2007] 1 A.C. 558 and *Sempra Metals Ltd v IRC* [2007] UKHL 34, [2008] 1 A.C. 561 although the recognition that the claimant taxpayer may rely on the ground of mistake of law to gain the benefit of the extended limitation period under the Limitation Act 1980 might suggest that there is no intrinsic objection to using the non-judicial review procedure. Simple interest can be awarded, under Supreme Court Act 1981 s.35A, in respect of such claims: *R. (Kemp) v Denbighshire Local Health Board* [2006] EWHC 181 (Admin), [2007] 1 W.L.R. 639.

489 *Woolwich Equitable Building Society v IRC* [1993] A.C. 70, 98 et seq., 121, 135–136, 140 CA; 165, 174, 178, 192, 196, 200–201 HL; *Air Canada v British Columbia* [1989] S.C.R. 1161, 1200; *David Securities Pty Ltd v Commonwealth Bank of Australia* [1992] 66 A.L.J.R. 768, 774–775. See above, para.29–039, below, paras 29–186—29–190. For the suggestion that only contractual compromise should be a defence see Burrows at pp.448–449. cf. Law Com. No.227, (1994), paras 2.25–2.38.

490 Below, paras 29–179 et seq. cf. the narrower defence in *Rural Municipality of Storthoaks v Mobil Oil Canada Ltd* [1975] 55 D.L.R. (3d) 1, 13.

491 *Woolwich* [1993] A.C. 70, 175–176. See also *Air Canada v British Columbia* (1989) 59 D.L.R. (4th) 161, 193–197. cf. 169 (Wilson J.); *Sargood Bros v Commonwealth* (1910–11) 11 C.L.R. 258, 303 (Isaacs J.). See also Law Com. Consultation Paper No.120, paras 3.70–3.73; Burrows at pp.451–454; Jones, *Restitution in Public and Private Law* (1991), pp.24–28. In *Deutsche Morgan Grenfell Group Plc v IRC* [2006] UKHL 49, [2007] 1 A.C. 558 the House of Lords rejected a defence that the money was paid when there was a settled view as to the state of the law: at [18] (Lord Hoffmann), and at [145] (Lord Walker).

492 [1993] A.C. 70, 177–178.

493 *Adminiztrazione delle Finanze dello Stato v SpA San Giorgio* (199–82) [1983] E.C.R. 3595. But now see *Marks and Spencer Plc v Commissioners of Customs and Excise* (309/06).

other than the payer, so that reimbursement would unjustly enrich the payer.[494] The provision in s.80(3) of the Value Added Tax Act 1994 that recovery of VAT should not be allowed if the payee can show that the *payer* would be unjustly enriched if he recovered the payment,[495] may reflect its *rationale*. However, it has been criticised[496] and arguments for a similar limit were not accepted by the High Court of Australia[497] or in the context of restitution in respect of money paid under an ultra vires contract.[498]

(h) *Compulsion*[499]

Compulsory transfer of benefit to the defendant. Where the claimant has transferred a benefit to the defendant by wrongful or illegitimate compulsion, or under extortion *colore officii*, the defendant is under an obligation to make restitution to the claimant. Usually the benefit transferred will be received directly by the defendant, but sometimes the benefit may take the form of the claimant paying a third party, the effect of which is to discharge a liability borne primarily or ultimately by the defendant.[500] In both situations the claim for restitution will fail if the transfer of the benefit can be considered to be voluntary.[501] 29–087

Unlawful or illegitimate compulsion. The question of what amounts to unlawful or illegitimate compulsion will depend on the circumstances of the particular case. Although the reported cases deal mainly with issues of duress of goods[502] and extortion *colore officii*,[503] duress of the person is included[504] and other forms of pressure on any rights of the person who pays, including economic 29–088

---

494 *Kapniki Mikhailidis AE v Idrima Kinonikon Aspaliseon (IKA)* (C–441/98) [2001] 1 C.M.L.R. 13 (partial repayment could be made in such cases). Under UK legislation the defence is available to the Customs even though the payments had been made owing to an error on their part: *RIBA Publications v Commissioners of Customs and Excise* [1999] B.V.C. 2201.

495 As amended by the Finance (No.2) Act 2005 s.3. See *Marks and Spencer Plc v Commissioners of Customs and Excise* (309/06) where the E.C.J. held that the English court had to consider the validity of the unjust enrichment defence in the light of the EC principles of equal treatement and fiscal neutrality. For the present operation of the defence see *Baines and Ernst Ltd v Commissioners For Her Majesty's Revenue and Customs* [2006] EWCA Civ 1040; *Weber's Wine World Handels GmbH v Abgabenberufungskommission Wien* (C147/01) [2005] All E.R. (EC) 224.

496 Rudden and Bishop (1981) 6 E.L.R. 243; Law Commission Consultation Paper No.120, paras 3.82–3.85.

497 *Mason v New South Wales* (1959) 102 C.L.R. 108, 136, 146; *Roxborough v Rothmans of Pall Mall Australia Ltd* (2002) 76 A.L.J.R. 203 High Ct of Australia.

498 *Kleinwort Benson Ltd v South Tyneside MBC* [1994] 4 All E.R. 972; *Kleinwort Benson Ltd v Birmingham CC* [1997] Q.B. 380. See also *Commissioner of State Revenue (Vic) v Royal Insurance Australia Ltd* (1994) 182 C.L.R. 51 and *Mutual Pools & Staff Pty Ltd v Commonwealth* (1994) 179 C.L.R. 155. See further above, para.29–027. cf. *Allied Air Conditioning v British Columbia* (1992) 76 B.C.L.R. 2d 218 (distinguishing specific and direct "passing on" of tax and merely treating it as a business cost).

499 Winfield (1944) 60 L.Q.R. 341; Beatson at Ch.5; Birks at pp.173 et seq.; Burrows at Ch.5; Goff and Jones at Ch.10; Virgo at Ch.9.

500 See below, para.29–099.

501 Below, para.29–109.

502 Below, para.29–090.

503 Below, para.29–094.

504 Below, para.29–089.

duress, will be recognised.[505] As a general rule, to constitute duress the pressure must be exerted by a threat to commit an unlawful act.[506] However, it has also been said that duress can exist where the threat is of lawful action provided the court regards the demand it is coupled with as illegitimate.[507] Although, in the absence of legislative guidance,[508] distinguishing legitimate from illegitimate demands is likely to be controversial, the courts may be assisted by drawing on cases of conspiracy where no unlawful means are used[509] and by having regard to usual trade practice. The coercive force[510] of the compulsion will depend on its immediacy,[511] on the ability of the payer to obtain legal advice or legal protection before making the payment,[512] and, in some circumstances, on the availability of an effective alternative remedy or course of action open to the payer.[513] It was sometimes said that economic duress had to coerce the claimant's

---

[505] e.g. threats of duress to goods will suffice: *Maskell v Horner* [1915] 3 K.B. 106 (see below, para.29–090) as will threats to commit other torts: *Universe Tankships Inc of Monrovia v International Transport Workers Federation* [1983] 1 A.C. 366. Threats to commit a breach of contract can amount to duress, and a payment in excess of the contract price which is made as the result of a coercive threat by the payee to commit a serious breach of his contractual obligations unless the excess payment is made, may be recovered in a restitutionary claim: see *North Ocean Shipping Co Ltd v Hyundai Construction Co Ltd* [1979] Q.B. 705; *B. & S. Contracts and Design Ltd v Victor Green Publications Ltd* [1984] I.C.R. 419; *The Alev* [1989] 1 Lloyd's Rep. 138; *Atlas Express Ltd v Kafco (Importers and Distributors) Ltd* [1989] Q.B. 833; *C.T.N. Cash and Carry Ltd v Gallagher Ltd* [1994] 4 All E.R. 714 and the Australian cases of *Nixon v Furphy* (1925) 25 S.R. (N.S.W.) 151 and *Sundell & Sons v Emm Yannoulatos (Overseas) Pty Ltd* (1956) 56 S.R. (N.S.W.) 323; cf. *Crescendo Management Pty Ltd v Westpac Banking Corp* (1988) 19 N.S.W.L.R. 40. See also *Pao On v Lau Yiu Long* [1980] A.C. 614. On economic duress see above, para.7–014; *D. & C. Builders Ltd v Rees* [1966] 2 Q.B. 617 (above, paras 3–136, 7–014—7–023).

[506] See *R. v Att-Gen for England and Wales* [2002] UKPC 22.

[507] *Universe Tankships Inc of Monrovia v International Transport Workers Federation* [1983] 1 A.C. 366, 384 (Lord Diplock), 401(Lord Scarman); *Dimskal S.S. Co Ltd v ITWF* [1992] 2 A.C. 152. See also *Thorne v Motor Trade Association* [1937] A.C. 797; *Norreys v Zeffert* [1939] 2 All E.R. 186; Birks at pp.177–179; Burrows at pp.230–234; Goff and Jones at pp.307–308, 329. cf. *C.T.N. Cash and Carry Ltd v Gallagher Ltd* [1994] 4 All E.R. 714; *Leyland Daf Ltd v Automotive Products Plc* [1994] 1 B.C.L.R. 244; *Royal Boskalis Westminster N.V. v Mountain* [1999] Q.B. 674, 730–731. Beatson at pp.129–134.

[508] Such as the Trade Union legislation in the *Universe Tankships* case [1983] 1 A.C. 366, although the threat there was to commit a tort.

[509] *Crofter Hand-Woven Harris Tweed Ltd v Veitch* [1942] A.C. 435; *Sorrell v Smith* [1925] A.C. 700, 712.

[510] *Skeate v Beale* (1841) 11 Ad. & E. 983, 990 ("the fear . . . does not deprive anyone of his free agency who possesses that ordinary degree of firmness which the law requires all to exert"). But see *Barton v Armstrong* [1976] A.C. 104.

[511] *Maskell v Horner* [1915] 3 K.B. 106, 118 (Lord Reading C.J.) ("under the compulsion of urgent and pressing necessity"). cf. *Twyford v Manchester Corp* [1946] Ch. 236, and *Somes v British Empire Shipping Co* (1860) 8 H.L.C. 338.

[512] *Maskell v Horner* [1915] 3 K.B. 106, 120. See below, para.29–090.

[513] The presence of an alternative remedy has been said to be irrelevant in cases involving detention of the payer's property (*Astley v Reynolds* (1731) 2 Str. 915, below, para.29–092; *Kanhaya Lal v National Bank of India* (1913) 29 T.L.R. 314, 315. cf. *Ashmole v Wainwright* (1842) 2 Q.B. 837, 845) but would appear to be relevant where there is no such detention (*Knibbs v Hall* (1794) Peake 276; *Twyford v Manchester Corp* [1946] Ch. 236, 241–242; *Pao On v Lau Yiu Long* [1980] A.C. 614, 635; *B. & S. Contracts and Design Ltd v Victor Green Publications Ltd* [1984] I.C.R. 419; *The Alev* [1989] 1 Lloyd's Rep. 138, 146–147; *Hennessy v Craigmyle & Co* [1986] I.C.R. 461. cf. *North Ocean Shipping v Hyundai Construction Co Ltd* [1979] Q.B. 705, 715, 719.

will so as to vitiate his consent,[514] but this approach has been criticised and the better view is to ask whether, where pressure has been applied, that pressure went beyond what the law considers legitimate.[515] If the payment amounts to a genuine compromise of a disputed claim honestly made by the payee,[516] or the payment is made in the course of or under threat of legal proceedings,[517] or the transaction is affirmed,[518] it cannot be recovered. Similarly, it appears, if the claimant cannot offer the defendant substantial counter-restitution.[519]

29–089 **Duress of the person.** Duress of the person[520] entitles a party to a contract to avoid it[521]; consequently, restitution of benefits conferred under the voidable contract will be ordered by the court, following rescission by the innocent party. Even if there has been no contract, benefits conferred on the defendant as the result of duress by him should, in principle, be recoverable from him by a claim in restitution.[522] The duress will usually amount to a tort and recovery can also be founded on the principles governing restitution for wrongdoing considered below.[523]

29–090 **Actual or threatened seizure or distress of the claimant's goods.** Lord Reading C.J. in the leading case of *Maskell v Horner*[524] said:

> "If a person pays money, which he is not bound to pay, under the compulsion of urgent and pressing necessity or of seizure, actual or threatened, of his goods, he can recover it as money had and received. The money is not paid under duress in the strict sense of the term, as that implies duress of person, but under the pressure of seizure or detention of goods which is analogous to that of duress."

In this case, the defendant owned a market and exacted from the plaintiff market tolls (to which he was not entitled) by threatening to distrain on the plaintiff's goods. The plaintiff paid the tolls under protest, but the Court of Appeal later

---

[514] *The Siboen and The Sibotre* [1976] 1 Lloyd's Rep. 293, 336; *North Ocean Shipping v Hyundai Construction Co Ltd* [1979] Q.B. 705, 717, 719; *Pao On v Lau Yiu Long* [1980] A.C. 614, 635.

[515] *Universe Tankships Inc of Monrovia v I.T.W.F.* [1983] 1 A.C. 366, 384, 400; *B. & S. Contracts and Design Ltd v Victor Green Publications Ltd* [1984] I.C.R. 419, 426–428; *Dimskal S.S. Co Ltd v I.T.W.F.* [1992] 2 A.C. 152, 165–166.

[516] *Atlee v Backhouse* (1838) 2 M. & W. 633; *Wakefield v Newbon* (1844) 6 Q.B. 276, 281; *Callisher v Bischoffsheim* (1870) L.R. 5 Q.B. 449; *Miles v New Zealand Alford Estate Co* (1885) 32 QBD 266, 291; *The Siboen and the Sibotre* [1976] 1 Lloyd's Rep. 293, 334. See above, paras 3–050—3–051.

[517] See below, para.29–098.

[518] *North Ocean Shipping Co Ltd v Hyundai Construction Co Ltd* [1979] Q.B. 705, 720–721; *B. & S. Contracts and Design Ltd v Victor Green Publications Ltd* [1984] I.C.R. 419, 428.

[519] See *Halpern v Halpern (Nos 1 and 2)* [2007] EWCA Civ 291, [2008] Q.B. 195.

[520] Above, para.7–011.

[521] Above, paras 7–053—7–055.

[522] In the analogous situation of duress of goods, there is ample authority permitting such recovery: see below, paras 29–090—29–093. cf. *Williams v Bayley* (1866) L.R. 1 H.L. 200; *Kaufman v Gerson* [1904] 1 K.B. 591.

[523] Below, paras 29–141 et seq.

[524] [1915] 3 K.B. 106, 118. See *Kanhaya Lal v National Bank of India* (1913) 29 T.L.R. 314; *Somes v British Empire Shipping Co* (1860) 8 H.L.C. 338.

upheld his claim to recover the payments on the ground that they were not voluntary. It would have been unreasonable to expect a man in the plaintiff's position to forgo the use of his goods while the matter was litigated.[525] Similarly, where a sheriff had seized certain goods, which were claimed by the assignees of a bankrupt as belonging to the bankrupt's estate, and in order to prevent a sheriff from proceeding to a sale, which he threatened to do, the assignees paid the sum claimed under the writ, it was held that they were entitled to recover such sum as money which had been paid by compulsion.[526]

29–091 **Distress for an excessive amount.** Where a distrainor demands an excessive payment before he will return the goods to their owner there is some doubt whether the distrainee may, without relying on his remedies of replevin or detinue, pay under protest and then sue in restitution to recover the excess.[527]

29–092 **Wrongful demand by defendant detaining goods.**[528] If chattels are wrongfully taken or detained from the claimant by the defendant, and money is paid to the defendant by the claimant simply for the purpose of recovering possession of the chattels, the money can be recovered by the claimant, since it was not a voluntary payment, especially if it was paid under protest.[529] Thus, in *Astley v Reynolds*,[530] where the claimant had pawned plate with the defendant and the latter would not part with it unless the claimant paid him more than legal interest, it was held that the excess paid to redeem the goods might be recovered, even though the claimant could have brought an action for trover on tendering the sum legally due to the defendant.[531] The same principle applies where a carrier refuses to deliver goods except on payment of excessive charges,[532] or where goods are

---

[525] The goods may be merely in the possession of the claimant, and not owned by him: *Fell v Whittaker* (1871) L.R. 7 Q.B. 120. cf. *Scarfe v Hallifax* (1840) 7 M. & W. 288. Duress of goods is also discussed, above, para.7–012.

[526] *Valpy v Manley* (1845) 1 C.B. 594. On the position where the money is paid under duress to an agent of a third person, *Oates v Hudson* (1851) 6 Ex. 346; *Owen & Co v Cronk* [1895] 1 Q.B. 265; *T.D. Keegan Ltd v Palmer* [1961] 2 Lloyd's Rep. 449, 459. See Vol.II, para.31–109. cf. the position where the claimant is coerced by the defendant to pay money to a third party: *Re Hooper and Grass' Contract* [1949] V.L.R. 269.

[527] See Woodfall, *Landlord and Tenant*, 28th edn, paras 1–0007 to 1–0008; Bullen, *Distress*, 2nd edn, pp.223–224 and the discussion in Winfield (1944) 60 L.Q.R. 345–346 of *Glynn v Thomas* (1856) 11 Exch. 870; *Loring v Warburton* (1858) E.B. & E. 507; *Fell v Whittaker* (1871) L.R. 7 Q.B. 120. cf. excessive demand on distress damage feasant: *Green v Duckett* (1883) 11 QBD 275.

[528] This is another instance where restitution for wrongdoing might also be available (see below, para.29–141) since the defendant would usually be liable in the tort of conversion.

[529] *Atlee v Backhouse* (1838) 3 M. & W. 633, 650. See also *Shaw v Woodcock* (1827) 7 B. & C. 73; *Green v Duckett* (1883) 11 QBD 275 (excessive sum demanded on distress damage feasant); *North v Walthamstow U.D.C.* (1898) 62 J.P. 836; *T.D. Keegan Ltd v Palmer* [1961] 2 Lloyd's Rep. 449; cf. *Maskell v Horner* [1915] 3 K.B. 106 (above, para.29–090).

[530] (1732) 2 Stra. 915.

[531] "The plaintiff might have such an immediate want of his goods, that an action of trover would not do his business" (*Astley* (1732) 2 Stra. 915, 916).

[532] Common Carrier: *Ashmole v Wainwright* (1842) 2 Q.B. 837; cf. *Skeate v Beale* (1841) 11 A. & E. 983; *G.W. Ry v Sutton* (1869) L.R. 4 H.L. 226 (below, para.29–097). See also Vol.II, para.36–016. Other carriers: *The Alev* [1989] 1 Lloyd's Rep. 138.

seized by a sheriff and the owner can redeem them only by paying him an amount in excess of the proper levy.[533]

Wrongful demand by defendant detaining title deeds. Where money was paid under protest by a mortgagor in order to obtain possession of his title deeds, which were withheld by the solicitor of the mortgagee in reliance on an unfounded claim of lien, it was held that the money might be recovered by a claim in restitution.[534] Similarly, where the solicitor of a mortgagee, who was about to sell, refused to stop the sale or deliver up the title deeds of the mortgaged property except on payment by the mortgagor of certain expenses with which he was not properly chargeable, it was held that the administratrix of the mortgagor, who had paid the excess under protest, could recover it.[535] 29–093

Extortion *colore officii*.[536] If a public officer demands an illegal or an excessive fee for performing duties imposed on him by law, it amounts to extortion *colore officii* and the fee or excess is recoverable by a claim in restitution.[537] It may also be recoverable under the principle laid down in *Woolwich Equitable Building Society v I.R.C.*[538] It is not yet clear whether that is an additional principle or subsumes *colore officii* cases.[539] A public officer is not on equal terms with a private citizen, who is likely to accept the correctness of an official demand and to believe that, unless he pays, he will suffer some penalty or exclusion from some benefit; it is likely to be held to be a payment under coercion if the official is in a position to prevent the payer from doing an act he wishes to do,[540] or to seize the goods of the payer.[541] But there may be extortion *colore officii* although the officer has not withheld a right or privilege in order to exact the fee,[542] and honestly believed that the fee was properly charged.[543] Thus a fee illegally demanded from a publican as a condition of granting his licence may be recovered[544]; as also may fees charged by a parish clerk, contrary to a statute, for extracts taken from a register book of burials and baptisms,[545] or 29–094

[533] *Scarfe v Hallifax* (1840) 7 M. & W. 288, 290.

[534] *Wakefield v Newbon* (1844) 6 Q.B. 276; *Turner v Deane* (1849) 3 Ex. 836; and see *Pratt v Vizard* (1833) 5 B. & Ad. 808; *Smith v Sleap* (1844) 12 M. & W. 585; *Oates v Hudson* (1851) 6 Ex. 346. cf. *Re Llewellin* [1891] 3 Ch. 145.

[535] *Close v Phipps* (1844) 7 M. & G. 586; and see *Fraser v Pendlebury* (1861) 31 L.J.C.P. 1. The PC has applied a similar rule to detention of land: *Kanhaya Lal v National Bank of India* (1913) 29 T.L.R. 314.

[536] Birks at pp.294–299; Burrows at pp.223–224, 436–438; Goff and Jones at pp.320–324; Virgo at pp.190, 405–407. On recovery of money paid by exploitation, see below, para.29–137.

[537] *Morgan v Palmer* (1824) 2 B. & C. 729; cf. *Traherne v Gardner* (1856) 5 E. & B. 913; *Hooper v Exeter Corp* (1887) 56 L.J.Q.B. 457 (harbour dues); *Marshall Shipping Co v Board of Trade* [1923] 2 K.B. 343; *R. v Brocklebank* [1925] 1 K.B. 52; *R. & W. Paul Ltd v The Wheat Commission* [1937] A.C. 139; *Mason v State of N.S.W.* (1959) 102 C.L.R. 108; *Bell Bros Pty Ltd v Shire of Serpentine-Jarrahdale* (1969) 44 A.L.J.R. 26.

[538] [1993] A.C. 70; above, para.29–083.

[539] For the view that it does not, see Goff and Jones at pp.322–324. For the view that it *could*, see Beatson (1993) 109 L.Q.R. 401, 404–410; Burrows at p.438; Virgo at p.407.

[540] e.g. *Morgan v Palmer* (1824) 2 B.C. 729; *Steele v Williams* (1853) 8 Ex. 625.

[541] e.g. *Atlee v Backhouse* (1838) 3 M. & W. 633.

[542] *Steele v Williams* (1853) 8 Ex. 625.

[543] *Morgan v Palmer* (1824) 2 B.C. 729.

[544] (1824) 2 B.C. 729.

[545] *Steele v Williams* (1853) 8 Ex. 625.

charges by an electricity company contravening statutory restrictions.[546] Similarly, a party to an arbitration may recover an excessive fee fixed by the arbitrator and paid to him in order to obtain delivery of the award.[547] The fact that the payer was acting under a mistake of law is no defence to an action for extortion *colore officii*, as where a sheriff claimed and was paid a larger fee than he was entitled to by law.[548] But in some circumstances, if no improper pressure or threat is used and the payer has full knowledge of all the facts, fees illegally collected by an official may be irrecoverable on the ground that they were paid voluntarily[549]; the court will assess the possible alternative courses of action open to the payer, such as how, if at all, would he have suffered if he had refused to pay and was the only way in which the authority could enforce its demand by suing the payer?[550]

29–095 **Express threat unnecessary.** The requirement, in some cases, that the authority accompany its demand with an express threat does not apply to the restitutionary right in the *Woolwich* case and has been criticised on two grounds. First, that demands made with the weight of an apparently valid governmental authority are far more coercive than demands made by private individuals whether or not there is:

> "... any actual threatened withholding of something to which the payer was entitled, or actual threatened impeding of him in the exercise of some right or liberty."[551]

Secondly, it is contrary to principles of public law for such an authority to keep money obtained in such a manner.[552] Even if there is no need for an express threat under the *colore officii* principle, it is still narrower than the restitutionary right in the *Woolwich* case which is not based on compulsion but on ultra vires. On the other hand, insofar as it applies to arbitrators and common carriers, *colore officii* may prove to apply to a wider class of payees.[553]

---

[546] *South of Scotland Electricity Board v British Oxygen Ltd (No.2)* [1959] 1 W.L.R. 587 (recovery not directed since facts not found), discussed in *Woolwich Equitable Building Society v IRC* [1993] A.C. 70, 133–134, 159–160, 165, 187–188.

[547] *Fernley v Branson* (1851) 20 L.J.Q.B. 178; *Barnes v Braithwaite* (1857) 2 H. & N. 569; cf. Arbitration Act 1950 s.19. See also *North Ocean Shipping Co Ltd v Hyundai Construction Co Ltd* [1979] Q.B. 705, 716.

[548] *Dew v Parsons* (1819) 2 B. & Ald. 562. On mistake of law, see above, paras 29–041 et seq.

[549] *Twyford v Manchester Corp* [1946] Ch. 236 (criticised by Marsh (1946) 62 L.Q.R. 333; Birks at pp.296–297). On voluntary payments see below, paras 29–109 et seq. cf. *R. v William Whiteley Ltd* (1909) 101 L.T. 741 (criticised by Munkman, *The Law of Quasi-Contracts* pp.39–40); *Sebel Products Ltd v Commissioners of Customs and Excise* [1949] Ch. 409. Note, however, that the plaintiff in *Maskell v Horner* [1915] 3 K.B. 106 (above, para.29–090) did not bring an action challenging the tolls until he had been paying them for 12 years.

[550] *Twyford v Manchester Corp* [1946] Ch. 236, 239, 242; *R. v William Whiteley Ltd* (1909) 101 L.T. 74.

[551] *Mason v New South Wales* (1959) 102 C.L.R. 108, 116–117 (Dixon J.). See also, at 126–127, 146; *Steele v Williams* (1853) 8 Ex. 625; *Hooper v Exeter Corp* (1887) 56 L.J.Q.B. 457; *Queens of the River S.S. Co Ltd v Conservators of the River Thames* (1899) 15 T.L.R. 474; *South of Scotland Electricity Board v British Oxygen Co Ltd (No.2)* [1959] 1 W.L.R. 587; *Rogers v Louth CC* [1981] I.R. 265. See further *Woolwich Equitable B.S. v IRC* [1993] A.C. 70, 173 (Lord Goff).

[552] Above, para.29–083.

[553] Above, para.29–094. See also Goff and Jones at pp.320–324.

Compliance with invalid local authority notices. A principle analogous to extortion *colore officii* allowed recovery of money expended where the claimants were under the impression that they were bound to comply with a notice from the local authority to repair a drain, and did so under pressure practically amounting to compulsion, although the notice was not a statutory one with which they were bound to comply.[554] 29–096

Compulsory payment of an excessive amount.[555] In *Great Western Ry v Sutton*[556] the railway refused to carry the claimant's goods unless he paid freight at an excessive rate not permitted by law; the House of Lords held that the claimant was entitled to recover the excess on the ground that, since the claimant could not have had his goods carried without meeting the railway's demand, it was a case of compulsion. Willes J. said: 29–097

> "When a man pays more than he is bound to do by law for the performance of a duty which the law says is owed to him for nothing, or for less than he has paid, there is a compulsion . . . in respect of which he is entitled to recover the excess by *condictio indebiti*, or action for money had and received."[557]

Payment made in the course of, or under the threat of, legal proceedings.[558] The general rule is that where a payment has been made in the course of legal proceedings, it is voluntary and irrecoverable; the same rule is generally true when legal proceedings are threatened.[559] In such cases legal advice can be taken, and if payment is made without doing so, the payer is deemed to have settled or compromised the dispute, "[t]here must be an end of litigation, otherwise there would be no security for any person".[560] However, if the payee 29–098

---

[554] *North v Walthamstow U.D.C.* (1898) 67 L.J.Q.B. 972. See also *Gebhardt v Saunders* [1892] 2 Q.B. 452; *Andrew v St Olave's Board of Works* [1898] 1 Q.B. 775; *Ellis v Bromley R.D.C.* (1899) 81 L.T. 224; *Wilson's Music & General Printing Co v Finsbury BC* [1908] 1 K.B. 563; cf. *Thompson and Norris Manufacturing Co Ltd v Hawes* (1895) 73 L.T. 369; *Oliver v Camberwell BC* (1904) 90 L.T. 285.

[555] Similar principles apply where the payee was legally obliged to act without payment: see extortion *colore officii*, above, para.29–094.

[556] (1869) L.R. 4 H.L. 226. cf. *South of Scotland Electricity Board v British Oxygen Co Ltd* [1959] 1 W.L.R. 587. On the position of a common carrier, see Vol.II, paras 36–007 et seq., especially para.36–016.

[557] (1869) L.R. 4 H.L. 226, 249. See also *Parker v G.W. Ry* (1844) 7 M. & G. 253; *Denaby Main Colliery Co Ltd v M.S. & L. Ry* (1885) 11 App. Cas. 97; *North Staffs Ry v Edge* [1920] A.C. 254. Recovery has been permitted although part of the excess was received by the defendant company as agent for a third party: *Parker v Bristol and Exeter Ry* (1851) 6 Ex. 702.

[558] See also the rule permitting the compromise of an invalid claim, above, paras 3–050—3–056; Beatson (1974) C.L.J. 97, 100–104; *Enrichment*, pp.100–103.

[559] *Marriot v Hampton* (1797) 7 T.R. 269; *Hamlet v Richardson* (1833) 9 Bing. 644; *Moore v Vestry of Fulham* [1895] 1 Q.B. 399; *Self v Hove Commissioners* [1895] 1 Q.B. 685, 690; *R. v William Whiteley Ltd* (1910) 101 L.T. 741; *Maskell v Horner* [1915] 3 K.B. 106, 121–122; *Sawyer and Vincent v Window Brace Ltd* [1943] K.B. 32; *Woolwich Equitable Building Society v IRC* [1993] A.C. 70, 98, 121, 135–136, 140, 165, 174, 178, 196, 198, 200–201. cf. *Rogers v Ingham* (1876) 3 Ch D 351; *Caird v Moss* (1886) 33 Ch D 22, 36; *Binder v Alachouzos* [1972] 2 Q.B. 151. (The rule also applies to payment in the course of foreign litigation: *Clydesdale Bank Ltd v Schroder & Co* [1913] 2 K.B. 1.) See generally above, para.7–050.

[560] *Marriot v Hampton* (1797) 7 T.R. 269; *Binder v Alachouzos* [1972] 2 Q.B. 151.

has acted fraudulently or illegally, such a payment may be recoverable[561]; and where money is paid under a void judgment, e.g. because an inferior court had no jurisdiction or because the correct procedure was not followed, it may be recovered.[562]

29–099 **Compulsory payments to a third person.**[563] In *Moule v Garrett*,[564] Cockburn C.J. approved the following statement from *Leake on Contracts*:

> "Where the plaintiff has been compelled by law to pay, or, being compellable by law, has paid money which the defendant was ultimately liable to pay, so that the latter obtains the benefit of the payment by the discharge of his liability; under such circumstances the defendant is held indebted to the plaintiff in the amount."

The payment made by the claimant must have discharged a legal liability of the defendant[565]; therefore, it must have been compulsory, since the general rule is that a *stranger* who pays another's debt to the creditor does not thereby obtain a discharge of the debtor's liability to the creditor: a voluntary payment is effective to discharge the debtor's liability only if it was made on his behalf and was subsequently ratified by him.[566] If, however, the claimant is compelled to make the payment to the third person, the cases cited in this section assume that the payment discharges the defendant's liability to the third person.[567] The compulsion may take the form of a secondary legal liability, but other forms of practical compulsion have also been recognised. It is sufficient, for instance, that the claimant was faced with the choice of either paying in order to recover possession of his chattel or being prevented from obtaining possession of it.[568] The payment of a third party's debt in order to release a security and perfect an independent right of reimbursement is a compulsory payment.[569] There are many

---

561 *Ward & Co v Wallis* [1900] 1 Q.B. 675. cf. *Pitt v Coomes* (1835) 2 A. & E. 459; *Duke de Cadaval v Collins* (1836) 4 A. & E. 858.

562 *Newdigate v Davy* (1701) 1 Ld. Raym. 742; *Farrow v Mayes* (1852) 18 Q.B. 516; *Re Smith* (1888) 20 QBD 321. cf. *O'Connor v Isaacs* [1956] 2 Q.B. 288.

563 Burrows at Ch.8; Goff and Jones at Ch.15; Virgo at pp.220–242; Winfield (1944) 60 L.Q.R. 341 (also his *Quasi-Contracts* (1952), pp.62–88). On compulsory payments to the defendant, see above, paras 29–087 et seq. and on duress or undue influence, which renders a contract voidable, see above, paras 7–001, 7–056, 29–089—29–093, below, paras 29–137—29–138.

564 (1872) L.R. 7 Ex. 101, 104 (which passage was in turn quoted with approval in *Brook's Wharf and Bull Wharf Ltd v Goodman Brothers* [1937] 1 K.B. 534, 543–544). See below, para.29–102. See also *Niru Battery Manufacturing Co v Maritime Freight Services Ltd* [2004] EWCA Civ 487, [2004] 2 All E.R. (Comm) 289 where the "principles of recoupment" were applied, although the effect was to recognise a restitutionary claim founded on the ground of legal compulsion. See also *Berghoff Trading Ltd v Swinbrook Developments Ltd* [2008] EWHC 1785 (Comm) (recognition right to recoupment from one debtor in favour of another).

565 See below, para.29–102.

566 *Simpson v Eggington* (1855) 10 Ex. 845, 847; *Smith v Cox* [1940] 2 K.B. 558. (These authorities were not considered in *Owen v Tate* [1976] Q.B. 402 (below, para.29–110).) See Goff and Jones at p.18 fn.16; Birks and Beatson (1976) 92 L.Q.R. 188–202; Beatson at pp.200–220 and below, para.29–115. But cf. Friedmann (1983) 99 L.Q.R. 534. On voluntary payments, see below, paras 29–109 et seq.

567 e.g. *Moule v Garrett* (1871–72) L.R. 7 Ex. 101; *Brook's Wharf and Bull Wharf Ltd v Goodman Bros* [1937] 1 K.B. 534, 544.

568 See below, paras 29–103—29–105.

569 *Kleinwort Benson Ltd v Vaughan* [1996] C.L.C. 620.

cases on what amounts to such a compulsory payment, and although the majority of reported cases are grouped under headings in the succeeding paragraphs, there may well be other miscellaneous cases of compulsory payments outside these headings.[570] The liability of a principal debtor to indemnify his surety[571] will also be discussed under this heading of compulsory payment, though a distinction might be drawn in that a surety in the first place voluntarily assumes potential liability for the debt.

Tortfeasor compelled to pay twice. Where a tortfeasor is compelled to pay damages to two or more claimants for wrongful interference with the same goods a statutory right to reimbursement arises under the Torts (Interference with Goods) Act 1977. Section 7(4) provides that: 29–100

> "... where, as the result of enforcement of a double liability, any claimant is unjustly enriched to any extent, he shall be liable to reimburse the wrongdoer to that extent."[572]

The defendant must be under a legal liability to pay the third person. If the defendant is under no legal liability to pay the money, he is not liable to make restitution to the claimant, although it may appear that indirectly the payment by the claimant has benefited the defendant.[573] So where a police authority was under a statutory obligation to pay constables while incapacitated through an injury received in the course of their duty, and a constable was injured by the negligence of the defendant, the Court of Appeal held that the authority could not recover from the defendant the wages paid to the constable during his period of incapacity, although the defendant had not been required to pay anything in respect of loss of earnings to settle the constable's claim for damages for negligence.[574] The defendant had paid to the constable all the damages he was 29–101

---

[570] e.g. *Kendal v Wood* (1871) L.R. 6 Ex. 243. See also payments made by necessity, below, paras 29–103, 29–112; *Owen v Tate* [1976] Q.B. 402, 412 (Scarman L.J.); *The "Zuhal K"* [1987] 1 Lloyd's Rep. 151. But cf. *Re Gasbourne Pty Ltd* [1984] V.R. 801, 840–845 (practical commercial compulsion not a ground for restitution). Quaere whether this is consistent with the development of economic duress, above, para.7–014. See also *Peel (Regional Municipality) v Canada* [1992] 3 S.C.R. 762 (local authority which was required by ultra vires statute to maintain delinquents not permitted to recover from federal government could not recover because benefit was incidental or collateral).

[571] Below, para.29–119. Analogous to this is the surety's right to claim contribution from a co-surety (below, para.29–123). Also analogous are other claims to contribution, such as the right of one joint tortfeasor to claim contribution from another (s.1(1) of the Civil Liability (Contribution) Act 1978) (below, para.29–121).

[572] The sub-section gives as an example of its operation the case where a converter of goods pays damages first to a finder and then to the true owner. The finder is unjustly enriched unless he accounts to the true owner who is himself then unjustly enriched and becomes liable to reimburse the converter.

[573] *Receiver for the Metropolitan Police District v Croydon Corp* [1957] 2 Q.B. 154 (*Receiver for the Metropolitan Police District v Tatum* [1948] 2 K.B. 68, though not referred to in this case, must be taken to have been impliedly overruled by it). See *Monmouthshire CC v Smith* [1956] 1 W.L.R. 1132; affirmed [1957] 2 Q.B. 154. See also *Re Nott and Cardiff Corp* [1918] 2 K.B. 146 reversed by the House of Lords on a different point: [1919] A.C. 337.

[574] *Receiver for the Metropolitan Police District v Croydon Corp* [1957] 2 Q.B. 154.

legally liable to pay, and so had not derived an unjust benefit through the authority's payment of wages.[575]

29–102 **The defendant must be primarily or ultimately liable to pay the third person.** In *Brook's Wharf and Bull Wharf Ltd v Goodman Bros*[576] Lord Wright said:

> "The essence of the rule is that there is a liability for the same debt resting on the plaintiff and the defendant and the plaintiff has been legally compelled to pay, but the defendant gets the benefit of the payment, because his debt is discharged either entirely or *pro tanto*, whereas the defendant is primarily liable to pay as between himself and the plaintiff."

In this case the plaintiffs, as bonded warehousemen, were compelled by statute to pay duties on skins stored with them by the defendants; since the defendants were primarily liable to pay these duties, they were required to reimburse the plaintiffs.

29–103 **Actual seizure of the claimant's goods in respect of the defendant's debt.**

> "Speaking generally, and excluding exceptional cases, where a person's goods are lawfully seized for another's debt, the owner of the goods is entitled to redeem them, and to be reimbursed by the debtor against the money paid to redeem them, and in the event of the goods being sold to satisfy the debt, the owner is entitled to recover the value of them from the debtor . . . The right to indemnity or contribution in these cases exists, although there may be no agreement to indemnify or contribute and although there may be, in that sense, no privity between the plaintiff and the defendant."[577]

Thus, where the claimant's goods, having been placed on the demised premises with the tenant's consent,[578] were distrained by the landlord for rent due from the tenant, and the claimant was obliged to pay the rent to redeem his goods, he was

---

[575] Lord Goddard C.J., *Croydon Corp* [1957] 2 Q.B. 154, 162, pointed out that the real loss sustained by the police authority was the loss of the constable's services, but that recovery for that loss by an action *per quod servitium amisit* was excluded because a constable was not a "servant" of the authority: *Att-Gen for New South Wales v Perpetual Trustee Co Ltd* [1955] A.C. 457. See, however, the recommendation of the 11th Report of the Law Reform Committee, Cmnd.2017.

[576] [1937] 1 K.B. 534, 544. This has been taken to mean that the claimant and the defendant must have been subject to a *common demand* for money, which the defendant was ultimately liable to pay: *Bonner v Tottenham and Edmonton Permanent Investment Building Society* [1899] 1 Q.B. 161, 171–174 but the cases on pressure falling short of secondary liability (below, paras 29–103—29–105) show that this is not so; *Whitham v Bullock* [1939] 2 K.B. 81, 85. See also Goff and Jones at pp.380–383, 439–440. *Bonner's* case itself can be explained on the ground that no debt was discharged. See also *Niru Battery Manufacturing Co v Milestone Trading Ltd (No.2)* [2004] EWCA Civ 487, [2004] 2 All E.R. (Comm) 289 where restitution was available even though the claimant and the defendant were not subject to a common demand.

[577] *Edmunds v Wallingford* (1885) 14 QBD 811, 814–815. See also *Dawson v Linton* (1822) 5 B. & Ald. 521; *Ex p. Elliot* (1838) 3 Deac. 343; *Johnson v Skafte* (1869) L.R. 4 Q.B. 700.

[578] If the plaintiff had, as a trespasser, placed his goods there without authority, his payment of rent to the landlord to redeem his goods would give him no right to indemnity from the tenant, since he would have: ". . . by his own voluntary act, and without any request of the defendant, express or implied, placed his goods in a position to enable the landlord to seize them." *England v Marsden* (1866) L.R. 1 C.P. 529, 533. In *Edmunds v Wallingford* (1884) 14 QBD 811, 816, the court thought that the decision in *England v Marsden* was wrong on the facts.

entitled to recover the rent from the tenant.[579] A similar situation arose where the mortgagees of some shares in a vessel paid a claim to redeem the vessel from arrest so that they could take possession under their mortgage; the co-owners of the vessel, who were liable to pay the claim, were compelled to repay the mortgagees.[580]

Effect of bankruptcy. The effect of the debtor's bankruptcy on a claim for restitution on this ground has been clarified by the Insolvency Act 1986. Formerly, a payment made to secure the release of goods lawfully distrained for the debt of a person who subsequently became bankrupt was neither provable in the bankruptcy nor barred by an order of discharge, since it was not a claim by reason of any contract or promise.[581] However, under the 1986 Act a liability arising out of an obligation to make restitution is a bankruptcy debt and is provable in the bankruptcy.[582] This will be so whether the payment is made before the commencement of the bankruptcy or after that time, since the Act provides that it is immaterial whether the liability is present or future, or certain or contingent.[583] 29–104

Threat to seize the claimant's goods in respect of the defendant's debt. The same principle applies where the third person threatens to levy distress on the claimant's goods to satisfy the defendant's debt. Thus if an underlessee, under threat of distress or eviction by the head lessor, pays ground rent due from his immediate lessor to the head lessor, the underlessee may recover it as money paid to the use of his immediate lessor.[584] In these circumstances, the Law of Distress Amendment Act 1908 enables the underlessee, by adopting a certain procedure, to avoid seizure of his goods. But where one underlessee of part of the premises comprised in the head lease has, under a threat of distress, paid the whole rent due under the head lease, he cannot recover from another underlessee, as money paid to his use, the proportion of rent due from him.[585] 29–105

Assignees of a lease. Despite the fact that there have been successive assignments of the term, the original lessee may still be held liable for rent or for breach of covenant under the terms of the lease. In *Moule v Garrett*[586] it was held that in these circumstances the original lessee may claim an indemnity from a 29–106

[579] *Exall v Partridge* (1799) 8 T.R. 308. See also *Bevan v Waters* (1828) 3 C. & P. 520.

[580] *The Orchis* (1890) 15 P.C. 38; *Johnson v Royal Mail Steam Packet Co* (1867) L.R. 3 C.P. 38. See also *The Heather Bell* [1901] P. 143; affirmed on another point, at 272.

[581] *Johnson v Skafte* (1869) L.R. 4 Q.B. 700. cf. *Re Button* [1907] 2 K.B. 180, 188, 190 (in respect of goods bailed to debtor).

[582] s.382(4).

[583] s.382(3).

[584] *Sapsford v Fletcher* (1792) 4 T.R. 511; *Jones v Morris* (1849) 3 Ex. 742, 747; *Underhay v Read* (1887) 20 QBD 209. The mere fact that the head lessor grants the underlessee time to pay does not prevent its being a compulsory payment: *Carter v Carter* (1829) 5 Bing. 406.

[585] *Hunter v Hunt* (1845) 1 C.B. 300. See also *Johnson v Wild* (1890) 44 Ch D 146 (below, para.29–122); Langan (1967) 31 Conv.(N.S.) 38; Goff and Jones at pp.381–383.

[586] (1872) L.R. 7 Ex. 101 (above, para.29–099). See Megarry and Wade, *The Law of Real Property*, 7th edn, p.936; Goff and Jones at pp.427–429. See also Law of Property Act 1925 s.77, as amended (implied covenant by assignee to indemnify against breach of covenant); *Dickinson UK Ltd v Zwebner* [1989] Q.B. 208; *Re Healing Research Trustee Ltd* [1992] 2 All E.R. 481.

subsequent assignee, even though each assignee may have covenanted expressly to indemnify his own assignor against any breach of covenant committed after the assignment to him. The original lessee's right of indemnity from a subsequent assignee will be of less importance in practice since the liability of both the original parties to a lease and of their assignees has been limited in respect of agreements for leases made or leases granted after January 1, 1996 by the Landlord and Tenant (Covenants) Act 1995.

29–107 **Other illustrations concerning land.** Another illustration of the general principle concerns a statutory notice served by a sanitary authority on the occupier of premises requiring[587] him to abate a nuisance; if the occupier pays for the required work to abate the nuisance, he may recover the cost from the owner of the premises if, as between the occupier and the owner, the owner is primarily liable.[588] Again, a tenant may obtain restitution from his landlord when the tenant is compelled to pay a tax which the landlord is ultimately liable to pay.[589] The same principle of restitution of a compulsory payment was applied where land charged with the repair of a bridge was occupied by a lessee; the occupier was, in the first instance, responsible to the public for the repair of the bridge, but he successfully claimed restitution from the owner in an action for money paid to the owner's use, since the owner was ultimately liable.[590]

29–108 **Bills of exchange.** If, when the indorser of a bill of exchange is sued by the holder, the indorser pays him the whole or part of the amount of the bill, the indorser can recover the amount paid from the acceptor as money paid to his use.[591]

29–109 **Voluntary payments.**[592] If the payment is regarded by the law as voluntary, it cannot normally[593] be recovered.[594] In one case Swinfen Eady J. said:

---

[587] cf. a mere recommendation: *Silles v Fulham BC* [1903] 1 K.B. 829.

[588] *Gebhardt v Saunders* [1892] 2 Q.B. 452, 456, 458 (reimbursement was granted on common law grounds, as well as under the relevant statute). See also the cases cited above, para.29–096; *Hackett v Smith* [1917] 2 I.R. 508.

[589] *Dawson v Linton* (1822) 5 B. & Ald. 521; cf. *Eastwood v McNab* [1914] 2 K.B. 361; *Hales v Freeman* (1819) 1 B. & B. 391. An illustration from a (now repealed) statutory provision was the right of a tenant who paid Sch.A tax to deduct the amount from his next payment of rent: Income Tax Act 1952 s.173; *Hill v Kirshenstein* [1920] 3 K.B. 556; cf. *Bernard and Shaw Ltd v Shaw* [1951] 2 All E.R. 267 (employer failed to deduct income tax under PAYE system, and was compelled to pay the same to the Revenue authorities: held, employer had no action to recover the tax paid from the employee). In *McCarthy v McCarthy and Stone Plc* [2007] EWCA Civ 664 tax paid by an employer under the PAYE system in respect of share options could not be deducted from salary because the employee had left the firm. It was held that the tax could be recovered from the former employee on the ground of legal compulsion because the former employee bore the ultimate liability for the tax. cf. the cases cited above, para.29–105.

[590] *Baker v Greenhill* (1842) 3 Q.B. 148. cf. *Macclesfield Corp v Great Central Ry* [1911] 2 K.B. 528.

[591] *Pownal v Ferrand* (1827) 6 B. & C. 439; cf. *Ex p. Bishop* (1880) 15 Ch D 400. But cf. ss.57 and 59(2) of the Bills of Exchange Act 1882 (Vol.II, para.34–125). See also Goff and Jones at pp.432–434.

[592] cf. cases where the request of the defendant to make the payment will be implied: below, paras 29–116—29–119.

[593] For exceptional circumstances in which a voluntary payment may be recovered, see below, para.29–112.

[594] See Birks at pp.102–103; Burrows at pp.283–286; Goff and Jones at pp.70–72, 430–435; Virgo at pp.39–40, 232–234; Hope (1929–1930) 15 Cornell L.Q. 25, 205. See, in addition to the cases cited

> "If A voluntarily pays B's debt, B is under no obligation to repay A. There must be a previous request, express or implied, to raise such an obligation, and in this respect I can see no difference between the discharge of a statutory liability and the discharge of a contractual liability."[595]

So where the claimant, drawer of a bill for the accommodation of the defendant, paid the holder a part of the bill after its dishonour, but without notice of dishonour and without any request from the defendant, this was held to be a voluntary payment which could not be recovered.[596] Again, the mere fact that a company promoter pays the fees and stamp duty on the registration of a company does not in itself entitle him to recover them from the company.[597] Where, without any request from the mortgagee, a mortgagor, who is the ultimate owner of the equity of redemption in a life insurance policy, pays a premium due on the policy in order to prevent its lapse, the mortgagor is not entitled to recover the amount from the mortgagee, despite the fact that the latter has benefited from the payment.[598] But a payment made under mistake is not a voluntary payment.[599]

Secondary liabilities voluntarily incurred. The principle of voluntariness applies to secondary liabilities that are voluntarily incurred. In *Owen v Tate*,[600] Scarman L.J. stated that: 29–110

> "If without an antecedent request a person assumes an obligation . . . for the benefit of another, the law will, as a general rule, refuse him a right of indemnity."

Thus, where, without consulting the debtor, a person guaranteed a debt in order to release a friend from an earlier guarantee in respect of the same debt, it was held that no action for restitution would lie. The principle also applies where the

---

below, *Stokes v Lewis* (1785) 1 T.R. 20; *Bates v Townley* (1848) 2 Ex. 152; *Re Cleadon Trust Ltd* [1939] Ch. 286; *Aktieselskabet Dampskibs Steinstad v William Pearson & Co* (1927) 137 L.T. 533; *Wilson v Audio-Visual Equipment Ltd* [1974] 1 Lloyd's Rep. 81. cf. *Pownal v Ferrand* (1827) 6 B. & C. 439, 443–444; *Owen v Tate* [1976] Q.B. 402, below, para.29–112; *Re Gasbourne Pty Ltd* [1984] V.R. 807; *Esso Petroleum Ltd v Hall Russell & Co* [1989] A.C. 643; *Kleinwort Benson Ltd v Vaughan* [1996] C.L.C. 620.

595 *Re National Motor Mail Coach Co Ltd* [1908] 2 Ch. 515, 520 (approved, 523).

596 *Sleigh v Sleigh* (1850) 5 Ex. 514 (distinguished in *Re Chetwynd's Estate* [1938] Ch. 13). cf. payment for honour supra protest (s.68(3) and (4) of the Bills of Exchange Act 1882; see Vol.II, para.34–144).

597 *Re National Motor Mail Coach Co Ltd* [1908] 2 Ch. 515 (see above, para.9–015).

598 *Falcke v Scottish Imperial Insurance Co* (1886) 34 Ch D 234 (below, para.29–115). cf. *Re Leslie* (1883) 23 Ch D 552 and note the developing law concerning restitution for interventions in cases of necessity and where an incontrovertible benefit is conferred, above, paras 29–022, 29–053, below, paras 29–130 et seq.

599 See also *Banque Financière de la Cité v Parc (Battersea) Ltd* [1999] 1 A.C. 221, below, para.29–173.

600 [1976] Q.B. 402, 411–412. The case has been criticised because it assumed, without considering and in the face of the authorities (above, para.29–099), that the payment discharged the debt. Had the authorities been considered it is arguable that a claim based on the acquiescence of the debtor (on which see above, para.29–021, below, para.29–116) would have succeeded; Birks and Beatson (1976) 92 L.Q.R. 188, 208–212; Beatson at pp.200–205. cf. Friedmann (1983) 99 L.Q.R. 534. There should, moreover, be no objection to the volunteer deriving rights against the debtor by assignment or subrogation. Goff and Jones at pp.138–140, 430–432; McCamus (1978) 16 Osgoode Hall L.J. 516, 550–559. Subrogation does not appear to have been argued in *Owen v Tate* on which, see Mercantile Law Amendment Act 1856 s.5; Burrows at pp.282–286.

intervener fulfils the defendant's obligation by performing a service. In one case,[601] the defendants were under a statutory duty to repair a road bridge over their canal, but refused to repair it when the claimants, who were the highway authority, called upon them to do so. The claimants then did the work themselves, but they were not able to recover from the defendants the cost incurred by them, since they were under no legal liability to repair the bridge, and accordingly had acted as mere volunteers.

29–111 **Payment under protest.** The fact that a protest is made at the time of payment may often indicate that a payment is not "voluntary", but the mere absence of a protest does not necessarily mean that a payment is voluntary. It is a question of fact whether the protests of the payer amount to no more than "grumbling acquiescence",[602] or whether the circumstances indicate a payment under protest, even where no express words are used.[603] Thus it is not a voluntary payment which:

> "... is made for the purpose of averting a threatened evil, and is made not with the intention of giving up a right but under an immediate necessity and with the intention of preserving the right to dispute the legality of the demand."[604]

(But the payments made in the course of, or under threat of, legal proceedings are not recoverable,[605] since the payer should take legal advice if he wishes to dispute his liability.) In one case, where a tenant at first protested against the refusal of his landlord to allow, as a deduction from rent due, land tax paid by the tenant, yet later during five successive years he paid the land tax without renewing his objection to the landlord, it was held that he could not recover any of the sums paid for land tax as money paid to the landlord's use, since they were voluntary payments.[606]

29–112 **Exceptional cases where a voluntary payment is recoverable.** A voluntary payment may be recoverable in the following exceptional circumstances:

(1) where the circumstances justify the inference of an implied request by the defendant to make the payment[607];

(2) where the special equitable doctrine accepted by the Court of Appeal in *Re Cleadon Trust Ltd*[608] applies:

---

601 *Macclesfield Corp v Great Central Ry* [1911] 2 K.B. 528. cf. above, para.29–107 and see *Procter & Gamble Phillipine Manufacturing Corp v Peter Cremer GmbH & Co* [1988] 3 All E.R. 843, 854–856 (recognition of incontrovertible benefit although not applicable on facts).

602 *Maskell v Horner* [1915] 3 K.B. 106, 119, 127. See also *Twyford v Manchester Corp* [1946] Ch. 236 (above, para.29–094); *R. v William Whiteley Ltd* (1909) 101 L.T. 741; *Woolwich Equitable Building Society v IRC* [1993] A.C. 70, 165, 174, 178, 192, 196, 200.

603 *Maskell v Horner* [1915] 3 K.B. 106, 119–120, 126.

604 [1915] 3 K.B. 106, 118.

605 See above, para.29–098.

606 *Spragg v Hammond* (1820) 2 Brod. & B. 59. cf. *Denby v Moore* (1817) 1 B. & Ald. 123.

607 See below, paras 29–116—29–117.

608 [1939] Ch. 286, 302. Discussed in Winfield, *Quasi-Contracts* (1952), pp.86–88 and Goff and Jones at p.166. See further below, para.29–173 (subrogation).

> "Where money is borrowed on behalf of a principal by an agent . . . though it turns out that his act has not been authorised, or ratified, or adopted by the principal, then, although the principal cannot be sued in law, yet in equity, to the extent to which the money borrowed has in fact been applied in paying legal debts and obligations of the principal, the lender is entitled to stand in the same position as if the money had originally been borrowed by the principal."

(3) where one person has innocently repaired or improved another's chattel, he may in some circumstances obtain restitution, directly or indirectly[609];

(4) where the doctrines of ratification in agency[610] and of agency of necessity[611] apply;

(5) where the claimant has reasonably intervened on behalf of the defendant in an emergency[612];

(6) although a "voluntary" payment to a third person which in fact benefits the defendant cannot normally create an obligation upon the defendant to indemnify the payer, there are dicta supporting a wider principle in *Owen v Tate*.[613] Scarman L.J. said[614] that, despite the general rule, if the intervener can show:

> ". . . that in the particular circumstances of the case there was some necessity for the obligation to be assumed, then the law will grant him a right of reimbursement if in all the circumstances it is just and reasonable to do so."

In the same case, Stephenson L.J. also assumed that there may be circumstances where a volunteer could recover if "it is obviously unjust that a debtor should be enriched by accepting the benefit".[615] Scarman L.J.'s formulation suggests that cases of necessitous intervention might suffice,[616] and it has been followed,[617] although Stephenson L.J. preferred not to give instances of the type of situation in which a "volunteer" may recover an indemnity[618] and Ormrod L.J. reserved his opinion on the whole question.[619]

Payment to a third party at the defendant's request. For many years, reimbursement has been available through the action "for money paid" to recover money paid by a person to a third person at the request,[620] express or implied, of the defendant, and with an undertaking, express or implied, on his 29–113

[609] See above, para.29–053 (cf. below, para.29–161).

[610] See Vol.II, paras 31–026 et seq.

[611] See below, para.29–130.

[612] See below, para.29–131.

[613] [1976] Q.B. 402 (noted (1975) 91 L.Q.R. 308; (1975) 38 M.L.R. 563; [1975] C.L.J. 202). See Birks and Beatson (1976) 92 L.Q.R. 188; cf. Friedmann (1983) 99 L.Q.R. 534.

[614] [1976] Q.B. 402, 411–412.

[615] [1976] Q.B. 402, 413.

[616] See also Goff and Jones at p.432.

[617] *The Zuhal K.* [1987] 1 Lloyd's Rep. 151. See also at *Re Berkeley Applegate Ltd* [1989] Ch. 32. cf. *Esso Petroleum Ltd v Hall Russell & Co* [1989] A.C. 643.

[618] [1976] Q.B. 402, 413.

[619] [1976] Q.B. 402, 414.

[620] cf. compulsory payments, above, paras 29–087, 29–099.

part to repay it[621]; and it is immaterial whether or not the defendant is relieved from a legal liability by the payment.[622] This type of claim is not obviously contractual, since the implied undertaking to repay is often fictional[623]; furthermore the claimant need not have been under any contractual obligation to make the payment, and the defendant's request may not have referred to a precise sum of money. The ground for recovery is akin to the principle of the law of agency which imposes on the principal an obligation to indemnify his agent against any liability which he may incur in the exercise of his authority.[624] However, although it is treated here for convenience, it is not necessarily restitutionary since the claimant will be entitled to be indemnified even though his payment has conferred no benefit on the defendant.[625]

29–114 **The payment must be to the use of the defendant.** The obligation to reimburse the claimant arises only when the money was paid to the use of the defendant. So if A by agreement with B binds himself to pay either to B or to a third party a sum of money which B is primarily liable to pay, and B is afterwards called upon to pay and does pay such sum, his only remedy against A is on the special agreement. For the money so paid by B, having been paid in discharge of his own liability, was not money paid to the use of A.[626]

29–115 **The payment must be made at the request of the defendant.** It is also necessary for the claimant to prove the defendant's express or implied request to the claimant to pay the money for his use. It is not sufficient to prove that the defendant was liable to a third person and that the claimant paid the third person: it must be proved that the claimant did so at the instance, either express or implied, of the defendant,[627] or, where the defendant had the option whether or not to ratify the payment, that he exercised his option to ratify it.[628] For no legal right to repayment will be established by the mere voluntary payment of the debt of another person; a man cannot make himself the creditor of another without his knowledge and consent,[629] except by the process of assignment.[630] The words of

---

[621] *Brittain v Lloyd* (1845) 14 M. & W. 762, 773; approved in *Lewis v Campbell* (1849) 8 C.B. 541, 547–548 and in *Re A Debtor* [1937] Ch. 156, 163. See also *Re H.P.C. Productions Ltd* [1962] Ch. 466, 487. The transfer of property with a marketable value may be equivalent to the payment of money: *Fahey v Frawley* (1890) 26 L.R.Ir. 78, 89–90.

[622] *Brittain v Lloyd* (1845) 14 M. & W. 762.

[623] cf. *Secretary of State v Bank of India Ltd* [1938] 2 All E.R. 797, 800 (see below, para.29–120).

[624] See Vol.II, para.31–160; also below, para.29–117.

[625] e.g. by discharging a liability of the defendant; *Brittain v Lloyd* (1845) 14 M. & W. 762; *Warlow v Harrison* (1858) 1 E. & E. 295, 317. There are, however, cases in which the claimant has been given a restitutionary right to reimbursement although there was also a contractual relationship between the parties which could have formed the basis of a claim for indemnity; Goff and Jones at pp.439–440.

[626] *Spencer v Parry* (1835) 3 A. & E. 331; *Lubbock v Tribe* (1838) 3 M. & W. 607.

[627] *Sleigh v Sleigh* (1850) 5 Ex. 514, 516.

[628] *Leigh v Dickeson* (1884) 15 QBD 60, 64–65.

[629] *Stokes v Lewis* (1785) 1 T.R. 20; *Owen v Tate* [1976] Q.B. 402 (discussed in (1976) 92 L.Q.R. 188); see also above, para.29–112; but see *Liggett (Liverpool) Ltd v Barclays Bank* [1928] 1 K.B. 48, for the liability of the defendant in equity, although the meaning, if not the decision, in this case is put into question by *Re Cleadon Trust Ltd* [1939] Ch. 286, 316–318, 326–327.

[630] See above, paras 19–001 et seq.

Bowen L.J. in *Falcke v Scottish Imperial Insurance Co*[631] have been frequently quoted:

> "The general principle is, beyond all question, that work and labour done or money expended by one man to preserve or benefit the property of another do not according to English law create any lien upon the property saved or benefited, nor, even if standing alone, create any obligation to repay the expenditure. Liabilities are not to be forced upon people behind their backs, any more than you can confer a benefit upon a man against his will . . .[632] There can, as it seems to me, according to the common law be only one principle upon which a claim for repayment can be based, and that is where you can find facts from which the law will imply a contract to repay or to give a lien."

Implied request by the defendant. The courts have often inferred from the circumstances an implied request by the defendant to the claimant to make the payment[633] especially where the money paid by the claimant was in discharge of a liability which the claimant had undertaken at the defendant's instance, or by his authority. Lord Greene M.R. has said: 29–116

> ". . . if a person knows that the consideration is being rendered for his benefit with an expectation that he will pay for it, then if he acquiesces in its being done, taking the benefit of it when done, he will be taken impliedly to have requested its being done; and that will import a promise to pay for it."[634]

In one case[635] the claimant, who had done work for the provisional committee of a projected railway company, had been induced by the defendant, a member of the committee, to sue certain other members of the committee for his bill. The claimant incurred legal costs in bringing those actions, which it was held he could recover from the defendant as money paid at his implied request. The implied request is normally inferred from the circumstances existing at the time of the intervention by the claimant who will otherwise be regarded as a volunteer. But even a volunteer, who initially takes the risk of getting no return, may be relieved of that risk by the acquiescence of his beneficiary who, provided he has an opportunity to choose:

> ". . . is bound by all the rules of honesty not to be quiescent, but actively to dissent, when he knows that others have for his benefit put themselves in a position of

[631] (1886) 34 Ch D 234, 248–249; *The Istros II* [1973] 2 Lloyd's Rep. 152, 157. But see *G.N. Ry v Swaffield* (1874) L.R. 9 Ex. 132 (carrier entitled to recover reasonable cost of caring for horse when consignee failed to take delivery of it); *Re Berkeley Applegate Ltd* [1989] Ch. 32 (allowance for expenses of administering trust property to liquidator); *Procter & Gamble Phillipine Manufacturing Corp v Peter Cremer GmbH & Co* [1988] 3 All E.R. 843, 854–855.

[632] e.g. *Sorrell v Paget* [1950] 1 K.B. 252.

[633] cf. cases where the claimant has rendered services to the defendant at his implied request (above, para.29–071), or has salvaged the defendant's ship or its cargo (below, para.29–136), or has performed services for the defendant in an emergency (below, para.29–131).

[634] *Re Cleadon Trust Ltd* [1939] Ch. 286, 299, citing 1 Sm. L.C., 13th edn, at 156; cf. *Unity Joint Stock Mutual Banking Association v King* (1858) 25 Beav. 72; cf. also cases where the defendant acquiesces in improvements to his land being made by the claimant: below, para.29–161.

[635] *Bailey v Haines* (1849) 13 Q.B. 815, 832. See also *Brewer Street Investments Ltd v Barclays Woollen Co Ltd* [1954] 1 Q.B. 428; *William Lacey (Hounslow) Ltd v Davis* [1957] 1 W.L.R. 932.

disadvantage, from which, if he speaks or acts at once, they can extricate themselves, but from which, after a lapse of time, they can no longer escape."[636]

Earlier paragraphs in the present chapter, on "compulsory payments to a third person",[637] cite a number of cases which could be regarded as falling within the scope of an implied undertaking to reimburse the claimant for money expended on the defendant's behalf.

29–117 **Payment by agent for principal.** From the relationship of principal and agent the law will imply a promise by which the principal undertakes to indemnify the agent in respect of all liabilities which the agent has properly incurred in the course of the agency.[638] If, by the custom of trade or of the Stock Exchange, an agent is obliged, without any default on his part, to pay money on account of a contract made for his principal, the law will imply a promise on the part of the latter to repay it as money which has been paid to his use; and this will be the case whether or not he was acquainted with the custom by which the agent's contracts were governed.[639] But if the expense was incurred by the agent as the result of some default on his own part, there is no such implied promise, although the loss is sustained in a matter connected with his agency.[640]

29–118 **Tenancy in common.** In ordinary circumstances it will be difficult to infer a request from one tenant in common to another to expend money upon the property held in common. If one tenant in common chooses to repair a house held in common, he cannot, without a previous express request from the co-owner, recover any part of the expense from him, however much the co-owner may be benefited.[641]

29–119 **Payment by guarantors.**[642] Where one person becomes a guarantor for another at his request, the law implies a promise by the latter that he will repay the guarantor whatever the guarantor may be compelled to pay the creditor; the guarantor may recover the amount paid to the creditor as money paid to the use

---

[636] *City Bank of Sydney v McLaughlin* (1909) 9 C.L.R. 615, 625 (in the context of agency of necessity). See also above, paras 3–093, 3–147—3–148, 29–002; *Phillips v Homfray* (1871) L.R. 6 Ch. App. 770, 778; *Brewer Street Investments Ltd v Barclays Woollen Co Ltd* [1954] 1 Q.B. 428, 431. See further *Stiles v Cooper* (1748) 3 Atk. 692; *Van der Berg v Giles* [1979] 2 N.Z.L.R. 111.

[637] Above, paras 29–099 et seq.

[638] See Vol.II, paras 31–160—31–161.

[639] *Westropp v Solomon* (1849) 8 C.B. 345; and see *Duncan v Hill* (1873) L.R. 8 Ex. 242; *Hartas v Ribbons* (1889) 22 QBD 254; *Hunt, Cox & Co v Chamberlain* (1896) 12 T.L.R. 186; *Beckhuson and Gibbs v Hamblet* [1900] 2 Q.B. 18. The custom must, of course, satisfy the test of reasonableness.

[640] *Allen v Wingrove* (1901) 17 T.L.R. 261; *Wilson v Audio-Visual Equipment Ltd* [1974] 1 Lloyd's Rep. 81. cf. *Bowlby v Bell* (1846) 3 C.B. 284.

[641] *Leigh v Dickeson* (1884) 15 QBD 60; *Re Jones* [1893] 2 Ch. 461, 476 et seq.; *Re Cook's Mortgage* [1896] 1 Ch. 923. On a partition, however, equity may take account of expenditure between tenants in common. (This represents the law prior to 1926 as regards tenants in common of land. After 1925 the legal estate will often be vested in the tenants in common as joint tenants on trust for sale and as trustees their liability may have been affected: Law of Property Act 1925 s.34.)

[642] On contracts of guarantee in general, see Vol.II, paras 44–001 et seq. On contribution between sureties, see below, para.29–123 and Vol.II, paras 44–111, 44–121—44–122.

of the debtor.[643] But if the debtor was not consulted before the guarantee was made, the guarantor cannot recover an indemnity from the debtor for the amount paid by the guarantor to the creditor[644] unless the guarantor had acted in a way which was "reasonably necessary" in the interests of the debtor and it was just and reasonable to grant a right of reimbursement.[645]

Indemnity against liability incurred when acting at the request of another. When an act,[646] which is neither manifestly illegal nor illegal to the knowledge of the person doing it, is done by one person at the request of another,[647] and the act turns out to be injurious to the rights of a third person, the person doing the act is entitled to an indemnity against his liability towards the third person, from the person who requested that the act should be done.[648] Thus, where the transferee under a forged transfer of stock requests the corporation to register the transfer to him, the transferee is obliged to indemnify the corporation against the consequences of the forgery.[649] 29–120

The right to contribution. At common law, apart from the cases discussed above[650] where a right to reimbursement arises in favour of a non-volunteer who discharges the obligation of another, a right to contribution will only arise when a person, who owes with another a duty to a third party and is liable with that other to a common demand, discharges more than his proportionate share of that duty.[651] The amount recoverable is determined by a broad rule of equity: 29–121

> "If, as between several persons or properties all equally liable at law to the same demand, it would be equitable that the burden should fall in a certain way, the court will so far as possible, having regard to the solvency of the different parties, see that, if that

[643] See Vol.II, para.44–111. The surety may also bring a *quia timet* action against the principal debtor: *Watt v Mortlock* [1964] Ch. 84.

[644] *Owen v Tate* [1976] Q.B. 402. (The guarantor might, however, obtain from the creditor an *assignment* of the debt: see (1975) 38 M.L.R. 563, 564–565 or, possibly, be *subrogated* to the creditor's rights, a point apparently not taken in the case; above, para.29–110.)

[645] *The Zuhal K.* [1987] 1 Lloyd's Rep. 151.

[646] One statement of the principle limits it to acts performed in the course of "a statutory or common law duty of a ministerial character": *Sheffield Corp v Barclay* [1905] A.C. 392, 399.

[647] The principle may apply even if the person acting was able to deliberate whether he should accede to the request: *Secretary of State v Bank of India Ltd* [1938] 2 All E.R. 797.

[648] *Sheffield Corp v Barclay* [1905] A.C. 392, 397 (citing the argument of Mr. Cave in *Dugdale v Lovering* (1875) L.R. 10 C.P. 196, 197) and 399; *Secretary of State v Bank of India Ltd* [1938] 2 All E.R. 797, 800; see also *Stathlorne S.S. Co Ltd v Andrew Weir & Co* (1934) 40 Com. Cas. 168. For a similar principle in the law of agency, see Vol.II, para.31–160; cf. *W. Cory & Son Ltd v Lambton and Hetton Collieries Ltd* (1916) 86 L.J.K.B. 401.

[649] *Sheffield Corp v Barclay* [1905] A.C. 392. See also *Att-Gen v Odell* [1906] 2 Ch. 47; *Bank of England v Cutler* [1908] 2 K.B. 208; *Secretary of State v Bank of India Ltd* [1938] 2 All E.R. 797; *Yeung Kai Yung v Hong Kong and Shanghai Banking Corp* [1981] A.C. 787.

[650] Above, paras 29–099—29–108. This is referred to as indemnity by the Law Commission: Law Com. No.79, 1977, para.16.

[651] See above, Ch.17; Burrows at 290–293; Goff and Jones at pp.379–383, 391; Virgo at 234–240. See also *Report on Contribution* (Law Com. No.79, 1977); Mitchell, *The Law of Contribution and Reimbursement* (2003).

burden is placed inequitably by the exercise of the legal right, its incidence should be afterwards adjusted."[652]

In general, persons who are liable to the same demand are made to share the burden of that liability equally.[653] This is subject to contrary agreement, since a claim to contribution may be modified or limited by a contractual provision. It will also not apply where the parties undertake a liability in unequal shares or up to differing limits, as for instance occurs in contracts of insurance and guarantee.[654] The rationale of the law of contribution is to ensure that one party is not unjustly enriched at the expense of the other.[655] The above rules still apply in respect of contribution proceedings between persons jointly liable for the same *debt* but the position of parties liable in respect of the same *damage*,[656] whether jointly or otherwise, is now governed by the Civil Liability (Contribution) Act 1978. In a case falling within that statute the rules of equity do not apply and the right to contribution is to be:

> "... such as may be found by the court to be just and equitable having regard to the extent of that person's responsibility for the damage in question."[657]

By s.6(1):

> "A person is liable in respect of any damage for the purposes of this Act if the person who suffered it (or anyone representing his estate or dependants) is entitled to recover compensation from him in respect of that damage (whatever the legal basis of his liability, whether tort, breach of contract, breach of trust or otherwise)."

---

[652] *Whitham v Bullock* [1939] 2 K.B. 81, 85 (quoting Rowlatt, *Principal and Surety*, 3rd edn, p.173.

[653] See Williams, *Joint Obligations* (1949), Ch.9; above, Ch.17; Law Comm. No.79, 1977, paras 13–15, 27–29.

[654] Vol.II, Ch.41, Ch.44.

[655] *Dubai Aluminium Co Ltd v Salaam* [2002] UKHL 48; [2003] 2 A.C. 366 at [76].

[656] *Royal Brompton Hospital NHS Trust v Hammond* [2002] UKHL 14, [2002] 1 W.L.R. 1397: "same damage" is not to be interpreted to mean "substantially or materially similar damage"; no glosses, extensive or restrictive to the natural and ordinary meaning of the words, are warranted. Damage does not mean "damages" but "harm". So a claim under the Act will not be available where one party is liable for breach of contract and the other for unjust enrichment. However, in *Niru Battery Manufacturing Co v Milestone Trading Ltd (No.2)* [2004] EWCA Civ 487, [2004] 2 All E.R. (Comm) 289 the Court of Appeal suggested that, if it had been necessary to decide the point, the dicta in *Royal Brompton Hospital Trust* concerning the meaning of "damage" were *obiter* and that it was bound by the earlier decision of the Court of Appeal in *Friends' Provident Life Office v Hillier Parker May and Rowden (A Firm)* [1997] Q.B. 85, which held that a claim for restitution could be treated as a claim for compensation for the purposes of the 1978 Act, so that claims for breach of contract or tort and for unjust enrichment could be treated as claims for the same damage. See also *City Index Ltd v Gawler* [2007] EWCA Civ 1382 where the remedy for the action of unconscionable receipt was characterised as compensatory so that the defendant to that claim could be considered to be liable for the same damage as tortfeasors.

[657] Civil Liability (Contribution) Act 1978 s.2(1). This follows the form of words in the Law Reform (Married Women and Tortfeasors) Act 1935 s.6(2), which it replaces, and the principles used in determining what is "just and equitable" under the 1935 Act will be relevant; see Law Commission No.79, 1977, paras 68–79. See also *Weaver v Commercial Process Co Ltd* (1947) 63 T.L.R. 466; *The Miraflores and The Abadesa* [1967] A.C. 826, 845. cf. *Collins v Herefordshire CC* [1947] K.B. 598.

The Act therefore covers liability arising out of breaches of different contractual obligations,[658] situations in which one person's liability is in contract but the other's is in tort,[659] situations where one person's liability is in either contract or tort and the other's is in unjust enrichment,[660] as well as the case where the liability of both persons is in tort.[661] The Act does not affect any express contractual provision regulating or excluding a right to contribution.[662] The effects of this Act are discussed in the chapter on Joint Obligations earlier in this work.[663]

The common law requirement: liability to a common demand. Apart from the statute, there can be no question of contribution where the parties are not liable to a common demand. In *Johnson v Wild*[664] a lessee assigned part of the land to the claimant for the residue of the term and gave the defendants an underlease of the other part of the land. In each case the lessee covenanted to pay the rent due to the head lessor, but on the lessee's bankruptcy the head lessor threatened to distrain on the claimant's part of the land, and the claimant paid the whole of the rent due under the head lease. Chitty J. held that the claimant had no right of contribution against the defendant: 29–122

> "Now he does not demand contribution from a person liable to a common demand, because the defendants are not liable for the rent; and the defendants are not only not liable for the rent but nobody can sue them in respect of this supposed liability unless it be the plaintiff; whereas, in a common demand for which two persons are liable, if one pays then there is a right of contribution on the part of the other who makes the payment against the one who does not."[665]

The main instances of contribution will now be outlined.[666] The purpose of collecting these instances is to facilitate the use of analogies, since an analogy taken from one category of contribution may well be useful in another category,[667] but it should be noted that the extent of the right to contribution will depend on whether the particular case is governed by the equitable rules or by the statutory discretion.

Guarantees. The leading illustration of contribution comes from the law relating to guarantors or sureties.[668] If several persons become sureties for the 29–123

[658] e.g. the facts of *McConnell v Lynch-Robinson* [1957] N.I. 70.

[659] e.g. *Batty v Metropolitan Realisations Ltd* [1978] Q.B. 554.

[660] *Friends' Provident Life Office v Hillier Parker May and Rowden (A Firm)* [1997] Q.B. 85. cf. fn.656, above.

[661] See Law Com. No.79, 1977. See *Clerk & Lindsell on Torts*, 19th edn (2006), paras 4–12 et seq. Similar provisions permit contribution between vessels responsible for collisions at sea: Merchant Shipping Act 1995 ss.187–189.

[662] Civil Liability (Contribution) Act 1978 s.7(3)(b).

[663] Above, Ch.17.

[664] (1890) 44 Ch D 146.

[665] (1890) 44 Ch D 146, 150.

[666] There is no right of contribution between tenants in common: above, para.29–118.

[667] e.g. *Spottiswoode's Case* (1855) 6 De G.M. & G. 345, 371–372.

[668] See Vol.II, paras 44–001 et seq.

same debt, either jointly or severally, and whether by the same or different instruments, and one surety pays more than his proportionate share of the debt, he may recover[669] from his co-sureties proportionate shares of the excess.[670] If, however, a surety has guaranteed the debtor's obligations in respect of matters other than the payment of money, for instance by entering a performance bond, the rules of equity do not apply and the right to contribution is governed by the exercise by the court of the statutory discretion.[671]

29–124 **Joint contractors or debtors.** Where two or more persons are joint contractors,[672] and one is required to perform more than his proportionate share of a common liability under the contract, he may recover contribution from the other joint contractors.[673] Thus, where several defendants to an action agreed to employ a solicitor to manage their defence on their joint responsibility, the one defendant who paid the solicitor's costs was held entitled to recover contributions from the others.[674] Likewise, when two parties employed an arbitrator and one, in taking up the award, paid the arbitrator's fees, he was entitled to recover half the fees from the other party.[675]

29–125 **Trustees.** Trustees who commit a breach of trust are jointly and severally liable for any resulting loss of the trust property. If one trustee is made responsible for more than his share of the loss, he may recover contribution from the other trustees,[676] but the former rule, which subjected a passive trustee, who allows his co-trustee to administer the trust, to equal liability has now been replaced by the statutory discretion to allow such contribution as is "just and equitable having regard to the extent of responsibility for the damage in question".[676a]

29–126 **Directors.** Directors who employ the assets of a company on an ultra vires undertaking are liable to indemnify the company in respect of any loss resulting; if one director pays more than his proportionate share of the loss, he may recover contribution from those of his co-directors who are also liable.[677] Again, the extent of the right to contribution is governed by the statutory discretion.

[669] In an action for contribution in the Chancery Division, or in a common law action for money paid to the defendant's use.

[670] See above, para.17–027, and Vol.II, paras 44–111 et seq.

[671] Civil Liability (Contribution) Act 1978 s.2(1) (discussed above, para.17–029).

[672] Or joint and several contractors.

[673] See above, para.17–027.

[674] *Edger v Knapp* (1843) 5 M. & G. 753.

[675] *Marsack v Webber* (1860) 6 H. & N. 1.

[676] *Bahin v Hughes* (1886) 31 Ch D 390; *Chillingworth v Chambers* [1896] 1 Ch. 685; *Robinson v Harkin* [1896] 2 Ch. 415.

[676a] Civil Liability (Contribution) Act 1978, s.2(1).

[677] *Spottiswoode's Case* (1855) 6 De G.M. & G. 345, 372; *Ashhurst v Mason* (1875) L.R. 20 Eq. 225; *Re Alexandra Palace Co* (1882) 21 Ch D 149; *Ramskill v Edwards* (1885) 31 Ch D 100. cf. *Walsh v Bardsley* (1931) 47 T.L.R. 564 (the breach of duty benefited only the director seeking contribution).

Partners. Partners are jointly liable for partnership debts and obligations[678] and one partner who bears more than his own share of a common obligation is entitled to contribution from the other partners,[679] although, if the partnership still subsists, the right to contribution may be enforced only in an action for a general partnership account.[680] 29–127

Insurers. Subject to the provisions of any special contribution clause in the relevant insurance policies,[681] one insurer who has paid more than his proportionate share of a single loss, where several insurance policies cover the same interest in the same property, may recover contribution from the other insurers.[682] 29–128

General average contribution. Parties to a common maritime adventure are required, by the principle of general average contribution, to contribute towards certain extraordinary losses or expenses incurred in time of peril in order to preserve the ship or its cargo.[683] All loss which arises in consequence of extraordinary sacrifices made or expenses incurred for the preservation of the ship and cargo comes within general average, and must be borne proportionately by all those who are interested.[684] 29–129

(i) *Necessity*[685]

Agency of necessity. Where there is a relationship of principal and agent (or a similar relationship) between the parties, and the agent, in an emergency, has acted reasonably to protect the interests of his principal, the principal is obliged to reimburse the agent his reasonable expenses incurred in so acting, despite the fact that the agent exceeded his authority.[686] The agent must show that it was 29–130

---

678 Partnership Act 1890 ss.9–12.

679 *Re Royal Bank of Australia, Robinson's Executors* (1856) 6 De G.M. & G. 572, 587–588; *Lindley and Banks on Partnership*, 18th edn, paras 20–04 et seq. cf. Partnership Act 1890 ss.24(1) and (2), 44.

680 *Sedgewick v Daniell* (1857) 2 H. & N. 319.

681 See *MacGillivray on Insurance Law*, 10th edn, para.23–52 for a standard form of such a clause.

682 *North British and Mercantile Insurance Co v London, Liverpool and Globe Insurance Co* (1876) 5 Ch D 569, 581; *Commercial Union Assurance Co Ltd v Hayden* [1977] Q.B. 804; *Legal & General Assurance Co Ltd v Drake Insurance Co Ltd* [1992] 1 Q.B. 877. cf. *Eagle Star Insurance Co Ltd v Provincial Insurance Plc* [1993] 3 All E.R. 1. See also the Marine Insurance Act 1906 s.80; *Arnould on Law of Marine Insurance and Average*, 16th edn, paras 406–407.

683 *Lowndes & Rudolf on General Average and York Antwerp Rules*, 12th edn; Arnould at Ch.26; *Carver on Carriage by Sea*, 13th edn, Ch.14.

684 *Birkley v Presgrave* (1801) 1 East 220, 228–229 (Lawrence J). cf. the Marine Insurance Act 1906 s.66(1). It has been doubted whether general average is a form of restitutionary liability: cf. *Milburn & Co v Jamaican Fruit Importing Co* [1900] 2 Q.B. 540, 548, and Winfield, *Province of the Law of Tort*, p.182. cf. Virgo at p.303 where the restitutionary claim is analysed in terms of necessitous intervention. See also Rose (1997) 113 L.Q.R. 569.

685 Burrows at Ch.9; Goff and Jones at Ch.17; Virgo at Ch.11.

686 See Vol.II, paras 31–034—31–036; Goff and Jones at pp.448–452; Merchant Shipping Act 1995 s.40; *Guildford BC v Hein* [2005] EWCA Civ 979 at [33] (Clarke L.J.) and [80] (Waller L.J.).

impracticable at the time of the emergency for him to get instructions from his principal.[687]

29–131 **Necessitous intervention on behalf of the defendant.** Except in cases of agency of necessity,[688] or of salvage,[689] English law has usually refused to give a remedy to a person who intervenes in the affairs of another, even where the purpose of his intervention is to benefit that other in an emergency or to rescue the other's property from danger.[690] There is, however, support[691] for the emergence of a principle that, in an emergency, provided the claimant has acted reasonably and bona fide in the interests of the defendant, in order to protect the defendant's property, health, or other important interests, the claimant may recover the expenses he incurred and, possibly, reasonable remuneration for his services. It is a condition for recovery that it was impracticable to obtain the defendant's instructions or authority.

29–132 **Acting in the public interest.** Where the public interest demands that the claimant should have acted, the courts are most likely to permit restitution. For instance, where circumstances make it reasonable that the claimant should voluntarily incur expense in burying a person, the executors of the deceased, if they have assets, are liable to repay the expenses incurred by the claimant.[692] Where a married woman dies leaving an estate sufficient to pay her funeral expenses, her executors (and not, as formerly, her husband) are now liable to pay them.[693] Similarly, when human life or limb is at risk, the courts are likely to award restitution to a claimant who has incurred expense or expended effort in a reasonable attempt to preserve life or limb. In a Canadian case,[694] a surgeon who intended to charge for his services was held entitled to recover remuneration

---

687 Vol.II, para.31–034.

688 Above, para.29–130.

689 See below, para.29–136. See also Merchant Shipping Act 1995 s.73(2) (obligation to repay expenses in bringing shipwrecked seamen ashore and burial expenses).

690 *Falcke v Scottish Imperial Insurance Co* (1886) 34 Ch D 234 (above, para.29–115); *Owen v Tate* [1976] Q.B. 402 (above, para.29–112); *China Pacific SA v Food Corp of India* [1982] A.C. 939, 961. See the discussion of "voluntary payments," above, paras 29–109 et seq.

691 Birks at pp.193–203; Hope (1929) 15 Cornell L.R. 25, 42–47; Jones (1977) 93 L.Q.R. 273; Goff and Jones at pp.452–466; Rose (1989) 9 O.J.L.S. 167; Stoljar (1989) 10 Int. Encly. Comp. Law Ch.17; The American Law Institute's *Restatement of the Law of Restitution, Quasi-contracts and Constructive Trusts* (1937), p.489; Virgo at p.29. See also *Owen v Tate* [1976] Q.B. 402, 411–412 (Scarman L.J.); *The Zuhal K.* [1987] 1 Lloyd's Rep. 151 (above, para.29–112, suggesting that necessity negatives "officiousness" or "voluntariness" in the case of discharge of another's obligation). cf. *The Goring* [1988] A.C. 831.

692 *Tugwell v Heyman* (1812) 3 Camp. 298; *Rogers v Price* (1829) 3 Y. & Jer. 28. See now Public Health (Control of Disease) Act 1984 ss.46–48.

693 *Rees v Hughes* [1946] K.B. 517. Quaere whether the husband is still liable, under the old common law rule, if his wife leaves insufficient estate to cover her funeral expenses. Before modern legislation altered the legal position of married women, the common law allowed a stranger who had, without any request from the husband, voluntarily incurred and paid such expenses in burying the wife, to recover them from the husband: see *Ambrose v Kerrison* (1851) 10 C.B. 776; *Jenkins v Tucker* (1788) 1 H.Bl. 90; cf. *Bradshaw v Beard* (1862) 12 C.B.(N.S.) 344 (deceased's brother).

694 *Matheson v Smiley* [1932] 2 D.L.R. 787. Quaere whether services rendered by a non-professional would justify recovery of remuneration for services.

for his professional services in his reasonable, but unsuccessful, attempt to revive a person who committed suicide. Legislation[695] in the United Kingdom entitles a hospital or doctor to charge for emergency treatment given after a road accident.

Analogous categories. There are a number of other situations where principles analogous to necessitous intervention have been used to justify restitution or reimbursement.[696] Where there is an existing or a previous relationship between the parties, the courts are naturally more willing to allow recovery.[697] Sometimes recovery might be permitted in an indirect way, as has been done in the cases where one person, acting innocently, has expended money or effort in repairing or improving a chattel belonging to another[698] or where an accident victim has recovered the value of nursing services rendered by a relative and holds the money for the relative.[699] For the principle of intervention to apply, there would need to be proof of a real "emergency" or "necessity"[700] to entitle the intervener to sue.[701] If the intervener was officious,[702] or thought that he was protecting his own interests,[703] or did not, at the time of his intervention on behalf of the other, intend to charge for it,[704] no recovery should be allowed. 29–133

[695] Road Traffic Act 1988 ss.157–159.

[696] e.g. the Bills of Exchange Act 1882 ss.65(1), 66(1) and 68(5) (acceptance of a bill of exchange for the honour of the drawer). See also *Re Berkeley Applegate Ltd* [1989] Ch. 32, below, para.29–157 and see *Procter & Gamble Phillipine Manufacturing Corp v Peter Cremer GmbH & Co* [1988] 3 All E.R. 843, 854–855 for support for the principle of recovery for incontrovertible benefit. See above, para.29–022.

[697] e.g. agency of necessity (above, para.29–130; Vol.II, para.31–034); the principle in *Re Cleadon Trust Ltd* [1939] Ch. 286, 302 (above, para.29–112); the supply of necessaries to persons under a disability (below, para.29–135); the recovery of expense incurred when the innocent party attempted to mitigate his loss following a breach of contract (above, para.26–105); the relationship of carrier and consignee (*G.N. Ry v Swaffield* (1874) L.R. 9 Ex. 132 (above, para.29–115)); and a quantum meruit claim when the bailee has acted reasonably in dealing with the goods following frustration of the contract (above, para.23–098).

[698] See above, paras 29–051 et seq.

[699] *Cunningham v Harrison* [1973] Q.B. 942, 952; *Donnelly v Joyce* [1974] Q.B. 454; *Mehmet v Perry* [1977] 2 All E.R. 529. But not where the carer is the tortfeasor: *Hunt v Severs* [1994] 2 A.C. 350; *Dimond v Lovell* [2002] 1 A.C. 384 HL (no recovery where provider of services intended to be paid but agreement unenforceable).

[700] cf. the concept of "necessity" in agency of necessity: above, para.29–130 and see *Re F. (Mental Patient: Sterilisation)* [1990] 2 A.C. 1, 75; *Re T. (Adult: Medical Treatment)* [1992] 3 W.L.R. 782. In the bailment cases of *Sachs v Miklos* [1948] 2 K.B. 23 and *Munro v Willmott* [1949] 1 K.B. 295, there was no real emergency to justify the bailee's sale of goods without communicating with the bailor and obtaining his authority (see above, para.29–052).

[701] cf. the dicta in *Owen v Tate* [1976] Q.B. 402, 411–412 (Scarman L.J.), 413 (Stephenson L.J.) (quoted above, para.29–111 which suggest that necessity may negative officiousness).

[702] cf. the situations covered by the Unsolicited Goods and Services Act 1971.

[703] In *Falcke v Scottish Imperial Insurance Co* (1886) 34 Ch D 234 (above, para.29–115) the intervener thought that he was preserving his own property. But cf. *Greenwood v Bennett* [1973] 1 Q.B. 195, and the other cases cited above, para.29–053.

[704] *Re F. (Mental Patient: Sterilisation)* [1990] 2 A.C. 1, 75. cf. *Re Rhodes* (1890) 44 Ch D 94 (necessaries supplied to a lunatic: see above, para.8–074, below, para.29–135); *Brown and Davis Ltd v Galbraith* [1972] 1 W.L.R. 997. cf. the Roman law principle that the onus should be on the defendant to show that the intervener intended to make no charge; *Ulpian*, D. 3.5.4; Goff and Jones at p.457.

29–134 **Reasonable and non-gratuitous intervention.** The need for the intervention to be reasonable and for the intervener to intend to charge for it will preclude the recovery of remuneration for services rendered in many cases and will restrict claims simply to reimbursement of expenses.[705] Where the intervener is a professional acting as such he will be more likely to recover remuneration.[706]

29–135 **Necessaries supplied to a minor, drunken person or person who lacks capacity to contract.** There are specific statutory obligations, which can be classified as restitutionary, namely the obligation of a minor or drunken person who is incompetent to contract to pay a reasonable price where necessaries are sold or delivered to him.[707] A similar, but wider, provision applies to a person who lacks mental capacity to contract for necessary goods or services who must pay a reasonable price for goods or services supplied.[707a]

29–136 **Salvage.**[708] The obligation of the owner of a ship or its cargo to pay compensation to a person who rescues it from peril is a good example of a restitutionary claim, as none of the elements of ordinary contract may exist, although in some cases there may be an opportunity for bargaining before the services are rendered.[709] But in many cases this is not so; the services are rendered and the question then is what are the salvors to be paid. In *The Five Steel Barges*[710] Sir James Hannen P. said:

> "The right to salvage may arise out of an actual contract; but it does not necessarily do so. It is a legal liability arising out of the fact that property has been saved, that the owner of the property who has had the benefit of it shall make remuneration to those who have conferred the benefit on him, notwithstanding that he has not entered into any contract on the subject."

In claims for saving life, the shipowner, in the interests of humanity, is compelled to pay for something from which he has derived no personal benefit.[711] In a

---

[705] *Shallcross v Wright* (1850) 12 Beav. 558, 561–562. Goff and Jones at p.457 support this on the ground that, apart from cases of maritime salvage, there is no urgent need to provide a real and positive incentive to take risks for the purpose of saving property. See further, Landes and Posner (1978) 7 J.Leg. Stud. 83.

[706] *Matheson v Smiley* [1932] 2 D.L.R. 787 (above, para.29–132); *J.D. White v Troups Transport* [1976] C.L.Y. 33 (below, para.29–136). See also the burial cases, above, para.29–132, from which it would appear that where the intervention takes the form of employing someone else to do the necessary act the two measures will not differ. See in particular *Ambrose v Kerrison* (1851) 10 C.B. 777.

[707] Sale of Goods Act 1979 s.3.

[707a] Mental Capacity Act 2005, s.7 (considered above, para.8–075).

[708] See *Kennedy and Rose on the Law of Salvage*, 6th edn (2002); Burrows at pp.309–310; Goff and Jones at Ch.18; Virgo at pp.301–303.

[709] *Semco Salvage & Marine Pte Ltd v Lancer Navigation Co Ltd* [1997] A.C. 455. In *The Troilus* [1950] P. 92, it was pointed out that salvage, an obligation imposed by law irrespective of any contract express or implied, must be distinguished from towage which only arises from an express or implied contract.

[710] (1890) 15 P.D. 142, 146.

[711] Kennedy and Rose at pp.13–14.

case[712] where "salvage" was claimed in respect of a policy of life insurance, Bowen L.J., after pointing out that neither a liability nor a benefit could be forced upon a man in order to create a legal obligation at common law, distinguished the law as regards salvage, general average and contribution on the ground that the maritime law differs from the common law: "no similar doctrine applies to things lost upon land, nor to anything except ships or goods in peril at sea".[713] But although salvage in tidal waters[714] is restricted to ships and their cargoes, there is some authority for a similar principle applicable to property on land. In an early case, where a person found timber where it had been carried by the tide, and brought it to safety, it was held that he had no lien on the timber for his trouble and expense.[715] The decision, however, probably leaves open the possibility that the finder could sue the owner of the timber in quantum meruit[716] for the value of his services. A carrier was able to recover reasonable expenses incurred in providing for the safety of the horse he carried when the consignee refused to take delivery of it.[717] In these cases the claimant was a bailee of the defendant's property. In such cases (including involuntary bailment[718]) the right to charge the property-owner for reasonable steps to preserve the property can be seen as the correlative of the bailee's duty to the owner in respect of the property.[719] However, recovery is not confined to cases of bailment. Thus, a crane hire firm, called in by the police, recovered a reasonable fee from a lorry owner for freeing the lorry which was stuck under a bridge.[720]

(j) *Exploitation*[721]

Undue influence.[722] Undue influence entitles a party to a contract to avoid it.[723] Consequently, restitution of benefits conferred under the voidable contract will be ordered by the court, following rescission by the innocent party. Equity may permit, as the result of setting aside a transaction, the recovery of benefits 29–137

[712] *Falcke v Scottish Imperial Insurance Co* (1886) 34 Ch D 234, 248–249.

[713] See *Sorrell v Paget* [1950] 1 K.B. 252 (claim for salvage of a heifer).

[714] *The Goring* [1988] A.C. 831. cf. [1987] Q.B. 687, 693, 707 for criticism of the restriction to tidal waters.

[715] *Nicholson v Chapman* (1793) 2 H.Bl. 254. The claim in *Falcke v Scottish Imperial Insurance Co* (1886) 34 Ch D 234 was also for a lien. cf. the position in tort where damages are recoverable by a person injured when trying to rescue property endangered by a fire caused by the defendant's negligence: *Hyett v G.W. Ry* [1948] 1 K.B. 345.

[716] See above, para.29–071.

[717] *G.N. Ry v Swaffield* (1874) L.R. 9 Ex. 132. During the carriage the carrier is under a duty to take reasonable care of the goods, and the case implies a continuation of this duty. It was cited with approval in *China Pacific SA v Food Corp of India* [1982] A.C. 939, 960.

[718] See Vol.II, para.33–036.

[719] *China Pacific SA v Food Corp of India* [1982] A.C. 939, 960. See also Birks at p.201.

[720] *J.D. White v Troups Transport* [1976] C.L.Y. 33. See *Waters v Weigall* (1795) 2 Anst. 575; Goff and Jones at p.456 fn.81.

[721] See Burrows at Chs 6 and 7; Goff and Jones at Chs 11 and 12; Virgo at Ch.10.

[722] Above, paras 7–056 et seq.

[723] Above, para.7–056. See *Yorkshire Bank Plc v Tinsley* [2004] EWCA Civ 816, [2004] 1 W.L.R. 2380.

conferred on the defendant following undue influence exercised by the defendant over the claimant.[724]

29–138 **Unconscionable bargains.** Equity may also grant relief from certain unconscionable bargains, especially where the claimant was suffering from a special disability or was placed in a special situation of disadvantage as against the defendant.[725]

3. RESTITUTION FOR WRONGS[726]

(a) *General Principles*

29–139 **Disgorgement for wrongs.** Where the defendant has benefited from the commission of a wrong a restitutionary remedy will sometimes be available to deprive the defendant of the benefit and to transfer it to the claimant. In such cases the remedy may sometimes literally be restitutionary, in the sense of restoring to the claimant what he has lost, or it may amount to disgorgement[727] where the defendant benefited without causing a loss to the claimant. In such circumstances there is nothing which can be restored. However, although there is no loss to the claimant in the sense of a diminution in his wealth, in some of these cases (typified by cases where the defendant has used the claimant's property to make a profit) the claimant will have lost the opportunity to charge the defendant

[724] *Allcard v Skinner* (1887) 36 Ch D 145; *Yorkshire Bank Plc v Tinsley* [2004] EWCA Civ 816, [2004] 1 W.L.R. 2380. See above, paras 7–098 et seq.

[725] *Earl of Chesterfield v Janssen* (1751) 2 Ves. Sen. 125, 157. See above, paras 7–126 et seq.; Vol.II, paras 38–192 et seq., 38–245; Goff and Jones at Ch.12; Bamforth [1995] L.M.C.L.Q. 538.

[726] Beatson, *The Use and Abuse of Restitution*, Ch.8; Birks at pp.39–44, Ch. X; Birks, *Civil Wrongs: A New World* (1991); Burrows at Ch.14; Goff and Jones at s.3; Virgo at Pt IV; Winfield, *Province of the Law of Tort* (1931), pp.168–176 (also *The Law of Quasi-Contracts* (1952), pp.91–102); Wright (1941) 57 L.Q.R. 184; Fridman (1955) 18 M.L.R. 1; Friedmann (1980) 80 Col.L.Rev. 504; Hedley (1984) 100 L.Q.R. 653. Note also the power of a criminal court, under s.148 of Powers of Criminal Courts (Sentencing) Act 2000, to order restitution upon conviction: *R. v Ferguson* [1970] 1 W.L.R. 1246; *R. v Church* (1970) 55 Cr. App. R. 65; *R. v Parker* [1970] 2 All E.R. 458. cf. *Malone v Metropolitan Police Commissioner* [1980] Q.B. 49. See generally *Profits of Crime and their Recovery* (Hodgson Committee) (1984), Ch.7. The courts are also empowered by s.130 of the Powers of Criminal Courts (Sentencing) Act 2000 to make a compensation order against a convicted offender: *R. v Inwood* (1975) 60 Cr. App. R. 70; *R. v Kneeshaw* [1975] Q.B. 57; *R. v Daly* [1974] 1 W.L.R. 133; *R. v Vivian* [1979] 1 All E.R. 48. Magistrates' courts may also make orders for the delivery of property in the possession of the police to the person appearing to be the owner: Police (Property) Act 1897; *Raymond Lyons & Co v Metropolitan Police Commissioner* [1975] Q.B. 321. See further Goff and Jones at Ch.38. The Proceeds of Crime Act 2002 creates a new statutory framework for the confiscation of assets of defendants convicted of a crime. Under the Act state officials can apply to the court to recover the proceeds of crime: see *Asset Recovery Agency v Singh* [2005] EWCA Civ 580, [2005] 1 W.L.R. 3747.

[727] Smith (1992) 71 Can. B.R. 672, 696. See also Edelman, *Gain-Based Damages: Contract, Tort, Equity and Intellectual Property* (2002); *Murad v Al-Saraj* [2005] EWCA Civ 1235 at [108] (Jonathan Parker L.J.).

for permission to carry on the activity which has led to the defendant's enrichment, which is mirrored by the amount the defendant saved in not having to pay the claimant.[728]

Nature of the obligation to make restitution. Two distinct analyses of restitution for wrongdoing can be identified. The first treats the restitutionary obligation as a secondary and parasitic obligation, which arises upon the violation of the primary obligation not to commit a wrong.[729] Alternatively, the cases are instances of situations in which one set of facts gives rise to two alternative but independent causes of action, one in wrongdoing and one in unjust enrichment.[730] Although the authorities appear to favour the former[731] (parasitic obligation), on that view it is difficult to see why factors which bar the claim founded on the wrong should not also bar the claim in restitution.[732] However, there are cases which are consistent only with the latter view.[733] The scope of the claim in restitution depends on which is adopted. If it is the former then it is a sine qua non that a wrong has been committed before restitutionary relief can be awarded, but if it is the latter then restitutionary relief should be available even though the wrong has not technically been committed.[734] The preferable view is that claims for restitution for wrongs are founded on the commission of a particular wrong 29–140

---

[728] e.g. *Strand Electric and Engineering Co Ltd v Brisford Entertainments Ltd* [1952] 2 Q.B. 246; *Penarth Dock Engineering Co v Pounds* [1963] 1 Lloyd's Rep. 359; *Seager v Copydex Ltd (No.2)* [1969] 1 W.L.R. 809. The first two cases concerned actions in tort in which relief in respect of such enrichment was described as restitutionary. See also below, paras 29–141 et seq. On actions in contract for relief in respect of such enrichment, see below, paras 29–151 et seq.; Beatson at pp.16–18; Goff and Jones at pp.519–534; *Surrey CC v Bredero Homes Ltd* [1993] 1 W.L.R. 1361 cf. *Jaggard v Sawyer* [1995] 1 W.L.R. 269. Cases of bribery of agents might be susceptible to this explanation because the principal is presumed to have foregone the opportunity of a higher sale price or a lower purchase price (*Hovenden v Millhoff* (1900) 83 L.T. 41, 43; *Industries & General Mortgage Co v Lewis* [1949] 2 All E.R. 573).

[729] *Oughton v Seppings* (1830) 1 B. & Ad. 241, 243; *Young v Marshall* (1831) 8 Bing. 43; *Turner v Camerons Coalbrook Steam Coal Co* (1850) 5 Ex. 932; *United Australia Ltd v Barclays Bank Ltd* [1941] 1 A.C. 18, 35; *Commercial Banking Co of Sydney v Mann* [1961] A.C. 1, 8. See also *Beaman v A.R.T.S. Ltd* [1948] 2 All E.R. 89, 92–93; *Redrow Homes Ltd v Bett Bros Plc* [1999] 1 A.C. 197.

[730] See, for instance, *Phillips v Homfray* (1883) 24 Ch D 439, 463; [1892] 1 Ch. 465, 470, 471; *Universe Tankships Inc of Monrovia v International Transport Workers Federation* [1983] 1 A.C. 366, 385, 401.

[731] See especially *United Australia Ltd v Barclays Bank Ltd* [1941] 1 A.C. 18, 18 and 35 and *Chesworth v Farrar* [1969] 1 Q.B. 407, 417.

[732] See *Chesworth v Farrar* [1969] 1 Q.B. 407 where the plaintiff was allowed to bring a restitutionary claim despite the fact that the tortious limitation period had passed.

[733] See below, para.29–150.

[734] *Heilbut & Rocca v Nevill* (1870) L.R. 5 C.P. 478 (technical requirements of tort not satisfied); *Asher v Wallis* (1707) 11 Mod. 146 (no action in trover because plaintiff had never possessed the money). See also *Anon* (1700) 12 Mod. 415. The cases on money obtained by fraud, deceit (below, para.29–147) and oppression (below, para.29–150) support this view because the action for money had and received antedated the development of the torts of deceit (Jackson, *The History of Quasi-Contract in English Law* (1936), pp.73–75) and intimidation (Beatson at p.221). See also *Mahesan v Malaysia Government Officers' Co-operative Housing Society Ltd* [1979] A.C. 374; *Universe Tankships Inc of Monrovia v International Transport Workers Federation* [1983] 1 A.C. 366, 385, 401; *National Trust Co v Gleason* (1879) 77 N.Y. 400, 403–404.

rather than on unjust enrichment.[735] Once it has been established that the wrong has been committed it is then necessary to determine whether the award of restitutionary remedies is appropriate. This will depend on the type of wrong which has been committed. On this interpretation of the law, restitutionary remedies would be available where the defendant has profited from the commission of certain torts,[736] and, exceptionally, for breach of contract,[737] equitable wrongdoing,[738] the commission of criminal acts[739] and, possibly, breach of statutory duties.[740]

(b) *Tort*

29–141 **"Waiver of tort".** If a person commits a tort and in so doing enriches himself by taking or using the property of another, the latter may, if certain conditions are satisfied, recover the value of that which has been wrongfully taken or used instead of suing for damages for the injury done. The remedies of compensation and restitution are not concurrent and the claimant is compelled to elect which he will pursue.[741] If he elects to seek restitution, he is said to "waive the tort".[742] Historically, there were a number of advantages of suing for restitution rather than damages,[743] e.g. avoidance of special pleading and of immunity from suit in tort,[744] a different period of limitation, the ability to prove for the claim in the tortfeasor's bankruptcy[745] and circumvention of the rule preventing survival of an action in tort against the estate of a tortfeasor. Some advantages may, however, continue today, such as the avoidance of the necessity to prove the actual loss suffered by the claimant (e.g. the exact value of goods lost through conversion) by claiming instead the sum received by the defendant.[746] Furthermore it may be

---

[735] *Macmillan Inc v Bishopsgate Investment Trust Plc (No.3)* [1995] 1 W.L.R. 978, 988 (Millett J.). The doctrine of waiver of tort is consistent with this interpretation; see below, para.29–141. cf. *Halifax Building Society v Thomas* [1996] Ch 217, 224 (Peter Gibson L.J.).

[736] See below, paras 29–142 et seq.

[737] See below, paras 29–151 et seq.

[738] See below, paras 29–155 et seq.

[739] Goff and Jones at Ch.38. See above, para.29–139 for statutory power to order restitution.

[740] *English v Dedham Vale Properties Ltd* [1978] 1 W.L.R. 93; Samuel (1978) 94 L.Q.R. 347, 350.

[741] On election, see below, para.29–146.

[742] This follows Keener, *A Treatise on the Law of Quasi-Contracts* (1893), p.159. The principle is fully discussed by the House of Lords in *United Australia Ltd v Barclays Bank Ltd* [1941] A.C. 1.

[743] Winfield, *Province of the Law of Tort* (1931), pp.143–146. cf. Goff and Jones at pp.803–808.

[744] e.g. the Crown's immunity before the Crown Proceedings Act 1947. See Williams, *Crown Proceedings* (1948), pp.11–13.

[745] See Law Reform (Miscellaneous Provisions) Act 1934 which was applied in *Chesworth v Farrar* [1967] 1 Q.B. 407. For the present position see, Insolvency Act 1986 s.382 and Insolvency Rules 1986 (SI 1986/1925) rr.13.1, 13.12.

[746] *King v Leith* (1787) 2 T.R. 141, 145; *Parker v Norton* (1796) 6 T.R. 695, 700; *Feltham v Terry* (1772) Lofft. 207, 208. This sum may exceed what could be recovered by claiming damages for loss suffered: *Bavins and Sims v London and South Western Bank Ltd* [1900] 1 Q.B. 270. See Marshall Evans (1966) 82 L.Q.R. 167–169.

possible to recover more than the loss sustained by claiming any profit made by the defendant which is attributable to the tort.[747] These last two may, however, be less important than they were in view of the relevance, in assessing damages in certain actions in tort, of the defendant's gain.[748]

29–142 **Which torts may give rise to a restitutionary claim.** Not all torts give rise to a claim for restitution, but only those where the tortfeasor receives a definite sum of money, or a definite benefit which can be readily assessed in money, and this benefit derives directly or indirectly from the claimant.[749] Restitutionary awards have most commonly been made in cases concerning what have been termed the "proprietary torts".[750] They have been made in the following cases: conversion[751] (as where the defendant tortiously takes the claimant's goods, sells them and receives the proceeds,[752] or wrongfully presents and collects the proceeds of his cheque[753]); other wrongful interference or trespass to goods[754] (which the defendant has turned into money,[755] or where the defendant tortiously takes and retains the claimant's money)[756]; trespass to land[757]; fraud or deceit[758]; intimidation[759]; inducing breach of contract[760]; passing off[761]; infringement of

---

[747] See below, para.29–145.

[748] See below, paras 29–144—29–145.

[749] *Hambly v Trott* (1776) 1 Cowp. 371, 376; *Phillips v Homfray* (1883) 24 Ch D 439; *Morris v Tarrant* [1971] 2 Q.B. 143, 160–162. See below, para.29–144.

[750] *Stoke on Trent CC v W. & J. Wass Ltd* [1988] 1 W.L.R. 1406, 1415 (no restitution where exclusive right to hold a market infringed); *Forsyth-Grant v Allen* [2008] EWCA Civ 505 (account of profits not available for tort of nuisance involving interference with right to light because this did not involve any misappropriation of the claimant's rights).

[751] *Re Simms* [1934] Ch. 1 (see below, para.29–145).

[752] *Lamine v Dorrell* (1706) 2 Ld. Raym. 1216; *Marsh v Keating* (1834) 1 Bing. N.C. 198, 215–216; *Phillips v Homfray* (1883) 24 Ch D 439, 462. cf. *Lake v Bayliss* [1974] 1 W.L.R. 1073 (see below, para.29–160).

[753] *Bavins and Sims v London and South Western Bank Ltd* [1900] 1 Q.B. 270; *Morison v London County and Westminster Bank Ltd* [1914] 3 K.B. 356, 365; *Fenton Textile Association v Thomas* (1929) 45 T.L.R. 264.

[754] It was also permitted for detinue, now abolished by the Torts (Interference with Goods) Act 1977. Although many aspects of detinue are still actionable under another head (s.2(2)), not all are: Palmer [1981] Conv.(N.S.) 62.

[755] *Oughton v Seppings* (1830) 1 B. & Ad. 241; *Rodgers v Maw* (1846) 15 M. & W. 444, 448; *Neate v Harding* (1851) 6 Ex. 349, 351.

[756] *Neate v Harding* (1851) 6 Ex. 349; *Bavins & Sims v London and South Western Bank Ltd* [1900] 1 Q.B. 270.

[757] *Powell v Rees* (1837) 7 A. & E. 426 (sale of coal extracted from land); *Bracewell v Appleby* [1975] Ch. 407 (damages in lieu of injunction took into account defendant's profits); *Ministry of Defence v Ashman* [1993] 2 E.G.L.R. 102; *Ministry of Defence v Thompson* [1993] 2 E.G.L.R. 107 (claim for *mesne* profit for trespass). See also Cooke (1994) 110 L.Q.R. 420; *Inverugie Investments Ltd v Hackett* [1995] 1 W.L.R. 713; *Horsford v Bird* [2006] UKPC 3, see Virgo (2006) 65 C.L.J. 272; *Murad v Al-Saraj* [2005] EWCA Civ 1235 at [108] (Jonathan Parker L.J.); *Field Common Ltd v Elmbridge BC* [2008] EWHC 2079 (Ch) (hypothetical negotiation measure adapted where trespass committed by defendant's tenants, characterised as restitutionary).

[758] Below, paras 29–147—29–149.

[759] Below, para.29–150.

[760] *Lightly v Clouston* (1808) 1 Taunt. 112; *Foster v Stewart* (1814) 3 M. & S. 191 (see the discussion of these cases in Winfield, *Quasi-Contracts* (1952), pp.98–99).

[761] *My Kinda Town v Soll* [1982] F.S.R. 147.

intellectual property rights[762]; usurpation of an office[763] and some miscellaneous actions.[764]

29–143 **Effect of statute.** If a statute is held to bar actions "in respect of any tortious act", the claimant cannot avoid the statute by "waiving" the tort and suing for restitution.[765] Where, however, the statute (or a common law rule) is held only to bar "actions in tort," it is still open to the claimant to sue in restitution[766] unless to allow him to do so would undermine the policy of the statutory (or common law) rule.[767] Moreover, where there is detailed legislation in an area, it has been said that "the courts should not indulge in parallel creativity by the extension of general common law principles".[768]

29–144 **The nature of the benefit.** In *Phillips v Homfray*[769] a majority of the Court of Appeal held that a trespass to land could only be waived so as to give a restitutionary remedy against the deceased tortfeasor's estate if the "property or the proceeds of property, belonging to another, have been appropriated by the

---

[762] Accounts of profits: *Hogg v Kirby* (1803) 8 Ves. J. 215, 223; *Colburn v Simms* (1843) 2 Ha. 543; *My Kinda Town Ltd v Soll* [1982] F.S.R. 147; *Potton Ltd v Yorkclose Ltd* [1990] F.S.R. 11. Damages and account of profits: Patents Act 1977 ss.61–62; Copyright, Designs and Patents Act 1988 ss.96, 97, 229. But cf. *Union Carbide Corp v B.P. Chemicals Ltd* [1998] F.S.R. 1, 6; *Redrow Homes Ltd v Bett Bros Plc* [1999] 1 A.C. 197.

[763] *Rowland v Hall* (1835) 1 Scott 539; *Hall v Swansea Corp* (1844) 5 Q.B. 526; *King v Alston* (1848) 12 Q.B. 971; *Shoubridge v Clark* (1852) 12 C.B. 335; *Wildes v Russell* (1866) L.R. 1 C.P. 722; *Osgood v Nelson* (1872) L.R. 5 H.L. 636. See also *Howard v Wood* (1679) 2 Lev. 245; *Lamine v Dorrell* (1705) 2 Ld. Raym. 1216 (after revocation of his grant of administration, an administrator of an estate is accountable for assets received); *Brown & Green Ltd v Hays* (1920) 36 T.L.R. 330 (above, para.9–059) (recovery of salary as a director paid to defendant whose appointment was not confirmed, but see *Craven-Ellis v Canons Ltd* [1936] 2 K.B. 403 (above, para.29–076) for quantum meruit in such circumstances); *Re Berkeley Applegate Ltd* [1989] Ch. 32.

[764] e.g. where the defendant falsely assumes to act as the claimant's agent and collects rent from his tenants: *Lightly v Clouston* (1808) 1 Taunt. 112, 115; *Asher v Wallis* (1707) 11 Mod. 146; *Hasser v Wallis* (1708) 1 Salk. 28. cf. *Kettlewell v Refuge Assistance Co* [1908] 1 K.B. 545; [1909] A.C. 243; or for unlawful eviction: Housing Act 1988 ss.27–28. Their appropriateness in nuisance has been recognised: *Carr-Saunders v Dick McNeill Associates* [1986] 1 W.L.R. 922 (although as there was no evidence of profit no award was made). cf. *Stoke-on-Trent City Council v W. & J. Wass Ltd* [1988] 1 W.L.R. 1406, 1410; *Forsyth-Grant v Allen* [2008] EWCA Civ 505, see above, fn.750.

[765] *R. v Brocklebank Ltd* [1925] 1 K.B. 52 (Indemnity Act 1920); *Hardie and Lane Ltd v Chiltern* [1928] 1 K.B. 663, 695 (Trade Disputes Act 1906 s.4). See also *Universe Tankships Inc of Monrovia v International Transport Workers Federation* [1983] 1 A.C. 366 HL; [1981] I.C.R. 129, 160–161 CA; Parker J., at 143–144 (Trade Union and Labour Relations Act 1974 s.13(1)).

[766] *Powell v Rees* (1837) 7 A. & E. 426; *Phillips v Homfray* (1883) 24 Ch D 439 (*actio personalis moritur cum persona*); *Chesworth v Farrar* [1967] 1 Q.B. 407 (Law Reform (Miscellaneous Provisions) Act 1934 s.1(3) as amended by Law Reform (Limitation of Actions) Act 1954 s.4).

[767] *Universe Tankships Inc of Monrovia v International Transport Workers Federation* [1983] 1 A.C. 366, 385, 401; *Dimskal S.S. Co SA v International Transport Workers Federation* [1992] 2 A.C. 152, 161–162, 166–167; *Union Carbide Corp v B.P. Chemicals Ltd* [1998] F.S.R. 1, 6 (restitution cannot supplement patent law).

[768] *Chief Constable of Leicestershire v M* [1989] 1 W.L.R. 20, 23 (Hoffmann J.). See also *Halifax B.S. v Thomas* [1996] Ch. 217, 229–230; *Union Carbide Corp v B.P. Chemicals Ltd* [1998] F.S.R. 1.

[769] (1883) 24 Ch D 439. For other stages of this litigation see (1871) 6 Ch. App. 770; (1890) 44 Ch D 694; affirmed [1892] 1 Ch. 465. See generally Swadling in Swadling and Jones (eds), *The Search for Principle: Essays in Honour of Lord Goff of Chieveley* (1999), pp.277–294.

deceased person and added to his own estate or moneys".[770] In that case the tortfeasor had made unauthorised use of roads over, and passages under, the plaintiff's land and this was held not to give rise to a remedy in restitution. This appropriation or accretion requirement has been criticised as confusing the role of personal and proprietary claims in restitution and as isolating the requirement of benefit from the question of what constitutes benefit in other restitutionary claims.[771] As Baggallay L.J., in a strong dissent, stated:

> "... a gain or acquisition to the wrongdoer by the work and labour of another does not necessarily, if it does at all, imply a diminution of the property of such other person."[772]

There are indications in the cases of a broader approach[773] and dicta suggesting that the rule in *Phillips v Homfray* should be discarded.[774] However, it has been followed at first instance.[775] In practice the rule should not prove a serious obstacle to a claimant since it is now possible to use the measure of the defendant's benefit (rather than what the claimant lost[776]) in an action in tort in respect of the wrongful use by the defendant of the claimant's land[777] or chattels.[778] The sum awarded in these cases, the reasonable hiring rate, should not be regarded as compensatory since it is calculated by reference to what the defendant has saved by not having to rent or hire, rather than what the claimant had lost. It is irrelevant that the owner suffered no loss because he

770 (1883) 24 Ch D 439, 454 (Bowen and Cotton L.JJ.). See also *Powell v Rees* (1837) 7 Ad. & El. 426. cf. *Kirk v Todd* (1882) 21 Ch D 484.

771 Goff and Jones at pp.804–806; Beatson at pp.224–230; Burrows at pp.473–475. cf. Gummow in Finn (ed.), *Essays on Restitution* (1990), pp.60–67; *Daniel v O'Leary* (1976) 14 N.B.R. (2d) 564 (quantum meruit awarded against trespasser who hooked his home on to plaintiff's sewage system so that his waste was processed at plaintiff's sewage farm).

772 (1883) 24 Ch D 439, 471–472. Goff and Jones at p.806, find his views compelling. See also *Restatement of Restitution* (1937), para.1(b).

773 *Lightly v Clouston* (1808) 1 Taunt. 112; *Rumsey v North Eastern Ry* (1863) 14 C.B.(N.S.) 641, 652. See also the claim of a principal against the person who bribed his agent for the amount of the bribe: *Hovenden & Sons v Millhoff* (1900) 83 L.T. 41, Vol.II, paras 31–074, 31–120; *Daniel v O'Leary* (1976) 14 N.B.R. (2d) 564.

774 *Nissan v Att-Gen* [1968] 1 Q.B. 286, 341, 352; [1970] A.C. 179, 228. But cf. 213, 236, 241. The rule has been rejected in certain jurisdictions in the United States provided the trespass to land was deliberate: *Edwards v Lee's Administrators* (1936) 265 Ky. 418; 96 S.W. 2d. 1028; *Red Raven Ash Coal Co v Bull* (1946) 39 S.E. 2d. 231; *Prosser and Keaton on the Law of Torts*, 5th edn, p.675.

775 *Morris v Tarrant* [1971] 2 Q.B. 143, 158, although Lane J. did recognise that the defendant had been "enriched by his free occupation of property". The case may reflect a policy of protecting spouses in possession of the matrimonial home pending divorce and a property settlement.

776 See *Horsford v Bird* [2006] UKPC 3, where damages for trespass to land were assessed with reference to the benefit obtained by the defendant from the trespass: at [12]. See Virgo (2006) C.L.J. 272 and Edelman (2006) L.Q.R. 391.

777 *Penarth Dock Engineering Co v Pounds* [1963] 1 Lloyd's Rep. 359; *Ministry of Defence v Ashman* [1993] 2 E.G.L.R. 102; *Ministry of Defence v Thompson* [1993] 2 E.G.L.R. 107; *Horsford v Bird* [2006] UKPC 3. See also *Severn Trent Water Ltd v Barnes* [2004] EWCA Civ 570; *Carr-Saunders v Dick McNeill Associates* [1986] 1 W.L.R. 922; *Anchor Brewhouse Developments Ltd v Berkeley House (Docklands) Developments Ltd* (1987) 284 E.G. 626; *Jaggard v Sawyer* [1995] 1 W.L.R. 269. cf. *Stoke-on-Trent CC v W. & J. Wass Ltd* [1988] 1 W.L.R. 1406 (nominal damages awarded).

778 *Strand Electric & Engineering Co Ltd v Brisford Entertainments Ltd* [1952] 2 Q.B. 246.

would not have used the property during the period of use by the defendant or could not have hired it out.[779] The argument that the owner has been deprived of the opportunity of charging a fee and that the remedy is therefore compensatory[780] is only realistic if it is clear that the owner would have been willing to do so.[781]

29–145 **Profits made by the defendant.** Apart from a reasonable hiring fee in respect of wrongful use of land or chattels, there is the question whether further profits[782] may be recoverable by suing for restitution rather than for damages. In some cases it will be difficult to attribute profits exclusively to the defendant's tort.[783] This may not be the case where the defendant has committed the tort deliberately,[784] but in such cases it is possible that exemplary damages will be awarded in tort.[785]

29–146 **Election of remedy.** The remedies in tort for damages and restitution are alternative, and the claimant cannot recover judgment on both, though he may pursue both remedies together.[786] The claimant does not elect one remedy merely by commencing an action in which he claims it[787]; as Lord Atkin said:

---

[779] *Strand Electric & Engineering Co Ltd v Brisford Entertainments Ltd* [1952] 2 Q.B. 246, 252, 254, 256–257; *Penarth Dock Engineering Co v Pounds* [1963] 1 Lloyd's Rep. 359, 361–362; *Swordheath Properties Ltd v Tabet* [1979] 1 W.L.R. 285. See the United States cases: *Amatrudi v Watson* (1952) 88 A. 2d 7 (defendant who benefited innocently from the use by a third party of the plaintiff's equipment liable for its reasonable rental value). See also *Restatement of Restitution* (1937), para.128 (p.533). cf. *Dilmitis v Niland* (1965) (3) S.A. 492 (no proof of extent of defendant's enrichment); *Stoke-on-Trent CC v W. & J. Wass* [1988] 1 W.L.R. 1406.

[780] *Strand Electric & Engineering Co Ltd v Brisford Entertainments Ltd* [1952] 2 Q.B. 246, per Somervell and Romer L.JJ.; *Hillesden Securities Ltd v Ryjack Ltd* [1983] 1 W.L.R. 959; *Anchor Brewhouse Developments Ltd v Berkeley House (Docklands) Developments Ltd* (1987) 284 E.G. 626, 633. See Sharpe & Waddams (1982) 2 O.J.L.S. 290.

[781] Hodder (1984) 42 U.Toronto Fac.L.Rev. 105; Burrows at p.477; Virgo at pp.457–458.

[782] As envisaged by *Strand Electric & Engineering Co Ltd v Brisford Entertainments* [1952] 2 Q.B. 246, 252, 255.

[783] *Re Simms* [1934] Ch. 1; Law Commission No.110, 1981 (Cmnd.8388), para.4.86; Birks at pp.351–355. cf. *My Kinda Town Ltd v Soll* [1982] F.S.R. 147; [1983] R.P.C. 407; *Colbeam Palmer Ltd v Stock Affiliates Pty Ltd* (1968) 122 C.L.R. 25.

[784] *Federal Sugar Refining Co v United States Sugar Equalisation Board* (1920) 268 F. 575; *Olwell v Nye & Nissen Co* (1883) 24 Ch D 439. There is apparently no English authority on the question and the rule in *Phillips v Homfray*, above, para.29–144, may prevent a restitutionary claim. Goff and Jones at p.815, cite the analogy of trade mark and patent cases to suggest that for knowing wrongdoing an account of profits might be allowed. See also breach of confidence: *Peter Pan Manufacturing Corp v Corsets Silhouette Ltd* [1964] 1 W.L.R. 96 (account of profits ordered where product could not have been manufactured without the confidential information). cf. *Seager v Copydex Ltd* [1967] 1 W.L.R. 923; *(No.2)* [1969] 1 W.L.R. 809 (payment for confidential information used innocently but negligently based on market value of information not profits); *Att-Gen v Guardian Newspapers* [1990] 1 A.C. 109. But see *English v Dedham Vale Properties Ltd* [1978] 1 W.L.R. 93, 111; *Universal Thermosensors Ltd v Hibben* [1992] 1 W.L.R. 840, 850–851.

[785] *Rookes v Barnard* [1964] A.C. 1129, 1220–1231; *Cassell & Co v Broome* [1972] A.C. 1027; *Kuddus v Chief Constable of Leicestershire* [2001] UKHL 29; [2002] 2 A.C. 127.

[786] *United Australia Ltd v Barclays Bank Ltd* [1941] A.C. 1; *Halifax B.S. v Thomas* [1996] Ch. 217; *Personal Representatives of Tang Man Sit v Capacious Investments Ltd* [1996] A.C. 514.

[787] [1941] A.C. 1. See also *Rice v Reed* [1900] 1 Q.B. 54; *Island Records Ltd v Tring International Plc* [1995] 3 All E.R. 444; cf. *Ernest Scragg & Sons Ltd v Perseverance Banking and Trust Co Ltd* [1973] 2 Lloyd's Rep. 101, 103.

> "I . . . think that on a question of alternative remedies no question of election arises until one or other claim has been brought to judgment. Up to that stage the plaintiff may pursue both remedies together, or pursuing one may amend and pursue the other; but he can take judgment only for the one, and his cause of action on both will then be merged in the one."[788]

However, Viscount Simon went further:

> "What would be necessary to constitute a bar . . . would be that, as the result of such judgment or otherwise, the appellant should have received satisfaction"[789]

and partial satisfaction may not suffice.[790] The claim in tort may, of course, be waived in other ways, such as by a genuine ratification of an agent's unauthorised act,[791] or by acceptance of the proceeds obtained by the defendant's tortious dealing with the claimant's property,[792] or by affirming a mortgage,[793] and the claimant cannot thereafter sue the wrongdoer in tort.[794] Similarly, where the claimant definitely elects in writing to treat the defendant as a wrongdoer and obtains damages from him on that footing, he cannot also maintain a claim for a further amount in restitution, based on approbation of the defendant's tortious act in using assets to make a profit for himself.[795]

Money obtained by fraud or deceit. An important instance of the award of restitutionary remedies is where the claimant uses a claim in restitution to recover money obtained from him by fraud or deceit.[796] It has been held that, while restitution is available in respect of money paid by the claimant to the defendant by virtue of the defendant's fraud or deceit, an account of the profits made by the defendant as a result of the fraud does not lie.[797] Thus, where the defendant obtained payment of a promissory note payable to the plaintiff, by means of a false or forged representation of authority from the plaintiff, the plaintiff was entitled to sue the defendant in restitution to recover the money which the defendant had received.[798] The defendant is liable to such an action even where 29–147

[788] *United Australia Ltd v Barclays Bank Ltd* [1941] A.C. 1, 30 (Lord Wright discussed the case in (1941) 57 L.Q.R. 184); *Mahesan v Malaysia Government Officers' Co-operative Housing Society Ltd* [1979] A.C. 374.

[789] [1941] A.C. 1, 21 (see also Lord Porter, 50).

[790] *Personal Representatives of Tang Man Sit v Capacious Investments Ltd* [1996] A.C. 514, 526.

[791] *Verschures Creameries Ltd v Hull and Netherlands S.S. Co Ltd* [1921] 2 K.B. 608 (tort action against agent barred by unsatisfied judgment against third party in quasi-contract). See also *John v Dodwell* [1918] A.C. 563, 570–571.

[792] *Lythgoe v Vernon* (1860) 5 H. & N. 180.

[793] *Halifax B.S. v Thomas* [1996] Ch. 217.

[794] *Smith v Baker* (1873) L.R. 8 C.P. 350; cf. *Smith v Hodson* (1791) 4 T.R. 211; *Roe v Mutual Loan Fund Ltd* (1887) 19 QBD 347.

[795] *Re Simms* [1934] Ch. 1, 20, 25–26. See also *Halifax B.S. v Thomas* [1996] Ch. 217, 227–228.

[796] See *Billing v Ries* (1841) Car. & M. 26; *Bonzi v Stewart* (1842) 4 M. & G. 295, 325. cf. avoidance of conveyances made with intent to defraud creditors: Law of Property Act 1925 s.173(1).

[797] *Halifax B.S. v Thomas* [1996] Ch. 217. Sed quaere? The case is perhaps better interpreted as one involving ratification of the tort. See Virgo at p.474.

[798] *Vaughan v Matthews* (1849) 13 Q.B. 187, 190.

the fraud was committed by his partner and agent, and not by him personally.[799] So where payments of premiums on a policy were continued by the plaintiff because of false representations by the defendant's agent, it was held that the premiums could be recovered by the plaintiff in a claim for restitution.[800] On the other hand, if the defendant obtains money by fraud from an agent, either the agent or his principal may recover it from him.[801]

29–148 **Services or property obtained by fraud.** If the defendant, without intending to pay for it, fraudulently induces the claimant to perform a service for him, the claimant may sue either for the tort of deceit, or in unjust enrichment for reasonable remuneration.[802] Where a sale by auction is advertised or stated by the auctioneer to be "without reserve", the secret employment by the vendor of a puffer to bid for him, without notice, renders the sale void and entitles the purchaser to recover his deposit from the auctioneer by a claim in restitution.[803]

29–149 **Limits on the right to rescind for fraud.** A person induced by fraud to enter into a contract under which he pays money may not rescind the contract and recover the price[804] if he can no longer restore the parties to the status quo ante (e.g. if he cannot return what he has received under the contract in the same condition as that in which he received it).[805] His only remedy is a claim for damages in an action for fraud.[806] The right to rescind may also be lost by affirmation.[807] Thus, if a person is induced to purchase an article by the seller's fraudulent misrepresentations about it, and after discovering the fraud he continues to deal with the article as his own, for example by selling it,[808] he cannot recover from the seller the price paid to him for it.[809] Again, if a party, after he has discovered a fraud which induced him to enter into a contract, voluntarily pays a sum of money under it with knowledge of the facts, he cannot claim a return of the money so paid.[810]

---

[799] *Crockford v Winter* (1807) 1 Camp. 124, 127; *Marsh v Keating* (1834) 1 Bing. N.C. 198 HL (discussed in *Jacobs v Morris* [1902] 1 Ch. 816).

[800] *Kettlewell v Refuge Assurance Co* [1908] 1 K.B. 545; [1909] A.C. 243; but cf. *Salata v Continental Insurance Co* [1948] 2 D.L.R. 663, where the agent was only authorised to solicit custom.

[801] *Holt v Ely* (1853) 1 E. & B. 795.

[802] *Rumsey v N.E. Ry* (1863) 14 C.B.(N.S.) 641; *Hill v Perrott* (1810) 3 Taunt. 274; *Abbotts v Barry* (1820) 2 Brod. & B. 369; *Collins v Brebner* [2000] Lloyd's Rep. P.N. 587, noted Elliott (2002) 65 M.L.R. 588.

[803] *Thornett v Haines* (1846) 15 M. & W. 367; *Green v Baverstock* (1863) 14 C.B.(N.S.) 204; *Parfitt v Jepson* (1877) 46 L.J.C.P. 529; and see Sale of Land by Auction Act 1867 ss.4–7. cf. solicitor suing, without authority, in the name of a nominal or imaginary claimant: *Dupen v Keeling* (1829) 4 C. & P. 102; see further, Vol.II, para.31–101.

[804] *Whittaker v Campbell* [1984] Q.B. 318, 327.

[805] Above, paras 6–115 et seq. But cf. *Logicrose Ltd v Southend United F.C. Ltd* [1988] 1 W.L.R. 1256. See also *Vadasz v Pioneer Concrete (SA) Pty Ltd* [1995] 185 C.L.R. 102; *Walker v W.A. Personnel Ltd* [2002] B.P.R. 621.

[806] *Clarke v Dickson* (1858) E.B. & E. 148.

[807] Above, para.6–124.

[808] *Halifax B.S. v Thomas* [1996] Ch. 217.

[809] *Campbell v Fleming* (1834) 1 A. & E. 40. See also *Law v Law* [1905] 1 Ch. 140, CA.

[810] *Miles v Dell* (1821) 3 Stark. 23, 26.

Money obtained by oppression or extortion. Money obtained by illegal oppression or extortion or by taking advantage of the weak and needy may be recovered.[811] This is another instance of a restitutionary remedy being awarded for an action in tort, since it is, in general, a tort to obtain money by unlawful intimidation.[812] Thus a claim lies against a broker to recover excessive charges on a distress for rent, paid by the tenant in order to prevent a sale, even though the tenant may have applied for and obtained time in consideration of his promise to pay the charges.[813] But where excessive charges are paid to satisfy a claim purporting to be made by virtue of a statute, but the person paying them is not oppressed or imposed on in any way, it depends on the interpretation of the particular statute whether he is entitled to recover the excess.[814] 29–150

(c) *Breach of Contract*[815]

Restitution for breach of contract. A defendant may make a gain from a breach of contract either by making a larger profit from a third party than he would have made from the other party had he performed[816] or by saving expense from its breach.[817] In general, the gain to a defendant from a breach of contract is irrelevant to the quantification of damages.[818] A claimant who suffers a smaller loss than the defendant's gain or who suffers injury of a non-pecuniary kind from the breach of contract will find a restitutionary award attractive, and, exceptionally, the defendant's gain is relevant to the quantification of damages. The 29–151

---

[811] *Lowry v Bourdieu* (1780) 2 Dougl. 468, 472; *Clarke v Shee* (1774) 1 Cowp. 197, 200; see also *Astley v Reynolds* (1732) 2 Stra. 915; *Re Judgment Summons (No.25 of 1952)* [1953] Ch. 1; *Re Majory* [1955] Ch. 600 (the threat of the final sanction of bankruptcy, when costs are wrongly demanded, may be extortion). For extortion *colore officii*, see above, para.29–094, for money obtained by wrongful demand, see above, paras 29–087 et seq., for unconscionable bargains, see above, para.29–138, and, for ultra vires receipts by tax and other public bodies, see above, para.29–083.

[812] On the tort of intimidation, see *Rookes v Barnard* [1964] A.C. 1129. But sed quaere whether "two party" intimidation is a tort: *J.T. Stratford & Son Ltd v Lindley* [1965] A.C. 269, 325; Harrison [1964] C.L.J. 159, 168; Hoffmann (1965) 81 L.Q.R. 116, 127–128. But see Beatson at pp.221 and 118–119. If it is not, these cases provide support for the view (above, para.29–140) that the claims in tort and restitution are entirely independent of each other. See also *Universe Tankships of Monrovia v International Transport Workers Federation* [1983] A.C. 366; *Dimskal S.S. Co SA v International Transport Workers Federation* [1992] 2 A.C. 152.

[813] *Hills v Street* (1828) 5 Bing. 37.

[814] *Green v Portsmouth Stadium* [1953] 2 Q.B. 190 (a charge contravening the Betting and Lotteries Act 1934 s.13, is not recoverable). On excessive charges paid to public authorities, see above, para.29–083.

[815] See generally, above, paras 26–020 et seq.; Burrows at pp.480–491; Goff and Jones at pp.519–534; Virgo at Ch.17. See also Friedmann (1980) 80 Col. L.Rev. 504, 513–529; Jones (1983) 99 L.Q.R. 442; Burrows, *Remedies for Torts and Breach of Contract*, 2nd edn (1994), pp.308–314; Birks [1987] L.M.C.L.Q. 421; *Aggravated, Exemplary and Restitutionary Damages*, (Law Com. No.247, 1998), Pt III; Smith [1999] 115 L.Q.R. 245.

[816] *Teacher v Calder* (1899) 1 F. 39, HL.

[817] *Tito v Waddell (No.2)* [1977] Ch. 106, above, para.26–016.

[818] *The Siboen* [1976] 1 Lloyd's Rep. 293, 337 (profits from alternative charter irrelevant); *Tito v Waddell (No.2)* [1977] Ch. 106, 332 (Megarry V.C.); *Surrey CC v Bredero Homes Ltd* [1993] 1 W.L.R. 1361. But see Goodhart [1995] Rest. L. Rev. 3; *Jaggard v Sawyer* [1995] 1 W.L.R. 269; *Nottingham University v Fishel* [2000] I.C.R. 1462. See, generally, above, para.26–020.

defendant's gain is relevant in sales of land,[819] where there has been a breach of a contractual duty of confidence[820] or a fiduciary duty[821] or where the breach of contract involves the use or interference with the claimant's property.[822] These are all cases of specifically enforceable contracts and it is arguable that the defendant's gains should be relevant in all such cases.

29–152 **Account of profits.** It has also been held that in an exceptional case, where specific enforcement and injunctions are inadequate remedies for a breach of contract or are not available, the court can require the defendant to account to the claimant for benefits received from a breach of contract even where the breach does not involve the use of or interference with the claimant's property:

> "The law recognises that a party to a contract may have an interest in performance which is not readily measurable in terms of money. On breach the innocent party suffers a loss. He fails to obtain the benefit promised by the other party to the contract. To him the loss may be as important as financially measurable loss, or more so. An award of damages, assessed by reference to financial loss, will not recompense him properly. For him a financially assessed measure of damages is inadequate."[823]

In determining whether to order an account of profits, the court will have regard to all the circumstances, including the subject matter of the contract, the purpose of the contractual provision which has been breached, the circumstances in which the breach occurred, the consequences of the breach and the circumstances in which relief is being sought. Lord Nicholls of Birkenhead (with whom Lord Goff and Lord Browne-Wilkinson agreed) stated that:

> "... a useful general guide, although not exhaustive, is whether the plaintiff had a legitimate interest in preventing the defendant's profit-making activities and, hence, in depriving him of his profit."[824]

---

[819] *Lake v Bayliss* [1974] 1 W.L.R. 1073; *Tito v Waddell (No.2)* [1977] Ch. 106, 332 (Megarry V.C.).

[820] *Peter Pan Manufacturing Corp v Corsets Silhouette Ltd* [1964] 1 W.L.R. 96. See also above, para.29–145.

[821] See *Reading v Att-Gen* [1951] A.C. 507. See also *Hospital Products Ltd v US Surgical Corp* (1984) 156 C.L.R. 41 (Australia).

[822] *Penarth Dock Engineering Co Ltd v Pound* [1963] 1 Lloyd's Rep. 359; *Wrotham Park Estate Co Ltd v Parkside Homes Ltd* [1974] 1 W.L.R. 798, 812–816 (damages in lieu of injunction for breach of restrictive covenant assessed at 5 per cent. of the profit made by the defendant builder on the basis that this was the sum that might reasonably have been demanded by the plaintiffs as a *quid pro quo* for relaxing the covenant); *Jaggard v Sawyer* [1995] 1 W.L.R. 269. See also Goodhart [1995] RLR 3; *Amec Developments v Jury's Hotel* Management [2001] E.G.L.R. 81. See also *O'Brien Homes Ltd v Lane* [2004] EWHC 303 (QB) where damages for breach of a collateral contract not to build more than three houses were assessed by reference to what the defendant would have been prepared to pay the claimant to be released from the contractual obligation. cf. *Surrey CC v Bredero Homes Ltd* [1993] 1 W.L.R. 1361, CA.

[823] *Att-Gen v Blake* [2001] 1 A.C. 268, 282 (Lord Nicholls). See also above, para.26–024. Lord Hobhouse dissented on the ground (at 298) that an account of profits, a remedy based on property rights, should not be given where the necessary property rights are absent. cf. *Hospitality Group Pty Ltd v Australian Rugby Football Union Ltd* [2001] F.C.A. 1040 (in Australia loss recoverable for breach of contract is limited to compensation); Campbell and Harris (2002) 22 L.S. 308; Campbell (2002) 65 M.L.R. 256.

[824] [2001] 1 A.C. 268, 285. See also Lord Steyn at 292 (defendant's position closely analogous to that of a fiduciary). cf. *R. v Att-Gen for England and Wales* [2003] UKPC 22.

The Crown was held to have such an interest in preventing a former member of the intelligence services who had undertaken not to divulge any official information gained as a result of his employment from profiting from breaches of the undertaking in an autobiography. He was therefore not entitled to receive the royalties which had been held by his publishers.

Attorney-General v Blake. In *Att-Gen v Blake*[825] their Lordships declined to give more specific guidance as to when an account of profits might be awarded for breach of contract. But they indicated that it would not in itself suffice that: (a) the breach was cyncial and deliberate; (b) the breach enabled the defendant to enter into a more profitable contract elsewhere; and (c) by entering into a new and more profitable contract the defendant put it out of his power to perform the contract with the claimant.[826] Their Lordships did not, moreover, consider the two categories suggested by the Court of Appeal for "restitutionary damages"[827] were satisfactory. The first, the case of "skimped" performance, where defendants fail to provide the full extent of the contracted services, was said not to fall within the scope of an account of profits as ordinarily understood. Nor was an account of profits needed in this context. Suppliers of inferior goods have to refund the difference in price as damages for breach of contract, and a similar approach should apply in cases where the defendant provided inferior and cheaper services than those contracted for.[828] The second category suggested by the Court of Appeal, where defendants profited by doing the very thing that they contracted not to do, was considered to be too widely defined because it embraced all express negative obligations.[829] 29–153

Subsequent developments. Subsequent cases indicate a liberal interpretation of when an account of profits will be available for breach of contract.[830] Most significantly, in *Experience Hendrix LLC v PPX Enterprises Inc*[831] the remedy of an account of profits was awarded where the defendant repeatedly breached a settlement agreement relating to the use of licensed material. However, the Court did not order the defendant to account for all the profits which derived from the breach, since the case was not considered to be exceptional. This was because, even though the case involved a deliberate breach of contract whereby the defendants did that which they had promised not to do and damages were an 29–154

[825] [2001] 1 A.C. 268.

[826] [2001] 1 A.C. 268, 286 (Lord Nicholls), 291 (Lord Steyn). See [1998] Ch. 439, 457, 458 CA.

[827] Lord Nicholls preferred ([2001] 1 A.C. 268, 284) to avoid this term.

[828] [2001] 1 A.C. 268, 285 (Lord Nicholls), 291 (Lord Steyn).

[829] [2001] 1 A.C. 268, 286 (Lord Nicholls), 291 (Lord Steyn).

[830] See *Esso Petroleum Co Ltd v Niad* [2001] All E.R. (D) 324 (Morritt V.C.): an account of profits was awarded in a commercial context where damages were an inadequate remedy, but cf. Beatson (2002) 118 L.Q.R. 377 contrasting this with a less liberal approach taken by commercial arbitrators (see *AB Corp v CD Co, The Sine Nomine* [2002] 1 Lloyd's Rep 805) and *WWW World Wide Fund for Nature v World Wrestling Federation Entertainment Inc* [2002] FSR 32; affirmed on different grounds [2002] FSR 33 CA.

[831] [2003] EWCA Civ 323, [2003] 1 All E.R. (Comm) 830. See above, paras 26–026 et seq.

inadequate remedy because it was not possible to quantify the loss suffered by the breach,[832] the case was not concerned with a sensitive subject such as national security, the defendants were not fiduciaries and the breaches occurred in a commercial context.[833] The remedy which was awarded was a reasonable sum assessed with reference to what the claimant would reasonably have demanded for the defendant's use of the material in breach of the agreement. In *WWF—World Wide Fund for Nature v World Wrestling Federation Entertainment Inc*[834] the claimant sought the award of a remedy to reflect its failure to make a bargain with the defendant to vary a compromise agreement, known as an award of damages on the *Wrotham Park* basis.[835] In previous proceedings[836] the claimant had unsuccessfully sought to amend its pleadings to claim an account of profits for breach of the settlement. The Court of Appeal held that it was an abuse of process now to seek *Wrotham Park* damages in separate proceedings, but it also recognised that both remedies were compensatory and so were juridically highly similar. Chadwick L.J. recognised[837] that the:

> "... two remedies should, I think, each be seen as a flexible response to the need to compensate the claimant for the wrong which has been done to him."

Whilst the characterisation of the *Wrotham Park* remedy is controversial, and may indeed be a remedy to compensate the claimant for loss suffered, the assertion that an account of profits is a compensatory remedy deprives the expression "compensatory damages" of any sensible meaning, since the remedy is assessed with reference to the defendant's gain arising from the breach of contract and not with the identification of the claimant's loss.

(d) *Equitable Wrongdoing*[838]

29–155 **Types of equitable wrongdoing.** Restitutionary remedies are available for a number of equitable wrongs including actions for breach of fiduciary duty[839] and breach of confidence.[840] A fiduciary who has profited from his breach of duty

---

[832] [2003] 1 All E.R. (Comm) 830, 843 (Mance L.J.).

[833] [2003] 1 All E.R. (Comm) 830. See also at 848 (Peter Gibson L.J.). cf. *Esso Petroleum Co Ltd v Niad* [2001] All E.R. (D) 324.

[834] [2007] EWCA Civ 286, [2008] 1 W.L.R. 445. See above, para.26–027.

[835] See above, para.29–151.

[836] [2002] F.S.R. 32.

[837] [2007] EWCA Civ 286, [2008] 1 W.L.R. 445 at [59].

[838] Burrows at pp.491–507; Goff and Jones at Chs 33, 34, 35; Virgo at Ch.18.

[839] *Regal (Hastings) Ltd v Gulliver* [1967] 2 A.C. 134n; *Boardman v Phipps* [1967] 2 A.C. 46; *Crown Dilmun, Dilmun Investments Ltd v Nicholas Sutton, Fulham River* [2004] EWHC 52 (Ch), [2004] 1 B.C.L.C. 468; *Re Quarter Master UK Ltd* Unreported July 15, 2004 (Paul Morgan Q.C.); *Murad v Al-Saraj* [2005] EWCA Civ 1235.

[840] *Peter Pan Manufacturing Corp v Corsets Silhouette Ltd* [1964] 1 W.L.R. 96; *Att-Gen v Guardian Newspapers Ltd (No.2)* [1990] 1 A.C. 109. See also Jones (1970) 86 L.Q.R. 463. In *LAC Minerals Ltd v International Cornoa Resources Ltd* (1989) 61 D.L.R. (4th) 14 profits were held on constructive trust.

will be liable to account for all the profits made, even if they would have been made had the defendant not breached his fiduciary duty.[841]

29–156 **Receipt of a bribe, secret profit or commission.** Where a fiduciary receives from a third party a bribe, secret profit or commission in connection with his principal's affairs, his principal may elect either to recover the bribe or damages for fraud (in respect of any loss he has sustained through the contract) from the agent.[842] The same principle holds in regard to the relationship of employer and employee.[843] Thus the Crown can recover secret bribes received by a police officer,[844] or secret payments received by a soldier for using his uniform illicitly to smuggle goods past civilian police[845]; the employer's right of recovery is not affected by the fact that the money was earned through a criminal act of the employee, nor by the fact that the employer has suffered no loss.[846] A wrongful payment does not have to induce a contract to be a bribe.[847] In equity, a person in a fiduciary position is held to be a constructive trustee of a profit resulting from that position for the benefit of the person to whom he is accountable.[848] The person who paid the bribe is also liable for dishonestly assisting a breach of fiduciary duty, but double recovery is not permitted and the principal can only recover the amount of the bribe and any additional loss he can prove however he chooses to frame his action and even if he sues both the agent and the briber.[849] Where, however, the principal rescinds the transaction tainted by a bribe he does not have to give credit for the amount of the bribe as part of his duty to make restitution of benefits received under the contract even where he has already recovered the bribe from the fiduciary.[850] A bribe is the payment of a secret

---

[841] *Murad v Al-Saraj* [2005] EWCA Civ 1235. See Conaglen [2006] C.L.J. 281.

[842] *Reading v Att-Gen* [1948] 1 K.B. 268, 276; [1949] 2 K.B. 232; [1951] A.C. 507; *Mahesan v Malaysia Government Officers' Co-operative Housing Society Ltd* [1979] A.C. 374, applying *United Australia Ltd v Barclays Bank Ltd* [1941] A.C. 1.

[843] *Boston Deep Sea Fishing & Ice Co Ltd v Ansell* (1888) 39 Ch D 339; *Lister v Stubbs* (1890) 45 Ch D 1. See Vol.II, paras 31–074 et seq. cf. *Meadow Schama & Co v C. Mitchel & Co* (1973) 228 E.G. 1511 (arrangement between estate agents after commission earned held not to amount to a secret commission); *Kelly v Cooper* [1993] A.C. 205.

[844] *Att-Gen v Goddard* (1929) 98 L.J.K.B. 743

[845] *Reading v Att-Gen* [1951] A.C. 507.

[846] [1951] A.C. 507.

[847] *Petrotrade Inc v Smith* [2000] 1 Lloyd's Rep. 486.

[848] *Regal (Hastings) Ltd v Gulliver* [1942] 1 All E.R. 378; [1967] 2 A.C. 134n; *Phipps v Boardman* [1967] 2 A.C. 46 (the agent or employee may, however, be entitled to some remuneration for his work and skill if he has acted openly: see below, para.29–157); *Industrial Development Consultants Ltd v Cooley* [1972] 1 W.L.R. 443; *Guinness Plc v Saunders* [1990] 2 A.C. 663; *Att-Gen for Hong Kong v Reid* [1994] 1 A.C. 324. In *Daraydan Holdings Ltd v Solland* [2004] EWHC 622 (Ch), [2005] Ch. 119 Lawrence Collins J. recognised that a defendant who had received a secret commission from the claimants in breach of fiduciary duty held that commission on constructive trust for the claimants, following the decision of the Privy Council in *Reid*.

[849] *Mahesan v Malaysia Government Officers' Co-operative Housing Society Ltd* [1979] A.C. 374, 382–383; *Arab Monetary Fund v Hashim (No.9)* [1993] 1 Lloyd's Rep. 543; *Petrotrade Inc v Smith* [2000] 1 Lloyd's Rep. 486; *Fyffes Group Ltd v Templeman* [2000] 2 Lloyd's Rep. 643. But see Tettenborn (1979) 95 L.Q.R. 68 and cf. Needham (1979) 95 L.Q.R. 536 (1979). See further Vol.II, para.31–074.

[850] *Logicrose Ltd v Southend United F.C. Ltd* [1988] 1 W.L.R. 1256.

commission: proof of corruptness or corrupt motive is not necessary in a civil action.[851]

29–157 **Equitable allowance.** Where a fiduciary is liable to account for a profit or commission resulting from his fiduciary position or arising out of his use of his principal's property or the trust property,[852] he may, if he has acted openly and honestly (albeit mistakenly), be entitled to some remuneration for his work and skill.[853] The factors which will incline a court to make such an allowance include whether the work would in any event have had to be done by the claimant and, the fact that the work has been of substantial benefit to the claimant.[854]

4. PROPRIETARY RESTITUTIONARY CLAIMS[855]

(a) *Establishing Proprietary Rights*

29–158 **Advantages of proprietary restitutionary claims.** The advantages of proprietary restitutionary claims include, first, that they may lie against an innocent recipient of the property, even where no personal claim, whether in tort, unjust enrichment, or equity, would lie against him[856]; secondly, if the recipient of the property is insolvent, the true owner may, subject to statutory requirements in certain cases,[857] claim specific property[858] in priority to the claims of general creditors[859]; thirdly, if the true owner traces his property into investments bearing interest, he will be entitled to claim the interest in addition.[860] Further, it is possible for a personal restitutionary remedy to be obtained by reliance on the

---

[851] *Industries and General Mortgage Co Ltd v Lewis* [1949] 2 All E.R. 573; Vol.II, para.31–074.

[852] Above, para.29–156; Vol.II, paras 31–120—31–122.

[853] *Phipps v Boardman* [1967] 2 A.C. 46, 104, 112; *O'Sullivan v Management Agency & Music Ltd* [1985] Q.B. 428; *Re Berkeley Applegate Ltd* [1989] Ch. 32. cf. *Guinness Plc v Saunders* [1990] 2 A.C. 663; *Nottingham University v Fishel* [2000] I.C.R. 1462; *James v Williams* [2000] Ch. 1 (constructive trustee of property who expends money on repairs and maintenance can deduct this from the amount payable to the beneficiary); *Murad v Al-Saraj* [2005] EWCA Civ 1235.

[854] *Re Berkeley Applegate Ltd* [1989] Ch. 32. The award of an equitable allowance was declined in *Re Quarter Master UK Ltd* Unreported July 15, 2004 on the ground that directors should not profit from their breach of fiduciary duty and that the directors concerned had not demonstrated special skills or taken unusual risks.

[855] Burrows at pp.60–77, Ch.2; Goff and Jones at Ch.2; Virgo at Pt V.

[856] *Sinclair v Brougham* [1914] A.C. 398; *International Sales & Agencies Ltd v Marcus* (1982) 34 C.M.L.R. 46. But cf. *Thavorn v Bank of Credit & Commerce International SA* [1985] 1 Lloyd's Rep. 259.

[857] e.g. the registration requirements of Companies Act 2006 ss.860–894; *Re Bond Worth Ltd* [1980] Ch. 228; *Borden (UK) Ltd v Scottish Timber Products Ltd* [1981] Ch. 25; *Re Peachdart Ltd* [1984] Ch. 131. But cf. *Clough Mill Ltd v Martin* [1985] 1 W.L.R. 111; *John Snow & Co Ltd v D.B.G. Woodcroft Ltd* [1985] B.C.L.C. 54.

[858] At common law it will not be possible, however, to ensure the return of the property *in specie*; below, para.29–170. See the discretion to order that a chattel be restored by the Torts (Interference with Goods) Act 1977 s.3.

[859] cf. claims for freezing orders which do not have this effect: *Cretanor Maritime Co Ltd v Irish Marine Management Ltd* [1978] 1 W.L.R. 966.

[860] *Re Diplock* [1948] Ch. 465, 517, 557; *Re Tilley's W.T.* [1967] Ch. 1179, 1193; *Foskett v McKeown* [2001] 1 A.C. 102.

vindication of the claimant's property rights.[861] This has the advantage that the claimant can obtain the restitution of value from an indirect recipient of the property, regardless of the fact that the recipient has not retained the property or its substitute.

Identifying a proprietary interest. Before a claimant can bring a proprietary restitutionary claim it is necessary to establish a proprietary interest, either at law or in equity. Where the claimant has transferred property, a legal proprietary interest may be retained where the claimant's intention to transfer the property can be considered to have been vitiated. For example, where the property was transferred as the result of a fundamental mistake, relating to the identity of the recipient[862] or the identity of the property,[863] then title will not pass. Similarly where property has been stolen, title will not pass.[864] A possessory title can be sufficient to found a proprietary restitutionary claim.[865] An equitable proprietary interest will be created either by an express trust or through the recognition of a resulting[866] or constructive trust. 29–159

Constructive trusts.[867] Equity has employed the mechansim of a trust in order to compel the "trustee" to convey property to the "beneficiary" where, quite apart from the intention of the parties, the rules of equity decide that property is in the wrong hands. The constructive trust arises by operation of law in a number of circumstances, including where the defendant has profited from a breach of fiduciary duty or trust,[868] where property has been obtained by 29–160

---

[861] See below, paras 29–170 and 29–172.

[862] *Citibank NA v Brown Shipley and Co Ltd* [1991] 2 All E.R. 690, 699 (Waller J.).

[863] *Ashwell* (1885) 16 QBD 190.

[864] This is the preferable explanation of *Lipkin Gorman (A Firm) v Karpnale Ltd* [1991] 2 A.C. 546, although the House of Lords based its decision on unjust enrichment. Now see *Foskett v McKeown* [2001] 2 A.C. 102. See also *OEM Plc v Schneider* [2005] EWHC 1072 (Ch) at [40] (Peter Clarke J.).

[865] *Costello v Chief Constable of Derbyshire Constabulary* [2001] 3 All E.R. 150.

[866] See *Air Jamaica v Charlton* [1999] 1 W.L.R. 1399, 1412 (Lord Millett); *Twinsectra Ltd v Yardley* [2002] 2 A.C. 164, 189 (Lord Millett); Chambers, *Resulting Trusts* (1997).

[867] Goff and Jones at pp.93–95, Ch.33; Underhill and Hayton, *Law of Trusts and Trustees*, 17th edn, Ch.7; *Snell's Equity*, 31st edn, pp.190–191, 468, Ch.22; Hanbury and Martin, *Modern Equity*, 17th edn, Ch.12; Elias, *Explaining Constructive Trusts* (1990); Oakley, *Constructive Trusts*, 3rd edn; Waters, *The Constructive Trust* (1964).

[868] See para.29–155, above. For leading cases, see e.g. *Keech v Sandford* (1726) Cas. t. King 61; *Re Knowles' Will Trusts* [1948] 1 All E.R. 866; *Bannister v Bannister* [1948] 2 All E.R. 133; *Reading v Att-Gen* [1951] A.C. 507, 516, 517; *Re Green* [1951] Ch. 148; *Hepburn v A. Tomlinson (Hauliers) Ltd* [1966] A.C. 451; *Phipps v Boardman* [1967] 2 A.C. 46 (above, para.29–156); *Guinness Plc v Saunders* [1990] 2 A.C. 663; *Selangor United Rubber Estates Ltd v Cradock* [1968] 1 W.L.R. 1555; *Industrial Development Consultants Ltd v Cooley* [1972] 1 W.L.R. 443; *Queensland Mines v Hudson* (1978) 18 A.L.R. 1; *New Zealand Netherland Society "Oranje" Inc v Kuys* [1973] 1 W.L.R. 1126 (PC: a special arrangement may displace what would otherwise be a potential fiduciary obligation); *Att-Gen (Hong Kong) v Reid* [1994] 1 A.C. 324 (PC: bribes) (above, para.29–156); approved in *Daraydan Holdings Ltd v Solland International Ltd* [2004] EWHC 622 (Ch) (Lawrence Collins J.); *Papamichael v National Westminster Bank* [2003] 1 Lloyd's Rep. 341, 371; *Clark v Cutland* [2003] EWCA Civ 810; *Sinclair Investment Holdings SA v Versailles Trade Finance Ltd* [2007] EWHC 915 (Ch), [2007] 2 All E.R. (Comm) 993 at [105] (Rimer J.). As to whether a constructive trust should be recognised where a defendant has breached confidence, see Tang (2003) L.S. 135, cf. *Att-Gen v Guardian Newspapers (No.2)* [1990] 1 A.C. 109, 288 (Lord Goff).

fraud,[869] or where the defendant has received property unconscionably, such as where the defendant is aware that money had been paid by or mistake,[870] or possibly where the payee was aware that there had already been a total failure of consideration.[871] This device has been extensively developed in the United States of America,[872] where such a trust is regarded as "purely a remedial institution"[873] and, although support has been expressed for the development of the remedial constructive trust in English law,[874] this notion of the trust has been rejected.[875] The constructive trust is significant in other areas. For instance, when a bailee, who has insured the goods bailed to him for their full value, receives payment from the insurers, he may retain so much as would cover his own interest in the goods, and is a trustee for the owner of the goods in respect of the balance.[876] Similarly, where the owner of real property agrees to sell it to a purchaser, he becomes a "qualified trustee" for the purchaser, with the result that if the owner later wrongfully sells the property to a second purchaser and receives the price from him, he is accountable to the first purchaser for the price as trust property to be transferred to the first purchaser upon his completing his obligations under the first contract.[877] The concept of a constructive trust has been used where there is a common intention of cohabitants that they should have an interest in their home.[878]

29–161 **Defendant's acquiescence in improvements to his land.** There are other equitable rules which may create equitable proprietary interests. For instance, where a person in occupation of the land of another expends money on the land

[869] *Westdeutsche Landesbank Girozentrale v Islington LBC* [1996] A.C. 669, 716 (Lord Browne-Wilkinson), at least where the transaction was void and not voidable: *Papamichael v National Westminster Bank* [2003] 1 Lloyd's Rep. 341, 374; *Halley v The Law Society* [2003] EWCA Civ 97 (contract was the instrument of fraud, rather than only induced by the fraud, and so was void); *Commerzbank AG v IMB Morgan Plc* [2004] EWHC 2771 (Ch), [2005] 1 Lloyd's Rep. 298 at [36] (Lawrence Collins J.); *Sinclair Investment Holdings SA v Versailles Trade Finance Ltd* [2005] EWCA Civ 722, [2006] 1 B.C.L.C. 66. cf. *Lonrho v Fayed (No.2)* [1992] 1 W.L.R. 1; *El Ajou v Dollar Land Holdings Plc* [1993] 3 All E.R. 717.

[870] [1996] A.C. 669, 715 (Lord Browne-Wilkinson). See also *Papamichael v National Westminster Bank* [2003] 1 Lloyd's Rep. 341, 372 (actual knowledge is required: at 373).

[871] *Re Farepak Food and Gifts Ltd* [2006] EWHC 3272, [2006] All E.R. (D) 265. See also *Nesté Oy v Lloyd's Bank Plc* [1983] 2 Lloyd's Rep. 658.

[872] Scott (1955) 71 L.Q.R. 39.

[873] Pound (1920) 33 Harv. L.R. 420, 421.

[874] *Westdeutsche Landesbank Girozentrale v Islington LBC* [1996] A.C. 669, 716 (Lord Browne-Wilkinson).

[875] *Re Polly Peck International (No.2)* [1998] 3 All E.R. 812, 823 (Mummery L.J.), 830 (Nourse L.J.). See also *Metall und Rohstoff AG v Donaldson, Lufkin and Jenrette Inc* [1990] 1 Q.B. 391, 474–480; *Halifax Building Society v Thomas* [1996] Ch. 217, 229 (Peter Gibson L.J.); *Cobbold v Bakewell Management Ltd* [2003] EWHC 2289 (Ch) at [17] (Rimer J.); *Sinclair Investment Holdings SA v Versailles Trade Finance Ltd* [2007] EWHC 915 (Ch), [2007] 2 All E.R. (Comm) 993 at [105] (Rimer J.). cf. *London Allied Holdings v Lee* [2007] EWHC 2061 (Ch) at [274] (Etherton J.).

[876] *Hepburn v A. Tomlinson (Hauliers) Ltd* [1966] A.C. 451 (Vol.II, paras 33–020, 41–010, 41–011). See also *The Albazero* [1977] A.C. 774.

[877] *Lake v Bayliss* [1974] 1 W.L.R. 1073. See also *English v Dedham Vale Properties Ltd* [1978] 1 W.L.R. 93.

[878] *Stack v Dowden* [2007] UKHL 17, [2007] 2 A.C. 432; Swadling (2007) L.Q.R. 511; Etherton (2008) C.L.J. 265. This has been extended to commercial arrangements: *Yaxley v Gotts* [2000] Ch. 162; *Banner Homes Group Plc v Luff Developments Ltd* [2000] Ch 372. See also *Yeoman's Row Management Ltd v Cobbe* [2008] UKHL 55.

(e.g. by building) in the expectation, induced or encouraged by the owner of the land, that he will be allowed to remain in occupation, an equity is created under which the court will protect his occupation of the land.[879] The nature of the relief will depend on the circumstances.[880]

(b) *Following and Tracing*

Following and tracing.[881] Where the claimant has a legal or equitable proprietary interest he will need to identify that interest in property which can be identified in the hands of the defendant. To do this the claimant as true owner of the property may "follow" the original property or "trace" the product or substitute of his property and then claim its recovery.[882] This process is recognised both at common law[883] and in equity,[884] each with its own limitations,[885] but tracing in equity is likely to prove more useful in practice because of the more extensive proprietary remedies available in equity. Despite calls for the assimilation of the tracing rules at law and in equity, they remain distinct.[886] **29–162**

Tracing at common law. At common law a claimant is permitted to trace and claim property in which he has a legal proprietary interest if it has not been mixed with other property but can be identified in a "physical"[887] sense, e.g. sovereigns **29–163**

[879] *Inwards v Baker* [1965] 2 Q.B. 29; *Chalmers v Pardoe* [1963] 1 W.L.R. 677; *Ward v Kirkland* [1966] 1 W.L.R. 601, 626–632; *Lee-Parker v Izzet* [1972] 1 W.L.R. 775, 780–781. cf. *E.R. Ives Investment Ltd v High* [1967] 2 Q.B. 379; *Siew Soon Wah v Yong Tong Hong* [1973] A.C. 836; *Dodsworth v Dodsworth* [1973] E.G. 233; *Crabb v Arun DC* [1976] Ch. 179 (one landowner encouraged the adjoining owner to act to his prejudice in the belief he would be given a right of way); *Jones v Jones* [1977] 1 W.L.R. 438; *Pascoe v Turner* [1979] 1 W.L.R. 431; *Grant v Edwards* [1986] Ch. 638; *Gillett v Holt* [2001] Ch. 210 *Yeoman's Row Management Ltd v Cobbe* [2008] UKHL 55. For earlier authorities, see *Dillwyn v Llewelyn* (1862) 4 De G.F. & J. 517; *Ramsden v Dyson* (1866) L.R. 1 H.L. 129; *Willmot v Barber* (1880) 15 Ch D 96; *Plimmer v Mayor of Wellington* (1884) 9 App. Cas. 699. See also Goff and Jones at pp.238–243; Allan (1963) 79 L.Q.R. 238; *Van den Berg v Giles* [1979] 2 N.Z.L.R. 111. cf. above, paras 3–139 et seq.

[880] [1965] 2 Q.B. 29.

[881] *Snell's Equity*, 31st edn, pp.683–690; Hanbury and Martin, *Modern Equity*, 17th edn, pp.684–716; Goff and Jones at pp.98–126; Birks at pp.358–375; Lawson, *Remedies of English Law*, 2nd edn, Ch.6; Smith, *The Law of Tracing* (1997); Wright (1936) 6 Camb. L.J. 305; Lord Denning (1949) 65 L.Q.R. 37; Maudsley (1959) 75 L.Q.R. 234; Babafemi (1971) 34 M.L.R. 12; Goode (1976) 92 L.Q.R. 360, 528; (1987) 103 L.Q.R. 433; Pearce (1976) 40 Conv.(N.S.) 277; Evans (1999) 115 L.Q.R. 469; Walker [2000] Rest. L. Rev. 573.

[882] *Foskett v McKeown* [2001] 1 A.C. 102, 128 and 139 (Lord Millett).

[883] *Re Diplock* [1948] Ch. 465, 518 et seq.; *Lipkin Gorman v Karpnale Ltd* [1991] 2 A.C. 548; *Trustee of the Property of F. C. Jones & Sons v Jones* [1997] Ch. 159. See also *Scott v Surman* (1742) Willes 400; *Taylor v Plumer* (1815) 3 M. & S. 562.

[884] *Sinclair v Brougham* [1914] A.C. 398; *Re Diplock* [1948] Ch. 465, 520 et seq.

[885] See below, paras 29–163, 29–164, 29–171, 29–172.

[886] *Shalson v Russo* [2003] EWHC 1637 (Ch), [2005] Ch. 281. In *Nelson v Larholt* [1948] 1 K.B. 339 at 343, Denning J. considered that common law and equity should be fused into one set of principles. See also *Bristol and West Building Society v Mothew* [1996] 4 All E.R. 698, 716 (Millett L.J.); *Foskett v McKeown* [2001] 1 A.C. 102, 129 (Lord Millett); Ulph [2007] R.L.R. 76.

[887] *Sinclair v Brougham* [1914] A.C. 398, 418 (Viscount Haldane L.C.). But cf. Matthews (1981) 34 C.L.P. 156; *Indian Oil Corp v Greenstone Shipping Co SA* [1988] Q.B. 345.

in a bag[888] or an entire chose in action, such as a bank balance[889] or a promissory note.[890] If another asset has been "purchased exclusively"[891] with the claimant's money, it is still identifiable at common law, because common law permits the owner of the original property to assert his title to the product in place of the original property[892] and to profits made from the exchanged property.[893] But in the case of money, identification has been held not to be possible if there was "admixture of other money".[894]

29–164 **Tracing in equity.** Tracing in equity is only possible where the claimant can establish that the defendant or a third party is in a fiduciary relationship to him which has been broken[895] and that he has an equitable proprietary interest in the relevant property.[896] Once this is established the beneficiary can trace the property into the hands of anyone, until either a bona fide purchaser for value without notice acquires the legal title to the property,[897] or the property ceases to be identifiable even in equity.[898] Thus, the beneficiary may recover his property from a person who purchases it for value, but with notice of the equitable interest, or from an innocent volunteer who takes the property without notice of the equitable interest but who does not give value for it,[899] for in these cases there is no bona fide purchaser for value.[900] If the trustee or fiduciary pays trust money into his private banking account which is overdrawn, and the bank, without

888 [1914] A.C. 398, 418 (Viscount Haldane L.C.).

889 *Banque Belge pour l'Etranger v Hambrouck* [1921] 1 K.B. 321; *Agip (Africa) Ltd v Jackson* [1991] 1 Ch. 547; *Lipkin Gorman v Karpnale Ltd* [1991] 2 A.C. 548.

890 *Scott v Surman* (1742) Willes 400.

891 *Re Diplock* [1948] Ch. 465, 519; *Re J. Leslie Engineers Co Ltd* [1976] 1 W.L.R. 292, 297 (Lord Parker). See also *Whitecomb v Jacob* (1710) Salk 160.

892 *Lipkin Gorman v Karpnale Ltd* [1991] 2 A.C. 548, 573 (Lord Goff). This process has been described as "ratification": *Re Diplock* [1948] Ch. 465, 518; *Sinclair v Brougham* [1914] A.C. 398, 441 (Lord Parker). This agency fiction is criticised by Lord Denning (1949) 65 L.Q.R. 37, 41–42; it was not accepted in *Taylor v Plumer* (1815) 3 M. & S. 562, nor in *Lipkin Gorman v Karpnale Ltd* 574 (Lord Goff). But cf. Goode (1976) 92 L.Q.R. 360, 367, fn.27; Khurshid and Matthews (1979) 95 L.Q.R. 78 for criticism of this "exchange product" theory and the view that the claimant will acquire no title to the new asset unless it has been transferred to the recipient as agent for him or the recipient appropriates the property to him.

893 *Trustee of the Property of F. C. Jones & Sons v Jones* [1992] Ch. 157.

894 *Re Diplock* [1948] Ch. 465, 518.

895 *Space Investments Ltd v Canadian Imperial Bank of Commerce Trust Co (Bahamas) Ltd* [1986] 1 W.L.R. 1072.

896 *Re Diplock* [1948] Ch. 465, 520–521, 529–530; *Westdeutsche Landesbank Girozentrale v Islington LBC* [1996] A.C. 669, 714, 716 (Lord Browne-Wilkinson). See also *Aluminium Industrie Vassen B.V. v Romalpa Aluminium Ltd* [1976] 1 W.L.R. 676; *Borden (UK) Ltd v Scottish Timber Products Ltd* [1981] Ch. 25; *Chase Manhattan Bank N.A. v Israel-British Bank (London) Ltd* [1981] Ch. 105; *Agip (Africa) Ltd v Jackson* [1991] Ch. 547; *Re Goldcorp Exchange Ltd* [1995] 1 A.C. 74; *Boscawen v Bajwa* [1996] 1 W.L.R. 328.

897 *Re Diplock* [1948] Ch. 465, 539, 544; *Cowan de Groot Properties Ltd v Eagle Trust Plc* [1994] 4 All E.R. 700, 767. The same limitation applies at common law: *Clarke v Shee* (1774) 1 Cowp. 197.

898 *Re Diplock* [1948] Ch. 465, 521, 546–550; *Borden (UK) Ltd v Scottish Timber Products Ltd* [1981] Ch. 25, 41–42; *R. v Preddy* [1996] A.C. 815, 834.

899 *Re Diplock* [1948] Ch. 465, 539. See also *Thorndike v Hunt* (1859) 3 De G. & J. 563; *Taylor v Blakelock* (1886) 32 Ch D 560; *Sinclair v Brougham* [1914] A.C. 398, 443–447 (Lord Parker). But cf. below, para.29–166 for the refusal to permit an equitable remedy which would operate unconscionably upon the volunteer.

900 See *Snell's Equity* at pp.65–78; Babafemi (1971) 34 M.L.R. 12, 22–28.

notice that it is trust money, uses it to pay off the overdraft, the right to trace is lost.[901]

Fiduciary relationship. The authorities requiring that there be a fiduciary relationship have been criticised[902] and courts have, on occasion, been willing to circumvent or manipulate the requirement.[903] Moreover, in some cases the finding that a fiduciary relationship exists has appeared to rest solely on the fact that it would be unconscionable for the recipient or his trustee in bankruptcy to retain the amount by which his assets had been increased.[904] However, the category of fiduciary relationships is broad[905] and the relationship need not originate in a consensual transaction.[906] Nor, apparently, need the property have been the subject of fiduciary obligations before it got into the wrong hands. Although the requirement of a fiduciary relationship has been reaffirmed by the House of Lords,[907] it was also stated[908] that stolen moneys are traceable in equity and that an equitable proprietary interest under a resulting or constructive trust will suffice. It therefore appears that the courts will continue to manipulate this requirement where they think it is appropriate. More recently the House of Lords has criticised but not rejected the fiduciary relationship requirement.[909] 29–165

Identifying property in equity. Equity may trace property beyond "the verge of actual identification",[910] into any specific asset purchased with it,[911] or into a 29–166

[901] *Thomson v Clydeside Bank* [1893] A.C. 282; *Coleman v Bucks & Oxon Union Bank* [1897] 2 Ch. 243; *Bishopsgate Investment Management Ltd v Homan* [1995] Ch. 211, 220; *Style Financial Services Ltd v Bank of Scotland* [1995] B.C.C. 785.

[902] Goff and Jones at pp.110–112 et seq.; Maudsley (1959) 75 L.Q.R. 234, 241–245; (1971) 19 Vanderbilt L.R. 1123, 1136; Babafemi (1971) 34 M.L.R. 12; Oakley (1975) 28 *Current Legal Problems* 64; Birks (1997) 11 Trust Law Internat. 2; Millet (1998) 114 LQR 399, 409.

[903] *El Ajou v Dollar Land Holdings Plc (No.1)* [1993] 3 All E.R. 717, 734 (Millett J.); *Bristol and West B.S. v Mothew* [1998] Ch. 1, 23 (Millett L.J.)

[904] *Sinclair v Brougham* [1914] A.C. 398, 441–444 (Lord Parker); *Chase Manhattan Bank N.A. v Israel-British Bank (London) Ltd* [1981] Ch. 105, above, para.29–160; *Clough Mill Ltd v Martin* [1985] 1 W.L.R. 111; *Re Goldcorp Exchange Ltd* [1995] 1 A.C. 74. See also *English v Dedham Vale Properties Ltd* [1978] 1 W.L.R. 93 (although the plaintiff there sought an account of profits rather than a proprietary remedy). But cf. *Borden (UK) Ltd v Scottish Timber Products Ltd* [1981] Ch. 25 for a more restrictive approach.

[905] Sealy [1962] C.L.J. 69; Goff and Jones at p.112, fn.93. For this purpose the relationship between, inter alia, solicitor and client, bailor and bailee, principal and agent will be regarded as fiduciary. An important factor in determining whether an agent is a fiduciary is whether he is under a duty to keep his own money separate from his principal's money. See also below, para.29–168.

[906] *Chase Manhattan Bank N.A. v Israel-British Bank (London) Ltd* [1981] Ch. 105, 119 (Goulding J.), discussed, Vol.II, para.34–136; *Westdeutsche Landesbank Girozentrale v Islngton LBC* [1996] A.C. 669, 716 (Lord Browne-Wilkinson). See also *Sinclair v Brougham* [1914] A.C. 398; *English v Dedham Vale Properties Ltd* [1978] 1 W.L.R. 93, 111; *Ex p. James* (1874) L.R. 9 Ch. App. 609, discussed, above, paras 20–022, 29–043; see further *Agip (Africa) Ltd v Jackson* [1991] Ch. 547 but cf. *Re Byfield* [1982] Ch. 267.

[907] *Westdeutsche Landesbank Girozentrale v Islington LBC* [1996] A.C. 669.

[908] [1996] A.C. 669, 716.

[909] *Foskett v McKeown* [2001] 1 A.C. 102. See also *Campden Hill Ltd v Chakrani* [2005] EWHC 911 (Ch) at [74] (Hart J.).

[910] *Sinclair v Brougham* [1914] A.C. 398, 459 (Lord Sumner). See also *Foskett v McKeown* [2001] 1 A.C. 102.

[911] *Lane v Dighton* (1762) Amb. 409; *Hopper v Conyers* (1866) L.R. 2 Eq. 549.

bank account even when it is mixed with other moneys[912]; "equity regarded the amalgam as capable, in proper circumstances, of being resolved into its component parts".[913] Accordingly, if the trustee mixes his own money with the trust money, the beneficiary can trace into the mixed fund or into any asset purchased with the mixed fund.[914] But even equity cannot trace property if its identity is finally lost, e.g. by being spent on living expenses such as a dinner,[915] being used to pay off a loan,[916] or by mixing heterogeneous goods in a manufacturing process wherein a wholly new product emerges.[917] Nor will equity permit tracing if it would operate in a harsh or unconscionable manner upon the volunteer, e.g. if a volunteer who innocently acquires trust property uses it to alter or improve his own land or buildings, the right to trace in equity is lost, since it would be inequitable to force the sale of his land.[918] The right to trace will also be lost if the recipient is a bona fide purchaser for value,[919] but it appears that the defence of change of position will not defeat a peropriertary restitutionary claim.[920]

29–167 **Withdrawals from a mixed fund in a bank account.** In *Clayton's Case*[921] it was held that the principle that moneys in a current bank account are presumed to have been paid out in the order in which they were paid in applies in equity where two trust funds, or trust money and a volunteer's own money, have been mixed in the same bank account.[922] Where, however, the application of the rule in *Clayton's Case* would be impracticable, is inconsistent with the presumed intentions of the parties (such as where the fund is intended to be a common investment fund), is inconsistent with the actual allocation of funds, or will result in injustice, it will not apply if there is a preferable alternative.[923] In such cases the rule in *Clayton's Case* will be easily displaced[924] and the court will incline to rateable division.[925] Moreover, where a trustee mixes his own money with trust

---

[912] *Re Diplock* [1948] Ch. 465, 520.

[913] [1948] Ch. 465, 520.

[914] [1948] Ch. 465, 539; *Re Hallett's Estate* (1880) 13 Ch D 696; *Re Pumfrey* (1882) 22 Ch D 255; *Re Oatway* [1903] 2 Ch. 356.

[915] *Re Diplock* [1948] Ch. 465, 521.

[916] [1948] Ch. 465, 548–550. (Sed quaere, if the loan was used to acquire a specific, identifiable asset.) See *Re J. Leslie Engineers Co Ltd* [1976] 1 W.L.R. 292, 300 (payments of debts).

[917] *Borden (UK) Ltd v Scottish Timber Products Ltd* [1981] Ch. 25, 41 but cf. *Clough Mills Ltd v Martin* [1985] 1 W.L.R. 111, below, para.29–168.

[918] *Re Diplock* [1948] Ch. 465, 546–548. (The alteration to the land or buildings may have been to suit the personal needs of the volunteer, so that there was no increase in the market value of the asset.).

[919] *Foskett v McKeown* [2001] 1 A.C. 102, 129 (Lord Millett).

[920] [2001] 1 A.C. 102. See Lord Millett in Edelman and Degeling (eds), *Equity in Commercial Law* (2005), pp.315 and 325.

[921] (1816) 1 Mer. 572. See McConville (1963) 79 L.Q.R. 388. It is uncertain whether this rule or the rule in *Re Hallett's Estate* (1880) 13 Ch D 696 (below, fn.926) applies where money has been paid under a mistake of fact.

[922] *Hancock v Smith* (1889) 41 Ch D 456, 461; *Re Stenning* [1895] 2 Ch. 433; *Re Hallett's Estate* (1880) 13 Ch D 696; *Re Diplock* [1948] Ch. 465, 552–554.

[923] *Barlow Clowes (International) Ltd v Vaughan* [1992] 4 All E.R. 22; *Russell-Cooke Trust Co v Prentis* [2002] EWHC 2227 (Ch); [2003] 2 All E.R. 478.

[924] In *Russell-Cooke Trust Co v Prentis* [2002] EWHC 2227 (Ch); [2003] 2 All E.R. 478, 495 the so-called "Rule" was described as the exception; *Commerzbank AG v IMB Morgan Plc* [2004] EWHC 2771 (Ch), [2005] 1 Lloyd's Rep. 298 at [50] (Lawrence Collins J.).

[925] *Barlow Clowes (International) Ltd v Vaughan* [1992] 4 All E.R. 22, 42, 44.

money in a bank account, the rule in *Clayton's Case* does not apply, and the trustee is taken to have drawn out first his own money, until his own money in the account is exhausted.[926] If the trustee draws out all the trust money, but later pays in money of his own, the beneficiary cannot trace this money in the account unless he can prove that the trustee intended to replace the trust money.[927] If the trustee or volunteer "unmixes" the trust money by earmarking a particular withdrawal as the trust money, the beneficiary may trace it into another asset purchased with the proceeds of the withdrawal.[928]

Reservation of title clauses: original goods and new products. The question of entitlement to trace has arisen in a commercial context where sellers of goods have sought to protect themselves from the consequences of their buyers' insolvency by including reservation of title clauses in the contract of sale.[929] It has been held that, where the purchaser holds the goods as a bailee, an appropriately drafted clause will entitle the unpaid seller to claim the goods and to trace into the identifiable proceeds of any further sale of the goods by the buyer.[930] The reservation of title clause must, however, ensure that the seller retains the beneficial ownership of the property. Although, for instance, allowing the buyer to sell the goods or to use them in a manufacturing process may be held to be inconsistent with this,[931] the seller may be held to have retained beneficial ownership and the entitlement to trace until the goods are sold or so used.[932] Where a reservation of title clause applies to the product of a manufacturing process it will normally be construed as creating a charge on the product by the buyer in favour of the seller rather than a reservation of beneficial ownership[933] and, as such, is subject to the registration requirements of the Companies Act 2006.[934] It has, however, been stated that in principle parties to a contract could 29–168

[926] *Re Hallett's Estate* (1880) 13 Ch D 696 CA; *James Roscoe (Bolton) Ltd v Winder* [1915] 1 Ch. 62. But cf. *Re Oatway* [1903] 2 Ch. 356 (money first drawn out and invested held to be traceable where remaining balance later dissipated).

[927] *James Roscoe (Bolton) Ltd v Winder* [1915] 1 Ch. 62; *Bishopsgate Investment Management Ltd v Homan* [1995] Ch. 211; *Goldcorp Exchange Ltd (In Receivership)* [1995] 1 A.C. 74, 107; *Campden Hill Ltd v Chakrani* [2005] EWHC 911 (Ch).

[928] *Re Diplock* [1948] Ch. 465, 551–552.

[929] See Goodhart and Jones (1980) 43 M.L.R. 489, 501–510; Goode (1976) 92 L.Q.R. 528, 547–552, 554–560 (discussion of the effect of such clauses in the context of the assignment of book debts and other receivables). See on reservation of title generally, below, Vol.II, paras 43–205 et seq.

[930] *Aluminium Industrie Vaasen B.V. v Romalpa Aluminium Ltd* [1976] 1 W.L.R. 676. For the limited nature of this right to trace, see *Borden (UK) Ltd v Scottish Timber Products Ltd* [1981] Ch. 25, 38–41. See also Davies [1984] L.M.C.L.Q. 49.

[931] *Borden (UK) Ltd v Scottish Timber Products Ltd* [1981] Ch. 25. See also *Re Bond Worth Ltd* [1980] Ch. 228.

[932] *Clough Mill Ltd v Martin* [1985] 1 W.L.R. 111; *John Snow & Co v D.B.G. Woodcroft Ltd* [1985] B.C.L.C. 54; *Re Peachdart Ltd* [1984] Ch. 131, 141; *Hendy Lennox (Industrial Engines) Ltd v Grahame Puttick Ltd* [1984] 1 W.L.R. 485, 492. See also *Four Point Garage Ltd v Carter* [1985] 3 All E.R. 12 (retention of title clause did not preclude implication of term authorising resale and passage of title to sub-buyer).

[933] *Clough Mill Ltd v Martin* [1985] 1 W.L.R. 111; *Re Peachdart Ltd* [1984] Ch. 131; *E. Pfeiffer Weinkellerei-Weinemkauf GmbH & Co v Arbuthnot Factors Ltd* [1988] 1 W.L.R. 150; *Re Weldtech Equipment Ltd* [1991] B.C.L.C. 393.

[934] ss.860–894. See above, paras 9–046.

provide that title in new goods created by a manufacturing process could directly vest in the sellers.[935]

29–169 **Proceeds of sale.** Where it is wished to trace into the proceeds of sale (even where no manufacturing process had occurred), it is necessary to show that the parties were in a fiduciary relationship.[936] The following factors have been said to assist in establishing such a relationship:

(a) an obligation to store the goods in a manner manifesting the seller's ownership;

(b) postponement of the passage of property until payment is made for the total indebtedness;

(c) provision that the seller obtains the benefit of any claims against a sub-purchaser;

(d) provision that the buyer act as agent for or on account of the seller; and

(e) an obligation on the buyer to keep the proceeds of sale separate from his own moneys and not to use them.[937]

(c) *Proprietary Restitutionary Claims*

29–170 **Claiming at common law.**[938] Where the claimant has traced a legal proprietary interest into property in the hands of the defendant, the claim at common law to vindicate this proprietary interest may take the form of a claim for wrongful interference with goods,[939] or a restitutionary claim for money had and received.[940] The scope of the remedy in tort in particular has been considerably widened in order to protect proprietary rights; for instance, an action for conversion is given to the person on whose bank account a cheque belonging to him is drawn without his authority,[941] the common law thus treating him as "owner" of

---

935 *Clough Mill Ltd v Martin* [1985] 1 W.L.R. 111, 119–120, 123–124.

936 *Hendy Lennox (Industrial Engines) Ltd v Grahame Puttick Ltd* [1984] 1 W.L.R. 485; *Re Andrabell* [1984] 3 All E.R. 407.

937 [1984] 1 W.L.R. 485. A fixed credit period has been held to be incompatible with (e).

938 See *OBG Ltd v Allan* [2007] UKHL 21, [2008] A.C. 1 at [308] (Baroness Hale).

939 e.g. *Miller v Race* (1758) 1 Burr. 452, 457–458; *Wookey v Pole* (1820) 4 B. & Ald. 1, 6. See also *Indian Oil Corp v Greenstone Shipping Co SA* [1988] Q.B. 345 (damages for short delivery of wrongfully mixed cargo).

940 e.g. *Clark v Shee* (1774) 1 Cowp. 197; *Reid v Rigby* [1894] 2 Q.B. 40; *Lipkin Gorman v Karpnale Ltd* [1991] 2 A.C. 548; *Trustee of the Property of F.C. Jones & Sons v Jones* [1997] Ch. 159.

941 *Morison v London County and Westminster Bank Ltd* [1914] 3 K.B. 356; *Lloyds Bank Ltd v Chartered Bank of India, Australia and China* [1929] 1 K.B. 40; *Midland Bank Ltd v Reckitt* [1933] A.C. 1; *Lloyds Bank Ltd v E.B. Savory & Co* [1933] A.C. 201. See now *OBG Ltd v Allan* [2007] UKHL 21, [2008] 1 A.C. 1 where some members of the House of Lords accepted that it was possible to convert intangible property such as debts and contractual rights (Lord Nicholls at [220]–[241]) and Baroness Hale (at [302]–[318])). Lords Hoffmann (at [94]–[107]) and Walker (at [271]) left the matter open for consideration by the Law Commission. Lord Brown, at [321]–[322] did not consider that it was possible to convert intangible property.

the cheque rather than "owner" of the intangible bank balance. These common law actions are, however, personal, in the sense that only a personal remedy is available, although the claim remains proprietary.[942] Common law tracing into a substitute "cannot be relied on so as to render an innocent recipient a wrongdoer".[943]

Limitations of common law proprietary claims. The limitations of the common law proprietary claims[944] are said to be as follows: 29–171

(1) the common law does not recognise equitable interests in property,[945] so that a beneficial interest under a trust cannot be claimed at law;

(2) at common law it is normally not possible to compel the return of the property *in specie* because the "device of a declaration of charge" is unknown to the common law[946];

(3) the common law cannot identify the claimant's money in a mixed fund. However, this does not mean that the remedy will be ineffective where the recipient of the property is insolvent since, if it comes into the hands of the trustee in bankruptcy, he will be personally liable even where he no longer has it.[947]

Claiming in equity. Equity recognises a variety of proprietary remedies to vindicate equitable proprietary rights, including a claim to a proportionate share of the property in the defendant's hands, recognition of an equitable charge over the property and subrogation. Where the claimant owns a proportionate share of the property in the defendant's hands, that share will be held on trust for the claimant. In *Foskett v McKeown*[948] it was held that where money subject to an express trust was fraudulently used to pay insurance premiums, the defrauded beneficiaries were entitled to trace the money wrongfully paid into the policy and its proceeds. Moreover, their remedy was not merely a lien to secure return of the misapplied money, but a share of the proceeds of the policy (a much larger sum) which was held on the original express trust for the beneficiaries. Where the property purchased by a "mixed" fund has increased in value, the charge will be for a proportionate part of the increased value, as well as for the amount of the 29–172

[942] *Trustee of the Property of F. C. Jones & Sons v Jones* [1997] Ch. 159, 168. See also Pearce (1976) 40 Conv.(N.S.) 277, 284.

[943] *Lipkin Gorman v Karpnale Ltd* [1991] 2 A.C. 548, 573, 583–588 (in respect of claims founded on conversion).

[944] *Re Diplock* [1948] Ch. 465, 519–520.

[945] *Re Diplock* [1948] Ch. 465.

[946] *Re Diplock* [1948] Ch. 465, 519. But see the discretion to order the return of a chattel under the Torts (Interference with Goods) Act 1977 s.3. On chattels, see Goff and Jones at pp.100–101, see further *Howard E. Perry & Co Ltd v British Rys Board* [1980] 1 W.L.R. 1375.

[947] *Giles v Perkins* (1807) East 12; *Scott v Surman* (1742) Willes 400; *Trustee of the Property of F.C. Jones & Sons v Jones* [1997] Ch. 159. See Pearce (1976) 40 Conv.(N.S.) 277, 284.

[948] [2001] 1 A.C. 102.

trust money.[949] If the trustee mixes the trust funds of two separate trusts, there is an equal equity in each beneficiary, so that the separate beneficiaries can trace and share pari passu, or enjoy pari passu any equitable lien or charge on an asset purchased with the mixed fund.[950] Any equitable charge may be enforced ultimately by sale of the assets.[951] If the trust money is received by a volunteer who then mixes it with his own money, the beneficiary may again trace his property, claiming a declaration of charge if necessary, but he must share the fund (or any asset purchased therewith) pari passu with the volunteer.[952]

29–173 **Subrogation.** By virtue of "subrogation" a person may, in certain situations, "step into the shoes" of another so as to enjoy the latter's legal position or his rights against a third person. Subrogation may arise from the express or implied agreement of the parties or by operation of law. In the latter situation subrogation may be triggered by the defendant's unjust enrichment[953] or by the vindication of property rights claim.[954] The right of an insurer who pays a claim under an indemnity policy in respect of a particular loss to be subrogated to and to enforce the rights of the insured person arising out of that loss against any third person[955] is founded upon contractual intention. So also, in general, is the entitlement of a guarantor who pays the debt of the principal debtor to require the creditor to give him the benefit of any security given by the principal debtor to the creditor[956] and of an indorser of a bill of exchange who pays the bill to claim analogous rights.[957] Where a loan to a minor has been expended on necessaries, the minor will be liable to pay the lender the amount so expended.[958] But in other cases the

[949] *Scott v Scott* (1963) 109 C.L.R. 649. cf. *Re Tilley's Will Trusts* [1967] Ch. 1179, 1193. The question whether the rule in *Re Hallett's Estate* (1880) 13 Ch D 696 (see above, para.29–167) applies where money paid under a mistake of fact to a person who is not a trustee was left open in *Chase Manhattan Bank N.A. v Israel-British Bank (London) Ltd* [1981] Ch. 105, 120 (Goudling J.) (on which, see Vol.II, para.34–136). It has been applied to such a case in the United States; *Re Berry* (1906) 147 F. 208. See further *Agip (Africa) Ltd v James* [1991] Ch. 547.

[950] *Re Diplock* [1948] Ch. 465, 533–534, 539; *Sinclair v Brougham* [1914] A.C. 398, 442 (Lord Parker) (above, para.9–025); *Barlow Clowes (International) Ltd v Vaughan* [1992] 4 All E.R. 22.

[951] *Re Diplock* [1948] Ch. 465, 546–547.

[952] *Re Diplock* [1948] Ch. 465, 534, 539; *Sinclair v Brougham* [1914] A.C. 398, 442–443 (Lord Parker).

[953] *Banque Financière de la Cité v Parc (Battersea) Ltd* [1999] 1 A.C. 221, where the claimant sought a personal remedy against a third party by means of subrogation; *Cheltenham and Gloucester Plc v Appleyard* [2004] EWCA Civ 291. See also *Niru Battery Manufacturing Co v Milestone Trading Ltd (No.2)* [2004] EWCA Civ 487, [2004] 2 All E.R. (Comm) 289, where the remedy of subrogation was ordered to prevent the defendant's unjust enrichment arising from the discharge of a liability owed by the defendant. It is unclear, however, why this remedy was sought or obtained since the claimant had a direct restitutionary claim to recover the value of the benefit obtained by the defendant and did not need to step into the shoes of any other party to bring such a claim.

[954] *Halifax Plc v Omar* [2002] EWCA Civ 121; *Eagle Star Insurance v Karasiewicz* [2002] EWCA Civ 940. See Midwinter [2003] L.M.C.L.Q. 6; *Filby v Mortgage Express (No.2) Ltd* [2004] EWCA Civ 759 (where, although the claim was characterised as grounded on unjust enrichment, the court treated it as a claim founded on the vindication of property rights).

[955] See Vol.II, para.41–091.

[956] See Vol.II, para.44–128, but see above, para.29–110 for the position of the officious guarantor.

[957] See Vol.II, para.34–127.

[958] See above, para.8–020; cf. above, paras 8–074—8–075.

foundation of a right to be subrogated can be characterised as restitutionary.[959] In such cases the rights are akin to other restitutionary rights, but subject to statute.[960] The contractual and restitutionary forms of subrogation have been said to be "radically different",[961] although the influence of contractual subrogation and of the implied contract theory of restitution has meant that the distinction has not always been maintained. Moreover, some types of transaction[962] may provide examples of both contractual and restitutionary subrogation. Examples of restitutionary subrogation include ultra vires or unauthorised borrowing used to discharge a debt.[963] Subrogation has also been sought by lenders where, for a variety of reasons, the loan is irrecoverable. Thus, where a loan on mortgage to a minor was void but the money lent was used to buy property, the lender was held to be entitled to a lien over the property by being "subrogated" to the position of the vendor who received the money.[964] Again, where an ultra vires loan is made to a company it has been held that the lender may be subrogated to the position of a creditor whose valid debt is discharged with the proceeds of the loan.[965] However, subrogation will not be permitted where it would frustrate the policy of the rule that invalidates the loan. Thus, a moneylender who financed a series of property transactions by loans that were unenforceable for non-compliance with statutory requirements was held not to be able to be subrogated to the security represented by the previously existing charges and unpaid vendors' liens that had been discharged by the loans.[966] To give relief by subrogation in such a case:

---

[959] *Banque Financière de la Cité v Parc (Battersea) Ltd* [1999] 1 A.C. 221, where subrogation was awarded as a remedy to reverse the defendant's unjust enrichment *Niru Battery Manfacturing Co v Milestone Trading Ltd (No.2)* [2004] EWCA Civ 487, [2004] 2 All E.R. (Comm) 289. See also Mitchell and Watterson, *Subrogation: Law and Practice*; (2007) Burrows at pp.104–127; Goff and Jones at Ch.3; Birks (1971) 34 M.L.R. 207; *Lord Napier and Ettrick v R. F. Kershaw Ltd* [1993] A.C. 713. Thus, a "volunteer" will not be subrogated: *Esso Petroleum Co Ltd v Hall Russell & Co Ltd* [1989] A.C. 643. See further *Boodle Hatfield & Co v British Films Ltd* [1986] P.C.C. 176; *Boscawen v Bajwa* [1996] 1 W.L.R. 328 (subrogation discussed under a restitutionary analysis); Mitchell [1995] L.M.C.L.Q. 451. See also *Kleinwort Benson Ltd v Vaughan* [1996] C.L.C. 620 CA. But cf. *Orakpo v Manson Developments Ltd* [1978] A.C. 95, 104, criticised (1978) 41 M.L.R. 330; *Re Byfield* [1982] Ch. 267.

[960] *Re T.H. Knitwear (Wholesale) Ltd* [1988] Ch. 275.

[961] *Banque Financierè de la Cité v Parc (Battersea) Ltd* [1999] 1 A.C. 221, 231 (Lord Hoffmann). See also *Cheltenham and Gloucester Plc v Appleyard* [2004] EWCA Civ 291 at [32] (Neuberger L.J.).

[962] e.g. guarantee, see above, para.29–110 (officious guarantor).

[963] Above, para.9–025 (ultra vires); *Bannatyne v D. & C. MacIver* [1906] 1 K.B. 103 (unauthorised borrowing by agent); but cf. the unauthorised payment of a debt by a "stranger": *Re Cleadon Trust Ltd* [1939] Ch. 286 (above, paras 29–099, 29–112).

[964] *Nottingham Permanent Benefit Building Society v Thurston* [1903] A.C. 6, above, para.8–066. See also *Filby v Mortgage Express (No.2)* [2004] EWCA Civ 759, where a mortgage was a nullity by virtue of a forged signature; and *Cheltenham and Gloucester Plc v Appleyard* [2004] EWCA Civ 291, where a mortgage had not been registered.

[965] *Re Cork and Youghal Ry* (1869) L.R. 4 Ch. App. 748; *Blackburn Benefit Building Society v Cunliffe, Brookes & Co* (1882) 22 Ch D 61; *Baroness Wenlock v River Dee Co* (1887) 19 QBD 155 (relief given where borrowed money used to pay debts accruing after dates of its receipt). But see *Re Cleadon Trust Ltd* [1939] Ch. 286, 322–344 for the requirement that the debtor must have adopted the benefit of the invalid loan.

[966] *Orakpo v Manson Investments Ltd* [1978] A.C. 95. See also *Burston Finance Ltd v Speirway Ltd* [1974] 1 W.L.R. 1648. Compare *Cheltenham and Gloucester Plc v Appleyard* [2004] EWCA Civ 291, where the claimant's mortgage had not been registered as required by statute but it was

> "... would be to enable the court to express a policy of its own in regard to moneylending transactions which would be in direct conflict with the policy of the [statute][967] itself."[968]

Where it is allowed, however, this form of subrogation may appear to differ from subrogation in the sense used in the insurance and guarantee cases in so far as the person entitled to be subrogated has, in some cases, only been allowed to succeed to the creditor's personal claim but not to take the benefit of any priority enjoyed by the creditor.[969] Subrogation rights may also be waived.[970] Principles relating to the award of the equitable remedy of subrogation were usefully summarised by the Court of Appeal in *Cheltenham and Gloucester Plc v Appleyard*.[971] These include that a lender cannot claim subrogation if he obtains all of the security for which he bargained[972] or where the lender bargained on the basis that no security would be received.[973]

29–174 **Personal restitutionary remedies.** Where the defendant has received property in which the claimant had an equitable proprietary interest, but the defendant no longer has that property or its traceable substitute, the claimant may sue the defendant in the action for unconscientious receipt.[974] The remedy which is awarded, namely the value of the property received, will be restitutionary.

---

subrogated to another mortgage because, inter alia, the claimant had not obtained the legal charge for which it had bargained but only an equitable charge and the failure to register was not the result of the claimant's negligence.

[967] Moneylenders Act 1927 s.6 (repealed by the Consumer Credit Act 1974).

[968] *Orakpo v Manson Investments Ltd* [1978] A.C. 95, 115. See also Megarry (1956) 72 L.Q.R. 480; Goff and Jones at p.137. This depends on whether a claim to this type of subrogation must be based on the presumed mutual intentions of the borrower and lender, for the statute only made a "security given by the borrower" unenforceable. For criticism of the decision in *Orakpo*, see (1978) 41 M.L.R. 330. See also *Re Byfield* [1982] Ch. 267.

[969] *Re Wrexham, Mold and Connah's Quay Ry* [1899] 1 Ch. 440; *Banque Financière de la Cité v Parc (Battersea) Ltd* [1999] 1 A.C. 221; *Cheltenham and Gloucester Plc v Appleyard* [2004] EWCA Civ 291 at [36] (Neuberger L.J.). See also *Bannatyne v D. & C. MacIver* [1906] 1 K.B. 108, 109. cf. *Paul v Speirway Ltd* [1976] 1 Ch. 220 which, by analogy, suggests that if the lender's money is to be used to discharge a secured loan the presumption is that he intended his loan to be secured. See also *Orakpo v Manson Investments Ltd* [1978] A.C. 95, 105; *McColl's Wholesale Pty Ltd v State Bank of N.S.W.* [1984] 3 N.S.W.L.R. 365, 369; Goff and Jones at pp.134–135, 171–175.

[970] *The Surf City* [1995] 2 Lloyd's Rep. 242.

[971] [2004] EWCA Civ 291 at [32]–[44] (Neuberger L.J.).

[972] *Capital Finance Co Ltd v* Stokes [1969] 1 Ch. 261.

[973] *Paul v Speirway Ltd (In Liquidation)* [1976] 1 W.L.R. 220.

[974] *Bank of Credit and Commerce International (Overseas) Ltd v Akindele* [2001] Ch. 437; *Papamichael v National Westminster Bank* [2003] 1 Lloyd's Rep. 341, 375: requiring proof of actual knowledge of the circumstances of the misapplication, rather than dishonesty. cf. *Farah Construction Pty Ltd v Say-Dee Pty* Ltd [2007] HCA 22; Ridge and Dietrich (2008) 124 L.Q.R. 26. See also *Criterion Properties Plc v Stratford UK Properties LLC* [2003] 1 W.L.R. 2108 (need to have regard to the defendant's actions and knowledge in the context of the commercial relationship as a whole to determine whether the test of unconscionability was satisfied; the House of Lords concluded that the case was not concerned with the question of unconscionability but whether directors had authority to sign an agreement: [2004] UKHL 28, [2004] 1 W.L.R. 1846). On the interpretation of the test of unconscionability see also *Crown Dilmun, Dilmun Investments Ltd v Nicholas Sutton, Fulham River* [2004] EWHC 52 (Ch), [2004] 1 B.C.L.C. 468 at [200] (Peter Smith J.). cf. *It's a Wrap (UK) Ltd v Gula* [2006] EWCA Civ 544, [2006] B.C.C. 626.

Alternatively the defendant may be liable for dishonest assistance,[975] but the remedy will typically be compensatory since it is usually assessed with reference to the claimant's loss rather than the defendant's gain.[976] Similarly, where the defendant has received property in which the claimant has a legal proprietary interest, but the defendant has not retained that property or its traceable substitute, the claimant can recover the value of the property received in an action for money had and received.[977]

Bona fide purchase defence.[978] Where a claimant brings a restitutionary claim to vindicate property rights, the claim may be defeated by a defence of bona fide purchase for value but not by a defence of change of position.[979] This is because the bona fide purchase defence defeats the claimant's proprietary interest. The defence of bona fide purchase is not available where the claim is a personal one for unjust enrichment.[980] 29–175

5. DEFENCES[981]

(a) *Estoppel*[982]

Nature of estoppel. In certain circumstances a person making a payment may be precluded from recovering it by an estoppel. He may, for instance, be estopped from subsequently alleging that he acted under a mistake. To raise an estoppel the payee must satisfy three conditions.[983] First, he must show that either the payer 29–176

---

[975] *Royal Brunei Airlines Sdn Bhd v Tan* [1995] 2 A.C. 378 (objective test of dishonesty: at 389 (Lord Nicholls)); *Twinsectra Ltd v Yardley* [2002] UKHL 12; [2002] 2 A.C. 164 (knowledge of circumstances of dishonesty required: at [20] (Lord Hoffmann) and at [35] (Lord Hutton)). Now see *Barlow Clowes International Ltd v Eurotrust International Ltd* [2005] UKPC 37, [2006] 1 W.L.R. 1476 (objective test of dishonesty). See also *Abou-Rahmah v Abacha* [2006] EWCA Civ 1492, [2007] 1 Lloyd's Rep. 115, and Virgo [2007] C.L.J. 22.

[976] *Sinclair Investment Holdings SA v Versailles Trade Finance Ltd* [2007] EWHC 915 (Ch), [2007] 2 All E.R. (Comm) 993 at [101] (Rimer J.).

[977] *Lipkin Gorman (A Firm) v Karpnale Ltd* [1991] 2 A.C. 548. Although the House of Lords analysed this claim with reference to the unjust enrichment principle, following the decision of the same court in *Foskett v McKeown* [2001] A.C. 102, it is better analysed with reference to the vindication of property rights principle. See Virgo, in Getzler (ed.), *Rationalizing Property, Equity and Trusts: Essays in Honour of Edward Burn* (2003), p.104; *OEM Plc v Schneider* [2005] EWHC 1072 (Ch).

[978] Burrows at pp.585–591; Goff and Jones at Ch.42; Virgo at Ch.22.

[979] *Foskett v McKeown* [2001] 1 A.C. 102, 129 (Lord Millett); *Papamichael v National Westminster Bank* [2003] 1 Lloyd's Rep. 341, 376. See Lord Millett in *Commercial Law in Equity.*

[980] *Papamichael v National Westminster Bank* [2003] 1 Lloyd's Rep. 341, 374.

[981] Burrows at Ch.15; Goff and Jones at Chs 39–44; Virgo at Pt VI; Grantham and Rickett [2008] C.L.J. 92. For the defence of limitation periods see above, Ch.28.

[982] Burrows at pp.529–538; Goff and Jones at pp.869–875; Spencer-Bower and Turner, *The Law Relating to Estoppel by Representation*, 3rd edn (1991); Jones (1957) 73 L.Q.R. 48, 49–53; Birks at pp.403, 410, 474; Virgo at pp.675–684.

[983] *United Overseas Bank v Jiwani* [1976] 1 W.L.R. 964, 968 (McKenna J.).

was under a duty to give him accurate information and failed to do so,[984] or that there was an unequivocal[985] misrepresentation made to him for which the payer was responsible.[986] Secondly, he must show that this inaccurate information led him to believe that he was entitled to treat the money as his own.[987] Thirdly, he must show that because of his mistaken belief he changed his position in a way which would make it inequitable to require him to repay the money.[988]

29–177 **Fact of payment in itself is insufficient.** The mere fact of payment by itself cannot give rise to an estoppel.[989] However, where there is inequality between the parties, as where the payer is uniquely well placed to know or ascertain the true state of accounts, it may be relatively easy to spell out a representation from the one-sidedness of the means of knowledge. Thus, where, after a computer had been fed with the wrong information by an employer who then overpaid one of his employees, it was conceded that, in the circumstances, there was a sufficient representation to found an estoppel.[990] Such situations, exemplified by the "pay-master" cases, are sometimes treated as instances of breach of a duty to inform the payee of the true state of the account rather than as representation cases.[991] In fact neither *Holt v Markham*[992] nor the old case of *Skyring v Greenwood*[993] turn on breach of duty. In *Holt v Markham* the claimant by letter claimed repayment of an excessive gratuity that he had mistakenly paid to the defendant. The defendant replied that the claim was unfounded and heard nothing further from the claimant for over two months. The Court of Appeal held that the claimant was:

> "... entitled to assume that his reply was regarded as satisfactory, and that he was at liberty to deal with the money as he pleased."[994]

Scrutton L.J. went further in not relying on the def[illegible] stated that:

[984] *Mercantile Bank of India Ltd v Central Bank of India Ltd* [1938] A.C. 287; *Moorgate Mercantile Co Ltd v Twitchings* [1977] A.C. 890, 903 (on facts, no duty found); *United Overseas Bank v Jiwani* [1976] 1 W.L.R. 964. On the question of whether estoppel by negligence is possible in the absence of a special relationship, see *R.E. Jones Ltd v Waring & Gillow Ltd* [1926] A.C. 670, 693; *Mercantile Credit Co Ltd v Hamblin* [1965] 2 Q.B. 242. cf. *Moorgate Mercantile Co Ltd v Twitchings*; *Tai Hing Cotton Mill Ltd v Lin Chong Hing Bank Ltd* [1986] A.C. 80. See also Consumer Credit Act 1974 s.172 which provides that certain statements made by a creditor, owner or trader are to bind him although provision exists for relief from the operation of the section to the extent that it "appears just in an appropriate case"; s.172(3).

[985] *Weld-Blundell v Synott* [1940] 2 K.B. 107, 114; *Moorgate Mercantile Co Ltd v Twitchings* [1977] A.C. 890.

[986] *R.E. Jones Ltd v Waring & Gillow Ltd* [1926] A.C. 670; *Deutsche Bank v Beriro & Co* (1895) 1 Com. Cas. 123, 255; *United Overseas Bank v Jiwani* [1976] 1 W.L.R. 964; *Avon CC v Howlett* [1983] 1 W.L.R. 605, 620.

[987] *Holt v Markham* [1923] 1 K.B. 504, 512; *Transvaal & Delagoa Bay Investment Co v Atkinson* [1944] 1 All E.R. 579, 585; *United Overseas Bank v Jiwani* [1976] 1 W.L.R. 964; *Avon CC v Howlett* [1983] 1 W.L.R. 605, and see Sheldon J. [1981] I.R.L.R. 447.

[988] See below, para.29–178.

[989] *R.E. Jones Ltd v Waring & Gillow Ltd* [1926] A.C. 670.

[990] *Avon CC v Howlett* [1983] 1 W.L.R. 605.

[991] *Weld-Blundell v Synott* [1940] 2 K.B. 107, 115.

[992] [1923] 1 K.B. 504.

[993] (1825) 4 B. & C. 281.

[994] *Holt v Markham* [1923] 1 K.B. 504, 512.

"The claimants represented to the defendant that he was entitled to a certain sum of money and paid it, and, after a lapse of time sufficient to enable mistakes to be detected and rectified, the defendant acted on the representation and spent the money."[995]

The representation in such cases has never been formulated with precision, but, in view of the need for a lapse of time before it may be acted upon, it is arguably a representation that reasonable care has been used in making and checking the payment.[996]

Reliance by payee. The third requirement of an estoppel, that the payee has changed his position so as to make it inequitable[997] to require him to repay the money, is clearly satisfied where he can establish that a particular expenditure has been incurred as a result of the receipt of the money and he is no longer able to recover the money. Examples include investing the money in a company that has since failed,[998] and irretrievably paying it over to a third party to whom the payee thought he was obliged to pay it.[999] However, in certain circumstances, a sufficient change of position to found an estoppel may occur without any obvious change in the payee's style of living. In one case an employee who had been overpaid for a period of some eighteen months and who had spent the money as part of his normal living expenses successfully raised an estoppel.[1000] The test is whether, but for the payment, the expenditure would have occurred. Thus, there may be circumstances in which even after all the money has been spent it would not be inequitable to require repayment.[1001] Conversely, in *Avon CC v Howlett*[1002] it was stated that, while a plea of estoppel should not enable a profit to be made, a payee who has relied on a representation should not be subjected to the difficult task of having "subsequently to recall and identify retrospectively in complete detail" alterations to his general mode of living, commitments undertaken and other transactions entered into. The operation of estoppel might, therefore, result in the payee returning less than the difference between the amount paid and the precise amount he proved he had irretrievably spent. This was stated to follow from the fact that estoppel by representation is a rule of evidence and does not operate pro tanto.[1003] However, the finding that the whole of the overpayment had in fact been spent and the recognition by the court that injustice would result if the sum sought to be recovered were so large as to bear no relation to the payee's detriment and that recovery in such circumstances 29–178

[995] *Holt v Markham* [1923] 1 K.B. 504, 514. See also the fuller report on this point in (1923) 128 L.T. 719, 726.

[996] See above, para.29–036; Birks [1972] C.L.P. 179, 194 et seq.

[997] *Kleinwort, Sons & Co v Dunlop Rubber Co* (1907) 97 L.T. 263, 264; *United Overseas Bank v Jiwani* [1976] 1 W.L.R. 964.

[998] *Holt v Markham* [1923] 1 K.B. 504.

[999] *Deutsche Bank v Beriro & Co* (1895) 1 Com. Cas. 123, 255.

[1000] *Avon CC v Howlett* [1983] 1 W.L.R. 605. See also *Skyring v Greenwood* (1825) 4 B. & C. 281, 289 (Abbott C.J.).

[1001] *United Overseas Bank v Jiwani* [1976] 1 W.L.R. 964, 968–969.

[1002] [1983] 1 W.L.R. 605.

[1003] *Avon CC v Howlett* [1983] 1 W.L.R. 605, 611, 621–624. For criticism see Burrows at pp.536–538; Goff and Jones at pp.870–873; Virgo at pp.681–682. See also *Lipkin Gorman v Karpnale Ltd* [1991] 2 A.C. 548, 579 (Lord Goff). cf. Fung and Ho (2001) 117 L.Q.R. 14.

might be unconscionable,[1004] suggests that in an appropriate case estoppel may nevertheless operate pro tanto.[1005]

(b) *Change of Position*[1006]

29–179 **Change of position as a separate defence.** In *Lipkin Gorman v Karpnale Ltd* the House of Lords recognised a broad defence of change of position. This was said to be:

> "... available to a person whose position has so changed that it would be inequitable in all the circumstances to require him to make restitution, or alternatively to make restitution in full."[1007]

The defence is said to be one of the general principles of the law of restitution[1008] and, even before the decision of the House of Lords, its supposed existence was used as a justification for widening the scope of recovery for mistake.[1009] Change of position is a wider defence than estoppel because it does not depend on breach of duty or misrepresentation by the payee. In one respect, however, it is narrower than estoppel in not recognising expenditure on everyday expenses.[1010] The broad formulation was explicitly chosen by the House of Lords to allow for the development of the defence on a case by case basis.[1011] In *Commerzbank AG v Gareth Price-Jones*[1012] Mummery L.J. recognised that "the decided cases steer a cautious course, aiming to avoid the dangers of a diffuse discretion and the restrictions of rigid rules". Munby J. stated that the defence was "intended to be a broadly stated concept of practical justice" and that "technicality and black

---

[1004] *Avon CC v Howlett* [1983] 1 W.L.R. 605, 612, 624–625.

[1005] As was recognised in *Scottish Equitable Plc v Derby* [2001] EWCA Civ 369; [2001] 3 All E.R. 818 and *National Westminster Bank Plc v Somer* [2001] EWCA Civ 970; [2002] 1 All E.R. 198. See also *Philip Collins Ltd v Davis* [2000] 3 All E.R. 808.

[1006] Burrows at pp.510–529; Goff and Jones at pp.845–869; Virgo at pp.689–714.

[1007] *Lipkin Gorman v Karpnale Ltd* [1991] 2 A.C. 548, 580 (Lord Goff). See also at 558 and 568. This case departed from the previous position on which see e.g. *Durrant v Ecclesiastical Commissioners* (1880) 6 QBD 234; *Larner v L.C.C.* [1949] 2 K.B. 683, 688–689; *Baylis v Bishop of London* [1913] Ch. 127; *Re Diplock* [1948] Ch. 465, 476; affirmed sub nom. *Minister of Health v Simpson* [1951] A.C. 251, 276. See also New Zealand Judicature Amendment Act 1958 s.94B; Restatement of Restitution para.142.

[1008] *R. v Tower Hamlets LBC Ex p. Chetnik Developments Ltd* [1988] A.C. 858.

[1009] *Barclays Bank Ltd v W. & J. Simms, Son and Cooke (Southern) Ltd* [1980] Q.B. 677, above, para.29–033; *Rover International Ltd v Cannon Film Sales Ltd (No.3)* [1989] 1 W.L.R. 912; *Midland Bank Plc v Brown Shipley & Co Ltd* [1991] 2 All E.R. 690, 701–702; *Rural Municipality of Storthoaks v Mobil Oil Canada Ltd* [1975] 55 D.L.R. (3d) 1; *David Securities Pty Ltd v Commonwealth of Australia* [1992] 66 A.L.J.R. 768. See also *Scottish Equitable Plc v Derby* [2001] 3 All E.R. 818. cf. Birks and Swadling [1999] All E.R. 319–320. See further McInnes (2002) 118 L.Q.R. 209.

[1010] *Lipkin Gorman v Karpnale* [1991] 2 A.C. 548, 559–560, 580 (Lord Goff); *National Westminster Bank Plc v Somer* [2002] 1 All E.R. 198, 213 (Potter L.J.); *Barros Mattos Jnr v McDaniels Ltd* [2004] EWHC 1188 (Ch), [2005] 1 W.L.R. 247 at [16] (Laddie J.).

[1011] See, e.g. *Dextra Bank & Trust Co Ltd v Bank of Jamaica* [2002] 1 All E.R. (Comm) 193 (PC).

[1012] [2003] EWCA Civ 1663, [2004] 1 P. & C.R.D. 15 at [32].

letter law are to be avoided".[1013] Where the basis of a claim is the unjust enrichment of the defendant then in principle the defence should be based on the extent of the defendant's enrichment and should apply to the extent that the enrichment has been erased.[1014] In the context of mistake, as the ground of recovery is wide and does not bar recovery by a negligent payer,[1015] it is particularly important to accept a broad defence. Moreover, although the evidential burden is on the defendant to establish the defence, it has been said that the court should beware of applying too strict a standard because it may be unrealistic to expect a defendant to produce conclusive evidence of a change of position, given that when he changed his position he can have had no expectation that he might thereafter have to prove that he did so and the reason why he did so.[1016] The defence does not apply where the restitutionary claim is founded on the vindication of the claimant's property rights rather than unjust enrichment, at least where the claimant seeks a proprietary remedy.[1017] It is unclear whether the defence applies to claims founded on restitution for wrongs. It has been suggested that the defence is not available where the defendant is a wrongdoer,[1018] although there is obiter dicta which indicates that the defence might be available to a restitutionary claim grounded on the tort of conversion.[1019]

Illustrations of change of position. The mere fact of having spent money or delivered property does not suffice to establish the defence.[1020] The paradigm case of change of position is where the payee has detrimentally relied on a payment made to him which he has received in good faith. For instance, where the recipient of a mistaken payment, acting in good faith, pays the money or part of it to charity or makes a purchase which he would not have made but for the payment, it is unjust to require him to make restitution to the extent that he has so changed his position.[1021] Thus, on the facts of *Lipkin Gorman v Karpnale Ltd*, where a person who had stolen money used it to gamble, the gaming club was not required to repay the entire amount gambled but only their net winnings from the 29–180

[1013] *Commerzbank AG v Gareth Prices-Jones* [2003] EWCA Civ 1663 at [48]. See also *Scottish Equitable Plc v Derby* [2001] EWCA Civ 369, [2001] 3 All E.R. 818, at [26], [34] (Robert Walker L.J.); *Niru Battery Manufacturing Co v Milestone Trading Ltd* [2002] EWHC (Comm) 1425, [2002] 2 All E.R. (Comm) 705, 743 (Moore-Bick J.).

[1014] So the defence is not available where money received is used to discharge a debt, since the defendant will remain enriched by the discharge of the debt: *Scottish Equitable Plc v Derby* [2001] EWCA Civ 369; [2001] 3 All E.R. 818 at [35] (Robert Walker L.J.); *National Bank of Egypt International Ltd v Oman Housing Bank SAOC* [2002] EWHC 1760 (Comm); [2003] 1 All E.R. (Comm) 246.

[1015] See above, para.29–036.

[1016] *Phillip Collins Ltd v Davis and Satterfield* [2000] 3 All E.R. 808. See also *Scottish Equitable Plc v Derby* [2001] EWCA Civ 369; [2001] 3 All E.R. 818; *National Westminster Bank Plc v Somer* [2001] EWCA Civ 970; [2002] 1 All E.R. 198, 215 (Potter L.J.).

[1017] *Foskett v McKeown* [2001] 1 A.C. 102, 129 (Lord Millett). See above, para.29–175.

[1018] *Lipkin Gorman (A Firm) v Karpnale Ltd* [1991] 2 AC 548, 580 (Lord Goff).

[1019] *Kuwait Airways Corp v Iraqi Airways Co (Nos 4 and 5)* [2002] UKHL 19; [2002] 2 A.C. 883, at [79] (Lord Nicholls). cf. Burrows at p.525.

[1020] *Rover International Ltd v Cannon Films Sales Ltd (No.3)* [1989] 1 W.L.R. 912. See also *United Overseas Bank v Jiwani* [1976] 1 W.L.R. 964, 968–969.

[1021] *Lipkin Gorman v Karpnale* [1991] 2 A.C. 548, 559 (Lord Bridge), 579 (Lord Goff). Where the item purchased has a second-hand value there is unjust enrichment to the extent of the second-hand value of that item, but where, for example, the money is spent on a holiday which leaves no by-product, the enrichment is erased by the change of position.

thief.[1022] In these cases the loss ought to lie where it falls, on the payer who has initiated the loss-causing event, at least where neither party is at fault. But if the payee has used the money to cover expenses which would have been incurred even if he had never received the payment in question, the defence will not be established.[1023] With regard to situations where the recipient has altered its position in "anticipatory reliance" on a payment, the Privy Council[1024] has held, obiter, that the defence of change of position is in principle available and confined cases of reliance on void contracts, where the defence failed, to their exceptional facts.[1025] The defence is founded on a principle of justice designed to protect the defendant from a claim to restitution in respect of a benefit received by him in circumstances in which it would be inequitable to pursue that claim, or to pursue it in full. Since an unjust enrichment claim can only be established if the expected payment has in any event been received by the defendant, giving effect to "anticipatory reliance" in that context will indeed operate to protect the security of an actual receipt.[1026] The change of position must, on the evidence, be referable in some way to the payment of the money.[1027]

29–181 **Link between receipt and specific expenditure unnecessary.** The broad defence as formulated by the House of Lords does not appear to require a link between specific expenditure and specific receipts.[1028] This means that deserving cases in which it would be difficult to show a specific link are not necessarily excluded. For instance, where a sick employee is erroneously paid his full salary instead of the reduced sick pay to which he is entitled and, as a consequence, the employee simply fails to adjust his outgoings in the light of his new income, or where it is difficult to characterise the expenditure as unusual, such as buying "a better cut of meat, maybe, from time to time, or something extra from the grocer",[1029] or where a person with a complicated pattern of expenditure cannot attribute any particular items to the payment,[1030] provided the payee can satisfy the court that expenditure has increased in line with income, it may be possible

---

[1022] *Lipkin Gorman v Karpnale* [1991] 2 A.C. 548, 559, 579–580 (Lord Goff). For the reason why the provision of gaming services was not regarded as good consideration see above, para.29–075.

[1023] *R.B.C. Dominion Securities Inc v Dawson* [1994] 111 D.L.R. (4th) 230.

[1024] *Dextra Bank & Trust Co Ltd v Bank of Jamaica* [2002] 1 All E.R. (Comm) 193 at [39]. The Court of Appeal expressly recognised that an anticipatory change of position is a good defence in *Commerzbank AG v Gareth Price-Jones* [2003] EWCA Civ 1663, [2004] 1 P. & C.R.D. 15 at [38] (Mummery L.J.) and [64] (Munby J.).

[1025] *South Tyneside MBC v Svenska International Plc* [1995] 1 All E.R. 545; *Barber v N.W.S. Bank* [1996] 1 W.L.R. 641; *State Bank of N.S.W. Ltd v Swiss Bank Corp* [1997] 6 Bank. L.R. 34. Nolan in Birks (ed.), *Laundering and Tracing* (1995), Ch.6.

[1026] *Dextra Bank & Trust Co Ltd v Bank of Jamaica* [2002] 1 All E.R. (Comm) 193 at [39].

[1027] *Phillip Collins Ltd v Davis and Satterfield* [2000] 3 All E.R. 808. See also *Scottish Equitable Plc v Derby* [2001] EWCA Civ 369, [2001] 3 All E.R. 818.

[1028] *Phillip Collins Ltd v Davis and Satterfield* [2000] 3 All E.R. 808. See also *Scottish Equitable Plc v Derby* [2001] EWCA Civ 369. cf. *Rural Municipality of Storthoaks v Mobile Oil Canada Ltd* [1976] 2 S.C.R. 147 where the defence failed because it was not proved that specific items of expenditure resulted from specific receipts. But reliance on the validity of the receipt must be established: *Rose v AIB Group (UK) Plc* [2003] EWHC 1737 (Ch), [2003] 2 B.C.L.C. 374.

[1029] *Avon CC v Howlett* [1981] I.R.L.R. 447, 449–450 (Sheldon J.); [1983] 1 W.L.R. 605, 622. See above, para.29–178.

[1030] *Avon CC v Howlett* [1981] I.R.L.R. 447.

to establish the defence.[1031] The broad test may also be able to deal with situations where the payee's loss is not due to his reliance on the payment but to some other factor, such as where the money mistakenly paid has been stolen from him or where its loss is the result of a natural event, such as a fire. While it is likely that hardship unrelated to the payment will be treated as irrelevant and will not establish the defence, in the case where the very notes are stolen or are consumed by fire, it is submitted that the defence should be available.[1032] In *Commerzbank AG v Gareth Price-Jones*[1033] the Court of Appeal recognised that a non-pecuniary change of position may be sufficient to establish the defence, although, on the facts of the case, the defendant's change of position in staying in his job rather than seeking more lucrative employment elsewhere was not sufficient for it to be inequitable to require him to make restitution, since there was no relevant connection between the anticipated receipt of money and the decision to stay in his job and that decision did not have a significant, precise or substantial impact on the defendant.

Similar defences. Prior to the recognition of the broad defence, in certain circumstances there were defences which could be rationalised[1034] as change of position. Thus, if an agent acting on behalf of a disclosed principal receives money paid under a mistake and pays the money to his principal before the payer claims recovery, the agent is not liable, since "the person who made the mistake is not without redress, but has his remedy over against the principal".[1035] This is 29–182

[1031] See *Home Office v Ayres* [1992] I.C.R. 175 (indications by EAT that spending money on normal living expenses, i.e. failing to adjust standard of living, would probably have qualified as a change of position); *Phillip Collins Ltd v Davis and Satterfield* [2000] 3 All E.R. 808. See also *David Securities Pty Ltd v Commonwealth Bank of Australia* (1992) 66 A.L.J.R. 768, 780–781; *Westdeutsche Landesbank Girozentrale v Islington LBC* (1993) 91 L.G.R. 325, 390–397 (Hobhouse J.) (while no need for link between specific expenditure and specific receipts, losses independent of or prior to the receipt of the benefit cannot be taken into account).

[1032] *Mistakes of Law and Ultra Vires Public Authority Receipts and Payments* (Cm.2731) (Law Com. No.227, 1994), para.2.21; Burrows at p.520; Goff and Jones at p.853, fn.69; Virgo at pp.699–701. cf. Birks [1991] L.M.C.L.Q. 473; Birks, *Restitution—The Future* (1991), pp.141–143; Watts, "Judicature Amendment Act 1958—Mistaken Payments" in (1993) *Contract Statutes Review* 25 N.Z.L.C. 191.

[1033] [2003] EWCA Civ 1663, [2004] 1 P. & C.R.D. 15 at [39], [40], [43] (Mummery L.J.) and [59] (Munby J.).

[1034] *Lipkin Gorman v Karpnale Ltd* [1991] 2 A.C. 548, 579 (Lord Goff).

[1035] *Buller v Harrison* (1777) 2 Cowp. 565, 566; *Continental Caoutchoue v Kleinwort* (1904) 90 L.T. 474, 476; *Gowers v Lloyds and National Provincial Foreign Bank Ltd* [1938] 1 All E.R. 766; *Agip (Africa) Ltd v Jackson* [1990] Ch. 265; affirmed [1991] Ch. 547; *Australia and New Zealand Banking Group Ltd v Westpac Banking Corp* (1988) 78 A.L.R. 157, 168; *Bank Tejarat v Hong Kong & Shanghai Banking Corp (CI) Ltd* [1995] 1 Lloyd's Rep 239; *National Bank of Egypt International Ltd v Oman Housing Bank SAOC* [2002] EWHC 1760 (Comm); [2003] 1 All E.R. (Comm) 246; Virgo at pp.685–689. See Vol.II, para.31–109. But see Burrows at pp.600–602; Goff and Jones at pp.876–880; Bant [2007] L.M.C.L.Q. 225 for the view that this is a distinct defence applicable under agency law. See also Millett (1991) 107 L.Q.R. 71, 76; Swadling in Birks (ed), *Laundering and Tracing* (1995), Ch.9. Note that this principle does not apply where the recipient is in the position of a trustee: *Baylis v Bishop of London* [1913] 1 Ch. 127; or received the money as a result of his own wrongdoing, or with knowledge that it resulted from another's wrongdoing: *Oates v Hudson* (1851) 6 Ex. 346.

now better treated as a rule for identifying the correct defendant.[1036] Another instance occurs where money is paid under a forged bill of exchange.[1037] Furthermore, the need to protect changes of position may well explain the denial of relief in some cases which appear to proceed on other grounds. *Boulton v Jones*,[1038] in which goods mistakenly supplied were consumed by the recipient, but where the recipient was held not to be liable to pay for them is one example. The "paymaster" cases[1039] may be another instance of the indirect operation of the defence in so far as it is difficult to accept them as true cases of estoppel.

29–183 **Bad faith.** In *Lipkin Gorman v Karpnale Ltd*[1040] Lord Goff recognised that the defence is not open to a defendant who has changed his position in bad faith, as where the defendant pays money away knowing of the facts which entitle the claimant to restitution. Beyond this situation it has been unclear what constitutes bad faith. The proper interpretation of bad faith for these purposes was considered by Moore-Bick J. in *Niru Battery Manufacturing Co v Milestone Trading Ltd*[1041] where it was held that bad faith includes, but is not confined to, dishonesty.[1042] It also includes "a failure to act in a commercially acceptable way and sharp practice that falls short of outright dishonesty".[1043] This will include a defendant who changes his position in circumstances where he has good reason to believe that there are facts which enable the claimant to claim restitution, such as that money was paid by mistake, and does not make inquiries of the payer. Moore-Bick J's interpretation was confirmed by the Court of Appeal where Clarke L.J. emphasised that the essential question is whether it would be inequitable or unconscionable to deny restitution.[1044] It has been suggested that the

---

[1036] *Portman Building Society v Hamlyn Taylor Neck* [1998] 4 All E.R. 202, 207 (Millett L.J.); *Niru Battery Manufacturing Co v Milestone Trading Ltd* [2002] EWHC (Comm) 1425; [2002] 2 All E.R. (Comm) 705, 740 (Moore-Bick J.).

[1037] *Price v Neal* (1762) 3 Burr. 1354; *Cocks v Masterman* (1829) 9 B. & C. 902; *London & River Plate Bank v Bank of Liverpool* [1896] 1 Q.B. 7; *Imperial Bank of Canada v Bank of Hamilton* [1903] A.C. 49; *National Westminster Bank Ltd v Barclays Bank International Ltd* [1975] Q.B. 654; Goff and Jones at pp.880–884.

[1038] (1857) 2 H. & N. 564. See also the requirement of restitutio in integrum for rescission for misrepresentation, above, paras 6–115 et seq. The requirement of total failure of consideration, above, paras 29–054 et seq. has also been justified because of the absence of a defence of change of position; *Whincup v Hughes* (1871) L.R. 6 C.P. 78, 82, 84. See also the "statutory recognition" of the defence in *B.P. Exploration Co (Libya) Ltd v Hunt (No.2)* [1979] 1 W.L.R. 783, 800.

[1039] See above, para.29–177.

[1040] [1991] 2 A.C. 548, 580. See also 560 (Lord Templeman). See Palmer [2005] R.L.R. 53

[1041] [2002] EWHC 1425 (Comm), [2002] 2 All E.R. (Comm) 705; approved [2003] EWCA Civ 1446.

[1042] See *Twinsectra Ltd v Yardley* [2002] UKHL 12; [2002] 2 A.C. 164 at [35] (Lord Hutton): the defendant must be aware that his conduct is dishonest by the standards of honest and reasonable people (in the context of the action for dishonest assistance in a breach of trust). See also Lord Hoffmann at [20]. cf. *Royal Brunei Airlines Sdn Bhd v Tan* [1995] 2 A.C. 378 and *Barlow Clowes International Ltd v Eurotrust International Ltd* [2005] UKPC 37, [2006] 1 W.L.R. 1476 (objective test of dishonesty).

[1043] [2002] EWHC 1425 (Comm); [2002] 2 All E.R. (Comm) 705, 741, approved [2003] EWCA Civ 1446. See also *McDonald v Coys of Kensington* [2004] EWCA Civ 47, [2004] 1 W.L.R. 2775 at [41] (Mance L.J.).

[1044] [2003] EWCA Civ 1446 at [152]. See also at [183] and [192] (Sedley L.J.). See also *Commerzbank AG v Gareth Price-Jones* [2003] EWCA Civ 1663, [2004] 1 P & C.R. D. 15 at [53] where Munby J. stated that this was an exercise in judicial evaluation rather than judicial discretion. cf. Birks (2004) 120 L.Q.R. 373, Burrows [2004] C.L.J. 276. See also *Abou-Ramah v Abacha* [2006]

defendant should have actual notice of the matters which relate to his good faith, although this was interpreted as including somebody who wilfully and recklessly failed to make such inquiries as an honest and reasonable person would make.[1045] Bad faith does not, however, include negligence.[1046] The defence is not available where a defendant's change of position is tainted since it involves the commission of an illegal act, other than where the illegality can be characterised as de minimis.[1047]

Relative fault. A further question concerns the effect of the relative fault of the parties in failing to avoid the mistaken payment and the reasonableness of the payee's conduct following the payment, for example where he suffers heavy losses as a result of making highly speculative investments, he incurs the expenses after becoming aware of the claimant's claim,[1048] or where he pays far over the odds for an item he particularly wants. It is submitted that it is the payee's *real* loss to which the law should look since individuals' perceptions of their own wealth are likely to influence the extent to which they are willing to take risks or are indifferent to price.[1049] It has been unclear whether the broad formulation in *Lipkin Gorman v Karpnale Ltd* would allow the payee's "contributory negligence" to be taken into account in determining the extent to which reliance can be placed on a change of position, as is the law in New Zealand,[1050] or whether, as appears to be the case under para.142(2) of the Restatement of Restitution, fault is only relevant to exclude the defence where the payee was clearly more at fault than the payer, a "relative fault" approach. The New Zealand approach has been criticised by law reform agencies which have considered this matter on the ground that it goes far beyond what is required to give effect to a change of position defence.[1051] The "contributory negligence" approach gives the court a power to split the loss between the two parties rather than simply determining whether the payee was clearly more at fault than the payer and, if not, simply refusing recovery to the extent of the payee's change of position. It has been argued that "a contributory negligence" approach involves too much uncertainty and complexity and is likely to hamper the settlement of disputes.[1052] The Privy Council in *Dextra Bank & Trust Co Ltd v Bank of Jamaica* accepted these criticisms and concluded that the New Zealand decisions show that when the defence is used to reflect relative fault it becomes unduly 29–184

EWCA Civ 1492, [2007] 1 Lloyd's Rep. 115, where it was held that bad faith had to be determined at the time of the defendant's change of position and is not concerned with the general nature of the defendant's conduct. See Virgo [2007] C.L.J. 22; Lee [2007] R.L.R. 135.

1045 *Papamichael v National Westminster Bank* [2003] 1 Lloyd's Rep. 341, 369 (Judge Chambers Q.C.).

1046 *Dextra Bank & Trust Co Ltd v Bank of Jamaica* [2002] 1 All E.R. (Comm) 193; *Niru Battery Manufacturing Co v Milestone Trading Ltd* [2002] 2 All E.R. (Comm) 705, 738; *Maersk Air Ltd v Expeditors International (UK) Ltd* [2003] 1 Lloyd's Rep. 491, 499.

1047 *Barros Mattos Jnr v McDaniels Ltd* [2004] EWHC 1188 (Ch), [2004] 3 All E.R. 299.

1048 *Sullivan v Lee* (1995) 95 B.C.L.R. (2d) 195.

1049 *Skyring v Greenwood* (1825) 4 B.C. 281, 289.

1050 *Thomas v Houston Corbett and Co* [1969] N.Z.L.R. 151.

1051 Law Commission Consultation Paper No.120, para.2.77; Law Reform Commission of British Columbia L.R.C. 51 (1981), p.79; Law Reform Committee of South Australia (84th Report, 1984), p.32. Law Reform Commission of New South Wales L.R.C. 53 (1987), para.5.35.

1052 Burrows at pp.522–524.

unstable.[1053] The Privy Council declined to recognise the propriety of introducing the concept of relative fault into this branch of the common law. Good faith on the part of the recipient was considered to be a sufficient requirement. The court was influenced by the fact that, in actions for the recovery of money paid under a mistake (the usual context in which the defence of change of position is invoked) it is well settled that the claimant may recover however careless he may have been in omitting to use due diligence.[1054] It would be strange if, in such circumstances, the defendant should find his conduct examined to ascertain whether he had been negligent, and still more so that the claimant's conduct should be examined for the purposes of assessing the relative fault of the parties. However, in *Commerzbank AG v Gareth Price-Jones*[1055] Munby J., whilst acknowledging that relative fault was irrelevant, was clearly influenced by the fact that the defendant changed his position as a result of his own negligent mistake, which was not shared or induced by the claimant, in reaching his conclusion that it was not equitable to allow the defendant to rely on the defence.

29–185 **Relationship between change of position and estoppel.** The flexibility of change of position may mean that it will be rare in the future for a defendant who has changed his position to plead that the claimant is estopped.[1056] While this may well be the case, the fact that estoppel will generally not operate pro tanto[1057] means that defendants may prefer it.[1058] But there are indications that the recognition of change of position which operates pro tanto means that it should no longer be possible to use estoppel to recover a sum that bears no relation to the payee's detriment.[1059] Another reason for a defendant preferring estoppel, at least until change of position is more fully developed, is that it may be easier to establish the defence where sums from a variety of sources have been spent but no particular item of expenditure can be ascribed to a particular payment, or where the payee, erroneously believing his income is higher than it is because of the payments, simply fails to adjust his outgoings to reflect his new

---

[1053] *Dextra Bank & Trust Co Ltd v Bank of Jamaica* [2002] 1 All E.R. (Comm) 193 at [45], accepting the view of Birks in Swadling (ed.), *Limits of Restitution: A Comparative Analysis*, p.41. See also *Niru Battery Manufacturing Co v Milestone Trading Ltd* [2002] EWHC (Comm) 1425, [2002] 2 All E.R. (Comm) 705, 738 (Moore-Bick J.).

[1054] *Kelly v Solari* (1841) 9 M. & W. 54, 59, above, para.29–036. Equally where the claimant might be considered to be negligent in failing to recover money from a third party: *Niru Battery Manufacturing Co v Milestone Trading Ltd* [2002] EWHC (Comm) 1425, [2002] 2 All E.R. (Comm) 705, 743 (Moore-Bick J.).

[1055] [2003] EWCA Civ 1663, [2004] 1 P & C.R.D. 15. See also *Niru Battery Manufacturing Co v Milestone Trading Ltd (No.2)* [2004] EWCA Civ 487 at [33] (Clarke L.J.).

[1056] Burrows at p.538; Goff and Jones at pp.873–875; Fung and Ho (2001) 9 R.L.R. 52; Wilken (2002) 54 Comm. Law. 73.

[1057] Above, para.29–178.

[1058] *Avon CC v Howlett* [1983] 1 W.L.R. 605, 612, 624–625. See above, para.29–178.

[1059] *R.B.C. Dominion Securities Inc v Dawson* (1994) 111 D.L.R. (4th) 230; *Boscawen v Bajura* [1996] 1 W.L.R. 328; *Phillip Collins Ltd v Davis and Satterfield* [2000] 3 All E.R. 808; *Scottish Equitable Plc v Derby* [2001] EWCA Civ 369; [2001] 3 All E.R. 818. But cf. the more recent decision of the CA in *National Westminster Bank Plc v Somer* [2001] EWCA Civ 970, [2002] 1 All E.R. 198 at [215] (Potter L.J.), [216] (Clarke L.J.), [219] (Peter Gibson L.J.).

income.[1060] The importance of estoppel will certainly diminish as the result of the introduction of a broad defence of change of position, but it is submitted that it is premature to regard it as redundant.

(c) *Settlement of an Honest Claim*

Settlement of an honest claim.[1061] A payment that is made in settlement of or submission to an honest claim, or as part of a compromise, cannot be recovered. Since greater doubts surround questions of law than questions of fact it is more likely that there will be a settlement or a compromise where the issue is one of law rather than one of fact. Although it has been stated that the precise limits of the settlement defence "have still to be clarified",[1062] the current position can be stated in the following way. First, where the payer knows or believes the money is not due but pays in any event, the money will not be recoverable on the ground of mistake.[1063] If a claim has been made and disputed but payment eventually made, whether in order to avoid threatened litigation or for some other reason such as to preserve good commercial relations or to secure some advantage, it will either be a compromise or a contractual submission to the claim. If there has been no overt dispute, the reason for irrecoverability may be more difficult to characterise as submission and is better analysed as waiver. In any event in such cases there is no mistake. 29–186

Payer has doubts but nevertheless pays. Where the payer has doubts but pays nevertheless, he is unlikely to be able to recover the payment: 29–187

> ". . . a state of doubt is different from that of mistake. A person who pays when in doubt takes the risk that he may be wrong."[1064]

Three situations must, however, be distinguished. First, if the payee has made a claim accompanied by a threat to sue, recovery will be denied.[1065] Secondly, where there has been no overt dispute, if the payer does not care which way that doubt is resolved but consciously makes a decision to pay, there will also be no recovery. In other cases recovery is unlikely, particularly where the payer's doubt

---

[1060] But note the more flexible approach adopted in *Phillip Collins Ltd v Davis and Satterfield* [2000] 3 All E.R. 808. See also *Scottish Equitable Plc v Derby* [2001] EWCA Civ 369, [2001] 3 All E.R. 818.

[1061] See generally *Restitution: Mistakes of Law and Ultra Vires Public Authority Receipts and Payments* (Law Com. No.227, 1994), paras 2.25–2.38. See also Andrews [1989] L.M.C.L.Q. 431; Arrowsmith, in Burrows (ed.), *Essays on the Law of Restitution* (1991); Virgo at pp.670–671.

[1062] *Kleinwort Benson Ltd v Lincoln CC* [1999] 2 A.C. 349, 413 (Lord Hope). See also at 373 (Lord Goff).

[1063] *David Securities Pty Ltd v Commonwealth Bank of Australia* (1992) 66 A.L.J.R. 768, 775, 778. See also *Kelly v Solari* (1841) 9 M. & W. 54, 59; *Maskell v Horner* [1915] 3 K.B. 106, 118; *Mason v New South Wales* (1959) 102 C.L.R. 108, 143.

[1064] *Kleinwort Benson Ltd v Lincoln CC* [1999] 2 A.C. 349, 410 (Lord Hope); *Cobbold v Bakewell Management Ltd* [2003] EWHC 2289 (Ch) at [19] (Rimer J.); *Brennan v Bolt Burdon* [2004] EWCA Civ 1017, [2005] Q.B. 303; *Deutsche Morgan Grenfell Plc v IRC* [2006] UKHL 49, [2007] 1 A.C. 558, above, para.29–035.

[1065] *Moore v Vestry of Fulham* [1895] 1 Q.B. 399; *David Securities Pty Ltd v Commonwealth Bank of Australia* (1992) 66 A.L.J.R. 768, 788 (Dawson J.).

concerns a crucial issue,[1066] but will depend on the degree of the doubt: while *some* doubt will not prevent recovery,[1067] the greater the doubt the less likely it is that recovery will be ordered. In the context of a question of law, a payer who adverted to the issue and nevertheless decided to make the payment is likely to be held to have been indifferent to what the law really was. Thirdly, if the payer would have paid in any event, any mistake would not have caused the payment and it would therefore not be recoverable on this ground.[1068]

29–188 **Payer has no doubts as to liability.** Where the payer pays by mistake but he has no doubts as to his liability he will prima facie recover.[1069] If, however, the payment is in response to a claim accompanied by a threat to sue, recovery will be denied even if the payer is mistaken.[1070] If, moreover, the payer has waived any claim to recover the money or has assumed the risk of any mistake, recovery will be denied. While in the context of mistake of fact it appears that a mistaken payer will only rarely be held to have so waived his right or assumed the risk, it is possible that courts may be more willing to hold that there has been a waiver in the context of mistake of law,[1071] perhaps because of the greater prevalence of doubtful questions of law, and particularly where the payer has adverted to the issue but decided to make the payment anyway.[1072]

29–189 **Compromise.** Recovery will also be denied if there has been a compromise of the claim. A compromise involves some degree of concession (or consideration) on each side, and this can include the forbearance to sue.[1073] Again, it may be binding regardless of the validity of the claim. This, of course, assumes that in cases where the only pressure on the party who makes the payment is the probabilty of being sued, the claimant bona fide believes he has a fair chance of

---

[1066] *Wason v Wareing* (1852) 15 Beav. 151; *Cushen v City of Hamilton* (1902) 4 Ont L.R. 265, 266, 270.

[1067] *Charfield v Paxton* (1799) 2 East 471. See also *Kleinwort Benson Ltd v Lincoln CC* [1999] 2 A.C. 349, 401 (Lord Hoffmann), 412 (Lord Hope); *Westdeutsche Landesbank Girozentrale v Islington LBC* [1994] 4 All E.R. 890, 934 (Hobhouse J) (need for "an actual conscious appreciation" for recovery to be barred).

[1068] *Home and Colonial Insurance Co Ltd v London Guarantee and Accident Co Ltd* (1928) 45 T.L.R. 134 (regarding the fact that in practice underwriters did not refuse to pay out on unstamped marine insurance policies, although they were not valid). See also *Kelly v Solari* (1841) 9 M. & W. 54, 59; *Maskell v Horner* [1915] 3 K.B. 106, 118; *Mason v New South Wales* (1959) 102 C.L.R. 108, 143; *Deutsche Morgan Grenfell Plc v IRC* [2006] UKHL 49, [2007] 1 A.C. 558, above, para.29–035.

[1069] Above, para.29–034. See also *Woolwich Equitable Building Society v IRC* [1993] A.C. 70, 192 (Lord Jauncey).

[1070] *David Securities Pty Ltd v Commonwealth Bank of Australia* (1992) 66 A.L.J.R. 768, 788 (Dawson J.); *Moore v Vestry of Fulham* [1895] 1 Q.B. 399; cf. *Re Roberts* [1905] 1 Ch. 704, 710–711.

[1071] See, e.g. *South Australia Cold Stores Ltd v Electricity Trust of South Australia* (1957) 98 C.L.R. 65, 73–5; Bryan (1993) 15 Syd L. Rev 461, 479–80, 481; *Kleinwort Benson Ltd v Lincoln CC* [1999] 2 A.C. 349, 401 (Lord Hoffmann), 409 (Lord Hope), 412 (Lord Hope).

[1072] *Avon CC v Howlett* [1983] 1 W.L.R. 605, 620; *Akt Dampskibbs Steinstad v William Pearson & Co* (1927) 137 L.T. 533; *Westdeutsche Landesbank Girozentrale v Islington LBC* [1994] 4 All E.R. 890.

[1073] *Callisher v Bischoffsheim* (1870) L.R. 5 Q.B. 449; *Cook v Wright* (1861) 1 B & S 559; *Atlee v Backhouse* (1838) 3 M. & W. 633. See generally, above paras 3–050—3–053.

success.[1074] A compromise may be invalidated by a mistake, but not where the compromise was agreed on the basis of an erroneous assumption about the law.[1075]

Payment following simple demand. A payment following a simple but mistaken demand can be recovered, as there is neither a compromise of nor a submission to an honest claim. For example, in *Baylis v Bishop of London*[1076] restitution was granted where the plaintiffs had paid a rentcharge under a mistake of fact to the sequestrator of a benefice, thinking that a lease was in force when in fact it had expired. Money cannot, however, be recovered for mistake if it was paid for reasons other than the mistake, as there is no causal link between mistake and payment.[1077] 29–190

6. MISCELLANEOUS RESTITUTIONARY CLAIMS

(a) *Account Stated*[1078]

Different meanings of the term "account stated". The term "account stated" is applied in at least three ways[1079]: 29–191

(i) To a claim by one party to payment of a definite amount, which is admitted to be correct by the other party. This is merely an admission of a debt out of court[1080] and is equivalent to a promise from which the existence of a debt may be inferred.[1081] Such an admission is only evidence[1082] of a debt, and can be rebutted[1083]; an item in an account stated of this type can be challenged or explained,[1084] or the admission can be rebutted by evidence that there was no consideration for the promise to pay. In order to have this evidential effect, the admission of liability must be unqualified and must relate to an existing debt.[1085]

[1074] *Llewellyn v Llewellyn* (1854) 3 Dow. & L. 318; *Longridge v Dorville* (1821) 5 B. & Ald. 117; *Haigh v Brooks* (1839) 10 Ad. E. 309.

[1075] *Brennan v Bolt Burdon* [2004] EWCA Civ 1017, [2005] Q.B. 303. See further above, para.5–055.

[1076] [1913] 1 Ch. 127.

[1077] Above, paras 29–034, 29–047.

[1078] Accounts stated are for convenience considered in this Chapter, although they cannot properly be classified as restitutionary claims in any technical sense, but only in a broadly descriptive sense. See in general Bullen & Leake and Jacob's *Precedents of Pleadings*, 14th edn, pp.187–191, 917–919; *Atkin's Court Forms*, 2nd edn (2002), Vol.I.

[1079] *Siqueira v Noronha* [1934] A.C. 332, 337.

[1080] (1921) 38 T.L.R. 134.

[1081] *Barker v Birt* (1842) 10 M. & W. 61; *Perry v Slade* (1845) 8 Q.B. 115.

[1082] It is not evidence unless the defendant clearly acknowledged that a definite sum was due from him: *Hughes v Thorpe* (1839) 5 M. & W. 656; *Lane v Hill* (1852) 18 Q.B. 252. See also *Fesenmayer v Adcock* (1847) 16 M. & W. 449 (an IOU).

[1083] e.g. by showing that it was made in error. See *Lubbock v Tribe* (1838) 3 M. & W. 607, 612–613. The admission places on the defendant the burden of proving that it was erroneous: *Camillo Tank S.S. Co Ltd v Alexandria Engineering Works* (1921) 38 T.L.R. 134, 141, 143.

[1084] *Wilson v Wilson* (1854) 14 C.B. 616.

[1085] *Burgh v Legge* (1839) 5 M. & W. 418, 421–422. See also *Tucker v Barrow* (1828) 7 B. & C. 623; *Wayman v Hilliard* (1830) 7 Bing. 101; *Warwick v Warwick* (1918) 34 T.L.R. 475.

(ii) The items in an account may have been settled and agreed on the basis of some new valuable consideration received by the party who admitted that he owed the agreed sum, e.g. where the repairers of a ship released it to the owners without exercising their lien for the cost of the repairs.[1086]

(iii) "A real account stated"[1087] is one in which the account includes items on both sides and the parties have agreed that there shall be a set-off and only the balance shall be payable. The:

> "... several items of claim are brought into account on either side, and, being set against one another, a balance is struck and the consideration for the payment of the balance is the discharge of the items on each side."[1088]

Though such an arrangement has been regarded as quasi-contractual, it is more properly described as "a promise for good consideration to pay the balance"[1089]; and the consideration is valid and the settlement is binding even though some of the debts may be statute-barred,[1090] or otherwise unenforceable.[1091] Fraud, however, will permit the questioning of an account stated[1092]:

> "The essence of an account stated [in this third sense] is not the character of the items on one side or the other, but the fact that there are cross items of account and that the parties mutually agree the several amounts of each and, by treating the items so agreed on the one side as discharging the items on the other side *pro tanto*, go on to agree that the balance only is payable ... Nor can it be material ... whether the balance of indebtedness is throughout, as it must be at the end, in favour of one side."[1093]

An account stated in this sense is a new cause of action for the purpose of limitation.[1094] But where there are no mutual debits and credits, in that the whole accounting is to be rendered by one party to the other, so that all the items are on one side only, there can be no account stated in this sense.[1095] For an account stated in the third sense there must be an "absolute acknowledgment" of the balance due to the claimant[1096] without any qualification.[1097] The debt must also be acknowledged by the defendant in his personal capacity: thus, where the defendants, directors of a company who were indebted to it, signed a balance-

---

1086 *Camillo Tank S.S. Co Ltd v Alexandria Engineering Works* (1921) 38 T.L.R. 134 HL.
1087 *Re Laycock v Pickles* (1863) 4 B. & S. 497, 506.
1088 (1863) 4 B. & S. 497.
1089 *Siqueira v Noronha* [1934] A.C. 332, 337.
1090 [1934] A.C. 332. See also *Ashby v James* (1843) 11 M. & W. 542 and above, para.28–129.
1091 *Re Laycock v Pickles* (1863) 4 B. & S. 497. See also *Dawson v Remnant* (1806) 6 Esp. 24.
1092 *Vagliano Bros v Bank of England* (1889) 22 QBD 103, 127; reversed on other grounds: *Bank of England v Vagliano Bros* [1891] A.C. 107.
1093 *Bushun Chand (A Firm) v Seth Girdhari Lal* (1934) 50 T.L.R. 465, 468 PC: accounts between moneylender and borrower can be the subject of an account stated in this sense in the same way as accounts between banker and customer.
1094 *Bushun Chand (A Firm) v Seth Girdhari Lal* (1934) 50 T.L.R. 465.
1095 *Anglo-American Asphalt Co Ltd v Crowley, Russell & Co Ltd* (1945) 173 L.T. 228.
1096 *Day v William Hill (Park Lane) Ltd* [1949] 1 K.B. 632, 641.
1097 *Calvert v Baker* (1838) 4 M. & W. 417. cf. *Chisman v Count* (1841) 2 M. & G. 307.

sheet of the company which showed the amount due by each defendant to the company, the balance-sheet was held not to be an account stated since the defendants had signed, not with the intention of contracting, but solely in performance of their duty as directors.[1098] Again, an arbitrator is not the agent of the parties to settle accounts between them: hence, his award is not an account stated between them.[1099]

Illegal or unenforceable debts. An account stated will not lie if the original debt is absolutely void because it is based on an illegal[1100] or immoral consideration, or is made void by statute[1101]: 29–192

> "I do not think that, where a contract from its nature can give rise to no valid claim, a claim upon it can be used to found an action upon an account stated."[1102]

Thus, an account stated will not lie for betting transactions rendered void by statute,[1103] or for items due under a policy of marine insurance rendered invalid by statute.[1104] On the other hand, the fact that a debt was originally unenforceable through lack of admissible evidence will not invalidate a subsequent account stated based on that debt.[1105] Similarly, where by the Trade Union Act 1871 a contract in restraint of trade between members of a trade union was not directly enforceable, it could nevertheless be the basis of a subsequent account stated.[1106] But there can be no claim on an account stated where a statutory condition precedent to recovery has not been fulfilled.[1107]

(b) *Account*[1108]

Liability to account. In this group of cases the defendant is under a liability imposed on him to account to the claimant in respect of money or property received from a third person; or the claimant is entitled to be subrogated to the rights of another against a third person.[1109] 29–193

[1098] *John Shaw & Sons (Salford) Ltd v Shaw* [1935] 2 K.B. 113 (the word "Directors" was appended to their signatures). See also *Petch v Lyon* (1846) 9 Q.B. 147.

[1099] *Bates v Townley* (1848) 2 Ex. 152.

[1100] *Rose v Savory* (1835) 2 Bing. N.C. 145.

[1101] *Cocking v Ward* (1845) 1 C.B. 858, 870.

[1102] *Joseph Evans & Co Ltd v Heathcote* [1918] 1 K.B. 418, 427. See also *Kennedy v Broun* (1863) 13 C.B.(N.S.) 677 (claim for barrister's fees).

[1103] *Law v Dearnley* [1950] 1 K.B. 400; *Alberg v Chandler* (1948) 64 T.L.R. 394.

[1104] *Re Home and Colonial Insurance Co Ltd* [1930] 1 Ch. 102, 130.

[1105] *Cocking v Ward* (1845) 1 C.B. 858, 868. This was an account stated of the first type discussed above, para.29–191. But a document which is inadmissible for want of a stamp in one capacity cannot be relied on as proof of an account stated: Stamp Act 1891 s.14(4).

[1106] *Joseph Evans & Co Ltd v Heathcote* [1918] 1 K.B. 418.

[1107] *Scadding v Eyles* (1846) 9 Q.B. 858.

[1108] cf. the remedy of account of profits which is available where the defendant has committed a wrong, such as breach of contract. See above, para.29–152. See also paras 29–155 et seq.

[1109] See above, para.29–173.

29–194 **General principle.** The principle of a line of cases[1110] may be stated as follows[1111]: where the defendant holds a fund on behalf of a third person (or acknowledges that he owes a debt to the third person[1112]), and the third person directs the defendant to pay the claimant out of the fund or debt, then, if the defendant accepts that direction and promises the claimant to pay him accordingly, the claimant may seek restitution from the defendant by an action for money had and received. In the nineteenth century, the emphasis on privity of contract led to confusion in the judgments on this principle,[1113] but Blackburn J. in *Griffin v Weatherby*[1114] laid it down that the claimant's remedy was distinct from contract:

> "Ever since the case of *Walker v Rostron,*[1115] it has been considered as settled law that where a person transfers to a creditor on account of a debt, whether due or not, a fund actually existing or accruing in the hands of a third person, and notifies the transfer to the holder of the fund, although there is no legal obligation on the holder to pay the amount of the debt to the transferee, yet the holder of the fund may, and if he does promise to pay to the transferee, then that which was merely an equitable right becomes a legal right in the transferee, founded on the promise; and the money becomes a fund received or to be received for and payable to the transferee, and when it has been received an action for money had and received to the use of the transferee lies at his suit against the holder."

29–195 ***Shamia v Joory.*** In *Shamia v Joory*[1116] the defendant owed Y some £1,300 as remuneration for services rendered, and when Y requested the defendant to pay £500 from this money to the plaintiff (Y's brother), the defendant agreed to do so and wrote to the plaintiff promising to send him the money. The plaintiff later received a cheque for £500 from the defendant, but owing to a technical irregularity the cheque was not met. Although the defendant promised to send the corrected cheque back to the plaintiff, it was not sent, and the plaintiff sued to recover the £500 as money had and received by the defendant to the use of the claimant. Barry J. held that although the £500 was to be a gift from Y to the plaintiff,[1117] the plaintiff could recover the money under the principle laid down by Blackburn J., above; there was a "fund" in the defendant's hands when he accepted Y's instructions and promised the claimant to pay him. Barry J. held

---

[1110] e.g. *Israel v Douglas* (1789) 1 H. Bl. 239; *Stevens v Hill* (1805) 5 Esp. 247; *Williams v Everett* (1811) 14 East. 582; *Lilly v Hays* (1836) 5 A. & E. 548; *Hamilton v Spottiswoode* (1849) 4 Ex. 200; *Griffin v Weatherby* (1868) L.R. 3 Q.B. 753; *Shamia v Joory* [1958] 1 Q.B. 448.

[1111] Jackson, *History of Quasi-Contract* (1936), pp.30–34, 92–103; Munkman, *The Law of Quasi-contracts* at pp.52–61; Davies (1959) 75 L.Q.R. 220; Goff and Jones at Ch.28. See also above, para.19–089.

[1112] *Shamia v Joory* [1958] 1 Q.B. 448 supports the application of the principle to a defendant who is a debtor and holds no identifiable "fund". See the criticism of Davies (1959) 75 L.Q.R. 220 and *Liversidge v Broadbent* (1859) 4 H. & N. 603, which was not cited in *Shamia v Joory.*

[1113] Davies (1959) 75 L.Q.R. 220 also shows the confusion which arose from the doctrines of consideration and of novation.

[1114] (1868) L.R. 3 Q.B. 753, 758–759.

[1115] (1842) 9 M. & W. 411.

[1116] [1958] 1 Q.B. 448.

[1117] In most of the earlier cases, the plaintiff was a creditor of the third person, and not a donee. But see *Fleet v Perrins* (1869) L.R. 4 Q.B. 500 (which was a "donee" case not cited in *Shamia v Joory* [1958] 1 Q.B. 448).

that there was no need for the third person to hand an identifiable sum of money to the defendant before there could be a "fund" in the hands of the defendant. He said[1118]:

> " . . . all that the law requires[1119] is that there must be in the hands of or accruing to the third person, either a sum of money, or a monetary liability, over which the transferor has a right of disposal. It matters not . . . from what source the liability arises, and I see no reason why it should not include a debt for money lent, or goods sold, or services rendered, or a debt of any kind; nor do I think that the situation can be altered if the debt is of a temporary nature, which in the ordinary course of things would shortly be extinguished by items of contra account, provided, of course, that the debt still exists at the date of the transfer and of the debtor's promise of payment made to the transferee."

It appears from this judgment that the "fund" need not be a specific sum, but may be a general "monetary liability". However, the extension of the principle in *Shamia v Joory* has not been applied in any subsequent reported case, and its authority remains in some doubt.

Distinct from assignment. This principle is distinct from the equitable assignment of a chose in action[1120] which takes immediate effect as between the assignor and assignee, without any notice to the debtor[1121]: the third party in *Shamia v Joory* did not transfer anything until the defendant accepted his instruction, and the defendant was not bound to accept the third party's instruction, nor to make any promise of payment to the claimant. The consent of the third party or debtor is essential before the principle in *Shamia v Joory* can apply,[1122] whereas in assignment it is irrelevant.[1123] 29–196

Stakeholders: deposit till a claim is ascertained. A stakeholder is an agent who is entitled, during the continuance of his authority from a party to some arrangement, to make payment, in accordance with that authority, of the money lodged with him by that party. Thus, if A deposits money in the hands of a stakeholder, until the extent of a claim which B has upon A can be ascertained, the stakeholder cannot, before the claim is ascertained, legally pay the amount to B upon his indemnity without the consent of A; if the stakeholder does so, A may maintain an action for money had and received against him without reference to B's claim.[1124] Where a stake was deposited with the defendant to abide the result of a sculling race, but there was no proper start and no race as contemplated, it 29–197

[1118] *Shamia v Joory* [1958] 1 Q.B. 448, 459.

[1119] But see Davies (1959) 75 L.Q.R. 220, who cites *Liversidge v Broadbent* (1859) 4 H. & N. 603 as authority for the proposition that where the claimant is a creditor of the third party he cannot sue the defendant without furnishing consideration.

[1120] See above, paras 19–020 et seq. A statutory assignment requires written notice to the debtor: above, para.19–016. The principle is also distinct from novation (see above, paras 19–086 et seq.), and from a completely constituted trust: Davies (1959) 75 L.Q.R. 220.

[1121] See above, para.19–020.

[1122] The principle seems to be an "attornment" of money, similar to the attornment of a chattel (see Vol.II, para.33–030).

[1123] For a discussion of the earlier cases, see Davies (1959) 75 L.Q.R. 220.

[1124] *Cowling v Beachum* (1823) 7 Moore 465; on the deposit of a cheque with a stakeholder, see *Wilkinson v Godefroy* (1839) 9 A. & E. 536.

was held that the claimant could recover his stake.[1125] The authority of the stakeholder may be withdrawn before he has acted on it: thus, it has been held that the Gaming Act 1892 did not prevent the recovery by the claimant of money deposited with a stakeholder to abide the result of a wager where the claimant demands his deposit back before it has been paid over by the stakeholder to the winner, since, until actual payment, the stakeholder remains the agent of the claimant in regard to the claimant's stake.[1126]

29–198 **Auctioneer, solicitor and estate agent as stakeholder.** On a sale of goods an auctioneer has implied authority to receive the sale proceeds[1127]; on a sale of an interest in land his only authority is to receive the deposit, unless he is expressly authorised otherwise.[1128] Generally he receives the deposit merely as a stakeholder, in which case he should retain it until the contract is either carried into effect or rescinded and the party entitled to the deposit ascertained.[1129] Where a deposit is paid to an auctioneer as a stakeholder, and the payment to the vendor is to depend on his making a good title to the property sold, the purchaser may, on the vendor failing to make out such title, recover the deposit from the auctioneer without giving him notice that he has rescinded the contract.[1130] Where a solicitor acting for a vendor receives the deposit as agent for the vendor, the law will not imply that he receives it as stakeholder (as in the case of an auctioneer); hence he is bound to pay the deposit to the vendor on demand.[1131] An estate agent who is authorised to find a purchaser for land is not (in the absence of express or implied authority to do so) authorised as agent for the owner to receive a pre-contract "deposit" from a potential purchaser.[1132]

1125 *Sadler v Smith* (1869) L.R. 5 Q.B. 40.

1126 *O'Sullivan v Thomas* [1895] 1 Q.B. 698; *Burge v Ashley Ltd* [1900] 1 Q.B. 744 CA. Such recovery was permitted before the Act: *Hampden v Walsh* (1876) 1 QBD 189; *Diggle v Higgs* (1877) 2 Ex. D. 422. See now the Gambling Act 2005, Vol.II, Ch.40. See further on the position of a stakeholder in respect of a wager, Vol.II, paras 40–043 et seq.

1127 *Williams v Millington* (1788) 1 H.Bl. 81.

1128 *Sykes v Giles* (1839) 5 M. & W. 645.

1129 *Harington v Hoggart* (1830) 1 B. & Ad. 577, 588–589. cf. *Skinner v The Trustee of the Property of Reed* [1967] Ch. 1194. A stakeholder is not accountable for any interest earned by the deposit while it is in his control, whereas an ordinary agent is so accountable: *Harington v Hoggart* (1850) 1 B. & Ad. 577, 587; *Potters (A Firm) v Loppert* [1973] Ch. 399. cf. *Brown v IRC* [1965] A.C. 244 (followed by the Solicitors Act 1974 s.33 (replacing the Solicitors Act 1965 s.8)).

1130 *Duncan v Cafe* (1837) 2 M. & W. 244.

1131 *Edgell v Day* (1865) L.R. 1 C.P. 80.

1132 *Sorrell v Finch* [1977] A.C. 728. Until a binding contract is made, the estate agent, on demand by the potential purchaser, must repay the "deposit" to him without reference to the vendor. See Vol.II, paras 31–109, 31–113. See also the Estate Agents Act 1979 ss.13, 14.

Part Ten
CONFLICT OF LAWS

Chapter 30

CONFLICT OF LAWS

		PARA.
1.	Preliminary considerations	30–001
2.	Common law: the doctrine of the proper law of a contract	30–005
3.	The Rome Convention	30–017
	(a) In general	30–017
	(b) Exclusions	30–030
	(c) Choice of law by the parties	30–047
	(d) Applicable law in the absence of choice by the parties	30–071
	(e) Certain consumer contracts and individual employment contracts	30–092
	(f) Voluntary assignments and subrogation	30–123
4.	The Rome I Regulation	30–130
	(a) In general	30–130
	(b) Exclusions	30–152
	(c) Habitual residence	30–164
	(d) Freedom of choice	30–170
	(e) Applicable law in the absence of choice	30–186
	(f) Contracts of carriage	30–209
	(g) Consumer contracts	30–231
	(h) Insurance contracts	30–252
	(i) Individual employment contracts	30–276
	(j) Voluntary assignment and contractual subrogation	30–288
	(k) Legal subrogation	30–293
	(l) Multiple liability	30–296
	(m) Set-off	30–299
5.	Scope of the applicable law	30–303
	(a) Material validity of the contract	30–304
	(b) Formal validity of the contract	30–310
	(c) Capacity	30–323
	(d) Particular issues: article 10	30–326
	(e) Burden of proof, etc.	30–351
	(f) Illegality and public policy	30–355
	(g) Foreign currency obligations	30–369

1. Preliminary Considerations

Introduction. A contract may be connected with several territorial jurisdictions because the parties to it reside in different countries, or because the contract is made in one country but is to be performed in a different country or concerns subject-matter which is situated in a different country, or for other reasons. In 30–001 such cases it may become necessary to determine which legal system is to govern the contract or a particular aspect of it, i.e. to determine what is the law applicable to the contract.[1]

30–002 **Sources of the law.** This chapter is concerned with the elucidation of the choice of law rules according to which the law applicable to a contract which is connected with more than one territorial jurisdiction is determined.[2] Originally, these rules were to be found in the common law as developed by the courts. According to these rules, a contract was governed by its "proper law".[3] These common law rules were first substantially reformulated as a result of the implementation in the United Kingdom of the Rome (EC) Convention on the Law Applicable to Contractual Obligations 1980 ("the Rome Convention") in the Contracts (Applicable Law) Act 1990. The rules of that Convention, as implemented in the Act of 1990, will apply to determine the law applicable to a contract which is entered into after April 1, 1991,[4] but before December 17, 2009. As from the latter date, the Rome Convention is replaced by Regulation (EC) 593/2008 of June 17, 2008 on the law applicable to contractual obligations (Rome I).[5] This Regulation (hereafter "the Rome I Regulation" or "the Regulation") arose out of a revision of the Rome Convention and will apply to determine the law applicable to contracts concluded after its date of application, December 17, 2009.[6]

30–003 **Structure of this Chapter.** This Chapter gives a brief account of the common law principles, by way of background, in section 2.[7] Section 3[8] seeks to analyse the provisions of the Rome Convention, since these will form the basis of the law until the Rome I Regulation takes effect. Section 4[9] provides a commentary on the Rome I Regulation, drawing attention to similarities and differences between the earlier Convention and the Regulation, as relevant. Section 5[10] explores the

---

[1] It will also be necessary to decide whether the court of the forum, i.e. the English court, has *jurisdiction* to entertain an action arising out of such a contract. On the issue of jurisdiction in such cases, see *Dicey, Morris and Collins on the Conflict of Laws*, 14th edn (2006), Chs 10–13; Cheshire and North, *Private International Law*, 13th edn (1999), Chs 10–14.

[2] It is not concerned with the rules as to the jurisdiction of English courts: see preceding note. Nor is it concerned with the rules relating to the recognition of foreign judgments, as to which see *Dicey, Morris and Collins*, Chs 14 and 15; Cheshire and North, Chs 15 and 16. The conflict of laws' aspects of arbitration (as to which see *Dicey, Morris and Collins* at Ch.16; Cheshire and North at Ch.17) are similarly excluded. For the conflict of laws with regard to negotiable instruments see below, paras 30–038—30–039 and Vol.II, paras 34–197 et seq. Some contracts for the sale of goods made on or after August 18, 1972, which are connected with several territorial jurisdictions may be governed by the provisions of the Uniform Law on International Sales Act 1967 and will not necessitate examination of the rules of the conflict of laws: Sch.I art.2. See Vol.II, para.43–003.

[3] See below, paras 30–005—30–016.

[4] The date on which the 1990 Act entered into force: see Rome Convention art.17; *Society of Lloyd's v Fraser* [1998] C.L.C. 1630, 1651.

[5] Regulation (EC) 593/2008 of June 17, 2008 on the law applicable to contractual obligations (Rome I) [2008] OJ L177/6.

[6] Rome I Regulation arts 28, 29.

[7] Below, paras 30–005 et seq.

[8] Below, paras 30–017 et seq.

[9] Below, paras 30–130 et seq.

[10] Below, paras 30–303 et seq.

scope of the applicable law and the relevance of other laws in the context of the incidents of the contract and the various issues which may arise in a contractual context. That section considers these matters from the perspective of the common law, the Rome Convention and the Rome I Regulation.

Terminology. The Rome Convention and the Rome I Regulation do not adopt the familiar terminology of the common law; in particular, they abandon the linguistic usage "proper law of a contract" and replace that usage with their own terminology. This terminology is variously, "applicable law," "law applicable to the contract," "governing law" or "law governing the contract." This terminology is used interchangeably in sections 3, 4 and 5 of the Chapter. The phrase "proper law of a contract" is, however, retained for the purpose of the discussion of the common law in section 2. 30–004

2. COMMON LAW: THE DOCTRINE OF THE PROPER LAW OF A CONTRACT[11]

Statement of the doctrine. The modern approach to the problem of determining the proper law of a contract involves the need to examine three possible situations.[12] If the parties have made an express choice of law in the contract itself, then, subject to certain limitations,[13] the law that they have chosen will govern. If there is no express choice, the court must examine all the facts surrounding the contract to determine whether there was an inferred or implied choice of law by the parties. In the absence of any choice, express or implied, the court ceases to look for the intention of the parties (since they are presumed to have no intention on the point) and proceeds, on objective grounds, to determine and apply "the system of law with which the transaction has the closest and most 30–005

[11] For more detailed accounts of the common law position, see the 26th edn of this work, Ch.30; *Dicey & Morris on the Conflict of Laws*, 11th edn (1987), Chs 32 and 33; Cheshire and North, *Private International Law*, 11th edn (1987), Ch.18.

[12] *Amin Rasheed Shipping Corp v Kuwait Insurance Co* [1984] A.C. 50, 51. For a short historical account of the development leading to this view, see *Dicey, Morris and Collins on the Conflict of Laws*, 14th edn (2006), paras 32–003—32–007. The detail may be traced through *Robinson v Bland* (1760) 2 Burr. 1077; *Lloyd v Guibert* (1865) L.R. 1 Q.B. 115: *P. & O. S.S. Co v Shand* (1865) 3 Moo. P.C. (N.S.) 272; *Chartered Mercantile Bank of India v Netherlands Co* (1883) 10 QBD 521; *Jacobs v Crédit Lyonnais* (1884) 12 QBD 589; *Re Missouri Steamship Co* (1889) 42 Ch D 321; *Hamlyn v Talisker Distillery* [1894] A.C. 202; *Spurrier v La Cloche* [1902] A.C. 446; *NV Kwik Hoo Tong Handel Maatschappij v James Finlay & Co* [1927] A.C. 604; *R. v International Trustee for the Protection of Bondholders AG* [1937] A.C. 500; *Mount Albert BC v Australasian, etc, Assurance Building Society Ltd* [1938] A.C. 224; *Vita Food Products Inc v Unus Shipping Co Ltd* [1939] A.C. 277; *Kahler v Midland Bank Ltd* [1950] A.C. 24; *Bonython v Commonwealth of Australia* [1951] A.C. 201; *The Assunzione* [1954] P. 150; *Re Helbert Wagg & Co Ltd's Claim* [1956] Ch. 323; *Re United Railway of the Havana and Regla Warehouses Ltd* [1960] Ch. 52 (affirmed sub nom. *Tomkinson v First Pennsylvania Banking and Trust Co* [1961] A.C. 1007); *James Miller and Partners Ltd v Whitworth Street Estates (Manchester) Ltd* [1970] A.C. 583; *Compagnie Tunisienne de Navigation SA v Compagnie d'Armement Maritime SA* [1971] A.C. 572; *Coast Lines Ltd v Hudig and Veder Chartering NV* [1972] 2 Q.B. 34; *Amin Rasheed Shipping Corp v Kuwait Insurance Co.*

[13] Below, paras 30–007—30–008.

real connection".[14] It is, however, often difficult to distinguish between the second and third approaches, i.e. implied choice and no choice, and the same decision may well be justified on either approach.[15] What is clear is that there must be a proper law and that it is not possible to have a contract which is not governed by some system of private law.[16] Furthermore, there must be a proper law from the time that the contract is made.[17] There cannot be a proper law which "floats", i.e. is not identified when the contract is made but which is left to be determined later by the unilateral act of one of the parties.[18] In determining the governing law at the time the contract was made, conduct or events subsequent to that date cannot be taken into account.[19] A contract can, however, validly provide for two proper laws, the second to be applied if the event on which the application of the first depends is negatived.[20] This would also support the view

---

[14] e.g. *Bonython v Commonwealth of Australia* [1951] A.C. 201, 219; *The Assunzione* [1954] P. 150; *Re United Railways of the Havana and Regla Warehouses Ltd* [1960] Ch. 52, 91–92, 115 (affirmed sub nom. *Tomkinson v First Pennsylvania Banking and Trust Co* [1961] A.C. 1007, 1068, 1081–1082); *Philipson-Stow v Inland Revenue Commissioners* [1961] A.C. 727, 760; *James Miller and Partners Ltd v Whitworth Street Estates (Manchester) Ltd* [1970] A.C. 583; *Compagnie d'Armement Maritime SA v Compagnie Tunisienne de Navigation SA* [1971] A.C. 572; *Coast Lines Ltd v Hudig and Veder Chartering NV* [1972] 2 Q.B. 34; *Amin Rasheed Shipping Corp v Kuwait Insurance Co* [1984] A.C. 50. Early decisions tended to express this idea in the language of the presumed intention of the parties rather than as a purely objective test which applied because of an absence of intent as to the applicable law. See, e.g. *Lloyd v Guibert* (1865) L.R. 1 Q.B. 115; *Mount Albert BC v Australasian, etc, Assurance Building Society Ltd* [1938] A.C. 224; *Kahler v Midland Bank Ltd* [1950] A.C. 24; *The Assunzione*.

[15] See the views of Lord Diplock and Lord Wilberforce in *Amin Rasheed Shipping Corp v Kuwait Insurance Co* [1894] A.C. 50. The former (speaking for the majority) treated the case as one of implied choice, the latter as one of no choice. See also *Armadora Occidental SA v Horace Mann Insurance Co* [1977] 1 W.L.R. 520 (implied choice) (affirmed 1098 (no choice)).

[16] *Amin Rasheed Shipping Corp v Kuwait Insurance Co* [1894] A.C. 50, 65. The proper law, at common law, must be the law of a country: *Musawi v R E International (UK) Ltd* [2007] EWHC 2981 (Ch); [2008] 1 Lloyd's Rep. 382.

[17] *Armar Shipping Co Ltd v Caisse Algérienne* [1981] 1 W.L.R. 207; *Black Clawson International Ltd v Papierwerke Waldhof-Aschaffenburgh AG* [1981] 2 Lloyd's Rep. 446, 456; *The Blue Wave* [1982] 1 Lloyd's Rep. 380, 385; *Cantieri Navali Riuniti S.p.A. v NV Omne Justitia* [1985] 2 Lloyd's Rep. 428, 435; *The Frank Pais* [1986] 1 Lloyd's Rep. 428, 435; *Star Shipping A.S. v China National Foreign Trade Transportation Corp* [1993] 2 Lloyd's Rep. 445. See also *XL Insurance v Owens Corning* [2000] 2 Lloyd's Rep. 500.

[18] *Armar Shipping Co Ltd v Caisse Algérienne* [1981] 1 W.L.R. 207, 215–216; *Astro Venturoso Compania Naviera v Hellenic Shipyards SA* [1983] 1 Lloyd's Rep. 12, 15; *E.I. Du Pont de Nemours v Agnew* [1987] 2 Lloyd's Rep. 585, 592; *Star Shipping A.S. v China National Foreign Trade Transportation Corp* [1993] 2 Lloyd's Rep. 445 (but there is no objection to an arbitration subject to a "floating" curial law).

[19] *James Miller and Partners Ltd v Whitworth Street Estates (Manchester) Ltd* [1970] A.C. 583, 603, 611, 614–615; *Compagnie d'Armement Maritime SA v Compagnie Tunisienne de Navigation SA* [1971] A.C. 572, 593, 595–596, 603; *Armar Shipping Co Ltd v Caisse Algérienne* [1981] 1 W.L.R. 207; *Amin Rasheed Shipping Corp v Kuwait Insurance Co* [1984] A.C. 50, 69. Such subsequent conduct may be relevant in determining whether the parties have entered a new collateral contract (*James Miller and Partners Ltd v Whitworth Street Estates (Manchester) Ltd* 603, 614–615; *Compagnie d'Armement Maritime SA v Compagnie Tunisienne de Navigation SA* 602–608) or as evidence of estoppel (*James Miller and Partners Ltd v Whitworth Street Estates (Manchester) Ltd* 611, 614–615). As to the position under the Rome Convention and the Rome I Regulation, see below, paras 30–054, 30–204. Effect will be given, however, to later changes in a foreign applicable law: see below, para.30–009.

[20] *Astro Venturoso Compania Naviera v Hellenic Shipyards SA* [1983] 2 Lloyd's Rep. 12.

that the proper law can be changed by the parties during the currency of the contract.[21]

Express choice of law. Determination of the proper law of the contract should not normally involve any difficulty if the parties have stipulated expressly which legal system is to apply to their agreement.[22] Where it is concluded that the choice of law by the parties is meaningless, the express choice will be ignored and the proper law determined by reference to any implied choice or, failing that, the most closely connected system of law.[23] An issue may arise as to the validity of the term which purports to choose the proper law. There is little direct authority on this issue. There is support of the application of English law as the law of the forum to the question,[24] but the better view is to apply the law that would govern if the choice is valid.[25] 30–006

Limitations on power to choose: common law. The parties' power to choose the proper law is limited, first, by virtue of an obscure judicial formula which requires that the choice must be "bona fide and legal".[26] The possible effect of this formula (which has never been applied in England to strike down a choice of law) is: 30–007

> "... that the parties cannot pretend to contract under one law in order to validate an agreement that clearly has its closest connection with another law. If, after having discovered that one particular provision was void under the proper law, they were to try to evade its consequences by claiming that the provision was subject to another legal system, their claim should not be considered as a bona fide expression of their intentions."[27]

---

[21] *James Miller and Partners Ltd v Whitworth Street Estates (Manchester) Ltd* [1970] A.C. 583, 603, 614; *Black Clawson International Ltd v Papierwerke Waldhof-Aschaffenburg AG* [1981] 2 Lloyd's Rep. 151, 153; *E.I. du Pont de Nemours v Agnew* [1987] 2 Lloyd's Rep. 585, 592; *Libyan Arab Foreign Bank v Bankers Trust Co* [1989] Q.B. 728, 747. cf. *Armar Shipping Co Ltd v Caisse Algérienne* [1981] 1 W.L.R. 207, 216. As to the position under the Rome Convention and the Rome I Regulation, see below, paras 30–058, 30–176.

[22] See, e.g. *Mackender v Feldia AG* [1967] 2 Q.B. 590; *Compagnie d'Armement Maritime SA v Compagnie Tunisienne de Navigation SA* [1971] A.C. 572.

[23] *Compagnie d'Armement Maritime SA v Compagnie Tunisienne de Navigation SA* [1969] 1 W.L.R. 1338 (reversed on a different view of the facts [1971] A.C. 572). Mere difficulty in ascertaining the chosen law will not render the choice ineffective: see, e.g. *The Blue Wave* [1982] 1 Lloyd's Rep. 151; *Star Shipping SA v China National Foreign Trade Transportation Corp* [1993] 2 Lloyd's Rep. 445.

[24] *Mackender v Feldia AG* [1967] 2 Q.B. 590, 598, 603, 605; *Chevron International Oil Co Ltd v A/S Sea Team* [1983] 2 Lloyd's Rep. 356, 358–458.

[25] See *Compagnia Naviera Micro SA v Shipley International Inc* [1982] 2 Lloyd's Rep. 351. This is the position under the Rome Convention arts 3(4) and 8 and the Rome I Regulation arts 3(5) and 10: see below, paras 30–059, 30–184.

[26] *Vita Food Products Inc v Unus Shipping Co Ltd* [1939] A.C. 277, 290.

[27] Cheshire and North, *Private International Law*, 11th edn (1987) p.454; see also, *Dicey & Morris on the Conflict of Laws*, 11th edn (1987), pp.1175–1176. And see *Boissevain v Weil* [1949] 1 K.B. 482, 490 (affirmed on other grounds [1950] A.C. 327); *English v Donnelly* (1958) S.C. 494; *Kay's Leasing Corp Pty Ltd v Fletcher* (1964) 116 C.L.R. 124, 143–144; *Golden Acres Ltd v Queensland Estates Ltd* [1969] St. R. Qd. 378 (affirmed on different grounds sub nom. *Freehold Land Investments Ltd v Queensland Estates Ltd* (1970) 123 C.L.R. 418); *Nike Information Systems Ltd v Avac Systems Ltd* (1979) 105 D.L.R. (3d) 455; *Greenshields Inc v Johnston* (1981) 119 D.L.R. (3d) 714 (appeal dismissed (1981) 131 D.L.R. (3d) 234); *Bank of Montreal v Snoxell* (1982) 143 D.L.R. (3d) 349.

Secondly, it has been said "that there must be no reason for avoiding [the choice] on the ground of public policy",[28] a limitation which is merely an example of the general principle that a foreign law will not be enforced if it offends English public policy.[29] Thirdly, it has sometimes been suggested that some sort of connection may possibly have to exist between the transaction and the chosen system of law, other than the mere fact that that law has been chosen.[30] The better view appears to be that no such connection need exist, though the absence of such a connection may be evidence that the choice of law is not "bona fide and legal" as described above.[31]

30–008 **Statutory limitations.** The power to choose a proper law may be restricted by statute. Thus, for example, the Unfair Contract Terms Act 1977 makes provision to prevent the use of choice of law clauses to evade the controls on exemption clauses imposed by the Act.[32] The controls cannot be evaded by the choice of the law of a country outside the United Kingdom as the governing law, if it either appears that the choice of law was imposed wholly or mainly to enable the party imposing it to evade the operation of the Act,[33] or where one of the parties dealt as consumer[34] and he was then habitually resident in the United Kingdom and the essential steps for the making of the contract were taken in the United Kingdom.[35] However, the controls in the 1977 Act do not apply where the law applicable to the contract is the law of a part of the United Kingdom only by reason of the choice of the parties,[36] nor do they apply to "international supply contracts".[37] Not all English statutes which express stringent social policy

---

[28] *Vita Food Products Inc v Unus Shipping Co Ltd* [1939] A.C. 277, 290.

[29] See generally *Dicey, Morris and Collins*, paras 5–002—5–006, 32–230—32–241; Cheshire and North, *Private International Law*, 13th edn (1999), pp.123–132, 584–586. And see below, paras 30–183, 30–355 et seq.

[30] *Boissevain v Weil* [1949] 1 K.B. 482, 490 (affirmed on other grounds [1950] A.C. 327); *Re Helbert Wagg & Co Ltd's Claim* [1956] Ch. 323, 341; *The Fehmarn* [1958] 1 W.L.R. 159. See also *The Hollandia* [1983] 1 A.C. 565, 576.

[31] *Vita Food Products Inc v Unus Shipping Co Ltd* [1939] A.C. 277, 290; *British Controlled Oilfields v Stagg* [1921] W.N. 31. There will often be good commercial grounds for choosing a geographically unconnected system, as, e.g. where the parties select a particular system of law because it is neutral: cf. *Steel Authority of India Ltd v Hind Metals Inc* [1984] 1 Lloyd's Rep. 405, 409; *Akai Pty Ltd v People's Insurance Co Ltd* [1998] 1 Lloyd's Rep. 90.

[32] See *Balmoral Group Ltd v Borealis (UK) Ltd* [2006] EWHC 1900 (Comm), [2006] 2 Lloyd's Rep. 629 at [436]–[448]. For detailed discussion, see *Benjamin's Sale of Goods*, 7th edn (2006), paras 25–090—25–100, 25–159—25–160; *Dicey, Morris and Collins*, paras 33–033—33–035, 33–126—33–128.

[33] Unfair Contract Terms Act 1977 s.27(2)(a).

[34] s.12.

[35] s.27(2)(b).

[36] s.27(1). See *Surzur Overseas Ltd v Ocean Reliance Shipping Co Ltd* [1997] C.L. 318. And see below, para.30–068. Note a similar provision in the (Australian) Insurance Contracts Act 1984 s.8, as to which see *Akai Pty Ltd v The People's Insurance Co Ltd* (1996) 188 C.L.R. 418 cf. *Akai Pty Ltd v People's Insurance Co Ltd* [1998] 1 Lloyd's Rep. 90. See also Late Payment of Commercial Debts (Interest) Act 1998 s.12, below, paras 30–341 et seq.

[37] Unfair Contract Terms Act 1977 s.26. On the meaning of "international supply contract", see *Ocean Chemical Transport Inc v Exnor Craggs Ltd* [2000] 1 All E.R. (Comm) 519; *Amiri Flight Authority v BAE Systems Plc* [2002] EWHC 2481 (Comm); [2003] 1 All E.R. (Comm) 1. See below, paras 30–068, 30–103.

contain (as does the Unfair Contract Terms Act[38]) any indication as to whether their provisions override a choice of a foreign law. Whether any particular statute, or provision thereof, has such an effect ultimately depends on the construction of the statute.[39]

30–009 **Incorporation by reference.**[40] There is a necessary distinction to be drawn between an express selection by the parties of the proper law to govern the whole contract and the incorporation into the contract of the provisions of some foreign legal system to govern some particular incident of the contract, such as the time at which property or risk should pass under a contract for the sale of goods. In these circumstances the provisions of the foreign law become terms of the contract and the reference to the foreign rules is a shorthand method of incorporating these rules into the contract rather than including a verbatim statement of the rules in the contract.[41] Nevertheless, the question whether a rule of foreign law has been effectively incorporated is a matter for the proper law of the contract. The importance of the distinction between selection of the proper law and incorporation of provisions of a foreign law into the contract by reference is seen most clearly where there is a change in the foreign law between the date of the contract and the time of the proceedings. The proper law selected is normally that of the country in question as existing from time to time with the changes that may befall it,[42] whilst if the provisions of a foreign law are incorporated they

[38] See too, Directive 93/13 on unfair terms in consumer contracts [1993] OJ L95/29 art.6(2), implemented in the United Kingdom in the Unfair Terms in Consumer Contracts Regulations 1999 (SI 1999/2083) as amended by SI 2000/1186, amending SI 1994/3159 reg.9; Directive 1997/7 on the protection of consumers in respect of "distance contracts" [1997] OJ L144/19 art.10(2), implemented in the United Kingdom by the Consumer Protection (Distance Selling) Regulations 2000 (SI 2000/2334) reg.25(5). cf. Directive 1999/44 on certain aspects of the sale of consumer goods and associated guarantees [1999] OJ L171/7 art.7(2). This provision is not reproduced in the Sale and Supply of Goods to Consumers Regulations 2002 (SI 2002/3045) and the application of the Regulations in the context of the conflict of laws appears to depend on Unfair Contract Terms Act 1977 ss.26 and 27. See below, para.30–103.

[39] See, e.g. *The Hollandia* [1983] A.C. 565 (no freedom to avoid operation of Carriage of Goods by Sea Act 1971 by choice of law clause); *English v Donnelly* (1958) S.C. 494 (Scottish hire-purchase legislation mandatory in effect); *Chiron Corp v Organon Teknika (No.2)* [1993] F.S.R. 567 (Patents Act 1977 s.44 applied to contract governed by foreign law); *DR Insurance Co v Central National Insurance Co* [1996] 1 Lloyd's Rep. 74 (Insurance Companies Act 1982 applied to reinsurance contracts whatever their proper law). See generally, *Dicey, Morris and Collins*, paras 32–132—32–137. As to the application of the Consumer Credit Act 1974 and orders made thereunder, see *Office of Fair Trading v Lloyds TSB Bank Plc* [2007] UKHL 48, [2007] 3 W.L.R. 733; *Dicey, Morris and Collins*, paras 33–036—33–041.

[40] *Dicey, Morris and Collins*, paras 32–088—32–090.

[41] *Ex p. Dever re Suse and Sibeth* (1887) 18 QBD 660; *Dobell & Co v Steamship Rossmore Co* [1895] 2 Q.B. 408; *Vita Food Products Inc v Unus Shipping Co Ltd* [1939] A.C. 277; *Ocean S.S. Co Ltd v Queensland State Wheat Board* [1941] 1 Q.B. 402; *Re Helbert Wagg & Co Ltd's Claim* [1956] Ch. 323; *Amin Rasheed Shipping Corp v Kuwait Insurance Co* [1984] A.C. 50, 69–70; *D R Insurance Co v Central Insurance Co* [1996] 1 Lloyd's Rep. 74, 81; *The Stolt Sydness* [1996] 1 Lloyd's Rep. 273; *Shamil Bank of Bahrain v Beximco Pharmaceuticals Ltd* [2004] EWCA Civ 19, [2004] 1 W.L.R. 1784; *Halpern v Halpern (Nos 1 and 2)* [2007] EWCA Civ 291, [2008] Q.B. 195 at [31]–[35] (both cases on the Rome Convention).

[42] *Re Chesterman's Trusts* [1923] 2 Ch. 466; *R. v International Trustee for the Protection of Bondholders AG* [1937] A.C. 500; *Kahler v Midland Bank Ltd* [1950] A.C. 24; *Zivnostenska Banka*

become terms of the contract as at the date of incorporation even though such foreign provisions may later be repealed or amended.[43]

30–010 **Implied choice of law.** Where there is no, or no valid, express choice of the proper law in the contract, the court may, nevertheless, be able to conclude that the parties have by implication (or by inference) come to an agreement[44] as to what should be the proper law.[45] Such an implication may be derived from a variety of factors surrounding the contract, the most usual being jurisdiction or arbitration clauses. If the parties agree that the courts of a particular country shall have jurisdiction over any claims made under the contract, that will give rise to a strong implication that the parties have chosen the law of that country as the proper law.[46] Similarly, if the contract contains a clause whereby the parties agree that any disputes shall be submitted to arbitration in a particular country, there is a powerful,[47] though not conclusive,[48] implication that the parties have selected the law of the country of arbitration as the proper law. A variety of other factors

---

v Frankman [1950] A.C. 57; *Jabbour v Custodian of Israeli Absentee Property* [1954] 1 W.L.R. 139; *Re Helbert Wagg & Co Ltd's Claim* [1956] Ch. 323; *Rossano v Manufacturers' Life Insurance Co* [1963] 2 Q.B. 352, 362.

[43] *Vita Food Products Inc v Unus Shipping Co Ltd* [1939] A.C. 277, 286.

[44] There must be actual agreement on the point: *James Miller and Partners Ltd v Whitworth Street Estates (Manchester) Ltd* [1970] A.C. 583, 603.

[45] *R. v International Trustee for the Protection of Bondholders AG* [1937] A.C. 500, 529–531; *Re United Railways of the Havana and Regla Warehouses* [1960] Ch. 52 (affirmed sub nom. *Tomkinson v First Pennsylvania Banking and Trust Co* [1961] A.C. 1007); *James Miller and Partners Ltd v Whitworth Street Estates (Manchester) Ltd* [1970] A.C. 583, 603; *Amin Rasheed Shipping Corp v Kuwait Insurance Co* [1984] A.C. 50.

[46] *Hamlyn & Co v Talisker Distillery* [1894] A.C. 202; *NV Kwik Hoo Tong Handel Maatschappij v James Finlay & Co* [1927] A.C. 604, 608; *Evans Marshall & Co Ltd v Bertola SA* [1973] 1 W.L.R. 349, 364; *The Komninos S* [1991] 1 Lloyd's Rep. 370. The effect of such a clause cannot be by-passed by attempting to formulate a claim in tort rather than in contract: *The Sindh* [1975] 1 Lloyd's Rep. 372.

[47] *Hamlyn & Co v Talisker Distillery* [1894] A.C. 202; *Spurrier v La Cloche* [1902] A.C. 446; *NV Kwik Hoo Tong Handel Maatschappij v James Finlay & Co* [1927] A.C. 604, 608; *Compagnie d'Armement Maritime SA v Compagnie Tunisienne de Navigation SA* [1971] A.C. 572; *The SLS Everest* [1981] 2 Lloyd's Rep. 389; *Compania Naviera Micro SA v Shipley International Inc* [1982] 2 Lloyd's Rep. 351; *Astro Venturoso Compania Naviera v Hellenic Shipyards SA* [1983] 1 Lloyd's Rep. 12; *Steel Authority of India Ltd v Hind Metals Inc* [1984] 1 Lloyd's Rep. 405. cf. *XL Insurance Ltd v Owens Corning* [2000] 2 Lloyd's Rep. 500 (insurance policy governed by New York law as a result of express choice, arbitration clause governed by English law since the parties had stipulated for arbitration in London under the Arbitration Act 1996).

[48] *Compagnie d'Armement Maritime SA v Compagnie Tunisienne de Navigation SA* [1971] A.C. 572 (disapproving *Tzortzis v Monark Link A/B* [1968] 1 W.L.R. 406 where the implication to be derived from an arbitration clause was treated as virtually conclusive); *The Elli 2* [1985] 2 Lloyd's Rep. 107, 117; *Star Shipping AS v China National Trade Transportation Corp* [1993] 2 Lloyd's Rep. 445; *C v D* [2007] EWCA Civ 1282, [2008] 1 Lloyd's Rep. 239. Where a clause provides for arbitration in a country other than that which is held to be that of the proper law, the curial law of the arbitration proceedings is that of the arbitration forum: *James Miller and Partners Ltd v Whitworth Street Estates (Manchester) Ltd* [1970] A.C. 583. See also *XL Insurance Ltd v Owens Corning* [2000] 2 Lloyd's Rep. 500. There is no reason why the curial law of an arbitration has to be fixed at the time of the arbitration agreement: *Star Shipping AS v China National Foreign Trade Transportation Corp*. On conflict of laws' aspects of arbitration see *Dicey, Morris and Collins*, Ch.16.

may also, in appropriate cases, give rise to an implication that the parties have made a choice of the proper law.

Relevant factors. Such factors have included the nature of the particular transaction,[49] the form of the documents made with respect to the transaction,[50] the style and terminology in which the contract is drafted,[51] the use of a particular language[52] (though this is a factor of minor importance[53]), the currency in which payment is to be made,[54] the use of a "follow London" clause,[55] the nature and location of the subject matter of the contract,[56] the residence[57] and, occasionally, the nationality[58] of the parties, a connection with a preceding transaction,[59] or, 30–011

---

[49] *Trade Indemnity Plc v Forsakringsaktiebolaget Njord* [1995] 1 All E.R. 796 (strong presumption that reinsurance contract written on London market is written on the basis of an implied or imputed English proper law); *DR Insurance Co v Central National Insurance Co* [1996] 1 Lloyd's Rep. 74 (when parties enter a particular market in order to transact business they can usually be taken to intend that their relationship will be governed by the system of law in force in that market unless they provide some clear indication to the contrary); *Tiernan v Magen Insurance Co Ltd* [2000] I.L. Pr. 517 (a case on the Rome Convention); *Ace Insurance SA-NV v Zurich Insurance Co of Europe* [2000] 2 Lloyd's Rep. 423, affirmed [2001] EWCA Civ 173, [2001] 1 Lloyd's Rep. 618; *Chase v Ram Technical Services Ltd* [2000] 2 Lloyd's Rep. 418. cf. *Commercial Union Assurance Co Plc v N R G Victory Reinsurance Ltd* [1998] 1 Lloyd's Rep. 80, 84–85 affirmed [1998] 2 All E.R. 434 (New York arbitration clause and service of suit clause indicated contrary intention); *King v Brandywine Reinsurance Co* [2005] EWCA Civ 235, [2005] 1 Lloyd's Rep. 655.

[50] *Chamberlain v Napier* (1880) 15 Ch D 614; *Re Missouri Steamship Co* (1889) 42 Ch D 321; *Rossano v Manufacturers' Life Insurance Co* [1963] 2 Q.B. 352; *James Miller and Partners Ltd v Whitworth Street Estates (Manchester) Ltd* [1970] A.C. 583; cf. *NV Handel My. J. Smits Import-Export v English Exporters (London) Ltd* [1955] 2 Lloyd's Rep. 69, 72 (affirmed [1955] 2 Lloyd's Rep. 317); *Compagnie d'Armement Maritime SA v Compagnie Tunisienne de Navigation SA* [1971] A.C. 572, 583.

[51] *Chatenay v Brazilian Submarine Telegraph Co Ltd* [1891] 1 Q.B. 79, 82; *Rossano v Manufacturers' Life Insurance Co* [1963] 2 Q.B. 352; *James Miller and Partners Ltd v Whitworth Street Estates (Manchester) Ltd* [1970] A.C. 583, 603, 608, 611–612; *Amin Rasheed Shipping Corp v Kuwait Insurance Co* [1984] A.C. 50.

[52] *Chatenay v Brazilian Submarine Telegraph Co Ltd* [1891] 1 Q.B. 79; *St Pierre v South American Stores (Gath and Chaves) Ltd* [1937] 2 All E.R. 349.

[53] *Compagnie d'Armement Maritime SA v Compagnie Tunisienne de Navigation SA* [1971] A.C. 572, 583, 594; *Sayers v International Drilling Co NV* [1971] 1 W.L.R. 1176, 1183–1184, 1186; *Coast Lines Ltd v Hudig and Veder Chartering NV* [1972] 2 Q.B. 34, 47, 50.

[54] *R. v International Trustee for the Protection of Bondholders AG* [1937] A.C. 500, 553; *The Assunzione* [1954] P. 150; *Rossano v Manufacturers' Life Insurance Co* [1963] 2 Q.B. 352; *Coast Lines Ltd v Hudig and Veder Chartering NV* [1972] 2 Q.B. 34, 47, 50; cf. *Re Helbert Wagg & Co Ltd's Claim* [1956] Ch. 323; *Sayers v International Drilling Co NV* [1971] 1 W.L.R. 1176, 1183, 1186.

[55] *Armadora Occidental SA v Horace Mann Insurance Co* [1977] 1 W.L.R. 1098. cf. *King v Brandywine Reinsurance Co* [2005] EWCA Civ 235, [2005] 1 Lloyd's Rep. 655.

[56] *Lloyd v Guibert* (1865) L.R. 1 Q.B. 115, 122–123; *British South Africa Co v De Beers Consolidated Mines Ltd* [1910] 1 Ch. 354, 383.

[57] *Jacobs v Crédit Lyonnais* (1884) 12 QBD 589; *Keiner v Keiner* [1952] 1 All E.R. 643.

[58] *Re Missouri Steamship Co* (1889) 42 Ch D 321, 328–329; *Sayers v International Drilling Co NV* [1971] 1 W.L.R. 1176, 1183.

[59] e.g. *The Adriatic* [1931] P. 241, 247; *R. v International Trustee for the Protection of Bondholders AG* [1937] A.C. 500, 554, 558; *The Freights Queen* [1977] 1 Lloyd's Rep. 140; *The Broken Hill Pty Co Ltd v Theodore Xenakis* [1982] 2 Lloyd's Rep. 304; *The Elli 2* [1985] 1 Lloyd's Rep. 107; *Turkiye Is Bankasi A.S. v Bank of China* [1993] 1 Lloyd's Rep. 132; *Wahda Bank v Arab Bank Plc* [1996] 1 Lloyd's Rep. 470; cf. *The Metamorphosis* [1953] 1 W.L.R. 543; *Forsikringsaktieselskapet Vesta v Butcher* [1989] A.C. 852; *Attock Cement Co Ltd v Romanian Bank for Foreign Trade* [1989] 1 W.L.R. 1147; *Gan Insurance Co Ltd v Tai Ping Insurance Co Ltd* [1999] 2 All E.R. (Comm) 54 (a case on

possibly, the fact that one of the parties is a government.[60] If one or more terms of the contract would be valid under one of two possible governing laws but invalid under the other, there is authority in favour of the view that the parties may be taken to have intended that their contract should be governed by the system of law by which it is valid.[61] However, it would seem that the fact that the contract is valid under one system of law is only evidence and not conclusive evidence as to the intention of the parties.[62]

30–012 **No choice of the proper law.** In cases where it is not possible to conclude that the parties have made an express or implied choice of the proper law, then it is necessary to abandon any reference to what the parties intended[63] and look for the law "with which the transaction has the closest and most real connection",[64] on objective grounds.[65] In this regard, all the facts and circumstances of the

---

the Rome Convention). See also *Groupama Navigation et Transports v Catatumbo C.A. Seguros* [2000] 2 All E.R. (Comm) 193.

[60] *R. v International Trustee for the Protection of Bondholders AG* [1937] A.C. 500, 554, 557.

[61] *P. & O. Steam Navigation Co v Shand* (1865) 3 Moo. P.C. (N.S.) 272; *Re Missouri S.S. Co* (1889) 42 Ch D 321, 341; *South African Breweries Ltd v King* [1899] 2 Ch. 173, 180–181; *Coast Lines Ltd v Hudig and Veder Chartering NV* [1972] 2 Q.B. 34, 44, 48; *S.C.F. Finance Co Ltd v Masri* [1986] 1 Lloyd's Rep. 293, 304.

[62] *British South Africa Co v De Beers Consolidated Mines Ltd* [1910] 2 Ch. 502, 513 (not of "much weight"); *Sayers v International Drilling Co NV* [1971] 1 W.L.R. 1176, 1184 (a "pointer," the importance of which "must not be exaggerated"); *Coast Lines Ltd v Hudig and Veder Chartering NV* [1972] 2 Q.B. 34, 50–51; contrast *Monterosso Shipping Co Ltd v International Transport Workers Federation* [1982] I.C.R. 675, 683–685 ("irrelevant").

[63] *Amin Rasheed Shipping Corp v Kuwait Insurance Co* [1984] A.C. 50. Rejection of any reference to the parties' intentions means that the fact that the contract would be valid under one system of law but not another is definitely irrelevant: *Monterosso Shipping Co Ltd v International Transport Workers Federation* [1982] I.C.R. 675, 683–685. Opinions may differ as to whether a case presents an example of "implied" choice or "no" choice: compare the contrasting views of Lord Diplock, speaking for the majority in *Amin Rasheed Shipping Corp v Kuwait Insurance Co* [1984] A.C. 50, 62–65, and Lord Wilberforce, 69; see also *DR Insurance Co v Central National Insurance Co* [1996] 1 Lloyd's Rep. 74; *Zebrarise Ltd v De Nieffe* [2004] EWHC 1842 (Comm), [2005] 1 Lloyd's Rep. 154.

[64] *Bonython v Commonwealth of Australia* [1951] A.C. 201, 219; *Tomkinson v First Pennsylvania Banking and Trust Co* [1961] A.C. 1007, 1068, 1081–1082; *James Miller and Partners Ltd v Whitworth Street Estates (Manchester) Ltd* [1970] A.C. 583; *Compagnie d'Armement Maritime SA v Compagnie Tunisienne de Navigation SA* [1971] A.C. 572; *Coast Lines Ltd v Hudig and Veder Chartering NV* [1972] 2 Q.B. 34; *Offshore International SA v Banco Central SA* [1977] 1 W.L.R. 399; *Power Curber International Ltd v National Bank of Kuwait* [1981] 1 W.L.R. 1233; *Amin Rasheed Shipping Corp v Kuwait Insurance Co* [1984] A.C. 50, 61; *Habib Bank Ltd v Central Bank of Sudan* [2006] EWHC 1767 (Comm), [2007] 1 W.L.R. 470.

[65] Where there is no choice of law by the parties, some older authorities purport to search for the "presumed intention" of the parties: see, e.g. *Lloyd v Guibert* (1865) L.R. 1 Q.B. 115, 120–123; *R. v International Trustee for the Protection of Bondholders AG* [1937] A.C. 500; *Mount Albert BC v Australasian Temperance and General Mutual Life Assurance Society* [1938] A.C. 224. In carrying out this exercise there was a tendency to resort to rebuttable presumptions, in favour, depending on the circumstances of the case, of, e.g. the law of the place of contracting (*Jacobs v Crédit Lyonnais* (1884) 12 QBD 589), the law of the place of performance (*Re Missouri S.S. Co* (1889) 42 Ch D 321; *Benaim & Co v Debono* [1924] A.C. 514), the law of the flag (*Lloyd v Guibert*; *The Assunzione* [1954] P. 150) or the *lex situs* of an immovable (*British South Africa Co v De Beers Consolidated Mines* [1910] 2 Ch. 502). The use of presumptions was rejected in *Coast Lines Ltd v Hudig and Veder Chartering NV* [1972] 2 Q.B. 34, 44, 47, 50. cf. the position under the Rome Convention and the Rome I Regulation, below, paras 30–072 et seq, 30–186 et seq.

contract should be examined.[66] Although the weight to be attached to relevant facts and circumstances will vary from case to case, the following may be mentioned as representative. The place where the contract was made,[67] the place where the contract has to be performed,[68] the nature of the legal personality of the parties,[69] the place of residence[70] or business[71] of the parties, the nature, subject-matter[72] and standard terms[73] of the contract, the situation of the funds which are available for the discharge[74] or security of the obligation,[75] the place where a bank must perform its obligation under a letter of credit,[76] or whether the contract is closely linked with another contract containing a choice of law clause.[77]

Connection of the transaction with a system of law. The proper law is usually defined as "the system of law with which the transaction has the closest 30–013

[66] e.g. *The Assunzione* [1954] P. 150; *Coast Lines Ltd v Hudig and Veder Chartering NV* [1972] 2 Q.B. 34.

[67] *P. & O. Steam Navigation Co v Shand* (1865) 3 Moo. P.C. (N.S.) 272; *Lloyd v Guibert* (1865) L.R. 1 Q.B. 115, 122; *Jacobs v Crédit Lyonnais* (1884) 12 QBD 589, 596–597, 600; *Re Missouri S.S. Co* (1889) 42 Ch D 321, 326, 338; *British South Africa Co v De Beers Consolidated Mines Ltd* [1910] 1 Ch. 354, 381; *Kahler v Midland Bank Ltd* [1950] A.C. 24; *Zivnostenska Banka v Frankman* [1950] A.C. 57; *Cantieri Navali Riuniti SpA v NV Omne Justitia* [1985] 2 Lloyd's Rep. 428, 433–435; cf. *Amin Rasheed Shipping Corp v Kuwait Insurance Co* [1984] A.C. 50, 62.

[68] e.g. *Lloyd v Guibert* (1865) L.R. 1 Q.B. 115, 122: *Re Missouri S.S. Co* (1889) 42 Ch D 321 at 341; *Chatenay v Brazilian Submarine Telegraph Co* [1891] 1 Q.B. 79, 83; *Hamlyn & Co v Talisker Distillery* [1894] A.C. 202; *Ralli Bros v Compania Naviera Sota y Aznar* [1920] 1 K.B. 614, 630, 631 (affirmed [1920] 2 K.B. 287); *Benaim & Co v Debono* [1924] A.C. 514, 520; *Adelaide Electric Supply Co Ltd v Prudential Assurance Co Ltd* [1934] A.C. 122, 145, 151; *James Miller and Partners Ltd v Whitworth Street Estates (Manchester) Ltd* [1970] A.C. 583; cf. *Amin Rasheed Shipping Corp v Kuwait Insurance Co* [1984] A.C. 50, 62–63.

[69] *R. v International Trustee for the Protection of Bondholders AG* [1937] A.C. 500, 531, 557, 574; *National Bank of Australia Ltd v Scottish Union and National Insurance Co* [1952] A.C. 493; *The Assunzione* [1954] P. 150.

[70] *Jacobs v Crédit Lyonnais* (1884) 12 QBD 589, 600, 602.

[71] *Re Anglo-Austrian Bank* [1920] 1 Ch. 69.

[72] e.g. whether it is a contract relating to land (*British South Africa Co v De Beers Consolidated Mines Ltd* [1910] 1 Ch. 354, 383) or a contract relating to a marriage settlement (*Re Fitzgerald* [1904] 1 Ch. 573, 587) or a contract of affreightment (*Re Missouri S.S. Co* (1889) 42 Ch D 321, 327); and see *Re United Railways of the Havana and Regla Warehouses Ltd* [1960] Ch. 52, 91.

[73] *Gill and Duffus Landauer Ltd v London Export Corp* [1982] 2 Lloyd's Rep. 627, 629.

[74] *Spurrier v La Cloche* [1902] A.C. 446, 450.

[75] *Bonython v Commonwealth of Australia* [1951] A.C. 201, 221 (loan secured on public revenue of self-governing colony).

[76] *Offshore International SA v Banco Central SA* [1977] 1 W.L.R. 399; *Power Curber International Ltd v National Bank of Kuwait* [1981] 1 W.L.R. 1233; *Turkiye Is Bankasi AS v Bank of China* [1993] 1 Lloyd's Rep. 132; *Minories Finance Ltd v Afribank Nigeria Ltd* [1995] 1 Lloyd's Rep. 134; *Bank of Credit and Commerce Hong Kong Ltd v Sonali Bank* [1995] 1 Lloyd's Rep. 227; *Bastone & Firminger Ltd v Nasima Enterprises (Nigeria) Ltd* [1996] C.L.C. 1902, 1910; *Habib Bank Ltd v Central Bank of Sudan* [2006] EWHC 1767 (Comm), [2007] 1 W.L.R. 470. See also *Bank of Baroda v Vysya Bank Ltd* [1994] 2 Lloyd's Rep. 87 (a case on the Rome Convention, below, para.30–075). cf. *Attock Cement Co Ltd v Romanian Bank for Foreign Trade* [1989] 1 W.L.R. 1147; *Wahda Bank v Arab Bank Plc* [1996] 1 Lloyd's Rep. 470.

[77] *The Njegos* [1936] P. 90; *The Broken Hill Proprietary Co v Xenakis* [1982] 2 Lloyd's Rep. 304; *Forsikringsaktieselskapet Vesta v Butcher* [1988] 3 W.L.R. 565 (affirmed on different grounds [1989] A.C. 852); *Mitsubishi Corp v Alafouzos* [1988] 1 Lloyd's Rep. 191. cf. *Gan Insurance Co Ltd v Tai Ping Insurance Co Ltd* [1999] 2 All E.R. (Comm) 54 (a case on the Rome Convention).

and most real connection".[78] However, it is not wholly clear whether the connection is to be with a "system of law" or with a "country". A number of earlier cases have preferred the latter criterion[79] but the weight of authority supports a connection with a "system of law".[80] The difference may be important when the geographical factors of the contract point to one country, whilst the legal factors point towards the legal system of another country as in the case of a contract to do building work in Scotland, the contractual documents for which were in English form.[81] It may be particularly relevant that one system of law under consideration has no provision dealing with the matter in issue.[82] Indeed, a more recent suggestion is that the two tests should be combined,[83] though this may well be difficult when they point to different solutions.[84]

30–014 **Transaction not contract.** It has been suggested that the connection with the system of law, or country, should be that of the "transaction" contemplated by the contract. This means the connection should be with what is to be done under the contract rather than just with the technical forms of the contract.[85]

30–015 **Splitting of the contract.**[86] Although almost all the incidents of a contract are governed by the proper law,[87] it has to be considered whether that proper law is to be the same for each incident and whether the obligations of both parties to the contract are to be governed by the same proper law, for it has been suggested that:

> "The fact that one aspect of a contract is to be governed by the law of one country does not necessarily mean that the law is to be the proper law of the contract as a whole."[88]

---

[78] *Bonython v Commonwealth of Australia* [1951] A.C. 201, at 219.

[79] *Boissevain v Weil* [1949] 1 K.B. 482, 490; *Tomkinson v First Pennsylvania Banking and Trust Co* [1961] A.C. 1007, 1068; *Philipson-Stow v IRC* [1961] A.C. 727, 760.

[80] *Bonython v Commonwealth of Australia* [1951] A.C. 201, 219; *Rossano v Manufacturers' Life Insurance Co* [1963] 2 Q.B. 352, 361, 368–369; *James Miller and Partners Ltd v Whitworth Street Estates (Manchester) Ltd* [1970] A.C. 583; *Coast Lines Ltd v Hudig and Veder Chartering NV* [1972] 2 Q.B. 34, 44, 46; *Amin Rasheed Shipping Corp v Kuwait Insurance Co* [1984] A.C. 50, 60, 71.

[81] *James Miller and Partners Ltd v Whitworth Street Estates (Manchester) Ltd* [1970] A.C. 583.

[82] *Islamic Arab Insurance Co v Saudi Egyptian American Reinsurance Co* [1987] 1 Lloyd's Rep. 315, 320.

[83] *James Miller and Partners Ltd v Whitworth Street Estates (Manchester) Ltd* [1970] A.C. 583, 603–604, 605–606, 614–616; *Compagnie d'Armement Maritime SA v Compagnie Tunisienne de Navigation SA* [1971] A.C. 572, 583; *Coast Lines Ltd v Hudig and Veder Chartering NV* [1972] 2 Q.B. 34, 50; *Monterosso Shipping Co Ltd v International Transport Workers Federation* [1982] I.C.R. 675. For the position under the Rome Convention and the Rome I Regulation, see below, paras 30–024, 30–145.

[84] e.g. *James Miller and Partners Ltd v Whitworth Street Estates (Manchester) Ltd* [1970] A.C. 583.

[85] *Coast Lines Ltd v Hudig and Veder Chartering NV* [1972] 2 Q.B. 34, 46.

[86] See McLachlan (1990) 61 B.Y.I.L. 311. For the position under the Rome Convention and the Rome I Regulation, see below, paras 30–056—30–057, 30–175.

[87] See below, paras 30–303 et seq.

[88] *Re United Railways of the Havana and Regla Warehouses* [1960] Ch. 52, 92; and see *Re Helbert Wagg & Co Ltd's Claim* [1956] Ch. 323, 340.

However the basic rule is that there will normally be no such "scission," for as Lord MacDermott said[89]:

> "It is doubtless true to say that the courts of this country will not split the contract in this sense readily or without good reason."

Nevertheless, there is some authority in the case of banking accounts of different aspects being governed by different laws[90]; and where a contract of reinsurance (governed by English law) was deemed to be "back to back" with the insurance contract (governed by Norwegian law), a clause in the former was construed as being intended by the parties to have the same effect as under Norwegian law.[91] The parties may, however, agree expressly that different contractual issues shall be governed by different laws.[92] The different obligations of the two parties to a contract will be governed by the same proper law[93] unless they have made an agreement, express or implied, to the contrary.[94]

Renvoi. The doctrine of renvoi[95] has no place in the law of contract.[96] Thus the proper law of the contract means the domestic rules of that law and not its rules of the conflict of laws. 30–016

[89] *Kahler v Midland Bank Ltd* [1950] A.C. 24, 42. See also *Centrax Ltd v Citibank NA* [1999] 1 All E.R. (Comm) 557.

[90] *Libyan Arab Foreign Bank v Bankers Trust Co* [1989] Q.B. 728; *Libyan Arab Foreign Bank v Manufacturers Hanover Trust Co* [1988] 2 Lloyd's Rep. 494; and see *Chamberlain v Napier* (1880) 15 Ch D 614; *British South Africa Co v De Beers Consolidated Mines Ltd* [1910] 1 Ch. 354, 383; Lord MacDermott, dissenting, in *Kahler v Midland Bank Ltd* [1950] A.C. 24, 42; *Re Helbert Wagg & Co Ltd's Claim* [1956] Ch. 323, 340; *Sayers v International Drilling Co NV* [1971] 1 W.L.R. 1176, 1180–1181; *Centrax Ltd v Citibank NA* [1999] 1 All E.R. (Comm) 557.

[91] *Forsikringsaktieselskapet Vesta v Butcher* [1988] 3 W.L.R. 565 (affirmed on different grounds [1989] A.C. 852). cf. *Gan Insurance Co Ltd v Tai Ping Insurance Co Ltd* [1999] 2 All E.R. (Comm) 54.

[92] *Hamlyn & Co v Talisker Distillery* [1894] A.C. 202; though see *Armar Shipping Co Ltd v Caisse Algérienne d'Assurance* [1981] 1 W.L.R. 207, 216; *XL Insurance Ltd v Owens Corning* [2000] 2 Lloyd's Rep. 500. Under the Uniform Laws on International Sales Act 1967, the parties are permitted to choose the uniform law to govern those aspects of their contract covered by that Act: Sch.1 arts 2 and 4. However, other aspects of their contract of sale of goods will be governed by the normal choice of law rules of the conflict of laws.

[93] *Zivnostenska Banka v Frankman* [1950] A.C. 57, 83.

[94] *Re Helbert Wagg & Co Ltd's Claim* [1956] Ch. 323, 340.

[95] *Dicey, Morris and Collins*, Ch.4; Cheshire and North, Ch.5.

[96] *Amin Rasheed Shipping Corp v Kuwait Insurance Co* [1984] A.C. 50, 61–62; *E.I. du Pont de Nemours v Agnew* [1987] 2 Lloyd's Rep. 582, 592. See also *Macmillan Inc v Bishopsgate Investment Trust Plc (No.3)* [1995] 1 W.L.R. 987, 1008 (Millett J.) affirmed on other grounds, [1996] 1 W.L.R. 387, see especially Staughton L.J., at 405; *Musawi v RE International (UK) Ltd* [2007] EWHC 2981 (Ch), [2008] 1 Lloyd's Rep. 326; cf. *Glencore International AG v Metro Trading International Inc* [2001] 1 Lloyd's Rep. 284, 296–297. And see below, paras 30–028, 30–146.

3. THE ROME CONVENTION[97]

(a) *In General*

30–017 **History and purpose.**[98] In 1980 the then Member States of the European Community concluded a Convention on the Law Applicable to Contractual Obligations. This Convention (which is known as the Rome Convention) was ratified by the United Kingdom in 1991 and was implemented in United Kingdom law in the Contracts (Applicable Law) Act 1990.[99] The provisions of the 1990 Act which give the force of law in the United Kingdom to the Rome Convention,[100] entered into force on April 1, 1991.[101] Consequently the rules of the Convention will apply to contracts falling within its scope which are entered into after that date[102] but before December 17, 2009, the date on which the Rome I Regulation enters into force.[103] Schedule 3 to the Act sets out the text of the Brussels Protocol which enables questions concerning the interpretation of the Rome Convention to be referred to the European Court of Justice.[104] Although

[97] *Dicey, Morris and Collins on the Conflict of Laws*, 14th edn (2006), Chs 32 and 33; Cheshire and North, *Private International Law*, 13th edn (1999), Ch.18; Fawcett, Harris and Bridge, *International Sale of Goods in the Conflict of Laws* (2005), Ch.13; Meeusen, Pertegas and Straetmans (eds), *The Enforcement of International Contracts in the European Union* (2004); Plender, *The European Contracts Convention*, 2nd edn (2001); Nygh, *Autonomy in International Contracts* (1999); Kaye, *The New Private International Law of Contract of the European Community* (1993); Lasok and Stone, *Conflict of Laws in the European Community* (1987), Ch.9; North (ed.), *Contract Conflicts* (1982); Fletcher, *Conflict of Laws and European Community Law* (1982), Ch.5; Anton, *Private International Law*, 2nd edn (1990), Ch.11; Diamond (1986) 216 *Recueil des Cours IV*, 233; North (1990) 220 *Recueil des Cours I*, 3, 176–205; North [1980] J.B.L. 392; Morse (1982) 2 Yb. Eur. L. 107; Jaffey (1984) 33 I.C.L.Q. 531; Williams (1986) 35 I.C.L.Q. 1. Extensive bibliographies will be found in Plender at Annex X and Kaye at pp.507–510.

[98] *Dicey, Morris and Collins*, paras 32–009 et seq; Cheshire and North at pp.535–536; Plender at Ch.1; North in North (ed.), *Contract Conflicts*, pp.4–9 reprinted in *Essays in Private International Law* (1993), p.23; Report on the Convention by Professors Giuliano and Lagarde [1980] OJ C282/1, 4–8 (hereafter Giuliano-Lagarde Report), as to which see below, para.30–020.

[99] Contracts (Applicable Law) Act 1990 s.2(1). The English text of the Convention is set out in Sch.1 to the Act "for ease of reference": s.2(4). Each language text is, however, equally authentic: Rome Convention art.33. For the French and German texts, see Plender at Annex II. For the French, German, Italian and Dutch texts, see Kaye at pp.478–505.

[100] Note the power to make reservations to arts 7(1) and 10(1)(e) in art.22 of the Convention. The UK has exercised this power so that arts 7(1) and 10(1)(e) do not have the force of law in the United Kingdom: Contracts (Applicable Law) Act 1990 s.2(2). See below, paras 30–033, 30–327.

[101] SI 1991/707.

[102] Rome Convention art.17, which provides that the Convention shall apply in a contracting state to contracts made after the date on which it has entered into force with respect to that State. Accordingly, contracts entered into *on or before* April 1, 1991, which will be rare, given the passage of time, will be governed by common law choice of law rules (as to which see above, paras 30–005 et seq).

[103] Rome I Regulation arts 28, 29.

[104] See below, para.30–019. Sch.2 to the Act contains the text of the Luxembourg Convention providing for accession to the Rome Convention by Greece. Sch.3A to the Act contains the text of the Funchal Convention providing for the accession to the Rome Convention by Spain and Portugal (see SI 1994/1900) which entered into force for the United Kingdom on December 1, 1997. Sch.3B to the Act contains the text of the 1996 Convention providing for the accession to the Rome Convention of Austria, Finland and Sweden (see SI 2000/1825), which came into force on January 1, 2001. A consolidated version of the text of the Rome Convention can be found in [1998] OJ C27/34.

the United Kingdom ratified the Brussels Protocol on implementing the Convention,[105] delay in ratification by Belgium[106] meant that it did not enter into force internationally until August 1, 2004 and was eventually implemented in United Kingdom law on March 1, 2005.[107]

The Rome Convention cannot be said to have been received with unequivocal enthusiasm in the United Kingdom.[108] Indeed there was much to be said for the view that the rules for choice of law in contract which had been developed by the common law constituted one of the most satisfactory and acceptable branches of the English conflict of laws.[109] This notwithstanding, the purpose of the Convention is, at a general level, to establish uniform choice of law rules so as to endeavour to achieve two principal aims. First, it was suggested that such uniformity was a necessary step on the route to achieving free movement of goods, services and capital amongst the Member States.[110] Secondly, the Convention was seen as a way of buttressing the work done in the Brussels Convention on Jurisdiction and the Enforcement of Judgments in Civil and Commercial Matters 1968 which is designed to establish uniform rules for the international jurisdiction of courts amongst the Member States.[111] One effect of that Convention is that it: 30–018

> "... enables the parties, in many matters, to reach agreements assigning jurisdiction and to choose among several courts. The outcome may be that preference is given to the court of a State whose law seems to offer a better solution to the proceedings. To prevent this 'forum shopping,' increase legal certainty, and anticipate more easily the law which will be applied, it would be advisable for the rules of conflict to be unified in fields of particular economic importance so that the same law is applied irrespective of the State in which the decision is given."[112]

---

105 See below, para.30–019.

106 Belgium finally ratified the Protocol on May 5, 2004.

107 SI 2004/3488. A Convention was signed on April 14, 2005 providing for the accession of the Czech Republic, Estonia, Cyprus, Latvia, Lithuania, Hungary, Malta, Poland, Slovenia and the Slovak Republic to the Rome Convention and the Brussels Protocol, but this is not yet in force. For the Recommendation for a Council Decision concerning the accession of Bulgaria and Romania, see COM(2007) 217 final. A consolidated version of the Convention and the Protocol is printed in [2005] OJ C334/11.

108 See F.A. Mann (1983) 32 I.C.L.Q. 265; (1991) 107 L.Q.R. 353; *Hansard*, HL Vol.515, cols 1467–1482; Vol.517, cols 1537–1541. It even provoked correspondence in *The Times*, a rare event in the conflict of laws: see F.A. Mann, *The Times*, December 4, 1989; P.M. North, *The Times*, December 19, 1989.

109 See *Hansard*, HL Vol.515, col.1482, per Lord Goff of Chieveley.

110 Speech of Director-General of the Internal Market and Approximation of Legislation at the European Commission (Mr. Vogelaar, as to whom see *Hansard*, HL Vol.515, col.1476) quoted in Giuliano-Lagarde Report, p.5.

111 Brussels Convention [1978] OJ L304/77, Cmnd.7395. See Giuliano-Lagarde Report, p.5. The Brussels Convention on Jurisdiction and the Enforcement of Judgments in Civil and Commercial Matters was replaced, as from March 1, 2002 for all Member States except Denmark, by Regulation 44/2001 on jurisdiction and the recognition and enforcement of judgments in civil and commercial matters [2001] OJ L12/1. The Regulation revises the text of the Convention. For implementation of the Regulation in the United Kingdom, see SI 2001/3929.

112 Brussels Convention [1978] OJ L304/77.

Justification of unification or harmonisation in these terms has not been uncritically accepted.[113] Nevertheless, it cannot be doubted that the Rome Convention has had, in its years in force, a significant effect in an area of the conflict of laws of great practical importance.

30–019 **Interpretation: European Court of Justice.** As will be seen in what follows, virtually all of the difficulties to which the Convention gives rise concern its interpretation. As explained above,[114] the Brussels Protocol confers jurisdiction on the European Court of Justice to give rulings on the interpretation of the Rome Convention, on any conventions for the accession of Member States of the European Communities, and on the Protocol itself.[115] As far as the United Kingdom is concerned, the House of Lords and other courts from which no further appeal is possible[116] and any other United Kingdom court when acting as an appeal court[117] may request a preliminary ruling on a question of interpretation if any of those courts consider that a decision on the question is necessary to enable it to give judgment in a case.[118] No national court is, however, bound to make such a reference.[119] Section 3 of the Contracts (Applicable Law) Act 1990 makes it clear that any question as to the meaning or effect of the Rome Convention shall, if not referred to the European Court in accordance with the Brussels Protocol, be determined in accordance with the principles laid down by, and any relevant decision of, the European Court.[120] There can be little doubt that the European Court will have regard to the objectives and scheme of the Convention in its approach to interpretation and that in so doing it will tend to provide autonomous, uniform meanings for the various terms or concepts used in the Convention.[121] Relevant decisions of the European Court

---

[113] Collins (1976) 25 I.C.L.Q. 35, reprinted in Collins, *Essays in International Litigation and The Conflict of Laws* (1994), p.409; Lipstein, in Lipstein (ed.), *Harmonisation of Private International Law by the EEC* (1978), p.1; Diamond (1986) *Recueil des Cours IV*, 216, 223, 246; Morse (1982) 2 Yb. Eur. L. 107, 108–110.

[114] See para.30–017.

[115] Brussels Protocol arts 1 and 2. No such rulings have yet been made. But see *Intercontainer Interfrigo (ICF) SC v Balkerende Oosthuisen BV* (C–133/08) (pending) [2008] OJ C 158/10.

[116] Brussels Protocol art.2(a).

[117] Brussels Protocol art.2(b).

[118] Brussels Protocol art.2 Preamble.

[119] Brussels Convention art.2. cf. the position under the Protocol to the Brussels Convention on Jurisdiction and the Enforcement of Judgments in Civil and Commercial Matters 1968 art.2(2), by virtue of which an appellate court from which no further appeal is possible was *required* to make a reference to the European Court. Under Council Regulation 44/2001 references to the European Court will no longer be under a separate Protocol, but will be under art.234 (formerly art.177) of the EC Treaty: references to the European Court under such a Regulation can only be made by a court or tribunal of a Member State against whose decisions there is no judicial remedy under national law: see arts 65 and 68. As to the position under the Rome I Regulation, see below, para.30–134.

[120] cf. Civil Jurisdiction and Judgments Act 1982 s.3(3).

[121] This is the normal practice in cases involving the Brussels Convention, above. See, e.g. *Dicey, Morris and Collins*, paras 11–061 et seq. See *Raiffeisen Zentralbank Osterreich AG v Five Star General Trading LLC* [2001] EWCA Civ 68, [2001] Q.B. 825. As to the link between the Brussels Convention and the Rome Convention, see the Preamble to the latter and *Ivenel v Schwab* (133/81) [1982] E.C.R. 1891. See also Forsyth and Moser (1996) 45 I.C.L.Q. 190. It is likely that cases decided by the European Court which do not involve the Rome Convention will provide, where appropriate, persuasive analogies: see Cheshire and North at pp.539–540. And see below, paras 30–031 et seq.

are binding on United Kingdom courts and judicial notice must be taken of any decision of, or expression of opinion by, that court as to the meaning or effect of the Rome Convention in relation to any question that is referred to it.[122]

Uniformity of interpretation and application. Since there is no *obligation* on national courts to refer questions to the European Court, the possibility exists of disparate interpretation amongst those courts. To reduce the likelihood of such a result, art.18 of the Rome Convention provides that in the interpretation and application of the uniform rules of the Convention, regard shall be had to their international character and to the desirability of achieving uniformity in their interpretation and application. United Kingdom courts have frequently referred to the need for uniform interpretation of the Rome Convention,[123] and have on occasion referred to decisions on the Convention rendered in other contracting states.[124] Additionally, if judgments given by the courts of a contracting state conflict with a judgment as to interpretation given by either the European Court or a court of another contracting state, power is given, in the Brussels Protocol, to the competent authority of the former contracting state to request the European Court to give a ruling on the conflict of interpretation.[125] Finally, s.3(3)(a) of the Contracts (Applicable Law) Act 1990 states that the Report on the Convention by Professors Giuliano and Lagarde ("Giuliano-Lagarde Report") may be considered in ascertaining the meaning or effect of any provision of the Convention.[126] The Report will doubtless play a significant role in the interpretation of the Convention if only because it is a document which negotiators representing Member States were able to revise (and into which, it may be noted, the United 30–020

[122] Contracts (Applicable Law) Act 1990 s.3(2).

[123] *Egon Oldendorff v Libera Corp (No.2)* [1996] 1 Lloyd's Rep. 380; *Credit Lyonnais v New Hampshire Insurance Co* [1997] 2 Lloyd's Rep. 1; *Raiffeisen Zentralbank Osterreich AG v Five Star General Trading LLC* [2001] EWCA Civ 68, [2001] Q.B. 825; *Samcrete Egypt Engineers and Contractors SAE v Land Rover Exports Ltd* [2001] EWCA Civ 2019, [2002] C.L.C. 533; *Bergmann v Kenburn Waste Management Ltd* [2002] EWCA Civ 2019, [2002] 2 F.S.R. 45; *Base Metal Trading Ltd v Shamurin* [2002] C.L.C. 322; *Ennstone Building Products Ltd v Stanger Ltd* [2002] EWCA Civ 916, [2002] 1 W.L.R. 359; *Iran Continental Shelf Oil Co v IRI International Corp* [2002] EWCA Civ 1024; *Caledonia Subsea Ltd v Microperi SRL* (2002) S.L.T. 1022.

[124] *Raiffeisen Zentralbank Osterreich AG v Five Star General Trading LLC* [2001] EWCA Civ 68; *Definitely Maybe (Touring) Ltd v Marek Lieberberg Konzertagentur GmbH* [2001] 1 W.L.R. 1745; *Samcrete Egypt Engineers and Contractors SAE v Land Rover Exports Ltd* [2001] EWCA Civ 2019; *Iran Continental Shelf Oil Co v IRI International Corp* [2002] EWCA Civ 1024; *Caledonia Subsea Ltd v Microperi SRL* (2002) S.L.T. 1022.

[125] Brussels Protocol art.3. No competent authority has yet been designated in the UK. The provision suggests that decisions of courts of other Contracting States may be of, at least, persuasive authority in the UK courts which, for this reason, should have regard to them. A joint Declaration to the Brussels Protocol (which does not appear in Sch.3 to the 1990 Act, but the text of which is reproduced in [1998] OJ C27/34, 50–51 and in Plender at Annex VI) provides a regime whereby Member States agree to exchange information as to decisions by national appellate courts on the Rome Convention through the offices of the European Court. For the latest text of the Declaration, see [2005] OJ C334/1, 19.

[126] For the text of the Report, see [1980] OJ C282/1; reprinted in North (ed.), pp.335–401; Plender at Annex IV. The opening words of s.3(3) make it clear that reference to the Report is without prejudice to any other material the court is permitted to look at. Despite the similarities between the Rome Convention and the common law, English courts should not place uncritical reliance on common law decisions in interpreting the Convention: see cases cited above fn.123; *Dicey, Morris and Collins*, para.32–020; Cheshire and North at p.542; cf. *Hansard*, HL Vol.515, col.1489.

Kingdom negotiators put revisions[127]). United Kingdom courts frequently refer to the Giuliano-Lagarde Report in interpreting the provisions of the Convention.[128]

30–021 **General scope of the Convention.** A number of general questions arise as to the scope of the Convention (as opposed to the specific questions which are included in or excluded from the Convention by the text of the instrument itself[129]).

30–022 **"Laws of different countries".** First, art.1(1) provides that the rules contained in the Rome Convention "shall apply to contractual obligations in any situation involving a choice between the laws of different countries". According to the Giuliano-Lagarde Report, such situations are those:

> ". . . which involve one or more elements foreign to the internal social system of a country (for example, the fact that one or all of the parties to the contract are foreign nationals or persons habitually resident abroad, the fact that the contract was made abroad, the fact that one or more of the obligations of the parties are to be performed in a foreign country, etc.), thereby giving the legal systems of several countries claims to apply."[130]

The situation contemplated thus seems to be the presence in a transaction of a foreign element of legal relevance according to customary notions of private international law. Such a relevant foreign element would appear to be present even if the only such element is the fact that a contract otherwise domestic in nature contains a choice of a foreign governing law.[131]

30–023 **Law specified need not be of a contracting state.** Secondly, art.2 of the Convention provides that any law specified by the Convention shall be applied whether or not it is the law of a contracting state. Taken with art.1(1), the effect of this is that it is not necessary that the countries whose laws are implicated in

---

[127] *Hansard*, HL Vol.513, col.1259.

[128] See *Raiffeisen Zentralbank Osterreich AG v Five Star General Trading LLC* [2001] EWCA Civ 68; *Print Concept GmbH v G.E.W. (EC)* [2001] EWCA Civ 352, [2002] C.L.C. 352; *Definitely Maybe (Touring) Ltd v Marek Lieberberg Konzertagentur GmbH* [2001] 1 W.L.R. 1745; *Aeolian Shipping SA v ISS Machinery Services Ltd* [2001] EWCA Civ 1162, [2001] 2 Lloyd's Rep. 641; *Samcrete Egypt Engineers and Contractors SAE v Land Rover Exports Ltd* [2001] EWCA Civ 2019; *Bergmann v Kenburn Waste Management Ltd* [2002] EWCA Civ 2019; *Ennnstone Building Products Ltd v Stanger Ltd* [2002] EWCA Civ 1024; *European Bank for Reconstruction & Development v Tekoglu* [2004] EWHC 846 (Comm); *Apple Corps v Apple Computer Inc* [2004] EWHC 768 (Ch), [2004] I.L. Pr. 597; *Base Metal Trading Ltd v Shamurin* [2004] EWCA Civ 1316, [2005] 1 W.L.R. 1167; *Opthalmic Innovations International (United Kingdom) Ltd v Opthalmic Innovations International Inc* [2004] EWHC 2948 (Ch), [2005] I.L. Pr. 10; *Caledonia Subsea Ltd v Microperi SRL* (2002) S.L.T. 1022; *Atlantic Telecom GmbH, Noter* (2004) S.L.T. 1031.

[129] See below, paras 30–030 et seq.

[130] Giuliano-Lagarde Report, p.10. The applicable law, as determined by the rules in the Convention, must be the law of a country: see *Shamil Bank of Bahrain v Beximco Pharmaceuticals Ltd* [2004] EWCA Civ 19, [2004] 1 W.L.R. 1784; *Halpern v Halpern (Nos 1 and 2)* [2007] EWCA Civ 291, [2008] Q.B. 195; *Musawi v RE International (UK) Ltd* [2007] EWHC 2981 (Ch), [2008] 1 Lloyd's Rep. 326. See below paras 30–048, 30–144.

[131] This would seem to follow from art.3(3) of the Rome Convention: see below, paras 30–061 et seq.

the problem be states which are parties to the Convention or Member States of the EC and that the rules of the Convention must be applied even if they point to a governing law which is neither the law of a contracting state nor the law of a Member State of the EC. The Convention will thus apply if the choice is between the law of England and the law of Brazil, or between the law of Brazil and the law of India,[132] as it will if the choice is between the law of the Netherlands and the law of Italy. Further, the application of the Convention, in a case where the forum is in the United Kingdom, does not depend on the situation having a factual link with another contracting state or with another Member State of the EC. The rules of the Convention will thus apply to all cases[133] brought in United Kingdom courts to which those rules, according to their terms, apply.[134]

Countries with more than one legal system. Thirdly, although art.1(1) refers to situations involving a choice between the law of different *countries*, the rules of the Convention are intended, also, to apply to situations involving a choice between two or more *legal systems* which may not necessarily be the same thing.[135] Article 19(1) of the Convention provides that where a state comprises territorial units, each of which has its own rules of law in respect of contractual obligations, each territorial unit shall be treated as a country for the purposes of identifying the applicable law.[136] Hence the rules of the Convention will apply to determine, for example, whether a contract is governed by the law of New York[137] or the law of California, whether a contract is governed by the law of California or the law of British Columbia, whether a contract is governed by the law of England or the law of Luxembourg, or whether a contract is governed by the law of Germany or the law of France. 30–024

Different parts of the United Kingdom. Fourthly, the Convention rules will apply in the case of conflicts between the laws of the different parts of the United 30–025

[132] *Bank of Baroda v Vysya Bank Ltd* [1994] 2 Lloyd's Rep. 412; *Egon Oldendorff v Libera Corp (No.2)* [1996] 1 Lloyd's Rep. 380 (law of England and law of Japan); *Gan Insurance Co Ltd v Tai Ping Insurance Co Ltd* [1999] 2 All E.R. (Comm) 54 (law of England and law of Taiwan); *Tiernan v Magen Insurance Co Ltd* [2000] I.L. Pr. 517 (law of England and law of Israel); *Aeolian Shipping SA v ISS Machinery Services Ltd* [2001] EWCA Civ 1162, [2001] 2 Lloyd's Rep. 641 (law of England and law of Japan); *Samcrete Egypt Engineers and Contractors SAE v Land Rover Exports Ltd* [2001 EWCA Civ 2019, [2002] C.L.C. 533 (law of England and law of Egypt).

[133] Including, it seems, cases where it is necessary to determine whether a contract is "governed by English law" for the purposes of CPR r.6.20(5)(a) which enables permission to be given for service of a claim form out of the jurisdiction: see *Bank of Baroda v Vysya Bank Ltd* [1994] 2 Lloyd's Rep. 87; *Egon Oldendorff v Libera Corp* [1995] 2 Lloyd's Rep. 64; *Burrows v Jamaica Private Power Co Ltd* [2002] 2 All E.R. (Comm) 374; *Dicey, Morris and Collins* para.30–027. According to CPR r.6.21(2A), the court will not give permission for such service "unless satisfied that England and Wales is the proper place in which to bring the claim".

[134] Giuliano-Lagarde Report, p.13. For criticism of this result by Lords Wilberforce and Goff, see *Hansard*, HL Vol.515, cols 1476–1482, Vol.517, cols 1537–1541.

[135] cf. *James Miller and Partners Ltd v Whitworth Street Estates (Manchester) Ltd* [1970] A.C. 583; above, para.30–013.

[136] See also Giuliano-Lagarde Report, p.10.

[137] See *Centrax Ltd v Citibank NA* [1999] 1 All E.R. (Comm) 557 (law of England or law of New York); *Iran Continental Shelf Oil Co v IRI International Corp* [2002] EWCA Civ 1024 (law of England or law of Texas).

Kingdom. For although art.19(2) does not require states within which different territorial units have their own rules of law in respect of contractual obligations to apply the Convention to conflicts between the laws of such units, the United Kingdom decided to apply those rules to intra-United Kingdom conflicts.[138] Accordingly, the rules of the Convention will apply to situations involving a choice between the laws of England and Wales, Scotland and Northern Ireland,[139] as the case may be, as well as to situations involving a choice between the laws of England and Germany.[140]

30–026 **Mandatory.** Lastly, it has been suggested that the parties to a contract may be able to exclude the application of the uniform rules contained in the Rome Convention by indicating a choice, in the contract, of "English law excluding the Act of 1990" (i.e. the Contracts (Applicable Law) Act 1990) or of English law as it was on the day before the 1990 Act entered into force.[141] This view cannot be accepted,[142] principally because the 1990 Act provides, in unambiguous terms, that the Convention shall have "the force of law" in the United Kingdom[143] and because it is stated in the Convention itself that the Convention:

> "… *shall* apply in a Contracting State to contracts made after the date on which this Convention has entered into force with respect to that State."[144]

The words of the Act denote the mandatory character of the rules, as a matter of English law,[145] while the words of the Convention clearly indicate a treaty obligation on the United Kingdom to implement the provisions of the Convention, which obligation has, of course, been discharged in the 1990 Act.

30–027 **Relationship with other Conventions and EC Law.** Article 21 of the Rome Convention stipulates that the Convention is not "to prejudice the application of international conventions to which a contracting state is, or becomes, a party".[146]

---

[138] Contracts (Applicable Law) Act 1990 s.2(3).

[139] For an example, see *Ennstone Building Products Ltd v Stanger Ltd* [2002] EWCA Civ 916, [2002] 1 W.L.R. 3059 (law of England or law of Scotland). In such cases it is probable that a UK appellate court could make a reference to the European Court under the Brussels Protocol: see *Dicey, Morris and Collins*, paras 32–029—32–030; Plender, pp.41–43. cf. *Kleinwort Benson Ltd v City of Glasgow District Council* (C–346/93) [1995] E.C.R. I–615 [1996] Q.B. 57.

[140] The German Länder would not have to be treated as separate legal systems under art.19(1) because German contract law is federal in nature: see *Dicey, Morris and Collins* para.32–029.

[141] F.A. Mann (1991) 107 L.Q.R. 353, a view perhaps not unconnected with the learned author's general hostility to the Convention. See above, para.30–018 fn.108.

[142] See *Halpern v Halpern (Nos 1 and 2)* [2007] EWCA Civ 291, [2008] Q.B. 195 at [21]–[24]; *Dicey, Morris and Collins*, para.32–044; *Benjamin's Sale of Goods*, 7th edn (2006), para.25–027; Hogan (1992) 108 L.Q.R. 12; North (1992) 3 King's Coll.L.J. 29, 38–40, reprinted in *Essays in Private International Law* (1993), p.171, 85–187.

[143] Contracts Act 1990 s.2(1) (subject only to s.2(2) and (3)).

[144] EC Treaty art.17 (emphasis supplied).

[145] Compare the same treatment of identical wording in the Carriage of Goods by Sea Act 1971, implementing the Hague-Visby Rules, in *The Hollandia* [1982] Q.B. 872 CA (affirmed [1983] A.C. 565). See also s.5 of and Sch.4 to the 1990 Act which amend legislation referring to the "proper law of a contract" so as to replace that terminology with words which reflect the Convention usage: and see above, para.30–004.

[146] See Plender, pp.15–18; Kaye, pp.367–370. See also arts 23, 24 and 25 of the Rome Convention.

Accordingly, existing and future conventions entered into by contracting states will apply in those states despite the existence of the Rome Convention.[147] Further, art.20 seeks to avoid conflicts between the Rome Convention regime and choice of law provisions contained in acts of the institutions of the European Communities or in national law harmonised in accordance with such acts by providing that the latter provisions shall take precedence over the rules contained in the Convention.[148]

No renvoi. Reflecting the common law,[149] art.15 of the Rome Convention excludes the doctrine of renvoi in providing that application of the law of any country specified by the Convention means "the application of the rules of law in force in that country other than its rules of private international law".[150] 30–028

Incorporation by reference. At common law, the parties were free to incorporate into the contract provisions of foreign law as part of the terms and conditions of the contract.[151] The Rome Convention does not appear to restrict their power to continue with such a device.[152] The principle of incorporation by reference only applies, however where the parties have sufficiently indicated the provisions of foreign law or international convention which are apt to be incorporated as terms of the contract. A broad reference to principles of Sharia law is insufficient to incorporate such principles.[153] 30–029

[147] The principal conventions envisaged in this provision would seem to be those concerning matters of private international law: see art.24 of the Rome Convention. See, e.g. the Hague Convention on the Law Applicable to International Sale of Goods of June 15, 1955 to which Denmark, France, Italy and Sweden but not the UK, are parties. Belgium has denounced this Convention. Art.21 is, however, broad enough to enable a State party to the Vienna Convention on the International Sale of Goods 1980 to continue to apply that Convention. A UK court *may* be required to apply the Vienna Convention if the law applicable to the contract pursuant to the Rome Convention is that of a country which is a party to the Vienna Convention and which would regard the latter Convention as applicable, but such a conclusion is controversial. It may equally be the case that, because of art.21, international conventions are only properly applicable as between contracting states which are parties thereto, with the consequence that since the UK is not a party to the Vienna Convention, it will be the contract law of the country (excluding the Vienna Convention) which will be applicable: this problem is distinct from that of *renvoi*, as to which, see above, para.30–016 and below, para.30–028. The power of the parties to a contract of sale to choose the Uniform Law on International Sales to govern the contract would not seem to be prejudiced by the Rome Convention since that power is conferred by statute (Uniform Law on International Sales Act 1967) and ULIS is not the law of a "country" for the purposes of the Rome Convention.

[148] See, e.g. the proposed Regulation concerning conflict of laws in employment relationships COM(1976) 75 final, which, if implemented, would have had that effect. The proposal was withdrawn in November 1981: see [1981] OJ C307/3. As to employment contracts, see below, paras 30–108 et seq.

[149] Above, para.30–010.

[150] Since the exclusion of *renvoi* prevents application of rules of private international law, it has no bearing on the issue concerning the application of the Vienna Convention discussed in fn.150, above, since that Convention establishes rules of substantive law rather than rules of private international law.

[151] Above, para.30–009.

[152] *Shamil Bank of Bahrain v Beximco Pharmaceuticals Ltd* [2004] EWCA Civ 19, [2004] 1 W.L.R. 1784; *Halpern v Halpern (Nos 1 and 2)* [2007] EWCA Civ 291, [2008] Q.B. 195 at [31]–[38]; *Dicey, Morris and Collins*, para.32–088.

[153] *Shamil Bank of Bahrain v Beximco Pharmaceuticals Ltd* [2004] EWCA Civ 19; see also *Halpern v Halpern* [2007] EWCA Civ 291 at [31]–[38].

(b) *Exclusions*[154]

30–030 **Introduction.** The specific scope of the provisions of the Rome Convention is set out in art.1. The general purport of art.1(1) has already been referred to but it is necessary to examine one additional question in relation to that provision, namely the meaning of "contractual obligations". For if an obligation is not a "contractual obligation" for the purposes of that provision, then the Convention does not apply even if the situation involves "a choice between the laws of different countries." Secondly, art.1(2) excludes certain types of contract and certain issues which are capable of arising in a contractual context from the scope of the Convention. The following paragraphs deal with these two questions.

30–031 **Meaning of "contractual obligations".** At a very general level, it can be said that since the Rome Convention is only concerned with contractual obligations, property rights and intellectual property are not covered by its provisions.[155] This observation, however, does not carry the matter much further and the Giuliano-Lagarde Report provides no additional guidance. Initially, however, it would seem to be generally accepted that an autonomous or Convention interpretation should be given to the expression "contractual obligations"[156] and that, thus, the expression should not necessarily be limited to obligations which the law of the English forum would regard as contractual.[157] But the precise ramifications of

---

[154] *Dicey, Morris and Collins on the Conflict of Laws*, 14th edn (2006), paras 32–031—32–042; Cheshire and North, *Private International Law*, 13th edn (1999), pp.543–544, 546–551; Fawcett, Harris and Bridge, *International Sale of Goods in the Conflict of Laws* (2005), Ch.18; Plender, *The European Contracts Convention*, 2nd edn (2001), Chs 3 and 4; Kaye, *The New Private International Law of Contract of the European Community* (1993), pp.98–106, 111–142.

[155] Giuliano-Lagarde Report, p.10. Thus, e.g. although the contractual aspects of a sale of goods will be governed by the Rome Convention, the proprietary aspects will not, and thus will be governed by the rules as to proprietary rights developed in the common law. See also *Glencore International AG v Metro Trading International Inc* [2001] 1 Lloyd's Rep. 284; *Raiffeisen Zentralbank Osterreich AG v Five Star General Trading LLC* [2001] EWCA Civ 68, [2001] Q.B. 825. On these rules, see *Benjamin's Sale of Goods*, 7th edn (2006), paras 25–121—25–155.

[156] *Raiffeisen Zentralbank Osterreich AG v Five Star General Trading LLC* [2001] EWCA Civ 68; *Base Metal Trading Ltd v Shamurin* [2004] EWCA Civ 1316, [2005] 1 W.L.R. 1157; see also *Atlantic Telecom GmbH, Noter* (2004) S.L.T. 1031. See *Dicey, Morris and Collins* para.32–023; Cheshire and North pp.543–546; Plender pp.49–54; Kaye pp.97–98. And see above, paras 1–007 et seq.

[157] *Raiffeisen Zentralbank Osterreich AG v Five Star General Trading LLC* [2001] EWCA Civ 68. cf. *Re Bonacina* [1912] 2 Ch. 394. See also the decisions of the European Court giving an independent meaning to the phrase "matters relating to contract" in art.5(1) of the Brussels Convention on Jurisdiction and the Enforcement of Judgments in Civil and Commercial Matters 1968: *Peters v ZNAV* (34/82) [1983] E.C.R. 987; *Arcado Sprl v Haviland SA* (9/87) [1988] E.C.R 1539; *Soc Handte et Cie GmbH v TMCS* (C–26/91) [1992] E.C.R. I–3967. Because of the different language used in art.5(1) of the 1968 Convention, such cases are only an approximate guide to the meaning of "contractual obligation" under the Rome Convention. It has been held that where A contracts with B to pay a sum of money to C, an action brought to enforce the obligation by C involves "matters relating to a contract" for the purposes of art.5(1) of the Lugano Convention on Jurisdiction and the Enforcement of Judgments in Civil and Commercial Matters 1988 (Civil Jurisdiction and Judgments Act 1982 Sch.3A): see *Atlas Shipping Agency (UK) Ltd v Suisse Atlantique Societe D'Armement Maritime SA* [1995] 2 Lloyd's Rep. 188. Whether the making of a contract was induced by a misrepresentation has also been held to fall within this provision, the relevant "obligation" for the purposes of art.5(1) being the obligation to avoid pre-contractual misrepresentation: see *Agnew v Lansforsakringsbolagens AB* [2000] 1 A.C. 268, not following on the latter point, *Trade Indemnity Plc v Forsakringsaktiebolaget Njord* [1995] 1 All E.R. 796. cf. *Fonderie Officine Meccaniche Tacconi SpA v Heinrich Wagner Sinto Maschinenfabrik GmbH (HWS)* (C–334/00) [2002] E.C.R.

this approach will only emerge through decided cases.[158] Additionally, it may be said that the Rome Convention does not apply to tortious obligations. But this observation does not help to resolve the proper classification of an obligation which is contractual under one relevant system of law but tortious under another relevant system of law, and presumably an autonomous or independent concept will have to be developed to deal with this situation as well.[159] This outcome will be all the more likely when the Rome II Regulation on the law applicable to non-contractual obligations[160] comes into effect since the term "non-contractual obligation" for the purpose of that Regulation must be understood as an autonomous concept, independent of meanings it may have in national law[161] and because it may become necessary to demarcate the respective scope of the Rome II Regulation and the Rome Convention, the meaning of "contractual obligation" in the latter instrument will similarly be interpreted in an autonomous fashion.

Concurrent liability. A rather different problem is presented when the forum (as is sometimes the case in English law, with employment contracts[162]) allows alternative claims in contract and tort. In such a case an English court has held[163] that there is nothing in the Rome Convention which precludes, say, an employee from framing his claim in tort if the tort choice of law rule is more advantageous to him than the rules of the Rome Convention.[164] When, however the Rome II 30–032

I–7357 (pre-contractual liability following from failure to conclude a contract not a matter of contract but a matter of tort, delict or quasi-delict within the meaning of art.5(3) of the Convention). The law applicable to non-contractual obligations falling within the principle of *culpa in contrahendo*, i.e. obligations arising out of dealings prior to the conclusion of the contract will be governed, when it enters into effect, by Regulation 864/2007 of July 11, 2007 on the law applicable to non-contractual obligations (Rome II) [2007] OJ L199/40 (hereafter "Rome II") art.1(2)(i) and art.12; see Rome I Regulation Recital 10; *Dicey, Morris and Collins, First Supplement to the Fourteenth Edition* (2007), paras S35–242—S35–247. See also Pertegas in Meeusen, Pertegas and Straetmans (eds), *Enforcement of International Contracts in the European Union* (2004), pp.175–190; Briggs [2003] L.M.C.L.Q. 12.

[158] For some speculative views, see Plender at pp.52–54; Kaye at pp.98–106. It has been doubted whether "public law" contracts, e.g. French administrative law contracts are covered: see Kaye at p.111; cf. *Dicey, Morris and Collins*, para.32–024. See also Whittaker (2000) 116 L.Q.R. 95 and above, para.1–007. As to unilateral contracts, see *Standard Bank Plc v Agrinvest International Inc* [2007] EWHC 2595 (Comm); Maher (2002) Jur. Rev. 317.

[159] cf. *Soc Handte et Cie GmbH v TMCS* [1992] E.C.R. I–3967.

[160] Regulation 864/2007.

[161] Recital 11 to the Rome II Regulation.

[162] As to which see below, paras 30–108 et seq.

[163] *Base Metal Trading Ltd v Shamurin* [2004] EWCA Civ 1316, [2005] 1 W.L.R. 1157; *Booth v Phillips* [2004] EWHC 1437 (Comm), [2004] 1 W.L.R. 3292. See *Dicey, Morris and Collins*, paras 33–084—33–085, 35–066; Fawcett, Harris and Bridge, *International Sale of Goods in the Conflict of Laws* (2005), Ch.20. See also *Ennstone Building Products Ltd v Stanger Ltd* [2002] EWCA Civ 916, [2002] 1 W.L.R. 3059. cf. *Kalfelis v Schroder* (189/87) [1988] E.C.R. 5565 holding such a claim to be contractual for the purposes of art.5(1) of the Brussels Convention.

[164] cf. *Matthews v Kuwait Bechtel Corp* [1959] 2 Q.B. 57; *Coupland v Arabian Gulf Oil Co* [1983] 1 W.L.R. 1136 (affirmed 1151); *Johnson v Coventry Churchill International Ltd* [1992] 3 All E.R. 14 (where the claim was made in tort only, the contract not being pleaded); *Base Metal Trading Ltd v Shamurin* [2004] EWCA Civ 1316. See also *Ennstone Building Products Ltd v Stanger Ltd* [2002] EWCA Civ 916. There is nothing in Pt III of the Private International Law (Miscellaneous Provisions) Act 1995, which contains the principal choice of law rules in tort in English law, which precludes an employee from relying on an alternative claim in contract if it is more advantageous to do so: see *Dicey, Morris and Collins* para.32–024. See also below, paras 30–121—30–122.

Regulation becomes applicable (i.e. in respect of proceedings commenced after January 11, 2009) it is highly unlikely that the claimant will have the option of framing a claim which is contractual as a claim in tort since the term "non-contractual obligation" in that Regulation must be understood as an autonomous concept independent of meanings it may have in national law so that the meanings of "contractual obligation" and "non-contractual obligation" are likely to be held to be mutually exclusive.[165]

30–033 **Restitution.** Finally, it would seem to be the case, in the United Kingdom at any rate, that the Rome Convention will not be applied to claims which are classified, according to English notions, as sounding in restitution (or quasi-contract[166]). This much is suggested by the power to make a reservation to art.10(1)(e) of the Convention, which refers the "consequences of nullity" of the contract to the law applicable to the contract,[167] which power was exercised by the United Kingdom[168] because such a question is not a matter of contract but one of restitution in United Kingdom legal systems.[169] Consistently with this, a majority of the House of Lords has held that a claim for money paid under a void contract was not a matter "relating to a contract" for the purposes of art.5(1) of the modified version of the Brussels Convention on Jurisdiction and the Enforcement of Judgments in Civil and Commercial Matters 1968[170] which is applicable as between the component parts of the United Kingdom.[171]

30–034 **Effect of Rome II Regulation.** When the Rome II Regulation takes effect it would seem that the consequences of nullity of a contract may be regarded as falling within art.10 of that Regulation which provides choice of law rules for determining the law applicable to non-contractual obligations arising out of unjust enrichment. The principal rule is that where such an obligation concerns a relationship between the parties, such as one arising out of a contract or a tort that is closely connected with the unjust enrichment, then the obligation shall be governed by the law that governs that relationship.[172] This will normally mean

[165] See Recital 11 and previous paragraph. And see *Kalfelis v Schroeder* (C–187/87) [1988] E.C.R. 5565. cf. *Trafigura Beheer BV v Kookmin Bank Co* [2006] EWHC 1450 (Comm), [2006] 2 Lloyd's Rep. 455.

[166] See Cheshire and North, pp.543, 671, 673; cf. Fawcett, Harris and Bridge, *International Sale of Goods in the Conflict of Laws* (2005), Ch.19. And below, para.30–327.

[167] Rome Convention art.22(1). Even Member States who do not make a reservation will, presumably, not apply the Convention to all aspects of restitution or quasi-contract but only to this aspect since they regard it as contractual.

[168] Contracts (Applicable Law) Act 1990 s.2(2).

[169] *Hansard*, HL Vol.513, cols 1258–1259. And see below, para.30–327.

[170] Civil Jurisdiction and Judgments Act 1982 Sch.4.

[171] *Kleinwort Benson Ltd v Glasgow City Council* [1999] 1 A.C. 153, reversing a majority decision of the Court of Appeal to the opposite effect: [1996] Q.B. 678. The European Court of Justice had earlier declined jurisdiction to interpret this version of the Brussels Convention: see *Kleinwort Benson Ltd v Glasgow City Council* (C–346/93) [1995] E.C.R. I–5615, [1996] Q.B. 547. See also *Raiffeisen Zentralbank Osterreich Aktiengesellshaft v National Bank of Greece SA* [1999] 1 Lloyd's Rep. 408. cf. *Caterpillar Financial Services Corp v SNC Passion* [2004] EWHC 569 (Comm), [2004] 2 Lloyd's Rep. 99 at [16].

[172] Rome II Regulation art.10(1). Art.10(2) and (3) provide default rules for cases where the applicable law cannot be determined on the basis of art.10(1) and 10(4) provides that where it is clear from all the circumstances of the case that the non-contractual obligation arising out of unjust enrichment is manifestly more closely connected with a country other than that indicated in art.10(1),

that the law applicable to the contract will be the applicable law in cases where the relationship between the parties arises out of a contract. It would also seem, however, that when the Rome I Regulation takes effect the issue will be submitted to the law applicable to the contract since art.12(1)(e) of the latter Regulation reproduces art.10(1)(e) of the Rome Convention and there is no power to make a reservation to any provision of a Regulation.[173]

Specifically excluded matters. Article 1(2) provides that the rules of the Rome Convention shall not apply to certain specified matters. These are discussed in the following paragraphs. 30–035

Capacity of natural persons. The Convention is not to apply to "questions involving the status or legal capacity of natural persons" subject to the operation of a special rule relating to the contractual capacity of such persons.[174] This special rule, contained in art.11, is discussed later in this Chapter.[175] The question of the law which determines the capacity of a natural person to enter into a contract will thus, in general, be governed by common law rules.[176] Essentially, this question was excluded because of disagreement between common law and civil law negotiators as to the proper classification of it. A common lawyer usually regards the matter as a contractual issue, whereas the civil lawyer regards it as an issue of status.[177] 30–036

Wills, succession, etc. Article 1(2)(b) excludes from the ambit of the Convention contractual obligations relating to wills and succession; rights in property arising out of a matrimonial relationship; rights and duties arising out of a family relationship, parentage, marriage or affinity, including maintenance obligations in respect of children who are not legitimate. The purpose of this is to exclude all matters of family law.[178] In relation to maintenance obligations, the exclusion extends only to contracts which are made by parties under a legal maintenance obligation, in performance of that obligation.[179] All other contractual obligations, even if they provide for maintenance of a member of the family to whom there are no legal maintenance obligations, would fall within the scope of the Convention.[180] The contractual effects of gifts apparently fall within the Convention, even when made within the family, unless they are covered by family law.[181] Contractual effects of gifts would also be excluded if they arise out of the law relating to succession or that relating to matrimonial property rights.[182] Although 30–037

(2), or (3), the law of that other country shall apply. See *Dicey, Morris and Collins on the Conflict of Laws, First Supplement to the Fourteenth Edition*, paras 34–014, 34–044.

[173] See below, para.30–328.

[174] Rome Convention art.1(2)(a).

[175] Below, para.30–324.

[176] Below, para.30–324.

[177] North in North (ed.), *Contract Conflicts* (1982), p.10, reprinted in *Essays in Private International Law* (1993), p.23; Bogdan in Meeusen, Pertegas and Straetmans (eds), *The Enforcement of International Contracts in the European Union* (2004), pp.211–223.

[178] Giuliano-Lagarde Report, p.10.

[179] Giuliano-Lagarde Report, p.10.

[180] Giuliano-Lagarde Report, p.10. See *Waldwiese Stiftung v Lewis* [2004] EWHC 2589 (Ch).

[181] Giuliano-Lagarde Report, p.10. See *Dicey, Morris and Collins*, para.32–033.

[182] Giuliano-Lagarde Report, pp.10–11. See *Tod v Barton* [2002] EWHC 264 (Ch); [2002] W.T.L.R. 469; *Halpern v Halpern* [2007] EWCA Civ. 291, [2007] 2 Lloyd's Rep. 56 at [23]

not specifically mentioned, matters relating to the custody of children are excluded since they fall within the realm of personal status and capacity.[183]

30–038 **Bills of exchange, cheques and promissory notes.** The rules of the Convention do not apply to bills of exchange, cheques and promissory notes.[184] To have included such obligations would have required "rather complicated special rules"[185] which would have been inappropriate in a Convention purporting to deal with contractual obligations in general. Further, many Member States (but not the United Kingdom) are parties to the Geneva Conventions which govern most of these areas.[186] And, in any event, such obligations are regarded as non-contractual in some Member States.[187] Bills, cheques and promissory notes will thus, in England, be dealt with under the relevant statutory and common law rules.[188]

30–039 **Other negotiable instruments.** The exclusion goes further than the obligations just mentioned for, in addition, "other negotiable instruments to the extent that the obligations under such other negotiable instruments arise out of their negotiable character"[189] are also excised from the ambit of the uniform rules.[190] Whether a document is to be classified as a negotiable instrument is not, however, a matter for the Convention but one for the law of the forum, including its rules of private international law.[191] But the exclusion only extends to those obligations which arise out of the negotiable character of documents so characterised: it would not, apparently, extend, e.g. to contracts pursuant to which such instruments are issued, or contracts for the purchase and sale of such instruments.[192]

30–040 **Arbitration agreements and agreements on the choice of court.** Of considerable practical significance is the exclusion from the scope of the Convention of arbitration agreements and agreements on the choice of court.[193] The exclusion was also a matter of some controversy within the group which negotiated the

(compromise of arbitration dealing with a dispute as to whether assets outside an estate should be brought into account in order that one party should gain a fair share could not be termed a contract relating to wills and succession).

[183] Giuliano-Lagarde Report, p.11.

[184] Rome Convention art.1(2)(c).

[185] Giuliano-Lagarde Report, p.11.

[186] Giuliano-Lagarde Report, p.11.

[187] Giuliano-Lagarde Report, p.11.

[188] See *Zebrarise Ltd v De Nieffe* [2004] EWHC 1842 (Comm), [2005] 1 Lloyd's Rep. 154; Vol.II, paras 34–197 et seq.

[189] Art.1(2)(c).

[190] For discussion, see *Dicey, Morris and Collins*, paras 33–323—33–332; Schultsz in North (ed.), *Contract Conflicts* (1982), pp.188–191; Plender, pp.65–67; Kaye, pp.117–118.

[191] Giuliano-Lagarde Report, p.11. cf. Schultsz in *Contract Conflicts*.

[192] Giuliano-Lagarde Report, p.11.

[193] Rome Convention art.1(2)(d). See *Tamil Nadu Electricity Board v ST-CMS Electric Co Private Ltd* [2007] EWHC 1713 (Comm), [2007] 2 All E.R. (Comm) 701 at [44]. And see *Halpern v Halpern (Nos 1 and 2)* [2007] EWCA Civ 291, [2008] Q.B. 195. For discussion, see *Dicey, Morris and Collins*, paras 32–035—32–037; Cheshire and North, pp.548–549; Plender, pp.67–74; Kaye, pp.118–121; Morse in Meeusen, Pertegas and Straetmans (eds), *The Enforcement of International Contracts in the European Union* (2004), pp.191–209. An arbitration or choice of court agreement may nonetheless be relevant in determining whether the parties have made a choice of law: see below, para.30–051.

Convention.[194] As far as arbitration agreements are concerned, the arguments for exclusion were the need to avoid an increase in the number of international conventions in this area,[195] that the concept of closest connection[196] was difficult to apply to arbitration agreements, that the procedural and contractual aspects of such agreements were difficult to separate and that since the Convention permitted "severability",[197] the arbitration clause could be treated as a distinct entity, apart from the contract, without any difficulty.[198] The result of the exclusion is that not only the procedural aspects but also the formation, validity and effect[199] of an arbitration agreement will have, seemingly, to be determined by common law rules, which is at best inconvenient, whereas the law applicable to the remaining part of the contract will be determined by the rules of the Convention.[200]

Choice of court agreements were excluded because the prevailing view in the negotiating group was that the matter lay within the realm of procedure, that rules of jurisdiction were a matter of public policy, that a court must determine the validity of such an agreement according to its own law rather than the law chosen,[201] that Convention rules would be frustrated if disputes were brought before courts of non-contracting states,[202] and, finally, that in relation to cases within the Community, most important matters (validity of the clause and form) are governed by art.17 of the Brussels Convention on Jurisdiction and the Enforcement of Judgments in Civil and Commercial Matters 1968.[203] The result is that this question will again be governed by common law rules.[204]

Questions governed by the law of companies, etc. Questions governed by the law of companies and other bodies corporate or unincorporate such as the 30–041

[194] Giuliano-Lagarde Report, pp.11–12. The UK argued strenuously for the inclusion of both matters.

[195] In fact only the New York Convention on the Recognition and Enforcement of Foreign Arbitral Awards touches upon the law applicable to an arbitration agreement (Arbitration Act 1996 s.103(2)(b)), and that only in the context of the recognition and enforcement of foreign awards.

[196] See below, para.30–071.

[197] See below, paras 30–056—30–057, 30–071.

[198] Giuliano-Lagarde Report, pp.11–12. As to "severability" of an arbitration clause, see *XL Insurance Ltd v Owens Corning* [2000] 2 Lloyd's Rep. 500; *Premium Nafta Products Ltd v Fili Shipping Co Ltd* [2007] UKHL 40.

[199] Giuliano-Lagarde Report, p.12; and see *XL Insurance Ltd v Owens Corning* [2002] 2 Lloyd's Rep. 500.

[200] In practice it may be that the law applicable to the contractual aspects of the arbitration agreement will normally be the same as that which governs the contract of which it forms part: *Dicey, Morris and Collins*, para.32–037; cf. Cheshire and North, pp.548–549.

[201] This is not the case in English law, in which the validity of such an agreement depends on the applicable law: see *Dicey, Morris and Collins*, para.12–090. cf. *Centrax Ltd v Citibank NA* [1999] 1 All E.R. (Comm) 557; *XL Insurance Ltd v Owens Corning* [2002] 2 Lloyd's Rep. 500; above, para.30–039.

[202] It is difficult not to regard this reason as incomprehensible, since, presumably, non-contracting states would not apply the Convention in any event.

[203] Giuliano-Lagarde Report, p.11. Apparently, according to the view there expressed: "[O]utstanding points, notably those relating to consent, do not arise in practice, having regard to the fact that Art.17 provides that these agreements shall be in writing." But see *Dicey, Morris and Collins*, paras 12–097—12–099, 16–017—16–027, 32–035—32–037.

[204] *Akai Pty Ltd v People's Insurance Co Ltd* [1998] 1 Lloyd's Rep. 90, 98. However, normally the law applicable to the choice of court agreement will be the same as that applicable to the contract of which it forms part: see fn.200, above.

creation, by registration or otherwise, legal capacity, internal organisation or winding up of companies and other bodies corporate or unincorporate and the personal liability of officers and members as such for the obligations of the company or body will not fall within the ambit of the Rome Convention.[205] The intention behind the provision is the exclusion of matters of contract which arise in the context of company law,[206] particularly in view of the work being done in the European Community on the harmonisation of company law.[207] Thus, for example, the question of the law applicable to the contractual capacity of a company will be governed by common law rules[208] and not by the Convention. On the other hand, an agreement by promoters to create a company is thought to fall within the scope of the Convention.[209]

30–042 **Power of agent to bind principal, etc.** Further excluded is the question of whether an agent is able to bind a principal, or an organ to bind a company or body corporate or unincorporate, to a third party.[210] The exclusion only affects the question of whether the principal is bound with regard to third parties by the acts of the agent (or organ of a company etc, as the case may be).[211] It is justified because the Convention permits parties a wide freedom to choose the applicable law of a contract,[212] a freedom which it was not thought appropriate to recognise in this context.[213] This matter will, therefore, continue to be governed by common law rules.[214] But the rules of the Convention will apply to determine the law which governs the contract (if any) between principal and agent,[215] and also,

---

[205] Rome Convention art.1(2)(e). See *Dicey, Morris and Collins*, paras 30–025—30–028; Benedetelli in Meeusen, Pertegas and Straetmans (eds), *The Enforcement of International Contracts in the European Union* (2004), pp.225–254.

[206] Giuliano-Lagarde Report, p.12.

[207] On this work, see Dine, *EC Company Law* (1991); Andenas and Kenyon-Slade (eds), *EC Financial Market Regulation and Company Law* (1993); Werlauff, *EC Company Law* (1993).

[208] *Base Metal Trading Ltd v Shamurin* [2004] EWCA Civ 1316, [2005] 1 W.L.R. 1157; *Continental Enterprises Ltd v Shandong Zucheng Foreign Trade Group Co* [2005] EWHC 92 (Comm); *Atlantic Telecom GmbH, Noter* (2004) S.L.T. 1031. See below, para.30–325. The exclusion of legal capacity concerns limitations on companies or firms, for example, in respect of acquisition of immovable property, but does not concern "*ultra vires* act by organs of the company or firm" (Giuliano-Lagarde Report, pp.12–13) which are excluded under Rome Convention art.1(2)(f): see below, paras 30–042, 30–325.

[209] Giuliano-Lagarde Report, p.12.

[210] Rome Convention art.1(2)(f).

[211] Giuliano-Lagarde Report, p.13.

[212] See below, paras 30–047 et seq.

[213] Giuliano-Lagarde Report, p.13.

[214] As to which, see *Dicey, Morris and Collins*, para.33R–428 et seq.

[215] Giuliano-Lagarde Report, p.13. For discussion, see *Dicey, Morris and Collins*, paras 33–405—33–425. Application of the common law rules on this matter may be affected by the Directive on Self-employed Commercial Agents [1986] OJ L382/17 implemented in England and Wales and Scotland by the Commercial Agents (Council Directive) Regulations 1993 (SI 1993/3053), as amended by SI 1993/3173 and SI 1998/2868 and in Northern Ireland by the Commercial Agents (Council Directive) Regulations (Northern Ireland) 1993 (SI 1993/483). The Regulations govern the relations between commercial agents and their principals and apply in respect of the activities of commercial agents in Great Britain (reg.1(2)). It is specifically provided that regs 3–22, which deal with the mutual rights and obligations of agent and principal, remuneration of the agent, the conclusion and termination of the agency contract and miscellaneous matters such as service of notices, do not apply where the parties have agreed that the agency contract is to be governed by the law of another Member State (reg.1(3)(a)). Conversely, regs 3–22 will apply where the law of another

it would seem, the law which governs the contract (if any) which the agent concludes with a third party.[216] Further excluded by art.1(2)(f) is the effect of ultra vires acts by an organ of a company or firm,[217] but the fact that this is said to be excluded under this provision rather than that dealing with company law (art.1(2)(e))[218] would appear to be of no practical significance.[219]

Trusts. Article 1(2)(g) excludes the constitution of trusts and the relationship between settlors, trustees and beneficiaries. Trusts in this context, are to be understood in the meaning which they bear in common law countries.[220] This readily explains their exclusion since, in the common law sense, a trust is not a contract.[221] In the civil law systems, however, institutions similar to the trust may fall within the Convention because they are normally contractual in origin.[222] According to the Giuliano-Lagarde Report, it will, nevertheless, be open to the judge to treat these civil law institutions in the same way as the institutions of the common law countries when the former exhibit the same characteristics as the latter.[223] **30–043**

Evidence and procedure. Article 1(2)(h) of the Convention excludes "evidence and procedure, without prejudice to Article 14", from the scope of the Convention. Article 14 (concerned with the law applicable to presumptions, burden of proof and mode of proof) is discussed below, paras 30–351—30–354. The Giuliano-Lagarde Report expresses the view that the exclusion of evidence and procedure "seems to require no comment".[224] Presumably it will be for national law to classify an issue as belonging to one or other of these categories.[225] But it must be borne in mind that a matter classified as evidential or procedural will be governed by the law of the forum. The possibility of disparate approaches to classification amongst the contracting states may thus constitute an **30–044**

Member State, corresponding to the Regulations, enables the parties to agree that the agency contract is to be governed by the law of a different Member State and the parties have agreed that it is to be governed by English law (reg.1(3)(b)). For consideration of some of the conflict of laws problems which arise in the context of the Directive and the Regulations, see *Ingmar GB Ltd v Eaton Leonard Technologies Inc* (381/98) [2000] E.C.R. I–9305, discussed by Verhagen (2002) 51 I.C.L.Q. 135. For further discussion, see Vol.II, para.31–017; *Bowstead and Reynolds on Agency*, 18th edn (2006), Ch.11; *Dicey, Morris and Collins*, paras 33–416—33–425; below, para.30–065. On the interpretation of the compensation provisions of the Regulations, see *Lonsdale v Howard & Hallam Ltd* [2007] UKHL 32, [2007] 1 W.L.R. 2055, Vol.II, para.31–147.

216 Giuliano-Lagarde Report, p.13. This conclusion is not free from difficulty: *Dicey, Morris and Collins*, para.33–443. See also *Presentaciones Musicales SA v Secunda* [1994] Ch. 271.

217 Giuliano-Lagarde Report, p.13.

218 Above, para.30–042.

219 *Dicey, Morris and Collins*, para.33–430.

220 Giuliano-Lagarde Report, p.13.

221 For choice of law rules in trusts, see *Dicey, Morris and Collins* at Ch.29. See *Tod v Barton* [2002] EWHC 264 (Ch), [2002] W.T.L.R. 469; *Chellaram v Chellaram (No.2)* [2002] EWHC 632 (Ch), [2002] 3 All E.R. 17.

222 Giuliano-Lagarde Report, p.13.

223 Giuliano-Lagarde Report, p.13. See the discussion in Plender at pp.78–80.

224 Giuliano-Lagarde Report, p.13.

225 See Cheshire and North, p.550 (stressing that English courts should not necessarily adopt the classifications applied in the common law in the context of the Convention).

obstacle to the uniformity of choice of law rules which the Convention seeks to achieve.[226]

30–045 **Insurance.** Article 1(3) of the Rome Convention provides that its rules:

> "... do not apply to contracts of insurance which cover risks situated in the territories of the Member States of the European Economic Community. In order to determine whether a risk is situated in these territories the court shall apply its internal law."[227]

The effect of this provision is as follows. Where the risk covered by the insurance contract is situated outside the territories of the Member States of the European Communities, the rules of the Rome Convention will apply.[228] Additionally, those rules will also apply to determine the law applicable to a contract of reinsurance since such contracts are specifically exempted from the exclusionary rule of art.1(3), even if the contract of reinsurance covers a risk which is situated in a Member State.[229] Where, however, the risk covered by a contract of insurance is situated in the territories of the Member States of the EC or, as from December 1, 2001, in an EEA Member State, the choice of law rules to determine the applicable law are to be found in special legal regimes for, respectively, non-life and life insurance, which regimes are based on Community Directives[230]

---

[226] Cheshire and North suggest that the principles of uniform interpretation (art.18, above, para.30–020) may be applied to avoid the danger of different states making different classifications. And see below, Section 5.

[227] Contrast the approach taken in the Rome I Regulation which provides, in art.7, choice of law rules for determining the law applicable to contracts of insurance, subject to the exclusion of a limited category of insurance contracts in art.1(2)(k): see below, paras 30–252 et seq.

[228] See *Crédit Lyonnais v New Hampshire Insurance Co* [1997] 2 Lloyd's Rep. 1; *American Motorists Insurance Co v Cellstar Corp* [2003] EWCA Civ 206; [2003] I.L. Pr. 370. For the application of the rules of the Rome Convention in this situation, see *Dicey, Morris and Collins*, r.214, paras 33–137 et seq.

[229] Rome Convention art.1(4). For application of the Convention rules to reinsurance, see *Dicey, Morris and Collins*, r.217, paras 33–210 et seq. The special choice of law rules for insurance contracts contained in the Rome I Regulation do not apply to contracts of reinsurance: see art.7(1), below, para.30–256.

[230] Second Council Directive on the co-ordination of laws, regulations and administrative provisions relating to direct insurance other than life insurance and laying down provisions to facilitate the effective exercise of the freedom to provide services: [1988] OJ L127/1, amending the First Council Directive [1973] OJ L228/3 (the Second Non-Life Insurance Directive); Third Council Directive on the co-ordination of laws, regulations and administrative provisions relating to direct insurance other than life insurance [1992] OJ L228/1, amending the First Council Directive and the Second Non-Life Insurance Directive, (the Third Non-Life Directive); Second Council Directive on the co-ordination of laws, regulations and administrative provisions relating to direct life assurance, laying down provisions to facilitate the effective exercise of freedom to provide services [1990] OJ L330/50, amending the First Council Directive [1979] OJ L63/1 (the Second Life Insurance Directive); Third Council Directive on the co-ordination of laws, regulations and administrative provisions relating to direct life assurance [1992] OJ L360/1, amending the First Council Directive and the Second Life Directive (the Third Life Directive). The choice of law rules are to be found respectively in art.7 of the Second Non-Life Insurance Directive, as amended by art.24 of the Third Non-Life Directive, and art.4 of the Second Life Insurance Directive. The Directives concerned with life insurance have been "recast" and amended in Directive 2002/83 [2002] OJ L345/1. See SI 2004/3379. The choice of law rules contained in art.32 of this Directive are the same as those which are already applicable.

which have been implemented in United Kingdom law.[231] The detail and complexity of these legal regimes precludes discussion here and the reader is referred to the appropriate source.[232]

Identification of *situs*. One issue which may, however, be appropriately dealt with here is as to the rules which are to be used for identifying the *situs* of a risk. The second sentence of art.1(3) requires the court to apply its "internal law"[233] to determine whether a risk is situated in the territories of Member States of the EC, which territories must now be taken to refer to the territories of the Member States of the European Economic Area.[234] Since, traditionally, the *situs* of a risk had played no role in United Kingdom insurance law, difficulties could have arisen in its identification. These difficulties are resolved by the existence of rules for this purpose in the Directives which are incorporated into United Kingdom law by the Financial Services and Markets Act 2000 (Law Applicable to Contracts of Insurance) Regulations 2001,[235] and by an amendment to the Contracts (Applicable Law) Act 1990 which provides that these rules constitute the relevant internal law in art.1(3) of the Rome Convention.[236] 30–046

---

[231] The choice of law rules contained in the directives are, with effect from December 1, 2001, implemented in the Financial Services and Markets Act 2000 (Law Applicable to Contracts of Insurance) Regulations 2001 (SI 2001/2635), as amended by SI 2001/3452. The Regulations apply to determine the law applicable to a contract of Insurance covering a risk situated in an EEA Member State: see in addition to the Regulations EEA Agreement (Agreement on the European Economic Area signed at Oporto on May 2, 1992 as adjusted by the Protocol signed at Brussels on March 17, 1993); European Economic Area Act 1993. The Directives were originally implemented in regulations amending the Insurance Companies Act 1982 which was repealed by the Financial Services and Markets Act 2000.

[232] *Dicey, Morris and Collins*, r.215, paras 33–159 et seq., r.216, paras 33–190 et seq.

[233] This excludes rules of private international law: Giuliano-Lagarde Report, p.13.

[234] See above, fn.230.

[235] SI 2001/2635, as amended by SI 2001/3542: above, fn.231.

[236] Contracts (Applicable Law) Act 1990 s.2(1)(a), as substituted by SI 2001/3649 art.320. According to the Financial Services and Markets Act 2000 (Law Applicable to Contracts of Insurance) Regulations 2001 (hereafter "the Regulations") where the contract relates to buildings or their contents (in so far as the contents are covered by the same policy) the risk covered by the contract is situated in the EEA state in which the property is situated: reg.2(2)(a). If the contract relates to vehicles of any type, the relevant EEA state is that of the registration of the vehicle: reg.2(2)(b). Where the contract covers travel or holiday risks and has a duration of four months or less, the relevant EEA state is that in which the policyholder entered into the contract: reg.2(2)(c). In any other case, if the policyholder is an individual, the EEA state where the risk covered by the contract is situated is that in which the policyholder resides on the date the contract is entered into (reg.2(2)(d)(i)) and the state in which an individual resides for these purposes is to be treated as being the country in which he has his habitual residence (reg.2(3)(a)). If the policyholder is not an individual the relevant EEA state is that in which the establishment (defined in reg.2(1)) of the policyholder too which the contract relates is situated on the date the contract is entered into: reg.2(2)(d)(ii). The scope of the choice of law rules for life insurance is defined by reference to these last two grounds. If the policyholder is an individual, the choice of law rules contained in the Regulations will apply if that individual is habitually resident in an EEA state: regs 2(1) and 2(2)(a). If the policyholder is, for example, a company insuring the lives of an employee or employees, the choice of law rules contained in the Regulations will apply if the establishment at which the employee is, or employees are, employed is situated in an EEA state: reg.2(1). For discussion, see *Dicey, Morris and Collins*, paras 33–144—33–146.

(c) *Choice of Law by the Parties*[237]

30–047 **The general principle.** The opening sentence of art.3(1) of the Rome Convention provides that a "contract shall be governed by the law chosen by the parties." The clear intent of this provision is to legitimise, for the purposes of the Convention, the principle of party autonomy.[238] Its effect is that the law chosen by the parties will govern the contract except to the extent that the power to choose is limited or restricted by other provisions of the Convention.[239]

30–048 **Choice must be of law of a country.** By way of introduction, it would first seem that parties may only choose a law of a country to govern the contract. This appears to follow from the terms of art.1(1) of the Convention.[240] Thus a choice of the principles of Sharia law will not be the choice of the law of a country.[241] Similarly, if the parties stipulate that the contract shall be governed by "general principles of law," or by "its own terms" or by the "*lex mercatoria*," such clauses will not amount to a choice of law.[242] In such cases, the applicable law will have to be determined as if the parties had made no choice of law, i.e. according to art.4 of the Convention[243]: and it will then be for the applicable law, as so identified, to determine whether a clause of this kind is effective.[244]

30–049 **Law neither pleaded nor proved.** Secondly, the question arises as to whether a court faced with a contract containing a choice of law is required to apply that law if that law is neither pleaded nor proved by either party. The use of the word "shall" in the first sentence of art.3(1) appears to carry a mandatory connotation. However, the English rule that foreign law must be pleaded and proved, failing which English law will be applied,[245] is a rule of evidence[246] or procedure[247] and,

---

[237] *Dicey, Morris and Collins on the Conflict of Laws*, 14th edn (2006), paras 30–062—30–103; Cheshire and North, *Private International Law*, 13th edn (1999), pp.552–564; Plender, *The European Contracts Convention*, 2nd edn (2001), Ch.5; Kaye, *The New Private International Law of Contract of the European Community* (1993), pp.147–170. As to the special rules in the Convention for Certain Consumer Contracts (art.5) and Individual Employment Contracts (art.6), see below, paras 30–092 et seq. As to insurance contracts, see above, paras 30–045—30–046. As to the Rome I Regulation, see below, paras 30–170 et seq.

[238] Giuliano-Lagarde Report, pp.15–16. For the background, see *Dicey, Morris and Collins*, paras 32–062—32–064.

[239] See below, paras 30–060 et seq.

[240] "Convention shall apply . . . in any situation involving a choice between the *laws of different countries*" [emphasis added]; *Shamil Bank of Bahrain v Beximco Pharmaceuticals Ltd* [2004] EWCA Civ 19, [2004] 1 W.L.R. 1784; *Halpern v Halpern (Nos 1 and 2)* [2007] EWCA Civ 291, [2008] Q.B. 195; *Musawi v RE International (UK) Ltd* [2007] EWHC 2981 (Ch), [2008] 1 Lloyd's Rep. 326. See above, paras 30–022—30–024.

[241] *Shamil Bank of Bahrain v Beximco Pharmaceuticals Ltd* [2004] EWCA Civ 19; *Musawi v RE International (UK) Ltd* [2007] EWHC 2881 (Ch). See also *Halpern v Halpern (Nos 1 and 2)* [2007] EWCA Civ 241 (Jewish law).

[242] *Dicey, Morris and Collins*, para.32–081; Cheshire and North at pp.559–560.

[243] Below, paras 30–071 et seq.

[244] See Plender at pp.56–57.

[245] *Dicey, Morris and Collins*, Ch.9; Fentiman, *Foreign Law in English Courts* (1998); Hartley (1996) 45 I.C.L.Q. 271; Fentiman (1992) 108 L.Q.R. 142.

[246] Fentiman (1992) 108 L.Q.R. 142.

[247] Giuliano-Lagarde Report, p.18.

as has been pointed out above,[248] such matters are excluded from the scope of the Convention by art.1(2)(h). It is suggested that the practice of the common law remains unchanged and that the court is not bound to apply a foreign applicable law which is neither pleaded nor proved by the parties.[249] However, this conclusion cannot be free from doubt in the light of the potential lack of harmony which it might introduce into the application of the Convention amongst the contracting states.[250]

Meaning of a "choice" of law: express. The second sentence of art.3(1) requires that the "choice must be express or demonstrated with reasonable certainty by the terms of the contract or the circumstances of the case." The first aspect of this formula recognises the efficacy of typical contractual terms such as the contact is to be "governed by"[251] or "construed in accordance with"[252] or "subject to"[253] a particular country's law, as apt to make a choice of law.[254] It appears, also, that an express oral agreement as to the applicable law will satisfy art.3(1).[255] 30–050

"Implied choice". More difficulty surrounds the second aspect of the formula.[256] The common law recognised that parties could impliedly choose the law to govern a contract and that an intention on their part to do so could be inferred from the terms and nature of the contract and from the general circumstances of the case.[257] However, art.3(1) requires that the parties choice be "demonstrated" and further that such demonstration be "with reasonable certainty", which might connote a stricter evidential standard than that involved in drawing an "inference" as to the parties' intentions at common law,[258] particularly when, according to the Giuliano-Lagarde Report, this aspect of the formula is supposed to reveal, in its application, that the parties have made a "real choice of law".[259] Having said that, it is necessary to bear in mind the need for uniform interpretation of the Convention.[260] This means that it is appropriate to adopt a purposive approach to interpretation which does not involve construing the 30–051

[248] Above, para.30–044.

[249] *Dicey, Morris and Collins*, paras 9–011, 32–060, 32–065; Cheshire and North, p.556.

[250] See Fentiman, *Foreign Law in English Courts* (1998), pp.87–96; Fentiman (1992) 108 L.Q.R. 142.

[251] See, e.g. *Vita Food Products Inc v Unus Shipping Co Ltd* [1939] A.C. 277.

[252] See, e.g. *The Torni* [1932] P.78.

[253] *Dicey, Morris and Collins*, para.32–078.

[254] cf. above, paras 30–005, 30–048.

[255] *Oakley v Ultra Vehicle Design Ltd* [2005] EWHC 872 (Ch), [2005] I.L. Pr. 747.

[256] *Dicey, Morris and Collins*, paras 32–091—32–099; Cheshire and North, pp.561–564; Plender, pp.92–100; Kaye, pp.150–154; Morse (1982) 2 Ybk. Eur.L. 107, 117.

[257] Above, paras 30–010—30–011.

[258] See Morse (1982) 2 Ybk. Eur. L. 107, 177. See above, paras 30–010—30–011.

[259] Giuliano-Lagarde Report, p.17. See *Egon Oldendorff v Libera Corp (No.2)* [1996] 1 Lloyd's Rep. 380; *Aeolian Shipping SA v ISS Machinery Services Ltd* [2001] EWCA Civ 1162, [2001] 2 Lloyd's Rep. 641; *Samcrete Egypt Engineers and Contractors SAE v Land Rover Exports Ltd* [2001] EWCA Civ 1162, [2002] C.L.C. 533; *Marubeni Hong Kong and South China Ltd v Mongolian Government* [2002] 2 All E.R. (Comm) 873; *American Motorists Insurance Co v Cellstar Corp* [2003] EWCA Civ 206; [2003] I.L. Pr. 370. See also *Travelers Casualty & Surety Co of Europe Ltd v Sun Life Assurance Co of Canada (UK) Ltd* [2004] EWHC 1704 (Comm), [2004] I.L. Pr. 793.

[260] Rome Convention art.18; *Raiffeisen Zentralbank Osterreich AG v Five Star General Trading LLC* [2001] EWCA Civ 68; [2001] Q.B. 825; *Samcrete Egypt Engineers and Contractors SAE v Land*

Convention in a narrow, literal fashion.[261] Overall however, the examples given in the Giuliano-Lagarde Report of circumstances which may suffice to demonstrate a choice of law with reasonable certainty, tend to indicate that the relevant factors are broadly similar to those which were capable of indicating an implied choice of law at common law.

> "For example, the contract may be in a standard form which is known to be governed by a particular system of law even though there is no express statement to this effect, such as a Lloyd's policy of marine insurance.[262] In other cases a previous course of dealing between the parties under contracts containing an express choice of law may leave the court in no doubt that the contract in question is to be governed by the law previously chosen where the choice of law clause has been omitted in circumstances which do not indicate a deliberate change of policy by the parties.[263] In some cases the choice of a particular forum may show in no uncertain manner that the parties intend the contract to be governed by the law of that forum, but this must always be subject to the other terms of the contract and all the circumstances of the case.[264] Similarly, references in the contract to specific Articles of the French Civil Code may leave the court in no doubt that the parties have deliberately chosen French law, although there

---

Rover Exports Ltd [2001] EWCA Civ 1162; *Iran Continental Shelf Oil Co v IRI International Corp* [2002] EWCA Civ 1024. Above, para.30–020.

[261] *Egon Oldendorff v Libera Corp (No.2)* [1996] 1 Lloyd's Rep. 380; *Raiffeisen Zentralbank Osterreich AG v Five Star General Trading LLC* [2001] EWCA Civ 68; *Samcrete Egypt Engineers and Contractors SAE v Land Rover Exports Ltd* [2001] EWCA Civ 1162; *Iran Continental Shelf Oil Co v IRI International Corp* [2002] EWCA Civ 1024; *Dicey, Morris and Collins*, para.32–080.

[262] See *Tiernan v Magen Insurance Co Ltd* [2000] I.L. Pr. 517 in which it was said that where a reinsurance contract was placed on the Lloyd's market in the usual way, the contract was on a Lloyd's form and contained London market clauses, such factors were sufficient to demonstrate with reasonable certainty a choice of English law for the purposes of art.3 of the Rome Convention. See also *Ace Insurance SA-NV v Zurich Insurance Co* [2000] 2 Lloyd's Rep. 423, affirmed [2001] EWCA Civ 173, [2001] 1 Lloyd's Rep. 618; *Evialis SA v S.I.A.T.* [2003] EWHC 863 (Comm), [2003] 2 Lloyd's Rep. 377; *Tonicstar Ltd v American Home Insurance Co* [2004] EWHC 1234 (Comm), [2005] Lloyd's Rep. I.R. 32; *Tryg Baltica International (UK) Ltd v Boston Compania De Seguros SA* [2004] EWHC 1186 (Comm), [2005] Lloyd's Rep. I.R. 40. cf. *Travelers Casualty and Surety Co of Canada v Sun Life Assurance Co of Canada (UK) Ltd* [2006] EWHC 2716 (Comm), [2007] Lloyd's Rep. I.R. 619; *Dornoch Ltd v Mauritius Union Assurance Co Ltd* [2006] EWCA Civ 389, [2006] 2 Lloyd's Rep. 475. In *Amin Rasheed Shipping Corp v Kuwait Insurance Co* [1984] A.C. 50, 62, where the use of a Lloyd's policy of marine insurance and the absence of any indigenous code of marine insurance law in Kuwait, the other possible applicable law, was held, at common law, to point to an intention to choose English law. cf. *DR Insurance Co v Central National Insurance Co* [1996] 1 Lloyd's Rep. 74. See above, paras 30–010—30–011.

[263] See *Aeolian Shipping SA v ISS Machinery Services Ltd* [2001] EWCA Civ 1162, [2001] 2 Lloyd's Rep. 641; cf. *Burrows v Jamaica Private Power Co Ltd* [2002] 1 All E.R. (Comm) 374. cf. above, para.30–011 fn.59.

[264] *Marubeni Hong Kong and South China Ltd v Mongolian Government* [2002] 2 All E.R. (Comm) 873. cf. *Burrows v Jamaica Private Power Co Ltd* [2002] 1 All E.R. (Comm) 374; *Samcrete Egypt Engineers and Contractors SAE v Land Rover Exports Ltd* [2001] EWCA Civ 2019, [2002] C.L.C. 533 (deletion of English jurisdiction and choice of law clause from draft contract indicates that parties had made no choice as to the governing law). And see cf. above, paras 30–010—30–011. In *The Komninos S.* [1991] 1 Lloyd's Rep. 371, the jurisdiction clause referred to "British" courts. This was construed as choice of English courts and English law ("[w]hatever the constitutional niceties, it seems to me altogether far-fetched, in truth a lawyer's point, to suppose that the parties can have intended to embrace the Courts of British dependencies overseas" and "scarcely less far-fetched to suppose that the parties can have meant or intended to embrace" the courts of Scotland or Northern Ireland: 374, per Bingham L.J.).

is no expressly stated choice of law.[265] Other matters that may impel the court to the conclusion that a real choice of law has been made might include an express choice of law in related transactions between the same parties,[266] or the choice of a place where disputes are to be settled by arbitration in circumstances indicating that the arbitrator should apply the law of that place."[267]

In the case of arbitration clauses it appears that the application of art.3(1) involves a shift of emphasis[268] from the approach which was found in the common law.[269] This results from the fact that, as stated in the extract from the Giuliano-Lagarde Report set out above, the circumstances surrounding the arbitration clause must indicate that it is the intention of the parties that the arbitrator should apply the law of the country in which the arbitration takes place, which is not quite the same test as was adopted in the common law.[270] In practice, however, it is unlikely that any material difference will emerge between the two approaches.[271] **30–052**

---

265 cf. *The Stensby* (1948) 64 T.L.R. 89; *Keiner v Keiner* [1952] 1 All E.R. 643; above, paras 30–010—30–011.

266 See *Samcrete Egypt Engineers and Contractors SAE v Land Rover Exports Ltd* [2001] EWCA Civ 2019. Contrast *Gan Insurance Co Ltd v Tai Ping Insurance Co Ltd* [1999] 2 All E.R. (Comm) 54 (fact that insurance policy was expressly governed by the law of Taiwan did not demonstrate with reasonable certainty an intention to choose Taiwanese law as the law applicable to an associated reinsurance policy which was made in England between English underwriters and brokers and thus was governed by English law). And see *Raiffeisen Zentralbank Osterreich Aktiengesellschaft v National Bank of Greece SA* [1999] 1 Lloyd's Rep. 408; *European Bank of Reconstruction & Development v Tekoglu* [2004] EWHC 846 (Comm). cf. *Re United Rys of the Havana and Regla Warehouses* [1960] Ch. 52, 94 (affirmed [1961] A.C. 1007). See also *Wahda Bank v Arab Bank Plc* [1996] 1 Lloyd's Rep. 470; cf. *Minories Finance Ltd v Afribank Nigeria Ltd* [1995] 1 Lloyd's Rep. 134; *Bank of Credit and Commerce Hong Kong Ltd v Sonali Bank* [1995] 1 Lloyd's Rep. 277; *Batstone & Firminger Ltd v Nasima Enterprises (Nigeria) Ltd* [1996] C.L.C. 1902, 1910.

267 Giuliano-Lagarde Report, p.17. cf. *Star Shipping SA v China National Foreign Trade Transportation Corp* [1993] 2 Lloyd's Rep. 445, and see *Dicey, Morris and Collins*, paras 32–096—32–098; above, para.30–010. The Report makes no reference to the relevance of an inference *in favorem negotii*: cf. above, para.30–011.

268 *Dicey, Morris and Collins*, paras 32–096—32–097 referred to with approval in *Egon Oldendorff v Libera Corp (No.2)* [1996] 1 Lloyd's Rep. 381. And see *Egon Oldendorff v Libera Corp (No.1)* [1995] 2 Lloyd's Rep. 64. See also Morse in Meeusen, Pertegas and Straetmans (eds), *The Enforcement of International Contracts in the European Union* (2004), pp.191, 204–206.

269 *Egon Oldendorff v Libera Corp (No.2)* [1996] 1 Lloyd's Rep. 381, 389–390.

270 Common law decisions did not always stress this additional factor, though there are dicta which refer to it: see, e.g. *Compagnie d'Armement Maritime SA v Compagnie Tunisienne de Navigation SA* [1971] A.C. 572, 579, 600, 605, 609.

271 *Egon Oldendorff v Libera Corp (No.2)* [1996] 1 Lloyd's Rep. 381, 390. In this case the parties had agreed to English arbitration by arbitrators conversant with shipping matters in respect of disputes arising out of a well-known English form of charterparty containing standard clauses and terminology with well-known meanings in English law. Although the parties were, respectively, German and Japanese, it was held that all of these factors pointed to an intention to choose English law for the purposes of art.3(1) of the Convention. The parties had chosen England as the place of arbitration because it was "neutral". Equally, they must have intended a "neutral" law to apply. The inference to be drawn, in favour of English law, will of course be stronger if the arbitration clause provides for arbitration in England before arbitrators of the London Maritime Arbitrators' Association, or before London brokers, or a London association or exchange. And see *Egon Oldendorff v Libera Corp (No.1)* [1995] 2 Lloyd's Rep. 64. cf. *XL Insurance Ltd v Owens Corning* [2000] 2 Lloyd's Rep. 500.

30–053 **Other relevant factors.** The extract from the Giuliano-Lagarde Report set out above[272] is expressly stated to provide examples of what might be taken to be indications as to the intent of the parties to choose a particular law as the governing law. There may, however, be other terms of the contract or other circumstances in the particular case which will point to the fact that the parties have made a "real choice of law".[273] Thus, for example, where a company based in a particular country concludes, in that country, through a broker based in the same country, a worldwide insurance policy on behalf of its subsidiaries with an insurer based in the same country, and the policy contains a term which imposes a one year period in which suit had to be brought unless such a limit was invalid by the law of the country in which the policy was issued in which case suit had to be commenced within the shortest limit of time permitted under the law of the latter country, the conclusion may well be drawn that the parties intended to make a real choice of the law of that country and that the term and the other circumstances demonstrated with reasonable certainty an intention to make such a choice.[274]

30–054 **Subsequent conduct.** At common law, it was not possible to take into account the conduct of the parties subsequent to the making of the contract in determining their intentions in relation to an implied choice of law.[275] The position under the Rome Convention is not clear. The Giuliano-Lagarde Report recognises that a choice of law may be deduced "in the light of all the facts".[276] It further concludes that where there is no choice of law, so that it is necessary to discover the law of the country with which the contract is most closely connected pursuant to art.4 of the Convention,[277] "it is also possible to take account of factors which supervened after the conclusion of the contract".[278] The better view, it is suggested, is that subsequent conduct may be taken into account in this context also to the extent that it points to the intentions of the parties at the time the contract was made.[279]

30–055 **"Implied" choice or "no" choice.** One difficulty in the common law, which remains under the Convention, is that of distinguishing between a case of "implied" choice of law and a case of "no" choice of law.[280] In the latter case,

---

[272] Above, para.30–051.

[273] Giuliano-Lagarde Report, p.17.

[274] *American Motorists Insurance Co v Cellstar Corp* [2003] EWCA Civ. 206; [2003] I.L. Pr. 370. See also *Travelers Casualty and Surety Co of Canada v Sun Life Assurance Co of Canada (UK) Ltd* [2006] EWHC 2716 (Comm), [2007] Lloyd's Rep. I.R. 619.

[275] *James Miller and Partners Ltd v Whitworth Street Estates (Manchester) Ltd* [1970] A.C. 583. See above, para.30–005.

[276] Giuliano-Lagarde Report, p.17.

[277] Below, paras 30–071 et seq.

[278] Giuliano-Lagarde Report, p.20.

[279] See *Dicey, Morris and Collins*, para.32–091; Plender, pp.97–99. This conclusion is supported by the fact that the common law approach is not accepted in other countries: see F.A. Mann (1973) 89 L.Q.R. 464. See also *Egon Oldendorff v Libera Corp (No.2)* [1996] 1 Lloyd's Rep. 380, 382.

[280] See *Tiernan v Magen Insurance Co Ltd* [2000] I.L. Pr. 517; *American Motorists Insurance Co v Cellstar Corp* [2003] EWCA Civ 206; [2003] I.L. Pr. 370; *Tryg Baltica International (UK) Ltd v Boston Compania De Seguros SA* [2004] EWHC 1186 (Comm), [2005] Lloyd's Rep. I.R. 40; *Cadre SA V Astra Asigurari* [2005] EWHC 2504 (Comm); *Travelers Casualty and Surety Co of Canada v Sun Life Assurance Co of Canada (UK) Ltd* [2006] EWHC 2716 (Comm), [2007] Lloyd's Rep. I.R.

art.4 will be used to determine the applicable law.[281] But opinions may legitimately differ on whether a particular case constitutes one in which a choice of law has been demonstrated with reasonable certainty or whether it is, in fact, one in which no choice of law has been made.[282] The obvious solution to this potential uncertainty is to include an express choice of law in the contract.

Partial choice of law. The first sentence of art.3(1) permits the parties to "select the law applicable to the whole or part only of the contract". The provision introduces into the Convention the notion of the splitting[283] of the contract, or severability[284] thereof, often described in the jargon of the conflict of laws as *dépeçage*,[285] whereby different aspects (or parts) of a contract may be governed by different laws. This notion was also recognised in the common law.[286] Its inclusion in the Convention was not, however, uncontroversial,[287] though ultimately it was accepted that permitting parties, in this way, to choose different laws to govern different parts of the contract or to make a choice of law in relation to one part and no choice in relation to another part or parts of the contract[288] could be justified as the logical conclusion of the principle of party autonomy in choice of law.[289] 30–056

The Giuliano-Lagarde Report provides some guidance as to how it is thought the provision is likely to operate. First, it appears that the contract must consist of several parts "which are separable and independent of each other from the legal and economic point of view".[290] Secondly, when the contract can be split in this sense: 30–057

619; *Dornoch Ltd v Mauritius Union Assurance Co Ltd* [2006] EWCA Civ 389, [2006] 2 Lloyd's Rep. 475. For the difficulty in the common law compare the views of Lords Diplock and Wilberforce in *Amin Rasheed Shipping Corp v Kuwait Insurance Co* [1984] A.C. 50. See above, para.30–012 fn.63.

281 Giuliano-Lagarde Report, p.17. Below, paras 30–071 et seq.

282 And compare the use of "reasonable certainty" in the English text with the phrase "*de façon certaine*" in the French text: see Anton, *Private International Law*, 2nd edn (1990), p.325.

283 cf. *Kahler v Midland Bank* [1950] A.C. 24, 42, per Lord MacDermott.

284 Giuliano-Lagarde Report, p.17. See also *XL Insurance Ltd v Owens Corning* [2000] 2 Lloyd's Rep. 500.

285 Giuliano-Lagarde Report, p.17. See generally, *Dicey, Morris and Collins*, paras 32–047—32–053; Cheshire and North, pp.553–554.

286 Above, para.30–015.

287 Giuliano-Lagarde Report, p.17.

288 Giuliano-Lagarde Report, pp.17, 20.

289 Giuliano-Lagarde Report, p.17. Contrast *CGU International Insurance Plc v Szabo* [2002] 1 All E.R. (Comm) 83 (no logical or commercially sensible basis on which words of an insurance policy defining the insured can be "severed" so as to be interpreted by different laws and given possibly different meanings); *American Motorists Insurance Co v Cellstar Corp* [2003] EWCA Civ 206; [2003] I.L. Pr. 370 at [20] ("neither the parties nor the Rome Convention could sensibly be taken to have intended to scissor up" a composite but single and probably multipartite insurance policy and to subject different aspects of it to different governing laws); *Travelers Casualty & Surety Co of Europe Ltd v Sun Life Assurance Co of Canada (UK) Ltd* [2004] EWHC 1704 (Comm), [2004] I.L. Pr. 793; *CGU International Insurance Plc v Astrazeneca Insurance Co Ltd* [2005] EWHC 2755 (Comm); [2006] 1 C.L.C. 162. For a sceptical view of *dépecage*, see the majority view of the Court of Appeal in *Centrax Ltd v Citibank NA* [1999] 1 All E.R. (Comm) 557 and contrast the dissenting judgment of Waller L.J. cf. *XL Insurance v Owens Corning* [2000] 2 Lloyd's Rep. 500.

290 Giuliano-Lagarde Report, p.17.

> "... the choice must be logically consistent, i.e. it must relate to elements in the contract which can be governed by different laws without giving rise to contradictions. For example, an 'index-linking clause' may be subject to a different law; on the other hand it is unlikely that repudiation of the contract for non-performance would be subjected to two different laws, one for the vendor and the other for the purchaser."[291]

If the chosen laws cannot be reconciled as a matter of logic, then neither choice of law is effective so that the law applicable to the contract will have to be determined according to art.4 of the Convention, as if the parties had made no choice of law at all.[292] Finally, where parties make a choice of law in relation to one part of the contract but no such choice in relation to the other part or parts, the law applicable to the latter part or parts will also have to be determined according to art.4 of the Convention.[293]

30–058 **Changing the applicable law.** At common law, it was uncertain whether the parties were free to change the law governing their contract and, if so, what law governed the question of whether they were able to make such a change.[294] Support, however, existed for the power to change,[295] such power to change being governed by English law as the law of the forum.[296] Article 3(2) of the Rome Convention provides a specific choice of law rule to deal with the question:

> "The parties may at any time agree to subject the contract to a law other than that which previously governed it, whether as a result of an earlier choice under this Article or of other provisions of this Convention. Any variation by the parties of the law to be applied made after the conclusion of the contract shall not prejudice its formal validity under Article 9 or adversely affect the rights of third parties."

In this formulation, it is necessary to emphasise the proviso as to formal validity of the contract[297] and the need to protect the rights of third parties who may be adversely affected by a change in the applicable law.[298] Subject to these points, however, the provision gives the parties to the contract maximum freedom as to the time when the ultimate choice of law is to be made since it confers on the parties such a wide freedom to change the applicable law.[299] This freedom extends to changing the applicable law when that law was chosen by the parties and to cases where the governing law which is changed was initially applicable by virtue of art.4 of the Convention.[300] The choice of law which purports to vary

---

[291] Giuliano-Lagarde Report, p.17.

[292] Giuliano-Lagarde Report, p.17. See below, paras 30–071 et seq.

[293] Giuliano-Lagarde Report, p.17 and p.20. See below, paras 30–071 et seq.

[294] Above, para.30–005.

[295] Above, para.30–005.

[296] See *Dicey, Morris and Collins*, paras 32–084—32–085.

[297] See below, paras 30–310 et seq.

[298] "The preservation of third-party rights appears to be entirely justified. In certain legal systems, a third-party may have acquired rights in consequence of a contract concluded between two other persons. These rights cannot be affected by a subsequent change in the choice of the applicable law": Giuliano-Lagarde Report, p.18.

[299] Giuliano-Lagarde Report, p.18.

[300] Giuliano-Lagarde Report, p.18.

or change the original governing law will, however, need to comply with the requirements of art.3(1) of the Convention.[301] The principle of the common law which requires that a contract have a governing law from its inception[302] is equally a principle of the Rome Convention which is unaffected by art.3(2). It would seem, however, that where the contract provides for two governing laws, the second to be applied if the event on which the application of the first depends is negatived,[303] then the applicable law can be said to be changed from the first to the second law, pursuant to art.3(2), when the relevant event comes about.[304]

Validity of choice of law. Article 3(4) refers the "existence and validity of the consent of the parties as to the choice of the applicable law" to the law which the parties purported to choose, i.e. the law which would be the chosen law if the choice of law were valid.[305] This so-called "bootstrap" rule would seem to enable one party to choose the law to govern consent to a choice of law.[306] However, it does not provide an answer in cases where there are conflicting standard forms of contract each referring to different applicable laws (or where one standard form contains a choice of law and the other does not). In such cases, it has been suggested that resort should be had to the law which would govern the contract if no choice of law had been made,[307] i.e. art.4 of the Convention. In any event, art.4 will determine the governing law if, according to the "bootstrap" rule, there is no valid choice of law in the contract itself.[308] 30–059

Limitations upon the choice. In general, the provisions of the Rome Convention will, in practice, give the parties a comparatively wide freedom to choose the applicable law.[309] There are, however, some provisions which place specific restraints limits upon this freedom. The tendency of these provisions, however, is to limit rather than invalidate in toto the choice of law.[310] These specific limitations are discussed in the following paragraphs. 30–060

---

301 Giuliano-Lagarde Report, p.18. See *Aeolian Shipping SA v ISS Machinery Services Ltd* [2001] EWCA Civ 1162, [2001] 2 Lloyd's Rep. 81. The power to change the governing law, pursuant to Rome Convention art.3(2), would seem to be distinct from any power to change which may exist, as a matter of procedure, in national law. An example in English law would be a case where parties do not rely on an applicable foreign law in their statements of case, in which case English law will apply: see Giuliano-Lagarde Report, p.18; above, para.30–049.

302 Above, para.30–005.

303 Above, para.30–005.

304 *Dicey, Morris and Collins*, paras 32–304 et seq.

305 Rome Convention arts 3(4), 8(1) (below, paras 30–304 et seq), 9(4) (below, paras 30–310 et seq). See *Egon Oldendorff v Libera Corp (No.1)* [1995] 2 Lloyd's Rep. 64; *Egon Oldendorff v Libera Corp (No.2)* [1996] 1 Lloyd's Rep. 380.

306 Cheshire and North, p.564.

307 *Dicey, Morris and Collins*, para.32–103. For further consideration of the problems generated by conflicting standard terms, see *Ferguson Shipbuilders Ltd v Voith Hydro GmbH* (2000) S.L.T. 229; Danneman in Rose (ed.), *Lex Mercatoria: Essays in Honour of Francis Reynolds* (2000), p.199.

308 Below, paras 30–071 et seq.

309 For discussion of the more stringent rules in relation to "certain consumer contracts" and "individual employment contracts", see below, paras 30–092 et seq.

310 A choice of law which is meaningless (cf. *Compagnie D'Armement Maritime SA v Compagnie Tunisienne de Navigation SA* [1970] A.C. 572, above, para.30–005) must be regarded as invalid (or ineffective at any rate) under the Convention. As to a choice which is not that of the law of a country, see above, para.30–048.

30–061 **Mandatory rules.** The Convention refers to the concept of "mandatory rule" in various provisions which will be discussed in this Chapter.[311] At this juncture, in connection with the power of the parties to choose the governing law, it is necessary to refer to art.3(3) which provides as follows:

> "The fact that the parties have chosen a foreign law, whether or not accompanied by the choice of a foreign tribunal, shall not, where all the other elements relevant to the situation at the time of the choice are connected with one country only, prejudice the application of rules of the law of that country which cannot be derogated from by contract, hereinafter called 'mandatory rules'."[312]

The purpose of this provision would seem, essentially, to be somewhat narrow. It is designed to prevent the evasion of mandatory rules, as defined in the Article, in relation to a contract which, but for a choice of foreign law, would be a purely domestic contract, by the simple device of including in the contract such a choice of foreign law.[313] Such a narrow situation does not appear to have arisen in any reported case at common law,[314] but the narrowness of art.3(3) is explicable by reference to the desire of the United Kingdom negotiators of the Convention to preserve the possibility of the parties choosing a foreign law although there was no other foreign element in the situation.[315] Such a possibility should only, thus, be restricted by the mandatory rules of the only other country which would otherwise be relevant to the situation.[316]

30–062 **Connection with one country only.** For art.3(3) to operate it is first necessary that all the elements (other than the choice of law and jurisdiction where present) relevant to the situation (not the contract) at the time of the choice are connected with *one* country only. Accordingly, the provision will not apply where, although at first sight the contract appears to be connected to one country only, there are other elements relevant to the "situation" (which goes beyond the contract itself) which are connected with another country or other countries. Having said that, it is not easy to determine in the abstract whether an element is "relevant" to the "situation". Such a conclusion may be reached if a seller manufactures goods in one country which are then sold in another country under a contract entirely connected with the latter country apart from the choice of the law of yet a different country. It is by no means certain that this is a situation which would not call art.3(3) into play, though it is suggested that art.3(3) should not apply here.[317] Conversely, it is likely that art.3(3) will apply if, say, an English buyer enters into

---

[311] See Rome Convention art.5 (below, paras 30–093 et seq); art.6 (below, paras 30–108 et seq); art.7(1) (below, para.30–063); art.7(2) (below, paras 30–066, 30–068); art.9(6) (below, para.30–133). For the position under the Rome I Regulation, see below, paras 30–177 et seq.

[312] See *Dicey, Morris and Collins*, paras 32–070—32–073, 32–132—32–134; Cheshire and North, pp.557–559; Plender, pp.104–107; Kaye, pp.159–168; Philip in North (ed.), *Contract Conflicts* (1982), p.81, at pp.95–97; Morse (1982) 2 Ybk. Eur. L. 107, 122–124.

[313] See Giuliano-Lagarde Report, p.18.

[314] Lasok and Stone, *Conflict of Laws in the European Community* (1987), pp.377–378.

[315] Giuliano-Lagarde Report, p.18.

[316] Giuliano-Lagarde Report, p.18. The application of Rome Convention art.3(3) was considered but rejected in *Caterpillar Financial Services Corp v SNC Passion* [2004] EWHC 569 (Comm), [2004] 2 Lloyd's Rep. 99. See also *Tamil Nadu Electricity Board v ST-CMS Electric Co Private Ltd* [2007] EWHC 1713, [2008] 1 Lloyd's Rep. 93 at [43]–[44].

[317] Lasok and Stone at pp.377–378; *Dicey, Morris and Collins*, para.32–071.

a contract with an English seller through the seller's website on the internet and the only foreign element (apart from a choice of foreign law) is the fact that the website is hosted by a third party in a foreign country, since the physical location of the server would not seem to be an element relevant to the situation.[318] Secondly, the time at which it must be ascertained whether the relevant elements are connected with one country only is the time at which the choice of law is made so that connections with other countries which materialise after that time must seemingly be ignored. Thirdly, although art.3(3) speaks literally of a choice of foreign law, it may apply, nonetheless, if parties to a contract have chosen English law if all the other elements relevant to the situation at the time of the choice are connected with a foreign country. Thus if all the other elements relevant to the situation are connected with Germany but the contract contains a choice of English law then the English court would have to apply German mandatory rules.[319] Likewise, if all the other elements relevant to the situation were connected with England, but the contract contains a choice of German law, the English court will have to apply any relevant English mandatory rules.

"Mandatory rules". The core difficulty with art.3(3) is, however, the concept of "mandatory rules". By way of purported definition, the provision describes them as rules "which cannot be derogated from by contract, hereinafter called 'mandatory rules' ". This wording might be thought to suggest that the concept of mandatory rules bears this meaning wherever these rules are referred to in other provisions of this Convention. Reference to such rules appears in art.5 (dealing with "certain consumer contracts"),[320] art.6 (dealing with "individual employment contracts"),[321] art.7(1) (which is of broader application) and art.7(2) (which concerns mandatory rules of the law of the forum[322]). Article 7(1) does not have the force of law in the United Kingdom[323] which renders unnecessary a detailed examination of its terms. However, comparison of arts 3(3) and 7(1) indicates that the Convention contemplates two kinds of mandatory rule.[324] Article 7(1) gives the courts of a country which implements the provision a 30–063

[318] cf. Directive 2000/31 on certain legal aspects of information society services, in particular electronic commerce in the Internal Market ("Directive on electronic commerce") [2000] OJ L178/1, Recital 19, not reproduced in the United Kingdom implementing legislation, the Electronic Commerce (EC Directive) Regulations 2002 (SI 2002/2013). See *Menashe Business Mercantile Ltd v William Hill Organisation Ltd* [2002] EWCA Civ 1702; [2003] 1 W.L.R. 1462. And see below, para.30–101.

[319] See *Caterpillar Financial Services Corp v SNC Passion* [2004] EWHC 569 (Comm), [2004] 2 Lloyd's Rep. 99. Presumably, the English court would not apply these rules unless they were pleaded and proved: see above, para.30–049.

[320] Below, paras 30–093 et seq.

[321] Below, paras 30–108 et seq.

[322] Below, para.30–068. See also Rome Convention art.9(6), below, para.30–314.

[323] Contracts (Applicable Law) Act 1990 s.2(2). Article 22 of the Convention permits contracting states to make a reservation to the application of this provision, which power the UK exercised on signing the Convention. See *Akai Pty Ltd v People's Insurance Co Ltd* [1998] 1 Lloyd's Rep. 90, 100; cf. art.9 of the Rome I Regulation, below, paras 30–178 et seq.

[324] *Dicey, Morris and Collins*, paras 32–132—32–143; Cheshire and North, pp.575–584; Plender at pp.106–107, 187–199; Kaye at pp.160–163, 167–168, 239–267; Philip in North (ed.), *Contract Conflicts* (1982), Ch.5; Jackson in North (ed.), *Contract Conflicts* (1982), Ch.4; Diamond (1986) 216 *Recueil des Cours IV* 233, 288–298; North (1990) 220 *Recueil des Cours I* 3, 191–194; Morse (1982) 2 Ybk. Eur. L. 107, 121–124, 142–147.

discretion, when applying under the Convention the law of one country, to give effect to:

> "... the mandatory rules of the law of another country with which the situation has a close connection, if and in so far as, under the law of the latter country, those rules must be applied whatever the law applicable to the contract."

It appears from this formulation that to be applied under art.7(1), a rule must not only be mandatory in the sense of art.3(3) but must also bear an additional quality, namely that it must also be a rule which must be applied whatever the law applicable to the contract. Accordingly, art.3(3) is concerned with securing the application of mandatory rules of a domestic nature, i.e. rules which cannot be derogated from in a purely domestic transaction, even by a choice of foreign law, but which can be derogated from in a contract which bears an international character.[325] On the other hand, art.7(1) entails the possibility, for courts of states which implement the provision, to apply mandatory rules of a higher order, namely rules which apply whatever law is applicable to the contract even when the contract is of an international character.[326]

30–064 **Rules not applicable if foreign law chosen.** When art.3(3) applies, its effect is that the choice of foreign law "shall not . . . prejudice" application of relevant mandatory rules. On one view, this wording might suggest that a rule is mandatory for this purpose even if, according to the law of the country of which it forms part, it is possible to contract out of it by a choice of foreign law. It is submitted, however, that art.3(3) does not have this effect. If the country of whose law the rule forms part would not apply the rule in the circumstances of the case then the rule is inapplicable in the context of art.3(3).[327]

30–065 **When is a rule mandatory?** Where an English court is faced with a problem involving art.3(3) and the possibility arises that foreign mandatory rules may apply, then whether a rule is mandatory for this purpose will depend on the view of it in the law of the country of which it forms part. Where it is alleged that an English mandatory rule is applicable, it will first be necessary to decide whether the particular rule in question does possess a mandatory character. A statute may give an express indication of whether,

---

[325] This view is supported by reference to the French text of the Convention. Mandatory rules in art.3(3) are described in that text as *"dispositions imperatives"*. Article 7 is, however, headed by the words "*Lois de Police*". The change in terminology reflects a distinction drawn in some Continental legal systems between the former class of laws from which derogation may be permitted in international contracts, and the latter class from which no derogation is permitted even in such contracts: Plender, p.106.

[326] For the historical origins of this provision, see F.A. Mann in Lipstein (ed.), *Harmonisation of Private International Law by the EEC* (1978), pp.31–32; *Dicey, Morris and Collins*, para.32–141. cf. the definition in art.9(1) of the Rome I Regulation, below, paras 30–180. And see *Arblade* (C–396/96) and *Leloup* (C–376/96) [1999] E.C.R. I–8453.

[327] *Dicey, Morris and Collins*, para.32–073; Morse (1982) 2 Ybk. Eur. L. 107, 123; cf. Cheshire and North, pp.576–577.

and to what extent, its provisions are mandatory,[328] but this is not always the case.[329] Further, it may be particularly difficult to determine whether any particular common law rule is mandatory. All that can be said with any degree of certainty is that, in the absence of any express indication, whether any given rule is mandatory will depend on the proper construction of the rule.[330]

Mandatory rules of English law. As far as English law is concerned, it is suggested that most rules possessing a mandatory character will be contained in legislation and these will also be rules which apply whatever the law applicable to the contract.[331] Accordingly, although art.3(3) is designed to secure application of "domestic" mandatory rules, and, a fortiori, internationally mandatory rules, there are unlikely to be many rules of domestic English contract law which will be treated as mandatory for the purposes of art.3(3). Thus, for example, it would be doubtful whether the requirement of consideration would be treated as mandatory,[332] though it is possible that the English rule against contractual penalties bears that character.[333] In contrast, statutory rules designed to give effect to 30–066

[328] See, e.g. Unfair Contract Terms Act 1977 s.27(2), above, para.30–008; Unfair Terms in Consumer Contracts Regulations 1999 (above, para.30–008). Reg.9 provides that the Regulations apply notwithstanding any contract term which applies or purports to apply the law of a non-Member State, if the contract has a close connection with the territories of the Member States. A virtually identical formula is found in the Consumer Protection (Distance Selling) Regulations 2000 (SI 2000/2334, as amended by SI 2005/689) reg.25(5). These Regulations implement Directive 97/7 on the protection of consumers in respect of distance contracts [1997] OJ L144/19. The same kind of provision is contained in Directive 1999/44 on certain aspects of the sale of consumer goods and associated guarantees [1999] OJ L171/12 art.7(2). Article 7(2) is not reproduced in the United Kingdom implementing legislation contained in the Sale and Supply of Goods to Consumers Regulations 2002 (SI 2002/3045). For the difficulties created by this omission, see below, para. 30–103. For similar anti-avoidance formulae, see Directive 2002/65 concerning the distance marketing of consumer financial services [2002] OJ L271/16 art.12(2), implemented in Financial Services (Distance Marketing) Regulations 2004 (SI 2004/ 2095) reg.16(3). For discussion, see *Benjamin's Sale of Goods*, 7th edn (2006), paras 25–101—25–118. See also Knofel (1998) 47 I.C.L.Q. 439. cf. Late Payment of Commercial Debts (Interest) Act 1998 s.12(2). Like the Directive which they implement (Council Directive on the co-ordination of the laws of the Member States relating to self-employed commercial agents [1986] OJ L382/17) the Commercial Agents (Council Directive) Regulations 1993 (SI 1993/3053, as amended by SI 1993/3173 and SI 1998/2868) contain no anti-avoidance provision. In *Ingmar G.B. Ltd v Eaton Leonard Technologies Inc* (C–381/98) [2002] E.C.R. I–9305 the European Court of Justice held that arts 17 and 18 of the Directive (implemented in regs 17 and 18 of the Regulations), which guarantee certain rights to commercial agents after the termination of the agency contract, must be applied, as mandatory rules, where the commercial agent carries out his activities in a Member State even though the principal is established in a non-Member State and a clause in the contract stipulates that the contract is to be governed by the law of that non-Member State. See *Dicey, Morris and Collins*, paras 33–416 et seq.; Verhagen [2002] 51 I.C.L.Q. 135; Vol.II, para.31–019.

[329] See, e.g. Consumer Credit Act 1974 s.75(1), considered in *Office of Fair Trading v Lloyds TSB Bank Plc* [2007] UKHL 48, [2008] 1 A.C. 316.

[330] cf. *The Hollandia* [1983] 1 A.C. 565; *Office of Fair Trading v Lloyds TSB Bank Plc* [2007] UKHL 48; *Trafigura Beheer BV v Mediterranean Shipping Co SA* [2007] EWCA Civ 794, [2007] 2 Lloyd's Rep. 622.

[331] See *Primetrade AG v Ythan Ltd* [2005] EWHC 2399 (Comm), [2006] 1 All E.R. 367 at [14]–[15] (Carriage of Goods by Sea Act 1992 is not mandatory and only applies if the law applicable to the contract is English law); Cheshire and North, p.579.

[332] cf. *Re Bonacina* [1912] 2 Ch. 394.

[333] cf. *Godard v Gray* (1870) L.R. 6 Q.B. 139. See *Dicey, Morris and Collins*, para.32–134.

important social policies, for example rules concerning consumer or employee protection, are more likely to be regarded as being of a mandatory nature.[334]

30–067 **Chosen law governs other issues.** Lastly, it must be emphasised that the application of art.3(3) does not strike down the choice of law in toto. The provision merely restricts application of the chosen law to the extent that the chosen law conflicts with relevant mandatory rules. To the extent that these mandatory rules are not prejudiced, the chosen law will continue to govern issues not covered by mandatory rules.[335]

30–068 **Mandatory rules of the law of the forum.** Article 7(2) of the Rome Convention provides that:

> "... nothing in this Convention shall restrict the application of the rules of the law of the forum in a situation where they are mandatory irrespective of the law otherwise applicable to the contract."[336]

As far as English courts are concerned, the provision will enable them to give effect to English rules of this nature so as to override the choice of law by the parties.[337] Rules envisaged as applicable through the principle are, notably, rules on cartels, competition and restrictive practices, consumer protection and certain rules concerning carriage.[338] To qualify for application, the relevant mandatory rules must be rules which cannot be derogated from even in an international transaction governed by a foreign law, as opposed to mandatory rules which are the subject-matter of art.3(3) where what are relevant are rules which are mandatory in a domestic context but which can, nevertheless, be avoided or restricted in application, by a choice of foreign law.[339] Whether any particular

---

[334] See below, paras 30–102 et seq., 30–112 et seq.

[335] cf. *The Hollandia* [1983] 1 A.C. 565.

[336] See *Dicey, Morris and Collins*, paras 32–135—32–137; Cheshire and North, pp.578–583.

[337] Some such rules may completely override the choice of law by the parties: see, e.g. Employment Rights Act 1996 s.204(1), below, para.30–114 et seq. Others may only restrict the power of the parties to avoid the relevant rules by a mere choice of law where English law would be applicable if there were no such choice: see, e.g. Unfair Contract Terms Act 1977 s.27(2), above, para.30–008. Contrast Unfair Contract Terms Act 1977 s.27(1), which provides that the controls on exemption clauses contained in the Act do not apply where the law applicable to the contract is the law of any part of the United Kingdom only by choice of the parties and apart from that choice would be the law of some country outside the United Kingdom. If a contract (other than one excluded from the 1977 Act by s.26, as to which see *Ocean Chemical Transport Inc v Exnor Craggs* [2001] 1 All E.R. (Comm) 519; *Amiri Flight Authority v B.A.E. Systems Plc* [2002] EWHC 2481 (Comm); [2003] 1 All E.R. (Comm) 1; *Balmoral Group Ltd v Borealis (UK) Ltd* [2006] EWHC 1900 (Comm), [2006] 2 Lloyd's Rep. 629 and Vol.II, para.43–110) contains a choice of English law, but the contract would be governed by a foreign law were the rules contained in art.4 of the Convention (below, paras 30–071 et seq.) to be applied, the controls contained in the Act will not form part of the applicable law: *Surzur Overseas Ltd v Ocean Reliance Shipping Co Ltd* [1997] C.L. 318. And see Late Payment of Commercial Debts (Interest) Act 1998 s.12(1), discussed below, paras 30–341 et seq.

[338] Giuliano-Lagarde Report, p.38. For a discussion of potentially mandatory rules contained in European Union legislation, see Knofel (1998) 47 I.C.L.Q. 439; Fallon and Francq in Basedow, Meier, Schnyder, Einhorn and Girsberger (eds), *Private Law in the International Arena: Liber Amicorum Kurt Siehr* (2000), p.155.

[339] See above, paras 30–063 et seq. cf. Rome Convention art.7(1), which does not have the force of law in the UK: above, para.30–063.

rule bears this overriding[340] character will, in the absence of any express indication in the rule itself,[341] depend on the proper construction of the relevant rule.[342]

30–069 **Public policy.**[343] Article 16 of the Rome Convention contains a general reservation to the application of a foreign law on the basis of public policy (*ordre public*):

> "The application of a rule of the law of any country specified by this Convention may be refused only if such application is manifestly incompatible with the public policy ('ordre public') of the forum."

This provision, although of general application, may also be resorted to to deny effect to a choice of law by the parties to the contract.[344] The expression "manifestly" is designed to indicate that there must be special grounds, of an exceptional nature, for the exclusion to apply.[345] It is also important to stress that the concept of public policy is not to be applied to a foreign law in the abstract. It may only be resorted to when a provision of foreign law, if applied to an actual case, would offend English public policy.[346] The terms of art.16 clearly warn against an ubiquitous application of the doctrine.[347]

30–070 **"Community public policy".** According to the Giuliano-Lagarde Report public policy, for the purposes of art.16 of the Rome Convention, includes "Community public policy" and the concept of the public policy of the English forum must be understood as embracing this European dimension.[348] The European Court of Justice has held, in the context of the Brussels Convention on

---

340 See *Dicey, Morris and Collins*, paras 1–053—1–061.

341 Employment Rights Act 1996 s.204(1); Unfair Contract Terms Act 1977 s.27(2); Unfair Terms in Consumer Contracts Regulations 1994 reg.7; Consumer Protection (Distance Selling) Regulations 2000 reg.25(5). cf. Sale and Supply of Goods to Consumers Regulations 2002. See below, para.31–103.

342 See *Ingmar G.B. Ltd v Eaton Leonard Technologies Inc* (C–381/98) [2000] E.C.R. I–9305; *Office of Fair Trading v Lloyds TSB Bank Plc* [2007] UKHL 48, [2008] 1 A.C. 316; *Duarte v Black & Decker Corp* [2007] EWHC 2720 (QB). cf. *Boissevain v Weil* [1949] 1 K.B. 482; *Corocraft Ltd v Pan American Airways Inc* [1969] 1 Q.B. 616; *The Hollandia* [1982] Q.B. 872 (affirmed [1983] 1 A.C. 565); *English v Donnelly* (1958) S.C. 494, not followed in *Hong Kong Shanghai (Shipping) Ltd v The Cavalry* [1987] H.K.L.R. 287; *Chiron Corp v Organon Teknika (No.2)* [1993] F.S.R. 567; *Kaye's Leasing Corp Pty Ltd v Fletcher* (1964) 116 C.L.R. 124; *Att-Gen's Reference No.1 of 1987* (1987) 47 SAS.R. 152; *DR Insurance Co v Central National Insurance Co* [1996] 1 Lloyd's Rep. 74. See also *Akai Pty Ltd v The People's Insurance Co Ltd* (1996) 188 C.L.R. 418; cf. *Akai Pty Ltd v People's Insurance Co Ltd* [1998] 1 Lloyd's Rep. 80. And see *Duncan v Motherwell Bridge and Engineering Co Ltd* (1952) S.C. 131, below, para.30–102.

343 *Dicey, Morris and Collins*, paras 32–230—32–241; Cheshire and North, pp.584–586; Plender, pp.199–201; Kaye, pp.345–350; below, paras 30–366 et seq.

344 See *Duarte v Black & Decker Corp* [2007] EWHC 2720 (QB). cf. above, para.30–007.

345 *Duarte v Black & Decker Corp* [2007] EWHC 2720 (QB); Giuliano-Lagarde Report, p.38.

346 Giuliano-Lagarde Report, p.38.

347 Giuliano-Lagarde Report, p.38. See also *Re COLT Telecom Group Plc* [2002] EWHC 2815 (Ch), [2003] B.P.I.R. 324; *Tekron Resources Ltd v Guinea Investment Co Ltd* [2003] EWHC 2577 (Comm), [2004] 2 Lloyd's Rep. 26.

348 Giuliano-Lagarde Report, p.38. See generally, Peruzzetto in Meeusen, Pertegas and Straetmans (eds), *The Enforcement of International Contracts in the European Union* (2004), pp.343–361; Meidanis (2005) E.L.Rev. 95.

Jurisdiction and the Enforcement of Judgments in Civil and Commercial Matters 1968[349] that fundamental principles of human rights, as contained in the European Convention on Human Rights, may inform the content of Community public policy,[350] a view which has been accepted in England.[351] The European Court has also indicated that it is for national courts to define the content of public policy, though the European Court may itself review the limits within which national courts may have recourse to that concept.[352]

(d) *Applicable Law in the Absence of Choice by the Parties*[353]

30–071 **General principle.** Article 4(1) of the Rome Convention provides as follows:

> "To the extent that the law applicable to the contract has not been chosen in accordance with Art.3, the contract shall be governed by the law of the country with which it is most closely connected."[354]

This proposition has a familiar ring to a common lawyer, since it reflects the general principle of the common law which was developed to deal with cases where the parties had made no choice of law in the contract itself.[355] The first general point to note is that art.4 envisages the possibility of a contract being governed in part by a law chosen by the parties and as to another part, by the law applicable through art.4, since art.4 operates to "the extent that" the parties have made no choice of law in the contract itself.[356] This concept of *dépeçage*[357] is extended in the second sentence of art.4(1) where it is stated that a "severable part of the contract" which has a closer connection with another country may, "by way of exception", be governed by the law of that country though the remaining part or parts of the contract will be governed by the law of the country

---

[349] Brussels Convention art.27(1). See Council Regulation 44/2001 on jurisdiction and the recognition and enforcement of judgments in civil and commercial matters art.34(1).

[350] *Krombach v Bamberski* (C–7/98) [2000] E.C.R. I–1935; [2001] Q.B. 709; *Regie National des Usines Renault SA v Maxicar SpA* (C–38/98) [2000] E.C.R. I–2973. See also *Eurofood IFSC Ltd* (C–341/04) [2006] E.C.R. I–3813, [2006] Ch. 508.

[351] *Maronier v Larmer* [2002] EWCA Civ 774; [2003] Q.B. 603. cf. *Oppenheimer v Cattermole* [1976] A.C. 249; *Kuwait Airways Corp v Iraqi Airways Co (Nos 4 and 5)* [2002] UKHL 19, [2002] 2 A.C. 883 at [15]–[29], [111]–[118], [135]–[149].

[352] *Krombach v Bamberski* (C–7/98) [2000] E.C.R. I–1935; *Regie National des Usines Renault SA v Maxicar SpA* (C–36/98) [2000] E.C.R. I–2973. See also *Eurofood IFSC Ltd* (C–341/04) [2006] E.C.R. I–3813.

[353] *Dicey, Morris and Collins on The Conflict of Laws*, 14th edn (2006), paras 32–108 et seq., 33–113 et seq., 33–150 et seq., 33–217 et seq., 33–229 et seq.; Cheshire and North, *Private International Law*, 13th edn (1999), pp.564–574; Plender, *The European Contracts Convention*, 2nd edn (2001), Ch.6; Kaye, *The New Private International Law of Contract of the European Community* (1993), pp.171–202; Hill (2004) 53 I.C.L.Q. 325; Atrill (2004) I.C.L.Q. 549. As to consumer contracts and employment contracts, see below, paras 30–092 et seq. As to insurance contracts, see above, paras 30–045—30–046. As to the position under the Rome I Regulation, see below, paras 30–186 et seq.

[354] For the meaning of "law of a country," see above, para.30–048 and below.

[355] See above, para.30–011.

[356] Giuliano-Lagarde Report, p.20. cf. above, paras 30–056—30–057.

[357] cf. above, paras 30–056—30–057.

with which it is, or they are, most closely connected. The Giuliano-Lagarde Report emphasises that the words "by way of exception" are to be interpreted in the sense that the courts must have regard to severability as seldom as possible.[358] Accordingly, it is likely that the second sentence of art.4(1) will be of limited importance in practice. The second general point to note is the opinion expressed in the Giuliano-Lagarde Report that in order to determine the law of the country with which the contract is most closely connected, it is possible to take account of factors which appear after the conclusion of the contract.[359] The third general point to emphasise is that the law applicable under art.4 of the Convention must be the law of a country and cannot, say, be a non-national body of rules or a system of religious law.[360]

Presumptions. Article 4 departs from the common law in establishing in art.4(2)–(4) a series of presumptions which are to be used to identify the law of the country with which the contract is most closely connected.[361] Specific presumptions are established for certain contracts regarding immovables[362] and contracts for the carriage of goods.[363] Article 4(2) establishes a controversial general presumption which will be applicable in cases involving most other types of contract.[364] However, these presumptions, where applicable, are to be disregarded if it appears from the circumstances as a whole that the contract is more closely connected with another country than it is with the country whose law is indicated by application of the presumption, in which case the law applicable to the contract will be the law of the former country.[365] These various elements of art.4 are discussed in the following paragraphs. 30–072

The general presumption. Article 4(2) provides as follows: 30–073

> "Subject to the provisions of paragraph 5 of this Article, it shall be presumed that the contract is most closely connected with the country where the party who is to effect the performance which is characteristic of the contract has, at the time of the conclusion of the contract, his habitual residence, or, in the case of a body corporate or unincorporate, its central administration. However, if the contract is entered into in the course of that party's trade or profession, that country shall be the country in which the principal place of business is situated or, where under the terms of the contract the performance is to

---

358 Giuliano-Lagarde Report, p.23. See also *Governor & Company of Bank of Scotland of the Mound v Butcher* Unreported July 28, 1998 CA; *Centrax Ltd v Citibank NA* [1999] 1 All E.R. (Comm) 557; *XL Insurance Ltd v Owens Corning* [2000] 2 Lloyd's Rep. 500; *CGU International Plc v Szabo* [2002] 1 All E.R. (Comm) 83; *American Motorists Insurance Co v Cellstar Corp* [2003] EWCA Civ 206, [2003] I.LPr. 370; *Travelers Casualty & Surety Co of Europe Ltd v Sun Life Assurance Co of Canada (UK) Ltd* [2004] EWHC 1704 (Comm), [2004] I.L. Pr. 793; *CGU International Insurance Plc v Astrazeneca Insurance Co Ltd* [2005] EWHC 2755 (Comm), [2006] 1 C.L.C. 162. Above, paras 30–056—30–057.

359 Giuliano-Lagarde Report, p.23. cf. above, paras 30–005, 30–054.

360 *Halpern v Halpern (Nos 1 and 2)* [2007] EWCA Civ 291, [2008] Q.B. 195. See also above, para.30–048.

361 Presumptions, once fashionable in English law, were eventually abandoned: *Coast Lines Ltd v Hudig & Veder Chartering NV* [1972] 2 Q.B. 34. See above, para.30–012.

362 Rome Convention art.4(3). See below, paras 30–082 et seq.

363 Rome Convention art.4(4). See below, paras 30–085 et seq.

364 See below, paras 30–073 et seq.

365 Rome Convention art.4(5). See below, paras 30–088 et seq.

be effected through a place of business other than the principal place of business, the country in which that other place of business is situated."

It can be seen that application of this rule involves, first, the identification of the "characteristic performance" of the contract in question. The law applicable to the contract will then, presumptively, be the law of the habitual residence or central administration (as the case may be) of the party who is to effect that characteristic performance. Secondly, however, if the contract is entered into in the course of the "characteristic performer's" trade or profession, then the applicable law will, presumptively, be the law of the characteristic performer's principal place of business. But where, thirdly, under the terms of the contract performance is to be effected through a place of business other than the characteristic performer's principal place of business, the applicable law will be, presumptively, the law of the country in which that other place of business is situated.

30–074 **Characteristic performance.**[366] The central concept of art.4(2) is that of the "characteristic performance" of a contract. The expression is not defined in the Convention itself and is a novel one for contracting states,[367] owing its origin to Swiss law.[368] Elucidation of the concept involves identifying specific contracts and then identifying in relation to each such contract the performance which characterises or typifies the relevant contract, in reality identifying the obligation which is peculiar to the contract under consideration.[369] The concept has been much criticised,[370] but is greeted with effusion in the Giuliano-Lagarde Report:

> ". . . this performance refers to the function which the legal relationship involved fulfils in the economic and social life of any country. The concept of characteristic performance essentially links the contract to the social and economic environment of which it forms part."[371]

Whether the reader will be persuaded by such claims remains to be seen.

30–075 **Performance for which payment due "characteristic".** According to the Giuliano-Lagarde Report, which purports to provide guidance to the application of the doctrine, identifying characteristic performance causes no difficulty in the

[366] *Dicey, Morris and Collins*, paras 32–113—32–117; Cheshire and North, pp.565–571; Plender, pp.113–119; Kaye, pp.178–183; Schultsz in North (ed.), *Contract Conflicts* (1982), p.185; Hill (2004) 53 I.C.L.Q. 325; Atrill (2004) 53 I.C.L.Q. 349; Diamond (1986) 216 *Recueil des Cours IV* 233, 273–276; Lasok and Stone, *Conflict of Laws in the European Community* (1987), pp.361–364; Morse (1982) 2 Ybk. Eur. L. 107, 126–131; Lipstein (1981) 3 Northwestern Journal Int'l. L. & Bus. 402; Jessurun d'Oliveira (1977) 25 Am. J. Comp. L. 303.

[367] cf. Giuliano-Lagarde Report, p.20.

[368] See Lipstein (1981) 3 Northwestern Journal Int'l L. & Bus. 402; *Dicey, Morris and Collins*, para.32–124.

[369] Giuliano-Lagarde Report, p.20.

[370] e.g. Lasok and Stone; Morse, (1982) 2 Ybk. Eur. L. 107; Jessurun d'Oliveira, (1977) 25 Am. J. Comp. L. 303.

[371] Giuliano-Lagarde Report, p.20.

case of unilateral contracts.[372] Since in such contracts only one party agrees to confer a benefit on another, the characteristic performance will be that of the party agreeing to confer the benefit.[373] More controversy surrounds the analysis of reciprocal or bilateral contracts in which each party has to perform obligations. The Report points out that the performance of:

> " . . . one of the parties in a modern economy usually takes the form of the payment of money. This is not, of course, the characteristic performance of the contract. It is the performance for which payment is due, i.e. depending on the type of contract, the delivery of goods, the granting of the right to make use of an item of property, the provision of a service, transport, insurance, banking operations, security etc, which usually constitutes the centre of gravity and the socio-economic function of the contractual transaction."[374]

This passage suggests that characteristic performance is a somewhat abstract notion: it is not the payment of money but performance for which such payment is due.

"Characteristic" performance not determinable. It does not follow from this that every contract not specifically dealt with in art.4(3) and (4) must have a characteristic performance. This is recognised in art.4(5) which provides that art.4(2) shall not apply if the characteristic performance cannot be determined.[375] One obvious example is that of a contract of barter or exchange.[376] It has been held that the characteristic performance of an agreement between two companies regulating the use of their respective trademarks cannot be determined.[377] It has also been suggested that certain kinds of joint venture agreements,[378] certain types of distributorship agreements,[379] and contracts between publisher and author[380] may similarly not have a particular performance which can be said to characterise them. Further, on occasion, the particular circumstances involved in a transaction may be such that it is not possible to determine the characteristic 30–076

[372] Giuliano-Lagarde Report, p.20. See Maher (2002) Jur. Rev. 317.

[373] See *Waldweise Stiftung v Lewis* [2004] EWHC 2589 (Ch) (gift); *Opthalmic Innovations International (United Kingdom) Ltd v Opthalmic Innovations International Inc* [2004] EWHC 2948 (Ch), [2005] I.L. Pr. 109 (indemnification agreement); *Ark Therapeutics Plc v True North Capital Ltd* [2005] EWHC 1585 (Comm), [2006] 1 All E.R. (Comm) 138 (letter of intent). cf. *Halpern v Halpern (Nos 1 and 2)* [2007] EWCA Civ 291, [2008] Q.B. 195 (compromise agreement); *Standard Bank Plc v Agrinvest International Inc* [2007] EWHC 2595 (Comm), [2008] 1 Lloyd's Rep. 532 (option agreement). See Maher (2002) Jur. Rev. 317; Kaye at p.181.

[374] Giuliano-Lagarde Report, p.20.

[375] See, further, below, paras 30–088 et seq.

[376] See, e.g. *Dicey, Morris and Collins*, para.32–124.

[377] *Apple Corps Ltd v Apple Computer Inc* [2004] EWHC 768 (Ch), [2004] I.L. Pr. 597.

[378] Kaye, p.182.

[379] See Collins in North (ed.), *Contract Conflicts* (1982), pp.206–210; *Dicey, Morris and Collins*, para.32–117; see Plender, pp.118–119 who cites a German decision (Dortmund L.G., April 8, 1985 [1989] I Prax 510) to this effect. cf. *Print Concept GmbH v GEW (EC) Ltd* [2001] EWCA Civ 352, [2002] C.L.C. 352 (characteristic performance of a distributorship agreement intended to be fulfilled by individual contracts of sale and purchase is that of the vendor).

[380] Kaye, p.182.

performance of the contract which is at the root of it.[381] In such cases the most closely connected law will have to be determined without the aid of any presumption.[382]

30–077 **Specific applications.** English courts have had some opportunities to consider the meaning of characteristic performance in the context of particular types of contracts. Drawing on the decisions and the passage from the Giuliano-Lagarde Report quoted above, the following conclusions may be reached. In a contract of sale, the characteristic performance is that of the seller[383]; in a contract which is in part for the sale of goods and in part for the supply of services, the characteristic performance is that of the seller/supplier[384]; in a contract for the supply of services, the characteristic performance is that of the supplier[385]; in a contract of hire, the characteristic performance will be that of the party who makes the item available for hire[386]; in a contract of insurance,[387] the characteristic performance is that of the insurer since he provides the service (cover) for which the insured pays his premium[388]; in a contract of reinsurance, the characteristic performance is that of the reinsurer[389]; in a contract between an insurance broker and an insurance company seeking reinsurance, the characteristic performance is that of the broker[390]; in a "bank to bank" contract under which one bank undertakes to make payment due under a separate agreement to another bank and to warrant that there has been no default under the loan agreement, the characteristic performance is that of the bank which makes the payment and provides the

---

[381] See *Governor and Company of the Bank of Scotland of the Mound v Butcher* Unreported July 28, 1998 CA (impossible to determine characteristic performance of a personal guarantee signed by two guarantors, one of whom was resident in Scotland and the other in England). Normally the characteristic performance of a guarantee will be that of the guarantor: see *Samcrete Egypt Engineers and Contractors SAE v Land Rover Exports Ltd* [2001] EWCA Civ 2019, [2002] C.L.C. 533. See below, para.30–077.

[382] See below, para.30–089.

[383] See *W. H. Martin Ltd v Feldbinder Spezialefahrzeugwerke GmbH* [1998] I.L. Pr. 794; *Print Concept GmbH v GEW (EC) Ltd* [2001] EWCA Civ 352, [2002] C.L.C. 352; *ISS Machinery Services Ltd v Aeolian Shipping SA* [2001] EWCA Civ 1162, [2001] 2 Lloyd's Rep. 641; *Iran Continental Shelf Oil Co v IRI International Oil Corp* [2002] EWCA Civ 1024, [2004] 2 C.L.C. 696; *Ferguson Shipbuilders Ltd v Voith Hydro GmbH* (2000) S.L.T. 229; *Societe Nouvelle des Papeteries de l' Aa SA v B.V. Machinefabrik BOA* (1992) NJ 750 (Dutch Hoge Raad), discussed by Struycken [1996] LMCLQ 18; *Dicey, Morris and Collins*, para.32–116; Plender, pp.117–118; *Benjamin's Sale of Goods*, 7th edn (2006), para.25–060. As to consumer sales, see below, paras 30–093 et seq.

[384] *Iran Continental Shelf Oil Co v IRI International Corp* [2002] EWCA Civ 1024.

[385] *Definitely Maybe (Touring) Ltd v Marek Lieberberg Konzertagentur GmbH* [2001] 1 W.L.R. 1754; *Ennstone Building Products Ltd v Stanger Ltd* [2002] EWCA Civ 916, [2002] 1 WLR 3059; *Caledonia Subsea Ltd v Microperi Srl* (2002) S.L.T. 1022.

[386] *Dicey, Morris and Collins*, para.33–114.

[387] But see above, paras 30–045—30–046.

[388] *Crédit Lyonnais v New Hampshire Insurance Co* [1997] 2 Lloyd's Rep. 1; *American Motorists Insurance Co v Cellstar Corp* [2003] EWCA Civ 206; [2003] I.L. Pr. 370; Giuliano-Lagarde Report, p.20; *Dicey, Morris and Collins*, para.33–150. An insurance contract may be a consumer contract: see below, paras 30–093 et seq.

[389] *Tiernan v Magen Insurance Co Ltd*; *Tonicstar Ltd v American Home Insurance Co* [2004] EWHC 1234 (Comm), [2005] Lloyd's Rep. I.R. 32; *Dornoch Ltd v Mauritius Union Assurance Co Ltd* [2006] EWCA Civ 389, [2006] 2 Lloyd's Rep. 475.

[390] *HIB Ltd v Guardian Insurance Co Ltd* [1997] 1 Lloyd's Rep. 412.

warranty[391]; in a contract between banker and customer, the characteristic performance is that of the bank[392]; in a letter of credit transaction,[393] separation of the various contracts involved reveals that the characteristic performance in the contract between the issuing bank and the buyer is that of the bank,[394] the characteristic performance in the contract between the issuing bank and the confirming bank is that of the confirming bank,[395] the characteristic performance in the contract between the confirming bank and the beneficiary is that of the confirming bank,[396] while the characteristic performance in the contract between the issuing bank and the beneficiary is that of the issuing bank[397]; in a contract of loan, the characteristic performance is that of the lender (since he provides the "service" for which repayment is due)[398]; in a contract between lawyer and client, the characteristic performance is that of the lawyer[399]; in a contract

[391] *Raiffeisen Zentralbank Osterreich Aktiengesellschaft v National Bank of Greece SA* [1999] 1 Lloyd's Rep. 408.

[392] *Sierra Leone Telecommunications Co Ltd v Barclays Bank Plc* [1998] 2 All E.R. 821; Giuliano-Lagarde Report, p.20; *Dicey, Morris and Collins*, para.33–305, with a full discussion of contracts between banker and customer, paras 33–298 et seq. A contract between a bank and a customer may be a consumer contract.

[393] See Morse [1994] L.M.C.L.Q. 560; Davenport and Smith [1994] 9 Butterworths Journal of International Banking and Financial Law 3.

[394] This follows from the authority cited in fn.374, above, since the provision of the credit is a service for the customer (buyer). See also *Bank of Baroda v Vysya Bank Ltd* [1994] 2 Lloyd's Rep. 87, 92.

[395] *Bank of Baroda v Vysya Bank Ltd* [1994] 2 Lloyd's Rep. 87, treating the contract as one of agency in which the characteristic performance was the adding of the confirmation to the credit. The same result is likely to ensue if the correspondent bank does not add its confirmation to the credit, since the contract is one of agency and the characteristic performance in such a contract is that of the agent: [1994] 2 Lloyd's Rep. 87, 93; *PT Pan Indonesia Bank Ltd Tbk v Marconi Communications International Ltd* [2005] EWCA Civ 235, [2007] 2 Lloyd's Rep. 72; Giuliano-Lagarde Report, p.20. See also *Bank of Credit and Commerce Hong Kong Ltd v Sonali Bank* [1995] 1 Lloyd's Rep. 223; *Batstone & Firminger Ltd v Nasima Enterprises (Nigeria) Ltd* [1996] C.L.C. 1902, 1910. cf. *European Asian Bank AG v Punjab and Sind Bank* [1981] 2 Lloyd's Rep. 651; *Habib Bank Ltd v Central Bank of Sudan* [2006] EWHC 1767 (Comm), [2006] 2 Lloyd's Rep. 44.

[396] *Bank of Baroda v Vysya Bank Ltd* [1994] 2 Lloyd's Rep. 87; *PT Pan Indonesia Bank Ltd Tbk v Marconi Communications International Ltd* [2005] EWCA Civ 235, [2007] 2 Lloyd's Rep. 72; *Trafigura Beheer BV v Kookmin Bank Co* [2005] EWHC 2350 (Comm); [2006] EWHC 1450 (Comm), [2006] 2 Lloyd's Rep. 455. This is because either the bank is providing a banking service (Giuliano-Lagarde Report, p.20) or because it is of the essence of a letter of credit that the confirming bank undertakes to pay the beneficiary (seller) on presentation of conforming documents ([1994] 2 Lloyd's Rep. 87, 92). See also *Bank of Credit and Commerce Hong Kong Ltd v Sonali Bank* [1995] 1 Lloyd's Rep. 223; *Batstone & Firminger Ltd v Nasima Enterprises (Nigeria) Ltd* [1996] C.L.C. 1902, 1910.

[397] *Bank of Baroda v Vysya Bank Ltd* [1994] 2 Lloyd's Rep. 87; *Trafigura Beheer BV v Kookmin Bank Co* [2005] EWHC 2350 (Comm); [2006] EWHC 1450 (Comm), [2006] 2 Lloyd's Rep. 455. It is highly likely that the presumptively applicable law (that of the country in which the issuing bank's principal place of business is situated) will be displaced, pursuant to art.4(5), in favour of the law of the country where payment is to be made against presentation of documents, since this is the country where the obligations of the issuing bank towards the beneficiary under the credit are to be performed; see below para.30–091.

[398] *Surzur Overseas Ltd v Ocean Reliance Shipping Co Ltd* [1997] C.L. 318 (bank loan); *Atlantic Telecom GmbH, Noter* (2004) S.L.T. 1031; Kaye, p.182. This conclusion may be questionable: Morse (1982) 2 Ybk. Eur. L. 107, 128. A loan may be a consumer contract: see below, paras 30–093 et seq.

[399] *Dicey, Morris and Collins*, para.32–117, citing a French decision reported in *Clunet* (1984) p.583. Such a contract may be a consumer contract: see below, paras 30–093 et seq.

between principal and agent, the characteristic performance is that of the agent[400]; in a distributorship contract intended to be fulfilled by individual contracts of sale and purchase, the characteristic performance is that of the vendor[401]; in a contract of guarantee, the characteristic performance is that of the guarantor[402]; in a contract of pledge, the characteristic performance is that of the pledgor (since he provides the relevant security)[403]; in a contract for storage (a bailment), the characteristic performance is that of the bailee[404]; in construction contracts, the characteristic performance is that of the builder[405]; in wagering contracts, the characteristic performance is that of the party who offers the facility for the placing of the wager[406]; in a contract whereby a person undertakes not to make or allow to be made any communication to any individual or company in the United Kingdom, the characteristic performance is that of the party who gives the undertaking[407]; in a contract of gift, the characteristic performance is that of the donor[408]; in a contract to provide an indemnity, the characteristic performance is that of the party who is to provide the indemnity[409]; in a compromise agreement, the characteristic performance is that of the party required to transfer assets[410]; in a contract whereby a bank grants an option to purchase promissory notes, the characteristic performance is that of the bank which is under an obligation to deliver the notes upon exercise of the option.[411]

30–078 **Applicable law.** Despite the central importance of characteristic performance, it is not the *place* of such performance which supplies the applicable law. Rather it is either the law of the country where the characteristic performer is habitually resident or, where the performer is a body corporate or unincorporate, its central

[400] *Albon v Naza Motor Trading Sdn Bhd* [1007] EWHC 9 (Ch), [2007] 1 W.L.R. 2489; Giuliano-Lagarde Report, p.209; *Dicey, Morris and Collins*, para.33–410; authorities cited in fn.396, above. But cf. above, para.30–076 (distributorship agreements). Such contracts may be consumer contracts: see below, paras 30–093 et seq.

[401] *Print Concept GmbH v GEW (EC) Ltd* [2001] EWCA Civ 352; [2002] C.L.C. 352. cf. above, para.30–076.

[402] *Samcrete Egypt Engineers and Contractors SAE v Land Rover Exports Ltd* [2001] EWCA Civ 2019; [2002] C.L.C. 533; Giuliano-Lagarde Report, p.20. Such a contract may be a consumer contract: see below, paras 30–093 et seq.

[403] *Dicey, Morris and Collins*, para.33–115, where it is pointed out that this conclusion is not uncontroversial. Such a contract may be a consumer contract: see below, paras 30–093 et seq.

[404] cf. Swiss Private International Law Act 1987 art.117(3)(d). Such a contract may be a consumer contract: see below, paras 30–093 et seq.

[405] *Dicey, Morris and Collins*, para.33–228. See *Ennstone Building Products Ltd v Stanger Ltd* [2002] EWCA Civ 916, [2002] 1 W.L.R. 3059. Such a contract may be a consumer contract: see below, paras 30–093 et seq.

[406] *Dicey, Morris and Collins*, para.33–454. Such a contract may be a consumer contract: see below, paras 30–093 et seq.

[407] *Bergmann v Kenburn Waste Management Ltd* [2002] EWCA Civ 98; [2002] F.S.R. 45.

[408] *Waldweise Stiftung v Lewis* [2004] EWHC 2589 (Ch).

[409] *Opthalmic Innovations International (United Kingdom) Ltd v Opthalmic Innovations International Inc* [2004] EWHC 2948 (Ch), [2005] I.L. Pr. 109.

[410] *Halpern v Halpern (Nos 1 and 2)* [2007] EWCA Civ 291, [2008] Q.B. 195. See also *Ark Therapeutics Plc v True North Capital Ltd* [2005] EWHC 1585 (Comm), [2006] 1 All E.R. (Comm) 138 (letter of intent).

[411] *Standard Bank Plc v Agrinvest International Inc* [2007] EWHC 2595 (Comm), [2008] 1 Lloyd's Rep. 532.

administration. If the contract is, however, entered into in the course of the characteristic performer's trade or profession, then a different set of connecting factors becomes relevant: in such circumstances, the applicable law will be the law of the country where the characteristic performer's principal place of business is situated or where under the terms of the contract the (characteristic) performance is to be effected through a place of business other than the principal place of business, the applicable law will be that of the country in which that other place of business is situated.[412] These various connecting factors are not defined in the Convention. It is likely, however, that they will receive an autonomous interpretation so as to achieve uniformity in the application of art.4(2).[413] The meaning given to analogous expressions in English case law, discussed below, is, thus, not conclusive as to their meaning under the Convention.[414] The relevant time for identifying each of the relevant connecting factors is the time at which the contract is concluded.

Habitual residence. English case law has not attributed a consistent meaning to this concept.[415] Outside the context of commercial law, it has been said that habitual residence refers to a person's abode in a particular country which he has adopted voluntarily and for settled purposes as part of the regular order of his life for the time being whether of short or long duration.[416] It seems possible that, on this basis, a person may have more than one habitual residence,[417] in which case, it has been suggested, the relevant habitual residence should be that of the place having the closest relationship to the contract and its performance, having regard to the circumstances known to, or contemplated by, the parties at any time before 30–079

---

412 Application of the presumption would point to the law of the characteristic performer's principal place of business unless *under the terms of the contract* performance must be effected through a place of business other than the principal place of business: *Ennstone Building Products Ltd v Stanger Ltd* [2002] EWCA Civ 916, [2002] 1 W.L.R. 3059. cf. *Iran Continental Shelf Oil Co v IRI International Corp* [2002] EWCA Civ 1024, [2004] 2 C.L.C. 696; *Trafigura Beheer BV v Kookmin Bank Co* [2005] EWHC 2350 (Comm); [2006] EWHC 1450 (Comm), [2006] 2 Lloyd's Rep. 455.

413 See *Raiffeisen Zentralbank Osterreich Aktiengesellschaft v National Bank of Greece SA* [1999] 1 Lloyd's Rep. 408.

414 *Dicey, Morris and Collins*, para.32–120. And see *Swaddling v Administration Officer* (C–90/97) [1999] E.C.R. I–1075 (consideration of meaning of habitual residence in the context of Council Regulation 1408/71 on the application of social security schemes to employed persons, to self-employed persons and to members of their families moving within the Community [1971] OJ L149/366, as amended).

415 *Dicey Morris, and Collins*, paras 6–125—6–130. As to the definition in art.19 of the Rome I Regulation, see below, paras 30–164 et seq.

416 *Kapur v Kapur* [1984] F.L.R. 920; *R. v Barnet LBC Ex p Nilish Shah* [1984] 2 A.C. 309; *Mark v Mark* [2005] UKHL 42, [2006] 1 A.C. 98. See also *Re M. (Minors) (Residence Order: Jurisdiction)* [1993] 1 F.L.R. 495; *A. v A (Child Abduction)* [1993] 2 F.L.R. 225; *D. v D. (Custody: Jurisdiction)* [1996] 1 F.L.R. 574; *Re S. (A Minor) (Custody: Habitual Residence)* [1998] A.C. 750; *Nessa v Chief Adjudication Officer* [1999] 1 W.L.R. 1937.

417 See *Ikimi v Ikimi* [2001] EWCA Civ 873, [2002] Fam. 72 (where spouses had consistently maintained two matrimonial homes in different jurisdictions, they could be habitually resident in both jurisdictions at the same time for the purposes of jurisdiction to grant a divorce under Domicile and Matrimonial Proceedings Act 1973 s.5(2)); *Mark v Mark* [2005] UKHL 42. See also *Leyvand v Barasch, The Times*, March 23, 2000 (possibility of ordinary residence in two countries, in the context of security for costs). cf. *Cameron v Cameron* (1996) S.L.T. 306 (person can only have one habitual residence, a view which is probably confined to the context of the Hague Convention on the Civil Aspects of Child Abduction 1980, implemented in Child Abduction and Custody Act 1985 Pt I: see *Dicey, Morris and Collins*, para.6–129.

or at the conclusion of the contract.[418] It is conceivable, also, that a person may be without any habitual residence.[419] In such circumstances it would seem that the applicable law will have to be determined without reference to the presumption in art.4(2).

30–080 **Central administration.** Where the characteristic performer is a body corporate or unincorporate, the law of the country where that party's "central administration" is situated may apply. This expression is not defined in the Convention, but, presumably, it will be given an autonomous meaning.[420] The nearest analogy in English law is the concept of "central management and control", as used, for example, in the Civil Jurisdiction and Judgments Act 1982,[421] but that Act also fails to supply a definition. Case law suggests that the question is one of fact, to be answered by an examination of the course of business or trading, reference to the place where the principal office is, to the place (or places) where the directors and shareholders reside (or meet) and where control over major policy decisions and business operations is actually exercised.[422]

30–081 **Principal place of business and place of business.** In the more likely situation where a body corporate or unincorporate, as characteristic performer, enters into a contract in the course of its trade or profession, the law of the place of central administration will be substituted by either the law of that party's principal place of business at the time of conclusion of the contract, or if that party's performance is to be effected through a place of business other than the principal place of business, the law of the country in which that other place of business is situated. "Principal place of business" and "place of business" are not defined in the Convention. While it is likely that each expression will be given an autonomous meaning, an analogy suggested by English law is with cases dealing with whether a corporation is present in England for the purpose of being subject to the in personam jurisdiction of the English courts.[423] These cases established that a place of business constitutes a place that is fixed and definite[424] and that the activity carried on at that place (which must be the business activity[425] of the corporation) must be carried on for a sufficient period of time

---

[418] See Plender, pp.131–132, relying on art.10(a) of the United Nations Convention on the International Sale of Goods 1980.

[419] *Hack v Hack* (1976) 6 Fam. Law 177; *Mark v Mark* [2005] UKHL 42, [2006] 1 A.C. 98; but cf. *Re J. (A Minor)(Abduction)* [1990] 2 A.C. 562.

[420] cf. Cheshire and North, p.571. The concept of "central administration" is adopted as one of the definitions of "domicile" in Council Regulation 44/2001 on jurisdiction and the recognition of judgments in civil and commercial matters art.60(1)(b), but the Regulation does not elaborate on its meaning. See also art.19(1) of the Rome I Regulation, below, para.30–165.

[421] s.42.

[422] cf. *The Rewia* [1991] 2 Lloyd's Rep. 325; see also *The Deichland* [1990] Q.B. 361; *Re Little Olympian Each Ways Ltd* [1995] 1 W.L.R. 560; *Dicey, Morris and Collins*, paras 30–005—30–006.

[423] *Dicey, Morris and Collins*, paras 11–115—11–125. See *Adams v Cape Industries Plc* [1990] Ch. 433, 523–531.

[424] *Saccharin Corp Ltd v Chemische Fabrik AG* [1911] 2 K.B. 516; *The Theodothos* [1977] 2 Lloyd's Rep. 428.

[425] See *South India Shipping Corp Ltd v Export-Import Bank of Korea* [1985] 1 W.L.R. 585.

for it to be characterised as a business.[426] Whether a particular place of business will be regarded as the "principal" such place will be a question of fact and degree.

Immovables.[427] Article 4(3) of the Rome Convention establishes a special presumption with regard to certain contracts concerning immovable property in the following terms: 30–082

> "Notwithstanding the provisions of paragraph 2 of this Article, to the extent that the subject matter of the contract is a right in immovable property or a right to use immovable property it shall be presumed that the contract is most closely connected with the country where the immovable property is situated."

It is important to delimit the scope of this provision. It is, first, confined to contracts which have as their subject matter rights in, or rights to use, immovable property. Thus, for example, it will not apply to contracts for the construction or repair of immovable property since "the main purpose of these contracts is the construction or repair rather than the immovable property itself".[428] A contract for the construction or repair of an immovable will thus be subject to the presumption in art.4(2).[429] Secondly, art.4(3) is concerned only with the contractual aspects of a transaction relating to immovables. The proprietary aspects will be subject to common law rules, since the Convention does not apply to proprietary matters.[430]

Severance. Since the presumption in favour of the *lex situs* applies "to the extent that" the contract has as its subject matter a right in or a right to use immovable property, a severable part of the contract which has that as its subject matter may be governed by art.4(3), whereas the remaining part or parts of the 30–083

---

[426] *Saccharin Corp Ltd v Chemische Fabrik AG* [1911] 2 K.B. 516; *South India Shipping Corp Ltd v Export-Import Bank of Korea* [1985] 1 W.L.R. 585; *Okura & Co Ltd v Forsbacka Jernverks A/B* [1914] 1 K.B. 715; *Domansa v Derin Shipping and Trading Co Inc* [2001] 1 Lloyd's Rep. 362. In the case of a bank account, performance, i.e. repayment of the sum deposited, is to be effected through the branch where the relevant account is kept and the country in which the branch is situated will be the relevant place of business: *Sierra Leone Telecommunications Co Ltd v Barclays Bank Plc* [1998] 2 All E.R. 821.

[427] *Dicey, Morris and Collins*, paras 33–224—33–247. As to the Rome I Regulation, see below, para.30–192.

[428] Giuliano-Lagarde Report, p.21.

[429] See *Ennstone Building Products Ltd v Stanger Ltd* [2002] EWCA Civ 916, [2002] 1 W.L.R. 3059. Above, para.30–077.

[430] Giuliano-Lagarde Report, p.10. The distinction between a contract to transfer land and an actual transfer of land, may, however, become blurred: see *British South Africa Co v De Beers Consolidated Mines Ltd* [1910] 2 Ch. 502, 512, 515, 522–524; see also *Webb v Webb* (C–294/92) [1994] E.C.R. I–1717, [1994] Q.B. 696; *Gaillard v Chekili* (C–518/99) [2001] E.C.R. I–2771; *Prazic v Prazic* [2006] EWCA Civ 497, [2006] 2 F.L.R. 1128; cf. *Re Hayward* [1997] Ch. 45; *Ashurst v Pollard* [2001] Ch. 595. As to the common law rules relating to the transfer of immovables, see *Dicey, Morris and Collins*, paras 23–062—23–074. Article 4(3) will not apply where the contractual obligation relating to immovables is excluded from the Convention by virtue of art.1: see above, paras 30–037 et seq. Such cases will be governed by common law rules. At common law the system of law with which a contract with regard to an immovable was most closely connected was sometimes said to be the *lex situs*: see, e.g. *British South Africa Co v De Beers Consolidated Mines Ltd*, 523. But, as is shown by that case, this was not an invariable rule. As to formal validity of the contract, see below, para.30–314.

contract may be governed by art.4(2). In view, however, of the view expressed in the Giuliano-Lagarde Report that severance should be resorted to on only the rarest of occasions,[431] cases of this kind are likely to be rare and may, in any event where appropriate, be the kind of cases in which a court will conclude that the presumption is rebutted, pursuant to art.4(5).

30–084 **Types of contracts for immovables.** Article 4(3) clearly applies, inter alios, to contracts to sell land[432]; agreements to rent premises[433]; and some timeshare arrangements.[434] It also seems to apply to short term tenancies and holiday lettings of apartments.[435]

30–085 **Contracts for the carriage of goods.**[436]

> "A contract for the carriage of goods shall not be subject to the presumption in paragraph 2. In such a contract if the country in which, at the time the contract is concluded, the carrier has his principal place of business is also the country in which the place of loading or the place of discharge or the principal place of business of the consignor is situated, it shall be presumed that the contract is most closely connected with that country. In applying this paragraph single voyage charter-parties and other contracts the main purpose of which is the carriage of goods shall be treated as contracts for the carriage of goods."[437]

The effect of this provision is that a contract for the carriage of goods (by whatever mode of transport) will be presumed to be most closely connected with

---

[431] Giuliano-Lagarde Report, p.23.

[432] cf. *Merwin Pastoral Co Pty Ltd v Moolpa Pastoral Co Pty Ltd* (1932) 48 C.L.R. 565.

[433] cf. *Sanders v Van der Putte* (73/77) [1977] E.C.R. 2383; *Dansommer A/S v Gotz* (C–8/98) [2000] E.C.R. I–393, [2001] 1 W.L.R. 1069.

[434] *Dicey, Morris and Collins*, paras 33–233, 33–244–33–247; Plender, p.130; see Timeshare Act 1992, as amended by Timeshare Regulations 1997 (SI 1997/1081) which implement in the United Kingdom EU Directive 94/97 [1994] OJ L280/83 on the protection of purchasers in respect of certain aspects of contracts relating to the purchase of the right to use immovable properties on a timeshare basis. Where the timeshare property is situated in a contracting state to the Brussels or Lugano Conventions on Jurisdiction and the Enforcement of Judgments in Civil and Commercial Matters, other than the United Kingdom, an English court may have no jurisdiction over a claim for misrepresentation or breach of contract brought by a timeshare purchaser against a timeshare owner since the claim may be one the object of which is a tenancy of immovable property, and such claims are subject to the exclusive jurisdiction of the *situs* of the immovable according to art.16(1) of each Convention: see *Klein v Rhodos Management Ltd* (C–73/04) [2005] E.C.R. I–867. Where however the timeshare purchaser has financed the purchase with money lent by a bank, art.16(1) does not impose this jurisdictional bar on a claim against the bank pursuant to the provisions of ss.56(2) and 75 of the Consumer Credit Act 1974 ("connected lender" liability, discussed Vol.II); *Jarrett v Barclays Bank* [1999] Q.B. 1, overruling *Lynch v Halifax Building Society and Royal Bank of Scotland Plc* [1995] C.C.L.R. 42; and see *Office of Fair Trading v Lloyds TSB Bank Plc* [2007] UKHL 48, [2008] 1 A.C. 316. The position would appear to be the same under Council Regulation 44/2001 art.22(1), above, para.30–018 fn.111. The Consumer Protection (Distance Selling) Regulations 2000 regs 7–20 do not apply to a contract which is a "timeshare agreement" within the meaning of the Timeshare Act 1992 and to which that Act applies: Consumer Protection (Distance Selling) Regulations 2000 reg.6(1).

[435] *Dicey, Morris and Collins*, para.33–233: cf. Plender, p.129. Contrast art.4(1)(c) and (d) of the Rome I Regulation, below para.30–192 and on timeshare arrangements, art.6(4)(c), below, para.30–236.

[436] *Dicey, Morris and Collins*, paras 33–264—33–292.

[437] Rome Convention art.4(4). For the position under art.5 of the Rome I Regulation, see below, paras 30–209 et seq.

the country in which the principal place of business of the carrier,[438] at the time of the conclusion of the contract, is situated, if that country is also the country in which either the place of loading,[439] or the place of discharge,[440] or the principal place of business of the consignor[441] is situated. Since the provision explicitly excludes the application of art.4(2) to contracts for the carriage of goods, where there is no relevant grouping of the factors identified in art.4(4) the applicable law will have to be determined without the aid of any presumption. A contract for the carriage of persons will, however, be subject to the presumption in art.4(2)[442] and, thus, it is conceivable that where there is a mixed contract for the carriage of goods and persons, the contract may have two different applicable laws.[443]

"Other contracts" involving carriage of goods. It is not clear, however, what is to be included in the expression "contract for the carriage of goods." While art.4(4) clearly states that a single voyage charter-party is to be treated as such a contract, less clarity surrounds the "other contracts the main purpose of which is the carriage of goods". It is likely (though the matter is controversial) that consecutive voyage charter-parties will fall within the provision,[444] as will contracts of carriage evidenced in a bill of lading,[445] though demise charters will not.[446] **30–086**

International conventions. It is important to remember that many aspects of international transport are governed by international conventions,[447] which will take precedence over the provisions of the Rome Convention when they are applicable.[448] **30–087**

[438] Where a party who contracts to carry goods for another does not carry them himself but arranges for a third party to do so, art.4(4) will apparently apply, since the term "carrier" means the party who undertakes to carry the goods whether or not he performs the carriage himself: Giuliano-Lagarde Report, p.22; see *Dicey, Morris and Collins*, para.33–271. As to the meaning of "principal place of business", see *Dicey, Morris and Collins*, para.33–272.

[439] The place of loading is that agreed at the time of the conclusion of the contract: Giuliano-Lagarde Report, p.22; *Dicey, Morris and Collins*, para.33–273.

[440] The place of discharge is that agreed at the time of the conclusion of the contract: see authorities in preceding note.

[441] "Consignor" apparently refers to "any person who consigns goods to the carrier": Giuliano-Lagarde Report, p.21. See *Dicey, Morris and Collins*, para.33–275. As to the meaning of "principal place of business," see *Dicey, Morris and Collins*, para.33–274 and above, para.30–081.

[442] *Dicey, Morris and Collins*, para.33–252. As to carriage of persons under the Rome I Regulation, see below, paras 30–221 et seq.

[443] Cheshire and North, p.572.

[444] See *Dicey, Morris and Collins*, para.33–266; cf. Schultsz in North (ed.), *Contract Conflicts* (1982), pp.185, 192, 198; Plender, p.133. And see *Intercontainer Interfrige (ICF) SC v Balkerende Oosthuisen BV* (C–133/08) (pending) [2008] OJ C 158/10.

[445] *Dicey, Morris and Collins*, para.33–267.

[446] Giuliano-Lagarde Report, p.21; *Scrutton on Charterparties*, 20th edn (1996), pp.14, fnn.6, 59–60. Art.4(2) will apply to such charters: *Dicey, Morris and Collins*, para.33–266.

[447] See Vol.II, paras 35–001 et seq. 36–078 et seq.

[448] Rome Convention art.21. See above, para.30–027; cf. *The Hollandia* [1983] 1 A.C 565; *Trafigura Beheer BV v Mediterranean Shipping Co SA* [2007] EWCA Civ 794, [2007] 2 Lloyd's Rep. 622.

30–088 **Non-application of the presumptions.** Article 4(5) of the Rome Convention provides that the presumption in art.4(2) shall not apply if the characteristic performance cannot be determined and that each of the three presumptions shall be disregarded if it appears from the circumstances as a whole that the contract is more closely connected with another country than it is with the country indicated by the presumption.

30–089 **Characteristic performance cannot be determined.** Where it is concluded that the contract is one for which the characteristic performance cannot be determined,[449] then the law of the country with which the contract is most closely connected will have to be determined without resort to any presumption. In such circumstances, the court will have regard to all the facts and circumstances surrounding the contract and its making: relevant facts and circumstances will be those treated as relevant in cases decided at common law.[450]

30–090 **Rebutting the presumptions.**[451] Each presumption set out in art.4 may be rebutted if it appears from the circumstances as a whole that the contract is more closely connected with another country than it is with the country whose law is indicated as applicable by virtue of the presumption.[452] The critical question, however, is as to the strength that will be attributed to the presumptions. The Giuliano-Lagarde Report states that paras (2)–(4) of art.4 are "only rebuttable presumptions"[453] and that art.4(5) "obviously leaves the judge a margin of discretion as to whether a set of circumstances exists in each specific case justifying the non-application of the presumption",[454] this being "the inevitable counterpart of a general conflict rule intended to apply to almost all types of contract",[455] but such remarks are not particularly revealing as to the weight to be attributed to the presumptions. The relationship between para.(2) and para.(5) of art.4 has proved to be controversial and has given rise to difficulty.[456] Early decisions expressed different and polarised views. Thus in England it was said, obiter, that art.4(5) means that the presumption is "displaced if the court concludes that it is not appropriate in the circumstances of any given case. This,

[449] *Apple Corps Ltd v Apple Computer Inc* [2004] EWHC 768 (Ch), [2004] I.L. Pr. 597. See above, para.30–076.

[450] *Apple Corps Ltd v Apple Computer Inc* [2004] EWHC 768 (Ch). See above, para.30–012.

[451] *Dicey, Morris and Collins*, paras 32–124 et seq., 33–117 et seq., 33–154—33–155, 33–220, 33–235—33–236, 33–277—33–278, 33–303 et seq., 33–412, 33–454; Cheshire and North, pp.573–574; Plender, pp.119–126; Kaye, pp.186–191; Hill (2004) 53 I.C.L.Q. 325; Atrill (2004) 53 I.C.L.Q. 549; Briggs (2001) 72 B.Y.I.L. 437, 465–470; Lagarde (1981) 22 Virginia J.Int.L. 91.

[452] Rome Convention art.4(5).

[453] Giuliano-Lagarde Report, p.23.

[454] Giuliano-Lagarde Report, p.22.

[455] Giuliano-Lagarde Report, p.22.

[456] For cases where Rome Convention art.4(2) has been applied without reference to art.4(5), see *W. H. Martin Ltd v Feldbinder Spezialfahrzeugwerke GmbH* [1998] I.L. Pr. 794; *Raiffeisen Zentralbank Osterreich Aktiengeesellschaft v National Bank of Greece SA* [1999] 1 Lloyd's Rep. 408; *Dinka Latchin v General Mediterranean Holdings SA* [2002] C.L.C. 330; *Print Concept GmbH v GEW (EC) Ltd* [2001] EWCA Civ 352, [2002] C.L.C. 352; *Ferguson Shipbuilders Ltd v Voith Hydro GmbH* (2000) S.L.T. 229. In *ISS Machinery Services Ltd v Aeolian Shipping SA* [2001] EWCA Civ 1162, [2001] 2 Lloyd's Rep. 641, the court determined the law of the country with which the contract was most closely connected without reference to art.4(2).

formally, makes the presumption very weak."[457] Conversely, the Dutch Hoge Raad decided that art.4(5) of the Rome Convention should be applied restrictively. On this view, the presumption in art.4(2) is the "main rule" which rule should only be disregarded if, in the special circumstances of the case, the place of business of the party who is to effect the characteristic performance "has no real significance as a connecting factor".[458] Further examination in English decisions reveals, however, support for the following propositions. First, the presumption in art.4(2) must be given "due weight".[459] Secondly:

> " . . . unless Art.4(2) is regarded as a rule of thumb which requires a preponderance of connecting factors to be established before the presumption can be disregarded, the intention of the Convention is likely to be subverted."[460]

This is because the presumptions were introduced into the Convention with a view to injecting a degree of certainty into the search for the law of the country with which the contract is most closely connected,[461] and it also therefore follows that the presumptions are not limited in effect to cases where all the other factors in the case point to an equal balance between two or more countries.[462] Thirdly, it is thus possible to state that the court will apply the presumptively applicable law unless satisfied on a balance of probabilities that the contract, having regard to the circumstances as a whole, is clearly more closely connected with another country[463] and that the burden of proving this lies on the party who asserts it.[464] Relevant circumstances are likely to include those treated as pointing to a close connection in cases decided at common law[465] and, additionally, factors which supervene after the conclusion of the contract.[466] Fourthly, however, the application of art.4(5) will be very much conditioned by the circumstances of particular

---

[457] *Credit Lyonnais v New Hampshire Insurance Co* [1997] 2 Lloyd's Rep. 1, 5, per Hobhouse L.J.

[458] *Societe Nouvelle des Papeteries de l'Aa v B.V. Machinefabriek BOA* (1992) N.J. 750. See on this case Struycken [1996] LMCLQ 18; Plender, pp.121–123. And see *Caledonia Subsea Ltd v Microperi Srl* (2002) S.L.T. 1022. See also *Intercontainer Interfrigo (ICF) SC v Balkerende Oosthuisen BV* (C–133/08) (pending) [2008] OJ C 158/10.

[459] *Definitely Maybe (Touring) Ltd v Marek Lieberberg Konzertagentur GmbH* [2001] 1 W.L.R. 1745, 1750. cf. *Caledonia Subsea Ltd v Microperi Srl* (2002) S.L.R. 1022.

[460] *Samcrete Egypt Engineers and Contractors SAE v Land Rover Exports Ltd* [2001] EWCA Civ 2019, [2002] C.L.C. 533 at [41]; *Ennstone Building Products Ltd v Stanger Ltd* [2002] EWCA Civ 916, [2002] 1 W.L.R. 3059 at [10]–[12]; *Iran Continental Shelf Oil Co v IRI International Corp* [2002] EWCA Civ 1024, [2004] 2 C.L.C. 696, [77]–[91]; *Waldweise Stiftung v Lewis* [2004] EWHC 2589 (Ch); *Opthalmic Innovations International (United Kingdom) Ltd v Opthalmic Innovations International Inc* [2004] EWHC 2948 (Ch), [2005] I.L. Pr. 109; see also *Bergmann v Kenburn Waste Management Ltd* [2002] EWCA Civ 98, [2002] F.S.R. 45. cf. *Caledonia Subsea Ltd v Microperi Srl* (2002) S.L.T. 1022.

[461] Giuliano-Lagarde Report, p.20; North in North (ed.), *Contract Conflicts* (1982), pp.3, 15, reprinted in *Essays in Private International Law* (1993), p.23.

[462] *Dicey, Morris and Collins*, para.33–125. And see *Caledonia Subsea Ltd v Microperi Srl* (2002) S.L.T. 1022.

[463] See cases cited in fn.460, above.

[464] *Definitely Maybe (Touring) Ltd v Marek Lieberberg Konzertagentur GmbH* [2001] 1 W.L.R. 1745; *Samcrete Egypt Engineers and Contractors SAE v Land Rover Exports Ltd* [2001] EWCA Civ 2019.

[465] Above, para.30–012.

[466] Giuliano-Lagarde Report, p.20. See above, para.30–054.

cases and general statements are of limited value.[467] There may, in some cases, be a tendency to regard the presumption as most easily rebutted in a case where the characteristic performance is to be effected in a country other than the country whose law is indicated by the presumption.[468]

30–091 This circumstance is of particular importance in the context of a letter of credit transaction. Here the operation of the presumption in art.4(2) will almost invariably mean that the contract between the issuing bank and the correspondent bank and that between the correspondent bank and the beneficiary will be governed by the law of the country in which the correspondent bank's principal place of business, or place of business, as the case may be, is situated.[469] However, in relation to the contract between the issuing bank and the beneficiary, the operation of the presumption would lead to application of the law of the country in which the issuing bank's principal place of business, or place of business, as the case may be, is situated, which places will not coincide with those of the correspondent bank.[470] In such a case:

> " . . . application of Art.4(2) would lead to an irregular and subjective position where the governing law of a letter of credit would vary according to whether one was looking at the position of the confirming bank or the issuing bank. It is of great importance to both beneficiaries and banks concerned in the issue and operation of letters of credit that there should be clarity and simplicity in such matters,"[471]

which clarity and simplicity could be achieved by invoking art.4(5) to secure application of the law of the country where the obligation to pay against presentation of conforming documents was to be performed.[472] This may not, of

---

[467] *Definitely Maybe (Touring) Ltd v Marek Lieberberg Konzertagentur GmbH* [2001] 1 W.L.R. 1745; *Samcrete Egypt Engineers and Contractors SAE v Land Rover Exports Ltd* [2001] EWCA Civ 2019; *Bergmann v Kenburn Waste Management Ltd* [2002] EWCA Civ 98; *Ennstone Building Products Ltd v Stanger Ltd* [2002] EWCA Civ 916. cf. *Caledonia Subsea Ltd v Microperi Srl* (2002) S.L.T. 1022. For circumstances in which the presumptions in art.4(3) and 4(4) may be rebutted, see *Dicey, Morris and Collins*, paras 33–235—33–236, 33–277—33–278.

[468] *Bank of Baroda v Vysya Bank Ltd* [1994] 2 Lloyd's Rep. 87; cases cited in preceding note; *Dicey, Morris and Collins*, para.32–127. And see *Ferguson Shipbuilders Ltd v Voith Hydro GmbH* (2000) S.L.T. 229.

[469] *Bank of Baroda v Vysya Bank Ltd* [1994] 2 Lloyd's Rep. 87; above, para.30–077; *PT Pan Indonesia Bank Ltd Tbk v Marconi Communications International Ltd* [2005] EWCA Civ 422, [2007] 2 Lloyd's Rep. 72 (letter of credit issued by Indonesian bank which became insolvent, confirmed by another Indonesian bank with no place of business in England, the credit to be advised through an English bank which did not confirm the credit, documents to be presented in England and payment to be made there, led to conclusion that although presumptively the contract between the beneficiary and the confirming bank was governed by Indonesian law, pursuant to art.4(2) of the Rome Convention, the above connections with England justified disregarding the presumption, pursuant to art.4(5). But (at [67]) there were no circumstances justifying displacement of the presumption in relation to the contract between the issuing bank and the confirming bank). See also *Bank of Credit and Commerce Hong Kong Ltd v Sonali Bank* [1995] 1 Lloyd's Rep. 227; *Batstone & Firminger Ltd v Nasima Enterprises (Nigeria) Ltd* [1996] C.L.C. 1902, 1910; *Habib Bank Ltd v Central Bank of Sudan* [2006] EWHC 1767 (Comm), [2006] 2 Lloyd's Rep. 412.

[470] *Bank of Baroda v Vysya Bank Ltd* [1994] 2 Lloyd's Rep. 87.

[471] [1994] 2 Lloyd's Rep. 87, 93, per Mance J.

[472] *Bank of Baroda v Vysya Bank Ltd* [1994] 2 Lloyd's Rep. 87; cf. *Offshore International SA v Banco Central SA* [1977] 1 W.L.R. 399. See also *PT Pan Indonesia Bank Ltd Tbk v Marconi Communications International Ltd* [2005] EWCA Civ 422.

course, be an inevitable outcome in every type of case in view of the fact that the presumption focuses on the *place of business*, etc., of the characteristic performer rather than on *the place of* the characteristic performance.[473]

(e) *Certain Consumer Contracts and Individual Employment Contracts*

Introduction. Articles 5 and 6 of the Rome Convention contain special rules for determining, respectively, the law applicable to certain consumer contracts and individual employment contracts. The central provisions of these articles are linked by a common underlying philosophy, namely that the consumer and the employee, respectively, are in a weaker position to the other contracting party. As such, the general choice of law rules contained in arts 3 and 4 of the Convention required modification so as to achieve, respectively, the aim of consumer and employee protection.[474] **30–092**

"Certain consumer contracts."[475] Article 5 contains the choice of law rules applicable to certain consumer contracts. These rules apply to a contract: **30–093**

> " . . . the object of which is the supply of goods or services to a person ('the consumer') for a purpose which can be regarded as being outside his trade or profession, or a contract for the provision of credit for that object."[476]

A more precise definition was avoided so as not to introduce conflict with definitions which are found in national law,[477] though it is likely that an autonomous meaning will be ascribed to contracts that fall within the provision.[478] In

---

[473] *Benjamin's Sale of Goods*, 7th edn (2006), para.25–066.

[474] Giuliano-Lagarde Report, pp.23, 25.

[475] *Dicey, Morris and Collins on The Conflict of Laws*, 14th edn (2006), paras 33–002—33–054; Plender, *The European Contracts Convention*, 2nd edn (2001), Ch.7; Kaye, *The New Private International Law of Contract of the European Community* (1993), pp.203–220; Basedow in Meeusen, Pertegas and Straetmans (eds), *The Enforcement of International Contracts in the European Union* (2004), pp.269–288; Straetmans in Meeusen, Pertegas and Straetmans (eds), *The Enforcement of International Contracts in the European Union* (2004), pp.295–322; Morse in Lomnicka and Morse (eds), *Contemporary Issues in Commercial Law* (1997), pp.117–135; Hartley in North (ed.), *Contract Conflicts* (1982), Ch. 6; Morse (1992) 41 I.C.L.Q. 1. Gillies (2007) 3 J. Priv. Int. L. 89; Tang (2007) 3 J. Priv. Int. L. 113. For the application of the provisions to contracts concluded "on-line", see below, paras 30–095 et seq. As to the position under art.6 of the Rome I Regulation, see below, paras 30–231 et seq. As to the correct validating of such contracts, see below, para.30–313.

[476] Rome Convention art.5(1). Thus, e.g. art.5 will not apply to contracts made by e.g. manufacturers or traders who buy goods or obtain services for business purposes, or to professionals who acquire goods or services for professional purposes: see Giuliano-Lagarde Report, p.23. For other difficulties in interpreting the language of art.5(1), see *Dicey, Morris and Collins*, paras 33–002—33–007.

[477] Giuliano-Lagarde Report, p.23. See the definition in Unfair Contract Terms Act 1977 s.12(1), above, paras 14–066 et seq.

[478] cf. *Société Bertrand v Paul Ott KG* (150/77) [1978] E.C.R. 143; *Shearson Lehmann Hutton Inc v TVB Treuhandgesellschaft für Vermogensverwaltung und Beteiligungen GmbH* (C–89/91) [1993] E.C.R. I–139; *Brenner v Dean Witter Reynolds Inc* (C–318/93) [1994] E.C.R. I–4725; *Benincasa v Dentalkit Srl* (C–269/95) [1997] E.C.R. I–3767; *Mietz v Intership Yachting Sneek B.V.* (C–99/96) [1999] E.C.R. I–2277; *Gabriel v Schlank & Schlick GmbH* (C–96/00) [2002] E.C.R. I–6367; *Engler v Janus Versand GmbH* (C–27/02) [2005] E.C.R. I–1481, [2005] I.L. Pr. 83; *Gruber v Bay Wa AG* (C–464/01) [2005] E.C.R. I–439, [2006] Q.B. 204. According to the Giuliano-Lagarde Report, p.23, the scope of the Article "should be interpreted in the light of its purpose which is to protect the weaker party and in accordance with other international instruments with the same purpose such as

terms, art.5 is capable of applying to a wide variety of contracts including contracts for the sale, hire or pledge of movables[479]; insurance contracts (to the extent that these are not excluded from the Convention)[480]; banking contracts; and wagering contracts. A contract which, for an exclusive price, provides for a combination of travel and accommodation (a so-called "package tour") is specifically made subject to the Article.[481] On the other hand, contracts of carriage are specifically excluded from the operation of art.5,[482] as are contracts for the supply of services where the services are to be supplied to the consumer exclusively in a country other than that in which he has his habitual residence.[483] Where a contract entered into by a consumer is not within the category of contracts covered by art.5, or art.5 is, for some other reason, inapplicable, the governing law will be determined by reference to the general choice of law rules contained in arts 3 and 4 of the Rome Convention.[484]

30–094 **Choice of law by the parties.** A key element in art.5 is the restriction on the effect of a choice of law contained in a contract which is subject to that Article. Notwithstanding art.3:

> "... a choice of law made by the parties shall not have the result of depriving the consumer of the protection afforded to him by the mandatory rules of the law of the country in which he has his habitual residence",

if any one of three specified conditions is satisfied.[485] The first condition is where, in the country of the consumer's habitual residence, the contract was preceded by a specific invitation addressed to the consumer, or by advertising, and the consumer had taken in the country of his habitual residence all the steps necessary on his part for the conclusion of the contract.[486] Any invitation must thus be specific to the particular consumer bringing this claim. As to "advertising", the Giuliano-Lagarde Report suggests that the other contracting party must have intended to advertise to the consumer in the latter's country of habitual

---

the Judgments Convention" (i.e. the Brussels Convention of 1968 on Jurisdiction and the Enforcement of Judgments in Civil and Commercial Matters, above, para.30–018). In the above mentioned cases the European Court has consistently stressed that "consumer" in the relevant provisions of the Brussels Convention should be strictly construed as limited to private final consumers who are not engaged in trade or professional activities. This will normally serve to exclude legal persons and traders, unless, possibly, such persons are acting entirely outside their trade or professional activities and can establish that they were in a weaker bargaining position in relation to the supplier. cf. *Chris Hart (Business Sales) Ltd v Niven* (1992) S.L.T. (Sh Ct) 53.

479 Sales of securities are excluded: Giuliano-Lagarde Report, p.23.

480 Rome Convention art.1(3). See Giuliano-Lagarde Report, p.23.

481 Rome Convention art.5(5). In Germany it has been held that a timeshare contract is not a contract the object of which is a supply of services for the purposes of Rome Convention art.5(1): BGH NJW 1997, 1697; Knöfel (1998) I.C.L.Q. 439, 443.

482 Rome Convention art.5(4)(a).

483 Rome Convention art.5(4)(b).

484 Above, paras 30–047 et seq.

485 Rome Convention art.5(2). See, in particular, *Dicey, Morris and Collins*, paras 33–009—33–113; Kaye, pp.216–218.

486 Rome Convention art.5(2), first indent.

residence[487]: if this view is accepted, the condition will be extremely restrictive in effect.[488] The provision refers to the "steps" necessary for the conclusion of the contract being taken in the consumer's country so as, apparently, to "avoid the classical problem of determining the place where the contract was concluded".[489] But this does not answer the question whether legal or factual steps are envisaged. To the extent that the Giuliano-Lagarde Report states that "steps" includes writing or any action taken in consequences of an offer or advertisement, the implication appears to be that factual steps are those contemplated.[490] According to the second condition, the effect of a choice of law will be limited, as described above, if the other party or his agent[491] received the consumer's order in the country where the consumer was habitually resident.[492] Although this condition overlaps with the first, the overlap is not complete: thus the second condition will apply:

> " . . . where the consumer has addressed himself to a stand of a foreign firm at a fair or exhibition taking place in the consumer's country or to a permanent branch or agency of a foreign firm established in the consumer's country even though the foreign firm has not advertised in the consumer's country in a way covered"[493]

by the first condition. The third condition is expressly limited to contracts for the sale of goods. The limits on the effect of a choice of law will also apply, in the case of a sale of goods, if the consumer travelled from the country of his habitual residence to another country and there gave his order, provided the consumer's journey was arranged by the seller for the purpose of inducing the consumer to buy.[494] The provision is intended to catch "cross-border excursion selling" (more common on the European Continent than in the United Kingdom[495]) whereby, for example, the owner of a store in one country arranges one-day bus trips for consumers in a neighbouring country to buy in his store.[496]

Application to contract concluded "on-line". Article 5 was drafted when the impact of the internet on the conclusion of contracts was unknown.[497] It is now common for consumers to conclude a contract with (it will be assumed in this discussion) a seller over the internet, so that the question arises as to how art.5 may be applied to such transactions. In light of the fact that the Rome Convention did not anticipate the internet, it is unsurprising that the application 30–095

---

[487] Giuliano-Lagarde Report, p.24. cf. *Standard Bank London Ltd v Apostolakis* [2002] C.L.C. 939; *Rayner v Davies* [2002] EWCA Civ 1880; [2003] 1 All E.R. (Comm) 394; *Gabriel v Schlank & Schlick GmbH* (C–96/00) [2002] E.C.R. I–6367.

[488] As to contracts concluded "on-line", see below, paras 30–095 et seq.

[489] Giuliano-Lagarde Report, p.24.

[490] Giuliano-Lagarde Report, p.24. Thus the fact that such factual steps (e.g. in relation to offer and acceptance) are deemed, as a matter of law, to occur elsewhere matters not. cf. Unfair Contract Terms Act 1977 s.27(2)(b), above, para.30–008.

[491] "Agent" is intended to refer to all persons acting on behalf of the trader: Giuliano-Lagarde Report, p.24.

[492] Rome Convention art.5(2), second indent.

[493] Giuliano-Lagarde Report, p.24.

[494] Rome Convention art.5(2), third indent.

[495] Giuliano-Lagarde Report, p.24; Plender, p.130; Kaye, p.149.

[496] Giuliano-Lagarde Report, p.24.

[497] See North (2001) 50 ICLQ 477, 503.

of art.5 in this context gives rise to considerable difficulty and, as will be seen below, the revised provision to be found in art.6 of the Rome I Regulation purports to take account of internet consumer transactions.[498] Nonetheless, it is proposed to offer some speculative remarks on the application of the text of the Rome Convention to such transactions.[499] For the purpose of the following discussion it is assumed that the eventual contract between the consumer and the seller is concluded on the seller's standard terms which contain an express choice of the law of a country other than that in which the consumer is habitually resident.[500] The chief difficulties revolve around the application of the first two conditions of art.5(2) in the internet context.[501]

30–096 **Article 5(2): first condition: specific invitation.** There would appear to be no difficulty in concluding that a specific invitation can be addressed to a consumer by a seller through electronic mail. Nonetheless, the provision requires the specific invitation to precede the conclusion of the contract and that the specific invitation be addressed to the consumer in the latter's country of habitual residence. These requirements raise the question of when and where a communication by electronic mail is received for these purposes. It is suggested that such a communication is received when it is accessed by the consumer and that it is immaterial that the communication is earlier received and stored on a server before it is accessed by the consumer.[502] Where a consumer accesses his electronic mail in the country in which he has his habitual residence, then it will be evident that he has received the specific invitation in that country. Difficulty arises, however, when the consumer accesses his electronic mail, as, for example, when travelling in a country other than that in which he habitually resides. Common sense suggests that the first condition in art.5(2) should continue to apply, since it is hard to justify relieving the seller of the legal risk which would otherwise be placed upon him by such a chance occurrence. It is, however, impossible to reconcile such an outcome with the actual wording of the provision, though a very bold interpretation of the language might enable the court to conclude that if the consumer did not act immediately on the invitation, retained the communication and then re-accessed it in the country of his habitual residence that circumstance could constitute receipt for the purposes of the provision.[503] It might also be argued that the provision gives rise to an evidential

[498] See below, paras 30–231 et seq.

[499] *Dicey, Morris and Collins*, paras 33–017—33–023; *Benjamin's Sale of Goods*, 7th edn (2006), paras 25–049—25–053; Plender at pp.147–149; Murray in Edwards and Waelde (eds), *Law & the Internet* (2000), p.17; Niemann (2000) 5 *Communications Law* 99; Kronke in Boele-Woelki and Kessedjian (eds), *Internet: Which Court Decides? Which Law Applies* (1998), p.65; Schu (1997) 5 *International Journal of Law and Information Technology* 192; Gillies (2007) 3 J. Priv. Int. L. 89; Tang (2007) 3 J. Priv. Int. L. 113.

[500] See, e.g. standard terms of amazon.co.uk (choice of the law of Luxembourg (*http://www.amazon.co.uk*); standard terms of amazon.fr. (choice of the law of Luxembourg (*http://www.amazon.fr.*)) [Accessed September 5, 2008.]

[501] See above, para.30–094. The terms of the third condition make it clear that it cannot apply to an internet contract: see above.

[502] Schu, pp.210–211. cf. Directive 2000/31 on certain legal aspects of information society services, in particular electronic commerce ("Directive on electronic commerce") [2000] OJ L178/1 art.11(1) and (3) and the UK implementing legislation, the Electronic Commerce (EC Directive) Regulations 2002 (SI 2002/2013) reg.11(2)(a).

[503] Schu, pp.210–211.

presumption that the consumer did receive the specific invitation in the country of his habitual residence which presumption it is incumbent on the seller to rebut.[504]

Article 5(2): first condition: advertising. A second considerable difficulty with the first condition in art.5(2) in the context of the present discussion relates to advertisements and websites. There can be little doubt that a website which seeks to promote a seller's products can constitute "advertising" for the purposes of the provision.[505] The problem is that such an advertisement can be accessed from most, if not all, parts of the world, thus, supposedly, opening up a seller to potential liability under a wide variety of foreign laws. On one view it can be argued that a seller should bear the risk of a choice of law in the contract being overridden by the mandatory rules of the consumer's habitual residence, since a seller must be aware of the potential reach of his website and because bearing this risk is part of cost of doing business on the internet, which must be balanced against the commercial benefits of doing business in this manner.[506] A rather narrower interpretation of the provision is, however, possible. This involves drawing an analogy with an example suggested in the Giuliano-Lagarde Report of a consumer who responds to an advertisement which appears in an American publication which has been sold in Germany. According to the Report, this situation would not fall within art.5 unless the advertisement had appeared in special editions of the publication intended for distribution in European countries.[507] This remark may be construed to indicate that the condition under discussion is only applicable if a consumer, either individually or more generally as a consumer, has been "targeted" in the country of his habitual residence by a seller.[508] This interpretation will not, of course, be easy to apply in the context of sales through websites which are, in principle, accessible throughout the world. If, however, the seller specifies that the site is only addressed to a particular country or countries, the conclusion can perhaps be drawn that consumers habitually resident in that country or those countries are covered by art.5, 30–097

[504] Schu, pp.210–211.

[505] *Dicey, Morris and Collins*, para.33–019; Plender, pp.146–147.

[506] *Dicey, Morris and Collins*, para.33–019. cf. *Dow Jones & Co Inc v Gutnick* [2002] H.C.A. 56; (2003) 210 C.L.R. 575; *King v Lewis* [2004] EWCA Civ 1329, [2005] I.L. Pr. 185. The Directive on electronic commerce (above, fn.502) and the Electronic Commerce (EC Directive) Regulations 2002 (above, fn.502) are generally thought to support a "country of origin" principle for regulating electronic commerce, a principle which might be thought to be inconsistent with interpreting art.5(2) in favour of the consumer. However, it is submitted that the Directive and the Regulations have no bearing on the matter under discussion for the following reasons: (1) the Directive and the Regulations are explicitly expressed not to apply to the freedom of the parties to choose the law applicable to their contract and to consumer contracts (art.3(3) and Annex, reg.4(4) and Sch.); (b) Recital 55 of the Directive (not reproduced in the Regulations) states that "this Directive cannot have the result of depriving the consumer of the protection afforded to him by the mandatory rules relating to contractual obligations of the law of the Member State in which he has his habitual residence"; (c) the Directive explicitly states that it does not establish additional rules of private international law (art.1(4) and Recital 23). The latter provisions are not reproduced in the Regulations, a highly questionable exclusion but one which does not detract from the proposition that the Directive and the Regulations are irrelevant in the present context.

[507] Giuliano-Lagarde Report, p.24.

[508] See Plender, pp.146–147. cf. *King v Lewis* [2004] EWCA Civ 1329, [2005] I.L. Pr. 185.

whereas consumers habitually resident elsewhere are not.[509] The same conclusion might be drawn if the material on the website is expressed in a language which is readily understood in relatively few countries. If there is no country based limitation stated on the website or if the material on it is expressed in a language which is readily understood in many countries (for example, English) then it will be hard to conclude that the seller was targeting any particular consumer or group of consumers but, rather, was directing its activities towards consumers world wide. In such a case, it seems appropriate to regard the seller rather than the consumer as bearing the legal risk and to conclude that the situation falls within art.5.[510]

30–098 **Article 5(2): first condition: "all the steps necessary".** The last requirement of the first condition is that the consumer takes in the country of his habitual residence all the steps necessary on his part for the conclusion of the contract. In relation to a contract concluded by electronic mail, this will involve a consumer sending relevant communications to the seller from the country of the consumer's habitual residence.[511] In relation to a response by a consumer to an advertisement on a seller's website, this, normally, will involve a consumer indicating his agreement to the terms and conditions by "clicking" on an appropriate icon on the relevant site which action must take place in the country of his habitual residence.[512]

30–099 **Article 5(2): second condition.** The second condition in art.5(2) also causes considerable difficulty in the case of contracts for the sale of goods since it requires that the other party or his agent received the consumer's order in the country in which the consumer is habitually resident and doubts may arise, first, as to the meaning of "agent" in this context and, secondly, as to where the order is "received".

30–100 **Article 5(2): second condition: "agent".** As to the meaning of "agent" it is submitted that neither a web server nor a passive third party service provider can be regarded as an agent of the seller for these purposes.[513] A server can be located anywhere and is a communications medium, the location of which is not necessarily related in any way to the seller's business. A passive third party service

---

[509] The seller may take technical steps to block access from particular countries or structure the transaction in such a way as to ascertain the consumer's habitual residence before any contract is concluded: see Gringras, *Laws of the Internet*, 2nd edn (2003), p.51.

[510] Such an interpretation would produce consistency with art.15(3) of Council Regulation 44/2001 (above, para.30–018) which provides that the rules of the Regulation concerned with consumers apply, inter alia, if: "the contract has been concluded with a person who pursues commercial or professional activities in the Member State of the consumer's domicile or, by any means, directs such activities to that Member State or to several States including that Member State, and the contract falls within the scope of those activities." For the virtually identical language adopted in art.6 of the Rome I Regulation, see below, paras 30–231 et seq.

[511] See Schu, p.215.

[512] See Niemann, p.100; Schu, p.192.

[513] Chissick and Kelman, *Electronic Commerce: Law and Practice*, 3rd edn (2002), para.4–35; Niemann 100. Nor, it is submitted, should so-called "electronic agents" be treated as agents for these purposes: cf. Wetzenboeck (2001) 9 *International Journal of Law and Information Technology* 204; Øren (2001) 9 *Journal of Law and Information Technology* 249.

provider merely provides a technical mechanism whereby the seller can pass information to potential customers. If, however, the third party service provider took action on behalf of the seller, such as processing orders, it might be possible to say that the provider was a "person acting on behalf of the trader"[514] and to conclude, in these circumstances, that the provider was an agent.[515]

Article 5(2): second condition: "received". It would appear, at least technically, that an order by electronic mail is "received" by the seller or his agent at the server where the mail is stored and that an order addressed to a website is "received" by the seller or his agent at the server on which the website is established.[516] If this is the meaning of "received" in this context, the order will be received in the country of the consumer's habitual residence only if the server is located in that country. Such a conclusion could produce unfortunate consequences, for example, in a case in which a consumer, habitually resident in England, approaches the English agent of a seller based, e.g. in France, and places his order on a website hosted for the agent by a third party in Brazil. If it is concluded that the order is received in Brazil, then the consumer could not rely on the mandatory rules of English law to the extent that they are more favourable to him than the rules of the foreign law expressly applicable to the contract.[517] It is suggested, admittedly without any authority, that such a result may be avoided by construing the country in which the order is "received" as the country in which the physical place of business of the seller or his agent from which the relevant server is accessed by the seller or his agent, as the case may be, is situated: if one of those places is the country in which the consumer is habitually resident, then the requirements of the provision should be regarded as satisfied, irrespective of whether the relevant server is also located in the same country.[518] 30–101

Mandatory rules. Provided the relevant contract falls within art.5 and provided one of the conditions discussed in the preceding paragraphs applies, the choice of law in the contract shall not have the result of "depriving" the consumer of the protection of the mandatory rules of the law of the country in which he is habitually resident. "Mandatory rules", for these purposes, would seem to be defined by reference to art.3(3)[519]: they are rules of the law of that country "which cannot be derogated from by contract" and it is not necessary in addition (though it will often be the case) that they are also rules which apply "whatever the law applicable to the contract".[520] In the context of art.5, such rules will relate to consumer protection.[521] 30–102

[514] Giuliano-Lagarde Report, p.24.

[515] Chissick and Kelman, pp.4–34.

[516] Schu, p.216.

[517] The example assumes that the first condition of Rome Convention art.5(2) is inapplicable.

[518] cf. Directive on electronic commerce (above, para.30–097) art.11(1) and Recital 19; Electronic Commerce (EC Directive) Regulations 2002 reg.11(2)(a); *Menashe Business Mercantile Ltd v William Hill Organization Ltd* [2002] EWCA Civ 1702, [2003] 1 W.L.R. 1462.

[519] Above, paras 30–061 et seq.

[520] cf. Rome Convention art.7(1) which does not have the force of law in the UK: Contracts (Applicable Law) Act 1990 s.2(2), above, para.30–063.

[521] Examples in English law might include the provisions of the Unfair Contract Terms Act 1977 and some provisions of the Consumer Credit Act 1974: see *Office of Fair Trading v Lloyds TSB Bank*

The relationship between these mandatory rules and the chosen law is, however, somewhat obscure. First, the rules of the chosen law may be more favourable to the consumer than the mandatory rules of the country of his habitual residence. In such circumstances, it cannot reasonably be said that the consumer is "deprived" of the protection of the mandatory rules of the country of his habitual residence since he is better off than he would have been had those rules been applied. Conversely, he would be deprived of the protection of those rules if the chosen law were less favourable to him than the mandatory rules of his habitual residence. Accordingly, the correct interpretation of art.5(2) is that it enables a consumer to rely on the mandatory rules of the law of his habitual residence if they are more favourable to him than the chosen law or on the chosen law if it is more favourable to him than the mandatory rules of the law of his habitual residence.[522] The law of the habitual residence thus defines the minimum, but not the maximum protection available to the consumer. This solution is, it is suggested, preferable to one which would allow the consumer to rely, cumulatively, on the mandatory rules of both the law of the habitual residence and the chosen law,[523] despite the potential difficulties which may be presented in deciding, in any given case, which set of rules is most favourable to the consumer. There seems to be no obvious justification in giving a consumer "double protection" just because the contract falls within art.5 of the Convention, and contains a choice of law.

30–103 **EC consumer protection legislation.** The European Community has produced a substantial body of law designed to protect consumers which has to be transposed into national law by Member States. Such legislation is generally mandatory in character, it being provided, normally, that the legislation cannot be avoided by the choice of the law of a non-Member State in the contract.[524] Three examples of English legislation implementing Community rules may be briefly mentioned here.[525] The Council Directive on unfair terms in consumer contracts

---

Plc [2007] UKHL 48, [2008] 1 A.C. 316 ("connected lender" liability under Consumer Credit Act 1974 s.75 applies in respect of all transactions entered into using credit cards issued under consumer credit agreements regulated by the 1974 Act whether they are entered into in the United Kingdom or elsewhere); *Dicey, Morris and Collins*, paras 33–033—33–042. See too below, para.30–103.

[522] See *Dicey, Morris and Collins*, para.33–014; Plender, p.149; Kaye, pp.212–214; Morse (1992) 41 I.C.L.Q. 1.

[523] cf. Philip in North (ed.), *Contract Conflicts* (1982), p.81, at p.99.

[524] See *Dicey, Morris and Collins*, paras 33–043—33–054; *Benjamin's Sale of Goods*, 7th edn (2006), paras 25–101—25–118; Plender, pp.152–157.

[525] For other examples, see Consumer Protection (Cancellation of Contracts Concluded away from Business Premises) Regulations 1987 (SI 1987/2117), as amended by SI 1988/958, and replaced by Cancellation of Contracts made in a Consumer's Home or Place of Work etc. Regulations 2008 (SI 2008/1816) implementing Council Directive 1985/577 to protect the consumer in respect of contracts negotiated away from business premises [1985] OJ L372/31, as to which see *Travel Vac SL v Sanchis* (C–423/97) [1999] E.C.R. I–2195; *Deutsche Bausparkasse Badenia AG* (C–350/03) [2005] E.C.R. I–9215; Enterprise Act 2002 Pt 8 (and see SI 2003/1374, SI 2003/1593), replacing; Stop Now Orders (EC Directive) Regulations 2001 (SI 2001/1422), implementing Directive 1998/27 on injunctions for the protection of consumers' interests [1998] OJ L166/51; Financial Services (Distance Marketing) Regulations 2004 (SI 2004/2095), implementing Directive concerning the distance marketing of consumer financial services [2002] OJ L271/16. See generally Regulation 2006/2004 on co-operation between national authorities responsible for the enforcement of consumer protection laws (the Regulation on consumer protection co-operation) [2004] OJ L346/1; Consumer Protection from Unfair Trading Regulations 2008 (SI 2008/ 1277), implementing Directive 2005/29 concerning unfair

is now implemented in the Unfair Terms in Consumer Contracts Regulations 1999.[526] The Regulations contain an anti-avoidance provision to the effect that the:

> "Regulations shall apply notwithstanding any contract term which applies or purports to apply the law of a non-Member State, if the contract has a close connection with the territory of the Member States".[527]

The Consumer Protection (Distance Selling) Regulations 2000[528] implement the Directive on the protection of consumers in respect of distance contracts.[529] The anti-avoidance provision in these Regulations is nearly, but not quite, identical to that contained in the 1999 Regulations and stipulates that the:

> "Regulations shall apply notwithstanding any contract term which applies or purports to apply the law of a non-Member State, if the contract has a close connection with the territory of a Member State."[530]

The Sale and Supply of Goods to Consumers Regulations 2002[531] implements the Directive on certain aspects of the sale of consumer goods and associated guarantees.[532] The anti-avoidance provision contained in the Directive[533] is not directly transposed into the Regulations which implement it, it being apparently thought that prevention of avoidance through a choice of law clause could be achieved by application of the anti-avoidance provision contained in the Unfair Contract Terms Act 1977.[534] Whether this is correct is highly questionable, not least because many cross-border consumer contracts will not fall within the 1977 Act because they will be "international supply contracts" within the meaning of s.26 of the Act and are thus excluded from the scope of that Act altogether.[535]

business-to-consumer commercial practices and amending Council Directive 84/450, Directives 97/7, 98/27 and 2002/65 and Regulation 2996/2004 (Unfair Commercial Practices Directive) [2005] OJ L149/22.

[526] SI 1999/2083, as amended by SI 2001/1186, revoking and replacing Unfair Terms in Consumer Contracts Regulations 1994 (SI 1994/3159). For the Directive see [1993] OJ L95/29. See above, paras 15–004—15–099. See also *Oceano Grupo Editorial SA v Rocio Murciano Quintero* (C–241/98 to C–244/98) [2000] E.C.R. 4941; *Mostaza Claro v Centro Movil Milenium SL* (C–168/05) [2006] E.C.R. I–10421; *Standard Bank London Ltd v Apostolakis* [2002] C.L.C. 939.

[527] Reg.9. For detailed discussion of this formula, see *Benjamin's Sale of Goods*, 7th edn (2006), paras 25–101—25–106. In *Commission of the European Communities v Kingdom of Spain* (C–70/03) [2004] E.C.R. I–7999 the European Court found that Spain had not properly transposed the anti-avoidance provision of the Directive into national law.

[528] SI 2000/2334, as amended by SI 2005/689. See above, fn.525.

[529] Directive on the protection of consumers in respect of distance contracts [1997] OJ L144/19.

[530] Reg.25(5). For detailed discussion of this formula, see *Benjamin's Sale of Goods*, 7th edn (2006), paras 25–107—25–110.

[531] SI 2002/3045. See above, fn.525.

[532] Directive on sale of consumer goods and associated guarantees [1999] OJ L171/12.

[533] 1999 Directive art.7(2).

[534] Unfair Contract Terms Act 1977 s.27(2), above, para.30–007. See Department of Trade and Industry, Consumer and Competition Policy Directorate, *Directive 1999/44/EC of the European Parliament and of the Council of May 25, 1999 on certain aspects of the sale of consumer goods and associated guarantees, Transposition Note*.

[535] For the detailed argument, see *Benjamin's Sale of Goods*, 7th edn (2006), paras 25–111—25–116; and see Law Commission, *Unfair Terms in Contracts* (Law Com. No.292, 2005), paras 7.4–7.6. For Unfair Contract Terms Act 1977 s.26, see above, para.30–068. It has been argued that Unfair Contract Terms Act 1977 s.26 is in breach of the EC Treaty art.12 in that it discriminates

30–104 **Rules which are mandatory irrespective of applicable law.** Independently of art.5, art.7(2) enables a court to restrict the scope of the chosen law through the application of English mandatory rules in a situation where those rules apply irrespective of the law applicable to the contract.[536] Unlike the mandatory rules applicable through art.5(2), these mandatory rules need not relate to consumer protection.

30–105 **Chosen law governs other issues.** Mandatory rules do not apply to strike down the chosen law in toto. The chosen law will apply to the extent that it does not conflict with any applicable mandatory rules.

30–106 **Habitual residence.** The meaning of this concept was discussed above, para.30–079 of this Chapter.

30–107 **Applicable law in the absence of choice.** Where a consumer contract falling within art.5 does not contain a choice of law, art.5(3) provides that notwithstanding art.4, the contract shall be governed by the law of the country in which the consumer has his habitual residence,[537] if it is entered into in circumstances giving rise to any one of the three conditions described above.[538] If none of those conditions exist or if the contract falls outside art.5, then the law applicable to the contract will be determined, in the absence of a choice satisfying art.3, according to the provisions of art.4 of the Convention.

30–108 **Individual employment contracts.**[539] Article 6 of the Rome Convention contains special choice of law rules which are expressed to apply to "individual

---

against purchasers who are nationals of EU Member States: see Burbidge [2000] N.L.J. 1544. The section may also be in breach of arts 28 and 29 of the Treaty as constituting a restriction on the free movement of goods and of art.49 as constituting a restriction on the free movement of services. See also *Philip Alexander Securities & Futures Ltd v Bamberger* [1997] I.L. Pr. 73.

536 cf. Lasok and Stone, *Conflict of Laws in the European Community* (1987), p.385.

537 Above, para.30–079.

538 Above, paras 30–094 et seq.

539 *Dicey, Morris and Collins on The Conflict of Laws*, 14th edn (2006), paras 33–059—33–102; Lasok and Stone, *Conflict of Laws in the European Community* (1987), pp.384–385; Plender, *The European Contracts Convention*, 2nd edn (2001), Ch.8; Kaye, *The New Private International Law of Contract of the European Community* (1993), pp.224–238; Polak in Meeusen, Pertegas and Straetmans (eds), *The Enforcement of International Contracts in the European Union* (2004), pp.323–342; Morse in North (ed.), *Contract Conflicts* (1982), Ch.7; Cavalier and Upex (2006) 55 I.C.L.Q. 587; Morse (1992) 41 I.C.L.Q. 1; Smith and Cromack (1993) 22 I.L.J. 1. In 1976 the European Commission published a proposal for a Regulation concerning conflict of laws in employment relationships: see COM(175) 653 final, discussed by Hepple in Lipstein (ed.), *Harmonisation of Private International Law by the EEC* (1978), p.390; Forde (1979) *Legal Issues of European Integration* 85. Had this proposal not been withdrawn in 1981 ([1981] OJ C307/3) and reached fruition it would have taken precedence over art.6 pursuant to art.20 of the Rome Convention, above, para.30–027. See also Directive 96/71 concerning the posting of workers in the framework of the provision of services [1997] OJ L18/1. This Directive has not been formally implemented in the United Kingdom by specific regulations, but it has been said that the repeal of the Employment Rights Act 1996 s.196 by the Employment Relations Act 1999 s.32(3) (below, para.30–109 fn.548) has facilitated implementation of the Directive by extending rights which are derived from European Union legislation (and also, presumably, English employment law) to workers who are "temporarily" working in Great Britain: see *Hansard*, HC Vol.336, col.32. This Directive takes precedence over the Rome Convention, pursuant to art.20 (above, para.30–027). See on the Directive *Mazzoleni and Inter Surveillance Assistance SARL* (C–165/98) [2001] E.C.R. I–2189; *Finalarte Sociedade de Construcao*

employment contracts". The policy which informs these provisions is the need to secure "more adequate protection for the party who from the socio-economic point of view is regarded as the weaker in the contractual relationship",[540] i.e. the employee. In particular, it was necessary to curb, in this context, the wide freedom to choose the applicable law permitted by art.3.[541] No doubt, the philosophy of employee protection will be influential in the interpretation and application of art.6.[542] Very broadly, art.6 permits the parties to choose the law to govern an employment contract, but provides that the choice of law cannot have the result of depriving the employee of the protection of the mandatory rules of the law which would be applicable were there no choice of law in the contract.[543] In the absence of a choice of law, the applicable law is, in general, that of the country in which the employee habitually carries out his work in performance of the contract even though he is temporarily employed in another country.[544] If he does not habitually carry out his work in any one country the applicable law will be that of the country in which the place of business through which he was engaged is situated.[545] But each of these rules will be displaced if it appears from the circumstances as a whole that the contract is more closely connected with another country, in which case the law of that other country will govern.[546]

Meaning of "employment contract". Article 6 contains no definition of the concept of "employment contract". That the Article is expressed to apply to "individual" employment contracts indicates that the provision is not intended to apply to collective agreements but only to contracts entered into by individual employees.[547] Accordingly, the law applicable to a collective agreement will be determined by reference to the general choice of law rules contained in arts 3 and 4 of the Convention.[548] 30–109

"Employment": autonomous meaning. More particularly, different legal systems may have different criteria or principles for determining whether a particular contract is an employment contract.[549] It is thus necessary to formulate 30–110

(C–49/98, C–50/98, C–52/98–C–54/98 & C–68/98, C–71/98) [2001] E.C.R. I–7831; *Portugaia Construcoes Ltd* (C–164/99) [2002] E.C.R. I–787; Smith and Villiers (1996) Jur. Rev. 167. As to the position under art.8 of the Rome I Regulation, see below, paras 30–276 et seq.

540 Giuliano-Lagarde Report, p.25.

541 Above, paras 30–058—30–067.

542 cf. the position with regard to "certain consumer contracts," above, paras 30–093 et seq.

543 Rome Convention art.6(1).

544 Rome Convention art.6(2)(a).

545 Rome Convention art.6(2)(b).

546 Rome Convention art.6(2), proviso.

547 Giuliano-Lagarde Report, p.25.

548 Plender, pp.159–162. cf. *Monterosso Shipping Corp Ltd v International Transport Workers Federation* [1982] I.C.R. 675; *Dimskal Shipping Co Ltd v International Transport Workers Federation* [1992] 2 A.C. 152. This may be an example of a contract for which the characteristic performance cannot be determined so that Rome Convention art.4(2) is not applicable. cf. above, paras 31–076, 31–089.

549 See Eörsi, "Private and Governmental Liability for the Tort of Employees and Organs" in Tunc (ed.), *International Encyclopedia of Comparative Law*, Vol.XI, Ch.4, pp.34–35. For the criteria in English domestic law, see Vol.II, paras 39–002 et seq.

an approach to the resolution of this problem for the purposes of art.6.[550] The obvious approach which suggests itself is the development of an autonomous meaning for the concept so as to secure uniformity of application amongst contracting states.[551] The danger with such an approach, however, is that the autonomous definition might result in a particular state's employment law being applied to a contract even though that state would not regard the contract as one of employment, or conversely, in a particular state's employment law not being applied to a contract even though that state's law regarded it as being a contract of employment: in either case the applicable law is distorted, a result which is only avoided if the autonomous definition accords with the definition which prevails in the relevant state's law.

30–111 **Alternative "classification" approach.** A different approach could be based in principles of classification. Here, however, the English court should not classify the contract according to the *lex fori*, i.e. according to its own criteria for determining whether a contract is one of employment. To do so would again risk the distortion of the applicable law if the forum's conception of a contract of employment did not correspond with that prevailing in the applicable law or vice versa. The risk referred to can, however, be minimised if the forum is prepared to classify the relevant contractual relationship according to the *lex causae*. On this view the English court should apply the rules of art.6 so as to determine the governing law and then decide whether, according to that law, the relevant contract is one of employment. If it is so classified, then the court should apply the rules of the applicable law concerned with employment contracts. If it is not so classified, the court should apply the general choice of law rules contained in arts 3 and 4 of the Convention to determine the applicable law. Although this approach is open to a considerable objection, viz that it necessitates determining the law applicable under art.6 before the process of classification has determined that art.6 is applicable, it has the merit of avoiding the distortion of the applicable

[550] See *Dicey, Morris and Collins*, paras 33–063—33–066; Plender, pp.162–164; Kaye, pp.222–223.

[551] See *Duarte v Black & Decker Corp* [2007] EWHC 2720 (QB), [2008] 1 All E.R. (Comm) 401; *Base Metal Trading Ltd v Shamurin* [2003] EWHC 2419 (Comm); [2004] 1 All E.R. (Comm) 159, reversed in part but not on this point, [2004] EWCA Civ 1316, [2005] 1 W.L.R. 1157; *Swithenbank Foods Ltd v Bowers* [2002] EWHC 2257 (QB); [2002] 2 All E.R. (Comm) 974; Kaye, pp.222–223; Anton, *Private International Law*, 2nd edn (1990), p.347. The Giuliano-Lagarde Report gives little guidance other than to say that art.6 covers void contracts and de facto employment relationships "in particular those characterised by failure to respect the contract imposed by law for the protection of employee": pp.25–26. The "Posted Workers" Directive (above, fn.539), provides that the definition of a worker for the purposes of the Directive is that which applies in the law of the Member State to whose territory the worker is posted: art.2(2). In construing art.5(1) of the Brussels Convention on Jurisdiction and the Enforcement of Judgments in Civil and Commercial Matters 1968, the European Court has shown itself to be aware of the special problems posed by employment contracts: see, e.g. *Ivenel v Schwab* (133/81) [1982] E.C.R. 1891; *Shenavai v Kreischer* (266/85) [1987] E.C.R. 239; *Mulox IBC Ltd v Geels* (C–125/92) [1993] E.C.R. I–4075; *Rutten v Cross Medical Ltd* (C–383/95) [1997] E.C.R. I–57, [1997] I.C.R. 715; *Weber v Universal Ogden Services Ltd* (C–37/00) [2002] E.C.R. I–2013; *Pugliese v Finmeccanica SpA* (C–437/00) [2003] I.L. Pr. 346. See also *Samengo-Turner v J & H Marsh & McLennan (Services) Ltd* [2007] EWCA Civ 723, [2007] I.L. Pr. 706; *WPP Holdings Italy SRL v Benatti* [2007] EWCA Civ 263, [2007] 1 W.L.R. 2310; Cavalier and Upex (2006) 55 I.C.L.Q. 587. And see above, para.1–007.

law which is inherent in other situations. Whether a *lex causae* approach[552] or an approach based on autonomous interpretation[553] cannot be regarded as settled, though it must be admitted that the autonomous approach is the most likely one to be adopted.[554]

Choice of law by the parties and mandatory rules. Although the parties may choose the law to govern an employment contract,[555] the effect of that choice is expressly limited by art.6(1) which provides that the choice of law shall not have the result of depriving the employee of the protection afforded to him by the mandatory rules of the country the law of which would be applicable to the contract were there no choice of law.[556] For these purposes, a "mandatory rule" bears the meaning given to that expression by art.3(3) of the Convention, i.e. such a rule is one which cannot be derogated from by contract[557] and it is not necessary, in addition, that the rule be a rule which applies irrespective of the law applicable to the contract[558] though some mandatory rules in the employment context may possess this additional characteristic.[559] The Giuliano-Lagarde Report informs that these mandatory rules: 30–112

> " . . . consist not only of the provisions relating to the contract of employment itself, but also provisions such as those concerning industrial safety and hygiene which are regarded in certain Member States as being provisions of public law."[560]

However, it will fall to the legal system of which the rule forms part to determine whether a rule is mandatory and also the circumstances in which the rule is mandatory.[561]

Mandatory rules of English law. In the English context, it has been held that the rules of English law in respect of restrictive covenants in employment contracts are not mandatory rules for the protection of employees for the purposes of art.6.[562] Such rules are part of the general law of restraint of trade which are, in turn, part of the general law of contract.[563] While it may be true that 30–113

---

552 Favoured by *Dicey, Morris and Collins*, para.33–065; Plender at pp.162–164.

553 Favoured by Anton, p.347; Kaye, p.223.

554 See *Duarte v Black & Decker Corp* [2007] EWHC 2720 (QB); *Samengo-Turner v JH Marsh & McLennan (Services) Ltd* [2007] EWCA Civ 723.

555 For an example, see *Roerig v Valiant Trawlers Ltd* [2002] EWCA Civ 21; [2002] 1 W.L.R. 2304 at [31]–[41]. The choice of law must satisfy the requirements of art.3(1): see *Base Metal Trading Ltd v Shamurin* [2003] EWHC 2419, [2004] 1 All E.R. (Comm) 159, reversed in part but not on this point, [2004] EWCA Civ 1316, [2005] 1 W.L.R. 1157; *Duarte v Black & Decker Corp* [2007] EWHC 2720 (QB); and see above, paras 30–047 et seq.

556 As to which, see below, paras 30–119—30–120.

557 Above, para.30–063.

558 cf. art.7(2), discussed below, para.30–118 and art.7(1), above, para.30–063 which does not have the force of law in the UK: Contracts (Applicable Law) Act 1990 s.2(2).

559 See statutes referred to in fn.565, below.

560 Giuliano-Lagarde Report, p.25.

561 See above, paras 30–063 et seq. Where the rule derives from European law, it may be mandatory even if there is no explicit indication in the rule itself: see *Bleuse v MBT Transport Ltd* (2007) UKEAT/339/07 (EAT).

562 *Duarte v Black & Decker Corp* [2007] EWHC 2720 (QB). Reliance was placed on the passage in the Giuliano-Lagarde Report, p.25, quoted in the preceding paragraph.

563 *Duarte v Black & Decker Corp* [2007] EWHC 2720.

covenants in employment contracts are harder to justify than covenants contained in commercial agreements, the rules applicable to both types of agreement are based on the principle of what is reasonably necessary to protect the covenantee's legitimate interest and not on the need to protect employees. Nonetheless, the law relating to such covenants has been said to be rooted in public policy so that where the employment contract is governed by a foreign law which would, in conflict with English law, regard the covenant as valid, the foreign law may be denied application on public policy grounds, pursuant to art.16 of the Convention.[564]

30–114 **Statutory rules.** Statutory rules which have the specific purpose of protecting employees, are, however, likely to qualify as mandatory rules for the purposes of art.6. Modern statutes often indicate this explicitly by stating that the statutory rules apply irrespective of the law which governs the contract of employment.[565] Where there is no such explicit indication in the statute itself, then whether a particular rule is mandatory will depend on the construction of the statute.[566]

30–115 **Territorial limitations.** Although a particular statutory right may be available irrespective of the law applicable to the contract of employment, the scope of the relevant right may be subject to a territorial limitation. Thus, for example, the Equal Pay Act 1970 applies only to employment at an establishment in Great Britain as defined in the Act.[567] Many of the principal statutory employment rights are contained in the Employment Rights Act 1996. Several provisions of the Act were originally expressed not to apply where the employee ordinarily worked outside Great Britain,[568] but this provision was repealed[569] without being replaced with any different limitation, thus leaving the proper scope of the statute

---

[564] *Duarte v Black & Decker Corp* [2007] EWHC 2720. See above, para.30–069 and below, paras 30–366 et seq.

[565] e.g. Equal Pay Act 1970 s.1(1), as amended by Sex Discrimination Act 1975 ss.1(11) and Contracts (Applicable Law) Act 1990 s.5 and Sch.4; Trade Union and Labour Relations (Consolidation) Act 1992 ss.285(2), 287, 289; Employment Rights Act 1996 Pt VIII ss.203, 204(1); National Minimum Wage Act 1998 s.25(1).

[566] e.g. Patents Act 1977 ss.39–43 (compensation provisions for employee's inventions probably mandatory); cf. *Chiron Corp v Organon Teknika Ltd (No.2)* [1993] F.S.R. 567 (Patents Act 1977 s.44, since repealed by Competition Act 1998 s.70, applies to contract governed by foreign law)); Sex Discrimination Act 1975 (mandatory); Race Relations Act 1976 (mandatory); Disability Discrimination Act 1995 (mandatory); Employment Equality (Religion and Belief) Regulations 2003 (SI 2003/1660, as amended by SI 2004/437, SI 2004/2520 and SI 2007/2269) (mandatory); Employment Equality (Sexual Orientation) Regulations 2003 (SI 2003/1661, as amended by SI 2004/2519 and SI 2007/ 2269) (mandatory); Employment Equality (Age) Regulations 2006 (SI 2006/1031) (mandatory); Equality Act 2006 (mandatory).

[567] Equal Pay Act 1970 s.1(1), as amended by Sex Discrimination Act 1975 s.8, Sex Discrimination Act 1975 s.10(1) and 10(1A) inserted by SI 2005/2467 reg.11. See for examples of similar limitations, Race Relations Act 1976 ss.4, 8(1) and 8(1A) and *Saggar v Ministry of Defence* [2005] EWCA Civ 413, [2005] I.C.R. 1073; Disability Discrimination Act 1995 ss.4, 68 and *Williams v University of Nottingham* [2007] I.R.L.R. 660 (EAT); cf. Equality Act (Sexual Orientation) Regulations 2007 (SI 2007/1263) reg.34. See generally *Dicey, Morris and Collins*, paras 33–096—33-103.

[568] s.196.

[569] Employment Relations Act 1999 s.32(3). Apparently the repeal was thought to facilitate implementation of the Posted Workers Directive (above, para.30–108). See *Dicey Morris and Collins*, para.33–091.

to judicial construction. In *Serco Ltd v Lawson*[570] the House of Lords had to decide on the proper reach of the provisions of the Employment Rights Act 1996 which provide for the right not to be unfairly dismissed. It was held that this depended on the construction of the relevant provisions in the light of the circumstances of the particular case. Primarily, the provisions apply where the employee is working in Great Britain at the time of the dismissal, as opposed to what was contemplated as the place of work at the time of the conclusion of the contract of employment. Where, however, the employee was a peripatetic worker working in several countries, such as an airline pilot, the work would be performed in Great Britain if the employee's base was in Great Britain at the time of the dismissal. As regards expatriate employees working overseas, the relevant provisions apply if a strong connection between the employment and Great Britain at the relevant time can be established. Such may be the case where an employee is posted abroad by a British employer for the purposes of a business carried on in Great Britain or where an expatriate employee is working in what is in effect an extra-territorial enclave in a foreign country (e.g. a military base). Although the House of Lords was careful to point out that the territorial reach of a statutory right might differ according to which particular right was in issue, it is likely that the principles in *Serco Ltd v Lawson*[571] will be held to apply to other rights contained in the Act.[572]

Rights derived from European law. Different principles apply where the relevant right in the Employment Rights Act 1996 derives from European law. Here there is an obligation to give direct effect to the European right through interpretation of the relevant English law with the consequence that *Serco Ltd v Lawson*[573] will not apply and the scope of the right may depend, instead, on whether the contract of employment is governed by English law or by the law of another Member State.[574] 30–116

Chosen law more favourable. Where the chosen law gives less protection to the employee than would the mandatory rules of the law of the country which would have been applicable in the absence of choice, then the mandatory rules of the latter law will prevail over the chosen law. Conversely, where the chosen 30–117

[570] *Serco Ltd v Lawson* [2006] UKHL 3, [2006] I.C.R. 250. See *Dicey, Morris and Collins*, paras 33–090—33–095.

[571] [2006] UKHL 3.

[572] See *Bleuse v MBT Transport Ltd* (2007) UKEAT/339/07 (EAT) (*Serco Ltd v Lawson* [2006] UKHL 3 applied to exclude claims for unfair dismissal and unlawful deductions from wages); *Ashbourne v Department of Education and Skills* (2007) UKEAT/0207/07 (EAT) (*Serco Ltd v Lawson* applied to scope of Fixed Term Employees (Prevention of Less Favourable Treatment) Regulations 2002).

[573] [2006] UKHL 3.

[574] *Bleuse v MBT Transport Ltd* (2007) UKEAT/339/07 (EAT) (right to paid annual leave under Working Time Regulations 1998 appliedwhere English law was the law applicable to the contract of employment). See also *Holis Metal Industries Ltd v GMB* (2007) UKEAT/0171/07/CEA (Transfer of Undertakings (Protection of Employment) Regulations 2006 and collective redundancy consultation obligations in Trade Union and Labour Relations (Consolidation) Act 1992 s.188, applies to transfer of a business which after transfer is based outside the United Kingdom). cf. *Williams v University of Nottingham* [2007] I.R.L.R. 660 (EAT); *Ashbourne v Department of Education and Skills* (2007) UKEAT/0207/07 (EAT).

law is more favourable to the employee than the mandatory rules of the law which would be applicable in the absence of choice, then it can hardly be said that the employee is "deprived" of the protection of mandatory rules since he is better off under the chosen law, so that the chosen law should prevail.[575] Where, however, the rules of the chosen law and the mandatory rules of the law which would be applicable in the absence of choice are not in direct conflict but offer different rights or remedies to an employee (say compensation for unfair dismissal[576] under the chosen law, in contrast with reinstatement[577] under the law applicable in the absent of choice) more difficulty arises. Article 6(1) merely says that the employee is not to be deprived of the protection of mandatory rules: it does not say he cannot have the benefit of the protective regime of both laws and since he would be deprived of reinstatement if he received only compensation, it could be said that he has been deprived of the protection of applicable mandatory rules. But it is difficult to accept that it was intended to benefit the employee in this way just because his contract contains a choice of law[578] and, therefore, it is suggested that the correct solution in such situations is to apply the law most favourable to the employee[579] despite the fact that it may not always be easy, in any given situation, to determine which law is most favourable.[580]

30–118 **Rules which are mandatory irrespective of applicable law.** It would seem implicit in art.6(1) that mandatory rules applicable thereunder should relate to the protection of employees. However, art.7(2) can also apply to employment contracts[581] to secure the application of English rules in a situation where they are mandatory irrespective of the law applicable to the contract. Such rules need not necessarily relate to employment protection, but many will.[582]

30–119 **Applicable law in absence of choice.** In effect art.6(2) supplies two presumptions as to what the applicable law will be in the absence of a choice of law, each presumption being rebuttable according to the proviso to art.6(2) if it appears from the circumstances as a whole that the contract is more closely connected with another country.[583] Where the employee habitually carries out his work in performance of the contract in a particular country then the law of that country will govern (subject to the proviso) even if the employee is temporarily employed in another country.[584] Article 6(2)(b) provides that if the employee does not

---

[575] cf. in relation to consumer contracts, above, para.30–102.
[576] See Vol.II, paras 39–232 et seq.
[577] See Vol.II, paras 39–229 et seq.
[578] cf. Philip in North (ed.), *Contract Conflicts* (1982), pp.81, 99–100. The principle of the "more favourable" law is recognised in the "Posted Workers" Directive (above, para.30–108 fn.539): see Preamble para.(18) and art.3(7).
[579] See *Bleuse v MBT Transport Ltd* (2007) UKEAT/339/07.
[580] *Dicey, Morris and Collins*, para.33–071; Plender, pp.167–169; Kaye, pp.228–229.
[581] cf. Lasok and Stone, *Conflict of Laws in the European Community* (1987), p.385.
[582] See, e.g. statutes referred to in fn.565, above. cf. *Duarte v Black & Decker Corp* [2007] EWHC 2720 (QB).
[583] Rome Convention art.6(2)(a).
[584] As to the meaning of "habitually carries out his work," see *Dicey, Morris and Collins*, paras 33–075—33–076; Plender, pp.169–173; Kaye, pp.233–235; Morse (1992) 41 I.C.L.Q. 1. cf. *Mulox IBC Ltd v Geels* (125/92) [1993] E.C.R. I–4075; *Rutten v Cross Medical Ltd* (C–385/95) [1997] E.C.R. I–57; *Weber v Universal Ogden Services Ltd* (C–37/00) [2002] E.C.R. I–2013; [2002] Q.B. 1189; *Pugliese v Finmeccanica SpA* (C–437/00) [2003] I.L. Pr. 346.

habitually carry out his work in any one country then the applicable law will (subject to the proviso) be the law of the country in which the place of business through which he was engaged is situated.[585] Article 6(2)(a) is thus concerned solely with the situation where the employee habitually carries out his work in one country only. Where the work is habitually carried out in more than one country, art.6(2)(b) applies: this will also be the case where the employee habitually carries out his work in no particular country or where he habitually carries out his work in a place which is not a country (e.g. on a ship or oil rig).[586]

If it appears from the circumstances as a whole that the contract is more closely connected with another country than it is with the country indicated by art.6(2)(a) or 6(2)(b), as the case may be, then the law of that other country will be the governing law. How easy it will be to displace art.6(2)(a) and 6(2)(b) will depend on the strength which will be accorded to those presumptive rules. It is possible to speculate (but no more than that) that the court will, in the spirit of art.6, give more weight to the presumptions if the law applicable through them would be more protective of the employee than would be the law which would govern if the proviso were invoked, and less weight to them if the converse was the case.[587] As to the factors which might serve to trigger the proviso, the law of the residence or centre of business operations of the employer might, in the case of an employer engaging employees of various nationalities in different parts of the world, be regarded as being more closely connected with the contract than the law indicated by the presumption.[588] But each case will depend on its particular facts.[589] **30–120**

Contract and tort. In English law an employee may elect to sue his employer, for injuries caused by the negligence of the employer, in either contract or tort.[590] There does not appear to be anything in the Rome Convention **30–121**

[585] See *Booth v Phillips* [2004] EWHC 1437 (Comm), [2004] 1 W.L.R. 3292. As to the meaning of "place of business through which he was engaged", see *Dicey, Morris and Collins*, para.33–077; Plender, pp.171–172; Kaye, pp.235–236; Morse (1992) 41 I.C.L.Q. 1. cf. *Sayers v International Drilling Co NV* [1971] 1 W.L.R. 1176.

[586] *Booth v Phillips* [2004] EWHC 1437 (Comm); Giuliano-Lagarde Report, p.26.

[587] cf. *Booth v Phillips* [2004] EWHC 1437 (Comm). See *Dicey, Morris and Collins*, para.33–078. cf. *Sayers v International Drilling Co NV* [1971] 1 W.L.R. 1176.

[588] In *Sayers v International Drilling Co NV* [1971] 1 W.L.R. 1176, it was held that the contract was most closely connected with Dutch law for this reason.

[589] *Base Metal Trading Ltd v Shamurin* [2003] EWHC (Comm) 2419, [2004] 1 All E.R. (Comm) 159, reversed in part, but not on this point, [2004] EWCA Civ 1316, [2005] 1 W.L.R. 1157. Other factors suggested as relevant in common law decisions include the residence and domicile of the employee (*South African Breweries v King* [1899] 2 Ch. 173 (affirmed [1990] 1 Ch. 273)) and the language and form of the contract (*South African Breweries v King*; *Sayers v International Drilling Co NV* [1971] 1 W.L.R. 1176; *Coupland v Arabian Gulf Oil Co* [1983] 1 W.L.R 1136 (affirmed [1983] 1 W.L.R. 1151)). If the contract is held to be governed by foreign law according to art.6(2), the English court may still apply any English mandatory rules by virtue of art.7(2): see above, para.30–118.

[590] e.g. *Matthews v Kuwait Bechtel Corp* [1959] 2 Q.B. 57; *Coupland v Arabian Gulf Oil Co* [1983] 1 W.L.R. 1136 (affirmed [1983] 1 W.L.R. 1151); *Roerig v Valiant Trawlers Ltd* [2002] EWCA Civ 21, [2002] 1 WLR 2304; *Base Metal Trading Ltd v Shamurin* [2003] EWHC (Comm) 2419, [2002] C.L.C. 322; *Booth v Phillips* [2004] EWHC 1437 (Comm), [2004] 1 W.L.R. 3292; contrast *Johnson*

which excludes this option.[591] The choice of law rules for torts are generally and, currently, to be found in Pt III of the Private International Law (Miscellaneous Provisions) Act 1995.[592] There is nothing in Pt III of the 1995 Act which indicates that an employee is not free to frame and pursue a claim in tort rather than contract if the case falls within Pt III and it is advantageous to do so. According to the general rule contained in the Act, the law applicable to a tort is the law of the country in which the events constituting the tort in question occur,[593] which rule may be displaced in favour of a different country's law in an appropriate case.[594] Application of these rules might, in particular situations, lead to a law which is more favourable to the employee than the law which might govern the contractual claim which he might have against his employer.[595]

30–122 **Effect of Rome II Regulation.** When the Rome II Regulation on the law applicable to non-contractual obligations becomes effective[596] it would seem that the claimant will not be able to frame the claim as a claim in tort if the law governing the tort would be more favourable to the claim than the law applicable to the contract.[597] This is because the expression "non-contractual obligations", which includes tort, must be given an autonomous meaning[598] and that meaning will, presumably, be distinct from an obligation which sounds in contract.

(f) *Voluntary Assignments and Subrogation*

30–123 **Voluntary assignments.** Article 12 of the Rome Convention provides choice of law rules relating to the voluntary assignment of rights. This provision, which is probably to the same effect as the common law,[599] will apply to assignments

---

v Coventry Churchill International Ltd [1992] 3 All E.R. 14 (action in tort only, case not framed in contract). See above, paras 1–169, 30–032.

[591] *Dicey, Morris and Collins*, paras 32–0025—32–026, 33–083—33–085.

[592] For discussion, see *Dicey, Morris and Collins*, Ch.35. But see the effect of the Rome II Regulation, below, para.30–122.

[593] Private International Law Act 1995 s.11(1), amplified in s.11(2).

[594] Private International Law Act 1995 s.12.

[595] The common law rule for choice of law in tort which is abolished by s.10(1)(a) of the 1995 Act, except in defamation and related cases (ss.9(3), 10, 13), normally favoured the defendant, because it required that the defendant's conduct be actionable as a tort by English law *and* civilly actionable by the law of the place where the tort was committed, at least as a general rule: see *Dicey, Morris and Collins*, paras 32–025—32–026, 33–083—33–085.

[596] Above, paras 30–032.

[597] Above, paras 30–032 and below, para.30–151.

[598] Rome II Regulation Recital 11. See above, para.30–032 and below, para.30–148.

[599] See *Lee v Abdy* (1886) 17 QBD 309; *Republic de Guatemala v Nunez* [1927] 1 K.B. 669; *Re Anziani* [1930] 1 Ch. 407; *Campbell Connelly & Co Ltd v Noble* [1963] 1 W.L.R. 252; *Trendtex Trading Corp v Crédit Suisse* [1982] A.C. 679; see also *Macmillan Inc v Bishopsgate Investment Trust Plc (No.3)* [1996] 1 W.L.R. 387; 26th edn of this work, para.2185; *Dicey, Morris and Collins on the Conflict of Laws*, 14th edn (2006) paras 24–051—24–054; Cheshire and North, *Private International Law*; Moshinsky (1992) 109 L.Q.R. 591; Struycken [1998] L.M.C.L.Q. 345. Where the right assigned arises under a contract excluded from the Convention under art.1, it is not clear whether art.12 or the common law applies, but since art.12 applies to voluntary assignments, involuntary assignments will be governed by common law rules: see *Dicey, Morris and Collins*, paras 24–055 et seq.; Cheshire and North, pp.963–965. Although art.12 applies to the assignment of non-contractual rights, it may not apply to non-contractual assignments of a voluntary nature (unless by way of gift, see Giuliano-Lagarde Report, p.10): see below, para.30–124. Such non-contractual voluntary assignments will be governed by common law rules (which apply the same principles as

made after April 1, 1991,[600] but before December 17, 2009, when it will be replaced by art.14 of the Rome I Regulation.[601]

Assignor and assignee. 30–124

"The mutual obligations of assignor and assignee under a voluntary assignment of a right against another person ('the debtor') are governed by the law which applies to the contract between assignor and assignee."[602]

Although the reference to "voluntary assignment" in this provision is not expressly limited to contractual assignments, the fact that the applicable law is that of the "contract between assignor and assignee" indicates that only contractual voluntary assignments are within art.12. The law applicable to the contract between assignor and assignee will be determined according to the rules of the Convention discussed earlier in this chapter.[603]

Assignability, etc. Article 12(2) provides that: 30–125

"The law governing the right to which the assignment relates determines its assignability, the relationship between the assignee and the debtor, the conditions under which the assignment can be invoked against the debtor and any question whether the debtor's obligations have been discharged."[604]

Accordingly, whether a right (which need not be of a contractual nature) is capable of being assigned will be determined by the law which creates the right.[605] That law will also govern the relationship between assignee and debtor.[606] Since that law also governs the conditions under which the assignment

---

art.12 in this field). Art.12 does not apply to the assignment of duties: Giuliano-Lagarde Report, p.35. For full discussion, see *Dicey, Morris and Collins*, paras 24–051—24–079; Plender, *The European Contracts Convention*, 2nd edn (2001), pp.223–229; Flessner and Verhagen, *Assignment in European Private International Law* (2006); Kieninger in Meeusen, Pertegas and Straetmans (eds), *The Enforcement of International Contracts in the European Union* (2004), pp.363–387. And see below, paras 30–124 et seq., 30–288 et seq.

[600] Rome Convention art.17. See above, para.30–017.

[601] See below, paras 30–288 et seq.

[602] Rome Convention art.12(1). See *Raiffeisen Zentralbank Osterreich AG v Five Star General Trading LLC* [2001] EWCA Civ 68, [2001] Q.B. 85 at [43] (art.12(1) regulates the position of assignor and assignee as between themselves); *Waldweise Stiftung v Lewis* [2004] EWHC 2589 (Ch).

[603] Above, paras 30–047 et seq. Where art.4(2) applies (see above, paras 30–071 et seq.) the characteristic performance appears to be that of the assignor.

[604] Logically, the question of assignability must be resolved before one reaches the question of the validity of the assignment—dealt with in art.12(1). For the reasons for the curious draftsmanship of art.12, see Giuliano-Lagarde Report, p.34.

[605] See *Waldweise Stiftung v Lewis* [2004] EWHC 2589 (Ch). See also *Peer International Corp v Termidor Music Publishers Ltd* [2003] EWCA Civ 1156, [2004] Ch. 212. cf. *Campbell Connelly and Co Ltd v Noble* [1963] 1 W.L.R. 252; *Trendtex Trading Corp v Crédit Suisse* [1982] A.C. 679, for the same rule at common law. If the right assigned is contractual, the applicable law wil be decided according to the rules of the Convention unless the relevant contract is excluded from the scope of the Convention: see above, paras 30–037 et seq.

[606] The relations between assignor and debtor (other than the issue of assignability), if a contract exists between them, will be governed by the law applicable to that contract identified by reference to the rules of the Convention: Giuliano-Lagarde Report, p.35.

can be invoked against the debtor and any question of whether the debtor's obligations have been discharged, it will determine questions of priorities as between competing valid assignments of the same debt (e.g. whether notice of the assignment must be given to the debtor).[607]

30–126 **Contract and property.** There is some controversy as to whether art.12 is applicable to the proprietary as well as the contractual effects of an assignment.[608] The issue received some consideration in *Raiffeisen Zentralbank Osterreich AG v Five Star General Trading LLC*.[609] A bank had taken an assignment of a policy of marine insurance, issued by French insurers but governed by English law, from a shipowner, as part of an arrangement whereby the bank lent money to the shipowner to assist in the purchase of a ship. The ship was lost and the bank sought to recover the insurance moneys from the insurers in proceedings to which the shipowner and cargo owner were parties, by invoking the assignment. The bank argued, on the basis of art.12(2) of the Rome Convention, that English law determined whether the assignment could be so invoked since English law governed the policy and was thus the law governing the right to which the assignment related, which under art.12(2) was the law which determined the conditions under which the assignment could be invoked against the debtor. Since the bank had given notice of the assignment to the insurers in accordance with English law, there was, argued the bank, no impediment to its claim. The cargo owners (who had obtained attachment orders in France of the insurance and proceeds) argued that art.12(2) of the Rome Convention had no application since the claim by the bank was proprietary in nature and the Convention only applied to contractual obligations.[610] The relevant applicable law was thus the *lex situs* of the right assigned[611] which in the instant case was French law and under French law the bank could not invoke the assignment against the insurers because it had not complied with a requirement of French law whereby notice of the assignment had to be given through a French bailiff. The Court of Appeal, adopting a broad interpretation of "contract", took the view that, for the purposes of the Rome Convention, the issue could legitimately be treated as a contractual one.[612] More particularly, art.12(2) "manifests the clear intention to embrace the issue and to state the appropriate law by which it must be determined".[613] Reinforcing the propositions set out in the previous paragraph, the court went on to say that by virtue of art.12(2):

---

[607] This was probably the common law rule: *Dicey, Morris and Collins*, para.24–054; Cheshire and North, pp.958–962; *Le Feuvre v Sullivan* (1855) 100 Moo. P.C. 1; *Kelly v Selwyn* [1905] Ch. 117; cf. *Republica de Guatemala v Nunez* [1927] 1 K.B. 669, 695 (obiter in favour of *lex fori*); Goode, *Commercial Law*, 2nd edn (1995), pp.1129–1130; Collier, *Conflict of Laws*, 3rd edn (2001), pp.258–259 (*lex situs* of debt).

[608] *Dicey, Morris and Collins*, para.24–064 takes the view that proprietary effects are included. Contrast Goode, 2nd edn (1995) pp.1129–1130 and Moshinsky (1992) 109 L.Q.R. 591, who take the view that they are not. See, generally, Plender at pp.223–229.

[609] [2001] EWCA Civ 68; [2001] Q.B. 825. For comment, see Plender, pp.226–229; Stevens in Bridge and Stevens (eds), *Cross-Border Security and Insolvency* (2001), pp.213–216; Stevens and Struycken (2002) 118 L.Q.R. 15; Briggs [2001] 72 B.Y.B.I.L. 461.

[610] See above, para.30–031.

[611] Relying, inter alia, on Goode, pp.1129–1130.

[612] [2001] EWCA Civ 68, [2001] Q.B. 825 at [34]–[43].

[613] [2001] EWCA Civ 68 at [43].

"... the contract giving rise to the obligation governs not merely its assignability, but also 'the relationship between the assignee and the debtor' and 'the conditions under which the assignment can be invoked against the debtor', as well as 'any question whether the debtor's obligations have been discharged'."[614]

The provision:

"... on its face ... treats as matters within its scope, and expressly provides for, issues both as to whether the debtor owes moneys to and must pay the assignee (their 'relationship') and under what 'conditions', e.g. as regards the giving of notice."[615]

Although the question was not considered by the Court of Appeal, the thrust of the decision would make it seem likely, as submitted in the previous paragraph, that the law governing the right assigned will also, pursuant to art.12(2), decide questions of priorities as between competing voluntary assignments of that right.[616]

Subrogation.[617] Article 13 of the Rome Convention contains a choice of law rule which is expressed to apply to "subrogation". However, in this context "subrogation" bears a limited meaning: art.13 is concerned only with cases where a creditor has a claim in *contract* against the debtor and a third person "has a duty to satisfy the creditor, or has in fact satisfied the creditor in discharge of that duty".[618] Thus the provision extends to a contract of guarantee where the guarantor has paid the creditor and is thus subrogated to the latter's rights against the debtor,[619] but not to subrogation by operation of law when the debt to be paid originates in a tort (e.g. where the insurer succeeds to the insured's right of action against the tortfeasor).[620] Although the extract from art.13(1) quoted above suggests that the third party must have a *duty* to satisfy the creditor, the Giuliano-Lagarde Report suggests that the provision may also apply to a situation in which a person has paid without "being obliged so to do by contract or law"[621] but by virtue of having an "economic interest recognised by law" as prevails in some legal systems.[622] But the Report follows this observation, extremely obscurely, 30–127

[614] [2001] EWCA Civ 68.

[615] [2001] EWCA Civ 68. The court referred to two decisions of the German Supreme Court to similar effect: see *Raiffeisen* [2001] EWCA Civ 68 at [49]–[50]; see also von Bar (1989) 53 RabelsZ 462. The court also referred to a decision of the Dutch Hoge Raad, discussed by Struycken [1998] L.M.C.L.Q. 345 and Koppenol-Laforce (1998) N.I.L.R. 129: see [2001] EWCA Civ 68, [2001] Q.B. 825 at [51]–[52]. And see Plender, pp.225–226.

[616] *Dicey, Morris and Collins*, para.24–062.

[617] See *Dicey, Morris and Collins*, para.32–211; Plender, pp.229–230; Takahashi, *Claims for Contribution and Reimbursement in an International Context* (2000), pp.78–82; Kaye, *The New Private International Law of Contract of the European Community* (1993), pp.327–330; Morse (1992) 2 Ybk. Eur. L. 107, 158. As to the position under the Rome I Regulation, see below, paras 30–288 et seq.

[618] Rome Convention art.13(1).

[619] Giuliano-Lagarde Report, p.35.

[620] Giuliano-Lagarde Report, p.35; *West Tankers Inc v RAS Riunione Adriatica di Sicurta SpA* [2005] EWHC 454 (Comm), [2005] 1 C.L.C. 347 (referred to the European Court by the House of Lords on a different point, [2007] UKHL 4, [2007] 1 Lloyd's Rep. 391).

[621] Giuliano-Lagarde Report, p.35.

[622] Giuliano-Lagarde Report, p.35.

by saying that the court "has a discretion in this respect", a comment which does little to clarify the position.

30–128 **Applicable law.** In circumstances falling within art.13(1):

> "... the law which governs the third person's duty to satisfy the creditor shall determine whether the third person is entitled to exercise against the debtor the rights which the creditor had against the debtor under the law governing their relationship and, if so, whether he may do so in full or only to a limited extent."[623]

Thus the law applicable to the relationship between creditor and debtor determines the rights which the former has against the latter. But the law which creates the duty in the third party to satisfy that creditor determines whether and to what extent, the third party is subrogated to those rights.[624]

30–129 **Co-debtors.** The rule described in the previous paragraph applies to cases where several persons (debtors) are subject to the same contractual claim and one of them has satisfied the creditor.[625] Thus, if one debtor satisfies the creditor, it is the law governing the duty which requires him to do this which will determine whether he is subrogated to the creditor's rights against the other debtors.

4. THE ROME I REGULATION

(a) *In General*

30–130 **History.** The provisions inserted into the EC Treaty by the Treaty of Amsterdam[626] which are concerned with the introduction of "measures in the field of judicial cooperation in civil matters" envisaged revisions of the Rome Convention.[627] In an action plan announced in December 1998, the Council and the Commission indicated an intention to:

> "... begin revision, where necessary, of certain provisions of the Convention on the Law Applicable to Contractual Obligations, taking into account special provisions on conflict of law rules in other Community instruments."[628]

In January 2003, the Commission issued a Green Paper "on the conversion of the Rome Convention of 1980 on the law applicable to contractual obligations into a Community instrument and its modernisation"[629] as part of a process of

---

[623] Rome Convention art.13(1).

[624] See *West Tankers Inc v RAS Riunione Adriatica di Sicurta SpA* [2005] EWHC 454 (Comm).

[625] Rome Convention art.13(2). As to the position under the Rome I Regulation, see below, paras 30–288 et seq.

[626] Treaty of Amsterdam art.65. See [1997] OJ C340/1.

[627] See, in particular, Treaty of Amsterdam art.65B.

[628] Action Plan [1999] OJ C19/1.

[629] Green Paper COM(2002) 654 final. See also the Opinion of the European Economic and Social Committee on the Green Paper [2004] OJ C108/1.

consultation on a wide variety of issues concerning the Convention.[630] The Hague Programme, adopted by the Council on November 5, 2004, called for work to be pursued actively on the rules of conflict of laws regarding contractual obligations (Rome I).[631] This resulted, in December 2005, in a proposal, presented by the Commission, for the conversion of the Rome Convention into a Regulation of the European Parliament and the Council.[632] After much debate and discussion, new provisions on the law applicable to contractual obligations were established in Regulation (EC) 593/2008 of June 17, 2008 on the law applicable to contractual obligations (Rome I)[633] (hereafter the "Rome I Regulation" or the "Regulation"). The Regulation entered into force on July 24, 2008[634] and will be applicable in the Member States in relation to contracts concluded on or after December 17, 2009.[635] As a Regulation, the Rome I Regulation is directly applicable and no United Kingdom legislation is required to bring it into effect.[636]

Position of the United Kingdom. The original position of the United Kingdom was that it would not, at the outset, participate in the adoption and application of the proposed Regulation.[637] The United Kingdom was, however, involved in discussions concerning the Commission's Proposal and continued to consider its position over the course of negotiations of the text. In July, 2008, the United Kingdom indicated its willingness to opt into the final instrument.[638] 30–131

Legal basis. The Commission's original Proposal and the eventual Rome I Regulation are based on art.61(c) of the EC Treaty[639] which enables the Council to adopt measures in the field of judicial cooperation in civil and commercial matters, as provided for in art.65, which refers to "measures in the field of judicial co-operation in civil matters with a cross-border impact[640]" to be taken "to the extent necessary for the proper functioning of the internal market".[641] Such measures may include "promoting the compatibility of the rules applicable 30–132

630 See also Communication from the *Commission to the European Parliament and the Council: A More Coherent European Contract Law: An Action Plan* COM(2003) 427 final.

631 Hague Programme [2005] OJ C53/1. See Recital 5 to the Rome I Regulation.

632 *Proposal for a Regulation of the European Parliament and the Council on the law applicable to contractual obligations (Rome I)* COM(2005) 650 final. For discussion of the Proposal, see Lando and Nielsen (2007) 3 J. Priv. Int. L. 89 and the Comments of the Max Planck Institute for Comparative and International Private Law in (2007) 71 *Rabels Zeitschrift* 225.

633 Rome I [2008] OJ L177/6.

634 Rome I art.29.

635 Rome I arts 28 and 29.

636 But see Rome I art.22(2). Legislation may be required to deal with the application or non-application of the Regulation in respect of conflicts between the laws of the component parts of the United Kingdom.

637 See Recital 18 to the Commission Proposal. See Recital 45 to the Regulation.

638 See Council of the European Union, Press Release, 11653/08 (Presse 205), p.26. This will, presumably, require amendment to Recital 45 to the Regulation. The decision was taken after consultation, based on Ministry of Justice, *Consultation Paper: Rome I—Should the UK opt in?* (April, 2008). Denmark did not take part in the adoption of the Regulation and is not bound by it or subject to its application: Recital 46 to the Regulation. Ireland did participate in the adoption of the Regulation: Recital 44.

639 See Preamble to the Regulation.

640 See Recital 1 to the Regulation.

641 See Recitals 1 and 6 to the Regulation.

in the Member States concerning the conflict of laws and of jurisdiction."[642] According to Recital 6 to the Regulation, the:

> ". . . proper functioning of the internal market creates a need, in order to improve the predictability of the outcome of litigation, certainty as to the law and the free movement of judgments, for the conflict-of-law rules in the Member States to designate the same national law irrespective of the country of the court in which the action is brought."[643]

While these remarks seem based on rhetoric rather than empirical research, it would seem that the "internal market" justification for harmonised conflict of laws rules is now too well established to be seriously challenged.

30–133 **The Rome I Regulation in outline.** Since the structure and scope of the Rome I Regulation differs considerably from the Rome Convention, it will be helpful, at the outset, to identify, in outline, the structure and subject matter of the Rome I Regulation. After an initial Preamble and 46 Recitals, the Regulation is arranged into four Chapters. Chapter I is concerned with scope. Chapter II headed "Uniform rules" contains the relevant choice of law rules for determining the law applicable to a contract consisting of: a general rule on freedom to choose the governing law (art.3); a general rule to determine the applicable law in the absence of choice (art.4); specific choice of law rules to determine the law applicable to contracts of carriage (art.5), consumer contracts (art.6), insurance contracts (art.7), and individual employment contracts (art.8). Article 9 is concerned with "overriding mandatory provisions". Articles 10–13 are concerned with specific issues: consent and material validity (art.10); formal validity (art.11); scope of the applicable law (art.12); and incapacity (art.13). Articles 14–17 deal respectively with: voluntary assignment and contractual subrogation (art.14); legal subrogation (art.15); multiple liability (art.16); and set-off (art.17). Chapter II concludes with a rule as to the burden of proof (art.18). Chapter III headed "other provisions", contains rules dealing with the following matters: the definition of "habitual residence" (art.19); the exclusion of *renvoi* (art.20); public policy (art.21); states with more than one legal system (art.22); relationship with other provisions of Community law (art.23); relationship with the Rome Convention (art.24); relationship with existing international conventions (arts 25 and 26); a review clause (art.27); and application in time (art.28). Chapter IV contains one provision concerned with date of entry into force and application (art.29).

30–134 **Interpretation.** The Rome I Regulation will be subject to interpretation by the European Court of Justice by way of a reference to that court under art.234 of the EC Treaty, but such a reference can only be made by a court or tribunal of a Member State against whose decisions there is no judicial remedy under national law.[644] Consequently, the task of interpreting the Regulation will largely fall on national courts. There are no explicit guides to interpretation in the

---

[642] See Recital 2 to the Regulation.

[643] See also Recitals 3 and 4 to the Regulation.

[644] See *Dicey, Morris and Collins on the Conflict of Laws*, 14th edn (2006), paras 11–019, 11–058 et seq.

Regulation itself, though on occasion guidance can be found in the Recitals.[645] The European Court and national courts will doubtless have regard to the need for uniformity in the interpretation and application of the Regulation amongst Member States and to this end will normally endeavour to attribute autonomous meanings to terms which are likely to have different meanings in the law of the Members States.[646] Furthermore it is suggested[647] that the substantive scope and the provisions of the Regulation should be consistent with Council Regulation 44/2001 on jurisdiction and the recognition and enforcement of judgments in civil and commercial matters (Brussels 1)[648] and Regulation 864/2007 on the law applicable to non-contractual obligations (Rome II).[649] It may also be possible to have regard to the Giuliano-Lagarde Report on the Rome Convention[650] where the terminology of the Regulation coincides with that contained in the Rome Convention or in circumstances where the somewhat different terminology of the Regulation is unlikely to imply any substantive change from that used in the Convention.[651]

Relationship with other provisions of Community law. Article 23 of the Regulation provides that subject to an exception in art.7, concerned with insurance contracts,[652] the Regulation does not prejudice the application of provisions of Community law which, in relation to particular matters, lay down conflict of laws rules relating to contractual obligations.[653] Recital 40[654] states that the Regulation should not prejudice the application of other instruments laying down provisions designed to contribute to the proper functioning of the internal market in so far as they cannot be applied in conjunction with the law designated by the rules contained in the Regulation, and further stipulates that the application of provisions of the applicable law designated by the rules of the Regulation should not restrict the free movement of goods and services regulated by Community instruments.[655] 30–135

Relationship with the Rome Convention. Article 24 makes provision for the relationship between the Regulation and the Rome Convention. It provides first,[656] that the Regulation will replace the Rome Convention in the Member 30–136

[645] e.g. Rome I Recitals 7–10. Reference is made to the Recitals at appropriate points in this section and in s.5.

[646] For exceptions see Rome I art.1(2)(b) and (c) and Recital 8. See below, paras 30–154—30–155.

[647] Rome I Recital 7.

[648] Regulation 44/2001 on jurisdiction in civil and commercial matters [2001] OJ L12/1. Above, para.30–018.

[649] Regulation 864/2007 on law applicable to non-contractual obligations [2007] OJ L199/40. Below para.30–148.

[650] Above, para.30–020.

[651] See e.g. in Rome I art.3(3), below, para.30–178, Recital 15.

[652] See below, paras 30–252 et seq. Specific choice of law rules for certain insurance contracts were to be found in a series of Directives. See above, para.30–045.

[653] See Rome I Recital 40, first and second sentences.

[654] Rome I Recital 40, third and fourth sentences.

[655] The example given is Directive 2000/31 on certain legal aspects of information society services, in particular electronic commerce, in the internal market (Directive on electronic commerce) [2000] OJ L178/1. See above, para.30–096.

[656] Rome I art.24(1).

States, except as regards the territories of the Member States which fall within the territorial scope of that Convention and to which the Regulation does not apply pursuant to art.299 of the EC Treaty. Secondly,[657] it provides that in so far as the Regulation replaces the provisions of the Rome Convention, any reference to the Convention shall be understood as a reference to the Regulation.

30–137 **Relationship with existing international conventions.** Article 25(1) provides that the Regulation shall not prejudice the application of international conventions to which one or more Member States are parties at the time the Regulation is adopted[658] and which lay down conflict of laws rules relating to contractual obligations. This notwithstanding, as between Member States, the Regulation takes precedence over conventions concluded exclusively between two or more such States in so far as such conventions concern matters covered by the Regulation.[659] Article 26(1)[660] requires Member States to notify the Commission of the aforementioned conventions by June 17, 2009 and after that date Member States are required to notify the Commission of all denunciations of such conventions. The Commission is obliged to publish in the Official Journal of the European Union within six months of receipt, a list of the aforementioned conventions and a list of denunciations.[661]

30–138 **Review clause.** Article 27 of the Rome I Regulation provides for review of certain matters arising in connection with the Regulation. No later than five years after the entry into force of the Regulation,[662] the Commission is required to submit to the European Economic and Social Committee a report on the application of the Regulation and if appropriate, the report shall be accompanied by proposals to adapt the Regulation.[663] The report is to include: (i) a study on the law applicable to insurance contracts and an assessment of the impact of the provisions to be introduced if any: and (ii) an evaluation on the application of art.6 (concerned with consumer contracts), in particular as regards the coherence of Community law in the field of consumer protection.[664] It is likely that review of the particular matters of insurance contracts and consumer contracts was prompted by the fact that these matters had proved controversial in the negotiation of the Regulation.[665] No later than two years after the entry into force of the Regulation, the Commission shall submit to the European Parliament, the Council and the European Economic and Social Committee a report on the question of the effectiveness of an assignment or subrogation of a claim against third parties and the priority of the assigned or subrogated claims over a right of another

[657] Rome I art.24(2).
[658] i.e. June 17, 2008.
[659] Rome I art.25(2). See Recital 41. According to Recital 42 the Commission will make a proposal to the European Parliament and the Council concerning the procedures and conditions according to which Member States would be entitled to negotiate and conclude on their own behalf agreements with third countries in individual and exceptional cases, concerning sectoral matters, containing provisions on the law applicable to contractual obligations.
[660] Rome I art.26 will apply from June 17, 2009.
[661] Rome I art.26(2).
[662] i.e. June 17, 2013.
[663] Rome I art.27(1).
[664] Rome I art.27(1)(a), (6).
[665] See below, paras 30–231 et seq., 30–252 et seq.

person, the report to be accompanied if appropriate, by a proposal to amend the Regulation and an assessment of the impact of the provisions to be introduced.[666] The requirement for review of these matters was similarly prompted by their controversial nature in the course of negotiations.[667]

General scope of the Regulation. A number of general questions arise as to the scope of the Regulation (as opposed to the specific questions which are included in or excluded from the Regulation by the text of the instrument).[668] The general scope of the Regulation is indicated in art.1(1) which provides that the Regulation: 30–139

> " . . . shall apply, in situations involving a conflict of laws, to contractual obligations in civil and commercial matters. It shall not apply, in particular, to revenue, customs or administrative matters."

This formulation (which is different from that contained in the equivalent provision of the Rome Convention)[669] reflects the language of: (a) Council Regulation 44/2001 on jurisdiction and the recognition and enforcement of judgments in civil and commercial matters ("Brussels I") (hereafter the "Judgments Regulation")[670]; and (b) Regulation 864/2007 on the law applicable to non-contractual obligations ("Rome II") (hereafter the "Rome II Regulation").[671] As explained above,[672] Recital 7 to the Regulation indicates that the substantive scope and the provisions of the Rome I Regulation should be consistent with those instruments which means that identical terminology in each instrument should be interpreted in the same way.

"Situations involving a conflict of laws". This expression seems to indicate that the situation must be one which implicates the need to make a choice of law in relation to a particular contractual obligation which falls within the provisions of the Regulation. 30–140

"Civil and commercial matters". This expression (found in the Judgments Regulation and the Rome II Regulation) must be interpreted in a manner consistent with each of those Regulations.[673] Very broadly a "civil and commercial matter" is a matter which raises an issue of private law, as opposed to public law. It may serve to exclude from the scope of the Regulation, public law contracts such as administrative contracts under French law.[674] The expression also seems 30–141

---

[666] Rome I art.27(2).

[667] See below, paras 30–288 et seq.

[668] See below, paras 30–152 et seq.

[669] See above, para.30–022.

[670] See above, para.30–018.

[671] See above, para.30–031 and below, para.30–148.

[672] See para.30–134.

[673] Recital 7 to the Rome I Regulation. See *Dicey, Morris and Collins*, paras 11–024 et seq.; *Dicey Morris and Collins, on The Conflict of Laws, First Supplement to the 14th Edition*, para.S35–175. Unlike the position in relation to the Judgments Regulation, the Rome II Regulation specifically excludes from its scope "the liability of the State for acts and omissions in the exercise of State authority" (art.1(1)). See *Dicey, Morris and Collins, First Supplement*, para.S35–176.

[674] cf. *Dicey, Morris and Collins*, para.32–024; Foyer, 1991 Clunet 605; Audit, *Droit International Privé*, 4th edn (2006), para.829.

to mean that the scope of the Regulation will be more limited than that of the Rome Convention which is not limited to civil and commercial matters. It is unclear whether it is also intended to exlude from the scope of the Regulation any contract to which a government is a party.[675] It is suggested, however, that where a government enters into a contract in the exercise of its peculiarly public powers, the Rome I Regulation will not apply.[676] Where, in contrast, a government enters into a contract acting, in effect, as a private party, it is possible that the Regulation will apply, but this is far from clear.[677]

30–142 **"Revenue, customs and administrative matters".** The exclusion of contractual obligations arising out of these matters from the scope of civil and commercial matters follows the Judgments Regulation[678] and the Rome II Regulation[679] and interpretation of their content should follow that adopted in relation to those instruments, particularly the Judgments Regulation.[680]

30–143 **Application of law of non-Member States.** Article 2 of the Regulation provides that any law specified by the Regulation shall be applied whether or not it is the law of a Member State.[681] Thus, the Regulation is to have "universal effect", as was the case with the Rome Convention.[682]

30–144 **Application of law of a country.** It is also legitimate to deduce from art.1(1) taken in conjunction with art.2 and other provisions of the Regulation, that the applicable law must be the law of a "country".[683] Thus it will not be possible for the applicable law to be a non-state body of law[684] or a system of religious law. In this respect the Regulation takes the same position as prevailed under the Rome Convention.[685]

30–145 **States with more than one legal system.** Where a state comprises several territorial units each of which has its own rules of law in respect of contractual obligations (e.g. the United States) each territorial unit is to be considered as a country for the purposes of identifying the applicable law under the Regulation.[686]

---

[675] See preceding note.

[676] cf. *Kleinworth Benson Ltd v Glasgow City Council* [1999] 1 A.C. 153.

[677] See *Dicey, Morris and Collins*, para.32–024.

[678] Judgments Regulation art.1(1).

[679] Rome II Regulation art.1(1).

[680] See *Dicey, Morris and Collins*, paras 11–026—11–028.

[681] Member State for these purposes means all the Member States except Denmark: Rome I art.1(3), subject to arts 3(4) and 7. See below, paras 30–179, 30–258.

[682] Above, para.30–023.

[683] See, e.g. Rome I arts 3–8.

[684] Rome I Recital 13 states that the Regulation does not preclude parties from incorporating by reference into their contract a non-state body or law or an international convention. More generally, incorporation by reference of foreign provisions of law into the contract (above, para.30–009) is also permitted. Recital 14 states that should the Community adopt in an appropriate legal instrument rules of substantive contract law, including standard terms and conditions, such instrument may provide that the parties may choose to apply these rules.

[685] Above, paras 30–048, 30–071.

[686] Rome I art.22(1). cf. the Rome Convention, above, para.30–022.

Renvoi. Article 20, headed "Exclusion of renvoi", provides that the application of the law of any country specified by the Regulation means the rules of law in force in that country other than its rules of private international law, unless provided otherwise in the Regulation. Renvoi is thus generally excluded. The exception appears to be limited to one provision (art.7(3)) concerned with insurance contracts.[687] 30–146

Meaning of "contractual obligations". The Regulation only applies to determine the law applicable to "contractual obligations", an expression that is not specifically defined in the Regulation itself. In general terms, subject to what is said below, the same observations may be made here as were made in relation to the meaning of the same expression in the Rome Convention.[688] There can be no doubt that the expression will be given an "autonomous" meaning and will, thus, not necessarily be limited to obligations which the law of the English forum would regard as contractual.[689] Equally, it is suggested that the basis of the autonomous meaning will be found to lie in an obligation which is voluntarily assumed by agreement between the parties.[690] 30–147

Meaning of "non-contractual obligations". The Rome II Regulation provides uniform choice of law rules for determining the law applicable to non-contractual obligations arising out of tort/delict, unjust enrichment, *culpa in contrahendo* and *negotiorum gestio*.[691] The meaning of contractual obligation for the purposes of the Rome I Regulation will necessarily involve delimiting the respective scope of the Rome I Regulation and the Rome II Regulation.[692] In this respect, attention may be drawn to three particular points. 30–148

Obligations arising out of pre-contractual dealings. Obligations arising out of pre-contractual dealings between the parties will be governed by art.12 of the Rome II Regulation dealing with *culpa in contrahendo*[693] and thus will not fall within the Rome I Regulation.[694] Article 12(1) of the Rome II Regulation provides, as a general rule, that the law applicable to a non-contractual obligation arising out of dealings prior to the conclusion of the contract, regardless of whether the contract was actually concluded or not, shall be the law that applies to the contract or would have been applicable to it had it been entered into.[695] Presumably the law that applies to the contract or would have been applicable to 30–149

---

[687] See below, para.30–272.

[688] Above, paras 30–031 et seq.

[689] Above, para.30–031.

[690] cf. *Base Metal Trading Ltd v Shamurin* [2004] EWCA Civ 1316, [2005] 1 W.L.R. 1157. See *Dicey, Morris and Collins*, para.30–023; above, para.30–031.

[691] For discussion, see *Dicey, Morris and Collins, First Supplement*, paras 34–005 et seq., paras S35–165 et seq.

[692] *Dicey, Morris and Collins, First Supplement*, paras 34–014, S35–242 et seq.

[693] For discussion, see *Dicey, Morris and Collins, First Supplement* at paras S35–242 et seq.

[694] Rome I art.1(2)(i); Recital 10 to the Rome I Regulation. For the purposes of the Rome II Regulation, *culpa in contrahendo* must be given an autonomous meaning: see Recital 30 to the latter Regulation.

[695] Rome II art.12(2) supplies a default rule applicable where the governing law cannot be determined by reference to art.12(1).

it had it been entered into, will have to be determined by reference to the choice of law rules contained in the Rome I Regulation.

30–150 **Consequences of nullity of a contract.** As discussed below,[696] art.12(1)(e) of the Rome I Regulation provides that the applicable law governs the consequences of nullity of the contract. As explained above earlier in this Chapter the Rome Convention allowed contracting states to make a reservation to this provision which the United Kingdom duly did, since in the view of United Kingdom legal systems this issue was to be classified not as contractual, but as restitutionary, in character.[697] No such reservation is permitted by the Rome I Regulation, and thus art.12(1)(e) will have to be applied. A question arises, however, because the Rome II Regulation contains in art.10[698] a choice of law rule concerning unjust enrichment into the category of which the consequences of nullity of the contract could be construed to fall. It is suggested, however, that this issue should be governed by the rules in the Rome I Regulation and not by art.10 of the Rome II Regulation, though it cannot be said that this conclusion is entirely clear. Article 10(1) of the Rome II Regulation provides that if a non-contractual obligation arising out of unjust enrichment, including payment of amounts wrongly received, concerns a relationship existing between the parties, such as one arising out of a contract or a tort/delict, that is closely connected with the unjust enrichment, it shall be governed by the law that governs that relationship.[699] This could be interpreted to mean that the consequences of nullity of a contract are governed by the law applicable to the contractual obligation out of which the unjust enrichment arises. Nonetheless, it is suggested that the relative scope of the Rome I Regulation and the Rome II Regulation will be determined to be mutually exclusive.

30–151 **Contract and tort.** In relation to the Rome Convention, it was held in England that where English law allowed concurrent claims in contract and tort, there was nothing in the Rome Convention to prevent a claimant from framing a claim in tort rather than contract if it was advantageous to do so.[700] It is suggested, however, that this option will not be available as between the choice of law rules contained in the two Regulations.[701] The scope of each Regulation will be determined to be mutually exclusive.

(b) *Exclusions*

30–152 **Specifically excluded matters.** Article 1(2) and art.1(3) of the Rome I Regulation specifically exclude certain matters from the material scope of the Regulation. Since many of these matters replicate the equivalent provisions in the

---

696 Para.30–328.

697 Above, paras 30–033 et seq.

698 For discussion, see *Dicey, Morris and Collins, First Supplement*, paras 34–005 et seq.

699 Rome II art.10(2)–(4) supplies default rules to be applied if the applicable law cannot be determined on the basis of art.10(1).

700 Above, para.30–032.

701 *Dicey, Morris and Collins, First Supplement*, para.S35–177.

Rome Convention, they will not be discussed in detail here.[702] The following paragraphs emphasis matters excluded where there are differences between the Rome Convention and the Regulation.

Capacity of natural persons. Article 1(2)(a) is in the same terms as art.1(2)(a) of the Rome Convention[703] and excludes questions involving the status or legal capacity of natural persons without prejudice to the special rule on incapacity contained in art.13 of the Regulation.[704] 30–153

Family relationships. The choice of law rules contained in the Regulation do not apply to obligations arising out of family relationships, and relationships deemed by the law applicable to such relationships to have comparable affects, including maintenance obligations. This provision, found in art.1(2)(b) of the Regulation, expresses, in somewhat different terms, part of art.1(2)(b) of the Rome Convention[705] which also excluded obligations arising out of family relationships. In the Regulation there is an additional exclusion of obligations arising out of relationships deemed by the law applicable to such relationships to have comparable effects to family relationships. Recital 8 to the Regulation states that "family relationships should cover parentage, marriage, affinity, and collateral relatives" and also states that the reference: 30–154

> " . . . to relationships having comparable effects to marriage and other family relationships should be interpreted in accordance with the law of the Member State in which the court is seised."

This would be apt to exclude civil partnerships as understood in English law.[706]

Matrimonial property regimes, etc. Article 1(2)(c) excludes obligations arising out of matrimonial property regimes, property regimes of relationships deemed by the law applicable to such relationships to have comparable effects to marriage, and wills and succession. Although in part, this provision is based on art.1(2)(b) of the Rome Convention,[707] there is a significant addition in that the exclusion is extended to property regimes arising out of relationships deemed to have comparable effects to marriage under the law applicable to such relationships. It will be for the law of the Member State in which the court is seised to determine whether the particular relationship has the necessary comparable effects.[708] 30–155

Bills of exchange etc. Article 1(2)(d) of the Regulation excludes obligations arising under bills of exchange, cheques and promissory notes and other negotiable instruments to the extent that the obligations under such other negotiable 30–156

---

702 See above, paras 30–035 et seq.
703 Above, para.30–036.
704 Rome I art.13 is discussed below, para.30–324.
705 Above, para.30–037.
706 Civil Partnerships Act 2004.
707 Above, para.30–037.
708 Recital 8 to the Rome I Regulation. For English law, see *Dicey, Morris and Collins on the Conflict of Laws*, 14th edn (2006), Ch. 28.

instruments arise out of their negotiable character. This provision is a replica of art.1(2)(c) of the Rome Convention.[709] Recital 9 to the Regulation states that obligations:

> "... under bills of exchange, cheques and promissory notes and other negotiable instruments should also cover bills of lading to the extent that the obligations under the bill of lading arise out of its negotiable character."

Thus, if under the relevant governing law a bill of lading is a negotiable instrument and the obligation in question arises out of its negotiable character, the rules contained in the Regulation will not apply.[710]

30–157 **Arbitration agreements and agreements on the choice of court.** Article 1(2)(e) excludes arbitration agreements and agreements on the choice of court from the scope of the Regulation. The provision replicates art.1(2)(d) of the Rome Convention.[711]

30–158 **Questions governed by the law of companies, etc.** Article 1(2)(f) excludes questions governed by the law of companies and other bodies corporate or unincorporated such as the creation, by registration or otherwise, legal capacity, internal organisation or winding up of companies and other bodies corporate or unincorporated and the personal liability of officers and members as such for the obligations of the company or body. With one minor linguistic change, of no substantial effect, (body "unincorporate" in the Rome Convention becomes body "unincorporated" in the Regulation), this provision reproduces art.1(2)(e) of the Rome Convention.[712]

30–159 **Power of agent to bind principal, etc.** According to art.1(2)(g), the Regulation does not apply to the question whether an agent is able to bind a principal, or an organ to bind a company or body corporate or unincorporated, in relation to a third party. With minor linguistic changes, of no substantial effect, art.1(2)(g) reproduces art.1(2)(f) of the Rome Convention.[713]

30–160 **Trusts.** Questions concerning the constitution of trusts and the relationship between settlors, trustees and beneficiaries, are excluded by art.1(2)(h) in terms which are identical with art.1(2)(g) of the Rome convention.[714]

30–161 **Evidence and procedure.** Article 1(3) of the Regulation, reproducing the effect of art.1(2)(h) of the Rome Convention[715] provides that the Regulation does

---

[709] Above, paras 30–038—30–039.

[710] See, for English law, *Dicey, Morris and Collins*, paras 33R–322 et seq.

[711] Above, para.30–040. As is pointed out below an arbitration clause or a jurisdiction clause may be relevant in determining whether a choice of law has been made for the purposes of art.3 of the Rome I Regulation: see below, para.30–174.

[712] Above, para.30–041.

[713] Above, para.30–042. The Commission's original Proposal contained choice of law rules in relation to agency: see art.7 of the Proposal.

[714] Above, para.30–043.

[715] Above, para.30–044.

not apply to evidence and procedure, without prejudice to art.18, concerned with the burden of proof.[716]

Pre-contractual dealings. As pointed out above,[717] art.1(2)(i) provides that the Regulation does not apply to obligations arising out of dealings prior to the conclusion of a contract. Such obligations are regarded as non-contractual obligations and thus will fall within art.12 of the Rome II Regulation.[718] Article 1(2)(j) has no counterpart in the Rome Convention. 30–162

Insurance. The Rome Convention contained no discrete rules for determining the law applicable to insurance contracts and indeed did not apply at all to determine the law applicable to an insurance contract covering risks situated in the territories of the European Community.[719] In contrast, art.7 of the Rome I Regulation contains elaborate choice of law rules for determining the law applicable to insurance contracts which are discussed later in this section.[720] There is however, in art.1(2)(j) of the Regulation an exclusion of a specific type of insurance from the Regulation regime, namely insurance contracts arising out of operations carried out by organisations other than undertakings referred to in art.2 of Directive 2002/83 concerning life insurance[721] the object of which is to provide benefits for employed or self-employed persons belonging to an undertaking or group of undertakings, or a trade or group of trades, in the event of death or survival or of discontinuance or curtailment of activity, or of sickness related to work or accidents at work.[722] 30–163

(c) *Habitual Residence*

Introduction. The Rome I Regulation makes frequent reference to the law of a party's habitual residence[723] and it will be convenient, at this point, to identify and discuss the definition of this concept which is to be found in art.19 of the Regulation. According to Recital 39 to the Regulation for "the sake of certainty there should be a clear definition of habitual residence, in particular for bodies corporate" which: 30–164

> " . . . should proceed on the basis of a single criterion; otherwise, the parties would be unable to foresee the law applicable to their situation."[724]

Companies, etc. For the purposes of the Regulation, art.19(1) provides that the habitual residence of companies and other bodies, corporate or unincorporated, shall be the place of central administration. "Central administration" 30–165

---

[716] Discussed above, paras 30–051 et seq.

[717] Above, para.30–149.

[718] See also Recital 10 to the Rome I Regulation.

[719] Above, para.30–045.

[720] Below, paras 30–252.

[721] Directive 2002/83 concerning life insurance [2002] OJ L345/1.

[722] See art.3(3) of Directive 2002/83, preceding note.

[723] Rome I arts 4, 5, 6, 7, 10 and 11.

[724] cf. Judgments Regulation art.60(1)(c); Rome II Regulation art.23. The Rome Convention did not contain a specific definition of habitual residence but makes reference to concepts employed in the definition found in art.19 of the Regulation. See above, paras 30–080 et seq.

will undoubtedly be given an autonomous meaning. It is an expression to be found, but not defined, in the Rome Convention. Some suggestions are made above as to the possible outlines of an autonomous meaning in the context of the discussion of the expression, as used in the Convention.[725]

30–166 **Branch, agency, etc.** Article 19(2) of the Regulation provides that where:

> "... the contract is concluded in the course of the operations of a branch, agency or any other establishment, or if, under the contract performance is the responsibility of such a branch, agency or establishment, the place where the branch, agency or any other establishment is located shall be treated as the place of habitual residence."[726]

It is unlikely that application of this provision will give rise to any particular difficulty in practice. It is likely, however, that the expression "branch, agency, or any other establishment" will be interpreted consistently with the same expression as found in art.5(5) of the Judgments Regulation.[727]

30–167 **Natural persons.** The Regulation provides that the "habitual residence of a natural person acting in the course of his business activity shall be his principal place of business".[728] "Principal place of business" will surely be given an autonomous meaning. Some suggestions as to the possible contours of this are made in the context of the discussion of the expression, as used in the Rome Convention, earlier in this Chapter.[729]

30–168 **Natural person not acting in the course of business.** No definition of habitual residence is provided in relation to a person who is not acting in the course of a business activity. Should this question arise for consideration, the solution will have to be found, it would seem, in general principles which will found the basis of an autonomous meaning.[730]

30–169 **Relevant time.** According to art.19(3) of the Regulation when determining a party's habitual residence the relevant point in time is to be the time of conclusion of the contract. It would seem that that point in time will have to be determined by reference to the law which is alleged to be applicable to the contract in question.[731]

(d) *Freedom of Choice*

30–170 **Introduction.** As is the case in the equivalent provision in the Rome Convention,[732] art.3 of the Rome I Regulation enshrines the principle of party autonomy

---

[725] Above, paras 30–079 et seq.

[726] There is no comparable provision in the Rome Convention. cf. Rome II Regulation art.23(1), second paragraph.

[727] See Recital 7 to the Rome I Regulation. See *Dicey, Morris and Collins on the Conflict of Laws*, 14th edn (2006), paras 11–309 et seq.

[728] Rome I art.19(1).

[729] Above, para.30–081.

[730] Some of these are identified and discussed in the context of the Rome Convention: see above, para.30–079.

[731] Rome I art.10(1): below, paras 30–304 et seq.

[732] Above, paras 30–047 et seq.

whereby parties may choose the law to govern a contract. The freedom of the parties to choose the governing law is described in Recital 11 to the Regulation as one of the "cornerstones" of the system of conflict of laws rules in matters of contractual obligations. Although art.3 of the Regulation reflects the same philosophy as art.3 of the Convention, there are differences in wording and detail between the two provisions to which attention is drawn in the following paragraphs.

General principle. Article 3(1) of the Regulation provides quite generally that a "contract shall be governed by the law chosen by the parties". The law chosen must be that of a country and it is not open to parties to choose, for example, a non-State body of law such as the "*lex mercatoria*" or "general principles of international commercial law".[733] It is, nonetheless, open to the parties to incorporate by reference into the contract a non-State body of law or an international convention.[734] Further, it would seem[735] that where the parties have chosen a foreign law to govern the contract, but do not plead or prove the content of the foreign law, then, at least in England, the court will apply English law since the principle that foreign law, as a fact, must be pleaded and proved is a rule of evidence or procedure to which the Regulation does not apply.[736] 30–171

Making the choice. The second sentence of art.3(1) provides, first, that the choice may be made expressly. In this respect the Regulation replicates the Rome Convention.[737] The provision then goes on to state that the choice may also be "clearly demonstrated by the terms of the contract or the circumstances of the case". This formula is different to that used in the Rome Convention which required that the choice be "demonstrated with reasonable certainty by the terms of the contract or the circumstances of the case".[738] 30–172

"Clearly demonstrated" etc. The change of language to "clearly demonstrated" would appear to be designed to impose a higher standard of indication that an "implied" choice of law has been made than that imposed by the Rome Convention.[739] The change in standard may be a response to suggestions that courts in some Member States were too liberal in, or inconsistent in, finding that a choice of law had been demonstrated with reasonable certainty under the Rome Convention formula,[740] suggestions which themselves may be questioned.[741] 30–173

---

733 See above, para.30–048.

734 Recital 13 to the Regulation, above, para.30–144. Should the Community adopt in an appropriate legal instrument rules of substantive contract law, including standard terms and conditions, such instrument may provide that the parties may choose to apply those rules: Recital 14, above, para.30–144.

735 Subject to the possibility that the European Court may take a different view.

736 Rome I art.1(3). Above, paras 30–049, 30–161.

737 Above, para.30–050.

738 Above, paras 30–051 et seq.

739 There is no Recital in the Regulation which indicates that this is the intention.

740 See Consultation Paper, para.50.

741 See Morse in Meeusen, Pertegas and Straetmans (eds), *The Enforcement of International Contracts in the European Union* (2004), p.191.

Whether the wording of art.3(1) of the Regulation will, in practice, produce significantly different outcomes in particular cases is open to doubt.[742]

30–174 **Relevant factors.** Subject to the potentially different standard referred to in the previous paragraph, there is no reason to doubt that the factors which were found to be relevant as indicating an "implied" choice of law under the Rome Convention[743] will be regarded as relevant in deciding whether a choice of law has been "clearly demonstrated" under the Regulation. It is worth noting that Recital 12 to the Regulation states that an:

> ". . . agreement of the parties to confer exclusive jurisdiction on one or more courts or tribunals of a Member State to determine disputes under the contract should be one of the factors to be taken into account in determining whether a choice of law was clearly demonstrated."[744]

There seems to be no reason, in principle, however, why an exclusive jurisdiction clause conferring jurisdiction on the courts of a non-member State should not have the same effect. And, further there is no reason to believe that the specific mention of a jurisdiction clause indicates an intention that arbitration clauses should not be relevant.[745]

30–175 **Partial choice of law.** The third sentence of art.3(1) provides that by "their choice the parties can select the law applicable to the whole or a part only of the contract". This repeats the equivalent provision of the Rome Convention, discussed earlier in this Chapter.[746]

30–176 **Changing the choice.** Article 3(2) of the Regulation provides that the:

> ". . . parties may at any time agree to subject the contract to a law other than that which previously governed it, whether as a result of an earlier choice under this Article or of other provisions of this Regulation. Any change in the law to be applied that is made after the conclusion of the contract shall not prejudice its formal validity under Article 11 or adversely affect the rights of third parties."

This (with minor differences of wording which have no substantive effect) reproduces art.3(2) of the Rome Convention, discussed earlier in this Chapter.[747]

30–177 **Limitations on choice.** Article 3 of the Rome I Regulation specifies two circumstances in which the effect of a choice of law by the parties may be

---

[742] What were "marginal" cases under the Rome Convention might be decided differently under the Regulation: see, e.g. *Marubeni Hong Kong and South China Ltd v Mongolian Government* [2002] 2 All E.R (Comm) 873. But whether this would be an inevitable or, indeed, desirable, outcome is far from clear.

[743] Above, paras 30–051 et seq.

[744] It is not clear whether this means that a non-exclusive jurisdiction clause cannot be relevant.

[745] Above, para.30–051. As to the relevance of subsequent conduct, see above, para.30–054.

[746] Above, paras 30–057 et seq.

[747] Above, para.30–058.

limited. The first, reflecting art.3(3) of the Rome Convention[748] (but differently worded), limits the effect of a choice in what may be described as "internal situations".[749] The second, which has no counterpart in the Rome Convention limits the effect of the choice by reference to certain provisions of Community law.[750] Additionally, the effect of a choice may be limited by "overriding mandatory provisions[751] and by reference to public policy.[752]

Article 3(3): internal situations. Article 3(3) of the Regulation provides that: 30–178

"... where all other elements relevant to the situation at the time of the choice are located in a country other than a country whose law has been chosen, the choice of the parties shall not prejudice the application of provisions of the law of that country which cannot be derogated from by agreement."

The change of wording from that adopted in the Rome Convention is, apparently, designed to bring the language into line, as far as possible, with art.14(2)[753] of the Rome II Regulation, art.14 of which allows the parties, in certain circumstances, to choose the law applicable to certain non-contractual obligations.[754] According to Recital 15 to the Regulation, the rule in art.3(3) applies whether or not the choice of law was accompanied by a choice of court or tribunal and the revised wording is not intended to indicate any substantial change, compared with art.3(3) of the Rome Convention, as discussed earlier in this Chapter.[755]

Article 3(4): Community law. Article 3(4) stipulates that where: 30–179

"... all other elements relevant to the situation at the time of the choice are located in one or more Member States, the parties' choice of applicable law other than that of a Member State shall not prejudice the application of provisions of Community law, where appropriate, as implemented in the Member State of the forum, which cannot be derogated from by agreement."

The effect of this provision is that where the elements relevant to the situation at the time of the choice[756] are limited only to Member States, the English forum must apply mandatory provisions of Community law, as implemented in the United Kingdom, where necessary, even if the contract is governed by the law of a non-Member State.[757] For the purposes of art.3(4) the term "Member State" means all the Member States, including Denmark.[758]

---

748 Above, paras 30–061 et seq.
749 Rome I art.3(3).
750 Rome I art.3(4).
751 Rome I art.9.
752 Rome I art.21
753 Recital 12 to the Rome I Regulation.
754 For discussion see *Dicey, Morris and Collins, First Supplement*, paras S35–248 et seq.
755 Above paras 30–061 et seq.
756 For discussion of this expression, see above, para.30–062.
757 cf. *Ingmar GB Ltd v Eaton Leonard Technologies Inc* (C–381/98) [2000] E.C.R. I–9305.
758 Rome I art.1(3).

30–180 **"Overriding mandatory provisions".** Article 9 of the Regulation imposes two potential limitations on the effect of a choice of law by reference to "overriding mandatory provisions". These are defined (or described) in art.9(1) as:

> "... provisions the respect for which is regarded as crucial by a country for safeguarding its public interests such as its political, social or economic organisation, to such an extent that they are applicable to any situation falling within their scope, irrespective of the law otherwise applicable to the contract under this Regulation."

It will be noted that the provisions which fall within art.9 must be provisions which apply irrespective of the law applicable to the contract.[759] They must be distinguished from "provisions which cannot be derogated from by agreement" referred to in art.3(3) and (4) and should be construed more restrictively.[760]

30–181 **Overriding mandatory provisions: law of the forum.** Article 9(2) of the Regulation stipulates that nothing "in this regulation shall restrict the application of the overriding mandatory provisions of the law of the forum". This provision replicates, in effect, though with different terminology, art.7(2) of the Rome Convention, as discussed earlier in this Chapter.[761]

30–182 **Overriding mandatory provisions: law of country of performance.** Article 9(3) of the Regulation contains a limited version of what was art.7(1) of the Rome Convention (which did not apply in the United Kingdom).[762] It provides that effect:

> "... may be given to the overriding mandatory provisions of the country where the obligations arising out of the contract have to be or have been performed, in so far as those overriding mandatory provisions render the performance of the contract unlawful. In considering whether to give effect to those provisions, regard shall be had to their nature and purpose and to the consequences of their application or non-application."

Article 9(3) imposes a potential limitation on the effect of a choice of law by reference to overriding provisions of the law of the country of performance where a contract, valid by its governing law, has to be or has been performed in a country where such performance would be or was illegal under that country's law. The provision, the application of which is discretionary, is discussed in detail later in this Chapter.[763]

30–183 **Public policy.** Article 21 of the Regulation, headed "[p]ublic policy of the forum" provides that the:

> "... application of a provision of the law of any country specified by this Regulation may be refused only if such application is manifestly incompatible with the public policy ("ordre public") of the forum."

---

759 Discussed below, para.30–361.
760 Recital 37 to the Regulation. See above, para.30–063 and below, para.30–361.
761 Above, para.30–068.
762 Above, para.30–068.
763 Below, paras 30–360 et seq.

This provision reproduces the effect of art.16 of the Rome Convention.[764] It is capable of limiting the effect of a choice of foreign law where the English court would regard that law as manifestly incompatible with English public policy. It is discussed in detail later in this Chapter.[765]

Consent to the choice of law. Article 3(5) of the Regulation reproduces art.3(4) of the Rome Convention.[766] According to art.3(5) the existence and validity of the consent of the parties as to the choice of the applicable law shall be determined in accordance with the provisions of arts 10, 11 and 13. As with art.3(4) of the Rome Convention, discussed earlier in this Chapter, the existence and validity of the consent of the parties to the choice of law is governed by the law the parties purported to choose.[767] 30–184

Party autonomy and particular contracts. The provisions relating to party autonomy in relation to contracts subject to special rules under the Regulation will be discussed in relation to each particular contract so subject.[768] 30–185

(e) *Applicable Law in the Absence of Choice*

Background. The Rome Convention established, as a general principle, that in the absence of choice, a contract should be governed by the law of the country with which it was most closely connected.[769] This law was to be discovered by reference to a general presumption pointing to the characteristic performer's habitual residence, central administration, principal place of business or place of business, as the case may be,[770] or by reference to specific presumptions in respect of contracts the subject matter of which is a right in immovable property or a right to use immovable property[771] and contracts for the carriage of goods.[772] The general presumption did not apply if the characteristic performance could not be determined and the presumption could be disregarded if it appeared from the circumstances as a whole that the contract was more closely connected with another country.[773] Article 4 of the Rome I Regulation, however, adopts a somewhat different structure. 30–186

Structure of article 4 of the Regulation. Article 4(1) of the Regulation provides, to the extent that the applicable law has not been chosen and subject to the choice of law rules applicable to particular contracts contained in arts 5–8, a series of rules for specific contracts. Where the contract is not covered by art.4(1) or where the elements of the contract would be covered by more than one of the types of contract referred to in art.4(1), art.4(2) provides that the contract will be 30–187

[764] Above, para.30–069; below, paras 30–366 et seq.
[765] Below, paras 30–366 et seq.
[766] Above, para.30–059.
[767] Above, para.30–059.
[768] Below, paras 30–209 et seq.
[769] Above, para.30–071.
[770] Above, paras 30–073 et seq.
[771] Above, paras 30–082 et seq.
[772] Above, paras 30–085 et seq.
[773] Above, paras 30–088 et seq.

governed by the law of the country where the party required to effect the characteristic performance of the contract has his habitual residence. Article 4(3) provides a rule of displacement whereby where it is clear from all the circumstances that the contract is manifestly more closely connected with a country other than that indicated in art.4(1) or (2), the law of that other country shall apply. Article 4(4) provides a "default rule" to the effect that where the applicable law cannot be determined pursuant to art.4(1) or 4(2), the contract shall be governed by the law of the country with which it is most closely connected. After examining the principles behind art.4 of the Regulation, the following paragraphs will discuss the various elements in this structure.

30–188 **Principles.** The approach taken in art.4 of the Rome Convention was an attempt to reconcile the competing requirements of certainty and flexibility in the determination of the applicable law. However, it appears to have been thought that the conceptual structure of art.4 of the Convention was undesirably complex and inherently uncertain, allowing national courts in Member States to interpret the provision in divergent ways.[775] Thus, for example, English courts have emphasised the flexibility of art.4 and have tended to place greater weight on the closest connection principle at the expense of the presumptions.[776] In contrast, Scottish courts and some continental courts have tended to emphasise the presumptions at the expense of the flexibility of the closest connection principle.[777] Divergent approaches have lead to uncertainty, particularly in the absence of any guidance from the European Court of Justice.[778] The approach taken in art.4 of the Regulation is to tighten the balance between flexibility and certainty with a view, also, to producing more uniform outcomes in the national courts of Member States.[779] This much is recognised in Recital 16 to the Regulation where it is stated that to:

> "... contribute to the general objective of this Regulation, legal certainty in the European judicial area, the conflict-of-law rules should be highly foreseeable. The courts should, however, retain a degree of discretion to determine the law that is most closely connected to the situation."

30–189 **Specific rules.** Article 4(1) of the Regulation provides that to the extent that the law applicable to the contract has not been chosen in accordance with art.3,[780] the law applicable to the contract shall be determined, in respect of certain

[774–775] Ministry of Justice, Consultation Paper, *Rome I—Should the UK opt in?* (April, 2008) (hereafter "Consultation Paper") para.50.

[776] See, e.g. *Samcrete Egypt Engineers and Contractors SAE v Land Rover Exports Ltd* [2001] EWCA Civ 2019, [2002] C.L.C. 533; above, para.30–090 et seq.

[777] See, e.g. *Caledonia Subsea Ltd v Microperi Srl* (2002) S.L.T. 1022; *Societe Nouvelle des Papeteries de l'Aa v BV Machinefabriek BOA* (1992) N.J. 750 (Dutch Hoge Raad); above, paras 30–090 et seq.

[778] Consultation Paper, para.50. But see *Intercontainer Interfrigo (ICF) SC v Balkerende Oosthuisen BV* (C–133/08) (pending) [2008] OJ C 158/10.

[779] Consultation Paper, para.51.

[780] Without prejudice to the particular contracts dealt with in Rome I arts 5 to 8.

identified contracts, as follows. It is likely that an autonomous meaning will be attributed to the contracts so identified where necessary.[781]

Sale of goods. Article 4(1)(a) provides that a contract for the sale of goods[782] shall be governed by the law of the country[783] where the seller has his habitual residence.[784] In effect, this reproduces in concrete form the outcome reached under art.4(2) of the Rome Convention.[785] 30–190

Provision of services. According to art.4(1)(b) a contract for the provision of services[786] shall be governed by the law of the country where the service provider has his habitual residence.[787] This specific rule reaches the same outcome as would application of art.4(2) of the Rome Convention.[788] 30–191

Immovables. Article 4(1)(c) stipulates that a contract relating to a right in rem in immovable property or to a tenancy of immovable property shall be governed by the law of the country where the property is situated. This is subject to an exception in art.4(1)(d) where it is provided that a tenancy of immovable property concluded for a temporary period of no more than six consecutive months shall be governed by the law of the country where the landlord has his habitual residence, provided that the tenant is a natural person and has his habitual residence in the same country.[789] It will be noted that neither provision requires that the immovable be situated in a Member State. Article 4(1)(c) is a rather different formulation to that found in art.4(3) of the Rome Convention,[790] while art.4(1)(d) has no counterpart in that Convention. Taken together, art.4(1)(c) and (d) appear to be based on art.22(1) of the Judgments Regulation which is in very similar terms, and is likely to be interpreted consistently with the latter provision so far as possible.[791] 30–192

Franchise contract. A franchise contract, according to art.4(2)(e), shall be governed by the law of the country where the franchisee has his habitual 30–193

[781] cf. Recital 17. It should be noted that these specific rules are not described as "presumptions". cf. Rome Convention art.4(2), above, para.30–072.

[782] According to Recital 17, the concept of "sale of goods" should be interpreted in the same way as when applying art.5 of Regulation 44/2001 (the Judgments Regulation) in so far as sale of goods is covered by that Regulation. As to sale of goods by auction, see below, para.30–195.

[783] i.e. the applicable law cannot be, say a religious law in this or in any other provision of Rome I art.4.

[784] As to the meaning of which, see above, paras 30–164 et seq.

[785] Above, para.30–077.

[786] According to Rome I Recital 17, the concept of "provision of services" should be interpreted in the same way as when applying art.5 of the Judgments Regulation in so far as provision of services is governed by that Regulation. Two specific contracts for the provision of services, franchise contracts and distribution contracts are dealt with separately: see below, paras 30–193, 30–194.

[787] As to the meaning of which, see above, paras 30–164 et seq.

[788] Above, para.30–077.

[789] As to the meaning of habitual residence, see above, paras 30–164 et seq.

[790] Above, para.30–082.

[791] See Recital 7 to the Rome I Regulation. For discussion of art.22(1) of the Judgments Regulation, see *Dicey, Morris and Collins on the Conflict of Laws*, 14th edn (2006), para.23–010 et seq., 23–029.

residence.[792] It is likely, although the question has not been decided, that the same outcome would be reached under art.4(2) of the Rome Convention.[793]

30–194 **Distribution contract.** Article 4(1)(f) deals with a distribution contract and provides that such a contract shall be governed by the law of the country where the distributor has his habitual residence.[794] It is likely, however, that where a "distribution" contract is to be fulfilled by individual contracts of sale and purchase, the applicable law will be determined by art.4(2) rather than by art.4(1)(f) since the elements of the contract are covered by art.4(1)(a) and art.4(1)(f).[795]

30–195 **Sale of goods by auction.** Article 4(1)(g) provides a specific rule for a contract for the sale of goods by auction. It stipulates that such a contract shall be governed by the law of the country where the auction takes place, if such a place can be determined. It may not be possible to determine where an auction takes place, in some situations, where the auction is conducted over the internet.[796]

30–196 **Contract concluded within multilateral system.** Article 4(1)(h) of the Regulation provides that:

> "... a contract concluded within a multilateral system which brings together or facilitates the bringing together of multiple third- party buying and selling interests in financial instruments, as defined by Article 4(1), point 17, of Directive 2004/39/EC, in accordance with non-discretionary rules and governed by a single law, shall be governed by that law."

This choice of law rule creates a specific rule for certain types of financial contract, as defined in the Markets in Financial Instruments Directive 2004 (MiFID),[797] art.4(1)(17).[798] Normally, such contracts will contain a choice of law by the parties.[799] However, it was felt that this rule was desirable in order to preserve the high degree of legal certainty required in international financial

---

[792] As to the meaning of habitual residence, see above, paras 30–164 et seq.

[793] cf. above, para.30–077.

[794] As to the meaning of habitual residence, see above, para.30–164 et seq.

[795] See below, para.30–199. Distribution contracts give rise to some difficulty under the Rome Convention: see above, para.30–076.

[796] Some contracts of this character may be consumer contracts subject to art.6 of the Regulation: see below, paras 30–231 et seq.

[797] Directive 2004/39 on markets in financial instruments, amending Council Directives 85/611 and Directive 2000/12 and repealing Council Directive 93/22: [2004] OJ L145/1. The Directive purports to provide a harmonised regulatory regime for investment services across the Member States of the European Economic Area.

[798] MiFID art.4(1)(17) defines these financial instruments by reference to Section C of Annex I to the Directive. Relevant financial instruments are: transferable securities; money-market instruments; units in collective investment undertakings; various forms of options, futures, swaps, forward rate agreements, and other derivative contracts; derivative instruments for the transfer of credit risk; and financial contracts for differences. As to the meaning of "multilateral trading facility" ("MTF"), for the purposes of the Directive, see art.4(1)(15). See, too, Recitals 18 and 30 to the Regulation.

[799] Consultation Paper, para.52.

systems of this character.[800] Article 4(1)(h) is designed to ensure that, in the absence of a choice of law by the parties to the contract, a single law will nonetheless govern the contract.[801]

30–197 **Contract not covered by article 4(1), etc.** According to art.4(2) of the Regulation where:

> "... the contract is not covered by paragraph 1[of Art. 4] or where the elements of the contract would be covered by more than one of points (a) to (h) of paragraph 1, the contract shall be governed by the law of the country where the party required to effect the characteristic performance of the contract has his habitual residence."[802]

This choice of law rule deals with two different situations as described below.

30–198 **Contract outside article 4(1).** Where the contract is not a specific contract identified in art.4(1), the contract will be governed by the law of the country where the party required to effect the characteristic performance of the contract has his habitual residence. First, it is likely that many contracts not specifically listed, as such, in art.4(1) will be regarded as contracts for the provision of services and thus will be covered by art.4(1)(b) of the Regulation. This may be true, for example, of a contract of hire; a contract between banker and customer; a contract of loan; a contract between lawyer and client; a contract between principal and agent, unless it is a distribution contract[803]; a contract of bailment; a construction contract; a wagering contract; and, probably, a reinsurance contract[804]; a contract of guarantee; and at least certain aspects of a letter of credit.[805] Secondly, if the contract is one in which this conclusion cannot be drawn, the characteristic performance of the contract will have to be identified. There is no reason to think that the concept of characteristic performance under the Regulation will be interpreted any differently to the way it was interpreted under art.4(2) of the Rome Convention.[806] Thirdly, the applicable law in respect of such a contract will then be that of the country where the party who is to effect that performance has his habitual residence, as defined in the Regulation.[807]

30–199 **Elements of contract covered by more than one point of article 4(1).** Article 4(2) of the Regulation also supplies a choice of law rule to deal with situations where the "elements of the contract would be covered by more than one of points (a) to (h)" of art.4(1). In such a situation the contract shall be governed by the law of the country where the party required to effect the characteristic performance of the contract has his habitual residence.[808]

---

[800] Consultation Paper, para.52.
[801] Consultation Paper, para.52.
[802] See Rome I Recital 19. As to the meaning of habitual residence, see above, paras 30–164 et seq.
[803] See above, para.30–077.
[804] Rome I art.7 (below, paras 30–252 et seq.) does not apply to reinsurance contracts.
[805] See below, para.30–252.
[806] Above, paras 30–074 et seq.
[807] Above, paras 30–164 et seq.
[808] As to the meaning of habitual residence, see above, paras 30–164 et seq.

30–200 **Scope of provision.** The type of situation envisaged by the second aspect of art.4(2) is one in which the contractual relationship between the parties involves rights and obligations which are capable of being categorised as falling within more than one of the specified types of contract in art.4(1).[809] An example might be a contract of sale and distributorship,[810] which is covered by art.4(1)(a) and (b).[811] The provision takes account of the possibility that a particular contractual relationship may not fall tidily into one category or another.

30–201 **Characteristic performance.** Application of the concept of characteristic performance in this situation is not, however, without difficulty since the characteristic performance of each contract covered may be different. The point is addressed to some extent, in Recital 19 to the Regulation which states that, in such situations, "the characteristic performance of the contract should be determined having regard to its *centre of gravity*".[812] The obvious question which arises is as to how the "centre of gravity" is to be determined. It may be that it will be taken to be the performance of the substantial or principal obligations under the contract, but even if this is correct, it may not necessarily be easy to determine, in any given case, what these obligations are to be taken to be.[813] It may also be that in the case of complex contracts it will not be possible to determine the characteristic performance so that the choice of law rule contained in art.4(4)[814] will come into play.

30–202 **Applicable law.** If it is possible to determine the characteristic performance of the contract in the situation under consideration, the applicable law will be that of the country in which the party who is to effect that performance has his habitual residence, as defined in the Regulation.[815]

30–203 **Rule of displacement.** Article 4(3) of the Regulation provides that where:

> "... it is *clear* from all the circumstances of the case that the contract is manifestly more closely connected with a country other than that indicated in paragraphs 1 or 2, the law of that other country shall apply."[816]

The purpose of this provision, described in Recital 20 to the Regulation as an "escape clause", is to permit a degree of flexibility[817] in cases where application of the law indicated by art.4(1) or (2), as the case may be, would not, for various possible reasons, produce appropriate results.[818] It will be noted, however, as indicated by the words emphasised in the provision, set out above, that art.4(3) is more tightly drawn than the equivalent provision in art.4(5) of the Rome

[809] See Recital 19 to the Regulation.
[810] See *Print Concept GmbH v GEW (EC) Ltd* [2001] EWCA Civ 352, [2002] C.L.C. 352; above, paras 30–076, 30–089.
[811] Above, paras 30–190 et seq.
[812] Emphasis added.
[813] cf. *Shenavai v Kreischer* (C–266/85) [1987] E.C.R. 239.
[814] See below, paras 30–206 et seq.
[815] Above, paras 30–164 et seq.
[816] Emphasis added.
[817] See Recital 16 to the Regulation.
[818] Consultation Paper, para.51.

Convention which permitted the presumptions in art.4(2)–(4) of the Convention to be disregarded if it appeared from the circumstances as a whole that the contract was more closely connected with another country.[819] The introduction of the words "clear" and "manifestly" appear to include an intention that the rules in art.4(1) and (2) should only be displaced in the clearest of cases.[820] Nonetheless, application, even of this language, involves a margin of appreciation in the context of particular cases and how it will be applied in particular cases remains to be seen.

Relevant factors. In order to determine whether it is clear that the contract is manifestly more closely connected with a country other than that indicated in art.4(1) or (2), account may be taken of "all the circumstances of the case". These would include, but are not necessarily limited to, factors which were regarded as relevant for this purpose in cases falling within the Rome Convention.[821] More specifically, Recital 20 to the Regulation states that "account should be taken inter alia of whether the contract in question has a very close relationship with another contract or contracts". The advice in this Recital may be of particular importance in respect of related contracts such as letters of credit or guarantees where it is of commercial importance that a single law be applied to a transaction rather than having different laws applying to the component parts of the transaction.[822] **30–204**

Applicable law. Where art.4(3) operates to displace the rules in art.4(1) and (2), the applicable law will be the law of the country with which the contract is manifestly more closely connected. **30–205**

Residual rule. Article 4(4) of the Regulation supplies what might be called a residual choice of law rule in the following terms: **30–206**

> "Where the applicable law cannot be determined pursuant to paragraphs 1 or 2, the contract shall be governed by the law of the country with which it is most closely connected."

The effect of this rule is explained in Recital 21 to the Regulation.

> "In the absence of choice, where the applicable law cannot be determined either on the basis of the fact that the contract can be categorised as one of the specified types or as being the law of the country of habitual residence of the party required to effect the characteristic performance of the contract, the contract should be governed by the law of the country with which it is most closely connected."

---

819 Above, paras 30–090 et seq.

820 This would be consistent with the policy of casting art.4(1) and (2) in the form of rules, rather than presumptions.

821 Above, paras 30–090 et seq.

822 Consultation Paper, para.54. cf. *Bank of Baroda v Vysya Bank Ltd* [1994] 2 Lloyd's Rep. 87; *PT Pan Indonesia Bank Ltd Tbk v Marconi Communications International Ltd* [2005] EWCA Civ 422, [2005] 2 All E.R (Comm) 325 (letters of credit); *Samcrete Egypt Engineers and Contractors SAE v Land Rover Exports Ltd* [2002] EWCA Civ 2019, [2002] C.L.C. 533, (guarantee); above, para.30–091.

This provision will prove of importance in relation to a contract which is not specified in art.4(1), or which is a complex contract made up of more than one contract specified in art.4(1), the characteristic performance of which cannot be determined under art.4(2). More obviously, it will be of importance in relation to contracts which do not have a characteristic performance, e.g. barter or exchange.[823]

30–207 **Relevant factors.** Article 4(4) does not in terms place any limits on the factors which may be taken into account in determining the law of the country with which the contract is most closely connected. Although all will depend on the particular circumstances of the case, generally, factors regarded for this purpose under art.4(5) of the Rome Convention may surely be taken into account.[824] More specifically, Recital 21 to the Regulation states that "account should be taken, inter alia, of whether the contract in question has a very close relationship with another contract or contracts". Article 4(4) clearly involves a margin of appreciation, depending on the circumstances of the case, as to the weight to be attributed to the various factors involved.[825]

30–208 **Applicable law.** Where art.4(4) of the Regulation is applicable, the applicable law is, obviously, the law of the country with which the contract is most closely connected.

(f) *Contracts of Carriage*

30–209 **Background.** As explained earlier in this Chapter, the Rome Convention, with one exception, provided no special rules relating to contracts of carriage.[826] Thus, party autonomy was permitted under the general rule in art.3 of the Rome Convention.[827] In the absence of a choice of law, art.4(4) of the Convention established a special presumption relating to contracts for the carriage of goods,[828] which presumption could be displaced by reference to art.4(5) of the Convention. Article 3 applied also to permit party autonomy in relation to contracts for the carriage of passengers.[829] In the absence of a choice of law, the relevant presumption was, in relation to a contract for the carriage of passengers, that stated in art.4(2) of the Convention, which would normally lead to the application of the law of the carrier's habitual residence, central administration, principal place of business or place of business, as the case may be,[830] but this presumption could, of course, be displaced by reference to art.4(5) of the Convention.[831] The choice of law rules for consumer contracts contained in art.5 of the Convention did not apply to contracts of carriage, subject to an exception

[823] cf. above, para.30–076.
[824] Above, paras 30–090 et seq.
[825] cf. above, para.30–203.
[826] Above, paras 30–085 et seq.
[827] Above, paras 30–047 et seq.
[828] Above, paras 30–085 et seq.
[829] Above, paras 30–047 et seq.
[830] Above, paras 30–071 et seq.
[831] Above, paras 30–088 et seq.

for so called package tours.[832] In contrast, at least generally, to the position under the Convention, art.5 of the Rome I Regulation provides more specific choice of law rules for contracts of carriage, the effect of which is explained in the following paragraphs.

Structure and scope of article 5. Article 5 of the Rome I Regulation applies to determine the law applicable to a contract of carriage of goods and to a contract for the carriage of passengers. In the absence of any contrary indication in the provision, it also seems to apply to carriage irrespective of the means of transport involved.[833] Article 5(1) is concerned with the choice of law rules applicable to contracts for the carriage of goods. It supplies a rule, not unlike the presumption contained in art.4(4) of the Rome Convention,[834] and based, broadly, on a combination of connecting factors, to determine the law applicable to the contract in the absence of a choice of law satisfying art.3 of the Regulation. Article 5(2) deals with the choice of law rules applicable to a contract for the carriage of passengers. This allows a more limited form of freedom to choose the applicable law designed to achieve an adequate level of protection of passengers.[835] In the absence of a choice of law, which complies with the provision, the determination of the applicable law is based, broadly, on a combination of connecting factors and not on the approach involved in the more general presumption, applicable to a variety of contracts, which is found in art.4(2) of the Rome Convention.[836] Article 5(3) of the Regulation provides a rule of displacement (or "escape clause") allowing displacement of the law of the country indicated, in the absence of choice, by art.5(1) or (2), where it is clear from all the circumstances of the case that the contract is manifestly more closely connected with another country. In such cases the applicable law will be the law of the other country.[837] A contract of carriage (with one limited exception) is not a consumer contract for the purposes of the Regulation.[838] Where, however, the contract is a mixed contract for the carriage of goods and passengers it is conceivable, that, in the absence of a choice of law governing the contract as a whole, the application of art.5(1) and (2) might result in the contract having two different applicable laws.[839] 30–210

International conventions. Many aspects of international transport are governed by international conventions to which Member States may be parties.[840] As pointed out above,[841] art.25(1) of the Regulation shall not prejudice the application of international conventions to which one or more Member States are parties 30–211

[832] Above, paras 30–093 et seq.

[833] cf. above, para.30–085.

[834] Above, paras 30–085 et seq.

[835] See Recital 32 to the Regulation.

[836] Above, paras 30–073 et seq.

[837] cf. above, para.30–088.

[838] Rome I art.6(4)(b), discussed below, para.30–235. The exception is in relation to "package tours". See too Recital 32.

[839] cf. above, para.30–199.

[840] See Vol II, Chs 35, 36; *Dicey, Morris and Collins*, paras 33–250 et seq., 33–286 et seq.

[841] See para.30–137.

at the time of the adoption of the Regulation[842] and "which lay down conflict-of-laws rules relating to contractual obligations". Most conventions concerning international transport contain uniform substantive law rules rather than conflict of laws rules[843] and thus it would seem that these conventions continue to apply, irrespective of the Regulation.[844] Rules contained in international conventions may also be regarded as overriding mandatory provisions of the law of the forum, applicable by virtue of art.9(2) of the Regulation.[845]

30–212 **Carriage of goods.** Article 5(1) of the Regulation provides as follows:

> "To the extent that the law applicable to a contract for the carriage of goods has not been chosen in accordance with Article 3, the law applicable shall be the law of the country of habitual residence of the carrier, provided that the place of receipt or the place of delivery or the habitual residence of the consignor is also situated in that country. If those requirements are not met, the law of the country where the place of delivery as agreed by the parties is situated shall apply."

The law applicable in the absence of choice under art.5(1) may be displaced by reference to the rule of displacement contained in art.5(3).[846]

30–213 **Meaning of contract for carriage of goods.** The meaning of "contract for the carriage of goods" is not defined in the text of the Regulation. However, Recital 22 to the Regulation states that in this regard:

> "... no change is intended with respect to Article 4(4), third sentence, of the Rome Convention. Consequently, single voyage charter parties and other contracts the main purpose of which is the carriage of goods should be treated as contracts for the carriage of goods."

One may deduce from this that "contract for the carriage of goods" has the same meaning under the Regulation as it has under the Convention, as discussed earlier in this Chapter.[847]

30–214 **Choice of law by the parties.** In accordance with art.3(1) of the Regulation, the parties to a contract for the carriage of goods are free to choose the law

---

[842] i.e. July 24, 2008, the date of entry into force, as opposed to December 17, 2009, the date of application. See arts 25–29.

[843] See references in fn.215.

[844] It may also be doubted whether conventions establishing uniform substantive rules, as opposed to choice of law rules, fall within art.25(2) where it is provided (see above, para.30–137) that the Regulation shall, as between Member States, take precedence over conventions concluded exclusively between two or more of them in so far as such conventions concern matters governed by the Regulation. This is because the Regulation is concerned with choice of applicable law, rather than uniform substantive law. And see Recital 41.

[845] cf. *The Hollandia* [1983] 1 A.C. 565; above, para.30–068; *Dicey, Morris and Collins*, para.33–286.

[846] Below, para.30–360.

[847] Above, paras 30–085 et seq. For more detail see *Dicey, Morris and Collins*, paras 33–265 et seq.

applicable to it subject to any constraints on that freedom imposed by other provisions of the Regulation.[848] The choice will often be made expressly,[849] but if it is not it will be necessary to enquire whether a choice has been clearly demonstrated by the terms of the contract or the circumstances of the case. The use of arbitration clauses, often contained in standard forms intimately linked to the law of a particular country may well be relevant factors,[850] but the outcome in any given case will ultimately depend on the particular circumstances of the case.

Applicable law in the absence of choice. To the extent that the applicable law has not been chosen in accordance with art.3, art.5(1) supplies choice of law rules for determining the applicable law. These consist of what may be called a "general rule" and a "residual rule". 30–215

General rule. Generally, the applicable law will be the law of the country of the habitual residence[851] of the carrier,[852] provided that the place of receipt or the place of delivery or the habitual residence[853] of the consignor[854] is *also* situated in that country. The "place of receipt" would seem to mean the place where the carrier receives the goods from the consignor.[855] The "place of delivery" would seem to mean the place where the carrier is required to deliver the goods.[856] Although it is not explicitly stated in the Regulation, it would also seem that the place of receipt and place of delivery are those agreed at the time of the conclusion of the contract.[857] 30–216

Meaning of "carrier". The meaning of "carrier" is not defined in the text of the Regulation. However, Recital 22 states that: 30–217

> ". . . the term 'carrier' should refer to the party to the contract who undertakes to carry the goods, whether or not he performs the carriage itself."

This reflects the position under the Rome Convention.[858]

---

848 Above, paras 30–060 et seq.

849 cf. *OT Africa Line Ltd v Magic Sportwear Corp* [2005] EWCA Civ 710, [2005] 2 Lloyd's Rep. 170.

850 See Giuliano-Lagarde Report, p.17; *Dicey, Morris and Collins*, para.33–268. See also Recital 12 (exclusive jurisdiction clause); above, para.30–174.

851 As to the meaning of which, see above, paras 30–164 et seq. Other concepts mentioned in art.5 which are not specifically defined should be given an autonomous meaning.

852 As to the meaning of which, see below, para.30–217.

853 As defined above, paras 30–164 et seq.

854 As to the meaning of which see below, para.30–218.

855 This expression seems to correspond to "place of loading" in art.4(4) of the Rome Convention. See above, para.30–085.

856 This expression seems to correspond to "place of discharge" in art.4(4) of the Rome Convention. See above, para.30–085.

857 cf. Giuliano-Lagarde Report, p.22.

858 See above, para.30–085.

30–218 **Meaning of "consignor".** The meaning of consignor, also, is not defined in the text of the Regulation. Recital 22, however, explains that "the term "consignor" should refer to any person who enters into a contract of carriage with the carrier".[859]

30–219 **Residual rule.** If the requirements in art.5(1), referred to above are not met, art.5(1) supplies a residual rule to the effect that "the law of the country where the place of delivery as agreed by the parties shall apply". It is not clear whether the relevant place of delivery agreed by the parties is that agreed upon at the time the contract is concluded or whether, if the parties subsequently agree on a different place of delivery, that different place may be the relevant place. Consistency with the general rule suggests the place originally agreed upon, but this conclusion might be thought to be unrealistic. Alternatively a subsequent agreement to change the place of delivery may be a relevant factor in determining whether the residual rule (or indeed the general rule) may be displaced by reference to art.5(3) of the Regulation.[860]

30–220 **Rule of displacement.** Article 5(3) provides that where:

> ". . . it is clear from all the circumstances of the case that the contract, in the absence of a choice of law is manifestly more closely connected with a country other than that indicated in paragraphs 1 or 2, the law of that other country shall apply."

This rule of displacement is formulated in terms which are to the same effect as those contained in art.4(3) of the Regulation. The rule attempts to address the need for certainty (as established by art.5(1)) and the need for flexibility in appropriate cases.[861]

30–221 **Carriage of passengers.** The Rome Convention contained no specific rule relating to contracts for the carriage of passengers, and dealt with the question through the application of the general rules contained in arts 3, 4(2) and 4(5) of the Convention.[862] In contrast art.5(2), in conjunction with art.5(3), of the Regulation seeks to take specific account of this matter.

30–222 **Principles.** Article 5(2) of the Regulation addresses two questions, namely the freedom to choose the applicable law and the question of the law applicable in the absence of choice. The provision restricts the power of the parties to choose the governing law by limiting the laws which may be chosen. This is with a view to ensuring an adequate level of protection for passengers.[863] Determination of the law applicable in the absence of choice is based on what can be called

---

[859] As to the position under the Rome Convention, see above, para.30–085.

[860] There seems to be no reason why events subsequent to the conclusion of the contract should not be taken into account in the application of art.5(3) and also, possibly, in the application of art.5(1). cf. above, para.30–054; *Dicey, Morris and Collins*, para.33–273.

[861] See Rome I Recital 16.

[862] Above, para.30–209. A contract for the carriage of passengers was not a consumer contract for the purposes of art.5 of the Rome Convention: art.5(4)(a) of the Convention: above, para.30–093.

[863] Rome I Recital 32 where it also stated (as it is in art.6(4)(b) of the Regulation itself) that art.6, dealing with consumer contracts, does not generally apply to contracts of carriage. And see Consultation Paper, para.57.

a general rule establishing a combination of connecting factors and what may be called a residual rule, applicable if such factors are not present. Both the general rule and the residual rule are subject to displacement under art.5(3) of the Regulation.

Choice of law by the parties. The principle of party autonomy in the context of contracts for the carriage of passengers is found in the second paragraph of art.5(2). This provides that the: 30–223

> "... parties may choose as the law applicable to the contract in accordance with Article 3 only the law of the country where: (a) the passenger has his habitual residence[864]; or (b) the carrier has his habitual residence[865]; or (c) the carrier has his place of central administration[866]; or (d) the place of departure is situated; or (e) the place of destination is situated."

The provisions at (d) and (e) do not require comment. Some brief remarks may usefully be made on the provisions at (a), (b) and (c).

Habitual residence of passenger. As pointed out earlier in this section, art.19(1) of the Regulation defines the habitual residence of a natural person acting in the course of his business activity as his principal place of business.[867] Where, however, as will commonly be the case, a passenger is not so acting, then the habitual residence of that natural person will have to be identified by reference to general principles.[868] 30–224

Habitual residence and central administration of carrier. Paragraph two of art.5(2) refers, in points (b) and (c), to the habitual residence and central administration of the carrier[869] as separate places, the laws of which may be chosen to govern the contract. At first sight this appears curious since art.19(1) defines the habitual residence of companies and other bodies corporate or unincorporated (which the carrier will normally be) as the place of central administration.[870] Article 19(2) of the Regulation, however, provides that where: 30–225

> "... the contract is concluded in the course of the operations of a branch, agency, or any other establishment, or if under the contract, performance is the responsibility of such a branch, agency or establishment, the place where the branch agency or any other establishment is located shall be treated as the place of habitual residence."[871]

In relation to an international carrier with branches, etc. in many different countries, it would be possible to choose, as the governing law, the country in

---

[864] See below, para.30–224.
[865] See below, para.30–224.
[866] See below, para.30–225.
[867] Above, para.30–167.
[868] Above, para.30–168. The relevant time for determining habitual residence is the time of conclusion of the contract: Rome I art.19(3).
[869] Carrier would seem to bear the same meaning in Rome I art.5(2) as it bears in art.5(1). See above, para.30–217.
[870] See above, para.30–165.
[871] See above, para.30–166.

which the branch, etc. is situated if the passenger's ticket is issued through that branch, etc. This could lead to a proliferation of possibly applicable laws in respect of contracts of passengers in relation to the same carriage.[872] Point (c) of art.5(2) avoids this outcome by focussing on the place of central administration only, usually the place where the head office is situated, thus implicitly excluding the application of art.19(2) of the Regulation.[873] Point (c) of art.5(2), of course, will cover situations where the ticket is issued through the carrier's place of central administration, i.e. the head office.[874]

30–226 **Making the choice.** Any choice of the laws of the countries available under art.5(2) must, of course, satisfy the requirements of art.3 of the Regulation.

30–227 **Applicable law in the absence of choice.** To the extent that the applicable law has not been chosen, as described in the previous paragraphs (which is perhaps unlikely in the case of a contract for the carriage of passengers) art.5(2) contains a choice of law rule to cover the situation. This choice of law rule may be broken up into what might be described as a "general rule" and a "residual rule".

30–228 **General rule.** Article 5(2) first stipulates that the applicable law, in the absence of choice:

> ". . . shall be the law of the country where the passenger has his habitual residence,[875] provided that either the place of departure or the place of destination is in that country."

This rule is, it seems, designed to reflect the interests of passengers.

30–229 **Residual rule.** If the requirements of the general rule are not met, art.5(2) goes on to provide that "the law of the country where the carrier has his habitual residence shall apply". For these purposes, it appears that habitual residence means what it is defined to mean in art.19 of the Regulation[876] and, thus, art.19(2) will also apply and is not excluded, as earlier discussed.[877]

30–230 **Rule of displacement.** The law applicable in the absence of choice under art.5(2) may be displaced by reference to art.5(3) where it is clear from all the circumstances of the case that the contract is manifestly more closely connected with a country other than that found to be applicable under art.5(2) in which case the law of the other country will apply. As is the case with art.5(1) and art.5(3), this serves the needs of certainty (supplied by art.5(2)) and the need for flexibility in appropriate cases.

---

872 Consultation Paper, para.59.

873 Consultation Paper, para.59. One suspects that, normally, the carrier's law will be chosen in the contract.

874 Consultation Paper, para.59.

875 As defined above, para.30–224.

876 Above, paras 30–165 et seq.

877 Above, para.30–225.

(g) *Consumer Contracts*

Background. Article 5 of the Rome Convention made particular provision for "certain consumer contracts".[878] Generally, such contracts (which were somewhat narrowly defined and from the category of which certain types of contract were excluded) were governed by the law chosen by the parties subject to the limitation that a choice of law could not have the effect of depriving the consumer of the protection of the mandatory rules of the law of the country in which the consumer had his habitual residence in certain (narrowly defined) situations.[879] In the absence of choice, the contract was governed by the law of the consumer's habitual residence if one of the situations where a choice of law would be controlled by reference to mandatory rules was present, but in other cases the applicable law in the absence of choice was governed by the general rule in art.4 of the Convention.[880] It was seen in the earlier discussion of art.5 of the Convention that it was particularly difficult to apply the provision to contracts concluded "on-line" and also that the provision supplied a somewhat limited degree of protection to consumers.[881] Article 6 of the Regulation makes fresh provision for consumer contracts endeavouring to take account, amongst other things, of the effect of electronic commerce on consumer transactions and the need for increased levels of consumer protection.[882] 30–231

Structure of article 6. Article 6(1) of the Regulation deals, firstly, with the definition of contracts to which art.6 applies,[883] excluding certain contracts which are not covered by art.6(1) as a result of art.6(4) of the Regulation,[884] and also stipulates that where art.6(1) applies the contract will be governed by the law of the country in which the consumer is habitually resident.[885] Article 6(2) allows the parties to choose the applicable law, but restricts that capacity by reference to provisions which the law of the country which would be applicable in the absence of choice, which cannot be derogated from by agreement.[886] If the requirements of art.6(1)(a) or (b) are not fulfilled and the contract is not excluded by virtue of art.6(4), the applicable law will be determined by art.6(3) of the Regulation.[887] There is no escape clause, as such, based on the principle that a contract within art.6 may be governed by the law of another country, when it is clear that the contract is manifestly more closely connected with a country other than that the law of which would be applicable under other provisions of art.6. The article thus seeks, as will be seen below, to achieve the purpose of protecting consumers. In addition, art.6(1) seeks to deal with consumer transactions involving electronic commerce.[888] 30–232

---

[878] See above, paras 30–093 et seq.
[879] Above, paras 30–094 et seq.
[880] Above, para.30–107.
[881] Above, paras 30–095 et seq.
[882] See Recitals 23 and 24 to the Regulation.
[883] Below, paras 30–239 et seq.
[884] Below, paras 30–233 et seq.
[885] Below, paras 30–239 et seq.
[886] Below, para.30–249.
[887] Below, para.30–249.
[888] Recital 24 to the Regulation.

30–233 **Specific exclusions.** Before considering the general scope of, and the provisions of, art.6 of the Regulation, it is necessary to draw attention to certain types of contract which are specifically excluded from the scope of the article, by art.6(4).

30–234 **Contract for the supply of services.** The special rules in art.6 do not apply, first, to contracts for the supply of services where the services are to be supplied to the consumer exclusively in a country other than that in which he has his habitual residence.[889] This reflects the exclusion of such contracts from art.5 of the Rome Convention.[890] The law applicable to such contracts will thus be determined by art.3 or 4 of the Regulation, as the case may be.[891]

30–235 **Contract of carriage.** Secondly, art.6. does not apply to:

> "... a contract of carriage other than a contract relating to package travel within the meaning of Council Directive 90/314/EEC of June 13, 1990 on package travel, package holidays and package tours."[892]

Unless, therefore, the contract of carriage relates to package travel, art.6 will not apply and the law applicable to the contract of carriage will be determined in accordance with art.5 of the Regulation.[893] Broadly speaking, a contract relates to package travel if it is a contract which, for an inclusive price, provides for a combination of travel and accommodation.[894] This exclusion generally reflects the position under the Rome Convention.[895]

30–236 **Immovable property, etc.** Thirdly, art.6(4)(c) of the Regulation excludes a:

> "... contract relating to a right in rem in immovable property other than a contract relating to the right to use immovable properties on a timeshare basis within the meaning of Directive 94/47/EC."[896]

Unless, therefore, the contract relates to the right to use immovable property on a timeshare basis, as defined in the Directive,[897] art.6 will not apply and the applicable law in such circumstances will be determined in accordance with art.3 of the Regulation, or, as the case may be, art.4 of the Regulation, in particular art.4(1)(c) and (d).[898]

---

[889] Rome I art.6(4)(a). As to the meaning of habitual residence, see above, paras 30–164 et seq.
[890] art.5(4)(b) of the Convention; above, para.30–093.
[891] Above, paras 30–170 et seq.
[892] Directive 90/314 on package travel [1990] OJ L158/59 art.6(4)(b). The Directive is implemented in the United Kingdom by the Package Travel, Package Holidays and Package Tours Regulations 1992 (SI 1992/3288).
[893] Above, paras 30–209 et seq.
[894] cf. Rome Convention art.5(4)(b) and (5); above, para.30–093.
[895] Above, para.30–093.
[896] Directive 94/47 [1994] OJ L280/83 implemented in the United Kingdom in Timeshare Regulations 1997 (SI 1997/1081), amending Timeshare Act 1992. See Recital 27 of the Rome I Regulation.
[897] See *Dicey, Morris and Collins on the Conflict of Laws*, 14th edn (2006), paras 33–233, 33–244 et seq.
[898] Above, paras 30–170 et seq.

Rights and obligations constituting a financial instrument, etc. Fourthly, art.6(4)(d) excludes the choice of law rules in art.6 in relation to: 30–237

> "... rights and obligations which constitute a financial instrument and rights and obligations constituting the terms and conditions governing the issuance or offer to the public and public take-over bids of transferable securities, and the subscription and redemption of units in collective investment undertakings, in so far as these activities do not constitute provision of a financial service."

The scope of this exclusion is explained in Recitals to the Regulation. Financial services such as investment services and ancillary services provided by a professional to a consumer, as referred to in sections A and B of Annex I to Directive 2004/29 (MiFID),[899] and contracts for the sale of units in collective investment undertakings, whether or not covered by Council Directive 85/611 on the co-ordination of laws, regulations and administrative provisions relating to collective investment in transferable securities (UCITS)[900] should be subject to art.6 of the Regulation. Consequently, when a reference is made to terms and conditions governing the issuance or offer to the public of transferable securities[901] or to the subscription and redemption of units in collective investment undertakings, that reference should *include* all aspects binding the issuer or the offeror to the consumer, but should *not include* those aspects involving provision of financial services.[902] Recital 28 states that it is important to ensure that rights and obligations which constitute a financial instrument[903] are not covered by the general rule applicable to consumer contracts, as that could lead to different laws being applicable to each of the instruments issued, therefore changing their nature and preventing their fungible trading and offering. Further, where ever such instruments are issued or offered, the contractual relationship between the issuer or the offeror and the consumer should not necessarily be subject to the

---

899 Directive 2004/29 [2004] OJ L145/1. Very broadly, s.A covers: reception and transmission of orders in relation to financial instruments; execution of orders on behalf of clients; dealing on own account; portfolio management; investment advice; underwriting and/or placement of financial instruments on a firm commitment basis; placing of financial instruments without a firm commitment basis; and the operation of multilateral trading facilities. In general terms s.B covers: safekeeping and administration of financial instruments and related matters; granting credits and loans to an investor in certain cases in relation to a transaction involving a financial instrument; advice to undertakings on capital structure, industrial strategy, and related matters and advice and services relating to mergers and acquisitions; foreign exchange services connected with the provision of investment services; investment research, financial analysis and other recommendations relating to transactions in financial instruments; services relating to underwriting; and certain investment services and activities related to derivatives. As to the meaning of "financial instrument", see below, fn.903.

900 Directive 85/611 on the co-ordination of laws relating to collective investment in transferable securities [1985] OJ L375/3, as amended by Directive 2005/1 [2005] OJ L79/9.

901 According to Recital 30 "transferable securities" are instruments referred to in Directive 2004/39 (MiDiD) art.4. These are, broadly, defined in art.4(18) as: shares and other securities equivalent to shares; bonds or other forms of securitised debt; and any other securities giving the right to acquire or sell any such transferable securities.

902 Rome I Recital 26. And see Consultation Paper, para.66.

903 According to Recital 3 "financial instruments" are instruments referred to in art.4 of Directive 2004/39 (MiFID). According to art.4(17) such instruments are those specified in Annex C to the Directive. Very broadly, these are: transferable securities; money market instruments, units in collective investment undertakings; certain options, futures, swaps, forward rate agreements and derivative contracts; derivative instruments for the transfer of credit risk; and financial contracts for differences.

mandatory application of the law of the consumer's habitual residence (a principal feature of the choice of law rules in art.6[904]) as there is a need to ensure uniformity in the terms and conditions of an issuance or offer.[905] Recital 29 states that for the purposes of the Regulation, references to rights and obligations constituting the terms and conditions governing the issuance, offers to the public or public take-over bids of transferable securities and references to the subscriptions and redemption of units in collective investment undertakings should include the terms governing amongst other things, the allocation of securities or units, rights in the event of over-subscription, withdrawal rights and similar matters in the context of the offer as well as those matters referred to in arts 10, 11, 12 and 13 of the Regulation,[906] thus ensuring that all relevant contractual aspects of an offer binding the issuer or the offeror to the consumer are governed by a single law.[907]

30–238 **Contract concluded within system falling within article 4(1)(9).** A contract falling within the scope of art.4(1)(h) of the Regulation,[908] is, finally, excluded from the scope of art.6.[909] The rationale for excluding contracts concluded within such multilateral systems is to ensure that the law of the country of habitual residence of the consumer will not interfere with the rules applicable to contracts concluded within such systems or with the operator of such systems.[910]

30–239 **Scope of, and general rule in, article 6.** The overall scope of art.6 and the general rule which it establishes are dealt with in art.6(1) which provides as follows:

> "Without prejudice to Articles 5 and 7, a contract concluded by a natural person for a purpose which can be regarded as being outside his trade or profession ("the consumer") with another person acting in the exercise of his trade or profession ("the professional") shall be governed by the law of the country where the consumer has his habitual residence, provided that the professional:
>
> (a) pursues his commercial or professional activities in the country where the consumer has his habitual residence, or
> (b) by any means directs such activities to that country or to several countries including that country,
>
> and the contract falls within the scope of such activities."

It will be noted that, subject to the excluded matters referred to earlier, to which must be added, contracts of insurance covered by art.7,[911] there is no particular

---

[904] See below, paras 30–239 et seq.
[905] Rome I Recital 28.
[906] Below, paras 30–304 et seq.
[907] See also Consultation paper, para.66. There is no exclusion equivalent to art.6(4)(d) of the Rome I Regulation in the Rome Convention.
[908] Above, para.30–196.
[909] Rome I art.6(4)(e)
[910] Rome I Recital 28. Recital 31 states that nothing in the Regulation shall prejudice the operation of a formal arrangement designated as a system under art.2(a) of Directive 98/26 on settlement finality in payment and securities settlement systems [1998] OJ L166/45. And see Consultation Paper, para.67.
[911] See also Rome I Recital 32.

restriction on scope based on category of the contract.[912] It is sufficient to bring art.6 into operation that the contract be concluded within the principles established in the provision.

Contract between consumer and professional. First, to be covered by art.6, the contract must be concluded by a consumer, who must be a natural person, for a purpose which can be regarded as being outside his trade or profession, with a professional, who may be a natural or legal person, but who must be acting in the course of his trade or profession.[913] This part (and other parts) of art.6(1) will, doubtless, be given an autonomous meaning which, in so far as possible, will be consistent with that given to similar provisions in art.15(1) of the Judgments Regulation[914] and which may reflect the fact that the consumer is the weaker party to the contract.[915] Following the approach of the European Court to the Judgments Regulation, it is possible that: (a) the provision will not apply to a contract which a natural person has concluded with a view to pursuing a trade in the future[916]; (b) the provision will not apply to a claim by an assignee of a consumer, where the assignee is acting in the course of its trade or professional activity[917]; and (c) that the provision will not apply where a natural person concludes a contract for purposes which are in part within, and in part outside his trade or profession, unless the trade, or professional purpose is so limited as to be negligible in the context of the overall supply.[918] 30–240

Habitual residence. If the contract falls within the scope of the principle identified in the previous paragraph, the law applicable to the contract will be the law of the consumer's habitual residence[919] provided one of the additional requirements in art.6(1)(a) or (b) are met. "Habitual residence" for these purposes, will have to be determined by reference to general principles since art.19(1) of the Regulation only defines the habitual residence of a natural person acting in the course of a business activity[920] and a natural person so acting cannot be a consumer. 30–241

"Pursues his commercial or professional activities", etc. Article 6(1)(a) will lead to the application of the law of the consumer's habitual residence if the professional pursues his commercial or professional activities in the country[921] where the consumer has his habitual residence. This provision would appear to 30–242

[912] cf. The position under the Rome Convention, above, para.30–093.

[913] cf. the Rome Convention art.5(1), above para.30–093.

[914] See Recitals 7 and 24 to the Regulation.

[915] See Recital 23 to the Regulation.

[916] See *Benincasa v Dentalkit Srl* (C–269/95) [1997] E.C.R. I–3767.

[917] See *Shearson Lehman Hutton Inc v TVB* (C–89/91) [1993] E.C.R. I–139.

[918] See *Gruber v Bay Wa AG* (C–464/01) [2005] E.C.R. I–439, [2006] 2 W.L.R. 205. See also *Gabriel v Schlank & Schick GmbH* (C–96/00) [2002] E.C.R. I–6367; *Verein für Konsumenteninformation v Henkel* (C–167/00) [2002] E.C.R I–8111; *Standard Bank London Ltd v Apostolakis* [2000] I.L. Pr. 766; *Standard Bank London Ltd v Apostolakis (No.2)* [2001] Lloyd's Rep. Bank. 240.

[919] And see Rome I art.6(2), below, para.30–250. The law of the consumer's habitual residence will also govern the formal validity of the contract: see art.11(4), below, para.30–320.

[920] Above, paras 30–167 et seq.

[921] Which need not be a Member State.

cover cases where the professional pursues his commercial or professional activities directly in the country of the consumer's habitual residence by carrying out those activities there at a place of business there. It would also seem to cover cases where the professional pursues the relevant activities in the country where the consumer is habitually resident through a branch, agency or other establishment which is situated in that country.[922] It is also necessary that the contract falls within the scope of relevant activities pursued in the country where the consumer is habitually resident.[923] Article 6(1)(a) of the Rome 1 Regulation is inspired by art.15(1)(c) of the Judgments Regulation concerned with jurisdiction in respect of consumer contracts, and, so far as possible, should be interpreted consistently with that provision.[924]

30–243 **"By any means directs such activities", etc.** Article 6(1)(b) will lead to the application of the law of the consumer's habitual residence if the professional by "any means directs his professional or commercial activities to that country or to several countries including that country" and the contract falls within the scope of such activities.[925] This provision is also inspired by art.15(1)(c) of the Judgments Regulation and should, so far as possible, be interpreted consistently with that article.[926] This aspect of art.6(1) is designed to take account of the development of distance selling techniques, particularly techniques involving electronic commerce.[927] The latter form of technique could not realistically be accommodated within the provisions of art.5 of the Rome Convention.[928] The key concept in art.6(1)(b) is that of "directs such activities", an expression which requires further elucidation. It will be convenient to consider "traditional" techniques for directing activities and those involving electronic commerce, separately.

30–244 **"Traditional" techniques.** Traditional distance techniques would include specific invitations to a consumer to purchase[929] which invitation is received by the consumer in the country where he is habitually resident. Such an invitation may be by mail order or by door-step selling.[930] Advertising in the country of the consumer's habitual residence (even if accompanied by advertising in other countries) would also be covered: such advertising might be through general dissemination in the press or by radio, television or mail order catalogue.[931] The notion of advertising may also cover offers made to a consumer in person through an agent or door-to-door salesman, if or to the extent that, this technique

[922] cf. art.19(3) of the Regulation, above, para.30–116. For these purposes, "agency" ought to include appointment of a commercial agent who receives orders, on behalf of the professional, in the country where the consumer is habitually resident: cf. Rome Convention art.5(2), second indent, above, para.30–094. See also *Ingmar GB Ltd v Eaton Leonard Technologies Inc* (C–381/98) [2000] E.C.R. I–9305; but contrast *Blanckaert and Willems PVBA v Trost* (139/80) [1981] E.C.R. 819 (independent commercial agent not an "agency" for the purposes of art.5(5)).

[923] See below, para.30–248.

[924] See Recitals 7 and 24 of the Rome I Regulation.

[925] See below, para.30–248.

[926] See Recitals 7 and 24 to the Rome I Regulation.

[927] Recital 24 to the Regulation.

[928] Above, paras 30–095 et seq.

[929] cf. Rome Convention art.5(2), first indent, above, paras 30–094, 30–096.

[930] *Dicey, Morris and Collins*, para.11–367.

[931] *Dicey, Morris and Collins*, para.11–367.

does not fall within art.6(1)(a).[932] It also seems that the notion of directing activities by such means involves some specific intent to advertise in the consumer's country of habitual residence[933] an intention the existence of which may be derived from the nature of the publication in an appropriate case.[934] It will be noted that art.6(1)(a) of the Regulation does not require, unlike the position under the Rome Convention,[935] that the consumer take in the country of his habitual residence all the steps necessary on his part for the conclusion of the contract.

Techniques involving electronic commerce. It has already been pointed out that it was only possible to accommodate developments in electronic commerce within art.5 of the Rome Convention with considerable artifice.[936] It was, in particular, the need to take account of these developments that prompted art.6(1) of the Regulation.[937] The more general and flexible character of art.6(1)(b) enables electronic techniques to be accommodated within art.6 with greater ease. However, the precise way in which the requirement of "directs" activities applies in this context is uncertain,[938] although the following suggestions may be made. 30–245

Electronic mail. Where a professional sends specific invitations or advertisements to a particular consumer or group of consumers in the country of habitual residence, there seems little doubt that art.6 will come into play provided a contract is concluded as a consequence.[939] This will be so whether or not the contract is concluded by traditional means (e.g. by a response from the consumer by letter or facsimile) or "on-line".[940] 30–246

Websites. It would seem clear that promotional material available on a professional's website can amount, in principle, to advertising.[941] More difficult, however, is when the availability of this material in the country of the consumer's habitual residence will be a consequence of the professional directing activities to that country. There is some (but not much) guidance in Recital 24 which invokes a joint declaration by the Council and Commission on art.15(1)(c) of the Judgments Regulation. According to this[942]: 30–247

---

932 Above, para.30–242.

933 cf. Rome Convention art.5(2), first indent; Giuliano-Lagarde Report, p.24; above paras 30–094, 30–096.

934 See preceding note. Thus, for example, such an intention could be derived when an advertisement is contained in a European edition of an American newspaper intended to circulate in European countries, including that where the consumer is habitually resident, but might not be so derived from the mere availability of an American newspaper (with no European edition) in such countries. It seems that so-called "cross-border excursion selling" (above, para.30–094) will also be covered.

935 Above, para.30–094.

936 Above, paras 30–095 et seq.

937 Recital 24 to the Regulation.

938 Consultation Paper, para.64.

939 See below, para.30–248.

940 See Explanatory Memorandum to the Commission's original Proposal, p.7. The difficulties, in this respect, in the application of the Rome Convention (above, paras 30–095 et seq.) will not arise.

941 For the Rome Convention, see above, para.30–097.

942 The passages of the joint declaration quoted in this paragraph are set out in Recital 24 to the Regulation.

> "... for Article 15(1)(c) to be applicable it is not sufficient for an undertaking to target its activities at the Member State of the consumer's residence, or at a number of Member States including that Member State; a contract must also be concluded within the framework of its activities."[943]

Further, the declaration also states that the:

> "... mere fact that an internet site is accessible is not sufficient for Article 15 to be applicable[944] although a factor will be that this internet site solicits the conclusion of distance contracts and that a contract has actually been concluded at a distance, by whatever means. In this respect, the language or currency which a website uses does not constitute a relevant factor."[945]

From these remarks it is possible to draw the following conclusions, as regards art.6(1)(b). First, the concept of targeted activity only becomes relevant where a contract is concluded at a distance (by whatever means) as a result of those activities.[946] Secondly, the website need not necessarily be an interactive one: if the site invites consumers to mail or fax orders then it aims to conclude distance contracts.[947] Thirdly, however, a site which offers information to potential consumers all over the world but, say, refers them to a local distributor or agent for the purpose of concluding the actual contract does not aim to conclude distance contracts.[948] Furthermore, art.6(1)(b) is not subject to any condition that the consumer has taken, in the country of his habitual residence, all the steps necessary on his part for the conclusion of the contract. This will reduce the difficulties encountered, in this respect, in the application of the Rome Convention.[949]

30–248 **Contract falls within scope of such activities.** Both art.6(1)(a) and art.6(1)(b) are subject to the condition that the contract falls within the scope of the relevant activities which are pursued in, or directed towards, the country where the consumer is habitually resident. As pointed out in the preceding paragraph, this is an important limitation on the scope of art.6(1) in the particular matter of electronic commerce. Beyond this, however, much is left to the courts of Member States and to the European Court, in identifying the scope of the provision with a view to producing certainty of outcome in what are likely, for the most part, to be relatively small claims.[950]

30–249 **Choice of law by the parties.** It is well known that contracts between professionals and consumers often, if not generally: (a) contain a choice of law

[943] See below, para.30–248.

[944] This possibility had been of considerable concern to the electronic commerce industry. The same concern was expressed in negotiations on the Rome I Regulation in that mere accessibility would have exposed the operator to liability under the law of any country in which the website was accessible.

[945] cf. above, para.30–097.

[946] See Explanatory Memorandum to the Commission's original Proposal, p.7.

[947] See preceding note.

[948] See fn.946.

[949] cf. above, para.30–098.

[950] See Recital 24 of the Rome I Regulation.

which; (b) is found in the professional's standard terms and conditions; which (c) applies the law of the professional's "country"; and which (d) is not normally open to negotiation by the consumer (assuming the consumer was even aware of it[951]). The original Proposal from the Commission did not permit, in effect, a choice of law in a consumer contract, and the only law that would be applicable under the Proposal would be the law of the consumer's habitual residence.[952] This was in contrast to art.5 of the Rome Convention which allowed a limited form of party autonomy[953] and caused concern in business sectors, particularly the small business and electronic commerce sectors which routinely provide goods and services to consumers in the European Union.[954] In consequence, art.6(2) of the Regulation provides that notwithstanding art.6(1), the parties may choose the law applicable to a contract which fulfils the requirements of art.6(1), in accordance with art.3 of the Regulation. Such:

> " . . . a choice may not, however, have the result of depriving the consumer of the protection afforded to him by provisions that cannot be derogated from by agreement by virtue of the law, which, in the absence of choice, would have been applicable on the basis of [art.6(1)]".

This, in effect, permits the limited autonomy recognised in art.5 of the Convention and prevents avoidance of compulsory provisions of the law of the country which would be applicable in the absence of choice, by the choice of another country's law.[955]

Application of articles 3 and 4. If the requirements of art.6(1)(a) or (b) are not fulfilled art.6(3) provides that the law applicable to a contract between a consumer and professional shall be determined pursuant to arts 3 and 4 of the Rome I Regulation, i.e. by the general rule governing choice of law by the parties[956] or, in the absence of a choice of law, by the general rule governing the determination of the law applicable in the absence of choice.[957] 30–250

Review clause. As already pointed out,[958] art.27(1) of the Regulation contains a review clause which requires the Commission to submit to the European Parliament, the Council and the European Economic and Social Committee a report on the application of the Rome I Regulation, that Report to be accompanied, if appropriate, by proposals to amend the Regulation. Explicitly, art.27(1)(b) requires the report to include an evaluation of the application of art.6, 30–251

---

[951] See above, para.30–095; see also Ch.15.

[952] See art.5 of the Proposal.

[953] Above, para.30–094.

[954] See Consultation Paper, para.61 where some of these concerns are referred to.

[955] As to these compulsory provisions (mandatory rules, rules which cannot be derogated from by agreement), see above paras 30–101 et seq. It is also possible that party autonomy may be further limited by overriding mandatory provisions (which are different from rules which cannot be derogated from by agreement) under art.9 of the Regulation: see above, paras 30–180 et seq. and below, paras 30–360 et seq. See also Recitals 25 and 37 of the Regulation.

[956] Above, paras 30–170 et seq.

[957] Above, paras 30–186 et seq.

[958] Above, para.30–138.

in particular as regards the coherence of Community law in the field of consumer protection.[959]

(h) *Insurance Contracts*

30–252 **Background.** The Rome Convention provided no discrete choice of law rules to determine the law applicable to insurance contracts. According to art.1(3) of the Convention, the rules contained in the Convention did not apply to contracts of insurance which covered risks situated in the territories of the Member States of the European Communities: in order to determine whether a risk was situated in those territories the court had to apply its internal law.[960] Where the risk was situated within the territories of the Member States, the relevant choice of law rules were to be found in Directives concerned with non-life insurance and life insurance[961] which were ultimately implemented in United Kingdom law in the Financial Services and Markets Act 2000 (Law Applicable to Contracts of Insurance) Regulations 2001.[962] It followed from this that arts 3, 4 and 5 of the Rome Convention applied to determine the law applicable to an insurance contract only in cases where the risk was situated outside the territories of the Member States.[963] Furthermore, the rules in Convention (unaffected by the Directives) applied to determine the law applicable to a reinsurance contract.[964] The result of this combination of different sources and the difficulties of demarcating their respective application was a complex and detailed (in the case of the Directives) body of rules, which were referred to earlier in this chapter,[965] but which, because of their detail and complexity were not considered in this Chapter.[966] In contrast, art.7 of the Rome I Regulation provides a discrete set of choice of law rules to determine the law applicable to insurance contracts. These choice of law rules are, in substance, a combination of and simplification (to some extent, at least) of the position under the Rome Convention and the Directives[967] and do not involve any significant changes. The following paragraphs attempt to identify the main principles and features of art.7.[968] It will be helpful, at the outset, to set out the structure of the article.

30–253 **Structure of article 7.** Article 7 consists of six paragraphs and several subparagraphs, dealing, respectively, with: scope (art.7(1)); the law applicable to a

---

[959] See also the Declaration by the French delegation relating to art.6 stating that in any revision of the Judgments Regulation, the provisions relating to jurisdiction must be consistent with art.6 of the Rome I Regulation: Council of the European Union, 2005/0261, CODEC 388 JUSTCIV 53, April 7, 2008.

[960] Rome Convention art.1(5); above, paras 30–045—30–046.

[961] Above, paras 30–045—30–046.

[962] Financial Services and Markets Act 2000 Regulations 2001 (SI 2001/2635, as amended by SI 2001/3452). The Directives, as implemented in the Regulations, applied where the risk was situated in an EEA Member State: see above, para.30–046.

[963] For discussion, see *Dicey, Morris and Collins on the Conflict of Laws*, 14th edn (2006), paras 33–136 et seq. And see above, paras 30–046 et seq.

[964] Rome Convention art.1(4).

[965] Above, paras 30–045—30–046.

[966] For the details, see *Dicey, Morris and Collins*, paras 33–136 et seq.

[967] Consultation Paper, paras 70–73.

[968] The details of the Directives, as implemented in the UK (above, fn.962) can be traced in *Dicey, Morris and Collins*, paras 33R–158 et seq.

contract covering a "large risk" within the meaning of the article (art.7(2)); the law applicable to an insurance contract other than a contract covering a large risk (art.7(3)); additional rules to determine the law applicable to insurance contracts covering risks for which a Member State imposes an obligation to take out insurance (art.7(4)); a provision clarifying, for the purposes of art.7(3) and 7(4), the situation where the insurance contract covers risks situated in more than one Member State (art.7(5)); and a provision indicating how the country in which the risk is situated is to be identified when it is necessary to do so for the purposes of the article (art.7(6)).

Scope. Article 7(1) of the Regulation stipulates that art.7 shall apply to insurance contracts referred to in art.7(2) (which deals with contracts covering "large risks"),[969] whether or not the risk covered is situated in a Member State,[970] and to all other insurance contracts covering risks situated inside the territory of the Member States.[971] It is specifically provided that art.7 does not apply to reinsurance contracts.[972] **30–254**

Exclusion in article 1(2)(j). By way of preliminary observation, it should be noted that, under art.1(2)(j), the Regulation does not apply at all, to insurance contracts which are the subject of that provision, as mentioned earlier in this section.[973] **30–255**

Reinsurance. Article 7 does not apply to reinsurance contracts. The law applicable to such contracts will therefore be determined by art.3 of the Regulation if the parties have made a choice of law satisfying that provision,[974] or, in the absence of a choice of law, by art.4 of the Regulation.[975] For the purposes of art.4(1) of the Regulation a contract of reinsurance would appear to be a contract for the provision of services and would thus be governed under the general rule by the law of the country where the reinsurer, as service provider, has his habitual residence.[976] Application of that law may be displaced under art.4(3) of the Regulation.[977] The purpose of art.7 of the Regulation is, inter alia, to take account, where appropriate, of the fact that it is thought that the insured is in a "weaker" position compared with the insurer.[978] That consideration is not relevant in relation to reinsurance contracts.[979] **30–256**

---

969 As defined by art.7(2), below, para.30–262.

970 As defined below, para.30–258.

971 As to where a risk is situated, see below, para.30–259.

972 Rome I art.7(1), second sentence.

973 Above, para.30–163.

974 Above, paras 30–170 et seq. cf. *Dicey, Morris and Collins*, paras 33–214 et seq.

975 Above, paras 30–186 et seq.

976 As to the meaning of habitual residence, see art.19. This outcome probably replicates art.4(2) of the Rome Convention when applied to contracts of reinsurance: see *Dicey, Morris and Collins*, paras 33–217 et seq. Presumably, reinsurance contract "includes a retrocession agreement", i.e. reinsurance of a contract of reinsurance: see *Dicey, Morris and Collins*, para.33R–209, fn.21.

977 Above, paras 30–203 et seq.

978 See Recitals 23 and 32 of the Regulation. A contract of insurance does not fall within the consumer contract provisions (art.6) of the Regulation: art.6(1) and Recital 32; above, para.30–239.

979 *Dicey, Morris and Collins*, para.33–210, fn.25.

30–257 **Situs of risk.** As a result of art.7(1) of the Regulation, the relevant choice of law rules for the purpose of art.7 depend, in part, on whether the insurance contract covers risks situated inside the territories of the Member States or risks situated in a non-Member State. Further, the choice of law rules in art.7, on occasion, refer to the law of the Member State in which the risk is situated. It is therefore convenient to identify the rules for determining the *situs* of a risk at this point.

30–258 **Meaning of "Member State".** Although, normally, Member State, for the purposes of the Regulation, means the Member States to which the Regulation applies i.e. Denmark is excluded,[980] art.1(4) of the Regulation provides that for the purposes of art.7, Member State means all the Member States so that Denmark is included. Thus, art.7 will apply where the *situs* of the risk is in Denmark.

30–259 **Rules for determination of situs of risk.** As regards non-life insurance, the country in which the risk is situated, is, according to art.7(6) of the Regulation, to be determined in accordance with art.2(d) of the Second Council Directive 88/357 on the coordination of laws, regulations and administrative provisions relating to direct insurance other than life insurance and laying down provisions to facilitate the effective exercise of freedom to provide services.[981] According to art.2(d) of the Directive, the Member State where the risk is situated means: the Member State in which the property is situated, where the insurance relates either to buildings or to buildings and their contents, in so far as the contents are covered by the same policy; the Member State of registration, where the insurance relates to vehicles of any type; the Member State where the policyholder took out the policy in the case of policies of a duration of four months or less covering travel or holiday risks, whatever the class concerned; and in all cases not explicitly covered by the foregoing provisions the Member State where the policyholder has his habitual residence or, if the policyholder is a legal person, the Member State where the latter's establishment[982] to which the contract relates, is situated. As regards life assurance, the country in which the risk is situated shall, according to art.6(4), be the country of commitment within the meaning of art.1(1)(g) of Directive 2002/83 concerning life assurance. Article 1(1)(g) defines Member State of the commitment as the Member State where the policyholder has his/her habitual residence or, if the policyholder is a legal person, the Member State were the latter's establishment[983] to which the contract relates, is situated.

30–260 **Choice of law rules applicable.** The following paragraphs seek to describe the relevant choice of law rules elating to contracts covering large risks, under

[980] Rome I art.1(4); above, para.30–131. Where the risk is situated in an EEA state rather than a Member State, it would seem that the choice of law rules contained in the Financial Services and Markets Act 2000 (Law Applicable to Contracts of Insurance) Regulations 2001 (SI 2001/2635), above, para.30–046, will apply.

[981] Directive 88/357 on the co-ordination of laws [1988] OJ L172/I.

[982] For the possible meaning of "establishment", see *Dicey, Morris and Collins*, para.33–160.

[983] Defined in art.1(1)(c) of the Directive as the head office, agency or branch of an undertaking.

art.7(2) of the Regulation, and the relevant choice of law rules relating to contracts covering other risks which are contained in art.7(3) of the Regulation.

Large risks. Article 7(2), first sub-para., of the Regulation provides that an: 30–261

> " . . . insurance contract covering a large risk as defined in Article 5(d) of the First Council Directive 73/239/EEC of July 24, 1973 on the co-ordination of laws, regulations and administrative provisions relating to the taking-up and pursuit of the business of direct insurance other than life assurance[984] shall be governed by the law chosen by the parties in accordance with Article 3 of this Regulation."

The second sub-para. of art.7(2) states that to:

> " . . . the extent that the applicable law has not been chosen by the parties, the insurance contract shall be governed by the law of the country where the insurer has his habitual residence. Where it is clear from all the circumstances that the contract is manifestly more closely connected with another country, the law of that other country shall apply."

Meaning of "large risk". According to art.5(d) of the Directive a large risk is defined as a risk which is classified as a risk relating to: damage or loss of, railway stock, aircraft, ships (sea, lake, river and canal vessels), goods in transit, aircraft liability, liability for ships (as above),[985] credit (covering general insolvency, export credit, instalment credit, mortgages, and agricultural credit), suretyship, (covering direct and indirect suretyship),[986] damage and loss to vechicles, certain events involving fire and natural forces, other damage to property, motor vechicle liability, general liability and miscellaneous financial loss.[987] 30–262

Choice of law by the parties. In relation to an insurance contract covering a large risk, as defined in the previous paragraph, the parties may choose the law[988] applicable to the contract in accordance with art.3 of the Regulation,[989] irrespective of the country in which the relevant risk covered is situated, as a result of art.7(2) of the Regulation. 30–263

Applicable law in absence of choice. The second sub-para. of art.7(2) stipulates that in the absence of a choice of law satisfying art.3 of the Regulation, the 30–264

---

984 Directive 73/239 on the co-ordination of laws [1973] OJ L228/3, as amended.

985 art.5(d)(i) of the Directive.

986 art.5(d)(ii) of the Directive, which is subject to the proviso that the policyholder is engaged professionally in an industrial or commercial activity or in one of the liberal professions and the risks related to such activity.

987 art.5(d)(iii) of the Directive, which is subject, inter alia, to the policyholder exceeding certain financial limits in respect of balance-sheet total, turnover and a stipulated average number of employees.

988 Which need not be the law of a Member State.

989 Above, paras 30–170 et seq. As to the position under the Rome Convention, see *Dicey, Morris, and Collins*, paras 33–148 et seq.

contract will be governed, as a general rule, by the law of the country[990] in which the insurer has his habitual residence.[991] This sub-paragraph also provides that where it is clear from all the circumstances of the case that the contract is manifestly more closely connected with another country, the law of that other country shall apply. This approach, in effect, reproduces art.4(1) and (3) of the Regulation in the specific context of insurance contracts covering large risks.[992]

30–265 **Other insurance contracts not falling within article 7(2).** Where the insurance contract is one which does not fall within art.7(2), the relevant choice of law rules are to be found in art.7(3) of the Regulation. As provided in art.7(1), these choice of law rules only apply to insurance contracts covering risks situated inside the territory of the Member States.[993] Article 7(3) of the Regulation is, however, capable of applying (unlike art.7(2) which only applies to non-life insurance) to life assurance. Essentially, non-life risks which are the subject of art.7(3) include the following: accident insurance; sickness insurance; legal expenses insurance; insurance for assistance; credit and suretyship insurance where the risks do *not* relate to a business carried on by the policyholder; and where the policyholder does not carry on a business which satisfies certain detailed requirements of the First Non-Life Directive,[994] land vehicle insurance, fire insurance, damage to property, motor vehicle liability, general liability (other than aircraft liability and liability for ships) and insurance against miscellaneous financial loss.[995]

30–266 **Choice of law by the parties.** Article 7(3) of the Regulation establishes a more limited form of party autonomy in relation to the classes of insurance contract referred to in the previous paragraph, by specifying the laws that may be chosen to govern the insurance contract under art.3 of the Regulation.

30–267 **Law of Member States where risk situated.** Article 7(3)(a) allows, first, the choice of the law of any Member State where the risk is situated at the time of the conclusion of the contract. This would seem to mean that where the risk is situated in more than one Member State, the law of any such state may be chosen.

30–268 **Habitual residence of policyholder.** The parties are permitted to choose, secondly, the law of the country where the policyholder has his habitual residence,[996] by art.7(3)(b) of the Regulation. It will be noted that the country the law of which may be chosen need not be a Member State.

[990] Which need not be a Member State.

[991] As defined above, paras 30–164 et seq.

[992] Above, paras 30–261 et seq. As to the position under the Rome Convention, see *Dicey, Morris, and Collins*, paras 33–150 et seq.

[993] Above, para.30–257. For discussion of these choice of law rules under the Directives, as implemented in the United Kingdom, see *Dicey, Morris and Collins*, paras 33R–158 et seq.

[994] Above, para.30–262.

[995] First Non-Life Directive art.5(d)(iii); above, para.30–262.

[996] As to the meaning of which, see above, paras 30–164 et seq.

Life assurance. As regards the case of life assurance, art.7(3)(c) allows, thirdly, choice of the law of the Member State of which the policyholder is a national. While this principle presents no problem where the policyholder is a national of a Member State which is a unitary state, its application creates difficulty in respect of the United Kingdom in that it requires determination of the national law of a British citizen.[997] Strictly speaking, there is no such law, at least in the field of contract, but only English law, Scottish law and Northern Irish law. And there appears to be no principle that determines what link must exist between an individual and a particular unit within the United Kingdom which can serve to demonstrate what the national law of a British citizen is to be.[998] It is possible, however, though the matter is far from clear, that the relevant "national" law will be that unit of the United Kingdom with which the individual is most closely connected to at the time of conclusion of the contract.[999] 30–269

Risks limited to events occurring in one Member State. Article 7(3)(d) provides that, fourthly, where the insurance contract covers risks limited to events occurring in a Member State other than the Member State where the risk is situated, the parties may choose the law of the former Member State. Presumably, this provision would permit a liability policy covering a lawyer qualified to practice in England and France to contain an effective choice of French law in relation to any indemnity for negligence in respect of advice on French law given in France (the policy being so limited) if the lawyer was habitually resident in England, where the risk would thus be situated.[1000] 30–270

Policyholder pursues commercial or industrial activity. Fifthly, art.7(3)(e) of the Regulation states that where the policyholder of a contract to which art.7(3) applies: 30–271

> "... pursues a commercial or industrial activity or a liberal profession and the insurance contract covers two or more risks which relate to those activities and are situated in different Member States",

the parties may choose the law of any of the Member States concerned or the law of the country of habitual residence of the policyholder.[1001]

Supplementary freedom of choice. The second sub-para. of art.7(3) of the Regulation provides that where, in the cases set out in art.7(3)(a), art.7(3)(b) and art.7(3)(e): 30–272

> "... the Member States referred to grant greater freedom of choice of the law applicable to the insurance contract, the parties may take advantage of that freedom."

---

[997] See on this question, *Dicey, Morris and Collins*, paras 3–201 et seq.

[998] See *Dicey, Morris and Collins*, para.33–202.

[999] See previous note. As to "dual nationality", see *Dicey, Morris and Collins*, para.33–203.

[1000] See *Dicey, Morris and Collins*, para.37–176, where it is also pointed out that it may not always be easy to determine whether the events insured against occurred in one Member State. Further, it is possible that the example given might fall within art.7(3)(e), below, para.30–271.

[1001] See *Dicey, Morris and Collins*, para.33–174.

This, it must be said, is a somewhat obscure provision, but the following points may be made. First, art.7(3)(b) of the Regulation does not require the policyholder to be habitually resident in a Member State: the provision refers to the "country" where the policyholder is habitually resident.[1002] It would, therefore, seem that art.7(3), second sub-para. is limited in scope, as regards, art.7(3)(b), to cases where the policyholder is habitually resident in a Member State. Secondly, the same conclusion would seem to follow in respect of art.7(3)(e) to the extent that that provision refers to the law of the "country" of habitual residence of the policyholder.[1003] Thirdly, the reference to the grant of greater freedom to choose the applicable law in the law of the Member States concerned is a reference to choice of law rules: thus a species of the doctrine of *renvoi* is introduced into the provision.[1004] Fourthly, however, it is not clear what choice of law rules are being referred to since the Rome I Regulation is the source of the relevant choice of law rules in all the Member States,[1005] and that Regulation limits the power to choose by reference to art.7. In the circumstances any conclusion on this issue must be speculative, but it is tentatively suggested that the reference in art.7(3), second sub-paragraph is to art.3 of the Regulation. Thus, if art.3 gives greater freedom of choice than the law which can be chosen under art.7(3)(a), art.7(3)(b) and 7(3)(e), the parties may take advantage of that freedom if the law of the Member States identified in art.7(3)(a), (b) and (e) so permit.[1006]

30–273 **Applicable law in the absence of choice.** Article 7(3), third sub-paragraph, provides that to the extent that the law applicable to the contract has not been chosen in accordance with art.7(3), the contract shall be governed by the law of the Member State in which the risk is situated at the time of conclusion to the contract. There is no escape clause allowing application of the law of another country (or Member State) if it is clear from all the circumstances of the case that the contract is manifestly more closely connected with that other country.[1007] For the purposes of art.7(3), third sub-para., art.7(5) provides that where the contract covers risks situated in more than one Member State, the contract "shall be considered as several contracts each relating to only one Member State".[1008] This might not be thought to be a particularly convenient solution.

30–274 **Risk situated in non-Member State, etc.** Article 7(3) only applies if the risk is situated in a Member State and also, together with art.7(5), deals with the situation where the risk is situated in more than one Member State. Where the risk is situated in a non-Member State then the law applicable to the insurance contract will, so it appears, be generally determined by reference to arts 3 and 4

[1002] See above, para.30–268.
[1003] See above, para.30–271.
[1004] See above, para.30–146.
[1005] The equivalent provision in Financial Services and Markets Act 2000 (Law Applicable to Contracts of Insurance) Regulations 2001 regs 4(5) and 7(3) provided that the choice of law rules of the Rome Convention were the rules referred to, rather than the rules contained in the Directives. See *Dicey, Morris and Collins*, paras 33–172 et seq.
[1006] cf. *Evialis SA v SIAT* [2003] EWHC 863 (Comm), [2003] 2 Lloyd's Rep. 377.
[1007] cf. Rome I art.7(2), second sub-para.
[1008] cf. *American Motorists Insurance Co v Cellstar Corp* [2003] EWCA Civ 206, [2003] I.L. Pr. 370.

of the Regulation[1009] unless the non-Member State is an EEA state, in which case it is possible that the applicable law will be determined by reference to the relevant provisions of the Financial Services and Markets Act 2000 (Law Applicable to Contracts of Insurance) Regulations 2001.[1010] Where the risk is situated in both a Member State and a non-Member State, then it may be, drawing an analogy with art.7(5), that the contract will be treated as a series of separate contracts with art.7(3) applying in respect of the risk situated in the Member State and arts 3 and 4 applying in so far as the risk is situated in a non-Member State. Where the risk is situated in both a Member State and an EEA State, then again the contract may be treated as a series of separate contracts with art.7(3) applying to the former situation and the 2001 Regulations applying to the latter situation. Where the risk is situated in two or more non-Member States, then the applicable law will be determined by reference to arts 3 and 4 of the Regulation, in respect of the contract as a whole, and there will, one would think, be no need to treat the contract as a series of separate contracts.[1011]

Compulsory insurance. Article 7(4) of the Regulation provides additional rules for contracts covering risks for which a Member State imposes an obligation to take out insurance. By virtue of art.7(4)(a), the insurance contract will not satisfy the obligation to take out insurance unless it complies with the specific provisions relating to that insurance laid down by the Member State that imposes the obligation. Where the law of the Member State in which the risk is situated and the law of the Member State imposing the obligation to take out insurance contradict each other, the latter shall prevail. For these purposes, where the contract covers risks situated in more than one Member State, art.7(5) provides that the contract shall be considered as constituting several contracts each relating to only one Member State.[1012] Article 7(4)(b), by way of derogation from art.7(2) and (3), permits a Member State to lay down that the insurance contract shall be governed by the law of the Member State that imposes the obligation to take out insurance. 30–275

(i) *Individual Employment Contracts*

Background. As regards the Rome Convention, determination of the law applicable to individual employment contracts was governed by art.6 of the Convention.[1013] Very generally, a choice of law in such a contract could not have the result of depriving the employee of the protection afforded to him by the mandatory rules of the law which would be applicable to the contract in the absence of choice.[1014] In the absence of choice, an employment contract would be governed by the law of the country in which the employee habitually carried 30–276

[1009] See Recital 33 of the Regulation above, paras 30–170 et seq.

[1010] Unless the Regulations are repealed consequent on the adoption of Rome I. For discussion, see *Dicey, Morris and Collins*, paras 33R–158 et seq.

[1011] Where the risk is situated in more than one EEA State, the matter will be governed by the 2001 Regulations.

[1012] Above, para.30–273.

[1013] Above, paras 30–108 et seq.

[1014] Rome Convention art.6(1), above, paras 30–112 et seq.

out his work in performance of the contract even if he was temporarily employed in another country,[1015] or, if the employee did not carry out his work in any one country, by the law of the country in which the place of business through which the employee was engaged was situated,[1016] unless it appeared from the circumstances as a whole that the contract was more closely connected with another country, in which case the contract was governed by the law of that country.[1017] These choice of law rules were discussed earlier in this Chapter.[1018] In relation to the Rome I Regulation, the relevant choice of law rules are to be found in art.8 of the Regulation. Article 8, essentially repeats art.6 of the Convention but contains some clarification of, and different terminology to, the latter provision. The philosophy behind art.8, is, however, identical to that behind art.6 of the Convention.[1019]

30–277 **Structure of article 8.** Article 8(1) provides a general rule allowing the parties to choose the governing law, but stipulates that the choice of law may not have the result of depriving the employee of the protection afforded to him by provisions which cannot be derogated from by agreement which are contained in the law that would be applicable in the absence of choice.[1020] Article 8(2), (3) and (4) provide the relevant rules for determining the law to be applied in the absence of a choice of law.[1021] This structure strongly reflects that of art.6 of the Rome Convention, as discussed in section 3 of this Chapter.[1022] The following paragraphs describe the main features of art.8 of the Regulation, concentrating in particular on any differences between art.8 and art.6 of the Convention.

30–278 **Meaning of individual employment contract.** Whatever the position is under art.6 of the Rome Convention,[1023] there can be no doubt that under art.8 of the Rome I Regulation the expression "individual employment contract" will be given an autonomous meaning.[1024] Further, that meaning should correspond, so far as possible, with the meaning given to the expression in the context of the Judgments Regulation.[1025] What the particular meaning will turn out to be may depend on the circumstances of the case but the following considerations may form the broad contours of an autonomous meaning.[1026] The first criterion identifying a contract of employment is the provision of services by one party

[1015] Rome Convention art.6(2)(a), above, paras 30–119 et seq.

[1016] Rome Convention art.6(2)(b) above, paras 30–119 et seq.

[1017] Rome Convention art.6(2), proviso.

[1018] Above, paras 30–108 et seq.

[1019] Above, para.30–108. See Recital 35 to the Rome I Regulation. Recital 34 states that art.8 should not prejudice the application of the overriding mandatory provisions of the country to which a worker is posted in accordance with Directive 96/71 concerning the posting of workers in the framework of the provision of services [1997] OJ L18/1, above, para.30–108.

[1020] cf. art.6(1) of the Rome Convention, above, para.30–112.

[1021] cf. art.6(2) of the Regulation, above, paras 30–119 et seq.

[1022] Above, paras 30–108 et seq.

[1023] Above, paras 30–119 et seq.

[1024] See *WPP Holdings Italy Srl v Benatti* [2007] EWCA Civ 263, [2007] 1 W.L.R. 263; *Samengo-Turner v J & H Marsh & McLennan (Services) Ltd* [2007] EWCA Civ 723, [2008] I.C.R. 18; *Duarte v Black & Decker Corp* [2007] EWHC 2720 (QB), [2008] 1 All E.R. (Comm) 401.

[1025] Judgments Regulation art.18. See Recital 7 to the Rome 1 Regulation. And see cases cited in preceding note.

[1026] *WPP Holdings Italy Srl v Benatti* [2007] EWCA Civ 263 at [46].

over a period of time for which remuneration is paid; the second criterion is the existence of control and direction over the provision of the services by the counterparty; and the third criterion is the integration to some extent of the provider of services within the organisational framework of the counterparty. These criteria are not, however, "hard edged" criteria which can be mechanistically applied, since there may, for example, be degrees of control and degrees of integration within the relevant organisational framework.[1027] And in applying these broad criteria regard must be had, particularly, to the terms of the contract.[1028]

Choice of law by the parties. Article 8(1) establishes that an individual employment contract shall be governed by the law chosen by the parties in accordance with art.3 of the Regulation.[1029] What is significant about the provision, is, however, that such a choice of law may not have the result of depriving the employee of the protection afford to him by provisions that cannot be derogated from by agreement under the law that would have been applied in the absence of choice. 30–279

"Provisions that cannot be derogated from by agreement". This expression corresponds to the expression "mandatory rules", as used in art.6(1) of the Rome Convention, which according to art.3(3) of the Convention are rules which "cannot be derogated from by contract.[1030] For the purposes of art.8(1) of the Regulation, likely relevant provisions will, it would appear, be those discussed in the context of the Rome Convention in section 3 of this Chapter.[1031] Further, analysis of the question of whether the employee has been "deprived" of the protection of a relevant provision would seem to involve the same process of reasoning as that discussed in connection with art.6(1) of the Rome Convention.[1032] 30–280

Applicable law in absence of choice. In the absence of a choice of law, the applicable law must be determined by reference to art.8(2) or (3) of the Regulation each of which is subject to a rule of displacement contained in art.8(4). 30–281

Country in which employee habitually carries out work, etc. Article 8(2) stipulates that to: 30–282

> "... the extent that the law applicable to the individual employment contract has not been chosen by the parties, the contract shall be governed by the law of the country in which, or failing that, from which the employee habitually carries out his work in performance of the contract. The country where the work is habitually carried out shall not be deemed to have changed if he is temporarily employed in another country."

[1027] *WPP Holdings Italy Srl v Benatti* [2007] EWCA Civ 263 at [47].

[1028] *WPP Holdings Italy Srl v Benatti* [2007] EWCA Civ 263 at [47].

[1029] Above, paras 30–170 et seq.

[1030] Above, para.30–063.

[1031] Above, paras 30–113 et seq. Where the relevant provision is derived from European law, it may have direct effect, independently of art.8(1); see Recitals 34 and 40 of the Regulation. And see above, para.30–116.

[1032] Above, para.30–117.

It will be noted that whereas art.6(2)(a) of the Rome Convention refers to the law of the country *in* which the employee carries out his work,[1033] as does art.8(2) of the Regulation, the Convention, in contrast to the Regulation does not refer to the law of the country *from* which the employee habitually carried out his work in performance of the contract. The effect of art.8(2) would seem to be as follows. If the employee habitually carries[1034] out his work in performance of the contract in one country, then that country's law will be, subject to art.8(4), the applicable law. If the employee habitually carries out his work in more than one country, or in no particular country, or in a place which is not a country[1035] then one must ask whether there is one country from which the employee habitually carries out his work in performance of the contract. An example of the latter situation might be the case of an airline pilot, based in one particular country who is required to fly aircraft to several different countries.[1036]

30–283 **Temporarily employed in another country.** The second sentence of art.8(2) is designed to ensure that the place where work is habitually carried out is not to be regarded as having changed if the employee is temporarily employed in another country. Recital 36 to the Regulation explains that:

> "... work carried out in another country should be regarded as temporary if the employee is expected to resume working in the country of origin after carrying out his tasks abroad. The conclusion of a new contract of employment with the original employer or an employer belonging to the same group of companies as the original employer should not preclude the employee from being regarded as carrying out his work in another country temporarily."

30–284 **Default rule.** Article 8(3) provides what might be called a "default" rule according to which if the applicable law cannot be determined by reference to art.8(2), the contract shall be governed by the law of the country where the place of business through which the employee was engaged is situated.[1037] This rule will apply where the employee habitually carries out his work in more than one country, or in no particular country, or in a place which is not a country *and* there is no one country *from* which he habitually carries out his work.

30–285 **Rule of displacement.** Article 8(4) provides that where:

> "... it appears from the circumstances as a whole that the contract is more closely connected with a country other than that indicated in paragraphs 2 or 3, the law of that other country shall apply."

This rule is modelled on the proviso to art.6(2) of the Rome Convention, as discussed earlier in this Chapter.[1038] It should be emphasised that there is no

---

1033 Above, para.30–119.

1034 As to the meaning of "habitually carries out his work" see references at para.30–119, fn.584, above.

1035 See above, para.30–119.

1036 cf. *Serco Ltd v Lawson* [2006] UKHL 3, [2006] I.C.R. 250; above, para.30–115.

1037 As to the meaning of "place of business through which the employee was engaged is situated", see above, para.30–120.

1038 Above, para.30–120.

requirement in art.8(4) that it must be "clear" from the circumstances as a whole that the contract is "manifestly" more closely connected with a country other than that indicated in art.8(2) or (3) to justify invocation of the rule of displacement.[1039] It may, therefore, in the context of employment contracts, be somewhat more easy to displace the application of the law found to govern the contract by reference, as the case may be, to art.8(2) or (3).[1040]

"Overriding mandatory provisions". It should finally be noted that it is conceivable that the effect of a choice of law or of the law that would be applicable in the absence of choice could be limited by reference to overriding mandatory provisions of the law of the forum or perhaps by relevant overriding mandatory provisions of the law of the country where the contract has been or has to be performed.[1041] **30–286**

Contract and tort. In English law, an employee may have alternative claims in contract or tort against his employer for, say, breach of contract or negligence, in respect of injuries suffered at work.[1042] As explained earlier in this Chapter, it is unlikely that this option will remain, as between the Rome I Regulation in respect of the contractual claim and the Rome II Regulation in respect of the non-contractual (tortious) claim, since the scope of each Regulation will be regarded as mutually exclusive.[1043] It is not entirely clear, however, whether such a claim will be regarded as contractual or tortious in character. It is suggested, with hesitation, that it should be regarded as arising out of a non-contractual obligation.[1044] **30–287**

(j) *Voluntary Assignment and Contractual Subrogation*

Background. Article 12 of the Rome Convention contained choice of law rules for determining the law applicable to "Voluntary assignment", as discussed earlier in this Chapter.[1045] Article 14 of the Rome I Regulation contains choice of law rules which are expressed to apply to determine the law applicable to "[v]oluntary assignment and contractual subrogation". The gestation of art.14 was not without controversy and it is therefore not surprising that it is one of the areas to be addressed in the review clause in the Regulation.[1046] Article 14(1) and (2), subject to some changes in drafting, reflect the substance of the equivalent rules in art.12(1) and (2) of the Rome Convention.[1047] Article 14(3) of the **30–288**

1039 cf. Rome I art.4(3); above, para.30–203.

1040 cf. Rome I art.4(4); above, para.30–203.

1041 See below, paras 30–360 et seq. In any event, in practice, the approach in art.8 will normally secure the application of these provisions.

1042 Above, para.30–121.

1043 Above, para.30–122.

1044 But cf. *Kalfelis v Schroeder* (189/87) [1988] E.C.R. 5565; *Source Ltd v TUV Rheinland Holding AG* [1998] Q.B. 54.

1045 Above, paras 30–123 et seq.

1046 Rome I art.27(2), above, para.30–138, below para.30–295. See Consultation Paper, paras 85–87. cf. the original Proposal of the Commission art.13.

1047 Consultation Paper, para.84.

Regulation is new and addresses, in part, the meaning of the concept of assignment.

30–289 **Meaning of "voluntary assignment" and "contractual subrogation".** There can be little doubt that the concept of "assignment" will be given an autonomous interpretation for the purposes of the Regulation. In this respect, art.14(3) provides that the:

> "... concept of assignment in this Article includes outright transfers of claims, transfers of claims by way of security and pledges or other security rights over claims."

It is also thought that the inclusion of "contractual subrogation" in art.14 (and the term is not to be found in art.12 of the Rome Convention) is designed to clarify the meaning of assignment by making a more general reference to the process by which claims are transferred. Contractual subrogation, in general terms, involves an agreement whereby a claim of a creditor who has been satisfied by a third party, subrogates the third party to the claim which the creditor would have had against the debtor. In some legal systems, this process, in effect, performs the function of an assignment[1048] and thus should be included in a provision dealing with voluntary assignment since it is a consensual process.[1049]

30–290 **Relationship between assignor and assignee.** Article 14(1) of the Regulation stipulates that the:

> "... relationship between assignor and assignee under a voluntary assignment or contractual subrogation of a claim against another person ('the debtor') shall be governed by the law that applies to the contract between the assignor and assignee under this Regulation."

Apart from the inclusion of contractual subrogation, this reproduces art.12(1) of the Rome Convention[1050] though with one other difference. Article 12(1) of the Convention referred to the "mutual obligations of assignor and assignee under a voluntary assignment", whereas art.14(1) of the Regulation refers to the "*relationship* between assignor and assignee under a voluntary assignee".[1051] The use

[1048] See, e.g. arts 1249 and 1250 of the French Civil Code. See generally, Friedmann and Cohen, *Payment of Another's Debt* in *International Encyclopedia of Comparative Law* (1985), Vol.X, Ch 10; Takahashi, *Claims for Contribution and Reimbursement in an International Context* (2000), pp.11–13, 77–82. And see Explanatory Memorandum to the Commission's original Proposal, comment on art.13 ("Voluntary assignment and contractual subrogation perform a similar economic function"); UNCITRAL Convention on the Assignment of Receivables in International Trade art.2 and Explanatory Note para.7 (an "assignment may be a contractual subrogation or a pledge-type transaction").

[1049] cf. Rome I art.15, discussed below, paras 30–293 et seq., dealing with "Legal subrogation". And see UNCITRAL Convention (preceding note), Explanatory Memorandum para.7 (assignment may not be a transfer by operation of law (e.g. statutory subrogation) or other non-contractual assignment).

[1050] For discussion of art.12(1) of the Convention (which applies equally to art.14(1) of the Regulation), see above, para.30–124.

[1051] Emphasis added.

of the term "relationship" is explained in Recital 38 to the Regulation, as follows:

> "In the context of a voluntary assignment, the term 'relationship' should make it clear that Article 14(1) also applies to the property aspects of an assignment, as between assignor and assignee, in legal orders where such aspects are treated separately from the aspects under the law of obligations. However, the term 'relationship' should not be understood as relating to any relationship that may exist between assignor and assignee. In particular, it should not concern preliminary questions as regards a voluntary assignment or a contractual subrogation. The term should be strictly limited to the aspects which are directly relevant to the voluntary assignment or contractual subrogation in question."

Assignability, etc. Article 14(2) of the Regulation states that the: **30–291**

> "... law governing *the assigned or subrogated claim* shall determine its assignability, the relationship between the assignee and the debtor, the conditions under which the assignment *or subrogation* can be invoked against the debtor and whether the debtor's obligations have been discharged."[1052]

Apart from the linguistic changes which have been italicised, but which do not bring about any substantive change, art.14(2) is a replica of art.12(2) of the Rome Convention, discussed in section 3 of this Chapter,[1053] and subject to what is said in the following paragraph, should be interpreted in the same way.

Priorities. In the earlier discussion of art.12(2) of the Rome Convention it was tentatively suggested that the question of priorities between competing assignments of the same debt could fall within art.12(2) and could thus be governed by the law governing the right to which the assignment related.[1054] This conclusion must now be regarded as unlikely to follow under the Regulation. First, the Commission's original Proposal contained a rule providing that whether the assignment or subrogation could be relied upon against third parties should be governed by the law of the assignor's or the author of the subrogation's habitual residence[1055] which might suggest that priorities were not covered by art.12(2). Secondly, the proposed rule provoked so much criticism that it was eliminated during the negotiations[1056] and the Consultation Paper expresses the view that the question of priorities is for national law.[1057] Thirdly, under the review clause the Commission is required to produce a report on the question of the effectiveness of an assignment or subrogation of a claim against third parties and the priority of the assigned or subrogated claim over a right of another person "the report to be accompanied, if appropriate, by a proposal to amend" the Regulation.[1058] This again suggests that these questions are not covered by the present text of art.14(2). **30–292**

1052 Emphasis added.
1053 Above, para.30–125.
1054 Above, paras 30–125—30–126.
1055 Proposal art.14(3).
1056 Consultation Paper, paras 85, 86.
1057 Consultation Paper, para.85.
1058 Rome I art.27(2). See also, Consultation Paper, para.87.

(k) *Legal Subrogation*

30–293 **Background.** Article 13 of the Rome Convention contained provisions expressed to apply to "[s]ubrogation", as discussed earlier in this Chapter.[1059] The principal rule was contained in art.13(1) while art.13(2) applied the same rule where several persons were subject to the same contractual claim and one of them had satisfied the debtor.[1060] Article 15 of the Regulation is expressed to apply to "[l]egal subrogation" and reproduces, with a minor linguistic change of no substantive effect, the text of art.13(1) of the Convention. Article 16 of the Regulation, headed "[m]ultiple liability" deals with cases where a creditor has a claim against several debtors who are liable for the same claim and one of them has already satisfied the claim in whole or in part, i.e. the situation dealt with in art.13(2) of the Convention.[1061] Article 16 is dealt with below.[1062]

30–294 **Article 15: Principle.** Article 15 of the Regulation provides that where:

> ". . . a person ('the creditor') has a contractual claim against another ('the debtor') and a third person has a duty to satisfy the creditor, or has in fact satisfied the creditor in discharge of that duty, the law which governs the third person's duty to satisfy the creditor shall determine whether and to what extent the third person is entitled to exercise against the debtor the rights which the creditor had against the debtor under the law governing their relationship."

This means, as was the case under art.13(1) of the Convention, that, in respect of a contractual claim[1063] the third person may seek to recover from the debtor, through being subrogated to the creditor's claim to the extent permitted by the law which governs his duty to satisfy the creditor.[1064] The text of the provision is discussed in the context of art.13(1) of the Convention and further discussion here is unnecessary.[1065]

30–295 **"Legal subrogation".** Article 15 only applies to "legal subrogation", i.e. to subrogation by operation of law and is to be distinguished from "contractual subrogation" which is part of the subject matter of art.14 of the Regulation.[1066] Thus, art.15 would apply to a contract of guarantee where the guarantor has paid the creditor and is thus subrogated to the latter's rights against the debtor.[1067] In some civil law systems, legal subrogation is known as "statutory subrogation".[1068]

[1059] Above, paras 30–127 et seq.

[1060] Above, para.30–129.

[1061] Rome Convention art.13(1) and (2) are discussed above, paras 30–127 et seq.

[1062] Below, paras 30–126 et seq.

[1063] i.e. Rome I Regulation art.15 will not apply to the question of whether an insured is subrogated to the rights of an insured who has been the victim of a tort.

[1064] Above, para.30–127.

[1065] Above, para.30–127.

[1066] Above, paras 30–288 et seq.

[1067] Above, para.30–127.

[1068] See, e.g. arts 1249, 1251 of the French Civil Code. See also the Commission's original Proposal art.14 and Explanatory Memorandum thereto.

(l) *Multiple Liability*

Principle. Article 16 of the Regulation (headed "Multiple liability") deals with a debtor's right to recourse from other debtors where the former debtor has paid the creditor in whole or in part. Reflecting art.13(2) of the Convention,[1069] it provides that if: 30–296

> "... a creditor has a claim against several debtors who are liable for the same claim, and one of the debtors has already satisfied the claim in whole or in part, the law governing the debtor's obligation towards the creditor also governs the debtor's right to claim recourse from the other debtors. The other debtors may rely on the defences they had against the creditor to the extent allowed by the law governing their obligations towards the creditor."

Right of recourse. It follows from the text of art.16 that where one debtor has already satisfied the creditors claim, whether he may obtain recourse against co-debtors liable for the same claim will be governed by the law applicable to the debtor's obligation towards the creditor, i.e. normally, the law applicable to the contract between the debtor and the creditor. The principle applies whether the debtor has satisfied the creditor in whole or in part.[1070] 30–297

Defences. The second sentence of art.16 of the Regulation (which is not found directly in art.13(2) of the Rome Convention)[1071] makes it clear that as against the debtor who seeks recourse, the co-debtors may rely on any defences they had against the debtor to the extent permitted by the law governing the co-debtors' obligations towards the creditor, i.e. normally the law applicable to the contract between the co-debtors and the creditor. 30–298

(m) *Set-off*

Background. The Rome Convention contained no specific rule relating to the law applicable to the right to set-off. However, it would seem likely that whether a debt is extinguished (or reduced) by set-off, is under the Convention, governed by the law applicable to the contract is determined by the applicable law, by virtue of art.10(1)(d) of the Convention which submits to the applicable law, amongst other things, the ways of extinguishing obligations.[1072] In contrast, art.17 of the Rome I Regulation contains a specific rule in relation to this matter. It provides that were: 30–299

> "... the right to set-off is not agreed by the parties, set-off shall be governed by the law applicable to the claim against which the right to set-off is asserted."

Meaning of "set-off". The meaning of "set-off" and the "right to set-off" is not defined in the Regulation, and, presumably, if necessary, the concept will be 30–300

1069 Above, para.30–129.
1070 cf. art.13(2) of the Rome Convention, above, para.30–129.
1071 Above, para.30–129.
1072 Below, para.30–345.

given an autonomous meaning. It is suggested, first, that if set-off is a claim of a certain kind which the defendant has against the claimant and which can conveniently be tried together with the claim against the defendant, or a counter-claim which can conveniently be tried with the claim against the defendant, then such a form of "set-off" will not fall within the scope of art.17, or, in any event, the scope of the applicable law. Whether a "set-off" of these kinds can be raised (if "set-off" is the correct description) is a question of procedure, governed by the *lex fori*,[1073] and the Regulation does not apply to matters of procedure.[1074] Conversely, a set-off (to borrow English legal terminology) may amount to an equity[1075] attaching to the claim directly and may operate in total or partial extinction of that claim.[1076] The question whether a set-off of the latter nature exists is one of substance governed by the relevant applicable law.[1077] It is set-off of this latter kind which is, it is suggested, a set-off or a right to set-off which falls within art.17.

30–301 **Set-off in insolvency proceedings.** The right to assert a set-off under art.17 of the Regulation must be distinguished from the right to assert a set-off in insolvency proceedings, at least where the insolvency proceedings fall within Council Regulation 1346/2000 on insolvency proceedings.[1078] This Regulation provides that, in proceedings which fall within it, the law of the State in which insolvency proceedings are opened will generally apply to determine the conditions under which set-offs may be invoked.[1079] By way of exception to this general rule, art.6(1) of the Regulation on Insolvency Proceedings establishes that:

> " . . . the opening of insolvency proceedings shall not affect the rights of creditors to demand the set-off of their claims against the claims of the debtor, where such a set-off is permitted by the law applicable to the insolvent debtor's claim. The effect of this rule is that where the law of the State of opening of insolvency proceedings does not permit set-off, then a creditor may nonetheless rely on set-off if set-off is permitted by the law which governs the insolvent debtor's claim against the creditor.[1080]

If the latter claim is contractual in nature, the law which governs it will be determined, when the Rome I Regulation takes effect, by choice of law rules in the Rome I Regulation, *not* including, it would seem, the rule in art.17 of the Regulation, since the Regulation on Insolvency Proceedings contains its own rule as to when set-off may be invoked.

[1073] *Dicey, Morris and Collins on the Conflict of Laws*, 14th edn (2006), para.7–032.

[1074] Rome I art.1(3); see above, para.30–161.

[1075] *Dicey, Morris and Collins*, para.7–032.

[1076] See preceding note where the example given is the *compensation de plein droit* in French law.

[1077] *Dicey, Morris and Collins*, para.7–032.

[1078] Regulation 1346/2000 on insolvency proceedings [2000] OJ L160/1. see generally *Dicey, Morris and Collins*, paras 30R–149 et seq.

[1079] Regulation 1346/2000 art.4(2)(d). See *Dicey, Morris and Collins*, para.30–026. As to the meaning of "[s]tate of the opening of insolvency proceedings", see arts 3 and 4(1) of the Regulation on insolvency proceedings.

[1080] See generally, *Dicey, Morris and Collins*, para.30–026.

Applicable law under article 17. Where the right to set-off is not agreed between the parties, set-off shall be governed by the law applicable to the contract creating the claim against which the right to set-off is asserted. 30–302

5. SCOPE OF THE APPLICABLE LAW

Introduction. This section seeks to identify the various issues which may be governed by the applicable law of the contract and to consider the extent to which laws other than the applicable law may be relevant to the determination of any of these issues in cases which fall, respectively, within the Rome Convention and the Rome I Regulation.[1081] In the background, it must be also borne in mind that other laws may impinge upon the scope of the applicable law through the operation, in particular, of arts 3(3), 5, 6, 7(2) and 16 of the Rome Convention and arts 3(3), 3(4), 6, 8, 9 and 21 of the Rome I Regulation, which were considered earlier in this Chapter. Formally, only art.10 of the Convention and art.12 of the Regulation are expressed to be concerned with the "scope of the applicable law". However, other provisions of the Convention, notably art.8 ("material validity"),[1082] art.9 ("formal validity"),[1083] art.11 ("incapacity")[1084] and art.14 ("burden of proof etc")[1085] and other provisions of the Regulation, notably art.10 ("consent and material validity"),[1086] art.11 ("formal validity"),[1087] art.13 ("incapacity")[1088] and art.18 ("burden of proof")[1089] also raise questions as to the relative competence of the applicable law and other relevant laws and thus are appropriate subjects for discussion in this section. 30–303

(a) *Material Validity of the Contract*[1090]

Article 8(1) of the Convention and article 10(1) of the Regulation. Article 8(1) of the Rome Convention which is expressed to apply to the "material validity" of the contract provides as follows: 30–304

> "The existence and validity of a contract, or of any term of a contract, shall be determined by the law which would govern it under this Convention if the contract or term were valid."

The terms of this provision are replicated in art.10(1) of the Regulation, save for the obvious fact that in the case of the Regulation, the governing law will be

---

[1081] Common law principles are referred to where relevant.
[1082] Below, para.30–304.
[1083] Below, paras 30–310 et seq.
[1084] Below, para.30–324.
[1085] Below, paras 30–352 et seq.
[1086] Below, paras 30–304 et seq.
[1087] Below, paras 30–310 et seq.
[1088] Below, para.30–324.
[1089] Below, paras 30–352 et seq.
[1090] *Dicey, Morris and Collins on the Conflict of Laws*, 14th edn (2006), paras 32–155—32–173; Cheshire and North, 13th edn (1999), pp.587–589; Plender, *The European Contracts Convention*, 2nd edn (2001) pp.205–210; Kaye, *The New Private International Law of Contract of the European Community* (1993), pp.269–279.

determined by the rules in the Regulation and the provisions in each instrument will be interpreted in the same manner. Material validity, for these purposes, thus includes[1091] the question of whether the contract has come into existence (i.e. matters relating to the formation,[1092] the validity of the contract and the terms thereof,[1093] and the validity of consent to the contract (e.g. questions of mistake, misrepresentation, duress or non-disclosure).[1094] Since arts 8(1) and 10(1) apply to the validity of the contract and its terms they will also apply to some (but not all) issues of legality of the contract.[1095] Where arts 8(1) or 10(1) apply, the relevant applicable law will be the law which would govern the contract under the Convention or the Regulation if the contract or term were valid, the "putative applicable law" or "putative governing law".[1096]

30–305 **Identification of "putative applicable law".** Since arts 8(1) and 10(1) stipulate that the governing law is the law which would apply, pursuant to the Convention or the Regulation, if the contract or term were valid, the putative governing law will be determined according to the rules for determining the applicable law which are contained in the Convention or the Regulation as the case may be. Accordingly, where the parties have made a choice of law in the contract and an issue of material validity arises, that chosen law will be the governing law.[1097] In the absence of such a choice the putative applicable law will be determined according to art.4 of the Convention or art.4 of the Regulation.[1098]

1091 See Cheshire and North, p.587.

1092 See below, paras 30–306 et seq.

1093 See below, para.30–309.

1094 See below, para.30–308.

1095 See below, paras 30–335 et seq.

1096 This was very much the approach of the common law: see 26th edn of this work, paras 2175–2177. See below, para.30–305. As to consent to choice of the applicable law (art.3(4) of the Convention, art.3(5) of the Regulation), see above, paras 30–059, 30–184.

1097 art.3(1) of, respectively, the Convention and the Regulation, above, paras 30–030 et seq., 30–170 et seq. See *Egon Oldendorff v Libera Corp (No.1)* [1995] 2 Lloyd's Rep. 64; see also *Egon Oldendorff v Libera Corp (No.2)* [1996] 1 Lloyd's Rep. 380; *Merrill Lynch Capital Services Inc v Municipality of Piraeus* [1997] C.L.C. 1214; *Credit Suisse First Boston (Europe) Ltd v Seagate Trading Co Ltd* [1999] 1 Lloyd's Rep. 784.

1098 Above, paras 30–071 et seq., 30–186 et seq. If the contract is subject to arts 5 or 6 of the Convention, the applicable law will be determined according to those provisions: see above, paras 30–092 et seq. If the contract is subject to arts 5, 6, 7 or 8 of the Regulation, the applicable law will be determined by those provisions: see above, paras 30–209 et seq. At common law, it was sometimes suggested that the "putative proper law" should be determined without reference to any choice of law made by the parties, i.e. on purely objective grounds (see, e.g. Cheshire and North, *Private International Law*, 11th edn (1987), pp.471–477), but this may have rested on a confusion between the putative proper law and the distinct concept of the proper law objectively determined. The weight of authority, however, supported the view that both an express and implied choice of law could constitute the putative proper law: see *The Parouth* [1982] 2 Lloyd's Rep. 351; *The Mariannina* [1983] 1 Lloyd's Rep. 12; *The T.S. Havprins* [1983] 2 Lloyd's Rep. 356; *The Iran Vojdan* [1984] 2 Lloyd's Rep. 380; *Dimskal Shipping Co SA v International Transport Workers Federation* [1992] 2 A.C. 152; *The Lake Avery* [1997] 1 Lloyd's Rep. 540; *Society of Lloyd's v Fraser* [1998] C.L.C. 1630, 1652; *Credit Suisse First Boston (Europe) Ltd v Seagate Trading Co Ltd* [1999] 1 Lloyd's Rep. 784. See also *Marc Rich & Co AG v Soc Italiana Impianti P.A.* [1989] 1 Lloyd's Rep. 548. cf. *Mackender v Feldia* [1967] Q.B. 590; *The Heidberg* [1994] 2 Lloyd's Rep. 287; *Dornoch Ltd v Mauritius Union Assurance Co Ltd* [2006] EWCA Civ 389, [2006] 2 Lloyd's Rep. 475; *Oceanic Sun Line Shipping Co Inc v Fay* (1988) 165 C.L.R. 197.

Formation of the contract. At common law, it was generally accepted that the question as to what minimum acts had to be performed to give rise to a contract was a matter for the "putative proper law" of the contract.[1099] This has been the subject of specific decision in relation to offer and acceptance[1100] and consideration.[1101] Article 8(1) of the Convention and art.10(1) of the Regulation thus repeat the common law rule in this regard in so far as they refer such matters to the putative applicable law.[1102] Article 8(2) of the Convention and art.10(2) of the Regulation however, create an exception to this general rule in the following identical terms: 30–306

> "Nevertheless a party may rely upon the law of the country in which he has his habitual residence to establish that he did not consent if it appears from the circumstances that it would not be reasonable to determine the effect of his conduct in accordance with the law specified in [art.8(1) of the Convention or art.10(1) of the Regulation]."

The purpose of this provision is to "solve the problem of the implications of silence by one party as to the formation of the contract",[1103] but it is not confined to that issue since the "word 'conduct' must be taken to cover both action and failure to act by the party in question".[1104] In deciding whether it would not be reasonable to determine the effect of a party's conduct in accordance with the putative applicable law, regard must be had to all the circumstances of the case and not only to the circumstances in which the party claiming not to have consented has acted.[1105] In this regard, the court should give particular consideration to the practices followed by the parties inter se as well as their previous business relationships.[1106] This suggests that art.8(2) and art.10(2) may be relied upon by both natural and legal persons.[1107] It is likely, however, that the provision will be more liberally applied in favour of natural persons than it will be in favour of commercial organisations.[1108] This much appears from the brief consideration given to the application of art.8(2) in *Egon Oldendorff v Libera*

[1099] See authorities cited in previous note; Jaffey (1975) 24 I.C.L.Q. 603; Libling (1979) 42 M.L.R. 169; Thomson (1980) 43 M.L.R. 650; Briggs [1990] L.M.C.L.Q. 192.

[1100] *Albeko Schumaschinen AG v Kamborian Shoe Machine Co* [1961] 111 L.J. 519. See also *The Parouth* [1982] 2 Lloyd's Rep. 351; *Union Transport Plc v Continental Lines SA* [1992] 1 W.L.R. 15, 23.

[1101] *Re Bonacina* [1912] 2 Ch. 394.

[1102] See *Egon Oldendorff v Libera Corp (No.1)* [1995] 2 Lloyd's Rep. 64; *The Epsilon Rosa (No.2)* [2002] EWHC 2033 (Comm), [2002] 2 Lloyd's Rep. 701, affirmed on other grounds, [2003] EWCA Civ 938, [2003] 2 Lloyd's Rep. 509; *Morin v Bonhams and Brooks Ltd* [2003] EWHC 467 (Comm), [2003] 2 All E.R. (Comm) 36; affirmed without reference to the point [2003] EWCA Civ 1802, [2004] 1 Lloyd's Rep. 702; *Horn Linie GmbH & Co v Panamerica Formas E Impresos* [2006] EWHC 373 (Comm), [2006] 2 Lloyd's Rep. 44.

[1103] Giuliano-Lagarde Report, p.28.

[1104] Giuliano-Lagarde Report, p.28.

[1105] Giuliano-Lagarde Report, p.28.

[1106] Giuliano-Lagarde Report, p.28.

[1107] As to the meaning of habitual residence in the context of the Rome I Regulation, see above paras 30–164 et seq.

[1108] See *Egon Oldendorff v Libera Corp (No.1)* [1995] 2 Lloyd's Rep. 64; *Horn Linie GmbH & Co v Panamericana Formas E Impresos* [2006] EWHC 373 (Comm), [2006] 2 Lloyd's Rep. 44.

Corp (No.1).[1109] Here it was assumed, without argument, that the Article could be relied on by a legal person and that the habitual residence of a Japanese corporation was in Japan. It was held that English law should apply to determine whether a clause providing for arbitration in London was incorporated into the contract because the contract was governed by English law. The defendants argued in favour of the application of art.8(2), contending that Japanese law governed, as the law of their habitual residence, claiming that it would be unreasonable to determine the effects of their conduct in accordance with English law.[1110] It was held, however, that it would be unreasonable not to apply English law and unreasonable to apply Japanese law. If the latter law was applied, that would in effect ignore the arbitration clause, a result which would not accord with normal commercial expectations. This supports the sensible conclusion that legal persons engaging in commercial transactions should receive little protection from art.8(2) of the Convention or art.10(2) of the Regulation in typical commercial situations and that what protection they might receive should be limited to unusual situations where the strict application of art.8(1) of the Convention or art.10(2) of the Regulation would produce a result which is *commercially unreasonable*.

30–307 Article 8(2) of the Convention and art.10(2) of the Regulation, it must be emphasised, only have the effect of releasing a party from a contract to which he would otherwise be bound under art.8(1) or 10(2). The provisions cannot have the effect of binding a party to a contract to which he would not be bound under the applicable law.[1111]

30–308 **Validity of consent.** The exceptional principle in art.8(2) and art.10(2) seems likely to be confined to the existence of consent, as opposed to the question of whether consent, admittedly given, was invalidated by mistake, misrepresentation, duress, undue influence or non-disclosure.[1112] Whether these factors vitiate consent would be a matter for the putative applicable law, pursuant to art.8(1) of the Rome Convention and art.10(1) of the Regulation.[1113]

[1109] *Egon Oldendorff v Libera Corp (No.1)* [1995] 2 Lloyd's Rep. 64; *Horn Linie GmbH & Co v Panamericana Formas E Impresos* [2006] EWHC 373 (Comm). See also *The Epsilon Rosa (No.2)* [2002] EWHC 2033 (Comm); *Morin v Bonhams and Brooks Ltd* [2003] EWHC 467 (Comm).

[1110] The onus of establishing that art.8(2) and, presumably, art.10(2) apply lies on the party who relies upon the provision: *Egon Oldendorff v Libera Corp (No.1)* [1995] 2 Lloyd's Rep. 64, 71; *The Epsilon Rosa (No.2)* [2002] EWHC 2033; *Horn Linie GmbH & Co v Panamericana formas E Impresos* [2006] EWHC 373 (Comm) (same principle applies in relation to consent to a jurisdiction clause and a choice of law clause).

[1111] *Egon Oldendorff v Libera Corp (No.1)* [1995] 2 Lloyd's Rep. 64, 71.

[1112] *The Epsilon Rosa (No.2)* [2002] EWHC 2033 (Comm), [2002] 2 Lloyd's Rep. 701, affirmed on other grounds, [2003] EWCA Civ 938; *Morin v Bonhams and Brooks Ltd* [2003] EWHC 467 (Comm), [2003] 2 All E.R. (Comm) 36; affirmed without reference to the point [2003] EWCA Civ 1802, [2004] 1 Lloyd's Rep. 702; *Halpern v Halpern (Nos 1 and 2)* [2007] EWCA Civ 291, [2008] Q.B. 195. cf. *Dimskal Shipping Co SA v International Transport Workers Federation* [1992] 2 A.C. 152, 168, per Lord Goff, who appears to regard economic duress as relating both to formation and validity of a contract. cf. *Dicey, Morris and Collins*, para.32–167; Cheshire and North, p.588.

[1113] *Halpern v Halpern (Nos 1 and 2)* [2007] EWCA Civ 291. cf. *Ark Therapeutics Plc v True North Capital Ltd* [2005] EWHC 1585 (Comm), [2006] 1 All E.R. (Comm) 138; *Credit Suisse First Boston (Europe) Ltd v Seagate Trading Co Ltd* [1999] 1 Lloyd's Rep. 784. This was the better view of the position at common law: see *Dimskal Shipping Co SA v International Transport Workers Federation* [1992] 2 A.C. 152; *Dicey, Morris and Collins*, paras 32–166—32–168; 26th edn of this

Validity of contract or terms. Whether the contract itself is materially (or essentially) valid is a matter for the law which would govern it if it were valid. Thus it would seem that art.8(1) of the Convention and art.10(1) of the Regulation will apply to determine the question, for example, of whether a contract is invalid as being in unreasonable restraint of trade.[1114] If the contract is illegal by its applicable law it will be unenforceable in England.[1115] The same principle applies to the material validity of a term of the contract.[1116] Thus, the validity of a term purporting to limit or exempt one party from liability will be governed by the law which would apply to the contract assuming the term were valid.[1117] In substance, this position is the same as that reached by the common law, though the cases tended to speak, in this context, of control by the "proper law" rather than the "putative proper law".[1118] 30–309

(b) *Formal Validity of the Contract*[1119]

Introduction. The position which ultimately came to be accepted at common law[1120] was that a contract was formally valid if it complied with the formal requirements of either the law applicable to the contract,[1121] or the law of the place where the contract was made.[1122] Article 9 of the Rome Convention 30–310

---

work, para.2175. Contrast *Mackender v Feldia* [1967] 2 Q.B. 590. cf. *The Lake Avery* [1997] 1 Lloyd's Rep. 540. As to the existence and validity of consent to a choice of law (art.3(4) of the Convention, art.3(5) of the Regulation), see above, paras 30–059, 30–184.

[1114] See *Duarte v Black & Decker Corp* [2007] EWHC 2720 (QB), [2008] 1 All E.R. (Comm) 401. cf. *Roussillon v Roussillon* (1880) 14 Ch D 351. The foreign law upholding or denying the validity of the contract may be refused application on the grounds of public policy: Rome Convention art.16, Rome I Regulation art.21, below, paras 30–366 et seq.

[1115] cf. *Kahler v Midland Bank Ltd* [1950] A.C. 24. For other aspects of illegality, see below, paras 30–355 et seq.

[1116] See *Egon Oldendorff v Libera Corp (No.1)* [1995] 2 Lloyd's Rep. 64. See also *Ark Therapeutics Plc v True North Capital Ltd* [2005] EWHC 1585 (Comm), [2006] 1 All E.R. (Comm) 138.

[1117] *Surzur Overseas Ltd v Ocean Reliance Shipping Co Ltd* [1997] C.L. 318; *Deepak Fertilisers and Petrochemicals Corp v ICI Chemicals & Polymers Ltd* [1998] 2 Lloyd's Rep. 139 reversed in part, but not on this point, [1999] 1 Lloyd's Rep. 387 CA; *Ocean Chemical Transport Inc v Exnor Craggs Ltd* [2000] 1 All E.R. (Comm) 519; *Amiri Flight Authority v BAE Systems Plc* [2002] EWHC 2481 (Comm), [2003] 1 All E.R. (Comm) 1. cf. *P. & O. Steam Navigation Co v Shand* (1865) 3 Moo. P.C. (N.S.) 272; *Re Missouri S.S. Co* (1889) 42 Ch D 321; *Jones v Oceanic Steam Navigation Co* [1924] 2 K.B. 730; *Sayers v International Drilling Co NV* [1971] 1 W.L.R. 1176; *Coast Lines Ltd v Hudig & Veder Chartering NV* [1972] 2 Q.B. 34; *Coupland v Arabian Gulf Oil Co* [1983] 1 W.L.R. 1136 (affirmed [1983] 1 W.L.R. 1153).

[1118] See 26th edn of this work, para.2183.

[1119] *Dicey, Morris and Collins on the Conflict of Laws*, 14th edn (2006) paras 32–176—32–186; Cheshire and North, *Private International Law*, 13th edn (1999), pp.589–592; Plender, *The European Contracts Convention*, 2nd edn (2001), pp.589–592; Kaye, *The New Private International Law of Contract of the European Community* (1993), pp.281–295; Lagarde in North (ed.), *Contract Conflicts* (1982), pp.51–54.

[1120] See 26th edn of this work, paras 2178–2180; *Dicey & Morris on the Conflict of Laws*, 11th edn (1987), pp.1207–1213.

[1121] *Van Grutten v Digby* (1862) 31 Beav. 561; *Re Bankes* [1902] 2 Ch. 333; *Viditz* v *O'Hagan* [1899] 2 Ch. 569, reversed on other grounds [1900] 2 Ch. 87. See also *Society of Lloyd's v Fraser* [1998] C.L.C. 1630, 1652.

[1122] *Guépratte v Young* (1851) 4 De G. & Sm. 217.

expresses the same principle as the general rule for formal validity.[1123] The Article contains, however, special rules concerning the formal validity of consumer contracts,[1124] certain contracts with regard to immovables[1125] and the formal validity of acts intended to have legal effect relating to an existing or contemplated contract.[1126] Article 11 of the Rome I Regulation is based on the same principles but because it is drafted in different language and contains additional principles, it is necessary to separate the discussion of this issue as between the two instruments. By way of prelude to that discussion, it is necessary to discuss an issue which is common to both instruments (and which, it is thought, will be dealt with in the same way in relation to each of them), namely, the meaning of the expression "formal validity".

30–311 **Meaning of formal validity.** A difficulty which obtained in the common law and one which persists under the Rome Convention and the Rome I Regulation concerns the requirements which are properly to be characterised as affecting formal validity. English common law had relatively few formal requirements and there was also a tendency to regard requirements which appeared, at first sight, to be formal, as questions of procedure to be governed by the *lex fori*,[1127] even though, had the requirement been treated as formal, its application would have been determined by the relevant governing law.[1128] Neither the Convention nor the Regulation provides any definition of formal requirements. The Giuliano-Lagarde Report suggests, however, that it is:

> ". . . nevertheless permissible to consider 'form', for the purposes of art.9, as including every external manifestation required on the part of a person expressing the will to be legally bound, and in the absence of which such expression of will would not be regarded as fully effective."[1129]

This observation, if accepted, indicates that it is possible that the category of formal requirements will expand at the expense of the category of procedure and evidence.[1130] Where a requirement (e.g. of writing) is imposed by the law of the

---

[1123] Rome Convention art.9(1)–(3). See below, para.30–312.

[1124] Rome Convention art.9(5). See below, para.30–313.

[1125] Rome Convention art.9(6). See below, para.30–314.

[1126] Rome Convention art.9(4). See below, para.30–315.

[1127] See *Leroux v Brown* (1852) 12 C.B. 801; *G. & H. Montage GmbH v Irvani* [1990] 1 W.L.R. 667, 684. For consideration of issues relating to formalities in the context of commercial transactions and electronic commerce, see Law Commission, *Electronic Commerce: Formal Requirements in Commercial Transactions, Advice from the Law Commission* (December 2001).

[1128] As in *Leroux v Brown* (1852) 12 C.B. 801 (Statute of Frauds 1677 s.4). This decision has been much criticised: see, e.g. *Monterosso Shipping Co Ltd v International Transport Workers Federation* [1982] I.C.R. 675. But it was approved in *G. & H. Montage GmbH v Irvani* [1990] 1 W.L.R. 667. See too, below, fn.1130.

[1129] Giuliano-Lagarde Report, p.29. This definition does not include the special requirements which have to be fulfilled where there are persons under a disability to be protected, such as the need in French law for the consent of a family council to an act for the benefit of a minor, or where an act is to be valid against third parties, for example the need in English law for a notice of statutory assignment of a chose in action: Giuliano-Lagarde Report, p.29.

[1130] The rules in the Rome Convention and the Rome I Regulation do not apply to evidence and procedure: above, paras 30–044, 30–161. This process might result in a reversal of *Leroux v Brown* (1852) 12 C.B. 801, since s.4 of the Statute of Frauds 1677 could be treated as a formal requirement, the applicability of which depends on art.9. A different approach would be to treat s.4 as subject to

forum with a view to protecting a party to a transaction who is presumed to be in a weaker bargaining position,[1131] such a requirement would seem to be neither formal nor procedural but substantive in effect.[1132] Under the Rome Convention and the Rome I Regulation, such requirements, if not contained in the applicable law, will nonetheless be applicable if they are construed as mandatory rules of the law of the forum, the application of which is required by art.7(2) of the Convention or art.9(2) of the Regulation.[1133]

Rome Convention: general rules. Where a contract is concluded between persons who are in the same country, the contract will be formally valid if it satisfies the formal requirements of the law which governs the contract under the Convention or the formal requirements of the law of the country where it is concluded.[1134] Where the contract is concluded between persons who are in different countries, the contract will be formally valid if it satisfies the formal requirements either of the law applicable to it under the Convention or the law of one of those different countries.[1135] Where the contract is concluded by an agent, the relevant country for the purpose of the foregoing rules is the country where the agent acts.[1136] 30–312

"Certain consumer contracts". The general rules concerning formal validity do not apply to a contract which falls within art.5 of the Convention if the contract is concluded in any of the circumstances described in art.5(2).[1137] In such circumstances the formal validity of the consumer contract is governed by the law of the country in which the consumer has his habitual residence.[1138] 30–313

Immovables.[1139] The formal validity of a contract with regard to an immovable is, in general, governed by the general rules relating to formal validity 30–314

---

art.14(2) (as to which, see below, para.30–315) which permits any act intended to have legal effect to be proved in any manner permitted by the law of the forum or in any manner permitted by the law which renders the contract formally valid under art.9, provided the mode of proof can be administered by the forum. If s.4 falls within this provision, *Leroux v Brown* would be reversed since the contract could have been proved by oral testimony under its French governing law: see *Dicey, Morris and Collins*, para.32–179; Lasok and Stone, *Conflict of Laws in the European Community* (1987), pp.366–367.

[1131] See, e.g. Consumer Credit Act 1974 ss.60–65.

[1132] cf. *English v Donnelly* (1958) S.C. 494, not followed in *Hong Kong Shipping Ltd v The Cavalry* [1987] H.K.L. Rep. 287; cf. *Kay's Leasing Corp Pty Ltd v Fletcher* (1964) 116 C.L.R. 124; *Golden Acres Ltd v Queensland Estates Ltd* [1969] St. R. Qd. 378 (affirmed on different grounds sub nom. *Freehold Land Investments Ltd v Queensland Estates Ltd* (1970) 123 C.L.R. 418); *Nike Information Systems Ltd v Avac Systems Ltd* (1979) 105 D.L.R. (3d) 455; *Greenshields Inc v Johnston* (1981) 119 D.L.R. (3d) 714 (appeal dismissed (1981) 131 D.L.R. (3d) 324); *Bank of Montreal v Snoxell* (1982) 143 D.L.R. (3d) 349.

[1133] Above, paras 30–068, 30–181.

[1134] Rome Convention art.9(1).

[1135] Rome Convention art.9(2).

[1136] Rome Convention art.9(3).

[1137] Rome Convention art.9(5). As to art.5, see above, paras 30–092 et seq.

[1138] Rome Convention art.9(5). As to the meaning of habitual residence, see above, para.30–079.

[1139] See *Dicey, Morris and Collins*, paras 33–240—33–243.

described above.[1140] However, art.9(6) of the Convention establishes an additional rule, in this respect, for contracts the subject matter of which is a right in or a right to use immovable property.[1141] Such a contract:

> "Shall be subject to the mandatory requirements of form of the law of the country where the property is situated if by that law those requirements are imposed irrespective of the country where the contract is concluded and irrespective of the law governing the contract."[1142]

The effect of this provision is to impose the mandatory requirements of form of the *lex situs*, which have the necessary characteristics, on the contract even though the contract is not concluded in the country where the immovable is situated and the law governing the contract is not that of the *lex situs*. Cases in which such rules exist are likely to be "rather rare".[1143]

30–315 **Acts intended to have legal effect.**

> "An act intended to have legal effect relating to an existing or contemplated contract is formally valid if it satisfies the formal requirements of the law which under the Convention governs or would govern the contract or of the law of the country where the act was done."[1144]

This provision covers unilateral acts, connected with a concluded contract, such as notice of termination, remission of a debt, declaration of rescission or repudiation,[1145] or such acts which are connected with a contemplated contract, for example an offer expressed to be open for a specified time.[1146]

30–316 **Effect of change of applicable law.** Article 3(2) of the Rome Convention enables the parties to a contract to change the law which governs it.[1147] However, the change in the applicable law shall not prejudice the formal validity of the

---

1140 See above, para.30–312.

1141 The scope of the provision is coterminous with that of art.4(3), above, para.30–082: see Giuliano-Lagarde Report, p.32.

1142 cf. Plender, p.212 who appears to maintain that art.9(6) is the only rule which deals with the formal validity of contracts the subject matter of which is a right in or a right to use immovable property so that art.9(1)–(4) is excluded. This suggestion cannot be accepted for the reasons given in *Dicey, Morris and Collins*, para.33–341.

1143 Giuliano-Lagarde Report, p.32. In relation to a contract for the sale or other disposition of English land, the Law of Property (Miscellaneous Provisions) Act 1989 s.2(1) is likely to be regarded as mandatory for the purposes of art.9(6): see *Dicey, Morris and Collins*, para.33–242.

1144 Rome Convention art.9(4).

1145 Giuliano-Lagarde Report, p.29. The requirement, in English law, that a contract unsupported by consideration must be by deed, would not seem to be a rule affecting formal validity, but would rather seem to be a rule of substance affecting the material validity of the contract, and would thus be applicable where the contract is, or would be, governed by English law. cf. *Re Bonacina* [1912] 2 Ch. 394. See above, paras 30–306 et seq.

1146 Lasok and Stone, *Conflict of Laws in the European Community* (1987), p.305; Kaye, p.291. Art.9(4) does not apply to public acts (e.g. the act of a notary in authenticating a transaction). The formal validity of such acts is governed by the general rules in Rome Convention art.9(1)–(3): Giuliano-Lagarde Report, p.29.

1147 Above, para.30–058.

contract.[1148] Thus, the contract is valid in respect of form, if it complies with the formal requirements of either the original governing law or the new governing law or the law of the country or countries where the parties were when they concluded the contract.[1149]

Effect of several applicable laws. Where a contract is subject to several applicable laws (either, e.g. because the parties have selected different laws to govern different parts of the contract pursuant to art.3(1),[1150] or because the court has, by way of exception, severed the contract pursuant to art.4(1)),[1151] the Guiliano-Lagarde Report suggests that, in relation to the issue of formal validity: 30–317

"... it would seem reasonable to apply the law applicable to the part of the contract most closely connected with the disputed condition on which its formal validity depends."[1152]

Rome I Regulation: general rules. Article 11(1) of the Rome I Regulation provides that a: 30–318

"... contract concluded between persons who, or whose agents are, in the same country at the time of its conclusion is formally valid if it satisfies the formal requirements of the law which governs it under this Regulation or of the law of the country where it is concluded."

This, in effect, is the same position as is taken in art.9(1), combined with art.9(3), of the Rome Convention.[1153] According to art.11(2):

"... a contract concluded between persons who, or whose agents, are in different countries at the time of its conclusion is formally valid if it satisfies the formal requirements of the law which governs it in substance under this Regulation or of the law of either of the countries where either of the parties or their agent is present at the time of the conclusion, or of the law of the country where either of the parties had his habitual residence at that time."

This provision reflects, first, art.9(2), combined with art.9(3) of the Convention.[1154] Secondly, unlike the Convention, however, art.11(2) of the Regulation also permits a reference to the law of either of the parties' habitual residence,[1155] as a law by which formal validity may be determined. In this respect, therefore, the Regulation is more liberal, as regards the applicable law to determine formal validity, than is the Convention.

1148 Rome Convention art.3(2), second sentence.
1149 Giuliano-Lagarde Report, p.30; Lagarde in North (ed.), *Contract Conflicts* (1982), pp.49, 52–53.
1150 Above, paras 30–056 et seq.
1151 Above, para.30–071.
1152 Giuliano-Lagarde Report, p.30.
1153 Above, para.30–312.
1154 Above, para.30–312.
1155 As to the meaning of which, see above paras 30–164 et seq.

30–319 **Unilateral acts.** Article 11(3) of the Regulation, reflecting a slightly different structure to art.9 of the Convention, then deals with unilateral acts "intended to have legal effect relating to an existing or contemplated contract". Such an act:

> "... is formally valid if it satisfies the formal requirements of the law which governs or would govern the contract in substance under this Regulation, or of the law of the country where the act was done, or of the law of the country where the person by whom it was done had his habitual residence at that time."

Although the equivalent provision in art.9(4) of the Rome Convention referred to an "act" rather than a "unilateral act", it appears that the Convention contemplated a unilateral act, so that no change of substance is intended by this linguistic difference.[1156] The difference between the Convention and the Regulation is, however, that the Regulation, in addition to the laws by which formal validity can be determined under the Convention, also permits formal validity to be determined by the law of the country where the person by whom the act was done had his habitual residence[1157] at the time the act was done. In this respect, therefore, the Regulation is also more liberal in its approach to formal validity than the Rome Convention.[1158]

30–320 **Consumer contracts.** Where contracts are consumer contracts falling within art.6 of the Regulation, art.11(4) of the Regulation provides that the "form of such contracts shall be governed by the law of the country where the consumer has his habitual residence" and excludes art.11(1)–(3).[1159] This provision is obviously different to that in the Rome Convention, because the Regulation defines consumer contracts and the circumstances in which the choice of law rules relating thereto will apply in a different manner.[1160] But each instrument employs the law of the consumer's habitual residence as the governing law.

30–321 **Immovables.** In general, the formal validity of a contract with regard to an immovable is governed, under the Regulation, by the general rules described above.[1161] Article 11(5) of the Regulation, however, establishes an additional rule, in this respect, in relation to "a contract the subject matter of which is a right in rem in immovable property or a tenancy of immovable property", a different formulation to that contained in art.9(6) of the Rome Convention, which is the equivalent provision to art.11(5).[1162] The formal validity of such a contract falling within art.11(5) of the Rome I Regulation shall be governed by:

1156 See above, para.30–315.

1157 As to the meaning of which, see above, paras 30–164 et seq.

1158 Above, para.30–312.

1159 As to the meaning of habitual residence, see above, paras 30–164 et seq.

1160 Above, paras 30–092 et seq.

1161 Subject to Rome I art.6(4)(c) excluding, for the most part, contracts relating to immovables from the consumer contract provisions in art.6, so that art.11(5) will not normally apply to the formal validity of such contracts.

1162 Above, para.30–314. See para.30–192, above, for the meaning of a "right *in rem* in immovable property or a tenancy of immovable property".

"... the requirements of form of the law of the country where the property is situated if by that law: (a) those requirements of form are imposed irrespective of the country where the contract is concluded and irrespective of the law governing the contract, and (b) those requirements cannot be derogated from by agreement."

The effect of this provision, notwithstanding the different terminology to that used in art.9(6) of the Rome Convention, is, it would seem, the same as that reached under the Convention.[1163]

Change of applicable law and several applicable laws. Where the parties agree to change the applicable law, pursuant to art.3(2) of the Regulation,[1164] the position appears to be the same as under the Rome Convention.[1165] Where the parties have selected the law applicable to a part only of the contract, under art.3(1) of the Regulation, and, say, the law applicable to the other part or parts, has to be determined by reference to art.4 of the Regulation,[1166] then again the position would appear to be the same as under the Rome Convention.[1167] 30–322

(c) *Capacity*[1168]

Introduction. Subject to an exception, discussed below,[1169] the uniform rules of the Rome Convention and the Rome I Regulation do not apply to questions involving the status or legal capacity of natural persons.[1170] Nor do the rules apply to the legal capacity of bodies corporate or unincorporate.[1171] Accordingly the law applicable to determine the contractual capacity of a natural person will, subject to the exception, be governed by common law rules, and the law governing the contractual capacity of a body corporate or unincorporate will be entirely governed by common law rules.[1172] 30–323

Natural persons. Despite contrary suggestions in older authorities,[1173] it is submitted that the contractual capacity of a natural person is governed by the law 30–324

1163 Above, para.30–314.

1164 Above, para.30–316.

1165 Above, para.30–317.

1166 Rome I art.4 does not, as such, permit "severance": cf. above, para.30–071.

1167 Above, para.30–317.

1168 See 26th edn of this work, para.2181; *Dicey, Morris and Collinson the Conflict of Laws*, 14th edn (2006), paras 30–021—30–023, 32–217—32–227; Cheshire and North, pp.592–595; Blaikie, 1984 S.L.T. 161.

1169 Below, para.30–324.

1170 arts 1(2)(a) of the Convention and of the Regulation. See above, paras 30–036, 30–153.

1171 art.1(2)(e) of the Convention and art.1(2)(f) of the Regulation. See above, paras 30–041, 30–158. And see art.1(2)(f) of the Convention and art.1(2)(g) of the Regulation, above, paras 30–042, 30–159.

1172 See authorities cited in fn.1168, above.

1173 In favour of the *lex loci contractus*, see *Simonin v Mallac* (1860) 2 Sw. & Tr. 67, 77; *Sottomayor v De Barros (No.2)* (1879) 5 P.D. 94, 100–101; *Baindail v Baindail* [1946] P. 122, 128; *McFeetridge v Stewarts and Lloyds Ltd* (1913) S.C. 773; *Bondholders Securities Corp v Manville* [1933] 4 D.L.R. 609; cf. *Male v Roberts* (1800) 3 Esp. 163. In favour of the law of the domicile, see *Sottomayor v De Barros (No.1)* (1877) 3 P.D. 1, 5; *Re Cooke's Trusts* (1887) 56 L.J. Ch. 637, 639; *Cooper v Cooper* (1883) 13 App. Cas. 88, 89, 100; *Viditz v O'Hagan* [1900] 2 Ch. 87.

applicable to the contract.[1174] In this context, however, the applicable law means that law objectively ascertained, without taking account of any choice of law in the contract itself.[1175] The one intrusion on this state of affairs is to be found in art.11 of the Convention and art.13 of the Regulation (entitled "incapacity") which provide as follows:

> "In a contract concluded between persons who are in the same country, a natural person who would have capacity under the law of that country may invoke his incapacity resulting from another law only if the other party to the contract was aware of this incapacity at the time of the conclusion of the contract or was not aware thereof as a result of negligence."[1176]

In terms, this rule is of limited effect. It only applies to contracts concluded between persons who are in the same country, one of whom must be a natural person who has capacity under that country's law, but who seeks to rely on a lack of capacity under the law of another country. That lack of capacity may only successfully be invoked if the other contracting party was aware of it or was unaware of it as a result of negligence.[1177]

30–325 **Corporations.** The contractual capacity of a corporation depends both on its constitution and on the law applicable to the contract which is concluded. Thus in so far as a corporation's capacity to enter into a contract depends on its constitution, the law of the country of incorporation is the governing law,[1178] though the corporation must also possess capacity under the law applicable to the

---

[1174] *Charron v Montreal Trust Co* (1958) 15 D.L.R. (2d) 240; see also *The Bodley Head Ltd v Flegon* [1972] 1 W.L.R. 68; *Marubeni Hong Kong and South China Ltd v Mongolian Government* [2002] 2 All E.R. (Comm) 873; and the authorities cited in fn.1168, above. It is possible that the law of the domicile would be applied if it would give capacity but the objective governing law would not: see *Dicey, Morris and Collins*, para.32–223.

[1175] See *Cooper v Cooper* (1883) 13 App. Cas. 88, 108; *Dicey, Morris and Collins*, para.32–224; Cheshire and North, p.593.

[1176] There is a slight difference in the wording of art.13 of the Regulation where "this incapacity" becomes "that incapacity", but the difference is of no substantive significance. Such a rule is not uncommon in civil law countries which regard contractual capacity as a matter of status to be governed by the personal law: see Giuliano-Lagarde Report, p.34.

[1177] The wording implies that the burden of proof lies on the party lacking capacity to show that the other party knew of the incapacity or should have known of it: Giuliano-Lagarde Report, p.34.

[1178] *Risdon Iron and Locomotive Works Ltd v Furniss* [1906] 1 K.B. 49, 56–57; *Banque Internationale de Commerce de Petrograd v Goukassow* [1923] 2 K.B. 682, 690–691; *Janred Properties Ltd v ENIT* [1989] 2 All E.R. 444; *J.H. Rayner (Mincing Lane) Ltd v Department of Trade and Industry* [1990] 2 A.C. 418; *Sierra Leone Telecommunications Co Ltd v Barclays Bank Plc* [1998] 2 All E.R. 821; *Merrill Lynch Capital Services Inc v Municipality of Piraeus* [1997] C.L.C. 1214; *Azov Shipping Co v Baltic Shipping Co* [1999] 2 Lloyd's Rep. 159; *Grupo Torras SA v Al-Sabah* [1999] C.L.C. 1469, reversed in part on other grounds, [2001] C.L.C. 221; *Continental Enterprises Ltd v Shandong Zucheng Foreign Trade Group Co* [2005] EWHC 92 (Comm); *Laemthong International Lines Co Ltd v Artis (No.3)* [2005] EWHC 1595 (Comm). See also *Marubeni Hong Kong and South China Ltd v Government of Mongolia* [2004] EWHC 472 (Comm), [2004] 2 Lloyd's Rep. 198, affirmed on other grounds, [2005] EWCA Civ 395, [2005] 1 W.L.R. 2497; Foreign Corporations Act 1991 s.1; Companies Act 2006 ss.43, 44, 45(1) and 51.

contract.[1179] It may, accordingly, be taken to lack capacity to enter into a contract if the law of the country of incorporation so holds because of a limitation on its powers under its constitution (e.g. the doctrine of ultra vires)[1180] or if the law applicable to the contract so holds on the basis of a principle of capacity which is unrelated to its constitutional powers.[1181] According to art.1(2)(e) of the Rome Convention and art.1(2)(f) of the Rome I Regulation, as pointed out above,[1182] the legal capacity of a corporation is not covered by the Convention or by the Regulation. But the Giuliano-Lagarde Report states that this reference is to limitations which may be imposed by law on companies or firms.[1183] It does not extend to ultra vires acts by organs of the company or firm,[1184] which are excluded by art.1(2)(f) of the Convention and art.1(2)(g) of the Regulation, which provide inter alia, that the Convention and the Regulation do not apply to the question whether an organ can bind a body corporate or unincorporate to a third party.[1185] Since the combined effect of respectively, art.1(2)(e), (f) and (g) is to exclude the contractual capacity of a corporation, however arising, exclusion of ultra vires acts under art.1(2)(f) or (g) rather than under art.1(2)(e) or (f) appears to produce no practical consequence, since in either case the common law rules described above will continue to apply.[1186]

(d) *Particular Issues: Article 10*[1187]

Introduction. Article 10(1) of the Rome Convention and art.12 of the Rome I Regulation, which are expressed in virtually identical language, and each of which is entitled "Scope of the applicable law", stipulates that the law applicable to a contract by virtue of the Convention or the Regulation will govern "in particular" the following matters: interpretation[1188]; performance[1189]; within the 30–326

[1179] See references in preceding note and: *General Steam Navigation Co v Guillou* (1843) 11 M. & W. 877; *Pickering v Stephenson* (1872) L.R. 14 Eq. 322; *Bateman v Service* (1881) 6 App. Cas. 386, 389; *Banco de Bilbao v Sancha and Rey* [1938] 2 K.B. 176; *National Bank of Greece and Athens SA v Metliss* [1958] A.C. 509; *Carl Zeiss Stiftung v Rayner & Keeler Ltd (No.2)* [1967] 1 A.C. 853.

[1180] cf. *Janred Properties Ltd v ENIT* [1989] 2 All E.R. 444.

[1181] There is little likelihood of this happening in practice where English law is the applicable law. The nearest English analogy is the now repealed law of Mortmain: see *Dicey, Morris and Collins*, para.30–022.

[1182] Above, paras 30–041, 30–158.

[1183] See Giuliano-Lagarde Report, p.12 where the example given is a limitation on power to acquire immovable property.

[1184] Giuliano-Lagarde Report, p.13. See, too, *Dicey, Morris and Collins*, paras 30–025—30–028.

[1185] Above, paras 30–042, 30–159.

[1186] art.11 of the Convention and art.13 of the Regulation (above, para.30–324) only apply to contracts entered into by natural persons.

[1187] See *Dicey, Morris and Collins on the Conflict of Laws*, 14th edn (2006), paras 32–189—32–210; Cheshire and North, *Private International Law*, 13th edn (1999), pp.595–600; Plender, *The European Contracts Convention*, 2nd edn (2001), pp.215–223; Kaye, *The New Private International Law of Contract of the European Community* (1993), pp.297–310; Lagarde in North (ed.), *Contract Conflicts* (1982), p.49, at pp.54–57.

[1188] Rome Convention art.10(1)(a), art.12(1)(a) of the Regulation.

[1189] Rome Convention art.10(1)(b), art.12(1)(b) of the Regulation. As to the "manner of performance", see art.10(2) of the Convention, art.12(2) of the Regulation.

limits of the powers conferred on the court by its procedural law, the consequences of breach, including the assessment of damages in so far as it is governed by rules of law[1190]; the various ways of extinguishing obligations, and prescription and limitation of actions,[1191] and the consequences of nullity of the contract.[1192]

30–327 **Rome Convention: consequences of nullity.** In relation to the last issue it must, however, be immediately pointed out that in cases falling within the Rome Convention, the applicable law will *not* be applied to determine the consequences of nullity of the contract in United Kingdom law. This is because the Convention recognises the power of contracting states to enter a reservation to this particular provision, which power was exercised by the United Kingdom.[1193] Accordingly, art.10(1)(e) does not have the force of law in the United Kingdom.[1194] In the law of United Kingdom jurisdictions the consequences of nullity of the contract belong to the law of restitution, and, as such, the relevant choice of law rules are those applicable to restitution rather those applicable to contractual obligations.[1195] This may, however be affected by the Rome II Regulation which contains choice of law rules on unjust enrichment which is apt to include the consequences of nullity of a contract, but this is most unclear as the latter concept is to be interpreted in an autonomous fashion and since, as pointed out below, the consequences of nullity of a contract are under the Rome I Regulation, a matter for the law applicable to the contract, it may well be that unjust enrichment under the Rome II Regulation on the law applicable to non-contractual obligations will be interpreted to exclude this issue from its scope.[1196]

30–328 **Rome I Regulation: consequences of nullity.** In contrast to the position under the Rome Convention, the law applicable to the contract under the Rome I Regulation will apply to determine the consequences of nullity of a contract[1197] and Member States have no power to make a reservation on the matter. This would seem to mean that, under the Rome I Regulation, the law applicable to the contract, or which would have been applicable to the contract had it been valid,[1198] will be the governing law rather than the rules governing unjust enrichment contained in the Rome II Regulation, because of the principle of

[1190] Rome Convention art.10(1)(c), art.12(1)(c) of the Regulation.
[1191] Rome Convention art.10(1)(d), art.12(1)(d) of the Regulation.
[1192] Rome Convention art.10(1)(e), art.12(1)(e) of the Regulation.
[1193] Rome Convention art.22(1)(b).
[1194] Contracts (Applicable Law) Act 1990 s.2(2).
[1195] See North in North (ed.), *Contract Conflicts* (1982), p.3, at pp.16–17; Giuliano-Lagarde Report, p.33; cf. *Caterpillar Financial Services Corp v SNC Passion* [2004] EWHC 569 (Comm), [2004] 2 Lloyd's Rep. 99 at [16]. On the choice of law rules applicable to restitution, see generally, *Dicey, Morris and Collins*, para.32–210, Ch.34 and *First Supplement* (2007), Ch.34; Cheshire and North, Ch.20; Panagopoulos, *Restitution in Private International Law* (2000); Rose (ed.), *Restitution and the Conflict of Laws* (1995); Dickinson [1996] LMCLQ 556. See also *Baring Bros & Co Ltd v Cunninghame DC*, *The Times*, September 30, 1996, [1997] C.L.C. 108 (Outer House of the Court of Session).
[1196] See above, para.30–034.
[1197] Rome I art.12(1)(e).
[1198] And see art.10(1) of the Regulation, above, para.30–305.

mutually exclusive interpretation, as between the Rome I Regulation and the Rome II Regulation, described above.[1199]

Overlapping categories. Questions may arise, of course, which overlap the particular categories of issue expressly referred to in art.10(1) of the Convention and art.12(1) of the Regulation. For example whether a contract has been frustrated may relate to interpretation, or performance, or to the extinguishing of obligations,[1200] while, in respect of the Rome I Regulation, the question may relate to the consequences of nullity of the contract.[1201] But since the applicable law governs all of these issues, no practical consequence can result from placing frustration (or any other overlapping question) in one category or another. 30–329

Non-exhaustive list. The list of issues in art.10(1) and art.12(1) is not intended to be exhaustive,[1202] so that in consequence, national courts may refer other issues which may arise in a contractual context to the law which governs the contract. Some of these issues are discussed at a later point.[1203] 30–330

Interpretation. At common law, a contract was construed and interpreted according to the canons of construction that prevailed in the law applicable to the contract.[1204] The same principle is adopted in the Rome Convention[1205] and in the Rome I Regulation.[1206] Thus the applicable law will determine the meaning to be given to particular words or phrases in the contract, for example the meaning of payment in "gold,"[1207] "pounds"[1208] or "shillings".[1209] 30–331

[1199] Above, para.30–150.

[1200] *Dicey, Morris and Collins*, para.32–190.

[1201] Rome I art.12(1)(e). The consequences which flow after it has been determined that the contract has been frustrated according to its applicable law will probably not be determined by the Rome Convention at all, because of the United Kingdom's reservation to art.10(1)(e), discussed above, paras 31–033, 30–327 above. And see below, para.30–347; *Benjamin's Sale of Goods*, 7th edn (2006), paras 25–176—25–177.

[1202] "The law applicable to a contract . . . shall govern *in particular*" [emphasis added].

[1203] Below, para.30–348.

[1204] e.g. *St Pierre v South American Stores Ltd* [1937] 3 All E.R. 349; *A.B. Bofors-Uva C.A.V. Ltd v A.B. Skandia Transport* [1982] 1 Lloyd's Rep. 410.

[1205] Rome Convention art.10(1)(a). And see *The Ikariada* [1999] 2 Lloyd's Rep. 365, 373; *OT Africa Line Ltd v Magic Sportswear Corp* [2005] EWCA Civ 710, [2005] 2 Lloyd's Rep. 170; *CGU International Insurance Plc v Astrazeneca Insurance Co* [2005] EWHC 2755 (Comm), [2006] C.L.C. 162.

[1206] Rome I art.12(1)(a).

[1207] cf. *St Pierre v South American Stores Ltd* [1937] 3 All E.R. 349. See also *Feist v Société Intercommunale Belge d'Electricité* [1934] A.C. 161; *Treseder-Griffin v Co-operative Insurance Society Ltd* [1956] 2 Q.B. 127; *The Rosa S.* [1989] Q.B. 419; *S.S. Pharmaceutical Co v Quantas Airways* [1991] 1 Lloyd's Rep. 288. See below, paras 30–369 et seq.

[1208] cf. *Bonython v Commonwealth of Australia* [1951] A.C. 201. See below, paras 30–369 et seq.

[1209] cf. *W.J. Alan & Co Ltd v El Nasr Export and Import Co* [1972] Q.B. 189. If, however, there is no doubt as to the identity of the currency referred to, then it is for the law of the country whose currency is mentioned to determine what is legal tender in that currency: this seems to rest on an "implied" choice of law (art.3(1) of the Rome Convention, above, para.30–051 and below, paras 30–370 et seq., art.3(1) of the Rome I Regulation, above, paras 30–172 et seq. and below, paras 30–370 et seq.) which implied choice may be limited to this question alone (i.e. the issue is "severed," see above, paras 30–056 et seq. and below, para.30–371) and submitted to its own governing law under art.3(1) of the Convention or the Regulation, as the case may be.) cf. *Pyrmont*

30–332 **Performance.** Article 10(1)(b) of the Rome Convention and art.12(1)(b) of the Rome I Regulation provide that the applicable law shall govern "performance" of the contract.[1210] The scope of these provisions must, initially, be delimited by reference to art.10(2) of the Convention and art.12(2) of the Regulation, each of which provide that in:

> "... relation to the manner of performance and the steps to be taken in the event of defective performance regard shall be had to the law of the country in which performance takes place."

The distinction between "performance" and "manner of performance" is the distinction between the substance of the obligation to be performed and the mode of performance of that obligation.[1211] Whereas the former matter is governed by the law applicable to the contract,[1212] the latter question is governed by the law of the place of performance[1213] which may be a law other than the governing law where the governing law is not that of the country in which the contract was to be performed.[1214] As far as "performance" is concerned, the Giuliano-Lagarde Report informs that it:

> "... appears to embrace the totality of the conditions, resulting from the law or from the contract, in accordance with which the acts essential for the fulfilment of the obligation must be performed ... ."[1215]

This observation lacks clarity but is rendered less difficult by the examples which follow, namely: the diligence with which the obligation must be performed; conditions relating to the place and time of performance; the extent to which the obligation can be performed by a person other than the party liable; the conditions as to performance of the obligation both in general and in relation to certain categories of obligation (joint and several obligations, alternative obligations, divisible and indivisible obligations, pecuniary obligations); where performance consists of the payment of a sum of money, the conditions relating to the discharge of the debtor who has made the payment, the appropriation of the payment, the receipt, etc.[1216]

30–333 **Manner of performance.** The foregoing issues must be distinguished from those which merely affect the "manner of performance" which are subject to

---

v Schott [1939] A.C. 145. See *Dicey, Morris and Collins*, para.36–009. As to currency questions, see further, below, paras 30–176—30–185.

[1210] *Import Export Metro Ltd v Compania Sud Americana de Vapores SA* [2003] EWHC 11 (Comm), [2003] 1 All E.R. (Comm) 703; *East West Corp v DKBS 1912 A/S* [2003] EWCA Civ 83; [2003] Q.B. 1509. As to illegality by the law of the place of performance, see below, paras 30–358 et seq.

[1211] *East West Corp v DKBS 1912 A/S* [2003] EWCA Civ 83, [2003] Q.B. 1509. This distinction was recognised in the common law. See *Jacobs v Crédit Lyonnais* (1884) 12 QBD 589; *Mount Albert BC v Australian Temperance & General Mutual Life Assurance Society* [1938] A.C. 224; *Bonython v Commonwealth of Australia* [1951] A.C. 201. See the 26th edn of this work, para.2184.

[1212] *Import Export Metro Ltd v Compania Sud Americana de Vapores SA* [2003] EWHC 11 (Comm); *East West Corp v DKBS 1912 A/S* [2003] EWCA Civ 83.

[1213] *East West Corp v DKBS 1912 A/S* [2003] EWCA Civ 83, [2003] Q.B. 1509.

[1214] *East West Corp v DKBS 1912 A/S* [2003] EWCA Civ 83, [2003] Q.B. 1509.

[1215] Giuliano-Lagarde Report, p.32.

[1216] Giuliano-Lagarde Report, pp.32–33.

art.10(2) of the Convention and art.12(2) of the Regulation. The latter expression is not defined in the Convention: no precise meaning is given to it in the various laws of contracting states, and, indeed, the drafting group was not prepared to provide a strict (or one might add, any) definition of it.[1217] In consequence, the Giuliano-Lagarde Report opines that it will be for the *lex fori* to determine what is meant by the expression.[1218] This view has, however, been challenged, it being suggested that it would be more appropriate to draw the distinction in a uniform manner on the basis of a Convention interpretation of the distinction.[1219] The latter view has much to be said for it. The expression "manner of performance" remains undefined in the Rome I Regulation. It is suggested, however, that in relation to this instrument, an autonomous interpretation is most likely to be preferred.

Examples. However the distinction is ultimately to be drawn, the Giuliano-Lagarde Report mentions, as examples of rules affecting the manner of performance: 30–334

> "... the rules governing public holidays, the manner in which goods are to be examined, and the steps to be taken if they are refused."[1220]

Thus, for example, if a contract governed by English law provides that the seller will deliver goods to the buyer in Paris "during usual business hours", it will be for French law to determine what business hours are "usual," since this relates to the manner of performance, but it will be for English law to determine whether performance of the contract is excused by force majeure.[1221] And if, pursuant to a contract governed by English law, a seller agrees to deliver goods to the buyer in Barcelona for export to Athens, Spanish law will determine whether an export licence is required, though English law will determine whether the seller or the buyer is contractually obliged to obtain a licence and whether, if no licence is obtained, one or other of the parties is in breach of contract.[1222] Equally, in a contract of sale, the applicable law will determine matters such as the person other than the buyer (if any) to whom delivery may be made, the identity and quantity of goods to be delivered, the nature of any additional duties of the seller in relation to the goods, and the documents, if any, that must be prepared and tendered by the seller.[1223] But questions relating to the mode of delivery such as the usages governing the unloading of goods at a particular port, will be regulated by the law of the place of performance.[1224]

[1217] Giuliano-Lagarde Report, p.33.

[1218] Giuliano-Lagarde Report, p.33.

[1219] *Dicey, Morris and Collins*, para.32–197.

[1220] Giuliano-Lagarde Report, p.33. See also *Import Export Metro Ltd v Compania Sud Americana de Vapores SA* [2003] EWHC 11 (Comm), [2003] 1 All E.R. (Comm) 703; *East West Corp v DKBS 1912 A/S* [2003] EWCA Civ 83, [2003] Q.B. 1509.

[1221] cf. *Jacobs v Crédit Lyonnais* (1884) 12 QBD 589; *Dicey, Morris and Collins*, para.32–199.

[1222] cf. *Pound & Co Ltd v Hardy & Co Inc* [1956] A.C. 588; *Dicey, Morris and Collins*, para.32–199.

[1223] See *Benjamin's Sale of Goods*, 7th edn (2006), para.25–156.

[1224] See *Import Export Metro Ltd v Compania Sud Americana de Vapores SA* [2003] EWHC 11 (Comm), [2003] 1 All E.R. (Comm) 703; *East West Corp v DKBS 1912 A/S* [2003] EWCA Civ 83; [2003] Q.B. 1509. cf. *Robertson v Jackson* (1845) 2 C.B. 412.

30–335 **Discretion.** Although the Convention and the Regulation perpetuate a distinction drawn in the common law between the "substance" of performance and the "manner" of such performance, there may be one difference between art.10(2) and art.12(2) and the position at common law. At common law, reference of matters affecting the manner of performance to the law of the place of performance seems to be a choice of law rule the application of which does not depend on any discretionary element. Article 10(2) and art.12(2), on the other hand, require simply that "regard shall be had" to the law of the country in which performance takes place. According to the Giuliano-Lagarde Report, the court:

> "May consider whether such law has any relevance to the manner in which the contract should be performed and has a discretion whether to apply it in whole or in part so as to do justice between the parties."[1225]

If this view is correct, the role and operation of art.10(2) and art.12(2) becomes somewhat uncertain in scope.

30–336 **Consequences of breach, etc.** According to art.10(1)(c) of the Rome Convention, the applicable law governs, within the limits of the powers conferred on the court by its procedural law, the consequences of breach including the assessment of damages in so far as it is governed by rules of law. The equivalent provision in art.12(1)(c) of the Rome I Regulation is largely expressed in identical language except that the expression "consequences of breach" becomes "the consequences of the total or partial breach of obligations". It would seem that it is most unlikely that any substantive change is intended by this different wording, since breach in art.10(1)(c) would surely be apt to cover either a total or partial breach. The expressions "consequences of breach" and "consequences of total or partial breach" are capable of wide interpretation.[1226] According to the Giuliano-Lagarde Report, which may be taken as a guide to the meaning of both expressions, the former expression refers to:

> ". . . the consequences which the law or the contract attaches to the breach of a contractual obligation, whether it is a matter of the liability of the party to whom the breach is attributable or of a claim to terminate the contract for breach. Any requirement of service of notice on the party to assume his liability also comes within this context."[1227]

The expressions would therefore appear to include the question of whether an innocent party has a right to treat the contract as repudiated or to rescind the

---

[1225] Giuliano-Lagarde Report, p.33.

[1226] See Kaye, pp.304–305. See also the Dutch case, *Buenaventura v Ocean Trade Co* [1984] E.C.C. 183, cited in Cheshire and North, p.598, where it was said (before the Rome Convention entered into force) that the expression must be construed widely, and could include strikes so that striking crew members on a Saudi Arabian ship lying at a Dutch port could be ordered to return to work on the ground that the strike was illegal under the governing law of the contract, the law of the Philippines: sed quaere. As to currency questions, see below, paras 30–369 et seq.

[1227] Giuliano-Lagarde Report, p.33. See also *Arcado v SA Haviland* (9/87) [1988] E.C.R. 1539, 1555 (art.10(1)(c) governs consequences of total or partial failure to comply with obligations under contract and consequently the contractual liability of the party responsible for breach); cf. *Kuwait Oil Tanker Co S.A.K v Al Bader* [2000] 2 All E.R. (Comm) 271, 333–334 (no view expressed as to whether right to claim interest was one of "the consequences of breach").

contract.[1228] The expressions (and the remaining words of art.10(1)(c) and art.12(1)(c)) also raise questions as to the effect of the applicable law on remedies, which questions are discussed in the two paragraphs which follow.

Damages. At common law a distinction is drawn between rules relating to remoteness of damage and heads of damages which are governed by the law applicable to the contract,[1229] and rules relating to the measure or quantification of damages which are governed by the *lex fori* since they are treated as a matter of procedure.[1230] It would seem incontrovertible that remoteness and heads of damage in contract are matters for the applicable law according to art.10(1)(c) and art.12(1)(c).[1231] More doubt surrounds the question of measure or quantification of damages. Article 10(1)(c) and art.12(1)(c) state that *assessment* of damages is a matter for the applicable law in so far as it is governed by rules of law. According to the Giuliano-Lagarde Report, this formulation is intended to exclude assessment of damages which is only concerned with questions of fact[1232] (e.g. arithmetical calculation of loss where the formula for such calculation is not dictated by rules of law). Where, however, a rule of law imposes a limit on compensation,[1233] or draws distinctions between penalties and liquidated damages,[1234] or provides a principle by which the measure of damages for, say, non-delivery of goods can be calculated,[1235] the applicability of the rule will depend on the governing law. In this context (as in other contexts in art.10(1)(c) and art.12(1)(c)) the scope of the applicable law is limited by "the powers conferred on the court by its procedural law". Thus, for example, an English court could refuse to award damages in the form of periodical payments as 30–337

[1228] *Dicey, Morris and Collins*, para.32–201; Kaye, p.305; *Benjamin's Sale of Goods*, 7th edn (2006), paras 25–178—25–202.

[1229] *D'Almedia Araujo Lda v Sir Frederick Becker & Co Ltd* [1953] 2 Q.B. 329 (where the question of the existence of a duty to mitigate damage was also said to be governed by the law applicable to the contract); *Livesley v Clemens Horst Co* [1925] 1 D.L.R. 159. A contractual term which limits the obligation to pay damages for a breach of contract or a statutory provision which is deemed to operate as such a term has been held to be substantive at common law: see *Cope v Doherty* (1858) 2 De G. &J. 614 at 626; *Allen J. Panozza & Co Pty Ltd v Allied Interstate (Qld) Pty Ltd* [1976] 2 N.S.W.L.R. 192, 196–197; *Harding v Wealands* [2006] UKHL 32, [2007] 2 A.C. 1 at [44]–[46]; and see *Stevens v Head* (1993) 176 C.L.R. 433, 458. See also *Boys v Chaplin* [1971] A.C. 356; *Dicey, Morris and Collins*, para.32–202; Cheshire and North, pp.85–88, 598–599.

[1230] *D'Almedia Araujo Lda v Sir Frederick Becker & Co Ltd* [1953] 2 Q.B. 328, 338; *Livesley v Clemens Horst Co* [1925] 1 D.L.R. 159; see also *Harding v Wealands* [2006] UKHL 32; *Boys v Chaplin* [1971] A.C. 356, 378, 381–382, 383, 394; *Edmunds v Simmonds* [2001] 1 W.L.R. 1003; *Hulse v Chambers* [2001] 1 W.L.R. 2386; *Roerig v Valiant Trawlers Ltd* [2002] EWCA Civ 21; [2002] 1 W.L.R. 2304; and works cited in preceding note. cf. *John Pfeiffer Pty Ltd v Rogerson* (2000) 203 C.L.R. 503; *Régie Nationale des Usines Renault SA v Zhang* (2003) 210 C.L.R. 491.

[1231] As would the existence of a duty to mitigate damage: cf. above, fn.1229.

[1232] Giuliano-Lagarde Report, p.33.

[1233] Giuliano-Lagarde Report, p.33. In *Harding v Wealands* [2006] UKHL 32, [2007] 2 A.C. 1 it was held that a statutory ceiling on damages in tort imposed by a foreign law was procedural rather than substantive and that the quantification of damages in tort was exclusively a matter for the law of the forum. But it was accepted that a contractual term which limits the obligation to pay damages for breach of contract or a statutory provision which is deemed to operate as such a term was substantive: [2006] UKHL 32 at [44]–[46] and above, fn.1229. In any event the views expressed in *Harding v Wealands*, above cannot affect the position under either the Rome Convention or the Rome I Regulation.

[1234] *Dicey, Morris and Collins*, para.32–201.

[1235] See, e.g. Sale of Goods Act 1979 ss.51(2) and (3); Vol.II, paras 43–419 et seq.

required by the law governing the contract, because there is no procedural machinery for making such an award.[1236]

30–338 **Other remedies.** Although the matter has received little discussion and is the subject of only scanty authority, it was generally stated that at common law the availability of the equitable remedies of specific performance or injunction was a matter for the *lex fori*.[1237] The position appears to be different under the Rome Convention and the Rome I Regulation, since the availability of a particular remedy would seem to be a consequence of breach which is referable to the applicable law pursuant to either art.10(1)(c) of the Convention or art.12(1)(c) of the Regulation.[1238] The applicable law should thus determine the availability of an injunction[1239] or a decree of specific performance. Such availability will, of course, be subject to the procedural proviso to both arts 10(1)(c) and 12(1)(c), i.e. to "the limits of the powers conferred on the court by its procedural law". Thus the English court could refuse, for example, a decree of specific performance if the order would require constant supervision by the court, according to English principles.[1240]

30–339 **Interest.** At common law, liability to pay contractual interest and the rate of interest payable in respect of a contractual debt were determined by the law applicable to the contract under which the debt was incurred.[1241] This is also the position under the Rome Convention and, it is submitted, under the Rome I Regulation though it would seem that this result is reached by reference to art.10(1)(b) of the Convention or art.12(1)(b) of the Regulation ("performance") since the liability to pay contractual interest and the rate thereof relate to the substance of the obligation to be performed.[1242] Where interest was claimed as damages for non-payment of a debt, the better view was that liability at common law similarly depended on the law applicable to the contract.[1243] The rate of

[1236] See Morse (1982) 2 Ybk. Eur. L. 107, 154–155; cf. *The Indian Grace* [1992] 1 Lloyd's Rep. 124, reversed, on other grounds, *sub nom. Republic of India v India S.S. Co* [1993] A.C. 410.

[1237] *Baschet v London Illustrated Standard Co* [1900] 1 Ch. 73; *Boys v Chaplin* [1971] A.C. 356, 394; *Dicey, Morris and Collins*, para.7–006. See also *Warner Brothers Pictures Inc v Nelson* [1937] 1 K.B. 209 where the point was neither raised nor discussed.

[1238] *Dicey, Morris and Collins*, para.32–201; Cheshire and North, p.599. *Dicta* in *Harding v Wealands* [2006] UKHL 32, [2007] 2 A.C. 1 at [32] suggest that the nature of the available remedy is a matter of procedure, at common law, but this cannot affect the position under either the Rome Convention or the Rome I Regulation.

[1239] This refers to a final injunction. The right to an interlocutory injunction would seem to be a matter of procedure for the *lex fori* as would other forms of interlocutory relief.

[1240] See above, fn.1238.

[1241] See e.g. *Mount Albert BC v Australasian Temperance & General Mutual Life Insurance Society* [1938] A.C. 224. As to other currency questions, see below, paras 30–370 et seq. For a discussion of pre-judgment interest in the conflict of laws, see Guest in Rose (ed.), *Lex Mercatoria: Essays in Honour of Francis Reynolds* (2000), p.271.

[1242] *Dicey, Morris and Collins*, paras 32–200, 33–383.

[1243] *Miliangos v George Frank (Textiles) Ltd (No.2)* [1977] Q.B. 489, 496–497; *Helmsing Schiffahrts GmbH v Malta Drydocks Corp* [1977] 2 Lloyd's Rep. 444, 449–450; *Lesotho Highlands Development Authority v Impregilo SpA* [2002] EWHC 2435 (Comm), [2003] 1 All E.R. (Comm) 22, affirmed without deciding this point, [2003] EWCA Civ 1159, [2003] 2 Lloyd's Rep. 497. The contrary view, that the question is a matter of procedure governed by the *lex fori*, was expressed in *Midland International Trade Services v Sudairy, Financial Times*, May 2, 1990 (Hobhouse J.) and in *Kuwait Oil Tanker Co SAK v Al Bader, The Independent*, January 11, 1999 (Moore-Bick J.). On

interest payable as damages was, however, governed by the *lex fori*.[1244] Under the Rome Convention, the right to claim interest as damages would seem to be a consequence of breach governed by the applicable law pursuant to art.10(1)(c) of the Convention and the same position would seem to prevail under art.12(1)(c) of the Rome I Regulation.[1245] It is also submitted that under the Convention and the Regulation the rate of such interest should continue to be a matter of procedure governed by the *lex fori*, a result which is not at variance with the terms of the Convention or the Regulation since neither instrument applies to procedure.[1246]

Exchange losses. The right to claim contractual interest and interest by way of damages must be distinguished from the question whether a contracting party who has paid a contractual debt after the due date is liable for exchange losses if the currency in which payment is expressed to be paid depreciates in value relative to the currency in which the other contracting party operates. The existence of such liability depended, at common law, on the law applicable to the contract.[1247] The same result should follow under the Rome Convention since the question relates to the consequences of breach, governed by the applicable law 30–340

appeal in the latter case, the Court of Appeal found it unnecessary to express a concluded view: see [2000] 2 All E.R. (Comm) 271, 339–344. In *Lesotho Highlands Development Authority v Impregilo SpA*, Morison J. preferred the view expressed in the text and in *Dicey, Morris and Collins*, paras 30–392—30–393, but the Court of Appeal, again found it unnecessary to express a concluded view. The House of Lords allowed an appeal from the decision of the Court of Appeal, [2003] UKHL 43, [2006] 1 A.C. 221, but no view was expressed on the point. The case was concerned with an arbitrator's power to award interest and it was held that Arbitration Act 1996 s.49(3) had not been expressly excluded by the parties. For an earlier but inconclusive case on the point, see *Zebrarise Ltd v De Nieffe* [2004] EWHC 1842 (Comm), [2005] 1 Lloyd's Rep. 154. In *Kuwait Oil Tanker Co SAK v Al Bader*, the Court of Appeal found it unnecessary to express a view on whether the right to claim compound interest should be regarded as substantive or procedural in nature.

1244 This is controversial: in favour, see *Rogers v Markel Corp* [2004] EWHC 1375 (QB), [2004] EWHC 2046 (QB); *Miliangos v George Frank (Textiles) Ltd (No.2)* [1977] Q.B. 489; against, see *Helmsing Schiffahrts GmbH v Malta Drydocks Corp* [1977] 2 Lloyd's Rep. 444. Since these decisions the Law Commission has conducted a thorough examination of the question and has concluded that the view expressed in the text should be preferred: see Law Com. No.124, 1983, paras 2.32, 3.55 and Law Com. Working Paper No.80, 1981, paras 4.22–4.27. See also, *The Pacific Colocotronis* [1981] 2 Lloyd's Rep. 40; *Swiss Bank Corp v State of New South Wales* (1993–94) 33 N.S.W.L.R. 63; *Dicey, Morris and Collins*, paras 33–397—33–399.

1245 Giuliano-Lagarde Report, p.32; *Dicey, Morris and Collins*, para.33–393. And see *Lesotho Highlands Development Authority v Impregilo SpA* [2000] EWHC 2435 (Comm). cf. *Kuwait Oil Tanker Co SAK v Al Bader* [2000] 2 All E.R. (Comm) 271, 333–334 (no view expressed on question of whether the right to claim interest by way of damages belonged to the "consequences of breach" for the purposes of art.10(1)(c) of the Rome Convention).

1246 *Lesotho Highlands Development Authority v Impregilo* [2003] EWCA Civ 1159, [2003] 2 Lloyd's Rep. 497, reversed, without reference to the point, [2005] UKHL] 43, [2006] 1 A.C. 221; Rome Convention art.1(2)(h); Rome I Regulation art.1(2)(i); *Dicey, Morris and Collins*, para.33–397.

1247 *President of India v Lips Maritime Corp* [1988] A.C. 395; *Ozalid Group (Export) Ltd v African Continental Bank Ltd* [1979] 2 Lloyd's Rep. 331; *International Minerals and Chemicals Corp v Karl O. Helm AG* [1986] 1 Lloyd's Rep. 81; *Rogers v Markel Corp* [2004] EWHC 2046 (QB); *Isaac Naylor & Sons Ltd v New Zealand Co-operative Wool Marketing Association Ltd* [1981] 1 N.Z.L.R. 361.

by virtue of art.10(1)(c) of the Convention and under the Rome I Regulation by virtue of art.12(1)(c).[1248]

30–341 **"Statutory interest".** The Late Payment of Commercial Debts (Interest) Act 1998[1249] makes provision with respect to interest on the late payment of certain debts. By virtue of Pt I of the Act, it is an implied term in a contract for the supply of goods or services where the purchaser and the supplier are each acting in the course of a business,[1250] other than an "excepted contract",[1251] that any "qualifying debt"[1252] created by the contract carries simple interest, referred to as "statutory interest",[1253] subject to and in accordance with Pt I of the Act.[1254] Part II of the Act describes the circumstances in which contract terms are permissible to oust or vary this right to statutory interest.[1255] Section 12 of the Act contains provisions dealing with the scope of the application of the Act in the context of cases involving the conflict of laws.[1256] According to s.12(1), the provisions of the Act do *not* have effect in relation to a contract governed by the law of a part of the United Kingdom by choice of the parties if: (a) there is no significant connection between the contract and that part of the United Kingdom; and (b) but for that choice the applicable law would be a foreign law, defined as the law of a country outside the United Kingdom.[1257] This would seem to mean that if the parties have chosen, say, English law to govern the contract in accordance with either art.3(1) of the Rome Convention or art.3(1) of the Rome I Regulation,[1258] but there is no significant connection between the contract and England, and, absent the choice of English law, the contract would, according to art.4 of the Convention or art.4 of the Regulation,[1259] be governed by the law of a country outside the United Kingdom, e.g. that of France, the provisions of the 1998 Act will not apply. This would appear to be the case even if the contract did have a significant connection with a part of the United Kingdom other than that whose law had been chosen in the contract, since the provision, in terms, requires the absence of a significant connection with the part whose law has been chosen. Conversely, the Act *will* apply where English law is chosen but, apart from that, the contract would be governed by the law of a country outside the United Kingdom, if there is, nonetheless, a significant connection between the contract

[1248] The cases in the preceding note establish that the question is one of remoteness of damage which is thus governed by the applicable law according to art.10(1)(c) of the Convention and art.12(1)(c) of the Regulation. See above, para.30–337; *Dicey, Morris and Collins*, para.36–084.

[1249] As amended by Late Payment of Commercial Debts Regulations 2002 (SI 2002/1674), fully in force from August 7, 2002. These Regulations partially implement Directive 2000/35 on combating late payment in commercial transactions [2000] OJ L200/35. See above, paras 26–172 et seq.

[1250] Late Payment of Commercial Debts (Interest) Act 1998 ss.1(1), 2(1), (2), (3), (7), 12(3).

[1251] Defined in s.2(5) and (7) as a consumer credit agreement within the meaning of the Consumer Credit Act 1974 (Vol.II, para.38–015), a contract intended to operate by way of mortgage, pledge, charge or other security and any other contract specified in an order made by the Secretary of State.

[1252] ss.1(1), 3(1).

[1253] s.1(2).

[1254] s.1(1).

[1255] ss.7–10.

[1256] cf. Unfair Contract Terms Act 1977 s.27, above, para.30–007.

[1257] s.12(3). cf. Unfair Contract Terms Act 1977 s.27(1), above, para.30–008.

[1258] Above, paras 30–047 et seq., 30–170 et seq.

[1259] Above, paras 30–071 et seq., 30–186 et seq.

and England. Section 12(1) thus envisages that a contract may have a *significant connection* with the part of the United Kingdom whose law has been chosen even though, pursuant to art.4 of the Rome Convention or art.4 of the Rome I Regulation, it is *most closely connected* with a country outside the United Kingdom. The factors which may be taken to constitute a significant connection are not identified in the Act and when such a connection will or will not be held to exist will depend on the circumstances of individual cases. However, by way of example, such a connection may be found to exist, in a contract of sale, where English law is chosen and England is also the place where the purchase price is to be paid, but apart from that choice of law the contract would be governed by the law of France pursuant to art.4(2) of the Rome Convention or art.4(1)(a) of the Rome I Regulation[1260] since France is the country in which the seller's principal place of business is situated. Further, the provisions of the Act would appear to apply if the law of one part of the United Kingdom is chosen in the contract, but in the absence of that choice the applicable law would be the law of another part of the United Kingdom. This result appears to ensue irrespective of whether a significant connection between the contract and the part of the United Kingdom whose law has been chosen does or does not exist. This is because s.12(1) only applies where in the absence of choice the contract would be governed by a foreign law[1261] and that law is, as pointed out above, defined as the law of a country outside the United Kingdom.[1262]

Section 12(2) of the 1998 Act is an anti-avoidance provision.[1263] It provides that the Act *has* effect in relation to a contract governed by a foreign law by choice of the parties if: (a) but for that choice, the applicable law would be the law of a part of the United Kingdom; *and* (b) there is no significant connection between the contract and any other country other than that part of the United Kingdom. The effect of the provision would seem to be that if, say, a contract contains a choice of French law satisfying art.3(1) of the Rome Convention or art.3(1) of the Rome I Regulation,[1264] but were it not for that choice, the applicable law would, under art.4 of the Convention or art.4 of the Regulation,[1265] be English law, the Act *will* apply unless the contract has a significant connection with a country other than England. That significant connection may be with the country whose law has been chosen, France in this example, or with a different foreign country, for example Luxembourg, or even with a part of the United Kingdom other than England, for example Scotland. For although the expression "country" is not defined in the Act, it is tolerably clear that the expression includes the different parts of the United Kingdom in s.12(2) since the subsection expressly refers to "any country other than that *part of the United Kingdom*" whose law has been chosen[1266] and that form of words is, in the above example, apt to include Scotland. What will be found to constitute a significant 30–342

[1260] Above, paras 30–071 et seq., 30–186 et seq.
[1261] s.12(1)(b).
[1262] s.12(3).
[1263] cf. Unfair Contract Terms Act 1977 s.27(2), above, para.30–008.
[1264] Above, paras 30–047 et seq., 30–170 et seq.
[1265] Above, paras 30–071 et seq., 30–186 et seq.
[1266] Emphasis added. cf. s.12(3), defining foreign law as the law of a country outside the *United Kingdom* (emphasis added). See also above, para.30–025.

connection for the purposes of the subsection will, as suggested above depend on the circumstances of the individual case, but, as was the case with s.12(1), it is clear that although the contract has its closest connection with the law of a particular part of the United Kingdom, the contract may, nonetheless, have a significant connection with a country other than that part of the United Kingdom.

30–343 Section 12(2) only controls the avoidance of the Act by a choice of foreign law, i.e. the law of a country outside the United Kingdom.[1267] Where, however, an issue arises in English proceedings involving a contract which contains a choice of the law of a different part of the United Kingdom, the Act would appear to apply on general principles,[1268] unless it is disapplied because the circumstances of the case fall within s.12(1).[1269] The Act also seems to apply where the contract contains no choice of law but, as a result of applying art.4 of the Rome Convention or art.4 of the Rome I Regulation,[1270] the applicable law is the law of a part of the United Kingdom.[1271]

30–344 The rate of statutory interest under the 1998 Act shall be that prescribed by the Secretary of State.[1272]

30–345 **Extinguishing obligations, etc.** Article 10(1)(d) of the Convention and art.12(1)(d) of the Regulation submit the various "ways of extinguishing obligations, and prescription and limitation of actions" to the applicable law. As to the various ways in which an obligation may be extinguished, it is possible that whether a contract has been discharged by performance or by frustration will fall under art.10(1)(b) or art.12(1)(b) ("performance") rather than art.10(1)(d) or art.12(1)(d), but this will make no practical difference since in either event the issue will be governed by the applicable law.[1273] Discharge (or extinction) by accord and satisfaction,[1274] moratorium,[1275] outbreak of war[1276] or legislation[1277]

[1267] s.12(3).

[1268] Above, para.30–025. The Act applies in England and Wales and in Scotland and is expressly stated to extend to Northern Ireland: s.17(5).

[1269] Above, para.30–341.

[1270] Above, paras 30–071 et seq., 30–186 et seq.

[1271] This is because the Act extends to each part of the United Kingdom.

[1272] s.6. A debt does not carry statutory interest if, or to the extent that it consists of a sum to which a right to interest or to charge interest applies by virtue of a statute other than the 1998 Act: s.3(2).

[1273] *Dicey, Morris and Collins*, para.32–204.

[1274] cf. *Ralli v Denistoun* (1851) 6 Ex. 488.

[1275] cf. *Re Helbert Wagg & Co Ltd's Claim* [1956] Ch. 323; *National Bank of Greece and Athens SA v Metliss* [1958] A.C. 509; *Adams v National Bank of Greece SA* [1961] A.C. 509. The distinct question raised in the last two cases as to whether there was a *successio in universum jus* on the amalgamation of the banks would not fall within either the Convention rules because of art.1(2)(e), or within the Regulation because of art.1(2)(f). That question will be determined according to the law of the place of incorporation: see further *The Rio Assu* [1999] 1 Lloyd's Rep. 201; *J.H. Rayner (Mincing Lane) Ltd v Cafenorte SA Importadora* [1999] 2 All E.R. (Comm) 577; *Eurosteel Ltd v Stinnes AG* [2000] 1 All E.R. (Comm) 964; *Astra SA Insurance and Reinsurance Co v Sphere Drake Insurance Ltd* [2000] 2 Lloyd's Rep. 550; *Dicey, Morris and Collins*, para.30–011.

[1276] cf. *Re Anglo-Austrian Bank* [1920] 1 Ch. 69.

[1277] cf. *Perry v Equitable Life Insurance Co* (1929) 45 T.L.R. 468; *R. v International Trustee for the Protection of Bondholders AG* [1937] A.C. 500; *Mount Albert BC v Australasian Temperance &*

would seem to fall within art.10(1)(d) of the Convention and within art.12(1)(d) of the Regulation[1278] and, as such, would be determined by the applicable law. Similarly, the question of whether a contractual debt or liability has been discharged by novation would be a matter for the law applicable to the contract which gives rise to the contractual debt or liability according to art.10(1)(d) or 12(1)(d), as the case may be.[1279] It would also seem likely that whether a debt has been extinguished by set-off is a matter for the applicable law by virtue of art.10(1)(d) of the Convention.[1280]

Set-off and the Rome I Regulation. As discussed earlier in this Chapter, art.17 of the Rome I Regulation provides a specific rule for determining the law applicable to set-off.[1281] 30–346

Prescription and limitation of actions. Article 10(1)(d) of the Convention and art.12(1)(d) of the Regulation also refer prescription and the limitation of actions to the applicable law. Although, at common law, there was a distinct tendency to classify the rules relating to limitation of actions as procedural and thus as a matter for the *lex fori*,[1282] a considerable inroad on this principle was made by the Foreign Limitation Periods Act 1984.[1283] Broadly speaking, that Act requires that the rules for the limitation of actions of the *lex causae*[1284] are to be applied, which means, in the case of contract, the limitation rules of the governing law[1285] and not those of the *lex fori*. The same principle is applied by art.10(1)(d) and art.12(1)(d). Where the Convention or the Regulation apply, the 30–347

General Mutual Life Assurance Society [1938] A.C. 224; *Re Helbert Wagg & Co Ltd's Claim* [1956] Ch. 323, 340.

1278 See *Dicey Morris and Collins*, paras 32–204—32–207. The same principle applied at common law: see *Wight v Eckhardt Marine GmbH* [2003] UKPC 37, [2004] 1 A.C. 147; 26th edn of this work, para.2192. For the special case of discharge by bankruptcy, see *Dicey, Morris and Collins*, paras 31–093—31–097, 31–114.

1279 See *Raiffeisen Zentralbank Osterreich AG v Five Star General Trading LLC* [2001] EWCA Civ 68, [2001] Q.B. 825 at [34]. cf. *Re United Railways of the Havana and Regla Warehouses Ltd* [1960] Ch. 52 (reversed on other grounds sub nom. *Tomkinson v First Pennsylvania Banking and Trust Co* [1961] A.C. 1007). See also *Wight v Eckhardt Marine GmbH* [2003] UKPC 37, [2003] 3 W.L.R. 414 at [13]–[14].

1280 *Dicey, Morris and Collins*, paras 7–032, 32–208. A set-off which is merely a claim of a certain kind which the defendant has against the plaintiff and which can be conveniently tried together with the plaintiff's claim against the defendant is procedural and thus a matter for the *lex fori* both at common law and under the Rome Convention: see *Meher v Dresser* (1864) 16 C.B. (N.S.) 646.

1281 See above, paras 30–299 et seq.

1282 As to the common law position, see *Dicey, Morris and Collins*, paras 7–047—7–048, 7–054; Cheshire and North, p.73. cf. *John Pfeiffer Pty Ltd v Rogerson* (2000) 203 C.L.R. 503 (obiter to effect that statutes of limitation substantive at common law).

1283 For comment, see *Dicey, Morris and Collins*, paras 7–049—7–051; Cheshire and North at p.73; Carter (1985) 101 L.Q.R. 68; Stone [1985] L.M.C.L.Q. 497. The 1984 Act implements recommendations of the Law Commission: see Law Com. No.114, 1982.

1284 Foreign Limitation Periods Act 1984 s.1(1).

1285 The foreign *lex causae* is defined to include both procedural and substantive rules in respect to limitation: Foreign Limitation Periods Act 1984 s.4. But *renvoi* is excluded: ss.1(5), 4(2). A foreign rule under which a limitation period is or may be extended or interrupted, in respect to the absence of a party from any specified jurisdiction or country, must be disregarded: s.2(3). If the *lex causae* confers a discretion, it should be exercised, so far as practicable, in the manner in which it is exercised in comparable cases by the courts of that country: s.2(4). English law will, however, determine the time at which proceedings have been commenced: s.1(3).

rules as to prescription and limitation of actions will be governed by the applicable law as a result of art.10(1)(d) or art.12(1)(d) rather than as a result of the 1984 Act.[1286] The Rome Convention, the Rome I Regulation and the Foreign Limitation Periods Act 1984 permit a foreign period of limitation to be denied application if its application would infringe public policy.[1287] According to s.2(2) of the 1984 Act, application of a foreign period of limitation conflicts with public policy:

> " . . . to the extent that its application would cause undue hardship to a person who is, or might be made, a party to the action or proceedings."

Although art.16 of the Rome Convention and art.21 of the Rome I Regulation require that the application of a foreign rule must be "manifestly incompatible with the public policy of the forum" it does not seek to define the content of the forum's public policy as such. Accordingly, the "undue hardship" aspect of public policy referred to in s.2(2) of the 1984 Act can in all probability[1288] be applied as part of English public policy through art.16 of the Convention or art.21 of the Regulation.[1289]

30–348 **Limitation in equity.**[1290] It is unclear (and there is no relevant authority) whether the equitable doctrines of laches and acquiescence or equivalent doctrines in foreign law are matters which relate to "prescription and limitation of actions" for the purposes of art.10(1)(d) and art.12(1)(d) or whether such doctrines relate to the "consequences of breach" within the meaning of art.10(1)(c) or art.12(1)(c) or whether such principles are matters of procedure and thus not within the scope of either of the foregoing rules. It is tentatively submitted that

---

[1286] See *Ennstone Building Products Ltd v Stanger Ltd* [2002] EWCA Civ 916, [2002] 1 W.L.R. 3059 at [5], [43]; *Dicey, Morris and Collins*, paras 7–052, 32–209. And see *Crédit Lyonnais v New Hampshire Insurance Co* [1997] 2 Lloyd's Rep. 1; *Zebrarise Ltd v De Nieffe* [2004] EWHC 1842 (Comm), [2005] 1 Lloyd's Rep. 154. as to restitutionary claims and the Foreign Limitation Periods Act 1984, see *Barros Mattos Junior v MacDaniels Ltd* [2004] EWHC 1323 (Ch), [2005] 1 W.L.R. 247.

[1287] Foreign Limitation Periods Act 1984 s.2(1), (2); Rome Convention art.16; Rome I Regulation art.21. And see below, paras 30–366 et seq. The 1984 Act is not intended to apply to periods of limitation referred to in the contract itself: see Law Com. No.114, 1982, para.4.52; *Dicey, Morris and Collins*, para.7–054. At common law such periods were probably substantive and thus referable to the law governing the contract: *Dicey, Morris and Collins*, para.7–054; cf. *Harding v Wealands* [2006] UKHL 32, [2007] 1 A.C. 1 at [44]–[46]; *Allan J. Panozza & Co Pty Ltd v Allied Interstate (Queensland) Pty Ltd* [1976] 2 N.S.W.L.R. 192. It is unclear whether such a clause would be regarded as affecting limitation of actions for the purpose of art.10(1)(d) or art.12(1)(d), but if it does not it would nevertheless be regarded as a way of extinguishing an obligation which is also governed by the applicable law according to each provision.

[1288] On undue hardship, see *The Komninos S.* [1990] 1 Lloyd's Rep. 541 (reversed but not on this point [1991] 1 Lloyd's Rep. 370 (undue hardship where defendants agreed to an extension of time which turned out to be ineffective under foreign *lex causae)); Jones v Trollope Colls Cementation Overseas Ltd*, *The Times*, January 26, 1990 (12 months' limitation period caused undue hardship where plaintiff had spent time in hospital and had been led to believe her claim would be met); *Arab Monetary Fund v Hashim* [1993] 1 Lloyd's Rep. 543 (impossible to hold that application of a three-year limitation period caused undue hardship).

[1289] *Dicey, Morris and Collins*, para.32–209.

[1290] See above, paras 28–134 et seq.

such doctrines should be accorded a substantive characterisation and should thus in principle be a matter for the governing law of the contract.[1291] It is also tentatively submitted that since these doctrines relate to the circumstances under which certain remedies are available, they should be regarded as falling within art.10(1)(c) and art.12(1)(c) rather than art.10(1)(d) and art.12(1)(d). If the contract is governed by a foreign law it will be for that foreign law to determine the circumstances in which a particular remedy is available, as a consequence of breach, including the issue of whether the claimant has acted in good time in seeking that remedy. It would appear to be unlikely that foreign rules on the latter question would extend beyond the powers conferred on the English court by its procedural law.

Consequences of nullity of contract. Although, according to art.10(1)(e), the consequences of nullity of the contract are governed by the applicable law, the United Kingdom has entered the permitted reservation to this provision so that art.10(1)(e) does not have the force of law in the United Kingdom.[1292] The consequences of nullity of the contract will be determined according to the choice of law rules applicable to restitutionary claims.[1293] As explained above, however, in cases falling within the Rome I Regulation, the applicable law, pursuant to the Regulation, will govern the consequences of nullity of the contract, as a result of art.12(1)(e) which is applicable in the United Kingdom.[1294] 30–349

Other unspecified issues. Article 10(1) and art.12(1) do not purport to provide a list of issues which is exhaustive of those intended to be governed by the applicable law.[1295] Courts in contracting states and Member States will thus be free to submit unspecified issues to that law. Thus it has been held, in the context of the Convention, that whether a person is a party to a contract is a matter for the applicable law.[1296] Amongst other unspecified issues are certain aspects of the effects of a contract,[1297] i.e. aspects of the rights and obligations of the parties under the contract (though some of these are covered by the nominated issues in art.10(1) and art.12(1)). More particularly, neither list explicitly refers to the extent to which the rights and obligations of the parties to the contract affect third parties. There seems no reason to doubt that this issue is a matter for the

---

[1291] cf. Foreign Limitation Periods Act 1984 s.4(3) which provides that the Act does not prevent the court, in the exercise of any discretion, from refusing equitable relief on the grounds of acquiescence or otherwise, but does require that, in applying the equitable rules, regard shall be had in particular to the provisions of a foreign applicable law. cf. Restatement, Second, Conflict of Laws, para.142 (substantive).

[1292] See above, paras 30–033, 30–327.

[1293] See preceding note.

[1294] Above, paras 30–034—30–328.

[1295] See above, para.30–143.

[1296] *Laemthong International Lines Co v ARTIS (No.3)* [2005] EWHC 1595 (Comm).

[1297] See Plender, pp.215–216; *Dicey, Morris and Collins*, para.32–190. As to set-off, see *Meridien Biao Bank GmbH v Bank of New York* [1997] 1 Lloyd's Rep. 437 and above, para.30–346; Rome I Regulation, art.17, above, paras 30–299 et seq.

applicable law,[1298] as it has been held to be at common law.[1299] Similarly, whether a defence, e.g. that of contributory negligence, to a contractual claim is available should depend on the law applicable to the contract,[1300] unless, on proper characterisation, the defence arises out of an aspect of the law which has its own rules of the conflict of laws which are different to the conflict of laws' rules governing contracts.[1301]

30–350 Two further issues, illegality and public policy, and foreign currency obligations, are reserved for special consideration in the concluding sub-sections of this chapter. The former presents special problems in the English conflict of laws while the latter goes beyond pure questions of the conflict of laws.[1302]

(e) *Burden of Proof, etc.*[1303]

30–351 **Generally.** Article 14 of the Rome Convention and art.18 of the Rome I Regulation each contain two provisions expressed to be applicable to burden of proof. One such provision deals, in effect, with the burden of proof and presumptions,[1304] the other with "contracts or acts intended to have legal effect".[1305]

30–352 **Burden of proof and presumptions.** Article 14(1) of the Convention and art.18(1) of the Regulation provide that the law governing the contract pursuant to the rules of the Convention or, as the case may be, the Regulation applies to the extent that it contains, in the "law of contract", the expression used in the Convention. or in "matters relating to contractual obligations", the expression used in the Regulation, rules which raise presumptions of law or determine the burden of proof. In relation to the burden of proof, the tendency of the common law was to characterise the burden of proof as a procedural matter to be governed by the *lex fori*.[1306] The effect of art.14(1) and art.18(1), however, is that the

[1298] See *Raiffeisen Zentralbank Osterreich AG v Five Star General Trading LLC* [2001] EWCA Civ 68, [2001] Q.B. 825 at [34]. This is subject to the exclusion of "the question of whether an agent is able to bind a principal, or an organ to bind a body corporate or unincorporate, to a third party": art.1(2)(f) of the Convention art.1(2)(g) of the Regulation, above, paras 30–042, 30–159. cf. *Atlas Shipping Agency (UK) Ltd v Suisse Atlantique Société D'Armement Maritime SA* [1995] 2 Lloyd's Rep. 188.

[1299] *Scott v Pilkington* (1862) 2 B. & S. 11. See 26th edn of this work, para.2177.

[1300] See *Meridien Biao Bank GmbH v Bank of New York* [1997] 1 Lloyd's Rep. 437.

[1301] *Meridien Biao Bank GmbH v Bank of New York* [1997] 1 Lloyd's Rep. 437 (set-off in insolvency proceedings). See also *Re Bank of Credit and Commerce International SA (No.10)* [1997] Ch. 213 (English rule on insolvency set-off (Insolvency Rules 1986 r.4.90) always to be applied in English insolvency proceedings). As to set-off and the Rome I Regulation, see art.17, above, paras 30–299 et seq.

[1302] Below, paras 30–355 et seq.

[1303] *Dicey, Morris and Collins on the Conflict of Laws*, 14th edn (2006), paras 7–027—7–028, 32–055—32–056; Cheshire and North, *Private International Law*, 13th edn (1999), p.78; Kaye, *The New Private International Law of Contract of the European Community* (1993), pp.331–341; Lasok and Stone, *Conflict of Laws in the European Community* (1987), pp.354–355; Morse (1982) 2 Ybk. Eur. L. 107, 156–157.

[1304] Rome Convention art.14(1), Rome I Regulation art.18(1), below, paras 30–352 et seq.

[1305] Rome Convention art.14(2), Rome I Regulation art.18(2), below, para.30–354.

[1306] e.g. *The Roberta* (1937) 58 Ll. L. Rep. 159. For criticism, see *Dicey, Morris and Collins*, para.7–027; Cheshire and North, p.78.

applicable law will determine the location of the burden of proof provided that the relevant rules for identifying its location are contained *in the law of contract*, for the purposes of the Convention, or involve *matters of contractual obligations*, for the purposes of the Regulation. The meaning of these italicised words is by no means clear, though it is suggested that the difference in formulation in, respectively, the Convention and the Regulation, is not intended to have any substantive effect and that each formulation should be construed in the same fashion. The Giuliano-Lagarde Report suggests that a rule relating to the burden of proof is a rule contained in the law of contract:

> "... to the extent that the law of contract determines it with regard to contractual obligations..., that is to say only to the extent to which the rules relating to the burden of proof are in effect rules of substance,"[1307]

as opposed to rules which are part of procedural law. The example given is art.1147 of the French Civil Code which provides that a debtor who has failed to fulfil his obligation shall be liable for damages "unless he shows that this failure is due to an extraneous cause outside his control".[1308]

In relation to presumptions, art.14(1) and art.18(1) only apply to presumptions of law.[1309] At common law, an irrebuttable presumption of law is regarded as substantive[1310]: it is probably the case that rebuttable resumptions of law bear the same characteristic.[1311] Article 14(1) and art.18(1) appear to contemplate the inclusion of both types of presumption under the aegis of the applicable law, subject to the relevant presumption being contained, again, in the law of contract. As far as irrebuttable presumptions of law are concerned, it is not easy to think of pertinent examples in the law of contract. This is because, in effect, an irrebuttable presumption of law is a rule of substantive law and what might, in 30–353

[1307] Giuliano-Lagarde Report, p.36.

[1308] Giuliano-Lagarde Report, p.36. For possible examples in English law see above, para.6–075 (Misrepresentation Act 1967 s.2(1)); paras 14–070, 14–088 (Unfair Contract Terms Act 1977 ss.11(5), 12(3)); para.15–047 (Unfair Terms in Consumer Contracts Regulations 1999 reg.5(4); for seller or supplier who claims that a term was individually negotiated to show that it was); para.43–137 (Consumer Credit Act 1974 s.171(4)(b); Consumer Protection (Distance Selling) Regulations 2000 reg.21(3); if in proceedings falling within reg.21(1) or (2), a consumer alleges that any use made of a payment card was not authorised by him it is for card issuer to prove that the use was authorised); (plaintiff has legal burden of proving fault when frustration pleaded as defence to action on contract: *Joseph Constantine S.S Line Ltd v Imperial Smelting Corp Ltd* [1942] A.C. 154); para.14–140 (burden of proof and force majeure clauses); para.25–022 (burden on party seeking to enforce altered instrument to show that alteration made in circumstances such as not to invalidate it); Vol.II, para.33–012 (burden of proving loss not caused by failure to take care rests on bailee); Vol.II, para.41–079 (insurance).

[1309] This is clearly stated in the text of Rome Convention art.14(1) and the Rome I Regulation, art.18(1). In some cases, however, a rule formulated as presumption of law in one legal system, may not be so formulated in another. In the Giuliano-Lagarde Report, p.36, reference is made to a procedural presumption: "[W]hereby the claim of a party who appears is deemed to be substantiated if the other party fails to appear, or the rule making silence on the party to an action with regard to the facts alleged by the other party equivalent to an admission of those facts," but neither of these rules involves any "presumption" in English law.

[1310] *Dicey, Morris and Collins*, para.7–029.

[1311] *Dicey, Morris and Collins*, para.7–029.

some legal systems, be formulated as an irrebuttable presumption of law,[1312] is more likely, in the English law of contract, to be formulated as a rule of substantive contract law.[1313] Examples of rebuttable presumptions spring more readily to mind and might include, in English law, the presumption of undue influence in relation to contracts between persons in a special relationship with one another (e.g. parent and child).[1314] Although this presumption may arise in other areas of the law, for example the law of trusts, that should not preclude it from being contained in the law of contract for the purposes of art.14(1) and art.18(1).[1315]

30–354 **Contract or act intended to have legal effect.** Article 14(2) of the Rome Convention and art.18(2) of the Rome I Regulation provide that a contract or act intended to have legal effect may be proved by any mode of proof recognised by the law of the forum or by any of the laws referred to in art.9 of the Convention or art.11 of the Regulation, under which that contract or act is formally valid, provided that such mode of proof can be administered by the forum. Thus, in English proceedings, a contract, or the terms thereof, may be proved by any method of proof available in English law. If a law applicable by virtue of art.9 or art.11[1316] would render the contract formally valid, the English court can allow any method of proof permitted by that law to the extent that such method of proof can be administered by the forum.[1317] According to the Giuliano-Lagarde Report, this proviso enables the court to disregard modes of proof which its law of procedure cannot generally allow, such as an affidavit, the testimony of a party, or common knowledge.[1318]

(f) *Illegality and Public Policy*[1319]

30–355 **Illegality.** The question of whether a contract is unenforceable or void for illegality justifies separate treatment because it involves reference to a number of

---

[1312] It is noteworthy that the Giuliano-Lagarde Report gives no examples.

[1313] See, e.g. Unfair Contract Terms Act 1977 s.12(2); Unfair Terms in Consumer Contracts Regulations 1999 reg.5(4), above, para.15–047.

[1314] Above, paras 7–072 et seq.

[1315] See text at fnn.1307–1308, above.

[1316] Above, para.30–352.

[1317] For the possible effect of this provision on *Leroux v Brown* (1852) 12 C.B. 801, see above, para.30–311 fn.1130.

[1318] See Giuliano-Lagarde Report, pp.36–37.

[1319] *Dicey, Morris and Collins on the Conflict of Laws*, 14th edn (2006), paras 5–009, 32–140—32–151, 32–230—32–241; Cheshire and North, *Private International Law*, 13th edn (1999), pp.123–132, 584–586, 600–603; Plender, *The European Contracts Convention*, 2nd edn (2001), Ch.9; Kaye, *The New Private International Law of Contract of the European Community* (1993), pp.239–268, 345–350; Peruzetto in Meeusen, Pertegas and Straetmans (eds), *The Enforcement of International Contracts in the European Union* (2004), pp.343–361. See above, paras 16–028 et seq. The separate questions of illegality and public policy in the conflict of laws are, nonetheless, closely linked and not always clearly distinguished: see *Royal Boskalis Westminster NV v Mountain* [1999] Q.B. 674; *Soleimany v Soleimany* [1999] Q.B. 785; *Westacre Investments Inc v Jugoimport-SDPR Holding Co Ltd* [1999] Q.B. 740 affirmed, [2000] Q.B. 288. cf. *Ispahani v Bank Melli Iran* [1998] Lloyd's Rep. Bank. 133; *Tekron Resources Ltd v Guinea Investment Co Ltd* [2004] EWHC 2577 (Comm), [2004] 2 Lloyd's Rep. 26; *Barros Mattos Junior v MacDaniels Ltd* [2004] EWHC 1188 (Ch), [2005] 1 W.L.R. 247; *Marlwood Commercial Inc v Kozeny* [2006] EWHC 872 (Comm); *Donegal International Ltd v Zambia* [2007] EWHC 197 (Comm), [2007] 1 Lloyd's Rep. 397.

different principles at common law[1320] and possible reference to several provisions of, respectively, the Rome Convention and the Rome I Regulation.

Illegality under applicable law. First, a contract is unenforceable for illegality to the extent that it is illegal under its governing law, according to common law rules,[1321] or, under the rules of the Rome Convention or the Rome I Regulation, illegal by the law which would be applicable to the contract if the contract (or term thereof) was valid.[1322] 30–356

Illegality under English law. Secondly, at common law, if any party in making or performing the contract commits, or assists another to commit, in England, a criminal offence under English law[1323] or commits abroad an act which is a criminal offence under English law by virtue of a statutory provision having extra-territorial operation,[1324] then even though the governing law is not English law, the contract is unenforceable in England by the party in question.[1325] In cases falling within the Rome Convention, this principle would seem to continue to have effect since the rules applicable by virtue of it appear to be mandatory rules of the law of the English forum which apply irrespective of the law applicable to the contract, so that, accordingly, art.7(2) may be invoked to secure their application.[1326] It would also seem that these rules are, for the purposes of the Rome I Regulation, overriding mandatory provisions the respect for which would be regarded as crucial by England for safeguarding its public interests and which would be applicable, irrespective of the law otherwise applicable to the contract under the Regulation.[1327] As such, art.9(2) of the Regulation may be invoked to secure their application.[1328] 30–357

Act illegal under law of country where to be performed. Thirdly, in *Ralli Bros v Compania Naviera Sota y Aznar*,[1329] the Court of Appeal established a common law rule that where an act required by a contract to be performed in a foreign country becomes illegal under that country's law, the contractual obligation to perform that act is discharged. Applying that principle, it was held that where under a contract governed by English law, charterers had agreed to pay freight in Spain to shipowners at a particular rate, and the Spanish government, 30–358

[1320] See 26th edn of this work, paras 2187–2191.

[1321] *Kahler v Midland Bank Ltd* [1950] A.C. 24; *Zivnostenska Banka v Frankman* [1950] A.C. 57; *Barros Mattos Junior v MacDaniels Ltd* [2004] EWHC 1188 (Comm), [2005] 1 W.L.R. 247. The rule rendering the contract illegal under the governing law will not be applied if to do so would infringe English public policy: see *The Playa Larga* [1983] 2 Lloyd's Rep. 171, 189–190; see also *Re Helbert Wagg & Co Ltd's Claim* [1956] Ch. 323, 345–346, 351–352. See below, paras 30–366 et seq.

[1322] Rome Convention art.8(1), art.10(1) of the Regulation, above paras 30–304 et seq. This is, again, subject to compliance of the applicable law with English public policy: below, paras 30–366 et seq.

[1323] e.g. *Clugas v Penaluna* (1791) 4 T.R. 466.

[1324] e.g. *Boissevain v Weil* [1950] A.C. 327; *Shanshal v Al-Kishtaini* [2001] EWCA Civ 264, [2001] 2 All E.R. (Comm) 601.

[1325] The relevant rule of English law must be one which is intended to affect the validity of contracts: see on this aspect of English domestic law, above, paras 16–014 et seq.

[1326] Above, para.30–066.

[1327] Rome I art.9(1), above para.30–180, below, para.30–361.

[1328] Above, para.30–181.

[1329] [1920] 2 K.B. 287.

after the conclusion of the contract, promulgated an order that freight should not exceed a fixed sum which was less than the agreed rate, the charterers were only obliged to pay the fixed rate rather than the agreed rate. The exact scope of this decision is, however, controversial. It has been suggested that the principle of *Ralli Bros* applies whether or not the contract is governed by English law.[1330] But the better view, it is submitted, is that for the principle to apply, the applicable law must, as it was in *Ralli Bros* itself, be English law.[1331] If the latter view is accepted, it follows that *Ralli Bros* established a principle of the domestic English law of contract relating to discharge by supervening illegality[1332] and does not establish a rule of the conflict of laws.[1333] Accordingly, the effect of illegality by the law of the place of performance where a contract is governed by a foreign law is a matter for that foreign law.[1334]

30–359 ***Ralli Bros* and The Rome Convention.** The next question which arises is as to the status of the principle in *Ralli Bros* in cases which fall within the Rome Convention. Since the United Kingdom has made a reservation to art.7(1) of the Convention, that article cannot be used to give effect, even as a matter of discretion, to the *Ralli Bros* principle.[1335] If the principle only applies, as suggested above and by a dictum in the Court of Appeal which found it unnecessary to express a final view on the point,[1336] where the contract is governed by English law, than it will operate, where relevant, if English law is the applicable law of the contract. But if, contrary to this view, it is eventually decided that the principle is of wider import so that it applies irrespective of the law applicable to the contract, it is difficult to accommodate it within the Convention. The first possibility is to argue that it can be applied pursuant to art.16,[1337] as a principle of English public policy, but it is doubtful whether the

---

1330 *Zivnostenska Banka v Frankman* [1950] A.C. 57, 78; *Mackender v Feldia* [1967] 2 Q.B. 590, 601; *R. v International Trustee for the Protection of Bondholders AG* [1937] A.C. 500, 519; *Kleinwort Sons & Co v Ungarische Baumwolle Industrie AG* [1939] 2 K.B. 678, 697–698; *Tamil Nadu Electricity Board v ST-CMS Electric Co Private Ltd* [2007] EWHC 1713 (Comm), [2007] 2 All E.R. (Comm) 701 at [46]–[47].

1331 *Kahler v Midland Bank Ltd* [1950] A.C. 24, 48; *Société Co-operative Suisse des Cereales, etc v Plata Cereal Co SA* (1949) 80 Ll. L. Rep. 530, 543–544: *Walton (Grain and Shipping) Ltd v British Italian Trading Co* [1959] 1 Lloyd's Rep. 223, 236; *Bangladesh Export Import Co Ltd v Sucden Kerry SA* [1995] 2 Lloyd's Rep. 1, 5; *Ispahani v Bank Melli Iran* [1998] Lloyd's Rep. Bank. 133; see also *Society of Lloyd's v Fraser* [1998] C.L.C. 1630, 1652; *Fox v Henderson Investment Fund Ltd* [1999] 2 Lloyd's Rep. 303; *Tekron Resources Ltd v Guinea Investment Co Ltd* [2004] EWHC 2577, [2004] 2 Lloyd's Rep. 26; *Continental Enterprises Ltd v Shandong Zucheng Foreign Trade Group Co* [2005] EWHC 95 (Comm); *Marlwood Commercial Inc v Kozeny* [2006] EWHC 872 (Comm); *Dicey, Morris and Collins*, paras 32–144—32–147; Cheshire and North, pp.601–602; F.A. Mann (1937) 18 B.Y.I.L. 97, 107–113; Morris (1953) 6 Vand. L. Rev. 510; Reynolds (1992) 108 L.Q.R. 553.

1332 See above, paras 23–024 et seq.

1333 See authorities in fn.1130, above.

1334 See authorities in fn.1130, above.

1335 Contracts (Applicable Law) Act 1990 s.2(2) and Sch.1 art.22, above, para.30–063. See on the status of the *Ralli Bros* rule in the Convention context, *Dicey, Morris and Collins*, paras 32–148—32–151; Reynolds, above.

1336 See *Ispahani v Bank Melli Iran* [1998] Lloyd's Rep. Bank. 133. See also *Royal Boskalis Westminster NV v Mountain* [1999] Q.B. 674, 733–734; *Tekron Resources v Guinea Investment Co Ltd* [2004] EWHC 2577; *Marlwood Commercial Inc v Kozeny* [2006] EWHC 872 (Comm).

1337 See below, paras 30–366 et seq.

principle bears the character of a rule of English public policy.[1338] Secondly, but more doubtfully, the principle of *Ralli Bros* could be construed as a mandatory rule of English law, applicable by virtue of art.7(2) of the Convention. Thirdly, but even more doubtfully, it has been suggested that the principle could be applied by virtue of art.10(2) of the Convention,[1339] but this is most unlikely since art.10(2) only submits to the law of the place of performance minor matters affecting the detail of performance rather than the substance of the obligation to be performed,[1340] and the latter, not the former, was what was at issue in the *Ralli Bros* case.

Effect of Rome I Regulation. To the extent that the principle in *Ralli Bros* is a rule of the domestic English law of contract (and this it is submitted is the better view), it will continue to apply in cases falling within the Rome I Regulation where, pursuant to the rules contained in the Regulation, English law is the law applicable to the contract. It is, however, unnecessary to consider whether the rule is of wider import, since the Regulation provides a specific rule enabling account to be taken of illegality by the law of the place of performance and the existence of this rule appears to mean that otherwise illegality by the law of the place of performance will only be relevant where, under the law applicable to the contract, account is taken of such illegality. Article 9(3) of the Regulation provides as follows: 30–360

> "Effect may be given to the overriding mandatory provisions of the law of the country where the obligations arising out of the contract have to be or have been performed, in so far as those overriding mandatory provisions render performance of the contract unlawful. In considering whether to give effect to those provisions, regard shall be had to their nature and purpose and to the consequences of their application or non-application."

The second sentence of this formulation is taken from art.7(1) of the Rome Convention, but the first sentence is of narrower import than the equivalent provision in the Convention which allowed effect to be given to the mandatory rules of the law of another country with which "the situation has a close connection".[1341] In contrast, art.9(3) of the Regulation only allows account to be taken of relevant rules of the place of performance. Thus art.9(3) only appears to be relevant where a contract, valid by its applicable law, is alleged to be invalid by reference to that provision.

"Overriding mandatory provisions". As explained earlier in this chapter, overriding mandatory provisions are defined in art.9(1) as: 30–361

> "... provisions the respect for which is regarded as crucial by a country for safeguarding its public interests, such as its political, social or economic organisation, to

[1338] See *Dicey, Morris and Collins*, para.32–150. If the only remedy provided by the foreign law compelled the defendant to act illegally in the place of performance, as opposed to paying damages elsewhere, this might justify invocation of public policy as a last resort. cf. *Royal Boskalis Westminster NV v Mountain* [1999] Q.B. 674, 733–734.

[1339] See Diamond (1986) 216 *Recueil des Cours* IV, 236, 296.

[1340] Above, paras 30–332 et seq.

[1341] Above, para.30–063, where it is also pointed out that art.7(1) of the Convention does not have the force of law in the United Kingdom.

> such an extent that they are applicable to any situation falling within their scope, irrespective of the law otherwise applicable to the contract"

under the Regulation.[1342] It will be noted that these rules are to be distinguished from "provisions which cannot be derogated from by agreement" referred to, for example, in art.3(3) of the Regulation,[1343] since they must possess the additional characteristic of being applicable irrespective of the law applicable to the contract. Such rules must be construed "more restrictively"[1344] than the rules referred to in art.3(3). But it would seem that art.9(1) necessarily entails the conclusion that it will be for the law of the country of which the rule forms part to determine whether it possesses the necessary characteristics and that the forum must scrutinise the rule to ensure that this is the case.[1345] Examples of potentially relevant rules might be provisions imposing economic sanctions on a particular country,[1346] rules imposing an embargo on exports to a particular country,[1347] rules imposing price, or exchange, controls[1348] and rules prohibiting cartels.[1349]

30–362 **Relevant country.** Article 9(3) allows effect to be given to overriding mandatory provisions of the "country where the obligations arising out of the contract have to be or have been performed". The relevant country (which need not be a Member State) may, thus be either the country where, as required by the contract, performance must take place, or the country where performance actually takes place if it is not required that performance take place there.[1350]

30–363 **Performance "unlawful".** The relevant overriding mandatory provisions must render performance unlawful. It would seem that performance may be unlawful for these purposes if, at the time the contract is concluded, it would be unlawful to perform the relevant obligations[1351] and where performance becomes unlawful, subsequent to the conclusion of the contract, by reason of, e.g. supervening legislation.[1352] It would appear, however, to be insufficient that performance of the obligations under the contract has been excused, e.g. by force majeure.[1353]

30–364 **Discretion.** Article 9(3) contains a discretionary principle, in the sense that the forum is not required to give effect to the relevant provisions. This much is

---

[1342] Above, para.30–178.
[1343] Above para.30–178.
[1344] Recital 37 to the Regulation.
[1345] cf. above, para.30–357.
[1346] cf. *Regazzoni v K.C. Sethia Ltd* [1956] 2 Q.B. 490; *Libyan Arab Foreign Bank v Bankers Trust Co* [1989] Q.B. 728.
[1347] cf. *Regazzoni v K.C. Sethia Ltd* [1956] 2 Q.B. 490; *Cie Europeene des Petroles SA v Sensor Nederland BV, The Hague, 1982* (1983) Int. Legal Mat. 66.
[1348] cf. *Ralli Bros v Compania Naviera Sota y Aznar* [1920] K.B. 287; *Ispahani v Bank Melli Iran* [1998] Lloyd's Rep. Bank. 133.
[1349] cf. *Dicey, Morris and Collins*, para.32–136.
[1350] cf. *Kahler v Midland Bank Ltd* [1950] A.C. 24 at 48; *Dicey, Morris and Collins*, para.32–145.
[1351] cf. *Regazzoni v K.C. Sethia Ltd* [1956] 2 Q.B. 490; *Foster v Driscoll* [1929] 1 K.B. 470.
[1352] cf. *Ralli Bros v Compania Naviera Sota y Aznar* [1920] K.B. 287.
[1353] cf. *Jacobs v Credit Lyonnais* (1884) 12 QBD 589.

clear from the opening words of the provision ("effect may be given") and from the second sentence of the provision where supposed guidance is given as to the considerations to be taken into account in considering whether to give effect to the relevant provisions. Although it is said that the application of the provision is envisaged only in exceptional circumstances,[1354] it cannot be said with any confidence that reference to the "nature and purpose" of the relevant provisions and to "the consequences of their application or non-application" provides sure guidance. How these formulae will be applied remains to be seen and will doubtless depend on the circumstances of individual cases. It is suggested, however, that the forum will take account of the extent to which the "public interests" of the country to which the provisions belong will be furthered by application of the rule in the instant case, a factor which will have to be balanced against the interest of the country whose law is applicable to the contract in upholding the contract, and, perhaps, to the interests of the forum in upholding a contract valid by its applicable law. It is also suggested that it is inappropriate for the forum to take account of purely political considerations and that account should primarily be taken of considerations of legal policy which affect the parties to the contract, but it is not obvious that either formula referred to above enables a clash of these interests to be easily resolved.[1355]

Illegality under other foreign law. Illegality under any foreign law, be it the law of one party's nationality,[1356] or of a country where performance may, but need not, take place,[1357] or of the place of contracting[1358] does not per se affect the enforceability of the contract either at common law or, because of the United Kingdom's reservation to art.7(1) of the Convention,[1359] under the provisions of the Rome Convention. Article 9(3) of the Rome I Regulation, likewise, does not allow illegality by the law of a party's nationality or the law of the place of contracting to affect the validity of the contract per se, but it does open up the possibility of application of the law of the place of performance where the obligations arising out of the contract have been, but do not have to be, performed in a particular country.[1360] 30–365

Public policy.[1361] It is axiomatic, and a general principle of the conflict of laws, that the forum will not apply a foreign law which is contrary to the public policy of the forum. The public policy principle may have the result of rendering 30–366

[1354] See Recital 37 to the Regulation.

[1355] See Chong (2006) 2 J. Priv. Int. L. 27; Dickinson (2007) 3 J. Priv. Int. L. 53.

[1356] *Kleinwort Sons & Co v Ungarische Baumwolle Industrie AG* [1939] K.B. 678; *Kahler v Midland Bank Ltd* [1950] A.C. 24, 48; *Toprak Mahsulleri Ofisi v Finagrain Compagnie Commerciale Agricole et Financière SA* [1979] 2 Lloyd's Rep. 98.

[1357] *Kahler v Midland Bank Ltd* [1950] A.C. 24, 36, 39, 48. And see *Zivnostenska Banka v Frankman* [1950] A.C. 57, 79; *Regazzoni v K.C. Sethia Ltd* [1956] 2 Q.B. 490, 514, 523; *Nile Co for the Export of Agricultural Crops v Bennett (Commodities) Ltd* [1986] 1 Lloyd's Rep. 555, 581. See also *Fox v Henderson Investment Fund Ltd* [1999] 2 Lloyd's Rep. 303.

[1358] *Vita Foods Products Inc v Unus Shipping Co Ltd* [1939] A.C. 277, 297–300. See F.A. Mann (1937) 18 B.Y.I.L. 97, 107–113. cf. *The Torni* [1932] P. 78; *Re Missouri S.S. Co Ltd* (1889) 42 Ch D 321, 336; *The Hollandia* [1983] 1 A.C. 565, 576.

[1359] See above, fn.1335.

[1360] Rome I art.9(3), above, para.30–364.

[1361] See also, above, paras 30–069 et seq., 30–183.

void or unenforceable a contract which is valid under its foreign governing law or it may result in the enforcement of a contract which is invalid by its governing law, if, in either case, the forum regards the public policy principle as applicable. The principle of public policy is recognised in art.16 of the Rome Convention which provides that the:

> "... application of a rule of law of any country specified by this Convention may be refused only if such application is manifestly incompatible with the public policy ('ordre public') of the forum."

and art.21 of the Rome I Regulation, which provides, subject to substituting the words "rules of the law of any country" with the words "a provision of the law of any country", to identical effect. These provisions clearly reflect the common law subject to the expression "manifestly incompatible", an expression designed to indicate that overzealous resort should not be made to the public policy doctrine.[1362] It is also important to stress that art.16, art.21 and the common law are concerned with public policy in the international sense, rather than the public policy in the domestic sense. Thus, for example, the fact that a contract, valid under its foreign governing law, lacks a requirement (e.g. consideration[1363]) which is essential to its validity under English law, is insufficient to render the public policy principle applicable.[1364] There must be some more fundamental objection to the application of a foreign law before public policy, in the international sense, may be invoked.[1365] Further, at common law and under art.16 of the Convention, it is the *application* of the foreign law in the circumstances of the case which must infringe English public policy rather than the *content* of the foreign law as such.[1366] The position will surely be the same under art.21 of the Rome I Regulation.

[1362] *Continental Enterprises Ltd v Shandong Zucheng Foreign Trade Group Co* [2005] EWHC 95 (Comm); Giuliano-Lagarde Report, p.38. In Recital 37 to the Rome I Regulation it is said that considerations "of public interest justify giving the courts of Member States the possibility, in exceptional circumstances, of applying exceptions based on public policy".

[1363] *Re Bonacina* [1912] 2 Ch. 394.

[1364] See, e.g. *Dicey, Morris and Collins*, para.32–236. The distinction is expressed by French jurists as one between *ordre public interne* and *ordre public international.*

[1365] *Re COLT Telecom Group Plc* [2002] EWHC 2815 (Ch), [2003] B.P.I.R. 324; *Continental Enterprises Ltd v Shandong Foreign Trade Group Co* [2005] EWHC 95 (Comm). Compare the language of Cardozo J. in *Loucks v Standard Oil Co of New York* (1918) 224 N.Y. 99, 120 N.E. 198: "If a foreign statute gives the right, the mere fact that we do not give a like right is no reason for refusing the plaintiff what belongs to him. We are not so provincial as to say that every solution of a problem is wrong because we deal with it otherwise at home."

[1366] There may be exceptional cases, however, where a foreign law involves such a serious infringement of human rights that it should not be recognised as law at all: see *Oppenheimer v Cattermole* [1976] A.C. 249. More generally on the relationship between public international law and public policy, see *Kuwait Airways Corp v Iraqi Airways Co (Nos 4 and 5)* [2002] UKHL 19, [2002] 2 A.C. 883 at [15]–[29]. See also *Royal Boskalis Westminster NV v Mountain* [1999] Q.B. 674; *Peer International Corp v Termidor Music Publishers Ltd* [2003] EWCA Civ 1156, [2004] Ch. 212. And see Collins (2002) 51 I.C.L.Q. 485. Public policy may also develop by reference to the European Convention on Human Rights incorporated into English law by the Human Rights Act 1998. For consideration of public policy in this context, see *Krombach v Bamberski* (C–7/98) [2000] E.C.R. I–1935, [2001] Q.B. 709; *Regie National des Usines Renault SA v Maxicar SpA* (C–38/98) [2000] E.C.R. I–2973; *Maronier v Larmer* [2002] EWCA Civ 774, [2003] Q.B. 620. See also *Eurofood IFSC Ltd* (C–341/04) [2006] E.C.R. I–3813, [2006] Ch. 508. If such a development is to occur proper allowance should be made for the fact that the case contains foreign elements which are such that the

Since the application of the doctrine of public policy must depend very much on the circumstances of individual cases, it is not possible to categorise the situations justifying its invocation with any precision. However, in the past, English courts have refused to enforce champertous contracts,[1367] contracts in restraint of trade,[1368] contracts involving trading with the enemy,[1369] and contracts involving collusive arrangements for a divorce.[1370] The principle will also apply where the parties make the contract with the intention that its performance should involve the commission in a foreign and friendly country of an act which would violate that country's laws.[1371] It has also been held that public policy is infringed where the contract, or circumstances in which it was made, render it incompatible with English ideas of justice and morality.[1372] Thus a contract governed by (and valid by) its foreign applicable law may be held unenforceable in England because it was entered into as a result of coercion.[1373] And where a contract governed by English law involved a transaction, to be performed abroad, 30–367

---

merits of the case should be governed by foreign law according to the normal principles of the conflict of laws. And see above, paras 30–069 et seq.

1367 *Grell v Levy* (1864) 16 C.B. (N.S.) 73; cf. *Trendtex Trading Corp v Crédit Suisse* [1982] A.C. 679; *Camdex International Ltd v Bank of Zambia* [1998] Q.B. 22; *Fraser v Buckle* [1996] 1 I.R. 1. Although champerty has ceased to be a crime or a tort in England, Criminal Law Act 1967 s.14, it will render a contract illegal: see above, paras 16–048 et seq.

1368 *Rousillon v Rousillon* (1880) 14 Ch D 351, which should be restricted to restraint of trade affecting trade in England. And see *Duarte v Black and Decker Corp* [2007] EWHC 2720 (QB), [2008] 1 All E.R. (Comm) 401, above, para.30–113.

1369 *Robson v Premier Oil and Pipe Line Co* [1915] 2 Ch. 124, 136; *Dynamit A/G v Rio Tinto Co Ltd* [1918] A.C. 260. See above, para.16–026.

1370 *Hope v Hope* (1857) 8 De G.M. & G. 731.

1371 *Regazzoni v K.C. Sethia Ltd* [1958] A.C. 301. And see *De Wutz v Hendricks* (1824) 2 Bing. 314; *Foster v Driscoll* [1929] 1 K.B. 470; *British Nylon Spinners v I.C.I. Ltd* [1955] Ch. 37, 52; *Euro-Diam Ltd v Bathurst* [1990] 1 Q.B. 1; *Royal Boskalis Westminster NV v Mountain* [1999] Q.B. 674; *Ispahani v Bank Melli Iran* [1998] Lloyd's Rep. Bank. 133; *Soleimany v Soleimany* [1999] Q.B. 785 (arbitration award based on such a contract unenforceable in England); *Westacre Investments Inc v Jugoimport-SDPR Holding Co Ltd* [1999] Q.B. 740, affirmed [2000] Q.B. 288 (public policy of sustaining international arbitration awards outweighed public policy of discouraging international commercial corruption); see also *Society of Lloyd's v Fraser* [1998] C.L.C. 1630, 1652; *Fox v Henderson Investment Fund Ltd* [1999] 2 Lloyd's Rep. 303. This rule applies, in all probability, to cases where a contract is governed by a foreign law as well as to cases where it is governed by English law (as was the case in *Regazzoni v K.C. Sethia Ltd*): see *Royal Boskalis Westminster NV v Mountain* [1999] Q.B. 674, 692, 703, 734–736; cf. *Ispahani v Bank Melli Iran*. It also applies where the object of the contract is to break the penal or revenue laws of a foreign country (*Regazzoni v K.C. Sethia Ltd*; *Re Emery's Investment Trusts* [1959] Ch. 410; *Euro-Diam Ltd v Bathurst*; *Soleimany v Soleimany*) or foreign exchange control legislation (*Kahler v Midland Bank Ltd* [1950] A.C. 24, 27; *Zivnostenska Banka v Frankman* [1950] A.C. 57, 72; *Re Helbert Wagg & Co Ltd's Claim* [1956] Ch. 323, 349, 351; *Re Lord Cable* [1977] 1 W.L.R. 7, 24; *Ispahani v Bank Melli Iran*, above). An English court will not *enforce* the penal or revenue or other public laws of a foreign country: see *Camdex International Ltd v Bank of Zambia* [1997] C.L.C. 714; *Dicey, Morris and Collins*, paras 5–020—5–040. See also *Barros Mattos Junior v MacDaniels Ltd* [2004] EWHC 118 (Ch), [2005] 1 W.L.R. 247; *Marlwood Commercial Inc v Kozeny* [2006] EWHC 872 (Comm); *Islamic Republic of Iran v Barakat Galleries Ltd* [2007] EWCA Civ 1374, [2008] 1 All E.R. 1177. As to exchange control in the conflict of laws, see *Dicey, Morris and Collins*, paras 36–062—36–077.

1372 *Kaufman v Gerson* [1904] 1 K.B. 591; *Royal Boskalis Westminster NV v Mountain* [1999] Q.B. 674. See also *Robinson v Bland* (1706) 2 Burr. 1077, 1084; *Re Missouri S.S. Co* (1889) 42 Ch. D. 321, 336. A contract to oust the jurisdiction of a foreign court (unlike one to oust the jurisdiction of the English court) is not contrary to public policy: cf. *Addison v Brown* [1954] 1 W.L.R. 779.

1373 *Royal Boskalis Westminster NV v Mountain* [1999] Q.B. 674; *Kaufman v Gerson* [1904] 1 K.B. 541. In the former case it was stated, at 689, 729, that the degree of coercion exercised in the

which was contrary to a head of English public policy based on general principles of morality, the same public policy applying in the country of performance, the contract was similarly unenforceable.[1374]

30–368 There is no reason to doubt that similar conclusions to the above may be reached by applying art.16 of the Rome Convention or art.21 of the Rome I Regulation subject, possibly, to the requirement that the application of foreign law be "manifestly incompatible" with public policy necessitating a more cautious view of the doctrine than was exhibited in some of the decisions rendered at common law, because the intention behind art.16 and art.21 is that public policy should be used in only exceptional circumstances.[1375] On the other hand, art.16 and art.21 import a new dimension into the content of public policy as understood in traditional English conflict of laws, for public policy, in these contexts, must be understood as including European Community public policy.[1376]

(g) *Foreign Currency Obligations*

30–369 **Scope of discussion.** The remaining paragraphs of this Chapter seek to identify and discuss particular problems of practical importance which may arise, in a contractual context, out of what may be loosely described as "foreign currency obligations".[1377] The separate treatment of these problems may be

---

particular case is relevant, and whether the degree of coercion exercised in the latter case would be regarded as sufficient today was questionable. In *Dimskal Shipping Co SA v International Transport Workers Federation* [1992] 2 A.C. 152, 158 it was held that whether a contract was void or voidable for duress depended on the law applicable to the contract, which was English law. However, if the law applicable to the contract is a foreign law and that law would regard the contract as valid despite the presence of duress of an unconscionable degree, the English court will refuse to enforce the contract on the grounds of public policy as happened in *Royal Boskalis Westminster NV v Mountain*, where a contract governed and valid by Iraqi law was procured by threats to use personnel as part of the "human shield" in the course of the Iraq-Kuwait conflict. In *Kaufman v Gerson*, a wife was held to have acted under duress by agreeing to pay sums to her husband's employer under a contract governed and valid by French law, on terms that the employer would refrain from bringing a criminal prosecution against the husband for misappropriation of the employer's funds, hardly duress of the same order.

[1374] *Lemenda Trading Co Ltd v African Middle East Petroleum Co Ltd* [1988] Q.B. 448. See also *Tekron Resources Ltd v Guinea Investment Co Ltd* [2003] EWHC 2577 (Comm), [2004] 2 Lloyd's Rep. 26; *Marlwood Commercial Inc v Kozeny* [2006] EWHC 872 (Comm); *Donegal International Ltd v Zambia* [2007] EWHC 197 (Comm), [2007] 1 Lloyd's Rep. 397.

[1375] *Continental Enterprises Ltd v Shandong Foreign Trade Group Co* [2005] EWHC 95 (Comm); Giuliano-Lagarde Report, p.38; Rome I Regulation Recital 37. Suspect decisions (at least on their facts) are, in particular, *Kaufman v Gerson* [1904] 1 K.B. 591; *Addison v Brown* [1954] 1 W.L.R. 779.

[1376] Giuliano-Lagarde Report, p.38. On the concept of European Community public policy, see *Krombach v Bamberski* (C–7/98) [2000] E.C.R. I–2973; [2001] Q.B. 709; *Regie National des Usines Renault SA v Maxicar SpA* (C–38/98) [2000] E.C.R. I–2973; *Maronier v Larmer* [2002] EWCA Civ 774; [2003] Q.B. 620; *Eurofood IFSC Ltd* (C–340/04) [2006] E.C.R. I–3813, [2006] Ch. 508; Meidanis (2005) 30 E.L. Rev. 95. See above, para.30–070.

[1377] See *Dicey, Morris and Collins on the Conflict of Laws*, 14th edn (2006), Ch.36; Cheshire and North, *Private International Law*, 13th edn (1999), pp.90–98. For an exhaustive account of the problems in this area, see *Mann on the Legal Aspect of Money*, 6th edn (Proctor, 2005). See too, Law Com. No.124, 1983, and above, paras 21–068 et seq.

justified, first, on the ground that the elucidation of some of these problems involves reference to various different provisions of the Rome Convention and the Rome I Regulation which can be most coherently treated together. Secondly, some of these problems require discussion of rules of English domestic law and procedure rather than rules of the conflict of laws in the strict sense.[1378]

Principle of nominalism. Where a debt is expressed in the currency of any particular country, the debtor is under an obligation to pay the nominal amount of the debt in whatever is legal tender at the time of payment according to the law of the country in whose currency the debt is expressed, irrespective of any fluctuation in exchange rates which affect that currency.[1379] This principle, the principle of nominalism, applies to claims for unliquidated damages as well as to debts.[1380] As a principle of English domestic law, the principle of nominalism applies to debts and contracts governed by English law.[1381] Where a debt or contract is governed by a foreign law, it will be for that law to determine whether the principle of nominalism applies[1382] but since the principle appears to form "part of the legal systems of all civilised countries"[1383] there is little likelihood of its being inapplicable in any given case. 30–370

Legal tender. The law of the country in whose currency a contractual debt is expressed will determine what is regarded as legal tender for the purpose of its discharge. This is probably because by referring to a particular country's currency, the parties agree (either impliedly, at common law,[1384] or by virtue of art.3(1) of the Rome Convention, or art.3(1) of the Rome I Regulation[1385]) that the law of that country will determine what constitutes the currency of that country. This result will ensue even if the contract as a whole is governed by a 30–371

[1378] As to interest, see above, paras 30–339 et seq.

[1379] The principle goes back to *Gilbert v Brett* (1604) Davis 18 (also known as the *Case de Mixt Moneys*). See too, *Re Chesterman's Trusts* [1923] 2 Ch. 466; *Ottoman Bank v Chakarian (No.2)* [1938] A.C. 260; *Pyrmont Ltd v Schott* [1939] A.C. 145; *Marrache v Ashton* [1943] A.C. 311. A party may, of course, be able to recover for exchange losses suffered as a result of late payment by the other party: see above, para.30–340. If the currency in which the debt is expressed is devalued between the date of the contract and the date when the payment is due, the question of whether the debt should be "revalorised" (i.e. whether a party should pay more to compensate for the devaluation) will be governed by the law applicable to the contract: *Anderson v Equitable Life Assurance Society of the United States* (1929) 45 T.L.R. 468; *Re Schnapper* [1936] 1 All E.R. 322; *Kornatzki v Oppenheimer* [1937] 4 All E.R. 133; Rome Convention art.10(1)(b); Rome I Regulation art.12(1)(b). See generally *Dicey, Morris and Collins*, paras 36–036—36–038. Parties may seek to guard against fluctuations in exchange rates by inserting a "gold clause" or similar "protective" clause into the contract: see *Dicey, Morris and Collins*, paras 36–041—36–049 and above, paras 21–068 et seq. On the implications of the implementation of a single European currency, see *Dicey, Morris and Collins*, paras 36–011—36–014; Mance [1997] European Business L. Rev. 266; Blair [1997] European Business L. Rev. 228.

[1380] *The Despina R.* [1979] A.C. 685, 698.

[1381] *Re Chesterman's Trusts* [1923] 2 Ch. 466.

[1382] *Dicey, Morris and Collins*, para.30–008. See *Société des Hôtels Le Touquet-Paris-Plage v Cummings* [1922] 1 K.B. 451.

[1383] *Dicey, Morris and Collins*, para.36–008.

[1384] *Re Chesterman's Trusts* [1923] Ch. 466, 483; see above, paras 30–011, 30–331.

[1385] i.e. this suffices to demonstrate a choice with reasonable certainty for the purposes of art.3(1) of the Convention or to clearly demonstrate a choice for the purposes of art.3(1) of the Rome I Regulation: see above, paras 30–051 et seq., 30–173 et seq.

different law: the question of what is the legal tender of the currency in which the contractual debt is expressed will be regarded as a severable part of the contract capable of being governed by its own applicable law which will be the law of the country in whose currency the debt is expressed.[1386] No other law can rationally determine what is meant by that currency.

30–372 **Money of account.** The "money of account" is the currency in which a debt is expressed or a liability to pay damages is calculated as opposed to the currency in which that debt or liability is to be discharged, described as the "money of payment".[1387] The former concept thus describes the currency in which the amount due is to be measured. Where the parties have not indicated in the contract itself the particular currency which is the money of account, the relevant currency must be identified by interpreting or construing the contract, the canons of interpretation or construction being those which prevail in the law which governs the contract.[1388] If English law is the applicable law, then in the absence of any intention emerging from the contract itself when construed according to English law,[1389] the parties will be presumed to have intended the currency of the country with which the contract is most closely connected.[1390] This may, but need not necessarily, be the country of the applicable law.[1391]

30–373 **Currency of damages.** Where damages are claimed for breach of contract, it may be necessary to determine the currency in which such damages are to be calculated, i.e. the money of account. In this context, however, the issue is not one of interpretation of the contract but rather one relating to the assessment of damages which, like interpretation, will be governed by the applicable law of the contract.[1392] If English law is the applicable law, it has been authoritatively stated that the:

> "[First] step must be to see whether, expressly or by implication, the contract provides an answer to the currency question. This may lead to selection of the 'currency of the contract.' If from the terms of the contract it appears that the parties have accepted a

[1386] Rome Convention, art.3(1) and Rome I Regulation art.3(1) which permit parties to select a law applicable to a part only of a contract: see above, paras 30–056 et seq., 30–175.

[1387] See *Dicey, Morris and Collins*, para.36–004.

[1388] Rome Convention art.10(1)(a); Rome I Regulation art.12(1)(a). *Adelaide Electric Supply Co Ltd v Prudential Assurance Co Ltd* [1934] A.C. 122; *Auckland Corp v Alliance Assurance Co Ltd* [1937] A.C. 587; *De Bueger v Ballantyne & Co* [1938] A.C. 452; *Bonython v Commonwealth of Australia* [1951] A.C. 201; *National Bank of Australasia Ltd v Scottish Union and National Insurance Co Ltd* [1952] A.C. 493; *National Mutual Life Association of Australasia Ltd v AG for New Zealand* [1956] A.C. 493.

[1389] See, e.g. *W.J. Alan & Co Ltd v El Nasr Export and Import Co* [1972] 2 Q.B. 189.

[1390] *Bonython v Commonwealth of Australia* [1951] A.C. 201; *National Bank of Australasia Ltd v Scottish Union and National Insurance Co Ltd* [1952] A.C. 493; *W.J. Alan & Co Ltd v El Nasr Export and Import Co* [1972] 2 Q.B. 189.

[1391] *Adelaide Electric Supply Co Ltd v Prudential Assurance Co Ltd* [1934] A.C. 122; *Bonython v Commonwealth of Australia* [1951] A.C. 201. The process of determining the money of account in English domestic law is similar to, but not, as these cases show, identical with the process of determining the law applicable to the contract according to English conflicts rules. See *Dicey, Morris and Collins*, paras 30–018—30–022.

[1392] Rome Convention art.10(1)(c); Rome I Regulation art.12(1)(c): *Services Europe Atlantique Sud v Stockholms Rederaktiebolag Svea* [1979] A.C. 685. See above, para.30–357.

currency as the currency of account and payment[1393] in respect of all transactions arising under the contract, then it would be proper to give a judgment for damages in that currency. . . . But there may be cases in which, although obligations under that contract are to be met in a specified currency, or currencies, the right conclusion may be that there is no intention shown that damages for breach of contract should be given in that currency or currencies. . . . If then the contract fails to provide a decisive interpretation, the damages should be calculated in the currency in which the loss was felt by the plaintiff or 'which most truly expresses his loss.' This is not limited to that in which it first or immediately arose. In ascertaining which this currency is the court must ask what is the currency, payment of which will as nearly as possible compensate the plaintiff in accordance with the principle of restitution, and whether the parties must be taken reasonably to have had this in contemplation."[1394]

Money of payment. The "money of payment" is the precise currency in which the debt or damages is actually payable. This, of course, need not necessarily be the money of account.[1395] Where there is no contractual stipulation as to the money of payment, it is, at common law, determined by the law of the country in which payment is made.[1396] This is because the question of what money tokens the debtor must tender to the creditor is one concerning the mode of performance which is, thus, referable to the law of the place of performance.[1397] Whether this principle continues to apply in cases falling within the Rome Convention or the Rome I Regulation depends upon the correct interpretation of art.10(2) of the Convention and art.12(2) of the Regulation.[1398] Each provision states, so far as relevant, that in relation to the "manner of performance . . . regard shall be had" to the law of the country in which performance takes place. One might reasonably surmise that "manner of performance" can be equated with "mode of performance" in the common law context and it would, on this assumption, appear that the common law rule survives, subject to the possibility that, because of the wording of art.10(2) and art.12(2), the rule is of 30–374

[1393] i.e. the money of account and the money of payment: see text at fn.1387, above and below, paras 30–374 et seq. For an example, see *Rogers v Markel Corp* [2004] EWHC 2046 (QB), although the contract in this case was governed by the law of Virginia which seems to be the same on this point as English law.

[1394] *Services Europe Atlantique Sud v Stockholms Rederaktiebolag Svea* [1979] A.C. 685. See *Bain v Field* (1920) 5 Ll. L. Rep. 16; *Ottoman Bank v Chakarian (No.1)* [1930] A.C. 277; *Kraut AG v Albany Fabrics Ltd* [1977] Q.B. 182; *Société Francaise Bunge SA v Belcan NV* [1985] 3 All E.R. 378; *Metaalhandel J.A. Magnus BV v Ardfields Transport Ltd* [1988] 1 Lloyd's Rep. 471; *The Texaco Melbourne* [1994] 1 Lloyd's Rep. 473 (loss felt in Ghanaian cedis and measured in that currency despite fall in rate of exchange from 2.75 cedis to dollar at date of breach to 375 at date of judgment; criticised by Knott [1994] L.M.C.L.Q. 311); *Virani Ltd v Manuel Revert Y Cia SA* [2003] EWCA Civ 1651, [2004] 2 Lloyd's Rep. 14. See also *B.P. Exploration Co (Libya) Ltd v Hunt (No.2)* [1981] 1 W.L.R. 232 (affirmed [1983] A.C. 352 (restitutionary award under Law Reform (Frustrated Contracts) Act 1943)).

[1395] See above, paras 30–372 et seq. The contract may expressly or impliedly stipulate, or one party may give the other an option to elect, that the money of account and money of payment should be different: see, e.g. *Woodhouse AC Israel Cocoa Ltd SA v Nigerian Produce Marketing Co Ltd* [1972] A.C. 741 (money of account Nigerian, buyers of goods given option to choose between paying in Nigerian currency or sterling).

[1396] *Adelaide Electric Supply Co Ltd v Prudential Assurance Co Ltd* [1934] A.C. 122; *Auckland Corp v Alliance Assurance Co Ltd* [1937] A.C. 587; *Mount Albert BC v Australasian etc. Life Assurance Society Ltd* [1930] A.C. 224.

[1397] *Dicey, Morris and Collins*, paras 36–053—36–056.

[1398] See above, paras 30–332 et seq.

a discretionary character which did not seem to be the case at common law.[1399] One cannot be certain of this conclusion, however, because the Giuliano-Lagarde Report does not include the money of payment among the examples of issues governed by art.10(2) of the Convention. In contrast the Report suggests that "where performance consists of the payment of a sum of money, the conditions relating to the discharge of the debtor who has made the payment"[1400] are governed by art.10(1)(b) of the Convention.[1401] It is likely, however, that this observation is intended only to refer to the money of account. Accordingly, the English courts should interpret art.10(2) to include this issue. It is also submitted that the same interpretation should be accorded to art.12(2) of the Rome I Regulation.

30–375 Where English law is the law of the country of payment, there is a presumption that the money of payment is the same as the money of account.[1402] If the former currency differs from the latter, the exchange rate between them should, it is submitted be determined by the law applicable to the contract since the relevant rate of exchange is an aspect of the quantum of money tokens to be rendered.[1403] A sum payable in England under a contract governed by English law may be paid in units of the money of account or in sterling[1404]: if payment is tendered in sterling the rate of exchange is the rate at which, on the date when payment is due, units of the money of account can be purchased in London at a recognised and accessible market, irrespective of the official rate of exchange.[1405]

30–376 **Judgments in foreign currency.** Until 1975 it had long been accepted that an English court could only order the payment of debts or damages in English currency; this was so whether the judgment stemmed from a breach of a contract whose applicable law was English or foreign.[1406] The amount due to the judgment creditor in foreign currency had to be converted into sterling at the appropriate exchange rate when the cause of action arose, for example the date

1399 See above, paras 30–332 et seq.

1400 Giuliano-Lagarde Report, pp.42, 43.

1401 Above, paras 30–332 et seq.; Rome I Regulation art.12(1)(b), above, paras 30–332 et seq.

1402 See *Auckland Corp v Alliance Assurance Co Ltd* [1937] A.C. 587.

1403 *Dicey, Morris and Collins*, paras 36–053—36–056.

1404 *Marrache v Ashton* [1943] A.C. 311; *Syndic for Khoury v Khayat* [1943] A.C. 507, 514; *Dicey, Morris and Collins*, para.36–004. cf. *National Bank of Australasia Ltd v Scottish Union and National Insurance Co Ltd* [1952] A.C. 493; *National Mutual Life Association of Australia Ltd v AG for New Zealand* [1956] A.C. 369. If payment in the foreign currency is impossible, the debtor must pay in sterling: he cannot choose to pay in the foreign currency and then claim that the obligation is discharged or suspended by reason of the impossibility: *Libyan Arab Foreign Bank v Bankers Trust Co* [1989] Q.B. 728.

1405 *Marrache v Ashton* [1943] A.C. 311; *Syndic for Khoury v Khayat* [1943] A.C. 507; *Barclays Bank International Ltd v Levin Brothers (Bradford) Ltd* [1977] Q.B. 270; *George Veflings Rederi A/S v President of India* [1979] 1 W.L.R. 59. *Graumann v Treitel* [1940] 2 All E.R. 188 may be explicable on the ground that German law was the applicable law of the contract (see *Dicey, Morris and Collins*, para.36–054). For a case where there was no recognised and accessible market and no commercial rate of exchange, see *Re Parana Plantations Ltd* [1946] 2 All E.R. 214.

1406 *Manners v Pearson* [1989] 1 Ch. 581; *Tomkinson v First Pennsylvania Banking and Trust Co* [1961] A.C. 1007.

of the breach of contract.[1407] This much-criticised[1408] rule was abandoned by the House of Lords in *Miliangos v George Frank (Textiles) Ltd*[1409] where the court gave judgment expressed in Swiss francs for the payment of a debt due in that currency. The principle underlying the decision was expressed thus by Lord Wilberforce:

> "... the creditor has no concern with pounds sterling: for him what matters is that a Swiss franc for good or ill should remain a Swiss franc."[1410]

As a result of the judicial developments which followed that landmark decision, it is now possible to state the law as to judgments in foreign currency with some degree of completeness.[1411] The court may give judgment for an amount expressed in foreign currency or its sterling equivalent at the date when the court authorises enforcement of the judgment[1412]—this latter being the closest practicable date to the date of actual payment, the ideal date for conversion. This rule applies to contractual actions whether the applicable law of the contract is foreign law[1413] or English law.[1414] It is clear that it is not restricted to claims for payment

[1407] e.g. *Di Ferdinando v Simon Smits & Co* [1920] 2 K.B. 409.

[1408] *The Teh Hu* [1970] P. 106, 124, 127; *Jugoslavenska Oceanska Plovidba v Castle Investment Co Inc* [1974] Q.B. 292; *Schorsch Meier GmbH v Hennin* [1975] Q.B. 416.

[1409] [1976] A.C. 443.

[1410] [1976] A.C. 443, 466.

[1411] These developments are not restricted to contractual claims but would appear to apply to all claims made in foreign currency—see, e.g. *The Despina R.* [1979] A.C. 685; *Hoffman v Sofaer* [1982] 1 W.L.R. 1350 (tort); *B.P. Exploration Co (Libya) Ltd v Hunt (No.2)* [1979] 1 W.L.R. 783, 840–841 (affirmed [1983] 2 A.C. 352 (restitution)); *Re Dynamics Corp of America* [1976] 1 W.L.R. 757; *Re Lines Bros Ltd* [1983] Ch. 1; *Re Lines Bros Ltd (No.2)* [1984] Ch. 438 (winding up); *Choice Investments Ltd v Jeromninon* [1981] 1 Q.B. 149 (garnishee order against English bank); *Re A Debtor (No.51–SD–1991)* [1992] 1 W.L.R. 1294 (debt in statutory demand under Insolvency Act 1986); *Carnegie v Giessen* [2005] EWCA Civ 191, [2005] 1 W.L.R. 2610 (charging order may be expressed in foreign currency); *Re Telewest Communications Plc* [2004] EWHC 924 (Ch), [2004] B.C.C. 342, affirmed [2004] EWCA Civ 728, [2005] B.C.C. 29 (to determine the number of shares to be transferred to claimants under scheme of arrangement pursuant to Companies Act 1985 s.425 (Companies Act 2006 ss.895 et seq.) it was necessary to express all claims covered by the scheme in a single currency and for this purpose sterling claims were to be converted into US dollars in accordance with average exchange rate). See, too, *Re Scandinavian Bank Group Plc* [1988] Ch. 87 (s.2(5)(a) of the Companies Act 1985 does not require company to have share capital only denominated in sterling). The principle in *Re Scandinavian Bank Group Plc* is now to be found in Companies Act 2006 s.542(3) which provides that shares in a limited company having a share capital may be denominated in any currency and different classes of shares may be denominated in different currencies, subject to s.765, concerned with the EC requirement that the amount needed for the authorised minimum capital of a public company must either be in sterling or euros.

[1412] *Miliangos v George Frank (Textiles) Ltd* [1976] A.C. 443; CPR para.40.2.3; and see *The Halcyon Skies* [1977] 1 Lloyd's Rep. 22; *George Veflings Rederi A/S v President of India* [1978] 1 W.L.R. 982 (affirmed [1979] 1 W.L.R. 59). For counterclaims, see *The Transoceanica Fransesca* [1987] 2 Lloyd's Rep. 155; *Smit Tak International Zeesleepen Bergingsbedriff BV v Selco Salvage Ltd* [1988] 2 Lloyd's Rep. 398. As to pleading claims in foreign currency, see CPR 1998 PD 16 para.12.1.

[1413] e.g. *Miliangos v George Frank (Textiles) Ltd* [1976] A.C. 443.

[1414] e.g. *Federal Commerce and Navigation Co Ltd v Tradax Export SA* [1977] Q.B. 324 (reversed on another ground [1978] A.C. 1); *Barclays Bank International Ltd v Levin Bros (Bradford) Ltd* [1977] Q.B. 270; *Services Europe Atlantique Sud v Stockholms Rederaktiebolag Svea* [1979] A.C. 685.

of debts[1415] but extends to claims for damages for breach of contract,[1416] whether the claim be for liquidated[1417] or unliquidated damages.[1418] The rules applicable to judgments have been held to be applicable to arbitration awards,[1419] though it may be that conversion is to be effected as at the date of the award,[1420] rather than at some date closer to that of payment. But the applicability of the rules to arbitral awards must now be read in the light of the decision of the House of Lords in *Lesotho Highlands Development Authority v Impregilo SpA*,[1421] discussed below.[1422]

30–377 The rule laid down in *Miliangos* is a rule of procedure, to be applied by English courts whatever may be the law applicable to the contract in issue.[1423] A judgment in foreign currency may be satisfied by payment of the sum due in that currency[1424] or by the appropriate sum in sterling converted as at "the date of payment", i.e. normally[1425] the date when the court authorises enforcement of the judgment in terms of sterling. There are a number of cases where a different conversion date is provided by statute.[1426]

30–378 The rate of interest on the judgment is a matter for the *lex fori*, even when the judgment is expressed in a foreign currency.[1427] By statute the English court may order that the rate of interest on foreign currency judgments shall be such rate as the court thinks fit.[1428]

1415 *Miliangos v George Frank (Textiles) Ltd* [1976] A.C. 443; *Barclays Bank International Ltd v Levin Brothers (Bradford) Ltd* [1977] Q.B. 270.

1416 *Services Europe Atlantique Sud v Stockholms Rederaktiebolag Svea* [1979] A.C. 685; *Société Francais Bunge SA v Belcan NV* [1985] 3 All E.R. 378.

1417 *Federal Commerce and Navigation Co Ltd v Tradax Export SA* [1977] Q.B. 324, 341–342, 349, 354 (reversed on another point [1978] A.C. 1).

1418 *Services Europe Atlantique Sud v Stockholms Rederaktiebolag Svea* [1979] A.C. 685; and see *Kraut AG v Albany Fabrics Ltd* [1977] Q.B. 182.

1419 *Jugoslavenska Oceanska Plovidba v Castle Investment Co Inc* [1974] Q.B. 292.

1420 [1974] Q.B. 292, 305; cf. *Miliangos v George Frank (Textiles) Ltd* [1976] A.C. 443, 469.

1421 [2005] UKHL 43, [2006] 1 A.C.221.

1422 See para.30–379.

1423 [1976] A.C. 443, 465; and see *The Despina R.* [1979] A.C. 685, 704. As a rule of procedure it is unaffected either by the Rome Convention or by the Rome I Regulation: see above, paras 30–044, 30–161.

1424 See CPR r.40.2.3.

1425 The appropriate date in the case of winding-up (both compulsory and voluntary) is that of the winding-up order or resolution: *Re Dynamics Corp of America* [1976] 1 W.L.R. 783; *Re Lines Bros Ltd* [1983] Ch. 1; *Re Lines Bros (No.2)* [1984] Ch. 438. See Insolvency Rules 1986 r.4.91 and in bankruptcy, where the relevant date is the date of the bankruptcy order r.6.111.

1426 See, e.g. Carriage by Air Act 1961 Sch.1 art.22(5) (date of judgment); see *Dicey, Morris and Collins*, para.36R–081.

1427 *Dicey, Morris and Collins*, para.33–400.

1428 Judgments Act 1838 s.17, as amended by Administration of Justice Act 1970 s.44 and SI 1998/2940; Administration of Justice Act 1970 s.44A, inserted by Private International Law (Miscellaneous Provisions) Act 1995 s.1(1). For judgments in the county court, see County Courts Act 1984 s.74(5A), inserted by Private International Law (Miscellaneous Provisions) Act 1995 s.2. The foregoing sections give effect to recommendations of the Law Commission: see Law Com. No.124, 1983, paras 4.1–4.15.

Arbitral awards. Section 48(4) of the Arbitration Act 1996 provides that unless otherwise agreed between the parties in writing,[1429] an arbitral tribunal may order the payment of a sum of money in any currency. The effect of this provision was considered by the House of Lords in *Lesotho Highland Development Authority v Impregilo SpA*.[1430] In the preferred view of Lord Steyn, the power of the tribunal under s.48(4) was unconstrained by the case law pre-dating the 1996 Act.[1431] In the alternative he held that the fact that the tribunal had rendered the award in a currency other than that of the contract did not constitute a serious irregularity in the award, pursuant to s.68 of the Act, which would justify setting the award aside. It was merely an error of law by the tribunal which could not be challenged.[1432] Lord Scott of Foscote and Lord Rodger of Earlsferry preferred the latter view. Lord Hoffmann had reservations in respect of Lord Steyn's preferred view but chose not to express an opinion on the point. Lord Phillips of Worth Matravers dissented. In the light of these opinions it would seem that Lord Steyn's alternative view commands a majority.[1433] 30–379

[1429] Arbitration Act 1996 s.5(1).

[1430] [2005] UKHL 43, [2006] 1 A.C. 221. And see *C v D* [2007] EWCA Civ 1282, [2008] 1 Lloyd's Rep. 239.

[1431] [2005] UKHL 43 at [22]. See *Jugoslavenska Oceanska Plovidba v Castle Investment Co Inc* [1974] Q.B. 292; above para.30–376.

[1432] [2005] UKHL 43 at [23].

[1433] As to an arbitral tribunal's power to award interest, see Arbitration Act 1996 s.49: Vol.II, para.32–119.

INDEX

NOTES

1. Location references are to chapters and paragraphs. This index refers to Volume I only. An index for Volumes I and II can be found in Volume II.

2. The specific entry method has been used, so that topics should be sought under their own names, not under the relevant major class. Cross-references are provided to lead to the main subdivisions of each class which are represented in the index.

Abandonment
rescission, 22–027
Abridgement (limitation periods)
agreements, by, 28–112
arbitration agreements, in, 28–115
exemption clauses, 28–113
statutory periods, 28–114
Absurdity
construction of terms, 12–055
Acceleration clauses
damages, 26–140
Acceptance
'battle of forms'
generally, 2–034
'last shot' doctrine, 2–037
reference to each party's conditions, 2–036
'usual conditions', 2–035
bilateral contracts
estate agents' contracts, 2–083—2–084
extent of liability, 2–086
generally, 2–085
cancellation, 2–062
communication of
exceptions, 2–047
generally, 2–045
methods, 2–046
conduct, by
generally, 2–030
relevant terms, 2–031
correspondence, by
'battle of forms', 2–034—2–037
generally, 2–032
inaccurate detail, 2–033
cross-offers, 2–044
distance contracts, 2–064
electronic mail, by, 2–051
fax, by, 2–051
garbled messages, 2–059
generally, 2–027
Acceptance—*cont.*
ignorance of offer, in
bilateral contracts, 2–042
unilateral contracts, 2–041
international sales, 2–063
letter, by
application of rule, 2–049—2–051
exceptions to rule, 2–052
general rule, 2–048
operation of rule, 2–053—2–061
motive, 2–043
multilateral contracts, 2–110
prescribed method, by
counter-offer, 2–066
generally, 2–065
purpose, 2–067
waiver, 2–068—2–069
post, by
application of rule, 2–049—2–051
distance contracts, 2–064
exceptions to rule, 2–052
general rule, 2–048
international sales, 2–063
operation of rule, 2–053—2–061
post-contract documents, 2–038
pre-contract documents
'battle of forms', 2–034—2–037
generally, 2–032
inaccurate detail, 2–033
sale of land, 2–110
silence, by
exceptions to rule, 2–072—2–077
general rule, 2–070—2–071
telegram, by
dictation, upon, 2–051
garbled, 2–059
generally, 2–048
telemessage, by
dictation, upon, 2–051
garbled, 2–059
generally, 2–048

Acceptance—*cont.*
telephone, by, 2–050
telex, by, 2–050
tender, by, 2–040
tenders, 2–039
time of
additional negotiations, 2–029
continuing negotiations, 2–028
unilateral contracts
continuing guarantees, 2–081
ignorance of offer, 2–041
introduction, 2–078
irrevocable credits, 2–082
part performance, 2–079—2–080
waiver
method of communication, 2–068—2–069
need for communication, 2–047
website trading, 2–051
Accord and satisfaction
bills of exchange, 22–020
compromise, 22–013
conditions
accord, 22–014
generally, 22–012—22–013
satisfaction, 22–015
consent orders, 22–024
consideration, 22–012
duress, 22–021
evidence, 22–022
form, 22–014
generally, 22–012
joint liability
generally, 22–019
introduction, 17–017
misrepresentation, 22–021
mistake, 22–021
part payment, 22–016
payment
creditor composition, by, 22–018
different terms, 22–017
generally, 21–052
partial, 22–016
third party, by, 22–018
pleading, 22–023
promissory notes, 22–020
proof, 22–022
rescission, 3–078
Account
assignment, 29–196
general principle, 29–194—29–195
introduction, 29–193
stakeholders, 29–197—29–198
Account of profits
fraudulent misrepresentation, 6–062
restitution, 29–152—29–154
undue influence, 7–100
Account stated
generally, 29–191
illegal debts, 29–192
Account stated—*cont.*
statute-barred debt, 28–129
unenforceable debts, 29–192
Acknowledgment
assignment, 19–089
debt
effect, 28–103
exclusions, 28–104
form, 28–094
general rule, 28–093
introduction, 28–092
nature, 28–095
parties, 28–100—28–102
pleading, 28–105
exemption clauses, 14–133
Acquiescence
applicable law, 30–348
limitation of actions, 28–136
"Act intended to have legal effect"
applicable law, 30–354
Act of state doctrine
generally, 11–007
"*Actio personalis moritur cum persona*"
bankruptcy, 20–001
Actual forbearance
See **Forbearance**
Actual undue influence
See also **Illegitimate pressure**
causation, 7–068
disregard of victim's interests, 7–067
generally, 7–064
independent and informed judgment, 7–065—7–066
Addition of parties
generally, 17–009
relevant persons
generally, 17–010
joint and several promisors, 17–011
Adjudication
unfair contract terms (consumer contracts), 15–072
Administration orders
contracts with companies, 9–053
Administrative law
CPR Part 54, 1–197
introduction, 1–193
RSC Order 53, 1–194—1–196
Administrators
payment, 21–049
Advancement
locus poenitentiae, 16–182—16–184
Advertisements
offers
bilateral contracts, 2–017
false statements, 2–020
rewards, 2–019
unilateral contracts, 2–018
Affirmation
effect, 24–010—24–012
estoppel, 24–007—24–008

Affirmation—*cont.*
generally, 24–003
nature, 24–004
rescission, 6–124—6–125
sale of goods, 22–004—22–005
undue influence, 7–097
waiver
election, by, 24–007—24–008
estoppel, by, 24–007—24–008
generally, 24–009
Agency
And see **Agents**
applicable law, 30–042
Crown contracts
generally, 10–009
liability of agent, 10–013
ostensible authority, 10–012
servant-agent issue, 10–011
unauthorised contracts, 10–011
warranty of authority, 10–014
privity of contract
generally, 18–012
sub-agency, 18–013
sub-agency, 18–013
true nature of document, evidence
2–122—12–115
unfair contract terms, 14–069
vicarious performance, 19–084
Agents
And see **Agency**
minors, 8–058—8–059
payments
by agent, 21–041
to agent, 21–043—21–044, 21–048
payments to third person, 29–117
recovery of payments, 16–192
signature of contract under LPA 1925, s.40
estate agent, 4–037
for both parties, 4–038
generally, 4–036
tender
tender by, 21–095
tender to, 21–094
"Agreed damages clauses"
damages
generally, 26–009
nature, 26–125—26–156
exemption clauses, 14–004
specific performance, 27–006
Agreement
And see under individual headings
acceptance
communication 2–045—2–046
generally, 2–027—2–044
prescribed method, by, 2–065—2–069
post, by, 2–048—2–064
silence, by, 2–070—2–077
unilateral contracts, 2–078—2–086
Agreement—*cont.*
certainty of terms
exceptions to rule, 2–140—2–146
general rule, 2–139
conditional
classification, 2–147—2–149
degrees of obligation, 2–150—2–156
consideration
adequacy 3–014—3–021
compromise, 3–046—3–056
contract as agreements, 1–005
deeds, 1–108
definitions, 3–004—3–013
existing duties, 3–061—3–075
forbearance to sue, 3–046—3–056
introduction, 3–001—3–003
movement 3–036—3–045
part payment of debt, 3–115—3–136
past, 3–026—3–035
proprietary estoppel, 3–137—3–164
special cases, 3–165—3–182
'valuable' consideration, 3–022—3–025
variation of terms, 3–076—3–114
contract as
enforcement, 1–006
existence, 1–004—1–005
generally, 1–001
problems with, 1–003—1–006
types, 1–003
incomplete agreements
continued operation of agreements, 2–115
contract to make contract, 2–134—2–138
facts to be ascertained, 2–133
in principle agreements, 2–112
lack of detail, 2–113—2–114
letters of intent, 2–125
subject to contract, 2–118—2–123
subject to execution of formal document, 2–116—2–117
subsequently completed agreements, 2–124
terms to be agreed, 2–126—2–132
intention
anger, agreements made in, 2–185—2–189
burden of proof, 2–159—2–160
collective agreements, 2–177
consumer guarantees, 2–167
discretion, 2–176
domestic agreements, 2–169—2–175
free passes, 2–178
generally, 2–158
giving effect to pre-existing rights, agreements, 2–180
goodwill agreements, 2–186
government policy statements, 2–179
impliedly negatived, 2–164

Agreement—*cont.*
intention—*cont.*
jest, agreements made in, 2–185—2–189
nature of relationship, 2–181—2–183
social agreements, 2–168
statements inducing contracts, 2–165—2–166
tests, 2–161—2–163
vague agreements, 2–184
offer
advertisements, by, 2–017—2–020
auctions, 2–011—2–013
conduct, by, 2–005
display, by, 2–014—2–016
generally, 2–003—2–004
inactivity, by, 2–006
invitation to treat, 2–007—2–010
place 2–025
share, 2–024
tender, by, 2–022—2–023
termination 2–087—2–109
ticket, by, 2–021
time 2–026
special cases, 2–110—2–111
Agreements
parties not to plead limitation
estoppel, 28–109
generally, 28–107—28–108
introduction, 28–106
terms, 28–110
Agreements for lease
specific performance, 27–040
Agreements in principle
generally, 2–112
"Agreements of minor importance"
"Agreements to negotiate"
incomplete agreements, 2–136—2–138
"Aids to interpretation"
illegality, 16–147—16–152
Alien enemies
claimant, as
exceptions, 11–029
generally, 11–027—11–028
common law, at
companies, 11–025
generally, 11–024
companies, 11–025
defendant, as, 11–030
illegal contracts, 11–032
limitation of actions, 11–031
statute, under, 11–026
Alterations to documents
See **Amendments**
Ambassadors
immunity from suit, 11–008—11–009
Ambiguity
construction of terms
Crown contracts, 12–086
generally, 12–083—12–085
Ambiguity—*cont.*
interpretation of document, evidence 12–125
Amendments
bills of exchange
introduction, 21–081
material change, 25–024
construction of terms
generally, 12–069
modifications, 12–075
deeds, 1–114
discharge
Bank of England notes, 25–025
immaterial alteration, 25–023
material alteration, 25–020—25–022
negotiable instruments, 25–024
joint liability, 17–022
Amenity
See **Loss of amenity**
"Anger"
agreements, and, 2–185—2–189
Animal feed
See **Feedingstuffs**
"Antecedent debt"
past consideration
bills of exchange, 3–034
generally, 3–031
Ante-natal care
See **Time off work**
Ante-nuptial settlements
capacity of parties, 8–069
Anticipatory breach
impossibility, 24–030—24–031
renunciation
breach accepted, 24–022—24–023
breach not accepted, 24–024—24–025
generally, 24–021
Applicable law
And see **Conflict of laws**
absence of choice by parties, in
carriage of goods contracts, 30–085—30–087
characteristic performance, 30–074—30–078
consumer contracts, for, 30–107
employment contracts, for, 30–119—30–120
general principle, 30–071
habitual residence, 30–079
immovables, 30–082—30–084
introduction, 30–055
non-application of presumptions, 30–088—30–089
place of business, 30–080—30–081
presumptions, 30–072—30–073
rebutting presumptions, 30–090—30–091
Rome I Regulation, and, 30–186—30–199

Applicable law—*cont.*
acquiescence, 30–348
act intended to have legal effect, 30–354
agent-principal disputes, 30–042
arbitration agreements
generally, 30–040
Rome I Regulation, and, 30–157
auction sales, 30–195
background
And see **Rome Convention**
generally, 30–017—30–029
bills of exchange
generally, 30–038—30–039
Rome I Regulation, and, 30–156
breach of contract, consequences of
damages, 30–337
exchange losses, 30–340
generally, 30–336
injunctions, 30–338
interest, 30–339—30–344
specific performance, 30–338
burden of proof, 30–351
capacity
bodies corporate, 30–325
generally, 30–036, 30–323
natural persons, 30–324
Rome I Regulation, and, 30–153
carriage of goods
generally, 30–085—30–087
Rome I Regulation, and, 30–212—30–220
characteristic performance
generally, 30–074—30–078
Rome I Regulation, and, 30–201—30–202
choice of law agreements
generally, 30–040
Rome I Regulation, and, 30–157
choice of law by parties
alteration, 30–058
consumer contracts, for, 30–092—30–107
employment contracts, for, 30–108—30–118
express choice, 30–050
generally, 30–047—30–048
implied choice, 30–051—30–055
limitations, 30–060—30–070
mandatory rules, 30–061—30–068
partial choice, 30–056—30–057
public policy, 30–070
Rome I Regulation, and, 30–170—30–185
validity, 30–059
company law
generally, 30–041
Rome I Regulation, and, 30–158
concurrent liability
employment contracts, 30–121

Applicable law—*cont.*
concurrent liability—*cont.*
generally, 30–032
Rome I Regulation, and, 30–151
consumer contracts, for
choice of law by parties, 30–094—30–106
formal validity of contract, 30–313
habitual residence, 30–106
introduction, 30–092
mandatory rules, 30–102—30–105
no choice of law by parties, 30–107
online contracts, 30–095—30–101
relevant contracts, 30–093
Rome I Regulation, and, 30–231—30–251
contract intended to have legal effect, 30–354
contracts of carriage
generally, 30–085—30–087
Rome I Regulation, and, 30–200—30–230
contractual obligations, 30–031
damages, 30–337
employment contracts, for
choice of law by parties, 30–112—30–118
concurrent liability, 30–121
generally, 30–108—30–111
no choice of law by parties, 30–119—30–120
Rome I Regulation, and, 30–276—30–287
territorial limitation, 30–115
evidence and procedure
generally, 30–044
Rome I Regulation, and, 30–161
exchange losses, 30–340
exclusions
agent-principal disputes, 30–042
arbitration agreements, 30–040
capacity of person, 30–036
choice of law agreements, 30–040
company law, 30–041
evidence and procedure, 30–044
generally, 30–030—30–035
insurance contracts, 30–045—30–046
matrimonial and similar rights, 30–037
negotiable instruments, 30–038—30–039
Rome I Regulation, and, 30–152—162
succession, 30–037
trusts, 30–043
wills, 30–037
extinguishing obligations, 30–345
foreign currency obligations
generally, 30–369—30–371

Applicable law—*cont.*
foreign currency obligations—*cont.*
money of account, 30–372—30–373
money of payment, 30–374—30–379
formal validity of contract
acts intended to have legal effect, 30–315—30–317
consumer contracts, 30–313
generally, 30–310—30–312
immovables, 30–314
Rome I Regulation, and, 30–318—30–322
habitual residence
generally, 30–079
Rome I Regulation, and, 30–164—30–169
illegality of contract
applicable law, under, 30–356
English law, under, 30–357
generally, 30–355
other foreign law, under, 30–365
place of performance of act, in, 30–358—30–364
immovables
formal validity of contract, 30–314
no choice of law by parties, 30–082—30–084
implied choice
distinction from no choice, 30–055
generally, 30–051—30–052
relevant factors, 30–053
subsequent conduct, 30–054
injunctions, 30–338
insurance contracts
generally, 30–045—30–046
Rome I Regulation, and, 30–252—30–275
interest
exchange losses, 30–340
generally, 30–339
statutory, 30–341—30–344
interpretation of contract, 30–331
introduction, 30–001—30–004
laches, 30–348
limitation of actions, 30–347—30–348
mandatory rules
application, 30–065
chosen law governs other issues, where, 30–067
connection with single country, 30–062
English law, 30–066
generally, 30–061
inapplicability, 30–064
law of the forum, 30–068
meaning, 30–063
material validity of contract
formation of contract, 30–306—30–307
generally, 30–304—30–305

Applicable law—*cont.*
material validity of contract—*cont.*
validity of consent, 30–308
validity of terms, 30–309
matrimonial and similar rights
generally, 30–037
Rome I Regulation, and, 30–155
money of account
currency of damages, 30–373
generally, 30–372
money of payment
generally, 30–374—30–375
judgments in foreign currency, 30–376—30–378
negotiable instruments
generally, 30–038—30–039
Rome I Regulation, and, 30–038—30–039
no choice of law by parties
carriage of goods contracts, 30–085—30–087
characteristic performance, 30–074—30–078
consumer contracts, for, 30–107
distinction from implied choice, 30–055
employment contracts, for, 30–119—30–120
general principle, 30–071
habitual residence, 30–079
immovables, 30–082—30–084
introduction, 30–055
non-application of presumptions, 30–088—30–089
place of business, 30–080—30–081
presumptions, 30–072—30–073
rebutting presumptions, 30–090—30–091
Rome I Regulation, and, 30–186—30–199
nominalism, 30–370
nullity of contract
consequences, 30–327—30–328
contract, and, 30–349
Rome I Regulation, and, 30–328
partial choice
generally, 30–056—30–057
Rome I Regulation, and, 30–175
performance of contract
discretion, 30–335
manner, 30–333—30–334
substance, 30–332
place of business, 30–080—30–081
prescription, 30–347—30–348
presumptions of law, 30–353
public policy
contract contrary to, 30–366—30–368
generally, 30–069—30–070
Rome I Regulation, and, 30–183

Applicable law—*cont.*
restitution, 30–033
Rome I Regulation, and
And see **Rome I Regulation**
applicable law in absence of choice, 30–186—30–199
consumer contracts, 30–231—30–251
contracts of carriage, 30–200—30–230
employment contracts, 30–276—30–287
exclusions, 30–152—30–163
formal validity of contract, 30–318—30–322
freedom of choice, 30–170—30–185
generally, 30–130—30–151
habitual residence, 30–164—30–169
illegality in place of performance of act, 30–360
insurance contracts, 30–252—30–275
multiple liability, 30–296—30–298
nullity of contract, 30–328
set-off, 30–299-30–302
subrogation, 30–288—30–295
unjust enrichment, 30–034
voluntary assignment, 30–288—30–292
scope
breach of contract, 30–336—30–344
burden of proof, 30–351—30–354
capacity, 30–323—30–325
extinguishing obligations, 30–345
foreign currency obligations, 30–369—30–379
formal validity of contract, 30–310—30–322
generally, 30–303
illegality of contract, 30–355—30–365
interpretation of contract, 30–331
limitation of actions, 30–347—30–348
material validity of contract, 30–304—30–309
nullity of contract, 30–327—30–328
other issues, 30–350
performance of contract, 30–332—30–335
prescription, 30–347—30–348
public policy, 30–366—30–368
Rome I Regulation, and, 30–139—30–151
set-off
generally, 30–346
Rome I Regulation, and, 30–299—30–301
specific performance, 30–338

Applicable law—*cont.*
subrogation
generally, 30–127—30–129
Rome I Regulation, and, 30–288—30–295
succession, 30–037
trusts
generally, 30–043
Rome I Regulation, and, 30–160
unjust enrichment, 30–034
voluntary assignment of rights
assignability, 30–125
generally, 30–123
mutual obligations, 30–124
property, 30–126
Rome I Regulation, and, 30–288—30–292
wills, 30–037
Apportionment
damages, 26–039
Apprenticeship contracts
See **Contracts of apprenticeship**
Appropriation (payments)
creditor's right, 21–061—21–062
current account, to, 21–066
debtor's right, 21–060
generally, 21–059
guaranteed debt, to, 21–064
instalment payments, 21–065
interest-bearing debt, to, 21–067
statute-barred debt, to, 21–063, 28–128
Arbitral proceedings
limitation of actions, 28–125
Arbitration
frustration, 23–097
interest, 26–183—26–184
limitation of actions
date from which time runs, 28–059—28–060
relevant period, 28–017
running of time, 28–067
ouster of jurisdiction, 16–045—16–047
unfair contract terms (consumer contracts), 15–072
Arbitration agreements
applicable law, 30–040
limitation of actions, 28–115
ouster of jurisdiction, 16–045—16–047
Articles of association
rectification, 5–135
"Ascertained goods"
See also **Unascertained goods**
specific performance, 27–016—27–018
Assessment of damages
See **Measure of damages**
Assignees
payment to third person, 29–106
Assignment
acknowledgment, 19–089

Assignment—*cont.*
assignable rights
champerty, 19–049—19–053
commercial contracts, 19–056
contracts with companies, 19–057
contractual prohibition, 19–043—19–046
generally, 19–042
personal contracts, 19–055
statutory prohibition, 19–047—19–048
bankruptcy, 20–021
choses in action, of
common law, at, 19–001
equity, in, 19–002
liability to account, 29–196
statute, under, 19–003
consent
conditional benefit, 19–079
generally, 19–077—19–078
pure benefit, 19–080
equitable assignment
conditions, 19–028—19–0
consideration, 19–027—19–037
distinction from statutory assignments, 19–004—19–006
enforcement, 19–038—19–041
formalities, 19–025—19–026
generally, 19–020
method, 19–021—19–024
generally, 1–125
introduction, 1–125
negotiability, 19–085
novation, 19–086—19–088
principles
assignable rights, 19–042—19–057
consent, 19–077—19–080
priority, 19–068—19–076
validity, 19–058—19–067
priority
equities, 19–070—19–076
generally, 19–068
notices, 19–069
restraint of trade, 16–099
statutory
conditions, 19–007—19–018
consideration, 19–019
distinction from equitable assignments, 19–004—19–006
generally, 19–007
types
equitable, 19–020—19–041
generally, 19–001—19–006
statutory, 19–007—19–019
unfair contract terms (consumer contracts), 15–085
validity
creditors, against, 19–065—19–067
generally, 19–058
liquidator, against, 19–065

Assignment—*cont.*
validity—*cont.*
personal representative, against, 19–059
trustee in bankruptcy, against, 19–060—19–064
vicarious performance
agency, 19–084
generally, 19–081—19–083
"Assignment of pay"
illegality, 16–022
Association for Payment Clearing Services
See **APACS**
Assumpsit
See **Writs of assumpsit**
Assumption of responsibility
contractual silence, 1–158—1–160
duty of care, 1–141
effect of liability, 1–143—1–144
fair, just and reasonable, 1–142
Henderson v Merrett, 1–138—1–139
inconsistency of contract, 1–140
introduction, 1–137
pure economic loss, 1–179
Athens Convention 1974
exemption clauses, 14–117
ATM cards
See **Debit cards**
Attorney, powers of
See **Powers of attorney**
"Auction rings"
generally, 16–135
Auctions
consideration, 3–174
offer
generally, 2–011
resale in case of dispute, 2–013
with reserve, 2–012
without reserve, 2–012
payment, 21–048
restraint of trade, 16–135
subject to contract, 2–122
unfair contract terms, 14–068
without reserve, 3–174
Auctioneers
stakeholders, as, 29–198
Auditors
contracts with companies, 9–062—9–063
"Automatic extension clause"
unfair contract terms (consumer contracts), 15–079

Bad faith
threats to break contract, 7–041
"Badly drafted contracts"
construction of terms, 12–056
Baggage
See **Luggage**

Bailment
exemption clauses
deliberate damage, 14–037
deposit, 14–034
misdelivery, 14–036
storage, 14–035
sub-contracting, 14–038
theft, 14–037
third parties, 14–054—14–055
Bank accounts
generally, 21–045—21–046
in-house, 21–047
"Bank notes"
material alteration, 25–025
Bankers Associated Clearing Services Ltd
See **BACS**
Bankers' commercial credits
See **Commercial credits**
Banknotes
material alteration, 25–025
Bankruptcy
action by bankrupt, 20–055
after-acquired property, 20–054
assignment, 20–021
benefit of contracts, 20–032—20–034
carrying on business of bankrupt, 20–056
choses in action, 20–026
compulsory payment to third party, 29–104
debts provable, 20–049
deeds of arrangement
generally, 20–051
surety, 20–052
discharge, 25–029
discharge of bankrupt
debts provable, 20–049
effect, 20–046—20–048
generally, 20–045
disclaimer of contracts, 20–035
extortionate credit transactions, 20–030
generally, 20–015—20–017
interference with course of justice, 16–042
joint liability, 17–024
limitation of actions, 28–070
matrimonial home, 20–036
post-bankruptcy contracts
action by bankrupt, 20–055
after-acquired property, 20–054
carrying on business of bankrupt, 20–056
generally, 20–053
pre-bankruptcy contracts
generally, 20–018—20–023
set-off, 20–040—20–044
"subject to equities", 20–039
vesting of property, 20–024—20–038
preferences, 20–029
Bankruptcy—*cont.*
provable debts, 20–049
remedies
contracting party, 20–037
employee, 20–038
schemes of arrangement
deeds of arrangement, 20–051—20–052
voluntary arrangements, 20–050
second bankruptcies, 20–057
set-off
generally, 20–040—20–041
mutual debts, 20–043—20–044
unliquidated damages, 20–042
"subject to equities", 20–039
transactions at an undervalue, 20–027—20–028
transactions defrauding creditors, 20–031
unjust enrichment, 29–104
voluntary arrangements, 20–050
Banks
undue influence
bank put on inquiry, 7–111—7–112
Barclays Bank v O'Brien, 7–106—7–108
conflicts of interest, 7–117—7–118
Etridge's case, 7–109—7–110
introduction, 7–105
jointly-owned homes, 7–123
legal advice, 7–115—7–116
loss of right to avoid, 7–122
procedure, 7–119
reasonable steps, 7–114
replacement mortgages, 7–121
spouse as party to transaction, 7–120
transactions not to advantage of surety, 7–113
Bar pupillage contracts
See **Pupillage**
"Battle of the forms"
generally, 2–034
'last shot' doctrine, 2–037
reference to each party's conditions, 2–036
'usual conditions', 2–035
"Beneficial contracts"
apprenticeship contracts
generally, 8–022—8–023
rescission, 8–024
education contracts, 8–027
employment contracts
generally, 8–025
other analogous contracts, 8–029
restraint of trade covenants, 8–026
introduction, 8–021
privity of contract, 18–012—18–013
Benefit of third party
See **Third party rights**

Benefits from crime
See **Proceeds of crime**
Benefits
illegality, 16–024
Betting contracts
See **Wagering contracts**
Bilateral contracts
acceptance
estate agents' contracts, 2–083—2–084
extent of liability, 2–086
generally, 2–085
generally, 1–079
offer by advertisements, 2–017
Bills of exchange
And see **Negotiable instruments**
accord and satisfaction, 22–020
alteration
introduction, 21–081
material change, 25–024
applicable law, 30–038—30–039
cancellation, 25–026
compulsory payment to third party, 29–108
consideration, 3–034
forgery, 21–078
loss
introduction, 21–080
material loss, 25–027
past consideration, 3–034
payment by
agent, from, 21–075
creditor's duties, 21–079
generally, 21–073
nature, 21–074
satisfaction, in, 21–077
security, as, 21–076
payment to third person, 29–108
release, 22–009
tender, 21–087
unjust enrichment, 29–108
"Binding contracts"
apprenticeship contracts
generally, 8–022—8–023
rescission, 8–024
education contracts, 8–027
employment contracts
generally, 8–025
other analogous contracts, 8–029
restraint of trade covenants, 8–026
generally, 8–021
introduction, 8–004
necessaries
examples, 8–016—8–018
generally, 8–007
goods sold and delivered, 8–010—8–012
loans, 8–020
meaning, 8–008
nature, 8–009
"Binding contracts"—*cont.*
necessaries—*cont.*
services, 8–013—8–014
spouse's needs, 8–019
trading contracts, 8–017—8–018
other analogous contracts, 8–029
Bodies corporate
See **Companies**
Bona fide purchaser
See **Purchasers without notice**
Boundary agreements
contracts for sale of land, 4–057
Breach of contract
And see under individual headings
conflict of laws
damages, 30–337
exchange losses, 30–340
generally, 30–336
injunctions, 30–338
interest, 30–339—30–344
specific performance, 30–338
damages
causation, 26–032—26–050
exchange rates, 26–159
interest, 26–167—26–184
mitigation of damage, 26–101—26–124
nature, 26–001—26–007
penalty damages, 26–125—26–156
remoteness, 26–051—26–100
tax, 26–157—26–166
types, 26–008—26–031
injunctions
damages, 27–077—27–079
express negative promises, 27–064—27–069
implied negative promises, 27–070—27–072
interim, 27–061
negative contracts, 27–060—27–063
refusal to contract, 27–073—27–076
limitation of actions
abridgement of period, 28–112—28–115
cause of action, 28–031—28–061
commencement of proceedings, 28–116—28–125
computation of period, 28–062—28–063
effect, 28–126—28–133
equitable remedies, 28–134—28–146
extension of period, 28–071—28–111
relevant period, 28–001—28–030
running of time, 28–064—28–070
remedies for
damages, 26–001—26–184
injunctions, 27–060—27–084
limitation of actions, 28–001—28–146

Breach of contract—*cont.*
remedies for—*cont.*
specific performance, 27–001—27–059
restitution
account of profits, 29–152—29–154
introduction, 29–151
specific performance
compensation, with, 27–054—27–058
generally, 27–001—27–004
limitations, 27–005—27–045
third parties, 27–049—27–053
Breach of trust
limitation of actions
date from which time runs, 28–057
relevant period, 28–019
Break clauses
time of the essence, 21–013
"Brewery agreements"
restraint of trade, 16–125—16–126
Bribes
restitution, 29–156
Burden of proof
applicable law, 30–352
discharge
material alteration, 25–022
under contract, 22–050
exemption clauses
reasonableness, 14–088
force majeure clauses
'delayed' clauses, 14–144
generally, 14–140
'hindered' clauses, 14–143
'prevented' clauses, 14–141—14–142
'rendered uneconomic' clauses, 14–145
illegality, 16–204
intention
express commercial agreements, 2–159
conduct, agreements inferred from, 2–160
negligent misrepresentation, 6–075
OFT proceedings, 15–097
presumed undue influence, 7–094
restraint of trade, 16–095—16–096
self-induced frustration, 23–065
unconscionable bargains, 7–135
unfair contract terms
dealing as a consumer, 14–070
reasonableness, 14–088
unfair contract terms (consumer contracts)
generally, 15–062—15–064
OFT proceedings, 15–097
"But for"
economic duress, 7–027
Cancellation
acceptance, 2–062
bills of exchange, 25–026
deeds, 25–026
discharge by frustration, 23–033—23–034
distance contracts, 2–064
revocation, 2–062
Capacity
ambassadors, 11–008—11–009
applicable law
bodies corporate, 30–325
generally, 30–323
introduction, 30–036
natural persons, 30–324
barristers, 11–29
consuls, 11–017
Crown contracts, 10–004
diplomats, 11–010—11–016
drunken persons
generally, 8–080
necessaries, liability for, 8–081
effect, 1–005
foreign heads of state, 11–008—11–009
foreign sovereign
common law, at, 11–001
human rights, 11–003
statute, under, 11–002—11–006
foreign states
common law, at, 11–001
human rights, 11–003
statute, under, 11–002—11–007
generally, 8–001
international organisations, 11–018—11–019
introduction, 1–125, 1–162
married women
ante-nuptial contracts, 8–069
generally, 8–068
mentally disordered persons
agency, 8–076
deeds, 8–071
evidence, 8–070
generally, 8–070—8–073
lasting powers of attorney, 8–078
necessaries, 8–074—8–075
statutory provisions, 8–077—8–079
minors
agency, 8–058—8–060
beneficial contracts, 8–021—8–029
binding contracts, 8–007—8–020
disposal of property, 8–065—8–067
generally, 8–002—8–006
parental liability, 8–061
restitution, 8–048—8–057
tortious liability, 8–046—8–047
voidable contracts, 8–030—8–045
trade unions, 9–081

Carriage by air
exemption clauses, 14–118
remoteness of damage, 26–089—26–090
Carriage by rail
deviation, 14–029
exemption clauses
delay, 14–030
generally, 14–116
misdelivery, 14–033
sub-contracting, 14–038
limitation of actions
relevant period, 28–025
running of time, 28–068
remoteness of damage, 26–089—26–090
Carriage by road
exemption clauses
delay, 14–030
generally, 14–116
misdelivery, 14–033
roadworthiness, 14–032
sub-contracting, 14–038
remoteness of damage, 26–089—26–090
Carriage by sea
classification
common law purposes, for, 1–071
statutory purposes, for, 1–069
delay, 14–030
deviation, 14–029
exemption clauses
deck, on, 14–031
delay, 14–030
deviation, 14–029
generally, 14–117
misdelivery, 14–033
seaworthiness, 14–032
sub-contracting, 14–038
frustration
generally, 23–047
'Suez Canal' cases, 23–048
limitation of actions, 28–022—28–023
remoteness of damage, 26–089—26–090
seaworthiness, 14–032
unfair contract terms, 14–106—14–107
Carriage of goods
air, by
And see **Carriage by air**
exemption clauses, 14–118
limitation of actions, 28–024
remoteness of damage, 26–089—26–090
applicable law, 30–085—30–087
discharge by frustration
generally, 23–047
'Suez Canal' cases, 23–048
exemption clauses
air, by, 14–118
Carriage of goods—*cont.*
exemption clauses—*cont.*
land, by, 14–029—14–033, 14–116
sea, by, 14–029—14–033, 14–117
limitation of actions
relevant period, 28–022—28–026
running of time, 28–068
rail, by
And see **Carriage by rail**
exemption clauses, 14–029—14–033, 14–116
limitation of actions, 28–025, 28–068
remoteness of damage, 26–089—26–090
remoteness of damage, 26–089—26–090
road, by
And see **Carriage by road**
exemption clauses, 14–029—14–033, 14–116
limitation of actions, 28–026, 28–068
remoteness of damage, 26–089—26–090
Rome I Regulation, and
applicable law in absence of choice, 30–215—30–218
"carrier", 30–217
choice of law by the parties, 30–214
"consignor", 30–218
generally, 30–212
meaning, 30–213
residual rule, 30–219
rule of displacement, 30–220
sea, by
And see **Carriage by sea**
exemption clauses, 14–029—14–033, 14–117
limitation of actions, 28–022—28–023
remoteness of damage, 26–089—26–090
"Causal connection"
enforcement against third parties, 18–143
Causation
actual undue influence, 7–068
damages
apportionment, 26–039
contributory negligence, 26–049—26–050
generally, 26–032—26–033
intervening act of plaintiff, 26–037—26–039
intervening act of third party, 26–034—26–036
intervening event, 26–040—26–041
intervening omission of plaintiff, 26–037—26–039

Causation—*cont.*
damages—*cont.*
loss of chance, 26–042—26–048
duress
duress to goods, 7–026
duress to person, 7–025
economic duress, 7–027—7–036
generally, 7–024
economic duress
additional elements, 7–029
"but for", 7–027
conclusion, 7–036
generally, 7–027
gravity of threat, 7–033
independent advice, 7–035
predominant cause, 7–030
protest, 7–034
reasonable alternative, 7–031—7–032
voluntary submission, 7–024
Cause of action estoppel
exceptional circumstances, 25–014
generally, 25–011
scope, 25–[illegible]
Certainty
conflicting provisions, 2–145
custom and trade usage
duty to resolve uncertainty, 2–143
generally, 2–141
meaningless terms, 2–144
reasonableness, 2–142
self-contradictory terms, 2–144
exceptions to rule
conflicting provisions, 2–145
custom, 2–141—2–144
generally, 2–140
trade usage, 2–141—2–144
vagueness in subsidiary term, 2–146
general rule, 2–139
specific performance, 27–042
vagueness in subsidiary term, 2–146
Champerty
assignment
generally, 19–049—19–053
right to litigate, 16–057—16–064
effect, 16–066
generally, 16–048—16–049
meaning, 16–054
other agreements, 16–065
solicitor and clients, 16–055—16–056
Chance
See **Sale of a chance**
Change of position
restitution
generally, 29–179—29–185
ultra vires demands, 29–086
undue influence, 7–103
Charge cards
payment, 21–082
Charitable companies
And see **Companies**
contracts, 9–005
ultra vires, 9–037
Charter companies
contracts with, 9–004
termination of offer, 2–108
Charterparties
frustration
other events, 23–044—23–044
requisition, 23–041—23–043
Change of law
mistake of law, 29–048
Chattels
enforcement against third parties, 18–137
restraint of trade, 16–130
Cheques
And see **Negotiable instruments**
alteration, 21–081
forgery, 21–078
loss, 21–080
payment by
agent, from, 21–075
creditor's duties, 21–079
generally, 21–073
nature, 21–074
satisfaction, in, 21–077
security, as, 21–076
privity of contract, 18–007
tender, 21–087
validity, 21–078
Children
And see **Minors**
capacity
agency, 8–058—8–060
beneficial contracts, 8–021—8–029
binding contracts, 8–007—8–020
disposal of property, 8–065—8–067
generally, 8–002—8–006
parental liability, 8–061
restitution, 8–048—8–057
tortious liability, 8–046—8–047
voidable contracts, 8–030—8–045
consideration, 3–166
limitation of actions
generally, 28–075
introduction, 28–074
joint claimants, 28–077
latent damage, 28–079
long-stop periods, 28–080
shorter extensions, 28–078
successive disabilities, 28–076
Choice of law
agreements, 30–040
applicable law
And see **Applicable law**
application, 30–002
background, 30–017—30–029

Choice of law—*cont.*
applicable law—*cont.*
choice of law by parties, 30–047—30–070
consumer contracts, 30–092—30–107
employment contracts, 30–108—30–122
exclusions, 30–030—30–046
no choice of law by parties, 30–071—30–091
scope, 30–303—30–379
subrogation, 30–127—30–129
voluntary assignment, 30–123—30–126
arbitration agreements, 30–040
common law
And see **Proper law of a contract**
express choice of law, 30–006—30–009
generally, 30–005
implied choice of law, 30–010—30–011
no choice of law, 30–012—30–016
generally, 1–125
governing law
And see **Applicable law**
application, 30–002
background, 30–017—30–029
choice of law by parties, 30–047—30–070
consumer contracts, 30–092—30–107
employment contracts, 30–108—30–122
exclusions, 30–030—30–046
no choice of law by parties, 30–071—30–091
scope, 30–303—30–379
subrogation, 30–127—30–129
voluntary assignment, 30–123—30–126
introduction, 30–001—30–004
post-30th March 1991 contracts
And see **Applicable law**
application, 30–002
background, 30–017—30–029
choice of law by parties, 30–047—30–070
consumer contracts, 30–092—30–107
employment contracts, 30–108—30–122
exclusions, 30–030—30–046
no choice of law by parties, 30–071—30–091
scope, 30–303—30–379
subrogation, 30–127—30–129
voluntary assignment, 30–123—30–126

Choice of law—*cont.*
pre-1st April 1991 contracts
And see **Proper law of a contract**
express choice of law, 30–006—30–009
generally, 30–005
implied choice of law, 30–010—30–011
no choice of law, 30–012—30–016
proper law
And see **Proper law of a contract**
express choice of law, 30–006—30–009
generally, 30–005
implied choice of law, 30–010—30–011
no choice of law, 30–012—30–016
Rome Convention 1980
And see **Applicable law**
application, 30–002
background, 30–017—30–029
choice of law by parties, 30–047—30–070
consumer contracts
employment contracts, 30–108—30–122
exclusions, 30–030—30–046
no choice of law by parties, 30–071—30–091
scope, 30–303—30–379
subrogation, 30–127—30–129
voluntary assignment, 30–123—30–126
Rome I Regulation, and
And see **Rome I Regulation**
applicable law in absence of choice, 30–186—30–199
consumer contracts, 30–231—30–251
contracts of carriage, 30–200—30–230
employment contracts, 30–276—30–287
exclusions, 30–152—30–163
formal validity of contract, 30–318—30–322
freedom of choice, 30–170—30–185
generally, 30–130—30–151
habitual residence, 30–164—30–169
illegality in place of performance of act, 30–360
insurance contracts, 30–252—30–275
multiple liability, 30–296—30–298
nullity of contract, 30–328
set-off, 30-299-30-302
subrogation, 30–288—30–295
unjust enrichment, 30–034

Choice of law—*cont.*
Rome I Regulation, and—*cont.*
voluntary assignment, 30–288—30–292
unfair contract terms (consumer contracts), 15–093
unfair contract terms, 14–113
Choses in action
assignment
common law, at, 19–001
equity, in, 19–002
statute, under, 19–003
bankruptcy, 20–026
liability to account, 29–196
Civil servants
intention, 2–182
"Classification of contracts"
effect, by
bilateral contracts, 1–079
generally, 1–078
synallagmatic contracts, 1–079
unenforceable contracts, 1–084
unilateral contracts, 1–079
void contracts, 1–080—1–081
voidable contracts, 1–082—1–083
form, by
distance contracts, 1–077
express contracts, 1–076
formal contracts, 1–075
generally, 1–074
implied contracts, 1–076
informal contracts, 1–075
generally, 1–067
parties, by, 1–073
subject-matter, by
commercial purposes, for, 1–072
common law purposes, for, 1–070—1–071
generally, 1–068
statutory purposes, for, 1–069
Classification of terms
See **Express terms**
Clergy
intention, 2–181
Clubs
generally, 9–072
members' clubs
election of members, 9–076—9–077
expulsion of members, 9–075
liability, 9–073
resignation of members, 9–078
status, 9–074
officers' mess, 9–079
proprietary clubs, 9–080
Coercion
And see **Undue influence**
generally, 7–056
Cohabitation
objects injurious to morality, 16–067—16–068
Collateral contracts
formal requirements
LPA 1925, s.40, 4–016
LP(MP)A 1989, s.2, 4–076
merger, 25–002
parol evidence, 12–103
part payment of debt, 3–127
privity of contract
cheque transactions, 18–007
consideration, 18–008
credit card transactions, 18–007
generally, 18–005
hire purchase, 18–006
intention, 18–009
proof of
consideration, 12–006
generally, 12–004—12–005
third parties, 12–007
subject to contract, 2–121
variation, 22–036
"Collateral guarantees"
exemption clauses, 14–134
"Collateral security"
negotiable instruments, 21–076
Collateral warranties
exemption clauses, 14–134
express terms, 12–033
Collective agreements
incorporation, 2–177
"Collusive divorce agreements"
interference with course of justice, 16–043
Commencement of proceedings
amendment of statements of case
counterclaims in, 28–122—28–123
defences in, 28–122—28–123
new claims in, 28–118—28–121
third party claims in, 28–124
arbitral proceedings, 28–125
legal proceedings, 28–116—28–117
Commercial contracts
assignment, 19–056
classification, 1–073
Commercial credits
acceptance, 2–082
irrevocable credits
acceptance, 2–082
consideration, 3–182
Common law (illegality)
crime, 16–014
evasion of obligations, 16–015
fraudulent intent, 16–017
objects injurious to good government
domestic affairs, 16–019—16–025
foreign affairs, 16–026—16–34
objects injurious to morality
cohabitation, 16–067—16–068
prostitution, 16–069
will revocation, 16–074

Common law (illegality)—*cont.*
objects injurious to proper working of justice
champertous agreements, 16–048, 16–054—16–066
concealment of crime, 16–035—16–038
interference with course of justice, 16–039—16–043
maintenance of litigation agreements, 16–048—16–053
ouster of jurisdiction, 16–044—16–047
restraint of trade
And see **Restraint of trade**
employer-employee, 16–104—16–115
horizontal agreements, 16–132—16–140
land or chattels, 16–128—16–131
partners, 16–119—16–120
scope, 16–075—16–103
statutory regulation, 16–141
vendor-purchaser, 16–116—16–118
vertical agreements, 16–121—16–127
scope, 16–005—16–013
torts, 16–018
waiver of rights, 16–016
Common mistake
Bell v Lever Bros, 5–028—5–032
compromise agreements, and, 5–055
consent orders, and, 5–056
construction of the contract
generally, 5–064—5–065
introduction, 5–016
contractual adventure rendered impossible, 5–052—5–053
equity, in, 5–057—5–063
elements, 5–037
generally, 5–001
impossibility, 5–043
introduction, 5–017
misrepresentation, 5–015
misrepresentor's reliance, and, 5–042
mistakes as to law
compromise agreements, 5–055
consent orders, 5–056
generally, 5–054
modern doctrine
conditions to render contract void, 5–038—5–053
post-*Bell v Lever Bros* position, 5–033—5–037
non-existence of state of affairs
not be attributable to fault of parties, 5–040
render performance impossible, 5–043
Common mistake—*cont.*
post-*Bell v Lever Bros* position, 5–033—5–037
pre-*Bell v Lever Bros* position, 5–018—5–027
quality of subject matter, 5–050—5–051
sale of goods never existed, 5–045
sale of property already belonging to buyer, 5–049
sale of thing ceased to exist, 5–044
seller should have known goods ceased to exist, 5–046—5–048
state of affairs, and
assumption as to existence, 5–038
non-existence, 5–040—5–043
warranty as to existence, 5–039
summary, 5–064—5–065
Companies
alien enemies, as, 11–025
applicable law, 30–325
attribution of acts, 9–007
Companies Act 2006, and, 9–003
contracts with
And see **Companies (contracts)**
auditors, 9–062—9–063
companies created by charter, 9–004
companies regulated by legislation, 9–006
companies created by statute, 9–005
directors, with, 9–055—9–059
members, 9–060—9–061
promoters, 9–054
third parties, 9–012—9–053
deeds, 9–010
directors' liability, 9–008
estoppel, 9–008
formal requirements
deeds, 9–010
generally, 9–009
limitation of actions, 28–004
name, 9–008
seal, 9–009
termination of offer
generally, 2–103—2–104
offeree, as, 2–105
offeror, as, 2–106—2–107
types, 9–001
Companies (contracts)
administration, in, 9–053
auditors, 9–062—9–063
companies created by charter, 9–004
companies created by statute, 9–005
companies regulated by legislation, 9–006
directors, with
employment contracts, 9–056—9–059
generally, 9–055

Companies (contracts)—*cont.*
managing directors, with
contract for term of years, 9–058
generally, 9–057
improper appointment, 9–059
members
allotment of shares, 9–060
effect of articles, 9–061
post-incorporation benefits, 9–017—9–018
pre-incorporation benefits, 9–016
pre-incorporation contracts
equity, in, 9–015
generally, 9–012—9–013
law, at, 9–014
promoters, 9–054
receivership, in
generally, 9–050—9–051
inducing breach of contract, 9–052
repudiation, 9–051
registration of charges, 9–046
statutory companies, 9–005
third parties
insolvency, 9–047—9–053
post-incorporation benefits, 9–017—9–019
pre-incorporation benefits, 9–016
pre-incorporation contracts, 9–012—9–015
registration of charges, 9–046
ultra vires, 9–020—9–045
ultra vires
And see **Ultra vires**
generally, 9–020—9–026
statutory modifications, 9–027—9–045
winding-up
disposal of property, 9–049
generally, 9–047
repudiation, 9–048
Company incorporation
unfair contract terms (consumer contracts), 15–028
Company law
applicable law, 30–041
Compensation
injunctions
generally, 27–063
statutory right, 27–062
specific performance
errors, 27–056—27–057
misdescription, 27–054—27–057
misrepresentation, 27–058
Competent authority agreements
unfair contract terms, 14–112
"Competition entries"
acceptance, 2–110
offer, 2–110
privity of contract, 18–011
Composite agreements
formal requirements, 4–067
Composition (creditors)
part payment of debt, 3–125
Compound interest
fraudulent misrepresentation, 6–065
Compromise
accord and satisfaction, 22–013
forbearance to sue
And see **Forbearance to sue**
actual forbearance, 3–057—3–060
introduction, 3–046
invalid and doubtful claims, 3–050—3–056
valid claims, 3–047—3–049
honest claim, of
generally, 29–189
introduction, 29–019
mistake of fact, 29–038
illegality, 16–013
mistake of fact, 29–038
restitution
generally, 29–189
introduction, 29–019
Compulsion
compliance with local authority notices, 29–096
distress of goods, 29–091
duress of the person
generally, 29–089
seizure of goods, 29–090
extortion colore officii
generally, 29–094
nature of threat, 29–095096
generally, 29–087
illegitimate compulsion, 29–088
payment made in course of legal proceedings, 29–098
payment of excessive amount, 29–097
payment to third person
assignees of lease, 29–106
generally, 29–099—29–100
legal liability to pay, 29–101
other examples, 29–107—29–129
primary liability to pay, 29–102
seizure of goods, 29–103—29–105
unlawful compulsion, 29–088
wrongful demand
detention of goods, on, 29–092
detention of title deeds, on, 29–093
Concealment
illegality, 16–035—16–038
limitation of actions
agent, 28–087
date from which time runs, 28–058
generally, 28–084—28–086
introduction, 28–081
Concentrations
See **Mergers**

"Concurrent conditions"
express terms, 12–029
Concurrent liability
conflict of laws
employment contracts, 30–121
generally, 30–032
damages, 26–005
limitation of actions, 28–033
Conditional contracts
classification, 2–147—2–149
contingent conditions
generally, 2–148
precedent, 2–149—2–156
subsequent, 2–149
contingent conditions precedent
effects of agreements subject to, 2–150—2–156
generally, 2–149
contingent conditions subsequent, 2–149
degrees of obligation, 2–150—2–156
generally, 2–147
promissory conditions, 2–148
specific performance, 27–039
validity of document, evidence 12–109
waiver, 2–157
Conditional payments
negotiable instruments, 21–074
"Conditional performance"
generally, 21–009
notices, 21–010
Conditions
See also **Warranties**
concurrent, 12–029
contingent, 12–027
generally, 2–148
precedent
effects of agreements subject to, 2–150—2–156
generally, 12–028
introduction, 2–149
promissory, 2–150, 12–027
satisfaction of one party, to, 2–154
subsequent, 2–149, 12–030
types
concurrent, 12–029
contingent, 12–027
generally, 12–019
meaning, 12–025—12–026
precedent, 12–028
promissory, 12–027
subsequent, 12–030
waiver, 2–157
Conditions precedent
effects of agreements subject to
duty not to prevent occurrence of event, 2–153—2–154
duty of reasonable diligence to effect event, 2–155
generally, 2–150
Conditions precedent—*cont.*
effects of agreements subject to—*cont.*
restricted right to withdraw, 2–152
unrestricted right to withdraw, 2–151
force majeure clauses, 14–150
generally, 12–028
introduction, 2–149
principal obligations, 2–156
'satisfaction', 2–154
subsidiary obligations, 2–156
waiver, 2–157
Conditions subsequent
generally, 12–030
introduction, 2–149
Conduct
acceptance
generally, 2–030
relevant terms, 2–031
offer
generally, 2–005
inactivity, 2–006
specific performance
failure to perform, 27–035
unfairness, 27–036
Confidentiality
Human Rights Act 1999, 1–065—1–066
presumed undue influence
generally, 7–079—7–081
husband-wife, 7–085
relevant relationships, 7–082—7–085
Conflict of interests
illegality
public employees, 16–020
ultra vires, 9–036
undue influence by third party, 7–117—7–118
Conflict of laws
applicable law
And see **Applicable law**
application, 30–002
background, 30–017—30–029
choice of law by parties, 30–047—30–070
consumer contracts, 30–092—30–107
employment contracts, 30–108—30–122
exclusions, 30–030—30–046
introduction, 1–169
no choice of law by parties, 30–071—30–091
scope, 30–303—30–379
subrogation, 30–127—30–129
voluntary assignment, 30–123—30–126
common law
And see **Proper law of a contract**
express choice of law, 30–006—30–009

Conflict of laws—*cont.*
common law—*cont.*
generally, 30–005
implied choice of law,
30–010—30–011
no choice of law, 30–012—30–016
generally, 1–125
governing law
And see **Applicable law**
application, 30–002
background, 30–017—30–029
choice of law by parties,
30–047—30–070
consumer contracts,
30–092—30–107
employment contracts,
30–108—30–122
exclusions, 30–030—30–046
no choice of law by parties,
30–071—30–091
scope, 30–303—30–379
subrogation, 30–127—30–129
voluntary assignment,
30–123—30–126
introduction, 30–001—30–004
jurisdiction, 1–168
negotiable instruments,
30–038—30–039
post-30th March 1991 contracts
And see **Applicable law**
application, 30–002
background, 30–017—30–029
choice of law by parties,
30–047—30–070
consumer contracts,
30–092—30–107
employment contracts,
30–108—30–121
exclusions, 30–030—30–046
no choice of law by parties,
30–071—30–091
scope, 30–303—30–379
subrogation, 30–127—30–129
voluntary assignment,
30–123—30–126
pre-1st April 1991 contracts
And see **Proper law of a contract**
express choice of law,
30–006—30–009
generally, 30–005
implied choice of law,
30–010—30–011
no choice of law, 30–012—30–016
proper law
And see **Proper law of a contract**
express choice of law,
30–006—30–009
generally, 30–005
implied choice of law,
30–010—30–011

Conflict of laws—*cont.*
proper law—*cont.*
no choice of law, 30–012—30–016
Rome Convention 1980
And see **Applicable law**
application, 30–002
background, 30–017—30–029
choice of law by parties,
30–047—30–070
consumer contracts,
30–092—30–107
employment contracts,
30–108—30–121
exclusions, 30–030—30–046
no choice of law by parties,
30–071—30–091
scope, 30–303—30–379
subrogation, 30–127—30–129
voluntary assignment,
30–123—30–126
Rome I Regulation, and
And see **Rome I Regulation**
applicable law in absence of choice,
30–186—30–199
consumer contracts,
30–231—30–251
contracts of carriage,
30–200—30–230
employment contracts,
30–276—30–287
exclusions, 30–152—30–163
formal validity of contract,
30–318—30–322
freedom of choice, 30–170—30–185
generally, 30–130—30–151
habitual residence, 30–164—30–169
illegality in place of performance of
act, 30–360
insurance contracts,
30–252—30–275
multiple liability, 30–296—30–298
nullity of contract, 30–328
set-off, 30–299-30–302
subrogation, 30–288—30–295
unjust enrichment, 30–034
voluntary assignment,
30–288—30–292
unfair contract terms
consumer contracts, 15–093
generally, 14–113
Consent to assignment
conditional benefit, 19–079
generally, 19–077—19–078
pure benefit, 19–080
Consent orders
accord and satisfaction, 22–024
misrepresentation, 6–113
rescission, 6–113
Consideration
accord and satisfaction, 22–012

Consideration—*cont.*
adequacy
generally, 3–014
inadequate sums, 3–020—3–021
nominal sums, 3–018—3–019
non-monetary, 3–015
objects of trifling value, 3–016—3–017
assignment
equitable, 19–027—19–037
statutory, 19–019
bar pupillage contracts, 3–038
benefit and detriment
generally, 3–004
nature, 3–006
sufficiency, 3–005
collateral contracts, 12–006
compromise
And see **Forbearance to sue**
actual forbearance, 3–057—3–060
introduction, 3–046
invalid and doubtful claims, 3–050—3–056
valid claims, 3–047—3–049
conditions, 3–012
contract as agreements, 1–005
deeds, 1–108
definition
benefit and detriment, 3–004—3–006
conditions, 3–012
generally, 3–007
invented consideration, 3–010
motive, 3–011
mutual promises, 3–009
performances, 3–008
promises, 3–008
discharge by agreements, 22–001
economic duress
generally, 7–019
non-contractual payments, 7–020
existing duties
And see **Existing duties**
duty imposed by contract with promisor, 3–065—3–071
duty imposed by contract with third party, 3–072—3–075
generally, 3–061
public duty, 3–062—3–064
features
generally, 3–001
value, 3–002—3–003
forbearance to sue
And see **Forbearance to sue**
actual, 3–057—3–060
introduction, 3–046
invalid and doubtful claims, 3–050—3–056
valid claims, 3–047—3–049
gambling chips, 3–016—3–017

Consideration—*cont.*
illusory
discretionary performance, 3–025
generally, 3–023
intended forbearance, 3–024
impossible, 3–023
inadequate sums, 3–020—3–021
introduction, 3–001—3–003
invented consideration
contracts for sale of land, 4–025
gambling chips, 3–016—3–017
generally, 3–010
more than one promisee, by
generally, 3–041
joint and several promisees, 3–044
joint promisees, 3–042
Law Commission proposals, 3–045
several promisees, 3–043
motive, 3–011
movement from promisee of
generally, 3–036
sufficiency of benefit and detriment, 3–037—3–045
mutual promises, 3–009
nominal sums, 3–018—3–019
non-monetary, 3–015
objects of trifling value
gambling chips, 3–016—3–017
generally, 3–016
part payment of debt
And see **Part payment of debt**
common law limitations, 3–118—3–127
equitable limitations, 3–128—3–136
general rule, 3–115—3–117
past
And see **Past consideration**
criteria, 3–027—3–035
generally, 3–026
performances, 3–008
privity of contract
collateral contracts, 18–008
joint liability, 18–018
movement from promisee, 18–016—18–017
promises, 3–008
proprietary estoppel
And see **Proprietary estoppel**
basis of liability, 3–139—3–143
conditions for liability, 3–144—3–148
effect, 3–149—3–164
general rule, 3–137—3–138
pupillage, 3–038
rescission of terms
each party has outstanding rights, 3–077
generally, 3–076
one party has outstanding rights, 3–078

Consideration—*cont.*
restraint of trade
generally, 3–166
introduction, 16–090
special cases
auctions without reserve, 3–174
defective promises, 3–165—3–169
'firm' offers, 3–172—3–173
gratuitous bailment, 3–177
gratuitous services, 3–178—3–181
irrevocable credits, 3–182
novation of partnership debt, 3–175—3–176
unilateral contracts, 3–170—3–171
specific performance
inadequacy, 27–033
lack 27–034
sufficiency of benefit and detriment
generally, 3–037—3–040
more than one promisee, 3–041—3–045
unjust enrichment
partial failure of consideration, 29–060—29–063
total failure of consideration, 29–055-29–059
validity of document, evidence 12–108
valuable consideration
generally, 3–022
illusory consideration, 3–023—3–025
impossible consideration, 3–023
variation of contractual duties
common law mitigation, 3–081—3–084
equitable mitigation, 3–085—3–114
generally, 3–076
types of variation, 3–079—3–080
waiver, 22–044
wrappers, 3–016
Construction contracts
agreements for lease, 27–028—27–029
damages for third party's loss, 18–053—18–066
frustration
delay, 23–050—23–051
generally, 23–049
limitation of actions, 28–054—28–055
Construction of legislation
See **Interpretation**
Construction of terms
See **Interpretation**
Constructive notice
ultra vires, 9–035
undue influence
bank put on inquiry, 7–111—7–112
Barclays Bank v O'Brien, 7–106—7–108
conflicts of interest, 7–117—7–118
Etridge's case, 7–109—7–110
Constructive notice—*cont.*
undue influence—*cont.*
introduction, 7–105
jointly-owned homes, 7–123
legal advice, 7–115—7–116
loss of right to avoid, 7–122
procedure, 7–119
reasonable steps, 7–114
replacement mortgages, 7–121
spouse as party to transaction, 7–120
transactions not to advantage of surety, 7–113
Constructive trusts
contracts for sale of land
generally, 4–077
proprietary estoppel, 4–081
damages, 26–021
proprietary estoppel, and
contracts for sale of land, 4–081
generally, 3–140
restitution, 29–160
"Consular staff"
immunity from suit
generally, 11–017
waiver, 11–022
Consumer contracts
common law, at
generally, 15–001
restrictions, 15–002
conflict of laws
choice of law by parties, 30–094—30–106
formal validity of contract, 30–313
habitual residence, 30–106
introduction, 30–092
mandatory rules, 30–102—30–105
no choice of law by parties, 30–107
online contracts, 30–095—30–101
relevant contracts, 30–093
damages
generally, 26–155
unfair contract terms, 26–156
definition, 1–009
exemption clauses
cancellation, 14–129
generally, 14–125—14–126
package holidays, 14–128
trading stamps, 14–127
online contracts
'advertising', 30–097
'agent', 30–100
'all the steps necessary', 30–098
first condition, 30–096—30–098
generally, 30–095
'received', 30–101
second condition, 30–099—30–101
'specific invitation', 30–096
restrictions on terms, 1–017
Rome I Regulation, and
background, 30–231

Consumer contracts—*cont.*
Rome I Regulation, and—*cont.*
choice of law by the parties, 30–249
consumer-professional contract, 30–240
contracts of carriage, 30–235
electronic commerce, 30–245
electronic mail, 30–246
exclusions, 30–233
general rule, 30–239
financial instruments, 30–237
habitual residence, 30–241
immovable property, 30–236
"pursues his commercial or professional activities", 30–242—30–243
review clause, 30–251
scope of Article, 30–239
structure of Article, 30–232
supply of services, 30–234
techniques used, 30–244—30–245
websites, 30–247
statutory regulation
generally, 15–003
UTCCA 1994, 15–004—15–077
UTCCA 1994
And see **Unfair contract terms (consumer contracts) Regulations 1994**
background, 15–004—15–010
choice of law, 15–093
fairness, 15–043—15–088
plain language, 15–089—15–092
relevant contracts, 15–011—15–029
relevant terms, 15–030—15–042
remedies, 15–094—15–099
Consumer credit agreements
unfair credit relationships
bankruptcy, 20–030
introduction, 7–138
unlicensed trading, 16–154—16–155
Consumer guarantees
intention, 2–167
"Contingent conditions"
generally, 2–148
precedent
And see **Contingent conditions precedent**
effects of agreements subject to, 2–150—2–156
generally, 2–149
subsequent
generally, 12–030
introduction, 2–149
waiver, 2–157
"Contingent conditions precedent"
effects of agreements subject to
duty not to prevent occurrence of event, 2–153—2–154
"Contingent conditions precedent"—*cont.*
effects of agreements subject to—*cont.*
duty of reasonable diligence to effect event, 2–155
generally, 2–150
restricted right to withdraw, 2–152
unrestricted right to withdraw, 2–151
force majeure clauses, 14–150
generally, 12–028
introduction, 2–149
principal obligations, 2–156
'satisfaction', 2–154
subsidiary obligations, 2–156
waiver, 2–157
"Continuing breaches"
damages, 26–015
limitation of actions, 28–035
Continuing guarantees
unilateral contracts, 2–081
Contra proferentem
construction of terms, 12–045
Contract terms
And see under individual headings
applicable law
common law, at, 30–005—30–016
generally, 30–001—30–004
Rome Convention, under, 30–017—30–129
scope, 30–303—30–379
conditions
And see **Conditions**
generally, 2–148
precedent, 2–149
promissory, 2–150
satisfaction of one party, to, 2–154
subsequent, 2–149
types, 12–019—12–030
waiver, 2–157
exemption
application, 14–025—14–038
common law control, 14–132—14–136
construction, 14–005—14–019
distance selling, 14–154
force majeure, 14–137—14–154
fundamental breach, 14–020—14–024
generally, 14–001—14–004
statutory regulation, 14–059—14–131
third parties, 14–039—14–058
express terms
classification, 12–019—12–040
construction, 12–041—12–094
extrinsic evidence, 12–095—12–133
form, 12–002—12–018
generally, 12–001
governing law
common law, at, 30–005—30–016

Contract terms—*cont.*
governing law—*cont.*
generally, 30–001—30–004
Rome Convention, under, 30–017—30–129
scope, 30–303—30–379
implied terms
generally, 13–002
nature, 13–001
purpose, 13–003—13–012
types, 13–013—13–035
misrepresentation, 6–004
proper law
common law, at, 30–005—30–016
generally, 30–001—30–004
Rome Convention, under, 30–017—30–129
scope, 30–303—30–379
unfair contract terms
introduction, 15–001—15–003
statutory regulation, 15–004—15–099
"Contract to make contract"
agreements to negotiate, 2–136—2–138
contract to execute document with agreed terms, 2–135
generally, 2–134
Contracting out
discharge by frustration
effect, 23–094
generally, 23–092
implicit provision, 23–093
waiver, 22–045
Contracts
And see under individual headings
agreement, as
enforcement, 1–006
existence, 1–004—1–005
generally, 1–001
problems with, 1–003—1–006
types, 1–003
binding force
generally, 1–019—1–020
limitations, 1–021
classification
distance contracts, 1–077
effect, by, 1–078—1–084
form, by, 1–074—1–077
generally, 1–067
parties, by, 1–073
subject-matter, by, 1–068—1–072
conveyances, 1–190
deeds
consideration, 1–108
delivery, 1–093—1–094
form, 1–087—1–107
other issues, 1–109—1–116
definitions
European, 1–007—1–009
introduction, 1–001
Contracts—*cont.*
definitions—*cont.*
problems with, 1–002—1–006
distance contracts, 1–077
European definitions
'consumer contract', 1–009
introduction, 1–007
'worker', 1–008
fairness
civil law systems, in, 1–025
common law systems, in, 1–024
English law, in, 1–026—1–034
introduction, 1–022—1–023
formal requirements
electronic communications, 4–005—4–006
electronic deeds, 4–008
electronic signatures, 4–007
estoppel, 4–004
generally, 4–001
non-compliance, 4–003
sale of land, 4–009—4–088
types, 4–002
formation
agreement, 2–003—2–157
consideration, 3–001—3–182
intention, 2–157—2–189
introduction, 2–001
objective test, 2–002
freedom of contract
discrimination, 1–016
European law, in, 1–013
generally, 1–011
modern common law, in, 1–012
qualifications, 1–014—1–018
refusal to enter contracts, 1–015
regulation of contractual environment, 1–018
restricted freedom as to terms, 1–017
generally, 1–001
good faith
civil law systems, in, 1–025
common law systems, in, 1–024
English law, in, 1–026—1–034
introduction, 1–022—1–023
Human Rights Act 1999
introduction, 1–035
post-1 October 2000 contracts, 1–044—1–066
pre-2 October 2000 contracts, 1–037—1–043
territorial impact, 1–036
principles
binding force of contract, 1–019—1–021
fairness, 1–022—1–034
freedom of contract, 1–011—1–018
good faith, 1–022—1–034
introduction, 1–010

Contracts—*cont.*
problems with
contract as agreement, 1–003—1–006
contract as promise, 1–002
promise, as
generally, 1–001
problems with, 1–002
property, as, 1–191
public bodies, with
capacity, 1–198
differences in rules, 1–201
Human Rights Act 1999, 1–199—1–200
public law
CPR Part 54, 1–197
introduction, 1–193
RSC Order 53, 1–194—1–196
restitution, 1–192
terms
exemption clauses, 14–001—14–154
express terms, 12–001—12–133
implied terms, 13–001—13–035
unfair contract terms, 15–001—15–077
torts
classification of actions, 1–118
concurrence of actions, 1–126—1–169
differences of rules, 1–119—1–125
generally, 1–117
influence on other relationships, 1–170—1–187
trusts, 1–188—1–189
Contracts for benefit of third party
See **Third party rights**
Contracts for necessaries
drunken persons, by, 8–081
intervention on behalf of defendant, 29–135
mentally disordered persons, by, 8–074
minors, by
examples, 8–016—8–018
generally, 8–007
goods sold and delivered, 8–010—8–012
loans, 8–020
meaning, 8–008
nature, 8–009
services, 8–013—8–014
trading contracts, 8–017—8–018
restitution, 29–135
spouse's needs, 8–019
Contracts for sale of land
formal requirements
background, 4–009
post-26th September 1989, 4–052—4–088
pre- 26th September 1989, 4–010—4–051
Contracts for sale of land—*cont.*
made on or after September 27, 1989
And see **Contracts for sale of land (s.2 LP(MP)A 1989)**
form of contracts, 4–069—4–072
generally, 4–052—4–053
non-compliance, effect 4–075—4–088
relevant contracts, 4–054—4–068
made on or before September 26, 1989
And see **Contracts for sale of land (s.40 LPA 1925)**
form of contracts, 4–022—4–040
generally, 4–010
non-compliance, effect 4–041—4–051
relevant contracts, 4–011—4–021
utmost good faith, 6–156—6–157
Contracts for sale of land (s.40 LPA 1925)
[*n.b. made on or before September 26, 1989*]
agents' signature
estate agent, 4–037
for both parties, 4–038
generally, 4–036
building materials, 4–019
collateral agreements, 4–016
consideration, 4–025
entire agreement clauses, 4–017
fixtures, 4–020
form of contracts
consideration, 4–025
generally, 4–022
parties, 4–023
signature, 4–031—4–040
subject-matter, 4–024
terms, 4–026
generally, 4–010
growing crops, 4–018
lost documents, and, 4–030
minerals, 4–019
non-compliance
part performance, 4–042—4–050
proprietary estoppel, 4–051
statute, under, 4–041
parol evidence, 4–029
part performance
effect of acts, 4–050
generally, 4–042—4–043
required acts, 4–044—4–049
parties, 4–023
proprietary estoppel, 4–051
purpose for which document prepared, 4–027
relevant dispositions and interests
building materials, 4–019
collateral agreements, 4–016
entire agreement clauses, 4–017
fixtures, 4–020

Contracts for sale of land (s.40 LPA 1925)—*cont.*
relevant dispositions and interests—*cont.*
generally, 4–011—4–014
growing crops, 4–018
minerals, 4–019
shooting rights, 4–021
things to be detached from land, 4–019
variation of contracts, 4–015
several documents, and, 4–028—4–029
shooting rights, 4–021
signature
agent, by, 4–036—4–039
alterations, 4–035
form, 4–034
generally, 4–031
intention, 4–033
position, 4–032
subject-matter, 4–024
terms, 4–026
things to be detached from land, 4–019
variation, 4–015
Contracts for sale of land (s.2 LP(MP)A 1989)
[*n.b. made on or after September 27, 1989*]
boundary agreements between neighbours, 4–057
collateral contracts, 4–076
composite agreements, 4–067
compromises, 4–065
conditions in planning agreements, 4–061
equitable leases, 4–060
equitable mortgages, 4–059
estoppel
convention, by, 4–079
generally, 4–078
promissory estoppel, 4–083
proprietary estoppel, 4–080—4–082
exchange of contracts, 4–071
excluded interests, 4–068
executed contracts, 4–084
form of contracts
generally, 4–069
signature, 4–072—4–074
terms, 4–070—4–071
generally, 4–052—4–053
'lock-out' agreements, 4–062
mutual wills, 4–063
non-compliance
collateral contracts, 4–076
constructive trusts, 4–077
estoppel, 4–078—4–083
executed contracts, 4–084
generally, 4–075
restitution, 4–084—4–088
options, 4–058
Contracts for sale of land (s.2 LP(MP)A 1989)—*cont.*
Part 36 settlements, 4–065
partnerships, 4–066
proceeds of sale of land, 4–064
promissory estoppel, 4–083
proprietary estoppel, 4–080—4–082
relevant dispositions and interests
boundary agreements between neighbours, 4–057
composite agreements, 4–067
compromises, 4–065
conditions in planning agreements, 4–061
equitable leases, 4–060
equitable mortgages, 4–059
generally, 4–054—4–055
'lock-out' agreements, 4–062
mutual wills, 4–063
options, 4–058
Part 36 settlements, 4–065
partnerships, 4–066
proceeds of sale of land, 4–064
variation of contracts, 4–056
restitution, 4–084—4–088
signature
agent, by, 4–074
generally, 4–072
meaning, 4–073
'subject to contract', 4–053
variation, 4–056
Contracts of apprenticeship
generally, 8–022—8–023
rescission, 8–024
Contracts of carriage
air, by
exemption clauses, 14–118
limitation of actions, 28–024
remoteness of damage, 26–089—26–090
applicable law, 30–085—30–087
discharge by frustration
generally, 23–047
'Suez Canal' cases, 23–048
exemption clauses
air, by, 14–118
land, by, 14–029—14–033, 14–116
sea, by, 14–029—14–033, 14–117
limitation of actions
relevant period, 28–022—28–026
running of time, 28–068
rail, by
exemption clauses, 14–029—14–033, 14–116
limitation of actions, 28–025, 28–068
remoteness of damage, 26–089—26–090
remoteness of damage, 26–089—26–090

Contracts of carriage—*cont.*
road, by
exemption clauses, 14–029—14–033, 14–116
limitation of actions, 28–026, 28–068
remoteness of damage, 26–089—26–090
Rome I Regulation, and
applicable law in absence of choice, 30–215—30–218
"carrier", 30–217
choice of law by the parties, 30–214
"consignor", 30–218
generally, 30–212
meaning, 30–213
residual rule, 30–219
rule of displacement, 30–220
sea, by
exemption clauses, 14–029—14–033, 14–117
limitation of actions, 28–022—28–023
remoteness of damage, 26–089—26–090
Contracts of employment
applicable law
choice of law by parties, 30–112—30–118
concurrent liability, 30–121
generally, 30–108—30–111
no choice of law by parties, 30–119—30–120
Rome I Regulation, and, 30–122
territorial limitation, 30–115
definition, 1–008
exemption clauses, 14–121—14–122
frustration, 23–023
implied terms, 13–019
limitation of actions, 28–028—28–030
minors
generally, 8–025
other analogous contracts, 8–029
restraint of trade covenants, 8–026
renunciation, 24–020
restraint of trade after expiry of
breach, 16–114
competition, 16–106
confidential information, 16–107—16–109
customer information, 16–108—16–110
generally, 16–104
limitations, 16–111—16–113
reasonableness, 16–105
trade secrets, 16–108
restraint of trade during currency of, 16–115
restrictions on terms
implied statutory terms, 1–017
Contracts of employment—*cont.*
restrictions on terms—*cont.*
standard commercial terms, 1–014
Rome I Regulation, and
applicable law in absence of choice, 30–281—30–283
background, 30–276
choice of law by parties, 30–279—30–280
concurrent claims, 30–287
default rule, 30–284
generally, 30–280—30–287
meaning, 30–278
non-derogable provisions, 30–280
overriding mandatory provisions, 30–286
principal place of work, 30–282
rule of displacement, 30–285
structure of Article, 30–277
temporary employment abroad, 30–283
specific performance, 27–022—27–023
unfair contract terms
consumer contracts, 15–028
generally, 14–108—14–109
Contracts of indemnity
And see **Contracts of suretyship**
payment to third person, 29–120
"Contracts of record"
generally, 1–075
Contracts of suretyship
joint liability, 17–021
misrepresentation, 6–158—6–161
Contracts under seal
deeds
And see **Deeds**
consideration, 1–108
delivery, 1–093—1–094
form, 1–087—1–107
other issues, 1–109—1–116
generally, 1–087
limitation of actions, 28–003
Contractual rights
property, as, 1–191
"Contractual silence"
assumption of responsibility, 1–158—1–160
general position, 1–157
introduction, 1–156
"Contradictory terms"
parol evidence, 12–100
"*Contrats d'adhésion*"
generally, 1–014
Contribution
amount, 17–031
assessment, 17–034
'damage', 17–029—17–030
effect of judgment, 17–032
generally, 17–027—17–028
joint debtors, 17–027

Contribution—*cont.*
limitation of actions
date from which time runs, 28–051
generally, 17–033
relevant period, 28–015
limits on right, 17–035
payment to third person
common law, at, 29–122
directors, 29–126
general average, 29–129
generally, 29–121
guarantees, 29–123
insurers, 29–128
joint contractors, 29–124
partners, 29–127
trustees, 29–125
restrictions, 17–035
'same damage', 17–029—17–030
Contributory negligence
damages, 26–049—26–050
fraudulent misrepresentation, 6–064
introduction, 1–166
negligent misrepresentation, 6–074
Conveyance
delivery
escrow, as an, 1–106
minors, 8–034
relationship with contracts, 1–190
restraint of trade, 16–129
"Co-operative marketing schemes"
restraint of trade, 16–127
Corporations
See **Companies**
"Corporations aggregate"
generally, 9–002
Corporations sole
generally, 9–002
Cost of completion
damages, 26–016—26–018
Costs
pleading illegality, 16–200
Counter-offers
termination of offer, 2–092
Counterclaims
discharge, 25–031
limitation of actions, 28–122—28–123
Courts (public authorities)
background, 1–043
construction of contracts, 1–061
common law developments, 1–060
exercise of judicial discretion, 1–059
implied terms, 1–062
introduction, 1–058
open-textured controls, 1–064
open-textured norms, 1–063
"Covenant not to sue"
joint liability, 17–017—17–020
release
generally, 22–006
joint contractors, 22–007
Cover notes
See **Temporary cover**
Credit cards
payment, 21–082
privity of contract, 18–007
tender, 21–088
"Creditors' liens"
statute-barred debt, 28–034
Crops
contracts for sale of land, 4–018
"Cross-offers"
acceptance, 2–044
Crown contracts
See **Government contracts**
"Culpa in contrahendo"
generally, 1–136
Custom and usage
duty to resolve uncertainty, 2–143
express terms
construction of terms,
12–058—12–059
extrinsic evidence, 12–127—12–130
extrinsic evidence
annex terms, to, 12–131
generally, 12–127—12–129
interpretation, for, 12–130
generally, 2–141
implied terms
collective agreements, 13–019
course of dealing, 13–022
generally, 13–018
human rights, 13–020
method of dealing, 13–021
meaningless terms, 2–144
reasonableness, 2–142
self-contradictory terms, 2–144

Damages
And see under individual headings
acceleration clauses, 26–140
agreed sum clauses
generally, 26–009
nature, 26–126—26–156
applicable law, 30–337
assessment
appeals, 26–030
generally, 26–007
time of assessment, 26–064—26–065
capital gains tax, 26–166
causation
apportionment, 26–039
contributory negligence,
26–049—26–050
generally, 26–032—26–033
intervening act of plaintiff,
26–037—26–039
intervening act of third party,
26–034—26–036
intervening event, 26–040—26–041

Damages—*cont.*
causation—*cont.*
intervening omission of plaintiff, 26–037—26–039
loss of chance, 26–042—26–048
completion cost, 26–016—26–018
concurrent liability, 26–005
conflict of laws, 30–337
consumer contracts
generally, 26–155
unfair contract terms, 26–156
continuing breaches, 26–015
contract for benefit of third party
promisee's loss, 18–047—18–048
third party's loss, 18–049—18–068
contributory negligence
non-statutory categories, 26–050
statutory categories, 26–049
cost of completion, 26–016—26–018
depriving defendant of profit
Att.-Gen. v. Blake, 26–024—26–025
disgorgement of profits, 26–026—26–029
introduction, 26–021—26–022
invasion of property interest, 26–023
disappointment, 26–083
disgorgement of profits
analogy with IPR, 26–029
generally, 26–026
partial, 26–027
total, 26–028
duress, 7–055
exchange rates
interest, 26–159
exemplary damages, 26–019
forfeiture of sums paid
express clause, 26–146—26–153
no express clause, 26–154
fraudulent misrepresentation
compound interest, 6–065
contributory negligence, 6–064
exemplary sums, 6–063
generally, 6–042
measure, 6–049—6–059
mitigation, 6–060
non-pecuniary losses, 6–061
relevant representations, 6–043—6–048
general damages, 26–006
generally, 1–122—1–124, 1–163—1–164
incentive clauses, 26–139
income tax
generally, 26–157
loss of profits, 26–163
mixed receipts, 26–165
salvage services, 26–164
wrongful dismissal, 26–158—26–162
inconvenience, 26–082

Damages—*cont.*
injunctions, and
assessment of damages, 27–079
generally, 27–077—27–078
introduction, 26–004
limits, 27–084
injury to feelings, 26–083
innocent misrepresentation
generally, 6–094—6–098
measure, 6–099—6–102
interest
Admiralty cases, 26–171
arbitration awards, 26–183—26–184
commercial debts, 26–172, 26–182
common law, at, 26–168—26–170
introduction, 26–168
judgment debts, 26–184
statute, under, 26–173—26–184
introduction, 1–122—1–124, 1–163—1–164
invasion of property interest, 26–023
invoicing back clauses, 26–144
limitation of liability clauses
charterparties, 26–143
generally, 26–142
liquidated damages
generally, 26–010—26–011
penalty sums, 26–125—26–156
unfair contract terms, 26–012
loss of amenity, 26–084—26–085
loss of enjoyment, 26–083
loss of future business, 26–071
loss of profits
carrier's liability, 26–070
seller's claim, 26–069
seller's liability, 26–066—26–068
loss of reputation, 26–086—26–087
mental distress, 26–083
misrepresentation
fraudulent, 6–042—6–066
generally, 6–041
innocent, 6–094—6–102
introduction, 1–133
negligent, 6–067—6–093
mitigation of damage
And see **Mitigation of damage**
avoidable loss, 26–103—26–114
avoided loss, 26–115—26–119
expenses of mitigation, 26–120—26–124
generally, 26–101
purpose, 26–102
national insurance contributions, 26–162
nature
'expectation' interest, 26–002
generally, 26–001
'performance' interest, 26–003
'reliance' interest, 26–002

Damages—*cont.*
negligent misrepresentation
burden of proof, 6–075
contributory negligence, 6–074
generally, 6–067—6–069
liable parties, 6–076—6–077
measure, 6–070—6–073
nervous shock, 26–083
nominal damages, 26–008
non-pecuniary loss
disappointment, 26–083
inconvenience, 26–082
injury to feelings, 26–083
loss of amenity, 26–084—26–085
loss of enjoyment, 26–083
loss of reputation, 26–086—26–087
mental distress, 26–083
nervous shock, 26–083
physical injury, 26–082
social discredit, 26–083
payment, 21–040
penalty clauses
And see **Penalty clauses**
fluctuating sums, 26–130
generally, 26–125—26–127
graduated sums, 26–135
minimum sums, 26–131
pre-estimate, 26–128—26–129
scope, 26–136—26–155
single sums, 26–132—26–134
unfair contract terms, 26–156
physical injury, 26–082
privity of contract, 18–035—18–036
prospective loss, 26–013—26–014
punitive damages, 26–019
purpose, 26–001
reimbursement clauses, 26–145
remoteness
And see **Remoteness of damage**
examples, 26–088—26–100
generally, 26–051—26–063
loss of profits, 26–066—26–071
non-pecuniary loss, 26–082—26–087
time of assessment, 26–064—26–065
wasted expenditure,
26–072—26–081
repairs, 26–016—26–018
rescission, 6–072—6–073
restitutionary damages, 26–025
sale of goods
And see **Damages (sale of goods)**
mitigation, 26–110—26–114
remoteness, 26–088
social discredit, 26–083
special damages, 26–006
specific performance
assessment of damages, 27–079
generally, 27–077—27–078
introduction, 26–004
limits, 27–084

Damages—*cont.*
substitute performance,
26–016—26–018
tax
capital gains tax, 26–166
income tax, 26–157—26–165
termination clauses, 26–141
third party beneficiaries, 26–031
types
agreed sum clauses, 26–009
cost of completion, 26–016—26–018
cost of repairs, 26–016—26–018
continuing breaches, 26–015
depriving defendant of profit,
26–020—26–029
exemplary damages, 26–019
generally, 26–006
liquidated damages,
26–010—26–012
nominal damages, 26–008
prospective loss, 26–013—26–014
repair costs, 26–016—26–018
restitutionary damages, 26–025
substitute performance,
26–016—26–018
unliquidated damages,
26–010—26–012
unfair contract terms
generally, 26–012
penalty clauses, 26–156
unliquidated damages
generally, 26–010—26–011
unfair contract terms, 26–012
vindictive damages, 26–019
wasted expenditure
currency exchange loss,
26–080—26–081
no transaction basis, 26–079
non-performance expenditure,
26–074—26–075
performance expenditure,
26–072—26–073
post-breach expenditure, 26–078
pre-contract expenditure,
26–076—26–077
Damages (sale of goods)
mitigation, 26–110—26–114
Dates
deeds, 1–103
Days
time of performance, 21–022
"Dealing as a consumer"
agents, and, 14–069
auctions, 14–068
burden of proof, 14–070
generally, 14–066
sale of goods, 14–067
tenders, 14–068
Death
discharge, 25–028

Death—*cont.*
frustration, 23–037
generally, 20–001
joint liability
joint contractor, 17–012
joint and several contractor, 17–013
personal representatives, actions against
bills of exchange, for, 20–011—20–012
carrying on business, on, 20–010
confirmation of contract, on, 20–009
distribution of estate, on, 20–013
generally, 20–005
leases, on, 20–008
payment of debts, for, 20–014
personal contracts, on, 20–006—20–007
personal representatives, actions by
damages, 20–003
generally, 20–002
time of accrual, 20–004
termination of offer
generally, 2–099
offeree, 2–101
offeror, 2–100
Debit transfers
See **Direct debits**
"Debt actions"
specific performance, 27–004
Debts (interest)
exemption clauses, 14–130
Deeds
alteration, 1–114
benefit, 1–109
companies
execution, 1–091
generally, 9–010
consideration, 1–108
date, 1–103
delivery
corporate bodies, and, 1–094
date, 1–103
escrow, as an, 1–105—1–107
generally, 1–093
discharge, 1–115
electronic documents, 1–088
escrow, as an
conveyances, 1–106
effect, 1–107
generally, 1–105
estoppel, 1–112
execution
after 14 September, 2005, 1–095—1–101
background, 1–087—1–088
between 31 July, 1989 and 14 September, 2005, 1–090—1–094
common aspects, 1–102—1–107
introduction, 1–089
Deeds—*cont.*
execution between 31 July, 1989 and 14 September, 2005
companies, by, 1–091
delivery, and, 1–093—1–094
individual, by, 1–090
introduction, 1–089
other persons, by, 1–092
form
execution, 1–089—1–107
generally, 1–087—1–088
generally, 1–087
limitation period, 1–116
merger, 1–113
minors, 8–006
non est factum, 1–111
restraint of trade, 16–089
third party rights, 1–110
variation, 1–115
Deeds of arrangement
generally, 20–051
surety, 20–052
Defective delivery
specific performance, 27–019
"Defective promises"
consideration
generally, 3–165—3–166
performance, 3–167
statutory restrictions, 3–168—3–169
contract for benefit of third party, 18–132
exemption clauses, 14–120
limitation of actions, 28–056
Defences
limitation of actions, 28–122—28–123
Delay
frustration
building contracts, 23–050—23–051
exceptions, 23–036
generally, 23–035
limitation of actions
awareness of facts, 28–140
generally, 28–139
mere delay, 28–142
prejudice to defendant, 28–141
offer, 2–005
presumed undue influence, 7–097
rectification, 5–127
specific performance, 27–045
undue influence, 7–097
Deletions (documents)
construction of terms, 12–069
"Deliberate breach"
failure of performance, 24–042
Delivery
conveyance, of
escrow, as an, 1–106
deeds
date, 1–103
escrow, as an, 1–105—1–107

Delivery—*cont.*
deeds—*cont.*
generally, 1–093
"*Dépeçage*"
And see **Applicable law**
generally, 30–071
Deposits
failure of consideration, 29–064—29–066
"Depriving defendant of profit"
Att.-Gen. v. Blake, 26–024—26–025
disgorgement of profits
analogy with IPR, 26–029
generally, 26–026
partial, 26–027
total, 26–028
introduction, 26–020
invasion of property interest, 26–023
Description
See **Correspondence with description**
Destruction of property
discharge by frustration, 23–005
Detention
goods, 29–092
title deeds, 29–093
Detriment
promissory estoppel, 3–094
proprietary estoppel, 3–147—3–148
total failure of consideration, 29–055
Diminution of price
See **Price reductions**
Diplomatic immunity
certificate of entitlement, 11–015
consular staff, and
generally, 11–017
waiver, 11–022
diplomatic agents, 11–011
diplomatic premises, 11–012
duration, 11–014
generally, 11–008—11–009
relevant persons
administrative, technical and service staff, 11–013
agents, 11–011
generally, 11–010
premises, 11–012
restrictions, 11–016
waiver, 11–022
Diplomatic premises
immunity from suit, 11–012
Diplomats
immunity from suit
generally, 11–017
waiver, 11–022
Directors
authority
generally, 9–032—9–033
limitations, 9–034
Directors—*cont.*
contracts
employment contracts, 9–056—9–059
generally, 9–055
ultra vires, 9–036
contribution, 29–126
duties, 9–030—9–031
interest in contract, 9–036
Turquand decision, 9–040—9–045
ultra vires, 9–036
"Disappointed beneficiary"
distinction from other cases, 18–037—18–039
generally, 18–025
"Disappointment"
damages, 26–083
Discharge
agreement, by
And see **Discharge (agreement)**
accord and satisfaction, 22–012—22–024
consideration, 22–001
contractual liability, 22–048—22–055
generally, 22–001—22–002
release, 21–003—21–011
rescission, 22–025—22–031
variation, 22–032—22–039
waiver, 22–040—22–047
accord and satisfaction
And see **Accord and satisfaction**
generally, 22–012—22–024
affirmation
And see **Affirmation**
effect, 24–010—24–012
generally, 24–003
nature, 24–004—24–009
alteration of document, by
Bank of England notes, 25–025
immaterial alteration, 25–023
material alteration, 25–020—25–022
negotiable instruments, 25–024
bankrupt, of
effect, 20–046—20–049
generally, 20–045
bankruptcy, by, 25–029
breach, by
And see **Discharge (breach of contract)**
consequences, 24–047—24–055
failure of performance, 24–034—24–046
generally, 24–001—24–017
impossibility, 24–028—24–033
renunciation, 24–018—24–027
cancellation of deed, by, 25–026
contract, under
express terms, 22–048—22–052
implied term, 22–054

Discharge—*cont.*
contract, under—*cont.*
notices, 22–051—22–052
unfair contract terms (consumer contracts), 22–048
waiver, 22–052—22–053
counterclaim, 25–031
death, by, 25–028
deeds, 1–115
express terms
burden of proof, 22–050
generally, 22–048–22–049
notices, 22–051—22–052
occurrence of event, 22–055
failure of performance
And see **Failure of performance**
generally, 24–034—24–046
frustration, by
And see **Frustration**
consequences, 23–070—23–098
examples, 23–020—23–057
generally, 23–001—23–006
limitations, 23–058—23–069
test, 23–007—23–019
implied terms, 22–054
impossibility
And see **Impossibility**
generally, 24–028—24–033
joint liability
accord and satisfaction, 17–017
performance, 17–014
release, 17–017—17–020
limitation, 25–032
loss of deed, by, 25–027
merger, by
And see **Merger**
generally, 25–001—25–019
post-termination obligations
generally, 24–049
guarantor, 24–055
guilty party, 24–052—24–054
innocent party, 24–050
release
And see **Release**
generally, 21–003—21–011
renunciation
And see **Renunciation**
generally, 24–018—24–027
rescission
And see **Rescission**
agreement, by, 22–025—22–031
breach of contract, for, 24–047
set-off, 25–031
variation
And see **Variation**
generally, 22–032—22–039
waiver
And see **Waiver**
generally, 22–040—22–047
winding-up, by, 25–030

Discharge (agreement)
accord and satisfaction
And see **Accord and satisfaction**
generally, 22–012—22–024
consideration, 22–001
contract, under
And see **Discharge under contract**
generally, 22–048—22–055
generally, 22–001—22–002
release
And see **Release**
generally, 21–003—21–011
rescission
And see **Rescission**
generally, 22–025—22–031
variation
And see **Variation**
generally, 22–032—22–039
waiver
And see **Waiver**
generally, 22–040—22–047

Discharge (breach of contract)
acceptance
generally, 24–013
reason, 24–014
affirmation
And see **Affirmation**
effect, 24–010—24–012
generally, 24–003
nature, 24–004—24–009
consequences
generally, 24–047—24–048
post-termination obligations, 24–049—24–055
pre-termination rights, 24–051
consequential breaches, 24–015
extinguishment, 24–001
failure of performance
And see **Failure of performance**
generally, 24–034—24–046
generally, 24–001—24–002
impossibility
And see **Impossibility**
generally, 24–028—24–033
post-termination obligations
generally, 24–049
guarantor, 24–055
guilty party, 24–052—24–054
innocent party, 24–050
renunciation
And see **Renunciation**
generally, 24–018—24–027
rescission
And see **Rescission**
generally, 24–047
introduction, 24–001
simultaneous breaches, 24–016
termination
generally, 24–047
introduction, 24–001

Discharge (breach of contract)—*cont.*
types
failure of performance, 24–034—24–046
impossibility, 24–028—24–033
renunciation, 24–018—24–027
Discharge (frustration)
arbitration, 23–097
background
adventure, 23–006
generally, 23–004
physical destruction of subject-matter, 23–005
building contracts
delay, 23–050—23–051
generally, 23–049
cancellation of expected event, 23–033—23–034
carriage of goods contracts
generally, 23–047
'Suez Canal' cases, 23–048
charterparties
other events, 23–044—23–044
requisition, 23–041—23–043
classification of cases
building contracts, 23–049—23–051
cancellation of expected event, 23–033—23–034
carriage of goods contracts, 23–047—23–048
charterparties, 23–041—23–044
contracts for sale of land, 23–057
delay, 23–035—23–036
generally, 23–020
leases, 23–052—23–056
outbreak of war, 23–030—23–032
personal contracts, 23–037—23–040
sale of goods, 23–047—23–048
sale of land, 23–057
subsequent legal changes, 23–022—23–023
supervening illegality, 23–024—23–029
compulsory service, 23–039
consequences
common law, at, 23–070—23–073
statute, under, 23–074—23–098
contracting out
effect, 23–094
generally, 23–092
implicit provision, 23–093
contracts for sale of land, 23–057
Davis Contractors test
application, 23–015—23–016
generally, 23–012—23–014
death, 23–037
delay
building contracts, 23–050—23–051
exceptions, 23–036
generally, 23–035
Discharge (frustration)—*cont.*
divisible contracts, 23–091
effect at common law
automatic discharge, 23–071
generally, 23–070
recovery of payments, 23–072—23–073
effect under statute
contracting out, 23–092—23–094
divisible contracts, 23–091
generally, 23–074—23–075
recovery of non-monetary benefits, 23–084—23–090
recovery of payments, 23–076—23–083
severable contracts, 23–091
supplementary provisions, 23–095—23–098
employment contracts, 23–023
excluded contracts, 23–096
force majeure, 23–003, 23–058
foreseeable event, 23–060
foreseen event, 23–059
generally, 23–001
hardship clause, 23–003, 23–058
ill health, 23–038
implied term test
generally, 23–010
objections, 23–011
impossibility
generally, 23–001
introduction, 24–033
imprisonment, 23–039
leases
consequences, 23–056
destruction of building, 23–053
generally, 23–052
interruption of use, 23–055
prohibition on use, 23–054
limitations
foreseeable event, 23–060
foreseen event, 23–059
generally, 23–058
partial impossibility, 23–066—23–069
self-induced event, 23–061—23–065
unforeseen event, 23–060
mistake, 23–002
outbreak of war
accrued rights, 23–031
executory contracts, 23–032
generally, 23–030
partial impossibility
force majeure, 23–067
generally, 23–066
Sainsbury v. Street, 23–068—23–069
personal contracts
compulsory service, 23–039
death, 23–037
ill health, 23–038

Discharge (frustration)—*cont.*
personal contracts—*cont.*
imprisonment, 23–039
other events, 23–040
physical destruction of subject-matter, 23–005
recovery of non-monetary benefits
generally, 23–084
identification of the benefit, 23–085—23–086
just sum, 23–090
valuing the benefit, 23–087—23–089
recovery of payments
allowance for expenses, 23–083
basis of proviso, 23–081
breaches before discharge, 23–079
burden of proof, 23–082
common law, at, 23–072—23–073
generally, 23–076—23–077
paid or payable, 23–078
time of discharge, 23–080
rescission, 23–071
sale of goods
generally, 23–047
'Suez Canal' cases, 23–048
sale of land, 23–057
scope, 23–003
self-induced event
burden of proof, 23–065
examples, 23–062—23–065
generally, 23–061
severability, 23–091
subsequent legal changes
employment contracts, 23–023
generally, 23–022
'Suez Canal' cases, 23–048
supervening illegality
foreign law, under, 23–027—23–029
generally, 23–024
statutory power, exercise 23–026
war, restrictions on outbreak 23–024—23–025
tenancies
consequences, 23–056
destruction of building, 23–053
generally, 23–052
interruption of use, 23–055
prohibition on use, 23–054
tests
Davis Contractors test, 23–012—23–016
differences between, 23–018
generally, 23–007—23–009
implied term test, 23–010—23–011
multi-factorial approach, 23–019
other, 23–017
unforeseen event, 23–060
war, restrictions on outbreak 23–024—23–025

"Disclaimer of contracts"
bankruptcy, 20–035
Disgorgement of profits
analogy with IPR, 26–029
generally, 26–026
partial, 26–027
total, 26–028
Display of goods
goods for sale
exceptional cases, 2–015
general rule, 2–014
menus, 2–016
Disposition of property
frustration, 23–057
implied terms
fitness for habitation, 13–015
generally, 13–031
remoteness of damage, 26–091—26–097
merger
generally, 25–003
lessee, to, 25–004
minors, 8–067
misrepresentation, 6–156—6–157
sale of land
And see **Contracts for the sale of land**
on or after September 27, 1989, 4–052—4–088
on or before September 26, 1989, 4–010—4–051
specific performance
generally, 27–007
unwritten contract, 27–037
unfair contract terms
consumer contracts, 15–014—15–018
generally, 14–105
unfair contract terms (consumer contracts)
consumer sales, 15–015
generally, 15–014
mortgage contracts, 15–016
other, 15–018
tenancies contracts, 15–017
"Disputed claims"
forbearance to sue, 3–054
part payment of debt, 3–118
Dispute resolution
part payment of debt, 3–118
Distance contracts
cancellation, 2–064
force majeure, 14–154
meaning, 1–077
Distress
unjust enrichment, 29–091
"Divisible contracts"
discharge by frustration, 23–091
failure of performance, 24–044
generally, 21–027

"Divisible contracts"—*cont.*
meaning, 21–037
Doctors
presumed undue influence, 7–077
Documentary credits
acceptance, 2–082
Documents under seal
See **Contracts under seal**
Domestic affairs
See **Objects injurious to domestic affairs**
Domestic agreements
See **Social and domestic agreements**
"Domination"
And see **Undue influence**
generally, 7–056
presumed undue influence, 7–072
"Doubtful claims"
forbearance to sue, 3–051
"Draft documents"
generally, 12–069
parol evidence, 12–096
Drunken persons
See **Intoxicated persons**
Drunkenness
See **Intoxication**
Duration (contracts)
implied terms, 13–027
Duress
accord and satisfaction, 22–021
basis of law
generally, 7–004—7–005
importance, 7–006
causation
duress to goods, 7–026
duress to person, 7–025
economic duress, 7–027—7–036
generally, 7–024
consideration, 7–019
counter-restitution of benefits, 7–054
damages, 7–055
economic duress
causation, 7–027—7–036
consideration, 7–019
different approaches, 7–021—7–023
generally, 7–014—7–018
legitimacy of the demand, 7–037—7–044
non-contractual payments, 7–020
effect
generally, 1–005
voidable, 1–082, 7–053
fraud, 7–007
generally, 7–003
goods, of
causation, 7–026
generally 7–012—7–013
unjust enrichment, 29–091
illegitimate pressure
effect, 7–009
Duress—*cont.*
illegitimate pressure—*cont.*
generally, 7–008
types, 7–010—7–019
introduction, 1–135
mistake, 7–007
nature
generally, 7–004—7–007
illegitimate pressure, 7–008—7–019
threats, 7–037—7–050
overview, 7–001
parties to
person suffering, 7–051
third party, 7–052
person, of
causation, 7–025
generally, 7–011
unjust enrichment, 29–089—29–090
pressure
generally, 7–008
types, 7–010—7–019
restitution
goods, 29–071—29–073
person, 29–070
threats
break contract, to, 7–038—7–044
commit otherwise lawful act, to, 7–045—7–046
commit unlawful act, to, 7–037
effect, 7–009
institute civil proceedings, to, 7–050
introduction, 7–008
not to contract, 7–047
prosecute, to, 7–048—7–049
types, 7–010
unfair commercial practices, and, 7–002
unjust enrichment
generally, 29–089
seizure of goods, 29–090
Duress of goods
causation, 7–026
generally 7–012
unjust enrichment, 29–091
"Duress of person"
causation, 7–025
generally, 7–011
unjust enrichment
generally, 29–089
seizure of goods, 29–090

"Ecclesiastical companies"
And see **Companies**
contracts, 9–005
generally, 9–001
Economic duress
And see **Duress**
causation
additional elements, 7–029
"but for", 7–027

Economic duress—*cont.*
causation—*cont.*
conclusion, 7–036
generally, 7–027
gravity of threat, 7–033
independent advice, 7–035
predominant cause, 7–030
protest, 7–034
reasonable alternative, 7–031—7–032
voluntary submission, 7–028
consideration
generally, 7–019
non-contractual payments, 7–020
different approaches
generally, 7–021
legitimacy of the demand, 7–023
special causal requirements, 7–022
generally, 7–014—7–018
legitimacy of the demand
break contract, to, 7–038—7–044
commit otherwise lawful act, to, 7–045—7–046
commit unlawful act, to, 7–037
institute civil proceedings, to, 7–050
introduction, 7–008
not to contract, 7–047
overview, 7–023
prosecute, to, 7–048—7–049
non-contractual payments, 7–020
special causal requirements, 7–022
Economic loss
case law
Balsamo v. Medici, 1–177
Hedley Byrne, 1–175, 1–179
Henderson v. Merrett, 1–180
Junior Books case, 1–176
Simaan General Contracting, 1–177
Smith v. Bush, 1–178
subsequent cases, 1–142
White v. Jones, 1–181
Williams v. Natural Life, 1–182—1–183
generally, 1–175
privity of contract, 18–031
"Economic threat"
duress, 1–135
"Education contracts"
incapacity, 8–027
"Effect classification"
bilateral contracts, 1–079
generally, 1–078
illegal contracts, 1–081
synallagmatic contracts, 1–079
unenforceable contracts, 1–084
unilateral contracts, 1–079
void contracts
effect, 1–081
generally, 1–080
"Effect classification"—*cont.*
voidable contracts
generally, 1–082
setting aside, 1–083
Ejusdem generis
common category, 12–088
generally, 12–087
use, 12–089—12–090
Electricity industry
contractual obligations, 1–013
Electronic communications
formal requirements, 4–005—4–006
Electronic commerce
Rome I Regulation, and, 30–245
Electronic contracts
'advertising', 30–097
'agent', 30–100
'all the steps necessary', 30–098
first condition, 30–096—30–098
generally, 30–095
'received', 30–101
second condition, 30–099—30–101
'specific invitation', 30–096
Electronic documents
deeds, 1–088
formal requirements, 4–008
Electronic mail
acceptance, 2–051
applicable law
'advertising', 30–097
'agent', 30–100
'all the steps necessary', 30–098
first condition, 30–096—30–098
generally, 30–095
'received', 30–101
second condition, 30–099—30–101
'specific invitation', 30–096
Rome I Regulation, and, 30–246
Electronic signatures
formal requirements, 4–007
E-mail
See **Electronic mail**
Employers' associations
restraint of trade, 16–133
Enemies
alien enemies
claimant, as, 11–027—11–029
common law, at, 11–024—11–025
companies, 11–025
defendant, as, 11–030
illegal contracts, 11–032
limitation of actions, 11–031
statute, under, 11–026
trading with the enemy
common law, at, 16–026
statute, under, 16–162—16–163
Enforcement (contract terms)
agreement, as, 1–006
consideration, 3–001

Enforcement (contract terms)—*cont.*
- fairness
  - generally, 1–020
  - relevance, 1–031—1–034
  - statutory authority, 1–021
- frustration, 1–020
- good faith
  - civil law systems, in, 1–025
  - common law systems, in, 1–024
  - English law, in, 1–026
  - fairness, 1–027—1–034
  - introduction, 1–022—1–023
- illegal transactions
  - *And see* **Enforcement (illegal contracts)**
  - benefits from crime, 16–168—16–175
  - collateral transactions, 16–176
  - *ex turpi causa*, 16–164—16–167
  - recovery of payments or property, 16–177—16–193
- inequality
  - generally, 1–020
  - statutory authority, 1–021
- nature of
  - generally, 1–019—1–020
  - good faith, 1–022—1–034
  - limitations, 1–021
- public policy
  - *And see* **Illegality**
  - common law, 16–003—16–141
  - introduction, 16–001—16–002
  - statute, 16–142—16–163
- unfairness
  - generally, 1–020
  - statutory authority, 1–021

Enforcement (illegal contracts)
- benefits from crime
  - court's discretion, 16–170
  - death at law, 16–172
  - generally, 16–168—16–169
  - indemnities, 16–173—16–175
  - suicide, 16–171
- collateral transactions, 16–176
- *ex turpi causa*
  - generally, 16–164
  - limitations, 16–167
  - tainted contracts, 16–165—16–166
- recovery of payments
  - agents, from, 16–192
  - fraud, 16–186
  - generally, 16–177
  - *in pari delicto*, 16–185
  - *locus poenitentiae*, 16–182—16–184, 16–188—16–190
  - marriage brokerage contracts, 16–191
  - mistake, 16–187
  - oppression, 16–186
  - trustees, by, 16–193

Enforcement (illegal contracts)—*cont.*
- recovery of property transferred
  - fraud, 16–186
  - generally, 16–178
  - limited interests, 16–179—16–181
  - *locus poenitentiae*, 16–182—16–184, 16–188—16–190
  - oppression, 16–186

Enforcement orders
- unfair contract terms (consumer contracts), 15–099

Enjoyment
- *See* **Loss of enjoyment**

Enrichment
- *See* **Unjust enrichment**

Enterprise Act 2002
- exemption clauses, 14–131

Entire agreement clauses
- contracts for sale of land, 4–017
- parol evidence, 12–104
- unfair contract terms (consumer contracts), 15–083

Entire contracts
- carriage of goods by sea, 21–034
- failure of performance, 24–043
- partial completion
  - acceptance, 21–035
  - carriage of goods by sea, 21–034
  - effect, 21–030—21–031
  - generally, 21–027—21–029
- substantial completion, 21–032—21–033

Equitable assignment
- conditions, 19–028
- consideration, 19–027—19–037
- distinction from statutory assignments, 19–004—19–006
- enforcement, 19–038—19–041
- formalities, 19–025—19–026
- generally, 19–020
- method, 19–021—19–024

Equitable compensation
- *See* **Equitable remuneration**

Equitable forbearance
- *See* **Forbearance**

Equitable leases
- *See* **Equitable tenancies**

Equitable mortgages
- generally, 4–059

Equitable remuneration
- undue influence, 7–101

Equitable tenancies
- generally, 4–060

"Equitable wrongdoing"
- allowance, 29–157
- bribes, 29–156
- commission, 29–156
- introduction, 29–155
- secret profit, 29–156

Escrow
conveyance, 1–106
deeds
effect, 1–107
generally, 1–105
Estate agents
contracts
generally, 2–083
sole agency, 2–084
negligent misrepresentation, 6–091
stakeholders, as, 29–198
Estoppel
acceptance by silence, 2–073
affirmation, 24–007—24–008
agreements of the parties not to plead limitation, 28–109
companies, 9–008
contracts for sale of land
collateral contracts, 4–076
convention, by, 4–079
generally, 4–078
promissory estoppel, 4–083
proprietary estoppel, 4–080—4–082
convention, by
And see **Estoppel by convention**
criteria, 3–108—3–109
effect, 3–111—3–114
generally, 3–107
deeds, 1–112
formal requirements, 4–004
innocent misrepresentation, 6–095
limitation of actions, 28–109
merger
And see **Estoppel by judgment**
exceptional circumstances, 25–014
foreign judgments, 25–018
generally, 25–011
requirements, 25–012
scope, 25–013
non est factum, 5–101
promissory estoppel
And see **Promissory estoppel**
effect, 3–096—3–097
generally, 3–085
introduction, 1–006
nature, 3–098—3–103
requirements, 3–086—3–095
proprietary estoppel
And see **Proprietary estoppel**
basis of liability, 3–139—3–143
conditions for liability, 3–144—3–148
effects, 3–149—3–164
general rule, 3–137—3–138
public authorities
exercise of statutory powers, and, 10–042
general principles, 10–039
public law, and, 10–043
statutory duty, 10–041
Estoppel—*cont.*
public authorities—*cont.*
ultra vires, and, 10–040
representation, by, 3–096
rescission, 6–126
restitution
generally, 29–176—29–178
introduction, 29–019
sale of land
collateral contracts, 4–076
convention, by, 4–079
generally, 4–078
promissory estoppel, 4–083
proprietary estoppel, 4–080—4–082
ultra vires
generally, 9–024
Turquand decision, 9–042
undue influence, 7–097
unilateral mistake, 5–082
waiver by, 22–040
Estoppel by convention
assumption of law, 3–110
contracts for sale of land, 4–079
effect
generally, 3–111
invalid terms, 3–114
new rights, creation 3–113
generally, 3–107
promissory estoppel, 3–112
requirements
communication, 3–109
generally, 3–108
"Estoppel by judgment"
exceptional circumstances, 25–014
foreign judgments *in personam*, 25–018
generally, 25–011
requirements, 25–012
scope, 25–013
Estoppel by representation
generally, 3–096
"Estoppel *per rem judicatam*"
exceptional circumstances, 25–014
foreign judgments *in personam*, 25–018
generally, 25–011
requirements, 25–012
scope, 25–013
Evidence
applicable law, 30–044
"*Ex contractu* actions"
generally, 1–118
"*Ex delicto* actions"
generally, 1–118
Excessive delivery
See **Defective delivery**
Exchange controls
illegality, 16–014
"Exchange losses"
applicable law, 30–340

Exchange of contracts
contracts for sale of land, 4–071
general rule
introduction, 2–119
mitigation, 2–120—2–123
mitigation of rule
auctions, 2–122
collateral agreements, 2–121
generally, 2–120
'lock-out' agreements, 2–121
provisional agreements, 2–123
tender, sales by, 2–122
sale of land, 4–071
Exchange rates
interest on damages, 26–159
Exemption clauses
And see **Unfair contract terms**
acknowledgment clauses, 14–133
agreed damages clauses, 14–004
animal feeding stuffs, 14–124
arbitration clauses, 14–004
bailment
deliberate damage, 14–037
deposit, 14–034
misdelivery, 14–036
storage, 14–035
sub-contracting, 14–038
theft, 14–037
third parties, 14–054—14–055
carriage by air, 14–118
carriage of goods by land
delay, 14–030
deviation, 14–029
generally, 14–116
misdelivery, 14–033
roadworthiness, 14–032
sub-contracting, 14–038
carriage of goods by sea
deck, on, 14–031
delay, 14–030
deviation, 14–029
generally, 14–117
misdelivery, 14–033
seaworthiness, 14–032
sub-contracting, 14–038
collateral guarantees, 14–134
collateral warranties, 14–134
construction of
And see **Construction of terms**
ambiguity, 14–005
burden of proof, 14–018—14–019
contra proferentem, 14–009
deliberate breach, 14–016—14–017
generally, 14–005—14–006, 14–025
inconsistency, 14–008
indemnity, 14–015
negligence, 14–010—14–014
purpose of contract, by reference to, 14–007—14–008
Exemption clauses—*cont.*
consumer contracts
cancellation, 14–129
common law, at, 15–001—15–002
generally, 14–125—14–126
package holidays, 14–128
statute, under, 15–003—15–077
trading stamps, 14–127
debt interest, 14–130
defective premises, 14–120
employment contracts, 14–121—14–122
Enterprise Act 2002, under, 14–131
fertilisers, 14–124
force majeure clauses
And see **Force majeure**
burden of proof, 14–140—14–146
generally, 14–137—14–139
introduction, 14–004
use, 14–147—14–152
fraud, 14–136
fundamental breaches
conclusion, 14–024
generally, 14–020
George Mitchell, 14–023
Photo Production v. Securicor, 14–022
Suisse Atlantique, 14–021
generally, 14–001
hire purchase, contracts for, 14–028
incorporation of
And see **Incorporation of terms**
generally, 14–002
insurance, contracts for, 14–119
interest on debts, 14–130
limitation of actions, 28–113
Misrepresentation Act 1967, under, 14–114
misrepresentations as to effect, 14–132
oral warranties, 14–134
reasonableness
generally, 14–135
UCTA 1977, 14–084—14–103
sale of goods
description, correspondence with, 14–027
fitness for purpose, 14–027
quality, 14–027
sample, correspondence with, 14–027
title, 14–026
statutory regulation
Misrepresentation Act 1967, 14–114
other, 14–115—14–131
UCTA 1977, 14–059—14–113
UTCCR 1994, 15–001—15–077
third parties
agency, 14–047—14–049
bailment, 14–054—14–055
benefit, 14–042—14–043

Exemption clauses—*cont.*
third parties—*cont.*
burden, 14–040—14–041
common law rule, 14–040—14–043
construction contracts, 14–056—14–058
exceptions, 14–045
excluded contracts, 14–044
introduction, 14–039
occupier's liability, 14–053
promise not to sue, 14–051
trust, 14–050
vicarious immunity, 14–046
voluntary assumption of risk, 14–053
types, 14–003
Unfair Contract Terms Act 1977, under
And see **Unfair Contract Terms Act 1977**
excluded contracts, 14–104—14–113
general provisions, 14–065—14–083
generally, 14–059—14–061
reasonableness, 14–084—14–103
relevant clauses, 14–062—14–064
Unfair Contract Terms (Consumer Contracts) Regulations 1994, under
And see **Unfair contract terms (consumer contracts)**
background, 15–004—15–010
choice of law, 15–093
fairness, 15–043—15–088
plain language, 15–089—15–092
relevant contracts, 15–011—15–029
relevant terms, 15–030—15–042
remedies, 15–094—15–099
unit trusts, 14–123
"Exclusive selling agreements"
restraint of trade, 16–127
"Executed compromises"
forbearance to sue, 3–056
Executed contracts
contracts for sale of land, 4–084
minors, 8–011
rescission, 6–133
Execution (deeds)
after 14 September, 2005, 1–095—1–101
background, 1–087—1–088
between 31 July, 1989 and 14 September, 2005
companies, by, 1–091
individual, by, 1–090
introduction, 1–089
other persons, by, 1–092
common aspects, 1–102—1–107
introduction, 1–089
Executors
payment, 21–049
Exemplary damages
fraudulent misrepresentation, 6–063
Exemplary damages—*cont.*
generally, 26–019
introduction, 1–123
Exemption clauses
See **Exclusion clauses**
"Existing duties"
duty imposed by contract with promisor
factual benefit, 3–068—3–069
generally, 3–065
no consideration, 3–066—3–067
other consideration, 3–070—3–071
duty imposed by contract with third party
generally, 3–072
performance of duty, 3–073—3–074
promise of performance of duty, 3–075
generally, 3–061
public duty
acts over and above, 3–063—3–064
generally, 3–062
"Expectation interest"
damages, 26–002
"Explanation of document"
equivocation, 12–124
generally, 12–117
identity of parties, 12–122
special meaning of words, 12–121
subject-matter, 12–123
subsequent acts, 12–126
surrounding circumstances, 12–118—12–120
Express terms
classification
conditions, 12–019, 12–025—12–030
fundamental terms, 12–021—12–024
intermediate terms, 12–020, 12–034—12–040
warranties, 12–019, 12–031—12–033
collateral contracts
consideration, 12–006
generally, 12–004—12–005
third parties, 12–007
conditions
concurrent conditions, 12–029
contingent, 12–027
generally, 12–019
meaning, 12–025—12–026
precedent, 12–028
promissory, 12–027
subsequent, 12–030
construction
ambiguity, 12–083—12–086
ejusdem generis, 12–087—12–090
general rules, 12–041—12–049
intention of parties, 12–072—12–082
ordinary meaning, 12–050—12–062
purpose of contract, 12–063—12–071

Express terms—*cont.*
construction—*cont.*
restrictions, 12–091—12–092
time stipulations, 12–093—12–094
extrinsic evidence
custom, 12–127—12–133
effectiveness of document, 12–106—12–112
explanation of document, 12–117—12–126
generally, 12–095
interpretation of document, 12–117—12–126
mercantile usage, 12–127—12–133
parol evidence, 12–096—12–105
true nature of document, 12–113—12–116
validity of document, 12–106—12–112
fundamental terms, 12–021—12–024
generally, 12–001
implied terms, 13–023
incorporation
course of dealing, by, 12–011
notices, 12–013—12–018
time, 12–010
trade custom, by, 12–012
intermediate terms
conclusion, 12–040
effect, 12–038—12–039
generally, 12–020
meaning, 12–034
nature, 12–035—12–037
proof
collateral contracts, 12–004—12–007
generally, 12–002
representations, 12–003
standard form contracts, 12–008—12–018
proper law
And see **Conflict of laws**
common law limitations, 30–007
generally, 30–006
statutory limitations, 30–008
representations, 12–003
standard form contracts
generally, 12–008
incorporation of terms, 12–010—12–018
relevant documents, 12–009
time stipulations
construction 12–093—12–094
intermediate term, 12–037
warranties
collateral, 12–033
election, upon, 12–032
generally, 12–019
meaning, 12–031
Expressio unius est exclusio alterius
construction of terms, 12–091
"Expressum facit cessare tacitum"
construction of terms, 12–092
Extended warranties
intention, 2–167
Extinguishment
discharge by breach, 24–001
Extortion
restitution, 29–150
Extortion colore officii
generally, 29–094
nature of threat, 29–095
Extortionate credit bargains
See also **Unfair credit relationships**
bankruptcy, 20–030
introduction, 7–138
Extrinsic evidence
custom
annex terms, to, 12–131
generally, 12–127—12–129
interpretation, for, 12–130
effectiveness of document
conditional contracts, 12–109
consideration, 12–108
fraud, 12–112
generally, 12–106—12–112
illegality, 12–112
explanation of document
ambiguity, 12–125
equivocation, 12–124
generally, 12–117
identity of parties, 12–122
special meaning of words, 12–121
subject-matter, 12–123
subsequent acts, 12–126
surrounding circumstances, 12–118—12–120
generally, 12–095
interpretation of document
ambiguity, 12–125
equivocation, 12–124
generally, 12–117
identity of parties, 12–122
special meaning of words, 12–121
subject-matter, 12–123
subsequent acts, 12–126
surrounding circumstances, 12–118—12–120
mercantile usage
annex terms, to, 12–133
generally, 12–127—12–129
interpretation, for, 12–132
parol evidence
collateral contracts, 12–103
contradictory terms, 12–100
entire agreement clauses, 12–104
excluded contracts, 12–101—12–102
exceptions, 12–097, 12–105
generally, 12–096
reform, 12–099
scope, 12–098

Extrinsic evidence—*cont.*
true nature of document
agency, 2–122—12–115
generally, 12–113
suretyship, 12–116
validity of document
conditional contracts, 12–109
consideration, 12–108
fraud, 12–112
generally, 12–106— 12–107

Failure of consideration
avoided insurance policy, 29–082
deposits, 29–064—29–065
illegal contracts
generally, 29–077
services rendered, 29–078
introduction, 29–054
minors' contracts, 29–081
part payments, 29–066
partial failure of consideration
common law, at, 29–061
divisible contract, in, 29–063
statute, under, 29–060
quantum meruit
additional work, 29–072
bad bargains, 29–068
contract price, 29–069
generally, 29–067
goods supplied, 29–070
introduction, 29–004
no fixed price, 29–071
services rendered, 29–070
substituted contract for services, 29–073
total failure of consideration
artificial distinctions, 29–057
detrimental reliance, 29–055
discharged contracts, 29–058—29–059
examples, 29–056
introduction, 29–054
reconsideration of requirement, 29–062
unenforceable contract
money paid, 29–079
work done, 29–080
void contract
absence of consideration, 29–075
generally, 29–074
goods supplied, 29–076
services rendered, 29–076

Fairness
civil law systems, in, 1–025
common law systems, in, 1–024
criteria
circumstances of conclusion of contract, 15–055
dependent contract, terms 15–057
generally, 15–053

Fairness—*cont.*
criteria—*cont.*
nature of goods and services, 15–054
other terms of contract, 15–056
English law, in
considering other parties' interests, 1–027
contractual interpretation, 1–031
equitable discretion, 1–034
express term as to good faith, 1–028
express term to act fairly, 1–030
express term to negotiate good faith, 1–029
implication of terms, 1–032
implied restrictions on broad commercial powers, 1–033
introduction, 1–026
statutory discretion, 1–034
test
appeals, 15–067
background, 15–045—15–036
burden of proof, 15–062—15–064
criteria, 15–053—15–057
First National Bank plc, 15–061—15–060
generally, 15–044
good faith, 15–058—15–060
imbalance in rights, 15–050—15–052
indicative list, 15–069—15–086
'neutral' assessment, 15–065—15–066
non-compliance, 15–086—15–088
OFT, 15–096
UK courts' interpretation, 15–068
threats to break contract, 7–042
unfair contract terms (consumer contracts)
generally, 15–043
relevant terms, 15–030—15–032
test, 15–044—15–088

"Family settlements"
misrepresentation, 6–155

Fatal accidents
limitation of actions, 28–007—28–008

Fax
acceptance, 2–051

Feedingstuffs
exemption clauses, 14–124

Feelings
See **Injury to feelings**

Fertilisers
exemption clauses, 14–124

"Figures"
construction of terms, 12–071

Financial assistance
ultra vires, 9–038

Financial loss
See **Economic loss**

Financial services
negligent misrepresentation, 6–090
Fire insurance
benefit of third party, 18–129
contract for benefit of third party, 18–129
"Firm offers"
consideration, 3–172—3–173
Fitness for habitation
leases, 13–016
sale of land, 13–015
Fitness for purpose
exclusion clauses, 14–027
Fixtures
contracts for sale of land, 4–020
Foakes v Beer
And see **Part payment of debt**
generally, 3–123
Forbearance
actual forbearance
causal connection, 3–059—3–060
generally, 3–057
period of forbearance, 3–058
causal connection
express request, 3–060
generally, 3–059
implied request, 3–060
disputed claims, 3–054
doubtful claims, 3–051
equity, in
And see **Promissory estoppel**
generally, 4–083
part payment of debt, 3–128—3–136
executed compromises, 3–056
introduction, 3–046
invalid claims
generally, 3–050
made in good faith, 3–052—3–053
part payment of debt
common law, at, 3–124
equity, in, 3–128—3–136
part payment of debt in equity
continuing obligations, 3–130—3–131
detriment, 3–135
effect, 3–129—3–133
extinctive effects, 3–132—3–133
inequity, 3–136
introduction, 3–128
nature of doctrine, 3–129
requirements, 3–134—3–136
valid claims
construction of releases, 3–048
other grounds for relief, 3–049
promise not to sue, 3–047
variation of terms
And see **Variation**
common law, 3–082—3–084
equity, 3–085—3–103
introduction, 3–081
Forbearance—*cont.*
void forbearances, 3–055
Force majeure
burden of proof
'delayed' clauses, 14–144
generally, 14–140
'hindered' clauses, 14–143
'prevented' clauses, 14–141—14–142
'rendered uneconomic' clauses, 14–145
conditions precedent, 14–150
'delayed' clauses, 14–144
distance selling, 14–154
frustration, 23–003, 23–058
generally, 14–137—14–139
'hindered' clauses, 14–143
introduction, 14–004
intermediate terms, 12–039
meaning
burden of proof, 14–140—14–145
generally, 14–137—14–139
specified events, 14–146
'prevented' clauses, 14–141—14–142
'rendered uneconomic' clauses, 14–145
sale of goods, 14–151
UCTA 1977, 14–152
use, 14–147—14–148
UTCCR 1994, 14–153
Foreign affairs
See **Objects injurious to foreign affairs**
Foreign currency transactions
arbitral awards, 30–379
currency of damages, 30–373
introduction, 30–369
foreign currency judgments, 30–376—30–378
legal tender, 30–371
money of account
currency of damages, 30–373
generally, 30–372
money of payment
generally, 30–374—30–375
judgments in foreign currency, 30–376—30–378
nominalism, 30–370
Foreign exchange
contracts in breach of controls, 1–084
Foreign governments
immunity from suit, 11–008—11–009
Foreign judgments
merger
generally, 25–016
in personam, 25–017—25–018
in rem, 25–019
Foreign sovereigns
See **Heads of state**

Foreign states
immunity from suit
act of state, 11–007
common law, at, 11–001
human rights, 11–003
statute, under, 11–002—11–006
waiver, 11–020
Forfeiture
damages
express clause, 26–146—26–153
no express clause, 26–154
proceeds of crime, 16–170
unconscionable bargains, 7–126
unfair contract terms (consumer contracts), 15–075
"Forfeiture rule"
benefits resulting from crime, 16–170
Forgery
bills of exchange, 21–078
Formal contracts
generally, 1–075
Formalities
companies
generally, 9–009
seal, 9–009
dispositions of land
background, 4–009
post-26th September 1989, 4–052—4–088
pre- 26th September 1989, 4–010—4–051
electronic communications, 4–005—4–006
electronic deeds, 4–008
electronic signatures, 4–007
estoppel, 4–004
generally, 4–001
non-compliance, 4–003
statutory
generally, 4–002
non-compliance, effect 4–003
types, 4–002
"Formal validity of contract"
acts intended to have legal effect, 30–315—30–317
consumer contracts
generally, 30–313
Rome I Regulation, 30–320
generally, 30–310—30–312
immovables
generally, 30–314
Rome I Regulation, 30–321
Rome I Regulation, and, 30–318—30–322
unilateral acts, 30–319
Formation of contract
And see under individual headings
acceptance
communication 2–045—2–046
generally, 2–027—2–044
Formation of contract—*cont.*
acceptance—*cont.*
prescribed method, by, 2–065—2–069
post, by, 2–048—2–064
silence, by, 2–070—2–077
unilateral contracts, 2–078—2–086
agreement
acceptance, 2–027—2–109
certainty of terms, 2–139—2–146
conditional, 2–147—2–157
incomplete, 2–112—2–138
offer, 2–003—2–026
special cases, 2–110—2–111
applicable law, 30–306—30–307
consideration
adequacy 3–014—3–021
definitions, 3–004—3–013
existing duties, 3–061—3–075
forbearance to sue, 3–047—3–056
introduction, 3–001—3–003
movement 3–036—3–045
part payment of debt, 3–115—3–136
past, 3–026—3–035
proprietary estoppel, 3–137—3–164
special cases, 3–165—3–182
'valuable' consideration, 3–022—3–025
variation of terms, 3–076—3–114
intention
anger, agreements made in, 2–185—2–189
burden of proof, 2–159—2–160
collective agreements, 2–177
consumer guarantees, 2–167
discretion, 2–176
domestic agreements, 2–169—2–175
free passes, 2–178
generally, 2–158
giving effect to pre-existing rights, agreements, 2–180
goodwill agreements, 2–186
government policy statements, 2–179
impliedly negatived, 2–164
jest, agreements made in, 2–185—2–189
nature of relationship, 2–181—2–183
social agreements, 2–168
statements inducing contracts, 2–165—2–166
tests, 2–161—2–163
vague agreements, 2–184
introduction, 2–001
material validity of contract, 30–306—30–307
objective test, 2–002
offer
advertisements, by, 2–017—2–020
auctions, 2–011—2–013
conduct, by, 2–005

Formation of contract—*cont.*
offer—*cont.*
display, by, 2–014—2–016
generally, 2–003—2–004
inactivity, by, 2–006
invitation to treat, 2–007—2–010
place 2–025
share, 2–024
tender, by, 2–022—2–023
termination 2–087—2–109
ticket, by, 2–021
time 2–026
termination of offer
death, by, 2–099—2–101
generally, 2–087
lapse of time, by, 2–095—2–097
occurrence of condition, by, 2–098
rejection, by, 2–092—2–094
supervening incapacity, by, 2–102—2–109
withdrawal, by, 2–088—2–091
Forms of action
generally, 1–118
Franchise agreements
restraint of trade, 16–120
Fraud
duress, 7–007
exemption clauses, 14–136
illegality, 16–017
limitation of actions
agent, 28–087
date from which time runs, 28–058
generally, 28–082—28–083
introduction, 28–081
misrepresentation, 6–003
objects illegal by common law or statute, 16–017
recovery of payments, 16–186
validity of document, 12–112
Fraudulent misrepresentation
account of profits, 6–062
agent, by, 6–048
contributory negligence, 6–064
damages
compound interest, 6–065
contributory negligence, 6–064
exemplary sums, 6–063
generally, 6–042
measure, 6–049—6–059
mitigation, 6–060
non-pecuniary losses, 6–061
relevant representations, 6–043—6–048
illegal contracts, 6–066
meaning
absence of honest belief, 6–044
ambiguity, 6–047
generally, 6–043
knowledge of falsity, 6–045
motive, 6–046
Fraudulent misrepresentation—*cont.*
measure of damages
entry into other losing transaction, 6–059
generally, 6–049
lost opportunity, 6–052
market value, fall in, 6–057—6–058
property value, fall in, 6–053—6–056
unforeseeable losses, 6–050—6–051
minor's age, of
bankruptcy debt, 8–052
generally, 8–051
release from obligations, 8–053
transfer of property, 8–054—8–057
"Free passes"
intention, 2–178
"Free services"
generally, 3–178
misfeasance, 3–180—3–181
negligence, 3–179
non-feasance, 3–180—3–181
Freedom of contract
discrimination, 1–016
European law, in, 1–013
generally, 1–011
modern common law, in, 1–012
qualifications
discrimination, 1–016
generally, 1–014
refusal to enter contracts, 1–015
regulation of contractual environment, 1–018
restricted freedom as to terms, 1–017
refusal to enter contracts, 1–015
regulation of contractual environment, 1–018
restricted freedom as to terms, 1–017
Freight forwarders
See **Forwarding agents**
Frustration
arbitration, 23–097
background
adventure, 23–006
generally, 23–004
physical destruction of subject-matter, 23–005
building contracts
delay, 23–050—23–051
generally, 23–049
cancellation of expected event, 23–033—23–034
carriage of goods contracts
generally, 23–047
'Suez Canal' cases, 23–048
charterparties
other events, 23–044—23–044
requisition, 23–041—23–043
classification of cases
building contracts, 23–049—23–051

Frustration—*cont.*
classification of cases—*cont.*
cancellation of expected event, 23–033—23–034
carriage of goods contracts, 23–047—23–048
charterparties, 23–041—23–044
delay, 23–035—23–036
generally, 23–020
leases, 23–052—23–056
outbreak of war, 23–030—23–032
personal contracts, 23–037—23–040
sale of goods, 23–047—23–048
sale of land, 23–057
subsequent legal changes, 23–022—23–023
supervening illegality, 23–024—23–029
compulsory service, 23–039
consequences
common law, at, 23–070—23–073
statute, under, 23–074—23–098
contracting out
effect, 23–094
generally, 23–092
implicit provision, 23–093
contracts for sale of land, 23–057
Davis Contractors test
application, 23–015—23–016
generally, 23–012—23–014
death, 23–037
delay
building contracts, 23–050—23–051
exceptions, 23–036
generally, 23–035
divisible contracts, 23–091
effect at common law
automatic discharge, 23–071
generally, 23–070
recovery of payments, 23–072—23–073
effect under statute
contracting out, 23–092—23–094
divisible contracts, 23–091
generally, 23–074—23–075
recovery of non-monetary benefits, 23–084—23–090
recovery of payments, 23–076—23–083
severable contracts, 23–091
supplementary provisions, 23–095—23–098
excluded contracts, 23–096
force majeure, 23–003, 23–058
foreseeable event, 23–060
foreseen event, 23–059
generally, 23–001
hardship clause, 23–003, 23–058
ill health, 23–038

Frustration—*cont.*
implied term test
generally, 23–010
objections, 23–011
impossibility
generally, 23–001
introduction, 24–033
imprisonment, 23–039
leases
consequences, 23–056
destruction of building, 23–053
generally, 23–052
interruption of use, 23–055
prohibition on use, 23–054
limitations
foreseeable event, 23–060
foreseen event, 23–059
generally, 23–058
partial impossibility, 23–066—23–069
self-induced event, 23–061—23–065
unforeseen event, 23–060
mistake, 23–002
outbreak of war
accrued rights, 23–031
executory contracts, 23–032
generally, 23–030
partial impossibility
force majeure, 23–067
generally, 23–066
Sainsbury v. Street, 23–068—23–069
personal contracts
compulsory service, 23–039
death, 23–037
ill health, 23–038
imprisonment, 23–039
other events, 23–040
physical destruction of subject-matter, 23–005
recovery of non-monetary benefits
generally, 23–084
identification of the benefit, 23–085—23–086
just sum, 23–090
valuing the benefit, 23–087—23–089
recovery of payments
allowance for expenses, 23–083
basis of proviso, 23–081
breaches before discharge, 23–079
burden of proof, 23–082
common law, at, 23–072—23–073
generally, 23–076—23–077
paid or payable, 23–078
time of discharge, 23–080
rescission, 23–071
sale of goods
generally, 23–047
'Suez Canal' cases, 23–048
sale of land, 23–057
scope, 23–003

Frustration—*cont.*
self-induced event
burden of proof, 23–065
examples, 23–062—23–065
generally, 23–061
severability, 23–091
subsequent legal changes
employment contracts, 23–023
generally, 23–022
'Suez Canal' cases, 23–048
supervening illegality
exercise of statutory power, 23–026
foreign law, under, 23–027—23–029
generally, 23–024
restrictions on outbreak of war, 23–024—23–025
tenancies
consequences, 23–056
destruction of building, 23–053
generally, 23–052
interruption of use, 23–055
prohibition on use, 23–054
tests
Davis Contractors test, 23–012—23–016
differences between, 23–018
generally, 23–007—23–009
implied term test, 23–010—23–011
multi-factorial approach, 23–019
other, 23–017
unforeseen event, 23–060
war, and, 23–024—23–025
Fundamental breach
exemption clauses
conclusion, 14–024
generally, 14–020
George Mitchell, 14–023
Photo Production v. Securicor, 14–022
Suisse Atlantique, 14–021
failure of performance, 24–041
"Fundamental mistake"
unjust enrichment, 29–033
Future loss
generally, 26–013—26–014
"Future possession"
enforcement against third parties, 18–147

"Gaming chips"
consideration, 3–016—3–017
Gaming contracts
See also **Gambling contracts**
See also **Wagering contracts**
[*n.b. prior to September 1, 2007*]
consideration, 3–169
mistake of fact, 29–038
"Garbled message"
acceptance, 2–059
Garnishee orders
And see **Third party debt orders**
payment, 21–051
Gas industry
contractual obligations, 1–013
General average
contribution, 29–129
General damages
generally, 26–006
Gifts
restitution, 29–019
"Gold clauses"
payment, 21–069—21–071
Good faith
civil law systems, in, 1–025
common law systems, in, 1–024
English law, in
considering other parties' interests, 1–027
contractual interpretation, 1–031
equitable discretion, 1–034
express term as to good faith, 1–028
express term to act fairly, 1–030
express term to negotiate good faith, 1–029
implication of terms, 1–032
implied restrictions on broad commercial powers, 1–033
introduction, 1–026
statutory discretion, 1–034
forbearance to sue, 3–052—3–053
introduction, 1–022—1–023
unfair contract terms
First National Bank plc, 15–048
generally, 15–058
other factors, 15–060
public services, 15–059
'significant imbalance', 15–046
Good government
See **Objects injurious to good government**
Goodwill
And see **Sale of goodwill**
generally, 2–186
Governing law
And see **Conflict of laws**
absence of choice by parties, in
carriage of goods contracts, 30–085—30–087
characteristic performance, 30–074—30–078
consumer contracts, for, 30–107
employment contracts, for, 30–119—30–120
general principle, 30–071
habitual residence, 30–079
immovables, 30–082—30–084
introduction, 30–055
non-application of presumptions, 30–088—30–089

Governing law—*cont.*
absence of choice by parties, in—*cont.*
place of business, 30–080—30–081
presumptions, 30–072—30–073
rebutting presumptions, 30–090—30–091
acquiescence, 30–348
act intended to have legal effect, 30–354
agent-principal disputes, 30–042
arbitration agreements, 30–040
background
And see **Rome Convention**
generally, 30–017—30–029
breach of contract, consequences of
damages, 30–337
exchange losses, 30–340
generally, 30–336
injunctions, 30–338
interest, 30–339—30–344
specific performance, 30–338
burden of proof, 30–352
capacity
bodies corporate, 30–325
generally, 30–323
introduction, 30–036
natural persons, 30–324
carriage of goods contracts, 30–085—30–087
choice of law agreements, 30–040
choice of law by parties
alteration, 30–058
consumer contracts, for, 30–092—30–107
employment contracts, for, 30–108—30–118
express choice, 30–050
generally, 30–047—30–048
implied choice, 30–051—30–055
limitations, 30–060—30–070
mandatory rules, 30–061—30–068
partial choice, 30–056—30–057
validity, 30–059
company law, 30–041
concurrent liability
employment contracts, 30–121
generally, 30–032
consumer contracts, for
choice of law by parties, 30–094—30–106
formal validity of contract, 30–313
habitual residence, 30–106
introduction, 30–092
mandatory rules, 30–102—30–105
no choice of law by parties, 30–107
online contracts, 30–095—30–101
relevant contracts, 30–093
contract intended to have legal effect, 30–354
contractual obligations, 30–031

Governing law—*cont.*
damages, 30–337
employment contracts, for
choice of law by parties, 30–112—30–118
concurrent liability, 30–121
generally, 30–108—30–111
no choice of law by parties, 30–119—30–120
Rome I Regulation, and, 30–122
territorial limitation, 30–115
exchange losses, 30–340
exclusions
agent-principal disputes, 30–042
arbitration agreements, 30–040
capacity of person, 30–036
choice of law agreements, 30–040
company law, 30–041
evidence and procedure, 30–044
generally, 30–030—30–035
insurance contracts, 30–045—30–046
matrimonial and similar rights, 30–037
negotiable instruments, 30–038—30–039
succession, 30–037
trusts, 30–043
wills, 30–037
evidence and procedure, 30–044
extinguishing obligations, 30–345
foreign currency obligations
generally, 30–369—30–371
money of account, 30–372—30–373
money of payment, 30–374—30–378
formal validity of contract
acts intended to have legal effect, 30–315—30–317
consumer contracts, 30–313
generally, 30–310—30–312
immovables, 30–314
Rome I Regulation, and, 30–318—30–322
habitual residence, 30–079
illegality of contract
applicable law, under, 30–356
English law, under, 30–357
generally, 30–355
other foreign law, under, 30–365
place of performance of act, in, 30–358—30–364
immovables
formal validity of contract, 30–314
no choice of law by parties, 30–082—30–084
implied choice
distinction from no choice, 30–055
generally, 30–051—30–052
relevant factors, 30–053
subsequent conduct, 30–054

Governing law—*cont.*
injunctions, 30–338
insurance contracts, 30–045—30–046
interest
exchange losses, 30–340
generally, 30–339
statutory, 30–341—30–344
interpretation of contract, 30–331
laches, 30–348
limitation of actions, 30–347—30–348
mandatory rules
application, 30–065
chosen law governs other issues, where, 30–067
connection with single country, 30–062
English law, 30–066
generally, 30–061
inapplicability, 30–064
law of the forum, 30–068
meaning, 30–063
material validity of contract
formation of contract, 30–306—30–307
generally, 30–304—30–305
validity of consent, 30–308
validity of terms, 30–309
matrimonial and similar rights, 30–037
negotiable instruments, 30–038—30–039
no choice of law by parties
carriage of goods contracts, 30–085—30–087
characteristic performance, 30–074—30–078
consumer contracts, for, 30–107
employment contracts, for, 30–119—30–120
general principle, 30–071
habitual residence, 30–079
immovables, 30–082—30–084
introduction, 30–055
non-application of presumptions, 30–088—30–089
place of business, 30–080—30–081
presumptions, 30–072—30–073
rebutting presumptions, 30–090—30–091
nominalism, 30–370
nullity of contract
consequences, 30–327—30–328
contract, and, 30–349
Rome I Regulation, and, 30–328
partial choice, 30–056—30–057
performance of contract
discretion, 30–335
manner, 30–333—30–334
substance, 30–332
place of business, 30–080—30–081
prescription, 30–347—30–348

Governing law—*cont.*
presumptions of law, 30–353
public policy, contract contrary to, 30–366—30–368
restitution, 30–033
scope
breach of contract, 30–336—30–344
burden of proof, 30–351—30–354
capacity, 30–323—30–325
extinguishing obligations, 30–345
foreign currency obligations, 30–369—30–379
formal validity of contract, 30–310—30–322
generally, 30–303
illegality of contract, 30–355—30–365
interpretation of contract, 30–331
limitation of actions, 30–347—30–348
material validity of contract, 30–304—30–309
nullity of contract, 30–327—30–328
other issues, 30–350
performance of contract, 30–332—30–335
prescription, 30–347—30–348
public policy, 30–366—30–368
specific performance, 30–338
set-off, 30–346
subrogation, 30–127—30–129
succession, 30–037
trusts, 30–043
unjust enrichment, 30–034
voluntary assignment of rights
assignability, 30–125
generally, 30–123
mutual obligations, 30–124
property, 30–126
wills, 30–037

Government contracts
See also **Public authorities**
agency
generally, 10–009
liability of agent, 10–013
ostensible authority, 10–012
servant-agent issue, 10–011
unauthorised contracts, 10–011
warranty of authority, 10–014
capacity, 10–004
fettering of discretion
express terms, 10–008
introduction, 10–007
injunctions, 10–019
interim remedies, 10–017
introduction, 10–001—10–003
Parliamentary control
express limitations, 10–005
implied limitations, 10–006

Government contracts—*cont.*
remedies
background, 10–015
Crown servants, against, 10–018—10–019
generally, 10–016
interim remedies, 10–017
"Grammatical errors"
construction of terms, 12–080
Gratuitous bailment
consideration, 3–177
Gratuitous services
generally, 3–178
misfeasance, 3–180—3–181
negligence, 3–179
non-feasance, 3–180—3–181
"Growing crops"
contracts for the sale of land, 4–018
Guarantees
effect, 1–084
past consideration, 3–027
Guarantors
payment to third person, 29–106
Guardians
presumed undue influence, 7–075

Habitual residence
applicable law, 30–079
Hadley v. Baxendale
actual knowledge
generally, 26–060
special circumstances, 26–061
assumption of risk, 26–062—26–063
degree of probability, 26–059
generally, 26–052—26–057
knowledge
actual, 26–060
imputed, 26–060
special circumstances, 26–061
relevant loss, 26–058
Hague Rules
exemption clauses, 14–117
Hardship
frustration, 23–003, 23–058
Heads of state
immunity from suit, 11–008—11–009
Himalaya clauses
agency, 14–047—14–049
Hire
See **Consumer hire**
Hire purchase
exemption clauses, 14–028
privity of contract, 18–006
unfair contract terms
dealing as a consumer, 14–067
implied terms, 14–078
reasonableness, 14–085
Holidays
implied terms, 13–034
negligent misrepresentation, 6–092
Home information packs
negligent misrepresentation, 6–093
Honours
See **Procurement of honours**
Horizontal agreements
auction rings, 16–135
employer's associations, 16–133
generally, 16–132
labour and services, 16–136—16–140
price-fixing agreements, 16–134
professional bodies, 16–139
trade unions, 16–136—16–140
House for sale advertisements
offer, 2–018
Human rights
confidentiality of contracts, 1–065—1–066
construction of legislation
background, 1–037—1–038
examples, 1–049
generally, 1–044
unenforceable contractual rights, 1–045
construction of contract terms, 12–049
courts as public authorities
background, 1–043
construction of contracts, 1–061
common law developments, 1–060
exercise of judicial discretion, 1–059
implied terms, 1–062
introduction, 1–058
open-textured controls, 1–064
open-textured norms, 1–063
custom trade and usage, 13–020
introduction, 1–035
post-1 October 2000 contracts
confidentiality of contracts, 1–065—1–066
construction of legislation, 1–044—1–051
courts as public authorities, 1–058—1–064
public authority contracts, 1–050—1–057
review of legislation, 1–044—1–051
pre-2 October 2000 contracts
accrued contractual rights, 1–037—1–038
courts as public authorities, 1–043
public authority contracts, 1–039—1–043
public authority contracts
background, 1–039—1–043
construction of contracts, 1–057
effect on contract, 1–056
hybrid bodies, 1–051—1–052
relevant authorities, 1–050
unlawful conclusion of contract, 1–054

Human rights—*cont.*
public authority contracts—*cont.*
unlawful manner of performance of contract, 1–055
unlawful refusal to contract, 1–053
review of legislation
background, 1–037—1–038
examples, 1–049
generally, 1–044
legitimacy, certainty and proportionality of interference with person's property, 1–048
unenforceable contractual rights, 1–045—1–047
sovereign immunity, 11–003
territorial impact, 1–036
Husband and wife
See **Spouses**

Ignorance (offers)
bilateral contracts, 2–042
unilateral contracts, 2–041
Ill health
frustration, 23–038
Illegal contracts
And see **Illegality**
alien enemies, 11–032
fraudulent misrepresentation, 6–066
generally, 1–081
unjust enrichment
generally, 29–077
services rendered, 29–078
"Illegal debts"
account stated, 29–192
Illegality
applicable law, under, 30–356
arbitration, 16–045—16–047
bankruptcy, 16–042
benefits from crime
court's discretion, 16–170
death at law, 16–172
generally, 16–168—16–169
indemnities, 16–173—16–175
suicide, 16–171
burden of proof, 16–204
champertous agreements
assignment of right to litigate, 16–057—16–064
effect, 16–066
generally, 16–048—16–049
meaning, 16–054
other agreements, 16–065
solicitor and clients, 16–055—16–056
collateral transactions, 16–176
collusive divorce agreements, 16–043
common law, at
generally, 16–003—16–004
injurious to good government, 16–019—16–034

Illegality—*cont.*
common law, at—*cont.*
injurious to morality and marriage, 16–067—16–075
injurious to proper working of justice, 16–035—16–066
objects illegal by common law or statute, 16–014—16–018
restraint of trade, 16–075—16–141
scope, 16–005—16–013
compromise, 16–013
concealment of crime, 16–035—16–038
conflict of laws
applicable law, under, 30–356
English law, under, 30–357
generally, 30–355
other foreign law, under, 30–365
place of performance of act, in, 30–358—30–364
costs, 16–200
domestic affairs, objects injurious to
assignment of pay, 16–022
negligent performance of duty, 16–023
procurement of benefits, 16–024
procurement of honours, 16–021
sale of public contracts, 16–019—16–020
sale of public office, 16–019—16–020
withdrawal of opposition to Bill, 16–025
effect
formation, 16–008
generally, 1–005, 16–007
performance, 16–009—16–012
enforcement of illegal transactions
benefits from crime, 16–168—16–175
collateral transactions, 16–176
ex turpi causa, 16–164—16–167
recovery of payments or property, 16–177—16–193
ex turpi causa non oritur actio
generally, 16–164
limitations, 16–167
tainted contracts, 16–165—16–166
foreign affairs, objects injurious to
contrary to foreign country's policy, 16–028
illegal under foreign law, 16–027, 16–031—16–034
legal foreign contract illegal under English law, 16–029—16–030
trading with the enemy, 16–026, 16–162—16–163
formation, as to, 16–008
fraud, 16–186
fraudulent misrepresentation, 6–066

Illegality—*cont.*
good government, objects injurious to
domestic affairs, 16–019—16–025
foreign affairs, 16–026—16–34
illegally performed contracts,
16–157—16–159
in pari delicto potior est conditio defendentis, 16–177
insolvency agreements
bankruptcy, 16–042
winding-up, 16–041
interference with course of justice
collusive divorce agreements,
16–043
generally, 16–039
insolvency agreements,
16–041—16–042
procurement of pardon, 16–040
introduction, 16–001—16–002
locus poenitentiae
advancement, 16–182—16–184
frustration, 16–190
generally, 16–188
performance, 16–189
maintenance agreements, 16–044
maintenance and champerty
effect, 16–053
generally, 16–048—16–049
justification, 16–051—16–052
meaning, 16–050
manner of performance, 16–153
marriage brokerage contracts
generally, 16–071
recovery of payments, 16–191
marriage, objects injurious to
brokerage contract, 16–071
contract to restrain marriage, 16–072
promise by married person, 16–070
surrender of parental responsibility,
16–074
money paid, recovery of
agents, from, 16–192
fraud, 16–186
generally, 16–177
in pari delicto, 16–185
locus poenitentiae, 16–182—16–184,
16–188—16–190
marriage brokerage contracts,
16–191
mistake, 16–187
oppression, 16–186
trustees, by, 16–193
morality
cohabitation, 16–067—16–068
prostitution, 16–069
will revocation, 16–074
objects illegal by common law or
statute
evasion of obligations, 16–015
crime, 16–014

Illegality—*cont.*
objects illegal by common law or
statute—*cont.*
fraudulent intent, 16–017
torts, 16–018
waiver of rights, 16–016
objects injurious to domestic affairs
assignment of pay, 16–022
negligent performance of duty,
16–023
procurement of benefits, 16–024
procurement of honours, 16–021
sale of public contracts,
16–019—16–020
sale of public office,
16–019—16–020
withdrawal of opposition to Bill,
16–025
objects injurious to foreign affairs
contrary to foreign country's policy,
16–028
illegal under foreign law, 16–027,
16–031—16–034
legal foreign contract illegal under
English law, 16–029—16–030
trading with the enemy, 16–026,
16–162—16–163
objects injurious to good government
domestic affairs, 16–019—16–025
foreign affairs, 16–026—16–34
objects injurious to marriage
brokerage contract, 16–071
contract to restrain marriage, 16–072
promise by married person, 16–070
surrender of parental responsibility,
16–074
objects injurious to morality
cohabitation, 16–067—16–068
prostitution, 16–069
will revocation, 16–074
objects injurious to proper working of
justice
champertous agreements, 16–048,
16–054—16–066
concealment of crime,
16–035—16–038
interference with course of justice,
16–039—16–043
maintenance of litigation agreements,
16–048—16–053
ouster of jurisdiction,
16–044—16–047
oppression, 16–186
ouster of jurisdiction
arbitration, 16–045—16–047
maintenance agreements, 16–044
parental responsibility, surrender
16–074
performance, as to
both parties ignorant of law, 16–012

Illegality—*cont.*
performance, as to—*cont.*
both parties know of objectionable features, 16–010
generally, 16–009
one party knows of objectionable features, 16–011
place of performance of act, in, 30–358—30–364
pleading 16–205
proper working of justice, objects injurious to
champertous agreements, 16–048, 16–054—16–066
concealment of crime, 16–035—16–038
interference with course of justice, 16–039—16–043
maintenance of litigation agreements, 16–048—16–053
ouster of jurisdiction, 16–044—16–047
public policy
generally, 16–003—16–004
scope, 16–005—16–013
recovery of property transferred
fraud, 16–186
generally, 16–178
limited interests, 16–179—16–181
locus poenitentiae, 16–182—16–184, 16–188—16–190
oppression, 16–186
repayments
agents, from, 16–192
fraud, 16–186
generally, 16–177
in pari delicto, 16–185
locus poenitentiae, 16–182—16–184, 16–188—16–190
marriage brokerage contracts, 16–191
mistake, 16–187
oppression, 16–186
trustees, by, 16–193
restraint of marriage, 16–072
restraint of trade
And see **Restraint of trade**
employer-employee, 16–104—16–115
horizontal agreements, 16–132—16–140
land or chattels, 16–128—16–131
partners, 16–119—16–120
scope, 16–075—16–103
statutory regulation, 16–141
vendor-purchaser, 16–116—16–118
vertical agreements, 16–121—16–127
severance
association's rules, 16–200

Illegality—*cont.*
severance—*cont.*
generally, 16–194—16–195
part of the consideration, 16–201
principles, 16–196—16–198
public policy, 16–202
restraint of trade, 16–199, 16–203
statute, under
aids to interpretation, 16–147—16–152
change of law, 16–161
generally, 16–142—16–146
illegally performed contracts, 16–157—16–159
manner of performance, 16–153
trading with the enemy, 16–162—16–163
unlicensed transactions, 16–154—16–155
unregistered contracts, 16–156
trading with the enemy
common law, at, 16–026
statute, under, 16–162—16–163
unlicensed transactions
consumer credit, 16–155
generally, 16–154
unregistered contracts, 16–156
validity of document, evidence 12–112
winding-up, 16–041
"Illegitimate pressure"
actual undue influence
causation, 7–068
disregard of victim's interests, 7–067
generally, 7–064
independent and informed judgment, 7–065—7–066
consideration, 7–019
duress of goods
causation, 7–026
generally 7–012
duress of person
causation, 7–025
generally, 7–011
economic duress
causation, 7–027—7–033
consideration, 7–019
different approaches, 7–021—7–023
generally, 7–014—7–018
legitimacy of the demand, 7–037—7–044
non-contractual payments, 7–020
effect, 7–009
generally, 7–008
Illiteracy
And see **Capacity of parties**
generally, 8–001
Illness
See **Ill health**
"Illusory consideration"
discretionary performance, 3–025

"Illusory consideration"—*cont.*
generally, 3–023
intended forbearance, 3–024
"Immaterial alterations"
discharge, 25–023
"Immovables"
conflict of laws
formal validity of contract, 30–314
no choice of law by parties, 30–082—30–084
Immunity from suit
ambassadors, 11–008—11–009
consular staff
generally, 11–017
waiver, 11–022
diplomatic staff
And see **Diplomatic immunity**
certificate of entitlement, 11–015
generally, 11–008—11–009
period of immunity, 11–014
relevant persons, 11–010—11–013
restrictions, 11–016
waiver, 11–022
foreign heads of state, 11–008—11–009
foreign sovereigns
common law, at, 11–001
human rights, 11–003
statute, under, 11–002—11–007
waiver, 11–020
foreign states
act of state, 11–007
common law, at, 11–001
human rights, 11–003
statute, under, 11–002—11–006
waiver, 11–020
heads of state, 11–008—11–009
international organisations
generally, 11–018
specialised agencies, 11–019
waiver, 11–023
sovereigns heads
common law, at, 11–001
human rights, 11–003
statute, under, 11–002—11–007
waiver, 11–020
waiver of
common law, at, 11–020
consular staff, 11–022
diplomatic staff, 11–022
international organisations, 11–023
statute, under, 11–021
Implied contracts
generally, 1–076
restitution
generally, 29–011
historical background, 29–007—29–009
Implied terms
contracts for sale of land
fitness for habitation, 13–015
generally, 13–031
contractual discretion, and, 13–026
custom, by
collective agreements, 13–019
course of dealing, 13–022
generally, 13–018
human rights, 13–020
method of dealing, 13–021
discharge under contract, 22–054
discretion, and, 13–026
duration of contract, 13–027
employment contracts, 13–019
express terms, 13–023
fitness for habitation
leases, 13–016
sale of land, 13–015
generally, 13–002
hire purchase, 13–029
leases
fitness for habitation, 13–016
licences, 13–028
multiple occupation housing
access, 13–017
nature, 13–001
occupation of premises
duty of care, 13–014
package holidays, 13–034
proper law
And see **Conflict of laws**
generally, 30–010
relevant factors, 30–010—30–011
purpose
completion of contract, 13–008
co-operation, 13–011
efficacy, 13–005—13–006
generally, 13–003
intention, 13–004
necessity, 13–009—13–010
obvious inference, 13–007
prevention of performance, 13–012
recitals, 13–024—13–025
sale of land
fitness for habitation, 13–015
generally, 13–031
supply of goods
debt payment, 13–035
generally, 13–030
supply of services, 13–032—13–033
trade usage, by
collective agreements, 13–019
course of dealing, 13–022
generally, 13–018
human rights, 13–020
method of dealing, 13–021
travel, 13–034
Impossibility
anticipatory breach, 24–030—24–031

Impossibility—*cont.*
consideration, 3–023
frustration
generally, 24–033
introduction, 23–001
generally, 24–028
nature
anticipatory breach, 24–030—24–031
non-cooperation, 24–032
renunciation, 24–029
specific performance, 27–041
Imprisonment
frustration, 23–039
Improvements
restitution
defendant's acquiescence, 29–161
In loco parentis
presumed undue influence, 7–075
"*In pari delicto potior est conditio defendentis*"
generally, 16–177
recovery of payments, 16–185
"In principle agreements"
generally, 2–112
"Inactivity"
offer, 2–006
Incapacity
See **Capacity**
"Incentive clauses"
damages, 26–139
Income tax
damages
generally, 26–157
loss of profits, 26–163
mixed receipts, 26–165
salvage services, 26–164
wrongful dismissal, 26–158—26–162
Incompatibility
liability arising during contractual term, 1–152—1–153
Incomplete agreements
continued operation of agreements, 2–115
contract to make contract
agreements to negotiate, 2–136—2–138
contract to execute document with agreed terms, 2–135
generally, 2–134
facts to be ascertained, 2–133
in principle, 2–112
lack of detail, 2–113—2–114
letters of comfort, 2–125
letters of intent, 2–125
options, 2–127
pre-emption rights, 2–127
subject to contract
And see **Subject to contract**
Incomplete agreements—*cont.*
subject to contract—*cont.*
exchange of contracts, 2–119—2–123
generally, 2–118
subject to execution of formal document
generally, 2–116
insurance agreements, 2–117
subsequently completed agreements, 2–124
terms to be agreed
determination criteria, 2–130—2–132
generally, 2–126—2–129
"Inconsistent clauses"
construction of terms, 12–078—12–079
"Inconsistent use"
construction of terms, 12–055
Inconvenience
damages, 26–082
Incorporation (contract terms)
course of dealing, by, 12–011
exemption clauses, 14–002
form of notices
generally, 12–017
statutory provision, 12–018
generally, 12–008
notices of
contents 12–013
form 12–017—12–018
sufficiency 12–014—12–016
proper law
And see **Conflict of laws**
generally, 30–009
relevant documents, 12–009
sufficiency of notices
generally, 12–014
onerous conditions 12–015
personal disability, 12–016
unusual conditions, 12–015
time, 12–010
trade custom, by, 12–012
"*Indebitatus assumpsit*"
restitution, 29–006
Indemnities
limitation of actions, 28–049
payment to third person, 29–120
Independent advice
presumed undue influence
adequacy, 7–096
generally, 7–095
unconscionable bargains, 7–134
undue influence by third party, 7–115—7–116
"Independent promise"
partial performance, 21–038
"Index-linking"
payment, 21–072
Inducing breach of contract
See **Procuring breach of contract**

Inequality of bargaining power
generally, 7–139
Infants
And see **Minors**
capacity
agency, 8–058—8–060
beneficial contracts, 8–021—8–029
binding contracts, 8–007—8–020
disposal of property, 8–065—8–067
generally, 8–002—8–006
parental liability, 8–061
restitution, 8–048—8–057
tortious liability, 8–046—8–047
voidable contracts, 8–030—8–045
consideration, 3–166
limitation of actions, 28–074—28–080
"Informal contracts"
generally, 1–075
"Informal gratuitous promises"
consideration, 3–002
Injunctions
compensation
generally, 27–063
statutory right, 27–062
conflict of laws, 30–338
contract for benefit of third party
promise not to compete, 18–069
promise not to sue, 18–070—18–071
Crown contracts, 10–019
damages
assessment of damages, 27–079
generally, 27–077—27–078
introduction, 26–004
limits, 27–084
express negative promises
non-personal services, 27–067
personal services, 27–064—27–066
restraint of trade, 27–068—27–069
implied negative promises
expulsion from associations, 27–072
generally, 27–070—27–071
interim, 27–061
limitation of actions, 28–018
negative contracts
compensation adequate, 27–062—27–063
generally, 27–060—27–061
personal services contracts, 27–064—27–067
refusal to contract
aiding and abetting a breach of injunction, 27–076
discrimination, 27–074
generally, 27–073
rules of trade association, 27–075
restraint of trade covenants
generally, 16–102, 27–068—27–069
interlocutory, 16–103
severable contracts, 27–069
Injury to feelings
generally, 26–083
introduction, 1–123
Innocent misrepresentation
damages
discretion, 6–102
generally, 6–094, 6–096
introduction, 1–133
measure, 6–099—6–101
restrictions, 6–097—6–098
estoppel, 6–095
generally, 1–131—1–132
measure of damages
bad bargains, 6–101
consequential loss, 6–100
generally, 6–099
rescission, 6–097—6–098
Innominate terms
classification
generally, 12–035
sale of goods transactions, 12–036
time stipulations, 12–037
conclusion, 12–040
effect
failure to perform on time, 12–038
force majeure clauses, 12–039
express terms, 12–036
generally, 12–020
meaning, 12–034
Insolvency
And see **Bankruptcy**
And see **Winding-up**
interference with course of justice
bankruptcy, 16–042
winding-up, 16–041
limitation of actions, 28–070
Insufficient delivery
See **Short delivery**
Insurance contracts
applicable law, 30–045—30–046
classification, 1–069
conflict of laws, 30–045—30–046
contract for benefit of third party
fire insurance, 18–129
life insurance, 18–126
marine insurance, 18–128
Motor Insurers' Bureau claims, 18–131
motor insurance, 18–127
persons with limited interest, 18–128
solicitors' indemnity insurance, 18–130
contribution, 29–128
exemption clauses, 14–119
fire insurance, 18–129
limitation of actions, 28–050
marine insurance, 18–128
misrepresentation
burden of proof, 6–150
continuing duty, 6–151

Insurance contracts—*cont.*
misrepresentation—*cont.*
introduction, 6–144
materiality, 6–145—6–149
statutory provisions, 6–152
motor insurance, 18–127
persons with limited interest, 18–128
Rome I Regulation, and
background, 30–252
compulsory insurance, 30–275
event in one member State, 30–270
exclusions, and, 30–163, 30–255
large risks, 30–260—30–264
life assurance, 30–269
"member State", 30–258
other insurance contracts, 30–265—30–275
reinsurance, 30–256
scope, 30–254
situs of risk, 30–257—30–259
structure of Article, 30–253
unjust enrichment, 29–082
Intellectual property rights
unfair contract terms, 14–105
"Intelligible language"
unfair contract terms (consumer contracts)
non-compliance, 15–091—15–092
relevant terms, 15–033
test, 15–089—15–090
Intention to create legal relations
agreements giving effect to pre-existing rights, 2–180
agreements made in anger, 2–185—2–189
agreements made in jest, 2–185—2–189
burden of proof
express commercial agreements, 2–159
conduct, 2–160
civil servants, 2–182
clergy, 2–181
collective agreements, 2–177
construction of terms
additions, 12–076
generally, 12–043—12–044, 12–072
grammatical errors, 12–080
inconsistent clauses, 12–078—12–079
modifications, 12–075
rejections, 12–077
reliance upon own breach, 12–082
repugnant clauses, 12–078
restrictions, 12–073
saving, 12–081
transpositions, 12–074
consumer guarantees, 2–167
discretion
performance, as to, 2–175
Intention to create legal relations—*cont.*
discretion—*cont.*
rescission, as to, 2–176
domestic agreements
adults sharing, between, 2–172—2–173
children and parents, between, 2–174
civil partners, between, 2–170
cohabitants, between, 2–171
introduction, 2–168
spouses, between, 2–169
free passes, 2–178
generally, 2–158
giving effect to pre-existing rights, 2–180
goodwill agreements, 2–186
government policy statements, 2–179
impliedly negatived, 2–164
jest and jokes, and, 2–185—2–189
mere representations, 2–166
nature of relationship
civil servants, 2–182
clergy, 2–181
police constables, 2–183
pre-existing rights, and, 2–180
puffs, 2–165
sham agreements, 2–186
social and domestic agreements
adults sharing, between, 2–172—2–173
children and parents, between, 2–174
civil partners, between, 2–170
cohabitants, between, 2–171
introduction, 2–168
spouses, between, 2–169
statements inducing contracts
mere representations, 2–166
puffs, 2–165
tests
negative expression, 2–162—2–163
objective, 2–161
vague agreements, 2–184
Intentional torts
enforcement against third parties, 18–144
Interest
Admiralty cases, 26–171
applicable law
exchange losses, 30–340
generally, 30–339
statutory, 30–341—30–344
arbitration awards, 26–183—26–184
commercial debts, on
generally, 26–172
late payment, 26–182
period, 26–173
rate, 26–173
common law, at, 26–168—26–170

Interest—*cont.*
damages
Admiralty cases, 26–171
arbitration awards, 26–183—26–184
commercial debts, 26–172, 26–182
common law, at, 26–167—26–170
introduction, 26–167
judgment debts, 26–184
right, as 26–182
statute, under, 26–173—26–182
debts, on
commercial debts, 26–172—26–173
generally, 26–174—26–184
exemption clauses, 14–130
foreign currency, in
exchange rates, 26–181
generally, 26–180
judgment debts, 26–184
late payment of commercial debts, 26–182
right, as 26–182
statute, under
applicable law, 30–341—30–344
exercise of discretion, 26–175
foreign currency, in, 26–180—26–181
generally, 26–174
late payment of commercial debts, 26–182
period, 26–176—26–177
rate, 26–178—26–179
Interests in land
see **Proprietary interests**
And see **Sale of land**
Interference with goods
restitution, 29–015
"Interfering with the course of justice"
collusive divorce agreements, 16–043
generally, 16–039
insolvency agreements
bankruptcy, 16–042
winding-up, 16–041
procurement of pardon, 16–040
Interim injunctions
generally, 27–061
Interim remedies
Crown contracts, 10–017
"Intermediate terms"
classification
generally, 12–035
sale of goods transactions, 12–036
time stipulations, 12–037
conclusion, 12–040
effect
failure to perform on time, 12–038
force majeure clauses, 12–039
express terms, 12–036
generally, 12–020
meaning, 12–034
International carriage by air
remoteness of damage, 26–089—26–090
"International conventions"
unfair contract terms, 14–111
International organisations
immunity from suit
generally, 11–018
specialised agencies, 11–019
waiver, 11–023
International relations
objects injurious to foreign affairs
contrary to foreign country's policy, 16–028
illegal under foreign law, 16–027, 16–031—16–034
legal foreign contract illegal under English law, 16–029—16–030
trading with the enemy, 16–026, 16–162—16–163
"International supply contracts"
unfair contract terms, 14–110
Interpretation
absurd use, 12–055
additions, 12–076
ambiguity
Crown contracts, 12–086
evidence, 12–125
generally, 12–083—12–085
badly drafted contracts, 12–056
Community directives, 12–054
contra proferentem, 14–009
custom, 12–058—12–059
draft documents, 12–069
ejusdem generis
common category, 12–088
generally, 12–087
use, 12–089—12–090
electronic documents, 12–048
equivocation, 12–124
established judicial construction, 12–053
evidence of
ambiguity, 12–125
conflict of laws, 30–331
equivocation, 12–124
generally, 12–117
identity of parties, 12–122
special meaning of words, 12–121
subject-matter, 12–123
subsequent acts, 12–126
surrounding circumstances, 12–118—12–120
exemption clauses
ambiguity, 14–005
burden of proof, 14–018—14–019
contra proferentem, 14–009
deliberate breach, 14–016—14–017
generally, 14–005—14–006, 14–025
inconsistency, 14–008

Interpretation—*cont*.
exemption clauses—*cont*.
indemnity, 14–015
negligence, 14–010—14–014
purpose of contract, 14–007—14–008
grammatical errors, 12–080
human rights, 12–049
identity of parties, 12–122
inconsistency, 14–008
inconsistent clauses, 12–078—12–079
inconsistent use, 12–055
intention of parties
additions, 12–076
generally, 12–043—12–044, 12–072
grammatical errors, 12–080
inconsistent clauses, 12–078—12–079
modifications, 12–075
rejections, 12–077
reliance upon own breach, 12–082
repugnant clauses, 12–078
restrictions, 12–073
saving, 12–081
transpositions, 12–074
introduction
generally, 12–041
intention, 12–043—12–044
method, 12–046
principles, 12–045
purpose, 12–042
legislation
background, 1–037—1–038
examples, 1–049
generally, 1–044
unenforceable contractual rights, 1–045
mercantile contracts, 12–057
method, 12–046—12–046
modifications, 12–075
ordinary meaning of words
absurd use, 12–055
badly drafted contracts, 12–056
Community directives, 12–054
custom, 12–058—12–059
established judicial construction, 12–053
general words, 12–062
generally, 12–050—12–051
inconsistent use, 12–055
mercantile contracts, 12–057
technical words, 12–052
principles, 12–045
purpose, 12–042
reference to draft documents, by, 12–069
reference to purpose of contract, by
alterations, 12–069
deletions, 12–069
draft documents, 12–069

Interpretation—*cont*.
reference to purpose of contract, by—*cont*.
figures, 12–071
generally, 12–063—12–065
printed documents, 12–070
recitals, 12–066
several documents, 12–067
supplemental documents, 12–068
reference to several documents, by, 12–067
reference to supplemental documents, by, 12–068
repugnant clauses, 12–078
restrictions, 12–091—12–092
restraint of trade, 16–097
several documents, 12–067
special meaning of words
evidence, 12–121
generally, 12–060
statutory definitions, 12–061
subject-matter, 12–123
subsequent acts, 12–126
supplemental documents, 12–068
surrounding circumstances, 12–118—12–120
technical words, 12–052
time stipulations, 12–093—12–094
transpositions, 12–074
"Intervening acts"
plaintiff, by, 26–037—26–039
third party, by, 26–034—26–036
Intervening events
damages, 26–040—26–041
"Intervening omissions"
damages, 26–037—26–039
Intervention
acting in public interest, 29–132
analogous categories, 29–133
generally, 29–131
necessaries, 29–135
non-gratuitous, 29–134
reasonableness, 29–134
Intimidation
pre-contractual liability, 1–135
privity of contract, 18–040—18–041
three-party, 1–172
Intoxication
effect, 1–082
Intoxicated persons
generally, 8–080
necessaries, liability for, 8–081
"Invalid claims"
forbearance to sue
generally, 3–050
good faith, made in, 3–052—3–053
"Invasion of property interest"
depriving defendant of profit, 26–023
Invitation to treat
distinction from offer, 2–010

Invitation to treat—*cont.*
generally, 2–007—2–008
menus, 2–016
self-service goods
exceptional cases, 2–015
general rule, 2–014
wording inconclusive, 2–009
"Invoicing back clauses"
damages, 26–144
"Irrevocable credits"
acceptance, 2–082
consideration, 3–182
Issue estoppel
exceptional circumstances, 25–014
foreign judgments *in personam*, 25–018
generally, 25–011
requirements, 25–012
scope, 25–013

"Jest"
intention to create legal relations, 2–185—2–189
Joinder
See **Addition of parties**
Joint and several liability
And see **Joint obligations**
generally, 17–005—17–006
meaning, 17–003
"Joint contractors"
contribution, 29–124
Joint creditors
payment, 21–049
Joint debtors
contribution, 17–027
Joint liability
accord and satisfaction
generally, 22–019
introduction, 17–017
alteration of document, 17–022
bankruptcy, 17–024
contract by person with himself, 17–007
contribution between joint debtors
amount, 17–031
assessment, 17–034
damage, 17–029—17–030
effect of judgment, 17–032
generally, 17–027—17–028
limitations of action, 17–033
limits on right, 17–035
covenant not to sue, 17–017—17–020
death
joint contractor, 17–012
joint and several contractor, 17–013
discharge
accord and satisfaction, 17–017
performance, 17–014
release, 17–017—17–020
generally, 17–005

Joint liability—*cont.*
introduction, 17–001—17–004
joinder of parties
generally, 17–009
relevant persons, 17–010—17–011
judgments
joint debtors, against, 17–015
joint and several debtors, against, 17–016
limitation of actions
contribution, 17–033
generally, 17–026
meaning, 17–002
minors, 17–008
release
generally, 22–007
introduction, 17–017—17–020
severance, 17–006
sureties, 17–021
voluntary arrangements with creditors, 17–025
"Joint obligations"
And see **Joint liability**
generally, 17–005
meaning, 17–002
"Jointly owned homes"
undue influence by third party, 7–123
Judgments and orders
limitation of actions, 28–016
merger
estoppel, 25–011—25–014
foreign, 25–016—25–019
generally, 25–007—25–008
ineffective, 25–0014
interest, 25–009
relevant judgments, 25–010
Judgment debts
interest, 26–184
Justice, objects injurious to proper working of
See **Objects injurious to proper working of justice**

Laches
applicable law, 30–348
limitation of actions, 28–137—28–138
Land
See **Contracts for sale of land**
See **Real property**
Language
And see **Capacity of parties**
lack of familiarity with, 8–001
"Lapse of time"
rescission, 6–127—6–128
termination of offer
conduct, 2–097
reasonable period, 2–096
specified period, 2–095
undue influence, 7–097

"Last shot doctrine"
'battle of the forms', 2–037
Lasting powers of attorney
And see **Powers of attorney**
capacity, 8–078
Latent damage
limitation of actions, 28–010—28–013
Law Commission
Privity of Contract: Contracts for the Benefit of Third Parties (No. 242, 1996)
generally, 18–001
introduction, 1–002
movement of consideration, 3–045
Law of Property Act 1925, s.40
agents' signature
estate agent, 4–037
for both parties, 4–038
generally, 4–036
consideration, 4–025
form of contracts
consideration, 4–025
generally, 4–022
parties, 4–023
signature, 4–031—4–040
subject-matter, 4–024
terms, 4–026
generally, 4–010
lost documents, and, 4–030
non-compliance
part performance, 4–042—4–050
proprietary estoppel, 4–051
statute, under, 4–041
parol evidence, 4–029
part performance
effect of acts, 4–050
generally, 4–042—4–043
required acts, 4–044—4–049
parties, 4–023
proprietary estoppel, 4–051
purpose for which document prepared, 4–027
relevant dispositions and interests
building materials, 4–019
collateral agreements, 4–016
entire agreement clauses, 4–017
fixtures, 4–020
generally, 4–011—4–014
growing crops, 4–018
minerals, 4–019
shooting rights, 4–021
things to be detached from land, 4–019
variation of contracts, 4–015
several documents, and, 4–028—4–029
signature
agent, by, 4–036—4–039
alterations, 4–035
form, 4–034
generally, 4–031
Law of Property Act 1925, s.40—*cont.*
signature—*cont.*
intention, 4–033
position, 4–032
subject-matter, 4–024
terms, 4–026
variation, 4–015
Law of Property (Miscellaneous Provisions) Act 1989, s.2
boundary agreements between neighbours, 4–057
collateral contracts, 4–076
composite agreements, 4–067
compromises, 4–065
conditions in planning agreements, 4–061
equitable leases, 4–060
equitable mortgages, 4–059
estoppel
convention, by, 4–079
generally, 4–078
promissory estoppel, 4–083
proprietary estoppel, 4–080—4–082
exchange of contracts, 4–071
excluded interests, 4–068
executed contracts, 4–084
form of contracts
generally, 4–069
signature, 4–072—4–074
terms, 4–070—4–071
generally, 4–052—4–053
'lock-out' agreements, 4–062
mutual wills, 4–063
non-compliance
collateral contracts, 4–076
constructive trusts, 4–077
estoppel, 4–078—4–083
executed contracts, 4–084
generally, 4–075
restitution, 4–084—4–088
options, 4–058
Part 36 settlements, 4–065
partnerships, 4–066
proceeds of sale of land, 4–064
promissory estoppel, 4–083
proprietary estoppel, 4–080—4–082
relevant dispositions and interests
boundary agreements between neighbours, 4–057
composite agreements, 4–067
compromises, 4–065
conditions in planning agreements, 4–061
equitable leases, 4–060
equitable mortgages, 4–059
generally, 4–054—4–055
'lock-out' agreements, 4–062
mutual wills, 4–063
options, 4–058
Part 36 settlements, 4–065

Law of Property (Miscellaneous Provisions) Act 1989, s.2—*cont.*
relevant dispositions and interests—*cont.*
partnerships, 4–066
proceeds of sale of land, 4–064
variation of contracts, 4–056
restitution, 4–084—4–088
signature
agent, by, 4–074
generally, 4–072
meaning, 4–073
'subject to contract', 4–053
variation, 4–056
"Lay corporations"
And see **Companies**
generally, 9–001
Leases
See also **Tenancies**
frustration
consequences, 23–056
destruction of building, 23–053
generally, 23–052
interruption of use, 23–055
prohibition on use, 23–054
implied terms
fitness for habitation, 13–016
minors, 8–033—8–035
remoteness of damage, 26–091—26–097
restraint of trade, 16–129
specific performance
agreements for, 27–040
generally, 27–047—27–048
introduction, 27–007
Legacies
statute-barred debt, 28–130
Legal advice
undue influence by third party, 7–115—7–116
Letters (acceptance)
application of rule
dictated communications, 2–051
generally, 2–049
instant communications, 2–050
exclusion of rule, 2–052
general rule
application, 2–049—2–051
exclusion, 2–052
introduction, 2–048
operation, 2–053—2–061
operation of rule
delayed letter, 2–055—2–056
first acceptor, 2–057
garbled messages, 2–059
generally, 2–053
lost letter, 2–055—2–056
misdirected letter, 2–058
uncommunicated withdrawal, 2–054
revocation, 2–060—2–061
Letters of comfort
See **Letters of intent**
Letters of intent
generally, 2–125
Licences
implied terms, 13–028
Liens
statute-barred debt, 28–034
Life insurance
contract for benefit of third party, 18–126
suicide, 16–171
Limit of liability
damages
charterparties, 26–143
generally, 26–142
unfair contract terms, 14–087
unfair contract terms (consumer contracts), 15–030
Limitation of actions
abridgement of period
agreements, by, 28–112
arbitration agreements, in, 28–115
exemption clauses, 28–113
statutory periods, 28–114
account stated, 28–129
acknowledgment of debt
effect, 28–103
exclusions, 28–104
form, 28–094
general rule, 28–093
introduction, 28–092
nature, 28–095
parties, 28–100—28–102
pleading, 28–105
acquiescence, 28–136
agreements of the parties not to plead the statute
estoppel, 28–109
generally, 28–107—28–108
introduction, 28–106
terms, 28–110
alien enemies, 11–031
applicable law, 30–347—30–348
appropriation of debt, 28–128
arbitration awards
date from which time runs, 28–059—28–060
relevant period, 28–017
running of time, 28–067
banker-customer relationship, 28–039
breach of trust
relevant period, 28–019
running of time, 28–057
building contracts, 28–054—28–055
carriage by air, 28–024
carriage by rail
relevant period, 28–025
running of time, 28–068

Limitation of actions—*cont.*
carriage by road
relevant period, 28–026
running of time, 28–068
carriage by sea, 28–022—28–023
commencement of proceedings
arbitral proceedings, 28–125
legal proceedings, 28–116—28–124
companies, 28–004
computation of period
commencement date, 28–062
termination date, 28–063
concealment
agent, 28–087
date from which time runs, 28–058
generally, 28–084—28–086
introduction, 28–081
concurrent liability, 28–033
continuing breach, 28–035
contribution
relevant period, 28–015
running of time, 28–051
counterclaims, 28–122—28–123
date from which time runs
arbitration awards, 28–059—28–060
banker-customer relationship, 28–039
building contracts, 28–054—28–055
burden of proof, 28–061
concurrent liability, 28–035
continuing breach, 28–035
contribution, 28–051
defective premises, 28–056
fiduciary duty, breach 28–057
fraud, 28–058
generally, 28–031—28–032
guarantees, 28–046—28–048
indemnities, 28–049
insurance, 28–050
loan of money, 28–036—28–038
misrepresentation, 28–034
mistake, 28–058
negotiable instruments, 28–041—28–045
overdraft, 28–040
sale of goods, 28–052
successive breach, 28–035
supply of services, 28–053
deduction from legacies, 28–130
deeds, 1–116
defective premises, 28–056
defences, 28–122—28–123
delay
awareness of facts, 28–140
generally, 28–139
mere delay, 28–142
prejudice to defendant, 28–141
discharge, 25–032
effect, 28–126—28–133
employment, 28–028—28–030

Limitation of actions—*cont.*
equitable remedies
acquiescence, 28–136
generally, 28–134—28–135
laches, 28–137—28–138
rectification, 28–146
rescission, 28–144
setting aside voluntary settlements, 28–145
specific performance, 28–143
extension of period
acknowledgment of debt, 28–092—28–105
agreements, by, 28–106—28–111
concealment, 28–081—28–091
disability, 28–074—28–080
fraud, 28–081—28–091
generally, 28–071—28–073
mistake, 28–081—28–091
part payment of debt, 28–092—28–105
personal injury, 28–072
persons under disability, 28–074—28–080
specialty debts, 28–092—28–105
fatal accidents, 28–007—28–008
fiduciary duty, breach of
relevant period, 28–019
running of time, 28–057
fraud
agent, 28–087
date from which time runs, 28–058
generally, 28–082—28–083
introduction, 28–081
guarantees, 28–046—28–048
indemnities, 28–049
injunctions, 28–018
insurance, 28–050
introduction, 1–124, 1–167
joint liability
contribution, 17–033
generally, 17–026
judgment, 28–016
laches, 28–137—28–138
latent damage, 28–010—28–013
legacies, 28–130
loan of money
bank deposits, 28–039
generally, 28–036—28–038
overdrafts, 28–040
relevant period, 28–014
misrepresentation, 28–034
mistake
date from which time runs, 28–058
generally, 28–088
introduction, 28–081
negligence, 28–010—28–013
negotiable instruments, 28–041—28–044
negotiations, 28–111

Limitation of actions—*cont.*
overdraft, 28–040
part payment of debt
effect, 28–103
exclusions, 28–104
general rule, 28–093
introduction, 28–092
nature, 28–05—28–099
parties, 28–100—28–102
pleading, 28–105
pending proceedings
counterclaims in, 28–122—28–123
defences in, 28–122—28–123
new claims in, 28–118—28–121
third party claims in, 28–124
personal injury
relevant period, 28–006—28–008
running of time, 28–072
persons under disability, 28–074—28–080
pleading 28–107
product liability, 28–009
rectification, 28–146
relevant period
arbitration awards, 28–017
breach of trust, 28–019
carriage by air, 28–024
carriage by rail, 28–025
carriage by road, 28–026
carriage by sea, 28–022—28–023
companies, 28–004
contribution, 28–015
employment, 28–028—28–030
fatal accidents, 28–007—28–008
fiduciary duty, 28–019
generally, 28–001
injunctions, 28–018
judgment, 28–016
loans, 28–014
negligence, 28–010—28–013
personal injury, 28–006—28–008
product liability, 28–009
sale of goods, 28–027
salvage services, 28–021
simple contracts, 28–002
specialty debts, 28–003
specific performance, 28–018
third parties, 28–005
trust, breach of, 28–019
rescission, 28–144
retainer, 28–131
running of time
arbitration awards, 28–067
carriage of goods, 28–068
generally, 28–064
insolvency, 28–070
personal representatives, 28–065—28–066
war, during, 28–069
sale of goods, 28–027, 28–052

Limitation of actions—*cont.*
salvage services, 28–021
securities, 28–045
set-off, 28–122—28–123
setting aside voluntary settlements, 28–145
simple contracts, 28–002
specialty debts, 28–003
specific performance, 28–018, 28–143
successive breach, 28–035
supply of services, 28–053
third party claims, 28–124
trust, breach of
relevant period, 28–019
running of time, 28–057
trustee's expenses, 28–132
Limited liability partnerships
termination of offer, 2–109
"Liquidated claims"
part payment of debt, 3–120
Liquidated damages
generally, 26–010—26–011
penalty sums
And see **Penalty clauses**
fluctuating sums, 26–130
generally, 26–125—26–127
graduated sums, 26–135
minimum sums, 26–131
pre-estimate, 26–128—26–129
scope, 26–136—26–155
single sums, 26–132—26–134
unfair contract terms, 26–156
unfair contract terms, 26–012
Literacy
And see **Capacity of parties**
generally, 8–001
Loans
limitation of actions
date from which time runs, 28–036—28–040
relevant period, 28–014
minors, 8–020
remoteness of damage, 26–099
specific performance, 27–012
Lockout agreements
contracts for sale of land, 4–062
subject to contract, 2–121
"*Locus poenitentiae*"
advancement, 16–182—16–184
frustration, 16–190
generally, 16–188
performance, 16–189
Loss of amenity
damages, 26–084—26–085
Loss of chance
damages, 26–042—26–048
Loss of documents
bills of exchange
introduction, 21–080
material loss, 25–027

Loss of documents—*cont.*
discharge, 25–027
Loss of enjoyment
damages, 26–083
Loss of profits
remoteness of damage
carrier's liability, 26–070
seller's claim, 26–069
seller's liability, 26–066—26–068
Loss of reputation
generally, 26–086—26–087
introduction, 1–123
"Lost documents"
contracts for sale of land, 4–030
"Lost instruments"
introduction, 21–080
material loss, 25–027

Maintenance agreements
ouster of jurisdiction, 16–044
Maintenance and champerty
See **Champerty**
Managing directors
contract for term of years, 9–058
generally, 9–057
improper appointment, 9–059
"Manifest disadvantage"
And see **Undue influence**
generally, 7–060—7–063
transaction not explicable by ordinary motives, 7–086—7–092
Marine insurance
classification, 1–069
contract for benefit of third party, 18–128
misrepresentation
burden of proof, 6–150
continuing duty, 6–151
generally, 6–144
materiality, 6–145—6–149
statutory provisions, 6–152
Marriage
brokerage contracts
injurious objects, 16–071
recovery of payments, 16–191
illegality
brokerage contracts, 16–071
contract to restrain marriage, 16–072
promise by married person, 16–070
surrender of parental responsibility, 16–074
repayments, 16–191
"Marriage brokerage contracts"
illegality, 16–071
recovery of payments, 16–191
"Marriage settlements"
contract for benefit of third party, 18–087
minors, 8–036
rectification, 5–134
Married women
capacity
ante-nuptial contracts, 8–069
generally, 8–068
Married persons
See **Spouses**
"Material alterations"
bank notes, 25–025
burden of proof, 25–022
generally, 25–020—25–021
negotiable instruments, 25–024
"Material validity"
formation of contract, 30–306—30–307
generally, 30–304—30–305
validity of consent, 30–308
validity of terms, 30–309
Matrimonial home
bankruptcy, 20–036
undue influence, 7–105—7–123
Matrimonial proceedings
applicable law, 30–037
"Meaningless terms"
custom and trade usage, 2–144
Measure of damages
appeals, 26–030
fraudulent misrepresentation
entry into other losing transaction, 6–059
generally, 6–049
lost opportunity, 6–052
market value, 6–057—6–058
property value, 6–053—6–056
unforeseeable losses, 6–050—6–051
generally, 26–007
innocent misrepresentation
bad bargains, 6–101
consequential loss, 6–100
generally, 6–099
negligent misrepresentation, 6–070—6–071
time of assessment, 26–064—26–065
"Members' clubs"
election of members, 9–076—9–077
expulsion of members, 9–075
liability, 9–073
resignation of members, 9–078
status, 9–074
Members of companies
See **Shareholders**
Mental distress
generally, 26–083
introduction, 1–123
Mental patients
consideration, 3–166
termination of offer, 2–102
Mentally disordered persons
capacity
agency, 8–076
deeds, 8–071
evidence, 8–070

Mentally disordered persons—*cont.*
capacity—*cont.*
generally, 8–070—8–073
lasting powers of attorney, 8–078
necessaries, 8–074—8–075
statutory provisions, 8–077—8–079
lasting powers of attorney, 8–078
"Menus"
offer, 2–016
Mere puffs
See **Puffs**
"Mere representations"
intention, 2–166
Merger
collateral contracts, 25–002
contracts for sale of land
generally, 25–003
lessee, to, 25–004
deeds, 1–113
estoppel by judgment
exceptional circumstances, 25–014
foreign judgments, 25–018
generally, 25–011
requirements, 25–012
scope, 25–013
foreign judgments
generally, 25–016
in personam, 25–017—25–018
in rem, 25–019
generally, 25–001
ineffective judgments, 25–0014
judgments
estoppel, 25–011—25–014
foreign, 25–016—25–019
generally, 25–007—25–008
ineffective, 25–0014
interest, 25–009
relevant judgments, 25–010
personal representatives
creditor as debtor's, 25–006
debtor as creditor's, 25–005
sale of land
generally, 25–003
lessee, to, 25–004
Minerals
contracts for the sale of land, 4–019
Minimum wage
See **National minimum wage**
Minors
agency, 8–058—8–059
capacity
agency, 8–058—8–060
contractual liability, 8–007—8–045
disposal of property, 8–065—8–067
generally, 8–002—8–006
parental liability, 8–061
restitution, 8–048—8–057
tortious liability, 8–046—8–047
claim procedure
generally, 8–062
Minors—*cont.*
claim procedure—*cont.*
joint liability, 8–063
pleading, 8–064
consideration, 3–166
contractual liability
And see **Minors (contractual liability)**
beneficial contracts, 8–021—8–029
binding contracts, 8–007—8–020
generally, 8–004—8–005
voidable contracts, 8–030—8–045
deeds, 8–006
disposal of land, 8–067
disposal of property
delivery, by, 8–065
grant, by, 8–066
fraudulent misrepresentation of age
bankruptcy debt, 8–052
generally, 8–051
release from obligations, 8–053
transfer of property, 8–054—8–057
joint liability, 17–008
land disposal, 8–067
meaning
generally, 8–002
very young children, 8–003
membership of societies, 8–060
parental liability, 8–061
property disposal
delivery, by, 8–065
grant, by, 8–066
release from obligations, 8–053
restitution
common law, at, 8–049
equity, in, 8–050
fraudulent gains, 8–051—8–057
generally, 8–048
sale of land, 8–067
societies, 8–060
specific performance, 27–047
tortious liability, 8–046—8–047
transfer of property, 8–054—8–057
Minors (contractual liability)
apprenticeship contracts
generally, 8–022—8–023
rescission, 8–024
beneficial contracts
apprenticeship, 8–022—8–024
education, 8–027
employment, 8–025—8–026
generally, 8–021
binding contracts
apprenticeship contracts, 8–022—8–024
education contracts, 8–027
employment contracts, 8–025—8–026
generally, 8–004
necessaries, 8–007—8–020

Minors (contractual liability)—*cont.*
binding contracts—*cont.*
other analogous contracts, 8–029
contracts for necessaries
examples, 8–016—8–018
generally, 8–007
goods sold and delivered, 8–010—8–012
loans, 8–020
meaning, 8–008
nature, 8–009
services, 8–013—8–014
spouse's needs, 8–019
trading contracts, 8–017—8–018
contracts of apprenticeship
generally, 8–022—8–023
rescission, 8–024
contracts of employment
generally, 8–025
other analogous contracts, 8–029
restraint of trade covenants, 8–026
conveyances, 8–033
education contracts, 8–027
employment contracts
generally, 8–025
other analogous contracts, 8–029
restraint of trade covenants, 8–026
executory contracts, 8–011
lease of land, 8–033—8–035
loans, 8–020
marriage settlements, 8–036
mixed contracts, 8–015
necessaries
examples, 8–016—8–018
generally, 8–007
goods sold and delivered, 8–010—8–012
loans, 8–020
meaning, 8–008
nature, 8–009
services, 8–013—8–014
spouse's needs, 8–019
trading contracts, 8–017—8–018
partnerships, 8–039
purchase of land, 8–033—8–034
ratification
examples, 8–043
generally, 8–042
procedure, 8–044
repudiation
effect of avoidance, 8–040
generally, 8–030—8–032
lease of land, 8–033—8–035
marriage settlements, 8–036
partnerships, 8–039
purchase of land, 8–033—8–034
share purchases, 8–037—8–038
time of avoidance, 8–041
restraint of trade, 8–026
secured tenancies, 8–035

Minors (contractual liability)—*cont.*
share purchases, 8–037—8–038
statutory tenancies, 8–035
trading contracts, 8–017—8–018
voidable contracts
generally, 8–005
ratified, which must be, 8–042—8–045
repudiated, which may be, 8–030—8–041

Misfeasance
gratuitous services, 3–180—3–181

Misrepresentation
accord and satisfaction, 22–021
'but for' causation, 6–035
conduct
concealing facts, 6–016
generally, 6–015
constructive notice
effect, 6–025—6–026
pleading, 6–027
continuity 6–019
contract terms, and, 6–004
criminal fraud, and, 6–003
damages
And see **Damages**
fraudulent misrepresentation, 6–042—6–066
generally, 6–040
innocent misrepresentation, 6–094—6–102
introduction, 1–133
negligent misrepresentation, 6–067—6–093
preliminary, 6–041
effect
continuity, 6–019
generally, 6–001
introduction, 1–005
voidable, 1–082
exclusion of liability
common law, at, 6–134
'no reliance' clauses, 6–135
statute, under, 6–136—6–141
exclusion of liability under Misrepresentation Act, s.3
clauses covering breach, 6–140
introduction, 6–136
'no reliance' clauses, 6–138
reasonableness, 6–139
scope, 6–137
exemption clauses, and, 14–132
fraud, and, 6–003
generally, 6–001—6–005
guarantees, 6–158—6–161
inducement
burden of proof, 6–033
generally, 6–032
multiple causes, 6–034
presumption, 6–036

Misrepresentation—*cont.*
insurance contracts
burden of proof, 6–150
continuing duty, 6–151
introduction, 6–144
materiality, 6–145—6–149
statutory provisions, 6–152
intention, 6–030—6–031
introduction, 1–131—1–132
limitation of actions, 28–034
materiality, 6–037
Misrepresentation Act, s.3
clauses covering breach, 6–140
introduction, 6–136
'no reliance' clauses, 6–138
reasonableness, 6–139
scope, 6–137
nature
generally, 6–006
non-disclosure, 6–014—6–019
statements of fact, 6–007—6–012
statements of law, 6–013
'no reliance' clauses
generally, 6–135
s.3 Misrepresentation Act, 6–138
non-disclosure
conduct, 6–015—6–016
general rule, 6–014
partial non-disclosure, 6–017—6–019
uberrimae fidei, 6–142—6–164
partial non-disclosure
continuity of representations, 6–019
generally, 6–017
representation ceases to be true, 6–018
parties to
representees, 6–028—6–040
representors, 6–021—6–027
release, 22–010
remedies
damages, 6–041—6–102
generally, 6–039—6–040
rescission, 6–103—6–133
representees
'but for' causation, 6–035
generally, 6–028
inducement, 6–032—6–034
intention, 6–030—6–031
material misrepresentation, 6–036
materiality, 6–037
presumption of inducement, 6–036
tort actions, 6–029
unforeseeable reliance, 6–038
representors
agents, 6–021—6–027
generally, 6–021
third party, 6–022
rescission
generally, 6–103—6–109

Misrepresentation—*cont.*
rescission—*cont.*
introduction, 6–039
liable parties, 6–112
procedure, 6–110—6–111
restrictions, 6–115—6–133
specific performance, 27–045
statements of fact
exceptions, 6–007—6–012
general rule, 6–006
statements of intention
belief as to future, 6–012
generally, 6–007
honest belief, 6–010
implied representation, 6–011
statements of law, 6–013
statements of mixed fact and law, 6–013
statements of opinion
belief as to future, 6–012
generally, 6–007
implied representation, 6–009
not honestly held, 6–008
sureties, 6–158—6–161
uberimae fidei contracts
contracts for sale of land, 6–156—6–157
family settlements, 6–155
general releases, 6–164
generally, 6–142—6–143
insurance contracts, 6–144—6–152
joint ventures, 6–163
partnership, 6–162
share subscription contracts, 6–153—6–154
sureties, 6–158—6–161
unfair commercial practices, and, 6–002

Mistake
accord and satisfaction, 22–021
common law, at, 5–010—5–011
common mistake
Bell v Lever Bros, 5–028—5–032
construction of the contract, 5–064—5–065
equity, in, 5–057—5–063
generally, 5–001
introduction, 5–017
misrepresentation, 5–015
mistakes as to law, 5–054—5–056
modern doctrine, 5–033—5–053
pre-*Bell v Lever Bros* position, 5–018—5–027
summary, 5–064—5–065
communication, in
introduction, 5–001
mutual misunderstanding, 5–071—5–073
underlying principles, 5–066—5–070
unilateral mistake, 5–074—5–100

Mistake—*cont.*
duress, 7–007
effects
generally, 5–009
introduction, 1–005
equity, in, 5–010—5–011
facts, as to, 5–005
fact, of
And see **Mistake of fact**
generally, 29–028—29–039
frustration, 23–002
identity, as to
face-to-face dealings, 5–092—5–093
inter praesentes, 5–096—5–097
introduction, 5–088
person, 5–089—5–091
reform proposals, 5–100
third parties, 5–098—5–099
written contract, where, 5–094—5–095
illegality, 16–187
introduction, 5–001—5–012
law, of
And see **Mistake of law**
generally, 29–040—29–051
legal relevance, 5–007
limitation of actions
date from which time runs, 28–058
generally, 28–088
introduction, 28–081
misrepresentation, 5–014—5–015
money paid under mistake of fact, 5–004
mutual misunderstanding
generally, 5–071—5–073
introduction, 5–001
non est factum
generally, 5–102
introduction, 5–002
meaning, 5–101
nature of mistake, 5–103—5–106
positive belief, and, 5–006
recovery of payments, 16–187
rectification of written agreements
And see **Rectification**
common mistake, 5–108—5–114
general principles, 5–122—5–136
generally, 5–107
introduction, 5–003
unilateral mistake, 5–115—5–121
specific performance, 27–045
terms, as to, 5–005
total failure of consideration, 5–019
types, 5–001
unconscionability, 5–013
unilateral mistake
contractual notices, in, 5–080
estoppel, 5–082
generally, 5–074—5–087
introduction, 5–001

Mistake—*cont.*
unilateral mistake—*cont.*
knowledge of other party, 5–074
mistaken identity, 5–088—5–100
ought to have been apparent, 5–075
rectification, 5–115—5–121
terms of contract, as to, 5–076—5–079
unjust enrichment
mistake of fact, 29–028—29–039
mistake of law, 29–040—29–051

Mistake of fact
burden of proof, 29–035
causative mistake, 29–034
compromise, 29–038
fundamental mistake, 29–033
good consideration, 29–037
introduction, 29–028
payer with means of knowledge, 29–036
prior notices and demand, 29–039
submission to claim, 29–038
'supposed liability' rule, 29–030—29–032

Mistake of law
abolition of bar, 29–046
change in law, 29–048
criticism of rule, 29–044
equitable relief, 29–043
examples, 29–041
exceptions, 29–042
generally, 29–040
improvements to another's goods
generally, 29–051
improver's claims, 29–053
owner's claims, 29–052
principles, 29–047
rejection of rule, 29–045
remedies
equitable, 29–050
personal and proprietary, 29–049
repairs to another's goods, 29–051

Mistaken identity
face-to-face dealings, 5–092—5–093
inter praesentes, 5–096—5–097
introduction, 5–088
person, as to, 5–089—5–091
reform proposals, 5–100
third parties, 5–098—5–099
written contract, where, 5–094—5–095

Mitigation
avoidable loss
generally, 26–103
impecuniosity of claimant, 26–105—26–108
reasonable steps, 26–104
sale of goods, 26–110—26–114
time of action, 26–109
avoided loss
generally, 26–115

Mitigation—*cont*.
avoided loss—*cont*.
independent transactions, 26–116—26–117
release for other use, 26–118—26–119
expenses
generally, 26–120—26–121
performance-related sums, 26–122—26–124
fraudulent misrepresentation, 6–060
general rules
generally, 26–101
purpose, 26–102
impecuniosity of claimant, 26–105—26–108
reasonable steps, 26–104
types
avoidable loss, 26–103—26–114
avoided loss, 26–115—26–119
expenses, 26–120—26–124
generally, 26–101
Modifications to documents
See **Amendments**
"Money of account"
currency of damages, 30–373
generally, 30–372
"Money of payment"
arbitral awards, 30–379
generally, 30–374—30–375
judgments in foreign currency, 30–376—30–378
Money paid, recovery of
See **Repayments**
Months
time of performance, 21–026
"Moral obligations"
past consideration, 3–032—3–033
Morality
cohabitation, 16–067—16–068
prostitution, 16–069
will revocation, 16–074
"Mortgage valuations"
privity of contract, 18–014—18–015
Mortgages
privity of contract, 18–014—18–015
undue influence, and, 7–121
valuations, 18–014—18–015
Motor Insurers' Bureau
contract for benefit of third party, 18–131
Motor insurance
contract for benefit of third party, 18–127
Multilateral contracts
offer and acceptance, 2–110
privity of contract, 18–010
Multiple occupation
implied terms, 13–017
Mutual misunderstanding
generally, 5–071—5–073
introduction, 5–001
"Mutual promises"
consideration, 3–009

National insurance contributions
damages, 26–162
Necessaries
drunken persons, by, 8–081
intervention on behalf of defendant, 29–135
mentally disordered persons, by, 8–074
minors, by
examples, 8–016—8–018
generally, 8–007
goods sold and delivered, 8–010—8–012
loans, 8–020
meaning, 8–008
nature, 8–009
services, 8–013—8–014
trading contracts, 8–017—8–018
restitution, 29–135
spouse's needs, 8–019
Necessity
generally, 29–130
intervention on behalf of defendant
acting in public interest, 29–132
analogous categories, 29–133
generally, 29–131
necessaries, 29–135
non-gratuitous, 29–134
reasonableness, 29–134
salvage, 29–136
Negligence
common law
Caparo Industries, 6–082
damages, 6–089
generally, 6–078
Hedley Byrne v. Heller, 6–081—6–084
Nocton v. Ashburton, 6–079—6–080
special relationships, 6–085—6–088
gratuitous services, 3–179
limitation of actions
latent damage, 28–010—28–013
mistake of law, 29–036
non est factum, 5–106
privity of contract
damages, 18–035—18–036
duty of care, 18–022—18–039
economic loss, 18–031
introduction, 1–174
physical harm, 18–031—18–032
rectification, 5–126
third party rights
damages, 18–035—18–036
duty of care, 18–022—18–039
economic loss, 18–031

Negligence—*cont.*
third party rights—*cont.*
physical harm, 18–031—18–032
Negligent misrepresentation
burden of proof, 6–075
contributory negligence, 6–074
damages
contributory negligence, 6–074
generally, 6–068—6–069
introduction, 1–133
liable parties, 6–076—6–077
measure, 6–070—6–071
generally, 6–067
financial services, 6–090
holiday description, 6–092
home information packs, 6–093
introduction, 1–131—1–132
property description, 6–091
rescission, 6–072—6–073
"Negotiability"
assignment, 19–085
Negotiable instruments
alteration
generally, 21–081
material, 25–024
applicable law, 30–038—30–039
cancellation, 25–026
conflict of laws, 30–038—30–039
forgery, 21–078
limitation of actions, 28–041—28–045
loss
introduction, 21–080
material loss, 25–027
payment
agent, from, 21–075
creditor's duties, 21–079
generally, 21–073
nature, 21–074
satisfaction, in, 21–077
security, as, 21–076
tender, 21–087
validity, 21–078
Negotiations
agreements to negotiate, 2–136—2–138
limitation of actions, 28–111
Nervous shock
See **Psychiatric harm**
"Newspaper advertisements"
offer, 2–017
"No reliance clauses"
generally, 6–135
s.3 Misrepresentation Act, 6–138
Nominal damages
generally, 26–008
specific performance, 27–009
"Nominal sums"
consideration, 3–018—3–019
"Nominalism"
foreign currency obligations, 30–370
Non-commercial agreements
classification, 1–073
"*Non-cumul*"
generally, 1–136
Non-disclosure
generally, 1–134
misrepresentation
conduct, 6–015—6–016
general rule, 6–014
partial non-disclosure,
6–017—6–019
uberrimae fidei, 6–142—6–164
Non est factum
deeds, 1–111
generally, 5–102
introduction, 5–002
meaning, 5–101
nature of mistake, 5–103—5–106
Nonfeasance
gratuitous services, 3–180—3–181
"Non-monetary benefits"
consideration, 3–015
unjust enrichment, 29–021—29–023
Non-pecuniary loss
disappointment, 26–083
inconvenience, 26–082
injury to feelings, 26–083
loss of amenity, 26–084—26–085
loss of enjoyment, 26–083
loss of reputation, 26–086—26–087
mental distress, 26–083
nervous shock, 26–083
physical injury, 26–082
social discredit, 26–083
"Non-statutory corporations"
And see **Companies**
generally, 9–001
Notes of the realm
See **Banknotes**
Novation
assignment, 19–086—19–088
consideration, 3–175—3–176
rescission, 22–031
"*Nudum pactum*"
release, 22–004
Nuisance
generally, 1–118
Nullity
applicable law
consequences, 30–327—30–328
contract, and, 30–349
Rome I Regulation, and, 30–328

Objects clause
ultra vires, 9–028
"Objects injurious to domestic affairs"
assignment of pay, 16–022
negligent performance of duty, 16–023
procurement of benefits, 16–024
procurement of honours, 16–021

"Objects injurious to domestic affairs"—*cont.*
sale of public contracts, 16–019—16–020
sale of public office, 16–019—16–020
withdrawal of opposition to Bill, 16–025
"Objects injurious to foreign affairs"
contrary to foreign country's policy, 16–028
illegal under foreign law, 16–027, 16–031—16–034
legal foreign contract illegal under English law, 16–029—16–030
trading with the enemy, 16–026, 16–162—16–163
"Objects injurious to good government"
objects injurious to domestic affairs
assignment of pay, 16–022
negligent performance of duty, 16–023
procurement of benefits, 16–024
procurement of honours, 16–021
sale of public contracts, 16–019—16–020
sale of public office, 16–019—16–020
withdrawal of opposition to Bill, 16–025
objects injurious to foreign affairs
contrary to foreign country's policy, 16–028
illegal under foreign law, 16–027, 16–031—16–034
legal foreign contract illegal under English law, 16–029—16–030
trading with the enemy, 16–026, 16–162—16–163
"Objects injurious to morality"
cohabitation, 16–067—16–068
prostitution, 16–069
revocation of wills, 16–074
"Objects injurious to proper working of justice"
champertous agreements
assignment of right to litigate, 16–057—16–064
effect, 16–066
generally, 16–048—16–049
meaning, 16–054
other agreements, 16–065
solicitor and clients, 16–055—16–056
concealment of crime, 16–035—16–038
interference with course of justice
collusive divorce agreements, 16–043
generally, 16–039
"Objects injurious to proper working of justice"—*cont.*
interference with course of justice—*cont.*
insolvency agreements, 16–041—16–042
procurement of pardon, 16–040
maintenance of litigation agreements
effect, 16–053
generally, 16–048—16–049
justification, 16–051—16–052
meaning, 16–050
ouster of jurisdiction
arbitration, 16–045—16–047
maintenance agreements, 16–044
"Objects of trifling value"
gambling chips, 3–016—3–017
generally, 3–016
Occupation
implied terms, 13–014
"Occurrence of condition"
termination of offer, 2–098
Offer
advertisements, by
bilateral contracts, 2–017
false statements, 2–020
rewards, 2–019
unilateral contracts, 2–018
auctions
generally, 2–011
resale in case of dispute, 2–013
with reserve, 2–012
without reserve, 2–012
conduct, by
generally, 2–005
inactivity, 2–006
delay, by, 2–005
display, by
goods for sale, 2–014—2–015
menus, 2–016
generally
definition, 2–003
state of mind of offeree, 2–004
inactivity, by, 2–006
invitation to treat
distinction from offer, 2–010
generally, 2–007—2–008
menus, 2–016
self-service goods, 2–014—2–015
wording inconclusive, 2–009
multilateral contracts, 2–110
place, 2–025
rejection
communication, 2–094
counter-offers, 2–092
information requests, 2–093
rewards, by, 2–019
sale of land, 2–110
shares, 2–024

Offer—*cont.*
tender, by
generally, 2–022
public procurement, 2–023
termination of
And see **Termination of offer**
death, by, 2–099—2–101
generally, 2–087
lapse of time, by, 2–095—2–097
occurrence of condition, by, 2–098
rejection, by, 2–092—2–094
supervening incapacity, by, 2–102—2–109
withdrawal, by, 2–088—2–091
ticket, by, 2–021
time 2–026
timetables, by, 2–021
withdrawal of
communication, 2–089—2–091
general rule, 2–088
Office of Fair Trading
application of fairness test, 15–096
burden of proof, 15–097
enforcement orders, 15–099
generally, 15–095
Officers' mess
contract with clubs, 9–079
"Officious acts"
restitution, 29–019
Online contracts
See **Electronic contracts**
Online gambling
See **Remote gambling**
"Open-textured controls"
courts as public authorities, 1–064
"Open-textured norms"
courts as public authorities, 1–063
Opposition
withdrawal of Bill, to, 16–025
Oppression
recovery of payments, 16–186
restitution, 29–150
"Opt out clause"
unfair contract terms (consumer contracts), 15–084
Options
formal requirements, 4–058
generally, 2–127
"Oral warranties"
exemption clauses, 14–134
Ordinary meaning
absurd use, 12–055
badly drafted contracts, 12–056
Community directives, 12–054
custom, 12–058—12–059
established judicial construction, 12–053
general words, 12–062
generally, 12–050—12–051
inconsistent use, 12–055
Ordinary meaning—*cont.*
mercantile contracts, 12–057
technical words, 12–052
Ostensible authority
See **Apparent authority**
Ouster clauses
arbitration, 16–045—16–047
maintenance agreements, 16–044
"Outbreak of war"
And see **Trading with the enemy**
frustration
accrued rights, 23–031
executory contracts, 23–032
generally, 23–030

Package holidays
implied terms, 13–034
negligent misrepresentation, 6–092
Pardons
interference with course of justice, 16–040
Parental liability
minors, for, 8–061
Parental responsibility
objects injurious to marriage, 16–074
Parents
presumed undue influence, 7–074
Parol evidence
collateral contracts, 12–103
contracts for sale of land, 4–029
contradictory terms, 12–100
entire agreement clauses, 12–104
excluded contracts, 12–101—12–102
exceptions, 12–097, 12–105
generally, 12–096
reform, 12–099
scope, 12–098
Parole
release, 22–004
Part payments
accord and satisfaction, 22–016
additional performance, 3–123
collateral contract, 3–127
common law limitations
additional performance, 3–123
collateral contract, 3–127
composition with creditors, 3–125
disputed claims, 3–118
forbearance to enforce cross-claims, 3–124
liquidated claims, 3–120
partly liquidated and unliquidated claims, 3–121
third party payment, 3–126
unliquidated claims, 3–119
variation of performance, 3–122
composition with creditors, 3–125
disputed claims, 3–118
effects of rule, 3–116—3–117

Part payments—*cont.*
equitable forbearance
continuing obligations, 3–130—3–131
detriment, 3–135
effect, 3–129—3–133
extinctive effects, 3–132—3–133
inequity, 3–136
introduction, 3–128
nature of doctrine, 3–129
requirements, 3–134—3–136
forbearance
common law limitation, 3–124
equitable limitation, 3–128—3–136
general rule
common law limitations, 3–118—3–127
effects, 3–116—3–117
equitable limitations, 3–128—3–136
generally, 3–115
limitation of actions
effect, 28–103
exclusions, 28–104
general rule, 28–093
introduction, 28–092
nature, 28–05—28–099
parties, 28–100—28–102
pleading, 28–105
limitations
common law, at, 3–118—3–127
equity, in, 3–128—3–136
liquidated claims, 3–120
partly liquidated and unliquidated claims, 3–121
third party, by, 3–126
unjust enrichment, 29–066
unliquidated claims, 3–119
variation in debtor's performance, 3–122
Part performance
contracts for sale of land
effect of acts, 4–050
generally, 4–042—4–043
required acts, 4–044—4–049
entire obligation, of
acceptance, 21–035
carriage of goods by sea, 21–034
effect, 21–030—21–031
generally, 21–027—21–029
unilateral contracts, 2–079—2–080
Partial failure of consideration
See **Failure of consideration**
"Partial frustration"
force majeure, 23–067
generally, 23–066
Sainsbury v. Street, 23–068—23–069
"Partial non-disclosure"
continuity of representations, 6–019
generally, 6–017
representation ceases to be true, 6–018
Parties
capacity
And see **Capacity**
drunken persons, 8–080—8–081
generally, 17–001
introduction, 1–125, 1–162
married women, 8–068—8–069
mentally disordered persons, 8–070—8–079
minors, 8–002—8–067
classification by, 1–073
contracts for sale of goods, 4–023
duress
person suffering, 7–051
third party, 7–052
misrepresentation
representee, 6–028—6–043
representor, 6–021—6–027
negligent misrepresentation, 6–076—6–077
privity of contract
agency contracts, 18–012—18–013
collateral contracts, 18–005—18–009
competitions, 18–011
generally, 18–004
mortgage valuations, 18–014—18–015
multilateral contracts, 18–010
rescission, 6–112
unfair contract terms (consumer contracts)
business, 15–021
consumer, 15–022—15–025
generally, 15–020
recipient, 15–025
seller, 15–021
supplier, 15–021
Partners
contracts for sale of land, 4–066
contribution, 29–127
payment, 21–049
Partnership agreements
minors, 8–039
misrepresentation, 6–162
restraint of trade, 16–119
Partnership debts
novation, 3–175—3–176
Partnerships
contracts for sale of land, 4–066
Passing on
unjust enrichment, 29–027
Past consideration
bills of exchange, 3–034
criteria
generally, 3–027
wording of promise, 3–028—3–035
generally, 3–026
wording of promise
acknowledgment of statute-barred debt, 3–035

Past consideration—*cont.*
wording of promise—*cont.*
antecedent debt, 3–031
bills of exchange, 3–034
generally, 3–028
moral obligation, 3–032—3–033
pre-promise act, 3–029
pre-promise request, 3–030
"Patent licences"
restraint of trade, 16–131
Paternity pay
See **Statutory paternity pay**
Patients
limitation of actions, 28–074—28–080
Payment
accord and satisfaction
creditor composition, by, 22–018
different terms, 22–017
generally, 21–052
partial, 22–016
third party, by, 22–018
administrators, to, 21–049
agent
payment by, 21–041
payment to, 21–043—21–044, 21–048
amount, 21–052
appropriation
creditor's right, 21–061—21–062
current account, to, 21–066
debtor's right, 21–060
generally, 21–059
guaranteed debt, to, 21–064
instalment payments, 21–065
interest-bearing debt, to, 21–067
statute-barred debt, to, 21–063
auctions, 21–048
bank accounts, to
generally, 21–045—21–046
in-house, 21–047
bankrupt, to, 21–050
bill of exchange, by
agent, from, 21–075
alteration, 21–081
creditor's duties, 21–079
forgery, 21–078
generally, 21–073
invalidity, 21–078
loss, 21–080
nature, 21–074
satisfaction, in, 21–077
security, as, 21–076
charge card, by, 21–082
cheque, by
agent, from, 21–075
alteration, 21–081
creditor's duties, 21–079
forgery, 21–078
generally, 21–073
invalidity, 21–078
Payment—*cont.*
cheque, by—*cont.*
loss, 21–080
nature, 21–074
satisfaction, in, 21–077
security, as, 21–076
credit card, by, 21–082
damages, 21–040
debt, 21–040
excessive amount, of, 29–097
executor, to, 21–049
garnishee orders, under, 21–051
generally, 21–039
gold clauses, 21–069—21–071
index-linking, 21–072
joint creditors, to, 21–049
made in course of legal proceedings, 29–098
method
contractually specified, 21–057
generally, 21–055
post, by, 21–056
negotiable instrument, by
agent, from, 21–075
alteration, 21–081
creditor's duties, 21–079
forgery, 21–078
generally, 21–073
invalidity, 21–078
loss, 21–080
nature, 21–074
satisfaction, in, 21–077
security, as, 21–076
partner, to, 21–049
personal representative, to, 21–049
place, 21–054
promissory estoppel, 21–052
promissory note, by
agent, from, 21–075
alteration, 21–081
creditor's duties, 21–079
forgery, 21–078
generally, 21–073
invalidity, 21–078
loss, 21–080
nature, 21–074
satisfaction, in, 21–077
security, as, 21–076
proof, 21–058
remoteness of damage, 26–098
restitution, 29–196
revalorization
generally, 21–068
gold clauses, 21–069—21–071
index-linking, 21–072
tender, by
And see **Tender**
generally, 21–083—21–096
third party
payment by, 21–041

Payment—*cont.*
third party—*cont.*
payment to, 21–042
time, 21–053
transfer to bank accounts, by
generally, 21–045—21–046
in-house, 21–047
trustee, to, 21–049
trustee in bankruptcy, to, 21–050
unjust enrichment
made in course of legal proceedings, 29–098
excessive amount, 29–097
Payment (third parties)
agent for principal, by, 29–117
assignees of lease, by, 29–106
bills of exchange, under, 29–108
contribution
common law, at, 29–122
directors, 29–126
general average, 29–129
generally, 29–121
guarantees, 29–123
insurers, 29–128
joint contractors, 29–124
partners, 29–127
trustees, 29–125
generally, 29–099—29–100
guarantors, by, 29–119
indemnity, under, 29–120
liability to pay
legal, 29–101
primary, 29–102
other examples, 29–107
request of third party, at, 29–113—29–116
seizure of goods, 29–103—29–105
tenancies in common, 29–118
voluntary payments, 29–109—29–112
Payment under protest
unjust enrichment, 29–111
Pay-when-paid clauses
See **Conditional payments**
Penalties
And see **Unconscionable bargains**
generally, 7–126
Penalty clauses
acceleration clauses, 26–140
consumer contracts
generally, 26–155
unfair contract terms, 26–156
fluctuating sums, 26–130
forfeiture of sums paid
express clause, 26–146—26–153
no express clause, 26–154
generally, 26–125—26–127
graduated sums, 26–135
incentive clauses, 26–139
invoicing back clauses, 26–144
Penalty clauses—*cont.*
limitation of liability clauses
charterparties, 26–143
generally, 26–142
minimum sums, 26–131
pre-estimate
damage, of, 26–129
generally, 26–128
reimbursement clauses, 26–145
single sums, 26–132—26–134
termination clauses, 26–141
unfair contract terms
generally, 26–156
introduction, 15–076
Performance
alternative methods, by
business option, 21–008
contractual option, 21–006—21–007
applicable law
discretion, 30–335
manner, 30–333—30–334
substance, 30–332
carriage by sea, 21–034
conditional
generally, 21–009
notices, 21–010
consideration, 3–008
divisible contract, of
generally, 21–027
meaning, 21–037
entire contracts, of
carriage of goods by sea, 21–034
partial completion, 21–027—21–036
substantial completion, 21–032—21–033
generally, 21–011—21–002
independent promise, 21–038
locus poenitentiae, 16–189
own benefit, of term for, 21–003
partial
And see **Part performance**
contracts for sale of land, 4–044—4–050
generally, 21–027—21–038
payment
And see **Payment**
appropriation, 21–059—21–067
credit card, by, 21–082
generally, 21–039—21–058
negotiable instrument, by, 21–073—21–081
revalorization, 21–068—21–072
place, 21–005
substituted, 21–004
tender
And see **Tender**
generally, 21–083—21–096
time
And see **Time of performance**
calculation, 21–023—21–026

Performance—*cont.*
time—*cont.*
fixed time, 21–019
meanings, 21–021—21–022
no fixed time, 21–020
time not of the essence, 21–018
time of the essence, 21–011—21–017
vicarious
And see **Vicarious performance**
agency, 19–084
generally, 19–081—19–083
introduction, 21–004
"Performance interest"
damages, 26–003
Personal injury
damages, 26–082
limitation of actions
extension of period, 28–072
relevant period, 28–006—28–008
Personal representatives
actions against
bills of exchange, for, 20–011—20–012
carrying on business, on, 20–010
confirmation of contract, on, 20–009
distribution of estate, on, 20–013
generally, 20–005
leases, on, 20–008
payment of debts, for, 20–014
personal contracts, on, 20–006—20–007
actions by
damages, 20–003
generally, 20–002
time of accrual, 20–004
assignment, 19–059
limitation of actions, 28–065—28–066
merger
creditor as debtor's, 25–006
debtor as creditor's, 25–005
payment, 21–049
"Personal services contracts"
discharge by frustration
compulsory service, 23–039
death, 23–037
ill health, 23–038
imprisonment, 23–039
other events, 23–040
injunctions, 27–064—27–066
specific performance
employment contracts, 27–022—27–023
generally, 27–046
other contracts, 27–024
Persons under disability
And see **Minors**
And see **Patients**
limitation of actions, 28–074—28–080
Perverting the course of justice
collusive divorce agreements, 16–043
generally, 16–039
insolvency agreements
bankruptcy, 16–042
winding-up, 16–041
procurement of pardon, 16–040
Petrol solus agreements
See **Solus agreements**
"Petrol stations"
offer, 2–014
restraint of trade, 16–122—16–124
Physical destruction
See **Destruction of property**
Physical injury
See **Personal injury**
"Physical threat"
duress, 1–135
Piece workers
See **Output workers**
Place of business
applicable law, 30–080—30–081
Place of performance
generally, 21–005
payment, 21–054
"Plain language"
unfair contract terms (consumer contracts)
non-compliance, 15–091—15–092
relevant terms, 15–033
test, 15–089—15–090
Pleadings
accord and satisfaction, 22–023
minors, 8–064
misrepresentation, 6–027
release, 22–011
Policy statements
government, and, 2–179
Possessory rights
enforcement against third parties, 18–146
Postal rule
application of rule
dictated communications, 2–051
generally, 2–049
instant communications, 2–050
distance contracts, 2–064
exclusion of rule, 2–052
general rule
application, 2–049—2–051
exclusion, 2–052
introduction, 2–048
operation, 2–053—2–061
international sales, 2–063
operation of rule
delayed letter, 2–055—2–056
first acceptor, 2–057
garbled messages, 2–059
generally, 2–053
lost letter, 2–055—2–056

Postal rule—*cont.*
operation of rule—*cont.*
misdirected letter, 2–058
uncommunicated withdrawal, 2–054
revocation, 2–060—2–061
"Potestative conditions"
unfair contract terms (consumer contracts), 15–074
"Pre-contractual liability"
culpa in contrahendo, 1–136
duress, 1–135
economic threat, 1–135
intimidation, 1–135
misrepresentation, 1–131—1–133
non-disclosure, 1–134
physical threat, 1–135
Pre-emption rights
generally, 2–127
Preferences
bankruptcy, 20–029
Pre-incorporation contracts
equity, in, 9–015
generally, 9–012—9–013
law, at, 9–014
Prescription
applicable law, 30–347—30–348
Presumed undue influence
affirmation, 7–097
burden of proof, 7–094
confidential relationship shown on the facts
generally, 7–079—7–081
husband-wife, 7–085
relevant relationships, 7–082—7–085
delay, 7–097
doctor-patient, 7–077
domination, 7–072
estoppel, 7–097
fiancé-fiancée, 7–077
guardian-ward, 7–075
husband-wife
generally, 7–085
manifest disadvantage, 7–087—7–090
in loco parentis, persons in, 7–075
independent advice, 7–095—7–096
introduction, 7–069—7–070
lapse of time, 7–097
nature of presumptions, 7–072
parent-child, 7–074
rebuttal
generally, 7–093—7–094
independent advice, 7–095—7–096
relevant relationships
doctor-patient, 7–077
fiancé-fiancée, 7–077
generally, 7–071—7–073
guardian-ward, 7–075
husband-wife, 7–085
in loco parentis, persons in, 7–075
Presumed undue influence—*cont.*
relevant relationships—*cont.*
other cases, 7–077
parent-child, 7–074
religious adviser-clients, 7–077
solicitor-clients, 7–076
trustee-beneficiary, 7–077
religious adviser-clients, 7–077
remedies
account of profits, 7–100
equitable compensation, 7–101
restitution, 7–098—7–099
sharing loss, 7–102—7–103
restitution, 7–098—7–099
solicitor-clients, 7–076
transaction not explicable by ordinary motives
generally, 7–086
manifest disadvantage, 7–087—7–092
trustee-beneficiary, 7–077
value of presumption, 7–078
Presumptions of law
applicable law, 30–353
legality, 16–204
Price fixing
restraint of trade, 16–134
Price of goods
See **Pricing**
Principles (contracts)
And see under individual headings
binding force of contract
generally, 1–019—1–020
limitations, 1–021
fairness
civil law systems, in, 1–025
common law systems, in, 1–024
English law, in, 1–026—1–034
introduction, 1–022—1–023
freedom of contract
discrimination, 1–016
European law, in, 1–013
generally, 1–011
modern common law, in, 1–012
qualifications, 1–014—1–018
refusal to enter contracts, 1–015
regulation of contractual environment, 1–018
restricted freedom as to terms, 1–017
good faith
civil law systems, in, 1–025
common law systems, in, 1–024
English law, in, 1–026—1–034
introduction, 1–022—1–023
introduction, 1–010
"Printed documents"
construction of terms, 12–070
Prisoners of war
limitation of actions, 28–069

Privity of contract
agency
generally, 18–012
sub-agency, 18–013
background
Beswick v. Beswick, 18–020
Tweddle v. Atkinson, 18–019
benefit of third party
And see **Third party rights**
effects, 18–043—18–076
exceptions, 18–077—18–132
building contract cases
distinction from other cases, 18–037—18–039
generally, 18–023—18–025
cancellation by third parties, 18–099—18–105
cheque transactions, 18–007
collateral contracts
cheque transactions, 18–007
consideration, 18–008
credit card transactions, 18–007
generally, 18–005
hire purchase, 18–006
intention, 18–009
common law, at
consideration, 18–016—18–018
development, 18–019—18–020
introduction, 18–003
parties, 18–004—18–015
rights of third party, 18–114—18–117
competitions, 18–011
consideration
collateral contracts, 18–008
joint liability, 18–018
movement from promisee, 18–016—18–017
Contracts for the Benefit of Third Parties (Law Com. No. 242, 1996)
generally, 18–001
introduction, 1–002
movement of consideration, 3–045
Contracts (Rights of Third Parties) Act 1999
cancellation by third party, 18–099—18–105
common law rights of third party, 18–114—18–117
double liability, 18–120
enforcement by third party, 18–088—18–098
exceptions to third party rights, 18–111—18–113
generally, 18–002
promisee's rights, 18–119
promisor's defences, 18–106—18–110

Privity of contract—*cont.*
Contracts (Rights of Third Parties) Act 1999—*cont.*
variation by third party, 18–099—18–105
credit card transactions, 18–007
defective premises, 18–132
'disappointed beneficiary' cases
distinction from other cases, 18–037—18–039
generally, 18–025
double liability, 18–120
enforcement against third parties
exceptions to rule, 18–134
general rule, 18–133
enforcement by third party, 18–088—18–098
equitable exceptions
marriage settlements, 18–087
trusts of promises, 18–078—18–086
exceptions
Contracts (Rights of Third Parties) Act 1999, 18–088—18–120
enforcement against third parties, and, 18–134
equitable, 18–078—18–087
generally, 18–077
statutory, 18–121—18–132
exemption clauses, 14–039
fire insurance, 18–129
general rule
consideration, 18–016—18–018
generally, 18–003
parties to agreements, 18–004—18–015
hire purchase, 18–006
interests in land, 18–122—18–125
intimidation, 18–040—18–041
life insurance, 18–126
marine insurance, 18–128
marriage settlements, 18–087
mortgage valuations, 18–014—18–015
Motor Insurers' Bureau claims, 18–131
motor insurance, 18–127—18–128
multilateral contracts, 18–010
negligence
damages, 18–035—18–036
duty of care, 18–022—18–039
economic loss, 18–031
introduction, 1–174
physical harm, 18–031—18–032
parties to agreements
agency contracts, 18–012—18–013
collateral contracts, 18–005—18–009
competitions, 18–011
generally, 18–004
mortgage valuations, 18–014—18–015
multilateral contracts, 18–010
persons with limited interest, 18–128

Privity of contract—*cont.*
promisee's rights, 18–119
promisor's defences, 18–106—18–110
reform
Contracts (Rights of Third Parties) Act 1999, 18–002
Law Commission Report 1996, 18–001
restitution
contract for benefit of third party, 18–045
generally, 29–023
third party rights, 18–042
scope
generally, 18–021
intimidation, 18–040—18–041
negligence, 18–022—18–039
restitution, 18–042
solicitors' indemnity insurance, 18–130
sporting competitions, 18–011
statutory exceptions
defective premises, 18–132
fire insurance, 18–129
interests in land, 18–122—18–125
introduction, 18–121
life insurance, 18–126
marine insurance, 18–128
Motor Insurers' Bureau claims, 18–131
motor insurance, 18–127
persons with limited interest, 18–128
solicitors' indemnity insurance, 18–130
sub-agency, 18–013
trusts of promises, 18–078—18–086
unjust enrichment
contract for benefit of third party, 18–045
generally, 29–023
third party rights, 18–042
variation by third party, 18–099—18–105
Proceeds of crime
court's discretion, 16–170
death at law, 16–172
'forfeiture rule', 16–170
generally, 16–168—16–169
indemnities, 16–173—16–175
life insurance, 16–171
suicide, 16–171
Proceeds of sale
contracts for sale of land, and, 4–064
"Procurement of honours"
illegality, 16–021
Procuring breach of contract
generally, 1–171
Professional bodies
restraint of trade, 16–139
Promises
consideration, 3–008
Promises—*cont.*
contract as
generally, 1–001
problems with, 1–002
failure of performance
dependent, 24–037
generally, 24–035
independent, 24–036
objects injurious to marriage, 16–070
past consideration
acknowledgment of statute-barred debt, 3–035
antecedent debt, 3–031
bills of exchange, 3–034
generally, 3–028
moral obligation, 3–032—3–033
pre-promise act, 3–029
pre-promise request, 3–030
without consideration, 3–013
"Promissory conditions"
conditional agreements, 2–148
express terms, 12–027
Promissory estoppel
comparison of
estoppel by convention, 3–112
estoppel by representation, 3–096
foreign rules, 3–106
promises with consideration, 3–105
proprietary estoppel, 3–160—3–163
waiver, 3–103—3–104
contracts for sale of land, 4–083
detriment, 3–094
effect
generally, 3–095—3–097
introduction, 1–006
inactivity, 3–092
inequity, 3–095
introduction, 3–085
nature, 3–098—3–103
payment, 21–052
pre-existing legal relationship, 3–088
promise
generally, 3–089
nature, 3–090—3–091
reliance, 3–093
representation
generally, 3–089
nature, 3–090—3–091
requirements
detriment, 3–094
generally, 3–086—3–087
inactivity, 3–092
inequity, 3–095
pre-existing legal relationship, 3–088
promise, 3–089—3–091
reliance, 3–093
sale of land, 4–083
Promissory notes
And see **Negotiable instruments**
accord and satisfaction, 22–020

Promissory notes—*cont.*
alteration, 21–081
cancellation, 25–026
forgery, 21–078
loss, 21–080
payment
agent, from, 21–075
creditor's duties, 21–079
generally, 21–073
nature, 21–074
satisfaction, in, 21–077
security, as, 21–076
release, 22–009
validity, 21–078
Promoters
company contracts with, 9–054
"Proper law of contract"
And see **Conflict of laws**
background, 30-001—30-004
express choice of law
common law limitations, 30–007
generally, 30–006
statutory limitations, 30–008
generally, 30–005
implied choice of law
generally, 30–010
relevant factors, 30–010—30–011
incorporation by reference of law, 30–009
no choice of law
generally, 30–012
relevant factors, 30–013—30–016
renvoi, 30–016
Proper working of justice
See **Objects injurious to proper working of justice**
Property disposal
See **Sale of land**
Property misdescriptions
negligent misrepresentation, 6–091
Property transfer
See **Transfer of land**
"Proprietary clubs"
contracts with clubs, 9–080
Proprietary estoppel
basis of liability
acts done in reliance, 3–141
alternative explanation, 3–142—3–143
constructive trust, 3–140
expenditure in reliance, 3–139
comparison of
contact, 3–164
promissory estoppel, 3–160—3–163
conditional operation, 3–153
constructive trusts, and
contracts for sale of land, 4–081
generally, 3–140
contracts for sale of land
s.40 LPA 1925, 4–051
Proprietary estoppel—*cont.*
contracts for sale of land—*cont.*
s.2 LP(MP)A 1989, 4–080—4–082
detriment, 3–147—3–148
effects
'equity' on the promisee, 3–150—3–159
revocability, 3–149
'equity' on the promisee
extent, 3–151—3–153
introduction, 3–150
remedy, 3–154—3–159
general rule, 3–137—3–138
operation, 3–150
remedy
balance of hardship, 3–159
conduct of promisor, 3–156
monetary compensation, 3–157—3–158
principled discretion, 3–154—3–155
requirements
detriment, 3–147—3–148
rights, 3–145
subject-matter, 3–146
type of promise, 3–144
revocability, 3–149
subject-matter of promise, 3–146
third party donee, 3–152
Proprietary interests
And see **Sale of land**
background, 4–009
contract for benefit of third party, 18–122—18–125
post-26th September 1989, 4–052—4–088
pre- 26th September 1989, 4–010—4–051
"Proprietary restitutionary claims"
bona fide purchase, 29–175
common law, at, 29–170—29–171
equity, in, 29–172
establishing rights, 29–158—29–161
personal remedies, 29–174
subrogation, 29–173
tracing
common law, at, 29–163
equity, in, 29–164—29–167
introduction, 29–162
proceeds of sale, 29–169
reservation of title, 29–168
Prospective loss
See **Future loss**
Prostitution
objects injurious to morality, 16–069
"Provisional agreements"
subject to contract, 2–123
Psychiatric harm
damages, 26–083
Public authorities
capacity, 1–198

Public authorities—*cont.*
differences in rules, 1–201
estoppel
exercise of statutory powers, and, 10–042
general principles, 10–039
public law, and, 10–043
statutory duty, 10–041
ultra vires, and, 10–040
fettering of discretion
compatibility test, 10–028
generally, 10–027
positive promises, 10–030
prioritisation of powers, 10–031
promises not to exercise powers, 10–029
Human Rights Act 1999
background, 1–039—1–043
construction of contracts, 1–057
effect on contract, 1–056
generally, 1–199—1–200
relevant authorities, 1–052
ultra vires rule, and, 10–033
unlawful conclusion of contract, 1–054
unlawful manner of performance of contract, 1–055
unlawful refusal to contract, 1–053
overview, 10–020
proper exercise of powers, 10–032
public procurement
domestic legislation, 10–030
EC law, 10–044—10–046
international agreements, 10–029
remedies, 10–045—10–046
relationship with contracts, 1–198—1–201
statutory powers to contract
ancillary power, 10–025
express powers, 10–021—10–022
implied powers, 10–023—10–026
incidental power, 10–025
tender process contracts
conditions, 10–036—10–037
contents, 10–038
factual conditions, 10–037
nature, 10–035
terms, 10–038
ultra vires
generally, 10–033
statutory reform, 10–034
unlawful conclusion of contract, 1–054
unlawful manner of performance of contract, 1–055
unlawful refusal to contract, 1–053
Public contracts
See also **Public authorities**
agency
generally, 10–009
liability of agent, 10–013
Public contracts—*cont.*
agency—*cont.*
ostensible authority, 10–012
servant-agent issue, 10–011
unauthorised contracts, 10–011
warranty of authority, 10–014
capacity, 10–004
fettering of discretion
express terms, 10–008
introduction, 10–007
illegality of sale, 16–019—16–020
injunctions, 10–019
interim remedies, 10–017
introduction, 10–001—10–003
Parliamentary control
express limitations, 10–005
implied limitations, 10–006
remedies
background, 10–015
Crown servants, against, 10–018—10–019
generally, 10–016
interim remedies, 10–017
Public law
See **Administrative law**
"Public office"
illegality of sale, 16–019—16–020
Public policy
champerty, 16–049
conflict of laws, 30–366—30–368
illegality of contracts, and
common law, 16–003—16–141
generally, 16–003—16–004
introduction, 16–001—16–002
statute, 16–142—16–163
maintenance and champerty, 16–049
scope, 16–005—16–013
severance, 16–202
restitution, 29–019
Public procurement
domestic legislation, 10–030
EC law, 10–044—10–046
international agreements, 10–029
remedies, 10–045—10–046
Puffs
intention, 2–165
Punitive damages
generally, 26–019
introduction, 1–123
Pupillage
consideration, 3–038
Purchase of own shares
ultra vires, 9–038
Purchasers without notice
restitution, 29–019
Pure economic loss
See **Economic loss**

Quantum meruit
additional work, 29–072

Quantum meruit—*cont.*
bad bargains, 29–068
contract price, 29–069
generally, 29–067
goods supplied, 29–070
introduction, 29–004
no fixed price, 29–071
services rendered, 29–070
substituted contract for services, 29–073
termination by breach, 29–067
Quantum valebant
introduction, 29–004
no fixed price, 29–071

"Rail tickets"
offer, 2–021
Ratification
minors
examples, 8–043
generally, 8–042
procedure, 8–044
ultra vires
common law, at, 9–024
statutory modifications, 9–039
Real property
disposition of
And see **Sale of land**
background, 4–009
post-26th September 1989, 4–052—4–088
pre- 26th September 1989, 4–010—4–051
minors
disposal, 8–067
lease, 8–033—8–035
misrepresentation, 6–156—6–157
restraint of trade
conveyances, 16–129
generally, 16–128
leases, 16–129
"Reasonable steps"
undue influence by third party, 7–114
Reasonableness
exemption clauses
generally, 14–135
Misrepresentation Act, s.3, 6–139
restraint of trade
construction of covenant, 16–097
determining factors, 16–098
generally, 16–092
parties' interests, 16–093—16–094
public interest, 16–095—16–096
solus petrol agreements, 16–123
unfair contract terms
appeals, 14–103
burden of proof, 14–088
case law, 14–089—14–099
courts' powers, 14–100—14–102
further factors, 14–086

Reasonableness—*cont.*
unfair contract terms—*cont.*
generally, 14–084
guidelines, 14–085
limits on amount, 14–087
"Receipt of goods"
unjust enrichment, 29–023
Receivership
companies in, contracts with
generally, 9–050—9–051
inducing breach of contract, 9–052
repudiation, 9–051
Recitals
construction of terms, 12–066
implied terms, 13–024—13–025
"Recovery of non-monetary benefits"
generally, 23–084
identification of the benefit, 23–085—23–086
just sum, 23–090
valuing the benefit, 23–087—23–089
"Recovery of payments"
See also **Repayments**
agents, from, 16–192
discharge by frustration
allowance for expenses, 23–083
basis of proviso, 23–081
breaches before discharge, 23–079
burden of proof, 23–082
common law, at, 23–072—23–073
generally, 23–076—23–077
paid or payable, 23–078
time of discharge, 23–080
fraud, 16–186
generally, 16–177
in pari delicto, 16–185
locus poenitentiae
advancement, 16–182—16–184
frustration, 16–190
generally, 16–188
performance, 16–189
marriage brokerage contracts, 16–191
mistake, 16–187
oppression, 16–186
trustees, by, 16–193
"Recovery of property transferred"
fraud, 16–186
generally, 16–178
limited interests, 16–179—16–181
locus poenitentiae
advancement, 16–182—16–184
frustration, 16–190
generally, 16–188
performance, 16–189
oppression, 16–186
Rectification
articles of association, 5–135
cancellation, and, 5–119—5–120
common mistake
clerical errors, and, 5–110

Rectification—*cont.*
common mistake—*cont.*
concluded agreements, 5–113
generally, 5–108
legal effect, as to, 5–109
outward expression of accord, 5–114
parol evidence, and, 5–111
recording of terms, in, 5–109
delay, and, 5–127
discretion of court, and, 5–125
general principles, 5–122—5–136
generally, 5–107
introduction, 5–003
limitation of actions, 28–146
literal disparity, 5–123
marriage settlements, 5–134
negligence, and, 5–126
payment of money under judgment, 5–129
procedure
generally, 5–131
jurisdiction of court, 5–132
proof of mistake, 5–122
restoration of parties to former position, 5–128
specific performance, 5–124
third parties, 5–130
unilateral mistake
cancellation, 5–119—5–120
contributing conduct, 5–117
generally, 5–115
inequity, 5–118
knowledge, 5–116
mistake known to have been made, 5–121
voluntary settlements, 5–136
Reduction of price
See **Price reductions**
References
See **Banking references**
See **Employment references**
"Refusal to contract"
injunctions
aiding and abetting a breach of injunction, 27–076
discrimination, 27–074
generally, 27–073
rules of trade association, 27–075
Registration
company charges, 9–046
Rejection
offer
communication, 2–094
counter-offers, 2–092
information requests, 2–093
Release
bills of exchange, 22–009
conditional, 22–008
covenant not to sue
generally, 22–006
Release—*cont.*
covenant not to sue—*cont.*
joint contractors, 22–007
deeds, 22–003
form, 22–005
joint liability
generally, 22–007
introduction, 17–017—17–020
methods
oral, 22–004
written, 22–003
misrepresentation, 22–010
pleading, 22–011
promissory notes, 22–009
"Reliance interest"
damages, 26–002
"Religious advisers"
presumed undue influence, 7–077
Remeasurement contracts
See **Measurement and value contracts**
Remedies
And see under individual headings
breach of contract
damages, 26–001—26–184
injunctions, 27–060—27–084
limitation of actions, 28–001—28–146
specific performance, 27–001—27–059
constructive trust, 26–021—26–022
Crown contracts
background, 10–015
Crown servants, against, 10–018—10–019
generally, 10–016
interim remedies, 10–017
damages
causation, 26–032—26–050
exchange rates, 26–159
interest, 26–167—26–184
mitigation of damage, 26–101—26–124
nature, 26–001—26–007
penalty damages, 26–125—26–156
remoteness, 26–051—26–100
tax, 26–157—26–166
types, 26–008—26–031
injunctions, 27–060—27–076
limitation of actions
abridgement of period, 28–112—28–115
cause of action, 28–031—28–061
commencement of proceedings, 28–116—28–125
computation of period, 28–062—28–063
effect, 28–126—28–133
equitable remedies, 28–134—28–146

Remedies—*cont.*
limitation of actions—*cont.*
extension of period, 28–071—28–111
relevant period, 28–001—28–030
running of time, 28–064—28–070
specific performance
compensation, with, 27–054—27–058
generally, 27–001—27–004
limitations, 27–005—27–045
third parties, 27–049—27–053
tracing, 26–021
Remoteness of damage
examples
carriage of goods, 26–089—26–090
lease of land, 26–091—26–097
loan of money, 26–099
payment of money, 26–098
sale of goods, 26–088
sale of land, 26–091—26–097
sale of shares, 26–100
generally, 26–051
Hadley v. Baxendale
actual knowledge of special circumstances, 26–061
assumption of risk, 26–062—26–063
degree of probability, 26–059
generally, 26–052—26–057
imputed knowledge, 26–060
relevant loss, 26–058
introduction, 1–165
loss of profits
carrier's liability, 26–070
seller's claim, 26–069
seller's liability, 26–066—26–068
non-pecuniary loss
disappointment, 26–083
inconvenience, 26–082
injury to feelings, 26–083
loss of amenity, 26–084—26–085
loss of enjoyment, 26–083
loss of reputation, 26–086—26–087
mental distress, 26–083
nervous shock, 26–083
physical injury, 26–082
social discredit, 26–083
time of assessment
generally, 26–064
interest, 26–065
wasted expenditure
currency exchange loss, 26–080—26–081
no transaction basis, 26–079
non-performance expenditure, 26–074—26–075
performance expenditure, 26–072—26–073
post-breach expenditure, 26–078
Remoteness of damage—*cont.*
wasted expenditure—*cont.*
pre-contract expenditure, 26–076—26–077
Rent reviews
generally, 2–132
"Renunciation"
actual breach
during course of performance, 24–027
generally, 24–026
anticipatory breach
breach accepted, 24–022—24–023
breach not accepted, 24–024—24–025
generally, 24–021
breach accepted
effect, 24–023
generally, 24–022
breach not accepted, 24–024—24–025
employment contracts, 24–020
form, 24–019
generally, 24–018
impossibility, 24–029
nature
actual breach, 24–026—24–027
anticipatory breach, 24–021—24–025
Repairs
damages, 26–016—26–018
Repayments
money paid under illegal contracts
agents, from, 16–192
fraud, 16–186
generally, 16–177
in pari delicto, 16–185
locus poenitentiae, 16–188—16–191
mistake, 16–187
oppression, 16–186
trustees, by, 16–193
Representations
See **Statements**
Representative actions
generally, 9–065
requirements
benefit of class, 9–070
common interest, 9–069
generally, 9–066
no new right of action, 9–067—9–068
Repudiation
employment contracts, 16–100—16–101
generally
And see **Discharge by breach**
consequences, 24–047—24–055
failure of performance, 24–034—24–046
generally, 24–001—24–017
impossibility, 24–028—24–033

Repudiation—*cont.*
generally—*cont.*
renunciation, 24–018—24–027
minors
effect of avoidance, 8–040
generally, 8–030—8–032
lease of land, 8–033—8–035
marriage settlements, 8–036
partnerships, 8–039
purchase of land, 8–033—8–034
share purchases, 8–037—8–038
time of avoidance, 8–041
restraint of trade, 16–100—16–101
"Repugnant clauses"
construction of terms, 12–078
Reputation
damages for loss
generally, 26–086—26–087
introduction, 1–123
Requests for information
termination of offer, 2–093
Rescission
abandonment, 22–027
affirmation, 6–124—6–125
agreement, by
abandonment, 22–027
effect, 22–026
form, 22–030
generally, 22–025
novation, 22–031
substitution of contract, 22–028—22–029
apprenticeships, 8–024
consent orders
misrepresentation, 6–113
consideration, 3–077—3–078
contract terms, 6–104—6–105
discharge by breach
generally, 24–047
introduction, 24–001
effect, 6–114
estoppel, 6–126
executed contracts, 6–133
frustration, 23–071
innocent misrepresentation, 6–097—6–098
lapse of time, 6–127—6–128
limitation of actions, 28–144
'mere equity', 6–130
misrepresentation
consent orders, 6–113
effect, 6–114
generally, 6–103—6–109
liable parties, 6–112
procedure, 6–110—6–111
restrictions, 6–115—6–133
mistake of law, 29–050
negligent misrepresentation, 6–072—6–073
novation, 22–031
Rescission—*cont.*
restitutio in integrum
alteration of subject-matter, 6–117—6–118
completion of services, 6–119—6–120
generally, 6–115—6–116
indemnity for obligations, 6–121—6–122
restrictions
affirmation, 6–124—6–125
estoppel, 6–126
executed contracts, 6–133
generally, 6–123
lapse of time, 6–127—6–128
'mere equity', 6–130
restitutio in integrum, 6–115—6–122
third party rights, 6–129—6–132
substitution of contract, 22–028—22–029
termination for breach, 6–106—6–108
variation, 22–034
Restitutio in integrum
alteration of subject-matter, 6–117—6–118
completion of services, 6–119—6–120
generally, 6–115—6–116
indemnity for obligations, 6–121—6–122
Restitution
account
assignment, 29–196
general principle, 29–194—29–195
introduction, 29–193
stakeholders, 29–197—29–198
account of profits, 29–152—29–154
account stated
generally, 29–191
illegal debts, 29–192
unenforceable debts, 29–192
auctioneers, 29–198
avoided insurance policy, 29–082
breach of contract
account of profits, 29–152—29–154
introduction, 29–151
bribes, 29–156
change of position, 29–179—29–185
classification, 29–004
common law, at, 29–002
compliance with local authority notices, 29–096
compromise, 29–189
compulsion
compliance with local authority notices, 29–096
distress of goods, 29–091
duress of the person, 29–089—29–090
extortion colore officii, 29–094–29–095

Restitution—*cont.*
compulsion—*cont.*
generally, 29–087
illegitimate, 29–088
payment made in course of legal proceedings, 29–098
payment of excessive amount, 29–097
payment to third person, 29–099—29–129
unlawful compulsion, 29–088
wrongful demand, 29–092—29–093
conflict of laws, 30–033
constructive trusts, 29–160
contract for benefit of third party, 18–045
contract for sale of goods, 4–084—4–088
damages, 26–025
defences
change of position, 29–179—29–185
compromise, 29–189
estoppel, 29–176—29–178
payment following demand, 29–190
settlement of honest claim, 29–186—29–188
deposits, 29–064—29–065
disgorgement of profits, 29–139
distress of goods, 29–091
duress of the person
generally, 29–089
seizure of goods, 29–090
equitable wrongdoing
allowance, 29–157
bribes, 29–156
commission, 29–156
introduction, 29–155
secret profit, 29–156
equity, in, 29–003
estate agents, 29–198
estoppel
generally, 29–176—29–178
introduction, 29–019
exploitation
unconscionable bargains, 29–138
undue influence, 29–137
extortion, 29–150
extortion colore officii
generally, 29–094
nature of threat, 29–095
failure of consideration
avoided insurance policy, 29–082
deposits, 29–064—29–065
illegal contracts, 29–077—29–078
introduction, 29–054
minors' contracts, 29–081
part payments, 29–066
partial failure of consideration, 29–060—29–063
quantum meruit, 29–067—29–073

Restitution—*cont.*
failure of consideration—*cont.*
total failure of consideration, 29–055—29–059
unenforceable contract, 29–079—29–080
void contract, 29–074—29–076
fraud
limitations, 29–149
obtaining money, 29–147
obtaining services, 29–148
historical background
generally, 29–005
implied promise, 29–007—29–009
indebitatus assumpsit, 29–006
illegal contracts
generally, 29–077
services rendered, 29–078
implied contract theory
generally, 29–011
historical background, 29–007—29–009
improvement to land
defendant's acquiescence, 29–161
intervention on behalf of defendant
acting in public interest, 29–132
analogous categories, 29–133
generally, 29–131
necessaries, 29–135
non-gratuitous, 29–134
reasonableness, 29–134
introduction
historical background, 29–005—29–009
nature of restitution, 29–001—29–004
theoretical basis, 29–010—29–017
minors
common law, at, 8–049
equity, in, 8–050
fraudulent gains, 8–051—8–057
generally, 8–048
mistake of fact, payment under
burden of proof, 29–035
causative mistake, 29–034
compromise, 29–038
fundamental mistake, 29–033
good consideration, 29–037
introduction, 29–028
payer with means of knowledge, 29–036
prior notices and demand, 29–039
submission to claim, 29–038
'supposed liability' rule, 29–030—29–032
mistake of law, payment under
abolition of bar, 29–046
change in law, 29–048
criticism of rule, 29–044
equitable relief, 29–043

Restitution—*cont.*
mistake of law, payment under—*cont.*
examples, 29–041
exceptions, 29–042
generally, 29–040
improvements to another's goods, 29–051—29–053
principles, 29–047
rejection of rule, 29–045
remedies, 29–049—29–050
repairs to another's goods, 29–051
nature of
common law, at, 29–002
equity, in, 29–003
generally, 29–001
necessity
generally, 29–130
intervention on behalf of defendant, 29–131—29–135
salvage, 29–136
oppression, 29–150
part payments, 29–066
partial failure of consideration
common law, at, 29–061
divisible contract, in, 29–063
statute, under, 29–060
passing on, 29–027
payment following demand, 29–190
payment made in course of legal proceedings, 29–098
payment of excessive amount, 29–097
payment to third person
assignees of lease, 29–106
generally, 29–099—29–100
legal liability to pay, 29–101
other examples, 29–107—29–129
primary liability to pay, 29–102
seizure of goods, 29–103—29–105
privity of contract
contract for benefit of third party, 18–045
generally, 29–026
third party rights, 18–042
proprietary claims
bona fide purchase defence, 29–175
common law, at, 29–170—29–171
equity, in, 29–172
establishing rights, 29–158—29–161
following, 29–162
personal remedies, 29–174
subrogation, 29–173
tracing, 29–162—29–169
quantum meruit
additional work, 29–072
bad bargains, 29–068
contract price, 29–069
generally, 29–067
goods supplied, 29–070
introduction, 29–004
no fixed price, 29–071

Restitution—*cont.*
quantum meruit—*cont.*
services rendered, 29–070
substituted contract for services, 29–073
quantum valebant, 29–004
relationship with contracts, 1–192
salvage, 29–136
secret profit, 29–156
seizure of goods
duress, 29–090
payment to third person, 29–103—29–105
settlement of honest claim, 29–186—29–188
solicitors, 29–198
stakeholders
auctioneers, 29–198
estate agents, 29–198
generally, 29–197
solicitors, 29–198
subrogation, 29–173
theoretical basis
alternative basis, 29–017
generally, 29–010—29–011
unjust enrichment, 29–012—29–016
tort, for
deceit, 29–147
effect of statute, 29–143
election of remedy, 29–146
extortion, 29–150
fraud, 29–147—29–149
introduction, 29–141
nature of benefit, 29–144
oppression, 29–150
profits made by defendant, 29–145
tortious acts, 29–142
total failure of consideration
artificial distinctions, 29–057
detrimental reliance, 29–055
discharged contracts, 29–058—29–059
examples, 29–056
introduction, 29–054
reconsideration of requirement, 29–062
tracing
common law, at, 29–163
equity, in, 29–164—29–167
introduction, 29–162
proceeds of sale, 29–169
reservation of title, 29–168
ultra vires receipts
defences, 29–086
demands, 29–083
introduction, 9–026
scope of right, 29–084
statutory provisions, 29–085
unconscionable bargains, 29–138

Restitution—*cont.*
undue influence
generally, 7–098—7–099
introduction, 29–137
unenforceable contract
money paid, 29–079
work done, 29–080
unjust enrichment
And see **Unjust enrichment**
background, 29–012—29–016
compulsion, 29–087—29–129
defences and bars, 29–019
elements, 29–018
'enrichment', 29–020—29–023
'expense of claimant', 29–025—29–027
exploitation, 29–137—29–138
failure of consideration, 29–054—29–082
grounds of restitution, 29–028
mistake, 29–028—29–053
necessity, 29–130—29–136
ultra vires receipts, 29–083—29–086
void contract
absence of consideration, 29–075
generally, 29–074
goods supplied, 29–076
services rendered, 29–076
writs of assumpsit, debt and account, 29–005
wrongful demand
detention of goods, on, 29–092
detention of title deeds, on, 29–093
wrongs, for
breach of contract, 29–151—29–154
disgorgement of profits, 29–139
equity, in, 29–155—29–157
general principles, 29–139—29–140
nature of obligation, 29–140
tort, 29–141—29–150
"Restitutionary damages"
generally, 26–025
"Restraint of marriage"
injurious objects, 16–072
Restraint of trade
assignment, 16–099
auction rings, 16–135
burden of proof, 16–095—16–096
chattels, 16–130
common law, at
employment, 16–104—16–115
horizontal agreements, 16–132—16–140
labour and services, 16–136—16–140
partnership, 16–119—16–120
sale of business, 16–116—16–118
scope, 16–075—16–103
supply of goods, 16–121—16–127, 16–132—16–135
Restraint of trade—*cont.*
common law, at—*cont.*
use of land, 16–128—16–131
vertical agreements, 16–121—16–127
commercial use of land, 16–128
competition abroad, 16–091
competition law
And see **Competition law**
generally, 16–141
consideration
generally, 16–090
introduction, 3–166
construction 16–097
conveyances, 16–129
co-operative marketing schemes, 16–127
deeds, 16–089
employer's associations, 16–133
employment contract, after expiry of
breach, 16–114
competition, 16–106
confidential information, 16–107—16–109
customer information, 16–108—16–110
generally, 16–104
limitations, 16–111—16–113
reasonableness, 16–105
trade secrets, 16–108
employment contract, during currency 16–115
exclusive purchasing agreements
solus petrol agreements, 16–122—16–124
tied public-houses, 16–125—16–126
exclusive selling agreements, 16–127
franchise agreements, 16–120
generally, 16–075
horizontal agreements
auction rings, 16–135
employer's associations, 16–133
generally, 16–132
price-fixing agreements, 16–134
professional bodies, 16–139
trade unions, 16–136—16–140
injunctions
generally, 27–068—27–069
interlocutory, 16–103
introduction, 16–102
labour and services, 16–136—16–140
land use
conveyances, 16–129
generally, 16–128
leases, 16–129
leases, 16–129
meaning, 16–077—16–078
minors, 8–026
parties' legitimate interests, 16–093—16–094

Restraint of trade—*cont.*
partnership agreements, 16–119
patent licences, 16–131
petrol agreements, 16–122—16–124
price-fixing agreements, 16–134
principles, 16–079—16–087
professional bodies, 16–139
property use
chattels, 16–130
patent licences, 16–131
patented articles, 16–131
public interest, 16–095—16–096
reasonableness
construction of covenant, 16–097
determining factors, 16–098
generally, 16–092
parties' legitimate interests, 16–093—16–094
public interest, 16–095—16–096
solus petrol agreements, 16–123
repudiation, 16–100—16–101
severance, 16–199, 16–203
solus petrol agreements, 16–122—16–124
statutory regulation, 16–141
supply and acquisition of goods
horizontal agreements, 16–132—16–135
vertical agreements, 16–121—16–127
supply of labour, 16–140
supply of services
generally, 16–138
professional work, 16–139
tied public-houses, 16–125—16–126
trade unions, 16–136—16–140
use of land
commercial land, 16–128
covenants in conveyance or lease, 16–129
vendor and purchaser of business
generally, 16–116—16–117
goodwill, 16–118
vertical agreements
co-operative marketing, 16–127
generally, 16–121
solus petrol agreements, 16–122—16–124
tied public-houses, 16–125—16–126
Retainers
statute-barred debt, 28–131
"Revalorisation"
generally, 21–068
gold clauses, 21–069—21–071
index-linking, 21–072
"Revocable contracts"
specific performance, 27–038
Revocation
acceptance, of
cancellation, 2–062
Revocation—*cont.*
acceptance, of—*cont.*
generally, 2–060—2–061
wills, of, 16–074
Rewards
offer, 2–019
Rome Convention 1980
background, 30–017—30–018
interpretation
generally, 30–019
uniformity, 30–020
provisions
And see **Applicable law**
choice of law by parties, 30–047—30–070
consumer contracts, 30–092—30–107
employment contracts, 30–108—30–121
exclusions, 30–030—30–046
no choice of law by parties, 30–071—30–091
subrogation, 30–127—30–129
voluntary assignment, 30–123—30–125
renvoi, 30–028
Rome I Regulation, and
And see **Rome I Regulation**
applicable law in absence of choice, 30–186—30–199
consumer contracts, 30–231—30–251
contracts of carriage, 30–200—30–230
employment contracts, 30–276—30–287
exclusions, 30–152—30–163
formal validity of contract, 30–318—30–322
freedom of choice, 30–170—30–185
generally, 30–130—30–151
habitual residence, 30–164—30–169
illegality in place of performance of act, 30–360
insurance contracts, 30–252—30–275
multiple liability, 30–296—30–298
nullity of contract, 30–328
set-off, 30–299-30–302
subrogation, 30–288—30–295
unjust enrichment, 30–034
voluntary assignment, 30–288—30–292
scope
choice between countries, 30–022—30–023
choice between systems, 30–024
choice within UK, 30–025
generally, 30–021
incorporation by reference, 30–029

Rome Convention 1980—*cont.*
scope—*cont.*
mandatory force, 30–026
relationship with other Conventions, 30–027
Rome I Regulation
And see **Rome Convention 1980**
"administrative matters", 30–142
agent-principal relationships, 30–159
applicable law in absence of choice
auction sales, 30–195
carriage of goods, 30–215—30–218
carriage of passengers, 30–227—30–228
characteristic performance, 30–201—30–202
contract not covered, 30–197
contract outside scope, 30–198
distribution contracts, 30–194
elements covered by more than one point, 30–199
employment contracts, 30–281—30–283
franchise contracts, 30–193
immovables, 30–192
introduction, 30–186
large insurance risks, 30–264
multilateral system, 30–196
principles, 30–188
provision of services, 30–191
residual rule, 30–206—30–208
rule of displacement, 30–203—30–205
sale of goods, 30–190
scope of provision, 30–200
specific rules, 30–189
structure of Article 4, 30–187
application of laws
country, of a, 30–144
non-member States, of, 30–143
arbitration agreements, 30–157
auction sales, 30–195
background, 30–130—30–131
bills of exchange, 30–156
capacity of natural persons, 30–153
carriage of goods
applicable law in absence of choice, 30–215—30–218
"carrier", 30–217
choice of law by the parties, 30–214
"consignor", 30–218
generally, 30–212
meaning, 30–213
residual rule, 30–219
rule of displacement, 30–220
carriage of passengers
applicable law in absence of choice, 30–227—30–228
central administration, 30–225

Rome I Regulation—*cont.*
carriage of passengers—*cont.*
choice of law by the parties, 30–223—30–226
generally, 30–221
habitual residence, 30–224—30–224
principles, 30–222
residual rule, 30–229
rule of displacement, 30–230
changing choice of law, 30–176
choice of court agreements, 30–157
choice of law by the parties
carriage of goods, 30–214
carriage of passengers, 30–223—30–226
changing choice of law, 30–176
"clearly demonstrated", 30–173
consent to choice of law, 30–184
consumer contracts, 30–249
employment contracts, 30–279—30–280
general principle, 30–171
introduction, 30–170
large insurance risks, 30–263
limitations on choice of law, 30–177—30–183
making choice of law, 30–172—30–173
other insurance contracts, 30–266
partial choice of law, 30–175
party autonomy, 30–185
"civil and commercial matters", 30–141
"clearly demonstrated", 30–173
Community law, and, 30–135
Community law restrictions, 30–179
company law issues, 30–158
concurrent claims
employment contracts, 30–287
generally, 30–151
consent to choice of law, 30–184
consumer contracts
background, 30–231
choice of law by the parties, 30–249
consumer-professional contract, 30–240
contracts of carriage, 30–235
electronic commerce, 30–245
electronic mail, 30–246
exclusions, 30–233
general rule, 30–239
financial instruments, 30–237
habitual residence, 30–241
immovable property, 30–236
"pursues his commercial or professional activities", 30–242—30–243
review clause, 30–251
scope of Article, 30–239
structure of Article, 30–232

Rome I Regulation—*cont*.
consumer contracts—*cont*.
supply of services, 30–234
techniques used, 30–244—30–245
websites, 30–247
contracts of carriage
background, 30–209
carriage of goods, 30–212—30–220
carriage of passengers, 30–221—30–230
consumer contracts, and, 30–235
international conventions, 30–211
scope of Article, 30–210
structure of Article, 30–210
"contractual obligations", 30–147
contractual subrogation
assignability, 30–291
assignee-assignor relationship, 30–290
background, 30–288
meaning, 30–289
priorities, 30–292
"customs matters", 30–142
distribution contracts, 30–194
EC law, and, 30–135
electronic commerce, 30–245
electronic mail, 30–246
employment contracts
applicable law in absence of choice, 30–281—30–283
background, 30–276
choice of law by parties, 30–279—30–280
concurrent claims, 30–287
default rule, 30–284
generally, 30–280—30–287
meaning, 30–278
non-derogable provisions, 30–280
overriding mandatory provisions, 30–286
principal place of work, 30–282
rule of displacement, 30–285
structure of Article, 30–277
temporary employment abroad, 30–283
evidence and procedure, 30–161
exclusions
agent-principal relationships, 30–159
arbitration agreements, 30–157
bills of exchange, 30–156
capacity of natural persons, 30–153
choice of court agreements, 30–157
company law issues, 30–158
evidence, 30–161
family relationships, 30–154
generally, 30–152
insurance, 30–163
matrimonial property, 30–155
pre-contractual dealings, 30–162
trusts, 30–160

Rome I Regulation—*cont*.
family relationships, 30–154
financial instruments, 30–237
formal validity of contract
change of applicable law, 30–322
consumer contracts, 30–320
general rules, 30–318
immovables, 30–321
unilateral acts, 30–319
franchise contracts, 30–193
freedom of choice
changing choice of law, 30–176
"clearly demonstrated", 30–173
consent to choice of law, 30–184
general principle, 30–171
introduction, 30–170
limitations on choice of law, 30–177—30–183
making choice of law, 30–172—30–173
partial choice of law, 30–175
party autonomy, 30–185
generally, 30–130—30–151
habitual residence
agencies, 30–166
branches, 30–166
companies, 30–165
consumer contracts, and, 30–241
introduction, 30–164
natural persons, 30–167—30–168
relevant time, 30–169
illegality in place of performance of act, 30–360
immovables
consumer contracts, 30–236
generally, 30–192
insurance contracts
background, 30–252
compulsory insurance, 30–275
event in one member State, 30–270
exclusions, and, 30–163, 30–255
large risks, 30–260—30–264
life assurance, 30–269
"member State", 30–258
other insurance contracts, 30–265—30–275
reinsurance, 30–256
scope, 30–254
situs of risk, 30–257—30–259
structure of Article, 30–253
internal situations, and, 30–178
international conventions, and, 30–137
interpretation, 30–134
large insurance risks
applicable law in absence of choice, 30–264
choice of law by parties, 30–263
generally, 30–261
meaning, 30–262

Rome I Regulation—*cont.*
'law of country of performance', 30–182
'law of the forum', 30–181
legal basis, 30–132
legal subrogation
background, 30–293
meaning, 30–295
principle, 30–294
limitations on choice of law
Community law restrictions, 30–179
internal situations, 30–178
introduction, 30–177
overriding mandatory provisions, 30–180—30–182
public policy, 30–183
making choice of law, 30–172—30–173
matrimonial property, 30–155
multiple liability
defences, 30–298
principle, 30–296
right of recourse, 30–298
non-contractual obligations
concurrent claims, 30–151
generally, 30–148
nullity of contract, 30–150
pre-contractual dealings, 30–149
nullity of contract
consequences, 30–150
generally, 30–328
other insurance contracts
applicable law in absence of choice, 30–273—30–275
choice of law by parties, 30–266—30–272
compulsory insurance, 30–275
generally, 30–265
habitual residence, 30–268
law of member State where risk situated, 30–267
life assurance, 30–269
limits on risks, 30–270
"pursues commercial or industrial activity", 30–271
supplementary freedom of choice, 30–272—30–274
overriding mandatory provisions
employment contracts, 30–286
introduction, 30–180
'law of country of performance', 30–182
'law of the forum', 30–181
overview, 30–133
partial choice of law, 30–175
party autonomy, 30–185
pre-contractual dealings
exclusions, and, 30–162
generally, 30–149
provision of services, 30–191

Rome I Regulation—*cont.*
public policy, 30–183
relationships with
Community law, 30–135
international conventions, 30–137
Rome Convention, 30–136
renvoi, 30–146
residence
agencies, 30–166
branches, 30–166
companies, 30–165
introduction, 30–164
natural persons, 30–167—30–168
relevant time, 30–169
residual rule
carriage of goods, 30–219
carriage of passengers, 30–229
generally, 30–206—30–208
"revenue matters", 30–142
review clause, 30–138
rule of displacement
carriage of goods, 30–220
carriage of passengers, 30–230
employment contracts, 30–285
generally, 30–203—30–205
sale of goods, 30–190
scope
"administrative matters", 30–142
"civil and commercial matters", 30–141
"contractual obligations", 30–147
"customs matters", 30–142
generally, 30–139
"non-contractual obligations", 30–148—30–151
renvoi, 30–146
"revenue matters", 30–142
"situations involving a conflict of laws", 30–140
states with more than one legal system, 30–145
"universal effect", 30–143
set-off
applicable law, 30–302
background, 30–299
insolvency proceedings, in, 30–301
introduction, 30–346
meaning, 30–300
"situations involving a conflict of laws", 30–140
specific choice of law rules
consumer contracts, 30–231—30–251
contracts of carriage, 30–200—30–230
employment contracts, 30–276—30–287
insurance contracts, 30–252—30–275
overview, 30–133

Rome I Regulation—*cont.*
states with more than one legal system, 30–145
structure, 30–133
subject-matter, 30–133
subrogation
contractual, 30–289—30–292
legal, 30–293—30–295
supply of services, 30–234
trusts, 30–160
"universal effect", 30–143
unjust enrichment, 30–034
voluntary assignment
assignability, 30–291
assignee-assignor relationship, 30–290
background, 30–288
meaning, 30–289
priorities, 30–292
websites, 30–247
Rome II Regulation
And see **Rome Convention 1980**
employment contracts, 30–122
interpretation of Rome I Regulation, and, 30–134

Safety of goods
See **Product safety**
Salaries
See **Wages**
Sale of goods
affirmation, 22–004—22–005
classification, 1–069
damages
mitigation, 26–110—26–114
remoteness, 26–088
discharge by frustration
generally, 23–047
'Suez Canal' cases, 23–048
exemption clauses
description, correspondence with, 14–027
fitness for purpose, 14–027
quality, 14–027
sample, correspondence with, 14–027
title, 14–026
force majeure clauses, 14–151
frustration
generally, 23–047
'Suez Canal' cases, 23–048
implied terms
debt payment, 13–035
export licences, 13–013
introduction, 13–029
innominate terms, 12–036
intermediate terms, 12–036
limitation of actions
date from which time runs, 28–052
relevant period, 28–027

Sale of goods—*cont.*
mitigation of damage, 26–110—26–114
remoteness of damage, 26–088
specific performance
ascertained goods, 27–016—27–018
defective delivery of goods, 27–019
generally, 27–013
specific goods, 27–016—27–018
unique goods, 27–014—27–015
unfair contract terms (consumer contracts), 15–012—15–013
unfair contract terms
dealing as a consumer, 14–067
implied terms, 14–078
reasonableness, 14–085
Sale of goodwill
specific performance, 27–043
Sale of land
discharge by frustration, 23–057
formal requirements
background, 4–009
post-26th September 1989, 4–052–4–088
pre- 26th September 1989, 4–010—4–051
frustration, 23–057
implied terms
fitness for habitation, 13–015
generally, 13–031
minors, 8–067
offer and acceptance, 2–110
remoteness of damage, 26–091—26–097
merger
generally, 25–003
lessee, to, 25–004
minors, by
delivery, by, 8–065
grant, by, 8–066
misrepresentation, 6–156—6–157
post-26th September 1989
And see **Contracts for sale of land (s.2 LP(MP)A 1989)**
form of contracts, 4–069—4–072
generally, 4–052—4–053
non-compliance, effect 4–075—4–088
relevant contracts, 4–054—4–068
pre- 26th September 1989
And see **Contracts for sale of land (s.40 LPA 1925)**
form of contracts, 4–022—4–040
generally, 4–010
non-compliance, effect 4–041—4–051
relevant contracts, 4–011—4–021
specific performance
generally, 27–007
unwritten contract, 27–037
unfair contract terms, 14–105

Sale of land—*cont.*
unfair contract terms (consumer contracts)
consumer sales, 15–015
generally, 15–014
mortgage contracts, 15–016
other, 15–018
tenancies contracts, 15–017
"Sale of public contracts"
illegality, 16–019—16–020
"Sale of public office"
illegality, 16–019—16–020
Sale by sample
exclusion clauses, 14–027
Sale of shares
See **Share sales**
"Salvage contracts"
limitation of actions, 28–021
restitution, 29–136
unconscionable bargains, 7–127
unfair contract terms, 14–106
Samples
See **Sale by sample**
Satisfaction
negotiable instruments, 21–077
Satisfactory quality
exclusion clauses, 14–027
Schemes of arrangement
deeds of arrangement
generally, 20–051
surety, 20–052
voluntary arrangements, 20–050
Secret profits
restitution, 29–156
Secured tenancies
minors, 8–035
Security
negotiable instruments, 21–076
Seizure
duress, 29–090
payment to third person, 29–103—29–105
"Self-contradictory terms"
custom and trade usage, 2–144
"Self-induced frustration"
burden of proof, 23–065
examples, 23–062—23–065
generally, 23–061
Self-service
offer, 2–014
Service
generally, 1–125
Service stations
offer, 2–014
restraint of trade, 16–122—16–124
Set-off
bankruptcy
generally, 20–040—20–041
mutual debts, 20–043—20–044
unliquidated damages, 20–042
Set-off—*cont.*
conflict of laws, and, 30–346
discharge, 25–031
Rome I Regulation, and
applicable law, 30–302
background, 30–299
insolvency proceedings, in, 30–301
introduction, 30–346
meaning, 30–300
Setting aside
voluntary settlements
limitation of actions, 28–145
restitution, 29–110
Settlement
honest claim, of
generally, 29–186—29–188
introduction, 29–019
mistake of fact, 29–038
Severability
discharge by frustration, 23–091
failure of performance, 24–044
generally, 21–027
injunctions, 27–069
meaning, 21–037
Several liability
And see **Joint obligations**
meaning, 17–001
"Severance"
association's rules, 16–200
generally, 16–194—16–195
joint liability, 17–006
part of the consideration, 16–201
principles, 16–196—16–198
public policy, 16–202
restraint of trade, 16–199, 16–203
Sham transactions
generally, 2–186
Share sales
remoteness of damage, 26–100
Shareholders
company contracts with
allotment of shares, 9–060
effect of articles, 9–061
ultra vires, 9–034
Shares
contracts for subscription
minors, 8–037—8–038
misrepresentation, 6–153—6–154
offer, 2–024
sales, 26–100
"Shelf displays"
offer, 2–014
"Shooting rights"
contracts for sale of land, 4–021
Signature
contracts for sale of land
LPA 1925, s.40, 4–031—4–039
LP(MP)A 1989, s.2, 4–072—4–074

Signature—*cont.*
contracts for sale of land (LPA 1925, s.40)
agent, by, 4–036—4–039
alterations, 4–035
form, 4–034
generally, 4–031
intention, 4–033
position, 4–032
contracts for sale of land (LP(MP)A 1989, s.2)
agent, by, 4–074
generally, 4–072
meaning, 4–073
non est factum
generally, 5–102
introduction, 5–002
meaning, 5–101
nature of mistake, 5–103—5–106
"Significant imbalance"
detriment of consumer, 15–050—15–052
generally, 15–046—15–049
Silence
contractual
assumption of responsibility, 1–158—1–160
general position, 1–157
introduction, 1–156
exceptions to rule
conduct, 2–076—2–077
offeree bound, 2–072—2–074
offeror bound, 2–075
general rule, 2–070—2–071
offeree bound
estoppel, 2–073
generally, 2–072
performance despite silence, 2–074
Social and domestic agreements
adults sharing, between, 2–172—2–173
children and parents, between, 2–174
civil partners, between, 2–170
cohabitants, between, 2–171
intention, 2–168
spouses, between, 2–169
"Social discredit"
damages, 26–083
Solicitors
indemnity insurance, 18–130
presumed undue influence, 7–076
stakeholders, as, 29–198
Solus agreements
restraint of trade, 16–122—16–124
Sovereign immunity
See **State immunity**
Special damages
generally, 26–006
Specialty contracts
See **Contracts under seal**
Specific goods
See also **Ascertained goods**
See also **Unascertained goods**
specific performance, 27–016—27–018
Specific performance
agreed sum clauses, 27–006
agreements for lease, 27–040
benefit of third party, contract for, 18–044
building services, contracts for, 27–028—27–029
compensation, with
errors, 27–056—27–057
misdescription, 27–054—27–057
misrepresentation, 27–058
conditional contracts, 27–039
conduct
failure to perform, 27–035
unfairness, 27–036
conflict of laws, 30–338
consideration
inadequacy, 27–033
lack 27–034
contracts for benefit of third party, 18–044
contracts for sale of land
generally, 27–007
unwritten contract, 27–037
contracts of employment, 27–022—27–023
damages
assessment, 27–079
generally, 27–077—27–083
introduction, 26–004
limits, 27–084
debt actions, 27–004
delay, 27–045
employment contracts, 27–022—27–023
generally, 27–001
goodwill, sale 27–043
impossibility, 27–041
lease of land
agreements for, 27–040
generally, 27–007, 27–047—27–048
limitation of actions, 28–018, 28–143
limitations
damages an adequate remedy, 27–005—27–019
generally, 27–002—27–003
other grounds, 27–030—27–045
unenforceable contracts, 27–020—27–029
loan of money, 27–012
minors, 27–047
misrepresentation, 27–045
mistake, 27–045
nominal damages, 27–009

Specific performance—*cont.*
personal services contracts
employment contracts, 27–022—27–023
generally, 27–046
other contracts, 27–024
rectification, 5–124
revocable contracts, 27–038
sale of goods
ascertained goods, 27–016—27–018
defective delivery of goods, 27–019
generally, 27–013
specific goods, 27–016—27–018
unique goods, 27–014—27–015
sale of land
generally, 27–007
unwritten contract, 27–037
severe hardship, 27–031
third parties
introduction, 27–049
promisee's claims, 27–051—27–052
third party's claims, 27–053
third party rights, 18–044
unenforceable contracts
building services, 27–028—27–029
carrying on an activity, 27–026
generally, 27–020
personal services, 27–022—27–024
unfairness, 27–032
vagueness, 27–042
Spouses
presumed undue influence
generally, 7–085
manifest disadvantage, 7–087—7–090
undue influence
bank put on inquiry, 7–111—7–112
Barclays Bank v O'Brien, 7–106—7–108
conflicts of interest, 7–117—7–118
Etridge's case, 7–109—7–110
introduction, 7–105
jointly-owned homes, 7–123
legal advice, 7–115—7–116
loss of right to avoid, 7–122
procedure, 7–119
reasonable steps, 7–114
replacement mortgages, 7–121
spouse as party to transaction, 7–120
transactions not to advantage of surety, 7–113
Stakeholders
restitution
auctioneers, 29–198
estate agents, 29–198
generally, 29–197
solicitors, 29–198
Standard forms of contracts
form of notices
generally, 12–017
Standard forms of contracts—*cont.*
form of notices—*cont.*
statutory provision, 12–018
generally, 12–008
incorporation of terms
course of dealing, by, 12–011
notices 12–013—12–018
time 12–010
trade custom, by, 12–012
notices of terms
contents 12–013
form 12–017—12–018
sufficiency 12–014—12–016
relevant documents, 12–009
sufficiency of notices
generally, 12–014
onerous conditions 12–015
personal disability, 12–016
unusual conditions, 12–015
unfair contract terms (consumer contracts), 15–031—15–032
State immunity
common law, at, 11–001
human rights, 11–003
statute, under
exceptions, 11–005—11–006
generally, 11–004
introduction, 11–002
waiver, 11–020
Statements
express terms, 12–030
mere representations, 2–166
puffs, 2–165
threats to break contract, 7–040
"Statements of the inevitable"
threats to break contract, 7–040
"Statute-barred debt"
past consideration, 3–035
"Statutory assignment"
conditions
absolute, 19–012—19–014
generally, 19–007
notices, 19–016—19–018
types of choses, 19–008—19–011
written, 19–015
consideration, 19–019
distinction from equitable assignments, 19–004—19–006
generally, 19–007
"Statutory corporations"
And see **Companies**
contracts, 9–005
generally, 9–001
"Statutory interest"
And see **Interest**
applicable law, 30–341—30–344
exercise of discretion, 26–175
foreign currency, in
exchange rates, 26–181
generally, 26–180

"Statutory interest"—*cont.*
generally, 26–174
late payment of commercial debts, 26–182
period, 26–176—26–177
rate, 26–178—26–179
Statutory tenancies
minors, 8–035
Sub-agents
privity of contract, 18–013
"Subject-matter classification"
commercial purposes, for, 1–072
common law purposes, for, 1–070—1–072
generally, 1–068
statutory purposes, for, 1–069
Subject to contract
auctions, 2–122
collateral agreements, 2–121
contracts for sale of land, 4–053
exchange of contracts, need for
general rule, 2–119
mitigation of rule, 2–120—2–123
generally, 2–118
'lock-out' agreements, 2–121
provisional agreements, 2–123
tender, sales by, 2–122
"Subject to equities"
bankruptcy, 20–039
"Submission to honest claim"
generally, 29–186—29–188
introduction, 29–019
mistake of fact, 29–038
Subrogation
applicable law, 30–127—30–129
restitution, 29–173
Rome I Regulation, and, 30–289—30–295
"Substituted performance"
damages, 26–016—26–018
generally, 21–004
Substitution
rescission, 22–028—22–029
Succession
applicable law, 30–037
unfair contract terms (consumer contracts), 15–028
"Successive breaches"
limitation of actions, 28–035
"Suez Canal cases"
discharge by frustration, 23–048
Suicide
life insurance, 16–171
"Supervening incapacity"
charter companies, 2–108
companies, of
generally, 2–103—2–104
offeree, as, 2–105
offeror, as, 2–106—2–107
limited liability partnerships, 2–109
"Supervening incapacity"—*cont.*
termination of offer
companies, 2–103—2–109
individuals, 2–102
Supervening prohibition
exercise of statutory power, 23–026
foreign law, under, 23–027—23–029
generally, 23–024
restrictions on outbreak of war, 23–024—23–025
"Supplier's discretion clause"
unfair contract terms (consumer contracts), 15–082
Supply of goods
implied terms
debt payment, 13–035
generally, 13–030
restraint of trade
horizontal agreements, 16–132—16–135
vertical agreements, 16–121—16–127
unfair contract terms (consumer contracts), 15–012—15–013
Supply of services
implied terms, 13–032—13–033
limitation of actions, 28–053
restraint of trade
generally, 16–138
professional work, 16–139
unfair contract terms (consumer contracts), 15–012—15–013
"Supposed liability rule"
mistake, 29–030—29–032
"Synallagmatic contracts"
generally, 1–079

Tax
damages
capital gains tax, 26–166
income tax, 26–157—26–165
"Technical words"
construction of terms, 12–052
"Telegram acceptance"
dictation, upon, 2–051
garbled message, 2–059
generally, 2–048
"Telemessage acceptance"
dictation, upon, 2–051
garbled message, 2–059
generally, 2–048
Telephones
acceptance, 2–050
Telex
acceptance, 2–050
Tenancies
classification
common law purposes, for, 1–070
statutory purposes, for, 1–069
formal requirements, 4–002

Tenancies—*cont.*
frustration
consequences, 23–056
destruction of building, 23–053
generally, 23–052
interruption of use, 23–055
prohibition on use, 23–054
Tenancies in common
payment to third person, 29–118
Tender
agent
tender by, 21–095
tender to, 21–094
amount, 21–085
conditional
generally, 21–091
protest, under, 21–092
credit card, by, 21–088
failure to comply, 21–096
generally, 21–083
legal currency, in, 21–086
money, 21–084
negotiable instrument, by, 21–087
offer
generally, 2–022
public procurement, 2–023
proof, 21–093
protest, under, 21–092
sale by
acceptance, 2–040
offer, 2–022
public procurement, 2–023
subject to contract, 2–122
unfair contract terms, 14–068
time 21–089—21–090
Tenders
acceptance, 2–039
Termination
breach of contract
damages, 26–141
rescission, 6–106—6–108
Termination (offers)
And see **Offer**
death, by
generally, 2–099
offeree, 2–101
offeror, 2–100
generally, 2–087
lapse of time, by
conduct, 2–097
reasonable period, 2–096
specified period, 2–095
occurrence of condition, by, 2–098
rejection, by
communication, 2–094
counter-offers, 2–092
information requests, 2–093
supervening incapacity, by
companies, 2–103—2–109
individuals, 2–102
Termination (offers)—*cont.*
withdrawal, by
communication, 2–089—2–091
general rule, 2–088
Terms and conditions
And see under individual headings
applicable law
common law, at, 30–005—30–016
generally, 30–001—30–004
Rome Convention, under,
30–017—30–129
scope, 30–303—30–379
conditions
And see **Conditions**
generally, 2–148
precedent, 2–149
promissory, 2–150
satisfaction of one party, to, 2–154
subsequent, 2–149
types, 12–019—12–030
waiver, 2–157
exemption
application, 14–025—14–038
common law control,
14–132—14–136
construction, 14–005—14–019
distance selling, 14–154
force majeure, 14–137—14–154
fundamental breach,
14–020—14–024
generally, 14–001—14–004
statutory regulation,
14–059—14–131
third parties, 14–039—14–058
express terms
classification, 12–019—12–040
construction, 12–041—12–094
extrinsic evidence, 12–095—12–133
form, 12–002—12–018
generally, 12–001
governing law
common law, at, 30–005—30–016
generally, 30–001—30–004
Rome Convention, under,
30–017—30–129
scope, 30–303—30–379
implied terms
generally, 13–002
nature, 13–001
purpose, 13–003—13–012
types, 13–013—13–035
proper law
common law, at, 30–005—30–016
generally, 30–001—30–004
Rome Convention, under,
30–017—30–129
scope, 30–303—30–379
unfair contract terms
introduction, 15–001—15–003

Terms and conditions—*cont.*
unfair contract terms—*cont.*
statutory regulation, 15–004—15–099
warranties
And see **Warranties**
collateral, 12–033
election, upon, 12–032
failure of performance, 24–038
generally, 12–019
meaning, 12–031
"Terms to be agreed"
determination criteria
generally, 2–130—2–131
rent review clauses, 2–132
exceptions to rule, 2–128—2–129
general rule, 2–126
options, 2–127
pre-emption rights, 2–127
Third parties
companies, contracts with
insolvency, 9–047—9–053
post-incorporation benefits, 9–017—9–019
pre-incorporation benefits, 9–016
pre-incorporation contracts, 9–012—9–015
registration of charges, 9–046
ultra vires, 9–020—9–045
contracts for benefit of
And see **Third party rights**
effects, 18–043—18–076
exceptions, 18–077—18–132
damages, 26–031
deeds, 1–110
enforcement against
exceptions to rule, 18–134
general rule, 18–133
scope of rule, 18–135—18–147
exemption clauses
agency, 14–047—14–049
bailment, 14–054—14–055
benefit, 14–042—14–043
burden, 14–040—14–041
common law rule, 14–040—14–043
construction contracts, 14–056—14–058
exceptions, 14–045
excluded contracts, 14–044
introduction, 14–039
occupier's liability, 14–053
promise not to sue, 14–051
trust, 14–050
vicarious immunity, 14–046
voluntary assumption of risk, 14–053
limitation of actions, 28–005
mistaken identity, 5–098—5–099
part payment of debt, 3–126
payment
payment by, 21–041

Third parties—*cont.*
payment—*cont.*
payment to, 21–042
privity of contract
And see **Privity of contract**
background, 18–019—18–020
general rule, 18–003—18–018
scope, 18–021—18–042
specific performance
introduction, 27–049
promisee's claims, 27–051—27–052
third party claims, 27–053
undue influence
constructive notice, 7–106—7–123
introduction, 7–104—7–105
other cases, 7–124
volunteers, 7–125
Third party claims
limitation of actions, 28–124
Third party debt orders
payment, 21–051
Third party rights
cancellation, 18–099—18–105
common law, at, 18–114—18–117
damages
promisee's loss, 18–047—18–048
third party's loss, 18–049—18–068
damages for third party's loss
building contracts, 18–053—18–066
criticism of general rule, 18–051
exceptions to rule, 18–052
general rule, 18–049—18–050
defective premises, 18–132
double liability, 18–120
effects
generally, 18–043
promisee's remedies, 18–044—18–071
enforcement, 18–088—18–098
equitable exceptions
marriage settlements, 18–087
trusts of promises, 18–078—18–086
exceptions
Contracts (Rights of Third Parties) Act 1999, 18–088—18–120
equitable, 18–078—18–087
generally, 18–077
statutory, 18–121—18–132
fire insurance, 18–129
generally, 18–002
injunctions
promise not to compete, 18–069
promise not to sue, 18–070—18–071
interests in land, 18–122—18–125
life insurance, 18–126
marine insurance, 18–128
marriage settlements, 18–087
Motor Insurers' Bureau claims, 18–131
motor insurance, 18–127
persons with limited interest, 18–128

Third party rights—*cont.*
promisee's remedies
agreed sum suit, 18–046
damages, 18–047—18–068
injunctions, 18–069—18–071
restitution, 18–045
specific performance, 18–044
promisee's rights, 18–119
promisor's defences, 18–106—18–110
restitution, 18–045
solicitors' indemnity insurance, 18–130
specific performance, 18–044
statutory exceptions
defective premises, 18–132
fire insurance, 18–129
interests in land, 18–122—18–125
introduction, 18–121
life insurance, 18–126
marine insurance, 18–128
Motor Insurers' Bureau claims, 18–131
motor insurance, 18–127
persons with limited interest, 18–128
solicitors' indemnity insurance, 18–130
statutory provisions
cancellation by third party, 18–099—18–105
common law rights of third party, 18–114—18–117
double liability, 18–120
enforcement by third party, 18–088—18–098
exceptions to third party rights, 18–111—18–113
generally, 18–002
promisee's rights, 18–119
promisor's defences, 18–106—18–110
variation by third party, 18–099—18–105
third party's loss
building contracts, 18–053—18–066
criticism of general rule, 18–051
exceptions to rule, 18–052
general rule, 18–049—18–050
trusts of promises, 18–078—18–086
variation, 18–099—18–105
Threats
break contract, to
bad faith, 7–041
conclusion, 7–043
fairness, 7–042
generally, 7–038—7–039
introduction, 1–145—1–146
statement of the inevitable, 7–040
summary, 7–044
commit otherwise lawful act, to, 7–045—7–046
commit unlawful act, to, 7–037
Threats—*cont.*
institute civil proceedings, to
generally, 7–050
unjust enrichment, 29–098
not to contract, 7–047
prosecute, to
generally, 7–048
stifling action, 7–049
unjust enrichment, 29–098
Three-party intimidation
See **Intimidation**
Tickets
offers, 2–021
Tie-ins
restraint of trade, 16–125—16–126
Time
'as soon as possible', 21–021
calculation
generally, 21–023
month, 21–026
period from, 21–024
period within, 21–025
construction of terms, 12–093—12–094
'day', 21–022
'directly', 21–021
failure of performance, 24–045
fixed time, 21–019
'forthwith', 21–021
meanings
'as soon as possible', 21–021
'day', 21–022
'directly', 21–021
'forthwith', 21–021
'month', 21–026
'month', 21–026
no fixed time, 21–020
payment, for, 21–053
performance, for
calculation, 21–023—21–026
fixed time, 21–019
meanings, 21–021—21–022
no fixed time, 21–020
time not of the essence, 21–018
time of the essence, 21–011—21–017
time not of the essence, 21–018
time of the essence
common law, at, 21–011
effect, 21–015—21–017
requirements, 21–013—21–014
statute, under, 21–012
Time of the essence
common law, at, 21–011
effect
generally, 21–015
loss of right to terminate, 21–016
equity, in, 21–011
notices making
effect, 21–017
generally, 21–014

Time of the essence—*cont.*
requirements
generally, 21–013
notices, 21–014
statute, under
exceptions, 21–013—21–014
generally, 21–012
Timesharing
contractual requirements, 4–002
Timetables
offer, 2–021
Tortious liability
minors, 8–046—8–047
restitution
deceit, 29–147
effect of statute, 29–143
election of remedy, 29–146
extortion, 29–150
fraud, 29–147—29–149
introduction, 29–141
nature of benefit, 29–144
oppression, 29–150
profits made by defendant, 29–145
tortious acts, 29–142
Torts
assignment, 1–125
capacity of parties, 1–125, 1–162
classification of actions, 1–118
concurrence of actions
historical background, 1–128—1–130
during contractual term, 1–136—1–169
generally, 1–126—1–127
pre-contractual liability, 1–131—1–136
conflict of laws
applicable law, 1–169
introduction, 1–125
jurisdiction, 1–168
contract terms, effect of
generally, 1–185
tortfeasor and another, between, 1–186
victim and another, between, 1–187
contributory negligence, 1–166
culpa in contrahendo, 1–136
damages, 1–122—1–124, 1–163—1–164
differences in rules
assignment, 1–125
capacity of parties, 1–125, 1–162
conflict of laws, 1–168—1–169
contributory negligence, 1–166
damages, 1–122—1–124, 1–163—1–164
generally, 1–119—1–121, 1–161
limitation of actions, 1–124, 1–167
remoteness of damage, 1–165
service of process, 1–125

Torts—*cont.*
duress, 1–135
during contractual term, liability arising
assumption of responsibility, 1–138—1–144
contractual silence, 1–156—1–160
differences in rules, 1–161—1–169
exclusion of liability, 1–151
generally, 1–137
immunity in law, 1–154—1–155
incompatibility of terms, 1–152—1–153
silence, 1–156—1–160
standards of care, 1–147—1–150
threat of breach of contract, 1–145—1–146
economic loss
case law, 1–176—1–184
generally, 1–175
economic threat, 1–135
generally, 1–117
inducing breach of contract, 1–171
influence on other relationships
effect of contract terms, 1–185—1–187
generally, 1–170
independent tort, 1–173
inducing breach of contract, 1–171
intimidation, 1–172
pure economic loss, 1–175—1–184
intimidation
pre-contractual liability, 1–135
three-party, 1–172
liability arising during contractual term
assumption of responsibility, 1–138—1–144
contractual silence, 1–156—1–160
differences in rules, 1–161—1–169
exclusion of liability, 1–151
generally, 1–137
immunity in law, 1–154—1–155
incompatibility of terms, 1–152—1–153
silence, 1–156—1–160
standards of care, 1–147—1–150
threat of breach of contract, 1–145—1–146
limitation of actions, 1–124, 1–167
misrepresentation
damages, 1–133
generally, 1–131—1–132
non-disclosure, 1–134
physical threat, 1–135
pre-contractual liability
culpa in contrahendo, 1–136
duress, 1–135
economic threat, 1–135
intimidation, 1–135
misrepresentation, 1–131—1–133
non-disclosure, 1–134

Torts—*cont.*
pre-contractual liability—*cont.*
physical threat, 1–135
procuring breach of contract, 1–171
pure economic loss
case law, 1–176—1–184
generally, 1–175
remoteness of damage, 1–165
service of process, 1–125
three-party intimidation, 1–172
Total failure of consideration
See **Failure of consideration**
Trade unions
capacity, 9–081—9–082
expulsion of members, 9–083
refusal of members, 9–084
restraint of trade, 16–136—16–140
rights of members, 9–085
Trade usage
And see **Custom and usage**
Trading with the enemy
common law, at, 16–026
statute, under, 16–162—16–163
Training
common law, at, 29–163
equity, in, 29–164—29–167
introduction, 29–162
proceeds of sale, 29–169
reservation of title, 29–168
Transactions at an undervalue
bankruptcy, 20–027—20–028
Transactions defrauding creditors
bankruptcy, 20–031
"Transpositions"
construction of terms, 12–074
Travel
See **Holidays**
Trespass
generally, 1–118
Trover
generally, 1–118
"True nature of document"
agency, 12–114—12–115
generally, 12–113
suretyship, 12–116
Trustee in bankruptcy
payment, 21–050
Trustees
contribution, 29–125
expenses, 28–132
payment, 21–049
presumed undue influence, 7–077
recovery of payments, 16–193
statute-barred debt, 28–132
Trusts
applicable law, 30–043
limitation of actions, 28–019
relationship with contracts,
1–188—1–189
Trusts—*cont.*
third party rights, 18–078—18–086

Uberrimae fidei
See **Utmost good faith**
Ultra vires
borrowing, 9–025
charitable companies, 9–037
common law, at
borrowing, 9–025
estoppel, 9–024
memorandum of association, 9–022
opinion of directors, 9–023
ratification, 9–024
restitution, 9–026
scope, 9–021
conflicts of interest, 9–036
constructive notice
public documents, 9–035
corporate capacity, 9–029
directors' authority
generally, 9–032—9–033
limitations, 9–034
directors' duties, 9–030—9–031
directors' interest in contract, 9–036
directors' liability, 9–040—9–045
estoppel
generally, 9–024
Turquand decision, 9–042
generally, 9–020
memorandum of association, 9–022
objects clause, 9–028
opinion of directors, 9–023
public authorities
generally, 10–033
statutory reform, 10–034
ratification
common law, at, 9–024
statutory modifications, 9–039
restitution, 9–026
shareholder rights, 9–034
statutory modifications
charitable companies, 9–037
conflicts of interest, 9–036
constructive notice, 9–035
corporate capacity, 9–029
directors' authority, 9–032—9–034
directors' duties, 9–030—9–031
directors' interest in contract, 9–036
directors' liability, 9–040—9–045
generally, 9–027
objects clause, 9–028
ratification of officer's unauthorised
act, 9–039
shareholder rights, 9–034
Turquand decision, 9–040—9–045
unjust enrichment
defences, 29–086
demands, 29–083
introduction, 9–026

Ultra vires—*cont.*
unjust enrichment—*cont.*
scope of right, 29–084
statutory provisions, 29–085
Unconscionability
conduct, 7–132—7–133
undue influence, 7–058
Unconscionable bargains
absence of independent advice, 7–134
burden of proof, 7–135
complainant's circumstances
generally, 7–131
poor and ignorant persons, 7–128
foreign law developments, 7–136
generally, 7–126
ignorant persons, 7–128
independent advice, 7–134
nature
absence of independent advice, 7–134
complainant's circumstances, 7–131
generally, 7–129
oppressive bargain, 7–130
unconscionable conduct, 7–132—7–133
oppressive bargain, 7–130
poor persons, 7–128
restitution, 29–138
salvage cases, 7–127
unconscionable conduct, 7–132—7–133
undue influence, 7–058
Undue influence
actual undue influence
causation, 7–068
disregard of victim's interests, 7–067
generally, 7–064
independent and informed judgment, 7–065—7–066
Barclays Bank v O'Brien, 7–106—7–108
basis of doctrine, 7–057
classes
actual, 7–064—7–068
generally, 7–059
presumed, 7–069—7–097
third party, 7–104—7–125
effect
generally, 1–005
voidable, 1–082
Etridge's case, 7–109—7–110
generally, 7–056—7–057
manifest disadvantage, 7–060—7–063
overview, 7–001
presumed undue influence
confidential relationships, 7–079—7–085
introduction, 7–069—7–070
rebuttal, 7–093—7–096
relevant relationships, 7–071—7–077
Undue influence—*cont.*
presumed undue influence—*cont.*
transaction not explicable by ordinary motives, 7–086—7–092
value of presumption, 7–078
remedies
account of profits, 7–100
affirmation, 7–097
equitable compensation, 7–101
restitution, 7–098—7–099
sharing loss, 7–102—7–103
restitution
generally, 7–098—7–099
introduction, 29–137
spouse, by
bank put on inquiry, 7–111—7–112
Barclays Bank v O'Brien, 7–106—7–108
conflicts of interest, 7–117—7–118
Etridge's case, 7–109—7–110
introduction, 7–105
jointly-owned homes, 7–123
legal advice, 7–115—7–116
loss of right to avoid, 7–122
procedure, 7–119
reasonable steps, 7–114
replacement mortgages, 7–121
spouse as party to transaction, 7–120
transactions not to advantage of surety, 7–113
surety, over, 7–105
third party, by
constructive notice, 7–106—7–123
introduction, 7–104—7–105
other cases, 7–124
volunteers, 7–125
unconscionable conduct, 7–058
unfair commercial practices, and, 7–002
"Unenforceable contracts"
account stated, 29–195
generally, 1–084
unjust enrichment
money paid, 29–079
work done, 29–080
Unfair commercial practices
duress, and, 7–002
misrepresentation, and, 6–002
undue influence, and, 7–002
Unfair credit relationships
bankruptcy, 20–030
introduction, 7–138
Unfair Contract Terms Act 1977
background, 14–059
burden of proof
dealing as a consumer, 14–070
reasonableness, 14–088
business liability
generally, 14–065

Unfair Contract Terms Act 1977—*cont.*
business liability—*cont.*
implied terms, 14–079
negligence, in, 14–071
carriage of goods by sea, contracts for, 14–106—14–107
choice of law clauses, 14–113
competent authority agreements, 14–112
consumer contracts, 7–137, 15–029
contracts for sale of land, 14–105
Contracts (Rights of Third Parties) Act 1999, 18–118
dealing as a consumer
agent, through, 14–069
auctions, 14–068
burden of proof, 14–070
generally, 14–066
sale of goods, 14–067
tender, sales by, 14–068
employment contracts, 14–108—14–109
force majeure clauses, 14–152
general provisions
anti-avoidance, 14–081—14–082
business liability, 14–065
contract, liability in, 14–072—14–074
dealing as a consumer, 14–066—14–070
effect of breach, 14–080
generally, 14–059
guarantees, 14–077
implied terms, 14–078—14–079
indemnity clauses, 14–075—14–076
limitations, 14–087
negligence, liability in, 14–071
voluntary assumption of risk, 14–083
generally, 14–059
hire purchase, contracts for
dealing as a consumer, 14–067
implied terms, 14–078
reasonableness, 14–085
insurance contracts, 14–105
intellectual property rights, contracts relating to, 14–105
international conventions, contracts governed by, 14–111
international supply contracts, 14–110
method of control, 14–060—14–061
reasonableness
appeals, 14–103
burden of proof, 14–088
case law, 14–089—14–099
courts' powers, 14–100—14–102
further factors, 14–086
generally, 14–084
guidelines, 14–085
limits on amount, 14–087
relevant clauses, 14–062—14–064

Unfair Contract Terms Act 1977—*cont.*
sale of goods
dealing as a consumer, 14–067
implied terms, 14–078
reasonableness, 14–085
sale of land, 14–105
salvage contracts, 14–106
third party rights, 18–118
Unfair contract terms
consumer contracts, in
And see **Unfair contract terms (consumer contracts)**
background, 15–004—15–010
choice of law, 15–093
fairness, 15–043—15–088
plain language, 15–089—15–092
relevant contracts, 15–011—15–029
relevant terms, 15–030—15–042
remedies, 15–094—15–099
damages
generally, 26–012
penalty clauses, 26–156
generally
And see **Unfair Contract Terms Act 1977**
excluded contracts, 14–104—14–113
general provisions, 14–065—14–083
generally, 14–059—14–061
reasonableness, 14–084—14–103
relevant clauses, 14–062—14–064
sale of goods
dealing as a consumer, 14–067
implied terms, 14–078
reasonableness, 14–085
Unfair contract terms (consumer contracts)
adjudication clauses, 15–094
arbitration clauses, 15–094
assignment clauses, 15–107
automatic extension clauses, 15–101
binding terms, 15–102
cancellation clauses, 15–099
choice of jurisdiction clauses, 15–095
choice of law clauses, 15–132
composite test of unfairness
basic test, 15–065—15–069
circumstances attending the conclusion of contract, 15–076
elements, 15–070—15–090
fair and equitable dealing, 15–080
good faith, 15–066—15–069
imbalance, 15–073
indicative list of unfair terms, 15–091—15–109
inducements to agree term, 15–080
introduction, 15–064
lack of plain or intelligent language, 15–077
language type, 15–088
nature of goods or services, 15–075

Unfair contract terms (consumer contracts)—*cont.*
composite test of unfairness—*cont.*
other dependent terms, 15–079
other terms of contract, 15–078
potential for unfairness, 15–072
price/quality ratio, 15–084
public services, 15–081
relative roles of courts and parties. 15–115—15–122
significant imbalance, 15–066—15–067
special order of goods, 15–080
strength of bargaining positions, 15–080
time limit for assessment, 15–110—15–114
vulnerable customers, 15–087
consumers
agents for non-consumers, 15–033
meaning, 15–028—15–031
suppliers, as, 15–032
contra proferentum, and, 15–131
'contract', 15–034—15–035
core terms, 15–049—15–063
customer's standard terms, 15–048
differences from UCTA 1977, 15–037
EC Directive
impact, 15–009
interpretation, 15–006—15–008
legislative history, 15–004
nature, 15–006—15–008
reform proposals, 15–010
status, 15–005
temporal application, 15–011—15–015
effect of finding term unfair, 15–123—15–128
entire agreement clauses, 15–105
excluded contract terms
fairness requirement, from, 15–045—15–063
scope of Regulations, from, 15–038—15–043
excluded contracts, 15–036
exclusion clauses, 15–093
fairness
bank charges, 15–059—15–060
composite test, 15–064—15–128
contract terms excluded from requirement, 15–045—15–063
core terms, 15–049—15–063
customer's standard terms, 15–048
definition of main subject-matter, 15–049
indicative list of unfair terms, 15–091—15–109
individually negotiated terms, 15–046—15–048
insurance contracts, 15–055

Unfair contract terms (consumer contracts)—*cont.*
fairness—*cont.*
introduction, 15–043
price, 15–049
relative roles of courts and parties. 15–115—15–122
time limit for assessment, 15–110—15–114
indicative list
adjudication clauses, 15–094
arbitration clauses, 15–094
assignment clauses, 15–107
automatic extension clauses, 15–101
binding terms, 15–102
cancellation clauses, 15–099
choice of jurisdiction clauses, 15–095
entire agreement clauses, 15–105
exclusion clauses, 15–093
introduction, 15–091—15–092
limitation clauses, 15–093
notice of indeterminate duration, 15–100
other terms, 15–108—15–109
penalty clauses, 15–098
potestative conditions, 15–096
supplier discretion clauses, 15–104
unbalanced forfeiture clauses, 15–097
unequal opt-out clauses, 15–106
variation clauses, 15–103
individually negotiated terms, 15–046—15–048
insurance contracts, 15–055
introduction, 15–001—15–003
limitation clauses, 15–093
notice of indeterminate duration, 15–100
Office of Fair Trading, 15–135
penalty clauses, 15–098
policing and monitoring
application of fairness test, 15–136
burden of proof, 15–137
enforcement orders, 15–139
generally, 15–133—15–134
Office of Fair Trading, 15–135
qualifying bodies, 15–138
potentially unfair terms
adjudication clauses, 15–094
arbitration clauses, 15–094
assignment clauses, 15–107
automatic extension clauses, 15–101
binding terms, 15–102
cancellation clauses, 15–099
choice of jurisdiction clauses, 15–095
entire agreement clauses, 15–105
exclusion clauses, 15–093
introduction, 15–091—15–092

Unfair contract terms (consumer contracts)—*cont.*
potentially unfair terms—*cont.*
limitation clauses, 15–093
notice of indeterminate duration, 15–100
other terms, 15–108—15–109
penalty clauses, 15–098
potestative conditions, 15–096
supplier discretion clauses, 15–104
unbalanced forfeiture clauses, 15–097
unequal opt-out clauses, 15–106
variation clauses, 15–103
potestative conditions, 15–096
price, 15–049
public authorities, and, 15–022
reasonableness test in UCTA, and, 15–090
relevant contracts
excluded contracts, 15–036
included contracts, 15–011—15–035
introduction, 15–016—15–017
sale of interest in land, 15–019—15–020
restitution, and, 15–126
"seller or supplier", 15–024—15–027
supplier discretion clauses, 15–104
temporal application, 15–011—15-015
UCTA 1977, and, 15–037
unbalanced forfeiture clauses, 15–097
unequal opt-out clauses, 15–106
variation clauses, 15–103
Unfair Terms in Consumer Contracts Directive 1993
duress, and, 7–137
exclusion clauses, and, 14–125
impact, 15–009
interpretation, 15–006—15–008
introduction, 1–009
legislative history, 15–004
nature, 15–006—15–008
reform proposals, 15–010
status, 15–005
temporal application, 15–012—15-015
unconscionable bargains, and, 7–137
Unfair relationships
bankruptcy, 20–030
introduction, 7–138
"Unfairness"
And see **Fairness**
generally, 1–020
specific performance, 27–032
statutory authority, 1–021
"Unforeseen events"
discharge by frustration, 23–060
Unilateral contracts
acceptance
acceptance, 2–079—2–080
continuing guarantees, 2–081
Unilateral contracts—*cont.*
acceptance—*cont.*
ignorance of offer, 2–041
introduction, 2–078
irrevocable credits, 2–082
part performance, 2–079—2–080
consideration, 3–170—3–171
generally, 1–079
offer by advertisements, 2–018
Unilateral mistake
contractual notices, in, 5–080
estoppel, 5–082
generally, 5–074—5–087
introduction, 5–001
knowledge of other party, 5–074
mistaken identity, 5–088—5–100
ought to have been apparent, 5–075
rectification
cancellation, 5–119—5–120
contributing conduct, 5–117
generally, 5–115
inequity, 5–118
knowledge, 5–116
mistake known to have been made, 5–121
terms of contract, as to, 5–076—5–079
Unincorporated associations
clubs
generally, 9–072
members' clubs, 9–073—9–077
officers' mess, 9–079
proprietary clubs, 9–080
generally, 9–064
members' clubs
election of members, 9–076—9–077
expulsion of members, 9–075
liability, 9–073
resignation of members, 9–078
status, 9–074
officers' mess, 9–079
proprietary clubs, 9–080
representative actions
generally, 9–065
requirements, 9–066—9–070
status, 9–071
trade unions
capacity, 9–081—9–082
expulsion of members, 9–083
refusal of members, 9–084
rights of members, 9–085
types
clubs, 9–072—9–080
trade unions, 9–081—9–085
Unit trusts
exemption clauses, 14–123
Unjust enrichment
applicable law, 30–034
avoided insurance policy, 29–082
background, 29–012—29–016

Unjust enrichment—*cont.*
compliance with local authority notices, 29–096
compulsion
compliance with local authority notices, 29–096
distress of goods, 29–091
duress of the person, 29–089—29–090
extortion colore officii, 29–094—29–095
generally, 29–087
illegitimate, 29–088
payment made in course of legal proceedings, 29–098
payment of excessive amount, 29–097
payment to third person, 29–099—29–129
unlawful compulsion, 29–088
wrongful demand, 29–092—29–093
conflict of laws, 30–034
defences and bars, 29–019
deposits, 29–064—29–065
distress of goods, 29–091
duress of the person
generally, 29–089
seizure of goods, 29–090
elements, 29–018
'enrichment', 29–020—29–023
'expense of claimant', 29–025—29–027
exploitation
unconscionable bargains, 29–138
undue influence, 29–137
extortion colore officii
generally, 29–094
nature of threat, 29–095
failure of consideration
avoided insurance policy, 29–082
deposits, 29–064—29–065
illegal contracts, 29–077—29–078
introduction, 29–054
minors' contracts, 29–081
part payments, 29–066
partial failure of consideration, 29–060—29–063
quantum meruit, 29–067—29–073
total failure of consideration, 29–055—29–059
unenforceable contract, 29–079—29–080
void contract, 29–074—29–076
grounds of restitution, 29–028
illegal contracts
generally, 29–077
services rendered, 29–078
intervention on behalf of defendant
acting in public interest, 29–132
analogous categories, 29–133

Unjust enrichment—*cont.*
intervention on behalf of defendant—*cont.*
generally, 29–131
necessaries, 29–135
non-gratuitous, 29–134
reasonableness, 29–134
mistake of fact
burden of proof, 29–035
causative mistake, 29–034
compromise, 29–038
fundamental mistake, 29–033
good consideration, 29–037
introduction, 29–028
payer with means of knowledge, 29–036
prior notices and demand, 29–039
submission to claim, 29–038
'supposed liability' rule, 29–030—29–032
mistake of law
abolition of bar, 29–046
change in law, 29–048
criticism of rule, 29–044
equitable relief, 29–043
examples, 29–041
exceptions, 29–042
generally, 29–040
improvements to another's goods, 29–051—29–053
principles, 29–047
rejection of rule, 29–045
remedies, 29–049—29–050
repairs to another's goods, 29–051
necessity
generally, 29–130
intervention on behalf of defendant, 29–131—29–135
salvage, 29–136
part payments, 29–066
partial failure of consideration
common law, at, 29–061
divisible contract, in, 29–063
statute, under, 29–060
passing on, 29–027
payment made in course of legal proceedings, 29–098
payment of excessive amount, 29–097
payment to third person
assignees of lease, 29–106
generally, 29–099—29–100
legal liability to pay, 29–101
other examples, 29–107—29–129
primary liability to pay, 29–102
seizure of goods, 29–103—29–105
payment under mistake of fact
burden of proof, 29–035
causative mistake, 29–034
compromise, 29–038
fundamental mistake, 29–033

Unjust enrichment—*cont.*
payment under mistake of fact—*cont.*
good consideration, 29–037
introduction, 29–028
payer with means of knowledge, 29–036
prior notices and demand, 29–039
submission to claim, 29–038
'supposed liability' rule, 29–030—29–032
payment under mistake of law
abolition of bar, 29–046
change in law, 29–048
criticism of rule, 29–044
equitable relief, 29–043
examples, 29–041
exceptions, 29–042
generally, 29–040
improvements to another's goods, 29–051—29–053
principles, 29–047
rejection of rule, 29–045
remedies, 29–049—29–050
repairs to another's goods, 29–051
quantum meruit
additional work, 29–072
bad bargains, 29–068
contract price, 29–069
generally, 29–067
goods supplied, 29–070
no fixed price, 29–071
services rendered, 29–070
substituted contract for services, 29–073
quantum valebant, 29–004
salvage, 29–136
seizure of goods
duress, 29–090
payment to third person, 29–103—29–105
total failure of consideration
artificial distinctions, 29–057
detrimental reliance, 29–055
discharged contracts, 29–058—29–059
examples, 29–056
introduction, 29–054
reconsideration of requirement, 29–062
ultra vires receipts
defences, 29–086
demands, 29–083
introduction, 9–026
scope of right, 29–084
statutory provisions, 29–085
unconscionable bargains, 29–138
undue influence
generally, 7–098—7–099
introduction, 29–137

Unjust enrichment—*cont.*
unenforceable contract
money paid, 29–079
work done, 29–080
void contract
absence of consideration, 29–075
generally, 29–074
goods supplied, 29–076
services rendered, 29–076
wrongful demand
detention of goods, on, 29–092
detention of title deeds, on, 29–093
"Unlicensed credit transactions"
illegality, 16–155
"Unliquidated claims"
part payment of debt, 3–119
"Unliquidated damages"
See also **Liquidated damages**
generally, 26–010—26–011
unfair contract terms, 26–012
"Unsoundness of mind"
effect, 1–082
"Ut res magis valeat cum pereat"
construction of terms, 12–081
Utilities
contractual obligations, 1–013
Utmost good faith
contracts for sale of land, 6–156—6–157
family settlements, 6–155
general releases, 6–164
generally, 6–142—6–143
joint ventures, 6–163
partnership, 6–162
share subscription contracts, 6–153—6–154
sureties, 6–158—6–161

"Vague agreements"
goodwill, 2–184
Vagueness
See **Certainty**
Validity (documents)
conditional contracts, 12–109
consideration, 12–108
fraud, 12–112
generally, 12–106—12–112
illegality, 12–112
"Valuable consideration"
generally, 3–022
illusory consideration, 3–023—3–025
impossible consideration, 3–023
Variation
agreement, by
consideration, 22–035
elucidation, 22–037
extra works, 22–038
form, 22–033
generally, 22–032
collateral contracts, 22–036

Variation—*cont.*
consideration
And see **Variation (consideration)**
common law mitigation, 3–081—3–084
equitable mitigation, 3–085—3–114
generally, 3–076
introduction, 22–035
types of variation, 3–079—3–080
contracts for sale of land
LPA 1925, s.40, 4–015
LP(MP)A 1989, s.2, 4–056
debtor's performance, 3–122
deeds, 1–115
elucidation, 22–037
extra works, 22–038
part payment of debt, 3–122
rescission, 22–034
types, 3–079—3–080
unfair contract terms (consumer contracts), 15–081, 22–039
unilateral power, 22–039
Variation (consideration)
common law mitigation
forbearance, 3–082—3–084
generally, 3–081
waiver, 3–081
equitable mitigation
And see **Promissory estoppel**
effect, 3–096—3–103
estoppel by convention, 3–107—3–114
estoppel by representation, 3–096
foreign jurisdictions, 3–106
generally, 3–085
promises with consideration, 3–105
requirements, 3–086—3–095
waiver, 3–103—3–104
forbearance at common law
generally, 3–082—3–084
introduction, 3–081
forbearance in equity
And see **Promissory estoppel**
generally, 3–085—3–103
general rule, 3–076
introduction, 22–035
part payment of debt, 3–122
requirement, 3–079—3–080
types of variation, 3–079—3–080
waiver
common law, at, 3–081
equity, in, 3–103—3–104
Vertical agreements
common law, at
co-operative marketing, 16–127
generally, 16–121
solus petrol agreements, 16–122—16–124
tied public-houses, 16–125—16–126
Vertical agreements—*cont.*
co-operative marketing agreements, 16–127
solus agreements, 16–122—16–124
tied public-houses, 16–125—16–126
Vicarious performance
agency, 19–084
generally, 19–081—19–083
introduction, 21–004
Vienna Convention 1980
acceptance, 2–063
"Vindictive damages"
generally, 26–019
Void contract (payments)
effect, 1–081
generally, 1–080
unjust enrichment
absence of consideration, 29–075
generally, 29–074
goods supplied, 29–076
services rendered, 29–076
Voidable contracts
generally, 1–082
minors
generally, 8–005
ratified, which must be, 8–042—8–045
repudiated, which may be, 8–030—8–041
ratification
examples, 8–043
generally, 8–042
procedure, 8–044
repudiation
effect of avoidance, 8–040
generally, 8–030—8–032
lease of land, 8–033—8–035
marriage settlements, 8–036
partnerships, 8–039
purchase of land, 8–033—8–034
share purchases, 8–037—8–038
time of avoidance, 8–041
setting aside, 1–083
"Voluntary acts"
restitution, 29–019
Voluntary arrangements
bankruptcy, 20–050
joint liability, 17–025
"Voluntary assignment of rights"
assignability, 30–125
generally, 30–123
mutual obligations, 30–124
property, 30–126
Voluntary payments
unjust enrichment, 29–109—29–112
"Voluntary settlements"
rectification, 5–136
Volunteers
undue influence, 7–125

Wagering contracts
See also **Gaming contracts**
[*n.b. prior to September 1, 2007*]
consideration, 3–169
mistake of fact, 29–038
Waiver
acceptance
method of communication, 2–068—2–069
need for communication, 2–047
affirmation
election, by, 24–007—24–008
estoppel, by, 24–007—24–008
generally, 24–009
agreements, by
consideration, 22–044
effect, 22–042—22–043
form, 22–041
generally, 22–040
breach, 22–047
condition for benefit of one party, of, 22–046
conditional agreements, 2–157
consideration, 22–044
contracting out, 22–045
discharge under contract
defects in notices, 22–052
right to terminate, 22–053
estoppel, by, 22–040
immunity from suit
common law, at, 11–020
consular staff, 11–022
diplomatic staff, 11–022
international organisations, 11–023
statute, under, 11–021
variation
common law, at, 3–081
equity, in, 3–103—3–104
War
discharge by frustration, 23–024—23–025
Warranties
collateral, 12–033
Warranties—*cont.*
election, upon, 12–032
failure of performance, 24–038
generally, 12–019
meaning, 12–031
Wasted expenditure
currency exchange loss, 26–080—26–081
no transaction basis, 26–079
non-performance expenditure, 26–074—26–075
performance expenditure, 26–072—26–073
post-breach expenditure, 26–078
pre-contract expenditure, 26–076—26–077
Water companies
contractual obligations, 1–013
Wills
applicable law, 30–037
objects injurious to morality, 16–074
Winding-up
company contracts with
disposal of property, 9–049
generally, 9–047
repudiation, 9–048
discharge, 25–030
limitation of actions, 28–070
Withdrawal (offer)
communication
exceptions, 2–091
generally, 2–089
method, 2–090
general rule, 2–088
"Writs of assumpsit, debt and account"
restitution, 29–005
"Wrongful demands"
detention of goods, on, 29–092
detention of title deeds, on, 29–093
Wrongful dismissal
renunciation, 24–020
Wrongful interference with goods
See **Interference with goods**